General Alphabetical Index
TO THE TOWNLANDS AND TOWNS, PARISHES AND BARONIES OF IRELAND

Based on the Census of Ireland for the Year 1851

Baltimore
GENEALOGICAL PUBLISHING CO., INC.
1986

Originally published: Dublin, 1861
Reprinted: Genealogical Publishing Co., Inc.
Baltimore, Maryland, 1984, 1986.
Library of Congress Catalogue Card Number 83-82450
International Standard Book Number 0-8063-1052-9
Made in the United States of America

Reprinted with the permission of
the Controller, Stationery Office, Dublin.

CENSUS OF IRELAND.

GENERAL ALPHABETICAL INDEX

TO THE

TOWNLANDS AND TOWNS, PARISHES, AND BARONIES

OF

IRELAND,

SHOWING

THE NUMBER OF THE SHEET OF THE ORDNANCE SURVEY MAPS IN WHICH
THEY APPEAR:

THE AREAS OF THE TOWNLANDS, PARISHES, AND BARONIES;

THE COUNTY, BARONY, PARISH, AND POOR LAW UNION IN WHICH THE TOWNLANDS ARE SITUATED:

AND

THE VOLUME AND PAGE OF THE TOWNLAND CENSUS OF 1851, WHICH CONTAINS
THE POPULATION AND NUMBER OF HOUSES IN 1841 AND 1851,
AND THE POOR LAW VALUATION IN 1851.

Presented to both Houses of Parliament by Command of Her Majesty.

DUBLIN:

PRINTED BY ALEXANDER THOM, 87 & 88, ABBEY-STREET,

FOR HER MAJESTY'S STATIONERY OFFICE.

1861.

CENSUS OF IRELAND.

TOWNLAND INDEX.

TO HIS EXCELLENCY GEORGE WILLIAM FREDERICK, EARL OF CARLISLE, K.G.,

&c.,   &c.,

LORD LIEUTENANT-GENERAL AND GENERAL GOVERNOR OF IRELAND.

MAY IT PLEASE YOUR EXCELLENCY,

I have the honour to submit for your Excellency's consideration an Index to the Townland Census of Ireland, which has been prepared in this Department. It gives, in alphabetical order, the name of every Townland, TOWN, and *Island* mentioned in the Census publications, and the number of the Sheet of the Maps of the Ordnance Survey in which the several denominations are to be found; also the area of each Townland, and the County, Barony, Parish, and Poor Law Union in which it is situated. The volume and page of the Townland Census, from which information may be procured as to the Population, and Houses, in 1841 and 1851, and the Poor Law Valuation, in 1851, are also given.

The Townland names are printed in Roman characters, the TOWNS in small CAPITALS, and *Islands*, which are *not* Townlands, in *Italics*.

Notes are appended, which state the quantity of water included within the area of each Townland, and the cases in which a Townland comprises one or more detached portions, or is divided by Municipal Boundaries into one or more parts. For example, the townland of " Abbeylands," in the parish of Ringcurran, barony of Kinsale, county of Cork, E.R., consists of five parts, containing an aggregate area of 106A. 3R. 32P.; and " Ayresfields," in the parish of St. Canice, barony of Crannagh, county of Kilkenny, having a total area of 43A. 1R. 4P., is made up of 16A. 2R. 26P. within, and the remainder without, the Municipal Boundary of the city of Kilkenny.

In order to facilitate the search for any townland having more than one name, such as " Ballydaly or Derrynagall," in the parish of Kilbride, barony of Ballycowan, King's County, it will be found under both names.

Indexes to the Parishes and Baronies follow the Townlands, so as to make the work form a complete topographical index of Ireland.

It would greatly increase the value of a publication of this nature if it were accompanied by a Glossary, or explanation of the Names, and an account of their origin. As an example of the interest which attaches to such an elucidation of the territorial divisions of the country, I beg to annex an extract from the Ordnance " Memoir of the City and North-Western Liberties of Londonderry;" and I may observe that the invaluable labours and researches of Dr. Petrie, Dr. O'Donovan, and Professor O'Curry have furnished ample material for this purpose, collected and arranged under the direction of Major-General Sir Thomas Larcom during the progress of the Ordnance Survey.

A 2

TEMPLEMORE.

The parish of Templemore, sometimes called Temple Derry [Ceampull Ohoιpe], and more anciently Derry [Oοιpe], or Derry Columbkille [Oοιpe Choluιm Cιlle], derives its first and most usual name—Templemore—from the Irish ceampull móp, or "great church"—ceampull [templum] being derived from the Latin, like most other Irish words expressive of Christian edifices, offices, rites, and ceremonies. This name was originally applied, in a popular sense, to the cathedral, or "great church" of Derry, in contradistinction from the smaller churches in its immediate vicinity; and, after the cathedral had become the parish church, its popular name—Templemore—was in a similar manner transferred to the parish. There is every reason, however, to believe that the use of this name is not of very ancient standing; for it appears from the Irish annals that the cathedral, or Templemore, was not erected till 1164, and it is probable that it was not used as a parish church till some centuries later. Its more ancient appellation—Derry—would therefore still be the more correct one, and it is generally so called in ecclesiastical records down to recent times.

The most ancient names of the district in which this parish [Templemore] is situated were Farran Neid—feapann Néιo, or the land of Neid,—and Tir Ely—Cιp Œιlιş, or the country of Aileach. Of these names the former is derived by Irish writers from Neid Mac Indai, a provincial king of the Tuatha-de-Dananns, who had his palace on the hill in Inishowen, now called the Grianan, or Grianan Ely, and anciently Œιleać Néιo,—and the latter name was derived from the palace of that monarch. At the commencement of the 5th century, when a large portion of Ireland was partitioned by the monarch Niall (called of the Nine Hostages,) among his twelve sons, this district became the patrimony of his son Eogan, or Owen, from whom it received the name of Inishowen—Inιp Eoşaιn, or Owen's Island—being nearly insulated by the two arms of the sea, called Lough Foyle and Lough Swilly. The ancient and natural southern boundary of this peninsula extended from Castleforward—anciently called Cúl-mac-an-cpeoin—on Lough Swilly, by Lough Lappan, now Port Lough, to Carrigins, on the Foyle, and included the whole of the present parish of Derry, or Templemore. After the erection of the abbey at Derry, by St. Columbkille, a portion of this ancient district, lying immediately adjacent to it, was given as a support to that establishment; and hence the territorial boundary of Inishowen, as a temporal lordship, became changed so as to exclude the island of Derry and the other church-lands. This change appears evident from the Inquisition taken at Derry, in 1609, before a jury composed of resident English, and of Irish natives of the principal ancient septs of the district, who were impannelled to ascertain among other matters the extent of the possessions of Sir John O'Doherty and his son Sir Cahir, as lords of Inishowen. Their return was, "that the auntient and knowne meares of the countrey of Inishowen, als O'Doghertie's countrey, to the south and southeast, are and have bene tyme out of mynde as followeth, viz. from the pte or braunch of Loughswilly on the west and southwest pte of Birt thorough the midst of a bog which extendeth to Loughlappan [O'Lappan's Lake], and soe thorough the midst of that lough, and soe alongst the midst of a small river, fallinge into Loughlappan, from a well or springe uppon Mullaghknockemona, and from the topp of that mountayne the meare extendeth thorough a small bogg which runeth alonge the topp of the hill of Ardenemahill, and soe to the top of the hill of Knockenagh, uppon the east pte of which hill ariseth the streame of Altbally Mᶜ Rowertie which runneth ameare betweene *Bally Mᶜ Rowertie* in *Enishowen* and pte of the lands of the Derry and Garrowgarle, to the cawsy, under Ellogh, and soe down thorough the bog to Loghswilly, and from the foresaid cawsy the meare of Inishowen aforesaid is thorough the midst of the bogg to Loughfoile."

Thus it appears certain that Sir John O'Doherty was in possession of all the townlands within the parish, the churchlands excepted, as belonging to his territory of Inishowen. These townlands were Ballyarnett, Ballymacgrorty, Coshquin, Laharden, and Elaghmore—all which were upon a surrender confirmed to him by letters patent in the 30th Elizabeth. In 1599 Sir John O'Doherty rebelled, and forfeited all Inishowen; but it was afterwards regranted to his son, Sir Cahir, "the said quarter of Ballyarnett, the half quarter of Laharden, on which the said castle of Coolemore is built, together with three hundred acres of land to the said castle allotted and apperteyninge, only excepted." In 1608 Sir Cahir also rebelled, and, his letters patent therefore becoming "null and voide," his whole property was granted to Arthur, Lord Chichester, of Belfast, by letters patent bearing date the 20th of November, in the 19th James I. It appears from an Inquisition, taken at Donegal in 1625, that Lord Chichester, being thus seized of these possessions, leased them to Faithfull Fortescue, Knt., Arthur Usher, Tristram Berrisford, and Charles Points, and to their heirs and assigns.

The townlands belonging to the abbey of St. Columbkille were *Ballougry, Ballymagowan, Ballynagard, Ballynashallog, Creevagh, Killea, Mullennan, Termonderry* (now *Londonderry*), and *Termonbacca*. These, with the exception of Ballynagard and Ballynashallog, formed the Fifteen Hundred Acres, or Quarter Lands.

The quarter of Craggin and Drumniurny, and the half-quarter of Courneglough—both which seem to be included in the present townlands of *Creggan* and *Edenballymore*—belonged to the bishop; and the townland of *Ballynagalliagh*, as its name imports, was a part of the property of the nunnery of Derry.—(See *Inquisition, taken at Derry in* 1609.)

It has not been discovered whether the townland of *Shantallow* was ecclesiastical or temporal property, as the name does not occur in the Inquisitions. The remaining rural townlands—*Cloughglass, Pennyburn, Sheriff's Mountain, Springhill,* and *Springtown*—are only modern subdivisions of earlier denominations.

The ancient topography of the district being thus pointed out, the next most important object of statistic research is the investigation of the orthography and etymology of the names of the townlands, into which the parish is now divided: and, as several of their constituent terms are of constant occurrence in Irish topography, it will be expedient to dilate on them when they first occur, especially as the view here taken of their origin differs in some important instances from that usually adopted.

It may also be necessary to premise that the term *townland* is now applied in a more general sense than anciently. The Irish designation baιle bιacać—victuallers', or farmers' town—originally denoted a tract of land, which constituted the thirtieth part of a cpιoća ceuo, or barony,—and all the lesser divisions were known by the various appellations of quarters, half-quarters, ballyboes, gneeves, tates, &c. In the Ordnance Maps, however, in accordance with the prevailing usage, all these names of subdivisions are discarded, and the term *townland* is applied to every such denomination, whether great or small.

The boundaries of the townlands laid down on the Ordnance Maps having, in accordance with the act 6 George IV. c. 99, been shewn by the local government, guided by the present usage in collecting the grand jury rates and cess, it will often happen that boundaries, so laid down on the Maps, do not exactly coincide with those of earlier denominations, and new subdivisions will sometimes occur. A great diversity is also found in the manner of spelling the early names of townlands, and their subdivisions, used in various authentic documents. The consideration of the etymology of these early names, and their collation with the most approved spelling in modern use, have therefore been a subject of anxious care, and the endeavour has been to adopt, as far as modern usage would permit, such a mode of spelling as would preserve the greatest identity with the best authorities; and, as a further aid in this identification, the various modes of spelling, with the authorities on which they rest, are given with the respective names.

CITY OF LONDONDERRY.

Cɪᴛʏ of Lᴏɴᴅᴏɴᴅᴇʀʀʏ.—Dᴇʀʀʏ, in Irish Ɗoɩꞃe—the popular name of the place—means literally a "place of oaks," but is also used to express a "thick wood:" it is so explained by Colgan (1645)—an Irish topographer of the highest authority—in his *Acta Sanctorum:* p. 566 [*rectè* 562]. This word, however, was not topographically used by the ancient Irish without the addition of some distinctive epithet, as in Ɗoɩꞃe Ɓꞃoꞃcaɩꝺ, Ɗoɩꞃe Ⱡóꞃáɩn, &c.: thus the original Pagan appellation of this place was Ɗoɩꞃe CaⱡꞬaɩc, or Derry-Calgach—the "oak wood of Calgach,"—*Calgach*, which signifies a "fierce warrior," being the proper name of a man in Pagan times, and rendered illustrious as *Galgacus* in the pages of Tacitus. In support of this etymology may be adduced the high authority of Adamnan—abbot of Iona, in the 7th century—who, in his Life of his predecessor, St. Columbkille, invariably calls this place "*Roboretum Calgagi*," in conformity with his habitual substitution of Latin equivalents for Irish topographical names. For a long period subsequent to the 6th century, in which a monastery was erected here by St. Columbkille, the name of Derry-Calgach prevailed; but, towards the latter end of the 10th century, it seems to have yielded to that of Derry-Columbkille—no other appearing in the Irish annals after that period. In subsequent ages, when the place had risen in importance above every other *Derry*, the distinctive epithet *Columbkille* was dropped as no longer necessary; and such is the effect of long established usage that the English prefix *London*—imperatively imposed by the original charter of James I., and preserved with pride by the colonists for a long time after—has likewise fallen into popular disuse. Indeed this mode of abbreviation is usual in Ireland, whenever the name of a place is compounded of two distinct and easily separable words: thus, in the counties of Antrim and Down, Carrickfergus is shortened into *Carrick*, Downpatrick into *Down*, Iniscourcy into *Inch*, &c.

It may, perhaps, not be unworthy of remark that the English prefix *London*, and the original Irish name *Derry*, are equally traceable to a Celtic—or, more correctly, Scythic—origin; and that by a curious coincidence, the word Lᴏɴᴅᴏɴ seems as graphically descriptive of the modern locality as Dᴇʀʀʏ was of the ancient. By Lʟᴜʏᴅ, and other British etymologists, it is interpreted the "town of ships," from *long* in British, and Irish, "ship,"—and *dinas* in British, or ɒún in Irish, "fortress,"—(the *dunum* of the Romans,) which is the root of the word "town," This derivation is, however, merely conjectural; and the Celtic compound Ⱡonn-ɒún, signifying a "strong fortress," is as likely to have been the original signification of Lᴏɴᴅᴏɴ. Either explanation is, however, curiously applicable to Londonderry, or Ⱡonnɒún-ɒoɩꞃe, which would mean in Irish what the English have really made the city—the "ship town," or "fortified town, of Derry;" and it may be added that an etymology similar to the former may be found in the name of an ancient fortress, a few miles higher up the river, called Ɗún na ⱠonꞬ—"fortress of ships," or "town of ships," as it has been preserved to the present time.

1. Cɪᴛʏ ᴏғ Lᴏɴᴅᴏɴᴅᴇʀʀʏ.

Considered as a townland, the City, or more correctly the Island, of Derry appears to have anciently borne the name of Tᴇʀᴍᴏɴᴅᴇʀʀʏ, or the Sanctuary of Derry, and to have constituted one of the seven quarters of *erenach* or *termon* land, called "the 1500 acres." Thus, in the license to grant leases, granted to Bishop Bramhall and the mayor and corporation of Londonderry by the lord lieutenant and privy council, in June, 1638, these seven townlands are thus enumerated:—

"Wᴇɴᴛᴡᴏʀᴛʜ, (Lord Lieutenant of Ireland)."

"Whereas there is an agreement for certain leases to be made by your supplicant, John Lord Bishop of Derry, unto the rest of your petitioners, *viz.*—To the Mayor and Commonalty of the seven quarters of land, called or known by the names of Moylenan alias Molenan, Ballyougery alias Ballydougery, Termanbackoe, Ballynegowan, Termonderry, Creevagh, and Killeagh, situate in the parish of Templemore alias Derry, within the liberties of the said city of Londonderry, at the yearly rent of £50." &c. &c.—"Signed by ten of the Council."—(*Concise View of the Irish Society:* p. 57.)

Though this name Termonderry was used in a loose and popular way to denote the whole of the *erenach* or *termon* lands of the monastery of Derry, it can scarcely admit of doubt that in the above list it was exclusively and properly applied to the Island, in which the original *termon*, or sanctuary, of the monastery was situated. In subsequent times, as appears from 3 and 4 Anne, the Island, as a townland, was omitted in the list of townlands called the "quarter lands," or "1500 acres," and which, even with this omission, contain in reality considerably more than that amount.

Of the word *termon* some fanciful etymologies, by Bishop Montgomery, will be found in page 51 of this Memoir. Some more recent writers have supposed that it was the same as *terra monachorum*, or the French *terre-moine*—the land of monks,—and others have derived it from the Latin *terra immunis*, free land, because it was unquestionably applied to land free from all claim of temporal lords. A more solid conjecture respecting its etymology has been given by Usher, who supposed it to have been derived from the Latin *terminus*, and that it signified an asylum, or sanctuary, "because such privileged places were usually designed by special marks, or bounds." It is probable indeed that they were always so, in accordance with the canon of the Irish synod, given by D'Achery:—"Let the *Terminus* of a holy place have marks about it: whenever you find the sign of the cross of Christ, do not do any injury." "Three persons consecrated a *Terminus* of a holy place—a king, a bishop, and the people." Such *termini*, or boundary-stones, still remain in the vicinity of many Irish *termons*. They are usually four in number, placed towards the cardinal points, and in the form of crosses; though occasionally they are pillar-stones, either plain, or having a cross cut upon them. From the application of the word *termon*, to signify a sanctuary, it afterwards came into general use to signify shelter, refuge, or protection, and is so employed by the Irish to the present day: "cɩꞬɩm ꞃáꝺ ꞇaꞃɩman, I require your protection, or I repair to you as my sanctuary."—(O'Bʀɪᴇɴ.) "ɒeɩꞇɩɓ ꞇeaꞃɩmaɩn, tutelary gods."—(*Id.*) It seems also to have been popularly applied to denote the lands belonging to a *termon*, in the same loose manner as *baile* was to those belonging to a habitation, and sometimes even, in a looser way, to an extensive district in which a sanctuary was situated, and which was believed to be under the protection of a patron saint. Thus in the Inquisition, taken at Lymmavaddy in 1609, the then parishes of Aghanloo, Drumachose, and Balteagh, are called by the name of "Termonconny," or the *termon* of St. Cainneach, though the *termon*, or sanctuary, was in reality limited to the church of Drumachose, which was popularly called *Termon Mac Teige*, from the family of that name, who were its hereditary *corbes*, or *erenachs*. [See *Parish of Drumachose.*] And though it is stated in the same Inquisition that land was called "termon or free," because it was free of all temporal exactions, it is obviously an error; for, though all *erenach* lands were equally exempted, none were called *termon* but such as had the privilege of sanctuary annexed to them. This appears clearly from several of the Inquisitions of the 7th James I. Thus, in the one above cited, it is stated:—"Further, the said jurors doe, upon their oathes, finde that the difference of termon, corbe, and herenagh, consisteth onlie in this, that the termon is the name of the land, and all termon land is herenagh land, and hath all the priviledges of herenagh land, but all herenagh land hath not alwaies as ample privileges as the termon lands." And again, in the Inquisition taken at Dungannon in the same year, the jurors "say, that termonland had the same beginninge as herenagh land, onelye they differ in that the termonland had often tymes more privileges, as sanctuarie and the like, which was not allowed to many of the herenaghes."

A 3

Dr. Lanigan was of opinion that the word *terminus*, in the ecclesiastical style, meant originally district, or territory (like *finis*), and that the idea of sanctuary was secondary. But, as already shewn, it does not appear that in Ireland church-lands were always called *termons*, or that the name was ever applied to any but those which had sanctuaries within them,—and it is always so understood by Colgan, the highest authority on the subject. And it may be observed that this word was applied to designate not only the church sanctuaries, but even those of the bards, or poets, &c. " Camden says, that it is a custom amongst the Irish nobility that each should have his own judges, antiquaries, poets, physicians, and musicians, to whom they granted *Termons*."— (KEATING : *Preface ;* p. 86.) "And what *Termons* they granted to the learned of Ireland."—(*Id.* p. 8.) The Irish had another word, which they used synonymously with this—nemineaⴆ, *sacred land*—and it is so translated by Colgan, and explained by O'Clery, as well as by Cormac Mac Cullenan, king of Munster, and archbishop of Cashel, in the 9th and 10th centuries. The Four Masters thus use it in speaking of the depredations of Sir Nicholas Malby, in 1582 :—" Neither the nemineaⴆ of the saint, or the poet, the wood, nor the desert, the valley, the town, nor the bawn, was available in sheltering the inhabitants from this captain and his people." As it is certain that among the Gaulish and British nations the druids, bards, &c., had their sanctuaries, or consecrated places, it is not improbable that these *termons* and *neveds*. in Ireland, had their origin in Pagan times, and therefore that the word *tearmann* may not be derived from the Latin, but be traceable rather to the parent of all the Indo-European languages—the Sanscrit. Such is the opinion of one of the most profound philologists of the present day—Professor Pictet, of Geneva—who thus expresses himself, respecting the remarks originally made on this word in the precursory impression of the present Memoir, in a letter to Mr. Petrie, dated " *Genève,* 13 *Mai,* 1836" :—

" Je prends la liberté de vous adresser à ce sujet une conjecture sur la vraie origine du mot *tearmann,* asylum, qui a été rapporté au latin *terminus,* lequel auroit été pris d'abord dans l' acception de territoire, district, puis de *church-land,* puis enfin de *sanctuaire,* et de *refuge.* (Voyez Ordnance Survey. Antiquities of the Parish. Etymolog. de Termonbacca.) J'avoue que j'ai quelques doutes sur ces transformations successives. Le sens *d'azyle,* de protection, me paroit être le plus ancien : dans le gallique écossais le mot *tearmunn* n' a pas d'autre signification, et il y a même un verbe *tearmunnaich,* protéger, défendre. Je crois que le latin *terminus* et l'irlandais *tearmann* se lient tous deux directement au sanscrit तर्मन् *tarman,* que Wilson traduit par *the top or term of the sacrificial post.* L'autel étant un lieu de refuge, un sanctuaire, le mot a conservé en irlandais le sens abstrait et dérivé, tandis que le latin *terminus* n' a gardé que la signification matérielle de *terme, borne.*"

It appears from the Inquisition taken at Derry in 1603, that the southern half of the Island of Derry then belonged to St. Columb's Monastery, and the northern half to the Nunnery—each containing by estimation, *half a small quarter* of land.

TOWNLANDS.

BALLOUGRY. Called *the quarter of Balliwirry* in the Inquisition taken at Derry in 1609 ; *Ballyougery alias Ballydougery* in the licence of the Lord Lieutenant to Bishop Bramhall, in 1638 ; *Ballywirry alias Ballyougry* in the Act 4 Anne; *Ballougry* by Sampson ; and *Ballyoogary* in the tithe-book. From the variety of forms which the latter part of this name assumes in ancient documents, and the want of historical evidence of its correct Irish orthography, it is impossible to offer any explanation but a useless conjectural one, as to its etymology, or original meaning.

The origin of the word *baile*, which enters so generally into Irish topographical names, has been the subject of a vast deal of learned conjecture. The advocates of the theory of a Phœnician colonization of Ireland, from General Vallancey down to Dr. Villanueva, have availed themselves of the support which their hypothesis seemed to derive from its apparent connexion with the name of Baal, the god of the Phœnicians, and the supposed deity of the ancient Irish ; while the earlier Irish writers content themselves with a simple explanation of its established meaning. Thus it is explained by the word ⴂⴎ, a place or locality, in the Book of Lecan (f. 164 ; p. b. ; col. a); translated *oppidum* by Archbishop Usher in his *Primordia* (p. 861), and by his cotemporary, Philip O'Sullevan Beare, in his History of the Irish Catholics (p. 159) ; *villa, vicus, vel burgum,* by Colgan in his *Acta Sanctorum* (p. 544 ; n. 2) ; and *villa, pagus, vel villata,* by Roderick O'Flaherty, in his Ogygia (p. 24).

The learned Dr. O'Brien has indeed remarked, in his Dictionary, that " this Celtic word *baille* and the Lat. *vallis* are originally the same, as the ancients always built their habitations in low, sheltered places, near Rivers or Rivulets." But this derivation, like those of the later etymologists already referred to, though ingenious and partly true, does not go far enough to be satisfactory ; or, to use the words of the learned William Baxter, " the origin of this name is to be sought from a more remote source."

" *Bel,* diminutive *Belin,*" observes this ingenious etymologist, " with all the Celts meant the *sun,* or *Apollo.* With the ancient Gauls, as appears from an inscription, *Abellio*—from the Greek 'Αϝηλιός. But the origin of this name is to be sought from a more remote source. Whatever was *round,* particularly the *head,* was called by the ancients either *Bâl,* or *Bêl,* and likewise *Bôl,* and *Bül.* Among the modern Persians the *skull* is called *Pola ;* and the Flemings use *Bolle* for the head. The Πόλος of the Greeks means *the crown of the head,* and Πολεῖν means *to turn.* Βῶλος, likewise, signifies a *round clod,* and what the English call *ball* [in Baxter's Latin *Pila,*] the Welch call *Bêl* [and the Irish *Meall*]. The Scoto-brigantes use *Bhêl* for the *head,* whence the English word *Bill* is derived, which signifies the *beak of a bird.* Figuratively, the Phrygians and the Thurian Greeks by Βάλλην understood a *king.* Hence also, in the Syriac dialects, Βαὰλ, Βηλ, and likewise Βὴλ, signifies *lord,* and hence also *God* and the *sun* [Irish *Mal,* and *Fal*—Hebrew *Milar*] ; and in some dialects ʽΗλ, and ʼΙλ, whence ʼΙλος, and the Greek ʽΗλιος, Ἥλιος, and Βήλιος ; and also the Celtic diminutives ʼΕλενος, Ϝέλενος, and Βέλενος, for the *sun,* and ʼΕλένη, Ϝελένη, and Βελένη, for the *moon.* In the Teutonic and Celto-Scythian dialects *Hol* and *Heil* have the same meaning [Sanscrit *Hailih*], whence is derived the adjective *Holig* or *Heilig,* which signifies *divine* or *holy,*—and, the aspiration being changed into the prepositive *S,* the Romans form their *Sol.*" And again, under the word *Bulæum* :—" We have also said, at the word *Bêl,* that it signified figuratively a *king,* but properly the *head.* It will therefore make no difference whether we write, according to the ancient dialects, *Bâl, Bêl, Bîl, Bôl, Bül ;* or *Mâl, Mêl, Mîl, Môl, Mül ;* or *Vâl, Vêl, Vîl, Vôl, Vü! ;* or *Fâl, Fêl, Fîl, Fôl, Fül ;* or finally, *Gâl, Gêl, Gîl, Gôl, Gül.* From *Gol* [in Baxter's Latin *Cranium,*] the Scoto-brigantes borrowed *Col,* the English *Skull,* and the Hebrews *Golgoleth,*—whence also the Syriac Γολγολθᾶ, and the Latin *Galea,* and *Galerus* [a *helmet*]. *Fal* also with the Scoto-brigantes means a *king,*—a word which the ancient Silures seem to have written indifferently *Bûl* and *Fûl.* Hence our *Bulæum* and *Caer Fyli,* or *Caer Fala,* which ought to be *Caer Bulach* and *Caer Falach,* meaning *royal city.*"

The justice of these observations will to the linguist at once appear obvious ; or, if a doubt of its extent occur, it will be immediately removed by a reference to the various words which, under the modifications above given, are found in the Celtic and Indo-European languages, to express objects into which the idea of rotundity enters. It will not, therefore, be considered visionary to inquire whether the Irish word *baile* (anglicized *bally,*) may not have had a similar origin. It will not admit of doubt that this word was originally applied to signify a *habitation*, and not *land*, though subsequently applied to denote the land belonging to a habitation, like *villa*, in the Law Latin,—and hence the constant recurrence of family names compounded with it when applied to townlands. In support of this fact numerous examples might be adduced from the most ancient Irish authorities, but the following entry in the Book of Kells, in the 11th century, is so decided as to make further evidence unnecessary:—"Muinrer Cennanra ro eopair Ard Camma .i. baile ui Uiorin cona muilinn ocur cona hepunn uili ocur baile ui Comgain cona hepunn uili ocur cona muiliunn do Dia ocur do Cholum cille," &c. "The family of Kells granted Ard-camma, i.e. Ballyheerin [O'Heerin's habitation], with its mill and with all ITS LAND, and Ballycoogan [O'Coogan's habitation], with all ITS LAND and with its mill, to God and to Columbkille," &c. Hence also the term baile biaraċ, literally *habitation of the* betagh, or *entertainer*, which was applied by the ancient Irish to signify a townland generally, as the modern Irish generally use the term baile taṁan for townland, and sometimes, especially in Munster, baile, absolutely, in the same sense, like *villa* in the Law Latin. Nor can it be questioned that in this sense of habitation, or village, the word *baile*, with all its modified changes, as *ball*, a *spot*, "balla, a wall,"—"ral, a wall, hedge, fold, circle" (O'REILLY), is referrible to the same source with the Welch *gual*, the English and German *wall*, the Icelandic or Gothic *bol*, the Latin *villa* (anciently written *vella*), *vallum*, *vallis*, and *ballium*, the Greek πόλις, and the Arabic *balad*. And, though this conjecture does not appear to have occurred to Baxter, it did not escape the critical mind of Pinkerton :—" This," he observes, " is another word, which might puzzle the most profound etymologist to determine, if really Celtic or Gothic. Nothing is more certain than that *Bal* and *Bally* are most frequent in Ireland, as initial of the names of towns ; and that *Baille*. in Irish, implies a city, town, or village. In Welch it means the head of a river flowing from a lake, as Twyne says [in Irish bel, from beal, or beul, a mouth] ; but, according to Price, a town. Davies doubts this last, except that it be from the Latin *Villa*, or the Arabic *Balad*, a town." " Nothing is also more certain, than that, in the Icelandic or Gothic, *Bol* is a town, or village. ' *Bol*. caput, πολος, Gr. bolwerk, *Bol*, rotundus.' Wachter. ' *Bal*, vide *Bol*.' *Id*. As the first towns were on the tops of hills, the consonance of *caput* and *rotundus* with a town is apparent. The Greek πόλος and πόλις are in singular agreement.' It is certain that *maol*, or *meall*, signifies in Ireland, as in Wales, a *round-shaped hill*, or *mountain* :—"meall, a hill, hillock, or any rising ground of a spherical shape" (O'BRIEN) : " meall, a globe, a ball, a lump, a mass, a heap" (O'REILLY). Pinkerton, however, is probably as much in error in supposing the first towns to have been on hills as O'Brien is in locating them in valleys ; at least it does not follow that towns, or habitations, took their name from the rotundity of hills, which are not always or necessarily round. And, if conjecture be allowed, it would appear to be more consistent with truth that the word originated in the circumstance of rotundity being connected with the primitive form of habitations in Ireland ; for it is certain that all the towns, inclosures, earthen works, fortresses, tombs, temples, and houses, in this country, before the introduction of Christianity, with the single exception of one constructed at Tara in the 3rd century, received this form : and it may be presumed that a similar mode was universal in the British Islands before the arrival of the Romans. St. Evin, a writer of the 6th century, in his Life of St. Patrick, makes a druid predict, that " one would come to Ireland, whose houses would be like the houses of the Romans, narrow and *angular* (*angustæ et* ANGULATÆ)"—a striking evidence that, previously to the introduction of Christianity into the island, no angular buildings were known.

In 1609 this townland was in the " occupation of John Howton."

BALLYARNET. Called *the quarter of Ballyarnell* in the Inquisition taken at Derry in 1609 ; *Ballyarnet* by Sampson ; and *Ballyarnett* in the tithe-book. The etymology of the latter part of this compound is uncertain : it would appear to be derived from the Irish family of O' hⱵaⱃnaoa, or Harnett, but this name is not found in the district.

BALLYMAGOWAN. Called *the half-quarter of Balliyam* in the Inquisition taken at Derry in 1609 ; and *Ballygan alias Ballygowan*, in the act 4 Anne. It is spelled *Ballinagowan* on Sampson's Map ; but *Ballymagowan*, the spelling adopted in the tithe-book, is now become the established name. The correct orthography is, however, *Ballynagananagh*, or baile na g-canánaċ—*the townland of the Canons*, or *Canonstown*—as it is written by the Four Masters at the year 1537, and as appears from an Inquisition taken at Derry in 1605, in which it is called the *Canons' Land*. In the Down Survey the northern part of this townland is marked as " many small parcels of land, belonging unto the City of Derry."

In 1609 this townland was in the " occupation of George Norman."

BALLYMAGRORTY. Called *Baile-meg-Rabhartaich* by Colgan ; *the quarter of Ballymᶜrewortie*, and *Bally Mᶜ Rowertie*, in the Inquisition taken at Derry in 1609 ; *the quarter of Ballymacrowretie, Bally mac-Roartie*, and *Ballymac-Rowrty*, in that taken at Lifford in 1621 ; *the quarter of Bally-Mac-Rowerty* in that taken at Donegal in 1625 ; and *Ballymagorty* in the Down Survey, but by mistake or ignorance. The signification is unquestionably *the town of* mac Róbaⱃtaⱨ, or *Mac Roverty*, now Magrorty—a family of the Kinel-owen, closely connected with the early ecclesiastical history of Derry, and probably *erenachs* here, as Colgan says there was a monastery anciently in this townland, the ruins of which were scarcely visible in his time (1647).—(*Triad. Thaum.* p. 495 ; col. 1.) Another branch of the Mac Rovertys, who were the keepers of the *Caah* of St. Columbkille, described by Sir William Betham in his Antiquarian Researches (— part 1.), gave name to *Baile-meg-Rabhartaich*, in the barony of Tirhugh.

BALLYNAGALLIAGH. Called *the half-quarter of Ballynecalliagh* in an Inquisition taken at Derry in 1602 ; *the quarter of Ballygalliagh* in that taken at Derry in 1609 ; *Ballynagaliagh* by Sampson ; and *Ballynagallagh* in the tithe-book. The meaning is unquestionably baile na g-cailleaċ, *the town of the nuns*, as it appears from the latter Inquisition that the jurors did, " upon their oathes, say and put [present] that there was a nunnery on the south side of the said cittie, in the iland of Derry, with a small garden or plott of ground called Garnegalliegh [ⱥaⱃóa na gcailleaċ, *the garden of the nuns*], and a quarter of land called Ballygalliagh to the said nunnery belonginge, and that the half quarter of land called Rossenegalliagh, lyinge in O'Chane's side, is parcell of the possessions of the said nunnery." Cailleaċ is the Irish word to denote an old woman who has borne no children, and also a nun. Cormac Mac Cullenan, fantastically derives it from the verb cail, to keep, and says it was a name for an old woman who keeps the house. Cailleaċ, when it signifies a *nun*, is derived from caille, Latin *vel-um, a veil*, or *cover*, q. d. *the veiled :* this rests on the authority of a very old Life of St. Bridget.

This townland has been in the possession of the Donegal family since 1620, but how it was acquired by them does not appear from the Inquisitions.

BALLYNAGARD. Called *Ballynagardie* in an Inquisition taken at Armagh previously to the settlement ; *the quarter of Ballinnegord* in one taken at Derry in 1602 ; *the quarter of Ballenegarde* in that taken at Derry in 1609 ; *Ballynagard* on Sampson's Map ; *Ballymagard* in his Memoir ; and *Ballynegard* in the tithe-book : *Ballymagard* has also, by corruption, become the popular name. The signification is probably baile na ⱥáⱃóa, *the town of the guard*, or *garrison :* thus *Stranagard*, in DESERTMARTIN, is named from a guard-house, a part of one wall of which still remains.

In 1609 this townland was in the " possession of capten Henrie Harte," whose descendant still retains it.

BALLYNASHALLOG. Called *the quarter of Gortneshalyg* in an Inquisition taken at Derry in 1602; *the quarter of Corneshalgagh* in that taken at Derry in 1609; *Ballynashanagh* on Sampson's Map, which means *town of the foxes*; and *Ballynashallog* in the tithe-book. The correct name is evidently ḃaıle na ṟealḃ, *the town of the chaces*, or *hunting*—a name synonymous with *Huntingdon*, in England. *Gortneshalyg*, or ᴳoṟᴈ na ṟealᴈ, means *the field of hunting*. The word *gort* is now understood in the north of Ireland to signify a glebe, but this meaning is not recognised by any Irish writer : Keating uses it to signify a tilled field, and O'Sullevan Beare translates it simply *ager*, and Colgan *prædium*.

It is obvious that in this sense the word is identified with the Welch *gardd*, Cornish *geare*, French *jardin*, Saxon *geard*, Gothic *gardr*, Latin *hortus*, a-*grum*, a-*ger*, a-*cra*, Greek ἀγρὸς, Sanscrit, a-*jirum*, Persian *gardah* (ploughed land—RICHARDSON), and Arabic *gaur*, or *gour*—(D'HERBELOT). But this sense of the word seems obviously derivative, or secondary, the original meaning being a circular inclosure :—"Goth. *garda*, a garden, from the Su. Goth. *gaerda*, to inclose, to hedge in.—(SERENIUS.) The same derivation is observable in other northern languages, v. Ludwig, Jura Feudorum, &c. p. 508. In like manner Mr. Horne Tooke deduces garden [Saxon *geard*,] from the Saxon *gyrdan*, to gird, to inclose."—(TODD's JOHNSON). The root of all these words seems to be the Persian *gird*, "a circle, round, orbit, circumference, circuit, rotundo"—(RICHARDSON) ; and hence, as in the word *bel*, already noticed, the various words in the Indo-European languages, expressing objects of a circular form, derived from this source—as the Persian *gardah*, a watch, guard ; Irish ᴈáṟoa ; Persian *garda*, wheeling round, encircling ; Greek γύρος ; Latin *gyrus*, and *gyro*, *circus*, and all its derivatives ; Irish cuaṟo—(O'REILLY) ; Cıṟ-ᴈoṟ, the ancient name of Stonehenge. Cormac Mac Cullenan thus derives the word ᴈṟıan, the common Irish name for the sun, the *Apollo Grynæus* of the Romans :—"ᴈṟıan a ᴈıṟanᴅo ᴄeṟṟam .ı. a cıṟcuıcu .ı. on cuaṟᴄuᴈaᴅ." "ᴈṟıan *a gyrando terram*, i.e. *a circuitû*, i.e. from its encircling the earth.' To the above may be added (with many others,) the following Irish words, collected from O'Brien's Dictionary, and Cormac's Glossary :—

Coṟ, a twist, a round or circular motion, a round hill : Latin *curvus*.

Cóṟ, a choir : Latin *chorus* ; *chorea*, the circular dance.

Coṟ, a round pit of water.

Coṟc, and coṟcán, a pot.

Coṟcóᴈ, a bee-hive.

Coıṟe, a cauldron, a whirlpool.

Coṟn, a horn, a drinking-cup : Latin *cornu* ; Greek κέρας ; Gothic *haúrn* ; Gaulish *carnon* ; Arabic *carnon* ; Syriac *carno*.

Coṟóın, a crown : Latin *corona* ; Greek κορώνη.

Ceıṟın, and Ceıṟnín, a dish, or platter.

Coṟᴄúıṟ, the border, or fringe, of a garment: English *garter*.

Caoṟ, a berry.

Cuaṟ, crooked : Welsh *guyr*.

Cuaıṟᴄ, a circulation, a circular visitation.

Cáṟn, a heap. "The true origin of the word caṟneaċ is from caṟn, a heap of stones, &c., on which the Druids or Pagan priests offered sacrifices to Belus ; whence the Armorics have the word *belec* to signify a priest."—(O'BRIEN.)

Caṟᴄ, and coıṟᴄ, the bark or rind of a tree, from the idea of circling : Latin *cortex*.

Caṟb, a basket : German *korb* ; Belgic *kerf*.

Caṟan, the crown of the head.

Caṟṟán, and Coṟṟán, a reaping-hook, derived from coṟ, a bend.

Caṟbaᴅ, the palate, or roof of the mouth.

Caṟbaᴅ, a chariot.

Cıoṟcaᴄ, a circle : Greek κίρκος ; Latin *circulus*, and *circus*.

Cṟoıᴅe, *q. d.* coṟoᴅe, the heart : Latin *cor* ; Greek καρδία.

Cṟo, a hovel, a fortress.

Cṟom, stooped, bent : Belgic *krom* ; German *krumb* (now *krumm*) ; Welch *krum*.

Cṟuınn, round : Welch *krun*.

Cṟuınne, the world—*orbis terrarum*.

Cṟıoṟ, *q. d.* cıṟıoṟ, a girdle : Armorican *guris* ; Welch *guregis* ; Cornish *grigis*.

Cṟıoṟ, cṟeaṟ, the sun : Phœnician *cares*.

ᴈaṟᴄ, a head.

ᴈaṟᴄán, a bonnet, a cap.

ᴈṟán, grain.

ᴈṟeıᴅeal, a griddle, *q. d.* girdle : British *gradell*, a grid-iron.

ᴈṟıoᴄ, *q. d.* ᴈṟıoᴄ, the sun.

ᴈṟaún, a hedge-hog.

The Irish caᴄaıṟ (pronounced *cahir*), a circular uncemented stone fort, and, figuratively, a city, appears also to be of the same stock :—"Brit. *kaer* ; Scythice, *car* ; Antiq. Saxon. *caerten* ; Goth. *gards* ; Cantab. *caria* ; Brit. *ker* ; Heb. קרת ; Phœn. and Pun. *kartha* ; Chaldaice, *kartha* ; and Syriace, *karitita* ; Græce, χαραξ. N. B. Malec-karthus, or Mel-karthus, i.e. king of the city, was an appellative of the Phœnician Hercules, said to be the founder of the city of Tyre.—(O'BRIEN). (And as the Phœnicians are acknowledged to have introduced their religion into the British Isles, hence probably the inscriptions to the god BEL-ATU-CADRUS, or BEL-ATA-CADER, *the father king of the city*, found in different parts of England, and so long a puzzle to the learned.) As in this sense no directly cognate word is found in Latin, the philologist, if he please, may add to the above the word *urbs*, its nearest parallel, which is derived by lexicographers from *urbum* (sometimes written *urvum*):—"*Nam urbare et orbare est circulo circumscribere*."—(SCALIGER.) It is not improbable that the Latins omitted the *c*, as in the word *ramus*, Celtic *craomh*, and as they rejected the *g* in *hortus*. Thus it might have been originally *curbus*, or *curvus*, next *curbs*, then, aspirating the *c*, *churbs*, next *hurbs*, and finally *urbs*. It is certain that many changes as remarkable may be found in other Latin words, from the aspiration or rejection of initial consonants. Finally :—if the two words *gort* and *baile*, which are so similar in several of their meanings, be not originally derived from different families of language, it is probable that the former originally denoted a *circle* or *girdle*, the latter a *ball* or *solid round*,—and that in course of time these primary ideas were sometimes abandoned, or neglected, in the derivative application of the words to objects of an orbicular and circular form.

In 1609 this townland was in the "occupation of Walter Tallon."

CLOUGHGLASS. This name does not appear in the Inquisitions. It is written *Cloughglass* by Sampson ; and *Cloghglss* [*Cloghglass*], and *Clochlass*, in the tithe-book. In the Down Survey the townland immediately to the north of *Edenballymore*, and evidently occupying the situation of this, is called *Knocktall*. *Cloughglass*, in Irish Cloċ ᴈlaṟ, means *green stone*. This small townland is probably a modern subdivision of some more extensive ancient denomination.

COSHQUIN. Called *the half-quarter of Costquoyne* in the Inquisition taken at Derry in 1609 ; *the half-quarter of Coskenie*, and *Coskeyne*, in that taken at Lifford in 1621 ; *Coshquin* by Sampson ; and *Cosquin* in the tithe-book. The orthography would at first sight seem obscure, but to a person acquainted with the general nomenclature of Ireland it will not appear inexplicable. The word coṟ is explained by O'Brien thus :—"Coṟ, the foot, the leg, is like the Greek πους, & the Latin *pes* ; the letters *C* and *P* being often commutable with respect to the Greek & Irish :" these are traceable to the Gothic, from which the English *foot* is evidently derived. From this word coṟ is formed the preposition coıṟ, or a-coıṟ (the preposition *a*, *at*, or *in*, being understood—), near to, hard by, alongside of, along, as coıṟ na ṟaınᴈe, by the sea, *i. e.* literally—by the foot of the sea. In like manner "láıṁ, from láṁ, the hand ;" as O'Brien remarks, "láıṁ ṟe, and láıṁ ṟıṟ, near at hand, close to, hard by. A barony in the county of Waterford bears the name of Coιρ bρίɟσe, *Coshbride,* i.e. along the Bride, from its stretching along the banks of a river of that name ; and another barony in the county of Limerick has derived the appellation of Coιρ Maɨʒe, *Coshma,* from its lying along the river Maig. In the county of Antrim the names of *Cushendun* and *Cushendall* are derived from two rivers, anciently, but not at present, called *Dun* and *Dall :* it is therefore highly probable that the stream that flows by this townland into Lough Swilly, the name of which is now lost, was anciently called cαoιn, or the beautiful (*amœna*—COLGAN), and that the townland received the appellation of coιρ cαoιne from its situation on its banks. Cαoιn would be a very appropriate Irish name for a stream, as such appellations are constantly given to them ; for example uιρce cαoιn, fair water, now *Eskaheen,* in Inishowen : ꝼιonn, white, or bright ; ʒlαn, and its diminutive ʒlαnόʒ, clean ; συb, black ; ꝼιonn ʒlαρ, the bright green, &c. Sampson explains *Coshquin* as rabbit's-foot ; but the Irish word which signifies rabbit is not *quin,* but *coinin* (coιnín).

CREEVAGH (UPPER and LOWER). Called *the quarter of Crivagh* in an Inquisition taken at Derry in 1602 ; *Crevagh* in that taken at Derry in 1609 ; *Creevagh* in the Act 4 Anne ; *Creevagh* by Sampson ; and *Creevy* in the tithe-book. It is an anglicizing of the Irish word cραοbαċ, which literally means *bushy,* but which is constantly used, in a topographical sense, to signify *bushy* or *shrubby land.* Respecting Cραοb, correctly Cραοṁ, O'Brien observes :—"Cράοṁ, a branch ; Lat. *ramus ;* either the Latins threw off the *c,* or the Celts prefixed it."

This townland was a possession of the abbey of Derry ; and was in 1609 in the "occupation of Denis O'Dery," who was probably the *erenach.* This family, called in Irish O'Oαιɟρe, which is now anglicized *Deery,* were a branch of the *Kinel-Owen,* and for many centuries hereditary *erenachs* of half the church-lands of the monastery of Derry, namely—those in the diocese of Raphoe.

CREGGAN. Called *the quarter of Craggin, Cargan,* and *Cregg,* in the Inquisition taken at Derry in 1609 ; and *Craggabell* in the Down Survey. Cρeαʒαn means *rocky ground.* [See *Edenballymore.*]

It is stated in the Down Survey that the half of *Craggabell* belonged to the church of Derry.

CULMORE. The fort is called *Cuil more* by O'Sullevan Beare ; and *Culmoore* by Pynnar ; and the place is called αn cúιl ṁόρ by the Four Masters ; the fort is called *Coolemore* in the Inquisition taken at Derry in 1609 ; and the townland, in which it stands, *the half-quarter of Laharden ;* it is called *Coolemore alias Culemore* in the charters of James 1., and Charles II. ; *Coulemore alias Culmore,* in that of Cromwell ; *Kilmore* in a manuscript in the Lambeth Library, the Southwell MSS., &c. ; and *Culmore* by Sampson. O'Sullevan Beare, in his account of the rebellion [*motus*] of Sir Cahir O'Doherty, translates *Cuil more* by *angulus magnus,* i.e. *great corner,* which is the true meaning, and descriptive of the locality. The two Irish words—cúl and cúιl—are sometimes confounded by Irish topographers ; they are, however, distinct—cúl signifying a back, or retired place, and cúιl a corner, or angle. Cúιl eαċραnn (now *Culfeighterin*), the name of the north-eastern corner of Antrim, affords another corroboration of the real meaning of this word. *Laharden*—in Irish leαt áρσán—the " *alias*" name of this townland, signifies *the half hill,* by which is meant a gently sloping hill.

EDENBALLYMORE. This townland is not named in the Inquisitions. It is called *Edenballimore,* and *Edenballymore,* in the Down Survey ; and *Edenballymore* by Sampson. The name is evidently eυσαn bαιle mόρ, which means *the large townland on the brow, or face, of the hill.* eυσαn bαιle is Brae-face-town ; and the adjectives mόρ, *large,* and beαʒ, *small,* were generally postfixed to the names of Irish townlands, when a denomination, originally one, was subdivided into a larger and smaller portion. Though this is the prevalent usage throughout Ireland there is no *Edenballybeg* to be now found in this neighbourhood.

The Irish word eυσαn is translated *frons* by Cormac Mac Cullenan, and generally signifies the human forehead, but when used topographically it signifies the brow of a hill—generally, but not always, the southern or sunny side ; and the opposite of cúl, the back, or northern side, of a hill. Keating defines the meaning of this word completely when he states that the river Barrow springs from the *eden,* or brow, of Slieve Bloom :—"1ρ ꝼolluρ ʒuρ αb ó heυσαn ρléιbe blαόmα σon leιτ ꝼoιρ σ'ꝼáραρ beαρbα."

Lluyd observes, "that the most common way [among the Britons,] of naming hills was by metaphors from the parts of the body," as *bron* the breast, *llygad* an eye, *geneu* the mouth, *braich* an arm, &c. In Ireland likewise places are found, which take their names from a comparison with almost every member of the human frame.

It appears from the Down Survey, which was finished in 1657, that 224 acres of this townland were then held under lease by Captain Alexander Staples, and 12 acres of the south-eastern corner of it " a controversie." It seems to have been included in the bishop's lands, called *the quarter of Craggin* and *Drumniurney,* and *the half-quarter of Courneglogh,* which lay on the northern side of the bog, near the Island of Derry.—(See *Inquisition, taken at Derry in* 1609.)

ELAGHMORE. Called in the most ancient Irish MSS. indifferently Cιleαċ and Oιleαċ (both which are pronounced *Ellagh,* according to the Ulster mode of pronouncing the diphthongs αι and oι, when short) ; and *the quarter of Ellaughmore,* and *Ellaghmore,* in the Inquisition taken at Lifford in 1621 (—the *l* being doubled, to secure the short sound of the *e*). It is written *Elaghmore* by Sampson, who remarks that the district is called *Ely.* A full explanation of this name will be found in the account of the Grianan of Aileach, and in that of the ruined castle of the O'Dohertys, which stands in this townland.

The adjective mόρ, *large,* is postfixed to the name of this townland, to distinguish it from the smaller townland of *Elaghbeg,* which lies to the west of it, outside the boundary of the county.

KILLEA. Called *the quarter of Killeigh* in an Inquisition taken at Derry in 1602 ; *the half-quarter of Kellegh* in that taken at Derry in 1609 ; *Killeigh alias Killeagh* in the Act 4 Anne ; *Keelagh* by Sampson, incorrectly ; and *Killea* in the tithe-book. The name may be an anglicizing either of Cιll lιατ, *grey church,* or, more probably, of Cιll ꝼιαch (pronounced *Killiagh*), *Fiach's church.* It is certain that Killeagh, in Meath, was thus derived, as St. Fiach is there venerated as the patron ; and it is most probable that the church owed its origin to another saint of that name, though no longer remembered in the district, as it appears from Mac Firbis's List of the Saints descended from Eogan, or Owen, the prince of this territory, that there were two bishops of the name in the 6th century—one a son, and the other a grandson of that prince.—(See MAC FIRBIS: p. 701.) The old church of Killea, which is situated in, and gave name to this townland, was anciently, according to Archbishop King's Visitation Book, one of five chapels-of-ease to the church of Derry—namely, Burt, Iniskehin, [Eskaheen, now Muff], Inch, Killeah [Killeagh], and (as he supposed) Grange. This church, however, was properly in the diocese of Raphoe, which, according to Bishop Downham's Visitation Book, extended in his time even into the Island of Derry,—and its name has been given to the adjacent parish in that diocese.

In 1609 this townland was in the "occupation of Francis White."

MULLENNAN. Called *the quarter of Moylenong,* in an Inquisition taken at Derry, in 1602 ; *the quarter of Mallennan* in that taken at Derry in 1609 ; *Mollenam* (erroneously for *Mollenan,*) in the Act 4 Anne ; *Mollenan* by Sampson ; and *Mullenan* in the tithe-book.

The meaning of this name is, possibly Muιlleαnn enna, *Enna* or *Anna's Mill*—Enna, or Annadh, being a male proper name, current in Ireland down to the 16th century. It appears at least certain that the word muιlleαnn (*molendinum*), a mill, forms the first part of the compound, as the ruins of a mill still exist in the townland.

As this word muilleann enters into the names of many ancient places in Ireland, it will not be irrelevant to give some account of the introduction of water-mills into the country.

It might be supposed from a passage in Dr. Ledwich (—see *Antiquities of Ireland* : p. 373,) that water-mills were nearly unknown in this island until a comparatively recent period,—but it would appear from early authorities that they were even more common in ancient than they are in modern times, when the mechanical force of the mill, and the facilities of communication by roads have been both increased. It is clear, from the Brehon Laws (*MSS. Trinity College: Class E ; Tab.* 3 ; *No.* 5), that they were common in the country at a very early period, and in the records of the grants of land to the monastery of Kells, preserved in its ancient Book, it would appear that, whenever the locality permitted, the *mill* was a common appendage to a *ballybetagh*, or ancient townland. For example :—"Muinτερ Cennanτa ρo eoραιη Αρo camma .i. baile ui Uroρín cona muiliuno ocuτ cona heρuno uili ocuτ baile ui Comτain cona heρuno uili ocuτ cona muiliuno oo Dia ocuτ oo Cholum cille," &c. "The family of Kells granted Ard-camma, i. e. Ballyheerin, with ITS MILL and with all its land, and Ballycoogan, with all its land and with ITS MILL, to God and to Columbkille," &c.—(*Book of Kells: MS. Trinity College.*) This grant was made in the middle of the 11th century, and similar notices occur in the Registry of Clonmacnoise about the same period. The charter also of lands granted to the monastery of Newry by King Muircheartach, or Mauritius M'Loughlin, about the year 1161, after enumerating the several townlands, adds "*Has terras cum* MOLENDINIS, *ex dono meo proprio, dictis monachis confirmavi,*" &c.—"(CLARENDON *MSS. in the British Museum :* vol. 45.—in *Ayscough's Catalogue* 4792.—*Plut. VIII. C. p.* 179.) The Lives of Irish Saints shew that mills were erected by ecclesiastics, shortly after the introduction of Christianity, as the mills of St. Senanus, St. Ciaran, St. Mochua, &c.—(See the Lives of these Saints.) The mills of St. Lucherin and St. Fechin are noticed by Giraldus Cambrensis ; and a mill at Fore, built on the ancient site of the latter, still exists, and is called St. Fechin's Mill.

The Annals of Tigernach, at the year 651, record that the two sons of Blamac (king of Ireland), son of Hugh Slaine, Donchad and Conall, were mortally wounded by the Lagenians in Maelodrain's mill.

The Four Masters also, at the year 998, record that a remarkable stone called *Lia-Ailbhe*, which stood on the plain of Moynalvy, in Meath, fell, and that the king, Maelsechlainn, made four mill-stones of it.

From the preceding authorities, as well as from the classical etymology of the name, in Ireland as in every other country of Europe, it might be supposed that water-mills were first introduced by Christian ecclesiastics. There is reason, however, to believe that their introduction is of higher antiquity. Cuan O'Lochain, chief poet and lawgiver of Ireland, whose death is recorded in the Annals of Tigernach, at the year 1024, states in his poem on the ruins then existing at Tara—that Cormac, the son of Art, chief monarch of Ireland in the 3rd century, had a beautiful *cumal*, or bond-maid, named Ciarnad, who was obliged to grind a certain quantity of corn every day with a *bro*, or quern,—but that the king, observing her beauty, took her into his house, *and sent across the sea* for a millwright (τuτ ραοη Muilinn τaρ móρ cuino), who constructed a mill on the stream of Nith, which flows from the fountain of Neamhnach to the north-east of Tara. The ancient Irish authorities all agree in stating that this was the *first* mill ever erected in Ireland ; and it is remarkable that this circumstance is still most vividly preserved by tradition, not only in the neighbourhood, where a mill still occupies its site, but also in most parts of Ireland. Tradition adds, that it was from the king of Scotland the Irish monarch obtained the millwright, and it can be shewn that the probability of its truth is strongly corroborated by that circumstance.

Professor Tennant, of St. Andrew's, in an ingenious Essay on Corn-mills, states, that "the first corn-mill driven by water was invented and set up by Mithridates, king of Cappadocia, the most talented, studious, and ingenious prince of any age or country. It was set up in the neighbourhood of his capital, or palace, about seventy years before the commencement of the Christian era. It was probably from this favourable circumstance of the invention of the water-mill, and the facility thereby afforded to the Cappadocian people for making cheap, good, and abundant flour, that the Cappadocian bakers obtained high celebrity, and were much in demand for two or three centuries posterior to the invention of mills, throughout all the Roman world. Coincident with the era of the inventor, as mentioned by Strabo, is the date of the Greek epigram on water-mills by Antipater, a poet of Syria, or Asia Minor, who is supposed to have lived sixty or eighty years before Christ. This epigram may be thus translated :—

" Ye maids who toil'd so faithful at the mill,
Now cease from work, and from these toils be still;
Sleep now till dawn, and let the birds with glee
Sing to the ruddy morn on bush and tree;
For what your hands perform'd so long, so true,
Ceres has charg'd the water-nymphs to do:
They come, the limpid sisters, to her call,
And on the wheel with dashing fury fall;
Impel the axle with a whirling sound,
And make the massy mill-stone reel around,
And bring the floury heaps luxuriant to the ground.

"The greater convenience and expedition in working of these water-mills soon made them be spread over the world. In about twenty or thirty years after their invention, one was set up on the Tiber. They must have been not uncommon in Italy in the age of Vitruvius, for he gives a description of them. Yet it is rather surprising that Pliny, whose eye nothing of art or nature escapes, has taken no notice of them."

This learned writer errs, however, respecting Pliny. The following passage is quite conclusive on this subject :—"*Major pars Italiæ ruido utitur pilo, rotis etiam quas aqua verset obiter, et molat.*"—(*Hist. Nat.* lib. 18 ; c. 10.) Whitaker shews that a water-mill was probably erected by the Romans at every stationary city in Roman Britain : they were certainly numerous during their time ; and this fact strongly corroborates the date assigned to the erection of the mill near Tara, as well as the tradition relative to its origin, derived most probably from the Roman portion of Scotland which lay nearest to Ireland, and which, during the reign of Cormac, was in the possession of the Picts.

In 1609 this townland was in the "occupation of John Woodes."

PENNYBURN. The name of this townland is thus spelled in every authority hitherto discovered, and must have been a name imposed by the English colony, as it is not of Irish origin. In the Teutonic dialects, according to Verstegan, *burn*, or *bourne*, signifies a stream. It has been added by the Scotch settlers to the names of several small rivers in the north of Ireland,—as in *Burndale*, the name of the celebrated river in Donegal, called *Daelia* in the Latin Lives of Columbkille, and Daoil by the Four Masters.

SHANTALLOW. This townland is not named in Sampson's Map, nor in any ancient document hitherto discovered : it is written *Shantallow* in the tithe-book. The meaning of the name is evidently Seán Talaṁ, *senex tellus*, i. e. *old land*,—but why it originally received such an appellation would be now difficult to ascertain : perhaps land a long time tilled might be so called, in contradistinction to contiguous land lately reclaimed.

SHERIFF'S MOUNTAIN. This townland is not mentioned in the Inquisitions, and, as its name indicates, is evidently a modern sub-denomination of some ancient quarter, or townland—most probably of *Ballymagrorty*. It was allotted to the sheriffs before a salary was annexed to their office.

SPRINGHILL. This townland also appears to be a sub-denomination of *Ballymagrorty*.

SPRINGTOWN. This townland appears to be a sub-denomination of *Ballymagrorty*, or *Shantallow*.

TERMONBACCA. Called *the quarter of Termonbackagh* in an Inquisition taken at Derry in 1602 ; *Termonbaccoe* in that taken at Derry in 1609 ; *Termonbacco* in the Act 4 Anne ; and *Tirmonbacca*, incorrectly, by Sampson.

The meaning is evidently ⅭeαⱤmαⱤn bαcαⅠⱫ—i. e., *the* termon *of the cripple*. But why it received the appellation *termon*, or the additional epithet of *bacca*, it would be now vain to conjecture, as after careful research no historical elucidation has been discovered.

In 1609 this townland was in the "possession of Sir Thomas Phillipps."

WHITEHOUSE or BALLYMAGRORTY. This townland is a sub-denomination of the *Ballymagrorty*, treated of above. The name *Whitehouse* is said to have been derived from an old English habitation, the ruins of which still remain.

In the "Preliminary Notice" to the Memoir, the historical importance of tracing the derivation of the Townland Names is noticed as follows :—

"Thus, a subject of the earliest necessity to the Maps themselves, afforded a basis for historic inquiries. The mode of spelling the names of places was peculiarly vague and unsettled, but on the Maps about to be constructed, it was desirable to establish a standard orthography, and for future reference, to identify the several localities with the names by which they had formerly been called; and as the townland, and other divisions under various denominations, have existed over the whole of Ireland from the earliest times, it soon became apparent, that a sufficient extension of the original orthographic inquiries, to trace all the mutations of each name, would be, in fact, to pass in review the local history of the whole country."

On this subject I beg to refer to a paper, written by Sir Thomas Larcom in 1846, on the "Territorial Divisions of the Country," which was published in the following year, by order of the Government, in the First Part of the "Relief Correspondence of the Commissioners of Public Works." This paper, I may observe, although professing to be merely an outline, contains much valuable matter in a concise form. It closes with a reference to the ancient manuscripts of the Brehon Laws, as the source from which incomparably the most valuable information on this subject generally is to be derived, "which it is very much to be desired the Government would publish, as they have the Laws of Howel Da, and the Saxon Laws." It is satisfactory to know that the publication of these ancient laws has been subsequently sanctioned, and is now in progress, the transcription, collation, and translation being understood to be already complete. With this national and historic work, the names of the Rev. Dr. Todd, the Very Rev. Dean Graves, and Dr. O'Donovan and Professor O'Curry, will ever be honorably associated ; and it is only to be hoped that the irreparable loss which Irish literature has sustained by the recent death of Dr. O'Donovan may not retard the editorial labours of the publication.

The "History of the Down Survey," edited by Sir Thomas Larcom for the Irish Archæological Society in 1851, is also interspersed with much interesting information relative to the several territorial denominations.

I also beg to refer to a paper on the "Townland Distribution of Ireland," which was read by the Rev. William Reeves, D.D., before the Royal Irish Academy in April last, and since published in the Proceedings of that body. In the course of this erudite and comprehensive paper the learned writer makes the following observations as to the great utility of the present publication :—

Entertaining the belief that the present townland names of Ireland not only preserve a great many ancient forms, but afford very interesting materials for philological deductions, both as regards the distribution of certain words, and the local varieties of the same word, feeling also the want of some comprehensive book of reference in the important work of the identification of ancient names, I undertook, in 1853, to compile an alphabetical index to all the townland names of Ireland, which I found to exceed sixty-two thousand in number. After a considerable amount of mechanical labour, I succeeded, in 1857, in producing the desired catalogue, in the form of these two large volumes which I have now the honour to exhibit to the meeting. The plan I adopted was, to divide the page into five columns, the first of which gave the townland ; the second, in the same line, the parish ; the third, the barony ; the fourth, the county ; and the fifth, open for the etymology, where attainable. I should have been glad to have given the acreable extent of each ; but the Addenda to the Census of 1841, from which I made my compilation, did not supply the desired information. It was my intention to have presented these books to the Academy as a work of public reference in topographical inquiry; but I lately learned that a similar index, containing all my items, and further supplying the areas, with a reference under each name to the sheet or sheets where it appeared on the Ordnance Survey, had been compiled from the Census of 1851, to which it was designed to serve as an alphabetical reference, and that it was likely, within a short time, to be published, and, of course, find its way to our library. It appeared to me, therefore, that it would be of no advantage to occupy a place in our shelves with an inferior production. It has, for several years, however, done good service, not only to the compiler, but some of his literary friends, who, in their difficulties, sought counsel of the "monster Index." The printed Index will form an invaluable book of reference, and I hope that its appearance will promote investigations into the interesting topography of our island : certainly the Census list of 1851, with its admirable details, and this Index to follow it, will prove a rich treasury of topographical illustration ; and ere long I hope to see the series on our shelves divested of their blue wrappers, and recommended to notice by a becoming exterior. It is impossible to over-estimate the importance of such a work as this to the topographer. Not only is he enabled hereby to trace to its proper position the site of an ancient church, or the field of a distant encounter, or the subject of an early grant, but he has also materials for the correction of etymological fallacies, and the establishment of a true standard of interpretation.

Endless are the curious applications and combinations of Irish words which such an Index presents to view. What a boon to Irish topography would the forthcoming compilation be, if it had but one column more, namely, an etymological one. There is no member of society, from the great landed proprietor down to the humblest antiquarian student, who would not welcome with delight the appearance of such a work. In some words considerable difficulty would attend the interpretation ; but the majority could be surely ascertained and safely expounded ; for it would be found that certain prevailing elements of composition pervaded the names to a great extent ; in which, as has already been observed, *Bally*, is so frequent; *Kill*, the first syllable of 2,890 names, representing, according to the combination, either *Cill* "cella," "church," or *Caille*, "sylva," "a wood ;" *Drum*, "dorsum," "a ridge," introduces 2,000 names ; *Knock*, "a hill," 1,600 ; *Lis*, "an enclosed abode," now called "a fort," 1,380 ; *Derry*, "an oak wood," 1,310 ; *Cluain*, "a meadow," 756, in the form *Clon*, and 924 in that of *Cloon*. The etymologicon, however, to be complete, would require a careful comparison of the old forms of the townland names, as found in Inquisitions, Patents, and kindred records, which were much purer than those now in use, as approaching nearer to the fountain head, and as current at a time when the Irish language was comparatively uninfluenced by foreign influence or intermixture.

I have thus indicated some of the various sources of information on this interesting subject, in the hope that those who have leisure will refer to the original documents ; and that by continued research the history which lies enshrined in local names may yet be preserved to the country, and rendered accessible to the public.

It is proper here to add, that since the publication of the first edition of the Ordnance Maps, power has been vested in the Lord Lieutenant and Privy Council to change the names and boundaries of townlands when the straightening of river courses, reclamation from the sea, or other circumstances, have rendered it necessary. The cases, however, will not be numerous, and no inconvenience or error from this cause need arise, if all the precautions required by the Acts of Parliament be, as they doubtless will be, duly observed.

I have the honour to be,

Your Excellency's very faithful servant,

WILLIAM DONNELLY,

Registrar-General.

HENRY WILKIE,
    Chief Clerk.

AGRICULTURAL AND EMIGRATION STATISTICS OFFICE,
    12*th December*, 1861.

CENSUS OF IRELAND

FOR THE YEAR

1851.

GENERAL ALPHABETICAL INDEX

TO THE

TOWNLANDS AND TOWNS OF IRELAND,

With the Number of the Sheet of the Ordnance Survey Maps in which they appear; the Areas of the Townlands in Statute Acres; the County, Barony, Parish, and Poor Law Union in which they are situated; also the Volume and Page of the Townland Census of 1851—which contain the Population and Number of Houses in 1841 and 1851, and the Poor Law Valuation in 1851.

₊ The names of Towns are printed in SMALL CAPITALS, and those of *Islands* which are not Townlands in *Italics*.

No. of Sheet of the Ordnance Survey Maps.	Townlands and Towns.	Area in Statute Acres.	County.	Barony.	Parish.	Poor Law Union in 1857.	Townland Census of 1851, Part I.	
		A. R. P.					Vol.	Page
34	Abartagh	34 2 32	Waterford	Decies within Drum	Clashmore	Youghal	II.	351
97	Abberanville	24 0 29	Galway	Athenry	Kiltullagh	Loughrea	IV.	4
93	Abbernadoorny	62 3 27	Donegal	Banagh	Killymard	Donegal	III.	111
58	Abbert	178 3 30*a*	Galway	Tiaquin	Monivea	Tuam	IV.	78
58, 59	Abbert Demesne	1,293 2 21*b*	Galway	Tiaquin	Monivea	Tuam	IV.	78
4	Abbeville	943 2 7	Tipperary, N.R.	Lower Ormond	Lorrha	Borrisokane	II.	285
118	Abbey	27 0 22	Cork, W.R.	Bantry	Kilmocomoge	Bantry	II.	119
116,117,125	Abbey	334 3 28	Galway	Leitrim	Ballynakill	Portumna	IV.	50
58	Abbey	875 3 7	Galway	Tiaquin	Abbeyknockmoy	Tuam	IV.	75
56	Abbey	222 3 21	Limerick	Coshlea	Kilflyn	Kilmallock	II.	240
13	Abbeycartron	219 2 20	Longford	Longford	Templemichael	Longford	I.	160
16	Abbeycartron	32 1 3	Roscommon	Roscommon	Elphin	Strokestown	IV.	209
18,19,22,23	Abbeyderg	867 2 21	Longford	Moydow	Taghsheenod	Ballymahon	I.	162
21	ABBEYDORNEY T.	—	Kerry	Clanmaurice	O'Dorney	Tralee	II.	173
4	Abbeydown	454 3 6	Wexford	Scarawalsh	Moyacomb	Shillelagh	I.	325
3	Abbey East	301 0 12	Clare	Burren	Abbey	Ballyvaghan	II.	11
47	Abbeyfarm	55 1 12	Limerick	Kilmallock	St.Peter's & St.Paul's	Kilmallock	II.	250
42, 51	Abbeyfeale East	1,350 3 23	Limerick	Glenquin	Abbeyfeale	Newcastle	II.	244
42	ABBEYFEALE T.	—	Limerick	Glenquin	Abbeyfeale	Newcastle	II.	244
42	Abbeyfeale West	718 2 4*c*	Limerick	Glenquin	Abbeyfeale	Newcastle	II.	244
86	Abbeyfield	18 0 36	Galway	Kilconnell	Kilconnell	Ballinasloe	IV.	40
107	Abbeygormacan	94 1 18	Galway	Longford	Abbeygormacan	Ballinasloe	IV.	56
33	Abbeygrey or Monasternalea	503 1 14	Galway	Killian	Athleague	Mountbellew	IV.	43
33	Abbeygrey or Monasternalea	157 3 37	Galway	Killian	Killeroran	Mountbellew	IV.	44
20	Abbeygrove	59 0 25	Kilkenny	Gowran	Blanchvilleskill	Kilkenny	I.	93
29	Abbeyhalfquarter	247 0 29	Sligo	Tireragh	Kilmoremoy	Ballina	IV.	235
107	Abbey Island	17 1 33	Donegal	Tirhugh	Kilbarron	Ballyshannon	III.	148
106	Abbey Island	83 1 23	Kerry	Dunkerron South	Kilcrohane	Cahersiveen	II.	183
20	Abbey Land	9 0 3	Cavan	Upper Loughtee	Urney	Cavan	III.	86
14	Abbeyland	68 3 19*d*	Kildare	Clane	Clane	Naas	I.	53
40	Abbeyland	144 2 3	Kildare	Kilkea and Moone	Castledermot	Athy	I.	59
15, 20	Abbey Land	9 0 11	Longford	Ardagh	Mostrim	Granard	I.	152
27	Abbeyland	92 2 23	Meath	Lower Duleek	Duleek	Drogheda	I.	195
25	Abbeyland	327 2 33	Meath	Lower Navan	Navan	Navan	I.	215
6, 7	Abbeyland	75 1 25	Westmeath	Corkaree	Multyfarnham	Mullingar	I.	263
11	Abbeyland and Charlestown or Ballynamonaster	230 1 6	Westmeath	Moygoish	Kilbixy	Mullingar	I.	279
100, 108	Abbeyland Great	812 1 6	Galway	Longford	Clonfert	Ballinasloe	IV.	56
101	Abbeyland Little	231 3 5	Galway	Longford	Clonfert	Ballinasloe	IV.	56
17	Abbeyland North	26 0 8	Galway	Dunmore	Dunmore	Tuam	IV.	33
112	Abbey-lands	20 3 14	Cork, E.R.	Kinsale	Kinsale	Kinsale	II.	100

(a) Including 3A. 2R. 16P. water.
(b) Including 12A. 3R. 24P. water.
(c) Including 6A. 3R. 5P. water.
(d) Including 5A. 3R. 32P. water.

No. of Sheet of the Ordnance Survey Maps.	Townlands and Towns.	Area in Statute Acres.	County.	Barony.	Parish.	Poor Law Union in 1857.	Townland Census of 1851, Part I.	
		A. R. P.					Vol.	Page
111, 112	Abbey-lands (in 5 pts.)	106 3 32a	Cork, E.R.	Kinsale	Ringcurran	Kinsale	II.	100
107	Abbeylands	173 0 34	Donegal	Tirhugh	Kilbarron	Ballyshannon	III.	148
47	Abbeylands	171 0 29	Kerry	Trughanacmy	Kilcolman	Killarney	II.	210
29	Abbeylands	105 0 35	Limerick	Connello Lower	Rathkeale	Rathkeale	II.	229
22	Abbeylands	40 1 30	Mayo	Tirawley	Killala	Killala	IV.	169
9, 10	Abbeylands	234 3 24b	Waterford	Gaultiere	Kilculliheen	Waterford	II.	363
40, 45	Abbeylands	115 2 34	Wicklow	Arklow	Arklow	Rathdrum	I.	341
17	Abbeyland South	22 3 14	Galway	Dunmore	Dunmore	Tuam	IV.	33
25	Abbeyland South	120 0 23	Meath	Lower Navan	Navan	Navan	I.	215
11	Abbeylara	296 0 12	Longford	Granard	Abbeylara	Granard	I.	154
11	ABBEYLARA T.	—	Longford	Granard	Abbeylara	Granard	I.	154
23, 29	Abbeyleix Demesne	1,321 3 14	Queen's Co.	Cullenagh	Abbeyleix	Abbeyleix	I.	238
23	ABBEYLEIX T.		Queen's Co.	Cullenagh	Abbeyleix	Abbeyleix	I.	238
123, 136	Abbeymahon	526 0 21	Cork, W.R.	Ibane and Barryroe	Abbeymahon	Clonakilty	II.	148
12	Abbey Park	14 3 38	Armagh	Armagh	Armagh	Armagh	III.	43
87, 88, 100	Abbeypark	283 2 12	Galway	Clonmacnowen	Clontuskert	Ballinasloe	IV.	24
93, 103	Abbeyquarter	193 1 6	Mayo	Costello	Annagh	Claremorris	IV.	137
14	Abbeyquarter North	54 1 11	Sligo	Carbury	St. John's	Sligo	IV.	223
14	Abbeyquarter South	111 3 11	Sligo	Carbury	St. John's	Sligo	IV.	223
23, 24, 27	Abbeyshrule	769 1 29c	Longford	Shrule	Abbeyshrule	Ballymahon	I.	165
31	Abbeyside	177 3 20	Waterford	Decies without Drum	Dungarvan	Dungarvan	II.	354
149	ABBEY STRAND T.	—	Cork, W.R.	West Carbery, (E.D.)	Tullagh	Skibbereen	II.	141
141	Abbeystrowry	428 0 17	Cork, W.R.	West Carbery, (E.D.)	Abbeystrowry	Skibbereen	II.	136
42	Abbeytown	263 1 30	Galway	Clare	Donaghpatrick	Tuam	IV.	19
29, 38	Abbeytown	124 2 22	Mayo	Tirawley	Crossmolina	Ballina	IV.	165
20	Abbeytown	350 1 15	Sligo	Leyny	Ballysadare	Sligo	IV.	230
83	ABBEY T.	—	Tipperary, S.R.	Iffa and Offa East	Inishlounaght	Clonmel	II.	313
15	Abbeyville	80 3 21	Dublin	Coolock	Kinsaley	Balrothery	I.	28
125	Abbeyville	95 1 0	Galway	Leitrim	Ballynakill	Portumna	IV.	50
39	Abbeyville or Ardlaherty	105 1 11	Sligo	Corran	Drumrat	Boyle	IV.	225
3	Abbey West	444 3 0	Clare	Burren	Abbey	Ballyvaghan	II.	11
13, 14	Abbotstown	101 3 6	Dublin	Castleknock	Castleknock	Dublin North	I.	23
18, 19	Abelstown	202 0 26	Meath	Upper Slane	Gernonstown	Navan	I.	224
14, 15	Abington	380 2 37	Limerick	Owneybeg	Abington	Limerick	II.	250
42	Ablintown	95 0 5	Wexford	Forth	Kildavin	Wexford	I.	310
26	Abcurragh	80 1 21	Fermanagh	Clanawley	Cleenish	Enniskillen	III.	189
26	Abohill	42 3 12	Fermanagh	Clanawley	Cleenish	Enniskillen	III.	189
9	Acantha	183 0 38	King's Co.	Ballycowan	Durrow	Tullamore	I.	127
7	Acarreagh	106 1 37	Louth	Upper Dundalk	Castletown	Dundalk	I.	177
9	Acaun	1 3 13	Carlow	Rathvilly	Rathvilly	Baltinglass	I.	12
65, 75	Achillbeg Island	330 3 19	Mayo	Burrishoole	Achill	Newport	IV.	117
32, 38	Achonry	3,157 0 28d	Sligo	Leyny	Achonry	Tobercurry	IV.	228
34, 39	Aclamon	477 2 26	Wexford	Shelburne	Tellarought	New Ross	I.	328
17, 20	Aclare	632 1 2	Carlow	Forth	Myshall	Carlow	I.	5
6	Aclare Cottage Demesne	304 1 21	Meath	Lower Slane	Drumcondra	Ardee	I.	222
6	Aclare House Demesne	303 3 3	Meath	Lower Slane	Drumcondra	Ardee	I.	222
36	ACLARE T.	—	Sligo	Leyny	Kilmacteige	Tobercurry	IV.	231
10, 13	Aclint	367 3 34	Louth	Ardee	Philipstown	Ardee	I.	174
58	Acraboy	159 0 5	Tipperary, S.R.	Clanwilliam	Solloghodmore	Tipperary	II.	310
9	Acragar	438 3 32	Kilkenny	Galmoy	Rathbeagh	Urlingford	II.	93
8	Acragar	647 0 25	Queen's Co.	Portnahinch	Ardea	Mountmellick	I.	243
22, 23	Acraroe	63 0 6	Kilkenny	Shillelogher	Tullaghanbrogue	Callan	I.	116
9	Acravally	31 1 28	Antrim	Cary	Culfeightrin	Ballycastle	III.	13
105	Acre Beg	44 1 21	Galway	Loughrea	Kilteskill	Loughrea	IV.	65
61	Acre East	154 2 5	Galway	Killian	Ahascragh	Mountbellew	IV.	42
31	Acre McCricket	4 3 2	Down	Lecale Lower	Kilclief	Downpatrick	III.	179
105, 115	Acre More	85 0 31	Galway	Loughrea	Kilteskill	Loughrea	IV.	65
69	Acrenakirka	51 3 14	Tipperary, S.R.	Middlethird	Mora	Cashel	II.	329
25	Acres	59 1 31	Cavan	Clanmahon	Denn	Cavan	III.	76
2, 3, 5	Acres	253 1 17	Clare	Burren	Drumcreehy	Ballyvaghan	II.	12
47	Acres	166 1 27	Clare	Ibrickan	Kilmacduane	Kilrush	II.	23
12	Acres	387 3 8e	Clare	Tulla Upper	Feakle	Tulla	II.	38
65	Acres	36 0 17	Cork, E.R.	Barrymore	Templenacarriga	Middleton	II.	58
22	Acres	159 3 24	Cork, E.R.	Duhallow	Kilmeen	Kanturk	II.	72
27, 35	Acres	141 0 36	Cork, E.R.	Fermoy	Litter	Fermoy	II.	80
124	Acres	85 3 8	Cork, E.R.	Kinsale	Ringrone	Kinsale	II.	100
6	Acres	53 3 38	Cork, E.R.	Orrery and Kilmore	Kilbolane	Kanturk	II.	108
108	Acres	275 0 15	Cork, W.R.	East Carbery,(W.D.)	Fanlobbus	Dunmanway	II.	131
107, 120	Acres	403 0 39	Cork, W.R.	West Carbery,(E.D.)	Dromdaleague	Skibbereen	II.	139
133	Acres	99 0 14	Cork, W.R.	West Carbery,(E.D.)	Kilmacabea	Skibbereen	II.	140

(a) Including 11A. 0R. 36P.; 4A. 0R. 0P.; 25A. 1R. 26P.; 7A. 3R. 16P. detached portions.
(b) Including 34A. 2R. 13P. within the Municipal Boundary.
(c) Including 8A. 1R. 34P. water.
(d) Including 14A. 0R. 26P. water.
(e) Including 4A. 3R. 0P. water.

No. of Sheet of the Ordnance Survey Maps.	Townlands and Towns.	Area in Statute Acres.			County.	Barony.	Parish.	Poor Law Union in 1857.	Townland Census of 1851, Part I.	
		A.	R.	P.					Vol.	Page
21	Acres	11	2	29	Fermanagh	Clanawley	Boho	Enniskillen	III.	189
27, 28	Acres	44	3	13a	Fermanagh	Magherastephana	Aghalurcher	Lisnaskea	III.	214
17, 30	Acres	8	3	36	Galway	Dunmore	Tuam	Tuam	IV.	35
94	Acres	4	3	27	Galway	Galway	Rahoon	Galway	IV.	37
125	Acres	23	3	34	Galway	Leitrim	Ballynakill	Loughrea	IV.	50
31	Acres	191	3	6	Galway	Tiaquin	Kilkerrin	Glennamaddy	IV.	76
44, 54	Acres	818	1	5	Kerry	Corkaguiny	Ballinvoher	Dingle	II.	173
1, 2	Acres	467	3	36	Kerry	Iraghticonnor	Kilconly	Listowel	II.	191
48, 58	Acres	77	2	37	Kerry	Magunihy	Aglish	Killarney	II.	199
29	Acres	56	1	20	Leitrim	Carrigallen	Cloone	Mohill	IV.	90
18	Acres	58	3	32	Leitrim	Drumahaire	Inishmagrath	Manorhamilton	IV.	95
23	Acres	37	1	4b	Leitrim	Leitrim	Kiltoghert	Car^k. on Shannon	IV.	100
35, 37	Acres	85	2	36	Leitrim	Mohill	Mohill	Mohill	IV.	107
52	Acres	162	3	10	Limerick	Glenquin	Killeedy	Kanturk	II.	245
9	Acres	38	0	11c	Longford	Granard	Clonbroney	Granard	I.	154
91	Acres	89	1	4	Mayo	Clanmorris	Mayo	Claremorris	IV.	135
19, 24	Acres	77	2	3	Monaghan	Cremorne	Ballybay	Castleblayney	III.	259
5	Acres	46	0	2	Monaghan	Monaghan	Tedavnet	Monaghan	III.	278
40	Acres	133	3	34	Roscommon	Ballintober South	Roscommon	Roscommon	IV.	190
10	Acres	125	2	39	Roscommon	Frenchpark	Kilmacumsy	Boyle	IV.	203
31	Acres	7	1	9	Waterford	Decies without Drum	Dungarvan	Dungarvan	II.	354
61	Acre West	11	1	13	Galway	Killian	Ahascragh	Mountbellew	IV.	42
18	Acton	22	0	31	Armagh	Orior Lower	Ballymore	Newry	III.	55
18	Acton T.	—			Armagh	Orior Lower	Ballymore	Newry	III.	56
142, 143	Adam's Island	1	3	31	Cork, W.R.	East Carbery,(W.D.)	Kilfaughnabeg	Skibbereen	II.	133
86	Adamstown	436	1	6	Cork, E.R.	Kerrycurrihy	Ballinaboy	Cork	II.	91
3, 4, 6, 7	Adamstown	565	3	11	Dublin	Balrothery West	Garristown	Dunshaughlin	I.	22
17	Adamstown	111	1	11	Dublin	Newcastle	Aderrig	Celbridge	I.	32
40	Adamstown	219	3	16	Limerick	Smallcounty	Athneasy	Kilmallock	II.	258
15, 18	Adamstown	311	3	33	Louth	Ardee	Drumcar	Ardee	I.	172
37	Adamstown	277	0	14	Meath	Lower Moyfenrath	Laracor	Trim	I.	210
29	Adamstown	289	3	14	Tipperary, N.R.	Eliogarty	Templemore	Thurles	II.	272
16, 17	Adamstown	247	3	20	Waterford	Middlethird	Kilmeadan	Waterford	II.	368
17	Adamstown	69	2	10	Waterford	Middlethird	Lisnakill	Waterford	II.	368
25, 32	Adamstown	551	3	14	Westmeath	Moycashel	Castletownkindalen	Mullingar	I.	277
25	Adamstown	35	0	3	Westmeath	Rathconrath	Conry	Mullingar	I.	282
30, 31	Adamstown	1,076	2	15	Wexford	Bantry	Adamstown	New Ross	I.	299
13	Adamstown Lower	189	1	25	Kilkenny	Crannagh	Tullaroan	Kilkenny	I.	87
13	Adamstown Upper	284	2	18	Kilkenny	Crannagh	Tullaroan	Kilkenny	I.	87
20, 29	Adamswood	302	1	18	Limerick	Connello Lower	Croagh	Rathkeale	II.	227
21	Adare	856	1	21	Limerick	Coshma	Adare	Croom	II.	241
21	Adare T.	—			Limerick	Coshma	Adare	Croom	II.	241
27	Addane	85	0	6	Tipperary, N.R.	Upper Ormond	Dolla	Nenagh	II.	290
30	Addanstown	155	0	12	Meath	Upper Navan	Trim	Trim	I.	216
18	Addergoole	114	1	23	Clare	Inchiquin	Kilkeedy	Corrofin	II.	25
23	Addergoole	2,658	3	25d	Galway	Ballynahinch	Ballynakill	Clifden	IV.	11
69	Addergoole	493	0	36	Galway	Clare	Annaghdown	Galway	IV.	16
44	Addergoole	151	1	39	Galway	Clare	Killererin	Tuam	IV.	20
99, 107	Addergoole	606	1	10	Galway	Longford	Abbeygormacan	Ballinasloe	IV.	56
81	Addergoole	942	0	16	Mayo	Costello	Aghamore	Claremorris	IV.	136
34	Addergoole	103	1	18	Queen's Co.	Clarmallagh	Aghmacart	Abbeyleix	I.	236
5	Addergoole Beg	161	1	7	Galway	Dunmore	Dunmore	Tuam	IV.	33
47	Addergoole or Knockmaria	227	0	22	Mayo	Tirawley	Addergoole	Castlebar	IV.	163
17	Addergoole More	278	3	37	Galway	Dunmore	Dunmore	Tuam	IV.	33
61, 74	Addergoole North	1,068	1	3e	Galway	Killian	Ahascragh	Ballinasloe	IV.	42
74	Addergoole South	54	3	8f	Galway	Clonmacnowen	Ahascragh	Ballinasloe	IV.	23
74	Addergoole West	53	2	23	Galway	Clonmacnowen	Ahascragh	Ballinasloe	IV.	23
9	Addergown	454	2	17	Kerry	Clanmaurice	Rattoo	Listowel	II.	173
10, 19	Adderville	752	3	18	Donegal	Inishowen East	Clonmany	Inishowen	III.	117
58	Adderwal	722	0	14g	Donegal	Boylagh	Inishkeel	Glenties	III.	112
9, 14	Addinstown	968	0	16	Westmeath	Delvin	Castletowndelvin	Castletowndelvin	I.	264
81	Addragool	149	1	2h	Galway	Moycullen	Moycullen	Galway	IV.	70
38	Addrigoole	102	3	31	Waterford	Decies within Drum	Lisgenan or Grange	Youghal	II.	352
17, 18	Addroon	148	1	12i	Clare	Inchiquin	Ruan	Corrofin	II.	28
11	Aderavoher	34	0	14	Sligo	Tireragh	Easky	Dromore, West	IV.	233
31	Aderoon	50	0	9	Leitrim	Leitrim	Kiltoghert	Car^k. on Shannon	IV.	190
103	Aderg	129	1	25	Mayo	Costello	Annagh	Claremorris	IV.	137
17	Aderrig	259	1	29	Dublin	Newcastle	Aderrig	Celbridge	I.	32
78	Admiran	135	2	30j	Donegal	Raphoe	Stranorlar	Stranorlar	III.	142
28, 29, 33	Adoon	699	3	37k	Leitrim	Mohill	Cloone	Mohill	IV.	105
26, 27	Adragool	231	1	13	Roscommon	Castlereagh	Kilkeevin	Castlereagh	IV.	200
24	Adramone Beg	92	2	36	Waterford	Decies without Drum	Kilrossanty,	Kilmacthomas	II.	357

(a) Including 4A. 2R. 7P. water.
(b) Including 2A. 1R. 19P. water.
(c) Including 10A. 0R. 35P. water.
(d) Including 4A. 1R. 9P. water.

(e) Including 25A. 0R. 16P. water.
(f) Including 1A. 1R. 24P. water.
(g) Including 10A. 3R. 10P. water.
(h) Including 42A. 3R. 3P. water.

(i) Including 3A. 3R. 6P. water.
(j) Including 8A. 3R. 17P. water.
(k) Including 57A. 3R. 30P. water.

CENSUS OF IRELAND FOR THE YEAR 1851.

No. of Sheet of the Ordnance Survey Maps.	Townlands and Towns.	Area in Statute Acres. A. R. P.	County.	Barony.	Parish.	Poor Law Union in 1857.	Townland Census of 1851, Part I. Vol.	Page
23, 24	Adramone More	118 2 32	Waterford	Decies without Drum	Kilrossanty,	Kilmacthomas	II.	357
40	Adraval	206 1 16	Kerry	Trughanacmy	Ballincuslane	Tralee	II.	206
103, 116	Adrigole	293 0 19	Cork, W.R.	Bear	Kilcaskan	Castletown	II.	122
133	Adrigool	450 1 0	Cork, W.R.	West Carbery, (E.D.)	Castlehaven	Skibbereen	II.	137
47, 48	Adrivale	460 3 4	Cork, W.R.	West Muskerry	Drishane	Millstreet	II.	155
42, 45	Adruel	120 1 25	King's Co.	Clonlisk	Kilcomin	Roscrea	I.	130
42	Afaddy or Silver-spring	165 0 27	Kilkenny	Iverk	Ballytarsney	Waterford	I.	105
42	Afaddy or Silver-spring	77 3 2	Kilkenny	Iverk	Pollrone	Waterford	I.	106
29	Affane	166 3 8a	Waterford	Decies without Drum	Affane	Lismore	II.	353
21, 29	Affane Hunter	200 2 15	Waterford	Decies without Drum	Affane	Lismore	II.	353
19, 27	Affick	1,679 0 15	Clare	Tulla Upper	Tulla	Tulla	II.	41
63	Affoley	165 2 4	Tipperary, S.R.	Slievardagh	Modeshil	Callan	II.	335
50, 53	Affollus	324 1 26	Meath	Upper Deece	Moyglare	Dunshaughlin	I.	194
10	Affouley	140 2 31	Kerry	Iraghticonnor	Galey	Listowel	II.	190
3	Afoley	122 3 8	Queen's Co.	Tinnahinch	Rearymore	Mountmellick	I.	249
16	Agall	72 0 34	King's Co.	Ballycowan	Lynally	Tullamore	I.	128
16	Agall	198 2 32	King's Co.	Ballycowan	Rahan	Tullamore	I.	128
19, 24	Aganlane or Parkmore	1,835 3 14	Antrim	Lower Glenarm	Layd	Ballycastle	III.	23
104	Aggard Beg	313 0 23	Galway	Dunkellin	Killora	Loughrea	IV.	31
96, 104	Aggard More,	333 1 8	Galway	Dunkellin	Killora	Loughrea	IV.	31
12, 16	Agha	783 0 21	Carlow	Idrone East	Agha	Carlow	I.	6
136	Agha	224 0 27	Cork, W.R.	Ibane and Barryroe	Lislee	Clonakilty	II.	149
15	Agha	261 2 37	Kilkenny	Gowran	Rathcoole	Kilkenny	I.	98
19	Aghabane	121 3 5b	Cavan	Tullyhunco	Kildallan	Cavan	III.	96
19	Aghabeg	283 2 9	Carlow	Idrone East	Sliguff	Carlow	I.	8
116	Aghabeg	267 0 37	Cork, W.R.	Bear	Killaconenagh	Castletown	II.	124
15	Aghabeg East	704 0 9	Kerry	Clanmaurice	Kiltomy	Listowel	II.	172
15	Aghabeg Middle	337 2 7	Kerry	Clanmaurice	Kiltomy	Listowel	II.	172
15	Aghabeg West	319 1 18	Kerry	Clanmaurice	Kiltomy	Listowel	II.	172
2	Aghabehy	537 2 16	Roscommon	Boyle	Kilronan	Boyle	IV.	196
22	Aghaboe	308 1 39	Queen's Co.	Clarmallagh	Aghaboe	Donaghmore	I.	235
17	Aghabog	93 2 16c	Monaghan	Dartree	Aghabog	Cootehill	III.	263
28	Aghaboneill	321 1 13d	Leitrim	Mohill	Fenagh	Mohill	IV.	106
43	Aghaboy	286 1 9e	Antrim	Upper Toome	Drummaul	Ballymena	III.	33
41	Aghaboy	116 0 20	Cavan	Clanmahon	Drumlumman	Granard	III.	76
7	Aghaboy	285 1 23	Cavan	Tullyhaw	Kinawley	Bawnboy	III.	92
40	Aghaboy	61 2 26	Fermanagh	Clankelly	Clones	Clones	III.	194
14, 15	Aghaboy	123 3 19	King's Co.	Garrycastle	Wheery or Killagally	Parsonstown	I.	139
10, 15	Aghaboy	161 1 14	Longford	Granard	Granard	Granard	I.	156
9	Aghaboy	442 1 36	Longford	Longford	Killoe	Longford	I.	158
9	Aghaboy	114 0 5	Monaghan	Monaghan	Kilmore	Monaghan	III.	275
6, 7	Aghaboy	83 0 17	Monaghan	Trough	Donagh	Monaghan	III.	281
27	Aghaboy Lower	289 1 17	Tyrone	Strabane Upper	Bodoney Lower	Gortin	III.	323
6	Aghaboy North	79 3 5	Monaghan	Monaghan	Tedavnet	Monaghan	III.	278
4, 7	Aghaboys	277 2 4	Louth	Lower Dundalk	Ballymascanlan	Dundalk	I.	175
8	Aghaboy South	156 2 30	Monaghan	Monaghan	Tedavnet	Monaghan	III.	278
27	Aghaboy Upper	361 0 27	Tyrone	Strabane Upper	Bodoney Lower	Gortin	III.	323
10, 11	Aghabrack	213 3 21	Longford	Granard	Granard	Granard	I.	156
6	Aghabrack	268 0 16	Tyrone	Strabane Lower	Donaghedy	Gortin	III.	320
24, 31	Aghabrack	127 0 0	Westmeath	Rathconrath	Conry	Mullingar	I.	282
10	Aghabrick	34 3 20	Monaghan	Monaghan	Tehallan	Monaghan	III.	280
7	Aghaburren	220 3 14	Cork, E.R.	Fermoy	Imphrick	Mallow	II.	80
48	Aghacarnaghan	279 2 7	Antrim	Upper Toome	Duneane	Antrim	III.	34
48	Aghacarnaghan, Part of	55 2 20	Antrim	Upper Toome	Duneane	Antrim	III.	34
63	Aghacarnan	450 2 21	Antrim	Upper Massereene	Ballinderry	Lisburn	III.	29
63	Aghacarnan	122 3 5	Antrim	Upper Massereene	Magheragall	Lisburn	III.	31
3	Aghacarra	587 1 26f	Roscommon	Boyle	Boyle	Boyle	IV.	193
54	Aghacarrible	146 0 25	Kerry	Corkaguiny	Kinard	Dingle	II.	179
39	Aghacashel	330 0 4	Cavan	Castlerahan	Lurgan	Oldcastle	II.	69
21, 24	Aghacashel	450 0 0	Leitrim	Leitrim	Kiltubbrid	Car^k. on Shannon	IV.	103
24	Aghacashlaun,	135 0 22	Leitrim	Leitrim	Kiltubbrid	Car^k. on Shannon	IV.	103
13	Aghaclay	98 1 27	Monaghan	Dartree	Aghabog	Monaghan	III.	263
6	Aghaclogha	118 1 31	Monaghan	Monaghan	Tedavnet	Monaghan	III.	278
27, 28	Aghacloghan	233 2 4	Monaghan	Farney	Donaghmoyne	Carrickmacross	III.	269
36	Aghaclogher	200 0 21	Roscommon	Roscommon	Cloonfinlough	Roscommon	IV.	208
29	Aghacocara	32 3 4	Westmeath	Brawny	St. Mary's	Athlone	I.	259
39, 40	Aghacolumb g	294 2 15	Tyrone	Dungannon Upper	Arboe	Cookstown	III.	305
6	Aghacommon	222 0 19	Armagh	Oneilland East	Seagoe	Lurgan	III.	50
31	Aghaconny	213 3 22h	Cavan	Clanmahon	Crosserlough	Cavan	III.	76
15	Aghacoora	260 0 26	Kerry	Clanmaurice	Kiltomy	Listowel	II.	172

(a) Including 4A. 1R. 18P. detached portion.
(b) Including 18A. 0R. 8P. water.
(c) Including 8A. 0P. 2P. water.
(d) Including 62A. 0R. 37P. water.
(e) Including 5A. 1R. 15P. water.
(f) Including 24A. 1R. 25P. water.
(g) Glebe of Arboe Parish.
(h) Including 0A. 1R. 27P. water.

No. of Sheet of the Ordnance Survey Maps.	Townlands and Towns.	Area in Statute Acres.			County.	Barony.	Parish.	Poor Law Union in 1857.	Townland Census of 1851, Part I.	
		A.	R.	P.					Vol.	Page
5, 6	Aghacordrinan .	440	3	3	Longford .	Granard . . .	Columbkille . .	Granard . .	I.	155
24	Aghacramphill .	130	2	24	Fermanagh .	Magherastephana .	Aghalurcher . .	Lisnaskea .	III.	214
37	Aghacreevy .	144	0	13	Cavan .	Clanmahon . .	Ballymachugh .	Cavan . .	III.	75
18, 19	Aghacross ..	355	0	23	Cork, E.R. .	Condons & Clangibbon	Aghacross . .	Mitchelstown .	II.	59
43, 49	Aghacullion .	214	3	0	Down .	Up. Iveagh, Lr. Part	Kilcoo . . .	Kilkeel . .	III.	173
28, 29, 33	Aghacully .	266	0	23	Antrim .	Lower Antrim .	Skerry . .	Ballymena .	III.	4
69, 70, 82	Aghacunna .	406	3	32	Cork, W.R. .	West Muskerry .	Kilnamartery .	Macroom . .	II.	159
58, 66	Aghacurreen .	412	1	32	Kerry .	Magunihy . .	Aghadoe . .	Killarney . .	II.	199
14	Aghacurreen .	761	3	16	Roscommon .	Frenchpark . .	Tibohine . .	Castlereagh .	IV.	204
88	Aghada . . .	488	0	21	Cork, E.R. .	Imokilly . . .	Aghada . .	Middleton .	II.	83
26	Aghadachor .	271	0	38	Donegal .	Kilmacrenan . .	Mevagh . .	Millford . .	III.	130
17, 18	Aghadaghly .	96	0	4	Donegal .	Kilmacrenan . .	Clondavaddog .	Millford . .	III.	124
88	AGHADA (LOWER) T.	—			Cork, E.R. .	Imokilly . . .	Aghada . .	Middleton .	II.	83
29	Aghadangan .	145	0	8	Roscommon .	Roscommon . .	Lissonuffy .	Strokestown .	IV.	211
25	Aghadark .	135	3	5	Leitrim .	Carrigallen . .	Oughteragh .	Bawnboy . .	IV.	91
41,42,49,50	Aghadarragh .	544	3	31	Tyrone .	Omagh East . .	Dromore . . .	Omagh . .	III.	311
20	Aghadaugh .	256	0	37	Westmeath .	Moyashel and Magh- eradernon . .	Rathconnell . .	Mullingar . .	I.	276
88	AGHADA (UPPER) T.	—			Cork, E.R. .	Imokilly . . .	Aghada . .	Middleton .	II.	83
29, 32	Aghadavoyle .	924	0	22	Armagh .	Orior Upper .	Killevy . . .	Newry . .	III.	57
63, 67	Aghadavy .	489	1	14	Antrim .	Upper Massereene .	Ballinderry .	Lisburn . .	III.	29
13	Aghade . .	266	2	26	Carlow .	Forth . . .	Aghade . .	Carlow . .	I.	3
13	Aghadegnan .	177	2	14	Longford .	Longford . . .	Templemichael .	Longford . .	I.	160
2, 4	Aghad.rrard East .	361	1	18	Leitrim .	Rosclogher . .	Rossinver .	Ballyshannon .	IV.	110
2, 4	Aghaderrard West .	217	0	25	Leitrim .	Rosclogher . .	Rossinver .	Ballyshannon .	IV.	110
1, 3	Aghaderry .	214	2	15	Monaghan .	Trough . . .	Errigal Trough .	Clogher . .	III.	283
14	Aghaderry .	397	3	17	Roscommon .	Frenchpark . .	Tibohine . .	Castlereagh .	IV.	204
33, 38	Aghaderryloman .	65	3	1	Fermanagh .	Knockninny . .	Kinawley . .	Lisnaskea . .	III.	201
73, 82	Aghadiffin .	950	0	20a	Mayo .	Costello . .	Kilmovee . .	Swineford . .	IV.	141
66	Aghadoe . .	348	3	0	Cork, E.R. .	Imokilly . . .	Killeagh . .	Youghal . .	II.	88
58, 59, 62, 63	Aghadolgan .	336	2	3	Antrim .	Upper Massereene .	Glenavy . .	Lisburn . .	III.	30
16	Aghadonagh .	211	1	10	King's Co. .	Ballycowan . .	Rahan . . .	Tullamore .	I.	128
15, 20	Aghadonagh .	84	0	33	Longford . .	Ardagh . .	Mostrim . .	Granard . .	I.	152
67	Aghadooey Glebe .	44	2	8	Mayo .	Burrishoole . .	Burrishoole . .	Newport . .	IV.	118
2, 9	Aghadoon . .	660	1	34	Mayo .	Erris . . .	Kilmore . .	Belmullet . .	IV.	145
31, 32	Aghadoon or Raven- field . . .	69	0	7	Cavan .	Upper Loughtee .	Denn . . .	Cavan . .	III.	83
42	Aghadouglas .	231	0	22	King's Co. .	Clonlisk . .	Ettagh . .	Roscrea . .	I.	130
100, 104	Aghadowey .	402	3	1	Donegal .	Tirhugh . . .	Drumhome . .	Donegal . .	III.	146
11, 18	Aghadowey .	441	0	30	Londonderry .	Coleraine . .	Aghadowey .	Coleraine . .	III.	229
141	Aghadown .	211	3	28b	Cork, W.R. .	West Carbery, (E.D.)	Aghadown .	Skibbereen .	II.	136
5	Aghadowry .	561	2	5	Longford .	Longford . . .	Killoe . . .	Longford . .	I.	158
25	Aghadreen .	516	2	11	Queen's Co. .	Cullenagh . .	Fossy or Timahoe .	Abbeyleix .	I.	240
16	Aghadreenagh .	177	2	21c	Cavan .	Tullygarvey . .	Annagh . .	Cootehill . .	III.	87
31	Aghadreenagh .	95	2	5	Cavan .	Upper Loughtee .	Denn . . .	Cavan . .	III.	83
26, 32	Aghadreenagh .	499	0	21	Cavan .	Upper Loughtee .	Lavey . . .	Cavan . .	III.	85
17, 18	Aghadreenan .	536	1	37	Donegal .	Kilmacrenan . .	Clondavaddog .	Millford . .	III.	124
25	Aghadreenan .	231	1	3	Monaghan .	Farney . . .	Donaghmoyne .	Castleblayney .	III.	269
50	Aghadreenan .	101	3	15	Tyrone .	Omagh East . .	Donacavey . .	Omagh . .	III.	310
35	Aghadreenan Glebe	42	2	12	Fermanagh .	Clankelly . .	Galloon . .	Lisnaskea .	III.	198
14	Aghadrestan .	563	2	22	Roscommon .	Frenchpark . .	Tibohine . .	Castlereagh .	IV.	204
78	Aghadrinagh .	355	0	7d	Mayo .	Carra . . .	Ballyhean .	Castlebar . .	IV.	125
39	Aghadrum . .	129	1	24e	Fermanagh .	Coole . . .	Galloon . .	Lisnaskea .	III.	199
28, 32	Aghadrumcarn .	257	1	30	Leitrim .	Mohill . . .	Mohill . . .	Mohill . .	IV.	107
1, 3	Aghadrumeru .	69	3	29	Monaghan .	Trough . . .	Errigal Trough .	Clogher . .	III.	283
32	Aghadrumderg .	45	2	30	Leitrim .	Mohill . . .	Mohill . . .	Mohill . .	IV.	107
16, 21	Aghadrumdoney .	111	2	1	Monaghan .	Dartree . .	Currin . . .	Clones . .	III.	265
66	Aghadrumglasny .	404	3	15	Antrim .	Upper Massereene .	Aghagallon .	Lurgan . .	III.	29
66, 67	Aghadrumglasny .	37	2	36	Antrim .	Upper Massereene .	Aghalee . .	Lurgan . .	III.	29
21, 22	Aghadrumgowna or Calf Field . .	230	3	18	Cavan .	Tullygarvey . .	Larah . .	Cootehill . .	III.	90
20	Aghadrumgullin .	99	3	13	Cavan .	Upper Loughtee .	Castleterra .	Cavan . .	III.	82
29, 30	Aghadruminshin .	275	0	7	Leitrim .	Carrigallen . .	Cloone . .	Mohill . .	IV.	90
18	Aghadrumkeen .	181	2	26	Monaghan .	Dartree . .	Aghabog . .	Cootehill . .	III.	263
17, 18	Aghadrumkeen .	132	2	16	Monaghan .	Dartree . .	Ematris . .	Cootehill . .	III.	266
35	Aghadrumsee and Killygorman .	263	3	8f	Fermanagh .	Clankelly . .	Clones . .	Clones . .	III.	104
64	Aghaduff . .	148	1	26	Cork, E.R. .	Barrymore . .	Kilquane . .	Cork . .	II.	55
42	Aghadulla . .	559	2	33g	Tyrone .	Omagh East . .	Drumragh . .	Omagh . .	III.	312
42	Aghadulla (Harper)	862	1	3	Tyrone .	Omagh East . .	Dromore . . .	Omagh . .	III.	311
2, 4	Aghadunvane .	671	3	9	Leitrim .	Rosclogher . .	Rossinver .	Ballyshannon .	IV.	110
37	Aghafad . .	69	3	27	Cavan .	Clanmahon . .	Ballymachugh .	Cavan . .	III.	75
13	Aghafad . .	22	2	9	Longford .	Ardagh . .	Ballymacormick .	Longford . .	I.	152
31	Aghafad . .	103	0	20	Monaghan .	Farney . . .	Killanny . .	Carrickmacross .	III.	271

(a) Including 15A. 1R. 34P. water.　(d) Including 9A. 0R. 25P. water.　(f) Including 11A. 0R. 16P. water.
(b) Including 3A. 0R. 16P. water.　(e) Including 26A. 2R. 4P. water.　(g) Including 1A. 0R. 37P. water.
(c) Including 4A. 0R. 5P. water.

No. of Sheet of the Ordnance Survey Maps	Townlands and Towns.	Area in Statute Acres.			County.	Barony.	Parish.	Poor Law Union in 1857.	Townland Census of 1851, Part I.	
		A.	R.	P.					Vol.	Page
51, 58	Aghafad .	1,036	1	27	Tyrone	Clogher .	Donacavey .	Omagh .	III.	294
45	Aghafad .	161	3	22	Tyrone	Dungannon Middle .	Pomeroy .	Cookstown .	III.	303
25	Aghafad .	333	1	18	Tyrone	Lower Strabane	Ardstraw .	Strabane .	III.	318
6	Aghafad .	713	3	38a	Tyrone	Lower Strabane	Donaghedy .	Gortin .	III.	320
72	Aghafadda	128	3	8	Galway	Tiaquin .	Monivea .	Loughrea .	IV.	78
117, 118	Aghafadda	71	2	32	Mayo	Kilmaine .	Ballinchalla .	Ballinrobe .	IV.	151
2	Aghafarnan	158	2	7	Meath	Lower Kells .	Enniskeen .	Kells .	I.	202
28, 29, 33	Aghafatten	210	3	23	Antrim	Lower Antrim .	Skerry .	Ballymena .	III.	4
6	Aghafin .	212	3	23	King's Co.	Garrycastle .	Lemanaghan .	Parsonstown .	I.	136
15	Aghafin .	347	3	3	Longford .	Ardagh .	Mostrim .	Granard .	I.	152
12	Aghafin .	184	1	22b	Monaghan	Dartree .	Clones .	Clones .	III.	264
16	Aghafin .	238	2	5	Queen's Co.	Upperwoods .	Offerlane .	Abbeyleix .	I.	250
2, 4	Aghafin .	561	1	17c	Roscommon	Boyle .	Kilronan .	Boyle .	IV.	196
30, 36	Aghafin .	115	2	31	Westmeath	Clonlonan .	Kilcleagh .	Athlone .	I.	261
16	Aghafin .	145	1	32	Westmeath	Kilkenny West .	Noughaval .	Ballymahon .	I.	274
136	Aghafore	307	1	14	Cork, W.R.	Ibane and Barryroe .	Abbeymahon .	Clonakilty .	II.	148
105	Aghafoy .	101	0	19d	Donegal .	Tirhugh .	Templecarn .	Donegal .	III.	148
9, 10	Aghafullim	142	2	35	Kildare .	Ikeathy&Oughterany	Clonshanbo .	Celbridge .	I.	57
38	Aghagad .	420	1	10	Roscommon	Athlone .	Fuerty .	Roscommon .	IV.	181
5	Aghagad .	417	2	9	Sligo	Carbury .	Drumcliff .	Sligo .	IV.	220
38, 39, 41	Aghagad Beg and Creemully .	940	2	38	Roscommon	Athlone .	Fuerty .	Roscommon .	IV.	181
88	Aghagadda	195	3	0	Kerry .	Iveragh .	Killemlagh .	Cahersiveen .	II.	196
6	Aghagaffert	149	2	23	Fermanagh	Lurg .	Magheraculmoney .	Lowtherstown .	III.	207
1, 3	Aghagah .	286	2	35	Longford .	Granard .	Killoe .	Granard .	I.	157
62, 66	Aghagallon	334	2	10	Antrim .	Upper Massereene .	Aghagallon .	Lurgan .	III.	29
35, 43	Aghagallon .	278	2	39e	Tyrone	Omagh East .	Cappagh .	Omagh .	III.	310
6	Aghagally	83	2	6	Monaghan	Monaghan .	Tedavnet .	Monaghan .	III.	278
18	Aghagashlan .	342	0	13f	Cavan .	Tullygarvey .	Drumgoon .	Cootehill .	III.	87
42	Aghagaskin .	779	1	17	Londonderry	Loughinsholin .	Magherafelt .	Magherafelt .	III.	243
12	Aghagaw .	69	0	31	Monaghan	Dartree .	Clones .	Clones .	III.	264
8	Aghagaw .	98	2	39g	Monaghan	Monaghan .	Tedavnet .	Monaghan .	III.	278
40	Aghagay .	45	2	21	Fermanagh	Coole .	Galloon .	Clones .	III.	199
32	Aghageena .	164	3	35h	Cavan .	Castlerahan .	Crosserlough .	Cavan .	III.	67
15	Aghagheigh .	75	0	7	Antrim .	Lower Glenarm .	Layd .	Ballycastle .	III.	22
53	Aghaginduff .	512	3	20	Tyrone	Dungannon Lower .	Killeeshil .	Dungannon .	III.	298
21, 23, 24, 3, 10	Aghaginny .	374	1	36	Leitrim .	Leitrim .	Kiltubbrid .	Cark. on Shannon	IV.	103
3, 10	Aghaglasheen .	1,522	3	6	Mayo .	Erris .	Kilmore .	Belmullet .	IV.	145
32	Aghaglass .	130	2	13	Monaghan	Farney .	Inishkeen .	Dundalk .	III.	271
11,12,20,21, 1, 2	Aghaglassan .	2,119	0	39	Donegal .	Inishowen East .	Culdaff .	Inishowen .	III.	118
1, 2	Aghaglinny North .	521	1	21	Clare .	Burren .	Gleninagh .	Ballyvaghan .	II.	12
2	Aghaglinny South .	461	3	37	Clare .	Burren .	Gleninagh .	Ballyvaghan .	II.	12
36, 37	Aghagogan .	949	2	34i	Tyrone	Omagh East .	Termonmaguirk .	Omagh .	III.	314
21, 26	Aghagoirick .	155	2	30	Cavan .	Upper Loughtee .	Larah .	Cavan .	III.	85
30, 31	Aghagoogy .	451	2	12	King's Co.	Eglish .	Eglish .	Parsonstown .	I.	134
118	Aghagooheen .	268	3	17	Cork, W.R.	West Carbery,(W.D.)	Kilmocomoge .	Bantry .	II.	144
88, 98	Aghagower .	445	2	34	Mayo	Burrishoole .	Aghagower .	Westport .	IV.	117
38, 41	Aghagower .	731	2	15j	Roscommon	Athlone .	Fuerty .	Roscommon .	IV.	181
88	AGHAGOWER T.	—			Mayo .	Burrishoole .	Aghagower .	Westport .	IV.	118
3	Aghagowla .	311	1	28	Roscommon	Boyle .	Boyle .	Boyle .	IV.	193
77	Aghagowla Beg	88	0	18	Mayo .	Burrishoole .	Kilmaclasser .	Westport .	IV.	121
77	Aghagowla More .	256	3	18k	Mayo .	Burrishoole .	Kilmaclasser .	Westport .	IV.	121
20,21,23,24	Aghagrania .	578	2	26	Leitrim .	Leitrim .	Kiltoghert .	Cark. on Shannon	IV.	100
5, 6, 9, 10	Aghagreagh .	1,145	1	21	Longford .	Granard .	Columbkille .	Granard .	I.	155
5, 6	Aghagrefin .	257	2	0	Fermanagh	Lurg .	Drumkeeran .	Lowtherstown .	III.	205
39	Aghagurty .	380	1	39	King's Co.	Ballybritt .	Seirkieran .	Parsonstown .	I.	126
5	Aghahannagh .	215	1	7	Fermanagh	Lurg .	Drumkeeran .	Lowtherstown .	III.	205
21	Aghaherrish .	277	0	1l	Fermanagh	Clanawley .	Boho .	Enniskillen .	III.	189
20, 21	Aghahoorin .	197	2	22	Fermanagh	Magheraboy .	Boho .	Enniskillen .	III.	209
46	Aghahull .	72	2	19	Donegal .	Kilmacrenan .	Aughnish .	Millford .	III.	122
32	Aghakee .	100	1	1	Cavan .	Castlerahan .	Crosserlough .	Cavan .	III.	67
21	Aghakeel .	46	0	18	Longford .	Rathcline .	Rathcline .	Ballymahon .	I.	164
14, 20	Aghakeeran .	211	2	32	Fermanagh	Magheraboy .	Devenish .	Enniskillen .	III.	210
6	Aghakeeran .	414	1	36	Longford .	Granard .	Columbkille .	Granard .	I.	155
13, 18	Aghakeeran and Kil-lashee .	371	1	9	Longford .	Moydow .	Killashee .	Longford .	I.	161
21, 24	Aghakilbrack .	360	2	10	Leitrim .	Leitrim, .	Kiltubbrid .	Cark. on Shannon	IV.	103
28	Aghakilconnell .	112	1	11m	Leitrim .	Leitrim .	Kiltoghert .	Cark. on Shannon	IV.	100
32	Aghakilfaughna .	36	0	37	Leitrim .	Mohill .	Mohill .	Mohill .	IV.	107
33	Aghakillymaud .	486	1	35	Fermanagh	Knockninny .	Kinawley .	Lisnaskea .	III.	201
23, 27	Aghakilmore .	137	2	15	Leitrim .	Leitrim .	Kiltubbrid .	Cark. on Shannon	IV.	103
6, 10	Aghakilmore .	604	0	0	Longford .	Granard .	Columbkille .	Granard .	I.	155
37	Aghakilmore Lower	252	1	7	Cavan .	Clanmahon .	Ballymachugh .	Cavan .	III.	75

(a) Including 19A. 2R. 38P. water.
(b) Including 11A. 2R. 4P. water.
(c) Including Islands.
(d) Including 6A. 1R. 16P. water.
(e) Including 5A. 1R. 28P. water.

(f) Including 12A. 2R. 6P. water.
(g) Including 7A. 3R. 36P. water.
(h) Including 12A. 0R. 35P. water.
(i) Including 0A. 3R. 34P. water.

(j) Including 3A. 1R. 16P. water.
(k) Including 6A. 1R. 18P. water.
(l) Including 2A. 3R. 25P. water.
(m) Including 4A. 1R. 11P. water.

No. of Sheet of the Ordnance Survey Maps.	Townlands and Towns.	Area in Statute Acres. A. R. P.	County.	Barony.	Parish.	Poor Law Union in 1857.	Townland Census of 1851, Part I. Vol.	Page
37	Aghakilmore Upper	77 3 26	Cavan	Clanmahon	Ballymachugh	Cavan	III.	75
6	Aghakine	553 3 31	Longford	Granard	Columbkille	Granard	I.	155
24	Aghakinmart	269 2 28	Tyrone	Omagh West	Longfield West	Castlederg	III.	316
7, 9	Aghakinnigh	460 2 23	Cavan	Tullyhaw	Kinawley	Bawnboy	III.	92
46, 47	Aghakinsallagh Glebe	120 2 11	Tyrone	Dungannon Middle	Tullyniskan	Dungannon	III.	304
24	Aghakista	256 3 24a	Monaghan	Cremorne	Aghnamullen	Castleblayney	III.	257
24	Aghaknock	180 2 15	Cavan	Tullyhunco	Killashandra	Cavan	III.	97
5	Aghalaan	116 1 5	Fermanagh	Lurg	Drumkeeran	Lowtherstown	III.	205
10, 11, 20,	Aghalacka	358 1 2	Limerick	Connello Lower	Askeaton	Rathkeale	II.	226
26	Aghalackan	482 1 26b	Cavan	Upper Loughtee	Annagelliff	Cavan	III.	81
129	Aghalahard	153 1 22	Mayo	Kilmaine	Cong	Ballinrobe	IV.	153
36	Aghalahard	150 3 6	Roscommon	Roscommon	Cloonfinlough	Roscommon	IV.	208
42	Aghalane	122 0 23c	Fermanagh	Knockninny	Kinawley	Lisnaskea	III.	201
11	Aghalane	353 2 0d	Tyrone	Strabane Upper	Bodoney Upper	Gortin	III.	324
26, 27	Aghalane	889 0 28e	Tyrone	Strabane Upper	Cappagh	Omagh	III.	325
47	Aghalarg	172 3 15	Tyrone	Dungannon Middle	Donaghenry	Cookstown	III.	300
47	Aghalarg Bog (recld.)	6 2 15	Tyrone	Dungannon Middle	Donaghenry	Cookstown	III.	300
4, 8	Aghalasty and Ankersland	307 0 31	Westmeath	Fore	St. Mary's	Castletowndelvin	I.	272
7, 19	Aghalateeve	434 0 19	Galway	Ballymoe	Kilbegnet	Glennamaddy	IV.	8
3, 4	Aghalateeve	1,061 2 16f	Leitrim	Rosclogher	Rossinver	Ballyshannon	IV.	110
32	Aghalattafraal	307 3 19g	Cavan	Upper Loughtee	Denn	Oldcastle	III.	83
26	Aghalattive	387 0 27h	Donegal	Kilmacrenan	Clondahorky	Dunfanaghy	III.	122
17, 27	Aghalatty	484 3 6	Donegal	Kilmacrenan	Mevagh	Millford	III.	130
10	Aghalaverty	77 0 19	Monaghan	Monaghan	Monaghan	Monaghan	III.	276
34	Aghaleag	166 3 6	Tyrone	Omagh East	Drumragh	Omagh	III.	312
6	Aghaleague	392 2 22	Fermanagh	Lurg	Magheraculmoney	Lowtherstown	III.	207
25, 26	Aghaleague	170 1 0	Leitrim	Carrigallen	Carrigallen	Bawnboy	IV.	89
25	Aghaleague	125 0 29	Leitrim	Carrigallen	Oughteragh	Bawnboy	IV.	91
14	Aghaleague	574 2 34	Mayo	Tirawley	Lackan	Killala	IV.	170
8, 9, 14	Aghaleck	228 0 23	Antrim	Cary	Ramoan	Ballycastle	III.	14
62, 63, 66	Aghalee	774 1 8	Antrim	Upper Massereene	Aghalee	Lurgan	III.	29
58	Aghalee Beg	71 2 18	Kerry	Magunihy	Aglish	Killarney	II.	199
58	Aghalee More	185 0 12	Kerry	Magunihy	Aghadoe	Killarney	II.	199
62	AGHALEE T.	—	Antrim	Upper Massereene	Aghalee	Lurgan	III.	29
34	Aghalenane	45 3 24	Sligo	Tirerrill	Tawnagh	Sligo	IV.	241
45, 53	Aghalenty	111 0 17	Donegal	Kilmacrenan	Aghanunshin	Letterkenny	III.	122
31	Aghalile	146 2 13	Monaghan	Farney	Magheross	Carrickmacross	III.	273
108, 109	Aghalinane	305 3 6	Cork, W.R.	East Carbery, (W.D.)	Kinneigh	Dunmanway	III.	134
39	Aghalion	491 3 25	Cavan	Castlerahan	Castlerahan	Oldcastle	III.	67
9	Aghalisk	122 0 38	Monaghan	Monaghan	Kilmore	Monaghan	III.	275
3	Aghaliskeevan	51 0 22	Monaghan	Trough	Errigal Trough	Monaghan	III.	283
64	Aghalislone	238 3 32	Antrim	Upper Belfast	Derryaghy	Lisburn	III.	10
64	Aghalislone	426 1 10	Antrim	Upper Massereene	Derryaghy	Lisburn	III.	30
8	Aghalissabeagh	93 3 10	Monaghan	Monaghan	Clones	Monaghan	III.	274
2	Aghaloughan	58 0 33	Meath	Lower Kells	Enniskeen	Kells	I.	202
47	Aghaloonteen	591 1 29	Mayo	Tirawley	Addergoole	Castlebar	IV.	162
31, 37	Aghaloory	770 0 0	Cavan	Clanmahon	Ballintemple	Cavan	III.	75
105	Aghalough	148 0 31	Donegal	Tirhugh	Templecarn	Donegal	III.	148
29	Aghalough	427 0 10i	Leitrim	Carrigallen	Cloone	Mohill	IV.	90
29	Aghalough	289 1 19j	Leitrim	Carrigallen	Drumreilly	Bawnboy	IV.	90
18	Aghalough	68 3 32	Monaghan	Dartree	Aghabog	Cootehill	III.	263
49	Aghaloughan	286 1 36	Antrim	Upper Toome	Drummaul	Antrim	III.	33
33, 39	Aghaloughan	228 1 22	Cavan	Castlerahan	Lurgan	Oldcastle	III.	69
17, 21	Aghaloughan	121 0 4	Longford	Rathcline	Rathcline	Longford	I.	164
7	Aghaloughan	138 1 34	Monaghan	Trough	Donagh	Monaghan	III.	281
23	Aghalougher	110 2 2	Tyrone	Omagh West	Termonamongan	Castlederg	III.	316
20	Aghalour	680 1 10	Roscommon	Frenchpark	Tibohine	Castlereagh	IV.	204
25, 29	Aghalum	984 1 35	Antrim	Lower Glenarm	Ardclinis	Larne	III.	21
28	Aghalun	75 2 32	Fermanagh	Magherastephana	Aghavea	Lisnaskea	III.	218
23	Aghalunny	493 1 6k	Tyrone	Omagh West	Termonamongan	Castlederg	III.	316
34	Aghalurcher Glebe	47 1 32	Fermanagh	Magherastephana	Aghalurcher	Lisnaskea	III.	214
16	Aghalusky	217 3 8	King's Co.	Ballycowan	Rahan	Tullamore	I.	128
69, 78, 79	Aghalusky	228 3 21	Mayo	Carra	Aglish	Castlebar	IV.	123
70, 71, 79,80	Aghalusky	571 3 17	Mayo	Gallen	Templemore	Castlebar	IV.	151
19	Aghalust	48 2 36	Longford	Moydow	Ballymacormick	Longford	I.	160
74, 83	Aghalustia	1,180 3 23	Roscommon	Frenchpark	Castlemore	Castlereagh	IV.	202
5	Aghama	45 3 13	Fermanagh	Lurg	Magheraculmoney	Lowtherstown	III.	207
3	Aghamackalinn	292 3 30	Monaghan	Trough	Errigal Trough	Clogher	III.	283
19	Aghamaddock	274 2 15	Queen's Co.	Stradbally	Stradbally	Athy	I.	247
25	Aghamafir	174 2 15	Queen's Co.	Ballyadams	Rathaspick	Athy	I.	232
23, 24	Aghamannan	116 3 10	Roscommon	Ballintober North	Kilglass	Strokestown	IV.	186
99	Aghamarta	378 3 13	Cork, E.R.	Kerricurrihy	Templebreedy	Kinsale	II.	93

(a) Including 8A. 2R. 29P. water.
(b) Including 5A. 3R. 16P. water.
(c) Including 6A. 3R. 24P. water.
(d) Including 4A. 3R. 10P. water.
(e) Including 2A. 1R. 26P. water.
(f) Including 2A. 0R. 8P. water.
(g) Including 14A. 2R. 8P. water.
(h) Including 5A. 3R. 25P. water.
(i) Including 28A. 1R. 36P. water.
(j) Including 0A. 3R. 6P. water.
(k) Including 7A. 1R. 35P. water.

No. of Sheet of the Ordnance Survey Maps.	Townlands and Towns.	Area in Statute Acres.	County.	Barony.	Parish.	Poor Law Union in 1857.	Townland Census of 1851, Part I.	
		A. R. P.					Vol.	Page.
9, 14	Aghameelan .	574 3 24a	Fermanagh .	Magheraboy .	Inishmacsaint . .	Ballyshannon .	III.	212
27, 28	Aghameelick .	397 2 9	King's Co. .	Coolestown .	Clonsast . .	Edenderry .	I.	132
11, 15	Aghameelta .	157 3 34	Leitrim .	Drumahaire .	Drumlease .	Manorhamilton.	IV.	94
11	Aghameelta Barr .	245 3 13	Leitrim .	Drumahaire .	Drumlease .	Manorhamilton.	IV.	94
5, 8	Aghameen .	343 0 18	Louth .	Lower Dundalk .	Ballymascanlan .	Dundalk .	I.	175
31	Aghameeny .	40 0 4	Leitrim .	Leitrim .	Kiltoghert .	Car^k. on Shannon	IV.	100
65	Aghamilkin .	194 1 36b	Tyrone .	Clogher .	Clogher .	Clogher .	III.	291
135	Aghamilla .	338 0 14	Cork, W.R. .	Ibane and Barryroe	Kilgarriff .	Clonakilty .	II.	149
12	Aghamoat .	8 1 21	Armagh .	Armagh .	Armagh . .	Armagh .	III.	43
20, 21	Aghamore . . .	709 3 6	Fermanagh .	Magheraboy .	Boho . .	Enniskillen .	III.	209
14	Aghamore .	76 1 32c	Fermanagh .	Magheraboy .	Inishmacsaint .	Ballyshannon .	III.	212
8	Aghamore .	130 0 11	King's Co. .	Kilcoursey .	Kilbride .	Tullamore .	I.	141
10	Aghamore .	113 1 30	King's Co. .	Lower Philipstown .	Croghan .	Edenderry .	I.	142
20	Aghamore .	93 3 2	Leitrim .	Drumahaire .	Inishmagrath .	Manorhamilton.	IV.	95
32, 35	Aghamore .	143 1 14	Leitrim .	Mohill . .	Annaduff .	Mohill .	IV.	105
33, 36	Aghamore .	281 3 39	Leitrim .	Mohill . .	Cloone .	Mohill .	IV.	105
37	Aghamore .	184 3 14	Leitrim .	Mohill . .	Mohill .	Mohill .	IV.	107
6	Aghamore .	222 2 22	Leitrim .	Rosclogher .	Killasnet .	Manorhamilton.	IV.	109
3	Aghamore .	179 2 12	Leitrim .	Rosclogher .	Rossinver .	Ballyshannon .	IV.	110
15, 16	Aghamore .	87 1 32	Longford .	Ardagh .	Street .	Granard .	I.	153
10	Aghamore .	124 3 5	Longford .	Granard . .	Clonbroney .	Granard .	I.	154
17	Aghamore .	108 0 17	Longford .	Rathcline .	Rathcline .	Longford .	I.	164
81, 82	Aghamore .	436 2 26	Mayo .	Costello . .	Aghamore .	Swineford .	IV.	136
87	Aghamore .	44 1 33	Mayo .	Murrisk . .	Oughaval .	Westport .	IV.	161
2, 5	Aghamore .	431 0 37	Meath .	Lower Kells .	Kilmainham .	Kells .	I.	203
11	Aghamore .	71 0 14	Queen's Co. .	Upperwoods .	Offerlane . .	Mountmellick .	I.	250
17	Aghamore .	200 1 38d	Roscommon .	Roscommon .	Aughrim . .	Car^k. on Shannon	IV.	207
29	Aghamore .	59 2 19	Roscommon .	Roscommon .	Lissonuffy .	Strokestown .	IV.	211
23	Aghamore .	330 2 6	Tyrone .	Omagh West .	Termonamongan .	Castlederg .	III.	316
28	Aghamore .	574 2 17	Westmeath .	Farbill . .	Killucan .	Mullingar .	I.	266
38	Aghamore .	32 3 5	Westmeath .	Moycashel .	Kilbeggan .	Tullamore .	I.	278
2	Aghamore or Ashbrook . .	22 0 27	Queen's Co. .	Tinnahinch .	Kilmanman .	Mountmellick .	I	248
20, 21	Aghamore Far .	853 0 35	Sligo .	Carbury . .	St. John's .	Sligo . .	IV.	223
2	Aghamore Lower .	313 1 17	Longford .	Granard . .	Columbkille .	Longford .	I.	155
14,15,20,21	Aghamore Near .	283 0 6	Sligo .	Carbury . .	St. John's .	Sligo .	IV.	223
34	Aghamore North .	84 2 37	Fermanagh .	Magherastephana .	Aghalurcher .	Lisnaskea .	III.	214
15	Aghamore North .	406 0 35	Kerry .	Clanmaurice .	Killahan .	Tralee .	II.	170
34	Aghamore South .	105 1 14	Fermanagh .	Magherastephana .	Aghalurcher .	Lisnaskea .	III.	214
15	Aghamore South .	563 1 35	Kerry .	Clanmaurice .	Killahan .	Tralee .	II.	170
5, 6	Aghamore Upper .	459 3 29	Longford .	Granard . .	Columbkille .	Granard .	I.	155
36	Aghamuck .	189 0 19	Roscommon .	Ballintober South .	Kilgefin .	Roscommon .	IV.	189
6	Aghamucky .	1,061 0 26	Kilkenny .	Fassadinin .	Castlecomer .	Castlecomer .	I.	88
13	Aghamuldowney .	739 1 3	Fermanagh .	Magheraboy .	Devenish .	Ballyshannon .	III.	210
15, 21	Aghanacrinna .	215 1 3	Kerry .	Clanmaurice .	Killahan .	Tralee .	II.	170
14	Aghanageeragh .	178 1 31	Longford .	Ardagh .	Ardagh . .	Longford .	I.	151
40	Aghanagh .	307 0 14	Sligo .	Tirerrill . .	Aghanagh .	Boyle . .	IV.	237
20	Aghanaglack .	1,379 3 0e	Fermanagh .	Clanawley .	Boho . .	Enniskillen .	III.	189
35	Aghanaglogh .	97 2 24	Fermanagh .	Clankelly .	Galloon . .	Lisnaskea .	III.	198
5	Aghanagran Lower .	491 1 17	Kerry .	Iraghticonnor .	Aghavallen .	Listowel .	II.	189
2, 5	Aghanagran Middle	741 2 32	Kerry .	Iraghticonnor .	Aghavallen .	Listowel .	II.	189
2	Aghanagran Upper .	322 3 23	Kerry .	Iraghticonnor .	Aghavallen .	Listowel .	II.	189
59, 60	Aghanahil .	223 1 23	Galway .	Tiaquin . .	Killoscobe .	Mountbellew .	IV.	77
14, 19	Aghanahown .	129 1 10	Longford .	Ardagh .	Ardagh . .	Longford .	I.	151
32, 38	Aghanamanagh or Commcenlonagh .	59 3 13	Westmeath .	Moycashel .	Newtown .	Mullingar .	I.	279
5	Aghanameena .	129 1 37	Monaghan .	Monaghan .	Tedavnet .	Monaghan .	III.	278
63	Aghanamoney .	263 0 4	Antrim .	Upper Massereene .	Ballinderry .	Lisburn .	III.	29
9	Aghananimy .	118 2 9	Monaghan .	Monaghan .	Monaghan .	Monaghan .	III.	276
16	Aghanapisha .	28 2 21	Westmeath .	Kilkenny West .	Noughaval .	Ballymahon .	I.	274
30	Aghanargit .	120 3 9	Westmeath .	Clonlonan .	Kilcleagh .	Athlone .	I.	261
41, 47	Aghanascortan .	28 1 27f	Meath .	Upper Moyfenrath .	Killyon . .	Edenderry .	I.	213
30	Aghanashanamore .	41 3 35	Westmeath .	Clonlonan .	Ballyloughloe .	Athlone .	I.	260
88	Aghanboy .	148 1 14	Kerry .	Iveragh . .	Killemlagh .	Cahersiveen .	II.	196
9	Aghancarnan .	185 0 7	King's Co. .	Ballycowan .	Durrow . .	Tullamore .	I.	127
31	Aghancarra .	46 0 1	Leitrim .	Leitrim .	Kiltoghert .	Car^k. on Shannon	IV.	100
39	Aghancon .	298 1 6	King's Co. .	Ballybritt .	Aghancon .	Roscrea .	I.	124
12	Aghancrossy .	55 2 37	Antrim .	Lower Dunluce .	Derrykeighan .	Ballymoney .	III.	16
21	Aghandunvarran .	513 2 7g	Down .	Lower Iveagh, Up.pt.	Hillsborough .	Lisburn .	III.	169
22	Aghaneenagh .	359 1 19	Cork, E.R. .	Duhallow .	Kilmeen . .	Kanturk .	II.	72
9	Aghanergill or Corglass .	93 0 1	Armagh .	Oneilland West .	Drumcree .	Lurgan .	III.	51
45, 46	Aghangaddy Glebe .	528 2 27	Donegal .	Kilmacrenan .	Aughnish .	Millford .	III.	122

(a) Including 17A. 0R. 39P. water.
(b) Including 2A. 2R. 0P. water.
(c) Including 13A. 2R. 18P. water.

(d) Including 8A. 3R. 24P. water.
(e) Including 9A. 1R. 6P. water.

(f) Including 10A. 1R. 5P. detached portion.
(g) Including 1A. 2R. 16P. water.

No. of Sheet of the Ordnance Survey Maps.	Townlands and Towns.	Area in Statute Acres. A. R. P.	County.	Barony.	Parish.	Poor Law Union in 1857.	Townland Census of 1851, Part I. Vol.	Page
1, 2, 3, 4	Aghanlish	982 1 19	Leitrim	Rosclogher	Rossinver	Ballyshannon	IV.	110
63	Aghanliss	341 2 11	Antrim	Upper Massereene	Ballinderry	Lisburn	III.	29
21, 26	Aghannagh	134 2 14	Fermanagh	Clanawley	Cleenish	Enniskillen	III.	189
6	Aghanoran	532 2 4	Longford	Granard	Columbkille	Granard	I.	155
12	Aghanore	144 1 10	Armagh	Armagh	Grange	Armagh	III.	44
25	Aghanrush	260 1 18	King's Co.	Geashill	Geashill	Tullamore	I.	139
17	Aghansillagh	544 1 24	Londonderry	Keenaght	Balteagh	NewTⁿLimavady	III.	234
18	Aghantaraghan	761 2 27	Armagh	Orior Lower	Ballymore	Newry	III.	55
13, 18	Aghantrah	177 2 15	Longford	Moydow	Ballymacormick	Longford	I.	160
2	Aghanure	171 3 9	Carlow	Carlow	Painestown	Carlow	I.	2
35	Aghanure	257 0 4	Kildare	Narragh and Reban West	Kilberry	Athy	I.	67
26	Aghanure	401 0 4	Queen's Co.	Ballyadams	Killabban	Athy	I.	231
36	Aghanursan	119 0 15a	Donegal	Kilmacrenan	Tullyfern	Milford	III.	132
23	Aghanvally	68 3 23	Longford	Moydow	Taghsheenod	Ballymahon	I.	162
26	Aghanvilla	72 2 7	King's Co.	Upper Philipstown	Ballykean	Mountmellick	I.	143
26	Aghanvilla	257 1 18	King's Co.	Upper Philipstown	Geashill	Mountmellick	I.	144
29, 30	Aghanvoneen	121 1 24	Westmeath	Clonlonan	Ballyloughloe	Athlone	I.	260
107	Aghany	59 3 38	Galway	Longford	Killimorbologue	Portumna	IV.	58
85, 95	Aghany	481 1 21b	Mayo	Murrisk	Kilgeever	Westport	IV.	159
28	Agharah	135 1 37	Cavan	Clankee	Knockbride	Bailieborough	III.	73
26	Agharahan	149 1 8	Cavan	Upper Loughtee	Annagelliff	Cavan	III.	81
20	Agharahan	185 3 17	Fermanagh	Magheraboy	Devenish	Enniskillen	III.	210
5	Agharainy	151 2 3	Fermanagh	Lurg	Magheraculmoney	Lowtherstown	III.	207
22	Agharainy	108 2 16	Fermanagh	Tirkennedy	Derryvullan	Enniskillen	III	220
46	Agharan	161 2 29	Tyrone	Dungannon Middle	Donaghmore	Dungannon	III.	301
21	Agharanagh	96 3 19	Longford	Rathcline	Rathcline	Longford	I.	164
23	Agharanagh	173 1 16	Longford	Shrule	Taghshinny	Ballymahon	I.	167
29, 30	Agharann	735 1 29c	Leitrim	Carrigallen	Cloone	Mohill	IV.	90
30, 36	Agharanny	25 0 4	Westmeath	Clonlonan	Kilcleagh	Athlone	I.	261
10, 14	Agharaskilly	550 0 9d	Cavan	Lower Loughtee	Tomregan	Bawnboy	III.	81
11	Aghards	67 2 6	Kildare	North Salt	Kildrought	Celbridge	I.	74
15	Aghareagh	60 2 6	Longford	Ardagh	Street	Granard	I.	153
13	Aghareagh	175 2 34	Longford	Longford	Templemichael	Longford	I.	160
17	Aghareagh	116 1 30	Monaghan	Dartree	Aghabog	Cootehill	III.	263
13	Aghareagh Bog	147 0 26	Longford	Longford	Templemichael	Longford	I.	160
22	Aghareagh East	294 1 10e	Monaghan	Dartree	Currin	Cootehill	III.	265
16, 21, 22	Aghareagh West	175 3 26	Monaghan	Dartree	Currin	Clones	III.	265
46, 54	Aghareany	341 0 32	Tyrone	Dungannon Middle	Donaghmore	Dungannon	III.	301
36	Agharevagh East	41 2 17	Westmeath	Clonlonan	Kilcleagh	Athlone	I.	261
35	Agharevagh West	24 0 31	Westmeath	Clonlonan	Kilcleagh	Athlone	I.	261
91, 101	Aghareville Lower	164 3 16	Mayo	Clanmorris	Kilcolman	Claremorris	IV.	133
91, 101	Aghareville Upper	233 2 5	Mayo	Clanmorris	Kilcolman	Claremorris	IV.	133
14	Agharickard	93 0 7	Longford	Ardagh	Templemichael	Longford	I.	153
72	Agharinagh	763 2 8	Cork, E.R.	East Muskerry	Inishcarra	Cork	II.	103
51	Agharonan	706 1 27	Tyrone	Clogher	Donacavey	Omagh	III.	294
35	Agharoosky	92 3 11	Fermanagh	Clankelly	Clones	Clones	III.	194
1, 2, 4	Agharoosky	346 3 38	Leitrim	Rosclogher	Rossinver	Ballyshannon	IV.	110
40	Agharoosky East	132 2 28	Fermanagh	Clankelly	Galloon	Clones	III.	198
40	Agharoosky West	125 1 9	Fermanagh	Coole	Galloon	Clones	III.	199
23, 24	Agharra	442 3 29f	Longford	Shrule	Agharra	Ballymahon	I.	166
1	Agharroo	398 2 34	Leitrim	Rosclogher	Rossinver	Ballyshannon	IV.	110
5	Agharrow	206 2 14	Sligo	Carbury	Ahamlish	Sligo	IV.	219
11	Agharue	715 1 32	Carlow	Idrone West	Tullowcreen	Carlow	I.	9
23	Aghascrebagh	159 0 32	Tyrone	Omagh West	Termonamongan	Castlederg	III.	316
19, 27	Aghascrebagh	483 2 26	Tyrone	Strabane Upper	Bodoney Lower	Gortin	III.	323
24, 25	Aghasessy	432 2 38	Tyrone	Strabane Lower	Ardstraw	Strabane	III.	318
78	Aghasheil	28 1 20	Donegal	Raphoe	Stranorlar	Stranorlar	III.	142
82	Aghataharn	542 1 2g	Mayo	Costello	Aghamore	Swineford	IV.	136
30	Aghatamy	94 3 22	Monaghan	Farney	Magheracloone	Carrickmacross	III.	272
25	Aghatawny Lower	101 1 29	Leitrim	Carrigallen	Oughteragh	Bawnboy	IV.	91
25	Aghatawny Upper	66 3 31	Leitrim	Carrigallen	Oughteragh	Bawnboy	IV.	91
20, 21	Aghateeduff	163 0 2	Cavan	Upper Loughtee	Castleterra	Cavan	III.	82
21	Aghateemore Glebe	13 0 13	Cavan	Upper Loughtee	Larah	Cavan	III.	85
26	Aghateggal or Ryefort	109 0 20	Cavan	Upper Loughtee	Denn	Cavan	III.	83
31	Aghaterry	90 3 37	Queen's Co.	Slievemargy	Killabban	Carlow	I.	245
28	Aghateskin	105 0 33	Monaghan	Farney	Donaghmoyne	Carrickmacross	III.	269
30, 36	Aghathomas	54 1 34	Meath	Upper Navan	Trim	Trim	I.	216
32, 37	Aghatirourke	2,019 0 31	Fermanagh	Clanawley	Killesher	Enniskillen	III.	192
17, 22	Aghatotan	202 3 26	Cavan	Tullygarvey	Kildrumsherdan	Cootehill	III.	89
12	Aghatubbrid	576 2 7	Donegal	Inishowen East	Culdaff	Inishowen	III.	118
88	Aghatubrid	992 1 28	Kerry	Iveragh	Caher	Cahersiveen	II.	193

(a) Including 21A. 1R. 0P. water.
(b) Including 18A. 2R. 15P. water.
(c) Including 78A. 3R. 0P. water.
(d) Including 22A. 2R. 29P. water.
(e) Including 22A. 3R. 4P. water.
(f) Including 14A. 1R. 13P. water.
(g) Including 112A. 3R. 1P. water.

No. of Sheet of the Ordnance Survey Maps.	Townlands and Towns.	Area in Statute Acres.			County.	Barony.	Parish.	Poor Law Union in 1857.	Townland Census of 1851, Part I.	
		A.	R.	P.					Vol.	Page
142	Aghatubrid Beg	156	0	36	Cork, W.R.	East Carbery (W.D.)	Kilfaughnabeg	Skibbereen	II.	132
142	Aghatubrid More	274	2	39	Cork, W.R.	East Carbery (W.D.)	Kilfaughnabeg	Skibbereen	II.	132
24	Aghavadden	213	3	6a	Leitrim	Leitrim	Fenagh	Mohill	IV.	100
21	Aghavadden	123	1	10	Longford	Rathcline	Cashel	Ballymahon	I.	163
32	Aghavaddy	92	0	33	Cavan	Upper Loughtee	Denn	Cavan	III.	83
19	Aghavadrin	183	0	1b	Cavan	Tullyhunco	Killashandra	Cavan	III.	97
22, 28	Aghavannagh Mountain	1,523	3	1	Wicklow	Ballinacor South	Moyne	Shillelagh	I.	350
28, 29	Aghavannagh (Ram)	1,026	1	22	Wicklow	Ballinacor South	Ballinacor	Rathdrum	I.	347
28, 29	Aghavannagh (Revell)	2,769	0	6	Wicklow	Ballinacor South	Ballinacor	Rathdrum	I.	347
28, 37	Aghavannan Far	179	2	27	Donegal	Kilmacrenan	Killygarvan	Millford	III.	128
28, 37	Aghavannan Near	102	3	3	Donegal	Kilmacrenan	Killygarvan	Millford	III.	128
8	Aghavanny	491	1	30c	Leitrim	Rosclogher	Cloonclare	Manorhamilton	IV.	109
36, 37	Aghavary	408	0	24	Antrim	Upper Toome	Ballyscullion Grange	Ballymena	III.	33
29, 33	Aghavas	343	2	8	Leitrim	Carrigallen	Cloone	Mohill	IV.	90
25	Aghavass	184	3	3	Fermanagh	Clanawley	Cleenish	Enniskillen	III.	189
28	Aghavea	131	3	37	Fermanagh	Magherastephana	Aghavea	Lisnaskea	III.	218
77	Aghaveagh	1,225	2	13d	Donegal	Raphoe	Kilteevoge	Stranorlar	III.	159
30, 39	Aghaveagh	375	3	37	Tyrone	Dungannon Upper	Tamlaght	Cookstown	III.	309
28	Aghavea Glebe	58	0	36	Fermanagh	Magherastephana	Aghavea	Lisnaskea	III	218
30, 36	Aghaveans,	615	1	38e	Cavan	Tullyhunco	Scrabby	Granard	III.	99
5, 9	Aghavellan or Richmount	123	1	13	Armagh	Oneilland West	Drumcree	Lurgan	III.	52
14, 15	Aghavilla	129	0	7f	Cavan	Lower Loughtee	Drumlane	Cavan	III.	79
30	Aghavilla	330	0	37	Leitrim	Carrigallen	Carrigallen	Mohill	IV.	89
28, 31	Aghavilla	117	1	19	Monaghan	Farney	Donaghmoyne	Carrickmacross	III.	269
119	Aghaville	515	1	33	Cork, W.R.	West Carbery (W.D.)	Caheragh	Skibbereen	II.	141
31	Aghaviller	208	3	8	Kilkenny	Knocktopher	Aghaviller	Thomastown	I.	110
16	Aghavilly	232	1	9	Armagh	Armagh	Lisnadill	Armagh	III.	45
51	Aghavilly	419	1	2	Down	Upper Iveagh, Up.pt.	Clonallan	Newry	III.	174
78	Aghavine	586	0	12	Cork, E.R.	Imokilly	Kilmacdonogh	Youghal	II.	88
2, 4	Aghavoghil	1,799	1	25	Leitrim	Rosclogher	Rossinver	Ballyshannon	IV.	110
14	Aghavoher	228	3	0g	Cavan	Lower Loughtee	Tomregan	Bawnboy	III.	81
36	Aghavoneen	169	2	37	Westmeath	Clonlonan	Kilcleagh	Athlone	I.	261
24	Aghavoory	279	3	37	Fermanagh	Magherastephana	Aghalurcher	Lisnaskea	III.	214
1	Aghavore	190	1	27	Fermanagh	Lurg	Drumkeeran	Lowtherstown	III.	205
30	Aghavore	584	1	30h	Leitrim	Carrigallen	Carrigallen	Mohill	IV.	89
60, 61, 71, 72	Aghavrin	667	1	11	Cork, W.R.	East Muskerry	Aghabulloge	Macroom	II.	153
11	Aghawaracahill	35	2	5	Roscommon	Ballintober North	Kilmore	Cark. on Shannon	IV.	186
9	Aghaward	281	0	12	Longford	Granard	Clonbroney	Granard	I.	154
61	Aghaward	251	3	35i	Mayo	Gallen	Toomore	Swineford	IV.	151
21, 22	Aghaway	328	2	6	Cavan	Tullygarvey	Larah	Cootehill	III.	90
31	Aghawee	448	1	0	Cavan	Clanmahon	Crosserlough	Cavan	III.	76
79	Aghawee	124	2	22	Donegal	Raphoe	Clonleigh	Strabane	III.	134
31	Aghaweely Lower	330	3	27	Cavan	Clanmahon	Ballintemple	Cavan	III.	75
31	Aghaweely Upper	231	1	36	Cavan	Clanmahon	Ballintemple	Cavan	III.	75
14	Aghaweenagh	375	0	38j	Cavan	Tullyhunco	Kildallan	Bawnboy	III.	96
38	Aghaweenagh	173	3	31	Fermanagh	Knockninny	Kinawley	Lisnaskea	III.	201
36	Aghawerriny	166	2	33	Roscommon	Ballintober South	Kilgefin	Roscommon	IV.	189
30, 34	Aghawillin	413	1	39	Leitrim	Carrigallen	Carrigallen	Mohill	IV.	89
22, 25	Aghawillin	83	1	15	Leitrim	Carrigallen	Drumreilly	Bawnboy	IV.	90
3, 6	Aghawinnaun	1,545	3	13	Clare	Burren	Oughtmama	Ballyvaghan	IV.	14
38, 42	Aghawonan	105	2	22	Cavan	Clanmahon	Kilbride	Oldcastle	III.	77
36, 45	Aghawoney	212	1	7k	Donegal	Kilmacrenan	Kilmacrenan	Millford	III.	128
29	Aghayalloge	571	3	7	Armagh	Orior Upper	Killevy	Newry	III.	57
91, 92	Aghayeevoge	346	1	31	Donegal	Banagh	Killybegs Upper	Glenties	III.	110
29	Aghclare	269	2	30	Kilkenny	Gowran	Graiguenamanagh	Thomastown	I.	95
31, 32	Aghcross	150	0	28	Queen's Co.	Slievemargy	Killabban	Carlow	I.	245
10, 11, 15, 16	Aghduff	159	3	33	Queen's Co.	Upperwoods	Offerlane	Mountmellick	I.	250
49	Aghee	249	1	13	Tyrone	Omagh East	Dromore	Omagh	III.	311
34	Aghee	138	1	7	Tyrone	Omagh East	Drumragh	Omagh	III.	312
24	Agheeghter	264	0	2	Fermanagh	Magherastephana	Aghalurcher	Lisnaskea	III.	214
25	Agheeshal	115	2	16	Monaghan	Farney	Donaghmoyne	Castleblayney	III.	269
22, 23	Aghenderry	170	3	15	Kilkenny	Shillelogher	Tullaghanbrogue	Callan	I.	116
67	Aghenis	358	3	4	Tyrone	Dungannon Lower	Aghaloo	Armagh	III.	296
42, 43, 48, 49	Agher	1,168	2	4	Meath	Upper Deece	Agher	Trim	I.	192
49	Agher	24	0	16	Meath	Upper Deece	Gallow	Trim	I.	193
5, 8	Agheracalkill	75	3	30	Monaghan	Monaghan	Tedavnet	Monaghan	III.	278
1	Agheragh	188	0	5	Meath	Lower Kells	Moybolgue	Kells	I.	203
5	Agherakeltan	176	2	23	Monaghan	Monaghan	Tedavnet	Monaghan	III.	278
19, 24	Agheralane	212	3	2	Monaghan	Cremorne	Ballybay	Castleblayney	III.	259
36, 45	Aghern East	328	0	9	Cork, E.R.	Kinnatalloon	Aghern	Fermoy	II.	97
36, 45	Aghern West	287	2	15	Cork, E.R.	Kinnatalloon	Aghern	Fermoy	II.	97

(a) Including 75A. 0R. 29P. water. (e) Including 87A. 1R. 36P. water. (i) Including 4A. 0R. 2P. water.
(b) Including 17A. 3R. 32P. water. (f) Including 5A. 0R. 9P. water. (j) Including 16A. 2R. 28P. water.
(c) Including 40A. 2R. 38P. water. (g) Including 10A. 1R. 13P. water. (k) Including 16A. 3R. 8P. water.
(d) Including 10A. 2R. 4P. water. (h) Including 41A. 0R. 8P. water.

No. of Sheet of the Ordnance Survey Maps.	Townlands and Towns.	Area in Statute Acres.	County.	Barony.	Parish.	Poor Law Union in 1857.	Townland Census of 1851, Part I.	
		A. R. P.					Vol.	Page
24	Aghfarrell	581 2 28	Dublin	Uppercross	Tallaght	Dublin South	I.	41
2	Aghfarrell	12 0 32	Wicklow	Lower Talbotstown	Kilbride	Naas	I.	361
149	Aghillaun	3 1 25	Cork, W.R.	West Carbery (E.D.)	Creagh	Skibbereen	II.	139
142	Aghills	732 3 29a	Cork, W.R.	West Carbery (E.D.)	Castlehaven	Skibbereen	II.	137
29	Aghilly and Lenynarnan	377 3 8	Donegal	Inishowen West	Fahan Lower	Inishowen	III.	120
18	Aghinaspick	231 3 21	Longford	Moydow	Moydow	Longford	I.	162
21	Aghincurk	1,165 2 4	Armagh	Fews Upper	Ballymyre	Newry	III.	48
38	Aghindaiagh	361 3 0	Fermanagh	Knockninny	Kinawley	Lisnaskea	III.	201
65	Aghindarragh East	278 2 8b	Tyrone	Clogher	Clogher	Clogher	III.	291
64	Aghindarragh West	248 0 6	Tyrone	Clogher	Clogher	Clogher	III.	291
38, 41	Aghindisert	167 2 3	Fermanagh	Knockninny	Tomregan	Lisnaskea	III.	203
58	Aghindrumman	159 0 15c	Tyrone	Clogher	Clogher	Clogher	III.	291
58, 64	Aghingowly	214 0 2	Tyrone	Clogher	Clogher	Clogher	III.	291
30	Aghinillard	179 0 29	Monaghan	Farney	Magheracloone	Carrickmacross.	III.	272
34	Aghinish	24 1 17	Fermanagh	Knockninny	Kinawley	Lisnaskea	III.	202
109	Aghinish	370 2 12	Mayo	Carra	Ballyovey	Ballinrobe	IV.	126
64	Aghinlark	253 0 36d	Tyrone	Clogher	Clogher	Clogher	III.	291
4, 8	Aghinlig	509 1 36	Armagh	Armagh	Loughgall	Armagh	III.	45
22, 23	Aghinraheen	319 2 35	Kilkenny	Shillelogher	Tullaghanbrogue	Callan	I.	116
58	Aghintain	86 1 29	Tyrone	Clogher	Clogher	Clogher	III.	291
10	Aghintamy	104 2 31	Monaghan	Monaghan	Monaghan	Monaghan	III.	276
35	Aghintass	138 2 14	Leitrim	Mohill	Annaduff	Mohill	IV.	105
37	Aghinteeduff	38 0 37	Leitrim	Mohill	Mohill	Mohill	IV.	107
14	Aghintemple	191 1 24	Longford	Ardagh	Ardagh	Longford	I.	151
31	Aghintober	36 0 30	Leitrim	Leitrim	Annaduff	Cark. on Shannon	IV.	99
53	Aghintober	122 1 30	Tyrone	Dungannon Middle	Donaghmore	Dungannon	III.	301
38	Aghintra	251 0 21	Fermanagh	Knockninny	Kinawley	Lisnaskea	III.	201
28	Aghinure	122 0 23	Fermanagh	Magherastephana	Aghalurcher	Lisnaskea	III.	214
10	Aghinver	157 2 2	Fermanagh	Lurg	Magheraculmoney	Lowtherstown	III.	207
12	Aghlacon	137 0 30e	Leitrim	Drumahaire	Cloonclare	Manorhamilton	IV.	93
31, 34	Aghlattacru	128 1 21	Monaghan	Farney	Magheracloone	Carrickmacross	III.	272
24	Aghleam	732 2 3	Mayo	Erris	Kilmore	Belmullet	IV.	145
53,54,61,62	Aghlehard	516 0 1	Donegal	Raphoe	Leck	Letterkenny	III.	140
94	Aghlem	234 3 9	Donegal	Tirhugh	Donegal	Donegal	III.	144
21, 24	Aghlin	237 1 17	Leitrim	Carrigallen	Oughteragh	Bawnboy	IV.	91
29, 30	Aghlisk	186 0 26	Galway	Dunmore	Tuam	Tuam	IV.	35
50	Aghlisk	248 2 39f	Tyrone	Omagh East	Dromore	Omagh	III.	311
36, 43	Aghlisnafin	809 1 16	Down	Lecale Upper	Kilmegan	Downpatrick	III.	181
22	Aghloonagh	59 2 2	Roscommon	Roscommon	Ogulla	Strokestown	IV.	212
34	Aghmacart	481 3 9	Queen's Co.	Clarmallagh	Aghmacart	Abbeyleix	I.	236
40	Aghmagree	521 2 32	Roscommon	Ballintober South	Kilteevan	Roscommon	IV.	189
25,26,28,29	Aghmakane	431 0 4g	Armagh	Orior Upper	Killevy	Newry	III.	57
24	Aghnakerr	256 2 19h	Monaghan	Cremorne	Aghnamullen	Castleblayney	III.	257
136	Aghmanister and Spital	153 1 7	Cork, W.R.	Ibane and Barryroe	Abbeymahon	Clonakilty	II.	148
4	Aghnablaney	345 0 22	Fermanagh	Lurg	Templecarn	Lowtherstown	III.	209
17	Aghnabohy	295 1 21	Westmeath	Rathconrath	Piercetown	Ballymahon	I.	283
7, 9	Aghnacally	760 1 16	Cavan	Tullyhaw	Kinawley	Bawnboy	III.	92
14	Aghnacally Glebe	34 1 0	Cavan	Tullyhaw	Templemichael	Longford	I.	153
27	Aghnacarra	99 3 9i	Fermanagh	Magherastephana	Derrybrusk	Lisnaskea	III.	219
35	Aghnachuill	37 3 10	Fermanagh	Clankelly	Clones	Clones	III.	194
18, 19	Aghnaclea	167 2 35	Monaghan	Monaghan	Kilmore	Monaghan	III.	275
6	Aghnacliff	236 3 13	Longford	Granard	Columbkille	Granard	I.	155
6	Aghnacloy	75 3 37	Armagh	Oneilland East	Shankill	Lurgan	III.	50
33, 38	Aghnacloy	131 1 24	Fermanagh	Knockninny	Kinawley	Lisnaskea	III.	201
28	Aghnacloy North	290 0 6	Fermanagh	Magherastephana	Aghavea	Lisnaskea	III.	218
28	Aghnacloy South	150 0 25	Fermanagh	Magherastephana	Aghavea	Lisnaskea	III.	218
34	Aghnaclue	70 2 32	Cavan	Clankee	Moybolgue	Bailieborough	III.	74
6	Aghnacollia	322 3 22	Cavan	Tullyhaw	Templeport	Bawnboy	III.	93
24	Aghnacor	157 3 30	Cavan	Tullyhunco	Killashandra	Cavan	III.	97
22	Aghnacranagh	42 2 37	Longford	Rathcline	Kilcommock	Ballymahon	I.	164
14, 19	Aghnacreevy	240 2 7	Cavan	Tullyhunco	Kildallan	Bawnboy	III.	96
32	Aghnacross	28 2 31	Leitrim	Mohill	Mohill	Mohill	IV.	107
21	Aghnacross	85 3 24	Longford	Rathcline	Cashel	Ballymahon	I.	163
30	Aghnacross	397 3 11	Queen's Co.	Cullenagh	Dysartgallen	Abbeyleix	I.	239
17, 18	Aghnacue	176 1 39	Monaghan	Dartree	Aghabog	Cootehill	III.	263
20	Aghnadamph	497 3 0	Monaghan	Cremorne	Muckno	Castleblayney	III.	261
21	Aghnadaragan	49 3 15	Cavan	Tullygarvey	Drung	Cootehill	III.	88
58, 59	Aghnadarragh	334 3 4	Antrim	Upper Massereene	Camlin	Antrim	III.	30
33	Aghnadore	287 2 21	Antrim	Lower Antrim	Racavan	Ballymena	III.	4
39	Aghnadrung	68 3 30	Cavan	Castlerahan	Lurgan	Oldcastle	III.	69
25	Aghnafarcan	135 3 34	Monaghan	Farney	Donaghmoyne	Castleblayney	III.	269

(a) Including 44A. 1R. 10P. water.　(d) Including 5A. 1R. 24P. water.　(g) Including 3A. 2R. 0P. water.
(b) Including 5A. 3R. 24P. water.　(e) Including 4A. 2R. 34P. water.　(h) Including 18A. 1R. 13P. water.
(c) Including 1A. 0R. 0P. water.　(f) Including 5A. 2R. 0P. water.　(i) Including 6A. 3R. 2P. water.

No. of Sheet of the Ordnance Survey Maps.	Townlands and Towns.	Area in Statute Acres. A. R. P.	County.	Barony.	Parish.	Poor Law Union in 1857.	Townland Census of 1851, Part I. Vol.	Page
10, 14	Aghnagap	217 0 30	Monaghan	Monaghan	Monaghan	Monaghan	III.	276
6, 7	Aghnagap	88 2 21	Monaghan	Trough	Donagh	Monaghan	III.	281
45, 53	Aghnagar	468 1 18	Tyrone	Dungannon Middle	Donaghmore	Dungannon	III.	301
44, 52	Aghnagar	467 2 25	Tyrone	Omagh East	Clogherny	Omagh	III.	310
6, 7, 10, 11	Aghnagarron	511 2 31	Longford	Granard	Granard	Granard	I.	156
40, 46, 47	Aghnagillagh	246 2 11	Meath	Upper Moyfenrath	Clonard	Edenderry	I.	213
44	Aghnaglea	228 3 4	Tyrone	Omagh East	Termonmaguirk	Omagh	III.	314
24, 25	Aghnaglear	626 0 25	Carlow	St. Mullin's Lower	St. Mullin's	New Ross	I.	13
25	Aghnaglogh	192 0 37	Cavan	Tullygarvey	Kildrumsherdan	Cootehill	III.	89
22	Aghnaglogh	172 3 8	Cavan	Upper Loughtee	Annagelliff	Cavan	III.	81
13	Aghnaglogh	221 0 16	Monaghan	Monaghan	Kilmore	Monaghan	III.	275
14	Aghnaglogh	149 2 32	Monaghan	Monaghan	Monaghan	Monaghan	III.	276
58	Aghnaglogh	263 2 23	Tyrone	Clogher	Clogher	Clogher	III.	291
23	Aghnagollop	250 1 27	Leitrim	Leitrim	Kiltoghert	Car^k. on Shannon	IV.	100
13	Aghnagore	388 3 30	Longford	Longford	Killashee	Longford	I.	158
23	Aghnagrane	332 2 26	Fermanagh	Magherastephana	Aghavea	Lisnaskea	III.	218
6	Aghnagrange	100 2 7	Roscommon	Boyle	Boyle	Boyle	IV.	193
36	Aghnagreggan	428 3 10	Tyrone	Omagh East	Termonmaguirk	Omagh	III.	314
44, 45	Aghnagross	107 2 18	King's Co.	Clonlisk	Dunkerrin	Roscrea	I.	130
15	Aghnaguig	70 3 27a	Cavan	Lower Loughtee	Annagh	Cavan	III.	78
3	Aghnaha	85 3 6	Monaghan	Trough	Errigal Trough	Monaghan	III.	283
4, 5	Aghnahaha	890 1 14	Leitrim	Rosclogher	Rossinver	Manorhamilton	IV.	110
31	Aghnahaia Glebe	107 1 26	Cavan	Upper Loughtee	Denn	Cavan	III.	83
13	Aghnaharna or Summerhill	134 2 18	Queen's Co.	Maryborough East	Borris	Mountmellick	I.	240
38	Aghnahederny	254 1 11	Cavan	Clanmahon	Kilbride	Cavan	III.	77
13	Aghnahily	204 2 9	Queen's Co.	Maryborough East	Dysartenos	Mountmellick	I.	241
13	Aghnahily Bog	49 0 11	Queen's Co.	Maryborough East	Dysartenos	Mountmellick	I.	241
40	Aghnahinch	200 1 18b	Fermanagh	Coole	Galloon	Clones	III.	199
53	Aghnahoe	396 3 1	Tyrone	Dungannon Lower	Killeeshil	Dungannon	III.	298
16	Aghnahola	93 0 9	Monaghan	Dartree	Currin	Clones	III.	265
31, 32, 37	Aghnahoo	720 2 8c	Fermanagh	Clanawley	Killesher	Enniskillen	III.	192
23, 24	Aghnahoo	142 1 22	Leitrim	Leitrim	Kiltubbrid	Car^k. on Shannon	IV.	103
4	Aghnahoo	391 3 26	Leitrim	Rosclogher	Rossinver	Manorhamilton	IV.	110
23	Aghnahoo	271 2 22	Tyrone	Omagh West	Termonamongan	Castlederg	III.	316
105	Aghnahoo Glebe	231 0 7	Donegal	Tirhugh	Templecarn	Donegal	III.	149
63, 64	Aghnahough	737 1 28	Antrim	Upper Massereene	Derryaghy	Lisburn	III.	30
37	Aghnahunshin	111 3 2	Leitrim	Mohill	Mohill	Mohill	IV.	107
8	Aghnahunshin	65 1 18	Monaghan	Monaghan	Tedavnet	Monaghan	III.	278
70	Aghnakeeragh	76 1 14	Donegal	Raphoe	Raphoe	Strabane	III.	140
15, 22	Aghnaleck	671 3 9	Down	Lower Iveagh, Lr. pt.	Annahilt	Lisburn	III.	167
27, 28	Aghnaloo	196 0 32d	Fermanagh	Magherastephana	Aghalurcher	Lisnaskea	III.	214
8, 9	Aghnamaddoo	199 2 39	Longford	Longford	Kiloe	Longford	I.	158
8, 9	Aghnamallagh	237 1 33	Monaghan	Monaghan	Drumsnat	Monaghan	III.	275
17	Aghnamard	55 1 7	Monaghan	Dartree	Killeevan	Clones	III.	267
22	Aghnameadle	590 1 39	Tipperary, N.R.	Upper Ormond	Aghnameadle	Nenagh	II.	288
14	Aghnameal	140 1 19	Monaghan	Cremorne	Clontibret	Monaghan	III.	259
19, 27	Aghnamirigan	378 1 16	Tyrone	Strabane Upper	Bodoney Lower	Gortin	III.	323
50	Aghnamoe	698 2 5e	Tyrone	Omagh East	Dromore	Omagh	III.	311
50, 51	Aghnamoira	565 1 25f	Down	Upper Iveagh, Up. pt.	Clonallan	Newry	III.	174
37	Aghnamona	207 0 6	Leitrim	Mohill	Mohill	Mohill	IV.	107
34	Aghnamoyle	297 3 3g	Tyrone	Omagh East	Drumragh	Omagh	III.	312
23	Aghnamullen	173 2 27h	Monaghan	Cremorne	Aghnamullen	Cootehill	III.	257
8, 16	Aghnananagh	400 3 19	King's Co.	Ballycowan	Kilbride	Tullamore	I.	127
5	Aghnaneane or Hermitage	198 1 35	Meath	Lower Kells	Moynalty	Kells	I.	203
36, 37	Aghnanereagh	286 1 10i	Tyrone	Omagh East	Termonmaguirk	Omagh	III.	314
9	Aghnasedagh	458 3 26j	Monaghan	Monaghan	Monaghan	Monaghan	III.	276
8	Aghnashalvy	33 0 1	Monaghan	Monaghan	Clones	Monaghan	III.	274
36	Aghnashammer	62 1 0	Fermanagh	Clankelly	Clones	Clones	III.	194
9	Aghnashannagh	386 1 17	Longford	Granard	Clonbroney	Granard	I.	154
18	Aghnashingan	95 2 4	Longford	Moydow	Kilcommock	Ballymahon	I.	161
19	Aghnasillagh	256 1 14	Longford	Moydow	Kilglass	Ballymahon	I.	161
18	Aghnaskea	43 3 38	Longford	Moydow	Killashee	Longford	I.	161
12	Aghnaskea	51 0 13k	Monaghan	Dartree	Killeevan	Clones	III.	267
45	Aghnaskea	240 3 21	Tyrone	Dungannon Middle	Pomeroy	Dungannon	III.	303
42	Aghnaskeagh	124 3 6	Cavan	Clanmahon	Kilbride	Oldcastle	III.	77
4	Aghnaskeagh	321 3 9	Louth	Lower Dundalk	Ballymascanlan	Dundalk	I.	175
20	Aghnaskerry	7 3 25	Cavan	Upper Loughtee	Urney	Cavan	III.	86
28	Aghnaskew	161 1 11	Fermanagh	Magherastephana	Aghalurcher	Lisnaskea	III.	214
23	Aghnaskew	162 3 11	Monaghan	Cremorne	Aghnamullen	Castleblayney	III.	257
16, 21	Aghnaskew	264 3 37	Monaghan	Dartree	Currin	Clones	III.	265
43	Aghnaskew Glebe	42 0 13	Fermanagh	Clankelly	Currin	Clones	III.	197

(a) Including 8A. 0R. 14P. water.
(b) Including 6A. 0R. 10P. water.
(c) Including 7A. 0R. 16P. water.
(d) Including 10A. 2R. 16P. Lough Corban.

(e) Including 2A. 2R. 19P. water.
(f) Including 7A. 0R. 8P. water.
(g) Including 0A. 3R. 34P. water.
(h) Including 6A. 2R. 9P. water.

(i) Including 2A. 3R. 29P. water.
(j) Including 9A. 1R. 8P. water.
(k) Including 7A. 2R. 6P. water.

No. of Sheet of the Ordnance Survey Maps.	Townlands and Towns.	Area in Statute Acres.	County.	Barony.	Parish.	Poor Law Union in 1857.	Townland Census of 1851, Part I.	
		A. R. P.					Vol.	Page
35, 36	Aghnasullivan	62 3 11	Westmeath	Clonlonan	Kilcleagh	Athlone	I.	261
3	Aghnasurn	70 3 28	Roscommon	Boyle	Kilbryan	Boyle	IV.	195
14	Aghnatrisk	277 1 22a	Down	Lower Iveagh, Up.pt.	Blaris	Lisburn	III.	169
1, 3	Aghnavar	53 0 21	Monaghan	Trough	Errigal Trough	Clogher	III.	283
20, 24	Aghnavealoge	356 3 38b	Longford	Ardagh	Rathreagh	Ballymahon	I.	153
19	Agho	916 1 19c	Fermanagh	Clanawley	Boho	Ballyshannon	III.	189
43	Aghody	207 2 25	King's Co.	Ballybritt	Aghancon	Roscrea	I.	124
24, 25	Aghoney	559 2 11	Queen's Co.	Cullenagh	Fossy or Timahoe	Abbeyleix	I.	240
25	Aghoo	92 2 12	Leitrim	Carrigallen	Drumreilly	Bawnboy	IV.	90
6, 7, 13, 14	Aghoo	508 3 7	Mayo	Tirawley	Doonfeeny	Killala	IV.	167
3	Aghoo	219 1 4	Roscommon	Boyle	Ardcarn	Boyle	IV.	192
27, 28	Aghoo	196 0 15	Sligo	Tirerrill	Kilmacallan	Sligo	IV.	239
25	Aghoo East	247 3 1	Leitrim	Carrigallen	Oughteragh	Bawnboy	IV.	91
11	Aghoos	897 3 34	Mayo	Erris	Kilcommon	Belmullet	IV.	143
25	Aghoo West	46 0 30	Leitrim	Carrigallen	Oughteragh	Bawnboy	IV.	91
88, 96, 97	Aghort	536 2 24	Kerry	Iveragh	Killemlagh	Cahersiveen	II.	196
13	Aghory	463 0 2	Armagh	Oneilland West	Kilmore	Armagh	III.	53
38	Aghoutereery	368 2 4	Cavan	Clanmahon	Kilbride	Cavan	III.	77
24	Aghowle Lower	325 2 3	Wicklow	Newcastle	Rathnew	Rathdrum	I.	354
42	Aghowle Lower	787 3 0	Wicklow	Shillelagh	Aghowle	Shillelagh	I.	356
24	Aghowle Upper	488 0 26	Wicklow	Newcastle	Rathnew	Rathdrum	I.	354
42	Aghowle Upper	556 0 12	Wicklow	Shillelagh	Aghowle	Shillelagh	I.	356
14	Aghpaudeen	7 0 16	Kildare	Clane	Killybegs	Naas	I.	54
36	Aghraboy	30 2 26	King's Co.	Ballybritt	Letterluna	Parsonstown	I.	126
3	Aghrafinigan	282 2 35	Roscommon	Boyle	Ardcarn	Boyle	IV.	192
90, 96	Aghragh	726 3 6	Donegal	Banagh	Glencolumbkille	Glenties	III.	105
33	Aghrane or Castle-kelly	751 2 8	Galway	Killian	Athleague	Mountbellew	IV.	43
33	Aghrane or Castle-kelly	564 3 37	Galway	Killian	Killeroran	Mountbellew	IV.	43
8, 13	Aghrunniaght	214 0 0	Antrim	Cary	Armoy	Ballycastle	III.	11
17	Aghsmear	466 1 21	Tipperary, N.R.	Ikerrin	Corbally	Roscrea	II.	275
81, 92	Aghtaboy	358 2 26	Mayo	Costello	Knock	Claremorris	IV.	142
38	Aghuldred	174 0 37	Westmeath	Moycashel	Kilbeggan	Tullamore	I.	278
19	Aghullaghy	48 1 32	Cavan	Tullyhunco	Killashandra	Cavan	III.	97
8	Aghwater	98 0 36	Carlow	Carlow	Grangeford	Carlow	I.	2
23	Aghyaran	735 2 31d	Tyrone	Omagh West	Termonamongan	Castlederg	III.	317
55	Aghyoghill	195 3 18	Down	Mourne	Kilkeel	Kilkeel	III.	182
109	Aghyohil Beg	94 2 36	Cork, W.R.	East Carbery (E.D.)	Desertserges	Bandon	II.	127
109	Aghyohil More	178 1 28	Cork, W.R.	East Carbery (E.D.)	Desertserges	Bandon	II.	127
38	Aghyoule	1,499 2 38	Fermanagh	Knockninny	Kinawley	Lisnaskea	III.	201
25	Aghyowla	112 0 12	Leitrim	Carrigallen	Oughteragh	Bawnboy	IV.	91
38	Aghyrassy	91 3 18	Westmeath	Moycashel	Newtown	Mullingar	I.	278
17	Aglish	413 3 36e	Clare	Inchiquin	Killinaboy	Corrofin	II.	26
72	Aglish	569 2 13f	Cork, E.R.	East Muskerry	Aglish	Macroom	II.	101
54	Aglish	187 2 19	Kerry	Corkaguiny	Minard	Dingle	II.	179
58	Aglish	201 2 16	Kerry	Magunihy	Aglish	Killarney	II.	199
20, 28	Aglish	307 3 1	Waterford	Coshmore and Coshbride	Lismore and Mocollop	Lismore	II.	344
29, 34	Aglish	302 0 30	Waterford	Decies within Drum	Aglish	Dungarvan	II.	349
42, 43	Aglish North	235 1 15	Kilkenny	Iverk	Aglish	Waterford	I.	105
42,43,45,46	Aglish South	291 3 7	Kilkenny	Iverk	Aglish	Waterford	I.	105
29, 34	AGLISH T.	—	Waterford	Decies within Drum	Aglish	Dungarvan	II.	349
103	Agloragh	274 1 22	Mayo	Costello	Annagh	Claremorris	IV.	137
15	Agolagh	138 3 10	Antrim	Lower Glenarm	Layd	Ballycastle	III.	22
117	Agrimhill	88 3 29	Galway	Longford	Lickmolassy	Portumna	IV.	60
14	Ahabeg	123 2 2	Limerick	Clanwilliam	Carrigparson	Limerick	II.	223
14	Ahabeg (Rose)	80 0 13	Limerick	Clanwilliam	Carrigparson	Limerick	II.	223
43	Ahaclare	218 1 21	Clare	Tulla Lower	Kilseily	Limerick	II.	36
14	Ahacore	164 3 24	Limerick	Owneybeg	Abington	Limerick	II.	250
45	Ahadagh	438 2 33	Limerick	Connello Upper	Kilmeedy	Newcastle	II.	233
50	Ahadallane	759 2 31	Cork, E.R.	Barretts	Donaghmore	Cork	II.	49
4	AHAFONA T.	—	Kerry	Iraghticonnor	Killehenny	Listowel	II.	19;
48, 58	Ahaga	215 0 21	Clare	Clonderalaw	Kilmihil	Kilrush	II.	17
135, 144	Ahagilla	110 3 4	Cork, W.R.	Ibane and Barryroe	Ardfield	Clonakilty	II.	148
121, 122, 134, 135	Ahagilla	316 0 7	Cork, W.R.	Ibane and Barryroe	Castleventry	Clonakilty	II.	148
143	Ahaglaslin	169 1 11	Cork, W.R.	Ibane and Barryroe	Castleventry	Clonakilty	II.	148
93	Ahaglugger	19 1 15	Galway	Galway	Rahoon	Galway	IV.	37
94	Ahakeera	620 2 39	Cork, W.R.	East Carbery (W.D.)	Fanlobbus	Dunmanway	II.	131
6	Ahalahana	809 3 23	Kerry	Iraghticonnor	Murher	Listowel	II.	193
122	Ahalisky	886 3 35	Cork, W.R.	East Carbery (E.D.)	Kilmaloda	Clonakilty	II.	129
4	Ahanagh	146 3 32	Longford	Longford	Mohill	Longford	I.	159
15, 24	Ahanaglogh	258 2 4	Waterford	Decies without Drum	Ballylaneen	Kilmacthomas	II.	354

(a) Including 1A. 2R. 32P. water.
(b) Including 6A. 0R. 8P. water.
(c) Including 33A. 2R. 12P. water.
(d) Including 12A. 2R. 22P. water.
(e) Including 30A. 2R. 39P. water.
(f) Including 3A. 1R. 16P. water.

CENSUS OF IRELAND FOR THE YEAR 1851.

No. of Sheet of the Ordnance Survey Maps.	Townlands and Towns.	Area in Statute Acres.	County.	Barony.	Parish.	Poor Law Union in 1857.	Townland Census of 1851, Part I.	
		A. R. P.					Vol.	Page
107	Ahanduff Beg	88 1 39	Galway . .	Longford . .	Killimorbologue .	Portumna . .	IV.	58
107	Ahanduff More	176 2 6	Galway . .	Longford . .	Killimorbologue .	Portumna . .	IV.	58
64, 72	Ahane . . .	404 1 3a	Kerry . .	Dunkerron North .	Knockane . .	Cahersiveen .	II.	181
57, 65	Ahane . . .	187 3 26	Kerry . .	Magunihy . .	Kilbonane . .	Killarney . .	II.	200
39	Ahane . . .	178 0 35	Kerry . .	Trughanacmy .	Ballymacelligott .	Tralee . .	II.	206
23	Ahane . . .	638 1 3	Kerry . .	Trughanacmy .	Castleisland .	Tralee . .	II.	208
31, 37	Ahane . . .	45 0 26	Tipperary, N.R.	Owney and Arra .	Kilnarath . .	Nenagh . .	II.	295
38	Ahane Beg .	158 0 15b	Cork, E.R.	Duhallow . .	Cullen . .	Millstreet . .	II.	70
31	Ahaneboy .	1,545 3 9	Kerry . .	Trughanacmy .	Castleisland .	Tralee . .	II.	208
38	Ahane Lower .	188 2 14c	Cork, E.R.	Duhallow . .	Cullen . .	Millstreet . .	II.	70
29, 38	Ahane Upper .	303 0 9	Cork, E.R.	Duhallow . .	Cullen . .	Millstreet . .	II.	70
79	Ahanroe . .	33 3 12	Mayo . .	Carra . .	Breaghwy .	Castlebar . .	IV.	126
26	Ahanure North	419 3 26	Kilkenny .	Kells . .	Coolaghmore .	Callan . .	I.	107
26	Ahanure South	375 0 31	Kilkenny .	Kells . .	Coolaghmore .	Callan . .	I.	107
94, 95, 102, 103	Ahapouleen .	187 1 10	Galway . .	Dunkellin .	Ballynacourty .	Galway . .	IV.	27
7	Ahare . . .	53 0 33	Wexford . .	Gorey . .	Kilcavan . .	Gorey . .	I.	317
7	Ahare . . .	267 0 14	Wexford . .	Gorey . .	Kilgorman .	Gorey . .	I.	318
53	Aharinaghbeg .	411 3 36	Clare . .	Tulla Lower .	Killokennedy .	Limerick . .	II.	35
53	Aharinaghmore	261 2 37	Clare . .	Tulla Lower .	O'Briensbridge .	Limerick . .	II.	37
8, 16	Aharney . .	344 3 8	King's Co. .	Ballycowan .	Kilbride . .	Tullamore .	I.	127
35	Aharney . .	608 3 27	Queen's Co. .	Clarmallagh .	Aharney . .	Abbeyleix .	I.	236
10	Ahascra . .	207 2 19	Kerry . .	Iraghticonnor .	Ballyconry .	Listowel . .	II.	190
61	Ahascragh East	123 0 13	Galway . .	Clonmacnowen .	Ahascragh .	Ballinasloe .	IV.	23
61, 74	AHASCRAGH T.	—	Galway . .	Kilconnell .	Ahascragh .	Ballinasloe .	IV.	39
61, 74	Ahascragh West	376 2 30	Galway . .	Kilconnell .	Ahascragh .	Ballinasloe .	IV.	38
24, 25	Ahasla . .	192 1 38	Clare . .	Inchiquin .	Dysert . .	Ennis . .	II.	24
18, 31	Ahaun . . .	181 2 16	Galway . .	Tiaquin . .	Kilkerrin .	Glennamaddy .	IV.	76
32	Ahaun . . .	848 1 29	Kerry . .	Trughanacmy .	Brosna . .	Tralee . .	II.	208
20	Ahaun . . .	99 3 13	Waterford .	Coshmore and Coshbride . .	Lismore and Mocollop	Lismore . .	II.	344
35, 36, 38	Ahaun . . .	128 2 7	Waterford .	Decies within Drum	Ardmore . . .	Dungarvan .	II.	349
20, 28	Ahaunboy North	261 1 17	Waterford .	Coshmore and Coshbride . .	Lismore and Mocollop	Lismore . .	II.	344
28	Ahaunboy South	117 1 34	Waterford .	Coshmore and Coshbride . .	Lismore and Mocollop	Lismore . .	II.	344
45	Ahaveheen .	399 1 31	Limerick . .	Connello Upper .	Cloncrew . .	Newcastle .	II.	232
44, 45	Ahawilk . .	1,010 2 2	Limerick . .	Glenquin . .	Mahoonagh .	Newcastle .	II.	246
101	Ahena . . .	256 1 24	Mayo . .	Clanmorris .	Tagheen . .	Claremorris .	IV.	135
72, 79	Ahenny . . .	655 2 12	Tipperary, S.R.	Iffa and Offa East .	Newtownlennan .	Carrick on Suir	II.	315
79	Ahenny Little .	84 0 11	Tipperary, S.R.	Slievardagh .	Newtownlennan .	Carrick on Suir	II.	335
84	Aherla Beg .	421 1 11	Cork, E.R.	East Muskerry .	Kilbonane .	Bandon . .	II.	104
84	Aherla More .	379 3 7	Cork, E.R.	East Muskerry .	Kilbonane .	Bandon . .	II.	104
44	Ahgloragh .	393 3 4	Galway . .	Dunmore . .	Tuam . .	Tuam . .	IV.	35
135	Ahidelake .	91 2 39	Cork, W.R.	Ibane and Barryroe	Island . .	Clonakilty .	II.	149
91, 92	Ahil Beg .	260 3 18	Cork, W.R.	Bantry . .	Kilmocomoge .	Bantry . .	II.	119
92	Ahildotia .	144 1 23	Cork, W.R.	Bantry . .	Kilmocomoge .	Bantry . .	II.	119
91, 92, 105, 106	Ahil More .	498 2 15	Cork, W.R.	Bantry . .	Kilmocomoge .	Bantry . .	II.	119
4	Ahimma . .	105 1 1	Kerry . .	Iraghticonnor .	Killehenny .	Listowel . .	II.	191
49, 57	Ahnagurra .	398 1 34	Limerick . .	Coshlea . .	Ballingarry .	Kilmallock .	II.	237
37	AHOGHILL T. .	—	Antrim . .	Lower Toome .	Ahoghill . .	Ballymena .	III.	32
92, 98	Aighan . .	132 3 30	Donegal . .	Banagh . .	Killaghtee .	Donegal . .	III.	109
82	Aighe . . .	758 1 23	Donegal . .	Banagh . .	Inishkeel .	Glenties . .	III.	106
23	Aillbrack .	169 3 26d	Clare . .	Ibrickan . .	Kilfarboy .	Ennistimon .	II.	22
32	Ailldavore .	228 3 24	Clare . .	Islands . .	Kilmaley .	Ennis . .	II.	30
17	Aille . . .	213 0 10	Galway . .	Dunmore .	Dunmore .	Tuam . .	IV.	33
93	Aille . . .	534 0 23e	Galway . .	Galway . .	Rahoon . .	Galway . .	IV.	37
106, 116	Aille . . .	379 0 38	Galway . .	Leitrim . .	Kilteskill .	Loughrea .	IV.	55
105	Aille . . .	29 3 24	Galway . .	Loughrea .	Killeenadeema .	Loughrea .	IV.	64
92	Aille . . .	798 2 36	Galway . .	Moycullen .	Killannin .	Galway . .	IV.	69
88, 89, 98, 99	Aille . . .	656 2 34f	Mayo . .	Burrishoole .	Aghagower .	Westport .	IV.	117
107, 108, 116	Aillebaun .	1,244 1 10	Mayo . .	Murrisk . .	Aghagower .	Westport .	IV.	158
48, 49	Aillebrack .	601 3 33g	Galway . .	Ballynahinch .	Ballindoon .	Clifden . .	IV.	10
45	Aillemore .	258 3 0	Clare . .	Tulla Lower .	Killaloe . .	Limerick . .	II.	35
95, 105	Aillemore .	714 1 17	Mayo . .	Murrisk . .	Killgeever .	Westport .	IV.	159
50	Aillenacally .	339 2 4	Galway . .	Ballynahinch .	Moyrus . .	Clifden . .	IV.	12
23	Aillenaveagh .	964 1 9h	Galway . .	Ballynahinch .	Omey . .	Clifden . .	IV.	14
69	Aillroe Beg .	68 0 29	Clare . .	Clonderalaw .	Kilfiddane .	Killadysert .	II.	15
69	Aillroe More .	231 2 18	Clare . .	Clonderalaw .	Kilfiddane .	Killadysert .	II.	15
20	Aillvaun . .	52 3 25	Clare . .	Tulla Upper .	Feakle . .	Scarriff . .	II.	38
5, 6	Aillwee . .	801 2 28	Clare . .	Burren . .	Abbey . .	Ballyvaghan .	II.	11
3	Aird . . .	354 3 26	Antrim . .	Cary . .	Billy . .	Ballycastle .	III.	12
29	Airgloony .	205 3 35	Galway . .	Dunmore . .	Tuam . .	Tuam . .	IV.	35

(a) Including 10A. 2R. 38P. water. (d) Including 5A. 3R. 39P. water. (g) Including 26A. 3R. 12P. water.
(b) Including 3A. 3R. 4P. water. (e) Including 13A. 2R. 13P. water. (h) Including 55A. 3R. 35P. water.
(c) Including 4A. 3R. 32P. water. (f) Including 14A. 2R. 13P. water.

No. of Sheet of the Ordnance Survey Maps.	Townlands and Towns.	Area in Statute Acres.			County.	Barony.	Parish.	Poor Law Union in 1857.	Townland Census of 1851, Part I.	
		A.	R.	P.					Vol.	Page
28	Akip	302	0	31	Queen's Co.	Clandonagh	Rathdowney	Donaghmore	I.	234
14	Alasty	398	3	29	Kildare	South Salt	Kill	Naas	I.	77
13	Alcrossagh	422	3	15	Antrim	Cary	Armoy	Ballycastle	III.	11
18, 26	Alderborough	152	3	32	King's Co.	Geashill	Geashill	Tullamore	I.	139
1	Alderford	251	2	37	Roscommon	Boyle	Kilronan	Boyle	IV.	196
64, 68	Alderwood	838	1	16	Tyrone	Clogher	Aghalurcher	Clogher	III.	291
47	Aldfreck	311	3	30	Antrim	Lower Belfast	Templecorran	Larne	III.	9
18, 19	Aldorough	306	0	11	Antrim	Upper Dunluce	Loughguile	Ballymoney	III.	20
44	Aldridge	96	1	38	Wexford	Shelburne	Templetown	New Ross	I.	328
32, 41	Aldworth	183	0	34	Cork, E.R.	Duhallow	Kilshannig	Mallow	II.	74
25	Alexander Reid	635	0	23	Meath	Skreen	Athlumney	Navan	I.	220
10	Alkill	124	1	24	Monaghan	Cremorne	Tehallan	Monaghan	III.	262
103	Alla	213	2	20	Donegal	Tirhugh	Kilbarron	Ballyshannon	III.	148
8	Allagesh	284	2	16	Monaghan	Monaghan	Tedavnet	Monaghan	III.	278
87, 96	Allaghee Beg (North)	25	2	30	Kerry	Iveragh	Killemlagh	Cahersiveen	II.	196
96	Allaghee Beg (South)	10	1	37	Kerry	Iveragh	Killemlagh	Cahersiveen	II.	196
96, 97	Allaghee More	487	3	30	Kerry	Iveragh	Killemlagh	Cahersiveen	II.	196
32	Allagh Island	4	0	9	Donegal	Kilmacrenan	Tullaghobegly	Dunfanaghy	III.	132
24	Allagour	83	0	0	Dublin	Uppercross	Tallaght	Dublin South	I.	41
22,23,28,29	Alla Lower	506	0	19	Londonderry	Tirkeeran	Cumber Upper	Londonderry	III.	249
93	Allaphreaghaun	228	3	16	Galway	Moycullen	Rahoon	Galway	IV.	72
11, 12	Allardstown	596	0	9	Louth	Louth	Killincoole	Dundalk	I.	184
6	Allardstown	82	2	30	Louth	Upper Dundalk	Dunbin	Dundalk	I.	178
22, 28	Alla Upper	315	1	23	Londonderry	Tirkeeran	Cumber Upper	Londonderry	III.	249
39	Allcollege	56	0	8	Meath	Skreen	Kilmoon	Dunshaughlin	I.	221
125, 131	Alleendarra East	890	0	9	Galway	Leitrim	Ballynakill	Loughrea	IV.	50
125, 131	Alleendarra West	1,684	1	33	Galway	Leitrim	Ballynakill	Loughrea	IV.	50
59	Alleen (Hogan)	358	1	0	Tipperary, S.R.	Clanwilliam	Donohill	Tipperary	II.	307
59	Alleen (Hogan)	16	3	10	Tipperary, S.R.	Clanwilliam	Rathlynin	Tipperary	II.	309
59	Alleen (Ryan)	29	0	32	Tipperary, S.R.	Clanwilliam	Donohill	Tipperary	II.	307
59	Alleen (Ryan)	90	1	31	Tipperary, S.R.	Clanwilliam	Rathlynin	Tipperary	II.	309
38	Allen	148	2	19	Tyrone	Dungannon Upper	Desertcreat	Cookstown	III.	307
14	Allenagh	91	1	22	Longford	Ardagh	Templemichael	Longford	I.	153
40	Allengort	103	0	18	Tipperary, N.R.	Kilnamanagh Upper	Moyaliff	Thurles	II.	279
48	Allenstown Big	176	3	4	Wexford	Forth	St. Iberius	Wexford	I.	314
24	Allenstown Demesne	652	3	36	Meath	Lower Navan	Martry	Kells	I.	215
48	Allenstown Little	64	0	22	Wexford	Forth	St. Iberius	Wexford	I.	314
13, 17	Allenswood	210	2	30	Dublin	Newcastle	Leixlip	Celbridge	I.	33
6	Allenswood	75	1	35	Kildare	North Salt	Confey	Celbridge	I.	74
12, 13	Allenwood Middle	312	2	17	Kildare	Connell	Kilmeage	Naas	I.	55
12, 13	Allenwood North	1,945	2	2	Kildare	Connell	Kilmeage	Naas	I.	55
12, 13	Allenwood South	1,243	2	3	Kildare	Connell	Kilmeage	Naas	I.	55
24,25,30,31	Allerstown or Mullaghmore	189	2	27	Meath	Lower Navan	Ardbraccan	Navan	I.	214
29	Alliganstown	493	3	37	Kildare	South Naas	Ballybought	Naas	I.	64
114, 127	Allihies	834	2	27	Cork, W.R.	Bear	Kilnamanagh	Castletown	II.	125
114	ALLIHIES T.	—			Cork, W.R.	Bear	Kilnamanagh	Castletown	II.	126
8, 12	Allistragh	147	1	31	Armagh	Armagh	Grange	Armagh	III.	44
73	Alloonbaun	388	3	17	Galway	Tiaquin	Ballymacward	Ballinasloe	IV.	75
73	Alloon Lower	81	3	10	Galway	Tiaquin	Ballymacward	Ballinasloe	IV.	75
60, 73	Alloon Upper	381	0	39	Galway	Tiaquin	Ballymacward	Ballinasloe	IV.	75
22	Allowan Island	2	1	22	Mayo	Tirawley	Ballysakeery	Ballina	IV.	165
32, 33	Ally	1,144	2	15	Tyrone	Omagh West	Longfield West	Castlederg	III.	316
116, 125	Allygola	226	3	9	Galway	Leitrim	Ballynakill	Loughrea	IV.	50
116, 125	Allykeolaun	316	0	37	Galway	Leitrim	Ballynakill	Loughrea	IV.	50
22	Almondstown	378	2	0	Louth	Ferrard	Clogher	Drogheda	I.	180
65, 73	Alohart	807	2	22	Kerry	Dunkerron North	Knockane	Killarney	II.	181
20	Alsmeed	281	0	21	Monaghan	Cremorne	Muckno	Castleblayney	III.	261
17	Alt	291	3	39	Mayo	Erris	Kilcommon	Belmullet	IV.	143
19	Altacamcosy	479	2	18a	Tyrone	Strabane Upper	Bodoney Lower	Gortin	III.	323
6, 7, 8, 9	Altachullion Lower	276	1	13	Cavan	Tullyhaw	Templeport	Bawnboy	III.	93
6, 8, 9	Altachullion Upper	272	3	32	Cavan	Tullyhaw	Templeport	Bawnboy	III.	93
65	Altadaven	614	3	11b	Tyrone	Clogher	Errigal Trough	Clogher	III.	296
93	Altadoo	487	3	2	Donegal	Banagh	Killymard	Donegal	III.	111
51,52,59,60	Altadush	525	0	9	Donegal	Kilmacrenan	Conwal	Letterkenny	III.	125
47, 55	Altaghaderry	557	3	5	Donegal	Raphoe	Killea	Londonderry	III.	138
28, 29	Altaghoney	1,163	2	6	Londonderry	Tirkeeran	Cumber Upper	Londonderry	III.	249
45, 53	Altaglushan	1,721	2	22	Tyrone	Dungannon Middle	Donaghmore	Dungannon	III.	301
24, 29	Altagoaghan	720	2	37c	Fermanagh	Magherastephana	Aghalurcher	Lisnaskea	III.	215
10, 15	Altagore	192	2	15	Antrim	Cary	Culfeightrin	Ballycastle	III.	13
7	Altagowlan	583	2	8	Roscommon	Boyle	Kilronan	Boyle	IV.	196
10	Altahalla	734	0	22	Donegal	Inishowen East	Clonmany	Inishowen	III.	117
19, 21	Altakeeran	806	2	8	Leitrim	Carrigallen	Oughteragh	Bawnboy	IV.	91

(a) Including 5A. 0R. 30P. water.   (b) Including 2A. 1R. 8P. water.   (c) Including 6A. 1R. 32P. water.

No. of Sheet of the Ordnance Survey Maps.	Townlands and Towns.	Area in Statute Acres.			County.	Barony.	Parish.	Poor Law Union in 1857.	Townland Census of 1851, Part I.	
		A.	R.	P.					Vol.	Page
7, 16	Altamira . .	216	1	5	Cork, E.R. .	Orrery and Kilmore	Liscarroll . .	Mallow . .	II.	109
44, 52	Altamooskan . .	1,165	2	37	Tyrone . .	Clogher . .	Errigal Keerogue	Clogher . .	III.	295
14, 15, 22, 23	Altamullan .	1,680	1	32	Tyrone . .	Omagh West .	Termonamongan .	Castlederg .	III.	317
34, 43	Altan . .	1,443	0	21a	Donegal . .	Kilmacrenan .	Tullaghobegly .	Dunfanaghy .	III.	131
44, 45	Altanagh .	971	2	0	Tyrone . .	Omagh East .	Termonmaguirk .	Omagh . .	III.	314
51, 58	Altanaveragh .	557	2	17	Tyrone . .	Clogher . .	Clogher . .	Clogher . .	III.	291
19	Altanelvick .	681	1	15	Sligo . .	Tireragh . .	Dromard . .	Dromore West .	IV.	233
12, 18	Altans . .	143	0	0	Sligo . .	Tireragh . .	Templeboy . .	Dromore West .	IV.	236
139, 148	Altar . .	295	1	7	Cork, W.R. .	West Carbery(W.D.)	Kilmoe . .	Skull . .	II.	144
13, 14, 18	Altarichard .	1,373	2	17	Antrim . .	Upper Dunluce	Loughguile . .	Ballymoney .	III.	20
11, 12	Altartate Glebe .	228	2	26	Monaghan .	Dartree . .	Clones . .	Clones . .	III.	264
10, 11, 19, 20	Altashane or Cabadooey .	1,591	0	18	Donegal . .	Inishowen East	Donagh . .	Inishowen .	III.	118
55, 63	Altaskin . .	107	3	16	Donegal . .	Raphoe . .	Taughboyne . .	Strabane . .	III.	143
6, 8	Altateskin . .	529	3	24	Cavan . .	Tullyhaw . .	Templeport . .	Bawnboy . .	III.	93
67, 76	Altatraght . .	647	1	16	Donegal . .	Raphoe . .	Kilteevoge . .	Stranorlar .	III.	139
12, 13	Altaturk . .	283	3	6	Armagh . .	Oneilland West	Loughgall . .	Armagh . .	III.	53
18, 19	Altaveedan North .	331	0	13	Antrim . .	Upper Dunluce	Loughguile . .	Ballymoney .	III.	20
18, 19	Altaveedan South .	345	2	11	Antrim . .	Upper Dunluce	Loughguile . .	Ballymoney .	III.	20
19, 20	Altavilla . .	274	.0	12	Limerick . .	Connello Lower	Lismakeery . .	Rathkeale .	II.	228
20	Altavilla .	55	3	18	Limerick . .	Connello Lower	Nantinan . .	Rathkeale .	II.	228
16	Altavilla . .	37	3	10	Queen's Co. .	Upperwoods .	Offerlane . .	Mountmellick .	I.	250
16	Altavra . .	686	1	29	Leitrim . .	Drumahaire .	Killarga . .	Manorhamilton	IV.	98
29	Altawark . .	749	1	1b	Fermanagh .	Magherastephana	Aghalurcher . .	Lisnaskea .	III.	215
71, 80	Altbaun . .	226	3	12	Mayo . .	Gallen . .	Bohola . .	Swineford .	IV.	147
26	Altbeagh . .	359	0	23	Cavan . .	Tullygarvey .	Larah . .	Cavan . .	III.	90
6, 7	Altbrean . .	325	0	35	Cavan . .	Tullyhaw . .	Kinawley . .	Bawnboy . .	III.	92
81, 90	Altclogh . .	275	2	0	Donegal . .	Banagh . .	Glencolumbkille .	Glenties . .	III.	105
52	Altcloghfin . .	1,366	2	20	Tyrone . .	Clogher . .	Errigal Keerogue	Clogher . .	III.	295
83, 92	Altcor . .	537	1	14	Donegal . .	Banagh . .	Inver . .	Donegal . .	III.	106
8	Altcrock . .	568	1	8	Cavan . .	Tullyhaw . .	Templeport . .	Bawnboy . .	III.	93
13	Altderg . .	905	2	36	Mayo . .	Tirawley . .	Kilfian . .	Killala . .	IV.	169
17	Altdoghal . .	559	1	1c	Tyrone . .	Strabane Lower	Ardstraw . .	Gortin . .	III.	318
27, 36	Altdrumman . .	1,830	1	27d	Tyrone . .	Omagh East .	Termonmaguirk .	Omagh . .	III.	314
17, 18	Altduff . .	660	0	29	Londonderry .	Coleraine . .	Errigal . .	Coleraine . .	III.	232
6, 7	Alteen . .	1,144	3	29	Cavan . .	Tullyhaw . .	Kinawley . .	Bawnboy . .	III.	92
16	Alteen . .	241	3	19	Leitrim . .	Drumahaire .	Inishmagrath .	Manorhamilton	IV.	95
16	Alteenacres Glebe .	38	3	24	Leitrim . .	Drumahaire .	Inishmagrath .	Manorhamilton	IV.	95
11	Alternan Park .	34	1	34	Sligo . .	Tireragh . .	Easky . .	Dromore West .	IV.	233
23, 32	Altgolan . .	721	2	1	Tyrone . .	Omagh West .	Termonamongan .	Castlederg .	III.	317
6	Altibrian . .	1,147	2	21	Londonderry .	Coleraine . .	Dunboe . .	Coleraine . .	III.	231
12, 13	Altidore Demesne .	186	3	25	Wicklow . .	Newcastle . .	Kilcoole . .	Rathdrum .	I.	351
12	Altidore Demesne .	76	0	28	Wicklow . .	Newcastle . .	Newcastle Upper .	Rathdrum .	I.	353
60	Altigarron . .	694	1	18	Antrim . .	Upper Belfast .	Shankill . .	Belfast . .	III.	10
6	Altikeeragh, . .	1,084	3	26	Londonderry .	Coleraine . .	Dunboe . .	Coleraine . .	III.	231
40, 46	Altilcvelly, . .	514	0	25	Antrim . .	Lower Belfast .	Raloo . .	Larne . .	III.	9
84, 85, 93, 94	Altilow, . .	1,092	3	14	Donegal . .	Banagh . .	Killymard . .	Donegal . .	III.	111
13, 17	Altimont, . .	146	1	31	Carlow . .	Forth . .	Aghade . .	Carlow . .	I.	3
59, 60	Altinierin, . .	913	3	35	Donegal . .	Kilmacrenan .	Conwal . .	Stranorlar .	III.	125
7, 9	Altinure, . .	265	2	7	Cavan . .	Tullyhaw . .	Templeport . .	Bawnboy . .	III.	93
29, 30	Altinure Lower .	149	0	36	Londonderry .	Tirkeeran . .	Banagher, now Learmount . .	Londonderry .	III.	247
29, 30	Altinure Upper .	322	0	8	Londonderry .	Tirkeeran . .	Banagher, now Learmount . .	Londonderry .	III.	247
20	Altiquin . .	95	3	21	Leitrim . .	Drumahaire .	Inishmagrath .	Manorhamilton .	IV.	95
6	Altishahane . .	744	0	25	Tyrone . .	Strabane Lower	Donaghedy . .	Gortin . .	III.	320
59, 60, 67, 68	Altlahan . .	1,235	0	28	Donegal . .	Raphoe . .	Kilteevoge . .	Stranorlar .	III.	139
79	Alt Lower . .	184	2	10	Donegal . .	Raphoe . .	Urney . .	Strabane . .	III.	144
29	Altmartin . .	123	3	12	Fermanagh .	Magherastephana	Aghalurcher . .	Lisnaskea .	III.	215
37, 45	Altmore (Alias) Barracktown . .	1,117	2	30	Tyrone . .	Dungannon Middle .	Pomeroy . .	Dungannon .	III.	304
19, 20	Altmore Lower .	96	3	16	Antrim . .	Lower Glenarm	Layd . .	Ballycastle .	III.	22
19	Altmore Upper .	153	3	28	Antrim . .	Lower Glenarm	Layd . .	Ballycastle .	III.	22
5	Altmush . .	105	2	3e	Meath . .	Lower Kells .	Cruicetown . .	Kells . .	I.	202
5	Altmush . .	203	3	34f	Meath . .	Morgallion . .	Nobber . .	Kells . .	I.	210
36, 45	Altnabrocky . .	4,682	2	11g	Mayo . .	Erris . .	Kilcommon . .	Belmullet .	IV.	143
6, 8	Altnadarragh . .	371	3	6	Cavan . .	Tullyhaw . .	Templeport . .	Bawnboy . .	III.	93
83	Altnagapple . .	454	2	8	Donegal . .	Banagh . .	Killybegs Lower .	Glenties . .	III.	110
83	Altnagapple or Mulmosog . .	766	2	21	Donegal . .	Banagh . .	Inishkeel . .	Glenties . .	III.	106
5	Altnageerog . .	145	3	16	Tyrone . .	Strabane Lower	Leckpatrick . .	Strabane . .	III.	321
20	Altnagelvin . .	292	2	31h	Londonderry .	Tirkeeran . .	Clondermot . .	Londonderry .	III.	247
52, 53	Altnagore . .	249	2	24	Tyrone . .	Clogher . .	Errigal Keerogue .	Clogher . .	III.	295
18, 19, 24	Altnahinch . .	1,339	1	39	Antrim . .	Kilconway . .	Loughguile . .	Ballymoney .	III.	27

(a) Including 98A. 1R. 36P. water. (d) Including 113A. 1R. 39P. water. (g) Including 45A. 3R. 13P. water.
(b) Including 20A. 0R. 8P. water.   (e) Including 0A. 3R. 37P. water.   (h) Including 1A. 1R. 1P. water.
(c) Including 4A. 3R. 32P. water.   (f) Including 32A. 2R. 32P. water.

No. of Sheet of the Ordnance Survey Maps.	Townlands and Towns.	Area in Statute Acres. A.	R.	P.	County.	Barony.	Parish.	Poor Law Union in 1857.	Townland Census of 1851, Part I. Vol.	Page
54	Annaghkeelaun	145	3	18	Galway	Moycullen	Kilcummin	Oughterard	IV.	66
41, 55	Annaghkeen	633	1	6	Galway	Clare	Killursa	Tuam	IV.	21
28	Annaghkeenty	166	2	17a	Leitrim	Leitrim	Kiltoghert	Cark. on Shannon	IV.	100
28	Annaghkeenty	72	2	25	Leitrim	Leitrim	Kiltubbrid	Cark. on Shannon	IV.	103
12, 17	Annaghkilly	246	0	13	Monaghan	Dartree	Clones	Clones	III.	264
17	Annaghlee	176	0	38	Cavan	Tullygarvey	Kildrumsherdan	Cootehill	III.	89
36	Annaghlee	97	2	5	Fermanagh	Clankelly	Clones	Clones	III.	195
2	Annagh Long	303	1	34	Wexford	Gorey	Kilnahue	Gorey	I.	318
18	Annagh Lower	176	2	22	Leitrim	Drumahaire	Drumreilly	Cark. on Shannon	IV.	95
2	Annagh Lower	295	2	27	Wexford	Gorey	Kilnahue	Gorey	I.	318
40	Annaghloy	143	2	21	Sligo	Tirerrill	Kilmactranny	Boyle	IV.	240
4	Annaghmacmanus	26	1	2	Armagh	Armagh	Loughgall	Armagh	III.	45
33	Annaghmaconway	258	3	11b	Leitrim	Mohill	Cloone	Mohill	IV.	105
33	Annaghmacullen	408	2	34	Leitrim	Mohill	Cloone	Mohill	IV.	105
20	Annaghmaghera	477	3	22	Roscommon	Castlereagh	Kilkeevin	Castlereagh	IV.	200
7	Annaghmagurthan	38	0	32	Roscommon	Boyle	Ardcarn	Cark. on Shannon	IV.	192
20, 27	Annaghmakeonan	378	3	36	Down	Lower Iveagh, Up. pt.	Donaghcloney	Lurgan	III.	169
46, 54	Annaghmakeown	353	2	15	Tyrone	Dungannon Middle	Donaghmore	Dungannon	III.	301
27, 30	Annaghmare	447	2	17c	Armagh	Fews Upper	Creggan	Castleblayney	III.	48
36	Annaghmartin	129	2	12	Fermanagh	Clankelly	Clones	Clones	III.	195
8, 12	Annaghmartin	150	3	33d	Monaghan	Monaghan	Drumsnat	Monaghan	III.	275
6	Annagh *McCann's*	191	2	34e	Louth	Louth	Louth	Dundalk	I.	184
2, 6	Annagh Middle	270	1	14	Wexford	Gorey	Kilnahue	Gorey	I.	318
10, 11	Annaghminnan	65	1	28	Louth	Louth	Louth	Dundalk	I.	184
40	*Annaghminnoge*	1	3	14	Galway	Moycullen	Kilcummin	Oughterard	IV.	68
7	Annaghmona	34	3	3	Roscommon	Boyle	Tumna	Cark. on Shannon	IV.	197
41	Annagh and Moneysterling	408	1	15	Londonderry	Loughinsholin	Desertmartin	Magherafelt	III.	240
48	Annaghmore	220	3	31	Antrim	Upper Toome	Duneane	Antrim	III.	34
4, 5	Annaghmore	786	0	19	Armagh	Oneilland West	Loughgall	Armagh	III.	53
97	Annagh More	468	1	31	Cork, E.R.	Kinalea	Inishannon	Bandon	II.	95
75, 76	Annagh More	869	0	6	Kerry	Magunihy	Killaha	Killarney	II.	202
24, 25, 32	Annaghmore	876	0	24f	King's Co.	Ballyboy	Killoughy	Tullamore	I.	123
13, 14	Annaghmore	258	3	22	King's Co.	Garrycastle	Tisaran	Parsonstown	I.	138
36	Annaghmore	499	3	34	Leitrim	Mohill	Cloone	Mohill	IV.	105
42	Annaghmore	546	2	29	Londonderry	Loughinsholin	Magherafelt	Magherafelt	III.	243
18	Annagh More	423	1	2	Longford	Moydow	Killashee	Longford	I.	161
14	Annagh More	446	2	17	Mayo	Tirawley	Kilfian	Killala	IV.	169
40	Annaghmore	151	2	33	Roscommon	Ballintober South	Kilteevan	Roscommon	IV.	189
23	Annaghmore	388	0	12g	Roscommon	Roscommon	Ogulla	Strokestown	IV.	212
43, 44	Annaghmore	486	2	19	Sligo	Coolavin	Kilfree	Boyle	IV.	224
26	Annagh More	616	1	32h	Sligo	Leyny	Kilvarnet	Tobercurry	IV.	231
26	Annaghmore	285	2	4i	Sligo	Tirerrill	Ballysadare	Tobercurry	IV.	237
60	Annagh More	193	0	22j	Tyrone	Dungannon Lower	Aghaloo	Dungannon	III.	296
47	Annaghmore	472	2	19	Tyrone	Dungannon Middle	Clonoe	Dungannon	III.	300
31	Annaghmore	365	0	10	Tyrone	Dungannon Upper	Arboe	Cookstown	III.	305
38	Annaghmore	139	3	37	Tyrone	Dungannon Upper	Desertcreat	Cookstown	III.	307
2, 6	Annagh More	295	3	8	Wexford	Gorey	Kilnahue	Gorey	I.	318
31, 36	Annaghmore and Annaghbeg	1,153	0	8	King's Co.	Eglish	Drumcullen	Parsonstown	I.	134
31, 32, 45, 46	Annaghmore East	1,056	0	3k	Galway	Tiaquin	Moylough	Mountbellew	IV.	79
43	Annaghmore Glebe	184	1	25l	Fermanagh	Coole	Drummully	Clones	III.	199
31, 45	Annaghmore West	857	1	37m	Galway	Tiaquin	Moylough	Mountbellew	IV.	79
43	Annaghmullin	158	1	36	Fermanagh	Coole	Drummully	Clones	III.	199
50	Annaghmurnin	42	1	17	Tyrone	Clogher	Donacavey	Omagh	III.	294
47, 55	Annaghnaboe	446	0	33	Tyrone	Dungannon Middle	Clonoe	Dungannon	III.	300
28	Annaghnamaddoo	203	0	15n	Leitrim	Leitrim	Kiltoghert	Cark. on Shannon	IV.	100
27, 28	Annaghneal	442	3	0o	Clare	Tulla Upper	Kilnoe	Tulla	II.	40
7	Annagh North	534	1	3	Cork, E.R.	Orrery and Kilmore	Churchtown	Mallow	II.	107
16	Annaghoash	93	1	23p	Cavan	Tullygarvey	Annagh	Cootehill	III.	87
39	Annaghone	272	3	24	Tyrone	Dungannon Middle	Donaghenry	Cookstown	III.	300
36	Annaghoney	131	2	34q	Leitrim	Mohill	Cloone	Mohill	IV.	105
38	Annaghquin	141	2	7	Tyrone	Dungannon Upper	Desertcreat	Cookstown	III.	307
16	Annaghraw	112	2	34	Monaghan	Dartree	Drummully	Clones	III.	266
67	Annaghroe	147	2	2	Tyrone	Dungannon Lower	Aghaloo	Armagh	III.	296
39	*Annaghroe Island*	22	1	3	Mayo	Tirawley	Kilbelfad	Ballina	IV.	168
41	Annaghs	565	0	17	Kilkenny	Ida	Shanbogh	New Ross	I.	104
66, 67	Annaghsallagh	512	3	1	Tyrone	Dungannon Lower	Aghaloo	Dungannon	III.	296
28	Annaghselherny	206	0	35r	Leitrim	Leitrim	Kiltoghert	Cark. on Shannon	IV.	100
7	Annagh South	190	3	12	Cork, E.R.	Orrery and Kilmore	Churchtown	Mallow	II.	107
38	Annaghteige	115	1	23	Tyrone	Dungannon Upper	Desertcreat	Cookstown	III.	307
39	*Annaghteige Island*	14	0	14	Mayo	Tirawley	Kilbelfad	Ballina	IV.	168
18	Annagh Upper	167	0	18	Leitrim	Drumahaire	Drumreilly	Cark. on Shannon	IV.	95

(a) Including 2A. 2R. 24P. water.
(b) Including 11A. 0R. 12P. water.
(c) Including 17A. 1R. 8P. water.
(d) Including 4A. 2R. 16P. water.
(e) Including 7A. 0R. 21P. water.
(f) Including 43A. 3R. 16P. water.
(g) Including 75A. 1R. 7P. water.
(h) Including 12A. 0R. 26P. water.
(i) Including 11A. 0R. 36P. water.
(j) Including 2A. 2R. 8P. of lake.
(k) Including 14A. 0R. 0P. water.
(l) Including 24A. 2R. 38P. water.
(m) Including 10A. 3R. 31P. water.
(n) Including 14A. 0R. 11P. water.
(o) Including 5A. 3R. 9P. water.
(p) Including 6A. 0R. 18P. water.
(q) Including 33A. 3R. 5P. water.
(r) Including 7A. 2R. 12P. water.

No. of Sheet of the Ordnance Survey Maps.	Townlands and Towns.	Area in Statute Acres. A.	R.	P.	County.	Barony.	Parish.	Poor Law Union in 1857.	Townland Census of 1851, Part I. Vol.	Page
24, 27	Altnamackan	621	2	15	Armagh	Fews Upper	Newtownhamilton	Castleblayney	III.	49
77, 85, 86	Altnapaste	2,362	1	31a	Donegal	Raphoe	Kilteevoge	Stranorlar	III.	139
29	Altnaponer	494	1	28	Fermanagh	Magherastephana	Aghalurcher	Lisnaskea	III.	215
5	Altnasheen	400	2	5	Cavan	Tullyhaw	Templeport	Enniskillen	III.	93
54, 55	Altnavannog,	138	1	10	Tyrone	Dungannon Middle	Clonfeacle	Dungannon	III.	298
59	Altnaveagh	315	3	20	Tyrone	Clogher	Clogher	Clogher	III.	291
26	Altnaveigh	483	0	18	Armagh	Orior Upper	Newry	Newry	III.	58
2	Altoghil	64	2	22	Roscommon	Boyle	Kilronan	Boyle	IV.	196
32	Altore	286	3	18	Roscommon	Castlereagh	Kiltullagh	Castlereagh	IV.	201
2	Altrest	255	0	7	Tyrone	Strabane Lower	Donaghedy	Strabane	III.	320
30	Alts	129	3	16	Monaghan	Farney	Magheracloone	Carrickmacross	III.	272
5, 6	Altshallan	289	2	34b	Cavan	Tullyhaw	Templeport	Enniskillen	III.	93
79, 88	Alt Upper	614	3	39	Donegal	Raphoe	Urney	Strabane	III.	144
21	Altvelid	151	1	33	Sligo	Tirerrill	Killerry	Sligo	IV.	239
47	Alva	178	0	9	Clare	Moyarta	Kilmacduane	Kilrush	II.	32
19	Alwories	406	0	34c	Tyrone	Strabane Upper	Bodoney Lower	Gortin	III.	323
16	Amberhill	448	0	35	Waterford	Middlethird	Kilmeadan	Waterford	II.	368
46	Ambrosetown	277	0	21	Wexford	Bargy	Ambrosetown	Wexford	I.	303
54, 56	America	291	0	6	Roscommon	Moycarn	Moore	Ballinasloe	IV.	206
20, 29	Amogan Beg	227	1	4	Limerick	Connello Lower	Croagh	Rathkeale	II.	227
29	Amogan More	511	2	17	Limerick	Connello Lower	Croagh	Rathkeale	II.	227
7	Amorset	119	1	38	Leitrim	Rosclogher	Killasnet	Manorhamilton	IV.	109
59	Anablaha	293	0	30	Kerry	Magunihy	Kilcummin	Killarney	II.	201
66, 67	Anacramp	241	2	1	Tyrone	Dungannon Lower	Aghaloo	Armagh	III.	296
61	Anagasna Glebe	146	2	12	Tyrone	Dungannon Middle	Clonfeacle	Dungannon	III.	298
17	Anaglog	373	1	17	Louth	Ardee	Kildemock	Ardee	I.	172
94	Anaharlick	353	3	13	Cork, W.R.	East Carbery, (W.D.)	Kinneigh	Dunmanway	II.	134
44	ANASCAUL T.	—			Kerry	Corkaguiny	Ballynacourty	Dingle	II.	174
16	Anatrim	5	3	4	Queen's Co.	Upperwoods	Offerlane	Mountmellick	I.	250
1, 4, 5	Anaverna or Ravensdale Park	2,343	0	18d	Louth	Lower Dundalk	Ballymascanlan	Dundalk	I.	176
57	Anbally	495	0	14	Galway	Clare	Kilmoylan	Tuam	IV.	22
57	ANBALLY T.	—			Galway	Clare	Kilmoylan	Tuam	IV.	22
37, 43	Andraid	748	3	29e	Antrim	Upper Toome	Drummaul	Ballymena	III.	33
41	Andresna	130	2	20	Sligo	Tirerrill	Kilmactranny	Boyle	IV.	240
57, 58	Anglesborough	709	2	32	Limerick	Coshlea	Galbally	Mitchelstown	II.	238
57, 58	Anglesborough	1,253	1	2	Limerick	Coshlea	Kilbeheny	Mitchelstown	II.	239
82	Angliham or Gortacallow	269	1	35	Galway	Galway	Oranmore	Galway	IV.	37
14	Anglode	62	1	13	Limerick	Clanwilliam	Caherconlish	Limerick	II.	222
57	Anglont	321	0	24	Kerry	Magunihy	Killorglin	Killarney	II.	204
40	Anglore	64	2	0	Kerry	Trughanacmy	Castleisland	Tralee	II.	208
119, 132	Angram	143	1	36	Cork, W.R.	WestCarbery, (E.D.)	Dromdaleague	Skibbereen	II.	139
30	Anhid East	119	1	6	Limerick	Coshma	Anhid	Croom	II.	241
30	Anhid West	378	2	38	Limerick	Coshma	Anhid	Croom	II.	241
100	Ankail	657	0	10	Kerry	Dunkerron South	Kilcrohane	Kenmare	II.	183
29	Ankersbower	58	1	22	Westmeath	Brawny	St. Mary's	Athlone	I.	259
4, 8	Ankersland and Aghalasty	307	0	31	Westmeath	Fore	St. Mary's	Castletowndelvin	I.	272
39, 40, 49	Anna Beg	169	3	34	Kerry	Trughanacmy	Killeentierna	Killarney	II.	211
32, 33	Annabella	393	0	28	Cork, E.R.	Fermoy	Mallow	Mallow	II.	81
9	Annaboe	354	0	14	Armagh	Oneilland West	Kilmore	Armagh	III.	53
10	Annacarney	168	1	35	Wicklow	Lower Talbotstown	Boystown	Baltinglass	I.	359
99, 113	Annacarriga	157	1	15	Cork, E.R.	Kinalea	Tracton	Kinsale	II.	97
7	Annacatty	115	1	28	Monaghan	Trough	Donagh	Monaghan	III.	281
36	Annachullion Glebe	171	0	24f	Fermanagh	Clankelly	Clones	Clones	III.	195
12	Annaclare	110	0	9	Armagh	Oneilland West	Grange	Armagh	III.	52
8	Annaclarey	86	2	18	Armagh	Tiranny	Eglish	Armagh	III.	59
4	Annacloghan	36	2	29	Roscommon	Boyle	Kilronan	Boyle	IV.	196
25, 28	Annacloghmullin	367	0	8	Armagh	Orior Upper	Killevy	Newry	III.	57
30, 37	Annacloy	1,152	0	15g	Down	Lecale Lower	Inch	Downpatrick	III.	179
14	Annacloy	195	2	25h	Down	Lower Iveagh, Up. pt.	Blaris	Lisburn	III.	169
8, 12	Annacramph	220	1	32	Armagh	Oneilland West	Grange	Armagh	III.	52
10	Annacramph	135	0	26	Monaghan	Monaghan	Tehallan	Monaghan	III.	280
3, 7	Annacrivey	509	3	19	Wicklow	Rathdown	Powerscourt	Rathdown	I.	356
31	Annacroff	322	0	25i	Monaghan	Farney	Killanny	Carrickmacross	III.	271
56, 57	Annadale	188	0	20	Kerry	Dunkerron North	Killorglin	Killarney	II.	181
30, 37	Annadorn	646	2	31j	Down	Kinelarty	Loughinisland	Downpatrick	III.	177
25	Annadrumman	190	3	9k	Monaghan	Cremorne	Clontibret	Castleblayney	III.	259
32	Annaduff	268	3	8l	Leitrim	Leitrim	Annaduff	Cark. on Shannon	IV.	99
32	Annaduff Glebe	482	2	0m	Leitrim	Leitrim	Annaduff	Cark. on Shannon	IV.	99
23	Annafarney	221	1	5n	Cavan	Clankee	Knockbride	Cootehill	III.	73
6	Annagally	149	2	27	Monaghan	Monaghan	Tedavnet	Monaghan	III.	278

(a) Including 14A. 1R. 26P. water.
(b) Including 7A. 1R. 9P. water.
(c) Including 3A. 1R. 0P. water.
(d) Including 7A. 1R. 3P. water.
(e) Including 21A. 0R. 0P. water.
(f) Including 12A. 2R. 0P. water.
(g) Including 14A. 1R. 12P. water.
(h) Including 2A. 1R. 33P. water.
(i) Including 29A. 2R. 18P. water.
(j) Including 27A. 0R. 8P. lake.
(k) Including 8A. 3R. 0P. water.
(l) Including 13A. 0R. 24P. water.
(m) Including 13A. 1R. 24P. water.
(n) Including 63A. 0R. 12P. water.

No. of Sheet of the Ordnance Survey Maps.	Townlands and Towns.	Area in Statute Acres. A. R. P.	County.	Barony.	Parish.	Poor Law Union in 1857.	Townland Census of 1851, Part I. Vol.	Page
49	Annagannihy	2,326 2 14	Cork, W.R.	East Muskerry	Aghabulloge	Macroom	II.	153
44	Annagap	328 1 39	Kerry	Corkaguiny	Ballynacourty	Dingle	II.	174
15	Annagar	404 0 36	Carlow	Idrone West	Oldleighlin	Carlow	I.	9
59	Annagarvey	118 0 36a	Tyrone	Clogher	Clogher	Clogher	III.	291
41, 49	Annagary	1,860 2 5b	Donegal	Boylagh	Templecrone	Glenties	III.	114
15	ANNAGASSAN T.	—	Louth	Ardee	Drumcar	Ardee	I.	172
20, 25	Annagelliff	134 2 1	Cavan	Upper Loughtee	Annagelliff	Cavan	III.	81
28, 29	Annagerril	124 3 22	Monaghan	Farney	Donaghmoyne	Carrickmacross	III.	269
9, 10	Annagh	236 2 3c	Armagh	Oneilland West	Drumcree	Lurgan	III.	51
11	Annagh	200 3 15	Armagh	Tiranny	Tynan	Armagh	III.	60
35	Annagh	76 3 24	Cavan	Clankee	Enniskeen	Bailieborough	III.	72
37	Annagh	132 3 31	Cavan	Clanmahon	Drumlumman	Granard	III.	76
15	Annagh	112 0 18d	Cavan	Lower Loughtee	Annagh	Cavan	III.	78
10	Annagh	389 3 35e	Cavan	Tullyhaw	Tomregan	Bawnboy	III.	96
24, 25	Annagh	95 3 26	Cavan	Upper Loughtee	Kilmore	Cavan	III.	84
30, 38	Annagh	524 1 32	Clare	Ibrickan	Kilmurry	Kilrush	II.	23
17	Annagh	68 0 29f	Clare	Inchiquin	Rath	Corrofin	II.	27
28	Annagh	272 3 28	Clare	Tulla Upper	Feakle	Scarriff	II.	38
27	Annagh	75 0 23g	Clare	Tulla Upper	Tulla	Tulla	II.	41
3, 10	Annagh	826 1 10	Donegal	Inishowen East	Clonmany	Inishowen	III.	117
57, 58	Annagh	619 3 2	Galway	Clare	Kilmoylan	Tuam	IV.	22
60, 73	Annagh	800 0 21	Galway	Kilconnell	Ballymacward	Mountbellew	IV.	39
123	Annagh	271 3 1h	Galway	Kiltartan	Kilbeacanty	Gort	IV.	47
37, 38	Annagh	1,178 0 21	Kerry	Trughanacmy	Annagh	Tralee	II.	205
47	Annagh	276 2 12	Kerry	Trughanacmy	Kiltallagh	Tralee	II.	212
30	Annagh	132 1 39	Leitrim	Carrigallen	Carrigallen	Bawnboy	IV.	89
13	Annagh	286 2 18	Leitrim	Drumahaire	Clooneclare	Manorhamilton	IV.	93
15	Annagh	163 0 37i	Leitrim	Drumahaire	Killarga	Manorhamilton	IV.	98
24	Annagh	118 0 29	Leitrim	Leitrim	Kiltubbrid	Cark. on Shannon	IV.	103
41, 49	Annagh	519 0 16	Limerick	Coshlea	Galbally	Mitchelstown	II.	238
6	Annagh	859 3 2	Limerick	Owneybeg	Abington	Limerick	II.	250
2, 5	Annagh	542 2 7j	Longford	Longford	Killoe	Longford	I.	158
26	Annagh	295 0 19k	Longford	Rathcline	Noughaval	Ballymahon	I.	164
10, 13	Annagh	73 1 24	Louth	Ardee	Philipstown	Ardee	I.	174
78	Annagh	298 1 24l	Mayo	Carra	Islandeady	Castlebar	IV.	128
93	Annagh	601 2 6m	Mayo	Costello	Aghamore	Swineford	IV.	136
9	Annagh	421 0 4	Mayo	Erris	Kilmore	Belmullet	IV.	145
117	Annagh	78 2 15	Mayo	Kilmaine	Ballinrobe	Ballinrobe	IV.	152
14	Annagh	850 2 35n	Meath	Fore	Moylagh	Oldcastle	I.	201
47	Annagh	282 1 30	Meath	Upper Moyfenrath	Clonard	Edenderry	I.	213
14, 19	Annagh	301 0 30	Monaghan	Cremorne	Clontibret	Monaghan	III.	259
8	Annagh	37 1 24	Monaghan	Monaghan	Drumsnat	Monaghan	III.	275
3, 6	Annagh	176 0 5	Monaghan	Trough	Errigal Trough	Monaghan	III.	283
16	Annagh	202 1 27	Queen's Co.	Upperwoods	Offerlane	Mountmellick	I.	250
18	Annagh	103 3 26	Roscommon	Ballintober North	Kilmore	Cark. on Shannon	IV.	186
3	Annagh	241 2 8o	Roscommon	Boyle	Kilronan	Boyle	IV.	196
26, 33	Annagh	541 1 36	Roscommon	Castlereagh	Kilkeevin	Castlereagh	IV.	200
46	Annagh	71 0 22	Sligo	Coolavin	Killaraght	Boyle	IV.	224
37	Annagh	518 1 29	Sligo	Leyny	Kilmacteige	Tobercurry	IV.	231
34	Annagh	188 3 32	Sligo	Tirerrill	Kilmacallan	Sligo	IV.	239
2, 5	Annagh	1,432 2 28	Tipperary, N.R.	Lower Ormond	Dorrha	Parsonstown	II.	283
9	Annagh	387 2 0p	Tipperary, N.R.	Lower Ormond	Kilbarron	Borrisokane	II.	284
4	Annagh	612 2 2q	Tipperary, N.R.	Lower Ormond	Lorrha	Borrisokane	II.	285
60	Annagh	131 2 31	Tyrone	Dungannon Lower	Aghaloo	Clogher	III.	296
61	Annagh	127 0 35	Tyrone	Dungannon Middle	Clonfeacle	Dungannon	III.	298
43	Annagh	215 1 31	Tyrone	Omagh East	Clogherny	Omagh	III.	310
22, 29	Annagh	810 1 3r	Westmeath	Kilkenny West	Kilkenny West	Athlone	I.	273
17	Annagh	289 2 28	Wexford	Gorey	Monamolin	Gorey	I.	321
24, 28	Annaghaderg	254 2 21s	Leitrim	Mohill	Fenagh	Mohill	IV.	106
41	Annaghalough	164 3 2t	Tyrone	Omagh West	Longfield West	Castlederg	III.	316
38	Annaghananam	162 1 25	Tyrone	Dungannon Upper	Desertcreat	Cookstown	III.	307
11	Annaghananny	232 1 22	Armagh	Tiranny	Tynan	Armagh	III.	60
5	Annaghanerrig	129 0 6	Tipperary, N.R.	Lower Ormond	Dorrha	Parsonstown	II.	283
10	Annaghanmoney	61 1 7	Louth	Ardee	Louth	Dundalk	I.	173
20	Annaghanoon	635 2 12	Down	Lower Iveagh, Up. pt.	Donaghcloney	Lurgan	III.	169
11	Annagharap	138 2 20	Armagh	Tiranny	Tynan	Armagh	III.	60
17	Annaghard	227 0 23u	Cavan	Tullygarvey	Drumgoon	Cootehill	III.	87
35, 36, 40	Annaghard	90 0 5	Fermanagh	Clankelly	Clones	Clones	III.	195
33, 39	Annagharnet	543 0 2v	Cavan	Castlerahan	Mullagh	Bailieborough	III.	70
17, 18	Annagharvey	1,074 3 12	King's Co.	Geashill	Geashill	Tullamore	I.	139
26	Annaghaskin	16 3 15	Dublin	Rathdown	Oldconnaught	Rathdown	I.	37
26	Annaghaskin	19 0 31	Dublin	Rathdown	Rathmichael	Rathdown	I.	37
28	Annaghasna	250 1 2	Leitrim	Leitrim	Kiltoghert	Cark. on Shannon	IV.	100

(a) Including 2A. 1R. 8P. water.
(b) Including 50A. 3R. 3P. water.
(c) Including 6A. 0R. 2P. water.
(d) Including 26A. 0R. 24P. water.
(e) Including 42A. 1R. 10P. water.
(f) Including 30A. 0R. 9P. water.
(g) Including 17A. 0R. 1P. water.
(h) Including 5A. 1R. 26P. water.
(i) Including 83A. 0R. 32P. water.
(j) Including 44A. 2R. 19P. water.
(k) Including 10A. 0R. 3P. water.
(l) Including 23A. 0R. 16P. water.
(m) Including 122A. 2R. 25P. water.
(n) Including 42A. 0R. 19P. water.
(o) Including 55A. 3R. 30P. water.
(p) Including 13A. 0R. 16P. water.
(q) Including 4A. 1R. 16P. water.
(r) Including 22A. 0R. 23P. water.
(s) Including 25A. 3R. 30P. water.
(t) Including 7A. 3R. 22P. water.
(u) Including 12A. 1R. 13P. water.
(v) Including 14A. 0R. 14P. water.

No. of Sheet of the Ordnance Survey Maps.	Townlands and Towns.	Area in Statute Acres. A. R. P.	County.	Barony.	Parish.	Poor Law Union in 1857.	Townland Census of 1851, Part I. Vol.	Page
64	Annagh (*Augher*)	95 1 37a	Tyrone	Clogher	Clogher	Clogher	III.	291
41	Annaghbane	264 3 33	Down	Upper Iveagh, Up. pt.	Donaghmore	Newry	III.	175
97	Annagh Beg	158 2 26	Cork, E.R.	Kinalea	Dunderrow	Kinsale	II.	94
74	Annaghbeg	720 1 23b	Galway	Clonmacnowen	Ahascragh	Ballinasloe	IV.	23
40	Annaghbeg	55 2 17	Galway	Moycullen	Kilcummin	Oughterard	IV.	66
31	Annaghbeg	305 3 32c	Galway	Tiaquin	Kilkerrin	Glennamaddy	IV.	76
59, 60	Annagh Beg	1,345 3 21	Kerry	Magunihy	Kilcummin	Killarney	II.	201
75, 76	Annagh Beg	729 1 4	Kerry	Magunihy	Killaha	Killarney	II.	202
18	Annagh Beg	186 3 12	Longford	Moydow	Killashee	Longford	I.	161
14	Annagh Beg	478 3 29	Mayo	Tirawley	Kilfian	Killala	IV.	169
7	Annaghbeg	64 0 2	Monaghan	Trough	Donagh	Monaghan	III.	281
7	Annaghbeg	249 1 16d	Roscommon	Boyle	Tumna	Cark. on Shannon	IV.	197
23	Annaghbeg	271 0 13e	Roscommon	Roscommon	Killukin	Strokestown	IV.	210
26	Annagh Beg	227 3 21f	Sligo	Leyny	Kilvarnet	Tobercurry	IV.	231
14	Annaghbeg	240 0 6	Tipperary, N.R.	Lower Ormond	Dromineer	Nenagh	II.	283
60	Annagh Beg	198 1 20g	Tyrone	Dungannon Lower	Carnteel	Dungannon	III.	297
46	Annaghbeg	139 2 34h	Tyrone	Dungannon Middle	Donaghmore	Dungannon	III.	301
55	Annaghbeg	275 2 24i	Tyrone	Dungannon Middle	Killyman	Dungannon	III.	303
31, 36	Annaghbeg and Annaghmore	1,153 0 8	King's Co.	Eglish	Drumcullen	Parsonstown	I.	134
46	Annaghbeg or Monasterredan	119 2 25j	Sligo	Coolavin	Kilcolman	Boyle	IV.	223
63, 64	Annagh (*Blessingbourne*)	124 1 2k	Tyrone	Clogher	Clogher	Clogher	III.	291
50, 51	Annaghbo	47 0 32	Tyrone	Clogher	Donacavey	Omagh	III.	294
7	Annagh Bogs	254 3 11	Cork, E.R.	Orrery and Kilmore	Churchtown	Mallow	II.	107
6	Annagh *Boltons*	150 0 14l	Louth	Louth	Louth	Dundalk	I.	184
11, 15	Annaghboy	138 1 38	Leitrim	Drumahaire	Killarga	Manorhamilton	IV.	98
12	Annaghboy or Rosebrook	42 0 0	Armagh	Armagh	Armagh	Armagh	III.	43
13	Annaghbrack	82 1 1	Monaghan	Monaghan	Drumsnat	Monaghan	III.	275
32	Annaghbrack Glebe	846 0 31m	King's Co.	Ballyboy	Killoughy	Tullamore	I.	123
28	Annaghbradican	243 2 33n	Leitrim	Leitrim	Kiltoghert	Cark. on Shannon	IV.	100
106	Annaghbride	345 1 24	Galway	Leitrim	Kilmeen	Loughrea	IV.	54
100, 108	Annaghcallow	282 2 9	Galway	Longford	Clonfert	Ballinasloe	IV.	56
27, 34	Annaghcarthy	255 1 19	Sligo	Tirerrill	Kilmacallan	Boyle	IV.	239
2	Annagh Central	340 3 9	Wexford	Gorey	Kilnahue	Gorey	I.	318
4, 8	Annaghcooleen	206 3 14	Longford	Longford	Mohill	Longford	I.	159
34	Annaghcor	142 2 13	Sligo	Tirerrill	Kilmacallan	Sligo	IV.	239
100	Annaghcorrib	841 3 27o	Galway	Longford	Clonfert	Ballinasloe	IV.	56
2	Annaghdaniel	199 0 8	Longford	Granard	Columbkille	Longford	I.	155
64	Annagh Demesne	121 0 27p	Tyrone	Clogher	Clogher	Clogher	III.	291
28, 29	Annaghderg Lower	103 3 15	Leitrim,	Mohill	Mohill	Mohill	IV.	107
28, 29	Annaghderg Upper	89 1 15	Leitrim	Mohill	Mohill	Mohill	IV.	107
56, 69	Annaghdown	686 3 12	Galway	Clare	Annaghdown	Galway	IV.	16
3	Annagh or Drumanilra	166 3 39	Roscommon	Boyle	Kilbryan	Boyle	IV.	195
15	Annaghduff	92 2 4q	Cavan	Upper Loughtee	Castleterra	Cavan	III.	82
16, 21	Annagheane	166 0 19r	Monaghan	Dartree	Currin	Clones	III.	265
27, 28	Annaghearly	268 2 28s	Leitrim	Leitrim	Kiltoghert	Cark. on Shannon	IV.	100
56	Annagh East	221 3 30	Galway	Clare	Annaghdown	Galway	IV.	16
47	Annagher	276 0 39	Tyrone	Dungannon Middle	Clonoe	Dungannon	III.	300
9	Annaghervy	67 3 29	Monaghan	Monaghan	Kilmore	Monaghan	III.	275
20	Annaghfin	53 1 37	Wexford	Ballaghkeen	Ballyhuskard	Enniscorthy	I.	291
30	Annaghgad	267 3 28	Armagh	Fews Upper	Creggan	Castleblayney	III.	48
2	Annaghgap	379 2 36	Wexford	Gorey	Kilnahue	Gorey	I.	318
18	Annaghgerry	111 0 25	Leitrim	Drumahaire	Inishmagrath	Manorhamilton	IV.	95
29	Annaghgortagh	171 0 7t	Westmeath,	Clonlonan	Ballyloughloe	Athlone	I.	260
40, 41	Annaghgowan	218 2 25	Sligo	Tirerrill	Kilmactranny	Boyle	IV.	240
34	*Annaghgowla Island*	34 1 13	Sligo	Tirerrill	Aghanagh	Boyle	IV.	237
57, 58	Annagh Hill	283 2 7	Galway	Clare	Kilmoylan	Tuam	IV.	22
80	Annagh Hill	154 1 24	Mayo	Gallen	Killedan	Swineford	IV.	149
2	Annagh Hill	303 0 14	Wexford	Gorey	Kilnahue	Gorey	I.	318
23, 28	Annaghierin	217 1 25u	Cavan	Clankee	Shercock	Bailieborough	III.	74
59	Annaghilla	177 3 22	Tyrone	Clogher	Errigal Keerogue	Clogher	III.	295
35	Annaghilly North	95 0 7	Fermanagh	Clankelly	Clones	Clones	III.	195
35, 36	Annaghilly South	80 2 23	Fermanagh	Clankelly	Clones	Clones	III.	195
59, 60	Annaghily More	1,017 1 13	Kerry	Magunihy	Aghadoe	Killarney	II.	199
29, 38	*Annagh Island*	32 3 8	Kerry	Trughanacmy	Annagh	Tralee	II.	205
43, 55, 56	Annagh Island	627 1 32	Mayo	Erris	Kilcommon	Newport	IV.	145
39	Annagh Island	52 1 8	Mayo	Tirawley	Kilbelfad	Ballina	IV.	168
87	*Annagh Island East*	47 3 35	Mayo	Murrisk	Oughaval	Westport	IV.	162
87	*Annagh Island Middle*	11 2 19	Mayo	Murrisk	Oughaval	Westport	IV.	162
87	*Annagh Island West*	17 1 12	Mayo	Murrisk	Oughaval	Westport	IV.	162
35, 40	Annaghkeel	70 3 32	Fermanagh	Clankelly	Clones	Clones	III.	195

(a) Including 1A. 1R. 24P. water.
(b) Including 2A. 0R. 24P. water.
(c) Including 0A. 3R. 3P. water.
(d) Including 18A. 2R. 39P. water.
(e) Including 22A. 2R. 31P. water.
(f) Including 1A. 0R. 9P. detached portion, and 8A. 0R. 17P. water.
(g) Including 3A. 3R. 3P. of lake.
(h) Including 1A. 2R. 8P. detached portion.
(i) Including 3A. 2R. 36P. water.
(j) Including 5A. 1R. 33P. water.
(k) Including 2A. 3R. 28P. water.
(l) Including 7A. 3R. 32P. water.
(m) Including 67A. 1R. 13P. water.
(n) Including 34A. 0R. 25P. water.
(o) Including 7A. 1R. 8P. water.
(p) Including 9A. 2R. 0P. water.
(q) Including 4A. 3R. 14P. water.
(r) Including 10A. 0R. 30P. water.
(s) Including 36A. 3R. 33P. water.
(t) Including 0A. 2R. 8P. water.
(u) Including 20A. 0R. 12P. water.

No. of Sheet of the Ordnance Survey Maps.	Townlands and Towns.	Area in Statute Acres.	County.	Barony.	Parish.	Poor Law Union in 1857.	Townland Census of 1851. Part I.	
		A. R. P.					Vol.	Page
2	Annagh Upper .	239 3 36	Wexford . .	Gorey . . .	Kilnahue . .	Gorey . .	I.	318
78	Annaghvaan .	311 2 31	Galway . .	Moycullen . .	Killannin . .	Oughterard .	IV.	70
3, 6	Annaghvacky .	369 3 35	Louth . .	Upper Dundalk .	Creggan . .	Dundalk . .	I.	177
56	Annagh West .	169 1 5	Galway . .	Clare . . .	Annaghdown .	Galway . .	IV.	16
40	Annaghwood .	22 0 33	Galway . .	Moycullen . .	Kilcummin . .	Oughterard .	IV.	66
18	Annaghybane .	169 0 1	Monaghan .	Dartree . . .	Ematris . . .	Cootehill .	III.	266
17, 18	Annaghyduff .	162 3 14	Monaghan .	Dartree . . .	Ematris . . .	Cootehill .	III.	266
46	Annaginny .	150 3 4	Tyrone . .	Dungannon Middle .	Donaghmore .	Dungannon .	III.	301
24, 25	Annagleve .	384 2 26	Monaghan .	Cremorne . .	Clontibret . .	Castleblayney .	III.	259
14, 15	Annaglogh .	293 0 29	Monaghan .	Cremorne . .	Clontibret . .	Castleblayney .	III.	259
38, 39	Annagloor .	417 1 19	Cork, E.R. .	Duhallow . .	Drishane . .	Millstreet .	II.	71
9	Annagola .	44 1 17	Monaghan .	Monaghan . .	Kilmore . . .	Monaghan .	III.	275
7	Annagola .	138 0 4	Monaghan .	Trough . . .	Donagh . . .	Monaghan .	III.	281
18, 24	Annagolan .	214 3 3	Wicklow . .	Newcastle . .	Derrylossary .	Rathdrum .	I.	351
36	Annagolgan .	177 3 24	Fermanagh .	Clankelly . .	Clones . . .	Clones . .	III.	195
27	Annagor . .	298 2 39	Meath . .	Lower Duleek .	Kilsharvan . .	Drogheda .	I.	196
9	Annagora . .	92 2 17	Armagh . .	Oneilland West .	Drumcree . .	Lurgan . .	III.	51
12, 17	Annagose . .	272 2 20a	Monaghan .	Dartree . . .	Aghabog . .	Clones . .	III.	263
8	Annahagh .	112 0 20	Armagh . .	Armagh . . .	Grange . . .	Armagh . .	III.	44
9	Annahagh .	161 3 2	Monaghan .	Monaghan . .	Monaghan . .	Monaghan .	III.	276
8, 9	Annahagh .	143 0 36b	Monaghan .	Monaghan . .	Tedavnet . .	Monaghan .	III.	278
8	Annahagh North .	47 1 23	Monaghan .	Monaghan . .	Clones . . .	Monaghan .	III.	274
8	Annahagh South .	121 2 34	Monaghan .	Monaghan . .	Clones . . .	Monaghan .	III.	274
28, 29	Annahaia .	641 1 20	Armagh . .	Orior Upper . .	Killevy . . .	Newry . .	III.	57
24	Annahaia .	138 0 34	Monaghan .	Cremorne . .	Aghnamullen .	Castleblayney .	III.	257
28	Annahaia .	111 3 29	Monaghan .	Farney . . .	Donaghmoyne .	Carrickmacross	III.	269
70, 71	Annahalabog .	259 0 25	Cork, W.R. .	West Muskerry .	Macloneigh . .	Macroom . .	II.	160
70, 71	Annahala East .	266 0 9	Cork, W.R. .	West Muskerry .	Macloneigh . .	Macroom . .	II.	160
70	Annahala West .	393 2 8	Cork, W.R. .	West Muskerry .	Macloneigh . .	Macroom . .	II.	160
20, 25	Annahale . .	146 1 35	Monaghan .	Cremorne . .	Clontibret . .	Castleblayney .	III.	259
48	Annahavil .	141 3 19	Londonderry .	Loughinsholin .	Arboe . . .	Magherafelt .	III.	238
48	Annahavil .	123 2 32	Londonderry .	Loughinsholin .	Derryloran . .	Magherafelt .	III.	240
38, 46	Annahavil .	359 0 25	Tyrone . .	Dungannon Upper .	Desertcreat .	Cookstown .	III.	307
34	Annahean .	389 1 8	Monaghan .	Farney . . .	Killanny . .	Carrickmacross	III.	271
36	Annahervy .	72 2 35	Fermanagh .	Clankelly . .	Clones . . .	Clones . .	III.	195
31, 37	Annaholty . .	1,485 1 14	Tipperary, N.R.	Owney and Arra .	Kilcomenty . .	Nenagh . .	II.	294
36	Annahone . .	98 0 29c	Fermanagh .	Clankelly . .	Clones . . .	Clones . .	III.	195
14	Annahuby .	134 0 18	Monaghan .	Cremorne . .	Clontibret . .	Monaghan .	III.	259
9	Annahugh . .	293 2 7	Armagh . .	Oneilland West .	Kilmore . . .	Armagh . .	III.	53
42	Annahunshigo .	553 0 3d	Down . .	Upper Iveagh, Lr. pt.	Drumballyroney .	Banbridge .	III.	172
40	Anna Island .	5 3 19	Donegal . .	Boylagh . . .	Templecrone .	Glenties .	III.	116
5, 9	Annakeera .	150 2 21	Armagh . .	Oneilland West .	Drumcree . .	Lurgan . .	III.	51
25	Annakisha .	51 1 17	Cork, E.R. .	Fermoy . . .	Carrigleamleary .	Mallow . .	II.	77
25	Annakisha North .	596 0 38	Cork, E.R. .	Fermoy . . .	Clenor . . .	Mallow . .	II.	78
25	Annakisha South .	271 3 16	Cork, E.R. .	Fermoy . . .	Clenor . . .	Mallow . .	II.	78
78	Annalecka .	55 3 33	Mayo . .	Carra . . .	Aglish . . .	Castlebar .	IV.	123
25	Annaleck Lower .	170 2 37	Kilkenny . .	Gowran . . .	Powerstown .	Thomastown .	I.	97
25	Annaleck Upper .	272 0 39	Kilkenny . .	Gowran . . .	Powerstown .	Thomastown .	I.	97
15	Annalecky .	125 3 12	Wicklow . .	Lower Talbotstown .	Dunlavin . .	Baltinglass .	I.	360
25	Annalittin .	299 3 21	Monaghan .	Cremorne . .	Clontibret . .	Castleblayney .	III.	259
6	Annaloist . .	285 0 2	Armagh . .	Oneilland East .	Seagoe . . .	Lurgan . .	III.	50
56	ANNALONG T. .	—	Down . .	Mourne . . .	Kilkeel . . .	Kilkeel . .	III.	183
32	Annalough .	115 2 21	Kildare . .	Narragh & Reban East	Narraghmore .	Athy . .	I.	66
8	Annaloughan .	1,078 2 23	Louth . .	Lower Dundalk .	Ballymascanlan .	Dundalk .	I.	175
59	Annaloughan .	285 1 38	Tyrone . .	Clogher . . .	Clogher . . .	Clogher .	III.	291
13, 18, 19	Annamacneill .	208 2 13	Monaghan .	Monaghan . .	Tullycorbet .	Monaghan .	III.	280
12	Annamakiff .	93 2 27	Monaghan .	Dartree . . .	Killeevan . .	Clones . .	III.	267
31, 34	Annamarran .	279 2 0	Monaghan .	Farney . . .	Killanny . .	Carrickmacross	III.	271
33, 34	Annamoe . .	375 2 34	King's Co. .	Upper Philipstown .	Clonyhurk . .	Mountmellick .	I.	143
40, 49	Anna More .	495 2 36	Kerry . .	Trughanacmy .	Killeentierna .	Killarney .	II.	211
8	Annamoy . .	197 0 24	Armagh . .	Tiranny . . .	Eglish . . .	Armagh . .	III.	59
23, 24, 27, 28	Annamult . .	1,351 2 2e	Kilkenny . .	Shillelogher .	Danesfort . .	Thomastown .	I.	114
19	Annaneese .	190 1 39f	Monaghan .	Cremorne . .	Ballybay . .	Castleblayney .	III.	259
13	Annareagh .	247 0 5	Armagh . .	Oneilland West .	Kilmore . . .	Armagh . .	III.	53
7	Annareagh North .	67 0 15	Monaghan .	Trough . . .	Donagh . . .	Monaghan .	III.	281
7, 10	Annareagh South .	244 2 26	Monaghan .	Trough . . .	Donagh . . .	Monaghan .	III.	281
13, 14	Annaroe . .	124 2 22	Monaghan .	Monaghan . .	Monaghan . .	Monaghan .	III.	270
4, 8	Annasamry .	415 0 29	Armagh . .	Oneilland West .	Loughgall . .	Armagh . .	III.	53
10, 14	Annaseeragh .	128 3 17	Monaghan .	Cremorne . .	Clontibret . .	Monaghan .	III.	259
36	Annashanco .	90 1 1	Fermanagh .	Clankelly . .	Clones . . .	Clones . .	III.	195
27	Annaskinnan .	511 2 30	Westmeath .	Farbill . . .	Killucan . .	Mullingar .	I.	266
29, 38	Annaslee . .	322 0 35	Donegal . .	Inishowen West .	Fahan Upper .	Londonderry .	III.	121
16	Annaveagh .	162 0 23	Monaghan .	Dartree . . .	Currin . . .	Clones . .	III.	265

(a) Including 22A. 2R. 32P. water.
(b) Including 11A. 0R. 0P. water.
(c) Including 16A. 1R. 23P. water.
(d) Including 11A. 2R. 19P. water.
(e) Including 21A. 1R. 32P. River Nore.
(f) Including 17A. 2R. 20P. water.

No. of Sheet of the Ordnance Survey Maps.	Townlands and Towns.	Area in Statute Acres.	County.	Barony.	Parish.	Poor Law Union in 1857.	Townland Census of 1851, Part I.	
		A. R. P.					Vol.	Page
14, 19	Annayalla . .	361 0 26a	Monaghan .	Cremorne . .	Clontibret . .	Castleblayney .	III.	259
107	Annees . . .	454 3 2b	Cork, W.R. .	EastCarbery,(W.D.)	Fanlobbus . .	Dunmanway .	II.	131
31	Anneeter Beg .	147 3 27c	Tyrone . .	Dungannon Upper .	Arboe . . .	Cookstown .	III.	305
31	Anneeter More .	152 1 1	Tyrone . .	Dungannon Upper .	Arboe . . .	Cookstown .	III.	305
112	Annefield . .	140 3 18	Cork, E.R. .	Kinalea . . .	Kinure . . .	Kinsale . .	II.	95
18	Annefield . .	4 3 21	Dublin . .	Rathdown . .	Donnybrook . .	Dublin South .	I.	35
37	Annefield . .	78 1 10	Kilkenny . .	Ida	Rosbercon . .	New Ross .	I.	103
119	Annefield . .	503 0 14	Mayo . .	Kilmaine . .	Kilcommon . .	Ballinrobe .	IV.	154
62, 70	Annesgift . .	318 2 15	Tipperary, S.R.	Middlethird . .	Rathcool . .	Cashel . .	II.	329
26	Annesgrove . .	412 3 5	Cork, E.R. .	Fermoy . . .	Castletownroche .	Fermoy , .	II.	77
25	Annestown . .	120 2 35	Waterford .	Middlethird . .	Dunhill . .	Kilmacthomas .	II.	366
25	ANNESTOWN T. .	—	Waterford .	Middlethird . .	Dunhill . .	Kilmacthomas .	II.	367
17	Anneville . .	91 0 34d	Clare . .	Inchiquin . .	Killinaboy . .	Corrofin . .	II.	26
32	Anneville . .	174 3 13e	Queen's Co. .	Slievemargy . .	Shrule . .	Carlow . .	I.	246
41, 47	Anneville or Clonard Old . . .	1,256 3 5f	Meath, . .	Upper Moyfenrath .	Clonard . . .	Edenderry .	I.	213
26	Anneville or Rathduff . . .	335 0 8	Westmeath .	Fartullagh . .	Moylisker . .	Mullingar .	I.	269
17	Annfield . .	19 0 38	Dublin . .	Castleknock . .	Castleknock . .	Dublin North .	I.	23
20, 24	Annfield . .	83 0 14	Kilkenny . .	Gowran . .	Dunbell . .	Kilkenny . .	I.	94
34, 40	Annfield . .	397 0 12	Tipperary, N.R.	Eliogarty . .	Inch . . .	Thurles . .	II.	270
75	Anngrove . .	297 2 38	Cork, E.R. .	Barrymore . .	Carrigtohill . .	Middleton .	II.	52
4	Annies . . .	129 2 8	Louth . .	Lower Dundalk .	Ballymascanlan .	Dundalk . .	I.	175
100, 110	Annies . . .	179 2 24	Mayo . .	Kilmaine . .	Robeen . .	Ballinrobe .	IV.	157
16	Annies . . .	268 0 26	Monaghan .	Dartree . .	Currin . . .	Clones . .	III.	265
66	Annistown . .	123 3 2	Cork, E.R. .	Imokilly . .	Mogeely . .	Middleton .	II.	89
7	Annsbrook . .	134 1 2	Dublin . .	Balrothery East .	Lusk . . .	Balrothery .	I.	20
18, 23	Anny . . .	467 3 35g	Monaghan .	Cremorne . .	Aghnamullen . .	Cootehill . .	III.	257
28	Anny . . .	161 0 10	Monaghan .	Farney . .	Donaghmoyne . .	Carrickmacross .	III.	269
9	Annyalty . .	129 0 36	Monaghan .	Monaghan . .	Tedavnet . .	Monaghan .	III.	278
20	Annyart . .	297 0 25	Monaghan .	Cremorne . .	Muckno . .	Castleblayney .	III.	261
8	Annyeeb . .	76 0 20	Monaghan .	Monaghan . .	Tedavnet . .	Monaghan .	III.	278
9	Annyerk . .	132 3 9	Monaghan .	Monaghan . .	Tedavnet . .	Monaghan .	III.	278
28	Anny Far and Near	378 1 24	Donegal . .	Kilmacrenan . .	Killygarvan . .	Milford . .	III.	128
36	Annynanum . .	61 2 12	Fermanagh .	Clankelly . .	Clones . . .	Clones . .	III.	195
36, 40	Anrittabeg . .	320 3 14	Roscommon .	Ballintober South .	Cloontuskert . .	Roscommon .	IV.	188
36	Anskert . .	339 3 12h	Leitrim . .	Mohill . .	Cloone . . .	Mohill . .	IV.	105
29	Anster . . .	40 0 23	Queen's Co. .	Clarmallagh . .	Aghaboe . . .	Abbeyleix .	I.	235
32, 35	Antfield . .	107 2 12	Leitrim . .	Mohill . .	Annaduff . .	Mohill . .	IV.	105
23	Anticur . .	903 1 30	Antrim . .	Kilconway . .	Rasharkin . .	Ballymena .	III.	27
78	Antigua or Lisnageeha . .	157 0 17i	Mayo . .	Carra . . .	Aglish . . .	Castlebar . .	IV.	124
35, 40	Antiville . .	165 0 25	Antrim . .	Upper Glenarm .	Larne . . .	Larne . .	III.	25
50	ANTRIM T. . .	—	Antrim . .	Upper Antrim .	Antrim . . .	Antrim . .	III.	5
18, 25	Antylstown . .	223 1 25	Meath . .	Lower Navan . .	Donaghmore . .	Navan . .	I.	214
29	Antynanum . .	450 2 6	Antrim . .	Lower Antrim .	Racavan, . .	Ballymena .	III.	4
23, 24	Anveyerg . .	205 3 26	Monaghan .	Cremorne . .	Aghnamullen . .	Castleblayney .	III.	257
40, 48	Aphort . .	340 0 0	Donegal . .	Boylagh . .	Templecrone . .	Glenties . .	III.	114
43	Applefort . .	29 1 23	Clare . .	Bunratty Upper .	Quin . . .	Tulla . .	II.	9
129	Apple Island . .	1 2 8	Galway . .	Kiltartan . .	Beagh . . .	Gort . .	IV.	46
37	Appletee . .	226 1 7	Antrim . .	Lower Antrim .	Connor . .	Ballymena .	III.	3
44, 45	Appletown . .	713 0 26	Limerick . .	Glenquin . .	Mahoonagh . .	Newcastle .	II.	246
16,17,24,25	Applevale . .	201 2 5	Clare . .	Inchiquin . .	Rath . . .	Corrofin . .	II.	27
79, 80	Ara . . .	495 2 20	Mayo . .	Gallen . .	Kildacommoge . .	Castlebar . .	IV.	148
39	Arabela . .	154 1 39	Kerry . .	Trughanacmy . .	Ballymacelligott .	Tralee . .	II.	206
3, 7	Araboy . .	430 0 22	Antrim . .	Cary . . .	Ballintoy . .	Ballycastle, .	III.	11
41	Araghty . .	577 2 31j	Roscommon .	Athlone . .	Athleague . .	Roscommon .	IV.	179
59, 67	Arbatt . . .	1,007 1 9	Donegal . .	Raphoe . .	Kilteevoge . .	Stranorlar .	III.	139
5	Arbourhill . .	136 1 17	Tipperary, N.R.	Lower Ormond .	Dorrha . .	Parsonstown, .	II.	283
62	Arbourhill . .	337 1 38	Tipperary, S.R.	Middlethird . .	Magorban . .	Cashel . .	II.	328
17	Archdeaconry Glebe	190 3 32	Meath . .	Upper Kells .	Kells . . .	Kells . .	I.	205
19	Archersgrove .	102 2 17k	Kilkenny . .	Shillelogher . .	St. Patrick's .	Kilkenny . .	I.	116
19	Archersleas .	147 3 25	Kilkenny . .	Shillelogher . .	St. Patrick's .	Kilkenny . .	I.	116
19	Archersrath . .	107 2 15	Kilkenny . .	Gowran . .	St. John's . .	Kilkenny . .	I.	98
45	Archerstown .	161 0 27	Meath . .	Ratoath . .	Donaghmore . .	Dunshaughlin .	I.	218
35	Archerstown .	734 3 8	Queen's Co. .	Clarmallagh . .	Aharney . .	Abbeyleix .	I.	236
41, 47	Archerstown .	482 1 39	Tipperary, N.R.	Eliogarty . .	Rahelty . .	Thurles . .	II.	272
8, 9	Archerstown .	822 0 17l	Westmeath .	Delvin . .	Castletowndelvin .	Castletowndelvin	I.	264
19	Archerstreet Lot .	88 3 29m	Kilkenny . .	Shillelogher . .	St. Canice . .	Kilkenny . .	I.	115
17, 18	Arch Hall . .	350 0 3	Meath . .	Morgallion . .	Clongill . .	Navan . .	I.	209
24	Archill . .	788 2 21	Tyrone . .	Strabane Lower .	Ardstraw . .	Castlederg .	III.	318
14	Arclintagh . .	145 2 3	Monaghan .	Cremorne . .	Clontibret . .	Monaghan .	III.	259
55	Ard . . .	106 0 29	Galway . .	Moycullen . .	Kilcummin . .	Oughterard .	IV.	66

(a) Including 3A. 3R. 31P. water.
(b) Including 3A. 2R. 32P. water.
(c) Including 0A. 3R. 21P. island.
(d) Including 21A. 2R. 11P. water.
(e) Including 2A. 2R. 20P. River Barrow.

(f) Including 0A. 2R. 31P. detached portion.
(g) Including 75A. 0R. 1P. water.
(h) Including 19A. 3R. 12P. water.
(i) Including 7A. 3R. 35P. water.
(j) Including 0A. 3R. 19P. water.

(k) Including 7A. 1R. 22P. River Nore.
(l) Including 11A. 1R. 26P. water.
(m) Area within the Municipal Boundary, 4A. 3R. 9P.

No. of Sheet of the Ordnance Survey Maps.	Townlands and Towns.	Area in Statute Acres.	County.	Barony.	Parish.	Poor Law Union in 1857.	Townland Census of 1851, Part I.	
		A. R. P.					Vol.	Page
26	Ard	816 3 33	King's Co.	Upper Philipstown	Geashill	Mountmellick	I.	144
27	Arda	217 0 29a	Fermanagh	Tirkennedy	Derryvullan	Enniskillen	III.	220
46	Ardabaun	83 2 2	Kerry	Trughanacmy	Kilgarrylander	Tralee	II.	210
13	Ardabrone	266 3 30	Sligo	Tireragh	Skreen	Dromore West	IV.	235
71	Ardacarha	301 1 31	Mayo	Gallen	Bohola	Swineford	IV.	147
51, 59	Ardachrin	1,369 3 15	Donegal	Kilmacrenan	Gartan	Letterkenny	III.	127
56,57,64,65	Ardacluckeen	320 2 5	Kerry	Dunkerron North	Killorglin	Killarney	II.	181
114	Ardacluggin	232 0 28	Cork, W.R.	Bear	Kilcatherine	Castletown	II.	123
29	Ardacong	200 3 2	Galway	Dunmore	Liskeevy	Tuam	IV.	35
123	Ardacrow	519 1 9	Cork, W.R.	East Carbery,(E.D.)	Rathclarin	Bandon	II.	129
17	Ardadam	121 0 17	Cork, E.R.	Fermoy	Doneraile	Mallow	II.	78
116	Ardagannive	86 0 6	Cork, W.R.	Bear	Killaconenagh	Castletown	II.	124
61	Ardaganny	416 1 14	Donegal	Raphoe	Leck	Letterkenny	III.	140
52	Ardagawna	242 2 9	Roscommon	Athlone	Drum	Athlone	IV.	180
14	Ardagh	177 3 36	Antrim	Cary	Ramoan	Ballycastle	III.	14
7	Ardagh	169 2 26	Cork, E.R.	Orrery and Kilmore	Shandrum	Kanturk	II.	109
115, 128	Ardagh	538 3 33	Cork, W.R.	Bear	Killaconenagh	Castletown	II.	124
149	Ardagh	211 3 4	Cork, W.R.	WestCarbery,(E.D.)	Aghadown	Skibbereen	II.	136
142	Ardagh	271 2 2	Cork, W.R.	WestCarbery,(E.D.)	Myross	Skibbereen	II.	140
3, 10	Ardagh	409 3 38	Donegal	Inishowen East	Clonmany	Inishowen	III.	117
54, 62	Ardagh	822 1 25	Donegal	Raphoe	Taughboyne	Strabane	III.	143
7	Ardagh	279 0 10	Galway	Ballymoe	Ballynakill	Glennamaddy	IV.	5
35, 36	Ardagh	1,052 3 22b	Galway	Ballynahinch	Ballindoon	Clifden	IV.	10
9	Ardagh	889 3 16	Kerry	Clanmaurice	Killury	Listowel	II.	170
58	Ardagh	199 3 34	Kerry	Magunihy	Kilcummin	Killarney	II.	201
66, 67	Ardagh	145 3 11c	Kerry	Magunihy	Killarney	Killarney	II.	202
25, 29	Ardagh	137 1 19	Leitrim	Leitrim	Fenagh	Mohill	IV.	100
28	Ardagh	75 2 3	Limerick	Shanid	Ardagh	Newcastle	II.	254
49	Ardagh	128 0 12	Londonderry	Loughinsholin	Ballinderry	Magherafelt	III.	239
23, 24	Ardagh	120 1 31	Louth	Ferrard	Tullyallen	Drogheda	I.	183
67	Ardagh	64 3 32	Mayo	Burrishoole	Burrishoole	Newport	IV.	118
30, 39	Ardagh	195 2 37	Mayo	Tirawley	Ardagh	Ballina	IV.	163
2, 3	Ardagh	524 3 19d	Meath	Lower Slane	Ardagh	Kells	I.	222
15	Ardagh	345 2 17	Roscommon	Frenchpark	Kilcolagh	Boyle	IV.	203
34	Ardagh	336 2 5	Sligo	Tirerrill	Kilmacallan	Sligo	IV.	239
134, 143	Ardagh East	430 0 4	Cork, W.R.	EastCarbery,(W.D.)	Ross	Clonakilty	II.	135
4, 5	Ardagh (Gilbride)	165 1 22	Leitrim	Rosclogher	Rossinver	Ballyshannon	IV.	110
14, 19	Ardaghmore or Glentop	1,508 0 28	Antrim	Cary	Culfeightrin	Ballycastle	III.	13
150	Ardagh North	158 0 8	Cork, W.R.	WestCarbery,(E.D.)	Tullagh	Skibbereen	II.	141
4, 5	Ardagh (Sheeran)	190 1 4	Leitrim	Rosclogher	Rossinver	Ballyshannon	IV.	110
150	Ardagh South	68 2 11	Cork, W.R.	WestCarbery,(E.D.)	Tullagh	Skibbereen	II.	141
28	ARDAGH T.	—	Limerick	Shanid	Ardagh	Newcastle	II.	255
19	ARDAGH T.	—	Longford	Ardagh	Ardagh	Longford	I.	151
134, 143	Ardagh West	143 0 16	Cork, W.R.	EastCarbery,(W.D.)	Ross	Clonakilty	II.	135
42	Ardaghy	372 1 23	Down	Upper Iveagh,Lr. pt.	Kilcoo	Kilkeel	III.	173
4, 5	Ardaghy	443 0 8	Louth	Lower Dundalk	Carlingford	Dundalk	I.	176
14	Ardaghy	320 1 24	Monaghan	Monaghan	Monaghan	Monaghan	III.	276
92	Ardaghy Glebe	119 2 7	Donegal	Banagh	Inver	Donegal	III.	106
13	Ardaghy Kill	100 2 31	Monaghan	Monaghan	Monaghan	Monaghan	III.	276
150	Ardagilla	73 2 32	Cork, W.R.	WestCarbery,(E.D.)	Creagh	Skibbereen	II.	138
15	Ardagullion	661 0 7	Longford	Granard	Granard	Granard	I.	156
60, 61	Ardahee	56 1 10	Donegal	Raphoe	Leck	Letterkenny	III.	140
129, 138	Ardahill	183 1 0	Cork, W.R.	WestCarbery,(W.D.)	Kilcrohane	Bantry	II.	143
28, 29	Ardakillin	554 1 29e	Roscommon	Roscommon	Killukin	Strokestown	IV.	210
14	Ardakip Beg	101 0 36	Leitrim	Drumahaire	Killanummery	Manorhamilton	IV.	97
14, 15	Ardakip More	199 0 38	Leitrim	Drumahaire	Killanummery	Manorhamilton	IV.	97
14	Ardaloo	401 3 12	Kilkenny	Fassadinin	Grangemaccomb	Kilkenny	I.	89
62	Ardamadane	237 0 38	Cork, E.R.	East Muskerry	Garrycloyne	Cork	II.	103
16	Ardamagh	424 0 33f	Cavan	Tullygarvey	Annagh	Cootehill	III.	87
33	Ardamore	128 0 24	Kerry	Corkaguiny	Kilmalkedar	Dingle	II.	178
44, 54	Ardamore	447 2 29	Kerry	Corkaguiny	Kinard	Dingle	II.	179
128, 129	Ardamullivan	514 0 6g	Galway	Kiltartan	Beagh	Gort	IV.	46
15	Ardan	277 0 34h	Cavan	Lower Loughtee	Drumlane	Cavan	III.	79
9, 17	Ardan	749 1 3	King's Co.	Ballycowan	Kilbride	Tullamore	I.	127
38	Ardan	196 3 17	Westmeath	Moycashel	Rahugh	Tullamore	I.	279
11	Ardanaffrin	82 2 33	Roscommon	Ballintober North	Kilmore	Car^k on Shannon	IV.	186
36	Ardanairy	564 0 21	Wicklow	Arklow	Ennereilly	Rathdrum	I.	344
107, 117	Ardane	96 1 20	Galway	Longford	Killimorbologue	Portumna	IV.	58
74	Ardane	2,319 1 28	Tipperary, S.R.	Clanwilliam	Templeneiry	Tipperary	II.	311
67	Ardaneanig	232 1 8	Kerry	Magunihy,	Killarney	Killarney	II.	202
10	Ardaneer	250 2 23	Limerick	Shanid	Shanagolden	Rathkeale	II.	258
82, 83	Ardaneneen	614 2 23	Cork, W.R.	West Muskerry	Kilmichael	Dunmanway	II.	158

(a) Including 61A. 0R. 18P. water.   (d) Including 15A. 1R. 31P. water.   (g) Including 14A. 3R. 2P. water.
(b) Including 57A. 1R. 37P. water.   (e) Including 88A. 3R. 6P. water.   (h) Including 51A. 2R. 5P. water.
(c) Including 5A. 1R. 33P. water.   (f) Including 13A. 0R. 31P. water.

No. of Sheet of the Ordnance Survey Maps.	Townlands and Towns.	Area in Statute Acres.	County.	Barony.	Parish.	Poor Law Union in 1857.	Townland Census of 1851, Part I.	
		A. R. P.					Vol.	Page
129, 130	Ardanenig	137 1 4	Cork, W.R.	WestCarbery,(W.D.)	Kilcrohane	Bantry	II.	143
42	Ardanew	414 1 11	Meath	Lower Moyfenrath	Rathmolyon	Trim	I.	211
23, 24	Ardanragh	556 3 0	Longford	Shrule	Agharra	Ballymahon	I.	166
32	Ardanreagh	85 0 24	Limerick	Coshma	Tullabracky	Kilmallock	II.	244
16	Ardaprior	794 0 38	Cork, E.R.	Orrery and Kilmore	Buttevant	Mallow	II.	107
73, 74	Ardara	482 0 24	Donegal	Banagh	Killybegs Lower	Glenties	III.	110
116, 129	Ardaragh East	197 3 18	Cork, W.R.	Bear	Killaconenagh	Castletown	II.	124
128, 129	Ardaragh West	84 2 16	Cork, W.R.	Bear	Killaconenagh	Castletown	II.	124
73, 74, 82	ARDARA T.	—	Donegal	Banagh	Killybegs Lower	Glenties	III.	110
29	Ardaravan	421 2 0	Donegal	Inishowen West	Fahan Lower	Inishowen	III.	120
53	Ardarawer	71 3 4	Donegal	Kilmacrenan	Aghanunshin	Letterkenny	III.	122
26	Ardardagh	234 0 26	Cavan	Upper Loughtee	Larah	Cavan	III.	85
73,74,85,86	Ardarostig	242 3 17	Cork, E.R.	Cork	Inishkenny	Cork	II.	64
43	Ardarou	369 2 7	Cork, E.R.	Barrymore	Ardnageehy	Fermoy	II.	50
19	Ardarragh	89 3 20	Cavan	Tullyhunco	Killashandra	Cavan	III.	97
41, 47	Ardarragh	456 1 9	Down	Lordship of Newry	Newry	Newry	III.	182
74, 86	Ardarrig	55 1 14	Cork, E.R.	Cork	Carrigaline	Cork	II.	63
15, 23	Ardarver	748 2 28a	Tyrone	Omagh West	Termonamongan	Castlederg	III.	317
27	Ardass	134 2 2	Roscommon	Castlereagh	Kilkeevin	Castlereagh	IV.	200
53, 54	Ardataggle	694 3 20	Clare	Tulla Lower	O'Briensbridge	Limerick	II.	37
38, 47	Ardatedaun	192 2 6	Kerry	Trughanacmy	Kiltallagh	Tralee	II.	212
31,32,36,37	Ardateggle	1,274 1 36	Queen's Co.	Slievemargy	Killeshin	Carlow	I.	245
50	Ardatinny	243 3 26	Tyrone	Clogher	Donacavey	Omagh	III.	294
94	Ardatowel	134 1 5b	Donegal	Tirhugh	Donegal	Donegal	III.	144
10	Ardatrave	45 0 16	Fermanagh	Lurg	Magheraculmoney	Lowtherstown	III.	207
13, 14	Ardattin	196 2 12	Carlow	Forth	Ardoyne	Carlow	I.	3
52	Ardaturr	86 2 17c	Donegal	Kilmacrenan	Gartan	Letterkenny	III.	127
105	Ardaturrish Beg	401 1 29	Cork, W.R.	Bantry	Kilmocomoge	Bantry	II.	119
105	Ardaturrish More	458 2 8	Cork, W.R.	Bantry	Kilmocomoge	Bantry	II.	119
43, 51	Ardaturr Mountain	539 1 5	Donegal	Kilmacrenan	Gartan	Letterkenny	III.	127
82,83,94,95	Ardaun	102 2 29	Galway	Dunkellin	Oranmore	Galway	IV.	31
27	Ardaun East	245 0 27	Galway	Ross	Cong	Oughterard	IV.	72
27	Ardaun West	210 1 12	Galway	Ross	Cong	Oughterard	IV.	72
42	Ardavagga	77 1 13	King's Co.	Clonlisk	Kilmurryely	Roscrea	I.	131
66, 73	Ardavullane	540 1 2	Tipperary, S.R.	Clanwilliam	Bruis	Tipperary	II.	305
44	Ardawarry	138 3 26	Galway	Clare	Killererin	Tuam	IV.	20
18, 19	Ardballan	333 0 14	Louth	Ferrard	Cloonmore	Drogheda	I.	180
37	Ardballymore	112 1 5	Westmeath	Moycashel	Ardnurcher or Horseleap	Tullamore	I.	276
84	Ardbane	321 1 36	Donegal	Banagh	Inver	Donegal	III.	106
7, 16	Ardbane	334 3 4	Donegal	Kilmacrenan	Mevagh	Milford	III.	130
78, 79	Ardbane	199 3 30	Tipperary, S.R.	Slievardagh	Garrangibbon	Carrick on Suir	II.	333
100	Ardbane or Laghy Barr	357 2 38	Donegal	Tirhugh	Drumhome	Donegal	III.	146
24	Ardbarren Lower	284 0 39	Tyrone	Omagh West	Ardstraw	Castlederg	III.	315
24	Ardbarren Upper	261 0 26	Tyrone	Omagh West	Ardstraw	Castlederg	III.	315
11	Ardbash	107 2 33	King's Co.	Coolestown	Ballynakill	Edenderry	I.	132
41	Ardbaun	51 0 32	Tipperary, N.R.	Eliogarty	Thurles	Thurles	II.	273
35	Ardbear	390 0 7	Galway	Ballynahinch	Moyrus	Clifden	IV.	12
13	Ardbearn	126 3 2	Carlow	Forth	Ballyellin	Carlow	I.	4
13	Ardbearn and Torman	121 2 3	Carlow	Forth	Kellistown	Carlow	I.	4
35	Ardbeg	150 2 21	Kerry	Corkaguiny	Stradbally	Dingle	II.	180
40, 43	Ardbeg	265 0 37	Kilkenny	Ida	Kilcolumb	Waterford	I.	102
99	Ardberreen	76 3 19	Galway	Longford	Killoran	Ballinasloe	IV.	59
19, 20	Ardboghil	119 1 16	Longford	Ardagh	Ardagh	Longford	I.	151
28, 29	Ardbohil	266 1 18	Limerick	Connello Lower	Rathkeale	Rathkeale	II.	229
90	Ardboley North	219 0 8	Mayo	Clanmorris	Balla	Castlebar	IV.	131
90	Ardboley South	218 3 4	Mayo	Clanmorris	Balla	Castlebar	IV.	131
18, 19	Ardbolies	197 1 29	Louth	Ferrard	Rathdrumin	Drogheda	I.	182
7	Ardboline	4 0 25	Sligo	Carbury	Drumcliff	Sligo	IV.	222
27	Ardbooly Lower	54 1 8	Clare	Tulla Upper	Tulla	Tulla	II.	41
27	Ardbooly Upper	68 0 32	Clare	Tulla Upper	Tulla	Tulla	II.	41
23	Ardborra	192 1 21	Westmeath	Kilkenny West	Drumraney	Ballymahon	I.	272
19	Ardboy	43 1 11	Kilkenny	Crannagh	St. Canice	Kilkenny	I.	87
24, 25	Ardbraccan	1,096 1 3	Meath	Lower Navan	Ardbraccan	Navan	I.	214
112	Ardbrack	203 1 18	Cork, E.R.	Kinsale	Ringcurran	Kinsale	II.	100
37	Ardbrackan or Wrightown	258 3 1	Meath	Lower Deece	Scurlockstown	Trim	I.	192
24	Ardbrennan	240 1 28	Westmeath	Rathconrath	Killare	Mullingar	I.	283
34, 35	Ardbrin	1,007 2 1	Down	Upper Iveagh,Up.pt.	Annaclone	Banbridge	III.	174
23	Ardbuckan	151 3 34	Westmeath	Kilkenny West	Drumraney	Ballymahon	I.	272
94, 108	Ardcahan	824 3 15	Cork, W.R.	East Carbery,(W.D.)	Fanlobbus	Dunmanway	II.	131
12,13,18,19	Ardcalf,	504 3 34	Meath	Upper Slane	Slane	Navan	I.	225

(a) Including 5A. 1R. 20P. water.   (b) Including 7A. 2R. 22P. detached portion.   (c) Including 8A. 3R. 24P. water.

No. of Sheet of the Ordnance Survey Maps.	Townlands and Towns.	Area in Statute Acres.	County.	Barony.	Parish.	Poor Law Union in 1857.	Townland Census of 1851, Part I.	
		A. R. P.					Vol.	Page
2, 3	Ardcame	264 2 34a	Tyrone	Strabane Lower	Donaghedy	Strabane	III.	320
47	Ardcanaght	1,118 3 24	Kerry	Trughanacmy	Kilgarry Lander	Tralee	II.	210
37	Ardcandrisk	83 2 39	Wexford	Shelmaliere West	Ardcandrisk	Wexford	I.	332
6	Ardcarn	631 3 17	Roscommon	Boyle	Ardcarn	Boyle	IV.	192
53, 54	Ardcarn	264 2 6b	Roscommon	Moycarn	Creagh	Ballinasloe	IV.	206
25	Ardcarney	178 2 30	Clare	Bunratty Upper	Templemaley	Ennis	II.	10
33	Ardcath	277 1 25	Meath	Upper Duleek	Ardcath	Drogheda	I.	197
33	ARDCATH T.	—	Meath	Upper Duleek	Ardcath	Drogheda	I.	197
37, 38	Ardcavan	308 1 25	Wexford	Shelmaliere East	Ardcavan	Wexford	I.	329
11	Ardchamoyle	49 3 29	Roscommon	Boyle	Tumna	Car^k. on Shannon	IV.	197
99	Ardchicken	61 2 28	Donegal	Tirhugh,	Donegal	Donegal	III.	144
20	Ardclinis	35 1 4	Antrim	Lower Glenarm	Ardclinis	Larne	III.	21
20	Ardclinis Mountain	439 0 25	Antrim	Lower Glenarm	Ardclinis	Larne	III.	21
14, 15	Ardclogh	150 3 37	Kildare	South Salt	Lyons	Celbridge	I.	77
39, 42	Ardclone	291 3 22	Kilkenny	Iverk	Fiddown	Carrick on Suir	I.	105
4, 16	Ardcloon	169 3 10	Galway	Dunmore	Addergoole	Tuam	IV.	32
60, 70, 71	Ardcloon	239 0 0	Mayo	Gallen	Templemore	Castlebar	IV.	151
45, 54	Ardcloony	459 0 35	Clare	Tulla Lower	Killaloe	Limerick	II.	35
111	Ardcloyne	157 1 11	Cork, E.R.	Kinsale	Tisaxon	Kinsale	II.	101
10	Ardcolagh	229 2 3	Roscommon	Frenchpark	Kilmacumsy	Boyle	IV.	203
2	Ardcollum	65 2 27	Roscommon	Boyle	Kilronan	Boyle	IV.	196
38	Ardcolm	131 0 29	Wexford	Shelmaliere East	Ardcolm	Wexford	I.	330
47	Ardcolman	171 0 15	Roscommon	Athlone	Dysart	Athlone	IV.	180
23	Ardcolum	49 1 4	Leitrim	Leitrim	Kiltoghert	Car^k. on Shannon	IV.	100
20	Ardconnell	233 0 26	Kerry	Clanmaurice	Kilmoyly	Tralee	II.	171
33, 39	Ardconnell	203 2 18	Sligo	Corran	Emlaghfad	Sligo	IV.	226
6	Ardconra	190 2 2	Roscommon	Boyle	Ardcarn	Boyle	IV.	192
136	Ardcoohig	109 3 22	Cork, W.R.	Ibane and Barryroe	Lislee	Clonakilty	II.	149
10	Ardcorcoran	54 0 25	Roscommon	Boyle	Boyle	Boyle	IV.	193
90	Ardcorky	251 2 9	Mayo	Clanmorris	Mayo	Castlebar	IV.	135
79, 88	Ardcost	955 1 30	Kerry	Iveragh	Killemlagh	Cahersiveen	II.	196
20, 26	Ardcotten	190 3 5c	Sligo	Leyny	Ballysadare	Sligo	IV.	230
26	Ardcree	171 2 28d	Sligo	Leyny	Kilvarnet	Tobercurry	IV.	231
48	Ardcrone	231 0 0	Kerry	Trughanacmy	Currans	Killarney	II.	209
15	Ardcrony	885 0 24	Tipperary, N.R.	Lower Ormond	Ardcrony	Nenagh	II.	281
9	Ardcullen	198 2 30	Kerry	Clanmaurice	Rattoo	Listowel	II.	173
9	Ardcullen-Marshes	168 3 30	Kerry	Clanmaurice	Rattoo	Listowel	II.	173
27	Ardcumber	161 2 25	Sligo	Tirerrill	Drumcolumb	Sligo	IV.	238
38	Ardcumber	36 2 20	Tyrone	Dungannon Upper	Derryloran	Cookstown	III.	306
26	Ardcurley	110 1 34e	Sligo	Tirerrill	Ballysadare	Sligo	IV.	237
67, 80	Ardderroo	844 2 18f	Galway	Moycullen	Killannin	Galway	IV.	69
38,39,52,53	Ardderrynagleragh	1,410 1 38g	Galway	Moycullen	Kilcummin	Oughterard	IV.	66
36	Arddrine	330 1 39	Limerick	Glenquin	Grange	Newcastle	II.	245
108, 121	Ardea	295 3 2h	Cork, W.R.	East Carbery (E.D.)	Ballymoney	Dunmanway	II.	127
100, 101	Ardea	608 1 5i	Kerry	Glanarought	Tuosist	Kenmare	II.	188
8	Ardeamush	163 0 10	Clare	Corcomroe	Killilagh	Ennistimon	II.	19
31, 40	Ardean	143 0 5j	Tyrone	Dungannon Upper	Arboe	Cookstown	III.	305
6, 10	Ardeash	156 3 34	Roscommon	Boyle	Ardcarn	Boyle	IV.	192
76	Ard East	217 2 32k	Galway	Ballynahinch	Moyrus	Clifden	IV.	12
46, 54	Ardee	363 1 3	Donegal,	Raphoe	Allsaints	Londonderry	III.	133
17	Ardee	80 1 0	Louth	Ardee	Ardee	Ardee	I.	171
103	Ardeelan Lower	110 3 25	Donegal	Tirhugh	Drumhome	Ballyshannon	III.	146
103	Ardeelan Upper	128 3 32	Donegal	Tirhugh	Drumhome	Ballyshannon	III.	146
59	Ardeen	360 1 25	Cork, W.R.	West Muskerry	Clondrohid	Macroom	II.	155
91	Ardeen	604 0 27	Kerry	Dunkerron South	Kilcrohane	Kenmare	II.	183
16	Ardeenloun East	295 3 38	Waterford	Middlethird	Newcastle	Waterford	II.	368
16	Ardeenloun West	210 3 36	Waterford	Middlethird	Newcastle	Waterford	II.	368
8, 9	Ardees Lower	173 2 24	Fermanagh	Magheraboy	Inishmacsaint	Ballyshannon	III.	212
8, 13	Ardees Upper	607 3 14	Fermanagh	Magheraboy	Inishmacsaint	Ballyshannon	III.	212
17	ARDEE T.	—	Louth	Ardee	Ardee	Ardee	I.	171
94	Ardeevin	96 3 3	Donegal	Tirhugh	Donegal	Donegal	III.	144
6	Ardeevin	95 1 21	Galway	Ballymoe	Boyounagh	Glennamaddy	IV.	6
27, 28	Ardeevin	515 3 0	Roscommon	Castlereagh	Baslick	Castlereagh	IV.	199
31	Ardellis Lower	163 0 22	Kildare	West Offaly	Fontstown	Athy	I.	72
31	Ardellis Upper	284 0 3	Kildare	West Offaly	Fontstown	Athy	I.	72
41	Ardenagh Great	277 3 2	Wexford	Shelmaliere West	Taghmon	Wexford	I.	334
41	Ardenagh Little	304 2 20	Wexford	Shelmaliere West	Taghmon	Wexford	I.	334
42	Arderra	583 2 12	Kilkenny	Iverk	Arderra	Waterford	I.	105
139, 148	Arderrawinny	702 2 18	Cork, W.R.	West Carbery(W.D.)	Skull	Skull	II.	145
74	Arderrow	140 2 26	Cork, E.R.	Cork	Rathcooney	Cork	II.	65
9	Arderry	210 1 19l	Cavan	Tullyhaw	Templeport	Bawnboy	III.	93
29	Arderry	236 1 28m	Leitrim	Carrigallen	Drumreilly	Bawnboy	IV.	90
98	Arderry	1,118 0 38	Mayo	Burrishoole	Aghagower	Westport	IV.	117

(a) Including 3A. 0R. 33P. water.
(b) Including 6A. 2R. 13P. water.
(c) Including 7A. 3R. 27P. water.
(d) Including 3A. 3R. 36P. water.
(e) Including 6A. 1R. 18P. water.

(f) Including 53A. 3R. 34P. water.
(g) Including 211A. 0R. 34P. water.
(h) Including 1A. 3R. 28P. Ballynacarriga Lough.
(i) Including 16A. 0R. 13P. water.

(j) Including 0A. 3R. 16P. island.
(k) Including 13A. 0R. 27P. water.
(l) Including 8A. 2R. 32P. Bunerky Lough.
(m) Including 7A. 2R. 9P. water.

E

No. of Sheet of the Ordnance Survey Maps.	Townlands and Towns.	Area in Statute Acres.	County.	Barony.	Parish.	Poor Law Union in 1857.	Townland Census of 1851, Part I.	
		A. R. P.					Vol.	Page
82	Arderry . . .	296 3 16a	Mayo . .	Costello . . .	Aghamore . .	Swineford . .	IV.	136
93	Arderry . . .	79 0 21	Mayo . .	Costello . .	Annagh . . .	Claremorris .	IV.	137
94, 100	Ardeskin . .	44 1 37	Donegal . .	Tirhugh . .	Donegal . .	Donegal . .	III.	144
5, 6	Ardess Glebe .	105 2 22	Fermanagh .	Lurg . . .	Magheraculmoney .	Lowtherstown .	III.	207
106,107,109,110	Ardfarn . . .	1,056 2 8	Donegal . .	Tirhugh . .	Inishmacsaint . .	Ballyshannon .	III.	147
20, 21	Ard'ert . . .	370 3 32	Kerry . .	Clanmaurice . .	Ardfert . .	Tralee . .	II.	167
20	Ardfert Oughter .	105 1 23	Kerry . .	Clanmaurice .	Ardfert . .	Tralee . .	II.	167
20	ARDFERT T. .	—	Kerry . .	Clanmaurice .	Ardf.rt . .	Tralee . .	II.	167
82, 88	Ardfinnan . .	267 2 25b	Tipperary, S.R.	Iffa and Offa West .	Ardfinnan . .	Clogheen . .	II.	316
88	ARDFINNAN T.	—	Tipperary, S.R.	Iffa and Offa West .	{ Ardfinnan } { Ballybacon }	Clogheen . .	II.	317
41	Ardfintan . .	177 1 28	Galway . .	Clare . .	Killursa . .	Tuam . .	IV.	21
9	Ardfrail . .	75 1 1	Meath, . .	Fore . . .	Kilbride . .	Oldcastle . .	I.	200
94	Ardfry . .	145 2 28	Galway . .	Dunkellin . .	Ballynacourty .	Galway . .	IV.	27
57	Ardgaineen .	616 2 31	Galway . .	Clare . .	Annaghdown . .	Tuam . .	IV.	16
17	Ardgallagher .	165 3 23	Roscommon .	Ballintober North .	Kilmore . .	Carkk. on Shannon	IV.	186
47	Ardgallin . .	111 1 20	Sligo . .	Coolavin . .	Killaraght . .	Boyle . .	IV.	224
8	Ardgart . .	269 0 16	Fermanagh .	Magheraboy . .	Inishmacsaint . .	Ballyshannon .	III.	212
16, 22	Ardgart . .	103 1 14	Fermanagh .	Tirkennedy . .	Magheracross . .	Enniskillen .	III.	223
16, 17	Ardgarvan . .	276 3 5c	Londonderry .	Keenaght . .	Drumachose . .	NewTn.Limavady	III.	235
83	Ardgeeha . .	78 2 20	Tipperary, S.R.	Iffa and Offa East .	St. Mary's, Clonmel	Clonmel . .	II.	316
77, 83	Ardgeeha Lower	109 1 12	Tipperary, S.R.	Iffa and Offa East .	Rathronan . .	Clonmel . .	II.	316
32	Ardgeehan . .	59 2 16	Down . .	Ards Upper . .	Ballyphilip . .	Downpatrick .	III.	159
77, 83	Ardgeeha Upper	122 1 7	Tipperary, S.R.	Iffa and Offa East .	Rathronan . .	Clonmel . .	II.	316
136	Ardgehane . .	448 1 4	Cork, W.R. .	Ibane and Barryroe .	Abbeymahon . .	Clonakilty . .	II.	148
150, 151	Ardgehane . .	177 3 1	Cork, W.R. .	West Carbery (E.D.)	Castlehaven . .	Skibbereen .	II.	137
5	Ardgillan Demesne .	178 1 8	Dublin . .	Balrothery East .	Balrothery . .	Balrothery . .	I.	19
107	Ardgillew . .	100 2 25	Donegal . .	Tirhugh . .	Kilbarron . .	Ballyshannon, .	III.	148
1	Ardginny . .	98 1 33	Monaghan .	Trough . .	Errigal Trough .	Clogher . .	III.	283
12, 18	Ardgivna . .	121 0 21	Sligo . .	Tireragh . .	Templeboy . .	Dromore West .	IV.	236
11, 20	Ardglare . .	239 1 3	Cork, E.R. .	Condons&Clangibbon	Brigown . .	Mitchelstown .	II.	59
7	Ardglass . .	42 0 19	Cork, E.R. .	Orrery and Kilmore	Aglishdrinagh .	Kilmallock . .	II.	106
7	Ardglass . .	498 3 20	Cork, E.R. .	Orrery and Kilmore .	Shandrum . .	Kilmallock . .	II.	109
17, 18	Ardglass . .	85 2 21	Donegal . .	Kilmacrenan . .	Clondavaddog .	Milford . .	III.	124
45	Ardglass . .	321 3 15	Down . .	Lecale Lower . .	Ardglass . .	Downpatrick .	III.	178
10	Ardglass . .	254 1 34	Roscommon .	Boyle . .	Ardcarn . .	Boyle . .	IV.	192
16	Ardglassan . .	90 3 7	Meath . .	Upper Kells . .	Kil-keer . .	Oldcastle . .	I.	206
45	ARDGLASS T. .	—	Down . .	Lecale Lower . .	Ardglass . .	Downpatrick .	III.	178
16	Ardglushin . .	137 3 22	Cavan . .	Tullygarvey . .	Annagh . .	Cootehill . .	III.	87
15	Ardgonnell . .	218 0 16	Armagh . .	Tiranny . .	Tynan . .	Armagh . .	III.	60
153	Ardgort . .	88 2 25	Cork, W.R. .	West Carbery (E.D.)	Clear-island . .	Skibbereen .	II.	138
20	Ardgoulbeg . .	180 1 1	Limerick . .	Connello Lower .	Nantinan . .	Rathkeale . .	II.	228
20	Ardgoul North .	192 3 6	Limerick . .	Connello Lower .	Nantinan . .	Rathk eale . .	II.	228
20	Ardgoul South .	176 0 30	Limerick . .	Connello Lower .	Nantinan . .	Rathkeale . .	II.	228
107, 108	Ardgraigue . .	284 1 14	Galway . .	Longford . .	Kiquain . .	Portumna . .	IV.	60
30, 31	Ardgreagh . .	569 0 0	Meath . .	Upper Navan . .	Kilcooly . .	Trim . .	I.	216
14, 20	Ardgregane . .	157 1 9	Tipperary, N.R.	Lower Ormond .	Monsea . .	Nenagh . .	II.	287
102	Ardgroom Inward .	1,456 1 14	Cork, W.R .	Bear . . .	Kilcatherine . .	Castletown .	II.	123
102	Ardgroom Outward	2,243 0 1d	Cork, W.R. .	Bear . .	Kilcatherine . .	Castletown .	II.	123
22	Ardground . .	431 0 36	Londonderry .	Tirkeeran . .	Cumber Lower .	Londonderry .	III.	248
61	Ardnoom . .	344 0 6e	Mayo . .	Gallen . .	Meelick . .	Swineford . .	IV.	150
15	Ardicoan . .	157 3 38	Antrim . .	Lower Glenarm .	Grange of Inispollan	Ballycastle .	III.	21
23, 24	Ardigon . .	483 2 36f	Down . .	Dufferin . .	Killyleagh . .	Downpatrick .	III.	167
3	Ardihannon . .	223 3 4	Antrim . .	Cary . .	Billy . .	Coleraine . .	III.	12
37, 44	Ardilea . .	279 3 24	Down . .	Kinelarty . .	Loughinisland .	Downpatrick .	III.	177
35	Ardillaun . .	8 2 30	Galway . .	Ballynahinch . .	Ballindoon, . .	Clifden . .	IV.	10
27	Ardillaun . .	6 3 35	Galway . .	Ross . .	Cong . .	Oughterard .	IV.	73
26	Ardillon . .	95 0 5	Westmeath .	Fartullagh . .	Lynn . .	Mullingar . .	I.	269
2, 3	Ardina . .	186 3 19	Londonderry .	Coleraine . .	Dunboe . .	Coleraine . .	III.	231
16, 24	Ardinarive . .	1,420 1 15	Londonderry .	Keenaght . .	Bovevagh . .	NewTn.Limavady	III.	235
85, 94	Ardinawark . .	324 2 26	Donegal . .	Tirhugh . .	Donegal . .	Donegal . .	III.	144
29	Ardinode . .	304 3 6g	Kildare . .	South Naas . .	Ballymore Eustace .	Naas . .	I.	64
29	Ardinode . .	208 3 28h	Kildare . .	South Naas . .	Jago . .	Naas . .	I.	65
140, 149	Ardintenant . .	117 2 9	Cork, W.R. .	West Carbery (W.D.)	Skull . .	Skull . .	II.	145
19	Ardivaghan . .	88 1 26	Westmeath .	Moyashel and Magh-eradernon .	Mullingar . .	Mullingar . .	I.	275
98, 106	Ardkearagh . .	362 2 13	Kerry . .	Dunkerron South .	Kilcrohane . .	Cahersiveen .	III.	183
39	Ardkeel . .	421 1 20	Roscommon .	Ballintober South .	Roscommon . .	Roscommon .	IV.	190
25	Ardkeen . .	461 3 4	Down . .	Ards Upper . .	Ardkeen . .	Downpatrick .	III.	159
76	Ardkeen . .	136 2 25	Mayo . .	Burrishoole . .	Kilmeena . .	Westport . .	IV.	121
28, 34	Ardkeen . .	143 2 31	Tipperary, N.R.	Eliogarty . .	Drom . .	Thurles . .	II.	269
10	Ardkeenagh . .	206 1 28	Roscommon .	Boyle . .	Estersnow . .	Boyle . .	IV.	194
22, 28	Ardkeenagh . .	202 3 32	Roscommon .	Roscommon . .	Kilcooley . .	Strokestown .	IV.	210

(a) Including 18A. 0R. 29P. water.   (d) Including 4A. 1R. 4P. Glenbeg Lough.   (g) Including 5A. 3R. 37P. water.
(b) Including 10A. 1R. 24P. water.   (e) Including 10A. 0R. 25P. water.   (h) Including 2A. 3R. 1P. water.
(c) Including 2A. 0R. 6P. water.   (f) Including 9A. 0R. 18P. water.

No. of Sheet of the Ordinance Survey Maps.	Townlands and Towns.	Area in Statute Acres.	County.	Barony.	Parish.	Poor Law Union in 1857.	Townland Census of 1851, Part I.	
		A. R. P.					Vol.	Page
22, 28	Ardkeenagh *Plunkett*	245 2 9	Roscommon	Roscommon	Kilcooley	Strokestown	IV.	210
51, 54	Ardkeenan	950 0 19	Roscommon	Athlone	Drum	Athlone	IV.	180
41	Ardkeeragh	275 2 16	Down	Upper Iveagh, Up. pt.	Donaghmore	Newry	III.	175
39	Ardkeeran	106 2 16	Sligo	Corran	Kilshalvy	Boyle	IV.	227
27, 34	Ardkeeran	310 3 33a	Sligo	Tirerrill	Kilmacallan	Sligo	IV.	239
3, 8	Ardkill	628 1 39	Kildare	Carbury	Ardkill	Edenderry	I.	51
22	Ardkill	566 0 12	Londonderry	Tirkeeran	Clondermot	Londonderry	III.	247
73, 74	Ardkill	446 1 21	Mayo	Costello	Castlemore,	Castlereagh	IV.	139
118, 119	Ardkill	431 2 32	Mayo	Kilmaine	Kilcommon	Ballinrobe	IV.	154
12	Ardkill	74 3 14	Sligo	Tireragh	Templeboy	Dromore West	IV.	236
31, 32	Ardkill Beg	169 0 2	Cavan	Upper Loughtee	Denn	Cavan	III.	83
94,95,103,109	Ardkilleen	405 2 10	Cork, W.R.	East Carbery (W.D.)	Kinneigh	Dunmanway	II.	134
31	Ardkill More	278 1 37	Cavan	Upper Loughtee	Denn	Cavan	III.	83
124, 125	Ardkilly	245 3 28	Cork, E.R.	Kinsale	Ringrone	Kinsale	II.	100
39,40,47,48	Ardkilmartin	409 3 25	Limerick	Kilmallock	St.Peter's & St.Paul's	Kilmallock	II.	250
25	Ardkirk	134 2 22	Monaghan	Farney	Donaghmoyne	Castleblayney	III.	269
3	Ardkirk	62 0 17	Monaghan	Trough	Errigal Trough	Clogher	III.	283
109	Ardkitt East	283 1 11	Cork, W.R.	East Carbery (E.D.)	Desertserges	Bandon	II.	127
109	Ardkitt West	407 2 4	Cork, W.R.	East Carbery (E.D.)	Desertserges	Bandon	II.	127
51	Ardkyle	261 3 3	Clare	Bunratty Lower	Feenagh	Ennis	II.	4
9, 22	Ardkyle	209 0 31	Galway	Ballynahinch	Ballynakill	Clifden	IV.	11
5	Ardla	136 2 30	Dublin	Balrothery East	Lusk	Balrothery	I.	20
57, 65	Ardlaghas	368 0 25	Kerry	Dunkerron North	Knockane	Killarney	II.	181
34, 35	Ardlagheen Beg	209 2 8	Roscommon	Ballymoe	Cloonygormican	Roscommon	IV.	191
34, 35	Ardlagheen More or Highlake	528 0 2	Roscommon	Ballymoe	Cloonygormican	Castlereagh	IV.	191
4, 12	Ardlahan	275 2 22b	Limerick	Kenry	Kildimo	Rathkeale	II.	249
39	Ardlaherty or Abbeyville	105 1 11	Sligo	Corran	Drumrat	Boyle	IV.	225
19, 20	Ardlaman	238 1 30	Limerick	Shanid	Kilbradran	Rathkeale	II.	255
58	Ardlaman	131 3 16	Tipperary, S.R.	Clanwilliam	Solloghodmore	Tipperary	II.	310
17	Ardlaraghan	101 2 38	Louth	Ardee	Mosstown	Ardee	I.	174
10, 11	Ardlavagh	165 2 7	Roscommon	Boyle	Killukin	Cark. on Shannon	IV.	195
17	Ardlea	157 0 26	Queen's Co.	Maryborough West	Clonenagh & Clonagheen	Abbeyleix	I.	242
26	Ardleag	117 1 35	Cork, E.R.	Fermoy	Wallstown	Mallow	II.	83
17	Ardleckna	192 1 9	Roscommon	Roscommon	Aughrim	Cark. on Shannon	IV.	207
71, 72	Ardlee	87 3 7	Mayo	Gallen	Kilconduff	Swineford	IV.	147
34	Ardlee	79 1 24	Sligo	Tirerrill	Drumcolumb	Sligo	IV.	238
27	Ardleebeg	81 3 31	Sligo	Tirerrill	Ballysumaghan	Sligo	IV.	238
99	Ardlenagh	64 0 19	Donegal	Tirhugh	Donegal	Donegal	III.	144
31, 37	Ardleny	507 1 28c	Cavan	Clanmahon	Ballintemple	Cavan	III.	75
35, 41	Ardline	259 2 9d	Sligo	Tirerrill	Kilmactranny	Boyle,	IV.	240
66, 67	Ardloman	441 3 27	Tipperary, S.R.	Clanwilliam	Clonpet	Tipperary	II.	306
47	Ardlona	127 3 7	Sligo	Coolavin	Killaraght	Boyle	IV.	224
11	Ardlonan	342 0 16	Meath	Lower Kells	Kilbeg	Kells	I.	202
14, 20	Ardlough	162 2 12	Londonderry	Tirkeeran	Clondermot	Londonderry	III.	247
25, 31	Ardlougher	430 3 8e	Cavan	Clanmahon	Denn	Cavan	III.	76
5	Ardlougher	194 3 23f	Cavan	Tullyhaw	Killinagh	Enniskillen	III.	91
14	Ardlougher	142 2 39	Cavan	Tullyhunco	Kildallan	Bawnboy	III.	96
83	Ardlougher	184 3 12	Donegal	Banagh	Killybegs Lower	Glenties	III.	110
11	Ardlougher	98 0 31	Fermanagh	Lurg	Derryvullan	Lowtherstown	III.	204
20	Ardlougher	125 0 18	Leitrim	Drumahaire	Inishmagrath	Manorhamilton	IV.	95
28, 32	Ardlougher	140 2 34g	Leitrim	Leitrim	Kiltoghert	Cark. on Shannon	IV.	100
17	Ardlougher	127 1 14	Roscommon	Roscommon	Aughrim	Cark. on Shannon	IV.	207
107, 110	Ardloughhill	376 2 25	Donegal	Tirhugh	Inishmacsaint	Ballyshannon	III.	147
39, 40	Ardlow	379 2 10h	Cavan	Castlerahan	Mullagh	Bailieborough	III.	70
34	Ardloy	154 2 26i	Sligo	Tirerrill	Tawnagh	Sligo	IV.	241
43, 52	Ardmaclancy	194 1 22	Clare	Bunratty Lower	Kilfinaghta	Tulla	II.	4
11, 17	Ardmacroan	67 0 21	Roscommon	Ballintober North	Kilmore	Cark. on Shannon	IV.	186
5	Ardmaghbreague	1,088 3 6	Meath	Lower Kells	Nobber	Kells	I.	204
1, 2	Ardmalin	1,980 2 13	Donegal	Inishowen East	Clonca	Inishowen	III.	116
139	Ardmanagh	757 0 25	Cork, W.R.	West Carbery (W.D.)	Skull,	Skull	II.	145
74	Ardmanning Beg	5 1 34	Cork, E.R.	Cork	St. Finbar's	Cork	II.	65
74	Ardmanning More	20 1 13	Cork, E.R.	Cork	St. Finbar's	Cork	II.	65
111, 112	Ardmartin	110 2 29	Cork, E.R.	Kinsale	Clontead	Kinsale	II.	99
52	Ardmayle	192 0 5	Tipperary, S.R.	Middlethird	Ardmayle	Cashel	II.	324
52, 53	Ardmayle East	256 3 30	Tipperary, S.R.	Middlethird	Ardmayle	Cashel	II.	324
52	Ardmayle West	262 1 25	Tipperary, S.R.	Middlethird	Ardmayle	Cashel	II.	324
47, 53	Ardmeelode	349 2 36	Kerry	Magunihy	Kilcolman	Killarney	II.	200
49, 50	Ardmeen	773 2 36j	Donegal	Boylagh	Templecrone	Glenties	III.	114
38	Ardmeen	239 1 15	Down	Lecale Upper	Down	Downpatrick	III.	180
25	Ardmeenan	212 0 10k	Leitrim	Carrigallen	Oughteragh	Bawnboy	IV.	91
17	ARDMILLAN T.	—	Down	Castlereagh Lower	Tullynakill	Newtownards	III.	164

(a) Including 8A. 3R. 16P. water.
(b) Including 28A. 0R. 23P. water.
(c) Including 11A. 3R. 26P. water.
(d) Including 7A. 1R. 0P. Lough Skean.

(e) Including 9A. 1R. 36P. water.
(f) Including 9A. 1R. 14P. water.
(g) Including 11A. 2R. 31P. water.
(h) Including 2A. 3R. 17P. water.

(i) Including 3A. 0R. 16P. water.
(j) Including 40A. 0R. 38P. water.
(k) Including 13A. 0R. 6P. water.

No. of Sheet of the Ordnance Survey Maps.	Townlands and Towns.	Area in Statute Acres.			County.	Barony.	Parish.	Poor Law Union in 1857.	Townland Census of 1851, Part I.	
		A.	R.	P.					Vol.	Page
25	Ardminnan .	143	1	12	Down .	Ards Upper .	Slanes .	Downpatrick .	III.	161
39	Ardminnan .	93	3	34	Sligo .	Corran .	Kilshalvy .	Boyle .	IV.	227
22, 27	Ardmone .	139	3	16	Cavan .	Clankee .	Drumgoon .	Cootehill .	III.	72
22, 27	Ardmone East	151	1	10	Cavan .	Clankee .	Knockbride .	Cootehill .	III.	73
56	Ardmoneel .	261	3	36	Kerry .	Trughanacmy .	Killorglin .	Killarney .	II.	211
8	Ardmoneen .	362	1	22	Cavan .	Tullyhaw .	Drumreilly .	Bawnboy .	III.	91
8, 9, 13	Ardmoneen .	364	3	27	Leitrim .	Drumahaire .	Cloonclare .	Manorhamilton	IV.	93
27	Ardmone West	237	3	1	Cavan .	Clankee .	Knockbride .	Cootehill .	III.	73
29	Ardmoney .	250	3	6	Fermanagh .	Magherastephana	Aghavea .	Lisnaskea .	III.	218
121	Ardmoran .	129	3	38	Mayo .	Kilmaine .	Kilmainebeg .	Ballinrobe .	IV.	155
54	Ardmore .	461	2	16	Antrim .	Lower Massereene .	Killead .	Antrim .	III.	28
2, 3	Ardmore .	333	2	10	Armagh .	Oneilland East .	Montiaghs .	Lurgan .	III.	49
16, 24	Ardmore .	118	1	36	Clare .	Corcomroe .	Clooney .	Ennistimon .	III.	18
75, 87	Ardmore .	285	3	1	Cork, E.R. .	Kerrycurrihy .	Marmullane .	Cork .	II.	92
2	Ardmore .	182	0	15	Cork, E.R. .	Orrery and Kilmore .	Rathgoggan .	Kilmallock .	II.	109
123	Ardmore .	223	0	24	Cork, W.R. .	Ibane and Barryroe .	Timoleague .	Clonakilty .	II.	151
39	Ardmore .	721	1	8	Donegal .	Inishowen West .	Muff .	Londonderry .	III.	121
23, 28	Ardmore .	178	0	26	Fermanagh .	Magherastephana .	Aghavea .	Lisnaskea .	III.	218
77	Ardmore .	497	3	23a	Galway .	Ballynahinch .	Moyrus .	Clifden .	IV.	12
35	Ardmore .	58	0	10	Galway .	Ballynahinch .	Omey .	Clifden .	IV.	14
99	Ardmore .	289	1	21b	Kerry .	Dunkerron South .	Kilcrohane .	Kenmare .	II.	183
31, 35	Ardmore .	241	0	2	Kildare .	Narragh & Reban W.	Kilberry .	Athy .	I.	67
41	Ardmore .	41	3	14	Limerick .	Coshlea .	Ballyscaddan .	Kilmallock .	II.	238
10, 17	Ardmore .	236	3	3	Londonderry .	Keenaght .	Balteagh .	New Tn Limavady	III.	234
20, 21, 22	Ardmore .	502	1	39	Londonderry .	Tirkeeran .	Clondermot .	Londonderry .	III.	247
16, 17	Ardmore .	143	0	30c	Mayo .	Erris .	Kilmore .	Belmullet .	IV.	145
88	Ardmore .	57	2	7	Mayo .	Murrisk .	Oughaval .	Westport .	IV.	161
38, 39	Ardmore .	702	1	2d	Roscommon .	Ballymoe .	Dunamon .	Roscommon .	IV.	191
5	Ardmore .	262	2	33	Roscommon .	Boyle .	Boyle .	Boyle .	IV.	193
10	Ardmore .	383	2	38	Roscommon .	Boyle .	Killukin .	Boyle .	IV.	195
9	Ardmore .	110	2	37	Roscommon .	Frenchpark .	Kilnamanagh .	Castlereagh .	IV.	204
2	Ardmore .	238	2	1	Tyrone .	Strabane Lower .	Donaghedy .	Strabane .	III.	320
19	Ardmore .	151	3	9	Westmeath .	Moyashel and Magh-eradernon .	Mullingar .	Mullingar .	I.	275
35	*Ardmore Island*	1	1	34	Galway .	Ballynahinch .	Omey .	Clifden .	IV.	15
16	Ardmore Point	93	0	3	Mayo .	Erris .	Kilmore .	Belmullet .	IV.	145
3	Ardmore or Windgap	76	0	36	Waterford .	Upperthird .	Dysert .	Carrick on Suir	II.	369
40	ARDMORE T. .	—			Waterford .	Decies within Drum	Ardmore .	Youghal .	II.	351
38	Ardmorney .	152	2	20	Westmeath .	Moycashel .	Newtown .	Mullingar .	I.	278
9	Ardmoyle .	188	3	12	Roscommon .	Frenchpark .	Kilnamanagh .	Boyle .	IV.	204
47	Ardmoyle .	260	1	11	Sligo .	Coolavin .	Killaraght .	Boyle .	IV.	224
25, 26	Ardmulchan .	1,156	1	9e	Meath .	Skreen .	Ardmulchan .	Navan .	I.	220
45, 48	Ardmullan .	628	1	9	Roscommon .	Athlone .	Cam .	Athlone .	IV.	179
94	Ardnablensk .	152	2	30	Donegal .	Tirhugh .	Donegal .	Donegal .	III.	144
112	Ardnaboha .	81	1	28	Cork, E.R. .	Kinalea .	Kilmonoge .	Kinsale .	II.	95
88, 100	Ardnabourkey .	341	2	0	Cork, E.R. .	Imokilly .	Corkbeg .	Midleton .	II.	86
33	Ardnaboy .	278	2	37	Wicklow .	Ballinacor South .	Hacketstown .	Shillelagh .	I.	348
14, 20	Ardnabrocky .	256	1	19f	Londonderry .	Tirkeeran .	Clondermot .	Londonderry .	III.	247
100, 100	Ardnacally .	355	0	3	Mayo .	Kilmaine .	Robeen .	Ballinrobe .	IV.	157
13, 14	Ardnacassagh .	168	1	18	Longford .	Ardagh .	Templemichael .	Longford .	I.	153
86, 87	Ardnacloghy .	62	3	31	Cork, E.R. .	Kerrycurrihy .	Carrigaline .	Cork .	II.	92
105	Ardnacloghy .	322	3	11	Cork, W.R. .	Bantry .	Kilmocomoge .	Bantry .	II.	119
96, 97	Ardnaclug .	202	0	0	Cork, W.R. .	East Carbery (E.D.)	Inishannon .	Bandon .	II.	128
14	Ardnacraa .	109	2	15	Clare .	Corcomroe .	Kilmacrehy .	Ennistimon .	II.	20
16	Ardnacrany North .	813	2	20	Westmeath .	Kilkenny West .	Noughaval .	Ballymahon .	I.	274
16, 23	Ardnacrany South .	162	0	2	Westmeath .	Kilkenny West .	Noughaval .	Ballymahon .	I.	274
36	Ardnacrohy .	243	0	12	Limerick .	Glenquin .	Monagay .	Newcastle .	II.	247
76	*Ardnacross Island*	2	2	36	Galway .	Ballynahinch .	Moyrus .	Clifden .	IV.	13
63	ARDNACRUSHA T. .	—			Clare .	Bunratty Lower .	St. Patrick's .	Limerick .	II.	7
54, 70	Ardnacrushy .	405	3	8	Cork, W.R. .	West Muskerry .	Clondrohid .	Macroom .	II.	155
15, 23	Ardnacullia North .	75	0	28	Clare .	Corcomroe .	Kilmanaheen .	Ennistimon .	II.	21
23	Ardnacullia South .	344	3	25	Clare .	Corcomroe .	Kilmanaheen .	Ennistimon .	II.	21
54	Ardnadiriin .	84	0	21	Donegal .	Raphoe .	Raymoghy .	Letterkenny .	III.	141
105	Ardnadoman East	71	1	19	Galway .	Loughrea .	Kilconickny .	Loughrea .	IV.	63
105	Ardnadoman West .	181	3	11	Galway .	Loughrea .	Kilconickny .	Loughrea .	IV.	63
16	Ardnagall .	259	1	35	Galway .	Dunmore .	Tuam .	Tuam .	IV.	35
103	Ardnagalliagh .	81	0	3	Donegal .	Tirhugh .	Drumhome .	Ballyshannon .	III.	146
78	Ardnagannagh .	195	3	25g	Donegal .	Raphoe .	Donaghmore .	Stranorlar .	III.	137
32, 33	Ardnagappary .	870	1	25	Donegal .	Kilmacrenan .	Tullaghobegly .	Dunfanaghy .	III.	131
105	Ardnagashel .	198	1	2	Cork, W.R. .	Bantry .	Kilmocomoge .	Bantry .	II.	119
94, 100	Ardnagassan .	153	3	32h	Donegal .	Tirhugh .	Donegal .	Donegal .	III.	144
51	Ardnagassane .	93	3	4	Tipperary, N.R.	Kilnamanagh Upper	Toem .	Tipperary .	II.	280
30	Ardnageeha .	311	3	35	Cork, E.R. .	Duhallow .	Cullen .	Millstreet .	II.	70

(a) Including 2A. 2R. 0P. water.
(b) Including 6A. 1R. 35P. water.
(c) Including 12A. 2R. 8P. water.

(d) Including 17A. 3R. 15P. water.
(e) Including 25A. 0R. 20P. water.
(f) Including 6A. 3R. 36P. water.

(g) Including 8A. 0R. 0P. water.
(h) Including 0A. 3R. 32P. water.

No. of Sheet of the Ordnance Survey Maps.	Townlands and Towns.	Area in Statute Acres.	County.	Barony.	Parish.	Poor Law Union in 1857.	Townland Census of 1851, Part I.	
		A. R. P.					Vol.	Page
27	Ardnageeha . .	211 2 36	Galway . .	Ross . . .	Cong . . .	Oughterard .	IV.	72
7, 8	Ardnageehy . .	361 1 3	Cork, E.R. .	Orrery and Kilmore	Rathgoggan . .	Kilmallock .	II.	109
118	Ardnageehy Beg	175 3 8	Cork, W.R. .	Bantry . . .	Kilmocomoge . .	Bantry . .	II.	119
53	Ardnageehy East	698 3 30	Cork, E.R. .	Barrymore . .	Ardnageehy . .	Fermoy . .	II.	50
118	Ardnageehy More .	229 2 12	Cork, W.R. .	Bantry . . .	Kilmocomoge . .	Bantry . .	II.	119
52, 53	Ardnageehy West .	477 2 13	Cork, E.R. .	Barrymore . .	Ardnageehy . .	Fermoy . .	II.	50
49, 50	Ardnagla . .	284 3 19	Clare . .	Clonderalaw .	Kilchreest . .	Killadysert .	II.	14
36, 37, 42	Ardnaglass . .	665 2 22	Antrim . .	Upper Toome .	Ballyscullion Grange	Ballymena .	III.	33
79	Ardnaglass . .	264 2 2	Donegal . .	Raphoe . .	Clonleigh . .	Strabane . .	III.	134
105	Ardnaglass . .	71 2 10	Donegal . .	Tirhugh . .	Templecarn . .	Donegal . .	III.	149
26, 33	Ardnaglass . .	332 0 34a	Sligo . .	Corran . . .	Emlaghfad . .	Sligo . .	IV.	226
5	Ardnaglass Lower .	109 0 37	Sligo . .	Carbury . .	Ahamlish . .	Sligo . .	IV.	219
5	Ardnaglass Upper .	87 3 1	Sligo . .	Carbury . .	Ahamlish . .	Sligo . .	IV.	219
38	Ardnaglew . .	351 2 22	Westmeath .	Moycashel . .	Kilbeggan . .	Tullamore .	I.	278
50,51,53,54	Ardnaglug . .	1,048 2 39	Roscommon .	Moycarn . . .	Moore . . .	Ballinasloe .	IV.	206
29	Ardnaglug . .	24 2 13	Westmeath .	Brawny . . .	St. Mary's . .	Athlone . .	I.	259
113, 122	Ardnagno . .	168 3 9	Galway . .	Kiltartan . .	Killinny . .	Gort . .	IV.	47
21	Ardnagor . .	137 1 28	Mayo . .	Tirawley . .	Rathreagh . .	Killala . .	IV.	171
16, 17	Ardnagowna . .	183 3 34b	Roscommon .	Roscommon . .	Elphin . .	Strokestown .	IV.	209
23	Ardnagragh . .	13 0 24	Westmeath .	Kilkenny West .	Drumraney . .	Ballymahon .	I.	272
23	Ardnagragh Digby .	650 3 4c	Westmeath .	Kilkenny West .	Drumraney . .	Ballymahon .	I.	272
23	Ardnagragh Gray .	261 1 4	Westmeath .	Kilkenny West .	Drumraney . .	Ballymahon .	I.	272
9	Ardnagreevagh .	161 2 32	Galway . .	Ballynahinch .	Ballynakill . .	Clifden . .	IV.	11
149, 150	Ardnagrena . .	158 3 29	Cork, W.R. .	West Carbery (E.D.)	Creagh . .	Skibbereen .	II.	138
149	Ardnagroghery .	90 2 1	Cork, W.R. .	West Carbery (E.D.)	Aghadown . .	Skibbereen .	II.	136
31	Ardnagross . .	128 0 32	Kildare . .	Narragh and Reban West . . .	Narraghmore . .	Athy . .	I.	68
1	Ardnagross . .	220 2 2	Westmeath .	Fore . . .	Lickbla . .	Granard . .	I.	270
14	Ardnaguniog .	389 0 16	Londonderry .	Tirkeeran . .	Faughanvale . .	Londonderry .	III.	249
15	Ardnahea . .	48 2 32	Clare . .	Corcomroe . .	Kilmacrehy . .	Ennistimon .	II.	20
89	Ardnahinch . .	149 1 37	Cork, E.R. .	Imokilly . .	Kilmahon . .	Middleton .	II.	89
25	Ardnahow . .	205 2 14	Waterford .	Middlethird . .	Reisk . .	Waterford .	II.	368
105	Ardnamanagh .	126 2 21	Cork, W.R. .	Bantry . . .	Kilmocomoge . .	Bantry . .	II.	119
55	Ardnamoghill .	59 1 29	Donegal . .	Raphoe . .	Killea . .	Londonderry .	III.	138
49, 50	Ardnamoher . .	597 0 8	Limerick . .	Coshlea . .	Galbally . .	Mitchelstown .	II.	238
27	Ardnamullagh	81 2 0	Roscommon .	Castlereagh . .	Ballintober . .	Castlereagh .	IV.	198
46, 47	Ardnamullan . .	657 1 16	Meath . .	Upper Moyfenrath .	Clonard . .	Edenderry .	I.	213
66	Ardnamweely . .	45 0 4	Kerry . .	Magunihy . .	Killarney . .	Killarney .	II.	202
39	Ardnanagh . .	221 3 34	Roscommon .	Ballintober South .	Roscommon . .	Roscommon .	IV.	190
29	Ardnanean . .	114 3 8	Limerick . .	Connello Lower .	Rathkeale . .	Rathkeale .	II.	229
51	Ardnanure . .	82 1 21	Roscommon .	Athlone . . .	Drum . . .	Athlone . .	IV.	180
30, 36	Ardnaponra . .	71 2 27	Westmeath .	Clonlonan . .	Kilmanaghan . .	Athlone . .	I.	262
29	Ardnapreaghaun .	91 0 32	Limerick . .	Connello Lower .	Croagh . .	Rathkeale .	II.	227
37	Ardnaree . .	172 1 18	Donegal . .	Kilmacrenan . .	Tullyfern . .	Millford . .	III.	132
29	Ardnaree or Shanaghy	522 2 4d	Sligo . .	Tireragh . .	Kilmoremoy . .	Ballina . .	IV.	235
29	ARDNAREE T. . .	—	Sligo . .	Tireragh . .	Kilmoremoy . .	Ballina . .	IV.	235
9	Ardnargle . .	105 3 4e	Londonderry .	Keenaght . .	Tamlaght-Finlagan	NewTⁿLimavady	III.	237
6	Ardnasallem . .	116 1 2	Monaghan .	Trough . . .	Donagh . .	Monaghan .	III.	281
54, 55	Ardnasillagh . .	244 0 21	Galway . .	Moycullen . .	Kilcummin . .	Oughterard .	IV.	66
58	Ardnasodan . .	111 1 37	Galway . .	Clare . . .	Kilmoylan . .	Tuam . .	IV.	22
70	Ardnasool . .	114 2 18	Donegal . .	Raphoe . .	Clonleigh . .	Strabane .	III.	134
29	Ardnaveagh . .	182 3 16	Limerick . .	Connello Lower .	Doondonnell . .	Rathkeale .	II.	228
27	Ardneeskan . .	105 2 28	Sligo . .	Tirerrill . .	Kilmacallen . .	Sligo . .	IV.	239
3, 8	Ardnehue . .	654 3 23	Carlow . .	Carlow . .	Killerrig . .	Carlow . .	I.	2
31	Ardnurcher . .	296 0 34	Westmeath .	Moycashel . .	Ardnurcher or Horseleap . . .	Mullingar .	I.	276
2	Ardnurcher Glebe .	80 1 18	King's Co. .	Kilcoursey . .	Ardnurcher or Horseleap . . .	Tullamore .	I.	140
66, 67	Ardo . . .	178 0 6	Tyrone . .	Dungannon Lower .	Aghaloo . .	Armagh . .	III.	296
60	Ardobireen . .	207 1 31	Tipperary, S.R.	Clanwilliam . .	Relickmurry and Athassel . .	Tipperary .	II.	309
40	Ardocheasty . .	172 0 0	Waterford .	Decies within Drum	Ardmore . .	Youghal .	II.	349
130, 131	Ardogeena . .	171 2 9	Cork, W.R. .	West Carbery(W.D.)	Durrus . .	Bantry . .	II.	142
12	Ardogelly . .	211 0 7	Sligo . .	Tireragh . .	Templeboy . .	Dromore West .	IV.	236
22, 26	Ardoghil . .	254 2 15	Longford . .	Ratheline . .	Shrule . .	Ballymahon .	I.	165
40	Ardoginna . .	425 2 5	Waterford .	Decies within Drum	Ardmore . .	Youghal .	II.	349
88	Ardogommon . .	233 0 10	Mayo . .	Burrishoole . .	Aghagower . .	Westport .	IV.	117
65, 66	Ardohill . .	61 1 19	Tipperary, S.R.	Clanwilliam . .	Emly . .	Tipperary .	II.	307
87, 88	Ardoley . .	143 2 6	Mayo . .	Murrisk . .	Oughaval . .	Westport .	IV.	161
15	Ardonan . .	136 2 13f	Cavan . .	Lower Loughtee .	Drumlane . .	Cavan . .	III.	79
11	Ardoohy . .	25 0 22	Cavan . .	Lower Loughtee .	Drumlane . .	Cavan . .	III.	79
5	Ardore . .	49 3 19	Fermanagh .	Lurg . . .	Drumkeeran . .	Lowtherstown .	III.	205
6	Ardore . .	146 1 8g	Fermanagh .	Lurg . . .	Magheraculmoney .	Lowtherstown .	III.	207
18	Ardoslough . .	410 3 12	Galway . .	Ballymoe . .	Boyounagh . .	Glennamaddy .	IV.	6

(a) Including 2A. 3R. 7P. water.　　　(d) Including 1A. 3R. 19P. River Moy.　　　(f) Including 4A. 0R. 0P. water.
(b) Including 4A. 0R. 10P. water.　　　(e) Including 4A. 1R. 4P. water.　　　(g) Including 8A. 1R. 4P. water.
(c) Including 4A. 2B. 24P. detached portion.

No. of Sheet of the Ordnance Survey Maps.	Townlands and Towns.	Area in Statute Acres.			County.	Barony.	Parish.	Poor Law Union in 1857.	Townland Census of 1851, Part I.	
		A.	R.	P.					Vol.	Page
30	Ardoughan	268	2	33	Mayo	Tirawley	Kilmoremoy	Ballina	IV.	170
36, 37	Ardough or Hunts-park	647	0	31	Queen's Co.	Slievemargy	Killabban	Carlow	I.	245
9	Ardoughter	864	0	39	Kerry	Clanmaurice	Killury	Listowel	II.	170
15, 28	Ardour	551	2	25	Galway	Dunmore	Kilconla	Tuam	IV.	35
9	Ardowen	173	3	28	Mayo	Erris	Kilmore	Belmullet	IV.	145
9	Ardowen Common	21	2	2	Mayo	Erris	Kilmore	Belmullet	IV.	145
37, 42	Ardoyne	971	1	·20	Wicklow	Shillelagh	Ardoyne	Shillelagh	I.	357
60	ARDOYNE T.	—			Antrim	Upper Belfast	Shankill	Belfast	III.	35
5	Ardpaddin	167	3	34a	Waterford	Glenahiry	Kilronan	Clonmel	II.	365
56	Ardpatrick	154	0	30	Limerick	Coshlea	Ardpatrick	Kilmallock	II.	236
11	Ardpatrick	174	1	39	Louth	Louth	Louth	Dundalk	I.	184
39	Ardpatrick	102	3	14	Tyrone	Dungannon Middle	Donaghenry	Cookstown	III.	300
103, 107	Ardpattan	95	3	29	Donegal	Tirhugh	Kilbarron	Ballyshannon	III.	148
24, 25	Ardquin	190	0	21b	Down	Ards Upper	Ardquin	Downpatrick	III.	159
24	Ardra	260	0	28c	Cavan	Tullyhunco	Killashandra	Cavan	III.	97
45	Ardra	390	2	13	Cork, E.R.	Barrymore	Britway	Fermoy	II.	51
142	Ardra	83	3	16	Cork, W.R.	West Carbery (E.D.)	Myross	Skibbereen	II.	140
5, 6	Ardra	770	0	37	Kilkenny	Fassadinin	Castlecomer	Castlecomer	I.	88
27	Ardra	392	1	37	King's Co.	Coolestown	Clonsast	Edenderry	I.	132
88	Ardra Beg	184	0	31	Cork, E.R.	Imokilly	Rostellan	Middleton	II.	90
27, 30	Ardragh	469	3	4d	Monaghan	Farney	Magheross	Carrickmacross	III.	273
49	Ardragh	120	2	19	Tipperary, S.R.	Slievardagh	Ballingarry	Callan	II.	331
106	Ardrah	477	2	21	Cork, W.R.	Bantry	Kilmocomoge	Bantry	II.	119
118	Ardrah	451	1	14	Cork, W.R.	West Carbery(W.D.)	Kilmocomoge	Bantry	II.	144
83	Ardrah	131	3	6	Cork, W.R.	West Muskerry	Kilmurry	Macroom	II.	159,
21	Ardrahan	488	1	11	Kerry	Clanmaurice	Killahan	Tralee	II.	170
21	Ardrahan	97	3	29	Kerry	Clanmaurice	Kilmoyly	Tralee	II.	171
114	Ardrahan North	35	0	22	Galway	Dunkellin	Ardrahan	Gort	IV.	26
113, 114	Ardrahan South	119	1	20	Galway	Dunkellin	Ardrahan	Gort	IV.	26
114	ARDRAHAN T.	—			Galway	Dunkellin	Ardrahan	Gort	IV.	27
39	Ardraheen Beg	99	2	24	Sligo	Corran	Kilshalvy	Boyle	IV.	227
39	Ardraheen More	129	1	26	Sligo	Corran	Kilshalvy	Boyle	IV.	227
49	Ardrahin	305	3	9	Limerick	Coshlea	Galbally	Mitchelstown	II.	238
141	Ardraly	475	1	35	Cork, W.R.	West Carbery (E.D.)	Aghadown	Skibbereen	II.	136
88	Ardra More	278	2	30	Cork, E.R.	Imokilly	Rostellan	Middleton	II.	90
99	Ardranny Beg	302	2	7	Galway	Clonmacnowen	Clontuskert	Ballinasloe	IV.	24
99	Ardranny More	197	2	26	Galway	Clonmacnowen	Clontuskert	Ballinasloe	IV.	24
40	Ardrass	235	0	36e	Mayo	Gallen	Attymass	Ballina	IV.	146
10, 11	Ardrass Lower	235	0	30	Kildare	North Salt	Killadoon	Celbridge	I.	74
10, 11, 14	Ardrass Upper	312	0	8f	Kildare	North Salt	Killadoon	Celbridge	I.	74
57, 65	Ardraw	197	1	31	Kerry	Dunkerron North	Knockane	Killarney	II.	181
8	Ardrea	166	0	15	Armagh	Oneilland West	Grange	Armagh	III.	52
33	Ardrea	161	1	31g	Sligo	Corran	Kilmorgan	Sligo	IV.	226
12	Ardreagh	297	2	6	Kilkenny	Galmoy	Urlingford	Urlingford	I.	93
11, 18	Ardreagh	196	2	22	Londonderry	Coleraine	Aghadowey	Coleraine	III.	229
35	Ardree	323	1	30h	Kildare	Kilkea and Moone	Ardree	Athy	I.	59
35, 37	Ardree	476	3	12i	Kildare	Kilkea and Moone	Tankardstown	Athy	I.	61
33, 39	Ardree	174	1	38	Sligo	Corran	Emlaghfad	Boyle	IV.	226
4, 8	Ardress East	322	3	36	Armagh	Oneilland West	Loughgall	Armagh	III.	53
4, 8	Ardress West	314	0	15	Armagh	Oneilland West	Loughgall	Armagh	III.	53
35	Ardrew	81	3	35	Kildare	Narragh & Reban W.	St. Johns	Athy	I.	68
44,45,54,55	Ardrinane	301	2	1	Kerry	Corkaguiny	Ballynacourty	Dingle	II.	174
8, 13	Ardristan	858	1	1	Carlow	Rathvilly	Ardristan	Carlow	I.	10
45	Ardroe	436	3	27	Kerry	Corkaguiny	Ballinvoher	Dingle	II.	173
23, 24	Ardroe	221	3	3	Limerick	Clanwilliam	Grean	Limerick	II.	224
101	Ardroe	93	3	18	Mayo	Clanmorris	Kilcolman	Claremorris	IV.	133
86, 87	Ardros	148	3	16	Galway	Kilconnell	Killallaghtan	Ballinasloe	IV.	41
29	Ardross	5	1	36	Wexford	Bantry	St. Marys	New Ross	I.	302
73	Ardrum	596	1	17	Cork, E.R.	East Muskerry	Inishcarra	Cork	II.	103
25	Ardrum	419	2	10	Leitrim	Carrigallen	Oughteragh	Bawnboy	IV.	91
28, 42, 43	Ardrumkilla	674	0	1	Galway	Clare	Belclare	Tuam	IV.	17
43	Ardrumkilla	35	1	12	Galway	Clare	Killower	Tuam	IV.	21
46	Ardrumman	500	0	32	Donegal	Kilmacrenan	Aughnish	Letterkenny	III.	122
48, 49	Ardrums Great	613	0	25	Meath	Upper Deece	Rathcore	Trim	I.	194
48	Ardrums Little	198	1	38	Meath	Upper Deece	Rathcore	Trim	I.	194
16, 24	Ardrush	147	3	25	Clare	Corcomroe	Clooney	Corrofin	II.	18
16, 26	Ards	559	2	8	Donegal	Kilmacrenan	Clondahorky	Dunfanaghy	III.	122
57, 65	Ards	92	0	11k	Kerry	Dunkerron North	Knockane	Killarney	II.	181
58, 66	Ards	211	3	17	Kerry	Magunihy	Aghadoe	Killarney	II.	199
18	Ards	395	3	5	Longford	Moydow	Kilcommock	Ballymahon	I.	161
31	Ardsallagh	665	1	14l	Meath	Lower Navan	Ardsallagh	Navan	I.	214
5	Ardsallagh	192	0	37	Roscommon	Boyle	Boyle	Boyle	IV.	193

(a) Including 2A. 2R. 0P. water.
(b) Including 17A. 2R. 11P. Lough Cowey.
(c) Including 25A. 0R. 18P. water.
(d) Including 5A. 3R. 7P. water.

(e) Including 54A. 3R. 5P. water.
(f) Including 7A. 2R. 16P. water.
(g) Including 2A. 1R. 3P. water.
(h) Including 5A. 3R. 20P. water.

(i) Including 10A. 1R. 0P. water.
(k) Including 2A. 0R. 29P. water.
(l) Including 20A. 1R. 26P. water.

No. of Sheet of the Ordnance Survey Maps.	Townlands and Towns.	Area in Statute Acres.			County.	Barony.	Parish.	Poor Law Union in 1857.	Townland Census of 1851. Part I.	
		A.	R.	P.					Vol.	Page
33, 39	Ardsallagh	161	1	31	Sligo	Corran	Toomour	Boyle	IV.	228
61, 62, 69, 70	Ardsallagh	150	1	30	Tipperary, S.R.	Middlethird	Rathcool	Cashel	II.	329
37	Ardsallagh	528	1	30	Waterford	Decies-within-Drum	Clashmore	Youghal	II.	351
39	Ardsallagh Beg	206	3	37	Roscommon	Ballintober South	Roscommon	Roscommon	IV.	190
39, 40	Ardsallagh More	270	1	14	Roscommon	Ballintober South	Roscommon	Roscommon	IV.	190
106	Ards Beg	188	3	30	Cork, W.R.	Bantry	Kilmocomoge	Bantry	II.	119
24, 33	Ards Beg	1,611	0	24a	Donegal	Kilmacrenan	Tullaghobegly	Dunfanaghy	III.	131
45	Ards Big	511	1	2	Donegal	Kilmacrenan	Conwal	Milford	III.	125
19	Ardscradaun	12	1	28	Kilkenny	Shillelogher	St. Patrick's	Kilkenny	I.	116
31, 35	Ardscull	1,188	3	8	Kildare	Narragh & Reban East	Moone	Athy	I.	66
66	Ardshanavooly	104	2	23	Kerry	Magunihy	Killarney	Killarney	II.	202
21	Ardshanbally	179	0	16	Limerick	Coshma	Adare	Croom	II.	241
4, 5	Ardshankill	358	3	12	Fermanagh	Lurg	Drumkeeran	Lowtherstown	III.	205
91	Ardsheelhane East	410	2	16	Kerry	Dunkerron South	Kilcrohane	Kenmare	II.	183
91, 100	Ardsheelhane West	276	1	25	Kerry	Dunkerron South	Kilcrohane	Kenmare	II.	183
57, 58	Ardskea Beg	716	3	17	Galway	Clare	Kilmoylan	Tuam	IV.	22
44	Ardskeagh	263	2	20	Clare	Tulla Lower	Kilseily	Limerick	II.	36
3, 8	Ardskeagh	210	1	38	Cork, E.R.	Fermoy	Ardskeagh	Mallow	II.	76
24	Ardskeagh	382	0	29	Cork, E.R.	Orrery and Kilmore	Buttevant	Mallow	II.	107
57	Ardskea More	430	1	20	Galway	Clare	Kilmoylan	Tuam	IV.	22
45	Ards Little	206	3	28	Donegal	Kilmacrenan	Conwal	Milford	III.	125
24	Ards More	160	0	6	Donegal	Kilmacrenan	Tullaghobegly	Dunfanaghy	III.	131
106	Ards More (East)	87	0	38	Cork, W.R.	Bantry	Kilmocomoge	Bantry	II.	119
33	Ardsmore Mountain	425	1	20b	Donegal	Kilmacrenan	Tullaghobegly	Dunfanaghy	III.	131
106	Ards More (West)	77	0	24	Cork, W.R.	Bantry	Kilmocomoge	Bantry	II.	119
42	Ardsollus	123	1	1	Clare	Bunratty Upper	Doora	Ennis	II.	8
47	Ardsreen	419	1	1	Sligo	Coolavin	Killaraght	Boyle	IV.	224
16, 17	Ardstraw	353	3	26c	Tyrone	Strabane Lower	Ardstraw	Strabane	III.	318
17	ARDSTRAW T.	—			Tyrone	Strabane Lower	Ardstraw	Strabane	III.	319
36, 37	Ardtanagh	477	2	4	Down	Kinelarty	Loughinisland	Downpatrick	III.	177
28	Ardtanagh	627	2	35	Down	Lower Iveagh, Lr. pt.	Dromara	Banbridge	III.	167
67	Ardteegalvaa	489	1	30	Kerry	Magunihy	Killaha	Killarney	II.	202
7	Ardternon	145	1	5d	Sligo	Carbury	Drumcliff	Sligo	IV.	220
45	Ardtole	431	3	29	Down	Lecale Lower	Ardglass	Downpatrick	III.	178
20	Ardtomin	94	2	13	Limerick	Connello Lower	Nantinan	Rathkeale	II.	228
27	Ardtonnagh	155	0	3e	Fermanagh	Clanawley	Cleenish	Enniskillen	III.	189
4	Ardtrasna	410	2	27	Sligo	Carbury	Drumcliff	Sligo	IV.	220
84, 85, 93, 94	Ardtully	505	1	9	Kerry	Glanarought	Kilgarvan	Kenmare	II.	187
8	Ardtully Beg	54	2	21	Louth	Lower Dundalk	Carlingford	Dundalk	I.	176
8, 9	Ardtully More	99	2	3	Louth	Lower Dundalk	Carlingford	Dundalk	I.	176
10	Arduc	212	1	8f	Cavan	Lower Loughtee	Drumlane	Cavan	III.	79
107	Ardultagh	182	1	31	Galway	Longford	Kilquain	Portumna	IV.	60
75	Ardun	250	0	9	Donegal	Boylagh	Inishkeel	Glenties	III.	112
33, 42	Arduns	2,901	2	5g	Donegal	Kilmacrenan	Tullaghobegly	Dunfanaghy	III.	131
25	Ardunsaghan	433	0	15h	Leitrim	Carrigallen	Drumreilly	Bawnboy	IV.	90
23, 28	Ardunshin	214	2	36	Fermanagh	Magherastephana	Aghavea	Lisnaskea	III.	218
58, 59	Ardunshin	163	3	14i	Tyrone	Clogher	Clogher	Clogher	III.	291
140	Ardura Beg	233	0	36	Cork W.R.	West Carbery (W.D.)	Kilcoe	Skull	II.	143
140	Ardura More	311	3	8	Cork W.R.	West Carbery (W.D.)	Kilcoe	Skull	II.	143
147	Arduslough	55	1	0	Cork W.R.	West Carbery (W.D.)	Kilmoe	Skull	II.	144
6	Ardvagh	307	3	3	Cavan	Tullyhaw	Templeport	Enniskillen	III.	93
83	Ardvally	160	2	18	Donegal	Banagh	Killybegs Lower	Glenties	III.	110
22	Ardvally	242	1	20	Sligo	Tireragh	Castleconor	Ballina	IV.	232
54	Ardvarna	18	3	20	Galway	Moycullen	Kilcummin	Oughterard	IV.	66
6	Ardvarna	172	1	16	Limerick	Clanwilliam	Killeenagarriff	Limerick	II.	224
7, 11	Ardvarness	366	3	16	Londonderry	Coleraine	Macosquin	Coleraine	III.	232
12	Ardvarney	823	1	24j	Leitrim	Drumahaire	Cloonclare	Manorhamilton	IV.	93
15	Ardvarney	169	2	14	Leitrim	Drumahaire	Killanummery	Manorhamilton	IV.	97
69	Ardvarney	377	1	9	Mayo	Carra	Aglish	Castlebar	IV.	123
121	Ardvarney	42	0	11	Mayo	Kilmaine	Kilmainebeg	Ballinrobe	IV.	155
21, 29	Ardvarney	147	3	17	Mayo	Tirawley	Maygawnagh	Killala	IV.	171
22	Ardvarney	21	2	19	Queen's Co.	Clandonagh	Aghaboe	Donaghmore	I.	232
34	Ardvarney	146	0	14k	Sligo	Tirerrill	Kilmacallan	Sligo	IV.	239
38, 39	Ardvarnish	132	3	27	Tyrone	Dungannon Upper	Derryloran	Cookstown	III.	306
61, 62, 69, 70	Ardvarnock Glebe	266	1	2	Donegal	Raphoe	Raphoe	Strabane	III.	140
25	Ardvarny	146	0	18	Cavan	Clanmahon	Denn	Cavan	III.	76
6	Ardvarny East	110	1	35	Fermanagh	Lurg	Magheraculmoney	Lowtherstown	III.	207
5, 6	Ardvarny West	143	2	19	Fermanagh	Lurg	Magheraculmoney	Lowtherstown	III.	207
28	Ardvone	56	1	19	Limerick	Shanid	Ardagh	Newcastle	II.	254
76	Ard West	405	0	7l	Galway	Ballynahinch	Moyrus	Clifden	IV.	12
17	Ardydonagan	490	0	8	Kerry	Clanmaurice	Duagh	Listowel	II.	168
30	Ardyduffy	87	3	20	Westmeath	Clonlonan	Ballyloughloe	Athlone	I.	260
118	Ardyhoolihane	85	0	29	Cork, W.R.	Bantry	Kilmocomoge	Bantry	II.	119

(a) Including 31A. 1R. 27P. water.
(b) Including 14A. 2R. 28P. water.
(c) Including 6A. 1R. 28P. water.
(d) Including 10A. 0R. 2P. water.

(e) Including 35A. 2R. 16P. water.
(f) Including 56A. 3R. 4P. water.
(g) Including 31A. 0R. 2P. water.
(h) Including 6A. 2R. 36P. water.

(i) Including 1A. 3R. 24P. water.
(j) Including 1A. 0R. 28P. water.
(k) Including 1A. 0R. 36P. water.
(l) Including 23A. 1R. 28P. water.

No. of Sheet of the Ordnance Survey Maps.	Townlands and Towns.	Area in Statute Acres.	County.	Barony.	Parish.	Poor Law Union in 1857.	Townland Census of 1851, Part I.	
		A. R. P.					Vol.	Page
32, 40	Ardykeohane . .	139 2 14	Limerick . .	Coshma . .	Bruff . .	Kilmallock .	II.	242
47	Ardyoul . .	67 1 25	Limerick . .	Kilmallock . .	St. Peter's & St. Paul's	Kilmallock .	II.	250
47, 57	Ardywanig . .	484 1 31	Kerry . .	Magunihy . .	Kilnanare . .	Killarney . .	II.	204
18	Argos . .	18 1 1	Dublin . .	Uppercross . .	St. Catherine's .	Dublin South .	I.	40
38	Arignagh . .	45 0 8	Roscommon .	Ballymoe . .	Oran . . .	Roscommon .	IV.	192
50	Arkeen Beg . .	302 1 33a	Galway . .	Ballynahinch . .	Moyrus . .	Clifden . .	IV.	12
36, 50	Arkeen More . .	518 3 12b	Galway . .	Ballynahinch . .	Moyrus . .	Clifden . .	IV.	12
40	Arklow . .	128 0 31	Wexford . .	Shelburne . .	Clonmines . .	New Ross . .	I.	327
40	Arklow . .	45 0 24	Wicklow . .	Arklow . .	Arklow . .	Rathdrum .	I.	341
40, 45	ARKLOW T. . .	—	Wicklow . .	Arklow . .	Arklow . .	Rathdrum .	I.	341
40	Arlands . .	184 3 31c	Donegal . .	Boylagh . .	Templecrone . .	Glenties . .	III.	114
32	ARLESS T. . .	—	Queen's Co. .	Slievemargy . .	Killaban . .	Carlow . .	I.	245
97, 98	Arlinstown . .	418 2 10	Cork, E.R. . .	Kinalea . .	Ballymartle . .	Kinsale . .	II.	94
28	Arlish . .	31 2 25	Fermanagh . .	Magherastephana .	Aghavea . .	Lisnaskea .	III.	218
37	Arlonstown . .	199 3 0	Meath . .	Skreen . .	Killeen . .	Dunshaughlin .	I.	221
26	Arm . .	823 1 39	Roscommon .	Castlereagh . .	Kilkeevin . .	Castlereagh .	IV.	200
20, 24	Armaghbrague . .	2,895 3 23	Armagh . .	Fews Upper . .	Lisnadill . .	Armagh . .	III.	49
12	ARMAGH T. . .	—	Armagh . .	Armagh . .	Armagh . .	Armagh . .	III.	43
53, 60	Armalughey . .	253 2 36	Tyrone . .	Dungannon Lower .	Carnteel . .	Clogher . .	III.	297
13	ARMOY T. . .	—	Antrim . .	Cary . .	Armoy . .	Ballycastle .	III.	11
46, 47	Armyhill . .	80 2 10	King's Co. . .	Clonlisk . .	Castletownely . .	Roscrea . .	I.	129
30, 36	Arnaghan . .	193 1 8	Cavan . .	Tullyhunco . .	Scrabby . .	Granard . .	III.	99
21	Arnasbrack . .	507 2 4d	Sligo . .	Tirerrill . .	Kilross . .	Sligo . .	IV.	241
29, 34	Arnestown . .	614 2 10	Wexford . .	Bantry . .	St. Mary's . .	New Ross .	I.	302
40, 41	Arnestown . .	294 2 32	Wexford . .	Shelmaliere West .	Ballingly . .	Wexford . .	I.	332
35	Arnots Grove . .	83 0 18e	Fermanagh . .	Clankelly . .	Clones . .	Clones . .	III.	195
28	Aroddy . .	235 3 37f	Leitrim . .	Leitrim . .	Fenagh . .	Mohill . .	IV.	100
43	Arodstown . .	1,038 2 25	Meath . .	Upper Deece . .	Kilmore . .	Dunshaughlin .	I.	193
42	Arpinstown . .	8 0 34	Wexford . .	Bargy . .	Kilmannan . .	Wexford . .	I.	306
15, 21	Arraghan . .	344 2 5	Roscommon .	Castlereagh . .	Kilcorkey . .	Castlereagh .	IV.	199
8	Arragh Beg . .	352 2 8	Tipperary, N.R. .	Lower Ormond .	Loughkeen . .	Borrisokane .	II.	286
5, 8	Arragh More . .	414 3 5	Tipperary, N.R. .	Lower Ormond .	Loughkeen . .	Parsonstown .	II.	286
25	Arraglen . .	1,086 1 24	Kerry . .	Corkaguiny . .	Cloghane . .	Dingle . .	II.	174
35, 36	Arraglen . .	877 3 20	Kerry . .	Corkaguiny . .	Killiney . .	Dingle . .	II.	177
12	Arragorteen . .	216 1 34	Wexford . .	Ballaghkeen . .	Killenagh . .	Gorey . .	I.	295
44	Arranagh . .	235 0 26	Limerick . .	Glenquin . .	Monagay . .	Newcastle . .	II.	247
6, 12	Arrigal . .	110 0 29	Meath . .	Morgallion . .	Nobber . .	Kells . .	I.	210
4	Arroo . .	371 2 30	Leitrim . .	Rosclogher . .	Rossinver . .	Ballyshannon .	IV.	110
33	Arrybreaga . .	167 2 39	Limerick . .	Coonagh . .	Oola . .	Tipperary . .	II.	235
8, 9	Arryheernabin . .	434 1 20g	Donegal . .	Kilmacrenan . .	Clondavaddog . .	Millford . .	III.	124
9	ARRYHEERNABIN T. .	—	Donegal . .	Kilmacrenan . .	Clondavaddog . .	Millford . .	III.	125
9	Artabrackagh . .	547 1 15	Armagh . .	Oneilland West .	Drumcree . .	Lurgan . .	III.	51
14, 15	Artaine (Domville) .	155 1 2	Dublin . .	Coolock . .	Artaine . .	Dublin North .	I.	26
15	Artaine East . .	29 2 7	Dublin . .	Coolock . .	Artaine . .	Dublin North .	I.	26
14, 15	Artaine North . .	164 3 36	Dublin . .	Coolock . .	Artaine . .	Dublin North .	I.	26
14,15,18,19	Artaine South . .	281 1 6	Dublin . .	Coolock . .	Artaine . .	Dublin North .	I.	26
14	Artaine West . .	124 3 3	Dublin . .	Coolock . .	Artaine . .	Dublin North .	I.	26
14, 15	ARTAINE T. . .	—	Dublin . .	Coolock . .	Killester . .	Dublin North .	I.	28
7, 8	Artasooly . .	198 0 14	Armagh . .	Tiranny . .	Eglish . .	Armagh . .	III.	59
64	Artclea . .	334 3 11	Tyrone . .	Clogher . .	Aghalurcher . .	Clogher . .	III.	291
20	Arthurstown . .	167 3 0	Kildare . .	South Salt . .	Kill . .	Naas . .	I.	77
11, 14	Arthurstown . .	502 2 34	Louth . .	Ardee . .	Tallanstown . .	Ardee . .	I.	175
14	Arthurstown Little .	73 2 36	Louth . .	Ardee . .	Tallanstown . .	Ardee . .	I.	175
44	ARTHURSTOWN T. .	—	Wexford . .	Shelburne . .	St. James and Dunbrody .	New Ross . .	I.	328
32	Artibrannan . .	112 2 11	Antrim . .	Lower Toome . .	Ahoghill . .	Ballymena . .	III.	31
2, 3, 6, 7	Articlave Lower .	196 3 3	Londonderry .	Coleraine . .	Dunboe . .	Coleraine . .	III.	231
6, 7	ARTICLAVE T. .	—	Londonderry .	Coleraine . .	Dunboe . .	Coleraine . .	III.	232
6	Articlave Upper .	177 0 37	Londonderry .	Coleraine . .	Dunboe . .	Coleraine . .	III.	231
3, 4, 7, 8	Articrunaght North	224 2 12	Londonderry .	N. E. Liberties of Coleraine . .	Ballyrashane . .	Coleraine . .	III.	245
4, 7, 8	Articrunaght South	159 2 4	Londonderry .	N. E. Liberties of Coleraine . .	Ballyrashane . .	Coleraine . .	III.	245
2, 6	Artidillon . .	106 2 5	Londonderry .	Coleraine . .	Dunboe . .	Coleraine . .	III.	231
14	Artidowney . .	49 2 17h	Cavan . .	Lower Loughtee .	Drumlane . .	Cavan . .	III.	79
17, 18, 22	Artiferrall . .	760 0 1	Antrim . .	Upper Dunluce .	Kilraghts . .	Ballymoney .	III.	19
21	Artiforty or Shanaghy Lower .	62 3 28	Antrim . .	Kilconway . .	Finvoy . .	Ballymoney .	III.	26
5	Artigarvan . .	175 0 27	Tyrone . .	Strabane Lower .	Leckpatrick . .	Strabane . .	III.	321
16	Artigoran . .	229 3 27	Antrim . .	Upper Dunluce .	Ballymoney . .	Ballymoney .	III.	18
9, 10	Artikelly . .	252 3 34	Londonderry .	Keenaght . .	Aghanloo . .	NewᵀⁿLimavady	III.	233
61, 69	Artikellys . .	144 0 25	Donegal . .	Raphoe . .	Convoy . .	Stranorlar .	III.	136
21	Artiloman . .	160 3 10	Antrim . .	Kilconway . .	Finvoy . .	Ballymoney .	III.	26
3	Artimacormick . .	143 1 34	Antrim . .	Cary . .	Ballintoy . .	Ballycastle .	III.	11

(a) Including 28A. 1R. 4P. water.
(b) Including 71A. 0R. 34P. water.
(c) Including 9A. 2R. 7P. water.

(d) Including 13A. 0R. 13P. water.
(e) Including 2A. 0R. 32P. water.
(f) Including 95A. 2R. 15P. water.

(g) Including 6A. 0R. 20P. water.
(h) Including 10A. 3R. 20P. water.

No of Sheet of the Ordnance Survey Maps.	Townlands and Towns.	Area in Statute Acres.	County.	Barony.	Parish.	Poor Law Union in 1857.	Townland Census of 1851, Part I.	
		A. R. P.					Vol.	Page
40	Artinagh	34 0 1	Fermanagh	Clankelly	Galloon	Clones	III.	198
124	Artiteige	337 3 20	Cork, W.R.	East Carbery (E.D.)	Templetrine	Kinsale	II.	130
42, 43, 48, 49	Artlone	133 0 32	Antrim	Upper Toome	Duneane	Antrim	III.	34
27	Artnacrea	200 0 28	Antrim	Kilconway	Dunaghy	Ballymena	III.	25
21, 22	Artnagross	184 3 32	Antrim	Kilconway	Finvoy	Ballymoney	III.	26
44	Artnagullian	692 2 14	Antrim	Antrim Lower	Connor	Antrim	III.	3
14	Artnalevery	278 3 35	Louth	Ardee	Charlestown	Ardee	I.	171
14	Artonagh	103 3 17	Cavan	Lower Loughtee	Drumlane	Cavan	III.	79
21, 22	Artonagh	409 1 38	Cavan	Tullygarvey	Larah	Cootehill	III.	90
11	Artoney	147 1 15	Louth	Louth	Louth	Dundalk	I.	184
37	Artramon	543 2 18	Wexford	Shelmaliere East	Artramon	Wexford	I.	330
43, 49	Artresnahan	267 1 17	Antrim	Upper Toome	Drummaul	Antrim	III.	33
135	Arundelmills	8 1 25	Cork, W.R.	Ibane and Barryroe	Templeomalus	Clonakilty	II.	150
135	ARUNDELMILLS T.	—	Cork, W.R.	Ibane and Barryroe {	Desert / Templeomalus }	Clonakilty	II. {	148 / 151
24, 30	ARVAGH T.	—	Cavan	Tullyhunco	Killashandra	Cavan	III.	99
35	Arvalee	827 3 0	Tyrone	Omagh East	Cappagh	Omagh	III.	310
22	Arywee	144 1 7	Limerick	Clanwilliam	Fedamore	Limerick	II.	223
6	Ash Big	144 2 58	Louth	Louth	Louth	Dundalk	I.	184
45	ASHBOURNE T.	—	Meath	Ratoath	Killegland	Dunshaughlin	I.	218
86	Ashbrook	469 2 36	Galway	Kilconnell	Killaan	Ballinasloe	IV.	41
70, 71	Ashbrook	142 3 28	Mayo	Gallen	Templemore	Castlebar	IV.	151
2	Ashbrook or Aghamore	22 0 27	Queen's Co.	Tinnahinch	Kilmanman	Mountmellick	I.	248
29	Ashbrook or Knocknabarnaboy	246 2 6	Roscommon	Roscommon	Lissonuffy	Strokestown	IV.	211
12	Ashbury	467 3 8	Tipperary, N.R.	Ikerrin	Roscrea	Roscrea	II.	276
21	Ashfield	32 3 33	Dublin	Uppercross	Clondalkin	Dublin South	I.	39
18, 19	Ashfield	449 1 4a	Galway	Ballymoe	Boyounagh	Glennamaddy	IV.	6
118	Ashfield	40 2 25	Galway	Longford	Tiranascragh	Portumna	IV.	62
60	Ashfield	406 1 3	Galway	Tiaquin	Ballymacward	Mountbellew	IV.	75
8	Ashfield	140 1 38	King's Co.	Ballycowan	Durrow	Tullamore	I.	127
26, 31, 32	Ashfield	1,045 1 13	Queen's Co.	Slievemargy	Killabban	Carlow	I.	245
128	Ashfield Demesne	463 2 29b	Galway	Kiltartan	Beagh	Gort	IV.	46
47	Ashfield or Screeboge	270 0 37	Meath	Upper Moyfenrath	Clonard	Edenderry	I.	213
53	Ashford	414 3 34c	Roscommon	Moycarn	Creagh	Ballinasloe	IV.	206
25	Ashford	71 3 11	Wicklow	Newcastle	Rathnew	Rathdrum	I.	354
27	Ashford or Cappacorcoge	178 3 0d	Galway	Ross	Cong	Oughterard	IV.	72
13	Ashfort	315 0 22	Limerick	Pubblebrien	Crecora	Limerick	II.	252
28	Ashglen or Glennafunshoge	68 0 19	Kilkenny	Gowran	Woolengrange	Thomastown	I.	100
15	Ashgrove	264 2 18e	Cavan	Lower Loughtee	Drumlane	Cavan	III.	79
76, 88	Ashgrove	177 2 13	Cork, E.R.	Barrymore	Templerobin	Cork	II.	58
33	Ashgrove	102 1 4	Cork, E.R.	Fermoy	Mallow	Mallow	II.	81
135	Ashgrove	174 1 30	Cork, W.R.	Ibane and Barryroe	Desert	Clonakilty	II.	148
30	Ashgrove	75 3 24	Kildare	West Offaly	Ballybrackan	Athy	I.	71
28, 36	Ashgrove	455 1 29	Limerick	Glenquin	Newcastle	Newcastle	II.	247
74	Ashgrove	306 3 12	Tipperary, S.R.	Clanwilliam	Templeneiry	Tipperary	II.	311
29	Ashgrove or Macnahanny	389 2 37	King's Co.	Garrycastle	Lusmagh	Parsonstown	I.	137
38, 39	Ash-hill	345 3 0	Kerry	Trughanacmy	Ballymacelligott	Tralee	II.	206
47	Ash Hill	257 1 18f	Limerick	Kilmallock	St. Peter's & St. Paul's	Kilmallock	II.	250
47, 53	Ash Hill	304 2 7	Tipperary, N.R.	Eliogarty	Moycarky	Thurles	II.	271
101	Ash Island	2 1 0	Donegal	Tirhugh	Templecarn	Donegal	III.	149
105	Ash Island	0 0 2	Galway	Loughrea	Killeenadeema	Loughrea	IV.	64
21	Ash Island	8 2 21	King's Co.	Garrycastle	Tisaran	Parsonstown	I.	138
3	Ash Island	0 0 7	Longford	Granard	Killoe	Granard	I.	157
3	Ash Islands	0 1 36	Roscommon	Boyle	Kilbryan	Boyle	IV.	195
25, 31	Ashlamaduff	699 2 34	Londonderry	Keenaght	Dungiven	New To Limavady	III.	236
15	Ashleypark	13 2 14	Tipperary, N.R.	Lower Ormond	Ardcrony	Nenagh	II.	281
14, 15	Ashleypark	403 3 24g	Tipperary, N.R.	Lower Ormond	Cloghprior	Nenagh	II.	282
14, 15	Ashleypark	82 1 6	Tipperary, N.R.	Lower Ormond	Knigh	Nenagh	II.	285
6	Ash Little	191 0 18	Louth	Louth	Louth	Dundalk	I.	184
33, 39	Ashpark	340 2 7	Meath	Upper Duleek	Piercetown	Dunshaughlin	I.	198
34	Ashpark	241 2 25	Roscommon	Ballymoe	Drumatemple	Castlereagh	IV.	191
4, 5	Ashpark	248 2 32	Tipperary, N.R.	Lower Ormond	Lorrha	Borrisokane	II.	285
6, 7	Ashroe	802 2 0	Limerick	Owneybeg	Abington	Limerick	II.	250
14, 18	Ashtown	270 3 12	Dublin	Castleknock	Castleknock	Dublin North	I.	23
35, 39	Ashtown	766 2 9	Kilkenny	Knocktopher	Fiddown	Carrick on Suir	II.	111
14, 15	Ashtown	1,066 3 9	Waterford	Decies without Drum	Fews	Kilmacthomas	II.	356
25	Ashtown	17 1 6	Wicklow	Arklow	Drumkay	Rathdrum	I.	342
25	Ashtown	128 1 26	Wicklow	Newcastle	Rathnew	Rathdrum	I.	354
12, 18	Ashtown or Ballinafunshoge	855 1 39	Wicklow	Ballinacor North	Derrylossary	Rathdrum	I.	346

(a) Including 1A. 0R. 15P. water.
(b) Including 23A. 1R. 21P. water.
(c) Including 20A. 3R. 4P. water.

(d) Including 11A. 1R. 23P. water.
(e) Including 35A. 1R. 29P. water.

(f) Including 25A. 3R. 6P. water.
(g) Including 31A. 1R. 28P. water.

F

No. of Sheet of the Ordnance Survey Maps.	Townlands and Towns.	Area in Statute Acres.			County.	Barony.	Parish.	Poor Law Union in 1857.	Townland Census of 1851, Part I.	
		A.	R.	P.					Vol.	Page
61	Ashwell's-lot .	93	3	21	Tipperary, S.R.	Middlethird	St. John Baptist	Cashel	II.	330
3	Ashwood Lower	183	1	10	Wexford	Gorey	Kilgorman	Gorey	I.	318
26	Ashwoods	87	2	33	Fermanagh	Magheraboy	Rossorry	Enniskillen	III.	214
21,22,26,27	Ashwoods or Woody Mullaghree .	168	1	9	Fermanagh	Magheraboy	Rossorry	Enniskillen	III.	214
3	Ashwood Upper	167	0	6	Wexford	Gorey	Kilgorman	Gorey	I.	318
7	Ask	398	3	33	Wexford	Gorey	Kilcavan .	Gorey	I.	317
27	Askabeg .	151	0	34	Wexford	Ballaghkeen	Castle-Ellis	Enniscorthy	I.	293
5, 10	Aska Beg	358	0	14	Wexford	Scarawalsh	Carnew	Gorey	I.	322
4	Askaheige	14	0	39	Wexford	Scarawalsh	Moyacomb	Shillelagh	I.	325
33,34,38,39	Askakeagh	832	2	25	Wicklow	Ballinacor South	Preban	Shillelagh	I.	350
2	Askakeel	82	3	20	Wexford	Gorey	Kilnahue	Gorey	I.	318
5, 10	Aska More	807	1	35	Wexford	Scarawalsh	Carnew	Gorey	I.	322
33, 34	Askanagap	490	2	15	Wicklow	Ballinacor South	Moyne	Shillelagh	I.	350
27	Askasilla	299	3	23	Wexford	Ballaghkeen	Castle-Ellis	Enniscorthy	I.	293
26	Aske .	52	2	17	Dublin	Rathdown	Oldconnaught .	Rathdown	I.	37
11, 20	Askeaton	640	1	30	Limerick	Connello Lower	Askeaton	Rathkeale	II.	226
11	ASKEATON T. .	—			Limerick	Connello Lower	Askeaton	Rathkeale	II.	227
39	Askill	77	3	32a	Fermanagh	Coole	Galloon	Clones	III.	199
2	Askill .	496	0	10	Leitrim	Rosclogher	Rossinver	Ballyshannon	IV.	110
49	Askillaun	200	0	4	Mayo	Gallen	Killasser .	Swineford	IV.	149
85,86,95,96	Askillaun	874	3	3	Mayo	Murrisk	Kilgeever	Westport .	IV.	159
10, 15	Askinamoe	320	1	8	Wexford	Scarawalsh	Ferns	Enniscorthy	I.	323
3	Askinch Lower	161	2	16	Wexford	Gorey	Inch	Gorey	I.	316
3	Askinch Upper	240	3	3	Wexford	Gorey	Inch	Gorey	I.	316
25	Askinfarney .	121	0	20	Wexford	Bantry	Rossdroit .	Enniscorthy	I.	301
24	Askinfarney .	199	0	21	Wexford	Bantry	Templeludigan	New Ross .	I.	303
17	Askingarran Lower	122	2	30	Wexford	Ballaghkeen	Donaghmore .	Gorey	I.	293
17	Askingarran Upper	192	1	8	Wexford	Ballaghkeen	Donaghmore .	Gorey	I.	293
45	Askintinny .	204	1	35	Wicklow	Arklow	Arklow .	Rathdrum	I.	341
13, 18	Askinvillar Lower	309	3	7	Wexford	Bantry	Killann .	Enniscorthy	I.	300
13, 18	Askinvillar Upper .	632	1	4	Wexford	Bantry	Killann .	Enniscorthy	I.	300
19	Askunshin	250	3	20	Wexford	Scarawalsh	Monart	Enniscorthy	I.	324
15	Asnagh .	449	2	15	Longford	Granard .	Granard .	Granard .	I.	156
35, 36	Assagart .	588	1	36	Wexford	Shelmaliere West	Kilgarvan	New Ross .	I.	334
47, 48	Assaly Great .	110	2	30	Wexford	Forth	Killinick .	Wexford .	I.	310
47	Assaly Little .	99	1	25	Wexford	Forth	Killinick .	Wexford .	I.	310
33	Assan .	138	1	32	Cavan	Castlerahan	Killinkere	Bailieborough .	III.	68
10, 16	Assaun .	127	1	21	Roscommon	Frenchpark	Creeve .	Car⁰. on Shannon	IV.	203
61	Asscarrick	0	0	33	Clare	Bunratty Lower	Clonloghan .	Ennis	II.	3
31	Assey .	429	3	36b	Meath	Lower Deece .	Assey .	Navan	I.	191
23	Assolas .	303	2	20	Cork, E.R.	Duhallow	Castlemagner .	Kanturk .	II.	67
17	Astagob .	93	0	27c	Dublin	Castleknock	Castleknock	Dublin, North .	I.	23
17	Astagob .	162	1	19d	Dublin	Castleknock	Clonsilla .	Celbridge .	I.	24
2	Astee East	607	1	33	Kerry	Iraghticonnor .	Aghavallen	Listowel .	II.	189
2	Astee West	697	2	13	Kerry	Iraghticonnor .	Aghavallen	Listowel .	II.	189
3	Astrish Beg .	37	2	5	Monaghan	Trough	Errigal Trough	Monaghan	III.	283
3	Astrish More .	77	0	20	Monaghan	Trough	Errigal Trough	Monaghan	III.	283
43	Atateemore or Black- neys	173	3	27	Kilkenny .	Ida .	Kilcolumb	Waterford	I.	102
22	Athabryanmore	642	3	24e	Tyrone	Omagh West .	Termonamongan	Castlederg	III.	317
60, 68	Athasselabbey North	416	1	10	Tipperary, S.R.	Clanwilliam	Relickmurry and Athassel	Tipperary	II.	309
60, 68	Athasselabbey South	399	1	28	Tipperary, S.R.	Clanwilliam	Relickmurry and Athassel	Tipperary	II.	309
29	ATHBOY T. .	—			Meath	Lune	Athboy .	Trim .	I.	207
33	Athcarne .	321	0	24	Meath	Upper Duleek .	Duleek .	Drogheda .	I.	197
18	Athclare .	271	2	13	Louth	Ferrard .	Dunleer .	Ardee .	I.	180
6	Athdown .	1,089	1	21	Wicklow	Lower Talbotstown .	Kilbride .	Naas .	I.	361
26, 34	Athea Lower .	552	0	7	Limerick .	Shanid	Rathronan	Newcastle	II.	257
34	ATHEA T. .	—			Limerick .	Shanid	Rathronan	Newcastle	II.	257
34	Athea Upper .	1,986	0	39	Limerick .	Shanid	Rathronan	Newcastle	II.	257
2	Athenboy .	69	2	36	Westmeath	Moygoish	Street .	Granard .	I.	281
84	Athenry .	65	2	11	Galway	Athenry .	Athenry .	Loughrea .	IV.	3
36	Athenry .	287	1	19f	Tyrone	Omagh East .	Termonmaguirk	Omagh .	III.	314
84	ATHENRY T. .	—			Galway	Athenry .	Athenry .	Loughrea .	IV.	4
17, 24	Athgaine Great	322	1	36	Meath	Lower Navan .	Balrathboyne .	Kells .	I.	214
17, 24	Athgaine Little	223	0	11	Meath	Upper Kells .	Balrathboyne .	Kells .	I.	204
24, 25	Athgarrett .	742	1	20	Kildare .	North Naas .	Rathmore .	Naas .	I.	62
9	Athgarvan .	53	0	29	Wicklow	Lower Talbotstown .	Hollywood .	Baltinglass .	I.	360
23, 28	Athgarvan and Black- rath	617	3	32g	Kildare .	Connell .	Greatconnell .	Naas .	I.	55
20, 21	Athgoe .	204	0	12	Dublin	Newcastle	Newcastle	Celbridge .	I.	34
20	Athgoe North .	246	3	30	Dublin	Newcastle	Newcastle	Celbridge .	I.	34

(a) Including 7A. 2R. 16P. water.
(b) Including 5A. 1R. 12P. water.
(c) Including 7A. 0R. 26P. water.

(d) Including 3A. 0R. 5P. water.
(e) Including 3A. 0R. 26P. water.

(f) Including 3A. 2R. 30P. water.
(g) Including 6A. 2R. 5P. water.

No. of Sheet of the Ordnance Survey Maps.	Townlands and Towns.	Area in Statute Acres. A. R. P.	County.	Barony.	Parish.	Poor Law Union in 1857.	Townland Census of 1851, Part I. Vol.	Page
20	Athgoe South	155 3 6	Dublin	Newcastle	Newcastle	Celbridge	I.	34
15	Athgreany	234 1 31	Wicklow	Lower Talbotstown	Hollywood	Baltinglass	I.	360
39	Athlacca North	492 2 16	Limerick	Coshna	Athlacca	Kilmallock	II.	241
39	Athlacca South	314 0 11	Limerick	Coshna	Athlacca	Kilmallock	II.	241
41	Athleague	325 1 15*a*	Roscommon	Athlone	Athleague	Roscommon	IV.	179
41	ATHLEAGUE T.	—	Roscommon	Athlone	Athleague	Roscommon	IV.	179
29	Athlone	378 1 3	Westmeath	Brawny	St. Mary's	Athlone	I.	259
52	Athlone & Bigmeadow	111 2 3	Roscommon	Athlone	St. Peter's	Athlone	IV.	184
52 ⎱ 29 ⎰	ATHLONE T.	—	⎰ Roscommon ⎱ Westmeath	Athlone	⎰ St. Peter's ⎱ St. Mary's	⎰ Athlone ⎱	⎰ IV. ⎱ I.	184 260
42	Athlummon	252 1 35	Tipperary, N.R.	Eliogarty	Rahelty	Thurles	II.	272
25	Athlumney	592 0 35*b*	Meath	Skreen	Athlumney	Navan	I.	220
63	Athlunkard	196 3 4	Clare	Bunratty Lower	St. Patrick's	Limerick	II.	6
35, 41	Athnid Beg	216 2 10	Tipperary, N.R.	Eliogarty	Athnid	Thurles	II.	269
35, 41	Athnid More	638 0 12	Tipperary, N.R.	Eliogarty	Athnid	Thurles	II.	269
16	Athroe	111 3 30	Roscommon	Roscommon	Shankill	Boyle	IV.	212
37	Athronan	75 3 30	Meath	Lower Deece	Kilmessan	Dunshaughlin	I.	192
37	Athronan	404 3 31	Meath	Skreen	Killeen	Dunshaughlin	I.	221
37, 51	Athry	1,613 3 29*c*	Galway	Ballynahinch	Moyrus	Clifden	IV.	12
35	Athy	52 2 8*d*	Kildare	Narragh & Reban W.	St. Johns	Athy	I.	68
35	Athy	162 1 15*e*	Kildare	Narragh & Reban W.	St. Michaels	Athy	I.	68
35	ATHY T.	—	Kildare	Narragh & Reban W. ⎰	⎱ Churchtown St. Johns St. Michaels ⎰	Athy	I.	⎰ 67 & 68 ⎰
29	Atnamollyboy	348 3 0	Fermanagh	Magherastephana	Aghalurcher	Lisnaskea	III.	215
40	Atshanboe (*Cahill*)	152 3 10	Tipperary, N.R.	Kilnamanagh Upper	Templebeg	Thurles	II.	279
40	Atshanboe (*Launders*)	336 0 1	Tipperary, N.R.	Kilnamanagh Upper	Templebeg	Thurles	II.	279
19	Attagh	599 0 6*f*	Tyrone	Strabane Upper	Bodoney Lower	Gortin	III.	323
42	Attaghmore	363 1 14	Tyrone	Omagh East	Donacavey	Omagh	III.	310
33	Attatantee	1,190 2 5	Donegal	Kilmacrenan	Tullaghobegly	Dunfanaghy	III.	131
26	Attateenoe Lower	81 0 21	Kilkenny	Kells	Coolaghmore	Callan	I.	107
26	Attateenoe Upper	133 3 18	Kilkenny	Kells	Coolaghmore	Callan	I.	107
89	Attavally	118 0 37	Mayo	Carra	Ballintober	Castlebar	IV.	124
18, 26	Attavally	816 1 32	Mayo	Erris	Kilcommon	Belmullet	IV.	143
80	Attavally	107 3 36	Mayo	Gallen	Killedan	Swineford	IV.	149
48	Atteagh	211 1 18	Roscommon	Athlone	Kiltoom	Athlone	IV.	182
16	Attiaghygrana	178 3 6	Roscommon	Frenchpark	Creeve	Cark. on Shannon	IV.	203
64	Attiantaggart	159 0 23	Mayo	Costello	Kilcolman	Castlereagh	IV.	141
60	Attiappleton	140 1 29*g*	Mayo	Carra	Turlough	Castlebar	IV.	130
22	Attiballa	55 0 9	Roscommon	Roscommon	Elphin	Strokestown	IV.	209
2	Attiblaney	59 0 19	King's Co.	Kilcoursey	Ardnurcher or Horseleap	Tullamore	I.	140
87, 99	Attibrassil	175 1 21	Galway	Clonmacnowen	Clontuskert	Ballinasloe	IV.	24
70	Atticahill	117 0 13	Mayo	Gallen	Kildacommoge	Castlebar	IV.	148
52, 55	Attical	396 0 2	Down	Mourne	Kilkeel	Kilkeel	III.	182
16, 22	Attichree	228 3 2	Sligo	Tireragh	Castleconor	Dromore West	IV.	232
22, 35	Atticlogh	392 3 30*h*	Galway	Ballynahinch	Omey	Clifden	IV.	14
14	Atticloghy	352 1 36	Mayo	Tirawley	Rathreagh	Killala	IV.	171
99	Atticoffey East	41 2 36	Galway	Clonmacnowen	Clontuskert	Ballinasloe	IV.	24
99	Atticoffey West	131 2 22*i*	Galway	Clonmacnowen	Clontuskert	Ballinasloe	IV.	24
10, 17	Atticonaun	551 2 23	Mayo	Erris	Kilcommon	Belmullet	IV.	143
38, 40	Atticonor	440 2 28	Westmeath	Moycashel	Rahugh	Tullamore	I.	279
53	Atticorra	399 3 36	Roscommon	Moycarn	Creagh	Ballinasloe	IV.	206
31	Attidavock	198 1 17*k*	Galway	Tiaquin	Kilkerrin	Glennamaddy	IV.	76
87	Attidermot	197 0 5	Galway	Kilconnell	Aughrim	Ballinasloe	IV.	39
22	Attiduff	97 0 25	Monaghan	Dartree	Ematris	Cootehill	III.	266
3	Attiduff	74 3 5	Monaghan	Trough	Errigal Trough	Monaghan	III.	283
4, 5	Attiduff	118 3 38	Sligo	Carbury	Drumcliff	Sligo	IV.	220
19, 32, 33	Attifarry	92 3 32	Galway	Killian	Athleague	Mountbellew	IV.	43
128	Attifineen	167 3 37	Galway	Kiltartan	Beagh	Gort	IV.	46
31	Attifinlay	78 0 11	Leitrim	Leitrim	Kiltoghert	Cark. on Shannon	IV.	101
5	Attiflynn	118 1 16	Galway	Ballymoe	Dunmore	Glennamaddy	IV.	7
117, 126	Attigara	116 1 29	Galway	Longford	Lickmolassy	Portumna	IV.	60
22	Attigoddaun	183 2 18*l*	Galway	Ballynahinch	Omey	Clifden	IV.	14
99	Attikee	105 2 4	Galway	Longford	Kiltormer	Ballinasloe	IV.	60
44	Attiknockan	249 2 11	Roscommon	Athlone	Tisrara	Roscommon	IV.	185
49	Attimachugh	542 2 33*m*	Mayo	Gallen	Killasser	Swineford	IV.	149
28	Attimanus	287 2 17*n*	Leitrim	Leitrim	Mohill	Mohill	IV.	104
72	Attimany	86 1 11	Galway	Tiaquin	Clonkeen	Loughrea	IV.	76
85	Attimonbeg	254 1 37	Galway	Tiaquin	Killimordaly	Loughrea	IV.	77
85	Attimonmore North	27 2 17	Galway	Tiaquin	Killimordaly	Loughrea	IV.	77
85	Attimonmore South	633 1 10	Galway	Kilconnell	Killimordaly	Loughrea	IV.	42
36	Attimurtagh	62 1 10	Westmeath	Clonlonan	Kilcleagh	Athlone	I.	261

(*a*) Including 8A. 3R. 0P. water.
(*b*) Including 22A. 2R. 29P. water.
(*c*) Including 201A. 3R. 2P. water.
(*d*) Including   6A. 0R. 12P. River Barrow.
(*e*) Including   6A. 0R. 19P. water.

(*f*) Including 6A. 0R. 17P. water.
(*g*) Including 15A. 1R. 0P. water.
(*h*) Including 8A. 0R. 28P. water.
(*i*) Including 9A. 1R. 10P. detached portion.
(*k*) Including 3A. 2R. 30P. water.

(*l*) Including 10A. 2R. 34P. water.
(*m*) Including 3A. 2R. 38P. water.
(*n*) Including 6A. 2R. 8P. water.

No. of Sheet of the Ordnance Survey Maps.	Townlands and Towns.	Area in Statute Acres.	County.	Barony.	Parish.	Poor Law Union in 1857.	Townland Census of 1851. Part I.	
		A. R. P.					Vol.	Page
51	Attinadague . .	579 0 9	Donegal . .	Kilmacrenan . .	Gartan . . .	Letterkenny .	III.	127
49, 50	Attinaskollia . .	89 0 32	Mayo . .	Gallen . .	Killasser . .	Swineford .	IV.	149
22	Attinkee . .	434 0 14	King's Co. .	Garrycastle . .	Gallen . .	Parsonstown .	I.	135
77	Attiquin . .	75 0 24	Cork, E.R. .	Imokilly . .	Ballyoughtera .	Middleton .	II.	84
77, 88	Attireesh . .	106 0 0	Mayo . .	Murrisk . .	Oughaval . .	Westport .	IV.	161
73	Attiregan . .	469 0 9	Galway . .	Kilconnell . .	Ballymacward .	Ballinasloe .	IV.	39
31	Attirory . .	245 3 39a	Leitrim . .	Leitrim . .	Kiltoghert . .	Cark.on Shannon	IV.	101
53, 54	Attirory . .	546 0 24b	Roscommon .	Moycarn . .	Creagh . .	Ballinasloe .	IV.	206
23	Attirowerty . .	498 2 7	Galway . .	Ballynahinch .	Ballynakill .	Clifden .	IV.	11
29	Attishane . .	206 1 16	Mayo . .	Tirawley . .	Crossmolina .	Ballina .	IV.	165
32	Attishane . .	233 0 21c	Roscommon .	Castlereagh .	Kiltullagh . .	Castlereagh .	IV.	201
29	Attishane (Joynt) .	148 2 5	Mayo . .	Tirawley . .	Crossmolina .	Ballina .	IV.	165
94	Attithomasrevagh .	81 0 19	Galway . .	Galway . .	Rahoon . .	Galway .	IV.	37
39	Attiville . .	68 1 29	Sligo . .	Corran . .	Kilshalvy . .	Boyle .	IV.	227
34	Attybaron . .	136 0 1	Fermanagh .	Magherastephana .	Aghalurcher . .	Lisnaskea .	III.	215
59	Attybrick . .	199 1 21	Tipperary, S.R.	Kilnamanagh Lower	Kilpatrick . .	Cashel .	II.	324
29	Attyclannabryan .	151 2 7	Fermanagh .	Magherastephana .	Aghalurcher . .	Lisnakea .	III.	215
23	Attycristora . .	290 3 4	Clare . .	Corcomroe . .	Kilmanaheen .	Ennistimon .	II.	21
12, 21	Attyflin . .	440 0 16	Limerick . .	Pubblebrien .	Killonahan .	Limerick .	II.	253
69	Attykit . .	492 0 16	Tipperary, S.R.	Middlethird . .	St. John Baptist .	Cashel .	II.	330
72, 79	Attyjames . .	169 2 22	Tipperary, S.R.	Slievardagh . .	Newtownlennan .	Carrick on Suir	II.	335
81, 82	Attyshonock . .	291 1 5d	Galway . .	Galway . .	Rahoon . .	Galway .	IV.	37
11	Attyslany North .	641 2 30e	Clare . .	Inchiquin . .	Kilkeedy . .	Corrofin .	II.	25
11	Attyslany South .	212 0 39f	Clare . .	Inchiquin . .	Kilkeedy . .	Corrofin .	II.	25
25	Attyterrila . .	186 1 3	Clare . .	Inchiquin . .	Dysert . .	Ennis .	II.	24
12, 15	Auburn . .	248 1 36	Dublin . .	Coolock . .	Kinsaley . .	Balrothery .	I.	28
22	Auburn . .	151 1 17g	Westmeath .	Kilkenny West .	Kilkenny West .	Athlone .	I.	273
81	Aubwee . .	37 2 34	Galway . .	Galway . .	Rahoon . .	Galway .	IV.	37
81	Aubwee . .	69 1 2	Galway . .	Moycullen . .	Moycullen . .	Galway .	IV.	70
56, 57, 69, 70	Aucloggeen . .	265 1 36	Galway . .	Clare . .	Annaghdown .	Galway .	IV.	16
38	Audleys Acre . .	8 0 0	Down . .	Lecale Upper .	Down . .	Downpatrick .	III.	180
31	Audleystown . .	604 2 11	Down . .	Lecale Lower .	Ballyculter .	Downpatrick .	III.	178
69, 81	Augeris . .	793 1 17	Cork, W.R. .	West Muskerry .	Inchigeelagh .	Macroom .	II.	156
34	Aughaboy . .	536 3 3	Antrim . .	Lower Glenarm .	Tickmacrevan .	Larne .	III.	23
114	Aughabrack . .	169 2 33	Cork, W.R. .	Bear . .	Kilcatherine .	Castletown .	II.	123
36	Aughacasla North .	260 3 39	Kerry . .	Corkaguiny . .	Killiney . .	Dingle .	II.	177
36	Aughacasla South .	111 0 28	Kerry . .	Corkaguiny . .	Killiney . .	Dingle .	II.	177
28	Aughadanove . .	337 2 9	Armagh . .	Orior Upper . .	Forkill . .	Newry .	III.	57
47	Aughagalla . .	208 1 15	Tyrone . .	Dungannon Middle .	Clonoe . .	Dungannon .	III.	300
57	Aughagarna . .	300 2 10	Clare . .	Moyarta . .	Kilmacduane .	Kilrush .	II.	32
69	Aughagault . .	180 3 16	Donegal . .	Raphoe . .	Convoy . .	Stranorlar .	III.	136
69	Aughagault Big .	266 2 2	Donegal . .	Raphoe . .	Convoy . .	Stranorlar .	III.	136
47	Aughagranna . .	105 0 8	Tyrone . .	Dungannon Middle .	Clonoe . .	Dungannon .	III.	300
129, 138	Aughaleigue Beg .	275 0 39	Cork, W.R. .	West Carbery (W.D.)	Kilcrohane .	Bantry .	II.	143
129, 138	Aughaleigue More .	285 1 23	Cork, W.R. .	West Carbery(W.D.)	Kilcrohane .	Bantry .	II.	143
37	Aughalin . .	565 0 32	Limerick . .	Glenquin . .	Clonelty . .	Newcastle .	II.	245
43	Aughalish . .	93 3 20	Antrim . .	Upper Toome .	Drummaul .	Antrim .	III.	33
29	Aughall Beg . .	127 0 22	Tipperary, N.R.	Ikerrin . .	Templeree .	Thurles .	II.	277
29	Aughall Middle .	142 3 22	Tipperary, N.R.	Ikerrin . .	Templeree .	Thurles .	II.	277
29	Aughall More . .	204 2 26	Tipperary, N.R.	Ikerrin . .	Templeree .	Thurles .	II.	277
47	Aughamullan . .	608 3 33	Tyrone . .	Dungannon Middle .	Clonoe . .	Dungannon .	III.	300
25, 28	Aughanduff . .	893 3 12	Armagh . .	Orior Upper . .	Forkill . .	Castleblayney .	III.	57
88	Aughane . .	78 1 33	Cork. E.R. .	Imokilly . .	Rostellan .	Middleton .	II.	90
35	Aughanna . .	88 0 32	Kerry . .	Corkaguiny . .	Stradbally .	Dingle .	II.	180
1	Aughans . .	55 0 14	Queen's Co. .	Tinnahinch . .	Castlebrack .	Mountmelick .	I.	248
7	Aughantarragh and Corr . .	743 2 3	Armagh . .	Tiranny . .	Eglish . .	Armagh .	III.	59
29	Aughareamlagh .	800 1 13	Antrim . .	Lower Glenarm .	Tickmacrevan .	Larne .	III.	23
19	Aughathlappa . .	355 1 36	Wexford . .	Scarawalsh . .	Monart . .	Enniscorthy .	I.	324
1, 2	Aughatubbrid or Chatsworth .	1,651 2 6	Kilkenny . .	Fassadinin . .	Castlecomer .	Castlecomer .	I.	88
88, 91	Aughavanlomaun .	827 0 5	Tipperary, S.R.	Iffa and Offa West .	Newcastle .	Clogheen .	II.	319
32	Aughavehir . .	503 3 9	Tipperary, N.R.	Owney and Arra .	Killoscully .	Nenagh .	II.	295
8	Aughavinna . .	71 0 27	Clare . .	Corcomroe . .	Killilagh . .	Ennistimon .	II.	19
22	Aughaward . .	105 2 23	Fermanagh .	Tirkennedy . .	Enniskillen .	Enniskillen .	III.	221
53	Aughboy . .	337 2 36	Clare . .	Tulla Lower .	Kiltenanlea .	Limerick .	II.	37
34, 39	Aughclare . .	508 1 8	Wexford . .	Shelburne . .	Ballybrazil .	New Ross .	I.	327
41	Aughermon . .	326 3 14	Wexford . .	Shelmaliere West .	Taghmon . .	Wexford .	I.	334
2, 9	Aughernagalliagh .	952 3 15	Mayo . .	Erris . .	Kilmore . .	Belmullet .	IV.	145
43, 44	Augherskea . .	656 2 8	Meath . .	Lower Deece .	Knockmark .	Dunshaughlin .	I.	192
59	Augher Tenements .	222 0 36h	Tyrone . .	Clogher . .	Clogher . .	Clogher .	III.	291
59	AUGHER T. . .	—	Tyrone . .	Clogher . .	Clogher . .	Clogher .	III.	293
27	Aughey . .	109 1 16i	Fermanagh .	Tirkennedy . .	Derryvullan .	Enniskillen .	III.	220

(a) Including islands.
(b) Including 0A. 3R. 30P. water.
(c) Including 12A. 3R. 27P. water.

(d) Including 15A. 0R. 8P. water.
(e) Including 4A. 3R. 13P. water.
(f) Including 7A. 1R. 32P. water.

(g) Including 27A. 2R. 0P. water.
(h) Including 1A. 0R. 32P. water.
(i) Including 6A. 2R. 17P. water.

No. of Sheet of the Ordnance Survey Maps.	Townlands and Towns.	Area in Statute Acres. A. R. P.	County.	Barony.	Parish.	Poor Law Union in 1857.	Townland Census of 1851. Part I. Vol.	Page
41	Aughfad . . .	435 3 8	Wexford . .	Shelmaliere West .	Coolstuff . . .	Wexford . .	I.	333
2, 6	Aughil . . .	207 3 33	Londonderry .	Keenaght . .	Magilligan . .	New Tⁿ Limavady	III.	236
46	Aughils . .	581 3 25	Kerry . .	Corkaguiny . .	Ballinvoher . .	Dingle . .	II.	173
18, 19	Aughine . . .	64 3 1	Longford . .	Moydow . .	Moydow . .	Longford . .	I.	162
60, 71	Aughinida . .	254 2 37	Cork, W.R. .	East Muskerry .	Aghabulloge . .	Macroom . .	II.	153
3	Aughinish . .	369 0 8	Clare . .	Burren . .	Oughtmama . .	Gort . .	II.	14
29	Aughinish . .	484 3 8	Clare . .	Tulla Lower . .	Ogonnelloe . .	Scarriff . .	II.	38
10	Aughinish East .	563 0 18	Limerick . .	Shanid . .	Robertstown . .	Rathkeale .	II.	257
3	AUGHINISH T. .	—	Clare . .	Burren . .	Oughtmama . .	Gort . .	II.	14
10	Aughinish West .	502 2 35	Limerick . .	Shanid . .	Robertstown . .	Rathkeale .	II.	257
40	Aughintober . .	227 0 25	Down . .	Upper Iveagh, Up.pt.	Donaghmore . .	Newry . .	III.	175
8	Aughiska Beg .	264 1 2	Clare . .	Corcomroe . .	Killilagh . .	Ennistimon .	II.	19
8	Aughiska More .	380 1 13a	Clare . .	Corcomroe . .	Killilagh . .	Ennistimon .	II.	19
68, 69	Aughkeely . .	919 3 13	Donegal . .	Raphoe . .	Convoy . .	Stranorlar .	III.	136
25	Aughkiletaun . .	462 1 1	Kilkenny . .	Gowran . .	Powerstown . .	Thomastown .	I.	97
14, 18	Aughlish . .	311 2 8	Armagh . .	Orior Lower . .	Ballymore . .	Banbridge .	III.	55
21	Aughlish . .	130 0 6	Fermanagh .	Clanawley . .	Cleenish . .	Enniskillen .	III.	189
30, 34	Aughlish . .	3,367 0 3	Londonderry .	Keenaght . .	Banagher . .	New Tⁿ Limavady	III.	234
54	Aughlish . .	142 2 13b	Tyrone . .	Dungannon Middle .	Donaghmore . .	Dungannon .	III.	301
29	Aughlish . .	252 2 26	Tyrone . .	Dungannon Upper .	Derryloran . .	Cookstown .	III.	306
3	Aughmore . .	200 0 9	Waterford . .	Upperthird . .	Rathgormuck . .	Carrick on Suir	II.	371
27	Aughmore . .	111 2 12	Wexford . .	Ballaghkeen . .	Killisk . .	Enniscorthy .	I.	296
48	Aughmore . .	39 2 25	Wexford . .	Forth . .	St. Iberius . .	Wexford . .	I.	314
59, 65	Aughnacarney .	175 1 19	Tyrone . .	Clogher . .	Clogher . .	Clogher . .	III.	291
40, 41	Aughnacaven . .	143 1 32	Down . .	Upper Iveagh, Up.pt.	Donaghmore . .	Newry . .	III.	175
31	Aughnacleagh .	325 2 34	Antrim . .	Lower Toome . .	Ahoghill . .	Ballymena .	III.	31
8	Aughnacloy . .	145 2 38	Armagh . .	Armagh . .	Grange . .	Armagh . .	III.	44
34	Aughnacloy . .	115 1 9	Down . .	Upper Iveagh, Up.pt.	Annaclone . .	Banbridge .	III.	174
8	Aughnacloy . .	172 0 26c	Monaghan .	Monaghan . .	Drumsnat . .	Monaghan .	III.	275
35	Aughnacloy . .	134 2 15	Sligo . .	Tirerrill . .	Kilmactranny .	Boyle . .	IV.	240
60	AUGHNACLOY T. .	—	Tyrone . .	Dungannon Lower .	Carnteel . .	Clogher . .	III.	298
55, 56	Aughnacrumpane .	105 3 12	Tipperary, S.R.	Slievardagh . .	Ballingarry . .	Callan . .	II.	331
38	Aughnacurraveel .	287 3 16	Waterford . .	Decies within Drum .	Clashmore . .	Youghal . .	II.	351
16, 23	Aughnadarragh .	552 3 34d	Down . .	Castlereagh Upper .	Killinchy . .	Downpatrick .	III.	165
13	Aughnadrumman .	139 2 8	Down . .	Lower Iveagh, Up. pt.	Moira . .	Lurgan . .	III.	170
13	Aughnafosker . .	126 2 6	Down . .	Lower Iveagh, Up. pt.	Moira . .	Lurgan . .	III.	170
26	Aughnagalley . .	170 3 24	Wexford . .	Ballaghkeen . .	Templeshannon .	Enniscorthy .	I.	298
41	Aughnagan . .	138 2 19	Wexford . .	Shelmaliere West .	Coolstuff . .	Wexford . .	I.	333
47, 53	Aughnagomaun .	1,297 0 35	Tipperary, S.R.	Middlethird . .	Ballysheehan . .	Cashel . .	II.	324
47, 51	Aughnagon . .	509 3 32e	Down . .	Upper Iveagh, Up. pt.	Clonallan . .	Newry . .	III.	174
20, 24	Aughnagurgan .	2,422 1 27f	Armagh . .	Armagh . .	Keady . .	Armagh . .	III.	45
28, 34	Aughnaheela . .	264 3 27	Tipperary, N.R.	Kilnamanagh Upper .	Glenkeen . .	Thurles . .	II.	278
10	Aughnaholle . .	96 3 27	Antrim . .	Cary . .	Culfeightrin . .	Ballycastle .	III.	13
55, 56	Aughnahoory . .	557 3 4	Down . .	Mourne . .	Kilkeel . .	Kilkeel . .	III.	182
31, 36	Aughnahoy . .	604 3 18	Antrim . .	Lower Toome . .	Ahoghill . .	Ballymena .	III.	31
55, 56	Aughnaloopy . .	382 3 6	Down . .	Mourne . .	Kilkeel . .	Kilkeel . .	III.	182
55	Aughnalyra . .	61 0 34	Cork, E.R. .	Barrymore . .	Clonmult . .	Middleton .	II.	53
2, 5, 6	Aughnamaulmeen .	219 3 21	Wexford . .	Gorey . .	Kilnahue . .	Gorey . .	I.	318
55, 59	Aughnamullan .	692 1 39	Antrim . .	Lower Massereene .	Killead . .	Antrim . .	III.	28
54	Aughnanure . .	244 1 11	Galway . .	Moycullen . .	Kilcummin . .	Oughterard .	IV.	66
10	Aughnasillagh .	164 2 23	Antrim . .	Cary . .	Culfeightrin . .	Ballycastle .	III.	13
28	Aughnaskeagh .	693 0 16	Down . .	Lower Iveagh, Lr. pt.	Dromara . .	Banbridge .	III.	167
41, 42	Aughnavallog . .	844 3 26	Down . .	Upper Iveagh, Lr. pt.	Drumballyroney .	Banbridge .	III.	172
25,26,34,35	Aughness . .	2,709 1 15g	Mayo . .	Erris . .	Kilcommon . .	Newport . .	IV.	143
46	Aughnish . .	682 1 33	Donegal . .	Kilmacrenan .	Aughnish . .	Millford . .	III.	122
37, 46	Aughnish Isle . .	66 2 39	Donegal . .	Kilmacrenan .	Aughnish . .	Millford . .	III.	122
11	Aughrafin . .	217 1 31	Armagh . .	Armagh . .	Eglish . .	Armagh . .	III.	44
10	Aughrim . .	247 1 33	Cavan . .	Tullyhaw . .	Tomregan . .	Bawnboy . .	III.	96
10, 11	Aughrim . .	616 1 32h	Clare . .	Inchiquin . .	Kilkeedy . .	Corrofin . .	II.	25
20, 28	Aughrim . .	543 3 38	Clare . .	Tulla Upper . .	Tomgraney . .	Scarriff . .	II.	40
6, 7	Aughrim . .	561 3 37	Cork, E.R. .	Orrery and Kilmore	Shandrum . .	Kanturk . .	II.	109
25	Aughrim . .	206 1 35	Fermanagh .	Clanawley . .	Cleenish . .	Enniskillen .	III.	189
21	Aughrim . .	134 1 37	Fermanagh .	Magheraboy . .	Devenish . .	Enniskillen .	III.	210
55	Aughrim . .	670 3 11	Down . .	Mourne . .	Kilkeel . .	Kilkeel . .	III.	182
6, 7	Aughrim . .	1,349 0 35	Kerry . .	Iraghticonnor .	Murher . .	Glin . .	II.	193
21	Aughrim . .	756 2 30	Kildare . .	West Offaly . .	Lackagh . .	Athy . .	I.	73
18, 19, 21	Aughrim . .	879 1 0	Leitrim . .	Drumahaire . .	Drumreilly . .	Cark. on Shannon	IV.	95
16	Aughrim . .	125 1 34	Leitrim . .	Drumahaire . .	Inishmagrath . .	Manorhamilton .	IV.	95
24	Aughrim . .	70 1 32	Leitrim . .	Leitrim . .	Kiltubrid . .	Cark. on Shannon	IV.	103
42, 47	Aughrim . .	373 2 12	Londonderry .	Loughinsholin .	Artrea . .	Magherafelt .	III.	238
17	Aughrim . .	347 0 33i	Roscommom .	Roscommon . .	Aughrim . .	Cark. on Shannon	IV.	207
23	Aughriman . .	174 3 17j	Leitrim . .	Leitrim . .	Kiltoghert . .	Cark. on Shannon	IV.	101
31	Aughriman South .	292 1 28	Leitrim . .	Leitrim . .	Kiltoghert . .	Cark. on Shannon	IV.	101

(a) Including 4A. 0R. 15P. water.
(b) Including 3A. 1R. 39P. water.
(c) Including 6A. 2R. 32P. water.
(d) Including 19A. 3R. 12P. water.

(e) Including 31A. 2R. 33P. water.
(f) Including 39A. 0R. 31P. water.
(g) Including 32A. 2R. 21P. water.

(h) Including 20A. 3R. 24P. water.
(i) Including 32A. 0R. 33P. water.
(j) Including 11A. 0R. 11P. water.

No. of Sheet of the Ordnance Survey Maps.	Townlands and Towns.	Area in Statute Acres.			County.	Barony.	Parish.	Poor Law Union in 1857.	Townland Census of 1851, Part I.	
		A.	R.	P.					Vol.	Page
28, 29	Aughrim Beg . .	160	2	28	Monaghan .	Farney . .	Donaghmoyne .	Carrickmacross	III.	269
47	Aughrimderg . .	263	3	3	Tyrone . .	Dungannon Middle .	Clonoe . .	Dungannon .	III.	300
25	Aughrim (Kelly) .	151	2	38a	Clare . .	Inchiquin . .	Dysert . .	Ennis . .	II.	24
34, 39	Aughrim Lower .	266	3	6	Wicklow .	Ballinacor South .	Ballykine .	Rathdrum .	I.	348
28	Aughrim More . .	227	0	0	Monaghan .	Farney . .	Donaghmoyne	Carrickmacross	III.	269
87	Aughrim Plots or Garrynamishaun .	125	2	37	Galway . .	Kilconnell . .	Aughrim . .	Ballinasloe .	IV.	39
25	Aughrim (Ross) .	136	2	7b	Clare . .	Inchiquin . .	Dysert . .	Corrofin . .	II.	24
25	Aughrim (Toohy) .	144	3	31c	Clare . .	Inchiquin . .	Dysert . .	Corrofin . .	II.	24
87	Aughrim T. . .	—			Galway . .	Kilconnell . .	Aughrim . .	Ballinasloe .	IV.	39
34	Aughrim Upper .	682	0	4	Wicklow . .	Ballinacor South .	Ballykine .	Rathdrum .	I.	348
33, 39	Aughris . . .	140	0	36	Sligo . .	Corran . . .	Cloonoghil .	Tobercurry .	IV.	225
12	Aughris . . .	515	2	27	Sligo . .	Tireragh . .	Templeboy .	Dromore West .	IV.	236
21	Aughrus Beg . .	443	1	30d	Galway . .	Ballynahinch . .	Omey . .	Clifden . .	IV.	14
21	Aughrus More . .	482	1	15e	Galway . .	Ballynahinch . .	Omey . .	Clifden . .	IV.	14
35	Aughry . . .	126	1	1	Leitrim . .	Mohill . . .	Annaduff .	Mohill . .	IV.	105
30, 39	Aught . . .	1,661	1	22	Donegal . .	Inishowen West .	Muff . .	Londonderry .	III.	121
19, 23	Aughtanny . .	171	2	9	Kilkenny .	Shillelogher . .	Castleinch or Inchyolaghan .	Kilkenny .	I.	114
36, 37	Aughterclooney .	462	2	1	Antrim . .	Upper Toome . .	Ahoghill . .	Ballymena .	III.	33
3, 6	Aughtermoy . .	235	1	24f	Tyrone . .	Strabane Lower .	Donaghedy .	Strabane .	III.	320
11, 12	Aughtreagh . .	88	1	38	Cavan . .	Tullygarvey . .	Annagh . .	Cavan . .	III.	87
2, 3	Aughullen . .	242	3	27	Wexford . .	Gorey . . .	Kilnenor . .	Gorey . .	I.	319
39	Aughvallydeag .	295	0	5	Tipperary, N.R.	Kilnamanagh Upper	Toem . .	Tipperary .	II.	280
34	Aughvolyshane .	154	2	13	Tipperary, N.R.	Kilnamanagh Upper	Glenkeen .	Thurles . .	II.	278
49, 50	Augullies . .	322	3	14g	Donegal . .	Boylagh . .	Templecrone .	Glenties . .	III.	114
21	Aulanebane . .	217	1	15	Kerry . .	Clanmaurice .	Killahan .	Tralee . .	II.	170
21	Aulaneduff . .	162	1	20	Kerry . .	Clanmaurice .	Killahan .	Tralee . .	II.	170
94	Aultagh . .	293	3	30	Cork, W.R. .	East Carbery (W.D.)	Kilmichael .	Dunmanway .	II.	134
94	Aultaghreagh .	206	1	26	Cork, W.R. .	East Carbery (W.D.)	Kilmichael .	Dunmanway .	II.	134
29, 30	Ault, alias Gowkstown .	367	2	14	Antrim . .	Lower Glenarm .	Tickmacrevan .	Larne . .	III.	23
44	Aunamihoonagh .	88	0	38	Cork, E.R. .	Barrymore . .	Rathcormack .	Fermoy . .	II.	57
21	Aungierstown and Ballybane . .	62	2	10	Dublin . .	Newcastle . .	Kilmactalway .	Celbridge .	I.	33
2, 6, 7	Aurora . . .	219	1	22	Wicklow . .	Rathdown . .	Powerscourt .	Rathdown .	I.	356
27	Auskurra Big .	39	3	31	Waterford .	Gaultiere . .	Killea . .	Waterford .	II.	363
27	Auskurra Little	9	0	18	Waterford .	Gaultiere . .	Killea . .	Waterford .	II.	363
14	Avalbane . .	167	0	30	Monaghan .	Cremorne . .	Clontibret .	Monaghan .	III.	259
14	Avalreagh . .	343	2	24	Monaghan .	Cremorne . .	Clontibret .	Monaghan .	III.	259
78	Avaltygort . .	197	2	39	Donegal . .	Raphoe . .	Donaghmore .	Stranorlar .	III.	137
66	Avenue . . .	67	2	8	Kerry . .	Magunihy . .	Killarney .	Killarney .	II.	202
76	Avery Island . .	2	3	37	Galway . .	Ballynahinch .	Moyrus . .	Clifden . .	IV	13
2, 6	Avish . . .	739	0	3	Londonderry .	Keenaght . .	Magilligan .	Newtn Limavady	III.	236
14	Avish . . .	144	2	0	Londonderry .	Tirkeeran . .	Clondermot .	Londonderry .	III.	247
3, 7	Avoley . . .	320	1	4	Queen's Co. .	Tinnahinch . .	Rosenallis .	Mountmellick .	I.	250
30, 35	Avondale . .	144	3	20	Wicklow . .	Ballinacor North .	Rathdrum .	Rathdrum .	I.	347
112, 113	Avough Island .	2	3	0	Galway . .	Kiltartan . .	Kinvarradoorus .	Gort . .	IV.	49
68, 76	Awnaskirtaun .	1,060	3	22	Kerry . .	Magunihy . .	Kilcummin .	Killarney .	II.	201
9	Ayle . . .	57	0	31	Kerry . .	Clanmaurice .	Rattoo . .	Listowel .	II.	173
50	Ayle . . .	73	1	16	Tipperary, S.R.	Clanwilliam . .	Solloghodmore .	Tipperary .	II.	310
50	Ayle . . .	545	2	23	Tipperary, S.R.	Clanwilliam . .	Toem . .	Tipperary .	II.	312
42	Ayleacotty . .	141	1	15	Clare . .	Bunratty Lower .	Tomfinlough .	Ennis . .	II.	7
27	Ayle Lower . .	367	3	9	Clare . .	Tulla Upper . .	Feakle . .	Scarriff .	II.	38
27	Ayle Upper . .	229	1	6	Clare . .	Tulla Upper . .	Feakle . .	Scarriff .	II.	38
38	Aylmerstown . .	250	1	39	Kildare . .	Kilkea and Moone .	Killelan .	Baltinglass .	I.	60
41	Aylwardstown .	555	1	24	Kilkenny .	Ida	Kilmakevoge .	Waterford .	I.	103
19	Ayresfields . .	43	1	4h	Kilkenny .	Crannagh . .	St. Canice .	Kilkenny .	I.	87 / 117
12, 15	Babeswood . .	100	0	25	Louth . .	Louth . . .	Dromiskin .	Dundalk . .	I.	183
42	Bachelorshall . .	48	3	19	Wexford . .	Forth . . .	Rathaspick .	Wexford . .	I.	312
88	Back . . .	39	0	5i	Galway . .	Clonmacnowen .	Kilcloony .	Ballinasloe .	IV.	25
9	Back . . .	273	1	24	Londonderry .	Keenaght . .	Tamlaghtfinlagan .	Newtn Limavady	III.	237
36, 43	Backaderry . .	1,763	1	27	Down . .	Upper Iveagh, Lr. pt.	Drumgooland .	Banbridge .	III.	172
27	Backan . . .	240	3	3k	Tyrone . .	Strabane Upper .	Bodoney Lower .	Gortin . .	III.	323
34	Backfarm . .	121	2	26	Tyrone . .	Omagh East, .	Drumragh .	Omagh . .	III.	312
5	Backfence . .	149	0	0l	Tyrone . .	Strabane Lower .	Leckpatrick .	Strabane .	III.	321
70	Backhill . .	13	2	0	Donegal . .	Raphoe . .	Clonleigh .	Strabane .	III.	134
19	Back of the Hill .	329	3	26	Longford . .	Ardagh . .	Ardagh . .	Longford . .	I.	151
24	Backhill . .	154	2	3	Tyrone . .	Omagh West . .	Ardstraw .	Castlederg .	III.	315
70	Backland . .	25	1	11	Donegal . .	Raphoe . .	Clonleigh .	Strabane .	III.	134
69, 78	Backlees . .	121	3	8	Donegal . .	Raphoe . .	Stranorlar .	Stranorlar .	III.	142

No. of Sheet of the Ordnance Survey Maps.	Townlands and Towns.	Area in Statute Acres.	County.	Barony.	Parish.	Poor Law Union in 1857.	Townland Census of 1851, Part I.	
		A. R. P.					Vol.	Page
39, 40, 47, 48	Back Lower .	433 3 7	Tyrone . .	Dungannon Upper .	Ballyclog, . .	Cookstown .	III.	306
21	Backnamullagh	463 1 12	Down . .	Lower Iveagh, Lr. pt.	Dromore . .	Lisburn . .	III.	168
84	Backpark .	109 1 38	Galway . .	Athenry . .	Kiltullagh .	Loughrea . .	IV.	4
16	Backsteel .	34 0 18	King's Co. .	Ballycowan .	Rahan . .	Tullamore .	I.	128
17	Backstown .	208 0 28	Dublin . .	Newcastle .	Aderrig . .	Celbridge .	I.	32
4, 9	Backtown .	210 0 21	Tyrone . .	Strabane Lower .	Urney . .	Strabane .	III.	322
47	Back Upper .	279 2 26	Tyrone . .	Dungannon Upper .	Ballyclog .	Cookstown .	III.	306
17	Backwestonpark .	138 3 24a	Dublin . .	Newcastle .	Aderrig . .	Celbridge .	I.	32
17	Backwestonpark .	40 2 9	Dublin . .	Newcastle .	Lucan . .	Celbridge .	I.	33
11	Backwestonpark .	87 1 34b	Kildare . .	South Salt .	Donaghcumper .	Celbridge .	I.	76
5	Backwood .	40 2 27	Fermanagh .	Lurg . .	Drumkeeran .	Lowtherstown .	III.	205
26, 33	Backwood .	420 3 23	King's Co. .	Upper Philipstown .	Ballykean .	Mountmellick .	I.	143
48	Baconstown .	1,097 3 8	Meath . .	Lower Moyfenrath .	Rathcore . .	Trim . .	I.	211
22	Badgerfort .	110 0 26	Limerick . .	Smallcounty .	Kilpeacon .	Croom . .	II.	260
24	Badgerhill .	237 2 3	Dublin . .	Newcastle . .	Rathcoole .	Celbridge .	I.	34
16	Badgerhill .	166 2 15	Queen's Co. .	Upperwoods .	Offerlane .	Mountmellick .	I.	250
22, 23	Badgerisland, .	94 3 21	Queen's Co. .	Upperwoods .	Offerlane .	Abbeyleix .	I.	250
28, 29	Badgerrock .	125 0 3	Kilkenny .	Gowran . .	Kilfane . .	Thomastown .	I.	96
16	BAGENALSTOWN T. .	—	Carlow . .	Idrone East .	Dunleckny .	Carlow . .	I.	7
18	Baggotrath . .	29 3 28c	Dublin . .	Dublin . .	Donnybrook .	Dublin South .	I.	30
18	Baggotrath East .	198 1 11	Dublin . .	Dublin . .	St. Peter's .	Dublin South .	I.	30
18	Baggotrath North .	27 3 30	Dublin . .	Dublin . .	St. Peter's .	Dublin South .	I.	30
18	BAGGOTRATH T. .	—	Dublin . .	Dublin . .	Donnybrook .	Dublin South .	I.	30
18	Baggotrath West .	44 1 14	Dublin . .	Uppercross .	St. Peter's .	Dublin South .	I.	41
32, 40	Baggotstown .	387 0 20	Limerick . .	Smallcounty .	Knockainy .	Kilmallock .	II.	260
21, 22	Baggotstown . .	165 2 14	Louth . .	Ferrard . .	Rathdrumin .	Drogheda . .	I.	182
32, 40	Baggotstown East .	457 1 36	Limerick . .	Smallcounty .	Knockainy .	Kilmallock .	II.	260
40	Baggotstown West .	460 2 14	Limerick . .	Smallcounty .	Knockainy .	Kilmallock .	II.	260
29	Baggottspark . .	95 3 34	Queen's Co. .	Clarmallagh .	Abbeyleix .	Abbeyleix .	I.	235
39	Baghloonagh .	64 2 4d	Sligo . .	Corran . .	Kilshalvy .	Boyle . .	IV.	227
45	Bahagha . .	588 2 15	Tipperary, N.R.	Kilnamanagh Upper	Doon . .	Tipperary .	II.	277
80	Bahaghs . .	794 0 37	Kerry . .	Iveragh . .	Killinane .	Cahersiveen .	II.	197
24, 26	Bahana . .	824 1 31e	Carlow . .	St. Mullins Lower .	St. Mullins .	New Ross .	I.	13
30	Bahana . .	240 0 2	Wicklow . .	Newcastle .	Kilcommon .	Rathdrum .	I.	351
7	Bahana . .	459 1 28	Wicklow . .	Rathdown .	Powerscourt .	Rathdown .	I.	356
34, 35	Bahana (King) .	278 1 8	Wicklow . .	Ballinacor South .	Ballykine .	Rathdrum .	I.	348
34, 35	Bahana (Whaley) .	620 0 6	Wicklow . .	Ballinacor South .	Ballykine .	Rathdrum .	I.	348
34	BAILIEBOROUGH T. .	—	Cavan . .	Clankee . .	Bailieborough .	Bailieborough .	III.	71
25	Bailis . .	127 1 17	Meath . .	Skreen . .	Athlumney .	Navan . .	I.	220
11	Bailyland .	34 2 20	Louth . .	Louth . .	Louth . .	Dundalk . .	I.	184
24	Bailypark .	28 0 4	Louth . .	Drogheda .	St. Peter's .	Drogheda .	I.	175
66, 67	Bakersclose .	24 2 19	Cork, E.R. .	Imokilly . .	Killeagh .	Youghal . .	II.	88
22, 25	Balally . .	834 3 5	Dublin . .	Rathdown .	Taney . .	Rathdown .	I.	38
91	Balbane . .	712 0 26f	Donegal . .	Banagh . .	Killybegs Upper .	Glenties . .	III.	110
31	Balbradagh .	394 1 8	Meath . .	Upper Navan .	Bective . .	Navan . .	I.	216
2, 5	Balbriggan .	332 1 33	Dublin . .	Balrothery East .	Balrothery .	Balrothery .	I.	19
2, 5	BALBRIGGAN T. .	—	Dublin . .	Balrothery East .	Balrothery .	Balrothery .	I.	19
31	Balbrigh . .	365 3 22	Meath . .	Upper Navan .	Bective . .	Navan . .	I.	216
14	Balbutcher .	141 2 17	Dublin . .	Coolock . .	Santry . .	Dublin North .	I.	29
12	Balcarrick .	203 3 17	Dublin . .	Nethercross .	Donabate .	Balrothery .	I.	30
16	Balcarrig .	318 3 10	Wexford . .	Gorey . .	Ballycanew .	Gorey . .	I.	315
16	Balcarrighill .	109 2 19	Wexford . .	Gorey . .	Ballycanew .	Gorey . .	I.	315
11	Balcultry .	93 2 35	Dublin . .	Nethercross .	Killossery .	Balrothery .	I.	31
5	Balcunnin .	580 1 27	Dublin . .	Balrothery East .	Lusk . .	Balrothery .	I.	20
14	Balcurris .	215 0 21	Dublin . .	Coolock . .	Santry . .	Dublin North .	I.	29
5, 8	Baldongan .	410 0 25g	Dublin . .	Balrothery East .	Baldongan .	Balrothery .	I.	19
21	Baldonnell Little .	28 0 9	Dublin . .	Newcastle .	Kilbride . .	Celbridge .	I.	33
21	Baldonnell Lower .	167 1 21	Dublin . .	Newcastle .	Kilbride . .	Celbridge .	I.	33
21	Baldonnell Upper .	229 3 17	Dublin . .	Newcastle .	Kilbride . .	Celbridge .	I.	33
15	Baldoyle . .	297 2 37	Dublin . .	Coolock . .	Baldoyle . .	Dublin North .	I.	26
37	Baldoyle or Curtistown Lower .	174 1 38	Meath . .	Lower Deece .	Kilmessan .	Dunshaughlin .	I.	192
15	BALDOYLE T. .	—	Dublin . .	Coolock . .	Baldoyle . .	Dublin North .	I.	26
7, 8	Baldrumman .	246 1 14h	Dublin . .	Balrothery East .	Lusk . .	Balrothery .	I.	20
7	Baldurgan .	243 1 30	Dublin . .	Nethercross .	Swords . .	Balrothery .	I.	32
3, 4	Baldwinstown .	792 2 10	Dublin . .	Balrothery West .	Garristown .	Dunshaughlin .	I.	22
47	Baldwinstown .	205 3 12	Wexford . .	Bargy . .	Kilcowan .	Wexford . .	I.	305
4 }	BALDWINSTOWN T. .	— {	Dublin . .	Balrothery West .	Garristown .	Dunshaughlin .	I.	22
47 }		{	Wexford . .	Bargy . .	Kilcowan .	Wexford . .	I.	305
49	Balfeaghan .	665 2 32	Meath . .	Upper Deece .	Balfeaghan .	Celbridge .	I.	193
22	Balfeddock .	116 0 31	Louth . .	Ferrard . .	Termonfeckin .	Drogheda .	I.	182
19	Balfeddock .	325 3 36	Meath . .	Slane Upper .	Monknewtown .	Drogheda .	I.	224
45, 51	Balfestown .	243 2 22	Meath . .	Ratoath . .	Ratoath . .	Dunshaughlin .	I.	219

(a) Including 4A. 0R. 32P. water.
(b) Including 1A. 3R. 20P. water.
(c) Including 12A. 0R. 17P. detached portions.
(d) Including 3A. 1R. 33P. water.
(e) Including 7A. 0R. 28P. River Barrow.
(f) Including 8A. 3R. 4P. water.
(g) Including 1A. 1R. 14P. detached portion.
(h) Including 6A. 2R. 26P. detached portion.

CENSUS OF IRELAND FOR THE YEAR 1851.

No. of Sheet of the Ordnance Survey Maps.	Townlands and Towns.	Area in Statute Acres. A. R. P.	County.	Barony.	Parish.	Poor Law Union in 1857.	Townland Census of 1851, Part I. Vol.	Page
1, 4	Balgaddy	155 0 24	Dublin	Balrothery East	Balscaddan	Balrothery	I.	20
17	Balgaddy	226 2 11	Dublin	Uppercross	Clondalkin	Dublin South	I.	39
18	Balgarrett	413 0 0	Westmeath	Moyashel and Magheradernon	Mullingar	Mullingar	I.	275
21, 24	Balgatheran	482 1 16a	Louth	Ferrard	Tullyallen	Drogheda	I.	183
27	Balgeen,	379 0 22	Meath	Upper Duleek	Kilsharvan	Drogheda	I.	198
31, 37	Balgeeth,	355 1 5	Meath	Lower Deece	Assey	Navan	I.	191
33	Balgeeth,	506 0 32	Meath	Upper Duleek	Ardcath	Drogheda	I.	197
16	Balgeeth,	299 2 9	Meath	Upper Kells	Burry	Kells	I.	205
31	Balgill,	248 3 26	Meath	Upper Navan	Bective	Navan	I.	216
10	Balgree,	492 2 39	Meath	Upper Kells	Kilskeer	Kells	I.	206
15	Balgriffin,	220 2 36	Dublin	Coolock	Balgriffin	Dublin North	I.	26
15	Balgriffin Park,	158 1 34	Dublin	Coolock	Balgriffin	Dublin North	I.	26
11	Balheary,	439 3 15	Dublin	Nethercross	Swords	Balrothery	I.	32
11, 12	Balheary Demesne,	160 2 14	Dublin	Nethercross	Swords	Balrothery	I.	32
12	Balief Lower	230 0 5	Kilkenny	Crannagh	Clomantagh	Urlingford	I.	85
8, 12	Balief Upper	253 1 36	Kilkenny	Crannagh	Clomantagh	Urlingford	I.	85
42, 46, 47	Balisland,	932 1 21	Wicklow	Shillelagh	Moyacomb	Shillelagh	I.	358
6	Balix Lower	537 0 32	Tyrone	Strabane Lower	Donaghedy	Gortin	III.	320
6, 11	Balix Upper	1,072 1 3	Tyrone	Strabane Lower	Donaghedy	Gortin	III.	320
27, 31	Balkinstown	302 3 14	Kildare	Offaly West	Nurney	Athy	I.	74
90	Balla	251 1 6	Mayo	Clanmorris	Balla	Castlebar	IV.	131
13	Ballabony	270 3 26	Louth	Ardee	Clonkeen	Ardee	I.	172
18, 19	Balladian	270 1 5	Monaghan	Cremorne	Ballybay	Castleblayney	III.	259
98, 112	Ballady	615 0 30	Cork, E.R.	Kinalea	Cullen	Kinsale	II.	94
9	Ballagan	470 0 38	Louth	Lower Dundalk	Carlingford	Dundalk	I.	176
42, 43	Ballagh	73 3 10	Clare	Bunratty Upper	Quin	Tulla	II.	9
16	Ballagh	1,052 0 37c	Clare	Corcomroe	Kilfenora	Ennistimon	II.	18
6	Ballagh	542 2 10	Cork, E.R.	Duhallow	Tullylease	Kanturk	II.	76
4	Ballagh	606 2 9	Donegal	Inishowen East	Clonca	Inishowen	III.	116
35	Ballagh	338 1 24	Fermanagh	Clankelly	Galloon	Lisnaskea	III.	198
43	Ballagh	78 1 21	Galway	Clare	Belclare	Tuam	IV.	17
81, 82	Ballagh	170 1 22	Galway	Galway	Rahoon	Galway	IV.	37
65	Ballagh	331 1 32	Kerry	Dunkerron North	Knockane	Killarney	II.	181
94, 95, 103	Ballagh	2,303 3 7	Kerry	Glanarought	Kilgarvan	Kenmare	II.	187
18	Ballagh	98 0 11	Kilkenny	Crannagh	Kilmanagh	Callan	I.	86
44	Ballagh	329 3 34	Limerick	Glenquin	Killeedy	Newcastle	II.	245
8	Ballagh	216 3 21	Longford	Longford	Clongesh	Longford	I.	157
21, 25	Ballagh	226 0 9d	Longford	Rathcline	Cashel	Ballymahon	I.	163
13	Ballagh	235 3 39	Monaghan	Monaghan	Drumsnat	Monaghan	III.	275
45	Ballagh	1,210 2 24e	Roscommon	Athlone	Rahara	Athlone	IV.	183
11, 17	Ballagh	169 0 0f	Roscommon	Ballintober North	Kilmore	Cark. on Shannon	IV.	187
36	Ballagh	183 3 14	Roscommon	Ballintober South	Kilgefin	Roscommon	IV.	189
5	Ballagh	335 2 18	Tipperary, N.R.	Lower Ormond	Loughkeen	Parsonstown	II.	286
67	Ballagh	787 2 36	Tipperary, S.R.	Clanwilliam	Templeneiry	Tipperary	II.	311
52	Ballagh	420 0 35	Tipperary, S.R.	Kilnamanagh Lower	Clonoulty	Cashel	II.	322
64	Ballagh	173 0 6g	Tyrone	Clogher	Clogher	Clogher	III.	291
66	Ballagh	345 2 6	Tyrone	Dungannon Lower	Aghaloo	Armagh	III.	296
31	Ballagh	82 3 27	Westmeath	Clonlonan	Kilcumreragh	Athlone	I.	262
19	Ballagh	217 2 27h	Westmeath	Moyashel and Magheradernon	Mullingar	Mullingar	I.	275
30	Ballagh	705 2 28	Wexford	Bantry	Adamstown	New Ross	I.	299
52	Ballagh	69 1 7	Wexford	Bargy	Tomhaggard	Wexford	I.	307
39	Ballagh	383 3 6	Wicklow	Ballinacor South	Kilpipe	Shillelagh	I.	349
27, 28	Ballaghabawbeg	427 1 5	Roscommon	Castlereagh	Baslick	Castlereagh	IV.	199
28	Ballaghabawmore	224 2 7	Roscommon	Roscommon	Ogulla	Strokestown	IV.	212
33	Ballaghablake	206 2 37	Wexford	Shelmaliere East	St. Margarets	Wexford	I.	331
8	Ballagh (Achmuty)	135 1 35	Longford	Longford	Clongesh	Longford	I.	157
9	Ballaghaclay	281 1 13	Carlow	Rathvilly	Clonmore	Shillelagh	I.	10
16	Ballaghaderneen	328 1 24	Carlow	Idrone East	Fennagh	Carlow	I.	7
74	Ballaghaderreen	349 1 29	Mayo	Costello	Kilcolman	Castlereagh	IV.	141
74	BALLAGHADERREENT.	—	Mayo	Costello	Kilcolman	Castlereagh	IV.	141
23,24,31,32	Ballaghaderry	54 1 28	King's Co.	Ballyboy	Killoughy	Tullamore	I.	123
11	Ballaghadigue	264 2 36	Kerry	Iraghticonnor	Listowel	Listowel	II.	192
119, 132	Ballaghadown North	235 3 27	Cork, W.R.	West Carbery,(W.D.)	Caheragh	Skibbereen	II.	141
132	Ballaghadown South	221 1 22	Cork, W.R.	West Carbery,(W.D.)	Caheragh	Skibbereen	II.	141
33, 41	Ballaghafadda East	113 2 14	Clare	Islands	Clareabbey	Ennis	II.	29
41	Ballaghafadda West	461 3 25i	Clare	Islands	Clareabbey	Ennis	II.	29
11	Ballaghaglash	261 3 11	Clare	Inchiquin	Kilkeedy	Corrofin	II.	25
2, 5	Ballaghalare,	213 3 31	Tyrone	Strabane Lower	Donaghedy	Strabane	III.	320
8, 14	Ballaghaline	186 2 35	Clare	Corcomroe	Killilagh	Ennistimon	II.	19
30	Ballaghalode	285 2 23	Galway	Ballymoe	Tuam	Tuam	IV.	10
29	Ballaghamuck	565 1 30	Mayo	Tirawley	Crossmolina	Ballina	IV.	165

(a) Including 9A. 0R. 26P. detached portion.
(b) Including 3A. 0R. 0P. water.
(c) Including 89A. 2R. 34P. water.

(d) Including 5A. 1R. 24P. water.
(e) Including 161A. 1R. 38P. water.
(f) Including 4A. 1R. 13P. water.

(g) Including 12A. 2R. 0P. water.
(h) Including 1A. 3R. 19P. water.
(i) Including 30A. 2R. 33P. water.

No. of Sheet of the Ordnance Survey Maps.	Townlands and Towns.	Area in Statute Acres.			County.	Barony.	Parish.	Poor Law Union in 1857.	Townland Census of 1851, Part I.	
		A.	R.	P.					Vol.	Page
39	Ballaghanea	398	0	9	Cavan	Castlerahan	Lurgan	Oldcastle	III.	69
39	*Ballaghanea Island*	5	0	31	Cavan	Castlerahan	Lurgan	Oldcastle	III.	70
49, 53	Ballaghanery	457	0	20	Down	Mourne	Kilkeel	Kilkeel	III.	182
49, 53	Ballaghanery Upper	1,580	3	26	Down	Mourne	Kilkeel	Kilkeel	III.	182
38	Ballaghanna	242	2	30	Cavan	Clanmahon	Kilbride	Cavan	III.	77
30, 35	Ballaghanoher	577	2	33	King's Co.	Garrycastle	Reynagh	Parsonstown	I.	137
94, 95	Ballaghanure	207	3	12	Cork, W.R.	East Carbery,(W.D.)	Kinneigh	Dunmanway	II.	134
27, 33	Ballagharahin	662	1	24	Queen's Co.	Clandonagh	Rathdowney	Donaghmore	I.	234
6	Ballagharea	314	3	39	Cork, E.R.	Orrery and Kilmore	Kilbolane	Kanturk	II.	108
19	Ballaghassaan	961	2	33	King's Co.	Upper Philipstown	Geashill	Edenderry	I.	144
1, 2	Ballaghaugeag East	257	3	18	Galway	Ballymoe	Kilcroan	Glennamaddy	IV.	8
1, 2, 6, 7	Ballaghaugeag West	384	3	20	Galway	Ballymoe	Kilcroan	Glennamaddy	IV.	8
31	Ballaghavorraga	201	2	25	Waterford	Decies without Drum	Clonea	Dungarvan	II.	354
45	Ballaghaweary	111	0	19	Meath	Ratoath	Greenoge	Dunshaughlin	I.	218
43	Ballaghbaun	268	3	2	Galway	Clare	Belclare	Tuam	IV.	17
21	Ballaghbeddy	164	1	28	Antrim	Kilconway	Finvoy	Ballymoney	III.	26
49	Ballaghbeg	2,510	1	5	Down	Upper Iveagh, Lower part	Kilcoo	Kilkeel	III.	173
34, 35, 42, 43	Ballaghbehy	1,438	1	35	Limerick	Glenquin	Abbeyfeale	Newcastle	II.	244
35, 43	Ballaghbehy North	1,152	3	19	Limerick	Glenquin	Abbeyfeale	Newcastle	II.	244
43	Ballaghbehy South	521	2	6	Limerick	Glenquin	Abbeyfeale	Newcastle	II.	244
33, 34	Ballaghboy	418	0	17	Clare	Bunratty Upper	Doora	Ennis	II.	8
25	Ballaghboy	101	1	9	Clare	Inchiquin	Ruan	Corrofin	II.	28
126	Ballaghboy	229	1	5	Cork, W.R.	Bear	Kilnamanagh	Castletown	II.	125
38, 41, 42	Ballaghboy	209	3	21	King's Co.	Clonlisk	Kilmurryely	Roscrea	I.	131
40, 45	Ballaghboy	718	0	3	Sligo	Tirerrill	Aghanagh	Boyle	IV.	237
55	Ballaghboy	592	3	35	Tipperary, S.R.	Slievardagh	Ballingarry	Callan	II.	331
53, 54, 61, 62	Ballaghboy	773	1	0	Tipperary, S.R.	Slievardagh	Graystown	Callan	II.	333
11	Ballaghboy	243	2	36	Wexford	Gorey	Liskinfere	Gorey	I.	320
16, 23	Ballaghboy or Fordstown	72	3	3	Meath	Upper Kells	Balrathboyne	Kells	I.	204
31	Ballagh or Boynehill	92	1	22*a*	Meath	Lower Navan	Navan	Navan	I.	215
52	Ballagh Burrow	38	0	38	Wexford	Bargy	Tomhaggard	Wexford	I.	307
18	Ballaghcloneen	285	0	22	Kilkenny	Crannagh	Tullaroan	Kilkenny	I.	87
15	Ballaghcullia	361	3	0	Roscommon	Castlereagh	Kilcorkey	Castlereagh	IV.	199
20, 33	Ballaghdacker	48	0	31*b*	Galway	Killian	Athleague	Mountbellew	IV.	43
45, 53	Ballaghderg	237	1	28	Donegal	Kilmacrenan	Conwal	Letterkenny	III.	125
43	Ballaghdorragh	325	2	37	Cavan	Castlerahan	Muntereonnaught	Oldcastle	III.	71
5	Ballaghdorragha	325	3	15	Galway	Ballymoe	Dunmore	Glennamaddy	IV.	7
31, 32	Ballaghduff	471	0	8	Galway	Tiaquin	Kilkerrin	Glennamaddy	IV.	76
99	Ballagh East	142	1	24	Galway	Clonmacnowen	Clontuskert	Ballinasloe	IV.	24
17	Ballagh East	80	2	30	Galway	Dunmore	Dunmore	Tuam	IV.	33
90	Ballaghfarna	187	2	35	Mayo	Carra	Drum	Castlebar	IV.	127
5, 8	Ballaghgar	295	3	19	Tipperary, N.R.	Lower Ormond	Loughkeen	Parsonstown	II.	286
3, 8	Ballaghgee Glebe	334	1	8*c*	Fermanagh	Lurg	Belleek	Ballyshannon	III.	203
15	Ballaghgowla	41	2	25	Longford	Ardagh	Street	Granard	I.	153
27	BALLAGHKEEN T.	—			Wexford	Ballaghkeen	Ballyhuskard	Enniscorthy	I.	292
22, 29	Ballaghkeeran Big	302	1	16	Westmeath	Kilkenny West	Kilkenny West	Athlone	I.	273
22, 29	Ballaghkeeran Little	30	0	13	Westmeath	Kilkenny West	Kilkenny West	Athlone	I.	273
15	Ballaghlyragh or Nealstown,	148	2	2	Queen's Co.	Upperwoods	Offerlane	Mountmellick	I.	250
39	Ballaghmoon	296	1	28	Kildare	Kilkea and Moone	Ballaghmoon	Athy	I.	59
39	Ballaghmoon Castle	266	0	32*d*	Kildare	Kilkea and Moone	Ballaghmoon	Athy	I.	59
12, 17	Ballaghmore	163	3	25	Antrim	Upper Dunluce	Ballymoney	Ballymoney	III.	18
17	Ballaghmore	471	0	5	Carlow	Forth	Myshall	Carlow	I.	5
21, 22	Ballaghmore	114	0	16*e*	Fermanagh	Magheraboy	Rossorry	Enniskillen	III.	214
19	Ballaghmore	172	0	13	Queen's Co.	Stradbally	Stradbally	Athy	I.	247
3, 7	Ballaghmore or Bushmills	107	1	35	Antrim	Lower Dunluce	Dunluce	Coleraine	III.	17
15, 21	Ballaghmore Lower	1,061	0	0*f*	Queen's Co.	Clandonagh	Kyle	Roscrea	I.	233
15	Ballaghmore Upper	503	2	28	Queen's Co.	Clandonagh	Kyle	Roscrea	I.	233
12	Ballaghnabehy	407	0	1	Leitrim	Drumahaire	Cloonclare	Manorhamilton	IV.	93
30	Ballaghnagearn	142	2	25	Monaghan	Farney	Magheracloone	Carrickmacross	III.	272
59	Ballaghnagrosheen	387	1	16	Galway	Tiaquin	Killoscobe	Mountbellew	IV.	77
58	Ballaghneed	390	2	29	Tyrone	Clogher	Clogher	Clogher	III.	291
71, 72	Ballaghoge	100	3	30	Tipperary, S.R.	Slievardagh	Grangemockler	Callan	II.	333
5, 8	Ballaghstown	219	1	13	Dublin	Balrothery East	Baldongan	Balrothery	I.	19
35, 36	Ballaghtalion	424	0	14	Meath	Lune	Kildalkcy	Trim	I.	208
52	BALLAGH T.	—			Tipperary, S.R.	Kilnamanagh Lower	Clonoulty	Cashel	II.	323
16, 21, 22	Ballaghveny	92	1	5	Tipperary, N.R.	Upper Ormond	Ballymackey	Nenagh	II.	289
87, 99	Ballagh West	163	2	15	Galway	Clonmacnowen	Clontuskert	Ballinasloe	IV.	24
17	Ballagh West	70	3	14	Galway	Dunmore	Dunmore	Tuam	IV.	33
12	Ballaghy	146	3	25	Armagh	Armagh	Eglish	Armagh	III.	44
2	Ballaghymurry	403	2	32	Galway	Ballymoe	Kilcroan	Glennamaddy	IV.	8

(*a*) Including 3A. 0R. 24P. water.
(*b*) Including 17A. 0R. 16P. water.
(*c*) Including 5A. 1R. 20P. water.
(*d*) Including 8A. 3R. 24P. water.
(*e*) Including 3A. 2R. 5P. water.
(*f*) Including 18A. 3R. 0P. water.

G

No. of Sheet of the Ordnance Survey Maps.	Townlands and Towns.	Area in Statute Acres.			County.	Barony.	Parish.	Poor Law Union in 1857.	Townland Census of 1851, Part I.	
		A.	R.	P.					Vol.	Page
67	Ballahacommane .	1,128	2	5	Kerry . .	Magunihy . .	Killarney . .	Killarney . .	II.	203
40	Ballahantouragh .	81	2	13	Kerry . .	Trughanacmy . .	Ballincuslane . .	Tralee . .	II.	206
49, 59	Ballahantouragh .	1,080	1	22	Kerry . .	Trughanacmy . .	Dysert . .	Tralee . .	II.	210
45, 54	Ballaheen . .	332	0	20	Cork, E.R. .	Barrymore . .	Britway . .	Middleton . .	II.	51
11	Ballair . .	217	1	1	Meath . .	Lower Kells . .	Newtown . .	Kells . .	I.	204
32	Ballakelly . .	136	3	10	Monaghan .	Farney . . .	Inishkeen . .	Dundalk . .	III.	271
8, 12	Ballalease North .	36	3	25	Dublin . .	Nethercross . .	Portraine . .	Balrothery . .	I.	31
12	Ballalease South .	14	2	28	Dublin . .	Nethercross . .	Portraine . .	Balrothery . .	I.	31
12	Ballalease West .	35	2	27	Dublin . .	Nethercross . .	Portraine . .	Balrothery . .	I.	31
10, 11	Ballallen . .	441	1	9a	Westmeath .	Moygoish . .	Kilbixy . .	Mullingar . .	I.	279
36, 37	Ballallog . .	362	2	32	Kilkenny . .	Ida . . .	Listerlin . .	New Ross . .	I.	103
10, 15	Ballaman . .	645	1	21	Wexford . .	Scarawalsh . .	Kilrush . .	Enniscorthy .	I.	324
35, 40	Ballanagh . .	423	1	34	Wicklow . .	Arklow . .	Castlemacadam .	Rathdrum . .	I.	342
14, 15	Ballany . .	452	0	33	Meath . .	Fore . .	Moylagh . .	Oldcastle . .	I.	201
7, 8	Ballany . .	440	0	9	Westmeath .	Fore . .	St. Feighins . .	Castletowndelvin .	I.	271
25, 28, 29	Ballard . .	997	3	38	Armagh . .	Orior Upper . .	Killevy . .	Newry . .	III.	57
46	Ballard . .	965	2	22b	Clare . .	Ibrickan . .	Killard . .	Kilrush . .	II.	23
17	Ballard . .	248	3	2c	Clare . .	Inchiquin . .	Killinaboy . .	Corrofin . .	II.	26
20, 28	Ballard . .	442	2	29	Cork, E.R. .	Condons&Clangibbon	Macroney . .	Fermoy . .	II.	63
115	Ballard . .	193	0	15	Cork, W.R. .	Bear . . .	Killaconenagh . .	Castletown . .	II.	124
80	Ballard . .	762	2	9	Donegal . .	Banagh . . .	Glencolumbkille	Glenties . .	III.	105
26, 27	Ballard . .	250	0	10	Galway . .	Ross . .	Cong . .	Oughterard .	IV.	72
17, 25	Ballard . .	409	0	7	King's Co. .	Ballycowan . .	Lynally . .	Tullamore . .	I.	128
19	Ballard . .	124	0	31	Sligo . .	Tireragh . .	Dromard . .	Dromore West .	IV.	233
18	Ballard . .	438	0	15	Westmeath .	Corkaree . .	Portloman . .	Mullingar . .	I.	263
37	Ballard . .	256	1	3	Westmeath .	Moycashel . .	Ardnurcher or Horse- leap . .	Tullamore . .	I.	276
17	Ballard . .	203	0	24	Westmeath .	Rathconrath . .	Rathconrath . .	Mullingar . .	I.	284
23, 24	Ballard . .	706	2	7	Wicklow . .	Ballinacor North .	Knockrath . .	Rathdrum . .	I.	347
30, 34, 35	Ballard . .	483	0	14	Wicklow . .	Ballinacor South .	Ballykine . .	Rathdrum . .	I.	348
42, 43	Ballard . .	140	2	4	Wicklow . .	Shillelagh . .	Aghowle . .	Shillelagh . .	I.	356
43	Ballard . .	705	3	4	Wicklow . .	Shillelagh . .	Carnew . .	Shillelagh . .	I.	357
30	Ballardan Great .	445	2	12	Meath . .	Upper Navan . .	Clonmacduff .	Trim . .	I.	216
30	Ballardan Little .	114	2	10	Meath . .	Upper Navan . .	Clonmacduff .	Trim . .	I.	216
24	Ballardbeg . .	242	0	5	Wicklow . .	Newcastle . .	Derrylossary .	Rathdrum . .	I.	351
102, 115	Ballard Commons .	668	2	26	Cork, W.R. .	Bear . . .	Killaconenagh . .	Castletown . .	II.	124
93	Ballard East .	65	1	39	Galway . .	Galway . .	Rahoon . .	Galway . .	IV.	37
123, 129	Ballardiggan . .	141	1	14	Galway . .	Kiltartan . .	Kilbeacanty . .	Gort . .	IV.	47
88	Ballard Lower .	702	2	31	Kerry . .	Iveragh . .	Prior . .	Cahersiveen .	II.	198
31	Ballard Lower .	63	1	32	Wicklow . .	Arklow . .	Dunganstown .	Rathdrum . .	I.	343
23, 24	Ballardpark . .	205	0	5	Wicklow . .	Ballinacor North .	Knockrath . .	Rathdrum . .	I.	347
88	Ballard Upper .	291	1	31	Kerry . .	Iveragh . .	Prior . .	Cahersiveen .	II.	198
30, 31	Ballard Upper .	214	0	23	Wicklow . .	Arklow . .	Dunganstown .	Rathdrum . .	I.	343
93	Ballard West .	29	3	33	Galway . .	Galway . .	Rahoon . .	Galway . .	IV.	37
48, 53	Ballard . .	84	1	27	Wexford . .	Forth . .	St. Margarets .	Wexford . .	I.	314
47, 52	Ballask . .	172	0	14	Wexford . .	Bargy . .	Kilturk . .	Wexford . .	I.	307
53	Ballask . .	68	1	32	Wexford . .	Forth . .	Carn . .	Wexford . .	I.	309
40, 41	Ballasport . .	466	1	5d	Meath . .	Upper Moyfenrath .	Clonard . .	Edenderry . .	I.	213
49	Ballastran . .	56	1	4	Meath . .	Upper Deece . .	Gallow . .	Trim . .	I.	193
90	BALLA T. .				Mayo . .	Clanmorris . .	Balla . .	Castlebar . .	IV.	132
8	Ballaverty . .	214	2	18	Louth . .	Lower Dundalk .	Carlingford . .	Dundalk . .	I.	176
86, 98	Ballca . .	930	2	34	Cork, E.R. .	Kerrycurrihy . .	Liscleary . .	Kinsale . .	II.	92
18	Balleaguy . .	191	0	19	Westmeath .	Moyashel and Ma- gheradernon . .	Mullingar . .	Mullingar . .	I.	275
8	Balleally East .	165	0	35	Dublin . .	Balrothery East .	Lusk . .	Balrothery . .	I.	20
8	Balleally West .	134	3	11	Dublin . .	Balrothery East .	Lusk . .	Balrothery . .	I.	20
49	Ballealy North .	111	2	22	Antrim . .	Upper Toome . .	Drummaul . .	Antrim . .	III.	33
49	Ballealy South .	136	3	16	Antrim . .	Upper Toome . .	Drummaul . .	Antrim . .	III.	33
37	Ballee . .	755	1	16	Antrim . .	Lower Antrim . .	Connor . .	Ballymena . .	III.	3
5	Ballee . .	540	0	10	Tyrone . .	Strabane Lower .	Leckpatrick . .	Strabane . .	III.	321
13, 22	Balleeghan . .	858	0	39	Donegal . .	Inishowen East .	Moville Lower .	Inishowen . .	III.	118
54	Balleeghan . .	313	1	10	Donegal . .	Raphoe . .	Raymoghy . .	Letterkenny .	III.	141
4	Balleeghan Lower .	265	2	20	Donegal . .	Inishowen East .	Clonca . .	Inishowen . .	III.	116
4, 5	Balleeghan Lower .	639	1	35e	Donegal . .	Inishowen East .	Culdaff . .	Inishowen . .	III.	118
4	Balleeghan Upper .	97	3	30	Donegal . .	Inishowen East .	Clonca . .	Inishowen . .	III.	116
4	Balleeghan Upper .	1,006	2	9	Donegal . .	Inishowen East .	Culdaff . .	Inishowen . .	III.	118
8	Balleek . .	318	2	15	King's Co. .	Ballycowen . .	Durrow . .	Tullamore . .	I.	127
9	Balleek Beg .	110	1	0	King's Co. .	Ballycowen . .	Durrow . .	Tullamore . .	I.	127
4	Balleelaghan . .	668	3	0	Donegal . .	Inishowen East .	Clonca . .	Inishowen . .	III.	116
32, 40	Balleen . .	353	2	39f	Clare . .	Islands . .	Kilmaley . .	Ennis . .	II.	30
106	Balleen . .	262	0	25	Kerry . .	Dunkerron South .	Kilcrohane . .	Cahersiveen .	II.	183
9	Balleen Little .	16	2	7	Kilkenny . .	Galmoy . .	Balleen . .	Urlingford . .	I.	91
9	Balleen Lower .	592	1	33	Kilkenny . .	Galmoy . .	Balleen . .	Urlingford . .	I.	91

(a) Including 3A. 2R. 32P. water.
(b) Including 33A. 1R. 27P. water.
(c) Including 9A. 2R. 29P. water.
(d) Including 3A. 2R. 24P. detached portions.
(e) Including 315A. 2R. 31P. detached portion.
(f) Including 1A. 3R. 29P. water.

No. of Sheet of the Ordnance Survey Maps.	Townlands and Towns.	Area in Statute Acres. A. R. P.	County.	Barony.	Parish.	Poor Law Union in 1857.	Vol.	Page
9	Balleen Upper or Baunmore	146 0 28	Kilkenny	Galmoy	Balleen	Urlingford	I.	91
16	Balleer	373 3 11	Armagh	Fews Lower	Lisnadill	Armagh	III.	46
30	Balleese Lower	222 3 15	Wicklow	Arklow	Kilcommon	Rathdrum	I.	345
30	Balleese Upper	169 2 7	Wicklow	Arklow	Kilcommon	Rathdrum	I.	345
30	Balleese Wood	134 0 32	Wicklow	Arklow	Kilcommon	Rathdrum	I.	345
34, 39	Balleeshal	256 2 35	Wicklow	Ballinacor South	Ballykine	Rathdrum	I.	348
27, 34	Balleevy	476 3 29	Down	Upper Iveagh, Up. pt.	Seapatrick	Banbridge	III.	176
31	Balleighteragh East	139 1 2	Waterford	Decies without Drum	Kilgobnet	Dungarvan	II.	357
31	Balleighteragh West	69 1 16	Waterford	Decies without Drum	Kilgobnet	Dungarvan	II.	357
27	Balleighter or Lowtown	395 0 1	Westmeath	Farbill	Killucan	Mullingar	I.	267
17, 18, 22	Ballenan	255 3 12	Armagh	Orior Lower	Loughgilly	Newry	III.	56
8, 13	Balleny	391 0 36	Antrim	Cary	Armoy	Ballycastle	III.	11
20, 21, 27, 28	Balleny	817 1 36	Down	Lower Iveagh, Lr. pt.	Dromore	Banbridge	III.	168
34	Ballestran	128 2 10	Meath	Upper Duleek	Stamullin	Drogheda	I.	198
18	Balleven	293 3 0	Kilkenny	Crannagh	Ballycallan	Kilkenny	I.	84
2	Ballew	27 0 23	Westmeath	Moygoish	Street	Granard	I.	281
8	Ballickmoyler	117 0 14	King's Co.	Kilcoursey	Kilbride	Tullamore	I.	141
32	Ballickmoyler	639 0 1	Queen's Co.	Slievemargy	Killabban	Carlow	I.	245
32	BALLICKMOYLER T.	—	Queen's Co.	Slievemargy	Killabban	Carlow	I.	245
31, 32	Ballickmoyler Upper	259 3 17	Queen's Co.	Slievemargy	Killabban	Carlow	I.	245
2, 8	Ballicknahee	328 3 33	King's Co.	Kilcoursey	Kilbride	Tullamore	I.	141
12, 18	Balliggan	303 1 12	Down	Ards Upper	Inishargy	Newtownards	III.	160
33, 37	Ballilogue	664 1 23	Kilkenny	Ida	The Rower	New Ross	I.	104
41, 42, 47	Ballin	227 0 0	Meath	Lower Moyfenrath	Rathmolyon	Trim	I.	211
37	Ballina	77 0 31	Cavan	Clanmahon	Ballymachugh	Cavan	III.	75
68	Ballina	553 3 7	Clare	Clonderalaw	Killofin	Killadysert	II.	16
82	Ballina	72 2 23	Cork, W.R.	West Muskerry	Kilmichael	Dunmanway	II.	158
17	Ballina	83 1 22a	Donegal	Kilmacrenan	Clondavaddog	Milford	III.	124
44, 58	Ballina	738 2 8	Galway	Clare	Killererin	Tuam	IV.	20
3	Ballina	839 3 0	Kildare	Carbury	Cadamstown	Edenderry	I.	51
8, 16	Ballina	955 1 17	King's Co.	Ballycowan	Rahan	Tullamore	I.	128
17, 18, 25, 26	Ballina	190 0 32	King's Co.	Geashill	Geashill	Tullamore	I.	139
22	Ballina	145 2 8	Longford	Rathcline	Cashel	Ballymahon	I.	163
26	Ballina	601 3 11b	Mayo	Erris	Kilcommon	Belmullet	IV.	143
118	Ballina	137 0 35c	Mayo	Kilmaine	Kilmainemore	Ballinrobe	IV.	155
30	Ballina	602 2 28	Mayo	Tirawley	Kilmoremoy	Ballina	IV.	170
41	Ballina	156 2 22	Meath	Upper Moyfenrath	Killyon	Trim	I.	213
12	Ballina	179 1 10	Queen's Co.	Maryborough East	Clonenagh and Clonagheen	Mountmellick	I.	241
11	Ballina	43 2 4	Queen's Co.	Upperwoods	Offerlane	Mountmellick	I.	250
47	Ballina	223 1 37	Roscommon	Athlone	Taghboy	Athlone	IV.	184
25	Ballina	270 0 39	Tipperary, N.R.	Owney and Arra	Templeachally	Nenagh	II.	297
18, 25	Ballina	261 1 25	Westmeath	Moyashel and Magheradernon	Mullingar	Mullingar	I.	275
33	Ballina	19 0 29d	Wexford	Ballaghkeen	Castle-ellis	Enniscorthy	I.	293
33	Ballina	237 1 32	Wexford	Shelmaliere East	Ardcolm	Wexford	I.	330
33	Ballina	112 2 5	Wexford	Shelmaliere East	Skreen	Wexford	I.	331
3, 7	Ballinab	253 0 34	Waterford	Upperthird	Mothel	Carrick on Suir	II.	370
45	Ballinabanoge	213 1 27	Wicklow	Arklow	Arklow	Rathdrum	I.	341
33	Ballinabarney	557 0 2	Kilkenny	Ida	The Rower	New Ross	I.	104
29	Ballinabarny	522 3 14	Wicklow	Ballinacor North	Knockrath	Rathdrum	I.	347
28	Ballinabarny	202 2 29	Wicklow	Upper Talbotstown	Donaghmore	Baltinglass	I.	362
28	Ballinabarny Gap	291 3 35	Wicklow	Upper Talbotstown	Donaghmore	Baltinglass	I.	362
30, 35	Ballinabarny North	302 0 33	Wicklow	Arklow	Castlemacadam	Rathdrum	I.	342
35	Ballinabarny South	112 3 0	Wicklow	Arklow	Castlemacadam	Rathdrum	I.	342
31, 37	Ballina or Bective	170 1 34e	Meath	Lower Deece	Balsoon	Trim	I.	191
97, 98	Ballinaboy	1,149 1 8	Cork, E.R.	Kinalea	Ballinaboy	Kinsale	II.	93
35	Ballinaboy	298 1 12f	Galway	Ballynahinch	Ballindoon	Clifden	IV.	10
40	Ballinaboy	96 1 6	Roscommon	Ballintober South	Roscommon	Roscommon	IV.	190
6, 7, 11, 12	Ballinabranagh	784 3 23g	Carlow	Idrone West	Cloydagh	Carlow	I.	9
40	Ballinabrannagh	165 1 4	Wicklow	Arklow	Kilbride	Rathdrum	I.	344
7	Ballinacarrig	313 3 5	Carlow	Carlow	Ballinacarrig	Carlow	I.	1
7	Ballinacarrig	234 3 5	Wexford	Ballaghkeen	Kiltennell	Gorey	I.	297
30, 35	Ballinacarrig Lower	306 2 3	Wicklow	Ballinacor North	Rathdrum	Rathdrum	I.	347
30, 35	Ballinacarrig Upper	316 3 13	Wicklow	Ballinacor North	Rathdrum	Rathdrum	I.	347
30, 34, 35	Ballinaclash	388 3 33	Wicklow	Ballinacor South	Ballykine	Rathdrum	I.	340
36	Ballinaclea	302 3 10	Wicklow	Arklow	Dunganstown	Rathdrum	I.	343
143	Ballinaclogh	210 2 26	Cork, W.R.	East Carbery, (W.D.)	Ross	Clonakilty	II.	135
60	Ballinaclogh	221 3 14	Tipperary, S.R.	Clanwilliam	Rathlynin	Tipperary	II.	309
60	Ballinaclogh	314 3 36	Tipperary, S.R.	Clanwilliam	Relickmurry and Athassel	Tipperary	II.	309
25, 31	Ballinaclogh	513 0 21	Wicklow	Arklow	Glenealy	Rathdrum	I.	344

(a) Including 5A. 3R. 24P. water.
(b) Including 12A. 0R. 21P. water.
(c) Including 3A. 0R. 14P. water.
(d) Including 8A. 0R. 28P. detached portion.
(e) Including 6A. 0R. 36P. water.
(f) Including 2A. 3R. 35P. water.
(g) Including 5A. 0R. 0P. River Barrow.

CENSUS OF IRELAND FOR THE YEAR 1851.

No. of Sheet of the Ordnance Survey Maps.	Townlands and Towns.	Area in Statute Acres.			County.	Barony.	Parish.	Poor Law Union in 1857.	Townland Census of 1851, Part I.	
		A.	R.	P.					Vol.	Page
24	Ballinaclogh Lower	440	2	9	Queen's Co.	Cullenagh	Fossy or Timahoe	Abbeyleix	I.	240
24	Ballinaclogh Upper	418	2	32	Queen's Co.	Cullenagh	Fossy or Timahoe	Abbeyleix	I.	240
6	Ballinacoola	399	0	21	Wexford	Gorey	Kilnahue	Gorey	I.	319
14	Ballinacoola	201	1	10	Wexford	Scarawalsh	Templeshanbo	Enniscorthy	I.	326
33	Ballinacoola Beg	81	3	35	Wexford	Shelmaliere East	Ardcolm	Wexford	I.	330
33	Ballinacoola More	140	2	7	Wexford	Shelmaliere East	Ardcolm	Wexford	I.	330
30	Ballinacooley	439	1	14	Wicklow	Newcastle	Glenealy	Rathdrum	I.	351
40	Ballinacor	200	3	0	Wicklow	Arklow	Kilbride	Rathdrum	I.	344
29	Ballinacor	2,117	2	38	Wicklow	Ballinacor South	Ballinacor	Rathdrum	I.	347
38	Ballinacor	174	2	2	Wicklow	Ballinacor South	Kilcommon	Shillelagh	I.	349
18	Ballinacorbeg	452	3	14	Wicklow	Ballinacor North	Derrylossary	Rathdrum	I.	346
17, 24	Ballinacor or Clonboy	371	0	9	Westmeath	Rathconrath	Killare	Mullingar	I.	283
31	Ballinacor East	271	1	25	Wicklow	Arklow	Dunganstown	Rathdrum	I.	343
31, 36	Ballinacor West	227	0	8	Wicklow	Arklow	Dunganstown	Rathdrum	I.	343
81	Ballinacostello	132	0	30	Mayo	Costello	Aghamore	Swineford	IV.	136
17	Ballinacrane	119	0	19	Wexford	Gorey	Kiltrisk	Gorey	I.	320
17	Ballinacrea	351	3	10	Carlow	Forth	Myshall	Carlow	I.	5
21, 27	Ballinacrow Lower	330	2	15	Wicklow	Upper Talbotstown	Rathbran	Baltinglass	I.	365
21	Ballinacrow Upper	256	3	21	Wicklow	Upper Talbotstown	Rathbran	Baltinglass	I.	365
12, 17	Ballinacur	253	3	13	Wexford	Ballaghkeen	Ardamine	Gorey	I.	291
11	Ballinacur	201	0	34	Wexford	Gorey	Liskinfere	Gorey	I.	320
111	Ballinacurra	314	2	24	Cork, E.R.	Kinsale	Clontead	Kinsale	II.	99
5	Ballinacurra (Bowman),	119	2	21a	Limerick	Pubblebrien	St. Michaels	Limerick	II.	254
5, 13	Ballinacurra (Hart)	196	3	9	Limerick	Pubblebrien	St. Michaels	Limerick	II.	254
5, 13	Ballinacurra (Weston)	290	2	23b	Limerick	Pubblebrien	St. Michaels	Limerick	II.	254
111	Ballinadee	329	0	6	Cork, W.R.	East Carbery, (E.D.)	Ballinadee	Bandon	II.	126
111	BALLINADEE T.	—			Cork, W.R.	East Carbery, (E.D.)	Ballinadee	Bandon	II.	126
13	Ballinadrum	335	3	0	Carlow	Forth	Fennagh	Carlow	I.	4
16, 17	Ballinadrummin	229	3	30	Wexford	Gorey	Monamolin	Gorey	I.	321
37, 51	Ballinafad	871	1	1c	Galway	Ballynahinch	Moyrus	Clifden	IV.	12
90	Ballinafad	306	2	12	Mayo	Carra	Drum	Castlebar	IV.	127
29	Ballinafad	272	2	36	Roscommon	Roscommon	Cloontinlough	Strokestown	IV.	208
40	Ballinafad	124	1	32	Sligo	Tirerrill	Aghanagh	Boyle	IV.	237
40	BALLINAFAD T.	—			Sligo	Tirerrill	Aghanagh	Boyle	IV.	237
23	Ballinafunshoge	678	2	17	Wicklow	Ballinacor North	Knockrath	Rathdrum	I.	347
12, 18	Ballinafunshoge or Ashtown	855	1	39	Wicklow	Ballinacor North	Derrylossary	Rathdrum	I.	346
17	Ballinagam Lower	191	0	25	Wexford	Ballaghkeen	Donaghmore	Gorey	I.	293
17	Ballinagam Upper	158	3	3	Wexford	Ballaghkeen	Donaghmore	Gorey	I.	293
29, 34	Ballinagappoge	656	2	5	Wicklow	Ballinacor South	Ballinacor	Rathdrum	I.	347
18	Ballinagar	362	2	23	King's Co.	Geashill	Geashill	Tullamore	I.	139
39, 41	Ballinagard	404	2	6	Roscommon	Ballintober South	Roscommon	Roscommon	IV.	190
18	BALLINAGAR T.	—			King's Co.	Geashill	Geashill	Tullamore	I.	140
21	Ballinagavna	109	2	26	Mayo	Tirawley	Kilfian	Killala	IV.	169
11, 16, 17	Ballinagee	2,934	2	4	Wicklow	Lower Talbotstown	Boystown	Naas	I.	359
7	Ballinagee	258	1	36	Wicklow	Rathdown	Powerscourt	Rathdown	I.	356
12	Ballinageeloge	170	0	10	Wexford	Ballaghkeen	Ardamine	Gorey	I.	291
10	Ballinagilky	331	3	6	Carlow	Rathvilly	Clonmore	Shillelagh	I.	10
22, 23	Ballinagoneen	940	0	28	Wicklow	Ballinacor North	Knockrath	Rathdrum	I.	347
20	Ballinagore	71	2	32	Tipperary, N.R.	Owney and Arra	Youghalarra	Nenagh	II.	297
39	Ballinagore	290	1	35	Wicklow	Arklow	Ballintemple	Rathdrum	I.	342
79	Ballinagran	334	1	8d	Mayo	Clanmorris	Balla	Castlebar	IV.	131
12	Ballinagrann Lower	211	2	29	Wexford	Ballaghkeen	Ardamine	Gorey	I.	291
12	Ballinagrann Upper	259	1	25	Wexford	Ballaghkeen	Ardamine	Gorey	I.	291
6, 9	Ballinagross	236	0	20e	Tipperary, N.R.	Lower Ormond	Kilbarron	Borrisokane	II.	284
45	Ballinagroun	182	0	30	Kerry	Corkaguiny	Ballinvoher	Dingle	II.	173
28	Ballinaha	118	2	35	Waterford	Cushmore and Coshbride	Tallow	Lismore	II.	348
40	Ballinaheese	86	1	8	Wicklow	Arklow	Kilbride	Rathdrum	I.	344
15, 21	Ballinahemery	58	0	18	Tipperary, N.R.	Upper Ormond	Ballymackey	Nenagh	II.	289
12, 18	Ballinahinch	194	2	7	Wicklow	Newcastle	Calary	Rathdrum	I.	350
25	Ballinahinch	227	0	15	Wicklow	Newcastle	Killiskey	Rathdrum	I.	352
13, 19	Ballinahinch Lower	178	0	39	Wicklow	Newcastle	Newcastle Upper	Rathdrum	I.	353
12, 13, 18, 19	Ballinahinch Middle	360	3	8	Wicklow	Newcastle	Newcastle Upper	Rathdrum	I.	353
12, 18	Ballinahinch Upper	736	2	32	Wicklow	Newcastle	Newcastle Upper	Rathdrum	I.	353
12	Ballinahorna	153	0	36	Wexford	Ballaghkeen	Killenagh	Gorey	I.	295
10	Ballinahown	709	1	25	Wicklow	Lower Talbotstown	Boystown	Naas	I.	359
30	Ballinakill	174	0	9	Queen's Co.	Cullenagh	Dysartgallen	Abbeyleix	I.	239
12	Ballinakill	215	1	0	Wexford	Ballaghkeen	Ardamine	Gorey	I.	291
16, 17	Ballinakill	96	2	25	Wexford	Gorey	Ballycanew	Gorey	I.	315
40	Ballinakill	319	2	19	Wicklow	Arklow	Kilbride	Rathdrum	I.	344
30	Ballinakill	826	1	31	Wicklow	Newcastle	Kilcommon	Rathdrum	I.	351

(a) Within the Municipal Boundary, 90A. 3R. 30P.
Without the Municipal Boundary, 28A. 2R. 31P.

(b) Within the Municipal Boundary, 82A. 2R. 5P.
Without the Municipal Boundary, 208A. 0R. 18P.

(c) Including 149A. 1R. 12P. water.
(d) Including 49A. 0R. 34P. water.
(e) Including 10A. 1R. 16P. water.

No. of Sheet of the Ordnance Survey Maps.	Townlands and Towns.	Area in Statute Acres.			County.	Barony.	Parish.	Poor Law Union in 1857.	Townland Census of 1851, Part I.	
		A.	R.	P.					Vol.	Page
30	BALLINAKILL T.	—			Queen's Co.	Cullenagh	Dysartgallen	Abbeyleix	I.	239
6, 11	Ballinalack	151	0	17a	Westmeath	Corkaree	Leny	Mullingar	I.	262
6	BALLINALACK T.	—			Westmeath	Corkaree	Leny	Mullingar	I.	263
25	Ballinalea	128	1	33	Wicklow	Newcastle	Rathnew	Rathdrum	I.	354
48	Ballinaleama	121	1	11	Galway	Ballynahinch	Ballindoon	Clifden	IV.	10
25	BALLINALEA T.	—			Wicklow	Newcastle	Rathnew	Rathdrum	I.	354
89	Ballinalecka	87	2	0	Mayo	Carra	Ballintober	Castlebar	IV.	124
9	Ballinalee or Saint-johnstown	161	3	10	Longford	Granard	Clonbroney	Granard	I.	154
9	BALLINALEE T.	—			Longford	Granard	Clonbroney	Granard	I.	155
11, 19	Ballinaleucra	111	1	11	Waterford	Coshmore and Coshbride	Lismore and Mocollop	Lismore	II.	344
33	Ballina Lower	96	2	4	Wexford	Ballaghkeen	Ballyvalloo	Enniscorthy	I.	292
26	Ballina Lower	342	0	25	Wexford	Ballaghkeen	Kilmallock	Enniscorthy	I.	296
44, 53	Ballinaltig	316	2	37	Cork, E.R.	Barrymore	Kilshanahan	Fermoy	II.	56
24	Ballinaltig	205	0	13	Cork, E.R.	Orrery and Kilmore	Ballyclough	Kanturk	II.	106
26	Ballinaltig Beg	159	1	4	Cork, E.R.	Fermoy	Castletownroche	Fermoy	II.	77
31	Ballinameesda Lower	224	2	18	Wicklow	Arklow	Dunganstown	Rathdrum	I.	343
31	BALLINAMEESDA T.	—			Wicklow	Arklow	Dunganstown	Rathdrum	I.	344
31	Ballinameesda Upper	204	2	12	Wicklow	Arklow	Dunganstown	Rathdrum	I.	343
2	Ballinaminton East	348	3	24	King's Co.	Kilcoursey	Kilmanaghan	Tullamore	I.	141
2	Ballinaminton West	136	0	21	King's Co.	Kilcoursey	Kilmanaghan	Tullamore	I.	141
38	Ballinamoe	271	0	7	King's Co.	Clonlisk	Kilmurrycly	Roscrea	I.	131
20	Ballinamoe	67	3	31	Tipperary, N.R.	Owney and Arra	Youghalarra	Nenagh	II.	297
21, 27	Ballinamona	439	3	16	Tipperary, N.R.	Upper Ormond	Kilkeary	Nenagh	II.	290
60	Ballinamona	177	1	7	Tipperary, S.R.	Kilnamanagh Lower	Oughterleague	Cashel	II.	324
60	Ballinamona	332	0	30	Tipperary, S.R.	Middlethird	Horeabbey	Cashel	II.	327
17	Ballinamona	348	0	1	Waterford	Gaultiere	Kilbarry	Waterford	II.	363
11, 12	Ballinamona	279	0	3	Wexford	Gorey	Ballycanew	Gorey	I.	315
11	Ballinamona	327	2	4	Wexford	Gorey	Toome	Gorey	I.	321
40	Ballinamona	331	1	29	Wicklow	Arklow	Castlemacadam	Rathdrum	I.	342
22	Ballinamona or Ballyellin	143	3	24	Carlow	Idrone East	Kiltennell	New Ross	I.	7
18	Ballinamore	240	0	35	Longford	Moydow	Ballymacormick	Longford	I.	160
80, 91	Ballinamore	1,276	1	16b	Mayo	Gallen	Killedan	Swineford	IV.	149
77,78,83,84	Ballinamore	312	3	39	Tipperary, S.R.	Iffa and Offa East	Kilsheelan	Clonmel	II.	314
25	BALLINAMORE T.	—			Leitrim	Carrigallen	Oughteragh	Fawnboy	IV.	93
33, 38	Ballinamorragh	155	3	4	Wexford	Shelmaliere East	Ardcolm	Wexford	I.	330
74	Ballinamought East	242	1	6c	Cork, E.R.	Cork	St. Annes Shandon	Cork	II.	65
74	Ballinamought West	209	3	14	Cork, E.R.	Municipal Borough of Cork	St. Annes Shandon	Cork	II.	65
28	Ballinanchor	118	1	27	Waterford	Coshmore and Coshbride	Lismore and Mocollop	Lismore	II.	344
48	Ballinanima (Brew)	203	0	20	Limerick	Coshlea	Kilfinnane	Kilmallock	II.	239
48	Ballinanima (D'Arcy)	378	3	26	Limerick	Coshlea	Kilfinnane	Kilmallock	II.	239
48	Ballinanima (Massy)	178	3	38	Limerick	Coshlea	Kilfinnane	Kilmallock	II.	239
29	Ballinanty	69	1	9	Wicklow	Ballinacor South	Ballinacor	Rathdrum	I.	347
9	Ballinapark	308	3	37d	Wexford	Scarawalsh	Kilrush	Enniscorthy	I.	324
35, 40	Ballinapark	147	2	35	Wicklow	Arklow	Castlemacadam	Rathdrum	I.	342
25	Ballinapark	310	3	0	Wicklow	Newcastle	Rathnew	Rathdrum	I.	354
6	Ballinapeaka	109	1	15	Galway	Ballymoe	Boyounagh	Glennamaddy	IV.	6
109, 122	Ballinard	589	3	1	Cork, W.R.	East Carbery (E.D.)	Desertserges	Clonakilty	II.	127
150	Ballinard	230	1	7	Cork, W.R.	West Carbery (E.D.)	Tullagh	Skibbereen	II.	141
31,32,40,41	Ballinard	1,048	2	28	Kerry	Trughanacmy	Ballincuslane	Tralee	II.	206
32	Ballinard	505	2	33	Limerick	Smallcounty	Ballinard	Kilmallock	II.	259
59, 60	Ballinard	209	2	32	Tipperary, S.R.	Clanwilliam	Rathlynin	Tipperary	II.	309
58, 66	Ballinard	254	3	14	Tipperary, S.R.	Clanwilliam	Shronell	Tipperary	II.	310
62, 70, 71	Ballinard	442	2	25	Tipperary, S.R.	Middlethird	Cloneen	Cashel	II.	325
21, 22	Ballinard	328	1	37	Wicklow	Upper Talbotstown	Donaghmore	Baltinglass	I.	362
38	Ballinarry	336	0	37	Down	Lecale Lower	Saul	Downpatrick	III.	179
122	BALLINASCARTY T.	—			Cork, W.R.	East Carbery (E.D.)	Kilmaloda	Clonakilty	II.	129
24	Ballinascorney Lower	177	1	7	Dublin	Uppercross	Tallaght	Dublin South	I.	41
24	Ballinascorney Upper	2,275	3	8	Dublin	Uppercross	Tallaght	Dublin South	I.	41
12, 13	Ballinashinnagh	172	1	32	Wicklow	Newcastle	Calary	Rathdrum	I.	350
43	Ballinasig	506	1	35	Kerry	Corkaguiny	Dingle	Dingle	II.	175
16	Ballinasilloge	82	0	0	Wexford	Gorey	Monamolin	Gorey	I.	321
39, 40	Ballinasilloge	387	2	32	Wicklow	Arklow	Ballintemple	Rathdrum	I.	342
33	Ballinasilloge	286	3	28	Wicklow	Ballinacor South	Hacketstown	Shillelagh	I.	348
41	Ballinaskea	478	2	22	Wicklow	Arklow	Ennereilly	Rathdrum	I.	344
22, 23	Ballinaskea	1,186	1	12e	Wicklow	Ballinacor South	Ballinacor	Rathdrum	I.	348
87, 88 } 53 }	BALLINASLOE T.	—			Galway Roscommon	Clonmacnowen Moycarn	Kilcloony Creagh }	Ballinasloe	IV.	25 206
12	Ballinasoostia	121	1	20	Wicklow	Newcastle	Calary	Rathdrum	I.	350
24, 31	Ballinaspick, or Bishopstown	1,572	3	6	Westmeath	Rathconrath	Killare	Mullingar	I.	283

(a) Including 10A. 2R. 16P. water.
(b) Including 9A. 0R. 6P. water.
(c) Within the Municipal Boundary, 236A. 2R. 28P.
  Without the Municipal Boundary, 5A. 2R. 18P.
(d) Including 4A. 3R. 34P. water.
(e) Including 6A. 3R. 20P. Arts Lough.

No. of Sheet of the Ordnance Survey Maps.	Townlands and Towns.	Area in Statute Acres.	County.	Barony.	Parish.	Poor Law Union in 1857.	Townland Census of 1851, Part I.	
		A. R. P.					Vol.	Page
28, 29	Ballinaspick North .	480 0 28	Waterford .	Coshmore and Coshbride . .	Lismore and Mocollop	Lismore . .	II.	344
28, 29	Ballinaspick South .	359 2 19a	Waterford .	Coshmore and Coshbride . .	Lismore and Mocollop	Lismore . .	II.	344
74	Ballinaspig Beg .	234 0 25	Cork, E.R. .	Cork . .	St. Finbars . .	Cork . .	II.	65
73, 74, 85	Ballinaspig More .	919 0 14	Cork, E.R. .	Cork . .	St. Finbars . .	Cork . .	II.	65
6	Ballinastack .	294 1 16	Galway .	Ballymoe . .	Boyounagh .	Glennamaddy .	IV.	6
90, 100	Ballinaster . .	153 3 29	Mayo .	Clanmorris .	Mayo . .	Claremorris .	IV.	135
6, 7, 11, 12	Ballinastoe . .	6,602 2 12b	Wicklow .	Ballinacor North .	Calary . .	Rathdrum .	I.	346
13, 14	Ballinastraw . .	300 1 35	Carlow .	Forth . .	Ardoyne . .	Carlow . .	I.	3
35, 40	Ballinastraw . .	159 1 37	Wicklow .	Arklow . .	Castlemacadam .	Rathdrum .	I.	342
24, 30	Ballinastraw . .	233 1 26	Wicklow .	Newcastle .	Kilcommon .	Rathdrum .	I.	351
16	Ballinastraw Lower	362 0 33	Wexford .	Gorey . .	Monamolin .	Gorey . .	I.	321
16	Ballinastraw Upper	340 2 20	Wexford .	Gorey . .	Monamolin .	Gorey . .	I.	321
17	Ballinastudd .	204 2 31	Wexford .	Gorey . .	Kiltrisk . .	Gorey . .	I.	320
142	Ballinatona . .	140 0 28c	Cork, W.R. .	West Carbery (E.D.)	Myross . .	Skibbereen .	II.	140
29, 30	Ballinatone Lower .	164 2 31	Wicklow .	Ballinacor South .	Ballinacor .	Rathdrum .	I.	348
29	Ballinatone Upper .	215 2 39	Wicklow .	Ballinacor South .	Ballinacor .	Rathdrum .	I.	348
30	BALLINA T. . .	—	Mayo .	Tirawley . .	Kilcremoy . .	Ballina . .	IV.	170
25	BALLINA T. . .	—	Tipperary, N.R.	Owney and Arra .	Templeachally .	Nenagh . .	II.	297
12	Ballinatray Lower .	257 2 28	Wexford .	Ballaghkeen .	Ardamine . .	Gorey . .	I.	291
12	Ballinatray Upper .	138 1 30	Wexford .	Ballaghkeen .	Ardamine . .	Gorey . .	I.	291
26	Ballinattin . .	297 0 32	Waterford .	Middlethird .	Drumcannon .	Waterford .	II.	366
69, 76	Ballinattin Lower .	238 2 29	Tipperary, S.R.	Middlethird .	Mora . .	Cashel . .	II.	329
69, 76	Ballinattin Upper .	306 1 29	Tipperary, S.R.	Middlethird .	Mora . .	Cashel . .	II.	329
33	Ballina Upper .	302 3 39	Wexford .	Ballaghkeen .	Ballyvalloo .	Enniscorthy .	I.	292
33	Ballina Upper .	20 2 38	Wexford .	Ballaghkeen .	Castle-ellis .	Enniscorthy .	I.	293
26, 27	Ballina Upper . .	214 2 0	Wexford .	Ballaghkeen .	Kilmallock .	Enniscorthy .	I.	296
25, 31	Ballinavary . .	680 3 11	Wexford .	Bantry . .	Clonmore .	Enniscorthy .	I.	300
118	Ballinaya . .	233 0 22	Mayo .	Kilmaine .	Ballinrobe .	Ballinrobe .	IV.	152
88	Ballinbeg . .	96 0 17	Cork, E.R. .	Imokilly . .	Aghada . .	Middleton .	II.	83
9	Ballinbranhig .	301 2 37	Kerry .	Clanmorris .	Rattoo . .	Listowel .	II.	173
64, 75	Ballinbrittig .	924 1 38	Cork, E.R. .	Barrymore .	Carrigtohill .	Middleton .	II.	52
8, 9	Ballinbrocky and Ballincrick .	449 0 33d	Donegal .	Kilmacrenan .	Clondavaddog .	Millford .	III.	124
8, 14	Ballincar . .	387 1 11	Sligo .	Carbury . .	Drumcliff .	Sligo . .	IV.	220
55	Ballincarroona .	96 1 20	Limerick .	Coshlea . .	Effin . .	Kilmallock .	II.	238
55	Ballincarroona .	63 1 3	Limerick .	Coshlea . .	Kilquane .	Kilmallock .	II.	240
40, 41	Ballincarroona .	610 3 8	Limerick .	Smallcounty .	Kilfrush . .	Kilmallock .	II.	260
88	Ballincarroonig .	244 0 25	Cork, E.R. .	Imokilly . .	Aghada . .	Middleton .	II.	83
21	Ballincash Lower	302 0 23	Wexford .	Ballaghkeen .	Kilcormick .	Enniscorthy .	I.	294
20, 21	Ballincash Upper .	486 2 39	Wexford .	Ballaghkeen .	Kilcormick .	Enniscorthy .	I.	294
24	Ballincassa .	67 2 30	Limerick .	Coonagh . .	Grean . .	Tipperary .	II.	235
2	Ballincastle . .	141 0 31	Sligo .	Carbury . .	Ahamlish .	Sligo . .	IV.	219
117	Ballinchalla .	365 0 29	Mayo .	Kilmaine .	Ballinchalla .	Ballinrobe .	IV.	151
44	Ballinclare . .	65 3 5	Kerry .	Corkaguiny .	Ballynacourty .	Dingle . .	II.	174
40,41,43,44	Ballinclare . .	324 3 24	Kilkenny .	Ida . .	Kilcolumb .	Waterford .	I.	102
6, 11	Ballinclare . .	57 1 18	Louth .	Upper Dundalk .	Louth . .	Dundalk .	I.	179
16	Ballinclare . .	241 1 18	Wexford .	Gorey . .	Ballycanew .	Gorey . .	I.	315
11	Ballinclare . .	402 3 30	Wexford .	Gorey . .	Toome . .	Gorey . .	I.	321
30, 31	Ballinclare . .	182 2 18	Wicklow .	Arklow . .	Dunganstown .	Rathdrum .	I.	343
11	Ballinclay . .	137 0 9	Wexford .	Gorey . .	Liskinfere .	Gorey . .	I.	320
31	Ballinclay Lower .	212 0 26	Wexford .	Bantry . .	Whitechurchglynn .	Wexford .	I.	303
31, 36	Ballinclay Upper .	291 3 25	Wexford .	Bantry . .	Whitechurchglynn .	Wexford .	I.	303
23	Ballinclea . .	72 2 33	Dublin .	Rathdown .	Kill . .	Rathdown .	I.	35
40, 41	Ballinclea . .	356 3 23	Wicklow .	Arklow . .	Kilbride . .	Rathdrum .	I.	344
21, 22	Ballinclea . .	310 3 21	Wicklow .	Upper Talbotstown	Donaghmore .	Baltinglass .	I.	362
14	Ballinclemesig .	289 1 18	Kerry .	Clanmaurice .	Ballyheige .	Tralee .	II.	167
14, 15	Ballinclemesig .	384 2 12	Kerry .	Clanmaurice .	Killury . .	Listowel .	II.	170
31	Ballincloghan .	239 2 2	King's Co. .	Ballyboy . .	Ballyboy . .	Parsonstown .	I.	123
16	Ballincloghan .	203 0 15	King's Co. .	Ballycowan .	Rahan . .	Tullamore .	I.	128
31	Ballincloghan Little	105 1 38	King's Co. .	Ballyboy . .	Ballyboy . .	Parsonstown .	I.	123
15	Ballincloher .	361 3 39	Kerry .	Clanmaurice .	Kilcaragh .	Listowel .	II.	169
15	Ballincloher East	291 0 33	Kerry .	Clanmaurice .	Kiltomy . .	Listowel .	II.	172
15	Ballincloher West	175 2 39	Kerry .	Clanmaurice .	Kiltomy . .	Listowel .	II.	172
142	Ballincolla . .	352 2 36	Cork, W.R. .	West Carbery (E.D.)	Myross . .	Skibbereen .	II.	141
42	Ballincolla . .	393 0 25	Kerry .	Corkaguiny .	Dunurlin .	Dingle . .	II.	176
73	Ballincollig .	746 0 22e	Cork, E.R. .	East Muskerry .	Carrigrohane .	Cork . .	II.	102
73	Ballincollig .	24 3 4	Cork, E.R. .	East Muskerry .	Kilnaglory .	Cork . .	II.	104
22, 30	Ballincollig .	626 0 13	Kerry .	Trughanacmy .	Obrennan .	Tralee .	II.	212
73	BALLINCOLLIG T. .	—	Cork, E.R. .	East Muskerry .	Carrigrohane .	Cork . .	II.	102
40	Ballincolloo .	387 2 24	Limerick .	Smallcounty .	Uregare . .	Kilmallock .	II.	261
136	Ballincollop .	95 3 19	Cork, W.R. .	Ibane and Barryroe .	Lislee . .	Clonakilty .	II.	149

(a) Including 5A. 0R. 32P. detached portion.　　(c) Including 10A. 0R. 11P. water.　　(e) Including 5A. 1R. 27P. water.
(b) Including 66A. 0R. 4P. Lough Tay.　　(d) Including 40A. 3R. 24P. water.

No. of Sheet of the Ordnance Survey Maps.	Townlands and Towns.	Area in Statute Acres.		County.	Barony.	Parish.	Poor Law Union in 1857.	Townland Census of 1851, Part I.	
		A.	R. P.					Vol.	Page
63, 74	Ballincolly . .	257	0 11	Cork, E.R. .	Cork . . .	St. Annes Shandon .	Cork . .	II.	65
47	Ballincolly . .	312	3 37	Limerick . .	Coshma . .	Hackmys . .	Kilmallock .	II.	243
15, 21	Ballincool . .	118	3 31	Roscommon .	Castlereagh .	Kilcorkey . .	Castlereagh .	IV.	199
4	Ballincor . .	194	0 0	Tipperary, N.R.	Lower Ormond .	Lorrha . .	Parsonstown .	II.	285
77	Ballincor . .	192	2 12	Tipperary, S.R.	Middlethird .	Colman . .	Cashel . .	II.	325
38, 42	Ballincor Demesne .	530	1 34	King's Co. .	Clonlisk . .	Kilmurryely .	Roscrea . .	I.	131
52	Ballincota . .	137	3 8	Kerry . .	Corkaguiny .	Ventry . .	Dingle . .	II.	180
136	Ballincourcey .	194	3 20	Cork, W.R. .	Ibane and Barry-roe	Templequinlan .	Clonakilty .	II.	151
77	Ballincourlea . .	144	3 3	Cork, E.R. .	Imokilly . .	Ightermurragh .	Middleton .	II.	87
84, 85	Ballincourneenig	385	0 25	Cork, E.R. .	East Muskerry .	Knockavilly .	Bandon . .	II.	104
16	Ballincraheen . .	215	2 0	Kerry . .	Clanmaurice .	Kiltomy . .	Listowel .	II.	172
48	Ballincrana . .	172	1 33	Limerick . .	Coshlea . .	Particles . .	Kilmallock .	II.	240
86	Ballincranig . .	363	2 25	Cork, E.R. .	Cork . . .	Ballinaboy .	Cork . .	II.	63
40, 43	Ballincrea . .	590	1 34g	Kilkenny . .	Ida . . .	Kilcolumb .	Waterford .	I.	102
43	BALLINCREA T. .	—		Kilkenny . .	Ida . . .	Kilcolumb .	Waterford .	I.	103
8, 9	Ballincrick and Bal-linbrocky . .	449	0 33b	Donegal . .	Kilmacrenan .	Clondavaddog .	Milford .	III.	124
63	Ballincrokig . .	168	3 11	Cork, E.R. .	Cork . . .	Rathcooney .	Cork . .	II.	65
63	Ballincrokig . .	111	3 35	Cork, E.R. .	Cork . . .	St. Annes Shandon .	Cork . .	II.	65
63, 64, 74	Ballincrossig . .	217	2 28	Cork, E.R. .	Cork . . .	Rathcooney .	Cork . .	II.	65
15	Ballincrossig . .	292	3 36	Kerry . .	Clanmaurice .	Rattoo . .	Listowel .	II.	173
39	Ballinculloo . .	207	2 8	Limerick . .	Coshma . .	Athlacca . .	Kilmallock .	II.	241
36	Ballincur . .	331	2 18	King's Co. .	Ballybritt .	Kinnitty . .	Parsonstown .	I.	125
16	Ballincur . .	339	0 36	King's Co. .	Ballycowan .	Rahan . .	Tullamore .	I.	128
26	Ballincur . .	174	2 16	Tipperary, N.R.	Upper Ormond .	Kilmore . .	Nenagh . .	II.	290
42	Ballincurra . .	59	2 32	Kilkenny . .	Iverk . .	Rathkieran .	Waterford .	I.	106
20	Ballincurra . .	285	3 19	Limerick . .	Connello Lower .	Croagh . .	Rathkeale .	II.	227
48	Ballincurra . .	163	0 0	Limerick . .	Coshlea . .	Kilbreedy Major .	Kilmallock .	II.	239
39	Ballincurra . .	412	1 12	Limerick . .	Coshma . .	Athlacca . .	Kilmallock .	II.	241
52	Ballincurra . .	310	0 5	Limerick . .	Smallcounty .	Ballynamona .	Kilmallock .	II.	259
27, 33	Ballincurra . .	399	1 33	Tipperary, N.R.	Upper Ormond .	Kilnaneave .	Nenagh . .	II.	291
17	Ballincurra . .	201	1 22	Westmeath .	Rathconrath .	Piercetown .	Ballymahon .	I.	283
43	Ballincurragh . .	158	0 24	Kilkenny . .	Ida . . .	Gaulskill . .	Waterford .	I.	102
42	Ballincurra North .	100	0 0	Kilkenny . .	Iverk . .	Arderra . .	Waterford .	I.	105
42	Ballincurra South .	93	1 11	Kilkenny . .	Iverk . .	Arderra . .	Waterford .	I.	105
54, 65	Ballincurrig . .	418	0 15	Cork, E.R. .	Barrymore .	Templebodan .	Middleton .	II.	58
74	Ballincurrig . .	306	1 19	Cork, E.R. .	Cork . . .	St. Finbars .	Cork . .	II.	65
34	Ballincurrig . .	417	1 30c	Cork, E.R. .	Fermoy . .	Monanimy .	Mallow . .	II.	81
88	Ballincurrig . .	200	2 27	Cork, E.R. .	Imokilly . .	Titeskin . .	Middleton .	II.	90
16	Ballincurrig . .	327	2 12	Cork, E.R. .	Orrery and Kilmore	Kilbroney .	Mallow . .	II.	109
124	Ballincurrig . .	281	0 30	Cork, W.R. .	Courceys . .	Ringrone . .	Kinsale . .	II.	147
136	Ballincurrig . .	128	1 25	Cork, W.R. .	Ibane and Barryroe	Lislee . .	Clonakilty .	II.	149
55	Ballincurry . .	260	1 37	Down . .	Upper Iveagh, Upper part	Kilbroney .	Kilkeel . .	III.	175
7	Ballincurry . .	633	0 5d	Galway . .	Ballymoe . .	Ballynakill .	Glennamaddy .	IV.	5
8, 9	Ballincurry . .	159	0 22	Longford . .	Longford . .	Killoe . .	Longford . .	I.	158
36	Ballincurry . .	192	1 19	Roscommon .	Ballintober South .	Kilgefin . .	Roscommon .	IV.	189
37,38,42,43	Ballincurry . .	985	1 35	Sligo . .	Leyny . .	Achonry . .	Tobercurry .	IV.	228
27	Ballincurry . .	119	2 30	Tipperary, N.R.	Upper Ormond .	Kilkenry . .	Nenagh . .	II.	290
54, 55	Ballincurry . .	420	3 25	Tipperary, S.R.	Slievardagh .	Crohane . .	Callan . .	II.	332
55	Ballincurry Upper .	52	3 38	Down . .	Upper Iveagh, Upper part	Kilbroney .	Kilkeel . .	III.	175
14	Ballindaggan . .	431	0 2	Wexford . .	Scarawalsh .	Templeshaubo .	Enniscorthy .	I.	326
14,15,19,20	Ballindagny and Cul-lyvore . .	291	2 12	Longford . .	Ardagh . .	Mostrim . .	Granard . .	I.	152
39	Ballindall . .	242	0 38	Roscommon .	Ballintober South .	Roscommon .	Roscommon .	IV.	190
15	Ballindam . .	41	3 31	Antrim . .	Cary . .	Culfeightrin .	Ballycastle .	III.	13
19	Ballindangan . .	662	3 13	Cork, E.R. .	Fermoy . .	Ballydeloughy .	Mitchelstown .	II.	76
35	Ballindarra . .	185	0 4	King's Co. .	Ballybritt .	Birr . .	Parsonstown .	I.	125
17	Ballindarragh . .	331	0 31	Armagh . .	Fews Lower .	Kilclooney .	Armagh . .	III.	46
113	Ballindeasig . .	464	0 18	Cork, E.R. .	Kinalea . .	Ballyfoyle .	Kinsale . .	II.	94
113	Ballindeasig . .	198	0 30	Cork, E.R. .	Kinalea . .	Nohaval . .	Kinsale . .	II.	96
52, 53, 63	Ballindeenisk . .	645	0 3	Cork, E.R. .	Barrymore .	Templeusque .	Cork . .	II.	59
112	Ballindeenisk . .	416	1 1	Cork, E.R. .	Kinalea . .	Kilmonoge .	Kinsale . .	II.	95
101, 111	Ballindell East .	81	1 5	Mayo . .	Clanmorris .	Crossboyne .	Claremorris .	IV.	132
111	Ballindell West .	49	3 25	Mayo . .	Clanmorris .	Crossboyne .	Claremorris .	IV.	132
103	Ballinderreen .	106	3 9	Galway . .	Dunkellin .	Drumacoo .	Gort . .	IV.	28
48	Ballinderrin . .	336	3 33e	Meath . .	Lower Moyfenrath .	Rathcore . .	Trim . .	I.	211
62, 63	Ballinderry . .	1,182	0 36f	Antrim . .	Upper Massereene .	Ballinderry .	Lurgan . .	III.	29
43	Ballinderry . .	544	1 17g	Galway . .	Clare . .	Cummer . .	Tuam . .	IV.	18
86	Ballinderry . .	496	2 37	Galway . .	Kilconnell .	Kilconnell .	Ballinasloe .	IV.	40
3	Ballinderry . .	593	1 1	Kildare . .	Carbury . .	Mylerstown .	Edenderry .	I.	52
49	Ballinderry . .	314	2 23	Londonderry .	Loughinsholin .	Ballinderry .	Magherafelt .	III.	239

(a) Including 11A. 0R. 16P. water.
(b) Including 40A. 3R. 24P. water.
(c) Including 10A. 1R. 29P. water.
(d) Including 10A. 1R. 24P. water.
(e) Including 24A. 1R. 19P. detached portion.
(f) Including 114A. 1R. 14P. Portmore Lough.
(g) Including 2A. 2R. 0P. water.

No. of Sheet of the Ordnance Survey Maps.	Townlands and Towns.	Area in Statute Acres.	County.	Barony.	Parish.	Poor Law Union in 1857.	Townland Census of 1851, Part I.	
		A. R. P.					Vol.	Page
36, 41	Ballinderry . .	390 3 39	Londonderry .	Loughinsholin .	Kilcronaghan . .	Magherafelt .	III.	241
47, 48	Ballinderry . .	491 2 13	Meath . .	Lower Moyfenrath .	Rathcore . .	Trim . .	I.	211
41	Ballinderry . .	239 3 18	Meath . .	Upper Moyfenrath .	Castlerickard . .	Trim . .	I.	213
35, 36	Ballinderry . .	1,411 2 26	Roscommon .	Ballintober South .	Kilbride . .	Roscommon .	II.	188
10	Ballinderry . .	318 0 8	Tipperary, N.R.	Lower Ormond .	Ardcrony . .	Borrisokane .	II.	281
6	Ballinderry . .	25 3 19	Tipperary, N.R.	Lower Ormond .	Finnoe . .	Borrisokane .	II.	283
6	Ballinderry . .	813 0 10	Tipperary, N.R.	Lower Ormond .	Kilbarron . .	Borrisokane .	II.	284
84, 85	Ballinderry . .	295 1 22a	Tipperary, S.R.	Iffa and Offa East .	Carrick . .	Carrick on Suir	II.	312
30, 31	Ballinderry . .	989 1 12b	Westmeath .	Clonlonan . .	Kilcumreragh .	Athlone . .	I.	262
19, 26	Ballinderry . .	452 2 33	Westmeath .	Moyashel and Ma-gheradernon .	Mullingar .	Mullingar .	I.	275
38	Ballinderry Big .	476 1 16	Westmeath .	Moycashel .	Kilbeggan .	Tullamore .	I.	278
37, 38	Ballinderry Little .	241 0 6	Westmeath .	Moycashel .	Kilbeggan .	Tullamore .	I.	278
30	Ballinderry Lower .	231 1 11	Wicklow . .	Ballinacor North .	Rathdrum .	Rathdrum .	I.	347
29, 30	Ballinderry Upper .	326 2 0	Wicklow . .	Ballinacor North .	Rathdrum .	Rathdrum .	I.	347
27	Ballindigny . .	95 1 13	Tipperary, N.R.	Upper Ormond .	Kilnaneave .	Nenagh . .	II.	291
7, 16	Ballindillanig .	326 2 35	Cork. E.R. .	Orrery and Kilmore	Churchtown .	Mallow . .	II.	107
37	Ballindinas . .	265 3 13	Wexford . .	Shelmaliere West .	Carrick . .	Wexford .	I.	332
112	Ballindine East .	127 2 14	Mayo . .	Clanmorris .	Crossboyne .	Claremorris .	IV.	132
111, 112	Ballindine North .	77 0 26	Mayo . .	Clanmorris .	Crossboyne .	Claremorris .	IV.	132
111, 112	BALLINDINE T. .	—	Mayo . .	Clanmorris .	Crossboyne .	Claremorris .	IV.	133
112	Ballindine West .	90 3 10	Mayo . .	Clanmorris .	Crossboyne .	Claremorris .	IV.	132
66, 77	Ballindinis . .	37 3 24	Cork, E.R. .	Imokilly . .	Ightermurragh .	Middleton .	II.	87
77	Ballindinis . .	2 1 33	Cork, E.R. .	Imokilly . .	Killeagh .	Middleton .	II.	88
66, 77	Ballindinis . .	110 0 10	Cork, E.R. .	Imokilly . .	Mogeely . .	Middleton .	II.	89
55	Ballindoalty .	212 0 34	Down . .	Upper Iveagh, Up.pt.	Kilbroney .	Kilkeel .	III.	175
55	Ballindoalty Upper .	78 0 18	Down . .	Upper Iveagh, Up.pt.	Kilbroney .	Kilkeel .	III.	175
21	Ballindollaghan (Crump) .	428 1 11	Roscommon .	Castlereagh .	Baslick . .	Castlereagh .	IV.	199
21	Ballindollaghan (Knox) .	298 1 37	Roscommon .	Castlereagh .	Baslick . .	Castlereagh .	IV.	199
82	Ballindoney . .	130 3 35	Tipperary, S.R.	Iffa and Offa West .	Ardfinnan .	Clogheen .	II.	316
24	Ballindoney . .	1,143 3 28	Wexford . .	Bantry . .	Templeludigan .	New Ross .	I.	303
82	Ballindoney East .	10 1 5	Tipperary, S.R.	Iffa and Offa West .	Derrygrath .	Clogheen .	II.	318
82	Ballindoney West .	584 1 8	Tipperary, S.R.	Iffa and Offa West .	Derrygrath .	Clogheen .	II.	318
51, 52	Ballindoo or Doo-castle . .	1,956 1 32c	Mayo . .	Costello . .	Kilturra . .	Swineford .	IV.	142
38	Ballindooganig .	201 3 26	Kerry . .	Trughanacmy .	Ballyseedy .	Tralee . .	II.	207
2, 3	Ballindoolin . .	856 2 13	Kildare . .	Carbury . .	Carrick . .	Edenderry .	I.	51
82	Ballindooly . .	497 0 8d	Galway . .	Galway . .	Oranmore .	Galway . .	IV.	37
34	Ballindoon . .	74 3 36	Sligo . .	Tirerrill . .	Killadoon .	Boyle . .	IV.	238
35	Ballindown . .	380 2 20	King's Co. .	Eglish . .	Eglish . .	Parsonstown .	I.	134
30	Ballindoyle . .	111 3 18	Wicklow . .	Arklow . .	Kilcommon .	Rathdrum .	I.	345
70	Ballindrait . .	103 1 27	Donegal . .	Raphoe . .	Clonleigh .	Strabane .	III.	134
70	BALLINDRAIT T. .	—	Donegal . .	Raphoe . .	Clonleigh .	Strabane .	III.	135
8	Ballindreen Irish .	231 2 12	Londonderry .	North East Liberties of Coleraine .	Ballyrashane .	Coleraine .	III.	245
8	Ballindreen Scotch .	310 0 19	Londonderry .	North East Liberties of Coleraine .	Ballyrashane .	Coleraine .	III.	245
71, 72	Ballindrehid . .	405 2 12	Mayo . .	Gallen . .	Kilconduff .	Swineford .	IV.	147
11	Ballindrehid . .	51 1 1	Roscommon .	Boyle . .	Killukin . .	Cark. on Shannon	IV.	195
98	Ballindresrough .	76 2 1	Cork, E.R. .	Kinalea . .	Ballymartle .	Kinsale .	II.	94
106	Ballindrimna .	250 1 15	Galway . .	Leitrim . .	Tynagh . .	Loughrea .	IV.	55
16	Ballindrinan . .	132 1 14	King's Co. .	Ballycowan .	Rahan . .	Tullamore .	I.	128
31, 32	Ballindrinnan . .	331 1 33	King's Co. .	Ballyboy . .	Ballyboy . .	Parsonstown .	I.	123
35, 36	Ballindrum . .	662 3 25	Kildare . .	Kilkea and Moone .	Narraghmore .	Athy . .	I.	61
46, 48	Ballindrum . .	684 0 4	Londonderry .	Loughinsholin .	Artrea . .	Magherafelt .	III.	238
20, 26	Ballindrumlea .	774 2 20	Roscommon .	Castlereagh .	Kilkeevin .	Castlereagh .	IV.	200
35	Ballindrumma .	241 0 33	Waterford .	Decies within Drum	Clashmore .	Youghal .	II.	351
46, 52	Ballindrummeen .	154 2 27	Tipperary, S.R.	Kilnamanagh Lower	Clonoulty .	Cashel .	II.	322
17	Ballindud . .	400 3 34	Waterford .	Gaultiere .	Kilbarry . .	Waterford .	II.	363
56	Ballinduff . .	297 2 3	Galway . .	Clare . .	Kilcoona .	Tuam . .	IV.	19
114	Ballinduff . .	238 3 26	Galway . .	Kiltartan .	Ardrahan .	Gort . .	IV.	45
11, 16	Ballindullagh Inward	220 2 28	Fermanagh .	Lurg . .	Derryvullan .	Lowtherstown .	III.	204
16	Ballindullagh Out-ward .	111 3 23	Fermanagh .	Lurg . .	Derryvullan .	Lowtherstown .	III.	204
6, 7, 11, 12	Ballindurrow . .	426 0 33	Westmeath .	Corkaree .	Multyfarnham .	Mullingar .	I.	265
3	Ballindysert . .	945 0 36	Waterford .	Upperthird .	Dysert . .	Carrick on Suir	II.	369
48	Balline . .	323 1 11	Limerick . .	Coshlea . .	Emlygrennan .	Kilmallock .	II.	238
40	Balline . .	212 3 12	Limerick . .	Smallcounty .	Athneasy .	Kilmallock .	II.	258
72	Ballineadig . .	1,034 0 21e	Cork, E.R. .	East Muskerry .	Aglish . .	Macroom .	II.	101
2, 3, 6, 7	Ballinealoe . .	565 0 31f	Westmeath .	Fore . .	Mayne . .	Granard .	I.	271
42	Ballineanig-castle-quarter .	171 0 21	Kerry . .	Corkaguiny .	Marhin . .	Dingle .	II.	179

(a) Including 7A. 0R. 34P. water.
(b) Including 6A. 0R. 0P. water.
(c) Including 7A. 2R. 35P. Cloonakillina Lough.
(d) Including 17A. 0R. 31P. water.
(e) Including 10A. 0R. 36P. water.
(f) Including 3A. 1R. 30P. water.

No. of Sheet of the Ordnance Survey Maps.	Townlands and Towns.	Area in Statute Acres.			County.	Barony.	Parish.	Poor Law Union in 1857.	Townland Census of 1851, Part I.	
		A.	R.	P.					Vol.	Page
20	Ballinlevane West	268	0	28a	Waterford	Coshmore and Coshbride	Lismore and Mocollop	Lismore	II.	344
3	Ballinlig	395	2	19	Kildare	Carbury	Kilrainy	Edenderry	I.	52
40, 41	Ballinlig	164	3	11	Meath	Upper Moyfenrath	Clonard	Edenderry	I.	213
39, 41	Ballinlig	381	3	32b	Roscommon	Athlone	Fuerty	Roscommon	IV.	181
42	Ballinlig	165	2	32	Roscommon	Athlone	Kilmeane	Roscommon	IV.	182
13, 19	Ballinlig	283	1	16	Sligo	Tireragh	Dromard	Dromore West	IV.	233
34,35,40,41	Ballinlig	261	3	16c	Sligo	Tirerrill	Kilmactranny	Boyle	IV.	240
9	Ballinlig	145	3	33	Westmeath	Delvin	Castletowndelvin	Castletowndelvin	I.	264
31	Ballinlig	157	3	10	Westmeath	Moycashel	Kilcumreragh	Athlone	I.	278
24	Ballinlig Lower	281	0	28	Westmeath	Rathconrath	Ballymore	Athlone	I.	281
24	Ballinlig Upper	248	0	24	Westmeath	Rathconrath	Ballymore	Athlone	I.	281
60	Ballinlina	272	1	29	Tipperary, S.R.	Clanwilliam	Relickmurry and Athassel	Tipperary	II.	309
98, 99	Ballinlining	75	3	28	Cork, E.R.	Kinalea	Carrigaline	Kinsale	II.	94
11, 18	Ballinlisheen	341	2	7d	Clare	Inchiquin	Kilkeedy	Corrofin	II.	25
26, 29	Ballinliss	505	0	13	Armagh	Orior Upper	Killevy	Newry	III.	57
34, 43	Ballinloghig	2,144	0	27	Kerry	Corkaguiny	Kilquane	Dingle	II.	179
14	Ballinloman	231	1	2	King's Co.	Garrycastle	Wheery or Killagally	Parsonstown	I.	139
45, 54	Ballinlongig	664	3	29	Limerick	Connello Upper	Dromcolliher	Newcastle	II.	232
34	Ballinlonty	356	0	11	Tipperary, N.R.	Eliogarty	Kilfithmone	Thurles	II.	270
15	Ballinlough	153	1	18e	Cavan	Lower Loughtee	Annagh	Cavan	III.	78
74	Ballinlough	312	0	22f	Cork, E.R.	Cork	St. Finbars	Cork	II.	65
133	Ballinlough	200	1	5g	Cork, W.R.	West Carbery (E.D.)	Kilmacabea	Skibbereen	II.	140
19, 20	Ballinlough	938	2	23h	Donegal	Inishowen West	Mintiaghs or Barr of Inch	Inishowen	III.	121
73	Ballinlough	93	1	6	Galway	Kilconnell	Ballymacward	Ballinasloe	IV.	39
125	Ballinlough	199	3	38i	Galway	Leitrim	Ballynakill	Loughrea	IV.	50
66	Ballinlough	109	2	1	Kerry	Dunkerron North	Aghadoe	Killarney	II.	181
42	Ballinlough	53	0	23	Kilkenny	Iverk	Rathkieran	Waterford	I.	106
38, 42, 43	Ballinlough	126	3	30	King's Co.	Clonlisk	Aghancon	Roscrea	I.	129
46	Ballinlough	350	3	38	King's Co.	Clonlisk	Borrisnafarney	Roscrea	I.	129
38, 42	Ballinlough	305	2	38	King's Co.	Clonlisk	Ettagh	Roscrea	I.	130
32, 33	Ballinlough	856	3	18	Limerick	Smallcounty	Ballinlough	Kilmallock	II.	259
10	Ballinlough	326	2	16j	Longford	Granard	Granard	Granard	I.	156
11	Ballinlough	147	1	6	Louth	Upper Dundalk	Louth	Dundalk	I.	179
77	Ballinlough	269	0	18k	Mayo	Burrishoole	Kilmeena	Westport	IV.	121
91	Ballinlough	500	2	32l	Mayo	Clanmorris	Mayo	Claremorris	IV.	135
14, 15, 22	Ballinlough	1,047	0	36m	Meath	Fore	Moylagh	Oldcastle	I.	201
44	Ballinlough	206	3	17	Meath	Ratoath	Dunshaughlin	Dunshaughlin	I.	218
24	Ballinlough	134	0	29	Queen's Co.	Cullenagh	Ballyroan	Abbeyleix	I.	239
13, 14	Ballinlough	210	0	24	Queen's Co.	Maryborough East	Kilteale	Mountmellick	I.	241
25	Ballinlough	189	1	20	Roscommon	Castlereagh	Kiltullagh	Castlereagh	IV.	201
22, 28	Ballinlough	512	1	28	Tipperary, N.R.	Upper Ormond	Aghnameadle	Nenagh	II.	288
60	Ballinlough	123	3	1	Tipperary, S.R.	Clanwilliam	Relickmurry and Athassel	Tipperary	II.	309
70, 77	Ballinlough	149	3	22	Tipperary, S.R.	Middlethird	Colman	Cashel	II.	325
16, 25	Ballinlough	284	2	0	Waterford	Decies without Drum	Kilbarrymeaden	Kilmacthomas	II.	356
9	Ballinlough	432	2	13n	Westmeath	Delvin	Killua	Castletowndelvin	I.	265
22	Ballinlough	159	1	9	Westmeath	Kilkenny West	Bunown	Athlone	I.	272
10	Ballinloughan	233	2	12	Antrim	Cary	Culfeightrin	Ballycastle	III.	13
6	Ballinloughan	211	3	34	Louth	Louth	Louth	Dundalk	I.	184
27, 28, 35	Ballinloughane	1,998	2	37	Limerick	Shanid	Ardagh	Newcastle	II.	254
19	Ballinloughane	195	2	22	Limerick	Shanid	Dunmoylan	Rathkeale	II.	255
83, 84	Ballinloughaun	364	2	16	Galway	Clare	Athenry	Galway	IV.	17
38	Ballinloughaun	322	3	11	Mayo	Tirawley	Crossmolina	Ballina	IV.	165
9, 10, 15, 16	Ballinlough Big	594	3	19	Meath	Upper Kells	Kilskeer	Kells	I.	206
67	Ballinlough East	26	3	4	Tipperary, S.R.	Clanwilliam	Templeneiry	Tipperary	II.	311
9, 10, 16	Ballinlough Little	526	2	26	Meath	Upper Kells	Kilskeer	Kells	I.	206
26	Ballinloughquarter	107	1	2	Roscommon	Castlereagh	Kiltullagh	Castlereagh	IV.	201
25	BALLINLOUGH T.	—			Roscommon	Castlereagh	Kiltullagh	Castlereagh	IV.	202
14	Ballinlough (Wadding)	294	3	18o	Westmeath	Delvin	Castletowndelvin	Castletowndelvin	I.	264
67	Ballinlough West	116	2	24	Tipperary, S.R.	Clanwilliam	Templeneiry	Tipperary	II.	311
21, 22	Ballinlow	205	2	37	Wexford	Ballaghkeen	Kilmuckridge	Gorey	I.	296
108, 118	Ballinlug	98	3	2	Galway	Longford	Tiranascragh	Portumna	IV.	62
17, 18	Ballinlug	316	3	21	Westmeath	Rathconrath	Rathconrath	Mullingar	I.	284
18, 19	Ballinlug East	511	2	22	Wexford	Bantry	Killann	Enniscorthy	I.	300
18	Ballinlug West	233	2	36	Wexford	Bantry	Killann	Enniscorthy	I.	300
136, 145	Ballinluig	183	0	19	Cork, W.R.	Ibane and Barryroe	Lislee	Clonakilty	II.	149
98, 112	Ballinluig East	233	1	8	Cork, E.R.	Kinalea	Ballyfeard	Kinsale	II.	93
98, 112	Ballinluig West	332	2	21	Cork, E.R.	Kinalea	Ballyfeard	Kinsale	II.	93
99	Ballinluska	255	3	20	Cork, E.R.	Kerrycurrihy	Templebreedy	Kinsale	II.	93
48, 56	Ballinlyna Lower	343	1	32	Limerick	Coshlea	Kilfinnane	Kilmallock	II.	239
56	Ballinlyna Upper	417	2	17	Limerick	Coshlea	Kilfinnane	Kilmallock	II.	239

(a) Including 5A. 2R. 0P. water.
(b) Including 12A. 0R. 10P. water.
(c) Including 8A. 2R. 0P. water.
(d) Including 3A. 3R. 35P. water.
(e) Including 15A. 1R. 31P. water.

(f) Including 37A. 1R. 35P. detached portion.
(g) Including 18A. 0R. 17P. water.
(h) Including 33A. 3R. 24P. water.
(i) Including 29A. 0R. 32P. water.
(j) Including 32A. 0R. 4P. water.

(k) Including 35A. 3R. 9P. water.
(l) Including 28A. 1R. 4P. water.
(m) Including 131A. 2R. 29P. water.
(n) Including 11A. 0R. 20P. water.
(o) Including 4A. 1R. 11P. water.

H 2

No. of Sheet of the Ordnance Survey Maps.	Townlands and Towns.	Area in Statute Acres.	County.	Barony.	Parish.	Poor Law Union in 1857.	Townland Census of 1851, Part I.	
		A. R. P.					Vol.	Page
28, 29	Ballinlyny	266 3 19	Limerick	Connello Lower	Kilscannell	Rathkeale	II.	228
14	Ballinn	243 0 23	Westmeath	Delvin	Castletowndelvin	Castletowndelvin	I.	264
32	Ballinookery	204 0 25	Cork, E.R.	Duhallow	Ballyclogh	Mallow	II.	67
51	Ballinooskny	190 2 39	Clare	Bunratty Lower	Clonloghan	Ennis	II.	3
51	Ballinooskny	98 1 14	Clare	Bunratty Lower	Kilmaleery	Ennis	II.	5
38, 39, 46, 47	Ballinoran	178 0 19	Limerick	Connello Upper	Bruree	Kilmallock	II.	231
29	Ballinorig East	329 1 7	Kerry	Trughanacmy	Ratass	Tralee	II.	213
29	Ballinorig South	275 2 14	Kerry	Trughanacmy	Ratass	Tralee	II.	213
29	Ballinorig West	132 3 38	Kerry	Trughanacmy	Ratass	Tralee	II.	213
122, 123 135, 136	Ballinoroher	757 0 5	Cork, W.R.	East Carbery (E.D.)	Templequinlan	Clonakilty	II.	130
22	Ballinoulart	407 1 30a	Wexford	Ballaghkeen	Donaghmore	Gorey	I.	293
19, 20	Ballinowlart North	177 3 26	King's Co.	Coolestown	Clonsast	Edenderry	I.	132
28	Ballinowlart South	458 3 34	King's Co.	Coolestown	Clonsast	Edenderry	I.	132
86, 98	Ballinphelic	564 3 0	Cork, E.R.	Kerrycurrihy	Liscleary	Kinsale	II.	92
85	Ballinphellic	726 2 16	Cork, E.R.	East Muskerry	Dunderrow	Cork	II.	103
44, 49	Ballinphile	149 1 0	Wexford	Shelburne	Templetown	New Ross	I.	328
7	Ballinphort	325 1 27	Westmeath	Corkaree	Multyfarnham	Mullingar	I.	263
57	Ballinphuil	369 3 3	Galway	Clare	Cummer	Tuam	IV.	18
30	Ballinphuill	142 3 35	Galway	Dunmore	Tuam	Tuam	IV.	35
98	Ballinphuill	119 2 6	Galway	Kilconnell	Grange	Loughrea	IV.	40
86	Ballinphuill	199 2 26	Galway	Kilconnell	Killallaghtan	Ballinasloe	IV.	41
6	Ballinphuill	285 0 39	Galway	Tiaquin	Boyounagh	Glennamaddy	IV.	76
31	Ballinphuill	190 1 29b	Galway	Tiaquin	Kilkerrin	Glennamaddy	IV.	76
101	Ballinphuill	123 2 1c	Mayo	Clanmorris	Kilcolman	Claremorris	IV.	133
93	Ballinphuill	58 3 32	Mayo	Costello	Bekan	Claremorris	IV.	138
5, 6	Ballinphuill	122 3 34	Roscommon	Boyle	Boyle	Boyle	IV.	193
27	Ballinphuill	60 3 30	Roscommon	Castlereagh	Kilkeevin	Castlereagh	IV.	200
8, 14	Ballinphuill	481 0 1	Roscommon	Frenchpark	Tibohine	Castlereagh	IV.	204
57	BALLINPHUIL T.	—	Galway	Clare	Cummer	Tuam	IV.	19
2	Ballinphull	77 1 25	Sligo	Carbury	Ahamlish	Sligo	IV.	219
4, 5, 8	Ballinphull	367 0 36	Sligo	Carbury	Drumcliff	Sligo	IV.	221
13, 19	Ballinphull	111 3 9	Sligo	Tireragh	Dromard	Dromore West	IV.	233
12, 18	Ballinphull	260 1 14	Sligo	Tireragh	Templeboy	Dromore West	IV.	236
34	Ballinphull	233 3 8d	Sligo	Tirerrill	Killadoon	Boyle	IV.	238
52, 62	Ballinphunta	374 1 26	Clare	Bunratty Lower	Kilfintinan	Limerick	II.	5
17	Ballinphunta	238 2 15	Clare	Inchiquin	Killinaboy	Corrofin	II.	26
14, 20	Ballinprior	488 1 36e	Kerry	Clanmaurice	Ardfert	Tralee	II.	167
33	Ballinra	100 0 25	Wexford	Ballaghkeen	Ballyvalloo	Enniscorthy	I.	292
33	Ballinra	179 3 32	Wexford	Ballaghkeen	Castle-ellis	Enniscorthy	I.	293
33	Ballinra	25 2 19	Wexford	Ballaghkeen	Skreen	Wexford	I.	298
28	Ballinrahin	375 0 9	King's Co.	Coolestown	Clonsast	Edenderry	I.	132
32	Ballinrahin	204 0 29	Queen's Co.	Slievemargy	Killabban	Carlow	I.	245
15, 16	Ballinrally	803 3 7	Queen's Co.	Upperwoods	Offerlane	Mountmellick	I.	251
52, 53, 55, 56	Ballinran	890 2 6	Down	Mourne	Kilkeel	Kilkeel	III.	182
54	Ballinran	195 1 14	Down	Upper Iveagh, Up. pt.	Kilbroney	Kilkeel	III.	175
42	Ballinrannig	143 1 15	Kerry	Corkaguiny	Marhin	Dingle	II.	179
52, 53	Ballinran Upper	550 1 26	Down	Mourne	Kilkeel	Kilkeel	III.	182
54	Ballinran Upper	80 3 22	Down	Upper Iveagh, Up. pt.	Kilbroney	Kilkeel	III.	175
11, 19	Ballinrath	560 0 0	King's Co.	Coolestown	Ballynakill	Edenderry	I.	132
86, 87	Ballinrea	888 2 22	Cork, E.R.	Cork	Carrigaline	Cork	II.	63
39	Ballinrea	212 2 8	Limerick	Coshma	Dromin	Kilmallock	II.	243
19	Ballinreaghan	138 0 34	Longford	Ardagh	Ardagh	Longford	I.	151
25	Ballinreask	49 3 21f	Louth	Ferrard	Beaulieu	Drogheda	I.	180
86	Ballinrea South	197 2 32	Cork, E.R.	Kerrycurrihy	Carrigaline	Cork	II.	92
19	Ballinree	831 3 31	Carlow	Idrone East	Sliguff	Carlow	I.	8
17	Ballinree	250 0 11	Cork, E.R.	Fermoy	Doneraile	Mallow	II.	78
35, 38	Ballinree	299 1 32	King's Co.	Ballybritt	Birr	Parsonstown	I.	125
35, 36	Ballinree	438 0 36	King's Co.	Eglish	Drumcullen	Parsonstown	I.	134
10	Ballinree	43 1 38	Limerick	Shanid	Shanagolden	Glin	II.	258
26	Ballinree	142 3 24	Queen's Co.	Ballyadams	Tankardstown	Athy	I.	232
21	Ballinree	153 3 9	Tipperary, N.R.	Upper Ormond	Ballymackey	Nenagh	II.	289
53	Ballinree	883 3 36	Tipperary, S.R.	Middlethird	Ballysheehan	Cashel	II.	324
60, 61	Ballinree	227 3 34	Tipperary, S.R.	Middlethird	St. Patricksrock	Cashel	II.	330
11	Ballinree	226 0 20	Wexford	Gorey	Toome	Gorey	I.	321
14, 19, 20	Ballinree and Ballymoat	310 1 11	Longford	Ardagh	Ardagh	Longford	I.	151
112	Ballinreenlanig	102 3 14	Cork, E.R.	Kinalea	Nohaval	Kinsale	II.	96
11	Ballinrees	180 2 5	Londonderry	Coleraine	Aghadowey	Coleraine	III.	229
6, 7	Ballinrees	594 2 32	Londonderry	Coleraine	Dunboe	Coleraine	III.	231
86	Ballinreeshig	419 1 36	Cork, E.R.	Kerrycurrihy	Killanully	Cork	II.	92
112	Ballinrichard	179 0 26	Cork, E.R.	Kinsale	Clontead	Kinsale	II.	99
7, 12	Ballinriddera	360 3 24	Westmeath	Corkaree	Multyfarnham	Mullingar	I.	263

(a) Including 8A. 1R. 15P. water.　　　　(c) Including 9A. 2R. 13P. water.　　　　(e) Including 13A. 3R. 0P. detached portion.
(b) Including 6A. 2R. 26P. water.　　　　(d) Including 33A. 0R. 33P. water.　　　　(f) Including 3A. 3R. 7P. detached portion.

No. of Sheet of the Ordnance Survey Maps.	Townlands and Towns.	Area in Statute Acres.	County.	Barony.	Parish.	Poor Law Union in 1857.	Townland Census of 1851, Part I.	
		A. R. P.					Vol.	Page
8	Ballinriddery or Knightstown	279 2 11	Queen's Co.	Portnahinch	Ardea	Mountmellick	I.	243
42	Ballinrig	106 3 21	Meath	Lower Moyfenrath	Laracor	Trim	I.	210
8	Ballinrink	964 1 19	Meath	Fore	Killeagh	Oldcastle	I.	201
39	Ballinroad	202 1 39	Waterford	Decies within Drum	Ardmore	Dungarvan	II.	349
31	Ballinroad	66 3 39	Waterford	Decies without Drum	Dungarvan	Dungarvan	II.	354
21	Ballinroad	427 3 6	Wexford	Ballaghkeen	Kilcormick	Enniscorthy	I.	294
27	Ballinroan Lower	179 1 12	Wicklow	Upper Talbotstown	Kilranelagh	Baltinglass	I.	364
27	Ballinroan Upper	183 0 10	Wicklow	Upper Talbotstown	Kilranelagh	Baltinglass	I.	364
118	Ballinrobe Demesne	286 3 36a	Mayo	Kilmaine	Ballinrobe	Ballinrobe	IV.	152
118	BALLINROBE T.	—	Mayo	Kilmaine	Ballinrobe	Ballinrobe	IV.	153
22	Ballinroche East	114 1 30	Limerick	Pubblebrien	Crecora	Croom	II.	252
21, 22	Ballinroche North	120 3 4	Limerick	Pubblebrien	Crecora	Croom	II.	252
19	Ballinroddy	302 3 29	Longford	Ardagh	Ardagh	Longford	I.	151
124	Ballinroe	110 0 30	Cork, W.R.	Courceys	Ringrone	Kinsale	II.	147
29, 30	Ballinroe	661 0 36	Tipperary, N.R.	Ikerrin	Templeree	Thurles	II.	277
124	Ballinroe East	45 0 32	Cork, E.R.	Kinsale	Ringrone	Kinsale	II.	101
134, 135, 136, 137	Ballinrooaun	100 0 39	Galway	Leitrim	Clonrush	Scarriff	IV.	52
98, 99	Ballinrooaun	361 2 14	Galway	Longford	Killoran	Ballinasloe	IV.	59
114	Ballinrooaun	104 2 10	Galway	Loughrea	Ardrahan	Loughrea	IV.	62
59	Ballinrooaun	648 2 38	Galway	Tiaquin	Moylough	Mountbellew	IV.	79
33	Ballinrooaun	353 2 23	Wexford	Ballaghkeen	Ballyvalloo	Enniscorthy	I.	292
33	Ballinrooaun	227 0 32	Wexford	Ballaghkeen	Skreen	Wexford	I.	298
6, 10	Ballinrooey	493 0 13	Longford	Granard	Abbeylara	Granard	I.	154
31	Ballinross	381 2 2	Roscommon	Castlereagh	Kiltullagh	Castlereagh	IV.	201
88, 100	Ballinrostig	282 3 24	Cork, E.R.	Imokilly	Rostellan	Middleton	II.	90
88	BALLINROSTIG T.	—	Cork, E.R.	Imokilly	Rostellan	Middleton	II.	90
135, 136	Ballinrougher	121 1 5	Cork, W.R.	East Carbery (E.D.)	Kilnagross	Clonakilty	II.	129
18, 19	Ballinruan	637 0 16b	Clare	Bunratty Upper	Inchicronan	Tulla	II.	8
71	Ballinruan	293 2 27	Tipperary, S.R.	Slievardagh	Grangemockler	Callan	II.	333
44, 49	Ballinruan	232 1 1	Wexford	Shelburne	Templetown	New Ross	I.	328
37, 45	Ballinruane	1,560 2 14	Limerick	Connello Upper	Kilmeady	Croom	II.	233
40, 45	Ballinruane	477 2 12	Wexford	Shelburne	Tintern	New Ross	I.	329
11	Ballinruddery	418 0 3c	Kerry	Clanmaurice	Finuge	Listowel	II.	169
7	Ballinruddery	256 0 32	Tipperary, N.R.	Lower Ormond	Aglishcloghane	Borrisokane	II.	281
11	Ballinrud East	108 0 8	Longford	Granard	Granard	Granard	I.	156
11	Ballinrud Glebe	41 1 14	Longford	Granard	Granard	Granard	I.	156
11	Ballinrud West	14 0 31	Longford	Granard	Granard	Granard	I.	156
73	Ballinrumpa	181 3 15	Mayo	Costello	Kilmovee	Swineford	IV.	141
17	Ballinrush	546 1 5	Carlow	Forth	Myshall	Carlow	I.	5
27	Ballinrush	370 3 17	Cork, E.R.	Condons & Clangibbon	Kilcrumper	Fermoy	II.	61
19, 27, 28	Ballinrush	604 0 12	Cork, E.R.	Condons & Clangibbon	Kilworth	Fermoy	II.	62
12, 18	Ballinrush	569 2 13d	Wicklow	Ballinacor North	Calary	Rathdrum	I.	346
40, 48	Ballinscaula	677 1 34	Limerick	Coshlea	Athneasy	Kilmallock	II.	237
32	Ballinscoola	63 3 11	Limerick	Smallcounty	Ballynamona	Kilmallock	II.	259
32	Ballinscoola	265 2 9	Limerick	Smallcounty	Kilcullane	Kilmallock	II.	260
46, 55	Ballinscurloge	633 0 34	Cork, E.R.	Kinnatalloon	Ballynoe	Fermoy	II.	97
97	Ballinskelligs	713 0 12	Kerry	Iveragh	Prior	Cahersiveen	II.	198
117	Ballinsmaul	109 0 9	Galway	Leitrim	Tynagh	Portumna	IV.	55
101, 102	Ballinsmaula	191 1 15	Mayo	Clanmorris	Kilcolman	Claremorris	IV.	133
124	Ballinspittle	12 2 2	Cork, W.R.	Courceys	Ringrone	Kinsale	II.	147
124	BALLINSPITTLE T.	—	Cork, W.R.	Courceys	Ringrone	Kinsale	II.	147
39, 40	Ballinstona North	418 0 9	Limerick	Coshma	Uregare	Kilmallock	II.	244
39, 40	Ballinstona South	141 1 34	Limerick	Smallcounty	Uregare	Kilmallock	II.	261
63	Ballintadder	122 3 11	Mayo	Costello	Kilbeagh	Swineford	IV.	140
91	Ballintaffy	637 3 0e	Mayo	Clanmorris	Kilcolman	Claremorris	IV.	133
9	Ballintaggart	592 1 26	Armagh	Oneilland West	Kilmore	Armagh	III.	53
87	Ballintaggart	100 3 17	Cork, E.R.	Kerrycurrihy	Carrigaline	Cork	II.	92
33, 34	Ballintaggart	503 0 15f	Down	Upper Iveagh, Up.pt.	Aghaderg	Banbridge	III.	173
45	Ballintaggart	162 0 23	Kerry	Corkaguiny	Ballinvoher	Dingle	II.	173
53	Ballintaggart	208 3 27	Kerry	Corkaguiny	Garfinny	Dingle	II.	176
32	Ballintaggart	280 2 38	Kildare	Narragh & Reban East	Davidstown	Athy	I.	66
11	Ballintaggart	177 3 30	Londonderry	Coleraine	Macosquin	Coleraine	III.	232
21	Ballintaggart	368 3 26	Queen's Co.	Clandonagh	Kyle	Donaghmore	I.	233
8	Ballintaggart	87 0 32	Queen's Co.	Portnahinch	Ardea	Mountmellick	I.	243
55, 56	Ballintaggart	1,281 0 28	Tipperary, S.R.	Slievardagh	Ballingarry	Callan	II.	331
33	Ballintaggart	148 0 5	Wexford	Ballaghkeen	Killisk	Enniscorthy	I.	296
85	Ballintannig	203 0 24	Cork, E.R.	Cork	Ballinaboy	Cork	II.	63
19	Ballintantassig	102 1 6	Cork, E.R.	Fermoy	Glanworth	Mitchelstown	II.	79
22, 27	Ballintarsan	221 3 5	Fermanagh	Tirkennedy	Derryvullan	Enniskillen	III.	220
13	Ballintarsna	128 2 26	Kilkenny	Crannagh	Tullaroan	Kilkenny	I.	87
36, 41	Ballintarton	104 1 14	Wexford	Shelmaliere West	Coolstuff	Wexford	I.	333

(a) Including 2A. 1R. 7P. water.
(b) Including 34A. 0R. 34P. water.
(c) Including 16A. 3R. 2P. water.
(d) Including 33A. 2R. 23P. Lough Dan.
(e) Including 13A. 1R. 30P. water.
(f) Including 31A. 3R. 5P. Lough Brickland.

No. of Sheet of the Ordnance Survey Maps.	Townlands and Towns.	Area in Statute Acres.			County.	Barony.	Parish.	Poor Law Union in 1857.	Townland Census of 1851, Part I.	
		A.	R.	P.					Vol.	Page
21	Ballintate	392	3	31	Armagh	Fews Upper	Ballymyre	Newry	III.	48
5	Ballintava	502	1	3	Galway	Ballymoe	Dunmore	Glennamaddy	IV.	7
31	Ballintaw	449	3	13	Limerick	Coshma	Croom	Croom	II.	242
30, 35	Ballintaylor Lower	503	0	18	Waterford	Decies without Drum	Whitechurch	Dungarvan	II.	361
30, 35	Ballintaylor Upper	82	3	29	Waterford	Decies without Drum	Whitechurch	Dungarvan	II.	361
16, 17	Ballinteane	270	1	14	Sligo	Tireragh	Kilglass	Dromore West	IV.	234
31	Ballintee	348	0	25	Kilkenny	Kells	Dunnamaggan	Callan	I.	108
22	Ballinteean	359	0	16a	Mayo	Tirawley	Ballysakeery	Ballina	IV.	164
110, 118	Ballinteeaun	321	3	29½	Mayo	Kilmaine	Ballinrobe	Ballinrobe	IV.	152
25	Ballinteenoe	456	0	25	Tipperary, N.R.	Owney and Arra	Kilmastulla	Nenagh	II.	295
22	Ballinteer	282	1	24	Dublin	Rathdown	Taney	Rathdown	I.	38
7	Ballinteer North	747	0	10	Londonderry	Coleraine	Macosquin	Coleraine	III.	232
7	Ballinteer South	363	2	15	Londonderry	Coleraine	Macosquin	Coleraine	III.	232
18	Ballintempan	87	0	25	Longford	Moydow	Ballymacormick	Longford	I.	160
20,21,24,25	Ballintemple	2,281	0	13	Armagh	Fews Upper	Ballymyre	Newry	III.	48
28, 29	Ballintemple	910	3	27	Armagh	Orior Upper	Killevy	Newry	III.	57
13,14,17,18	Ballintemple	970	2	6	Carlow	Forth	Ardoyne	Carlow	I.	3
31	Ballintemple	344	0	22	Cavan	Clanmahon	Ballintemple	Cavan	III.	75
74	Ballintemple	292	2	20c	Cork, E.R.	Cork	St. Finbars	Cork	II.	65
135	Ballintemple	268	0	23	Cork, W.R.	Ibane and Barryroe	Templeomalus	Clonakilty	II.	150
25	Ballintemple	259	2	1	Donegal	Kilmacrenan	Tullaghobegly	Dunfanaghy	III.	131
82	Ballintemple	286	3	32	Galway	Dunkellin	Oranmore	Galway	IV.	31
42, 52	Ballintemple	146	2	36	Kerry	Corkaguiny	Dunquin	Dingle	II.	176
44	Ballintemple	853	0	34	King's Co.	Clonlisk	Templeharry	Roscrea	I.	132
18,19,26,27	Ballintemple	314	1	38	King's Co.	Upper Philipstown	Geashill	Tullamore	I.	144
17,18,25,26	Ballintemple	759	0	3	Londonderry	Coleraine	Errigal	Coleraine	III.	232
61	Ballintemple	314	0	8d	Mayo	Gallen	Meelick	Swineford	IV.	150
29	Ballintemple	110	2	24e	Roscommon	Roscommon	Cloonfinlough	Strokestown	IV.	208
7	Ballintemple	267	2	16	Sligo	Carbury	Drumcliff	Sligo	IV.	221
59, 60	Ballintemple	622	1	22	Tipperary, S.R.	Kilnamanagh Lower	Ballintemple	Cashel	II.	322
62. 70	Ballintemple	211	2	3	Tipperary, S.R.	Middlethird	Rathcool	Cashel	II.	329
40	Ballintemple	479	1	24	Wicklow	Arklow	Ballintemple	Rathdrum	I.	342
74	BALLINTEMPLE T.	—			Cork, E.R.	Cork	St. Finbars	Cork	II.	66
20	Ballintempo	489	0	27	Fermanagh	Clanawley	Cleenish	Enniskillen	III.	189
55	Ballinteosig	815	1	36	Cork, E.R.	Imokilly	Ardagh	Youghal	II.	83
31	Ballinter	433	1	23f	Meath	Lower Deece	Assey	Navan	I.	191
45	Ballintermon	312	3	27	Kerry	Corkaguiny	Ballynacourty	Dingle	II.	174
44	Ballinterry	311	1	35	Cork, E.R.	Barrymore	Gortroe	Fermoy	II.	54
35	Ballinteskin	506	1	5	Kilkenny	Knocktopher	Aghaviller	Carrick on Suir	I.	110
5	Ballinteskin	607	1	35	Louth	Lower Dundalk	Carlingford	Dundalk	I.	176
19	Ballinteskin	765	3	14	Queen's Co.	Stradbally	Timogue	Athy	I.	248
34	Ballinteskin	352	2	23	Wexford	Shelburne	Whitechurch	New Ross	I.	329
31	Ballinteskin	707	2	9	Wicklow	Arklow	Glenealy	Rathdrum	I.	344
7, 12	Ballinteskin	94	0	19g	Wicklow	Rathdown	Calary	Rathdown	I.	355
7	Ballinteskin	235	0	19	Wicklow	Rathdown	Kilmacanoge	Rathdown	I.	355
5	Ballintillan	118	1	25	Meath	Lower Kells	Kilbeg	Kells	I.	202
11	Ballintim	178	1	12	Wexford	Gorey	Toome	Gorey	I.	321
36	Ballintim	46	0	21	Wicklow	Arklow	Redcross	Rathdrum	I.	345
14	Ballintine	190	1	15h	Down	Castlereagh Upper	Blaris	Lisburn	III.	164
18	Ballintine	309	0	12	Kildare	Connell	Kilmeage	Naas	I.	55
17	Ballintise	222	1	36	Galway	Dunmore	Dunmore	Tuam	IV.	33
52	Ballintlea	423	2	3i	Kerry	Corkaguiny	Ventry	Dingle	II.	180
40	Ballintlea	279	1	1	Kilkenny	Knocktopher	Rossinan	Waterford	I.	113
19	Ballintlea	862	1	1	Queen's Co.	Ballyadams	Ballyadams	Athy	I.	231
23	Ballintlea	473	2	15	Waterford	Decies without Drum	Kilrossanty	Kilmacthomas	II.	357
6	Ballintlea	237	3	22	Wexford	Gorey	Kilnahue	Gorey	I.	319
36, 41	Ballintlea	145	1	38	Wexford	Shelmaliere West	Coolstuff	Wexford	I.	333
36, 41, 42	Ballintlea	134	1	29	Wexford	Shelmaliere West	Taghmon	Wexford	I.	334
18, 24, 25	Ballintlea Lower	335	2	39	Queen's Co.	Cullenagh	Fossy or Timahoe	Abbeyleix	I.	240
52	Ballintlea North	29	0	10	Clare	Bunratty Lower	Kilfintinan	Limerick	II.	5
8, 9, 18	Ballintlea North	951	0	10	Cork, E.R.	Fermoy	Doneraile	Mallow	II.	78
39	Ballintlea North	176	2	30	Waterford	Decies within Drum	Ardmore	Dungarvan	II.	349
52	Ballintlea South	272	1	26	Clare	Bunratty Lower	Kilfintinan	Limerick	II.	5
9, 18	Ballintlea South	952	1	36	Cork, E.R.	Fermoy	Doneraile	Mallow	II.	78
39	Ballintlea South	114	1	22	Waterford	Decies within Drum	Ardmore	Dungarvan	II.	349
24	Ballintlea Upper	279	0	22	Queen's Co.	Cullenagh	Fossy or Timahoe	Abbeyleix	I.	240
63, 64	Ballintleave	391	1	12	Kerry	Iveragh	Killorglin	Killarney	II.	197
56, 63, 64	Ballintleave Commons	677	0	10j	Kerry	Iveragh	Killorglin	Killarney	II.	197
42	Ballintleva	301	3	36	Galway	Clare	Killower	Tuam	IV.	21
90, 91	Ballintleva	549	3	29k	Galway	Moycullen	Kilcummin	Galway	IV.	66
60	Ballintleva	297	1	24	Galway	Tiaquin	Killosolan	Mountbellew	IV.	78

(a) Including 21A. 0R. 29P. water.　　(e) Including 37A. 1R. 5P. water.　　(i) Including 5A. 0R. 8P. water.
(b) Including 1A. 1R. 33P. water.　　(f) Including 13A. 3R. 4P. water.　　(j) Including 18A. 1R. 38P. water.
(c) Including 2A. 0R. 15P. detached portion.　　(g) Including 0A. 2R. 27P. detached portion.　　(k) Including 21A. 0R. 27P. water.
(d) Including 14A. 0R. 34P. water.　　(h) Including 1A. 0R. 34P. water.

No. of Sheet of the Ordnance Survey Maps.	Townlands and Towns.	Area in Statute Acres.			County.	Barony.	Parish.	Poor Law Union in 1857.	Townland Census of 1851. Part I.	
		A.	R.	P.					Vol.	Page
77	Ballintleva	423	0	32	Mayo	Burrishoole	Kilmaclasser	Westport	IV.	121
91	Ballintleva	134	2	13	Mayo	Clanmorris	Mayo	Castlebar	IV.	135
26	Ballintlevy	137	1	30	Westmeath	Fartullagh	Enniscoffey	Mullingar	I.	268
10, 19	Ballintlieve	521	0	3a	Donegal	Inishowen West	Mintiaghs or Barr of Inch	Inishowen	III.	121
31	Ballintlieve	308	1	38b	Down	Lecale Lower	Ballyculter	Downpatrick	III.	178
10	Ballintlieve	208	3	34	Meath	Lower Kells	Moynalty	Kells	I.	203
21, 29, 30	Ballintobeenig	377	3	28	Kerry	Trughanacmy	Ratass	Tralee	II.	213
23	Ballintober	331	0	24	Cork, E.R.	Duhallow	Castlemagner	Kanturk	II.	67
97,98,111,112	Ballintober	251	0	2t	Cork, E.R.	Kinalea	Ballymartle	Kinsale	II.	94
57	Ballintober	203	2	11	Galway	Clare	Cummer	Tuam	IV.	18
86	Ballintober	25	0	10	Galway	Kilconnell	Kilconnell	Ballinasloe	IV.	40
86	Ballintober	132	3	0	Galway	Kilconnell	Killallaghtan	Ballinasloe	IV.	41
35, 39	Ballintober	261	2	3	Kilkenny	Knocktopher	Killahy	Waterford	I.	112
48,49,56,57	Ballintober	1,633	0	34	Limerick	Coshlea	Darragh	Kilmallock	II.	238
89, 99	Ballintober	358	3	6c	Mayo	Carra	Ballintober	Castlebar	IV.	124
21, 29	Ballintober	415	2	14	Mayo	Tirawley	Kilfian	Killala	IV.	169
27, 34	Ballintober	58	3	39	Roscommon	Castlereagh	Ballintober	Castlereagh	IV.	198
31	Ballintober	530	0	6	Westmeath	Moycashel	Kilcumreragh	Athlone	I.	278
29, 30	Ballintober	385	2	24	Wexford	Bantry	Ballyanne	New Ross	I.	299
9, 10	Ballintober	377	2	10	Wicklow	Talbotstown Lower	Hollywood	Baltinglass	I.	360
23	Ballintober (Bonny)	172	2	29	Longford	Moydow	Taghsheenod	Ballymahon	I.	162
98	Ballintober East	269	1	8	Galway	Leitrim	Kilreekill	Ballinasloe	IV.	54
44	Ballintober East	349	3	14	Limerick	Glenquin	Killeedy	Newcastle	II.	245
23	Ballintober (Rock)	67	1	0	Longford	Moydow	Taghsheenod	Ballymahon	I.	162
44	Ballintober South	132	1	33	Limerick	Glenquin	Killeedy	Newcastle	II.	245
98	Ballintober West	248	2	5	Galway	Leitrim	Kilreekill	Loughrea	IV.	54
44	Ballintober West	121	3	33	Limerick	Glenquin	Killeedy	Newcastle	II.	245
49	Ballintoghee	125	1	18	Meath	Upper Deece	Agher	Trim	I.	192
31	Ballintogher	776	3	19	Down	Lecale Lower	Saul	Downpatrick	III.	179
16	Ballintogher	211	2	33	Kerry	Clanmaurice	Dysert	Listowel	II.	169
26	Ballintogher	313	2	7	King's Co.	Upper Philipstown	Ballykean	Mountmellick	I.	143
26	Ballintogher	153	2	17	King's Co.	Upper Philipstown	Geashill	Tullamore	I.	144
15	Ballintogher	287	3	1d	Meath	Fore	Moylagh	Oldcastle	I.	201
5, 9	Ballintogher	604	1	25	Queen's Co.	Portnahinch	Lea	Mountmellick	I.	244
54	Ballintogher	551	3	37	Tipperary, S.R.	Slievardagh	Graystown	Cashel	II.	333
54	Ballintogher	275	3	22	Tipperary, S.R.	Slievardagh	Killenaule	Cashel	II.	334
21	BALLINTOGHER T.	—			Sligo	Tirerrill	Killerry	Sligo	IV.	239
45	Ballintombay	125	2	30	Wicklow	Arklow	Arklow	Rathdrum	I.	341
29, 30	Ballintombay Lower	439	1	35	Wicklow	Ballinacor North	Knockrath	Rathdrum	I.	347
29, 30	Ballintombay Upper	581	0	3	Wicklow	Ballinacor North	Knockrath	Rathdrum	I.	347
104	Ballintooey	205	3	23e	Donegal	Tirhugh	Drumhome	Donegal	III.	146
23, 31	Ballintoor	169	3	27	Waterford	Decies without Drum	Kilgobnet	Dungarvan	II.	357
12	Ballintoppan	83	1	17	Monaghan	Dartree	Clones	Monaghan	III.	264
15	Ballintore	287	0	6	Wexford	Scarawalsh	Kilbride	Enniscorthy	I.	323
77	Ballintotis	438	0	15	Cork, E.R.	Imokilly	Ballyoughtera	Middleton	II.	84
21	Ballintotty	761	0	36	Tipperary, N.R.	Upper Ormond	Lisbunny	Nenagh	II.	292
4	Ballintoy	274	1	35f	Antrim	Cary	Ballintoy	Ballycastle	III.	11
4	Ballintoy Demesne	505	3	14	Antrim	Cary	Ballintoy	Ballycastle	III.	12
4	BALLINTOY T.	—			Antrim	Cary	Ballintoy	Ballycastle	III.	12
40, 48	Ballintra	1,676	0	12g	Donegal	Boylagh	Templecrone	Glenties	III.	114
103	Ballintra	34	2	37	Donegal	Tirhugh	Drumhome	Ballyshannon	III.	146
29, 32	Ballintra	113	3	11	Monaghan	Farney	Inishkeen	Dundalk	III.	271
2, 3	Ballintrae	104	1	39	Antrim	Lower Dunluce	Dunluce	Coleraine	III.	17
100	Ballintra East	59	2	2	Cork, E.R.	Imokilly	Corkbeg	Middleton	II.	86
36, 44	Ballintrain	729	1	17	Tyrone	Omagh East	Termonmaguirk	Omagh	III.	314
13	Ballintrane	121	1	32	Carlow	Forth	Fennagh	Carlow	I.	4
12, 13	Ballintrane	547	3	16	Carlow	Forth	Templepeter	Carlow	I.	5
103	BALLINTRA T.	—			Donegal	Tirhugh	Drumhome	Ballyshannon	III.	147
100	Ballintra West	70	1	2	Cork, E.R.	Imokilly	Corkbeg	Middleton	II.	86
20	Ballintredida	141	1	32	Limerick	Connello Lower	Nantinan	Rathkeale	II.	228
98	Ballintrideen	232	3	19	Cork, E.R.	Kinalea	Ballyfeard	Kinsale	II.	93
88	Ballintrim	210	1	22	Cork, E.R.	Imokilly	Titeskin	Middleton	II.	90
39	Ballintrofaun	57	2	36	Sligo	Corran	Kilshalvy	Boyle	IV.	227
21	Ballintruer Beg	111	2	12	Wicklow	Upper Talbotstown	Donaghmore	Baltinglass	I.	362
21	Ballintruer More	182	2	3	Wicklow	Upper Talbotstown	Donaghmore	Baltinglass	I.	362
51	Ballintry	161	2	15	Meath	Dunboyne	Kilbride	Dunshaughlin	I.	200
19	Ballintubbert	510	3	34	Queen's Co.	Ballyadams	Ballyadams	Athy	I.	231
36	Ballintubbrid	375	3	3	Limerick	Glenquin	Monagay	Newcastle	II.	247
27, 28	Ballintubbrid	179	3	2	Wexford	Ballaghkeen	Ballyvaldon	Enniscorthy	I.	292
76	Ballintubbrid East	391	2	5	Cork, E.R.	Barrymore	Mogeesha	Middleton	II.	57
76	Ballintubbrid West	367	0	9	Cork, E.R.	Barrymore	Mogeesha	Middleton	II.	57
10, 11	Ballintue	669	3	8	Westmeath	Moygoish	Kilmacnevan	Mullingar	I.	280

(a) Including 1A. 1R. 28P. water.
(b) Including 5A. 1R. 20P. Great Dam.
(c) Including 4A. 0R. 36P. water.

(d) Including 8A. 3R. 4P. water.
(e) Including 11A. 1R. 28P. water.

(f) Including 3A. 1R. 24P. Sheep Island.
(g) Including 20A. 1R. 25P. water.

No. of Sheet of the Ordnance Survey Maps.	Townlands and Towns.	Area in Statute Acres.	County.	Barony.	Parish.	Poor Law Union in 1857.	Townland Census of 1851, Part I.	
		A. R. P.					Vol.	Page
55	Ballintur	226 1 36	Down	Upper Iveagh, Up.pt.	Kilbroney	Kilkeel	III.	175
41	Ballinturly	367 2 24	Roscommon	Athlone	Fuerty	Roscommon	IV.	181
34, 35	Ballinturly	408 3 3	Roscommon	Ballymoe	Cloonygormican	Roscommon	IV.	191
14, 15	Ballinturner or Mountfin Lower	437 0 27a	Wexford	Scarawalsh	Ballycarney	Enniscorthy	I.	322
55	Ballintur Upper	140 0 26	Down	Upper Iveagh, Up.pt.	Kilbroney	Kilkeel	III.	175
122	Ballinulty	254 2 24	Mayo	Kilmaine	Kilmainemore	Ballinrobe	IV.	155
58	Ballinulty	632 1 16	Tipperary, S.R.	Clanwilliam	Cullen	Tipperary	II.	306
6	Ballinulty Lower	299 1 22	Longford	Granard	Columbkille	Granard	I.	155
6, 10	Ballinulty Upper	311 1 24	Longford	Granard	Columbkille	Granard	I.	155
54	Ballinunty	218 2 33	Tipperary, S.R.	Slievardagh	Graystown	Urlingford	II.	333
48, 54	Ballinunty	241 3 27	Tipperary, S.R.	Slievardagh	Kilcooly	Urlingford	II.	333
54	BALLINUNTY T.	—	Tipperary, S.R.	Slievardagh	{ Kilcooly	Urlingford	II. }	334
					{ Killenaule	Cashel	II. }	
6	Ballinurd	219 2 37b	Louth	Upper Dundalk	Barronstown	Dundalk	I.	177
45, 54	Ballinure	304 1 39	Cork, E.R.	Barrymore	Gortroe	Fermoy	II.	54
74, 75	Ballinure	482 2 6	Cork, E.R.	Cork	St. Finbars	Cork	II.	65
16	Ballinure	218 3 26	Kildare	Offaly East	Rathangan	Edenderry	I.	70
53	Ballinure	853 1 22	Tipperary, S.R.	Slievardagh	Graystown	Cashel	II.	333
34, 35	Ballinure	79 2 39	Waterford	Decies within Drum	Clashmore	Youghal	II.	351
31	Ballinure	58 0 15	Waterford	Decies without Drum	Dungarvan	Dungarvan	II.	354
19	Ballinure	284 2 6	Wexford	Scarawalsh	Monart	Enniscorthy	I.	324
14	Ballinure or Ballyhealy	884 2 38	Westmeath	Delvin	Castletowndelvin	Castletowndelvin	I.	264
79	Ballinurra	886 1 29	Tipperary, S.R.	Iffa and Offa East	Newtownlennan	Carrick on Suir	II.	315
31	Ballinva	132 0 16	Kilkenny	Knocktopher	Aghaviller	Thomastown	I.	110
21	Ballinvack	116 0 22	Wexford	Ballaghkeen	Kilnamanagh	Gorey	I.	297
12, 18	Ballinvalla or Sleamaine	540 3 19	Wicklow	Ballinacor North	Calary	Rathdrum	I.	346
36	Ballinvallig	112 1 3	Limerick	Glenquin	Monagay	Newcastle	II.	247
13, 17	Ballinvally	216 3 18	Carlow	Forth	Ballon	Carlow	I.	3
17, 18	Ballinvally	427 1 10	Carlow	Forth	Barragh	Enniscorthy	I.	4
15, 20, 21	Ballinvally	1,030 2 21	Gowran	Gowran	Kilmacahill	Kilkenny	I.	97
25	Ballinvally	1,473 0 9	King's Co.	Geashill	Geashill	Tullamore	I.	139
9, 15	Ballinvally	575 0 3	Meath	Fore	Oldcastle	Oldcastle	I.	202
32	Ballinvally	85 1 19	Sligo	Leyny	Achonry	Tobercurry	IV.	228
25	Ballinvally	234 0 32	Sligo	Leyny	Killoran	Tobercurry	IV.	230
8, 13	Ballinvally	264 3 23	Westmeath	Delvin	Castletowndelvin	Castletowndelvin	I.	264
21	Ballinvally	61 0 5	Wexford	Ballaghkeen	Kilnamanagh	Gorey	I.	297
16, 17	Ballinvally	277 3 5	Wexford	Gorey	Monamolin	Gorey	I.	321
39, 44	Ballinvally	211 1 8	Wicklow	Arklow	Killahurler	Rathdrum	I.	345
38	Ballinvally East	252 1 12	Sligo	Corran	Cloonoghill	Tobercurry	IV.	225
22	Ballinvally and Kiltennell	298 0 10	Carlow	Idrone East	Kiltennell	New Ross	I.	7
40	Ballinvally Lower	188 2 8	Wicklow	Arklow	Killahurler	Rathdrum	I.	345
35, 36	Ballinvally Lower	251 0 24	Wicklow	Arklow	Redcross	Rathdrum	I.	345
38	Ballinvally or Roadstown	213 1 34	Sligo	Corran	Cloonoghill	Tobercurry	IV.	225
39, 40	Ballinvally Upper	168 2 34	Wicklow	Arklow	Killahurler	Rathdrum	I.	345
35	Ballinvally Upper	201 3 0	Wicklow	Arklow	Redcross	Rathdrum	I.	345
35	Ballinvally (Valentine)	386 1 33	Wicklow	Arklow	Castlemacadam	Rathdrum	I.	342
38	Ballinvally West	66 3 9	Sligo	Corran	Cloonoghill	Tobercurry	IV.	225
35	Ballinvally (Wisdom)	382 1 7	Wicklow	Arklow	Castlemacadam	Rathdrum	I.	342
40, 48	Ballinvana	369 2 9	Limerick	Coshlea	Athneasy	Kilmallock	II.	237
40, 48	Ballinvana	126 2 26	Limerick	Coshlea	Emlygrennan	Kilmallock	II.	238
40	Ballinva North	101 0 7	Kilkenny	Knocktopher	Killahy	Waterford	I.	112
111	Ballinvard	132 0 10	Cork, E.R.	Kinsale	Clontead	Kinsale	II.	99
121	Ballinvard	199 2 28	Cork, W.R.	East Carbery (W.D.)	Kilmean	Clonakilty	II.	133
39	Ballinvariscal	405 2 34	Kerry	Trughanacmy	Nohaval	Tralee	II.	212
98, 99	Ballinvarosig	203 0 33	Cork, E.R.	Kinalea	Carrigaline	Kinsale	II.	94
63	Ballinvarrig	795 1 31	Cork, E.R.	Cork	Whitechurch	Cork	II.	66
99, 113	Ballinvarrig	392 3 21	Cork, E.R.	Kinalea	Tracton	Kinsale	II.	97
48	Ballinvarrig	151 3 30	Kerry	Magunihy	Molahiffe	Killarney	II.	204
45	Ballinvarrig East	21 0 32	Cork, E.R.	Barrymore	Gortroe	Fermoy	II.	54
67	Ballinvarrig Lower	188 1 0	Cork, E.R.	Imokilly	Clonpriest	Youghal	II.	84
67	Ballinvarrig Upper	304 3 23	Cork, E.R.	Imokilly	Clonpriest	Youghal	II.	84
44, 45	Ballinvarrig West	196 3 25	Cork, E.R.	Barrymore	Gortroe	Fermoy	II.	54
33	Ballinvarry	121 1 34	Kilkenny	Ida	The Rower	Thomastown	I.	104
33	Ballinvarry English	449 1 35	Kilkenny	Ida	The Rower	Thomastown	I.	104
33	Ballinvarry Irish	157 3 9	Kilkenny	Ida	The Rower	Thomastown	I.	104
51, 59	Ballinvasa	224 3 2	Tipperary, S.R.	Clanwilliam	Donohill	Tipperary	II.	307
40	Ballinva South	60 1 00	Kilkenny	Knocktopher	Killahy	Waterford	I.	112
21, 22	Ballinveala	352 3 32	Limerick	Pubblebrien	Crecora	Croom	II.	252
66	Ballinvee	120 3 4	Tipperary, S.R.	Clanwilliam	Tipperary	Tipperary	II.	312

(a) Including 6A. 3R. 9P. water.　　　　　　　(b) Including 0A. 3R. 8P. water.

No. of Sheet of the Ordnance Survey Maps.	Townlands and Towns.	Area in Statute Acres.	County.	Barony.	Parish.	Poor Law Union in 1857.	Townland Census of 1851, Part I.	
		A. R. P.					Vol.	Page
36	Ballinveelig . .	147 0 22	Cork, E. R. .	Condons & Clangibbon	Clondulane . .	Fermoy . .	II.	60
24, 30	Ballinvegga . .	521 0 37	Wexford . .	Bantry . . .	Ballyanne . .	New Ross . .	I.	299
73, 85	Ballinveiltig . .	205 2 22	Cork, E. R. .	Cork . . .	Inishkenny . .	Cork . . .	II.	64
29	Ballinvella . .	223 1 35	Waterford .	Coshmore and Coshbride . .	Lismore and Mocollop	Lismore . .	II.	344
27	Ballinvella . .	251 0 24	Waterford .	Gaultiere . .	Kilmacleague .	Waterford . .	II.	364
22, 28	Ballinveny . .	849 1 22	Tipperary, N. R.	Upper Ormond .	Aghnameadle .	Nenagh . .	II.	288
69, 70	Ballinvilla . .	275 3 28a	Mayo . .	Carra . . .	Aglish . . .	Castlebar . .	IV.	123
112	Ballinvilla . .	436 1 12	Mayo . .	Clanmorris . .	Kilvine . .	Claremorris . .	IV.	134
10, 11	Ballinvilla . .	406 1 1b	Roscommon .	Boyle . . .	Killummod . .	Carkⁿ. on Shannon	IV.	196
10, 15	Ballinvilla . .	53 0 39	Tipperary, N. R.	Lower Ormond .	Ardcrony . .	Nenagh . .	II.	281
102	Ballinvilla Demesne	76 3 32	Mayo . .	Costello . .	Bekan . . .	Claremorris . .	IV.	138
64	Ballinvinny North .	265 0 25	Cork, E. R. .	Barrymore . .	Killaspugmullane .	Cork . . .	II.	55
64	Ballinvinny South .	325 0 26	Cork, E. R. .	Barrymore . .	Killaspugmullane .	Cork . . .	II.	55
72, 79	Ballinvir . . .	369 1 23	Tipperary, S. R.	Slievardagh . .	Templemichael .	Carrick on Suir	II.	336
20	Ballinvira . .	26 0 23	Limerick . .	Connello Lower .	Cappagh . .	Rathkeale . .	II.	227
20	Ballinvira . .	413 2 18	Limerick . .	Connello Lower .	Croagh . . .	Rathkeale . .	II.	227
20	Ballinvirick . .	278 2 7	Limerick . .	Connello Lower .	Nantinan . .	Rathkeale . .	II.	229
79	Ballinvoash . .	180 0 13	Mayo . .	Carra . . .	Turlough . .	Castlebar . .	IV.	130
44	Ballinvogig . .	174 3 15	Kerry . .	Corkaguiny . .	Minard . .	Dingle . .	II.	179
20, 28	Ballinvoher . .	1,261 3 3	Cork, E. R. .	Condons & Clangibbon	Kilworth . .	Fermoy . .	II.	62
26	Ballinvoher . .	637 2 6	Cork, E. R. .	Fermoy . . .	Castletownroche .	Fermoy . .	II.	77
88	Ballinvoher . .	23 3 28	Cork, E. R. .	Imokilly . .	Ballintemple .	Middleton . .	II.	84
88	Ballinvoher . .	247 3 12	Cork, E. R. .	Imokilly . .	Cloyne . .	Middleton . .	II.	85
42	Ballinvoher . .	124 2 25	Galway . .	Clare . . .	Donaghpatrick .	Tuam . .	IV.	19
57, 70, 71	Ballinvoher . .	136 2 22	Galway . .	Clare . . .	Lackagh . .	Galway . .	IV.	22
20	Ballinvoher . .	72 2 27	Kerry . .	Clanmaurice . .	Ardfert . .	Tralee . .	II.	167
15	Ballinvoher . .	148 1 15	Kerry . .	Clanmaurice . .	Kiltomy . .	Listowel . .	II.	172
26	Ballinvoher . .	193 2 39	King's Co. .	Upper Philipstown .	Ballykean . .	Mountmellick .	I.	143
3, 11	Ballinvoher . .	367 3 15	Limerick . .	Kenry . . .	Iverus . .	Rathkeale . .	II.	248
19	Ballinvoher . .	42 2 24	Longford . .	Moydow . .	Moydow . .	Longford . .	I.	162
71	Ballinvoher . .	98 1 19	Mayo . .	Gallen . .	Meelick . .	Swineford . .	IV.	150
9	Ballinvoher . .	177 2 35	Roscommon .	Boyle . . .	Eastersnow . .	Boyle . .	IV.	194
9	Ballinvoher . .	192 2 22	Roscommon .	Frenchpark . .	Kilnamanagh .	Boyle . .	IV.	204
8, 14	Ballinvoher . .	177 1 25	Sligo . .	Carbury . .	Drumcliff . .	Sligo . .	IV.	221
33	Ballinvoher . .	198 2 38	Sligo . .	Corran . .	Toomour . .	Sligo . .	IV.	228
77	Ballinvoher . .	208 3 20	Tipperary, S. R.	Iffa and Offa East .	Kilgrant . .	Clonmel . .	II.	314
9, 10	Ballinvoher . .	112 1 17	Waterford .	Gaultiere . .	Kilculliheen .	Waterford . .	II.	363
47	Ballinvoher North .	236 0 20	Galway . .	Killian . .	Killeroran . .	Mountbellew .	IV.	43
47	Ballinvoher South .	355 0 8	Galway . .	Killian . .	Killeroran . .	Mountbellew .	IV.	43
113	Ballinvologe . .	220 0 30	Cork, E. R. .	Kinalea . .	Ballyfoyle . .	Kinsale . .	II.	94
8, 17	Ballinvonear . .	1,429 0 2	Cork, E. R. .	Fermoy . . .	Doneraile . .	Mallow . .	II.	78
29	Ballinvosherig East .	82 3 35	Kerry . .	Trughanacmy .	Ratass . .	Tralee . .	II.	213
29	Ballinvosherig West .	84 3 15	Kerry . .	Trughanacmy .	Ratass . .	Tralee . .	II.	213
85, 86	Ballinvoultig . .	189 2 35	Cork, E. R. .	Cork . . .	Inishkenny . .	Cork . . .	II.	64
43, 53	Ballinvownig . .	324 1 33	Kerry . .	Corkaguiny . .	Garfinny . .	Dingle . .	II.	176
88	Ballinvoy . .	117 2 2	Mayo . .	Burrishoole . .	Aghagower . .	Westport . .	IV.	117
98	Ballinvragnosig .	239 3 39	Cork, E. R. .	Kinalea . .	Cullen . .	Kinsale . .	II.	94
124	Ballinvredig . .	248 1 10	Cork, W. R. .	Courceys . .	Ringrone . .	Kinsale . .	II.	147
48	Ballinvreena . .	752 3 23	Limerick . .	Coshlea . .	Ballingarry . .	Kilmallock . .	II.	237
48	Ballinvreena . .	154 0 6	Limerick . .	Coshlea . .	Emlygrennan .	Kilmallock . .	II.	238
65	Ballinvreena . .	379 0 39	Tipperary, S. R.	Clanwilliam . .	Emly . . .	Tipperary . .	II.	307
85, 86	Ballinvrinsig . .	319 1 28	Cork, E. R. .	Cork . . .	Inishkenny . .	Cork . . .	II.	64
63	Ballinvriskig . .	689 3 7	Cork, E. R. .	Cork . . .	St. Michaels .	Cork . . .	II.	66
136	Ballinvrokig . .	246 0 3	Cork, W. R. .	Ibane and Barryroe .	Lislee . .	Clonakilty . .	II.	149
124	Ballinvronig . .	319 1 1	Cork, W. R. .	East Carbery (E.D.) .	Templetrine .	Kinsale . .	II.	130
28	Ballinvulla . .	59 0 7	Limerick . .	Connello Lower .	Clonagh . .	Rathkeale . .	II.	227
28	Ballinvulla . .	45 1 21	Limerick . .	Connello Lower .	Kilbradran . .	Rathkeale . .	II.	228
36	Ballinvullin . .	382 0 0	Limerick . .	Glenquin . .	Mahoonagh . .	Newcastle . .	II.	246
22	Ballinvunnia . .	91 0 0	Wexford . .	Ballaghkeen . .	Donaghmore .	Gorey . .	I.	293
22	Ballinvunnia . .	41 0 13	Wexford . .	Ballaghkeen . .	Kiltrisk . .	Gorey . .	I.	297
86	Ballinvuskig . .	494 3 13	Cork, E. R. .	Cork . . .	Killanully . .	Cork . .	II.	64
33, 42	Ballinvuskig East .	150 3 8	Cork, E. R. .	Fermoy . . .	Rahan . .	Mallow . .	II.	82
33, 42	Ballinvuskig West .	500 2 26	Cork, E. R. .	Fermoy . . .	Rahan . .	Mallow . .	II.	82
15	Ballinwear . .	171 1 21	Tipperary, N. R.	Lower Ormond .	Kilruane . .	Nenagh . .	II.	285
44, 45, 53, 54	Ballinwillin . .	351 3 11	Cork, E. R. .	Barrymore . .	Gortroe . .	Fermoy . .	II.	54
10, 19	Ballinwillin . .	138 3 32	Cork, E. R. .	Condons & Clangibbon	Brigown . .	Mitchelstown .	II.	59
88	Ballinwillin . .	140 0 36	Cork, E. R. .	Imokilly . .	Cloyne . .	Middleton . .	II.	85
112	Ballinwillin . .	112 3 20	Cork, E. R. .	Kinalea . .	Kinure . .	Kinsale . .	II.	95
112	Ballinwillin . .	11 2 39	Cork, E. R. .	Kinalea . .	Nohaval . .	Kinsale . .	II.	96
38, 46	Ballinwillin . .	179 1 12	Limerick . .	Connello Upper .	Bruree . .	Kilmallock . .	II.	231
29	Ballinwillin . .	145 3 1	Waterford .	Coshmore & Coshbride	Lismore and Mocollop	Lismore . .	II.	344
27	Ballinwing . .	279 2 14	Leitrim . .	Leitrim . . .	Kiltoghert . .	Carkⁿ. on Shannon	IV.	101

(a) Including 13A. 0R. 37P. water.　　　　　(b) Including 26A. 2R. 7P. water.

I

No. of Sheet of the Ordnance Survey Maps.	Townlands and Towns.	Area in Statute Acres. A. R. P.	County.	Barony.	Parish.	Poor Law Union in 1857.	Townland Census of 1851, Part I. Vol.	Page
38	Ballinwire	258 2 29	Westmeath	Moycashel	Kilbeggan	Tullamore	I.	278
36	Ballinwully	164 0 2	Roscommon	Ballintober South	Kilgefin	Roscommon	IV.	189
4	Balliny North	225 3 12	Clare	Burren	Killonaghan	Ballyvaghan	II.	13
4	Balliny South	209 2 1	Clare	Burren	Killonaghan	Ballyvaghan	II.	13
12	Ballisk	53 0 33	Dublin	Nethercross	Portraine	Balrothery	I.	31
8, 12	Ballisk Common	95 3 29	Dublin	Nethercross	Portraine	Balrothery	I.	31
12	BALLISK T.	—	Dublin	Nethercross	Portraine	Balrothery	I.	31
123	Ballisnahyny	315 3 33	Mayo	Kilmaine	Kilmainebeg	Ballinrobe	IV.	155
123	Ballisnahyny	839 2 35a	Mayo	Kilmaine	Shrule	Ballinrobe	IV.	158
36	Ballitore	637 2 36	Kildare	Narragh & Reban East	Timolin	Baltinglass	I.	67
36	BALLITORE T.	—	Kildare	Narragh & Reban East	Timolin	Baltinglass	I.	67
22, 30	Balliver	483 3 20	King's Co.	Garrycastle	Gallen	Parsonstown	I.	135
35, 41	Ballivor	768 0 37	Meath	Lune	Killaconnigan	Trim	I.	208
35	BALLIVOR T.	—	Meath	Lune	Killaconnigan	Trim	I.	208
13, 17	Ballon	322 1 23	Carlow	Forth	Ballon	Carlow	I.	3
39	Ballonaghan or Harristown	75 1 30	Sligo	Corran	Kilshalvy	Boyle	IV.	227
13	BALLON T.	—	Carlow	Forth	Ballon	Carlow	I.	3
41	Balloo	341 3 15b	Antrim	Lower Belfast	Islandmagee	Larne	III.	8
50, 55	Balloo	560 0 15	Antrim	Lower Massereene	Muckamore (Grange of)	Antrim	III.	28
2, 6	Balloo	533 0 0	Down	Ards Lower	Bangor	Newtownards	III.	157
16, 17	Balloo	474 2 11	Down	Dufferin	Killinchy	Downpatrick	III.	166
16	Balloo	272 2 5	Longford	Ardagh	Street	Granard	I.	153
2	Balloo Lower	383 1 29	Down	Ards Lower	Bangor	Newtownards	III.	157
27, 28	Ballooly	428 3 18	Down	Upper Iveagh, Lr. pt.	Garvaghy	Banbridge	III.	172
99	Ballooly	18 1 31	Galway	Longford	Kiltormer	Ballinasloe	IV.	60
99	Ballooly (Eyre)	38 0 24	Galway	Longford	Killoran	Ballinasloe	IV.	59
99	Ballooly (Kelly)	56 3 35	Galway	Longford	Killoran	Ballinasloe	IV.	59
99	Ballooly (McDermott)	74 1 24	Galway	Longford	Killoran	Ballinasloe	IV.	59
34, 35	Balloolymore	916 0 21	Down	Upper Iveagh, Lr. pt.	Garvaghy	Banbridge	III.	172
29	Balloonagh	48 2 39	Kerry	Trughanacmy	Tralee	Tralee	II.	213
13	Balloonigan	154 1 14	Down	Lower Iveagh, Up.pt.	Moira	Lurgan	III.	170
21, 27	Balloony	132 0 35	Roscommon	Castlereagh	Baslick	Castlereagh	IV.	199
8, 9	Balloor	425 2 16c	Donegal	Kilmacrenan	Clondavaddog	Milford	III.	124
78	Balloor	151 0 5	Mayo	Carra	Breaghwy	Castlebar	IV.	126
72, 81	Balloor	168 2 20	Mayo	Costello	Aghamore	Swineford	IV.	136
86	Balloor	179 1 16	Mayo	Murrisk	Kilgeever	Westport	IV.	159
72, 81	Balloorclerhy	475 3 1d	Mayo	Gallen	Killedan	Swineford	IV.	149
99	Balloor East	145 0 12	Mayo	Carra	Ballintober	Castlebar	IV.	124
89	Balloor West	80 0 6	Mayo	Carra	Ballintober	Castlebar	IV.	124
7, 8	Ballough	398 2 26e	Dublin	Balrothery East	Lusk	Balrothery	I.	20
21, 22, 29, 30	Balloughadalla	635 3 18f	Mayo	Tirawley	Ballysakeery	Ballina	IV.	164
35	Balloughly	282 3 26	Cavan	Clankee	Enniskeen	Bailieborough	III.	72
20	Balloughry	670 3 0	Londonderry	North West Liberties of Londonderry	Templemore	Londonderry	III.	246
9, 10	Ballought	250 3 17g	Tyrone	Strabane Lower	Ardstraw	Strabane	III.	318
11, 16	Balloughter	246 1 15	Wexford	Gorey	Toome	Gorey	I.	321
26, 27	Balloughter or Hightown	1,283 1 16	Westmeath	Farbill	Killucan	Mullingar	I.	267
46	Balloughton	420 0 30	Wexford	Bargy	Kilcavan	Wexford	I.	305
6, 7	Ballowen or Ramsfortpark	324 3 31	Wexford	Gorey	Kilmakilloge	Gorey	I.	318
28	Balloy	384 3 26	Meath	Upper Duleek	Stamullin	Drogheda	I.	198
24, 28	Ballsallagh	1,213 3 28	Antrim	Lower Antrim	Skerry	Ballymena	III.	4
18	Ballsbridge	32 3 37	Dublin	Dublin	Donnybrook	Dublin South	I.	30
18	BALLSBRIDGE T.	—	Dublin	Dublin	Donnybrook	Dublin South	I.	30
20	Ballsgrove	26 0 23	Louth	Municipal Borough of Drogheda	St. Marys	Drogheda	I.	185
20	Ballsgrove	84 1 14	Meath	Drogheda	St. Marys	Drogheda	I.	194
8, 9	Ballug	147 0 27	Louth	Lower Dundalk	Carlingford	Dundalk	I.	176
15	Ballure	81 0 33	Antrim	Lower Glenarm	Grange of Inispollan	Ballycastle	III.	21
15	Ballure	169 0 4h	Sligo	Carbury	Calry	Sligo	IV.	220
8	Ballustree	95 0 30	Dublin	Balrothery East	Lusk	Balrothery	I.	20
19	Ballyadack North	196 2 14	Cork, E.R.	Condons&Clangibbon	Kilphelan	Mitchelstown	II.	62
19	Ballyadack South	113 3 15	Cork, E.R.	Condons&Clangibbon	Kilphelan	Mitchelstown	II.	62
76	Ballyadam	256 3 16	Cork, E.R.	Barrymore	Carrigtohill	Middleton	II.	52
16	Ballyadam	104 3 22	Cork, E.R.	Orrery and Kilmore	Churchtown	Mallow	II.	107
25	Ballyadam	115 3 9	Down	Ards Upper	Castleboy	Downpatrick	III.	160
14, 23	Ballyadam	197 3 1	Limerick	Clanwilliam	Caherconlish	Limerick	II.	222
20	Ballyadam	75 2 11	Limerick	Connello Lower	Nantinan	Rathkeale	II.	229
25	Ballyadam	990 1 0	Waterford	Middlethird	Kelsk	Waterford	II.	368
21, 22, 27, 28	Ballyadam	430 1 1	Wexford	Ballaghkeen	Kilmuckridge	Gorey	I.	296
31, 32	Ballyadams	93 2 33	Kildare	Narragh & Reban East	Narraghmore	Athy	I.	66

(a) Including 8A. 1R. 10P. water.
(b) Including 12A. 1R. 8P. water.
(c) Including 13A. 0R. 12P. water.
(d) Including 5A. 0R. 36P. water.
(e) Including 3A. 3R. 27P. detached portions.
(f) Including 66A. 1R. 18P. water.
(g) Including 1A. 0R. 36P. water.
(h) Including 14A. 0R. 17P. water.

No. of Sheet of the Ordnance Survey Maps.	Townlands and Towns.	Area in Statute Acres.	County.	Barony.	Parish.	Poor Law Union in 1857.	Townland Census of 1851, Part I.	
		A. R. P.					Vol.	Page
41	Ballyadams	268 1 27a	Meath	Moyfenrath Upper	Killyon	Trim	I.	213
19	Ballyadams	575 1 27	Queen's Co.	Ballyadams	Ballyadams	Athy	I.	231
9	Ballyadding	302 2 2	Queen's Co.	Portnahinch	Lea	Mountmellick	I.	244
48	Ballyaddragh	85 2 19	Wexford	Forth	Kilrane	Wexford	I.	311
26	Ballyadeen	553 0 26	Cork, E.R.	Fermoy	Castletownroche	Fermoy	II.	77
15	Ballyagan	96 3 20	Antrim	Lower Glenarm	Layd	Ballycastle	III.	22
18	Ballyagan	523 1 7	Londonderry	Coleraine	Desertoghill	Coleraine	III.	230
56, 57	Ballyaghagan	527 1 30	Antrim	Upper Belfast	Shankill	Belfast	III.	10
16, 23	Ballyagherty	376 0 39b	Down	Castlereagh Upper	Saintfield	Lisburn	III.	166
9, 15	Ballyaghlis	302 2 37	Down	Castlereagh Upper	Drumbeg	Lisburn	III.	164
51	Ballyagholy	682 0 5	Down	Upper Iveagh, Upper part	Kilbroney	Newry	III.	175
3, 11	Ballyaglish	259 3 25	Limerick	Kenry	Iverus	Rathkeale	II.	248
42	Ballyaglisha	191 0 26	Kerry	Corkaguiny	Dunurlin	Dingle	II.	176
46	Ballyagran	321 0 15	Limerick	Connello Upper	Corcomohide	Croom	II.	232
46	BALLYAGRAN T.	—	Limerick	Connello Upper	Corcomohide	Croom	II.	232
39, 45	Ballyalbanagh	2,253 2 25	Antrim	Upper Antrim	Ballycor	Larne	III.	6
23	Ballyalgan	664 3 34	Down	Dufferin	Killyleagh	Downpatrick	III.	167
6	Ballyalicock	279 1 5	Down	Ards Lower	Newtownards	Newtownards	III.	158
8, 15	Ballyalla	272 3 39c	Clare	Corcomroe	Kilshanny	Ennistimon	II.	21
104	Ballyalla	156 1 35	Donegal	Tirhugh	Drumhome	Donegal	III.	146
9, 14	Ballyalla	221 0 39	Tipperary, N.R.	Lower Ormond	Killodiernan	Nenagh	II.	284
5	Ballyallaban	752 0 29	Clare	Burren	Rathborney	Ballyvaghan	II.	14
3	Ballyallaght	164 0 32	Antrim	Cary	Billy	Ballycastle	III.	12
76	Ballyallavoe	86 0 16	Tipperary, S.R.	Iffa and Offa West	Caher	Clogheen	II.	317
25, 33	Ballyallia	295 2 26d	Clare	Bunratty Upper	Templemaley	Ennis	II.	10
29	Ballyallinan North	619 3 17	Limerick	Connello Lower	Rathkeale	Rathkeale	II.	229
29	Ballyallinan South	666 2 32	Limerick	Connello Lower	Rathkeale	Rathkeale	II.	229
10	Ballyalloly	419 1 23e	Down	Castlereagh Lower	Comber	Newtownards	III.	161
159	Ballyally	193 0 32f	Cork, W.R.	West Carbery (E D.)	Creagh	Skibbereen	II.	138
10	Ballyaltikilligan	338 3 6	Down	Castlereagh Lower	Comber	Newtownards	III.	161
5	Ballyalton	148 1 31	Down	Castlereagh Lower	Comber	Newtownards	III.	161
5	Ballyalton	150 1 5	Down	Castlereagh Lower	Newtownards	Newtownards	III.	163
38	Ballyalton	240 0 38	Down	Lecale Lower	Ballee	Downpatrick	III.	178
53	Ballyameenboght	68 0 10	Kerry	Corkaguiny	Dingle	Dingle	II.	175
53	Ballyameentrant	118 0 32	Kerry	Corkaguiny	Kildrum	Dingle	II.	177
19, 20	Ballyan	396 3 3	Limerick	Shanid	Kilbradran	Rathkeale	II.	255
89	Ballyandreen	74 0 33	Cork, E.R.	Imokilly	Ballintemple	Middleton	II.	84
45	Ballyandreen	175 1 16	Kerry	Corkaguiny	Ballinvoher	Dingle	II.	173
89	BALLYANDREEN T.	—	Cork, E.R.	Imokilly	Kilmahon	Middleton	II.	89
25	Ballyandrew	428 1 31	Cork, E.R.	Fermoy	Doneraile	Mallow	II.	78
10	Ballyandrew	389 2 18	Wexford	Scarawalsh	Ferns	Enniscorthy	I.	323
10	Ballyandrew	191 0 36	Wexford	Scarawalsh	Kilrush	Enniscorthy	I.	324
18, 19	Ballyane	184 1 24	Limerick	Shanid	Kilmoylan	Glin	II.	256
123	Ballyaneen North	138 1 17	Galway	Kiltartan	Kiltartan	Gort	IV.	48
123	Ballyaneen South	130 0 26	Galway	Kiltartan	Kiltartan	Gort	IV.	48
39	Ballyania	356 2 26	Limerick	Coshma	Uregare	Kilmallock	II.	244
61,62,72,73	Ballyanly	498 2 8	Cork, E.R.	East Muskerry	Inisbcarra	Cork	II.	103
76	Ballyannan	363 0 8	Cork, E.R.	Barrymore	Mogeesha	Middleton	II.	57
18, 19	Ballyannan	1,306 1 7	Donegal	Inishowen West	Desertegny	Inishowen	III.	120
29, 30	Ballyanne	714 3 6	Wexford	Bantry	Ballyanne	New Ross	I.	299
17	Ballyanny	42 2 19	Armagh	Fews Lower	Mullaghbrack	Armagh	III.	47
14	Ballyanny Lower	390 2 39	Tipperary, N.R.	Lower Ormond	Knigh	Nenagh	II.	285
14	Ballyannymore	369 3 39	Tipperary, N.R.	Lower Ormond	Knigh	Nenagh	II.	285
14, 20	Ballyanny Upper	239 2 13	Tipperary, N.R.	Lower Ormond	Knigh	Nenagh	II.	285
26	Ballyanrahan	270 1 3	Tipperary, N.R.	Upper Ormond	Kilmore	Nenagh	II.	290
12	Ballyanrahan East	316 0 27	Limerick	Pubblebrien	Kilkeedy	Limerick	II.	252
12	Ballyanrahan West	105 3 13	Limerick	Pubblebrien	Kilkeedy	Limerick	II.	252
46, 55	Ballyanthony	273 0 9	Cork, E.R.	Kinnatalloon	Mogeely	Youghal	II.	98
91, 97	Ballyara	900 2 3	Donegal	Banagh	Killybegs Upper	Glenties	III.	110
59, 60	Ballyara	300 2 39	Galway	Tiaquin	Killoscobe	Mountbellew	IV.	77
37	Ballyara or Falduff	239 0 25	Sligo	Leyny	Achonry	Tobercurry	IV.	228
37, 38	Ballyara (Knox)	383 2 8	Sligo	Leyny	Achonry	Tobercurry	IV.	228
54	Ballyard	207 2 30	Cork, E.R.	Barrymore	Britway	Middleton	II.	51
55	Ballyard	349 2 16	Cork, E.R.	Barrymore	Clonmult	Middleton	II.	53
29	Ballyard	148 0 6	Kerry	Trughanacmy	Annagh	Tralee	II.	205
31	Ballyard	630 0 36	Tipperary, N.R.	Owney and Arra	Kilcomenty	Nenagh	II.	294
49, 50, 57	Ballyard	351 3 4	Tyrone	Omagh East	Kilskeery	Lowtherstown	III.	313
22	Ballyard	84 3 6	Waterford	Decies without Drum	Whitechurch	Lismore	II.	361
6	Ballyardan	103 0 21	Roscommon	Boyle	Ardcarn	Boyle	IV.	192
7	Ballyard or Bellair	1,262 3 24	King's Co.	Garrycastle	Lemanaghan	Parsonstown	I.	136
55, 57	Ballyardel	348 0 16	Down	Mourne	Kilkeel	Kilkeel	III.	182
16	Ballyards	538 0 0	Armagh	Armagh	Lisnadill	Armagh	III.	45

(a) Including 9A. 0R. 8P. water.
(b) Including 1A. 3R. 2P. water.
(c) Including 1A. 2R. 27P. water.
(d) Including 56A. 0R. 26P. water.
(e) Including 29A. 3R. 27P. water.
(f) Including 6A. 0R. 8P. water.

I 2

No. of Sheet of the Ordnance Survey Maps.	Townlands and Towns.	Area in Statute Acres.			County.	Barony.	Parish.	Poor Law Union in 1857.	Townland Census of 1851, Part I.	
		A.	R.	P.					Vol.	Page
116	Ballyargadaun	486	0	20	Galway	Leitrim	Leitrim	Loughrea	IV.	55
118	Ballyargadaun	205	2	15	Mayo	Kilmaine	Ballinchalla	Ballinrobe	IV.	151
118	Ballyargadaun	161	1	5	Mayo	Kilmaine	Kilmolara	Ballinrobe	IV.	156
18	Ballyargan	197	3	21a	Armagh	Orior Lower	Ballymore	Banbridge	III.	55
20, 21, 31	Ballyargus	1,368	1	1b	Donegal	Inishowen East	Moville Upper	Inishowen	III.	119
46	Ballyarkane Eighter	500	2	25	Kerry	Trughanacmy	Kilgarrylander	Dingle	II.	210
37, 46	Ballyarkane Oughter	670	1	3	Kerry	Trughanacmy	Kilgarrylander	Dingle	II.	210
13	Ballyarnet	603	2	27c	Londonderry	North West Liberties of Londonderry	Templemore	Londonderry	III.	246
50, 55	Ballyarnot	320	3	4	Antrim	Lower Massereene	Muckamore (Grange of)	Antrim	III.	28
45	Ballyarr	446	1	30	Donegal	Kilmacrenan	Tullyfern	Millford	III.	132
45	Ballyarra	744	1	28	Cork, E.R.	Barrymore	Castlelyons	Fermoy	II.	53
78, 87	Ballyarrell	862	0	25d	Donegal	Raphoe	Donaghmore	Stranorlar	III.	137
45	Ballyarr Glebe	231	1	17	Donegal	Kilmacrenan	Tullyfern	Millford	III.	132
14, 15	Ballyart	320	0	8	Limerick	Clanwilliam	Caherconlish	Limerick	II.	222
70	Ballyart	70	2	30	Mayo	Carra	Turlough	Castlebar	IV.	130
17	Ballyart	382	1	25	Wexford	Gorey	Kiltrisk	Gorey	I.	320
7	Ballyartan	71	0	5	Londonderry	North East Liberties of Coleraine	Coleraine	Coleraine	III.	246
22, 28	Ballyartan	786	1	24	Londonderry	Tirkeeran	Cumber Upper	Londonderry	III.	249
14	Ballyartella	231	2	8	Tipperary, N.R.	Lower Ormond	Dromineer	Nenagh	II.	283
14	Ballyartella	54	0	21	Tipperary, N.R.	Lower Ormond	Monsea	Nenagh	II.	287
27, 35	Ballyarthur	126	3	35	Cork, E.R.	Condons&Clangibbon	Fermoy	Fermoy	II.	60
10	Ballyarthur	852	3	17	Cork, E.R.	Condons&Clangibbon	Marshalstown	Mitchelstown	II.	63
40	Ballyarthur	448	2	11	Wicklow	Arklow	Castlemacadam	Rathdrum	I.	342
68, 69	Ballyartney	395	2	18	Clare	Clonderalaw	Killofin	Killadysert	II.	16
12	Ballyashea	210	3	16e	Limerick	Kenry	Kildimo	Rathkeale	II.	249
24, 25, 33	Ballyasheea	500	1	5	Clare	Inchiquin	Kilnamona	Ennis	II.	27
38, 42	Ballyatty	379	1	6	King's Co.	Clonlisk	Ettagh	Roscrea	I.	130
12	Ballyatwood	270	1	37	Down	Ards Upper	Ballywalter	Newtownards	III.	160
48, 52	Ballyaughian	2,218	2	6	Down	Upper Iveagh, Lr. pt.	Clonduff	Newry	III.	171
29, 30	Ballyaukeen	299	2	6	Kerry	Trughanacmy	Ballymacelligott	Tralee	II.	206
10	Ballyavelin North	113	2	21	Londonderry	Keenaght	Drumachose	NewTnLimavady	III.	235
10	Ballyavelin South	23	1	36	Londonderry	Keenaght	Balteagh	NewTnLimavady	III.	234
25, 26	Ballyavill	569	0	31	King's Co.	Geashill	Geashill	Tullamore	I.	139
82, 94	Ballybaan Beg	441	1	23	Galway	Galway	St. Nicholas	Galway	IV.	38
82, 94	Ballybaan More	222	0	36	Galway	Galway	St. Nicholas	Galway	IV.	38
84	Ballybackagh	318	1	23	Galway	Clare	Athenry	Galway	IV.	17
114	Ballybackagh	78	3	28	Galway	Loughrea	Ardrahan	Loughrea	IV.	62
121	Ballybackagh	83	0	0	Mayo	Kilmaine	Kilmainebeg	Ballinrobe	IV.	155
15	Ballybahallagh	1,077	3	25	Cork, E.R.	Duhallow	Churchtown	Kanturk	II.	67
14	Ballybailie	324	3	38	Louth	Ardee	Ardee	Ardee	I.	171
88	Ballyballinaun	192	0	26f	Mayo	Burrishoole	Aghagower	Westport	IV.	118
43, 57	Ballybanagher	270	1	36g	Galway	Clare	Cummer	Tuam	IV.	18
108, 109	Ballybanaun Mountain	472	0	14	Mayo	Carra	Ballyovey	Ballinrobe	IV.	126
15, 16	Ballybane	488	0	37	Cork, E.R.	Duhallow	Kilbrin	Kanturk	II.	71
89	Ballybane	491	1	23	Cork, E.R.	Imokilly	Cloyne	Middleton	II.	85
17, 21	Ballybane	208	1	0	Dublin	Uppercross	Clondalkin	Dublin South	I.	39
48	Ballybane	262	2	0	Kerry	Magunihy	Molahiffe	Killarney	II.	204
46	Ballybane	405	2	16	Limerick	Connello Upper	Corcomohide	Croom	II.	232
31	Ballybane	87	0	20	Limerick	Coshma	Tullabracky	Kilmallock	II.	244
21	Ballybane and Aungierstown	62	2	10	Dublin	Newcastle	Kilmactalway	Celbridge	I.	33
131	Ballybane East	847	3	21	Cork, W.R.	West Carbery (W.D.)	Skull	Skull	II.	145
25, 32	Ballybane Lower	151	0	3	Roscommon	Castlereagh	Kiltullagh	Castlereagh	IV.	201
25, 32	Ballybane (Reynolds)	145	1	15	Roscommon	Castlereagh	Kiltullagh	Castlereagh	IV.	201
25, 32	Ballybane Upper	92	2	31	Roscommon	Castlereagh	Kiltullagh	Castlereagh	IV.	201
131	Ballybane West	610	1	30	Cork, W.R.	West Carbery (W.D.)	Skull	Skull	II.	145
43	Ballybannan	577	3	39	Down	Lecale Upper	Kilmegan	Downpatrick	III.	181
7, 12	Ballybannon	416	0	8	Carlow	Carlow	Killerrig	Carlow	I.	2
26	Ballybanoge	285	2	24	Wexford	Ballaghkeen	Edermine	Enniscorthy	I.	294
11	Ballybanoge	289	3	17	Wexford	Gorey	Toome	Gorey	I.	321
7, 12	Ballybar Lower	465	0	19	Carlow	Carlow	Clonmelsh	Carlow	I.	1
5	Ballybarnes	255	1	19	Down	Castlereagh Lower	Newtownards	Newtownards	III.	163
32	Ballybarney	394	2	12	Kildare	Narragh & Reban East	Davidstown	Athy	I.	66
7, 12	Ballybarrack	428	0	19	Louth	Upper Dundalk	Ballybarrack	Dundalk	I.	177
7, 12	Ballybar Upper	491	3	36	Carlow	Carlow	Clonmelsh	Carlow	I.	1
25, 31	Ballybatter or Balreask New	114	0	37h	Meath	Lower Navan	Navan	Navan	I.	215
16	Ballybaun	990	1	99	Clare	Corcomroe	Killenora	Corrofin	II.	16
42, 56	Ballybaun	154	1	10	Galway	Clare	Kilcoona	Tuam	IV.	19
104	Ballybaun	115	2	5	Galway	Dunkellin	Ardrahan	Gort	IV.	26

(a) Including 5A. 2R. 30P. water.   (d) Including 5A. 1R. 25P. water.   (g) Including 14A. 0R. 16P. water.
(b) Including 10A. 3R. 27P. water.   (e) Including 2A. 1R. 13P. water.   (h) Including 1A. 1R. 24P. water.
(c) Including 1A. 2R. 26P. water.   (f) Including 9A. 3R. 23P. water.

No. of Sheet of the Ordnance Survey Maps.	Townlands and Towns.	Area in Statute Acres. A. R. P.	County.	Barony.	Parish.	Poor Law Union in 1857.	Townland Census of 1851, Part I. Vol.	Page
60, 61	Ballybaun	236 3 3	Galway	Kilconnell	Ahascragh	Mountbellew	IV.	38
86	Ballybaun	154 2 5	Galway	Kilconnell	Killallaghtan	Ballinasloe	IV.	41
46, 47	Ballybaun	287 3 7	Galway	Killian	Killian	Mountbellew	IV.	44
122, 128	Ballybaun	247 2 24	Galway	Kiltartan	Kilmacduagh	Gort	IV.	47
97	Ballybaun	229 1 14	Galway	Loughrea	Kilconickny	Loughrea	IV.	63
104	Ballybaun	139 2 21	Galway	Loughrea	Killogilleen	Loughrea	IV.	64
58	Ballybaun	271 3 0	Galway	Tiaquin	Abbeyknockmoy	Tuam	IV.	75
59, 72	Ballybaun	219 0 11	Galway	Tiaquin	Moylough	Mountbellew	IV.	79
20	Ballybaun	115 0 11	Limerick	Connello Lower	Nantinan	Rathkeale	II.	229
102, 112	Ballybaun	314 1 5	Mayo	Costello	Annagh	Claremorris	IV.	137
9, 10	Ballybaun	97 2 26	Roscommon	Boyle	Boyle	Boyle	IV.	193
27, 33	Ballybaun	168 2 30	Wexford	Ballaghkeen	Killisk	Enniscorthy	I.	296
18	Ballybaun	457 0 15	Wexford	Bantry	Templeludigan	New Ross	I.	303
7	Ballybawn Lower	148 0 25	Wicklow	Rathdown	Kilmacanoge	Rathdown	I.	355
7	Ballybawn Upper	24 1 0	Wicklow	Rathdown	Kilmacanoge	Rathdown	I.	355
19	BALLYBAY T.	—	Monaghan	Cremorne	Ballybay	Castleblayney	III.	259
17, 18	Ballybeagh	1,124 1 27	Kilkenny	Crannagh	Tullaroan	Kilkenny	I.	87
10	Ballybeen	421 0 21	Down	Castlereagh Lower	Comber	Newtownards	III.	161
5	Ballybeen	442 0 33	Down	Castlereagh Lower	Dundonald	Belfast	III.	162
2	Ballybeeny	140 3 29	Tyrone	Strabane Lower	Donaghedy	Strabane	III.	320
31,32,36,37	Ballybeg	425 2 14	Antrim	Toome Lower	Ahoghill	Ballymena	III.	31
33, 41	Ballybeg	318 0 29a	Clare	Islands	Clareabbey	Ennis	II.	29
19	Ballybeg	248 2 36	Cork, E.R.	Condons&Clangibbon	Brigown	Mitchelstown	II.	59
19	Ballybeg	92 2 19	Cork, E.R.	Condons&Clangibbon	Glanworth	Mitchelstown	II.	61
24, 25	Ballybeg	746 0 13	Cork, E.R.	Orrery and Kilmore	Buttevant	Mallow	II.	107
123, 124	Ballybeg	261 2 36	Cork, W.R.	East Carbery (E.D.)	Kilbrittain	Bandon	II.	128
38	Ballybeg	176 0 17	Down	Lecale Lower	Dunsfort	Downpatrick	III.	179
43	Ballybeg	173 2 34	Kerry	Corkaguiny	Dingle	Dingle	II.	175
42, 52	Ballybeg	188 3 2	Kerry	Corkaguiny	Ventry	Dingle	II.	180
30	Ballybeg	76 3 21	Kerry	Trughanacmy	Ballymacelligott	Tralee	II.	206
48, 49	Ballybeg	708 0 14	Kerry	Trughanacmy	Killeentierna	Killarney	II.	211
37	Ballybeg	233 3 29	Kilkenny	Ida	Rosbercon	New Ross	I.	103
42	Ballybeg	398 3 14	King's Co.	Clonlisk	Ettagh	Roscrea	I.	130
3, 10	Ballybeg	927 3 38	King's Co.	Lower Philipstown	Croghan	Edenderry	I.	142
24	Ballybeg	114 0 11	Limerick	Clanwilliam	Dromkeen	Limerick	II.	223
25	Ballybeg	158 3 23	Limerick	Coonagh	Oola	Tipperary	II.	235
40	Ballybeg	162 3 17	Limerick	Smallcounty	Uregare	Kilmallock	II.	261
19, 23	Ballybeg	250 1 26	Longford	Moydow	Taghsheenod	Ballymahon	I.	162
103	Ballybeg	119 0 2	Mayo	Costello	Annagh	Claremorris	IV.	137
26	Ballybeg	102 3 21b	Mayo	Erris	Kilcommon	Belmullet	IV.	143
39	Ballybeg	388 3 33c	Mayo	Tirawley	Ballynahaglish	Ballina	IV.	164
14	Ballybeg	716 3 14	Mayo	Tirawley	Rathreagh	Killala	II.	171
17, 24	Ballybeg	339 1 15	Meath	Upper Kells	Balrathboyne	Kells	I.	204
26	Ballybeg	127 0 37	Queen's Co.	Ballyadams	Tankardstown	Athy	I.	232
29	Bally Beg	53 0 19	Roscommon	Roscommon	Lissonuffy	Strokestown	IV.	211
28	Ballybeg	257 2 22	Roscommon	Roscommon	Ogulla	Strokestown	IV.	212
14	Ballybeg	86 2 20	Sligo	Carbury	Killaspugbrone	Sligo	IV.	222
11	Ballybeg	135 2 21	Sligo	Tireragh	Easky	Dromore West	IV.	233
48	Bally Beg	1,691 0 37	Tipperary, N.R.	Eliogarty	Twomileborris	Thurles	II.	273
22, 28	Ballybeg	730 0 15	Tipperary, N.R.	Upper Ormond	Aghnameadle	Nenagh	II.	288
59	Ballybeg	29 0 35	Tipperary, S.R.	Clanwilliam	Kilmucklin	Tipperary	II.	309
76, 77	Ballybeg	129 2 18	Tipperary, S.R.	Iffa and Offa East	Newchapel	Clonmel	II.	315
82, 88	Ballybeg	302 1 22d	Tipperary, S.R.	Iffa and Offa West	Tullaghmelan	Clogheen	II.	321
47	Ballybeg	362 0 5	Tyrone	Dungannon Middle	Clonoe	Dungannon	III.	300
17	Ballybeg	267 2 33	Waterford	Gaultiere	Kilbarry	Waterford	II.	363
30, 31	Ballybeg	244 3 39e	Westmeath	Clonlonan	Kilcumreragh	Athlone	I.	262
7, 8	Ballybeg	226 0 27	Westmeath	Fore	Faughalstown	Castletowndelvin	I.	269
26	Ballybeg	87 1 35	Wexford	Ballaghkeen	Ballyhuskard	Enniscorthy	I.	291
36	Ballybeg	101 2 21	Wexford	Bantry	Whitechurch Glynn	Wexford	I.	303
47, 48	Ballybeg	155 1 2	Wexford	Forth	Ballymore	Wexford	I.	308
10	Ballybeg	1,970 0 37	Wexford	Scarawalsh	Ferns	Gorey	I.	323
38, 39	Ballybeg	891 0 18	Wicklow	Ballinacor South	Kilcommon	Shillelagh	I.	349
25	Ballybeg	231 2 28	Wicklow	Newcastle	Rathnew	Rathdrum	I.	354
24, 25	Ballybeg Big	1,204 0 38	Carlow	St. Mullins Lower	St. Mullins	New Ross	I.	13
17, 25	Ballybeg East	417 1 31	Cork, E.R.	Orrery and Kilmore	Buttevant	Mallow	II.	107
29	Ballybeggan	254 2 33	Kerry	Trughanacmy	Ratass	Tralee	II.	213
37	Ballybeggane	283 1 29	Limerick	Connello Upper	Cloncagh	Newcastle	II.	231
27, 33	Ballybeg Great	226 1 26	Wexford	Ballaghkeen	Killisk	Enniscorthy	I.	296
94	*Ballybeg Island*	6 1 4	Mayo	Murrisk	Kilgeever	Westport	IV.	161
12	Ballybeg or Leagh	148 1 23	Carlow	Forth	Tullowmagimma	Carlow	I.	5
24	Ballybeg Little	127 3 17	Carlow	St. Mullins Lower	St. Mullins	New Ross	I.	13
46	Ballybegly	237 1 33	Donegal	Raphoe	Allsaints	Londonderry	III.	133
46	Ballybegly Little	162 3 14	Donegal	Raphoe	Allsaints	Letterkenny	III.	133

(a) Including 29A. 3R. 6P. water.
(b) Including 11A. 3R. 19P. water.
(c) Including 12A. 2R. 7P. water.
(d) Including 6A. 0R. 20P. water.
(e) Including 17A. 0R. 12P. water.

No. of Sheet of the Ordnance Survey Maps.	Townlands and Towns.	Area in Statute Acres.	County.	Barony.	Parish.	Poor Law Union in 1857.	Townland Census of 1851, Part I.	
		A. R. P.					Vol.	Page
17, 25	Ballybeg Middle .	493 3 39	Cork, E.R. .	Orrery and Kilmore	Buttevant . .	Mallow . .	II.	107
33	Ballybeg Small .	199 2 36	Wexford .	Ballaghkeen . .	Killisk . .	Enniscorthy .	I.	296
16,17,24,25	Ballybeg West .	438 2 35	Cork, E.R. .	Orrery and Kilmore	Buttevant . .	Mallow . .	II.	107
50	Ballybentragh .	402 1 6	Antrim .	Upper Antrim .	Nilteen Grange	Antrim . .	III.	6
9	Ballyberidagh North	124 1 32	Antrim .	Cary . . .	Culfeightrin .	Ballycastle .	III.	13
9	Ballyberidagh South	165 2 28	Antrim .	Cary . . .	Culfeightrin .	Ballycastle .	III.	13
25, 26	Ballybetagh . .	464 3 37	Dublin .	Rathdown . .	Kiltiernan .	Rathdown .	I.	36
39, 45	Ballybin . . .	574 0 33	Meath .	Ratoath . .	Cookstown .	Dunshaughlin .	I.	217
44	Ballybin . . .	207 0 33	Meath .	Ratoath . .	Ratoath . .	Dunshaughlin .	I.	219
3	Ballybinaby . .	485 3 4	Louth .	Upper Dundalk .	Roche . .	Dundalk . .	I.	179
48	Ballybing . .	37 1 17	Wexford .	Forth . .	Kilscoran .	Wexford . .	I.	311
3, 4, 8	Ballybit Big . .	656 0 31	Carlow .	Rathvilly . .	Rathvilly . .	Baltinglass .	I.	12
3, 4	Ballybit Little .	119 3 8	Carlow .	Rathvilly . .	Rathvilly . .	Baltinglass .	I.	12
19	Ballybla . .	272 2 25	Wicklow .	Newcastle . .	Killiskey . .	Rathdrum .	I.	352
6	Ballyblack . .	640 2 31	Down .	Ards Lower .	Greyabbey .	Newtownards .	III.	158
6	Ballyblack . .	450 0 35	Down .	Ards Lower .	Newtownards .	Newtownards .	III.	158
32	Ballyblack . .	79 1 27	Down .	Ards Upper .	Ballyphilip .	Downpatrick .	III.	159
6, 11	Ballyblack Little .	279 1 7	Down .	Ards Lower .	Greyabbey .	Newtownards .	III.	158
6	Ballyblagh . .	162 2 20	Armagh .	Oneilland East .	Shankill . .	Lurgan . .	III.	50
39	Ballyblagh . .	205 3 29	Tyrone .	Dungannon Upper .	Ballyclog .	Cookstown .	III.	306
24	Ballyblake . .	21 2 21	Carlow .	St. Mullins Lower .	St. Mullins .	New Ross . .	I.	13
23	Ballyblake . .	179 2 34	Limerick . .	Clanwilliam . .	Caherelly . .	Limerick . .	II.	222
40	Ballyblaugh . .	172 1 8	Down .	Upper Iveagh, Upper part . .	Donaghmore .	Newry . .	III.	175
35	Ballyblood . .	1,396 1 24a	Clare . .	Tulla Upper . .	Tulla . .	Tulla . .	II.	41
68, 77	Ballybobaneen .	401 3 31b	Donegal . .	Raphoe . .	Kilteevoge .	Stranorlar .	III.	139
22	Ballyboden . .	125 3 12	Dublin .	Rathdown . .	Whitechurch .	Dublin South .	I.	38
22	BALLYBODEN T. .	—	Dublin .	Rathdown . .	Whitechurch .	Dublin South .	I.	38
98	Ballybodonnell .	184 2 32	Donegal .	Banagh . .	Killaghtee .	Donegal . .	III.	109
26, 35	Ballyboe . .	78 3 14c	Donegal .	Kilmacrenan .	Clondahorky .	Dunfanaghy .	III.	122
37	Ballyboe . .	15 2 5	Donegal .	Kilmacrenan .	Killygarvan .	Millford . .	III.	128
25	Ballyboe . .	442 2 15	Donegal .	Kilmacrenan .	Raymunterdoney	Dunfanaghy .	III.	131
45, 46	Ballyboe . .	69 1 12	Donegal .	Kilmacrenan .	Tullyfern .	Millford . .	III.	132
55	Ballyboe . .	90 0 18	Donegal .	Raphoe . .	Allsaints .	Londonderry .	III.	133
69	Ballyboe . .	65 3 31	Donegal .	Raphoe . .	Convoy . .	Stranorlar .	III.	136
61	Ballyboe . .	131 3 10	Donegal .	Raphoe . .	Leck . .	Letterkenny .	III.	140
54	Ballyboe . .	75 2 17	Donegal .	Raphoe . .	Raymoghy .	Letterkenny .	III.	141
62	Ballyboe . .	168 1 27	Donegal .	Raphoe . .	Taughboyne .	Strabane .	III.	143
77, 78	Ballyboe . .	615 2 17	Tipperary, S.R. .	Iffa and Offa East .	Temple-etney .	Clonmel . .	II.	316
53	Ballyboe Glencar .	146 1 26	Donegal .	Kilmacrenan .	Conwal . .	Letterkenny .	III.	125
53	Ballyboe Lisnenan .	30 0 38	Donegal .	Kilmacrenan .	Conwal . .	Letterkenny .	III.	125
34	Ballyboe Mountain .	1,091 2 25	Donegal .	Kilmacrenan .	Raymunterdoney	Dunfanaghy .	III.	131
45, 53	Ballyboencurragh .	142 3 29	Donegal .	Kilmacrenan .	Aghanunshin .	Letterkenny .	III.	122
77, 78	Ballybofey . .	453 0 2d	Donegal .	Raphoe . .	Stranorlar .	Stranorlar .	III.	142
78	BALLYBOFEY T. .	—	Donegal .	Raphoe . .	Stranorlar .	Stranorlar .	III.	143
79	Ballybogan . .	124 2 10e	Donegal .	Raphoe . .	Clonleigh .	Strabane .	III.	134
112	Ballybogey . .	183 1 37	Cork, E.R. .	Kinalea . .	Nohaval . .	Kinsale . .	II.	96
60, 61	Ballyboggan . .	336 3 30	Galway .	Kilconnell .	Ahascragh .	Mountbellew .	IV.	38
84, 85	Ballyboggan . .	534 1 29	Galway .	Kilconnell .	Moñivea . .	Loughrea .	IV.	42
46, 47	Ballyboggan . .	1,236 3 28	Meath .	Upper Moyfenrath .	Ballyboggan .	Edenderry .	I.	212
37	Ballyboggan . .	202 1 32	Wexford .	Shelmaliere West .	Carrick . .	Wexford . .	I.	332
32, 37	Ballyboggan Lower	395 2 12	Wexford .	Shelmaliere East .	Tikillin . .	Wexford . .	I.	331
14, 18	Ballyboggan North .	31 1 26	Dublin .	Castleknock .	Finglas . .	Dublin North .	I.	24
14, 18	Ballyboggan South .	104 1 8	Dublin .	Castleknock .	Finglas . .	Dublin North .	I.	24
32	Ballyboggan Upper	218 3 5	Wexford .	Shelmaliere East .	Tikillin . .	Wexford . .	I.	331
7	Ballyboghil . .	384 3 8	Dublin .	Balrothery West .	Ballyboghil .	Balrothery .	I.	22
12	Ballyboghilbo .	339 1 35	Down .	Ards Lower .	Greyabbey .	Newtownards .	III.	158
7	BALLYBOGHIL T. .	—	Dublin .	Balrothery West .	Ballyboghil .	Balrothery .	I.	22
41, 50	Ballyboght . .	439 2 21	Cork, E.R. .	Duhallow .	Kilshannig .	Mallow . .	II.	74
23	Ballybogy . .	555 2 25	Antrim .	Kilconway .	Dunaghy .	Ballymena .	III.	25
11, 12	Ballybogy . .	434 2 33	Antrim .	Lower Dunluce .	Dunluce . .	Ballymoney .	III.	17
47	Ballyboher . .	59 1 32	Wexford .	Forth . .	Ballymore .	Wexford . .	I.	308
47	Ballyboher . .	45 1 17	Wexford .	Forth . .	Ishartmon .	Wexford . .	I.	309
46	Ballybokeel . .	111 0 19	Donegal .	Kilmacrenan .	Aughnish .	Millford . .	III.	122
9, 18	Ballybolagan and Drumavohy .	350 3 17	Donegal .	Kilmacrenan .	Clondavaddog .	Millford . .	III.	124
52	Ballybolauder .	275 0 2	Donegal .	Kilmacrenan .	Conwal . .	Letterkenny .	III.	125
39,40,45,46	Ballyboley . .	2,968 0 1	Antrim .	Upper Antrim .	Ballycor . .	Larne . .	III.	6
35, 40	Ballyboley . .	294 0 12	Antrim .	Upper Glenarm .	Larne . .	Larne . .	III.	25
6, 11	Ballyboley . .	783 0 20	Down .	Ards Lower .	Greyabbey .	Newtownards .	III.	158
37	Ballybollen . .	277 1 25	Antrim .	Upper Toome .	Ahoghill .	Ballymena .	III.	33
81, 45	Ballybollen . .	425 3 28	Antrim .	Upper Toome .	Drummaul .	Ballymena .	III.	33
32, 41	Ballyboneill . .	120 1 25	Cork, E.R. .	Duhallow .	Kilshannig .	Mallow . .	II.	74

No. of Sheet of the Ordnance Survey Maps.	Townlands and Towns.	Area in Statute Acres.			County.	Barony.	Parish.	Poor Law Union in 1857.	Townland Census of 1851, Part I.	
		A.	R.	P.					Vol.	Page
31	Ballyboodan .	276	2	38	Kilkenny .	Knocktopher .	Knocktopher .	Thomastown .	I.	112
29	Ballyboodin .	472	3	17	Queen's Co.	Clarmallagh .	Aghmacart .	Abbeyleix .	I.	236
6, 7	Ballybornagh .	730	3	23	Clare .	Inchiquin .	Kilkeedy .	Corrofin .	II.	25
24, 25	Ballyboro .	204	0	31	Wexford .	Bantry .	Killegney .	Enniscorthy .	I.	301
68	Ballybotemple .	137	2	22a	Donegal .	Raphoe .	Kilteevoge .	Stranorlar .	III.	139
18	Ballybough .	112	1	34b	Dublin .	Coolock .	Clonturk .	Dublin North .	I.	26
70	Ballybough .	163	0	37	Tipperary, S.R.	Middlethird .	Rathcool .	Cashel .	II.	329
39	Ballyboughan .	261	1	25	Roscommon .	Ballintober South .	Roscommon .	Roscommon .	IV.	190
8	Ballyboughlin .	105	2	1c	King's Co.	Kilcoursey .	Kilbride .	Tullamore .	I.	141
56	Ballybought .	379	3	2	Antrim .	Lower Belfast .	Shankill .	Belfast .	III.	9
29	Ballybought .	517	1	30	Kildare .	Naas South .	Ballybought .	Naas .	I.	64
35	Ballybought .	48	3	2d	Kildare .	Narragh&RebanWest	St. Johns .	Athy .	I.	68
8, 9	Ballybought .	913	2	12	King's Co.	Ballycowan .	Durrow .	Tullamore .	I.	127
47	Ballybought .	136	1	18	Wexford .	Bargy .	Kilmore .	Wexford .	I.	306
18	BALLYBOUGH T. .	—			Dublin .	Coolock .	Clonturk .	Dublin North .	I.	27
43	Ballybowler North .	488	1	35	Kerry .	Corkaguiny .	Garfinny .	Dingle .	II.	176
43	Ballybowler South .	434	1	25	Kerry .	Corkaguiny .	Garfinny .	Dingle .	II.	176
104, 114	Ballyboy .	136	1	21	Galway .	Dunkellin .	Ardrahan .	Gort .	IV.	26
29	Ballyboy .	671	2	7e	Galway .	Dunmore .	Kilbennan .	Tuam .	IV.	34
128	Ballyboy .	363	1	9	Galway .	Kiltartan .	Beagh .	Gort .	IV.	46
31	Ballyboy .	296	3	31	King's Co.	Ballyboy .	Ballyboy .	Parsonstown .	I.	123
30	Ballyboy .	225	2	12	King's Co.	Garrycastle .	Reynagh .	Parsonstown .	I.	137
11	Ballyboy .	261	2	11	Longford .	Granard .	Abbeylara .	Granard .	I.	154
29	Ballyboy .	392	0	20	Meath .	Lune .	Athboy .	Trim .	I.	207
24, 30	Ballyboy .	330	0	28	Meath .	Lune .	Rathmore .	Trim .	I.	208
40	Ballyboy .	523	2	15	Tipperary, N.R.	Kilnamanagh Upper	Upperchurch .	Thurles .	II.	280
66, 67	Ballyboy .	190	3	30	Tyrone .	Dungannon Lower .	Aghaloo .	Armagh .	III.	296
15	Ballyboy .	707	2	7	Waterford .	Decies without Drum	Fews .	Kilmacthomas .	II.	356
18	Ballyboy .	169	3	10	Westmeath .	Corkaree .	Portloman .	Mullingar .	I.	263
47	Ballyboy .	148	3	0	Wexford .	Forth .	Ballymore .	Wexford .	I.	308
10, 15	Ballyboy .	506	2	12	Wexford .	Scarawalsh .	Ballycarney .	Enniscorthy .	I.	322
23, 29	Ballyboy .	1,023	3	1	Wicklow .	Ballinacor North .	Knockrath .	Rathdrum .	I.	347
87	Ballyboy East .	725	2	22	Tipperary, S.R.	Iffa and Offa West .	Tullaghorton .	Clogheen .	II.	321
17	Ballyboylands Lower	165	0	36	Antrim .	Upper Dunluce .	Ballymoney .	Ballymoney .	III.	18
17	Ballyboylands Upper	278	1	6	Antrim .	Upper Dunluce .	Ballymoney .	Ballymoney .	III.	18
93, 99	Ballyboyle .	107	1	28	Donegal .	Banagh .	Killymard .	Donegal .	III.	111
99	*Ballyboyle Island* .	30	2	33	Donegal .	Banagh .	Killymard .	Donegal .	III.	112
15, 22	Ballyboy or Lowpark	262	0	27	Westmeath .	Kilkenny West .	Kilkenny West .	Athlone .	I.	273
31	BALLYBOY T. .	—			King's Co.	Ballyboy .	Ballyboy .	Parsonstown .	I.	123
87	Ballyboy West .	595	1	7	Tipperary, S.R.	Iffa and Offa West .	Tullaghorton .	Clogheen .	II.	321
15	Ballybrack .	142	2	21	Antrim .	Lower Glenarm .	Layd .	Ballycastle .	III.	22
22, 23	Ballybrack .	544	3	7	Carlow .	St. Mullins Lower .	Ballyellin .	New Ross .	I.	13
53	Ballybrack .	347	2	23	Clare .	Tulla Lower .	O'Briensbridge .	Limerick .	II.	37
52	Ballybrack .	1,127	1	39	Cork, E.R.	Barrymore .	Dunbulloge .	Cork .	II.	54
74, 86	Ballybrack .	17	2	11	Cork, E.R.	Cork .	Carrigaline .	Cork .	II.	64
25	Ballybrack .	406	2	39	Cork, E.R.	Fermoy .	Caherduggan .	Mallow .	II.	77
148	Ballybrack .	121	0	30	Cork, W.R.	West Carbery (W.D.)	Skull .	Skull .	II.	145
13, 22	Ballybrack .	448	3	2	Donegal .	Inishowen East .	Moville Lower .	Inishowen .	III.	118
25	Ballybrack .	890	2	0	Dublin .	Rathdown .	Kilgobbin .	Rathdown .	I.	35
26	Ballybrack .	174	0	32	Dublin .	Rathdown .	Killiney .	Rathdown .	I.	36
34	Ballybrack .	1,221	2	39	Kerry .	Corkaguiny .	Kilquane .	Dingle .	II.	179
98	Ballybrack .	134	2	17	Kerry .	Dunkerron South .	Kilcrohane .	Cahersiveen .	II.	183
48, 58	Ballybrack .	316	2	1	Kerry .	Magunihy .	Aglish .	Killarney .	II.	199
47	Ballybrack .	390	0	22	Kerry .	Magunihy .	Kilnanare .	Killarney .	II.	204
12	Ballybrack .	308	1	8	Kildare .	Carbury .	Kilpatrick .	Edenderry .	I.	52
5, 10	Ballybrack .	292	2	2	Kildare .	Ikeathy and Oughterany .	Clonshanbo .	Celbridge .	I.	57
45	Ballybrack .	530	3	33	King's Co.	Clonlisk .	Roscrea .	Roscrea .	I.	131
51	Ballybrack .	238	0	39	Tipperary, S.R.	Kilnamanagh Lower	Donohill .	Tipperary .	II.	323
34	Ballybrack .	179	2	8	Waterford .	Coshmore & Coshbride	Kilcockan .	Lismore .	II.	343
15, 16	Ballybrack .	735	1	5	Waterford .	Decies without Drum	Rossmire .	Kilmacthomas .	II.	359
40	Ballybrack .	232	0	27	Wexford .	Shelmaliere West .	Clongeen .	New Ross .	I.	332
23, 31	Ballybrackan Little	230	1	29	King's Co.	Ballyboy .	Ballyboy .	Parsonstown .	I.	123
23, 31	Ballybrackan or Ridgemount .	513	1	35	King's Co.	Ballyboy .	Ballyboy .	Parsonstown .	I.	123
33	Ballybrack Beg .	199	3	35	Wicklow .	Upper Talbotstown .	Kiltegan .	Baltinglass .	I.	364
45, 46	Ballybracken .	738	1	10	Antrim .	Lower Belfast .	Ballynure .	Larne .	III.	7
44, 45	Ballybracken .	337	0	27	Antrim .	Upper Antrim .	Kilbride .	Antrim .	III.	6
12	Ballybracken .	97	2	22	Wexford .	Ballaghkeen .	Ardamine .	Gorey .	I.	291
33	Ballybrack More .	302	1	22	Wicklow .	Upper Talbotstown .	Kiltegan .	Baltinglass .	I.	364
81	Ballybrada .	341	2	24f	Tipperary, S.R.	Iffa and Offa West .	Caher .	Clogheen .	II.	317
18, 19	Ballybraddin .	890	0	0	Antrim .	Upper Dunluce .	Loughguile .	Ballymoney .	III.	20
41	Ballybraghy .	160	2	32	Kilkenny .	Ida .	Kilcoan .	Waterford .	I.	102

(a) Including 3A. 1R. 11P. water.
(b) Including 10A. 0R. 12P. swamp.
(c) Including 19A. 1R. 16P. detached portion.
(d) Including 1A. 2R. 12P. River Barrow.
(e) Including 47A. 0R. 5P. water.
(f) Including 7A. 2R. 31P. water.

No. of Sheet of the Ordnance Survey Maps.	Townlands and Towns.	Area in Statute Acres.			County.	Barony.	Parish.	Poor Law Union in 1857.	Townland Census of 1851. Part I.	
		A.	R.	P.					Vol.	Page
89	Ballybraher	84	3	2	Cork, E.R.	Imokilly	Ballyoughtera	Middleton	II.	84
89	Ballybraher	194	3	14	Cork, E.R.	Imokilly	Cloyne	Middleton	II.	85
89	Ballybraher	374	0	10	Cork, E.R.	Imokilly	Kilmahon	Middleton	II.	89
23, 29	Ballybraid	897	0	8	Wicklow	Ballinacor North	Knockrath	Rathdrum	I.	347
17	Ballybrakes	266	3	27	Antrim	Upper Dunluce	Ballymoney	Ballymoney	III.	18
29, 37	Ballybran	274	2	34	Clare	Tulla Lower	Ogonnelloe	Scariff	II.	38
88, 100	Ballybranagan	317	2	14	Cork, E.R.	Imokilly	Titeskin	Middleton	II.	90
113	Ballybranagan	153	0	17	Galway	Kiltartan	Kinvarradoorus	Gort	IV.	49
89	Ballybranagh	218	3	35	Cork, E.R.	Imokilly	Cloyne	Middleton	II.	85
25, 32	Ballybranigan	185	2	0	Down	Ards Upper	Ballytrustan	Downpatrick	III.	160
23, 27	Ballybranigan	283	3	28	Longford	Ratheline	Shrule	Ballymahon	I.	165
30	Ballybrannagh	143	1	7	Kerry	Trughanacmy	Ballymacelligott	Tralee	II.	206
38	Ballybrannagh Lower	325	3	32	Down	Lecale Lower	Ballee	Downpatrick	III.	178
38, 45	Ballybrannagh Upper	346	0	22	Down	Lecale Lower	Ballee	Downpatrick	III.	178
8, 12	Ballybrannan	152	3	6	Armagh	Oneilland West	Grange	Armagh	III.	52
19	Ballybrannis	149	3	18	Wexford	Scarawalsh	Monart	Enniscorthy	I.	324
88	Ballybrassil	222	1	12	Cork, E.R.	Barrymore	Templerobin	Cork	II.	58
42, 45	Ballybrassil	260	1	34	Kilkenny	Iverk	Pollrone	Waterford	I.	106
31, 35	Ballybray	427	1	32	Kilkenny	Knocktopher	Kilkeasy	Thomastown	I.	112
46	Ballybray	240	2	20	Tyrone	Dungannon Middle	Donaghmore	Dungannon	III.	301
34, 39	Ballybrazil	386	2	0	Wexford	Shelburne	Ballybrazil	New Ross	I.	327
13	Ballybreagh	455	2	14	Armagh	Oneilland West	Kilmore	Armagh	III.	53
17, 24	Ballybredagh	183	3	38	Down	Dufferin	Killinchy	Downpatrick	III.	166
8, 9, 15, 16	Ballybreen	713	1	6	Clare	Corcomroe	Kilfenora	Ennistimon	II.	18
19	Ballybreen	365	1	23	Wexford	Scarawalsh	Templeshanbo	Enniscorthy	I.	326
13	Ballybregagh	399	3	34	Antrim	Upper Dunluce	Loughguile	Ballymoney	III.	20
27	Ballybregagh	268	1	17	Wexford	Ballaghkeen	Castle-ellis	Enniscorthy	I.	293
16, 25	Ballybregin	149	3	39	Waterford	Middlethird	Dunhill	Kilmacthomas	II.	366
13	Ballybrennan	58	2	36	Limerick	Clanwilliam	Cahernarry	Limerick	II.	222
33	Ballybrennan	461	3	8	Sligo	Corran	Emlaghfad	Sligo	IV.	226
32	Ballybrennan	405	3	18	Westmeath	Moycashel	Castletownkindalen	Mullingar	I.	277
25, 31	Ballybrennan	997	0	2	Wexford	Bantry	Kilcowanmore	Enniscorthy	I.	300
48	Ballybrennan Big	160	0	15	Wexford	Forth	Ballybrennan	Wexford	I.	308
48	Ballybrennan Little	143	3	17	Wexford	Forth	Ballybrennan	Wexford	I.	308
16, 25	Ballybrennock	353	2	16	Waterford	Middlethird	Reisk	Waterford	II.	368
3	Ballybrew	594	3	18	Wicklow	Rathdown	Powerscourt	Rathdown	I.	356
99	Ballybrian	178	2	26	Galway	Clonmacnowen	Killallaghtan	Ballinasloe	IV.	26
34,35,41,42	Ballybrick	1,393	0	12	Down	Upper Iveagh, Lr.pt.	Drumballyroney	Banbridge	III.	172
87	Ballybricken	53	0	30	Cork, E.R.	Kerryeurrihy	Barnahely	Cork	II.	91
23	Ballybricken East	31	2	7	Limerick	Clanwilliam	Caherelly	Limerick	II.	222
23	Ballybricken East	185	2	12	Limerick	Clanwilliam	Inch St. Lawrence	Limerick	II.	224
23	Ballybricken North	167	3	31	Limerick	Clanwilliam	Caherelly	Limerick	II.	222
23	Ballybricken South	345	2	6	Limerick	Clanwilliam	Caherelly	Limerick	II.	222
23	Ballybricken West	321	0	14	Limerick	Clanwilliam	Inch St. Lawrence	Limerick	II.	224
31	Ballybrickoge	465	0	18	Westmeath	Moycashel	Kilcumrreagh	Athlone	I.	278
39	Ballybride	486	0	24	Roscommon	Ballintober South	Roscommon	Roscommon	IV.	190
36, 45	Ballybride Lower	339	1	5	Cork, E.R.	Kinnatalloon	Knockmourne	Fermoy	II.	98
36	Ballybride Upper	342	2	32	Cork, E.R.	Kinnatalloon	Knockmourne	Fermoy	II.	98
57	Ballybrien	519	1	25	Limerick	Coshlea	Ballylanders	Mitchelstown	II.	237
10	Ballybrien	236	0	36	Longford	Granard	Granard	Granard	I.	156
58	Ballybrien	55	2	21	Tipperary, S.R.	Clanwilliam	Solloghodmore	Tipperary	II.	310
40, 45	Ballybriest	1,009	1	9a	Londonderry	Loughinsholin	Lissan	Magherafelt	III.	242
38	Ballybrinoge	192	1	29	Mayo	Tirawley	Crossmolina	Ballina	IV.	165
6	Ballybrissell	265	3	16	Londonderry	Keenaght	Aghanloo	New TⁿLimavady	III.	233
35	Ballybristy	403	0	6	Tipperary, N.R.	Eliogarty	Loughmoe West	Thurles	II.	271
82	Ballybrit	325	2	18	Galway	Galway	St. Nicholas	Galway	IV.	38
11, 18	Ballybritain	385	3	8	Londonderry	Coleraine	Aghadowey	Coleraine	III.	229
39, 43	Ballybritt	591	3	39	King's Co.	Ballybritt	Aghancon	Roscrea	I.	124
11	Ballybrittan	942	2	21	King's Co.	Warrenstown	Ballymacwilliam	Edenderry	I.	144
5, 9	Ballybrittas	914	3	7	Queen's Co.	Portnahinch	Lea	Mountmellick	I.	244
31	Ballybrittas	2	0	2	Wexford	Bantry	Clonmore	Enniscorthy	I.	300
25, 31	Ballybrittas	382	3	12	Wexford	Bantry	Kilcowanmore	Enniscorthy	I.	300
9	BALLYBRITTAS T.	—			Queen's Co.	Portnahinch	Lea	Mountmellick	I.	244
48	Ballybro	105	1	27	Wexford	Forth	Rosslare	Wexford	I.	313
11, 12	Ballybrocky	144	2	15	Armagh	Tiranny	Eglish	Armagh	III.	59
98, 106	Ballybroder	135	2	33	Galway	Loughrea	Kilmeen	Loughrea	IV.	65
97, 98 105, 106 }	Ballybroder	372	1	6	Galway	Loughrea	Loughrea	Loughrea	IV.	65
31	Ballybroder	95	0	25	Westmeath	Clonlonan	Kilcumrreagh	Athlone	I.	262
38, 40	Ballybroder	243	1	20	Westmeath	Moycashel	Durrow	Tullamore	I.	277
25	Ballybrody	179	1	36	Clare	Inchiquin	Dysert	Ennis	II.	24
45, 46	Ballybrogan	591	2	0	Roscommon	Athlone	St. Johns	Athlone	IV.	183
36, 37	Ballybroghan	1,368	1	25	Clare	Tulla Lower	Ogonnelloe	Scariff	II.	38

(a) Including 69A. 3R. 38P. Lough Fea.

No. of Sheet of the Ordnance Survey Maps.	Townlands and Towns.	Area in Statute Acres.	County.	Barony.	Parish.	Poor Law Union in 1857.	Townland Census of 1851, Part I.	
		A. R. P.					Vol.	Page
28	Ballybroghan . .	134 2 36	Roscommon	Roscommon . .	Kilcooley . .	Strokestown .	IV.	210
93	Ballybrollaghan .	366 1 35	Donegal . .	Banagh . .	Inver . .	Donegal . .	III.	106
12	Ballybrolly . .	135 1 0	Armagh . .	Armagh . .	Eglish . .	Armagh . .	III.	44
16, 20	Ballybrolly . .	237 0 31	Armagh . .	Fews Lower .	Lisnadill .	Armagh . .	III.	46
21	Ballybroman . .	260 2 9	Kerry . .	Clanmaurice . .	O'Dorney . .	Tralee . .	II.	172
12, 13, 16	Ballybrommell .	373 0 9	Carlow . .	Idrone East .	Fennagh . .	Carlow . .	I.	7
12	BALLYBROMMELL T.	—	Carlow . .	Idrone East . .	Fennagh . .	Carlow . .	I.	7
57, 70	Ballybrone . .	770 0 29	Galway . .	Clare . .	Athenry . .	Galway . .	IV.	17
79	Ballybronoge . .	196 1 25	Tipperary, S.R.	Slievardagh .	Newtownlennan	Carrick on Suir	II.	335
12, 21	Ballybronoge North	92 2 16	Limerick . .	Pubblebrien .	Killonahan .	Limerick . .	II.	253
12, 21	Ballybronoge South	167 0 21	Limerick . .	Pubblebrien .	Killonahan .	Limerick . .	II.	253
23	Ballybrood . .	357 3 11	Limerick . .	Clanwilliam .	Ballybrood .	Limerick . .	II.	221
22, 30	Ballybroony . .	842 0 33a	Mayo . .	Tirawley .	Ballysakeery .	Ballina . .	IV.	164
22, 28	Ballybrophy . .	564 2 19	Queen's Co. .	Clandonagh .	Aghaboe . .	Donaghmore .	I.	232
52	Ballybroughan .	116 2 9	Clare . .	Bunratty Lower	Kilfintinan .	Limerick . .	II.	5
29, 37	Ballybrown . .	138 0 21	Limerick . .	Connello Lower	Rathkeale .	Rathkeale .	II.	229
29, 37	Ballybrown . .	136 2 7	Limerick . .	Glenquin .	Clonelty . .	Rathkeale .	II.	245
12	Ballybrown . .	325 3 6	Limerick . .	Pubblebrien .	Kilkeedy .	Limerick . .	II.	252
31	Ballybrown . .	104 3 31	Westmeath .	Moycashel .	Castletownkindalen	Mullingar .	I.	277
44	Ballybrowney Lower	179 0 4	Cork, E.R. .	Barrymore .	Rathcormack .	Fermoy . .	II.	57
44	Ballybrowney-mountain . .	240 1 2	Cork, E.R. .	Barrymore .	Rathcormack .	Fermoy . .	II.	57
44	Ballybrowney Upper	166 1 34	Cork, E.R. .	Barrymore .	Rathcormack .	Fermoy . .	II.	57
7, 8	Ballybruncullin .	290 1 27	King's Co. .	Ballycowan .	Rahan . .	Tullamore .	I.	128
58	Ballybrunoge . .	45 1 16	Tipperary, S.R.	Clanwilliam .	Cullen . .	Tipperary .	II.	306
38	Ballybrusa or Brucetown . .	104 1 28	Waterford .	Decies within Drum	Lisgenan or Grange	Youghal . .	II.	352
38	Ballybrusa East .	128 0 5	Waterford .	Decies within Drum	Lisgenan or Grange	Youghal . .	II.	352
38	Ballybrusa West .	227 3 33	Waterford .	Decies within Drum	Lisgenan or Grange	Youghal . .	II.	352
12	Ballybryan . .	543 3 8	Down . .	Ards Lower .	Greyabbey .	Newtownards .	III.	158
4, 11	Ballybryan . .	346 0 35	King's Co. .	Warrenstown .	Ballymacwilliam	Edenderry .	I.	144
25, 31	Ballybuckley . .	227 2 26	Wexford . .	Bantry . .	Clonmore .	Enniscorthy .	I.	300
113, 122	Ballybuck North .	342 0 1	Galway . .	Kiltartan .	Killinny . .	Gort . .	IV.	47
122	Ballybuck South .	223 3 0	Galway . .	Kiltartan .	Killinny . .	Gort . .	IV.	47
28, 34	Ballybuggy . .	537 0 15	Queen's Co. .	Clandonagh .	Rathdowney .	Donaghmore .	I.	234
99, 103	Ballybulgan . .	174 2 27	Donegal . .	Tirhugh . .	Drumhome .	Donegal . .	III.	146
79	Ballybun . .	327 0 10	Donegal . .	Raphoe . .	Donaghmore .	Strabane . .	III.	137
16, 17	Ballybunden and Kilmood . .	921 0 9	Down . .	Castlereagh Lower .	Kilmood . .	Newtownards .	III.	163
35, 44	Ballybuninabber .	1,222 3 19	Donegal . .	Kilmacrenan .	Kilmacrenan .	Milford . .	III.	128
4	Ballybunnion . .	371 3 22	Kerry . .	Iraghticonnor .	Killehenny .	Listowel . .	II.	191
4	BALLYBUNNION T. .	—	Kerry . .	Iraghticonnor .	Killehenny .	Listowel . .	II.	191
23	Ballybur . .	32 1 32	Kilkenny . .	Shillelogher .	Tuilaghanbrogue	Callan . .	I.	116
85	Ballyburden Beg .	255 1 6	Cork, E.R. .	East Muskerry	Kilnaglory .	Cork . .	II.	104
85	Ballyburden More .	312 1 25	Cork, E.R. .	East Muskerry	Kilnaglory .	Cork . .	II.	104
93	Ballyburke . .	127 1 5	Galway . .	Galway . .	Rahoon . .	Galway . .	IV.	37
23	Ballybur Lower .	275 0 17	Kilkenny . .	Shillelogher .	Ballybur . .	Kilkenny .	I.	113
4, 11	Ballyburly . .	431 3 11	King's Co. .	Warrenstown .	Ballyburly .	Edenderry .	I.	144
40	Ballyburn Lower .	367 2 16	Kildare . .	Kilkea and Moone .	Killelan . .	Athy . .	I.	60
40	Ballyburn Upper .	252 2 0	Kildare . .	Kilkea and Moone .	Killelan . .	Athy . .	I.	60
23	Ballybur Upper .	392 1 16	Kilkenny . .	Shillelogher .	Ballybur . .	Kilkenny .	I.	113
26	Ballybush . .	10 1 28	Kilkenny . .	Shillelogher .	Killaloe . .	Callan . .	I.	115
77, 89	Ballybutler . .	327 3 1	Cork, E.R. .	Imokilly . .	Garryvoe .	Middleton .	II.	86
6, 7	Ballybuttle . .	423 3 5b	Down . .	Ards Lower .	Donaghadee .	Newtownards .	III.	157
25	Ballycabus . .	130 3 38	Kilkenny . .	Gowran . .	Powerstown .	Thomastown .	I.	97
10	Ballycadden Lower .	162 3 10	Wexford . .	Scarawalsh .	Kilrush . .	Enniscorthy .	I.	324
10	Ballycadden Upper .	225 1 39	Wexford . .	Scarawalsh .	Kilrush . .	Enniscorthy .	I.	324
5	Ballycaghan . .	385 0 14	Kildare . .	Ikeathy and Oughterany .	Cloncurry . .	Celbridge .	I.	56
11	Ballycaghan . .	275 0 30	Londonderry .	Coleraine .	Aghadowey .	Coleraine .	III.	229
123	Ballycahalan . .	461 0 1	Galway . .	Kiltartan .	Kilbeacanty .	Gort . .	IV.	47
8	Ballycahan . .	141 1 2	Clare . .	Corcomroe .	Kililagh . .	Ennistimon .	II.	19
37, 38, 40	Ballycahan . .	368 0 21	Westmeath .	Moycashel .	Durrow . .	Tullamore .	I.	277
151	Ballycahane . .	122 2 4	Cork, W.R. .	West Carbery (E.D.)	Castlehaven .	Skibbereen .	II.	137
11	Ballycahane . .	254 3 22	Limerick . .	Kenry . .	Kilcornan .	Rathkeale .	II.	249
25, 31	Ballycahane . .	241 3 22	Tipperary, N.R.	Owney and Arra	Killoscully .	Nenagh . .	II.	295
8	Ballycahane . .	836 0 36	Waterford .	Upperthird .	Guilcagh . .	Carrick on Suir	II.	370
22	Ballycahane Lower .	255 1 0	Limerick . .	Pubblebrien .	Ballycahane .	Croom . .	II.	251
22	Ballycahane Middle	247 2 7	Limerick . .	Pubblebrien .	Ballycahane .	Croom . .	II.	251
22	Ballycahane Upper .	418 3 7c	Limerick . .	Pubblebrien .	Ballycahane .	Croom . .	II.	251
5	Ballycahill . .	519 3 31	Clare . .	Burren . .	Drumcreehy .	Ballyvaghan .	II.	12
117	Ballycahill . .	156 1 32	Galway . .	Longford .	Killimorbologue .	Portumna .	IV.	58
40	Ballycahill . .	596 3 15	Limerick . .	Smallcounty .	Hospital . .	Kilmallock .	II.	260
40, 41	Ballycahill . .	405 0 18	Tipperary, N.R.	Eliogarty .	Ballycahill .	Thurles . .	II.	269

(a) Including 1A. 2R. 32P. water.　　　　(b) Including 13A. 3R. 32P. of mill-pond.　　　　(c) Including 2A. 3R. 8P. water.

K

No. of Sheet of the Ordnance Survey Maps.	Townlands and Towns.	Area in Statute Acres.			County.	Barony.	Parish.	Poor Law Union in 1857.	Townland Census of 1851, Part I.	
		A.	R.	P.					Vol.	Page
23, 29	Ballycahill . .	1,028	2	2	Tipperary, N.R.	Eliogarty .	Templemore .	Thurles . .	II.	272
20	Ballycahill . .	232	1	17	Tipperary, N.R.	Upper Ormond .	Kilmore . .	Nenagh . .	II.	290
30, 36	Ballycahillroe .	222	1	30	Westmeath .	Clonlonan .	Kilcleagh .	Athlone . .	I.	261
62	Ballycairn . .	473	1	26	Antrim . .	Upper Massereene .	Aghagallon .	Lurgan . .	III.	29
3, 7	Ballycairn . .	200	0	31	Londonderry .	Coleraine .	Killowen .	Coleraine .	III.	232
51	Ballycalket . .	79	2	20	Antrim . .	Lower Belfast .	Ballylinny .	Antrim . .	III.	7
9	Ballycallaghan .	283	0	38	King's Co. .	Ballycowan .	Durrow . .	Tullamore .	I.	127
22, 28	Ballycallaghan .	301	0	30	Londonderry .	Tirkeeran .	Cumber Upper .	Londonderry .	III.	249
18, 28	Ballycallan . .	604	3	8	Donegal . .	Kilmacrenan .	Clondavaddog .	Millford . .	III.	124
18, 22	Ballycallan . .	331	0	37	Kilkenny .	Crannagh .	Ballycallan .	Kilkenny .	I.	84
25	Ballycalleen . .	149	0	8	Leitrim . .	Leitrim . .	Fenagh . .	Mohill . .	IV.	100
13, 17	Ballycallon or Clon- bulloge . .	139	1	5	Carlow . .	Forth . .	Fennagh . .	Carlow . .	I.	4
51, 61	Ballycally . .	516	2	21	Clare . .	Bunratty Lower .	Kilconry .	Ennis . .	II.	4
100, 110	Ballycally . .	784	2	2a	Mayo . .	Carra . .	Burriscarra .	Ballinrobe .	IV.	127
32	Ballycam . .	119	1	0	Down . .	Ards Upper .	Ballyphilip .	Downpatrick .	III.	159
45	Ballycam . .	248	1	1	Down . .	Lecale Upper .	Bright . .	Downpatrick .	III.	180
32	Ballycampion .	148	0	27	Limerick .	Coshma .	Bruff . .	Kilmallock .	II.	242
46, 52	Ballycamusk .	596	2	27	Tipperary, N.R.	Eliogarty .	Holycross .	Thurles . .	II.	270
13	Ballycanal . .	167	1	30	Down . .	Lower Iveagh, Up.pt.	Moira . .	Lurgan . .	III.	170
3, 11	Ballycanauna .	273	1	3	Limerick .	Kenry . .	Iveruss . .	Rathkeale .	II.	248
11,12,16, 17	Ballycanew .	366	0	16	Wexford .	Gorey . .	Ballycanew .	Gorey . .	I.	315
16, 17	BALLYCANEW T.	—			Wexford .	Gorey . .	Ballycanew .	Gorey . .	I.	316
53, 63	Ballycannan .	96	1	35	Clare . .	Bunratty Lower .	St. Patricks .	Limerick .	II.	6
53	Ballycannan East .	219	0	7	Clare . .	Bunratty Lower .	St. Munchins .	Limerick .	II.	6
53, 63	Ballycannan North .	65	0	4	Clare . .	Bunratty Lower .	St. Munchins .	Limerick .	II.	6
53, 63	Ballycannan West .	318	2	18	Clare . .	Bunratty Lower .	St. Munchins .	Limerick .	II.	6
34, 43	Ballycanneen .	601	1	16	Kerry . .	Corkaguiny .	Dingle . .	Dingle . .	II.	175
73	Ballycannon .	216	0	22	Cork, E.R.	Cork . .	Currykippane .	Cork . .	II.	64
13, 18	Ballycannon .	362	1	11	Kilkenny .	Crannagh .	Ballinamara .	Kilkenny .	I.	84
20, 29	Ballycannon .	252	3	16	Limerick .	Connello Lower .	Croagh . .	Rathkeale .	II.	227
4, 5	Ballycanon .	589	3	26	Kildare .	Ikeathy&Oughterany	Cloncurry .	Celbridge .	I.	56
10, 18	Ballycanvan Big .	366	2	15	Waterford .	Gaultiere .	Kill St. Nicholas .	Waterford .	II.	364
18	Ballycanvan Little .	3	1	37	Waterford .	Gaultiere .	Kill St. Nicholas .	Waterford .	II.	364
15	Ballycapple . .	814	1	37	Tipperary, N.R.	Lower Ormond .	Modreeny .	Borrisokane .	II.	286
30,31,35,36	Ballycapple . .	252	2	37	Wicklow .	Arklow . .	Dunganstown .	Rathdrum .	I.	343
30, 31	Ballycapple Hill .	97	3	8	Wicklow .	Arklow . .	Dunganstown .	Rathdrum .	I.	343
15	Ballyapplewood .	209	0	31	Tipperary, N.R.	Lower Ormond .	Modreeny .	Borrisokane .	II.	286
47	Ballycappoge .	293	0	29	Wexford .	Bargy . .	Mulrankin .	Wexford .	I.	307
42, 51	Ballycar . .	932	3	23b	Clare . .	Bunratty Lower .	Tomfinlough .	Ennis . .	II.	7
79	Ballycarbery East .	235	0	9	Kerry . .	Iveragh . .	Caher . .	Cahersiveen .	II.	193
79	Ballycarbery South .	159	2	1	Kerry . .	Iveragh . .	Caher . .	Cahersiveen .	II.	193
79	Ballycarbery West .	184	2	28	Kerry . .	Iveragh . .	Caher . .	Cahersiveen .	II.	193
136	Ballycardeen .	62	0	16	Cork, W.R.	Ibane and Barryroe	Lislee . .	Clonakilty .	II.	150
9	Ballycarn . .	457	0	18c	Down . .	Castlereagh Upper .	Drumbo . .	Lisburn . .	III.	164
48	Ballycarn . .	396	3	0	Meath . .	Lower Moyfenrath .	Rathcore .	Trim . .	I.	211
33	Ballycarn . .	284	1	4	Tipperary, N.R.	Upper Ormond .	Dolla . .	Nenagh . .	II.	290
106	Ballycarnahan .	426	1	5	Kerry . .	Dunkerron South .	Kilcrohane .	Cahersiveen .	II.	183
18	Ballycarnan .	832	2	10	Queen's Co. .	Maryborough East .	Kilcolmanbane .	Mountmellick .	I.	241
66	Ballycarnane .	162	0	0	Cork, E.R.	Imokilly .	Killeagh .	Youghal .	II.	88
26	Ballycarnane .	225	1	21	Waterford .	Middlethird .	Drumcannon .	Waterford .	II.	366
7	Ballycarney . .	321	0	13	Carlow . .	Carlow . .	Ballinacarrig .	Carlow . .	I.	1
12	Ballycarney . .	139	1	7	Limerick .	Pubblebrien .	Kilkeedy .	Limerick .	II.	252
15	Ballycarney . .	739	1	27d	Wexford .	Scarawalsh .	Ballycarney .	Enniscorthy .	I.	322
15	Ballycarngannon .	632	0	21	Down . .	Castlereagh Upper .	Drumbo . .	Lisburn . .	III.	164
52, 53	Ballycar North .	459	0	23	Clare . .	Tulla Lower .	O'Briensbridge .	Limerick .	II.	37
90	Ballycarra . .	184	3	13	Mayo . .	Carra . .	Drum . .	Castlebar .	IV.	127
14	Ballycarran .	296	1	0	Kilkenny .	Crannagh .	Odagh . .	Kilkenny .	I.	86
48	Ballycarran .	94	3	17	Wexford .	Forth . .	Ballybrennan .	Wexford .	I.	308
12, 21	Ballycarrane .	274	0	9	Limerick .	Pubblebrien .	Croom . .	Limerick .	II.	252
41, 47	Ballycarrane .	238	1	31	Tipperary, N.R.	Eliogarty .	Thurles . .	Thurles . .	II.	273
14	Ballycarran Little .	112	0	10	Kilkenny .	Crannagh .	Odagh . .	Kilkenny .	I.	86
63	Ballycarrickmaddy .	424	1	28	Antrim . .	Upper Massereene .	Magheragall .	Lisburn . .	III.	31
19, 20	Ballycarridoge .	150	3	25	Tipperary, N.R.	Owney and Arra .	Castletownarra .	Nenagh . .	II.	294
30	Ballycarrigeen .	60	0	5	Wicklow .	Ballinacor North .	Rathdrum .	Rathdrum .	I.	347
15, 16	Ballycarrigeen Lower	376	3	27	Wexford .	Gorey . .	Kilcormick .	Enniscorthy .	I.	317
16	Ballycarrigeen Upper	242	3	7	Wexford .	Gorey . .	Kilcormick .	Enniscorthy .	I.	317
25, 26	Ballycarroll .	244	2	28e	Clare . .	Bunratty Upper .	Templemaley .	Corrofin .	II.	10
13, 14	Ballycarroll .	777	2	27	Queen's Co. .	Maryborough East .	Kilteale .	Mountmellick .	I.	241
5, 9	Ballycarroll .	391	3	11	Queen's Co. .	Portnahinch .	Lea . .	Mountmellick .	I.	244
68	Ballycarron . .	561	2	39	Tipperary, S.R.	Clanwilliam .	Relickmurry and Athassel .	Tipperary .	II.	309
38	Ballycarroon .	203	0	13	Mayo . .	Tirawley .	Crossmolina .	Ballina .	IV.	165

(a) Including 19A. 0R. 29P. water.   (c) Including 2A. 3R. 28P. water.   (e) Including 17A. 0R. 32P. water.
(b) Including 17A. 2R. 4P. water.   (d) Including 6A. 1R. 12P. water.

No. of Sheet of the Ordnance Survey Maps.	Townlands and Towns.	Area in Statute Acres.			County.	Barony.	Parish.	Poor Law Union in 1857.	Townland Census of 1851, Part I.	
		A.	R.	P.					Vol.	Page
1	Ballycarry	298	2	2	Antrim	Cary	Rathlin Island	Ballycastle	III.	15
47	Ballycarry North West	459	3	23	Antrim	Lower Belfast	Templecorran	Larne	III.	9
47	Ballycarry South West	361	3	18	Antrim	Lower Belfast	Templecorran	Larne	III.	9
47	BALLYCARRY T.	—			Antrim	Lower Belfast	Templecorran	Larne	III.	9
53	Ballycar South	357	0	26	Clare	Tulla Lower	O'Briensbridge	Limerick	II.	37
33	Ballycartlan	159	0	28	Monaghan	Farney	Magheracloone	Carrickmacross	III.	272
5, 6	Ballycarton	463	2	24a	Londonderry	Keenaght	Aghanloo	New Tᵉ Limavady	III.	233
5	Ballycarton	130	3	8b	Londonderry	Keenaght	Magilligan	New Tᵉ Limavady	III.	236
29, 38	Ballycarty	182	3	3	Kerry	Trughanacmy	Ballyseedy	Tralee	II.	207
42, 56	Ballycasey	413	1	1	Galway	Clare	Kilcoona	Tuam	IV.	19
12	Ballycasey	631	0	12	Limerick	Kenry	Kildimo	Croom	II.	249
7	Ballycasey	289	3	9	Tipperary, N.R.	Lower Ormond	Uskane	Borrisokane	II.	288
51	Ballycasey Beg	115	3	30	Clare	Bunratty Lower	Drumline	Ennis	II.	3
51, 61	Ballycasey More	367	1	17	Clare	Bunratty Lower	Drumline	Ennis	II.	3
16	Ballycasheen	332	3	18	Clare	Inchiquin	Killinaboy	Corrofin	II.	26
66, 67	Ballycasheen	353	2	32	Kerry	Magunihy	Killarney	Killarney	II.	203
17	Ballycashin	609	3	3	Waterford	Middlethird	Kilburne	Waterford	II.	367
52, 63	Ballycaskin	230	3	34	Cork, E.R.	Barrymore	Whitechurch	Cork	II.	59
16	Ballycassidy	83	1	39	Fermanagh	Tirkennedy	Trory	Enniskillen	III.	223
6, 11	Ballycastle	495	3	26	Down	Ards Lower	Greyabbey	Newtownards	III.	158
5, 9	Ballycastle	292	3	1c	Londonderry	Keenaght	Aghanloo	New Tᵉ Limavady	III.	233
7, 14	Ballycastle	298	3	10	Mayo	Tirawley	Doonfeeny	Killala	IV.	167
8	BALLYCASTLE T.	—			Antrim	Cary	Ramoan	Ballycastle	III.	15
7	BALLYCASTLE T.	—			Mayo	Tirawley	Doonfeeny	Killala	IV.	167
89	Ballycatoo	266	1	34	Cork, E.R.	Imokilly	Ballintemple	Middleton	II.	84
124	Ballycatteen	325	3	25	Cork, W.R.	Courceys	Templetrine	Kinsale	II.	147
123	Ballycatteen	338	0	28	Cork, W.R.	East Carbery (E.D.)	Rathclarin	Bandon	II.	129
5, 12	Ballycharry	996	1	22	Donegal	Inishowen East	Culdaff,	Inishowen	III.	118
26	Ballychristal	20	3	14	King's Co.	Upper Philipstown	Ballykean	Tullamore	I.	143
26	Ballychristal	381	1	5	King's Co.	Upper Philipstown	Geashill	Tullamore	I.	144
7	Ballyclaber	190	1	32	Londonderry	North East Liberties of Coleraine	Coleraine	Coleraine	III.	246
67	Ballyclamasy	39	1	13	Cork, E.R.	Imokilly	Youghal	Youghal	II.	90
27	Ballyclamay	413	1	29	Longford	Shrule	Forgney	Ballymahon	I.	166
54, 58	Ballyclan	522	2	29	Antrim	Lower Massereene	Killead	Antrim	III.	28
9, 16	Ballyclancahill	238	1	39	Clare	Corcomroe	Kilfenora	Corrofin	II.	18
38	Ballyclander Lower	204	2	18	Down	Lecale Lower	Ballee	Downpatrick	III.	178
38	Ballyclander Upper	224	0	24	Down	Lecale Lower	Ballee	Downpatrick	III.	178
45	Ballyclare	209	3	31	Antrim	Lower Belfast	Ballynure	Antrim	III.	7
45, 51	Ballyclare	1,013	1	39d	Antrim	Upper Antrim	Donegh Grange	Antrim	III.	6
14	Ballyclare	559	0	20	King's Co.	Garrycastle	Whery or Killagally	Parsonstown	I.	139
18	Ballyclare	30	2	29	Longford	Moydow	Ballymacormick	Longford	I.	160
13, 18	Ballyclare	115	3	13	Longford	Moydow	Killashee	Longford	I.	161
41	Ballyclare	466	0	32	Meath	Upper Moyfenrath	Castlerickard	Trim	I.	213
37	Ballyclare	283	1	15	Roscommon	Ballintober South	Cloontuskert	Roscommon	IV.	188
37	*Ballyclare Island*	2	1	7	Roscommon	Ballintober South	Cloontuskert	Roscommon	IV.	188
45	BALLYCLARE T.	—			Antrim	Lower Belfast / Upper Antrim	Ballynure / Donegh Grange	Antrim	III.	7 / 6
44, 45, 50	Ballyclaverty	339	0	37	Antrim	Upper Antrim	Donegore	Antrim	III.	6
15	Ballycleagh	103	0	0	Antrim	Cary	Culfeightrin	Ballycastle	III.	13
16, 17, 23	Ballycleary	323	0	8	Queen's Co.	Upperwoods	Offerlane	Abbeyleix	I.	251
52	Ballycleary	224	3	3	Wexford	Bargy	Kilturk	Wexford	I.	307
28	Ballyclement	89	0	5	Waterford	Coshmore & Coshbride	Kilwatermoy	Lismore	II.	343
35	Ballyclemock	1,340	1	22	Wexford	Shelmaliere West	Newbawn	New Ross	I.	334
76, 77	Ballyclerahan	1,014	0	11	Tipperary, S.R.	Iffa and Offa East	Ballyclerahan	Clonmel	II.	312
76, 77	BALLYCLERAHAN T.	—			Tipperary, S.R.	Iffa and Offa East	Ballyclerahan	Clonmel	II.	312
113	Ballyclery	708	0	13	Galway	Dunkellin	Killeenavarra	Gort	IV.	30
45	Ballyclery	402	2	33	King's Co.	Clonlisk	Roscrea	Roscrea	I.	131
13	Ballyclider	191	2	38	Queen's Co.	Maryborough East	Straboe	Mountmellick	I.	241
63	Ballyclogh	241	3	0	Antrim	Upper Massereene	Magheragall	Lisburn	III.	31
27	Ballyclogh	686	0	26	Cork, E.R.	Fermoy	Glanworth	Fermoy	II.	79
46	Ballyclogh	112	3	9	Cork, E.R.	Kinnatalloon	Mogeely	Fermoy	II.	98
24	Ballyclogh	302	1	32	Cork, E.R.	Orrery and Kilmore	Ballyclogh	Mallow	II.	106
6	Ballyclogh	203	3	15	Limerick	Clanwilliam	Kilmurry	Limerick	II.	224
10, 19	Ballyclogh	490	0	36	Limerick	Connello Lower	Lismakeery	Rathkeale	II.	228
13	Ballyclogh	361	1	1	Limerick	Pubblebrien	Knocknagaul	Limerick	II.	253
11	Ballyclogh	139	0	29	Wexford	Gorey	Toome	Gorey	I.	321
28, 33	Ballycloghan	498	2	6	Antrim	Lower Antrim	Skerry	Ballymena	III.	4
49	Ballycloghan	115	3	12	Antrim	Upper Toome	Duneane	Antrim	III.	34
4, 5	Ballycloghan	633	1	1	Down	Castlereagh Lower	Holywood	Belfast	III.	162
16	Ballycloghan	558	0	11	Down	Castlereagh Lower	Killinchy	Newtownards	III.	163
19	Ballycloghan	208	3	3	Longford	Moydow	Kilglass	Ballymahon	I.	161

(a) Including 1ᴬ. 3ᴿ. 24ᴾ. water.
(b) Including 2ᴬ. 1ᴿ. 23ᴾ. water.
(c) Including 5ᴬ. 3ᴿ. 27ᴾ. water.
(d) Including 2ᴬ. 2ᴿ. 31ᴾ. water.

K 2

No. of Sheet of the Ordnance Survey Maps.	Townlands and Towns.	Area in Statute Acres.	County.	Barony.	Parish.	Poor Law Union in 1857.	Townland Census of 1851, Part I.	
		A. R. P.					Vol.	Page
7	Ballyclogh (*Centre*) .	172 3 2	Antrim .	Lower Dunluce .	Dunluce . . .	Coleraine . .	III.	17
23, 30	Ballycloghduff . .	230 1 39	Westmeath .	Kilkenny West .	Drumraney . .	Athlone . .	I.	272
23, 30	Ballycloghduff (*Molston*) . . .	288 0 1	Westmeath .	Kilkenny West .	Drumraney . .	Athlone . .	I.	272
79, 80, 91	Ballyclogher . .	824 0 20*a*	Mayo . .	Clanmorris . .	Balla . . .	Castlebar . .	IV.	131
24	Ballyclogher . .	83 3 38	Westmeath .	Rathconrath . .	Killare . . .	Mullingar . .	I.	283
50	Ballycloghessy . .	119 2 36	Clare . .	Islands . . .	Clondagad . .	Killadysert . .	II.	29
38	Ballyclogh Lower .	37 1 15	Limerick . .	Connello Upper .	Bruree . . .	Kilmallock . .	II.	231
7	Ballyclogh (*North*) .	77 0 0	Antrim . .	Lower Dunluce .	Dunluce . . .	Coleraine . .	III.	17
36	Ballyclogh North .	186 1 9	Wicklow . .	Arklow . . .	Dunganstown . .	Rathdrum . .	I.	343
7	Ballyclogh (*North Centre*) . .	78 0 26	Antrim . .	Lower Dunluce .	Dunluce . . .	Coleraine . .	III.	17
7	Ballyclogh (*South*) .	76 2 12	Antrim . .	Lower Dunluce .	Dunluce . . .	Coleraine . .	III.	17
36	Ballyclogh South .	93 2 28	Wicklow ..	Arklow . . .	Dunganstown . .	Rathdrum . .	I.	343
7	Ballyclogh (*South Centre*) . .	68 2 14	Antrim . .	Lower Dunluce .	Dunluce . . .	Coleraine . .	III.	17
24	BALLYCLOGH T. .	—	Cork, E.R. .	Orrery and Kilmore	Ballyclogh . .	Mallow . .	II.	106
38, 46	Ballyclogh Upper .	174 1 7	Limerick . .	Connello Upper .	Bruree . . .	Kilmallock . .	II.	231
2, 3	Ballycloby . .	456 1 35	Waterford .	Upperthird . .	Dysert . . .	Carrick on Suir .	II.	369
32	Ballyclosh, . .	458 2 17	Antrim . .	Lower Toome .	Ahoghill . .	Ballymena . .	III.	31
11	Ballyclough . .	265 2 29	Londonderry .	Coleraine . .	Aghadowey . .	Coleraine . .	III.	229
22	Ballyclovan . .	192 0 35	Kilkenny . .	Callan . . .	Callan . . .	Callan . .	I.	83
22	Ballyclovan Meadows	42 0 9	Kilkenny . .	Callan . . .	Callan . . .	Callan . .	I.	83
36	Ballycluane . .	131 3 37	Limerick . .	Glenquin . .	Monagay . .	Newcastle . .	II.	247
27	Ballycoam . .	100 2 5	Kilkenny . .	Knocktopher . .	Ennisnag . .	Thomastown . .	I.	111
17	Ballycoardra . .	89 2 11	Waterford .	Gaultiere . .	Drumcannon . .	Waterford . .	II.	362
32	Ballycocksoost . .	801 1 6	Kilkenny . .	Gowran . .	Inistiogue . .	Thomastown . .	I.	96
31	Ballycoe . . .	155 0 39	Waterford .	Decies without Drum	Dungarvan . .	Dungarvan . .	II.	354
12	Ballycoffey or Ballyhoy . . .	241 2 13	Armagh . .	Armagh . . .	Lisnadill . .	Armagh . .	III.	45
97	Ballycoghlan . .	266 1 2	Cork, E.R. .	Kinalea . . .	Innishannon . .	Bandon . .	II.	95
47	Ballycogly . .	226 2 11	Wexford . .	Forth . .	Mayglass . .	Wexford . .	I.	312
58, 65	Ballycohy . .	524 2 31	Tipperary, S.R. .	Clanwilliam .	Shronell . .	Tipperary . .	II.	310
42	Ballycolgan . .	192 0 30	Galway . .	Clare . . .	Kilkilvery . .	Tuam . .	IV.	20
11	Ballycolgan . .	328 2 28	King's Co. .	Coolestown . .	Ballynakill . .	Edenderry . .	I.	132
11	Ballycolgan . .	169 3 2	King's Co. .	Coolestown . .	Monasteroris . .	Edenderry . .	I.	133
29	Ballycolla . .	373 0 36	Queen's Co. .	Clarmallagh . .	Aghaboe . . .	Abbeyleix . .	I.	235
29	Ballycolla . .	52 1 36	Queen's Co. .	Clarmallagh . .	Killermogh . .	Abbeyleix . .	I.	238
29	Ballycolla Heath .	285 3 20	Queen's Co. .	Clarmallagh . .	Killermogh . .	Abbeyleix . .	I.	238
29	BALLYCOLLA T. .	—	Queen's Co. .	Clarmallagh . .	Aghaboe . . .	Abbeyleix . .	I.	236
60, 64	Ballycollin . .	883 1 15	Antrim . .	Upper Belfast .	Derryaghy . .	Lisburn . .	III.	10
30	Ballycollin . .	256 1 18	King's Co. .	Eglish . .	Eglish . . .	Parsonstown . .	I.	134
17, 25, 26	Ballycollin . .	357 3 0	King's Co. .	Geashill . .	Geashill . . .	Tullamore . .	I.	139
31	Ballycollin Lower .	147 1 8	King's Co. .	Ballyboy . .	Ballyboy . . .	Parsonstown . .	I.	123
31	Ballycollin Upper .	233 2 35	King's Co. .	Ballyboy . .	Ballyboy . . .	Parsonstown . .	I.	123
9	Ballycolliton . .	399 0 14	Tipperary, N.R. .	Lower Ormond .	Kilbarron . .	Borrisokane . .	II.	284
55	Ballycolman . .	467 0 2	Cork, E.R. .	Imokilly . .	Ardagh . . .	Youghal . .	II.	83
4, 5, 9, 10	Ballycolman . .	588 0 24*b*	Tyrone . .	Strabane Lower .	Urney . . .	Strabane . .	III.	322
7, 12	Ballycomclone . .	337 3 12	Wexford . .	Ballaghkeen . .	Kiltennell . .	Gorey . .	I.	297
61, 69	Ballycomisk . .	308 1 34	Tipperary, S.R. .	Middlethird . .	St. Patricksrock .	Cashel . .	II.	330
46	Ballycomlargy . .	185 1 39	Londonderry .	Loughinsholin . .	Desertlyn . .	Magherafelt . .	III.	240
131	Ballycommane . .	1,349 0 17	Cork. W.R. .	West Carbery (W.D.)	Durrus . . .	Bantry . .	II.	142
15	Ballycommon . .	33 3 16	Kildare . .	South Salt . .	Clonaghlis . .	Celbridge . .	I.	76
37	Ballycommon . .	122 2 5	Kilkenny . .	Ida . . .	The Rower . .	New Ross . .	I.	104
17, 18	Ballycommon . .	1,249 2 16	King's Co. .	Lower Philipstown .	Ballycommon . .	Tullamore . .	I.	142
14, 20	Ballycommon . .	350 3 39	Tipperary, N.R. .	Lower Ormond .	Monsea . . .	Nenagh . .	II.	287
3	Ballycomoyle . .	465 0 38	Westmeath .	Fore . . .	Rathgarve . .	Castletowndelvin .	I.	271
10	Ballycomy . .	269 0 16	Kilkenny . .	Fassadinin . .	Dysart . . .	Castlecomer . .	I.	89
11, 19	Ballycon . .	469 0 31	King's Co. .	Coolestown . .	Ballynakill . .	Edenderry . .	I.	132
1	Ballyconagan . .	168 0 19	Antrim . .	Cary . . .	Rathlin Island .	Ballycastle, . .	III.	15
21, 22	Ballyconboy . .	879 2 32	Roscommon .	Castlereagh. . .	Kilcorkey . .	Castlereagh . .	IV.	199
37	Ballycondon . .	213 3 6	Waterford .	Coshmore and Coshbride	Templemichael .	Youghal . .	II.	348
33, 34, 37	Ballycondon Commons . .	554 1 29	Waterford .	Coshmore and Coshbride	Templemichael .	Youghal . .	II.	348
39, 40, 48, 49	Ballycong . .	582 2 28*c*	Mayo . .	Gallen . . .	Attymass . .	Ballina . .	IV.	146
3	Ballyconlore . .	151 2 2	Wexford . .	Gorey . . .	Inch . . .	Gorey . .	I.	316
3	Ballyconlore . .	173 2 31	Wexford . .	Gorey . . .	Kilcavan . .	Gorey . .	I.	317
3	Ballyconlore . .	98 1 21	Wexford . .	Gorey . . .	Kilnenor . .	Gorey . .	I.	319
41, 55	Ballyconlought . .	291 0 32	Galway . .	Clare . . .	Cargin . . .	Tuam . .	IV.	18
36	Ballyconnaught . .	204 3 26	Kilkenny . .	Ida . . .	Dysertmoon . .	New Ross . .	I.	101
42	Ballyconneely . .	224 0 8	Clare . .	Bunratty Lower .	Kilnasoolagh . .	Ennis . .	II.	6
10	Ballyconneely .	1,000 1 20*d*	Galway . .	Ballynahinch . .	Ballindoon . .	Clifden . .	IV.	10
24, 25	Ballyconnell . .	598 2 26	Donegal . .	Kilmacrenan . .	Raymunterdoney .	Dunfanaghy . .	III.	131
123	Ballyconnell . .	245 3 33	Galway . .	Kiltartan . .	Kilbeacanty . .	Gort . .	IV.	47

(*a*) Including 5A. 3R. 17P. water. (*c*) Including 89A. 1R. 12P. water. (*d*) Including 119A. 1R. 31P. water.
(*b*) Including 22A. 2R. 11P. water.

No. of Sheet of the Ordnance Survey Maps.	Townlands and Towns.	Area in Statute Acres.			County.	Barony.	Parish.	Poor Law Union in 1857.	Townland Census of 1851, Part I.	
		A.	R.	P.					Vol.	Page
21	Ballyconnell . .	362	2	21	Kerry . .	Clanmaurice . .	Kilflyn . . .	Listowel . .	II.	170
4, 7	Ballyconnell . .	1,019	0	9a	Sligo . .	Carbury . .	Drumcliff . .	Sligo . .	IV.	221
37	Ballyconnell . .	946	1	23	Wicklow . .	Shillelagh . .	Crecrin . . .	Shillelagh . .	I.	357
10	BALLYCONNELL T. .	—			Cavan . .	Tullyhaw . .	Tomregan . .	Bawnboy . .	III.	96
7	BALLYCONNELL T. .	—			Sligo . .	Carbury . .	Drumcliff . .	Sligo . .	IV.	222
31, 32	Ballyconnelly . .	497	1	11	Antrim . .	Lower Toome .	Ahoghill . .	Ballymena .	III.	31
37	Ballyconnelly . .	562	3	15	Donegal . .	Kilmacrenan .	Tullyfern . .	Millford . .	III.	132
53, 61	Ballyconnelly . .	149	2	13	Donegal . .	Raphoe . .	Leck . . .	Letterkenny .	III.	140
22, 30	Ballyconnery Lower	156	2	8	Waterford .	Decies without Drum	Kilgobnet . .	Dungarvan .	II.	357
22, 23, 30, 31	Ballyconnery Upper	224	0	32	Waterford .	Decies without Drum	Kilgobnet . .	Dungarvan .	II.	357
41, 46	Ballyconnick . .	206	3	22	Wexford . .	Bargy . .	Ballyconnick .	Wexford . .	I.	304
27, 33	Ballyconnigar Lower	469	2	5	Wexford . .	Ballaghkeen .	Ballyvaldon .	Enniscorthy .	I.	292
27, 33	Ballyconnigar Upper	320	2	22	Wexford . .	Ballaghkeen .	Ballyvaldon .	Enniscorthy .	I.	292
5, 8, 9	Ballyconnoe North .	545	0	15	Clare . .	Burren . .	Killeany . .	Ballyvaghan .	II.	13
8, 9	Ballyconnoe South .	802	1	31	Clare . .	Burren . .	Killeany . .	Ballyvaghan .	II.	13
27	Ballyconnor . .	649	2	13	Tipperary, N.R.	Upper Ormond .	Aghnameadle .	Nenagh . .	II.	288
48	Ballyconor Big .	74	2	39	Wexford . .	Forth . .	Kilrane . .	Wexford . .	I.	311
48	Ballyconor Little .	79	2	32	Wexford . .	Forth . .	Kilrane . .	Wexford . .	I.	311
4, 5, 9	Ballyconra . .	1,153	2	32	Kilkenny . .	Galmoy . .	Aharney . .	Urlingford .	I.	91
6	Ballyconran . .	459	1	39	Wexford . .	Scarawalsh . .	Carnew . .	Gorey . .	I.	322
10	Ballyconry . .	181	2	2	Clare . .	Burren . .	Carran . .	Ballyvaghan .	II.	11
2	Ballyconry . .	789	3	30	Clare . .	Burren . .	Drumcreehy .	Ballyvaghan .	II.	12
9, 10	Ballyconry . .	166	3	18	Kerry . .	Iraghticonnor .	Ballyconry . .	Listowel . .	II.	190
66	Ballyconry . .	164	1	13	Tipperary, S.R.	Clanwilliam .	Shronell . .	Tipperary .	II.	310
32	Ballyconway . .	485	3	20	Kilkenny . .	Knocktopher .	Jerpointchurch .	Thomastown .	I.	111
36	Ballyconway . .	162	2	23	Limerick . .	Glenquin . .	Monagay . .	Newcastle .	II.	247
39, 40	Ballycoog Lower .	452	3	17	Wicklow . .	Arklow . .	Ballintemple .	Rathdrum .	I.	342
39, 40	Ballycoog Upper .	311	1	18	Wicklow . .	Arklow . .	Ballintemple .	Rathdrum .	I.	342
3	Ballycook . .	484	1	39	Carlow . .	Rathvilly . .	Kineagh . .	Baltinglass .	I.	11
19	Ballycoolan . .	722	0	32	Queen's Co. .	Stradbally . .	Timogue . .	Athy . .	I.	248
40	Ballycooleen . .	272	0	37	Wicklow . .	Arklow . .	Castlemacadam .	Rathdrum .	I.	342
13, 14	Ballycoolen . .	511	0	14	Dublin . .	Castleknock .	Cloghran . .	Dublin North .	I.	24
28	Ballycoolid . .	497	3	13	Queen's Co. .	Clandonagh .	Donaghmore .	Donaghmore .	I.	233
105, 115	Ballycoony . .	305	3	14	Galway . .	Loughrea . .	Killeenadeema .	Loughrea . .	IV.	64
30, 35	Ballycoos&Ballygawn	1,058	0	28	Antrim . .	Upper Glenarm .	Carncastle .	Larne . .	III.	24
6, 7	Ballycopeland . .	474	1	21b	Down . .	Ards Lower .	Donaghadee .	Newtownards .	III.	157
22	Ballycoppigan . .	108	1	13	Carlow . .	Idrone East .	Clonygoose .	Carlow . .	I.	6
45	Ballycor . . .	600	0	16	Antrim . .	Upper Antrim .	Ballycor . .	Antrim . .	III.	6
20	Ballycor . . .	331	1	33	Westmeath .	Moyashel and Magheradernon . .	Rathconnell .	Mullingar .	I.	270
20, 28	Ballycorban . .	857	3	25	Clare . .	Tulla Upper .	Tomgraney .	Scarriff . .	II.	46
125	Ballycorban . .	120	0	29	Galway . .	Leitrim . .	Ballynakill .	Loughrea . .	IV.	50
48	Ballycorboys Big .	97	3	5	Wexford . .	Forth . .	Killinick . .	Wexford . .	I.	310
48	Ballycorboys Little .	41	2	22	Wexford . .	Forth . .	Killinick . .	Wexford . .	I.	310
24	Ballycore . .	69	1	34	Kerry . .	Ballyboy . .	Killoughy . .	Tullamore .	I.	123
13	Ballycore . .	148	2	23	Longford . .	Moydow . .	Killashee . .	Longford . .	I.	161
20	Ballycore . .	266	3	14	Wicklow . .	Upper Talbotstown .	Rathtoole . .	Baltinglass .	I.	365
33	Ballycorey . .	156	0	38c	Clare . .	Bunratty Upper .	Templemaley .	Ennis . .	II.	10
50	Ballycorick . .	510	2	5	Clare . .	Islands . .	Clondagad .	Killadysert .	II.	29
6, 11	Ballycorkey . .	402	2	19d	Westmeath .	Moygoish . .	Kilbixy . .	Mullingar .	I.	279
25, 26	Ballycorman . .	213	2	15	Queen's Co. .	Ballyadams .	Killabban . .	Athy . .	I.	231
17	Ballycormick . .	127	2	4	Antrim . .	Upper Dunluce .	Ballymoney .	Ballymoney .	III.	18
16, 19	Ballycormick . .	370	3	14	Carlow . .	Idrone East .	Lorum . .	Carlow . .	I.	8
16, 19	Ballycormick . .	166	3	38	Carlow . .	Idrone East .	Sliguff . .	Carlow . .	I.	8
46	Ballycormick . .	263	2	37	King's Co. .	Clonlisk . .	Borrisnafarney .	Roscrea . .	I.	129
18, 19	Ballycormick . .	446	3	8	Limerick . .	Shanid . .	Shanagolden .	Glin . .	II.	258
12	Ballycormick . .	199	1	23	Queen's Co. .	Maryborough West	Clonenagh and Clonagheen . .	Mountmellick .	I.	242
7	Ballycormuck . .	265	2	38	Tipperary, N.R.	Lower Ormond .	Aglishcloghane .	Borrisokane .	II.	281
77	Ballycornane . .	188	0	23	Tipperary, S.R.	Iffa and Offa East .	Newchapel .	Clonmel . .	II.	315
45	Ballycorney . .	347	3	4	Clare . .	Tulla Lower .	Killaloe . .	Limerick . .	II.	35
25	Ballycorrigan . .	210	0	36	Tipperary, N.R.	Owney and Arra .	Templeachally .	Nenagh . .	II.	297
26	Ballycorus . .	232	2	22	Dublin . .	Rathdown . .	Rathmichael .	Rathdown .	I.	37
42	Ballycoshone Lower	179	3	13	Down . .	Upper Iveagh, Lr. pt.	Clonduff . .	Newry . .	III.	171
48	Ballycoshone Upper	236	0	19	Down . .	Upper Iveagh, Lr. pt.	Clonduff . .	Newry . .	III.	171
15	Ballycoshown . .	208	3	21	Limerick . .	Coonagh . .	Doon . .	Tipperary .	II.	234
8	Ballycoskery . .	819	2	0	Cork, E.R.	Orrery and Kilmore .	Aglishdrinagh .	Kilmallock .	II.	106
9, 17	Ballycosney . .	324	0	1	King's Co. .	Ballycowan .	Kilbride . .	Tullamore .	I.	127
14, 15	Ballycotteen North	904	2	16e	Clare . .	Corcomroe .	Kilmacrehy .	Ennistimon .	II.	20
14, 15	Ballycotteen South	274	3	21	Clare . .	Corcomroe .	Kilmacrehy .	Ennistimon .	II.	20
89	Ballycottin . .	466	3	10	Cork, E.R.	Imokilly . .	Cloyne . .	Middleton .	II.	85
89	*Ballycottin Island*	9	0	7	Cork, E.R.	Imokilly . .	Cloyne . .	Middleton .	II.	85
89	*Ballycottin Island (Small)*	4	3	23	Cork, E.R.	Imokilly . .	Cloyne . .	Middleton .	II.	85

(a) Including 8A. 0R. 25P. water.
(b) Including 12A. 0R. 7P. of mill-pond.
(c) Including 10A. 1R. 34P. water.
(d) Including 30A. 1R. 24P. water.
(e) Including 4A. 3R. 24P. water.

No. of Sheet of the Ordnance Survey Maps	Townlands and Towns	Area in Statute Acres.	County.	Barony.	Parish.	Poor Law Union in 1857.	Townland Census of 1851, Part I.	
		A. R. P.					Vol.	Page
89	BALLYCOTTIN T. . .	—	Cork, E.R. .	Imokilly . . .	Cloyne . . .	Middleton .	II.	86
26	Ballycourcy Beg .	281 0 28	Wexford .	Ballaghkeen .	Ballyhuskard .	Enniscorthy .	I.	291
26	Ballycourcy More .	445 3 10	Wexford .	Ballaghkeen .	Ballyhuskard .	Enniscorthy .	I.	291
9	Ballycourdra . .	14 2 17	Waterford .	Gaultiere .	St. Johns Without .	Waterford .	II.	365
9	BALLYCOURDRA T. .	—	Waterford .	Gaultiere .	St. Johns Without .	Waterford .	II.	365
37, 38	Ballycowan . .	490 3 29	Antrim . .	Lower Antrim .	Connor . .	Ballymena .	III.	3
9	Ballycowan . .	778 2 3a	Down . .	Castlereagh Upper .	Drumbo . .	Lisburn .	III.	164
2, 3	Ballycowan . .	173 2 4	Kildare . .	Carbury . .	Nurney . .	Edenderry .	I.	53
16	Ballycowan . .	364 2 24	King's Co. .	Ballycowan . .	Kilbride . .	Tullamore .	I.	127
48	Ballycowan . .	118 2 7	Wexford . .	Forth . . .	Kilscoran .	Wexford .	I.	311
7	Ballycoyle . .	154 0 15	Wicklow .	Rathdown .	Powerscourt .	Rathdown .	I.	356
16	Ballycraddock .	349 2 0	Waterford .	Middlethird .	Dunhill . .	Waterford .	II.	366
14	Ballycraggan .	330 3 2b	Tipperary, N.R.	Lower Ormond .	Killodiernan .	Nenagh .	II.	284
22	Ballycragh . .	102 2 13	Dublin . .	Uppercross .	Tallaght . .	Dublin South .	I.	41
61, 62	Ballycraheen .	260 1 8	Cork, E.R. .	Barretts . .	Donaghmore .	Cork .	II.	49
2, 6	Ballycraig Lower .	186 3 31	Antrim . .	Lower Dunluce .	Dunluce . .	Coleraine .	III.	17
6	Ballycraig Upper .	98 1 1	Antrim . .	Lower Dunluce .	Dunluce . .	Coleraine .	III.	17
51	Ballycraigy . .	947 0 26	Antrim . .	Lower Belfast .	Carnmoney .	Belfast .	III.	7
50	Ballycraigy . .	215 3 27	Antrim . .	Upper Antrim .	Antrim . .	Antrim .	III.	5
35, 40	Ballycraigy . .	478 0 2	Antrim . .	Upper Glenarm .	Larne . .	Larne .	III.	25
4	Ballycramsy .	146 3 19	Donegal . .	Inishowen East .	Clonca . .	Inishowen .	III.	116
73	Ballycrana . .	382 3 20	Tipperary, S.R.	Clanwilliam .	Clonbeg . .	Tipperary .	II.	305
18, 25	Ballycran Beg .	394 3 17	Down . .	Ards Upper .	Ardkeen . .	Downpatrick .	III.	159
37, 38	Ballycrane . .	175 3 29	Wexford . .	Shelmaliere East .	Ardcolm . .	Wexford .	I.	330
18, 25	Ballycran More .	593 2 21	Down . .	Ards Upper .	Ardkeen . .	Newtownards .	III.	159
10, 16	Ballycreelly . .	603 3 2c	Down . .	Castlereagh Lower .	Comber . .	Newtownards .	III.	161
22	Ballycreen . .	628 2 3	Down . .	Lower Iveagh, Lr. pt.	Magheradrool .	Lisburn .	III.	168
34	Ballycreen Lower .	385 1 36	Wicklow .	Ballinacor South .	Ballinacor .	Rathdrum .	I.	348
29, 34	Ballycreen Upper .	953 2 38	Wicklow .	Ballinacor South .	Ballinacor .	Rathdrum .	I.	348
23, 27	Ballycregagh .	728 1 1	Antrim . .	Kilconway .	Dunaghy . .	Ballymena .	III.	25
13, 18	Ballycregagh Lower	315 1 25	Antrim . .	Upper Dunluce .	Loughguile .	Ballymoney .	III.	20
13	Ballycregagh Upper	308 2 18	Antrim . .	Upper Dunluce .	Loughguile .	Ballymoney .	III.	20
48	Ballycreggan . .	344 1 37	Roscommon .	Athlone . .	Kiltoom . .	Athlone .	IV.	182
37, 38	Ballycreggy . .	443 0 5	Antrim . .	Lower Antrim .	Ballyclug . .	Ballymena .	III.	3
73	Ballycrehane .	407 2 18	Tipperary, S.R.	Clanwilliam .	Clonbeg . .	Tipperary .	II.	305
89	Ballycrenane .	297 2 15	Cork, E.R. .	Imokilly . .	Cloyne . .	Middleton .	II.	85
77, 78, 89	Ballycrenane .	511 2 37	Cork, E.R. .	Imokilly . .	Kilcredan .	Middleton .	II.	87
66	Ballycrenane Beg .	102 3 18	Cork, E.R. .	Imokilly . .	Mogeely . .	Middleton .	II.	89
27	Ballycrenode .	18 0 22	Tipperary, N.R.	Upper Ormond .	Ballymaclogh .	Nenagh .	II.	290
27	Ballycrenode .	354 0 21	Tipperary, N.R.	Upper Ormond .	Kilkeary . .	Nenagh .	II.	290
34	Ballycrighan .	191 2 38	Clare . .	Bunratty Upper .	Clooney . .	Ennis .	II.	7
17	Ballycrine . .	323 3 26	Tipperary, N.R.	Ikerrin . .	Corbally . .	Roscrea .	II.	275
24, 25, 26	Ballycrinnigan .	1,223 3 4	Carlow . .	St. Mullins Lower .	St. Mullins .	New Ross .	I.	13
47	Ballycrispin . .	79 1 3	Kerry . .	Trughanacmy .	Kiltallagh .	Tralee .	II.	212
2	Ballycroghan . .	375 0 23	Down . .	Ards Lower .	Bangor . .	Newtownards .	III.	157
7	Ballycrogue . .	370 1 22	Carlow . .	Carlow . .	Ballycrogue .	Carlow .	I.	1
37	Ballycrompane .	182 3 18	Waterford .	Decies within Drum	Clashmore .	Youghal .	II.	351
41	Ballycronan Beg .	264 0 0	Antrim . .	Lower Belfast .	Islandmagee .	Larne .	III.	8
41	Ballycronan More .	356 3 22	Antrim . .	Lower Belfast .	Islandmagee .	Larne .	III.	8
13	Ballycrone . .	76 3 24	Wicklow .	Newcastle .	Newcastle Lower .	Rathdrum .	I.	353
89	Ballycroneen East .	7 2 32	Cork, E.R. .	Imokilly . .	Cloyne . .	Middleton .	II.	85
88, 89, 100	Ballycroneen West .	401 2 25	Cork, E.R. .	Imokilly . .	Cloyne . .	Middleton .	II.	85
48	Ballycronigan . .	103 1 9	Wexford .	Forth . .	Kilrane . .	Wexford .	I.	311
48	Ballycronigan . .	84 2 18	Wexford .	Forth . .	St. Helens .	Wexford .	I.	313
14	Ballycronog . .	69 1 33	Monaghan .	Monaghan .	Monaghan .	Monaghan .	III.	276
37, 41	Ballycrony . .	498 3 2	Kilkenny .	Ida . .	Ballygurrim .	New Ross .	I.	101
2	Ballycross . .	83 3 16	Down . .	Ards Lower .	Donaghadee .	Newtownards .	III.	157
27	Ballycross . .	692 2 25	Down . .	Lower Iveagh, Lr. pt.	Magherally .	Banbridge .	III.	168
47	Ballycross . .	273 3 29	Wexford .	Bargy . .	Kilmore . .	Wexford .	I.	306
8	Ballycrossal . .	166 0 0	Queen's Co. .	Portnahinch .	Ardea . .	Mountmellick .	I.	243
118	Ballycrossaun .	211 3 11	Galway . .	Longford .	Tiranascragh .	Portumna .	IV.	62
19	Ballycroum . .	332 1 22	Clare . .	Tulla Upper .	Feakle . .	Tulla .	II.	38
101, 102	Ballycrovane .	550 2 31d	Cork, W.R. .	Bear . .	Kilcatherine .	Castletown .	II.	123
101	*Ballycrovane Island* .	4 0 5	Cork, W.R. .	Bear . .	Kilcatherine .	Castletown .	II.	123
101	*Ballycrovane Little* .	1 1 38	Cork, W.R. .	Bear . .	Kilcatherine .	Castletown .	II.	123
97, 98	Ballycroy . .	226 2 25	Donegal . .	Banagh . .	Killaghtee .	Donegal .	III.	109
10, 17	Ballycrum . .	1,032 1 34	Londonderry .	Keenaght .	Drumachose .	NewT° Limavady .	III.	235
18	Ballycrumlin . .	88 2 13	King's Co. .	Geashill .	Geashill . .	Tullamore .	I.	139
12	Ballycrummy . .	79 1 38	Armagh . .	Armagh . .	Armagh . .	Armagh .	III.	43
21, 22	Ballycrune . .	608 2 35e	Down . .	Lower Iveagh, Lr. pt.	Annahilt . .	Lisburn .	III.	167
38	Ballycruttle . .	212 1 32	Down . .	Lecale Lower .	Ballee . .	Downpatrick .	III.	179
8, 9, 13, 14	Ballycrystal . .	1,779 1 24	Wexford . .	Scarawalsh .	Templeshanbo .	Enniscorthy .	I.	326
22, 23	Ballycuddahy . .	231 1 28	Queen's Co. .	Clarmallagh .	Aghaboe . .	Abbeyleix .	I.	235

(a) Including 0A. 3R. 12P. water.
(b) Including 2A. 2R. 30P. water.
(c) Including 0A. 1R. 22P. water.
(d) Including 12A. 0R. 28P. water.
(e) Including 5A. 0R. 25P. water.

No. of Sheet of the Ordnance Survey Maps.	Townlands and Towns.	Area in Statute Acres.			County.	Barony.	Parish.	Poor Law Union in 1857.	Townland Census of 1851. Part I.	
		A.	R.	P.					Vol.	Page
18	Ballycuddihy . .	575	1	32	Kilkenny . .	Crannagh . .	Tullaroan . .	Kilkenny . .	I.	87
8	Ballycuddihy . .	408	0	17	Kilkenny . .	Galmoy . .	Fertagh . .	Urlingford . .	I.	92
104, 105, 115	Ballycuddy . .	301	2	27	Galway . .	Dunkellin . .	Kilchreest . .	Loughrea . .	IV.	28
20, 26	Ballycuddy Beg .	41	2	25	Tipperary, N.R.	Owney and Arra .	Burgesbeg . .	Nenagh . .	II.	293
26	Ballycuddy More .	98	2	39	Tipperary, N.R.	Owney and Arra .	Burgesbeg . .	Nenagh . .	II.	293
18, 26	Ballycue . .	442	0	14	King's Co. .	Geashill . .	Geashill . .	Tullamore .	I.	139
37	Ballycuggaran .	601	3	39	Clare . .	Tulla Lower .	Killaloe . .	Scarriff . .	II.	35
81	Ballycuirke East .	130	1	8a	Galway . .	Moycullen . .	Moycullen . .	Galway . .	IV.	70
68, 81	Ballycuirke West .	323	3	11b	Galway . .	Moycullen . .	Moycullen . .	Galway . .	IV.	71
12	Ballyculhane . .	382	3	23	Limerick . .	Kenry . .	Kildimo . .	Rathkeale .	II.	249
46	Ballycullane . .	236	1	6	Cork, E.R. .	Kinnatalloon . .	Mogeely . .	Fermoy . .	II.	98
45	Ballycullane . .	420	0	30	Kerry . .	Corkaguiny . .	Ballinvoher . .	Dingle . .	II.	173
60, 68	Ballycullane . .	455	3	18	Kerry . .	Magunihy . .	Kilcummin . .	Killarney . .	II.	201
35	Ballycullane . .	449	3	17	Kildare . .	Narragh & RebanEast	Tankardstown .	Athy . .	I.	66
39, 40	Ballycullane . .	346	0	14	Limerick . .	Coshlea . .	Kilbreedy Major .	Kilmallock .	II.	239
39, 47	Ballycullane . .	286	1	25	Limerick .	Kilmallock . .	St.Peter's & St.Paul's	Kilmallock .	II.	250
22, 31	Ballycullane . .	736	2	35	Limerick . .	Smallcounty . .	Glenogra . .	Croom . .	II.	259
34, 35	Ballycullane . .	263	0	21	Waterford .	Decies within Drum	Aglish . .	Dungarvan .	II.	349
6	Ballycullane . .	178	0	13	Waterford .	Upperthird . .	Rathgormuck .	Carrick on Suir	II.	371
40	Ballycullane . .	544	2	37	Wexford . .	Shelburne . .	Tintern . .	New Ross .	I.	329
30, 35	Ballycullane Beg .	200	3	37	Waterford .	Decies without Drum	Dungarvan .	Dungarvan .	II.	355
40	Ballycullane Lower	237	2	26	Kildare . .	Kilkea and Moone .	Kineagh . .	Baltinglass .	I.	60
17	Ballycullane Lower	163	2	8	Limerick . .	Shanid . .	Kilfergus . .	Glin . .	II.	255
30, 35	Ballycullane More .	285	2	36	Waterford .	Decies without Drum	Dungarvan .	Dungarvan .	II.	355
40	Ballycullane Upper	290	3	19	Kildare . .	Kilkea and Moone .	Kineagh . .	Baltinglass .	I.	60
17	Ballycullane Upper	324	1	16	Limerick . .	Shanid . .	Kilfergus . .	Glin . .	II.	255
8, 15	Ballycullaun . .	101	2	39	Clare . .	Corcomroe . .	Killilagh . .	Ennistimon .	II.	19
31	Ballyculleen . .	429	2	6	Limerick . .	Coshma . .	Croom . .	Croom . .	II.	242
11	Ballycullen . .	175	2	27	Roscommon .	Boyle . .	Killukin . .	Cark. on Shannon	IV.	195
35	Ballycullcen . .	258	3	10	Sligo . .	Tirerrill . .	Kilmactranny .	Boyle . .	IV.	240
16, 24	Ballyculleeny . .	148	1	20	Clare . .	Corcomroe . .	Clooney . .	Corrofin . .	II.	18
43, 52	Ballycullen . .	314	2	23	Clare . .	Bunratty Lower .	Kilfinaghta . .	Limerick . .	II.	4
5	Ballycullen . .	324	2	34	Down . .	Castlereagh Lower .	Newtownards .	Newtownards .	III.	163
22	Ballycullen . .	112	0	36	Dublin . .	Uppercross . .	Tallaght . .	Dublin South .	I.	41
10, 19	Ballycullen . .	263	1	14	Limerick . .	Connello Lower .	Lismakeery . .	Rathkeale .	II.	228
24	Ballycullen . .	1,237	3	39	Wicklow . .	Newcastle . .	Rathnew . .	Rathdrum .	I.	354
136	Ballycullenane .	54	2	18	Cork, W.R. .	Ibane and Barryroe	Lislee . .	Clonakilty .	II.	150
8	Ballycullenbeg .	599	0	11	Queen's Co. .	Portnahinch . .	Ardea . .	Mountmellick .	I.	243
8	Ballycullen or Drumask . .	86	1	15	Armagh . .	Armagh . .	Clonfeacle . .	Armagh . .	III.	43
8	Ballycullen or Shanmullagh . .	239	0	27	Armagh . .	Armagh . .	Clonfeacle . .	Armagh . .	III.	43
63, 71	Ballycullin . .	817	0	25	Tipperary, S.R.	Slievardagh . .	Kilvemnon . .	Callan . .	II.	334
25	Ballycullinan . .	166	1	14c	Clare . .	Inchiquin . .	Dysert . .	Ennis . .	II.	24
60, 64	Ballycullo . .	384	2	6	Antrim . .	Upper Belfast .	Shankill . .	Lisburn . .	III.	10
103	Ballyculloo . .	131	0	39d	Galway . .	Dunkellin . .	Kilcolgan . .	Gort . .	IV.	28
34, 38	Ballyculter Lower .	255	3	21	Down . .	Lecale Lower .	Ballyculter .	Downpatrick .	III.	178
31	Ballyculter Upper .	296	1	16c	Down . .	Lecale Lower .	Ballyculter .	Downpatrick .	III.	178
1, 5	Ballycultraw . .	825	1	26	Down . .	Castlereagh Lower .	Holywood . .	Belfast . .	III.	162
7	Ballycumber . .	453	0	24	King's Co. .	Garrycastle . .	Lemanaghan .	Parsonstown .	I.	136
33, 38	Ballycumber North	283	3	31	Wicklow . .	Ballinacor South .	Kilcommon .	Shillelagh .	I.	349
38	Ballycumber South	584	2	5	Wicklow . .	Ballinacor South .	Kilcommon .	Shillelagh .	I.	349
7	BALLYCUMBER T. .	—			King's Co. .	Garrycastle . .	Lemanaghan .	Parsonstown .	I.	137
13	Ballycummin . .	697	3	20	Limerick . .	Pubblebrien . .	Mungret . .	Limerick . .	II.	253
18	Ballycummin . .	124	0	34	Roscommon .	Ballintober North .	Kilmore . .	Cark. on Shannon	IV.	187
11	Ballycummin . .	220	1	13	Sligo . .	Tireragh . .	Easky . .	Dromore West .	IV.	233
140	Ballycummisk . .	191	2	39	Cork, W.R. .	WestCarbery(W.D.)	Skull . .	Skull . .	II.	145
51	Ballycunneen . .	163	0	28	Clare . .	Bunratty Lower .	Drumline . .	Ennis . .	II.	3
50, 61	Ballycunningham .	641	2	37	Cork, E.R. .	East Muskerry .	Donaghmore .	Macroom . .	II.	102
78, 84	Ballycurkeen . .	310	2	17	Tipperary, S.R.	Iffa and Offa East .	Kilmurry . .	Carrick on Suir	II.	314
13	Ballycurragh . .	80	1	11	Carlow . .	Forth . .	Gilbertstown .	Carlow . .	I.	4
39	Ballycurragh . .	405	2	14	King's Co. .	Ballybritt . .	Aghancon . .	Roscrea . .	I.	124
33, 34	Ballycurragh . .	588	2	30	Wicklow . .	Ballinacor South .	Moyne . .	Shillelagh .	I.	350
5	Ballycurraghan .	77	1	31	Kildare . .	North Salt . .	Laraghbryan .	Celbridge .	I.	75
66, 67	Ballycurraginny .	311	2	16	Cork, E.R. .	Imokilly . .	Killeagh . .	Youghal . .	II.	88
34	Ballycurrane . .	251	3	5	Kerry . .	Corkaguiny . .	Kilquane . .	Dingle . .	II.	179
65	Ballycurrane . .	331	1	37	Tipperary, S.R.	Clanwilliam . .	Emly . .	Tipperary .	II.	307
35, 38	Ballycurrane . .	223	3	14	Waterford .	Decies within Drum	Ardmore . .	Youghal . .	II.	349
35, 38	Ballycurrane North	162	1	31	Waterford .	Decies within Drum	Clashmore .	Youghal . .	II.	351
35, 38	Ballycurrane South	232	0	23	Waterford .	Decies within Drum	Clashmore .	Youghal . .	II.	351
65	Ballycurrany East .	175	0	5	Cork, E.R. .	Barrymore . .	Ballycurrany .	Middleton .	II.	51
65	Ballycurrany West .	244	0	20	Cork, E.R. .	Barrymore . .	Ballycurrany .	Middleton .	II.	51
58, 68	Ballycurraun . .	209	3	17	Clare . .	Clonderalaw .	Kilmurray . .	Kilrush . .	II.	17

No. of Sheet of the Ordnance Survey Maps.	Townlands and Towns.	Area in Statute Acres.	County.	Barony.	Parish.	Poor Law Union in 1857.	Townland Census of 1851, Part I.	
		A. R. P.					Vol.	Page
64, 75	Ballycurreen . .	375 0 29	Cork, E. R.	Barrymore . .	Carrigtohill . .	Middleton . .	II.	52
74, 86	Ballycurreen . .	612 2 34	Cork, E.R.	Cork . .	St. Finbar's . .	Cork . .	II.	65
36, 39	Ballycurreen North	335 3 14	Waterford .	Decies within Drum	Ballymacart . .	Dungarvan . .	II.	351
36, 39	Ballycurreen South	318 3 5	Waterford .	Decies within Drum	Ballymacart . .	Dungarvan . .	II.	351
37, 41	Ballycurrin . .	348 2 10	Kilkenny .	Ida	Listerlin . .	New Ross . .	I.	103
123	Ballycurrin Demesne	557 2 26	Mayo .	Kilmaine . .	Shrule . . .	Ballinrobe . .	IV.	158
19, 25	Ballycurry Demesne	352 2 30	Wicklow .	Newcastle . .	Kiliskey . .	Rathdrum . .	I.	352
51	Ballycushan . .	228 2 27	Antrim .	Upper Belfast . .	Templepatrick . .	Antrim . .	III.	10
122	Ballycusheen . .	765 2 10	Mayo .	Kilmaine . .	Kilmainmore . .	Ballinrobe . .	IV.	155
24	Ballycushen . .	190 3 29	Cork, E.R.	Orrery and Kilmore	Ballyclogh . .	Mallow . .	II.	106
54, 55	Ballycushion . .	104 2 9	Donegal .	Raphoe . .	Taughboyne . .	Londonderry .	III.	143
48	Ballycushlane Big .	72 1 37	Wexford .	Forth . . .	Ladysisland . .	Wexford . .	I.	311
48	Ballycushlane Little	83 2 19	Wexford .	Forth . . .	Ladysisland . .	Wexford . .	I.	311
44, 53	Ballyda . .	287 2 11	Cork, E.R.	Barrymore . .	Gortroe . .	Fermoy . .	II.	54
23	Ballyda . .	339 2 39	Kilkenny .	Shillelogher . .	Danesfort . .	Thomastown .	I.	114
34	Ballydaff . .	225 0 37	Tipperary, N.R.	Kilnamanagh Upper	Glenkeen . .	Thurles . .	II.	278
34	Ballydague . .	1,130 3 26a	Cork, E.R.	Fermoy . .	Kilcummer . .	Fermoy . .	II.	80
26	Ballydaheen . .	303 1 34	Cork, E.R.	Fermoy . .	Wallstown . .	Mallow . .	II.	83
67	Ballydaheen . .	16 3 29	Cork, E.R.	Imokilly . .	Ardagh . .	Youghal . .	II.	83
67	Ballydaheen . .	132 0 39	Cork, E.R.	Imokilly . .	Clonpriest . .	Youghal . .	II.	84
2	Ballydaheen . .	215 0 15	Cork, E.R.	Orrery and Kilmore	Shandrum . .	Kilmallock . .	II.	109
32	Ballydaheen . .	195 0 5	Limerick .	Coshma . .	Bruff . . .	Kilmallock . .	II.	242
33	Ballydahin . .	281 1 30b	Cork, E.R.	Fermoy . .	Mallow . .	Mallow . .	II.	81
25	Ballydallagh . .	41 1 34	Kildare .	Naas South . .	Ballymore Eustace .	Naas . .	I.	64
38, 47	Ballydaly . .	1,089 1 35c	Cork, W.R.	West Muskerry .	Drishane . .	Millstreet . .	II.	155
125	Ballydaly . .	46 2 0	Galway .	Leitrim . .	Ballynakill . .	Loughrea . .	IV.	50
15	Ballydaly . .	273 1 30	King's Co.	Garrycastle . .	Wheery or Killagally	Parsonstown .	I.	139
40	Ballydaly . .	69 1 11	Limerick .	Smallcounty .	Knockainy . .	Kilmallock . .	II.	260
28	Ballydaly . .	268 1 15d	Roscommon .	Roscommon . .	Killukin . .	Strokestown .	IV.	210
17	Ballydaly or Derrynagall . .	464 2 33	King's Co.	Ballycowan . .	Kilbride . .	Tullamore . .	I.	127
12	Ballydane . .	142 0 4	Wexford .	Ballaghkeen . .	Ardamine . .	Gorey . .	I.	291
54	Ballydangan . .	53 1 26	Roscommon .	Moycarn . .	Moore . . .	Ballinasloe . .	IV.	206
56	Ballydaniel . .	1,157 0 16	Cork, E.R.	Imokilly . .	Ardagh . .	Youghal . .	II.	83
78	Ballydaniel . .	408 2 4	Cork, E.R.	Imokilly . .	Kilmacdonogh . .	Youghal . .	II.	88
13, 14	Ballydaniel . .	377 1 25	Kilkenny .	Crannagh . .	Odagh . .	Kilkenny . .	I.	86
11	Ballydaniel . .	351 2 38	Wexford .	Gorey . .	Toome . .	Gorey . .	I.	321
75, 87	Ballydaniel Beg .	80 1 19	Cork, E.R.	Barrymore . .	Templerobin . .	Cork . .	II.	58
75,76,87,88	Ballydaniel More .	367 2 21e	Cork, E.R.	Barrymore . .	Templerobin . .	Cork . .	II.	58
44, 45	Ballydargan . .	420 2 12	Down .	Lecale Upper .	Bright . .	Downpatrick .	III.	180
6, 11	Ballydarragh . .	511 0 10	Wexford .	Gorey . .	Kilnahue . .	Gorey . .	I.	319
69, 70	Ballydarrig . .	178 0 6	Kerry .	Iveragh . .	Kilinane . .	Cahersiveen .	II.	197
16, 17	Ballydarton . .	212 1 19	Carlow .	Idrone East . .	Fennagh . .	Carlow . .	I.	7
37	Ballydasoon . .	130 0 14	Waterford .	Coshmore and Coshbride .	Templemichael . .	Youghal . .	II.	348
1	Ballydavey . .	610 2 9	Down .	Castlereagh Lower .	Holywood . .	Belfast . .	III.	162
88, 89	Ballydavid . .	148 0 35	Cork, E.R.	Imokilly . .	Cloyne . .	Middleton . .	II.	85
106	Ballydavid . .	339 1 6	Galway .	Leitrim . .	Kilcooly . .	Loughrea . .	IV.	54
33	Ballydavis . .	429 1 3	Kerry .	Corkaguiny . .	Kilquane . .	Dingle . .	II.	179
47, 48	Ballydavid . .	831 2 18	Tipperary, N.R.	Eliogarty . .	Twomileborris . .	Thurles . .	II.	273
67, 74, 75	Ballydavid . .	1,686 2 26	Tipperary, S.R.	Clanwilliam . .	Templeneiry . .	Tipperary . .	II.	311
71	Ballydavid . .	621 3 24	Tipperary, S.R.	Slievardagh .	Kilvemnon . .	Callan . .	II.	334
18	Ballydavid . .	227 2 12	Waterford .	Gaultiere . .	Crooke . .	Waterford . .	II.	362
17, 24	Ballydavid . .	99 1 5	Westmeath .	Rathconrath . .	Killare . .	Ballymahon . .	I.	283
84	Ballydavid Middle .	201 0 7	Galway .	Athenry . .	Athenry . .	Galway . .	IV.	3
84	Ballydavid North .	197 2 23	Galway .	Athenry . .	Athenry . .	Galway . .	IV.	3
84	Ballydavid South .	477 3 32	Galway .	Athenry . .	Athenry . .	Loughrea . .	IV.	3
34	Ballydavin . .	102 1 23	Queen's Co.	Clarmallagh . .	Rathdowney . .	Abbeyleix . .	I.	238
13	Ballydavis . .	934 0 29	Queen's Co.	Maryborough East .	Straboe . .	Mountmellick . .	I.	241
90	Ballydavock . .	78 3 15	Mayo .	Carra . .	Drum . .	Castlebar . .	IV.	127
45	Ballydaw . .	55 0 32	Cork, E.R.	Barrymore . .	Britway . .	Fermoy . .	II.	51
45	Ballydaw . .	123 0 20	Cork, E.R.	Barrymore . .	Knockmourne . .	Fermoy . .	II.	56
40, 43	Ballydaw . .	506 1 10	Kilkenny .	Iverk . . .	Kilmacow . .	Waterford . .	I.	105
19	Ballydaw or Davidstown . .	328 2 18	Wexford .	Scarawalsh . .	Monart . .	Enniscorthy .	I.	324
48, 49	Ballydawley . .	407 2 16	Londonderry .	Loughinsholin .	Tamlaght . .	Magherafelt .	III.	243
20, 21	Ballydawley . .	792 1 1f	Sligo .	Tirerrill . .	Kilross . .	Sligo . .	IV.	241
48	Ballydawley (alias) Crosspatrick . .	257 3 39	Londonderry .	Loughinsholin .	Artrea . .	Magherafelt .	III.	238
20	Ballydawmore . .	187 3 34	Wexford .	Scarawalsh . .	Clone . .	Enniscorthy .	I	322
20	Ballydawmore . .	49 2 36	Wexford .	Scarawalsh . .	Templeshannon .	Enniscorthy .	I.	326
1, 9	Ballyday . .	164 2 16	Wexford .	Gorey . .	Kilpipe . .	Gorey . .	I	320
15	Ballydeely . .	154 3 14	Clare .	Corcomroe . .	Kilshanny . .	Ennistimon .	II.	21
58	Ballydeenlea . .	134 1 14	Kerry .	Magunihy . .	Kilcummin . .	Killarney . .	II.	201

(a) Including 15A. 1R. 4R. water.   (c) Including 2A. 1R. 0P. water.   (e) Including 23A. 3R. 23P. detached portion.
(b) Including 7A. 2R. 32P. water.   (d) Including 5A. 3R. 3P. water.   (f) Including 49A. 3R. 3P. water.

No. of Sheet of the Ordnance Survey Maps.	Townlands and Towns.	Area in Statute Acres.	County.	Barony.	Parish.	Poor Law Union in 1857.	Townland Census of 1851, Part I.	
		A. R. P.					Vol.	Page
140	Ballydehob . .	188 3 30	Cork, W.R. .	West Carbery (W.D.)	Skull . . .	Skull . .	II.	145
140	BALLYDEHOB T. .	—	Cork, W.R. .	West Carbery (W.D.)	Skull . . .	Skull . .	II.	147
19	Ballydeloughy .	656 3 31	Cork, E.R. .	Fermoy . . .	Ballydeloughy .	Mitchelstown .	II.	76
16	Ballyderg . .	486 3 21	Londonderry .	Keenaght . .	Tamlaght Finlagan .	NewT⁰Limavady	III.	237
39	Ballyderg . .	395 1 2a	Mayo . .	Tirawley . .	Ballynahaglish .	Ballina . .	IV.	164
25	Ballydermody .	313 2 25	Waterford .	Middlethird .	Reisk . .	Waterford .	II.	368
25, 26	Ballydermodybog .	112 3 32	Waterford .	Middlethird .	Reisk . .	Waterford .	II.	368
104	Ballydermot .	358 3 18	Donegal . .	Tirhugh . . .	Drumhome .	Donegal . .	III.	146
19, 20	Ballydermot .	878 0 17	King's Co. .	Coolestown . .	Clonsast . .	Edenderry .	I.	132
37, 42	Ballydermot .	470 2 26	Londonderry .	Loughinsholin .	Ballyscullion .	Magherafelt .	III.	239
7	Ballydermot . .	74 1 18	Wexford . .	Gorey . . .	Kilcavan . .	Gorey . .	I.	317
28, 36	Ballyderown . .	460 2 9b	Cork, E.R. .	Condons and Clangibbon .	Kilcrumper .	Fermoy . .	II.	61
51	Ballydesland .	310 1 5	Down . .	Upper Iveagh, Up. pt.	Clonallan .	Newry . .	III.	174
93	Ballydevitt .	253 1 0	Donegal . .	Banagh . . .	Killymard .	Donegal . .	III.	111
11	Ballydevitt .	185 3 10	Londonderry .	Coleraine . .	Aghadowey .	Coleraine . .	III.	229
93	Ballydevitt Beg .	202 2 35	Donegal . .	Banagh . . .	Killymard .	Donegal . .	III.	111
32	Ballydicken Lower .	54 0 30	Wexford . .	Sh. lmaliere East .	Tikillin . .	Wexford . .	I.	331
32, 37	Ballydicken Upper .	156 3 38	Wexford . .	Shelmaliere East .	Tikillin . .	Wexford . .	I.	331
78, 84	Ballydine . .	445 2 13c	Tipperary, S.R. .	Iffa and Offa East .	Kilmurry . .	Carrick on Suir	II.	314
78, 84	Ballydine . .	311 3 18d	Tipperary, S.R. .	Iffa and Offa East .	Kilsheelan .	Clonmel . .	II.	314
52	Ballydine . .	60 0 18	Tipperary, S.R. .	Middlethird . .	Ardmayle . .	Cashel . .	II.	324
25	Ballydineen .	190 1 35	Cork. E.R. .	Fermoy . . .	Caherduggan .	Mallow . .	II.	77
25	Ballydineen .	161 3 3	Cork, E.R. .	Fermoy . . .	Doneraile . .	Mallow . .	II.	78
7	Ballydivity . .	333 3 20	Antrim . .	Lower Dunluce .	Derrykeighan .	Ballymoney .	III.	16
147	Ballydivlin . .	649 3 26	Cork, W.R. .	West Carbery (W.D.)	Kilmoe . .	Skull . .	II.	144
21, 22	Ballydogherty .	385 2 20	Armagh . .	Orior Lower . .	Loughgilly .	Newry . .	III.	56
9	Ballydollaghan .	272 1 35	Down . .	Castlereagh Upper .	Drumbo . .	Lisburn . .	III.	164
9	Ballydollaghan .	377 3 25	Down . .	Castlereagh Upper .	Knockbreda .	Lisburn . .	III.	165
116, 117	Ballydonagh .	105 3 6	Galway . .	Leitrim . .	Tynagh . .	Portumna .	IV.	55
99, 100	Ballydonagh .	629 2 4	Galway . .	Longford . .	Kiltormer .	Ballinasloe .	IV.	60
44, 45	Ballydonagh . .	666 2 24	King's Co. .	Clonlisk . .	Templeharry .	Roscrea . .	I.	132
59	Ballydonagh . .	173 3 7	Tipperary, S.R. .	Clanwilliam .	Donohill . .	Tipperary .	II.	307
1, 5	Ballydonagh . .	462 2 6e	Waterford .	Glenahiry . .	Kilronan . .	Clonmel . .	II.	365
29	Ballydonagh .	62 3 38	Westmeath .	Clonlonan . .	Kilcleagh . .	Athlone . .	I.	261
8	Ballydonagh .	94 1 10	Wicklow . .	Rathdown . .	Delgany . .	Rathdown .	I.	355
28, 36	Ballydonaghan .	1,141 0 27	Clare . .	Tulla Upper . .	Kilnoe . .	Scarriff . .	II.	40
54, 55, 65, 66	Ballydonagh Beg .	177 0 0	Cork, E.R. .	Barrymore . .	Dungourney .	Middleton .	II.	54
54, 55, 66	Ballydonagh More .	438 1 0	Cork, E.R. .	Barrymore . .	Dungourney .	Middleton .	II.	54
55, 59	Ballydonaghy .	2,418 3 14	Antrim . .	Upper Massereene .	Camlin . .	Antrim . .	III.	30
10	Ballydonaghy .	122 1 8	Armagh . .	Oneilland East .	Seagoe . .	Lurgan . .	III.	50
111	Ballydonaghy .	223 3 16	Cork, E.R. .	Kinalea . . .	Leighmoney .	Kinsale . .	II.	96
2	Ballydonaghy .	234 3 13f	Tyrone . .	Strabane Lower .	Leckpatrick .	Strabane .	III.	321
13	Ballydonarea .	78 2 0	Wicklow . .	Newcastle . .	Kilcoole . .	Rathdrum .	I.	351
13	Ballydonarea .	273 3 11	Wicklow . .	Newcastle . .	Newcastle Lower .	Rathdrum .	I.	353
114, 127	Ballydonegan .	535 0 7	Cork, W.R. .	Bear . . .	Kilnamanagh .	Castletown .	II.	125
30, 34	Ballydonegan .	2,383 0 23	Londonderry .	Tirkeeran . .	Banagher . .	NewT⁰Limavady	III.	247
127	BALLYDONEGAN T. .	—	Cork, W.R. .	Bear . . .	Kilnamanagh .	Castletown .	II.	126
37	Ballydonety .	265 0 29g	Down . .	Lecale Upper .	Down . .	Downpatrick .	III.	180
26	Ballydonfin .	383 0 35	Wexford . .	Ballaghkeen .	Ballyhuskard .	Enniscorthy .	I.	291
20	Ballydonigan .	271 3 14	Wexford . .	Scarawalsh .	Clone . .	Enniscorthy .	I.	322
37, 44	Ballydonnell . .	415 2 3h	Down . .	Lecale Upper . .	Down . .	Downpatrick .	III.	180
8	Ballydonnell . .	136 3 39	Kilkenny . .	Galmoy . .	Erke . .	Urlingford .	I.	92
28	Ballydonnell . .	108 0 32	Kilkenny . .	Gowran . .	Ballylinch .	Thomastown .	I.	93
45	Ballydonnell . .	350 1 10	Limerick . .	Glenquin . .	Mahoonagh .	Newcastle .	II.	246
47, 49	Ballydonnell . .	424 2 6	Londonderry .	Loughinsholin .	Ballinderry .	Magherafelt .	III.	239
22, 25	Ballydonnell . .	164 3 30	Louth . .	Ferrard . . .	Termonfeckin .	Drogheda .	I.	182
46, 52	Ballydonnell . .	155 0 39	Meath . .	Upper Moyfenrath .	Castlejordan .	Edenderry .	I.	212
55, 63	Ballydonnell . .	893 1 15	Tipperary, S.R. .	Shevardagh .	Lismalin . .	Callan . .	II.	335
35	Ballydonnell . .	415 0 16	Wicklow . .	Arklow . .	Redcross . .	Rathdrum .	I.	345
56	Ballydonnellan .	401 1 2	Galway . .	Clare . .	Kilcoona . .	Tuam . .	IV.	19
88	Ballydonnellan .	59 3 9	Mayo . .	Burrishoole .	Aghagower .	Westport .	IV.	118
98	Ballydonnellan East	296 0 21	Galway . .	Kilconnell . .	Killallaghtan .	Ballinasloe .	IV.	41
98	Ballydonnellan West	273 1 16	Galway . .	Kilconnell . .	Killallaghtan .	Ballinasloe .	IV.	41
5, 6, 10	Ballydonnell North	560 3 20	Wicklow . .	Lower Talbotstown	Blessington .	Naas . .	I.	358
6, 11	Ballydonnell South	1,279 2 4	Wicklow . .	Lower Talbotstown	Blessington .	Naas . .	I.	358
26	Ballydonnelly .	317 1 34	Antrim . .	Kilconway . .	Rasharkin .	Ballymoney .	III.	27
42, 43	Ballydonnelly .	611 3 24	Antrim . .	Upper Toome .	Duneane . .	Ballymena .	III.	34
8	Ballydonohoe .	217 0 7	Clare . .	Burren . .	Kilmoon . .	Ballyvaghan .	II.	13
32	Ballydonohoe .	259 3 24i	Clare . .	Islands . .	Kilmaley . .	Ennis . .	II.	31
5, 10	Ballydonohoe .	816 1 0	Kerry . .	Iraghticonnor .	Galey . .	Listowel . .	II.	190
56	Ballydonohoe .	207 3 34	Limerick . .	Coshlea . .	Kilflyn . .	Kilmallock .	II.	240
17	Ballydonohoe .	403 0 20	Limerick . .	Shanid . .	Kilfergus . .	Glin . .	II.	255

(a) Including 6A. 1R. 6P. water.
(b) Including 14A. 3R. 10P. River Blackwater.
(c) Including 6A. 1R. 27P. water.

(d) Including 4A. 3R. 21P. water.
(e) Including 10A. 3R. 8P. water.
(f) Including 6A. 1R. 29P. water.

(g) Including 3A. 2R. 0P. water.
(h) Including 2A. 2R. 16P. water.
(i) Including 9A. 3R. 9P. water.

L

No. of Sheet of the Ordnance Survey Maps.	Townlands and Towns.	Area in Statute Acres.			County.	Barony.	Parish.	Poor Law Union in 1857.	Townland Census of 1851, Part I.	
		A.	R.	P.					Vol.	Page
11, 12	Ballydoo . . .	191	2	32	Armagh . .	Armagh . . .	Eglish . . .	Armagh . .	III.	44
47	Ballydoo . . .	254	0	34	Down . .	Upper Iveagh, Up. pt.	Drumgath . .	Newry . .	III.	175
73	Ballydoogan . .	252	1	36	Galway . .	Kilconnell . .	Fohanagh . .	Mountbellew .	IV.	39
106	Ballydoogan . .	690	2	2	Galway . .	Leitrim . .	Kilmeen . .	Loughrea . .	IV.	54
14	Ballydoogan . .	281	3	16	Sligo . .	Carbury . . .	St. Johns . .	Sligo . .	IV.	223
30	Ballydoogan . .	532	0	8	Westmeath .	Clonlonan . .	Ballyloughloe .	Athlone . .	I.	260
16, 22	Ballydoolagh . .	773	2	14a	Fermanagh .	Tirkennedy . .	Magheracross .	Enniskillen .	III.	223
3, 4	Ballydoole . .	464	1	37	Limerick . .	Kenry . . .	Ardcanny . .	Rathkeale .	II.	248
3	Ballydoole . .	46	1	5	Limerick . .	Kenry . . .	Chapelrussell .	Rathkeale .	II.	248
34, 38, 39	Ballydooley . .	415	1	26	Roscommon .	Ballymoe . .	Oran . . .	Roscommon .	IV.	192
26	Ballydoolough .	719	3	20b	Galway . .	Ross . . .	Ross . . .	Oughterard .	IV.	73
12	Ballydoonan . .	252	1	8	Down . .	Ards Lower . .	Donaghadee .	Newtownards .	III.	157
21	Ballydooneen . .	99	3	6	Kerry . .	Clanmaurice .	Odorney . .	Tralee . .	II.	172
9	Ballydoora . .	36	2	21	Clare . .	Burren . .	Carran . .	Ballyvaghan .	II.	11
19, 28	Ballydoorlis . .	141	2	14	Limerick . .	Shanid . .	Kilcolman . .	Glin . .	II.	255
36, 37	Ballydoorty . .	415	3	16	Limerick . .	Glenquin . .	Mahoonagh .	Newcastle .	II.	246
18, 19	Ballydoreen . .	202	1	36	Wicklow . .	Newcastle . .	Killiskey . .	Rathdrum .	I.	352
5, 6	Ballydorey . .	60	0	28	Westmeath .	Moygoish . .	Rathaspick .	Granard .	I.	280
36	Ballydorgan . .	499	2	21c	Cork, E.R. .	Condons&Clangibbon	Castlelyons .	Fermoy . .	II.	60
17	Ballydorn . .	355	2	22	Down . .	Dufferin . .	Killinchy . .	Newtownards .	III.	166
68	Ballydotia . .	311	3	35	Galway . .	Moycullen . .	Moycullen . .	Galway . .	IV.	71
43	Ballydotia East .	130	2	39	Galway . .	Clare . .	Belclare . .	Tuam . .	IV.	17
43	Ballydotia West .	124	3	29	Galway . .	Clare . .	Belclare . .	Tuam . .	IV.	17
32	Ballydowan . .	51	0	7	Kilkenny . .	Knocktopher .	Derrynahinch .	Thomastown .	I.	111
24, 32	Ballydowane East .	188	2	5	Waterford .	Decies without Drum	Ballylaneen .	Kilmacthomas .	II.	354
24, 32	Ballydowane West .	197	3	19	Waterford .	Decies without Drum	Ballylaneen .	Kilmacthomas .	II.	354
17	Ballydowd . .	153	3	19d	Dublin . .	Newcastle . .	Esker . .	Celbridge .	I.	33
13	Ballydowel Big .	489	0	27	Kilkenny . .	Crannagh . .	Ballinamara .	Kilkenny .	I.	84
13	Ballydowel Little .	230	0	38	Kilkenny . .	Crannagh . .	Ballinamara .	Kilkenny .	I.	84
31	Ballydowling . .	162	2	24	Wicklow . .	Arklow . .	Dunganstown .	Rathdrum .	I.	343
30	Ballydowling . .	202	2	8	Wicklow . .	Ballinacor North .	Rathdrum . .	Rathdrum .	I.	347
24, 30	Ballydowling . .	524	3	13	Wicklow . .	Newcastle . .	Glenealy . .	Rathdrum .	I.	351
29, 30	Ballydowling Hill .	262	0	16	Wicklow . .	Ballinacor North .	Rathdrum . .	Rathdrum .	I.	347
41	Ballydown . .	210	1	8	Antrim . .	Lower Belfast .	Islandmagee .	Larne . .	III.	8
27, 34	Ballydown . .	529	2	20	Down . .	Upper Iveagh, Up. pt.	Seapatrick . .	Banbridge .	III.	176
26	Ballydownan . .	1,016	1	35	King's Co. .	Geashill . . .	Geashill . .	Tullamore .	I.	139
60, 64	Ballydownfine .	748	0	34	Antrim . .	Upper Belfast .	Shankill . .	Belfast . .	III.	10
124	Ballydownis . .	73	3	35	Cork, W.R. .	East Carbery (E.D.)	Ringrone . .	Kinsale . .	II.	130
124	Ballydownis East .	42	2	20	Cork, W.R. .	East Carbery (E.D.)	Templetrine .	Kinsale . .	II.	130
124	Ballydownis West .	60	0	8	Cork, W.R. .	East Carbery (E.D.)	Templetrine .	Kinsale . .	II.	130
66	Ballydowny . .	91	3	9	Kerry . .	Magunihy . .	Aghadoe . .	Killarney .	II.	199
26	Ballydoyle . .	776	3	17	Cork, E.R. .	Fermoy . .	Castletownroche .	Fermoy . .	II.	77
69	Ballydoyle . .	581	2	14	Tipperary, S.R.	Middlethird .	St. Patricksrock .	Cashel . .	II.	330
47	Ballydoyle . .	95	0	35	Wexford . .	Forth . .	Mayglass . .	Wexford . .	I.	312
11	Ballydrain . .	362	3	6e	Down . .	Castlereagh Lower .	Tullynakill . .	Newtownards .	III.	163
48	Ballydrane . .	57	2	22	Wexford . .	Forth . .	Rosslare . .	Wexford . .	I.	313
75	Ballydrehid . .	1,985	3	6	Tipperary, S.R.	Clanwilliam . .	Killardry . .	Tipperary .	II.	308
66	Ballydribbeen . .	80	2	9	Kerry . .	Magunihy . .	Killarney . .	Killarney .	II.	203
14	Ballydrinan . .	32	2	18	Tipperary, N.R.	Lower Ormond .	Dromineer . .	Nenagh . .	II.	283
14	Ballydrinan . .	176	2	35	Tipperary, N.R.	Lower Ormond .	Monsea . .	Nenagh . .	II.	287
81	Ballydrinan . .	157	2	20f	Tipperary, S.R.	Iffa and Offa West .	Tubbrid . .	Clogheen . .	II.	320
66	Ballydrisheen . .	59	0	22	Kerry . .	Magunihy . .	Killarney . .	Killarney .	II.	203
17, 26	Ballydrislane . .	272	0	0	Waterford .	Middlethird .	Drumcannon .	Waterford .	II.	366
16, 17	Ballydrohid . .	310	1	27	King's Co. .	Ballycowan . .	Kilbride . .	Tullamore .	I.	127
13, 18	Ballydrum . .	184	3	1	Longford .	Moydow . . .	Killashee . .	Longford .	I.	161
62	Ballydrum . .	346	3	37g	Mayo . .	Gallen . . .	Kilconduff . .	Swineford .	IV.	147
35,36,42,43	Ballydrumman .	650	1	33	Down . .	Upper Iveagh, Lr. pt.	Drumgooland .	Banbridge .	III.	172
35	Ballyduag . .	154	3	31	Tipperary, N.R.	Eliogarty . .	Loughmoe East .	Thurles . .	II.	271
61	Ballyduagh . .	249	1	27	Tipperary, S.R.	Middlethird .	Railstown . .	Cashel . .	II.	329
61	Ballyduagh . .	66	0	22	Tipperary, S.R.	Middlethird .	St. Patricksrock .	Cashel . .	II.	330
12	Ballyduane . .	127	3	10	Limerick . .	Pubblebrien .	Mungret . .	Limerick . .	II.	253
22	Ballyduane East .	141	2	7	Cork, E.R. .	Duhallow . .	Clonfert . .	Kanturk . .	II.	67
22	Ballyduane South .	157	2	35	Cork, E.R. .	Duhallow . .	Clonfert . .	Kanturk . .	II.	67
22	Ballyduane West .	255	3	11	Cork, E.R. .	Duhallow . .	Clonfert . .	Kanturk . .	II.	68
22, 28	Ballyduboy . .	210	2	27	Wexford . .	Ballaghkeen .	Killincooly . .	Gorey . .	I.	295
51,52,56,57	Ballyduff . .	667	3	14	Antrim . .	Lower Belfast .	Carnmoney .	Belfast . .	III.	7
9	Ballyduff . .	310	0	26	Carlow . .	Rathvilly . .	Clonmore . .	Shillelagh .	I.	10
34	Ballyduff . .	103	3	23h	Clare . .	Bunratty Upper .	Kilraghtis . .	Ennis . .	II.	9
34	Ballyduff . .	237	2	29	Cork, E.R. .	Fermoy . .	Monanimy . .	Mallow . .	II.	81
89	Ballyduff . .	316	3	9	Cork, E.R. .	Imokilly . .	Cloyne . .	Middleton .	II.	85
35, 44	Ballyduff . .	1,070	2	39	Kerry . .	Corkaguiny .	Ballyduff . .	Dingle . .	II.	174
23, 31	Ballyduff . .	1,430	3	26	Kerry . .	Trughanacmy .	Castleisland .	Tralee . .	II.	208
25, 29	Ballyduff . .	167	2	32	Kilkenny . .	Gowran . .	Graiguenamanagh .	Thomastown .	I.	95

(a) Including 45A. 1R. 16P. water.　　　(d) Including 23A. 0R. 28P. detached portion.　　　(g) Including 3A. 2R. 17P. water.
(b) Including 21A. 1R. 26P. water.　　　(e) Including 1A. 0R. 30P. water.　　　(h) Including 5A. 2R. 17P. water.
(c) Including 4A. 2R. 4P. water.　　　(f) Including 1A. 0R. 32P. water.

No. of Sheet of the Ordnance Survey Maps.	Townlands and Towns.	Area in Statute Acres.	County.	Barony.	Parish.	Poor Law Union in 1857.	Townland Census of 1851, Part I.	
		A. R. P.					Vol.	Page
32	Ballyduff	234 2 29a	Kilkenny	Gowran	Inistioge	Thomastown	I.	96
43	Ballyduff	498 1 4	King's Co.	Ballybritt	Roscrea	Roscrea	I.	126
16, 17	Ballyduff	622 0 4	King's Co.	Ballycowan	Kilbride	Tullamore	I.	127
6	Ballyduff	519 2 30	King's Co.	Garrycastle	Clonmacnoise	Parsonstown	I.	135
18, 26	Ballyduff	375 3 19	King's Co.	Upper Philipstown	Geashill	Tullamore	I.	144
57	Ballyduff	506 3 9	Limerick	Coshlea	Ballylanders	Mitchelstown	II.	237
15	Ballyduff	509 2 15	Queen's Co.	Clandonagh	Kyle	Roscrea	I.	233
19	Ballyduff	190 3 28	Queen's Co.	Stradbally	Curraclone	Athy	I.	246
14	Ballyduff	262 2 29	Queen's Co.	Stradbally	Moyanna	Mountmellick	I.	247
5	Ballyduff	554 0 12	Tipperary, N.R.	Lower Ormond	Dorrha	Parsonstown	II.	283
20	Ballyduff	133 0 9b	Waterford	Coshmore&Coshbride	Lismore and Mocollop	Lismore	II.	344
30	Ballyduff	196 1 25	Waterford	Decies without Drum	Dungarvan	Dungarvan	II.	355
27	Ballyduff	87 1 12	Wexford	Ballaghkeen	Meelnagh	Gorey	I.	297
16	Ballyduff	182 1 19	Wexford	Gorey	Ballycanew	Gorey	I.	315
16, 21	Ballyduff	90 1 10	Wexford	Gorey	Monamolin	Gorey	I.	321
14	Ballyduff	332 1 32	Wexford	Scarawalsh	Ballycarney	Enniscorthy	I.	322
10	Ballyduff	711 2 29	Wexford	Scarawalsh	Kilcomb	Gorey	I.	323
45	Ballyduff	146 2 10	Wicklow	Arklow	Arklow	Rathdrum	I.	341
32	Ballyduff Beg	612 2 19	Clare	Inchiquin	Inagh	Ennistimon	II.	24
30	Ballyduff Beg	100 3 37	Waterford	Decies without Drum	Dungarvan	Dungarvan	II.	355
21	Ballyduffbeg	87 3 0	Wexford	Ballaghkeen	Kilnamanagh	Gorey	I.	297
11	Ballyduffbeg	247 0 39	Wexford	Gorey	Toome	Gorey	I.	321
26	Ballyduff (Blake)	59 2 36c	Clare	Bunratty Upper	Templemaley	Ennis	II.	10
8, 16	Ballyduff East	527 3 3	Waterford	Middlethird	Kilmeadan	Waterford	II.	368
20	Ballyduff Lower	322 3 34d	Waterford	Coshmore&Coshbride	Lismore and Mocollop	Lismore	II.	344
17	Ballyduff Lower	173 1 33	Wexford	Ballaghkeen	Ardamine	Gorey	I.	291
19	Ballyduff Lower	145 0 26	Wicklow	Newcastle	Killiskey	Rathdrum	I.	352
24, 32, 33	Ballyduff More	506 0 33	Clare	Inchiquin	Inagh	Ennistimon	II.	24
30	Ballyduff More	246 1 29e	Waterford	Decies without Drum	Dungarvan	Dungarvan	II.	355
40, 45	Ballyduff North	102 3 9	Wicklow	Arklow	Arklow	Rathdrum	I.	341
26, 34	Ballyduff (Paterson)	100 0 23f	Clare	Bunratty Upper	Templemaley	Ennis	II.	10
18	Ballyduff South	541 0 14	King's Co.	Geashill	Geashill	Tullamore	I.	139
40, 45	Ballyduff South	172 0 17	Wicklow	Arklow	Arklow	Rathdrum	I.	341
9	BALLYDUFF T.	—	Kerry	Clanmaurice	Rattoo	Listowel	II.	173
20	BALLYDUFF T.	—	Waterford	Coshmore&Coshbride	Lismore and Mocollop	Lismore	II.	348
20, 28	Ballyduff Upper	297 3 15	Waterford	Coshmore&Coshbride	Lismore and Mocollop	Lismore	II.	344
17	Ballyduff Upper	223 1 3	Wexford	Ballaghkeen	Ardamine	Gorey	I.	291
18, 19	Ballyduff Upper	310 1 14	Wicklow	Newcastle	Killiskey	Rathdrum	I.	352
16	Ballyduff West	343 2 15	Waterford	Middlethird	Kilmeadan	Waterford	II.	368
1, 2, 3	Ballyduffy	730 2 35g	Longford	Granard	Killoe	Granard	I.	157
38, 47	Ballyduffy	167 2 20	Mayo	Tirawley	Addergoole	Castlebar	IV.	162
29	Ballyduffy	223 1 3	Roscommon	Roscommon	Lissonuffy	Strokestown	IV.	211
37	Ballydugan	622 0 20h	Down	Lecale Upper	Down	Downpatrick	III.	180
19	Ballydugan	947 2 3	Down	Lower Iveagh, Up.pt.	Tullylish	Lurgan	III.	171
48	Ballydugeannan	397 3 4	Antrim	Toome Upper	Duneane	Antrim	III.	34
71, 72	Ballyduggan	417 0 29	Tipperary, S.R.	Slievardagh	Kilvemnon	Callan	II.	334
16	Ballyduhig	518 1 7	Kerry	Clanmaurice	Kilshenane	Listowel	II.	171
44, 53	Ballyduhig	237 3 24	Limerick	Glenquin	Killeedy	Newcastle	II.	245
86	Ballyduhig North	283 2 31	Cork, E.R.	Cork	Carrigaline	Cork	II.	64
86	Ballyduhig South	233 3 27	Cork, E.R.	Kerrycurrihy	Carrigaline	Cork	II.	92
47	Ballydulany	415 3 19	Down	Upper Iveagh, Up.pt.	Clonallan	Newry	III.	174
75, 87	Ballydulea	146 2 27	Cork, E.R.	Barrymore	Templerobin	Cork	II.	58
26	Ballydullaghan	466 1 23	Londonderry	Coleraine	Desertoghill	Ballymoney	III.	230
18, 19	Ballydun	200 2 17	Kilkenny	Crannagh	Ballycallan	Kilkenny	I.	84
48,49,58,59	Ballyduneen	1,080 1 4	Clare	Clonderalaw	Kilmihil	Kilrush	II.	17
48	Ballydungan	106 3 32	Wexford	Forth	Kilscoran	Wexford	I.	311
29, 38	Ballydunlea	1,065 3 4	Kerry	Trughanacmy	Annagh	Tralee	II.	205
43	Ballydunmaul	401 0 9	Antrim	Upper Toome	Drummaul	Ballymena	III.	33
7, 15	Ballydurn	1,149 0 5	Waterford	Upperthird	Mothel	Carrick on Suir	III.	370
8	Ballydurnian	149 0 20	Antrim	Cary	Ramoan	Ballycastle	III.	14
47	Ballydusker	89 3 22	Wexford	Forth	Killinick	Wexford	I.	310
135	Ballyduvane	264 3 10	Cork, W.R.	Ibane and Barryroe	Kilgarriff	Clonakilty	II.	149
135	Ballyduvane	225 3 35	Cork, W.R.	Ibane and Barryroe	Kilkerranmore	Clonakilty	II.	149
30, 39	Ballydwyer East	184 3 3	Kerry	Trughanacmy	Ballymacelligott	Tralee	II.	206
30, 39	Ballydwyer Middle	136 2 19	Kerry	Trughanacmy	Ballymacelligott	Tralee	II.	206
30, 39	Ballydwyer West	179 1 22	Kerry	Trughanacmy	Ballymacelligott	Tralee	II.	206
88	Ballydwyre	136 1 39	Cork, E.R.	Imokilly	Rostellan	Middleton	II.	90
23	Ballydyan	542 3 22	Down	Castlereagh Upper	Kilmore	Downpatrick	III.	165
14, 15	Ballyea	40 0 5	Clare	Corcomroe	Kilmacrehy	Ennistimon	II.	20
41	Ballyea	257 1 11	Clare	Islands	Killone	Ennis	II.	30
28	Ballyea	153 0 32	Kerry	Trughanacmy	Ballynahaglish	Tralee	II.	207
29	Ballyea	140 1 30	Limerick	Connello Lower	Croagh	Rathkeale	II.	227
29, 37	Ballyea	541 1 32	Limerick	Connello Lower	Rathkeale	Rathkeale	II.	229

(a) Including 5A. 2R. 37P. River Nore.
(b) Including 2A. 1R. 8P. water.
(c) Including 1A. 1R. 29P. water.
(d) Including 13A. 2R. 8P. water.
(e) Including 5A. 0R. 35P. detached portion.
(f) Including 2A. 0R. 19P. water.
(g) Including 20A. 3R. 34P. water.
(h) Including 17A. 1R. 28P. water.

L 2

No. of Sheet of the Ordnance Survey Maps.	Townlands and Towns.	Area in Statute Acres.			County.	Barony.	Parish.	Poor Law Union in 1857.	Townland Census of 1851, Part I.	
		A.	R.	P.					Vol.	Page
22, 31	Ballyea . . .	476	2	33	Limerick . .	Smallcounty . .	Fedamore . .	Croom . .	II.	259
1	Ballyea . . .	662	3	33	Tipperary, N.R.	Lower Ormond .	Dorrha . .	Parsonstown .	II.	283
81	Ballyea . . .	98	2	24	Tipperary. S.R.	Iffa and Offa West .	Tubbrid . . .	Clogheen . .	II.	320
21	Ballyea East . .	135	0	22	Waterford .	Coshmore&Coshbride	Lismore and Mocollop	Lismore . .	II.	344
11	Ballyeafy . .	478	3	13	Waterford .	Coshmore&Coshbride	Lismore and Mocollop	Lismore . .	II.	344
4, 9	Ballyeagh . .	563	0	17	Kerry . .	Iraghticonnor .	Killehenny . .	Listowel . .	II.	191
24	Ballyealan . .	191	0	15	King's Co. .	Ballyboy . . .	Killoughy . .	Tullamore . .	I.	123
24	Ballyea North .	474	3	39	Clare . .	Inchiquin . .	Inagh . . .	Ennistimon . .	II.	24
25	Ballyea North .	335	1	17	Tipperary. N.R.	Owney and Arra .	Templeachally .	Nenagh . .	II.	297
51, 52	Ballyearl . .	1,096	2	23	Antrim . .	Lower Belfast . .	Ballylinny . .	Antrim . .	III.	7
24	Ballyea South .	1,109	0	1	Clare . .	Inchiquin . .	Inagh . . .	Ennistimon . .	II.	24
25	Ballyea South .	138	0	10	Tipperary, N.R.	Owney and Arra .	Templeachally .	Nenagh . .	II.	297
45	Ballyeaston . .	851	2	2	Antrim . .	Upper Antrim .	Ballycor . .	Antrim . .	III.	6
45	BALLYEASTON T. .	—			Antrim . .	Upper Antrim .	Ballycor . .	Antrim . .	III.	6
37	Ballyeaton . .	115	0	29	Wexford . .	Shelmaliere West .	Ardcandrisk . .	Wexford . .	I.	332
21	Ballyea West .	131	0	10	Waterford .	Coshmore&Coshbride	Lismore and Mocollop	Lismore . .	II.	344
29	Ballyeawood .	246	1	1	Limerick . .	Connello Lower .	Rathkeale . .	Rathkeale . .	II.	229
76, 77	Ballyedekin . .	257	0	31a	Cork, E.R. .	Imokilly . .	Middleton . .	Middleton . .	II.	89
37, 41	Ballyeden . .	129	3	38	Kilkenny . .	Ida . . .	Shanbogh . .	New Ross . .	I.	104
25, 31	Ballyeden . .	766	1	14	Wexford . .	Bantry . . .	Rossdroit . .	Enniscorthy .	I.	301
11, 16	Ballyeden . .	149	0	16	Wexford . .	Gorey . . .	Toome . . .	Gorey . . .	I.	321
98	Ballyederlan .	307	0	38	Donegal . .	Banagh . . .	Killaghtee . .	Donegal . .	III.	109
38, 47	Ballyederowen .	629	0	14	Donegal . .	Inishowen West .	Burt . . .	Londonderry .	III.	119
5	Ballyedmond . .	417	3	23	Carlow . .	Rathvilly . .	Hacketstown . .	Shillelagh . .	I.	11
65	Ballyedmond . .	236	1	35	Cork. E.R. .	Barrymore . .	Templenacarriga .	Middleton . .	II.	58
54, 55	Ballyedmond . .	255	1	21	Down . .	Upper Iveagh, Up. pt.	Kilbroney . .	Kilkeel . .	III.	175
31	Ballyedmond . .	650	1	15	Galway . .	Ballymoe . .	Clonbern . .	Glennamaddy .	IV.	6
34	Ballyedmond . .	197	3	38	Queen's Co .	Clandonagh . .	Erke . . .	Donaghmore .	I.	233
21	Ballyedmond . .	41	0	37	Wexford . .	Ballaghkeen . .	Kilnamanagh . .	Gorey . .	I.	297
16, 21	Ballyedmond . .	143	1	9	Wexford . .	Ballaghkeen . .	Monamolin . .	Gorey . .	I.	298
65	Ballyedmond Little	162	2	4	Cork. E.R. .	Barrymore . .	Templenacarriga .	Middleton . .	II.	58
25, 26	Ballyedmonduff .	1,011	3	32	Dublin . .	Rathdown . .	Kilgobbin . .	Rathdown . .	I.	35
54, 55	Ballyedmond Upper	92	1	1	Down . .	Upper Iveagh, Up. pt.	Kilbroney . .	Kilkeel . .	III.	175
39	Ballyedock . .	214	2	13	Wexford . .	Shelburne . .	Kilmokea . .	New Ross . .	I.	327
32	Ballyedock or Carrstown	244	2	4	Down . .	Ards Upper . .	Witter . . .	Downpatrick .	III.	161
38	Ballyedock Lower .	70	2	16	Down . .	Lecale Lower . .	Dunsfort . .	Downpatrick .	III.	179
38, 45	Ballyedock Upper .	405	2	20	Down . .	Lecale Lower . .	Dunsfort . .	Downpatrick .	III.	179
41, 47	Ballyedward . .	469	2	17	Antrim . .	Lower Belfast . .	Glynn . . .	Larne . .	III.	8
40	Ballyedward . .	225	0	20	Antrim . .	Upper Glenarm .	Kilwaughter . .	Larne . .	III.	25
11	Ballyedward . .	45	0	22	Westmeath . .	Corkaree . .	Tyfarnham . .	Mullingar . .	I.	264
38	Ballyeelinan . .	265	0	6	Waterford .	Decies within Drum	Lisgenan or Grange	Youghal . .	II.	352
12, 18	Ballyeeskeen . .	240	0	1	Sligo . .	Tireragh . .	Templeboy . .	Dromore West .	IV.	236
10	Ballyegan . .	728	2	36	Kerry . .	Iraghticonnor .	Galey . . .	Listowel . .	II.	190
30, 39	Ballyegan . .	384	3	0	Kerry . .	Trughanacmy .	Nohaval . .	Tralee . .	II.	212
38	Ballyegan . .	799	2	9	King's Co. .	Clonlisk . .	Kilcolman . .	Parsonstown .	I.	130
46, 47, 48, 49	Ballyeglish . .	324	3	20	Londonderry .	Loughinsholin .	Artrea . . .	Magherafelt .	III.	238
19, 28	Ballyegny . .	168	1	21	Limerick . .	Shanid . .	Rathronan . .	Glin . . .	II.	257
28	Ballyegny Beg .	116	0	23	Limerick . .	Connello Lower .	Clonagh . .	Glin . . .	II.	227
19, 28	Ballyegny More .	240	3	4	Limerick . .	Connello Lower .	Clonagh . .	Glin . . .	II.	227
10, 11, 17, 18	Ballyeighter . .	470	0	36b	Clare . .	Inchiquin . .	Kilkeedy . .	Corrofin . .	II.	25
87	Ballyeighter . .	249	2	21	Galway . .	Clonmacnowen .	Aughrim . .	Ballinasloe .	IV.	24
123	Ballyeighter . .	257	1	21	Galway . .	Kiltartan . .	Kilbeacanty .	Gort . . .	IV.	47
115, 116	Ballyeighter . .	153	0	27	Galway . .	Leitrim . .	Kilteskill . .	Loughrea . .	IV.	55
29, 30	Ballyeighter . .	231	2	15	King's Co. .	Garrycastle . .	Reynagh . .	Parsonstown .	I.	138
74	Ballyeighter (Dowdall) . .	142	0	19	Galway . .	Clonmacnowen .	Aghascragh . .	Ballinasloe .	IV.	23
74	Ballyeighter (Mahon)	214	2	16c	Galway . .	Clonmacnowen .	Aghascragh . .	Ballinasloe .	IV.	24
55	Ballyeightragh .	306	1	4	Cork, E.R. .	Barrymore . .	Clonmult . .	Middleton . .	II.	53
42, 43	Ballyeightragh .	222	3	18	Kerry . .	Corkaguiny .	Dingle . .	Dingle . .	II.	175
42, 43	Ballyeightragh .	187	2	39	Kerry . .	Corkaguiny .	Kildrum . .	Dingle . .	II.	177
38	Ballyelan . .	532	1	35	Limerick . .	Connello Upper .	Ballingarry . .	Croom . .	II.	230
25	Ballyeland . .	491	1	11	Wexford . .	Bantry . . .	Clonmore . .	Enniscorthy .	I.	300
76, 88	Ballyellane . .	169	3	17	Cork, E.R. .	Barrymore . .	Templerobin . .	Cork . .	II.	58
48	Ballyell Big . .	128	2	35	Wexford . .	Forth . . .	Kilscoran . .	Wexford . .	I.	311
15	Ballyellery . .	256	1	34	Clare . .	Corcomroe . .	Killaspuglonane .	Ennistimon .	II.	19
3	Ballyellin . .	115	2	5	Wexford . .	Gorey . . .	Kilgorman . .	Gorey . .	I.	318
10	Ballyellinan . .	229	0	10	Limerick . .	Connello Lower .	Lismakeery . .	Rathkeale .	II.	228
22	Ballyellin or Ballinamona . .	143	3	24	Carlow . .	Idrone East . .	Kiltennell . .	New Ross . .	I.	7
3	Ballyellin Lower .	100	0	32	Wexford . .	Gorey . . .	Inch . . .	Gorey . .	I.	316
19, 22	Ballyellin and Tomdarragh .	1,067	3	35d	Carlow . .	Idrone East . .	Ballyellin . .	Carlow . .	I.	6
19	BALLYELLIN T. .	—			Carlow . .	Idrone East . .	Ballyellin . .	Carlow . .	I.	6
3	Ballyellin Upper .	120	3	1	Wexford . .	Gorey . . .	Inch . . .	Gorey . .	I.	316

(a) Including 2A. 3R. 0P. water.   (c) Including 6A. 3R. 0P. water.   (d) Including 25A. 1R. 16P. River Barrow.
(b) Including 60A. 3R. 35P. water.

No. of Sheet of the Ordnance Survey Maps.	Townlands and Towns.	Area in Statute Acres.	County.	Barony.	Parish.	Poor Law Union in 1857.	Townland Census of 1851, Part I.	
		A. R. P.					Vol.	Page
17	Ballyellis	562 3 30	Cork, E.R.	Fermoy	Doneraile	Mallow	II.	78
33	Ballyellis	332 2 37a	Cork, E.R.	Fermoy	Mallow	Mallow	II.	81
26	Ballyellis	13 2 16	Cork, E.R.	Fermoy	Templeroan	Mallow	II.	82
26	Ballyellis	132 1 11	Cork, E.R.	Fermoy	Wallstown	Mallow	II.	83
8	Ballyellis	165 3 6	Kilkenny	Galmoy	Erke	Urlingford	I.	92
5	Ballyellis	84 0 17	Wexford	Scarawalsh	Carnew	Gorey	I.	322
48	Ballyell Little	66 0 27	Wexford	Forth	Kilscoran	Wexford	I.	311
63	Ballyellough	637 0 12	Antrim	Upper Masserecne	Magheragall	Lisburn	III.	31
4	Ballyelly	540 1 27	Clare	Burren	Killonaghan	Ballyvaghan	II.	13
46	Ballyelly	102 0 1	Donegal	Kilmacrenan	Aughnish	Milford	III.	122
29	Ballyenaghty	190 2 11	Kerry	Trughanacmy	Clogherbrien	Tralee	II.	209
18, 19	Ballyenahan North	693 3 36	Cork, E.R.	Condons &Clangibbon	Derryvillane	Mitchelstown	II.	60
18, 19	Ballyenahan South	593 1 13	Cork, E.R.	Fermoy	Derryvillane	Mitchelstown	II.	78
11	Ballyengland Lower	450 2 22	Limerick	Connello Lower	Askeaton	Rathkeale	II.	226
11	Ballyengland Upper	461 3 9	Limerick	Connello Lower	Askeaton	Rathkeale	II.	226
36	Ballyerk	306 1 20	Tipperary, N.R.	Eliogarty	Moyne	Thurles	II.	271
42, 48	Ballyerk	233 2 2	Tipperary, N.R.	Eliogarty	Twomileborris	Thurles	II.	273
54	Ballyerra	299 2 30	Cork, E.R.	Barrymore	Templebodan	Middleton	II.	58
46	Ballyerrin	175 0 11	Cork, E.R.	Kinnatalloon	Mogeely	Fermoy	II.	98
18	Ballyesborough	788 3 29	Down	Ards Upper	St. Andrews alias Bal- lyhalbert	Newtownards	III.	161
29, 34	Ballyeustace	18 0 9	Wicklow	Ballinacor South	Ballykine	Rathdrum	I.	348
11	Ballyewry	193 3 26	Down	Ards Lower	Greyabbey	Newtownards	III.	158
19, 20	Ballyfad	76 0 31	Antrim	Lower Glenarm	Layd	Ballycastle	III.	22
3	Ballyfad	145 0 8	Wexford	Gorey	Inch	Gorey	I.	316
3	Ballyfad	214 3 28	Wexford	Gorey	Kilnenor	Gorey	I.	319
62	Ballyfadeen Beg	234 0 8	Cork, E.R.	Barretts	Grenagh	Cork	II.	49
51, 62	Ballyfadeen More	468 3 34	Cork, E.R.	Barretts	Grenagh	Cork	II.	49
39	Ballyfahy	404 3 20	Sligo	Corran	Kilturra	Tobercurry	IV.	227
23	Ballyfair	140 3 16	Kildare	Offaly East	Ballysax	Naas	I.	69
29, 30	Ballyfallon or New- town	650 1 11	Meath	Lune	Athboy	Trim	I.	207
53	Ballyfane	85 0 6	Wexford	Forth	Carn	Wexford	I.	309
12	Ballyfaris	125 3 3	Sligo	Tireragh	Templeboy	Dromore West	IV.	236
91, 92	Ballyfarnagh	358 2 34	Mayo	Clanmorris	Kilcolman	Claremorris	IV.	133
1	BALLYFARNAN T.	—	Roscommon	Boyle	Kilronan	Boyle	IV.	197
33	Ballyfarnoge	226 0 2	Wexford	Ballaghkeen	Killisk	Enniscorthy	I.	296
34, 39	Ballyfarnoge	58 2 22	Wexford	Shelburne	Ballybrazil	New Ross	I.	327
34, 39	Ballyfarnoge	264 3 18	Wexford	Shelburne	Whitechurch	New Ross	I.	329
24	Ballyfarrell	533 2 11	King's Co.	Ballyboy	Killoughy	Tullamore	I.	123
2	Ballyfarrell	105 2 5	Queen's Co.	Tinnahinch	Kilmanman	Mountmellick	I.	248
26	Ballyfarsoon	177 3 3	Kildare	Offaly West	Monasterevin	Athy	I.	73
40	Ballyfasy Lower	349 0 11	Kilkenny	Ida	Kilbride	Waterford	I.	102
40	Ballyfasy Upper	647 2 12	Kilkenny	Ida	Kilbride	Waterford	I.	102
4, 9, 10	Ballyfatten	522 0 32b	Tyrone	Strabane Lower	Urney	Strabane	III.	322
15	Ballyfaudeen	629 3 21	Clare	Corcomroe	Killaspuglonane	Ennistimon	II.	19
49, 57	Ballyfauskeen	679 3 3	Limerick	Coshlea	Ballylanders	Mitchelstown	II.	237
49, 57	Ballyfauskeen	156 0 24	Limerick	Coshlea	Galbally	Mitchelstown	II.	238
19	Ballyfeanan or Bally- whinnin	134 2 16	Carlow	Idrone East	Ballyellin	Carlow	I.	6
19, 22	Ballyfeanan or Bally- whinnin	273 3 12	Carlow	Idrone East	Clonygoose	Carlow	I.	6
16, 17, 23	Ballyfeenaun or Tul- lylin	1,498 3 29	Sligo	Tireragh	Castleconor	Dromore West	IV.	232
23, 24	Ballyfeeny	654 1 32	Roscommon	Ballintober North	Kilglass	Strokestown	IV.	186
23	Ballyfeeny	117 3 8	Roscommon	Roscommon	Bumlin	Strokestown	IV.	208
57	Ballyfeerode	493 3 32	Limerick	Coshlea	Darragh	Kilmallock	II.	238
33	Ballyfereen	179 0 37	Kilkenny	Ida	The Rower	New Ross	I.	104
7, 12	Ballyferis	434 1 7	Down	Ards Upper	Ballywalter	Newtownards	III.	160
18	Ballyfermot Lower	316 0 3	Dublin	Uppercross	Ballyfermot	Dublin South	I.	39
17, 18	Ballyfermot Upper	334 0 37	Dublin	Uppercross	Ballyfermot	Dublin South	I.	39
42	Ballyferriter	469 0 31	Kerry	Corkaguiny	Dunurlin	Dingle	II.	176
42	Ballyfilibeen	491 0 11	Cork, E.R.	Barretts	Mourneabbey	Mallow	II.	50
88	Ballyfin	5 2 36	Cork, E.R.	Imokilly	Cloyne	Middleton	II.	85
88, 89	Ballyfin	355 0 32	Cork, E.R.	Imokilly	Inch	Middleton	II.	87
7	Ballyfin	239 2 29	Queen's Co.	Maryborough West	Clonenagh and Clo- nagheen	Mountmellick	I.	242
16	Ballyfin	132 3 36	Wexford	Gorey	Ballycanew	Gorey	I.	315
64	Ballyfinaghy	701 2 15	Antrim	Upper Belfast	Drumbeg	Lisburn	III.	10
10	Ballyfinboy	67 2 26	Tipperary, N.R.	Lower Ormond	Finnoe	Borrisokane	II.	283
12	Ballyfin Demesne	566 2 0c	Queen's Co.	Maryborough West	Clonenagh and Clon- agheen	Mountmellick	I.	242
19	Ballyfinegan	120 0 35	Galway	Ballymoe	Kilbegnet	Glennamaddy	IV.	8
27, 34	Ballyfinegan	438 0 1	Roscommon	Castlereagh	Ballintober	Castlereagh	IV.	198

(a) Including 8A. 2R. 0P. water.   (b) Including 14A. 0R. 0P. water.   (c) Including 26A. 0R. 0P. water.

No. of Sheet of the Ordnance Survey Maps.	Townlands and Towns.	Area in Statute Acres.			County.	Barony.	Parish.	Poor Law Union in 1857.	Townland Census of 1851, Part I.	
		A.	R.	P.					Vol.	Page
26	Ballyfinnan	237	0	1	Queen's Co.	Slievemargy	Killabban	Carlow	I.	245
47, 48	Ballyfinnane	508	1	35	Kerry	Maguniny	Molahiffe	Killarney	II.	204
53, 63	Ballyfinneen	252	0	8	Clare	Bunratty Lower	St. Patricks	Limerick	II.	6
30	Ballyfinoge	179	0	36	Kerry	Trughanacmy	Ballymacelligott	Tralee	II.	206
42	Ballyfinoge Great	230	3	14	Wexford	Forth	Kilmacree	Wexford	I.	311
42	Ballyfinoge Little	155	0	6	Wexford	Forth	Kilmacree	Wexford	I.	311
25	Ballyfinragh	253	0	38a	Down	Ards Upper	Witter	Downpatrick	III.	161
106	Ballyfintan	328	2	24	Galway	Leitrim	Abbeygormacan	Loughrea	IV.	50
12	Ballyfin Upper	1,757	3	35	Queen's Co.	Maryborough West	Clonenagh and Clonagheen	Mountmellick	I.	242
51	Ballyfireen	234	3	14	Cork, E.R.	Barretts	Grenagh	Cork	II.	49
24, 33	Ballyfirreen North	44	0	14	Limerick	Coonagh	Oola	Tipperary	II.	235
33	Ballyfirreen South	13	1	3	Limerick	Coonagh	Oola	Tipperary	II.	235
31, 36	Ballyflanigan	171	1	20	Wicklow	Arklow	Dunganstown	Rathdrum	I.	343
77, 78	Ballyfleming	264	3	28	Cork, E.R.	Imokilly	Kilmacdonagh	Youghal	II.	88
30	Ballyfliugh	234	3	13	Kilkenny	Kells	Coolaghmore	Callan	I.	107
5, 9	Ballyfodrin	101	0	10	Armagh	Oneilland West	Drumcree	Lurgan	III.	51
37	Ballyfoile Lower	113	3	15	Kilkenny	Ida	Dysartmoon	New Ross	I.	101
37	Ballyfoile Upper	207	2	37	Kilkenny	Ida	Dysartmoon	New Ross	I.	101
1, 2, 6	Ballyfolan	848	0	39	Wicklow	Lower Talbotstown	Kilbride	Naas	I.	361
30	Ballyfoleen North	201	0	9	Limerick	Connello Upper	Kilfinny	Croom	II.	233
30	Ballyfoleen South	232	3	18	Limerick	Connello Upper	Kilfinny	Croom	II.	233
16	Ballyfoley	287	3	7	Wexford	Scarawalsh	Kilbride	Enniscorthy	I.	323
16	Ballyfoley Little	133	1	7	Wexford	Scarawalsh	Kilbride	Enniscorthy	I.	323
16	Ballyfolliard	392	0	23	Tyrone	Strabane Lower	Ardstraw	Castlederg	III.	318
38, 39	Ballyfookeen	604	1	8	Limerick	Connello Upper	Bruree	Kilmallock	II.	231
21	Ballyfookoon	157	3	23	Limerick	Coshma	Killonahan	Croom	II.	243
47	Ballyforau	477	0	38a	Roscommon	Athlone	Taghboy	Athlone	IV.	184
46	Ballyfore	523	2	16	Antrim	Lower Belfast	Raloo	Larne	III.	9
3, 10	Ballyfore	618	2	3	King's Co.	Lower Philipstown	Croghan	Edenderry	I.	142
46, 52	Ballyfore	153	3	15	Meath	Upper Moyfenrath	Castlejordan	Edenderry	I.	212
11	Ballyfore Big	209	3	22	King's Co.	Coolestown	Ballynakill	Edenderry	I.	132
11	Ballyfore Little	42	1	0	King's Co.	Coolestown	Ballynakill	Edenderry	I.	132
48	Ballyforlea	97	1	5	Londonderry	Loughinsholin	Derryloran	Magherafelt	III.	240
48	Ballyforlea	148	0	27	Londonderry	Loughinsholin	Lissan	Magherafelt	III.	242
4	Ballyformoyle	727	3	25c	Roscommon	Boyle	Ardcarn	Boyle	IV.	192
2, 6	Ballyfotherly	539	2	0	Down	Ards Lower	Bangor	Newtownards	III.	157
87	Ballyfouloo	140	1	7	Cork, E.R.	Kerrycurrihy	Monkstown	Cork	II.	93
32	Ballyfounder	139	0	11	Down	Ards Upper	Ballytrustan	Downpatrick	III.	160
61	Ballyfowloo	369	0	18	Tipperary, S.R.	Middlethird	St. Patricksrock	Cashel	II.	330
113	Ballyfoyle	382	3	15	Cork, E.R.	Kinalea	Ballyfoyle	Kinsale	II.	94
14, 15	Ballyfoyle	1,431	2	14	Kilkenny	Gowran	Kilmadum	Kilkenny	I.	97
26	Ballyfoyle	730	1	17d	Queen's Co.	Ballyadams	Killabban	Athy	I.	231
5	Ballyfoyle	433	3	19	Wicklow	Lower Talbotstown	Kilbride	Naas	I.	361
28, 36	Ballyfraley	257	1	5	Limerick	Glenquin	Grange	Newcastle	II.	245
14	Ballyfree	119	1	31	Sligo	Carbury	St. Johns	Sligo	IV.	223
30	Ballyfree East	43	1	12	Wicklow	Newcastle	Glenealy	Rathdrum	I.	351
24, 30	Ballyfree West	254	2	14	Wicklow	Newcastle	Glenealy	Rathdrum	I.	351
18	Ballyfrench	260	3	21	Down	Ards Upper	St. Andrews, alias Ballyhalbert	Newtownards	III.	161
6, 7	Ballyfrenis	266	2	17	Down	Ards Lower	Donaghadee	Newtownards	III.	157
49	Ballyfroota	486	2	6	Limerick	Coshlea	Ballingarry	Kilmallock	II.	237
46	Ballyfrory	260	2	8	Wexford	Bargy	Bannow	Wexford	I.	304
41, 42	Ballyfruit	168	1	19e	Galway	Clare	Kilkilvery	Tuam	IV.	20
18	Ballyfrunk	279	1	30	Kilkenny	Crannagh	Ballycallan	Kilkenny	I.	84
29	Ballygaddy	189	0	15	Galway	Dunmore	Kilbennan	Tuam	IV.	34
16	Ballygaddy	116	0	17	Kildare	Offaly East	Rathangan	Edenderry	I.	70
39	Ballygaddy	361	3	23	King's Co.	Ballybritt	Seirkieran	Parsonstown	I.	126
38	Ballygaddy	427	2	37	King's Co.	Clonlisk	Kilcolman	Parsonstown	I.	130
73, 74	Ballygaggin	126	3	17	Cork, E.R.	Cork	St. Finbars	Cork	II.	65
30	Ballygagin (Crawford)	178	0	28	Waterford	Decies without Drum	Kilrush	Dungarvan	II.	358
30, 31	Ballygagin (Garde)	151	2	8	Waterford	Decies without Drum	Kilrush	Dungarvan	II.	358
35	Ballygahan Lower	85	2	21	Wicklow	Arklow	Castlemacadam	Rathdrum	I.	342
35	Ballygahan Upper	251	3	13	Wicklow	Arklow	Castlemacadam	Rathdrum	I.	342
21	Ballygalane	106	2	3	Waterford	Coshmore&Coshbride	Lismore and Mocollop	Lismore	II.	344
21	Ballygalane Upper	136	2	23	Waterford	Coshmore&Coshbride	Lismore and Mocollop	Lismore	II.	344
41	Ballygalda or Trust	596	3	27	Roscommon	Ballintober South	Roscommon	Roscommon	IV.	190
25	Ballygalget	289	0	6f	Down	Ards Upper	Witter	Downpatrick	III.	161
14	Ballygall	85	2	1	Dublin	Castleknock	Finglas	Dublin North	I.	24
14	Ballygall	49	3	34	Dublin	Coolock	Glasnevin	Dublin North	I.	27
45, 51	Ballygallagh	503	3	9	Antrim	Lower Belfast	Ballylinny	Antrim	III.	7
60	Ballygallan	1,008	1	6g	Donegal	Raphoe	Conwal	Stranorlar	III.	137
35	Ballygalley	769	3	28	Antrim	Upper Glenarm	Carncastle	Larne	III.	24

(a) Including 6A. 2R. 32P. Lough.   (d) Including 15A. 3R. 27P. River Barrow.   (f) Including 10A. 1R. 9P. Lough.
(b) Including 35A. 2R. 1P. water.   (e) Including 9A. 2R. 15P. water.   (g) Including 31A. 1R. 5P. water.
(c) Including 8A. 2R. 14P. water.

No. of Sheet of the Ordnance Survey Maps.	Townlands and Towns.	Area in Statute Acres.			County.	Barony.	Parish.	Poor Law Union in 1857.	Townland Census of 1851. Part I.	
		A.	R.	P.					Vol.	Page
3	Ballygallin .	57	2	23	Londonderry .	North East Liberties of Coleraine . .	Ballyaghran . .	Coleraine . .	III.	244
29, 32, 33	Ballygallon .	338	1	39a	Kilkenny .	Gowran . . .	Inistioge . . .	Thomastown .	I.	96
38	Ballygallum .	164	2	10	Down .	Lecale Upper .	Bright . .	Downpatrick .	III.	180
30, 31	Ballygally .	934	1	22	Down .	Lecale Lower .	Inch . .	Downpatrick .	III	179
40	Ballygally .	420	0	15	Galway .	Moycullen .	Kilcummin . .	Oughterard .	IV.	66
20	Ballygally .	149	2	3b	Waterford .	Coshmore&Coshbride	Lismore and Mocollop	Lismore . .	II.	344
20	Ballygally East	167	2	12c	Waterford .	Coshmore&Coshbride	Lismore and Mocollop	Lismore . .	II.	344
20	Ballygally West	96	1	3d	Waterford .	Coshmore&Coshbride	Lismore and Mocollop	Lismore . .	II.	344
24, 30	Ballygalvert .	1,200	1	5	Wexford .	Bantry . .	Clonleigh . .	New Ross .	I.	300
70	Ballygambon .	451	0	25	Tipperary, S.R.	Middlethird . .	Baptistgrange .	Cashel .	II.	325
30	Ballygambon Lower	212	0	30	Waterford .	Decies without Drum	Whitechurch . .	Dungarvan .	II.	361
30	Ballygambon Upper	284	3	17	Waterford .	Decies without Drum	Whitechurch . .	Dungarvan .	II.	361
47	Ballygamboon Lower	201	0	9	Kerry .	Trughanacmy .	Kiltallagh . .	Tralee .	II.	212
38, 47	Ballygamboon Upper	1,076	3	24	Kerry .	Trughanacmy .	Kiltallagh . .	Tralee .	II.	212
41, 42	Ballygammane .	274	1	29	Tipperary, N.R.	Eliogarty . .	Thurles . .	Thurles .	II.	273
60, 64	Ballygammon .	121	0	29	Antrim .	Upper Belfast .	Shankill . .	Belfast .	III.	10
11, 16	Ballygan Lower .	132	3	27	Antrim .	Upper Dunluce .	Ballymoney .	Ballymoney .	III.	18
33, 34	Ballyganneen .	362	0	18	Kerry .	Corkaguiny .	Kilquane . .	Dingle .	II.	179
9	Ballyganner North .	644	3	10	Clare .	Burren . .	Noughaval . .	Ballyvaghan .	II.	13
9, 16	Ballyganner South .	578	0	13	Clare .	Burren . .	Noughaval . .	Corrofin .	II.	13
30	Ballygannon .	299	2	9	Wicklow .	Ballinacor North .	Rathdrum .	Rathdrum .	I.	347
13	Ballygannon .	322	0	2	Wicklow .	Newcastle .	Kilcoole . .	Rathdrum .	I.	351
30	Ballygannon Beg .	315	1	27	Wicklow .	Arklow . .	Dunganstown .	Rathdrum .	I.	343
30	Ballygannon More .	315	2	16	Wicklow .	Arklow . .	Dunganstown .	Rathdrum .	I.	343
11, 16	Ballygan Upper .	140	2	2	Antrim .	Upper Dunluce .	Ballymoney .	Ballymoney .	III.	18
8	Ballygan Upper .	18	0	26	Londonderry .	North East Liberties of Coleraine . .	Ballymoney . .	Ballymoney .	III.	245
33	Ballygar . .	293	1	14	Galway .	Killian . .	Killeroran . .	Mountbellew .	IV.	43
19	Ballygar . .	77	1	7	Longford .	Ardagh . .	Ardagh . .	Longford .	I.	151
10	Ballygargan .	304	2	12	Armagh .	Oneilland East .	Seagoe . .	Lurgan .	III.	50
53	Ballygarra .	58	1	15	Wexford .	Forth . .	Carn . .	Wexford .	I.	309
26	Ballygarran .	667	0	20	Kerry .	Trughanacmy .	Ballynahaglish .	Tralee .	II.	207
24	Ballygarran .	237	2	4	Waterford .	Decies without Drum	Ballylaneen .	Kilmacthomas .	II.	354
18, 27	Ballygarran .	412	2	26	Waterford .	Gaultiere . .	Kilmacleague .	Waterford .	II.	364
25	Ballygarran .	224	2	37	Waterford .	Middlethird .	Islandikane .	Waterford .	II.	367
16	Ballygarran .	410	0	18	Waterford .	Middlethird .	Newcastle .	Waterford .	II.	368
5, 6	Ballygarran .	145	3	6	Westmeath .	Moygoish .	Rathaspick .	Granard .	I.	280
21, 22	Ballygarran .	221	2	1	Wexford .	Ballaghkeen .	Kilmuckridge .	Gorey .	I.	296
25, 26	Ballygarrane .	347	3	25	Cork, E.R.	Fermoy . .	Clenor . .	Mallow .	II.	78
81	Ballygarrane .	211	2	15	Tipperary, S.R.	Iffa and Offa West .	Tubbrid . .	Clogheen .	II.	320
52	Ballygarrane .	122	0	27	Tipperary, S.R.	Kilnamanagh Lower	Kilmore . .	Cashel .	II.	323
82	Ballygarraun .	173	1	38e	Galway .	Galway . .	Oranmore .	Galway .	IV.	37
104, 105	Ballygarraun .	667	1	9	Galway .	Loughrea .	Isertkelly .	Loughrea .	IV.	63
84	Ballygarraun North	224	1	34	Galway .	Athenry .	Athenry .	Loughrea .	IV.	3
84	Ballygarraun South	238	0	7	Galway .	Athenry .	Athenry .	Loughrea .	IV.	3
84	Ballygarraun West .	250	3	27	Galway .	Athenry .	Athenry .	Loughrea .	IV.	3
45	Ballygarreen .	100	1	16	Clare .	Tulla Lower .	Killaloe .	Scarriff .	II.	35
17	Ballygarret .	115	3	21	Kerry .	Clanmaurice .	Duagh .	Listowel .	II.	168
16	Ballygarret .	181	1	1	Kerry .	Clanmaurice .	Kilfeighny .	Listowel .	II.	169
36	Ballygarret .	206	2	36	Kerry .	Corkaguiny .	Kilgobban .	Tralee .	II.	177
3, 7	Ballygarret .	133	3	30	Waterford .	Upperthird .	Mothel . .	Carrick on Suir	II.	370
13	Ballygarret .	55	1	38	Wicklow .	Newcastle .	Newcastle Upper .	Rathdrum .	I.	353
13	Ballygarret or Sandbrook .	258	3	25	Carlow .	Forth . .	Ballon . .	Carlow .	I.	3
33	Ballygarrett .	216	2	37f	Cork, E.R.	Fermoy . .	Mallow . .	Mallow .	II.	81
20	Ballygarrett .	123	1	6	King's Co.	Coolestown .	Clonsast . .	Edenderry .	I.	132
17	Ballygarrett .	161	3	9	Wexford .	Ballaghkeen .	Donaghmore .	Gorey .	I.	293
6	Ballygarrett .	284	3	24	Wexford .	Gorey . .	Kilnahue .	Gorey .	I.	319
45	Ballygarrett .	43	3	10	Wexford .	Shelburne .	Fethard . .	New Ross .	I.	327
45	Ballygarrett .	167	0	32	Wexford .	Shelburne .	Tintern . .	New Ross .	I.	329
17	Ballygarrett Little .	91	0	25	Wexford .	Ballaghkeen .	Donaghmore .	Gorey .	I.	293
110	Ballygarries .	183	1	0	Mayo .	Kilmaine .	Robeen . .	Ballinrobe .	IV.	157
95	Ballygarriff .	127	1	3	Galway .	Dunkellin .	Killeely . .	Gort .	IV.	29
60, 70	Ballygarriff .	217	1	10	Mayo .	Carra . .	Turlough . .	Castlebar .	IV.	130
109	Ballygarry .	128	3	15	Mayo .	Carra . .	Ballyovey .	Ballinrobe .	IV.	126
15	Ballygarry .	120	3	39	Mayo .	Tirawley .	Kilcummin .	Killala .	IV.	168
28	Ballygarth .	327	2	24	Meath .	Upper Duleek .	Ballygarth .	Drogheda .	I.	197
33	BALLYGAR T.	—			Galway .	Killian . .	Killeroran .	Mountbellew .	IV.	44
86	Ballygarvan .	1,251	3	34	Cork, E.R.	Kerrycurrihy .	Carrigaline .	Cork .	II.	92
12, 18	Ballygarvan .	543	2	24	Down .	Ards Upper .	Inishargy .	Newtownards .	III.	160
40	Ballygarvan .	681	1	26	Wexford .	Shelburne .	Owenduff .	New Ross .	I.	328
29	Ballygarvan Glebe .	298	0	31	Queen's Co.	Clarmallagh .	Aghaboe . .	Abbeyleix .	II.	235

(a) Including 2A. 0R. 26P. River Nore.
(b) Including 4A. 0R. 18P. water.

(c) Including 6A. 2R. 16P. water.
(d) Including 2A. 2R. 0P. water.

(e) Including 3A. 1R. 15P. water.
(f) Including 5A. 0R. 32P. water.

No. of Sheet of the Ordnance Survey Maps.	Townlands and Towns.	Area in Statute Acres.			County.	Barony.	Parish.	Poor Law Union in 1857.	Townland Census of 1851, Part I.	
		A.	R.	P.					Vol.	Page
14	Ballygarve . .	463	0	31	Longford . .	Longford . .	Killoe . .	Longford . .	I.	158
32, 33	Ballygarvey . .	547	0	5	Antrim . .	Lower Toome . .	Kirkinriola . .	Ballymena .	III.	32
5, 10	Ballygarvey . .	261	0	3	Westmeath	Moygoish .	Rathaspick .	Mullingar .	I.	280
48	Ballygarvey . .	180	3	17	Wexford . .	Forth . .	Kilscoran . .	Wexford . .	I.	311
5	Ballygarveybeg .	530	1	35a	Westmeath	Moygoish .	Rathaspick .	Mullingar .	I.	280
25, 32	Ballygarvigan .	234	1	29	Down . .	Ards Upper .	Ballyphilip .	Downpatrick .	III.	159
8	Ballygasey . .	205	2	35	Armagh . .	Oneilland West .	Loughgall .	Armagh . .	III.	53
21, 27	Ballygasheen .	741	2	7	Tipperary, N.R.	Upper Ormond .	Ballymaclogh .	Nenagh . .	II.	290
18	Ballygassan . .	200	0	6b	Clare . .	Bunratty Upper .	Inchicronan .	Ennis . .	II.	8
8	Ballygassoon . .	145	2	37	Armagh . .	Armagh . .	Grange . .	Armagh . .	III.	44
8, 9	Ballygastell . .	503	0	5	Clare . .	Burren . .	Killeany . .	Ballyvaghan .	II.	13
105	Ballygasty . .	280	1	15	Galway . .	Loughrea . .	Loughrea . .	Loughrea . .	IV.	65
30	Ballygate . .	38	3	26	Roscommon .	Ballintober North .	Termonbarry .	Strokestown .	IV.	187
51	Ballygatta and Cor-									
	raree . .	525	0	33	Roscommon .	Athlone . .	Taghmaconnell .	Athlone . .	IV.	185
29	Ballygauge Beg .	341	3	34	Queen's Co. .	Clarmallagh .	Killermogh .	Abbeyleix .	I.	238
29	Ballygauge More .	319	1	6	Queen's Co. .	Clarmallagh .	Killermogh .	Abbeyleix .	I.	238
52, 60	Ballygawley . .	71	3	1	Donegal . .	Raphoe . .	Conwal . .	Letterkenny .	III.	137
18	Ballygawley . .	273	0	21	Londonderry	Coleraine . .	Aghadowey .	Coleraine . .	III.	229
52, 53, 59, 60	Ballygawley . .	123	0	14	Tyrone . .	Clogher . .	Errigal Keerogue .	Clogher . .	III.	295
52, 59	BALLYGAWLEY T. .	—			Tyrone . .	Clogher . .	Errigal Keerogue .	Clogher . .	III.	296
30, 35	Ballygawn and Bal-									
	lycoos . .	1,058	0	28	Antrim . .	Upper Glenarm .	Carncastle .	Larne . .	III.	24
36, 37	Ballygay . .	349	1	4c	Donegal . .	Kilmacrenan .	Tullyfern .	Millford .	III.	132
128, 133	Ballygeagin .	109	2	18	Galway . .	Kiltartan . .	Beagh . .	Gort . .	IV.	46
48, 56	Ballygeagoge .	349	3	25	Limerick . .	Coshlea . .	Particles .	Kilmallock .	II.	240
21	Ballygeale . .	206	3	12	Limerick . .	Coshma . .	Adare . .	Croom . .	II.	241
21	Ballygeale . .	201	2	15	Limerick . .	Coshma . .	Killonahan .	Croom . .	II.	243
50	Ballygeana . .	643	0	3	Limerick . .	Coshlea . .	Galbally .	Mitchelstown .	II.	238
89	Ballygeany . .	234	0	32	Cork, E.R. .	Imokilly . .	Cloyne . .	Middleton .	II.	85
31	Ballygeardra .	793	0	35	Kilkenny . .	Knocktopher .	Knocktopher .	Thomastown .	I.	112
17, 24	Ballygeegan .	617	1	2d	Down . .	Dufferin . .	Killinchy .	Downpatrick .	III.	166
23, 29	Ballygeehin Lower .	523	0	35	Queen's Co. .	Clarmallagh .	Aghaboe . .	Abbeyleix .	I.	235
23	Ballygeehin Upper .	402	3	10	Queen's Co. .	Clarmallagh .	Aghaboe . .	Abbeyleix .	I.	235
36, 44	Ballygeel . .	365	2	14	Limerick . .	Glenquin . .	Monagay .	Newcastle .	II.	247
68, 69	Ballygeery East .	250	1	39	Clare . .	Clonderalaw .	Killofin . .	Killadysert .	II.	16
68	Ballygeery West .	229	0	32	Clare . .	Clonderalaw .	Killofin . .	Killadysert .	II.	16
32, 36	Ballygegan . .	158	1	12	Kilkenny . .	Gowran . .	Inistioge . .	Thomastown .	I.	96
25	Ballygelagh . .	629	3	29	Down . .	Ards Upper .	Ardkeen . .	Downpatrick .	III.	159
3	Ballygelagh East .	147	0	4	Londonderry	North East Liberties of Coleraine .	Ballyaghran .	Coleraine . .	III.	244
3	Ballygelagh West .	132	0	29	Londonderry	North East Liberties of Coleraine .	Ballyaghran .	Coleraine . .	III.	244
33, 38	Ballygelly . .	892	3	35	Antrim . .	Lower Antrim .	Racavan . .	Ballymena .	III.	4
69	Ballygerald East .	504	3	18	Tipperary, S.R.	Middlethird .	Knockgraffon .	Cashel . .	II.	328
69	Ballygerald West .	34	1	19	Tipperary, S.R.	Middlethird .	Knockgraffon .	Cashel . .	II.	328
48	Ballygerry . .	139	3	36	Wexford . .	Forth . .	Kilrane . .	Wexford . .	I.	311
23	Ballygibbagh . .	75	3	24	Longford . .	Moydow . .	Taghsheenod .	Ballymahon .	I.	162
62	Ballygibbon . .	450	2	18	Cork, E.R. .	East Muskerry .	Garrycloyne .	Cork . .	II.	103
66	Ballygibbon . .	208	0	14	Cork, E.R. .	Imokilly . .	Mogeely . .	Middleton .	II.	89
15	Ballygibbon . .	622	3	17	Tipperary, N.R.	Upper Ormond .	Ballygibbon .	Nenagh . .	II.	289
18, 24	Ballygibbon . .	213	0	9	Wexford . .	Bantry . .	Templeludigan .	New Ross . .	I.	303
7, 8	Ballygibbon East .	568	0	29	Kildare . .	Carbury . .	Carrick . .	Edenderry .	I.	51
2, 7	Ballygibbon West .	758	0	13	Kildare . .	Carbury . .	Carrick . .	Edenderry .	I.	51
20	Ballygiblin . .	192	0	13	Cork, E.R. .	Condons&Clangibbon	Brigown . .	Mitchelstown .	II.	59
24	Ballygiblin . .	442	3	3	Cork, E.R. .	Duhallow . .	Castlemagner .	Kanturk . .	II.	67
30, 35	Ballygilbert . .	713	3	29	Antrim . .	Upper Glenarm .	Carncastle .	Larne . .	III.	24
1	Ballygilbert . .	368	1	6	Down . .	Castlereagh Lower .	Bangor . .	Newtownards .	III.	161
45	Ballygilbert . .	273	2	25	Down . .	Lecale Upper .	Bright . .	Downpatrick .	III.	180
11, 12	Ballygilcash . .	259	0	20	Sligo . .	Tireragh . .	Kilmacshalgan .	Dromore West .	IV.	234
10	Ballygilchrist .	263	0	22	Longford . .	Granard . .	Granard . .	Granard . .	I.	156
8	Ballygilgan . .	875	2	27	Sligo . .	Carbury . .	Drumcliff .	Sligo . .	IV.	221
3	Ballygillaheen .	246	0	3	Queen's Co. .	Tinnahinch .	Rearymore .	Mountmellick .	I.	249
47, 48	Ballygillane . .	327	2	26	Limerick . .	Coshlea . .	Ballingaddy .	Kilmallock .	II.	237
48	Ballygillane Big .	158	2	20	Wexford . .	Forth . .	Kilrane . .	Wexford . .	I.	311
48	Ballygillane Little .	128	3	30	Wexford . .	Forth . .	Kilrane . .	Wexford . .	I.	311
35, 36	Ballygillaroe . .	132	0	27	Wicklow . .	Arklow . .	Redcross .	Rathdrum .	I.	345
49	Ballygillen Beg .	383	0	33	Londonderry	Loughinsholin .	Artrea . .	Magherafelt .	III.	238
49	Ballygillen More .	347	2	10	Londonderry	Loughinsholin .	Artrea . .	Magherafelt .	III.	238
13	Ballygillin . .	168	2	11	Westmeath	Delvin . .	Killulagh .	Castletowndelvin .	I.	266
25	Ballygillistown .	315	0	39	Wexford . .	Bantry . .	Rossdroit .	Enniscorthy .	I.	301
1	Ballygill Middle .	244	0	9	Antrim . .	Cary . .	Rathlin Island .	Ballycastle .	III.	15
1	Ballygill North .	149	8	14	Antrim . .	Cary . .	Rathlin Island .	Ballycastle .	III.	15
1	Ballygill South .	145	2	21	Antrim . .	Cary . .	Rathlin Island .	Ballycastle .	III.	15

(a) Including 105A. 1R. 1P. water.   (c) Including 23A. 2R. 12P. water.   (d) Including 27A. 0R. 24P. water.
(b) Including 8A. 1R. 19P. water.

No. of Sheet of the Ordnance Survey Maps.	Townlands and Towns.	Area in Statute Acres.			County.	Barony.	Parish.	Poor Law Union in 1857.	Townland Census of 1851, Part I.	
		A.	R.	P.					Vol.	Page
17, 18	Ballygiltenan Lower	490	3	10	Limerick .	Shanid . .	Kilfergus .	Glin . .	II.	255
17, 18	Ballygiltenan North	135	1	10	Limerick .	Shanid . .	Kilfergus .	Glin . .	II.	255
17,18,26,27	Ballygiltenan Upper	1,110	1	36	Limerick .	Shanid . .	Kilfergus .	Glin . .	II.	255
98	Ballyginnane .	394	3	31	Cork, E.R. .	Kerrycurrihy .	Liscleary .	Kinsale .	II.	92
54	Ballyginniff .	438	2	4	Antrim .	Lower Massereene .	Killead . .	Antrim .	III.	28
43	Ballyginny .	522	1	27	Down .	Upper Iveagh, Lr. pt.	Maghera . .	Kilkeel .	III.	173
42	Ballygirreen .	541	3	19	Clare .	Bunratty Lower .	Kilnasoolagh .	Ennis .	II.	6
50, 61	Ballygirriha .	683	3	16	Cork, E.R. .	East Muskerry .	Donaghmore .	Macroom .	II.	102
47	Ballygittle .	169	0	29	Tyrone .	Dungannon Middle .	Clonoe . .	Dungannon .	III.	300
18, 27	Ballyglan .	381	1	14	Waterford .	Gaultiere .	Kill St. Nicholas .	Waterford .	II.	364
44, 45	Ballyglasheen .	334	0	35	Kerry .	Corkaguiny .	Ballinvoher .	Dingle .	II.	173
67	Ballyglasheen .	370	0	5	Tipperary, S.R.	Clanwilliam .	Kilfeakle .	Tipperary .	II.	308
78	Ballyglasheen .	249	0	35	Tipperary, S.R.	Iffa and Offa East .	Kilsheelan .	Clonmel .	II.	314
78	Ballyglasheen Little	83	1	21	Tipperary, S.R.	Iffa and Offa East .	Kilsheelan .	Clonmel .	II.	314
53, 63	Ballyglass .	360	2	2	Clare . .	Bunratty Lower .	St. Patricks .	Limerick .	II.	6
34, 42	Ballyglass .	252	1	33	Clare . .	Bunratty Upper .	Doora . .	Ennis .	II.	8
51	Ballyglass .	355	1	12	Cork, E R. .	Barretts . .	Grenagh . .	Cork .	II.	49
70	Ballyglass .	195	2	11	Galway .	Clare . .	Athenry . .	Galway .	IV.	17
74	Ballyglass .	145	3	15	Galway .	Clonmacnowen .	Ahascragh .	Ballinasloe .	IV.	24
73, 86	Ballyglass .	560	0	7	Galway .	Kilconnell .	Kilconnell .	Ballinasloe .	IV.	40
125	Ballyglass .	44	3	23	Galway .	Leitrim . .	Ballynakill .	Loughrea .	IV.	50
135	Ballyglass .	44	0	23	Galway .	Leitrim . .	Clonrush .	Scarriff .	IV.	52
117, 126	Ballyglass .	211	0	34	Galway .	Leitrim . .	Tynagh . .	Portumna .	IV.	55
72	Ballyglass .	722	2	20	Galway .	Tiaquin . .	Clonkeen .	Loughrea .	IV.	76
7	Ballyglass .	301	0	20	Leitrim .	Rosclogher .	Killasnet .	Manorhamilton	IV.	109
77	Ballyglass .	306	2	13	Mayo .	Burrishoole .	Kilmaclasser .	Westport .	IV.	121
100	Ballyglass .	171	3	28a	Mayo .	Carra . .	Toughty .	Ballinrobe .	IV.	130
111, 119	Ballyglass .	894	0	5	Mayo .	Clanmorris .	Crossboyne .	Claremorris .	IV.	132
102	Ballyglass .	270	1	7	Mayo .	Clanmorris .	Kilcolman .	Claremorris .	IV.	133
72, 81	Ballyglass .	72	0	39	Mayo .	Costello . .	Aghamore .	Swineford .	IV.	136
74	Ballyglass .	307	1	14	Mayo .	Costello . .	Kilmovee .	Swineford .	IV.	141
10	Ballyglass .	243	0	3	Mayo .	Erris . .	Kilmore . .	Belmullet .	IV.	145
71	Ballyglass .	154	0	36	Mayo .	Gallen . .	Kilconduff .	Swineford .	IV.	147
120, 121	Ballyglass .	244	2	18	Mayo .	Kilmaine . .	Ballinchalla .	Ballinrobe .	IV.	151
7	Ballyglass .	357	3	35	Mayo .	Tirawley . .	Doonfeeny .	Killala .	IV.	167
21, 29	Ballyglass .	125	3	10	Mayo .	Tirawley . .	Moygawnagh .	Killala .	II.	171
21	Ballyglass .	85	2	10	Queen's Co. .	Clandonagh .	Skirk . .	Donaghmore .	I.	235
47	Ballyglass .	270	3	38	Roscommon .	Athlone . .	Dysart . .	Athlone .	IV.	180
42	Ballyglass .	77	1	15b	Roscommon .	Athlone . .	Killinvoy .	Roscommon .	IV.	181
42, 45	Ballyglass .	300	0	24	Roscommon .	Athlone . .	Kahara . .	Roscommon .	IV.	183
36, 37	Ballyglass .	294	3	14	Roscommon .	Ballintober South .	Cloontuskert .	Roscommon .	IV.	188
21	Ballyglass .	2,000	2	0	Roscommon .	Castlereagh .	Baslick . .	Castlereagh .	IV.	199
28	Ballyglass .	495	3	21	Roscommon .	Roscommon .	Killukin .	Strokestown .	IV.	210
15	Ballyglass .	135	3	10	Sligo .	Carbury . .	Calry . .	Sligo .	IV.	220
31, 32	Ballyglass .	473	3	8	Sligo .	Leyny . .	Achonry .	Tobercurry .	IV.	228
17	Ballyglass .	180	1	15	Sligo .	Tireragh . .	Kilglass . .	Dromore West .	IV.	234
12, 18	Ballyglass .	469	3	38	Sligo .	Tireragh . .	Kilmacshalgan .	Dromore West .	IV.	234
19	Ballyglass .	143	3	19	Westmeath .	Moyashel and Magheradernon .	Mullingar .	Mullingar .	I.	275
18	Ballyglass .	152	1	9	Westmeath .	Rathconrath .	Rathconrath .	Mullingar .	I.	284
47, 50	Ballyglass (Dodwell)	298	0	9	Roscommon .	Athlone . .	Dysart . .	Athlone .	IV.	180
104	Ballyglass East .	254	1	14	Galway .	Dunkellin .	Ardrahan .	Loughrea .	IV.	26
63	Ballyglass East	213	0	8	Mayo .	Costello . .	Kilbeagh .	Swineford .	IV.	140
20	Ballyglass East	403	3	24	Roscommon .	Frenchpark .	Tibohine .	Castlereagh .	IV.	204
66, 67	Ballyglassin .	475	0	13	Cork, E R. .	Imokilly . .	Killeagh .	Youghal .	II.	88
19, 23	Ballyglassin .	375	1	28	Longford .	Shrule . .	Kilglass . .	Ballymahon .	I.	166
103	Ballyglass Lower .	211	2	18	Mayo .	Costello . .	Annagh . .	Claremorris .	IV.	137
35	Ballyglass Lower .	177	3	39	Roscommon .	Ballymoe .	Cloonygormican .	Roscommon .	IV.	191
67	Ballyglass Lower .	91	0	8	Tipperary. S.R.	Clanwilliam .	Clonpet . .	Tipperary .	II.	306
67	Ballyglass Lower .	25	1	32	Tipperary, S.R.	Clanwilliam .	Cordangan .	Tipperary .	II.	306
74	Ballyglass (Mahon) .	274	1	6	Galway .	Clonmacnowen .	Ahascragh .	Ballinasloe .	IV.	24
7	Ballyglass Middle .	68	0	37	Galway .	Ballymoe .	Kilcroan . .	Glennamaddy .	IV.	8
103	Ballyglass Middle .	316	3	27	Mayo .	Costello . .	Annagh . .	Claremorris .	IV.	137
2, 7	Ballyglass North .	195	0	36	Galway .	Ballymce .	Kilcroan . .	Glennamaddy .	IV.	8
39	Ballyglassoon .	160	2	7	Kilkenny .	Iverk . .	Fiddown .	Carrick on Suir	I.	105
6, 7	Ballyglass South .	555	0	37	Galway .	Ballymoe .	Kilcroan .	Glennamaddy .	IV.	8
35	Ballyglass Upper .	545	2	31c	Roscommon .	Ballymoe .	Cloonygormican .	Roscommon .	IV.	191
67	Ballyglass Upper .	228	3	8	Tipperary, S.R.	Clanwilliam .	Clonpet . .	Tipperary .	II.	306
67	Ballyglass Upper .	106	2	7	Tipperary, S.R.	Clanwilliam .	Cordangan .	Tipperary .	II.	306
6, 7	Ballyglass West .	184	1	14	Galway, .	Ballymoe .	Kilcroan . .	Glennamaddy .	IV.	8
113	Ballyglass West .	335	0	16	Galway, .	Dunkellin .	Ardrahan .	Gort .	IV.	26
63	Ballyglass West .	74	1	10	Mayo .	Costello . .	Kilbeagh .	Swineford .	IV.	140
19, 20	Ballyglass West .	283	0	22	Roscommon .	Frenchpark .	Tibohine . .	Castlerengh .	IV.	204

(a) Including 2A. 3R. 16P. water.   (b) Including 2A. 3R. 36P. water.   (c) Including 12A. 0R. 20P. water.

M

No. of Sheet of the Ordnance Survey Maps.	Townlands and Towns.	Area in Statute Acres. A. R. P.	County.	Barony.	Parish.	Poor Law Union in 1857.	Townland Census of 1851, Part I. Vol.	Page
56, 67	Ballyglavin	272 0 21	Cork, E.R.	Imokilly	Ardagh	Youghal	II.	83
10, 11	Ballyglighorn	182 0 6	Down	Castlereagh Lower	Tullynakill	Newtownards	III.	163
24, 25	Ballyglisheen	746 1 0	Carlow	St. Mullins Lower	St. Mullins	New Ross	I.	13
24	Ballyglishen	158 0 28	Queen's Co.	Cullenagh	Ballyroan	Abbeyleix	I.	239
44	Ballyglissane	203 1 37	Cork, E.R.	Barrymore	Rathcormack	Fermoy	II.	57
57, 58	Ballyglooneen	427 3 8	Galway	Clare	Kilmoylan	Tuam	IV.	22
28, 29, 33, 34	Ballygobban	560 3 3	Wicklow	Ballinacor South	Moyne	Shillelagh	I.	350
12, 17	Ballygobbin	172 1 22	Antrim	Upper Dunluce	Ballymoney	Ballymoney	III.	18
58	Ballygodoon	330 2 13	Tipperary, S.R.	Clanwilliam	Solloghodmore	Tipperary	II.	310
17, 26	Ballygoghlan	893 1 29	Limerick	Shanid	Kilfergus	Glin	II.	255
56, 57	Ballygolan	274 2 39	Antrim	Lower Belfast	Carnmoney	Belfast	III.	7
88, 98	Ballygolman	337 0 26a	Mayo	Murrisk	Aghagower	Westport	IV.	158
8	Ballygoly	187 0 10	Louth	Lower Dundalk	Ballymascanlan	Dundalk	I.	175
37	Ballygoman	320 0 21	Wexford	Shelmaliere West	Carrick	Wexford	I.	332
60	Ballygomartin	647 3 32	Antrim	Upper Belfast	Shankill	Belfast	III.	10
70	Ballygommon	238 1 11	Mayo	Carra	Kildacommoge	Castlebar	IV.	129
79	Ballygonigan	154 2 8	Donegal	Raphoe	Donaghmore	Strabane	III.	137
21	Ballygonnell	80 2 28	Fermanagh	Magheraboy	Devenish	Enniskillen	III.	210
31	Ballygonnell	198 1 34	Wicklow	Arklow	Drumkay	Rathdrum	I.	342
48	Ballygonny Beg	165 1 17	Londonderry	Loughinsholin	Arboe	Magherafelt	III.	238
48	Ballygonny Beg	149 2 38	Londonderry	Loughinsholin	Tamlaght	Magherafelt	III.	243
48	Ballygonny More	214 0 11	Londonderry	Loughinsholin	Arboe	Magherafelt	III.	238
48	Ballygonny More	259 0 26	Londonderry	Loughinsholin	Tamlaght	Magherafelt	III.	243
9	Ballygoonaun	487 3 36	Clare	Corcomroe	Kilfenora	Ennistimon	II.	18
6, 11	Ballygoran	353 3 17	Kildare	North Salt	Laraghbryan	Celbridge	I.	75
42, 45	Ballygorey	488 3 9	Kilkenny	Iverk	Portnascully	Waterford	I.	106
45	BALLYGOREY T.	—	Kilkenny	Iverk	Portnascully	Waterford	I.	106
47, 48	Ballygorian Beg	500 0 27	Down	Upper Iveagh, Lr. pt.	Clonduff	Newry	III.	171
47	Ballygorian More	672 1 28	Down	Upper Iveagh, Lr. pt.	Clonduff	Newry	III.	171
21, 22	Ballygorman	390 2 23	Armagh	Lower Orior	Loughgilly	Newry	III.	56
2	Ballygorman	799 2 36	Donegal	Inishowen East	Clonca	Inishowen	III.	116
18	Ballygormill North	137 2 1	Queen's Co.	Maryborough East	Fossy or Timahoe	Abbeyleix	I.	241
18	Ballygormill South	257 1 29	Queen's Co.	Cullenagh	Fossy or Timahoe	Abbeyleix	I.	240
43	Ballygortagh	297 0 35	Meath	Upper Deece	Kilmore	Dunshaughlin	I.	193
53	Ballygortagh	113 3 9	Roscommon	Moycarn	Creagh	Ballinasloe	IV.	206
15	Ballygorteen	976 1 29	Kilkenny	Gowran	Shankill	Kilkenny	I.	99
17	Ballygorteen	318 3 18	Tipperary, N.R.	Ikerrin	Corbally	Roscrea	II.	275
68, 75	Ballygorteen	505 0 38	Tipperary, S.R.	Clanwilliam	Clonbullogue	Tipperary	II.	306
58, 59	Ballygortgarve	241 2 6	Antrim	Upper Massereene	Camlin	Antrim	III.	30
21	Ballygortin	182 1 34	Wexford	Ballaghkeen	Killincooly	Gorey	I.	295
23, 24	Ballygoskin	401 3 26	Down	Dufferin	Killyleagh	Downpatrick	III.	167
45, 46	Ballygow	327 1 19	Wexford	Bargy	Bannow	Wexford	I.	304
45, 50	Ballygow	291 0 19	Wexford	Shelburne	St. James and Dunbrody	New Ross	I.	328
40, 46	Ballygowan	877 1 5	Antrim	Lower Belfast	Ballynure	Larne	III.	7
40, 46	Ballygowan	614 0 19	Antrim	Lower Belfast	Raloo	Larne	III.	9
44	Ballygowan	338 3 34	Antrim	Upper Antrim	Donegore	Antrim	III.	6
12	Ballygowan	70 2 17b	Carlow	Idrone West	Cloydagh	Carlow	I.	9
12	Ballygowan	282 3 30c	Carlow	Idrone West	Tullowcreen	Carlow	I.	9
10, 16	Ballygowan	302 3 6d	Down	Castlereagh Lower	Comber	Newtownards	III.	161
16	Ballygowan	380 3 6	Down	Castlereagh Lower	Killinchy	Newtownards	III.	163
9	Ballygowan	200 0 5	Down	Castlereagh Upper	Drumbeg	Lisburn	III.	164
20, 21	Ballygowan	504 3 0	Down	Lower Iveagh, Up. pt.	Moira	Lurgan	III.	170
55	Ballygowan	124 2 22	Down	Mourne	Kilkeel	Kilkeel	III.	182
26, 27, 33, 34	Ballygowan	431 2 8	Down	Upper Iveagh, Up. pt.	Aghaderg	Banbridge	III.	173
125	Ballygowan	741 2 12	Galway	Leitrim	Ballynakill	Loughrea	IV.	50
17	Ballygowan	314 3 8	Louth	Ardee	Shanlis	Ardee	I.	174
102	Ballygowan	88 1 32	Mayo	Clanmorris	Kilcolman	Claremorris	IV.	133
21	Ballygowan	308 2 18	Mayo	Tirawley	Rathreagh	Killala	II.	171
34	Ballygowan	424 0 18	Tyrone	Omagh East	Drumragh	Omagh	III.	312
34, 35	Ballygowan (Ponsonby)	395 1 15	Kilkenny	Kells	Kilmaganny	Carrick on Suir	I.	109
30, 31, 34, 35	Ballygowan (Reade)	374 2 0	Kilkenny	Kells	Kilmaganny	Callan	I.	109
28	Ballygowdan	84 0 32	Queen's Co.	Clarmallagh	Aghaboe	Abbeyleix	I.	235
29, 35	Ballygowlan	90 1 7	Westmeath	Brawny	St. Mary's	Athlone	I.	259
10, 11	Ballygowloge	201 2 0e	Kerry	Iraghticonnor	Listowel	Listowel	II.	192
25, 26	Ballygown	403 1 4	Cork, E.R.	Fermoy	Clenor	Mallow	II.	78
39	Ballygown	405 2 2	Kilkenny	Iverk	Fiddown	Carrick on Suir	I.	105
9	Ballygowney	651 2 32	Kilkenny	Galmoy	Coolcashin	Urlingford	I.	92
9	Ballygowney	265 3 35	Kilkenny	Galmoy	Sheffin	Urlingford	I.	93
26	Ballygown North	15 0 32	Tipperary, N.R.	Upper Ormond	Kilmore	Nenagh	II.	290
26	Ballygown South	83 0 30	Tipperary, N.R.	Upper Ormond	Kilmore	Nenagh	II.	290
40, 45	Ballygowny	161 2 9	Wexford	Shelburne	Tintern	New Ross	I.	329

(a) Including 14A. 3R. 21P. water. (c) Including 4A. 1R. 32P. River Barrow. (e) Including 8A. 0R. 17P. water.
(b) Including 2A. 3R. 32P. River Barrow. (d) Including 42A. 0R. 12P. detached portion.

No. of Sheet of the Ordnance Survey Maps.	Townlands and Towns.	Area in Statute Acres.			County.	Barony.	Parish.	Poor Law Union in 1857.	Townland Census of 1851, Part I.	
		A.	R.	P.					Vol.	Page
16	Ballygrace . .	322	2	7	Cork, E.R. .	Orrery and Kilmore	Churchtown . .	Mallow . .	II.	107
16	Ballygrady North .	354	1	18	Cork, E.R. .	Duhallow . .	Kilbrin . . .	Kanturk . .	II.	71
16, 24	Ballygrady South .	298	0	18	Cork, E.R. .	Duhallow . .	Kilbrin . . .	Kanturk . .	II.	71
18	Ballygraffan . .	398	1	3	Down . .	Ards Upper .	St. Andrews, alias Ballyhalbert . .	Newtownards .	III.	161
10	Ballygraffan . .	212	3	15a	Down . .	Castlereagh Lower .	Kilmood . . .	Newtownards .	III.	163
20, 21	Ballygraigue . .	197	3	34	Tipperary, N.R. .	Upper Ormond .	Nenagh . . .	Nenagh . .	II.	292
2, 6	Ballygrainey . .	700	0	11	Down . .	Ards Lower .	Bangor . . .	Newtownards .	III.	157
1	Ballygrainey . .	424	3	10	Down . .	Castlereagh Lower .	Holywood . .	Belfast . .	III.	162
19, 22	Ballygraney . .	65	2	29	Carlow . .	Idrone East .	Ballyellin . .	Carlow . .	I.	6
52	Ballygrangans .	270	2	12	Wexford . .	Bargy . . .	Kilmore . .	Wexford . .	I.	306
6, 11	Ballygrangee . .	331	2	3	Down . .	Ards Lower .	Greyabbey . .	Newtownards .	III.	158
20, 26	Ballygrania . .	218	1	25	Sligo . .	Tirerrill . .	Kilross . . .	Sligo . .	IV.	241
72	Ballygrany . .	151	0	8	Galway . .	Tiaquin . .	Ballymacward .	Loughrea . .	IV.	75
27	Ballygreany . .	441	0	22	Kildare . .	Offaly West .	Duneany . .	Athy . .	I.	72
14	Ballygreany . .	160	1	25	Monaghan . .	Cremorne . .	Clontibret . .	Monaghan .	III.	259
39, 40	Ballygree . .	141	1	26	Kerry . .	Trughanacmy . .	Dysert . . .	Tralee . .	II.	210
40	Ballygreek . .	134	1	26	Kilkenny . .	Knocktopher .	Rosinan . . .	Waterford . .	I.	113
46	Ballygreen . .	151	1	14	Donegal . .	Kilmacrenan .	Aughnish . .	Milford . .	III.	122
59	Ballygreenan . .	191	3	31	Tyrone . .	Clogher . .	Clogher . . .	Clogher . .	III.	291
12, 18	Ballygreighan .	582	2	36	Sligo . .	Tireragh . .	Templeboy . .	Dromore West .	IV.	236
18	Ballygreighan Barr .	523	1	9	Sligo . .	Tireragh . . .	Templeboy . .	Dromore West .	IV.	236
10, 11, 16, 17	Ballygrenane . .	547	2	11b	Kerry . .	Clanmaurice .	Finuge . . .	Listowel . .	II.	169
38	Ballygrennan . .	950	2	13	Limerick . .	Connello Upper .	Ballingarry . .	Croom . .	II.	230
40, 48	Ballygrennan . .	437	0	12	Limerick . .	Coshlea . .	Kilbreedy Major .	Kilmallock .	II.	239
30	Ballygrennan . .	267	1	33	Limerick . .	Coshma . .	Croom . . .	Croom . .	II.	242
32, 39, 40	Ballygrennan . .	698	3	37	Limerick . .	Coshma . .	Uregare . . .	Kilmallock .	II.	244
5	Ballygrennan . .	309	3	38	Limerick . .	Pubblebrien .	St. Munchins . .	Limerick . .	II.	254
26, 34	Ballygriffin . .	532	2	34c	Cork, E.R. .	Fermoy . .	Monanimy . .	Mallow . .	II.	81
93, 102	Ballygriffin . .	418	0	33	Kerry . .	Glanarought . .	Kenmare . .	Kenmare . .	II.	185
43, 46	Ballygriffin . .	167	0	19	Kilkenny . .	Iverk . . .	Kilmacow . .	Waterford . .	I.	105
21, 22	Ballygriffin . .	103	2	34	Limerick . .	Coshma . .	Killeenoghty . .	Croom . .	II.	243
60	Ballygriffin . .	382	2	15	Tipperary, S.R. .	Clanwilliam .	Ballygriffin . .	Tipperary . .	II.	305
60	Ballygriffin . .	10	2	7	Tipperary, S.R. .	Clanwilliam .	Relickmurry and Athassel .	Tipperary . .	II.	309
40, 45	Ballygriffin . .	263	0	17	Wicklow . .	Arklow . .	Arklow . . .	Rathdrum . .	I.	341
25	Ballygriffy North .	391	0	24	Clare . .	Inchiquin . .	Dysert . . .	Ennis . .	II.	24
25	Ballygriffy South .	479	3	1	Clare . .	Inchiquin . .	Dysert . . .	Ennis . .	II.	24
26	Ballygriggan . .	155	1	7	Cork, E.R. .	Fermoy . .	Wallstown . .	Mallow . .	II.	83
26	Ballygrillihan .	217	3	16	Cork, E.R. .	Fermoy . .	Castletownroche .	Fermoy . .	II.	77
99	Ballygrissane . .	271	0	24	Cork, E.R. .	Kerrycurrihy . .	Carrigaline . .	Kinsale . .	II.	92
51	Ballygrogan . .	481	3	36	Cork, E.R. .	Barretts . .	Grenagh . .	Cork . .	II.	49
62, 73	Ballygrohan . .	97	1	18	Cork, E.R. .	Cork . . .	Currykippane . .	Cork . .	II.	64
22, 23	Ballygroll . .	334	0	22	Londonderry .	Tirkeeran .	Cumber Lower .	Londonderry .	III.	248
84, 85	Ballygroman Lower .	495	2	21	Cork, E.R. .	East Muskerry .	Desertmore . .	Bandon . .	II.	102
85	Ballygroman Upper .	589	0	21	Cork, E.R. .	East Muskerry .	Desertmore . .	Bandon . .	II.	102
13	Ballygroobany .	277	0	27	Armagh . .	Fews Lower .	Mullaghbrack . .	Armagh . .	III.	47
43, 49	Ballygrooby . .	691	0	7d	Antrim . .	Upper Toome .	Drummaul . .	Antrim . .	III.	33
29, 38	Ballygroogan . .	340	1	39	Tyrone . .	Dungannon Upper .	Derryloran . .	Cookstown .	III.	306
1	Ballygrot . .	721	1	0	Down . .	Castlereagh Lower .	Bangor . . .	Newtownards .	III.	161
46, 47, 48	Ballygruby . .	613	2	23	Londonderry .	Loughinsholin .	Artrea . . .	Magherafelt .	III.	238
55, 56, 66	Ballygrunna . .	170	3	27	Cork, E.R. .	Imokilly . .	Ardagh . .	Youghal . .	II.	83
39, 47	Ballygubba North .	247	2	16	Limerick . .	Coshma . .	Tankardstown .	Kilmallock .	II.	244
39, 47	Ballygubba South .	389	2	7	Limerick . .	Coshma . .	Tankardstown .	Kilmallock .	II.	244
33	Ballygub New .	1,553	1	34	Kilkenny . .	Ida . . .	Clonamery . .	Thomastown .	I.	101
33	BALLYGUB NEW T. .	—			Kilkenny . .	Ida . . .	Clonamery . .	Thomastown .	I.	101
33	Ballygub Old . .	252	3	31	Kilkenny . .	Ida . . .	Clonamery . .	Thomastown .	I.	101
15	Ballygudden . .	95	3	3	Londonderry .	Tirkeeran .	Faughanvale . .	Londonderry .	III.	249
24	Ballyguddin . .	230	0	38	Londonderry .	Keenaght . .	Dungiven . .	New Tn Limavady .	III.	236
38	Ballyguileataggle .	483	1	13	Limerick . .	Connello Upper .	Ballingarry . .	Croom . .	II.	230
38	Ballyguilebeg . .	95	0	32	Limerick . .	Connello Upper .	Ballingarry . .	Croom . .	II.	230
25, 31	Ballyguile Beg . .	249	0	18	Wicklow . .	Arklow . .	Kilpoole . .	Rathdrum . .	I.	345
25, 31	Ballyguile More .	398	0	16	Wicklow . .	Arklow . . .	Kilpoole . .	Rathdrum . .	I.	345
70	Ballyguin . .	114	1	12	Mayo . .	Carra . . .	Turlough . .	Castlebar . .	IV.	130
35	Ballyguiry . .	261	0	9	Waterford . .	Decies within Drum .	Ardmore . .	Dungarvan .	II.	349
30, 35	Ballyguiry East .	109	3	28	Waterford . .	Decies without Drum .	Dungarvan . .	Dungarvan .	II.	355
30, 35	Ballyguiry West .	316	2	27	Waterford . .	Decies without Drum .	Dungarvan . .	Dungarvan .	II.	355
45	Ballygulleen . .	422	0	2	Limerick . .	Glenquin . .	Mahoonagh . .	Newcastle .	II.	246
6	Ballygullen . .	378	1	22	Wexford . .	Gorey . .	Kilnahue . .	Gorey . .	I.	319
11	Ballygullen . .	171	0	27	Wexford . .	Gorey . . .	Liskinfere . .	Gorey . .	I.	320
47	Ballygullick . .	106	1	8	Wexford . .	Forth . . .	Ishartmon . .	Wexford . .	I.	309
20, 27	Ballygunaghan .	432	3	37	Down . .	Lower Iveagh Up. pt.	Donaghcloney . .	Lurgan . .	III.	169
114, 115	Ballygunneen . .	456	1	30	Galway . .	Loughrea . .	Killinan . . .	Loughrea . .	IV.	64

(a) Including 5A. 1R. 31P. water.   (c) Including 17A. 2R. 17P. water.   (d) Including 9A. 1R. 7P. water.
(b) Including 8A. 2R. 1P. water.

M 2

No. of Sheet of the Ordnance Survey Maps.	Townlands and Towns.	Area in Statute Acres.	County.	Barony.	Parish.	Poor Law Union in 1857.	Townland Census of 1851, Part I.	
		A. R. P.					Vol.	Page
18	Ballygunnercastle	282 3 25	Waterford	Gaultiere	Ballygunner	Waterford	II.	362
18	Ballygunnermore	654 2 18	Waterford	Gaultiere	Ballygunner	Waterford	II.	362
18	Ballygunnertemple	278 1 6	Waterford	Gaultiere	Ballygunner	Waterford	II.	362
47, 49	Ballygurk	178 3 38	Londonderry	Loughinsholin	Artrea	Magherafelt	III.	238
47, 48, 49	Ballygurk	160 0 30	Londonderry	Loughinsholin	Tamlaght	Magherafelt	III.	243
14	Ballyguy	199 1 35	Limerick	Clanwilliam	Abington	Limerick	II.	221
14	Ballyguy	29 1 34	Limerick	Clanwilliam	Clonkeen	Limerick	II.	223
9, 18	Ballyguyroe North	830 0 23	Cork, E.R.	Fermoy	Farahy	Mitchelstown	II.	79
18	Ballyguyroe South	339 2 34	Cork. E.R.	Fermoy	Farahy	Mitchelstown	II.	79
11	Ballyhack	80 2 16	Dublin	Nethercross	Kilsallaghan	Balrothery	I.	31
18	Ballyhack	59 2 21	Kilkenny	Crannagh	Ballycallan	Kilkenny	I.	84
44, 45	Ballyhack	341 3 17	Meath	Ratoath	Ratoath	Dunshaughlin	I.	219
38, 39	Ballyhack	142 2 8	Meath	Skreen	Kilmoon	Dunshaughlin	I.	221
44	Ballyhack	267 0 28	Wexford	Shelburne	St.James & Dunbrody	New Ross	I.	328
4	Ballyhackamore	417 3 8	Down	Castlereagh Lower	Holywood	Belfast	III.	162
4	BALLYHACKAMORE T.	—	Down	Castlereagh Lower	Holywood	Belfast	III.	163
45	Ballyhackbeg	234 2 37	Wexford	Shelburne	Tintern	New Ross	I.	329
2, 6	Ballyhacket Glena- horry	392 1 6	Londonderry	Coleraine	Dunboe	Coleraine	III.	231
6	Ballyhacket Lisa- willing	489 2 3	Londonderry	Coleraine	Dunboe	Coleraine	III.	231
3	Ballyhacket Lower	462 1 5	Carlow	Rathvilly	Kineagh	Baltinglass	I.	11
2, 6	Ballyhacket Magilli- gan	369 2 0	Londonderry	Coleraine	Dunboe	Coleraine	III.	231
35	Ballyhackett	341 2 31	Antrim	Upper Glenarm	Carncastle	Larne	III.	24
2, 6	Ballyhacket Tober- claw	89 2 36	Londonderry	Coleraine	Dunboe	Coleraine	III.	231
3	Ballyhacket Upper	268 1 16	Carlow	Rathvilly	Kineagh	Baltinglass	I.	11
44	BALLYHACK T.	— —	Wexford	Shelburne	St.James & Dunbrody	New Ross	I.	328
15, 16	Ballyhaddock	388 2 38	Wexford	Gorey	Ferns	Enniscorthy	I.	316
40	Ballyhade	287 3 18	Kildare	Kilkea and Moone	Castledermot	Carlow	I.	59
7, 10	Ballyhaden	147 1 18	Tipperary, N.R.	Lower Ormond	Borrisokane	Borrisokane	II.	282
30	Ballyhad Lower	259 1 30	Wicklow	Ballinacor North	Rathdrum	Rathdrum	I.	347
24, 30	Ballyhad Upper	209 0 2	Wicklow	Ballinacor North	Rathdrum	Rathdrum	I.	347
43, 49	Ballyhafry	380 1 18	Down	Upper Iveagh, Lr. pt.	Kilcoo	Kilkeel	III.	173
6, 11	Ballyhaft	283 1 17	Down	Ards Lower	Newtownards	Newtownards	III.	158
9	Ballyhagan	156 3 32	Armagh	Oneilland West	Kilmore	Armagh	III.	53
8	Ballyhagan	1,115 0 34	Kildare	Carbury	Carbury	Edenderry	I.	51
55	Ballyhaght	401 3 10	Limerick	Coshlea	Kilquane	Kilmallock	II.	240
37	Ballyhahil	497 3 25	Limerick	Connello Upper	Cloncagh	Newcastle	II.	231
18	Ballyhahill	605 3 24	Limerick	Shanid	Kilmoylan	Glin	II.	256
18	BALLYHAHILL T.	—	Limerick	Shanid	Kilmoylan	Glin	II.	256
16	BALLYHAISE T.	—	Cavan	Upper Loughtee	Castleterra	Cavan	III.	83
18	Ballyhalbert	648 2 1	Down	Ards Upper	St. Andrews, alias Ballyhalbert	Newtownards	III.	161
18	BALLYHALBERT T.	—	Down	Ards Upper	St. Andrews, alias Ballyhalbert	Newtownards	III.	161
55	Ballyhale	352 1 11	Galway	Clare	Cargin	Tuam	IV.	18
31, 32	Ballyhale	368 3 18	Kilkenny	Knocktopher	Derrynahinch	Thomastown	I.	111
31, 32	BALLYHALE T.	— —	Kilkenny	Knocktopher	Derrynahinch	Thomastown	I.	111
26, 30	Ballyhall	279 1 3	Kilkenny	Kells	Ballytobin	Callan	I.	107
44	Ballyhallaghan	266 0 35	Tyrone	Omagh East	Clogherny	Omagh	III.	310
16	Ballyhally	144 0 10	Cavan	Tullygarvey	Drung	Cootehill	III.	88
108	Ballyhalwick	576 1 39	Cork, W.R.	East Carbery (W.D.)	Fanlobbus	Dunmanway	II.	131
45, 51	Ballyhamage	394 3 23	Antrim	Upper Antrim	Kilbride	Antrim	III.	6
14	Ballyhamilton	163 1 35	Wexford	Scarawalsh	Templeshanbo	Enniscorthy	I.	326
28, 33	Ballyhamlet	247 1 39	Waterford	Coshmore and Cosh- bride	Kilwatermoy	Lismore	II.	343
29	Ballyhammon	127 1 36	Roscommon	Roscommon	Lissonuffy	Strokestown	IV.	211
40	Ballyhampton	222 2 8	Antrim	Upper Glenarm	Kilwaughter	Larne	III.	25
98, 112	Ballyhamsane	262 2 9	Cork, E.R.	Kinalea	Ballyfeard	Kinsale	II.	93
45	Ballyhamsherry	383 1 16	Cork, E.R.	Barrymore	Castlelyons	Fermoy	II.	53
124	Ballyhander	303 3 38	Cork, W.R.	Courceys	Ringrone	Kinsale	II.	147
28	Ballyhander	149 2 29	Waterford	Coshmore and Cosh- bride	Tallow	Lismore	II.	348
85, 97	Ballyhandle	398 0 7	Cork, E.R.	Kinalea	Knockavilly	Bandon	II.	96
25	Ballyhandy	74 3 36	Westmeath	Rathconrath	Dysart	Mullingar	I.	283
33	Ballyhane	362 2 16	Tipperary, N.R.	Upper Ormond	Kilnaneave	Nenagh	II.	291
21,22,29,30	Ballyhane	407 2 21	Waterford	Decies without Drum	Affane	Lismore	II.	353
22, 30	Ballyhane	133 0 33	Waterford	Decies without Drum	Whitechurch	Lismore	II.	361
24, 30	Ballyhanedin	1,032 0 32	Londonderry	Tirkeeran	Banagher	New Tⁿ Limavady	III.	247
50	Ballyhane East	109 3 2	Tipperary, N.R.	Kilnamanagh Upper	Toem	Tipperary	II.	280
1	Ballyhane Lower	360 0 1	Cork, E.R.	Orrery and Kilmore	Kilbolane	Kanturk	II.	108
1	Ballyhane Upper	167 0 5	Cork, E.R.	Orrery and Kilmore	Kilbolane	Kanturk	II.	108

No. of Sheet of the Ordnance Survey Maps.	Townlands and Towns.	Area in Statute Acres.			County.	Barony.	Parish.	Poor Law Union in 1857.	Townland Census of 1851, Part I.	
		A.	R.	P.					Vol.	Page
50	Ballyhane West	108	1	15	Tipperary, N.R.	Kilnamanagh Upper	Toem	Tipperary	II.	280
85	Ballyhank	318	3	25	Cork, E.R.	East Muskerry	Kilnaglory	Cork	II.	104
111	Ballyhankeen	373	3	11	Mayo	Clanmorris	Crossboyne	Claremorris	IV.	132
107	Ballyhanna	221	0	20a	Donegal	Tirhugh	Inishmacsaint	Ballyshannon	III.	147
6	Ballyhanna	432	3	37	Londonderry	Keenaght	Aghanloo	New Tᵒ Limavady	III.	233
34, 42	Ballyhannan North	184	3	3	Clare	Bunratty Upper	Quin	Ennis	II.	10
42	Ballyhannan South	221	0	24	Clare	Bunratty Upper	Quin	Ennis	II.	10
10	Ballyhannon	275	3	14	Armagh	Oneilland East	Seagoe	Lurgan	III.	50
48	Ballyhanruck	309	1	7b	Mayo	Tirawley	Kilbelfad	Ballina	IV.	167
117	Ballyhanry	137	0	23	Galway	Longford	Lickmolassy	Portumna	IV.	60
5, 10	Ballyhanwood	643	2	12c	Down	Castlereagh Lower	Comber	Newtownards	III.	161
58	Ballyhar	282	0	28	Kerry	Magunihy	Kilcredane	Killarney	II.	200
31	Ballyhara	123	2	26	Wicklow	Arklow	Drumkay	Rathdrum	I.	342
31, 36	Ballyhara	60	0	32	Wicklow	Arklow	Dunganstown	Rathdrum	I.	343
19	Ballyhard	621	0	36	Galway	Ballymoe	Boyounagh	Glennamaddy	IV.	6
24	Ballyharigan	773	3	0	Londonderry	Keenaght	Bovevagh	New Tᵒ Limavady	III.	235
32	Ballyharmon	158	3	26	Queen's Co.	Slievemargy	Killeshin	Carlow	I.	245
6	Ballyharney	577	1	29d	Westmeath	Corkaree	Lackan	Mullingar	I.	262
63, 74	Ballyharoon	178	1	32	Cork, E.R.	Cork	Rathcooney	Cork	II.	65
25	Ballyharraghan	104	1	21e	Clare	Inchiquin	Ruan	Corrofin	II.	28
36	Ballyharrahan	309	0	39	Waterford	Decies within Drum	Ringagonagh	Dungarvan	II.	352
37	Ballyharran Lower	117	3	30	Wexford	Shelmaliere East	Tikillin	Wexford	I.	331
37	Ballyharran Upper	156	3	13	Wexford	Shelmaliere East	Tikillin	Wexford	I.	331
41	Ballyharry	224	2	25	Antrim	Lower Belfast	Islandmagee	Larne	III.	8
6	Ballyharry	193	3	38	Down	Ards Lower	Newtownards	Newtownards	III.	158
51	Ballyhartfield	479	0	35	Antrim	Upper Belfast	Ballymartin	Antrim	III.	9
47, 52	Ballyharty	249	0	30	Wexford	Bargy	Kilmore	Wexford	I.	306
50, 55	Ballyharvey Lower	223	3	34	Antrim	Lower Massereene	Muckamore,Grange of	Antrim	III.	28
50, 55	Ballyharvey Upper	154	1	22	Antrim	Lower Massereene	Muckamore,Grange of	Antrim	III.	28
7	Ballyhaskin	349	1	17	Down	Ards Lower	Donaghadee	Newtownards	III.	157
46,47,54,55	Ballyhasky	314	0	1	Donegal	Raphoe	All Saints	Londonderry	III.	133
24	Ballyhass	247	0	18	Cork, E.R.	Duhallow	Castlemagner	Kanturk	II.	67
32	Ballyhast	517	3	10	Westmeath	Moycashel	Castletownkindalen	Mullingar	I.	277
41	Ballyhast	337	3	6	Wexford	Gorey	Liskinfere	Gorey	I.	320
10, 15	Ballyhasty	330	1	19	Tipperary, N.R.	Lower Ormond	Modreeny	Borrisokane	II.	286
31	Ballyhattan	102	3	16	Westmeath	Moycashel	Ardnurcher or Horseleap	Mullingar	I.	276
4, 7	Ballyhaugh	514	0	17	Tipperary, N.R.	Lower Ormond	Aglishcloghane	Borrisokane	II.	281
32	Ballyhaukish	110	2	31	Limerick	Smallcounty	Knockainy	Kilmallock	II.	260
93	BALLYHAUNIS T.	—			Mayo	Costello	Annagh Bekan	Claremorris	IV.	{138 {139
5	Ballyhavil	22	2	7	Dublin	Balrothery East	Lusk	Balrothery	I.	20
27, 28	Ballyhaw	227	0	32f	Westmeath	Farbill	Killucan	Mullingar	I.	266
2, 3, 7	Ballyhay	221	3	32	Cork, E.R.	Fermoy	Ballyhay	Mallow	II.	76
2, 6	Ballyhay	843	1	6g	Down	Ards Lower	Donaghadee	Newtownards	III.	157
14	Ballyhays	135	1	29h	Kildare	Naas North	Whitechurch	Naas	I.	63
43	Ballyheabought	743	0	7	Kerry	Corkaguiny	Dingle	Dingle	II.	175
25	Ballyheadon	212	2	4	Waterford	Middlethird	Dunhill	Kilmacthomas	II.	366
14	Ballyhealy or Ballinure	884	2	38	Westmeath	Delvin	Castletowndelvin	Castletowndelvin	I.	264
52	Ballyhealycastle	89	3	30	Wexford	Bargy	Kilturk	Wexford	I.	307
40	Ballyhealy or Hollybrook Demesne	285	2	6	Sligo	Tirerrill	Aghanagh	Boyle	IV.	237
52	Ballyhealy North	147	2	0	Wexford	Bargy	Kilturk	Wexford	I.	307
52	Ballyhealy South	133	3	37	Wexford	Bargy	Kilturk	Wexford	I.	307
79, 88	Ballyhearny East	194	3	12	Kerry	Iveragh	Valencia	Cahersiveen	II.	198
78,79,87,88	Ballyhearny West	346	3	4	Kerry	Iveragh	Valencia	Cahersiveen	II.	198
4, 11	Ballyheashill	601	2	20	King's Co.	Warrenstown	Ballymacwilliam	Edenderry	I.	144
2	Ballyheather	257	0	12i	Tyrone	Strabane Lower	Donaghedy	Strabane	III.	320
25	Ballyhee	210	2	11j	Clare	Bunratty Upper	Templemaley	Ennis	II.	10
14, 15	Ballyheean	136	1	23	Clare	Corcomroe	Kilmacrehy	Ennistimon	II.	20
97	Ballyheedy	263	3	6	Cork, E.R.	Kinalea	Ballinaboy	Kinsale	II.	93
37	Ballyheefy	243	3	16	Clare	Tulla Lower	Ogonnelloe	Scarriff	II.	38
37	Ballyheelan	89	1	22	Cavan	Clanmahon,	Ballymachugh	Cavan	III.	75
29	Ballyheen	156	0	19	Tipperary N.R.	Eliogarty	Templemore	Thurles	II.	272
23	Ballyheen Middle	142	3	30	Cork, E.R.	Duhallow	Kilbrin	Kanturk	II.	71
23	Ballyheen North	142	1	28	Cork, E.R.	Duhallow	Kilbrin	Kanturk	II.	71
61	Ballyheens	134	2	15	Tipperary S.R.	Middlethird	Ballysheehan	Cashel	II.	324
23	Ballyheen South	154	2	1	Cork, E.R.	Duhallow	Kilbrin	Kanturk	II.	71
37	Ballyheeny	381	3	7	Waterford	Decies within Drum	Clashmore	Youghal	II.	351
37	Ballyheeny	278	0	16	Waterford	Decies within Drum	Kinsalebeg	Youghal	II.	351
94, 104	Ballyheer	498	2	3k	Mayo	Murrisk	Kilgeever	Westport	IV.	161
119	Ballyheeragh (Caslane)	302	0	22l	Mayo	Kilmaine	Kilcommon	Ballinrobe	IV.	154

(a) Including 20A. 0R. 16P. water.
(b) Including 25A. 3R. 36P. water.
(c) Including 0A. 2R. 28P. water.
(d) Including 23A. 3R. 9P. water.

(e) Including 3A. 2R. 38P. water.
(f) Including 10A. 2R. 2P. detached portion.
(g) Including 2A. 0R. 10P. detached portions.
(h) Including 3A. 1R. 33P. water.

(i) Including 2A. 2R. 30P. water.
(j) Including 7A. 2R. 2P. water.
(k) Including 19A. 2R. 36P. detached portion.
(l) Including 6A. 0R. 18P. water.

No. of Sheet of the Ordnance Survey Maps.	Townlands and Towns.	Area in Statute Acres.	County.	Barony.	Parish.	Poor Law Union in 1857.	Townland Census of 1851, Part I.	
		A. R. P.					Vol.	Page
119	Ballyheeragh (*St. Leger*) . .	303 1 24	Mayo . .	Kilmaine . .	Kilcommon . .	Ballinrobe .	IV.	154
17	Ballyheerin . .	291 0 3	Donegal . .	Kilmacrenan . .	Clondavaddog .	Millford . .	III.	124
28	Ballyhegadon Glebe	166 3 27	Queen's Co. .	Clandonagh . .	Donaghmore .	Donaghmore .	I.	233
24	Ballyhegan . .	132 1 0	Carlow . .	St. Mullins Lower .	St. Mullins .	New Ross .	I.	13
3, 6	Ballyhehan . .	492 2 12	Clare . .	Burren . .	Abbey . .	Ballyvaghan .	II.	11
41, 42	Ballyheifer . .	317 3 21	Londonderry .	Loughinsholin .	Magherafelt .	Magherafelt .	III.	243
14	Ballyheige . .	351 2 26	Kerry . .	Clanmaurice .	Ballyheige .	Tralee . .	II.	167
33	Ballyheige . .	248 2 22	Wexford . .	Ballaghkeen .	Skreen . .	Wexford . .	I.	298
14	BALLYHEIGE T. .	—	Kerry . .	Clanmaurice .	Ballyheige .	Tralee . .	II.	168
87	Ballyhemiken . .	58 0 9	Cork, E.R. .	Kerrycurrihy .	Liscleary .	Cork . .	II.	92
15	Ballyhemikin . .	160 1 21	Kerry . .	Clanmaurice .	Kilmoyly .	Tralee . .	II.	171
7	Ballyhemlin . .	180 1 8	Antrim . .	Lower Dunluce .	Billy . .	Coleraine .	III.	16
18	Ballyhemlin . .	419 3 20	Down . .	Ards Upper .	St. Andrews *alias* Ballyhalbert .	Newtownards .	III.	161
19	Ballyhendricken, .	491 3 6	Kilkenny . .	Crannagh . .	Ballycallan .	Kilkenny .	I.	84
38, 39	Ballyhenebery .	463 3 16	Kilkenny . .	Iverk . .	Owning . .	Carrick on Suir	I.	106
38	Ballyhenebery .	85 2 12	Kilkenny . .	Iverk . .	Whitechurch .	Carrick on Suir	I.	107
75, 76	Ballyhenebery .	157 3 27	Tipperary, S.R.	Iffa and Offa West .	Caher . .	Clogheen .	II.	317
4, 8	Ballyhenna . .	387 1 32	Clare . .	Burren . .	Kilmoon .	Ballyvaghan .	II.	13
61	Ballyhennessy .	218 0 12	Clare . .	Bunratty Lower	Kilconry . .	Ennis . .	II.	4
61	Ballyhennessy .	142 1 25	Cork, E.R. .	East Muskerry .	Donaghmore, .	Macroom . .	II.	102
16	Ballyhennessy .	417 1 16	Kerry . .	Clanmaurice .	Dysert . .	Listowel .	II.	169
75	Ballyhennick . .	220 2 36	Cork. E.R. .	Barrymore .	Caherlag .	Cork . .	II.	52
86	Ballyhennigan .	166 1 22	Wexford . .	Shelmaliere West	Taghmon .	Wexford . .	I.	334
6	Ballyhenny . .	256 3 29	Down . .	Ards Lower .	Newtownards .	Newtownards .	III.	158
51, 52, 56	Ballyhenry .	642 3 38	Antrim . .	Lower Belfast .	Carnmoney .	Belfast . .	III.	7
24,25,31,32	Ballyhenry .	206 1 28	Down . .	Ards Upper .	Ardquin . .	Downpatrick .	III.	159
15, 21	Ballyhenry . .	93 3 30	Kerry . .	Clanmaurice .	Killahan . .	Tralee . .	II.	170
121	Ballyhenry . .	38 0 17	Mayo . .	Kilmaine . .	Kilmainemore .	Ballinrobe .	IV.	155
17	Ballyhenry . .	233 2 33	Tipperary, N.R.	Ikerrin . .	Bourney . .	Roscrea .	II.	274
19, 25	Ballyhenry . .	198 2 22	Wicklow . .	Newcastle .	Killiskey . .	Rathdrum .	I.	352
121, 122	Ballyhenry or Caraun	168 2 9	Mayo . .	Kilmaine . .	Kilmainebeg .	Ballinrobe .	IV.	155
5	Ballyhenry East .	282 3 18*d*	Londonderry .	Keenaght . .	Aghanloo .	New T^n Limavady	III.	233
31	*Ballyhenry Island* .	4 1 5	Down . .	Ards Upper .	Ardquin . .	Downpatrick .	III.	159
5, 10	Ballyhenry Major .	304 1 11	Down . .	Castlereagh Lower .	Comber . .	Newtownards .	III.	161
10	Ballyhenry Minor .	119 0 10	Down . .	Castlereagh Lower .	Comber . .	Newtownards .	III.	161
5, 9	Ballyhenry West .	287 0 16	Londonderry .	Keenaght . .	Tamlaghtfinlagan .	New T^n Limavady	III.	237
61	Ballyherberry . .	569 0 8	Tipperary, S.R.	Middlethird .	Ballysheehan .	Cashel . .	II.	324
12, 16	Ballyheridan .	332 2 22	Armagh . .	Armagh . .	Lisnadill . .	Armagh . .	III.	45
112	Ballyherkin Lower .	30 2 39	Cork, E.R. .	Kinalea . .	Nohaval . .	Kinsale .	II.	96
112	Ballyherkin Upper .	38 1 29	Cork, E.R. .	Kinalea . .	Nohaval . .	Kinsale .	II.	96
25, 32	Ballyherly . .	227 3 19*c*	Down . .	Ards Upper .	Ardquin . .	Downpatrick .	III.	159
14, 22	Ballyherragh . .	269 1 36	Clare . .	Corcomroe .	Kilmacrehy .	Ennistimon .	II.	20
86	Ballyherrig . .	121 2 25	Wicklow . .	Arklow . .	Dunganstown .	Rathdrum .	I.	343
7	Ballyhest . .	135 3 34	Waterford .	Upperthird .	Mothel . .	Carrick on Suir	II.	370
24	Ballyhest East .	55 2 32	Cork, E.R. .	Duhallow .	Kilbrin . .	Kanturk .	II.	71
23, 24	Ballyhest West .	88 1 2	Cork, E.R. .	Duhallow .	Kilbrin . .	Kanturk .	II.	71
52, 63	Ballyhesty . .	249 3 38	Cork, E.R. .	Cork . .	Dunbulloge .	Cork . .	II.	64
75	Ballyhetterick .	15 0 8	Cork, E.R. .	Barrymore .	Clonmel . .	Cork . .	II.	53
18	Ballyheyland . .	112 0 39	Queen's Co. .	Cullenagh .	Ballyroan .	Abbeyleix .	I.	239
18	Ballyheyland . .	431 2 21	Queen's Co. .	Cullenagh .	Kilcolmanbane .	Abbeyleix .	I.	240
20	Ballyhibbin . .	108 1 31	Limerick . .	Connello Lower .	Nantinan .	Rathkeale .	II.	229
7, 12	Ballyhibistock Lower	157 3 23	Antrim . .	Lower Dunluce .	Derrykeighan .	Ballymoney .	III.	16
7, 12	Ballyhibistock Upper	133 0 23	Antrim . .	Lower Dunluce .	Derrykeighan .	Ballymoney .	III.	16
34	Ballyhickey . .	385 2 20	Clare . .	Bunratty Upper .	Clooney . .	Tulla . .	II.	7
82	Ballyhickey . .	103 1 21	Tipperary, S.R.	Iffa and Offa West .	Rochestown .	Clogheen .	II.	319
37	Ballyhide . .	487 0 10	Queen's Co. .	Slievemargy .	Killeshin .	Carlow . .	I.	245
8	Ballyhiernan . .	825 1 37*d*	Donegal . .	Kilmacrenan .	Clondavaddog .	Millford . .	III.	124
39	Ballyhiernaun .	274 2 38	Mayo . .	Tirawley .	Ballynahaglish .	Ballina . .	IV.	164
136	Ballyhigeen . .	57 0 11	Cork, W.R. .	Ibane and Barryroe .	Lislee . .	Clonakilty .	II.	150
27	Ballyhigh . .	89 3 29	Wexford . .	Ballaghkeen .	Meelnagh .	Gorey . .	I.	297
18, 19	Ballyhighland .	874 2 7	Wexford . .	Bantry . .	Rossdroit .	Enniscorthy .	I.	301
53	Ballyhiho . .	81 2 31	Wexford . .	Forth . .	Tacumshin .	Wexford . .	I.	314
47, 53	Ballyhill . .	860 2 24	Antrim . .	Lower Belfast .	Kilroot . .	Larne . .	III.	9
23	Ballyhill . .	45 2 38	Fermanagh .	Magherastephana .	Aghavea . .	Lisnaskea .	III.	218
55,56,59,60	Ballyhill Lower .	579 0 1	Antrim . .	Lower Massereene .	Killead . .	Antrim . .	III.	28
42, 51	Ballyhilloge . .	954 0 22	Cork, E.R. .	Barretts . .	Grenagh . .	Cork . .	II.	49
55, 56	Ballyhill Upper .	403 3 16	Antrim . .	Lower Massereene .	Killead . .	Antrim . .	III.	28
77, 89	Ballyhimilcin .	318 1 11	Cork, E.R. .	Imokilly . .	Garryvoe .	Middleton .	II.	86
14, 20	Ballyhimilcin .	445 0 22	Tipperary, N.R.	Lower Ormond .	Monsea . .	Nenagh . .	II.	287
76	Ballyhimilcin .	279 1 20	Tipperary, S.R.	Iffa and Offa East .	Newchapel .	Clonmel . .	II.	313
5, 10	Ballyhimmin . .	347 0 0	Kilkenny . .	Fassadinin .	Kilmacar .	Castlecomer .	I.	90

No. of Sheet of the Ordnance Survey Maps.	Townlands and Towns.	Area in Statute Acres.	County.	Barony.	Parish.	Poor Law Union in 1857.	Townland Census of 1851, Part I.
		A. R. P.					Vol. Page
35, 39	Ballyhimmin . .	239 1 19	Kilkenny . .	Knocktopher . .	Killahy . . .	Waterford .	I. 112
26	Ballyhimock . .	351 2 14	Cork, E.R. .	Fermoy . . .	Castletownroche .	Fermoy . .	II. 77
134	Ballyhinch . .	718 0 36	Galway . .	Leitrim . . .	Clonrush . .	Scariff .	IV. 52
27	Ballyhindon . .	264 3 3	Cork, E.R. .	Fermoy . . .	Kilcrumper . .	Fermoy . .	II. 80
82	Ballyhine . .	206 3 13	Mayo . .	Costello . . .	Aghamore . .	Swineford .	IV. 136
37	Ballyhine . .	141 2 10	Wexford . .	Shelmaliere West .	Kilbrideglynn . .	Wexford . .	I. 334
39, 47	Ballyhinnaught .	455 2 37	Limerick . .	Connello Upper .	Bruree . .	Kilmallock .	II. 231
28	Ballyhinode . .	93 3 5	Queen's Co. .	Clarmallagh . .	Aghaboe . . .	Donaghmore .	I. 235
48	Ballyhire . .	178 0 17	Wexford . .	Forth . . .	St. Helens . .	Wexford . .	I. 313
20, 26	Ballyhisky . .	193 2 39	Tipperary, N.R.	Owney and Arra .	Burgesbeg . .	Nenagh . .	II. 293
10, 16	Ballyhist . .	509 3 21	Meath . .	Upper Kells . .	Kilskeer . .	Kells . .	I. 206
87	Ballyhist . .	124 3 24	Tipperary, S.R.	Iffa and Offa West .	Ballybacon . .	Clogheen . .	II. 317
87	Ballyhistbeg .	110 3 31	Tipperary, S.R.	Iffa and Offa West .	Tullaghorton . .	Clogheen . .	II. 321
37	Ballyhit . . .	38 3 0	Wexford . .	Shelmaliere West .	Kilbrideglynn . .	Wexford . .	I. 334
48	Ballyhitt . .	86 1 11	Wexford . .	Forth . . .	Ladysisland . .	Wexford . .	I. 311
67	Ballyhobert . .	316 3 21	Cork, E.R. .	Imokilly . . .	Youghal . . .	Youghal . .	II. 90
23	Ballyhobin . .	265 0 24	Limerick . .	Clanwilliam . .	Ballybrood . .	Limerick . .	II. 221
41, 44	Ballyhobuck . .	281 2 24	Kilkenny . .	Ida	Kilcolumb . .	Waterford .	I. 102
3	Ballyhoe . . .	410 0 12a	Meath . .	Lower Slane . .	Drumconrath . .	Ardee . .	I. 222
98	Ballyhogan . .	349 0 8	Galway . .	Leitrim . . .	Abbeygormacan .	Loughrea . .	IV. 50
14	Ballyhogan . .	344 0 30	Tipperary, N.R.	Lower Ormond .	Knigh . . .	Nenagh . .	II. 285
20	Ballyhogan . .	189 0 21	Tipperary, N.R.	Owney and Arra .	Burgesbeg . .	Nenagh . .	II. 293
31, 32	Ballyhoge . .	1,489 1 26	Wexford . .	Shelmaliere West .	Ballyhoge . .	Enniscorthy .	I. 332
81	Ballyhohan . .	146 3 4	Tipperary, S.R.	Iffa and Offa West .	Tubbrid . . .	Clogheen . .	II. 320
65	Ballyholahan East .	424 0 36	Tipperary, S.R.	Clanwilliam . .	Emly . . .	Tipperary . .	II. 307
65	Ballyholahan West .	242 3 28	Tipperary, S.R.	Clanwilliam . .	Emly . . .	Tipperary . .	II. 307
29	Ballyholan . .	339 3 4	Sligo . . .	Tireragh . . .	Kilmoremoy . .	Ballina . .	IV. 235
62	Ballyholey Far .	622 0 33	Donegal . .	Raphoe . . .	Raphoe . . .	Letterkenny .	III. 140
62	Ballyholey Near .	197 1 28	Donegal . .	Raphoe . . .	Raphoe . . .	Strabane . .	III. 140
16	Ballyhollaghan .	67 3 28	Roscommon .	Frenchpark . .	Creeve . . .	Car*k*. on Shannon	IV. 203
46, 47, 50, 51	Ballyholland Lower	291 3 13	Down . .	Lordship of Newry .	Newry . . .	Newry . .	III. 182
50, 51	Ballyholland Upper	363 3 28	Down . .	Lordship of Newry .	Newry . . .	Newry . .	III. 182
23	Ballyholly . .	981 3 13	Londonderry .	Tirkeeran . .	Cumber Upper .	New T*n*Limavady	III. 249
2	Ballyholme . .	325 3 30	Down . .	Ards Lower . .	Bangor . . .	Newtownards .	III. 157
6	Ballyhome . .	516 2 0	Antrim . .	Lower Dunluce .	Dunluce . . .	Coleraine . .	III. 17
11	Ballyhomin . .	345 1 23	Limerick . .	Connello Lower .	Askeaton . .	Rathkeale .	II. 226
20	Ballyhomock . .	223 2 12	Limerick . .	Connello Lower .	Nantinan . .	Rathkeale .	II. 229
14	Ballyhomra . .	432 3 20	Down . .	Lower Iveagh, Upper part . . .	Ida	Hillsborough .	III. 169
40, 43	Ballyhomuck . .	385 3 26	Kilkenny . .	Ida	Dunkitt . .	Waterford .	I. 101
63, 71	Ballyhomuck . .	345 1 17	Tipperary, S.R.	Middlethird . .	Cloneen . .	Cashel . .	II. 325
9	Ballyhomulta . .	155 0 31	Clare . .	Corcomroe . .	Kilfenora . .	Ennistimon .	II. 18
40, 46	Ballyhone . .	468 3 38	Antrim . .	Lower Belfast . .	Glynn . . .	Larne . .	III. 8
65	Ballyhone . .	308 0 4	Tipperary, S.R.	Clanwilliam . .	Emly . . .	Tipperary . .	II. 307
35, 44	Ballyhoneen . .	1,100 3 36b	Kerry . .	Corkaguiny . .	Ballyduff . .	Dingle . .	II. 174
77	Ballyhonock . .	347 3 34c	Cork, E.R. .	Imokilly . . .	Ightermurragh .	Middleton . .	II. 87
78	Ballyhonock . .	106 0 10	Cork, E.R. .	Imokilly . . .	Kilmacdonogh .	Youghal . .	II. 88
17	Ballyhoo . .	300 1 31	Waterford .	Gaultiere . .	Kilbarry . . .	Waterford .	II. 363
23	Ballyhoodane . .	305 1 28	Limerick . .	Clanwilliam . .	Inch St. Lawrence .	Limerick . .	II. 224
88, 100	Ballyhook . .	439 1 25	Cork, E.R. .	Imokilly . . .	Corkbeg . .	Middleton . .	II. 86
20, 21	Ballyhook . .	209 3 15	Wicklow . .	Upper Talbotstown .	Rathbran . .	Baltinglass .	I. 365
21	Ballyhook Demesne	200 1 25	Wicklow . .	Upper Talbotstown .	Rathbran . .	Baltinglass .	I. 365
21	Ballyhook Hill .	271 0 24	Wicklow . .	Upper Talbotstown .	Rathbran . .	Baltinglass .	I. 365
99	Ballyhoolahan . .	61 0 24	Galway . .	Clonmacnowen .	Aughrim . .	Ballinasloe .	IV. 24
17	Ballyhoolahan . . .	106 2 15	Limerick . .	Shanid . . .	Loghill . . .	Glin . .	II. 256
22	Ballyhoolahan East .	235 3 39	Cork, E.R. .	Duhallow . .	Kilmeen . .	Kanturk . .	II. 72
22	Ballyhoolahan Middle	418 2 5	Cork, E.R. .	Duhallow . .	Kilmeen . .	Kanturk . .	II. 72
22, 30	Ballyhoolahan West	694 0 27	Cork, E.R. .	Duhallow . .	Kilmeen . .	Kanturk . .	II. 72
85, 97	Ballyhooleen . .	614 2 7	Cork, E.R. .	East Muskerry .	Ballinaboy . .	Cork . .	II. 101
14	Ballyhoolivan . .	177 2 24	Longford . .	Granard . .	Killoe . . .	Granard . .	I. 157
26, 34	Ballyhooly North .	585 1 21d	Cork, E.R. .	Fermoy . . .	Ballyhooly . .	Fermoy . .	II. 76
26, 27, 34, 35	Ballyhooly South .	1,176 1 9e	Cork, E.R. .	Fermoy . . .	Ballyhooly . .	Fermoy . .	II. 76
34, 35	BALLYHOOLY T. .	—	Cork, E.R. .	Fermoy . . .	Ballyhooly . .	Fermoy . .	II. 76
100	Ballyhoose . .	283 1 20	Galway . .	Longford . .	Clonfert . .	Ballinasloe .	IV. 56
16	Ballyhorahan . .	207 1 11	Queen's Co. .	Upperwoods . .	Offerlane . .	Mountmellick .	I. 251
11	Ballyhoreen . .	213 2 0	Westmeath .	Moygoish . .	Kilbixy . . .	Mullingar .	I. 279
9	Ballyhorgan . .	296 3 13	Kerry . .	Clanmaurice . .	Rattoo . . .	Listowel . .	II. 173
16	Ballyhorgan East .	510 1 13	Kerry . .	Clanmaurice . .	Dysert . . .	Listowel . .	II. 169
9	Ballyhorgan Marshes	137 1 9	Kerry . .	Clanmaurice . .	Rattoo . . .	Listowel . .	II. 173
16	Ballyhorgan South .	266 1 14	Kerry . .	Clanmaurice . .	Dysert . . .	Listowel . .	II. 169
16	Ballyhorgan West .	225 3 38	Kerry . .	Clanmaurice . .	Dysert . . .	Listowel . .	II. 169
17	Ballyhork . .	243 2 13f	Donegal . .	Kilmacrenan . .	Clondavaddog . .	Millford . .	III. 124
38, 39	Ballyhornan . .	330 1 17	Down . .	Lecale Lower . .	Dunsfort . . .	Downpatrick .	III. 179

No. of Sheet of the Ordnance Survey Maps.	Townlands and Towns.	Area in Statute Acres.	County.	Barony.	Parish.	Poor Law Union in 1857.	Townland Census of 1851, Part I.	
		A. R. P.					Vol.	Page
38, 39	BALLYHORNAN T. .	—	Down . .	Lecale Lower . .	Dunsfort . . .	Downpatrick .	III.	179
12, 13	Ballyhorsey . .	55 1 22	Wicklow . .	Newcastle . .	Kilcoole . . .	Rathdrum . .	I.	351
15, 21	Ballyhose . .	210 1 4	Fermanagh .	Magheraboy . .	Devenish . .	Enniskillen .	III.	210
38, 45	Ballyhosset . .	363 0 17	Down . .	Lecale Lower .	Ballee . . .	Downpatrick .	III.	178
38, 45	Ballyhosset Milltown	294 0 36	Down . .	Lecale Lower . .	Ballee . . .	Downpatrick .	III.	178
48	Ballyhote . .	82 3 17	Wexford . .	Forth . . .	Kilrane . .	Wexford . .	I.	311
27	Ballyhought . .	23 2 8	Wexford . .	Ballaghkeen . .	Castle-ellis .	Enniscorthy .	I.	293
134	Ballyhoulahan .	77 2 27	Cork, W.R. .	East Carbery (W.D.)	Ross . . .	Clonakilty .	II.	135
7, 17	Ballyhoura . .	838 0 32	Cork, E.R. .	Fermoy . .	Imphrick . .	Mallow . .	II.	80
31, 32	Ballyhourigan .	514 1 35	Tipperary, N.R. .	Owney and Arra .	Killoscully . .	Nenagh . .	II.	295
18	Ballyhourode . .	107 2 38	Cork, E.R. .	Fermoy . . .	Templeroan .	Mallow . .	II.	82
26	Ballyhow . .	80 2 37	Tipperary, N.R. .	Upper Ormond .	Kilmore . .	Nenagh . .	II.	290
33	Ballyhow Beg .	74 0 5	Wexford . .	Shelmaliere East	Skreen . . .	Wexford . .	I.	331
33	Ballyhow Lower .	110 1 30	Wexford . .	Shelmaliere Eat .	Skreen . . .	Wexford . .	I.	331
92	Ballyhowly . .	242 2 12	Mayo . .	Clanmorris . .	Knock . . .	Claremorris .	IV.	135
33	Ballyhow Middle .	151 2 19	Wexford . .	Shelmaliere East .	Skreen . .	Wexford . .	I.	331
51	Ballyhowne . .	282 1 13	Antrim . .	Lower Belfast .	Ballylinny .	Antrim . .	III.	7
52	Ballyhowne . .	583 0 14	Antrim . .	Lower Belfast .	Carnmoney .	Belfast . .	III.	7
15	Ballyhoy . .	60 2 13	Dublin . .	Coolock . .	Raheny . .	Dublin North .	I.	28
12	Ballyhoy or Bally- coffey . . .	241 2 13	Armagh . .	Armagh . . .	Lisnadill . .	Armagh . .	III.	45
2	Ballyhubbo . .	114 3 12	Cork, E.R. .	Orrery and Kilmore	Rathgoggan . .	Kilmallock .	II.	109
21	Ballyhubbock . .	156 0 22	Wexford . .	Ballaghkeen . .	Kilmuckridge .	Gorey . .	I.	296
21	Ballyhubbock . .	26 1 39	Wexford . .	Ballaghkeen . .	Meelnagh . .	Enniscorthy .	I.	297
21	Ballyhubbock Lower	145 3 13	Wicklow . .	Upper Talbotstown .	Donaghmore . .	Baltinglass .	I.	362
21, 27	Ballyhubbock Upper	244 0 9	Wicklow . .	Upper Talbotstown .	Donaghmore . .	Baltinglass .	I.	363
16	Ballyhubbock or Up- ton . . .	260 2 14	Carlow . .	Idrone East . .	Fennagh . .	Carlow . .	I.	7
29, 30	Ballyhubert . .	327 2 21	Roscommon .	Roscommon . .	Lissonuffy . .	Strokestown .	IV.	211
47	Ballyhudda . .	142 3 38	Tipperary, N.R. .	Eliogarty . .	Moycarky . .	Thurles . .	II.	271
11	Ballyhug . .	350 2 39	Westmeath .	Moygoish . .	Kilbixy . .	Mullingar .	I.	279
14	Ballyhugh . .	333 2 8a	Cavan . .	Lower Loughtee .	Drumlane . .	Cavan . .	III.	79
122, 128	Ballyhugh . .	311 0 10	Galway . .	Kiltartan . .	Kilmacduagh .	Gort . .	IV.	47
10, 11, 19	Ballyhugh . .	396 0 8	King's Co. .	Coolestown . .	Monasteroris .	Edenderry .	I.	133
53, 54	Ballyhugh . .	31 2 9	Roscommon .	Moycarn . .	Creagh . .	Ballinasloe .	IV.	206
11, 19	Ballyhugh or Spring- field . .	185 2 22	King's Co. .	Coolestown . .	Ballynakill . .	Edenderry .	I.	132
34	Ballyhullagh .	261 1 9	Fermanagh .	Clankelly . .	Galloon . . .	Lisnaskea .	III.	198
112	Ballyhullen Keague	47 3 28	Cork, E.R. .	Kinalea . . .	Nohaval . .	Kinsale . .	II.	96
7	Ballyhunsley North .	110 1 20	Antrim . .	Lower Dunluce .	Dunluce . .	Coleraine . .	III.	17
7, 12	Ballyhunsley South .	220 0 29	Antrim . .	Lower Dunluce .	Dunluce . .	Coleraine . .	III.	17
7	Ballyhuppahane .	1,203 2 30	Queen's Co. .	Tinnahinch . .	Rosenallis . .	Mountmellick .	I.	250
29	Ballyhurly . .	225 2 26	Clare . .	Tulla Lower . .	Ogonnelloe .	Scarriff . .	II.	38
80	Ballyhurrow . .	1,118 2 5	Tipperary, S.R. .	Iffa and Offa West .	Shanrahan . .	Clogheen . .	II.	319
24	Ballyhurst . .	51 0 21	Limerick . .	Coonagh . .	Ballynaclogh . .	Tipperary .	II.	233
14	Ballyhurtim . .	112 3 32	Wicklow . .	Upper Talbotstown .	Rathsallagh .	Baltinglass .	I.	365
15, 16	Ballyhussa . .	616 0 35	Waterford .	Decies without Drum	Rossmire . .	Kilmacthomas .	II.	359
41	Ballyhust . .	220 2 17	Wexford . .	Shelmaliere West .	Coolstuff . .	Wexford . .	I.	333
59, 67	Ballyhusty . .	511 3 1	Tipperary, S.R. .	Clanwilliam . .	Templenoe . .	Tipperary .	II.	311
136	Ballyhutch . .	55 1 20	Cork, W.R. .	Ibane and Barryroe .	Lislee . .	Clonakilty .	II.	150
27	Ballyhutherland .	362 0 6	Antrim . .	Kilconway . .	Grange of Dundermot	Ballymena .	III.	26
52	Ballyickeen . .	172 3 20	Kerry . .	Corkaguiny . .	Dunquin . . .	Dingle . .	II.	176
52	Ballyickeen Com- mons . .	25 0 4	Kerry . .	Corkaguiny . .	Dunquin . . .	Dingle . .	II.	176
138	Ballyieragh . .	578 2 11	Cork, W.R. .	West Carbery (W.D.)	Kilcrohane . .	Bantry . .	II.	143
153	Ballyieragh North .	240 1 13b	Cork, W.R. .	West Carbery (E.D.)	Clear-island . .	Skibbereen .	II.	138
153	Ballyieragh South .	202 1 39	Cork, W.R. .	West Carbery (E.D.)	Clear-island . .	Skibbereen .	II.	138
32	Ballyillaun . .	491 0 10c	Clare . .	Islands . . .	Kilmaley . .	Ennis . .	II.	31
22	Ballyine . .	476 0 4	Carlow . .	St. Mullins Lower .	Ullard . . .	New Ross .	I.	13
27,28,35,36	Ballyine . . .	874 0 2	Limerick . .	Shanid . . .	Ardagh . . .	Newcastle .	II.	254
20, 21	Ballyin Lower .	305 0 38d	Waterford .	Coshmore and Cosh- bride . . .	Lismore and Mocollop	Lismore . .	II.	344
8	Ballyinsheen Beg .	157 2 21	Clare . .	Burren . . .	Kilmoon . . .	Ballyvaghan .	II.	13
8	Ballyinsheen More .	173 1 29	Clare . .	Burren . . .	Kilmoon . . .	Ballyvaghan .	II.	13
20, 21	Ballyin Upper .	159 1 7	Waterford .	Coshmore and Cosh- bride . . .	Lismore and Mocollop	Lismore . .	II.	344
65	Ballyiriston . .	621 3 21	Donegal . .	Boylagh . . .	Inishkeel . .	Glenties . .	III.	112
150	Ballyisland . .	101 2 28	Cork, W.R. .	West Carbery (E.D.)	Creagh . .	Skibbereen .	II.	138
38	BALLYJAMESDUFF T.	—	Cavan . .	Castlerahan . .	Castlerahan . .	Oldcastle .	III.	67
118	Ballyjennings .	218 0 14	Mayo . .	Kilmaine . .	Kilmainemore . .	Ballinrobe .	IV.	155
25	Ballyjohnboy . .	113 1 19	Kilkenny . .	Gowran . . .	Ullard . . .	Thomastown .	I.	100
11, 12	Ballykale . .	268 0 34	Wexford . .	Ballaghkeen . .	Kilmakilloge .	Gorey . .	I.	296
5, 8	Ballykea . . .	420 1 9e	Dublin . .	Balrothery East .	Lusk . . .	Balrothery .	I.	20
43	Ballykeaghra . .	282 1 33	Galway . .	Clare . . .	Cummer . . .	Tuam . .	IV.	18

(a) Including 8A. 2R. 4P. water.
(b) Including 11A. 1R. 23P. Lough Errul.

(c) Including 16A. 2R. 39P. water.
(d) Including 14A. 2R. 16P. water.

(e) Including 13A. 3R. 14P. detached portion.

No. of Sheet of the Ordnance Survey Maps.	Townlands and Towns.	Area in Statute Acres.			County.	Barony.	Parish.	Poor Law Union in 1857.	Townland Census of 1851. Part I.	
		A.	R.	P.					Vol.	Page
13, 17	Ballykealey	106	1	5d	Carlow	Forth	Ballyellin	Carlow	I.	4
13	Ballykealey	212	3	1b	Carlow	Forth	Fennagh	Carlow	I.	4
13, 17	Ballykealey	326	3	10c	Carlow	Forth	Kellistown	Carlow	I.	4
14	Ballykealy	172	0	6	Kerry	Clanmaurice	Kilmoyly	Tralee	II.	171
30	Ballykealy	293	1	14	King's Co.	Eglish	Eglish	Parsonstown	I.	134
28	Ballykealy	83	0	4	Limerick	Shanid	Rathronan	Glin	II.	257
35	Ballykealy	768	1	15	Queen's Co.	Clarmallagh	Aghmacart	Abbeyleix	I.	236
35	Ballykealy	48	3	32	Queen's Co.	Clarmallagh	Aharney	Abbeyleix	I.	236
26	Ballykean	899	0	38	King's Co.	Upper Philipstown	Ballykean	Mountmellick	I.	143
35	Ballykean (Annesley)	260	2	28	Wicklow	Arklow	Redcross	Rathdrum	I.	346
30, 35, 36	Ballykean (Penrose)	375	2	22	Wicklow	Arklow	Redcross	Rathdrum	I.	346
35	Ballykean (Stringer)	190	1	29	Wicklow	Arklow	Redcross	Rathdrum	I.	346
19	Ballykearney	225	1	31	Cork, E.R.	Condons &Clangibbon	Killgulane	Mitchelstown	II.	61
26, 27	Ballykeating	437	2	27	Cork, E.R.	Fermoy	Glanworth	Fermoy	II.	79
22	Ballykeefe	14	0	3	Kilkenny	Crannagh	Kilmanagh	Callan	I.	86
22	Ballykeefe	213	0	39	Kilkenny	Crannagh	Tullaghanbrogue	Callan	I.	87
5, 13	Ballykeefe	546	3	2	Limerick	Pubblebrien	Mungret	Limerick	II.	253
22	Ballykeefe Bog	306	1	11	Kilkenny	Crannagh	Killaloe	Callan	I.	86
22	Ballykeefecastle	293	2	34	Kilkenny	Crannagh	Tullaghanbrogue	Callan	I.	87
22	Ballykeefe Hill	230	3	22	Kilkenny	Crannagh	Tullaghanbrogue	Callan	I.	87
32,33,37,38	Ballykeel	594	3	24	Antrim	Lower Antrim	Ballyclug	Ballymena	III.	3
47	Ballykeel	381	3	20	Antrim	Lower Belfast	Islandmagee	Larne	III.	8
2, 6	Ballykeel	214	3	28	Antrim	Lower Dunluce	Dunluce	Coleraine	III.	17
40	Ballykeel	414	1	5d	Antrim	Upper Glenarm	Kilwaughter	Larne	III.	25
66	Ballykeel	220	1	36	Antrim	Upper Massereene	Aghagallon	Lurgan	III.	29
28	Ballykeel	156	3	12	Armagh	Orior Upper	Forkhill	Newry	III.	57
9, 10	Ballykeel	589	0	9	Down	Castlereagh Lower	Comber	Newtownards	III.	161
1, 5	Ballykeel	685	0	33	Down	Castlereagh Lower	Holywood	Belfast	III.	162
10, 16	Ballykeel	703	2	39	Down	Castlereagh Lower	Kilmood	Newtownards	III.	163
37	Ballykeel	308	1	33c	Down	Lecale Upper	Down	Downpatrick	III.	180
21, 22	Ballykeel	1,112	1	18f	Down	Lower Iveagh, Lr. pt.	Dromore	Lisburn	III.	168
26, 27	Ballykeel	319	3	38	Down	Lower Iveagh, Lr. pt.	Seapatrick	Banbridge	III.	169
20	Ballykeel	303	0	27g	Down	Lower Iveagh,Up. pt.	Magheralin	Lurgan	III.	170
56	Ballykeel	912	3	37	Down	Mourne	Kilkeel	Kilkeel	III.	182
42, 48	Ballykeel	567	3	20	Down	Upper Iveagh, Lr. pt	Clonduff	Newry	III.	171
41, 47	Ballykeel	575	1	30	Down	Upper Iveagh, Up.pt.	Drumgath	Newry	III.	175
44	Ballykeel	328	0	0	Tyrone	Omagh East	Clogherny	Omagh	III.	310
17,18,25,26	Ballykeel	442	0	37h	Tyrone	Strabane Upper	Cappagh	Omagh	III.	325
4, 9	Ballykeelan	136	2	7	Kildare	Ikeathy and Oughterany	Cloncurry	Celbridge	I.	56
14, 21	Ballykeel Artifinny	640	0	7i	Down	Lower Iveagh,Up. pt.	Hillsborough	Lisburn	III.	169
53, 63	Ballykeelaun	264	3	2	Clare	Bunratty Lower	St. Patricks	Limerick	II.	6
14	Ballykeel Edenagonnell	240	1	18	Down	Lower Iveagh, Up.pt.	Blaris	Lisburn	III.	169
14, 21	Ballykeel Edenagonnell	221	2	29	Down	Lower Iveagh,Up. pt.	Hillsborough	Lisburn	III.	169
15, 22	Ballykeel Lougherne	578	2	22j	Down	Lower Iveagh, Lr. pt.	Annahilt	Lisburn	III.	167
9	Ballykeel North	592	1	8	Clare	Corcomroe	Kilfenora	Ennistimon	II.	18
9, 16	Ballykeel South	424	3	8	Clare	Corcomroe	Kilfenora	Ennistimon	II.	18
9	Ballykeen	160	2	24	Londonderry	Keenaght	Tamlaght Finlagan	New T. Limavady	III.	237
16	Ballykeenaghan	357	3	19	King's Co.	Ballycowan	Rahan	Tullamore	I.	128
17	Ballykeenan	351	0	0	Carlow	Forth	Barragh	Carlow	I.	4
22, 24	Ballykeenan	361	3	32	Carlow	St. Mullins Lower	Ullard	New Ross	I.	13
45	Ballykeeran	801	1	3	Donegal	Kilmacrenan	Kilmacrenan	Millford	III.	128
97	Ballykeeran	331	3	35	Galway	Longhrea	Lickerrig	Loughrea	IV.	65
22, 29	Ballykeeran	415	1	36	Westmeath	Brawny	St. Mary's	Athlone	I.	259
39	Ballykeeroge	271	2	39	Wexford	Shelburne	Kilmokea	New Ross	I.	327
39	Ballykeerogebeg	422	2	39	Wexford	Shelburne	Kilmokea	New Ross	I.	327
39	Ballykeecrogemore	759	1	9	Wexford	Shelburne	Ballybrazil	New Ross	I.	327
5, 6, 10, 11	Ballykeery	940	3	7	Tyrone	Strabane Lower	Donaghedy	Strabane	III.	320
22	Ballykeevan	81	2	4	Queen's Co.	Clandonagh	Aghaboe	Donaghmore	I.	232
6	Ballykeevican	35	2	24	Roscommon	Boyle	Kilbryan	Boyle	IV.	195
50	Ballykeevin	346	0	28	Tipperary, S.R.	Clanwilliam	Solloghodmore	Tipperary	II.	311
50	Ballykeevin	65	0	37	Tipperary, S.R.	Clanwilliam	Toem	Tipperary	II.	312
63	Ballykelly	315	2	6	Antrim	Upper Massereene	Ballinderry	Lisburn	III.	29
43, 44	Ballykelly	821	2	5	Clare	Tulla Lower	Kilseily	Limerick	II.	36
27	Ballykelly	414	3	21	Down	Lower Iveagh, Lr. pt.	Seapatrick	Banbridge	III.	169
21	Ballykelly	391	1	24	Kildare	Offaly West	Lackagh	Athy	I.	73
36, 37	Ballykelly	136	2	30	King's Co.	Ballybritt	Letterluna	Parsonstown	I.	126
9	Ballykelly	365	2	31	Londonderry	Keenaght	Tamlaght Finlagan	New T. Limavady	III.	237
18	Ballykelly	803	2	34	Tipperary, N.R.	Ikerrin	Bourney	Roscrea	II.	274
53	Ballykelly	243	0	6	Tipperary, S.R.	Middlethird	Ballysheehan	Cashel	II.	324
26	Ballykelly	370	3	9	Wexford	Ballaghkeen	Kilmallock	Enniscorthy	I.	296

(a) Including 44A. 1R. 16P. detached portion.
(b) Including 6A. 1R. 21P. water.
(c) Including 0A. 0R. 37P. water.
(d) Including 6A. 0R. 36P. water.

(e) Including 1A. 3R. 24P. water.
(f) Including 45A. 3R. 31P. water.
(g) Including 7A. 2R. 6P. water.

(h) Including 4A. 2R. 32P. water.
(i) Including 9A. 1R. 18P. water.
(j) Including 36A. 0R. 32P. water.

N

No. of Sheet of the Ordnance Survey Maps.	Townlands and Towns.	Area in Statute Acres.	County.	Barony.	Parish.	Poor Law Union in 1857.	Townland Census of 1851, Part I.	
		A. R. P.					Vol.	Page
42	Ballykelly . .	152 1 31	Wexford . .	Forth . . .	Killiane . . .	Wexford . .	I.	310
34	Ballykelly . .	2 3 38	Wexford . .	Shelburne . .	Ballybrazil . .	New Ross . .	I.	327
34, 39	Ballykelly . .	607 2 32	Wexford . .	Shelburne . .	Whitechurch . .	New Ross . .	I.	329
43	Ballykelly . .	406 0 36	Wicklow . .	Shillelagh . .	Carnew . . .	Shillelagh .	I.	357
9	Ballykelly Level (Intake)	1,002 1 4	Londonderry .	Keenaght . .	Tamlaght Finlagan .	New T⁰ Limavady	III.	237
9	BALLYKELLY T.	—	Londonderry .	Keenaght . .	Tamlaght Finlagan .	New T⁰ Limavady	III.	238
48	Ballykelsh . .	62 0 7	Wexford . .	Forth . . .	Kilscoran . .	Wexford . .	I.	311
88, 100	Ballykenefick .	195 2 18	Cork, E.R. .	Imokilly . . .	Inch . . .	Middleton . .	II.	87
19, 27	Ballykenly . .	141 3 16	Cork, E.R. .	Condons&Clangibbon	Glanworth . .	Mitchelstown .	II.	61
36	Ballykenna . .	586 0 36	Kilkenny . .	Ida . . .	Dysartmoon . .	New Ross . .	I.	101
55, 59	Ballykennedy . .	598 3 31	Antrim . .	Lower Massereene .	Killead . . .	Antrim . .	III.	28
37	Ballykennedy . .	362 1 21	Antrim . .	Lower Toome . .	Ahoghill . .	Ballymena . .	III.	31
30	Ballykennedy . .	60 1 37	Waterford . .	Decies without Drum	Whitechurch . .	Dungarvan . .	II.	361
37	Ballykennedy North	130 3 24	Limerick . .	Connello Upper .	Cloncagh . .	Newcastle . .	II.	231
37	Ballykennedy South	324 0 37	Limerick . .	Connello Upper .	Cloncagh . .	Newcastle . .	II.	231
2	Ballykenneen Lower	329 2 21	Queen's Co. .	Tinnahinch . .	Kilmanman . .	Mountmellick .	I.	249
2	Ballykenneen Upper	261 2 19	Queen's Co. .	Tinnahinch . .	Kilmanman . .	Mountmellick .	I.	249
2, 4	Ballykenny . .	278 3 24	Donegal . .	Inishowen East .	Clonca . . .	Inishowen . .	III.	116
37	Ballykenny . .	151 0 12	Donegal . .	Kilmacrenan . .	Tullyfern . .	Milford . .	III.	132
44	Ballykenny . .	463 1 1	Limerick . .	Glenquin . .	Killeedy . .	Newcastle . .	II.	245
8, 13	Ballykenny . .	308 3 27	Longford . .	Longford . .	Clongesh . .	Longford . .	I.	157
28	Ballykenry . .	197 1 33	Limerick . .	Connello Lower .	Clonagh . .	Rathkeale . .	II.	227
8, 13	Ballykenver . .	228 2 23	Antrim . .	Cary . . .	Armoy . . .	Ballycastle .	III.	11
24	Ballykeoghan . .	69 2 34	Kilkenny . .	Gowran . .	Kilfane . .	Thomastown .	I.	96
24	Ballykeoghan . .	45 0 32	Kilkenny . .	Gowran . .	Tullaherin . .	Thomastown .	I.	100
40, 43	Ballykeoghan . .	381 3 24	Kilkenny . .	Ida . . .	Dunkitt . .	Waterford . .	I.	101
31	Ballykeppoge . .	96 2 2	Wicklow . .	Arklow . . .	Dunganstown . .	Rathdrum . .	I.	343
48	Ballykereen .	130 3 30	Wexford . .	Forth . . .	Ballybrennan . .	Wexford . .	I.	308
76, 77	Ballykergan . .	1,319 1 24	Donegal . .	Raphoe . . .	Kilteevoge . .	Stranorlar . .	III.	139
54, 55	Ballykerin . .	348 0 38	Tipperary, S.R. .	Slievardagh . .	Crohane . .	Callan . .	II.	332
22	Ballykerin Lower .	125 0 37	Waterford . .	Decies without Drum	Modelligo . .	Dungarvan . .	II.	359
22	Ballykerin Middle .	183 0 2	Waterford . .	Decies without Drum	Modelligo . .	Dungarvan . .	II.	359
22	Ballykerin Upper .	235 1 7	Waterford . .	Decies without Drum	Modelligo . .	Dungarvan . .	II.	359
23,24,31,32	Ballykeroge Big .	447 0 3	Waterford . .	Decies without Drum	Kilrossanty . .	Kilmacthomas .	II.	357
23	Ballykeroge Little .	158 3 36	Waterford . .	Decies without Drum	Kilrossanty . .	Kilmacthomas .	II.	357
90	Ballykerrigan . .	56 1 17	Mayo . . .	Clanmorris . .	Balla . . .	Castlebar . .	IV.	131
50, 60, 61	Ballykerwick . ' .	287 0 16	Cork, E.R. .	East Muskerry .	Donaghmore . .	Macroom . .	II.	102
57, 67	Ballykett . .	1,018 0 17	Clare . . .	Moyarta . .	Kilrush . .	Kilrush . .	II.	33
37	Ballykevan East .	147 2 34	Limerick . .	Connello Upper .	Ballingarry . .	Newcastle . .	II.	230
37	Ballykevan West .	194 3 37	Limerick . .	Connello Upper .	Ballingarry . .	Newcastle . .	II.	230
8, 9	Ballykieran or Frankford .	457 2 34	Kilkenny . .	Galmoy . .	Balleen . .	Urlingford . .	I.	91
37	Ballykilbeg . .	288 1 29a	Down . .	Lecale Upper .	Down . . .	Downpatrick .	III.	180
14, 19	Ballykilcavan . .	296 0 28	Queen's Co. .	Stradbally . .	Curraclone . .	Athy . .	I.	246
23, 24	Ballykilcline . .	610 2 6b	Roscommon .	Ballintober North .	Kilglass . .	Strokestown .	IV.	186
2	Ballykilcross . .	76 2 27	King's Co. .	Kilcoursey . .	Kilbride . .	Tullamore . .	I.	141
45	Ballykildea . .	261 2 5	Clare . . .	Tulla Lower . .	Killaloe . .	Scariff . .	II.	35
2	Ballykildevin . .	105 0 12	Westmeath .	Moygoish . .	Street . . .	Granard . .	I.	281
9	Ballykilduff Lower .	253 0 20	Carlow . .	Rathvilly . .	Haroldstown . .	Shillelagh .	I.	11
9	Ballykilduff Upper .	313 3 15	Carlow . .	Rathvilly . .	Haroldstown . .	Shillelagh .	I.	11
40, 43	Ballykillaboy . .	350 1 30	Kilkenny . .	Ida . . .	Dunkitt . .	Waterford . .	I.	101
43	Ballykillaboy . .	64 0 29	Kilkenny . .	Ida . . .	Gaulskill . .	Waterford . .	I.	102
113, 122	Ballykilladea . .	135 2 17	Galway . .	Kiltartan . .	Killinny . .	Gort . .	IV.	47
33, 40	Ballykillageer Lower	302 0 39	Wicklow . .	Arklow . . .	Ballintemple . .	Rathdrum . .	I.	342
39, 40	Ballykillageer Upper	372 1 1	Wicklow . .	Arklow . . .	Ballintemple . .	Rathdrum . .	I.	342
4	Ballykillane . .	297 0 1	Carlow . .	Rathvilly . .	Hacketstown . .	Shillelagh .	I.	11
8	Ballykillane . .	447 3 22	Queen's Co. .	Portnahinch . .	Coolbanagher . .	Mountmellick .	I.	244
1, 2	Ballykillare . .	429 3 22c	Down . .	Castlereagh Lower .	Bangor . .	Newtownards .	III.	161
24, 25	Ballykillavane . .	284 2 14	Wicklow . .	Newcastle . '.	Glencaly . .	Rathdrum . .	I.	351
42	Ballykilleen . .	355 0 6	King's Co. .	Clonlisk . .	Kilmurryely . .	Roscrea . .	I.	131
11,12,19,20	Ballykilleen . .	1,229 3 36	King's Co. .	Coolestown . .	Ballynakill . .	Edenderry . .	I.	132
2	Ballykilleen . .	391 1 30	King's Co. .	Kilcoursey . .	Ardnurcher or Horseleap . .	Tullamore . .	I.	140
103, 113	Ballykilleen . .	649 0 8	Mayo . . .	Costello . .	Annagh . .	Claremorris .	IV.	137
32, 37	Ballykillen . .	160 1 17	Queen's Co. .	Slievemargy . .	Killeshin . .	Carlow . .	I.	245
42	Ballykilliane . .	255 0 29	Wexford . .	Forth . . .	Killiane . .	Wexford . .	I.	310
78, 79	Ballykill Lower .	132 0 24	Mayo . . .	Carra . .	Breaghwy . .	Castlebar . .	IV.	126
100	Ballykillowen . .	1,066 0 18	Donegal . .	Tirhugh . .	Drumhome . .	Donegal . .	III.	146
78, 79	Ballykill Upper .	81 1 38	Mayo . . .	Carra . .	Breaghwy . .	Castlebar . .	IV.	127
33, 39	Ballykilmore . .	330 3 0	Westmeath .	Fartullagh . .	Newtown . .	Mullingar . .	I.	269
8, 16	Ballykilmurry . .	779 1 20	King's Co. .	Ballycowan . .	Kilbride . .	Tullamore . .	I.	127
38	Ballykilmurry .	110 0 10	Waterford .	Decies within Drum	Ardmore . .	Dungarvan . .	II.	349
38	Ballykilmurry .	59 1 23	Waterford . .	Decies within Drum	Lisgenan or Grange .	Youghal . .	II.	352

(a) Including 1A. 2R. 32P. water.   (b) Including 3A. 1R. 18P. water.   (c) Including 17A. 0R. 13P. detached portion.

No. of Sheet of the Ordinance Survey Maps.	Townlands and Towns.	Area in Statute Acres.	County.	Barony.	Parish.	Poor Law Union in 1857.	Townland Census of 1851, Part I.	
		A. R. P.					Vol.	Page
14, 23	Ballykilmurry .	205 2 0	Waterford .	Decies without Drum	Kilrossanty . .	Kilmacthomas .	II.	357
33	Ballykilmurry Lower	382 1 35	Wicklow . .	Upper Talbotstown .	Kiltegan . .	Baltinglass .	I.	364
23	Ballykilmurry Upper	220 3 39	Wicklow . .	Upper Talbotstown .	Kiltegan . .	Baltinglass .	I.	364
32	Ballykilroe . .	457 3 6	Westmeath .	Moycashel . .	Castletownkindalen	Mullingar .	I.	277
42	Ballykilty .	597 1 32	Clare . .	Bunratty Upper .	Quin . .	Tulla .	II.	10
67	Ballykilty . .	335 3 10	Cork, E.R. .	Imokilly . . .	Clonpriest . .	Youghal .	II.	84
3	Ballykilty Lower .	284 2 31	Wexford . .	Gorey . . .	Inch . . .	Gorey .	I.	316
3	Ballykilty Upper .	165 0 28	Wexford . .	Gorey . . .	Inch . . .	Gorey .	I.	316
17	Ballykinard . .	103 1 38	Donegal . .	Kilmacrenan . .	Clondavaddog .	Milford .	III.	124
5	Ballykinash . .	473 3 26	Tipperary, N.R. .	Lower Ormond .	Loughkeen .	Parsonstown .	II.	286
101,102,112	Ballykinava . .	1,001 2 35	Mayo . .	Clanmorris . .	Kilcolman .	Claremorris .	IV.	133
22	Ballykine . .	333 3 5	Down . .	Kinelarty . .	Dromara . .	Lisburn .	III.	176
78	Ballykinealy . .	329 0 31	Cork, E.R. .	Imokilly . . .	Kilmacdonogh .	Youghal .	II.	88
22	Ballykine Lower .	598 3 33a	Down . .	Kinelarty . .	Magheradrool .	Lisburn .	III.	177
120	Ballykine Lower .	455 3 38b	Mayo . .	Kilmaine . .	Cong . .	Oughterard .	IV.	153
22, 29	Ballykine Upper .	689 1 23	Down . .	Kinelarty . .	Magheradrool .	Lisburn .	III.	177
120	Ballykine Upper .	159 1 14	Mayo . .	Kilmaine . .	Cong . .	Ballinrobe .	IV.	153
24	Ballyking . .	192 0 23	Queen's Co. .	Cullenagh . .	Ballyroan .	Abbeyleix .	I.	239
31	Ballykinlalee .	386 1 25	Tipperary, N.R. .	Owney and Arra .	Kilcomenty .	Nenagh .	II.	294
37, 44	Ballykinler Lower .	440 1 10	Down . .	Lecale Upper .	Ballykinler .	Downpatrick .	III.	180
44	Ballykinler Middle .	555 3 28	Down . .	Lecale Upper .	Ballykinler .	Downpatrick .	III.	180
44	Ballykinler Upper .	1,042 1 15	Down . .	Lecale Upper .	Ballykinler .	Downpatrick .	III.	180
13, 14	Ballykinlettragh .	1,864 0 19	Mayo . .	Tirawley . .	Kilfian . .	Killala .	IV.	169
17	Ballykinnacorra North	242 1 27	Clare . .	Inchiquin . .	Rath . .	Corrofin .	II.	27
17, 25	Ballykinnacorra South	141 0 10c	Clare . .	Inchiquin . .	Rath . .	Corrofin .	II.	27
17	Ballykinsella . .	408 1 25	Waterford .	Middlethird . .	Drumcannon .	Waterford .	II.	366
9	Ballykinvarga . .	174 0 2	Clare . .	Corcomroe . .	Kilfenora .	Ennistimon .	II.	18
56	Ballykissane . .	236 3 18	Kerry . .	Trughanacmy . .	Killorglin .	Killarney .	II.	211
58	Ballykisteen . .	178 2 25	Tipperary, S.R. .	Clanwilliam .	Solloghodmore .	Tipperary .	II.	311
24	Ballykitt . .	219 1 12	Cork, E.R. .	Orrery and Kilmore .	Ballyclogh .	Mallow .	II.	106
44, 45	Ballyknavin . .	387 2 3	Clare . .	Tulla Lower .	O'Briensbridge .	Limerick .	II.	37
8	Ballyknick . .	171 0 9	Armagh . .	Oneilland West .	Grange . .	Armagh .	III.	52
13, 14	Ballyknock . .	295 3 7	Armagh . .	Orior Lower .	Kilmore . .	Banbridge .	III.	56
26	Ballyknock . .	500 2 12	Carlow . .	St. Mullins Lower .	St. Mullins .	New Ross .	I.	13
33	Ballyknock . .	243 2 29	Clare . .	Inchiquin . .	Kilnamona .	Ennis .	II.	27
55	Ballyknock . .	165 1 20	Cork, E.R. .	Imokilly . . .	Ardagh . .	Youghal .	II.	83
89	Ballyknock . .	115 3 1	Cork, E.R. .	Imokilly . . .	Cloyne . .	Middleton .	II.	85
66	Ballyknock . .	279 3 23	Cork, E.R. .	Imokilly . . .	Dungourney .	Middleton .	II.	86
100	Ballyknock . .	167 3 39	Cork, E.R. .	Imokilly . . .	Trabolgan .	Middleton .	II.	90
55	Ballyknock . .	405 3 21	Cork, E.R. .	Kinnatalloon .	Ballynoe . .	Fermoy .	II.	97
13,14,20,21	Ballyknock . .	1,204 3 39	Down . .	Lower Iveagh, Up.pt.	Moira . .	Lurgan .	III.	170
115	Ballyknock . .	9 1 36	Galway . .	Loughrea . .	Killeenadeema .	Loughrea .	IV.	64
115	Ballyknock . .	66 1 39	Galway . .	Loughrea . .	Kilteskill . .	Loughrea .	IV.	65
37	Ballyknock . .	457 0 22	Kilkenny . .	Ida . . .	Dysartmoon .	New Ross .	i.	101
32, 36	Ballyknock . .	981 1 10	Londonderry .	Loughinsholin .	Killelagh .	Magherafelt .	III.	241
18, 22	Ballyknock . .	212 0 29	Longford . .	Moydow . .	Kilcommock .	Ballymahon .	I.	161
59	Ballyknock . .	825 3 23d	Mayo . .	Tirawley . .	Addergoole .	Castlebar .	IV.	162
6, 7	Ballyknock . .	709 2 11	Mayo . .	Tirawley . .	Doonfeeny .	Killala .	IV.	167
53, 61	Ballyknock . .	250 0 27	Tipperary, S.R. .	Middlethird . .	St. Patricksrock .	Cashel .	II.	330
37	Ballyknock . .	163 1 37	Waterford .	Coshmore and Coshbride .	Templemichael .	Youghal .	II.	348
17	Ballyknock . .	322 3 13	Waterford .	Middlethird . .	Drumcannon .	Waterford .	II.	366
3	Ballyknock . .	487 1 32	Waterford .	Upperthird . .	Mothel . . .	Carrick on Suir	II.	370
41	Ballyknock . .	262 1 17	Wexford . .	Shelmaliere West .	Ballymitty .	Wexford .	I.	332
16, 17	Ballyknockan . . .	337 3 13	Carlow . .	Idrone East . .	Fennagh . .	Carlow .	I.	7
11, 12, 16	Ballyknockan . .	240 0 36e	Carlow . .	Idrone West . .	Wells . .	Carlow .	I.	10
16	Ballyknockan . .	646 3 32f	Down . .	Castlereagh Upper .	Saintfield . .	Lisburn .	III.	166
42	Ballyknockan . .	386 3 34	King's Co. .	Clonlisk . . .	Ettagh . .	Roscrea .	I.	130
18, 26	Ballyknockan . .	232 0 6	King's Co. .	Geashill . .	Geashill . .	Tullamore .	I.	139
18	Ballyknockan . .	558 1 27	Queen's Co. .	Maryborough East .	Kilcolmanbane .	Mountmellick .	I.	241
27	Ballyknockan . .	272 3 23	Wexford . .	Ballaghkeen . .	Castle-ellis .	Enniscorthy .	I.	293
25	Ballyknockan . .	78 1 10	Wexford . .	Bantry . .	Rossdroit .	Enniscorthy .	I.	301
48	Ballyknockan . .	78 1 36	Wexford . .	Forth . .	Kilrane . .	Wexford .	I.	311
48	Ballyknockan . .	60 0 1	Wexford . .	Forth . .	St. Margaret's .	Wexford .	I.	314
48	Ballyknockan . .	85 1 0	Wexford . .	Forth . .	St. Michael's .	Wexford .	I.	314
10	Ballyknockan . .	1,112 2 6	Wicklow . .	Lower Talbotstown .	Boystown .	Naas .	I.	359
28	Ballyknockan . .	174 1 6	Wicklow . .	Upper Talbotstown .	Kiltegan . .	Baltinglass .	I.	364
24, 25	Ballyknockan Beg .	197 2 27	Wicklow . .	Newcastle . .	Glenealy . .	Rathdrum .	I.	351
42	Ballyknockane .	497 2 36	Cork, E.R. .	Barretts . .	Mourneabbey .	Mallow .	II.	50
46, 55	Ballyknockane .	212 2 27	Cork, E.R. .	Kinnatalloon .	Mogeely . .	Youghal .	II.	98
30	Ballyknockane .	145 2 26	Limerick . .	Connello Upper .	Ballingarry .	Croom .	II.	230
29, 30	Ballyknockane .	724 3 7	Tipperary, N.R. .	Ikerrin . .	Templetouhy .	Thurles .	II.	277
16, 22	Ballyknockane .	296 0 8	Tipperary, N.R. .	Upper Ormond .	Ballymackey .	Nenagh .	II.	289

(a) Including 18A. 2R. 20P. water.
(b) Including 11A. 3R. 11P. water.
(c) Including 0A. 0R. 29P. water.
(d) Including 19A. 3R. 4P. water.
(e) Including 13A. 3R. 26P. River Barrow.
(f) Including 19A. 1R. 16P. water.

No. of Sheet of the Ordnance Survey Maps.	Townlands and Towns.	Area in Statute Acres.	County.	Barony.	Parish.	Poor Law Union in 1857.	Townland Census of 1851, Part I.	
		A. R. P.					Vol.	Page
71, 78	Ballyknockane	1,562 3 32	Tipperary, S.R.	Iffa and Offa East	Temple-etney	Clonmel	II.	316
87	Ballyknockane	356 2 28	Tipperary, S.R.	Iffa and Offa West	Tullaghorton	Clogheen	II.	321
30, 35	Ballyknockan Lower	153 0 33	Wicklow	Ballinacor North	Tullaghorton	Rathdrum	I.	347
24	Ballyknockan More	392 0 8	Wicklow	Newcastle	Glenealy	Rathdrum	I.	351
16, 17	BALLYKNOCKAN T.	—	Carlow	Idrone East	Fennagh	Carlow	I.	7
10	BALLYKNOCKAN T.	—	Wicklow	Lower Talbotstown	Boystown	Naas	I.	359
30, 35	Ballyknockan Upper	302 0 14	Wicklow	Ballinacor North	Rathdrum	Rathdrum	I.	347
40	Ballyknockbeg	196 1 13	Kilkenny	Knocktopher	Killahy	Waterford	I.	112
18	Ballyknock (Big)	312 2 30	Antrim	Upper Dunluce	Loughguile	Ballymoney	III.	20
26	Ballyknockcrumpin	109 0 5	Carlow	St. Mullins Lower	St. Mullins	New Ross	I.	13
43, 47	Ballyknocker	302 2 30	Wicklow	Shillelagh	Carnew	Shillelagh	I.	357
43, 47	Ballyknocker East	31 1 36	Wicklow	Shillelagh	Moyacomb	Shillelagh	I.	358
43, 47	Ballyknocker West	53 2 0	Wicklow	Shillelagh	Moyacomb	Shillelagh	I.	358
18	Ballyknock (Little)	167 0 35	Antrim	Upper Dunluce	Loughguile	Ballymoney	III.	20
31	Ballyknock Lower	256 1 6	Waterford	Decies without Drum	Kilgobnet	Dungarvan	II.	357
35	Ballyknockmore	223 1 14	Kilkenny	Knocktopher	Lismateige	Thomastown	I.	113
55	Ballyknock North	317 1 38	Cork, E.R.	Kinnatalloon	Ballynoe	Fermoy	II.	97
55	Ballyknock South	600 3 28	Cork, E.R.	Kinnatalloon	Ballynoe	Fermoy	II.	97
23, 31	Ballyknock Upper	430 3 37	Waterford	Decies without Drum	Kilgobnet	Dungarvan	II.	357
38	Ballyla	91 2 21	Wexford	Shelmaliere East	Ardcolm	Wexford	I.	330
14, 22	Ballylaan	235 0 24	Clare	Corcomroe	Kilmacrehy	Ennistimon	II.	20
63, 67	Ballylacky	250 1 21	Antrim	Upper Massereene	Ballinderry	Lisburn	III.	29
7	Ballylacy	204 2 10	Wexford	Gorey	Kilcavan	Gorey	I.	317
81, 87	Ballylaffin	295 0 15	Tipperary, S.R.	Iffa and Offa West	Tubbrid	Clogheen	II.	320
15	Ballylaffin	190 0 25	Wicklow	Upper Talbotstown	Rathsallagh	Baltinglass	I.	365
46	Ballylagan	479 1 12	Antrim	Lower Belfast	Ballynure	Larne	III.	7
11, 12	Ballylagan	149 0 11	Londonderry	Coleraine	Macosquin	Coleraine	III.	232
59	Ballylagan	158 2 14	Tyrone	Clogher	Errigal Keerogue	Clogher	III.	295
3	Ballylagan North	113 0 25	Londonderry	North East Liberties of Coleraine	Ballywillin	Coleraine	III.	245
3, 4	Ballylagan South	140 0 12	Londonderry	North East Liberties of Coleraine	Ballywillin	Coleraine	III.	245
37	Ballylaghnan	516 2 33	Clare	Tulla Lower	Ogonnelloe	Scarriff	II.	38
61, 71	Ballylahan	283 3 38a	Mayo	Gallen	Templemore	Castlebar	IV.	151
21	Ballylahiff	216 2 10	Kerry	Clanmaurice	O'Dorney	Tralee	II.	172
25	Ballylahiff	294 2 15	Limerick	Coonagh	Oola	Tipperary	II.	235
28, 36	Ballylahiff	147 0 26	Limerick	Glenquin	Newcastle	Newcastle	II.	247
114	Ballylahy	154 0 24	Galway	Kiltartan	Kilthomas	Gort	IV.	49
35, 36	Ballylahy	266 2 5	Tipperary, N.R.	Ikerrin	Templetouhy	Thurles	II.	277
26	Ballylame	220 1 18	Londonderry	Coleraine	Desertoghill	Ballymoney	III.	230
89	Ballylanders	322 1 11	Cork, E.R.	Imokilly	Ballintemple	Middleton	II.	84
49	Ballylanders	755 1 9	Limerick	Coshlea	Ballylanders	Mitchelstown	II.	237
49	BALLYLANDERS T.	—	Limerick	Coshlea	Ballylanders	Mitchelstown	II.	237
17, 21	Ballylane	1,150 1 20b	Armagh	Fews Lower	Kilclooney	Armagh	III.	46
38	Ballylane	237 1 8	Waterford	Decies within Drum	Lisgenan or Grange	Youghal	II.	352
34	Ballylane East	320 1 21	Wexford	Bantry	Oldross	New Ross	I.	301
24	Ballylaneen	433 1 24	Waterford	Decies without Drum	Ballylaneen	Kilmacthomas	II.	354
24	BALLYLANEEN T.	—	Waterford	Decies without Drum	Ballylaneen	Kilmacthomas	II.	354
34	Ballylane West	334 0 38	Wexford	Bantry	Oldross	New Ross	I.	301
38	Ballylangadon	318 0 16	Waterford	Decies within Drum	Lisgenan or Grange	Youghal	II.	352
96, 110	Ballylangley	288 2 28	Cork, W.R.	East Carbery (E.D.)	Ballymodan	Bandon	II.	126
136	Ballylangy	192 2 8	Cork, W.R.	Ibane and Barryroe	Lislee	Clonakilty	II.	150
44	Ballylanigan	99 3 12	Limerick	Glenquin	Killeedy	Newcastle	II.	245
63	Ballylanigan (Cramer)	258 2 33	Tipperary, S.R.	Slievardagh	Kilvemnon	Callan	II.	334
63, 64	Ballylanigan (Pennefather)	216 0 8	Tipperary, S.R.	Slievardagh	Kilvemnon	Callan	II.	334
40, 45	Ballylannan	548 1 33	Wexford	Shelmaliere West	Ballylannan	New Ross	I.	332
33	Ballylannidy	193 2 15	Clare	Islands	Drumcliff	Ennis	II.	29
113, 114	Ballylara	267 1 22	Galway	Dunkellin	Ardrahan	Gort	IV.	26
26	Ballylarkin	161 3 32	Kilkenny	Shillelogher	Killaloe	Callan	I.	115
3	Ballylarkin	203 0 29	Wexford	Gorey	Inch	Gorey	I.	316
13	Ballylarkin Lower	370 0 8	Kilkenny	Crannagh	Ballylarkin	Kilkenny	I.	85
13	Ballylarkin Upper	540 2 11	Kilkenny	Crannagh	Ballylarkin	Kilkenny	I.	85
79	Ballylast	7 3 28	Donegal	Raphoe	Clonleigh	Strabane	III.	134
79	Ballylast	155 0 12c	Donegal	Raphoe	Urney	Strabane	III.	144
2, 5	Ballylaw	272 2 4	Tyrone	Strabane Lower	Leckpatrick	Strabane	III.	321
21	Ballylawn	746 1 30	Donegal	Inishowen East	Moville Upper	Inishowen	III.	119
46, 54	Ballylawn	428 3 24	Donegal	Raphoe	Raymoghy	Letterkenny	III.	141
14	Ballylea	257 3 11	Wicklow	Upper Talbotstown	Dunlavin	Baltinglass	I.	364
59, 60	Ballyleaan	543 3 5d	Clare	Clonderalaw	Killadysert	Killadysert	II.	15
64, 65	Ballyleagh	118 0 20	Cork, E.R.	Barrymore	Lisgoold	Middleton	II.	56
17	Ballyleagry	426 1 3	Londonderry	Keenaght	Balteagh	New Town Limavady	III.	234
37	Ballyleague	374 1 6	Roscommon	Ballintober South	Cloontuskert	Roscommon	IV.	188

(a) Including 9A. 2R. 30P. water.   (c) Including 2A. 1R. 0P. water.   (d) Including 1A. 3R. 24P. water.
(b) Including 9A. 3R. 8P. water.

No. of Sheet of the Ordnance Survey Maps.	Townlands and Towns.	Area in Statute Acres.			County.	Barony.	Parish.	Poor Law Union in 1857.	Townland Census of 1851, Part I.	
		A.	R.	P.					Vol.	Page
11	Ballyleakin	277	1	3	King's Co.	Coolestown	Ballynakill	Edenderry	I.	132
65	Ballyleary	158	1	31	Cork, E.R.	Barrymore	Carrigtohill	Middleton	II.	52
75, 87	Ballyleary	332	2	8	Cork, E.R.	Barrymore	Clonmel	Cork	II.	53
9	Ballyleck	155	2	27	Monaghan	Monaghan	Kilmore	Monaghan	III.	275
6, 7	Ballyleckan	290	3	37	Antrim	Lower Dunluce	Dunluce	Coleraine	III.	17
65, 73	Ballyledder	1,157	3	29	Kerry	Dunkerron North	Knockane	Killarney	II.	181
69	Ballylee	71	1	18	Galway	Clare	Annaghdown	Galway	IV.	16
114, 123	Ballylee	219	2	39	Galway	Kiltartan	Kiltartan	Gort	IV.	48
114, 123	Ballylee	82	0	5	Galway	Kiltartan	Kilthomas	Gort	IV.	49
17	Ballyleen	415	2	3	Carlow	Forth	Ballon	Carlow	I.	3
117	Ballyleen	176	3	38	Galway	Leitrim	Tynagh	Portumna	IV.	55
16, 25	Ballyleen	481	3	2	Waterford	Middlethird	Dunhill	Kilmacthomas	II.	366
3	Ballyleese North	185	0	26	Londonderry	North East Liberties of Coleraine	Ballyaghran	Coleraine	III.	244
3	Ballyleese South	72	2	6	Londonderry	North East Liberties of Coleraine	Ballyaghran	Coleraine	III.	244
3	Ballyleese West Quarter	64	3	7	Londonderry	North East Liberties of Coleraine	Ballyaghran	Coleraine	III.	244
27	Ballylegan	387	0	16	Cork, E.R.	Fermoy	Glanworth	Fermoy	II.	79
76	Ballylegan	262	0	8	Tipperary, S.R.	Iffa and Offa West	Caher	Clogheen	II.	317
16, 17, 25, 26	Ballylegat	166	0	11	Waterford	Middlethird	Reisk	Waterford	II.	368
25, 26	Ballylehane Lower	812	2	39	Queen's Co.	Ballyadams	Killabban	Carlow	I.	231
25, 31	Ballylehane Upper	832	2	22	Queen's Co.	Ballyadams	Killabban	Carlow	I.	231
3, 4, 8 9	Ballylehaun	418	3	11	Kilkenny	Galmoy	Glashare	Urlingford	I.	92
1, 5	Ballyleidy	443	1	24	Down	Castlereagh Lower	Bangor	Newtownards	III.	161
85	Ballyleigh	445	3	28	Cork, E.R.	East Muskerry	Inishkenny	Cork	II.	104
23, 24	Ballyleigh	1,248	0	0	Wexford	Bantry	St. Mullins	New Ross	I.	303
6	Ballyleighery Lower	518	0	37	Londonderry	Keenaght	Magilligan	NewtⁿLimavady	III.	236
5, 6	Ballyleighery Upper	723	2	3	Londonderry	Keenaght	Magilligan	NewtⁿLimavady	III.	236
33	Ballylemin	69	3	38	Wexford	Ballaghkeen	Skreen	Wexford	I.	298
30	Ballylemon	118	0	18	Waterford	Decies without Drum	Whitechurch	Dungarvan	II.	361
30	Ballylemon Lower	102	1	19	Waterford	Decies without Drum	Whitechurch	Dungarvan	II.	361
22, 30	Ballylemon Upper	97	2	13	Waterford	Decies without Drum	Whitechurch	Dungarvan	II.	361
30	Ballylemonwood	116	3	12	Waterford	Decies without Drum	Whitechurch	Dungarvan	II.	361
31, 38	Ballylenagh	238	3	6	Down	Lecale Lower	Ballyculter	Downpatrick	III.	178
9	Ballylenaghan	598	1	28a	Down	Castlereagh Upper	Knockbreda	Lisburn	III.	165
16, 25	Ballylenane	256	3	11	Waterford	Middlethird	Dunhill	Kilmacthomas	II.	366
62	Ballylennan	334	0	21	Donegal	Raphoe	Taughboyne	Strabane	III.	143
122	Ballylennan	56	2	3	Galway	Kiltartan	Kilmacduagh	Gort	IV.	47
16, 24	Ballylennan Mercer	66	3	23	Tyrone	Omagh West	Urney	Castlederg	III.	318
16, 24	Ballylennan Scott	204	3	20	Tyrone	Omagh West	Urney	Castlederg	III.	318
2, 3	Ballylennon	321	1	39	Carlow	Carlow	Urglin	Carlow	I.	3
10, 18	Ballylennon	499	3	10	King's Co.	Lower Philipstown	Kilclonfert	Tullamore	I.	142
42, 43	Ballylenully	212	1	4	Antrim	Upper Toome	Duneane	Antrim	III.	34
9, 13	Ballyleny	434	3	35	Armagh	Oneilland West	Kilmore	Armagh	III.	53
20	Ballyleny	283	3	35	Down	Lower Iveagh, Up. pt.	Magheralin	Lurgan	III.	170
6, 7	Ballylerane	179	0	37	Wicklow	Rathdown	Powerscourt	Rathdown	I.	356
9	Ballylessan	520	2	31b	Down	Castlereagh Upper	Drumbo	Lisburn	III.	164
37, 38	Ballylesson	504	1	29	Antrim	Lower Antrim	Ballyclug	Ballymena	III.	3
40	Ballylesson	360	3	25	Antrim	Lower Belfast	Glynn	Larne	III.	8
54	Ballylevin	196	1	31	Donegal	Raphoe	Raymoghy	Letterkenny	III.	141
25, 26	Ballylevin	493	1	9	King's Co.	Geashill	Geashill	Tullamore	I.	139
40	Ballyliamgow	183	0	18	Wexford	Shelmaliere West	Inch	New Ross	I.	333
47	Ballylibernagh	168	1	26	Wexford	Bargy	Mulrankin	Wexford	I.	307
144	Ballylibert	109	3	28	Cork, W.R.	Ibane and Barryroe	Rathbarry	Clonakilty	II.	150
105	Ballylicky	131	3	18	Cork, W.R.	Bantry	Kilmocomoge	Bantry	II.	119
52	Ballyliddan East	64	0	35	Clare	Bunratty Lower	Kilfintinan	Limerick	II.	5
52	Ballyliddan West	222	2	26	Clare	Bunratty Lower	Kilfintinan	Limerick	II.	5
29	Ballylier	45	1	24	King's Co.	Garrycastle	Lusmagh	Parsonstown	I.	137
3, 10	Ballyliffin	594	3	32	Donegal	Inishowen East	Clonmany	Inishowen	III.	117
3. 10	BALLYLIFFIN T.	—			Donegal	Inishowen East	Clonmany	Inishowen	III.	117
49	Ballylifford	534	0	35	Londonderry	Loughinsholin	Ballinderry	Magherafelt	III.	239
8	Ballylig	229	3	22	Antrim	Cary	Ramoan	Ballycastle	III.	14
23	Ballylig	289	0	0	Antrim	Kilconway	Killagan	Ballymoney	III.	27
28, 33	Ballylig	508	1	38	Antrim	Lower Antrim	Skerry	Ballymena	III.	4
41	Ballylig	331	2	19	Antrim	Lower Belfast	Glynn	Larne	III.	8
45	Ballylig	255	2	9	Down	Lecale Upper	Bright	Downpatrick	III.	180
33	Ballyligpatrick	617	0	37	Antrim	Lower Antrim	Racavan	Ballymena	III.	4
18	Ballylimp	366	1	3	Down	Ards Upper	Ballywalter	Newtownards	III.	160
37, 46	Ballylin	465	1	11	Donegal	Kilmacrenan	Aughnish	Milford	III.	122
14, 15	Ballylin	583	2	23	King's Co.	Garrycastle	Wheery or Killagally	Parsonstown	I.	139
29	Ballylin	328	0	0	Limerick	Connello Lower	Croagh	Rathkeale	II.	227
19	Ballylin	108	1	34	Limerick	Shanid	Kilbradran	Rathkeale	II.	255

(a) Including 1A. 2R. 3P. River Lagan.　　　　(b) Including 0A. 2R. 35P. water.

No. of Sheet of the Ordnance Survey Maps.	Townlands and Towns.	Area in Statute Acres.			County.	Barony.	Parish.	Poor Law Union in 1857.	Townland Census of 1851. Part I.	
		A.	R.	P.					Vol.	Page
19	Ballylin . . .	197	3	30	Limerick . .	Shanid . . .	Kilmoylan . .	Rathkeale . .	II.	256
28	Ballylin . . .	483	1	38	Limerick . .	Shanid . . .	Rathronan . .	Newcastle . .	II.	257
7	Ballylina . .	46	2	14	Tipperary, N.R.	Lower Ormond .	Ballingarry . .	Borrisokane .	II.	282
7	Ballylina East .	221	2	11	Tipperary, N.R.	Lower Ormond .	Uskane . . .	Borrisokane .	II.	288
44	Ballylinane .	198	0	37	Limerick . .	Glenquin . . .	Monagay . .	Newcastle . .	II.	247
7, 10	Ballylina West .	521	3	7	Tipperary, N.R.	Lower Ormond .	Uskane . .	Borrisokane .	II.	288
24	Ballylinch . .	395	0	12	Waterford . .	Decies without Drum	Stradbally . .	Kilmacthomas .	II.	360
28	Ballylinch Demesne	817	1	4a	Kilkenny . .	Gowran . .	Ballylinch . .	Thomastown .	I.	93
150	Ballylinchy . .	796	1	18	Cork, W.R. .	West Carbery (E.D.)	Tullagh . .	Skibbereen .	II.	141
26	Ballyline . . .	499	3	1b	Clare . .	Bunratty Upper .	Kilraghtis . .	Ennis . .	II.	9
9, 10	Ballyline . .	137	0	3i	Clare . .	Burren . . .	Carran . .	Corrofin . .	II.	11
22	Ballyline . .	360	0	27	Kilkenny . .	Shillelogher . .	Killaloe . .	Callan . .	I.	115
104	Ballylin East .	174	0	25	Galway . .	Dunkellin . .	Killogilleen .	Loughrea . .	IV.	31
5, 6	Ballyline East .	318	0	18	Kerry . .	Iraghticonnor .	Aghavallen . .	Listowel . .	II.	189
5, 6	Ballyline West .	1,667	1	22	Kerry . .	Iraghticonnor .	Aghavallen . .	Listowel . .	II.	189
24	Ballyling . .	455	0	11	Carlow . .	St. Mullins Lower .	St. Mullins . .	New Ross . .	I.	13
66, 77	Ballyling . .	114	3	19	Cork, E.R. .	Imokilly . . .	Ightermurragh .	Middleton . .	II.	87
5	Ballylinnen .	659	0	12	Kilkenny . .	Fassadinin . .	Castlecomer . .	Castlecomer .	I.	88
3	Ballylinny . .	161	1	34	Antrim . .	Cary . . .	Billy . .	Coleraine . .	III.	12
51	Ballylinny . .	405	1	34	Antrim . .	Lower Belfast .	Ballylinny . .	Antrim . .	III.	7
21, 22	Ballylintagh .	684	3	5	Down . .	Lower Iveagh, Lr. pt.	Annahilt . .	Lisburn . .	III.	167
11	Ballylintagh .	130	2	14	Londonderry .	Coleraine . .	Aghadowey . .	Coleraine . .	III.	229
11	Ballylintagh .	121	0	29	Londonderry .	Coleraine . .	Macosquin . .	Coleraine . .	III.	232
104	Ballylin West .	245	2	19	Galway . .	Dunkellin . .	Killogilleen .	Loughrea . .	IV.	31
44, 45	Ballylion . .	342	1	24c	Roscommon .	Athlone . .	Cam . .	Athlone . .	IV.	179
21	Ballylion Bawn .	38	3	18	Wicklow . .	Lower Talbotstown .	Donard . .	Baltinglass .	I.	359
21	Ballylion Lower .	179	3	34	Wicklow . .	Lower Talbotstown .	Donard . .	Baltinglass .	I.	359
21	Ballylion Upper .	137	2	21	Wicklow . .	Lower Talbotstown .	Donard . .	Baltinglass .	I.	359
5	Ballylisbredan .	467	1	10	Down . .	Castlereagh Lower .	Dundonald . .	Newtownards .	III.	162
27	Ballylisheen .	10	3	16	Tipperary, N.R.	Upper Ormond .	Ballymaclogh .	Nenagh . .	II.	290
27	Ballylisheen .	11	1	14	Tipperary, N.R.	Upper Ormond .	Dolla . .	Nenagh . .	II.	290
27	Ballylisheen .	209	3	6	Tipperary, N.R.	Upper Ormond .	Kilnaneave . .	Nenagh . .	II.	291
9, 13, 14	Ballylisk . .	342	3	39	Armagh . .	Orior Lower . .	Kilmore . .	Banbridge .	III.	56
22, 29	Ballylone Big .	545	1	0	Down . .	Kinelarty . .	Magheradrool .	Downpatrick .	III.	177
22	Ballylone Little	418	1	29d	Down . .	Kinelarty . .	Magheradrool .	Downpatrick .	III.	177
89	Ballylongane .	175	0	8	Cork, E.R. .	Imokilly . . .	Kilmahon . .	Middleton . .	II.	89
14	Ballylongane .	527	0	18	Kerry . .	Clanmaurice . .	Ballyheige . .	Tralee . .	II.	167
12, 21	Ballylongford .	282	0	24	Limerick . .	Kenry . . .	Adare . .	Croom . .	II.	248
2, 3	BALLYLONGFORD T.	—			Kerry . .	Iraghticonnor .	Aghavallen . .	Listowel . .	II.	189
31	Ballylonnan .	116	2	38	King's Co. .	Ballyboy . .	Ballyboy . .	Parsonstown .	I.	123
42	Ballylonnan .	313	1	36	King's Co. .	Clonlisk . .	Kilmurryely . .	Roscrea . .	I.	131
12	Ballyloo . . .	688	1	19	Carlow . .	Carlow . . .	Tullowmagimma .	Carlow . .	I.	2
12	Ballyloo . . .	3	3	0	Carlow . .	Idrone East . .	Nurney . .	Carlow . .	I.	8
41	Ballylooby . .	446	1	38	Limerick . .	Coshlea . .	Galbally . .	Mitchelstown .	II.	238
64	Ballyloohane .	29	3	27	Cork, E.R. .	Barrymore . .	Kilquane . .	Cork . .	II.	55
3, 8	Ballylopen . .	210	2	24	Cork, E.R. .	Fermoy . . .	Ardskeagh . .	Mallow . .	II.	76
3, 8	Ballylopen . .	425	3	38	Cork, E.R. .	Fermoy . . .	Kilquane . .	Mallow . .	II.	80
40	Ballyloran . .	276	2	38	Antrim . .	Upper Glenarm .	Larne . .	Larne . .	III.	25
11	Ballylosky . .	705	2	38	Donegal . .	Inishowen East .	Donagh . .	Inishowen .	III.	118
22	Ballylougan .	322	0	8	King's Co. .	Garrycastle . .	Gallen . .	Parsonstown .	I.	135
7	Ballylough . .	256	1	12	Antrim . .	Lower Dunluce .	Billy . .	Coleraine . .	III.	16
17, 18	Ballylough . .	289	0	6e	Antrim . .	Upper Dunluce .	Kilraghts . .	Ballymoney .	III.	19
36, 43	Ballylough . .	911	2	12f	Down . .	Lecale Upper . .	Kilmegan . .	Downpatrick .	III.	181
19, 20, 26, 27	Ballylough . .	425	2	0	Down . .	Lower Iveagh, Up. pt.	Seapatrick . .	Lurgan . .	III.	171
40, 46	Ballylough . .	520	0	14	Down . .	Upper Iveagh, Up. pt.	Donaghmore .	Newry . .	III.	175
15, 20	Ballylough . .	444	0	3	Wexford . .	Scarawalsh . .	Ferns . .	Enniscorthy .	I.	323
32	Ballyloughan .	514	0	4	Antrim . .	Lower Toome . .	Ahoghill . .	Ballymena .	III.	31
13	Ballyloughan .	483	1	2	Armagh . .	Oneilland West .	Kilmore . .	Armagh . .	III.	53
16, 19	Ballyloughan .	462	0	10	Carlow . .	Idrone East . .	Sliguff . .	Carlow . .	I.	8
92, 97, 98	Ballyloughan .	422	0	28	Donegal . .	Banagh . .	Killaghtee . .	Glenties . .	III.	109
10	Ballyloughan .	335	2	1	Down . .	Castlereagh Lower .	Comber . .	Newtownards .	III.	161
10	Ballyloughan .	119	1	7	Kildare . .	Ikeathy and Oughterany . .	Clonshanbo . .	Celbridge . .	I.	57
48	Ballyloughan .	552	3	17	Londonderry .	Loughinsholin .	Derryloran . .	Magherafelt .	III.	240
31	Ballyloughan .	173	0	33	Monaghan .	Farney . .	Magheracloone .	Carrickmacross	III.	272
7	Ballyloughan .	74	2	16	Wexford . .	Gorey . .	Kilmakilloge .	Gorey . .	I.	318
114, 123	Ballyloughaun .	98	2	14	Galway . .	Kiltartan . .	Kiltartan . .	Gort . .	IV.	48
94	BALLYLOUGHAUN T.	—			Galway . .	Galway . . .	St. Nicholas . .	Galway . .	IV.	38
7	Ballylough Beg .	137	1	19	Antrim . .	Lower Dunluce .	Billy . .	Coleraine . .	III.	16
18, 27	Ballyloughbeg .	337	2	26g	Waterford . .	Gaultiere . .	Kilmacleague .	Waterford . .	II.	364
43	Ballyloughlin .	410	1	32	Down . .	Upper Iveagh, Lr. pt.	Maghera . .	Kilkeel . .	III.	173
2, 6	Ballyloughlin .	120	0	27	Wexford . .	Gorey . .	Kilnahue . .	Gorey . .	I.	319
13	Ballyloughlin .	132	3	16	Wicklow . .	Newcastle . .	Newcastle Lower .	Rathdrum . .	I.	353

(a) Including 17A. 0R. 22P. River Nore.　　(d) Including 5A. 3R. 23P. water.　　(f) Including 6A. 2R. 32P. water.
(b) Including 32A. 1R. 1P. water.　　(e) Including 3A. 1R. 0P. water.　　(g) Including 3A. 0R. 0P. water.
(c) Including 13A. 3R. 13P. water.

No. of Sheet of the Ordnance Survey Maps.	Townlands and Towns.	Area in Statute Acres.	County.	Barony.	Parish.	Poor Law Union in 1857.	Townland Census of 1851, Part I.	
		A. R. P.					Vol.	Page
7	Ballylough More	362 0 31	Antrim	Lower Dunluce	Billy	Coleraine	III.	16
18, 27	Ballyloughmore	279 0 15a	Waterford	Gaultiere	Kilmacomb	Waterford	II.	364
12, 21	Ballyloughnaan	263 0 19	Limerick	Pubblebrien	Croom	Croom	II.	252
5	Ballyloughnane	238 0 30	Tipperary, N.R.	Lower Ormond	Loughkeen	Parsonstown	II.	286
4, 5	Ballyloughran	87 2 33	Kerry	Iraghticonnor	Lisselton	Listowel	II.	192
32	Ballyloundash	316 3 3	Limerick	Smallcounty	Ballinard	Kilmallock	II.	259
6, 11	Ballylow	1,643 0 35	Wicklow	Talbotstown Lower	Blessington	Naas	I.	358
17	Ballylower	189 1 4	Carlow	Forth	Ballon	Carlow	I.	3
32	Ballylowra	342 2 2	Kilkenny	Knocktopher	Jerpointchurch	Thomastown	I.	111
44	Ballylucas	303 2 1	Down	Lecale Upper	Rathmullan	Downpatrick	III.	181
22	Ballylucas	226 1 12	Fermanagh	Tirkennedy	Enniskillen	Enniskillen	III.	221
26,27,32,33	Ballylucas	291 3 14	Wexford	Ballaghkeen	Killisk	Enniscorthy	I.	296
26,27,32,33	Ballylucas	345 3 1	Wexford	Ballaghkeen	Kilmallock	Enniscorthy	I.	296
144	Ballyluck	177 1 2	Cork, W.R.	Ibane and Barryroe	Island	Clonakilty	II.	149
24	Ballyluddy	141 1 24	Limerick	Coonagh	Ballynaclogh	Tipperary	II.	233
23, 24	Ballylug	503 0 4	Wicklow	Ballinacor North	Knockrath	Rathdrum	I.	347
5	Ballylugnagon	269 3 23	Roscommon	Boyle	Boyle	Boyle	IV.	193
41	Ballylumford	264 0 10	Antrim	Lower Belfast	Islandmagee	Larne	III.	8
36, 37	Ballylummin	1,139 2 20	Antrim	Lower Toome	Ahoghill	Ballymena	III.	31
99	Ballyluoge	415 3 28	Galway	Clonmacnowen	Killoran	Ballinasloe	IV.	26
43	Ballylurgan	611 2 35b	Antrim	Upper Toome	Drummaul	Antrim	III.	33
48, 49	Ballylurgan	161 1 22	Antrim	Upper Toome	Duneane	Antrim	III.	34
22	Ballylurkin	164 1 30	Wexford	Ballaghkeen	Killincooly	Gorey	I.	295
12	Ballylusk	410 0 36	Queen's Co.	Maryborough West	Clonenagh and Clonagheen	Mountmellick	I.	242
12	Ballylusk	145 2 35	Wexford	Ballaghkeen	Ardamine	Gorey	I.	291
2, 6	Ballylusk	274 0 39	Wexford	Gorey	Kilnahue	Gorey	I.	319
14	Ballylusk	265 1 28	Wexford	Scarawalsh	Templeshanbo	Enniscorthy	I.	326
23, 24	Ballylusk	336 1 39	Wicklow	Ballinacor North	Knockrath	Rathdrum	I.	347
24, 25	Ballylusk	378 1 9	Wicklow	Newcastle	Rathnew	Rathdrum	I.	354
45	Ballylusky	612 2 35	Cork, E.R.	Kinnatalloon	Aghern	Fermoy	II.	97
33, 42	Ballylusky	161 1 36	Kerry	Corkaguiny	Kilmalkedar	Dingle	II.	178
40	Ballylusky	325 1 27	Kilkenny	Knocktopher	Kilbeacon	Waterford	I.	111
21, 22	Ballylusky	26 3 15	Limerick	Coshma	Croom	Croom	II.	242
21, 22	Ballylusky	142 3 26	Limerick	Coshma	Killonahan	Croom	II.	243
10, 15	Ballylusky	732 3 32	Tipperary, N.R.	Lower Ormond	Ardcrony	Borrisokane	II.	281
54, 62	Ballylusky	345 3 23	Tipperary, S.R.	Middlethird	Magowry	Cashel	II.	328
26	Ballylynan	585 3 9	Queen's Co.	Ballyadams	Killabban	Athy	I.	231
26	BALLYLYNAN T.	—	Queen's Co.	Ballyadams	Killabban	Athy	I.	231
85	Ballylynch	314 2 33	Tipperary, S.R.	Iffa and Offa East	Carrick	Carrick on Suir	II.	312
86, 98	Ballymabilla	867 0 22	Galway	Kilconnell	Killallaghtan	Ballinasloe	IV.	41
27	Ballymabin	291 2 22	Waterford	Gaultiere	Killea	Waterford	II.	363
8, 14	Ballymacad	549 2 17	Meath	Fore	Killeagh	Oldcastle	I.	201
40	Ballymacadam	172 2 12	Kerry	Trughanacmy	Castleisland	Tralee	II.	208
82	Ballymacadam(Austin)	2 1 29	Tipperary, S.R.	Iffa and Offa West	Caher	Clogheen	II.	317
82	Ballymacadam East	63 2 36	Tipperary, S.R.	Iffa and Offa West	Caher	Clogheen	II.	317
75, 81, 82	Ballymacadam West	447 3 34	Tipperary, S.R.	Iffa and Offa West	Caher	Clogheen	II.	317
53	Ballymacadoyle	430 3 19	Kerry	Corkaguiny	Dingle	Dingle	II.	175
67, 68	Ballymacady	427 0 15	Tipperary, S.R.	Clanwilliam	Kilfeakle	Tipperary	II.	308
24	Ballymacaffry	37 1 16	Fermanagh	Magherastephana	Aghalurcher	Lisnaskea	III.	215
25	Ballymacahara	204 1 16	Wicklow	Newcastle	Rathnew	Rathdrum	I.	354
92, 93	Ballymacahil	382 3 32	Donegal	Banagh	Inver	Donegal	III.	106
8, 13	Ballymacahil and Derries	428 3 15	Westmeath	Delvin	Kilcumny	Castletowndelvin	I.	265
34	Ballymacahill	292 0 10c	Clare	Bunratty Upper	Kilraghtis	Ennis	II.	9
22, 23	Ballymacaldrack	1,246 2 4d	Antrim	Kilconway	Finvoy	Ballymoney	III.	26
45, 46	Ballymacall	213 2 30	Tyrone	Dungannon Middle	Pomeroy	Dungannon	III.	304
35	Ballymacallen	214 0 10e	Cork, E.R.	Fermoy	Killathy	Fermoy	II.	80
17	Ballymacallen	579 0 27	Westmeath	Ratheonrath	Killare	Ballymahon	I.	283
25	Ballymacallion	838 1 28	Londonderry	Keenaght	Dungiven	NewTnLimavady	III.	236
13	Ballymacan	200 0 0	Meath	Upper Slane	Grangegeeth	Ardee	I.	224
64, 68	Ballymacan	1,684 3 36f	Tyrone	Clogher	Clogher	Clogher	III.	291
16	Ballymacanab	513 1 21	Armagh	Fews Lower	Lisnadill	Armagh	III.	46
26	Ballymacanallen	677 0 19	Down	Lower Iveagh, Up.pt.	Tullylish	Lurgan	III.	171
20	Ballymacanally	182 3 13	Down	Lower Iveagh, Up.pt.	Magheralin	Lurgan	III.	170
14, 15	Ballymacandrew Nth.	132 3 25	Kerry	Clanmaurice	Kilmoyly	Tralee	II.	171
15, 21	Ballymacandrew Sth.	155 2 38	Kerry	Clanmaurice	Kilmoyly	Tralee	II.	171
88	Ballymacandrick	228 0 1	Cork, E.R.	Imokilly	Cloyne	Middleton	II.	85
88	Ballymacandrick	155 0 25	Cork, E.R.	Imokilly	Inch	Middleton	II.	87
47	Ballymacandy	204 3 21	Kerry	Trughanacmy	Kilcolman	Killarney	II.	210
48, 53	Ballymacane	113 2 7	Wexford	Forth	Tacumshin	Wexford	I.	314
15, 21	Ballymacaquim East	435 1 36	Kerry	Clanmaurice	Killahan	Tralee	II.	170
15, 21	Ballymacaquim West	192 2 5	Kerry	Clanmaurice	Killahan	Tralee	II.	170

(a) Including 33A. 0R. 32P. water.
(b) Including 11A. 2R. 11P. water.
(c) Including 6A. 0R. 32P. water.
(d) Including 5A. 1R. 12P. water.
(e) Including 6A. 0R. 17P. water.
(f) Including 4A. 3R. 30P. water.

No. of Sheet of the Ordnance Survey Maps.	Townlands and Towns.	Area in Statute Acres.			County.	Barony.	Parish.	Poor Law Union in 1857.	Townland Census of 1851, Part I.	
		A.	R.	P.					Vol.	Page
29, 34	Ballymacar . .	610	2	33	Wexford .	Bantry . . .	Oldross . .	New Ross . .	I.	301
22, 23	Ballymacaramery .	778	1	18a	Down .	Castlereagh Upper .	Saintfield . .	Lisburn . .	III.	166
33, 40	Ballymacaratty Beg	457	2	14b	Down .	Upper Iveagh, Up. pt.	Donaghmore .	Newry . .	III.	175
33, 40	Ballymacaratty More	340	2	18c	Down .	Upper Iveagh,Up. pt.	Donaghmore .	Newry . .	III.	175
5	Ballymacarbry .	865	3	9	Waterford .	Glenahiry . .	Kilronan . .	Clonmel . .	II.	365
51	Ballymacarney .	515	2	16	Meath .	Dunboyne . .	Kilbride . .	Dunshaughlin .	I.	200
29	Ballymacarn North .	969	3	39	Down .	Kinelarty . .	Magheradrool .	Downpatrick .	III.	177
29	Ballymacarn South .	767	3	3d	Down .	Kinelarty . .	Magheradrool .	Downpatrick .	III.	177
4	Ballymacarret .	575	3	39	Down .	Castlereagh Upper .	Knockbreda .	Belfast . .	III.	165
4	BALLYMACARRET T.	—			Down .	Castlereagh Upper .	Knockbreda .	Belfast . .	III.	165
24	Ballymacarron .	226	2	19	Down .	Dufferin . .	Killyleagh .	Downpatrick .	III.	167
29	Ballymacarry . .	556	0	23	Donegal .	Inishowen West .	Fahan Lower .	Inishowen .	III.	120
29	Ballymacarry Lower	225	3	3	Donegal .	Inishowen West .	Fahan Lower .	Inishowen .	III.	120
17	Ballymacartan .	129	2	27	Westmeath .	Rathconrath .	Killare . .	Ballymahon .	I.	283
13, 22	Ballymacarthur .	794	1	38	Donegal .	Inishowen East .	Moville Lower .	Inishowen .	III.	118
15	Ballymacartle . .	84	0	8	Dublin .	Coolock . .	Balgriffin .	Dublin North .	I.	26
39	Ballymacart Lower .	228	1	23	Waterford .	Decies within Drum	Ballymacart .	Dungarvan .	II.	351
39	Ballymacart Upper	591	2	31	Waterford .	Decies within Drum	Ballymacart .	Dungarvan .	II.	351
12	Ballymacashel .	90	1	27	Limerick .	Pubblebrien .	Mungret . .	Limerick . .	II.	253
16	Ballymacashen .	688	2	11e	Down .	Dufferin . .	Killinchy .	Downpatrick .	III.	166
67	Ballymacask . .	249	2	1	Cork, E.R. .	Imokilly . .	Youghal . .	Youghal . .	II.	90
2, 3, 5, 6	Ballymacasy . .	508	2	3	Kerry . .	Iraghticonnor .	Aghavallen .	Listowel . .	II.	189
10	Ballymacataggart .	122	0	14	Fermanagh .	Lurg . .	Derryvullan .	Lowtherstown .	III.	204
13, 19, 20	Ballymacateer .	732	2	30	Down .	Lower Iveagh, Up.pt.	Magheralin .	Lurgan . .	III.	170
33	Ballymacaula . .	183	0	27	Clare . .	Islands . .	Drumcliff .	Ennis . .	II.	29
33, 41	Ballymacaula . .	101	1	14	Clare . .	Islands . .	Kilmaley .	Ennis . .	II.	31
101, 105	Ballymacavany .	634	2	12	Donegal .	Tirhugh . .	Templecarn .	Donegal . .	III.	149
29	Ballymacave . .	264	0	15	Limerick .	Connello Lower .	Croagh . .	Rathkeale .	II.	227
124, 125	Ballymacaw . .	200	2	39	Cork, E.R. .	Kinsale . . .	Ringrone . .	Kinsale . .	II.	101
27	Ballymacaw . .	539	1	0	Waterford .	Gaultiere . .	Rathmoylan .	Waterford .	II.	364
106, 107	Ballymacaward .	605	0	19	Donegal .	Tirhugh . .	Kilbarron .	Ballyshannon .	III.	148
16, 17	Ballymacawley .	1,026	0	10	Armagh .	Fews Lower .	Kilclooney .	Armagh . .	III.	46
13	Ballymacbredan .	189	1	9	Down .	Lower Iveagh,Up.pt.	Magheralin .	Lurgan . .	III.	170
15	Ballymacbrennan .	741	3	5	Down .	Castlereagh Upper .	Drumbo . .	Lisburn . .	III.	164
13, 20	Ballymacbrennan .	298	2	32	Down .	Lower Iveagh,Up.pt.	Magheralin .	Lurgan . .	III.	170
26, 29	Ballymacdermot .	715	1	11	Armagh .	Orior Upper .	Killevy . .	Newry . .	III.	57
20	Ballymacdoe . .	44	0	3	Antrim .	Lower Glenarm .	Layd . .	Ballycastle .	III.	22
11	Ballymacdonagh .	143	0	16	Limerick .	Kenry . .	Kilcornan .	Rathkeale .	II.	249
36	Ballymacdonnell .	636	3	13	Clare . .	Tulla Lower .	Killuran . .	Tulla . .	II.	36
39	Ballymacdonnell .	177	3	25	Kerry . .	Trughanacmy .	Killeentierna .	Killarney .	II.	211
1, 4	Ballymacegan . .	1,849	0	17	Tipperary, N.R.	Lower Ormond .	Lorrha . .	Borrisokane .	II.	285
1	*Ballymacegan Island*	33	2	17	Tipperary, N.R.	Lower Ormond .	Lorrha . .	Borrisokane .	II.	285
39	Ballymacelligott .	97	3	11	Kerry . .	Trughanacmy .	Ballymacelligott	Tralee . .	II.	206
38	Ballymacfarrane .	481	1	34	Roscommon .	Ballymoe . .	Dunamon .	Roscommon .	IV.	191
7, 12	Ballymacfin . .	363	2	29	Antrim .	Lower Dunluce .	Billy . .	Ballymoney .	III.	16
9	Ballymacforban .	109	3	27	Monaghan .	Monaghan . .	Monaghan .	Monaghan .	III.	276
121	Ballymacgibbon N. .	236	3	34	Mayo . .	Kilmaine . .	Cong . .	Ballinrobe .	IV.	153
121, 123	Ballymacgibbon S. .	375	2	4f	Mayo . .	Kilmaine . .	Cong . .	Ballinrobe .	IV.	153
7	Ballymachugh .	357	1	35	Mayo . .	Tirawley . .	Kilbride . .	Killala . .	IV.	168
38	Ballymachugh .	352	1	3	Westmeath .	Moycashel .	Newtown .	Mullingar .	I.	298
32, 36	Ballymacilcurr .	341	0	27	Londonderry .	Loughinsholin .	Maghera . .	Magherafelt .	III.	242
54, 55	Ballymacilhoyle .	446	3	28	Antrim .	Lower Massereene .	Killead . .	Antrim . .	III.	28
62	Ballymacilrany .	325	2	8	Antrim .	Upper Massereene .	Aghagallon .	Lurgan . .	III.	29
37	Ballymacilroy . .	341	2	33	Antrim .	Upper Toome .	Drummaul .	Ballymena .	III.	33
18	Ballymacjordan .	257	3	5g	Kerry . .	Clanmaurice .	Duagh . .	Listowel . .	II.	168
13	Ballymackan . .	284	3	18	Queen's Co. .	Maryborough East .	Straboe . .	Mountmellick .	I.	241
61	Ballymackane . .	30	0	6	Tipperary, S.R.	Middlethird .	St. Patricksrock .	Cashel . .	II.	330
22, 23	Ballymack (*Desart*)	374	1	14	Kilkenny .	Shillelogher .	Burnchurch .	Callan . .	I.	113
38, 39	Ballymackea Beg .	639	0	30	Clare . .	Ibrickan . .	Kilmurry .	Kilrush . .	II.	23
38	Ballymackea More .	494	1	27	Clare . .	Ibrickan . .	Kilmurry .	Kilrush . .	II.	23
30	Ballymackeamore .	535	1	31	Limerick .	Connello Upper .	Kilfinny . .	Croom . .	II.	233
137	Ballymackean .	295	0	21	Cork, W.R. .	Courceys . .	Ringrone . .	Kinsale . .	II.	147
137	BALLYMACKEAN T. .	—			Cork, W.R. .	Courceys . .	Ringrone . .	Kinsale . .	II.	147
21, 29	Ballymackeehola .	1,334	1	15	Mayo . .	Tirawley . .	Ballysakeery .	Ballina . .	IV.	164
90	Ballymackeogh .	230	0	11	Mayo . .	Clanmorris .	Balla . .	Castlebar .	IV.	131
31, 37	Ballymackeogh .	1,002	1	29	Tipperary, N.R.	Owney and Arra .	Kilvellane .	Nenagh . .	II.	296
36	Ballymackesy . .	182	1	0	Limerick .	Glenquin . .	Monagay . .	Newcastle .	II.	247
25	Ballymackesy .	516	3	12	Wexford .	Bantry . .	Chapel . .	Enniscorthy .	II.	299
21	Ballymackey . .	162	3	21	Tipperary, N.R.	Upper Ormond .	Ballymackey .	Nenagh . .	II.	289
23	Ballymack (*Flood*)	200	2	25	Kilkenny .	Shillelogher .	Burnchurch .	Callan . .	I.	113
55, 66	Ballymackibbot .	171	3	27	Cork, E.R. .	Imokilly . . .	Ardagh . .	Youghal . .	II.	89
64, 73	Ballymackilduff .	364	0	7h	Donegal .	Boylagh . .	Inishkeel .	Glenties . .	III.	112
61	Ballymackilduff .	264	3	18	Tyrone .	Dungannon Middle .	Clonfeacle .	Dungannon .	III.	298

(a) Including 30A. 3R. 20P. water. (d) Including 56A. 3R. 39P. water. (g) Including 4A. 1R. 4P. water.
(b) Including 2A. 3R. 24P. water. (e) Including 4A. 0R. 8P. water. (h) Including 24A. 0R. 21P. water.
(c) Including 3A. 1R. 11P. water. (f) Including 8A. 3R. 19P. water.

No. of Sheet of the Ordnance Survey Maps.	Townlands and Towns.	Area in Statute Acres.	County.	Barony.	Parish.	Poor Law Union in 1857.	Townland Census of 1851, Part I.	
							Vol.	Page
		A. R. F.						
36	Ballymackillagill	398 0 3	Kilkenny	Knocktopher	Listerlin	New Ross	I	113
8, 12	Ballymackilmurry	143 1 28	Armagh	Armagh	Grange	Armagh	III.	44
35	Ballymackilreiny	992 2 23	Down	Upper Iveagh, Lr. pt.	Drumgooland	Banbridge	III.	172
52	Ballymackilroy	679 0 26	Tyrone	Clogher	Errigal Keerogue	Clogher	III.	295
34	Ballymackilroy or Mullaghkeel	119 2 27	Fermanagh	Magherastephana	Aghalurcher	Lisnaskea	III.	217
20	Ballymackinroe	298 2 19a	Cavan	Upper Loughtee	Annagelliff	Cavan	III.	81
7	Ballymacky	76 0 38	Wexford	Gorey	Kilcavan	Gorey	I.	317
7	Ballymacky	6 1 7	Wexford	Gorey	Kilgorman	Gorey	I.	318
23	Ballymaclanigan	899 0 13	Londonderry	Tirkeeran	Cumber Upper	NewTⁿLimavady	III.	249
34	Ballymaclare	257 2 29	Wexford	Shelburne	Whitechurch	New Ross	I.	329
2	Ballymaclary	635 0 20	Londonderry	Keenaght	Magilligan	NewTⁿLimavady	III.	236
35	Ballymaclawrence	226 3 4b	Cork, E.R.	Fermoy	Killathy	Fermoy	II.	80
3	Ballymaclevennon East	190 2 5	Londonderry	North East Liberties of Coleraine	Ballywillin	Coleraine	III.	245
3	Ballymaclevennon West	172 0 16	Londonderry	North East Liberties of Coleraine	Ballywillin	Coleraine	III.	245
19, 23	Ballymaclifford	104 3 26	Longford	Ardagh	Kilglass	Ballymahon	I.	152
14, 22	Ballymaclinaun	171 2 7	Clare	Corcomroe	Kilmacrehy	Ennistimon	II.	20
10, 18	Ballymaclode	374 2 27	Waterford	Gaultiere	Ballygunner	Waterford	II.	362
42	Ballymacloon East	162 3 0	Clare	Bunratty Upper	Quin	Tulla	II.	10
42	Ballymacloon North	9 3 14	Clare	Bunratty Upper	Quin	Tulla	II.	10
42	Ballymacloon West	123 2 34	Clare	Bunratty Upper	Quin	Tulla	II.	10
62, 63	Ballymaclose	446 2 28	Antrim	Upper Massereene	Ballinderry	Lisburn	III.	29
79, 80, 90	Ballymacloughlin	113 0 18	Mayo	Clanmorris	Balla	Castlebar	IV.	131
30	Ballymacmague East	177 1 6	Waterford	Decies without Drum	Dungarvan	Dungarvan	II.	355
30	Ballymacmague Nth.	252 3 35	Waterford	Decies without Drum	Dungarvan	Dungarvan	II.	355
30, 31	Ballymacmague Sth.	315 3 17	Waterford	Decies without Drum	Dungarvan	Dungarvan	II.	355
30	Ballymacmague West	194 0 11	Waterford	Decies without Drum	Dungarvan	Dungarvan	II.	355
13	Ballymacmaine	209 2 24	Down	Lower Iveagh, Up.pt.	Magheralin	Lurgan	III.	170
58	Ballymacmary	315 1 13	Antrim	Lower Massereene	Killead	Antrim	III.	28
3	Ballymacmoriarty	860 1 10	Donegal	Inishowen East	Clonmany	Inishowen	III.	117
32, 38	Ballymacmorris	485 1 26	Westmeath	Moycashel	Kilbeggan	Tullamore	I.	278
33, 34	Ballymacmoy	638 0 19c	Cork, E.R.	Fermoy	Monanimy	Mallow	II.	81
23, 31	Ballymacmurragh	399 0 28	Cork, E.R.	Duhallow	Castlemagner	Kanturk	II.	67
39	Ballymacmurragh	533 0 35	King's Co.	Ballybritt	Kinnitty	Parsonstown	I.	125
25	Ballymacnamee	181 0 34	Down	Ards Upper	Ballytrustan	Downpatrick	III.	160
51	Ballymacnevin	91 3 53	Clare	Bunratty Lower	Kilmaleery	Ennis	II.	5
78	Ballymacoda	552 1 15	Cork, E.R.	Imokilly	Kilmacdonogh	Youghal	II.	88
78	BALLYMACODA T.	—	Cork, E.R.	Imokilly	Kilmacdonogh	Youghal	II.	88
3, 6	Ballymacolgan	173 0 22	Meath	Slane Lower	Drumcondra	Ardee	I.	222
50	Ballymacoll	608 3 3	Meath	Dunboyne	Dunboyne	Dunshaughlin	I.	199
45, 51	Ballymacoll Little	301 0 9	Meath	Dunboyne	Dunboyne	Dunshaughlin	I.	199
37	Ballymacombs Beg	655 3 9	Londonderry	Loughinsholin	Ballyscullion	Magherafelt	III.	239
37, 38	Ballymacombs More	954 0 22	Londonderry	Loughinsholin	Ballyscullion	Magherafelt	III.	239
4, 9	Ballymaconaghy	681 1 27	Down	Castlereagh Upper	Knockbreda	Belfast	III.	165
51	Ballymaconaghy	240 3 31	Down	Upper Iveagh, Up pt	Clonallan	Newry	III.	174
28, 33	Ballymaconey	217 1 20	Wicklow	Upper Talbotstown	Kiltegan	Baltinglass	I.	364
25	Ballymacon and Ferganstown	695 3 0d	Meath	Skreen	Athlumney	Navan	I.	220
25	Ballymaconna	326 0 14	Clare	Bunratty Upper	Kilraghtis	Ennis	II.	9
2	Ballymaconnell	495 3 37	Down	Ards Lower	Bangor	Newtownards	III.	157
22, 26	Ballymaconnelly	835 2 35	Antrim	Kilconway	Rasharkin	Ballymoney	III.	27
22, 35	Ballymaconry or Kingstown Glebe	78 1 37	Galway	Ballynahinch	Omey	Clifden	IV.	15
61	Ballymacoo	243 0 26	Cork, E.R.	East Muskerry	Inishcarra	Cork	II.	103
41	Ballymacooda	513 1 32e	Clare	Islands	Kilmaley	Ennis	II.	31
53	Ballymacool	470 2 26	Donegal	Kilmacrenan	Conwal	Letterkenny	III.	125
21, 29	Ballymacoolaghan	220 3 28	King's Co.	Garrycastle	Lusmagh	Parsonstown	I.	137
66	Ballymacooly Beg	163 3 34	Cork, E.R.	Imokilly	Mogeely	Middleton	II.	89
66	Ballymacooly More	270 3 24	Cork, E.R.	Imokilly	Mogeely	Middleton	II.	89
27	Ballymacoonoge	196 2 13	Wexford	Ballaghkeen	Killisk	Enniscorthy	I.	296
59	Ballymacorcoran	226 2 22	Cork, W.R.	West Muskerry	Clondrohid	Macroom	II.	155
2	Ballymacormick	351 1 20	Down	Ards Lower	Bangor	Newtownards	III.	157
21	Ballymacormick	700 0 19	Down	Lower Iveagh, Lr. pt	Dromore	Banbridge	III.	168
63, 64, 68	Ballymacoss	464 1 38	Antrim	Upper Massereene	Derryaghy	Lisburn	III.	30
89	Ballymacotter	260 3 27	Cork, E.R.	Imokilly	Ballintemple	Middleton	II.	84
122, 135	Ballymacowen	522 2 27	Cork, W.R.	East Carbery (E.D.)	Kilnagross	Clonakilty	II.	129
33, 37	Ballymacpeake Lower	662 3 25	Londonderry	Loughinsholin	Tamlaght O'Crilly	Magherafelt	III.	243
37	Ballymacpeake Upper	1,107 3 22	Londonderry	Loughinsholin	Maghera	Magherafelt	III.	242
90	Ballymacphadin	256 0 19	Donegal	Banagh	Kilcar	Glenties	III.	108
41	Ballymacpherson	166 3 9	Londonderry	Loughinsholin	Desertmartin	Magherafelt	III.	240
35	Ballymacphilip	333 2 24	Cork, E.R.	Fermoy	Killathy	Fermoy	II.	80
24	Ballymacpierce	222 2 31	Cork, E.R.	Duhallow	Kilbrin	Kanturk	II.	71

No. of Sheet of the Ordnance Survey Maps	Townlands and Towns	Area in Statute Acres.			County.	Barony.	Parish.	Poor Law Union in 1857.	Townland Census of 1851, Part I.	
		A.	R.	P.					Vol.	Page
39	Ballymacpierce	257	3	34	Kerry	Trughanacmy	Nohaval	Killarney	II.	212
56	Ballymacprior	226	1	35	Kerry	Trughanacmy	Killorglin	Killarney	II.	211
14, 20	Ballymacquin Lower	471	0	25a	Kerry	Clanmaurice	Ardfert	Tralee	II.	167
14, 20	Ballymacquin Upper	200	2	36	Kerry	Clanmaurice	Ardfert	Tralee	II.	167
78	Ballymacrah	367	2	24b	Mayo	Carra	Aglish	Castlebar	IV.	123
136	Ballymacraheen	113	2	3	Cork, W.R.	Ibane and Barryroe	Lislee	Clonakilty	II.	150
9	Ballymacran	153	0	39	Londonderry	Keenaght	Tamlaght Finlagan	New T. Limavady	III.	237
10	Ballymacrandal	169	2	3	Armagh	Oneilland East	Seagoe	Lurgan	III.	50
15	Ballymacravan	375	2	32	Clare	Corcomroe	Kilshanny	Ennistimon	II.	21
2, 6	Ballymacrea Lower	93	1	32	Antrim	Lower Dunluce	Dunluce	Coleraine	III.	17
6	Ballymacrea Upper	53	3	0	Antrim	Lower Dunluce	Dunluce	Coleraine	III.	17
124	Ballymacredmond	61	2	14	Cork, W.R.	Courceys	Ringrone	Kinsale	II.	147
136, 145	Ballymacredmond	500	2	7	Cork, W.R.	Ibane and Barryroe	Lislee	Clonakilty	II.	150
47	Ballymacredmond	146	3	16	Mayo	Tirawley	Addergoole	Castlebar	IV.	162
39, 48	Ballymacredmond	335	0	35	Mayo	Tirawley	Ballynahaglish	Ballina	IV.	164
16, 17, 23, 24	Ballymacreely	1,342	0	34c	Down	Dufferin	Killinchy	Downpatrick	III.	166
14, 23	Ballymacreese	455	1	3	Limerick	Clanwilliam	Ludden	Limerick	II.	225
59, 62, 63	Ballymacrevan	364	0	6	Antrim	Upper Massereene	Ballinderry	Lisburn	III.	29
58, 59	Ballymacrevan	551	1	34	Antrim	Upper Massereene	Camlin	Antrim	III.	30
59, 63	Ballymacricket	335	3	3	Antrim	Upper Massereene	Glenavy	Lisburn	III.	30
67	Ballymacrinan	475	2	9d	Clare	Clonderalaw	Killimer	Kilrush	II.	16
25	Ballymacrogan East	115	1	21	Clare	Inchiquin	Ruan	Corrofin	II.	28
25	Ballymacrogan West	101	1	4e	Clare	Inchiquin	Ruan	Corrofin	II.	28
10	Ballymacroly	62	3	16	Longford	Granard	Granard	Granard	I.	156
24	Ballymacromwell	218	1	14	Down	Dufferin	Killyleagh	Downpatrick	III.	167
30, 31	Ballymacrory	145	2	22	Limerick	Coshma	Anhid	Croom	II.	241
30, 31	Ballymacrory	237	0	25	Limerick	Coshma	Croom	Croom	II.	242
2	Ballymacrory	39	2	1	Queen's Co.	Tinnahinch	Rearymore	Mountmellick	I.	249
26, 33	Ballymacrossan	609	3	30	King's Co.	Upper Philipstown	Ballykean	Mountmellick	I.	143
26, 33	Ballymacrossan	625	3	24	King's Co.	Upper Philipstown	Geashill	Mountmellick	I.	144
150	Ballymacrown	663	2	23	Cork, W.R.	West Carbery (E.D.)	Tullagh	Skibbereen	II.	141
7	Ballymacruise	381	1	27	Down	Ards Lower	Donaghadee	Newtownards	III.	157
23	Ballymacshane	72	0	19	Longford	Shrule	Agharra	Ballymahon	I.	166
55	Ballymacshaneboy	51	2	0	Limerick	Coshlea	Effin	Kilmallock	II.	238
55	Ballymacshaneboy	706	3	37	Limerick	Coshlea	Kilquane	Kilmallock	II.	240
9, 16	Ballymacsherron	335	2	34	Mayo	Erris	Kilmore	Belmullet	IV.	145
136, 145	Ballymacshoneen	233	0	7	Cork, W.R.	Ibane and Barryroe	Lislee	Clonakilty	II.	150
37	Ballymacshoneen	5	1	12	Wexford	Shelmaliere East	Kilpatrick	Wexford	I.	330
37	Ballymacshoneen	17	2	20	Wexford	Shelmaliere East	Tikillin	Wexford	I.	331
45	Ballymacsimon	426	2	5	Cork, E.R.	Kinnatalloon	Aghern	Fermoy	II.	97
27, 28	Ballymacsimon	241	1	12	Wexford	Ballaghkeen	Killincooly	Enniscorthy	I.	295
24, 25	Ballymacsimon	419	1	30	Wicklow	Newcastle	Glenealy	Rathdrum	I.	351
65	Ballymacsliney	341	3	19	Cork, E.R.	Barrymore	Templenacarriga	Middleton	II.	58
31	Ballymacsradeen East	268	2	37	Limerick	Coshma	Monasteranenagh	Croom	II.	243
30, 31	Ballymacsradeen West	345	3	5	Limerick	Pubblebrien	Monasteranenagh	Croom	II.	253
29, 30, 38, 39	Ballymacthomas	395	1	3	Kerry	Trughanacmy	Ballyseedy	Tralee	II.	207
15, 21	Ballymacue	115	1	33	Tipperary, N.R.	Upper Ormond	Kilruane	Nenagh	II.	292
7, 11	Ballymacully Lower	212	3	30	Armagh	Tiranny	Eglish	Armagh	III.	59
11	Ballymacully Upper	249	3	34	Armagh	Tiranny	Eglish	Armagh	III.	59
35	Ballymacurly North	193	3	25	Roscommon	Ballymoe	Cloonygormican	Roscommon	IV.	191
35	Ballymacurly South	697	0	20	Roscommon	Ballymoe	Cloonygormican	Roscommon	IV.	191
56, 67	Ballymacurtaun	53	1	19	Clare	Moyarta	Kilrush	Kilrush	II.	33
125	Ballymacus	252	1	0	Cork, E.R.	Kinsale	Ringcurran	Kinsale	II.	100
48	Ballymacushin	12	2	0	Wexford	Forth	Ballybrennan	Wexford	I.	308
48	Ballymacushin	112	3	10	Wexford	Forth	Kilscoran	Wexford	I.	311
73	Ballymacward	223	1	21	Galway	Tiaquin	Ballymacward	Ballinasloe	IV.	75
59, 63	Ballymacward Lower	927	1	4	Antrim	Upper Massereene	Derryaghy	Lisburn	III.	30
59, 60, 63, 64	Ballymacward Upper	1,454	3	14	Antrim	Upper Massereene	Derryaghy	Lisburn	III.	30
4, 11	Ballymacwilliam	396	2	4	King's Co.	Warrenstown	Ballymacwilliam	Edenderry	I.	144
14	Ballymacwilliam	119	0	14	Longford	Ardagh	Templemichael	Longford	I.	153
135, 136	Ballymacwilliam East	104	0	30	Cork, W.R.	Ibane and Barryroe	Templeomalus	Clonakilty	II.	150
135, 136	Ballymacwilliam Sth.	18	2	7	Cork, W.R.	Ibane and Barryroe	Templeomalus	Clonakilty	II.	150
135	Ballymacwilliam West	71	1	34	Cork, W.R.	Ibane and Barryroe	Templeomalus	Clonakilty	II.	150
21	Ballymad	64	2	11	Meath	Lower Duleek	Colp	Drogheda	I.	194
21, 28	Ballymad	111	3	37	Meath	Lower Duleek	Julianstown	Drogheda	I.	196
45, 46	Ballymadder	215	2	4	Wexford	Bargy	Bannow	Wexford	I.	304
31	Ballymaddock	30	0	32	King's Co.	Ballyboy	Ballyboy	Parsonstown	I.	123
24	Ballymaddock	452	2	37	Queen's Co.	Cullenagh	Abbeyleix	Abbeyleix	I.	238
13, 14	Ballymaddock	689	3	33	Queen's Co.	Stradbally	Kilteale	Athy	I.	247
11	Ballymadeer	147	3	37	Kildare	South Salt	Stacumny	Celbridge	I.	78
55	Ballymadeerfy	499	1	25	Down	Mourne	Kilkeel	Kilkeel	III.	182
2	Ballymadigan	160	0	20	Londonderry	Coleraine	Dunboe	Coleraine	III.	231
67, 78	Ballymadog	365	3	28	Cork, E.R.	Imokilly	Clonpriest	Youghal	II.	84

(a) Including 55A. 2R. 11P. water.
(b) Including 2A. 0R. 20P. water.
(c) Including 23A. 3R. 19P. water.
(d) Including 3A. 0R. 12P. water.
(e) Including 4A. 2R. 32P. water.

No. of Sheet of the Ordnance Survey Maps	Townlands and Towns	Area in Statute Acres.			County.	Barony.	Parish.	Poor Law Union in 1857.	Townland Census of 1851, Part I.	
		A.	R.	P.					Vol.	Page
12	Ballymadrough	544	2	31	Dublin	Nethercross	Swords	Balrothery	I.	32
6	Ballymadun	785	0	29	Dublin	Balrothery West	Ballymadun	Dunshaughlin	I.	22
3, 4, 8, 9	Ballymagaghran	277	2	28a	Fermanagh	Lurg	Belleek	Ballyshannon	III.	203
8, 17	Ballymagahy Mountain	140	3	5	Donegal	Kilmacrenan	Clondavaddog	Millford	III.	124
17	Ballymagahy North	126	2	1b	Donegal	Kilmacrenan	Clondavaddog	Millford	III.	124
17	Ballymagahy South	197	1	19c	Donegal	Kilmacrenan	Clondavaddog	Millford	III.	124
20, 21	Ballymaganlis	115	0	0	Down	Lower Iveagh, Lr. pt.	Dromore	Banbridge	III.	168
29	Ballymagan Upper & Lower & Clonblosk	481	0	17	Donegal	Inishowen West	Fahan Lower	Inishowen	III.	120
13, 20	Ballymagaraghan	555	2	8	Down	Lower Iveagh, Up.pt.	Moira	Lurgan	III.	170
12, 13	Ballymagarghy	387	0	25d	Donegal	Inishowen East	Culdaff	Inishowen	III.	118
12, 13	Ballymagaraghy	268	1	18	Donegal	Inishowen East	Moville Lower	Inishowen	III.	118
2, 6	Ballymagarry	599	3	8	Antrim	Lower Dunluce	Dunluce	Coleraine	III.	17
60	Ballymagaury	617	2	33e	Antrim	Upper Belfast	Shankill	Belfast	III.	10
55	Ballymagart	202	1	31	Down	Mourne	Kilkeel	Kilkeel	III.	182
32	Ballymagarvey	442	1	12	Meath	Lower Duleek	Ballymagarvey	Navan	I.	194
10	Ballymagaughey	77	3	34f	Down	Castlereagh Lower	Comber	Newtownards	III.	161
13	Ballymagauran	327	2	27g	Cavan	Tullyhaw	Templeport	Bawnboy	III.	93
2	Ballymagee	358	2	25	Down	Ards Lower	Bangor	Newtownards	III.	157
52, 55	Ballymageogh	1,345	0	0	Down	Mourne	Kilkeel	Kilkeel	III.	182
18	Ballymageragh	170	2	2	Louth	Ardee	Cappoge	Ardee	I.	171
45	Ballymageraghty	276	0	22	Galway	Tiaquin	Moylough	Mountbellew	IV.	79
8	Ballymagerny	263	1	9	Armagh	Oneilland West	Loughgall	Armagh	III.	53
4, 5	Ballymaghan	461	3	8	Down	Castlereagh Lower	Holywood	Belfast	III.	162
48	Ballymaghery	419	1	29	Down	Upper Iveagh, Lr. pt.	Clonduff	Newry	III.	171
13	Ballymaghery	34	3	25	Westmeath	Delvin	Killagh	Castletowndelvin	I.	265
33	Ballymaghroe	352	0	10	Wicklow	Ballinacor South	Hacketstown	Shillelagh	I.	348
33	Ballymaghroe	414	3	36	Wicklow	Ballinacor South	Moyne	Shillelagh	I.	350
18,19,24,25	Ballymaghroe	686	1	15	Wicklow	Newcastle	Killiskey	Rathdrum	I.	352
52, 60	Ballymagig or Barrack	140	1	24	Donegal	Raphoe	Conwal	Letterkenny	III.	137
50, 51	Ballymagillin	143	1	14h	Meath	Dunboyne	Dunboyne	Dunshaughlin	I.	199
49	Ballymagillin	192	1	22	Meath	Upper Deece	Moyglare	Celbridge	I.	194
13	Ballymagin	860	0	7	Down	Lower Iveagh, Up.pt.	Magheralin	Lurgan	III.	170
36, 43	Ballymaginaghy	1,185	1	0	Down	Upper Iveagh, Lr. pt.	Drumgooland	Banbridge	III.	172
74	Ballymaging or Castlemore	285	1	28	Mayo	Costello	Castlemore	Castlereagh	IV.	139
13	Ballymagirril	156	2	15	Cavan	Tullyhaw	Templeport	Bawnboy	III.	93
5, 10	Ballymaglaff	809	1	18	Down	Castlereagh Lower	Comber	Newtownards	III.	162
27	Ballymaglancy	50	3	21	Galway	Ross	Cong	Oughterard	IV.	72
28	Ballymaglancy	195	3	27	Roscommon	Ballymoe	Cloonygormican	Castlereagh	IV.	191
22	Ballymaglane	156	3	30	Louth	Ferrard	Termonfeckin	Drogheda	I.	182
44, 50	Ballymaglassan	426	3	16	Meath	Ratoath	Ballymaglassan	Dunshaughlin	I.	217
22, 29	Ballymaglave North	514	2	22	Down	Kinelarty	Magheradrool	Downpatrick	III.	177
29	Ballymaglave South	785	1	28	Down	Kinelarty	Magheradrool	Downpatrick	III.	177
10, 17	Ballymaglavy	803	3	39i	Westmeath	Rathconrath	Piercetown	Mullingar	I.	283
5, 6	Ballymaglin	365	3	29j	Londonderry	Keenaght	Aghanloo	New T^n Limavady	III.	233
1, 2	Ballymagoland	473	0	0	Londonderry	Keenaght	Magilligan	New T^n Limavady	III.	236
33	Ballymagooly	187	1	37k	Cork, E.R.	Fermoy	Rahan	Mallow	II.	82
33	BALLYMAGOOLY T.	—			Cork, E.R.	Fermoy	Rahan	Mallow	II.	82
5	Ballymagorry	289	1	19	Tyrone	Strabane Lower	Leckpatrick	Strabane	III.	321
5	BALLYMAGORRY T.	—			Tyrone	Strabane Lower	Leckpatrick	Strabane	III.	322
98	Ballymagowan	298	0	35	Donegal	Banagh	Killaghtee	Donegal	III.	109
20	Ballymagowan	381	3	3	Londonderry	North West Liberties of Londonderry	Templemore	Londonderry	III.	246
58, 59	Ballymagowan	285	3	30	Tyrone	Clogher	Clogher	Clogher	III.	291
17, 27	Ballymagowan Lower	267	2	13	Donegal	Kilmacrenan	Clondavaddog	Millford	III.	124
17, 27	Ballymagowan Upper	340	0	0	Donegal	Kilmacrenan	Clondavaddog	Millford	III.	124
15	Ballymagree	44	1	31	Tipperary, N.R.	Upper Ormond	Kilruane	Nenagh	II.	292
5	Ballymagreehan	188	1	9	Down	Castlereagh Lower	Newtownards	Newtownards	III.	163
42, 43	Ballymagreehan	1,243	1	20l	Down	Upper Iveagh, Lr. pt.	Drumgooland	Banbridge	III.	172
24	Ballymagrine	222	2	2	Roscommon	Ballintober North	Termonbarry	Strokestown	IV.	187
104	Ballymagrorty	1,101	1	21m	Donegal	Tirhugh	Drumhome	Ballyshannon	III.	146
13, 20	Ballymagrorty	648	3	21	Londonderry	North West Liberties of Londonderry	Templemore	Londonderry	III.	246
103	Ballymagrorty Irish	410	0	6n	Donegal	Tirhugh	Drumhome	Ballyshannon	III.	146
103	Ballymagrorty Scotch	534	1	9o	Donegal	Tirhugh	Drumhome	Ballyshannon	III.	146
13, 20	Ballymagrorty or White House	1,072	0	1	Londonderry	North West Liberties of Londonderry	Templemore	Londonderry	III.	247
25	Ballymague	432	0	1	Cork, E.R.	Fermoy	Caherduggan	Mallow	II.	77
42, 47	Ballymaguigan	1,028	3	6	Londonderry	Loughinsholin	Artrea	Magherafelt	III.	238
42, 47	BALLYMAGUIGAN T.	—			Londonderry	Loughinsholin	Artrea	Magherafelt	III.	238
5, 8	Ballymaguire	190	2	37	Dublin	Balrothery East	Lusk	Balrothery	I.	20
39	Ballymaguire	264	2	14	Tyrone	Dungannon Upper	Arboe	Cookstown	III.	305

(a) Including 6A. 1R. 24P. water.
(b) Including 2A. 3R. 25P. water.
(c) Including 9A. 1R. 31P. water.
(d) Including 0A. 1R. 2P. detached portion.
(e) Including 10A. 0R. 16P. water.

(f) Including 0A. 3R. 19P. water.
(g) Including 77A. 3R. 3P. water.
(h) Including 27A. 3R. 22P. detached portion.
(i) Including 6A. 3R. 27P. Inny River.
(j) Including 1A. 3R. 11P. water.

(k) Including 6A. 2R. 32P. water.
(l) Including 26A. 0R. 13P. water.
(m) Including 96A. 2R. 34P. water.
(n) Including 29A. 3R. 20P. water.
(o) Including 4A. 2R. 19P. water.

No. of Sheet of the Ordnance Survey Maps.	Townlands and Towns.	Area in Statute Acres. A. R. P.	County.	Barony.	Parish.	Poor Law Union in 1857.	Townland Census of 1851, Part I. Vol.	Page
85, 86	Ballymah	369 3 13	Cork, E.R.	Cork	Inishkenny	Cork	II.	64
27	Ballymahon	276 1 29a	Longford	Rathcline	Shrule	Ballymahon	I.	165
41	Ballymahon	235 1 17b	Meath	Moyfenrath Upper	Castlerickard	Trim	I.	213
27	BALLYMAHON T.	—	Longford	{ Rathcline / Shrule	Shrule / Noughaval }	Ballymahon	I. {	165 / 166
9	Ballymahony	451 3 4	Clare	Burren	Noughaval	Ballyvaghan	II.	13
24	Ballymaice	170 2 21	Dublin	Uppercross	Tallaght	Dublin South	I.	41
17	Ballymakaily	108 3 21	Dublin	Newcastle	Kilmactalway	Celbridge	I.	33
5	Ballymakane	232 3 33	Meath	Lower Kells	Moynalty	Kells	I.	203
78	Ballymakeagh	333 2 20	Cork, E.R.	Imokilly	Kilmacdonogh	Youghal	II.	88
66, 77	Ballymakeagh Beg	177 1 29	Cork, E.R.	Imokilly	Killeagh	Youghal	II.	88
66, 67	Ballymakeagh More	377 1 6	Cork, E.R.	Imokilly	Killeagh	Youghal	II.	88
11	Ballymakealy Lower	113 1 29	Kildare	North Salt	Killadoon	Celbridge	I.	74
11	Ballymakealy Upper	149 1 11	Kildare	North Salt	Killadoon	Celbridge	I.	74
5	Ballymakee	357 1 4c	Waterford	Glenahiry	Kilronan	Clonmel	II.	365
13, 14	Ballymakeegan	243 2 34	Longford	Ardagh	Ballymacormick	Longford	I.	152
58	Ballymakeery	463 0 18	Cork, W.R.	West Muskerry	Ballyvourney	Macroom	II.	154
28	Ballymakeery	92 0 28	Limerick	Shanid	Rathronan	Glin	II.	257
25	Ballymakeever	129 0 32	Londonderry	Keenaght	Dungiven	NewTⁿLimavady	III.	236
28	Ballymakegoge	756 2 36	Kerry	Trughanacmy	Ballynahaglish	Tralee	II.	207
4, 5, 7, 8	Ballymakellett	1,148 0 38	Louth	Lower Dundalk	Ballymascanlan	Dundalk	I.	175
28	Ballymakenny	71 0 2	Fermanagh	Magherastephana	Aghalurcher	Lisnaskea	III.	215
21	Ballymakenny	421 0 26d	Louth	Drogheda	Ballymakenny	Drogheda	I.	175
13	Ballymakeonan	585 2 32e	Down	Lower Iveagh,Up. pt.	Magheralin	Lurgan	III.	170
9	Ballymakeown	127 0 4	Armagh	Oneilland West	Drumcree	Lurgan	III.	51
10	Ballymalady	343 0 36f	Down	Castlereagh Lower	Comber	Newtownards	III.	162
53	Ballymaleel	156 3 8	Donegal	Kilmacrenan	Aghanunshin	Letterkenny	III.	122
25, 26, 33, 34	Ballymaley	342 0 9g	Clare	Bunratty Upper	Templemaley	Ennis	II.	10
57	Ballymalis	502 1 0h	Kerry	Magunihy	Kilbonane	Killarney	II.	200
89	Ballymaloe Beg	170 2 15	Cork, E.R.	Imokilly	Kilmahon	Middleton	II.	89
77, 89	Ballymaloe More	241 2 31	Cork, E.R.	Imokilly	Kilmahon	Middleton	II.	89
28, 29, 36, 37	Ballymalone	1,153 2 7	Clare	Tulla Upper	Tomgraney	Scarriff	II.	40
25	Ballymalone Beg	157 3 34	Tipperary, N.R.	Owney and Arra	Templeachally	Nenagh	II.	297
25	Ballymalone More	414 0 27	Tipperary, N.R.	Owney and Arra	Templeachally	Nenagh	II.	297
26, 28	Ballyman	463 3 27	Dublin	Rathdown	Oldconnaught	Rathdown	I.	37
21, 24	Ballymana	444 2 10	Dublin	Uppercross	Tallaght	Dublin South	I.	41
17	Ballymanaggin	149 0 35	Dublin	Uppercross	Clondalkin	Dublin South	I.	39
104	Ballymanagh	96 2 39	Galway	Dunkellin	Killogilleen	Loughrea	IV.	31
88, 100	Ballymanagh	449 0 5	Galway	Longford	Clontuskert	Ballinasloe	IV.	58
79, 88	Ballymanagh	181 0 5	Kerry	Iveragh	Valencia	Cahersiveen	II.	198
30	Ballymanagh	187 0 31	Mayo	Tirawley	Ardagh	Ballina	IV.	163
119	Ballymangan	282 0 5	Mayo	Kilmaine	Kilcommon	Ballinrobe	IV.	154
14	Ballymanus	549 0 34	Queen's Co.	Stradbally	Curraclone	Athy	I.	246
1, 3	Ballymanus	486 0 33	Westmeath	Fore	Rathgarve	Castletowndelvin	I.	271
34	Ballymanus	1,077 3 2	Wicklow	Ballinacor South	Kilpipe	Shillelagh	I.	349
24, 25, 30, 31	Ballymanus Lower	152 3 32	Wicklow	Newcastle	Glenealy	Rathdrum	I.	351
24, 30	Ballymanus Upper	629 0 30	Wicklow	Newcastle	Glenealy	Rathdrum	I.	351
23	Ballymany	506 2 34	Kildare	Offally East	Ballymany	Naas	I.	69
113, 114	Ballymaquiff North	249 0 33	Galway	Dunkellin	Ardrahan	Gort	IV.	26
113, 114	Ballymaquiff South	108 1 12	Galway	Kiltartan	Ardrahan	Gort	IV.	45
25, 33	Ballymaquiggin	273 2 35i	Clare	Bunratty Upper	Templemaley	Ennis	II.	10
52	Ballymaquin	186 0 35j	Donegal	Kilmacrenan	Gartan	Letterkenny	III.	127
31	Ballymaquirk	360 3 17k	Cork, E.R.	Duhallow	Dromtarriff	Kanturk	II.	71
113, 114	Ballymarcahaun	194 3 4	Galway	Kiltartan	Ardrahan	Gort	IV.	45
114	Ballymariscal	80 2 10	Galway	Dunkellin	Ardrahan	Gort	IV.	26
42, 43	Ballymarkahan	486 0 32	Clare	Bunratty Upper	Quin	Tulla	II.	10
37, 38	Ballymarlagh	400 2 18	Antrim	Lower Antrim	Ballyclug	Ballymena	III.	3
42, 43	Ballymarroge	393 0 0	Wicklow	Shillelagh	Mullinacuff	Shillelagh	I.	358
32	Ballymarter	216 1 22	Down	Ards Upper	Witter	Downpatrick	III.	161
51	Ballymartin	751 3 15	Antrim	Upper Belfast	Ballymartin	Antrim	III.	9
19	Ballymartin	493 0 29	Carlow	Idrone East	Clonygoose	Carlow	I.	6
65, 66	Ballymartin	569 0 20	Cork, E.R.	Barrymore	Dungourney	Middleton	II.	54
51, 62	Ballymartin	354 3 4	Cork, E.R.	East Muskerry	Grenagh	Cork	II.	103
17	Ballymartin	310 1 18l	Down	Castlereagh Lower	Tullynakill	Newtownards	III.	163
56	Ballymartin	351 3 15	Down	Mourne	Kilkeel	Kilkeel	III.	182
117, 118	Ballymartin	68 3 33	Galway	Longford	Lickmolassy	Portumna	IV.	60
5	Ballymartin	875 3 30	Kilkenny	Fassadinin	Donaghmore	Castlecomer	I.	89
36, 40	Ballymartin	821 2 36	Kilkenny	Knocktopher	Listerlin	New Ross	I.	113
3, 11	Ballymartin	390 3 25	Limerick	Kenry	Kilcornan	Rathkeale	II.	249
22	Ballymartin	250 2 14	Limerick	Pubblebrien	Monasteranenagh	Croom	II.	253
118, 121	Ballymartin	327 2 16m	Mayo	Kilmaine	Kilmainemore	Ballinrobe	IV.	155
23	Ballymartin	257 0 27	Roscommon	Ballintober North	Kilglass	Strokestown	IV.	186
33	Ballymartin	91 2 15	Wexford	Shelmaliere East	Ardcavan	Wexford	I.	329

(a) Including 7A. 3R. 30P. water.
(b) Including 9A. 2R. 0P. water.
(c) Including 15A. 0R. 0P. water.
(d) Including 11A. 1R. 1P. detached portion.
(e) Including 99A. 1R. 1P. detached portion.

(f) Including 10A. 1R. 3P. water.
(g) Including 37A. 2R. 24P. water.
(h) Including 10A. 0R. 7P. water.
(i) Including 14A. 3R. 13P. water.

(j) Including 70A. 0R. 21P. water.
(k) Including 5A. 0R. 32P. River Blackwater.
(l) Including 4A. 2R. 4P. water.
(m) Including 28A. 3R. 6P. water.

No. of Sheet of the Ordnance Survey Maps.	Townlands and Towns.	Area in Statute Acres.			County.	Barony.	Parish.	Poor Law Union in 1857.	Townland Census of 1851, Part I.	
		A.	R.	P.					Vol.	Page
39, 41	Ballymartin Beg	113	0	3	Roscommon	Ballintober South	Roscommon	Roscommon	IV.	190
39, 40	Ballymartin More	249	3	10	Roscommon	Ballintober South	Roscommon	Roscommon	IV.	190
28	Ballymartin North	237	0	25	Waterford	Coshmore&Coshbride	Lismore & Mocollop	Lismore	II.	344
28	Ballymartin South	180	2	20	Waterford	Coshmore&Coshbride	Lismore & Mocollop	Lismore	II.	344
98	Ballymartle	317	0	32	Cork, E.R.	Kinalea	Ballymartle	Kinsale	II.	94
8, 12	Ballymartrim Etra	134	3	28	Armagh	Armagh	Eglish	Armagh	III.	44
8, 12	Ballymartrim Otra	131	2	3	Armagh	Armagh	Eglish	Armagh	III.	44
4, 16	Ballymary	41	0	16	Galway	Dunmore	Addergoole	Tuam	IV.	32
4, 7	Ballymascanlan	210	2	38	Louth	Lower Dundalk	Ballymascanlan	Dundalk	I.	175
7	Ballymassy	281	3	10	Tipperary, N.R.	Lower Ormond	Aglishcloghane	Borrisokane	II.	281
7	Ballymassy Little	41	3	14	Tipperary, N.R.	Lower Ormond	Aglishcloghane	Borrisokane	II.	281
12	Ballymastone	129	3	28	Dublin	Nethercross	Portraine	Balrothery	I.	31
55, 56	Ballymather Lower	509	1	0	Antrim	Lower Massereene	Killead	Antrim	III.	28
56	Ballymather Upper	247	3	29	Antrim	Lower Massereene	Killead	Antrim	III.	28
42	Ballymatoskerty	390	3	3	Antrim	Upper Toome	Duneane	Ballymena	III.	34
10, 11, 15	Ballymaurice	455	0	0	Longford	Granard	Granard	Granard	I.	156
63	Ballymave	425	1	16	Antrim	Upper Massereene	Magheragall	Lisburn	III.	31
17, 25	Ballymee	212	0	26	Cork, E.R.	Fermoy	Caherduggan	Mallow	II.	77
21, 22	Ballymeelish	228	3	3	Queen's Co.	Clandonagh	Skirk	Donaghmore	I.	235
11	Ballymeeny	108	1	0	Sligo	Tireragh	Easky	Dromore West	IV.	233
11	Ballymeeny, *Armstrong*	288	1	27	Sligo	Tireragh	Easky	Dromore West	IV.	233
11	Ballymeeny, *Hillas*, or Carrownabinna	175	3	14	Sligo	Tireragh	Easky	Dromore West	IV.	233
11	Ballymeeny, *Jones*	218	1	38	Sligo	Tireragh	Easky	Dromore West	IV.	233
28, 33	Ballymena	963	0	37	Antrim	Lower Antrim	Skerry	Ballymena	III.	4
1, 5	Ballymenagh	845	3	29	Down	Castlereagh Lower	Holywood	Belfast	III.	162
38	Ballymenagh	292	1	17	Down	Lecale Lower	Dunsfort	Downpatrick	III.	179
11	Ballymenagh	265	2	10	Londonderry	Coleraine	Aghadowey	Coleraine	III.	229
26	Ballymenagh	255	0	31	Londonderry	Coleraine	Desertoghill	Ballymoney	III.	230
46	Ballymenagh	248	1	27a	Tyrone	Dungannon Middle	Tullyniskan	Dungannon	III.	304
29	Ballymenagh	204	3	31	Tyrone	Dungannon Upper	Derryloran	Cookstown	III.	306
45, 51, 52	Ballymena Little	837	1	6	Antrim	Lower Belfast	Ballynure	Larne	III.	7
32	BALLYMENA T.	—			Antrim	Lower Toome	Kirkinriola	Ballymena	III.	33
116	Ballymerret	285	3	18	Galway	Leitrim	Leitrim	Loughrea	IV.	55
25	Ballymerrigan	385	1	37	Wicklow	Newcastle	Glenealy	Rathdrum	I.	351
83	Ballymichael	530	3	23	Cork, W.R.	West Muskerry	Kilmurry	Macroom	II.	159
8	Ballymichael	166	1	17	Donegal	Kilmacrenan	Clondavaddog	Milfford	III.	124
37	Ballymichael	41	0	18	Wexford	Shelmaliere West	Ardcandrisk	Wexford	I.	332
13, 18	Ballymichan	138	1	19	Longford	Moydow	Ballymacormick	Longford	I.	160
5, 9	Ballymihil	152	3	34	Clare	Burren	Kilcorney	Ballyvaghan	II.	12
71	Ballymiles	141	0	3	Mayo	Gallen	Meelick	Swineford	IV.	150
11, 12	Ballyminaun	165	2	35	Wexford	Gorey	Liskinfere	Gorey	I.	320
47, 48	Ballyminaun Big	114	2	36	Wexford	Forth	Killinick	Wexford	I.	310
11, 12	Ballyminaunhill	198	3	1	Wexford	Gorey	Liskinfere	Gorey	I.	320
47	Ballyminaun Little	70	2	12	Wexford	Forth	Killinick	Wexford	I.	310
2	Ballyminetragh	584	1	13	Down	Ards Lower	Bangor	Newtownards	III.	157
13	Ballyminion	291	2	38	Longford	Ardagh	Ballymacormick	Longford	I.	152
16, 17	Ballyministragh	784	0	2b	Down	Castlereagh Lower	Kilmood	Newtownards	III.	163
25, 32	Ballyminnish	192	1	27c	Down	Ards Upper	Ardquin	Downpatrick	III.	159
28, 29	Ballyminoge	448	1	24	Clare	Tuila Upper	Tomgraney	Scarriff	II.	40
37	Ballyminstra	620	0	30	Antrim	Upper Toome	Ahoghill	Ballymena	III.	33
47	Ballymintan	104	0	0	Roscommon	Athlone	Dysart	Athlone	IV.	180
59	Ballyminymore	372	3	36	Antrim	Upper Massereene	Glenavy	Lisburn	III.	30
5	Ballymiscaw	853	0	5	Down	Castlereagh Lower	Dundonald	Belfast	III.	162
4, 5	Ballymisert	360	2	18	Down	Castlereagh Lower	Holywood	Belfast	III.	162
41	Ballymitty	241	3	23	Wexford	Shelmaliere West	Ballymitty	Wexford	I.	332
29, 43, 44	Ballymoat	418	3	12	Galway	Dunmore	Tuam	Tuam	IV.	35
16, 17	Ballymoat	279	2	1	Waterford	Middlethird	Reisk	Waterford	II.	368
24, 25, 30	Ballymoat	185	3	24	Wicklow	Newcastle	Glenealy	Rathdrum	I.	351
14, 19, 20	Ballymoat and Ballinree	310	1	11	Longford	Ardagh	Ardagh	Longford	I.	151
28	Ballymoat Lower	184	1	38	Waterford	Coshmore&Coshbride	Kilwatermoy	Lismore	II.	343
28, 33	Ballymoat Upper	165	2	21	Waterford	Coshmore&Coshbride	Kilwatermoy	Lismore	II.	343
2	BALLYMOE T.	—			Galway	Ballymoe	Drumatemple	Glennamaddy	IV.	7
46, 47	Ballymoghan Beg	404	1	12	Londonderry	Loughinsholin	Magherafelt	Magherafelt	III.	243
47	Ballymoghan More	505	2	6	Londonderry	Loughinsholin	Magherafelt	Magherafelt	III.	243
16,17, 22, 23	Ballymoghany	816	2	25	Sligo	Tireragh	Castleconor	Dromore West	IV.	232
13	Ballymogue	211	3	15	Carlow	Forth	Ballon	Carlow	I.	3
13	Ballymogue	127	3	18	Carlow	Forth	Templepeter	Carlow	I.	5
17	Ballymoheen	181	3	20	Tipperary, N.R.	Ikerrin	Rathnaveoge	Roscrea	II.	276
44	Ballymoloney	783	1	38	Clare	Tulla Lower	Killokennedy	Limerick	II.	35
8	Ballymona	422	2	9	Tipperary, N.R.	Lower Ormond	Ballingarry	Borrisokane	II.	282
25, 31	Ballymonan	285	0	29	Londonderry	Keenaght	Dungiven	NewᵀⁿLimavady	III.	236
70	Ballymonaster	143	3	33	Donegal	Raphoe	Clonleigh	Strabane	III.	134

(a) Including 2A. 0R. 24P. water.　　　(b) Including 3A. 3R. 17P. water.　　　(c) Including 9A. 1R. 6P. water.

No. of Sheet of the Ordnance Survey Maps	Townlands and Towns.	Area in Statute Acres.	County.	Barony.	Parish.	Poor Law Union in 1857.	Townland Census of 1851. Part I.	
		A. R. P.					Vol.	Page
70, 83	Ballymoneen . .	583 0 20	Galway . .	Clare . . .	Lackagh . . .	Galway . .	IV.	22
104	Ballymoneen . .	146 3 8	Galway . .	Loughrea . .	Killogilleen . .	Loughrea . .	IV.	64
38	Ballymoneen . .	157 2 32	Mayo . .	Tirawley . .	Crossmolina . .	Ballina . .	IV.	165
16, 22	Ballymoneen . .	253 1 25	Sligo . .	Tireragh . .	Castleconor . .	Dromore West .	IV.	232
35, 40	Ballymoneen . .	418 0 11	Wicklow . .	Arklow . . .	Castlemacadam .	Rathdrum . .	I.	342
18	Ballymoneen . .	362 0 5	Wicklow . .	Newcastle . .	Killiskey . .	Rathdrum . .	I.	352
93	Ballymoneen East .	37 0 31	Galway . .	Galway . . .	Rahoon . . .	Galway . .	IV.	37
93	Ballymoneen West .	87 2 29	Galway . .	Galway . . .	Rahoon . . .	Galway . .	IV.	37
41	Ballymoney . .	328 0 22	Antrim . .	Lower Belfast .	Islandmagee . .	Larne . .	III.	8
60, 64	Ballymoney . .	538 2 36	Antrim . .	Upper Belfast .	Shankill . .	Belfast . .	III.	10
46, 47	Ballymoney . .	376 1 8	Donegal . .	Inishowen West .	Burt . . .	Londonderry .	III.	119
7, 12	Ballymoney . .	206 1 8	Down . .	Ards Lower . .	Donaghadee . .	Newtownards .	III.	157
1, 5	Ballymoney . .	448 1 3	Down . .	Castlereagh Lower .	Newtownards . .	Newtownards .	III.	163
27	Ballymoney . .	390 2 5	Down . .	Lower Iveagh, Lr. pt.	Magherally . .	Banbridge .	III.	168
27	Ballymoney . .	411 2 37	Down . .	Lower Iveagh, Lr. pt.	Seapatrick . .	Banbridge .	III.	169
42	Ballymoney . .	500 3 29a	Down . .	Upper Iveagh, Lr. pt.	Kilcoo . .	Kilkeel . .	III.	173
51, 54	Ballymoney . .	303 2 5	Down . .	Upper Iveagh, Up. pt.	Kilbroney . .	Kilkeel . .	III.	175
2, 6	Ballymoney . .	115 1 6	Londonderry .	Coleraine . .	Dunboe . .	Coleraine . .	III.	231
10	Ballymoney . .	89 1 17	Londonderry .	Keenaght . .	Aghanloo . .	NewTnLimavady	III.	233
24, 30	Ballymoney . .	1,278 3 37	Londonderry .	Keenaght . .	Bovevagh . .	NewTnLimavady	III.	235
31	Ballymoney . .	345 3 25	Wicklow . .	Arklow . .	Dunganstown . .	Rathdrum . .	I.	343
40, 41	Ballymoney . .	256 2 10	Wicklow . .	Arklow . .	Kilbride . .	Rathdrum . .	I.	344
29,30,34,35	Ballymoney . .	188 0 39	Wicklow . .	Ballinacor South .	Ballykine . .	Rathdrum . .	I.	348
7	Ballymoney Lower .	236 1 29	Wexford . .	Ballaghkeen . .	Kiltennell . .	Gorey . .	I.	297
59	Ballymoneymore .	146 0 1	Antrim . .	Upper Massereene .	Glenavy . .	Lisburn . .	III.	30
17	Ballymoney North .	173 2 37	Galway . .	Dunmore . .	Dunmore . .	Tuam . .	IV.	33
17	Ballymoney South .	259 2 12	Galway . .	Dunmore . .	Dunmore . .	Tuam . .	IV.	33
17	BALLYMONEY T. .	—	Antrim . .	Upper Dunluce .	Ballymoney . .	Ballymoney .	III.	19
7	Ballymoney Upper .	185 0 27	Wexford . .	Ballaghkeen . .	Kiltennell . .	Gorey . .	I.	297
23, 32	Ballymongan . .	1,172 3 37b	Tyrone . .	Omagh West . .	Termonamongan .	Castlederg .	III.	317
25, 33	Ballymongaun .	104 2 2	Clare . .	Inchiquin . .	Kilnamona . .	Ennis . .	II.	27
45	Ballymongaun .	86 2 32	Limerick . .	Connello Upper .	Cloncrew . .	Newcastle . .	II.	232
45	Ballymongaun .	68 3 6	Limerick . .	Connello Upper .	Dromcolliher .	Newcastle . .	II.	232
45,46,54,55	Ballymonteen . .	482 1 14	Cork. E.R. .	Kinnatalloon . .	Ballynoe . .	Fermoy . .	II.	97
37	Ballymontenagh .	258 0 9	Antrim . .	Upper Toome . .	Ahoghill . .	Ballymena .	III.	33
21, 29	Ballymoodranagh .	146 0 4	Waterford . .	Coshmore and Coshbride . .	Lismore and Mocollop	Lismore . .	II.	344
16	Ballymoon . .	415 3 28	Carlow . .	Idrone East . .	Dunleckny . .	Carlow . .	I.	6
90, 91	Ballymoon . .	309 2 31	Donegal . .	Banagh . . .	Kilcar . .	Glenties . .	III.	108
18, 26	Ballymooney .	586 0 38	King's Co. .	Geashill . . .	Geashill . .	Tullamore .	I.	139
13	Ballymooney .	337 3 20	Queen's Co. .	Maryborough East .	Straboe . .	Mountmellick .	I.	241
15	Ballymooney . .	714 1 33	Wicklow . .	Lower Talbotstown .	Donard . .	Baltinglass .	I.	359
16	Ballymoran . .	393 2 18	Armagh . .	Fews Lower . .	Lisnadill . .	Armagh . .	III.	46
11	Ballymoran . .	32 1 37	King's Co. .	Coolestown . .	Ballynakill . .	Edenderry .	I.	132
11	Ballymoran . .	368 2 15	King's Co. .	Coolestown . .	Monasteroris . .	Edenderry .	I.	133
14	Ballymore . .	676 3 26	Armagh . .	Orior Lower . .	Ballymore . .	Banbridge .	III.	55
87, 88	Ballymore . .	343 0 5	Cork, E.R. .	Barrymore . .	Templerobin . .	Cork . .	II.	58
110, 111, 123, 124	Bally More . .	418 2 0	Cork, W.R. .	East Carbery (E.D.) .	Kilbrittain . .	Bandon . .	II.	128
89, 90, 96	Ballymore . .	927 3 32c	Donegal . .	Banagh . . .	Glencolumbkille .	Glenties . .	III.	105
103, 113	Ballymore . .	368 2 16	Galway . .	Dunkellin . .	Killeenavarra . .	Gort . .	IV.	30
96	Ballymore . .	384 3 33	Galway . .	Dunkellin . .	Killora . .	Loughrea .	IV.	31
26	Ballymore . .	43 2 15	Kerry . .	Corkaguiny . .	Cloghane . .	Dingle . .	II.	174
2	Ballymore . .	158 2 36	Leitrim . .	Rosclogher . .	Rossinver . .	Ballyshannon .	IV.	110
16	Ballymore . .	386 3 38	Londonderry .	Keenaght . .	Tamlaght Finlagan .	NewTnLimavady	III.	237
10	Ballymore . .	551 0 88	Longford . .	Granard . .	Granard . .	Granard . .	I.	156
40	Ballymore . .	599 0 13d	Mayo . .	Gallen . . .	Attymass . .	Ballina . .	IV.	146
44	Ballymore . .	157 3 6	Meath . .	Ratoath . .	Ratoath . .	Dunshaughlin .	I.	219
29	Bally More . .	192 2 32	Roscommon .	Roscommon . .	Lissonuffy . .	Strokestown .	IV.	211
52	Ballymore . .	1,228 1 33	Tipperary, S.R. .	Kilnamanagh Lower .	Clonoulty . .	Cashel . .	II.	322
23, 24	Ballymore . .	676 1 18e	Westmeath . .	Rathconrath . .	Ballymore . .	Ballymahon .	I.	281
33	Ballymore . .	231 0 17	Wexford . .	Ballaghkeen . .	Skreen . .	Wexford . .	I.	298
16	Ballymore . .	451 3 28	Wexford . .	Scarawalsh . .	Kilbride . .	Enniscorthy .	I.	323
16	Ballymore Demesne	364 1 0	Wexford . .	Scarawalsh . .	Kilbride . .	Enniscorthy .	I.	323
52, 53	Ballymore East .	121 1 15	Kerry . .	Corkaguiny . .	Kildrum . .	Dingle . .	II.	177
9, 10	Ballymore East or Corbally . .	395 2 21	Roscommon .	Boyle . . .	Boyle . . .	Boyle . .	IV.	193
24, 25, 29	Ballymore Eustace East . .	919 0 8f	Kildare . .	Naas South . .	Ballymore Eustace .	Naas . .	I.	64
29	BALLYMORE EUSTACE T.	—	Kildare . .	Naas South . .	Ballymore Eustace .	Naas . .	I.	64
29	Ballymore Eustace West . .	381 1 23g	Kildare . .	Naas South . .	Ballymore Eustace .	Naas . .	I.	64
24, 25	Ballymorefinn .	532 0 39	Dublin . .	Uppercross . .	Tallaght . .	Dublin South .	I.	41
16, 26	Ballymore Lower .	343 0 1	Donegal . .	Kilmacrenan . .	Clondahorky . .	Dunfanaghy .	III.	122

(a) Including 19A. 3R. 28P. water.
(b) Including 6A. 0R. 14P. water.
(c) Including 12A. 0R. 33P. water.

(d) Including 19A. 2R. 22P. water.
(e) Including 31A. 0R. 0P. water.

(f) Including 25A. 1R. 32P. detached portions, and 10A. 1R. 11P. water.
(g) Including 17A. 3R. 3P. water.

No. of Sheet of the Ordnance Survey Maps.	Townlands and Towns.	Area in Statute Acres.			County.	Barony.	Parish.	Poor Law Union in 1857.	Townland Census of 1851, Part I.	
		A.	R.	P.					Vol.	Page
100	Ballymore Lower .	366	2	38	Galway . .	Longford . .	Clonfert . . .	Ballinasloe .	IV.	56
42, 43	Ballymorereagh .	473	3	3	Kerry . .	Corkaguiny .	Dingle . .	Dingle . .	II.	175
24	BALLYMORE T. .	—			Westmeath .	Rathconrath . {	Ballymore Killare . }	Ballymahon .	I. {	282 283
26	Ballymore Upper .	160	2	38	Donegal . .	Kilmacrenan .	Clondahorky .	Dunfanaghy .	III.	122
100, 108	Ballymore Upper .	246	1	39	Galway . .	Longford . .	Clonfert . . .	Ballinasloe .	IV.	56
52, 53	Ballymore West .	179	3	17	Kerry . .	Corkaguiny .	Kildrum . .	Dingle . .	II.	177
5, 9	Ballymore West .	427	2	13	Roscommon .	Boyle . .	Boyle . . .	Boyle . .	IV.	193
10, 15	Ballymorgan . .	122	0	5	Wexford . .	Scarawalsh .	Ballycarney .	Enniscorthy .	I.	322
17	Ballymorin . .	290	0	11	Westmeath .	Rathconrath .	Ballymorin .	Mullingar .	I.	282
51	Ballymorisheen .	824	1	38	Cork, E.R. .	Barretts . .	Grenagh . .	Cork . .	II.	49
17	Ballymorran . .	474	0	1	Down . .	Dufferin . .	Killinchy . .	Downpatrick .	III.	165
62	Ballymorris . .	639	2	23	Clare . .	Bunratty Lower .	Kilfintinan .	Limerick . .	II.	5
40	Ballymorris . .	42	3	25	Kilkenny . .	Knocktopher .	Killahy . .	Waterford .	I.	112
4, 5	Ballymorris . .	904	3	16	Queen's Co. .	Portnahinch .	Lea . . .	Mountmellick .	I.	244
68, 75	Ballymorris . .	286	3	2	Tipperary, S.R. .	Clanwilliam .	Killardry . .	Tipperary .	II.	308
82, 88	Ballymorris . .	59	3	9	Tipperary, S.R. .	Iffa and Offa West .	Tullaghmelan .	Clogheen .	II.	321
25, 26	Ballymorris . .	196	2	34	Waterford . .	Middlethird .	Reisk . .	Waterford .	II.	368
31	Ballymorris . .	272	3	32	Wexford . .	Bantry . .	Ballyhoge .	Enniscorthy .	I.	299
37, 42	Ballymorris . .	142	0	24	Wexford . .	Forth . .	St. Peters .	Wexford . .	I.	314
8	Ballymorris . .	25	2	4	Wicklow . .	Rathdown .	Bray . .	Rathdown .	I.	354
20	Ballymorrisheen .	144	1	1	Limerick . .	Connello Lower .	Nantinan . .	Rathkeale .	II.	229
28	Ballymorrisheen .	126	0	5	Limerick . .	Glenquin . .	Grange . .	Newcastle .	II.	245
34, 39, 40	Ballymorris Lower .	208	1	37	Wicklow . .	Ballinacor South .	Ballykine .	Rathdrum .	I.	348
34,35,39,40	Ballymorris Upper .	288	3	25	Wicklow . .	Ballinacor South .	Ballykine .	Rathdrum .	I.	348
87	Ballymot . .	109	3	28	Cork, E.R. .	Kerrycurrihy .	Monkstown .	Cork . .	II.	93
59	Ballymote . .	406	2	16	Antrim . .	Upper Massereene .	Glenavy . .	Lisburn . .	III.	30
33	Ballymote . .	38	2	12	Sligo . .	Corran . .	Emlaghfad .	Sligo . .	IV.	226
38	Ballymote Lower .	172	3	28	Down . .	Lecale Upper .	Down . .	Downpatrick .	III.	180
37, 38	Ballymote Middle .	169	2	8	Down . .	Lecale Upper .	Down . .	Downpatrick .	III.	180
33	BALLYMOTE T. .	—			Sligo . .	Corran . .	Emlaghfad .	Sligo . .	IV.	226
37, 38	Ballymote Upper .	110	2	39	Down . .	Lecale Upper .	Down . .	Downpatrick .	III.	180
20	Ballymoty Beg .	302	1	37	Wexford . .	Ballaghkeen .	Ballyhuskard .	Enniscorthy .	I.	291
20	Ballymoty More .	270	2	20	Wexford . .	Ballaghkeen .	Ballyhuskard .	Enniscorthy .	I.	291
32	Ballymount . .	315	0	38	Kildare . .	Narragh & Reban East	Usk . .	Naas . .	I.	67
84	Ballymountain .	431	3	20	Cork, E.R. .	East Muskerry .	Knockavilly .	Bandon . .	II.	104
110, 111	Ballymountain .	533	1	39	Cork, W.R. .	East Carbery (E.D.) .	Inishannon .	Bandon . .	II.	128
43	Ballymountain .	392	0	4	Kilkenny . .	Ida . .	Dunkitt . .	Waterford .	I.	101
21, 22	Ballymount Great .	280	0	35a	Dublin . .	Uppercross .	Clondalkin .	Dublin South .	I.	39
21, 22	Ballymount Little .	37	1	11	Dublin . .	Uppercross .	Clondalkin .	Dublin South .	I.	39
3	Ballymoy . .	264	3	17	Antrim . .	Cary . .	Billy . .	Ballycastle .	III.	12
49	Ballymoyle . .	476	2	21	Londonderry .	Loughinsholin .	Tamlaght .	Magherafelt .	III.	243
7	Ballymoyle . .	175	2	7	Queen's Co. .	Tinnahinch .	Rosenallis .	Mountmellick .	I.	250
35,36,40,41	Ballymoyle . .	495	3	22	Wicklow . .	Arklow . .	Ennereilly .	Rathdrum .	I.	344
24	Ballymoylin . .	265	3	8	Roscommon .	Ballintober North .	Kilglass . .	Strokestown .	IV.	186
19, 20	Ballymoylin . .	257	3	2	Tipperary, N.R. .	Owney and Arra .	Youghalarra .	Nenagh . .	II.	297
38, 47	Ballymoyock . .	320	1	9	Mayo . .	Tirawley . .	Addergoole .	Castlebar .	IV.	162
46	Ballymuckleheany .	208	0	27	Londonderry .	Loughinsholin .	Desertlyn .	Magherafelt .	III.	240
33	Ballymuck or Pluckhimin . .	156	2	9	Meath . .	Upper Duleek .	Piercetown .	Dunshaughlin .	I.	198
37, 43, 44	Ballymuckvea .	556	0	33	Antrim . .	Lower Antrim .	Connor . .	Ballymena .	III.	3
29, 34	Ballymuddy . .	148	0	7	Waterford . .	Coshmore &Coshbride	Kilwatermoy .	Lismore . .	II.	343
30	Ballymulalla East .	198	1	25	Waterford . .	Decies without Drum	Whitechurch .	Dungarvan .	II.	361
30	Ballymulalla West .	200	0	0	Waterford . .	Decies without Drum	Whitechurch .	Dungarvan .	II.	361
43, 52	Ballymulcashel .	689	1	37b	Clare . .	Bunratty Lower .	Kilfinaghta .	Tulla . .	II.	4
47	Ballymulderg Beg .	700	0	23	Londonderry .	Loughinsholin .	Artrea . .	Magherafelt .	III.	238
47	Ballymulderg More .	434	3	14	Londonderry .	Loughinsholin .	Artrea . .	Magherafelt .	III.	238
7	Ballymuldorry .	261	0	33c	Sligo . .	Carbury . .	Drumcliff .	Sligo . .	IV.	221
41	Ballymuldrogh .	168	1	23d	Antrim . .	Lower Belfast .	Islandmagee .	Larne . .	III.	8
122	Ballymulfaig . .	164	0	10	Galway . .	Kiltartan . .	Kilmacduagh .	Gort . .	IV.	47
1, 5	Ballymulholland .	393	3	13	Londonderry .	Keenaght . .	Magilligan .	NewTⁿLimavady	III.	236
1	Ballymullan . .	752	0	6e	Down . .	Castlereagh Lower .	Bangor . .	Newtownards .	III.	161
14, 15	Ballymullan .	585	3	21	Down . .	Castlereagh Upper .	Blaris . .	Lisburn . .	III.	164
40	Ballymullanny .	81	0	32	Sligo . .	Tirerrill . .	Aghanagh .	Boyle . .	IV.	237
10, 17	Ballymullarty .	464	3	34	Tyrone . .	Strabane Lower .	Ardstraw .	Strabane .	III.	318
91	Ballymullavil . .	106	1	29	Mayo . .	Clanmorris .	Mayo . .	Claremorris .	IV.	135
48	Ballymulvill . .	202	3	11	Roscommon .	Athlone . .	Kiltoom . .	Athlone . .	IV.	182
114	Ballymulen . .	142	1	31	Galway . .	Loughrea . .	Killinan . .	Loughrea .	IV.	64
30	Ballymulen . .	84	2	6	Kerry . .	Trughanacmy .	O'Brennan .	Tralee . .	II.	212
29	Ballymullen . .	29	2	6	Kerry . .	Trughanacmy .	Ratass . .	Tralee . .	II.	213
10, 18	Ballymullen . .	302	1	35	King's Co. .	Lower Philipstown .	Kilclonfert .	Tullamore .	I.	142
23,24,29,30	Ballymullen . .	1,003	0	23	Queen's Co. .	Cullenagh . .	Abbeyleix .	Abbeyleix .	I.	238
27	Ballymullen (Stubber) .	75	1	34	Queen's Co. .	Clandonagh .	Rathdowney .	Donaghmore .	I.	234

(a) Including 9A. 3R. 16P. detached portion.
(b) Including 52A. 0R. 0P. water.
(c) Including 5A. 3R. 10P. water.
(d) Including 7A. 1R. 20P. water.
(e) Including 22A. 2R. 35P. water.

No. of Sheet of the Ordnance Survey Maps	Townlands and Towns	Area in Statute Acres.			County	Barony	Parish	Poor Law Union in 1857.	Townland Census of 1851, Part I.	
		A.	R.	P.					Vol.	Page
27	Ballymullen (Warrensford)	54	2	24	Queen's Co.	Clandonagh	Rathdowney	Donaghmore	I.	234
47	Ballymulligan	580	2	16	Londonderry	Loughinsholin	Artrea	Magherafelt	III.	238
35, 40	Ballymullock	421	2	2	Antrim	Upper Glenarm	Grange of Killyglen	Larne	III.	24
17	Ballymully	319	1	2	Londonderry	Keenaght	Balteagh	NewTⁿLimavady	III.	234
46	Ballymully	340	3	2	Londonderry	Loughinsholin	Desertlyn	Magherafelt	III.	240
38, 39	Ballymully Glebe	144	2	22	Tyrone	Dungannon Upper	Desertcreat	Cookstown	III.	307
35,36,41,42	Ballymulmore	521	0	36d	Meath	Moyfenrath Lower	Trim	Trim	I.	211
25, 26	Ballymulqueeny	176	0	5	Clare	Bunratty Upper	Templemaley	Ennis	II.	10
27	Ballymulrennan	102	1	37	Roscommon	Castlereagh	Kilkeevin	Castlereagh	IV.	200
5	Ballymultimber	331	0	27	Londonderry	Keenaght	Magilligan	NewTⁿLimavady	III.	236
47, 49	Ballymultrea	470	0	33	Londonderry	Loughinsholin	Ballinderry	Magherafelt	III.	239
27	Ballymulvey	451	1	16b	Longford	Ratheline	Shrule	Ballymahon	I.	165
14	Ballymun	365	0	0	Dublin	Coolock	Santry	Dublin North	I.	29
107, 110	Ballymunterhiggin	754	3	39	Donegal	Tirhugh	Inishmacsaint	Ballyshannon	III.	147
26, 32	Ballymurn Lower	181	3	31	Wexford	Ballaghkeen	Kilmallock	Enniscorthy	I.	296
26, 32	Ballymurn Upper	198	0	29	Wexford	Ballaghkeen	Kilmallock	Enniscorthy	I.	296
60	Ballymurphy	1,433	0	5	Antrim	Upper Belfast	Shankill	Belfast	III.	10
8	Ballymurphy	424	0	37	Carlow	Rathvilly	Tullowphelim	Carlow	I.	12
22	Ballymurphy	94	0	21	Carlow	St. Mullins Lower	St. Mullins	New Ross	I.	13
9	Ballymurphy	452	3	23	Clare	Burren	Noughaval	Ballyvaghan	II.	13
11, 12	Ballymurphy	396	3	33	Down	Ards Lower	Greyabbey	Newtownards	III.	158
31, 32	Ballymurphy	345	0	22	Down	Ards Upper	Ardquin	Downpatrick	III.	159
22	Ballymurphy	744	2	10c	Down	Lower Iveagh, Lr. pt.	Annahilt	Lisburn	III.	167
123	Ballymurphy	26	2	23	Galway	Kiltartan	Kiltartan	Gort	IV.	48
22	Ballymurphy	118	2	10	Limerick	Pubblebrien	Crecora	Croom	II.	252
14	Ballymurphy	77	2	26	Mayo	Tirawley	Lackan	Killala	IV.	170
44	Ballymurphy	230	3	9	Meath	Ratoath	Dunshaughlin	Dunshaughlin	I.	218
39, 40	Ballymurphy	255	0	21	Tyrone	Dungannon Upper	Arboe	Cookstown	III.	305
36, 45	Ballymurphy Lower	194	0	34	Cork, E.R.	Barrymore	Knockmourne	Fermoy	II.	56
85	Ballymurphy North	506	0	20	Cork, E.R.	Kinalea	Knockavilly	Bandon	II.	96
85, 97	Ballymurphy South	532	1	35	Cork, E.R.	Kinalea	Knockavilly	Bandon	II.	96
22	BALLYMURPHY T.	—			Carlow	St. Mullins Lower	St. Mullins	New Ross	I.	13
36	Ballymurphy Upper	332	2	28	Cork. E.R.	Barrymore	Knockmourne	Fermoy	II.	56
25	Ballymurragh	167	1	8	Kilkenny	Gowran	Ullard	Thomastown	I.	100
21	Ballymurragh	66	1	36	Wexford	Ballaghkeen	Killincooly	Gorey	I.	295
21	Ballymurragh	72	3	23	Wexford	Ballaghkeen	Kilnamanagh	Gorey	I.	297
48	Ballymurragh	35	3	33	Wexford	Forth	Kilscoran	Wexford	I.	311
35,36,43,44	Ballymurragh East	824	2	33	Limerick	Glenquin	Monagay	Newcastle	II.	247
43	Ballymurragh West	385	0	30	Limerick	Glenquin	Monagay	Newcastle	II.	247
42	Ballymurray	322	0	11	Roscommon	Athlone	Kilmeane	Roscommon	IV.	182
22	Ballymurray	291	2	34	Roscommon	Roscommon	Elphin	Strokestown	IV.	209
25,26,32,33	Ballymurray	235	2	23	Sligo	Leyny	Kilvarnet	Tobercurry	IV.	231
47, 48	Ballymurreen	367	2	25	Tipperary, N.R.	Eliogarty	Ballymurreen	Thurles	II.	269
25	Ballymurrin	236	0	17	Waterford	Decies without Drum	Kilbarrymeaden	Kilmacthomas	II.	356
31	Ballymurrin Lower	194	2	25	Wicklow	Arklow	Dunganstown	Rathdrum	I.	343
31	Ballymurrin Upper	210	1	18	Wicklow	Arklow	Dunganstown	Rathdrum	I.	343
38	Ballymurry	186	3	4	Down	Lecale Lower	Ballee	Downpatrick	III.	178
97	Ballymurry	177	1	26	Galway	Athenry	Kiltullagh	Loughrea	IV.	4
30	Ballymurry	89	3	18	Westmeath	Clonlonan	Ballyloughloe	Athlone	I.	260
27	Ballymurry	207	1	13	Wexford	Ballaghkeen	Ballyhuskard	Enniscorthy	I.	291
53	Ballymurry	73	0	6	Wexford	Forth	Tacumshin	Wexford	I.	314
51	Ballymurtagh	77	3	17	Clare	Bunratty Lower	Clonloghan	Ennis	II.	3
20	Ballymurtagh	195	2	21	Wexford	Scarawalsh	Clone	Enniscorthy	I.	322
35	Ballymurtagh	172	0	3	Wicklow	Arklow	Castlemacadam	Rathdrum	I.	342
47	Ballynaas Great	103	2	9	Wexford	Forth	Rathmacknee	Wexford	I.	313
47	Ballynaas Little	58	3	25	Wexford	Forth	Rathmacknee	Wexford	I.	313
73, 74	Ballynabanaba	442	1	28	Galway	Kilconnell	Fohanagh	Ballinasloe	IV.	39
30, 31, 38	Ballynabane	412	2	32	Limerick	Coshma	Croom	Croom	II.	242
23, 29	Ballynabanoge	542	2	16	Wexford	Bantry	Ballyanne	New Ross	I.	299
15, 24	Ballynabanoge North	240	1	3	Waterford	Decies without Drum	Ballylaneen	Kilmacthomas	II.	354
24	Ballynabanoge South	404	3	10	Waterford	Decies without Drum	Ballylaneen	Kilmacthomas	II.	354
31	Ballynabarna	240	1	31	Kildare	Narragh and Reban West	Narraghmore	Athy	I.	68
2	Ballynabarney	720	3	26	Wexford	Gorey	Kilpipe	Gorey	I.	320
51, 56	Ballynabarnish	706	1	7	Antrim	Lower Belfast	Templepatrick	Antrim	III.	9
41, 47	Ballynabarny	567	1	30d	Meath	Upper Moyfenrath	Clonard	Trim	I.	213
20	Ballynabarny	466	3	34e	Wexford	Scarawalsh	Templeshannon	Enniscorthy	I.	326
23, 31	Ballynabarny	745	3	4	Wicklow	Newcastle	Glenealy	Rathdrum	I.	351
86, 98	Ballynabearna	533	1	23	Cork, E.R.	Kinalea	Ballinaboy	Kinsale	II.	93
28	Ballynabearna	352	0	34	Limerick	Shanid	Ardagh	Newcastle	II.	254
23, 24	Ballynabearna	803	3	38	Wexford	Bantry	St. Mullins	New Ross	I.	303
9, 10	Ballynaberny	532	0	27	Wexford	Scarawalsh	Kilrush	Enniscorthy	I.	324

(a) Including 6A. 2R. 8P. water.　　　　(c) Including 1A. 0R. 4P. water.　　　　(e) Including 1t. 3R. 20P. water.
(b) Including 13A. 1R. 8P. water.　　　　(d) Including 11A. 2R. 28P. River Boyne.

No. of Sheet of the Ordnance Survey Maps.	Townlands and Towns.	Area in Statute Acres.			County.	Barony.	Parish.	Poor Law Union in 1857.	Townland Census of 1851, Part I.	
		A.	R.	P.					Vol.	Page
25, 33	Ballynabinnia . .	214	0	17	Clare . .	Inchiquin . .	Kilnamona . .	Ennis . .	II.	7
87, 96	Ballynabloun .	225	2	29	Kerry . .	Iveragh . .	Killemlagh . .	Cahersiveen .	II.	196
76	Ballynabointra	338	3	12	Cork, E.R. .	Barrymore . .	Carrigtohill .	Middleton . .	II.	52
10, 18	Ballynabola .	236	3	22	Waterford .	Gaultiere . .	Kill St. Nicholas .	Waterford . .	II.	364
35	Ballynabola .	626	2	14	Wexford . .	Bantry . .	Kilscanlan . .	New Ross . .	I.	301
12	Ballynaboley .	380	0	8a	Carlow . .	Idrone East .	Killinane . .	Carlow . .	I.	7
10, 14	Ballynaboley .	216	1	25	Kildare . .	Clane . .	Clane . .	Naas . .	I.	53
24	Ballynaboley .	685	1	29	Kilkenny . .	Gowran . .	Tullaherin .	Thomastown .	I.	100
39, 42	Ballynaboley .	865	1	37	Kilkenny . .	Iverk . .	Ullid . .	Waterford . .	I.	107
7, 11	Ballynaboll .	351	1	39	Leitrim . .	Drumahaire .	Drumlease . .	Manorhamilton .	IV.	94
22, 29, 30	Ballynaboll .	277	0	11	Mayo . .	Tirawley . .	Ballysakeery .	Ballina . .	IV.	164
26	Ballynaboll .	468	2	32	Sligo . .	Tirerrill . .	Ballysadare .	Sligo . .	IV.	237
78	Ballynaboll North	64	0	9	Mayo . .	Carra . .	Aglish . .	Castlebar . .	IV.	123
78	Ballynaboll South	121	1	7	Mayo . .	Carra . .	Aglish . .	Castlebar . .	IV.	123
8	Ballynaboola .	192	0	34	Cork, E.R. .	Fermoy . .	Ballyhay . .	Mallow . .	II.	76
8	Ballynaboola West .	257	3	23	Cork, E.R. .	Fermoy . .	Ballyhay . .	Mallow . .	II.	76
124, 125	Ballynabooly .	227	0	17	Cork, E.R. .	Kinsale . .	Kilroan . .	Kinsale . .	II.	100
43	Ballynabooly .	234	0	13	Kerry . .	Corkaguiny .	Dingle . .	Dingle . .	II.	175
58, 59, 71	Ballynaboorkagh .	319	2	6	Galway . .	Tiaquin . .	Monivea . .	Tuam . .	IV.	78
52	Ballynabortagh .	1,003	3	22	Cork, E.R. .	Barrymore . .	Dunbulloge .	Cork . .	II.	54
7, 16	Ballynaboul .	362	3	9	Cork, E.R. .	Orrery and Kilmore .	Churchtown .	Mallow . .	II.	107
39, 40	Ballynaboul .	92	0	4	Kerry . .	Trughanacmy .	Castleisland .	Tralee . .	II.	208
20, 27	Ballynabragget .	390	3	26	Down . .	Lower Iveagh, Up.pt.	Donaghcloney .	Lurgan . .	III.	169
23, 25	Ballynabranagh or Walshstown .	465	0	6	Carlow . .	St. Mullins Lower .	St. Mullins .	New Ross . .	I.	13
5	Ballynabrannagh .	58	1	3	Fermanagh .	Lurg . .	Drumkeeran .	Lowtherstown .	III.	205
64	Ballynabrannagh East .	225	0	24	Cork, E.R. .	Barrymore . .	Ballycurrany .	Middleton . .	II.	51
64	Ballynabrannagh West	89	1	30	Cork, E.R. .	Barrymore . .	Ballycurrany .	Middleton . .	II.	51
70	Ballynabreen .	245	1	18	Donegal . .	Raphoe . .	Clonleigh . .	Strabane . .	III.	134
91, 101	Ballynabrehon North	296	1	10b	Mayo . .	Clanmorris .	Kilcolman . .	Claremorris .	IV.	133
91, 101	Ballynabrehon South	317	0	10c	Mayo . .	Clanmorris .	Kilcolman . .	Claremorris .	IV.	133
29	Ballynabrennagh Lr.	221	0	22	Kerry . .	Trughanacmy .	Ratass . .	Tralee . .	II.	213
29	Ballynabrennagh Up.	242	0	13	Kerry . .	Trughanacmy .	Ratass . .	Tralee . .	II.	213
26, 32	Ballynabrigadane .	214	2	7	Wexford . .	Ballaghkeen .	Kilmallock .	Enniscorthy .	I.	296
20	Ballynabrock .	347	0	30	Cork, E.R. .	Condons&Clangibbon	Brigown . .	Mitchelstown .	II.	59
2	Ballynabrock .	64	0	21	Sligo . .	Carbury . .	Ahamlish . .	Sligo . .	IV.	219
6, 11	Ballynabrocky .	3,613	1	17	Wicklow . .	Lower Talbotstown .	Blessington .	Naas . .	I.	358
36	Ballynabrone .	94	1	32	Clare . .	Tulla Lower .	Killuran . .	Tulla . .	II.	36
33	Ballynabuck .	309	1	27	Kerry . .	Corkaguiny .	Kilquane . .	Dingle . .	II.	179
103	Ballynabucky .	331	3	34	Galway . .	Dunkellin .	Killeely . .	Gort . .	IV.	29
114, 123	Ballynabucky .	117	0	8	Galway . .	Kiltartan . .	Kilthomas .	Gort . .	IV.	49
2	Ballynabwee .	208	0	24	Tyrone . .	Strabane Lower .	Donaghedy .	Strabane . .	III.	320
19	Ballynacaheragh .	248	1	26	Cork, E.R. .	Condons&Clangibbon	Glanworth .	Mitchelstown .	II.	61
11, 20	Ballynacaheragh .	350	0	26	Limerick .	Connello Lower .	Askeaton . .	Rathkeale . .	II.	226
33, 34	Ballynacaird .	1,716	0	19	Antrim . .	Lower Antrim .	Racavan . .	Ballymena .	III.	4
126	Ballynacallagh	412	0	33	Cork, W.R. .	Bear . .	Kilnamanagh .	Castletown .	II.	125
126	BALLYNACALLAGH T.	—			Cork, W.R. .	Bear . .	Kilnamanagh .	Castletown .	II.	126
50	Ballynacally .	213	1	29	Clare . .	Clonderalaw .	Kilchreest .	Killadysert .	II.	14
28	Ballynacally .	89	3	6	Limerick . .	Shanid . .	Ardagh . .	Newcastle .	II.	254
11, 18	Ballynacally Beg .	564	1	8	Londonderry .	Coleraine .	Aghadowey .	Coleraine . .	III.	229
11, 18	Ballynacally More .	484	3	34	Londonderry .	Coleraine .	Aghadowey .	Coleraine . .	III.	229
50	BALLYNACALLY T. .	—			Clare . .	Clonderalaw .	Kilchreest .	Killadysert .	II.	15
11	Ballynacanon .	346	1	24	Londonderry .	Coleraine .	Macosquin .	Coleraine . .	III.	232
24	Ballynacanty .	537	2	14	King's Co. .	Ballyboy .	Killoughy .	Tullamore .	I.	123
30, 31	Ballynacard .	391	3	2	King's Co. .	Eglish . .	Eglish . .	Parsonstown .	I.	134
16	Ballynacarhagh .	563	3	23	Clare . .	Corcomroe .	Kiltoraght .	Ennistimon .	II.	22
121	Ballynacarragh .	172	3	17	Mayo . .	Kilmaine . .	Kilmainemore .	Ballinrobe .	IV.	155
103, 104	Ballynacarrick .	859	3	9	Donegal . .	Tirhugh . .	Drumhome .	Ballyshannon .	III.	146
107	Ballynacarrick .	141	0	23	Donegal . .	Tirhugh . .	Kilbarron .	Ballyshannon .	III.	148
91	Ballynacarrick .	284	3	37	Mayo . .	Clanmorris .	Kilcolman . .	Claremorris .	IV.	133
104	Ballynacarrick, Barr of	475	1	13	Donegal . .	Tirhugh . .	Drumhome .	Ballyshannon .	III.	146
38	Ballynacarrick Lower	465	0	0	Kildare . .	Kilkea and Moone .	Killelan . .	Baltinglass .	I.	60
38	Ballynacarrick Upper	187	1	14	Kildare . .	Kilkea and Moone .	Killelan . .	Baltinglass .	I.	60
31, 32	Ballynacarrig . .	1,223	1	39	King's Co. .	Ballyboy .	Ballyboy . .	Parsonstown .	I.	123
32	Ballynacarrig . .	102	1	36	Wexford . .	Shelmaliere East .	Ballynaslaney .	Enniscorthy .	I.	330
32	Ballynacarrig . .	283	0	7	Wexford . .	Shelmaliere East .	Kilpatrick .	Enniscorthy .	I.	330
31, 36	Ballynacarriga .	560	3	20	Wicklow . .	Arklow . .	Dunganstown .	Rathdrum .	I.	343
27	Ballynacarriga .	238	2	10	Cork, E.R. .	Condons&Clangibbon	Kilcrumper .	Fermoy . .	II.	61
66	Ballynacarriga .	237	2	7	Cork, E.R. .	Imokilly . .	Killeagh . .	Youghal . .	II.	88
67	Ballynacarriga .	27	3	37	Cork, E.R. .	Imokilly . .	Youghal . .	Youghal . .	II.	90
126	Ballynacarriga .	464	0	5	Cork, W.R. .	Bear . .	Kilnamanagh .	Castletown .	II.	125
108	Ballynacarriga .	124	1	7d	Cork, W.R. .	East Carbery (E.D.)	Ballymoney .	Dunmanway .	II.	127
4, 12	Ballynacarriga .	845	2	1e	Limerick . .	Kenry . .	Ardcanny . .	Rathkeale .	II.	248
77	Ballynacarriga .	306	2	12f	Mayo . .	Burrishoole .	Kilmaclasser .	Westport . .	IV.	121

(a) Including 2A. 3R. 0R. River Barrow.
(b) Including 6A. 1R. 24P. water.
(c) Including 12A. 1R. 17P. water.
(d) Including 5A. 3R. 0P. Ballynacarriga Lough.
(e) Including 7A. 1R. 4P. water.
(f) Including 8A. 0R. 38P. water.

P

No. of Sheet of the Ordnance Survey Maps.	Townlands and Towns.	Area in Statute Acres.			County.	Barony.	Parish.	Poor Law Union in 1857.	Townland Census of 1851, Part I.	
		A.	R.	P.					Vol.	Page
69, 78	Ballynacarriga	191	3	35a	Mayo	Carra	Aglish	Castlebar	IV.	123
39	Ballynacarriga	66	3	6	Sligo	Corran	Kilshalvy	Boyle	IV.	227
126	BALLYNACARRIGA T.	—			Cork, W.R.	Bear	Kilnamanagh	Castletown	II.	126
58	Ballynacarrig East	196	1	39	Kerry	Magunihy	Aglish	Killarney	II.	199
58	Ballynacarrig West	180	1	10	Kerry	Magunihy	Aglish	Killarney	II.	199
10, 11	Ballynacarrigy	146	3	23	Westmeath	Moygoish	Kilbixy	Mullingar	I.	279
11	Ballynacarrigy Old	175	2	37	Westmeath	Moygoish	Kilbixy	Mullingar	I.	279
10, 11	BALLYNACARRIGY T.	—			Westmeath	Moygoish	Kilbixy	Mullingar	I.	280
10	Ballynacarrow	327	0	35b	Westmeath	Moygoish	Kilmacnevan	Mullingar	I.	280
17,18,24,25	Ballynacarrow	660	2	37c	Westmeath	Rathconrath	Rathconrath	Mullingar	I.	284
26, 33	Ballynacarrow North	442	3	36d	Sligo	Leyny	Kilvarnet	Tobercurry	IV.	231
26, 33	Ballynacarrow South	275	1	4e	Sligo	Leyny	Kilvarnet	Tobercurry	IV.	232
30	Ballynacarry	124	3	2	Armagh	Fews Upper	Creggan	Castleblayney	III.	48
34, 37	Ballynaclash	283	3	4	Waterford	Decies within Drum	Clashmore	Youghal	II.	351
33	Ballynaclash	171	1	5	Wexford	Ballaghkeen	Ballyvalloo	Enniscorthy	I.	292
33	Ballynaclash	102	1	36	Wexford	Ballaghkeen	Killila	Enniscorthy	I.	295
65	Ballynaclashy	406	3	33	Cork, E.R.	Barrymore	Ballycurrany	Middleton	II.	51
31	Ballynacleigh	158	2	4	Leitrim	Leitrim	Kiltoghert	Car^k on Shannon	IV.	101
70	Ballynaclera	6	2	28	Tipperary, S.R.	Middlethird	Kiltinan	Clonmel	II.	328
15	Ballynacliffy	486	0	31	Westmeath	Kilkenny West	Kilkenny West	Athlone	I.	273
18	Ballynaclin	222	1	17	Westmeath	Moyashel and Magheradernon	Mullingar	Mullingar	I.	275
86	Ballynaclogh	427	1	38	Galway	Kilconnell	Killallaghtan	Ballinasloe	IV.	41
24	Ballynaclogh	290	3	33	Limerick	Coonagh	Ballynaclogh	Tipperary	II.	233
21, 27	Ballynaclogh	1,094	1	28	Tipperary, N.R.	Upper Ormond	Ballynaclogh	Nenagh	II.	290
17, 26	Ballynaclogh North	305	0	36	Waterford	Middlethird	Reisk	Waterford	II.	368
17, 26	Ballynaclogh South	314	0	9	Waterford	Middlethird	Reisk	Waterford	II.	368
94, 102	Ballynacloghy	370	1	23	Galway	Dunkellin	Ballynacourty	Galway	IV.	27
63	Ballynacloghy	315	2	29	Tipperary, S.R.	Slievardagh	Isertkieran	Callan	II.	333
6	Ballynaclonagh	254	1	12	Westmeath	Corkaree	Multyfarnham	Mullingar	I.	263
78	Ballynacloona	400	1	4	Tipperary, S.R.	Iffa and Offa East	Kilmurry	Carrick on Suir	II.	314
2	Ballynaclose	143	2	9	Meath	Lower Kells	Enniskeen	Kells	I.	202
31	Ballynaclosha	140	0	37	Armagh	Fews Upper	Creggan	Dundalk	III.	48
82	Ballynacloy	218	2	36	Mayo	Costello	Aghamore	Swineford	IV.	136
29	Ballynacloy	272	1	3	Mayo	Tirawley	Crossmolina	Ballina	IV.	165
65, 66	Ballynacole	320	3	1	Cork, E.R.	Barrymore	Dungourney	Middleton	II.	54
23	Ballynacoolagh	371	3	30	Wexford	Bantry	St. Mullins	New Ross	I.	303
49	Ballynacooley	167	0	15	Antrim	Upper Toome	Duneane	Antrim	III.	34
39	Ballynacooly	158	2	15	Kilkenny	Knocktopher	Killahy	Waterford	I.	112
6	Ballynacor	320	0	21	Armagh	Oneilland East	Seagoe	Lurgan	III.	50
78	Ballynacor	700	1	21	Donegal	Raphoe	Donaghmore	Stranorlar	III.	137
13, 14	Ballynacor	730	0	20	Westmeath	Delvin	Killulagh	Castletowndelvin	I.	266
76	Ballynacorra	119	2	19	Cork, E.R.	Imokilly	Middleton	Middleton	II.	89
23	Ballynacorra	232	1	1	Westmeath	Rathconrath	Ballymore	Ballymahon	I.	281
32	Ballynacorra(Davies)	111	2	0	Galway	Killian	Killian	Mountbellew	IV.	44
76	Ballynacorra East	155	3	39	Cork, E.R.	Imokilly	Middleton	Middleton	II.	89
32	Ballynacorra(Ffrench)	349	1	26	Galway	Killian	Killian	Mountbellew	IV.	44
32	Ballynacorra (Netterville)	110	2	17	Galway	Killian	Killian	Mountbellew	IV.	44
76	BALLYNACORRA T.	—			Cork, E.R.	Imokilly	Middleton	Middleton	II.	89
76	Ballynacorra West	251	0	36	Cork, E.R.	Imokilly	Middleton	Middleton	II.	89
32	Ballynacoska	246	3	30	Westmeath	Moycashel	Castletownkindalen	Mullingar	I.	277
98, 112	Ballynacourty	614	3	23	Cork, E.R.	Kinalea	Cullen	Kinsale	II.	94
95, 103	Ballynacourty	469	3	31	Galway	Dunkellin	Ballynacourty	Galway	IV.	27
44	Ballynacourty	362	2	21	Kerry	Corkaguiny	Ballynacourty	Dingle	II.	174
6	Ballynacourty	109	1	24	Limerick	Clanwilliam	Stradbally	Limerick	II.	226
56, 57	Ballynacourty	1,035	2	11	Limerick	Coshlea	Darragh	Kilmallock	II.	238
3, 11	Ballynacourty	410	0	26	Limerick	Kenry	Iveruss	Rathkeale	II.	248
66, 73	Ballynacourty	1,054	2	9	Tipperary, S.R.	Clanwilliam	Clonbeg	Tipperary	II.	305
29	Ballynacourty	154	0	8	Waterford	Decies within Drum	Aglish	Dungarvan	II.	349
31	Ballynacourty	359	0	24	Waterford	Decies without Drum	Dungarvan	Dungarvan	II.	355
30	Ballynacourty	242	3	9	Waterford	Decies without Drum	Whitechurch	Dungarvan	II.	361
36	Ballynacourty North	69	2	11	Waterford	Decies within Drum	Ringagonagh	Dungarvan	II.	352
36	Ballynacourty South	194	2	24	Waterford	Decies within Drum	Ringagonagh	Dungarvan	II.	352
59, 63	Ballynacoy	694	3	0	Antrim	Upper Massereene	Glenavy	Lisburn	III.	30
42, 51	Ballynacragga	426	0	13	Clare	Bunratty Lower	Kilnasoolagh	Ennis	II.	6
59, 60	Ballynacragga	201	1	6	Clare	Clonderalaw	Killadysert	Killadysert	II.	15
10	Ballynacragga	229	3	30	Limerick	Shanid	Shanagolden	Glin	II.	258
10	Ballynacragga North	51	1	10	Limerick	Shanid	Robertstown	Glin	II.	257
10	Ballynacragga South	31	3	31	Limerick	Shanid	Robertstown	Glin	II.	257
24, 33	Ballynacraig	348	2	38	Donegal	Kilmacrenan	Tullaghobegly	Dunfanaghy	III	131
30	Ballynacraig	511	2	21	Down	Lecale Lower	Inch	Downpatrick	III.	179
46, 50	Ballynacraig	682	0	1	Down	Lordship of Newry	Newry	Newry	III.	182

(a) Including 17A. 2R. 30P. water.
(b) Including 9A. 3R. 6P. water.
(c) Including 23A. 1R. 10P. water.
(d) Including 21A. 2R. 15P. water.
(e) Including 3A. 3R. 26P. water.

No. of Sheet of the Ordnance Survey Maps.	Townlands and Towns.	Area in Statute Acres.			County.	Barony.	Parish.	Poor Law Union in 1857.	Townland Census of 1851, Part I.	
		A.	R.	P.					Vol.	Page
49	Ballynacraigy	125	2	31	Antrim	Upper Toome	Drummaul	Antrim	III.	33
8	Ballynacree	110	0	33	Meath	Fore	Killeagh	Oldcastle	I.	201
58, 66	Ballynacree	500	3	39	Tipperary, S.R.	Clanwilliam	Emly	Tipperary	II.	307
7	Ballynacree	173	0	27	Wexford	Gorey	Kilgorman	Gorey	I.	318
16, 17	Ballynacree Beg	133	1	5	Antrim	Upper Dunluce	Ballymoney	Ballymoney	III.	18
16	Ballynacree More	342	3	2	Antrim	Upper Dunluce	Ballymoney	Ballymoney	III.	18
16	Ballynacree Skein	185	0	34	Antrim	Upper Dunluce	Ballymoney	Ballymoney	III.	18
55	Ballynacregga	234	1	22	Galway	Clare	Cargin	Tuam	IV.	18
57	Ballynacreg North	224	1	34	Galway	Clare	Cummer	Tuam	IV.	18
57	Ballynacreg South	440	0	3	Galway	Clare	Cummer	Tuam	IV.	18
11	Ballynacroghy or Gallowstown	358	0	0	Westmeath	Moygoish	Kilbixy	Mullingar	I.	279
34, 38	Ballynacronny	425	1	17	Kilkenny	Iverk	Owning	Carrick on Suir	II.	106
36, 37	Ballynacross	308	0	7	Londonderry	Loughinsholin	Maghera	Magherafelt	III.	242
11	Ballynacross	392	3	8	Longford	Granard	Granard	Granard	I.	156
3	Ballynacross	141	2	10	Tyrone	Strabane Lower	Donaghedy	Strabane	III.	320
38	Ballynacroy	142	1	0	Tyrone	Dungannon Upper	Desertcreat	Cookstown	III.	307
75, 87	Ballynacrusha	380	3	19	Cork, E.R.	Barrymore	Clonmel	Cork	II.	53
112	Ballynacubby	35	2	24	Cork, E.R.	Kinsale	Kinsale	Kinsale	II.	100
112	Ballynacubby	39	0	19	Cork, E.R.	Kinsale	Ringcurran	Kinsale	II.	100
40	Ballynacullia	124	2	37	Roscommon	Ballintober South	Roscommon	Roscommon	IV.	190
30, 31	Ballynacurra	217	0	32	King's Co.	Eglish	Eglish	Parsonstown	I.	134
3	Ballynacurra	536	0	22	Waterford	Upperthird	Mothel	Carrick on Suir	II.	370
105, 115	Ballynacurragh	535	2	25	Galway	Loughrea	Kilchreest	Loughrea	IV.	63
21	Ballynadeige	81	3	24	Waterford	Coshmore&Coshbride	Lismore and Mocollop	Lismore	II.	344
63	Ballynadolly	635	2	27	Antrim	Upper Massereene	Magheragall	Lisburn	III.	31
54,55,58,59	Ballynadrentagh	1,251	1	3	Antrim	Lower Massereene	Killead	Antrim	III.	28
7, 8	Ballynadrideen	642	1	13	Cork, E.R.	Orrery and Kilmore	Aglishdrinagh	Kilmallock	II.	106
29, 35	Ballynadrimna	838	1	27	Meath	Lune	Kildalkey	Trim	I.	208
28	Ballynadrishoge	158	2	26	Wexford	Ballaghkeen	Ballyvaldon	Enniscorthy	I.	292
13	Ballynadrone	111	2	1	Down	Lower Iveagh, Up. pt.	Magheralin	Lurgan	III.	170
66	Ballynadruckilly	179	3	18	Tipperary, S.R.	Clanwilliam	Lattin	Tipperary	II.	309
1, 3	Ballynadrumny	263	0	33	Kildare	Carbury	Ballynadrumny	Edenderry	I.	51
9, 13	Ballynafagh	1,154	2	35a	Kildare	Clane	Ballynafagh	Naas	I.	53
88	Ballynafarsid	120	0	22	Cork, E.R.	Imokilly	Aghada	Middleton	II.	83
36	Ballynafauna	256	3	36	Cork, E.R.	Condons&Clangibbon	Clondulane	Fermoy	II.	60
36	BALLYNAFAUNA T.	—			Cork, E.R.	Condons&Clangibbon	Clondulane	Fermoy	II.	60
39	Ballynafeagh	81	2	5	Tyrone	Dungannon Upper	Arboe	Cookstown	III.	305
32	Ballynafeaha	167	0	32b	Cork, E.R.	Duhallow	Ballyclogh	Mallow	II.	67
23	Ballynafearagh	71	2	7	Westmeath	Rathconrath	Ballymore	Athlone	I.	281
18	Ballynafearagh	163	0	1	Westmeath	Rathconrath	Churchtown	Mullingar	I.	282
36	Ballynafeeragh (1st Division)	64	1	27	Meath	Upper Navan	Trim	Trim	I.	216
36	Ballynafeeragh (2nd Division)	13	0	20	Meath	Upper Navan	Trim	Trim	I.	216
12, 13	Ballynafeigh	245	0	37	Antrim	Lower Dunluce	Derrykeighan	Ballymoney	III.	16
34, 41	Ballynafern	778	0	14	Down	Upper Iveagh, Up. pt.	Annaclone	Banbridge	III.	174
48	Ballynafoy	37	2	8	Antrim	Upper Toome	Duneane	Antrim	III.	34
11, 12	Ballynafid	290	0	25	Westmeath	Corkaree	Leny	Mullingar	I.	262
11, 12	Ballynafid	108	3	26c	Westmeath	Corkaree	Portnashangan	Mullingar	I.	263
31, 36	Ballynafie	348	0	25	Antrim	Lower Toome	Ahoghill	Ballymena	III.	31
3, 7	Ballynafina	257	1	2	Waterford	Upperthird	Rathgormuck	Carrick on Suir	II.	371
33	Ballynafineshoge	209	1	9	Waterford	Coshmore&Coshbride	Kilwatermoy	Lismore	II.	343
4, 9	Ballynafoy	821	1	3	Down	Castlereagh Upper	Knockbreda	Belfast	III.	165
34	Ballynafoy	901	1	16	Down	Upper Iveagh, Up. pt.	Annaclone	Banbridge	III.	174
102	Ballynafullia	249	3	1	Kerry	Glanarought	Tuosist	Kenmare	II.	188
29, 35	Ballynafunshin	38	3	24	Queen's Co.	Clarmallagh	Attanagh	Abbeyleix	I.	237
29, 35	Ballynafunshin	64	3	38	Queen's Co.	Clarmallagh	Rosconnell	Abbeyleix	I.	238
23	Ballynagabog	86	1	35	Antrim	Kilconway	Loughguile	Ballymoney	III.	27
41	Ballynagale	265	1	37	Wexford	Bargy	Taghmon	Wexford	I.	307
26, 32	Ballynagall	717	3	31	Queen's Co.	Slievemargy	Killabban	Carlow	I.	245
12	Ballynagall	813	1	19d	Westmeath	Corkaree	Portnashangan	Mullingar	I.	263
12	Ballynagall	16	3	2e	Westmeath	Corkaree	Tyfarnham	Mullingar	I.	264
8	Ballynagall	358	0	9	Westmeath	Delvin	Kilcumny	Castletowndelvin	I.	265
3	Ballynagall	175	0	17	Westmeath	Fore	Lickbla	Granard	I.	270
3	Ballynagall	33	1	24	Westmeath	Fore	Rathgarve	Granard	I.	271
12	Ballynagall	24	3	6f	Westmeath	Moyashel and Magheradernon	Rathconnell	Mullingar	I.	276
30, 31	Ballynagall	286	2	14	Westmeath	Moycashel	Kilcumreragh	Athlone	I.	278
44, 45	Ballynagallagh	184	2	33	Down	Lecale Upper	Bright	Downpatrick	III.	180
32	Ballynagallagh	475	2	7g	Limerick	Smallcounty	Knockainy	Kilmallock	II.	260
16	Ballynagalliagh	509	2	0	Armagh	Fews Lower	Lisnadill	Armagh	III.	46
13	Ballynagalliagh	647	0	37	Londonderry	North West Liberties of Londonderry	Templemore	Londonderry	III.	246

(a) Including 21A. 1R. 16P. water.
(b) Including 6A. 0R. 37P. water.
(c) Including 7A. 1R. 32P. water.

(d) Including 12A. 2R. 0P. water.
(e) Including 11A. 2R. 8P. water.

(f) Including 6A. 0R. 32P. water.
(g) Including 20A. 3R. 0P. Lough Gur.

No. of Sheet of the Ordnance Survey Maps.	Townlands and Towns.	Area in Statute Acres.			County.	Barony.	Parish.	Poor Law Union in 1857.	Townland Census of 1851, Part I.	
		A.	R.	P.					Vol.	Page
8	Ballynagalliagh	756	2	23	Sligo	Carbury	Drumcliff	Sligo	IV.	221
22, 26, 27	Ballynagalliagh or Mayfield	303	1	22	Kildare	Offaly West	Duneany	Athy	I.	72
3	Ballynagall Little	114	0	2	Westmeath	Fore	Lickbla	Granard	I.	270
24	Ballynagally	424	2	1	Limerick	Coonagh	Aglishcormick	Tipperary	II.	233
24	Ballynagally	81	3	2	Limerick	Coonagh	Grean	Tipperary	II.	235
46	Ballynagalshy	124	2	6	Meath	Upper Moyfenrath	Castlejordan	Edenderry	I.	212
13, 14	Ballynagappagh	716	1	20a	Kildare	Clane	Clane	Naas	I.	53
42	Ballynagappoge	488	0	11	Down	Upper Iveagh, Lr. pt.	Clonduff	Newry	III.	171
125	Ballynagar	108	2	33	Galway	Leitrim	Ballynakill	Loughrea	IV.	50
124, 137	Ballynagaragh	297	2	30	Cork, W.R.	Courceys	Templetrine	Kinsale	II.	147
64, 75	Ballynagarbragh	232	1	30	Cork, E.R.	Barrymore	Caherlag	Cork	II.	52
30	Ballynagarbry	147	2	3	Westmeath	Clonlonan	Ballyloughloe	Athlone	I.	260
30	Ballynagarbry (Mulloch)	76	3	16	Westmeath	Clonlonan	Ballyloughloe	Athlone	I.	260
30	Ballynagarbry (Pim)	137	2	13	Westmeath	Clonlonan	Ballyloughloe	Athlone	I.	260
9	Ballynagard	288	0	23	Antrim	Cary	Culfeightrin	Ballycastle	III.	13
1	Ballynagard	161	1	3	Antrim	Cary	Rathlin Island	Ballycastle	III.	15
50, 60	Ballynagard	516	0	16	Clare	Clonderalaw	Kilchreest	Killadysert	II.	14
13, 14	Ballynagard	424	3	22b	Londonderry	North West Liberties of Londonderry	Templemore	Londonderry	III.	246
13, 22	Ballynagarde	134	0	33	Limerick	Clanwilliam	Caheravally	Limerick	II.	221
13,14,22,23	Ballynagarde	368	2	14	Limerick	Clanwilliam	Cahernarry	Limerick	II.	222
22	Ballynagarde	156	2	4	Limerick	Clanwilliam	Fedamore	Limerick	II.	223
9, 10, 15, 16	Ballynagare	991	2	6	Kerry	Clanmaurice	Dysert	Listowel	II.	169
89, 90	Ballynagarha	189	3	18	Mayo	Carra	Ballyhean	Castlebar	IV.	125
26	Ballynagarr	257	0	10	Queen's Co.	Ballyadams	Killabban	Athy	I.	231
9, 15	Ballynagarrick	964	0	15	Down	Castlereagh Upper	Drumbo	Lisburn	III.	164
38	Ballynagarrick	222	1	35	Down	Lecale Lower	Saul	Downpatrick	III.	179
19, 25	Ballynagarrick	862	0	13	Down	Lower Iveagh, Up.pt.	Tullylish	Lurgan	III.	171
18, 19	Ballynagarry	166	2	3	Monaghan	Monaghan	Kilmore	Monaghan	III.	275
42, 47	Ballynagarve	418	3	33	Londonderry	Loughinsholin	Artrea	Magherafelt	III.	238
21	Ballynagarvy	181	3	36	Antrim	Kilconway	Finvoy	Ballymoney	III.	26
13, 18	Ballynagashel	316	0	22	Antrim	Upper Dunluce	Loughguile	Ballymoney	III.	20
15	Ballynagassan	174	1	33c	Louth	Ardee	Drumcar	Ardee	I.	172
65	Ballynagaul	129	3	13	Cork, E.R.	Barrymore	Dungourney	Middleton	II.	54
64	Ballynagaul	305	2	6	Cork, E.R.	Barrymore	Kilquane	Cork	II.	55
17	Ballynagaul	573	0	17	Limerick	Shanid	Kilfergus	Glin	II.	256
36	Ballynagaul Beg	63	2	21	Waterford	Decies within Drum	Ringagonagh	Dungarvan	II.	352
36	BALLYNAGAULBEG or RINGVILLE T.	—			Waterford	Decies within Drum	Ringagonagh	Dungarvan	II.	353
36	Ballynagaul More	117	0	37	Waterford	Decies within Drum	Ringagonagh	Dungarvan	II.	352
37, 42	Ballynagee	95	0	34	Wexford	Forth	St. Peters	Wexford	I.	314
95	Ballynageecha	214	3	29	Galway	Dunkellin	Oranmore	Galway	IV.	31
33, 34	Ballynageehy	518	0	34	Cork, E.R.	Fermoy	Monanimy	Mallow	II.	81
54	Ballynageeragh	332	0	8	Antrim	Lower Massereene	Killead	Antrim	III.	28
96	Ballynageeragh	175	3	28	Galway	Dunkellin	Kilconierin	Loughrea	IV.	29
25	Ballynageeragh	439	2	37	Waterford	Middlethird	Dunhill	Kilmacthomas	II.	366
7, 8	Ballynageragh	324	1	30	Cork, E.R.	Fermoy	Imphrick	Mallow	II.	80
15, 16	Ballynageeragh	529	3	36	Kerry	Clanmaurice	Kilcaragh	Listowel	II.	169
17	Ballynagh	87	0	36	King's Co.	Ballycowan	Lynally	Tullamore	I.	128
62,63,66,67	Ballynaghten	333	3	9	Antrim	Upper Massereene	Aghalee	Lurgan	III.	29
10	Ballynaghy	83	3	26	Armagh	Oneilland East	Seagoe	Lurgan	III.	50
25	Ballynagigla	241	3	12	Waterford	Decies without Drum	Monksland	Kilmacthomas	II.	359
20, 21, 29	Ballynagilly	1,874	1	31	Tyrone	Dungannon Upper	Lissan	Cookstown	III.	309
15, 28	Ballynagittagh	259	3	26	Galway	Dunmore	Kilconla	Tuam	IV.	35
69, 77, 78	Ballynaglack	197	0	3	Donegal	Raphoe	Stranorlar	Stranorlar	III.	142
100	Ballynaglea	177	0	8	Mayo	Carra	Touaghty	Ballinrobe	IV.	130
29	Ballynagleragh	359	0	32	Clare	Tulla Lower	Ogonnelloe	Scarriff	II.	38
66	Ballynagleragh	340	0	23	Tipperary, S.R.	Clanwilliam	Bruis	Tipperary	II.	305
38	Ballynagleragh	98	3	33	Waterford	Decies within Drum	Ardmore	Youghal	II.	349
22	Ballynagleragh	70	1	10	Waterford	Decies without Drum	Modelligo	Dungarvan	II.	359
5, 9	Ballynaglogh	96	0	23	Antrim	Cary	Culfeightrin	Ballycastle	III.	13
64	Ballynaglogh	164	3	28	Cork, E.R.	Barrymore	Ballycurrany	Middleton	II.	51
103, 107	Ballynaglogh	101	1	3	Donegal	Tirhugh	Kilbarron	Ballyshannon	III.	148
33, 39	Ballynaglogh	125	1	31	Sligo	Corran	Cloonoghil	Tobercurry	IV.	225
27	Ballynaglogh	67	0	28	Wexford	Ballaghkeen	Ballyvaldon	Enniscorthy	I.	292
27	Ballynaglogh	68	3	10	Wexford	Ballaghkeen	Killila	Enniscorthy	I.	295
41	Ballynaglogh	194	1	39	Wexford	Bargy	Ballyconnick	Wexford	I.	314
37	Ballynaglogh	143	2	12	Wexford	Shelmaliere West	Ardcandrisk	Wexford	I.	332
52	Ballynaglogh East	808	0	18	Cork, E.R.	Barrymore	Dunbulloge	Cork	II.	54
53	Ballynaglogh West	883	2	16	Cork, E.R.	Barrymore	Dunbulloge	Cork	II.	54
8	Ballynag Lower	150	1	20	Londonderry	North East Liberties of Coleraine	Ballyrashane	Coleraine	III.	245

(a) Including 1A. 2R. 19P. detached portion.   (b) Including 0A. 3R. 34P. water.   (c) Including 14A. 3R. 19P. water.

No. of Sheet of the Ordnance Survey Maps.	Townlands and Towns.	Area in Statute Acres.	County.	Barony.	Parish.	Poor Law Union in 1857.	Townland Census of 1851, Part I.	
		A. R. P.					Vol.	Page
16	Ballynagolan . .	256 2 36	Armagh . .	Armagh . . .	Derrynoose . .	Armagh . .	III.	44
24, 25	Ballynagonnaghtagh	317 3 21	Clare . .	Inchiquin . .	Dysert . . .	Ennis . .	II.	24
20	Ballynagool . .	350 3 38	Limerick . .	Connello Lower .	Croagh . . .	Rathkeale . .	II.	227
12	Ballynagor . .	328 0 11	Antrim . .	Lower Dunluce .	Billy . . .	Ballymoney . .	III.	16
21	Ballynagor . .	419 3 10	Mayo . .	Tirawley . .	Moygawnagh . .	Killala . .	II.	171
44	Ballynagore . .	83 1 28	Cork, E.R. .	Barrymore . .	Rathcormack . .	Fermoy . .	II.	57
32	Ballynagore . .	58 2 0	Westmeath .	Moycashel . .	Castletownkindalen	Mullingar . .	I.	277
27	Ballynagore . .	106 0 36	Wexford . .	Ballaghkeen . .	Castle-ellis . .	Enniscorthy . .	I.	293
27	Ballynagore . .	191 3 34	Wexford . .	Ballaghkeen . .	Killila . . .	Enniscorthy . .	I.	295
32	BALLYNAGORE T. .	—	Westmeath .	Moycashel . .	Newtown . .	Mullingar . .	I.	279
25	Ballynagorkagh .	144 3 31	Waterford .	Middlethird . .	Dunhill . . .	Kilmacthomas .	II.	366
14	Ballynagoshen .	267 0 22	Longford . .	Longford . .	Killoe . . .	Longford . .	I.	158
47	Ballynagoul . .	963 3 1	Limerick . .	Coshma . .	Hackmys . .	Kilmallock . .	II.	243
5, 9	Ballynagowan .	498 3 0a	Armagh . .	Oneilland West .	Drumcree . .	Lurgan . .	III.	51
6	Ballynagowan .	80 2 8	Limerick . .	Clanwilliam . .	Killeenagarriff .	Limerick . .	II.	224
6	Ballynagowan .	14 1 4	Limerick . .	Clanwilliam . .	Stradbally . .	Limerick . .	II.	226
39, 47	Ballynagowan Lower, Alias Bellsgrove .	194 1 1	Tyrone . .	Dungannon Upper .	Ballyclog . .	Cookstown . .	III.	306
39, 47	Ballynagowan Upper, Alias Bellmount .	202 1 17	Tyrone . .	Dungannon Upper .	Ballyclog . .	Cookstown . .	III.	306
41	Ballynagown . .	188 3 33	Londonderry .	Loughinsholin .	Desertmartin . .	Magherafelt . .	III.	240
17, 18	Ballynagraigue .	382 0 8	Kerry . .	Clanmaurice . .	Duagh . . .	Listowel . .	II.	168
30, 35	Ballynagrallagh .	414 0 39	Wexford . .	Bantry . .	Newbawn . .	New Ross . .	I.	301
96	Ballynagran . .	197 2 8	Galway . .	Dunkellin . .	Killeeneen . .	Gort . .	IV.	30
105, 115	Ballynagran . .	131 3 30	Galway . .	Loughrea . .	Kilchreest . .	Loughrea . .	IV.	63
31, 36	Ballynagran . .	152 3 35	Wicklow . .	Arklow . .	Dunganstown . .	Rathdrum . .	I.	343
25, 31	Ballynagran . .	232 1 27	Wicklow . .	Arklow . .	Glenealy . .	Rathdrum . .	I.	344
66	Ballynagrana . .	417 1 26	Tipperary, S.R.	Clanwilliam . .	Emly . . .	Tipperary . .	II.	307
85	Ballynagrana . .	279 1 19	Tipperary, S.R.	Iffa and Offa East .	Carrick . .	Carrick on Suir .	II.	312
85	Ballynagrana . .	253 0 18	Tipperary, S.R.	Iffa and Offa East .	Newtownlennan .	Carrick on Suir .	II.	315
18, 26	Ballynagranagh .	275 0 16b	Clare . .	Bunratty Upper .	Inchicronan . .	Tulla . .	II.	8
32	Ballynagranagh .	414 3 25	Limerick . .	Smallcounty . .	Ballinlough . .	Kilmallock . .	II.	259
22	Ballynagrane . .	275 1 39c	Carlow . .	Idrone East . .	Clonygoose . .	Carlow . .	I.	6
8	Ballynagranshy .	170 1 8	Meath . .	Fore . .	Killeagh . .	Oldcastle . .	I.	201
18	Ballynagreagh .	159 0 10	Armagh . .	Orior Lower . .	Ballymore . .	Newry . .	III.	55
33	Ballynagreanagh .	362 1 12	Limerick . .	Coonagh . .	Kilteely . .	Tipperary . .	II.	235
49, 60	Ballynagree East .	1,320 1 9	Cork, W.R. .	West Muskerry .	Macroom . .	Macroom . .	II.	160
115	Ballynagreeve .	306 2 24	Galway . .	Loughrea . .	Killcenadeema .	Loughrea . .	IV.	64
49, 60	Ballynagree West .	1,345 2 3	Cork, W.R. .	West Muskerry .	Macroom . .	Macroom . .	II.	160
18	Ballynagrena . .	123 2 23	Louth . .	Ferrard . .	Dysart . .	Drogheda . .	I.	181
30, 31	Ballynagrenia .	608 3 26	Westmeath .	Moycashel . .	Kilcumreragh .	Athlone . .	I.	278
34, 41	Ballynagross . .	368 3 7	Down . .	Upper Iveagh, Up.pt.	Annaclone . .	Banbridge . .	III.	174
38	Ballynagross Lower	295 1 26	Down . .	Lecale Lower . .	Ballee . .	Downpatrick . .	III.	178
38	Ballynagross Upper	285 3 31	Down . .	Lecale Lower . .	Ballee . .	Downpatrick . .	III.	178
85, 86	Ballynagrumoolia .	424 3 21	Cork, E.R. .	Kerrycurrihy . .	Ballinaboy . .	Cork . .	II.	91
29, 30	Ballynaguila . .	459 2 8	Limerick . .	Connello Lower .	Croagh . .	Rathkeale . .	II.	227
13, 22	Ballynaguilkee Lower	331 3 3	Waterford .	Decies without Drum	Seskinan . .	Lismore . .	II.	360
13	Ballynaguilkee Upper	404 0 13	Waterford .	Decies without Drum	Seskinan . .	Lismore . .	II.	360
6	Ballynaguilla . .	396 1 28	Cork, E.R. .	Duhallow . .	Tullylease . .	Kanturk . .	II.	76
30, 35	Ballynaguilsha .	448 3 17	King's Co. .	Eglish . .	Eglish . .	Parsonstown . .	I.	134
47	Ballynagun East .	548 0 34	Clare . .	Moyarta . .	Kilmacduane .	Kilrush . .	II.	32
47	Ballynagun West .	415 1 38	Clare . .	Moyarta . .	Kilmacduane .	Kilrush . .	II.	32
8	Ballynag Upper .	146 0 1	Londonderry .	North East Liberties of Coleraine .	Ballyrashane .	Coleraine . .	III.	245
59	Ballynagurragh .	195 3 7	Tyrone . .	Clogher . .	Clogher . .	Clogher . .	III.	291
32	Ballynagussaun .	203 1 7	Kildare . .	Narragh and Reban East . .	Fontstown . .	Athy . .	I.	66
39	Ballynahaglish .	189 3 30d	Mayo . .	Tirawley . .	Ballynahaglish .	Ballina . .	IV.	164
30	Ballynahaha . .	462 2 27	Limerick . .	Connello Upper .	Ballingarry . .	Croom . .	II.	230
17	Ballynahaia . .	117 3 5	Cavan . .	Tullygarvey . .	Drumgoon . .	Cootehill . .	III.	88
18, 26	Ballynahalisk . .	531 0 17	Cork, E.R. .	Fermoy . .	St. Nathlash . .	Mitchelstown .	II.	82
12	Ballynahallee . .	168 3 13	Limerick . .	Kenry . .	Kildimo . .	Rathkeale . .	II.	249
68	Ballynahallia . .	668 2 33	Galway . .	Moycullen . .	Moycullen . .	Galway . .	IV.	71
40	Ballynahallia . .	338 3 7	Kerry . .	Trughanacmy . .	Ballincuslane' .	Tralee . .	II.	206
20	Ballynahallin . .	358 1 13e	Wexford . .	Scarawalsh . .	St. Marys, Enniscorthy	Enniscorthy .	I.	325
39	Ballynaharda . .	266 1 1	Waterford .	Decies within Drum	Ardmore . .	Dungarvan . .	II.	349
27, 28	Ballynahask . .	29 0 33	Wexford . .	Ballaghkeen . .	Ballyvaldon . .	Enniscorthy . .	I.	292
27, 28	Ballynahask . .	210 1 32	Wexford . .	Ballaghkeen . .	Killincooly . .	Enniscorthy . .	I.	295
27	Ballynahask . .	30 1 33	Wexford . .	Ballaghkeen . .	Meelnagh . .	Enniscorthy . .	I.	297
57	Ballynahatten .	333 0 3	Down . .	Mourne . .	Kilkeel . .	Kilkeel . .	III.	182
4, 7	Ballynahattin .	105 2 38	Louth . .	Upper Dundalk .	Dundalk . .	Dundalk . .	I.	178
60	Ballynahattina .	269 3 32	Galway . .	Tiaquin . .	Killosolan . .	Mountbellew .	IV.	78
9	Ballynahatty . .	257 1 32f	Down . .	Castlereagh Upper .	Drumbo . .	Lisburn . .	III.	164
42, 43	Ballynahatty . .	236 1 27g	Tyrone . .	Omagh East . .	Drumragh . .	Omagh . .	III.	312

(a) Including 13A. 2R. 4P. water.
(b) Including 17A. 3R. 9P. water.
(c) Including 6A. 1R. 2P. River Barrow.

(d) Including 1A. 0R. 7P. water.
(e) Including 9A. 2R. 14P. water.

(f) Including 2A. 2R. 10P. water.
(g) Including 4A. 3R. 23P. water.

No. of Sheet of the Ordnance Survey Maps.	Townlands and Towns.	Area in Statute Acres.			County.	Barony.	Parish.	Poor Law Union in 1857.	Towaland Census of 1851. Part I.	
		A.	R.	P.					Vol.	Page
20	Ballynahaville	65	0	2	Antrim	Lower Glenarm	Layd	Ballycastle	III.	22
45, 53	Ballynahaye	1,451	2	39	Tyrone	Dungannon Lower	Killeeshil	Dungannon	III.	298
28	Ballynaheglish	89	0	15	Roscommon	Ballymoe	Cloonygormican	Castlereagh	IV.	191
55	Ballynaheila	94	1	27	Cork, E.R.	Imokilly	Ardagh	Youghal	II.	83
30	Ballynahemery	159	0	12	Waterford	Decies without Drum	Whitechurch	Dungarvan	II.	361
10	Ballynahery	240	0	19	Londonderry	Keenaght	Drumachose	NewTⁿLimavady	III.	235
117	Ballynaheskeragh	431	1	13	Galway	Longford	Killimorbologue	Portumna	IV.	58
24	Ballynahila	190	0	4	Waterford	Decies without Drum	Ballylaneen	Kilmacthomas	II.	354
11	Ballynahillen	284	2	1	Wexford	Gorey	Liskinfere	Gorey	I.	320
2, 6	Ballynahimmy	498	1	21	Queen's Co.	Tinnahinch	Kilmanman	Mountmellick	I.	249
35, 44	Ballynahina	890	2	25	Cork, E.R.	Barrymore	Rathcormack	Fermoy	II.	57
63	Ballynahina	737	3	32	Cork, E.R.	Cork	Kilcully	Cork	II.	64
13	Ballynahinch	462	2	23	Armagh	Oneilland West	Kilmore	Armagh	III.	53
27,28,35,36	Ballynahineh	725	3	28a	Clare	Tulla Upper	Kilnoe	Tulla	II.	40
22, 29	Ballynahinch	775	3	11b	Down	Kinelarty	Magheradrool	Downpatrick	III.	177
36	Ballynahinch	790	1	32c	Galway	Ballynahinch	Moyrus	Clifden	IV.	12
29, 30	Ballynahinch	80	2	31	Kerry	Trughanacmy	Ballymacelligott	Tralee	II.	206
1, 2	Ballynahinch	105	2	24d	King's Co.	Kilcoursey	Kilcumreragh	Tullamore	I.	141
40, 48	Ballynahinch	962	1	30	Limerick	Coshlea	Knocklong	Kilmallock	II.	240
21	Ballynahinch	425	1	32	Longford	Rathcline	Cashel	Ballymahon	I.	163
8, 11	Ballynahinch	260	1	9e	Tipperary, N.R.	Lower Ormond	Ballingarry	Borrisokane	II.	282
31	Ballynahinch	467	1	27	Tipperary, N.R.	Owney and Arra	Kilcomenty	Nenagh	II.	294
52, 60	Ballynahinch	1,409	0	32	Tipperary, S.R.	Clanwilliam	Ballygriffin	Tipperary	II.	305
22	BALLYNAHINCH T.	—			Down	Kinelarty	Magheradrool	Downpatrick	III.	177
106	Ballynahistil	191	2	1	Galway	Leitrim	Kilcooly	Loughrea	IV.	54
96, 97	Ballynahivnia	161	2	5	Galway	Loughrea	Kilconierin	Loughrea	IV.	64
29, 38	Ballynahone	882	3	13	Donegal	Inishowen West	Fahan Upper	Londonderry	III.	121
4	Ballynahone	300	3	39	Monaghan	Trough	Errigal Trough	Monaghan	III.	283
30, 39	Ballynahone	107	0	13	Tyrone	Dungannon Upper	Artrea	Cookstown	III.	305
12, 16	Ballynahone Beg	302	3	33	Armagh	Armagh	Lisnadill	Armagh	III.	45
36	Ballynahone Beg	571	2	35	Londonderry	Loughinsholin	Maghera	Magherafelt	III.	242
12	Ballynahone More	598	2	18	Armagh	Armagh	Armagh	Armagh	III.	43
36, 41	Ballynahone More	1,453	0	0	Londonderry	Loughinsholin	Termoneeny	Magherafelt	III.	244
10	Ballynahoogh or Cavetown	319	3	0f	Roscommon	Boyle	Estersnow	Boyle	IV.	195
29	Ballynahoulort	373	3	6	Kerry	Trughanacmy	Tralee	Tralee	II.	213
43	Ballynahow	63	3	24	Kerry	Corkaguiny	Cloghane	Dingle	II.	174
42, 52	Ballynahow	65	3	31	Kerry	Corkaguiny	Dunquin	Dingle	II.	176
25, 34	Ballynahow	1,954	3	32	Kerry	Corkaguiny	Kilquane	Dingle	II.	179
87, 96	Ballynahow	175	0	35	Kerry	Iveragh	Killemlagh	Cahersiveen	II.	196
41	Ballynahow	1,379	1	15	Tipperary, N.R.	Eliogarty	Ballycahill	Thurles	II.	269
33, 34	Ballynahow	145	0	8	Tipperary, N.R.	Kilnamanagh Upper	Glenkeen	Thurles	II.	278
66	Ballynahow	332	2	36	Tipperary, S.R.	Clanwilliam	Bruis	Tipperary	II.	305
70	Ballynahow Beg	83	3	14	Kerry	Iveragh	Killinane	Cahersiveen	II.	197
42	BallynahowCommons	176	1	1	Kerry	Corkaguiny	Dunquin	Dingle	II.	176
70	Ballynahow More	441	3	24	Kerry	Iveragh	Killinane	Cahersiveen	II.	197
27	Ballynahow(Murrogh)	122	1	26	Cork, E.R.	Condons&Clangibbon	Glanworth	Fermoy	II.	61
4, 8	Ballynahown	1,041	2	30	Clare	Corcomroe	Killilagh	Ennistimon	II.	19
103	Ballynahown	135	1	15	Cork, W.R.	Bear	Kilcaskan	Castletown	II.	122
97	Ballynahown	98	2	8	Galway	Athenry	Lickerrig	Loughrea	IV.	5
99	Ballynahown	72	0	20	Galway	Clonmacnowen	Aughrim	Ballinasloe	IV.	24
93	Ballynahown	267	0	39	Galway	Moycullen	Rahoon	Galway	IV.	72
48	Ballynahown	343	1	35	Limerick	Coshlea	Ballingaddy	Kilmallock	II.	237
21, 30	Ballynahown	132	3	35	Limerick	Coshma	Croom	Croom	II.	242
36	Ballynahown	131	0	11	Limerick	Glenquin	Monagay	Newcastle	II.	247
2, 6	Ballynahown	369	1	27	Queen's Co.	Tinnahinch	Kilmanman	Mountmellick	I.	249
35	Ballynahown	723	1	6	Westmeath	Clonlonan	Kilcleagh	Athlone	I.	261
21	Ballynahown	145	0	27	Wexford	Ballaghkeen	Killincooly	Gorey	I.	295
21	Ballynahown	172	1	22	Wexford	Ballaghkeen	Kilnamanagh	Gorey	I.	297
19, 32	Ballynahowna	358	0	5	Galway	Ballymoe	Kilbegnet	Glennamaddy	IV.	8
46	Ballynahowna	81	3	29	Galway	Killian	Ballynakill	Mountbellew	IV.	43
123	Ballynahowna	257	3	38	Galway	Loughrea	Kilthomas	Gort	IV.	65
15	Ballynahowna	286	1	0	Roscommon	Castlereagh	Kilcorkey	Castlereagh	IV.	199
11	Ballynahowna	386	1	1	Sligo	Tireragh	Kilmacshalgan	Dromore West	IV.	234
93	Ballynahown East	63	2	20	Galway	Galway	Rahoon	Galway	IV.	37
91	Ballynahown North	206	1	11g	Galway	Moycullen	Killannin	Galway	IV.	69
91	Ballynahown South	616	3	11h	Galway	Moycullen	Killannin	Galway	IV.	69
35	Ballynahownwood	1,083	2	20	Westmeath	Clonlonan	Kilcleagh	Athlone	I.	261
27	Ballynahow (Spiers)	174	2	31	Cork, E.R.	Condons&Clangibbon	Glanworth	Fermoy	II.	61
50	Ballynahulla	1,510	3	25	Kerry	Trughanacmy	Ballincuslane	Tralee	II.	206
36, 45	Ballynahunt	662	3	19	Kerry	Corkaguiny	Ballinvoher	Dingle	II.	173
19, 29	Ballynakeeloge	258	1	23	Donegal	Inishowen West	Fahan Lower	Inishowen	III.	120
21	Ballynakelly	155	2	23	Dublin	Newcastle	Rathcoole	Celbridge	I.	34

(a) Including 113A. 1R. 12P. water.
(b) Including 9A. 3R. 20P. water.
(c) Including 130A. 3R. 21P. water.
(d) Including 7A. 3R. 0P. water.
(e) Including 10A. 3R. 32P. water.
(f) Including 75A. 3R. 7P. water.
(g) Including 10A. 3R. 19P. water.
(h) Including 95A. 0R. 31P. water.

No. of Sheet of the Ordnance Survey Maps.	Townlands and Towns.	Area in Statute Acres. A. R. P.	County.	Barony.	Parish.	Poor Law Union in 1857.	Townland Census of 1851, Part I. Vol.	Page
16, 19	Ballynakill	364 0 2	Carlow	Idrone East	Dunleckny	Carlow	I.	6
9	Ballynakill	493 1 23	Carlow	Rathvilly	Clonmore	Shillelagh	I.	10
21	Ballynakill	86 2 4	Fermanagh	Magheraboy	Devenish	Enniskillen	III.	210
7	Ballynakill	287 0 35	Galway	Ballymoe	Ballynakill	Glennamaddy	IV.	5
129	Ballynakill	385 3 13*a*	Galway	Kiltartan	Beagh	Gort	IV.	46
125	Ballynakill	146 1 21	Galway	Leitrim	Ballynakill	Loughrea	IV.	50
108, 109	Ballynakill	596 0 18	Galway	Longford	Clonfert	Ballinasloe	IV.	56
1, 3	Ballynakill	735 1 21	Kildare	Carbury	Ballynadrumny	Edenderry	I.	51
4	Ballynakill	590 3 9	Kildare	Ikeathy and Oughterany	Cloncurry	Celbridge	I.	56
29	Ballynakill	274 3 18	Kilkenny	Gowran	Graiguenamanagh	Thomastown	I.	95
40	Ballynakill	306 2 11	Kilkenny	Knocktopher	Rossinan	Waterford	I.	113
44, 45, 46, 47	Ballynakill	496 1 13	King's Co.	Clonlisk	Cullenwaine	Roscrea	I.	129
11, 19	Ballynakill	426 1 13	King's Co.	Coolestown	Ballynakill	Edenderry	I.	132
18, 26	Ballynakill	1,055 3 8	King's Co.	Upper Philipstown	Geashill	Tullamore	I.	144
30	Ballynakill	467 0 28	Limerick	Connello Upper	Kilfinny	Croom	II.	233
12, 13	Ballynakill	525 2 8	Longford	Moydow	Killashee	Longford	I.	161
48	Ballynakill	812 3 12	Meath	Lower Moyfenrath	Rathcore	Trim	I.	211
46, 52	Ballynakill	184 1 31	Meath	Upper Moyfenrath	Ballyboggan	Edenderry	I.	212
27	Ballynakill	139 1 18	Queen's Co.	Clandonagh	Rathdowney	Donaghmore	I.	234
31, 32	Ballynakill	688 0 17	Queen's Co.	Slievemargy	Killabban	Carlow	I.	245
2	Ballynakill	130 3 17	Queen's Co.	Tinnahinch	Kilmanman	Mountmellick	I.	249
27	Ballynakill	254 1 29	Sligo	Tirerrill	Ballynakill	Sligo	IV.	237
17	Ballynakill	707 0 39	Tipperary, N.R.	Ikerrin	Rathnaveoge	Roscrea	II.	276
14, 22, 23	Ballynakill	438 1 3	Waterford	Decies without Drum	Kilgobnet	Dungarvan	II.	357
10, 18	Ballynakill	358 2 19	Waterford	Gaultiere	Ballynakill	Waterford	II.	362
36	Ballynakill	676 0 6	Westmeath	Clonlonan	Kilcleagh	Athlone	I.	261
7	Ballynakill	282 3 11	Westmeath	Corkaree	Multyfarnham	Mullingar	I.	263
22	Ballynakill	139 0 3	Westmeath	Kilkenny West	Kilkenny West	Athlone	I.	273
15, 16	Ballynakill	351 1 23	Wexford	Scarawalsh	Kilbride	Enniscorthy	I.	323
14, 19	Ballynakill	824 3 31	Wexford	Scarawalsh	Monart	Enniscorthy	I.	324
64	Ballynakilla	509 0 5	Cork, E.R.	Barrymore	Ballycurrany	Middleton	II.	51
44, 45	Ballynakilla	227 1 11	Cork, E.R.	Barrymore	Gortroe	Fermoy	II.	54
116, 117	Ballynakilla	32 0 14	Cork, W.R.	Bear	Kilcaskan	Castletown	II.	122
115, 128	Ballynakilla	1,010 0 3	Cork, W.R.	Bear	Killaconenagh	Castletown	II.	124
44	Ballynakilla	170 3 15	Galway	Clare	Killererin	Tuam	IV.	20
58	Ballynakilla	335 2 28	Galway	Tiaquin	Abbeyknockmoy	Tuam	IV.	75
2	Ballynakilla East	889 3 8	Cork, E.R.	Orrery and Kilmore	Shandrum	Kanturk	II.	109
2	Ballynakilla West	626 3 18	Cork, E.R.	Orrery and Kilmore	Shandrum	Kanturk	II.	109
7	Ballynakillbeg	328 0 24	Carlow	Carlow	Urglin	Carlow	I.	3
36	Ballynakill Beg	147 2 13	Limerick	Glenquin	Mahoonagh	Newcastle	II.	246
2	Ballynakill Big	312 1 16	King's Co.	Kilcoursey	Ardnurcher or Horseleap	Tullamore	I.	140
41	Ballynakillew	108 3 9	Galway	Clare	Cargin	Tuam	IV.	18
136, 137	Ballynakillew	84 0 19	Galway	Leitrim	Clonrush	Scarriff	IV.	52
110	Ballynakillew	121 2 10*b*	Mayo	Kilmaine	Ballinrobe	Ballinrobe	IV.	152
39	Ballynakillew	47 2 6	Sligo	Corran	Kilshalvy	Boyle	IV.	227
100, 104	Ballynakillew Mountain	1,470 0 20*c*	Donegal	Tirhugh	Drumhome	Donegal	III.	146
2	Ballynakill Little	104 3 6	King's Co.	Kilcoursey	Ardnurcher or Horseleap	Tullamore	I.	140
8, 12	Ballynakill Lower	338 1 23	Kildare	Carbury	Kilpatrick	Edenderry	I.	52
36, 37	Ballynakill More	405 1 18	Limerick	Glenquin	Mahoonagh	Newcastle	II.	246
8, 12	Ballynakill Upper	542 3 7	Kildare	Carbury	Kilpatrick	Edenderry	I.	52
22	Ballynakill Upper	42 3 3	Westmeath	Kilkenny West	Kilkenny West	Athlone	I.	273
37	Ballynakilly	686 2 19	Donegal	Inishowen West	Inch	Londonderry	III.	121
52	Ballynakilly	408 3 20	Donegal	Kilmacrenan	Conwal	Letterkenny	III.	125
81	Ballynakilly	217 2 34	Kerry	Iveragh	Dromod	Cahersiveen	II.	194
71	Ballynakilly	117 2 3	Kerry	Iveragh	Glanbehy	Cahersiveen	II.	195
47, 55	Ballynakilly	406 1 30	Tyrone	Dungannon Middle	Killyman	Dungannon	III.	303
38	Ballynakilly	151 0 24	Tyrone	Dungannon Upper	Desertcreat	Cookstown	III.	307
63, 71	Ballynakilly Lower	673 1 86	Kerry	Iveragh	Glanbehy	Cahersiveen	II.	195
63, 71	Ballynakilly Upper	743 0 0	Kerry	Iveragh	Glanbehy	Cahersiveen	II.	195
25, 26, 28, 29	Ballynalack	484 0 11*d*	Armagh	Orior Upper	Killevy	Newry	III.	57
39	Ballynalack	148 2 22	King's Co.	Ballybritt	Kinnitty	Parsonstown	I.	125
55	Ballynalacka	122 1 16	Galway	Clare	Cargin	Tuam	IV.	18
4, 8	Ballynalackan	340 1 35	Clare	Corcomroe	Killilagh	Ennistimon	II.	19
14	Ballynalackan	162 1 4	Clare	Corcomroe	Kilmacrehy	Ennistimon	II.	20
28, 36	Ballynalacken	529 2 15	Cork, E.R.	Condons & Clangibbon	Leitrim	Fermoy	II.	62
34, 35	Ballynalacken	289 0 17	Kerry	Corkaguiny	Cloghane	Dingle	II.	175
5	Ballynalacken	940 0 5	Kilkenny	Fassadinin	Donaghmore	Castlecomer	I.	89
49	Ballynalacken	312 0 29	Limerick	Coshlea	Ballingarry	Kilmallock	II.	237
66	Ballynalahagh	405 0 21	Cork, E.R.	Imokilly	Killeagh	Youghal	II.	88
32	Ballynalahagh	31 2 2	Limerick	Smallcounty	Knockainy	Kilmallock	II.	260

(*a*) Including 29A. 1R. 13P. water.
(*b*) Including 5A. 3R. 5P. water.
(*c*) Including 21A. 0R. 27P. water.
(*d*) Including 42A. 2R. 13P. water.

No. of Sheet of the Ordnance Survey Maps.	Townlands and Towns.	Area in Statute Acres.	County.	Barony.	Parish.	Poor Law Union in 1857.	Townland Census of 1851, Part I.	
		A. R. P.					Vol.	Page
31	Ballynalahessery Nth.	123 1 32	Waterford	Decies without Drum	Dungarvan	Dungarvan	II.	355
31	Ballynalahessery Sth.	101 1 35	Waterford	Decies without Drum	Dungarvan	Dungarvan	II.	355
32, 46	Ballynalahy	249 1 5	Galway	Killian	Killian	Mountbellew	IV.	44
67	Ballynalargy	224 1 36	Antrim	Upper Massereene	Magheragall	Lisburn	III.	31
67	Ballynalargy	274 3 14	Antrim	Upper Massereene	Magheramesk	Lisburn	III.	31
18	Ballynaleck	332 2 10	Armagh	Orior Lower	Ballymore	Newry	III.	55
14	Ballynaleck	217 0 24	Mayo	Tirawley	Lackan	Killala	IV.	170
32, 37	Ballynaleck	26 2 39	Wexford	Shelmaliere East	Artramon	Wexford	I.	330
48, 49	Ballynaleney (part of)	227 0 24	Antrim	Upper Toome	Drummaul	Antrim	III.	33
48	Ballynaleney (part of)	148 0 9	Antrim	Upper Toome	Drummaul	Antrim	III.	33
21	Ballynalick	448 2 2	Tipperary, N.R.	Upper Ormond	Lisbunny	Nenagh	II.	292
19, 23	Ballynalina	290 2 19	Kilkenny	Shillelogher	St. Canice	Kilkenny	I.	115
34, 35	Ballynalinagh	536 3 8	Kilkenny	Kells	Tullahought	Carrick on Suir	I.	110
12,13,21,22	Ballynally	756 3 30	Donegal	Inishowen East	Moville Lower	Inishowen	III.	118
16	Ballynaloan	140 0 39a	Tyrone	Strabane Lower	Ardstraw	Castlederg	III.	318
23	Ballynalone	23 3 1	Westmeath	Kilkenny West	Drumraney	Ballymahon	I.	272
16, 23	Ballynalone	263 3 8	Westmeath	Kilkenny West	Noughaval	Ballymahon	I.	274
17,18,22,23	Ballynaloob	1,153 3 37	Antrim	Upper Dunluce	Killagan	Ballymoney	III.	19
56	Ballynalough	551 0 37	Antrim	Upper Belfast	Templepatrick	Antrim	III.	10
113	Ballynalougha	161 3 30	Cork, E.R.	Kinalea	Nohaval	Kinsale	II.	96
20	Ballynalougher	99 3 0	Antrim	Lower Glenarm	Layd	Ballycastle	III.	22
97	Ballynalouhy	371 1 26	Cork, E.R.	Kinalea	Ballymartle	Kinsale	II.	94
26	Ballynalour	768 3 1	Carlow	St. Mullins Lower	St. Mullins	New Ross	I.	13
123	Ballynalty	632 1 10b	Mayo	Kilmaine	Shrule	Ballinrobe	IV.	158
2, 3, 6, 7	Ballynalug	1,327 0 17	Queen's Co.	Tinnahinch	Rearymore	Mountmellick	I.	249
2	Ballynalurgan	155 1 15	Meath	Morgallion	Enniskeen	Kells	I.	209
38	Ballynalynagh	273 2 22	Mayo	Tirawley	Crossmolina	Ballina	IV.	165
9	Ballynamaddoo	233 2 38	Cavan	Tullyhaw	Templeport	Bawnboy	III.	93
52	Ballynamaddree	470 0 32	Cork, E.R.	Barrymore	St. Michaels	Cork	II.	57
27	Ballynamaddy	183 3 0	Antrim	Kilconway	Grange of Dundermot	Ballymena	III.	26
8	Ballynamaghery	184 2 28	Louth	Lower Dundalk	Carlingford	Dundalk	I.	176
41	Ballynamagna	676 2 38	Down	Upper Iveagh, Lr. pt.	Drumballyroney	Banbridge	III.	172
6	Ballynamallaght	1,213 3 21	Tyrone	Strabane Lower	Donaghedy	Gortin	III.	320
78	Ballynaman	114 1 7	Donegal	Raphoe	Donaghmore	Stranorlar	III.	137
67, 76	Ballynaman	692 1 7	Donegal	Raphoe	Kilteevoge	Stranorlar	III.	139
23	Ballynamanagh	219 3 32	Longford	Moydow	Taghsheenod	Ballymahon	I.	162
95, 103	Ballynamanagh East	591 3 13	Galway	Dunkellin	Ballynacourty	Galway	IV.	27
95, 103	Ballynamanagh West	396 1 33	Galway	Dunkellin	Ballynacourty	Galway	IV.	27
15	Ballynamannan	42 1 18	Cavan	Lower Loughtee	Drumlane	Cavan	III.	79
104	Ballynamannin	203 2 27	Galway	Dunkellin	Killora	Loughrea	IV.	31
38	Ballynamanoge	538 0 36	Wicklow	Ballinacor South	Kilcommon	Shillelagh	I.	349
122, 123	Ballynamantan	100 3 2	Galway	Kiltartan	Kiltartan	Gort	IV.	48
89	Ballynamarroge	406 1 32c	Mayo	Burrishoole	Islandeady	Westport	IV.	121
97, 111	Ballynamaul	282 1 6	Cork, E.R.	Kinalea	Ringcurran	Kinsale	II.	96
58, 59	Ballynamaunagh	333 1 30	Kerry	Magunihy	Kilcummin	Killarney	II.	201
3	Ballynameagh	500 3 14	Westmeath	Fore	Lickbla	Granard	I.	270
30	Ballynameclagh	192 1 19	Waterford	Decies without Drum	Whitechurch	Dungarvan	II.	361
21	Ballynameeltoge	305 1 19	Leitrim	Carrigallen	Oughteragh	Bawnboy	IV.	91
18, 26	Ballynameen	325 1 9	Londonderry	Coleraine	Desertoghill	Coleraine	III.	230
18	BALLYNAMEEN T.	—	Londonderry	Coleraine	Desertoghill	Coleraine	III.	231
17	Ballynamenagh Nth. or Cummingstown	151 0 28	Antrim	Upper Dunluce	Ballymoney	Ballymoney	III.	18
38	Ballynamertinagh	336 2 15	Waterford	Decies within Drum	Ardmore	Youghal	II.	349
66	Ballynametagh	238 1 1	Cork, E.R.	Imokilly	Mogeely	Middleton	II.	89
87	Ballynametagh	165 1 16	Cork, E.R.	Kerrycurrihy	Carrigaline	Cork	II.	92
39	Ballynametagh	86 1 31	Kilkenny	Iverk	Fiddown	Carrick on Suir	I.	105
15	Ballynameta or Wood Park	234 3 27	Armagh	Tiranny	Tynan	Armagh	III.	60
19	Ballynaminnan	364 1 39	Wexford	Scarawalsh	Templeshanbo	Enniscorthy	I.	326
30	Ballynamintra Lower	42 0 9	Waterford	Decies without Drum	Whitechurch	Dungarvan	II.	361
30	Ballynamintra Middle	84 0 23	Waterford	Decies without Drum	Whitechurch	Dungarvan	II.	361
30	Ballynamintra Upper	261 1 21	Waterford	Decies without Drum	Whitechurch	Dungarvan	II.	361
16	Ballynamire	38 1 36	Carlow	Idrone East	Fennagh	Carlow	I.	7
16	Ballynamire	323 2 27	King's Co.	Ballycowan	Kilbride	Tullamore	I.	127
21	Ballynamire	53 2 8	Wexford	Ballaghkeen	Kilnamanagh	Gorey	I.	297
87	Ballynamockagh	262 1 37	Galway	Clonmacnowen	Kilcloony	Ballinasloe	IV.	25
23	Ballynamoe	74 2 13	Tipperary, N.R.	Ikerrin	Rathnaveoge	Roscrea	II.	276
48	Ballynamoloogh	220 3 26	Limerick	Coshlea	Ballingaddy	Kilmallock	II.	237
34	Ballynamona	341 3 20	Cavan	Clankee	Moybolgue	Bailieborough	III.	74
42	Ballynamona	416 0 24	Cork, E.R.	Barretts	Mourneabbey	Mallow	II.	50
19, 20	Ballynamona	370 3 4	Cork, E.R.	Condons & Clangibbon	Brigown	Mitchelstown	II.	59
35	Ballynamona	196 2 9	Cork, E.R.	Condons & Clangibbon	Clondulane	Fermoy	II.	60
24	Ballynamona	114 1 13	Cork, E.R.	Duhallow	Castlemagner	Kanturk	II.	67

(a) Including 0A. 3R. 14P. water.   (b) Including 18A. 2R. 17P. water.   (c) Including 2A. 2R. 13P. water.

No. of Sheet of the Ordnance Survey Maps.	Townlands and Towns.	Area in Statute Acres.			County.	Barony.	Parish.	Poor Law Union in 1857.	Townland Census of 1851, Part I.	
		A.	R.	P.					Vol.	Page
27	Ballynamona	424	2	33	Cork, E.R.	Fermoy	Glanworth	Fermoy	II.	79
18	Ballynamona	295	0	20	Cork, E.R.	Fermoy	Templeroan	Mallow	II.	82
89	Ballynamona	462	0	24	Cork, E.R.	Imokilly	Kilmahon	Middleton	II.	89
111	Ballynamona	273	0	23	Cork, E.R.	Kinsale	Dunderrow	Kinsale	II.	99
136	Ballynamona	235	3	11	Cork, W.R.	Ibane and Barryroe	Lislee	Clonakilty	II.	150
30	Ballynamona	89	3	8	Galway	Dunmore	Tuam	Tuam	IV.	35
134, 136	Ballynamona	147	3	38	Galway	Leitrim	Clonrush	Scarriff	IV.	52
116	Ballynamona	169	0	35	Galway	Leitrim	Duniry	Portumna	IV.	53
27	Ballynamona	54	1	16	Galway	Ross	Cong	Oughterard	IV.	72
58	Ballynamona	215	3	10	Galway	Tiaquin	Abbeyknockmoy	Tuam	IV.	75
59	Ballynamona	427	1	16	Galway	Tiaquin	Moylough	Mountbellew	IV.	79
20	Ballynamona	53	0	30	Kilkenny	Gowran	Blackrath	Kilkenny	I.	93
20	Ballynamona	53	0	29	Kilkenny	Gowran	Clara	Kilkenny	I.	94
43	Ballynamona	155	3	17	Kilkenny	Ida	Dunkitt	Waterford	I.	101
41	Ballynamona	79	3	21	Kilkenny	Ida	Kilcolumb	Waterford	I.	102
27, 28, 32	Ballynamona	389	3	34	Kilkenny	Knocktopher	Jerpointchurch	Thomastown	I.	111
9	Ballynamona	494	1	30	King's Co.	Ballycowan	Durrow	Tullamore	I.	127
11	Ballynamona	93	0	22	King's Co.	Warrenstown	Ballyburly	Edenderry	I.	144
41, 49	Ballynamona	565	0	3	Limerick	Coshlea	Galbally	Mitchelstown	II.	238
11, 20	Ballynamona	438	1	0	Limerick	Kenry	Kilcornan	Rathkeale	II.	249
32	Ballynamona	844	3	31	Limerick	Smallcounty	Ballynamona	Kilmallock	II.	259
40	Ballynamona	267	2	15	Limerick	Smallcounty	Uregare	Kilmallock	II.	261
71,72,80,81	Ballynamona	583	0	39	Mayo	Gallen	Killedan	Swineford	IV.	149
15	Ballynamona	240	2	10	Meath	Fore	Loughcrew	Oldcastle	I.	201
43	Ballynamona	150	3	27	Meath	Lower Deece	Galtrim	Trim	I.	191
10, 16	Ballynamona	225	2	3	Meath	Upper Kells	Dulane	Kells	I.	205
15	Ballynamona	357	0	2a	Sligo	Carbury	Calry	Sligo	IV.	220
48	Ballynamona	193	2	9	Tipperary, N.R.	Eliogarty	Twomileborris	Thurles	II.	273
10	Ballynamona	195	1	35	Tipperary, N.R.	Lower Ormond	Finnoe	Borrisokane	II.	283
78	Ballynamona	555	1	18	Tipperary, S.R.	Iffa and Offa East	Kilmurry	Carrick on Suir	II.	314
81	Ballynamona	206	1	8	Tipperary, S.R.	Iffa and Offa West	Caher	Clogheen	II.	317
88	Ballynamona	156	2	34b	Tipperary, S.R.	Iffa and Offa West	Molough	Clogheen	II.	318
38, 40	Ballynamona	464	1	15	Waterford	Decies within Drum	Ardmore	Youghal	II.	349
9	Ballynamona	33	2	10	Waterford	Middlethird	Killoteran	Waterford	II.	367
28	Ballynamona	87	2	1	Wexford	Ballaghkeen	Ballyvaldon	Enniscorthy	I.	292
27	Ballynamona	243	2	9	Wexford	Ballaghkeen	Castle-ellis	Enniscorthy	I.	293
28	Ballynamona	200	2	18	Wexford	Ballaghkeen	Killincooly	Enniscorthy	I.	295
39	Ballynamona	459	2	7	Wexford	Shelburne	Kilmokea	New Ross	I.	327
35, 40	Ballynamona	346	1	4	Wexford	Shelmaliere West	Clongeen	New Ross	I.	332
36	Ballynamona	161	1	22	Wicklow	Arklow	Redcross	Rathdrum	I.	346
27	Ballynamonabeg	29	1	33	Wexford	Ballaghkeen	Castle-ellis	Enniscorthy	I.	293
27	Ballynamonabeg	155	2	5	Wexford	Ballaghkeen	Killisk	Enniscorthy	I.	296
36	Ballynamona Glebe	113	0	23	King's Co.	Eglish	Drumcullen	Parsonstown	I.	134
47	Ballynamona Lower	159	0	20	Kerry	Trughanacmy	Kiltallagh	Tralee	II.	212
39	Ballynamona Lower	400	3	8	Waterford	Decies within Drum	Ardmore	Dungarvan	II.	349
11	Ballynamonaster or Charlestown and Abbeyland	230	1	6	Westmeath	Moygoish	Kilbixy	Mullingar	I.	279
43	BALLYNAMONA T.	—			Kilkenny	Ida	Dunkitt	Waterford	I.	101
38, 47	Ballynamona Upper	297	1	13	Kerry	Trughanacmy	Kiltallagh	Tralee	II.	212
39	Ballynamona Upper	337	1	35	Waterford	Decies within Drum	Ardmore	Dungarvan	II.	349
17	Ballynamoney	292	0	34	Antrim	Upper Dunluce	Ballymoney	Ballymoney	III.	18
27	Ballynamongaree	201	1	20	Cork, E.R.	Fermoy	Glanworth	Fermoy	II.	79
6	Ballynamony	467	2	22	Armagh	Oneilland East	Seagoe	Lurgan	III.	50
37	Ballynamony	82	3	26	Cavan	Clanmahon	Ballymachugh	Cavan	III.	75
37, 38	Ballynamony	141	2	5	Kildare	Kilkea and Moone	Kilkea	Athy	I.	60
26, 30	Ballynamony	74	1	35	Leitrim	Carrigallen	Carrigallen	Bawnboy	IV.	89
27, 31	Ballynamony	99	3	28	Leitrim	Leitrim	Kiltoghert	Cark. on Shannon	IV.	101
16	Ballynamony	171	0	26	Wexford	Gorey	Ballycanew	Gorey	I.	315
8, 9	Ballynamony, Bradshaw	106	0	0	Louth	Lower Dundalk	Carlingford	Dundalk	I.	176
9	Ballynamony, Murphy	175	3	21	Louth	Lower Dundalk	Carlingford	Dundalk	I.	176
43	Ballynamorahan	104	0	11	Kilkenny	Ida	Gaulskill	Waterford	I.	102
22	Ballynamore	493	1	25	Londonderry	Tirkeeran	Cumber Lower	Londonderry	III.	248
92	Ballynamought	542	0	13	Cork, W.R.	Bantry	Kilmocomoge	Bantry	II.	119
42	Ballynamountain	89	3	8	Kilkenny	Iverk	Rathkieran	Waterford	I.	107
27	Ballynamoyntragh	702	0	30	Waterford	Gaultiere	Kilmacleague	Waterford	II.	364
66	Ballynamrossagh	700	0	2	Tipperary, S.R.	Clanwilliam	Bruis	Tipperary	II.	305
16	Ballynamuck	75	3	7	Cork, E.R.	Orrery and Kilmore	Churchtown	Mallow	II.	107
105	Ballynamucka	68	1	16	Galway	Dunkellin	Kilconickny	Loughrea	IV.	29
31	Ballynamuck East	37	2	0	Waterford	Decies without Drum	Kilrush	Dungarvan	II.	358
31	Ballynamuck Middle	142	0	7	Waterford	Decies without Drum	Kilrush	Dungarvan	II.	358
30, 31	Ballynamuck West	181	2	11	Waterford	Decies without Drum	Kilrush	Dungarvan	II.	358

(a) Including 4A. 2R. 38P. water.   (b) Including 3A. 3R. 6P. water.

Q

No. of Sheet of the Ordnance Survey Maps.	Townlands and Towns.	Area in Statute Acres.			County.	Barony.	Parish.	Poor Law Union in 1857.	Townland Census of 1851, Part I.	
		A.	R.	P.					Vol.	Page
29	Ballynamucky	389	2	1	Limerick	Connello Lower	Rathkeale	Croom	II.	229
28	Ballynamuddagh	933	3	30	Cork, E.R.	Condons&Clangibbon	Leitrim	Fermoy	II.	62
35	Ballynamuddagh	250	2	0	Cork, E.R.	Fermoy	Killathy	Fermoy	II.	80
99	Ballynamuddagh	214	0	32	Galway	Clonmacnowen	Killallaghtan	Ballinasloe	IV.	26
100, 108	Ballynamuddagh	273	0	5	Galway	Longford	Donanaghta	Portumna	IV.	58
17, 18	Ballynamuddagh	250	3	17	Kerry	Clanmaurice	Duagh	Listowel	II.	168
28	Ballynamuddagh	103	1	39	Limerick	Connello Lower	Clonagh	Rathkeale	II.	227
49, 50, 58	Ballynamuddagh	619	2	37	Limerick	Coshlea	Galbally	Mitchelstown	II.	238
39	Ballynamuddagh	476	2	1	Limerick	Coshma	Dromin	Kilmallock	II.	243
17	Ballynamuddagh	221	2	28	Limerick	Shanid	Kilfergus	Glin	II.	256
90, 100	Ballynamuddagh	162	2	36	Mayo	Carra	Rosslee	Ballinrobe	IV.	130
17	Ballynamuddagh	444	3	3	Queen's Co.	Maryborough West	Clonenagh and Clonagheen	Abbeyleix	I.	242
82, 88	Ballynamuddagh	135	3	12	Tipperary, S.R.	Iffa and Offa West	Tullaghmelan	Clogheen	II.	321
36	Ballynamuddagh	639	0	4	Westmeath	Clonlonan	Kilcleagh	Athlone	I.	261
26, 27	Ballynamuddagh	450	0	9	Wexford	Ballaghkeen	Ballyhuskard	Enniscorthy	I.	291
8	Ballynamuddagh	470	1	13	Wicklow	Rathdown	Bray	Rathdown	I.	354
26	Ballynamuddagh T.	—			Wexford	Ballaghkeen	Ballyhuskard	Enniscorthy	I.	292
3, 4, 8, 9	Ballynamullagh	611	3	35	Kildare	Carbury	Mylerstown	Edenderry	I.	52
48, 49	Ballynamullan (pt. of)	255	3	34	Antrim	Upper Toome	Duneane	Antrim	III.	34
48	Ballynamullan (pt. of)	151	1	22	Antrim	Upper Toome	Duneane	Antrim	III.	34
35	Ballynamullan	950	3	38	Tyrone	Strabane Upper	Cappagh	Omagh	III.	325
31	Ballynamullen	49	2	14	Westmeath	Moycashel	Ardnurcher or Horseleap	Mullingar	I.	276
13	Ballynamult	136	2	12	Waterford	Decies without Drum	Seskinan	Lismore	II.	360
34,35,37,38	Ballynamultina	540	1	35	Waterford	Decies within Drum	Clashmore	Youghal	II.	351
106	Ballynamurdoon	200	2	14	Galway	Leitrim	Abbeygormacan	Loughrea	IV.	50
15	Ballynamurragh Nth.	151	3	23	Tipperary, N.R.	Lower Ormond	Kilruane	Nenagh	II.	285
15	Ballynamurragh Sth.	222	2	23	Tipperary, N.R.	Upper Ormond	Kilruane	Nenagh	II.	292
42, 43	Ballynana	294	1	2	Kerry	Corkaguiny	Kilmalkedar	Dingle	II.	178
63, 67	Ballynanaghten	415	3	18	Antrim	Upper Massereene	Aghalee	Lurgan	III.	29
5, 10	Ballynancoran	370	0	25	Wexford	Scarawalsh	Carnew	Gorey	I.	322
45	Ballynane	500	0	0	Kerry	Corkaguiny	Ballinvoher	Dingle	II.	173
9, 17	Ballynaneashagh	333	2	8	Waterford	Gaultiere	Kilbarry	Waterford	II.	363
99	Ballynaneening	209	2	17	Cork, E.R.	Kerrycurrihy	Kilpatrick	Kinsale	II.	92
44, 45	Ballynanelagh	241	1	39	Cork, E.R.	Barrymore	Gortroe	Fermoy	II.	54
64	Ballynanelagh	433	0	31	Cork, E.R.	Barrymore	Kilquane	Cork	II.	55
99, 109	Ballynanerroon Beg	77	1	2	Mayo	Carra	Ballyovey	Ballinrobe	IV.	126
99, 109	Ballynanerroon More	255	3	38	Mayo	Carra	Ballyovey	Ballinrobe	IV.	126
48, 52	Ballynanny	1,698	2	24	Down	Upper Iveagh, Lr. pt.	Clonduff	Newry	III.	171
34	Ballynanny	538	1	3	Down	Upper Iveagh, Up.pt.	Annaclone	Banbridge	III.	174
26, 32	Ballynanoose	617	2	33	Tipperary, N.R.	Owney and Arra	Killoscully	Nenagh	II.	295
5	Ballynant	66	3	0	Fermanagh	Lurg	Magheraculmoney	Lowtherstown	III.	207
31	Ballynanty	404	1	24	Limerick	Coshma	Tullabracky	Kilmallock	II.	244
5	Ballynanty Beg	68	2	35a	Limerick	Pubblebrien	Killeely	Limerick	II.	253
5	Ballynanty More	121	0	9	Limerick	Pubblebrien	Killeely	Limerick	II.	253
5	Ballynanultagh	196	3	27	Roscommon	Boyle	Boyle	Boyle	IV.	193
85	Ballynanulty	254	0	14	Galway	Tiaquin	Killimordaly	Loughrea	IV.	77
11	Ballynanum	125	1	19	King's Co.	Coolestown	Ballynakill	Edenderry	I.	132
59	Ballynany	201	1	22	Tyrone	Clogher	Errigal Keerogue	Clogher	III.	295
58	Ballynapark	274	0	6	Galway	Clare	Killererin	Tuam	IV.	20
36	Ballynapark	193	1	11	Wicklow	Arklow	Dunganstown	Rathdrum	I.	343
29,30,34,35	Ballynaparka	235	2	4	Waterford	Decies within Drum	Aglish	Dungarvan	II.	349
29	Ballynaparka	221	3	4	Waterford	Decies within Drum	Kilmolash	Dungarvan	II.	351
28	Ballynaparka North	172	0	10	Cork, E.R.	Condons&Clangibbon	Leitrim	Fermoy	II.	62
28, 36	Ballynaparka South	123	0	23	Cork, E.R.	Condons&Clangibbon	Leitrim	Fermoy	II.	62
63	Ballynaparson	283	0	25	Cork, E.R.	Barrymore	Templeusque	Cork	II.	59
25, 26	Ballynapierce	385	2	7	Wexford	Bantry	St. John's	Enniscorthy	I.	302
59	Ballynapottoge	107	0	35	Tyrone	Dungannon Lower	Carnteel	Clogher	III.	297
26, 35	Ballynaquilly	456	1	0	Tyrone	Strabane Upper	Cappagh	Omagh	III.	325
62	Ballynaraha	277	1	22	Cork, E.R.	East Muskerry	Garrycloyne	Cork	II.	103
26, 27	Ballynaraha	269	2	16	Cork, E.R.	Fermoy	Glanworth	Fermoy	II.	79
40, 41	Ballynaraha	290	1	14	Kilkenny	Ida	Kilmakevoge	Waterford	I.	103
39	Ballynaraha	91	2	26	Mayo	Tirawley	Ballynahaglish	Ballina	IV.	164
78, 84	Ballynaraha	713	1	11b	Tipperary, S.R.	Iffa and Offa East	Kilsheelan	Clonmel	II.	314
29	Ballynaraha	187	1	17	Waterford	Coshmore&Coshbride	Lismore and Mocollop	Lismore	II.	344
52	Ballynaraha North	86	0	8	Kerry	Corkaguiny	Dunquin	Dingle	II.	176
39	Ballynaraha North	38	3	30	Kilkenny	Knocktopher	Killahy	Waterford	I.	112
52	Ballynaraha South	46	2	9	Kerry	Corkaguiny	Dunquin	Dingle	II.	176
39, 40	Ballynaraha South	181	3	36	Kilkenny	Knocktopher	Killahy	Waterford	I.	112
38, 39	Ballynaraw North	56	3	36	Sligo	Corran	Cloonoghill	Tobercurry	IV.	225
38, 39	Ballynaraw South	382	2	6	Sligo	Corran	Cloonoghill	Tobercurry	IV.	225
50	Ballynare	25	1	30	Meath	Upper Deece	Culmullin	Dunshaughlin	I.	193

(a) Within the Municipal Boundary, 1A. 2R. 17P.; without the Municipal Boundary, 67A. 0R. 18P.   (b) Including 12A. 1R. 6P. water.

No. of Sheet of the Ordnance Survey Maps.	Townlands and Towns.	Area in Statute Acres.			County.	Barony.	Parish.	Poor Law Union in 1857.	Townland Census of 1851, Part I.	
		A.	R.	P.					Vol.	Page
24, 27	Ballynarea	384	0	37	Armagh	Fews Upper	Newtownhamilton	Castleblayney	III.	49
30, 39	Ballynargan	204	3	28	Tyrone	Dungannon Upper	Arboe	Cookstown	III.	305
20, 21	Ballynaris	986	2	21	Down	Lower Iveagh, Lr. pt.	Dromore	Banbridge	III.	168
37	Ballynarooga Beg	72	0	16	Limerick	Connello Upper	Cloncagh	Newcastle	II.	231
37	Ballynarooga Beg (East)	131	0	10	Limerick	Connello Upper	Ballingarry	Croom	II.	230
37	Ballynarooga Beg (West)	209	2	11	Limerick	Connello Upper	Ballingarry	Croom	II.	230
37	Ballynarooga More (North)	117	2	0	Limerick	Connello Upper	Cloncagh	Newcastle	II.	231
37	Ballynarooga More (South)	427	3	7	Limerick	Connello Upper	Cloncagh	Newcastle	II.	231
75	Ballynaroon	194	0	8	Cork, E.R.	Barrymore	Caherlag	Cork	II.	52
24, 32	Ballynarrid	244	3	0	Waterford	Decies without Drum	Ballylaneen	Kilmacthomas	II.	354
46	Ballynarry	405	2	33	Antrim	Lower Belfast	Ballynure	Larne	III.	7
5	Ballynarry	579	3	2	Armagh	Oneilland West	Tartaraghan	Lurgan	III.	54
19, 28, 29	Ballynarry	640	1	31	Donegal	Inishowen West	Fahan Lower	Inishowen	I.I.	120
7	Ballynarry Lower	262	3	23	Antrim	Lower Dunluce	Billy	Coleraine	III.	16
7, 12	Ballynarry Upper	190	2	23	Antrim	Lower Dunluce	Derrykeighan	Ballymoney	III.	16
34, 40	Ballynary	201	0	19	Sligo	Tirerrill	Kilmactranny	Boyle	IV.	240
52, 59	Ballynasaggart	159	3	22	Tyrone	Clogher	Errigal Keerogue	Clogher	III.	295
29	Ballynasare	121	0	35	Kerry	Trughanacmy	Clogherbrien	Tralee	II.	209
44	Ballynasare Beg	71	3	29	Kerry	Corkaguiny	Minard	Dingle	II.	179
44, 54	Ballynasare Lower	376	0	12	Kerry	Corkaguiny	Minard	Dingle	II.	179
44	Ballynasare Mountain	617	0	36	Kerry	Corkaguiny	Minard	Dingle	II.	179
51, 52	Ballynascall	94	3	17	Donegal	Kilmacrenan	Gartan	Letterkenny	III.	127
1	Ballynascarry	628	1	15	Westmeath	Fore	Foyran	Granard	I.	270
12	Ballynascarry(Butler)	40	3	6	Kilkenny	Crannagh	Tubbridbritain	Urlingford	I.	87
12	Ballynascarry (Gore)	216	1	17	Kilkenny	Crannagh	Tubbridbritain	Urlingford	I.	87
66, 77	Ballynascarty	477	1	2	Cork, E.R.	Imokilly	Ballyoughtera	Middleton	II.	84
104	Ballynascragh	97	0	35	Dunkellin	Dunkellin	Killogilleen	Loughrea	IV.	31
10	Ballynascraw	329	3	6	Longford	Granard	Clonbroney	Granard	I.	154
124	Ballynascubbig	272	1	15	Cork, W.R.	East Carbery (E.D.)	Templetrine	Kinsale	II.	130
34, 35	Ballynasculloge	80	2	17	Kildare	Narragh and Reban West	Churchtown	Athy	I.	67
5	Ballynasculloge Lower	376	3	27	Wicklow	Lower Talbotstown	Blessington	Naas	I.	358
5	Ballynasculloge Upper	773	2	35	Wicklow	Lower Talbotstown	Blessington	Naas	I.	358
10, 11	Ballynash	80	0	6	Limerick	Connello Lower	Askeaton	Rathkeale	II.	226
13, 14	Ballynashallog	523	0	18a	Londonderry	North West Liberties of Londonderry	Templemore	Londonderry	III.	246
17, 18	Ballynashannagh	214	3	15	Donegal	Kilmacrenan	Clondavaddog	Milford	III.	124
9, 10, 18	Ballynash (Bishop)	417	1	7	Limerick	Shanid	Shanagolden	Glin	II.	258
9, 10	Ballynash (Clare)	381	0	6	Limerick	Shanid	Shanagolden	Glin	II.	258
39, 45	Ballynashee	1,315	0	14	Antrim	Upper Antrim	Rashee	Antrim	III.	7
35	Ballynashee	1,165	0	1	Sligo	Tirerrill	Kilmactranny	Boyle	IV.	240
70	Ballynasheeoge	178	1	29	Galway	Clare	Lackagh	Galway	IV.	22
38	Ballynashig	149	1	13	Limerick	Connello Upper	Ballingarry	Croom	II.	230
19, 22	Ballynasilloge	386	3	23	Carlow	Idrone East	Clonygoose	Carlow	I.	6
24, 25	Ballynasissala	334	1	22	Waterford	Decies without Drum	Monksland	Kilmacthomas	II.	359
42, 48	Ballynaskea	1,507	3	34	Meath	Lower Moyfenrath	Rathcore	Trim	I.	211
34, 41	Ballynaskeagh	665	1	3	Down	Upper Iveagh, Up.pt.	Aghaderg	Banbridge	III.	173
8, 13	Ballynaskeagh	381	2	22	Westmeath	Delvin	Castletowndelvin	Castletowndelvin	I.	264
20, 21	Ballynaskeagh	334	2	6	Westmeath	Delvin	Killagh	Castletowndelvin	I.	265
64	Ballynaskeha	186	1	1	Cork, E.R.	Barrymore	Lisgoold	Middleton	II.	56
31	Ballynaskeha Beg	49	3	19	Waterford	Decies without Drum	Dungarvan	Dungarvan	II.	355
31	Ballynaskeha More	65	2	4	Waterford	Decies without Drum	Dungarvan	Dungarvan	II.	355
9	Ballynaskreena	311	2	12	Kerry	Clanmaurice	Killury	Listowel	II.	170
32	Ballynaslaney	355	2	37	Wexford	Shelmaliere East	Ballynaslaney	Enniscorthy	I.	330
32	Ballynaslaney	7	3	20	Wexford	Shelmaliere East	Kilpatrick	Enniscorthy	I.	330
4	Ballynaslee	668	2	9	Kilkenny	Galmoy	Durrow	Urlingford	I.	92
99, 109	Ballynaslee	101	2	32	Mayo	Carra	Ballyovey	Ballinrobe	IV.	126
8, 9	Ballynaslost	303	2	2	Donegal	Kilmacrenan	Clondavaddog	Milford	III.	124
21, 29	Ballynasollus	261	3	14	Tyrone	Dungannon Upper	Derryloran	Cookstown	III.	306
20, 21, 28, 29	Ballynasollus	1,076	1	2	Tyrone	Dungannon Upper	Kildress	Cookstown	III.	308
10, 11	Ballynasollus	925	0	17	Tyrone	Strabane Upper	Bodoney Upper	Gortin	III.	324
59, 60	Ballynasooragh Eighter	144	1	31	Galway	Tiaquin	Killoscobe	Mountbellew	IV.	77
59, 60	Ballynasooragh Oughter	249	0	5	Galway	Tiaquin	Killoscobe	Mountbellew	IV.	77
16	Ballynasrah	311	3	7	King's Co.	Ballycowan	Kilbride	Tullamore	I.	127
29	Ballynasrah	927	3	22	King's Co.	Garrycastle	Lusmagh	Parsonstown	I.	137
25	Ballynasrah	574	0	11	King's Co.	Geashill	Geashill	Tullamore	I.	140
9, 17	Ballynasrah or Tinnycross	510	2	28	King's Co.	Ballycowan	Kilbride	Tullamore	I.	127
103	Ballynastaig	175	2	4	Galway	Dunkellin	Killeely	Gort	IV.	29
122	Ballynastaig	214	2	2b	Galway	Kiltartan	Kilmacduagh	Gort	IV.	47

(a) Including 1A. 1R. 7P. water.   (b) Including 4A. 2R. 22P. water.

Q 2

No. of Sheet of the Ordnance Survey Maps.	Townlands and Towns.	Area in Statute Acres.	County.	Barony.	Parish.	Poor Law Union in 1857.	Townland Census of 1851, Part I.	
		A. R. P.					Vol.	Page
91, 101	Ballynastangford Lower	143 2 37	Mayo . .	Clanmorris . .	Kilcolman . .	Claremorris .	IV.	133
101	Ballynastangford Upper	99 3 18	Mayo . .	Clanmorris . .	Kilcolman . .	Claremorris .	IV.	133
48, 49	Ballynastick . .	380 3 30	Tipperary, S.R.	Slievardagh . .	Buolick . .	Urlingford .	II.	332
103	Ballynastockagh .	268 1 15	Mayo . .	Costello . .	Annagh . .	Claremorris .	IV.	137
10	Ballynastockan .	1,504 3 26	Wicklow . .	Lower Talbotstown .	Boystown . .	Naas . .	I.	359
3, 4, 7	Ballynastraid . .	387 3 17	Antrim . .	Cary . .	Ballintoy . .	Ballycastle .	III.	12
26	Ballynastraw . .	750 2 0	Wexford . .	Ballaghkeen .	Ballyhuskard .	Enniscorthy .	I.	291
4, 9	Ballynastraw . .	795 3 11	Wexford . .	Scarawalsh .	Moyacomb .	Shillelagh .	I.	325
43,44,57,58	Ballynastuckaun .	426 1 36	Galway . .	Clare . .	Kilmoylan .	Tuam . .	IV.	22
38	Ballynasuddery and Shureen . .	171 0 36	Westmeath .	Moycashel .	Kilbeggan .	Tullamore .	I.	278
48	Ballynatona . .	278 0 22	Cork, W.R. .	West Muskerry .	Drishane .	Millstreet .	II.	155
49	Ballynatona . .	251 0 28	Limerick . .	Coshlea . .	Galbally . .	Mitchelstown .	II.	238
58, 60	Ballynatona . .	309 1 3	Limerick . .	Coshlea . .	Kilbeheny .	Mitchelstown .	II.	239
86, 89	Ballynatona . .	395 0 16	Tipperary, S.R.	Iffa and Offa West .	Shanrahan .	Clogheen .	II.	319
5, 6	Ballynatona . .	690 1 18	Wicklow . .	Lower Talbotstown .	Blessington .	Naas . .	I.	358
68, 77	Ballynatone . .	272 1 20a	Donegal . .	Raphoe . .	Kilteevoge .	Stranorlar .	III.	139
21	Ballynatone . .	108 2 4	Wicklow . .	Upper Talbotstown	Rathbran .	Baltinglass .	I.	365
76, 88	Ballynatra . .	83 2 26	Cork, E.R. .	Barrymore . .	Templerobin .	Cork . .	II.	58
138	Ballynatra . .	39 1 23	Cork, W.R. .	WestCarbery (W.D.)	Kilcrohane .	Bantry .	II.	143
33, 34, 37	BallynatrayCommons	737 0 6	Waterford .	Coshmore&Coshbride	Templemichael .	Youghal .	II.	348
34, 37	Ballynatray Demesne	1,158 3 17	Waterford .	Coshmore&Coshbride	Templemichael .	Youghal .	II.	348
7, 16	Ballynatrilla . .	237 3 36	Cork, E.R. .	Orrery and Kilmore	Kilbroney .	Mallow .	II.	109
22	Ballynattin . .	229 0 31	Carlow . .	Idrone East .	Kiltennell .	Carlow .	I.	7
55	Ballynattin . .	373 1 7	Cork, E.R. .	Kinnatalloon .	Ballynoe .	Fermoy .	II.	97
45	Ballynattin . .	150 3 9	Wicklow . .	Arklow . .	Arklow . .	Rathdrum .	I.	341
18, 26	Ballynatubbrit .	447 1 31	Tyrone . .	Strabane Upper .	Cappagh . .	Omagh .	III.	325
152	Ballynaule . .	91 0 25	Cork, W.R. .	West Carbery (W.D.)	Kilmoe . .	Skull .	II.	144
31, 37	Ballynavaddog .	180 3 10	Meath . .	Lower Deece .	Balsoon . .	Trim .	I.	191
37	Ballynavaddog .	84 2 20	Meath . .	Lower Deece .	Trubley . .	Trim .	I.	192
9	Ballynavally . .	298 3 8b	Down . .	Castlereagh Upper .	Drumbo . .	Lisburn .	III.	164
65	Ballynaveen . .	425 1 22	Tipperary, S.R.	Clanwilliam .	Emly . .	Tipperary .	II.	307
34	Ballynavenooragh .	636 1 24	Kerry . .	Corkaguiny .	Kilquane .	Dingle .	II.	179
10	Ballynavin . .	484 1 26	Tipperary, N.R.	Lower Ormond .	Modreeny .	Borrisokane .	II.	286
42, 46	Ballynavortha . .	320 0 8	Wicklow . .	Shillelagh .	Moyacomb .	Shillelagh .	I.	358
18	Ballynawall and Drum . . .	108 2 35	Donegal . .	Kilmacrenan .	Clondavaddog .	Millford .	III.	124
21,22,26,27	Ballyneage or Hybla	641 2 30	Kildare . .	Offally West .	Duneany .	Athy .	I.	72
56, 67	Ballyneague . .	222 0 25	Cork, E.R. .	Imokilly . .	Ardagh . .	Youghal .	II.	83
7	Ballyneal . .	346 0 18	Waterford .	Upperthird .	Mothel . .	Carrick on Suir	II.	370
37	Ballyneale . .	167 0 11	Kilkenny . .	Ida . .	Dysartmoon .	New Ross .	I.	101
37	Ballyneale . .	341 2 8	Kilkenny . .	Ida . .	Listerlin .	New Ross .	I.	103
37, 38	Ballyneale . .	656 3 34	Limerick . .	Connello Upper .	Ballingarry .	Croom .	II.	230
3	Ballyneaner . .	652 1 20	Tyrone . .	Strabane Lower .	Donaghedy .	Strabane .	III.	320
42, 43	Ballynearla . .	467 1 31	Kilkenny . .	Iverk . .	Kilmacow .	Waterford .	I.	105
15	Ballyneary . .	32 1 18	Cavan . .	Lower Loughtee .	Annagh . .	Cavan .	III.	78
33, 37	Ballynease-helton .	387 0 16	Londonderry .	Loughinsholin .	Ballyscullion .	Magherafelt .	III.	239
33, 37, 38	Ballynease-macpeake	867 1 11	Londonderry .	Loughinsholin .	Ballyscullion .	Magherafelt .	III.	239
37	Ballynease-strain .	395 2 35	Londonderry .	Loughinsholin .	Ballyscullion .	Magherafelt .	III.	239
54	Ballyneddan . .	129 3 18	Down . .	Upper Iveagh,Up. pt.	Kilbroney .	Kilkeel .	III.	175
54	Ballyneddan Upper .	117 3 38	Down . .	Upper Iveagh,Up. pt.	Kilbroney .	Kilkeel .	III.	175
30	Ballyneena . .	163 2 22	King's Co. .	Garrycastle .	Reynagh .	Parsonstown .	I.	138
109	BALLYNEEN T. .	—	Cork, W.R. .	East Carbery, (E.D.)	Ballymoney .	Dunmanway .	II.	127
14	Ballyneety . .	94 0 24	Limerick . .	Clanwilliam .	Cahernarry .	Limerick .	II.	222
33	Ballyneety . .	105 2 38	Limerick . .	Coonagh . .	Oola . .	Tipperary .	II.	235
19, 28	Ballyneety . .	295 0 17	Limerick . .	Shanid . .	Kilbradran .	Rathkeale .	II.	255
29	Ballyneety . .	310 3 0	Mayo . .	Tirawley . .	Crossmolina .	Ballina .	IV.	165
82, 88	Ballyneety . .	63 3 13	Tipperary, S.R.	Iffa and Offa West .	Ardfinnan .	Clogheen .	II.	316
82, 88	Ballyneety . .	331 3 8	Tipperary, S.R.	Iffa and Offa West .	Neddans .	Clogheen .	II.	319
82	Ballyneety . .	97 0 32	Tipperary, S.R.	Iffa and Offa West .	Tullaghmelan .	Clogheen .	II.	321
29, 34	Ballyneety . .	209 3 15	Waterford .	Coshmore&Coshbride	Kilwatermoy .	Lismore .	II.	343
31	Ballyneety . .	343 2 27	Waterford .	Decies without Drum	Kilgobnet .	Dungarvan .	II.	357
33	Ballyneety North .	164 1 20	Limerick . .	Coonagh . .	Templebredon .	Tipperary .	II.	236
33	Ballyneety South .	228 3 13	Limerick . .	Coonagh . .	Templebredon .	Tipperary .	II.	236
14	BALLYNEETY T. .	—	Limerick . .	Clanwilliam .	Cahernarry .	Limerick .	II.	223
70	Ballyneggin . .	180 3 24	Mayo . .	Carra . .	Aglish . .	Castlebar .	IV.	123
51	Ballyneill . .	155 2 26	Tipperary, S.R.	Clanwilliam ·	Donohill .	Tipperary .	II.	307
78,79,84,85	Ballyneill . .	825 1 28	Tipperary, S.R.	Iffa and Offa East .	Kilmurry .	Carrick on Suir	II.	314
8	Ballyneillan . .	21 2 11	Clare . .	Burren . .	Kilmoon .	Ballyvaghan .	II.	13
33	Ballyneillan . .	166 2 35	Clare . .	Inchiquin .	Kilnamona .	Ennis .	II.	27
47, 49	Ballyneill Beg . .	472 1 7	Londonderry .	Loughinsholin .	Artrea .	Magherafelt .	III.	238
47	Ballyneill More .	639 2 14	Londonderry .	Loughinsholin .	Artrea .	Magherafelt .	III.	200
14	Ballynelahillan .	331 1 27	Wexford . .	Scarawalsh .	Monart . .	Enniscorthy .	I.	324

(a) Including 5A. 3R. 35P. water.　　　(b) Including 8A. 1R. 24P. water.

No. of Sheet of the Ordnance Survey Maps.	Townlands and Towns.	Area in Statute Acres.			County.	Barony.	Parish.	Poor Law Union in 1857.	Townland Census of 1851, Part I.	
		A.	R.	P.					Vol.	Page
45	Ballynella	169	2	14	Cork, E.R.	Barrymore	Knockmourne	Fermoy	II.	56
27	Ballynellard	390	1	17	Wexford	Ballaghkeen	Castle-ellis	Enniscorthy	I.	293
27	Ballynellard	50	1	13	Wexford	Ballaghkeen	Killila	Enniscorthy	I.	295
21	Ballynelligan Glebe	67	2	11	Waterford	Coshmore&Coshbride	Lismore and Mocollop	Lismore	II.	344
46, 47	Ballynenagh	500	0	14	Londonderry	Loughinsholin	Artrea	Magherafelt	III.	238
63	Ballynennan	122	3	16	Tipperary, S.R.	Middlethird	Drangan	Cashel	II.	326
63	Ballynennan (*Lloyd*)	609	2	29	Tipperary, S.R.	Middlethird	Drangan	Cashel	II.	326
40	Ballynera	104	1	12	Tipperary, N.R.	Kilnamanagh Upper	Moyaliff	Thurles	II.	279
13	Ballynerrin	244	0	23	Wicklow	Newcastle	Kilcoole	Rathdrum	I.	351
25	Ballynerrin	290	1	12	Wicklow	Newcastle	Rathnew	Rathdrum	I.	354
25	Ballynerrin Lower	245	0	26	Wicklow	Arklow	Drumkay	Rathdrum	I.	342
25, 31	Ballynerrin Upper	187	2	13	Wicklow	Arklow	Drumkay	Rathdrum	I.	342
19, 20	Ballynerroon East	150	2	24*a*	Waterford	Coshmore&Coshbride	Lismore and Mocollop	Lismore	II.	344
19	Ballynerroon West	142	0	12*b*	Waterford	Coshmore&Coshbride	Lismore and Mocollop	Lismore	II.	344
5, 6	Ballynery	779	2	28*c*	Armagh	Oneilland East	Montiaghs	Lurgan	III.	49
7	Ballyness	209	2	29	Antrim	Lower Dunluce	Billy	Coleraine	III.	16
7	Ballyness	137	3	38	Antrim	Lower Dunluce	Dunluce	Coleraine	III.	17
24, 25	Ballyness	349	0	20	Donegal	Kilmacrenan	Tullaghobegly	Dunfanaghy	III.	131
7	Ballyness	124	0	26	Londonderry	Coleraine	Macosquin	Coleraine	III.	232
17, 25	Ballyness	2,191	0	15	Londonderry	Keenaght	Dungiven	New Tⁿ Limavady	III.	236
58, 64	Ballyness	798	3	20	Tyrone	Clogher	Clogher	Clogher	III.	291
34	Ballyness Mountain	1,306	2	3*d*	Donegal	Kilmacrenan	Tullaghobegly	Dunfanaghy	III.	131
11, 12	Ballynester	191	1	21	Down	Ards Lower	Greyabbey	Newtownards	III.	158
6, 7	Ballynestragh	166	0	20	Wexford	Gorey	Kilcavan	Gorey	I.	317
3, 7	Ballynestragh Demesne	401	3	15	Wexford	Gorey	Kilcavan	Gorey	I.	317
43, 52	Ballynevan	154	0	13*e*	Clare	Bunratty Lower	Kilfinaghta	Limerick	II.	4
34, 35	Ballynevin	267	3	32	Queen's Co.	Clarmallagh	Aghmacart	Abbeyleix	I.	236
77, 78	Ballynevin	230	3	8	Tipperary, S.R.	Iffa and Offa East	Killaloan	Clonmel	II.	314
3, 7	Ballynevin	697	0	38	Waterford	Upperthird	Mothel	Carrick on Suir	II.	370
23	Ballynevoga	324	3	33	Waterford	Decies without Drum	Kilrossanty	Kilmacthomas	II.	357
31	Ballynew	307	3	27	Clare	Ibrickan	Kilfarboy	Ennistimon	II.	22
9, 22	Ballynew	493	3	16*f*	Galway	Ballynahinch	Ballynakill	Clifden	IV.	11
56	Ballynew	140	0	39	Galway	Clare	Kilcoona	Tuam	IV.	19
99	Ballynew	24	0	34	Galway	Clonmacnowen	Clontuskert	Ballinasloe	IV.	24
117, 118	Ballynew	160	0	38	Galway	Longford	Lickmolassy	Portumna	IV.	60
69, 70, 78	Ballynew	98	2	29	Mayo	Carra	Aglish	Castlebar	IV.	123
101	Ballynew	119	0	16	Mayo	Clanmorris	Kilcolman	Claremorris	IV.	133
101	Ballynew	174	1	35	Mayo	Clanmorris	Tagheen	Claremorris	IV.	135
37, 44	Ballynewport	287	2	19	Down	Lecale Upper	Rathmullan	Downpatrick	III.	181
13	Ballynewry	413	1	18*g*	Armagh	Fews Lower	Muliaghbrack	Armagh	III.	47
48, 49	Ballynewy	537	0	29	Londonderry	Loughinsholin	Artrea	Magherafelt	III.	238
26,27,32,33	Ballynian	537	2	11	Londonderry	Loughinsholin	Tamlaght O'Crilly	Ballymoney	III.	243
32	Ballynichol	201	2	7	Down	Ards Upper	Ballytrustan	Downpatrick	III.	160
10	Ballynichol	289	3	31	Down	Castlereagh Lower	Comber	Newtownards	III.	162
29	Ballynicole	197	1	28	Waterford	Decies within Drum	Kilmolash	Dungarvan	II.	351
124	Ballynidon	182	1	34	Cork, E.R.	Kinsale	Ringrone	Kinsale	II.	101
66, 67	Ballynilard	702	0	35	Tipperary, S.R.	Clanwilliam	Tipperary	Tipperary	II.	312
19, 28	Ballynisky	213	2	13	Limerick	Connello Lower	Clonagh	Rathkeale	II.	227
42	Ballynocker	388	3	32	Londonderry	Loughinsholin	Magherafelt	Magherafelt	III.	243
1	Ballynoe	80	3	2	Antrim	Cary	Rathlin Island	Ballycastle	III.	15
44, 50	Ballynoe	816	2	26	Antrim	Upper Antrim	Donegore	Antrim	III.	6
32	Ballynoe	524	1	23	Clare	Inchiquin	Inagh	Ennistimon	II.	24
87	Ballynoe	254	1	19	Cork, E.R.	Barrymore	Clonmel	Cork	II.	53
53	Ballynoe	237	0	14	Cork, E.R.	Barrymore	Gortroe	Fermoy	II.	54
35	Ballynoe	148	0	1	Cork, E.R.	Condons&Clangibbon	Fermoy	Fermoy	II.	60
63	Ballynoe	297	3	12	Cork, E.R.	Cork	Rathcooney	Cork	II.	65
23	Ballynoe	169	0	37	Cork, E.R.	Duhallow	Kilbrin	Kanturk	II.	71
32, 40, 41	Ballynoe	291	1	0	Cork, E.R.	Duhallow	Kilshannig	Mallow	II.	74
18	Ballynoe	327	0	33	Cork, E.R.	Fermoy	Farahy	Mitchelstown	II.	79
86	Ballynoe	204	2	31	Cork, E.R.	Kerrycurrihy	Ballinaboy	Cork	II.	91
98	Ballynoe	195	0	20	Cork, E.R.	Kinalea	Ballyfeard	Kinsale	II.	93
46	Ballynoe	243	2	5	Cork, E.R.	Kinnatalloon	Ballynoe	Fermoy	II.	97
2, 3	Ballynoe	187	0	33	Down	Ards Lower	Donaghadee	Newtownards	III.	157
37	Ballynoe	205	3	25	Down	Lecale Upper	Bright	Downpatrick	III.	180
14, 15	Ballynoe	238	1	20	Kerry	Clanmaurice	Killury	Listowel	I I.	171
37, 38	Ballynoe	661	1	22	Limerick	Connello Upper	Ballingarry	Croom	II.	230
39	Ballynoe	118	3	31	Limerick	Connello Upper	Bruree	Kilmallock	II.	231
37	Ballynoe	666	0	27	Limerick	Glenquin	Clonelty	Newcastle	II.	245
37	Ballynoe	126	2	2	Limerick	Glenquin	Mahoonagh	Newcastle	II.	246
12, 13	Ballynoe	158	1	26	Limerick	Pubblebrien	Mungret	Limerick	II.	253
20, 21	Ballynoe	196	1	19	Waterford	Coshmore&Coshbride	Lismore and Mocollop	Lismore	II.	344
27	Ballynoe East	92	2	6	Cork, E.R.	Condons&Clangibbon	Glanworth	Fermoy	II.	61
21	Ballynoe East	155	2	4	Waterford	Coshmore&Coshbride	Lismore and Mocollop	Lismore	II.	344

(a) Including 11A. 2R. 33P. water.
(b) Including 9A. 3R. 16P. water.
(c) Including 11A. 1R. 6P. of Lough Gullion, and 14A. 2R. 19P. of River Bann.
(d) Including 69A. 2R. 29P. water.

(e) Including 28A. 2R. 1P. water.
(f) Including 15A. 2R. 16P. water.
(g) Including 7A. 3R. 5P. water.

No. of Sheet of the Ordnance Survey Maps.	Townlands and Towns.	Area in Statute Acres.	County.	Barony.	Parish.	Poor Law Union in 1857.	Townland Census of 1851, Part I.	
		A.　R.　P.					Vol.	Page
13	Ballynoe or Newtown	573　2　22	Carlow	Forth	Ardoyne	Carlow	I.	3
46	BALLYNOE T.	—	Cork, E.R.	Kinnatalloon	Ballynoe	Fermoy	II.	97
27	Ballynoe West	44　2　3	Cork, E.R.	Fermoy	Glanworth	Fermoy	II.	79
19, 20	Ballynoe West	291　1　37	Waterford	Coshmore&Coshbride	Lismore and Mocollop	Lismore	II.	344
11,12,15,16	Ballynolan	76　0　33	Carlow	Idrone West	Oldleighlin	Carlow	I.	9
13	Ballynolan	87　1　32	Kilkenny	Crannagh	Ballinamara	Kilkenny	I.	84
11, 12	Ballynolan	119　0　8	Limerick	Kenry	Kildimo	Rathkeale	II.	249
87	Ballynomasna	383　2　16	Tipperary, S.R.	Iffa and Offa West	Tubbrid	Clogheen	II.	320
54, 65	Ballynona North	1,215　1　27	Cork, E.R.	Barrymore	Dungourney	Middleton	II.	54
65, 66	Ballynona South	410　1　0	Cork, E.R.	Barrymore	Dungourney	Middleton	II.	54
2, 5	Ballynoneen	820　3　35	Kerry	Iraghticonnor	Aghavallen	Listowel	II.	189
88	Ballynookery	395　2　6	Cork, E.R.	Imokilly	Aghada	Middleton	II.	83
36, 40	Ballynoony East	417　2　31	Kilkenny	Knocktopher	Kilbeacon	Waterford	I.	111
36, 40	Ballynoony West	1,326　2　19	Kilkenny	Knocktopher	Kilbeacon	Waterford	I.	111
73, 85	Ballynora	879　0　14	Cork, E.R.	Cork	Kilnaglory	Cork	II.	65
7	Ballynoran	275　3　16	Cork, E.R.	Orrery and Kilmore	Aglishdrinagh	Kilmallock	II.	106
84	Ballynoran	607　1　26a	Tipperary, S.R.	Iffa and Offa East	Kilmurry	Carrick on Suir	II.	314
15	Ballynorig East	432　0　4	Kerry	Clanmaurice	Kilmoyly	Tralee	II.	171
14, 15	Ballynorig West	438　3　30	Kerry	Clanmaurice	Kilmoyly	Tralee	II.	171
11	Ballynort	657　3　17	Limerick	Connello Lower	Askeaton	Rathkeale	II.	226
54	Ballynorthland De-mesne	117　2　11b	Tyrone	Dungannon Middle	Drumglass	Dungannon	III.	302
67	Ballynote East	301　0　36	Clare	Moyarta	Kilrush	Kilrush	II.	33
67	Ballynote West	433　1　15	Clare	Moyarta	Kilrush	Kilrush	II.	33
23, 24	Ballynough	314　1　9	Tipperary, N.R.	Ikerrin	Bourney	Roscrea	II.	274
14	Ballynowlan	221　0　1	Queen's Co.	Stradbally	Moyanna	Athy	I.	247
5, 6, 10, 11	Ballynultagh	2,889　2　33	Wicklow	Lower Talbotstown	Boystown	Naas	I.	359
43	Ballynultagh	1,719　3　37	Wicklow	Shillelagh	Mullinacuff	Shillelagh	I.	358
33, 38	Ballynulto	568　0　36	Antrim	Lower Antrim	Glenwhirry	Ballymena	III.	4
13	Ballynunnery	191　2　18	Carlow	Forth	Gilbertstown	Carlow	I.	4
33, 37	Ballynunry	349　2　27	Kilkenny	Ida	The Rower	New Ross	I.	104
35, 36	Ballynure	584　0　20	Londonderry	Loughinsholin	Ballynascreen	Magherafelt	III.	238
12, 17	Ballynure	150　3　39	Monaghan	Dartree	Killeevan	Clones	III.	267
22	Ballynure	175　0　0	Wexford	Ballaghkeen	Kilmuckridge	Gorey	I.	296
14, 20	Ballynure	182　3　6	Wicklow	Upper Talbotstown	Ballynure	Baltinglass	I.	361
20	Ballynure Demesne	294　0　29	Wicklow	Upper Talbotstown	Ballynure	Baltinglass	I.	361
20	Ballynure Park	122　3　35	Wicklow	Upper Talbotstown	Ballynure	Baltinglass	I.	361
45	BALLYNURE T.	—	Antrim	Lower Belfast	Ballynure	Larne	III.	7
14	Ballyoan	299　0　6c	Londonderry	Tirkeeran	Clondermot	Londonderry	III.	247
32, 38	Ballyoban	78　1　7	Westmeath	Moycashel	Kilbeggan	Tullamore	I.	278
12	Ballyobegan	564　2　34	Down	Ards Upper	Inishargy	Newtownards	III.	160
54	Ballyogaha East	81　0　33	Cork, E.R.	Barrymore	Gortroe	Fermoy	II.	54
54	Ballyogaha North	79　0　19	Cork, E.R.	Barrymore	Gortroe	Fermoy	II.	55
54	Ballyogaha West	607　3　31	Cork, E.R.	Barrymore	Gortroe	Fermoy	II.	55
26	Ballyogan	683　2　5d	Clare	Bunratty Upper	Kilraghtis	Ennis	II.	9
26	Ballyogan	111　1　1	Dublin	Rathdown	Tully	Rathdown	I.	38
29, 33	Ballyogan	1,225　3　26e	Kilkenny	Gowran	Graiguenamanagh	Thomastown	I.	95
17	Ballyogan	570　0　26	Sligo	Tireragh	Kilglass	Dromore West	IV.	234
17	Ballyogan Beg	204　2　2	Clare	Inchiquin	Ruan	Corrofin	II.	28
17, 18	Ballyogan More	527　1　22f	Clare	Inchiquin	Ruan	Corrofin	II.	28
13, 14	Ballyogartha	66　1　21	Limerick	Clanwilliam	Cahernarry	Limerick	II.	222
15, 24	Ballyogarty	222　2　11	Waterford	Decies without Drum	Ballylaneen	Kilmacthomas	II.	354
16	Ballyoghagan	342　2　16	Donegal	Kilmacrenan	Mevagh	Millford	III.	130
7	Ballyoglagh	806　2　19	Antrim	Cary	Billy	Ballycastle	III.	12
3, 4	Ballyoliver	498　2　4	Carlow	Rathvilly	Rathvilly	Baltinglass	I.	12
1, 3	Ballyonan	603　0　39g	Kildare	Carbury	Ballynadrumny	Edenderry	I.	51
5	Ballyonan	851　0　10	Louth	Lower Dundalk	Carlingford	Dundalk	I.	176
55, 56	Ballyonan or Do-naghboy	775　3　6	Clare	Moyarta	Kilfearagh	Kilrush	II.	32
89	Ballyonane	111　0　37	Cork, E.R.	Imokilly	Cloyne	Middleton	II	85
54	Ballyoneen	171　1　31	Cork, E.R.	Barrymore	Gortroe	Fermoy	II.	55
54	Ballyoneen	108　0　30	Cork, E.R.	Barrymore	Templebodan	Middleton	II.	58
9	Ballyoran	136　1　6	Armagh	Oneilland West	Drumcree	Lurgan	III.	51
35, 36	Ballyoran	575　2　23	Cork, E.R.	Barrymore	Castlelyons	Fermoy	II.	53
5	Ballyoran	228　3　29	Down	Castlereagh Lower	Dundonald	Newtownards	III.	162
23, 31	Ballyoran	350　2　34	King's Co.	Ballyboy	Ballyboy	Parsonstown	I.	123
11	Ballyoran	237　3　33	Louth	Louth	Louth	Dundalk	I.	184
86, 87	Ballyorban	564　2　2	Cork, E.R.	Cork	Carrigaline	Cork	II.	64
20	Ballyore	123　1　34	Londonderry	Tirkeeran	Clondermot	Londonderry	III.	247
38	Ballyorgan	319　2　8	Down	Lecale Lower	Rathmullan	Downpatrick	III.	179
56	Ballyorgan	356　0　23	Limerick	Coshlea	Kilfiyn	Kilmallock	II.	240
56	BALLYORGAN T.	—	Limerick	Coshlea	Kilfiyn	Kilmallock	II.	240
21	Ballyorley Lower	275　1　35	Wexford	Gorey	Kilcormick	Enniscorthy	I.	317

(a) Including 13A. 0R. 27P. water.
(b) Including 4A. 2R. 2P. water.
(c) Including 3A. 2R. 22P. water.
(d) Including 34A. 1R. 34P. water.
(e) Including 20A. 0R. 18P. River Barrow.
(f) Including 18A. 2R. 18P. water.
(g) Including 2A. 2R. 10P. detached portion.

No. of Sheet of the Ordnance Survey Maps.	Townlands and Towns.	Area in Statute Acres.			County.	Barony.	Parish.	Poor Law Union in 1857.	Townland Census of 1851, Part I.	
		A.	R.	P.					Vol.	Page
21	Ballyorley Upper	309	2	14	Wexford	Gorey	Kilcormick	Enniscorthy	I.	317
7	Ballyorney	68	1	10	Wicklow	Rathdown	Kilmacanoge	Rathdown	I.	355
19, 20	Ballyorril	568	2	28	Wexford	Scarawalsh	Monart	Enniscorthy	I.	324
34	Ballyortla North	109	3	6	Clare	Bunratty Upper	Doora	Ennis	II.	8
34	Ballyortla South	54	3	12	Clare	Bunratty Upper	Doora	Ennis	II.	8
5	Ballyoskill	1,053	1	19	Kilkenny	Fassadinin	Attanagh	Castlecomer	I.	88
5	Ballyoskill	480	1	16	Kilkenny	Fassadinin	Kilmenan	Castlecomer	I.	90
18	Ballyote	127	1	34	Westmeath	Moyashel and Magheradernon	Dysart	Mullingar	I.	274
17	Ballyoughna	380	3	34	Wexford	Gorey	Kiltrisk	Gorey	I.	320
74	Ballyoughter	317	3	13	Mayo	Costello	Kilcolman	Castlereagh	IV.	141
40	Ballyoughter	171	1	25	Tipperary, N.R.	Kilnamanagh Upper	Moyaliff	Thurles	II.	279
2, 5	Ballyoughter	482	0	17	Tipperary, N.R.	Lower Ormond	Dorrha	Parsonstown	II.	283
150	Ballyoughtera	156	2	23	Cork, W.R.	West Carbery (E.D.)	Creagh	Skibbereen	II.	138
42	Ballyoughteragh Nth.	436	2	37	Kerry	Corkaguiny	Dunurlin	Dingle	II.	176
42	Ballyoughteragh Sth.	420	2	34	Kerry	Corkaguiny	Dunurlin	Dingle	II.	176
27	Ballyoughtra	283	0	31	Clare	Tulla Upper	Tulla	Tulla	II.	41
47, 57	Ballyoughtragh Nth.	211	2	17	Kerry	Trughanacmy	Kilcolman	Killarney	II.	210
47, 57	Ballyoughtragh Sth.	314	1	28	Kerry	Trughanacmy	Kilcolman	Killarney	II.	210
27	Ballyoughtra (O'Callaghan)	121	2	31	Clare	Tulla Upper	Tulla	Tulla	II.	41
11	Ballyoulster	73	2	38	Kildare	South Salt	Donaghcumper	Celbridge	I.	76
9, 10	Ballyouneen	656	2	17	Kerry	Iraghticonnor	Rattoo	Listowel	II.	193
21, 30	Ballyouragan	236	1	27	Limerick	Coshma	Dysert	Croom	II.	243
132	Ballyourane	535	1	29	Cork, W.R.	West Carbery (W.D.)	Caheragh	Skibbereen	II.	141
17	Ballyowen	547	1	7	Dublin	Newcastle	Esker	Celbridge	I.	33
10	Ballyowen	493	1	28	King's Co.	Lower Philipstown	Kilclonfert	Tullamore	I.	142
10	Ballyowen	69	2	20	King's Co.	Lower Philipstown	Killaderry	Tullamore	I.	142
44	Ballyowen	175	2	34	Limerick	Glenquin	Killeedy	Newcastle	II.	245
23	Ballyowen	99	2	25	Queen's Co.	Clarmallagh	Aghaboe	Abbeyleix	I.	235
13, 20	Ballyowen	160	0	10	Westmeath	Delvin	Killagh	Castletowndelvin	I.	265
6	Ballyowen	290	2	19	Wexford	Gorey	Kilnahue	Gorey	I.	319
40, 45	Ballyowen	352	1	39	Wexford	Shelmaliere West	Ballylannan	New Ross	I.	332
61	Ballypadeen	143	0	9	Tipperary, S.R.	Middlethird	St. Patricksrock	Cashel	II.	330
51	Ballypalady	630	0	7	Antrim	Upper Belfast	Ballymartin	Antrim	III.	9
9, 14	Ballypatrick	2,171	1	26	Antrim	Cary	Culfeightrin	Ballycastle	III.	13
17	Ballypatrick	130	3	23	Antrim	Upper Dunluce	Ballymoney	Ballymoney	III.	18
39	Ballypatrick	38	3	14	Kilkenny	Iverk	Fiddown	Carrick on Suir	I.	105
34, 35	Ballypatrick	544	3	4	Tipperary, N.R.	Eliogarty	Inch	Thurles	II.	270
71, 78	Ballypatrick	825	3	27	Tipperary, S.R.	Iffa and Offa East	Temple-etney	Clonmel	II.	316
39	Ballyphensan	199	1	13	Roscommon	Ballintober South	Roscommon	Roscommon	IV.	190
74	Ballyphehane	128	2	38	Cork, E.R.	Cork	St. Finbars	Cork	II.	65
74	Ballyphehane	205	1	39	Cork, E.R.	Cork	St. Nicholas	Cork	II.	66
78	Ballypherode	331	0	26	Cork, E.R.	Imokilly	Kilmacdonogh	Youghal	II.	88
23	Ballyphilibeen	225	1	29	Cork, E.R.	Duhallow	Kilbrin	Kanturk	II.	72
63	Ballyphilip	313	0	11	Cork, E.R.	Cork	Rathcooney	Cork	II.	65
32	Ballyphilip	180	3	32	Down	Ards Upper	Ballyphilip	Downpatrick	III.	159
13	Ballyphilip	247	0	39	Kilkenny	Crannagh	Ballylarkin	Kilkenny	I.	85
43	Ballyphilip	435	3	28	King's Co.	Ballybritt	Aghancon	Roscrea	I.	124
23, 24	Ballyphilip	299	2	9	Limerick	Clanwilliam	Aglishcormick	Limerick	II.	221
30,31,38,39	Ballyphilip	644	3	33	Limerick	Coshma	Croom	Croom	II.	242
20, 26	Ballyphilip	339	2	22	Tipperary, N.R.	Upper Ormond	Kilmore	Nenagh	II.	291
58	Ballyphilip	172	1	28	Tipperary, S.R.	Clanwilliam	Solloghodmore	Tipperary	II.	311
49, 55	Ballyphilip	417	3	7	Tipperary, S.R.	Slievardagh	Ballingarry	Callan	II.	331
54	Ballyphilip	221	0	15	Tipperary, S.R.	Slievardagh	Crohane	Callan	II.	332
25	Ballyphilip	212	0	1	Waterford	Middlethird	Reisk	Kilmacthomas	II.	368
9, 14	Ballyphilip	433	3	7	Wexford	Scarawalsh	St. Mary's Newtownbarry	Enniscorthy	I.	325
13	Ballyphilip	64	3	36	Wicklow	Newcastle	Newcastle Lower	Rathdrum	I.	353
34	Ballyphilip East	224	0	37	Waterford	Coshmore&Coshbride	Kilcockan	Lismore	II.	343
34	Ballyphilip West	351	3	22	Waterford	Coshmore&Coshbride	Kilcockan	Lismore	II.	343
29, 30	Ballyphillips	422	2	11	Tipperary, N.R.	Ikerrin	Templeree	Thurles	II.	277
24	Ballypickas Lower or Bernardsgrove	207	3	14	Queen's Co.	Cullenagh	Ballyroan	Abbeyleix	I.	239
24, 30	Ballypickas Upper	297	3	15	Queen's Co.	Cullenagh	Ballyroan	Abbeyleix	I.	239
17,18,20,21	Ballypierce	626	2	35	Carlow	St. Mullins Upper	Barragh	Shillelagh	I.	14
2	Ballypierce	159	2	14	Cork, E.R.	Orrery and Kilmore	Rathgoggan	Kilmallock	II.	109
36	Ballypierce	333	0	10	Limerick	Glenquin	Newcastle	Newcastle	II.	247
59, 63	Ballypitmave	580	2	19	Antrim	Upper Massereene	Glenavy	Lisburn	III.	30
40	Ballyplimoth	232	0	35	Kerry	Trughanacmy	Ballincuslane	Tralee	II.	206
44	Ballyplunt	375	0	16	Down	Lecale Upper	Rathmullan	Downpatrick	III.	181
41, 47	Ballypollard	270	3	3	Antrim	Lower Belfast	Glynn	Larne	III.	8
86	Ballyporeen	150	1	21	Tipperary, S.R.	Iffa and Offa West	Templetenny	Clogheen	II.	320
86	BALLYPOREEN T.	—			Tipperary, S.R.	Iffa and Offa West	Templetenny	Clogheen	II	320

No. of Sheet of the Ordnance Survey Maps.	Townlands and Towns.	Area in Statute Acres.	County.	Barony.	Parish.	Poor Law Union in 1857.	Townland Census of 1851, Part I.	
		A. R. P.					Vol.	Page
18, 23	Ballyportery North	345 3 39	Antrim	Upper Dunluce	Loughguile	Ballymoney	III.	20
18, 23	Ballyportery South	272 1 30	Antrim	Upper Dunluce	Loughguile	Ballymoney	III.	20
17	Ballyportry North	455 2 0a	Clare	Inchiquin	Killinaboy	Corrofin	II.	26
17	Ballyportry South	284 0 17b	Clare	Inchiquin	Killinaboy	Corrofin	II.	26
9	Ballyprecas	943 0 22	Wexford	Scarawalsh	St. Mary's Newtown-barry	Enniscorthy	I.	325
19	Ballyprior	250 1 28	Queen's Co.	Stradbally	Timogue	Athy	I.	248
41	Ballyprior Beg	241 2 6	Antrim	Lower Belfast	Islandmagee	Larne	III.	8
41	Ballyprior More	253 0 22	Antrim	Lower Belfast	Islandmagee	Larne	III.	8
21, 27	Ballyquaid Glebe	203 0 0	Queen's Co.	Clandonagh	Skirk	Donaghmore	I.	235
27	Ballyquane	188 1 1	Cork, E.R.	Fermoy	Dunmahon	Fermoy	II.	79
54, 55	Ballyquillin	578 1 31	Antrim	Lower Massereene	Killead	Antrim	III.	28
28, 29	Ballyquin	256 3 37	Clare	Tulla Upper	Tomgraney	Scarriff	II.	40
26, 35	Ballyquin	308 3 35	Kerry	Corkaguiny	Cloghane	Dingle	II.	175
40	Ballyquin	544 2 23	Kilkenny	Knocktopher	Rossinan	Waterford	I.	113
16, 17	Ballyquin	516 2 18c	Londonderry	Keenaght	Balteagh	New T⁸ Limavady	III.	234
38	Ballyquin	219 0 34	Waterford	Decies within Drum	Lisgenan or Grange	Youghal	II.	352
3, 4, 7	Ballyquin	471 0 30	Waterford	Upperthird	Fenoagh	Carrick on Suir	II.	369
44	Ballyquin Beg	269 0 14	Clare	Tulla Lower	Killokennedy	Limerick	II.	35
9	BallyquinlevanLower	80 2 19	Tipperary, N.R.	Lower Ormond	Finnoe	Borrisokane	II.	283
9	BallyquinlevanUpper	104 2 28	Tipperary, N.R.	Lower Ormond	Finnoe	Borrisokane	II.	283
44	Ballyquin More	253 2 28	Clare	Tulla Lower	Killokennedy	Limerick	II.	35
32, 39	Ballyquintin	246 0 6	Down	Ards Upper	Witter	Downpatrick	III.	161
26	BALLYQUIN T.	—	Kerry	Corkaguiny	Cloghane	Dingle	II.	175
66	Ballyquirk	198 3 22	Cork. E.R.	Imokilly	Killeagh	Youghal	II.	88
20	Ballyquirk	523 2 8	Kilkenny	Gowran	Gowran	Kilkenny	I.	95
36	Ballyquirk	260 3 27	Limerick	Glenquin	Monagay	Newcastle	II.	247
4, 7	Ballyquirk	1,023 0 2	Tipperary, N.R.	Lower Ormond	Lorrha	Borrisokane	II.	285
27	Ballyquiveen	100 3 23	Tipperary, N.R.	Upper Ormond	Ballynaclogh	Nenagh	II.	290
21	Ballyrafter	188 3 14	Waterford	Coshmore&Coshbride	Lismore and Mocollop	Lismore	II.	344
21	Ballyrafter Flats	94 2 25	Waterford	Coshmore&Coshbride	Lismore and Mocollop	Lismore	II.	344
14	Ballyrafton	283 0 27	Kilkenny	Fassadinin	Dunmore	Kilkenny	I.	89
40	Ballyraggan	714 3 28	Kildare	Kilkea and Moone	Graney	Baltinglass	I.	60
4, 5, 9, 10	Ballyragget	715 1 25	Kilkenny	Fassadinin	Donaghmore	Castlecomer	I.	89
10	BALLYRAGGET T.	—	Kilkenny	Fassadinin	Donaghmore	Castlecomer	I.	89
44	Ballyrahan	146 1 14	Kilkenny	Ida	Kilcolumb	Waterford	I.	102
6	Ballyrahan	202 3 26	Wexford	Gorey	Kilnahue	Gorey	I.	319
43	Ballyraheen	721 1 23	Wicklow	Shillelagh	Mullinacuff	Shillelagh	I.	358
22	Ballyrahin	192 2 1	Wexford	Ballaghkeen	Killincooly	Gorey	I.	295
53	Ballyraine	315 3 24	Donegal	Kilmacrenan	Conwal	Letterkenny	III.	126
40	Ballyraine Lower	74 1 26	Wicklow	Arklow	Arklow	Rathdrum	I.	341
40	Ballyraine Middle	229 2 36	Wicklow	Arklow	Arklow	Rathdrum	I.	341
40, 45	Ballyraine Upper	153 3 32	Wicklow	Arklow	Arklow	Rathdrum	I.	341
5, 10	Ballyrainey	445 3 13	Down	Castlereagh Lower	Dundonald	Newtownards	III.	162
31	Ballyrandle	41 1 7d	Waterford	Decies without Drum	Clonea	Dungarvan	II.	354
47, 48	Ballyrane	112 2 12	Wexford	Forth	Killinick	Wexford	I.	310
9, 10	Ballyrankin	557 2 30e	Wexford	Scarawalsh	Kilrush	Enniscorthy	I.	324
26	Ballyrannel	343 0 35	Wexford	Ballaghkeen	Ballyhuskard	Enniscorthy	I.	291
12	Ballyratahan Lower	133 1 30	Antrim	Lower Dunluce	Derrykeighan	Ballymoney	III.	16
12	Ballyratahan Upper	215 0 9	Antrim	Lower Dunluce	Derrykeighan	Ballymoney	III.	16
12	Ballyrath	147 3 4	Armagh	Armagh	Armagh	Armagh	III.	43
21	Ballyrattan	837 2 9	Donegal	Inishowen East	Moville Upper	Inishowen	III.	119
6, 7	Ballyrawer	336 0 13	Down	Ards Lower	Donaghadee	Newtownards	III.	157
47	Ballyraymeen Lower	131 3 3	Kerry	Trughanacmy	Kiltallagh	Tralee	II.	212
38, 47	Ballyraymeen Upper	239 1 33	Kerry	Trughanacmy	Kiltallagh	Tralee	II.	212
55, 66	Ballyre	660 2 20	Cork, E.R.	Imokilly	Dangandonovan	Middleton	II.	86
12	Ballyrea	226 0 14	Armagh	Armagh	Armagh	Armagh	III.	43
21	Ballyrea	180 3 17	Wexford	Ballaghkeen	Kilnamanagh	Gorey	I.	297
44, 53	Ballyready	383 2 24	Cork, E.R.	Barrymore	Rathcormack	Fermoy	II.	57
27	Ballyreagh	603 0 1	Antrim	Kilconway	Dunaghy	Ballymena	III.	25
18	Ballyreagh	370 0 9	Armagh	Orior Lower	Ballymore	Newry	III.	55
6	Ballyreagh	333 2 26	Down	Ards Lower	Newtownards	Newtownards	III.	158
28	Ballyreagh	137 1 11	Fermanagh	Magherastephana	Aghavea	Lisnaskea	III.	218
16,17,22,23	Ballyreagh	1,858 3 6f	Fermanagh	Tirkennedy	Derrybrusk	Enniskillen	III.	220
3	Ballyreagh	190 1 29	Londonderry	North East Liberties of Coleraine	Ballywillin	Coleraine	III.	245
38	Ballyreagh	237 0 27	Tyrone	Dungannon Upper	Derryloran	Cookstown	III.	306
7	Ballyreagh	222 2 39	Wicklow	Rathdown	Powerscourt	Rathdown	I.	356
9, 10	Ballyreaghan	239 0 8	Longford	Granard	Clonbroney	Granard	I.	154
5, 9	Ballyreagh Lower	201 1 3	Antrim	Cary	Culfeightrin	Ballycastle	III.	13
5, 9	Ballyreagh Upper	218 0 37	Antrim	Cary	Culfeightrin	Ballycastle	III.	13
65	Ballyreardon	57 1 5	Cork, E.R.	Barrymore	Templenacarriga	Middleton	II.	58
21	Ballyreask	266 1 34	Wicklow	Upper Talbotstown	Donaghmore	Baltinglass	I.	363

(a) Including 28A. 1R. 9P. water.
(b) Including 32A. 3R. 23P. water.
(c) Including 5A. 1R. 13P. water.
(d) Including 9A. 2R. 32P. detached portion.
(e) Including 4A. 1R. 37P. water.
(f) Including 17A. 1R. 19P. water.

No. of Sheet of the Ordnance Survey Maps.	Townlands and Towns.	Area in Statute Acres.			County.	Barony.	Parish.	Poor Law Union in 1857.	Townland Census of 1851, Part I.	
		A.	R.	P.					Vol.	Page
24	Ballyredding North	235	0	20	Kilkenny	Gowran	Treadingstown	Thomastown	I.	99
24	Ballyredding South	53	3	8	Kilkenny	Gowran	Treadingstown	Thomastown	I.	99
24	Ballyredding West	18	3	36a	Kilkenny	Shillelogher	Treadingstown	Thomastown	I.	116
37	Ballyreddy	316	2	11	Kilkenny	Ida	Dysartmoon	New Ross	I.	101
18	Ballyredmond	807	3	33	Carlow	St. Mullins Upper	Moyacomb	Shillelagh	I.	14
2	Ballyree	233	3	11	Down	Ards Lower	Bangor	Newtownards	III.	157
16	Ballyreehan East	213	0	27	Kerry	Clanmaurice	Kilfeighny	Listowel	II.	169
15, 16	Ballyreehan West	248	3	14	Kerry	Clanmaurice	Kilfeighny	Listowel	II.	169
31	Ballyreesode	140	3	7	Limerick	Coshma	Bruff	Kilmallock	II.	242
64, 75	Ballyregan	207	3	23	Cork, E.R.	Barrymore	Carrigtohill	Middleton	II.	52
89	Ballyregan	193	0	35	Cork, E.R.	Imokilly	Cloyne	Middleton	II.	85
5	Ballyregan	522	2	9	Down	Castlereagh Lower	Dundonald	Belfast	III.	162
36	Ballyregan	104	2	0	Limerick	Glenquin	Mahoonagh	Newcastle	II.	246
22	Ballyregan	457	3	6	Limerick	Pubblebrien	Ballycahane	Croom	II.	251
10	Ballyregan	88	1	35	Louth	Ardee	Killanny	Dundalk	I.	173
48	Ballyregan	119	0	34	Wexford	Forth	Ballymore	Wexford	I.	308
6, 11	Ballyregan	229	0	3	Wexford	Gorey	Rossminoge	Gorey	I.	321
16	Ballyregan	415	3	9	Wexford	Scarawalsh	Kilbride	Enniscorthy	I.	323
111	Ballyregan Beg	188	0	31	Cork, E.R.	Kinalea	Ringcurran	Kinsale	II.	96
32, 37	Ballyregan or Fairyhill	133	2	28	Wexford	Shelmaliere East	Artramon	Wexford	I.	330
97, 111	Ballyregan More	434	1	23	Cork, E.R.	Kinalea	Ringcurran	Kinsale	II.	96
22	Ballyreilly	260	2	9	Queen's Co.	Clandonagh	Aghaboe	Donaghmore	I.	232
36	Ballyreilly	99	1	27	Waterford	Decies within Drum	Ringagonagh	Dungarvan	II.	353
48	Ballyreilly	116	0	37	Wexford	Forth	Kilrane	Wexford	I.	311
7, 12	Ballyremon Commons	641	3	39	Wicklow	Rathdown	Calary	Rathdown	I.	355
31, 38	Ballyrenan	130	2	2b	Down	Lecale Lower	Ballee	Downpatrick	III.	178
30, 31, 37	Ballyrenan	604	3	27c	Down	Lecale Lower	Inch	Downpatrick	III.	179
17, 25	Ballyrenan	723	1	23	Tyrone	Strabane Lower	Ardstraw	Strabane	III.	318
21, 22	Ballyrevagh	236	1	5	Longford	Rathcline	Cashel	Ballymahon	I.	163
47, 50	Ballyrevagh & Porteen	305	1	4	Roscommon	Athlone	Dysart	Athlone	IV.	181
50	Ballyrevagh West and Porteen	363	0	38d	Roscommon	Athlone	Dysart	Athlone	IV.	181
85	Ballyrichard	234	3	6	Tipperary, S.R.	Iffa and Offa East	Carrick	Carrick on Suir	II.	312
85	Ballyrichard	222	2	38	Tipperary, S.R.	Iffa and Offa East	Newtownlennan	Carrick on Suir	II.	315
63	Ballyrichard	415	1	28	Tipperary, S.R.	Middlethird	Drangan	Cashel	II.	326
40, 41	Ballyrichard	253	2	8	Wicklow	Arklow	Kilbride	Rathdrum	I.	344
65, 76	Ballyrichard Beg	107	1	22	Cork, E.R.	Barrymore	Carrigtohill	Middleton	II.	52
65, 76	Ballyrichard More	285	0	17	Cork, E.R.	Barrymore	Carrigtohill	Middleton	II.	52
51, 59	Ballyrickane	147	3	28	Tipperary, S.R.	Clanwilliam	Donohill	Tipperary	II.	307
10, 11	Ballyrickard	397	0	30	Down	Castlereagh Lower	Comber	Newtownards	III.	162
40	Ballyrickard Beg	511	0	22	Antrim	Lower Belfast	Raloo	Larne	III.	9
42, 43	Ballyrickard Beg	191	0	34	King's Co.	Clonlisk	Aghancon	Roscrea	I.	129
40, 46	Ballyrickard More	770	2	21	Antrim	Lower Belfast	Raloo	Larne	III.	9
42, 43	Ballyrickard More	172	1	5	King's Co.	Clonlisk	Aghancon	Roscrea	I.	129
10	Ballyrickard North	324	2	9	Tipperary, N.R.	Lower Ormond	Ardcrony	Borrisokane	II.	281
15	Ballyrickard South	343	3	28	Tipperary, N.R.	Lower Ormond	Ardcrony	Nenagh	II.	281
14	Ballyrider	488	1	10	Queen's Co.	Stradbally	Moyanna	Athy	I.	247
25	Ballyridley	236	0	5e	Down	Ards Upper	Ardquin	Downpatrick	III.	159
47	Ballyriff	552	2	10	Londonderry	Loughinsholin	Artrea	Magherafelt	III.	238
48, 56	Ballyriggin	336	1	7	Limerick	Coshlea	Kilfinnane	Kilmallock	II.	239
45	Ballyrihy	1,034	0	8	King's Co.	Clonlisk	Dunkerrin	Roscrea	I.	130
9	Ballyring Lower	172	0	2	Kilkenny	Galmoy	Sheffin	Urlingford	I.	93
9	Ballyring Upper	350	1	25	Kilkenny	Galmoy	Sheffin	Urlingford	I.	93
65	Ballyriorthy	157	3	8	Cork, E.R.	Imokilly	Dungourney	Middleton	II.	86
133	Ballyriree	434	0	16	Cork, W.R.	West Carbery, (E.D.)	Kilmacabea	Skibbereen	II.	140
43, 44	Ballyrishteen	692	3	5	Kerry	Corkaguiny	Garfinny	Dingle	II.	176
10	Ballyrisk Beg	121	1	14	Londonderry	Keenaght	Drumachose	NewTⁿLimavady	III.	235
10	Ballyrisk More	146	2	22	Londonderry	Keenaght	Drumachose	NewTⁿLimavady	III.	235
147, 148	Ballyrisode	591	1	6	Cork, W.R.	West Carbery (W.D.)	Kilmoe	Skull	II.	144
25	Ballyristeen	351	2	39	Waterford	Decies without Drum	Monksland	Kilmacthomas	II.	359
22	Ballyroan	9	3	31	Dublin	Rathdown	Rathfarnham	Dublin South	I.	37
22	Ballyroan	114	1	6	Dublin	Uppercross	Tallaght	Dublin South	I.	41
18, 24	Ballyroan	1,335	0	29	Queen's Co.	Cullenagh	Ballyroan	Abbeyleix	I.	239
13	Ballyroan	167	1	35	Queen's Co.	Maryborough East	Straboe	Mountmellick	I.	241
34	Ballyroan	79	1	4	Tipperary, N.R.	Kilnamanagh Upper	Glenkeen	Thurles	II.	278
24	BALLYROAN T.	—			Queen's Co.	Cullenagh	Ballyroan	Abbeyleix	I.	239
45	Ballyrobert	169	0	10	Cork, E.R.	Barrymore	Castlelyons	Fermoy	II.	53
53, 54	Ballyrobert	374	2	31	Cork, E.R.	Barrymore	Gortroe	Fermoy	II.	55
45	Ballyrobert	133	2	26	Cork, E.R.	Barrymore	Knockmourne	Fermoy	II.	56
54	Ballyrobert	28	0	21	Cork, E.R.	Barrymore	Templebodan	Middleton	II.	58
1	Ballyrobert	460	1	17	Down	Castlereagh Lower	Holywood	Belfast	III.	162
20, 21	Ballyrobert	100	3	2	Kerry	Clanmaurice	Kilmoyly	Tralee	II.	171
51	Ballyrobert, Grange of	883	2	17	Antrim	Lower Belfast	Templepatrick	Antrim	III.	9

(a) Including 0A. 1R. 37P. River Nore.
(b) Including 46A. 3R. 30P. detached portion.
(c) Including 13A. 3R. 26P. water.
(d) Including 28A. 1R. 29P. water.
(e) Including 26A. 2R. 33P. Lough Cowey.

R

No. of Sheet of the Ordnance Survey Maps	Townlands and Towns.	Area in Statute Acres.	County.	Barony.	Parish.	Poor Law Union in 1857.	Townland Census of 1851, Part I.	
		A. R. P.					Vol.	Page
23	Ballyroberts . .	146 2 34	Kilkenny . .	Shillelogher . .	Burnchurch . .	Callan . .	I.	113
50, 55	Ballyrobin . .	1,343 0 39	Antrim . .	Lower Massereene .	Killead . .	Antrim . .	III.	28
12	Ballyrobin . .	285 1 15	Antrim . .	Upper Dunluce .	Ballymoney . .	Ballymoney . .	III.	18
28	Ballyrobin . .	244 1 3	Limerick . .	Connello Lower .	Kilscannell . .	Rathkeale . .	II.	228
59	Ballyrobin . .	82 1 19	Tipperary, S.R.	Clanwilliam . .	Donohill . .	Tipperary . .	II.	307
58, 66	Ballyrobin . .	275 1 36	Tipperary, S.R.	Clanwilliam . .	Kilcornan . .	Tipperary . .	II.	308
9	Ballyrobin . .	322 0 24	Waterford . .	Gaultiere . .	Kilculliheen . .	Waterford . .	II.	363
16, 25	Ballyrobin . .	265 2 19	Waterford . .	Middlethird . .	Dunhill . .	Kilmacthomas . .	II.	366
89	Ballyrobin North .	82 3 14	Cork, E.R. .	Imokilly . .	Ballintemple . .	Middleton . .	II.	84
89	Ballyrobin South .	361 3 15	Cork, E.R. .	Imokilly . .	Ballintemple . .	Middleton . .	II.	84
7, 12	Ballyrock Irish .	381 2 23	Antrim . .	Lower Dunluce .	Ballyrashane . .	Coleraine . .	III.	15
7	Ballyrock Scotch .	146 3 9	Antrim . .	Lower Dunluce .	Ballyrashane . .	Coleraine . .	III.	15
16	Ballyroddy . .	634 2 31	Roscommon .	Roscommon . .	Shankill . .	Boyle . .	IV.	212
52	Ballyroe . .	228 3 33	Clare . .	Bunratty Lower .	Kilfinaghta . .	Limerick . .	II.	4
52	Ballyroe . .	74 0 27	Clare . .	Bunratty Lower .	Kilfintinan . .	Limerick . .	II.	5
89	Ballyroe . .	225 3 28	Cork, E.R. .	Imokilly . .	Cloyne . .	Middleton . .	II.	85
7	Ballyroe . .	392 2 37	Cork, E.R. .	Orrery and Kilmore	Aglishdrinagh .	Kilmallock . .	II.	106
133	Ballyroe . .	271 3 0a	Cork, W.R. .	East Carbery (W.D.)	Kilmacabea . .	Skibbereen . .	II.	133
6	Ballyroe . .	171 3 36	Galway . .	Ballymoe . .	Templetogher . .	Glennamaddy . .	IV.	9
33, 34	Ballyroe . .	148 2 13	Kerry . .	Corkaguiny . .	Kilquane . .	Dingle . .	II.	179
29	Ballyroe . .	128 2 4	Kerry . .	Trughanacmy . .	Ardfert . .	Tralee . .	II.	205
37	Ballyroe . .	356 1 2	Kildare . .	Kilkea and Moone .	Tankardstown .	Athy . .	I.	61
34	Ballyroe . .	427 0 17	Kildare . .	Narragh and Reban West . .	Churchtown . .	Athy . .	I.	67
13	Ballyroe . .	171 0 4	Kilkenny . .	Crannagh . .	Freshford . .	Kilkenny . .	I.	85
28	Ballyroe . .	61 0 15	Kilkenny . .	Gowran . .	Columbkille . .	Thomastown . .	I.	94
31, 36	Ballyroe . .	230 0 25	King's Co. .	Eglish . .	Drumcullen . .	Parsonstown . .	I.	134
18	Ballyroe . .	132 2 28	Limerick . .	Shanid . .	Loghill . .	Glin . .	II.	256
92	Ballyroe . .	91 1 28b	Mayo . .	Costello . .	Knock . .	Claremorris . .	IV.	142
52	Ballyroe . .	154 3 36	Tipperary, S.R.	Middlethird . .	Ardmayle . .	Cashel . .	II.	324
34	Ballyroe . .	67 0 32	Waterford . .	Coshmore&Coshbride	Kilcockan . .	Lismore . .	II.	343
26	Ballyroe . .	199 1 31	Wexford . .	Ballaghkeen . .	Edermine . .	Enniscorthy . .	I.	294
27, 33	Ballyroe (Annesley).	220 2 8	Wexford . .	Ballaghkeen . .	Castle-ellis . .	Enniscorthy . .	I.	293
27	Ballyroebeg . .	106 2 1	Wexford . .	Ballaghkeen . .	Castle-ellis . .	Enniscorthy . .	I.	293
10	Ballyroebuck . .	574 3 24	Wexford . .	Scarawalsh . .	Kilrush . .	Enniscorthy . .	I.	324
29, 30, 38	Ballyroe East .	169 0 37	Limerick . .	Connello Upper .	Ballingarry . .	Croom . .	II.	230
13	Ballyroe (Grace) .	220 2 35	Kilkenny . .	Crannagh . .	Tullaroan . .	Kilkenny . .	I.	87
48, 56	Ballyroe Lower .	343 0 18	Limerick . .	Coshlea . .	Kilfinnane . .	Kilmallock . .	II.	239
29	Ballyroe Lower .	162 2 2	Wexford . .	Bantry . .	St. Mary's . .	New Ross . .	I.	302
13	Ballyroe (Maher) .	201 0 2	Kilkenny . .	Crannagh . .	Tullaroan . .	Kilkenny . .	I.	87
27, 33	Ballyroe (Nunn) .	239 1 37	Wexford . .	Ballaghkeen . .	Castle-ellis . .	Enniscorthy . .	I.	293
56	Ballyroe Upper .	351 1 20	Limerick . .	Coshlea . .	Kilfinnane . .	Kilmallock . .	II.	240
29	Ballyroe Upper .	152 2 20	Wexford . .	Bantry . .	St. Mary's . .	New Ross . .	I.	302
29,30,37,38	Ballyroe West .	99 2 35	Limerick . .	Connello Upper .	Ballingarry . .	Croom . .	II.	230
5	Ballyrogan . .	363 1 17	Down . .	Castlereagh Lower .	Newtownards . .	Newtownards . .	III.	163
18	Ballyrogan . .	535 3 34	Londonderry .	Coleraine . .	Errigal . .	Coleraine . .	III.	232
36	Ballyrogan Lower .	321 1 11	Wicklow . .	Arklow . .	Redcross . .	Rathdrum . .	I.	346
55	Ballyrogan or Mourne Park . .	1,141 3 3	Down . .	Mourne . .	Kilkeel . .	Kilkeel . .	III.	182
36	Ballyrogan Upper .	221 1 18	Wicklow . .	Arklow . .	Redcross . .	Rathdrum . .	I.	346
47, 49	Ballyrogully . .	367 0 28	Londonderry .	Loughinsholin .	Artrea . .	Magherafelt . .	III.	238
5	Ballyrohan . .	178 1 39	Waterford . .	Glenahiry . .	Kilronan . .	Clonmel . .	II.	365
7	Ballyrolly . .	253 3 12	Down . .	Ards Lower . .	Donaghadee . .	Newtownards . .	III.	157
37	Ballyrolly . .	310 2 35c	Down . .	Lecale Upper . .	Down . .	Downpatrick . .	III.	180
14	Ballyronan . .	236 0 13	Kerry . .	Clanmaurice . .	Ballyheige . .	Tralee . .	II.	167
13	Ballyronan . .	155 2 29	Wicklow . .	Newcastle . .	Kilcoole . .	Rathdrum . .	I.	351
47	Ballyronan Beg .	189 0 16	Londonderry .	Loughinsholin .	Ballinderry . .	Magherafelt . .	III.	239
47	Ballyronan More .	695 3 34	Londonderry .	Loughinsholin .	Artrea . .	Magherafelt . .	III.	238
47	BALLYRONAN T. .	—	Londonderry .	Loughinsholin .	Artrea . .	Magherafelt . .	III.	238
35, 42	Ballyroney . .	1,241 2 39d	Down . .	Upper Iveagh, Lr. pt.	Drumballyroney .	Banbridge . .	III.	172
32	Ballyrooaun . .	83 0 4	Wexford . .	Ballaghkeen . .	Ballynaslaney . .	Enniscorthy . .	I.	292
45	Ballyrooaun . .	91 3 35	Wicklow . .	Arklow . .	Arklow . .	Rathdrum . .	I.	341
138	Ballyroon . .	115 1 25	Cork, W.R. .	West Carbery (W.D.)	Kilcrohane . .	Bantry . .	II.	143
138	Ballyroon Mountain	466 2 37	Cork, W.R. .	West Carbery (W.D.)	Kilcrohane . .	Bantry . .	II.	143
8	Ballyroosky . .	289 3 19	Donegal . .	Kilmacrenan . .	Clondavaddog . .	Milford . .	III.	124
8	Ballyroosky Island .	8 2 32	Donegal . .	Kilmacrenan . .	Clondavaddog . .	Milford . .	III.	125
8	BALLYROOSKY T. .	—	Donegal . .	Kilmacrenan . .	Clondavaddog . .	Milford . .	III.	125
29	Ballyrory . .	426 3 14	Londonderry .	Tirkeeran . .	Cumber Upper .	Londonderry . .	III.	249
2	Ballyrory . .	236 0 30	Wexford . .	Gorey . .	Kilpipe . .	Gorey . .	I.	320
7	Ballyross . .	352 2 5	Wicklow . .	Rathdown . .	Powerscourt . .	Rathdown . .	I.	356
22, 24	Ballyroughan Big .	283 2 26	Carlow . .	St. Mullins Lower .	Ullard . .	New Ross . .	I.	13
22	Ballyroughan Little	81 1 34	Carlow . .	St. Mullins Lower .	Ullard . .	New Ross . .	I.	13
43	Ballyroughan North	113 1 7e	Clare . .	Bunratty Upper .	Quin . .	Tulla . .	II.	10

(a) Including 18A. 1R. 35P. water.
(b) Including 8A. 1R. 15P. water.
(c) Including 4A. 2R. 32P. water.
(d) Including 52A. 0R. 32P. water.
(e) Including 2A. 2R. 30P. water.

No. of Sheet of the Ordnance Survey Maps.	Townlands and Towns.	Area in Statute Acres. A. R. P.	County.	Barony.	Parish.	Poor Law Union in 1857.	Townland Census of 1851, Part I. Vol.	Page
43	Ballyroughan South	172 3 37	Clare	Bunratty Upper	Quin	Tulla	II.	10
79, 90	Ballyrourke	145 0 1	Mayo	Clanmorris	Balla	Castlebar	IV.	131
118, 121	Ballyrourke	49 1 15	Mayo	Kilmaine	Ballinchalla	Ballinrobe	IV.	151
7, 10	Ballyrourke	358 3 10	Tipperary, N.R.	Lower Ormond	Uskane	Borrisokane	II.	288
44	Ballyrowragh	322 3 18	Kilkenny	Ida	Kilcolumb	Waterford	I.	102
124	Ballyrub	57 1 17	Cork, W.R.	Courceys	Ringrone	Kinsale	II.	147
103, 104	Ballyruddelly or Lis-mintan	377 3 1	Donegal	Tirhugh	Drumhome	Donegal	III.	146
18	Ballyruin	439 0 37	Queen's Co.	Cullenagh	Ballyroan	Abbeyleix	I.	239
12	Ballyrune	187 3 1	Limerick	Kenry	Kildimo	Rathkeale	III.	249
10, 16	Ballyrush	539 1 10	Down	Castlereagh Lower	Comber	Newtownards	III.	162
29	Ballyrush	99 0 39	Monaghan	Farney	Inishkeen	Dundalk	III.	271
40	Ballyrush	205 0 7	Wicklow	Arklow	Kilfahurler	Rathdrum	I.	345
4	Ballyrushboy	96 2 11	Down	Castlereagh Upper	Knockbreda	Belfast	III.	165
24	Ballyrusheen	378 0 32	Cork, E.R.	Duhallow	Kilbrin	Kanturk	II.	72
20	Ballyrusheen	94 0 30	Tipperary, N.R.	Owney and Arra	Youghalarra	Nenagh	II.	297
32	Ballyrusley	231 2 6	Down	Ards Upper	Ballyphilip	Downpatrick	III.	159
37	Ballyrussel	147 1 23	Waterford	Coshmore&Coshbride	Templemichael	Youghal	II.	348
77, 89	Ballyrussell	299 0 26	Cork, E.R.	Imokilly	Cloyne	Middleton	II.	85
5, 10	Ballyrussell	453 1 15	Down	Castlereagh Lower	Comber	Newtownards	III.	162
51	Ballyrussell	278 2 20	Down	Upper Iveagh, Up. pt.	Clonallan	Newry	III.	174
30, 35	Ballyruther	273 2 6	Antrim	Upper Glenarm	Carncastle	Larne	III.	24
12	Ballyryan	125 2 5	Carlow	Carlow	Tullowmagimma	Carlow	I.	2
12	Ballyryan	397 0 30	Carlow	Idrone East	Nurney	Carlow	I.	8
4, 8	Ballyryan	594 1 6	Clare	Corcomroe	Killilagh	Ennistimon	II.	19
58	Ballyryan East	176 3 8	Tipperary, S.R.	Clanwilliam	Solloghodmore	Tipperary	II.	311
58	Ballyryan West	254 0 39	Tipperary, S.R.	Clanwilliam	Solloghodmore	Tipperary	II.	311
40, 46	Ballyryland	238 1 13	Antrim	Lower Belfast	Raloo	Larne	III.	9
20	Ballysadare	208 0 17a	Sligo	Tirerrill	Ballysadare	Sligo	IV.	237
20	BALLYSADARE T.	—	Sligo	{ Leyny { Tirerrill	Ballysadare	Sligo	IV.	{230 {238
97, 98	Ballysaggart	125 1 11	Donegal	Banagh	Killaghtee	Donegal	III.	109
54	Ballysaggart	110 2 34	Tyrone	Dungannon Middle	Donaghmore	Dungannon	III.	301
21, 29	Ballysaggart Beg (East)	223 3 31	Waterford	Coshmore&Coshbride	Lismore and Mocollop	Lismore	II.	344
21, 29	Ballysaggart Beg Glebe	59 1 14	Waterford	Coshmore&Coshbride	Lismore and Mocollop	Lismore	II.	344
29	Ballysaggartbeghill	316 2 3	Waterford	Coshmore&Coshbride	Lismore and Mocollop	Lismore	II.	344
21, 29	Ballysaggart Beg (West)	186 1 2	Waterford	Coshmore&Coshbride	Lismore and Mocollop	Lismore	II.	344
20	Ballysaggartmore	311 0 37	Waterford	Coshmore&Coshbride	Lismore and Mocollop	Lismore	II.	344
22	Ballysakeery	436 1 25	Mayo	Tirawley	Ballysakeery	Ballina	IV.	164
46	Ballysalla	294 0 18	Limerick	Connello Upper	Corcomohide	Croom	II.	232
8	Ballysallagh	150 1 30	Clare	Corcomroe	Killilagh	Ennistimon	II.	19
53, 54, 64	Ballysallagh	198 1 28	Cork, E.R.	Barrymore	Lisgoold	Middleton	II.	56
3	Ballysallagh	63 1 35	Cork, E.R.	Orrery and Kilmore	Hackmys	Kilmallock	II.	108
3	Ballysallagh	280 2 22	Cork, E.R.	Orrery and Kilmore	Rathgoggan	Kilmallock	II.	109
38	Ballysallagh	256 1 3	Down	Lecale Lower	Ballee	Downpatrick	III.	178
21, 28	Ballysallagh	573 1 31	Down	Lower Iveagh, Lr. pt.	Dromore	Banbridge	III.	168
15	Ballysallagh	617 2 14	Kilkenny	Gowran	Kilderry	Kilkenny	I.	96
23	Ballysallagh	274 0 29	Limerick	Clanwilliam	Caherelly	Limerick	II.	222
38, 40	Ballysallagh	376 2 1	Waterford	Decies within Drum	Kinsalebeg	Youghal	II.	351
23, 30	Ballysallagh	246 0 35	Westmeath	Kilkenny West	Drumraney	Athlone	I.	272
51	Ballysallagh East	400 1 21	Clare	Bunratty Lower	Kilnasoolagh	Ennis	II.	6
36	Ballysallagh East	189 2 38	Wicklow	Arklow	Dunganstown	Rathdrum	I.	343
11	Ballysallagh (Fox)	286 1 25	Westmeath	Moygoish	Kilbixy	Mullingar	I.	279
5, 10	Ballysallagh Lower	319 2 32	Carlow	Rathvilly	Hacketstown	Shillelagh	I.	11
1, 5	Ballysallagh Major	934 3 32	Down	Castlereagh Lower	Bangor	Newtownards	III.	161
1, 5	Ballysallagh Minor	401 0 17	Down	Castlereagh Lower	Bangor	Newtownards	III.	161
11	Ballysallagh (Taite)	254 1 35	Westmeath	Moygoish	Kilbixy	Mullingar	I.	279
5, 10	Ballysallagh Upper	358 0 26	Carlow	Rathvilly	Hacketstown	Shillelagh	I.	11
42, 51	Ballysallagh West	457 2 31	Clare	Bunratty Lower	Kilnasoolagh	Ennis	II.	6
36	Ballysallagh West	87 1 13	Wicklow	Arklow	Dunganstown	Rathdrum	I.	343
3	Ballysally	1 2 11	Londonderry	North East Liberties of Coleraine	Ballyaghran	Coleraine	III.	244
3, 7	Ballysally	491 0 39	Londonderry	North East Liberties of Coleraine	Coleraine	Coleraine	III.	246
48	Ballysampson	152 2 26	Wexford	Forth	Tacumshin	Wexford	I.	314
50	Ballysavage	335 3 16	Antrim	Upper Antrim	Donegore	Antrim	III.	6
28	Ballysax Great	772 0 22	Kildare	Offaly East	Ballysax	Naas	I.	69
28	Ballysaxhills	446 3 18	Kildare	Offaly East	Ballysax	Naas	I.	69
28	Ballysax Little	271 2 38	Kildare	Offaly East	Ballysax	Naas	I.	69
28	Ballysaxplain	383 3 30	Kildare	Offaly East	Ballysax	Naas	I.	69
64, 65	Ballyscally	418 2 15b	Tyrone	Clogher	Clogher	Clogher	III.	292
12	Ballyscandal	133 2 27	Armagh	Armagh	Eglish	Armagh	III.	44
26	Ballyscanlan	143 3 36c	Clare	Bunratty Upper	Inchicronan	Tulla	II.	8

(a) Including 05A. R 36P. water. (b) Including 4A. 1R. 5P. water. (c) Including 3A. 0R. 25P. water.

R 2

No. of Sheet of the Ordnance Survey Maps.	Townlands and Towns.	Area in Statute Acres.	County.	Barony.	Parish.	Poor Law Union in 1857.	Townland Census of 1851, Part I.	
		A. R. P.					Vol.	Page
38	Ballyscanlan . .	253 2 25	Mayo . .	Tirawley . .	Crossmolina . .	Ballina . .	IV.	165
6, 9	Ballyscanlan . .	285 1 0	Tipperary, N.R.	Lower Ormond .	Kilbarron . .	Borrisokane . .	II.	284
26	Ballyscanlan . .	881 1 29a	Waterford . .	Middlethird . .	Islandikane . .	Waterford . .	II.	367
36	Ballyscanlan Lower	361 0 18b	Donegal . .	Kilmacrenan . .	Kilmacrenan .	Milford . .	III.	129
36, 45	Ballyscanlan Upper	404 0 34c	Donegal . .	Kilmacrenan . .	Kilmacrenan . .	Milford . .	III.	129
5	Ballyscannel . .	423 3 11	Sligo . .	Carbury . .	Ahamlish . .	Sligo . .	IV.	219
7	Ballyscartin . .	314 1 14	Wexford . .	Ballaghkeen .	Kilmakilloge . .	Gorey . .	I.	296
36	Ballyscarvan . .	253 2 19	Westmeath . .	Clonlonan . .	Kilcleagh . .	Athlone . .	I.	261
63	Ballyscolly . .	512 0 20	Antrim . .	Upper Massereene .	Ballinderry . .	Lisburn . .	III.	29
21	Ballyscough . .	111 0 26	Wexford . .	Ballaghkeen . .	Meelnagh . .	Gorey . .	I.	298
5	Ballyscullion . .	315 1 9	Londonderry .	Keenaght . .	Magilligan . .	NewTⁿLimavady	III.	236
36, 42	Ballyscullion East .	929 2 12	Antrim . .	Upper Toome . .	Ballyscullion . .	Ballymena . .	III.	33
37, 42	Ballyscullion West .	1,101 3 3	Londonderry .	Loughinsholin .	Ballyscullion .	Magherafelt . .	III.	239
116	Ballyscully . .	131 1 3	Galway . .	Leitrim . .	Duniry . .	Loughrea . .	IV.	53
55	Ballysculty . .	480 3 9	Antrim . .	Lower Massereene .	Killead . .	Antrim . .	III.	28
29, 38	Ballyseedy . .	440 3 32	Kerry . .	Trughanacmy .	Ballyseedy .	Tralee . .	II.	208
47, 52	Ballyseskin . .	226 0 17	Wexford . .	Bargy . .	Kilmore . .	Wexford . .	I.	306
59	Ballysessy . .	299 3 16	Antrim . .	Upper Massereene .	Camlin . .	Antrim . .	III.	30
58, 59	Ballyshanaghill .	507 1 0	Antrim . .	Upper Massereene .	Camlin . .	Antrim . .	III.	30
17, 18, 20	Ballyshancarragh .	301 3 0	Carlow . .	St. Mullins Upper .	Barragh . .	Shillelagh . .	I.	14
9	Ballyshane . .	603 0 13	Carlow . .	Rathvilly . .	Crecrin . .	Shillelagh . .	I.	11
17	Ballyshane . .	245 2 4	Cork, E.R. .	Fermoy . .	Doneraile . .	Mallow . .	II.	78
100	Ballyshane . .	458 3 2	Cork, E.R. .	Imokilly . .	Inch . .	Middleton . .	II.	87
32	Ballyshane . .	319 3 9	Kilkenny . .	Gowran . .	Inistioge . .	Thomastown . .	I.	96
36	Ballyshane . .	432 3 11	King's Co. .	Ballybritt . .	Kinnitty . .	Parsonstown . .	I.	125
28	Ballyshane . .	177 3 16	King's Co. .	Coolestown . .	Clonsast . .	Edenderry . .	I.	132
22	Ballyshane . .	126 3 6	King's Co. .	Garrycastle . .	Gallen . .	Parsonstown .	I.	135
56, 57	Ballyshane . .	489 2 16	Limerick . .	Coshlea . .	Darragh . .	Kilmallock . .	II.	238
36	Ballyshane . .	137 3 9	Limerick . .	Glenquin . .	Killeedy . .	Newcastle . .	II.	245
22	Ballyshane . .	71 2 18	Limerick . .	Pubblebrien . .	Kilpeacon .	Croom . .	II.	253
79	Ballyshane . .	233 3 29	Mayo . .	Carra . .	Breaghwy . .	Castlebar . .	IV.	127
21	Ballyshane . .	59 1 25	Wexford . .	Ballaghkeen .	Kilnamanagh . .	Gorey . .	I.	297
32	Ballyshane . .	97 1 6	Wexford . .	Shelmaliere East .	Artramon . .	Wexford . .	I.	330
34	Ballyshane . .	939 3 3	Wicklow . .	Ballinacor South .	Ballykine . .	Rathdrum . .	I.	348
55	Ballyshanedehey .	341 1 4	Limerick . .	Coshlea . .	Kilquane . .	Kilmallock . .	II.	240
9	Ballyshaneduff or The Derries .	618 3 16	Queen's Co. .	Portnahinch . .	Lea . .	Mountmellick . .	I.	244
8	Ballyshannon . .	141 3 1	Kildare . .	Carbury . .	Ardkill . .	Edenderry . .	I.	51
28	Ballyshannon . .	227 3 39d	Kildare . .	Offaly West . .	Ballyshannon . .	Athy . .	I.	72
35	Ballyshannon . .	497 3 34	Wexford . .	Shelmaliere West .	Newbawn . .	New Ross . .	I.	334
28, 32	Ballyshannon Demesne	161 0 11	Kildare . .	Offaly West .	Ballyshannon . .	Athy . .	I.	72
107	BALLYSHANNON T. .	—	Donegal . .	Tirhugh . .	{ Inishmacsaint Kilbarron }	Ballyshannon . .	III.	{ 147 148 }
9	Ballyshanny . .	269 2 4	Clare . .	Corcomroe . .	Kilfenora . .	Ennistimon . .	II.	18
20, 22	Ballyshasky . .	306 2 30	Londonderry .	Tirkeeran . .	Clondermot .	Londonderry . .	III.	247
11	Ballyshaun . .	314 1 26	Wexford . .	Gorey . . .	Toome . .	Gorey . .	I.	321
104	Ballyshea . .	413 1 14	Galway . .	Dunkellin . .	Killinan . .	Loughrea . .	IV.	30
51	Ballysheeda . .	10 2 17	Tipperary, S.R.	Kilnamanagh Lower	Aghacrew . .	Tipperary . .	II.	322
51	Ballysheeda . .	581 0 18	Tipperary, S.R.	Kilnamanagh Lower	Donohill . .	Tipperary . .	II.	323
122, 128	Ballysheedy . .	365 3 9	Galway . .	Kiltartan . .	Kilmacduagh . .	Gort . .	IV.	47
13	Ballysheedy East .	180 1 38	Limerick . .	Clanwilliam . .	St. Nicholas . .	Limerick . .	II.	225
13	Ballysheedy West .	120 3 26	Limerick . .	Clanwilliam . .	St. Nicholas . .	Limerick . .	II.	225
81, 86, 87	Ballysheehan . .	244 0 31	Tipperary, S.R.	Iffa and Offa West .	Shanrahan . .	Clogheen . .	II.	319
53	Ballysheehan . .	403 2 16	Tipperary, S.R.	Middlethird . .	Ballysheehan .	Cashel . .	II.	325
73, 74	Ballysheehy . .	122 3 14	Cork, E.R. .	Cork . .	Currykippane .	Cork . .	II.	64
30	Ballysheeman . .	93 2 10	Wicklow . .	Ballinacor North .	Knockrath . .	Rathdrum . .	I.	347
30	Ballysheeman . .	61 2 20	Wicklow . .	Ballinacor North .	Rathdrum . .	Rathdrum . .	I.	347
21	Ballysheen . .	668 1 28	Kerry . .	Clanmaurice . .	O'Dorney . .	Tralee . .	II.	172
53	Ballysheen . .	130 3 18	Wexford . .	Forth . .	Carn . .	Wexford . .	I.	309
47	Ballysheen . .	154 2 4	Wexford . .	Forth . .	Killinick . .	Wexford . .	I.	310
52	Ballysheen Beg .	131 3 33	Clare . .	Bunratty Lower .	Kilfinaghta . .	Tulla . .	II.	4
43, 52	Ballysheen More .	684 3 5	Clare . .	Bunratty Lower .	Kilfinaghta . .	Tulla . .	II.	4
25, 33	Ballyshehan . .	275 2 24	Cork, E.R. .	Fermoy . .	Carrigleamleary .	Mallow . .	II.	77
34, 35	Ballysheil . .	385 3 32	Down . .	Upper Iveagh, Up. pt.	Annaclone . .	Banbridge . .	III.	174
14, 22	Ballysheil . .	231 0 11	King's Co. .	Garrycastle . .	Gallen . .	Parsonstown . .	I.	136
13, 17	Ballysheil Beg .	302 1 3	Armagh . .	Orior Lower . .	Ballymore . .	Banbridge . .	III.	55
13, 17, 18	Ballysheil More .	339 0 15	Armagh . .	Orior Lower . .	Ballymore . .	Banbridge . .	III.	55
41	Ballyshelin . .	206 3 26	Wexford . .	Shelmaliere West .	Taghmon . .	Wexford . .	I.	324
121	Ballyshingadaun .	286 1 0	Mayo . .	Kilmaine . .	Kilmolara . .	Ballinrobe . .	IV.	156
85	Ballyshoneen . .	524 3 18	Cork, E.R. .	East Muskerry .	Corbally . .	Cork . .	II.	102
61, 62	Ballyshoneen . .	685 0 1	Cork, E.R. .	East Muskerry .	Inishcarra .	Cork . .	II.	102
24	Ballyshoneen . .	23 0 21	Limerick . .	Coonagh . .	Oola . .	Tipperary . .	II.	235
18, 27	Ballyshoneen . .	231 0 12	Waterford . .	Gaultiere . .	Kilmacleague . .	Waterford . .	II.	364

(a) Including 11ᴀ. 2ʀ. 0ᴘ. water.   (c) Including 29ᴀ. 0ʀ. 20ᴘ. water.   (d) Including 13ᴀ. 1ʀ. 38ᴘ. detached portion.
(b) Including 14ᴀ. 0ʀ. 0ᴘ. water.

No. of Sheet of the Ordnance Survey Maps.	Townlands and Towns.	Area in Statute Acres. A. R. P.	County.	Barony.	Parish.	Poor Law Union in 1857.	Townland Census of 1851, Part I. Vol.	Page
11	Ballyshonickbane	275 1 17	Limerick	Kenry	Kilcornan	Rathkeale	II.	249
55	Ballyshonikin	453 0 7	Limerick	Coshlea	Effin	Kilmallock	II.	238
18	Ballyshonock	531 3 28	Cork, E.R.	Fermoy	Farahy	Mitchelstown	II.	79
16	Ballyshonock	848 0 20	Waterford	Decies without Drum	Rossmire	Kilmacthomas	II.	359
4	Ballyshonock	287 3 21a	Wexford	Scarawalsh	Moyacomb	Shillelagh	I.	325
38, 43	Ballyshonog	575 3 8	Wicklow	Ballinacor South	Kilcommon	Shillelagh	I.	349
126	Ballyshrule	223 2 33	Galway	Longford	Lickmolassy	Portumna	IV.	60
9, 10, 18, 19	Ballyshurdane	381 3 30	Cork, E.R.	Condons & Clangibbon	Templemolaga	Mitchelstown	II.	63
32	Ballysilla	335 1 11	Wexford	Ballaghkeen	Kilmallock	Enniscorthy	I.	296
32	Ballysillagh	70 0 17	Wexford	Ballaghkeen	Edermine	Enniscorthy	I.	294
56, 60	Ballysillan Lower	323 0 35	Antrim	Upper Belfast	Shankill	Belfast	III.	10
56, 60	Ballysillan Upper	988 1 0	Antrim	Upper Belfast	Shankill	Belfast	III.	10
41	Ballysimon	300 3 14	Cork, E.R.	Duhallow	Kilshannig	Mallow	II.	74
65	Ballysimon	149 1 8	Cork, E.R.	Imokilly	Dungourney	Middleton	II.	86
5, 13	Ballysimon	166 2 6	Limerick	Clanwilliam	Kilmurry	Limerick	II.	224
59	Ballysimon	35 3 10	Tipperary, S.R.	Clanwilliam	Kilmucklin	Tipperary	II.	309
20	Ballysimon	310 0 32	Wexford	Scarawalsh	Clone	Enniscorthy	I.	322
13	Ballysimon Commons	38 2 25	Limerick	Clanwilliam	Derrygalvin	Limerick	II.	223
5, 13	Ballysimon (Dickson)	24 0 22	Limerick	Clanwilliam	Derrygalvin	Limerick	II.	223
5, 13	Ballysimon (Staunton)	123 3 19	Limerick	Clanwilliam	Derrygalvin	Limerick	II.	223
14, 19	Ballysize	206 1 18	Kildare	Clane	Brideschurch	Naas	I.	53
9	Ballysize Lower	191 0 36	Wicklow	Talbotstown Lower	Hollywood	Baltinglass	I.	360
9	Ballysize Upper	112 1 31	Wicklow	Talbotstown Lower	Hollywood	Baltinglass	I.	360
8, 9	Ballyskeagh	430 0 8	Down	Castlereagh Upper	Lambeg	Lisburn	III.	166
71	Ballyskeagh	130 1 30	Galway	Tiaquin	Monivea	Tuam	IV.	78
5	Ballyskeagh	514 0 24	Tyrone	Strabane Lower	Leckpatrick	Strabane	III.	321
5	Ballyskeagh High	669 2 9	Down	Castlereagh Lower	Newtownards	Newtownards	III.	163
5	Ballyskeagh Low	372 3 33	Down	Castlereagh Lower	Newtownards	Newtownards	III.	163
52, 63	Ballyskerdane	162 0 33	Cork, E.R.	Barrymore	St. Michaels	Cork	II.	57
78	Ballyskibbole	83 2 7	Cork, E.R.	Imokilly	Kilmacdonogh	Youghal	II.	88
68	Ballyslatteen	488 0 22	Tipperary, S.R.	Clanwilliam	Relickmurry & Athassel	Tipperary	II.	309
26,27,34,35	Ballyslattery or New-grove	754 0 12b	Clare	Tulla Upper	Tulla	Tulla	II.	41
30	Ballyslavin	268 3 23	King's Co.	Garrycastle	Reynagh	Parsonstown	I.	138
17	Ballyslea	192 2 17	Tipperary, N.R.	Ikerrin	Rathnaveoge	Roscrea	II.	276
3	Ballyslough	164 1 19	Waterford	Upperthird	Kilmoleran	Carrick on Suir	II.	370
5	Ballysmuttan Lower	198 3 3	Wicklow	Lower Talbotstown	Blessington	Naas	I.	358
5, 6	Ballysmuttan Upper	347 0 27	Wicklow	Lower Talbotstown	Blessington	Naas	I.	358
40	Ballysnod	589 1 29	Antrim	Lower Belfast	Inver	Larne	III.	8
16, 17	Ballysooghan North	600 3 15	Kildare	Offaly East	Rathangan	Edenderry	I.	70
16, 17	Ballysooghan South	177 2 8	Kildare	Offaly East	Rathangan	Edenderry	I.	70
26	Ballysooragh	51 1 32	Fermanagh	Clanawley	Cleenish	Enniskillen	III.	189
34, 39	Ballysop	353 1 21	Wexford	Shelburne	Ballybrazil	New Ross	I.	327
29, 30	Ballysorrell Big	523 0 36	Tipperary, N.R.	Ikerrin	Killavinoge	Roscrea	II.	275
23,24,29,30	Ballysorrell Little	369 0 23	Tipperary, N.R.	Ikerrin	Killavinoge	Roscrea	II.	275
88	Ballysovane	84 2 2	Cork, E.R.	Imokilly	Aghada	Middleton	II.	83
9	Ballyspallan	204 3 35	Londonderry	Keenaght	Tamlaght Finlagan	New Tn Limavady	III.	237
8	Ballyspellan	1,075 3 32	Kilkenny	Galmoy	Fertagh	Urlingford	I.	92
7	Ballyspellane North	208 0 14	Tipperary, N.R.	Lower Ormond	Uskane	Borrisokane	II.	288
7	Ballyspellane South	141 3 23	Tipperary, N.R.	Lower Ormond	Uskane	Borrisokane	II.	288
66, 67	Ballyspillane	29 1 3	Kerry	Magunihy	Killarney	Killarney	II.	203
65	Ballyspillane East	325 0 17	Cork, E.R.	Barrymore	Ballyspillane	Middleton	II.	51
65	Ballyspillane West	455 2 1	Cork, E.R.	Barrymore	Ballyspillane	Middleton	II.	51
25	Ballyspurge	212 0 33	Down	Ards Upper	Slanes	Downpatrick	III.	161
25	Ballysroonagh	171 1 38c	Fermanagh	Clanawley	Cleenish	Enniskillen	III.	189
45	Ballystanly	494 3 27	King's Co.	Clonlisk	Dunkerrin	Roscrea	I.	130
14	Ballysteen	279 1 39	Clare	Corcomroe	Kilmacrehy	Ennistimon	II.	20
3, 11	Ballysteen	307 2 6	Limerick	Kenry	Iveruss	Rathkeale	II.	248
19	Ballysteen	220 2 38	Limerick	Shanid	Kilbradran	Glin	II.	255
10, 11, 15	Ballysteena	176 3 27	Tipperary, N.R.	Lower Ormond	Modreeny	Borrisokane	II.	286
5, 10	Ballystockart	628 3 28	Down	Castlereagh Lower	Comber	Newtownards	III.	162
31, 38	Ballystokes	209 1 25	Down	Lecale Lower	Ballee	Downpatrick	III.	178
11	Ballystrahan	152 2 31	Dublin	Nethercross	Finglas	Balrothery	I.	30
7, 8	Ballystrane	98 2 33d	Dublin	Balrothery East	Lusk	Balrothery	I.	20
60	Ballystrang	442 3 20	Donegal	Raphoe	Conwal	Letterkenny	III.	137
44	Ballystraw	177 0 1	Wexford	Shelburne	Templetown	New Ross	I.	328
37, 38	Ballystrew	271 1 9	Down	Lecale Upper	Down	Downpatrick	III.	180
11	Ballystrig	297 3 30	King's Co.	Warrenstown	Ballyburly	Edenderry	I.	144
7	Ballystrone	391 1 30	Londonderry	Coleraine	Dunboe	Coleraine	III.	231
14	Ballystruam	100 1 27	Dublin	Coolock	Santry	Dublin North	I.	29
47	Ballystrudder	255 2 32	Antrim	Lower Belfast	Islandmagee	Larne	III.	8
38	Ballysudden	179 1 12	Tyrone	Dungannon Upper	Derryloran	Cookstown	III.	306
31, 38	Ballysugagh	529 3 19e	Down	Lecale Lower	Saul	Downpatrick	III.	179

(a) Including 6A. 0R. 30P. water.
(b) Including 13A. 3R. 38P. water.
(c) Including 7A. 1R. 22P. water.
(d) Including 6A. 0R. 31P. detached portions.
(e) Including 11A. 3R. 14P. water.

No. of Sheet of the Ordnance Survey Maps.	Townlands and Towns.	Area in Statute Acres. A. R. P.	County.	Barony.	Parish.	Poor Law Union in 1857.	Townland Census of 1851, Part I. Vol.	Page
21, 27	Ballysumaghan	485 2 33a	Sligo	Tirerrill	Ballysumaghan	Sligo	IV.	238
16	Ballysundrivan	357 1 4	Roscommon	Frenchpark	Creeve	Cark. on Shannon	IV.	203
13, 18	Ballytaggart	540 0 37	Antrim	Upper Dunluce	Loughguile	Ballymoney	III.	20
12	Ballytarsna	785 0 28	Carlow	Carlow	Nurney	Carlow	I.	2
8, 15	Ballytarsna	407 0 35	Clare	Corcomroe	Kilshanny	Ennistimon	II.	21
16, 21	Ballytarsna	213 0 8	Kilkenny	Gowran	Shankill	Kilkenny	I.	99
36	Ballytarsna	694 0 4	Kilkenny	Knocktopher	Derrynahinch	Thomastown	I.	111
23	Ballytarsna	465 3 36	Queen's Co.	Cullenagh	Abbeyleix	Abbeyleix	I.	238
16, 22	Ballytarsna	667 3 7	Queen's Co.	Upperwoods	Offerlane	Abbeyleix	I.	251
76, 77	Ballytarsna	104 3 29	Tipperary, S.R.	Iffa and Offa East	Newchapel	Clonmel	II.	315
27	Ballytarsna	482 3 10	Wexford	Ballaghkeen	Meelnagh	Enniscorthy	I.	298
5, 10	Ballytarsna	505 0 7	Wexford	Scarawalsh	Carnew	Gorey	I.	322
40	Ballytarsna	382 0 8	Wexford	Shelburne	Owenduff	New Ross	I.	328
53	Ballytarsna (Hackett)	1,190 3 13	Tipperary, S.R.	Middlethird	Ballysheehan	Cashel	II.	325
21, 27	Ballytarsna Little	79 0 37	Wexford	Ballaghkeen	Meelnagh	Enniscorthy	I.	298
42	Ballytarsney	361 0 17	Kilkenny	Iverk	Ballytarsney	Waterford	I.	105
42	Ballytarsney	71 2 31	Kilkenny	Iverk	Pollrone	Waterford	I.	106
42	Ballytarsney	55 0 4	Kilkenny	Iverk	Rathkieran	Waterford	I.	107
3	Ballytaylor	157 1 25	Antrim	Cary	Billy	Coleraine	III.	12
15	Ballyteerim	147 3 13	Antrim	Cary	Culfeightrin	Ballycastle	III.	13
25	Ballyteernau	161 3 23	Clare	Inchiquin	Dysert	Ennis	II.	24
13	Ballytegan	192 1 5	Queen's Co.	Maryborough East	Borris	Mountmellick	I.	240
7	Ballytegan	332 1 5	Wexford	Gorey	Kilcavan	Gorey	I.	317
7	Ballyteganpark	126 0 32	Wexford	Gorey	Kilcavan	Gorey	I.	317
8	Ballyteige	266 2 4	Clare	Burren	Kilmoon	Ballyvaghan	II.	13
4, 9	Ballyteige	162 1 16	Kildare	Ikeathy and Oughterany	Scullogestown	Celbridge	I.	58
58, 68	Ballyteige	472 1 18	Mayo	Tirawley	Addergoole	Castlebar	IV.	162
22	Ballyteige	117 3 30	Wexford	Ballaghkeen	Kilmuckridge	Gorey	I.	296
52	Ballyteige	169 0 32	Wexford	Bargy	Kilmore	Wexford	I.	306
16	Ballyteige	208 1 21	Wexford	Gorey	Ballycanew	Gorey	I.	315
30	Ballyteige	131 0 36	Wicklow	Ballinacor North	Knockrath	Rathdrum	I.	347
33, 34	Ballyteige	552 2 29	Wicklow	Ballinacor South	Moyne	Shillelagh	I.	350
17	Ballyteige Big	483 2 18	King's Co.	Lower Philipstown	Ballycommon	Tullamore	I.	142
46, 51, 52	Ballyteige Burrow	666 2 10	Wexford	Bargy	Kilmore	Wexford	I.	306
9	Ballyteigeduff or Jamestown	699 1 4	Queen's Co.	Portnahinch	Lea	Mountmellick	I.	244
17, 18	Ballyteige East	307 1 17b	Clare	Inchiquin	Ruan	Corrofin	II.	28
19, 22	Ballyteigelca	367 2 30c	Carlow	Idrone East	Ballyellin	Carlow	I.	6
19, 22	Ballyteigelea	194 3 24	Carlow	Idrone East	Clonygoose	Carlow	I.	6
22	Ballyteigelea	72 2 0	Carlow	Idrone East	Ullard	Carlow	I.	8
17	Ballyteige Little	357 0 12	King's Co.	Lower Phillipstown	Ballycommon	Tullamore	I.	142
38	Ballyteige Lower	339 0 16	Limerick	Connello Upper	Bruree	Kilmallock	II.	231
12, 13, 17	Ballyteige North	876 3 34	Kildare	Connell	Kilmeage	Naas	I.	55
12, 13, 17, 18	Ballyteige South	543 2 14	Kildare	Connell	Kilmeage	Naas	I.	55
38, 46	Ballyteige Upper	404 2 16	Limerick	Connello Upper	Bruree	Kilmallock	II.	231
17	Ballyteige West	264 2 37d	Clare	Inchiquin	Ruan	Corrofin	II.	28
99	Ballyterrim	216 1 21	Galway	Clonmacnowen	Killallaghtan	Ballinasloe	IV.	26
52	Ballythomas	128 2 31	Cork, E.R.	Barrymore	St. Michaels	Cork	II.	57
32	Ballythomas	197 2 15	Cork, E.R.	Duhallow	Ballyclogh	Mallow	II.	67
112	Ballythomas	88 0 38	Cork, E.R.	Kinsale	Clontead	Kinsale	II.	99
14	Ballythomas	217 3 39	Queen's Co.	Stradbally	Kilteale	Mountmellick	I.	247
10, 14, 15	Ballythomas	153 1 18	Tipperary, N.R.	Lower Ormond	Ardcrony	Nenagh	II.	281
3, 7	Ballythomas	602 0 11	Waterford	Upperthird	Mothel	Carrick on Suir	II.	370
2	Ballythomas	355 2 23	Wexford	Gorey	Kilpipe	Gorey	I.	320
111	Ballythomas East	135 2 33	Cork. E.R.	Kinsale	Dunderrow	Kinsale	II.	99
1, 2	Ballythomashill	646 3 24	Wexford	Gorey	Kilpipe	Gorey	I.	320
111	Ballythomas West	106 2 11e	Cork, E.R.	Kinsale	Dunderrow	Kinsale	II.	99
88, 100	Ballytibbot	292 3 37	Cork, E.R.	Imokilly	Inch	Middleton	II.	87
88, 100	Ballytigeen	119 2 34	Cork, E.R.	Imokilly	Corkbeg	Middleton	II.	86
16, 17	Ballytimmin	149 2 24	Carlow	Idrone East	Fennagh	Carlow	I.	7
14	Ballytivnan	203 2 35	Sligo	Carbury	Calry	Sligo	IV.	220
14	BALLYTIVNAN T.	—	Sligo	Carbury	Calry	Sligo	IV.	220
41	Ballytober	249 3 31f	Antrim	Lower Belfast	Islandmagee	Larne	III.	8
34, 35	Ballytober	963 1 30	Antrim	Upper Glenarm	Carncastle	Larne	III.	24
6, 7	Ballytober East	190 3 15	Antrim	Lower Dunluce	Dunluce	Coleraine	III.	17
6, 7	Ballytober West	202 3 17	Antrim	Lower Dunluce	Dunluce	Coleraine	III.	17
26, 27, 30, 31	Ballytobin	298 0 1	Kilkenny	Kells	Ballytobin	Callan	I.	107
71	Ballytohil	25 1 6	Tipperary, S.R.	Slievardagh	Grangemockler	Carrick on Suir	II.	333
71	Ballytohil	185 3 23	Tipperary, S.R.	Slievardagh	Kilvennon	Carrick on Suir	II.	334
30	Ballytoohey	878 2 36	Roscommon	Ballintober North	Tormonbarry	Strokestown	IV.	181
75, 84, 85	Ballytoohy Beg	121 1 4	Mayo	Murrisk	Kilgeever	Westport	IV.	161
75, 85	Ballytoohy More	526 0 10	Mayo	Murrisk	Kilgeever	Westport	IV.	161

(a) Including 8A. 1R. 30P. water.
(b) Including 16A. 0R. 32P. water.
(c) Including 6A. 0R. 5P. River Barrow.
(d) Including 36A. 0R. 4P. water.
(e) Including 0A. 1R. 12P. corporation ground.
(f) Including 33A. 1R. 38P. water.

No. of Sheet of the Ordnance Survey Maps.	Townlands and Towns.	Area in Statute Acres.	County.	Barony.	Parish.	Poor Law Union in 1857.	Townland Census of 1851, Part I.	
		A. R. P.					Vol.	Page
21, 27	Ballytoole Lower	267 1 30	Wicklow	Upper Talbotstown	Donaghmore	Baltinglass	I.	363
27	Ballytoole Upper	238 2 30	Wicklow	Upper Talbotstown	Donaghmore	Baltinglass	I.	363
41, 42, 45	Ballytoran	178 1 37	King's Co.	Clonlisk	Kilcomin	Roscrea	I.	130
48, 53	Ballytory Lower	147 1 4	Wexford	Forth	Tacumshin	Wexford	I.	314
48	Ballytory Upper	141 0 29	Wexford	Forth	Tacumshin	Wexford	I.	315
53	Ballytra	89 1 34	Wexford	Forth	Carn	Wexford	I.	309
16, 21	Ballytracey	453 0 36	Wexford	Gorey	Kilcormick	Enniscorthy	I.	317
32, 37	Ballytramon	336 1 33	Wexford	Shelmaliere East	Ardcavan	Wexford	I.	329
36	Ballytrasna	419 2 25	Cork, E.R.	Barrymore	Castlelyons	Fermoy	II.	53
75	Ballytrasna	382 0 14	Cork, E.R.	Barrymore	Little Island	Cork	II.	56
65	Ballytrasna	297 3 38	Cork, E.R.	Barrymore	Templenacarriga	Middleton	II.	58
89	Ballytrasna	66 0 16	Cork, E.R.	Imokilly	Kilmahon	Middleton	II.	89
71, 83	Ballytrasna	514 1 0a	Cork, W.R.	West Muskerry	Kilmurry	Macroom	II.	159
29	Ballytrasna	321 2 34	Galway	Dunmore	Tuam	Tuam	IV.	35
42, 52	Ballytrasna	110 1 8	Kerry	Corkaguiny	Ventry	Dingle	II.	180
58	Ballytrasna	174 2 36	Kerry	Magunihy	Aglish	Killarney	II.	199
24	Ballytrasna	342 3 16	Limerick	Coonagh	Grean	Tipperary	II.	235
10	Ballytrasna	52 0 20	Louth	Ardee	Killanny	Dundalk	I.	173
9	Ballytrasna	36 2 23	Louth	Lower Dundalk	Carlingford	Dundalk	I.	176
118	Ballytrasna	239 0 38	Mayo	Kilmaine	Kilmolara	Ballinrobe	IV.	156
6	Ballytrasna	251 1 35	Roscommon	Boyle	Boyle	Boyle	IV.	194
30, 35	Ballytrasna	165 2 22	Wicklow	Ballinacor North	Rathdrum	Rathdrum	I.	347
87	Ballytrehy	139 0 37	Tipperary, S.R.	Iffa and Offa West	Tullaghorton	Clogheen	II.	321
48	Ballytrent	107 2 29	Wexford	Forth	Kilrane	Wexford	I.	311
43	Ballytresna	723 0 20b	Antrim	Upper Toome	Drummaul	Ballymena	III.	33
24, 31	Ballytrim	226 1 20	Down	Dufferin	Killyleagh	Downpatrick	III.	167
39	Ballytrisnane	281 1 26	Waterford	Decies within Drum	Ardmore	Dungarvan	II.	349
8	Ballytroddan	281 1 30	Armagh	Armagh	Clonfeacle	Armagh	III.	43
59	Ballytromery	353 0 5	Antrim	Upper Massereene	Camlin	Antrim	III.	30
9, 17	Ballytruckle	273 3 39	Waterford	Gaultiere	St. Johns Without	Waterford	II.	365
9	BALLYTRUCKLE T.	—	Waterford	Gaultiere	St. Johns Without	Waterford	II.	365
9	Ballytrue	160 1 18	Armagh	Oneilland West	Kilmore	Armagh	III.	53
31	Ballytrust	250 3 23	Cavan	Clanmahon	Ballintemple	Cavan	III.	75
32	Ballytrustan	222 1 26	Down	Ards Upper	Ballytrustan	Downpatrick	III.	160
38	Ballytrustan	315 2 8	Down	Lecale Lower	Ballee	Downpatrick	III.	178
31	Ballytrust Lower	79 1 2c	Cavan	Clanmahon	Ballintemple	Cavan	III.	75
22, 26	Ballytunn	184 2 37	Antrim	Kilconway	Finvoy	Ballymoney	III.	26
36	Ballytunny	142 2 11	Wicklow	Arklow	Ennereilly	Rathdrum	I.	344
99	Ballyturick	64 1 13	Galway	Longford	Kiltormer	Ballinasloe	IV.	60
123, 129	Ballyturin	866 0 39d	Galway	Kiltartan	Kilbeacanty	Gort	IV.	47
55	Ballytweedy	498 2 22	Antrim	Lower Massereene	Killead	Antrim	III.	28
8	Ballytyrone	273 3 17e	Armagh	Oneilland West	Loughgall	Armagh	III.	53
11	Ballyurnanellan	73 0 21	Down	Ards Lower	Greyabbey	Newtownards	III.	158
57, 67	Ballyurra	318 3 2	Clare	Moyarta	Kilrush	Kilrush	II.	33
56, 60	Ballyutoag	3,895 1 18	Antrim	Upper Belfast	Templepatrick	Belfast	III.	10
144	Ballyva	210 2 15	Cork, W.R.	Ibane and Barryroe	Ardfield	Clonakilty	II.	148
135	Ballyvackey	293 3 23	Cork, W.R.	Ibane and Barryroe	Kilkerranmore	Clonakilty	II.	149
68	Ballyvada	335 3 39	Tipperary, S.R.	Clanwilliam	Relickmurry and Athassel	Tipperary	II.	309
8, 16	Ballyvadd	420 0 37	Waterford	Decies without Drum	Rossmire	Kilmacthomas	II.	359
64	Ballyvaddan	319 2 36f	Tyrone	Clogher	Clogher	Clogher	III.	292
24, 25	Ballyvadden	574 2 13	Waterford	Decies without Drum	Monksland	Kilmacthomas	II.	359
21	Ballyvadden	219 2 23	Wexford	Ballaghkeen	Kilmuckridge	Gorey	I.	296
11	Ballyvaddock	70 2 23	Limerick	Connello Lower	Askeaton	Rathkeale	II.	226
11	Ballyvaddock	117 1 21	Limerick	Kenry	Iveruss	Rathkeale	II.	248
29	Ballyvaddy	1,293 3 30	Antrim	Lower Glenarm	Tickmacrevan	Larne	III.	23
61, 67	Ballyvaddy	242 0 12	Tyrone	Dungannon Lower	Aghaloo	Dungannon	III.	296
11	Ballyvade	224 0 39	Westmeath	Corkaree	Leny	Mullingar	I.	262
61, 62	Ballyvadin	477 0 1	Tipperary, S.R.	Middlethird	Magorban	Cashel	II.	328
62	Ballyvadin	176 0 25	Tipperary, S.R.	Middlethird	Rathcool	Cashel	II.	329
62, 63	Ballyvadlea	272 1 36	Tipperary, S.R.	Middlethird	Cloneen	Cashel	II.	325
63	Ballyvadlea	316 1 38	Tipperary, S.R.	Slievardagh	Isertkieran	Callan	II.	333
36	Ballyvadona	400 0 37	Cork, E.R.	Condons &Clangibbon	Clondulane	Fermoy	II.	60
2, 5	Ballyvaghan	163 0 16	Clare	Burren	Drumcreehy	Ballyvaghan	II.	12
5	BALLYVAGHAN T.	—	Clare	Burren	Drumcreehy	Ballyvaghan	II.	12
7, 16	Ballyvaheen	153 0 13	Cork, E.R.	Orrery and Kilmore	Churchtown	Mallow	II.	107
107	Ballyvaheen	93 1 7	Galway	Longford	Abbeygormacan	Ballinasloe	IV.	56
77	Ballyvaheen	194 0 5	Tipperary, S.R.	Iffa and Offa East	Newchapel	Clonmel	II.	315
26, 32	Ballyvake	340 3 35	Wexford	Ballaghkeen	Edermine	Enniscorthy	I.	294
15, 20	Ballyvaldon	475 1 30	Kilkenny	Gowran	Shankill	Kilkenny	I.	99
27, 28	Ballyvaldon	467 2 29	Wexford	Ballaghkeen	Ballyvaldon	Enniscorthy	I.	292
46	Ballyvallagh	723 0 9	Antrim	Lower Belfast	Raloo	Larne	III.	9
7, 8	Ballyvallikin	530 0 26	Waterford	Upperthird	Guilcagh	Carrick on Suir	II.	370

No. of Sheet of the Ordnance Survey Maps.	Townlands and Towns.	Area in Statute Acres.	County.	Barony.	Parish.	Poor Law Union in 1857.	Townland Census of 1851, Part I.	
		A. R. P.					Vol.	Page
36, 37	Ballyvalloge . .	184 0 21	Wexford . .	Shelmaliere West .	Ardcandrisk . .	Wexford . .	I.	332
33	Ballyvalloo Lower .	302 3 10	Wexford . .	Ballaghkeen . .	Ballyvalloo . .	Enniscorthy .	I.	292
24	Ballyvalloona . .	258 2 1	Waterford . .	Decies without Drum	Stradbally . .	Kilmacthomas .	II.	360
33	Ballyvalloo Upper .	421 2 2	Wexford . .	Ballaghkeen . .	Ballyvalloo . .	Enniscorthy .	I.	292
17	Ballyvally . .	185 0 21	Armagh . .	Orior Lower . .	Loughgilly . .	Newry . .	III.	56
37, 45	Ballyvally . .	373 2 19	Clare . .	Tulla Lower . .	Killaloe . .	Scarriff . .	II.	35
47, 51	Ballyvally . .	936 0 4	Down . .	Upper Iveagh, Up.pt.	Clonallan . .	Newry . .	III.	174
27, 34	Ballyvally . .	1,060 3 11	Down . .	Upper Iveagh, Up.pt.	Seapatrick . .	Banbridge .	III.	176
24, 25	Ballyvalode . .	152 3 22	Limerick . .	Coonagh . .	Doon . .	Tipperary .	II.	234
24, 25	Ballyvalode . .	249 1 6	Limerick . .	Coonagh . .	Oola . .	Tipperary .	II.	235
51	Ballyvaloon . .	592 3 26	Cork, E.R. .	Barretts . .	Grenagh . .	Cork . .	II.	49
88, 100	Ballyvaloon . .	210 1 27	Cork, E.R. .	Imokilly . .	Corkbeg . .	Middleton .	II.	86
31, 36	Ballyvaltron . .	346 2 8	Wicklow . .	Arklow . .	Dunganstown . .	Rathdrum .	I.	343
58, 62	Ballyvanen . .	517 1 6	Antrim . .	Upper Massereene .	Glenavy . .	Lisburn . .	III.	30
37	Ballyvange . .	262 0 6	Down . .	Lecale Upper . .	Down . .	Downpatrick .	III.	180
8, 9	Ballyvangour . .	131 0 35	Carlow . .	Rathvilly . .	Ardoyne . .	Shillelagh .	I.	10
18, 26	Ballyvanna . .	266 2 9	Clare . .	Bunratty Upper .	Inchicronan . .	Ennis . .	II.	8
28, 36	Ballyvannan . .	714 1 14	Clare . .	Tulla Upper . .	Tomgraney . .	Scarriff . .	II.	41
40	Ballyvannan . .	50 3 8	Kildare . .	Kilkea and Moone .	Castledermot . .	Athy . .	I.	59
27	Ballyvanran . .	250 0 5	Tipperary, N.R. .	Upper Ormond .	Ballynaclogh . .	Nenagh . .	II.	290
8, 15	Ballyvara . .	204 2 16	Clare . .	Corcomroe . .	Killilagh . .	Ennistimon .	II.	19
12	Ballyvareen . .	314 3 23	Limerick . .	Kenry . .	Kildimo . .	Rathkeale .	II.	249
26, 27, 33	Ballyvarley . .	751 2 16	Down . .	Lower Iveagh, Lr. pt.	Aghaderg . .	Banbridge .	III.	167
1, 2, 5, 6	Ballyvarnet . .	1,152 0 25	Down . .	Ards Lower . .	Bangor . .	Newtownards .	III.	157
27	Ballyvarney . .	197 1 4	Kildare . .	Offaly West . .	Walterstown . .	Athy . .	I.	74
45	Ballyvaroge . .	235 3 14	Wexford . .	Shelburne . .	Fethard . .	New Ross .	I.	327
6, 14	Ballyvarra . .	478 3 19	Limerick . .	Clanwilliam . .	Killeenagarriff .	Limerick . .	II.	224
63	Ballyvarra . .	153 1 35	Tipperary, S.R. .	Middlethird . .	Drangan . .	Cashel . .	II.	326
6, 14	Ballyvarra Wood .	206 1 28	Limerick . .	Clanwilliam . .	Killeenagarriff .	Limerick . .	II.	224
44	Ballyvarring . .	242 2 3	Kilkenny . .	Ida . . .	Kilcolumb . .	Waterford .	I.	102
23, 31	Ballyvaskin North .	482 1 0	Clare . .	Ibrickan . .	Kilfarboy . .	Ennistimon .	II.	22
22,23,30,31	Ballyvaskin South .	232 1 30	Clare . .	Ibrickan . .	Kilfarboy . .	Ennistimon .	II.	22
38	Ballyvass . .	765 1 9	Kildare . .	Kilkea and Moone .	Castledermot . .	Athy . .	I.	59
56	Ballyvaston . .	423 0 23	Antrim . .	Lower Belfast .	Shankill . .	Belfast . .	III.	9
44, 45	Ballyvaston . .	355 0 18	Down . .	Lecale Upper . .	Rathmullan . .	Downpatrick .	III.	181
36	Ballyvatheen . .	103 2 13	Kilkenny . .	Knocktopher . .	Kilbeacon . .	Waterford .	I.	112
53, 64	Ballyvatta . .	575 1 31	Cork, E.R. .	Barrymore . .	Ballycurrany . .	Middleton .	II.	51
13	Ballyvaughan . .	217 2 1	Tipperary, N.R. .	Owney and Arra .	Castletownarra .	Nenagh . .	II.	294
77	Ballyvaughan . .	355 3 22	Tipperary, S.R. .	Iffa and Offa East .	Kilgrant . .	Clonmel . .	II.	314
53, 56	Ballyveagh Beg .	608 2 7	Down . .	Mourne . .	Kilkeel . .	Kilkeel . .	III.	182
53	Ballyveagh Beg Upper	353 3 32	Down . .	Mourne . .	Kilkeel . .	Kilkeel . .	III.	182
53, 56	Ballyveagh More .	857 2 11	Down . .	Mourne . .	Kilkeel . .	Kilkeel . .	III.	183
53	Ballyveagh More Upper .	156 2 29	Down . .	Mourne . .	Kilkeel . .	Kilkeel . .	III.	183
13	Ballyveal . .	196 3 9	Carlow . .	Forth . .	Kellistown . .	Carlow . .	I.	4
20, 28	Ballyvecane Lower .	322 1 17a	Waterford . .	Coshmore&Coshbride	Lismore and Mocollop	Lismore . .	II.	344
28	Ballyvecane Upper .	149 3 37	Waterford . .	Coshmore&Coshbride	Lismore and Mocollop	Lismore . .	II.	344
26	Ballyveelick . .	183 2 19	Cork, E.R. .	Fermoy . .	Castletownroche .	Mallow . .	II.	77
22	Ballyveelish . .	160 0 17	Limerick . .	Pubblebrien .	Crecora . .	Croom . .	II.	252
77	Ballyveelish North .	219 0 30	Tipperary, S.R. .	Iffa and Offa East .	Newchapel . .	Clonmel . .	II.	315
77	Ballyveelish South .	150 3 3	Tipperary, S.R. .	Iffa and Offa East .	Newchapel . .	Clonmel . .	II.	315
9	Ballyveely . .	604 0 23	Antrim . .	Cary . .	Ramoan . .	Ballycastle .	III.	14
18	Ballyveely Lower .	277 3 5	Antrim . .	Upper Dunluce .	Loughguile . .	Ballymoney .	III.	20
18	Ballyveely Upper .	256 3 17	Antrim . .	Upper Dunluce .	Loughguile . .	Ballymoney .	III.	20
39	Ballyveeny . .	360 3 8	Tyrone . .	Dungannon Upper .	Ballyclog . .	Cookstown .	III.	306
88	Ballyveera . .	149 2 27	Tipperary, S.R. .	Iffa and Offa West .	Ballybacon . .	Clogheen .	II.	317
60, 70, 71	Ballyveerane . .	444 0 13	Cork, W.R. .	West Muskerry .	Macroom . .	Macroom .	II.	160
3	Ballyvelaghan . .	311 3 16	Clare . .	Burren . .	Abbey . .	Ballyvaghan .	II.	11
39	Ballyvelig . .	425 3 27	Wexford . .	Shelburne . .	St. James and Dunbrody .	New Ross .	I.	328
25	Ballyvelligan . .	50 1 30	Antrim . .	Lower Glenarm .	Ardclinis . .	Larne . .	III.	21
17, 25, 26	Ballyvellon . .	130 2 3	Waterford . .	Middlethird .	Reisk . .	Waterford .	II.	368
29	Ballyvelly . .	179 2 7	Kerry . .	Trughanacmy .	Tralee . .	Tralee . .	II.	213
12, 13	Ballyveloge . .	354 2 30	Limerick . .	Pubblebrien .	Kilkeedy . .	Limerick . .	II.	252
94	Ballyvelone East .	256 2 22	Cork, W.R. .	East Carbery (W.D.)	Kinneigh . .	Dunmanway .	II.	134
94	Ballyvelone West .	422 3 26	Cork, W.R. .	East Carbery (W.D.)	Kinneigh . .	Dunmanway .	II.	134
7, 8	Ballyvelton Lower .	165 1 27	Londonderry .	North East Liberties of Coleraine	Ballyrashane .	Coleraine .	III.	245
7, 8	Ballyvelton Upper .	119 3 3	Londonderry .	North East Liberties of Coleraine	Ballyrashane .	Coleraine .	III.	245
9, 10, 14, 15	Ballyvennaght . .	2,041 0 11b	Antrim . .	Cary . .	Culfeightrin .	Ballycastle .	III.	13
7	Ballyvennox . .	364 2 15	Londonderry .	Coleraine . .	Macosquin . .	Coleraine .	III.	233
87	Ballyverassa . .	127 2 29	Tipperary, S.R. .	Iffa and Offa West .	Tubbrid . .	Clogheen .	II.	320
2	Ballyvergal . .	109 2 22	Carlow . .	Carlow . .	Urglin . .	Carlow . .	I.	3

(a) Including 4A. 0R. 0P. water.　　　　　(b) Including 9A. 0R. 39P. water.

No. of Sheet of the Ordnance Survey Maps.	Townlands and Towns.	Area in Statute Acres.			County.	Barony.	Parish.	Poor Law Union in 1857.	Townland Census of 1851, Part I.	
		A.	R.	P.					Vol.	Page
67	Ballyvergan East	207	2	26	Cork, E.R.	Imokilly	Youghal	Youghal	II.	90
67	Ballyvergan West	368	0	29	Cork, E.R.	Imokilly	Youghal	Youghal	II.	90
26, 34	Ballyvergin	288	1	9	Clare	Bunratty Upper	Clooney	Tulla	II.	7
35, 36	Ballyvergin	549	1	17	Wexford	Shelmaliere West	Kilgarvan	New Ross	I.	334
41	Ballyverneen	273	0	4	Kilkenny	Ida	Ballygurrim	New Ross	I.	101
40	Ballyvernstown	505	0	24	Antrim	Lower Belfast	Glynn	Larne	III.	8
34	Ballyverroge	423	0	18	Wexford	Shelburne	Whitechurch	New Ross	I.	329
4, 8	Ballyversall	365	0	27	Londonderry	North East Liberties of Coleraine	Ballyrashane	Coleraine	III.	245
51, 56	Ballyvesey	625	3	27	Antrim	Lower Belfast	Carnmoney	Belfast	III.	7
41	Ballyveskil	417	1	9	Clare	Islands	Clareabbey	Ennis	II.	29
2, 3, 6, 7	Ballyvester	598	1	37	Down	Ards Lower	Donaghadee	Newtownards	III.	157
21	Ballyvicknacally	735	3	3	Down	Lower Iveagh, Lr. pt.	Dromore	Banbridge	III.	168
38	Ballyvicmaha	249	0	10	Mayo	Tirawley	Crossmolina	Ballina	IV.	165
67, 74	Ballyviggane	89	3	33	Tipperary, S.R.	Clanwilliam	Templeneiry	Tipperary	II.	311
45	Ballyviggis	135	2	10	Down	Lecale Upper	Bright	Downpatrick	III.	180
14, 20	Ballyvillane	131	3	12	Tipperary, N.R.	Lower Ormond	Nenagh	Nenagh	II.	287
25, 33	Ballyviniter Lower	400	2	6	Cork, E.R.	Fermoy	Mallow	Mallow	II.	81
25, 33	Ballyviniter Middle	464	3	14	Cork, E.R.	Fermoy	Mallow	Mallow	II.	81
25	Ballyviniter Upper	547	2	31	Cork, E.R.	Fermoy	Mallow	Mallow	II.	81
67, 74	Ballyvirane	253	3	35	Tipperary, S.R.	Clanwilliam	Templeneiry	Tipperary	II.	311
143	Ballyvireen	287	0	26	Cork, W.R.	East Carbery (W.D.)	Ross	Clonakilty	II.	135
57	Ballyvirrane	302	0	19	Kerry	Magunihy	Kilcolman	Killarney	II.	200
57, 65	Ballyvistea	629	2	32	Tipperary, S.R.	Clanwilliam	Emly	Tipperary	II.	307
64	Ballyvisteale	250	3	34	Cork, E.R.	Barrymore	Ballydeloher	Cork	II.	51
64	BallyvistealeDemesne	55	2	22	Cork, E.R.	Barrymore	Ballydeloher	Cork	II.	51
9, 18	Ballyvisteen	388	1	31	Cork, E.R.	Condons&Clangibbon	Kildorrery	Mitchelstown	II.	61
15	Ballyvlin	92	1	29	King's Co.	Garrycastle	Wheery or Killagally	Parsonstown	I.	139
11, 20	Ballyvockoge	357	2	29	Limerick	Connello Lower	Nantinan	Rathkeale	II.	229
50, 51, 61, 62	Ballyvodane	140	3	11	Cork, E.R.	East Muskerry	Donaghmore	Macroom	II.	102
18, 26	Ballyvoddy	354	0	23	Cork, E.R.	Fermoy	St. Nathlash	Mitchelstown	II.	82
76	Ballyvodock East	533	0	36	Cork, E.R.	Barrymore	Mogeesha	Middleton	II.	57
76	Ballyvodock West	399	0	8	Cork, E.R.	Barrymore	Mogeesha	Middleton	II.	57
8	Ballyvoe	246	3	3	Clare	Corcomroe	Killilagh	Ennistimon	II.	19
33	Ballyvoe	303	3	8	Clare	Islands	Kilmaley	Ennis	II.	31
70	Ballyvoge	587	3	17	Cork, W.R.	West Muskerry	Kilnamartry	Macroom	II.	159
147	Ballyvoge Beg	100	1	38	Cork, W.R.	West Carbery (W.D.)	Kilmoe	Skull	II.	144
147	Ballyvoge More	240	0	29	Cork, W.R.	West Carbery(W.D.)	Kilmoe	Skull	II.	144
28	Ballyvoghan	459	1	28	Limerick	Shanid	Rathronan	Newcastle	II.	257
22	Ballyvoghan	249	3	17	Wicklow	Upper Talbotstown	Donaghmore	Baltinglass	I.	363
28	Ballyvoghlaun or Middlemount	434	0	22	Queen's Co.	Clarmallagh	Coolkerry	Donaghmore	I.	237
11	Ballyvogue	224	2	34	Limerick	Kenry	Kilcornan	Rathkeale	II.	249
16, 25	Ballyvohalane	423	1	9	Waterford	Decies without Drum	Kilbarrymeaden	Kilmacthomas	II.	356
59	Ballyvohane	301	2	2	Clare	Clonderalaw	Killadysert	Killadysert	II.	15
122	Ballyvoher	159	2	20	Galway	Kiltartan	Kilmacduagh	Gort	IV.	47
109	Ballyvoige	278	1	4	Cork, W.R.	East Carbery (E.D.)	Desertserges	Clonakilty	II.	127
45	Ballyvolane	361	1	14	Cork, E.R.	Barrymore	Britway	Fermoy	II.	51
74	Ballyvolane	317	2	35a	Cork, E.R.	Cork	St. Anne's Shandon	Cork	II.	65
111, 124	Ballyvolane	333	1	17	Cork, W.R.	East Carbery (E.D.)	Ballinadee	Bandon	II.	126
19	Ballyvolan Lower	216	2	15	Wicklow	Newcastle	Killiskey	Rathdrum	I.	352
19	Ballyvolan Upper	56	1	8	Wicklow	Newcastle	Killiskey	Rathdrum	I.	352
13	Ballyvolden	56	0	14	Carlow	Forth	Ballon	Carlow	I.	3
6	Ballyvollane	318	0	8	Limerick	Clanwilliam	Stradbally	Limerick	II.	226
58, 59	Ballyvollen	321	1	32	Antrim	Upper Massereene	Camlin	Antrim	III.	30
27	Ballyvolock	148	2	18	Cork, E.R.	Condons&Clangibbon	Glanworth	Fermoy	II.	61
30, 38	Ballyvologe	282	0	7	Limerick	Connello Upper	Ballingarry	Croom	II.	230
87	Ballyvoloon	265	1	18	Cork, E.R.	Barrymore	Clonmel	Cork	II.	53
139	Ballyvonane	235	0	3	Cork, W.R.	West Carbery(W.D.)	Skull	Skull	II.	145
46, 47, 60, 61	Ballyvoneen	211	3	27	Galway	Kilconnell	Killosolan	Mountbellew	IV.	42
73	Ballyvoneen	59	1	15	Galway	Tiaquin	Ballymacward	Ballinasloe	IV.	75
4	Ballyvoneen	612	2	27	Kildare	Ikeathy&Oughterany	Cloncurry	Celbridge	I.	56
24	Ballyvoneen	170	1	13	Limerick	Coonagh	Grean	Tipperary	II.	235
41	Ballyvoneen	185	1	27	Tipperary, N.R.	Eliogarty	Holycross	Thurles	II.	270
63	Ballyvoneen	274	2	12	Tipperary, S.R.	Slievardagh	Modeshil	Callan	II.	335
60	Ballyvongane	237	1	19	Cork, W.R.	East Muskerry	Aghinagh	Macroom	II.	153
34, 42	Ballyvonnavaun	106	0	17	Clare	Bunratty Upper	Doora	Ennis	II.	8
34, 42	Ballyvonnavaun	316	2	5	Clare	Islands	Clareabbey	Ennis	II.	29
55	Ballyvoodane	275	3	9	Limerick	Coshlea	Ballingaddy	Kilmallock	II.	237
55	Ballyvoodane	48	3	24	Limerick	Coshlea	Effin	Kilmallock	II.	238
27	Ballyvoodock	283	2	16	Wexford	Ballaghkeen	Ballyvaldon	Enniscorthy	I.	292
27	Ballyvoodrane	214	2	4	Wexford	Ballaghkeen	Ballyvaldon	Enniscorthy	I.	292
32	Ballyvool	467	1	5	Kilkenny	Gowran	Inistioge	Thomastown	I.	96

(a) { Within the Municipal Boundary, 11A. 3R. 28P.
{ Without the Municipal Boundary, 305A. 3R. 7P.

S

No. of Sheet of the Ordnance Survey Maps.	Townlands and Towns.	Area in Statute Acres. A. R. P.	County.	Barony.	Parish.	Poor Law Union in 1857.	Vol.	Page
15	Ballyvooly	109 1 28	Antrim	Lower Glenarm	Layd	Ballycastle	III.	22
24, 32	Ballyvoony	356 2 9	Waterford	Decies without Drum	Stradbally	Kilmacthomas	II.	360
14, 15	Ballyvora	410 1 20	King's Co.	Garrycastle	Wheery or Killagally	Parsonstown	I.	139
58, 59	Ballyvorally	487 2 18	Antrim	Upper Massereene	Glenavy	Lisburn	III.	30
112, 113	Ballyvorane	175 1 18	Cork, E.R.	Kinalea	Ballyfoyle	Kinsale	II.	94
112	Ballyvorane North	161 3 5	Cork, E.R.	Kinalea	Nohaval	Kinsale	II.	96
112, 113	Ballyvorane South	312 0 21	Cork, E.R.	Kinalea	Nohaval	Kinsale	II.	96
14, 15	Ballyvorda	207 1 20	Clare	Corcomroe	Kilmacrehy	Ennistimon	II.	20
18	Ballyvoreen	229 1 9	Waterford	Gaultiere	Kilmacomb	Waterford	II.	364
43	Ballyvorgal Beg	71 1 25	Clare	Tulla Lower	Clonlea	Limerick	II.	34
43	Ballyvorgal North	113 0 13	Clare	Tulla Lower	Clonlea	Limerick	II.	34
43	Ballyvorgal South	306 0 5	Clare	Tulla Lower	Clonlea	Limerick	II.	34
7, 15	Ballyvorheen	832 1 35	Limerick	Owneybeg	Abington	Limerick	II.	250
25, 33	Ballyvorisheen	157 0 15	Cork, E.R.	Fermoy	Rahan	Mallow	II.	82
66, 77	Ballyvorisheen	121 2 13	Cork, E.R.	Imokilly	Mogeely	Middleton	II.	89
16	Ballyvorisheen	151 0 3	Cork, E.R.	Orrery and Kilmore	Kilbroney	Mallow	II.	109
52	Ballyvorisheen East	367 2 32	Cork, E.R.	Barrymore	Dunbulloge	Cork	II.	54
52	Ballyvorisheen West	592 3 4	Cork, E.R.	Barrymore	Dunbulloge	Cork	II.	54
23	Ballyvorneen	337 3 2	Limerick	Clanwilliam	Caherconlish	Limerick	II.	222
27	Ballyvoskillakeen	113 1 35	Cork, E.R.	Fermoy	Kilcrumper	Fermoy	II.	80
24, 33	Ballyvouden	225 2 19	Limerick	Coonagh	Kilteely	Kilmallock	II.	235
52, 62	Ballyyoughallan	175 0 36	Clare	Bunratty Lower	Killeely	Limerick	II.	5
37, 40, 41	Ballyvoulera or Moulerstown	323 1 26	Kilkenny	Ida	Kilcoan	Waterford	I.	102
48	Ballyvouskill	495 1 3	Cork, W.R.	West Muskerry	Drishane	Millstreet	II.	155
5, 9	Ballyvoy	269 1 12	Antrim	Cary	Culfeightrin	Ballycastle	III.	13
31, 32	Ballyvoyle	527 0 12	Waterford	Decies without Drum	Stradbally	Kilmacthomas	II.	360
21	Ballyraghan	183 3 29	Wicklow	Upper Talbotstown	Donaghmore	Baltinglass	I.	363
23, 24	Ballyvranneen	430 1 27	Clare	Corcomroe	Clooney	Ennistimon	II.	18
111	Ballyvrin Lower	60 1 15	Cork, E.R.	Kinsale	Dunderrow	Kinsale	II.	99
111	Ballyvrin Upper	80 2 20	Cork, E.R.	Kinalea	Dunderrow	Kinsale	II.	94
14, 15	Ballyvrislaun	304 1 8	Clare	Corcomroe	Kilmacrehy	Ennistimon	II.	20
26	Ballyvroghaun Eighter	95 1 14	Clare	Bunratty Upper	Clooney	Tulla	II.	7
26	Ballyvroghaun Oughter	313 1 21	Clare	Bunratty Upper	Clooney	Tulla	II.	7
40	Ballyvulhane	315 0 15	Limerick	Coshma	Uregare	Kilmallock	II.	244
41	Ballyvullagan	123 3 27	Clare	Islands	Killone	Ennis	II.	30
103	Ballyvullaun	192 2 34	Galway	Dunkellin	Drumacoo	Gort	IV.	28
24, 25	Ballywaddan	158 3 29	Down	Ards Upper	Ardquin	Downpatrick	III.	159
36, 40	Ballywairy	322 0 2	Kilkenny	Ida	Kilbride	Waterford	I.	102
40	Ballywairy	160 1 11	Kilkenny	Ida	Kilcoan	Waterford	I.	102
25	Ballywallon	221 0 10	Down	Ards Upper	Ardquin	Downpatrick	III.	159
25	*Ballywallon Island*	30 0 29	Down	Ards Upper	Ardquin	Downpatrick	III.	159
26	Ballywalter	282 2 17	Cork, E.R.	Fermoy	Wallstown	Mallow	II.	83
12	Ballywalter	437 0 13	Down	Ards Upper	Ballywalter	Newtownards	III.	160
38	Ballywalter	297 0 31	Down	Lecale Lower	Ballee	Downpatrick	III.	178
22, 26	Ballywalter	230 1 4	Kilkenny	Callan	Callan	Callan	I.	63
19, 20	Ballywalter	190 0 38	Longford	Ardagh	Ardagh	Longford	I.	151
121	Ballywalter	220 2 26	Mayo	Kilmaine	Kilmolara	Ballinrobe	IV.	156
110	Ballywalter	181 3 15	Mayo	Kilmaine	Robeen	Ballinrobe	IV.	157
60	Ballywalter	293 0 2	Tipperary, S.R.	Kilnamanagh Lower	Oughterleague	Cashel	II.	324
63, 71	Ballywalter	562 0 34	Tipperary, S.R.	Slievardagh	Kilvemnon	Callan	II.	334
12	Ballywalter	160 0 25	Wexford	Ballaghkeen	Killenagh	Gorey	I.	295
11, 12, 17	Ballywalter Beg	249 3 27	Wexford	Ballaghkeen	Killenagh	Gorey	I.	295
26	Ballywalter Demesne	128 1 14	Cork, E.R.	Fermoy	Wallstown	Mallow	II.	83
51	Ballywalter, Grange of	320 1 37	Antrim	Lower Belfast	Ballylinny	Antrim	III.	7
12, 16, 17	Ballywalter More	319 1 4	Wexford	Ballaghkeen	Killenagh	Gorey	I.	295
12	BALLYWALTER T.	—	Down	Ards Upper	Ballywalter	Newtownards	III.	160
7, 8	Ballywaltrin	114 3 7	Wicklow	Rathdown	Bray	Rathdown	I.	354
25	Ballyward	314 1 20	Down	Ards Upper	Ardkeen	Downpatrick	III.	159
35, 42	Ballyward	623 0 12*a*	Down	Upper Iveagh, Lr. pt.	Drumgooland	Banbridge	III.	172
54	Ballyward	148 2 13	Tyrone	Dungannon Middle	Donaghmore	Dungannon	III.	301
5	Ballyward	345 1 3	Wicklow	Lower Talbotstown	Blessington	Naas	I.	358
38	Ballywarren	347 0 4	Down	Lecale Upper	Down	Downpatrick	III.	180
5, 17	Ballywataire	237 1 34	Galway	Ballymoe	Dunmore	Glennamaddy	IV.	7
37	Ballywater	66 2 23	Wexford	Shelmaliere East	Tikillin	Wexford	I.	331
22	Ballywater Lower	441 3 2	Wexford	Ballaghkeen	Donaghmore	Gorey	I.	293
27	Ballywatermoy	321 0 8	Antrim	Lower Toome	Ahoghill	Ballymena	III.	31
22	Ballywater Upper	109 3 22	Wexford	Ballaghkeen	Donaghmore	Gorey	I.	293
6	Ballywatt East	116 1 19	Antrim	Lower Dunluce	Ballyrashane	Coleraine	III.	15
117	Ballywatteen and Knockauneeyin	367 0 13	Galway	Longford	Tynagh	Portumna	IV.	02
16, 17	Ballywattick Lower	100 2 19	Antrim	Upper Dunluce	Ballymoney	Ballymoney	III.	18
16, 17	Ballywattick Middle	98 3 34	Antrim	Upper Dunluce	Ballymoney	Ballymoney	III.	18

(*a*) Including 46A. 2R. 0P. water.

No. of Sheet of the Ordnance Survey Maps.	Townlands and Towns.	Area in Statute Acres. A. R. P.	County.	Barony.	Parish.	Poor Law Union in 1857.	Townland Census of 1851, Part I. Vol.	Page
12, 16, 17	Ballywattick Upper	137 0 10	Antrim	Upper Dunluce	Ballymoney	Ballymoney	III.	18
6, 11	Ballywatticock	524 0 9	Down	Ards Lower	Newtownards	Newtownards	III.	158
6	Ballywatt Leggs	167 0 3	Antrim	Lower Dunluce	Ballyrashane	Coleraine	III.	15
6	Ballywatt West	129 2 23	Antrim	Lower Dunluce	Ballyrashane	Coleraine	III.	15
50, 51	Ballywee	295 3 34	Antrim	Upper Antrim	Donegore	Antrim	III.	6
45, 51	Ballywee	298 3 22	Antrim	Upper Antrim	Kilbride	Antrim	III.	6
26, 27	Ballyweeaun	680 2 23a	Galway	Ross	Ross	Oughterard	IV.	73
119, 122	Ballyweela	380 0 10	Mayo	Kilmaine	Kilcommon	Ballinrobe	IV.	154
8	Ballyweelin	276 1 35	Sligo	Carbury	Drumcliff	Sligo	IV.	221
42, 48	Ballyweely	246 2 10	Down	Upper Iveagh, Lr. pt.	Clonduff	Newry	III.	171
18, 23	Ballyweeny	644 0 33	Antrim	Upper Dunluce	Loughguile	Ballymoney	III.	20
21, 29	Ballywelligan	168 3 32	Waterford	Coshmore&Coshbride	Lismore and Mocollop	Lismore	II.	345
36, 37	Ballywether	211 1 9	Wexford	Shelmaliere West	Kilbrideglynn	Wexford	I.	334
19	Ballywhinnin or Ballyfeanan	134 2 16	Carlow	Idrone East	Ballyellin	Carlow	I.	6
19, 22	Ballywhinnin or Ballyfeanan	273 3 12	Carlow	Idrone East	Clonygoose	Carlow	I.	6
7	Ballywhiskin	165 0 30	Down	Ards Lower	Donaghadee	Newtownards	III.	157
24, 31	Ballywhite	249 0 5	Down	Ards Upper	Ardquin	Downpatrick	III.	159
65	Ballywholan	2,004 3 9b	Tyrone	Clogher	Clogher	Clogher	III.	292
39	Ballywholan	387 1 32	Tyrone	Dungannon Upper	Ballyclog	Cookstown	III.	306
25	Ballywhollart	147 3 18	Down	Ards Upper	Witter	Downpatrick	III.	161
32	Ballywierd	203 3 21	Down	Ards Upper	Ballytrustan	Downpatrick	III.	160
42	Ballywiheen	417 1 19	Kerry	Corkaguiny	Marhin	Dingle	II.	179
6, 7	Ballywildrick Lower	211 1 2	Londonderry	Coleraine	Dunboe	Coleraine	III.	231
6, 7	Ballywildrick Upper	271 2 22	Londonderry	Coleraine	Dunboe	Coleraine	III.	231
87	Ballywilliam	156 1 20	Cork, E.R.	Barrymore	Templerobin	Cork	II.	58
89	Ballywilliam	363 3 6	Cork, E.R.	Imokilly	Ballintemple	Middleton	II.	84
98	Ballywilliam	207 1 28	Cork, E.R.	Kinalea	Cullen	Kinsale	II.	94
111, 124	Ballywilliam	348 3 7	Cork, E.R.	Kinsale	Tisaxon	Kinsale	II.	101
2, 3	Ballywilliam	312 1 25	Down	Ards Lower	Donaghadee	Newtownards	III.	157
10	Ballywilliam	219 3 3c	Down	Castlereagh Lower	Comber	Newtownards	III.	162
23, 31	Ballywilliam	170 0 11	King's Co.	Ballyboy	Ballyboy	Parsonstown	I.	123
38, 39	Ballywilliam	90 0 36	King's Co.	Ballybritt	Ettagh	Roscrea	I.	125
39	Ballywilliam	236 1 0	King's Co.	Ballybritt	Roscomroe	Parsonstown	I.	126
42, 45	Ballywilliam	190 1 16	King's Co.	Clonlisk	Kilcomin	Roscrea	I.	130
35	Ballywilliam	531 2 17	King's Co.	Eglish	Eglish	Parsonstown	I.	134
7, 11	Ballywilliam	218 1 8	Londonderry	Coleraine	Macosquin	Coleraine	III.	233
26	Ballywilliam	229 2 4	Tipperary, N.R.	Owney and Arra	Burgesbeg	Nenagh	II.	293
13, 19	Ballywilliam	213 0 23	Tipperary, N.R.	Owney and Arra	Castletownarra	Nenagh	II.	294
86, 89	Ballywilliam	475 2 31	Tipperary, S.R.	Iffa and Offa West	Templetenny	Clogheen	II.	320
23, 24	Ballywilliam	736 0 13	Wexford	Bantry	Templeludigan	New Ross	I.	303
7	Ballywilliam	288 3 20	Wexford	Gorey	Kilcavan	Gorey	I.	317
29	Ballywilliam Demesne	212 2 7	Limerick	Connello Lower	Rathkeale	Rathkeale	II.	229
29	Ballywilliam North	150 3 8	Limerick	Connello Lower	Rathkeale	Rathkeale	II.	229
31, 32	Ballywilliamreagh	210 2 20	King's Co.	Ballyboy	Ballyboy	Parsonstown	I.	123
16	Ballywilliamroe	1,074 2 8	Carlow	Idrone East	Dunleckny	Carlow	I.	6
14, 15	Ballywilliamroe	232 2 22	Wexford	Scarawalsh	Monart	Enniscorthy	I.	324
29	Ballywilliam South	259 3 21	Limerick	Connello Lower	Rathkeale	Rathkeale	II.	229
40, 46	Ballywillin	382 1 26	Antrim	Lower Belfast	Raloo	Larne	III.	9
6	Ballywillin	194 2 23	Antrim	Lower Dunluce	Ballywillin	Coleraine	III.	15
35	Ballywillin	299 0 36	Antrim	Upper Glenarm	Carncastle	Larne	III.	24
23, 24	Ballywillin	724 0 31d	Down	Dufferin	Killyleagh	Downpatrick	III.	167
40	Ballywillin	172 0 39	Fermanagh	Clankelly	Galloon	Clones	III.	198
11, 18	Ballywillin	114 0 17	Londonderry	Coleraine	Aghadowey	Coleraine	III.	229
11	Ballywillin	364 3 34	Longford	Granard	Granard	Granard	I.	156
3	Ballywillin Bog	196 1 37	Londonderry	North East Liberties of Coleraine	Ballywillin	Coleraine	III.	245
36	Ballywillwill	930 0 32	Down	Upper Iveagh, Lr. pt.	Kilmegan	Downpatrick	III.	173
9	Ballywilly	197 2 12	Armagh	Oneilland West	Kilmore	Armagh	III.	53
16	Ballywindelland Lr.	107 2 1	Antrim	Upper Dunluce	Ballymoney	Ballymoney	III.	18
8, 12	Ballywindelland Lr.	65 3 31	Londonderry	North East Liberties of Coleraine	Ballymoney	Ballymoney	III.	245
11, 16	Ballywindelland Upr.	44 3 22	Antrim	Upper Dunluce	Ballymoney	Ballymoney	III.	18
8, 12	Ballywindelland Upr.	200 2 36	Londonderry	North East Liberties of Coleraine	Ballymoney	Ballymoney	III.	245!
96	Ballywinna	415 1 20	Galway	Dunkellin	Killora	Loughrea	IV.	31
29	Ballywinterrourke	478 1 20	Limerick	Connello Lower	Rathkeale	Rathkeale	II.	229
29	Ballywinterrourkewood	348 3 3	Limerick	Connello Lower	Rathkeale	Rathkeale	II.	229
66, 73	Ballywire	558 0 16	Tipperary, S.R.	Clanwilliam	Clonbeg	Tipperary	II.	305
33	Ballywish	43 0 1	Wexford	Shelmaliere East	Ardcavan	Wexford	I.	329
48	Ballywitch	83 2 35	Wexford	Forth	St. Helens	Wexford	I.	313

(a) Including 20A. 2R. 35P. water.
(b) Including 15A. 2R. 10P. water.

(c) Including 2A. 0R. 7P. water.
(d) Including 26A. 2R. 0P. water.

S 2

No. of Sheet of the Ordnance Survey Maps.	Townlands and Towns.	Area in Statute Acres.	County.	Barony.	Parish.	Poor Law Union in 1857.	Townland Census of 1851, Part I.	
		A.　R.　P.					Vol.	Page
56	Ballywonard . .	344　2　18	Antrim . .	Lower Belfast .	Shankill . .	Belfast . .	III.	9
38	Ballywoodan . .	587　2　3	Down . .	Lecale Lower .	Saul . .	Downpatrick .	III.	179
44, 50	Ballywoodock . .	411　0　3	Antrim . .	Upper Antrim .	Donegore . .	Antrim . .	III.	6
2	Ballywoodock . .	184　0　26	Londonderry .	Coleraine . .	Dunboe . .	Coleraine . .	III.	231
2, 3	Ballywoolen . .	238　1　21	Londonderry .	Coleraine . .	Dunboe . .	Coleraine . .	III.	231
14, 21	Ballyworfy . .	583　3　11	Down . .	Lower Iveagh, Up.pt.	Hillsborough .	Lisburn . .	III.	169
9, 10, 13	Ballyworkan . .	978　0　30	Armagh . .	Oneilland West .	Drumcree . .	Lurgan . .	III.	51
95	Ballywulash or Crinnage . .	401　0　10	Galway . .	Dunkellin . .	Killora . .	Loughrea . .	IV.	31
10	Balnagall . .	112　1　10	Longford . .	Granard . .	Granard . .	Granard . .	I.	156
16	Balnagon Lower .	723　2　17	Meath . .	Upper Kells . .	Kilskeer . .	Kells . .	I.	206
16	Balnagon Upper .	659　2　23	Meath . .	Upper Kells . .	Kilskeer . .	Kells . .	I.	206
19	Balnamona or Charlestown }	94　2　1	Westmeath .	Moyashel and Magheradernon .	Mullingar .	Mullingar . .	I.	275
4, 8	Balnavine . .	297　3　14	Westmeath .	Fore . . .	St. Marys . .	Castletowndelvin	I.	272
42	Bal of Dookinelly (Calcy) . .	189　2　22	Mayo . .	Burrishoole . .	Achill . .	Newport . .	IV.	117
9, 15	Balrath . . .	360　0　11	Meath . .	Fore . . .	Diamor . .	Oldcastle . .	I.	200
26, 32	Balrath . . .	635　2　5	Meath . .	Lower Duleek .	Piercetown .	Navan . .	I.	196
3	Balrath . . .	392　1　8	Meath . .	Lower Slane .	Drumcondra .	Ardee . .	I.	222
29	Balrath . . .	356　0　1	Meath . .	Lune . . .	Athboy . .	Trim . .	I.	207
11	Balrath . . .	278　3　33	Westmeath .	Corkaree . .	Portloman . .	Mullingar . .	I.	263
1, 3	Balrath . . .	180　0　6	Westmeath .	Fore . . .	Lickbla . .	Granard . .	I.	270
32	Balrath . . .	132　1　32	Westmeath .	Moycashel . .	Castletownkindalen	Mullingar .	I.	277
18, 25	Balrath . . .	925　2　20a	Westmeath .	Rathconrath .	Churchtown .	Mullingar .	I.	282
17	Balrath . . .	215　0　9	Westmeath .	Rathconrath .	Rathconrath .	Mullingar .	I.	284
24	Balrathboyne Glebe	412　2　26	Meath . .	Upper Kells . .	Balrathboyne .	Kells . .	I.	204
16	Balrath Demesne .	703　2　31	Meath . .	Upper Kells . .	Burry . .	Kells . .	I.	205
13, 20	Balrath East .	386　1　3	Westmeath .	Moyashel and Magheradernon .	Rathconnell .	Mullingar .	I.	276
14	Palrath North .	182　2　16	Westmeath .	Delvin . .	Castletowndelvin	Castletowndelvin	I.	264
13	Balrath North .	73　3　20	Westmeath .	Moyashel and Magheradernon .	Rathconnell .	Mullingar .	I.	276
14	Balrath South .	353　3　1	Westmeath .	Delvin . .	Castletowndelvin	Castletowndelvin	I.	264
13, 20	Balrath West .	96　1　35	Westmeath .	Moyashel and Magheradernon .	Rathconnell .	Mullingar .	I.	276
12, 13	Balreagh . .	827　1　5	Westmeath .	Moyashel and Magheradernon .	Rathconnell .	Mullingar .	I.	276
31, 37	Balreask . . .	406　2　18	Meath . .	Lower Deece . .	Balsoon . .	Trim . .	I.	191
11, 17	Balreask . . .	525　0　35	Meath . .	Lower Kells .	Emlagh . .	Kells . .	I.	202
25, 31	Balreask New or Ballybatter .	114　0　37b	Meath . .	Lower Navan .	Navan . .	Navan . .	I.	215
25, 31	Balreask Old .	989　1　4c	Meath . .	Lower Navan .	Navan . .	Navan . .	I.	215
4, 7	Balregan . .	184　1　30	Louth . .	Upper Dundalk .	Castletown .	Dundalk . .	I.	177
13, 19	Balrenny . .	606　3　7	Meath . .	Upper Slane .	Grangegeeth .	Ardee . .	I.	224
4	Balrickard . .	208　0　8	Dublin . .	Balrothery West .	Hollywood .	Balrothery .	I.	23
41, 42, 56	Balrickard . .	270　1　9	Galway . .	Clare . .	Cargin . .	Tuam . .	IV.	18
4, 7	Balriggan . .	437　3　23d	Louth . .	Upper Dundalk .	Faughart . .	Dundalk . .	I.	178
3	Balrinnet . .	402　0　33	Kildare . .	Carbury . .	Nurney . .	Edenderry .	I.	53
6	Balrobin . .	214　2　15	Louth . .	Upper Dundalk .	Barronstown .	Dundalk . .	I.	177
56	Balrobuck Beg .	336　0　17	Galway . .	Clare . .	Annaghdown .	Tuam . .	IV.	16
56	Balrobuck More .	259　3　31	Galway . .	Clare . .	Annaghdown .	Tuam . .	IV.	16
11, 18	Balroe . .	525　3　32	Westmeath .	Moygoish . .	Kilbixy . .	Mullingar .	I.	279
5	Balrothery . .	62　1　12	Dublin . .	Balrothery East .	Balrothery .	Balrothery .	I.	19
5	BALROTHERY T. .	—	Dublin . .	Balrothery East .	Balrothery .	Balrothery .	I.	19
20, 27	Balrowan (Pakenham)	144　0　9	Westmeath .	Farbill . .	Killucan . .	Mullingar .	I.	266
20, 27	Balrowan (Rowley) and Kerinstown .	747　0　14	Westmeath .	Farbill . .	Killucan . .	Mullingar .	I.	267
24	Balruntagh . .	241　2　0	Meath . .	Lune . .	Rathmore .	Trim . .	I.	208
27	Balsaran . .	124　2　30	Meath . .	Lower Duleek .	Duleek . .	Drogheda .	I.	195
18	Balsaw . .	651　2　1	Meath . .	Morgallion .	Kilberry . .	Navan . .	I.	209
1, 4	Balscaddan . .	333　1　15e	Dublin . .	Balrothery East .	Balscaddan .	Balrothery .	I.	20
1	BALSCADDAN T. .	—	Dublin . .	Balrothery East .	Balscaddan .	Balrothery .	I.	20
11	Balscott . .	117　1　36	Kildare . .	South Salt .	Stacumny .	Celbridge .	I.	78
14	Balseskin . .	123　1　34	Dublin . .	Castleknock .	Finglas . .	Dublin North .	I.	24
6	Balsitric . .	282　2　35	Meath . .	Lower Slane .	Loughbrackan .	Ardee . .	I.	223
31	Balsoon . .	209　1　26f	Meath . .	Lower Deece .	Balsoon . .	Trim . .	I.	191
12, 16	Baltarran . .	231　1　28	Armagh . .	Armagh . .	Lisnadill . .	Armagh . .	III.	45
15	Balteagh . .	436　0　17	Armagh . .	Armagh . .	Tynan . .	Armagh . .	III.	46
6	Balteagh . .	239　1　1	Armagh . .	Oneilland East .	Seagoe . .	Lurgan . .	III.	50
7, 11	Balteagh Lower .	554　1　21	Londonderry	Coleraine .	Macosquin .	Coleraine .	III.	233
6, 7, 10, 11	Balteagh Upper .	902　1　8	Londonderry	Coleraine .	Macosquin .	Coleraine .	III.	233
147	Balteen . .	605　0　29	Cork, W.R. .	West Carbery (W.D.)	Kilmoe . .	Skull . .	II.	144
148	Balteen . .	101　3　28	Cork, W.R. .	West Carbery (W.D.)	Skull . .	Skull . .	II.	145

(a) Including 8A. 1R. 8P. water.　　　(c) Including 6A. 1R. 16P. water.　　　(e) Including 5A. 2R. 16P. detached portion.
(b) Including 1A. 1R. 24P. water.　　　(d) Including 9A. 1R. 30P. detached portion.　　　(f) Including 11A. 1R. 4P. water.

No. of Sheet of the Ordnance Survey Maps.	Townlands and Towns.	Area in Statute Acres.			County.	Barony.	Parish.	Poor Law Union in 1857.	Townland Census of 1851, Part I.	
		A.	R.	P.					Vol.	Page
108	Balteenbrack .	432	0	27	Cork, W.R.	East Carbery (W.D.)	Fanlobbus	Dunmanway	II.	131
144	Balteenbrack .	58	0	4	Cork, W.R.	Ibane and Barryroe	Ardfield .	Clonakilty	II.	148
144	Balteenbrack .	33	2	12	Cork, W.R.	Ibane and Barryroe	Island	Clonakilty	II.	149
46	Baltigeer	459	2	37	Meath	Upper Moyfenrath .	Castlejordan	Edenderry	I.	212
149, 150	Baltimore	615	2	21	Cork, W.R.	West Carbery (E.D.)	Tullagh .	Skibbereen	II.	141
150	BALTIMORE T.	—			Cork, W.R.	West Carbery (E.D.)	Tullagh .	Skibbereen	II.	141
123	Baltinakin	333	1	8	Cork, W.R.	East Carbery (E.D.)	Kilbrittain	Bandon .	II.	128
27	Baltinglass East	221	2	9	Wicklow .	Upper Talbotstown .	Baltinglass	Baltinglass	I.	362
27	BALTINGLASS T.	—			Wicklow	Upper Talbotstown .	Baltinglass	Baltinglass	I.	362
26, 27	Baltinglass West	210	0	29	Wicklow .	Upper Talbotstown .	Baltinglass	Baltinglass	I.	362
46	Baltinoran	507	1	34	Meath	Upper Moyfenrath .	Castlejordan	Edenderry	I.	212
21	Baltovin .	25	0	10	Kerry	Clanmaurice .	Killahan .	Tralee	II.	170
21	Baltovin .	135	3	25	Kerry	Clanmaurice .	Kilmoyly	Tralee	II.	171
15, 21	Baltovin .	114	2	34	Kerry	Clanmaurice .	O'Dorney	Tralee	II.	172
10	Baltracey	707	1	17	Kildare	Ikeathy and Oughterany .	Balraheen	Celbridge	I.	56
10, 24	Baltracey	175	2	19a	Kildare	Naas North	Tipper	Naas	I.	63
5	Baltrasna	251	3	3	Dublin	Balrothery East	Holmpatrick .	Balrothery	I.	20
3, 6	Baltrasna	94	3	11	Dublin	Balrothery West	Ballymadun .	Dunshaughlin .	I.	22
17	Baltrasna	247	3	21	Louth	Ardee .	Ardee .	Ardee .	I.	171
8, 9, 14, 15	Baltrasna	1,537	0	10	Meath	Fore	Moylagh .	Oldcastle .	I.	201
11	Baltrasna	270	1	10	Meath	Lower Kells .	Moynalty	Kells	I.	203
45	Baltrasna	456	0	28	Meath	Ratoath .	Ratoath .	Dunshaughlin .	I.	219
43	Baltrasna	383	1	36	Meath	Upper Deece .	Culmullin	Dunshaughlin .	I.	193
43	Baltrasna	107	0	23	Meath	Upper Deece .	Kilmore .	Dunshaughlin .	I.	193
30, 36	Baltrasna	145	1	6	Westmeath	Clonlonan .	Kilcleagh	Athlone .	I.	261
19, 26	Baltrasna	788	2	29	Westmeath	Moyashel and Magheradernon	Mullingar .	Mullingar .	I.	275
22, 25	Baltray .	436	2	1	Louth	Ferrard .	Termonfeckin .	Drogheda	I.	182
25	BALTRAY T.	—			Louth	Ferrard .	Termonfeckin .	Drogheda	I.	183
34	Baltreagh	246	3	26	Fermanagh	Clankelly	Galloon .	Lisnaskea .	III.	198
5, 10	Baltyboys Lower or Boystown .	1,142	2	23b	Wicklow .	Lower Talbotstown .	Boystown	Naas	I.	359
10	Baltyboys Upper or Boystown .	810	1	0	Wicklow .	Lower Talbotstown .	Boystown	Naas	I.	359
24, 25	Baltydaniel East	646	1	23	Cork, E.R.	Fermoy .	Caherduggan .	Mallow .	II.	77
25	Baltydaniel West	410	3	33	Cork, E.R.	Fermoy .	Caherduggan .	Mallow .	II.	77
6	Baltyfarrell .	172	2	35	Wexford .	Gorey	Kilnahue .	Gorey .	I.	319
9	Baltylum .	145	3	35	Armagh .	Oneilland West .	Drumcree .	Lurgan .	III.	51
18	Baltynanima .	629	0	6	Wicklow .	Ballinacor North .	Derrylossary .	Rathdrum .	I.	346
92	Balwoges	524	2	39c	Donegal .	Banagh .	Killaghtee .	Donegal .	III.	109
74	Banada .	580	1	21	Roscommon .	Frenchpark .	Kilcolman .	Castlereagh .	IV.	203
37	Banada .	915	1	24	Sligo .	Leyny .	Kilmacteige .	Tobercurry .	IV.	231
26	Banagher .	495	1	7	Cavan .	Upper Loughtee .	Denn .	Cavan .	III.	83
21	Banagher .	148	0	55	Fermanagh	Magheraboy .	Devenish .	Enniskillen .	III.	210
16	Banagher .	399	0	24	Galway .	Dunmore .	Liskeevy .	Tuam .	IV.	35
39	Banagher .	221	3	34	Kilkenny .	Iverk .	Fiddown .	Carrick on Suir .	I.	105
10	Banagher .	416	0	13d	Leitrim .	Drumahaire .	Drumlease .	Manorhamilton .	IV.	94
8, 15	Banagher .	130	3	7e	Mayo .	Tirawley .	Kilcummin .	Killala .	IV.	108
27	Banagher .	344	0	20	Westmeath	Farbill .	Killucan .	Mullingar .	I.	266
21, 29	Banagher or Kylebeg	307	0	11	King's Co.	Garrycastle .	Reynagh .	Parsonstown .	I.	138
21, 29	BANAGHER T.	—			King's Co.	Garrycastle .	Reynagh .	Parsonstown .	I.	138
8	Bananstown .	31	2	39f	Westmeath	Delvin .	Kilcumny .	Castletowndelvin	I.	265
60	Banard .	626	0	36	Kerry	Magunihy .	Kilcummin .	Killarney .	II.	201
27	BANBRIDGE T.	—			Down	Upper Iveagh, Up. pt.	Seapatrick .	Banbridge	III.	176
35,36,43,44	Bancran .	769	3	28g	Tyrone .	Omagh East .	Termonmaguirk .	Omagh .	III.	314
35, 40	Bancran Glebe	750	1	7	Londonderry	Loughinsholin .	Ballynascreen .	Magherafelt .	III.	208
110	BANDON T.	—			Cork, W.R.	East Carbery (E.D.) / Kinalmeaky . / Kinalmeaky .	Ballymodan . / Ballymodan . / Kilbrogan .	Bandon .	II.	127 / 151 / 152
74	Banduff . .	292	1	34	Cork, E.R.	Cork	Rathcooney .	Cork	II.	65
44	Baneena North .	100	3	27	Cork, E.R.	Barrymore .	Gortroe .	Fermoy .	II.	55
44, 53	Baneena South .	116	0	38	Cork, E.R.	Barrymore .	Gortroe .	Fermoy .	II.	55
25	Banefune .	127	0	5	Cork, E.R.	Fermoy .	Caherduggan .	Mallow .	II.	77
16, 22	Banemore .	1,246	2	21	Kerry	Clanmaurice .	Kilfeighny .	Listowel .	II.	169
13	Banemore .	74	0	22	Limerick .	Clanwilliam .	St. Nicholas .	Limerick .	II.	225
53, 54	Banemore .	402	0	36	Limerick .	Glenquin .	Killeedy .	Newcastle .	II.	245
76	Baneshane .	249	3	14	Cork, E.R.	Barrymore .	Mogeesha .	Middleton .	II.	57
24	Banestown .	93	2	26	Meath	Lower Navan .	Martry .	Kells .	I.	215
66, 75	Banganboy .	619	3	38	Donegal .	Boylagh .	Inishkeel .	Glenties .	III.	112
19	Banghill . .	74	1	32h	Longford .	Ardagh .	Ardagh .	Longford .	I.	151
18, 26	Bangor . .	762	1	6	Mayo .	Erris .	Kilcommon .	Belmullet .	IV.	143
1	Bangor Bog .	13	2	12	Down	Ards Lower .	Bangor .	Newtownards .	III.	157
1	Bangor Bog .	18	3	13	Down	Castlereagh Lower .	Bangor .	Newtownards .	III.	161

(a) Including 7A. 1R. 1P. detached portion.
(b) Including 28A. 2R. 12P. water.
(c) Including 2A. 2R. 0P. water.
(d) Including 16A. 3R. 32P. water.
(e) Including 3A. 3R. 38P. water.
(f) Including 1A. 2R. 18P. water.
(g) Including 7A. 1R. 27P. water.
(h) Including 26A. 1R. 19P. detached portion.

No. of Sheet of the Ordnance Survey Maps.	Townlands and Towns.	Area in Statute Acres. A. R. P.	County.	Barony.	Parish.	Poor Law Union in 1857.	Townland Census of 1851, Part I. Vol.	Page
80, 81	Bangort .	1,269 1 7a	Donegal .	Banagh .	Glencolumbkille .	Glenties .	III.	105
2	BANGOR T.	—	Down .	Ards Lower .	Bangor .	Newtownards .	III.	157
116	Bank .	95 3 3	Cork, W.R.	Bear .	Killaconenagh .	Castletown .	II.	124
59	Bank .	52 3 28	Tyrone .	Clogher .	Clogher .	Clogher .	III.	232
21	Bankerstown .	68 0 28	Louth .	Ferrard .	Mullary .	Drogheda .	I.	181
14, 18	Bankfarm .	45 3 15	Dublin .	Coolock .	Glasnevin .	Dublin North .	I.	27
25	Banktown .	185 2 14	Louth .	Ferrard .	Beaulieu .	Drogheda .	I.	180
20	Banna East .	236 1 8	Kerry .	Clanmaurice .	Kilmoyly .	Tralee .	II.	171
15	Bannagagole .	526 2 23	Carlow .	Idrone West .	Oldleighlin .	Carlow .	I.	9
23, 31	Bannagh .	251 2 10	Cork, E.R.	Duhallow .	Castlemagner .	Kanturk .	II.	67
13, 18	Bannaghbane .	150 3 11	Monaghan .	Monaghan .	Kilmore .	Monaghan .	III.	275
5	Bannagh Beg .	516 2 36	Fermanagh .	Lurg .	Drumkeeran .	Lowtherstown .	III.	205
5	Bannagh More .	171 3 8	Fermanagh .	Lurg .	Drumkeeran .	Lowtherstown .	III.	205
13	Bannaghroe .	141 0 18	Monaghan .	Monaghan .	Kilmore .	Monaghan .	III.	275
9	Bannagroe .	30 1 17	Wicklow .	Lower Talbotstown .	Hollywood .	Baltinglass .	I.	360
76	Bannamore .	46 3 24	Tipperary, S.R.	Iffa and Offa West .	Mortlestown .	Clogheen .	II.	318
20	Banna-mountain .	633 1 4	Kerry .	Clanmaurice .	Kilmoyly .	Tralee .	II.	171
20	Banna South .	197 2 0	Kerry .	Clanmaurice .	Kilmoyly .	Tralee .	II.	171
20	Banna West .	231 0 31	Kerry .	Clanmaurice .	Kilmoyly .	Tralee .	II.	171
3	Bannbrook Lower .	80 3 36	Londonderry .	Coleraine .	Dunboe .	Coleraine .	III.	231
3, 7	Bannbrook Upper .	30 2 19	Londonderry .	Coleraine .	Dunboe .	Coleraine .	III.	231
70	Bannixtown .	441 0 39	Tipperary, S.R.	Middlethird .	Coolmundry .	Cashel .	II.	326
45, 50	Bannow .	389 1 24	Wexford .	Bargy .	Bannow .	Wexford .	I.	304
45	Bannow Island .	1 0 0	Clare .	Tulla Lower .	Killaloe .	Scarriff .	II.	35
45	Bannow Island .	143 2 18	Wexford .	Bargy .	Bannow .	Wexford .	I.	304
45	Bannow Moor .	120 3 39	Wexford .	Bargy .	Bannow .	Wexford .	I.	304
11	Bannpark .	185 3 7	Wexford .	Gorey .	Rossminoge .	Gorey .	I.	321
11	Banntown .	217 3 5	Wexford .	Gorey .	Liskinfere .	Gorey .	I.	320
105	Bannus .	99 0 17b	Donegal .	Tirhugh .	Templecarn .	Donegal .	III.	149
20	Banoge .	572 3 39	Down .	Lower Iveagh, Up. pt.	Donaghcloney .	Lurgan .	III.	169
12	Banoge .	310 2 35	Wexford .	Ballaghkeen .	Kiltennell .	Gorey .	I.	297
47, 48	Banoge .	82 2 7	Wexford .	Forth .	Ballymore .	Wexford .	I.	308
44	Banoge Beg .	49 2 3	Kerry .	Corkaguiny .	Minard .	Dingle .	II.	179
12	Banogehill .	197 2 4	Wexford .	Ballaghkeen .	Kilmakilloge .	Gorey .	I.	296
44	Banoge North .	628 3 33	Kerry .	Corkaguiny .	Minard .	Dingle .	II.	179
44	Banoge South .	325 3 25	Kerry .	Corkaguiny .	Minard .	Dingle .	II.	179
79, 91	Banraghbaun North .	383 0 15c	Galway .	Moycullen .	Killannin .	Galway .	IV.	69
91	Banraghbaun South .	915 3 23d	Galway .	Moycullen .	Killannin .	Galway .	IV.	69
13	Banragh Island .	9 0 27	King's Co. .	Garrycastle .	Clonmacnoise .	Parsonstown .	I.	135
18	Banse Glebe .	322 2 39	Kilkenny .	Crannagh .	Kilmanagh .	Callan .	I.	86
41	Bansha .	296 0 30	Clare .	Islands .	Killone .	Ennis .	II.	30
11	Bansha .	104 0 25	Limerick .	Kenry .	Kilcornan .	Rathkeale .	II.	249
67	Bansha East .	125 2 5	Tipperary, S.R.	Clanwilliam .	Templeneiry .	Tipperary .	II.	311
56, 57	Banshagh .	310 1 2	Kerry .	Trughanacmy .	Killorglin .	Killarney .	II.	211
67	BANSHA T.	—	Tipperary, S.R.	Clanwilliam .	Templeneiry .	Tipperary .	II.	311
67	Bansha West .	509 2 11	Tipperary, S.R.	Clanwilliam .	Templeneiry .	Tipperary .	II.	311
20	Banshee .	162 2 28	Dublin .	Newcastle .	Newcastle .	Celbridge .	I.	34
67	Banshy .	44 3 33	Cork, E.R.	Imokilly .	Youghal .	Youghal .	II.	90
31	Banteer .	1,020 3 37e	Cork, E.R.	Duhallow .	Clonmeen .	Kanturk .	II.	69
31	BANTEER T.	—	Cork, E.R.	Duhallow .	Clonmeen .	Kanturk .	II.	70
15	Bantis .	531 0 2	Tipperary, N.R.	Upper Ormond .	Ballygibbon .	Nenagh .	II.	289
13, 18	Bantry Commons .	1,640 2 4	Wexford .	Bantry .	Killann .	Enniscorthy .	I.	300
18, 24	Bantry Commons .	545 3 22	Wexford .	Bantry .	St. Mullins .	New Ross .	I.	303
18, 24	Bantry Commons .	1,514 2 10	Wexford .	Bantry .	Templeludigan .	New Ross .	I.	303
118	BANTRY T.	—	Cork, W.R.	Bantry .	Kilmocomoge .	Bantry .	II.	122
70, 77	Baptistgrange .	458 0 6	Tipperary, S.R.	Middlethird .	Baptistgrange .	Cashel .	II.	183
21	Barabona .	293 0 7	Louth .	Ferrard .	Monasterboice .	Drogheda .	I.	181
16	Baragh .	214 2 22	Fermanagh .	Tirkennedy .	Magheracross .	Lowtherstown .	III.	223
25	Baraghilly .	76 0 19	Antrim .	Lower Glenarm .	Layd .	Ballycastle .	III.	22
18	Baraghy .	247 0 9f	Cavan .	Tullygarvey .	Drumgoon .	Cootehill .	III.	88
5, 12	Baralty .	1,190 1 11	Mayo .	Erris .	Kilcommon .	Belmullet .	IV.	143
19	Barard .	1,274 2 1	Antrim .	Lower Glenarm .	Layd .	Ballycastle .	III.	22
22, 23	Baravore .	1,205 1 21	Wicklow .	Ballinacor South .	Ballinacor .	Rathdrum .	I.	348
23	BARAVORE T.	—	Wicklow .	Ballinacor South .	Ballinacor .	Rathdrum .	I.	348
19,20,25,26	Barbaha .	785 0 59	Tipperary, N.R.	Owney and Arra .	Youghalarra .	Nenagh .	II.	297
36, 44	Barbane .	503 3 15	Clare .	Tulla Lower .	Killokennedy .	Limerick .	II.	35
8, 13	Barbavilla Demesne .	581 1 14	Westmeath .	Fore .	St. Feighins .	Castletowndelvin .	I.	271
44	Barbersfort .	387 1 36	Galway .	Clare .	Killererin .	Tuam .	IV.	20
13	Barberstown .	166 1 25	Dublin .	Castleknock .	Clonsilla .	Celbridge .	I.	24
11	Barberstown .	144 2 2	Dublin .	Coolock .	St. Margaret's .	Dublin North .	I.	29
10	Barberstown .	139 1 4	Kildare .	North Salt .	Straffan .	Celbridge .	I.	75
10	Barberstown Lower .	199 2 19	Kildare .	North Salt .	Straffan .	Celbridge .	I.	75
10	Barberstown Upper .	152 3 35	Kildare .	North Salt .	Straffan .	Celbridge .	I.	75

(a) Including 21A. 3R. 12P. water.
(b) Including 10A. 1R. 16P. water.
(c) Including 21A. 1R. 6P. water.
(d) Including 138A. 1R. 39P. water.
(e) Including 19A. 1R. 36P. River Blackwater.
(f) Including 22A. 3R. 8P. water.

No. of Sheet of the Ordnance Survey Maps.	Townlands and Towns.	Area in Statute Acres.			County.	Barony.	Parish.	Poor Law Union in 1857.	Townland Census of 1851, Part I.	
		A.	R.	P.					Vol.	Page
39, 40	Barcam	659	0	34	King's Co.	Ballybritt	Kinnitty	Parsonstown	I.	125
7, 8	Barchuillia Commons	243	0	29	Wicklow	Rathdown	Kilmacanoge	Rathdown	I.	355
38, 42	Barconny (Cuppage)	181	0	22	Cavan	Castlerahan	Castlerahan	Oldcastle	III.	67
38, 42	Barconny (Grattan)	44	2	15	Cavan	Castlerahan	Castlerahan	Oldcastle	III.	67
38, 42	Barconny (Massereene)	35	3	10	Cavan	Castlerahan	Castlerahan	Oldcastle	III.	67
42	Barconny (Nugent)	297	3	34	Cavan	Castlerahan	Castlerahan	Oldcastle	III.	67
38, 42	Barconny (Robinson)	138	0	11	Cavan	Castlerahan	Castlerahan	Oldcastle	III.	67
72, 73	Barcull	702	1	32	Mayo	Costello	Kilmovee	Swineford	IV.	141
3	Barcullin	111	2	8	Roscommon	Boyle	Ardcarn	Boyle	IV.	192
37, 38	Bardahessiagh	583	3	26	Tyrone	Dungannon Upper	Desertcreat	Cookstown	III.	307
10, 11	Bardanstown	304	1	16a	Westmeath	Moygoish	Rathaspick	Mullingar	I.	280
57,58,68,69	Bardinch	391	3	14	Cork, W.R.	West Muskerry	Ballyvourney	Macroom	II.	154
26	Barefield or Gortlumman	170	1	12	Clare	Bunratty Upper	Templemaley	Ennis	II.	10
16	Barfordstown	284	1	14	Meath	Upper Kells	Burry	Kells	I.	205
80, 81	Bargarriff	344	0	9	Cork, W.R.	West Muskerry	Inchigeelagh	Dunmanway	II.	156
135	Bargarriff	196	1	17b	Galway	Leitrim	Clonrush	Scarriff	IV.	52
103	Bargarriff	458	0	27	Mayo	Costello	Annagh	Claremorris	IV.	137
17	Bargowla	288	0	8	Leitrim	Drumahaire	Inishmagrath	Manorhamilton	IV.	95
47	Bargy	62	2	14	Wexford	Bargy	Tomhaggard	Wexford	I.	307
42	Bargy Commons	732	0	2	Wexford	Bargy	Kilmaanan	Wexford	I.	306
93	Barheen	126	0	34c	Mayo	Costello	Annagh	Claremorris	IV.	137
35	Barkersford	128	0	0	Kildare	Narragh and Reban West	Kilberry	Athy	I.	67
82	Barkillew	246	3	10	Donegal	Banagh	Inishkeel	Glenties	III.	106
7	Barkmill	250	1	27	Queen's Co.	Maryborough West	Clonenagh & Clonagheen	Mountmellick	I.	242
37	Barlahan	935	1	3	King's Co.	Ballybritt	Letterluna	Parsonstown	I.	126
12, 16	Barlear	600	0	8d	Leitrim	Drumahaire	Killarga	Manorhamilton	IV.	98
123	Barleyfield	795	3	11	Cork, W.R.	East Carbery (E.D.)	Rathclarin	Bandon	II.	129
14. 15	Barleyhill	835	2	9	Cork, E.R.	Duhallow	Clonfert	Kanturk	II.	68
71	Barleyhill	638	1	8	Mayo	Gallen	Bohola	Swineford	IV.	147
2, 3	Barleyhill	772	2	4e	Meath	Lower Slane	Ardagh	Kells	I.	222
134	Barleyhill East	348	1	16	Cork, W.R.	East Carbery(W.D.)	Ross	Clonakilty	II.	135
134, 143	Barleyhill West	306	0	6	Cork, W.R.	East Carbery (W.D.)	Ross	Clonakilty	II.	135
58	Barleymount East	213	1	26	Kerry	Magunihy	Aglish	Killarney	II.	199
58	Barleymount Middle	85	2	28	Kerry	Magunihy	Aglish	Killarney	II.	199
58	Barleymount West	252	0	15	Kerry	Magunihy	Aglish	Killarney	II.	199
41	Barloughra	132	2	28	Clare	Islands	Killone	Ennis	II.	30
18	Barmeath	312	3	5	Louth	Ferrard	Dysart	Drogheda	I.	181
15	Barmeen	59	1	32	Antrim	Cary	Culfeightrin	Ballycastle	III.	13
16, 21	Barmona	195	1	39	Wexford	Ballaghkeen	Monamolin	Gorey	I.	298
20	Barmona	100	2	38	Wexford	Scarawalsh	Clone	Enniscorthy	I.	322
31, 36	Barmoney	835	1	23	Wexford	Bantry	Whitechurchglynn	Wexford	I.	303
97	Barna	429	2	24	Cork, E.R.	Kinalea	Inishannon	Bandon	II.	95
132	Barna	302	1	35	Cork, W.R.	West Carbery(W.D.)	Caheragh	Skibbereen	II.	141
18, 19	Barna	295	1	0	Galway	Ballymoe	Boyounagh	Glennamaddy	IV.	6
93	Barna	124	3	26	Galway	Galway	Rahoon	Galway	IV.	37
128, 133	Barna	134	0	16	Galway	Kiltartan	Beagh	Gort	IV.	46
49, 50	Barna	1,571	2	24	Kerry	Trughanacmy	Ballincuslane	Tralee	II.	206
13	Barna	193	1	36	Kilkenny	Crannagh	Clomantagh	Urlingford	I.	85
13	Barna	91	1	26	Kilkenny	Crannagh	Fertagh	Urlingford	I.	85
44, 45	Barna	162	3	24	King's Co.	Clonlisk	Dunkerrin	Roscrea	I.	130
49, 50	Barna	970	1	36	Limerick	Coshlea	Galbally	Mitchelstown	II.	238
120	Barna	193	1	12	Mayo	Kilmaine	Ballinchalla	Ballinrobe	IV.	151
31, 37	Barna	334	0	27	Tipperary, N.R.	Owney and Arra	Kilvellane	Nenagh	II.	296
150	Barnabah	47	2	5	Cork, W.R.	West Carbery (E.D.)	Tullagh	Skibbereen	II.	141
105	Barnabaun	66	1	39	Mayo	Murrisk	Kilgeever	Westport	IV.	159
32	Barnabaun	308	1	18	Tipperary, N.R.	Owney and Arra	Killoscully	Nenagh	II.	295
57, 70	Barnaboy	299	1	35	Galway	Clare	Athenry	Galway	IV.	17
41, 42	Barnaboy	209	3	30	Galway	Clare	Kilkilvery	Tuam	IV.	20
125	Barnaboy	280	2	36	Galway	Leitrim	Ballynakill	Loughrea	IV.	50
100	Barnaboy	169	3	35	Galway	Longford	Clontuskert	Ballinasloe	IV.	58
23, 31	Barnaboy	384	2	37	King's Co.	Ballyboy	Ballyboy	Parsonstown	I.	123
10	Barnaboy	656	3	7	King's Co.	Lower Philipstown	Kilclonfert	Tullamore	I.	142
74	Barnaboy	353	2	36	Mayo	Costello	Castlemore	Castlereagh	IV.	139
15	Barnaboy	265	1	5	Queen's Co.	Clandonagh	Kyle	Roscrea	I.	233
9, 15	Barnaboy	191	0	38	Roscommon	Frenchpark	Kilnamanagh	Castlereagh	IV.	204
19	Barnabrack	151	1	21f	Sligo	Tireragh	Dromard	Dromore West	IV.	233
77, 89	Barnabrow	342	3	10	Cork, E.R.	Imokilly	Cloyne	Middleton	II.	85
72	Barnacahoge	1,316	2	36	Mayo	Costello	Kilbeagh	Swineford	IV.	140
42	Barnacashel	119	3	33	Wicklow	Shillelagh	Aghowle	Shillelagh	I.	356
14	Barnacawley	836	1	36	Roscommon	Frenchpark	Tibohine	Castlereagh	IV.	204

(a) Including 19A. 2R. 36P. water.
(b) Including 3A. 3R. 0P. water.
(c) Including 10A. 1R. 30P. water.
(d) Including 11A. 2R. 4P. water.
(e) Including 2A. 0R. 8P. water.
(f) Including 4A. 2R. 21P. water.

No. of Sheet of the Ordnance Survey Maps.	Townlands and Towns.	Area in Statute Acres.	County.	Barony.	Parish.	Poor Law Union in 1857.	Townland Census of 1851, Part I.	
		A. R. P.					Vol.	Page
40	Barnacleagh East .	190 0 39	Wicklow . .	Arklow . . .	Killahurler . .	Rathdrum . .	I.	345
40	Barnacleagh North .	173 1 26	Wicklow . .	Arklow . . .	Killahurler . .	Rathdrum . .	I.	345
40, 45	Barnacleagh South .	171 1 35	Wicklow . .	Arklow . . .	Killahurler . .	Rathdrum . .	I.	345
12, 18	Barnacoghil . .	295 3 15	Sligo . .	Tireragh . .	Templeboy . .	Dromore West .	IV.	236
39	Barnacole . .	120 3 28	Kilkenny . .	Iverk . . .	Tubbrid . .	Carrick on Suir	I.	107
17	Barnacor . .	354 3 34a	Longford . .	Rathcline . .	Rathcline . .	Longford . .	I.	164
26	Barnacor . .	294 3 16b	Longford . .	Rathcline . .	Shrule . . .	Ballymahon .	I.	165
19	Barnacoyle Big .	218 3 23	Wicklow . .	Newcastle . .	Killiskey . .	Rathdrum . .	I.	352
19	Barnacoyle Little .	21 0 1	Wicklow . .	Newcastle . .	Killiskey . .	Rathdrum . .	I.	352
87	Barnacragh . .	57 0 12	Galway . .	Clonmacnowen .	Kilcloony . .	Ballinasloe .	IV.	25
82	Barnacranny . .	101 3 8	Galway . .	Galway . . .	Rahoon . .	Galway . .	IV.	37
17, 18	Barnacrow . .	342 1 14	Kildare . .	Connell . . .	Rathernan . .	Naas . .	I.	56
4, 11	Barnacuillew . .	243 2 18	Mayo . .	Erris . . .	Kilcommon . .	Belmullet .	IV.	143
45	Barnacullen . .	397 1 30	Roscommon .	Athlone . . .	Rahara . .	Roscommon .	IV.	183
22, 25	Barnacullia . .	247 0 6	Dublin . .	Rathdown . .	Kilgobbin . .	Rathdown .	I.	35
22	Barnacurra . .	508 0 26	Cork, E.R. .	Duhallow . .	Clonfert . .	Kanturk . .	II.	68
33, 47	Barnacurra . .	162 2 34	Galway . .	Killian . . .	Killian . .	Mountbellew .	IV.	44
43	Barnacurragh . .	352 1 8	Galway . .	Dunmore . .	Tuam . . .	Tuam . .	IV.	35
4	Barnadarrig . .	157 0 20	Kerry . .	Iraghticonnor . .	Killehenny . .	Listowel . .	II.	191
23	Barnadarrig . .	310 0 2	Queen's Co. .	Maryborough West .	Clonenagh and Clonagheen .	Abbeyleix .	I.	242
107	Barnaderg . .	1,131 0 18c	Mayo . .	Murrisk . . .	Oughaval . .	Westport .	IV.	161
5	Barnaderg . .	464 0 3	Sligo . .	Carbury . .	Drumcliff . .	Sligo . .	IV.	221
44	Barnaderg North .	308 1 3	Galway . .	Clare . . .	Killererin . .	Tuam . .	IV.	20
44	Barnaderg South .	152 3 1	Galway . .	Clare . . .	Killererin . .	Tuam . .	IV.	20
82, 83	Barnadivane . .	215 1 17	Cork, W.R. .	West Muskerry .	Kilmichael . .	Dunmanway .	II.	158
82,83,94,95	Barnadivane (Kneeves)	237 1 33	Cork, W.R. .	West Muskerry .	Kilmichael . .	Dunmanway .	II.	158
31, 35	Barnadown . .	551 0 38	Kilkenny . .	Knocktopher . .	Aghaviller . .	Thomastown .	I.	110
1, 2	Barnadown . .	311 3 30	Wexford . .	Gorey . . .	Kilpipe . .	Gorey . .	I.	320
11	Barnadown Lower .	291 2 32	Wexford . .	Gorey . . .	Liskinfere . .	Gorey . .	I.	320
11	Barnadown Upper .	169 2 2	Wexford . .	Gorey . . .	Liskinfere . .	Gorey . .	I.	320
54	Barnagarrane . .	495 1 35	Limerick . .	Glenquin . .	Killagholehane .	Newcastle .	II.	245
105	Barnagearagh . .	171 0 28	Cork, W.R. .	Bantry . . .	Kilmocomoge .	Bantry . .	II.	119
67	Barnageehy East .	247 1 9	Cork, E.R. .	Imokilly . .	Youghal . .	Youghal . .	II.	90
67	Barnageehy West .	217 0 31	Cork, E.R. .	Imokilly . .	Youghal . .	Youghal . .	II.	90
5	Barnageeragh . .	186 2 31	Dublin . .	Balrothery East .	Holmpatrick . .	Balrothery .	I.	20
73	Barnagore . .	201 0 9	Cork, E.R. .	East Muskerry .	Athnowen . .	Cork . .	II.	101
27, 33	Barnagore . .	484 3 10	Tipperary N.R. .	Upper Ormond .	Dolla . .	Nenagh . .	II.	290
39,40,53,54	Barnagorteeny . .	728 2 26d	Galway . .	Moycullen . .	Kilcummin . .	Oughterard .	IV.	66
15	Barnagouloge . .	109 0 29	Tipperary, N.R. .	Lower Ormond .	Modreeny . .	Borrisokane .	II.	286
141	Barnagowlane . .	151 1 23	Cork, W.R. .	West Carbery (E.D.)	Abbeystrowry . .	Skibbereen .	II.	136
106	Barnagowlane East .	963 2 35	Cork, W.R. .	West Carbery (E.D.)	Dromdaleague .	Skibbereen .	II.	139
106	Barnagowlane West	817 0 7	Cork, W.R. .	West Carbery (E.D.)	Dromdaleague .	Skibbereen .	II.	139
12	Barnagree . .	56 3 0	Tipperary, N.R. .	Ikerrin . .	Roscrea . .	Roscrea . .	II.	276
91	Barnagreggaun . .	480 0 33	Mayo . .	Clanmorris . .	Mayo . .	Claremorris .	IV.	135
46, 47	Barnagrotty . .	474 0 6	King's Co. .	Clonlisk . .	Borrisnafarney .	Roscrea . .	I.	129
23	Barnagrow . .	267 0 9e	Cavan . .	Clankee . .	Drumgoon . .	Cootehill .	III.	72
81	Barnagurry . .	572 3 9f	Mayo . .	Costello . .	Aghamore . .	Swineford .	IV.	136
22	Barnahallia . .	85 3 12g	Galway . .	Ballynahinch .	Omey . .	Clifden . .	IV.	14
20, 21	Barnahask . .	466 1 10	Carlow . .	Forth . . .	Barragh . .	Enniscorthy .	I.	4
33	Barnahask . .	159 2 3	Wexford . .	Shelmaliere East .	St. Margaret's .	Wexford . .	I.	331
22, 23	Barnahaskin . .	217 0 14	Carlow . .	Idrone East .	Kiltennell . .	New Ross .	I.	7
87	Barnahely . .	451 2 14	Cork, E.R. .	Kerrycurrihy . .	Barnahely . .	Cork . .	II.	91
81	Barnahesker . .	217 1 4h	Mayo . .	Costello . .	Aghamore . .	Swineford .	IV.	136
29, 38	Barnahone and Owenkillew .	584 2 37	Donegal . .	Inishowen West .	Fahan Lower . .	Inishowen .	III.	120
89	Barnahown . .	1,437 2 33	Tipperary S.R. .	Iffa and Offa West .	Templetenny . .	Clogheen .	II.	320
3, 13	Barnahowna . .	1,325 3 24i	Galway . .	Ross . . .	Ballinrobe . .	Ballinrobe .	IV.	72
99	Barnakillew . .	134 2 9	Mayo . .	Carra . . .	Ballintober . .	Castlebar .	IV.	124
9	Barnakilly . .	95 2 18	Londonderry .	Tirkeeran . .	Faughanvale . .	NewT⁣Limavady	III.	250
12, 13	Barnakyle . .	394 0 22	Limerick . .	Pubblebrien . .	Mungret . .	Limerick . .	II.	253
6	Barnalackan . .	104 1 10	Fermanagh . .	Lurg . . .	Magheraculmoney .	Lowtherstown .	III.	207
29	Barnalascaw . .	18 2 32	Tipperary, N.R. .	Eliogarty . .	Templemore . .	Thurles . .	II.	272
30, 36	Barnalisheen . .	703 2 8	Tipperary, N.R. .	Ikerrin . .	Templetouhy . .	Thurles . .	II.	277
62, 72	Barnalyra . .	796 0 28	Mayo . .	Costello . .	Kilbeagh . .	Swineford .	IV.	140
16, 23	Barnamaghery . .	646 0 17	Down . .	Castlereagh Upper .	Killinchy . .	Downpatrick .	III.	165
23	Barnamaghery . .	775 2 6	Down . .	Castlereagh Upper .	Kilmore . .	Downpatrick .	III.	165
28, 33	Barnameelia . .	397 1 11	Wicklow . .	Ballinacor South .	Moyne . .	Shillelagh .	I.	350
20, 21	Barnameenagh . .	1,492 3 10	Leitrim . .	Leitrim . . .	Kiltoghert . .	Carr on Shannon	IV.	101
20	Barnameenagh West	349 1 0	Leitrim . .	Leitrim . . .	Kiltoghert . .	Carr on Shannon	IV.	101
7	Barnamire . .	267 1 11	Wicklow . .	Rathdown . .	Powerscourt . .	Rathdown .	I.	336
12, 16	Barnamuinga . .	303 2 33	Wicklow . .	Shillelagh . .	Moyacomb . .	Shillelagh .	I.	358
10	Barnan . .	460 2 27	King's Co. .	Lower Philipstown .	Kilclonfert . .	Tullamore .	I.	142

(a) Including 34A. 3R. 4P. water.   (d) Including 5A. 0R. 30P. water.   (g) Including 4A. 0R. 24P. water.
(b) Including 15A. 2R. 25P. water.   (e) Including 42A. 0R. 1P. water.   (h) Including 2A. 2R. 34P. water.
(c) Including 10A. 1R. 26P. water.   (f) Including 11A. 0R. 32P. water.   (i) Including 23A. 2R. 25P. water.

No. of Sheet of the Ordnance Survey Maps.	Townlands and Towns.	Area in Statute Acres. A. R. P.	County.	Barony.	Parish.	Poor Law Union in 1857.	Townland Census of 1851, Part I. Vol.	Page
41	Barnanageeha	397 1 21	Clare	Islands	Killone	Ennis	II.	30
58, 59	Barnanalleen	239 3 21	Tipperary, S.R.	Clanwilliam	Solloghodmore	Tipperary	II.	311
23, 24, 36	Barnanang	1,199 2 19	Galway	Ballynahinch	Moyrus	Clifden	IV.	12
28, 29	Barnane	2,166 3 5	Tipperary, N.R.	Ikerrin	Barnane-ely	Roscrea	II.	274
28, 29	Barnane	191 2 1	Tipperary, N.R.	Ikerrin	Killea	Roscrea	II.	275
23	Barnankile	295 0 18	Waterford	Decies without Drum	Kilrossanty	Kilmacthomas	II.	357
36	Barnanoraun	895 1 21	Galway	Ballynahinch	Moyrus	Clifden	IV.	12
23, 36	Barnanoraun	366 2 28a	Galway	Ballynahinch	Omey	Clifden	IV.	14
7	Barnanstown	183 3 9	Dublin	Balrothery West	Westpalstown	Balrothery	I.	23
12, 17	Barnaran	174 3 17	Kildare	Offaly East	Cloncurry	Edenderry	I.	69
22	Barnaree	81 0 27	Wexford	Gorey	Kiltrisk	Gorey	I.	320
33	Barnariddery	142 2 25	Wexford	Ballaghkeen	Ballyvalloo	Enniscorthy	I.	292
5, 8	Barnarobin	795 0 35	Sligo	Carbury	Drumcliff	Sligo	IV.	221
22	Barnasallagh	146 1 22	Queen's Co.	Clandonagh	Aghaboe	Donaghmore	I.	232
65	Barnashillane	78 0 30	Cork, E.R.	Barrymore	Baliyspillane	Middleton	II.	51
26	Barnaslingan	188 3 13	Dublin	Rathdown	Rathmichael	Rathdown	I.	37
14	Barnasrahy	275 2 12	Sligo	Carbury	Killaspugbrone	Sligo	IV.	222
68, 69	Barnastang	300 3 8	Mayo	Carra	Islandeady	Westport	II.	128
94	Barnastooka	1,216 1 25	Kerry	Glanarought	Kilgarvan	Kenmare	II.	187
139	Barnatonicane	261 2 30	Cork, W.R.	West Carbery (W.D.)	Skull	Skull	II.	145
93	BARNA T.	—	Galway	Galway	Rahoon	Galway	IV.	38
17	Barnaveddoge	93 3 27	Louth	Ardee	Dromin	Ardee	I.	172
55, 56	Barnaviddane	261 0 2	Cork, E.R.	Imokilly	Ardagh	Youghal	II.	83
25, 29	Barnaviddaun North	97 1 30	Kilkenny	Gowran	Ullard	Thomastown	I.	100
29	Barnaviddaun South	58 1 20	Kilkenny	Gowran	Ullard	Thomastown	I.	100
73, 74	Barnavihall	354 0 38	Galway	Kilconnell	Kilconnell	Ballinasloe	IV.	40
53	Barnawheel	33 2 27b	Wexford	Forth	Carn	Wexford	I.	309
24, 30	Barnbawn	343 3 25	Wicklow	Newcastle	Kilcommon	Rathdrum	I.	351
82	Barn Demesne	612 3 15	Tipperary, S.R.	Iffa and Offa East	Innishlounaght	Clonmel	II.	313
76, 82	Barn Demesne	71 1 11	Tipperary, S.R.	Iffa and Offa East	Newchapel	Clonmel	II.	315
31	Barndonagh	115 3 3	Monaghan	Farney	Magheross	Carrickmacross	III.	273
20	Barne	200 0 1	Longford	Ardagh	Mostrim	Granard	I.	152
35, 36	Barnes Lower	754 2 17c	Donegal	Kilmacrenan	Kilmacrenan	Millford	III.	129
12, 19	Barnes Lower	446 3 2d	Tyrone	Strabane Upper	Bodoney Upper	Gortin	III.	324
35	Barnes Upper	1,082 3 34e	Donegal	Kilmacrenan	Kilmacrenan	Millford	III.	129
12, 19	Barnes Upper	628 1 14f	Tyrone	Strabane Upper	Bodoney Upper	Gortin	III.	324
94, 95	Barnesyneilly	542 1 33	Donegal	Tirhugh	Drumhome	Donegal	III.	146
53, 64	Barnetstown	360 1 20	Cork, E.R.	Barrymore	Kilquane	Cork	II.	55
19	Barney	360 1 38	Longford	Ardagh	Ardagh	Longford	I.	151
79	Barney	193 2 18	Mayo	Carra	Breaghwy	Castlebar	IV.	127
19	Barneygole	269 0 24	Longford	Ardagh	Ardagh	Longford	I.	151
78	Barnfield	78 3 6	Cork, E.R.	Imokilly	Ightermurragh	Middleton	II.	87
11	Barnhall	224 2 29	Kildare	North Salt	Leixlip	Celbridge	I.	75
4	Barnhill	199 2 21	Carlow	Rathvilly	Rathvilly	Baltinglass	I.	12
13	Barnhill	190 3 29	Dublin	Castleknock	Clonsilla	Celbridge	I.	24
34	Barnhill	51 1 4	Fermanagh	Magherastephana	Aghalurcher	Lisnaskea	III.	215
40	Barnhill	99 2 29	Kildare	Kilkea and Moone	Graney	Athy	I.	60
39	Barnhill	180 0 29	Roscommon	Ballintober South	Roscommon	Roscommon	IV.	190
40	Barnhill East	119 3 16	Kildare	Kilkea and Moone	Castledermot	Athy	I.	59
14	Barnhill Lower	139 2 20	Mayo	Tirawley	Lackan	Killala	IV.	170
14	Barnhill Upper	373 1 39	Mayo	Tirawley	Lackan	Killala	IV.	170
40	Barnhill West	213 2 34	Kildare	Kilkea and Moone	Castledermot	Athy	I.	59
5, 9	Barnish	104 2 1	Antrim	Cary	Culfeightrin	Ballycastle	III.	13
44	Barnish	920 3 32	Antrim	Lower Antrim	Connor	Antrim	III.	3
43, 49	Barnish	170 1 27	Antrim	Upper Toome	Drummaul	Antrim	III.	34
6, 7	Barnland	158 0 24	Wexford	Gorey	Kilcavan	Gorey	I.	317
67,68,74,75	Barnlough	916 2 19	Tipperary, S.R.	Clanwilliam	Templeneiry	Tipperary	II.	311
41, 47	Barnmeen	823 3 31	Down	Upper Iveagh, Up. pt.	Drumgath	Newry	III.	175
75, 76	Barnora	264 1 1g	Tipperary, S.R.	Iffa and Offa West	Caher	Clogheen	II.	317
99, 100	Barnpark	79 1 34	Galway	Clonmacnowen	Clontuskert	Ballinasloe	IV.	24
41	Barntick	490 0 18h	Clare	Islands	Clareabbey	Ennis	II.	29
37	Barntown	194 1 21i	Wexford	Shelmaliere West	Carrick	Wexford	I.	332
46	Barnwellsgrove	174 3 25j	Galway	Killian	Ballynakill	Mountbellew	IV.	43
12	Barnwellstown	132 1 26	Meath	Lower Slane	Killary	Ardee	I.	223
27, 28	Barny and Bealady	264 3 5	Queen's Co.	Clandonagh	Rathdowney	Donaghmore	I.	234
101, 102	Barnycarroll	253 1 19k	Mayo	Clanmorris	Kilcolman	Claremorris	IV.	133
42	Baronagh	378 3 23	Tyrone	Omagh East	Donacavey	Omagh	III.	310
14	Baronrath	372 2 15	Kildare	Naas North	Whitechurch	Naas	I.	63
17, 25	Barons Court	885 0 32l	Tyrone	Strabane Lower	Ardstraw	Strabane	III.	318
32	Baronsland	201 0 8	Kildare	Kilcullen	Kilcullen	Naas	I.	58
24	Baronsland	36 2 11	Kilkenny	Gowran	Tullaherin	Thomastown	I.	100
24	Baronsland	83 2 37m	Kilkenny	Gowran	Woolengrange	Thomastown	I.	100
43, 44	Baronstown	68 3 2	Meath	Lower Deece	Knockmark	Dunshaughlin	I.	192

(a) Including 7A. 0R. 0P. water.
(b) Including 2A. 0R. 15P. detached portion.
(c) Including 63A. 0R. 3P. water.
(d) Including 4A. 1R. 20P. water.
(e) Including 3A. 1R. 27P. Lough Grennan.

(f) Including 5A. 0R. 6P. water.
(g) Including 5A. 0R. 25P. water.
(h) Including 31A. 2R. 32P. water.
(i) Including 2A. 0R. 11P. detached portion.

(j) Including 2A. 0R. 4P. water.
(k) Including 4A. 0R. 32P. water.
(l) Including 150A. 3R. 3P. water.
(m) Including 2A. 2R. 24P. detached portion.

T

No. of Sheet of the Ordnance Survey Maps.	Townlands and Towns.	Area in Statute Acres.	County.	Barony.	Parish.	Poor Law Union in 1857.	Townland Census of 1851, Part I.	
		A. R. P.					Vol.	Page
32	Baronstown . .	61 2 13	Meath . .	Skreen . . .	Skreen . . .	Dunshaughlin .	I.	221
35	Baronstown . .	512 1 3	Tipperary, N.R.	Eliogarty . .	Loughmoe East .	Thurles . .	II.	271
11	Baronstown . .	160 2 15	Westmeath .	Moygoish . .	Kilbixy . .	Mullingar .	I.	279
6, 11	Baronstown Demesne	929 3 8a	Westmeath .	Moygoish . .	Kilbixy . .	Mullingar .	I.	279
18	Baronstown East .	435 2 21	Kildare . .	Connell . .	Rathernan . .	Naas . .	I.	56
20	Baronstown Lower .	233 3 34	Wicklow . .	Upper Talbotstown .	Ballynure . .	Baltinglass .	I.	361
20	Baronstown Upper .	281 1 9	Wicklow . .	Upper Talbotstown .	Ballynure . .	Baltinglass .	I.	361
18	Baronstown West .	354 0 24b	Kildare . .	Connell . .	Rathernan . .	Naas . .	I.	56
39	Barrabehy . .	539 0 6	Kilkenny . .	Iverk . . .	Tubbrid . .	Carrick on Suir	I.	107
7	Barracashlaun .	287 3 6	Leitrim . .	Rosclogher . .	Killasnet . .	Manorhamilton	IV.	109
45	Barrack . . .	70 0 16	Donegal . .	Kilmacrenan . .	Conwal . .	Letterkenny .	III.	126
26, 27, 35	Barrack . . .	269 1 13	Kerry . .	Corkaguiny . .	Stradbally .	Dingle . .	II.	180
52, 60	Barrack or Ballymagig . . .	140 1 24	Donegal . .	Raphoe . .	Conwal . .	Letterkenny .	III.	137
13	Barrack Bog . .	14 0 10	Longford . .	Ardagh . .	Ballymacormick .	Longford . .	I.	152
1, 2, 3	Barrackcroghan .	201 2 22	Wexford . .	Gorey . .	Kilnenor . .	Gorey . .	I.	319
112	Barrackgreen . .	3 2 23	Cork, E.R. .	Kinsale . .	Kinsale . .	Kinsale . .	II.	100
68	Barrackhill . .	106 2 23c	Mayo . .	Burrishoole . .	Burrishoole . .	Newport . .	IV.	118
18	Barrackhill (Barton)	97 2 31	Kilkenny . .	Crannagh . .	Ballycallan . .	Kilkenny . .	I.	84
18, 19	Barrackhill (Cranesborough) . .	67 2 2	Kilkenny . .	Crannagh . .	Ballycallan . .	Kilkenny . .	I.	84
79	Barrackland . .	144 2 22d	Mayo . .	Carra . . .	Manulla . .	Castlebar .	IV.	129
16	Barrack North . .	12 2 6e	Mayo . .	Erris . . .	Kilmore . .	Belmullet .	IV.	145
7	Barrackpark . .	30 2 1	Leitrim . .	Rosclogher . .	Killasnet . .	Manorhamilton	IV.	109
35	Barrackquarter or Ross . . .	160 1 24	Queen's Co. .	Clarmallagh . .	Aghmacart . .	Abbeyleix .	I.	236
16	Barrack South . .	174 1 34	Mayo . .	Erris . . .	Kilmore . .	Belmullet .	IV.	145
37, 45	Barracktown (Alias) Altmore . .	117 2 30	Tyrone . .	Dungannon Middle .	Pomeroy . .	Dungannon .	III.	304
14	Barracree . .	373 0 38	Waterford .	Decies without Drum	Ki'gobnet . .	Dungarvan .	II.	357
14	Barracreemountain Lr.	417 0 10	Waterford .	Decies without Drum	Kilgobnet . .	Dungarvan .	II.	357
14	Barracreemountain Up.	590 0 10	Waterford .	Decies without Drum	Kilgobnet . .	Dungarvan .	II.	357
40	Barracurragh . .	168 1 0	Tipperary, N.R.	Kilnamanagh Upper	Ballycahill . .	Thurles . .	II.	277
2	Barracurragh . .	265 3 6	Wexford . .	Gorey . .	Kilcavan . .	Gorey . .	I.	317
55	Barradaw . .	706 0 13	Cork, E.R. .	Imokilly . .	Dangandonovan .	Middleton .	II.	86
21, 26	Barraderra . .	190 2 19	Kildare . .	Offaly West . .	Monasterevin .	Athy . .	I.	73
90	Barraderry . .	765 0 4f	Galway . .	Moycullen . .	Killannin . .	Oughterard .	IV.	69
27, 32	Barraderry East .	100 1 0	Wicklow . .	Upper Talbotstown	Kilranelagh .	Baltinglass .	I.	364
27, 32	Barraderry North .	152 2 0	Wicklow . .	Upper Talbotstown	Kilranelagh .	Baltinglass .	I.	364
27, 32	Barraderry West .	435 0 38	Wicklow . .	Upper Talbotstown	Kilranelagh .	Baltinglass .	I.	364
2, 6	Barradoos . .	415 1 17	Queen's Co. .	Tinnahinch . .	Kilmanman .	Mountmellick .	I.	249
2, 6	Barradrum . .	416 3 6	Westmeath .	Moygoish . .	Street . .	Granard . .	I.	281
102	Barraduff . .	341 2 33	Kerry . .	Glanarought . .	Kenmare . .	Kenmare .	II.	185
5	Barraduff . .	164 0 22	Kerry . .	Iraghticonnor . .	Lisselton . .	Listowel .	II.	192
67, 68	Barraduff . .	408 1 39	Kerry . .	Magunihy . .	Aghadoe . .	Killarney .	II.	199
45, 54	Barrafohona . .	967 1 2	Cork, E.R. .	Barrymore . .	Britway . .	Middleton .	II.	51
105, 115	Barragarraun . .	192 0 36	Galway . .	Loughrea . .	Killeenadeema .	Loughrea .	IV.	64
17	Barragh . . .	120 2 17	Carlow . .	Forth . .	Barragh . .	Enniscorthy .	I.	4
16, 17	Barragh . . .	235 2 2g	Cavan . .	Tullygarvey . .	Kildrumsherdan .	Cootehill .	III.	89
18	Barragh Beg . .	60 0 4	Leitrim . .	Drumahaire . .	Inishmagrath .	Manorhamilton	IV.	95
4, 5	Barragh Beg . .	217 2 14	Longford . .	Longford . .	Killoe . .	Longford . .	I.	158
17, 18	Barragh More . .	144 3 26	Leitrim . .	Drumahaire . .	Inishmagrath .	Manorhamilton	IV.	95
5	Barragh More . .	434 3 18	Longford . .	Longford . .	Killoe . .	Longford . .	I.	158
16, 21	Barraglan . .	312 2 17	Wexford . .	Ballaghkeen . .	Monamolin .	Gorey . .	I.	298
97	Barraglanna . .	1,267 3 19h	Mayo . .	Murrisk . .	Oughaval . .	Westport .	IV.	161
49, 50	Barrahaurin . .	2,527 1 8	Cork, E.R. .	East Muskerry .	Donaghmore .	Macroom .	II.	102
27, 28	Barrahill . .	294 2 30	Queen's Co. .	Clandonagh . .	Rathdowney .	Donaghmore .	I.	234
29	Barrakilla . .	201 3 95	Kerry . .	Trughanacmy . .	Ballymacelligot .	Tralee . .	II.	207
1, 3	Barran . . .	852 0 28	Cavan . .	Tullyhaw . .	Killinagh . .	Enniskillen .	III.	91
5, 6	Barran . . .	299 0 18	Tyrone . .	Strabane Lower .	Donaghedy . .	Strabane .	III.	320
19, 20	Barranafaddock .	112 2 13	Waterford .	Coshmore&Coshbride	Lismore andMocollop	Lismore . .	II.	345
16	Barranagh East .	266 3 0i	Mayo . .	Erris . . .	Kilmore . .	Belmullet .	IV.	145
16	Barranagh Island .	63 0 28	Mayo . .	Erris . . .	Kilmore . .	Belmullet .	IV.	146
33	Barranaghs . .	901 2 8	King's Co. .	Upper Philipstown	Clonyhurk . .	Mountmellick .	I.	143
16	Barranagh West .	95 3 19j	Mayo . .	Erris . . .	Kilmore . .	Belmullet .	IV.	145
44	Barranahash . .	290 0 33	Cork, E.R. .	Barrymore . .	Rathcormack .	Fermoy . .	II.	57
36	Barranaleaha . .	123 1 35	Waterford .	Decies within Drum	Ardmore . .	Dungarvan .	II.	349
35, 36	Barranalira . .	135 0 6	Waterford .	Decies without Drum	Dungarvan . .	Dungarvan .	II.	355
20	Barranamanoge .	212 0 35	Waterford .	Coshmore&Coshbride	Lismore andMocollop	Lismore . .	II.	345
21	Barranarran Lower .	63 1 34	Mayo . .	Tirawley . .	Kilfian . .	Killala . .	IV.	169
21	Barranarran Upper .	168 1 8	Mayo . .	Tirawley . .	Kilfian . .	Killala . .	IV.	169
5	Barranashingaun .	244 1 8	Waterford .	Glenahiry . .	Kilronan . .	Clonmel . .	II.	365
36, 39	Barranastook . .	419 3 21	Waterford .	Decies within Drum	Ardmore . .	Dungarvan .	II.	349
30, 35	Barranastook Lower	436 1 21	Waterford .	Decies without Drum	Whitechurch .	Dungarvan .	II.	361

(a) Including 6A. 3R. 33P. water.
(b) Including 69A. 0R. 14P. detached portion.
(c) Including 2A. 2R. 17P. water.
(d) Including 5A. 2R. 8P. water.

(e) Including 3A. 0R. 16P. water.
(f) Including 58A. 3R. 11P. water.
(g) Including 15A. 1R. 14P. water.

(h) Including 58A. 2R. 28P. water.
(i) Including 10A. 2R. 24P. water.
(j) Including 14A. 0R. 16r. water.

No. of Sheet of the Ordnance Survey Maps.	Townlands and Towns.	Area in Statute Acres.			County.	Barony.	Parish.	Poor Law Union in 1857.	Townland Census of 1851, Part I.	
		A.	R.	P.					Vol.	Page
30, 35	Barranastook Upper	107	2	18	Waterford	Decies without Drum	Whitechurch	Dungarvan	II.	361
35, 40	Barranisky East	167	3	3	Wicklow	Arklow	Kilbride	Rathdrum	I.	344
35, 40	Barranisky West	332	0	17	Wicklow	Arklow	Kilbride	Rathdrum	I.	344
69	Barranny	1,181	1	30	Galway	Clare	Annaghdown	Galway	IV.	16
5	Barratitoppy Lower	265	1	20	Monaghan	Monaghan	Tedavnet	Monaghan	III.	278
5	Barratitoppy Upper	657	3	20	Monaghan	Monaghan	Tedavnet	Monaghan	III.	278
39, 40	Barratleva	480	3	7	Galway	Moycullen	Kilcummin	Oughterard	IV.	66
32	Barratober or Farmhill	131	0	24	Wexford	Shelmaliere East	Artramon	Wexford	I.	330
6	Barratogher	166	0	15	Westmeath	Moygoish	Russagh	Granard	I.	280
116	Barratoor	250	3	1	Galway	Leitrim	Ballynakill	Loughrea	IV.	50
104,113,114	Barratreana	187	0	3	Galway	Dunkellin	Ardrahan	Gort	IV.	26
22	Barratrough or Streamstown	1,000	3	8a	Galway	Ballynahinch	Omey	Clifden	IV.	15
2	Barravakeen	535	2	9	Waterford	Upperthird	Killaloan	Clonmel	II.	370
30	Barravally	149	3	33	Kilkenny	Kells	Kilmaganny	Callan	I.	109
18, 24	Barravally	112	3	13	Roscommon	Ballintober North	Kilglass	Strokestown	IV.	186
33	Barravey	260	0	0b	Tyrone	Omagh West	Longfield West	Castlederg	III.	316
26	Barravie	166	3	4	Tipperary, N.R.	Upper Ormond	Kilmore	Nenagh	II.	291
69, 70	Barravilla	93	1	37	Galway	Clare	Annaghdown	Galway	IV.	16
33	Barrawinga	188	3	8	Queen's Co.	Clandonagh	Rathdowney	Donaghmore	I.	234
23	Barr Cregg	346	2	8	Londonderry	Tirkeeran	Cumber Upper	Londonderry	III.	249
101	Barreel	238	1	21	Mayo	Clanmorris	Tagheen	Claremorris	IV.	135
10	Barreen	295	1	9	Kildare	Ikeathy and Oughterany	Balraheen	Celbridge	I.	56
102	Barrees	1,098	2	20	Cork, W.R.	Bear	Kilcatherine	Castletown	II.	123
136	Barreragh	110	2	2	Cork, W.R.	Ibane and Barryroe	Lislee	Clonakilty	II.	150
24, 25	Barretstown	509	3	21	Kildare	Naas South	Tipperkevin	Naas	I.	65
69, 70	Barrettsgrange	358	2	22	Tipperary, S.R.	Middlethird	Barrettsgrange	Cashel	II.	325
85,86,97,98	Barrettshill and Rearour	608	1	11	Cork, E.R.	Kerrycurrihy	Ballinaboy	Cork	II.	91
83	Barrettspark	251	3	1	Galway	Clare	Athenry	Galway	IV.	17
29	Barrettspark	15	1	32	Wexford	Bantry	St. Mary's	New Ross	I.	302
16	Barrettsplot East	118	2	5c	Mayo	Erris	Kilmore	Belmullet	IV.	145
16	Barrettsplot West	54	3	32d	Mayo	Erris	Kilmore	Belmullet	IV.	145
14, 19	Barrettstown	366	1	38e	Kildare	Clane	Brideschurch	Naas	I.	53
18	Barrettstown	1,145	2	9f	Kildare	Connell	Oldconnell	Naas	I.	56
27, 31	Barrettstown	576	2	17g	Kildare	Knocktopher	Knocktopher	Thomastown	I.	112
70	Barrettstown	372	0	31	Tipperary, S.R.	Middlethird	Barrettsgrange	Cashel	II.	325
25	Barrettstown	261	0	28	Westmeath	Rathconrath	Dysart	Mullingar	I.	283
25, 26	Barrevagh	783	1	35	Galway	Ross	Ross	Oughterard	IV.	73
32	Barrinagh	268	1	15	Roscommon	Castlereagh	Kiltullagh	Castlereagh	IV.	201
16	Barrinagh	116	2	23	Roscommon	Roscommon	Shankill	Strokestown	IV.	212
41, 42	Barrinclay	408	1	37	Cork, E.R.	Barretts	Mourneabbey	Mallow	II.	50
18	Barristown	280	2	25	Waterford	Gaultiere	Kill St. Nicholas	Waterford	II.	364
49, 50	Barrockstown	269	0	0	Meath	Upper Deece	Moyglare	Celbridge	I.	194
19	Barroe	33	1	13	Longford	Moydow	Moydow	Longford	I.	162
63	Barroe	774	1	16	Mayo	Costello	Kilbeagh	Swineford	IV.	140
14	Barroe	135	3	17	Mayo	Tirawley	Lackan	Killala	IV.	170
14, 15	Barroe	194	3	19	Sligo	Carbury	Calry	Sligo	IV.	220
34	Barroe Lower	161	3	24	Sligo	Tirerrill	Killadoon	Boyle	IV.	238
34	Barroe North	140	2	33	Sligo	Tirerrill	Killadoon	Boyle	IV.	238
34, 40	Barroe South	98	0	7	Sligo	Tirerrill	Killadoon	Boyle	IV.	238
34	Barroe Upper	284	1	9	Sligo	Tirerrill	Killadoon	Boyle	IV.	238
34	Barr of Ballyconnell or Devlin	1,129	3	33	Donegal	Kilmacrenan	Raymunterdoney	Dunfanaghy	III.	131
104	Barr of Ballynacarrick	475	1	13	Donegal	Tirhugh	Drumhome	Ballyshannon	III.	146
9	Barr of Bolustymore	346	3	12h	Fermanagh	Magheraboy	Inishmacsaint	Ballyshannon	III.	212
8, 9, 13, 14	Barr of Drumbadmeen	514	1	14i	Fermanagh	Magheraboy	Inishmacsaint	Ballyshannon	III.	212
13,14,19,20	Barr of Drumgormly	196	2	35	Fermanagh	Magheraboy	Devenish	Ballyshannon	III.	210
12	Barr of Farrow	844	3	26j	Leitrim	Drumahaire	Cloonclare	Manorhamilton	IV.	93
38	Barr of Kilmackilvenny or Monreagh	930	2	37	Donegal	Inishowen West	Fahan Upper	Londonderry	III.	121
7	Barr of Shancurragh	53	3	3	Leitrim	Rosclogher	Killasnet	Manorhamilton	IV.	110
13, 19	Barr of Slattinagh	244	0	19	Fermanagh	Magheraboy	Devenish	Ballyshannon	III.	210
8, 13	Barr of Slawin	240	3	12k	Fermanagh	Magheraboy	Inishmacsaint	Ballyshannon	III.	212
3, 7	Barroge	66	2	14	Wexford	Gorey	Kilgorman	Gorey	I.	318
11	Barrogstown	155	2	21	Kildare	North Salt	Laraghbryan	Celbridge	I.	75
6, 11	Barrogstown East	89	1	24	Kildare	North Salt	Donaghmore	Celbridge	I.	74
6, 11	Barrogstown West	119	0	31	Kildare	North Salt	Donaghmore	Celbridge	I.	74
27	Barronsknock	10	2	2	Kilkenny	Kells	Kells	Callan	I.	108
6	Barronstown	513	1	8	Louth	Upper Dundalk	Barronstown	Dundalk	I.	177
58	Barronstown (Laffan)	234	3	17	Tipperary, S.R.	Clanwilliam	Tipperary	Tipperary	II.	312
58, 66	Barronstown (Ormond)	255	3	26	Tipperary, S.R.	Clanwilliam	Shronell	Tipperary	II.	310

(a) Including 16A. 1R. 23P. water.
(b) Including 0A. 2R. 22P. water.
(c) Including 7A. 0R. 29P. water.
(d) Including 9A. 2R. 11P. water.

(e) Including 3A. 0R. 24P. River Liffey.
(f) Including 9A. 1R. 39P. water.
(g) Including 26A. 3R. 10P. detached portions.
(h) Including 37A. 2R. 22P. water.

(i) Including 43A. 0R. 6P. water.
(j) Including 3A. 3R. 16P. water.
(k) Including 5A. 3R. 39P. water.

T 2

No of Sheet of the Ordnance Survey Maps.	Townlands and Towns.	Area in Statute Acres.	County.	Barony.	Parish.	Poor Law Union in 1857.	Townland Census of 1851, Part I.	
		A. R. P.					Vol.	Page
58, 66	Barronstown(*Ormond*)	157 0 7	Tipperary, S.R.	Clanwilliam	Tipperary	Tipperary	II.	312
12, 19	Barroosky	1,951 2 13	Mayo	Erris	Kilcommon	Belmullet	IV.	143
20, 28	Barrow	876 2 27	Kerry	Trughanacmy	Ardfert	Tralee	II.	205
35	Barrowford	105 1 16a	Kildare	Narragh and Reban West	Kilberry	Athy	I.	67
20, 26	Barrowhouse	616 3 7b	Queen's Co.	Ballyadams	Tankardstown	Athy	I.	232
21, 25	Barrowmount	725 0 1c	Kilkenny	Gowran	Grangesilvia	Thomastown	I.	95
38	Barr or Ramoan	206 3 28	Fermanagh	Knockninny	Kinawley	Lisnaskea	III.	201
8, 12	Barrs East	436 2 20	Leitrim	Drumahaire	Cloonclare	Manorhamilton	IV.	93
25, 38	Barrslievenaroy	602 1 30	Galway	Ross	Ross	Oughterard	IV.	73
8, 12	Barrs West	397 0 10	Leitrim	Drumahaire	Cloonclare	Manorhamilton	IV.	93
54	Barrusheen	114 3 11	Galway	Moycullen	Kilcummin	Oughterard	IV.	66
23	Barry	149 0 20	Longford	Shrule	Kilcommock	Ballymahon	I.	166
23	Barry	242 0 13	Longford	Shrule	Taghshinny	Ballymahon	I.	167
49, 52	Barry Beg	768 1 20	Roscommon	Athlone	Kiltoom	Athlone	IV.	182
49	Barry More	1,140 2 12	Roscommon	Athlone	Kiltoom	Athlone	IV.	182
150, 151	Barryroe	235 2 27	Cork, W.R.	West Carbery (E.D.)	Castlehaven	Skibbereen	II.	137
131	Barryroe	685 2 11	Cork, W.R.	West Carbery (W.D.)	Skull	Skull	II.	145
10	Barrysbrook	892 3 11d	King's Co.	Lower Philipstown	Ballyburly	Edenderry	I.	142
75, 76	Barryscourt	699 0 9	Cork, E.R.	Barrymore	Carrigtohill	Middleton	II.	52
32, 40	Barrysfarm	99 0 12	Limerick	Smallcounty	Hospital	Kilmallock	II.	260
136	Barryshall	579 1 13	Cork, W.R.	Ibane and Barryroe	Timoleague	Clonakilty	II.	151
20	Barrysmountain	208 1 38	Waterford	Coshmore and Coshbride	Lismore and Mocollop	Lismore	II.	345
11, 12	Barrysparks	138 0 37	Dublin	Nethercross	Swords	Balrothery	I.	32
45, 46	Barrystown	519 0 0	Wexford	Bargy	Bannow	Wexford	I.	304
23	Barry T.	—	Longford	Shrule	Taghshinny	Ballymahon	I.	167
50	Barstown	198 3 24	Meath	Upper Deece	Culmullin	Dunshaughlin	I.	193
53	Bartleystown	66 0 0	Clare	Tulla Lower	Kiltenanlea	Limerick	II.	37
31	Bartonsfarm	64 2 0	Kilkenny	Knocktopher	Aghaviller	Thomastown	I.	110
65	Bartoose	378 2 38	Tipperary, S.R.	Clanwilliam	Emly	Tipperary	II.	307
16	Bartragh	398 2 19	Sligo	Tireragh	Castleconor	Dromore West	IV.	232
15, 22	Bartragh Island	316 3 34	Mayo	Tirawley	Killala	Killala	IV.	170
33	Bartramstown	349 1 34	Meath	Upper Duleek	Ardcath	Drogheda	I.	197
10	Bartrauve	600 2 10	Mayo	Erris	Kilmore	Belmullet	IV.	145
23	Baskethill	226 2 11	Limerick	Clanwilliam	Caherconlish	Limerick	II.	222
43	Basketstown	199 0 8	Meath	Lower Deece	Galtrim	Trim	I.	191
11, 12	Baskill	686 2 15	Donegal	Inishowen East	Culdaff	Inishowen	III.	118
15	Baskin	139 3 8	Dublin	Coolock	Cloghran	Balrothery	I.	26
29, 35	Baskinagh Lower	232 2 16	Meath	Lune	Kildalkey	Trim	I.	208
29, 35	Baskinagh Upper	315 2 24	Meath	Lune	Kildalkey	Trim	I.	208
23	Baskin High	661 3 32	Westmeath	Kilkenny West	Drumraney	Ballymahon	I.	272
23	Baskin Low	598 3 1	Westmeath	Kilkenny West	Drumraney	Ballymahon	I.	272
21	Baslick	129 2 9	Roscommon	Castlereagh	Baslick	Castlereagh	IV.	199
98	Baslickane	487 0 26	Kerry	Dunkerron South	Kilcrohane	Cahersiveen	II.	183
52	Bastardstown	191 2 6	Wexford	Bargy	Kilmore	Wexford	I.	306
6	Batestown	88 2 38	Meath	Lower Slane	Siddan	Ardee	I.	223
37	Batterjohn	33 0 39e	Meath	Lower Deece	Kiltale	Dunshaughlin	I.	192
36, 42	Batterstown	267 0 32f	Meath	Lower Moyfenrath	Trim	Trim	I.	211
25	Batterstown	154 1 35	Meath	Lower Navan	Donaghmore	Navan	I.	214
41	Batterstown	140 1 37	Meath	Lune	Killaconnigan	Trim	I.	208
49	Batterstown	134 0 6	Meath	Upper Deece	Rodanstown	Celbridge	I.	194
7	BATTLEBRIDGE T.	—	Roscommon	Boyle	Tumna	Car*k.* on Shannon	IV.	198
39, 40, 44	Battlefield	644 1 34g	Sligo	Corran	Toomour	Boyle	IV.	228
62	*Battle Island*	0 1 13	Clare	Bunratty Lower	Kilfintinan	Limerick	II.	5
32, 36	Battlemount	781 1 27	Kildare	Narragh and Reban East	Narraghmore	Athy	I.	66
44, 45	Battlestown	1,291 0 5	Wexford	Shelburne	St. James and Dunbrody	New Ross	I.	328
18	Battsland	49 2 34	Louth	Ferrard	Dunleer	Ardee	I.	180
13	Battstown	437 3 29	Westmeath	Delvin	Killulagh	Castletowndelvin	I.	266
26	Bauck	193 2 12	Carlow	St. Mullins Lower	St. Mullins	New Ross	I.	13
82	Baulbrack	317 3 7	Cork, W.R.	West Muskerry	Kilmichael	Dunmanway	II.	158
14, 19	Baun	157 0 4	Kilkenny	Gowran	St. John's	Kilkenny	I.	98
13	Baunacloka	124 3 16	Limerick	Pubblebrien	Mungret	Limerick	II.	253
33	Baunaghra	1,045 0 24	Queen's Co.	Clandonagh	Erke	Donaghmore	I.	233
31	Baunanattin	22 3 2	Kilkenny	Knocktopher	Knocktopher	Thomastown	I.	112
9, 13	Baunaniska	242 1 2	Kilkenny	Crannagh	Freshford	Kilkenny	I.	85
25	Baunastackaun	123 2 34	Kilkenny	Gowran	Graiguenamanagh	Thomastown	I.	95
31	Baunatillaun	14 2 27	Kilkenny	Kells	Dunnamaggan	Callan	I.	108
56	Baunatlea	59 2 3	Limerick	Coshlea	Ballingaddy	Kilmallock	II.	227
97	Baunavollaboy	20 3 15	Kilkenny	Shillelogher	Stonecarthy	Thomastown	I.	115
8	Baunballinlough	601 3 21	Kilkenny	Galmoy	Erke	Urlingford	I.	92
22	Baunbrack	63 0 20	Queen's Co.	Clarmallagh	Aghaboe	Donaghmore	I.	235

(a) Including 4A. 0R. 10P. water.   (d) Including 5A. 0R. 20P. water.   (f) Including 6A. 3R. 20P. water.
(b) Including 7A. 0R. 20P. River Barrow.   (e) Including 20A. 2R. 38P. detached portions.   (g) Including 3A. 0R. 30P. water.
(c) Including 15A. 0R. 38P. River Barrow.

No. of Sheet of the Ordnance Survey Maps.	Townlands and Towns.	Area in Statute Acres.	County.	Barony.	Parish.	Poor Law Union in 1857.	Townland Census of 1851, Part I.	
		A. R. P.					Vol.	Page
26	Bauneen . .	59 0 19	Kilkenny . .	Kells . . .	Coolaghmore . .	Callan . .	I.	107
27	Baunemon . .	148 0 26	Kilkenny . .	Kells . . .	Kells . . .	Callan . .	I.	108
34	Baunfree . .	230 1 25	Kilkenny . .	Kells . . .	Tullahought . .	Carrick on Suir	I.	110
18, 19	Baungarriff . .	162 1 21	Kilkenny . .	Crannagh . .	Ballycallan . .	Kilkenny . .	I.	84
38	Baungarriff . .	148 2 6	Kilkenny . .	Iverk . . .	Whitechurch . .	Carrick on Suir	I.	107
8	Baungarrow . .	163 3 0	Kilkenny . .	Galmoy . .	Fertagh . .	Urlingford .	I.	92
17	Baunkyle . .	475 2 23a	Clare . .	Inchiquin . .	Killinaboy . .	Corrofin . .	II.	26
15	Baunleath . .	62 3 26	Carlow . .	Idrone West .	Oldleighlin . .	Carlow . .	I.	9
23	Baunlusk . .	216 2 27	Kilkenny . .	Shillelogher .	Grange . .	Kilkenny . .	I.	114
56	Baunmore . .	226 3 30	Clare . .	Moyarta . .	Kilfearagh .	Kilrush . .	II.	32
84	Baunmore . .	211 1 2	Galway . .	Athenry . .	Athenry . .	Loughrea . .	IV.	3
70	Baunmore . .	121 2 28	Galway . .	Clare . .	Annaghdown .	Galway . .	IV.	16
16	Baunmore . .	109 3 7	Galway . .	Dunmore . .	Dunmore . .	Tuam . .	IV.	33
7, 8, 12	Baunmore . .	3,092 0 8	Kilkenny . .	Galmoy . .	Erke . .	Urlingford .	I.	92
20	Baunmore . .	101 1 27	Kilkenny . .	Gowran . .	Clara . .	Kilkenny . .	I.	94
48, 56	Baunmore .	494 1 13	Limerick . .	Coshlea . .	Ballingaddy .	Kilmallock .	II.	237
9	Baunmore or Balleen Upper . .	146 0 28	Kilkenny . .	Galmoy . .	Balleen . .	Urlingford .	I.	91
40	Baunnageeragh .	159 3 11	Limerick . .	Smallcounty .	Uregare . .	Kilmallock .	II.	261
40	Baunnageloge . .	175 3 27	Kilkenny . .	Ida . .	Dunkitt . .	Waterford .	I.	101
10	Baunnanooneeny .	250 1 5	Cork, E.R. .	Condons&Clangibbon	Marshalstown .	Mitchelstown .	II.	63
18	Baunnaraha . .	224 0 21	Kilkenny . .	Crannagh . .	Ballycallan .	Kilkenny . .	I.	84
23	Baunoge . . .	933 3 15b	Galway . .	Ballynahinch .	Ballynakill .	Clifden . .	IV.	11
105	Baunoge . . .	109 3 22	Galway, . .	Loughrea . .	Loughrea . .	Loughrea . .	IV.	65
22, 26	Baunoge . . .	159 1 22	Kilkenny . .	Callan . .	Callan . .	Callan . .	I.	83
28	Baunoge . . .	91 0 28	Queen's Co. .	Clarmallagh .	Aghaboe . .	Donaghmore .	I.	235
24, 25	Baunogemeely .	586 1 26	Queen's Co. .	Cullenagh . .	Fossy or Timahoe .	Abbeyleix .	I.	240
8	Baunogenasraid .	231 2 20	Carlow . .	Carlow . .	Grangeford . .	Carlow . .	I.	2
8	Baunogephlure .	314 1 8	Carlow . .	Carlow . .	Grangeford . .	Carlow . .	I.	2
60	Baunoges . .	337 1 18	Galway . .	Tiaquin . .	Ballymacward .	Mountbellew .	IV.	75
99	Baunoges . .	245 3 7c	Mayo . .	Carra . .	Ballintober .	Castlebar . .	IV.	124
17	Baunoges North .	50 0 22	Galway . .	Ballymoe . .	Dunmore . .	Glennamaddy .	IV.	7
17	Baunoges South .	23 2 37	Galway . .	Ballymoe . .	Dunmore . .	Tuam . .	IV.	7
23	Baunoulagh . .	53 3 12	Cork, E.R. .	Duhallow . .	Castlemagner .	Kanturk . .	II.	67
114	Baunragh . .	26 2 1	Galway . .	Kiltartan . .	Kiltartan . .	Gort . .	IV.	48
11, 15	Baunreagh . .	712 2 20	Carlow . .	Idrone West .	Oldleighlin . .	Carlow . .	I.	9
39, 40	Baunreagh . .	76 0 21	Cork, W.R. .	West Muskerry .	Kilcorney . .	Millstreet .	II.	158
26	Baunreagh . .	6 2 24	Kilkenny . .	Callan . .	Callan . .	Callan . .	I.	83
30	Baunreagh . .	175 0 10	Kilkenny . .	Kells . .	Kilmaganny .	Callan . .	I.	109
34	Baunreagh . .	153 0 32	Kilkenny . .	Kells . .	Tullahought .	Callan . .	I.	110
27	Baunreagh . .	158 2 33	Kilkenny . .	Shillelogher .	Stonecarthy .	Thomastown .	I.	115
19	Baunreagh . .	151 2 27	Kilkenny . .	Shillelogher .	St. Patrick's .	Kilkenny . .	I.	116
10,11,19,20	Baunreagh . .	117 2 15	Limerick . .	Connello Lower .	Askeaton . .	Rathkeale .	II.	226
6, 11	Baunreagh . .	1,834 0 23	Queen's Co. .	Upperwoods .	Offerlane . .	Mountmellick .	I.	251
18	Baunree . .	90 0 29	Queen's Co. .	Cullenagh . .	Ballyroan . .	Abbeyleix .	I.	239
18	Baunree . .	111 3 34	Queen's Co. .	Cullenagh . .	Fossy or Timahoe .	Abbeyleix .	I.	240
8	Baunrickeen .	119 3 39	Kilkenny . .	Galmoy . .	Fertagh . .	Urlingford .	I.	92
22	*Baunrosmore* .	9 2 53	Mayo . .	Tirawley . .	Killala . .	Killala . .	IV.	170
52	Baunskeha . .	909 2 13	Kilkenny . .	Gowran . .	Jerpoint West .	Thomastown .	I.	96
32	BAUNSKEHA T. .	—	Kilkenny . .	Gowran . .	Jerpoint West .	Thomastown .	I.	96
26	Baunta . .	90 3 7	Kilkenny . .	Callan . .	Callan . .	Callan . .	I.	83
25	Bauntabarna . .	75 3 13	Kilkenny . .	Gowran . .	Graiguenamanagh .	Thomastown .	I.	95
26	Baunta Commons .	418 1 23	Kilkenny . .	Callan . .	Callan . .	Callan . .	I.	83
50	Baunteen . .	431 1 28	Limerick . .	Coshlea . .	Galbally . .	Mitchelstown .	II.	238
126, 132	Bauntia . .	203 2 13	Galway . .	Leitrim . .	Ballynakill .	Portumna .	IV.	50
32	Bauntlieve . .	285 1 30	Clare . .	Inchiquin . .	Inagh . .	Ennistimon .	II.	25
116	Baunyknav . .	148 0 15	Galway . .	Leitrim . .	Ballynakill .	Loughrea .	IV.	50
19,20,27,28	Bauragegaun . .	769 3 32	Clare . .	Tulla Upper .	Feakle . .	Scarriff . .	II.	38
26, 32	Bauraglanna . .	1,355 3 23	Tipperary, N.R.	Owney and Arra .	Killoscully . .	Nenagh . .	II.	295
6, 7	Bauragoogeen . .	391 2 29	Kerry . .	Iraghticonnor .	Murher . .	Glin . .	II.	193
27	Bauraneag . .	691 1 19	Limerick . .	Shanid . .	Dunmoylan .	Newcastle .	II.	255
132	Bauravilla . .	579 0 38	Cork, W.R. .	West Carbery (W.D.)	Caheragh . .	Skibbereen .	II.	142
101, 102) 109, 110)	Baurearagh . .	1,966 0 37	Kerry . .	Glanarought .	Kilcaskan . .	Kenmare . .	II.	186
84	Baurearagh . .	750 1 2	Kerry . .	Glanarought .	Kilgarvan . .	Kenmare . .	II.	187
26	Baurela . .	122 2 10	Wexford . .	Ballaghkeen .	Ballyhuskard .	Enniscorthy .	I.	291
119	Baurgarriff . .	167 0 0	Cork, W.R. .	West Carbery (E.D.)	Dromdaleague .	Skibbereen .	II.	139
118	Baurgorm . .	613 3 5	Cork, W.R. .	West Carbery (W.D.)	Kilmocomoge .	Bantry . .	II.	144
110, 123	Baurleigh . .	885 0 37	Cork, W.R. .	East Carbery (E.D.)	Kilbrittain .	Bandon . .	II.	128
38	Baurnadomeeny .	1,270 1 24	Tipperary, N.R.	Owney and Arra .	Abington . .	Nenagh . .	II.	293
15	Baurnafea . .	1,159 1 14	Kilkenny . .	Gowran . .	Shankill . .	Kilkenny . .	I.	99
49, 57, 58	Baurnagurrahy .	398 0 3	Limerick . .	Coshlea . .	Galbally . .	Mitchelstown .	II.	238
119, 120	Baurnahulla .	746 3 32	Cork, W.R. .	West Carbery (E.D.)	Dromdaleague .	Skibbereen .	II.	139

(a) Including 63A. 0R. 38P. water. (b) Including 19A. 0R. 0P. water. (c) Including 28A. 3R. 13P. water.

No. of Sheet of the Ordnance Survey Maps.	Townlands and Towns.	Area in Statute Acres.	County.	Barony.	Parish.	Poor Law Union in 1857.	Townland Census of 1851. Part I.	
		A. R. P.					Vol.	Page
21	Baurnalicka . .	449 3 3	Limerick . .	Connello Upper .	Adare . . .	Rathkeale .	II.	230
5, 9	Baur North . .	123 3 25	Clare . .	Burren . .	Kilcorney . .	Ballyvaghan .	II.	12
20, 28	Baurroe . .	440 2 36	Clare . .	Tulla Upper . .	Feakle . .	Scarriff .	II.	38
28	Baurroe . .	331 1 14	Tipperary, N.R.	Upper Ormond .	Latteragh . .	Nenagh .	II.	292
28	BAURROE T. . .	—	Clare . .	Tulla Upper . .	Feakle . .	Scarriff .	II.	40
5, 9	Baur South . .	111 3 25	Clare . .	Burren . .	Kilcorney . .	Ballyvaghan .	II.	12
60	Baurstookeen . .	34 0 30	Tipperary, S.R.	Clanwilliam .	Relickmurry & Athassel	Tipperary .	II.	310
84, 85	Bausheen . .	701 3 3	Kerry . .	Glanarought . .	Kilgarvan . .	Kenmare .	II.	187
18, 19	Bauteogue . .	159 3 9	Queen's Co. .	Stradbally . .	Dysartenos . .	Athy .	I.	247
104	Bauttagh . .	43 1 12	Galway . .	Dunkellin . .	Killogilleen . .	Loughrea .	IV.	31
29	Bauville Keeloges and Clonglash .	727 3 22	Donegal . .	Inishowen West .	Fahan Lower . .	Inishowen .	III.	120
96, 97	Bavan . .	395 1 17	Donegal . .	Banagh . .	Kilcar . .	Glenties .	III.	108
47	Bavan . .	455 1 4	Down . .	Upper Iveagh, Up.pt.	Clonallan . .	Newry .	III.	174
4, 5	Bavan . .	514 1 35	Louth . .	Lower Dundalk .	Carlingford . .	Dundalk .	I.	176
37, 41	Bawn . .	121 1 3	Cavan . .	Clanmahon . .	Drumlumman .	Granard .	III.	76
19	Bawn . .	142 1 30a	Cavan . .	Tullyhunco . .	Killashandra .	Cavan .	III.	97
116	Bawn . .	205 1 6	Cork, W.R. .	Bear . .	Kilcaskan . .	Castletown .	II.	122
27	Bawn . .	127 3 22	Kildare . .	Offaly West . .	Harristown . .	Athy .	I.	72
14	Bawn . .	145 1 28	Leitrim . .	Drumahaire . .	Killanummery .	Manorhamilton	IV.	97
8, 9	Bawn . .	381 0 9	Longford . .	Longford . .	Killoe . .	Longford .	I.	158
18, 19	Bawn . .	538 3 2	Longford . .	Moydow . .	Moydow . .	Longford .	I.	162
14, 15	Bawn . .	220 3 6	Louth . .	Louth . .	Mansfieldstown .	Ardee .	I.	185
118	Bawn . .	109 3 38	Mayo . .	Kilmaine . .	Ballinrobe . .	Ballinrobe .	IV.	152
11	Bawn . .	234 2 22	Meath . .	Lower Kells . .	Moynalty . .	Kells .	I.	203
14	Bawn . .	338 2 34	Queen's Co. .	Stradbally . .	Curraclone . .	Athy .	I.	246
20, 26	Bawn . .	346 2 17	Tipperary, N.R.	Upper Ormond .	Kilmore . .	Nenagh .	II.	291
20	Bawn . .	145 3 33	Tipperary, N.R.	Upper Ormond .	Nenagh . .	Nenagh .	II.	292
16	Bawn . .	55 3 8	Westmeath .	Kilkenny West .	Noughaval . .	Ballymahon	I.	274
31	Bawnabraher .	18 3 39	Waterford .	Decies without Drum	Dungarvan . .	Dungarvan .	II.	355
36	Bawnacarrigaun .	63 0 5	Waterford .	Decies without Drum	Dungarvan . .	Dungarvan .	II.	355
10	Bawnachaulig .	194 0 5	Kerry . .	Iraghticonnor .	Dysert . .	Listowel .	II.	190
38	Bawnacommera .	110 2 1	Waterford .	Decies within Drum	Lisgenan or Grange	Youghal .	II.	352
22	Bawnacouma .	227 0 24	Limerick . .	Smallcounty . .	Kilpeacon . .	Croom .	II.	260
66	Bawnadoune .	104 2 7	Cork, E.R. .	Imokilly . .	Dungourney . .	Middleton .	II.	86
29	Bawnagappul .	57 0 39	Waterford .	Coshmore&Coshbride	Lismore and Mocollop	Lismore .	II.	345
38	Bawnagarrane .	257 0 6	Waterford .	Decies within Drum	Lisgenan or Grange	Youghal .	II.	352
48	Bawnagh . .	140 2 3	Limerick . .	Coshlea . .	Kilbreedy Major .	Kilmallock .	II.	239
49, 59	Bawnaglanna .	498 0 5	Kerry . .	Trughanacmy .	Killeentierna .	Killarney .	II.	211
112	Bawnagoynig . .	104 2 17	Cork, E.R. .	Kinalea . .	Kinure . .	Kinsale .	II.	95
31	Bawnahila . .	29 0 0	Waterford .	Decies without Drum	Kilrush . .	Dungarvan .	II.	358
20	Bawnakey . .	150 1 32	Tipperary, N.R.	Owney and Arra .	Youghalarra .	Nenagh .	II.	297
131, 140	Bawnaknockane .	297 1 0	Cork, W.R. .	West Carbery (W.D.)	Skull . .	Skull .	II.	145
41	Bawnanattin .	34 0 37	Tipperary, N.R.	Eliogarty . .	Thurles . .	Thurles .	II.	273
19	Bawnanearla .	58 3 33	Cork, E.R. .	Condons&Clangibbon	Kilphelan . .	Mitchelstown .	II.	62
22	Bawnaneel .	165 0 7	Cork, E.R. .	Duhallow . .	Kilmeen . .	Kanturk .	II.	72
102, 115	Bawnard . .	156 3 0	Cork, W.R. .	Bear . .	Kilcatherine . .	Castletown .	II.	123
60	Bawnard . .	541 0 33	Kerry . .	Magunihy . .	Nohavaldaly .	Killarney .	II.	205
38	Bawnard . .	50 1 14	Waterford .	Decies within Drum	Lisgenan or Grange	Youghal .	II.	352
2	Bawnard . .	134 0 27b	Waterford .	Upperthird . .	Killaloan . .	Clonmel .	II.	370
76	Bawnard East .	142 1 3	Cork, E.R. .	Imokilly . .	Middleton . .	Middleton .	II.	89
76	Bawnard West .	207 1 32	Cork, E.R. .	Imokilly . .	Middleton . .	Middleton .	II.	89
17	Bawnaree .	178 2 18	Queen's Co. .	Maryborough West .	Clonenagh and Clonagheen	Abbeyleix .	I.	242
40, 49	Bawnaskehy .	514 0 3	Kerry . .	Trughanacmy .	Castleisland .	Tralee .	II.	208
59	Bawnatanaknock .	382 3 22	Cork, W.R. .	West Muskerry .	Clondrohid . .	Macroom .	II.	155
31	Bawnatanavoher .	27 0 36	Waterford .	Decies without Drum	Kilrush . .	Dungarvan .	II.	358
69	Bawnatanvoher .	25 0 18	Tipperary, S.R.	Middlethird .	Kilbragh . .	Cashel .	II.	327
71	Bawnatemple .	181 1 37	Cork, E.R. .	East Muskerry .	Cannaway . .	Macroom .	II.	102
112, 115	Bawnavota . .	233 0 28c	Cork, E.R. .	Kinsale . .	Ringcurran . .	Kinsale .	II.	100
63	Bawnavrona Lower .	236 3 11	Tipperary, S.R.	Slievardagh . .	Kilvemnon . .	Callan .	II.	334
63	Bawnavrona Upper .	173 1 4	Tipperary, S.R.	Slievardagh . .	Kilvemnon . .	Callan .	II.	334
9	Bawnboy . .	336 1 29	Cavan . .	Tullyhaw . .	Templeport . .	Bawnboy .	III.	93
119	Bawnboy . .	257 3 5	Cork, W.R. .	West Carbery (W.D.)	Caheragh . .	Skibbereen .	II.	142
29	Bawnboy . .	291 3 36	Kerry . .	Trughanacmy .	Clogherbrien .	Tralee .	II.	209
9	BAWNBOY T. .	—	Cavan . .	Tullyhaw . .	Templeport . .	Bawnboy .	III.	96
68	Bawnbrack . .	168 2 22	Tipperary, S.R.	Clanwilliam . .	Relickmurry & Athassel	Tipperary .	II.	310
20	Bawnbrack . .	22 1 3	Waterford .	Coshmore&Coshbride	Lismore and Mocollop	Lismore .	II.	345
2, 5	Bawnbreakey .	175 1 36d	Meath . .	Lower Kells . .	Moybolgue . .	Kells .	I.	203
9	Bawndaw . .	63 2 28	Waterford .	Middlethird . .	Killoteran . .	Waterford .	II.	367
124	Bawnea . .	355 2 15	Cork, W.R. .	East Carbery (E.D.)	Ringrone . .	Kinsale .	II.	130
124	Bawnea . .	112 0 10	Cork, W.R. .	East Carbery (E.D.)	Templetrine . .	Kinsale .	II.	130
21, 22	Bawnfoun . .	187 3 26	Waterford .	Decies without Drum	Affane . .	Lismore .	II.	353

(a) Including 26A. 1R. 2P. water.   (c) Including 1A. 2R. 17P. detached portion.
(b) Including 7A. 0R. 1P. water.   (d) Including 22A. 1R. 15P. water.

No. of Sheet of the Ordnance Survey Maps.	Townlands and Towns.	Area in Statute Acres.			County.	Barony.	Parish.	Poor Law Union in 1857.	Townland Census of 1851. Part I.	
		A.	R.	P.					Vol.	Page
133	Bawnfune	148	0	19	Cork, W.R.	West Carbery (E.D.)	Kilmacabea	Skibbereen	II.	140
1, 5	Bawnfune	631	1	16	Waterford	Glenahiry	Kilronan	Clonmel	II.	365
17	Bawnfune	285	1	37	Waterford	Middlethird	Kilburne	Waterford	II.	367
141, 150	Bawngare	141	0	26	Cork, W.R.	West Carbery (E.D.)	Aghadown	Skibbereen	II.	136
97	Bawngoula	13	3	32	Cork, E.R.	Kinalea	Dunderrow	Kinsale	II.	94
31	Bawnhubbamaddereen	77	0	12	Kilkenny	Kells	Dunnamaggan	Callan	I.	108
132	Bawnishal	365	2	18	Cork, W.R.	West Carbery(W.D.)	Caheragh	Skibbereen	II.	142
151	Bawnishall	385	3	23a	Cork, W.R.	West Carbery (E.D.)	Castlehaven	Skibbereen	II.	137
70	Bawnkeal	17	3	18	Tipperary, S.R.	Middlethird	Coolmundry	Cashel	II.	326
150	Bawnlahan	183	1	26	Cork, W.R.	West Carbery (E.D.)	Castlehaven	Skibbereen	II.	137
142	Bawnlahan	411	2	38	Cork, W.R.	West Carbery (E.D.)	Myross	Skibbereen	II.	141
34	Bawnlaur	102	3	38	Waterford	Coshmore&Coshbride	Kilcockan	Lismore	II.	343
49	Bawnlea	259	2	23	Tipperary, S.R.	Slievardagh	Kilcooly	Urlingford	II.	333
97	Bawnleigh	365	0	13	Cork, E.R.	Kinalea	Ballymartle	Kinsale	II.	94
40	Bawnluskaha	132	2	4	Kerry	Trughanacmy	Castleisland	Tralee	II.	208
70	Bawnmacshane	17	1	9	Tipperary, S.R.	Middlethird	Cloneen	Cashel	II.	325
17, 18, 23, 24	Bawnmadrum	347	3	17	Tipperary, N.R.	Ikerrin	Bourney	Roscrea	II.	274
17, 18	Bawnmadrum North	301	1	23	Tipperary, N.R.	Ikerrin	Bourney	Roscrea	II.	274
67	Bawnmore	41	1	31	Cork, E.R.	Imokilly	Youghal	Youghal	II.	91
59, 60	Bawnmore	515	1	22	Cork, W.R.	West Muskerry	Clondrohid	Macroom	II.	155
14, 20	Bawnmore	578	1	3	Kerry	Clanmaurice	Kilmoyly	Tralee	II.	171
26	Bawnmore	247	2	28	King's Co.	Geashill	Geashill	Tullamore	I.	140
10	Bawnmore	154	3	31	Tipperary, N.R.	Lower Ormond	Uskane	Borrisokane	II.	288
52	Bawnmore	569	1	10	Tipperary, S.R.	Middlethird	Ardmayle	Cashel	II.	324
21, 29	Bawnmore	63	2	28	Waterford	Coshmore&Coshbride	Lismore and Mocollop	Lismore	II.	345
29	Bawnmore	101	2	16	Wexford	Bantry	St. Mary's	New Ross	I.	302
15	Bawnmore North	443	1	35	Cork, E.R.	Duhallow	Kilbrin	Kanturk	II.	72
15	Bawnmore South	729	1	1	Cork, E.R.	Duhallow	Kilbrin	Kanturk	II.	72
42	Bawnmore or Stone-park	101	1	5	Galway	Clare	Donaghpatrick	Tuam	IV.	19
19	Bawn Mountain	283	1	28	Longford	Moydow	Moydow	Longford	I.	162
73	Bawnnafinny	143	2	12	Cork, E.R.	East Muskerry	Carrigrohanebeg	Cork	II.	102
62, 73	Bawnnafinny	80	2	22b	Cork, E.R.	East Muskerry	Garrycloyne	Cork	II.	103
36	Bawnnaglogh	81	2	16	Cork, E.R.	Condons&Clangibbon	Clondulane	Fermoy	II.	60
142	Bawnnagollopy	134	1	4	Cork, W.R.	West Carbery (E.D.)	Abbeystrowry	Skibbereen	II.	136
142, 151	Bawnnagollopy	53	2	16	Cork, W.R.	West Carbery (E.D.)	Castlehaven	Skibbereen	II.	137
132	Bawnnahow North	229	0	32	Cork, W.R.	West Carbery (E.D.)	Dromdaleague	Skibbereen	II.	139
132	Bawnnahow South	207	1	28	Cork, W.R.	West Carbery (E.D.)	Dromdaleague	Skibbereen	II.	139
22, 30	Bawnavinnoge	235	0	21	Waterford	Decies without Drum	Modelligo	Lismore	II.	359
24	Bawnoge	263	2	26	Kildare	Naas South	Tipperkevin	Naas	I.	65
16	Bawnoge	273	0	20	Wicklow	Lower Talbotstown	Boystown	Baltinglass	I.	359
26, 27	Bawnoge	206	1	25	Wicklow	Upper Talbotstown	Baltinglass	Baltinglass	I.	362
28	Bawnoge	146	2	24	Wicklow	Upper Talbotstown	Kiltegan	Baltinglass	I.	364
17	Bawnoges	28	0	15	Dublin	Uppercross	Clondalkin	Dublin South	I.	39
10, 14	Bawnoges	230	3	17	Kildare	North Salt	Straffan	Celbridge	I.	75
30, 31	Bawnoges	171	1	6c	Westmeath	Clonlonan	Kilmanaghan	Athlone	I.	262
42, 48	Bawnreagh	436	2	6	Tipperary, S.R.	Slievardagh	Buolick	Urlingford	II.	332
71	Bawnrickard	211	3	8	Tipperary, S.R.	Slievardagh	Kilvemnon	Callan	II.	334
131, 140	Bawnshanaclogh	194	0	18	Cork, W.R.	West Carbery(W.D.)	Skull	Skull	II.	145
21	Bawntaaffe	280	1	28	Louth	Ferrard	Monasterboice	Drogheda	I.	181
41	Bawntameena	131	2	13	Tipperary, N.R.	Eliogarty	Thurles	Thurles	II.	273
13	Bawntanameenagh	110	1	6	Kilkenny	Crannagh	Freshford	Kilkenny	I.	85
48	Bawntard North	205	3	21	Limerick	Kilmallock	St. Peter's & St. Paul's	Kilmallock	II.	250
48	Bawntard South	142	1	16	Limerick	Kilmallock	St. Peter's & St. Paul's	Kilmallock	II.	250
31	Bawn or Williams-town	265	2	13	Meath	Lower Navan	Ardsallagh	Navan	I.	214
20	Bay	203	0	6	Antrim	Lower Glenarm	Ardclinis	Larne	III.	21
25, 29	Bay	461	1	36	Antrim	Lower Glenarm	Tickmacrevan	Larne	III.	23
13, 14	Bay	188	3	36	Dublin	Castleknock	Mulhuddart	Dublin North	I.	25
10	Baybush	196	3	32	Kildare	North Salt	Straffan	Celbridge	I.	75
10	Baybush	70	0	5	Kildare	North Salt	Taghadoe	Celbridge	I.	76
45	Bayhill	58	3	15	Donegal	Kilmacrenan	Tullyfern	Milford	III.	132
10, 15, 16	Bayland	299	2	11	Wexford	Scarawalsh	Ferns	Enniscorthy	I.	323
40, 45	Baylestown	236	2	9	Wexford	Shelburne	Tintern	New Ross	I.	329
38, 47	Baylet	265	0	14	Donegal	Inishowen West	Inch	Londonderry	III.	121
22	Baynanagh	131	3	22	Tipperary, N.R.	Upper Ormond	Aghnameadle	Nenagh	II.	288
19	Baysland	71	2	5	Kildare	South Salt	Haynestown	Naas	I.	77
31	Baysrath	222	2	16	Kilkenny	Kells	Dunnamaggan	Callan	I.	108
31	Baysrath	4	1	22	Kilkenny	Knocktopher	Dunnamaggan	Thomastown	I.	111
7, 8	Bayswell	620	2	21	Kilkenny	Galmoy	Erke	Urlingford	I.	92
45, 51	Baytown	356	3	4d	Meath	Dunboyne	Kilbride	Dunshaughlin	I.	200
50	Baytownpark	323	2	24	Meath	Dunboyne	Dunboyne	Dunshaughlin	I.	199
21	Beabus	270	2	19	Limerick	Coshma	Drehidtarsna	Croom	II.	242

(a) Including 4A. 2R. 17P. detached portion.
(b) Including 5A. 0R. 23P. water.

(c) Including 9A. 0R. 20P. water.
(d) Including 58A. 2R. 16P. detached portion.

No. of Sheet of the Ordnance Survey Maps.	Townlands and Towns.	Area in Statute Acres.			County.	Barony.	Parish.	Poor Law Union in 1857.	Townland Census of 1851, Part I.	
		A.	R.	P.					Vol.	Page
118	Beach	317	2	27	Cork, W.R.	Bantry	Kilmocomoge	Bantry	II.	119
37	Beaconstown	522	2	18	Kildare	Kilkea and Moone	Kilkea	Athy	I.	60
73	Beagh	380	2	18	Donegal	Boylagh	Inishkeel	Glenties	III.	112
23	Beagh	175	2	14a	Fermanagh	Tirkennedy	Enniskillen	Enniskillen	III.	221
16, 17	Beagh	503	0	22	Fermanagh	Tirkennedy	Magheracross	Enniskillen	III.	223
5, 6	Beagh	629	1	5b	Galway	Ballymoe	Templetogher	Glennamaddy	IV.	9
15,16,28,29	Beagh	650	1	3	Galway	Dunmore	Kilconla	Tuam	IV.	35
123, 129	Beagh	331	3	18	Galway	Kiltartan	Beagh	Gort	IV.	46
39, 43	Beagh	666	3	23	King's Co.	Ballybritt	Roscomroe	Parsonstown	I.	126
15, 17	Beagh	725	0	22	Leitrim	Drumahaire	Killanummery	Manorhamilton	IV.	97
3	Beagh	256	1	0	Limerick	Kenry	Iveruss	Rathkeale	II.	248
27	Beagh	311	0	36c	Monaghan	Cremorne	Aghnamullen	Castleblayney	III.	257
28	Beagh	130	0	34	Monaghan	Farney	Donaghmoyne	Carrickmacross	III.	269
30	Beagh	174	3	29d	Monaghan	Farney	Magheracloone	Carrickmacross	III.	272
28, 31	Beagh	152	1	33	Monaghan	Farney	Magheross	Carrickmacross	III.	273
9, 13	Beagh	82	0	2	Monaghan	Monaghan	Monaghan	Monaghan	III.	276
26, 27	Beagh	413	0	8	Roscommon	Castlereagh	Kilkeevin	Castlereagh	IV.	200
64	Beagh	109	1	20	Tyrone	Clogher	Aghalurcher	Clogher	III.	291
51	Beagh	445	1	6	Tyrone	Omagh East	Clogherny	Omagh	III.	310
35, 43	Beagh	291	1	20e	Tyrone	Omagh East	Drumragh	Omagh	III.	312
10	Beagh	386	3	19	Tyrone	Strabane Lower	Ardstraw	Strabane	III.	318
64	Beagha	847	1	26f	Galway	Ballynahinch	Moyrus	Clifden	IV.	12
29, 30	Beaghbaun	107	3	32	Galway	Dunmore	Dunmore	Tuam	IV.	33
28, 42	Beagh Beg	362	0	32	Galway	Clare	Donaghpatrick	Tuam	IV.	19
30, 34	Beagh Beg	265	1	4	Leitrim	Carrigallen	Carrigallen	Mohill	IV.	89
54	Beaghbeg	101	1	5	Roscommon	Moycarn	Creagh	Ballinasloe	IV.	206
28	Beaghbeg	307	2	36	Tyrone	Dungannon Upper	Kildress	Cookstown	III.	308
15	Beagh Big	153	0	14	Fermanagh	Magheraboy	Inishmacsaint	Enniskillen	III.	212
53, 54	Beagh (Brabazon)	446	2	19	Roscommon	Moycarn	Creagh	Ballinasloe	IV.	206
30	Beagh (Browne)	97	0	19	Galway	Dunmore	Dunmore	Tuam	IV.	33
35, 36, 49	Beaghcauneen	664	3	35g	Galway	Ballynahinch	Ballindoon	Clifden	IV.	10
30	Beagh (Donnellan)	111	3	29	Galway	Dunmore	Dunmore	Tuam	IV.	33
33	Beagh Glebe	654	1	34	Cavan	Castlerahan	Killinkere	Bailieborough	III.	68
129	Beagh Island	4	2	8	Galway	Kiltartan	Beagh	Gort	IV.	46
13	Beagh (Kearns)	118	1	3h	Monaghan	Monaghan	Monaghan	Monaghan	III.	276
15	Beagh Little	118	3	17i	Fermanagh	Magheraboy	Inishmacsaint	Enniskillen	III.	212
66	Beaghmore	607	1	11j	Donegal	Boylagh	Inishkeel	Glenties	III.	112
28, 42	Beagh More	2,316	2	11k	Galway	Clare	Donaghpatrick	Tuam	IV.	19
30, 34	Beagh More	545	2	29l	Leitrim	Carrigallen	Carrigallen	Mohill	IV.	89
20, 28	Beagh-more	1,883	1	37	Tyrone	Dungannon Upper	Kildress	Cookstown	III.	308
53, 54	Beagh (Naghten)	33	2	27	Roscommon	Moycarn	Creagh	Ballinasloe	IV.	206
28	Beagho	146	0	13	Fermanagh	Tirkennedy	Cleenish	Enniskillen	III.	219
29	Beaghroe	39	3	24	Galway	Dunmore	Dunmore	Tuam	IV.	33
29, 30	Beaghroe	135	0	14	Galway	Dunmore	Tuam	Tuam	IV.	35
14, 19	Beaghs	4,343	1	35	Antrim	Lower Glenarm	Grange of Layd	Ballycastle	III.	22
36	Beagh (Spiritual)	238	3	24	Londonderry	Loughinsholin	Maghera	Magherafelt	III.	242
32	Beagh (Temporal)	302	2	24	Londonderry	Loughinsholin	Maghera	Magherafelt	III.	242
54	Beagh (Trench)	121	0	16	Roscommon	Moycarn	Creagh	Ballinasloe	IV.	206
20, 21	Beaghy	187	3	15m	Cavan	Upper Loughtee	Annagelliff	Cavan	III.	81
26	Beaghy	454	1	18n	Cavan	Upper Loughtee	Lavey	Cavan	III.	85
14	Beaghy	150	2	38	Clare	Corcomroe	Kilmacrehy	Ennistimon	II.	20
78	Beaghy Island	9	2	18	Galway	Ballynahinch	Moyrus	Clifden	IV.	13
78	Beaghy North	6	3	24	Galway	Ballynahinch	Moyrus	Clifden	IV.	13
52	Beak	68	0	12	Wexford	Bargy	Kilmore	Wexford	I.	306
'148	Beakeen	99	1	34	Cork, W.R.	West Carbery (W.D.)	Skull	Skull	II.	145
41, 47	Beakstown	728	3	34	Tipperary, N.R.	Eliogarty	Holycross	Thurles	II.	270
38	Bealaclave	815	0	4	Tipperary, N.R.	Owney and Arra	Abington	Nenagh	II.	293
78	Bealadangan	998	1	17o	Galway	Moycullen	Killannin	Oughterard	IV.	69
121, 134	Beald East	445	2	10	Cork, W.R.	Ibane and Barryroe	Kilkerranmore	Clonakilty	II.	149
121, 134	Beald West	573	3	17	Cork, W.R.	Ibane and Barryroe	Kilkerranmore	Clonakilty	II.	149
27, 28	Bealady and Barny	264	3	5	Queen's Co.	Clandonagh	Rathdowney	Donaghmore	I.	234
38, 39	Bealagrellagh	72	3	13	Kerry	Trughanacmy	Ballymacelligott	Tralee	II.	206
17, 20	Bealalaw	553	2	4	Carlow	Forth	Myshall	Carlow	I.	5
32, 40	Bealcragga	869	2	37	Clare	Islands	Kilmaley	Ennis	II.	31
83	Bealdarrig	578	1	36	Kerry	Dunkerron North	Templenoe	Kenmare	II.	182
29	Bealduvroga	477	2	23	Limerick	Connello Lower	Rathkeale	Croom	II.	229
1, 2	Beal East	476	3	15	Kerry	Iraghticonnor	Kilconly	Listowel	II.	191
71	Bealick	361	3	14	Cork, W.R.	West Muskerry	Macroom	Macroom	II.	160
17	Bealickania	108	0	21	Clare	Inchiquin	Ruan	Corrofin	II.	28
10, 16	Bealkelly	173	3	28p	Kerry	Clanmaurice	Finuge	Listowel	II.	169
29	Bealkelly (Eyre)	201	2	9	Clare	Tulla Lower	Ogonnelloe	Scarriff	II.	38
29, 37	Bealkelly (Purdon)	862	3	16	Clare	Tulla Lower	Ogonnelloe	Scarriff	II.	38
8	Beallough	447	3	8	Waterford	Upperthird	Guilcagh	Carrick on Suir	II.	370

(a) Including 3A. 0R. 28P. water.
(b) Including 10A. 2R. 32P. water.
(c) Including 13A. 3R. 12P. water.
(d) Including 20A. 0R. 1P. water.
(e) Including 1A. 1R. 22P. water.
(f) Including 12A. 0R. 22P. water.

(g) Including 72A. 3R. 34P. water.
(h) Including 6A. 1R. 8P. water.
(i) Including 5A. 0R. 0P. water.
(j) Including 29A. 3R. 32P. water.
(k) Including 49A. 1R. 18P. water.

(l) Including 28A. 2R. 22P. water.
(m) Including 5A. 2R. 21P. Beaghy Lough.
(n) Including 7A. 1R. 29P. water.
(o) Including 26A. 3R. 16P. water.
(p) Including 11A. 1R. 31P. water.

No. of Sheet of the Ordnance Survey Maps	Townlands and Towns.	Area in Statute Acres.			County.	Barony.	Parish.	Poor Law Union in 1857.	Townland Census of 1851, Part I.	
		A.	R.	P.					Vol.	Page
1	Beal Middle . .	184	3	3	Kerry . .	Iraghticonnor .	Kilconly . .	Listowel . .	II.	191
54	Bealnalappa . .	31	1	32	Galway . .	Moycullen .	Kilcummin .	Oughterard .	IV.	66
25	Bealnalicka . .	389	3	17a	Clare . .	Inchiquin .	Ruan . .	Corrofin . .	II.	28
17	Bealragh . .	398	0	32	Roscommon .	Roscommon .	Aughrim .	Carᵗ.on Shannon	IV.	207
1	Beal West . .	141	1	16	Kerry . .	Iraghticonnor .	Kilconly . .	Listowel . .	II.	191
67, 78	Beanfield . .	274	2	34	Cork, E.R. .	Imokilly . .	Clonpriest .	Youghal . .	II.	84
20	Beanfield . .	63	2	6	Sligo . .	Carbury . .	Kilmacowen .	Sligo . .	IV.	222
122	Beanhill North .	108	3	10	Cork, W.R. .	East Carbery (E.D.)	Kilnagross .	Clonakilty .	II.	129
122	Beanhill South .	134	3	39	Cork, W.R. .	East Carbery (E.D.)	Kilnagross .	Clonakilty .	II.	129
6	Beardiville . .	213	2	33	Antrim . .	Lower Dunluce .	Ballywillin .	Coleraine .	III.	15
33	Bearforest Lower .	104	0	14	Cork, E.R. .	Fermoy . .	Mallow . .	Mallow . .	II.	81
33	Bearforest Upper .	121	2	24	Cork, E.R. .	Fermoy . .	Mallow . .	Mallow . .	II.	81
39	Bearlough . .	245	1	23	Sligo . .	Corran . .	Drumrat . .	Boyle . .	IV.	225
43	Bearlough . .	137	0	17	Wexford . .	Forth . .	Rosslare . .	Wexford . .	I.	313
26	Bearnafunshin .	342	3	38b	Clare . .	Bunratty Upper .	Kilraghtis .	Ennis . .	II.	9
10	Bearney Glebe .	612	3	35c	Tyrone . .	Strabane Lower .	Camus . .	Strabane . .	III.	320
39	Bearvaish . .	257	3	18	Sligo . .	Corran . .	Drumrat . .	Boyle . .	IV.	225
34, 35	Beatin . .	182	2	30	Kilkenny .	Iverk . .	Owning . .	Carrick on Suir	I.	106
8	Beau . .	76	2	29	Dublin . .	Balrothery East .	Lusk . .	Balrothery .	I.	20
4, 5	Beaufield . .	280	1	4	Wexford . .	Scarawalsh .	Moyacomb .	Shillelagh .	I.	325
65	Beaufort . .	171	3	12d	Kerry . .	Dunkerron North .	Knockane .	Killarney .	II.	181
98	Beaugreen Glebe .	120	0	38	Donegal . .	Banagh . .	Killaghtee .	Donegal . .	III.	109
25	Beaulieu . .	464	0	18e	Louth . .	Ferrard . .	Beaulieu . .	Drogheda . .	I.	180
14	Beaumont . .	86	1	37	Dublin . .	Coolock . .	Coolock . .	Dublin North .	I.	27
27	Beaumont . .	31	2	16	Meath . .	Lower Duleek .	Duleek . .	Drogheda . .	I.	195
27	Beaumont . .	174	0	20	Meath . .	Upper Duleek .	Duleek . .	Drogheda . .	I.	197
8, 12	Beaverstown .	444	3	1	Dublin . .	Nethercross .	Portraine .	Balrothery .	I.	31
28	Beckfield . .	267	3	20	Queen's Co. .	Clandonagh .	Rathdowney .	Donaghmore .	I.	234
28	Beckfield North .	5	0	17	Queen's Co. .	Clandonagh .	Bordwell . .	Donaghmore .	I.	233
28	Beckfield South .	4	3	39	Queen's Co. .	Clarmallagh .	Bordwell . .	Donaghmore .	I.	237
34	Beckscourt . .	75	3	20	Cavan . .	Clankee . .	Bailieborough .	Bailieborough .	III.	71
47	Beckville . .	30	2	32	Wexford . .	Bargy . .	Kilcowan .	Wexford . .	I.	305
31	Bective . .	521	1	36f	Meath . .	Upper Navan .	Bective . .	Navan . .	I.	216
31, 37	Bective or Ballina .	170	1	34g	Meath . .	Lower Deece .	Balsoon . .	Trim . .	I.	191
43, 44	Bedfanstown .	104	1	24	Meath . .	Lower Deece .	Knockmark .	Dunshaughlin .	I.	192
10, 11	Bedford . .	943	1	15	Kerry . .	Iraghticonnor .	Galey . .	Listowel . .	II.	190
21	Bedlesshill . .	38	0	31	Dublin . .	Uppercross .	Clondalkin .	Dublin South .	I.	39
85, 86	Beech Hill . .	580	0	27	Galway . .	Kilconnell .	Grange . .	Loughrea .	IV.	40
29	BeechmountDemesne	249	3	39h	Limerick . .	Connello Lower .	Rathkeale .	Rathkeale .	II.	229
15	Beechwood . .	242	2	13	Dublin . .	Coolock . .	Portmarnock .	Balrothery .	I.	28
80	Beefan . .	112	1	22	Donegal . .	Banagh . .	Glencolumbkille .	Glenties . .	III.	105
80	Beefan and Garveross Mountain .	228	0	5	Donegal . .	Banagh . .	Glencolumbkille .	Glenties . .	III.	105
86	Beefield . .	42	3	25	Galway . .	Kilconnell .	Killaan . .	Ballinasloe .	IV.	41
99	Beefpark . .	53	0	19	Donegal . .	Banagh . .	Killymard .	Donegal . .	III.	111
41, 50	Beenalaght .	488	0	0	Cork, E.R. .	Duhallow .	Kilshannig .	Mallow . .	II.	74
48,49,58,59	Beenateevaun .	494	2	0	Kerry . .	Trughanacmy .	Killeentierna .	Killarney .	II.	211
53	Beenbane . .	235	2	2	Kerry . .	Corkaguiny .	Garfinny . .	Dingle . .	II.	176
98	Beenbane . .	264	2	8	Kerry . .	Iveragh . .	Dromod . .	Cahersiveen .	II.	194
22	Beennageeha .	364	2	30	Kerry . .	Trughanacmy .	O'Brennan .	Tralee . .	II.	212
10	Beennameclane .	171	1	9	Kerry . .	Iraghticonnor .	Dysert . .	Listowel . .	II.	190
41, 50	Beennanweel East .	506	3	1	Cork, E.R. .	Duhallow .	Kilshannig .	Mallow . .	II.	74
41, 50	Beennanweel West .	419	1	36	Cork, E.R. .	Duhallow .	Kilshannig .	Mallow . .	II.	74
11, 12	Beennanaspuck .	580	0	30	Kerry . .	Iraghticonnor .	Knockanure .	Listowel . .	II.	192
34, 43	Beennaskehy .	349	2	13	Cork, E.R. .	Fermoy . .	Monanimy .	Mallow . .	II.	81
40	Beenreagh . .	255	2	35	Cork, W.R. .	West Muskerry .	Kilcorney .	Millstreet .	II.	158
12	Beerhill . .	62	3	5	Antrim . .	Lower Dunluce .	Derrykeighan .	Ballymoney .	III.	16
67	Beetle Island North .	2	0	9	Mayo . .	Burrishoole .	Burrishoole .	Newport . .	IV.	120
67	Beetle Island South .	1	2	35	Mayo . .	Burrishoole .	Burrishoole .	Newport . .	IV.	120
63	Beeverstown .	370	3	32	Tipperary, S.R.	Slievardagh .	Isertkieran .	Callan . .	II.	338
50, 51, 58	Befflaght . .	1,725	0	2i	Donegal . .	Boylagh . .	Lettermacward .	Glenties . .	III.	114
38	Begerin Island .	21	2	35	Wexford . .	Shelmaliere East .	St. Margaret's .	Wexford . .	I.	331
30, 35	Begerin (Lloyd) .	200	2	17	Wexford . .	Bantry . .	Oldross . .	New Ross . .	I.	301
29,30,34,35	Begerin (Loftus) .	359	0	37	Wexford . .	Bantry . .	Oldross . .	New Ross . .	I.	301
18	Beggarsbush . .	116	2	21	Dublin . .	Dublin . .	Donnybrook .	Dublin South .	I.	30
29, 30	Beggarstown .	156	1	37	King's Co. .	Garrycastle .	Lusmagh .	Parsonstown .	I.	137
50	Beggstown . .	173	0	26	Meath . .	Dunboyne .	Dunboyne .	Dunshaughlin .	I.	199
26, 33	Beggstown . .	81	3	12	Westmeath .	Fartullagh .	Kilbride . .	Mullingar .	II.	268
51	Beginish . .	32	2	18	Kerry . .	Corkaguiny .	Dunquin . .	Dingle . .	II.	176
79	Beginish . .	217	1	32	Kerry . .	Iveragh . .	Caher . .	Cahersiveen .	II.	193
27, 28	Beglieve . .	475	0	5	Cavan . .	Clankee . .	Knockbride .	Bailieborough .	III.	73
13	Begnagh . .	449	0	1	Longford .	Moydow . .	Killashee .	Longford . .	I.	161
28, 29	Begny . .	909	2	2j	Down . .	Lower Iveagh, Lr. pt.	Dromara . .	Lisburn . .	III.	167

(a) Including 0A. 1R. 34P. water.
(b) Including 20A. 0R. 8P. water.
(c) Including 2A. 0R. 4P. water.
(d) Including 10A. 3R. 23P. water.

(e) Including 9A. 0R. 16P. water.
(f) Including 13A. 3R. 26P. water.
(g) Including 6A. 0R. 36P. water.

(h) Including 3A. 3R. 33P. water.
(i) Including 67A. 3R. 32P. water.
(j) Including 30A. 0R. 27P. water.

U

No. of Sheet of the Ordnance Survey Maps.	Townlands and Towns.	Area in Statute Acres.			County.	Barony.	Parish.	Poor Law Union in 1857.	Townland Census of 1851, Part I.	
		A.	R.	P.					Vol.	Page
20, 21, 24	Begrath	521	3	36	Louth	Ferrard	Tullyallen	Drogheda	I.	183
6, 12	Begsreeve	174	1	3	Meath	Lower Slane	Siddan	Ardee	I.	223
2	Behabane	484	0	6a	Westmeath	Moygoish	Street	Granard	I.	281
3	Behagh	448	2	21	Clare	Burren	Oughtmama	Ballyvaghan	II.	14
108	Behagh	497	3	2	Cork, W.R.	East Carbery (W.D.)	Fanlobbus	Dunmanway	II.	131
98, 106, 107	Behaghane	737	1	16	Kerry	Dunkerron South	Kilcrohane	Cahersiveen	II.	183
17, 23	Behaghglass	363	2	26	Tipperary, N.R.	Ikerrin	Bourney	Roscrea	II.	274
94	Behagullane	810	3	25	Cork, W.R.	East Carbery (W.D.)	Fanlobbus	Dunmanway	II.	131
11	Behamore(Hawkshaw)	527	1	32	Tipperary, N.R.	Lower Ormond	Modreeny	Borrisokane	II.	286
11	Behamore (Smith)	643	2	2	Tipperary, N.R.	Lower Ormond	Modreeny	Borrisokane	II.	286
58, 60	Behanagh	320	1	27	Limerick	Coshlea	Kilbeheny	Mitchelstown	II.	239
60, 71	Beheena	255	0	35	Cork, W.R.	East Muskerry	Aghinagh	Macroom	II.	153
37, 46	Beheenagh	875	2	15	Kerry	Corkaguiny	Kilgobban	Tralee	II.	177
68	Beheenagh	269	1	13	Kerry	Magunihy	Kilcummin	Killarney	II.	201
23	Beheenagh	325	3	7	Kerry	Trughanacmy	Castleisland	Tralee	II.	208
30	Beheenagh	294	1	33	Kerry	Trughanacmy	O'Brennan	Tralee	II.	212
16, 17	Beheens East	244	1	32	Kerry	Clanmaurice	Kilshenane	Listowel	II.	171
16, 17	Beheens West	287	3	37	Kerry	Clanmaurice	Kilshenane	Listowel	II.	171
43	Behernagh	771	1	36	Cavan	Castlerahan	Munterconnaught	Oldcastle	III.	71
44	Behernagh	141	1	35	King's Co.	Clonlisk	Dunkerrin	Roscrea	I.	130
44	Behernagh Lower	89	2	28	Cork, E.R.	Barrymore	Rathcormack	Fermoy	II.	57
44	Behernagh Upper	186	2	5	Cork, E.R.	Barrymore	Rathcormack	Fermoy	II.	57
24, 30	Behy	334	3	17	Cavan	Tullyhunco	Killashandra	Cavan	III.	97
107	Behy	869	3	28b	Donegal	Tirhugh	Kilbarron	Ballyshannon	III.	148
29	Behy	292	0	34	Mayo	Tirawley	Crossmolina	Ballina	IV.	165
6, 13	Behy	2,561	1	31	Mayo	Tirawley	Doonfeeny	Killala	IV.	167
3, 4	Behy	196	2	5c	Roscommon	Boyle	Ardcarn	Boyle	IV.	192
9, 10	Behy	210	1	13	Roscommon	Boyle	Boyle	Boyle	IV.	194
27, 34	Behy	203	1	11	Sligo	Tirerrill	Tawnagh	Sligo	IV.	241
39	Behybaun	103	3	36	Mayo	Tirawley	Ballynahaglish	Ballina	IV.	164
29	Behy Beg	490	0	37	Sligo	Tireragh	Kilmoremoy	Ballina	IV.	235
29	Behy More	293	3	1	Sligo	Tireragh	Kilmoremoy	Ballina	IV.	235
58, 64	Beigh Glebe	243	3	14	Tyrone	Clogher	Clogher	Clogher	III.	292
32, 37	Beihy	645	2	19	Fermanagh	Clanawley	Killesher	Enniskillen	III.	192
36, 38	Beihy	1,016	3	33	Leitrim	Mohill	Cloone	Mohill	IV.	105
92, 102	Bekan	632	1	34d	Mayo	Costello	Bekan	Claremorris	IV.	138
13	Beladd	118	2	31	Queen's Co.	Maryborough East	Borris	Mountmellick	I.	240
13	Beladd	109	0	14	Queen's Co.	Maryborough East	Straboe	Mountmellick	I.	241
47, 49	Belagherty	424	0	4	Londonderry	Loughinsholin	Ballinderry	Magherafelt	III.	239
78,79,87,88	Belalt	593	1	18	Donegal	Raphoe	Donaghmore	Strabane	III.	137
105	Belalt North	1,354	3	5e	Donegal	Tirhugh	Templecarn	Donegal	III.	149
104, 105	Belalt South	1,850	2	34f	Donegal	Tirhugh	Templecarn	Donegal	III.	149
36, 38	Belan	1,197	2	10	Kildare	Kilkea and Moone	Belan	Athy	I.	59
15	Belcamp	70	3	25	Dublin	Coolock	Balgriffin	Dublin North	I.	26
14, 15	Belcamp	269	1	37	Dublin	Coolock	Santry	Dublin North	I.	29
87	Belclare	131	0	11	Mayo	Murrisk	Oughaval	Westport	IV.	161
36	Belclare	690	3	15	Sligo	Leyny	Kilmacteige	Tobercurry	IV.	231
25	Belcoo East	109	0	4	Fermanagh	Clanawley	Cleenish	Enniskillen	III.	189
25	Belcoo West	133	1	34	Fermanagh	Clanawley	Cleenish	Enniskillen	III.	189
41	Belcruit	1,398	2	5g	Donegal	Boylagh	Templecrone	Glenties	III.	114
4	Beldaragh	154	2	32	Dublin	Balrothery West	Hollywood	Balrothery	I.	23
6	Belderg	81	0	29	Monaghan	Trough	Donagh	Monaghan	III.	281
40	Belderg	21	0	20	Roscommon	Ballintober South	Kilteevan	Roscommon	IV.	189
5, 6	Belderg Beg	757	3	39	Mayo	Tirawley	Doonfeeny	Killala	IV.	167
5, 6	Belderg More	2,750	1	32	Mayo	Tirawley	Doonfeeny	Killala	IV.	167
46	Belderny North	202	3	12	Galway	Killian	Moylough	Mountbellew	IV.	45
46, 60	Belderny South	408	1	28	Galway	Killian	Moylough	Mountbellew	IV.	45
20, 28	Beleevna Beg	386	3	25	Tyrone	Dungannon Upper	Kildress	Cookstown	III.	308
20	Beleevna More	1,637	3	30	Tyrone	Dungannon Upper	Kildress	Cookstown	III.	308
102	Belesker	153	2	39	Mayo	Costello	Bekan	Claremorris	IV.	138
65	Belfarsad	695	0	22h	Mayo	Burrishoole	Achill	Newport	IV.	117
61	BELFAST T.	—			Antrim	Upper Belfast	Shankill	Belfast	III.	35
21	Belgard	323	0	9	Dublin	Uppercross	Tallaght	Dublin South	I.	41
5, 10	Belgard	287	3	23	Kildare	Ikeathy and Oughterany	Clonshanbo	Celbridge	I.	57
24	Belgard, Deer Park	123	3	35	Dublin	Uppercross	Tallaght	Dublin South	I.	41
6	Belgarrow	177	2	32	Londonderry	Coleraine	Dunboe	Coleraine	III.	231
48, 49, 61	Belgarrow	578	1	6	Mayo	Gallen	Toomore	Swineford	IV.	151
4	Belgee	130	2	9i	Dublin	Balrothery West	Hollywood	Balrothery	I.	23
112	BELGOOLY T.	—			Cork, E.R.	Kinalea	Kilmonoge	Kinsale	II.	95
10	Belgree	13	3	22	Dublin	Castleknock	Mulhuddart	Dunshaughlin	I.	25
51	Belgree	546	3	15	Meath	Dunboyne	Kilbride	Dunshaughlin	I.	200
76, 88	Belgrove	334	3	31	Cork, E.R.	Barrymore	Templerobin	Cork	II.	58

(a) Including 15A. 2R. 30P. water.
(b) Including 17A. 1R. 8P. water.
(c) Including 6A. 2R. 3P. water.
(d) Including 12A. 1R. 35P. water.
(e) Including 70A. 1R. 10P. water.
(f) Including 53A. 3R. 37P. water.
(g) Including 131A. 1R. 7P. water.
(h) Including 21A. 1R. 17P. water.
(i) Including 6A. 2R. 27P. detached portion.

No. of Sheet of the Ordnance Survey Maps.	Townlands and Towns.	Area in Statute Acres. A. R. P.	County.	Barony.	Parish.	Poor Law Union in 1857.	Townland Census of 1851, Part I. Vol.	Page
15	Belhavel . . .	111 1 17a	Leitrim .	Drumahaire .	Killarga . .	Manorhamilton	IV.	98
9	Belin . . .	257 1 35b	Queen's Co. .	Portnahinch .	Lea . . .	Mountmellick .	I.	244
7	Belinstown . .	338 2 37	Dublin . .	Balrothery West .	Ballyboghil .	Balrothery .	I.	22
7, 8, 11, 12	Belinstown . .	475 2 29	Dublin . .	Nethercross .	Swords . .	Balrothery .	I.	32
15	Bella . . .	280 1 18	Roscommon .	Frenchpark .	Kilcolagh .	Boyle . .	IV.	203
89	Bellaburke . .	500 0 16	Mayo . .	Carra . . .	Ballintober .	Castlebar . .	IV.	124
34	Bellacagher . .	485 2 13	Roscommon .	Ballymoe .	Drumatemple .	Castlereagh .	IV.	191
16	Bellaconeen . .	57 1 6	Galway . .	Dunmore .	Addergoole .	Tuam . .	IV.	32
27, 36	Bellacorick . .	800 3 32c	Mayo . .	Erris . .	Kilcommon .	Belmullet .	IV.	143
101, 111	Belladaff . .	138 3 25	Mayo . .	Clanmorris .	Tagheen . .	Claremorris .	IV.	135
21	Belladooan . .	433 3 37	Mayo . .	Tirawley .	Kilfian . .	Killala . .	IV.	169
20	Belladrihid . .	279 3 8	Sligo . .	Tirerrill . .	Ballysadare .	Sligo . .	IV.	237
86	Bellafa . .	6 2 32	Galway . .	Kilconnell .	Grange . .	Loughrea .	IV.	40
17	Bellafarney . .	558 2 7	Sligo . .	Tireragh . .	Kilmacshalgan .	Dromore West .	IV.	234
20, 33	Bellagad or Rookwood	316 3 20d	Galway . .	Killian . .	Athleague .	Mountbellew .	IV.	43
73	Bellaganny . .	48 3 18	Donegal . .	Banagh . .	Inishkeel .	Glenties . .	III.	106
27	Bellagart . .	87 2 30	Leitrim . .	Leitrim . .	Kiltoghert .	Cark. on Shannon	IV.	101
44, 56	Bellagarvaun . .	1,543 3 14	Mayo . .	Erris . .	Kilcommon .	Newport . .	IV.	143
37, 38	Bellageeher . .	445 0 30	Leitrim . .	Mohill . .	Mohill . .	Mohill . .	IV.	107
11, 12	Bellagelly North .	2,528 2 25	Mayo . .	Erris . .	Kilcommon .	Belmullet .	IV.	143
11, 12	Bellagelly South .	3,409 1 8	Mayo . .	Erris . .	Kilcommon .	Belmullet .	IV.	143
23, 27	Bellaghy . .	737 1 3	Antrim . .	Kilconway .	Rasharkin .	Ballymena .	III.	27
37	BELLAGHY T. . .	—	Londonderry .	Loughinsholin .	Ballyscullion .	Magherafelt .	III.	240
53	Bellagill . .	197 3 4e	Roscommon .	Moycarn .	Creagh . .	Ballinasloe .	IV.	206
13, 14	Bellaheady or Ross-bressal . .	222 0 5f	Cavan . .	Tullyhunco .	Kildallan .	Bawnboy . .	III.	96
23	Bellaheen . .	96 3 0	Waterford .	Decies without Drum .	Kilrossanty .	Kilmacthomas .	II.	357
42	Bellahy . .	196 3 35	Sligo . .	Leyny . .	Achonry . .	Tobercurry .	IV.	228
42	BELLAHY T. .	—	Sligo . .	Leyny . .	Achonry . .	Tobercurry .	IV.	230
29	Bellair . .	127 0 3	Antrim . .	Lower Glenarm .	Tickmacrevan .	Larne . .	III.	23
7	Bellair or Ballyard .	1,262 3 24	King's Co. .	Garrycastle .	Lemanaghan .	Parsonstown .	I.	136
2	Bellair or Cappana-pinion . .	83 3 22	Queen's Co. .	Tinnahinch .	Kilmanman .	Mountmellick .	I.	249
29, 33	Bellakiltyfea . .	696 1 29g	Leitrim . .	Mohill . .	Cloone . .	Mohill . .	IV.	105
86, 96	Bellakip . .	1,015 2 25	Mayo . .	Murrisk . .	Kilgeever .	Westport .	IV.	159
9, 13	Bellaleenan . .	222 0 29	Cavan . .	Tullyhaw .	Templeport .	Bawnboy . .	III.	93
115	Bellalegaun . .	82 2 2	Galway . .	Loughrea .	Killcenadeema .	Loughrea . .	IV.	64
17	Bellamont Forest .	870 3 2h	Cavan . .	Tullygarvey .	Drumgoon .	Cootehill .	III.	88
27	Bellanaboy . .	276 1 17	Leitrim . .	Leitrim . .	Kiltoghert .	Cark. on Shannon	IV.	101
11	Bellanaboy . .	1,050 1 32	Mayo . .	Erris . .	Kilcommon .	Belmullet .	IV.	143
23, 24	Bellanaboy . .	2,259 2 5	Sligo . .	Tireragh . .	Kilmacshalgan .	Dromore West .	IV.	234
58	Bellanaboy or Derry-nacarrow East . .	99 0 23	Donegal . .	Boylagh . .	Lettermacward .	Glenties .	III.	114
121	Bellanabriscaun .	58 0 6	Mayo . .	Kilmaine .	Kilmainebeg .	Ballinrobe .	IV.	155
16, 21	Bellanacargy . .	229 2 3	Cavan . .	Tullygarvey .	Drung . .	Cootehill .	III.	88
16	BELLANACARGY T. .	—	Cavan . .	Tullygarvey .	Drung . .	Cootehill .	III.	89
41	Bellanacarrow . .	120 1 5i	Roscommon .	Athlone . .	Fuerty . .	Roscommon .	IV.	181
50, 62	Bellanacurra . .	93 1 32j	Mayo . .	Gallen . .	Killasser .	Swineford .	IV.	149
8	Bellanadohy . .	48 1 14	Fermanagh .	Lurg . .	Belleek . .	Ballyshannon .	III.	203
9	Bellanagall . .	109 1 15	Monaghan .	Monaghan .	Monaghan .	Monaghan .	III.	276
15, 21	Bellanagare . .	316 2 2	Roscommon .	Castlereagh .	Kilcorkey .	Castlereagh .	IV.	199
15	BELLANAGARE T. .	—	Roscommon .	Castlereagh .	Kilcorkey .	Castlereagh .	IV.	200
28, 42	Bellanagarraun . .	531 1 4k	Galway . .	Clare . .	Donaghpatrick .	Tuam . .	IV.	19
34	Bellanagarrigeeny or Castlebaldwin . .	64 2 17	Sligo . .	Tirerrill .	Kilmacallan .	Sligo . .	IV.	239
39	Bellanalack . .	193 2 21	Sligo . .	Corran . .	Kilturra . .	Tobercurry .	IV.	227
30	Bellanalack . .	194 3 20	Westmeath .	Clonlonan .	Ballyloughloe .	Athlone . .	I.	260
27	Bellanaleck . .	277 1 30l	Fermanagh .	Clanawley .	Cleenish . .	Enniskillen .	III.	189
100, 110	Bellanaloob . .	499 1 20	Mayo . .	Kilmaine .	Robeen . .	Ballinrobe .	IV.	157
16	Bellanamallard . .	23 3 9	Fermanagh .	Tirkennedy .	Magheracross .	Lowtherstown .	III.	223
16	BELLANAMALLARD T.	—	Fermanagh .	Tirkennedy .	Magheracross .	Lowtherstown .	III.	223
7	Bellanaman . .	72 3 15	Monaghan .	Trough . .	Donagh . .	Monaghan .	III.	281
59, 67	Bellanamore . .	923 0 13m	Donegal . .	Boylagh . .	Inishkeel .	Glenties .	III.	112
51, 52	Bellanamullia . .	421 3 19	Roscommon .	Athlone . .	St. Peter's .	Athlone . .	IV.	184
29	Bellanamullia . .	104 0 32	Roscommon .	Roscommon .	Bumlin . .	Strokestown .	IV.	208
25	Bellananagh . .	136 2 1	Cavan . .	Clanmahon .	Kilmore . .	Cavan . .	III.	78
25	BELLANANAGH T. .	—	Cavan . .	Clanmahon .	Kilmore . .	Cavan . .	III.	78
42, 54	Bellanasally . .	833 2 31n	Mayo . .	Burrishoole .	Achill . .	Newport . .	IV.	117
45, 53	Bellanascaddan . .	337 0 30	Donegal . .	Kilmacrenan .	Kilmacrenan .	Letterkenny .	III.	129
33	Bellanascarrow East .	138 3 30o	Sligo . .	Corran . .	Toomour .	Sligo . .	IV.	228
33	Bellanascarrow West .	149 2 10p	Sligo . .	Corran . .	Toomour .	Sligo . .	IV.	228
34	Bellanascarva . .	112 2 21	Sligo . .	Tirerrill . .	Kilmacallan .	Sligo . .	IV.	239
51	Bellaneeny . .	140 0 24	Roscommon .	Athlone . .	Taghmaconnell .	Athlone . .	IV.	185
69	Bellanierin . .	183 1 2q	Mayo . .	Carra . .	Turlough .	Castlebar .	IV.	130

(a) Including 27A. 0R. 32P. water.
(b) Including 9A. 3R. 25P. River Barrow.
(c) Including 17A. 1R. 24P. water.
(d) Including 22A. 1R. 0P. water.
(e) Including 11A. 3R. 38P. water.
(f) Including 10A. 0R. 0P. water.

(g) Including 7A. 2R. 8P. water.
(h) Including 144A. 2R. 9P. water.
(i) Including 4A. 2R. 6P. water.
(j) Including 1A. 1R. 8P. water.
(k) Including 15A. 0R. 33P. water.
(l) Including 28A. 1R. 10P. water.

(m) Including 12A. 1R. 16P. water.
(n) Including 62A. 0R. 14P. water.
(o) Including 11A. 3R. 33P. water.
(p) Including 0A. 3R. 10P. water.
(q) Including 17A. 0R. 19P. water.

No. of Sheet of the Ordnance Survey Maps.	Townlands and Towns.	Area in Statute Acres.	County.	Barony.	Parish.	Poor Law Union in 1857.	Townland Census of 1851, Part I. Vol.	Page
		A. R. P.					Vol.	Page
22	Bellanira or Iceford	81 1 4	Sligo	Tireragh	Castleconor	Ballina	IV.	232
14, 15	Bellanode	106 2 30	Sligo	Carbury	Calry	Sligo	IV.	220
9	BELLANODE T.	—	Monaghan	Monaghan	Tedavnet	Monaghan	III.	280
26	Bellanumera	119 2 5a	Mayo	Erris	Kilcommon	Belmullet	IV.	143
15	Bellanurly	93 2 32	Sligo	Carbury	Calry	Sligo	IV.	220
3, 7	Bellany	241 3 14	Londonderry	Coleraine	Dunboe	Coleraine	III.	231
5	Bellarena	199 1 31b	Londonderry	Keenaght	Magilligan	New Tn Limavady	III.	236
34	Bellarush	194 2 35	Sligo	Tirerril	Kilmacallan	Sligo	IV.	239
46	Bellary	77 0 39	Wexford	Bargy	Duncormick	Wexford	I.	304
14	Bellasallagh	155 2 37	Mayo	Tirawley	Rathreagh	Killala	II.	171
48, 60	Bellass	370 3 24c	Mayo	Tirawley	Ballynahaglish	Ballina	IV.	164
7	Bellasses	171 0 27	Londonderry	North East Liberties of Coleraine	Coleraine	Coleraine	III.	246
87	Bellataleen	438 2 24	Mayo	Murrisk	Oughaval	Westport	IV.	161
27	BELLATRAIN T.	—	Monaghan	Cremorne	Aghnamullen	Castleblayney	III.	259
52	Bellaugh	354 2 24	Roscommon	Athlone	St. Peter's	Athlone	IV.	184
52	BELLAUGH T.	—	Roscommon	Athlone	St. Peter's	Athlone	IV.	184
6	Bellavally Lower	1,014 3 15	Cavan	Tullyhaw	Templeport	Enniskillen	III.	94
6	Bellavally Upper	709 0 33	Cavan	Tullyhaw	Templeport	Enniskillen	III.	94
70	Bellavary	660 1 10d	Mayo	Gallen	Kildacommoge	Castlebar	IV.	148
70	BELLAVARY T.	—	Mayo	Gallen	Kildacommoge	Castlebar	IV.	148
94	Bellavaum	181 3 29	Mayo	Murrisk	Kilgeever	Westport	IV.	161
103	Bellaveel	66 1 8	Mayo	Costello	Annagh	Claremorris	IV.	137
44, 56, 57	Bellaveeny	3,649 2 24e	Mayo	Erris	Kilcommon	Newport	IV.	143
15	Bellawillinbeg	89 0 7	Sligo	Carbury	Calry	Sligo	IV.	220
97, 98	Bellayarha North	491 0 21	Galway	Loughrea	Bullaun	Loughrea	IV.	63
97, 98	Bellayarha South	410 0 19	Galway	Loughrea	Bullaun	Loughrea	IV.	63
22	Bellcotton	123 2 2	Louth	Ferrard	Termonfeckin	Drogheda	I.	182
27, 32	Bellee	419 3 6	Antrim	Lower Toome	Kirkinriola	Ballymena	III.	32
25	Belleek	994 3 8	Armagh	Orior Upper	Loughgilly	Newry	III.	58
35	Belleek	312 2 21	Galway	Ballynahinch	Omey	Clifden	IV.	14
30	Belleek	210 3 37	Mayo	Tirawley	Kilmoremoy	Ballina	IV.	170
15	Belleek	237 2 23	Meath	Fore	Loughcrew	Oldcastle	I.	201
25	BELLEEK T.	—	Armagh	Orior Upper	Loughgilly	Newry	III.	58
8	BELLEEK T.	—	Fermanagh	Lurg	Belleek	Ballyshannon	III.	204
20	Belleen Lower	182 2 17	Tipperary, N.R.	Lower Ormond	Monsea	Nenagh	II.	287
20	Belleen Upper	192 1 34	Tipperary, N.R.	Lower Ormond	Monsea	Nenagh	II.	287
9	Bellegrove	702 2 35	Queen's Co.	Portnahinch	Lea	Mountmellick	I.	244
27, 33	Belleisle	470 1 35f	Fermanagh	Tirkennedy	Cleenish	Lisnaskea	III.	219
3	Bellemont More	107 1 6	Londonderry	North East Liberties of Coleraine	Ballyaghran	Coleraine	III.	244
3	Bellemont North	56 1 6	Londonderry	North East Liberties of Coleraine	Ballyaghran	Coleraine	III.	244
3	Bellemont South	62 2 27	Londonderry	North East Liberties of Coleraine	Ballyaghran	Coleraine	III.	244
29	Belleville	32 3 1	Tipperary, N.R.	Eliogarty	Templemore	Thurles	II.	272
21	Belleville	140 3 13	Waterford	Decies without Drum	Affane	Lismore	II.	353
71	Belleville Demesne	245 1 8	Galway	Clare	Monivea	Galway	IV.	23
6, 9	Bellevue	643 3 22	Tipperary, N.R.	Lower Ormond	Kilbarren	Borrisokane	II.	284
8, 13	Bellevue Demesne	15 1 23	Wicklow	Newcastle	Kilcoole	Rathdrum	I.	351
8, 13	Bellevue Demesne	603 1 25	Wicklow	Rathdown	Delgany	Rathdown	I.	355
32	Bellew	357 1 32	Meath	Skreen	Rathfeigh	Dunshaughlin	I.	221
36	Bellewstown	481 0 18g	Meath	Lower Moyfenrath	Trim	Trim	I.	211
31	Bellewstown	298 2 38	Meath	Lower Navan	Rataine	Navan	I.	215
27	Bellewstown	1,276 1 8	Meath	Upper Duleek	Duleek	Drogheda	I.	197
101	Bellfield	73 3 39	Mayo	Clanmorris	Kilcolman	Claremorris	IV.	133
26, 33	Bellfield or Brannockstown	455 2 23	Westmeath	Fartullagh	Enniscoffey	Mullingar	I.	268
10	Bellgrove	130 2 36	Tipperary, N.R.	Lower Ormond	Finnoe	Borrisokane	II.	283
46	Bellgrove	219 0 28	Wexford	Bargy	Duncormick	Wexford	I.	304
46	Bellgrovecross	129 1 38	Wexford	Bargy	Duncormick	Wexford	I.	304
36, 39	Bellhill	281 2 0	King's Co.	Ballybritt	Seirkieran	Parsonstown	I.	126
65	Bellia	318 2 36	Clare	Moyarta	Moyarta	Kilrush	II.	34
65	BELLIA T.	—	Clare	Moyarta	Moyarta	Kilrush	II.	34
24, 25	Bellina	160 0 22	Donegal	Kilmacrenan	Tullaghobegly	Dunfanaghy	III.	131
38, 39	Belline & Rogerstown	648 2 38	Kilkenny	Iverk	Fiddown	Carrick on Suir	I.	105
20	Bellisk or Waterford	22 3 7	Antrim	Lower Glenarm	Layd	Ballycastle	III.	22
12	Bellisle	282 3 33	Antrim	Lower Dunluce	Derrykeighan	Ballymoney	III.	16
10	Bellmount	178 0 20	Carlow	Rathvilly	Clonmore	Shillelagh	I.	10
40	Bellmount	133 0 13	Fermanagh	Clankelly	Galloon	Clones	III.	198
39, 47	Bellmount alias Ballynagowen Upper	909 1 17	Tyrone	Dungannon Upper	Ballyclog	Cookstown	III.	306
29	Bellmount or Cloggernagh	50 0 3	Roscommon	Roscommon	Lissonuffy	Strokestown	IV.	211

(a) Including 4A. 3R. 34P. water.
(b) Including 4A. 1R. 4P. water.
(c) Including 15A. 2R. 29P. water.
(d) Including 3A. 3R. 39P. water.
(e) Including 56A. 3R. 6P. water.
(f) Including 87A. 3R. 12P. water.
(g) Including 10A. 1R. 0P. water.

No. of Sheet of the Ordnance Survey Maps.	Townlands and Towns.	Area in Statute Acres.	County.	Barony.	Parish.	Poor Law Union in 1857.	Townland Census of 1851, Part I.	
		A. R. P.					Vol.	Page
18, 25	Bellmount or Curristown	195 2 29	Westmeath	Moyashel and Magheradernon	Mullingar	Mullingar	I.	275
14, 22	Bellmount or Lisderg	420 2 18	King's Co.	Garrycastle	Tisaran	Parsonstown	I.	138
83, 84	Bellmount Lower	474 2 5	Cork, E.R.	East Muskerry	Moviddy	Bandon	II.	105
83, 84	Bellmount Upper	720 2 27	Cork, E.R.	East Muskerry	Moviddy	Bandon	II.	105
10	Bellpark	116 1 15	Tipperary, N.R.	Lower Ormond	Finnoe	Borrisokane	II.	283
36	Bellpark	118 1 29	Wicklow	Arklow	Dunganstown	Rathdrum	I.	343
37	Bellsgrove	306 3 23	Cavan	Clanmahon	Ballymachugh	Cavan	III.	75
39, 47	Bellsgrove *alias* Ballynagowan Lower	194 1 1	Tyrone	Dungannon Upper	Ballyclog	Cookstown	III.	306
9, 10	Bellshill	158 0 19	Carlow	Rathvilly	Clonmore	Shillelagh	I.	10
6	Bellspark	21 1 8	Roscommon	Boyle	Boyle	Boyle	IV.	194
9	Bellspark	71 3 3	Tyrone	Strabane Lower	Urney	Strabane	III.	322
5, 7, 8	Bellurgan	1,435 3 6	Louth	Lower Dundalk	Ballyboys	Dundalk	I.	175
4, 7	Bellurgan	562 3 35	Louth	Lower Dundalk	Castletown	Dundalk	I.	177
18, 26	Bellury	504 0 36	Londonderry	Coleraine	Desertoghill	Coleraine	III.	230
19	Bellview	24 1 5	Westmeath	Moyashel and Magheradernon	Mullingar	Mullingar	I.	275
25	Bellville	364 0 18	Cavan	Clanmahon	Kilmore	Cavan	III.	78
44, 52	Bellville or Gartan	174 0 19*a*	Donegal	Kilmacrenan	Gartan	Letterkenny	III.	127
15, 16	Belmont	1,905 1 29*b*	Galway	Dunmore	Liskeevy	Tuam	IV.	35
8	Belmont Demesne	54 0 16	Wicklow	Rathdown	Delgany	Rathdown	I.	355
9	Belmount	148 3 4	Waterford	Gaultiere	Kilculliheen	Waterford	II.	363
10, 17	Belmullet	319 3 19	Mayo	Erris	Kilcommon	Belmullet	IV.	143
10	BELMULLET T.	—	Mayo	Erris	Kilcommon	Belmullet	IV.	145
59	Belnaclogh	171 1 7	Tyrone	Clogher	Clogher	Clogher	III.	292
51	Belnagarnan	148 2 32	Tyrone	Clogher	Donacavey	Omagh	III.	294
17, 20	Belpatrick	1,513 3 6	Louth	Ferrard	Collon	Ardee	I.	180
37, 38	Belpere	749 1 30	Meath	Skreen	Killeen	Dunshaughlin	I.	221
31, 37	Belpere	86 1 29	Meath	Skreen	Skreen	Dunshaughlin	I.	221
25, 32	Belra	185 1 6	Sligo	Leyny	Achonry	Tobercurry	IV.	229
60	Belragh	193 0 12	Tyrone	Dungannon Lower	Carnteel	Clogher	III.	297
18	Belraugh	368 2 23	Londonderry	Coleraine	Errigal	Coleraine	III.	232
51	Belrea	277 1 11	Roscommon	Athlone	Drum	Athlone	IV.	180
85, 97	Belrose	454 0 13	Cork, E.R.	East Muskerry	Knockavilly	Bandon	II.	104
95	Belrose Lower	226 2 19	Cork, W.R.	East Carbery (W.D.)	Kinneigh	Bandon	II.	134
95	Belrose Upper	433 2 33	Cork, W.R.	East Carbery (W.D.)	Kinneigh	Bandon	II.	134
44	Belshamstown	106 3 27	Meath	Ratoath	Rathregan	Dunshaughlin	I.	219
17	Beltacken	136 0 16	Westmeath	Rathconrath	Templepatrick	Ballymahon	I.	284
70	Beltany	295 2 34	Donegal	Raphoe	Raphoe	Strabane	III.	140
51, 52, 59	Beltany	469 3 1	Tyrone	Clogher	Clogher	Clogher	III.	292
17, 25	Beltany	702 2 22*c*	Tyrone	Strabane Upper	Cappagh	Omagh	III.	325
24, 33	Beltany Lower	394 2 8	Donegal	Kilmacrenan	Tullaghobegly	Dunfanaghy	III.	131
33, 42	Beltany Mountain	1,067 3 24*d*	Donegal	Kilmacrenan	Tulloghobegly	Dunfanaghy	III.	131
33	Beltany Upper	201 1 37	Donegal	Kilmacrenan	Tulloghobegly	Dunfanaghy	III.	131
25	Beltichburne	196 2 13*e*	Louth	Ferrard	Beaulieu	Drogheda	I.	180
28, 29	Beltonanean	856 1 30	Tyrone	Dungannon Upper	Kildress	Cookstown	III.	308
46	Beltoy	108 1 36	Antrim	Lower Belfast	Glynn	Larne	III.	8
46	Beltoy	238 3 25	Antrim	Lower Belfast	Raloo	Larne	III.	9
59, 69	Beltra	1,989 2 27	Mayo	Carra	Islandeady	Castlebar	IV.	128
7, 8	Beltra	215 3 9	Mayo	Tirawley	Kilcummin	Killala	IV.	168
7	Beltra	22 1 16	Mayo	Tirawley	Lackan	Killala	IV.	170
18	Beltrim	962 1 3*f*	Tyrone	Strabane Upper	Bodoney Lower	Gortin	III.	323
11, 15	BELTURBET T.	—	Cavan	Lower Loughtee	Annagh	Cavan	III.	79
75	Belvelly	417 3 10*g*	Cork, E.R.	Barrymore	Clonmel	Cork	II.	53
37	Belvidere	171 1 2	Cork, E.R.	Kinnatalloon	Knockmourne	Fermoy	II.	98
26	Belvidere	42 0 37	Westmeath	Fartullagh	Moylisker	Mullingar	I.	269
35	Belview	99 0 30*h*	Kildare	Narragh&RebanWest	Kilberry	Athy	I.	67
15, 16	Belview	280 3 4	Meath	Fore	Diamor	Oldcastle	I.	200
27	Belview or Drumcoo	161 2 32*i*	Fermanagh	Tirkennedy	Enniskillen	Enniskillen	III.	222
99, 100	Belview or Lissareaghaun	969 2 25	Galway	Longford	Kiltormer	Ballinasloe	IV.	60
9	Belville	171 0 7	Kilkenny	Crannagh	Garranamanagh	Urlingford	I.	86
12, 18	Belville	439 0 23	Sligo	Tireragh	Kilmacshalgan	Dromore West	IV.	234
29, 30	Belville	242 0 22	Westmeath	Clonlonan	Ballyloughbloe	Athlone	I.	260
43	Belvoir	465 0 39	Clare	Tulla Lower	Clonlea	Limerick	II.	34
43	Belvoir Demesne	348 0 24	Clare	Tulla Lower	Clonlea	Limerick	II.	34
4, 8	Ben	458 0 12*j*	Westmeath	Fore	St. Feighins	Castletowndelvin	I.	271
47	Benagh	680 0 38*k*	Down	Lordship of Newry	Newry	Newry	III.	182
8	Benagh	233 3 24	Louth	Lower Dundalk	Carlingford	Dundalk	I.	176
57	Benagh Lower	154 2 33	Down	Mourne	Kilkeel	Kilkeel	III.	183
55, 57	Benagh Upper	281 3 36	Down	Mourne	Kilkeel	Kilkeel	III.	183
32	Benalbit & Derryroe	407 3 17	Westmeath	Moycashel	Castletownkindalen	Mullingar	I.	277
12	Benamore	186 3 29	Tipperary, N.R.	Ikerrin	Roscrea	Roscrea	II.	276

(*a*) Including 87A. 3R. 0P. water.
(*b*) Including 82A. 3R. 37P. water.
(*c*) Including 7A. 2R. 25P. water.
(*d*) Including 6A. 0R. 0P. water.

(*e*) Including 7A. 2R. 37P. detached portion.
(*f*) Including 3A. 3R. 3P. water.
(*g*) Including 4A. 0R. 32P. detached portion.
(*h*) Including 3A. 0R. 24P. water.

(*i*) Including 24A. 3R. 9P. water.
(*j*) Including 18A. 2R. 26P. water.
(*k*) Including 6A. 0R. 37P. water.

No. of Sheet of the Ordnance Survey Maps.	Townlands and Towns.	Area in Statute Acres.			County.	Barony.	Parish.	Poor Law Union in 1857.	Townland Census of 1851, Part I.	
		A.	R.	P.					Vol.	Page
97, 98	Ben Beg . . .	304	3	13	Galway . .	Loughrea . .	Grange . . .	Loughrea .	IV.	63
61	Benburb . . .	185	1	37	Tyrone . .	Dungannon Middle .	Clonfeacle . .	Dungannon .	III.	298
61	BENBURB T. . .	—			Tyrone . .	Dungannon Middle .	Clonfeacle . .	Dungannon .	III.	300
13	Bendinstown . .	215	2	33	Carlow . .	Forth . . .	Ballyellin . .	Carlow . .	I.	4
16, 17	Bendooragh . .	261	2	28	Antrim . .	Upper Dunluce .	Ballymoney .	Ballymoney .	III.	18
134	Benduff . . .	432	2	1	Cork, W.R. .	East Carbery (W.D.)	Ross . . .	Clonakilty .	II.	135
40, 49	Beneden . . .	666	2	6	Clare . . .	Islands . . .	Clondagad .	Killadysert .	II.	29
20	Benedin . . .	246	1	38	Tipperary, N.R.	Upper Ormond .	Nenagh . .	Nenagh . .	II.	292
33	Benfield . . .	137	1	37	King's Co. .	Upper Philipstown .	Clonyhurk . .	Mountmellick .	I.	143
38	Bengeery . . .	221	1	36	Mayo . .	Tirawley . .	Crossmolina .	Ballina . .	IV.	165
83, 95	Bengour East .	1,217	2	33	Cork, W.R. .	Kinalmeaky . .	Murragh . .	Bandon . .	II.	152
95	Bengour West .	1,348	2	20	Cork, W.R. .	Kinalmeaky . .	Murragh . .	Bandon . .	II.	152
7	Benisonlodge or Bratty	449	1	6	Westmeath .	Fore . . .	St. Feighins .	Castletowndelvin	I.	271
6, 12	Benjerstown . .	583	2	3	Meath . .	Lower Slane .	Siddan . . .	Ardee . .	I.	223
97, 98	Ben More . .	636	3	14	Galway . .	Loughrea . .	Grange . . .	Loughrea .	IV.	63
9	Benmore . .	223	3	15	Kerry . .	Clanmaurice .	Rattoo . . .	Listowel .	II.	173
31	Benmore . .	217	0	27	Roscommon .	Castlereagh . .	Kiltullagh . .	Castlereagh .	IV.	201
2	Bennarees . .	244	3	5	Londonderry .	Coleraine . .	Dunboe . .	Coleraine .	III.	231
7	Bennekerry . .	268	1	23	Carlow . .	Carlow . . .	Ballinacarrig .	Carlow . .	I.	1
7	Bennekerry . .	361	3	9	Carlow . .	Carlow . . .	Urglin . . .	Carlow . .	I.	3
35, 37	Bennetsbridge .	416	3	38	Kildare . .	Narragh&RebanWest	St. John's . .	Athy . . .	I.	68
50	Bennetstown . .	139	0	8	Meath . .	Dunboyne . .	Dunboyne . .	Dunshaughlin .	I.	199
24	Bennettsbridge .	403	3	14a	Kilkenny . .	Gowran . . .	Treadingstown .	Thomastown .	I.	99
23, 24	Bennettsbridge .	450	2	4b	Kilkenny . .	Shillelogher . .	Danesfort . .	Thomastown .	I.	114
24	BENNETTSBRIDGE T.	—			Kilkenny . .	{ Gowran . . .	Treadingstown . }	Thomastown .	I.	{ 99
						Shillelogher . .	Danesfort . . }			114
29	Bennettsknock .	7	0	28	Wexford . .	Bantry . . .	St. Mary's . .	New Ross .	I.	302
26	Bennettsmeadow .	2	2	6	Kilkenny . .	Callan . . .	Callan . . .	Callan . .	I.	83
48	Bennettstown . .	115	3	33	Wexford . .	Forth . . .	Tacumshin . .	Wexford . .	I.	315
2	Benone . . .	396	1	28	Londonderry .	Keenaght . .	Magilligan . .	NewT.ᵃLimavady	III.	236
35, 36	Benraw . . .	860	0	6	Down . .	Upper Iveagh, Lr. pt.	Drumgooland .	Banbridge .	III.	172
47	Bentra . . .	647	2	27	Antrim . .	Lower Belfast .	Templecorran .	Larne . .	III.	9
12	Benvardin . .	946	3	6	Antrim . .	Lower Dunluce .	Dunluce . .	Ballymoney .	III.	17
25	Benvoy . . .	193	3	26	Waterford .	Middlethird . .	Dunhill . .	Kilmacthomas .	II.	366
17	Benwilt . . .	265	2	4c	Cavan . .	Tullygarvey . .	Drumgoon . .	Cootehill .	III.	88
43, 44	Beragh . . .	481	1	5	Tyrone . .	Omagh East . .	Clogherny . .	Omagh . .	III.	310
25	Beragh . . .	736	3	17	Tyrone . .	Strabane Upper .	Cappagh . .	Omagh . .	III.	325
44	BERAGH T. . .	—			Tyrone . .	Omagh East . .	Clogherny . .	Omagh . .	III.	310
60	*Berger's Island* .	7	3	31	Clare . . .	Clonderalaw . .	Killadysert .	Killadysert .	II.	16
29, 30	Berkeley . .	374	0	25	Wexford . .	Bantry . . .	Ballyanne . .	New Ross .	I.	299
54, 55	Bernagh . . .	174	1	7	Tyrone . .	Dungannon Middle .	Killyman . .	Dungannon .	III.	303
28	Bernagh . . .	165	2	33	Wicklow . .	Upper Talbotstown .	Kiltegan . .	Baltinglass .	I.	364
24	Bernardsgrove or Ballypickas Lower	207	3	14	Queen's Co. .	Cullenagh . .	Ballyroan . .	Abbeyleix .	I.	239
15	*Bernards Island* .	2	0	5	Sligo . .	Carbury . .	Calry . . .	Sligo . .	IV.	220
5	Berneens . .	627	2	7	Clare . . .	Burren . . .	Rathborney .	Ballyvaghan .	II.	14
30	Bernyhill . .	212	2	4	Cavan . .	Tullyhunco . .	Scrabby . .	Granard . .	III.	99
38	Berrillstown . .	381	3	5	Meath . .	Skreen . . .	Trevet . . .	Dunshaughlin .	I.	222
61, 72	Berrings . . .	1,056	3	12	Cork, E.R. .	East Muskerry .	Inishcarra . .	Cork . .	II.	103
14	Berrymount . .	134	2	26	Cavan . .	Lower Loughtee .	Tomregan . .	Bawnboy . .	III.	81
16	Berrysfort . .	98	0	37d	Tyrone . .	Omagh West . .	Urney . . .	Castlederg .	III.	318
30,31,34,35	Bert Demesne . .	192	2	28e	Kildare . .	Narragh&RebanWest	Kilberry . .	Athy . . .	I.	67
33	Beshellstown . .	223	2	25	Meath . .	Upper Duleek .	Clonalvy . .	Drogheda .	I.	197
21, 22	Bessborough . .	24	3	2	Tipperary, N.R.	Upper Ormond .	Ballymackey .	Nenagh . .	II.	289
15	Bessbrook . .	87	0	2f	Cavan . .	Lower Loughtee .	Annagh . .	Cavan . .	III.	78
19	Bessmount . .	258	0	19	Wexford . .	Scarawalsh . .	Monart . .	Enniscorthy .	I.	324
24	Bessville . . .	40	2	35	Westmeath .	Rathconrath . .	Killare . .	Mullingar .	I.	283
2	Bestfield or Dungans-town . . .	55	2	37g	Carlow . .	Carlow . . .	Carlow . . .	Carlow . .	I.	1
2	Bestfield or Dungans-town . . .	101	2	33h	Carlow . .	Carlow . . .	Painestown .	Carlow . .	I.	2
9, 10, 13, 14	Betaghstown . .	621	3	29	Kildare . .	Clane . . .	Clane . . .	Naas . .	I.	53
22	Betaghstown . .	175	0	34	Louth . .	Ferrard . .	Termonfeckin .	Drogheda .	I.	182
21	Betaghstown . .	537	3	0	Meath . .	Lower Duleek .	Colp . . .	Drogheda .	I.	194
24	Betaghstown . .	228	0	35	Meath . .	Lower Navan . .	Ardbraccan .	Navan . .	I.	214
24	Betaghstown . .	277	0	27	Meath . .	Lower Navan . .	Balrathboyne .	Kells . .	I.	214
32	Betal . . .	159	3	18	Roscommon .	Castlereagh . .	Kiltullagh . .	Castlereagh .	IV.	201
15	Bethlehem . .	182	2	25i	Westmeath .	Kilkenny West .	Kilkenny West .	Athlone .	I.	273
3	Bettyfield or Rickets-town . . .	198	2	12	Carlow . .	Rathvilly . .	Kineagh . .	Baltinglass .	I.	12
30	Bettyspark . .	30	2	10	Galway . .	Dunmore . .	Dunmore . .	Tuam . .	IV.	33
00	Bettyville . .	100	0	10j	Cork, E.R. .	Condons&Clangibbon	Clondulane .	Fermoy . .	II.	60
23	Bettyville . .	302	2	21	Cork, E.R. .	Duhallow . .	Castlemagner .	Kanturk . .	II.	67
7	Bettyville . .	144	3	37	Dublin . .	Balrothery East .	Lusk . . .	Balrothery .	I.	20

(a) { Including 137A. 1R. 4P. detached portions.
{ Including 11A. 0R. 35P. River Nore.
(b) Including 12A. 3R. 3P. River Nore.
(c) Including 2A. 0R. 24P. water.

(d) Including 1A. 3R. 23P. water.
(e) Including 5A. 3R. 12P. water.
(f) Including 14A. 0R. 20P. water.
(g) Including 3A. 1R. 0P. River Barrow.

(h) Including 6A. 3R. 14P. River Barrow.
(i) Including 29A. 1R. 8P. water.
(j) Including 3A. 3R. 16P. water.

No. of Sheet of the Ordnance Survey Maps.	Townlands and Towns.	Area in Statute Acres. A. R. P.	County.	Barony.	Parish.	Poor Law Union in 1857.	Townland Census of 1851, Part I. Vol.	Page
15, 19	Bettyville	96 3 14	Dublin	Coolock	Raheny	Dublin North	I.	28
29	Bewley	300 0 27	Waterford	Decies without Drum	Kilmolash	Lismore	II.	357
20, 27	Bey Beg	405 2 37	Meath	Lower Duleek	Colp	Drogheda	I.	194
20, 27	Bey More	806 3 23	Meath	Lower Duleek	Colp	Drogheda	I.	194
79	Bicketstown or Tir-nagushoge	140 0 4	Donegal	Raphoe	Donaghmore	Strabane	III.	138
6	Biddyford	241 3 36	Limerick	Clanwilliam	Killeenagarriff	Limerick	II.	224
40	Bigbog	228 2 13	Kildare	Kilkea and Moone	Castledermot	Athy	I.	59
19	Bigbog	137 2 28	Kilkenny	Crannagh	Ballycallan	Kilkenny	I.	84
18, 19	Bigbog	206 2 4	Queen's Co.	Stradbally	Dysartenos	Athy	I.	247
17	Bigfurze	113 3 21	Westmeath	Rathconrath	Rathconrath	Mullingar	I.	284
42, 56	Biggera Beg	362 1 36	Galway	Clare	Annaghdown	Tuam	IV.	16
42,43,56,57	Biggera More	306 3 37	Galway	Clare	Annaghdown	Tuam	IV.	16
2, 6	Big Glebe	165 2 5	Londonderry	Coleraine	Dunboe	Coleraine	III.	231
61	Bigg's-Lot & Owen's	143 0 27	Tipperary, S.R.	Middlethird	St. John Baptist	Cashel	II.	330
5, 9	Bighouse	188 1 10	Antrim	Cary	Culfeightrin	Ballycastle	III.	13
108, 118	Bigisland	168 3 23	Galway	Longford	Meelick	Portumna	IV.	61
89	*Big Island*	9 .0 21	Galway	Moycullen	Killannin	Oughterard	IV.	70
27	*Big Island*	44 1 36	Galway	Ross	Ross	Oughterard	IV.	74
41	Bigisland	34 0 8	Meath	Upper Moyfenrath	Kilyon	Trim	I.	213
46,47	*Big Island*	28 3 28	Wexford	Bargy	Kilcowan	Wexford	I.	305
38	Big Island	124 3 38	Wexford	Shelmaliere East	St. Margaret's	Wexford	I.	331
54	Big Isle	175 2 28	Donegal	Raphoe	Raymoghy	Letterkenny	III.	141
141	Bigmarsh	174 1 6	Cork, W.R.	West Carbery (E.D.)	Aghadown	Skibbereen	III.	136
26	Bigmeadow	14 1 4	Kilkenny	Callan	Callan	Callan	I.	83
22	Bigmeadow	38 0 7	Kilkenny	Crannagh	Killaloe	Callan	I.	86
52	Bigmeadow and Ath-lone	111 2 3	Roscommon	Athlone	St. Peter's	Athlone	IV.	184
104	Bigpark	106 1 28a	Donegal	Tirhugh	Drumhome	Donegal	III.	146
27, 28	Bigpark	261 1 37	Tipperary, N.R.	Upper Ormond	Latteragh	Nenagh	II.	292
17	Bigsland	18 2 24	Louth	Ardee	Smarmore	Ardee	I.	174
6, 7	Bigstown	453 1 34	Meath	Lower Slane	Siddan	Ardee	I.	223
51	*Big Venture*	4 3 9	Clare	Bunratty Lower	Kilmaleery	Ennis	II.	5
5	Bigwood	81 1 17	Fermanagh	Lurg	Drumkeeran	Lowtherstown	III.	205
4	Bigwood	154 3 28	Fermanagh	Lurg	Templecarn	Lowtherstown	III.	209
38	Bigwood	170 1 4	King's Co.	Ballybritt	Kilcolman	Parsonstown	I.	125
1, 3	Bigwood	442 3 0	Westmeath	Fore	Lickbla	Granard	I.	270
23	Bigwood	81 2 24	Wexford	Bantry	St. Mullins	New Ross	I.	303
65,66,76,77	Bilberry	609 1 11	Cork, E.R.	Barrymore	Inchinabacky	Middleton	II.	55
13	*Bilberry Island*	6 3 3	Fermanagh	Magheraboy	Devenish	Ballyshannon	III.	211
33	*Bilberry Island*	4 1 20	Fermanagh	Tirkennedy	Cleenish	Lisnaskea	III.	220
40	*Bilberry Island*	2 1 10	Galway	Moycullen	Kilcummin	Oughterard	IV.	68
9, 13	*Bilberry Island*	2 2 36	Leitrim	Drumahaire	Cloonclare	Manorhamilton	IV.	94
15	Bilboa	847 1 36	Limerick	Coonagh	Doon	Tipperary	II.	234
26	Billa	245 1 20	Sligo	Leyny	Ballysadare	Sligo	IV.	230
105	Billary	47 1 21	Donegal	Tirhugh	Templecarn	Donegal	III.	149
12	Billary	60 2 35	Monaghan	Dartree	Clones	Clones	III.	264
33	Billary	166 1 12b	Tyrone	Omagh West	Longfield West	Castlederg	III.	316
19	Billeady	237 1 3	Monaghan	Cremorne	Clontibret	Castleblayney	III.	259
126	Billeragh	211 2 13	Cork, W.R.	Bear	Kilnamanagh	Castletown	II.	125
10, 16	Billeragh	420 2 30	Kerry	Clanmaurice	Kilshenane	Listowel	II.	171
20, 28	Billeragh East	905 3 21	Cork, E.R.	Condons & Clangibbon	Macroney	Fermoy	II.	63
20, 28	Billeragh West	810 1 10	Cork, E.R.	Condons & Clangibbon	Macroney	Fermoy	II.	63
33	Billis	288 0 39	Cavan	Castlerahan	Killinkere	Bailieborough	III.	68
20	Billis	261 2 3	Cavan	Upper Loughtee	Annagelliff	Cavan	III.	81
6	Billis	252 1 30	Monaghan	Trough	Donagh	Monaghan	III.	281
9	Billises	115 2 31c	Monaghan	Monaghan	Tedavnet	Monaghan	III.	278
13, 14	Billistown	419 1 31	Westmeath	Delvin	Castletowndelvin	Castletowndelvin	I.	264
14	Billoos	370 3 32	Mayo	Tirawley	Lackan	Killala	IV.	170
7	Billy or Curramoney	358 2 2	Antrim	Lower Dunluce	Billy	Coleraine	III.	16
54	Billymore or Car-rowntober	303 3 6	Galway	Moycullen	Kilcummin	Oughterard	IV.	66
10	Billywood	491 1 30	Meath	Lower Kells	Moynalty	Kells	I.	203
28	Bin	25 0 36	Donegal	Kilmacrenan	Killygarvan	Millford	III.	128
22	Binbane	127 0 35	Cavan	Tullygarvey	Kildrumsherdan	Cootehill	III.	89
19	Binbawn	108 2 9	Queen's Co.	Stradbally	Curraclone	Athy	I.	246
6	Binbunniff	320 1 25	Tyrone	Strabane Lower	Donaghedy	Gortin	III.	320
22	Bindoo	222 0 12	Cavan	Tullygarvey	Kildrumsherdan	Cootehill	III.	89
67,68,76,77	Bindoo	154 0 20	Donegal	Raphoe	Kilteevoge	Stranorlar	III.	139
48	Bing	94 1 27	Wexford	Forth	St. Helens	Wexford	I.	313
39	Binganagh	104 0 14	Sligo	Corran	Drumrat	Boyle	IV.	225
84	Bingarra	347 1 39	Galway	Tiaquin	Monivea	Loughrea	IV.	78
25	Bingfield or Gortna-shangan Lower	123 1 14	Cavan	Clanmahon	Kilmore	Cavan	III.	78

(a) Including 4A. 3R. 24P. water.   (b) Including 0A. 1R. 19P. water.   (c) Including 3A. 0R. 16P. water.

No. of Sheet of the Ordnance Survey Maps.	Townlands and Towns.	Area in Statute Acres.	County.	Barony.	Parish.	Poor Law Union in 1857.	Townland Census of 1851, Part I.	
		A. R. P.					Vol.	Page
9, 16, 17	Binghamstown	715 2 31a	Mayo	Erris	Kilmore	Belmullet	IV.	145
16	BINGHAMSTOWN T.	—	Mayo	Erris	Kilmore	Belmullet	IV.	146
50, 51	Bingorms	1,687 1 17b	Donegal	Kilmacrenan	Gartan	Dunfanaghy	III.	127
7	Binkeeragh	296 3 23	Cavan	Tullyhaw	Kinawley	Bawnboy	III.	93
76	Binmore	285 0 29	Donegal	Raphoe	Kilteevoge	Stranorlar	III.	139
24	Binmore	133 1 8	Monaghan	Cremorne	Aghnamullen	Castleblayney	III.	257
10	Binmore Glebe	42 2 9	Fermanagh	Magheraboy	Inishmacsaint	Ballyshannon	III.	212
45	Binmuck	222 2 28	Roscommon	Athlone	St. Johns	Athlone	IV.	183
84	Binn	89 1 11	Galway	Tiaquin	Monivea	Loughrea	IV.	78
23, 29	Binn	581 1 32	Londonderry	Tirkeeran	Cumber Upper	Londonderry	III.	249
19, 27	Binnafreaghan	1,328 3 30c	Tyrone	Strabane Upper	Bodoney Lower	Gortin	III.	323
23,24,32,33	Binnawooda	517 2 11d	Tyrone	Omagh West	Ardstraw	Castlederg	III.	315
2, 3	Binnelly	199 0 37e	Tyrone	Strabane Lower	Donaghedy	Strabane	III.	320
3, 10	Binnion	513 2 16	Donegal	Inishowen East	Clonmany	Inishowen	III.	117
62, 63	Binnion	170 1 23	Donegal	Raphoe	Taughboyne	Strabane	III.	143
97	Binroe	189 3 30	Donegal	Banagh	Killaghtee	Glenties	III.	109
97	Binroe	185 1 17	Donegal	Banagh	Killybegs Upper	Glenties	III.	110
58	Binvoran	794 3 16	Clare	Clonderalaw	Kilmurry	Killadysert	II.	17
77	Birbeg Island	2 3 11	Galway	Ballynahinch	Moyrus	Clifden	IV.	14
19	Birchfield	158 0 21	Kilkenny	Shillelogher	St. Patrick's	Kilkenny	I.	116
91, 101	Birchfield	112 3 29	Mayo	Clanmorris	Kilcolman	Claremorris	IV.	133
12	Birchgrove	63 1 35	Tipperary, N.R.	Ikerrin	Corbally	Roscrea	II.	275
45	Birchgrove	185 2 17	Tipperary, N.R.	Kilnamanagh Upper	Doon	Tipperary	II.	277
54, 55	Birchhall or Curraveha	116 2 8	Galway	Moycullen	Kilcummin	Oughterard	IV.	67
50	Birch Hill	97 0 26	Antrim	Upper Antrim	Antrim	Antrim	III.	5
94	Birchhill	207 3 3	Donegal	Tirhugh	Donegal	Donegal	III.	144
40	Birchhill	277 1 32	Tipperary, N.R.	Kilnamanagh Upper	Templebeg	Thurles	II.	279
134, 135	Birchpark	48 2 28	Galway	Leitrim	Clonrush	Scarriff	IV.	52
34	Birchwood	176 1 10	Kilkenny	Kells	Tullahought	Carrick on Suir	I.	110
3	Birchwood	201 2 15	Queen's Co.	Tinnahinch	Rearymore	Mountmellick	I.	249
18, 19	Birchwood	157 3 30	Wicklow	Newcastle	Killiskey	Rathdrum	I.	352
105	Bircog	94 1 36	Donegal	Tirhugh	Templecarn	Donegal	III.	149
6	Birdhill	224 2 11	Meath	Lower Slane	Drumcondra	Ardee	I.	222
25, 31	Birdhill	1,956 3 7	Tipperary, N.R.	Owney and Arra	Kilcomenty	Nenagh	II.	294
147	Bird Island	2 1 5	Cork, W.R.	West Carbery (W.D.)	Kilmoe	Skull	II.	144
17	Bird Island	1 0 14	Down	Ards Upper	Ardkeen	Downpatrick	III.	159
17	Bird Island	2 2 10	Down	Castlereagh Lower	Tullynakill	Newtownards	III.	163
108	Bird Island	4 1 35	Kerry	Glanarought	Tuosist	Kenmare	II.	189
99	Bird Island	0 0 27	Mayo	Carra	Ballintober	Castlebar	IV.	125
21	Birds Island	4 0 5	King's Co.	Garrycastle	Reynagh	Parsonstown	I.	138
70	Birdstown	126 3 12	Donegal	Raphoe	Clonleigh	Strabane	III.	134
48, 53	Birdstown	12 3 16	Wexford	Forth	St. Margaret's	Wexford	I.	314
38	Birdstown Demesne	266 0 28	Donegal	Inishowen West	Fahan Upper	Londonderry	III.	121
29, 30	Birmingham Demesne	398 0 22	Galway	Dunmore	Tuam	Tuam	IV.	35
89	Birmore Island	32 1 30	Galway	Ballynahinch	Moyrus	Clifden	IV.	14
17	Birnaghs	455 1 37f	Tyrone	Strabane Lower	Ardstraw	Strabane	III.	318
103	Birra	168 0 17g	Donegal	Tirhugh	Drumhome	Ballyshannon	III.	146
35	Birragh	197 0 7h	Cavan	Clankee	Enniskeen	Bailieborough	III.	72
3	Birrinagh	336 3 23i	Longford	Granard	Killoe	Granard	I.	157
35	BIRR or PARSONSTOWN T.		King's Co.	Ballybritt	Birr	Parsonstown	I.	125
8	Bishopland	29 1 28	Dublin	Balrothery East	Lusk	Balrothery	I.	20
32, 33	Bishopland	60 0 30	Wexford	Ballaghkeen	St. Nicholas	Enniscorthy	I.	298
38	Bishops Court	246 0 26	Down	Lecale Lower	Dunsfort	Downpatrick	III.	179
18	Bishopscourt	318 1 32	Waterford	Gaultiere	Kilcaragh	Waterford	II.	363
14, 15	Bishopscourt Lower	249 3 12	Kildare	South Salt	Oughterard	Naas	I.	78
9	Bishopscourt North	85 0 16	Kerry	Clanmaurice	Rattoo	Listowel	II.	173
9	Bishopscourt South	144 1 24	Kerry	Clanmaurice	Rattoo	Listowel	II.	173
14,15,19,20	Bishopscourt Upper	409 3 17	Kildare	South Salt	Oughterard	Naas	I.	78
19	Bishops Demesne	54 0 9j	Kilkenny	Crannagh	St. Canice	Kilkenny	I.	87
48	Bishopsfield	21 3 30	Limerick	Coshlea	Emlygrennan	Kilmallock	II.	238
14, 19	Bishopsfurze	71 0 26	Kilkenny	Crannagh	St. Canice	Kilkenny	I.	87
43	Bishopshall	240 3 21	Kilkenny	Ida	Gaulskill	Waterford	I.	102
24, 25, 29	Bishopshill Commons	58 2 13	Kildare	Naas South	Ballymore Eustace	Naas	I.	64
55	Bishop's Island	3 0 0	Clare	Moyarta	Kilfearagh	Kilrush	II.	32
53	Bishops-island	587 2 3	Cork, E.R.	Barrymore	Ardnageehy	Fermoy	II.	50
53	Bishop's Island	19 1 6	Cork, E.R.	Barrymore	Kilquane	Cork	II.	55
26	Bishop's Island	0 1 7	Donegal	Kilmacrenan	Clondahorky	Dunfanaghy	III.	123
33	Bishopsknock	27 0 9	Kilkenny	Ida	The Rower	New Ross	I.	104
25, 29	Bishopsland	561 3 6k	Kildare	Naas South	Ballymore Eustace	Naas	I.	64
22	Bishopsland	115 2 22	Kildare	Offaly East	Kildare	Naas	I.	70
55	Bishopsland	190 0 22	Kilkenny	Ida	Clonamery	Thomastown	I.	101
29	Bishopsland	44 3 17	Wexford	Bantry	St. Mary's	New Ross	I.	302
25, 29	Bishopslane	87 3 37l	Kildare	Naas South	Ballymore Eustace	Naas	I.	64

(a) Including 22A. 0R. 18P. water.
(b) Including 35A. 3R. 21P. water.
(c) Including 11A. 2R. 25P. water.
(d) Including 2A. 3R. 36P. water.
(e) Including 3A. 0R. 25P. water.

(f) Including 13A. 1R. 27P. water.
(g) Including 2A. 2R. 6P. water.
(h) Including 1A. 5R. 12P. water.
(i) Including 5A. 1R. 36P. water.

(j) { Within the Municipal Boundary, 14A. 3R. 7P. / Without the Municipal Boundary, 39A. 1R. 2P. }
(k) { Including 11A. 3R. 0P. water. / Including 5A. 0R. 21P. detached portion. }
(l) Including 1A. 0R. 27P. detached portion.

No. of Sheet of the Ordnance Survey Maps.	Townlands and Towns.	Area in Statute Acres.	County.	Barony.	Parish.	Poor Law Union in 1857.	Townland Census of 1851. Part I.	
		A. R. P.					Vol.	Page
24	Bishopslough East .	15 2 17	Kilkenny . .	Gowran . . .	Tullaherin . .	Thomastown .	I.	100
24	Bishopslough Newtown	574 0 37	Kilkenny . .	Gowran . . .	Tullaherin . .	Thomastown .	I.	100
24	Bishopslough South	189 3 25	Kilkenny . .	Gowran . . .	Tullaherin . .	Thomastown .	I.	100
24	Bishopslough West .	98 3 25	Kilkenny . .	Gowran . . .	Tullaherin . .	Thomastown .	I.	100
13	Bishopsmeadows .	50 2 31	Kilkenny . .	Crannagh . .	Odagh . . .	Kilkenny . .	I.	86
19	Bishopsmeadows .	32 0 22a	Kilkenny . .	Crannagh . .	St. Canice . .	Kilkenny . .	I.	87
74	Bishop's-mill-lands .	52 0 5b	Cork, E.R. .	Cork . . .	St. Finbars . .	Cork . .	II.	65
40	Bishopsmountain .	404 3 28	Kilkenny . .	Ida . . .	Rossinan . .	Waterford .	I.	104
2	Bishopsquarter .	266 3 1	Clare . .	Burren . . .	Drumcreehy . .	Ballyvaghan .	II.	12
3, 7	Bishopstown .	591 1 2	Waterford .	Upperthird . .	Mothel . . .	Carrick on Suir	II.	370
24, 31	Bishopstown or Ballinaspick . .	1,572 3 6	Westmeath .	Rathconrath .	Killare . . .	Mullingar . .	I.	283
11	Bishopswood . .	68 3 3	Dublin . .	Castleknock .	Finglas . . .	Dublin North .	I.	24
34	Bishopswood . .	438 0 10	King's Co. .	Upper Philipstown .	Clonyhurk . .	Mountmellick .	I.	143
51, 52	Bishopswood . .	1,053 0 2	Tipperary, S.R.	Kilnamanagh Lower	Kilmore . .	Cashel . .	II.	323
95	Blabreenagh . .	358 2 17c	Donegal . .	Tirhugh . . .	Drumhome . .	Donegal . .	III.	146
19	Black . . .	122 2 19	Waterford .	Coshmore&Coshbride	Lismore & Mocollop	Lismore . .	II.	345
12	Black Abbey . .	471 2 17	Down . .	Ards Lower . .	Greyabbey . .	Newtownards .	III.	158
21	Blackabbey . .	103 1 39	Limerick . .	Coshma . .	Adare . . .	Croom . .	II.	241
29	Blackacre . .	63 3 38	Galway . .	Dunmore . .	Tuam . . .	Tuam . .	IV.	35
35	Blackbog . .	426 0 3	Kilkenny . .	Kells . . .	Kilmaganny . .	Carrick on Suir	I.	109
37	Blackbog . .	31 2 14	Waterford .	Decies within Drum	Clashmore . .	Youghal . .	II.	351
13	Blackbottom . .	117 0 29	Kilkenny . .	Crannagh . .	Killahy . .	Urlingford . .	I.	86
30	Blackbull . .	115 0 23	King's Co. .	Garrycastle . .	Reynagh . . .	Parsonstown .	I.	138
26	Black Bull or Gallon-bulloge . .	45 0 5	Cavan . .	Upper Loughtee .	Denn . . .	Cavan . .	III.	83
39	Blackcastle . .	173 2 21	Kildare . .	Kilkea and Moone .	Dunmanoge . .	Athy . .	I.	59
25	Blackcastle . .	149 3 32	Meath . .	Lower Navan .	Donaghmore . .	Navan . .	I.	214
42	Blackcastle . .	191 2 28	Tipperary, N.R.	Eliogarty . .	Twomileborris .	Thurles . .	II.	273
76	Blackcastle . .	53 1 3	Tipperary, S.R.	Iffa and Offa East .	Inishlounaght .	Clonmel . .	II.	313
69	Blackcastle . .	528 2 37	Tipperary, S.R.	Middlethird . .	St. Patricksrock .	Cashel . .	II.	330
25	Blackcastle Demesne	395 0 56d	Meath . .	Lower Navan .	Donaghmore . .	Navan . .	I.	214
35	Blackcave North .	173 2 11	Antrim . .	Upper Glenarm .	Larne . . .	Larne . .	III.	25
35, 40	Blackcave South .	178 0 30	Antrim . .	Upper Glenarm .	Larne . . .	Larne . .	III.	25
15, 20	Blackchurch . .	220 2 1	Kildare . .	South Salt . .	Kilteel . . .	Naas . .	I.	77
49	Blackcommon .	50 0 11	Tipperary, S.R.	Slievardagh . .	Ballingarry . .	Callan . .	II.	331
49	Blackcommon .	118 0 13	Tipperary, S.R.	Slievardagh . .	Kilcooly . .	Urlingford . .	II.	333
43	Blackcut . .	199 3 4	Meath . .	Lower Deece .	Galtrim . . .	Trim . .	I.	191
17	Blackditch . .	137 1 39	Dublin . .	Uppercross . .	Ballyfermot . .	Dublin South .	I.	39
27	Blackditch . .	344 2 21	Kildare . .	Offaly West . .	Nurney . . .	Athy . .	I.	74
27	Blackditch . .	16 3 33e	Meath . .	Lower Duleek .	Duleek . .	Drogheda . .	I.	195
27	Blackditch . .	82 3 12f	Meath . .	Upper Duleek .	Duleek . .	Drogheda . .	I.	197
41	Blackditch . .	158 2 5	Meath . .	Upper Moyfenrath .	Castlerickard . .	Trim . .	I.	213
31	Blackditch . .	150 1 30	Wicklow . .	Arklow . . .	Drumkay . .	Rathdrum . .	I.	342
19	Blackditch . .	220 0 23	Wicklow . .	Newcastle . .	Killiskey . .	Rathdrum . .	I.	352
19	Blackditch . .	365 0 39	Wicklow . .	Newcastle . .	Newcastle Lower .	Rathdrum . .	I.	353
10	Blackditches Lower	158 1 34	Wicklow . .	Lower Talbotstown .	Boystown . .	Baltinglass .	I.	359
10, 16	Blackditches Upper	157 3 35	Wicklow . .	Lower Talbotstown .	Boystown . .	Baltinglass .	I.	359
20	Blackdown . .	151 1 3	Kildare . .	South Salt . .	Kilteel . . .	Naas . .	I.	77
3	Blackfallow . .	87 0 7	Roscommon .	Boyle . . .	Ardcarn . . .	Boyle . .	IV.	192
34	Blackford . .	197 1 29	Kildare . .	Narragh and Reban West . . .	Churchtown . .	Athy . .	I.	67
14, 19	Blackford . .	278 1 11	Queen's Co. .	Stradbally . .	Curraclone . .	Athy . .	I.	246
14	Blackfort . .	245 2 4	Tipperary, N.R.	Lower Ormond .	Killodiernan . .	Nenagh . .	II.	284
43	Blackfort . .	183 2 20	Tyrone . .	Clogher . . .	Donacavey . .	Omagh . .	III.	294
36	Blackfriary (1st Division) . . .	9 2 21	Meath . .	Upper Navan .	Trim . . .	Trim . .	I.	216
36	Blackfriary (2nd Division) . . .	278 0 21g	Meath . .	Upper Navan .	Trim . . .	Trim . .	I.	216
104	Blackgarden . .	179 1 20	Galway . .	Dunkellin . .	Kilconickny . .	Loughrea . .	IV.	29
15	Blackgardens . .	122 3 0	Leitrim . .	Drumahaire . .	Killarga . . .	Manorhamilton	IV.	98
5	Blackhall . .	169 0 20	Dublin . .	Balrothery East .	Balrothery . .	Balrothery .	I.	19
14	Blackhall . .	614 0 6h	Kildare . .	Naas North . .	Bodenstown . .	Naas . .	I.	62
24	Blackhall . .	345 3 15	Kildare . .	Naas North . .	Rathmore . .	Naas . .	I.	62
32	Blackhall . .	396 0 39	Kildare . .	Narragh and Reban East . . .	Davidstown . .	Athy . .	I.	66
21, 22	Blackhall . .	173 3 1i	Louth . .	Ferrard . . .	Termonfeckin . .	Drogheda .	I.	182
36	Blackhall . .	602 0 31	Wexford . .	Bantry . . .	Whitechurchglynn .	Wexford . .	I.	303
45	Blackhall . .	113 2 28	Wexford . .	Bargy . . .	Bannow . . .	Wexford . .	I.	304
50	Blackhall Big .	417 2 28	Meath . .	Ratoath . .	Ballymaglassan .	Dunshaughlin .	I.	217
50	Blackhall Little .	201 2 35	Meath . .	Ratoath . .	Ballymaglassan .	Dunshaughlin .	I.	217
46, 47	Black Hill . .	517 1 19	Antrim . .	Lower Belfast . .	Templecorran . .	Larne . .	III.	9
9	Blackhill . .	204 2 11	Carlow . .	Rathvilly . .	Clonmore . .	Shillelagh .	I.	10
23	Blackhill . .	59 1 39	Fermanagh .	Tirkennedy . .	Enniskillen . .	Enniskillen .	III.	221

(a) { Including 2A. 1R. 24P. River Nore.
Within the Municipal Boundary, 31A. 3R. 36P.
Without the Municipal Boundary, 0A. 0R. 26P.
(b) Including 1A. 2R. 14P. water.

(c) Including 9A. 0R. 25P. water.
(d) Including 23A. 2R. 9P. water.
(e) Including 2A. 1R. 3P. detached portion.
(f) Including 4A. 2R. 0P. detached portion.

(g) Including 6A. 0R. 12P. water.
(h) Including 12A. 0R. 27P. water.
(i) Including 6A. 1R. 9P. detached portion.

No. of Sheet of the Ordnance Survey Maps.	Townlands and Towns.	Area in Statute Acres.	County.	Barony.	Parish.	Poor Law Union in 1857.	Townland Census of 1851, Part I.	
		A. R. P.					Vol.	Page
15, 20	Blackhill	175 3 24	Kildare	South Salt	Oughterard	Naas	I.	78
15	Blackhill	85 1 35	Wicklow	Lower Talbotstown	Dunlavin	Baltinglass	I.	360
23	Blackhills	201 1 17	Queen's Co.	Cullenagh	Abbeyleix	Abbeyleix	I.	238
34	Blackhills Lower	235 2 26	Cavan	Clankee	Moybolgue	Bailieborough	III.	74
34	Blackhills Upper	172 2 4	Cavan	Clankee	Moybolgue	Bailieborough	III.	74
42	Blackhorse	64 1 25	Wexford	Forth	Drinagh	Wexford	I.	309
112	Blackhorsefield	15 0 34	Cork, E.R.	Kinsale	Kinsale	Kinsale	II.	100
117	*Black Island*	1 0 8	Mayo	Kilmaine	Ballinchalla	Ballinrobe	IV.	152
20	Black Island	109 3 30	Monaghan	Cremorne	Muckno	Castleblayney	III.	262
23	Black Island	194 3 30a	Monaghan	Dartree	Ematris	Cootehill	III.	266
26, 33	Blackislands or Windmill	152 0 29	Westmeath	Fartullagh	Enniscoffey	Mullingar	I.	268
16	Blackknock	288 2 37	Waterford	Middlethird	Kilmeadan	Waterford	II.	368
36	Blackland	32 3 16	Donegal	Kilmacrenan	Tullyfern	Milford	III.	132
8	Blackland	151 2 34	Dublin	Balrothery East	Lusk	Balrothery	I.	20
63	Blacklands	109 1 30	Tyrone	Clogher	Clogher	Clogher	III.	292
12	Blackmiles	151 2 32	Westmeath	Corkaree	Stonehall	Mullingar	I.	263
22	Blackmillershill	114 2 19	Kildare	Offaly East	Dunmurry	Naas	I.	69
41	Blackmoor	95 0 15	Wexford	Bargy	Kilmannan	Wexford	I.	306
15	Blackmoor	303 2 29	Wicklow	Lower Talbotstown	Donard	Baltinglass	I.	359
60	Black Mountain	707 2 7	Antrim	Upper Belfast	Shankill	Belfast	III.	10
8	Blackmountain	347 0 27	Leitrim	Drumahaire	Cloonclare	Manorhamilton	IV.	93
43	Blackneys or Atateemore	173 3 27	Kilkenny	Ida	Kilcolumb	Waterford	I.	102
35	Blackories	45 1 36	Westmeath	Clonlonan	Kilcleagh	Athlone	I.	261
4, 9	Blackparks	33 1 27	Kerry	Iraghticonnor	Lisselton	Listowel	II.	192
35	Blackparks	51 0 32	Kildare	Narragh&RebanWest	St. Johns	Athy	I.	68
61, 62	Blackpatch	154 3 13	Mayo	Gallen	Killasser	Swineford	IV.	149
16, 22	Blackpits	315 2 4	Wicklow	Upper Talbotstown	Donaghmore	Baltinglass	I.	363
46	Blackpool	38 0 27	Cork, E.R.	Kinnatalloon	Mogedly	Fermoy	II.	98
32	Blackrath	1,156 1 4	Kildare	Narragh&RebanEast	Narraghmore	Athy	I.	66
23, 28	Blackrath and Athgarvan	617 3 32b	Kildare	Connell	Greatconnell	Naas	I.	55
13	Blackraw	341 0 11	Monaghan	Monaghan	Drumsnat	Monaghan	III.	275
69	Blackrepentance	96 1 3	Donegal	Raphoe	Raphoe	Strabane	III.	140
71	Blackrock	9 0 37	Donegal	Raphoe	Clonleigh	Strabane	III.	134
23	Blackrock	3 1 1	Dublin	Dublin	Monkstown	Rathdown	I.	30
23	Blackrock	107 2 12	Dublin	Rathdown	Booterstown	Rathdown	I.	35
114	Blackrock	125 3 3	Galway	Loughrea	Kilthomas	Loughrea	IV.	65
23	Blackrock	233 3 8c	Leitrim	Leitrim	Kiltoghert	Cark. on Shannon	IV.	101
41	*Black Rock*	3 0 18	Mayo	Erris	Kilmore	Belmullet	IV.	146
114	*Black Rock*	3 2 24	Mayo	Murrisk	Inishbofin	Clifden	IV.	159
28	Blackrock	308 2 30	Wicklow	Ballinacor South	Moyne	Shillelagh	I.	330
5	Blackrock	221 0 12	Wicklow	Lower Talbotstown	Blessington	Naas	I.	358
74	BLACKROCK T.	—	Cork, E.R.	Cork	St. Finbars	Cork	II.	66
23	BLACK ROCK T.	—	Dublin	{ Dublin } { Rathdown }	Monkstown	Rathdown	I.	{ 30 } { 37 }
12	BLACK ROCK T.	—	Louth	Upper Dundalk	Haggardstown	Dundalk	I.	178
42	Blacksessagh	151 2 20d	Tyrone	Omagh East	Drumragh	Omagh	III.	312
36, 45	Black's Glen	167 0 37	Donegal	Kilmacrenan	Tullyfern	Milford	III.	132
41	Blackshade	118 2 20	Meath	Upper Moyfenrath	Killyon	Trim	I.	213
9	Blackslee	519 3 2	Fermanagh	Magheraboy	Inishmacsaint	Ballyshannon	III.	212
26	Blackstaff	23 3 5	Kilkenny	Callan	Callan	Callan	I.	83
45	Blackstairs	207 3 17	Tipperary, N.R.	Kilnamanagh Upper	Toem	Tipperary	II.	280
13, 18	Blackstairs Commons	532 1 18	Wexford	Bantry	Killann	Enniscorthy	I.	300
27, 28	Blackstep	183 3 14	Cavan	Clankee	Knockbride	Bailieborough	III.	73
17	Blackstick	66 3 34	Louth	Ardee	Ardee	Ardee	I.	171
100	Blacksticks	104 0 33	Galway	Longford	Clonfert	Ballinasloe	IV.	56
46	Blackstone	100 2 35	Wexford	Bargy	Killag	Wexford	I.	306
20	Blackstoops	203 0 7e	Wexford	Scarawalsh	St.MarysEnniscorthy	Enniscorthy	I.	325
22, 23	Blackthorn	115 3 33	Dublin	Rathdown	Tully	Rathdown	I.	38
60	*Blackthorn Island*	4 2 5	Clare	Clonderalaw	Killadysert	Killadysert	II.	16
60	*Blackthorn Island South*	2 2 3	Clare	Clonderalaw	Killadysert	Killadysert	II.	16
46	Blacktown	135 2 38	Tyrone	Dungannon Middle	Tullyniskan	Dungannon	III.	304
18	Blacktrench	334 3 23	Kildare	Connell	Oldconnell	Naas	I.	56
53	Blackwater	251 1 39	Clare	Bunratty Lower	St. Patricks	Limerick	II.	6
38, 39	Blackwater	143 2 9	Meath	Ratoath	Crickstown	Dunshaughlin	I.	217
27	BLACKWATER T.	—	Wexford	Ballaghkeen	{ Ballyvaldon } { Killila }	Enniscorthy	I.	{ 292 } { 295 }
8	Blackwatertown or Lisbofin	259 0 31	Armagh	Armagh	Clonfeacle	Armagh	III.	43
0	BLACKWATERTOWN T.	—	Armagh	Armagh	Clonfeacle	Armagh	III.	44
112	*Black Weir*	1 1 33	Galway	Kiltartan	Kinvarradoorus	Gort	IV.	49
24	Blackwell	160 2 29	Kilkenny	Gowran	Tullaherin	Thomastown	I.	100

(a) Including 35A. 3R. 36P. water.
(b) Including 6A. 2R. 5P. water.
(c) Including 7A. 1R. 28P. water.
(d) Including 3A. 3R. 11P. water.
(e) Including 4A. 1R. 4P. water.

No. of Sheet of the Ordnance Survey Maps.	Townlands and Towns.	Area in Statute Acres.			County.	Barony.	Parish.	Poor Law Union in 1857.	Townland Census of 1851, Part I.	
		A.	R.	P.					Vol.	Page
13	Blackwood	44	1	24	Kildare	Clane	Downings	Naas	I.	54
13	Blackwood	421	1	14a	Kildare	Clane	Timahoe	Naas	I.	54
31, 35	Blackwood	661	0	33	Kildare	Narragh&RebanWest	Kilberry	Athy	I.	67
9	Blackwood	375	1	36	Kilkenny	Galmoy	Rathbeagh	Urlingford	I.	93
16	Blackwood	192	3	16	King's Co.	Ballycowan	Rahan	Tullamore	I.	128
3	Blagh	211	1	6	Londonderry	North East Liberties of Coleraine	Coleraine	Coleraine	III.	246
31	Blainroe Lower	273	1	31	Wicklow	Arklow	Kilpoole	Rathdrum	I.	345
31	Blainroe Upper	242	0	27	Wicklow	Arklow	Kilpoole	Rathdrum	I.	345
79	Blairstown	289	1	12	Donegal	Raphoe	Donaghmore	Stranorlar	III.	137
28	Blakefield	528	2	34	Tipperary, N.R.	Upper Ormond	Aghnameadle	Nenagh	II.	288
7	Blakes Lower	227	1	38	Londonderry	Coleraine	Dunboe	Coleraine	III.	231
4	Blakesmountain	525	3	16	Clare	Burren	Killonaghan	Ballyvaghan	II.	13
13	Blakestown	104	3	6	Dublin	Castleknock	Clonsilla	Celbridge	I.	24
17	Blakestown	118	1	28	Kildare	Connell	Feighcullen	Naas	I.	55
5, 6, 11	Blakestown	206	0	15	Kildare	North Salt	Laraghbryan	Celbridge	I.	75
17	Blakestown	39	2	37	Kildare	Offaly East	Feighcullen	Edenderry	I.	70
17	Blakestown	381	0	30	Louth	Ardee	Shanlis	Ardee	I.	174
9	Blakestown Lower	138	1	36b	Wicklow	Lower Talbotstown	Hollywood	Naas	I.	360
9, 10	Blakestown Upper	152	1	11	Wicklow	Lower Talbotstown	Hollywood	Naas	I.	360
7	Blakes Upper	118	3	3	Londonderry	Coleraine	Dunboe	Coleraine	III.	231
13, 17	Blanchardstown	454	3	5	Dublin	Castleknock	Castleknock	Dublin North	I.	23
13	BLANCHARDSTOWN T.	—			Dublin	Castleknock	Castleknock	Dublin North	I.	24
17	Blanchfieldsbog	168	0	39	Kilkenny	Crannagh	Tubbridbritain	Urlingford	I.	87
19	Blanchfieldsland	116	2	3	Kilkenny	Gowran	St. John's	Kilkenny	I.	98
20	Blanchville Demesne	179	3	2	Kilkenny	Gowran	Blanchvilleskill	Kilkenny	I.	93
20	Blanchvilleskill	98	3	11	Kilkenny	Gowran	Gowran	Kilkenny	I.	95
20	Blanchvilleskill	31	2	13	Kilkenny	Gowran	Tiscoffin	Kilkenny	I.	99
20	Blanchvillespark	902	2	29	Kilkenny	Gowran	Gowran	Kilkenny	I.	95
20, 24	Blanchvillestown	396	3	28	Kilkenny	Gowran	Blanchvilleskill	Kilkenny	I.	93
20	Blanchvillestown	105	2	5	Kilkenny	Gowran	Gowran	Kilkenny	I.	95
22	Blane	269	1	37	Wicklow	Upper Talbotstown	Donaghmore	Baltinglass	I.	363
15	Blaney East	117	3	15	Fermanagh	Magheraboy	Inishmacsaint	Enniskillen	III.	212
15	Blaney West	53	0	0	Fermanagh	Magheraboy	Inishmacsaint	Enniskillen	III.	212
46, 47	Blanket Nook (Intake)	246	0	0c	Donegal	Inishowen West	Burt	Londonderry	III.	119
46, 47	Blanket Nook (Intake)	660	3	14c	Donegal	Raphoe	Allsaints	Londonderry	III.	134
14	Blaris	543	3	25d	Down	Castlereagh Upper	Blaris	Lisburn	III.	164
62, 73	Blarney	206	1	38e	Cork, E.R.	East Muskerry	Garrycloyne	Cork	II.	103
62	BLARNEY T.				Cork, E.R.	East Muskerry	Garrycloyne	Cork	II.	103
51, 61	Blasket Island Great	1,020	3	12	Kerry	Corkaguiny	Dunquin	Dingle	II.	176
41	Blastknock	224	3	17	Wexford	Shelmaliere West	Taghmon	Wexford	I.	334
35	Bleach	90	3	21f	Kildare	Narragh&RebanWest	St. John's	Athy	I.	68
29	Bleach	31	1	29	Waterford	Decies within Drum	Aglish	Dungarvan	II.	349
19	Bleachgreen	12	2	0g	Kilkenny	Gowran	St. John's	Kilkenny	I.	98
20, 26	Bleachgreen	58	0	16h	Sligo	Leyny	Ballysadare	Sligo	IV.	230
32	Bleachlands	56	3	15	Wexford	Ballaghkeen	Ballynaslaney	Enniscorthy	I.	292
23	Bleachlawn	80	2	16	Westmeath	Kilkenny West	Drumraney	Ballymahon	I.	272
68	Bleachyard	87	2	0i	Mayo	Burrishoole	Burrishoole	Newport	IV.	118
59	Blean	308	1	0j	Clare	Clonderalaw	Killadysert	Killadysert	II.	15
84	Blean	223	3	11	Galway	Athenry	Athenry	Loughrea	IV.	3
22	Blean	429	1	29	Tipperary, N.R.	Upper Ormond	Aghnameadle	Nenagh	II.	288
21	Bleanahource	58	2	30	Waterford	Decies without Drum	Affane	Lismore	II.	353
17, 21	Bleanavoher	325	0	34	Longford	Rathcline	Rathcline	Longford	I.	164
32	Bleanbeg	381	1	17	Tipperary, N.R.	Owney and Arra	Kilnarath	Nenagh	II.	295
20, 25	Bleancup	118	2	11k	Cavan	Upper Loughtee	Kilmore	Cavan	III.	84
39	Bleanish Island	112	0	16	Fermanagh	Coole	Galloon	Lisnaskea	III.	200
35	Bleankillew or Furnace	177	1	19l	Leitrim	Mohill	Annaduff	Mohill	IV.	105
58, 68	Bleanmore	221	3	14	Clare	Clonderalaw	Kilmurry	Kilrush	II.	17
56	Bleanmore Island	34	2	3	Mayo	Erris	Kilcommon	Newport	IV.	145
32, 46	Bleannagloos	373	2	20	Galway	Killian	Killian	Mountbellew	IV.	44
55	Bleanoran or Burnthouse	132	0	33	Galway	Moycullen	Killannin	Oughterard	IV.	69
15	Bleanphuttoge	160	3	34	Westmeath	Kilkenny West	Kilkenny West	Athlone	I.	273
13, 14	Bleantasour	921	3	37	Waterford	Decies without Drum	Seskinan	Dungarvan	II.	360
13, 14	Bleantasour Mountain	700	1	22	Waterford	Decies without Drum	Seskinan	Dungarvan	II.	360
19	Bleary	911	3	25	Down	Lower Iveagh, Up.pt.	Tullylish	Lurgan	III.	171
71, 72	Bleenaleen Lower	161	2	14	Tipperary, S.R.	Slievardagh	Garrangibbon	Carrick on Suir	II.	333
71, 72	Bleenaleen Upper	165	0	12	Tipperary, S.R.	Slievardagh	Garrangibbon	Carrick on Suir	II.	333
50	Bleerick	60	3	31	Antrim	Upper Antrim	Antrim	Antrim	III.	5
29, 38	BLENNERVILLE T.	—			Kerry	Trughanacmy	Annagh	Tralee	II.	205
28, 29	Blessington	206	1	7	Kilkenny	Gowran	Columbkille	Thomastown	I.	94
28, 29	Blessington	104	2	26	Kilkenny	Gowran	Inistioge	Thomastown	I.	96
28, 29	Blessington	120	2	26	Kilkenny	Gowran	Kilfane	Thomastown	I.	96

(a) Including 10A. 6R. 30P. Reservoir.
(b) Including 1A. 2R. 39P. water.
(c) The area of this Intake does not appear on the Ordnance Maps; that here given is from the "Tenement Valuation."
(d) Including 9A. 0R. 2P. water.
(e) Including 8A. 3R. 1P. water.
(f) Including 3A. 3R. 8P. River Barrow.
(g) Including 2A. 0R. 36P. River Nore.
(h) Including 2A. 2R. 37P. water.
(i) Including 1A. 2R. 33P. water.
(j) Including 31A. 2R. 1P. water.
(k) Including 16A. 1R. 37P. water.
(l) Including 6A. 2R. 18P. water.

No. of Sheet of the Ordnance Survey Maps	Townlands and Towns.	Area in Statute Acres.	County.	Barony.	Parish.	Poor Law Union in 1857.	Townland Census of 1851, Part I.	
		A. R. P.					Vol.	Page
5	Blessington	136 0 7	Wicklow	Lower Talbotstown	Blessington	Naas	I.	358
5	Blessington Demesne	411 3 3	Wicklow	Lower Talbotstown	Blessington	Naas	I.	358
5	BLESSINGTON T.	—	Wicklow	Lower Talbotstown	Blessington	Naas	I.	358
118	Blessingtown	81 3 12	Mayo	Kilmaine	Kilmainemore	Ballinrobe	IV.	155
10	Blindennis	90 0 36	Carlow	Rathvilly	Hacketstown	Shillelagh	I.	11
15	Blindwell	1,412 0 31a	Galway	Dunmore	Kilconla	Tuam	IV.	35
35	Blindwood	142 3 10	Wicklow	Arklow	Redcross	Rathdrum	I.	346
28, 31	Blittoge	171 2 23	Monaghan	Farney	Donaghmoyne	Carrickmacross	III.	269
110, 111	Bloomfield	821 3 32b	Mayo	Kilmaine	Robeen	Ballinrobe	IV.	157
28	Bloomfield	113 3 35	Roscommon	Roscommon	Kilcooley	Strokestown	IV.	210
25, 26	Bloomfield	158 0 5	Wexford	Bantry	St. John's	Enniscorthy	I.	302
59	Bloomhill	74 0 23	Tyrone	Clogher	Errigal Keerogue	Clogher	III.	295
42	Bloomhill	96 2 5	Wexford	Forth	Rathmacknee	Wexford	I.	313
6	Bloomhill or Cloncraff	1,626 3 30	King's Co.	Garrycastle	Clonmacnoise	Parsonstown	I.	135
46	Bloomhill Demesne	92 3 22	Tyrone	Dungannon Middle	Tullyniskan	Dungannon	III.	304
17	Bloomry	17 0 28c	Tyrone	Strabane Lower	Ardstraw	Gortin	III.	318
17	Bloomsberry	111 3 2	Meath	Upper Kells	Donaghpatrick	Kells	I.	205
17	Bloomsberry	108 0 26	Meath	Upper Kells	Kells	Kells	I.	205
24, 32	Blossomfort	508 3 5	Cork, E.R.	Orrery and Kilmore	Ballyclogh	Mallow	II.	106
64	Blossomgrove	409 0 37	Cork, E.R.	Barrymore	Ballydeloher	Cork	II.	51
43	Blossomhill	92 2 23	Kilkenny	Ida	Dunkitt	Waterford	I.	101
20, 29	Blossomhill	296 3 26d	Limerick	Connello Lower	Rathkeale	Rathkeale	II.	229
11	Blossomhill	164 1 10e	Limerick	Kenry	Kilcornan	Rathkeale	II.	249
17, 18	Bluebell	261 3 2	Dublin	Uppercross	Drimnagh	Dublin South	I.	40
19, 24	Bluebell	135 2 1	Kildare	Naas North	Naas	Naas	I.	62
22	Blueford	416 0 15	Cork, E.R.	Duhallow	Clonfert	Kanturk	II.	68
23	Bluepool	50 3 35	Cork, E.R.	Duhallow	Castlemagner	Kanturk	II.	67
142, 151	Bluid East	104 3 27	Cork, W.R.	West Carbery (E.D.)	Castlehaven	Skibbereen	II.	137
142, 151	Bluid West	183 0 18	Cork, W.R.	West Carbery (E.D.)	Castlehaven	Skibbereen	II.	137
21	Blundelstown	157 1 13	Dublin	Newcastle	Clondalkin	Celbridge	I.	33
31, 32	Blundelstown	162 3 33	Meath	Skreen	Templekeeran	Navan	I.	222
26	Blunnick	208 3 18	Fermanagh	Clanawley	Killesher	Enniskillen	III.	192
48	Blunsheens	69 0 22	Wexford	Forth	Ballybrennan	Wexford	I.	308
29	Blyry Lower	355 2 12	Westmeath	Brawny	St. Mary's	Athlone	I.	259
29	Blyry Upper	43 1 24	Westmeath	Brawny	St. Mary's	Athlone	I.	259
28, 29	Boadaun	289 1 27	Galway	Dunmore	Kilconla	Tuam	IV.	35
18, 23	Boagh	365 2 23	Cavan	Tullygarvey	Drumgoon	Cootehill	III.	88
98, 99	Boardee	600 1 10	Cork, E.R.	Kinalea	Tracton	Kinsale	II.	97
23	Boardsland	79 0 9	Westmeath	Kilkenny West	Kilkenny West	Athlone	I.	273
19, 26	Boardstown	114 0 12	Westmeath	Moyashel and Magheradernon	Mullingar	Mullingar	I.	275
24	Boarheeny	103 3 4	Limerick	Coonagh	Doon	Tipperary	II.	234
7	Boarmanshill	569 2 9	Limerick	Owneybeg	Abington	Limerick	II.	250
19	Boarmona	94 3 10	Wexford	Scarawalsh	Templeshanbo	Enniscorthy	I.	326
101	Boat Island	2 1 0	Donegal	Tirhugh	Templecarn	Donegal	III.	149
42	Bobsgrove	313 3 4	Cavan	Clanmahon	Kilbride	Oldcastle	III.	77
15	Bobsville	170 0 36	Meath	Fore	Diamor	Oldcastle	I.	200
14	Bocade Glebe	271 3 14	Cavan	Tullyhunco	Kildallan	Bawnboy	III.	96
104	Bocarnagh	335 3 36	Cork, W.R.	Bear	Kilcaskan	Bantry	II.	122
64, 74	Bockagh	448 2 8	Mayo	Costello	Kilcolman	Castlereagh	IV.	141
6, 11	Bockagh	1,448 3 12	Queen's Co.	Upperwoods	Offerlane	Mountmellick	I.	251
39	Bockan Island	10 2 17	Fermanagh	Knockninny	Kinawley	Lisnaskea	III.	203
53	Bockets	667 0 5	Tyrone	Dungannon Lower	Killeeshil	Dungannon	III.	298
27	Bocks Lower	316 0 23f	Monaghan	Farney	Donaghmoyne	Carrickmacross	III.	269
27	Bocks Middle	255 3 31	Monaghan	Farney	Donaghmoyne	Carrickmacross	III.	269
27	Bocks Upper	336 3 10	Monaghan	Farney	Donaghmoyne	Carrickmacross	III.	269
10	Bocombra	108 2 22	Armagh	Oneilland East	Seagoe	Lurgan	III.	50
6	Boconnell	175 0 21	Armagh	Oneilland East	Seagoe	Lurgan	III.	50
77	Bocullin	118 1 0g	Mayo	Burrishoole	Kilmeena	Westport	IV.	121
24	Bodal	170 1 0	Kilkenny	Gowran	Dungarvan	Kilkenny	I.	94
23	Bodalmore	314 0 26	Kilkenny	Shillelogher	Outrath	Kilkenny	I.	115
21, 26	Bodarra Big	124 1 35	Fermanagh	Magheraboy	Rossorry	Enniskillen	III.	214
21, 26	Bodarra Little	71 2 33	Fermanagh	Magheraboy	Rossorry	Enniskillen	III.	214
38	Bodeen	198 3 28	Meath	Ratoath	Kilbrew	Dunshaughlin	I.	218
14, 19	Bodenstown	380 1 35	Kildare	Naas North	Bodenstown	Naas	I.	62
39, 44	Boderan	489 2 9	Wexford	Shelburne	Killesk	New Ross	I.	327
33	Bodingtown	272 0 4	Meath	Upper Duleek	Clonalvy	Drogheda	I.	197
41	Bodoney	331 3 0	Tyrone	Omagh East	Dromore	Omagh	III.	311
56, 57	Bodoney	506 1 3	Tyrone	Omagh East	Kilskeery	Enniskillen	III.	313
3	Bodorragha	142 1 24	Roscommon	Boyle	Kilbryan	Boyle	IV.	195
2, 4	Bodorragha	203 1 0	Roscommon	Boyle	Kilronan	Boyle	IV.	196
101, 105	Boceshil	937 3 31h	Donegal	Tirhugh	Templecarn	Donegal	III.	149
25	Boceshil	203 3 6i	Leitrim	Carrigallen	Drumreilly	Bawnboy	IV.	90

(a) Including 65A. 0R. 30P. water. (d) Including 9A. 1R. 26P. water. (g) Including 25A. 0R. 2P. water.
(b) Including 9A. 3R. 2P. water. (e) Including 2A. 1R. 33P. water. (h) Including 10A. 0R. 7P. water.
(c) Including 2A. 3R. 1P. water. (f) Including 18A. 1R. 15P. water. (i) Including 7A. 1R. 8P. water.

No. of Sheet of the Ordnance Survey Maps.	Townlands and Towns.	Area in Statute Acres.			County.	Barony.	Parish.	Poor Law Union in 1857.	Townland Census of 1851. Part I.	
		A.	R.	P.					Vol.	Page
32	Boeeshil . .	80	2	2	Leitrim .	Mohill . .	Mohill . .	Mohill .	IV.	107
87	Bofara . .	132	1	28	Mayo .	Murrisk . .	Aghagower .	Westport .	IV.	158
9, 10	Bofealan . .	78	1	28	Cavan .	Tullyhaw . .	Templeport .	Bawnboy .	III.	94
47, 59	Bofeenaun . .	659	0	10a	Mayo .	Tirawley . .	Addergoole .	Castlebar .	IV.	162
101, 102	Bofickil . .	420	2	12	Cork, W.R. .	Bear . .	Kilcatherine .	Castletown .	II.	123
25	Bog . .	190	0	36	Waterford .	Decies without Drum	Kilbarrymeaden	Kilmacthomas .	II.	356
70	Bogagh . .	214	0	31	Donegal .	Raphoe . .	Raphoe . .	Strabane .	III.	140
21	Bogagh . .	168	1	24	Londonderry .	Tirkeeran .	Clondermot .	Londonderry .	III.	247
90	Bogagh Glebe .	596	1	15	Donegal .	Banagh . .	Kilcar .	Glenties .	III.	108
91	Bogare . .	687	1	5	Kerry .	Dunkerron South .	Kilcrohane .	Kenmare .	II.	183
53	Bogay . .	91	2	7	Donegal .	Kilmacrenan .	Aghanunshin .	Letterkenny .	III.	122
47, 55	Bogay Glebe .	156	1	29	Donegal .	Raphoe . .	Allsaints . .	Londonderry .	III.	134
55	Bogbane . .	148	3	28	Tyrone .	Dungannon Middle .	Killyman .	Dungannon .	III.	303
26	Bog Commons .	93	1	32	Kilkenny .	Kells . .	Coolaghmore .	Callan .	I.	107
35	Bogderrics .	412	0	14	King's Co. .	Eglish . .	Eglish . .	Parsonstown .	I.	134
47	Bog East . .	105	3	25	Wexford .	Forth . .	Mayglass . .	Wexford .	I.	312
27, 33	Bogesky . .	305	1	31	Cavan .	Upper Loughtee .	Lavey . .	Cavan .	III.	85
12, 21	Boggagh . .	139	1	2	Waterford .	Coshmore&Coshbride	Lismore & Mocollop	Lismore .	II.	345
11, 12	Boggaghbaun .	626	1	29	Waterford .	Coshmore&Coshbride	Lismore & Mocollop	Lismore .	II.	345
36	Boggagh (Conran) .	150	1	26	Westmeath .	Clonlonan .	Kilcleagh .	Athlone .	I.	261
11, 12	Boggaghduff .	453	1	9	Waterford .	Coshmore&Coshbride	Lismore & Mocollop	Lismore .	II.	345
36	Boggagh Eighter .	234	3	24	Westmeath .	Clonlonan .	Kilcleagh .	Athlone .	I.	261
36	Boggagh (Fury) .	106	1	12	Westmeath .	Clonlonan .	Kilcleagh .	Athlone .	I.	261
36	Boggagh (Malone) .	89	2	39	Westmeath .	Clonlonan .	Kilcleagh .	Athlone .	I.	261
13, 17	Boggan . .	267	1	16	Carlow .	Forth . .	Ballon . .	Carlow .	I.	3
17	Boggan . .	230	3	39	Carlow .	Forth . .	Barragh . .	Carlow .	I.	4
17	Boggan . .	460	2	24	Kilkenny .	Crannagh .	Tullaroan .	Kilkenny .	I.	87
5	Boggan . .	119	2	22	Meath .	Lower Kells .	Moybolgue .	Kells .	I.	203
40, 42	Bogganfin . .	163	1	31	Roscommon .	Athlone . .	Kilmeane .	Roscommon .	IV.	182
49, 52	Bogganfin . .	292	2	4	Roscommon .	Athlone . .	Kiltoom . .	Athlone .	IV.	182
49, 52	Bogganfin . .	105	3	15	Roscommon .	Athlone . .	St. Peter's .	Athlone .	IV.	184
52	BOGGANFIN T. .	—			Roscommon .	Athlone . .	St. Peter's .	Athlone .	IV.	184
50, 53	Bogganstown .	211	0	15	Meath .	Dunboyne .	Dunboyne .	Dunshaughlin .	I.	199
43, 44	Bogganstown .	395	3	31	Meath .	Upper Deece .	Culmullin .	Dunshaughlin .	I.	193
42, 43	Bogganstown Lower	37	2	8	Wexford .	Forth . .	Drinagh . .	Wexford .	I.	309
42	Bogganstown Upper	26	1	35	Wexford .	Forth . .	Drinagh . .	Wexford .	I.	309
105, 115	Boggaun . .	98	1	31	Galway .	Loughrea .	Kilchreest .	Loughrea .	IV.	63
21	Boggaun . .	108	3	18	Leitrim .	Carrigallen .	Oughteragh .	Bawnboy .	IV.	91
11	Boggaun . .	984	1	30	Leitrim .	Drumahaire .	Cloonlogher .	Manorhamilton .	IV.	94
23	Boggaun . .	102	1	39	Tipperary, N.R. .	Ikerrin .	Killavinoge .	Roscrea .	II.	275
30	Boggaunreagh .	86	0	3	King's Co. .	Garrycastle .	Reynagh . .	Parsonstown .	I.	138
32	Boggauns . .	416	0	26	Galway .	Ballymoe .	Kilbegnet .	Glennamaddy .	IV.	8
32	Boggauns . .	420	0	3	Galway .	Killian .	Killian . .	Mountbellew .	IV.	44
95	Boggra . .	184	1	14	Cork, W.R. .	Kinalmeaky .	Templemartin .	Bandon .	II.	152
59	Boggy . .	678	1	28	Mayo .	Tirawley . .	Addergoole .	Castlebar .	IV.	163
11	Boggyheary .	90	2	2	Dublin .	Nethercross .	Killossery .	Balrothery .	I.	31
46, 47, 59	Boghadoon .	1,197	0	0	Mayo .	Tirawley . .	Addergoole .	Castlebar .	IV.	163
27, 31	Boghall . .	344	0	11	Kildare .	Offaly West .	Harristown .	Athy .	I.	72
8, 9	Boghil . .	371	1	23	Clare .	Corcomroe .	Kilfenora .	Ennistymon .	II.	19
18, 19	Boghilboy .	228	1	1	Londonderry .	Coleraine .	Desertoghill .	Coleraine .	III.	230
3, 7	Boghill . .	341	2	39	Londonderry .	North East Liberties of Coleraine .	Coleraine .	Coleraine .	III.	246
68, 69	Boghilmore Island .	8	0	1	Galway .	Moycullen .	Moycullen .	Galway .	IV.	71
12, 13	Boghlone . .	306	3	31	Queen's Co. .	Maryborough East .	Clonenagh&Clonagheen	Mountmellick .	I.	241
16	Boghouse . .	77	2	36	Carlow .	Idrone East .	Fennagh . .	Carlow .	I.	7
63,64,73,74	Boghtaduff .	931	3	4	Mayo .	Costello .	Castlemore .	Castlereagh .	IV.	139
45	Bogland . .	109	3	34	Wicklow .	Arklow . .	Arklow . .	Rathdrum .	I.	341
99	Bogpark . .	138	0	4	Galway .	Clonmacnowen .	Clontuskert .	Ballinasloe .	IV.	24
98	Bogside . .	35	2	0	Donegal .	Banagh . .	Killaghtee .	Donegal .	III.	109
46	Bogstown or Moydrum	369	0	11	Meath .	Upper Moyfenrath .	Clonard . .	Edenderry .	I.	213
26	Bogtown . .	811	0	16	King's Co. .	Upper Philipstown .	Ballykean .	Mountmellick .	I.	143
2	Bogtown . .	169	3	20	Londonderry .	Coleraine .	Dunboe . .	Coleraine .	III.	231
14	Bogtown . .	273	0	22	Louth .	Ardee . .	Mapastown .	Ardee .	I.	173
22	Bog and Warren .	97	0	1	Wexford .	Ballaghkeen .	Donaghmore .	Gorey .	I.	293
47	Bog West . .	177	3	3	Wexford .	Forth . .	Mayglass . .	Wexford .	I.	312
36	Bogwood or Carrowntogher .	200	3	38	Roscommon .	Ballintober South .	Kilgefin . .	Roscommon .	IV.	189
115, 124	Bohaboy . .	637	0	11	Galway .	Loughrea .	Killeenadeema .	Loughrea .	IV.	64
99	Bohacogram .	1,044	2	10	Kerry .	Dunkerrin South .	Kilcrohane .	Kenmare .	II.	183
82	Bohacullia . .	699	1	5	Kerry .	Dunkerrin South .	Templenoe .	Kenmare .	II.	185
23	Bohadoonmountain .	828	1	19	Waterford .	Decies without Drum	Kilgobnet .	Dungarvan .	II.	357
22, 23	Bohadoon North .	316	0	1	Waterford .	Decies without Drum	Kilgobnet .	Dungarvan .	II.	357
22, 23	Bohadoon South .	584	1	14	Waterford .	Decies without Drum	Kilgobnet .	Dungarvan .	II.	357

(a) Including 7A. 0R. 12P. water.

No. of Sheet of the Ordnance Survey Maps.	Townlands and Towns.	Area in Statute Acres.			County.	Barony.	Parish.	Poor Law Union in 1857.	Townland Census of 1851, Part I.	
		A.	R.	P.					Vol.	Page
27	Bohagh	533	1	34	Roscommon	Castlereagh	Ballintober	Castlereagh	IV.	198
64, 74	Bohalas	494	3	16	Mayo	Costello	Castlemore	Castlereagh	IV.	139
15	Bohammer	134	2	2	Dublin	Coolock	Balgriffin	Dublin North	I.	26
80	Bohamore	328	0	12	Mayo	Gallen	Bohola	Swineford	IV.	147
69, 78	Bohanboy	394	1	19	Donegal	Raphoe	Donaghmore	Stranorlar	III.	137
45	Bohard	434	0	10	Limerick	Connello Upper	Kilmeedy	Newcastle	II.	233
60	Bohard	344	1	13	Tyrone	Dungannon Lower	Aghaloo	Dungannon	III.	296
14, 17	Boharnamoe	390	2	15	Louth	Ardee	Ardee	Ardee	I.	171
35, 40	Bohasset	78	3	8	Fermanagh	Clankelly	Galloon	Clones	III.	198
134	Bohatch North	1,090	3	30	Galway	Leitrim	Inishcaltra	Scarriff	IV.	53
134	Bohatch South	453	1	17	Galway	Leitrim	Inishcaltra	Scarriff	IV.	53
24	Bohattan	108	0	0	Fermanagh	Magherastephana	Aghalurcher	Lisnaskea	III.	215
26	Bohaun	443	0	13	Galway	Ross	Ross	Oughterard	IV.	73
80, 81	Bohaun	226	2	4	Mayo	Costello	Knock	Claremorris	IV.	142
98, 99	Bohaun North	845	2	32	Mayo	Carra	Ballintober	Ballinrobe	IV.	124
98, 99, 108	Bohaun South	728	1	16	Mayo	Carra	Ballintober	Ballinrobe	IV.	124
38, 52	Boheeshal	2,542	2	25a	Galway	Ballynahinch	Moyrus	Clifden	IV.	12
72	Boheeshil	497	3	24	Kerry	Dunkerron North	Knockane	Cahersiveen	II.	181
87, 97, 98	Boheh	424	3	22	Mayo	Murrisk	Aghagower	Westport	IV.	158
96	Boheh	360	1	29	Mayo	Murrisk	Oughaval	Westport	IV.	161
77, 78	Bohehs	109	0	37	Mayo	Carra	Islandeady	Westport	IV.	128
44	Boheolan	170	3	20	Donegal	Kilmacrenan	Conwal	Letterkenny	III.	126
116	Boher	36	0	38	Cork, W.R.	Bear	Killaconenagh	Castletown	II.	124
14	Boher	308	2	19	Limerick	Clanwilliam	Abington	Limerick	II.	221
58	Boher	208	0	14	Limerick	Coshlea	Kilbeheny	Mitchelstown	II.	239
25	Boher	442	0	7	Tipperary, N.R.	Owney and Arra	Kilmastulla	Nenagh	II.	295
48	Boher	31	2	13	Wexford	Forth	St. Helens	Wexford	I.	313
30	Boheradurrow	213	2	36	King's Co.	Garrycastle	Reynagh	Parsonstown	I.	138
24	Boheragaddy	250	1	1	Kilkenny	Gowran	Tullaherin	Thomastown	I.	100
35	Boheragh	194	1	10	Tyrone	Strabane Upper	Cappagh	Omagh	III.	325
52	Boherard	301	0	36	Cork, E.R.	Barrymore	Dunbulloge	Cork	II.	54
22	Boherard	229	2	39	Meath	Fore	Killallon	Oldcastle	I.	200
22	Boherard	491	2	19	Queen's Co.	Clarmallagh	Aghaboe	Abbeyleix	I.	235
31, 36	Boherard	104	1	27	Waterford	Decies without Drum	Dungarvan	Dungarvan	II.	355
51	Boheraroan	42	2	6	Clare	Bunratty Lower	Tomfinlough	Ennis	II.	7
51	BOHERAROAN T.	—			Clare	Bunratty Lower	Tomfinlough	Ennis	II.	7
16, 24	Boherascrub East	282	0	35	Cork, E.R.	Orrery and Kilmore	Buttevant	Mallow	II.	107
16, 24	Boherascrub West	527	1	23	Cork, E.R.	Orrery and Kilmore	Buttevant	Mallow	II.	107
27	Boherash	259	2	25	Cork, E.R.	Fermoy	Glanworth	Fermoy	II.	79
59	Boheravendrum	80	1	13	Tipperary, S.R.	Clanwilliam	Tipperary	Tipperary	II.	312
26	Boherawarraga	8	3	4	Kilkenny	Kells	Coolaghmore	Callan	I.	107
22, 30	Boherawillin	289	1	29	Waterford	Decies without Drum	Modelligo	Lismore	II.	359
32	Boherbannagh	299	1	23	Galway	Killian	Killian	Mountbellew	IV.	44
31	Boherbaun Lower	462	2	12	Kildare	Offaly West	Harristown	Athy	I.	72
27, 31	Boherbaun Upper or Monapheeby	374	1	24	Kildare	Offaly West	Harristown	Athy	I.	72
8, 15	Boherboy	325	2	31	Clare	Corcomroe	Killilagh	Ennistimon	II.	19
21	Boherboy	245	3	36	Dublin	Newcastle	Saggart	Celbridge	I.	34
79, 80	Boherboy	148	3	35	Kerry	Iveragh	Caher	Cahersiveen	II.	193
39, 48	Boherboy	247	1	33	Kerry	Trughanacmy	Currans	Killarney	II.	209
35	Boherboy	109	3	23	King's Co.	Ballybritt	Birr	Parsonstown	I.	125
11	Boherboy	78	0	1b	Limerick	Kenry	Kilcornan	Rathkeale	II.	249
71	Boherboy	1,085	2	20	Tipperary, S.R.	Slievardagh	Kilvemnon	Callan	II.	334
21	Boherboy	154	2	3	Waterford	Coshmore&Coshbride	Lismore and Mocollop	Lismore	II.	345
38	Boherboy	212	1	8	Waterford	Decies within Drum	Ardmore	Dungarvan	II.	349
15	Boherboy	189	1	28	Wicklow	Lower Talbotstown	Dunlavin	Baltinglass	I.	360
21	Boherboyrea	179	0	21	Waterford	Coshmore&Coshbride	Lismore and Mocollop	Lismore	II.	345
22, 30	BOHERBOY T.	—			Cork, E.R.	Duhallow	Kilmeen	Kanturk	II.	73
44	Boherbrack	468	2	5c	Kerry	Corkaguiny	Kinard	Dingle	II.	179
21	Boherbraddagh	156	3	35	Limerick	Connello Lower	Clonshire	Rathkeale	II.	227
16	Boherbullog	60	2	21	Clare	Inchiquin	Rath	Corrofin	II.	27
41	Bohercarron	317	3	5	Limerick	Coshlea	Galbally	Mitchelstown	II.	238
61	Boherclogh	14	1	18	Tipperary, S.R.	Middlethird	St. John Baptist	Cashel	II.	330
53	Bohercreen	2	1	7	Wexford	Forth	Carn	Wexford	I.	309
58,59,66,67	Bohercrow	828	0	34	Tipperary, S.R.	Clanwilliam	Tipperary	Tipperary	II.	312
42	Bohercuill	269	1	38	Galway	Clare	Kilcoona	Tuam	IV.	19
38	Boherdeel	182	0	2	King's Co.	Ballybritt	Birr	Parsonstown	I.	125
27	Boherderroge	119	2	28	Cork, E.R.	Fermoy	Kilcrumper	Fermoy	II.	89
25	Boherdotia	169	0	32	Limerick	Coonagh	Oola	Tipperary	II.	235
16	Boherduff	489	0	19	Carlow	Idrone East	Dunleckny	Carlow	I.	6
105	Boherduff	163	0	20	Galway	Dunkellin	Kilconickny	Loughrea	IV.	29
23	Boherduff	164	2	5	Limerick	Clanwilliam	Caherelly	Limerick	II.	222
161	Boherduff	51	1	16	Mayo	Clanmorris	Kilcolman	Claremorris	IV.	133

(a) Including 165A. 1R. 9P. water.   (b) Including 1A. 0R. 9P. water.   (c) Including 2A. 1P. 11P. water.

No. of Sheet of the Ordnance Survey Maps.	Townlands and Towns.	Area in Statute Acres. A. R. P.	County.	Barony.	Parish.	Poor Law Union in 1857.	Townland Census of 1851, Part I. Vol.	Page
58	Boherduff	63 3 30	Tipperary, S.R.	Clanwilliam	Cullen	Tipperary	II.	307
77, 83	Boherduff	121 0 39	Tipperary, S.R.	Iffa and Offa East	Rathronan	Clonmel	II.	316
13	Bohereen	101 3 25	Limerick	Clanwilliam	Donaghmore	Limerick	II.	223
13	Bohereen	40 2 23	Limerick	Clanwilliam	St. Nicholas	Limerick	II.	225
49	Bohereenkyle	190 0 27	Limerick	Coshlea	Ballingarry	Kilmallock	II.	237
48	Bohereens	106 1 19	Kerry	Magunihy	Molahiffe	Killarney	II.	204
7	Boherfadda or Parkaree	285 1 11	King's Co.	Garrycastle	Lemanaghan	Parsonstown	I.	137
14	Bohergar	280 0 21	Limerick	Clanwilliam	Abington	Limerick	II.	221
39	Bohergarve	152 2 12	Roscommon	Ballintober South	Roscommon	Roscommon	IV.	190
27, 28	Bohergoy Lower	363 3 36	Kildare	Offaly East	Ballysax	Naas	I.	69
27, 28	Bohergoy Upper	236 3 27	Kildare	Offaly East	Ballysax	Naas	I.	69
49	Boherhallagh	641 2 26	Mayo	Gallen	Toomore	Swineford	IV.	151
10	Boherhole	465 3 23	Kildare	Ikeathy&Oughterany	Mainham	Celbridge	I.	58
17	Boherkill	431 0 34	Kildare	Offaly East	Rathangan	Naas	I.	70
13	Boherkyle	44 1 0	Kilkenny	Crannagh	Freshford	Kilkenny	I.	85
25	Boherkyle	301 3 29	Kilkenny	Gowran	Powerstown	Thomastown	I.	97
2	Boherlea	237 2 34	Meath	Lower Kells	Kilmainham	Kells	I.	203
10	Boherleigh	174 3 34	Tipperary, N.R.	Lower Ormond	Finnoe	Borrisokane	II.	284
13, 22	Boherload	394 2 21	Limerick	Clanwilliam	Cahervally	Limerick	II.	221
27	Boherlody	102 2 8	Tipperary, N.R.	Upper Ormond	Dolla	Nenagh	II.	290
24	BOHERMEEN T.	—	Meath	Lower Navan	{ Ardbraccan ; Martry }	{ Navan ; Kells }	I.	{ 214 ; 215 }
16	Bohermore	468 1 38	Carlow	Idrone East	Dunleckny	Carlow	I.	6
29	Bohermore	46 2 34	Kilkenny	Gowran	Graiguenamanagh	Thomastown	I.	95
19	Bohermore	351 3 30	Longford	Ardagh	Ardagh	Longford	I.	151
133	Bohernabredagh	113 2 20	Cork, W.R.	West Carbery (E.D.)	Dromdaleague	Skibbereen	II.	139
21,22,24,25	Bohernabreena	231 2 38	Dublin	Uppercross	Tallaght	Dublin South	I.	41
20	Bohernacross	92 2 18	Longford	Ardagh	Ardagh	Longford	I.	151
16	Bohernaghty	272 2 13	Queen's Co.	Upperwoods	Offerlane	Abbeyleix	I.	251
47,48,55,56	Bohernagore	629 1 30	Limerick	Coshlea	Ballingaddy	Kilmallock	II.	237
87	Bohernagore East	59 3 28	Tipperary, S.R.	Iffa and Offa West	Tullaghorton	Clogheen	II.	321
87, 90	Bohernagore West	1,321 1 34a	Tipperary, S.R.	Iffa and Offa West	Tullaghorton	Clogheen	II.	321
24	Bohernagraga	185 1 12	Limerick	Coonagh	Oola	Tipperary	II.	235
24	Bohernagraga	26 0 26	Limerick	Coonagh	Tuoghcluggin	Tipperary	II.	236
7, 8	Bohernagrisna	360 1 6	King's Co.	Ballycowan	Rahan	Tullamore	I.	128
9	Bohernameeltoge	130 3 0	Longford	Longford	Killoe	Longford	I.	158
41	Bohernamona	162 2 10	Tipperary, N.R.	Eliogarty	Thurles	Thurles	II.	273
74, 80, 81	Bohernarnane	1,355 2 38	Tipperary, S.R.	Iffa and Offa West	Tubbrid	Clogheen	II.	320
22, 23, 28	Bohernarude	532 3 13	Tipperary, N.R.	Ikerrin	Killea	Roscrea	II.	275
32	Bohernasear	89 2 15	Queen's Co.	Slievemargy	Killeshin	Carlow	I.	245
21	Bohernastrekaun or Killure	253 0 36	Kilkenny	Gowran	Wells	Kilkenny	I.	100
116	Bohernoe	27 2 13	Cork, W.R.	Bear	Killaconenagh	Castletown	II.	124
20	Boherphilip	74 2 23	Kildare	South Salt	Kill	Naas	I.	77
2	Boherquill	173 0 20	Westmeath	Moygoish	Street	Granard	I.	281
21	Boherroe	368 1 5	Kerry	Clanmaurice	O'Dorney	Tralee	II.	172
24	Boherroe	242 1 18	Limerick	Clanwilliam	Aglishcormick	Limerick	II.	221
24	Boherroe	121 2 3	Limerick	Clanwilliam	Grean	Limerick	II.	224
16	Boherroe	35 2 36	Roscommon	Frenchpark	Creeve	Car". on Shannon	IV.	203
29, 30	Boherstooka	169 0 39	Wexford	Bantry	Ballyanne	New Ross	I.	299
31	Boherygeela	352 3 3	Limerick	Smallcounty	Glenogra	Croom	II.	259
31	Boherygeela	248 0 23	Limerick	Smallcounty	Tullabracky	Croom	II.	261
26	Bohevny	192 0 17	Fermanagh	Clanawley	Cleenish	Enniskillen	III.	189
9	Bohevny	353 3 11	Fermanagh	Magheraboy	Inishmacsaint	Ballyshannon	III.	212
32	Bohilla	223 2 7	Kilkenny	Gowran	Inistioge	Thomastown	I.	96
77	Bohillane	284 0 25	Cork, E.R.	Imokilly	Bohillane	Middleton	II.	84
45	Bohirril	233 2 21	Donegal	Kilmacrenan	Conwal	Letterkenny	III.	126
45	Bohirril Park	95 2 15	Donegal	Kilmacrenan	Conwal	Letterkenny	III.	126
79	Bohoge	243 3 11b	Mayo	Carra	Manulla	Castlebar	·IV.	129
92, 93	Bohogerawer	161 0 0c	Mayo	Costello	Bekan	Claremorris	IV.	138
71	Bohola	565 2 9	Mayo	Gallen	Bohola	Swineford	IV.	147
121, 122, 134	Bohona	229 0 22	Cork, W.R.	Ibane and Barryroe	Castleventry	Clonakilty	II.	148
134, 143	Bohonagh	368 3 15	Cork, W.R.	East Carbery (W.D.)	Ross	Clonakilty	II.	135
92	Bohoona East	418 1 8	Galway	Moycullen	Killannin	Galway	IV.	69
92	Bohoona West	494 2 38	Galway	Moycullen	Killannin	Galway	IV.	69
19, 24	Bohora	106 1 4	Cavan	Tullyhunco	Killashandra	Cavan	III.	97
35, 40	Bohora	109 3 27	Fermanagh	Coole	Galloon	Clones	III.	199
23	Bohulkin	77 3 38	Fermanagh	Tirkennedy	Enniskillen	Enniskillen	III.	221
37, 38	Bohullion or Glack	296 0 20	Donegal	Inishowen West	Inch	Londonderry	III.	121
47	Bohullion Lower	629 2 0	Donegal	Inishowen West	Burt	Londonderry	III.	119
47	Bohullion Upper	661 1 0	Donegal	Inishowen West	Burt	Londonderry	III.	119
58, 59, 68	Bohyodaun	157 3 8d	Clare	Clonderalaw	Killofin	Killadysert	II.	16
11	Boihy	885 0 37	Leitrim	Drumahaire	Drumlease	Manorhamilton	IV.	94

(a) Including 7A. 1R. 24P. Bay Lough.   (c) Including 2A. 3R. 32P. water.   (d) Including 10A. 2R. 32P. water.
(b) Including 11A. 0R. 34P. water.

No. of Sheet of the Ordnance Survey Maps.	Townlands and Towns.	Area in Statute Acres.			County.	Barony.	Parish.	Poor Law Union in 1857.	Townland Census of 1851, Part I.	
		A.	R.	P.					Vol.	Page
21, 22	Boira North	251	2	3	Wexford	Gorey	Kiltrisk	Gorey	I.	320
21, 22	Boira South	355	0	3	Wexford	Gorey	Kiltrisk	Gorey	I.	320
32	*Bo Island*	4	1	2	Donegal	Kilmacrenan	Tullaghobegly	Dunfanaghy	III.	132
37	Bolabaun	278	1	38	Wexford	Shelmaliere West	Killurin	Wexford	I.	334
14	Bola Beg	429	1	30	Wexford	Scarawalsh	Templeshanbo	Enniscorthy	I.	326
27	Bolaboy Beg	184	1	24	Wexford	Ballaghkeen	Castle-ellis	Enniscorthy	I.	293
27	Bolaboy Beg	28	0	6	Wexford	Ballaghkeen	Meelnagh	Enniscorthy	I.	298
27	Bolaboy More	369	2	15	Wexford	Ballaghkeen	Meelnagh	Enniscorthy	I.	298
3	Bolabradda	160	0	12	Wexford	Gorey	Inch	Gorey	I.	316
23, 24, 29, 30	Bolacaheer	174	2	19	Wexford	Bantry	Ballyanne	New Ross	I.	299
15	Bolacaheer	308	1	14	Wexford	Scarawalsh	Ferns	Enniscorthy	I.	323
6	Bolacreen	336	0	24	Wexford	Gorey	Kilnahue	Gorey	I.	319
16	Bolacreen	336	3	14	Wexford	Scarawalsh	Kilbride	Enniscorthy	I.	323
9, 14	Boladurragh	727	1	28	Wexford	Scarawalsh	Templeshanbo	Enniscorthy	I.	326
125, 126 } 131, 132 }	Bolag	433	1	33	Galway	Leitrim	Ballynakill	Loughrea	IV.	50
30	Bolagh Lower	152	3	39	Wicklow	Arklow	Dunganstown	Rathdrum	I.	343
24, 33	Bolaght	692	3	17*a*	Tyrone	Omagh West	Ardstraw	Castlederg	III.	315
30	Bolagh Upper	171	0	15	Wicklow	Arklow	Dunganstown	Rathdrum	I.	343
49	Bolakeale	294	0	38	Tipperary, S.R.	Slievardagh	Ballingarry	Callan	II.	331
14	Bola More	288	3	14	Wexford	Scarawalsh	Templeshanbo	Enniscorthy	I.	326
54, 61	Boland	190	3	30	Tyrone	Dungannon Middle	Clonfeacle	Dungannon	III.	298
14	Bolandstown	252	0	13	Westmeath	Delvin	Castletowndelvin	Castletowndelvin	I.	264
12	Bolane	281	3	24	Limerick	Kenry	Kildimo	Rathkeale	II.	249
2, 6	Bolany	300	2	24	Wexford	Gorey	Kilnahue	Gorey	I.	319
4	Bolarry	68	3	38	Roscommon	Boyle	Kilronan	Boyle	IV.	196
1, 2, 8	Bolart North	117	1	38	King's Co.	Kilcoursey	Kilmanaghan	Tullamore	I.	141
8	Bolart South	300	3	10	King's Co.	Kilcoursey	Kilmanaghan	Tullamore	I.	141
10	Bolea	206	0	2	Londonderry	Keenaght	Drumachose	New T⁰ Limavady	III.	235
140	Boleagh	252	2	35	Cork, W.R.	West Carbery (W.D.)	Kilcoe	Skull	II.	143
12	Boleany	191	3	9	Wexford	Ballaghkeen	Ardamine	Gorey	I.	291
18	Boleran	546	1	38	Londonderry	Coleraine	Errigal	Coleraine	III.	232
13	Boley	294	3	9	Cavan	Tullyhaw	Templeport	Bawnboy	III.	94
118	Boley	72	2	14	Galway	Longford	Kilmalinoge	Portumna	IV.	59
118	Boley	60	0	25	Galway	Longford	Lickmolassy	Portumna	IV.	60
25	Boley	1,090	2	3	Queen's Co.	Ballyadams	Rathaspick	Athy	I.	232
23, 29	Boley	804	0	39	Queen's Co.	Cullenagh	Abbeyleix	Abbeyleix	I.	238
11, 16	Boley	322	1	28	Wexford	Gorey	Ballycanew	Gorey	I.	316
40	Boley	1,193	2	31	Wexford	Shelburne	Owenduff	New Ross	I.	328
42, 43	Boley	660	0	39	Wicklow	Shillelagh	Aghowle	Shillelagh	I.	356
27	Boley	231	1	5	Wicklow	Upper Talbotstown	Baltinglass	Baltinglass	I.	362
71, 80	Boleyard	425	1	32	Mayo	Gallen	Kildacommoge	Castlebar	IV.	148
17	Boleybaun	193	1	20	Leitrim	Drumahaire	Inishmagrath	Manorhamilton	IV.	95
3	Boleybaun	155	1	3	Wexford	Gorey	Kilcavan	Gorey	I.	317
30	Boleybawn	603	2	15	Queen's Co.	Cullenagh	Dysartgallen	Abbeyleix	I.	239
43	Boleybawn	303	2	23	Wicklow	Shillelagh	Crosspatrick	Shillelagh	I.	357
115, 124	Boleybeg	520	0	15	Galway	Loughrea	Killeenadeema	Loughrea	IV.	64
29	Boleybeg	593	0	0	Kildare	Naas South	Jago	Naas	I.	65
32, 36	Boleybeg	521	1	23	Kildare	Narragh & Reban East	Narraghmore	Athy	I.	66
31	Boleybeg	90	3	25	Kildare	Offaly West	Fontstown	Athy	I.	72
101, 111	Boleybeg	432	2	37*b*	Mayo	Clanmorris	Tagheen	Claremorris	IV.	135
24	Boleybeg	715	3	1	Queen's Co.	Cullenagh	Dysartgallen	Abbeyleix	I.	239
81, 93	Boleybeg East	153	1	36	Galway	Galway	Rahoon	Galway	IV.	37
107, 117	Boleybeg & Killimor	105	3	32	Galway	Longford	Killimorbologue	Portumna	IV.	59
81, 93	Boleybeg West	58	0	10	Galway	Galway	Rahoon	Galway	IV.	37
8, 12	Boleyboy	1,634	2	3	Leitrim	Rosclogher	Cloonclare	Manorhamilton	IV.	109
112	Boleyboy	549	1	19	Mayo	Clanmorris	Kilvine	Claremorris	IV.	134
82	Boleyboy	136	2	20	Mayo	Costello	Aghamore	Swineford	IV.	136
62	Boleyboy	64	0	30	Mayo	Gallen	Killasser	Swineford	IV.	149
16	Boleybrack	212	1	35	Leitrim	Drumahaire	Killarga	Manorhamilton	IV.	98
87, 97	Boleybrian	176	2	37	Mayo	Murrisk	Aghagower	Westport	IV.	158
27	Boleycarrigeen	297	3	10	Wicklow	Upper Talbotstown	Kilranelagh	Baltinglass	I.	364
115	Boleycurheen	95	0	37	Galway	Loughrea	Killeenadeema	Loughrea	IV.	64
96	Boleydorragha	20	3	36	Galway	Dunkellin	Kilconierin	Loughrea	IV.	29
48	Boleyduff	119	3	31	Roscommon	Athlone	Taghmaconnell	Athlone	IV.	185
59	Boleyglass	384	1	16	Mayo	Tirawley	Addergoole	Castlebar	IV.	163
31	Boley Great	438	1	15	Kildare	Narragh & Reban East	Fontstown	Athy	I.	66
34	Boleyhill	110	1	32	Fermanagh	Magherastephana	Aghalurcher	Lisnaskea	III.	215
30	Boleylaan	139	2	26	Galway	Dunmore	Tuam	Tuam	IV.	35
31	Boley Little	251	2	10	Kildare	Narragh & Reban East	Fontstown	Athy	I.	66
23	Boley Lower	425	3	14	Queen's Co.	Cullenagh	Clonenagh and Clonaghoon	Abbeyleix	I.	239
11	Boley Lower	225	2	25	Wexford	Gorey	Rossminoge	Gorey	I.	321

(*a*) Including 0A. 1R. 9P. water.　　　　(*b*) Including 15A. 3R. 12P. water.

No. of Sheet of the Ordnance Survey Maps.	Townlands and Towns.	Area in Statute Acres.	County.	Barony.	Parish.	Poor Law Union in 1857.	Townland Census of 1851, Part I.	
		A. R. P.					Vol.	Page
27	Boleylug	151 1 38	Wicklow	Upper Talbotstown	Baltinglass	Baltinglass	I.	362
17, 20	Boleymaguire	858 0 9	Leitrim	Drumahaire	Inishmagrath	Manorhamilton	IV.	95
119	Boleymeelagh	186 1 17	Mayo	Kilmaine	Kilcommon	Ballinrobe	IV.	154
98	Boleymore	59 1 31	Galway	Kilconnell	Grange	Loughrea	IV.	40
27, 28	Boleymount	193 2 13	Sligo	Tirerrill	Killerry	Sligo	IV.	239
134	Boleynagoagh North	614 3 23	Galway	Leitrim	Clonrush	Scarriff	IV.	52
134,135,136	Boleynagoagh South	248 2 32	Galway	Leitrim	Clonrush	Scarriff	IV.	52
107, 117	Boleynaminna	184 3 23	Galway	Longford	Tynagh	Portumna	IV.	62
132	Boleynanollag	135 1 11	Galway	Leitrim	Ballynakill	Portumna	IV.	50
9, 18	Boleynanoultagh	589 2 30	Cork, E.R.	Condons&Clangibbon	Kildorrery	Mitchelstown	II.	61
81	Boleynasruhaun	167 3 28	Galway	Galway	Rahoon	Galway	IV.	37
18	Boleynass Lower	226 1 9	Wicklow	Newcastle	Killiskey	Rathdrum	I.	352
18	Boleynass Upper	159 2 14	Wicklow	Newcastle	Killiskey	Rathdrum	I.	352
114, 115,) 123, 124 }	Boleyneendorrish	2,168 1 21	Galway	Loughrea	Ardrahan	Gort	IV.	62
129, 133	Boleyphaudeen	198 0 1	Galway	Kiltartan	Beagh	Gort	IV.	46
107	Boleyroe	159 2 26	Galway	Longford	Abbeygormacan	Portumna	IV.	56
64	Boleysillagh	516 0 25	Mayo	Costello	Kilcolman	Castlereagh	IV.	141
19, 32	Boleythomas	238 2 4	Galway	Ballymoe	Kilbegnet	Glennamaddy	IV.	8
23	Boley Upper	600 0 27	Queen's Co.	Maryborough West	Clonenagh&Clonagheen	Abbeyleix	I.	242
11	Boley Upper	206 0 39	Wexford	Gorey	Rossminoge	Gorey	I.	321
68	Boleyvaunaun	29 2 33	Galway	Moycullen	Killannin	Oughterard	IV.	69
25	Bolganard	74 1 38a	Leitrim	Carrigallen	Oughteragh	Bawnboy	IV.	91
37	Bolgerstown	130 3 38	Wexford	Shelmaliere West	Ardcandrisk	Wexford	I.	332
15, 16	Bolie	855 2 15	Londonderry	Tirkeeran	Faughanvale	Newᵀ Limavady	III.	250
20	Bolies	154 2 32	Londonderry	Tirkeeran	Clondermot	Londonderry	III.	247
15	Bolies	299 0 22	Louth	Ardee	Kilsaran	Ardee	I.	173
58	Bolies	418 3 31	Tyrone	Clogher	Clogher	Clogher	III.	292
5, 10	Bolinahaney	605 2 4	Wexford	Scarawalsh	Kilrush	Enniscorthy	I.	324
36	Bolinarra	278 3 34	Westmeath	Clonlonan	Kilcleagh	Athlone	I.	261
10,11,15,16	Bolinaspick	237 0 12	Wexford	Scarawalsh	Ferns	Enniscorthy	I.	323
32, 33	Bolingbrook	782 1 21	Tipperary, N.R.	Upper Ormond	Kilmore	Nenagh	II.	291
65, 66, 75	Bolinglanna	2,930 2 12b	Mayo	Burrishoole	Achill	Newport	IV.	117
16	Bolinready	303 1 3	Wexford	Gorey	Ballycanew	Gorey	I.	316
101, 102	Bolinree	116 1 24	Mayo	Clanmorris	Kilcolman	Claremorris	IV.	133
41	Bolinree	122 1 25	Roscommon	Athlone	Kilmeane	Roscommon	IV.	182
5, 10	Bolinrush	913 3 4	Wexford	Scarawalsh	Carnew	Gorey	I.	322
49	Bolintlea	1,058 1 17	Tipperary, S.R.	Slievardagh	Ballingarry	Callan	II.	331
56	Bolinsheen	251 3 17	Galway	Clare	Annaghdown	Tuam	IV.	16
80, 92	Boliska Eighter	1,401 2 35c	Galway	Moycullen	Killannin	Galway	IV.	69
80, 92	Boliska Oughter	1,669 1 19d	Galway	Moycullen	Killannin	Galway	IV.	69
25	Bollarney Murragh	32 2 5	Wicklow	Newcastle	Rathnew	Rathdrum	I.	354
25	Bollarney North	139 2 38	Wicklow	Newcastle	Rathnew	Rathdrum	I.	354
25	Bollarney South	34 0 38	Wicklow	Newcastle	Rathnew	Rathdrum	I.	354
9	Boluagree	92 1 29	Queen's Co.	Portnahinch	Lea	Mountmellick	I.	244
49, 59	Bolooghra	1,064 3 26	Clare	Clonderalaw	Kilfiddane	Killadysert	II.	15
5, 6	Boloona	147 3 32	Clare	Burren	Oughtmama	Ballyvaghan	II.	14
55	Boltnaconnell	522 1 22	Antrim	Lower Massereene	Killead	Antrim	III.	28
21	Bolton	391 0 20	Armagh	Orior Lower	Loughgilly	Newry	III.	56
38	Bolton	438 0 27	Kildare	Kilkea and Moone	Killelan	Baltinglass	I.	60
26	Bolton	133 1 8	Kilkenny	Callan	Callan	Callan	I.	83
16	Boltown	854 3 20	Meath	Upper Kells	Kilskeer	Kells	I.	206
96,97,104,105	Bolus	425 0 9	Kerry	Iveragh	Killemlagh	Cahersiveen	II.	196
9	Bolusty Beg	689 0 15e	Fermanagh	Magheraboy	Inishmacsaint	Ballyshannon	III.	212
9	Bolusty More	143 3 36	Fermanagh	Magheraboy	Inishmacsaint	Ballyshannon	III.	212
9	Bolusty More Barr of	346 3 12f	Fermanagh	Magheraboy	Inishmacsaint	Ballyshannon	III.	212
36	Bolyconor	140 1 1	Westmeath	Clonlonan	Kilcleagh	Athlone	I.	261
24,25,33,34	Bomackatall Lower	1,124 0 13g	Tyrone	Omagh West	Longfield West	Castlederg	III.	316
24, 33	Bomackatall Upper	823 2 16h	Tyrone	Omagh West	Longfield West	Castlederg	III.	316
2	Bomahas	58 3 21	Leitrim	Rosclogher	Rossinver	Ballyshannon	IV.	110
53, 61	Bomany	210 3 6	Donegal	Raphoe	Conwal	Letterkenny	III.	137
31	Bonabrocka	213 2 17	Wicklow	Arklow	Dunganstown	Rathdrum	I.	343
17	Bonaghmore	149 0 26	Kildare	Offaly East	Rathangan	Edenderry	I.	71
7	Bonagooga	56 3 2	Tipperary, N.R.	Lower Ormond	Uskane	Borrisokane	II.	288
17, 23	Bonagortbaun	179 1 34	Tipperary, N.R.	Ikerrin	Bourney	Roscrea	II.	274
36	Bonagrew	171 2 6	Wicklow	Arklow	Dunganstown	Rathdrum	I.	343
36	Bonagrew Little	15 0 1	Wicklow	Arklow	Dunganstown	Rathdrum	I.	343
5, 9	Bonamargy	87 0 25	Antrim	Cary	Culfeightrin	Ballycastle	III.	13
51	Bonarea	462 3 19	Tipperary, S.R.	Kilnamanagh Lower	Aghacrew	Tipperary	II.	322
13	Bonatouk or Monatouk	135 3 30	Waterford	Decies without Drum	Seskinan	Lismore	II.	360
15	Bondville or Tullybrick Etra	298 1 3	Armagh	Tiranny	Tynan	Armagh	III.	60
37	Bonecastle	336 3 37	Down	Lecale Upper	Down	Downpatrick	III.	180

(a) Including 9A. 2R. 24P. water.
(b) { Including 35A. 2R. 8P. water.
     { Including 5A. 0R. 25P. detached portion.
(c) Including 156A. 2R. 15P. water.
(d) Including 171A. 0R. 7P. water.
(e) Including 6A. 0R. 15P. water.
(f) Including 37A. 2R. 22P. water.
(g) Including 17A. 3R. 13P. water.
(h) Including 1A. 2R. 39P. water.

No. of Sheet of the Ordnance Survey Maps.	Townlands and Towns.	Area in Statute Acres.			County.	Barony.	Parish.	Poor Law Union in 1857.	Townland Census of 1851, Part I.	
		A.	R.	P.					Vol.	Page
24	Boneill . . .	150	0	25	Leitrim . .	Mohill . . .	Fenagh . .	Mohill . .	IV.	106
38, 44	Bonestown . .	321	0	33	Meath . .	Ratoath . .	Dunshaughlin .	Dunshaughlin .	I.	218
2, 6	Boneyclassagh .	137	0	32	Antrim . .	Lower Dunluce .	Dunluce . .	Coleraine . .	III.	17
31	Bonfield . .	33	0	4	Meath . .	Lower Deece .	Balsoon . .	Navan . .	I.	191
24	Bonnanaboigh .	154	2	25	Londonderry .	Keenaght . .	Bovevagh . .	New T.ⁿLimavady	III.	235
14, 19	Bonnetsrath . .	269	2	7	Kilkenny . .	Gowran . .	St. Johns . .	Kilkenny . .	I.	98
14, 19	Bonnetstown . .	574	2	28	Kilkenny . .	Crannagh . .	St. Canice . .	Kilkenny . .	I.	87
99	*Bonniamillish Island*	3	1	21	Mayo . .	Carra . .	Ballyovey . .	Ballinrobe . .	IV.	126
14, 15	Bonnybrook . .	87	1	34	Dublin . .	Coolock . .	Coolock . .	Dublin North .	I.	27
22	Bonnybrook . .	119	3	18	Fermanagh .	Tirkennedy . .	Derrybrusk . .	Enniskillen .	III.	220
92	Bonnyglen . .	98	1	15	Donegal . .	Banagh . .	Inver . .	Donegal . .	III.	107
26, 27	Boocaun . . .	160	3	18	Galway . .	Ross . .	Ross . .	Oughterard .	IV.	73
27, 40	*Booey* . .	6	1	6	Galway . .	Ross . .	Cong . .	Oughterard .	IV.	73
1, 2	Bookalagh . .	680	0	35	Galway . .	Ballymoe . .	Kilcroan . .	Glennamaddy .	IV.	8
11	Bookaun (*Browne*) .	84	3	0	Sligo . .	Tireragh . .	Easky . .	Dromore West .	IV.	233
11	Bookaun (*Tottenham*)	79	2	5	Sligo . .	Tireragh . .	Easky . .	Dromore West .	IV.	233
115	Bookeen . . .	391	1	10	Galway . .	Loughrea . .	Killeenadeema .	Loughrea . .	IV.	64
97	Bookeen North .	38	2	28	Galway . .	Athenry . .	Lickerrig . .	Loughrea . .	IV.	5
97	Bookeen South .	399	0	14	Galway . .	Dunkellin . .	Lickerrig . .	Loughrea . .	IV.	31
41, 50	Boola . . .	403	2	26	Cork, E.R. .	Duhallow . .	Kilshannig . .	Mallow . .	II.	74
79, 88	Boola . . .	127	2	18	Kerry . .	Iveragh . .	Caher . .	Cahersiveen .	II.	193
54	Boola . . .	408	2	8	Limerick . .	Glenquin . .	Killagholehane .	Newcastle .	II.	245
17	Boola . . .	376	3	16	Tipperary, N.R.	Ikerrin . .	Bourney . .	Roscrea . .	II.	274
17	Boola . . .	163	0	17	Tipperary, N.R.	Ikerrin . .	Corbally . .	Roscrea . .	II.	275
21	Boola . . .	162	3	26	Waterford .	Coshmore&Coshbride	Lismore and Mocollop	Lismore . .	II.	345
34, 37	Boola . . .	452	1	8	Waterford .	Coshmore&Coshbride	Templemichael .	Youghal . .	II.	348
2	Boola . . .	642	0	24	Waterford .	Upperthird . .	Kilsheelan .	Clonmel . .	II.	370
33	Boolabane . .	280	3	12	Tipperary, N.R.	Upper Ormond .	Templederry .	Nenagh . .	II.	293
17, 23	Boolabaun . .	742	1	29	Tipperary, N.R.	Ikerrin . .	Bourney . .	Roscrea . .	II.	274
25	Boolabaun . .	783	0	6	Wexford . .	Bantry . .	Rossdroit . .	Enniscorthy .	I.	301
6, 7	Boolabeg . .	325	1	18	Waterford .	Upperthird . .	Rathgormuck .	Carrick on Suir	II.	371
36, 42	Boolabeha . .	535	1	16	Tipperary, N.R.	Eliogarty . .	Moyne . .	Thurles . .	II.	271
5	Boolabrien Lower .	318	1	0	Waterford .	Glenahiry . .	Kilronan . .	Clonmel . .	II.	365
1, 5	Boolabrien Upper .	575	0	24	Waterford .	Glenahiry . .	Kilronan . .	Clonmel . .	II.	365
36	Boolabwee . .	119	1	10	Cork, E.R. .	Condons&Clangibbon	Clondulane . .	Fermoy . .	II.	60
6, 7	Boolacloghagh .	907	0	34	Waterford .	Upperthird . .	Rathgormuck .	Carrick on Suir	II.	371
48	Boolacullane . .	668	0	10	Kerry . .	Magunihy . .	Molahiffe . .	Killarney . .	II.	204
10	Booladurragha .	98	1	36	Cork, E.R. .	Condons&Clangibbon	Marshalstown .	Mitchelstown .	II.	63
46	Booladurragha North	289	1	11	Cork, E.R. .	Kinnatalloon .	Ballynoe . .	Fermoy . .	II.	97
46	Booladurragha South	270	3	11	Cork, E.R. .	Kinnatalloon .	Ballynoe . .	Fermoy . .	II.	97
49	Boolagare . .	543	0	27*a*	Galway . .	Ballynahinch .	Ballindoon .	Clifden . .	IV.	10
14, 20	Boolagelagh . .	66	2	37	Tipperary, N.R.	Lower Ormond .	Monsea . .	Nenagh . .	II.	287
70, 77, 78	Boolagh . .	179	3	28	Tipperary, S.R.	Middlethird .	Kiltinan . .	Clonmel . .	II.	328
20	Boolaglass . .	464	0	33	Limerick . .	Connello Lower .	Nantinan . .	Rathkeale .	II.	229
19, 20	Boolaglass . .	328	3	21	Tipperary, S.R.	Owncy and Arra .	Youghalarra .	Nenagh . .	II.	297
88, 91	Boolahallagh . .	1,014	1	3	Tipperary, S.R.	Iffa and Offa West .	Newcastle .	Clogheen . .	II.	319
97	Boolakeel . .	191	0	25	Kerry . .	Iveragh . .	Prior . .	Cahersiveen .	II.	198
29, 30	Boolakeel . .	173	0	16	King's Co. .	Garrycastle .	Reynagh . .	Parsonstown .	I.	138
10	Boolakelly . .	144	1	26	Cork, E.R. .	Condons&Clangibbon	Marshalstown .	Mitchelstown .	II.	63
74, 80	Boolakennedy .	1,047	2	37	Tipperary, S.R.	Iffa and Offa West .	Shanrahan . .	Clogheen . .	II.	319
80	Boolakennedy .	41	2	37	Tipperary, S.R.	Iffa and Offa West .	Tubbrid . .	Clogheen . .	II.	320
29	Boolakiley . .	204	1	4	Waterford .	Coshmore&Coshbride	Lismore and Mocollop	Lismore . .	II.	345
52	Boolanacausk .	307	0	33	Clare . .	Bunratty Lower .	Killeely . .	Limerick . .	II.	5
91, 100	Boolananave . .	416	0	6	Kerry . .	Dunkerron South .	Kilcrohane .	Kenmare . .	II.	183
49, 50, 57, 58	Boolanlisheen .	742	0	24	Limerick . .	Coshlea . .	Galbally . .	Mitchelstown .	II.	238
39, 45	Boolanunane . .	335	1	33	Tipperary, N.R.	Kilnamanagh Upper	Toem . . .	Tipperary .	II.	280
7	Boolard . .	200	3	38	Cork. E.R. .	Orrery and Kilmore	Shandrum . .	Kilmallock .	II.	109
22	Boolard . .	372	2	27	Galway . .	Ballynahinch .	Omey . .	Clifden . .	IV.	14
22	*Boolard Island* .	12	2	30	Galway . .	Ballynahinch .	Omey . .	Clifden . .	IV.	15
18, 23, 24	Boolareagh . .	543	1	4	Tipperary, N.R.	Ikerrin . .	Bourney . .	Roscrea . .	II.	274
30, 36	Boolaree . .	63	3	3	Tipperary, N.R.	Ikerrin . .	Templetouhy .	Thurles . .	II.	277
20	Boolaroe . .	47	3	8	Tipperary, N.R.	Owney and Arra .	Youghalarra .	Nenagh . .	II.	297
48, 58	Boolasallagh . .	303	2	12	Kerry . .	Magunihy . .	Aglish . .	Killarney . .	II.	199
32	Boolatin . .	567	2	37	Tipperary, N.R.	Owney and Arra .	Kilbscnlly .	Nenagh . .	II.	295
23	Boolattin . .	810	1	12	Waterford .	Decies without Drum	Kilrossanty .	Kilmacthomas .	II.	357
24, 32	Boolavaun . .	178	0	20	Clare . .	Inchiquin . .	Inagh . .	Ennistimon .	II.	25
13	Boolavonteen .	560	2	8	Waterford .	Decies without Drum	Seskinan . .	Dungarvan .	II.	360
22	Boolavoord . .	205	3	28	Limerick . .	Smallcounty .	Fedamore . .	Croom . .	III.	259
1, 5	Boolawater . .	122	3	29	Fermanagh .	Lurg . .	Drumkeeran .	Lowtherstown .	III.	205
16, 17	Booldurragh . .	104	2	5	Carlow . .	Idrone East .	Myshall . .	Carlow . .	I.	8
97	Booleen . . .	494	0	14	Tipperary, S.R.	Slievardagh . .	Templeuuhy .	Tipperary .	II.	211
14	Booleenshare .	545	3	14	Kerry . .	Clanmaurice .	Ballyheige .	Tralee . .	II.	167
44, 49	Booley . .	227	1	29	Wexford . .	Shelburne . .	Templetown .	New Ross .	I.	328

(*a*) Including 81A. 1R. 27P. water.

No. of Sheet of the Ordnance Survey Maps.	Townlands and Towns.	Area in Statute Acres.	County.	Barony.	Parish.	Poor Law Union in 1857.	Townland Census of 1851, Part I.	
		A. R. P.					Vol.	Page
45, 51	Boolies	213 2 32	Meath	Dunboyne	Kilbride	Dunshaughlin	I.	200
9	Boolies	892 3 12	Meath	Fore	Oldcastle	Oldcastle	I.	202
16	Boolies	199 2 27	Meath	Upper Kells	Burry	Kells	I.	205
18, 25	Boolies	234 3 5	Meath	Upper Kells	Donaghpatrick	Navan	I.	205
33	Boolies Great	388 0 24	Meath	Upper Duleek	Duleek	Drogheda	I.	197
27, 33	Boolies Little	234 1 6	Meath	Upper Duleek	Duleek	Drogheda	I.	197
30, 35	Boolinarig Big	543 1 30	King's Co.	Eglish	Eglish	Parsonstown	I.	134
35	Boolinarig Little	87 3 21	King's Co.	Eglish	Eglish	Parsonstown	I.	134
35	Boolinarig School Land	86 0 7	King's Co.	Eglish	Eglish	Parsonstown	I.	134
31	Boolinrudda	463 3 23	Clare	Inchiquin	Inagh	Ennistimon	II.	25
10	Boolnadrum	270 3 19	Wexford	Scarawalsh	Kilrush	Enniscorthy	I.	324
118	Boolteenagh	146 3 27	Cork, W.R.	Bantry	Durrus	Bantry	II.	119
38, 47	Boolteens East	917 0 6	Kerry	Trughanacmy	Kilgarrylander	Tralee	II.	210
37,38,46,47	Boolteens West	1,086 3 23	Kerry	Trughanacmy	Kilgarrylander	Tralee	II.	210
26	Boolteeny	327 1 3	Tipperary, N.R.	Upper Ormond	Kilmore	Nenagh	II.	291
39, 40	Booltiagh	796 1 25a	Clare	Islands	Kilmaley	Ennis	II.	31
16	Booltinaghadine	303 1 14	Clare	Inchiquin	Killinaboy	Corrofin	II.	26
59	Booltydoolan	404 1 11	Clare	Clonderalaw	Killadysert	Killadysert	II.	15
22, 23	Booly	261 3 38	Kilkenny	Shillelogher	Burnchurch	Callan	I.	113
150	Boolybane	97 1 2	Cork, W.R.	West Carberry, E.D.	Creagh	Skibbereen	II.	138
63	Boolybeg	184 1 3	Cork, E.R.	Cork	Whitechurch	Cork	II.	66
40	Boolybrien	261 1 33	Clare	Islands	Kilmaley	Ennis	II.	31
9	Boolycreen	34 0 19	Wexford	Scarawalsh	St. Marys Newtownbarry	Enniscorthy	I.	325
31	Boolyduff	312 2 31	Clare	Inchiquin	Inagh	Ennistimon	II.	25
35	Boolyglass	876 0 2	Kilkenny	Knocktopher	Aghaviller	Carrick on Suir	I.	110
35	BOOLYGLASS T.	—	Kilkenny	Knocktopher	Aghaviller	Carrick on Suir	I.	111
41, 47	Boolykeagh	322 1 32b	Meath	Upper Moyfenrath	Clonard	Trim	I.	213
30,31,39,40	Boolymore	1,031 1 1c	Cork, E.R.	Duhallow	Drumtarriff	Millstreet	II.	71
40	Boolynagleragh	769 1 34	Clare	Islands	Kilmaley	Killadysert	II.	31
40, 49	Boolynaknockaun	720 3 24	Clare	Islands	Kilmaley	Ennis	II.	31
31	Boolynamiscaun	279 1 39	Clare	Inchiquin	Inagh	Ennistimon	II.	25
39,40,48,49	Boolynamweel	770 1 37	Clare	Clonderalaw	Kilmihil	Kilrush	II.	17
9	Boolynavoughran	375 1 17	Wexford	Scarawalsh	St. Marys Newtownbarry	Enniscorthy	I.	325
40	Boolyneaska	628 0 16d	Clare	Islands	Kilmaley	Ennis	II.	31
62, 73	Boolypatrick	232 0 36	Cork, E.R.	East Muskerry	Garrycloyne	Cork	II.	103
6, 11	Boolyrathornan or Tomard	286 3 16	Carlow	Idrone West	Tullowcreen	Carlow	I.	9
18, 19	Boolyshea	168 3 3	Kilkenny	Crannagh	St. Canice	Kilkenny	I.	87
6, 11	Boolyvannanan	383 1 17	Carlow	Idrone West	Tullowcreen	Carlow	I.	9
45	Booragh	223 3 6	Donegal	Kilmacrenan	Conwal	Milford	III.	126
23	Booterstown	146 2 24	Dublin	Rathdown	Booterstown	Rathdown	I.	35
23	BOOTERSTOWN T.	—	Dublin	Rathdown	Booterstown	Rathdown	I.	35
12	Bootown	399 0 39	Antrim	Lower Dunluce	Dunluce	Ballymoney	III.	17
11, 12	Bootown	211 0 11	Antrim	Upper Dunluce	Ballymoney	Ballymoney	III.	18
11, 12	Bootown	75 2 22	Down	Ards Lower	Greyabbey	Newtownards	III.	158
6	Bootown	183 1 32	Down	Ards Lower	Newtownards	Newtownards	III.	158
13	Bootstown (Connor)	186 1 16	Kilkenny	Crannagh	Ballinamara	Kilkenny	I.	84
13	Bootstown (Cox)	199 1 0	Kilkenny	Crannagh	Ballinamara	Kilkenny	I.	84
24	Boraghy	188 2 36e	Monaghan	Cremorne	Aghnamullen	Castleblayney	III.	257
41	Boraheen	107 3 33	Meath	Upper Moyfenrath	Killyon	Trim	I.	213
25, 27	Boranaraltry	639 2 19	Dublin	Rathdown	Kiltiernan	Rathdown	I.	36
33	Borderreen	37 3 34	King's Co.	Upper Philipstown	Clonyhurk	Mountmellick	I.	143
6, 11	Bordowin	439 3 12	Queen's Co.	Upperwoods	Offerlane	Mountmellick	I.	251
23	Bordwell Big	180 2 12	Queen's Co.	Clarmallagh	Bordwell	Donaghmore	I.	237
28	Bordwell Little	80 2 9	Queen's Co.	Clarmallagh	Bordwell	Donaghmore	I.	237
58	Boreen	98 1 27	Tipperary, S.R.	Clanwilliam	Solloghodmore	Tipperary	II.	311
17	Borehovel	104 2 26	Wexford	Ballaghkeen	Killenagh	Gorey	I.	295
11	Boretree Island East	1 1 38	Down	Ards Lower	Greyabbey	Newtownards	III.	158
31	Borheen	43 3 7	Waterford	Decies without Drum	Dungarvan	Dungarvan	II.	355
83	Borheenduff	17 3 34	Tipperary, S.R.	Iffa and Offa East	St. Marys, Clonmel	Clonmel	II.	316
46	Borheenduff	92 1 33	Tipperary, S.R.	Kilnamanagh Lower	Clogher	Cashel	II.	322
7	Borim	181 2 25	Cavan	Tullyhaw	Kinawley	Bawnboy	III.	93
32, 33	Borkill Beg	453 2 5	Wicklow	Upper Talbotstown	Kiltegan	Baltinglass	I.	364
32, 33	Borkill More	594 1 3	Wicklow	Upper Talbotstown	Kiltegan	Baltinglass	I.	364
3	Borleagh	206 3 13	Wexford	Gorey	Kilcavan	Gorey	I.	317
3	Borleagh Demesne	188 0 19	Wexford	Gorey	Kilcavan	Gorey	I.	317
22, 28	Bornacourtia	89 2 17	Wexford	Ballaghkeen	Killincooly	Enniscorthy	I.	295
13	Borniagh Island	3 3 10	King's Co.	Garrycastle	Clonmacnoise	Parsonstown	I.	135
4, 5	Borough	172 2 21	Carlow	Rathvilly	Hacketstown	Shillelagh	I.	11
32	Borough	172 3 9	Kildare	Offaly West	Kilrush	Athy	I.	72
4	Borough of Charlemont	210 2 39	Armagh	Armagh	Loughgall	Armagh	III.	45

(a) Including 30A. 0R. 4P. water.
(b) Including 5A. 2R. 0P. River Boyne.
(c) Including 12A. 3R. 36P. water.
(d) Including 14A. 2R. 34P. water.
(e) Including 9A. 0R. 6P. water.

No. of Sheet of the Ordnance Survey Maps	Townlands and Towns	Area in Statute Acres. A. R. P.	County.	Barony.	Parish.	Poor Law Union in 1857.	Townland Census of 1851, Part I. Vol.	Page
27	Borraghaun	178 0 8	Queen's Co.	Clandonagh	Rathsaran	Donaghmore	I.	234
3, 6	Borranstown	625 1 24	Dublin	Balrothery West	Ballymadun	Dunshaughlin	I.	22
19, 22	Borris	1,221 2 12a	Carlow	Idrone East	Clonygoose	Carlow	I.	6
42, 48	Borris	1,325 3 27b	Tipperary, N.R.	Eliogarty	Twomileborris	Thurles	II.	273
12, 17	Borris	64 3 22	Tipperary, N.R.	Ikerrin	Roscrea	Roscrea	II.	276
10	Borris	288 0 0	Wexford	Scarawalsh	Kilrush	Enniscorthy	I.	324
12	Borrisbeg	218 2 29	Kilkenny	Galmoy	Urlingford	Urlingford	I.	93
29	Borrisbeg	488 3 12	Tipperary, N.R.	Eliogarty	Templemore	Thurles	II.	272
14	Borris Big	41 0 13	Kilkenny	Fassadinin	Odagh	Kilkenny	I.	91
13	Borris Great	529 3 20	Queen's Co.	Maryborough East	Borris	Mountmellick	I.	240
21, 22	BORRIS-IN-OSSORY T.	—	Queen's Co.	Clandonagh	Aghaboe	Donaghmore	I.	233
34	Borrisland North	47 2 18	Tipperary, N.R.	Kilnamanagh Upper	Glenkeen	Thurles	II.	278
34	Borrisland South	92 1 13	Tipperary, N.R.	Kilnamanagh Upper	Glenkeen	Thurles	II.	278
14	Borris Little	7 3 19	Kilkenny	Fassadinin	Odagh	Kilkenny	I.	91
13	Borris Little	419 1 29	Queen's Co.	Maryborough East	Borris	Mountmellick	I.	240
12	Borrismore	1,087 0 7	Kilkenny	Galmoy	Borrismore	Urlingford	I.	92
22, 28	Borrisnafarney	1,567 2 21	Tipperary, N.R.	Ikerrin	Borrisnafarney	Roscrea	II.	274
22, 23	Borrisnoe	1,365 1 22	Tipperary, N.R.	Ikerrin	Bourney	Roscrea	II.	274
10	BORRISOKANE T.	--	Tipperary, N.R.	Lower Ormond	Borrisokane	Borrisokane	II.	282
34	BORRISOLEIGH T.	--	Tipperary, N.R.	Kilnamanagh Upper	Glenkeen	Thurles	II.	279
22	BORRIS T.	—	Carlow	Idrone East	Clonygoose	Carlow	I.	6
26	Borrmount	348 1 1	Wexford	Bantry	Clonmore	Enniscorthy	I.	300
35	Bosallagh	51 0 3	Fermanagh	Clankelly	Clones	Clones	III.	195
61	Boscabell	268 1 5	Tipperary, S.R.	Middlethird	St. Patricksrock	Cashel	II.	330
28	Boshinny	87 3 28	Fermanagh	Tirkennedy	Cleenish	Enniskillen	III.	219
14, 23	Boskill	280 2 16	Limerick	Clanwilliam	Caherconlish	Limerick	II.	222
48	Bosnetstown	784 1 33	Limerick	Coshlea	Kilfinnane	Kilmallock	II.	240
14, 15	Boston	488 3 2	Kildare	South Salt	Oughterard	Naas	I.	78
23	Boston	33 1 11	Queen's Co.	Upperwoods	Offerlane	Abbeyleix	I.	251
11	Boston	96 2 0	Tipperary, N.R.	Lower Ormond	Ballingarry	Borrisokane	II.	282
17	Bostoncommon	32 1 25	Kildare	Offaly East	Cloncurry	Edenderry	I.	69
17	Bostoncommon	24 0 27	Kildare	Offaly East	Feighcullen	Edenderry	I.	70
17	Boston or Coolballyogan	144 1 29	Queen's Co.	Maryborough West	Abbeyleix	Abbeyleix	I.	242
52	Boston or Moneennagliggin North	129 1 28	Clare	Bunratty Lower	Killcely	Limerick	II.	5
18	Botanic Garden	30 0 0	Dublin	Coolock	Glasnevin	Dublin North	I.	27
34	Botera Lower	311 1 1c	Tyrone	Omagh East	Drumragh	Omagh	III.	312
34	Botera Upper	357 0 36	Tyrone	Omagh East	Drumragh	Omagh	III.	312
61	Bothaul	332 3 4	Mayo	Gallen	Meelick	Swineford	IV.	150
51, 63	Botinny	527 3 3	Mayo	Costello	Kilbeagh	Swineford	IV.	140
13, 20	Bottier	468 2 38	Down	Lower Iveagh, Up.pt.	Moira	Lurgan	III.	170
9	Bottlehill	202 1 21	Armagh	Oneilland West	Kilmore	Armagh	III.	53
32	Bottom	205 1 0	Antrim	Lower Toome	Kirkinriola	Ballymena	III.	32
96	Bottom	100 0 13	Galway	Athenry	Athenry	Loughrea	IV.	3
40	Bottomstown	773 1 15	Limerick	Smallcounty	Knockainy	Kilmallock	II.	260
2, 6	Bottomy	810 0 16d	Westmeath	Moygoish	Street	Granard	I.	281
3, 4	Bough	403 0 8	Carlow	Rathvilly	Rahill	Baltinglass	I.	12
8, 9	Bough	140 1 10	Monaghan	Monaghan	Tedavnet	Monaghan	III.	278
47	Boughil	432 0 8	Galway	Killian	Taghboy	Mountbellew	IV.	45
19, 28	Boughilbo	505 0 29	Limerick	Shanid	Kilcolman	Glin	II.	255
12	Boughill	167 2 38	Monaghan	Dartree	Killeevan	Clones	III.	267
5, 8	Boughkeel	64 2 7	Monaghan	Monaghan	Tedavnet	Monaghan	III.	278
21	Boulabally	211 1 3	Limerick	Coshma	Adare	Croom	II.	241
34,35,40,41	Bouladuff	252 3 17	Tipperary, N.R.	Eliogarty	Inch	Thurles	II.	270
98	Boulaling	238 0 36	Cork, E.R.	Kinalea	Cullen	Kinsale	II.	94
57	Boulanimrish	140 1 0	Kerry	Magunihy	Kilbonane	Killarney	II.	200
6, 7	Bouleevin	944 0 9	Clare	Inchiquin	Kilkeedy	Corrofin	II.	25
70	Boulerdah	479 0 27	Kerry	Iveragh	Killinane	Cahersiveen	II.	197
109	Boulteen	212 2 33	Cork, W.R.	East Carbery (E.D.)	Desertserges	Bandon	II.	127
42, 45	Boultry	116 3 29	King's Co.	Clonlisk	Kilcomin	Roscrea	I.	130
67, 76	Boultypatrick	1,133 0 13	Donegal	Raphoe	Kilteevoge	Stranorlar	III.	139
117	Bouluskeagh or Flowerhill	321 3 8	Galway	Longford	Tynagh	Portumna	IV.	62
147	Boulysallagh	252 1 6	Cork, W.R.	West Carbery(W.D.)	Kilmoe	Skull	II.	144
6	Bounla Islands	4 0 19f / 6 3 18g	Tipperary, N.R.	Lower Ormond	Kilbarron	Borrisokane	II.	284
18, 19	Bovagh	306 3 11	Londonderry	Coleraine	Aghadowey	Coleraine	III.	229
9, 10	Bovally	338 1 37	Londonderry	Keenaght	Drumachose	NewtⁿLimavady	III.	235
41	Boveagh	393 0 30	Londonderry	Loughinsholin	Desertmartin	Magherafelt	III.	240
55	Bovean	349 2 34c	Tyrone	Dungannon Middle	Killyman	Dungannon	III.	303
26, 27	Bovedy	908 2 0	Londonderry	Coleraine	Tamlaght O'Crilly	Ballymoney	III.	233
38, 42	Boveen	1,089 1 3	King's Co.	Clonlisk	Kilcolman	Parsonstown	I.	130
33, 34	Bovennett	128 0 3	Down	Upper Iveagh, Up. pt.	Aghaderg	Banbridge	III.	173

(a) Including 8A. 2R. 2P. River Barrow.
(b) Including 2A. 2R. 2P. detached portions.
(c) Including 0A. 3R. 13P. water.
(d) Including 11A. 3R. 16P. water.
(e) Including 4A. 0R. 38P. water.

No. of Sheet of the Ordnance Survey Maps.	Townlands and Towns.	Area in Statute Acres.			County.	Barony.	Parish.	Poor Law Union in 1857.	Townland Census of 1851, Part I.	
		A.	R.	P.					Vol.	Page
16, 24	Bovevagh	1,220	2	4	Londonderry	Keenaght	Bovevagh	New T^n Limavady	III.	235
25, 31	Boviel	563	1	18	Londonderry	Keenaght	Dungiven	New T^n Limavady	III.	236
46, 60	Bovinion	771	1	7	Galway	Killian	Moylough	Mountbellew	IV.	45
63, 64	Bovolcan	582	2	17	Antrim	Upper Massereene	Derryaghy	Lisburn	III.	30
79	Bovroughaun	1,750	2	23d	Galway	Moycullen	Killannin	Galway	IV.	69
21	Bowara	80	0	23	Fermanagh	Magheraboy	Rossorry	Enniskillen	III.	214
34	Bowarran	62	2	23	Fermanagh	Clankelly	Galloon	Lisnaskea	III.	198
18, 23	Bowelk	129	3	37	Monaghan	Cremorne	Aghnamullen	Cootehill	III.	257
31	Bowersacre	1	3	4b	Kilkenny	Knocktopher	Knocktopher	Thomastown	I.	112
5	Bow Hill	93	3	33	Dublin	Balrothery East	Balrothery	Balrothery	I.	19
41	Bowling Green	31	1	22	Tipperary, N.R.	Eliogarty	Thurles	Thurles	II.	273
29	Bowling Green	8	1	17	Wexford	Bantry	St. Mary's	New Ross	I.	302
63, 71	Boyagh	243	2	27	Donegal	Raphoe	Clonleigh	Strabane	III.	134
10, 11	Boyaghan	148	1	9	Fermanagh	Lurg	Derryvullan	Lowthertown	III.	204
16, 17	Boyanagh	161	1	3	Roscommon	Roscommon	Aughrim	Car^k. on Shannon	IV.	207
22	Boyanagh	96	1	31	Roscommon	Roscommon	Elphin	Strokestown	IV.	209
30	Boyanaghcalry	128	0	10	Westmeath	Clonlonan	Ballyloughloe	Athlone	I.	260
30, 36	Boyanagh (*Earl*)	111	1	0	Westmeath	Clonlonan	Kilcleagh	Athlone	I.	261
30, 36	Boyanagh (*Malone*)	175	1	33	Westmeath	Clonlonan	Kilcleagh	Athlone	I.	261
2	Boyannagh	465	0	12	Leitrim	Rosclogher	Rossinver	Ballyshannon	IV.	110
99	Boycestown	158	1	29	Cork, E.R.	Kerrycurrihy	Carrigaline	Kinsale	II.	92
5	Boycetown	592	0	26	Kildare	Ikeathy&Oughterany	Kilcock	Celbridge	I.	57
19	Boycetown	202	2	31	Louth	Ferrard	Port	Drogheda	I.	182
37, 43	Boycetown	313	2	31c	Meath	Lower Deece	Galtrim	Trim	I.	191
39, 47	Boyd's Farm	50	1	9	Tyrone	Dungannon Middle	Donaghenry	Cookstown	III.	300
78	*Boyd's Islands* {	3 0	1 2	10 29	Mayo	Carra	Aglish	Castlebar	IV.	124
40	Boydstown	393	3	16	Antrim	Upper Glenarm	Kilwaughter	Larne	III.	25
24, 25, 31	Boyerstown	434	0	31	Meath	Lower Navan	Ardbraccan	Navan	I.	214
18, 23	Boyher	149	1	4	Monaghan	Dartree	Ematris	Cootehill	III.	266
28	Boyhill	184	1	32	Fermanagh	Magherastephana	Aghavea	Lisnaskea	III.	218
84, 96	Boyhill	180	0	9	Galway	Athenry	Athenry	Loughrea	IV.	3
40, 49	Boyhollagh	1,085	3	14d	Mayo	Gallen	Attymass	Ballina	IV.	146
2	Boyle	48	2	37	Queen's Co.	Tinnahinch	Rearymore	Mountmellick	I.	249
6	BOYLE T.	—			Roscommon	Boyle	Boyle	Boyle	IV.	194
2	Boynagh	171	0	7	Meath	Lower Kells	Enniskeen	Kells	I.	202
5	Boynagh	444	0	1e	Meath	Lower Kells	Kilmainham	Kells	I.	203
2	Boynaghbought	157	3	4	Meath	Lower Kells	Enniskeen	Kells	I.	202
31	Boynehill or Ballagh	92	1	22f	Meath	Lower Navan	Navan	Navan	I.	215
70	Boyogonnell	112	0	33	Mayo	Carra	Turlough	Castlebar	IV.	130
57, 65	Boyoughter	1,075	3	16g	Donegal	Boylagh	Lettermacward	Glenties	III.	114
6	Boyounagh Beg	325	0	39	Galway	Tiaquin	Boyounagh	Glennamaddy	IV.	76
6, 18	Boyounagh More	714	3	16	Galway	Tiaquin	Boyounagh	Glennamaddy	IV.	76
5, 10	Boystown or Baltyboys Lower	1,142	2	23h	Wicklow	Lower Talbotstown	Boystown	Naas	I.	359
10	Boystown or Baltyboys Upper	810	1	0	Wicklow	Lower Talbotstown	Boystown	Naas	I.	359
68	Boytonrath	991	2	23	Tipperary, S.R.	Middlethird	Boytonrath	Cashel	II.	325
41	Braade	349	1	4i	Donegal	Boylagh	Templecrone	Glenties	III.	114
71	Braade	245	1	18	Donegal	Raphoe	Clonleigh	Strabane	III.	134
9, 14	Braade	1,417	0	16j	Fermanagh	Magheraboy	Inishmacsaint	Ballyshannon	III.	212
81, 90	Braade Lower	878	2	18k	Donegal	Banagh	Glencolumbkille	Glenties	III.	105
81, 90	Braade Upper	728	3	29l	Donegal	Banagh	Glencolumbkille	Glenties	III.	105
9	*Braadillaun*	4	2	8	Galway	Ballynahinch	Ballynakill	Clifden	IV.	12
18	Brabstown	200	2	35	Kilkenny	Crannagh	Tullaroan	Kilkenny	I.	87
36	Brabstown	151	2	11	Kilkenny	Ida	Listerlin	New Ross	I.	103
31, 35, 36	Bracaghreilly	1,157	1	10	Londonderry	Loughinsholin	Maghera	Magherafelt	III.	242
28, 29, 34	Braccas	97	0	25	Queen's Co.	Clarmallagh	Aghmacart	Abbeyleix	I.	236
50, 51	Bracetown	146	1	18	Meath	Dunboyne	Dunboyne	Dunshaughlin	I.	199
9,10,13,14	Brackagh	760	1	9m	Armagh	Orior Lower	Kilmore	Banbridge	III.	56
17	Brackagh	184	1	3	Armagh	Orior Lower	Loughgilly	Newry	III.	56
21	Brackagh	75	1	11	Fermanagh	Magheraboy	Devenish	Enniskillen	III.	210
2	Brackagh	319	3	35	Kildare	Carbury	Carrick	Edenderry	I.	51
16, 24	Brackagh	95	3	38	King's Co.	Ballyboy	Killoughy	Tullamore	I.	123
24	Brackagh	86	3	20	King's Co.	Ballycowan	Lynally	Tullamore	I.	128
7, 15	Brackagh	272	3	27	King's Co.	Ballycowan	Rahan	Tullamore	I.	128
2	Brackagh	159	2	33	King's Co.	Kilcoursey	Kilcumreragh	Tullamore	I.	141
18, 19	Brackagh	535	3	25	King's Co.	Upper Philipstown	Geashill	Edenderry	I.	144
40, 45	Brackagh	637	0	17	Londonderry	Loughinsholin	Ballynascreen	Magherafelt	III.	238
45	Brackagh	48	1	39	Londonderry	Loughinsholin	Lissan	Magherafelt	III.	242
19	Brackagh	160	1	36	Monaghan	Cremorne	Clontibret	Castleblayney	III.	259
25	Brackagh	201	3	14	Monaghan	Farney	Donaghmoyne	Castleblayney	III.	269
3	Brackagh	179	2	35	Monaghan	Trough	Errigal Trough	Monaghan	III.	283
52	Brackagh	313	1	6	Tyrone	Clogher	Errigal Keerogue	Clogher	III.	295

(a) Including 155A. 0R. 37P. water.
(b) Including 0A. 1R. 38P. detached portion.
(c) Including 12A. 0R. 3P. detached portions.
(d) Including 3A. 0R. 14P. water.
(e) Including 14A. 0R. 16P. water.
(f) Including 3A. 0R. 24P. water.
(g) Including 23A. 0R. 33P. water.
(h) Including 26A. 2R. 12P. water.
(i) Including 7A. 0R. 0P. water.
(j) Including 46A. 2R. 31P. water.
(k) Including 15A. 3R. 4P. water.
(l) Including 24A. 1R. 25P. water.
(m) Including 13A. 1R. 9P. water.

No. of Sheet of the Ordnance Survey Maps.	Townlands and Towns.	Area in Statute Acres.			County.	Barony.	Parish.	Poor Law Union in 1857.	Townland Census of 1851, Part I.	
		A.	R.	P.					Vol.	Page
49, 56	Brackagh	91	2	0	Tyrone	Omagh East	Kilskeery	Lowtherstown	III.	313
26, 33	Brackagh	179	2	24	Westmeath	Fartullagh	Carrick	Mullingar	I.	267
16	Brackagh	47	0	19	Westmeath	Kilkenny West	Noughaval	Ballymahon	I.	274
37, 38	Brackagh Castle	27	1	18	Westmeath	Moycashel	ArdnurcherorHorsleap	Tullamore	I.	276
40, 41	Brackaghlislea	1,247	3	18	Londonderry	Loughinsholin	Kilcronaghan	Magherafelt	III.	241
13, 20	Brackagh North	1,446	1	14	Tyrone	Strabane Upper	Bodoney Lower	Gortin	III.	323
41, 46	Brackagh Slieve Gallion	712	3	5	Londonderry	Loughinsholin	Desertmartin	Magherafelt	III.	240
27	Brackagh South	326	3	8a	Tyrone	Strabane Upper	Bodoney Lower	Gortin	III.	323
106	Brackaharagh	514	0	18	Kerry	Dunkerron South	Kilcrohane	Cahersiveen	II.	183
41	Brackanrainey	204	0	26	Meath	Upper Moyfenrath	Castlerickard	Trim	I.	213
7	Brackary Beg	302	1	10	Leitrim	Roselogher	Killasnet	Manorhamilton	IV.	109
7	Brackary More	314	2	17b	Leitrim	Roselogher	Killasnet	Manorhamilton	IV.	109
46, 47	Brackaville	235	1	21	Tyrone	Dungannon Middle	Donaghenry	Dungannon	III.	300
58, 60	Brackbaun	351	0	12	Limerick	Coshlea	Kilbeheny	Mitchelstown	II.	239
127	Brackcloon	198	1	2	Cork, W.R.	Bear	Kilnamanagh	Castletown	II.	125
32, 38	Brackcloonagh	164	0	36	Sligo	Corran	Cloonoghill	Tobercurry	IV.	225
53, 56	Brackenagh East	441	0	7	Down	Mourne	Kilkeel	Kilkeel	III.	183
53	Brackenagh East Up.	379	3	8	Down	Mourne	Kilkeel	Kilkeel	III.	183
53, 56	Brackenagh West	606	0	19	Down	Mourne	Kilkeel	Kilkeel	III.	183
53	Brackenagh West Up.	263	3	13	Down	Mourne	Kilkeel	Kilkeel	III.	183
63	Brackenhill	443	0	33	Antrim	Upper Massereene	Ballinderry	Lisburn	III.	29
11	Brackenstown	221	3	0	Dublin	Nethercross	Swords	Balrothery	I.	32
11	Brackernagh	214	0	30	Wexford	Gorey	Ballycanew	Gorey	I.	316
87	Brackernagh(Clancarty)	85	1	39	Galway	Clonmacnowen	Kilcloony	Ballinasloe	IV.	25
87	Brackernagh (Persse)	108	3	29	Galway	Clonmacnowen	Kilcloony	Ballinasloe	IV.	25
87	BRACKERNAGH T.	—			Galway	Clonmacnowen	Kilcloony	Ballinasloe	IV.	25
116	Brackery	108	3	23	Galway	Leitrim	Duniry	Loughrea	IV.	53
117	Brackery North	124	2	30	Galway	Leitrim	Tynagh	Portumna	IV.	55
117, 126	Brackery South	197	0	36	Galway	Leitrim	Tynagh	Portumna	IV.	55
22	Brackfield	438	0	8	Londonderry	Tirkeeran	Cumber Lower	Londonderry	III.	248
47	Brackhill	536	2	26	Kerry	Trughanacmy	Kilcolman	Killarney	II.	210
10, 14	Brackin	102	0	28	Kilkenny	Fassadinin	Mayne	Kilkenny	I.	90
41	Bracklagh	247	0	14c	Cavan	Clanmahon	Drumlumman	Granard	III.	76
16	Bracklagh	52	3	23	Cavan	Tullygarvey	Drung	Cootehill	III.	88
18	Bracklagh	115	3	17	Galway	Ballymoe	Clonbern	Glennamaddy	IV.	6
1, 2	Bracklagh	397	2	37	Galway	Ballymoe	Kilcroan	Glennamaddy	IV.	8
29, 30	Bracklagh	168	0	1	Galway	Dunmore	Dunmore	Tuam	IV.	33
29	Bracklagh	7	3	22	Galway	Dunmore	Tuam	Tuam	IV.	35
116	Bracklagh	216	2	33	Galway	Leitrim	Duniry	Portumna	IV.	53
102	Bracklagh	487	2	28	Mayo	Costello	Bekan	Claremorris	IV.	139
63	Bracklagh	190	2	18	Mayo	Costello	Kilbeagh	Swineford	IV.	140
97, 98	Bracklagh	140	2	13	Mayo	Murrisk	Aghagower	Westport	IV.	158
58, 59	Bracklagh	1,773	3	4	Mayo	Tirawley	Addergoole	Castlebar	IV.	163
93	Bracklaghboy	263	2	37	Mayo	Costello	Bekan	Claremorris	IV.	139
116	Bracklagh Grange	98	1	18	Galway	Leitrim	Duniry	Loughrea	IV.	53
9	Brackley	618	3	23d	Cavan	Tullyhaw	Templeport	Bawnboy	III.	94
28, 34	Bracklin	166	3	11	Cavan	Clankee	Bailieborough	Bailieborough	III.	71
28, 34	Bracklin	536	2	26	Cavan	Clankee	Enniskeen	Bailieborough	III.	72
6	Bracklin	174	2	3	Fermanagh	Lurg	Drumkeeran	Lowtherstown	III.	205
8, 20	Bracklin	458	0	24e	Galway	Ballymoe	Dunamon	Roscommon	IV.	7
13,14,20,21	Bracklin	2,730	2	9	Westmeath	Delvin	Killulagh	Castletowndelvin	I.	266
9	Bracklin Big	1,069	3	5	King's Co.	Lower Philipstown	Ballycommon	Tullamore	I.	142
9	Bracklin Little	601	0	6	King's Co.	Lower Philipstown	Ballycommon	Tullamore	I.	142
14, 15	Bracklon	623	2	15	Longford	Ardagh	Mostrim	Granard	I.	152
5	Bracklone	303	0	23	Queen's Co.	Portnahinch	Lea	Mountmellick	I.	244
42, 43	Brackloney	234	0	5	Cavan	Castlerahan	Castlerahan	Oldcastle	III.	67
85, 97	Brackloon	840	1	13	Galway	Athenry	Killimordaly	Loughrea	IV.	4
17, 30	Brackloon	364	1	21f	Galway	Ballymoe	Clonbern	Tuam	IV.	6
58	Brackloon	83	2	20	Galway	Clare	Killererin	Tuam	IV.	20
57, 58	Brackloon	300	2	11	Galway	Clare	Kilmoylan	Tuam	IV.	22
113	Brackloon	65	2	17	Galway	Dunkellin	Killeenavarra	Gort	IV.	30
86	Brackloon	76	1	33	Galway	Kilconnell	Grange	Loughrea	IV.	40
98	Brackloon	215	2	19	Galway	Kilconnell	Killallaghtan	Ballinasloe	IV.	41
100, 101 } 108, 109 }	Brackloon	288	2	14	Galway	Longford	Clonfert	Ballinasloe	IV.	56
44, 45, 55	Brackloon	754	3	6	Kerry	Corkaguiny	Ballynacourty	Dingle	II.	174
91, 100	Brackloon	615	3	38	Kerry	Dunkerron South	Kilcrohane	Kenmare	II.	183
6	Brackloon	66	1	38	Limerick	Clanwilliam	Stradbally	Limerick	II.	226
24	Brackloon	66	0	24	Limerick	Coonagh	Tuoghcluggin	Tipperary	II.	236
71, 72	Brackloon	576	1	9	Mayo	Gallen	Kilconduff	Swineford	IV.	147
122	Brackloon	128	2	10	Mayo	Kilmaine	Kilmaiaemore	Ballinrobe	IV.	155
122	Brackloon	146	2	6	Mayo	Kilmaine	Shrule	Ballinrobe	IV.	158

(a) Including 3A. 3R. 0P. water.   (c) Including 14A. 3R. 37P. water.   (e) Including 12A. 0R. 21P. water.
(b) Including 4A. 1R. 5P. water.   (d) Including 56A. 2R. 3P. Brackley Lough.   (f) Including 45A. 3R. 24P. water.

No. of Sheet of the Ordnance Survey Maps.	Townlands and Towns.	Area in Statute Acres. A. R. P.	County.	Barony.	Parish.	Poor Law Union in 1857.	Townland Census of 1851, Part I. Vol.	Page
87, 88, 97	Brackloon	334 0 6	Mayo	Murrisk	Aghagower	Westport	IV.	158
39	Brackloon	447 3 15	Roscommon	Athlone	Fuerty	Roscommon	IV.	181
7	Brackloon	32 1 35	Roscommon	Boyle	Tumna	Boyle	IV.	197
27, 34	Brackloon	336 3 36	Roscommon	Castlereagh	Ballintober	Castlereagh	IV.	198
21	Brackloon	553 1 9	Roscommon	Castlereagh	Kilcorkey	Castlereagh	IV.	199
15, 16	Brackloon	542 1 19	Roscommon	Roscommon	Shankill	Boyle	IV.	212
30	Brackloonagh	69 1 19	Mayo	Tirawley	Ardagh	Ballina	IV.	163
51, 63	Brackloonagh North	187 0 38	Mayo	Costello	Kilbeagh	Swineford	IV.	140
63	Brackloonagh South	207 0 32	Mayo	Costello	Kilbeagh	Swineford	IV.	140
97	Brackloonbeg	436 1 32	Galway	Athenry	Kiltullagh	Loughrea	IV.	4
93	Brackloon East	127 1 8a	Mayo	Costello	Bekan	Claremorris	IV.	139
93	Brackloon North	488 2 29b	Mayo	Costello	Bekan	Claremorris	IV.	139
93	Brackloon South	307 2 7c	Mayo	Costello	Bekan	Claremorris	IV.	139
92	Brackloon West	495 3 20d	Mayo	Costello	Bekan	Claremorris	IV.	139
17	Brackly	357 0 25	Armagh	Fews Lower	Kilclooney	Armagh	III.	46
19	Brackly	286 3 4e	Armagh	Tiranny	Keady	Armagh	III.	60
24	Brackly	331 0 28f	Monaghan	Cremorne	Aghnamullen	Castleblayney	III.	257
28	Brackly	171 2 2g	Monaghan	Farney	Donaghmoyne	Carrickmacross	III.	269
11	Bracknagh	164 2 17	Armagh	Armagh	Eglish	Armagh	III.	44
27, 28	Bracknagh	597 1 7	King's Co.	Coolestown	Clonsast	Edenderry	I.	132
24, 31	Bracknahevla	344 2 5	Westmeath	Rathconrath	Killare	Mullingar	I.	283
31	Bracknamuckley	488 2 20	Antrim	Lower Toome	Ahoghill	Ballymena	III.	31
9	Brackney	92 2 9	Antrim	Cary	Culfeightrin	Ballycastle	III.	13
34	Brackney	308 1 21	Kildare	Narragh&RebanWest	Churchtown	Athy	I.	67
31,32,39,40	Brackvoan	118 2 15	Limerick	Coshma	Bruff	Kilmallock	II.	242
48	Brackwanshagh	355 3 29	Mayo	Tirawley	Kilbelfad	Ballina	IV.	167
82	Bracky	283 1 38	Donegal	Banagh	Inishkeel	Glenties	III.	106
27	Bracky	112 3 22	Fermanagh	Tirkennedy	Derryvullan	Enniskillen	III.	220
35, 36	Bracky	1,122 0 2h	Tyrone	Omagh East	Termonmaguirk	Omagh	III.	314
24	Brackyle	487 0 13	Limerick	Coonagh	Oola	Tipperary	II.	235
14	Braddocks	183 2 37	Monaghan	Monaghan	Tullycorbet	Monaghan	III.	280
142	Brade	591 2 33i	Cork, W.R.	West Carbery (E.D.)	Myross	Skibbereen	II.	141
11	Bradkeel	511 2 21	Tyrone	Strabane Upper	Bodoney Upper	Gortin	III.	324
17	Bradock Island	1 1 11	Down	Dufferin	Killinchy	Downpatrick	III.	166
44	Bradystown	91 1 7	Meath	Ratoath	Ratoath	Dunshaughlin	I.	219
28	Brae	199 0 32	Antrim	Lower Antrim	Skerry	Ballymena	III.	4
62, 70	Braehead	131 3 21	Donegal	Raphoe	Raphoe	Strabane	III.	140
47	Braestown	60 3 6	Wexford	Forth	Mayglass	Wexford	I.	312
34, 39	Braetown	1,222 3 27	Antrim	Lower Antrim	Glenwhirry	Ballymena	III.	4
2, 3, 5	Bragan	2,359 3 14j	Monaghan	Trough	Errigal Trough	Clogher	III.	283
15	Braganstown	1,266 2 15	Louth	Ardee	Stabannan	Ardee	I.	174
25	Braghan	36 2 36	Louth	Ferrard	Termonfeckin	Drogheda	I.	182
130	Brahalish	782 2 1	Cork, W.R.	West Carbery (W.D.)	Durrus	Bantry	II.	142
27	Brallistown	242 1 23	Kildare	Offaly East	Kildare	Naas	I.	70
27	Brallistown Commons	5 1 20	Kildare	Offaly East	Kildare	Naas	I.	70
27	Brallistown Little	4 1 32	Kildare	Offaly East	Kildare	Naas	I.	70
24, 25	Bramblestown	1,442 1 12	Kilkenny	Gowran	Dungarvan	Thomastown	I.	94
26, 33	Branchfield	501 2 16k	Sligo	Corran	Kilmorgan	Sligo	IV.	226
45	Brandane	242 0 12	Wexford	Bargy	Bannow	Wexford	I.	304
29	Brandondale	65 3 0l	Kilkenny	Gowran	Graiguenamanagh	Thomastown	I.	95
29, 33	Brandonhill	1,654 0 23	Kilkenny	Gowran	Graiguenamanagh	Thomastown	I.	95
33	Brandonhill	1,057 1 3	Kilkenny	Ida	The Rower	Thomastown	I.	104
20	Brandonwell	457 0 37	Kerry	Clanmaurice	Ardfert	Tralee	II.	167
29	Brandra	195 3 2	Queen's Co.	Cullenagh	Abbeyleix	Abbeyleix	I.	238
9	Brandrum	215 2 21	Monaghan	Monaghan	Kilmore	Monaghan	III.	275
5	Branganstown	281 3 39	Kildare	Ikeathy and Oughterany	Kilcock	Celbridge	I.	57
37	Branganstown	297 1 26	Meath	Lower Deece	Galtrim	Trim	I.	191
4, 5, 9, 10	Braniel	616 2 14	Down	Castlereagh Upper	Knockbreda	Belfast	III.	165
24	Brankill	463 3 31m	Cavan	Tullyhunco	Killashandra	Cavan	III.	97
10, 11	Brankill (Flood)	78 0 30	Cavan	Lower Loughtee	Drumlane	Cavan	III.	79
11	Brankill (Lanesborough)	138 3 9n	Cavan	Lower Loughtee	Drumlane	Cavan	III.	79
25	Brannanstown	268 3 14	Meath	Skreen	Kilcarn	Navan	I.	220
34, 39	Brannish	115 0 0o	Fermanagh	Coole	Galloon	Lisnaskea	III.	199
18	Brannock	333 1 2	Armagh	Orior Lower	Ballymore	Newry	III.	55
110	Brannock Island	48 2 12	Galway	Aran	Inishmore	Galway	IV.	3
29	Brannockstown	137 1 17p	Kildare	Naas South	Brannockstown	Naas	I.	64
29	Brannockstown	114 2 5	Kildare	Naas South	Gilltown	Naas	I.	65
36, 42	Brannockstown	918 3 35q	Meath	Lower Moyfenrath	Trim	Trim	I.	211
26, 33	Brannockstown or Bellfield	455 2 23	Westmeath	Fartullagh	Enniscoffey	Mullingar	I.	268
60	Branny	228 2 16	Tyrone	Dungannon Lower	Carnteel	Clogher	III.	297
24	Branra	60 1 18r	Leitrim	Leitrim	Fenagh	Mohill	IV.	100

(a) Including 4A. 3R. 37P. water.
(b) Including 28A. 1R. 1P. water.
(c) Including 9A. 2R. 2P. water.
(d) Including 40A. 2R. 10P. water.
(e) Including 7A. 1R. 0P. water.
(f) Including 4A. 3R. 30P. water.

(g) Including 14A. 3R. 28P. water.
(h) Including 2A. 2R. 16P. water.
(i) Including 1A. 1R. 16P. water.
(j) Including 6A. 2R. 2P. water.
(k) Including 3A. 2R. 25P. water.
(l) Including 9A. 2R. 18P. River Barrow.

(m) Including 77A. 1R. 3P. water.
(n) Including 11A. 2R. 7P. water.
(o) Including 25A. 1R. 2P. water.
(p) Including 8A. 0R. 20P. water.
(q) Including 6A. 2R. 4P. water.
(r) Including 9A. 2R. 32P. water.

No. of Sheet of the Ordnance Survey Maps.	Townlands and Towns.	Area in Statute Acres.			County.	Barony.	Parish.	Poor Law Union in 1857.	Townland Census of 1851, Part I.	
		A.	R.	P.					Vol.	Page
112	Branraduff . .	229	2	32	Mayo . .	Clanmorris . .	Crossboyne .	Claremorris .	IV.	132
38	Branstown . .	393	2	29	Meath . .	Skreen . .	Trevet . .	Dunshaughlin .	I.	222
59	Branter . . .	51	3	14	Tyrone . .	Clogher . .	Clogher . .	Clogher . .	III.	292
7	Bratty or Benisonlodge	449	1	6	Westmeath .	Fore . .	St. Feighns .	Castletowndelvin	I.	271
6	Bratwell . .	428	2	11	Londonderry .	Coleraine .	Dunboe . .	Coleraine . .	III.	231
17	Braudphark . .	236	2	27	Leitrim . .	Drumahaire .	Inishmagrath .	Manorhamilton	IV.	95
16,17,22,23	Braumaddra . .	379	2	19	Kerry . .	Clanmaurice .	Kilfeighny .	Listowel . .	II.	169
17	Bravallen . .	229	0	28	Antrim . .	Upper Dunluce	Ballymoney .	Ballymoney .	III.	18
87	Bray . . .	823	3	31	Kerry . .	Iveragh . .	Valencia . .	Cahersiveen .	II.	198
4, 8	Bray . . .	334	0	7	Wicklow . .	Rathdown .	Bray . .	Rathdown .	I.	354
26, 28	Bray Commons .	57	1	13a	Dublin . .	Rathdown .	Oldconnaught .	Rathdown .	I.	37
4	Bray Commons .	8	2	6	Wicklow . .	Rathdown .	Bray . .	Rathdown .	I.	354
35	Bray Lower . .	326	3	5	Kildare . .	Kilkea and Moone	St. Michael's .	Athy . .	I.	61
6	Braysland . .	57	0	26	Meath . .	Lower Slane .	Siddan . .	Ardee . .	I.	223
12, 13	Braystown . .	216	2	22	Meath . .	Lower Slane .	Killary . .	Ardee . .	I.	223
18, 19	Braystown . .	179	3	21	Meath . .	Upper Slane .	Gernonstown .	Navan . .	I.	224
4	Bray T. . .	—			Wicklow . .	Rathdown .	Bray . .	Rathdown .	I.	355
35	Bray Upper . .	240	0	17	Kildare . .	Kilkea and Moone	St. Michael's .	Athy . .	I.	61
11	Brazil . . .	216	2	29	Dublin . .	Nethercross .	Killossery .	Balrothery .	I.	31
54, 55	Bready . . .	322	2	12	Donegal . .	Raphoe . .	Taughboyne .	Londonderry .	III.	143
30	Breaffy North .	243	2	22	Clare . .	Ibrickan . .	Kilfarboy .	Ennistimon .	II.	22
30	Breaffy South .	360	3	23	Clare . .	Ibrickan . .	Kilfarboy .	Ennistimon .	II.	22
10	Breagh . . .	257	1	30b	Armagh . .	Oneilland East	Seagoe . .	Lurgan . .	III.	50
5	Breagh . . .	240	1	17	Armagh . .	Oneilland West	Drumcree .	Lurgan . .	III.	51
5	Breagh . . .	355	1	4	Armagh . .	Oneilland West	Tartaraghan .	Lurgan . .	III.	54
15	Breaghey . .	396	1	6	Armagh . .	Tiranny . .	Tynan . .	Armagh . .	III.	60
36	Breaghmore . .	827	0	1	King's Co. .	Ballybritt .	Seirkieran .	Parsonstown .	I.	126
109	Breaghna . .	333	0	31	Cork, W.R. .	East Carbery (E.D.)	Desertserges .	Bandon . .	II.	127
16, 22	Breagho . .	398	3	32	Fermanagh .	Tirkennedy .	Enniskillen .	Enniskillen .	III.	221
58	Breaghva . .	325	1	28	Clare . .	Clonderalaw .	Kilmurry .	Kilrush . .	II.	17
49	Breaghva . .	383	0	28	Clare . .	Islands . .	Clondagad .	Killadysert .	II.	29
57	Breaghva . .	252	1	3	Clare . .	Moyarta . .	Kilrush . .	Kilrush . .	II.	33
65	Breaghva . .	469	2	36	Clare . .	Moyarta . .	Moyarta . .	Kilrush . .	II.	34
49	Breaghva East .	96	0	38	Clare . .	Clonderalaw .	Kilchreest .	Killadysert .	II.	14
49	Breaghva West .	377	1	38	Clare . .	Clonderalaw .	Kilchreest .	Killadysert .	II.	14
79	Breaghwy . .	52	1	28	Mayo . .	Carra . .	Breaghwy .	Castlebar .	IV.	127
4, 5	Breaghwy . .	371	1	9	Sligo . .	Carbury . .	Ahamlish .	Sligo . .	IV.	219
29	Breaghwy . .	1,420	0	31	Sligo . .	Tireragh . .	Kilmoremoy .	Ballina . .	IV.	235
21	Breaghwyanteean .	411	0	38	Mayo . .	Tirawley . .	Kilfian . .	Killala . .	IV.	169
21	Breaghwyanurlaur .	331	2	14	Mayo . .	Tirawley . .	Kilfian . .	Killala . .	IV.	169
16	Breaghy . .	303	3	1	Donegal . .	Kilmacrenan .	Clondahorky .	Dunfanaghy .	III.	122
45	Breaghy . .	403	3	14	Donegal . .	Kilmacrenan .	Conwal . .	Milford . .	III.	126
45	Breaghy . .	65	1	10	Donegal . .	Kilmacrenan .	Tullyfern .	Milford . .	III.	132
70, 79	Breaghy . .	160	3	0	Donegal . .	Raphoe . .	Donaghmore .	Strabane .	III.	137
10, 15	Breaghy . .	167	2	8	Longford . .	Granard . .	Clonbroney .	Granard . .	I.	154
31	Breagura . .	38	2	31	Wicklow . .	Arklow . .	Dunganstown .	Rathdrum .	I.	343
89	Brehig . .	208	0	20	Kerry . .	Iveragh . .	Dromod . .	Cahersiveen .	II.	194
40, 49	Brehig . .	804	2	39	Kerry . .	Trughanacmy .	Ballincuslane .	Tralee . .	II.	206
64	Breakly . .	111	1	1	Tyrone . .	Clogher . .	Aghalurcher .	Clogher . .	III.	291
20	Breanabeg . .	313	0	39	Roscommon .	Castlereagh .	Kilkeevin .	Castlereagh .	IV.	200
19, 20	Breanamore . .	580	0	5	Roscommon .	Frenchpark .	Tibohine . .	Castlereagh .	IV.	204
27	Breandrim . .	177	3	33	Galway . .	Ross . .	Cong . .	Oughterard .	IV.	72
14	Breandrum . .	63	1	3	Cavan . .	Tullyhunco .	Kildallan .	Bawnboy . .	III.	96
20	Breandrum . .	134	0	20	Cavan . .	Upper Loughtee	Kilmore . .	Cavan . .	III.	84
28	Breandrum . .	110	1	7	Fermanagh .	Magherastephana	Aghavea . .	Lisnaskea .	III.	218
22	Breandrum . .	143	2	3c	Fermanagh .	Tirkennedy .	Enniskillen .	Enniskillen .	III.	221
70	Breandrum . .	62	3	33	Mayo . .	Gallen . .	Kildacommoge .	Castlebar .	IV.	148
5	Breandrum . .	161	1	9	Roscommon .	Boyle . .	Boyle . .	Boyle . .	IV.	194
28	Breandrum (King) .	99	2	12d	Leitrim . .	Mohill . .	Mohill . .	Mohill . .	IV.	107
28	Breandrum (Peyton) .	173	3	10	Leitrim . .	Mohill . .	Mohill . .	Mohill . .	IV.	107
70, 79	Breandrum or Windsor	215	1	3	Mayo . .	Carra . .	Breaghwy .	Castlebar .	IV.	127
21	Breaninch . .	10	2	12	King's Co. .	Garrycastle .	Lusmagh .	Parsonstown .	I.	137
64, 72, 73	Breanlee . .	1,166	2	29e	Kerry . .	Dunkerron North	Killorglin .	Cahersiveen .	II.	181
4	Breanletter . .	606	3	25f	Roscommon .	Boyle . .	Ardcarn .	Boyle . .	IV.	192
82	Breanloughaun .	149	0	15	Galway . .	Dunkellin .	Oranmore .	Galway . .	IV.	31
17	Breanra . .	138	1	11	Galway . .	Ballymoe .	Dunmore .	Tuam . .	IV.	7
4, 8	Breanrisk . .	254	1	7	Longford . .	Longford .	Clongesh .	Longford . .	I.	157
5	Breanriskcullew .	254	2	17	Longford . .	Longford .	Killoe . .	Longford . .	I.	158
32, 35	Breanross . .	125	0	36	Leitrim . .	Mohill . .	Mohill . .	Mohill . .	IV.	107
33, 36	Breanross North .	244	1	15g	Leitrim . .	Mohill . .	Cloone . .	Mohill . .	IV.	105
36	Breanross South .	299	2	39	Leitrim . .	Mohill . .	Cloone . .	Mohill . .	IV.	105
66	Breansha . .	158	1	11	Tipperary, S.R.	Clanwilliam .	Emly . .	Tipperary .	II.	307
66, 67	Breansha Beg .	76	1	4	Tipperary, S.R.	Clanwilliam .	Clonpet . .	Tipperary .	II.	306

(a) Including 15A. 2R. 1P. detached portion.   (d) Including 2A. 0R. 26P. water.   (f) Including 3A. 1R. 38P. water.
(b) Including 3A. 1R. 26P. water.   (e) Including 39A. 0R. 14P. water.   (g) Including 9A. 2R. 12P. water.
(c) Including 4A. 3R. 10P. water.

No. of Sheet of the Ordnance Survey Maps.	Townlands and Towns.	Area in Statute Acres.			County.	Barony.	Parish.	Poor Law Union in 1857.	Townland Census of 1851, Part I.	
		A.	R.	P.					Vol.	Page
47	Breanshagh	138	2	9	Kerry	Magunihy	Molahiffe	Killarney	II.	204
67	Breansha More	231	2	15	Tipperary, S.R.	Clanwilliam	Clonpet	Tipperary	II.	306
19	Breany	801	1	36	Longford	Ardagh	Kilglass	Longford	I.	152
14, 15	Breastagh	271	0	7a	Mayo	Tirawley	Templemurry	Killala	IV.	171
38	Breast Island	3	2	23	Wexford	Shelmaliere East	St. Margaret's	Wexford	I.	331
38	Breast Island, Little	0	2	19	Wexford	Shelmaliere East	St. Margaret's	Wexford	I.	331
42	Brecart	441	2	22b	Antrim	Upper Toome	Duneane	Ballymena	III.	34
28, 33	Breckagh	648	0	18	Antrim	Lower Antrim	Skerry	Ballymena	III.	4
12, 17	Breckagh	213	1	3	Antrim	Upper Dunluce	Ballymoney	Ballymoney	III.	18
50	Breckinish	5	2	18	Clare	Bunratty Lower	Kilmaleery	Ennis	II.	5
51	Breckinish	81	3	30	Clare	Bunratty Lower	Kilmaleery	Ennis	II.	5
9	Breda	471	0	11c	Down	Castlereagh Upper	Knockbreda	Lisburn	III.	165
56	Bredagh	345	0	37	Galway	Clare	Kilcoona	Tuam	IV.	19
60	Bredagh	257	2	24	Galway	Kilconnell	Killosolan	Mountbellew	IV.	42
43	Bredagh	51	2	5	King's Co.	Ballybritt	Aghancon	Roscrea	I.	124
30	Bredagh	230	2	4d	Leitrim	Carrigallen	Carrigallen	Mohill	IV.	89
47	Bredagh	380	3	8	Roscommon	Athlone	Dysart	Athlone	IV.	180
45	Bredagh	291	0	25	Roscommon	Athlone	Kiltoom	Athlone	IV.	182
4	Bredagh	642	2	12e	Tipperary, N.R.	Lower Ormond	Lorrha	Borrisokane	II.	285
28	Bredagh	283	1	28	Tipperary, N.R.	Upper Ormond	Latteragh	Nenagh	II.	292
31, 32	Bredagh	69	2	9	Westmeath	Moycashel	Castletownkindalen	Mullingar	I.	277
12, 21	Bredagh Glen	873	0	17	Donegal	Inishowen East	Moville Lower	Inishowen	III.	118
2	Bree	1,151	1	12	Donegal	Inishowen East	Clonca	Inishowen	III.	116
20, 25	Bree	152	3	8	Monaghan	Cremorne	Muckno	Castleblayney	III.	261
25, 31	Bree	498	2	13	Wexford	Bantry	Clonmore	Enniscorthy	I.	300
55, 56	Breeda	1,274	0	23	Cork, E.R.	Imokilly	Ardagh	Youghal	II.	83
13, 14	Breen	1,240	0	32	Antrim	Cary	Armoy	Ballycastle	III.	11
61, 69	Breen	114	2	20	Donegal	Raphoe	Convoy	Stranorlar	III.	136
9, 10	Breen	339	3	1f	Tyrone	Strabane Lower	Ardstraw	Strabane	III.	318
52, 60	Breenagh	886	3	8	Donegal	Kilmacrenan	Conwal	Letterkenny	III.	126
25	Breenaun	1,069	1	25	Galway	Ross	Ross	Oughterard	IV.	73
105, 106	Breeny Beg	161	0	20	Cork, W.R.	Bantry	Kilmocomoge	Bantry	II.	119
106	Breeny More	351	2	23	Cork, W.R.	Bantry	Kilmocomoge	Bantry	II.	119
14, 20	Breeoge	424	0	17	Sligo	Carbury	Kilmacowen	Sligo	IV.	222
50	Breeole	290	1	3	Roscommon	Athlone	Dysart	Athlone	IV.	181
50	Breeole West	73	0	36g	Roscommon	Athlone	Dysart	Athlone	IV.	181
91	Brees	242	2	5	Mayo	Clanmorris	Mayo	Castlebar	IV.	135
47	Breesheen North	116	2	19	Limerick	Kilmallock	St. Peter's & St. Paul's	Kilmallock	II.	250
47	Breesheen South	191	3	1	Limerick	Kilmallock	St. Peter's & St. Paul's	Kilmallock	II.	250
34	Bregaun	243	2	32	Kilkenny	Kells	Tullahought	Carrick on Suir	I.	110
16	Bregoge	701	1	39	Cork, E.R.	Orrery and Kilmore	Bregoge	Mallow	II.	106
36, 37	Bregorteen	205	0	7	Wexford	Shelmaliere West	Kilbrideglynn	Wexford	I.	334
70	Brehaun	211	2	33	Cork, W.R.	West Muskerry	Kilnamartry	Macroom	II.	159
15	Brehoge	123	0	10	King's Co.	Garrycastle	Wheery or Killagally	Parsonstown	I.	139
1, 2	Bremore	742	3	18	Dublin	Balrothery East	Balrothery	Balrothery	I.	19
24	Brenan	634	0	29	Waterford	Decies without Drum	Stradbally	Kilmacthomas	II.	360
26	Brenanstown	327	2	14	Dublin	Rathdown	Tully	Rathdown	I.	38
39	Brenar	311	1	20	Kilkenny	Iverk	Fiddown	Carrick on Suir	I.	105
25	Brennanshill	196	1	23	Queen's Co.	Stradbally	Tullomoy	Athy	I.	248
71, 78	Brenormore	1,892	3	39	Tipperary. S.R.	Iffa and Offa East	Garrangibbon	Carrick on Suir	II.	313
98	Brenter	224	0	4	Donegal	Banagh	Inver	Donegal	III.	107
15, 22	Bresagh	508	0	32h	Down	Castlereagh Upper	Saintfield	Lisburn	III.	166
3	Breslanstown	480	0	30	Meath	Lower Slane	Drumcondra	Ardee	I.	222
50	Brettens Walls	44	2	30	Antrim	Upper Antrim	Antrim	Antrim	III.	5
32	Brewel East, or Merville	418	0	35	Kildare	Narragh & Reban East	Usk	Naas	I.	67
32	Brewel West	301	1	33	Kildare	Narragh & Reban East	Usk	Naas	I.	67
15	Brewershill	88	2	35	Wicklow	Lower Talbotstown	Dunlavin	Baltinglass	I.	360
67	Brewsterfield	216	3	8	Kerry	Magunihy	Killaha	Killarney	II.	202
8, 13	Brianstown	314	1	23	Longford	Longford	Clongesh	Longford	I.	157
18	Briarhill	81	3	31	Louth	Ferrard	Dysart	Drogheda	I.	181
28	Briarleas	384	2	32	Meath	Upper Duleek	Moorechurch	Drogheda	I.	198
82	Brick	185	0	6	Tipperary, S.R.	Iffa and Offa West	Tullaghmelan	Clogheen	II.	321
20	Brickana	200	2	20	Kilkenny	Gowran	Gowran	Kilkenny	I.	95
44	Brickanagh	545	2	11	King's Co.	Clonlisk	Templeharry	Roscrea	I.	132
34, 40	Brickeen	234	3	39	Sligo	Tirerrill	Kilmacallan	Sligo	IV.	239
74	Brickeen Island	19	1	34	Kerry	Magunihy	Killarney	Killarney	II.	203
18	Brickeens	146	1	10	Longford	Moydow	Ballymacormick	Longford	I.	161
102	Brickeens	368	0	23	Mayo	Costello	Bekan	Claremorris	IV.	139
61	Brickendown	507	2	27	Tipperary, S.R.	Middlethird	Brickendown	Cashel	II.	325
36	Bricketstown	514	0	9	Wexford	Bantry	Whitechurchglynn	Wexford	I.	303
47, 55	Brickfield	423	2	4	Limerick	Coshlea	Effin	Kilmallock	II.	238
52, 62	Brickhill East	252	2	14i	Clare	Bunratty Lower	Kilfintinan	Limerick	II.	5

(a) Including 5A. 0R. 15P. water.
(b) Including 147A. 1R. 19P. Creagh Bog.
(c) Including 3A. 3R. 12P. River Lagan.
(d) Including 10A. 0R. 24P. water.
(e) Including 1A. 0R. 20P. water.
(f) Including 8A. 2R. 20P. water.
(g) Including 9A. 2R. 38P. water.
(h) Including 47A. 2R. 19P. water.
(i) Including 5A. 3R. 2P. water.

Z

No. of Sheet of the Ordnance Survey Maps.	Townlands and Towns.	Area in Statute Acres.	County.	Barony.	Parish.	Poor Law Union in 1857.	Townland Census of 1851, Part I.	
		A. R. P.					Vol.	Page
52, 62	Brickhill West	564 0 16a	Clare	Bunratty Lower	Kilfintinan	Limerick	II.	5
74	Brick Island	2 0 11	Cork, E.R.	Cork	Carrigaline	Cork	II.	64
20	Brickkilns	176 3 12	Londonderry	Tirkeeran	Clondermot	Londonderry	III.	247
34	Brickland	367 0 39b	Down	Upper Iveagh, Up. pt.	Aghaderg	Banbridge	III.	173
34, 40	Bricklieve	545 3 29	Sligo	Tirerrill	Drumcolumb	Sligo	IV.	238
17	Brickpark	40 1 4	Wexford	Ballaghkeen	Killenagh	Gorey	I.	295
29	Bridane Lower	235 2 35	Waterford	Coshmore&Coshbride	Lismore and Mocollop	Lismore	II.	345
29	Bridane Upper	147 3 22	Waterford	Coshmore&Coshbride	Lismore and Mocollop	Lismore	II.	345
45	BRIDEBRIDGE T.	—	Cork, E.R.	Barrymore	Castlelyons	Fermoy	II.	53
37	Bridepark	81 3 4	Cork, E.R.	Kinnatalloon	Knockmourne	Fermoy	II.	98
43, 44	Bridestown	905 0 8	Cork, E.R.	Barrymore	Ardnageehy	Fermoy	II.	50
48	Brideswell	263 0 19	Roscommon	Athlone	Cam	Athlone	IV.	179
47	Brideswell	170 1 39	Wexford	Bargy	Mulrankin	Wexford	I.	307
5, 6	Brideswell Big	637 0 10	Wexford	Scarawalsh	Carnew	Gorey	I.	322
21	Brideswell Commons	8 2 13	Dublin	Uppercross	Clondalkin	Dublin South	I.	39
5, 6	Brideswell Little	331 0 6	Wexford	Scarawalsh	Carnew	Gorey	I.	322
8	Bridetree	28 3 9	Dublin	Balrothery East	Lusk	Balrothery	I.	20
3	Bridgecartron or Derrycashel	362 1 33	Roscommon	Boyle	Ardcarn	Boyle	IV.	192
45	Bridge End or Drummonaghan	229 0 19	Donegal	Kilmacrenan	Tullyfern	Millford	III.	132
77	Bridgefield	196 0 15	Cork, E.R.	Imokilly	Ightermurragh	Middleton	II.	87
38	Bridgeland	66 0 11	Wicklow	Ballinacor South	Kilcommon	Shillelagh	I.	349
44	Bridgeland East	44 2 37	Cork, E.R.	Barrymore	Rathcormack	Fermoy	II.	57
44	Bridgeland West	46 0 36	Cork, E.R.	Barrymore	Rathcormack	Fermoy	II.	57
116	Bridgepark	45 0 31	Galway	Leitrim	Ballynakill	Loughrea	IV.	50
37	Bridgequarter	33 0 11	Waterford	Coshmore&Coshbride	Templemichael	Youghal	II.	348
30	Bridgequarter	236 1 10	Waterford	Decies without Drum	Whitechurch	Dungarvan	II.	361
73	Bridgestown	276 3 34	Cork, E.R.	East Muskerry	Inishcarra	Cork	II.	103
77	Bridgetown	177 3 21	Cork, E.R.	Imokilly	Ightermurragh	Middleton	II.	87
16, 24	Bridgetown	317 1 10c	Tyrone	Omagh West	Urney	Castlederg	III.	318
7	Bridgetown	410 1 0	Waterford	Upperthird	Mothel	Carrick on Suir	II.	370
25	Bridgetown	41 1 36	Wexford	Bantry	Clonmore	Enniscorthy	I.	300
34	Bridgetown Lower	553 3 31d	Cork, E.R.	Fermoy	Bridgetown	Fermoy	II.	77
47	Bridgetown North	29 3 31	Wexford	Bargy	Mulrankin	Wexford	I.	307
47	Bridgetown South	130 2 14	Wexford	Bargy	Mulrankin	Wexford	I.	307
44,45,53,54	BRIDGETOWN T.	—	Clare	Tulla Lower	O'Briensbridge	Limerick	II.	38
47	BRIDGETOWN T.	—	Wexford	Bargy	Mulrankin	Wexford	I.	307
26, 34	Bridgetown Upper	540 1 9	Cork, E.R.	Fermoy	Bridgetown	Fermoy	II.	77
72, 73	Bridia	327 2 25	Kerry	Dunkerron North	Knockane	Killarney	II.	181
24, 29	Briencan	217 2 4	Kildare	Naas South	Ballymore Eustace	Naas	I.	64
6	Brieny's Island	2 0 35	Tipperary, N.R.	Lower Ormond	Kilbarron	Borrisokane	II.	284
45	Brierfield	77 3 26	Galway	Tiaquin	Moylough	Mountbellew	IV.	79
28	Brierfield	288 2 30e	Roscommon	Ballymoe	Cloongormican	Castlereagh	IV.	191
45, 59	Brierfield (Blake)	138 0 18	Galway	Tiaquin	Abbeyknockmoy	Tuam	IV.	75
44, 45, 59	Brierfield (Burke)	362 1 8	Galway	Tiaquin	Abbeyknockmoy	Tuam	IV.	75
45	Brierfield North	37 3 14	Galway	Tiaquin	Abbeyknockmoy	Tuam	IV.	75
44,45,58.59	Brierfield South	551 0 3	Galway	Tiaquin	Abbeyknockmoy	Tuam	IV.	75
45	Brierfield (Stevens)	136 2 27	Galway	Tiaquin	Abbeyknockmoy	Tuam	IV.	75
44, 45, 59	Brierfield (Toole)	204 2 13	Galway	Tiaquin	Abbeyknockmoy	Tuam	IV.	75
1, 14	Brierfort	358 2 14	Galway	Ballymoe	Templetogher	Glennamaddy	IV.	9
39	Brigh	202 1 39	Tyrone	Dungannon Upper	Ballyclog	Cookstown	III.	306
45	Bright	336 2 17	Down	Lecale Upper	Bright	Downpatrick	III.	180
19	Brigown	688 3 17	Cork, E.R.	Condons&Clangibbon	Brigown	Mitchelstown	II.	59
109	Brimnoge	2 3 0	Galway	Longford	Meelick	Portumna	IV.	61
23, 24	Brinlack	1,292 3 29f	Donegal	Kilmacrenan	Tullaghobegly	Dunfanaghy	III.	131
96	Brinny	440 2 17	Cork, E.R.	Kinalea	Brinny	Bandon	II.	94
17, 22	Briscarnagh	253 0 8	Monaghan	Dartree	Currin	Cootehill	III.	265
12	Briscloonagh	460 3 35	Leitrim	Drumahaire	Cloonclare	Manorhamilton	IV.	93
12	Briscula	68 2 25	Queen's Co.	Maryborough West	Clonenagh&Clonagheen	Mountmellick	I.	242
6, 11	Brisha	828 3 3	Queen's Co.	Upperwoods	Offerlane	Mountmellick	I.	251
25	Brishey	877 2 25	Londonderry	Keenaght	Dungiven	NewTⁿLimavady	III.	236
26, 27	Briska	3,636 1 29g	Mayo	Erris	Kilcommon	Belmullet	IV.	143
12	Briska Beg	267 1 6	Limerick	Pubblebrien	Kilkeedy	Limerick	II.	252
18, 19	Briskagh	462 2 38	Limerick	Shanid	Kilmoylan	Glin	II.	256
18	Briskalagh	85 1 36	Kilkenny	Crannagh	Tullaroan	Kilkenny	I.	88
14, 15, 24	Briska Lower	208 0 11	Waterford	Decies without Drum	Kilrossanty	Kilmacthomas	II.	357
12	Briska More	264 2 27	Limerick	Pubblebrien	Kilkeedy	Limerick	II.	252
14, 23	Briska Upper	147 1 5	Waterford	Decies without Drum	Kilrossanty	Kilmacthomas	II.	357
8	Briskil	333 0 24	Longford	Longford	Clongesh	Longford	I.	157
57, 58	Brisla East	684 2 26	Clare	Moyarta	Kilmacduane	Kilrush	IV.	32
5	Brislagh	490 2 16	Roscommon	Boyle	Boyle	Boyle	IV.	194
57	Brisla West	456 1 29	Clare	Moyarta	Kilmacduane	Kilrush	II.	32

(a) Including 3A. 1R. 20P. water.
(b) Including 16A. 1R. 18P. Lough Brickland.
(c) Including 3A. 3R. 8P. water.

(d) Including 22A. 3R. 26P. water.
(e) Including 15A. 0R. 19P. water.

(f) Including 8A. 2R. 10P. water.
(g) Including 42A. 3R. 7P. water.

No. of Sheet of the Ordnance Survey Maps.	Townlands and Towns.	Area in Statute Acres.	County.	Barony.	Parish.	Poor Law Union in 1857.	Townland Census of 1851, Part I.	
		A. R. P.					Vol.	Page
113	Britfieldstown	432 2 33	Cork, E.R.	Kinalea	Ballyfoyle	Kinsale	II.	94
54, 55	British	806 1 24	Antrim	Lower Massereene	Killead	Antrim	III.	28
9, 10	Britonstown	306 0 30a	Wicklow	Lower Talbotstown	Hollywood	Naas	I.	360
32, 41	Brittas	494 0 29b	Cork, E.R.	Duhallow	Kilshannig	Mallow	II.	74
135	Brittas	11 2 30	Cork, W.R.	Ibane and Barryroe	Ardfield	Clonakilty	II.	148
135	Brittas	2 1 27	Cork, W.R.	Ibane and Barryroe	Island	Clonakilty	II.	149
135	Brittas	26 1 38	Cork, W.R.	Ibane and Barryroe	Kilkerranmore	Clonakilty	II.	149
13, 18	Brittas	551 2 7	Kilkenny	Crannagh	Tullaroan	Kilkenny	I.	88
14, 15	Brittas	274 1 20	Limerick	Clanwilliam	Caherconlish	Limerick	II.	222
18, 21	Brittas	338 3 39	Louth	Ferrard	Carrickbaggot	Drogheda	I.	180
111, 119	Brittas	149 3 14	Mayo	Kilmaine	Kilcommon	Ballinrobe	IV.	154
5	Brittas	561 2 23	Meath	Morgallion	Nobber	Kells	I.	210
8	Brittas	327 2 21	Queen's Co.	Portnahinch	Ardea	Mountmellick	I.	243
2	Brittas	492 3 2	Queen's Co.	Tinnahinch	Kilmanman	Mountmellick	I.	249
35, 41	Brittas	1,004 1 4	Tipperary, N.R.	Eliogarty	Thurles	Thurles	II.	273
78	Brittas	324 0 38	Tipperary, S.R.	Iffa and Offa East	Kilmurry	Carrick on Suir	II.	314
60	Brittas	268 0 14	Tipperary, S.R.	Middlethird	St. Patricksrock	Cashel	II.	330
22, 23	Brittas	269 2 38	Westmeath	Kilkenny West	Kilkenny West	Athlone	I.	273
12, 19	Brittas	185 0 23	Westmeath	Moyashel and Magheradernon	Rathconnell	Mullingar	I.	276
48	Brittas	128 3 31	Wexford	Forth	Kilscoran	Wexford	I.	311
36	Brittas	626 3 38	Wicklow	Arklow	Dunganstown	Rathdrum	I.	343
1	Brittas	245 1 32	Wicklow	Lower Talbotstown	Kilbride	Naas	I.	361
22	Brittas	413 0 16	Wicklow	Upper Talbotstown	Donaghmore	Baltinglass	I.	363
24	Brittas Big	140 1 4	Dublin	Uppercross	Tallaght	Naas	I.	41
22	Brittasdryland	611 3 7	Kilkenny	Crannagh	Kilmanagh	Callan	I.	86
24	Brittas Little	250 2 34	Dublin	Uppercross	Tallaght	Naas	I.	41
135	Brittas North	62 2 26	Cork, W.R.	Ibane and Barryroe	Island	Clonakilty	II.	149
41	Brittasroad	141 1 26	Tipperary, N.R.	Eliogarty	Thurles	Thurles	II.	273
135, 144	Brittas South	55 2 5	Cork, W.R.	Ibane and Barryroe	Island	Clonakilty	II.	149
19	Brittstown	155 2 28	Meath	Upper Slane	Slane	Navan	I.	225
45, 54	Britway	225 3 13	Cork, E.R.	Barrymore	Britway	Fermoy	II.	51
36	Broad	17 2 8	Meath	Upper Navan	Trim	Trim	I.	216
19, 24	Broadfield	401 0 13	Kildare	Naas North	Naas	Naas	I.	62
44	BROADFORD T.	—	Clare	Tulla Lower	Kilseily	Limerick	II.	37
54	BROADFORD T.	—	Limerick	Glenquin	Killagholehane	Newcastle	II.	245
22	Broadlands or Knockafarson	230 0 7	Mayo	Tirawley	Ballysakeery	Ballina	IV.	164
70	Broadlea	171 2 24	Donegal	Raphoe	Raphoe	Strabane	III.	140
29	Broadleas Commons	465 2 14c	Kildare	Naas South	Ballymore Eustace	Naas	I.	64
14, 17	Broadlough	168 2 11	Louth	Ardee	Ardee	Ardee	I.	171
11	Broadmeadow	206 2 30d	Dublin	Nethercross	Swords	Balrothery	I.	32
26	Broadmore	102 3 25	Kilkenny	Callan	Callan	Callan	I.	83
69	Broadpath	185 1 22	Donegal	Raphoe	Convoy	Stranorlar	III.	136
38, 40	Broadstown	265 0 37	Kildare	Kilkea and Moone	Graney	Baltinglass	I.	60
48	BROADWAY T.	—	Wexford	Forth	St. Iberius	Wexford	I.	314
37, 42	Broagh	540 0 22	Londonderry	Loughinsholin	Termoneeny	Magherafelt	III.	244
30, 37	Broaghclogh or Murvaclogher	648 1 15	Down	Kinelarty	Kilmore	Downpatrick	III.	177
24	Brobrohan	166 2 20	Fermanagh	Magherastephana	Aghalurcher	Lisnaskea	III.	215
28	Brocka	53 2 33	Queen's Co.	Clarmallagh	Kildellig	Donaghmore	I.	238
50	Brockagh	1,575 0 17e	Donegal	Boylagh	Templecrone	Glenties	III.	114
34, 35	Brockagh	870 0 13f	Donegal	Kilmacrenan	Clondahorky	Dunfanaghy	III.	123
68	Brockagh	825 3 11	Donegal	Raphoe	Kilteevoge	Stranorlar	III.	139
62	Brockagh	198 2 19	Donegal	Raphoe	Taughboyne	Strabane	III.	143
26	Brockagh	173 3 16	Fermanagh	Clanawley	Cleenish	Enniskillen	III.	189
17	Brockagh	829 0 39	Fermanagh	Tirkennedy	Enniskillen	Enniskillen	III.	221
57, 58	Brockagh	444 1 14	Galway	Clare	Cummer	Tuam	IV.	18
96	Brockagh	115 2 37	Galway	Dunkellin	Killeeneen	Gort	IV.	30
30	Brockagh	216 2 16g	Galway	Dunmore	Tuam	Tuam	IV.	35
82	Brockagh	239 3 35	Galway	Galway	Oranmore	Galway	IV.	37
13	Brockagh	514 0 35	Kildare	Clane	Timahoe	Naas	I.	54
15	Brockagh	28 0 28	Leitrim	Drumahaire	Killarga	Manorhamilton	IV.	98
17, 25, 26	Brockagh	950 1 7	Londonderry	Coleraine	Errigal	Coleraine	III.	232
14, 15, 23	Brockagh	564 0 27	Londonderry	Tirkeeran	Cumber Lower	Londonderry	III.	248
77	Brockagh	183 2 26	Mayo	Burrishoole	Kilmaclasser	Westport	III.	121
2	Brockagh	620 3 11h	Queen's Co.	Tinnahinch	Kilmanman	Mountmellick	I.	249
13, 19	Brockagh	137 2 22	Sligo	Tireragh	Skreen	Dromore West	IV.	235
6	Brockagh	547 0 16	Tipperary, N.R.	Lower Ormond	Kilbarron	Borrisokane	II.	284
46	Brockagh	280 0 0	Tipperary, S.R.	Kilnamanagh Lower	Clogher	Cashel	II.	322
12, 19	Brockagh	342 1 38	Westmeath	Moyashel and Magheradernon	Mullingar	Mullingar	I.	275
17, 23, 32	Brockagh	4,811 0 30i	Wicklow	Ballinacor North	Derrylossary	Rathdrum	I.	346
2	Brockaghbeg	95 1 15	Queen's Co.	Tinnahinch	Kilmanman	Mountmellick	I.	249

(a) Including 3A. 1R. 21P. water.
(b) Including 2A. 1R. 6P. water.
(c) Including 10A. 2R. 19P. water.

(d) Including 81A. 2R. 33P. detached portion.
(e) Including 113A. 3R. 10P. water.
(f) Including 72A. 0R. 32P. water.

(g) Including 34A. 2R. 16P. water.
(h) Including 31A. 1R. 13P. water.
(i) Including 33A. 1R. 24P. Lough Nahanagan.

No. of Sheet of the Ordnance Survey Maps.	Townlands and Towns.	Area in Statute Acres. A. R. P.	County.	Barony.	Parish.	Poor Law Union in 1857.	Townland Census of 1851, Part I. Vol.	Page
26	Brockaghboy	1,191 3 21	Londonderry	Coleraine	Errigal	Coleraine	III.	232
13	Brockagh Lower	243 3 22	Leitrim	Drumahaire	Cloonclare	Manorhamilton	IV.	93
14	Brockaghs	757 3 32	Antrim	Lower Glenarm	Grange of Layd	Ballycastle	III.	22
13	Brockagh Upper	250 0 34	Leitrim	Drumahaire	Cloonclare	Manorhamilton	IV.	93
45	Brockernagh	123 3 27	King's Co.	Clonlisk	Dunkerrin	Roscrea	I.	130
25	Brockey	80 2 20	Dublin	Rathdown	Kiltiernan	Rathdown	I.	36
42, 48	Brockish pt. of Cargin	93 3 11	Antrim	Upper Toome	Duneane	Antrim	III.	34
5	Brocklagh	378 1 25	Longford	Longford	Killoe	Longford	I.	158
32, 37	Brocklamont	634 3 27	Antrim	Lower Toome	Ahoghill	Ballymena	III.	31
14, 19	Brockleypark	277 2 12	Queen's Co.	Stradbally	Stradbally	Athy	I.	247
16, 17	Brocklis	349 0 33a	Tyrone	Strabane Lower	Ardstraw	Strabane	III.	318
16	Brockly	96 1 21	Cavan	Tullygarvey	Annagh	Cootehill	III.	87
27	Brockna	348 1 4	Wicklow	Upper Talbotstown	Kilranelagh	Baltinglass	I.	364
12	Brockra	844 2 19	Queen's Co.	Maryborough West	Clonenagh and Clonagheen	Mountmellick	I.	242
27	Brockry	78 1 8	Queen's Co.	Clandonagh	Rathdowney	Donaghmore	I.	234
30, 31	Brocorrow	505 2 12	Wexford	Bantry	Adamstown	New Ross	I.	299
67	Brodeen	37 1 12	Tipperary, S.R.	Clanwilliam	Corroge	Tipperary	II.	306
70	Brodeen	229 1 20	Tipperary, S.R.	Middlethird	Redcity	Cashel	II.	329
121, 122, 123	Brodullagh North	249 2 32b	Mayo	Kilmaine	Shrule	Ballinrobe	IV.	158
122, 123	Brodullagh South	502 2 29	Mayo	Kilmaine	Shrule	Ballinrobe	IV.	158
12, 13	Broemountain	387 0 17	Waterford	Decies without Drum	Lickoran	Lismore	II.	358
12, 13	Broemountain	437 1 36	Waterford	Decies without Drum	Seskinan	Lismore	II.	360
11, 14	Broghan	338 2 12	Dublin	Castleknock	Finglas	Dublin North	I.	24
64	Brogher	245 1 26	Mayo	Costello	Kilcolman	Castlereagh	IV.	141
2	Brogherla Big	170 0 23	Queen's Co.	Tinnahinch	Kilmanman	Mountmellick	I.	249
2	Brogherla Little	67 0 24	Queen's Co.	Tinnahinch	Kilmanman	Mountmellick	I.	249
2	Broghill North	579 2 14	Cork, E.R.	Orrery and Kilmore	Ballyhay	Kilmallock	II.	106
2	Broghill South	195 2 20	Cork, E.R.	Orrery and Kilmore	Ballyhay	Kilmallock	II.	106
9	Broglasco	353 1 3	Londonderry	Keenaght	Tamlaght Finlagan	NewT'nLimavady	III.	237
19, 20	Broguestown	122 3 30	Kildare	South Salt	Kill	Naas	I.	77
9	Broharris	248 1 6	Londonderry	Keenaght	Tamlaght Finlagan	NewT'nLimavady	III.	237
9	Broighter	152 0 11	Londonderry	Keenaght	Tamlaght Finlagan	NewT'nLimavady	III.	237
8, 13	Brollagh	577 3 27c	Fermanagh	Magheraboy	Inishmacsaint	Ballyshannon	III.	212
13	Bromley	71 2 6	Wicklow	Newcastle	Kilcoole	Rathdrum	I.	351
1, 4	Bromore East	192 3 1	Kerry	Iraghticonnor	Kilconly	Listowel	II.	191
1, 4	Bromore West	267 2 36	Kerry	Iraghticonnor	Kilconly	Listowel	II.	191
12	Bronagh	590 0 7	Leitrim	Drumahaire	Cloonclare	Manorhamilton	IV.	93
28	BROOKEBOROUGH T.	—	Fermanagh	Magherastephana	Aghavea	Lisnaskea	III.	219
40	Brookend	500 0 17	Tyrone	Dungannon Upper	Arboe	Cookstown	III.	305
32	Brookfield	338 1 26	Fermanagh	Clanawley	Killesher	Enniskillen	III.	192
16,17,24,25	Brookfield	289 2 13	King's Co.	Ballycowan	Lynally	Tullamore	I.	128
6, 9	Brookfield	212 1 3	Tipperary, N.R.	Lower Ormond	Kilbarron	Borrisokane	II.	284
42	Brookfield	25 2 32	Wexford	Forth	Rathaspick	Wexford	I.	312
64	Brookhill	60 3 35	Cork, E.R.	Barrymore	Ballydeloher	Cork	II.	51
4	Brookhill	253 0 23	Fermanagh	Lurg	Templecarn	Lowtherstown	III.	209
65	Brookhill	331 0 16	Kerry	Dunkerron North	Knockane	Killarney	II.	181
101, 191	Brookhill	101 0 21	Mayo	Clanmorris	Crossboyne	Claremorris	IV.	132
17	Brooklawn	45 0 25d	Dublin	Uppercross	Palmerston	Dublin South	I.	40
34	Brookley	80 2 39	Tipperary, N.R.	Eliogarty	Drom	Thurles	II.	269
64	Brooklodge	475 3 18	Cork, E.R.	Barrymore	Ballydeloher	Cork	II.	51
67	Brooklodge	6 3 10	Cork, E.R.	Imokilly	Youghal	Youghal	II.	91
22	Brooklodge	52 0 6	Waterford	Decies without Drum	Modelligo	Lismore	II.	359
57, 58	Brooklodge Demesne	204 1 27	Galway	Clare	Killererin	Tuam	IV.	20
64	Brooklodge Lower	70 3 27	Cork, E.R.	Barrymore	Ballydeloher	Cork	II.	51
64	BROOKLODGE T.	—	Cork, E.R.	Barrymore	Ballydeloher	Cork	II.	51
64	Brooklodge Upper	348 3 5	Cork, E.R.	Barrymore	Ballydeloher	Cork	II.	51
107, 108	Brookpark	78 3 39	Cork, W.R.	East Carbery (W.D.)	Fanlobbus	Dunmanway	II.	131
39, 48, 49	Brookpark	750 3 13	Cork, W.R.	West Muskerry	Kilcorney	Millstreet	II.	158
12, 13	Brookvale	67 2 27	Monaghan	Monaghan	Drumsnat	Monaghan	III.	275
64	Brookville	117 2 13	Cork, E.R.	Barrymore	Ballydeloher	Cork	II.	51
15	Brookville	172 0 0	Dublin	Coolock	Coolock	Dublin North	I.	27
8, 9	Broom-beg	287 2 34	Antrim	Cary	Ramoan	Ballycastle	III.	14
7	Broomfield	73 2 7	Dublin	Balrothery East	Lusk	Balrothery	I.	21
17	Broomfield	24 3 7e	Dublin	Castleknock	Clonsilla	Celbridge	I.	24
12	Broomfield	96 3 19	Dublin	Coolock	Portmarnock	Balrothery	I.	28
13	Broomfield	588 2 0	Meath	Upper Slane	Collon	Ardee	I.	224
25	Broomfield	49 1 14	Wicklow	Newcastle	Killiskey	Rathdrum	I.	352
65, 76	Broomfield East	444 0 9	Cork, E.R.	Imokilly	Middleton	Middleton	II.	89
15, 21	Broomfields	99 2 18	Wicklow	Lower Talbotstown	Donard	Baltinglass	I.	359
65, 76	Broomfield West	365 0 21	Cork, E.R.	Imokilly	Middleton	Middleton	II.	89
25	Broomhall	168 1 4	Wicklow	Newcastle	Rathnew	Rathdrum	I.	354
19	Broomhill	289 1 35	Cork, E.R.	Condons & Clangibbon	Kilgullane	Mitchelstown	II.	61

No. of Sheet of the Ordnance Survey Maps.	Townlands and Towns.	Area in Statute Acres. A. R. P.	County.	Barony.	Parish.	Poor Law Union in 1857.	Townland Census of 1851, Part I. Vol.	Page
54	Broomhill	50 3 38	Tipperary, S.R.	Slievardagh	Crohane	Callan	II.	332
49	Broomhill	364 2 35	Wexford	Shelburne	Templetown	New Ross	I.	328
8, 9	Broom-more	674 3 14	Antrim	Cary	Ramoan	Ballycastle	III.	14
25	Broom Quarter	68 1 13a	Down	Ards Upper	Castleboy	Downpatrick	III.	160
14	Broomville or Clona-chona	236 2 39	Carlow	Forth	Ardoyne	Carlow	I.	3
15	Brootally	528 3 8	Armagh	Armagh	Derrynoose	Armagh	III.	44
42	Brosna	248 0 35	King's Co.	Clonlisk	Kilmurryely	Roscrea	I.	131
24, 32	Brosna East	616 3 10	Kerry	Trughanacmy	Brosna	Tralee	II.	208
24, 32	BROSNA T.	—	Kerry	Trughanacmy	Brosna	Tralee	II.	208
42	BROSNA T.	—	King's Co.	Clonlisk	Kilmurryely	Roscrea	I.	131
24, 32	Brosna West	804 3 13	Kerry	Trughanacmy	Brosna	Tralee	II.	208
61	Brossloy	133 1 35	Tyrone	Dungannon Middle	Cionfeacle	Dungannon	III.	298
18	Brottonstown	212 2 30	Westmeath	Moyashel and Magh-eradernon	Mullingar	Mullingar	I.	275
18	Brottonstown Little	59 3 22	Westmeath	Moyashel and Magh-eradernon	Mullingar	Mullingar	I.	275
17	Brough	141 0 26	Cork, E.R.	Fermoy	Doneraile	Mallow	II.	78
61, 62	Broughadowey	289 2 30	Tyrone	Dungannon Middle	Clonfeacle	Dungannon	III.	298
23, 31	Broughal	3,785 2 17b	King's Co.	Ballyboy	Ballyboy	Parsonstown	I.	123
16	Broughan	269 3 2	Armagh	Fews Lower	Lisnadill	Armagh	III.	46
30	Broughane	742 3 11	Kerry	Trughanacmy	Castleisland	Tralee	II.	208
5, 9	Broughanlea	199 1 31	Antrim	Cary	Culfeightrin	Ballycastle	III.	13
23	Broughanore	255 1 26	Antrim	Kilconway	Killagan	Ballymoney	III.	27
4	Broughattin	68 3 25	Louth	Lower Dundalk	Ballymascanlan	Dundalk	I.	175
21	Broughderg	165 1 38	Cavan	Upper Loughtee	Larah	Cavan	III.	85
28, 29	Broughderg	236 3 29	Fermanagh	Magherastephana	Aghavea	Lisnaskea	III.	218
20	Broughderg	4,239 1 35	Tyrone	Dungannon Upper	Lissan	Cookstown	III.	309
32	Broughdone	392 0 9	Antrim	Lower Toome	Ahoghill	Ballymena	III.	31
17	Brougher	422 3 31	Fermanagh	Tirkennedy	Enniskillen	Enniskillen	III.	221
40, 45	Brougher	612 0 20	Sligo	Corran	Toomour	Boyle	IV.	228
4, 8	Broughgammon	547 2 36	Antrim	Cary	Ballintoy	Ballycastle	III.	12
9	Broughills Hill	67 2 33	Wicklow	Lower Talbotstown	Hollywood	Baltinglass	I.	360
3, 4	Broughillstown	428 2 28	Carlow	Rathvilly	Rahill	Baltinglass	I.	12
9	Broughmore	168 1 18	Antrim	Cary	Culfeightrin	Ballycastle	III.	13
67	Broughmore	314 1 19c	Antrim	Upper Massereene	Blaris	Lisburn	III.	30
32, 33	Broughshane Lower	290 1 36	Antrim	Lower Antrim	Racavan	Ballymena	III.	4
33	BROUGHSHANE T.	—	Antrim	Lower Antrim	Racavan	Ballymena	III.	4
33	Broughshane Upper	585 1 21d	Antrim	Lower Antrim	Racavan	Ballymena	III.	4
9	Browley East	41 3 4e	Waterford	Middlethird	Trinity Without	Waterford	II.	369
9	Browley West	46 1 14	Waterford	Middlethird	Trinity Without	Waterford	II.	369
4	Brownbog	209 1 15	Carlow	Rathvilly	Hacketstown	Shillelagh	I.	11
13	Brownbog	31 2 4	Longford	Longford	Templemichael	Longford	I.	160
51	Brownbog	50 0 8	Tipperary, N.R.	Kilnamanagh Upper	Toem	Tipperary	II.	280
40	Browndod	485 1 25	Antrim	Lower Belfast	Inver	Larne	III.	8
44	Browndod	975 2 6	Antrim	Upper Antrim	Donegore	Antrim	III.	6
80	Brownespark	19 3 9	Mayo	Gallen	Killedan	Swineford	IV.	149
61	Brownhall	77 3 18	Donegal	Raphoe	Conwal	Letterkenny	III.	137
103, 104	Brownhall Demesne	311 1 31f	Donegal	Tirhugh	Drumhome	Donegal	III.	146
90	Brownhall Demesne	604 0 38g	Mayo	Clanmorris	Mayo	Castlebar	IV.	135
11	Brownhill	84 1 13	Fermanagh	Lurg	Derryvullan	Lowtherstown	III.	204
5	Brownhill	125 1 29	Tyrone	Strabane Lower	Leckpatrick	Strabane	III.	321
30	Brownhill and Cullen	212 2 18h	Leitrim	Carrigallen	Carrigallen	Bawnboy	IV.	89
39	Brownhills	115 0 33	King's Co.	Ballybritt	Aghancon	Roscrea	I.	124
74	Browningstown	65 3 24	Cork, E.R.	Cork	St. Finbars	Cork	II.	65
75	Brown Island	8 1 10	Cork, E.R.	Barrymore	Carrigtohill	Middleton	II.	52
37	Brownknowe	104 1 24	Donegal	Kilmacrenan	Tullyfern	Milford	III.	133
35	Brownmountain	134 0 33	Kilkenny	Iverk	Owning	Carrick on Suir	I.	106
66	Brown or Rabbit Island	12 0 35	Kerry	Magunihy	Aghadoe	Killarney	II.	199
50	Brownrath	162 2 23	Meath	Ratoath	Ballymaglassan	Dunshaughlin	I.	217
21	Brownsbarn	688 3 35	Dublin	Newcastle	Saggart	Celbridge	I.	34
28, 32	Brownsbarn	492 1 25i	Kilkenny	Gowran	Famma	Thomastown	I.	94
36	Brownscastle	224 1 33	Wexford	Shelmaliere West	Taghmon	Wexford	I.	334
7	Brownscross	164 1 8	Dublin	Balrothery West	Clonmethan	Balrothery	I.	22
38	Brownscurragh	86 0 34	Westmeath	Moycashel	Kilbeggan	Tullamore	I.	278
32,33,36,37	Brownsford	871 0 14	Kilkenny	Ida	Dysartmoon	New Ross	I.	101
122	Brownsisland	547 0 20	Mayo	Kilmaine	Kilmainemore	Ballinrobe	IV.	155
112	Brownsmills	2 2 17	Cork, E.R.	Kinsale	Ringcurran	Kinsale	II.	100
112	BROWNSMILLS T.	—	Cork, E.R.	Kinsale	Ringcurran	Kinsale	II.	100
99	Brownstown	146 2 7	Cork, E.R.	Kerrycurrihy	Kilpatrick	Kinsale	II.	92
144	Brownstown	246 3 20	Cork, W.R.	Ibane and Barryroe	Ardfield	Clonakilty	II.	148
7	Brownstown	186 3 11	Dublin	Balrothery West	Hollywood	Balrothery	I.	23
7	Brownstown	246 0 6	Dublin	Nethercross	Swords	Balrothery	I.	32

(a) Including 2A. 0R. 22P. Lough.
(b) Including 89A. 3R. 38P. water.
(c) Including 1A. 3R. 6P. water.
(d) Including 0A. 2R. 25P. detached portion.

(e) { Within the Municipal Boundary 21A. 0R. 39P.
{ Without the Municipal Boundary 20A. 2R. 5P.
(f) Including 5A. 0R. 32P. water.

(g) Including 43A. 0R. 12P. water.
(h) Including 2A. 2R. 22P. water.
(i) Including 21A. 3R. 0P. River Nore.

No. of Sheet of the Ordnance Survey Maps	Townlands and Towns.	Area in Statute Acres.			County.	Barony.	Parish.	Poor Law Union in 1857.	Townland Census of 1851, Part I.	
		A.	R.	P.					Vol.	Page
17, 21	Brownstown . .	114	3	18	Dublin . .	Newcastle . .	Kilmactalway .	Celbridge . .	I.	33
23,24,28,29	Brownstown . .	379	0	24	Kildare . .	Naas South . .	Carnalway . .	Naas . .	I.	64
34	Brownstown . .	137	0	2	Kildare . .	Narragh&RebanWest	Churchtown . .	Athy . .	I.	67
13	Brownstown . .	83	0	14	Kilkenny . .	Crannagh . .	Clashacrow .	Kilkenny . .	I.	85
14, 19	Brownstown . .	537	3	10	Kilkenny . .	Gowran . . .	St. John's . .	Kilkenny . .	I.	98
37	Brownstown . .	655	0	20	Kilkenny . .	Ida . . .	Dysartmoon . .	New Ross . .	I.	101
37	Brownstown . .	110	0	5	Kilkenny . .	Ida . . .	Listerlin . .	New Ross . .	I.	103
35	Brownstown . .	105	0	17	Kilkenny . .	Knocktopher . .	Aghaviller . .	Carrick on Suir	I.	110
23	Brownstown . .	209	3	33	Kilkenny . .	Shillelogher . .	Castleinch or Inchyolaghan . .	Kilkenny . .	I.	114
44, 46	Brownstown . .	464	3	8	King's Co. . .	Clonlisk . . .	Cullenwaine . .	Roscrea . .	I.	129
21	Brownstown . .	613	0	7	Louth . .	Ferrard . .	Drumshallon . .	Drogheda . .	I.	180
36	Brownstown . .	52	3	13	Meath . .	Lower Moyfenrath .	Laracor . .	Trim . .	I.	210
12, 13	Brownstown . .	236	1	1	Meath . .	Lower Slane . .	Killary . .	Ardee . .	I.	223
50	Brownstown . .	330	0	30	Meath . .	Ratoath . .	Ballymaglassan .	Dunshaughlin .	I.	217
44	Brownstown . .	114	1	21	Meath . .	Ratoath . .	Ratoath . .	Dunshaughlin .	I.	219
26, 32	Brownstown . .	949	1	15	Meath , . .	Skreen . .	Brownstown . .	Navan . .	I.	220
35	Brownstown . .	428	2	35	Tipperary, N.R.	Eliogarty . .	Loughmoe East .	Thurles . .	II.	271
26, 27	Brownstown . .	413	2	17	Waterford . .	Gaultiere . .	Rathmoylan . .	Waterford . .	II.	364
8	Brownstown . .	837	0	33	Westmeath . .	Delvin . .	Castletowndelvin .	Castletowndelvin	I.	264
47	Brownstown . .	117	0	10	Wexford . .	Bargy . .	Kilcowan . .	Wexford . .	I.	305
35	Brownstown . .	624	2	33	Wexford . .	Shelmaliere West .	Newbawn . .	New Ross . .	I.	334
110	Brownstown or Donnageaga . .	343	3	13	Mayo . .	Kilmaine . .	Robeen . .	Ballinrobe . .	IV.	157
28	Brownstown Great .	376	1	26	Kildare . .	Offaly East . .	Ballysax . .	Naas . .	I.	69
28	Brownstown Little .	78	3	19	Kildare . .	Offaly East . .	Ballysax . .	Naas . .	I.	69
28	Brownstown Lower .	283	3	16	Kildare . .	Offaly East . .	Carn . .	Naas . .	I.	69
28	Brownstown Upper .	238	1	34	Kildare . .	Offaly East . .	Carn . .	Naas . .	I.	69
4	Brownswood . .	718	2	18	Waterford . .	Upperthird . .	Fenoagh . .	Carrick on Suir	II.	369
26	Brownswood . .	519	0	4	Wexford . .	Ballaghkeen . .	Templeshannon .	Enniscorthy .	I.	298
81, 82	Brownville . .	155	3	31a	Galway . .	Galway . .	Rahoon . .	Galway . .	IV.	37
17	Bruce . . .	54	2	0	Wexford . .	Gorey . .	Donaghmore . .	Gorey . .	I.	316
17	Bruce . . .	93	1	0	Wexford . .	Gorey . .	Kiltrisk . .	Gorey . .	I.	320
38	Brucetown or Ballybrusa . .	104	1	28	Waterford . .	Decies within Drum	Lisgenan or Grange	Youghal . .	II.	352
7, 8	Bruckana . .	787	1	28	Kilkenny . .	Galmoy . .	Erke . .	Urlingford . .	I.	92
104	Brucken . .	72	0	13	Galway . .	Dunkellin . .	Killogilleen . .	Loughrea . .	IV.	31
98	Bruckless . .	219	0	8	Donegal . .	Banagh . .	Killaghtee . .	Donegal . .	III.	109
23	Bruffea . .	49	0	37	Limerick . .	Clanwilliam . .	Inch St. Lawrence .	Limerick . .	II.	224
31, 32, 40	Bruff . . .	398	2	39	Limerick . .	Coshma . .	Bruff . .	Kilmallock . .	II.	242
81	Bruff . . .	131	3	7	Mayo . .	Costello . .	Aghamore . .	Swineford . .	IV.	136
32	BRUFF T. . .	—			Limerick . .	Coshma . .	Bruff . .	Kilmallock . .	II.	242
5	Brughas . .	68	0	0	Armagh . .	Oneilland West .	Tartaraghan . .	Armagh . .	III.	54
21	Brughas . .	141	0	14	Fermanagh . .	Magheraboy . .	Rossory . .	Enniskillen . .	III.	214
66	Bruis . . .	177	0	0	Tipperary, S.R.	Clanwilliam . .	Bruis . .	Tipperary . .	II.	305
143	Brulea . . .	167	1	29	Cork. W.R. . .	East Carbery (W.D.)	Kilfaughnabeg .	Skibbereen . .	II.	132
24, 29	Brumlin . .	54	0	31	Kildare . .	Naas South . .	Ballymore Eustace .	Naas . .	I.	64
76, 77. 82	Brunswick . .	87	2	35	Tipperary, S.R.	Iffa and Offa East .	Newchapel . .	Clonmel . .	II.	315
39	Bruree . . .	142	3	32	Limerick . .	Connello Upper .	Bruree . .	Kilmallock . .	II.	231
39	BRUREE T. . .	—			Limerick . .	Connello Upper .	Bruree . .	Kilmallock . .	II.	231
30, 35, 36	Bruscarnagh . .	122	3	33	Fermanagh . .	Clankelly . .	Clones . .	Clones . .	III.	195
43, 44	Bruse . . .	153	3	10	Cavan . .	Castlerahan . .	Loughan or Castlekeeran . .	Oldcastle . .	III.	69
24, 30	Bruse . . .	605	3	6	Cavan . .	Tullyhunco . .	Killashandra . .	Cavan . .	III.	97
84,85,96,97	Brusk . . .	259	1	29	Galway . .	Athenry . .	Kiltullagh . .	Loughrea . .	IV.	4
31	Brusky . . .	152	3	20	Cavan . .	Clanmahon . .	Ballintemple . .	Cavan . .	III.	75
51	Bruslee . . .	462	0	31	Antrim . .	Lower Belfast . .	Ballylinny . .	Antrim . .	III.	7
21, 27	Brusselstown . .	360	2	6	Wicklow . .	Upper Talbotstown .	Donaghmore . .	Baltinglass . .	I.	363
20,21,27,28	Brutonstown . .	200	0	21	Westmeath . .	Farbill . .	Killucan . .	Mullingar . .	I.	266
20	Brutonstown Little .	68	0	38	Westmeath . .	Farbill . .	Killucan . .	Mullingar . .	I.	266
11, 17	Bryan Beg . .	42	1	19	Roscommon . .	Roscommon . .	Aughrim . .	Car.k on Shannon	IV.	207
23	Bryanbeg Lower .	87	2	0	Westmeath . .	Kilkenny West .	Drumraney . .	Ballymahon . .	I.	272
23	Bryanbeg Upper .	107	0	26	Westmeath . .	Kilkenny West .	Drumraney . .	Ballymahon . .	I.	272
17	Bryandrum . .	128	3	24	Armagh . .	Fews Lower . .	Mullaghbrack . .	Armagh . .	III.	47
14	Bryanlitter . .	223	3	13	Monaghan . .	Cremorne . .	Clontibret . .	Monaghan . .	III.	259
11, 17	Bryan More . .	84	1	17	Roscommon . .	Roscommon . .	Aughrim . .	Car.k on Shannon	IV.	207
23	Bryanmore Lower .	152	3	23	Westmeath . .	Kilkenny West .	Drumraney . .	Ballymahon . .	I.	272
23	Bryanmore Upper .	115	2	18	Westmeath . .	Kilkenny West .	Drumraney . .	Ballymahon . .	I.	273
10	Bryanstown . .	198	2	38	Kildare . .	North Salt . .	Taghadoe . .	Celbridge . .	I.	76
20	Bryanstown . .	589	2	31	Meath . .	Drogheda . .	St. Mary's . .	Drogheda . .	I.	194
49	Bryanstown . .	326	1	16	Meath . .	Upper Deece . .	Moyglare . .	Celbridge . .	I.	194
19	Bryanstown . .	275	1	4	Meath . .	Upper Slane . .	Slane . .	Navan . .	I.	225
25	Bryanstown . .	612	2	30	Westmeath . .	Moyashel and Magheradernon . .	Dysart . . .	Mullingar . .	I.	274

(a) Including 13A. 0R. 3P. water.

No. of Sheet of the Ordnance Survey Maps.	Townlands and Towns.	Area in Statute Acres.	County.	Barony.	Parish.	Poor Law Union in 1857.	Townland Census of 1851, Part I.	
		A. R. P.					Vol.	Page
40	Bryanstown	441 2 10	Wexford	Shelmaliere West	Clongeen	New Ross	I.	332
45, 46	Bryantang	435 0 20a	Antrim	Lower Belfast	Ballynure	Larne	III.	7
16	Buavanagh	153 1 36	Cork, E.R.	Orrery and Kilmore	Bregoge	Mallow	II.	106
21	Buckandhounds	75 2 30	Dublin	Uppercross	Clondalkin	Dublin South	I.	39
76	Buckfield	238 1 3	Mayo	Burrishoole	Kilmeena	Westport	IV.	121
15, 16	Buckhill Barr	193 2 39	Leitrim	Drumahaire	Cloonlogher	Manorhamilton	IV.	94
14	Buckill	827 2 7	Roscommon	Frenchpark	Tibohine	Castlereagh	IV.	204
9	*Buck Island*	2 0 29	Fermanagh	Lurg	Belleek	Ballyshannon	III.	204
34	Buckna	1,595 2 34	Antrim	Lower Antrim	Racavan	Ballymena	III.	4
2, 4	Buckode	333 1 12	Leitrim	Rosclogher	Rossinver	Ballyshannon	IV.	110
94	Buckree	183 0 39	Cork, W.R.	East Carbery (W.D.)	Kinneigh	Dunmanway	II.	134
88	Buckstown	234 0 13	Cork, E.R.	Imokilly	Aghada	Middleton	II.	83
2, 6	Buckstown	234 2 2	Wexford	Gorey	Carnew	Gorey	I.	316
88	Buckwaria	119 3 15	Mayo	Murrisk	Aghagower	Westport	IV.	158
58, 59	Buddaghauns	507 3 2	Kerry	Magunihy	Kilcummin	Killarney	II.	201
108	Buddrimeen	227 1 23	Cork, W.R.	East Carbery (E.D.)	Ballymoney	Dunmanway	II.	127
108	Budellagh and Cloghbrack	166 2 20	Galway	Longford	Donanaghta	Portumna	IV.	58
59, 60	Budore	1,657 2 19	Antrim	Upper Massereene	Tullyrusk	Lisburn	III.	31
54, 62	Buffanagh	566 1 15	Tipperary, S.R.	Middlethird	Kilconnell	Cashel	II.	327
7, 15	Buffanoky	852 3 23	Limerick	Owneybeg	Doon	Limerick	II.	251
67	Buffy	567 3 8b	Galway	Moycullen	Killannin	Oughterard	IV.	69
14	Buggan	201 2 14	Fermanagh	Magheraboy	Devenish	Enniskillen	III.	210
11, 16	Bughorn	182 1 0	Queen's Co.	Upperwoods	Offerlane	Mountmellick	I.	251
29	Bulcaun	109 1 37	Galway	Dunmore	Kilconla	Tuam	IV.	35
63	Bulcaun	173 0 22	Mayo	Costello	Kilbeagh	Swineford	IV.	140
40	Bulgaden	139 3 17	Limerick	Coshlea	Kilbreedy Major	Kilmallock	II.	239
40, 48	Bulgaden Eady	372 2 22	Limerick	Coshlea	Kilbreedy Major	Kilmallock	II.	239
40	Bulgadenhall	223 0 14	Limerick	Smallcounty	Uregare	Kilmallock	II.	261
36, 37	Bulgan	562 2 25	Wexford	Bantry	Whitechurchglynn	Wexford	I.	303
57	Bullaun	747 2 12	Galway	Clare	Kilmoylan	Tuam	IV.	22
97	Bullaun	141 0 5	Galway	Loughrea	Bullaun	Loughrea	IV.	63
20	Bullaun	70 3 37	Limerick	Connello Lower	Nantinan	Rathkeale	II.	229
122	Bullaun	54 0 10	Mayo	Kilmaine	Moorgagagh	Ballinrobe	IV.	157
34, 35	Bullaun	121 0 28	Sligo	Tirerrill	Killadoon	Boyle	IV.	238
114	Bullaunagh	99 1 0	Galway	Kiltartan	Kilthomas	Gort	IV.	49
114	Bullaunagh	178 3 35	Galway	Loughrea	Ardrahan	Gort	IV.	62
77, 88	Bullaunmeneen	273 2 2c	Mayo	Burrishoole	Aghagower	Westport	IV.	118
13	Bullford	186 1 8	Wicklow	Newcastle	Kilcoole	Rathdrum	I.	351
32	Bullhill	272 1 3	Kildare	Narragh & Reban East	Davidstown	Athy	I.	66
14	Bulligs	60 1 26	Cavan	Lower Loughtee	Drumlane	Cavan	III.	79
23	Bullock	347 2 27	Dublin	Rathdown	Monkstown	Rathdown	I.	36
14	Bullockhill	196 3 1	Kilkenny	Fassadinin	Kilmademoge	Kilkenny	I.	90
150	*Bullock Island*	14 1 4	Cork, W.R.	West Carbery (E.D.)	Creagh	Skibbereen	II.	138
21	Bullock Island	83 3 9	King's Co.	Garrycastle	Gallen	Parsonstown	I.	136
6	*Bullock Island*	11 2 14	Roscommon	Boyle	Ardcarn	Boyle	IV.	193
19	Bullockpark	40 2 19	Kildare	Naas North	Tipper	Naas	I.	63
69	Bullockpark	119 3 25	Tipperary, S.R.	Middlethird	Tullamain	Cashel	II.	331
24	Bullock Park	398 0 14	Tyrone	Omagh West	Longfield West	Castlederg	III.	316
23	BULLOCK T.	—	Dublin	Rathdown	Monkstown	Rathdown	I.	37
12	Bullogbrean	255 1 20d	Monaghan	Dartree	Clones	Clones	III.	264
62	Bullsfarm	34 1 38	Clare	Bunratty Lower	Killeely	Limerick	II.	5
45	Bullstown	287 1 28	Meath	Ratoath	Donaghmore	Dunshaughlin	I.	218
29	Bumlin	257 3 8	Roscommon	Roscommon	Bumlin	Strokestown	IV.	208
32	Bumper Lodge or Mullan	57 1 16	Fermanagh	Clanawley	Killesher	Enniskillen	III.	193
15	Bun	230 1 2e	Cavan	Lower Loughtee	Urney	Cavan	III.	81
39	Bun	144 2 20f	Fermanagh	Coole	Galloon	Clones	III.	199
23	Bun	320 0 6	King's Co.	Garrycastle	Gallen	Parsonstown	I.	136
13	Bunacloy	40 1 22	Longford	Moydow	Killashee	Longford	I.	161
118	Bunacrower	151 0 33	Mayo	Kilmaine	Kilmainemore	Ballinrobe	IV.	155
22	Bunacum	210 2 23	Tipperary, N.R.	Upper Ormond	Aghnameadle	Nenagh	II.	288
43, 55	Bunacurry	1,226 3 0g	Mayo	Burrishoole	Achill	Newport	IV.	117
89, 90	Bunaderreen	703 1 11	Kerry	Iveragh	Dromod	Cahersiveen	II.	194
11	Bunagarha	833 1 32h	Kerry	Iraghticonnor	Listowel	Listowel	II.	192
15, 16	Bunagarraun	242 2 26	Galway	Dunmore	Kilbennan	Tuam	IV.	34
43	Bunaglanna	247 0 29	Cork, E.R.	Barrymore	Ardnageehy	Fermoy	II.	50
23, 24	Bunakeeran	643 3 8	King's Co.	Ballyboy	Killoughy	Tullamore	I.	123
18, 19	Bunalough	47 1 32	Longford	Moydow	Moydow	Longford	I.	162
12	Bunalty	954 1 13	Mayo	Erris	Kilcommon	Belmullet	IV.	143
132, 141	Bunalunn	435 2 33	Cork, W.R.	West Carbery (W.D.)	Caheragh	Skibbereen	II.	142
31	Bunanagh	161 0 2	Westmeath	Moycashel	Ardnurcher or Horseleap	Mullingar	I.	276
4	Bunanass	134 2 9	Longford	Longford	Mohill	Longford	I.	159

(a) Including 22A. 0R. 22P. water.
(b) Including 24A. 3R. 14P. water.
(c) Including 15A. 3R. 1P. water.

(d) Including 12A. 0R. 30P. water.
(e) Including 45A. 3R. 38P. water.
(f) Including 15A. 0R. 30P. water.

(g) Including 4A. 3R. 13P. water.
(h) Including 12A. 1R. 2P. water.

No. of Sheet of the Ordnance Survey Maps.	Townlands and Towns.	Area in Statute Acres.			County.	Barony.	Parish.	Poor Law Union in 1857.	Townland Census of 1851, Part I.	
		A.	R.	P.					Vol.	Page
30	Bunaneraghtish	337	2	0a	Mayo	Tirawley	Ardagh	Ballina	IV.	163
10	Bunaninver	213	3	21	Fermanagh	Lurg	Derryvullan	Lowtherstown	III.	204
65	Bunanioo	1,809	2	2b	Mayo	Burrishoole	Achill	Newport	IV.	117
42	Bunanraun	87	1	5	Galway	Clare	Kilkilvery	Tuam	IV.	20
108	Bunanumera	232	2	37	Cork, W.R.	East Carbery (E.D.)	Ballymoney	Dunmanway	II.	127
11	Bunanumery	44	0	3	Cavan	Lower Loughtee	Drumlane	Cavan	III.	79
53	Bunargate	66	1	26c	Wexford	Forth	Tacumshin	Wexford	I.	315
53	Bunargate Strand	23	1	34d	Wexford	Forth	Tacumshin	Wexford	I.	315
53	Bunarge	17	0	31	Wexford	Forth	Carn	Wexford	I.	309
2	Bunastick	69	0	32	Queen's Co.	Tinnahinch	Kilmanman	Mountmellick	I.	249
16, 24	Bunaterin	258	3	25	King's Co.	Ballyboy	Killoughy	Tullamore	I.	123
24	Bunaterin	26	0	21	King's Co.	Ballycowan	Lynally	Tullamore	I.	128
56	Bunatober	461	2	23	Galway	Clare	Annaghdown	Tuam	IV.	16
60, 61	Bunavan	165	2	19	Galway	Kilconnell	Ahascragh	Mountbellew	IV.	38
118	Bunavaunish	186	2	28	Mayo	Kilmaine	Ballinchalla	Ballinrobe	IV.	151
46	Bunaveela	1,112	0	8e	Mayo	Tirawley	Crossmolina	Ballina	IV.	165
24	Bunavie	253	3	19	Limerick	Coonagh	Grean	Tipperary	II.	235
35	Bunavory	158	1	24	Clare	Tulla Upper	Tulla	Tulla	II.	41
41, 49	Bunawack	375	0	23f	Donegal	Boylagh	Templecrone	Glenties	III.	114
17, 25	Bunawillin	271	2	31g	Mayo	Erris	Kilcommon	Belmullet	IV.	143
32	Bunbeg	65	3	28	Donegal	Kilmacrenan	Tullaghobegly	Dunfanaghy	III.	131
73, 82, 83	Bunbinnia	1,546	2	14h	Kerry	Dunkerron North	Knockane	Killarney	II.	181
29	Bunboggan	132	1	20	Meath	Lune	Athboy	Trim	I.	207
46	Buncam	25	2	0	Galway	Killian	Killian	Mountbellew	IV.	44
89	Buncam East	103	2	30i	Mayo	Carra	Ballyhean	Castlebar	IV.	125
78, 89	Buncam North	64	1	14	Mayo	Carra	Ballyhean	Castlebar	IV.	125
89	Buncam West	109	3	11j	Mayo	Carra	Ballyhean	Castlebar	IV.	125
53	Buncarrick	90	3	21	Wexford	Forth	Carn	Wexford	I.	309
41	Buncraggy	424	3	22	Clare	Islands	Clareabbey	Ennis	II.	29
29	BUNCRANA T.	—			Donegal	Inishowen West	Fahan Lower	Inishowen	III.	120
98	Buncronan	126	3	8	Donegal	Banagh	Inver	Donegal	III.	107
75	Buncroobog	250	0	18	Donegal	Boylagh	Inishkeel	Glenties	III.	112
17	Buncrowey	183	0	12	Sligo	Tireragh	Kilmacshalgan	Dromore West	IV.	234
14	Buncurrig	505	3	29k	Kerry	Clanmaurice	Ballyheige	Tralee	II.	167
33	Bundarragh	176	3	12	Leitrim	Carrigallen	Cloone	Mohill	IV.	90
29	Bundeeleen	231	1	10	Mayo	Tirawley	Crossmolina	Ballina	IV.	165
17	Bunderg	184	1	36l	Tyrone	Strabane Lower	Ardstraw	Strabane	III.	318
18, 20	Bundiveen	38	2	29	Leitrim	Drumahaire	Inishmagrath	Manorhamilton	IV.	95
9	Bundoon	65	0	21	Longford	Longford	Killoe	Longford	I.	158
106	BUNDORAN T.	—			Donegal	Tirhugh	Inishmacsaint	Ballyshannon	III.	147
115	Bundorragha	767	0	28	Mayo	Murrisk	Kilgeever	Westport	IV.	159
115	BUNDORRAGHA T.	—			Mayo	Murrisk	Kilgeever	Westport	IV.	161
9	Bundouglas	88	0	15	Galway	Ballynahinch	Ballynakill	Clifden	IV.	11
1	Bunduff	47	1	36	Leitrim	Rosclogher	Rossinver	Ballyshannon	IV.	110
102, 112	Bunduff	180	3	11	Mayo	Costello	Annagh	Claremorris	IV.	137
2, 3	Bunduff	893	2	0	Sligo	Carbury	Ahamlish	Sligo	IV.	219
60	Bunduvowen	554	0	27	Mayo	Carra	Turlough	Castlebar	IV.	130
17	Bunglasha	216	3	30	Kerry	Clanmaurice	Duagh	Listowel	II.	168
63, 64, 72	Bunglasha North	249	3	16	Kerry	Iveragh	Glanbehy	Cahersiveen	II.	195
63,64,71,72	Bunglasha South	341	2	15	Kerry	Iveragh	Glanbehy	Cahersiveen	II.	195
91	Bungosteen	78	1	26	Donegal	Banagh	Killybegs Upper	Glenties	III.	110
13, 19	Buninna	124	3	36	Sligo	Tireragh	Dromard	Dromore West	IV.	233
10, 15	Buninubber	128	1	36	Fermanagh	Lurg	Trory	Lowtherstown	III.	209
6	Bunkey	88	0	32	Limerick	Clanwilliam	Killeenagarriff	Limerick	II.	224
1, 6	Bunkey	112	0	1	Limerick	Clanwilliam	Stradbally	Limerick	II.	226
61, 62	Bunkilla	393	2	21	Cork, E.R.	East Muskerry	Donaghmore	Macroom	II.	102
32	Bunkilleen	89	2	23m	Leitrim	Mohill	Mohill	Mohill	IV.	107
32	Bunkimalta	1,441	2	7	Tipperary, N.R.	Owney and Arra	Killoscully	Nenagh	II.	295
35	Bunlacken	213	3	1	Queen's Co.	Clarmallagh	Aghmacart	Abbeyleix	I.	236
10	Bunlahy	177	2	33	Longford	Granard	Granard	Granard	I.	156
10	BUNLAHY T.	—			Longford	Granard	Granard	Granard	I.	157
141	Bunlick	123	1	38	Cork, W.R.	West Carbery (E.D.)	Creagh	Skibbereen	II.	138
5, 13	Bunlicky	169	0	27	Limerick	Pubblebrien	Mungret	Limerick	II.	253
29, 30	Bunlougher	468	0	30	Fermanagh	Clankelly	Clones	Clones	III.	195
28, 29	Bunlougher	423	1	36n	Fermanagh	Magherastephana	Aghavea	Lisnaskea	III.	218
24, 25	BUNMAHON T.	—			Waterford	Decies without Drum	Ballylaneen	Kilmacthomas	II.	354
29, 35	Bunmichael	79	0	10	Fermanagh	Clankelly	Clones	Clones	III.	195
35, 36, 44	Bunmore East	1,899	2	38	Mayo	Erris	Kilcommon	Newport	IV.	143
35, 44	Bunmore West	2,215	3	28	Mayo	Erris	Kilcommon	Newport	IV.	143
52	Bunnabinnia North	60	1	18	Clare	Bunratty Lower	Kilfinaghta	Limerick	II.	4
52	Bunnabinnia South	988	2	30	Clare	Bunratty Lower	Kilfinaghta	Limerick	II.	4
35	Bunnablaneybane	194	0	24	Fermanagh	Clankelly	Clones	Clones	III.	195
42	Bunnaconeen	119	1	6	Galway	Clare	Kilkilvery	Tuam	IV.	20

(a) Including 6A. 0R. 18P. water.
(b) Including 10A. 3R. 6P. water.
(c) Including 5A. 0R. 20P. water.
(d) Including 0A. 1R. 32P. water.
(e) Including 48A. 1R. 10P. water.

(f) { Including 55A. 3R. 35P. Island Trairagh.
{ Including 146A. 0R. 5P. water.
(g) Including 9A. 0R. 0P. water.
(h) Including 31A. 1R. 29P. water.
(i) Including 10A. 0R. 1P. water.

(j) Including 10A. 3R. 24P. water.
(k) Including 46A. 0R. 16P. water.
(l) Including 7A. 2R. 12P. water.
(m) Including 14A. 2R. 3P. water.
(n) Including 8A. 0R. 19P. water.

No. of Sheet of the Ordnance Survey Maps.	Townlands and Towns.	Area in Statute Acres.	County.	Barony.	Parish.	Poor Law Union in 1857.	Townland Census of 1851, Part I.	
		A. R. P.					Vol.	Page
42	Bunnacranagh	1,329 1 25	Sligo	Leyny	Achonry	Tobercurry	IV.	229
93	Bunnadober	231 0 36	Mayo	Costello	Bekan	Claremorris	IV.	139
117, 118	Bunnadober	160 2 8	Mayo	Kilmaine	Ballinchalla	Ballinrobe	IV.	151
40	Bunnadober	199 0 35	Sligo	Tirerrill	Aghanagh	Boyle	IV.	237
9	Bunnadober	147 3 38	Tipperary N.R.	Lower Ormond	Cloghprior	Borrisokane	II.	282
19	Bunnafedia	376 2 11	Sligo	Tireragh	Dromard	Dromore West	IV.	233
48	Bunnafinglas	316 1 12a	Mayo	Gallen	Attymass	Ballina	IV.	146
121, 123	Bunnafollistran	936 2 33b	Mayo	Kilmaine	Shrule	Ballinrobe	IV.	158
19, 27	Bunnagappagh	615 0 24	King's Co.	Upper Philipstown	Geashill	Tullamore	I.	144
29	Bunnageddy	176 3 14	Roscommon	Roscommon	Lissonuffy	Strokestown	IV.	211
53	Bunnagee	140 0 15	Donegal	Raphoe	Leck	Letterkenny	III.	140
54, 67	Bunnagippaun	331 2 29c	Galway	Moycullen	Kilcummin	Oughterard	IV.	66
123, 124	Bunnaglass	387 3 36	Galway	Kiltartan	Kilthomas	Gort	IV.	49
21	Bunnagurragh	52 0 9	Carlow	Forth	Barragh	Enniscorthy	I.	4
33, 34	Bunnahesco	230 0 33	Fermanagh	Magherastephana	Aghalurcher	Lisnaskea	III.	215
56	Bunnahevelly Beg	139 0 38	Galway	Clare	Annaghdown	Tuam	IV.	16
56, 57	Bunnahevelly More	547 1 11	Galway	Clare	Annaghdown	Tuam	IV.	16
29	Bunnahinly	434 0 13	Westmeath	Brawny	St. Mary's	Athlone	I.	259
9, 10, 14, 15	Bunnahone	157 0 7d	Fermanagh	Magheraboy	Inishmacsaint	Ballyshannon	III.	212
18	Bunnahow	157 2 25e	Clare	Bunratty Upper	Inchicronan	Gort	II.	8
17	Bunnahowen	448 3 20	Mayo	Erris	Kilcommon	Belmullet	IV.	143
51, 64	Bunnahown	671 3 29	Galway	Ballynahinch	Moyrus	Clifden	IV.	12
56, 66	Bunnahowna	859 3 25f	Mayo	Burrishoole	Burrishoole	Newport	IV.	118
39, 53	Bunnakill	541 2 27g	Galway	Moycullen	Kilcummin	Oughterard	IV.	66
47	Bunnamayne	883 0 7	Donegal	Inishowen West	Burt	Londonderry	III.	119
84	Bunnamohaun	889 2 6	Mayo	Murrisk	Kilgeever	Westport	IV.	161
39	Bunnamuck	150 2 2	Sligo	Corran	Drumrat	Boyle	IV.	225
23, 29	Bunnamucka	221 2 10h	Roscommon	Roscommon	Killukin	Strokestown	IV.	210
17	Bunnanagat North	25 3 18	Clare	Inchiquin	Killinaboy	Corrofin	II.	26
17	Bunnanagat South	125 3 9	Clare	Inchiquin	Killinaboy	Corrofin	II.	26
22	Bunnanilra	411 1 32	Sligo	Tireragh	Castleconor	Dromore West	IV.	232
52	Bunnaribba	121 0 8	Roscommon	Athlone	St. Peter's	Athlone	IV.	184
6	Bunnaruddee	315 0 7	Kerry	Iraghticonnor	Aghavallen	Listowel	II.	189
42	Bunnasillagh	237 2 30i	Galway	Clare	Donaghpatrick	Tuam	IV.	19
128, 129	Bunnasrah	373 0 16	Galway	Kiltartan	Beagh	Gort	IV.	46
18	Bunnaton	587 3 39	Donegal	Kilmacrenan	Clondavaddog	Millford	III.	124
34, 43	Bunnatreesruhan	1,978 0 22	Donegal	Kilmacrenan	Gartan	Dunfanaghy	III.	127
29	Bunnavally	114 0 2	Westmeath	Brawny	St. Mary's	Athlone	I.	259
11, 24, 25	Bunnaviskaun	1,592 3 18	Galway	Ross	Ross	Oughterard	IV.	73
34, 35	Bunneill	154 1 8	Fermanagh	Clankelly	Galloon	Lisnaskea	III.	198
33	Bunnianstown	67 2 26	Meath	Upper Duleek	Ardcath	Drogheda	I.	197
29	Bunnisnagapple	619 2 38	Fermanagh	Magherastephana	Aghavea	Lisnaskea	III.	218
16	Bunnoe	197 0 14	Cavan	Tullygarvey	Drung	Cootehill	III.	88
33, 34	Bunnow	191 1 19	Clare	Bunratty Upper	Doora	Ennis	II.	8
32	Bunny Beg	254 0 7	Leitrim	Leitrim	Mohill	Mohill	IV.	104
31, 40	Bunnyconnellan East	2,212 2 10j	Mayo	Gallen	Kilgarvan	Ballina	IV.	148
31, 40	Bunnyconnellan West	507 3 36	Mayo	Gallen	Kilgarvan	Ballina	IV.	148
32	Bunny More Lower	51 3 3	Leitrim	Leitrim	Mohill	Mohill	IV.	104
32	Bunny More Upper	95 0 34	Leitrim	Leitrim	Mohill	Mohill	IV.	104
34	Bunnynubber	157 3 10k	Tyrone	Strabane Upper	Cappagh	Omagh	III.	325
56, 57	Bunoghanaun	472 0 4	Galway	Clare	Annaghdown	Tuam	IV.	16
11	Bunowen	1,452 1 28l	Galway	Ballynahinch	Ballynakill	Clifden	IV.	11
86	Bunowen	171 0 34	Mayo	Murrisk	Kilgeever	Westport	IV.	159
3	Bunowen	508 3 11m	Tyrone	Strabane Lower	Donaghedy	Strabane	III.	320
49	Bunowen Beg	566 1 18n	Galway	Ballynahinch	Ballindoon	Clifden	IV.	10
126	*Bunowen Island*	0 2 32	Galway	Longford	Lickmolassy	Portumna	IV.	61
49	Bunowen More	243 2 11o	Galway	Ballynahinch	Ballindoon	Clifden	IV.	10
22	Bunown	357 0 39	Westmeath	Kilkenny West	Bunown	Athlone	I.	272
11	Bunowna	135 3 22	Sligo	Tireragh	Easky	Dromore West	IV.	233
51,52,61,62	Bunratty East	394 2 0p	Clare	Bunratty Lower	Bunratty	Ennis	II.	3
51, 61, 62	Bunratty West	416 2 39	Clare	Bunratty Lower	Bunratty	Ennis	II.	3
88	Bunrawer	271 2 21	Mayo	Burrishoole	Aghagower	Westport	IV.	118
10	Bunreagh	263 1 27	Roscommon	Boyle	Killummod	Boyle	IV.	196
29	Bunree	41 3 23	Sligo	Tireragh	Kilmoremoy	Ballina	IV.	235
29	BUNREE T.	—	Sligo	Tireragh	Kilmoremoy	Ballina	IV.	235
24	Bunrevagh	318 1 10	Leitrim	Leitrim	Kiltubbrid	Car^k. on Shannon	IV.	103
30, 35	Bunrevan	182 3 14	King's Co.	Garrycastle	Lusmagh	Parsonstown	I.	137
66	Bunrower	197 3 9q	Kerry	Magunihy	Aghadoe	Killarney	II.	199
3, 10	Bunsallagh	946 3 19	King's Co.	Lower Philipstown	Croghan	Edenderry	I.	142
38, 52	Bunscanniff	1,102 2 10r	Galway	Moycullen	Kilcummin	Oughterard	IV.	66
8, 13	Bunshanacloney	396 1 19	Antrim	Cary	Armoy	Ballycastle	III.	11
102	Bunskellig	512 1 38s	Cork, W.R.	Bear	Kilcatherine	Castletown	II.	124
29	Buntalloon	33 3 39	Kerry	Trughanacmy	Tralee	Tralee	II.	213

(a) Including 11A. 2R. 17P. water.
(b) Including 1A. 3R. 10P. water.
(c) Including 7A. 0R. 3P. water.
(d) Including 11A. 1R. 33P. water.
(e) Including 18A. 2R. 2P. water.
(f) Including 18A. 2R. 4P. detached portion.
(g) Including 8A. 0R. 30P. water.

(h) Including 10A. 3R. 35P. water.
(i) Including 31A. 1R. 6P. water.
(j) Including 9A. 3R. 22P. water.
(k) Including 2A. 0R. 14P. water.
(l) Including 15A. 0R. 29P. water.
(m) Including 3A. 0R. 23P. water.

(n) Including 59A. 0R. 6P. water.
(o) Including 23A. 0R. 22P. water.
(p) Including 8A. 1R. 19P. detached portion.
(q) Including 10A. 0R. 16P. water.
(r) Including 10A. 0R. 16P. water.
(s) Including 199A. 3R. 17P. water.
(s) Including 15A. 0R. 27P. Glenbeg Lough.

No. of Sheet of the Ordnance Survey Maps.	Townlands and Towns.	Area in Statute Acres.	County.	Barony.	Parish.	Poor Law Union in 1857.	Townland Census of 1851, Part I.	
		A. R. P.					Vol.	Page
42,43,48,49	Buolick . . .	496 1 39	Tipperary, S.R.	Slievardagh . .	Buolick . . .	Urlingford . .	II.	332
11	Burdautien . .	113 1 10a	Monaghan	Dartree . . .	Clones . . .	Clones . . .	III.	264
11	Burfits Hill . .	61 1 22	Fermanagh .	Lurg . . .	Derryvullan .	Lowtherstown .	III.	204
16	Burgage . . .	83 2 24b	Carlow . .	Idrone West .	Wells . . .	Carlow . .	I.	10
15	Burgage . . .	78 3 19	Dublin . .	Coolock . .	Balgriffin . .	Dublin North .	I.	26
5	Burgage More .	671 1 19c	Wicklow . .	Lower Talbotstown .	Burgage . .	Naas . .	I.	359
5	Burgage Moyle .	322 2 13d	Wicklow . .	Lower Talbotstown .	Burgage . .	Naas . .	I.	359
83	Burgagery-lands East	263 2 32e	Tipperary, S.R.	Iffa and Offa East .	St. Marys, Clonmel	Clonmel . .	II.	316
83	Burgagery-lands West	592 1 6f	Tipperary, S.R.	Iffa and Offa East .	St. Marys, Clonmel	Clonmel . .	II.	316
76, 88	Burgary . . .	60 3 23	Cork, E.R. .	Imokilly . .	Cloyne . .	Middleton . .	II.	85
134, 143	Burgatia . . .	742 2 17	Cork, W.R. .	East Carbery (W.D.)	Ross . . .	Clonakilty . .	II.	135
31	Burgery . . .	60 3 24g	Waterford .	Decies without Drum	Dungarvan .	Dungarvan . .	II.	355
81	Burges . . .	120 2 0	Tipperary, S.R.	Iffa and Offa West .	Whitechurch .	Clogheen . .	II.	321
19, 25, 26	Burgesbeg . .	619 1 27	Tipperary, N.R.	Owney and Arra .	Burgesbeg . .	Nenagh . .	II.	294
76	Burgesland . .	117 2 26	Cork, E.R. .	Barrymore . .	Carrigtohill .	Middleton . .	II.	52
88	Burgesland . .	214 1 6	Tipperary, S.R.	Iffa and Offa West .	Molough . .	Clogheen . .	II.	318
2, 6	Burgesland . .	137 2 25	Westmeath .	Moygoish . .	Street . .	Granard . .	I.	281
67	Burges Lower .	443 0 33	Cork, E.R. .	Imokilly . .	Clonpriest . .	Youghal . .	II.	84
81, 87	Burges Mansion .	177 2 32	Tipperary, S.R.	Iffa and Offa West .	Tubbrid . .	Clogheen . .	II.	320
81	Burges New . .	153 2 22	Tipperary, S.R.	Iffa and Offa West .	Tubbrid . .	Clogheen . .	II.	320
37, 38	Burgess . . .	27 1 28	Wexford . .	Shelmaliere East .	Ardcavan . .	Wexford . .	I.	329
25	Burgessacre . .	22 3 19	Cavan . .	Upper Loughtee .	Urney . .	Cavan . .	III.	86
20,21,28,29	Burgessanchor .	37 0 20	Waterford .	Coshmore&Coshbride	Lismore & Mocollop	Lismore . .	II.	345
67	Burges Upper .	101 1 19	Cork, E.R. .	Imokilly . .	Clonpriest . .	Youghal . .	II.	84
81	Burges West . .	259 0 17	Tipperary, S.R.	Iffa and Offa West .	Tubbrid . .	Clogheen . .	II.	320
18	*Burial Island* .	0 3 19	Down . .	Ards Upper . .	St. Andrews, alias Ballyhalbert .	Newtownards .	III.	161
25	Burkeen . . .	63 3 27	Wicklow . .	Newcastle . .	Rathnew . .	Rathdrum . .	I.	354
39, 40	Burkestown . .	290 2 37	Wexford . .	Shelburne . .	Tintern . .	New Ross . .	I.	329
90	Burnafaunia . .	73 1 39	Mayo . .	Carra . .	Drum . .	Castlebar . .	IV.	128
9	Burnally . . .	169 3 11h	Londonderry .	Keenaght . .	Tamlaght Finlagan .	NewTnLimavady	III.	237
23	Burnchurch . .	588 0 22	Kilkenny . .	Shillelogher .	Burnchurch .	Callan . .	I.	113
54	Burnchurch . .	377 3 5	Tipperary, S.R.	Slievardagh .	St. John Baptist .	Cashel . .	II.	336
23, 27	Burnchurch Viper .	227 1 36	Kilkenny . .	Shillelogher .	Burnchurch .	Callan . .	I.	113
80, 86	Burncourt . .	301 1 14	Tipperary, S.R.	Iffa and Offa West .	Shanrahan .	Clogheen . .	II.	319
86	BURNCOURT T. .	—	Tipperary, S.R.	Iffa and Offa West .	Shanrahan .	Clogheen . .	II.	320
26	Burnellstown . .	113 2 31	Westmeath .	Fartullagh .	Lynn . .	Mullingar .	I.	269
39	Burnew . . .	179 0 9	Cavan . .	Castlerahan .	Killinkere .	Bailieborough .	III.	68
42	Burnfort . . .	538 3 19	Cork, E.R. .	Barretts . .	Mourneabbey .	Mallow . .	II.	50
53	Burnham East .	135 2 0	Kerry . .	Corkaguiny .	Dingle . .	Dingle . .	II.	175
53	Burnham West .	95 2 15	Kerry . .	Corkaguiny .	Dingle . .	Dingle . .	II.	175
17, 20, 22	Burnquarter . .	454 1 14	Antrim . .	Upper Dunluce .	Ballymoney .	Ballymoney .	III.	18
25	Burnside . . .	38 1 10	Antrim . .	Lower Glenarm .	Ardclinis .	Larne . .	III.	21
45	Burnside . . .	153 0 18	Antrim . .	Upper Antrim .	Kilbride . .	Antrim . .	III.	6
70	Burnside . . .	161 2 33	Donegal . .	Raphoe . .	Raphoe . .	Strabane . .	III.	140
29, 30	Burns Libbert .	106 3 7	Antrim . .	Lower Glenarm .	Tickmacrevan .	Larne . .	III.	24
94	Burns Mountain .	255 3 37i	Donegal . .	Banagh . .	Killymard .	Donegal . .	III.	111
19, 20	Burntfurze . .	131 3 16	Kildare . .	South Salt . .	Haynestown .	Naas . .	I.	77
14, 19	Burntfurze . .	32 3 18	Kilkenny . .	Crannagh . .	St. Canice .	Kilkenny . .	I.	87
63	Burnthaw . .	108 3 2	Donegal . .	Raphoe . .	Taughboyne .	Strabane . .	III.	143
55	BurnthouseorBleanoran	132 0 33	Galway . .	Moycullen .	Killannin .	Oughterard .	IV.	69
48	*Burnt Island* .	7 0 28	Mayo . .	Tirawley . .	Kilbelfad . .	Ballina . .	IV.	168
11, 16	Burntwood Big .	292 3 38	Tipperary, N.R.	Lower Ormond .	Modreeny . .	Borrisokane .	II.	286
11	Burntwood Little .	120 1 30	Tipperary, N.R.	Lower Ormond .	Modreeny . .	Borrisokane .	II.	286
123	Burrane . . .	410 0 15	Cork, W.R. .	East Carbery (E.D.)	Kilmaloda .	Clonakilty .	II.	129
68	Burrane Lower .	698 3 6	Clare . .	Clonderalaw .	Killimer . .	Kilrush . .	II.	16
68	Burrane Upper .	361 0 31	Clare . .	Clonderalaw .	Killimer . .	Kilrush . .	II.	16
28	Burrellspark . .	24 1 39j	Kilkenny . .	Gowran . .	Thomastown .	Thomastown .	I.	99
4	Burren . . .	271 0 28	Cavan . .	Tullyhaw . .	Killinagh .	Enniskillen .	III.	91
13	Burren . . .	943 2 4k	Cavan . .	Tullyhaw . .	Templeport .	Bawnboy . .	III.	94
49, 50	Burren . . .	663 1 13	Clare . .	Clonderalaw .	Kilchreest .	Killadysert .	II.	15
123, 136	Burren . . .	639 1 27	Cork, W.R. .	East Carbery (E.D.)	Rathclarin .	Bandon . .	II.	129
51	Burren . . .	743 2 14l	Down . .	Upper Iveagh, Up. pt.	Clonallan .	Newry . .	III.	174
22, 29	Burren . . .	1,231 0 1m	Down . .	Kinelarty . .	Dromara . .	Lisburn . .	III.	176
18	Burren . . .	405 3 6	Louth . .	Ferrard . .	Dunleer . .	Ardee . .	I.	180
59, 69	Burren . . .	1,875 0 5	Mayo . .	Carra . .	Aglish . .	Castlebar . .	IV.	123
100	Burren . . .	188 1 25	Mayo . .	Carra . .	Toughty . .	Ballinrobe .	IV.	130
43	Burrenbane . .	565 1 24	Down . .	Upper Iveagh, Lr. pt.	Kilcoo . .	Kilkeel . .	III.	173
2	Burren Beg . .	231 1 39	Londonderry .	Coleraine . .	Dunboe . .	Coleraine .	III.	231
39	Burrencarragh .	140 3 10	Cavan . .	Castlerahan .	Lurgan . .	Oldcastle . .	III.	69
49, 59	Burrenfadda . .	945 3 4	Clare . .	Clonderalaw .	Kilfiddane .	Killadysert .	II.	15
9, 6	Burren More . .	153 0 2	Londonderry .	Coleraine . .	Dunboe . .	Coleraine .	III.	231
39, 43	Burrenrea . .	146 2 36	Cavan . .	Castlerahan .	Lurgan . .	Oldcastle . .	III.	69

(a) Including 6A. 0R. 30P. water.
(b) Including 5A. 0R. 0P. River Barrow.
(c) Including 21A. 3R. 35P. water.
(d) Including 5A. 2R. 35P. water.
(e) {Within the Borough Boundary, 91A. 2R. 18P. / Including 4A. 0R. 8P. water. / Without the Borough Boundary, 172A. 0R. 14P. / Including 0A. 3R. 0P. water.

(f) {Within the Borough Boundary, 201A. 3R. 22P. / Including 7A. 2R. 8P. water. / Without the Borough Boundary, 390A. 1R. 21P. / Including 3A. 2R. 6P. water.
(g) Including 14A. 3R. 6P. detached portion.
(h) Including 0A. 2R. 21P. water.

(i) Including 7A. 0R. 34P. water.
(j) Including 2A. 0R. 28P. River Nore.
(k) Including 110A. 2R. 20P. water.
(l) Including 6A. 0R. 8P. water.
(m) Including 10A. 3R. 32P. water.

No. of Sheet of the Ordnance Survey Maps.	Townlands and Towns.	Area in Statute Acres. A. R. P.	County.	Barony.	Parish.	Poor Law Union in 1857.	Townland Census of 1851, Part I. Vol.	Page
43	Burrenreagh . .	691 2 1	Down . .	Upper Iveagh, Lr. pt.	Kilcoo . . .	Kilkeel . .	III.	173
5	Burrenwee . .	64 1 15	Clare . .	Burren . . .	Rathborney . .	Ballyvaghan .	II.	14
79	Burris . .	224 0 9a	Mayo . .	Carra . . .	Manulla . .	Castlebar . .	IV.	129
111	Burris . .	29 1 29	Mayo . .	Clanmorris . .	Crossboyne . .	Claremorris .	IV.	132
112	Burris . .	345 1 24	Mayo . .	Clanmorris . .	Kilvine . .	Claremorris .	IV.	134
100	Burriscarra . .	259 0 24	Mayo . .	Carra . . .	Burriscarra .	Ballinrobe .	IV.	127
40	Burr Island . .	2 3 28	Galway . .	Ross . . .	Cong . .	Oughterard .	IV.	73
125	Burroge . .	99 3 35	Galway . .	Leitrim . .	Ballynakill .	Loughrea .	IV.	50
105, 115	Burroge . .	475 3 31	Galway . .	Loughrea . .	Killeenadeema .	Loughrea .	IV.	64
15	Burrow . .	257 1 17	Dublin . .	Coolock . .	Howth . .	Dublin North .	I.	27
15	Burrow . . .	588 0 1	Dublin . .	Coolock . . .	Portmarnock .	Balrothery .	I.	28
8	Burrow . . .	264 0 15	Dublin . .	Nethercross . .	Portraine . .	Balrothery .	I.	31
2	Burrow . . .	95 0 8	King's Co. .	Kilcoursey . .	Ardnurcher or Horse-leap . . .	Tullamore .	I.	140
53	Burrow . . .	155 1 7	Wexford . .	Forth . . .	Carn . . .	Wexford . .	I.	309
43	Burrow . . .	188 2 37	Wexford . .	Forth . . .	Rosslare . .	Wexford . .	I.	313
48	Burrow . . .	12 2 24	Wexford . .	Forth . . .	St. Helens .	Wexford . .	I.	313
5	Burrow . . .	246 2 0	Wexford . .	Scarawalsh . .	Carnew . .	Gorey . .	I.	322
20	Burrow . . .	182 2 21	Wicklow . .	Upper Talbotstown .	Ballynure . .	Baltinglass .	I.	361
2	Burrow or Glenna-nummer . .	97 1 22	King's Co. .	Kilcoursey . .	Kilcumreragh .	Tullamore .	I.	141
6	Bursan . . .	406 1 8	Cavan . .	Tullyhaw . .	Templeport .	Enniskillen .	III.	94
38, 47	Burt Level (Intake)	1,430 0 0b	Donegal . .	Inishowen West .	Burt . . .	Londonderry .	III.	119
2, 3	Burtonhall Demesne	162 1 29	Carlow . .	Carlow . . .	Killerrig . .	Carlow . .	I.	2
2	Burtonhall Demesne	121 1 28	Carlow . .	Carlow . . .	Urglin . .	Carlow . .	I.	3
40	Burtonhall Demesne	318 0 32	Kildare . .	Kilkea and Moone .	Castledermot .	Carlow . .	I.	59
62	Burtonhill . .	34 1 39	Clare . .	Bunratty Lower .	Killeely . .	Limerick . .	II.	5
7, 16	Burton Park . .	156 2 12	Cork, E.R. .	Orrery and Kilmore	Churchtown .	Mallow . .	II.	107
48	Burtonport . .	32 3 24	Donegal . .	Boylagh . .	Templecrone .	Glenties . .	III.	115
32	Burtonstown . .	473 0 16	Meath . .	Lower Duleek .	Ballymagarvey .	Navan . .	I.	194
35, 36	Burtown Big . .	783 2 27	Kildare . .	Kilkea and Moone .	Moone . .	Athy . .	I.	61
35, 36	Burtown Little .	438 2 11	Kildare . .	Kilkea and Moone .	Moone . .	Athy . .	I.	61
50	Bush . . .	191 3 21	Antrim . .	Upper Antrim .	Antrim . .	Antrim . .	III.	5
53	Bush . . .	20 0 21	Wexford . .	Forth . . .	Carn . .	Wexford . .	I.	309
48	Bush . . .	97 3 21	Wexford . .	Forth . . .	St. Michael's .	Wexford . .	I.	314
21	Bushelloaf . .	55 3 34	Dublin . .	Uppercross . .	Clondalkin .	Dublin South .	I.	39
7, 8	Busherstown .	688 2 8	Carlow . .	Carlow . . .	Killerrig . .	Carlow . .	I.	2
41	Busherstown .	344 1 37	Kilkenny . .	Ida . . .	Ballygurrim .	New Ross .	I.	101
45, 47	Busherstown .	712 2 32	King's Co. .	Clonlisk . .	Castletownely .	Roscrea . .	I.	129
46	Busherstown .	254 0 39	Wexford . .	Bargy . . .	Kilcavan . .	Wexford . .	I.	305
47	Busherstown .	50 3 3	Wexford . .	Forth . . .	Mayglass . .	Wexford . .	I.	312
95	Bushfield . .	290 2 36	Galway . .	Dunkellin . .	Oranmore .	Galway . .	IV.	31
97	Bushfield . .	204 1 22	Galway . .	Loughrea . .	Kilconickny .	Loughrea .	IV.	63
111, 119	Bushfield . .	193 3 21	Mayo . .	Kilmaine . .	Kilcommon .	Ballinrobe .	IV.	154
27, 28, 35	Bushfield . .	388 0 35	Roscommon .	Ballymoe . .	Cloonygormican .	Castlereagh .	IV.	191
21, 22	Bushfield . .	152 1 12	Wicklow . .	Upper Talbotstown .	Donaghmore .	Baltinglass .	I.	363
22	Bushfield or Magher-naskeagh . .	258 0 33	Queen's Co. .	Clandonagh . .	Aghaboe . .	Donaghmore .	I.	232
3	Bushfoot or Lissan-duff . .	225 2 3	Antrim . .	Lower Dunluce .	Dunluce . .	Coleraine .	III.	17
62	Bush Island . .	5 3 1	Clare . .	Bunratty Lower .	Kilfintinan .	Limerick . .	II.	5
50	Bush Island . .	1 2 13	Clare . .	Islands . . .	Clondagad .	Killadysert .	II.	29
95	Bush Island . .	0 2 16	Galway . .	Dunkellin . .	Ballynacourty .	Galway . .	IV.	27
110	Bush Island . .	1 3 3	Mayo . .	Kilmaine . .	Robeen . .	Ballinrobe .	IV.	158
68	Bush Island . .	0 2 32	Mayo . .	Tirawley . .	Addergoole .	Castlebar .	IV.	163
3, 7	Bushmills or Ballagh-nore . . .	107 1 35	Antrim . .	Lower Dunluce .	Dunluce . .	Coleraine .	III.	17
3, 7	Bushmills or Magh-eraboy . . .	23 3 36	Antrim . .	Cary . . .	Billy . . .	Coleraine .	III.	12
3, 7	BUSHMILLS T. .	—	Antrim . .	{ Cary . . . { Lower Dunluce .	{ Billy . . . { Dunluce . .	{ Ballycastle { Coleraine .	III.	{ 13 { 18
48	Bushmount . .	276 1 35	Kerry . .	Magunihy . .	Molahiffe .	Killarney .	II.	204
30	Bushpark . .	229 2 9	Wexford . .	Bantry . .	Oldross . .	New Ross .	I.	301
27	Bushtameen . .	26 3 29	Kilkenny . .	Kells . . .	Kilree . .	Callan . .	I.	109
6, 18	Bushtown . .	181 0 21	Galway . .	Ballymoe . .	Boyounagh .	Glennamaddy .	IV.	6
7	Bushtown . .	166 1 37	Londonderry .	Coleraine . .	Macosquin .	Coleraine .	III.	233
101	Bushy Island .	22 3 37	Galway . .	Longford . .	Clonfert . .	Ballinasloe .	IV.	57
136	Bushy Island .	16 2 21	Galway . .	Leitrim . .	Inishcaltra .	Scarriff . .	IV.	54
3, 11	Bushyisland . .	153 3 37	Limerick . .	Kenry . .	Kilcornan .	Rathkeale .	II.	249
21	Bushy Island .	1 3 14	Longford . .	Ratheline . .	Ratheline .	Longford .	I.	164
33	Bushypark . .	335 0 39	Clare . .	Islands . . .	Drumcliff .	Ennis . .	II.	29
44	Bushypark . .	296 0 6	Cork, E.R. .	Barrymore . .	Kilshanahan .	Fermoy . .	II.	56
82	Bushypark . .	91 0 39c	Galway . .	Galway . .	Rahoon . .	Galway . .	IV.	37
27, 31	Bushypark . .	278 0 7	Kildare . .	Offaly West .	Kilrush . .	Athy . .	I.	72

(a) Including 35A. 2R. 36P. water.   (b) The area of this Intake does not appear on the Ordnance Maps; that here given is from the "Tenement Valuation."
(c) Including 7A. 3R. 21P. water.

2 A 2

No. of Sheet of the Ordnance Survey Maps.	Townlands and Towns.	Area in Statute Acres.			County.	Barony.	Parish.	Poor Law Union in 1857.	Townland Census of 1851, Part I.	
		A.	R.	P.					Vol.	Page
40, 41	Buskhill . .	165	2	18	Down . .	Upper Iveagh, Up. pt.	Donaghmore . .	Newry . .	III.	175
20	Bustyhill . .	216	2	39	Dublin . .	Newcastle . .	Newcastle . .	Celbridge . .	I.	34
18	Butchersarms . .	36	2	5	Dublin . .	Uppercross . .	St. James . .	Dublin South .	I.	41
15	BUTLERSBRIDGE T.	—			Cavan . .	Upper Loughtee .	Castleterra . .	Cavan . .	III.	83
47	Butlersfarm . .	63	2	31	Tipperary, N.R.	Eliogarty . .	Moycarky . .	Thurles . .	II.	271
8, 9	Butlersgrange . .	735	3	20	Carlow . .	Rathvilly . .	Tullowphelim . .	Carlow . .	I.	12
21	Butlersgrove . .	207	2	32	Kilkenny . .	Gowran . .	Kilmacahill . .	Kilkenny . .	I.	97
70	Butler's-land . .	72	0	8	Tipperary, S.R.	Middlethird . .	Coolmundry . .	Cashel . .	II.	326
29, 34	Butlersland . .	92	0	35	Wexford . .	Bantry . .	St. Mary's . .	New Ross . .	I.	302
29	Butlerslodge . .	20	3	39	Tipperary, N.R.	Eliogarty . .	Templemore . .	Thurles . .	II.	272
76, 77	Butlerstown . .	174	2	38a	Cork, E.R.	Imokilly . . .	Middleton . .	Middleton . .	II.	89
111	Butlerstown . .	78	2	20	Cork, E.R.	Kinsale . . .	Clontead . .	Kinsale . .	II.	99
136	Butlerstown . .	372	0	2	Cork, W.R.	Ibane and Barryroe .	Lislee . . .	Clonakilty . .	II.	150
11, 12	Butlerstown . .	228	1	24	Meath . .	Morgallion . .	Castletown . .	Navan . .	I.	209
50	Butlerstown . .	108	2	38	Meath . .	Upper Deece . .	Moyglare . .	Dunshaughlin .	I.	194
78, 84	Butlerstown . .	409	3	24	Tipperary, S.R.	Iffa and Offa East .	Kilmurry . .	Carrick on Suir	II.	314
78	Butlerstown . .	109	1	9	Tipperary, S.R.	Iffa and Offa East .	Kilsheelan . .	Clonmel . .	II.	314
47	Butlerstown . .	44	2	33	Wexford . .	Forth . . .	Ballymore . .	Wexford . .	I.	308
47	Butlerstown . .	103	0	30	Wexford . .	Forth . . .	Ishartmon . .	Wexford . .	I.	309
48, 53	Butlerstown . .	171	3	9	Wexford . .	Forth . . .	St. Iberius . .	Wexford . .	I.	314
64	Butlerstown Great .	245	3	23	Cork, E.R.	Barrymore . .	Ballydeloher . .	Cork . .	II.	51
64	Butlerstown Little .	124	1	1	Cork, E.R.	Barrymore . .	Ballydeloher . .	Cork . .	II.	51
9, 17	Butlerstown North .	414	0	34	Waterford . .	Middlethird . .	Kilburne . .	Waterford . .	II.	367
17	Butlerstown South .	366	1	5	Waterford . .	Middlethird . .	Kilburne . .	Waterford . .	II.	367
136	BUTLERSTOWN T. .	—			Cork, W.R.	Ibane and Barryroe .	Lislee . .	Clonakilty . .	II.	150
30	Butlerswood . .	470	2	5	Kilkenny . .	Kells . . .	Killamery . .	Callan . .	I.	108
22	Butterfield . .	250	0	8	Dublin . .	Rathdown . .	Rathfarnham . .	Dublin South .	I.	37
5	Butterhill . .	407	3	25	Wicklow . .	Lower Talbotstown .	Blessington . .	Naas . .	I.	358
37	Butterhouse or									
	Mountland . .	107	2	32	Meath . .	Lower Deece . .	Scurlockstown .	Trim . .	I.	192
16	Butterisland . .	180	0	27	Queen's Co. .	Upperwoods . .	Offerlane . .	Abbeyleix . .	I.	251
1, 2	Butter Mountain .	935	2	36	Wicklow . .	Lower Talbotstown .	Kilbride . .	Naas . .	I.	361
14	Butterstream Commons . .	0	3	32	Kildare . .	Clane . . .	Clane . . .	Naas . .	I.	53
17	Buttevant . .	51	0	5	Cork, E.R.	Orrery and Kilmore	Buttevant . .	Mallow . .	II.	107
16, 17	BUTTEVANT T. .	—			Cork, E.R.	Orrery and Kilmore	Buttevant . .	Mallow . .	II.	107
13	Buzzardstown . .	298	3	6	Dublin . .	Castleknock . .	Mulhuddart . .	Dublin North .	I.	25
17	Byblox . . .	100	1	15	Cork, E.R.	Fermoy . . .	Doneraile . .	Mallow . .	II.	78
5	Byrnesgrove . .	725	3	6	Kilkenny . .	Fassadinin . .	Kilmacar . .	Castlecomer .	I.	90
21	Byrneshill . .	171	1	32	Wicklow . .	Upper Talbotstown .	Freynestown . .	Baltinglass .	I.	364
70	Byrneskill . .	137	0	31	Tipperary, S.R.	Middlethird . .	Coolmundry . .	Cashel . .	II.	326
24, 25	Byturn . .	206	3	6	Tyrone . .	Strabane Lower .	Ardstraw . .	Strabane . .	III.	318
10,11,19,20	Cabadooey or Altashane . .	1,591	0	18	Donegal . .	Inishowen East .	Donagh . .	Inishowen . .	III.	118
4	Cabinhill . .	81	3	4	Dublin . .	Balrothery West .	Naul . . .	Balrothery . .	I.	23
38	Cabinhill . .	206	3	31	Meath . .	Ratoath . .	Ratoath . .	Dunshaughlin .	I.	219
23, 26	Cabinteely . .	267	0	22	Dublin . .	Rathdown . .	Kill . . .	Rathdown . .	I.	35
26	CABINTEELY T. .	—			Dublin . .	Rathdown . .	Killiney . . / Tully . .	Rathdown . .	I.	{36 {38
7	Cabintown . .	193	0	31	Mayo . .	Tirawley . .	Kilbride . .	Killala . .	IV.	168
35	Cabra . . .	599	2	13b	Cavan . .	Clankee . .	Enniskeen . .	Bailieborough .	III.	72
52	Cabra Brook . .	270	2	1	Donegal . .	Kilmacrenan .	Conwal . .	Letterkenny .	III.	126
27, 32	Cabragh . .	211	1	15	Antrim . .	Lower Toome .	Kirkinriola . .	Ballymena .	III.	32
17, 22	Cabragh . .	294	3	12	Antrim . .	Upper Dunluce .	Ballymoney .	Ballymoney .	III.	18
8, 12	Cabragh . .	182	0	30	Armagh . .	Armagh . . .	Grange . .	Armagh . .	III.	44
17	Cabragh . .	24	2	20	Armagh . .	Fews Lower . .	Mullaghbrack . .	Armagh . .	III.	47
13	Cabragh . .	372	3	28	Armagh . .	Oneilland West .	Mullaghbrack . .	Banbridge . .	III.	54
11	Cabragh . .	113	2	30	Armagh . .	Tiranny . .	Eglish . .	Armagh . .	III.	59
17, 18	Cabragh . .	205	2	17	Cavan . .	Tullygarvey . .	Drumgoon . .	Cootehill . .	III.	88
17	Cabragh . .	188	3	14	Cavan . .	Tullygarvey . .	Kildrumsherdan	Cootehill . .	III.	89
59	Cabragh . .	398	1	15	Cork, W.R.	West Muskerry .	Clondrohid . .	Macroom . .	II.	155
14,15,21,22	Cabragh . .	865	0	16	Down . .	Lower Iveagh, Up. pt.	Hillsborough . .	Lisburn . .	III.	169
42	Cabragh . .	268	2	33	Down . .	Upper Iveagh, Lr. pt.	Clonduff . .	Newry . .	III.	171
47	Cabragh . .	319	1	13	Down . .	Upper Iveagh, Up. pt.	Clonallan . .	Newry . .	III.	174
7	Cabragh . .	157	0	3	Dublin . .	Balrothery West .	Clonmethan . .	Balrothery . .	I.	22
14, 18	Cabragh . .	457	0	17	Dublin . .	Castleknock . .	Castleknock . .	Dublin North .	I.	24
18	Cabragh . .	102	2	20	Dublin . .	Castleknock . .	Finglas . .	Dublin North .	I.	24
18	Cabragh . .	24	1	11	Dublin . .	Coolock . .	Grangegorman .	Dublin North .	I.	27
37, 42	Cabragh . .	298	1	38	Londonderry .	Loughinsholin .	Termoneeny . .	Magherafelt .	III.	244
61	Cabragh . .	168	3	0	Mayo . .	Gallen . .	Toomore . .	Swineford . .	IV.	151
38	Cabragh . .	255	3	38c	Mayo . .	Tirawley . .	Crossmolina . .	Ballina . .	IV.	165
31,32,37,38	Cabragh . .	642	2	13	Meath . .	Skreen . .	Tara . . .	Navan . .	I.	222

(a) Including 17A. 1R. 14P. water.   (b) Including 2A. 1R. 27P. water.   (c) Including 2A. 1R. 28P. water.

No of Sheet of the Ordnance Survey Maps.	Townlands and Towns.	Area in Statute Acres.			County.	Barony.	Parish.	Poor Law Union in 1857.	Townland Census of 1851, Part I.	
		A.	R.	P.					Vol.	Page
10	Cabragh	397	2	8	Meath	Upper Kells	Loughan or Castlekeeran	Kells	I.	206
24	Cabragh	307	3	35	Monaghan	Cremorne	Ballybay	Castleblayney	III.	259
13	Cabragh	122	1	34	Monaghan	Monaghan	Drumsnat	Monaghan	III.	275
19, 25	Cabragh	1,129	1	37	Sligo	Leyny	Killoran	Tobercurry	IV.	230
10, 11	Cabragh	854	1	30	Sligo	Tireragh	Kilglass	Dromore West	IV.	234
35	Cabragh	450	3	19	Sligo	Tirerrill	Shancough	Boyle	IV.	241
47	Cabragh	589	0	25	Tipperary, N.R.	Eliogarty	Fertiana	Thurles	II.	269
53	Cabragh	347	0	38	Tyrone	Dungannon Lower	Killeeshil	Dungannon	III.	298
49, 56	Cabragh	825	0	27	Tyrone	Omagh East	Kilskeery	Lowtherstown	III.	313
7	Cabragh or Cavanmore	135	0	6	Antrim	Lower Dunluce	Billy	Coleraine	III.	16
10	Cabraghkeel	284	0	17	Sligo	Tireragh	Kilglass	Dromore West	IV.	234
52	Cabra Glebe	236	1	4	Donegal	Kilmacrenan	Conwal	Letterkenny	III.	126
30, 31	Cabry	927	1	36	Donegal	Inishowen East	Moville Upper	Inishowen	III.	119
59	Cackanode	221	3	13	Cork, W.R.	West Muskerry	Clondrohid	Macroom	II.	155
42	Cackinish	235	1	14a	Fermanagh	Knockninny	Kinawley	Lisnaskea	III.	201
3	Cadamstown	1,154	2	10	Kildare	Carbury	Cadamstown	Edenderry	I.	51
31,32,36,37	Cadamstown	863	1	12	King's Co.	Ballybritt	Letterluna	Parsonstown	I.	126
18	Caddagh	296	3	6	Monaghan	Cremorne	Tullycorbet	Monaghan	III.	262
13	Caddagh	182	2	5b	Westmeath	Delvin	Castletowndelvin	Castletowndelvin	I.	264
15	Caddagh Glebe	216	0	4	Leitrim	Drumahaire	Killanummery	Manorhamilton	IV.	97
21	Caddellbrook	216	0	27	Roscommon	Castlereagh	Baslick	Castlereagh	IV.	199
6	Caddelstown	68	2	10	Meath	Lower Slane	Loughbrackan	Ardee	I.	223
6	Caddelstown	43	2	10	Meath	Lower Slane	Siddan	Ardee	I.	223
69	Caddlestown	158	1	24	Tipperary, S.R.	Middlethird	Knockgraffon	Cashel	II.	328
43	Caddy	309	2	22c	Antrim	Upper Toome	Drummaul	Ballymena	III.	34
61	Cadian	642	0	2d	Tyrone	Dungannon Middle	Clonfeacle	Dungannon	III.	298
5	Cady	147	3	15	Fermanagh	Lurg	Magheraculmoney	Lowtherstown	III.	207
38	Cady	104	1	21	Tyrone	Dungannon Upper	Desertcreat	Cookstown	III.	307
38, 47	Caffoley	394	1	5	Mayo	Tirawley	Addergoole	Ballina	IV.	163
18	Cah	820	0	6	Londonderry	Coleraine	Errigal	Coleraine	III.	232
8	Cahanagh	181	0	35	Longford	Longford	Clongesh	Longford	I.	157
22, 23	Cahard	511	2	36e	Down	Castlereagh Upper	Kilmore	Downpatrick	III.	165
19	Caheny	378	2	27	Londonderry	Coleraine	Aghadowey	Coleraine	III.	229
19	CAHENY T.	—			Londonderry	Coleraine	Aghadowey	Coleraine	III.	230
18,19,26,27	Caher	587	3	6	Clare	Bunratty Upper	Inchicronan	Tulla	II.	8
29	Caher	372	3	34	Clare	Tulla Lower	Ogonnelloe	Scarriff	II.	38
55	Caher	226	0	23	Cork, E.R.	Kinnatalloon	Mogeely	Youghal	II.	98
105	Caher	74	0	21	Cork, W.R.	Bantry	Kilmocomoge	Bantry	II.	119
121, 122	Caher	315	2	21	Cork, W.R.	East Carbery (W.D.)	Kilmeen	Clonakilty	II.	133
108	Caher	616	1	38	Cork, W.R.	East Carbery (W.D.)	Kinneigh	Dunmanway	II.	134
135, 144	Caher	135	2	17	Cork, W.R.	Ibane and Barryroe	Ardfield	Clonakilty	II.	148
138	Caher	253	0	22	Cork, W.R.	West Carbery (W.D.)	Kilcrohane	Bantry	II.	143
146,147,152	Caher	465	3	33	Cork, W.R.	West Carbery (W.D.)	Kilmoe	Skull	II.	144
37, 38	Caher	747	1	28f	Galway	Ballynahinch	Moyrus	Clifden	IV.	12
87	Caher	66	2	27	Galway	Clonmacnowen	Kilcloony	Ballinasloe	IV.	25
117	Caher	58	1	12	Galway	Longford	Killimorbologue	Portumna	IV.	58
117, 126	Caher	163	0	37	Galway	Longford	Lickmolassy	Portumna	IV.	60
36	Caher	109	3	31	Kerry	Corkaguiny	Killiney	Dingle	II.	177
85, 94	Caher	427	0	14	Kerry	Glanarought	Kilgarvan	Kenmare	II.	187
58, 66	Caher	178	2	24	Kerry	Magunihy	Aghadoe	Killarney	II.	199
81	Caher	564	1	19	Mayo	Costello	Aghamore	Swineford	IV.	136
117	Caher	121	1	34	Mayo	Kilmaine	Ballinrobe	Ballinrobe	IV.	152
111	Caher	181	2	23	Mayo	Kilmaine	Kilcommon	Ballinrobe	IV.	151
118	Caher	81	2	22	Mayo	Kilmaine	Kilmainemore	Ballinrobe	IV.	155
86, 96	Caher	417	3	10	Mayo	Murrisk	Kilgeever	Westport	IV.	159
26	Caher	350	3	30	Roscommon	Castlereagh	Kilkeevin	Castlereagh	IV.	200
19	Caher	188	2	20	Roscommon	Frenchpark	Tibohine	Castlereagh	IV.	204
26	Caher	168	2	18	Waterford	Middlethird	Islandikane	Waterford	II.	367
75	Caherabbey Lower	439	2	30g	Tipperary, S.R.	Iffa and Offa West	Caher	Clogheen	II.	317
75	Caherabbey Upper	615	2	23h	Tipperary, S.R.	Iffa and Offa West	Caher	Clogheen	II.	317
45	Caheracruttera	574	1	33	Kerry	Corkaguiny	Ballinvoher	Dingle	II.	174
96	Caheradangan	80	2	17	Galway	Dunkellin	Killora	Loughrea	IV.	31
15	Caheraderry	368	1	1	Clare	Corcomroe	Killaspuglonane	Ennistimon	II.	19
96	Caheradine	233	3	33	Galway	Dunkellin	Killeeneen	Gort	IV.	30
119, 132	Caheragh	664	2	23	Cork, W.R.	West Carbery (W.D.)	Caheragh	Skibbereen	II.	142
40	Caheragh	435	2	9	Kerry	Trughanacmy	Castleisland	Tralee	II.	208
17, 18	Caheragh	461	1	32	Limerick	Shanid	Kilfergus	Glin	II.	256
39, 48	Caheraghacullin	252	0	38	Clare	Moyarta	Kilmacduane	Kilrush	II.	32
28, 42	Caherakeeny	269	1	30	Galway	Clare	Donaghpatrick	Tuam	IV.	19
97	Caherakilleen	89	2	26	Galway	Dunkellin	Kilconierin	Loughrea	IV.	29
104	Caheraloggy East	77	3	33	Galway	Dunkellin	Killeely	Gort	IV.	29
103, 104	Caheraloggy West	132	0	18	Galway	Dunkellin	Killeely	Gort	IV.	29
13	Caheranardrish	124	0	32	Limerick	Pubblebrien	Mungret	Limerick	II.	253

(a) Including 28A. 3R. 13P. water.
(b) Including 3A. 1R. 32P. water.
(c) Including 12A. 2R. 36P. water.

(d) Including 2A. 3R. 11P. water.
(e) Including 5A. 0R. 18P. water.
(f) Including 10A. 3R. 2P. water.

(g) Including 13A. 2R. 17P. water.
(h) Including 1A. 3R. 18P. water.

No. of Sheet of the Ordnance Survey Maps.	Townlands and Towns.	Area in Statute Acres.			County.	Barony.	Parish.	Poor Law Union in 1857.	Townland Census of 1851, Part I.	
		A.	R.	P.					Vol.	Page
103, 104	Caherapheepa	165	0	33	Galway	Dunkellin	Killeeneen	Gort	IV.	30
18, 26	Caheraphuca	305	2	0	Clare	Bunratty Upper	Inchicronan	Tulla	II.	8
42, 52	Caherard	199	0	28	Kerry	Corkaguiny	Kildrum	Dingle	II.	177
21	Caherass	268	1	4	Limerick	Coshma	Croom	Croom	II.	242
70, 71	Caherateemore North	552	3	28	Galway	Clare	Lackagh	Galway	IV.	22
70,71,83,84	Caherateemore South	369	1	39	Galway	Clare	Lackagh	Galway	IV.	22
103,113,114	Caherateige	343	3	29	Galway	Dunkellin	Ardrahan	Gort	IV.	26
52	Caheratrant	297	3	32	Kerry	Corkaguiny	Ventry	Dingle	II.	180
114	Caheratrim	250	0	33	Galway	Dunkellin	Ardrahan	Gort	IV.	26
105, 115	Caheratrim	458	0	30	Galway	Loughrea	Killeenadeema	Loughrea	IV.	64
102, 115	Caheravart	52	2	19	Cork, W.R.	Bear	Kilcatherine	Castletown	II.	124
50	Caheraveelane	234	1	2	Cork, E.R.	Duhallow	Kilshannig	Mallow	II.	74
148	Caheravirane	137	0	35	Cork, W.R.	West Carbery (W.D.)	Skull	Skull	II.	145
57	Caheravoley	412	1	21	Galway	Clare	Kilmoylan	Tuam	IV.	22
118, 119	Caheravoostia	351	0	13	Mayo	Kilmaine	Kilcommon	Ballinrobe	IV.	154
113	Caherawoneen North	370	2	6	Galway	Kiltartan	Kinvarradoorus	Gort	IV.	49
113	Caherawoneen South	485	1	18	Galway	Kiltartan	Kinvarradoorus	Gort	IV.	49
25, 33	Caherbannagh	420	3	10	Clare	Inchiquin	Kilnamona	Ennis	II.	27
8	Caherbarnagh	183	1	4	Clare	Burren	Kilmoon	Ennistimon	II.	13
14, 15	Caherbarnagh	382	1	8	Clare	Corcomroe	Kilmacrehy	Ennistimon	II.	20
38, 47	Caherbarnagh	3,626	2	22	Cork, W.R.	West Muskerry	Drishane	Millstreet	II.	155
89, 98	Caherbarnagh	295	2	21	Kerry	Iveragh	Dromod	Cahersiveen	II.	194
60	Caherbaroul	426	0	25	Cork, W.R.	East Muskerry	Aghabulloge	Macroom	II.	153
61	Caherbaun	334	2	37	Tipperary, S.R.	Middlethird	Kilconnell	Cashel	II.	327
1	Caherbaun	167	2	19	Waterford	Glenahiry	Inishlounaght	Clonmel	II.	365
134	Caherbeg	375	2	23	Cork, W.R.	East Carbery (W.D.)	Rathbarry	Clonakilty	II.	135
59	Caherbirrane	717	3	14	Cork, W.R.	West Muskerry	Clondrohid	Macroom	II.	155
16	Caherblonick North	298	2	0	Clare	Inchiquin	Killinaboy	Corrofin	II.	26
16	Caherblonick South	192	1	8	Clare	Inchiquin	Killinaboy	Corrofin	II.	26
42, 43, 52	Caherboshina	444	1	29	Kerry	Corkaguiny	Kildrum	Dingle	II.	177
13	Caherbrack	426	0	21	Waterford	Glenahiry	Kilronan	Clonmel	II.	365
29	Caherbreagh	387	1	12	Kerry	Trughanacmy	Ballymacelligott	Tralee	II.	207
128, 129	Caherbrian	34	1	4	Galway	Kiltartan	Beagh	Gort	IV.	46
83	Caherbriskaun	373	3	36	Galway	Clare	Athenry	Galway	IV.	17
128	Caherbroder	354	0	37a	Galway	Kiltartan	Beagh	Gort	IV.	46
17	Caherbullaun	408	2	16b	Clare	Inchiquin	Killinaboy	Corrofin	II.	26
52	Caherbullig	323	2	17	Kerry	Corkaguiny	Ventry	Dingle	II.	180
95, 96	Caherbulligin	160	1	5	Galway	Dunkellin	Killeeneen	Gort	IV.	30
4, 5	Caherbullog	1,060	0	36	Clare	Burren	Kilmoon	Ballyvaghan	II.	13
34	Cahercalla	147	1	28	Clare	Bunratty Upper	Quin	Tulla	II.	10
48	Cahercannavan	778	2	4	Clare	Clonderalaw	Kilmihil	Kilrush	II.	17
58, 69	Cahercarney	88	2	28	Cork, W.R.	West Muskerry	Ballyvourney	Macroom	II.	154
113	Cahercarney	445	3	23	Galway	Kiltartan	Kinvarradoorus	Gort	IV.	49
25	Caherclanchy	131	3	33	Clare	Inchiquin	Dysert	Ennis	II.	24
4, 5, 8, 9	Cahercloggaun	239	0	35	Clare	Burren	Kilmoon	Ballyvaghan	II.	13
38	Caherclogh	199	0	35	Limerick	Connello Upper	Corcomohide	Croom	II.	232
77	Caherclogh	614	3	22	Tipperary, S.R.	Iffa and Offa East	Lisronagh	Clonmel	II.	315
113, 122	Cahercon	427	0	37	Galway	Kiltartan	Killinny	Gort	IV.	47
14, 23	Caherconlish	209	3	18	Limerick	Clanwilliam	Caherconlish	Limerick	II.	222
14	CAHERCONLISH T.	—			Limerick	Clanwilliam	Caherconlish	Limerick	II.	222
9	Caherconnell	260	3	11	Clare	Burren	Kilcorney	Ballyvaghan	II.	12
51, 52	Caher (Connell)	943	2	7c	Limerick	Glenquin	Abbeyfeale	Newcastle	II.	244
7	Caherconnor	213	3	7	Cork, E.R.	Fermoy	Imphrick	Mallow	II.	80
23	Caherconreafy	70	0	10	Limerick	Clanwilliam	Aglishcormick	Limerick	II.	221
25	Cahercoreaun	144	1	28	Clare	Inchiquin	Rath	Corrofin	II.	27
96	Cahercormick	35	1	15	Galway	Dunkellin	Kilconierin	Loughrea	IV.	29
23, 32	Cahercorney	719	0	36	Limerick	Smallcounty	Cahercorney	Kilmallock	II.	259
105	Cahercrea East	326	2	27	Galway	Loughrea	Killeenadeema	Loughrea	IV.	64
105	Cahercrea West	92	1	10	Galway	Loughrea	Killeenadeema	Loughrea	IV.	64
96	Cahercrin	325	2	26	Galway	Dunkellin	Killeeneen	Loughrea	IV.	30
118	Cahercroobeen	64	1	27	Mayo	Kilmaine	Ballinrobe	Ballinrobe	IV.	152
30	Cahercullenagh Lower	283	3	37	Kerry	Trughanacmy	Ballymacelligott	Tralee	II.	207
30	Cahercullenagh Upper	520	3	4	Kerry	Trughanacmy	Ballymacelligott	Tralee	II.	207
16, 22	Caher (Custodia)	358	1	39	Queen's Co.	Upperwoods	Offerlane	Abbeyleix	I.	251
15	Caherdague	40	2	30	Longford	Ardagh	Street	Granard	I.	153
70	Caherdaha	208	0	4	Cork, W.R.	West Muskerry	Kilnamartry	Macroom	II.	159
113, 114	Caherdaly	221	1	25	Galway	Dunkellin	Ardrahan	Gort	IV.	26
106	Caherdaniel	452	3	13	Kerry	Dunkerron South	Kilcrohane	Cahersiveen	II.	183
118	Caherdaniel East	119	1	25	Cork, W.R.	Bantry	Kilmocomoge	Bantry	II.	119
118	Caherdaniel West	96	1	4	Cork, W.R.	Bantry	Kilmocomoge	Bantry	II.	119
5	Caherdavin	94	1	7	Limerick	Pubblebrien	St. Munchins	Limerick	II.	254
48, 58	Caherdean	243	3	21	Kerry	Magunihy	Kilcredane	Killarney	II.	200
54	Caherdesert	235	0	32	Cork, E.R.	Barrymore	Gortroe	Fermoy	II.	55

(a) Including 3A. 3R. 37P. water.　　　　(b) Including 51A. 3R. 16P. water.　　　　(c) Including 5A. 3R. 16P. water.

No. of Sheet of the Ordnance Survey Maps.	Townlands and Towns.	Area in Statute Acres.	County.	Barony.	Parish.	Poor Law Union in 1857.	Townland Census of 1851, Part I.	
		A. R. P.					Vol.	Page
42, 43	Caherdorgan North	216 2 39	Kerry	Corkaguiny	Kilmalkedar	Dingle	II.	178
42	Caherdorgan South	105 3 6	Kerry	Corkaguiny	Kilmalkedar	Dingle	II.	178
47, 48	Caherdowney	1,173 0 24	Cork, W.R.	West Muskerry	Drishane	Millstreet	II.	155
19, 27	Caherdrinny	826 1 24	Cork, E.R.	Condons&Clangibbon	Glanworth	Mitchelstown	II.	61
19	Caherdrinny	22 2 30	Cork, E.R.	Condons&Clangibbon	Kilphelan	Mitchelstown	II.	62
104	Caherduff	97 3 18	Galway	Dunkellin	Ardrahan	Gort	IV.	26
120, 121	Caherduff	376 3 1	Mayo	Kilmaine	Cong	Ballinrobe	IV.	153
54	Caherduggan	115 0 26	Cork, E.R.	Barrymore	Gortroe	Fermoy	II.	55
54	Caherduggan Demesne	149 1 0	Cork, E.R.	Barrymore	Templebodan	Middleton	II.	58
54	Caherduggan East	59 0 7	Cork, E.R.	Barrymore	Templebodan	Middleton	II.	58
25	Caherduggan North	334 0 19	Cork, E.R.	Fermoy	Caherduggan	Mallow	II.	77
25	Caherduggan South	468 0 37	Cork, E.R.	Fermoy	Caherduggan	Mallow	II.	77
54	Caherduggan West	104 0 13	Cork, E.R.	Barrymore	Templebodan	Middleton	II.	58
40, 41, 50	Caherea	825 1 26	Clare	Islands	Clondagad	Killadysert	II.	29
41	Caherea	29 1 20	Clare	Islands	Kilmaley	Ennis	II.	31
15	Cahercamore	261 3 38	Clare	Corcomroe	Kilshanny	Ennistimon	II.	21
93	Caher East	483 3 26	Kerry	Glanarought	Kenmare	Kenmare	II.	185
118	Caheredmond	156 1 20	Mayo	Kilmaine	Ballinrobe	Ballinrobe	IV.	152
40	Cahereen East	8 0 3	Kerry	Trughanacmy	Castleisland	Tralee	II.	208
40	Cahereen West	109 0 22	Kerry	Trughanacmy	Castleisland	Tralee	II.	208
70	Cahereighterrush	277 3 20	Kerry	Iveragh	Killinane	Cahersiveen	II.	197
23	Caherelly East	724 0 35	Limerick	Clanwilliam	Caherelly	Limerick	II.	222
23	Caherelly West	419 3 6	Limerick	Clanwilliam	Caherelly	Limerick	II.	222
113,121,122	Cahererillan	498 3 21	Galway	Kiltartan	Killinny	Gort	IV.	47
9,10,16,17	Caherfadda	432 2 7	Clare	Inchiquin	Killinaboy	Corrofin	II.	26
27, 46	Caherfealane	1,038 1 4	Kerry	Trughanacmy	Kilgarrylander	Tralee	II.	210
46	Caherfealane-marsh	64 2 20	Kerry	Trughanacmy	Kilgarrylander	Tralee	II.	210
47	Caherfeenick North	459 2 22	Clare	Moyarta	Kilmacduane	Kilrush	II.	32
47	Caherfeenick South	469 0 28	Clare	Moyarta	Kilmacduane	Kilrush	II.	32
96	Caherfinesker	250 1 27	Galway	Athenry	Athenry	Loughrea	IV.	3
96	Caherfurvaus	188 2 37	Galway	Dunkellin	Killeeneen	Gort	IV.	30
74	Cahergal	204 0 0a	Cork, E.R.	Cork	St. Annes Shandon	Cork	II.	65
135	Cahergal	27 3 21	Cork, W.R.	Ibane and Barryroe	Desert	Clonakilty	II.	148
135	Cahergal	61 1 5	Cork, W.R.	Ibane and Barryroe	Templeomalus	Clonakilty	II.	150
142	Cahergal	268 2 24b	Cork, W.R.	West Carbery (E.D.)	Myross	Skibbereen	II.	141
129, 138	Cahergal	121 3 12	Cork, W.R.	West Carbery(W.D.)	Kilcrohane	Bantry	II.	143
41, 55, 56	Cahergal	248 3 32	Galway	Clare	Cargin	Tuam	IV.	18
44	Cahergal	260 2 2	Galway	Clare	Killererin	Tuam	IV.	20
104	Cahergal	83 3 20	Galway	Dunkellin	Killogilleen	Loughrea	IV.	31
26, 27	Cahergal	251 2 24c	Galway	Ross	Ross	Oughterard	IV.	73
67, 68	Cahergal	75 1 36	Mayo	Burrishoole	Burrishoole	Newport	IV.	118
19	Cahergal	210 2 9	Waterford	Coshmore&Coshbride	Leitrim	Lismore	II.	344
114, 115, 127, 128	Cahergarriff	341 0 35	Cork, W.R.	Bear	Killaconenagh	Castletown	II.	124
113, 122	Caherglassaun	273 1 15d	Galway	Kiltartan	Ardrahan	Gort	IV.	45
113	Caherglassaun	241 1 18	Galway	Kiltartan	Kinvarradoorus	Gort	IV.	49
69,70,82,83	Cahergowan or Summerfield	841 0 25	Galway	Dunkellin	Claregalway	Galway	IV.	27
9, 10	Cahergrillaun	90 0 33	Clare	Burren	Carran	Ballyvaghan	II.	11
51, 52	Caher (Huyes)	716 3 6e	Limerick	Glenquin	Abbeyfeale	Newcastle	II.	244
121	Caherhemush	134 1 17	Mayo	Kilmaine	Ki'molara	Ballinrobe	IV.	156
29, 37	Caherhenesy	235 3 13	Limerick	Connello Upper	Ballingarry	Croom	II.	230
97	Caherhenryhoe	467 0 26	Galway	Loughrea	Kilconickny	Loughrea	IV.	63
5, 8	Caherhoereigh	225 2 16	Tipperary, N.R.	Lower Ormond	Loughkeen	Parsonstown	II.	286
43	Caherhugh	239 0 30	Galway	Clare	Belclare	Tuam	IV.	17
28, 36	Caherhurly	2,060 2 20	Clare	Tulla Upper	Kilnoe	Scarriff	II.	40
29	Caher Island	13 3 11	Clare	Tulla Lower	Ogonnelloe	Scarriff	II.	38
94	Caher Island	128 1 3	Mayo	Murrisk	Kilgeever	Westport	IV.	161
59	Caherkeegane	397 2 37	Cork, W.R.	West Muskerry	Clondrohid	Macroom	II.	155
114	Caherkeen	1,044 1 37	Cork, W.R.	Bear	Kilcatherine	Castletown	II.	124
114	CAHERKEEN T.	—	Cork, W.R.	Bear	Kilcatherine	Castletown	II.	124
113, 114	Caherkelly	166 3 17	Galway	Dunkellin	Ardrahan	Gort	IV.	26
70	Caherkereen	386 3 25	Cork, W.R.	West Muskerry	Kilnamartry	Macroom	II.	159
8	Caherkinallia	284 3 30f	Clare	Corcomroe	Killilagh	Ennistimon	II.	19
8	Caherkinallia	179 1 0	Clare	Corcomroe	Kilshanny	Ennistimon	II.	21
42	Caherkine	161 2 17g	Clare	Bunratty Lower	Tomfinlough	Ennis	II.	7
96	Caherkinmonwee	38 3 16	Galway	Dunkellin	Kilconierin	Loughrea	IV.	29
121	Caherkirky	434 2 5	Cork, W.R.	East Carbery (W.D.)	Kilmeen	Clonakilty	II.	133
42,43,51,52	Caher (Lane)	885 3 23h	Limerick	Glenquin	Abbeyfeale	Newcastle	II.	244
135, 144	Caherlarhig	197 1 9	Cork, W.R.	Ibane and Barryroe	Island	Clonakilty	II.	149
105	Caherlavine	191 1 0	Galway	Loughrea	Loughrea	Loughrea	IV.	65
69	Caherlea	114 0 12	Galway	Clare	Annaghdown	Galway	IV.	16
43, 57	Caherlea	188 0 23	Galway	Clare	Belclare	Tuam	IV.	17

(a) { Within the Municipal Boundary, 202A. 2R. 14P. / Without the Municipal Boundary, 1A. 1R. 26P.
(b) Including 4A. 2R. 16P. water.
(c) Including 5A. 3R. 14P. water.
(d) Including 18A. 1R. 3P. water.
(e) Including 5A. 2R. 24P. water.
(f) Including 1A. 1R. 6P. water.
(g) Including 11A. 3R. 8P. water.
(h) Including 11A. 2R. 0P. water.

No. of Sheet of the Ordnance Survey Maps.	Townlands and Towns.	Area in Statute Acres.			County.	Barony.	Parish.	Poor Law Union in 1857.	Townland Census of 1851, Part I.	
		A.	R.	P.					Vol.	Page
83	Caherlea . . .	147	3	36	Galway . .	Dunkellin . .	Claregalway . .	Galway . .	IV.	27
46	Caherlean . .	400	2	15	Clare . .	Ibrickan . .	Killard . .	Kilrush . .	II.	23
38	Caherleheen . .	64	0	7	Kerry . .	Trughanacmy .	Ballyseedy . .	Tralee . .	II.	208
38	Caherleheen . .	826	2	30	Kerry . .	Trughanacmy .	Ratass . .	Tralee . .	II.	213
70, 71	Caherlehillan .	709	2	3	Kerry . .	Iveragh . . .	Killinane . .	Cahersiveen .	II.	197
26, 27, 31	Caherlesk . .	1,162	3	28	Kilkenny . .	Kells . . .	Ballytobin . .	Callan . .	I.	107
52	Caherlevoy . .	1,715	3	4	Limerick . .	Glenquin . .	Killeedy . .	Newcastle . .	II.	245
23	Caherline . .	354	1	7	Limerick . .	Clanwilliam .	Ballybrood . .	Limerick . .	II.	221
114	Caherlinny . .	166	2	8	Galway . .	Loughrea . .	Killinan . .	Loughrea . .	IV.	64
71	Caherlissakill .	748	3	24	Galway . .	Tiaquin . .	Monivea . .	Tuam . .	IV.	78
34, 35	Caherloghan . .	423	0	26	Clare . .	Bunratty Upper .	Clooney . .	Tulla . .	II.	7
15	Caherlooskaun .	27	0	5	Clare . .	Corcomroe . .	Kilshanny . .	Ennistimon .	II.	21
17	Caherlough . .	350	2	12	Clare . .	Inchiquin . .	Ruan . .	Corrofin . .	II.	28
117, 120	Caherloughlin .	252	1	4	Mayo . .	Kilmaine . .	Ballinchalla . .	Ballinrobe .	IV.	151
148	Caherlusky . .	153	2	10	Cork, W.R. .	West Carbery(W.D.) .	Skull . .	Skull . .	II.	145
42	Caherlustraun .	156	0	4	Galway . .	Clare . .	Donaghpatrick .	Tuam . .	IV.	19
5, 9	Cahermaan . .	427	3	20	Clare . .	Burren . .	Killeany . .	Ballyvaghan .	II.	13
41	Cahermacanally .	199	0	32	Galway . .	Clare . .	Killursa . .	Tuam . .	IV.	21
16	Cahermackateer .	192	3	37	Clare . .	Inchiquin . .	Killinaboy . .	Corrofin . .	II.	26
9, 10	Cahermackirilla .	287	2	39	Clare . .	Burren . .	Carran . .	Ballyvaghan .	II.	11
8	Cahermaclanchy .	227	0	37	Clare . .	Corcomroe . .	Killilagh . .	Ennistimon .	II.	19
5, 9	Cahermacnaghten .	734	0	37	Clare . .	Burren . .	Rathborney . .	Ballyvaghan .	II.	14
16	Cahermacon . .	140	0	9	Clare . .	Inchiquin . .	Killinaboy . .	Corrofin . .	II.	26
17, 25	Cahermacrea . .	398	1	0a	Clare . .	Inchiquin . .	Ruan . .	Corrofin . .	II.	28
8	Cahermacrusheen .	168	0	4	Clare . .	Corcomroe . .	Killilagh . .	Ennistimon .	II.	19
121	Cahermaculick .	459	2	19b	Mayo . .	Kilmaine . .	Moorgagagh . .	Ballinrobe .	IV.	157
5	Cahermacun . .	152	3	0	Clare . .	Burren . .	Rathborney . .	Ballyvaghan .	II.	14
5, 9	Cahermakerrila .	471	0	4	Clare . .	Burren . .	Killeany . .	Ballyvaghan .	II.	13
17, 25	Cahermee . .	275	3	31	Cork, E.R. .	Fermoy . .	Caherduggan . .	Mallow . .	II.	77
127	Cahermeeleboe .	530	2	18	Cork, W.R. .	Bear . .	Kilnamanagh . .	Castletown .	II.	125
9, 16	Caherminnaun East .	27	0	7	Clare . .	Corcomroe . .	Kilfenora . .	Ennistimon .	II.	19
9, 16	Caherminnaun West .	212	3	19	Clare . .	Corcomroe . .	Kilfenora . .	Corrofin . .	II.	19
92, 106	Cahermoanteen .	257	0	37	Cork, W.R. .	Bantry . .	Kilmocomoge . .	Bantry . .	II.	119
76	Cahermone . .	171	0	15	Cork, E.R. .	Imokilly . .	Middleton . .	Middleton . .	II.	89
29	Cahermoneen . .	28	2	36	Kerry . .	Trughanacmy .	Tralee . .	Tralee . .	II.	213
40, 41	Cahermore . .	315	1	24	Clare . .	Islands . .	Kilmaley . .	Ennis . .	II.	31
134	Cahermore . .	488	0	10	Cork, W.R. .	East Carbery (W.D.) .	Ross . .	Clonakilty .	II.	135
113, 122	Cahermore . .	247	1	17c	Galway . .	Kiltartan . .	Ardrahan . .	Gort . .	IV.	45
113	Cahermore . .	262	0	26	Galway . .	Kiltartan . .	Kinvarradoorus .	Gort . .	IV.	49
39	Cahermore . .	89	3	4	Kerry . .	Trughanacmy .	Ballymacelligott .	Tralee . .	II.	207
56	Cahermorris . .	501	1	0	Galway . .	Clare . . .	Annaghdown . .	Tuam . .	IV.	16
129, 138	Caher-mountain .	221	2	10	Cork, W.R. .	West Carbery(W.D.) .	Kilcrohane . .	Bantry . .	II.	143
28	Cahermoyle . .	457	0	3	Limerick . .	Shanid . .	Rathronan . .	Rathkeale .	II.	257
92	Cahermuckee . .	706	0	13	Cork, W.R. .	Bantry . .	Kilmocomoge . .	Bantry . .	II.	119
39, 48	Cahermurphy . .	2,419	2	3	Clare . .	Clonderalaw .	Kilmihil . .	Kilrush . .	II.	17
13, 20	Caher (Murphy) .	579	0	14	Clare . .	Tulla Upper . .	Feakle . .	Scarriff . .	II.	38
74, 84	Cahernabane . .	476	3	39d	Kerry . .	Dunkerron South .	Knockane . .	Killarney . .	II.	184
118	Cahernablauhy .	151	0	35	Mayo . .	Kilmaine . .	Ballinrobe . .	Ballinrobe .	IV.	152
121, 123	Cahernabrock .	612	2	16e	Mayo . .	Kilmaine . .	Shrule . .	Ballinrobe .	IV.	158
118	Cahernabudogy .	67	0	10	Mayo . .	Kilmaine . .	Ballinrobe . .	Ballinrobe .	IV.	152
68, 69	Cahernacaha . .	733	3	31	Cork, W.R. .	West Muskerry .	Inchigeelagh . .	Macroom . .	II.	156
118	Cahernacreevy .	87	2	20	Mayo . .	Kilmaine . .	Ballinrobe . .	Ballinrobe .	IV.	152
105, 106, 118, 119	Cahernacrin . .	484	3	36f	Cork, W.R. .	Bantry . .	Kilmocomoge . .	Bantry . .	II.	119
73, 74, 83	Cahernaduv . .	131	3	3	Kerry . .	Dunkerron South .	Knockane . .	Killarney . .	II.	184
97, 98	Cahernagarry .	818	3	10	Galway . .	Leitrim . .	Kilreekill . .	Loughrea . .	IV.	54
106	Cahernageeha . .	355	0	9	Kerry . .	Dunkerron South .	Kilcrohane . .	Cahersiveen .	II.	183
18, 19, 27, 28	Cahernagh . .	475	0	37	Limerick . .	Shanid . .	Dunmoylan . .	Glin . .	II.	255
6	Cahernagh East .	110	1	12	Cork, E.R. .	Duhallow . .	Tullylease . .	Kanturk . .	II.	76
6	Cahernagh (Leland) .	141	2	16	Cork, E.R. .	Duhallow . .	Tullylease . .	Kanturk . .	II.	76
6	Cahernagh (Morgel) .	200	0	24	Cork, E.R. .	Duhallow . .	Tullylease . .	Kanturk . .	II.	76
58	Cahernaglass . .	416	2	7	Galway . .	Tiaquin . .	Monivea . .	Tuam . .	IV.	78
117, 118	Cahernagollum .	180	3	32	Mayo . .	Kilmaine . .	Ballinchalla . .	Ballinrobe .	IV.	151
105	Cahernagormuck .	82	3	15	Galway . .	Loughrea . .	Loughrea . .	Loughrea . .	IV.	65
44	Cahernagry . .	83	1	2	Galway . .	Clare . .	Killererin . .	Tuam . .	IV.	20
118, 121	Cahernagry East .	76	0	24	Mayo . .	Kilmaine . .	Kilmolara . .	Ballinrobe .	IV.	156
118, 121	Cahernagry West .	199	3	38	Mayo . .	Kilmaine . .	Kilmolara . .	Ballinrobe .	IV.	156
50	Cahernahallia .	827	2	8	Tipperary, N.R. .	Kilnamanagh Upper .	Toem . .	Tipperary .	II.	280
42	Cahernaheeny .	146	2	38	Galway . .	Clare . .	Kilkilvery . .	Tuam . .	IV.	20
70	Cahernahoon . .	177	2	19	Galway . .	Clare . .	Lackagh . .	Tuam . .	IV.	22
13	Cahernaleague .	401	3	5	Waterford .	Decies without Drum .	Seskinan . .	Dungarvan .	II.	360
97	Cahernalee . .	187	3	13	Galway . .	Dunkellin . .	Kilconierin . .	Loughrea . .	IV.	29
103, 113	Cahernalinsky .	104	2	14g	Galway . .	Dunkellin . .	Killeenavarra . .	Gort . .	IV.	30

(a) Including 34A. 1R. 33P. water.   (d) Including 6A. 1R. 38P. water.   (f) Including 17A. 3R. 27P. water.
(b) Including 50A. 3R. 35P. water.   (e) Including 6A. 1R. 21P. water.   (g) Including 3A. 3R. 16P. water.
(c) Including 1A. 3R. 4P. water.

No. of Sheet of the Ordnance Survey Maps.	Townlands and Towns.	Area in Statute Acres.	County.	Barony.	Parish.	Poor Law Union in 1857.	Townland Census of 1851, Part I.	
		A. R. P.					Vol.	Page
34	Cahernalough .	177 1 22	Clare . .	Bunratty Upper .	Kilraghtis . .	Ennis . .	II.	9
118	Cahernamallaght .	249 3 31	Mayo . .	Kilmaine . .	Ballinrobe . .	Ballinrobe .	IV.	152
97, 105	Cahernaman .	279 0 10	Galway . .	Loughrea . .	Kilconickny .	Loughrea .	IV.	63
70	Cahernaman .	503 2 17	Kerry . .	Iveragh . .	Killinane . .	Cahersiveen .	II.	197
88	Cahernamart .	162 0 10	Mayo . .	Murrisk . .	Oughaval . .	Westport .	IV.	161
25	Cahernamona .	43 1 6	Clare . .	Inchiquin . .	Rath . .	Corrofin .	II.	27
97	Cahernamona .	56 0 32	Galway . .	Loughrea . .	Kilconickny .	Loughrea .	IV.	63
97, 105	Cahernamuck East .	236 2 6	Galway . .	Loughrea . .	Kilconickny .	Loughrea .	IV.	63
97	Cahernamuck West	116 1 35	Galway . .	Loughrea . .	Kilconickny .	Loughrea .	IV.	63
66	Cahernane .	75 1 10a	Kerry . .	Magunihy . .	Aghadoe . .	Killarney .	II.	199
66	Cahernane . .	188 3 32b	Kerry . .	Magunihy . .	Killarney .	Killarney .	II.	203
87	Cahernaran Island .	4 0 25	Mayo . .	Murrisk . .	Oughaval . .	Westport .	IV.	162
13, 14	Cahernarry (Cripps)	218 1 19	Limerick . .	Clanwilliam .	Cahernarry .	Limerick .	II.	222
13, 14	Cahernarry (Keane)	259 2 39	Limerick . .	Clanwilliam .	Cahernarry .	Limerick .	II.	222
70, 83	Cahernashilleeny .	679 0 38	Galway . .	Clare . .	Lackagh . .	Galway .	IV.	22
21	Cahernead .	131 3 0	Kerry . .	Clanmaurice .	Killahan . .	Tralee .	II.	170
118, 121	Cahernichole East .	133 1 39	Mayo . .	Kilmaine . .	Ballinchalla .	Ballinrobe .	IV.	152
118, 121	Cahernichole West .	73 2 32	Mayo . .	Kilmaine . .	Ballinchalla .	Ballinrobe .	IV.	152
31	Caherogan .	423 2 8	Clare . .	Ibrickan . .	Kilfarboy . .	Ennistimon .	II.	22
118	Caherogullane .	292 1 2	Cork, W.R.	West Carbery (W.D.)	Kilmocomoge .	Bantry .	II.	144
130, 139	Caherolickane .	240 2 33	Cork, W.R. .	West Carbery (W.D.)	Skull . .	Skull .	II.	145
105	Caheronaun .	251 3 4	Galway . .	Loughrea . .	Loughrea . .	Loughrea .	IV.	65
103	Caherpeak East .	390 1 34	Galway . .	Dunkellin .	Kilcolgan . .	Gort .	IV.	28
103	Caherpeak West .	405 3 35c	Galway . .	Dunkellin .	Kilcolgan . .	Gort .	IV.	28
58	Caherphuca .	260 0 13	Galway . .	Tiaquin . .	Abbeyknockmoy .	Tuam .	IV.	75
45	Caherpierce .	503 0 11	Kerry . .	Corkaguiny .	Ballinvoher .	Dingle .	II.	174
19, 20	Caher (Power) .	313 3 21	Clare . .	Tulla Upper .	Feakle . .	Scarriff .	II.	38
42	Caherquin .	164 2 26	Kerry . .	Corkaguiny .	Dunurlin . .	Dingle .	II.	176
16, 22	Caher (Retrenched) .	446 1 27	Queen's Co.	Upperwoods .	Offerlane . .	Abbeyleix .	I.	251
122	Caherrevagh and Cloonnameeltoge .	623 0 14	Mayo . . .	Kilmaine . .	Kilmainemore .	Ballinrobe .	IV.	155
19, 20	Caher (Rice) .	478 1 9	Clare . .	Tulla Upper .	Feakle . .	Scarriff .	II.	38
117, 120	Caherrobert .	191 3 19	Mayo . .	Kilmaine . .	Ballinchalla .	Ballinrobe .	IV.	152
84	Caherroyn .	269 1 2	Galway . .	Athenry . .	Athenry . .	Loughrea .	IV.	3
30	Caherrush .	373 1 25	Clare . .	Ibrickan . .	Kilmurry . .	Kilrush .	II.	23
89, 98	Cahersavane .	621 1 18	Kerry . .	Iveragh . .	Dromod . .	Cahersiveen .	II.	194
42	Caherscooby .	153 3 15d	Clare . .	Bunratty Lower .	Tomfinlough .	Ennis .	II.	7
33,34,42,43	Caherscullibeen .	322 0 4	Kerry . .	Corkaguiny .	Kilmalkedar .	Dingle .	II.	178
34	Cahershaughnessy .	250 1 32	Clare . .	Bunratty Upper .	Clooney . .	Ennis .	II.	7
16	Cahersherkin .	608 3 39	Clare . .	Corcomroe .	Clooney . .	Ennistimon .	II.	18
79	Cahersiveen .	255 0 19	Kerry . .	Iveragh . .	Caher . .	Cahersiveen .	II.	193
79	CAHERSIVEEN T. .	—	Kerry . .	Iveragh . .	Caher . .	Cahersiveen .	II.	194
104	Caherskeehaun .	101 1 14	Galway . .	Dunkellin .	Killogilleen .	Loughrea .	IV.	31
29	Caherslee .	40 2 26	Kerry . .	Trughanacmy .	Tralee . .	Tralee .	II.	213
51, 61	Caherteige .	400 1 7	Clare . .	Bunratty Lower .	Clonloghan .	Ennis .	II.	3
97, 105	Cahertinny .	270 3 10	Galway . .	Loughrea . .	Kilconickny .	Loughrea .	IV.	63
75	CAHER T. . .	—	Tipperary, S.R.	Iffa and Offa West .	Caher . .	Clogheen .	II.	318
33, 38	Caherty . .	946 1 6	Antrim . .	Lower Antrim .	Ballyclug . .	Ballymena .	III.	3
16, 25	Caheruane .	698 2 9	Waterford .	Decies without Drum	Kilbarrymeaden .	Kilmacthomas .	II.	356
14	Caherulla .	557 1 21	Kerry . .	Clanmaurice .	Ballyheige .	Tralee .	II.	167
77	Caherultan .	122 2 30e	Cork, E.R. .	Imokilly . .	Ballyoughtera .	Middleton .	II.	84
138	Caherurlagh .	30 2 29	Cork, W.R. .	West Carbery (W.D.)	Kilcrohane .	Bantry .	II.	143
138	Caherurlagh Mountain North .	27 0 15	Cork, W.R. .	West Carbery (W.D.)	Kilcrohane .	Bantry .	II.	143
138	Caherurlagh Mountain South .	23 3 0	Cork, W.R. .	West Carbery (W.D.)	Kilcrohane .	Bantry .	II.	143
13	Cahervally .	60 2 24	Limerick . .	Pubblebrien .	Knocknagaul .	Limerick .	II.	253
59, 60	Cahervillahowe .	513 2 29	Tipperary, S.R.	Clanwilliam .	Kilfeakle . .	Tipperary .	II.	308
60	Cahervillahowe .	171 1 33	Tipperary, S.R.	Clanwilliam .	Relickmurry and Athassel .	Tipperary .	II.	310
105	Caherwalter .	65 2 35	Galway . .	Loughrea . .	Loughrea . .	Loughrea .	IV.	65
103, 104	Caherweelder .	479 3 32	Galway . .	Dunkellin .	Killeely . .	Gort .	IV.	29
29, 38	Caherweesheen .	137 3 20	Kerry . .	Trughanacmy .	Annagh . .	Tralee .	II.	205
93	Caher West .	234 1 28	Kerry . .	Glanarought .	Kenmare . .	Kenmare .	II.	185
119	Caherwiclaun .	326 3 0	Mayo . .	Kilmaine . .	Kilmainemore .	Ballinrobe .	IV.	155
10	Cahery . .	256 1 9	Londonderry .	Keenaght . .	Drumachose .	New T. Limavady	III.	235
14, 15	Caherycahill .	150 1 33	Clare . .	Corcomroe .	Kilmacrehy .	Ennistimon .	II.	20
15	Caherycoosaun .	298 1 13	Clare . .	Corcomroe .	Kilshanny .	Ennistimon .	II.	21
21	Cahills Island .	1 0 30	King's Co. .	Garrycastle .	Lusmagh . .	Parsonstown .	I.	137
59, 69	Cahiracon .	615 1 29f	Clare . .	Clonderalaw .	Kilfiddane .	Killadysert .	II.	15
59, 69	Cahiracon .	506 0 17	Clare . .	Clonderalaw .	Killadysert .	Killadysert .	II.	15
33, 41	Cahircalla Beg .	232 3 20	Clare . .	Islands . .	Drumcliff .	Ennis .	II.	29
33, 41	Cahircalla More .	518 2 6	Clare . .	Islands . .	Drumcliff .	Ennis .	II.	29
22, 31	Cahirduff .	388 1 38	Limerick . .	Pubblebrien .	Monasteranenagh .	Croom .	II.	253

(a) Including 6A. 1R. 24P. water. (c) Including 8A. 2R. 17P. water. (e) Including 2A. 2R. 19P. Lough Aderry.
(b) Including 5A. 2R. 32P. water. (d) Including 2A. 2R. 16P. water. (f) Including 10A. 3R. 16P. water.

2 B

No. of Sheet of the Ordinance Survey Maps.	Townlands and Towns.	Area in Statute Acres.			County.	Barony.	Parish.	Poor Law Union in 1857.	Townland Census of 1851, Part I.	
		A.	R.	P.					Vol.	Page
31	Cahirguillamore	238	2	2	Limerick	Coshma	Tullabracky	Croom	II.	244
31	Cahirguillamore	427	1	13	Limerick	Smallcounty	Glenogra	Croom	II.	259
38, 39	Cahoo	165	3	32	Tyrone	Dungannon Middle	Donaghenry	Cookstown	III.	300
6	Cahore	158	3	8	Fermanagh	Lurg	Drumkeeran	Lowtherstown	III.	205
40	Cahore	638	2	34	Londonderry	Loughinsholin	Ballynascreen	Magherafelt	III.	238
17, 22	Cahore	275	2	31	Wexford	Ballaghkeen	Donaghmore	Gorey	I.	293
19	Caim	642	3	11	Wexford	Scarawalsh	Monart	Enniscorthy	I.	324
11	Cain	128	2	22	Wexford	Gorey	Liskinfere	Gorey	I.	320
17	Cakestown Glebe	222	2	10	Meath	Kells Upper	Kells	Kells	I.	205
7, 8, 12, 13	Calary Lower	771	0	11	Wicklow	Rathdown	Calary	Rathdown	I.	355
7, 12	Calary Upper	554	0	21	Wicklow	Rathdown	Calary	Rathdown	I.	355
22, 23	Caldanagh	872	2	34	Antrim	Kilconway	Finvoy	Ballymoney	III.	26
6	Caldavnet	143	1	8	Monaghan	Monaghan	Tedavnet	Monaghan	III.	278
11	Caldragh	52	2	35	Cavan	Lower Loughtee	Drumlane	Cavan	III.	79
38	Caldragh	275	1	1	Fermanagh	Knockninny	Kinawley	Enniskillen	III.	201
27	Caldragh	92	3	30	Leitrim	Leitrim	Kiltoghert	Carkon Shannon	IV.	101
8, 13	Caldragh	132	1	27	Longford	Longford	Clongesh	Longford	I.	157
92	Caldragh	170	0	34a	Mayo	Costello	Knock	Claremorris	IV.	142
16	Caldragh	212	1	22	Roscommon	Frenchpark	Kilmacumsy	Boyle	IV.	203
23	Caldragh	198	2	4	Roscommon	Roscommon	Kiltrustan	Strokestown	IV.	211
18	Caldraghmore	176	3	39	Longford	Moydow	Ballymacormick	Longford	I.	160
59	Caldrum	114	2	36	Tyrone	Clogher	Clogher	Clogher	III.	292
15	Caldrum Glebe	173	0	6	Fermanagh	Magheraboy	Inishmacsaint	Enniskillen	III.	212
16, 22	Caldrymoran	131	0	22	Roscommon	Roscommon	Shankill	Strokestown	IV.	212
67	Caledon	232	0	26½	Tyrone	Dungannon Lower	Aghaloo	Armagh	III.	296
67	CALEDON T.	—			Tyrone	Dungannon Lower	Aghaloo	Armagh	III.	297
64	Calehane	135	3	27	Cork, E.R.	Barrymore	Ballydeloher	Cork	II.	51
1	Calf Field	102	2	12	Kildare	Carbury	Ballynadrumny	Edenderry	I.	51
21, 22	Calf Field or Aghadrumgowna	230	3	18	Cavan	Tullygarvey	Larah	Cootehill	III.	90
40	*Calf Island*	5	0	4	Donegal	Boylagh	Templecrone	Glenties	III.	116
17	*Calf Island*	3	1	0	Down	Ards Upper	Ardkeen	Newtownards	III.	159
49	*Calf Island*	1	3	23	Galway	Ballynahinch	Ballindoon	Clifden	IV.	10
126	*Calf Island*	2	0	32	Galway	Longford	Lickmolassy	Portumna	IV.	61
76	*Calf Island*	8	3	28	Mayo	Burrishoole	Kilmeena	Westport	IV.	122
149	Calf Island East	77	1	34	Cork, W.R.	West Carbery (E.D.)	Aghadown	Skibbereen	II.	136
149	Calf Island Middle	63	3	10	Cork, W.R.	West Carbery (W.D.)	Skull	Skull	II.	145
149	Calf Island West	62	0	24	Cork. W.R.	West Carbery (W.D.)	Skull	Skull	II.	145
18	Calfpark	10	2	14	Longford	Moydow	Ballymacormick	Longford	I.	160
3	Calfstown	272	2	39	Kildare	Carbury	Mylerstown	Edenderry	I.	52
10, 13	Calga	257	3	3	Louth	Ardee	Philipstown	Ardee	I.	174
49	Calgath	414	3	33	Meath	Upper Deece	Rodanstown	Celbridge	I.	194
92	Calhame	396	3	10c	Donegal	Banagh	Killaghtee	Donegal	III.	109
24, 25	Calhame	118	1	36	Donegal	Kilmacrenan	Tullaghobegly	Dunfanaghy	III.	131
70	Calhame	90	2	5	Donegal	Raphoe	Clonleigh	Strabane	III.	134
78	Calhame	296	2	12	Donegal	Raphoe	Donaghmore	Stranorlar	III.	137
61	Calhame	125	2	26	Donegal	Raphoe	Leck	Letterkenny	III.	140
79, 88	Calhame	229	1	12	Donegal	Raphoe	Urney	Strabane	III.	144
45, 53	Calhame or Fallard	269	2	16	Donegal	Kilmacrenan	Conwal	Letterkenny	III.	126
61, 69	Calhame or Montgomery's Fort	146	2	35	Donegal	Raphoe	Convoy	Stranorlar	III.	136
17	Calheme	266	1	9	Antrim	Upper Dunluce	Ballymoney	Ballymoney	III.	18
5	Calheme	146	0	2	Tyrone	Strabane Lower	Camus	Strabane	III.	320
26, 32	Calkill	201	1	32	Fermanagh	Clanawley	Killesher	Enniskillen	III.	192
25, 34	Calkill	451	3	38d	Tyrone	Strabane Upper	Cappagh	Omagh	III.	325
86	Calla	28	2	28	Mayo	Murrisk	Kilgeever	Westport	IV.	159
86, 96	Callacoon	529	3	7	Mayo	Murrisk	Kilgeever	Westport	IV.	159
18	Callaghane	447	2	34	Waterford	Gaultiere	Ballygunner	Waterford	II.	362
8, 13	Callagheen	928	3	39e	Fermanagh	Magheraboy	Inishmacsaint	Ballyshannon	III.	212
13, 14	Callaghs	335	0	37f	Cavan	Tullyhunco	Kildallan	Bawnboy	III.	96
64	Callahaniska	394	1	7g	Kerry	Iveragh	Glanbehy	Killarney	II.	195
45	Callahow	260	1	25	Limerick	Connello Upper	Cloncrew	Newcastle	II.	232
28	Callahy	512	0	13h	Clare	Tulla Upper	Tomgraney	Scarriff	II.	41
69	Callan	393	1	29	Donegal	Raphoe	Convoy	Stranorlar	III.	136
69	Callanacor	86	0	19	Donegal	Raphoe	Convoy	Stranorlar	III.	136
46,47,56,57	Callanafersy East	848	3	19	Kerry	Trughanacmy	Kilcolman	Killarney	II.	210
46, 56	Callanafersy West	779	1	32	Kerry	Trughanacmy	Kilcolman	Killarney	II.	210
37	Callanagh Lower	276	1	18	Cavan	Clanmahon	Drumlumman	Granard	III.	76
37	Callanagh Middle	167	1	28	Cavan	Clanmahon	Drumlumman	Granard	III.	77
37	Callanagh Upper	159	2	31	Cavan	Clanmahon	Drumlumman	Granard	III.	77
64	Callancruck	1,032	3	24i	Galway	Ballynahinch	Moyrus	Clifden	IV,	12
26	Callan North	21	2	10	Kilkenny	Callan	Callan	Callan	I.	83
26	Callan South	96	0	15	Kilkenny	Callan	Callan	Callan	I.	83

(a) Including 34A. 3R. 26P. water.
(b) Including 4A. 2R. 22P. of Lake.
(c) Including 4A. 0R. 30P. water.
(d) Including 5A. 2R. 0P. water.
(e) Including 1A. 1R. 23P. water.
(f) Including 2A. 2R. 0P. water.
(g) Including 2A. 3R. 16P. water.
(h) Including 20A. 1R. 12P. water.
(i) Including 69A. 3R. 18P. water.

No. of Sheet of the Ordnance Survey Maps.	Townlands and Towns.	Area in Statute Acres.			County.	Barony.	Parish.	Poor Law Union in 1857.	Townland Census of 1851, Part I.	
		A.	R.	P.					Vol.	Page
26	CALLAN T.	—			Kilkenny	Callan	Callan	Callan	I.	84
147	Callaros Eighter	169	3	39	Cork, W.R.	West Carbery (W.D.)	Kilmoe	Skull	II.	144
147	Callaros Oughter	500	0	22	Cork, W.R.	West Carbery (W.D.)	Kilmoe	Skull	II.	144
22, 23	Callary or Mount-merrion	376	1	5	Dublin	Rathdown	Taney	Rathdown	I.	38
61, 62	Callas	352	0	12	Cork, E.R.	East Muskerry	Inishcarra	Cork	II.	103
116	Callatra	124	3	10	Galway	Leitrim	Ballynakill	Loughrea	IV.	50
96, 110	Callatrim	625	1	38	Cork, W.R.	Kinalmeaky	Kilbrogan	Bandon	II.	152
13	Calliagh	237	1	29	Monaghan	Dartree	Aghabog	Monaghan	III.	263
21	Calliaghadoo	449	3	18	Mayo	Tirawley	Moygawnagh	Killala	II.	171
7	Calliaghstown	128	2	14	Dublin	Balrothery West	Westpalstown	Balrothery	I.	23
27	Calliaghstown	410	3	2	Meath	Lower Duleek	Kilsharvan	Drogheda	I.	196
16	Calliaghstown	219	3	28	Meath	Upper Kells	Kells	Kells	I.	205
18	Calliaghstown	401	2	18	Westmeath	Moygoish	Kilmacnevan	Mullingar	I.	280
16, 23	Calliaghstown	1,015	1	25	Westmeath	Rathconrath	Ballymore	Ballymahon	I.	281
24	Calliaghstown Lower	230	0	2	Dublin	Newcastle	Rathcoole	Celbridge	I.	34
24	Calliaghstown Upper	313	2	24	Dublin	Newcastle	Rathcoole	Celbridge	I.	34
51	Calliaghwee	55	2	12	Meath	Dunboyne	Dunboyne	Dunshaughlin	I.	199
25	Callisnagh	211	3	1	Antrim	Lower Glenarm	Ardclinis	Larne	III.	21
15	Callisnagh	76	3	38	Antrim	Lower Glenarm	Layd	Ballycastle	III.	22
30	Calloughs	260	1	33a	Leitrim	Carrigallen	Carrigallen	Mohill	IV.	89
14	Callow	85	1	22	Fermanagh	Magheraboy	Inishmacsaint	Ballyshannon	III.	212
49, 62	Callow	997	1	15b	Galway	Ballynahinch	Ballindoon	Clifden	IV.	10
73	Callow	336	2	12c	Galway	Kilconnell	Kilconnell	Ballinasloe	IV.	40
20	Callow	450	2	4	Limerick	Connello Lower	Nantinan	Rathkeale	II.	229
49, 61	Callow	1,242	0	0d	Mayo	Gallen	Killasser	Swineford	IV.	149
108	Callow Beg	67	0	35	Galway	Longford	Meelick	Portumna	IV.	61
55	Callowbeg	282	1	39	Roscommon	Athlone	Drum	Athlone	IV.	180
58, 67, 68	Callowbrack	624	0	38	Mayo	Burrishoole	Burrishoole	Newport	IV.	118
77	Callowfinish	803	3	10e	Galway	Ballynahinch	Moyrus	Clifden	IV.	12
38	Callowhill	95	1	2	Fermanagh	Knockninny	Kinawley	Lisnaskea	III.	201
25	Callowhill	309	0	15f	Leitrim	Carrigallen	Oughteragh	Bawnboy	IV.	91
21	Callowhill	178	2	12	Monaghan	Dartree	Currin	Clones	III.	265
18, 19	Callowhill Lower	241	2	29	Wicklow	Newcastle	Newcastle Upper	Rathdrum	I.	353
18, 19	Callowhill Upper	361	3	8	Wicklow	Newcastle	Newcastle Upper	Rathdrum	I.	353
108, 118	Callow More	120	0	33	Galway	Longford	Meelick	Portumna	IV.	61
55, 68	Callownamuck	581	1	28	Galway	Moycullen	Kilcummin	Oughterard	IV.	66
55	Callownaskeagh	1	1	0	Galway	Clare	Cargin	Tuam	IV.	18
8, 9	Callow or Runnawillin	632	1	24g	Roscommon	Frenchpark	Kilnamanagh	Castlereagh	IV.	204
52	Calluragh	159	3	5	Clare	Bunratty Lower	Kilfintinan	Limerick	II.	5
18, 19	Calluragh	858	2	38h	Clare	Bunratty Upper	Inchicronan	Tulla	II.	8
15	Calluragh East	163	3	13	Clare	Corcomroe	Kilmanaheen	Ennistimon	II.	21
23	Calluragh South	296	1	28	Clare	Corcomroe	Kilmanaheen	Ennistimon	II.	21
15	Calluragh West	134	0	29	Clare	Corcomroe	Kilmanaheen	Ennistimon	II.	21
22	Callystown	680	0	0	Louth	Ferrard	Clogher	Drogheda	I.	180
36, 41	Calmore	283	2	10	Londonderry	Loughinsholin	Kilcronaghan	Magherafelt	III.	241
16	Calone	325	3	24	Armagh	Fews Lower	Lisnadill	Armagh	III.	46
44	Calteraun	260	0	12	Sligo	Coolavin	Kilfree	Boyle	IV.	224
46, 60	Caltra	651	2	31	Galway	Tiaquin	Killosolan	Mountbellew	IV.	78
42	Caltragh	129	0	18	Galway	Clare	Belclare	Tuam	IV.	17
42, 56	Caltragh	83	3	34	Galway	Clare	Kilkilvery	Tuam	IV.	20
42	Caltragh	537	2	9	Galway	Clare	Killower	Tuam	IV.	21
87	Caltragh	135	2	36	Galway	Kilconnell	Aughrim	Ballinasloe	IV.	39
100	Caltragh	505	2	33	Galway	Longford	Clonfert	Ballinasloe	IV.	56
72	Caltragh	140	0	30	Galway	Tiaquin	Clonkeen	Loughrea	IV.	76
101	Caltragh	109	2	28	Mayo	Clanmorris	Crossboyne	Claremorris	IV.	132
45	Caltragh	132	1	1	Roscommon	Athlone	Rahara	Roscommon	IV.	183
40	Caltragh	54	0	31	Roscommon	Ballintober South	Cloontuskert	Roscommon	IV.	188
14	Caltragh	155	1	6	Sligo	Carbury	St. John's	Sligo	IV.	223
11, 17, 23	Caltragh	1,969	1	28i	Sligo	Tireragh	Easky	Dromore West	IV.	233
13, 19	Caltragh	151	2	39	Sligo	Tireragh	Skreen	Dromore West	IV.	235
21, 22	Caltragh Beg	188	2	2	Longford	Rathcline	Cashel	Ballymahon	I.	163
45	Caltraghbeg	74	0	18	Roscommon	Athlone	Cam	Athlone	IV.	179
72, 85	Caltraghbreedy	168	2	18	Galway	Kilconnell	Killimordaly	Loughrea	IV.	42
59	Caltraghcreen	227	2	31	Galway	Tiaquin	Killoscobe	Mountbellew	IV.	77
47, 61	Caltraghduff	350	3	33	Galway	Killian	Taghboy	Mountbellew	IV.	45
74	Caltraghlea	482	2	39	Galway	Clonmacnowen	Kilgerrill	Ballinasloe	IV.	25
21, 22	Caltragh More	206	0	0	Longford	Rathcline	Cashel	Ballymahon	I.	163
60	Caltrapallas	40	3	13j	Galway	Tiaquin	Killosolan	Mountbellew	IV.	78
60	CALTRA T.	—			Galway	Tiaquin	Killosolan	Mountbellew	IV.	78
63	Calveagh Lower	221	1	23	Mayo	Costello	Kilbeagh	Castlereagh	IV.	140
63	Calveagh Upper	162	0	27	Mayo	Costello	Kilbeagh	Castlereagh	IV.	140
28, 32	Calverstown	786	2	33	Kildare	Narragh & Reban East	Davidstown	Athy	I.	66

(a) Including 25A. 1R. 34P. water.
(b) Including 177A. 1R. 18P. water.
(c) Including 9A. 0R. 36P. water.
(d) Including 77A. 3R. 12P. water.

(e) Including 119A. 3R. 36F. water.
(f) Including 4A. 2R. 6P. water.
(g) Including 7A. 1R. 21P. water.

(h) Including 16A. 2R. 9P. water.
(i) Including 4A. 3R. 0P. Lough Scorrew.
(j) Including 3A. 0R. 32P. detached portion.

No. of Sheet of the Ordnance Survey Maps.	Townlands and Towns.	Area in Statute Acres.	County.	Barony.	Parish.	Poor Law Union in 1857.	Townland Census of 1851, Part I.	
		A. R. P.					Vol.	Page
32, 33	Calverstown . .	406 1 10	Westmeath .	Fartullagh .	Clonfad . .	Mullingar .	I.	268
32	Calverstown Demesne	223 0 22	Kildare .	Narragh & Reban East	Davidstown .	Athy . .	I.	66
32	Calverstown Little .	407 2 0	Kildare .	Narragh & Reban East	Davidstown .	Athy . .	I.	66
33	Cam . . .	163 0 31	Fermanagh .	Knockninny .	Kinawley .	Lisnaskea .	III.	201
10, 11	Cam . . .	1,472 3 5	Londonderry .	Coleraine .	Macosquin .	Coleraine .	III.	233
15, 20	Cam . . .	406 3 3	Longford .	Ardagh .	Mostrim .	Granard .	I.	152
48	Cam . . .	1,009 1 37	Roscommon .	Athlone .	Cam . .	Athlone .	IV.	179
16, 17, 22, 23	Camaderry or Sevenchurches . .	4,518 3 38a	Wicklow .	Ballinacor North	Derrylossary .	Rathdrum .	I.	346
19	Camagh . .	452 1 30	Armagh .	Armagh .	Derrynoose .	Armagh .	III.	44
13	Camagh . .	162 2 31b	Cavan .	Tullyhaw .	Templeport .	Bawnboy .	III.	94
22, 25	Camagh . .	303 0 37c	Leitrim .	Carrigallen .	Oughteragh .	Bawnboy .	IV.	91
16	Camagh . .	387 1 9d	Longford .	Granard .	Abbeylara .	Granard .	I.	154
2, 5	Camagh . .	355 0 13	Longford .	Longford .	Killoe .	Longford .	I.	158
2, 3	Camagh . .	678 2 22e	Westmeath .	Fore .	Lickbla .	Granard .	I.	270
38	Camagh . .	50 3 31	Westmeath .	Moycashel .	Kilbeggan .	Tullamore .	I.	278
30, 33	Camaghy . .	272 3 23	Monaghan .	Farney .	Magheracloone .	Carrickmacross	III.	272
45	Camaghy . .	442 2 2	Tyrone .	Dungannon Middle .	Pomeroy .	Dungannon .	III.	304
10	Camalier . .	91 3 38	Cavan .	Lower Loughtee .	Drumlane .	Cavan .	III.	79
17	Camalt . .	57 0 24	Leitrim .	Drumahaire .	Inishmagrath .	Manorhamilton	IV.	95
22	Camara . .	228 1 2	Wicklow .	Talbotstown Upper .	Donaghmore .	Baltinglass .	I.	363
22	Camarahill North .	251 3 1	Wicklow .	Talbotstown Upper .	Donaghmore .	Baltinglass .	I.	363
22	Camarahill South .	229 2 13	Wicklow .	Talbotstown Upper .	Donaghmore .	Baltinglass .	I.	363
31, 36	Camaross . .	1,385 1 30	Wexford .	Shelmaliere West .	Kilgarvan .	New Ross .	I.	334
44	Camas . .	398 2 16	Limerick .	Glenquin .	Killeedy .	Newcastle .	II.	245
44	Camas . .	670 1 31	Limerick .	Glenquin .	Monagay .	Newcastle .	II.	247
31	Camas North .	704 0 29	Limerick .	Smallcounty .	Monasteranenagh .	Croom .	II.	261
31, 39	Camas South .	438 1 7	Limerick .	Smallcounty .	Monasteranenagh .	Kilmallock .	II.	261
53	Camblestown .	48 3 18	Donegal .	Kilmacrenan .	Aghanunshin .	Letterkenny .	III.	122
7	Cambrickville . .	43 1 1	Louth .	Upper Dundalk .	Dundalk . .	Dundalk .	I.	178
7, 12	Camcloon . .	535 0 35	Queen's Co. .	Maryborough West .	Clonenagh and Clonagheen . .	Mountmellick .	I.	242
23	Camcloon . .	171 3 6	Queen's Co. .	Upperwoods .	Offerlane .	Abbeyleix .	I.	251
54	Camcloon . .	194 0 19	Roscommon .	Moycarn .	Moore .	Ballinasloe .	IV.	206
68	Camcloon Beg .	135 2 25f	Mayo .	Burrishoole .	Burrishoole .	Newport .	IV.	118
68	Camcloon More .	83 1 12	Mayo .	Burrishoole .	Burrishoole .	Newport .	IV.	118
11, 17	Camcuill . .	564 3 0	Sligo .	Tireragh .	Kilmacshalgan .	Dromore West .	IV.	234
19, 32	Camderry . .	468 1 16	Galway .	Ballymoe .	Kilbegnet .	Glennamaddy .	IV.	8
12	Camderry . .	786 1 4g	Leitrim .	Drumahaire .	Cloonclare .	Manorhamilton	IV.	93
41, 42	Camderry . .	119 0 6	Tyrone .	Omagh East .	Dromore .	Omagh .	III.	311
80	Camderrynabinnia .	222 3 25	Mayo .	Gallen .	Killedan .	Swineford .	IV.	149
59, 67	Camea . .	172 2 28	Tipperary, S.R. .	Clanwilliam .	Kilfeakle .	Tipperary .	II.	308
22	Camenabologue .	1,043 0 24h	Wicklow .	Ballinacor South .	Knockrath .	Rathdrum .	I.	350
9	Cameron (Island) .	66 2 12	Tipperary, N.R. .	Lower Ormond .	Kilbarron .	Borrisokane .	II.	284
115	Cametringane . .	41 2 15	Cork, W.R. .	Bear .	Kilaconenagh .	Castletown .	II.	124
17, 18	Camgart . .	452 2 22	Fermanagh .	Tirkennedy .	Enniskillen .	Enniskillen .	III.	221
100, 108	Camgort and Corballymore . .	140 0 23	Galway .	Longford .	Donanaghta .	Portumna .	IV.	58
12, 13	Camheen . .	185 3 28	Limerick .	Pubblebrien .	Mungret .	Limerick .	II.	253
120	Camillaun . .	1 0 36	Mayo .	Kilmaine .	Cong . .	Ballinrobe .	IV.	154
120, 123	Camillaun or Holy Island . .	4 1 11	Mayo .	Kilmaine .	Cong . .	Ballinrobe .	IV.	154
114	Caminches . .	249 0 23	Cork, W.R. .	Bear .	Kilnamanagh .	Castletown .	II.	125
3, 7	Camira Glebe . .	276 2 11	Queen's Co. .	Tinnahinch .	Rosenallis .	Mountmellick .	I.	250
9	Camla . .	154 2 0	Monaghan .	Monaghan .	Monaghan .	Monaghan .	III.	276
50, 51	Camlagh . .	620 0 29	Roscommon .	Athlone .	Taghmaconnell .	Ballinasloe .	IV.	185
38	Camletter . .	156 1 0	Fermanagh .	Knockninny .	Kinawley .	Lisnaskea .	III.	201
107	Camlin . .	166 2 22i	Donegal .	Tirhugh .	Kilbarron .	Ballyshannon .	III.	148
9, 10	Camlin . .	274 0 17	Roscommon .	Boyle .	Estersnow .	Boyle .	IV.	195
17	Camlin . .	637 3 12	Tipperary, N.R. .	Ikerrin .	Corbally .	Roscrea .	II.	275
34	Camlin . . .	578 3 19	Wexford .	Bantry .	Oldross .	New Ross .	I.	301
14, 15	Camlisk Beg .	59 1 23	Longford .	Ardagh .	Mostrim .	Granard .	I.	152
14, 15	Camlisk More .	147 0 0	Longford .	Ardagh .	Mostrim .	Granard .	I.	152
26	CAMLOUGH T. .	—	Armagh .	Orior Upper .	Killevy .	Newry .	III.	58
25, 28	Camly (Ball) .	439 3 11	Armagh .	Fews Upper .	Newtownhamilton .	Castleblayney .	III.	49
25	Camly Macullagh .	1,029 2 29	Armagh .	Fews Upper .	Newtownhamilton .	Castleblayney .	III.	49
25	Cammanagh . .	1,241 1 12	Galway .	Ross .	Ross . .	Oughterard .	IV.	73
66	Cammoge . .	88 2 31	Clare .	Moyarta .	Moyarta .	Kilrush .	II.	34
22	Cammoge . .	535 1 34	Roscommon .	Roscommon .	Elphin .	Strokestown .	IV.	209
24, 25	Camnish . .	358 1 11	Londonderry .	Keenaght .	Bovevagh .	NewTᵃLimavady	III.	235
11, 16	Camolin . .	336 1 13	Wexford .	Scarawalsh .	Toome .	Gorey .	I.	326
10, 11	Camolin Park . ,	974 2 7	Wexford .	Scarawalsh .	Kilcomb .	Gorey .	I.	323
11	CAMOLIN T. .	—	Wexford .	Scarawalsh .	Toome .	Gorey .	I.	326
43	Camowen . .	478 1 8j	Tyrone .	Omagh East .	Cappagh .	Omagh .	III.	310

(Including 51A. 1R. 24P. Loughnahanagan.
(a) ⎨ Including 48A. 1R. 16P. Upper Lake.
(Including 7A. 2R. 24P. Lower Lake.
(b) Including 5A. 0R. 33P. water.

(c) Including 14A. 2R. 20P. water.
(d) Including 4A. 0R. 0P. water.
(e) Including 16A. 3R. 28P. water.
(f) Including 2A. 2R. 16P. water.

(g) Including 3A. 3R. 30P. water.
(h) Including 1A. 1R. 17P. water.
(i) Including 12A. 2R. 20P. water.
(j) Including 2A. 3R. 34P. water.

No. of Sheet of the Ordnance Survey Maps.	Townlands and Towns.	Area in Statute Acres.	County.	Barony.	Parish.	Poor Law Union in 1857.	Townland Census of 1851. Part I.	
							Vol.	Page
		A. R. P.						
107	Camp . . .	55 1 35	Donegal . .	Tirhugh . . .	Kilbarron . .	Ballyshannon .	III.	148
36, 37	Camp . . .	226 1 10	Kerry . .	Corkaguiny . .	Kilgobban . .	Tralee . .	II.	177
39	Camp . . .	356 2 4	Kerry . .	Trughanacmy . .	Castleisland . .	Tralee . .	II.	208
29, 38	Camp . . .	160 0 8	Kerry . .	Trughanacmy . .	Ratass . . .	Tralee . .	II.	213
39	Camp East . .	109 0 18	Kerry . .	Trughanacmy . .	Castleisland . .	Tralee . .	II.	208
112	Camphill . .	16 1 2	Cork, E.R. .	Kinsale . . .	Clontead . . .	Kinsale . .	II.	99
16	Camphill . .	232 2 19	Queen's Co. .	Upperwoods . .	Offerlane . .	Abbeyleix .	I.	251
29	Camphire . .	546 2 1	Waterford . .	Coshmore&Coshbride	Lismore & Mocollop	Lismore . .	II.	345
29	Camphirehill . .	79 1 25	Waterford . .	Coshmore&Coshbride	Lismore & Mocollop	Lismore . .	II.	345
29	*Camphire Island*	3 2 32	Waterford . .	Decies within Drum	Aglish . . .	Dungarvan .	II.	349
1	Camplagh . .	162 0 8	Fermanagh . .	Lurg . . .	Drumkeeran . .	Lowtherstown .	III.	205
5	Camplany . .	76 1 18	Fermanagh . .	Lurg . . .	Magheraculmoney .	Lowtherstown .	III.	207
14	Campsey Lower	413 3 23*a*	Londonderry .	Tirkeeran . .	Faughanvale .	Londonderry .	III.	250
14	Campsey Upper	315 2 12	Londonderry .	Tirkeeran . .	Faughanvale .	Londonderry .	III.	250
35	Campsie . . .	260 2 10*b*	Tyrone . .	Omagh East . .	Cappagh . .	Omagh . .	III.	310
17	Campstown . .	229 2 20	Cavan . .	Tullygarvey . .	Kildrumsherdan .	Cootehill .	III.	89
16	Camross . . .	384 1 33	Queen's Co. .	Upperwoods . .	Offerlane . .	Mountmellick .	I.	251
33	Camross . . .	218 2 3	Sligo . .	Corran . . .	Emlaghfad . .	Sligo . .	IV.	226
39	Cams . . .	818 1 8	Roscommon . .	Athlone . .	Fuerty . .	Roscommon .	IV.	181
34	Cams . . .	376 2 23	Sligo . .	Tirerrill . .	Tawnagh . .	Sligo . .	IV.	241
9	Camteige . .	226 3 27	Wexford . .	Scarawalsh . .	St. Marys Newtown-barry . .	Enniscorthy .	I.	325
135, 144	Camus . . .	367 3 27	Cork, W.R. .	Ibane and Barryroe .	Kilkerranmore .	Clonakilty .	II.	149
144	Camus . . .	320 3 7	Cork, W.R. .	Ibane and Barryroe .	Rathbarry . .	Clonakilty .	II.	150
79	Camus . . .	35 1 30	Donegal . .	Raphoe . .	Clonleigh . .	Strabane .	III.	134
108	Camus . . .	250 2 15	Galway . .	Longford . .	Meelick . .	Portumna .	IV.	61
14, 22	Camus . . .	128 0 5	King's Co. .	Garrycastle . .	Tisaran . .	Parsonstown .	I.	138
7, 8, 11, 12	Camus . . .	900 1 6	Londonderry .	Coleraine . .	Macosquin . .	Coleraine .	III.	233
52, 60	Camus . . .	246 2 13	Tipperary, S.R. .	Middlethird . .	Ardmayle . .	Cashel . .	II.	324
52, 60	Camus . . .	777 2 19	Tipperary, S.R. .	Middlethird . .	St. Patricksrock .	Cashel . .	II.	330
10	Camus . . .	392 0 5*c*	Tyrone . .	Strabane Lower .	Camus . . .	Strabane .	III.	320
65, 66	Camus Eighter .	1,830 0 15*d*	Galway . .	Moycullen . .	Kilcummin . .	Oughterard .	IV.	66
7	Camus MacosquinGlebe	57 3 22	Londonderry .	Coleraine . .	Macosquin . .	Coleraine .	III.	233
65, 66	Camus Oughter .	1,498 1 24*e*	Galway . .	Moycullen . .	Kilcummin . .	Oughterard .	IV.	66
111	Canagullen . .	555 2 23*f*	Kerry . .	Glanarought . .	Tuosist . .	Kenmare .	II.	188
52	Canal and Banks .	28 3 12*g*	Roscommon .	Athlone . .	St. Peter's . .	Athlone .	IV.	184
126	Canalmore . .	265 2 25	Cork, W.R. .	Bear . . .	Kilnamanagh .	Castletown .	II.	125
127	Canalough . .	441 3 31	Cork, W.R. .	Bear . . .	Kilnamanagh .	Castletown .	II.	125
4	Canary . . .	347 0 28	Armagh . .	Oneilland West .	Clonfeacle . .	Armagh . .	III.	51
18	Canbeg . . .	171 2 29*h*	Leitrim . .	Drumahaire . .	Inishmagrath . .	Manorhamilton .	IV.	95
10, 11	Canbo . . .	315 3 7*i*	Roscommon . .	Boyle . .	Killummod . .	Car^k. on Shannon	IV.	196
81	Canbrack . .	264 3 19*j*	Mayo . .	Gallen . .	Killedan . .	Swineford .	IV.	149
80, 89	Canburrin . .	1,293 0 25	Kerry . .	Iveragh . .	Caher . . .	Cahersiveen .	II.	193
26	Candlefield . .	140 0 20	Roscommon .	Castlereagh . .	Kiltullagh . .	Castlereagh .	IV.	201
29, 32	Candlefort . .	127 3 6	Monaghan . .	Farney . .	Inishkeen . .	Dundalk .	III.	271
69, 70	Candroma . .	456 0 8	Cork, W.R. .	West Muskerry .	Clondrohid . .	Macroom .	II.	155
71	Canearagh . .	949 0 9	Kerry . .	Iveragh . .	Glanbehy . .	Cahersiveen .	II.	195
46	Caneese . . .	375 0 31	Londonderry .	Loughinsholin . .	Lissan . .	Magherafelt .	III.	242
100, 108	Canfee . . .	195 0 9	Kerry . .	Glanarought . .	Tuosist . .	Kenmare .	II.	188
12,13,25,26	Cangarrow . .	543 2 3	Galway . .	Ross . .	Ross . . .	Oughterard .	IV.	73
41, 42	Cangort Demesne .	511 0 27	King's Co. .	Clonlisk . .	Shinrone . .	Roscrea .	I.	131
41, 42	Cangort Park .	373 0 3	King's Co. .	Clonlisk . .	Shinrone . .	Roscrea .	I.	131
49	Cangullia . .	789 1 31	Kerry . .	Trughanacmy . .	Castleisland . .	Tralee . .	II.	208
18	Cangy . . .	123 0 24	Louth . .	Ardee . .	Cappoge . .	Ardee . .	I.	171
32	Cankeel . . .	39 2 22	Leitrim . .	Leitrim . .	Annaduff . .	Mohill . .	IV.	99
101, 109	Cankilly . . .	392 2 12	Galway . .	Longford . .	Clonfert . .	Ballinasloe .	IV.	56
82	Canknoogheda .	359 1 33	Kerry . .	Dunkerron North .	Knockane . .	Cahersiveen .	II.	182
25	Cannaboe . .	129 0 23	Leitrim . .	Carrigallen . .	Oughteragh . .	Bawnboy .	IV.	91
26	Cannafahy . .	31 0 3	Kilkenny . .	Callan . .	Callan . .	Callan . .	I.	83
17	Cannaghanally .	326 0 3	Sligo . .	Tireragh . .	Kilmacshalgan .	Dromore West .	IV.	234
5	Cannagola Beg .	133 1 15	Armagh . .	Oneilland West .	Drumcree . .	Lurgan . .	III.	51
5	Cannagola More .	223 0 27	Armagh . .	Oneilland West .	Drumcree . .	Lurgan . .	III.	51
10	Cannakill . .	209 3 31	King's Co. .	Lower Phillipstown	Croghan . .	Edenderry .	I.	142
40	*Cannaver Island* .	9 3 23	Galway . .	Ross . .	Cong . .	Oughterard .	IV.	73
147	Cannawee . .	113 3 19	Cork, W.R. .	West Carbery(W.D.)	Kilmoe . .	Skull . .	II.	144
29	Cannonsfield . .	16 0 33	Westmeath .	Brawny . .	St. Mary's . .	Athlone .	I.	259
8	Cannonsquarter .	199 0 27	Carlow . .	Rathvilly . .	Fennagh . .	Carlow . .	I.	11
17	Cannonstown . .	210 2 12	Kildare . .	Connell . .	Feighcullen . .	Naas . .	I.	55
16, 17	Cannonstown . .	111 3 19	Meath . .	Kells Upper . .	Kells . .	Kells . .	I.	205
28, 34	Cannonstown . .	262 3 20	Queen's Co. .	Clarmallow . .	Aghmacart . .	Abbeyleix .	I.	336
15, 16	Cannorstown(*Chapman*)	67 1 23	Westmeath .	Kilkenny West .	Noughaval . .	Ballymahon .	I.	274
15, 16	Cannorstown (*Hogan*)	45 0 24	Westmeath .	Kilkenny West .	Noughaval . .	Ballymahon .	I.	274
22	Cannow . . .	321 0 29	Wicklow . .	Talbotstown Upper .	Donaghmore .	Baltinglass .	I.	363

(*a*) Including 39A. 2R. 13P. water.
(*b*) Including 14A. 0R. 27P. water.
(*c*) Including 23A. 2R. 32P. water.
(*d*) Including 85A. 2R. 10P. water.

(*e*) Including 59A. 0R. 9P. water.
(*f*) Including 25A. 1R. 20P. water.
(*g*) Including 11A. 0R. 14P. water.

(*h*) Including 9A. 1R. 16P. water.
(*i*) Including 57A. 0R. 33P. water.
(*j*) Including 9A. 2R. 17P. water.

No. of Sheet of the Ordnance Survey Maps.	Townlands and Towns.	Area in Statute Acres.			County.	Barony.	Parish.	Poor Law Union in 1857.	Townland Census of 1851, Part I.	
		A.	R.	P.					Vol.	Page
22	Cannow Mountain	1,128	2	2	Wicklow	Upper Talbotstown	Donaghmore	Baltinglass	I.	363
5	Canoneill	113	1	3	Armagh	Oneilland West	Drumcree	Lurgan	III.	51
60	Canon Island	270	3	27	Clare	Clonderalaw	Killadysert	Killadysert	II.	16
21,22,24,25	Canonstown	254	0	18	Louth	Ferrard	Termonfeckin	Drogheda	I.	182
50	Canower	271	3	15	Galway	Ballynahinch	Moyrus	Clifden	IV.	12
54	Canrawer East	14	3	33	Galway	Moycullen	Kilcummin	Oughterard	IV.	66
54	Canrawer West	146	2	7a	Galway	Moycullen	Kilcummin	Oughterard	IV.	66
90	Canrooska	590	0	30	Cork, W.R.	Bear	Kilcaskan	Bantry	II.	122
103	Canshanavoe	1,365	0	6b	Cork, W.R.	Bear	Kilcaskan	Castletown	II.	122
35, 43	Cant	250	1	37	Clare	Bunratty Upper	Quin	Tulla	II.	10
70	Canteeny	145	1	10	Galway	Clare	Lackagh	Galway	IV.	22
44	Cantogher	150	2	26	Limerick	Glenquin	Killeedy	Newcastle	II.	245
52	Cantra	145	0	6	Kerry	Corkaguiny	Ventry	Dingle	II.	180
30	Canty	319	3	8	Waterford	Decies without Drum	Whitechurch	Dungarvan	II.	361
16	Cantytrindle	154	0	3	Fermanagh	Lurg	Derryvullan	Lowtherstown	III.	204
80, 89	Canuig	1,267	1	28	Kerry	Iveragh	Dromod	Cahersiveen	II.	194
97	Canuig	450	2	39	Kerry	Iveragh	Prior	Cahersiveen	II.	198
18	Canvarstown	373	1	29	Kilkenny	Crannagh	Tullaroan	Kilkenny	I.	88
34, 39	Capanagh	1,043	0	24	Antrim	Upper Glenarm	Kilwaughter	Larne	III.	25
3, 6, 7	Capard	2,548	3	31	Queen's Co.	Tinnahinch	Rosenallis	Mountmellick	I.	250
14	Capdoo	122	3	24c	Kildare	Clane	Clane	Naas	I.	53
14	Capdoo Commons	113	3	35	Kildare	Clane	Clane	Naas	I.	53
8	Cape Castle	348	1	12	Antrim	Cary	Ramoan	Ballycastle	III.	14
78	Capel Island	10	1	1	Cork, E.R.	Imokilly	Kilmacdonogh	Youghal	II.	88
117, 118	Capira	204	0	29	Galway	Longford	Lickmolassy	Portumna	IV.	60
22	Caplahard	56	1	36d	Westmeath	Kilkenny West	Kilkenny West	Athlone	I.	273
29	Caplevane	260	2	14	King's Co.	Garrycastle	Lusmagh	Parsonstown	I.	137
75, 85	Capnagower	214	1	25	Mayo	Murrisk	Kilgeever	Westport	IV.	161
43	Cappa	38	3	36	Kerry	Corkaguiny	Dingle	Dingle	II.	175
82	Cappa	371	0	3e	Kerry	Dunkerron South	Templenoe	Kenmare	II.	185
15, 21	Cappa	284	1	34	Tipperary, N.R.	Upper Ormond	Ballymackey	Nenagh	II.	289
3	Cappabeg	299	0	14	Queen's Co.	Tinnahinch	Rosenallis	Mountmellick	I.	250
46	Cappaboggan	211	3	10	Meath	Moyfenrath Upper	Castlejordan	Edenderry	I.	212
92	Cappaboy Beg	633	2	32	Cork, W.R.	Bantry	Kilmocomoge	Bantry	II.	119
92	Cappaboy More	782	0	8	Cork, W.R.	Bantry	Kilmocomoge	Bantry	II.	119
20	Cappacannaun	681	0	1	Clare	Tulla Upper	Tomgraney	Scarriff	II.	41
122	Cappacasheen	364	2	1	Galway	Kiltartan	Killinny	Gort	IV.	47
89	Cappacharnaun	292	1	25	Mayo	Carra	Ballintober	Castlebar	IV.	124
40	Cappaclogh	66	1	13	Tipperary, N.R.	Kilnamanagh Upper	Templebeg	Thurles	II.	279
36	Cappaclogh East	220	0	33	Kerry	Corkaguiny	Kilgobban	Tralee	II.	177
36	Cappaclogh West	214	1	34	Kerry	Corkaguiny	Kilgobban	Tralee	II.	177
27	Cappacorcoge	136	0	30	Galway	Ross	Cong	Oughterard	IV.	72
27	Cappacorcoge or Ashford	178	3	0f	Galway	Ross	Cong	Oughterard	IV.	72
117	Cappacuilla	116	1	33	Galway	Longford	Tynagh	Portumna	IV.	62
117	Cappacur	345	0	20	Galway	Leitrim	Tynagh	Portumna	IV.	55
110, 118	Cappacurry	315	1	5g	Mayo	Kilmaine	Ballinrobe	Ballinrobe	IV.	152
30	Cappadavock	287	1	23h	Galway	Ballymoe	Tuam	Tuam	IV.	10
25	Cappadine	139	3	13	Tipperary, N.R.	Owney and Arra	Kilnarath	Nenagh	II.	295
107, 120	Cappadineen	106	2	30	Cork, W.R.	East Carbery (W.D.)	Fanlobbus	Dunmanway	II.	131
70, 77, 78	Cappadrummin	152	2	16	Tipperary, S.R.	Middlethird	Kiltinan	Clonmel	II.	328
134, 136	Cappaduff	510	2	17	Galway	Leitrim	Inishcaltra	Scarriff	IV.	53
31, 32	Cappaduff	170	0	14	Westmeath	Moycashel	Ardnurcher or Horseleap	Mullingar	I.	276
23	Cappafaulish	87	1	8	Kilkenny	Shillelogher	Tullaghanbrogue	Callan	I.	116
26	Cappafeean	375	0	14i	Clare	Bunratty Upper	Inchicronan	Tulla	II.	8
65	Cappaganneen	496	3	30	Kerry	Dunkerron North	Knockane	Killarney	II.	181
41	Cappagarraun	100	0	28	Clare	Islands	Killone	Ennis	II.	30
40	Cappagarriff	50	0	25	Galway	Moycullen	Kilcummin	Oughterard	IV.	66
30	Cappagh	172	1	8	Armagh	Fews Upper	Creggan	Castleblayney	III.	48
17	Cappagh	229	3	24	Carlow	Forth	Ballon	Carlow	I.	3
19	Cappagh	212	3	26j	Cavan	Tullyhunco	Kildallan	Cavan	III.	97
6	Cappagh	770	3	7	Clare	Burren	Carran	Ballyvaghan	II.	11
67	Cappagh	203	1	7	Clare	Moyarta	Kilrush	Kilrush	II.	33
35	Cappagh	334	3	10	Cork, E.R.	Fermoy	Killathy	Fermoy	II.	80
34	Cappagh	283	1	34	Cork, E.R.	Fermoy	Monanimy	Mallow	II.	81
111, 112	Cappagh	322	2	29	Cork, E.R.	Kinsale	Ringcurran	Kinsale	II.	100
96	Cappagh	343	2	27k	Donegal	Banagh	Glencolumbkille	Glenties	III.	105
34	Cappagh	476	2	39	Down	Upper Iveagh, Up. pt.	Annaclone	Banbridge	III.	174
17	Cappagh	194	0	35	Dublin	Uppercross	Clondalkin	Dublin South	I.	39
99	Cappagh	101	3	9	Galway	Clonmacnowen	Clontuskert	Ballinasloe	IV.	24
5	Cappagh	834	0	23	Galway	Dunmore	Dunmore	Tuam	IV.	33
81, 93	Cappagh	401	0	33	Galway	Galway	Rahoon	Galway	IV.	37

(a) Including 6A. 2R. 0P. water.
(b) Including 46A. 1R. 10P. water.
(c) Including 4A. 0R. 34P. water.
(d) Including 0A. 2R. 21P. water.

(e) Including 29A. 2R. 9P. water.
(f) Including 11A. 1R. 23P. water.
(g) Including 2A. 3R. 22P. water.
(h) Including 33A. 3R. 39P. water.

(i) Including 70A. 0R. 11P. water.
(j) Including 13A. 2R. 10P. water.
(k) Including 16A. 1R. 0P. detached portion.

No. of Sheet of the Ordnance Survey Maps.	Townlands and Towns.	Area in Statute Acres. A. R. P.	County.	Barony.	Parish.	Poor Law Union in 1857.	Townland Census of 1851. Part I. Vol.	Page
74, 87	Cappagh . . .	423 3 5	Galway . .	Kilconnell . .	Kilgerrill . .	Ballinasloe .	IV.	40
32	Cappagh . . .	387 0 39	Galway . .	Killian . . .	Kilhan . .	Mountbellew .	IV.	44
125, 126	Cappagh . . .	326 3 19	Galway . .	Leitrim . . .	Ballynakill . .	Loughrea . .	IV.	50
126	Cappagh . . .	469 2 39	Galway . .	Leitrim . . .	Tynagh . .	Portumna .	IV.	55
118	Cappagh . . .	444 3 31	Galway . .	Longford . .	Tiranascragh . .	Portumna .	IV.	62
18,19,31,32	Cappagh . . .	657 1 16a	Galway . .	Tiaquin . . .	Kilkerrin . .	Glennamaddy .	IV.	76
22	Cappagh . . .	518 1 4	Kerry . .	Clanmaurice . .	Kilflyn . .	Tralee . .	II.	170
26, 35	Cappagh . . .	190 2 34	Kerry . .	Corkaguiny . .	Cloghane . .	Dingle . .	II.	175
65	Cappagh . . .	110 0 4	Kerry . .	Dunkerron North .	Killorglin . .	Killarney .	II.	181
65	Cappagh . . .	248 0 22	Kerry . .	Dunkerron North .	Knockane . .	Killarney .	II.	181
93, 94, 102	Cappagh . . .	383 1 25	Kerry . .	Glanarought . .	Kenmare . .	Kenmare . .	II.	185
80	Cappagh . . .	720 2 13	Kerry . .	Iveragh . . .	Killinane . .	Cahersiveen .	II.	197
75	Cappagh . . .	1,253 1 1b	Kerry . .	Magunihy . .	Killaha . .	Killarney .	II.	202
4	Cappagh . . .	886 3 30	Kildare . .	Ikeathy&Oughterany	Cloncurry . .	Celbridge .	I.	57
19	Cappagh . . .	140 2 3	Kilkenny . .	Crannagh . .	St. Canice . .	Kilkenny .	I.	87
28,29,32,33	Cappagh . . .	730 2 0c	Kilkenny .	Gowran . . .	Inistioge . .	Thomastown .	I.	96
43	Cappagh . . .	128 2 7	Kilkenny . .	Ida . . .	Gaulskill . .	Waterford .	I.	102
41	Cappagh . . .	161 2 32	Kilkenny . .	Ida . . .	Kilcoan . .	Waterford .	I.	102
32, 36	Cappagh . . .	516 1 6	Kilkenny . .	Knocktopher . .	Jerpointchurch .	Thomastown .	I.	111
27, 28	Cappagh . . .	128 3 17	King's Co. .	Coolestown . .	Clonsast . .	Edenderry .	I.	132
9, 10	Cappagh . . .	161 2 27	King's Co. .	Lower Philipstown .	Kilclonfert . .	Tullamore .	I.	142
32	Cappagh . . .	103 2 14	Leitrim . .	Mohill . . .	Mohill . .	Mohill . .	IV.	107
20	Cappagh . . .	786 2 22	Limerick . .	Connello Lower .	Cappagh . .	Rathkeale .	II.	227
69	Cappagh . . .	284 2 38d	Mayo . .	Carra . . .	Aglish . .	Castlebar .	IV.	123
82	Cappagh . . .	315 2 32	Mayo . .	Costello . . .	Aghamore . .	Swinford .	IV.	136
12	Cappagh . . .	52 1 0	Monaghan .	Dartree . . .	Clones . .	Clones . .	III.	264
22	Cappagh . . .	163 2 18	Queen's Co. .	Clandonagh . .	Aghaboe . .	Donaghmore .	I.	232
36	Cappagh . . .	153 0 17	Roscommon .	Ballintober South .	Kilgefin . .	Roscommon .	IV.	189
74	Cappagh . . .	47 2 29	Roscommon .	Frenchpark . .	Castlemore . .	Castlereagh .	IV.	202
29	Cappagh . . .	65 0 33	Roscommon .	Roscommon . .	Kilbride . .	Strokestown .	IV.	210
34	Cappagh . . .	173 1 0	Sligo . .	Corran . . .	Kilmorgan . .	Sligo . .	IV.	226
25	Cappagh . . .	556 0 28	Sligo . .	Leyny . . .	Killoran . .	Tobercurry .	IV.	230
51	Cappagh . . .	460 1 32	Tipperary, N.R.	Kilnamanagh Upper	Toem . .	Tipperary .	II.	280
51	Cappagh . . .	48 1 23	Tipperary, S.R.	Kilnamanagh Lower	Donohill . .	Tipperary .	II.	323
55, 56	Cappagh . . .	519 2 2	Tipperary, S.R.	Slievardagh . .	Ballingarry . .	Callan . .	II.	331
72	Cappagh . . .	54 1 20	Tipperary, S.R.	Slievardagh . .	Templemichael .	Carrick on Suir	II.	336
45	Cappagh . . .	464 0 11	Tyrone . .	Dungannon Middle .	Pomeroy . .	Dungannon .	III.	304
40	Cappagh . . .	67 2 28	Waterford .	Decies within Drum	Lisgenan or Grange	Youghal . .	II.	352
30	Cappagh . . .	401 0 14	Waterford .	Decies without Drum	Whitechurch . .	Dungarvan .	II.	361
6	Cappagh . . .	1,138 1 6e	Westmeath .	Moygoish . .	Russagh . .	Mullingar .	I.	280
34	Cappagh . . .	583 2 23	Wicklow . .	Ballinacor South .	Ballinacor . .	Rathdrum .	I.	348
135	Cappagha	74 0 8	Galway . .	Leitrim . . .	Clonrush . .	Scarriff . .	IV.	52
20, 21	Cappaghabaun Mountain .	1,254 3 26	Clare . .	Tulla Upper . .	Moynoe . .	Scarriff . .	II.	40
20, 21	Cappaghabaunpark .	684 2 3	Clare . .	Tulla Upper . .	Moynoe . .	Scarriff . .	II.	40
30	Cappaghauneen .	58 0 22	Westmeath .	Clonlonan . .	Ballyloughloe .	Athlone . .	I.	260
115	Cappaghavuckee .	89 0 5	Cork, W.R. .	Bear . . .	Killaconenagh .	Castletown .	II.	124
26, 34	Cappagh Beg .	215 2 4	Clare . .	Bunratty Upper .	Kilraghtis . .	Ennis . .	II.	9
131, 132	Cappagh Beg .	474 2 2	Cork, W.R. .	West Carbery,(W.D.)	Skull . .	Skull . .	II.	145
112, 113, 121, 122	Cappagh Beg .	247 3 4	Galway . .	Kiltartan . .	Killinny . .	Gort . .	IV.	47
3	Cappagh Beg .	49 1 22	Londonderry .	North East Liberties of Coleraine	Ballyaghran .	Coleraine .	III.	244
30	Cappaghbrack .	208 1 17	Westmeath .	Clonlonan . .	Ballyloughloe .	Athlone . .	I.	260
52	Cappaghcastle .	75 3 12	Clare . .	Bunratty Lower .	Kilfinaghta . .	Ennis . .	II.	4
125	Cappaghcon .	91 0 29	Galway . .	Leitrim . . .	Ballynakill . .	Loughrea .	IV.	50
125	Cappaghconbeg .	62 1 38	Galway . .	Leitrim . . .	Ballynakill . .	Loughrea .	IV.	50
125	Cappaghcon East .	127 2 22	Galway . .	Leitrim . . .	Ballynakill . .	Loughrea .	IV.	50
125	Cappaghcon West .	131 1 26	Galway . .	Leitrim . . .	Ballynakill . .	Loughrea . .	IV.	50
53	Cappaghcreen .	20 1 31	Meath . .	Dunboyne . .	Dunboyne . .	Dunshaughlin .	I.	199
109, 117	Cappaghduff East .	458 3 5	Mayo . .	Carra . . .	Ballyovey . .	Ballinrobe .	IV.	126
108,109,117	Cappaghduff West .	514 3 6	Mayo . .	Carra . . .	Ballyovey . .	Ballinrobe .	IV.	126
58	Cappagh East .	541 0 20	Cork, W.R. .	West Muskerry .	Ballyvourney .	Macroom . .	II.	154
140, 149	Cappaghglass .	426 3 26	Cork, W.R. .	West Carbery(W.D.)	Skull . .	Skull . .	II.	145
17, 24	Cappaghjuan .	90 3 34	Westmeath .	Rathconrath . .	Ballymorin . .	Mullingar .	I.	282
10	Cappaghkenne ly .	413 2 18	Clare . .	Burren . . .	Carran . .	Ballyvaghan .	II.	11
12	Cappagh (Kilgarialy)	70 1 26	Monaghan .	Dartree . . .	Clones . .	Clones . .	III.	264
52	Cappaghlodge .	347 3 11	Clare . .	Bunratty Lower .	Kilfinaghta . .	Ennis . .	II.	4
26, 34	Cappagh More .	263 1 16f	Clare . .	Bunratty Upper .	Kilraghtis . .	Ennis . .	II.	9
131	Cappagh More .	382 1 13	Cork, W.R. .	West Carbery (W.D.)	Skull . .	Skull . .	II.	145
112,121,122	Cappagh More .	473 2 19	Galway . .	Kiltartan . .	Killiny . .	Gort . .	IV.	47
3	Cappagh More .	90 1 38	Londonderry .	North East Liberties of Coleraine	Ballyaghran .	Coleraine .	III.	244
71	Cappaghmore .	612 3 11	Tipperary, S.R.	Slievardagh . .	Cloneen . .	Callan . .	II.	332

(a) Including 3A. 0R. 2¹P. water.
(b) Including 10A. 3R. 25P. water.
(c) Including 4A. 3R. 33P. River Nore.
(d) Including 3A. 1R. 31P. water.
(e) Including 118A. 1R. 32P. water.
(f) Including 3A. 1R. 38P. water.

No. of Sheet of the Ordnance Survey Maps.	Townlands and Towns.	Area in Statute Acres. A. R. P.	County.	Barony.	Parish.	Poor Law Union in 1857.	Townland Census of 1851, Part I. Vol.	Page
84, 85	Cappaghmoyle	231 0 28	Galway . .	Tiaquin . .	Monivea . .	Loughrea . .	IV.	78
140	Cappaghnacallee	228 0 14	Cork, W.R. .	West Carbery(W.D.)	Skull . .	Skull . .	II.	145
26, 27	Cappaghnagapple or Petersburgh .	655 0 36	Galway . .	Ross . .	Ross . .	Oughterard .	IV.	73
63	Cappaghnagarrane .	425 1 31	Tipperary, S.R.	Slievardagh .	Isertkieran .	Callan . .	II.	333
16	Cappaghnahoran or Windsor .	269 3 4	Queen's Co. .	Upperwoods .	Offerlane .	Abbeyleix .	I.	252
85	Cappaghnanool	429 2 11	Galway . .	Kilconnell .	Killimordaly .	Loughrea .	IV.	42
52	Cappagh North	187 2 4	Clare . .	Bunratty Lower .	Kilfinaghta .	Ennis . .	II.	4
96	Cappagh North	40 3 9	Galway . .	Dunkellin .	Kilconierin .	Loughrea .	IV.	29
101	Cappagh North	116 3 31	Mayo . .	Clanmorris .	Tagheen .	Claremorris .	IV.	135
7, 12, 13	Cappagh North	523 0 38	Queen's Co. .	Maryborough East .	Clonenagh and Clonagheen .	Mountmellick .	I.	241
37,38,51,52	Cappaghoosh .	2,160 2 39	Galway . .	Ballynahinch .	Moyrus . .	Clifden . .	IV.	12
51, 59	Cappaghrattin	170 3 28	Tipperary, S.R.	Clanwilliam .	Donohill . .	Tipperary .	II.	307
52	Cappagh South	232 2 9	Clare . .	Bunratty Lower .	Kilfinaghta .	Ennis . .	II.	4
96	Cappagh South	37 0 2	Galway . .	Dunkellin .	Kilconierin .	Loughrea .	IV.	29
101	Cappagh South	124 3 25	Mayo . .	Clanmorris .	Tagheen .	Claremorris .	IV.	135
12, 17	Cappagh South	488 2 20	Queen's Co. .	Maryborough West .	Clonenagh&Clonagheen	Mountmellick .	I.	242
20	CAPPAGH T.	—	Limerick . .	Connello Lower .	Cappagh . .	Rathkeale .	II.	227
58	Cappagh West	312 1 14	Cork, W.R. .	West Muskerry .	Ballyvourney .	Macroom .	II.	154
51	CAPPAGH WHITE T.	—	Tipperary, N.R.	Kilnamanagh Upper	Toem . .	Tipperary .	II.	280
24, 31, 32	Cappagowlan .	508 1 15	King's Co. .	Ballyboy . .	Killoughy .	Tullamore .	I.	124
33, 34	Cappahard .	193 3 22	Clare . .	Bunratty Upper .	Templemaley .	Ennis . .	II.	10
22, 26	Cappahayden .	589 1 21	Kilkenny . .	Shillelogher .	Killaloe . .	Callan . .	I.	115
26	Cappahenry .	12 0 6	Kilkenny . .	Callan . .	Callan . .	Callan . .	I.	83
26	Cappahenry East	49 2 13	Kilkenny . .	Callan . .	Callan . .	Callan . .	I.	83
53, 54	Cappakea .	452 0 28	Clare . .	Tulla Lower .	O'Briensbridge .	Limerick .	II.	37
9, 14	Cappakeel .	1,527 2 4	Queen's Co. .	Portnahinch .	Coolbanagher .	Mountmellick .	I.	244
118	Cappakeela .	11 3 33	Galway . .	Longford .	Tiranascragh .	Portumna .	IV.	62
11, 16	Cappakilleen .	160 2 9	Tipperary, N.R.	Lower Ormond .	Modreeny .	Borrisokane .	II.	286
109, 110	Cappaknockane .	585 3 28	Cork, W.R. .	Kinalmeaky .	Desertserges .	Bandon . .	II.	152
17, 18	Cappalahan .	796 1 25	Tipperary, N.R.	Ikerrin . .	Bourney . .	Roscrea .	II.	274
18	Cappalahan .	17 2 25	Tipperary, N.R.	Ikerrin . .	Corbally . .	Roscrea .	II.	275
35, 43	Cappalaheen .	374 0 10a	Clare . .	Tulla Lower .	Clonlea . .	Tulla . .	II.	34
38	Cappalahy .	241 2 24	Westmeath .	Moycashel .	Durrow . .	Tullamore .	I.	277
7	Cappalane .	193 2 33	Queen's Co. .	Tinnahinch .	Rosenallis .	Mountmellick .	I.	250
26	Cappalauna .	21 2 24	Kilkenny . .	Kells . .	Mallardstown .	Callan . .	I.	110
36	Cappalea . .	40 3 14	Clare . .	Tulla Lower .	Killuran . .	Tulla . .	II.	36
32, 33	Cappalea North	252 2 7	Clare . .	Islands . .	Kilmaley . .	Ennis . .	II.	31
33	Cappalea South	186 3 24	Clare . .	Islands . .	Kilmaley . .	Ennis . .	II.	31
103, 116	Cappaleigh North	123 1 1	Cork, W.R. .	Bear . .	Kilcaskan .	Castletown .	II.	122
116	Cappaleigh South	115 2 19	Cork, W.R. .	Bear . .	Kilcaskan .	Castletown .	II.	122
56	Cappaleitrim .	524 3 2	Roscommon .	Moycarn . .	Moore . .	Ballinasloe .	IV.	206
33, 34	Cappalinnan .	426 1 25	Queen's Co. .	Clandonagh .	Rathdowney .	Donaghmore .	I.	234
48, 49	Cappalisheen .	226 1 11	Roscommon .	Athlone . .	Kiltoom . .	Athlone . .	IV.	182
1, 3	Cappalough .	478 2 9	Queen's Co. .	Tinnahinch .	Castlebrack .	Mountmellick .	I.	248
16	Cappaloughan .	159 3 38	King's Co. .	Ballycowan .	Rahan . .	Tullamore .	I.	128
17, 23	Cappaloughlin or Clonard	1,592 0 19	Queen's Co. .	Maryborough West	Clonenagh and Clonagheen . .	Abbeyleix .	I.	242
108	Cappaluane .	41 1 5	Galway . .	Longford .	Clonfert . .	Portumna .	IV.	57
32	Cappalug .	342 1 16	Queen's Co. .	Slievemargy .	Killeshin .	Carlow . .	I.	245
18, 26	Cappamore .	192 1 6	Clare . .	Bunratty Upper .	Inchicronan .	Ennis . .	II.	8
72	Cappamore .	79 1 20	Kerry . .	Dunkerron North .	Knockane .	Cahersiveen .	II.	181
98	Cappamore .	273 0 1	Kerry . .	Dunkerron South .	Kilcrohane .	Cahersiveen .	II.	183
83,84,92,93	Cappamore .	636 2 32b	Kerry . .	Glanarought .	Kenmare .	Kenmare .	II.	185
62, 70	Cappamore .	225 2 37	Kerry . .	Iveragh . .	Killinane .	Cahersiveen .	II.	197
15	Cappamore .	190 3 37	Limerick . .	Coonagh .	Doon . .	Limerick .	II.	234
15	CAPPAMORE T.	—	Limerick . .	Owneybeg .	Tuogh . .	Limerick .	II.	251
52	Cappamurragh .	388 3 23	Tipperary, S.R.	Kilnamanagh Lower	Clonoulty .	Cashel . .	II.	322
32	Cappanaboe .	177 3 12	Queen's Co. .	Slievemargy .	Killeshin .	Carlow . .	I.	245
133	Cappanabohy .	231 2 8	Cork, W.R. .	West Carbery (E.D.)	Kilmacabea .	Skibbereen .	II.	140
82	Cappanabornia .	12 3 8	Galway . .	Galway . .	St. Nicholas .	Galway . .	IV.	38
105, 106	Cappanaboul .	260 2 33c	Cork, W.R. .	Bantry . .	Kilmocomoge .	Bantry . .	II.	119
91	Cappanabrick .	254 2 24	Cork, W.R. .	Bantry . .	Kilmocomoge .	Bantry . .	II.	119
12	Cappanacleare .	175 1 26	Queen's Co. .	Maryborough West .	Clonenagh and Clonagheen .	Mountmellick .	I.	242
23	Cappanacloghy .	574 3 36	Queen's Co. .	Maryborough West .	Clonenagh and Clonagheen .	Abbeyleix .	I.	242
3, 13	Cappanacreha .	1,855 0 18d	Galway . .	Ross . .	Ballinchalla .	Ballinrobe .	IV.	72
92	Cappanacush East .	684 0 0	Kerry . .	Dunkerron South .	Templenoe .	Kenmare .	II.	185
32	Cappanacush Island .	19 0 35	Kerry . .	Dunkerron South .	Templenoe .	Kenmare .	II.	185
92	Cappanacush West .	495 0 13	Kerry . .	Dunkerron South .	Templenoe .	Kenmare .	II.	185
39	Cappanafaraha .	244 2 34	Limerick . .	Coshma . .	Bruree . .	Kilmallock .	II.	242

(a) Including 73A. 1R. 27P. water.   (c) Including 5A. 0R. 26P. water.   (d) Including 92A. 2R. 4P. water.
(b) Including 4A. 1R. 27P. water.

No. of Sheet of the Ordnance Survey Maps.	Townlands and Towns.	Area in Statute Acres.			County.	Barony.	Parish.	Poor Law Union in 1857.	Townland Census of 1851, Part I.	
		A.	R.	P.					Vol.	Page
19, 20	Cappanafeacle	260	2	17	Queen's Co.	Ballyadams	Ballyadams	Athy	I.	231
49, 50	Cappanageeragh	312	1	15	Clare	Islands	Clondagad	Killadysert	II.	29
18	Cappanageeragh	294	3	31	King's Co.	Geashill	Geashill	Tullamore	I.	140
107	Cappanaghtan	321	3	1	Galway	Longford	Abbeygormacan	Ballinasloe	IV.	56
39	Cappanaglogh	119	0	28	Mayo	Tirawley	Kilbelfad	Ballina	IV.	167
6, 15	Cappanagoul	509	1	39	Cork, E.R.	Duhallow	Knocktemple	Kanturk	II.	75
2	Cappanagraigue	86	2	2	Queen's Co.	Tinnahinch	Kilmanman	Mountmellick	I.	249
71	Cappanagraun	259	2	25	Cork, W.R.	East Muskerry	Aghinagh	Macroom	II.	153
89, 90	Cappanagroun	558	0	31*a*	Kerry	Iveragh	Dromod	Cahersiveen	II.	194
6, 7	Cappanahanagh	648	3	34	Limerick	Owneybeg	Abington	Limerick	II.	250
25, 31	Cappanakeady	373	1	6	Tipperary, N.R.	Owney and Arra	Kilmastulla	Nenagh	II.	295
25	Cappanakilla	161	2	26	Clare	Inchiquin	Dysert	Ennis	II.	24
52	Cappanalaght	86	2	27	Clare	Bunratty Lower	Kilfinaghta	Limerick	II.	4
52	Cappanalaght	116	0	3	Clare	Bunratty Lower	Kilfintinan	Limerick	II.	5
39	Cappanalaurabaun	184	1	2	Galway	Moycullen	Kilcummin	Oughterard	IV.	66
40	Cappanaleigh	107	0	18	Tipperary, N.R.	Kilnamanagh Upper	Upperchurch	Thurles	II.	280
118	Cappanaloha East	68	1	6	Cork, W.R.	Bantry	Kilmocomoge	Bantry	II.	119
118	Cappanaloha West	68	3	3	Cork, W.R.	Bantry	Kilmocomoge	Bantry	II.	119
7	Cappanalosset	386	1	23	King's Co.	Garrycastle	Lemanaghan	Parsonstown	I.	136
80	Cappanaminna	99	0	9	Cork, W.R.	West Muskerry	Inchigeelagh	Macroom	II.	156
2, 8	Cappanamorath	28	3	18	King's Co.	Kilcoursey	Kilbride	Tullamore	I.	141
32	Cappanamrogue	179	1	16	Queen's Co.	Slievemargy	Killeshin	Carlow	I.	245
7	Cappanamuck	82	1	33	Tipperary, N.R.	Lower Ormond	Aghlishcloghane	Borrisokane	II.	281
36	Cappananee	101	0	35	Kerry	Corkaguiny	Killiney	Dingle	II.	177
38, 46	Cappananty	529	1	10	Limerick	Connello Upper	Corcomohide	Croom	II.	232
103, 116	Cappanaparka East	171	0	5	Cork, W.R.	Bear	Kilcaskan	Castletown	II.	122
103, 116	Cappanaparka West	273	3	7	Cork, W.R.	Bear	Kilcaskan	Castletown	II.	122
18	Cappanapeasta	805	2	19*b*	Clare	Bunratty Upper	Inchicronan	Ennis	II.	8
2	Cappanapinion or Bellair	83	3	22	Queen's Co.	Tinnahinch	Kilmanman	Mountmellick	I.	249
122	Cappanapisha North	121	0	38	Galway	Kiltartan	Kilmacduagh	Gort	IV.	48
122	Cappanapisha South	165	1	2	Galway	Kiltartan	Kilmacduagh	Gort	IV.	48
17	Cappanargid	1,450	1	3	Kildare	Offaly East	Cloncurry	Edenderry	I.	69
11	Cappanarrow	385	0	17	Queen's Co.	Upperwoods	Offerlane	Mountmellick	I.	251
24, 30	Cappanashannagh	263	3	24	Queen's Co.	Cullenagh	Dysartgallen	Abbeyleix	I.	239
44	Cappanaslish	510	2	29	Clare	Tulla Lower	Killokennedy	Limerick	II.	35
7	Cappanasmear	454	1	0	Tipperary, N.R.	Lower Ormond	Terryglass	Borrisokane	II.	287
85	Cappanasruhaun	675	0	14	Galway	Kilconnell	Killimordaly	Loughrea	IV.	42
105	Cappanavar	44	2	20	Cork, W.R.	Bantry	Kilmocomoge	Bantry	II.	119
59	Cappanavarnoge	482	3	36	Clare	Clonderalaw	Killadysert	Killadysert	II.	15
94	Cappanaveagh	50	2	13	Galway	Galway	Rahoon	Galway	IV.	37
33, 34	Cappanavilla	189	2	25	Tipperary, N.R.	Kilnamanagh Upper	Upperchurch	Thurles	II.	280
81	Cappanclare	181	1	30	Cork, W.R.	West Muskerry	Inchigeelagh	Dunmanway	II.	156
17	Cappancur	1,933	1	13	King's Co.	Geashill	Geashill	Tullamore	I.	140
3	Cappaneary	197	2	10	Queen's Co.	Tinnahinch	Rosenallis	Mountmellick	I.	250
38	Cappanihane	770	3	12	Limerick	Connello Upper	Corcomohide	Croom	II.	232
34	Cappanilly	19	0	12	Tipperary, N.R.	Kilnamanagh Upper	Glenkeen	Thurles	II.	278
22, 29	Cappankelly	137	1	35	Westmeath	Brawny	St. Mary's	Athlone	I.	259
85	Cappanlivane	265	0	37	Kerry	Glanarought	Kilgarvan	Kenmare	II.	187
1, 3	Cappanlug	151	0	2	Queen's Co.	Tinnahinch	Castlebrack	Mountmellick	I.	248
15	Cappanouk	983	1	11	Limerick	Owneybeg	Abington	Limerick	II.	250
96, 104	Cappanraheen	79	0	38	Galway	Dunkellin	Killora	Loughrea	IV.	31
12	Cappanrush	309	1	21	Queen's Co.	Maryborough West	Clonenagh and Clonagheen	Mountmellick	I.	242
38	Cappanrush	381	2	25	Westmeath	Moycashel	Rahugh	Tullamore	I.	279
30	Cappantack	88	0	3*c*	Westmeath	Clonlonan	Kilmanaghan	Athlone	I.	262
72, 73	Cappanthlarrig	310	3	8	Kerry	Dunkerron North	Knockane	Killarney	II.	181
56	Cappantogher	268	3	34	Roscommon	Moycarn	Moore	Ballinasloe	IV.	206
31	Cappantruhaun	277	3	23	Galway	Ballymoe	Dunmore	Glennamaddy	IV.	7
135	Cappantruhaun	119	3	5	Galway	Leitrim	Clonrush	Scarriff	IV.	52
12, 13	Cappaphaudeen	1,516	0	37	Cork, E.R.	Duhallow	Kilmeen	Kanturk	II.	72
70	Capparanny	248	2	16	Mayo	Carra	Turlough	Castlebar	IV.	130
114, 123	Cappard Demesne	471	1	13	Galway	Loughrea	Kilthomas	Gort	IV.	65
28	Capparoe	646	2	19*d*	Clare	Tulla Upper	Tomgraney	Scarriff	II.	41
73	Capparoe	325	1	5	Kerry	Dunkerron North	Knockane	Killarney	II.	181
92	Capparoe	385	1	8	Kerry	Dunkerron South	Templenoe	Kenmare	II.	185
12, 21	Capparoe	55	1	2	Limerick	Kenry	Adare	Croom	II.	248
26	Capparoe	288	2	29	Tipperary, N.R.	Upper Ormond	Kilmore	Nenagh	II.	291
2	Capparogan	70	3	28	Queen's Co.	Tinnahinch	Kilmanman	Mountmellick	I.	249
118, 127	Cappasallagh	634	1	33	Galway	Longford	Kilmalinoge	Portumna	IV.	59
26	Cappass	56	2	32	Kilkenny	Callan	Callan	Callan	I.	83
86, 98	Cappataggle	390	0	37	Galway	Kilconnell	Killallaghtan	Ballinasloe	IV.	41
53	Cappateemore East	260	0	8	Clare	Bunratty Lower	St. Munchin's	Limerick	II.	6
52, 53	Cappateemore West	180	2	15	Clare	Bunratty Lower	St. Munchin's	Limerick	II.	6

(*a*) Including 77A. 1R. 1P. water.
(*b*) Including 33A. 1R. 23P. water.
(*c*) Including 4A. 3R. 28P. water.
(*d*) Including 7A. 2R. 19P. water.

2 C

No. of Sheet of the Ordnance Survey Maps.	Townlands and Towns.	Area in Statute Acres.	County.	Barony.	Parish.	Poor Law Union in 1857.	Townland Census of 1851, Part I.	
		A. R. P.					Vol.	Page
35	Cappateige	492 1 4	Kerry	Corkaguiny	Stradbally	Dingle	II.	180
74, 75	Cappauniac	1,563 1 29	Tipperary, S.R.	Clanwilliam	Clonbullogue	Tipperary	II.	306
75	Cappauniac	736 2 31	Tipperary, S.R.	Clanwilliam	Killardry	Tipperary	II.	308
122	Cappavarna	51 3 29	Galway	Kiltartan	Kilmacduagh	Gort	IV.	48
86	Cappaveha	179 2 30	Galway	Kilconnell	Killallaghtan	Ballinasloe	IV.	41
70, 79	Cappavicar North	171 1 32	Mayo	Carra	Turlough	Castlebar	IV.	130
79	Cappavicar South	174 3 14	Mayo	Carra	Turlough	Castlebar	IV.	130
53, 63	Cappavilla North	384 3 27	Clare	Tulla Lower	Kiltenanlea	Limerick	II.	37
63	Cappavilla South	159 0 27	Clare	Tulla Lower	Kiltenanlea	Limerick	II.	37
17	Cappawater	97 3 12	Carlow	Forth	Myshall	Carlow	I.	5
88	Cappawee	308 3 18	Kerry	Iveragh	Killemlagh	Cahersiveen	II.	196
54	Cappayuse	324 2 13	Roscommon	Moycarn	Moore	Ballinasloe	IV.	206
135	Cappeen	36 3 4	Cork, W.R.	East Carbery (E.D.)	Kilgarriff	Clonakilty	II.	128
94	Cappeen East	435 1 34	Cork, W.R.	East Carbery (W.D.)	Kinneigh	Dunmanway	II.	134
94	Cappeen West	315 2 15	Cork, W.R.	East Carbery (W.D.)	Kinneigh	Dunmanway	II.	134
7	Cappercullen	358 0 36	Limerick	Owneybeg	Abington	Limerick	II.	250
14, 17	Cappocksgreen	194 3 0	Louth	Ardee	Ardee	Ardee	I.	171
23, 27, 28	Cappog	268 2 9a	Cavan	Clankee	Knockbride	Bailieborough	III.	73
26, 27	Cappog	101 3 12b	Fermanagh	Clanawley	Rossorry	Enniskillen	III.	194
12, 17	Cappog	87 2 10	Monaghan	Dartree	Killeevan	Clones	III.	267
9	Cappog	112 3 28	Monaghan	Monaghan	Tedavnet	Monaghan	III.	278
14	Cappoge	698 0 5	Dublin	Castleknock	Castleknock	Dublin North	I.	24
18	Cappoge	400 2 10	Louth	Ardee	Cappoge	Ardee	I.	171
63	Cappoge	245 0 11	Tipperary, S.R.	Slievardagh	Kilvemnon	Callan	II.	334
18	Cappoley	441 3 15	Queen's Co.	Maryborough East	Kilcolmanbane	Mountmellick	I.	241
35	Capponellan	429 0 37	Queen's Co.	Clarmallagh	Durrow	Abbeyleix	I.	237
21	Cappoquin	86 2 18	Waterford	Coshmore&Coshbride	Lismore and Mocollop	Lismore	II.	345
21	Cappoquin Demesne	223 1 5	Waterford	Coshmore&Coshbride	Lismore and Mocollop	Lismore	II.	345
21	CAPPOQUIN T.	—	Waterford	Coshmore&Coshbride	Lismore and Mocollop	Lismore	II.	348
77, 78	Cappry	744 0 10c	Donegal	Raphoe	Stranorlar	Stranorlar	III.	142
77	Cappry (Graham)	25 0 6	Donegal	Raphoe	Stranorlar	Stranorlar	III.	142
63	Cappulcorragh	545 0 26	Mayo	Costello	Kilbeagh	Swineford	IV.	140
2	Cappusteen	29 2 30	Queen's Co.	Tinnahinch	Kilmanman	Mountmellick	I.	249
27	Cappy	129 0 4d	Fermanagh	Tirkennedy	Derrybrusk	Enniskillen	III.	220
64, 72	Cappyantanvally	317 3 27	Kerry	Dunkerron North	Knockane	Cahersiveen	II.	181
90, 104	Cappyaughna	136 0 4	Cork, W.R.	Bear	Kilcaskan	Bantry	II.	122
2	Cappydonnell Big	159 1 25	King's Co.	Kilcoursey	Ardnurcher or Horse-leap	Tullamore	I.	140
2	Cappydonnell Little	120 2 1	King's Co.	Kilcoursey	Ardnurcher or Horse-leap	Tullamore	I.	140
17, 18	Cappyroe	548 3 13	King's Co.	Geashill	Geashill	Tullamore	I.	140
37	Capragh	85 0 14	Cavan	Clanmahon	Ballymachugh	Cavan	III.	76
28, 31	Capragh	147 1 16c	Monaghan	Farney	Donaghmoyne	Carrickmacross	III.	269
36	Capranny	113 0 35	Meath	Upper Navan	Trim	Trim	I.	216
27, 28	Caran	312 3 21	Roscommon	Ballymoe	Cloonygormican	Castlereagh	IV.	191
34	Caran	334 1 12	Roscommon	Ballymoe	Drumatemple	Castlereagh	IV.	191
16	Caran	100 1 7	Roscommon	Frenchpark	Kilmacumsy	Boyle	IV.	203
103	Caranavoodaun	102 0 14	Galway	Dunkellin	Kilcolgan	Gort	IV.	28
28, 35	Caran Bog	39 3 8	Roscommon	Ballymoe	Cloonygormican	Castlereagh	IV.	191
26, 27	Caran or Enniscoffey	1,421 2 4	Westmeath	Fartullagh	Enniscoffey	Mullingar	I.	268
16	Caranlea	92 1 38	Roscommon	Frenchpark	Kilmacumsy	Boyle	IV.	203
70	Caraun	124 2 5	Galway	Clare	Lackagh	Galway	IV.	22
71	Caraun	282 2 3	Galway	Clare	Monivea	Galway	IV.	23
102	Caraun	359 2 23	Mayo	Clanmorris	Kilcolman	Claremorris	IV.	133
121, 122	Caraun or Ballyhenry	168 2 9	Mayo	Kilmaine	Kilmainebeg	Ballinrobe	IV.	155
85, 97	Caraun Beg	246 2 35	Galway	Kilconnell	Killimordaly	Loughrea	IV.	42
83, 84	Caraunduff	193 2 3	Galway	Clare	Athenry	Galway	IV.	17
106	Caraunduff	155 3 19	Galway	Leitrim	Kilmeen	Loughrea	IV.	54
70	Caraunkeelwy	116 3 7	Galway	Clare	Lackagh	Galway	IV.	22
5, 6	Caraun or Kilmaca-hill	408 1 8	Westmeath	Moygoish	Rathaspick	Mullingar	I.	280
85, 97	Caraun More	353 2 35	Galway	Kilconnell	Killimordaly	Loughrea	IV.	42
14, 15	Carbad Beg	72 0 13	Mayo	Tirawley	Templemurry	Killala	IV.	171
14, 15	Carbad More	321 2 7	Mayo	Tirawley	Templemurry	Killala	IV.	171
26	Carbalintober	277 2 33	Londonderry	Coleraine	Desertoghill	Ballymoney	III.	230
22	Carberry Island	2 1 36	Westmeath	Brawny	St. Mary's	Athlone	I.	259
36	Carberrystown	345 2 31	Meath	Lower Moyfenrath	Trim	Trim	I.	211
138, 139	Carbery Island	26 0 27	Cork, W.R.	West Carbery (W.D.)	Skull	Skull	II.	145
9	Carbullion	170 3 7f	Londonderry	Keenaght	Aghanloo	New Tn Limavady	III.	233
8	Carbury	671 1 0	Kildare	Carbury	Carbury	Edenderry	I.	51
26, 27	Carclunty	758 1 0	Antrim	Kilconway	Rasharkin	Ballymena	III.	27
47, 48, 51, 52	Carcullion	1,453 1 21	Down	Upper Iveagh, Lr. pt.	Clonduff	Newry	III.	171
14	Cardiffsbridge	143 1 6	Dublin	Castleknock	Finglas	Dublin North	I.	24

(a) Including 3A. 1R. 33P. water.
(b) Including 3A. 1R. 2P. water.
(c) Including 6A. 3R. 26P. water.
(d) Including 8A. 1R. 13P. water.
(e) Including 10A. 1R. 27P. water.
(f) Including 7A. 3R. 0P. water.

No. of Sheet of the Ordnance Survey Maps.	Townlands and Towns.	Area in Statute Acres.			County.	Barony.	Parish.	Poor Law Union in 1857.	Townland Census of 1851, Part I.	
		A.	R.	P.					Vol.	Page
14	Cardiffcastle	252	3	18	Dublin	Castleknock	Finglas	Dublin North	I.	24
35	Cardington	85	1	4	Kildare	Narragh&RebanWest	Churchtown	Athy	I.	67
35	Cardington Demesne	96	0	25a	Kildare	Narragh&RebanWest	Churchtown	Athy	I.	67
13, 14	Cardistown	230	1	1	Louth	Ardee	Clonkeen	Ardee	I.	172
32	Cardonaghy	302	2	17	Antrim	Lower Toome	Ahoghill	Ballymena	III.	31
13, 19	Cardrath	558	3	38	Meath	Upper Slane	Grangegeeth	Ardee	I.	224
11	Cardtown	531	3	34	Queen's Co.	Upperwoods	Offerlane	Mountmellick	I.	251
11, 12	Cardy	513	0	11	Down	Ards Lower	Greyabbey	Newtownards	III.	158
34, 40	Carew	131	1	9	Tipperary, N.R.	Kilnamanagh Upper	Upperchurch	Thurles	II.	280
77	Carewswood	112	1	25	Cork, E.R.	Imokilly	Ightermurragh	Middleton	II.	87
9	Carey Mill	69	0	39	Antrim	Cary	Culfeightrin	Ballycastle	III.	13
36	Careysville	291	0	19b	Cork, E.R.	Condons&Clangibbon	Clondulane	Fermoy	II.	60
41	Cargabane	240	1	10c	Down	Upper Iveagh, Up.pt.	Donaghmore	Newry	III.	175
20, 24	Cargaclogher	490	0	0	Armagh	Armagh	Keady	Armagh	III.	45
15, 22	Cargacreevy	708	1	27	Down	Kinelarty	Annahilt	Lisburn	III.	176
15	Cargacroy	688	1	0	Down	Castlereagh Upper	Drumbo	Lisburn	III.	164
12	Cargagh	24	2	17	Armagh	Armagh	Armagh	Armagh	III.	43
33	Cargagh	286	3	26	Cavan	Castlerahan	Killinkere	Bailieborough	III.	68
26, 32	Cargagh	1,038	1	4	Cavan	Upper Loughtee	Lavey	Cavan	III.	85
38	Cargagh	96	2	9	Down	Lecale Lower	Ballyculter	Downpatrick	III.	178
37	Cargagh	247	1	38	Down	Lecale Upper	Down	Downpatrick	III.	180
59, 65	Cargagh	134	2	19	Tyrone	Clogher	Clogher	Clogher	III.	292
23, 24	Cargaghbane	238	1	30	Monaghan	Cremorne	Aghnamullen	Castleblayney	III.	257
24, 25	Cargaghdoo	302	3	1	Monaghan	Cremorne	Aghnamullen	Castleblayney	III.	257
28	Cargaghlisnanarney	194	0	17	Monaghan	Farney	Donaghmoyne	Carrickmacross	III.	269
27	Cargaghmore	264	0	9	Monaghan	Farney	Magheross	Carrickmacross	III.	273
27, 30	Cargaghoge	568	1	14	Monaghan	Farney	Magheross	Carrickmacross	III.	273
19	Cargaghramer	198	2	23	Monaghan	Monaghan	Tullycorbet	Monaghan	III.	281
19	Cargalisgorran	250	3	5	Armagh	Tiranny	Derrynoose	Armagh	III.	59
24	Cargan	693	1	5	Antrim	Kilconway	Dunaghy	Ballymena	III.	25
8	Carganamuck	97	1	26	Armagh	Armagh	Grange	Armagh	III.	44
14	Cargans	695	1	24	Armagh	Orior Lower	Ballymore	Banbridge	III.	55
48	Cargin	156	0	10	Antrim	Upper Toome	Duneane	Antrim	III.	34
55	Cargin	138	3	33	Galway	Clare	Cargin	Tuam	IV.	18
28	Cargin Demesne	394	3	39	Roscommon	Roscommon	Ogulla	Strokestown	IV.	212
22	Cargygray	470	0	13d	Down	Lower Iveagh, Lr. pt.	Annahilt	Lisburn	III.	167
21	Carha	108	3	4	Cavan	Tullygarvey	Larah	Cootehill	III.	90
78	Carha	508	1	11	Mayo	Carra	Islandeady	Westport	IV.	128
31	Carha	835	2	31	Mayo	Gallen	Kilgarvan	Ballina	IV.	148
25	Carha	1,062	0	20	Sligo	Leyny	Killoran	Tobercurry	IV.	230
79	Carhan Lower	200	0	12	Kerry	Iveragh	Caher	Cahersiveen	II.	193
79, 80	Carhan Upper	553	2	17	Kerry	Iveragh	Caher	Cahersiveen	II.	194
27	Carheen	75	0	3	Clare	Tulla Upper	Feakle	Scarriff	II.	39
104	Carheen	159	1	5	Galway	Dunkellin	Killogilleen	Loughrea	IV.	31
109	Carheen	186	2	7	Mayo	Carra	Ballyovey	Ballinrobe	IV.	126
96	Carheenadiveane	205	1	4	Galway	Dunkellin	Killeeneen	Gort	IV.	30
42	Carheenard	274	2	26	Galway	Clare	Donaghpatrick	Tuam	IV.	19
57, 67	Carheenbrack	635	1	8e	Mayo	Burrishoole	Burrishoole	Newport	IV.	118
106	Carheendoo	73	0	23	Galway	Leitrim	Leitrim	Loughrea	IV.	55
70	Carheenlea	506	1	17	Galway	Clare	Lackagh	Galway	IV.	22
96	Carheennascovoge	166	2	35	Galway	Dunkellin	Killeeneen	Loughrea	IV.	30
42, 43	Carheens	425	1	24	Galway	Clare	Belclare	Tuam	IV.	17
79	Carheens	108	2	1	Mayo	Carra	Breaghwy	Castlebar	IV.	127
123	Carheens	252	1	28	Mayo	Kilmaine	Cong	Ballinrobe	IV.	153
57	Carheenshowagh	307	0	37	Galway	Clare	Cummer	Tuam	IV.	18
70	Carheeny	94	0	0	Galway	Clare	Annaghdown	Galway	IV.	16
70	Carheeny	62	0	39	Galway	Clare	Lackagh	Galway	IV.	22
4, 12	Carheeny	228	2	25	Limerick	Kenry	Kildimo	Rathkeale	II.	249
133	Carheenybaun	278	0	24f	Galway	Kiltartan	Beagh	Gort	IV.	46
128, 133	Carheeny Beg	166	1	24	Galway	Kiltartan	Beagh	Gort	IV.	46
128, 133	Carheeny More	264	2	29g	Galway	Kiltartan	Beagh	Gort	IV.	46
25	Carhoo	228	1	16	Clare	Inchiquin	Dysert	Ennis	II.	24
75	Carhoo	97	1	15	Cork, E.R.	Barrymore	Carrigtohill	Middleton	II.	52
63, 74	Carhoo	211	1	32	Cork, E.R.	Cork	Whitechurch	Cork	II.	66
18	Carhoo	97	0	5	Cork, E.R.	Fermoy	Kildorrery	Mitchelstown	II.	80
66, 67	Carhoo	192	3	17	Cork, E.R.	Imokilly	Killeagh	Youghal	II.	88
144	Carhoo	32	0	12	Cork, W.R.	Ibane and Barryroe	Ardfield	Clonakilty	II.	148
135	Carhoo	269	3	15	Cork, W.R.	Ibane and Barryroe	Kilgarriff	Clonakilty	II.	149
123, 136	Carhoo	534	3	19	Cork, W.R.	Ibane and Barryroe	Timoleague	Clonakilty	II.	151
65	Carhoobeg	225	0	14	Kerry	Dunkerron North	Knockane	Killarney	II.	181
11	Carhooearagh	1,370	0	15	Kerry	Iraghticonnor	Knockanure	Listowel	II.	192
53	Carhoo East	158	0	22	Kerry	Corkaguiny	Dingle	Dingle	II.	175
135	Carhoogarriff	281	3	35	Cork, W.R.	East Carbery (E.D.)	Kilnagross	Clonakilty	II.	129

(a) Including 3A. 3R. 14P. River Barrow.
(b) Including 20A. 2R. 10P. water.
(c) Including 13A. 3R. 8P. Loughorne.
(d) Including 2A. 2R. 33P. water.
(e) Including 2A. 3R. 26P. water.
(f) Including 17A. 2R. 33P. water.
(g) Including 26A. 0R. 22P. water.
(h) Including 6A. 3R. 24P. water.

No. of Sheet of the Ordnance Survey Maps.	Townlands and Towns.	Area in Statute Acres.	County.	Barony.	Parish.	Poor Law Union in 1857.	Townland Census of 1851, Part I.	
		A. R. P.					Vol.	Page
133, 134	Carhoogarriff .	401 1 28	Cork, W.R.	East Carbery (W.D.)	Kilmacabea	Skibbereen	II.	133
33	Carhookeal	16¼ 0 14	Cork, E.R.	Fermoy	Mallow	Mallow	II.	81
71, 72	Carhoo Lower	284 2 1a	Cork, E.R.	East Muskerry	Magourney	Macroom	II.	105
84, 93	Carhoomeengar East	223 1 5	Kerry	Glanarought	Kenmare	Kenmare	II.	185
84, 93	Carhoomeengar West	249 2 23	Kerry	Glanarought	Kenmare	Kenmare	II.	185
128	Carhoon .	88 3 19	Galway	Kiltartan	Beagh	Gort .	IV.	46
107, 117	Carhoon .	245 2 9	Galway	Longford	Tynagh	Portumna	IV.	62
153	Carhoona	42 0 15	Cork, W.R.	West Carbery (E.D.)	Clear-island	Skibbereen	II.	138
3	Carhoona	593 2 31	Kerry	Iraghticonnor	Kilnaughtin	Glin .	II.	191
65	Carhoonahone .	805 2 24	Kerry	Dunkerron North	Knockane	Killarney .	II.	181
3	Carhoonakilla .	161 2 3	Kerry	Iraghticonnor	Kilnaughtin	Glin .	II.	191
3	Carhoonakineely .	316 2 7	Kerry	Iraghticonnor	Kilnaughtin	Glin .	II.	191
5, 10	Carhoonaknock East	103 1 25	Kerry	Iraghticonnor	Galey	Listowel .	II.	190
10	Carhoonaknock West	89 2 15	Kerry	Iraghticonnor	Galey	Listowel	II.	190
42,43,52,53	Carhoonaphuca .	163 2 36	Kerry	Corkaguiny	Kildrum .	Dingle	II.	177
110	Carhoon East .	273 1 19	Cork, W.R.	Kinalmeaky	Kilbrogan	Bandon	II.	152
50	Carhoonoe .	305 1 17	Kerry	Magunihy	Nohavaldaly .	Killarney .	II.	205
97, 98	Carhoo North .	161 2 2	Cork, E.R.	Kinalea .	Ringcurran	Kinsale	II.	96
95,96,109,110	Carhoon West	530 3 5	Cork, W.R.	Kinalmeaky	Kilbrogan	Bandon	II.	152
97, 111	Carhoo South .	175 3 9	Cork, E.R.	Kinalea .	Ringcurran	Kinsale	II.	96
71, 72	Carhoo Upper .	199 0 13	Cork, E.R.	East Muskerry	Magourney	Macroom .	II.	105
121, 122	Carhoovauler .	561 2 32	Cork, W.R.	East Carbery (E.D.)	Desertserges	Clonakilty	II.	127
53	Carhoo West .	181 0 25	Kerry	Corkaguiny	Dingle	Dingle	II.	175
61	Carhue .	391 0 39	Cork, E.R.	East Muskerry	Inishcarra	Cork .	II.	103
41	Carickaleese .	202 3 38	Fermanagh	Knockninny	Tomregan	Lisnaskea	III.	203
16	*Car Island*	19 1 19	Fermanagh	Tirkennedy	Trory .	Enniskillen	III.	224
60, 68	Cark .	2,684 2 32b	Donegal .	Raphoe .	Convoy .	Stranorlar	III.	136
17, 18	Carker .	239 0 38	Cork, E.R.	Fermoy .	Doneraile	Mallow .	II.	78
49	Carker .	938 2 31	Kerry	Trughanacmy .	Ballincuslane	Tralee	II.	206
17	Carkerbeg .	245 2 13	Cork, E.R.	Fermoy .	Doneraile	Mallow .	II.	78
8, 9, 17, 18	Carker Middle .	514 1 39	Cork, E.R.	Fermoy .	Doneraile	Mallow .	II.	78
8, 9	Carker North .	1,109 1 20	Cork, E.R.	Fermoy .	Doneraile	Mallow .	II.	78
10	Carkfree .	191 1 4c	Roscommon	Boyle .	Estersnow	Boyle .	IV.	195
101	Carks .	447 2 0	Kerry	Glanarought	Tuosist	Kenmare .	II.	188
48	Carlane .	480 2 32	Antrim	Upper Toome .	Duneane .	Antrim .	III.	34
17,18,27,28	Carlan Lower .	257 2 30	Donegal .	Kilmacrenan .	Clondavaddog .	Millford .	III.	124
11	Carlanstown .	324 0 22	Meath .	Lower Kells .	Kilbeg .	Kells .	I.	202
1, 3	Carlanstown .	1,349 1 11d	Westmeath	Fore .	Lickbla .	Granard .	I.	270
11	CARLANSTOWN T.	—	Meath .	Lower Kells .	Kilbeg .	Kells .	I.	203
27, 28	Carlan Upper .	389 3 2	Donegal .	Kilmacrenan .	Clondavaddog .	Millford .	III.	124
16	Carlaragh .	115 0 10	Londonderry	Keenaght .	Tamlaght Finlagan .	NewTⁿLimavady	III.	237
5, 8, 9	Carlingford, Liberties of	2,321 3 2	Louth .	Dundalk Lower	Carlingford .	Dundalk .	I.	176
5	CARLINGFORD T.	—	Louth .	Dundalk Lower	Carlingford .	Dundalk .	I.	177
87,88,99,100	Carlislefort .	140 0 2	Cork, E.R.	Imokilly .	Corkbeg .	Middleton .	II.	86
7	Carlow .	978 0 26e	Carlow .	Carlow .	Carlow .	Carlow .	I.	1
7	CARLOW T.	—	Carlow .	Carlow .	Carlow .	Carlow .	I.	1
37	Carmacmoin .	152 3 37	Antrim .	Lower Toome .	Ahoghill .	Ballymena .	III.	31
36	Carmagrim .	919 2 38	Antrim .	Lower Toome .	Ahoghill .	Ballymena .	III.	31
22, 23	Carmanhall .	117 2 8	Dublin .	Rathdown .	Tully .	Rathdown .	I.	38
23, 26	Carmanhall and Leopardstown	277 2 35	Dublin .	Rathdown .	Tully .	Rathdown .	I.	38
55	Carmavy, Grange of	789 0 27	Antrim .	Lower Massereene .	Killead .	Antrim .	III.	28
46	Carmean .	238 0 39	Londonderry	Loughinsholin .	Desertlyn .	Magherafelt .	III.	240
47, 51	Carmeen .	562 3 27	Down .	Upper Iveagh.Up. pt.	Clonallan .	Newry .	III.	174
27	Carmoney .	598 2 24f	Donegal .	Kilmacrenan .	Kilmacrenan .	Millford .	III.	129
14	Carmoney .	144 2 24	Londonderry	Tirkeeran .	Faughanvale .	Londonderry .	III.	250
48	Carmorn .	73 3 30	Antrim .	Upper Toome .	Duneane .	Antrim .	III.	34
6	Carn .	193 1 37	Armagh .	Oneilland East .	Seagoe .	Lurgan .	III.	50
38	Carn .	265 1 17	Cavan .	Castlerahan .	Castlerahan .	Oldcastle .	III.	67
14	Carn .	227 2 28g	Cavan .	Tullyhunco .	Kildallan .	Bawnboy .	III.	96
26, 32	Carn .	262 1 6	Cavan .	Upper Loughtee .	Denn .	Cavan .	III.	83
78, 87	Carn .	904 0 6h	Donegal .	Raphoe .	Donaghmore .	Stranorlar .	III.	137
101, 105	Carn .	791 2 35	Donegal .	Tirhugh .	Templecarn .	Donegal .	III.	149
21	Carn .	122 3 14	Fermanagh	Clanawley .	Boho .	Enniskillen .	III.	189
33, 38	Carn .	243 2 32	Fermanagh	Knockninny .	Kinawley .	Lisnaskea .	III.	201
6	Carn .	176 1 17	Fermanagh	Lurg .	Magheraculmoney .	Lowtherstown .	III.	207
17	Carn .	177 1 32	Fermanagh	Tirkennedy .	Enniskillen .	Enniskillen .	III.	221
105	Carn .	225 1 3	Galway .	Loughrea .	Loughrea .	Loughrea .	IV.	65
28	Carn .	276 2 7i	Kildare .	Offaly East .	Carn .	Naas .	I.	69
25, 31	Carn .	1,361 0 30	Londonderry	Keenaght .	Dungiven .	NewTⁿLimavady	III.	236
14, 20	Carn .	214 0 34j	Londonderry	Tirkeeran .	Clondermot .	Londonderry .	III.	247
19, 23	Carn .	287 1 15	Longford .	Shrule .	Kilglass .	Ballymahon .	I.	166
99	Carn .	505 1 12	Mayo .	Carra .	Ballintober .	Castlebar .	IV.	124

(a) Including 9A. 1R. 13P. water.
(b) Including 25A. 3R. 14P. water.
(c) Including 0A. 3R. 6P. water.
(d) Including 10A. 3R. 26P. water.

(e) Including 12A. 2R. 20P. River Barrow.
(f) Including 5A. 3R. 9P. water.
(g) Including 7A. 0R. 0P. water.

(h) Including 4A. 0R. 15P. water.
(i) Including 1A. 3R. 18P. detached portion.
(j) Including 6A. 2R. 12P. water.

No. of Sheet of the Ordnance Survey Maps.	Townlands and Towns.	Area in Statute Acres.			County.	Barony.	Parish.	Poor Law Union in 1857.	Townland Census of 1851, Part I.	
		A.	R.	P.					Vol.	Page
78, 79	Carn . . .	128	1	24	Mayo . .	Carra . . .	Breaghwy . .	Castlebar . .	IV.	127
62, 72	Carn . . .	158	1	13	Mayo . .	Costello . .	Kilbeagh . .	Swineford . .	IV.	140
72	Carn . . .	367	0	0	Mayo . .	Gallen . . .	Kilconduff . .	Swineford . .	IV.	147
117, 118,⎫ 120, 121⎬	Carn . . .	212	1	23	Mayo . .	Kilmaine . .	Ballinchalla . .	Ballinrobe . .	IV.	152
117, 118	Carn . . .	94	3	21	Mayo . .	Kilmaine . .	Ballinrobe . .	Ballinrobe . .	IV.	152
14	Carn . . .	620	2	39	Mayo . .	Tirawley . .	Lackan . .	Killala . .	IV.	170
21	Carn . . .	239	3	32	Mayo . .	Tirawley . .	Moygawnagh . .	Killala . .	II.	171
12, 13, 18	Carn . . .	319	2	18	Monaghan .	Dartree . .	Aghabog . .	Monaghan . .	III.	263
11	Carn . . .	145	1	7	Monaghan .	Dartree . .	Clones . .	Clones . .	III.	264
9, 10	Carn . . .	60	1	1	Monaghan .	Monaghan . .	Tehallan . .	Monaghan . .	III.	280
1	Carn . . .	166	0	16	Westmeath .	Fore . . .	Foyran . .	Granard . .	I.	270
3	Carn . . .	724	0	29	Westmeath .	Fore . . .	Mayne . .	Granard . .	I.	271
24, 25	Carn . . .	733	3	27	Westmeath .	Rathconrath .	Conry . .	Mullingar . .	I.	282
64, 76, 77	Carna . .	1,080	1	32a	Galway . .	Ballynahinch .	Moyrus . .	Clifden . .	IV.	12
53	Carna . .	25	0	18	Wexford . .	Forth . . .	Carn . .	Wexford . .	I.	309
4	Carnaboy . .	162	0	21	Londonderry .	North East Liberties of Coleraine .	Ballywillin . .	Coleraine . .	III.	245
25	Carnacally . .	100	1	33	Armagh . .	Orior Upper . .	Forkill . .	Newry . .	III.	57
30	Carnacally . .	427	1	36	Down . .	Castlereagh Upper .	Kilmore . .	Downpatrick . .	III.	165
40,41,46,47	Carnacally . .	516	0	34	Down . .	Lordship of Newry .	Newry . .	Newry . .	III.	182
2, 5	Carnacally . .	299	2	18	Meath . .	Lower Kells . .	Kilmainham . .	Kells . .	I.	203
43, 49	Carnacavill . .	536	0	30	Down . .	Upper Iveagh, Lr. pt.	Maghera . .	Kilkeel . .	III.	173
6, 12	Carnacop . .	317	1	32	Meath . .	Morgallion . .	Castletown . .	Navan . .	I.	209
20, 21	Carnafarn . .	342	0	38	Londonderry .	Tirkeeran . .	Clondermot . .	Londonderry . .	III.	247
37	Carnafeagh . .	103	3	0	Donegal . .	Kilmacrenan .	Killygarvan . .	Milford . .	III.	128
12	Carnaff . . .	268	3	21	Antrim . .	Lower Dunluce .	Derrykeighan . .	Ballymoney . .	III.	16
23	Carnagall . .	314	0	29	Antrim . .	Kilconway . .	Loughguile . .	Ballymoney . .	III.	27
34	Carnagarve . .	618	2	32	Cavan . .	Castlerahan . .	Killinkere . .	Bailieborough . .	III.	68
13, 22	Carnagarve . .	743	2	26	Donegal . .	Inishowen East .	Moville Lower . .	Inishowen . .	III.	118
26	Carnagat . .	210	3	23	Armagh . .	Orior Upper . .	Killevy . .	Newry . .	III.	58
58	Carnagat . .	446	0	6	Tyrone . .	Clogher . .	Clogher . .	Clogher . .	III.	292
18	Carnageeragh .	204	0	9	Antrim . .	Upper Dunluce .	Kilraghts . .	Ballymoney . .	III.	19
34, 35	Carnagh . .	753	3	0	Wexford . .	Bantry . .	Carnagh . .	New Ross . .	I.	299
37, 38	Carnaghan . .	279	0	32	Donegal . .	Inishowen West .	Inch . .	Londonderry . .	fII.	121
45, 46	Carnagh East . .	864	2	2	Roscommon .	Athlone . .	St. Johns . .	Athlone . .	IV.	183
56, 59, 60	Carnaghliss . .	1,464	3	25	Antrim . .	Lower Massereene .	Killead . .	Antrim . .	III.	28
36, 37	Carnagh Lower .	361	0	19	Cavan . .	Clanmahon . .	Drumlumman . .	Granard . .	III.	77
37, 38	Carnaghts . .	382	1	25	Antrim . .	Lower Antrim .	Connor . .	Ballymena . .	III.	3
36, 37	Carnagh Upper .	277	3	3	Cavan . .	Clanmahon . .	Drumlumman . .	Granard . .	III.	77
45	Carnagh West .	459	0	27	Roscommon .	Athlone . .	St. Johns . .	Athlone . .	IV.	183
26, 27	Carnagore . .	137	0	36	Donegal . .	Kilmacrenan .	Mevagh . .	Milford . .	III.	130
3, 6	Carnagribban .	329	1	5	Tyrone . .	Strabane Lower .	Donaghedy . .	Strabane . .	III.	320
20	Carnahagh . .	53	3	37	Antrim . .	Lower Glenarm .	Layd . .	Ballycastle . .	III.	22
58, 64	Carnahinny . .	69	3	28	Tyrone . .	Clogher . .	Clogher . .	Clogher . .	III.	292
85	Carnakelly . .	70	2	39	Galway . .	Athenry . .	Kiltullagh . .	Loughrea . .	IV.	5
84, 85	Carnakelly North .	788	2	24	Galway . .	Kilconnell . .	Kiltullagh . .	Loughrea . .	IV.	42
84, 85	Carnakelly South .	383	1	3	Galway . .	Kilconnell . .	Kiltullagh . .	Loughrea . .	IV.	42
15	Carnakilly Lower .	254	1	17	Londonderry .	Tirkeeran . .	Faughanvale . .	Londonderry . .	III.	250
15	Carnakilly Upper .	144	3	23	Londonderry .	Tirkeeran . .	Faughanvale . .	Londonderry . .	III.	250
21, 22	Carnakit . .	410	3	17	Roscommon .	Castlereagh . .	Baslick . .	Castlereagh . .	IV.	199
29, 34	Carnalbanagh .	1,628	2	36	Antrim . .	Lower Glenarm .	Tickmacrevan . .	Larne . .	III.	23
3	Carnalbanagh . .	51	1	11	Londonderry .	North East Liberties of Coleraine .	Ballyaghran . .	Coleraine . .	III.	244
13	Carnalbanagh East .	22	3	3	Down . .	Lower Iveagh, Up. pt.	Moira . .	Lurgan . .	III.	170
13	Carnalbanagh West	11	3	25	Down . .	Lower Iveagh, Up. pt.	Moira . .	Lurgan . .	III.	170
1, 2	Carnalea . .	266	1	21	Down . .	Ards Lower . .	Bangor . .	Newtownards . .	III.	157
51	Carnalea . .	229	3	29	Tyrone . .	Clogher . .	Donacavey . .	Omagh . .	III.	294
41, 49	Carnalea . .	530	1	3	Tyrone . .	Omagh East . .	Dromore . .	Omagh . .	III.	311
28, 31	Carnally . .	811	2	0	Armagh . .	Fews Upper . .	Creggan . .	Dundalk . .	III.	48
3	Carnalridge . .	109	0	7	Londonderry .	North East Liberties of Coleraine .	Ballywillin . .	Coleraine . .	III.	245
11	Carnalughoge .	108	1	22	Louth . .	Louth . .	Louth . .	Dundalk . .	I.	184
24, 29	Carnalway . .	752	3	15b	Kildare . .	Naas South . .	Carnalway . .	Naas . .	I.	64
34	Carnalynch . .	468	2	37	Cavan . .	Castlerahan . .	Killinkere . .	Bailieborough . .	III.	68
14	Carnamaddy . .	294	2	29	Antrim . .	Lower Glenarm .	Grange of Layd .	Ballycastle . .	III.	22
18, 23	Carnamenagh . .	581	2	35	Antrim . .	Kilconway . .	Loughguile . .	Ballymoney . .	III.	27
53	Carnamogagh Lower	393	0	39	Donegal . .	Kilmacrenan .	Conwal . .	Letterkenny . .	III.	126
53	Carnamogagh Upper	210	1	30	Donegal . .	Kilmacrenan .	Conwal . .	Letterkenny . .	III.	126
35, 36	Carnamoney . .	934	3	12	Londonderry .	Loughinsholin .	Ballynascreen . .	Magherafelt . .	III.	238
29,30,38,39	Carnamoyle . .	2,927	1	29	Donegal . .	Inishowen West .	Muff . .	Londonderry . .	III.	121
4, 5	Carnamuck . .	225	1	18	Down . .	Castlereagh Upper .	Knockbreda . .	Belfast . .	III.	165
9, 15, 16	Carnamuff . .	1,172	0	7	Londonderry .	Tirkeeran . .	Faughanvale . .	NewTᵃLimavady	III.	250
19, 20	Carnan . .	267	0	27	Longford . .	Ardagh . .	Ardagh . .	Longford . .	I.	151

(a) Including 109ᴀ. 0ʀ. 28ᴘ. water.   (b) Including 20ᴀ. 2ʀ. 8ᴘ. water.

No. of Sheet of the Ordnance Survey Maps.	Townlands and Towns.	Area in Statute Acres.	County.	Barony.	Parish.	Poor Law Union in 1857.	Townland Census of 1851, Part I.	
		A. R. P.					Vol.	Page
39, 47	Carnan	465 3 13	Tyrone	Dungannon Upper	Arboe	Cookstown	III.	305
30, 31, 35	Carnanbane	1,581 3 22	Londonderry	Keenaght	Banagher	NewTⁿLimavady	III.	234
29	Carnanbane	300 3 0	Londonderry	Tirkeeran	Cumber Upper, now Learmount	Londonderry	III.	249
7, 12	Carnanbregagh	107 1 5	Louth	Upper Dundalk	Ballybarrack	Dundalk	I.	177
22	Carnane	455 2 15	Limerick	Smallcounty	Fedamore	Croom	II.	259
51	Carnanee	385 2 0	Antrim	Lower Belfast	Ballymartin	Antrim	III.	7
20	Carnanee	28 1 10	Antrim	Lower Glenarm	Layd	Ballycastle	III.	22
3	Carnanee	53 3 39	Londonderry	North East Liberties of Coleraine	Ballyaghran	Coleraine	III.	244
19	Carnanransy	339 1 25	Tyrone	Strabane Upper	Bodoney Lower	Gortin	III.	323
7	Carnanreagh	120 2 7	Antrim	Lower Dunluce	Billy	Coleraine	III.	16
29	Carnanreagh	888 3 3	Londonderry	Tirkeeran	Cumber Upper, now Learmount	Londonderry	III.	249
34	Carnans Lower	206 1 27	Cavan	Clankee	Moybolgue	Bailieborough	III.	74
34	Carnans Upper	150 2 33	Cavan	Clankee	Moybolgue	Bailieborough	III.	74
104	Carnanthomas	58 2 18	Galway	Dunkellin	Killora	Loughrea	IV.	31
47	Carnany	337 2 18	Down	Upper Iveagh, Up.pt.	Drumgath	Newry	III.	175
17	Carnany Lower	99 3 34	Antrim	Upper Dunluce	Ballymoney	Ballymoney	III.	18
17	Carnany Upper	187 1 15	Antrim	Upper Dunluce	Ballymoney	Ballymoney	III.	18
10, 11, 18	Carnargan	310 1 27a	Tyrone	Strabane Upper	Bodoney Upper	Gortin	III.	324
10	Carnaross	139 0 25	Meath	Upper Kells	Loughan or Castlekeeran	Kells	I.	206
51	Carnarousk	46 1 28	Tyrone	Clogher	Donacavey	Omagh	III.	294
38	Carnashannagh	270 0 10	Donegal	Inishowen West	Fahan Upper	Londonderry	III.	121
15	Carnasheeran	124 3 32	Antrim	Lower Glenarm	Layd	Ballycastle	III.	22
10	Carnasure	399 2 25	Down	Castlereagh Lower	Comber	Newtownards	III.	162
44	Carnatreantagh	448 0 1	Donegal	Kilmacrenan	Conwal	Letterkenny	III.	126
8	Carnaun	638 3 7	Clare	Corcomroe	Killilagh	Ennistimon	II.	19
25	Carnaun	147 1 20	Clare	Inchiquin	Rath	Corrofin	II.	27
57, 67	Carnaun	496 1 11	Clare	Moyarta	Kilrush	Kilrush	II.	33
84	Carnaun	486 1 0	Galway	Athenry	Athenry	Galway	IV.	3
29	Carnaun	58 2 39	Galway	Dunmore	Tuam	Tuam	IV.	35
98	Carnaun	98 2 25	Galway	Leitrim	Kilreekill	Loughrea	IV.	54
16	Carnavanaghan	632 3 32	Armagh	Fews Lower	Kilclooney	Armagh	III.	46
29	Carnave	116 1 14	Antrim	Lower Glenarm	Tickmacrevan	Larne	III.	23
24	Carnaveagh	458 0 27b	Monaghan	Cremorne	Aghnamullen	Castleblayney	III.	257
17	Carnaveagh	102 2 31	Tyrone	Strabane Lower	Ardstraw	Gortin	III.	318
34, 40	Carnaweeleen	210 3 24	Sligo	Corran	Toomour	Sligo	IV.	228
22, 26	Carnbane	200 0 19c	Armagh	Orior Upper	Newry	Newry	III.	58
14	Carnbane	527 3 12	Down	Lower Iveagh, Up.pt.	Blaris	Lisburn	III.	169
9, 15	Carnbane	69 1 4	Meath	Fore	Loughcrew	Oldcastle	I.	201
13	Carnbane	82 2 33	Monaghan	Monaghan	Drumsnat	Monaghan	III.	275
94	Carnbeagh North	89 2 24	Donegal	Tirhugh	Donegal	Donegal	III.	145
94	Carnbeagh South	60 2 11	Donegal	Tirhugh	Donegal	Donegal	III.	145
27	Carn-beg	153 1 13	Antrim	Kilconway	Dunaghy	Ballymena	III.	25
23	Carnbeg	95 3 12	Antrim	Kilconway	Killagan	Ballymoney	III.	27
4, 7	Carn Beg	135 1 7	Louth	Upper Dundalk	Dundalk	Dundalk	I.	178
82, 93	Carn Beg	164 0 18	Mayo	Costello	Aghamore	Swineford	IV.	136
91, 97	Carn Beg Glebe	58 3 35	Donegal	Banagh	Killaghtee	Glenties	III.	109
7	Carnbore	355 3 30	Antrim	Lower Dunluce	Billy	Ballymoney	III.	16
32	Carnboy	236 0 1d	Donegal	Boylagh	Templecrone	Glenties	III.	115
47, 53	Carnbrock	249 0 35	Antrim	Lower Belfast	Templecorran	Larne	III.	9
18,19,23,24	Carnbuck	2,629 2 25	Antrim	Kilconway	Loughguile	Ballymoney	III.	27
8, 14, 15	Carncash	198 2 17	Sligo	Carbury	Calry	Sligo	IV.	220
21	Carnclogh	330 2 0	Mayo	Tirawley	Moygawnagh	Killala	II.	171
27, 28	Carncoagh	716 2 32	Antrim	Lower Antrim	Skerry	Ballymena	III.	4
12	Carncoggy	172 3 25	Antrim	Lower Dunluce	Derrykeighan	Ballymoney	III.	16
3	Carncolp	177 2 33	Antrim	Cary	Billy	Ballycastle	III.	12
38, 44	Carncone	337 0 2	Antrim	Lower Antrim	Connor	Antrim	III.	3
16, 24	Carncorran Glebe	243 3 10	Tyrone	Omagh West	Ardstraw	Castlederg	III.	315
46	Carncose	495 0 0	Londonderry	Loughinsholin	Desertmartin	Magherafelt	III.	240
39, 40	Carncreagh	839 2 13	Clare	Islands	Kilmaley	Ennis	II.	31
12	Carncullagh Lower	173 2 4	Antrim	Lower Dunluce	Derrykeighan	Ballymoney	III.	16
12	Carncullagh Middle	104 1 17	Antrim	Lower Dunluce	Derrykeighan	Ballymoney	III.	16
12	Carncullagh Upper	431 3 21	Antrim	Lower Dunluce	Derrykeighan	Ballymoney	III.	16
8	Carn or Curraghane	740 0 27	Queen's Co.	Portnahinch	Coolbanagher	Mountmellick	I.	244
46	Carndaisy	617 0 5	Londonderry	Loughinsholin	Desertlyn	Magherafelt	III.	230
4, 10, 11	Carndoagh	607 3 7	Donegal	Inishowen East	Donagh	Inishowen	III.	118
11	CARNDONAGH T.	—	Donegal	Inishowen East	Donagh	Inishowen	III.	118
11, 12	Carndougan	134 1 5	Londonderry	Coleraine	Macosquin	Coleraine	III.	233
15	Carndreen	177 1 39	Tyrone	Omagh West	Termonamongan	Castlederg	III.	317
4	Carnduff	147 2 21	Antrim	Cary	Ramoan	Ballycastle	III.	14
40	Carnduff	408 1 0	Antrim	Lower Belfast	Inver	Larne	III.	8

(a) Including 2A. 2R. 15P. water.
(b) Including 23A. 0R. 32P. water.
(c) Including 5A. 2R. 32P. water.
(d) Including 11A. 1R. 28P. water.

No. of Sheet of the Ordnance Survey Maps.	Townlands and Towns.	Area in Statute Acres.			County.	Barony.	Parish.	Poor Law Union in 1857.	Townland Census of 1851, Part I.	
		A.	R.	P.					Vol.	Page
46	Carneal	673	2	28	Antrim	Lower Belfast	Raloo	Larne	III.	9
37	Carnearney	201	3	29	Antrim	Lower Toome	Ahoghill	Ballymena	III.	31
44	Carnearny	1,091	1	33	Antrim	Lower Antrim	Connor	Antrim	III.	3
8	Carneatly	639	3	32	Antrim	Carey	Ramoan	Ballycastle	III.	14
17	Carneatly	288	2	19	Antrim	Upper Dunluce	Ballymoney	Ballymoney	III.	18
2, 6	Carneety	78	0	32	Londonderry	Coleraine	Dunboe	Coleraine	III.	231
16	Carnelrussel	36	1	10	Meath	Upper Kells	Kilskeer	Oldcastle	I.	206
37, 38	Carnenny	305	0	3	Tyrone	Dungannon Upper	Desertcreat	Cookstown	III.	307
27, 33	Carnes East	307	2	28	Meath	Upper Duleek	Duleek	Drogheda	I.	197
27, 33	Carnes West	300	0	3	Meath	Upper Duleek	Duleek	Drogheda	I.	197
10, 17	Carnet	161	2	31	Londonderry	Keenaght	Balteagh	NewTⁿLimavady	III.	234
28, 35	Carnew	925	1	38	Down	Lower Iveagh, Lr. Pt.	Garvaghy	Banbridge	III.	168
47	Carnew	936	2	19	Wicklow	Shillelagh	Carnew	Shillelagh	I.	357
47	CARNEW T.	—			Wicklow	Shillelagh	Carnew	Shillelagh	I.	357
9, 10, 15	Carneybeg	350	0	19	Tipperary, N.R.	Lower Ormond	Cloghprior	Borrisokane	II.	282
9, 10	Carneybrack	123	0	10	Tipperary, N.R.	Lower Ormond	Cloghprior	Borrisokane	II.	282
9, 10	Carneycastle	176	3	37	Tipperary, N.R.	Lower Ormond	Cloghprior	Borrisokane	II.	282
9, 10	Carney, Commons of	280	2	32	Tipperary, N.R.	Lower Ormond	Finnoe	Borrisokane	II.	284
22, 26	Carney Hill	114	1	37	Antrim	Kilconway	Finvoy	Ballymoney	III.	26
7	Carney Hill	113	2	10	Down	Ards Lower	Donaghadee	Newtownards	III.	158
27	Carneyhill	169	2	32	Fermanagh	Clanawley	Cleenish	Enniskillen	III.	189
40	Carneyhome	204	2	19	Fermanagh	Clankelly	Clones	Clones	III.	195
46, 47	Carneyhough	342	3	28	Down	Lordship of Newry	Newry	Newry	III.	182
8	Carney (Jones)	57	3	17	Sligo	Carbury	Drumcliff	Sligo	IV.	221
8	Carney (O'Beirne)	76	1	26	Sligo	Carbury	Drumcliff	Sligo	IV.	221
12	Carneys Island	109	1	21a	Monaghan	Dartree	Clones	Clones	III.	264
8	CARNEY T.	—			Sligo	Carbury	Drumcliff	Sligo	IV.	222
9, 10	Carneywoodlands	411	3	4	Tipperary, N.R.	Lower Ormond	Cloghprior	Borrisokane	II.	282
12, 13	Carnfeogue	209	1	36	Antrim	Lower Dunluce	Derrykeighan	Ballymoney	III.	16
26	Carnfinton	544	1	6	Antrim	Kilconway	Rasharkin	Ballymoney	III.	27
9, 10	Carn (Fowler)	675	3	29	Mayo	Erris	Kilmore	Belmullet	IV.	145
35	Carnfunnock	193	3	34	Antrim	Upper Glenarm	Carncastle	Larne	III.	24
30	Carnfyan	28	3	9	Westmeath	Clonlonan	Ballyloughloe	Athlone	I.	260
18, 28	Carngarrow	313	0	31	Donegal	Kilmacrenan	Clondavaddog	Millford	III.	124
34	Carnglass	405	1	20	Waterford	Coshmore & Coshbride	Kilcockan	Lismore	II.	343
6, 11	Carnglass Beg	84	0	25	Antrim	Lower Dunluce	Ballyrashane	Coleraine	III.	15
6	Carnglass More	106	0	28	Antrim	Lower Dunluce	Ballyrashane	Coleraine	III.	15
43, 44, 49, 50	Carngranny	260	1	33	Antrim	Upper Toome	Antrim	Antrim	III.	33
36, 37	Carn High	471	3	27b	Donegal	Kilmacrenan	Tullyfern	Millford	III.	133
46	Carnhill	85	3	10	Donegal	Kilmacrenan	Aughnish	Millford	III.	122
8	Carnhill	100	2	37	Dublin	Balrothery East	Lusk	Balrothery	I.	21
11	Carnhill	597	3	12	Mayo	Erris	Kilcommon	Belmullet	IV.	143
38	Carnin	390	3	23	Cavan	Castlerahan	Castlerahan	Oldcastle	III.	67
32	Carniny	206	3	34	Antrim	Lower Toome	Ahoghill	Ballymena	III.	31
9, 14	Carnirk	312	0	15c	Fermanagh	Magheraboy	Inishmacsaint	Ballyshannon	III.	212
45	Carnisk	179	0	22	Donegal	Kilmacrenan	Conwal	Millford	III.	126
45	Carnisk	54	2	13	Donegal	Kilmacrenan	Tullyfern	Millford	III.	133
33	Carnkeeran	322	1	17	Antrim	Lower Antrim	Skerry	Ballymena	III.	4
17	Carnkenny	629	2	27d	Tyrone	Strabane Lower	Ardstraw	Strabane	III.	318
59, 63	Carnkilly Lower	132	3	25	Antrim	Upper Massereene	Glenavy	Lisburn	III.	30
59	Carnkilly Upper	72	1	3	Antrim	Upper Massereene	Glenavy	Lisburn	III.	30
3, 7	Carnkirk	587	0	15e	Antrim	Cary	Billy	Ballycastle	III.	12
8, 13	Carnkirn	231	3	27	Antrim	Cary	Grange of Drumtullagh	Ballycastle	III.	14
39, 45	Carnlea	1,096	1	33	Antrim	Antrim Upper	Rashee	Antrim	III.	7
27	Carnlea	597	2	10	Antrim	Lower Toome	Kirkinriola	Ballymena	III.	32
7, 8	Carnlelis	432	3	5	Antrim	Cary	Ballintoy	Ballycastle	III.	12
67	Carnlougherin	301	1	16	Antrim	Upper Massereene	Magheramesk	Lisburn	III.	31
25	Carnlough North	143	1	25	Antrim	Lower Glenarm	Ardclinis	Larne	III.	21
25	Carnlough South	33	3	13f	Antrim	Lower Glenarm	Ardclinis	Larne	III.	21
25	CARNLOUGH T.	—			Antrim	Lower Glenarm	Ardclinis / Tickmacreevan	Larne	III.	21 / 24
37, 45, 46	Carn Low	222	0	26	Donegal	Kilmacrenan	Tullyfern	Millford	III.	133
5, 6	Carnmaclean	186	0	22	Cavan	Tullyhaw	Templeport	Enniskillen	III.	94
42, 43	Carnmallow	129	2	14	Clare	Bunratty Upper	Quin	Tulla	II.	10
46	Carnmeen	362	3	15	Down	Lordship of Newry	Newry	Newry	III.	182
56, 57	Carnmoney	456	1	28	Antrim	Lower Belfast	Carnmoney	Belfast	III.	7
56	Carnmoney Bog	96	0	33	Antrim	Lower Belfast	Carnmoney	Belfast	III.	7
56, 57	Carnmoney Glebe	82	2	36	Antrim	Lower Belfast	Carnmoney	Belfast	III.	7
4	Carnmoon	110	0	10	Antrim	Cary	Ramoan	Ballycastle	III.	14
7	Carnmoon	256	1	5	Antrim	Lower Dunluce	Billy	Ballymoney	III.	16
27	Carn-more	161	1	24	Antrim	Kilconway	Dunaghy	Ballymena	III.	25
29, 35	Carnmore	349	3	24	Fermanagh	Clankelly	Clones	Clones	III.	195
83	Carnmore	169	2	38	Galway	Clare	Athenry	Galway	IV.	17

(a) Including 4A. 0R. 33P. water.
(b) Including 13A. 0R. 18P. water.

(c) Including 12A. 3R. 39P. water.
(d) Including 7A. 0R. 4P. water.

(e) Including 9A. 0R. 15P. water.
(f) Including 1A. 1R. 1P. Mill Tenement.

No. of Sheet of the Ordnance Survey Maps.	Townlands and Towns.	Area in Statute Acres.	County.	Barony.	Parish.	Poor Law Union in 1857.	Townland Census of 1851, Part I.	
		A. R. P.					Vol.	Page
4, 7	Carn More	72 0 17	Louth	Upper Dundalk	Dundalk	Dundalk	I.	178
82, 93	Carn More	196 2 27	Mayo	Costello	Aghamore	Swineford	IV.	136
83	Carnmore East	88 2 1	Galway	Clare	Claregalway	Galway	IV.	18
91,92,97,98	Carn More Glebe	140 1 24	Donegal	Banagh	Killaghtee	Glenties	III.	109
83	Carnmore West	2,186 0 34	Galway	Dunkellin	Claregalway	Galway	IV.	27
9	Carn (Nash)	649 0 37a	Mayo	Erris	Kilmore	Belmullet	IV.	145
16	Carnoge	27 3 11	Cavan	Upper Loughtee	Castleterra	Cavan	III.	82
26	Carnony	185 1 21	Tyrone	Strabane Upper	Cappagh	Omagh	III.	325
15	Carnoughter	787 2 9	Tyrone	Omagh West	Termonamongan	Castlederg	III.	317
69, 70, 79	Carnowen	1,672 2 29	Donegal	Raphoe	Donaghmore	Strabane	III.	137
12	Carnowen	144 0 11	Monaghan	Dartree	Killeevan	Clones	III.	267
2	Carnowry	236 3 0	Londonderry	Keenaght	Magilligan	NewTⁿLimavady	III.	236
29, 30	Carnpark	868 3 27	Westmeath	Clonlonan	Ballyloughloe	Athlone	I.	260
5	Carnquill	157 0 35	Monaghan	Monaghan	Tedavnet	Monaghan	III.	278
14	Carnreagh	383 2 21	Down	Lower Iveagh, Up. pt.	Blaris	Lisburn	III.	169
6	Carnroe	108 2 4	Louth	Upper Dundalk	Dunbin	Dundalk	I.	178
16, 17	Carnroe	622 2 0	Monaghan	Dartree	Currin	Clones	III.	265
28	Carns	391 0 1	Roscommon	Roscommon	Ogulla	Strokestown	IV.	212
14, 15	Carns	349 2 13	Sligo	Carbury	St. John's	Sligo	IV.	223
36, 37	Carns	330 2 1	Sligo	Leyny	Kilmacteige	Tobercurry	IV.	231
17, 23	Carns	1,164 3 24	Sligo	Tireragh	Castleconor	Dromore West	IV.	232
4, 8	Carnsampson	497 2 3	Antrim	Cary	Ramoan	Ballycastle	III.	14
14	Carns (Duke)	76 2 29	Sligo	Carbury	St. John's	Sligo	IV.	223
62	Carnshannagh	296 2 16	Donegal	Raphoe	Taughboyne	Strabane	III.	143
3	Carnside	175 3 37	Antrim	Cary	Billy	Ballycastle	III.	12
41	Carnspindle	217 3 6	Antrim	Lower Belfast	Islandmagee	Larne	III.	8
33, 34	Carnstroan	935 1 25	Antrim	Lower Antrim	Racavan	Ballymena	III.	4
51, 52	Carntall	1,085 3 10	Antrim	Lower Belfast	Ballylinny	Antrim	III.	7
58	Carntall Beg	96 3 4	Tyrone	Clogher	Clogher	Clogher	III.	292
58	Carntall More	161 3 26	Tyrone	Clogher	Clogher	Clogher	III.	292
60	Carnteel	235 2 35b	Tyrone	Dungannon Lower	Carnteel	Dungannon	III.	297
60	CARNTEEL T.	—	Tyrone	Dungannon Lower	Carnteel	Dungannon	III.	298
31	CARN T.	—	Londonderry	Keenaght	Dungiven	NewTⁿLimavady	III.	236
21	Carntown	427 0 21	Louth	Drogheda	Ballymakenny	Drogheda	I.	175
21	Carntown	86 3 0	Louth	Drogheda	St. Peter's	Drogheda	I.	175
105	Carntressy	502 1 28c	Donegal	Tirhugh	Templecarn	Donegal	III.	149
28, 34	Carntrone	192 1 4	Fermanagh	Magherastephana	Aghavea	Lisnaskea	III.	218
97	Carntullagh	217 2 24	Donegal	Banagh	Killybegs Upper	Glenties	III.	110
19	Carntullagh	616 0 16d	Leitrim	Drumahaire	Drumreilly	Carᵏ.on Shannon	IV.	95
25, 26	Carnuff Great and Kingstown	561 3 10	Meath	Skreen	Ardmulchan	Navan	I.	220
25, 26	Carnuff Little and Haystown	1,005 1 0	Meath	Skreen	Ardmulchan	Navan	I.	220
32	Carnyarra	600 1 2	Sligo	Leyny	Achonry	Tobercurry	IV.	229
9	Carnybrogan	82 3 24	Westmeath	Delvin	Castletowndelvin	Castletowndelvin	I.	264
17, 18	Carolina	207 3 19e	Cavan	Tullygarvey	Drumgoon	Cootehill	III.	88
17	Carolina	152 3 19f	Monaghan	Dartree	Aghabog	Cootehill	III.	263
33, 34	Carony	417 0 5g	Tyrone	Omagh West	Longfield East	Omagh	III.	315
13, 17	Carpenterstown	166 3 11	Dublin	Castleknock	Castleknock	Dublin North	I.	24
3, 4	Carpenterstown	794 3 34h	Westmeath	Fore	St. Feighins	Castletowndelvin	I.	271
15	Carr	729 3 35	Down	Castlereagh Upper	Drumbo	Lisburn	III.	164
21	Carr	296 3 34i	Fermanagh	Magheraboy	Devenish	Enniskillen	III.	210
59	Carr	214 2 34	Tyrone	Clogher	Clogher	Clogher	III.	292
40, 43	Carra	264 2 33	Fermanagh	Clankelly	Drummully	Clones	III.	197
106	Carra	444 0 26	Galway	Leitrim	Killoran	Loughrea	IV.	54
98	Carra	1,466 0 12	Galway	Loughrea	Killaan	Loughrea	IV.	64
8	Carrachor	63 3 25	Monaghan	Monaghan	Tedavnet	Monaghan	III.	278
6	Carracloghan	166 3 10	Louth	Upper Dundalk	Inishkeen	Dundalk	I.	179
13	Carracloghy	171 3 24	Antrim	Lower Dunluce	Derrykeighan	Ballymoney	III.	16
15, 23	Carracoghan	357 1 24j	Tyrone	Omagh West	Termonamongan	Castlederg	III.	317
28	Carradoan	90 0 29	Donegal	Kilmacrenan	Killygarvan	Milford	III.	128
21, 27	Carradooan	106 1 7	Roscommon	Castlereagh	Kilkeevin	Castlereagh	IV.	200
33, 41	Carradoo Glebe	312 3 34	Tyrone	Omagh West	Longfield West	Castlederg	III.	316
33, 41	Carradowa Glebe	197 2 26	Tyrone	Omagh West	Longfield West	Castlederg	III.	316
92	Carraduffy	250 2 30	Donegal	Banagh	Inver	Donegal	III.	107
76, 82	Carragaun	114 1 29	Tipperary, S.R.	Iffa and Offa West	Derrygrath	Clogheen	II.	318
123	Carragh	283 3 10	Galway	Kiltartan	Kilbeacanty	Gort	IV.	47
18, 19	Carragh	457 1 14	Kildare	Clane	Carragh	Naas	I.	53
10, 11	Carragh	279 2 9	Longford	Granard	Granard	Granard	I.	156
103	Carraghadoo	429 3 30k	Galway	Dunkellin	Kilcolgan	Gort	IV.	28
26	Carraghs East	454 0 22	Roscommon	Castlereagh	Kiltullagh	Castlereagh	IV.	201
26	Carraghs West	321 1 14	Roscommon	Castlereagh	Kiltullagh	Castlereagh	IV.	201
70	Carraghy	271 3 16	Galway	Clare	Annaghdown	Galway	IV.	16

(a) Including 4A. 3R. 2P. water.
(b) Including 7A. 1R. 11P. water.
(c) Including 11A. 2R. 4P. water.
(d) Including 4A. 0R. 10P. water.

(e) Including 6A. 0R. 12P. water.
(f) Including 7A. 0R. 16P. water.
(g) Including 4A. 0R. 20P. water.
(h) Including 83A. 0R. 34P. water.

(i) Including 73A. 0R. 13P. water.
(j) Including 2A. 3R. 11P. water.
(k) Including 18A. 1R. 22P. water.

No. of Sheet of the Ordnance Survey Maps.	Townlands and Towns.	Area in Statute Acres.			County.	Barony.	Parish.	Poor Law Union in 1857.	Townland Census of 1851, Part I.	
		A.	R.	P.					Vol.	Page
40	Carragraigue	1,552	2	17	Cork, E.R.	Duhallow	Dromtarriff	Millstreet	II.	71
26, 34	Carrahan	236	2	21	Clare	Bunratty Upper	Clooney	Tulla	II.	7
20, 28	Carrahane Lower	1,008	2	19	Kerry	Clanmaurice	Ardfert	Tralee	II.	167
20	Carrahane Upper	156	3	31	Kerry	Clanmaurice	Ardfert	Tralee	II.	167
26	Carrahil	220	3	33a	Clare	Bunratty Upper	Inchicronan	Ennis	II.	8
76	*Carra Island*	2	2	38	Galway	Ballynahinch	Moyrus	Clifden	IV.	14
92	Carrakeel	78	2	25	Donegal	Banagh	Inver	Donegal	III.	107
14	Carrakeel	383	2	8b	Londonderry	Tirkeeran	Clondermot	Londonderry	III.	247
43	Carrakeelty Beg	120	0	12	Cavan	Castlerahan	Lurgan	Oldcastle	III.	69
43	Carrakeelty More	124	2	32	Cavan	Castlerahan	Lurgan	Oldcastle	III.	69
37	Carraleena	16	0	36	Donegal	Kilmacrenan	Killygarvan	Millford	III.	128
42, 47	Carraloan (*Glebe*)	403	2	17	Londonderry	Loughinsholin	Artrea	Magherafelt	III.	238
11, 12	Carramoreen	69	1	34	Cavan	Tullygarvey	Annagh	Cavan	III.	67
27, 30	Carran	309	3	10	Armagh	Fews Upper	Creggan	Castleblayney	III.	48
17	Carran	167	1	5	Armagh	Lower Orior	Loughgilly	Newry	III.	56
9	Carran	261	0	19	Clare	Burren	Carran	Ballyvaghan	II.	11
91, 105	Carran	485	0	4	Cork, W.R.	Bantry	Kilmocomoge	Bantry	II.	120
22	Carran	39	1	20	Fermanagh	Tirkennedy	Enniskillen	Enniskillen	III.	221
68	Carran	394	3	26	Kerry	Magunihy	Kilcummin	Killarney	II.	201
24	Carran	289	0	23	Kilkenny	Gowran	Dunbell	Kilkenny	I.	94
24	Carran	179	1	11	Kilkenny	Gowran	Tullaherin	Thomastown	I.	100
9, 10, 16, 17	Carran	266	1	31	Londonderry	Keenaght	Drumachose	NewT⁰Limavady	III.	235
59	Carran	99	1	35	Tyrone	Clogher	Errigal Keerogue	Clogher	III.	295
49, 56	Carran	458	3	33c	Tyrone	Omagh East	Kilskeery	Lowtherstown	III.	313
79	Carranadore	136	3	33d	Donegal	Raphoe	Donaghmore	Strabane	III.	137
8	Carran Beg	291	3	25e	Fermanagh	Magheraboy	Inishmacsaint	Ballyshannon	III.	212
10	Carranboy	96	3	13	Fermanagh	Lurg	Derryvullan	Lowtherstown	III.	204
10	Carranduff	361	2	18	Sligo	Tireragh	Kilglass	Dromore West	IV.	234
15, 21	Carran East	181	1	32f	Fermanagh	Magheraboy	Devenish	Enniskillen	III.	210
22	Carran Little	7	2	23	Fermanagh	Tirkennedy	Derryvullan	Enniskillen	III.	220
8	Carran More	210	3	6	Fermanagh	Magheraboy	Inishmacsaint	Ballyshannon	III.	212
11, 18	Carranrallagh	209	2	37	Londonderry	Coleraine	Aghadowey	Coleraine	III.	229
19	Carranroe	153	1	30	Londonderry	Coleraine	Aghadowey	Ballymoney	III.	229
14	Carranroe	397	1	19	Wexford	Scarawalsh	Monart	Enniscorthy	I.	324
33, 37	Carranroe Lower	144	3	31	Kilkenny	Ida	The Rower	New Ross	I.	104
33, 37	Carranroe Upper	281	3	13	Kilkenny	Ida	The Rower	New Ross	I.	104
6, 7, 11, 12	Carrans and Tates Park	132	3	35	Louth	Upper Dundalk	Dunbin	Dundalk	I.	178
27	Carranstown	647	1	8	Meath	Lower Duleek	Duleek	Drogheda	I.	195
35	Carranstown Great	564	2	16	Meath	Lune	Killaconnigan	Trim	I.	208
35	Carranstown Little	122	2	38	Meath	Lune	Killaconnigan	Trim	I.	208
18	Carran, Upper & Lower	309	1	8	Donegal	Kilmacrenan	Clondavaddog	Millford	III.	124
13, 19	Carran West	654	2	36	Fermanagh	Magheraboy	Devenish	Ballyshannon	III.	210
9	Carrarea	141	3	0	Carlow	Rathvilly	Clonmore	Shillelagh	I.	10
8	Carraun	283	0	20	Leitrim	Rosclogher	Cloonclare	Manorhamilton	IV.	109
31, 32	Carraun	350	0	34	Sligo	Leyny	Achonry	Tobercurry	IV.	229
37	Carraun	275	1	3	Sligo	Leyny	Kilmacteige	Tobercurry	IV.	231
22	Carraun	528	2	22	Sligo	Tireragh	Castleconor	Dromore West	IV.	232
71	Carraunrevagh	80	1	17	Galway	Tiaquin	Monivea	Tuam	IV.	78
129	Carravilleen	242	3	34	Cork, W.R.	West Carbery (W.D.)	Kilcrohane	Bantry	II.	143
1	Carravinally	116	0	37g	Antrim	Cary	Rathlin Island	Ballycastle	III.	15
1	Carravindoon	188	3	31h	Antrim	Cary	Rathlin Island	Ballycastle	III.	15
23, 28, 29	Carrawaystick	1,178	0	12i	Wicklow	Ballinacor South	Knockrath	Rathdrum	I.	350
9	Carrhill	222	3	9j	Wexford	Scarawalsh	Moyacomb	Enniscorthy	I.	325
10	Carrick	167	0	18k	Armagh	Oneilland East	Seagoe	Lurgan	III.	50
39, 43	Carrick	557	0	11	Cavan	Castlerahan	Munterconnaught	Oldcastle	III.	71
41	Carrick	498	1	5	Cavan	Clanmahon	Drumlumman	Granard	III.	77
44, 52	Carrick	642	0	34	Donegal	Kilmacrenan	Conwal	Letterkenny	III.	126
17, 27	Carrick	635	0	6	Donegal	Kilmacrenan	Mevagh	Millford	III.	130
23, 24, 32	Carrick	1,206	1	12l	Donegal	Kilmacrenan	Tullaghobegly	Dunfanaghy	III.	131
79	Carrick	397	3	39m	Donegal	Raphoe	Donaghmore	Stranorlar	III.	137
14	Carrick	125	0	32n	Fermanagh	Magheraboy	Inishmacsaint	Ballyshannon	III.	212
2, 7	Carrick	689	2	34	Kildare	Carbury	Carrick	Edenderry	I.	52
17, 18	Carrick	359	1	6	Kildare	Connell	Rathernan	Naas	I.	56
22, 30	Carrick	671	2	24	King's Co.	Garrycastle	Gallen	Parsonstown	I.	136
4	Carrick	1,408	1	26	King's Co.	Warrenstown	Castlejordan	Edenderry	I.	145
32, 35	Carrick	292	3	36o	Leitrim	Leitrim	Annaduff	Carkᵏ. on Shannon	IV.	99
28	Carrick	108	0	14	Leitrim	Leitrim	Kiltubbrid	Carkᵏ. on Shannon	IV.	103
33	Carrick	82	2	34	Leitrim	Mohill	Mohill	Mohill	IV.	107
16	Carrick	674	2	9	Londonderry	Keenaght	Bovevagh *now* Carrick	NewT⁰Limavady	III.	235
40, 49	Carrick	196	1	8p	Mayo	Gallen	Attymass	Ballina	IV.	147
80, 81	Carrick	421	3	5q	Mayo	Gallen	Killedan	Swineford	IV.	149

(a) Including 29A. 3R. 23P. water.
(b) Including 18A. 3R. 32P. water.
(c) Including 3A. 1R. 0P. water.
(d) Including 1A. 2R. 6P. water.
(e) Including 10A. 1R. 14P. water.
(f) Including 16A. 0R. 8P. water.

(g) Including 6A. 0R. 28P. Lough.
(h) Including 18A. 0R. 36P. Lough.
(i) Including 4A. 0R. 26P. Kelly's Lough.
(j) Including 4A. 1R. 16P. water.
(k) Including 5A. 0R. 17P. water.
(l) Including 18A. 0R. 17P. water.

(m) Including 9A. 2R. 10P. water.
(n) Including 4A. 0R. 6P. water.
(o) Including 40A. 2R. 32P. water.
(p) Including 19A. 2R. 25P. water.
(q) Including 17A. 2R. 8P. water.

2 D

No. of Sheet of the Ordnance Survey Maps.	Townlands and Towns.	Area in Statute Acres. A. R. P.	County.	Barony.	Parish.	Poor Law Union in 1857.	Townland Census of 1851, Part I. Vol.	Page
16	Carrick	250 2 39	Meath	Kells Upper	Kilskeer	Kells	I.	206
45, 48	Carrick	610 1 22a	Roscommon	Athlone	Cam	Athlone	IV.	179
45, 48	Carrick	219 3 19	Roscommon	Athlone	Kiltoom	Athlone	IV.	182
25	Carrick	424 1 24	Roscommon	Castlereagh	Kiltullagh	Castlereagh	IV.	201
12, 17	Carrick	608 0 30	Tipperary, N.R.	Ikerrin	Roscrea	Roscrea	II.	276
11	Carrick	44 0 26	Tipperary, N.R.	Lower Ormond	Ballingarry	Borrisokane	II.	282
9	Carrick	87 0 10b	Tipperary, N.R.	Lower Ormond	Kilbarron	Borrisokane	II.	284
14	Carrick	161 2 30	Tipperary, N.R.	Lower Ormond	Monsea	Nenagh	II.	287
27	Carrick	3 1 21	Tipperary, N.R.	Upper Ormond	Latteragh	Nenagh	II.	292
33, 41	Carrick	363 3 18	Tyrone	Omagh West	Longfield West	Castlederg	III.	316
6, 11	Carrick	303 0 1c	Westmeath	Corkaree	Lackan	Mullingar	I.	262
26, 33	Carrick	1,058 3 38	Westmeath	Fartullagh	Carrick	Mullingar	I.	267
4, 8	Carrick	331 2 3d	Westmeath	Fore	St. Mary's	Castletowndelvin	I.	272
16	Carrick	173 3 25	Westmeath	Kilkenny West	Noughaval	Ballymahon	I.	274
45, 46	Carrick	189 3 22	Wexford	Bargy	Bannow	Wexford	I.	304
38	Carrick	316 2 14	Wicklow	Ballinacor South	Kilcommon	Shillelagh	I.	349
31	Carrickabane	167 3 13e	Cavan	Clanmahon	Crosserlough	Cavan	III.	76
41	Carrickabane	190 1 39f	Cavan	Clanmahon	Drumlumman	Granard	III.	77
19	Carrickabolie	229 2 4g	Armagh	Tiranny	Derrynoose	Armagh	III.	59
25,26,31,32	Carrickaboy Glebe	166 1 35	Cavan	Upper Loughtee	Denn	Cavan	III.	83
3	Carrickabraghy	441 2 39	Donegal	Inishowen East	Clonmany	Inishowen	III.	117
26	Carrickabweehan	65 0 37	Fermanagh	Clanawley	Cleenish	Enniskillen	III.	189
102, 103	Carrickacat	196 2 14	Mayo	Costello	Annagh	Claremorris	IV.	137
6	Carrickacreagh	67 0 19	Louth	Louth	Louth	Dundalk	I.	184
14	Carrickacroghery	172 2 25	Leitrim	Drumahaire	Drumlease	Manorhamilton	IV.	94
27	Carrickacroman	1,425 3 22h	Cavan	Tullygarvey	Larah	Cootehill	III.	91
32, 38	Carrickacroy	236 0 8	Cavan	Castlerahan	Crosserlough	Cavan	III.	67
25	Carrickacullion	89 2 11	Armagh	Fews Upper	Newtownhamilton	Castleblayney	III.	49
16, 24	Carrickadartan	130 3 7	Tyrone	Omagh West	Ardstraw	Castlederg	III.	315
62	Carrickadawson	383 2 26	Donegal	Raphoe	Taughboyne	Strabane	III.	143
14	Carrickaderry	194 1 18	Monaghan	Cremorne	Clontibret	Monaghan	III.	259
11	Carrickadooan	43 1 13	Louth	Louth	Louth	Dundalk	I.	184
27	Carrickadooey	266 1 3i	Monaghan	Farney	Magheross	Carrickmacross	III.	273
6	Carrickadorrish	373 3 23	Longford	Granard	Columbkille	Granard	I.	155
4	Carrickadraan	113 1 0	Roscommon	Boyle	Kilronan	Boyle	IV.	196
25	Carrickadrantan	60 1 25	Fermanagh	Clanawley	Cleenish	Enniskillen	III.	189
16	Carrickadustara	226 2 8	Waterford	Middlethird	Kilmeadan	Waterford	II.	368
11	Carrickafodan	777 3 23j	Donegal	Inishowen East	Donagh	Inishowen	III.	118
25	Carrickagarvan	185 2 24	Monaghan	Cremorne	Clontibret	Castleblayney	III.	259
6	Carrickagreany	197 1 7	Fermanagh	Lurg	Magheraculmoney	Lowthertstown	III.	207
27	Carrickaheenan	66 0 16k	Fermanagh	Tirkennedy	Cleenish	Enniskillen	III.	219
24	Carrickahilla	427 0 36	Waterford	Decies without Drum	Stradbally	Kilmacthomas	II.	360
23, 32	Carrickaholten	1,030 3 1l	Tyrone	Omagh West	Termonamongan	Castlederg	III.	317
37, 41	Carrickakillew	287 1 18	Cavan	Clanmahon	Drumlumman	Granard	III.	77
59, 60	Carrickalangan	1,085 3 37	Donegal	Raphoe	Conwal	Stranorlar	III.	137
24	Carrickaldragh	229 0 21	Monaghan	Cremorne	Aghnamullen	Castleblayney	III.	257
28	Carrickaldreen	231 0 16	Armagh	Orior Upper	Forkill	Newry	III.	57
6	Carrickallan	181 0 12	Louth	Louth	Louth	Dundalk	I.	184
22, 27	Carrickallen	504 1 1m	Cavan	Tullygarvey	Larah	Cootehill	III.	91
25	Carrickaloughan	76 3 19	Fermanagh	Clanawley	Cleenish	Enniskillen	III.	189
12	Carrickaloughran	20 1 23	Armagh	Armagh	Grange	Armagh	III.	44
6	Carrickalust	61 2 26	Louth	Upper Dundalk	Barronstown	Dundalk	I.	177
17	Carrickalwy	333 2 13n	Cavan	Tullygarvey	Kildrumsherdan	Cootehill	III.	89
30	Carrickamone	118 3 14	Armagh	Fews Upper	Creggan	Castleblayney	III.	48
25	Carrickananny	159 3 15	Armagh	Orior Upper	Loughgilly	Newry	III.	58
14	Carrickanass	216 2 36	Mayo	Tirawley	Lackan	Killala	IV.	170
20	Carrickane	89 2 16	Cavan	Upper Loughtee	Annagelliff	Cavan	III.	81
68	Carrickaneady	247 3 24	Mayo	Burrishoole	Burrishoole	Newport	IV.	118
15	Carrickaneagh	203 3 7	Tipperary, N.R.	Lower Ormond	Kilruane	Nenagh	II.	285
17, 22	Carrickanearla	178 0 28	Kildare	Offaly East	Dunmurry	Naas	I.	69
38	Carrickanee	371 0 10o	Donegal	Inishowen West	Inch	Londonderry	III.	121
23	Carrickaneha	259 1 31	Westmeath	Kilkenny West	Drumraney	Ballymahon	I.	273
7	Carrickaness	200 3 13	Armagh	Tiranny	Eglish	Armagh	III.	59
33	Carrickaness	97 3 5p	Tyrone	Omagh West	Longfield West	Castlederg	III.	316
33	Carrickanoran	214 3 15	Kilkenny	Ida	The Rower	Thomastown	I.	104
13	Carrickanoran	139 0 32	Monaghan	Monaghan	Monaghan	Monaghan	III.	276
14	Carrickanure	225 1 4	Monaghan	Cremorne	Clontibret	Monaghan	III.	259
16	Carrickanure	631 1 1	Waterford	Middlethird	Newcastle	Waterford	II.	368
10	Carrickanurroo	190 2 8q	Leitrim	Drumahaire	Drumlease	Manorhamilton	IV.	94
23, 24	Carrickaport	148 1 5r	Leitrim	Leitrim	Kiltubbrid	Cark. on Shannon	IV.	103
41	Carrickard	184 3 15	Sligo	Tirerrill	Kilmactranny	Boyle	IV.	240
24	Carrickarea	172 3 27	Waterford	Decies without Drum	Stradbally	Kilmacthomas	II.	360
24, 25	Carrickaready	323 2 34	Waterford	Decies without Drum	Monksland	Kilmacthomas	II.	359

(a) Including 80A. 3R. 32P. water.
(b) Including 2A. 2R. 8P. water.
(c) Including 0A. 0R. 35P. water.
(d) Including 96A. 3R. 21P. water.
(e) Including 0A. 2R. 3P. water.
(f) Including 6A. 1R. 6P. water.
(g) Including 3A. 1R. 10P. water.
(h) Including 43A. 3R. 24P. water.
(i) Including 8A. 2R. 7P. water.
(j) Including 1A. 2R. 23P. detached portion.
(k) Including 10A. 1R. 24P. water.
(l) Including 10A. 0R. 33P. water.
(m) Including 6A. 0R. 16P. water.
(n) Including 11A. 3R. 28P. water.
(o) Including 21A. 3R. 20P. reclaimed land.
(p) Including 2A. 1R. 7P. water.
(q) Including 1A. 0R. 18P. water.
(r) Including 18A. 3R. 11P. water.

No. of Sheet of the Ordnance Survey Maps.	Townlands and Towns.	Area in Statute Acres.	County.	Barony.	Parish.	Poor Law Union in 1857.	Vol.	Page
		A. R. P.						
17, 27	Carrickart .	870 0 39a	Donegal .	Kilmacrenan .	Mevagh .	Millford .	III.	130
27, 30	Carrickartagh .	354 2 20	Monaghan .	Farney .	Magheross .	Carrickmacross	III.	273
17	CARRICKART T.	—	Donegal .	Kilmacrenan .	Mevagh .	Millford .	III.	131
34	Carrickashedoge .	249 3 10	Monaghan .	Farney .	Magheracloone .	Carrickmacross	III.	272
20	Carrickaslane .	517 0 5b	Monaghan .	Cremorne .	Muckno .	Castleblayney .	III.	261
31, 32	Carrickastickan .	863 1 11	Armagh .	Orior Upper .	Forkill .	Newry .	III.	57
3, 6	Carrickastuck .	229 2 28	Louth .	Upper Dundalk .	Philipstown .	Dundalk .	I.	179
91	Carrickataggart .	518 3 3c	Donegal .	Banagh .	Killybegs Upper .	Glenties .	III.	110
2, 3	Carrickatane .	486 2 27	Tyrone .	Strabane Lower .	Donaghedy .	Strabane .	III.	320
21	Carrickateane .	152 2 10	Cavan .	Upper Loughtee .	Castleterra .	Cavan .	III.	82
26	Carrickateane .	99 1 14	Leitrim .	Carrigallen .	Carrigallen .	Bawnboy .	IV.	89
5	Carrickateane .	205 2 0	Longford .	Granard .	Clonbroney .	Granard .	I.	154
24	Carrickatee .	594 1 4d	Monaghan .	Cremorne .	Aghnamullen .	Castleblayney .	III.	257
51	Carrickatimpan .	2,356 3 13	Donegal .	Kilmacrenan .	Gartan .	Letterkenny .	III.	127
83	Carrickatlieve Glebe	1,824 2 36e	Donegal .	Banagh .	Killybegs Lower .	Glenties .	III.	110
32	Carrickatober .	213 1 2	Cavan .	Upper Loughtee .	Denn .	Cavan .	III.	83
10	Carrickavallan .	209 2 38	Louth .	Ardee .	Killanny .	Dundalk .	I.	173
17, 26	Carrickavarahane .	214 2 20f	Waterford .	Middlethird .	Reisk .	Waterford .	II.	368
104	Carrickavea .	1 3 8	Mayo .	Murrisk .	Kilgeever .	Westport .	IV.	161
38, 39	Carrickavee .	296 1 18	Cavan .	Castlerahan .	Castlerahan .	Oldcastle .	III.	67
24	Carrickaveilty .	392 0 27	Monaghan .	Cremorne .	Aghnamullen .	Castleblayney .	III.	257
27	Carrickaveril .	21 0 3	Leitrim .	Leitrim .	Kiltoghert .	Car*. on Shannon	IV.	101
29, 33	Carrickavoher .	476 3 22	Leitrim .	Carrigallen .	Cloone .	Mohill .	IV.	90
28	Carrickavoley .	101 2 31	Monaghan .	Farney .	Donaghmoyne .	Carrickmacross	III.	269
65	Carrickavoy .	24 3 10g	Tyrone .	Clogher .	Clogher .	Clogher .	III.	292
65	Carrickavoy .	108 1 24	Tyrone .	Clogher .	Errigal Trough .	Clogher .	III.	296
26	Carrickavrantry .	407 2 28	Waterford .	Middlethird .	Islandikane .	Waterford .	II.	367
26	Carrickavrantry Nth.	184 0 2	Waterford .	Middlethird .	Kilbride .	Waterford .	II.	367
26	Carrickavrantry Sth.	231 1 29	Waterford .	Middlethird .	Kilbride .	Waterford .	II.	367
29, 35	Carrickawick .	730 2 25	Fermanagh .	Magherastephana .	Aghalurcher .	Lisnaskea .	III.	215
6, 7	Carrickayne .	980 2 21	Tyrone .	Strabane Lower .	Donaghedy .	Gortin .	III.	320
18, 21	Carrickbaggot .	487 1 1	Louth .	Ferrard .	Carrickbaggot .	Drogheda .	I.	180
54, 62	Carrickballydooey .	119 2 34	Donegal .	Raphoe .	Raymoghy .	Letterkenny .	III.	141
54	Carrickballydooey Glebe	50 1 37	Donegal .	Raphoe .	Raymoghy .	Letterkenny .	III.	141
26, 33	Carrickbanagher .	1,329 3 28	Sligo .	Tirerrill .	Ballysadare .	Sligo .	IV.	237
24	Carrickbarrahane .	224 2 38	Waterford .	Decies without Drum	Stradbally .	Kilmacthomas .	II.	360
48, 60	Carrickbarrett .	206 3 24	Mayo .	Tirawley .	Addergoole .	Castlebar .	IV.	163
23	Carrickbaun .	123 3 4h	Leitrim .	Leitrim .	Kiltoghert .	Car*.on Shannon	IV.	101
21	Carrickbeg .	126 3 19	Fermanagh .	Magheraboy .	Boho .	Enniskillen .	III.	209
27	Carrickbeg .	44 1 35	Longford .	Shrule .	Noughaval .	Ballymahon .	I.	166
45, 48	Carrickbeg .	173 1 27i	Roscommon .	Athlone .	Cam .	Athlone .	IV.	179
44	Carrickbeg .	85 0 12	Roscommon .	Athlone .	Tisrara .	Roscommon .	IV.	185
3	Carrickbeg .	800 2 0	Waterford .	Upperthird .	Kilmoleran .	Carrick on Suir .	II.	370
3	CARRICKBEG T.	—	Waterford .	Upperthird .	Kilmoleran .	Carrick on Suir .	II.	370
104	Carrickboorla .	1 3 0	Mayo .	Murrisk .	Kilgeever .	Westport .	IV.	161
107	Carrickboy .	225 0 12j	Donegal .	Tirhugh .	Inishmacsaint .	Ballyshannon .	III.	147
19, 23	Carrickboy .	149 0 2	Longford .	Shrule .	Kilglass .	Ballymahon .	I.	166
18, 22	Carrickbrack .	213 1 14	Armagh .	Orior Lower .	Ballymore .	Newry .	III.	55
69, 70	Carrickbrack .	516 2 39	Donegal .	Raphoe .	Convoy .	Stranorlar .	III.	136
69, 70	Carrickbrack .	72 0 23	Donegal .	Raphoe .	Raphoe .	Stranorlar .	III.	140
26	Carrickbrackan .	440 2 30	Armagh .	Orior Upper .	Killevy .	Newry .	III.	58
5	Carrickbrannan .	133 1 19	Cavan .	Tullyhaw .	Killinagh .	Enniskillen .	III.	91
99,100,103,104	Carrickbreeny .	267 0 12	Donegal .	Tirhugh .	Drumhome .	Donegal .	III.	146
32	Carrickbroad .	1,200 0 14	Armagh .	Orior Upper .	Killevy .	Newry .	III.	58
33, 41	Carrickbwee Glebe .	278 2 20	Tyrone .	Omagh West .	Longfield West .	Castlederg .	III.	316
1	Carrickcarnan .	350 2 13	Louth .	Lower Dundalk .	Ballymascanlan .	Dundalk .	I.	175
30, 31	Carrickclevan .	248 2 12	Cavan .	Clanmahon .	Ballintemple .	Cavan .	III.	75
25, 26	Carrickcloghan .	406 0 20	Armagh .	Orior Upper .	Killevy .	Newry .	III.	58
41	Carrickcloney .	500 1 26	Kilkenny .	Ida .	Kilmakevoge .	Waterford .	I.	103
82	Carrickconeen .	338 3 34	Tipperary, S.R.	Iffa and Offa East .	Inishlounaght .	Clonmel .	II.	313
27	Carrickcoola .	268 3 18	Sligo .	Tirerrill .	Ballynakill .	Sligo .	IV.	237
23	Carrickcreeny .	549 2 28k	Cavan .	Clankee .	Shercock .	Bailieborough .	III.	74
1, 2	Carrickcroghery .	179 3 37	Fermanagh .	Lurg .	Drumkeeran .	Lowtherstown .	III.	205
26	Carrickcroppan .	364 3 3	Armagh .	Orior Upper .	Killevy .	Newry .	III.	58
47	Carrickcrossan .	403 2 18	Down .	Upper Iveagh, Up.pt.	Clonallan .	Newry .	III.	174
27	Carrick (Dawson) .	154 3 22	Tipperary, N.R.	Upper Ormond .	Templedowney .	Nenagh .	II.	293
19	Carrickdexter .	374 1 0l	Meath .	Upper Slane .	Slane .	Navan .	I.	225
33, 40	Carrickdrumman .	208 1 25	Down .	Upper Iveagh, Up.pt.	Aghaderg .	Banbridge .	III.	174
23, 24	Carrickduff .	425 3 24	Armagh .	Tiranny .	Keady .	Armagh .	III.	60
21	Carrickduff .	697 3 12m	Carlow .	Forth .	Barragh .	Enniscorthy .	I.	4
6, 10	Carrickduff .	390 2 7	Longford .	Granard .	Abbeylara .	Granard .	I.	154
21	CARRICKDUFF T.	—	Carlow .	Forth .	Barragh .	Enniscorthy .	I.	4
9	Carrick East .	126 2 25	Cavan .	Tullyhaw .	Templeport .	Bawnboy .	III.	94

(a) Including 9A. 0R. 29P. water.
(b) Including 6A. 0R. 30P. water.
(c) Including 8A. 2R. 31P. water.
(d) Including 14A. 0R. 31P. water.
(e) Including 16A. 3R. 19P. water.

(f) Including 4A. 2R. 24P. water.
(g) Including 0A. 3R. 24P. water.
(h) Including 7A. 2R. 27P. water.
(i) Including 13A. 0R. 16P. water.

(j) Including 7A. 2R. 34P. water.
(k) Including 105A. 1R. 9P. water.
(l) Including 6A. 1R. 11P. water.
(m) Including 13A. 2R. 14P. River Slaney.

No. of Sheet of the Ordnance Survey Maps.	Townlands and Towns.	Area in Statute Acres.			County.	Barony.	Parish.	Poor Law Union in 1857.	Townland Census of 1851, Part I.	
		A.	R.	P.					Vol.	Page
99, 100	Carrick East . .	121	1	35	Donegal . .	Tirhugh . . .	Drumhome . .	Donegal . .	III.	146
26, 27	Carrick East . .	600	1	9	Galway . .	Ross . . .	Cong . . .	Oughterard . .	IV.	72
16, 17	Carrick East .	348	0	21a	Londonderry .	Keenaght . .	Balteagh now Carrick	New Tn Limavady	III.	234
23	Carrickedmond .	245	1	10	Longford . .	Moydow . .	Taghsheenod . .	Ballymahon .	I.	162
4	Carrickedmond .	574	1	13	Louth . .	Upper Dundalk .	Faughart . .	Dundalk . .	I.	178
6, 7	Carrickeeny . .	773	3	17	Leitrim . .	Rosclogher . .	Killasnet . .	Manorhamilton	IV.	109
33	Carrickeeshill .	298	3	4	Cavan . .	Castlerahan . .	Killinkere . .	Bailieborough .	III.	68
27	Carrickevy . .	58	3	8b	Leitrim . .	Leitrim . .	Kiltoghert . .	Cark. on Shannon	IV.	101
10	Carrickfad . .	425	1	12	Leitrim . .	Drumahaire . .	Drumlease . .	Manorhamilton	IV.	94
52	Carrickfergus . .	65	3	36	Antrim . .	Carrickfergus .	Carrickfergus .	Larne . .	III.	11
52	CARRICKFERGUS T.	—			Antrim . .	Carrickfergus .	Carrickfergus .	Larne . .	III.	11
32, 41	Carrickfin . .	213	3	30c	Donegal . .	Boylagh . .	Templecrone . .	Glenties . .	III.	115
22	Carrickfin . .	154	0	12	Westmeath . .	Kilkenny West .	Kilkenny West .	Athlone . .	I.	273
25	Carrickgallogly .	263	3	29	Armagh . .	Orior Upper . .	Loughgilly . .	Newry . .	III.	58
34	Carrickglass . .	118	1	4	Sligo . .	Tirerrill . .	Killadoon . .	Boyle . .	IV.	239
9, 14	CarrickglassDemesne	144	2	20	Longford . .	Ardagh . .	Templemichael .	Longford . .	I.	153
14	CarrickglassDemesne	434	2	35	Longford . .	Longford . .	Killoe . . .	Longford . .	I.	158
7	Carrickgooan . .	258	0	11	Leitrim . .	Rosclogher . .	Killasnet . .	Manorhamilton	IV.	109
33, 34	Carrickgorman .	343	3	38	Cavan . .	Castlerahan . .	Killinkere . .	Bailieborough .	III.	68
40	Carrickhawna .	275	2	11	Sligo . .	Corran . .	Toomour . .	Boyle . .	IV.	228
114	Carrickheelia . .	1	1	2	Mayo . .	Murrisk . .	Inishbofin . .	Clifden . .	IV.	159
14, 20	Carrickhenry . .	290	3	36	Sligo . .	Carbury . .	St. John's . .	Sligo . .	IV.	223
12, 15	Carrickhill . .	263	2	21	Dublin . .	Coolock . .	Portmarnock .	Balrothery . .	I.	28
79	Carrick Hill . .	107	0	15	Mayo . .	Carra . .	Breaghwy . .	Castlebar . .	IV.	127
9, 15	Carrickhugh . .	157	0	6	Londonderry .	Tirkeeran . .	Faughanvale .	New Tn Limavady	III.	250
17	Carrickilla . .	85	2	7	Roscommon .	Roscommon . .	Aughrim . .	Cark. on Shannon	IV.	207
44	Carrickinab . .	267	0	18	Down . .	Lecale Upper .	Tyrella . .	Downpatrick .	III.	181
24	Carrickinare . .	479	2	5	Monaghan . .	Cremorne . .	Ballybay . .	Castleblayney .	III.	259
40	Carrickinnane .	65	0	31	Kilkenny . .	Ida . . .	Rossinan . .	Waterford . .	I.	104
33	Carrickittle . .	525	2	18	Limerick . .	Smallcounty . .	Kilteely . .	Kilmallock . .	II.	260
65	Carrickkildavnet	184	3	2	Mayo . .	Burrishoole . .	Achill . . .	Newport . .	IV.	117
17	Carricklane . .	265	3	12	Armagh . .	Fews Lower . .	Kilclooney . .	Armagh . .	III.	46
15, 19	Carricklane . .	382	3	22d	Armagh . .	Tiranny . .	Tynan . .	Armagh . .	III.	60
28	Carricklane . .	110	2	21	Monaghan . .	Farney . .	Donaghmoyne .	Carrickmacross	III.	269
37	Carricklawn . .	83	2	23	Wexford . .	Shelmaliere West .	Carrick . .	Wexford . .	I.	332
6	Carrickleagh . .	91	1	29	Louth . .	Louth . .	Louth . .	Dundalk . .	I.	184
2, 3, 5, 6	Carrickleck . .	1,192	1	27	Meath . .	Morgallion . .	Enniskeen . .	Kells . .	I.	209
4	Carricklee . .	237	1	33e	Tyrone . .	Strabane Lower .	Urney . .	Strabane . .	III.	322
11	Carrickleitrim .	307	3	20	Leitrim . .	Drumahaire . .	Cloonclare . .	Manorhamilton	IV.	93
17	Carricklom . .	82	1	22	Roscommon .	Roscommon . .	Aughrim . .	Cark. on Shannon	IV.	207
60	Carricklongfield .	443	1	21f	Tyrone . .	Dungannon Lower .	Aghaloo . .	Dungannon .	III.	296
35	Carrickloughmore .	186	0	23	Tipperary, N.R.	Eliogarty . .	Loughmoe West .	Thurles . .	II.	271
90	Carrick Lower .	607	3	0	Donegal . .	Banagh . .	Glencolumbkille .	Glenties . .	III.	105
102, 103	Carrickmacantire .	232	0	3	Mayo . .	Costello . .	Annagh . .	Claremorris .	IV.	137
25	Carrickmacflaherty	114	3	6	Fermanagh .	Clanawley . .	Cleenish . .	Enniskillen .	III.	189
30, 31	Carrickmaclim .	217	2	30	Monaghan . .	Farney . .	Magheross . .	Carrickmacross	III.	273
34	Carrickmacosker .	239	0	30	Fermanagh .	Magherastephana .	Aghalurcher . .	Lisnaskea . .	III.	215
31	CARRICKMACROSS T.	—			Monaghan . .	Farney . .	Magheross . .	Carrickmacross	III.	274
33	Carrickmacrourk Island	3	2	18	Fermanagh .	Tirkennedy . .	Cleenish . .	Lisnaskea . .	III.	220
26	Carrickmacsparrow	197	3	9	Fermanagh .	Clanawley . .	Cleenish . .	Enniskillen .	III.	190
51	Carrickmacstay .	516	2	13	Down . .	Upper Iveagh, Up. pt.	Clonallan . .	Newry . .	III.	174
15	Carrickmaddyroe .	801	3	11	Down . .	Castlereagh Upper .	Killaney . .	Lisburn . .	III.	165
77, 78, 86	Carrickmagrath .	888	1	27	Donegal . .	Raphoe . .	Donaghmore . .	Stranorlar .	III.	137
2, 3	Carrickmaguirk .	348	0	26	Longford . .	Granard . .	Columbkille . .	Granard . .	I.	155
76, 77	Carrickmahon .	472	0	7	Donegal . .	Raphoe . .	Kilteevoge . .	Stranorlar .	III.	139
25	Carrickmakeegan .	349	2	28	Leitrim . .	Carrigallen . .	Drumreilly . .	Bawnboy . .	IV.	90
16	Carrickmannan .	1,430	0	17g	Down . .	Castlereagh Upper .	Killinchy . .	Newtownards .	III.	165
21, 31	Carrickmaquigley .	832	0	21h	Donegal . .	Inishowen East .	Moville Upper .	Inishowen . .	III.	119
27	Carrick (Maunsell) .	136	0	2	Tipperary, N.R.	Upper Ormond .	Templedowney .	Nenagh . .	II.	293
31	Carrickmerlin . .	85	1	9	Kilkenny . .	Knocktopher . .	Aghaviller . .	Thomastown .	I.	110
26, 39	Carrick Middle .	370	2	31	Galway . .	Ross . . .	Cong . . .	Oughterard .	IV.	72
26	Carrickmines Great	545	1	0	Dublin . .	Rathdown . .	Tully . .	Rathdown . .	I.	38
23, 26	Carrickmines Little	125	2	16	Dublin . .	Rathdown . .	Tully . .	Rathdown . .	I.	38
21	Carrickmoran . .	90	1	10	Longford . .	Ratheline . .	Cashel . .	Ballymahon .	I.	163
16	Carrickmore . .	274	0	16i	Cavan . .	Upper Loughtee .	Castleterra . .	Cavan . .	III.	82
63	Carrickmore . .	471	3	38	Donegal . .	Raphoe . .	Taughboyne . .	Strabane . .	III.	143
12	Carrickmore . .	128	3	5	Monaghan . .	Dartree . .	Clones . .	Clones . .	III.	264
6	Carrickmore . .	431	3	26	Roscommon .	Boyle . .	Boyle . .	Boyle . .	IV.	194
36	Carrickmore . .	915	0	5j	Tyrone . .	Omagh East . .	Termonmaguirk .	Omagh . .	III.	314
28	Carrickmourne .	300	0	17	Kilkenny . .	Gowran . .	Columbkille . .	Thomastown .	I.	94
9	Carrickmoyragh .	376	0	6	Longford . .	Longford . .	Clongesh . .	Longford . .	I.	157
6, 11	Carrickmullan .	229	1	11	Louth . .	Louth . .	Louth . .	Dundalk . .	I.	184
15	Carrickmurray . .	55	0	38	Leitrim . .	Drumahaire . .	Killarga . .	Manorhamilton	IV.	98

(a) Including 5A. 1R. 36P. water.
(b) Including 11A. 1R. 9P. water.
(c) Including 10A. 2R. 27P. water.
(d) Including 3A. 1R. 9P. water.

(e) Including 6A. 2R. 18P. water.
(f) Including 5A. 2R. 32P. water.
(g) Including 30A. 2R. 10P. water.

(h) Including 9A. 3R. 14P. water.
(i) Including 4A. 0R. 36P. water.
(j) Including 5A. 3R. 9P. water.

No. of Sheet of the Ordnance Survey Maps	Townlands and Towns.	Area in Statute Acres.			County.	Barony.	Parish.	Poor Law Union in 1857.	Townland Census of 1851. Part I.	
		A.	R.	P.					Vol.	Page
23	Carricknabrack .	80	0	3	Leitrim . .	Leitrim . . .	Kiltoghert .	Car^k. on Shannon	IV.	101
35	Carricknabrattoge .	352	3	10	Fermanagh .	Magherastephana .	Aghalurcher .	Lisnaskea .	III.	215
31, 37	Carricknabrick .	98	3	17	Cavan . .	Clannahon . .	Drumlumman .	Granard . .	III.	77
2	Carricknabrone .	123	3	31	Waterford .	Upperthird . .	Killaloan .	Clonmel . .	II.	370
22	Carricknadarriff .	636	3	12a	Down . .	Lower Iveagh, Lr. pt.	Annahilt . .	Lisburn . .	III.	167
25, 28	Carricknagalliagh .	221	1	14	Armagh . .	Orior Upper . .	Killevy . . .	Newry . .	III.	58
44	Carricknagat .	134	3	31	Roscommon .	Athlone . .	Tisrara . .	Roscommon .	IV.	185
20	Carricknagat .	284	0	8b	Sligo . .	Leyny . .	Ballysadare .	Sligo . .	IV.	230
21, 27	Carricknagat .	136	0	17	Sligo . .	Tirerrill . .	Ballysumaghan .	Sligo . .	IV.	238
25, 28	Carricknagavna .	588	0	30	Armagh . .	Orior Upper . .	Forkill . .	Newry . .	III.	57
34	Carricknagoan .	143	3	14c	Monaghan .	Farney . . .	Magheracloone .	Carrickmacross	III.	272
91	Carricknagore .	127	1	2	Donegal .	Banagh . .	Killybegs Upper .	Glenties . .	III.	110
23	Carricknagower .	334	2	10	Westmeath .	Rathconrath .	Ballymore .	Ballymahon .	I.	281
35, 41	Carricknagrip .	131	3	11	Sligo . .	Tirerrill . .	Kilmactranny .	Boyle . .	IV.	240
3	Carricknagrow .	679	3	7d	Cavan . .	Tullyhaw . .	Killinagh .	Enniskillen .	III.	91
103, 104, 108	Carricknahorna .	2,337	1	6e	Donegal .	Tirhugh . .	Kilbarron .	Ballyshannon .	III.	148
40	Carricknahorna East	631	1	22	Sligo . .	Tirerrill . .	Aghanagh .	Boyle . .	IV.	237
40	Carricknahorna West	643	2	17	Sligo . .	Tirerrill . .	Aghanagh .	Boyle . .	IV.	237
36	Carricknakielt .	390	2	18	Londonderry .	Loughinsholin .	Termoneeny .	Magherafelt .	III.	244
27, 33	Carricknamaddoo .	624	1	13	Cavan . .	Upper Loughtee .	Killinkere .	Cavan . .	III.	84
78	Carricknamanna .	689	3	0f	Donegal . .	Raphoe . .	Donaghmore .	Stranorlar .	III.	137
62	Carricknamart .	440	2	17	Donegal . .	Raphoe . .	Raymoghy .	Letterkenny .	III.	141
91	Carricknamoghil .	533	1	0g	Donegal . .	Banagh . .	Killybegs Upper .	Glenties . .	III.	110
26	Carricknaseer .	169	1	2	Fermanagh .	Clanawley .	Cleenish . .	Enniskillen .	III.	190
21	Carricknashanagh .	172	3	18	Louth . .	Ferrard . .	Drumshallon .	Drogheda . .	I.	180
79	Carricknashane .	134	2	6	Donegal . .	Raphoe . .	Donaghmore .	Stranorlar .	III.	137
64	*Carricknashee* .	3	0	6	Donegal . .	Boylagh . .	Inishkeel .	Glenties . .	III.	114
4	Carricknashee .	33	2	36	Roscommon .	Boyle . .	Kilronan . .	Boyle . .	IV.	196
22, 27	Carricknashoke .	330	0	34	Cavan . .	Tullygarvey .	Larah . .	Cootehill .	III.	91
70, 71	Carricknaslate .	90	0	9	Donegal . .	Raphoe . .	Clonleigh .	Strabane .	III.	134
33	Carricknaveagh .	337	1	6	Cavan . .	Castlerahan .	Killinkere .	Bailieborough .	III.	68
15	Carricknaveagh .	969	1	36	Down . .	Castlereagh Upper .	Killaney . .	Lisburn . .	III.	165
26, 32	Carricknaveddan .	160	1	27	Cavan . .	Upper Loughtee .	Lavey . .	Cavan . .	III.	85
29	Carrickobreen .	472	3	16	Westmeath .	Brawny . .	St. Mary's .	Athlone .	I.	259
15	Carrickoghil .	72	0	31	Leitrim . .	Drumahaire .	Killarga . .	Manorhamilton	IV.	98
9	Carrickone . .	73	3	2	Tyrone . .	Strabane Lower .	Urney . .	Strabane . .	III.	322
15	Carrickoneilleen .	198	2	32	Sligo . .	Carbury . .	Calry . .	Sligo . .	IV.	220
31	CARRICK ON SHANNON T. (part of) .	—			Leitrim . .	Leitrim . . .	Kiltoghert .	Car^k. on Shannon	IV.	103
11	CARRICK ON SHANNON T. (part of) .	—			Roscommon .	Boyle . .	Killukin . .	Car^k. on Shannon	IV.	196
85	CARRICK ON SUIR T.	—			Tipperary, S.R.	Iffa and Offa East .	Carrick . .	Carrick on Suir	II.	313
1, 5	Carrickoughter .	266	0	29	Fermanagh .	Lurg . .	Drumkeeran .	Lowtherstown .	III.	205
27	Carrick (*Peacocke*) .	99	3	8	Tipperary, N.R.	Upper Ormond .	Templedowney .	Nenagh . .	II.	293
9	Carrickphierish .	140	3	26	Waterford .	Middlethird .	Killoteran .	Waterford .	II.	367
16	Carrickphilip .	634	0	20	Waterford .	Middlethird .	Newcastle .	Waterford .	II.	368
29	Carrickpolin .	535	3	23	Fermanagh .	Magherastephana .	Aghalurcher .	Lisnaskea .	III.	215
39	Carrickrathmullin .	154	2	16	Sligo . .	Corran . .	Drumrat . .	Boyle . .	IV.	225
15	Carrickreagh .	411	0	38	Fermanagh .	Magheraboy .	Devenish .	Enniskillen .	III.	210
9, 13	Carrickrevagh .	535	1	14	Leitrim . .	Drumahaire .	Cloonclare .	Manorhamilton	IV.	93
6	Carrickrobin .	246	1	15h	Louth . .	Upper Dundalk .	Barronstown .	Dundalk . .	I.	177
105	Carrickrory .	614	2	2i	Donegal . .	Tirhugh . .	Templecarn .	Donegal . .	III.	149
40, 46	Carrickrovaddy .	366	0	17	Down . .	Upper Iveagh, Up.pt.	Donaghmore .	Newry . .	III.	175
25, 28	Carrickrovaddy or Dorsy (*Macdonald*)	570	1	20	Armagh . .	Fews Upper . .	Newtownhamilton .	Castleblayney .	III.	49
18	Carricksaggart .	234	1	22	Waterford .	Gaultiere . .	Crooke . .	Waterford .	II.	362
19	Carricksallagh .	62	3	30	Queen's Co. .	Stradbally .	Stradbally .	Athy . .	I.	247
78	Carrickshandrum .	185	1	38j	Donegal . .	Raphoe . .	Donaghmore .	Stranorlar .	III.	137
31	Carrickshock Commons . .	47	2	33	Kilkenny . .	Knocktopher .	Knocktopher .	Thomastown .	I.	112
13	Carrickslaney .	452	2	11	Carlow . .	Forth . . .	Aghade . .	Carlow . .	I.	3
13	Carrickslaney .	12	3	20	Carlow . .	Forth . . .	Ballon . .	Carlow . .	I.	3
27	Carrickslavan .	124	2	5	Leitrim . .	Leitrim . . .	Kiltoghert .	Car^k. on Shannon	IV.	101
5	Carrickspringan .	518	3	24	Meath . .	Lower Kells .	Moynalty .	Kells . .	I.	203
45, 46	CARRICK T. . .	—			Wexford . .	Bargy . . .	Bannow . .	Wexford . .	VI.	304
12	Carricktroddan .	24	1	36	Armagh . .	Armagh . .	Grange . .	Armagh . .	I.	44
90	Carrick Upper .	807	1	23k	Donegal . .	Banagh . .	Glencolumbkille .	Glenties . .	III.	105
100	Carrick Upper and Lower Barr .	1,142	3	16l	Donegal . .	Tirhugh . .	Drumhome .	Donegal . .	III.	146
6	Carrick West .	157	1	7	Cavan . .	Tullyhaw . .	Templeport .	Enniskillen .	III.	94
99, 100	Carrick West .	142	0	29	Donegal . .	Tirhugh . .	Drumhome .	Donegal . .	III.	146
26	Carrick West .	336	2	36	Galway . .	Ross . . .	Cong . .	Oughterard .	IV.	73
36	Carrickybressil .	148	3	25	Donegal . .	Kilmacrenan .	Kilmacrenan .	Millford . .	III.	129
29	Carrickyheenan .	926	1	20	Fermanagh .	Magherastephana .	Aghavea . .	Lisnaskea .	III.	218

No. of Sheet of the Ordnance Survey Maps.	Townlands and Towns.	Area in Statute Acres.	County.	Barony.	Parish.	Poor Law Union in 1857.	Townland Census of 1851, Part I.	
		A.　R.　P.					Vol.	Page
29	Carrickykelly .	290　3　7	Monaghan	Farney . .	Inishkeen . .	Dundalk . .	III.	271
52	Carrickynaghtan .	293　0　34	Roscommon	Athlone . .	Drum . .	Athlone . .	IV.	180
52	Carrickynaghtan and Garrynagawna Bog	973　2　18	Roscommon	Athlone . .	Drum . .	Athlone . .	IV.	180
52	Carrickyscanlan .	161　3　33	Donegal .	Kilmacrenan .	Conwal . .	Letterkenny .	III.	126
48	Carriff Island . .	7　3　6	Donegal .	Boylagh . .	Templecrone .	Glenties . .	III.	116
43	Carrig . . .	325　2　31	Cork, E.R.	Barrymore . .	Ardnageehy .	Fermoy . .	II.	50
102, 115	Carrig . . .	47　3　0	Cork, W.R.	Bear . . .	Kilcatherine .	Castletown .	II.	124
116	Carrig . . .	42　3　4	Cork, W.R.	Bear . . .	Killaconenagh .	Castletown .	II.	124
122	Carrig . . .	410　3　22	Cork, W.R.	East Carbery (E.D.)	Kilmaloda .	Clonakilty .	II.	129
122	Carrig . . .	165　1　15	Cork, W.R.	East Carbery (E.D.)	Templequinlan .	Clonakilty .	II.	130
132	Carrig . . .	97　3　9	Cork, W.R.	West Carbery (W.D.)	Caheragh . .	Skibbereen .	II.	142
80	Carrig . . .	119　3　34	Cork, W.R.	West Muskerry .	Inchigeelagh .	Macroom . .	II.	156
33, 42	Carrig . . .	151　3　12	Kerry . .	Corkaguiny .	Kilmalkedar .	Dingle . .	II.	178
25	Carrig . . .	189　0　39	Wexford .	Bantry . .	Clonmore . .	Enniscorthy .	I.	300
1, 2	Carrig . . .	437　3　39	Wexford .	Gorey . .	Kilpipe . .	Gorey . .	I.	320
5	Carrig . . .	381　3　5	Wicklow .	Lower Talbotstown .	Boystown . .	Naas . .	I.	359
35, 36	Carrigabrick . .	221　2　30a	Cork, E.R.	Condons&Clangibbon	Clondulane .	Fermoy . .	II.	60
43, 44	Carrigabruse . .	207　1　20	Cavan .	Castlerahan .	Loughan or Castle-keeran . .	Oldcastle . .	III.	69
19, 20	Carrigabruse . .	123　2　20	Wexford .	Scarawalsh .	Monart . .	Enniscorthy .	I.	324
20	Carrigabruse . .	14　2　0	Wexford .	Scarawalsh .	St.MarysEnniscorthy	Enniscorthy .	I.	325
138, 147	Carrigacat & Milleen	838　2　27	Cork, W.R.	West Carbery (W.D.)	Kilmoe . .	Skull . .	II.	144
48	Carrigacooleen .	599　0　5	Cork, W.R.	West Muskerry .	Drishane . .	Millstreet .	II.	155
88	Carrigacrump . .	195　3　37	Cork, E.R.	Imokilly . .	Inch . .	Middleton .	II.	87
34	Carrigacunna . .	510　1　21b	Cork, E.R.	Fermoy . .	Monanimy .	Mallow . .	II.	81
10, 16	Carrigacurra . .	995　3　0	Wicklow .	Lower Talbotstown .	Boystown . .	Baltinglass .	I.	359
146, 147	Carrigacurriheen .	234　2　5	Cork, W.R.	West Carbery (W.D.)	Kilmoe . .	Skull . .	II.	144
35	Carrigadaggan .	233　0　25	Wexford .	Bantry . .	Newbawn . .	New Ross .	I.	301
36	Carrigadav . .	984　0　3	Kerry . .	Corkaguiny .	Killiney . .	Dingle . .	II.	178
71	Carrigadrohid . .	559　1　25c	Cork, W.R.	East Muskerry .	Aghinagh . .	Macroom . .	II.	153
2	Carrigafoyle . .	221　0　32	Kerry . .	Iraghticonnor .	Aghavallen .	Listowel . .	II.	189
66	Carrigafreaghane .	79　1　39	Kerry . .	Magunihy . .	Killarney . .	Killarney . .	II.	203
84, 96	Carrigafroca . .	122　2　15	Cork, W.R.	Kinalmeaky .	Templemartin .	Bandon . .	II.	152
1, 4	Carrigagh . .	356　0　4	Meath . .	Lower Kells .	Moynalty . .	Kells . .	I.	203
5, 10	Carrigagh . .	233　2　35	Westmeath .	Moygoish . .	Rathaspick .	Mullingar .	I.	280
76	Carrigagour . .	124　2　6	Cork, E.R.	Imokilly . .	Middleton .	Middleton .	II.	89
9	Carrigagown North	159　2　28	Tipperary, N.R.	Lower Ormond .	Kilbarron .	Borrisokane .	II.	284
9	Carrigagown South	137　3　6	Tipperary, N.R.	Lower Ormond .	Kilbarron .	Borrisokane .	II.	284
121, 134	Carrigagrenane .	470　1　6	Cork, W.R.	East Carbery (W.D.)	Ross . .	Clonakilty .	II.	135
49, 60	Carrigagulla . .	2,292　3　37	Cork, W.R.	West Muskerry .	Macroom . .	Macroom . .	II.	160
36	Carrigaha . .	155　1　36	Kerry . .	Corkaguiny .	Killiney . .	Dingle . .	II.	178
65	CARRIGAHOLT T. .	—	Clare . .	Moyarta . .	Moyarta . .	Kilrush . .	II.	34
38	Carrigaline . .	380　1　0d	Cork, E.R.	Duhallow . .	Nohavaldaly .	Millstreet .	II.	75
87	Carrigaline . .	84　0　29	Cork, E.R.	Kerrycurrihy .	Liscleary .	Cork . .	II.	92
87	Carrigaline East .	332　1　24	Cork, E.R.	Kerrycurrihy .	Carrigaline .	Cork . .	II.	92
87	Carrigaline Middle .	406　1　27	Cork, E.R.	Kerrycurrihy .	Carrigaline .	Cork . .	II.	92
87, 99	CARRIGALINE T. .	—	Cork, E.R.	Kerrycurrihy .	Carrigaline Kilmoney }	Kinsale . .	II.	92
86, 87	Carrigaline West .	458　0　34	Cork, E.R.	Kerrycurrihy .	Carrigaline .	Cork . .	II.	92
30	CARRIGALLEN T. .	—	Leitrim . .	Carrigallen .	Carrigallen .	Mohill . .	IV.	90
78	Carrigaloe . .	297　1　36	Tipperary, S.R.	Iffa and Offa East .	Kilcash . .	Clonmel . .	II.	313
87	CARRIGALOE T. .	—	Cork, E.R.	Barrymore . .	Clonmel . .	Cork . .	II.	53
31	Carrigan . .	313　0　28e	Cavan .	Clanmahon .	Ballintemple .	Cavan . .	III.	75
14, 15	Carrigan . .	94　0　27f	Cavan .	Lower Loughtee .	Drumlane .	Cavan . .	III.	79
14	Carrigan . .	102　1　5g	Cavan .	Lower Loughtee .	Tomregan .	Bawnboy .	III.	81
20	Carrigan . .	1,286　1　19h	Fermanagh .	Magheraboy .	Boho . .	Enniskillen .	III.	209
15	Carrigan . .	24　1　14	Fermanagh .	Magheraboy .	Devenish . .	Enniskillen .	III.	210
22	Carrigan . .	106　1　10i	Fermanagh .	Magheraboy .	Rossorry . .	Enniskillen .	III.	214
68	Carriganagh . .	637　3　19	Tipperary, S.R.	Clanwilliam .	Clonbullogue .	Tipperary .	II.	306
17	Carriganard . .	163　1　12	Waterford .	Gaultiere . .	Kilbarry . .	Waterford .	II.	363
55, 56	Carriganass . .	211　2　6	Cork, E.R.	Imokilly . .	Ardagh . .	Youghal . .	II.	83
92, 105, 106	Carriganass . .	307　0　18	Cork, W.R.	Bantry . .	Kilmocomoge .	Bantry . .	II.	120
23	Carriganattin . .	134　3　2	Limerick .	Clanwilliam .	Rochestown .	Limerick . .	II.	225
45	Carrigan Beg .	131　1　27	Roscommon .	Athlone . .	St. John's .	Athlone . .	IV.	183
65, 76	Carrigane . .	432　3　9	Cork, E.R.	Barrymore . .	Carrigtohill .	Middleton .	II.	52
53	Carrigane . .	188　3　32	Cork, E.R.	Barrymore . .	Lisgoold . .	Middleton .	II.	56
11	Carrigane . .	799　2　16	Cork, E.R.	Condons&Clangibbon	Brigown . .	Mitchelstown .	II.	59
32	Carrigane . .	177　1　28j	Cork, E.R.	Duhallow . .	Roskeen . .	Kanturk . .	II.	75
73	Carrigane . .	35　1　14	Cork, E.R.	East Muskerry .	Athnowen .	Cork . .	II.	101
2	Carrigane . .	198　1　16	Kerry . .	Iraghticonnor .	Aghavallen .	Listowel . .	II.	189
19	Carrigane . .	151　2　12k	Waterford .	Coshmore&Coshbride	Lismore and Mocollop	Lismore . .	II.	343
12	Carriganeagh . .	197　3　27	Wexford .	Ballaghkeen .	Kilmakilloge .	Gorey . .	I.	296

(a) Including 5A. 1R. 15P. water.　　　(e) Including 0A. 1R. 38P. water.　　　(i) Including 8A. 0R. 21P. water.
(b) Including 18A. 3R. 14P. water.　　　(f) Including 6A. 3R. 31P. water.　　　(j) Including 0A. 2R. 16P. water.
(c) Including 16A. 2R. 20P. water.　　　(g) Including 3A. 1R. 17P. water.　　　(k) Including 7A. 0R. 23P. water.
(d) Including 6A. 1R. 20P. water.　　　(h) Including 31A. 0R. 13P. water.

No. of Sheet of the Ordnance Survey Maps	Townlands and Towns.	Area in Statute Acres.	County.	Barony.	Parish.	Poor Law Union in 1857.	Townland Census of 1851, Part I.	
		A. R. P.					Vol.	Page
12, 21	Carriganes	1,013 1 25	Cork, E.R.	Duhallow	Nohavaldaly	Kanturk	II.	75
48, 59	Carriganimmy	1,227 0 33	Cork, W.R.	West Muskerry	Clondrohid	Macroom	II.	155
70	Carriganine	120 2 6	Cork, W.R.	West Muskerry	Macroom	Macroom	II.	160
60	Carriganish	432 1 16	Cork, W.R.	East Muskerry	Aghinagh	Macroom	II.	153
19	Carriganleigh	69 2 39	Cork, E.R.	Condons&Clangibbon	Kilgullane	Mitchelstown	II.	61
45	Carrigan More	461 2 39	Roscommon	Athlone	St. John's	Athlone	IV.	183
122	Carriganookery	94 3 18	Cork, W.R.	East Carbery (E.D.)	Kilnagross	Clonakilty	II.	129
86	Carriganroe	337 2 35	Tipperary, S.R.	Iffa and Offa West	Shanrahan	Clogheen	II.	319
28, 31	Carrigans	511 3 0a	Armagh	Orior Upper	Forkill	Newry	III.	57
55	Carrigans	129 0 36	Donegal	Raphoe	Killea	Londonderry	III.	138
40	Carrigans	124 1 8	Fermanagh	Clankelly	Galloon	Clones	III.	198
6	Carrigans	142 1 38b	Monaghan	Trough	Donagh	Monaghan	III.	281
17, 25, 26	Carrigans	859 2 39c	Tyrone	Strabane Upper	Cappagh	Omagh	III.	325
33	Carrigans Lower	528 3 4	Sligo	Corran	Emlaghfad	Sligo	IV.	226
38, 39	Carrigans Park	248 2 11	Roscommon	Ballymoe	Dunamon	Roscommon	IV.	191
55	Carrigans T.	—	Donegal	Raphoe	Killea	Londonderry	III.	139
33	Carrigans Upper	950 1 3d	Sligo	Corran	Emlaghfad	Sligo	IV.	226
43, 44	Carriganurra	393 2 6	Kilkenny	Ida	Kilcolumb	Waterford	I.	102
70	Carrigaphooca	205 2 38	Cork, W.R.	West Muskerry	Clondrohid	Macroom	II.	155
66, 77	Carrigarostig	103 3 26	Cork, E.R.	Imokilly	Ightermurragh	Middleton	II.	87
14	Carrigarreely	214 3 38	Limerick	Clanwilliam	Caherconlish	Limerick	II.	222
44	Carrigasimon	247 2 29	Cavan	Castlerahan	Loughan or Castle-keeran	Oldcastle	III.	69
81	Carrigataha	291 0 16e	Tipperary, S.R.	Iffa and Offa West	Tubbrid	Clogheen	II.	320
28	Carrigatheme	252 1 0	Wicklow	Ballinacor South	Kiltegan	Baltinglass	I.	350
71	Carrigathou	224 2 22	Cork, W.R.	East Muskerry	Aghinagh	Macroom	II.	153
31, 35	Carrigatna	338 0 1	Kilkenny	Kells	Kilmaganny	Callan	I.	109
76, 77	Carrigatogher	128 1 20	Cork, E.R.	Imokilly	Cloyne	Middleton	II.	85
20, 26	Carrigatogher (Abbott)	447 2 9f	Tipperary, N.R.	Owney and Arra	Burgesbeg	Nenagh	II.	294
20	Carrigatogher Bog (Abbott)	28 1 15	Tipperary, N.R.	Owney and Arra	Burgesbeg	Nenagh	II.	294
20	Carrigatogher Bog (Harding)	11 1 15	Tipperary, N.R.	Owney and Arra	Burgesbeg	Nenagh	II.	294
20	Carrigatogher Bog (Ryan)	21 2 25	Tipperary, N.R.	Owney and Arra	Burgesbeg	Nenagh	II.	294
20	Carrigatogher(Harding)	274 1 36g	Tipperary, N.R.	Owney and Arra	Burgesbeg	Nenagh	II.	294
20, 26	Carrigatogher (Ryan)	356 1 20h	Tipperary, N.R.	Owney and Arra	Burgesbeg	Nenagh	II.	294
36	Carrigatoortane	170 0 30i	Cork, E.R.	Condons&Clangibbon	Clondulane	Fermoy	II.	60
22	Carrigaun (Hely)	73 3 34	Waterford	Decies without Drum	Modelligo	Lismore	II.	359
22	Carrigaun(Mansfield)	189 2 30	Waterford	Decies without Drum	Modelligo	Dungarvan	II.	359
18, 26	Carrigaunroe	410 1 17	Cork, E.R.	Fermoy	Templeroan	Mallow	II.	82
76	Carrigaveema	299 3 4	Kerry	Magunihy	Killaha	Killarney	II.	202
86	Carrigavisteal	380 0 13	Tipperary, S.R.	Iffa and Offa West	Templetenny	Clogheen	II.	320
17	Carrigavoe	160 1 7	Waterford	Gaultiere	Kill St. Lawrence	Waterford	II.	363
124	Carrigavulleen	251 0 34	Cork, W.R.	Courceys	Ringrone	Kinsale	II.	147
67,68,75,76	Carrigawannia	241 3 14	Kerry	Magunihy	Killaha	Killarney	II.	202
77	Carrigawillin	48 2 14	Tipperary, S.R.	Iffa and Offa East	Lisronagh	Clonmel	II.	315
133	Carrigbaun	285 3 5	Cork, W.R.	East Carbery (W.D.)	Kilmacabea	Skibbereen	II.	133
133	Carrigbaun	298 1 35	Cork, W.R.	West Carbery (E.D.)	Drinagh	Skibbereen	II.	139
68	Carrigbaun	342 1 32	Cork, W.R.	West Muskerry	Inchigeelagh	Macroom	II.	156
16	Carrig Beg	258 0 21	Carlow	Idrone East	Dunleckny	Carlow	I.	6
24, 25	Carrig Beg	403 0 19	Limerick	Coonagh	Castletown	Tipperary	II.	234
6, 11	Carrigbeg	237 2 5	Wexford	Gorey	Kilnahue	Gorey	I.	319
6, 11	Carrigbeg	250 1 25	Wexford	Gorey	Rossminoge	Gorey	I.	321
105, 118	Carrigboy	87 2 30	Cork, W.R.	Bantry	Kilmocomoge	Bantry	II.	120
116	Carrigboy	0 0 8	Cork, W.R.	Bear	Kilcaskan	Castletown	II.	122
130, 131	Carrigboy	116 1 6	Cork, W.R.	West Carbery (W.D.)	Durrus	Bantry	II.	142
82, 94	Carrigboy	989 0 33	Cork, W.R.	West Muskerry	Kilmichael	Dunmanway	II.	158
14	Carrigbrack	724 3 5	Waterford	Decies without Drum	Seskinan	Dungarvan	II.	360
110	Carrigcannon	59 0 31	Cork, W.R.	East Carbery (E.D.)	Ballymodan	Bandon	II.	126
124	Carrigcannon	122 1 32	Cork, W.R.	East Carbery (E.D.)	Ringrone	Kinsale	II.	130
22	Carrigcannon	962 1 14	Kerry	Clanmaurice	Kilfeighny	Listowel	II.	169
14, 15	Carrigcastle	268 2 13	Cork, E.R.	Duhallow	Clonfert	Kanturk	II.	68
24	Carrigcastle	436 3 3	Waterford	Decies without Drum	Ballylaneen	Kilmacthomas	II.	354
41, 42	Carrigcleena Beg	314 3 6	Cork, E.R.	Duhallow	Kilshannig	Mallow	II.	74
41	Carrigcleena More	632 1 25	Cork, E.R.	Duhallow	Kilshannig	Mallow	II.	74
93, 94	Carrigdangan	618 2 2	Cork, W.R.	West Muskerry	Kilmichael	Dunmanway	II.	158
83	Carrigdarrery	204 2 29	Cork, W.R.	West Muskerry	Kilmurry	Macroom	II.	159
33	Carrig Demesne	279 3 5j	Cork, E.R.	Fermoy	Carrigleamleary	Mallow	II.	77
18,19,26,27	CarrigdownaneLower	310 0 38	Cork, E.R.	Fermoy	Carrigdownane	Mitchelstown	II.	77
26	CarrigdownaneUpper	302 3 37	Cork, E.R.	Fermoy	Carrigdownane	Mitchelstown	II.	77
33, 42	Carrigduff	791 0 1	Cork, E.R.	Barretts	Mourneabbey	Mallow	II.	50
40, 49	Carrigduff	1,305 2 26	Cork, W.R.	West Muskerry	Kilcorney	Millstreet	II.	158
83, 84, 92	Carrig East	1,013 1 29k	Kerry	Dunkerrin South	Templenoe	Kenmare	II.	185

(a) Including 5A. 1R. 8P. water.
(b) Including 4A. 3R. 35P. water.
(c) Including 15A. 3R. 15P. water.
(d) Including 2A. 1R. 7P. water.

(e) Including 5A. 2R. 34P. water.
(f) Including 47A. 1R. 15P. detached portions.
(g) Including 30A. 1R. 0P. detached portions.
(h) Including 18A. 3R. 36P. detached portions.

(i) Including 8A. 2R. 32P. water.
(j) Including 17A. 2R. 26P. water.
(k) Including 9A. 1R. 11P. water.

No. of Sheet of the Ordnance Survey Maps.	Townlands and Towns.	Area in Statute Acres.			County.	Barony.	Parish.	Poor Law Union in 1857.	Townland Census of 1851. Part I.	
		A.	R.	P.					Vol.	Page
4, 12	Carrig East	135	0	37	Limerick	Pubblebrien	Kilkeedy	Limerick	II.	252
84	Carrigeen	284	0	7	Cork, E.R.	East Muskerry	Moviddy	Bandon	II.	105
17	Carrigeen	367	0	23	Cork, E.R.	Fermoy	Doneraile	Mallow	II.	78
98, 112	Carrigeen	133	3	16	Cork, E.R.	Kinalea	Cullen	Kinsale	II.	94
7	Carrigeen	328	2	10	Cork, E.R.	Orrery and Kilmore	Churchtown	Mallow	II.	107
108	Carrigeen	210	2	1	Cork, W.R.	East Carbery (E.D.)	Ballymoney	Dunmanway	II.	127
136	Carrigeen	247	2	30	Cork, W.R.	Ibane and Barryroe	Lislee	Clonakilty	II.	150
21, 24	Carrigeen	164	1	22	Dublin	Newcastle	Rathcoole	Celbridge	I.	34
24	Carrigeen	301	0	5a	Kerry	Trughanacmy	Brosna	Tralee	II.	208
14	Carrigeen	105	3	23b	Kildare	Clane	Clane	Naas	I.	53
13, 14	Carrigeen	450	2	20	Kilkenny	Crannagh	Odagh	Kilkenny	I.	86
15	Carrigeen	518	0	39	Kilkenny	Gowran	Rathcoole	Kilkenny	I.	98
27, 31	Carrigeen	107	2	20	Kilkenny	Knocktopher	Jerpointchurch	Thomastown	I.	111
31	Carrigeen	46	3	23	Kilkenny	Knocktopher	Knocktopher	Thomastown	I.	112
24, 32	Carrigeen	89	0	23	King's Co.	Ballyboy	Killoughy	Tullamore	I.	124
30	Carrigeen	123	2	1	King's Co.	Eglish	Eglish	Parsonstown	I.	134
14, 15	Carrigeen	230	3	10	Leitrim	Drumahaire	Killanummery	Manorhamilton	IV.	97
32	Carrigeen	203	3	19	Mohill	Mohill	Mohill	Mohill	IV.	107
58	Carrigeen	602	3	22	Limerick	Coshlea	Kilbeheny	Mitchelstown	II.	239
21, 30	Carrigeen	673	2	5	Limerick	Coshma	Dysert	Croom	II.	243
31	Carrigeen	307	2	35	Limerick	Smallcounty	Monasteranenagh	Croom	II.	261
20, 24	Carrigeen	302	1	16	Longford	Ardagh	Rathreagh	Ballymahon	I.	153
18	Carrigeen	94	1	14	Longford	Moydow	Ballymacormick	Longford	I.	160
23	Carrigeen	48	0	12	Longford	Moydow	Taghsheenod	Ballymahon	I.	162
18	Carrigeen	110	0	13	Queen's Co.	Stradbally	Fossy or Timahoe	Athy	I.	247
14	Carrigeen	186	0	35	Queen's Co.	Stradbally	Kilteale	Mountmellick	I.	247
17,18,23,24	Carrigeen	430	2	10	Roscommon	Ballintober North	Kilglass	Strokestown	IV.	186
7	Carrigeen	74	2	14d	Roscommon	Boyle	Tumna	Car^{k.}on Shannon	IV.	197
15	Carrigeen	193	0	24e	Roscommon	Frenchpark	Kilcolagh	Boyle	IV.	203
16	Carrigeen	184	1	36	Roscommon	Roscommon	Shankill	Boyle	IV.	212
39	Carrigeen	24	0	14	Sligo	Corran	Kilshalvy	Boyle	IV.	227
41	Carrigeen	157	1	6	Tipperary, N.R.	Eliogarty	Thurles	Thurles	II.	273
34	Carrigeen	202	2	23	Tipperary, N.R.	Kilnamanagh Upper	Glenkeen	Thurles	II.	278
21	Carrigeen	64	1	35	Tipperary, N.R.	Upper Ormond	Lisbunny	Nenagh	II.	292
83	Carrigeen	44	3	15	Tipperary, S.R.	Iffa and Offa East	St. Mary's Clonmel	Clonmel	II.	316
75, 81	Carrigeen	170	0	18f	Tipperary, S.R.	Iffa and Offa West	Caher	Clogheen	II.	317
46	Carrigeen	218	0	17	Tipperary, S.R.	Kilnamanagh Lower	Clonoulty	Cashel	II.	322
69	Carrigeen	323	1	3	Tipperary, S.R.	Middlethird	Knockgraffon	Cashel	II.	328
62	Carrigeen	140	0	25	Tipperary, S.R.	Middlethird	Rathcool	Cashel	II.	329
34, 37	Carrigeen	422	3	2	Waterford	Coshmore&Coshbride	Templemichael	Youghal	II.	348
35	Carrigeen	46	3	30	Waterford	Decies within Drum	Ardmore	Dungarvan	II.	349
36	Carrigeen	119	0	5	Waterford	Decies within Drum	Ringagonagh	Dungarvan	II.	353
21, 29	Carrigeen	256	0	28	Waterford	Decies without Drum	Affane	Lismore	II.	353
16, 25	Carrigeen	365	2	17	Waterford	Decies without Drum	Kilbarrymeaden	Kilmacthomas	II.	356
15	Carrigeen	727	1	28	Waterford	Decies without Drum	Rossmire	Kilmacthomas	II.	360
6	Carrigeen	840	2	19	Waterford	Upperthird	Rathgormuck	Carrick on Suir	II.	371
15, 16	Carrigeen	219	2	37	Wexford	Gorey	Kilcormick	Enniscorthy	I.	317
15	Carrigeenacreeha	207	1	1	Roscommon	Frenchpark	Kilcolagh	Boyle	IV.	203
15	Carrigeenagappul	79	2	14	Roscommon	Frenchpark	Kilcolagh	Boyle	IV.	203
22	Carrigeenagappul	325	1	4g	Roscommon	Roscommon	Kilcooley	Strokestown	IV.	210
5	Carrigeenagowna	196	1	37	Roscommon	Boyle	Boyle	Boyle	IV.	194
37	Carrigeenagowna	139	0	8	Sligo	Leyny	Kilmacteige	Tobercurry	IV.	231
117	*Carrigeenagur*	1	2	25	Mayo	Kilmaine	Ballinchalla	Ballinrobe	IV.	152
34,35,40,41	Carrigeenblike	231	3	3h	Sligo	Tirerrill	Kilmactranny	Boyle	IV.	240
35, 41	Carrigeenboy	296	0	29i	Sligo	Tirerrill	Kilmactranny	Boyle	IV.	240
21	Carrigeenboy	29	1	13	Sligo	Tirerrill	Kilross	Sligo	IV.	241
10	Carrigeencarragh	264	1	30j	Roscommon	Boyle	Estersnow	Boyle	IV.	195
11, 15	Carrigeencor	900	0	24k	Leitrim	Drumahaire	Drumlease	Manorhamilton	IV.	94
67	Carrigeencullia	1,485	2	31	Kerry	Magunihy	Killarney	Killarney	II.	203
29	Carrigeendaniel	106	3	39	Kerry	Trughanacmy	Tralee	Tralee	II.	213
117	*Carrigeendaroe*	3	2	0	Mayo	Kilmaine	Ballinchalla	Ballinrobe	IV.	152
17	Carrigeenduff	81	0	21l	Roscommon	Roscommon	Aughrim	Car^{k.} on Shannon	IV.	207
11, 17, 18	Carrigeenduff	3,514	2	1m	Wicklow	Ballinacor North	Derrylossary	Rathdrum	I.	346
37, 46	Carrigeen East	320	3	3	Cork, E.R.	Kinatalloon	Knockmourne	Fermoy	II.	98
96, 104	Carrigeen East	429	1	3	Galway	Dunkellin	Killeely	Gort	IV.	29
20	*Carrigeenfadda*	0	1	4	Sligo	Carbury	Kilmacowen	Sligo	IV.	222
20	*Carrigeengare*	0	0	9	Sligo	Carbury	Kilmacowen	Sligo	IV.	222
8, 12	Carrigeengeare	97	0	34	Leitrim	Rosclogher	Cloonclare	Manorhamilton	IV.	109
76	*Carrigeenglass North*	3	1	19	Mayo	Burrishoole	Kilmeena	Westport	IV.	122
76	*Carrigeenglass South*	0	3	20	Mayo	Burrishoole	Kilmeena	Westport	IV.	122
116, 147	Carrigeengour	132	2	8	Cork, W.R.	West Carbery (W.D.)	Kilmoe	Skull	II.	144
37	Carrigeenhill	355	0	23	Cork, E.R.	Kinnatalloon	Knockmourne	Fermoy	II.	98
38	Carrigeenhill	211	2	19	Kildare	Kilkea and Moone	Kineagh	Baltinglass	I.	60

(a) Including 9A. 0R. 27P. water.
(b) Including 5A. 2R. 21P. water.
(c) Including 42A. 1R. 19P. water.
(d) Including 2A. 3R. 19P. water.
(e) Including 56A. 2R. 38P. water.

(f) Including 4A. 0R. 17P. water.
(g) Including 15A. 2R. 30P. water.
(h) Including 5A. 0R. 28P. water.
(i) Including 14A. 0R. 7P. Lough Skean.
(j) Including 13A. 3R. 2P. water.

(k) Including 66A. 2R. 0P. water.
(l) Including 30A. 3R. 1P. water.
(m) Including 90A. 2R. 22P. Lough Dan.

No. of Sheet of the Ordnance Survey Maps.	Townlands and Towns.	Area in Statute Acres.			County.	Barony.	Parish.	Poor Law Union in 1857.	Townland Census of 1851, Part I.	
		A.	R.	P.					Vol.	Page
120	*Carrigeen Middle*	1	0	29	Mayo	Kilmaine	Ballinchalla	Ballinrobe	IV.	152
33, 39	Carrigeenmore	264	2	4	Sligo	Corran	Emlaghfad	Sligo	IV.	226
50, 58	Carrigeen Mountain	2,082	1	1	Limerick	Coshlea	Kilbeheny	Mitchelstown	II.	239
23	Carrigeennageragh Big	259	2	12	Waterford	Decies without Drum	Kilrossanty	Kilmacthomas	II.	358
23	Carrigeennageragh Little	83	3	29	Waterford	Decies without Drum	Kilrossanty	Kilmacthomas	II.	358
24	Carrigeennahaha	181	2	4	Waterford	Decies without Drum	Stradbally	Kilmacthomas	II.	360
120	*Carrigeennakeelagh*	12	1	20	Mayo	Kilmaine	Cong	Ballinrobe	IV.	154
76	Carrigeennamoe	29	0	29	Cork, E.R.	Imokilly	Middleton	Middleton	II.	89
38	Carrigeen North	440	2	22	Kildare	Kilkea and Moone	Kineagh	Baltinglass	I.	60
17	Carrigeens	117	2	39	Longford	Rathcline	Rathcline	Longford	I.	164
42	Carrigeens	174	0	1	Roscommon	Athlone	Kilmeane	Roscommon	IV.	182
4, 7	Carrigeens	330	0	27	Sligo	Carbury	Drumcliff	Sligo	IV.	221
11, 17	Carrigeens	70	0	6	Sligo	Tireragh	Kilmacshalgan	Dromore West	IV.	234
26	Carrigeensallagh	65	3	8	Sligo	Tirerrill	Ballysadare	Sligo	IV.	237
77	Carrigeensharragh	291	3	1	Tipperary, S.R.	Middlethird	Baptistgrange	Clonmel	II.	325
17, 18	Carrigeenshinnagh	877	1	13a	Wicklow	Ballinacor North	Derrylossary	Rathdrum	I.	346
38, 40	Carrigeen South	397	0	20	Kildare	Kilkea and Moone	Kineagh	Baltinglass	I.	60
37, 46	Carrigeen West	135	3	10	Cork, E.R.	Kinnatalloon	Knockmourne	Fermoy	II.	98
96, 104	Carrigeen West	350	1	37	Galway	Dunkellin	Killeely	Gort	IV.	29
24	Carrigeenwood	393	1	2	Kerry	Trughanacmy	Brosna	Tralee	II.	208
133	Carrigeeny	311	0	17	Cork, W.R.	West Carbery (E.D.)	Kilmacabea	Skibbereen	II.	140
15	Carrigeenynaghtan	382	1	8	Roscommon	Frenchpark	Kilcolagh	Boyle	IV.	203
53, 56	Carrigenagh	673	3	27	Down	Mourne	Kilkeel	Kilkeel	III.	183
52, 53	Carrigenagh Upper	536	0	25	Down	Mourne	Kilkeel	Kilkeel	III.	183
51	Carrigerry	156	1	37	Clare	Bunratty Lower	Kilconry	Ennis	II.	4
121,133,134	Carrigfadda	614	2	14	Cork, W.R.	East Carbery (W.D.)	Ross	Clonakilty	II.	135
141	Carrigfadda	318	3	3	Cork, W.R.	West Carbery (E.D.)	Abbeystrowry	Skibbereen	II.	136
134, 143	Carrigfadeen	138	1	37	Cork, W.R.	Ibane and Barryroe	Rathbarry	Clonakilty	II.	150
20, 25, 26	Carriggal	355	0	38	Tipperary, N.R.	Owney and Arra	Burgesbeg	Nenagh	II.	294
12	Carriggower	900	0	35	Wicklow	Newcastle	Calary	Rathdrum	I.	350
28, 32	Carrighill Lower	149	0	24	Kildare	Offaly West	Ballyshannon	Athy	I.	72
28, 32	Carrighill Upper	161	1	39	Kildare	Offaly West	Ballyshannon	Athy	I.	72
142	Carrigillihy	253	2	7	Cork, W.R.	West Carbery (E.D.)	Myross	Skibbereen	II.	141
142	CARRIGILLIHY T.	—			Cork, W.R.	West Carbery (E.D.)	Myross	Skibbereen	II.	141
71, 81	Carriginane	770	0	15	Kerry	Iveragh	Glanbehy	Cahersiveen	II.	195
2	Carrig Island	231	1	38	Kerry	Iraghticonnor	Aghavallen	Listowel	II.	189
27	Carrigkerry	722	2	30	Limerick	Shanid	Ardagh	Newcastle	II.	254
89	Carrigkilter	155	1	7	Cork, E.R.	Imokilly	Ballintemple	Middleton	II.	84
30	Carriglea	202	1	12	Waterford	Decies without Drum	Whitechurch	Dungarvan	II.	361
10, 18	Carriglea	160	3	1	Waterford	Gaultiere	Kill St. Nicholas	Waterford	II.	364
24	Carriglead	446	1	39b	Carlow	St. Mullins Lower	St. Mullins	New Ross	I.	13
18, 26	Carrigleagh	287	3	3	Cork, E.R.	Fermoy	Templeroan	Mallow	II.	82
18, 26	Carrigleagh	246	3	18	Cork, E.R.	Fermoy	Wallstown	Mallow	II.	83
11	Carriglegan	365	2	15	Wexford	Scarawalsh	Kilcomb	Gorey	I.	323
39, 48	Carrigleigh	97	0	37	Cork, W.R.	West Muskerry	Drishane	Millstreet	II.	156
81	Carrigleigh	246	1	10	Cork, W.R.	West Muskerry	Inchigeelagh	Macroom	II.	156
23, 29	Carriglineen	998	3	13	Wicklow	Ballinacor North	Knockrath	Rathdrum	I.	347
17	Carriglong	266	3	19	Waterford	Middlethird	Drumcannon	Waterford	II.	366
27	Carrig Lower	184	1	21	Wicklow	Upper Talbotstown	Kiltegan	Baltinglass	I.	364
88	Carriglusky	29	3	5	Cork, E.R.	Imokilly	Cloyne	Middleton	II.	85
88	Carriglusky	79	3	25	Cork, E.R.	Imokilly	Inch	Middleton	II.	87
143	Carriglusky	63	1	26	Cork, W.R.	East Carbery (W.D.)	Kilfaughnabeg	Skibbereen	II.	132
25	Carrigmacoge	27	3	32	Wexford	Bantry	Clonmore	Enniscorthy	I.	300
20	Carrigmadden	301	0	37	Tipperary, N.R.	Owney and Arra	Youghalarra	Nenagh	II.	297
37	Carrigmannon	207	1	30	Wexford	Shelmaliere West	Killurin	Wexford	I.	334
147	Carrigmanus	78	0	31	Cork, W.R.	West Carbery (W.D.)	Kilmoe	Skull	II.	144
13, 14	Carrigmartin	195	1	39	Limerick	Clanwilliam	Cahernarry	Limerick	II.	222
23	Carrigmoorna	105	0	23	Waterford	Decies without Drum	Kilrossanty	Kilmacthomas	II.	358
16	Carrig More	179	2	27	Carlow	Idrone East	Dunleckny	Carlow	I.	6
36,37,45,46	Carrigmore	282	0	17	Cork, E.R.	Kinnatalloon	Knockmourne	Fermoy	II.	98
25	Carrig More	363	3	15	Tipperary, S.R.	Coonagh	Castletown	Tipperary	II.	234
86, 87	Carrigmore	354	2	27	Tipperary, S.R.	Iffa and Offa West	Shanrahan	Clogheen	II.	319
30, 31	Carrigmore	162	3	0	Wicklow	Arklow	Dunganstown	Rathdrum	I.	343
27	Carrig Mountain	224	1	22	Wicklow	Upper Talbotstown	Kiltegan	Baltinglass	I.	364
81, 82	Carrignacurra	446	1	26	Cork, W.R.	West Muskerry	Inchigeelagh	Dunmanway	II.	156
68, 69, 80	Carrignadoura	422	3	25	Cork, W.R.	West Muskerry	Inchigeelagh	Macroom	II.	156
19	Carrignafecka	98	1	6	Carlow	Idrone East	Sliguff	Carlow	I.	8
30	Carrignafeela	81	0	26	Kerry	Trughanacmy	Ballymacelligott	Tralee	II.	207
30	Carrignafeela	108	0	21	Kerry	Trughanacmy	O'Brennan	Tralee	II.	212
87	Carrignafoy	328	0	31	Cork, E.R.	Barrymore	Templerobin	Cork	II.	58
118	Carrignagat	27	2	3	Cork, W.R.	Bantry	Kilmocomoge	Bantry	II.	120

(a) Including 33A. 0R. 17P. Lough Dan.　　　　(b) Including 5A. 3R. 28P. River Barrow.

2 E

No. of Sheet of the Ordnance Survey Maps.	Townlands and Towns.	Area in Statute Acres.			County.	Barony.	Parish.	Poor Law Union in 1857.	Townland Census of 1851, Part I.	
		A.	R.	P.					Vol.	Page
1	Carrignagower . .	205	1	12	Wicklow . .	Lower Talbotstown	Kilbride . . .	Naas . . .	I.	361
21	Carrignagower East	155	3	10	Waterford .	Coshmore&Coshbride	Lismore andMocollop	Lismore . .	II.	345
21	Carrignagower West	158	1	21	Waterford .	Coshmore&Coshbride	Lismore and Mocollop	Lismore . .	II.	345
35	Carrignagroghera .	335	2	7	Cork, E.R. .	Condons&Clangibbon	Fermoy . . .	Fermoy . .	II.	60
93	Carrignahihilan .	119	2	16	Kerry . .	Glanarought . .	Kenmare . .	Kenmare . .	II.	186
70	Carrignamaddry .	285	2	3	Cork, W.R. .	West Muskerry	Clondrohid . .	Macroom . .	II.	155
61, 72	Carrignamuck .	363	3	3	Cork, E.R. .	East Muskerry	Magourney . .	Macroom . .	II.	105
80, 81, 93	Carrignamuck .	302	2	22	Cork, W.R. .	West Muskerry	Inchigeelagh . .	Dunmanway .	II.	156
33	Carrignamuck .	452	2	16	Wicklow . .	Ballinacor South	Hacketstown .	Shillelagh .	I.	348
19	Carrignamuck Lower	231	3	19	Wicklow . .	Newcastle . .	Killiskey . .	Rathdrum .	I.	352
18, 19	Carrignamuck Upper	291	3	9	Wicklow . .	Newcastle . .	Killiskey . .	Rathdrum .	I.	352
28, 33	Carrignamweel .	448	1	27	Wicklow . .	Ballinacor South	Hacketstown .	Shillelagh .	I.	348
82	Carrignaneelagh .	154	0	29	Cork, W.R. .	West Muskerry	Inchigeelagh . .	Macroom . .	II.	156
15	Carrignanonshagh .	139	1	14	Waterford .	Decies without Drum	Rossmire . .	Kilmacthomas .	II.	359
66, 77	Carrignashinny .	372	2	22	Cork, E.R. .	Imokilly . .	Mogeely . .	Middleton .	II.	89
52, 63	Carrignavar . .	372	3	18	Cork, E.R. .	Barrymore . .	Dunbulloge . .	Cork . . .	II.	54
52, 63	CARRIGNAVAR T. .	—			Cork, E.R. .	Barrymore . .	Dunbulloge . .	Cork . . .	II.	54
74	Carrignaveagh .	20	1	26a	Cork, E.R. .	Cork . . .	St. Marys Shandon	Cork . . .	II.	111
65	Carrigogna . .	272	2	35	Cork, E.R. .	Barrymore . .	Templenacarriga .	Middleton .	II.	58
4, 12	Carrigogunnel .	136	3	4	Limerick . .	Pubblebrien . .	Kilkeedy . .	Limerick . .	II.	252
8	Carrigolagh . .	126	3	21b	Fermanagh .	Magheraboy . .	Inishmacsaint .	Ballyshannon .	III.	212
59	Carrigonirtane .	334	2	12	Cork, W.R. .	West Muskerry	Clondrohid . .	Macroom . .	II.	155
33	Carrigoon . .	329	2	27c	Cork, E.R. .	Fermoy . . .	Rahan . . .	Mallow . .	II.	82
7	Carrigoona Commons East . . .	97	3	15	Wicklow . .	Rathdown . .	Kilmacanoge . .	Rathdown .	I.	355
7	Carrigoona Commons West . . .	102	1	1	Wicklow . .	Rathdown . .	Kilmacanoge . .	Rathdown .	I.	355
33	Carrigoon Beg . .	187	2	18d	Cork, E.R. .	Fermoy . . .	Mallow . . .	Mallow . .	II.	81
33	Carrigoon More .	161	2	13e	Cork, E.R. .	Fermoy . . .	Mallow . . .	Mallow . .	II.	81
51	Carrigoran . .	241	3	3	Clare . .	Bunratty Lower	Kilnasoolagh . .	Ennis . .	II.	6
16	Carrigpark . .	128	2	12	Carlow . .	Idrone East . .	Dunleckny . .	Carlow . .	I.	6
25, 33	Carrigpark . .	309	2	37	Cork, E.R. .	Fermoy . . .	Carrigleamleary .	Mallow . .	II.	77
14	Carrigparson . .	283	3	1	Limerick .	Clanwilliam . .	Carrigparson . .	Limerick . .	II.	223
75	Carrigrenan . .	80	3	12	Cork, E.R. .	Barrymore . .	Little Island . .	Cork . . .	II.	56
109	Carrigroe . .	276	3	32	Cork, W.R. .	East Carbery (E.D.)	Desertserges . .	Bandon . .	II.	127
134, 135 ⎫ 143, 144 ⎬	Carrigroe . .	559	2	31	Cork, W.R. .	Ibane and Barryroe	Rathbarry . .	Clonakilty .	II.	150
28, 33	Carrigroe . .	61	0	26	Waterford .	Coshmore&Coshbride	Tallow . . .	Lismore . .	II.	348
30	Carrigroe . .	240	0	17	Waterford .	Decies without Drum	Whitechurch . .	Dungarvan .	II.	361
17	Carrigroe . .	93	3	37	Waterford .	Gaultiere . .	Kilbarry . . .	Waterford .	II.	363
13	Carrigroe . .	149	1	36	Waterford .	Glenahiry . .	Kilronan . . .	Clonmel . .	II.	365
17, 18	Carrigroe . .	562	0	0f	Wicklow . .	Ballinacor North	Derrylossary .	Rathdrum .	I.	346
38	Carrigroe . .	329	0	30	Wicklow . .	Ballinacor South	Moyne . . .	Shillelagh .	I.	350
73, 74	Carrigrohane . .	1,543	2	14g	Cork, E.R. .	Cork . . .	Carrigrohane . .	Cork . . .	II.	64
73	Carrigrohanebeg .	156	2	38h	Cork, E.R. .	East Muskerry	Carrigrohanebeg .	Cork . . .	II.	102
90	Carrigrour . .	241	1	0	Cork, W.R. .	Bear . . .	Kilcaskan . .	Bantry . .	II.	122
76	Carrigshane . .	278	2	25	Cork, E.R. .	Imokilly . .	Middleton . .	Middleton .	II.	89
105	Carrigskeewaun .	142	2	7	Mayo . .	Murrisk . .	Kilgeever . .	Westport .	IV.	159
107	Carrigskullihy .	381	0	21	Cork, W.R. .	East Carbery (W.D.)	Fanlobbus . .	Dunmanway .	II.	131
60	Carrigthomas . .	347	1	3	Cork, W.R. .	East Muskerry	Aghabulloge . .	Macroom . .	II.	153
142	Carrigtishane . .	217	1	33	Cork, W.R. .	West Carbery (E.D.)	Castlehaven . .	Skibbereen .	II.	137
75, 76	Carrigtohill . .	566	2	7	Cork, E.R. .	Barrymore . .	Carrigtohill . .	Middleton .	II.	52
75, 76	CARRIGTOHILL T. .	—			Cork, E.R. .	Barrymore . .	Carrigtohill . .	Middleton .	II.	52
17, 24	Carrigullian . .	371	1	17i	Down . .	Dufferin . .	Killinchy . .	Downpatrick .	III.	166
10	Carrigullin . .	497	2	33j	Tyrone . .	Strabane Lower	Camus . . .	Strabane .	III.	320
31	Carrigunane . .	159	3	36	Wexford . .	Bantry . .	Kilcowanmore .	Enniscorthy .	I.	300
27	Carrig Upper . .	183	2	26	Wicklow . .	Upper Talbotstown	Kiltegan . .	Baltinglass .	I.	364
83	Carrig West . .	699	1	9k	Kerry . .	Dunkerron South .	Templenoe . .	Kenmare . .	II.	185
4, 12	Carrig West . .	612	3	11	Limerick . .	Pubblebrien . .	Kilkeedy . .	Limerick . .	II.	252
73	Carrigyknaveen .	234	0	1l	Cork, E.R. .	East Muskerry	Inishcarra . .	Cork . . .	II.	103
31	Carrintaggart . .	153	1	8m	Down . .	Lecale Lower . .	Ballyculter . .	Downpatrick .	III.	178
13	Carrivcashel . .	399	0	23	Antrim . .	Upper Dunluce	Loughguile . .	Ballymoney .	III.	20
34	Carrive . . .	1,300	0	1	Antrim . .	Lower Glenarm	Tickmacrevan .	Larne . .	III.	23
28, 31	Carrive . . .	901	2	22	Armagh . .	Orior Upper . .	Forkill . . .	Newry . .	III.	57
26	Carrivekeeny . .	187	3	6	Armagh . .	Orior Upper . .	Killevy . . .	Newry . .	III.	58
26, 29	Carrivemaclone .	194	1	5	Armagh . .	Orior Upper . .	Killevy . . .	Newry . .	III.	58
20	Carrivemurphy Mountain . .	509	0	39	Antrim . .	Lower Glenarm	Ardclinis . .	Larne . .	III.	21
25	Carrivereagh . .	435	1	9	Antrim . .	Lower Glenarm	Ardclinis . .	Larne . .	III.	21
11, 12	Carrivetragh . .	181	3	14n	Monaghan .	Dartree . .	Clones . . .	Clones . .	III.	264
19	Carroghill . .	305	1	16	Donegal . .	Inishowen West	Mintiaghs or Barr of Inch . . .	Inishowen .	III.	121
51	Carrogs . . .	572	0	5o	Down . .	Upper Iveagh, Up. pt.	Clonallan . .	Newry . .	III.	174
60	Carrollspark . .	41	0	10	Tipperary, S.R.	Middlethird . .	St. Patricksrock .	Cashel . .	II.	330

(a) Included in the parish of St. Mary's Shandon.
(b) Including 1A. 3R. 20P. water.
(c) Including 6A. 1R. 24P. water.
(d) Including 4A. 2R. 32P. water.
(e) Including 4A. 3R. 0P. water.
(f) Including 64A. 0R. 28P. Lough Dan.
(g) Including 25A. 1R. 2P. water.
(h) Including 0A. 2R. 9P. River Lee.
(i) Including 20A. 2R. 28P. water.
(j) Including 1A. 1R. 13P. water.
(k) Including 4A. 3R. 20P. water.
(l) Including 7A. 0R. 1P. water.
(m) Including 3A. 3R. 10P. Great Dam.
(n) Including 11A. 2R. 1P. water.
(o) Including 14A. 1R. 3P. water.

No. of Sheet of the Ordnance Survey Maps.	Townlands and Towns.	Area in Statute Acres.			County.	Barony.	Parish.	Poor Law Union in 1857.	Townland Census of 1851, Part I.	
		A.	R.	P.					Vol.	Page
58, 59	Carron . . .	98	0	28	Tipperary, S.R.	Clanwilliam . .	Solloghod-beg . .	Tipperary . .	II.	310
58, 59	Carron . . .	300	2	39	Tipperary, S.R.	Clanwilliam . .	Tipperary . .	Tipperary . .	II.	312
69	Carron . . .	481	1	23	Tipperary, S.R.	Middlethird . .	St. John Baptist .	Cashel . .	II.	330
35	Carronadavderg	357	2	26	Waterford .	Decies within Drum	Ardmore . .	Youghal .	II.	349
35	Carronahyla . .	157	3	2	Waterford .	Decies within Drum	Ardmore . .	Dungarvan .	II.	349
35	Carronbeg .	230	0	21	Waterford .	Decies within Drum	Ardmore . .	Youghal . .	II.	350
19	Carrons . .	316	0	1	Limerick . .	Shanid . .	Kilcolman . .	Glin . .	II.	255
38	Carrontlieve .	118	2	37	Donegal .	Inishowen West .	Fahan Upper . .	Londonderry .	III.	121
25	Carrontreemall	180	2	4	Fermanagh .	Clanawley . .	Cleenish . .	Enniskillen .	III.	190
51	Carrow . .	127	3	7	Clare .	Bunratty Lower .	Kilmaleery . .	Ennis . .	II.	5
57	Carrow . . .	231	1	3	Clare .	Moyarta . . .	Kilmacduane .	Kilrush . .	II.	32
58, 60	Carrow . . .	501	3	7	Limerick . .	Coshlea . .	Kilbeheny . .	Mitchelstown .	II.	239
30	Carrow . . .	278	0	8	Limerick . .	Coshma . .	Croom . .	Croom . .	II.	242
14	Carrow . .	273	3	38	Tipperary, N.R.	Lower Ormond .	Monsea . .	Nenagh .	II.	287
26	Carrow . .	314	0	11	Tipperary, N.R.	Upper Ormond .	Kilmore . .	Nenagh . .	II.	291
88	Carrow . .	84	2	10	Tipperary, S.R.	Iffa and Offa West .	Ballybacon . .	Clogheen .	II.	317
45, 51, 52	Carrow . . .	1,600	2	36	Tipperary, S.R.	Kilnamanagh Lower	Donohill . .	Cashel . .	II.	323
53	Carrow . . .	183	3	14	Tipperary, S.R.	Middlethird . .	Ballysheehan . .	Cashel . .	II.	325
109	Carrowneeragh	191	0	13a	Mayo .	Carra . .	Ballyovey . .	Ballinrobe .	IV.	126
39	Carrowanree . .	79	2	37	Wexford .	Shelburne . .	Killesk . .	New Ross .	I.	327
71	Carroward . .	448	2	0	Mayo .	Gallen . .	Bohola . .	Swineford .	IV.	147
44	Carroward . .	292	1	21	Roscommon .	Athlone . .	Tisrara . .	Roscommon .	IV.	185
28, 29	Carroward . .	209	1	11	Roscommon .	Ballintober South .	Kilbride . .	Roscommon .	IV.	188
36	Carroward . .	90	1	20	Roscommon .	Ballintober South .	Kilgefin . .	Roscommon .	IV.	189
11	Carroward . .	101	1	19	Roscommon .	Boyle . .	Killukin . .	Car^{k.} on Shannon	IV.	195
29	Carroward . .	221	0	31	Roscommon .	Roscommon . .	Lissonuffy . .	Strokestown .	IV.	211
19	Carroward . .	530	1	28	Sligo .	Tireragh . .	Dromard . .	Dromore West .	IV.	233
54	Carroward East	224	0	17	Limerick . .	Connello Upper .	Dromcolliher .	Newcastle .	II.	232
54	Carroward West	420	3	27	Limerick . .	Connello Upper .	Dromcolliher .	Newcastle .	II.	232
33	CARROWARREN T. .	—			Clare .	Islands . .	Drumcliff . .	Ennis . .	II.	30
38	Carrowbaghran	121	0	32	Down .	Lecale Lower .	Ballee . .	Downpatrick .	III.	178
51	Carrowbane .	169	1	36	Clare .	Bunratty Lower .	Kilmaleery . .	Ennis . .	II.	5
58, 68	Carrowbane .	458	0	25	Clare .	Clonderalaw .	Kilmurry . .	Kilrush . .	II.	17
44, 45	Carrowbane .	218	2	17	Down .	Lecale Upper .	Bright . .	Downpatrick .	III.	180
15	Carrowbane .	95	1	36	Roscommon .	Frenchpark . .	Tibohine . .	Castlereagh .	IV.	204
14, 20	Carrowbane .	100	3	4	Tipperary, N.R.	Owney and Arra .	Youghalarra . .	Nenagh . .	II.	297
9, 18	Carrowbane Beg	135	2	32	Limerick . .	Shanid . .	Loghill . .	Glin . .	II.	256
9, 18	Carrowbane More .	337	0	2	Limerick . .	Shanid . .	Loghill . .	Glin . .	II.	256
8, 12	Carrowbarra . .	78	0	38	Monaghan .	Monaghan . .	Clones . .	Monaghan .	III.	274
12	Carrowbarra Island .	22	3	7	Monaghan .	Monaghan . .	Clones . .	Monaghan .	III.	274
36, 37	Carrowbaun . .	615	2	37	Clare .	Tulla Lower .	Killaloe . .	Scarriff .	II.	35
16	Carrowbaun . .	156	1	35	Galway .	Dunmore .	Dunmore . .	Tuam . .	IV.	33
29	Carrowbaun . .	197	1	28	Galway .	Dunmore .	Tuam . .	Tuam . .	IV.	35
97	Carrowbaun . .	239	2	1	Galway .	Loughrea .	Lickerrig . .	Loughrea .	IV.	65
27	Carrowbaun . .	164	3	26	Galway .	Ross . .	Cong . .	Oughterard .	IV.	73
68	Carrowbaun . .	60	3	13	Mayo .	Burrishoole .	Burrishoole . .	Newport .	IV.	118
82	Carrowbaun . .	231	0	27	Mayo .	Costello . .	Aghamore . .	Swineford .	IV.	136
61, 71, 72	Carrowbaun . .	321	3	33	Mayo .	Gallen . .	Meelick . .	Swineford .	IV.	150
88	Carrowbaun . .	491	0	30b	Mayo .	Murrisk . .	Oughaval . .	Westport .	IV.	161
36, 40	Carrowbaun . .	140	0	34	Roscommon .	Ballintober South .	Kilbride . .	Roscommon .	IV.	188
28	Carrowbaun . .	376	3	4c	Roscommon .	Ballymoe . .	Cloonygormican .	Castlereagh .	IV.	191
1	Carrowbaun . .	130	2	28	Roscommon .	Boyle . .	Kilronan . .	Boyle . .	IV.	196
27	Carrowbaun . .	239	2	18	Roscommon .	Castlereagh .	Ballintober .	Castlereagh .	IV.	198
21	Carrowbaun . .	128	0	6	Roscommon .	Castlereagh .	Baslick . .	Castlereagh .	IV.	199
114, 123	Carrowbaun East	84	2	20	Galway .	Kiltartan .	Kiltartan . .	Gort . .	IV.	48
114	Carrowbaun West .	99	3	21	Galway .	Kiltartan .	Kiltartan . .	Gort . .	IV.	48
18	Carrowbawn . .	164	3	6	Wicklow .	Newcastle .	Killiskey . .	Rathdrum .	I.	352
12	Carrowbeg .	464	0	33	Donegal .	Inishowen East .	Moville Lower .	Inishowen .	III.	118
41	Carrowbeg .	238	0	7	Galway .	Clare . .	Killursa . .	Tuam . .	IV.	21
9	Carrowbeg .	147	0	36	Longford .	Longford . .	Clongesh . .	Longford .	I.	157
21	Carrow Beg .	225	1	3d	Longford .	Rathcline .	Cashel . .	Ballymahon .	I.	163
89	Carrowbeg .	308	2	16e	Mayo .	Burrishoole .	Islandeady . .	Westport .	IV.	121
76, 77	Carrowbeg .	137	2	37	Mayo .	Burrishoole .	Kilmeena . .	Westport .	IV.	121
112	Carrowbeg .	107	1	18	Mayo .	Clanmorris .	Crossboyne .	Claremorris .	IV.	132
92, 102	Carrowbeg .	626	1	4	Mayo .	Clanmorris .	Kilcolman .	Claremorris .	IV.	133
103	Carrow Beg .	144	3	20	Mayo .	Costello . .	Annagh . .	Claremorris .	IV.	137
72,73,81,82	Carrowbeg .	1,104	1	1f	Mayo .	Costello . .	Kilmovee . .	Swineford .	IV.	141
61, 62	Carrowbeg .	101	0	33	Mayo .	Gallen . .	Kilconduff . .	Swineford .	IV.	147
62	Carrowbeg .	197	1	13g	Mayo .	Gallen . .	Killasser . .	Swineford .	IV.	149
88	Carrowbeg .	118	3	25	Mayo .	Murrisk . .	Oughaval . .	Westport .	IV.	161
4	Carrowbeg .	82	2	18	Roscommon .	Boyle . .	Kilronan . .	Boyle . .	IV.	196
61	Carrowbeg .	280	0	18	Tyrone .	Dungannon Middle .	Clonfeacle .	Dungannon .	III.	298
101	Carrowbeg East	137	2	27h	Mayo .	Clanmorris .	Crossboyne .	Claremorris .	IV.	132

(a) Including 17A. 0R. 0P. detached portion.
(b) Including 6A. 0R. 34P. water.
(c) Including 15A. 3R. 10P. water.
(d) Including 9A. 3R. 26P. water.
(e) Including 4A. 1R. 20P. water.
(f) Including 13A. 0R 2P. water.
(g) Including 4A. 0R. 10P. water.
(h) Including 6A. 0R. 5F. water.

No. of Sheet of the Ordnance Survey Maps.	Townlands and Towns.	Area in Statute Acres.	County.	Barony.	Parish.	Poor Law Union in 1857.	Townland Census of 1851, Part I.	
		A. R. P.					Vol.	Page
67	Carrowbeg (*Fergus*)	49 0 8	Mayo	Burrishoole	Burrishoole	Newport	IV.	118
56	Carrowbeg North	110 3 7	Galway	Clare	Annaghdown	Galway	IV.	16
42, 43	Carrowbeg North	186 0 19	Galway	Clare	Belclare	Tuam	IV.	17
67	Carrowbeg North	138 2 35a	Mayo	Burrishoole	Burrishoole	Newport	IV.	118
56, 69	Carrowbeg South	122 0 29	Galway	Clare	Annaghdown	Galway	IV.	16
43	Carrowbeg South	178 2 18	Galway	Clare	Belclare	Tuam	IV.	17
67,68,76,77	Carrowbeg South	112 0 28	Mayo	Burrishoole	Burrishoole	Newport	IV.	118
101	Carrowbeg West	41 2 35	Mayo	Clanmorris	Crossboyne	Claremorris	IV.	132
19	Carrowbehy	838 3 19b	Roscommon	Frenchpark	Tibohine	Castlereagh	IV.	204
20	Carrowblagh	2,414 2 39	Donegal	Inishowen East	Donagh	Inishowen	III.	118
12	Carrowblagh	745 2 20	Donegal	Inishowen East	Moville Lower	Inishowen	III.	118
12	Carrowblagh or Leckemy	935 3 35	Donegal	Inishowen East	Moville Lower	Inishowen	III.	118
19	Carrowbleagh East	82 1 7	Sligo	Tireragh	Dromard	Dromore West	IV.	233
19	Carrowbleagh West	38 3 31	Sligo	Tireragh	Dromard	Dromore West	IV.	233
46	Carrowblough Beg	232 1 25	Clare	Ibrickan	Killard	Kilrush	II.	23
46, 56	Carrowblough More	594 3 17	Clare	Ibrickan	Killard	Kilrush	II.	23
2, 4	Carrowboy	142 1 24	Leitrim	Rosclogher	Rossinver	Ballyshannon	IV.	111
28	Carrowboy	93 2 29	Roscommon	Ballintober South	Kilbride	Roscommon	IV.	188
100	Carrowbrack	96 2 7c	Mayo	Kilmaine	Mayo	Ballinrobe	IV.	157
19	Carrowbreedoge	28 3 1	Limerick	Shanid	Kilmoylan	Rathkeale	II.	256
13	Carrowbrickeen	230 0 15	Sligo	Tireragh	Skreen	Dromore West	IV.	235
69, 78	Carrowbrinoge	365 3 26d	Mayo	Carra	Aglish	Castlebar	IV.	123
82	Carrowbrowne	861 3 1	Galway	Galway	Oranmore	Galway	IV.	37
13, 14	Carrowbunnaun	242 1 3	Sligo	Carbury	Killaspugbrone	Sligo	IV.	222
76, 87	Carrowcally	109 1 33	Mayo	Burrishoole	Kilmeena	Westport	IV.	122
61,62,71,72	Carrowcanada	497 2 15	Mayo	Gallen	Kilconduff	Swineford	IV.	147
25	Carrowcanon	459 2 34	Donegal	Kilmacrenan	Raymunterdoney	Dunfanaghy	III.	131
16, 22	Carrowcardin	456 3 9	Sligo	Tireragh	Castleconor	Dromore West	IV.	232
38	Carrowcarlan	81 0 27	Fermanagh	Knockninny	Kinawley	Lisnaskea	III.	201
31	Carrowcarlin	130 1 20	Down	Lecale Lower	Saul	Downpatrick	III.	179
32	Carrowcarragh	279 0 26	Sligo	Leyny	Achonry	Tobercurry	IV.	229
46	Carrowcashel	288 0 6	Donegal	Kilmacrenan	Aughnish	Millford	III.	122
27	Carrowcashel	217 3 20	Sligo	Tirerrill	Drumcolumb	Sligo	IV.	238
28, 35	Carrowcashel	801 2 26	Sligo	Tirerrill	Kilmactranny	Boyle	IV.	240
12	Carrowcaslan	115 1 0	Sligo	Tireragh	Skreen	Dromore West	IV.	235
71	Carrowcastle	294 1 13	Mayo	Gallen	Bohola	Castlebar	IV.	147
40	Carrowcastle	810 2 8e	Mayo	Gallen	Kilgarvan	Ballina	IV.	148
33	Carrowcauly or Earlsfield	115 0 20	Sligo	Corran	Emlaghfad	Sligo	IV.	226
86	Carrowclaggan	94 2 23	Mayo	Murrisk	Kilgeever	Westport	IV.	159
5, 9	Carrowclare	343 1 10	Londonderry	Keenaght	Tamlaght Finlagan	NewTᵃLimavady	III.	237
32	Carrowclare	109 1 8	Sligo	Leyny	Achonry	Tobercurry	IV.	229
105	Carrowclogh	152 0 24	Galway	Dunkellin	Kilconickny	Loughrea	IV.	29
19	Carrowclogh	105 1 26	Limerick	Shanid	Kilmoylan	Rathkeale	II.	256
67	Carrowclogh	68 3 29	Tipperary, S.R.	Clanwilliam	Cordangan	Tipperary	II.	306
38	Carrowcloghagh	162 0 27	Mayo	Tirawley	Crossmolina	Ballina	IV.	165
8	Carrowcloghan	281 0 13	Antrim	Cary	Grange of Drumtullagh	Ballycastle	III.	14
89	Carrowclogher	334 2 4f	Mayo	Carra	Ballyhean	Castlebar	IV.	125
29	Carrowclogher	251 2 2	Roscommon	Roscommon	Cloonfinlough	Strokestown	IV.	208
25	Carrowclooneen	194 0 27	Sligo	Leyny	Killoran	Tobercurry	IV.	230
2	Carrowclough	93 3 25	Waterford	Upperthird	Dysert	Carrick on Suir	II.	369
2	Carrowclough	130 0 7	Waterford	Upperthird	Rathgormuck	Carrick on Suir	II.	371
17	Carrowcoller	444 0 21	Sligo	Tireragh	Kilglass	Dromore West	IV.	234
61	Carrowcolman	267 2 1	Tyrone	Dungannon Middle	Clonfeacle	Dungannon	III.	299
40	Carrowconeen	72 0 1	Mayo	Gallen	Kilgarvan	Ballina	IV.	148
42	Carrowconlaun	140 1 20	Galway	Clare	Donaghpatrick	Tuam	IV.	19
70	Carrowconnell	104 2 29	Mayo	Gallen	Kildacommoge	Castlebar	IV.	148
112	Carrowconor	213 3 25	Mayo	Clanmorris	Crossboyne	Claremorris	IV.	132
19	Carrowconor	161 2 29	Sligo	Tireragh	Dromard	Dromore West	IV.	233
92, 102	Carrowcor	124 0 19	Mayo	Costello	Knock	Claremorris	IV.	142
7	Carrowcor	362 3 39	Mayo	Tirawley	Kilbride	Killala	IV.	168
12	Carrowcor	71 1 36	Sligo	Tireragh	Templeboy	Dromore West	IV.	236
29, 37	Carrowcore	202 3 1	Clare	Tulla Lower	Ogonnelloe	Scarriff	II.	38
24, 28	Carrowcowan	358 2 39	Antrim	Kilconway	Dunaghy	Ballymena	III.	25
11, 18	Carrowcraheen	136 3 34	Clare	Inchiquin	Kilkeedy	Corrofin	II.	25
116	Carrowcreevanagh	156 2 3	Galway	Leitrim	Duniry	Loughrea	IV.	53
13, 18	Carrowcrin	282 0 38	Antrim	Upper Dunluce	Loughguile	Ballymoney	III.	20
116	Carrowcrin	120 2 9	Galway	Leitrim	Ballynakill	Loughrea	IV.	50
14	Carrowcrin	235 0 14	Leitrim	Drumahaire	Killanummery	Manorhamilton	IV.	97
30	Carrowcrin	227 2 30	Mayo	Tirawley	Ardagh	Ballina	IV.	163
36, 40	Carrowcrin	274 2 17	Roscommon	Ballintober South	Kilbride	Roscommon	IV.	188
16	Carrowcrin	29 0 1	Roscommon	Frenchpark	Kilmacumsy	Boyle	IV.	203

(a) Including 12A. 1R. 13P. water.
(b) Including 2A. 0R. 16P. water.
(c) Including 10A. 3R. 32P. water.
(d) Including 8A. 1R. 13P. water.
(e) Including 4A. 1R. 20P. water.
(f) Including 0A. 0R. 8P. water.

No. of Sheet of the Ordnance Survey Maps.	Townlands and Towns.	Area in Statute Acres.	County.	Barony.	Parish.	Poor Law Union in 1857.	Townland Census of 1851, Part I.	
		A. R. P.					Vol.	Page
20	Carrowcrin	116 3 24	Sligo	Carbury	Kilmacowen	Sligo	IV.	222
21, 27	Carrowcrin	165 1 20	Sligo	Tirerrill	Ballysumaghan	Sligo	IV.	238
8	Carrowcroey	202 3 10	Antrim	Cary	Ballintoy	Ballycastle	III.	12
31, 40	Carrowcrom	477 3 21	Mayo	Gallen	Kilgarvan	Ballina	IV.	148
40, 45	Carrowcrory	561 2 0a	Sligo	Corran	Toomour	Boyle	IV.	228
11, 17, 18	Carrowcuill	184 1 0	Roscommon	Ballintober North	Kilmore	Carᵇ. on Shannon	IV.	187
14	Carrowcuilleen	899 0 31	Mayo	Tirawley	Lackan	Killala	IV.	170
17	Carrowculleen	238 3 9	Galway	Dunmore	Dunmore	Tuam	IV.	33
18, 19, 24	Carrowculleen	1,079 2 31b	Sligo	Tireragh	Skreen	Dromore West	IV.	235
17	Carrowculleen(Hoare)	28 0 18	Galway	Dunmore	Dunmore	Tuam	IV.	33
26, 33	Carrowcushely	384 0 31	Sligo	Corran	Emlaghfad	Sligo	IV.	226
29	Carrowcushlaun	442 0 36c	Sligo	Tireragh	Kilmoremoy	Ballina	IV.	235
29	Carrowcushlaun West	17 2 24d	Sligo	Tireragh	Kilmoremoy	Ballina	IV.	235
40, 49	Carrowdoogan	498 0 29	Mayo	Gallen	Attymass	Ballina	IV.	147
6,7	CARROWDORE T.	—	Down	Ards Lower	Donaghadee	Newtownards	III.	158
26	Carrowdotia	229 1 24	Clare	Bunratty Upper	Kilraghtis	Ennis	II.	9
67	Carrowdotia North	323 0 24	Clare	Clonderalaw	Killimer	Kilrush	II.	16
67	Carrowdotia South	472 0 31	Clare	Clonderalaw	Killimer	Kilrush	II.	16
13, 14	Carrowdough	366 0 24	Sligo	Carbury	Killaspugbrone	Sligo	IV.	222
45	Carrowdressex	59 1 14	Down	Lecale Upper	Kilclief	Downpatrick	III.	181
15	Carrowduff	680 0 14	Clare	Corcomroe	Killaspuglonane	Ennistimon	II.	19
15	Carrowduff	296 0 33	Clare	Corcomroe	Kilshanny	Ennistimon	II.	21
30, 31	Carrowduff	604 0 29	Clare	Ibrickan	Kilmurry	Ennistimon	II.	23
24	Carrowduff	206 2 1	Clare	Inchiquin	Rath	Corrofin	II.	27
3	Carrowduff	155 3 37	Leitrim	Rosclogher	Rossinver	Ballyshannon	IV.	111
51	Carrowduff&Garbally	924 1 32	Roscommon	Athlone	Taghmaconnell	Athlone	IV.	185
27,28,34,35	Carrowduff Lower	333 3 25	Roscommon	Ballymoe	Cloonygormican	Castlereagh	IV.	191
34, 35	Carrowduff Upper	192 3 31	Roscommon	Ballymoe	Cloonygormican	Castlereagh	IV.	191
21	Carrowdunican	68 2 39	Longford	Rathcline	Cashel	Ballymahon	I.	163
19	Carrowdurneen	190 0 15	Sligo	Tireragh	Skreen	Dromore West	IV.	235
22	Carrowea	68 0 4	Tipperary, N.R.	Upper Ormond	Ballymackey	Nenagh	II.	289
50	Carroweeny	408 1 27	Mayo	Gallen	Killasser	Swineford	IV.	149
34	Carroweighter	216 3 8	Roscommon	Ballymoe	Oran	Roscommon	IV.	192
46, 47	Carrowen	435 2 8	Donegal	Inishowen West	Burt	Londonderry	III.	119
29, 37	Carrowena	352 3 22	Clare	Tulla Lower	Ogonnelloe	Scarriff	II.	38
8, 15	Carroweragh	552 1 23	Clare	Corcomroe	Kilshanny	Ennistimon	II.	21
10	Carrowfarnaghan	163 1 34e	Cavan	Lower Loughtee	Drumlane	Cavan	III.	79
59, 72	Carrowferrikeen	79 0 0	Galway	Tiaquin	Moylough	Mountbellew	IV.	79
13, 19	Carrowflatley or Carrownaglogh	121 3 5	Sligo	Tireragh	Dromard	Dromore West	IV.	233
57, 58, 67	Carrowfree	551 2 21	Clare	Moyarta	Kilrush	Kilrush	II.	33
61, 71	Carrowgallda	463 0 33f	Mayo	Gallen	Templemore	Swineford	IV.	151
34,35,42,43	Carrowgar	294 3 27	Clare	Bunratty Upper	Quin	Tulla	II.	10
23	Carrowgar	281 2 16	Clare	Corcomroe	Kilmanaheen	Ennistimon	II.	21
42	Carrowgar	186 2 9	Clare	Islands	Clareabbey	Ennis	II.	29
29, 37	Carrowgar	175 1 15	Clare	Tulla Lower	Ogonnelloe	Scarriff	II.	38
36	Carrowgar	127 2 32	Limerick	Glenquin	Grange	Newcastle	II.	245
34	Carrowgarragh	107 3 35g	Fermanagh	Magherastephana	Aghalurcher	Lisnaskea	III.	215
123, 129	Carrowgarriff	291 3 29	Galway	Kiltartan	Beagh	Gort	IV.	46
26, 39	Carrowgarriff	659 0 12	Galway	Ross	Cong	Oughterard	IV.	73
22	Carrowgarriff	150 2 11	Waterford	Decies without Drum	Colligan	Dungarvan	II.	354
22	Carrowgarriff Beg	145 3 6	Waterford	Decies without Drum	Colligan	Dungarvan	II.	354
22	Carrowgarriff More	321 1 5	Waterford	Decies without Drum	Colligan	Dungarvan	II.	354
113	Carrowgarriff North	128 1 17	Galway	Dunkellin	Ardrahan	Gort	IV.	26
113	Carrowgarriff South	344 3 34	Galway	Dunkellin	Ardrahan	Gort	IV.	26
16	Carrowgarry	328 3 35	Sligo	Tireragh	Castleconor	Dromore West	IV.	232
65	Carrowgarve	206 1 12	Mayo	Burrishoole	Achill	Newport	IV.	117
91	Carrowgarve	201 1 28	Mayo	Clanmorris	Balla	Castlebar	IV.	131
48	Carrowgarve	214 3 21	Mayo	Tirawley	Kilbelfad	Ballina	IV.	167
34	Carrowgarve	200 0 14	Roscommon	Ballymoe	Oran	Roscommon	IV.	192
27	Carrowgarve	156 3 33	Roscommon	Castlereagh	Kilkeevin	Castlereagh	IV.	200
14	Carrowgarve	536 0 25	Roscommon	Frenchpark	Tibohine	Castlereagh	IV.	204
28	Carrowgarve	474 3 26	Roscommon	Roscommon	Ogulla	Strokestown	IV.	212
29	Carrowgarve North	315 2 0	Mayo	Tirawley	Crossmolina	Ballina	IV.	165
37, 38	Carrowgarve South	676 2 27	Mayo	Tirawley	Crossmolina	Ballina	IV.	165
19, 25	Carrowgavneen	648 0 4h	Sligo	Leyny	Killoran	Tobercurry	IV.	230
13	Carrowgilhooly	202 1 7	Sligo	Tireragh	Skreen	Dromore West	IV.	235
19	Carrowgilpatrick	156 1 31	Sligo	Tireragh	Dromard	Dromore West	IV.	233
22	Carrowgobbadagh	94 2 0	Roscommon	Roscommon	Elphin	Strokestown	IV.	209
20	Carrowgobbadagh	226 3 8	Sligo	Carbury	Kilmacowen	Sligo	IV.	222
44	Carrowgorm	214 3 22	Galway	Tiaquin	Killererin	Tuam	IV.	77
71	Carrowgowan	168 2 28	Mayo	Gallen	Bohola	Castlebar	IV.	147
16, 22	Carrowgun	116 1 19	Sligo	Tireragh	Castleconor	Dromore West	IV.	232

(a) Including 5ᴀ. 1ʀ. 26ᴘ. water.
(b) Including 21ᴀ. 1ʀ. 23ᴘ. water.
(c) Including 13ᴀ. 3ʀ. 9ᴘ. River Moy.

(d) Including 4ᴀ. 3ʀ. 2ᴘ. River Moy.
(e) Including 7ᴀ. 0ʀ. 19ᴘ. water.
(f) Including 15ᴀ. 0ʀ. 1ᴘ. water.

(g) Including 7ᴀ. 1ʀ. 5ᴘ. water.
(h) Including 6ᴀ. 2ʀ. 10ᴘ. water.

No. of Sheet of the Ordnance Survey Maps.	Townlands and Towns.	Area in Statute Acres.	County.	Barony.	Parish.	Poor Law Union in 1857.	Townland Census of 1851, Part I.	
		A.　R.　P.					Vol.	Page
100	Carrowhall　.　.	152　1　37	Mayo　.　.	Carra　.　.	Rosslee　.　.	Ballinrobe　.	IV.	130
9	Carrowhatta　.	127　2　25	Monaghan　.	Monaghan　.	Tedavnet　.	Monaghan　.	III.	278
103	Carrowhawny　.	118　0　8	Mayo　.　.	Costello　.　.	Annagh　.　.	Claremorris　.	IV.	138
27	Carrowhekeen　.	225　1　33	Galway　.	Ross　.　.	Cong　.　.	Oughterard　.	IV.	73
73, 86	Carrowholla　.	515　0　34	Galway　.	Kilconnell　.	Ballymacward　.	Ballinasloe　.	IV.	39
28, 34	Carrowhony　.　.	146　3　25	Fermanagh　.	Magherastephana　.	Aghalurcher　.	Lisnaskea　.	III.	215
16	Carrowhubbuck Nth.	251　0　7	Sligo　.　.	Tireragh　.	Kilglass　.　.	Dromore West.	IV.	234
16	Carrowhubbuck Sth.	552　1　15	Sligo　.　.	Tireragh　.　.	Kilglass　.　.	Dromore West.	IV.	234
13, 22	Carrowhugh　.　.	633　3　7	Donegal　.	Inishowen East	Moville Lower	Inishowen　.	III.	118
90	Carrowjames　.	176　0　3	Mayo　.　.	Carra　.　.	Drum　.　.	Castlebar　.	IV.	128
31, 37	Carrowkeale　.	439　2　5	Tipperary, N.R.	Owney and Arra	Kilvellane　.	Nenagh　.　.	II.	296
45, 51, 52	Carrowkeale　.	395　0　13	Tipperary, S.R.	Kilnamanagh Lower	Donohill　.　.	Cashel　.　.	II.	323
8, 15	Carrowkeel　.	278　3　1	Clare　.　.	Corcomroe　.	Kilshanny　.	Ennistimon　.	II.	21
23, 30, 31	Carrowkeel　.	206　0　22	Clare　.　.	Ibrickan　.　.	Kilfarboy　.	Ennistimon　.	II.	22
30, 31	Carrowkeel　.	110　0　7	Donegal　.	Inishowen East	Moville Upper	Inishowen　.	III.	119
27, 28	Carrowkeel　.	177　0　19	Donegal　.	Kilmacrenan　.	Tullyfern　.	Milford　.　.	III.	133
23	Carrowkeel　.	207　3　12	Fermanagh　.	Tirkennedy　.	Enniskillen　.	Enniskillen　.	III.	221
97	Carrowkeel　.	373　2　4	Galway　.	Athenry　.　.	Kiltullagh　.	Loughrea　.	IV.	5
20	Carrowkeel　.	185　0　8	Galway　.	Ballymoe　.	Dunamon　.	Roscommon　.	IV.	7
17	Carrowkeel　.	526　2　32	Galway　.	Ballymoe　.	Dunmore　.	Glennamaddy.	IV.	7
99	Carrowkeel　.	139　1　33	Galway　.	Clonmacnowen　.	Clontuskert　.	Ballinasloe　.	IV.	24
83, 95	Carrowkeel　.	44　3　23	Galway　.	Dunkellin　.	Oranmore　.	Galway　.　.	IV.	32
106, 116	Carrowkeel　.	253　2　37	Galway　.	Leitrim　.　.	Leitrim　.　.	Loughrea　.	IV.	55
27	Carrowkeel　.	129　2　27	Galway　.	Ross　.　.	Cong　.　.	Oughterard　.	IV.	73
45	Carrowkeel　.	103　0　27	Galway　.	Tiaquin　.　.	Moylough　.	Mountbellew　.	IV.	79
6	Carrowkeel　.	391　2　24	King's Co.	Garrycastle　.	Clonmacnoise.	Parsonstown　.	I.	135
4	Carrowkeel　.	128　3　5	Leitrim　.	Rosclogher　.	Rossinver　.	Manorhamilton	IV.	111
6	Carrowkeel　.	18　0　12	Limerick　.	Clanwilliam　.	Killeenagarriff　.	Limerick　.　.	II.	224
6	Carrowkeel　.	21　2　10	Limerick　.	Clanwilliam　.	Stradbally　.	Limerick　.　.	II.	226
88	Carrowkeel　.	54　3　7	Mayo　.　.	Burrishoole　.	Aghagower　.	Westport　.	IV.	118
67	Carrowkeel　.	87　0　0a	Mayo　.　.	Burrishoole　.	Burrishoole　.	Newport　.	IV.	118
89, 90, 100	Carrowkeel　.	141　2　32	Mayo　.　.	Carra　.　.	Burriscarra　.	Castlebar　.	IV.	127
79	Carrowkeel　.	137　2　34	Mayo　.　.	Carra　.　.	Manulla　.　.	Castlebar　.	IV.	129
70	Carrowkeel　.	173　2　39	Mayo　.　.	Carra　.　.	Turlough　.	Castlebar　.	IV.	130
101, 111	Carrowkeel　.	146　3　8	Mayo　.　.	Clanmorris　.	Tagheen　.　.	Claremorris　.	IV.	135
17	Carrowkeel　.	455　3　39	Mayo　.　.	Erris　.　.	Kilcommon　.	Belmullet　.	IV.	143
71	Carrowkeel　.	185　2　11	Mayo　.　.	Gallen　.　.	Bohola　.　.	Swineford　.	IV.	147
118	Carrowkeel　.	281　1　4	Mayo　.　.	Kilmaine　.	Kilmolara　.	Ballinrobe　.	IV.	156
87	Carrowkeel　.	109　2　9	Mayo　.　.	Murrisk　.　.	Oughaval　.	Westport　.	IV.	161
47	Carrowkeel　.	386　1　12	Mayo　.　.	Tirawley　.	Addergoole　.	Castlebar　.	IV.	163
29, 38	Carrowkeel　.	285　1　35b	Mayo　.　.	Tirawley　.	Crossmolina　.	Ballina　.　.	IV.	165
14, 21	Carrowkeel　.	184　2　7	Mayo　.　.	Tirawley　.	Rathreagh　.	Killala　.　.	IV.	171
10	Carrowkeel　.	138　3　23	Monaghan　.	Monaghan　.	Tehallan　.　.	Monaghan　.	III.	280
39, 41	Carrowkeel　.	285　1　18	Roscommon　.	Athlone　.　.	Fuerty　.　.	Roscommon　.	IV.	181
45	Carrowkeel　.	156　3　1	Roscommon　.	Athlone　.　.	Rahara　.　.	Roscommon　.	IV.	183
47	Carrowkeel　.	242　0　1	Roscommon　.	Athlone　.　.　.	Taghboy　.	Athlone　.　.	IV.	184
28	Carrowkeel　.	38　3　11	Roscommon　.	Ballintober South	Kilbride　.　.	Roscommon　.	IV.	188
9, 10	Carrowkeel　.	135　2　33	Roscommon　.	Boyle　.　.	Estersnow　.	Boyle　.　.	IV.	195
27	Carrowkeel　.	154　1　2	Roscommon　.	Castlereagh　.	Baslick　.　.	Castlereagh　.	IV.	199
27	Carrowkeel　.	173　2　36	Roscommon　.	Castlereagh　.	Kilkeevin　.	Castlereagh　.	IV.	200
16	Carrowkeel　.	23　1　29	Roscommon　.	Frenchpark　.	Kilmacumsy.	Boyle　.　.	IV.	203
9	Carrowkeel　.	138　2　16	Roscommon　.	Frenchpark　.	Kilnamanagh.	Boyle　.　.	IV.	204
17	Carrowkeel　.	122　1　4	Roscommon　.	Roscommon　.	Clooncraff　.	Strokestown　.	IV.	208
28	Carrowkeel　.	78　1　36	Roscommon　.	Roscommon　.	Ogulla　.　.	Strokestown　.	IV.	212
14, 20	Carrowkeel　.	464　3　39c	Sligo　.　.	Carbury　.　.	Kilmacowen　.	Sligo　.　.	IV.	222
33	Carrowkeel　.	213　3　0	Sligo　.　.	Corran　.　.	Emlaghfad　.	Tobercurry　.	IV.	226
38	Carrowkeel　.	231　3　5	Sligo　.　.	Leyny　.　.	Achonry　.	Tobercurry　.	IV.	229
19	Carrowkeel　.	149　2　37	Sligo　.　.	Tireragh　.	Dromard　.	Dromore West.	IV.	233
34, 40	Carrowkeel　.	521　2　19	Sligo　.　.	Tirerrill　.　.	Aghanagh　.	Boyle　.　.	IV.	237
27	Carrowkeel　.	124　0　21	Sligo　.　.	Tirerrill　.　.	Ballynakill　.	Sligo　.　.	IV.	237
34	Carrowkeel　.	217　3　23	Sligo　.　.	Tirerrill　.　.	Tawnagh　.	Sligo　.　.	IV.	241
17	Carrowkeelanahglass	390　1　29	Galway　.	Ballymoe　.	Dunmore　.	Glennamaddy.	IV.	7
18	Carrowkeel Beg　.	104　1　1	Clare　.　.	Bunratty Upper	Inchicronan　.	Ennis　.　.	II.	8
24, 32	Carrowkeel East　.	275　0　20	Clare　.　.	Inchiquin　.	Inagh　.　.	Ennistimon　.	II.	25
92,93,102,103	Carrowkeel East　.	206　3　17	Mayo　.　.	Costello　.　.	Annagh　.　.	Claremorris　.	IV.	138
8, 17	Carrowkeel Glebe　.	307　3　11	Donegal　.	Kilmacrenan　.	Clondavaddog.	Milford　.　.	III.	124
8	Carrowkeel Glebe　.	64　3　26d	Fermanagh　.	Lurg　.　.	Belleek　.　.	Ballyshannon	III.	203
18, 26	Carrowkeel More　.	199　3　17	Clare　.　.	Bunratty Upper	Inchicronan　.	Ennis　.　.	II.	8
111	Carrowkeel North　.	426　3　20e	Mayo　.　.	Kilmaine　.	Kilcommon　.	Ballinrobe　.	IV.	154
119	Carrowkeel South　.	100　1　19	Mayo　.　.	Kilmaine　.	Kilcommon　.	Ballinrobe　.	IV.	154
10, 17	Carrowkeel Upper　.	125　1　11f	Roscommon　.	Roscommon　.	Clooncraff　.	Strokestown　.	IV.	208
24, 32	Carrowkeel West　.	521　0　36g	Clare　.　.	Inchiquin　.	Inagh　.　.	Ennistimon　.	II.	25
102, 112	Carrowkeel West　.	164　1　35	Mayo　.　.	Costello　.　.	Annagh　.　.	Claremorris　.	IV.	138

(a) Including 31A. 1R. 11P. detached portion.　　　(d) Including 6A. 0R. 18P. water.　　　(f) Including 5A. 0R. 0P. water.
(b) Including 3A. 2R. 19P. Brackloon Lough.　　　(e) Including 15A. 3R. 30P. water.　　　(g) Including 27A. 0R. 23P. water.
(c) Including 7A. 3R. 0P. water.

No. of Sheet of the Ordnance Survey Maps.	Townlands and Towns.	Area in Statute Acres.			County.	Barony.	Parish.	Poor Law Union in 1857.	Townland Census of 1851, Part I.	
		A.	R.	P.					Vol.	Page
48	Carrowkeeny	348	3	17	Roscommon	Athlone	Kiltoom	Athlone	IV.	182
87	Carrowkeeran	86	1	27	Mayo	Murrisk	Oughaval	Westport	IV.	161
48, 51	Carrowkeeran	303	0	7a	Roscommon	Athlone	Taghmaconnell	Athlone	IV.	185
22, 30	Carrowkelly	305	2	8	Mayo	Tirawley	Ballysakeery	Ballina	IV.	164
97, 98, 107	Carrowkennedy	381	3	24	Mayo	Murrisk	Aghagower	Westport	IV.	158
39, 48	Carrowkeribly	1,737	0	34b	Mayo	Gallen	Attymass	Ballina	IV.	147
7	Carrowkibbock Lower	177	0	20	Mayo	Tirawley	Doonfeeny	Killala	IV.	167
7, 14	Carrowkibbock Upper	333	1	8	Mayo	Tirawley	Doonfeeny	Killala	IV.	167
50	Carrowkilla	226	0	22	Clare	Clonderalaw	Kilchreest	Killadysert	II.	15
113	Carrowkilleen	472	0	34	Galway	Kiltartan	Killinny	Gort	IV.	47
101, 102	Carrowkilleen	129	3	11	Mayo	Clanmorris	Kilcolman	Claremorris	IV.	133
100, 110	Carrowkilleen	295	0	21	Mayo	Kilmaine	Robeen	Ballinrobe	IV.	157
37, 38	Carrowkilleen	800	0	28	Mayo	Tirawley	Crossmolina	Ballina	IV.	165
38, 39	Carrowlagan	410	0	34	Clare	Ibrickan	Kilmurry	Kilrush	II.	23
18	Carrowlaur	103	1	39	Leitrim	Drumahaire	Inishmagrath	Manorhamilton	IV.	95
13	Carrowlaverty	445	0	12	Antrim	Cary	Armoy	Ballycastle	III.	11
31, 32	Carrowleagh	3,143	3	5	Mayo	Gallen	Kilgarvan	Ballina	IV.	148
31	Carrowleana	196	2	2	Galway	Tiaquin	Kilkerrin	Glennamaddy	IV.	76
3, 7	Carrowleigh	204	2	0	Waterford	Upperthird	Rathgormuck	Carrick on Suir	II.	371
111	Carrowlena	84	1	11	Mayo	Clanmorris	Crossboyne	Claremorris	IV.	132
50	Carrowliam Beg	311	2	33	Mayo	Gallen	Killasser	Swineford	IV.	149
50	Carrowliam More	330	3	11c	Mayo	Gallen	Killasser	Swineford	IV.	149
5, 9	Carrowlinan	359	2	22	Longford	Granard	Clonbroney	Granard	I.	154
100	Carrowlisdooaun	211	1	18d	Mayo	Carra	Touaghty	Ballinrobe	IV.	130
13	Carrowloughan East	92	3	6	Sligo	Tireragh	Skreen	Dromore West	IV.	235
13	Carrowloughan West	79	3	34e	Sligo	Tireragh	Skreen	Dromore West	IV.	235
39	Carrowloughlin	201	1	2	Sligo	Corran	Cloonoghil	Tobercurry	IV.	225
9, 15	Carrowlustia	214	1	29	Sligo	Carbury	Calry	Sligo	IV.	220
68, 81	Carrowlustraun	116	2	22	Galway	Moycullen	Moycullen	Galway	IV.	71
12	Carrowmably	173	3	29	Sligo	Tireragh	Kilmacshalgan	Dromore West	IV.	234
10, 11	Carrowmacbryan	543	0	33	Sligo	Tireragh	Easky	Dromore West	IV.	233
39	Carrowmaclenany	111	2	15f	Sligo	Corran	Toomour	Boyle	IV.	228
70	Carrowmacloughlin	242	2	13g	Mayo	Carra	Turlough	Castlebar	IV.	130
87	Carrowmacloughlin	600	2	12	Mayo	Murrisk	Oughaval	Westport	IV.	161
22	Carrowmacmea	251	0	9	Fermanagh	Tirkennedy	Enniskillen	Enniskillen	III.	221
29	Carrowmacowan	333	2	13	Galway	Dunmore	Kilbennan	Tuam	IV.	34
12	Carrowmacrory	91	1	28	Sligo	Tireragh	Templeboy	Dromore West	IV.	236
7, 14	Carrowmacshane	306	0	20	Mayo	Tirawley	Lackan	Killala	IV.	170
35	Carrowmaculla	373	3	10	Fermanagh	Clankelly	Galloon	Lisnaskea	III.	198
5	Carrowmanagh	449	1	7	Galway	Dunmore	Dunmore	Tuam	IV.	33
73	Carrowmanagh	300	1	21	Galway	Kilconnell	Kilconnell	Ballinasloe	IV.	40
54	Carrowmanagh	140	1	9	Galway	Moycullen	Kilcummin	Oughterard	IV.	66
44	Carrowmanagh	181	3	1	Galway	Tiaquin	Killererin	Tuam	IV.	77
21, 29	Carrowmanagh	206	1	7	King's Co.	Garrycastle	Lusmagh	Parsonstown	I.	137
18	Carrowmanagh	169	1	33	Longford	Moydow	Ballymacormick	Longford	I.	160
8, 15	Carrowmanagh North	210	3	34	Clare	Corcomroe	Kilshanny	Ennistimon	II.	21
8, 15	Carrowmanagh South	294	2	8	Clare	Corcomroe	Kilshanny	Ennistimon	II.	21
104	Carrowmaneen	111	0	17	Galway	Dunkellin	Killeely	Gort	IV.	29
25	Carrowmannan	1,117	1	16	Armagh	Orior Upper	Loughgilly	Newry	III.	58
101	Carrowmarley	171	1	16	Mayo	Clanmorris	Crossboyne	Claremorris	IV.	132
42	Carrowmeer	184	0	3h	Clare	Bunratty Lower	Tomfinlough	Ennis	II.	7
42	Carrowmeer	286	3	34	Clare	Bunratty Upper	Quin	Ennis	II.	10
12	Carrowmenagh	713	0	35	Donegal	Inishowen East	Moville Lower	Inishowen	III.	118
5	Carrowmenagh	180	1	17	Londonderry	Keenaght	Tamlaght Finlagan	New Tⁿ Limavady	III.	237
32, 36	Carrowmenagh	643	3	39	Londonderry	Loughinsholin	Killelagh	Magherafelt	III.	241
83, 95	Carrowmoneash	344	1	18	Galway	Dunkellin	Oranmore	Galway	IV.	32
43, 44	Carrowmoneen	573	0	14	Galway	Dunmore	Tuam	Tuam	IV.	35
36	Carrowmoneen	185	2	25	Roscommon	Ballintober South	Kilgefin	Roscommon	IV.	189
16	Carrowmoneen	135	1	20	Roscommon	Frenchpark	Kilcolagh	Boyle	IV.	203
13	Carrowmoney	59	1	27	Armagh	Fews Lower	Mullaghbrack	Armagh	III.	47
109	Carrowmoney	285	1	10	Mayo	Carra	Ballyovey	Ballinrobe	IV.	126
42, 45	Carrowmoney	421	1	29	Roscommon	Athlone	Rahara	Roscommon	IV.	183
12	Carrowmoran	115	1	4	Sligo	Tireragh	Templeboy	Dromore West	IV.	236
9, 10	Carrowmore	980	2	27	Cavan	Tullyhaw	Tomregan	Bawnboy	III.	96
52	Carrowmore	284	1	3	Clare	Bunratty Lower	Kilfintinan	Limerick	II.	5
47	Carrowmore	384	0	31	Clare	Ibrickan	Killard	Kilrush	II.	23
29	Carrowmore	333	3	9	Clare	Tulla Upper	Moynoe	Scarriff	II.	40
4	Carrowmore	839	2	27i	Donegal	Inishowen East	Clonca	Inishowen	III.	116
11, 12	Carrowmore	798	2	34	Donegal	Inishowen East	Culdaff	Inishowen	III.	118
34	Carrowmore	152	3	30	Fermanagh	Clankelly	Galloon	Lisnaskea	III.	198
28, 42	Carrowmore	127	3	33	Galway	Clare	Donaghpatrick	Tuam	IV.	19
102, 103	Carrowmore	345	2	11	Galway	Dunkellin	Ballynacourty	Galway	IV.	27
105	Carrowmore	346	2	5	Galway	Dunkellin	Kilconickny	Loughrea	IV.	29

(a) Including 52A. 3R. 24P. water.
(b) Including 108A. 3R. 36P. water.
(c) Including 7A. 1R. 7P. water.

(d) Including 14A. 0R. 24P. water.
(e) Including 6A. 1R. 27P. water.
(f) Including 2A. 3R. 24P. water.

(g) Including 33A. 0R. 23P. water.
(h) Including 31A. 3R. 21P. water.
(i) Including 26A. 2R. 6P. detached portion.

No. of Sheet of the Ordnance Survey Maps.	Townlands and Towns.	Area in Statute Acres.	County.	Barony.	Parish.	Poor Law Union in 1857.	Townland Census of 1851, Part I.	
		A.　R.　P.					Vol.	Page
87	Carrowmore . .	756　1　15a	Galway . .	Kilconnell . .	Aughrim . .	Ballinasloe .	IV.	39
73	Carrowmore . .	286　0　33	Galway . .	Kilconnell . .	Kilconnell . .	Ballinasloe .	IV.	40
106, 116	Carrowmore . .	176　1　9	Galway . .	Leitrim . .	Duniry . .	Loughrea .	IV.	53
105, 106	Carrowmore . .	282　3　3	Galway . .	Leitrim . .	Kilmeen . .	Loughrea .	IV.	54
97, 98	Carrowmore . .	576　1　16	Galway . .	Loughrea . .	Bullaun . .	Loughrea .	IV.	63
58	Carrowmore . .	515　2　11	Galway . .	Tiaquin . .	Monivea . .	Tuam .	IV.	78
59	Carrowmore . .	251　1　4	Galway . .	Tiaquin . .	Moylough . .	Mountbellew .	IV.	79
37	Carrow More . .	330　0　34	Limerick . .	Connello Upper .	Cloncagh . .	Newcastle .	II.	231
21	Carrow More . .	87　2　35	Longford . .	Rathcline . .	Cashel . .	Ballymahon .	I.	163
68, 77	Carrowmore . .	193　0　26b	Mayo . .	Burrishoole . .	Burrishoole . .	Newport .	IV.	118
79	Carrowmore . .	239　1　36c	Mayo . .	Carra . .	Manulla . .	Castlebar .	IV.	129
101	Carrowmore . .	163　2　9	Mayo . .	Clanmorris . .	Crossboyne ,. .	Claremorris .	IV.	132
101, 111	Carrowmore . .	144　3　23	Mayo . .	Clanmorris . .	Tagheen . .	Claremorris .	IV.	135
103	Carrow More . .	166　1　39	Mayo . .	Costello . .	Annagh . .	Claremorris .	IV.	138
92	Carrowmore . .	613　3　6	Mayo . .	Costello . .	Knock . .	Claremorris .	IV.	142
11, 18	Carrowmore . .	1,356　0　39	Mayo . .	Erris . .	Kilcommon . .	Belmullet .	IV.	143
71	Carrowmore . .	263　0　35	Mayo . .	Gallen . .	Bohola . .	Swineford .	IV.	147
49, 50	Carrowmore . .	349　3　23	Mayo . .	Gallen . .	Killasser . .	Swineford .	IV.	149
118	Carrowmore . .	134　0　15	Mayo . .	Kilmaine . .	Ballinrobe . .	Ballinrobe .	IV.	152
119	Carrowmore . .	322　0　4	Mayo . .	Kilmaine . .	Kilcommon . .	Ballinrobe .	IV.	154
122	Carrowmore . .	445　1　14	Mayo . .	Kilmaine . .	Kilmainemore .	Ballinrobe .	IV.	155
118	Carrowmore . .	308　1　15	Mayo . .	Kilmaine . .	Kilmainemore .	Ballinrobe .	IV.	156
121	Carrowmore . .	89　1　37	Mayo . .	Kilmaine . .	Moorgagagh .	Ballinrobe .	IV.	157
98	Carrowmore . .	467　1　28d	Mayo . .	Murrisk . .	Aghagower .	Westport .	IV.	158
85, 86, 96	Carrowmore . .	688　3　9	Mayo . .	Murrisk . .	Kilgeever .	Westport .	IV.	159
39	Carrowmore . .	358　3　24	Mayo . .	Tirawley . .	Kilbelfad . .	Ballina .	IV.	167
7	Carrowmore . .	432　1　30	Mayo . .	Tirawley . .	Kilbride . .	Killala .	IV.	168
14	Carrowmore . .	478　2　39	Mayo . .	Tirawley . .	Lackan . .	Killala .	IV.	170
47	Carrowmore . .	195　3　7	Roscommon .	Athlone . .	Taghboy . .	Athlone .	IV.	184
11, 17	Carrowmore . .	127　3　4	Roscommon .	Ballintober North .	Kilmore . .	Cark.on Shannon	IV.	187
40	Carrowmore . .	583　3　10	Roscommon .	Ballintober South .	Roscommon .	Roscommon .	IV.	190
6, 10	Carrowmore . .	212　3　29	Roscommon .	Boyle . .	Ardcarn . .	Boyle .	IV.	192
6, 10	Carrowmore . .	179　3　12	Roscommon .	Boyle . .	Kilbryan .	Boyle .	IV.	195
10, 16	Carrowmore . .	456　3　27	Roscommon .	Boyle . .	Killummod .	Cark.on Shannon	IV.	196
1, 2, 3, 4	Carrowmore . .	25　2　19e	Roscommon .	Boyle . .	Kilronan . .	Boyle .	IV.	196
27	Carrowmore . .	166　3　9	Roscommon .	Castlereagh . .	Kilkeevin . .	Castlereagh .	IV.	200
14, 20	Carrowmore . .	494　0　36	Sligo . .	Carbury . .	Kilmacowan .	Sligo .	IV.	222
32	Carrowmore . .	384　2　16	Sligo . .	Leyny . .	Achonry . .	Tobercurry .	IV.	229
28, 35	Carrowmore . .	1,157　3　14	Sligo . .	Tirerrill . .	Shancough .	Boyle .	IV.	241
46	Carrowmore (Cheevers)	101　3　15	Galway . .	Killian . .	Killian . .	Mountbellew .	IV.	44
99	Carrowmore East .	65　2　22	Galway . .	Clonmacnowen .	Clontuskert .	Ballinasloe .	IV.	24
20, 30	Carrowmore or Glentogher . .	5,784　3　38	Donegal . .	Inishowen East .	Donagh . .	Inishowen .	III.	118
46	Carrowmore (Kelly)	51　3　5	Galway . .	Killian . .	Killian . .	Mountbellew .	IV.	44
55	Carrowmoreknock .	555　0　19	Galway . .	Moycullen . .	Kilcummin .	Oughterard .	IV.	66
61, 62	Carrowmoremoy .	331　0　0f	Mayo . .	Gallen . .	Killasser . .	Swineford .	IV.	149
38, 47	Carrowmore North .	347　3　27g	Clare . .	Ibrickan . .	Killard . .	Kilrush .	II.	23
90	Carrowmore North .	275　1　26h	Mayo . .	Carra . .	Drum . .	Castlebar .	IV.	128
46,47,56,57	Carrowmore South .	2,026　0　38	Clare . .	Ibrickan . .	Killard . .	Kilrush .	II.	23
90	Carrowmore South .	46　0　36i	Mayo . .	Carra . .	Drum . .	Castlebar .	IV.	128
19	Carrowmore or Tanrego East . .	167　2　5	Sligo . .	Tireragh . .	Dromard . .	Dromore West .	IV.	233
122	CARROWMORE T.	—	Mayo . .	Kilmaine . .	Kilmainemore .	Ballinrobe .	IV.	156
99	Carrowmore West .	116　2　18	Galway . .	Clonmacnowen .	Clontuskert .	Ballinasloe .	IV.	24
102, 112	Carrowmore West .	261　1　21	Mayo . .	Costello . .	Annagh . .	Claremorris .	IV.	138
19	Carrowmorris . .	151　3　17	Sligo . .	Tireragh . .	Dromard . .	Dromore West .	IV.	233
5	Carrowmuddle .	325　1　34j	Londonderry .	Keenaght . .	Tamlaght Finlagan	NewTnLimavady	III.	237
38	Carrowmullin . .	301　2　32	Donegal . .	Inishowen West .	Fahan Upper .	Londonderry .	III.	121
104, 105	Carrowmunna .	190　0　4	Galway . .	Dunkellin . .	Killogilleen .	Loughrea .	IV.	31
17	Carrowmunniagh .	227　1　39	Galway . .	Dunmore . .	Dunmore . .	Tuam .	IV.	33
45,46,48,49	Carrowmurragh .	791　1　37	Roscommon .	Athlone . .	Kiltoom . .	Athlone .	IV.	182
24, 25	Carrowmurray .	1,185　2　10	Sligo . .	Leyny . .	Achonry . .	Tobercurry .	IV.	229
19, 25	Carrownabanny .	808　0　16k	Sligo . .	Leyny . .	Killoran . .	Tobercurry .	IV.	230
11	Carrownabinna or Ballymeeny (Hillas)	175　3　14	Sligo . .	Tireragh . .	Easky . .	Dromore West .	IV.	233
45	Carrownabo . .	330　3　36l	Galway . .	Tiaquin . .	Moylough . .	Mountbellew .	IV.	79
13, 19	Carrownaboll . .	271　1　36	Sligo . .	Tireragh . .	Skreen . .	Dromore West .	IV.	235
39	Carrownabrickna .	605　0　32	Roscommon .	Ballintober South .	Roscommon .	Roscommon .	IV.	190
25, 26	Carrownacarrick .	460　2　35	Sligo . .	Leyny . .	Killoran . .	Tobercurry .	IV.	230
31, 38	Carrownacaw . .	285　3　6	Down . .	Lecale Lower .	Ballee . .	Downpatrick .	III.	178
77, 88	Carrownaclea . .	308　1　38m	Mayo . .	Burrishoole . .	Islandeady .	Westport .	IV.	121
95	Carrownaclsigha .	177　1　05	Sligo . .	Leyny . .	Killoran . .	Tobercurry .	IV.	230
15, 16, 23	Carrownaclogh .	413　1　9	Clare . .	Corcomroe . .	Clooney . .	Ennistimon .	II.	18

(a) Including 5A. 1R. 12P. water.　　　(f) Including 10A. 0R. 27P. water.　　　(j) Including 25A. 3R. 21P. water.
(b) Including 5A. 0R. 18P. water.　　　(g) Including 40A. 1R. 8P. water.　　　(k) Including 16A. 2R. 33P. of Loughs.
(c) Including 46A. 0R. 31P. water.　　　(h) Including 7A. 3R. 38P. water.　　　(l) Including 6A. 1R. 6P. water.
(d) Including 41A. 2R. 31P. water.　　　(i) Including 0A. 2R. 24P. water.　　　(m) Including 6A. 2R. 18P. water.
(e) Including 9A. 0R. 29P. water.

No of Sheet of the Ordnance Survey Maps.	Townlands and Towns.	Area in Statute Acres. A. R. P.	County.	Barony.	Parish.	Poor Law Union in 1857.	Townland Census of 1851, Part I. Vol.	Page
14, 20	Carrownaclogh North	73 0 13	Tipperary, N.R.	Owney and Arra	Youghalarra	Nenagh	II.	297
20	Carrownaclogh South	3 0 1	Tipperary, N.R.	Owney and Arra	Youghalarra	Nenagh	II.	297
18, 26	Carrownacloghy	302 1 26a	Clare	Bunratty Upper	Inchicronan	Ennis	II.	8
100	Carrownacon	264 3 16b	Mayo	Carra	Burriscarra	Ballinrobe	IV.	127
33,34,39,40	Carrownacreevy	195 2 37	Sligo	Corran	Toomour	Sligo	IV.	228
24, 25, 32	Carrownacreevy	1,614 2 39	Sligo	Leyny	Achonry	Tobercurry	IV.	229
19	Carrownacreevy	160 1 16	Sligo	Tireragh	Dromard	Dromore West	IV.	233
12	Carrownacreevy	106 3 30	Sligo	Tireragh	Templeboy	Dromore West	IV.	236
103	Carrownacreggaun	123 3 35	Galway	Dunkellin	Drumacoo	Gort	IV.	28
59	Carrownacregg East	185 1 28	Galway	Tiaquin	Killoscobe	Mountbellew	IV.	77
45, 59	Carrownacregg West	272 1 36	Galway	Tiaquin	Killoscobe	Mountbellew	IV.	77
41, 55	Carrownacrogh	316 2 13	Galway	Clare	Killursa	Tuam	IV.	21
70	Carrownacross	110 0 29	Mayo	Gallen	Kildacommoge	Castlebar	IV.	148
71	Carrownacross	115 2 22	Mayo	Gallen	Meelick	Swineford	IV.	150
71, 72	Carrownaculla	347 0 30	Mayo	Gallen	Kilconduff	Swineford	IV.	147
28, 35	Carrownadargny	1,667 0 11	Sligo	Tirerrill	Shancough	Boyle	IV.	241
47	Carrownadurly	274 1 34	Roscommon	Athlone	Taghboy	Athlone	IV.	184
21	Carrownaff	225 0 16	Donegal	Inishowen East	Moville Upper	Inishowen	III.	119
108	Carrownafinnoge	220 2 1	Galway	Longford	Meelick	Portumna	IV.	61
46	Carrownafreevy	403 2 19	Galway	Killian	Killian	Mountbellew	IV.	44
46	Carrownagannive	353 0 2	Galway	Killian	Ballynakill	Mountbellew	IV.	43
36	Carrownaganonagh	1,015 0 37c	Donegal	Kilmacrenan	Kilmacrenan	Milford	III.	129
32, 46	Carrownagappul	1,058 3 26	Galway	Killian	Ballynakill	Mountbellew	IV.	43
9	Carrownagappul	217 1 8	Roscommon	Boyle	Estersnow	Boyle	IV.	195
37	Carrownagappul	132 2 6	Sligo	Leyny	Kilmacteige	Tobercurry	IV.	231
34	Carrownagark	214 2 21	Sligo	Tirerrill	Tawnagh	Sligo	IV.	241
16	Carrownagarraun	216 1 13	Clare	Inchiquin	Rath	Corrofin	II.	27
43	Carrownagarraun	93 1 6	Galway	Dunmore	Tuam	Tuam	IV.	35
29	Carrownagarry	372 0 33	Galway	Dunmore	Tuam	Tuam	IV.	35
6	Carrownagashel	178 1 19	Roscommon	Boyle	Ardcarn	Boyle	IV.	192
4, 15, 16	Carrownageeha	241 0 0d	Galway	Dunmore	Liskeevy	Tuam	IV.	35
22, 28	Carrownageelaun	185 3 36	Roscommon	Roscommon	Ogulla	Strokestown	IV.	212
34	Carrownageeloge	185 0 22	Roscommon	Ballymoe	Oran	Roscommon	IV.	192
49	Carrownageeragh	33 0 17	Mayo	Gallen	Killasser	Swineford	IV.	149
80	Carrownageeragh	269 1 16e	Mayo	Gallen	Killedan	Swineford	IV.	149
6, 10	Carrownageeragh	295 0 5	Roscommon	Boyle	Boyle	Boyle	IV.	194
20	Carrownageeragh or Stonehall	208 2 6	Sligo	Leyny	Ballysadare	Sligo	IV.	230
21	Carrownagh	870 1 14f	Sligo	Tirerrill	Killery	Sligo	IV.	239
23	Carrownagiltagh	231 3 28	Fermanagh	Tirkennedy	Enniskillen	Enniskillen	III.	221
27, 28	Carrownagilty	763 0 9	Sligo	Tirerrill	Kilmacallan	Boyle	IV.	239
17	Carrownaglearagh	516 0 13g	Roscommon	Roscommon	Aughrim	Cark. on Shannon	IV.	207
25	Carrownagleragh	182 0 9	Sligo	Leyny	Killoran	Tobercurry	IV.	230
85, 97	Carrownaglogh	257 3 37	Galway	Athenry	Killimordaly	Loughrea	IV.	4
7, 8, 19, 20	Carrownaglogh	601 3 25h	Galway	Ballymoe	Dunamon	Roscommon	IV.	7
1, 4	Carrownaglogh	2,294 0 30	Mayo	Erris	Kilcommon	Belmullet	IV.	143
31, 32	Carrownaglogh	3,515 0 29	Mayo	Gallen	Kilgarvan	Ballina	IV.	148
6, 7	Carrownaglogh	183 1 19	Tipperary, N.R.	Lower Ormond	Terryglass	Borrisokane	II.	287
13, 19	Carrownaglogh or Carrowflatley	121 3 5	Sligo	Tireragh	Dromard	Dromore West	IV.	233
10, 11	Carrownagoul	751 2 1i	Clare	Inchiquin	Kilkeedy	Corrofin	II.	25
36	Carrownagowan	986 2 24	Clare	Tulla Lower	O'Briensbridge	Scarriff	II.	38
97	Carrownagower	183 0 4	Galway	Dunkellin	Lickerrig	Loughrea	IV.	31
100	Carrownagreggaun	200 3 21	Mayo	Carra	Burriscarra	Ballinrobe	IV.	127
39	Carrownagry North	358 2 35	Clare	Ibrickan	Kilmurry	Kilrush	II.	23
39	Carrownagry South	293 2 21	Clare	Ibrickan	Kilmurry	Kilrush	II.	23
19	Carrownaguivna East	8 2 34	Sligo	Tireragh	Dromard	Dromore West	IV.	233
19	Carrownaguivna West	35 2 32	Sligo	Tireragh	Dromard	Dromore West	IV.	233
23	Carrownagullagh	170 3 16	Roscommon	Roscommon	Kiltrustan	Strokestown	IV.	211
17	Carrownagur	339 1 2j	Galway	Ballymoe	Dunmore	Glennamaddy	IV.	7
118, 121	Carrownagurraun	50 0 1	Mayo	Kilmaine	Kilmolara	Ballinrobe	IV.	156
100	Carrownahaltore	34 1 20	Mayo	Carra	Touaghty	Ballinrobe	IV.	130
80, 91	Carrownahaun	531 3 32	Mayo	Clanmorris	Balla	Castlebar	IV.	132
42, 43, 57	Carrownaherick East	112 0 22	Galway	Clare	Belclare	Tuam	IV.	17
42,43,56,57	Carrownaherick West	111 0 15	Galway	Clare	Belclare	Tuam	IV.	17
15	Carrownahooan East	221 2 28	Clare	Corcomroe	Kilshanny	Ennistimon	II.	21
15	Carrownahooan West	219 0 22	Clare	Corcomroe	Kilshanny	Ennistimon	II.	21
73	Carrownakelly	40 2 4	Galway	Kilconnell	Ballymacward	Ballinasloe	IV.	39
41, 55	Carrownakib	517 3 17	Galway	Clare	Killursa	Tuam	IV.	21
42, 51	Carrownakilly	366 0 36h	Clare	Bunratty Lower	Tomfinlough	Ennis	II.	7
36, 37	Carrownakilly	879 1 14	Clare	Tulla Lower	Killaloe	Scarriff	II.	35
118	Carrownakilly	57 2 23	Mayo	Kilmaine	Kilmolara	Ballinrobe	IV.	156
12, 13	Carrownaknockan	102 0 21	Sligo	Tireragh	Skreen	Dromore West	IV.	235

(a) Including 38A. 2R. 19P. water.
(b) Including 58A. 3R. 30P. water.
(c) Including 8A. 1R. 18P. water.
(d) Including 1A. 3R. 8P. water.

(e) Including 9A. 0R. 3P. water.
(f) Including 8A. 2R. 35P. Lough Lumman.
(g) Including 20A. 0R. 38P. water.
(h) Including 32A. 1R. 8P. water.

(i) Including 26A. 3R. 10P. water.
(j) Including 4A. 2R. 16P. water.
(k) Including 13A. 3R. 8P. water.

2 F

No. of Sheet of the Ordnance Survey Maps.	Townlands and Towns.	Area in Statute Acres.			County.	Barony.	Parish.	Poor Law Union in 1857.	Townland Census of 1851, Part I.	
		A.	R.	P.					Vol.	Page
13	Carrownaknockaun .	266	1	7	Roscommon	Frenchpark .	Tibohine	Castlereagh	IV.	204
28, 29, 35	Carrownalassan	1,241	0	3	Roscommon	Ballintober South	Kilbride .	Roscommon	IV.	188
24, 31, 32	Carrownaleck .	724	2	25	Sligo	Leyny .	Achonry .	Tobercurry	IV.	229
110, 118	Carrownalecka .	278	0	39	Mayo	Kilmaine .	Ballinrobe .	Ballinrobe	IV.	152
52	Carrownalegaun	66	3	3	Clare	Bunratty Lower	Feenagh .	Ennis .	II.	4
25	Carrownalegg .	38	2	39	Fermanagh	Clanawley .	Cleenish .	Enniskillen	III.	190
69, 70	Carrownaltore	138	1	34	Mayo	Carra .	Aglish .	Castlebar .	IV.	123
88	Carrownalurgan	267	0	4	Mayo	Murrisk .	Oughaval .	Westport .	IV.	161
5, 6	Carrownamaddoo	479	2	21	Sligo	Carbury .	Ahamlish .	Sligo .	IV.	219
20	Carrownamaddoo	433	2	3	Sligo	Carbury .	St. John's .	Sligo .	IV.	223
19	Carrownamaddoo .	406	1	5	Sligo	Tireragh .	Skreen .	Dromore West .	IV.	235
10, 17	Carrownamaddra .	309	3	32	Clare	Inchiquin .	Killinaboy .	Corrofin .	II.	26
112, 113	Carrownamaddra .	774	1	23	Galway	Kiltartan .	Kinvarradoorus	Gort .	IV.	49
47	Carrownamaddy .	386	3	33	Donegal .	Inishowen West	Burt .	Londonderry	III.	119
25, 26. 34	Carrownamaddy .	2,198	2	13a	Donegal .	Kilmacrenan .	Clondahorky .	Dunfanaghy .	III.	123
42,43,45,46	Carrownamaddy .	427	2	4	Roscommon	Athlone .	St. John's .	Athlone .	IV.	183
17, 23	Carrownamaddy .	421	1	23b	Roscommon	Roscommon .	Creeve .	Strokestown	IV.	209
92	Carrownamallaght .	334	1	24c	Mayo	Costello .	Knock .	Claremorris .	IV.	142
114	Carrownamona .	135	1	27	Galway	Kiltartan .	Ardrahan .	Gort .	IV.	45
16, 22	Carrownamorheeny .	139	1	16	Roscommon	Roscommon .	Shankill .	Strokestown	IV.	212
96, 97	Carrownamorrissy .	202	0	39	Galway .	Dunkellin .	Kilconierin .	Loughrea .	IV.	29
2	Carrownanalt .	216	0	28	Roscommon	Boyle .	Kilronan .	Boyle .	IV.	196
41, 42	Carrownanelly	346	0	9	Clare	Islands .	Clareabbey .	Ennis .	II.	29
33	Carrownanty .	125	1	36	Sligo	Corran .	Emlaghfad .	Sligo .	IV.	226
70	Carrownaraha .	468	0	8	Mayo	Gallen .	Templemore .	Castlebar .	IV.	151
36	Carrownasaul .	279	0	15d	Donegal .	Kilmacrenan .	Kilmacrenan .	Millford .	III.	129
5	Carrownaseer North	397	0	26	Galway .	Dunmore .	Dunmore .	Tuam .	IV.	33
5, 17	Carrownaseer South	224	1	10	Galway .	Dunmore .	Dunmore .	Tuam .	IV.	33
29	Carrownaskeagh .	190	2	12	Roscommon	Roscommon .	Cloonfinlough .	Strokestown	IV.	208
28	Carrownaskeagh .	182	0	28	Roscommon	Roscommon .	Ogulla .	Strokestown	IV.	212
25	Carrownaskeagh .	715	0	10e	Sligo	Leyny .	Killoran .	Tobercurry .	IV.	230
101	Carrownaskeha .	118	1	2	Mayo	Clanmorris .	Kilcolman .	Claremorris .	IV.	133
32	Carrownateewaun .	122	2	8	Sligo	Leyny .	Killoran .	Tobercurry .	IV.	230
47	Carrownaun .	78	3	19	Sligo	Coolavin .	Killaraght .	Boyle .	IV.	224
123	Carrownavohanaun .	131	3	19	Galway .	Kiltartan .	Kiltartan .	Gort .	IV.	48
65	Carrownaweelaun .	847	0	38	Clare .	Moyarta .	Moyarta .	Kilrush .	II.	34
32	Carrownaworan .	249	0	30	Sligo	Leyny .	Achonry .	Tobercurry .	IV.	229
56, 57	Carrowncalla North	314	1	35	Clare .	Moyarta .	Kilrush .	Kilrush .	II.	33
56,57,66,67	Carrowncalla South	816	2	28	Clare .	Moyarta .	Kilrush .	Kilrush .	II.	33
16	Carrowncaran .	96	1	31	Roscommon	Frenchpark .	Kilmacumsy .	Boyle .	IV.	203
30, 31	Carrowncashlane .	56	3	18	Waterford	Decies without Drum	Dungarvan .	Dungarvan .	II.	355
23, 31	Carrowncashlane .	123	1	3	Waterford	Decies without Drum	Kilgobnet .	Dungarvan .	II.	357
48	Carrowncloghan .	207	3	5	Roscommon	Athlone .	Kiltoom .	Athlone .	IV.	182
16	Carrowncully .	184	0	16	Roscommon	Frenchpark .	Kilmacumsy .	Boyle .	IV.	203
69, 78	Carrowncurry .	152	0	14f	Mayo	Carra .	Aglish .	Castlebar .	IV.	123
80, 91	Carrowndangan .	543	2	24g	Mayo	Gallen .	Killedan .	Swineford .	IV.	150
28, 35	Carrowndangan .	323	2	18h	Roscommon	Ballymoe .	Cloonygormican .	Castlereagh .	IV.	191
1, 6	Carrownderry .	272	2	32	Galway .	Ballymoe .	Templetogher .	Glennamaddy .	IV.	9
45	Carrownderry .	554	0	24	Roscommon	Athlone .	Kiltoom .	Athlone .	IV.	183
42	Carrowndrisha .	458	1	30	Roscommon	Athlone .	Killinvoy .	Roscommon .	IV.	181
67	Carrowndulla .	156	0	29i	Galway .	Moycullen .	Kilcummin .	Oughterard .	IV.	66
73	Carrownea .	115	0	25	Galway .	Kilconnell .	Ballymacward .	Ballinasloe .	IV.	39
73	Carrownea Lower .	129	3	30	Galway .	Kilconnell .	Ballymacward .	Ballinasloe .	IV.	39
1, 6	Carrowneany .	235	0	9	Galway .	Ballymoe .	Templetogher .	Glennamaddy .	IV.	9
73	Carrownea Upper .	129	3	3	Galway .	Kilconnell .	Ballymacward .	Ballinasloe .	IV.	39
82, 92, 93	Carrowneden .	572	2	15	Mayo .	Costello .	Aghamore .	Swineford .	IV.	136
102, 112	Carrowneden .	416	0	36	Mayo .	Costello .	Annagh .	Claremorris .	IV.	138
49, 61	Carrowneden .	555	2	2	Mayo .	Gallen .	Killasser .	Swineford .	IV.	149
7	Carrowneden .	216	3	4	Mayo .	Tirawley .	Kilbride .	Killala .	IV.	168
24, 25	Carrowneden .	801	2	39	Sligo .	Leyny .	Achonry .	Tobercurry .	IV.	229
16	Carrowneden .	208	2	10	Sligo .	Tireragh .	Kilglass .	Dromore West .	IV.	234
52	Carrownerribul .	63	2	31	Clare .	Bunratty Lower	Kilfintinan .	Limerick .	II.	5
16	Carrowngarry .	77	1	32	Roscommon	Frenchpark .	Kilmacumsy .	Boyle .	IV.	203
58	Carrowniska North .	425	2	28	Clare .	Clonderalaw .	Kilmurry .	Killadysert .	II.	17
58	Carrowniska South .	295	1	14	Clare .	Clonderalaw .	Kilmurry .	Killadysert .	II.	17
95, 96	Carrownisky .	979	2	20j	Mayo .	Murrisk .	Kilgeever .	Westport .	IV.	159
7	Carrownisky .	400	2	16	Mayo .	Tirawley .	Doonfeeny .	Killala .	IV.	167
31, 40	Carrownlabaun .	731	0	27	Mayo .	Gallen .	Kilgarvan .	Ballina .	IV.	148
73	Carrownlacka .	720	0	19	Mayo .	Costello .	Kilmovee .	Swineford .	IV.	142
25	Carrownleam .	227	3	4	Sligo .	Leyny .	Killoran .	Tobercurry .	IV.	230
119	Carrownlisheen .	1,131	1	35k	Galway .	Aran .	Inishmaan .	Galway .	IV.	3
36	Carrownlobaun .	264	1	5	Sligo .	Leyny .	Kilmacteige .	Tobercurry .	IV.	231
112	Carrownlough .	363	1	18l	Mayo .	Clanmorris .	Crossboyne .	Claremorris .	IV.	132

(a) Including 42A. 0R. 31P. water.
(b) Including . 3A. 1R. 30P. water.
(c) Including 13A. 2R. 20P. water.
(d) Including 3A. 3R. 30P. water.

(e) Including 7A. 1R. 9P. of Loughs.
(f) Including 1A. 2R. 18P. water.
(g) Including 14A. 2R. 21P. water.
(h) Including 2A. 1R. 24P. water.

(i) Including 16A. 3R. 24P. water.
(j) Including 22A. 0R. 10P. water.
(k) Including 16A. 1R. 24P. water.
(l) Including 12A. 2R. 24P. water.

No. of Sheet of the Ordnance Survey Maps.	Townlands and Towns.	Area in Statute Acres.	County.	Barony.	Parish.	Poor Law Union in 1857.	Townland Census of 1851, Part I. Vol.	Page
		A. R. P.						
25, 32	Carrownloughan	512 1 5	Sligo	Leyny	Killoran	Tobercurry	IV.	230
93	Carrownluggaun	45 3 2	Mayo	Costello	Bekan	Claremorris	IV.	139
48	Carrownolan	277 0 21	Roscommon	Athlone	Kiltoom	Athlone	IV.	183
3	Carrownoona	423 1 25	Leitrim	Rosclogher	Rossinver	Ballyshannon	IV.	111
21	Carrownphull	83 2 35	Longford	Rathcline	Rathcline	Longford	I.	164
59, 67	Carrownreddy	297 3 37a	Tipperary, S.R.	Clanwilliam	Tipperary	Tipperary	II.	312
26	Carrownree	413 2 17b	Sligo	Corran	Emlaghfad	Sligo	IV.	226
13, 19	Carrownree	297 3 2	Sligo	Tireragh	Skreen	Dromore West	IV.	235
28	Carrownrinny	70 0 25	Roscommon	Roscommon	Kilcooley	Strokestown	IV.	210
28	Carrownrinny	70 2 7	Roscommon	Roscommon	Killukin	Strokestown	IV.	210
11	Carrownrod	489 2 11	Sligo	Tireragh	Easky	Dromore West	IV.	233
57	Carrownrooaun	134 1 25	Galway	Clare	Annaghdown	Tuam	IV.	16
11	Carrownrush	322 3 27	Sligo	Tireragh	Easky	Dromore West	IV.	233
12	Carrownrush	148 1 30	Sligo	Tireragh	Kilmacshalgan	Dromore West	IV.	234
119	Carrownskehaun	241 1 18	Mayo	Clanmorris	Crossboyne	Claremorris	IV.	132
23, 24	Carrownskeheen	207 0 38	Roscommon	Ballintober North	Kilglass	Strokestown	IV.	186
27	Carrownspurraun	475 3 7	Sligo	Tirerrill	Kilmacallan	Sligo	IV.	239
17, 30	Carrowntanlis	249 0 32c	Galway	Dunmore	Tuam	Tuam	IV.	35
47	Carrowntarriff	454 1 17d	Roscommon	Athlone	Taghboy	Athlone	IV.	184
24	Carrowntassona	174 2 5	Waterford	Decies without Drum	Ballylaneen	Kilmacthomas	II.	354
32	Carrowntawa	170 0 14	Sligo	Leyny	Achonry	Tobercurry	IV.	229
26, 33	Carrowntawy	233 3 2	Sligo	Leyny	Kilvarnet	Tobercurry	IV.	232
13	Carrownteane	88 0 26	Sligo	Tireragh	Skreen	Dromore West	IV.	235
23	Carrowntedaun	433 3 8	Clare	Corcomroe	Kilmanaheen	Ennistimon	II.	21
80	Carrownteeaun	314 3 9	Mayo	Gallen	Killedan	Swineford	IV.	150
119	Carrowntemple	1,121 1 7	Galway	Aran	Inishman	Galway	IV.	3
43	Carrowntemple	104 2 5	Galway	Clare	Belclare	Tuam	IV.	17
44	Carrowntemple	128 0 16	Roscommon	Athlone	Tisrara	Roscommon	IV.	185
43, 44, 46	Carrowntemple	767 2 10	Sligo	Coolavin	Kilfree	Boyle	IV.	224
71, 80	Carrowntleva	383 3 22	Mayo	Gallen	Bohola	Swineford	IV.	147
44	Carrowntlieve	405 2 3e	Roscommon	Athlone	Tisrara	Roscommon	IV.	185
98	Carrowntober	136 0 26	Galway	Leitrim	Abbeygormacan	Loughrea	IV.	50
63	Carrowntober	235 3 21	Mayo	Costello	Kilbeagh	Swineford	IV.	140
32, 37, 38	Carrowntober	651 0 15	Sligo	Leyny	Achonry	Tobercurry	IV.	229
54	Carrowntober or Billymore	303 3 6	Galway	Moycullen	Kilcummin	Oughterard	IV.	66
71, 84	Carrowntober East	566 1 31	Galway	Athenry	Athenry	Galway	IV.	3
18, 19, 31	Carrowntober East	1,049 0 23f	Galway	Tiaquin	Kilkerrin	Glennamaddy	IV.	76
79	Carrowntober Eighter	93 0 20	Mayo	Carra	Manulla	Castlebar	IV.	129
79, 90	Carrowntober Oughter	100 1 7	Mayo	Carra	Manulla	Castlebar	IV.	129
84	Carrowntober West	200 3 23	Galway	Athenry	Athenry	Galway	IV.	3
18, 31	Carrowntober West	375 2 29	Galway	Tiaquin	Kilkerrin	Glennamaddy	IV.	76
16	Carrowntogher	113 0 11	Roscommon	Frenchpark	Kilmacumsy	Boyle	IV.	203
36	Carrowntogher or Bogwood	200 3 38	Roscommon	Ballintober South	Kilgefin	Roscommon	IV.	189
4, 16	Carrowntomush	204 2 19	Galway	Dunmore	Addergoole	Tuam	IV.	32
22	Carrowntoosan	111 1 37	Roscommon	Roscommon	Ogulla	Strokestown	IV.	212
16	Carrowntootagh	182 1 36	Galway	Dunmore	Addergoole	Tuam	IV.	32
28, 29	Carrowntornan	144 0 4	Roscommon	Ballintober South	Kilbride	Roscommon	IV.	188
39	Carrowntreila	426 1 27g	Mayo	Tirawley	Ballynahaglish	Ballina	IV.	164
17	Carrowntryla	729 2 9h	Galway	Ballymoe	Dunmore	Glennamaddy	IV.	7
29	Carrowntryla	132 1 33	Roscommon	Roscommon	Cloonfinlough	Strokestown	IV.	208
121	Carrownturly	163 0 32	Mayo	Kilmaine	Kilmainebeg	Ballinrobe	IV.	155
45	Carrownure	53 1 28	Roscommon	Athlone	Kiltoom	Athlone	IV.	183
50, 51	Carrownure	129 2 3	Roscommon	Athlone	Taghmaconnell	Ballinasloe	IV.	185
46	Carrownure Lower	180 0 17	Roscommon	Athlone	St. John s	Athlone	IV.	183
46	Carrownure Upper	162 1 5	Roscommon	Athlone	St. John's	Athlone	IV.	183
44	Carrownurlar	86 3 0	Roscommon	Athlone	Taghboy	Roscommon	IV.	184
9	Carrownurlar	102 3 25	Roscommon	Frenchpark	Kilnamanagh	Castlereagh	IV.	204
16,17,22,23	Carrownurlar	356 2 39	Roscommon	Roscommon	Elphin	Strokestown	IV.	209
16, 17, 23	Carrownurlar	488 2 32	Sligo	Tireragh	Castleconor	Dromore West	IV.	232
12	Carrownurlar	112 3 3	Sligo	Tireragh	Skreen	Dromore West	IV.	235
4, 15	Carrownurlaur	1,583 0 7	Galway	Dunmore	Liskeevy	Tuam	IV.	35
79	Carrownurlaur	151 2 24	Mayo	Carra	Breaghwy	Castlebar	IV.	127
47	Carrownurlaur	131 2 28	Sligo	Coolavin	Killaraght	Boyle	IV.	224
23	Carrownvally	137 3 15	Roscommon	Roscommon	Killukin	Strokestown	IV.	210
4	Carrownycleary	97 3 10	Clare	Corcomroe	Killilagh	Ennistimon	II.	19
28	Carrownyclowan	826 2 8	Sligo	Tirerrill	Shancough	Boyle	IV.	241
8, 13	Carrowoaghtragh	833 2 4	Tyrone	Strabane Upper	Bodoney Upper	Gortin	III.	324
123	Carrowoughteragh	234 0 5	Mayo	Kilmaine	Kilmainebeg	Ballinrobe	IV.	155
11	Carrowpadeen	143 0 38	Sligo	Tireragh	Easky	Dromore West	IV.	233
17	Carrowpadeen East	324 0 11i	Galway	Dunmore	Dunmore	Tuam	IV.	33
17	Carrowpadeen West	198 2 25	Galway	Dunmore	Dunmore	Tuam	IV.	33

(a) Including 12A. 1R. 8P. water.
(b) Including 10A. 1R. 4P. water.
(c) Including 6A. 0R. 16P. water.

(d) Including 3A. 1R. 4P. water.
(e) Including 14A. 3R. 18P. water.
(f) Including 4A. 2R. 36P. water.

(g) Including 13A. 2R. 11P. water.
(h) Including 8A. 2R. 8P. water.
(i) Including 3A. 0R. 16P. water.

No. of Sheet of the Ordnance Survey Maps.	Townlands and Towns.	Area in Statute Acres.			County.	Barony.	Parish.	Poor Law Union in 1857.	Townland Census of 1851, Part I.	
		A.	R.	P.					Vol.	Page
43	Carrowpeter . .	45	3	37	Galway . .	Dunmore . .	Tuam . .	Tuam . .	IV.	35
45, 46	Carrowphadeen .	544	1	33	Roscommon .	Athlone . .	St. John's . .	Athlone . .	IV.	183
3	Carrowreagh . .	136	3	33	Antrim . .	Cary . .	Billy . .	Ballycastle .	III.	12
8	Carrowreagh .	443	2	5	Antrim . .	Cary . .	Grange of Drumtullagh . .	Ballycastle .	III.	14
22	Carrowreagh . .	636	3	8	Antrim . .	Kilconway . .	Finvoy . .	Ballymoney .	III.	26
34, 35	Carrowreagh .	196	0	20	Cavan . .	Clankee . .	Enniskeen . .	Bailieborough .	III.	72
11, 20	Carrowreagh . .	1,803	3	29	Donegal . .	Inishowen East .	Donagh . .	Inishowen . .	III.	118
47	Carrowreagh . .	1,242	2	27	Donegal . .	Inishowen West .	Burt . .	Londonderry .	III.	119
28	Carrowreagh . .	465	3	29	Donegal . .	Kilmacrenan .	Clondavaddog .	Millford . .	III.	124
5	Carrowreagh . .	687	0	25	Down . .	Castlereagh Lower .	Dundonald . .	Belfast . .	III.	162
97	Carrowreagh . .	169	0	27	Galway . .	Athenry . .	Killimordaly .	Loughrea . .	IV.	4
57	Carrowreagh . .	139	3	4	Galway . .	Clare . .	Cummer . .	Tuam . .	IV.	18
16	Carrowreagh . .	258	2	20	Galway . .	Dunmore . .	Dunmore . .	Tuam . .	IV.	33
73	Carrowreagh . .	416	1	15	Galway . .	Kilconnell .	Fohanagh . .	Ballinasloe .	IV.	39
98	Carrowreagh . .	258	2	4	Galway . .	Longford . .	Killoran . .	Ballinasloe .	IV.	59
18	Carrowreagh . .	65	1	23	Londonderry .	Coleraine . .	Desertoghill .	Coleraine . .	III.	230
5	Carrowreagh . .	218	3	8	Londonderry .	Keenaght . .	Magilligan . .	NewTⁿLimavady	III.	236
5, 9	Carrowreagh . .	222	0	38	Londonderry .	Keenaght . .	Tamlaght Finlagan .	NewTⁿLimavady	III.	237
102	Carrowreagh . .	253	1	4	Mayo . .	Clanmorris .	Kilcolman . .	Claremorris .	IV.	133
93	Carrowreagh . .	304	1	23a	Mayo . .	Costello . .	Bekan . .	Claremorris .	IV.	139
31, 40	Carrowreagh . .	791	0	9	Mayo . .	Gallen . .	Kilgarvan . .	Ballina . .	IV.	148
80	Carrowreagh . .	901	3	38b	Mayo . .	Gallen . .	Killedan . .	Swineford .	IV.	150
61, 71	Carrowreagh . .	203	1	21	Mayo . .	Gallen . .	Meelick . .	Swineford .	IV.	150
118	Carrowreagh . .	86	0	10	Mayo . .	Kilmaine . .	Kilmainemore .	Ballinrobe .	IV.	156
22	Carrowreagh . .	169	0	15	Mayo . .	Tirawley . .	Ballysakeery .	Ballina . .	IV.	164
22	Carrowreagh . .	293	2	12	Queen's Co. .	Clarmallagh .	Aghaboe . .	Donaghmore .	I.	235
10, 15	Carrowreagh . .	209	3	36	Queen's Co. .	Upperwoods .	Offerlane . .	Mountmellick .	I.	251
41	Carrowreagh . .	464	2	21	Roscommon .	Athlone . .	Athleague . .	Roscommon .	IV.	179
50	Carrowreagh . .	682	1	1	Roscommon .	Athlone . .	Taghmaconnell .	Ballinasloe .	IV.	185
11	Carrowreagh . .	385	3	30c	Roscommon .	Boyle . .	Killummod . .	Carᵏ. on Shannon	IV.	196
27	Carrowreagh . .	235	3	33	Roscommon .	Castlereagh .	Ballintober .	Castlereagh .	IV.	198
15, 21	Carrowreagh . .	675	1	22	Roscommon .	Castlereagh .	Kilcorkey . .	Castlereagh .	IV.	199
32	Carrowreagh . .	237	0	31	Roscommon .	Castlereagh .	Kiltullagh . .	Castlereagh .	IV.	201
9, 15	Carrowreagh . .	385	3	36	Roscommon .	Frenchpark .	Kilnamanagh .	Castlereagh .	IV.	204
16, 17	Carrowreagh . .	655	1	36	Roscommon .	Roscommon .	Aughrim . .	Carᵏ. on Shannon	IV.	207
33	Carrowreagh . .	182	0	27d	Sligo . .	Corran . .	Cloonoghill .	Tobercurry .	IV.	225
40	Carrowreagh . .	415	1	38	Sligo . .	Corran . .	Toomour . .	Boyle . .	IV.	228
30, 36	Carrowreagh . .	1,308	1	10e	Sligo . .	Leyny . .	Kilmacteige .	Tobercurry .	IV.	231
13	Carrowreagh . .	289	0	29	Sligo . .	Tireragh . .	Skreen . .	Dromore West .	IV.	235
34	Carrowreagh . .	256	2	37	Sligo . .	Tirerrill . .	Kilmacallan .	Sligo . .	IV.	239
36	Carrowreagh . .	219	3	24	Wexford . .	Shelmaliere West .	Kilgarvan . .	New Ross . .	I.	334
37, 38	Carrowreagh (Cooper)	954	2	26	Sligo . .	Leyny . .	Achonry . .	Tobercurry .	IV.	229
3, 4	Carrowreagh or Craignacally . .	497	0	23	Donegal . .	Inishowen East .	Clonmany . .	Inishowen . .	III.	117
29, 35	Carrowreagh and Dereen . .	524	0	3	Queen's Co. .	Clarmallagh .	Aghmacart . .	Abbeyleix . .	I.	236
49, 59	Carrowreagh East .	743	2	37	Clare . .	Clonderalaw .	Kilfiddane . .	Killadysert .	II.	15
58, 71	Carrowreagh East .	744	1	22	Galway . .	Tiaquin . .	Abbeyknockmoy .	Tuam . .	IV.	75
36	Carrowreagh or Keelcurragh . .	53	0	14	Roscommon .	Ballintober South .	Kilgefin . .	Roscommon .	IV.	189
31,32,37,38	Carrowreagh (Knox)	623	2	10	Sligo . .	Leyny . .	Achonry . .	Tobercurry .	IV.	229
100	Carrowreaghmony .	148	1	13	Mayo . .	Carra . .	Toughty . .	Ballinrobe .	IV.	130
3	Carrowreagh Mountain . . .	155	0	35	Antrim . .	Cary . .	Billy . .	Ballycastle .	III.	12
58, 59	Carrowreagh West .	1,107	1	20	Clare . .	Clonderalaw .	Kilfiddane . .	Killadysert .	II.	15
71	Carrowreagh West .	8	3	20	Galway . .	Clare . .	Abbeyknockmoy .	Tuam . .	IV.	16
32	Carrowreilly . .	390	2	32	Sligo . .	Leyny . .	Achonry . .	Tobercurry .	IV.	229
97	Carrowrevagh .	266	3	21	Galway . .	Dunkellin .	Kilconierin .	Loughrea . .	IV.	29
4	Carrowrevagh . .	368	2	6	Leitrim . .	Rosclogher .	Rossinver . .	Manorhamilton	IV.	111
97, 98	Carrowrevagh . .	907	2	28f	Mayo . .	Murrisk . .	Aghagower .	Westport . .	IV.	158
17	Carrowrevagh Beg .	97	1	3	Galway . .	Dunmore . .	Tuam . .	Tuam . .	IV.	36
17, 30	Carrowrevagh More	222	0	8	Galway . .	Dunmore . .	Tuam . .	Tuam . .	IV.	36
35	Carrowroe . .	330	2	33	Clare . .	Bunratty Upper .	Quin . .	Tulla . .	II.	10
6	Carrowroe . .	199	2	32	Galway . .	Ballymoe . .	Templetogher .	Glennamaddy .	IV.	9
125	Carrowroe . .	190	2	6	Galway . .	Leitrim . .	Ballynakill .	Loughrea . .	IV.	50
106	Carrowroe . .	399	0	0	Galway . .	Leitrim . .	Kilcooly . .	Loughrea . .	IV.	54
17, 21	Carrowroe . .	347	2	8	Longford . .	Rathcline . .	Rathcline . .	Longford . .	I.	164
39, 40	Carrowroe . .	496	2	13	Roscommon .	Ballintober South .	Roscommon .	Roscommon .	IV.	190
14	Carrowroe . .	178	3	39	Sligo . .	Carbury . .	St. John's . .	Sligo . .	IV.	223
17, 30	Carrowroe East .	144	0	18	Galway . .	Ballymoe . .	Dunmore . .	Tuam . .	IV.	7
97	Carrowroe North .	129	3	26	Galway . .	Athenry . .	Lickerrig . .	Loughrea . .	IV.	5
78, 90	Carrowroe North .	2,288	3	28g	Galway . .	Moycullen .	Kilcummin .	Oughterard .	IV.	66
97	Carrowroe South .	19	3	19	Galway . .	Dunkellin .	Lickerrig . .	Loughrea . .	IV.	31

No. of Sheet of the Ordnance Survey Maps.	Townlands and Towns.	Area in Statute Acres.	County.	Barony.	Parish.	Poor Law Union in 1857.	Townland Census of 1851. Part I.	
		A. R. P.					Vol.	Page
90	Carrowroe South	995 0 28a	Galway	Moycullen	Kilcummin	Oughterard	IV.	66
17, 30	Carrowroe West	469 0 10	Galway	Ballymoe	Dunmore	Tuam	IV.	7
78	Carrowroe West	1,081 0 16b	Galway	Moycullen	Kilcummin	Oughterard	IV.	66
70	Carrowroger	133 0 38	Mayo	Gallen	Kildacommoge	Castlebar	IV.	148
25	Carrowrory	131 0 1	Longford	Rathcline	Cashel	Ballymahon	I.	163
67	Carrowsallagh	331 1 22c	Mayo	Burrishoole	Burrishoole	Newport	IV.	118
82	Carrowscoltia	146 3 6	Mayo	Costello	Aghamore	Swineford	IV.	136
106	Carrowshanbally	295 0 23	Galway	Leitrim	Abbeygormacan	Loughrea	IV.	50
47	Carrowskeheen	419 2 2	Mayo	Tirawley	Addergoole	Castlebar	IV.	163
110	Carrowslattery	184 0 12	Mayo	Kilmaine	Robeen	Ballinrobe	IV.	157
104	Carrowsteelagh	148 3 0	Galway	Loughrea	Killogilleen	Loughrea	IV.	64
8, 15	Carrowsteelagh	273 3 17	Mayo	Tirawley	Kilcummin	Killala	IV.	168
101	Carrowsteelaun	237 0 7	Mayo	Clanmorris	Crossboyne	Claremorris	IV.	132
39, 41	Carrowstellan	149 1 37	Roscommon	Athlone	Fuerty	Roscommon	IV.	181
17, 21	Carrowstrawly	190 3 33	Longford	Rathcline	Rathcline	Longford	I.	164
4	Carrowteige	403 0 33	Mayo	Erris	Kilcommon	Belmullet	IV.	143
77	Carrowtootagh	218 0 24d	Mayo	Burrishoole	Islandeady	Westport	IV.	121
13, 22	Carrowtrasna	808 3 9	Donegal	Inishowen East	Moville Lower	Inishowen	III.	119
44	Carrowtrasna	1,003 3 28e	Donegal	Kilmacrenan	Gartan	Letterkenny	III.	127
15	Carrowtrasna	230 3 24f	Mayo	Tirawley	Kilcummin	Killala	IV.	168
48	Carrowvaneen	245 3 36	Mayo	Tirawley	Kilbelfad	Ballina	IV.	167
31, 38	Carrowvanny	146 0 2	Down	Lecale Lower	Saul	Downpatrick	III.	179
24	Carrowvere	183 3 32	Clare	Inchiquin	Rath	Ennistimon	II.	27
37, 42	Carrowwilkin	481 0 28	Sligo	Leyny	Achonry	Tobercurry	IV.	229
32	Carrstown or Ballyedock	244 2 4	Down	Ards Upper	Witter	Downpatrick	III.	161
27	Carry	267 2 37g	Fermanagh	Tirkennedy	Derryvullan	Enniskillen	III.	220
9, 18	Carryblagh	218 0 37	Donegal	Kilmacrenan	Clondavaddog	Millford	III.	124
61	Carrycastle	500 2 38h	Tyrone	Dungannon Middle	Clonfeacle	Dungannon	III.	299
58, 64	Carryclogher	252 0 20	Tyrone	Clogher	Clogher	Clogher	III.	292
40	Carrycole	329 2 25	Wicklow	Arklow	Kilbride	Rathdrum	I.	344
46	Carrydarragh	366 2 14	Londonderry	Loughinsholin	Desertlyn	Magherafelt	III.	240
10	Carrydoo	315 2 9	Londonderry	Keenaght	Drumachose	NewTn Limavady	III.	235
9, 15	Carryduff	596 0 27	Down	Castlereagh Upper	Drumbo	Lisburn	III.	164
53, 61	Carrygally	145 2 28	Donegal	Raphoe	Leck	Letterkenny	III.	140
46	Carrygalt	112 3 11	Donegal	Kilmacrenan	Aughnish	Millford	III.	122
57	Carryglass	589 0 38	Tyrone	Clogher	Donacavey	Omagh	III.	294
19	Carryhugh	430 0 38	Armagh	Armagh	Derrynoose	Armagh	III.	44
2, 3, 6	Carryreagh	261 3 29	Down	Ards Lower	Donaghadee	Newtownards	III.	158
22, 23	Carsan	161 0 16	Monaghan	Dartree	Ematris	Cootehill	III.	266
16, 23	Carsonstown	1,036 3 33i	Down	Castlereagh Upper	Saintfield	Downpatrick	III.	166
27	Carsrock	138 1 20	Wicklow	Upper Talbotstown	Baltinglass	Baltinglass	I.	362
21	Carstown	326 2 36	Louth	Ferrard	Ballymakenny	Drogheda	I.	179
21, 22	Carstown	731 2 11	Louth	Ferrard	Termonfeckin	Drogheda	I.	182
101	Carta	961 3 6	Galway	Longford	Clonfert	Ballinasloe	IV.	57
21	Cartanstown	288 1 10	Louth	Ferrard	Drumshallon	Drogheda	I.	180
13	Cartenstown	133 3 22	Westmeath	Delvin	Killulagh	Castletowndelvin	I.	266
28	Cartersbog	13 1 2	Kildare	Kilcullen	Kilcullen	Naas	I.	58
4, 5	Carthage	1,497 2 21	Donegal	Inishowen East	Culdaff	Inishowen	III.	118
149	Carthy's Island,	7 0 34	Cork, W.R.	West Carbery (W.D.)	Skull	Skull	II.	145
6	Carton Demesne,	963 3 4j	Kildare	North Salt	Laraghbryan	Celbridge	I.	75
25	Cartoon	67 0 32	Longford	Rathcline	Cashel	Ballymahon	I.	163
14, 15	Cartoon	212 1 28k	Mayo	Tirawley	Killala	Killala	IV.	169
68	Cartoor	165 3 28	Galway	Moycullen	Moycullen	Galway	IV.	71
96	Cartoor	132 2 34	Mayo	Murrisk	Oughaval	Westport	IV.	161
21	Cartoorbeg	73 3 26l	Galway	Ballynahinch	Omey	Clifden	IV.	15
27	Cartown	93 2 33	Leitrim	Leitrim	Kiltoghert	Cark. on Shannon	IV.	101
3, 4	Cartown	170 0 6	Limerick	Kenry	Ardcanny	Rathkeale	II.	248
3	Cartron	36 3 5	Clare	Burren	Abbey	Ballyvaghan	II.	11
7, 19	Cartron	133 3 33	Galway	Ballymoe	Kilbegnet	Roscommon	IV.	8
9, 22	Cartron	241 0 24m	Galway	Ballynakinch	Ballynakill	Clifden	IV.	11
57, 69, 70	Cartron	137 3 19	Galway	Clare	Annaghdown	Tuam	IV.	16
43	Cartron	124 3 37	Galway	Clare	Belclare	Tuam	IV.	17
99	Cartron	114 2 10	Galway	Clonmacnowen	Killallaghtan	Ballinasloe	IV.	26
103	Cartron	157 1 20	Galway	Dunkellin	Drumacoo	Gort	IV.	28
113	Cartron	236 3 15	Galway	Dunkellin	Killeenavarra	Gort	IV.	30
95	Cartron	119 0 8	Galway	Dunkellin	Oranmore	Galway	IV.	32
16	Cartron	145 2 15	Galway	Dunmore	Addergoole	Tuam	IV.	32
15, 28	Cartron	85 3 29	Galway	Dunmore	Kilconla	Tuam	IV.	35
30	Cartron	367 1 11	Galway	Dunmore	Tuam	Tuam	IV.	36
86	Cartron	20 3 15	Galway	Kilconnell	Grange	Loughrea	IV.	40
60	Cartron	55 1 26	Galway	Kilconnell	Killosolan	Mountbellew	IV.	42
33	Cartron	277 2 10	Galway	Killian	Killeroran	Mountbellew	IV.	43

(a) Including 39A. 0R. 9P. water.
(b) Including 54A. 1R. 28P. water.
(c) Including 2A. 2R. 17P. water.
(d) Including 40A. 2R. 28P. water.
(e) Including 76A. 3R. 29P. water.

(f) Including 3A. 1R. 22P. water.
(g) Including 43A. 0R. 0P. water.
(h) Including 29A. 2R. 0P. water.
(i) Including 3A. 2R. 16P. water.

(j) Including 42A. 0R. 32P. water.
(k) Including 5A. 1R. 8P. water.
(l) Part of Omey Island.
(m) Including 47A. 3R. 31P. water.

No. of Sheet of the Ordnance Survey Maps.	Townlands and Towns.	Area in Statute Acres. A. R. P.	County.	Barony.	Parish.	Poor Law Union in 1857.	Townland Census of 1851, Part I. Vol.	Page
113	Cartron	129 2 13	Galway	Kiltartan	Kinvarradoorus	Gort	IV.	49
134, 135	Cartron	73 2 39	Galway	Leitrim	Clonrush	Scarriff	IV.	52
116	Cartron	210 3 24	Galway	Leitrim	Duniry	Loughrea	IV.	53
104, 105	Cartron	250 2 35	Galway	Loughrea	Killogilleen	Loughrea	IV.	64
91	Cartron	111 0 21	Galway	Moycullen	Killannin	Galway	IV.	69
71	Cartron	91 2 20	Galway	Tiaquin	Monivea	Tuam	IV.	78
8	Cartron	59 0 13	King's Co.	Ballycowan	Durrow	Tullamore	I.	127
10	Cartron	145 2 25	Leitrim	Drumahaire	Drumlease	Manorhamilton	IV.	94
28, 32	Cartron	83 2 39	Leitrim	Leitrim	Mohill	Mohill	IV.	104
10	Cartron	708 1 9	Longford	Granard	Granard	Granard	I.	156
27	Cartron	230 3 39	Longford	Shrule	Noughaval	Ballymahon	I.	166
55,56,65,66	Cartron	1,886 2 19a	Mayo	Burrishoole	Achill	Newport	IV.	117
68, 77	Cartron	227 0 5	Mayo	Burrishoole	Kilmaclasser	Westport	IV.	121
79, 90	Cartron	60 3 12	Mayo	Carra	Manulla	Castlebar	IV.	129
101	Cartron	126 2 35	Mayo	Clanmorris	Kilcolman	Claremorris	IV.	133
93	Cartron	279 3 9b	Mayo	Costello	Aghamore	Swineford	IV.	136
102,103,112	Cartron	87 2 20	Mayo	Costello	Annagh	Claremorris	IV.	138
62	Cartron	460 0 13	Mayo	Costello	Kilbeagh	Swineford	IV.	140
24	Cartron	76 1 5	Mayo	Erris	Kilmore	Belmullet	IV.	145
40	Cartron	125 2 6c	Mayo	Gallen	Attymass	Ballina	IV.	147
49, 50	Cartron	501 2 6	Mayo	Gallen	Killasser	Swineford	IV.	149
80	Cartron	147 3 36	Mayo	Gallen	Killedan	Swineford	IV.	150
117	Cartron	129 2 9	Mayo	Kilmaine	Ballinrobe	Ballinrobe	IV.	152
47	Cartron	47 3 9	Mayo	Tirawley	Addergoole	Castlebar	IV.	163
42	Cartron	46 0 3	Roscommon	Athlone	Killinvoy	Roscommon	IV.	181
45	Cartron	190 1 27	Roscommon	Athlone	Kiltoom	Athlone	IV.	183
48,49,51,52	Cartron	163 2 21	Roscommon	Athlone	St. Peter's	Athlone	IV.	184
44	Cartron	201 2 13	Roscommon	Athlone	Tisrara	Roscommon	IV.	185
28	Cartron	78 0 24	Roscommon	Ballintober South	Kilbride	Roscommon	IV.	188
36	Cartron	61 0 31	Roscommon	Ballintober South	Kilgefin	Roscommon	IV.	189
35	Cartron	70 2 29	Roscommon	Ballymoe	Cloonygormican	Roscommon	IV.	191
34	Cartron	58 3 26	Roscommon	Ballymoe	Drumatemple	Castlereagh	IV.	191
3	Cartron	109 0 18	Roscommon	Boyle	Ardcarn	Boyle	IV.	192
11	Cartron	277 0 22	Roscommon	Boyle	Killummud	Cark. on Shannon	IV.	196
10, 16	Cartron	117 2 28	Roscommon	Frenchpark	Creeve	Cark. on Shannon	IV.	203
22	Cartron	286 3 7	Roscommon	Roscommon	Elphin	Strokestown	IV.	209
22, 28	Cartron	65 1 27	Roscommon	Roscommon	Kilcooley	Strokestown	IV.	210
14	Cartron	105 3 28	Sligo	Carbury	Calry	Sligo	IV.	220
11, 17	Cartron	140 1 7	Sligo	Tireragh	Kilglass	Dromore West	IV.	234
12, 18	Cartron	103 3 18	Sligo	Tireragh	Templeboy	Dromore West	IV.	236
40, 45	Cartron	215 1 18	Sligo	Tirerrill	Aghanagh	Boyle	IV.	237
15	Cartron	126 1 18d	Westmeath	Kilkenny West	Noughaval	Athlone	I.	274
25	Cartron	115 3 7	Westmeath	Moyashel and Magheradernon	Mullingar	Mullingar	I.	275
12	Cartron	10 0 15	Westmeath	Moyashel and Magheradernon	Rathconnell	Mullingar	I.	276
18	Cartron	355 3 26	Westmeath	Moygoish	Templeoran	Mullingar	I.	281
20	Cartronabree	126 3 16	Sligo	Carbury	Kilmacowan	Sligo	IV.	222
13	Cartronageeragh	237 1 32	Longford	Ardagh	Ballymacormick	Longford	I.	152
2, 4	Cartronaglogh	143 0 15	Roscommon	Boyle	Kilronan	Boyle	IV.	196
16, 22	Cartronagor	146 2 4	Roscommon	Roscommon	Shankill	Strokestown	IV.	212
6, 10	Cartronamarkey	266 1 18	Longford	Granard	Abbeylara	Granard	I.	154
7	Cartronatemple	188 0 31	Leitrim	Rosclogher	Killasnet	Manorhamilton	IV.	109
2	Cartronavally	197 0 26	Roscommon	Boyle	Kilronan	Boyle	IV.	196
34	Cartronavally	21 2 7	Sligo	Tirerrill	Killadoon	Boyle	IV.	239
14	Cartronawar	278 1 0	Longford	Ardagh	Ardagh	Longford	I.	151
22	Cartronawar	95 1 15	Longford	Ratheline	Kilcommock	Ballymahon	I.	164
20	Cartronbeg	43 3 20	Leitrim	Drumahaire	Inishmagrath	Manorhamilton	IV.	95
8	Cartron Beg	117 2 21	Roscommon	Frenchpark	Tibohine	Castlereagh	IV.	204
14	Cartron Big	180 0 6	Longford	Ardagh	Templemichael	Longford	I.	153
11	Cartronbore	226 3 28	Longford	Granard	Granard	Granard	I.	156
99	Cartronbower	233 1 15	Mayo	Carra	Ballintober	Castlebar	IV.	124
22, 26	Cartronboy	136 2 28	Longford	Ratheline	Shrule	Ballymahon	I.	165
22, 23	Cartonbrack	272 3 10	Longford	Ratheline	Kilcommock	Ballymahon	I.	164
40	Cartron (Brett)	70 2 15	Roscommon	Ballintober South	Roscommon	Roscommon	IV.	190
10, 15	Cartroncar	210 3 19	Longford	Granard	Granard	Granard	I.	156
16	Cartroncaran	26 1 19	Roscommon	Frenchpark	Kilmacumsy	Boyle	IV.	203
16	Cartroncarrowntogher	152 1 15	Roscommon	Frenchpark	Kilmacumsy	Boyle	IV.	203
40	Cartron (Coote)	119 3 20	Roscommon	Ballintober South	Roscommon	Roscommon	IV.	190
23	Cartroncoragh	310 3 7	Westmeath	Kilkenny West	Drumraney	Ballymahon	I.	273
15, 16	Cartroncroy	226 2 7	Westmeath	Kilkenny West	Noughaval	Ballymahon	I.	274
73	Cartrondoogan	338 1 19	Galway	Kilconnell	Fohanagh	Mountbellew	IV.	39
73	Cartrondoogan	189 3 32	Galway	Kilconnell	Kilconnell	Ballinasloe	IV.	40

(a) Including 21A. 3R. 35P. water.
(b) Including 87A. 1R. 12P. water.
(c) Including 6A. 2R. 0P. water.
(d) Including 30A. 3R. 0P. water.

No. of Sheet of the Ordnance Survey Maps.	Townlands and Towns.	Area in Statute Acres.	County.	Barony.	Parish.	Poor Law Union in 1857.	Townland Census of 1851, Part I.	
		A. R. P.					Vol.	Page
77, 78	Cartronduff	194 1 11	Mayo	Burrishoole	Islandeady	Westport	IV.	121
26, 27	Cartronduffy	143 0 6	Sligo	Tirerrill	Kilross	Sligo	IV.	241
47	Cartronearl	121 2 5	Galway	Killian	Killeroran	Mountbellew	IV.	43
1, 6	Cartron East	36 1 39	Galway	Ballymoe	Templetogher	Glennamaddy	IV.	9
9	Cartron East	194 0 22	King's Co.	Ballycowan	Kilbride	Tullamore	I.	127
23	Cartronfin	52 1 23	Longford	Shrule	Taghshinny	Ballymahon	I.	167
36, 37, 41	Cartronfree	312 0 3	Cavan	Clanmahon	Drumlumman	Granard	III.	77
122	Cartron (French)	50 2 26	Mayo	Kilmaine	Kilmainemore	Ballinrobe	IV.	156
26	Cartronganny	177 0 5	Westmeath	Fartullagh	Mullingar	Mullingar	I.	269
4, 8	Cartrongar	52 2 12	Longford	Longford	Clongesh	Longford	I.	157
19	Cartrongarrow	490 2 24	Longford	Moydow	Ardagh	Longford	I.	160
7, 8	Cartrongibbagh	348 2 3	Leitrim	Rosclogher	Rossinver	Manorhamilton	IV.	111
33	Cartrongilbert	248 2 10	Mayo	Erris	Kilmore	Belmullet	IV.	145
38	Cartrongilbert	88 0 14	Mayo	Tirawley	Crossmolina	Ballina	IV.	165
2	Cartron Glebe	141 0 32	King's Co.	Kilcoursey	Kilcumreragh	Tullamore	I.	141
5, 9	Cartrongolan	441 0 10	Longford	Longford	Killoe	Longford	I.	158
17, 18	Cartron (Hartland)	228 1 9	Roscommon	Ballintober North	Kilmore	Carᵏ. on Shannon	IV.	187
14	Cartron (Honoria Duff)	35 0 13	Sligo	Carbury	Killaspugbrone	Sligo	IV.	222
21	Cartronhugh	327 0 29	Sligo	Tirerrill	Killerry	Sligo	IV.	239
30	Cartronkeel	58 0 2	Westmeath	Clonlonan	Kilcleagh	Athlone	I.	261
22	Cartronkeel	93 1 29	Westmeath	Kilkenny West	Kilkenny West	Athlone	I.	273
2, 3	Cartronkillerdoo	99 2 19	Sligo	Carbury	Ahamlish	Sligo	IV.	219
47	Cartronkilly	194 0 15a	Roscommon	Athlone	Dysart	Athlone	IV.	181
11, 12	Cartron (King)	113 0 25b	Roscommon	Ballintober North	Kilmore	Carᵏ. on Shannon	IV.	187
122	Cartron (Kirwan)	52 0 17	Mayo	Kilmaine	Kilmainemore	Ballinrobe	IV.	156
91	Cartronlahan	1,013 0 31c	Galway	Moycullen	Kilcummin	Galway	IV.	66
13	Cartronlebagh	199 0 16	Longford	Longford	Templemichael	Longford	I.	160
121, 122	Cartron (Lindsay)	129 3 12	Mayo	Kilmaine	Kilmainemore	Ballinrobe	IV.	156
14	Cartron Little	117 0 8	Longford	Ardagh	Templemichael	Longford	I.	153
49	Cartronmacmanus	147 0 21	Mayo	Gallen	Killasser	Swineford	IV.	149
14	Cartron More	392 3 14	Roscommon	Frenchpark	Tibohine	Castlereagh	IV.	204
8	Cartronmore	529 1 21	Sligo	Carbury	Drumcliff	Sligo	IV.	221
101, 102	Cartronnacross	202 0 22	Mayo	Clanmorris	Kilcolman	Claremorris	IV.	133
8, 9	Cartronnagilta	244 1 28	Cavan	Tullyhaw	Templeport	Bawnboy	III.	94
117, 126	Cartron North	74 3 39	Galway	Leitrim	Ballynakill	Portumna	IV.	51
82	Cartron North	227 3 19	Mayo	Costello	Aghamore	Swineford	IV.	136
12	Cartronofarry East	15 0 13	Sligo	Tireragh	Templeboy	Dromore West	IV.	236
12	Cartronofarry South	10 1 13	Sligo	Tireragh	Templeboy	Dromore West	IV.	236
12	Cartronofarry West	42 3 6	Sligo	Tireragh	Templeboy	Dromore West	IV.	236
36	Cartron or Old Glebe	54 3 28	Roscommon	Ballintober South	Kilgefin	Roscommon	IV.	189
42	Cartronperagh	32 1 39	Roscommon	Athlone	Killinvoy	Roscommon	IV.	181
33	Cartron (Percival)	33 3 20	Sligo	Corran	Emlaghfad	Tobercurry	IV.	226
33	Cartron (Phibbs)	31 2 37	Sligo	Corran	Emlaghfad	Tobercurry	IV.	226
2, 3	Cartronplank	188 0 27	Sligo	Carbury	Ahamlish	Sligo	IV.	219
21	Cartronrathroe	77 2 10	Mayo	Tirawley	Kilfian	Killala	IV.	169
15	Cartronreagh	224 2 16	Longford	Ardagh	Clonbroney	Granard	I.	152
30, 44	Cartronroe	362 1 7	Galway	Dunmore	Tuam	Tuam	IV.	36
33	Cartronroe	133 0 33d	Sligo	Corran	Cloonoghil	Tobercurry	IV.	225
34	Cartronroe	148 0 5	Sligo	Tirerrill	Kilmacallan	Sligo	IV.	239
13	Cartrons	316 0 23	Longford	Longford	Clongesh	Longford	I.	157
22	Cartrons	252 1 4	Longford	Moydow	Kilcommock	Ballymahon	I.	161
35, 36	Cartrons	300 2 31	Westmeath	Clonlonan	Kilcleagh	Athlone	I.	261
98	Cartronsheela	98 3 32	Galway	Kilconnell	Aughrim	Ballinasloe	IV.	39
125	Cartron South	71 1 6	Galway	Leitrim	Ballynakill	Loughrea	IV.	51
90	Cartronstanton	33 3 9	Mayo	Carra	Drum	Castlebar	IV.	128
21	Cartrontaylor	202 0 5	Sligo	Tirerrill	Killerry	Sligo	IV.	239
27, 28	Cartrontonlena	255 0 19	Sligo	Tirerrill	Kilmacallan	Sligo	IV.	239
112	Cartrontrellick	188 0 22	Galway	Kiltartan	Kinvarradoorus	Gort	IV.	49
29	Cartrontroy	105 0 31	Westmeath	Brawny	St. Mary's	Athlone	I.	259
6	Cartron West	44 0 30	Galway	Ballymoe	Templetogher	Glennamaddy	IV.	9
16	Cartron West	82 2 32	King's Co.	Ballycowan	Kilbride	Tullamore	I.	127
5, 8	Cartronwilliamoge	247 3 34	Sligo	Carbury	Drumcliff	Sligo	IV.	221
23	Carysfort	75 0 5	Dublin	Rathdown	Stillorgan	Rathdown	I.	37
15, 25	Casey Glebe	124 0 10	Donegal	Kilmacrenan	Raymunterdoney	Dunfanaghy	III.	131
16, 20	Cashel	427 2 11	Armagh	Fews Lower	Lisnadill	Armagh	III.	46
28	Cashel	642 1 16	Armagh	Orior Upper	Forkill	Castleblayney	III.	57
19, 22	Cashel	294 0 33	Carlow	Idrone East	Kiltennel	Carlow	I.	7
23	Cashel	137 3 37	Cavan	Clankee	Drumgoon	Cootehill	III.	72
25	Cashel	226 0 18	Cavan	Clanmahon	Crosserlough	Cavan	III.	76
3, 5	Cashel	169 0 21	Cavan	Tullyhaw	Killinagh	Enniskillen	III.	91
134	Cashel	448 0 29	Cork, W.R.	East Carbery (W.D.)	Kilmacabea	Skibbereen	II.	133
80, 89, 90	Cashel	1,230 0 16e	Donegal	Banagh	Glencolumbkille	Glenties	III.	105
82, 83	Cashel	760 1 35	Donegal	Banagh	Inishkeel	Glenties	III.	106

(a) Including 5A. 3R. 16P. water.
(b) Including 14A. 2R. 8P. water.
(c) Including 5A. 2R. 26P. water.
(d) Including 16A. 3R. 27P. water.
(e) Including { 10A. 0R. 5P. detached portion.
{ 40A. 0R. 14P. water.

No. of Sheet of the Ordnance Survey Maps.	Townlands and Towns.	Area in Statute Acres. A. R. P.	County.	Barony.	Parish.	Poor Law Union in 1857.	Townland Census of 1851, Part I. Vol.	Page
11	Cashel	762 0 1	Donegal	Inishowen East	Culdaff	Inishowen	III.	118
11, 20	Cashel	1,449 2 12	Donegal	Inishowen East	Donagh	Inishowen	III.	118
26, 35	Cashel	1,010 0 9a	Donegal	Kilmacrenan	Kilmacrenan	Dunfanaghy	III.	129
24, 33	Cashel	336 3 6	Donegal	Kilmacrenan	Tullaghobegly	Dunfanaghy	III.	131
68, 77	Cashel	183 0 17	Donegal	Raphoe	Kilteevoge	Stranorlar	III.	139
103, 107	Cashel	687 1 25	Donegal	Tirhugh	Kilbarron	Ballyshannon	III.	148
15	Cashel	90 2 30	Fermanagh	Magheraboy	Inishmacsaint	Enniskillen	III.	212
51	Cashel	1,281 2 21b	Galway	Ballynahinch	Moyrus	Clifden	IV.	12
6, 18	Cashel	594 1 32	Galway	Tiaquin	Boyounagh	Glennamaddy	IV.	76
39	Cashel	227 3 27	Kilkenny	Iverk	Clonmore	Carrick on Suir	I.	105
19	Cashel	39 0 15c	Kilkenny	Shillelogher	St. Canice	Kilkenny	I.	115
15	Cashel	222 3 32	Leitrim	Drumahaire	Killanummery	Manorhamilton	IV.	97
35	Cashel	350 2 6	Leitrim	Mohill	Mohill	Mohill	IV.	107
11	Cashel	344 0 23	Londonderry	Coleraine	Macosquin	Coleraine	III.	233
31	Cashel	385 2 32	Londonderry	Keenaght	Dungiven	New Tⁿ Limavady	III.	236
21	Cashel	312 3 21	Longford	Rathcline	Cashel	Ballymahon	I.	163
54, 55	Cashel	1,687 3 0	Mayo	Burrishoole	Achill	Newport	IV.	117
88, 89	Cashel	366 2 5d	Mayo	Burrishoole	Islandeady	Westport	IV.	121
68, 69	Cashel	305 1 23e	Mayo	Carra	Islandeady	Castlebar	IV.	128
63, 73	Cashel	417 2 21	Mayo	Costello	Kilbeagh	Swineford	IV.	140
61	Cashel	589 2 30f	Mayo	Gallen	Toomore	Swineford	IV.	151
110	Cashel	394 2 36g	Mayo	Kilmaine	Robeen	Ballinrobe	IV.	157
15	Cashel	312 2 9h	Mayo	Tirawley	Kilcummin	Killala	IV.	168
19	Cashel	298 0 20	Meath	Upper Slane	Slane	Navan	I.	225
14, 19	Cashel	549 1 33	Monaghan	Cremorne	Clontibret	Castleblayney	III.	260
18	Cashel	884 0 0	Queen's Co.	Cullenagh	Ballyroan	Abbeyleix	I.	239
16, 22	Cashel	234 3 7	Queen's Co.	Upperwoods	Offerlane	Abbeyleix	I.	251
1	Cashel	196 1 10	Roscommon	Boyle	Kilronan	Boyle	IV.	196
15	Cashel	86 0 8	Roscommon	Castlereagh	Kilcorkey	Castlereagh	IV.	199
25	Cashel	136 1 32	Roscommon	Castlereagh	Kiltullagh	Castlereagh	IV.	201
45	Cashel	260 3 13	Sligo	Coolavin	Killaraght	Boyle	IV.	224
61	Cashel	32 0 21	Tipperary, S.R.	Middlethird	St. John Baptist	Cashel	II.	330
27	Cashel	1,261 1 5	Tyrone	Strabane Upper	Bodoney Lower	Gortin	III.	323
9, 14	Cashel	113 3 19	Wexford	Scarawalsh	St. Marys Newtownbarry	Enniscorthy	I.	325
103, 104, 107, 108	Cashelard	2,740 1 39i	Donegal	Tirhugh	Kilbarron	Ballyshannon	III.	148
74	Cashelard	227 0 35	Mayo	Costello	Castlemore	Castlereagh	IV.	140
8	Cashelaveela	287 0 28	Leitrim	Rosclogher	Cloonclare	Manorhamilton	IV.	109
5	Cashelbane	214 0 32	Cavan	Tullyhaw	Killinagh	Enniskillen	III.	91
109, 110	Cashel Beg	459 2 7	Cork, W.R.	Kinalmeaky	Desertserges	Bandon	II.	152
21	Cashelbeg	167 2 26	Longford	Rathcline	Rathcline	Longford	I.	164
12, 18	Cashelboy	151 3 14	Sligo	Tireragh	Templeboy	Dromore West	IV.	236
90, 96	Cashelcarn	247 1 16	Donegal	Banagh	Kilcar	Glenties	III.	108
64, 74	Cashelcolaun	206 2 15	Mayo	Costello	Castlemore	Castlereagh	IV.	140
109, 110	Cashel Commons	101 2 17	Cork, W.R.	Kinalmeaky	Desertserges	Bandon	II.	152
97	Cashelcummin	44 3 13	Donegal	Banagh	Killybegs Upper	Glenties	III.	110
63, 73	Cashelduff	702 0 7	Mayo	Costello	Kilbeagh	Swineford	IV.	140
35, 36, 45	Casheleenan	931 3 9j	Donegal	Kilmacrenan	Kilmacrenan	Millford	III.	129
102	Cashelenny	660 2 23h	Donegal	Tirhugh	Templecarn	Donegal	III.	149
130, 139	Cashelfean	1,005 3 7	Cork, W.R.	West Carbery (W.D.)	Skull	Skull	II.	145
98	Cashelfean	279 0 34	Donegal	Banagh	Killaghtee	Donegal	III.	109
6	Cashelfinoge or Lugnamuddagh	211 2 36	Roscommon	Boyle	Boyle	Boyle	IV.	194
5, 8	Cashelgarran	457 0 4	Sligo	Carbury	Drumcliff	Sligo	IV.	221
45	Cashelgay	274 0 15	Donegal	Kilmacrenan	Kilmacrenan	Letterkenny	III.	129
8	Cashel Glebe	130 0 39	Donegal	Kilmacrenan	Clondavaddog	Millford	III.	124
64, 65	Cashelgolan	463 1 7	Donegal	Boylagh	Inishkeel	Glenties	III.	112
79	Cashelin	207 0 11	Donegal	Raphoe	Donaghmore	Strabane	III.	137
122, 135	Cashelisky	368 3 19	Cork, W.R.	East Carbery (E.D.)	Island	Clonakilty	II.	128
108	Cashelkeelty	595 2 35	Kerry	Glanarought	Tuosist	Kenmare	II.	188
107	Cashellackan	82 3 8	Donegal	Tirhugh	Kilbarron	Ballyshannon	III.	148
73, 74	Cashellahenny	242 0 17	Mayo	Costello	Kilmovee	Swineford	IV.	142
70	Cashel Lower	151 1 10	Mayo	Carra	Turlough	Castlebar	IV.	130
35, 36	Cashelmeehan	794 3 15	Roscommon	Ballintober South	Kilbride	Roscommon	IV.	188
109, 110	Cashel More	654 2 13	Cork, W.R.	Kinalmeaky	Desertserges	Bandon	II.	152
26	Cashelmore	280 1 11	Donegal	Kilmacrenan	Clondahorky	Dunfanaghy	III.	123
13, 19	Cashelnadrea	377 2 39	Fermanagh	Magheraboy	Devenish	Ballyshannon	III.	210
21	Cashelnagole	150 1 3	Roscommon	Castlereagh	Kilcorkey	Castlereagh	IV.	199
33	Cashelnagor	1,352 3 29l	Donegal	Kilmacrenan	Tullaghobegly	Dunfanaghy	III.	131
77, 95, 96	Cashelnavean	1,046 1 3m	Donegal	Raphoe	Stranorlar	Stranorlar	III.	142
25, 32	Cashel North	266 3 8	Sligo	Leyny	Achonry	Tobercurry	IV.	229
83	Cashelodogherty	106 1 20	Donegal	Banagh	Killybegs Lower	Glenties	III.	110

(a) Including 95A. 1R. 25P. water.
(b) Including 24A. 0R. 7P. water.
(c) { Within the Municipal Boundary, 8A. 0R. 10P. / Without the Municipal Boundary, 31A. 0R. 5P.
(d) Including 9A. 1R. 25P. water.
(e) Including 12A. 0R. 23P. water.
(f) Including 16A. 0R. 26P. water.
(g) Including 3A. 2R. 30P. water.
(h) Including 12A. 3R. 26P. water.
(i) Including 158A. 2R. 38P. water.
(j) Including 32A. 2R. 23P. water.
(k) Including 52A. 3R. 14P. water.
(l) Including 45A. 3R. 25P. water.
(m) Including 61A. 1R. 17P. water.

No. of Sheet of the Ordnance Survey Maps.	Townlands and Towns.	Area in Statute Acres.			County.	Barony.	Parish.	Poor Law Union in 1857.	Townland Census of 1851, Part I.	
		A.	R.	P.					Vol.	Page
92	Casheloogary	920	3	21	Donegal	Banagh	Inver	Donegal	III.	107
17, 18	Cashelpreaghan	232	3	24	Donegal	Kilmacrenan	Clondavaddog	Milford	III.	124
52	Cashelreagh	214	3	30	Donegal	Kilmacrenan	Conwal	Letterkenny	III.	126
92, 98	Cashelreagh Glebe	230	0	14	Donegal	Banagh	Killaghtee	Glenties	III.	109
82, 93	Cashels	63	3	25	Mayo	Costello	Aghamore	Swineford	IV.	136
45,46,53,54	Cashelshanaghan	845	1	14	Donegal	Kilmacrenan	Aughnish	Letterkenny	III.	122
37, 38	Cashel South	832	1	3	Sligo	Leyny	Achonry	Tobercurry	IV.	229
28, 35	Casheltauna	335	2	30	Roscommon	Ballintober South	Kilbride	Roscommon	IV.	188
39	Cashel or Tobernafauna	79	2	0	Kilkenny	Iverk	Fiddown	Carrick on Suir	I.	105
81	Casheltourly	331	3	14a	Mayo	Costello	Aghamore	Swineford	IV.	136
36, 37	Casheltown	671	3	39	Antrim	Lower Toome	Ahoghill	Ballymena	III.	31
92, 98	Casheltown	431	3	11	Donegal	Banagh	Killaghtee	Donegal	III.	109
51, 52	Casheltown	253	0	27b	Donegal	Kilmacrenan	Gartan	Letterkenny	III.	127
61	CASHEL T.	—			Tipperary, S.R.	Middlethird	{ St. John Baptist { St. Patricksrock	Cashel	II.	{330 {331
43, 51	Casheltown Mountain	391	1	13	Donegal	Kilmacrenan	Gartan	Letterkenny	III.	127
70	Cashel Upper	244	2	7	Mayo	Carra	Turlough	Castlebar	IV.	130
83	Cashla	292	0	6	Galway	Clare	Athenry	Galway	IV.	17
83	Cashla	282	3	26	Galway	Clare	Lackagh	Galway	IV.	22
81	Cashlagh	801	3	7	Kerry	Iveragh	Dromod	Cahersiveen	II.	194
14	Cashlan	256	0	5	Antrim	Lower Glenarm	Layd	Ballycastle	III.	22
12	Cashlan	201	3	13	Monaghan	Dartree	Killeevan	Monaghan	III.	267
121	Cashlancran	267	0	38	Mayo	Kilmaine	Kilmolara	Ballinrobe	IV.	156
28	Cashlan East	143	0	33	Monaghan	Farney	Donaghmoyne	Carrickmacross	III.	269
28	Cashlan West	158	0	37	Monaghan	Farney	Donaghmoyne	Carrickmacross	III.	269
58	Cashlaundarragh	255	2	5	Galway	Tiaquin	Moniva	Tuam	IV.	78
9	Cashleen	350	1	39	Galway	Ballynahinch	Ballynakill	Clifden	IV.	11
25, 26	Cashlieve	281	2	33	Roscommon	Castlereagh	Kiltullagh	Castlereagh	IV.	201
120	Cashloura	560	3	4	Cork, W.R.	West Carbery (E.D.)	Drinagh	Skibbereen	II.	139
25	Cashty	408	0	14	Tyrone	Strabane Lower	Ardstraw	Strabane	III.	318
34	Caskum	646	2	38	Down	Upper Iveagh, Up. pt.	Aghaderg	Banbridge	III.	174
3	Caslanakirka	179	1	4c	Westmeath	Fore	Rathgarve	Castletowndelvin	I.	271
19	Casorna	558	2	27d	Tyrone	Strabane Upper	Bodoney Lower	Gortin	III.	323
11, 15	Cassagh	245	2	5	Kilkenny	Gowran	Mothell	Kilkenny	I.	97
27, 33	Cassan	85	2	20e	Fermanagh	Tirkennedy	Cleenish	Enniskillen	III.	219
58, 68	Cassarnagh	682	0	39	Clare	Clonderalaw	Kilmurry	Kilrush	II.	17
41	Cassestown	506	3	28	Tipperary, N.R.	Eliogarty	Rahelty	Thurles	II.	272
11	Cassidy	109	0	28	Fermanagh	Lurg	Derryvullan	Lowtherstown	III.	204
13	Castaheany	302	3	36	Dublin	Castleknock	Clonsilla	Celbridge	I.	24
5, 6, 18	Castle	479	1	10	Galway	Ballymoe	Dunmore	Glennamaddy	IV.	7
76	Castleaffy	131	3	14	Mayo	Burrishoole	Kilmeena	Westport	IV.	122
22	Castleannesley	266	0	35	Wexford	Ballaghkeen	Kilmuckridge	Gorey	I.	296
7	Castlearmstrong	442	0	24	King's Co.	Garrycastle	Lemanaghan	Parsonstown	I.	136
5, 6, 10, 11	Castleaverry	343	0	6	Down	Castlereagh Lower	Comber	Newtownards	III.	162
34	Castlebaldwin or Bellanagarrigeeny	64	2	17	Sligo	Tirerrill	Kilmacallan	Sligo	IV.	239
34	Castle Balfour Demesne	201	0	8f	Fermanagh	Magherastephana	Aghalurcher	Lisnaskea	III.	215
53	Castlebane	73	3	0	Donegal	Kilmacrenan	Aghanunshin	Letterkenny	III.	122
15, 25	Castlebane	59	2	29	Donegal	Kilmacrenan	Clondahorky	Dunfanaghy	III.	123
78	Castlebane	122	1	24	Donegal	Raphoe	Stranorlar	Stranorlar	III.	142
16, 24	Castlebane	158	0	20	Tyrone	Omagh West	Ardstraw	Castlederg	III.	315
53, 63	Castlebank	372	0	16	Clare	Bunratty Lower	St. Patricks	Limerick	II.	6
32, 36	Castlebanny	2,071	1	10	Kilkenny	Knocktopher	Derrynahinch	Thomastown	I.	111
72	Castlebarnagh	245	2	30	Mayo	Gallen	Kilconduff	Swineford	IV.	147
10, 18	Castlebarnagh Big	220	1	21	King's Co.	Lower Philipstown	Killaderry	Tullamore	I.	142
10	Castlebarnagh Little	74	1	5	King's Co.	Lower Philipstown	Killaderry	Tullamore	I.	142
42	Castlebarrett	122	2	30	Cork, E.R.	Barretts	Mourneabbey	Mallow	II.	50
78	CASTLEBAR T.	—			Mayo	Carra	Aglish	Castlebar	IV.	124
5, 9	Castlebaun	256	2	26	Longford	Granard	Clonbroney	Granard	I.	154
10	Castlebeg	139	0	32	Down	Castlereagh Lower	Dundonald	Newtownards	III.	162
45	Castlebellew	300	0	16	Galway	Tiaquin	Moylough	Mountbellew	IV.	79
15	Castlebellingham	1,038	2	34	Louth	Ardee	Gernonstown	Ardee	I.	172
15	CASTLEBELLINGHAM T.	—			Louth	Ardee	Gernonstown	Ardee	I.	172
110	Castlebernard	398	1	5	Cork, W.R.	Kinalmeaky	Ballymodan	Bandon	II.	151
86	Castlebin East	308	1	38	Galway	Kilconnell	Killaan	Ballinasloe	IV.	41
86	Castlebin North	291	1	24	Galway	Kilconnell	Killaan	Ballinasloe	IV.	41
86	Castlebin South	147	3	36	Galway	Kilconnell	Killaan	Ballinasloe	IV.	41
34, 35	Castleblagh	1,516	3	6g	Cork, E.R.	Fermoy	Ballyhooly	Fermoy	II.	76
69	Castleblake	533	2	19	Tipperary, S.R.	Middlethird	Mora	Cashel	II.	329
60	Castleblakeney	105	3	10	Galway	Tiaquin	Killosolan	Mountbellew	IV.	78
60	CASTLEBLAKENEY T.	—			Galway	Tiaquin	Killosolan	Mountbellew	IV.	78
54	Castleblaugh	264	1	22	Donegal	Raphoe	Raymoghy	Londonderry	III.	141
20	CASTLEBLAYNEY T.	—			Monaghan	Cremorne	Muckno	Castleblayney	III.	262

(a) Including 1A. 1R. 13P. water.
(b) Including 4A. 0R. 7P. water.
(c) Including 10A. 3R. 16P. water.
(d) Including 2A. 3R. 4P. water.
(e) Including 17A. 2R. 26P. water.
(f) Including 12A. 0R. 16P. water.
(g) Including 18A. 1R. 6P. water.

2 G

No. of Sheet of the Ordnance Survey Maps.	Townlands and Towns.	Area in Statute Acres.	County.	Barony.	Parish.	Poor Law Union in 1857.	Townland Census of 1851, Part I.	
		A. R. P.					Vol.	Page
19	Castleblunden . .	190 0 28	Kilkenny . .	Shillelogher . .	St. Patrick's . .	Kilkenny . .	I.	116
24, 25	Castleboro Demesne .	745 0 21	Wexford . .	Bantry . .	Killegney . .	Enniscorthy .	I.	301
25	Castleboy . .	151 2 3	Down . .	Ards Upper .	Castleboy . .	Downpatrick .	III.	160
114	Castleboy . .	456 3 34	Galway . .	Loughrea . .	Killinan . .	Loughrea . .	IV.	64
31, 37	Castleboy . .	6 1 31	Meath . .	Skreen . .	Skreen . .	Dunshaughlin .	I.	221
31, 37	Castleboy . .	86 2 37	Meath . .	Skreen . .	Tara . .	Navan . .	I.	222
1	Castlebrack . .	179 0 20	Queen's Co. .	Tinnahinch . .	Castlebrack . .	Mountmellick .	I.	248
32, 33	Castlebridge . .	57 0 1	Wexford . .	Shelmaliere East .	Ardcavan . .	Wexford . .	I.	329
32, 37, 38	Castlebridge . .	38 2 30	Wexford . .	Shelmaliere East .	Ardcolm . .	Wexford . .	I.	330
32, 37	CASTLEBRIDGE T. .	—	Wexford . .	Shelmaliere East . { Ardcavan . . / Ardcolm . . / Tikillin . . }		Wexford . .	I. {	330 / 330 / 330 / 331 }
9, 14, 15	Castlebrock . .	239 2 37a	Longford . .	Granard . .	Clonbroney . .	Granard . .	I.	154
10, 14	Castlebrown or Clon- gowes . . }	704 0 36	Kildare . .	{ Ikeathy and Ough- terany . . }	Mainham . .	Celbridge . .	I.	58
99, 100	Castleburke . .	207 0 9	Mayo . .	Carra . .	Ballintober . .	Castlebar . .	IV.	124
99, 100	Castlecarra . .	496 1 39	Mayo . .	Carra . .	Burriscarra . .	Ballinrobe . .	IV.	127
8	Castlecarragh . .	366 3 38	Louth . .	Lower Dundalk .	Carlingford . .	Dundalk . .	I.	176
31, 37	Castlecarragh or Cas- tlerock . . .	1,132 3 20b	Sligo . .	Leyny . .	Kilmacteige . .	Tobercurry . .	IV.	231
7	Castlecat . .	173 3 29	Antrim . .	Lower Dunluce .	Billy . .	Coleraine . .	III.	16
54	CASTLECAULFIELD T.	—	Tyrone . .	Dungannon Middle .	Donaghmore . .	Dungannon . .	III.	302
24	Castlecluggin . .	127 0 17	Limerick . .	Coonagh . .	Tuoghcluggin .	Tipperary . .	II.	236
31, 32	Castlecolumb . .	364 2 37	Kilkenny . .	Knocktopher . .	Knocktopher . .	Thomastown . .	I.	112
5	Castlecomer . .	81 0 22	Kilkenny . .	Fassadinin . .	Castlecomer . .	Castlecomer . .	I.	88
5	CASTLECOMER T. .	—	Kilkenny . .	Fassadinin . .	Castlecomer . .	Castlecomer . .	I.	89
1	CASTLECONNELL T. .	—	Limerick . .	Clanwilliam . .	Stradbally . .	Limerick . .	II.	226
11	Castleconor . .	212 0 22	Queen's Co. .	Upperwoods . .	Offerlane . .	Mountmellick .	I.	251
22	Castleconor . .	239 1 0	Sligo . .	Tireragh . .	Castleconor . .	Ballina . .	IV.	232
56	Castleconway . .	91 3 34	Kerry . .	Trughanacmy . .	Killorglin . .	Killarney . .	II.	211
28	Castlecooke . .	597 2 37	Cork, E.R. .	Condons&Clangibbon	Macroney . .	Fermoy . .	II.	63
22, 27	Castle Coole . .	529 0 17c	Fermanagh . .	Tirkennedy . .	Derryvullan . .	Enniskillen . .	III.	220
47	Castlecooly . .	298 3 3	Donegal . .	Inishowen West .	Burt . .	Londonderry .	III.	119
38, 39	Castlecoote . .	524 0 31d	Roscommon . .	Athlone . .	Fuerty . .	Roscommon . .	IV.	181
8	Castlecor . .	382 2 37	Meath . .	Fore . .	Kilbride . .	Oldcastle . .	I.	200
23, 24	Castlecor Demesne .	548 3 24	Cork, E.R. .	Duhallow . .	Kilbrin . .	Kanturk . .	II.	72
26, 27	Castlecore . .	268 1 12e	Longford . .	Rathcline . .	Shrule . .	Ballymahon .	I.	165
25	Castlecosby or Kevit Upper . .	136 1 33	Cavan . .	Clanmahon . .	Kilmore . .	Cavan . .	III.	78
32	Castlecosker . .	509 3 35	Kilkenny . .	Gowran . .	Jerpoint West .	Thomastown . .	I.	96
76	Castlecoyne . .	77 1 2	Tipperary, S.R. .	Iffa and Offa West .	Mortlestown . .	Clogheen . .	II.	318
25	Castlecraddock . .	311 2 1	Waterford . .	Middlethird . .	Dunhill . .	Kilmacthomas .	II.	366
25	Castlecraddockbog .	50 0 4	Waterford . .	Middlethird . .	Dunhill . .	Kilmacthomas .	II.	366
24, 33	Castlecraig . .	545 3 10f	Tyrone . .	Omagh West .	Longfield West .	Castlederg . .	III.	316
26	Castlecranna . .	373 2 36	Tipperary, N.R. .	Owney and Arra .	Kilmastulla . .	Nenagh . .	II.	295
41, 49	Castlecreagh . .	250 2 26	Limerick . .	Coshlea . .	Galbally . .	Mitchelstown .	II.	238
56, 69	Castlecreevy . .	405 1 1	Galway . .	Clare . .	Annaghdown . .	Galway . .	IV.	16
43, 52	Castlecrine . .	576 2 25	Clare . .	Bunratty Lower .	Kilfinaghta . .	Limerick . .	II.	4
72	Castlecrunnoge . .	159 3 18	Mayo . .	Gallen . .	Kilconduff . .	Swineford . .	IV.	147
2, 6	Castlecuffe . .	1,273 2 14	Queen's Co. .	Tinnahinch . .	Kilmanman . .	Mountmellick .	I.	249
114	Castledaly . .	228 0 9	Galway . .	Loughrea . .	Ardrahan . .	Gort . .	IV.	62
11	Castledamph . .	929 1 14g	Tyrone . .	Strabane Upper .	Bodoney Upper .	Gortin . .	III.	324
20, 21	Castledargan . .	988 1 7h	Sligo . .	Tirerrill . .	Kilross . .	Sligo . .	IV.	241
42	CASTLE DAWSON T.	—	Londonderry .	Loughinsholin .	Magherafelt . .	Magherafelt .	III.	243
36	Castle Demesne . .	96 2 21	Limerick . .	Glenquin . .	Newcastle . .	Newcastle . .	II.	247
16	CASTLEDERG T. .	—	Tyrone . .	Omagh West .	Urney . .	Castlederg . .	III.	318
38, 40	Castledermot . .	120 3 26	Kildare . .	Kilkea and Moone .	Castledermot . .	Athy . .	I.	59
38, 40	CASTLEDERMOT T. .	—	Kildare . .	Kilkea and Moone .	Castledermot . .	Athy . .	I.	59
109, 122	Castlederry . .	148 0 19	Cork, W.R. .	East Carbery (E.D.) .	Desertserges . .	Clonakilty .	II.	127
14	Castledillon Lower .	163 2 10i	Kildare . .	South Salt . .	Castledillon . .	Celbridge . .	I.	76
10,11,14,15	Castledillon Upper .	358 2 15j	Kildare . .	South Salt . .	Castledillon . .	Celbridge . .	I.	76
26	Castledoe . .	221 3 0k	Donegal . .	Kilmacrenan . .	Clondahorky . .	Dunfanaghy .	III.	123
106, 119	Castledonovan . .	123 3 27	Cork, W.R. .	West Carbery (E.D.) .	Dromdaleague .	Skibbereen .	III.	139
62	Castledowey . .	502 1 23	Donegal . .	Raphoe . .	Raymoghy . .	Strabane . .	III.	141
62	Castledowey . .	43 3 22	Donegal . .	Raphoe . .	Taughboyne . .	Strabane . .	III.	143
20	Castledown . .	520 3 4	Westmeath . .	Farbill . .	Killucan . .	Mullingar . .	I.	266
46, 47	Castledrum . .	707 2 8	Kerry . .	Trughanacmy . .	Kilgarrylander .	Tralee . .	II.	210
29, 35	Castledurrow De- mesne . .	829 1 22	Queen's Co. .	Clarmallagh . .	Durrow . .	Abbeyleix .	I.	237
71, 84	Castle Ellen . .	379 2 34	Galway . .	Athenry . .	Athenry . .	Galway . .	IV.	3
20	Castle Ellis . .	195 0 34	Kilkenny . .	Gowran . .	Gowran . .	Kilkenny . .	I.	95
27	Castleellis . .	130 0 23	Wexford . .	Ballaghkeen . .	Castle-ellis . .	Enniscorthy .	I.	293
41, 47	Castle Enigan . .	253 3 20	Down . .	Lordship of Newry .	Newry . .	Newry . .	III.	182
14, 15	Castle-erkin North .	287 0 11	Limerick . .	Clanwilliam . .	Caherconlish .	Limerick . .	II.	222

(a) Including 0A. 3R. 22P. water.
(b) Including 8A. 3R. 0P. water.
(c) Including 47A. 1R. 34P. water.
(d) Including 28A. 3R. 17P. water.

(e) Including 5A. 1R. 2P. water.
(f) Including 5A. 3R. 28P. water.
(g) Including 7A. 2R. 4P. water.
(h) Including 16A. 0R. 39P. water.

(i) Including 7A. 1R. 32P. water.
(j) Including 4A. 1R. 24P. water.
(k) Including 4A. 1R. 11P. water.

No. of Sheet of the Ordnance Survey Maps.	Townlands and Towns.	Area in Statute Acres.			County.	Barony.	Parish.	Poor Law Union in 1857.	Townland Census of 1851, Part I.	
		A.	R.	P.					Vol.	Page
14, 15, 23	Castle-erkin South	246	2	15	Limerick	Clanwilliam	Caherconlish	Limerick	II.	222
10, 11	Castle Espie	255	1	10	Down	Castlereagh Lower	Tullynakill	Newtownards	III.	163
26, 27	Castle Eve	548	1	11	Kilkenny	Shillelogher	Earlstown	Callan	I.	114
11	Castlefarm	52	2	30	Dublin	Nethercross	Kilsallaghan	Balrothery	I.	31
11	Castlefarm	35	3	29	Dublin	Nethercross	Swords	Balrothery	I.	32
5, 17	Castlefarm	192	2	20	Galway	Dunmore	Dunmore	Tuam	IV.	33
48	Castlefarm	258	3	2	Kerry	Magunihy	Molahiffe	Killarney	II.	204
32	Castlefarm	139	2	2	Kildare	Narragh & RebanEast	Fontstown	Athy	I.	66
32	Castlefarm	166	3	32	Kildare	Offaly West	Kilrush	Athy	I.	72
32	Castlefarm	142	3	1	Limerick	Smallcounty	Ballynamona	Kilmallock	II.	259
32	Castlefarm	595	1	38	Limerick	Smallcounty	Hospital	Kilmallock	II.	260
50, 51	Castlefarm	803	2	20	Meath	Dunboyne	Dunboyne	Dunshaughlin	I.	199
39, 47	Castle Farm	205	1	33	Tyrone	Dungannon Middle	Donaghenry	Cookstown	III.	301
42	Castlefergus	376	3	13	Clare	Bunratty Upper	Doora	Ennis	II.	8
46, 47, 61	Castle Ffrench	443	1	39	Galway	Kilconnell	Killosolan	Mountbellew	IV.	42
47	Castle Ffrench East	369	2	31	Galway	Killian	Ahascragh	Mountbellew	IV.	42
47, 61	Castle Ffrench West	336	2	38	Galway	Kilconnell	Ahascragh	Mountbellew	IV.	39
1	Castlefield	284	3	18	Galway	Ballymoe	Templetogher	Glennamaddy	IV.	9
24	Castlefield	196	1	38	Kilkenny	Gowran	Tullaherin	Thomastown	I.	100
32, 36, 37	Castlefield	78	3	1	King's Co.	Ballybritt	Letterluna	Parsonstown	I.	126
79	Castlefinn	152	0	23a	Donegal	Raphoe	Donaghmore	Strabane	III.	137
79	CASTLEFINN T.	—			Donegal	Raphoe	Donaghmore	Strabane	III.	138
28	Castlefish	210	1	8	Kildare	Kilcullen	Kilcullen	Naas	I.	58
27	Castlefleming (Giles)	380	3	32	Queen's Co.	Clandonagh	Rathdowney	Donaghmore	I.	234
27	Castlefleming or Heath	329	3	20	Queen's Co.	Clandonagh	Rathdowney	Donaghmore	I.	234
27	Castlefleming(Manly)	83	1	30	Queen's Co.	Clandonagh	Rathdowney	Donaghmore	I.	234
27	Castlefleming (Stubber)	206	0	27	Queen's Co.	Clandonagh	Rathdowney	Donaghmore	I.	234
40	Castlefogarty	403	0	10	Tipperary, N.R.	Kilnamanagh Upper	Ballycahill	Thurles	II.	277
8	Castleforbes Demesne	1,347	1	24	Longford	Longford	Clongesh	Longford	I.	157
46, 47, 55	Castleforward Demesne	321	1	2	Donegal	Raphoe	Allsaints	Londonderry	III.	134
143	Castlefreke	324	0	17b	Cork, W.R.	Ibane and Barryroe	Rathbarry	Clonakilty	II.	150
143, 144	Castlefreke-island	245	1	32c	Cork, W.R.	Ibane and Barryroe	Rathbarry	Clonakilty	II.	150
143, 144	Castlefreke-warren	178	2	0d	Cork, W.R.	Ibane and Barryroe	Rathbarry	Clonakilty	II.	150
10	Castlegaddery	371	3	38	Westmeath	Rathconrath	Rathconrath	Mullingar	I.	284
3	Castlegal	461	3	34	Sligo	Carbury	Ahamlish	Sligo	IV.	219
9	Castlegal	562	1	17	Sligo	Carbury	Drumcliff	Sligo	IV.	221
35, 36	Castlegannon	972	3	0	Kilkenny	Knocktopher	Derrynahinch	Thomastown	I.	111
95, 103	Castlegar	289	2	31	Galway	Dunkellin	Killeely	Gort	IV.	29
82	Castlegar	528	3	20e	Galway	Galway	St. Nicholas	Galway	IV.	38
46	Castlegar	799	1	3	Galway	Killian	Ballynakill	Mountbellew	IV.	43
101	Castlegar	270	2	11	Mayo	Clanmorris	Kilcolman	Claremorris	IV.	133
15, 24	Castlegarde	500	1	20	Limerick	Coonagh	Doon	Tipperary	II.	234
24, 28	Castlegarden	1,018	0	35	Kilkenny	Gowran	Kilfane	Thomastown	I.	96
61, 74	Castlegar East	927	0	8	Galway	Killian	Ahascragh	Ballinasloe	IV.	42
61, 74	Castlegar West	311	0	31	Galway	Clonmacnowen	Ahascragh	Ballinasloe	IV.	24
38	Castlegore	1,245	0	23	Antrim	Lower Antrim	Connor	Antrim	III.	3
16, 24	Castlegore	446	1	17f	Tyrone	Omagh West	Urney	Castlederg	III.	318
5, 6	Castlegowan	256	2	25	Sligo	Carbury	Ahamlish	Sligo	IV.	219
13	Castlegrace	331	2	24	Carlow	Forth	Aghade	Carlow	I.	3
13	Castlegrace	139	0	21	Carlow	Forth	Ballon	Carlow	I.	3
87	Castlegrace	540	0	2	Tipperary, S.R.	Iffa and Offa West	Tullaghorton	Clogheen	II.	321
19	Castlegrange	306	2	9	Wicklow	Newcastle	Killiskey	Rathdrum	I.	352
27, 36	Castlegregory	250	3	10	Kerry	Corkaguiny	Killiney	Dingle	II.	178
27, 36	CASTLEGREGORY T.	—			Kerry	Corkaguiny	Killiney	Dingle	II.	178
11	Castlegrey	129	0	28	Limerick	Kenry	Kilcornan	Rathkeale	II.	249
27	Castlegrogan	211	1	23	Queen's Co.	Clandonagh	Rathsaran	Donaghmore	I.	234
16, 29	Castlegrove East	261	0	17g	Galway	Dunmore	Kilbennan	Tuam	IV.	34
16, 29	Castlegrove West	357	1	3	Galway	Dunmore	Kilbennan	Tuam	IV.	34
42, 43	Castlehacket	902	0	33	Galway	Clare	Killower	Tuam	IV.	21
8	Castleharrison	239	2	4	Cork, E.R.	Orrery and Kilmore	Ballyhay	Kilmallock	II.	106
151	Castlehaven	202	3	0	Cork, W.R.	West Carbery (E.D.)	Castlehaven	Skibbereen	II.	137
31, 36	Castlehaystown	442	3	12	Wexford	Bantry	Whitechurchglynn	Wexford	I.	303
70	Castlehiggins	22	1	21	Tipperary, S.R.	Middlethird	Coolmundry	Cashel	II.	326
44, 56	Castlehill	1,188	3	29	Mayo	Erris	Kilcommon	Newport	IV.	143
38, 47	Castlehill	414	2	32	Mayo	Tirawley	Addergoole	Ballina	IV.	163
38	Castlehill	349	1	1	Mayo	Tirawley	Crossmolina	Ballina	IV.	165
34	Castlehill	203	3	30	Tipperary, N.R.	Kilnamanagh Upper	Glenkeen	Thurles	II.	278
59	Castlehill Demesne	149	1	32h	Tyrone	Clogher	Clogher	Clogher	III.	292
12	Castleholding	90	2	34	Tipperary, N.R.	Ikerrin	Roscrea	Roscrea	II.	276
35	Castlehoward	210	0	22	Wicklow	Arklow	Castlemacadam	Rathdrum	I.	342
35	Castlehyde	213	0	35i	Cork, E.R.	Condons&Clangibbon	Fermoy	Fermoy	II.	60
35	Castlehyde East	340	0	27j	Cork, E.R.	Condons&Clangibbon	Litter	Fermoy	II.	62
35	Castlehyde West	103	2	25k	Cork, E.R.	Fermoy	Litter	Fermoy	II.	80

(a) Including 6A. 0R. 15P. water.
(b) Including 15A. 2R. 39P. water.
(c) Including 14A. 2R. 33P. water.
(d) Including 9A. 2R. 16P. water.

(e) Including 9A. 2R. 24P. water.
(f) Including 8A. 0R. 20P. water.
(g) Including 16A. 1R. 24P. water.
(h) Including 21A. 2R. 8P. water.

(i) Including 10A. 2R. 27P. water.
(j) Including 7A. 0R. 0P. water.
(k) Including 2A. 1R. 8P. water.

No. of Sheet of the Ordnance Survey Maps.	Townlands and Towns.	Area in Statute Acres.	County.	Barony.	Parish.	Poor Law Union in 1857.	Townland Census of 1851, Part I.	
		A. R. P.					Vol.	Page
72, 73	Castleinch	372 0 22a	Cork, E.R.	East Muskerry	Athnowen	Cork	II.	101
19, 23	Castleinch or Inchyolaghan	} 447 2 27	Kilkenny	Shillelogher	Castleinch or Inchyolaghan	Kilkenny	I.	114
11	Castle Irvine Demesne	433 3 1	Fermanagh	Lurg	Derryvullan	Lowtherstown	III.	204
150	Castle Island	3 1 14	Cork, W.R.	West Carbery (E.D.)	Creagh	Skibbereen	II.	139
149	Castle Island	121 3 24	Cork, W.R.	West Carbery (W.D.)	Skull	Skull	II.	145
31	Castle Island	112 2 15	Down	Lecale Lower	Saul	Downpatrick	III.	179
129	Castle Island	8 0 29	Galway	Kiltartan	Beagh	Gort	IV.	46
38	Castle Island	4 2 21	Mayo	Tirawley	Crossmolina	Ballina	IV.	167
40	CASTLEISLAND T.	—	Kerry	Trughanacmy	Castleisland	Tralee	II.	209
72	Castlejohn	364 0 23	Tipperary, S.R.	Slievardagh	Templemichael	Carrick on Suir	II.	336
46, 52	Castlejordan	546 2 14	Meath	Upper Moyfenrath	Castlejordan	Edenderry	I.	212
82	Castlekeale	75 3 0	Tipperary, S.R.	Iffa and Offa West	Ardfinnan	Clogheen	II.	316
19	Castlekeely	637 0 38b	Kildare	Clane	Brideschurch	Naas	I.	53
10, 16	Castlekeeran	714 2 32	Meath	Upper Kells	Loughan or Castlekeeran	Kells	I.	206
25, 26, 27	Castlekelly	2,797 1 20	Dublin	Uppercross	Tallaght	Dublin South	I.	41
21	Castlekelly	511 3 26	Kilkenny	Gowran	Kilmacahill	Kilkenny	I.	97
33	Castlekelly or Aghrane	751 2 8	Galway	Killian	Athleague	Mountbellew	IV.	43
33	Castlekelly or Aghrane	564 3 37	Galway	Killian	Killeroran	Mountbellew	IV.	43
25, 26	Castlekevin	394 0 14	Cork, E.R.	Fermoy	Clenor	Mallow	II.	78
18, 24	Castlekevin	1,148 1 27	Wicklow	Ballinacor North	Derrylossary	Rathdrum	I.	346
13,14,17,18	Castleknock	1,020 0 13c	Dublin	Castleknock	Castleknock	Dublin North	I.	24
18	Castleknock (part of Phoenix Park)	787 2 39d	Dublin	Castleknock	Castleknock	Dublin North	I.	24
17	CASTLEKNOCK T.	—	Dublin	Castleknock	Castleknock	Dublin North	I.	24
7, 8, 14, 15	Castlelackan Demesne	292 3 31	Mayo	Tirawley	Lackan	Killala	IV.	170
43	Castlelake	205 1 27e	Clare	Bunratty Lower	Kilfinaghta	Limerick	II.	4
60	Castlelake	402 2 23	Tipperary, S.R.	Middlethird	Relickmurry and Athassel	Cashel	II.	330
83, 84	Castlelambert	588 1 10	Galway	Clare	Athenry	Galway	IV.	17
17	Castle-land	67 2 6	Cork, E.R.	Orrery and Kilmore	Buttevant	Mallow	II.	107
5	Castleland	58 2 19	Dublin	Balrothery East	Balrothery	Balrothery	I.	19
22	Castleland	265 1 25	Roscommon	Roscommon	Ogulla	Strokestown	IV.	212
2, 3, 7	Castleland	133 1 39	Wexford	Gorey	Kilcavan	Gorey	I.	317
15	Castleland	227 0 17	Wexford	Scarawalsh	Ferns	Enniscorthy	I.	323
33	Castlelands	226 2 37f	Cork, E.R.	Fermoy	Mallow	Mallow	II.	81
125	Castlelands	23 2 18	Cork, E.R.	Kinsale	Ringrone	Kinsale	II.	101
109	Castlelands	224 2 29	Cork, W.R.	East Carbery (W.D.)	Kinneigh	Bandon	II.	134
20, 21	Castlelands	382 1 26g	Waterford	Coshmore and Coshbride	Lismore & Mocollop	Lismore	II.	345
29	Castleleiny	322 2 27	Tipperary, N.R.	Ikerrin	Templeree	Thurles	II.	277
6	Castlelishen	282 0 29	Cork, E.R.	Orrery and Kilmore	Kilbolane	Kanturk	II.	108
24, 25, 33	Castlelloyd	95 2 39	Limerick	Coonagh	Oola	Tipperary	II.	235
24, 32	Castlelohort Demesne	223 2 11	Cork, E.R.	Duhallow	Castlemagner	Kanturk	II.	67
33	Castlelost	635 0 27	Westmeath	Fartullagh	Castlelost	Mullingar	I.	268
33	Castlelost West	538 2 14	Westmeath	Fartullagh	Castlelost	Mullingar	I.	268
66	Castlelough	125 1 21	Kerry	Magunihy	Killarney	Killarney	II.	203
13, 19	Castlelough	601 3 26	Tipperary, N.R.	Owney and Arra	Castletownarra	Nenagh	II.	294
123	Castle Lower	79 0 37	Cork, W.R.	Ibane and Barryroe	Timoleague	Clonakilty	II.	151
38	Castleoye	165 2 34	Sligo	Leyny	Achonry	Tobercurry	IV.	229
90	Castlelucas	58 2 32	Mayo	Carra	Rosslee	Castlebar	IV.	130
18, 21	Castlelumny	347 2 13	Louth	Ferrard	Mullary	Drogheda	I.	181
45	CASTLELYONS T.	—	Cork, E.R.	Barrymore	Castlelyons	Fermoy	II.	53
35, 40	Castlemacadam	192 3 25	Wicklow	Arklow	Castlemacadam	Rathdrum	I.	342
22	Castlemacauliffe	214 2 5	Cork, E.R.	Duhallow	Clonfert	Kanturk	II.	68
101, 111	Castlemagarret North	262 2 28	Mayo	Clanmorris	Crossboyne	Claremorris	IV.	132
111	Castlemagarretpark New	507 1 39	Mayo	Clanmorris	Crossboyne	Claremorris	IV.	132
111	Castlemagarretpark Old	170 0 3	Mayo	Clanmorris	Crossboyne	Claremorris	IV.	132
23, 24	Castlemagner	241 3 39	Cork, E.R.	Duhallow	Castlemagner	Kanturk	II.	67
31, 38	Castlemahon	343 3 5	Down	Lecale Lower	Ballyculter	Downpatrick	III.	178
47	Castlemaine	9 1 27h	Kerry	Trughanacmy	Kiltallagh	Tralee	II.	212
47	CASTLEMAINE T.	—	Kerry	Trughanacmy	Kiltallagh	Tralee	II.	212
1, 5	Castlemarket	665 2 27	Kilkenny	Fassadinin	Rosconnell	Castlecomer	I.	91
1, 5	Castlemarket East	59 3 23	Kilkenny	Fassadinin	Attanagh	Castlecomer	I.	88
5	Castlemarket West	9 2 9	Kilkenny	Fassadinin	Attanagh	Castlecomer	I.	88
97, 98	Castlemartin	442 3 35i	Kildare	Kilcullen	Kilcullen	Naas	I.	59
17, 24	Castlemartin	408 3 11	Meath	Lower Navan	Martry	Kells	I.	215
77	Castlemartyr	648 3 35	Cork, E.R.	Imokilly	Ballyoughtera	Middleton	II.	84
77	Castlemartyr	30 0 0	Cork, E.R.	Imokilly	Mogeely	Middleton	II.	89

(a) Including 3A. 2R. 29P. water.
(b) Including 8A. 2R. 22P. water.
(c) Including 11A. 2R. 12P. water.
(d) Including 0A. 1R. 4P. water. The remainder of the Phœnix Park is in the Parishes of Chapelizod and St. James's; the entire Park contains 1,752A. 3R. 21P.
(e) Including 11A. 2R. 33P. water.
(f) Including 11A. 0R. 8P. water.
(g) Including 17A. 1R. 12P. water.
(h) Including 0A. 2R. 15P. detached portion.
(i) Including 10A. 0R. 26P. water.

No. of Sheet of the Ordnance Survey Maps.	Townlands and Towns.	Area in Statute Acres.			County.	Barony.	Parish.	Poor Law Union in 1857.	Townland Census of 1851, Part I.	
		A.	R.	P.					Vol.	Page
77	CASTLEMARTYR T. .	—			Cork, E.R.	Imokilly . . }	Ightermurragh } Mogeely . . }	Middleton .	II.	} 87 } 90
76, 88	Castlemary . .	587	0	27	Cork, E.R.	Imokilly . . .	Inch . . .	Middleton .	II.	87
29	Castlematrix . .	228	2	0	Limerick . .	Connello Lower .	Rathkeale .	Rathkeale .	II.	229
147	Castlemehigan .	118	1	36	Cork, W.R.	West Carbery (W.D.)	Kilmoe . .	Skull . .	II.	144
2, 3	Castlemellan .	457	0	35a	Tyrone .	Strabane Lower .	Donaghedy .	Strabane . .	III.	320
49, 56	Castlemervyn Demesne	363	0	24	Tyrone .	Omagh East .	Kilskeery .	Lowherstown .	III.	313
37	Castlemiles .	265	0	7	Waterford .	Coshmore&Coshbride	Templemichael .	Youghal . .	II.	348
34	Castlemitchell North	723	0	29	Kildare .	Narragh&Reban West	Churchtown .	Athy . .	I.	67
34	Castlemitchell South	327	0	25	Kildare .	Narragh&Reban West	Churchtown .	Athy . .	I.	67
8, 13	Castlemore .	938	0	23	Carlow .	Rathvilly .	Fennagh . .	Carlow . .	I.	11
83, 84	Castlemore .	356	3	28	Cork, E.R.	East Muskerry .	Moviddy . .	Bandon . .	II.	105
74	Castlemore or Bally- maging .	285	1	28	Mayo .	Costello . .	Castlemore .	Castlereagh .	IV.	139
31, 35	Castlemorris .	513	2	30	Kilkenny .	Knocktopher .	Aghaviller .	Thomastown .	I.	110
30, 44	Castlemoyle .	198	3	36	Galway .	Dunmore .	Killererin .	Tuam . .	IV.	35
29	Castlemoyle .	42	2	33	Wexford .	Bantry . .	St. Mary's .	New Ross .	I.	302
52, 53	Castlemoyle North .	142	1	1	Tipperary, S.R.	Middlethird .	Ardmayle .	Cashel . .	II.	324
52, 53	Castlemoyle South .	130	2	5	Tipperary, S.R.	Middlethird .	Ardmayle .	Cashel . .	II.	324
5, 13	Castlemungret .	327	1	20	Limerick .	Pubblebrien .	Mungret . .	Limerick .	II.	254
15	Castlenageeha .	169	0	37	Mayo .	Tirawley .	Kilcummin .	Killala . .	IV.	168
3	Castlenagree .	275	3	10	Antrim .	Cary . .	Billy . .	Ballycastle .	III.	12
96	Castlenalact .	454	3	17	Cork, W.R.	Kinalmeaky .	Brinny . .	Bandon . .	II.	151
96	Castlenalact .	274	1	29	Cork, W.R.	Kinalmeaky .	Templemartin .	Bandon . .	II.	152
106	Castlenancy .	363	2	37	Galway .	Leitrim . .	Abbeygormacan .	Loughrea .	IV.	50
30, 37	Castlenavan .	669	3	22	Down .	Kinelarty .	Loughinisland .	Downpatrick .	III.	177
29	Castlenode .	220	2	21	Roscommon .	Roscommon .	Bumlin . .	Strokestown .	IV.	208
10, 15	Castlenugent .	500	3	21	Longford .	Ardagh . .	Granard . .	Granard . .	I.	152
56	Castleoliver .	786	3	20	Limerick .	Coshlea . .	Particles . .	Kilmallock .	II.	240
21	Castleore .	644	2	21	Sligo .	Tirerrill .	Killerry . .	Sligo . .	IV.	239
53	Castlepaliser .	30	3	11	Wexford .	Forth . .	Carn . .	Wexford .	I.	309
15	Castle Park .	17	1	22	Antrim .	Cary . .	Culfeightrin .	Ballycastle .	III.	13
48	Castlepark .	644	3	5b	Clare .	Clonderalaw .	Kilmihil . .	Kilrush .	II.	17
125	Castlepark .	415	3	18	Cork, E.R.	Kinsale .	Ringrone .	Kinsale . .	II.	101
114	Castlepark .	50	2	36	Galway .	Loughrea .	Isertkelly .	Loughrea .	IV.	63
60	Castlepark .	214	0	4	Tipperary, S.R.	Clanwilliam .	Relickmurry and Athassel .	Tipperary .	II.	310
19	Castleparks .	269	0	34	Meath .	Upper Slane .	Slane . .	Navan . .	I.	225
27	Castleplunket .	393	1	29	Roscommon .	Castlereagh .	Baslick . .	Castlereagh .	IV.	199
27	CASTLEPLUNKET T.	—			Roscommon .	Castlereagh .	Baslick . .	Castlereagh .	IV.	199
148	Castlepoint .	85	1	38	Cork, W.R.	West Carbery (W.D.)	Skull . .	Skull . .	II.	145
99	CASTLEPOINT T. .	—			Cork, E.R.	Kerrycurrihy .	Templebreedy .	Kinsale . .	II.	93
16	Castlepole .	325	0	21	Meath .	Upper Kells .	Loughan or Castle- keeran . .	Kells . .	I.	206
24, 30	Castlepoles .	503	2	17	Cavan .	Tullyhunco .	Killashandra .	Cavan . .	III.	97
3, 7	CASTLEPOLLARD T. .	—			Westmeath .	Fore . .	Rathgarve .	Castletowndelvin	I.	271
8, 17	Castlepook North .	1,455	1	36	Cork, E.R.	Fermoy . .	Doneraile .	Mallow . .	II.	78
17	Castlepook South .	541	3	22	Cork, E.R.	Fermoy . .	Doneraile .	Mallow . .	II.	78
18	Castlequarter .	578	1	27c	Antrim .	Upper Dunluce .	Loughguile .	Ballymoney .	III.	20
52	Castlequarter .	211	3	2	Clare .	Bunratty Lower .	Kilfintinan .	Limerick .	II.	5
15	Castlequarter .	177	2	12	Clare .	Corcomroe .	Kilmanaheen .	Ennistimon .	II.	21
18	Castlequarter .	361	2	21d	Clare .	Inchiquin .	Kilkeedy .	Corrofin .	II.	25
66	Castlequarter .	311	3	24	Cork, E.R.	Barrymore .	Dungourney .	Middleton .	II.	54
38	Castlequarter .	110	2	9	Donegal .	Inishowen West .	Fahan Upper .	Londonderry .	III.	121
37,38,46,47	Castlequarter .	295	2	16	Donegal .	Inishowen West .	Inch . .	Londonderry .	III.	121
69	Castlequarter .	107	2	23e	Galway .	Clare . .	Annaghdown .	Galway . .	IV.	16
122	Castlequarter .	343	3	11	Galway .	Kiltartan .	Kilmacduagh .	Gort . .	IV.	48
1, 2	Castlequarter .	189	1	21	Kerry .	Iraghticonnor .	Kilconly .	Listowel .	II.	191
58, 60	Castlequarter .	254	3	26	Limerick .	Coshlea . .	Kilbeheny .	Mitchelstown .	II.	239
22	Castlequarter .	197	3	1	Limerick .	Smallcounty .	Fedamore .	Croom . .	II.	259
21	Castlequarter .	187	2	35	Queen's Co.	Clandonagh .	Skirk . .	Donaghmore .	I.	235
35	Castlequarter .	133	1	11	Queen's Co.	Clarmallagh .	Aghmacart .	Abbeyleix .	I.	236
32	Castlequarter .	262	3	13	Roscommon .	Castlereagh .	Kiltullagh .	Castlereagh .	IV.	201
34	Castlequarter .	238	1	24	Tipperary, N.R.	Kilnamanagh Upper	Glenkeen .	Thurles .	II.	278
21, 22	Castlequarter .	126	1	16	Tipperary, N.R.	Upper Ormond .	Aghnameadle .	Nenagh .	II.	288
54	Castlequarter .	181	0	16	Tipperary, S.R.	Slievardagh .	Killenaule .	Cashel .	II.	334
23, 24, 31	Castlequarter .	157	3	1	Waterford .	Decies without Drum	Kilrossanty .	Kilmacthomas .	II.	358
22	Castlequarter .	64	2	17	Waterford .	Decies without Drum	Modelligo .	Dungarvan .	II.	359
5	Castlequarter .	73	1	3	Waterford .	Glenahiry .	Kilronan .	Clonmel .	II.	365
9	Castlequarter .	224	1	6f	Wexford .	Scarawalsh .	Kilrush .	Enniscorthy .	I.	324
27	Castlequarter .	180	3	23	Wicklow .	Upper Talbotstown .	Donaghmore .	Baltinglass .	I.	363
11	Castlequarter Kil- keedy . .	124	2	10	Clare .	Inchiquin .	Kilkeedy .	Corrofin .	II.	25
69, 79	Castlequin .	1,192	1	25	Kerry .	Iveragh . .	Caher . .	Cahersiveen .	II.	194

(a) Including 2A. 1R. 38P. water.
(b) Including 13A. 1R. 5P. water.
(c) Including 38A. 3R. 19P. Lough Guile, and 18A. 3R. 23P. Small Loughs.

(d) Including 11A. 0R. 8P. water.
(e) Including 16A. 1R. 11P. water.
(f) Including 7A. 2R. 13P. water.

No. of Sheet of the Ordnance Survey Maps.	Townlands and Towns.	Area in Statute Acres.	County.	Barony.	Parish.	Poor Law Union in 1857.	Townland Census of 1851, Part I.	
		A.　R.　P.					Vol.	Page
38	Castlerahan	504　0　16	Cavan	Castlerahan	Castlerahan	Oldcastle	III.	67
8, 9	Castleraw	259　3　1	Armagh	Oneilland West	Kilmore	Armagh	III.	53
19	Castlerea	150　1　19	Longford	Moydow	Moydow	Longford	I.	162
4, 9	Castlereagh	405　2　26	Down	Castlereagh Upper	Knockbreda	Belfast	III.	165
6, 7	Castlereagh	318　1　4	King's Co.	Garrycastle	Lemanaghan	Parsonstown	I.	136
112	Castlereagh	309　1　38	Mayo	Clanmorris	Crossboyne	Claremorris	IV.	132
14,15,21,22	Castlereagh	470　3　35	Mayo	Tirawley	Killala	Killala	IV.	169
26	Castlereagh	148　3　9	Roscommon	Castlereagh	Kilkeevin	Castlereagh	IV.	200
5, 13	Castlereagh	368　3　33	Waterford	Glenahiry	Kilronan	Clonmel	II.	365
26	CASTLEREAGH T.	—	Roscommon	Castlereagh	Kilkeevin	Castlereagh	IV.	201
19	Castlerea Mountain	458　2　12	Longford	Moydow	Moydow	Ballymahon	I.	162
30, 34	Castlereban North	696　1　34a	Kildare	Narragh&RebanWest	Churchtown	Athy	I.	67
34	Castlereban South	221　0　28	Kildare	Narragh&RebanWest	Churchtown	Athy	I.	67
76	Castleredmond	486　3　33	Cork, E.R.	Imokilly	Middleton	Middleton	II.	89
77	Castlerichard	293　1　38	Cork, E.R.	Imokilly	Ightermurragh	Middleton	II.	87
41, 42	Castlerickard	974　3　27b	Meath	Upper Moyfenrath	Castlerickard	Trim	I.	213
6, 11	Castlering	209　0　25	Louth	Louth	Louth	Dundalk	I.	184
45, 47	Castleroan	525　0　27	King's Co.	Clonlisk	Dunkerrin	Roscrea	I.	130
21	Castleroberts	783　1　0	Limerick	Coshma	Adare	Croom	II.	241
31, 37	Castlerock or Castlecarragh	1,132　3　20c	Sligo	Leyny	Kilmacteige	Tobercurry	IV.	231
18, 26	Castleroddy Glebe	432　2　10	Tyrone	Strabane Upper	Cappagh	Omagh	III.	325
7	Castleroe	418　1　25	Londonderry	Coleraine	Macosquin	Coleraine	III.	233
37, 39	Castleroe East	295　1　17	Kildare	Kilkea and Moone	Dunmanoge	Athy	I.	59
37, 39	Castleroe West	512　0　33	Kildare	Kilkea and Moone	Dunmanoge	Athy	I.	59
25	Castlerogy	150　2　14d	Leitrim	Carrigallen	Oughteragh	Bawnboy	IV.	91
71, 72	Castleroyan	514　0　21	Mayo	Gallen	Kilconduff	Swineford	IV.	147
21, 27	Castleruby	271　2　11	Roscommon	Castlereagh	Baslick	Castlereagh	IV.	199
21	Castleruddery Lower	328　1　25	Wicklow	Upper Talbotstown	Donaghmore	Baltinglass	I.	363
21	Castleruddery Upper	199　2　27	Wicklow	Upper Talbotstown	Donaghmore	Baltinglass	I.	363
17,18,25,26	Castlesaffron	485　2　8	Cork, E.R.	Fermoy	Doneraile	Mallow	II.	78
21	Castlesallagh	248　2　7	Wicklow	Upper Talbotstown	Donaghmore	Baltinglass	I.	363
48, 51	Castlesampson	1,560　1　2e	Roscommon	Athlone	Taghmaconnell	Athlone	IV.	185
11	Castlesaunderson Demesne	932　1　38f	Cavan	Tullygarvey	Annagh	Cavan	III.	87
16	Castlesessagh	165　0　7g	Tyrone	Omagh West	Urney	Castlederg	III.	318
10, 14	Castleshane Demesne	379　1　36	Monaghan	Monaghan	Monaghan	Monaghan	III.	276
8, 14	Castleshannon	238　2　28	Kerry	Clanmaurice	Ballyheige	Tralee	II.	167
8, 14	Castleshannon	386　2　31	Kerry	Clanmaurice	Killury	Listowel	II.	171
14	Castlesheela	123　2　39	Tipperary, N.R.	Lower Ormond	Dromineer	Nenagh	II.	283
72	Castlesheenaghan	392　2　15	Mayo	Gallen	Meelick	Swineford	IV.	150
14, 19	Castlesize	218　0　27h	Kildare	Naas North	Bodenstown	Naas	I.	62
37, 44	Castleskreen	334　0　32	Down	Lecale Upper	Bright	Downpatrick	III.	180
32	Castlesow	95　0　6	Wexford	Shelmaliere East	Tikillin	Wexford	I.	331
41	Castlestrange	802　2　33i	Roscommon	Athlone	Fuerty	Roscommon	IV.	181
27	Castletalbot	183　0　8	Wexford	Ballaghkeen	Killila	Enniscorthy	I.	295
10	Castletate	7　1　29	Louth	Ardee	Louth	Dundalk	I.	173
103, 104	Castletaylor North	267　3　9	Galway	Dunkellin	Ardrahan	Gort	IV.	26
104, 114	Castletaylor South	431　1　21	Galway	Dunkellin	Ardrahan	Gort	IV.	26
27	Castleteheen	575　0　17	Roscommon	Castlereagh	Baslick	Castlereagh	IV.	199
1, 2, 3, 4	Castletenison Demesne	600　0　0j	Roscommon	Boyle	Kilronan	Boyle	IV.	196
21	Castleterra	141　3　39	Cavan	Upper Loughtee	Castleterra	Cavan	III.	82
19	Castleterry	288　3　15	Cork, E.R.	Fermoy	Ballydeloughy	Mitchelstown	II.	76
55	Castlethird	213　0　17	Donegal	Raphoe	Taughboyne	Londonderry	III.	143
31, 36	Castletimon	467　0　3	Wicklow	Arklow	Dunganstown	Rathdrum	I.	343
22, 26	Castletobin	85　1　24	Kilkenny	Callan	Callan	Callan	I.	83
26	Castletobin East	11　2　7	Kilkenny	Callan	Callan	Callan	I.	83
26	Castletobin West	67　2　8	Kilkenny	Callan	Callan	Callan	I.	83
6	Castletogher	429　0　15	Galway	Ballymoe	Templetogher	Glennamaddy	IV.	9
7	Castletoodry	194　2　21	Londonderry	Coleraine	Killowen	Coleraine	III.	232
61	Castletorrison	342　3　34	Donegal	Raphoe	Convoy	Stranorlar	III.	136
45, 46	Castletown	591　3　36	Antrim	Lower Belfast	Ballynure	Larne	III.	7
47	Castletown	347　3　39	Antrim	Lower Belfast	Islandmagee	Larne	III.	8
7, 12	Castletown	485　0　9	Carlow	Carlow	Tullowmagimma	Carlow	I.	2
34	Castletown	146　2　37	Clare	Bunratty Upper	Doora	Ennis	II.	8
10	Castletown	238　3　6	Clare	Burren	Carran	Ballyvaghan	II.	11
66	Castletown	394　0　9	Cork, E.R.	Imokilly	Mogeely	Middleton	II.	89
112	Castletown	102　0　10	Cork, E.R.	Kinalea	Kinure	Kinsale	II.	95
95	Castletown	464　2　12	Cork, W.R.	East Carbery (W.D.)	Kinneigh	Dunmanway	II.	134
62, 63	Castletown	381　3　36	Donegal	Raphoe	Taughboyne	Strabane	III.	143
16, 29	Castletown	140　0　16	Galway	Dunmore	Tuam	Tuam	IV.	36
122, 123	Castletown	253　1　22	Galway	Kiltartan	Kiltartan	Gort	IV.	48
106, 107	Castletown	123　1　5	Galway	Longford	Abbeygormacan	Ballinasloe	IV.	56

(a) Including 17A. 1R. 0P. River Barrow.
(b) Including 1A. 0R. 20P. water.
(c) Including 8A. 3R. 0P. water.
(d) Including 3A. 1R. 32P. water.
(e) Including 7A. 1R. 24P. water.
(f) Including 35A. 3R. 29P. water.
(g) Including 1A. 3R. 8P. water.
(h) Including 9A. 3R. 35P. water.
(i) Including 18A. 2R. 6P. water.
(j) Including 87A. 3R. 31P. water.

No. of Sheet of the Ordnance Survey Maps.	Townlands and Towns.	Area in Statute Acres.	County.	Barony.	Parish.	Poor Law Union in 1857.	Townland Census of 1851, Part I.	
		A. R. P.					Vol.	Page
18, 31	Castletown	381 3 7	Galway	Tiaquin	Kilkerrin	Glennamaddy	IV.	76
21, 22	Castletown	197 1 37	Kerry	Clanmaurice	Kilflyn	Listowel	II.	170
11	Castletown	647 3 34a	Kildare	North Salt	Kildrought	Celbridge	I.	74
3, 8	Castletown	860 2 29	Kilkenny	Galmoy	Erke	Urlingford	I.	92
34, 38	Castletown	987 1 21	Kilkenny	Iverk	Whitechurch	Carrick on Suir	I.	107
35, 38	Castletown	529 3 14	King's Co.	Ballybritt	Birr	Parsonstown	I.	125
7, 8, 15	Castletown	744 3 5	King's Co.	Ballycowan	Rahan	Tullamore	I.	128
7	Castletown	67 0 2	Leitrim	Rosclogher	Killasnet	Manorhamilton	IV.	109
38, 46	Castletown	1,472 2 10	Limerick	Connello Upper	Corcomohide	Croom	II.	232
3, 11	Castletown	433 3 35	Limerick	Kenry	Kilcornan	Rathkeale	II.	249
18, 21	Castletown	126 1 18	Louth	Ferrard	Mullary	Drogheda	I.	181
7	Castletown	377 2 2	Louth	Upper Dundalk	Castletown	Dundalk	I.	177
118	Castletown	155 1 26	Mayo	Kilmaine	Ballinchalla	Ballinrobe	IV.	152
123	Castletown	624 2 35	Mayo	Kilmaine	Cong	Ballinrobe	IV.	153
7	Castletown	285 1 20	Mayo	Tirawley	Kilbride	Killala	IV.	168
7, 8	Castletown	372 2 20	Mayo	Tirawley	Lackan	Killala	IV.	170
36, 42	Castletown	689 1 12	Meath	Lower Moyfenrath	Rathmolyon	Trim	I.	211
29	Castletown	540 2 10b	Meath	Lune	Athboy	Trim	I.	207
11, 12	Castletown	780 3 0	Meath	Morgallion	Castletown	Navan	I.	209
28	Castletown	370 2 8	Queen's Co.	Clandonagh	Donaghmore	Donaghmore	I.	233
15, 21	Castletown	186 0 0	Queen's Co.	Clandonagh	Kyle	Donaghmore	I.	233
26	Castletown	298 0 17	Queen's Co.	Slievemargy	Killabban	Carlow	I.	245
10	Castletown	70 3 25	Roscommon	Frenchpark	Creeve	Cark. on Shannon	IV.	203
11	Castletown	394 3 14	Sligo	Tireragh	Easky	Dromore West	IV.	233
36, 42	Castletown	730 1 16	Tipperary, N.R.	Eliogarty	Moyne	Thurles	II.	271
9	Castletown	317 3 35	Tipperary, N.R.	Lower Ormond	Kilbarron	Borrisokane	II.	284
8	Castletown	99 1 14	Tipperary, N.R.	Lower Ormond	Loughkeen	Parsonstown	II.	286
13, 19	Castletown	529 2 0	Tipperary, N.R.	Owney and Arra	Castletownarra	Nenagh	II.	294
50, 51	Castletown	215 2 29	Tyrone	Clogher	Donacavey	Omagh	III.	294
60	Castletown	272 1 35c	Tyrone	Dungannon Lower	Carnteel	Dungannon	III.	297
5	Castletown	349 0 13	Tyrone	Strabane Lower	Leckpatrick	Strabane	III.	321
4	Castletown	185 1 5d	Tyrone	Strabane Lower	Urney	Strabane	III.	322
25	Castletown	547 3 24e	Tyrone	Strabane Upper	Cappagh	Omagh	III.	325
17, 18	Castletown	585 1 30	Waterford	Middlethird	Drumcannon	Waterford	II.	366
35, 36	Castletown	498 1 14	Westmeath	Clonlonan	Kilcleagh	Athlone	I.	261
25, 32	Castletown	691 2 33	Westmeath	Moycashel	Castletownkindalen	Mullingar	I.	277
47	Castletown	92 3 16	Wexford	Bargy	Kilmore	Wexford	I.	306
53	Castletown	119 3 4	Wexford	Forth	Carn	Wexford	I.	309
3, 7	Castletown	219 0 13	Wexford	Gorey	Kilgorman	Gorey	I.	318
115	CASTLETOWN BEAR-HAVEN T.	—	Cork, W.R.	Bear	Killaconenagh	Castletown	II.	125
8	Castletowncooley	1,211 2 18	Louth	Lower Dundalk	Carlingford	Dundalk	I.	176
9, 13, 14	Castletowndelvin	471 3 23	Westmeath	Delvin	Castletowndelvin	Castletowndelvin	I.	264
14	CASTLETOWNDELVIN T.	—	Westmeath	Delvin	Castletowndelvin	Castletowndelvin	I.	265
36, 37	Castletown & Glinsk	900 2 32	King's Co.	Ballybritt	Kinnitty	Parsonstown	I.	125
18	Castletown Kilberry	418 1 38	Meath	Morgallion	Kilberry	Navan	I.	209
1	Castletown Lower	426 1 10	Westmeath	Fore	Lickbla	Granard	I.	270
15	Castletown Monea	139 0 11	Fermanagh	Magheraboy	Devenish	Enniskillen	III.	210
11	Castletownmoor	449 1 31	Meath	Lower Kells	Staholpmog	Kells	I.	204
26	Castletownroche	804 3 17	Cork, E.R.	Fermoy	Castletownroche	Fermoy	II.	77
26	CASTLETOWNROCHE T.	—	Cork, E.R.	Fermoy	Castletownroche	Fermoy	II.	78
142, 151	Castletownsend	315 2 2	Cork, W.R.	West Carbery (E.D.)	Castlehaven	Skibbereen	II.	137
142	CASTLETOWNSEND T.	—	Cork, W.R.	West Carbery (E.D.)	Castlehaven	Skibbereen	II.	138
31	Castletown Tara	799 0 21	Meath	Skreen	Tara	Navan	I.	222
95	CASTLETOWN T.	—	Cork, W.R.	East Carbery (W.D.)	Kinneigh	Dunmanway	II.	135
16	CASTLETOWN T.	—	Queen's Co.	Upperwoods	Offerlane	Abbeyleix	I.	252
32	CASTLETOWN T.	—	Westmeath	Moycashel	Castletownkindalen	Mullingar	I.	277
1	Castletown Upper	231 0 12	Westmeath	Fore	Lickbla	Granard	I.	270
86	Castletreasure	827 0 22	Cork, E.R.	Cork	Carrigaline	Cork	II.	64
23	Castletrench	429 3 22	Queen's Co.	Upperwoods	Offerlane	Abbeyleix	I.	251
5, 6	Castletroy	293 0 37	Limerick	Clanwilliam	Kilmurry	Limerick	II.	224
96	Castleturvin	388 1 1	Galway	Athenry	Athenry	Loughrea	IV.	3
123	Castle Upper	103 1 37	Cork, W.R.	Ibane and Barryroe	Timoleague	Clonakilty	II.	151
27, 34	Castlevennon	423 3 18f	Down	Upper Iveagh, Lr. pt.	Garvaghy	Banbridge	III.	172
134	Castleventry	544 0 17	Cork, W.R.	East Carbery (W.D.)	Castleventry	Clonakilty	II.	131
75	Castleview	122 1 17	Cork, E.R.	Barrymore	Little Island	Cork	II.	56
37	Castleview	181 2 36	Cork, E.R.	Kinnatalloon	Knockmourne	Fermoy	II.	98
40	Castleview	35 1 7	Kerry	Trughanacmy	Castleisland	Tralee	II.	208
29	Castleview	67 1 32	Queen's Co.	Clarmallagh	Durrow	Abbeyleix	I.	237
31,32,37,38	Castlewaller	2,425 2 1	Tipperary, N.R.	Owney and Arra	Kilnarath	Nenagh	II.	295
31	Castleward	530 0 0	Down	Lecale Lower	Ballyculter	Downpatrick	III.	178
20	Castlewarden	221 2 33	Dublin	Newcastle	Newcastle	Celbridge	I.	34
15	Castlewarden North	467 0 3	Kildare	South Salt	Oughterard	Naas	I.	78

(a) Including 7A. 2R. 24P. water.
(b) Including 29A. 1R. 39P. detached portion.
(c) Including 2A. 2R. 3P. of Lake.
(d) Including 2A. 3R. 0P. water.
(e) Including 18A. 3R. 23P. water.
(f) Including 10A. 0R. 29P. Corbet Lough.

No. of Sheet of the Ordnance Survey Maps.	Townlands and Towns.	Area in Statute Acres.	County.	Barony.	Parish.	Poor Law Union in 1857.	Townland Census of 1851, Part I.	
		A. R. P.					Vol.	Page
15	Castlewarden South	112 3 33	Kildare . .	South Salt . .	Oughterard . .	Naas . . .	I.	78
15	Castlewarren . .	1,046 0 8	Kilkenny .	Gowran . .	Tiscoffin . .	Kilkenny . .	I.	99
3	Castlewarren .	797 3 5	Tyrone . .	Strabane Lower .	Donaghedy . .	Strabane . .	III.	320
43	Castlewellan . .	737 1 25	Down . .	Upper Iveagh, Lr. pt.	Kilmegan . .	Downpatrick .	III.	173
43	CASTLEWELLAN T. .	—	Down . .	Upper Iveagh, Lr. pt.	Kilmegan . .	Downpatrick .	III.	173
5, 6	Castlewhite . .	234 0 33	Wexford . .	Scarawalsh . .	Carnew . .	Gorey . .	I.	322
26	Castlewidenham .	184 3 14	Cork, E.R. .	Fermoy . .	Castletownroche .	Fermoy . .	II.	77
23, 24	Castlewilder . .	269 0 35a	Longford . .	Shrule . .	Agharra . .	Ballymahon .	I.	166
29, 35	Castlewood . .	337 0 36	Queen's Co. .	Clarmallagh . .	Durrow . .	Abbeyleix .	I.	237
45	Castleworkhouse .	224 3 25	Wexford . .	Shelburne . .	Tintern . .	New Ross .	I.	329
53	Castlewray . .	144 1 14	Donegal . .	Kilmacrenan . .	Aghanunshin .	Letterkenny .	III.	122
8	Castlewrixon . .	99 1 19	Cork, E.R. .	Orrery and Kilmore	Imphrick . .	Kilmallock .	II.	108
7, 8	Castlewrixon South	867 0 26	Cork, E.R. .	Orrery and Kilmore	Imphrick . .	Kilmallock .	II.	108
47, 55	Castruse . .	433 2 26	Donegal . .	Raphoe . .	Allsaints . .	Londonderry .	III.	134
90, 100	Catfort . .	165 0 3	Mayo . .	Carra . .	Drum . .	Castlebar .	IV.	128
54, 62	Cathaganstown .	521 0 6	Tipperary, S.R.	Slievardagh . .	Killenaule . .	Cashel . .	II.	334
15	Catherine's Isle .	2 0 1	Donegal . .	Kilmacrenan . .	Clondahorky .	Dunfanaghy .	III.	123
6	Catherinestown .	114 1 3	Kildare . .	North Salt . .	Laraghbryan .	Celbridge . .	I.	75
26	Catherinestown .	667 1 12	Westmeath .	Fartullagh . .	Lynn . .	Mullingar .	I.	269
40, 43	Catsrock . .	117 0 27	Kilkenny . .	Ida . . .	Kilcolumb . .	Waterford .	I.	102
31, 35	Catstown . .	536 3 23	Kilkenny . .	Knocktopher . .	Aghaviller . .	Thomastown .	I.	110
33, 36	Cattan . .	1,187 3 10b	Leitrim . .	Mohill . .	Cloone . .	Mohill . .	IV.	105
10	Cattogs . .	364 2 30c	Down . .	Castlereagh Lower .	Comber . .	Newtownards .	III.	162
51	Cattor . .	192 0 15	Tyrone . .	Clogher . .	Donacavey .	Clogher . .	III.	294
25	Cauhoo . .	371 3 22	Cavan . .	Upper Loughtee .	Kilmore . .	Cavan . .	III.	84
24, 30	Caul . .	579 1 37	Roscommon .	Ballintober North .	Kilglass . .	Strokestown .	IV.	186
18, 26	Caulhame . .	199 2 37	Londonderry .	Coleraine . .	Desertoghill .	Coleraine . .	III.	230
67, 68	Caulicaun . .	12 0 19	Mayo . .	Burrishoole . .	Burrishoole . .	Newport . .	IV.	118
50	Caulside . .	67 0 16	Antrim . .	Upper Antrim .	Antrim . .	Antrim . .	III.	5
44,45,50,51	Caulstown . .	231 1 24	Meath . .	Dunboyne . .	Dunboyne . .	Dunshaughlin .	I.	199
27	Caulstown . .	195 0 24	Meath . .	Lower Duleek .	Duleek . .	Drogheda .	I.	195
27	Caulstown . .	57 0 27	Meath . .	Upper Duleek .	Duleek . .	Drogheda .	I.	197
71	Caum . .	421 3 28d	Cork, W.R. .	East Muskerry .	Aghinagh . .	Macroom . .	II.	153
11, 20	Caumglen . .	273 0 34	Waterford .	Coshmore&Coshbride	Lismore and Mocollop	Lismore . .	II.	345
99	Caunteens . .	710 0 28	Kerry . .	Dunkerron South .	Kilcrohane .	Cahersiveen .	II.	183
23	Cauran . .	127 1 26	Westmeath .	Kilkenny West .	Drumraney .	Ballymahon .	I.	273
60	Caurans Lower .	243 0 32	Mayo . .	Carra . .	Turlough . .	Castlebar .	IV.	130
60	Caurans Upper or Oughterard .	119 3 38e	Mayo . .	Carra . .	Turlough . .	Castlebar .	IV.	130
20	Caureen . .	110 3 1	Kildare . .	Naas North . .	Rathmore .	Naas . .	I.	62
8	Causanagh . .	297 0 21	Armagh . .	Oneilland West .	Loughgall . .	Armagh . .	III.	53
8	Causestown . .	110 3 31	Dublin . .	Balrothery East .	Lusk . .	Balrothery .	I.	21
29	Causestown . .	669 3 0f	Meath . .	Lune . .	Athboy . .	Trim . .	I.	207
18	Causestown . .	404 0 27	Meath . .	Upper Slane .	Stackallan .	Navan . .	I.	225
15	CAUSEWAY T. .	—	Kerry . .	Clanmaurice .	Killury . .	Listowel . .	II.	171
51, 58, 59	Cauteen . .	148 1 16	Tipperary, S.R.	Clanwilliam . .	Solloghodmore .	Tipperary .	II.	311
7	Cavan . .	146 1 19	Antrim . .	Lower Dunluce .	Billy . .	Coleraine .	III.	16
9	Cavan . .	166 0 19	Armagh . .	Oneilland West .	Kilmore . .	Armagh . .	III.	53
98	Cavan . .	120 0 14	Donegal . .	Banagh . .	Killaghtee .	Donegal . .	III.	109
70, 71	Cavan . .	126 2 31	Donegal . .	Raphoe . .	Clonleigh .	Strabane .	III.	134
107	Cavan . .	85 3 32	Donegal . .	Tirhugh . .	Kilbarron .	Ballyshannon .	III.	148
42, 48	Cavan . . .	180 1 2	Down . .	Upper Iveagh, Lr. pt.	Clonduff . .	Newry . .	III.	171
42	Cavan . . .	213 0 31	Down . .	Upper Iveagh, Lr. pt.	Drumballyroney .	Newry . .	III.	172
18	Cavan . . .	148 0 10	Leitrim . .	Drumahaire .	Inishmagrath .	Manorhamilton .	IV.	95
32	Cavan . . .	143 0 16	Leitrim . .	Mohill . .	Mohill . .	Mohill . .	IV.	107
9	Cavan . . .	135 0 5	Longford . .	Granard . .	Clonbroney .	Granard . .	I.	154
12	Cavan . . .	92 3 19	Louth . .	Upper Dundalk .	Dunbin . .	Dundalk .	I.	178
12	Cavan . . .	147 0 37	Louth . .	Upper Dundalk .	Haynestown .	Dundalk .	I.	178
118	Cavan . . .	247 1 31	Mayo . .	Kilmaine . .	Ballinrobe .	Ballinrobe .	IV.	152
11, 12	Cavan . . .	175 3 29	Monaghan .	Dartree . .	Clones . .	Clones . .	III.	264
65	Cavan . . .	199 1 3g	Tyrone . .	Clogher . .	Clogher . .	Clogher . .	III.	292
55	Cavan . . .	219 2 33	Tyrone . .	Dungannon Middle .	Killyman . .	Dungannon .	III.	303
42, 50	Cavan . . .	419 1 23	Tyrone . .	Omagh East .	Donacavey .	Omagh . .	III.	310
15, 16	Cavan . . .	356 0 38	Tyrone . .	Omagh West .	Urney . .	Castlederg .	III.	318
58	Cavanacark . .	410 0 36	Tyrone . .	Clogher . .	Clogher . .	Clogher . .	III.	292
12, 16	Cavanacaw . .	398 1 37	Armagh . .	Armagh . .	Lisnadill . .	Armagh . .	III.	45
63	Cavanacaw . .	85 3 15	Donegal . .	Raphoe . .	Taughboyne .	Strabane .	III.	143
37	Cavanacaw . .	192 0 25	Tyrone . .	Dungannon Middle .	Pomeroy . .	Cookstown .	III.	304
34	Cavanacaw . .	116 3 19	Tyrone . .	Omagh East .	Drumragh .	Omagh . .	III.	312
34, 42	Cavanacaw Lower .	228 3 13	Tyrone . .	Omagh East .	Drumragh .	Omagh . .	III.	312
34	Cavanacaw Upper .	293 2 28	Tyrone . .	Omagh East .	Drumragh .	Omagh . .	III.	312
70	Cavanacor . .	85 1 3	Donegal . .	Raphoe . .	Clonleigh .	Strabane .	III.	134
22	Cavanacross . .	303 3 29h	Fermanagh .	Tirkennedy . .	Derryvullan .	Enniskillen .	III.	220

(a) Including 5A. 1R. 35P. water.
(b) Including 36A. 0R. 36P. water.
(c) Including 4A. 1R. 28P. water.
(d) Including 11A. 3R. 2P. water.
(e) Including 13A. 0R. 4P. water.
(f) Including 40A. 1R. 14P. detached portions.
(g) Including 7A. 2R. 6P. water.
(h) Including 3A. 1R. 32P. water.

No. of Sheet of the Ordnance Survey Maps.	Townlands and Towns.	Area in Statute Acres.	County.	Barony.	Parish.	Poor Law Union in 1857.	Townland Census of 1851, Part I.	
		A. R. P.					Vol.	Page
8	Cavanacross	28 2 17	Monaghan	Monaghan	Clones	Monaghan	III.	274
35, 40	Cavanacurragh	26 1 16	Fermanagh	Coole	Galloon	Clones	III.	199
15, 19	Cavanagarvan	443 1 25	Armagh	Armagh	Tynan	Armagh	III.	46
23, 24, 28	Cavanagarvan	55 2 9	Fermanagh	Magherastephana	Aghalurcher *	Lisnaskea	III.	215
23, 28	Cavanagarvan	54 3 3a	Fermanagh	Magherastephana	Aghavea	Lisnaskea	III.	218
13	Cavanagarvan	279 0 23	Monaghan	Monaghan	Kilmore	Monaghan	III.	275
31	Cavanageeragh	72 2 9	Monaghan	Farney	Magheross	Carrickmacross	III.	273
10, 14	Cavanagh	275 0 30b	Cavan	Tullyhaw	Tomregan	Bawnboy	III.	96
40, 43	Cavanagh	70 0 14	Fermanagh	Coole	Drummully	Clones	III.	199
16, 17	Cavanagrow	757 0 28	Armagh	Fews Lower	Kilclooney	Armagh	III.	46
25	Cavanaguillagh	132 2 29	Monaghan	Cremorne	Clontibret	Castleblayney	III.	260
37	Cavanakeeran	894 2 18	Tyrone	Dungannon Middle	Pomeroy	Cookstown	III.	304
21	Cavanakeery	23 0 8	Fermanagh	Magheraboy	Devenish	Enniskillen	III.	210
21, 25	Cavanakill	1,473 3 19	Armagh	Fews Upper	Ballymyre	Newry	III.	48
24	Cavanaleck	304 3 39c	Fermanagh	Magherastephana	Aghalurcher	Lisnaskea	III.	215
22	Cavanaleck	58 0 6	Fermanagh	Tirkennedy	Enniskillen	Enniskillen	III.	221
5, 10	Cavanalee	1,096 3 33d	Tyrone	Strabane Lower	Camus	Strabane	III.	320
16	Cavanalough Glebe	404 0 13e	Fermanagh	Tirkennedy	Magheracross	Enniskillen	III.	223
56, 57	Cavanamara	484 1 1	Tyrone	Omagh East	Kilskeery	Lowtherstown	III.	313
3	Cavananore	219 1 18	Louth	Upper Dundalk	Creggan	Dundalk	I.	177
11, 15	Cavanapole	181 2 6	Armagh	Tiranny	Tynan	Armagh	III.	60
9	Cavanaquill	101 3 27	Cavan	Tullyhaw	Templeport	Bawnboy	III.	94
16, 21	Cavanarainy	184 1 2	Cavan	Tullygarvey	Drung	Cootehill	III.	88
12	Cavanavally	30 0 21	Monaghan	Dartree	Killeevan	Clones	III.	267
79	Cavanaweery	129 1 11f	Donegal	Raphoe	Urney	Strabane	III.	144
11	Cavanballaghy	240 3 13	Armagh	Tiranny	Eglish	Armagh	III.	59
67	Cavanboy	120 2 6	Tyrone	Dungannon Lower	Aghaloo	Armagh	III.	296
25	Cavancarragh	41 2 11	Fermanagh	Clanawley	Cleenish	Enniskillen	III.	190
22, 23	Cavancarragh	837 0 27g	Fermanagh	Tirkennedy	Derryvullan	Enniskillen	III.	220
3	Cavan (Cope)	87 3 16	Monaghan	Trough	Errigal Trough	Monaghan	III.	283
38	Cavancoulter	84 3 18	Cavan	Clanmahon	Kilbride	Oldcastle	III.	77
2	Cavancreagh	237 1 17h	Tyrone	Strabane Lower	Donaghedy	Strabane	III.	320
10	Cavancreevy	221 0 3	Monaghan	Cremorne	Clontibret	Monaghan	III.	260
16, 24	Cavandarragh	362 0 36	Tyrone	Strabane Lower	Ardstraw	Castlederg	III.	318
15	Cavandoogan	223 1 33	Armagh	Tiranny	Tynan	Armagh	III.	60
25	Cavanfin	66 1 32	Cavan	Clanmahon	Kilmore	Cavan	III.	78
103. 107	Cavangarden	299 2 26i	Donegal	Tirhugh	Kilbarron	Ballyshannon	III.	148
60	Cavankilgreen	414 1 13	Tyrone	Dungannon Lower	Carnteel	Clogher	III.	297
3	Cavanleckagh	67 2 34	Monaghan	Trough	Errigal Trough	Monaghan	III.	283
78	Cavan Lower	434 0 31j	Donegal	Raphoe	Donaghmore	Stranorlar	III.	137
25	Cavanmore	106 2 33	Fermanagh	Clanawley	Cleenish	Enniskillen	III.	190
3	Cavanmore	77 0 17	Monaghan	Trough	Errigal Trough	Monaghan	III.	283
7	Cavanmore or Cabragh	135 0 6	Antrim	Lower Dunluce	Billy	Coleraine	III.	16
1, 3	Cavan (Moutray)	185 1 24	Monaghan	Trough	Errigal Trough	Clogher	III.	283
59, 60	Cavan O'Neill	82 0 0k	Tyrone	Dungannon Lower	Carnteel	Clogher	III.	297
28, 37	Cavanoneill	258 2 12	Tyrone	Dungannon Upper	Kildress	Cookstown	III.	308
118	Cavanquarter	137 1 1	Mayo	Kilmaine	Ballinrobe	Ballinrobe	IV.	152
25,26,31,32	Cavanreagh	116 2 27	Fermanagh	Clanawley	Killesher	Enniskillen	III.	192
40	Cavanreagh	1,731 1 18	Londonderry	Loughinsholin	Ballynascreen	Magherafelt	III.	238
16	Cavanreagh	86 2 36	Monaghan	Dartree	Currin	Clones	III.	265
9, 10	Cavanreagh	41 2 33	Monaghan	Monaghan	Tehallan	Monaghan	III.	280
44	Cavanreagh	670 3 28	Tyrone	Omagh East	Termonmaguirk	Omagh	III.	314
11	Cavanrobert	77 3 21	Louth	Ardee	Tallanstown	Ardee	I.	175
23, 24	Cavans	237 2 29	Fermanagh	Magherastephana	Aghavea	Lisnaskea	III.	218
33	Cavansallagh	82 0 36	Tyrone	Omagh West	Longfield West	Castlederg	III.	316
12	Cavansheath	212 3 15	Queen's Co.	Maryborough West	Clonenagh and Clonagheen	Mountmellick	I.	242
28	Cavanskeldragh	76 0 17	Cavan	Clankee	Knockbride	Bailieborough	III.	73
16	Cavantillycormick	359 3 22	Fermanagh	Tirkennedy	Magheracross	Enniskillen	III.	223
27	Cavantimahon	214 1 25l	Cavan	Clankee	Knockbride	Cootehill	III.	73
20, 25	CAVAN T.	—	Cavan	Upper Loughtee	Urney	Cavan	III.	86
25, 26	Cavantreeduff	149 3 32	Fermanagh	Clanawley	Cleenish	Enniskillen	III.	190
69, 78	Cavan Upper	578 1 10	Donegal	Raphoe	Donaghmore	Stranorlar	III.	137
16,17,21,22	Cavany	188 1 5	Monaghan	Dartree	Currin	Clones	III.	265
42	Cave	199 1 5	Galway	Clare	Killower	Tuam	IV.	21
72, 73	Cave	590 1 0	Galway	Kilconnell	Ballymacward	Ballinasloe	IV.	39
93	Cave	155 1 9m	Mayo	Costello	Bekan	Claremorris	IV.	139
10, 18	Cavemount or Mullalough	778 1 6	King's Co.	Lower Philipstown	Kilclonfert	Tullamore	I.	142
9, 14	Cavestown and Rosmead	1,346 0 17	Westmeath	Delvin	Castletowndelvin	Castletowndelvin	I.	264
10	Cavetown or Ballynahoogh	319 3 0n	Roscommon	Boyle	Estersnow	Boyle	IV.	195

(a) Including 3A. 0R. 23P. detached portion.
(b) Including 7A. 3R. 15P. water.
(c) Including 11A. 1R. 30P. water.
(d) Including 2A. 3R. 30P. water.
(e) Including 9A. 0R. 30P. water.

(f) Including 1A. 3R. 27P. water.
(g) Including 5A. 1R. 5P. water.
(h) Including 2A. 0R. 34P. water.
(i) Including 12A. 0R. 36P. water.
(j) Including 8A. 1R. 26P. water.

(k) Including 7A. 0R. 5P. detached portion.
(l) Including 3A. 0R. 9P. water.
(m) Including 16A. 1R. 23P. water.
(n) Including 75A. 3R. 7P. water.

No. of Sheet of the Ordnance Survey Maps.	Townlands and Towns.	Area in Statute Acres.	County.	Barony.	Parish.	Poor Law Union in 1857.	Townland Census of 1851, Part I.	
		A. R. P.					Vol.	Page
52	Cavey	217 0 31	Tyrone	Clogher	Errigal Keerogue	Clogher	III.	295
13, 14, 20	Caw	277 3 26	Londonderry	Tirkeeran	Clondermot	Londonderry	III.	247
119, 120	Ceancullig	687 0 1	Cork, W.R.	West Carbery (E.D.)	Dromdaleague	Skibbereen	II.	140
24	Cecilstown	239 2 37	Cork, E.R.	Duhallow	Castlemagner	Kanturk	II.	67
24	CECILSTOWN T.	—	Cork, E.R.	Duhallow	Castlemagner	Kanturk	II.	67
11	Celbridge	212 0 37a	Kildare	North Salt	Kildrought	Celbridge	I.	74
11	Celbridgeabbey	119 0 21b	Kildare	North Salt	Kildrought	Celbridge	I.	74
11	Celbridge Abbey	13 3 32c	Kildare	South Salt	Donaghcumper	Celbridge	I.	76
11	CELBRIDGE T.	—	Kildare	{ North Salt { South Salt	{ Kildrought { Donaghcumper }	Celbridge	I.	{ 74 { 76
15, 20	Cellarstown East	167 3 22d	Kilkenny	Gowran	St. John's	Kilkenny	I.	98
19, 20	Cellarstown Lower	100 0 25	Kilkenny	Gowran	St. John's	Kilkenny	I.	98
20	Cellarstown Upper	87 2 7	Kilkenny	Gowran	St. John's	Kilkenny	I.	98
14,15,19,20	Cellarstown West	299 2 0	Kilkenny	Gowran	St. John's	Kilkenny	I.	98
19	Censure	103 2 15	Dublin	Coolock	Howth	Dublin North	I.	27
44, 45	Chacefield	153 0 2	Sligo	Coolavin	Kilfree	Boyle	IV.	224
51	Chadville	185 1 39	Tipperary, S.R.	Clanwilliam	Donohill	Tipperary	II.	307
38	Chaffpool	287 3 15	Sligo	Leyny	Achonry	Tobercurry	IV.	229
39, 47	Chain Island	2 2 22	Mayo	Tirawley	Crossmolina	Ballina	IV.	167
33	Chalkhill	174 2 37	Tipperary, N.R.	Upper Ormond	Templederry	Nenagh	II.	293
23	Chamberlainstown	588 3 10	Meath	Upper Kells	Girley	Kells	I.	205
69, 76	Chamberlainstown	294 0 24	Tipperary, S.R.	Middlethird	Outeragh	Cashel	II.	329
29	Chambersland	68 2 25	Wexford	Bantry	St. Mary's	New Ross	I.	302
18	Chamberstown	379 3 6	Meath	Upper Slane	Rathkenny	Navan	I.	225
65	Chancellorsland	231 3 20	Tipperary, S.R.	Clanwilliam	Emly	Tipperary	II.	307
76, 77	Chancellorstown Lower	422 0 38	Tipperary, S.R.	Iffa and Offa East	Newchapel	Clonmel	II.	315
76	Chancellorstown Upper	314 2 3	Tipperary, S.R.	Iffa and Offa East	Newchapel	Clonmel	II.	315
2	Chancery	123 3 38	Westmeath	Moygoish	Street	Granard	I.	281
6, 11	Chanonrock	645 2 2	Louth	Louth	Louth	Dundalk	I.	184
20	Chanonstown	234 3 31	Westmeath	Farbill	Killucan	Mullingar	I.	266
22	Chanterhill or Moneynoe Glebe	126 1 3	Fermanagh	Tirkennedy	Enniskillen	Enniskillen	III.	222
35	Chanterlands	70 3 14	Kildare	Narragh&RebanWest	St. Michaels	Athy	I.	68
16	Chanterland or Windmillpark	103 2 6	Roscommon	Roscommon	Elphin	Strokestown	IV.	209
57, 65	Chantersland	216 3 33	Tipperary, S.R.	Clanwilliam	Emly	Tipperary	II.	307
25, 31	Chapel	743 0 1	Wexford	Bantry	Chapel	Enniscorthy	I.	299
52	Chapel	90 0 22	Wexford	Bargy	Kilmore	Wexford	I.	306
35, 36	Chapel	189 1 20	Wicklow	Arklow	Redcross	Rathdrum	I.	346
16	Chapelbride	213 0 32	Meath	Upper Kells	Burry	Kells	I.	205
31, 32	Chapelfarm	192 0 18	Kildare	Offaly West	Kilrush	Athy	I.	72
58	Chapelfield	20 2 30	Galway	Tiaquin	Abbeyknockmoy	Tuam	IV.	75
28	Chapelhill	3 2 0	Queen's Co.	Clarmallagh	Aghaboe	Abbeyleix	I.	235
28	Chapelhill	104 2 19	Queen's Co.	Clarmallagh	Bordwell	Abbeyleix	I.	237
118	Chapel Island	9 3 3	Cork, W.R.	Bantry	Kilmocomoge	Bantry	II.	120
11	Chapel Island	25 3 26	Down	Ards Lower	Greyabbey	Newtownards	III.	158
31	Chapel Island	12 1 16	Down	Lecale Lower	Ballyculter	Downpatrick	III.	178
48	Chapel Island	10 3 24	Galway	Ballynahinch	Ballindoon	Clifden	IV.	10
118	Chapel Island (Little)	5 3 3	Cork, W.R.	Bantry	Kilmocomoge	Bantry	II.	120
18	Chapelizod	67 1 28e	Dublin	Castleknock	Chapelizod	Dublin North	I.	24
18	Chapelizod (part of Phœnix Park)	465 1 7f	Dublin	Castleknock	Chapelizod	Dublin North	I.	24
18	CHAPELIZOD T.	—	Dublin	{ Castleknock { Uppercross	{ Chapelizod { Palmerston	{ Dublin North { Dublin South	I.	{ 24 { 40
29	Chapel Land	82 3 5	Meath	Lune	Athboy	Trim	I.	207
88, 99, 100	Chapelpark	245 1 35	Galway	Clonmacnowen	Clontuskert	Ballinasloe	IV.	24
40	Chapel Quarter	7 0 27	Kerry	Trughanacmy	Castleisland	Tralee	II.	208
7	Chapelstown	466 3 39	Carlow	Carlow	Clonmelsh	Carlow	I.	1
28	CHAPELTOWN T.	—	Kerry	Trughanacmy	Ballynahaglish	Tralee	II.	207
4	Charlemont, Borough of	210 2 39	Armagh	Armagh	Loughgall	Armagh	III.	45
4	CHARLEMONT T.	—	Armagh	Armagh	Loughgall	Armagh	III.	46
40	Charlesfield	684 3 31	Cork, E.R.	Duhallow	Clonmeen	Kanturk	II.	69
13	Charlesland	198 2 39	Wicklow	Newcastle	Kilcoole	Rathdrum	I.	351
14	Charlestown	56 2 36	Dublin	Castleknock	Finglas	Dublin North	I.	24
43	Charlestown	278 0 20g	Kilkenny	Ida	Dunkitt	Waterford	I.	101
13	Charlestown	292 3 33	King's Co.	Garrycastle	Clonmacnoise	Parsonstown	I.	135
14	Charlestown	514 0 32	Louth	Ardee	Charlestown	Ardee	I.	171
11, 12	Charlestown	167 1 34	Roscommon	Ballintober North	Kilmore	Cark. on Shannon	IV.	187
11	Charlestown and Abbeyland or Ballynamonaster	260 1 0	Westmeath	Moygoish	Kilbixy	Mullingar	I.	279
19	Charlestown or Ballnamona	94 2 1	Westmeath	{ Moyashel and Magheradernon	Mullingar	Mullingar	I.	275

(a) Including 2A. 2R. 0P. water.
(b) Including 7A. 0R. 16P. water.
(c) Including 8A. 3R. 38P. water.
(d) Including 0A. 2R. 10P. detached portion.
(e) Including 8A. 2R. 16P. water.

(f) The remainder of the Phœnix Park is in the Parishes of Castleknock and St. James's; the entire Park contains 1,752A. 3R. 21P.
(g) Including 7A. 3R. 0P. water.

No. of Sheet of the Ordnance Survey Maps.	Townlands and Towns.	Area in Statute Acres.	County.	Barony.	Parish.	Poor Law Union in 1857.	Townland Census of 1851. Part I. Vol.	Page
		A. R. P.					Vol.	Page
47	Charlestown or Pollnamucka	88 0 10	Galway	Killian	Killeroran	Mountbellew	IV.	43
2	CHARLESTOWN T.	—	Armagh	Oneilland East	Montiaghs	Lurgan	III.	50
8	CHARLESTOWN T.	—	King's Co.	Kilcoursey	Kilbride	Tullamore	I.	141
19	Charleville	59 3 4	Dublin	Coolock	Raheny	Dublin North	I.	28
15, 18	Charleville	510 3 32	Louth	Ardee	Stabannan	Ardee	I.	174
16, 17	Charleville Demesne	1,140 3 4a	King's Co.	Ballycowan	Lynally	Tullamore	I.	128
7	Charleville Demesne	196 2 35	Wicklow	Rathdown	Kilmacanoge	Rathdown	I.	355
15, 21	Charleville or Raheen	219 1 5	Queen's Co.	Clandonagh	Kyle	Donaghmore	I.	233
2, 3	CHARLEVILLE T.	—	Cork, E.R.	Orrery and Kilmore	Rathgoggan	Kilmallock	II.	109
6	Charstown	222 2 8	Dublin	Balrothery West	Ballymadun	Dunshaughlin	I.	22
19	Charterschoolland	34 0 9	Kilkenny	Gowran	St. John's	Kilkenny	I.	98
36	Charterschoolland	15 0 5	Meath	Lower Moyfenrath	Trim	Trim	I.	211
61	Charterschool Land	50 1 25	Tipperary, S.R.	Middlethird	St. John Baptist	Cashel	II.	330
13	Chathamhall	189 0 23	Antrim	Lower Dunluce	Derrykeighan	Ballymoney	III.	16
1, 2	Chatsworth or Aughatubbrid	1,651 2 6	Kilkenny	Fassadinin	Castlecomer	Castlecomer	I.	88
10	Cheekpoint	199 1 24	Waterford	Gaultiere	Faithlegg	Waterford	II.	362
10	CHEEKPOINT T.	—	Waterford	Gaultiere	Faithlegg	Waterford	II.	362
72, 78, 79	Cheesemount	157 0 24	Tipperary, S.R.	Slievardagh	Garrangibbon	Carrick on Suir	III.	333
21	Cheeverstown	345 1 34	Dublin	Uppercross	Clondalkin	Dublin South	I.	39
45, 51	Cheeverstown	81 2 0	Meath	Ratoath	Ratoath	Dunshaughlin	I.	219
98	Chelsea	206 2 35	Galway	Kilconnell	Killallaghtan	Ballinasloe	IV.	41
42, 47	Cherriestown	106 3 32	Wexford	Bargy	Kilmannan	Wexford	I.	306
8, 12	Cherrybrook	135 2 16	Leitrim	Rosclogher	Cloonclare	Manorhamilton	IV.	109
93	Cherryfield	70 2 21	Mayo	Costello	Bekan	Claremorris	IV.	139
16, 22	Cherryfield or Drishaghan	174 0 2	Roscommon	Roscommon	Shankill	Strokestown	IV.	212
11, 14	Cherryhound	112 3 17	Dublin	Castleknock	Ward	Dublin North	I.	25
25	Cherry Island	3 3 24	Leitrim	Carrigallen	Carrigallen	Bawnboy	IV.	90
27, 31	Cherrymills	158 0 11	Kildare	Offaly West	Harristown	Athy	I.	72
107	Cherrymount	167 1 23b	Donegal	Tirhugh	Kilbarron	Ballyshannon	III.	148
27	Cherrymount	54 3 5	Kilkenny	Shillelogher	Stonecarthy	Thomastown	I.	115
37	Cherrymount	245 1 3	Waterford	Coshmore&Coshbride	Templemichael	Youghal	II.	348
35	Cherrymount	106 1 18	Wicklow	Arklow	Castlemacadam	Rathdrum	I.	342
18	Cherry Orchard	11 2 17c	Dublin	Uppercross	St. Nicholas Without	Dublin South	I.	41
19, 20	Cherryorchard	116 1 30	Wexford	Scarawalsh	Monart	Enniscorthy	I.	324
20	Cherryorchard	1 1 38	Wexford	Scarawalsh	St. Marys Enniscorthy	Enniscorthy	I.	325
10	Cherryvalley	354 3 15d	Down	Castlereagh Lower	Comber	Newtownards	III.	162
42	Cherryvalley	214 2 11	Meath	Lower Moyfenrath	Rathmolyon	Trim	I.	211
22	Cherryville	472 3 12	Kildare	Offaly West	Lackagh	Athy	I.	73
26	Cherrywood	95 1 22	Dublin	Rathdown	Killiney	Rathdown	I.	36
86	Chetwynd	287 1 34	Cork, E.R.	Cork	St. Finbars	Cork	II.	65
27, 34	Chevychase or Derrynadarragh	349 2 19	King's Co.	Coolestown	Clonsast	Edenderry	I.	132
43	Chimneyfield	141 0 8	Cork, E.R.	Barrymore	Ardnageehy	Fermoy	II.	50
53	Chour	39 1 18e	Wexford	Forth	Carn	Wexford	I.	309
9, 10	Christendom	188 3 32f	Waterford	Gaultiere	Kilculliheen	Waterford	II.	363
17	Christianstown	507 3 1	Kildare	Connell	Feighcullen	Naas	I.	55
11, 14	Christianstown	499 3 34	Louth	Louth	Darver	Dundalk	I.	183
8	Christianstown	330 0 6	Westmeath	Fore	St. Mary's	Castletowndelvin	I.	272
4	Churchacres	70 1 33g	Roscommon	Boyle	Kilronan	Boyle	IV.	196
38	Church Ballee	202 0 20	Down	Lecale Lower	Ballee	Downpatrick	III.	178
20	Churchclara	335 1 39	Kilkenny	Gowran	Clara	Kilkenny	I.	94
9	Churchfield	112 1 39	Antrim	Cary	Culfeightrin	Ballycastle	III.	13
44	Churchfield	100 3 35	Kerry	Corkaguiny	Kinard	Dingle	II.	179
24	Churchfield	6 1 14	Leitrim	Leitrim	Fenagh	Mohill	IV.	100
10	Churchfield	100 1 26h	Limerick	Shanid	Shanagolden	Rathkeale	II.	258
92	Churchfield	403 3 34	Mayo	Costello	Knock	Claremorris	IV.	142
87	Churchfield	30 3 24	Mayo	Murrisk	Oughaval	Westport	IV.	161
16	Churchfield	46 1 25	Queen's Co.	Upperwoods	Offerlane	Abbeyleix	I.	251
59	Churchfield	108 0 19	Tipperary, S.R.	Clanwilliam	Donohill	Tipperary	II.	307
3, 13, 14	Churchfield Lower	373 0 38	Galway	Ross	Ballinrobe	Ballinrobe	IV.	72
3, 13	Churchfield Upper	355 0 14	Galway	Ross	Ballinrobe	Ballinrobe	IV.	72
85, 94	Churchground	641 0 10	Kerry	Glanarought	Kilgarvan	Kenmare	II.	187
29, 30	Church Hill	99 3 19	Cork, E.R.	Duhallow	Cullen	Millstreet	II.	70
44, 52	Church Hill	269 1 28	Donegal	Kilmacrenan	Gartan	Letterkenny	III.	127
23	Church Hill	262 1 10	Kilkenny	Shillelogher	Grange	Kilkenny	I.	114
16, 24	Church Hill	102 1 3	King's Co.	Ballycowan	Rahan	Tullamore	I.	128
20	Church Hill	174 3 2	Monaghan	Cremorne	Muckno	Castleblayney	III.	261
7	Church Hill	114 0 33	Roscommon	Boyle	Ardcarn	Carr. on Shannon	IV.	192
32, 38	Church Hill	214 3 39	Sligo	Corran	Cloonoghil	Tobercurry	IV.	225
3	Church Hill	133 2 27	Tyrone	Strabane Lower	Donaghedy	Strabane	III.	320
47	Church Hill Glebe	66 3 23	Meath	Upper Moyfenrath	Clonard	Edenderry	I.	213

(a) Including 54A. 2R. 10P. water.
(b) Including 6A. 2R. 30P. water.
(c) { Within the Municipal Boundary, 6A. 1R. 38P. / Without the Municipal Boundary, 5A. 0R. 19P.
(d) Including 1A. 2R. 6P. water.
(e) Including 3A. 2R. 39P. detached portion.
(f) { Within the Municipal Boundary, 11A. 3R. 38P. / Without the Municipal Boundary, 176A. 3R. 34P.
(g) Including 31A. 0R. 35P. water.
(h) Including 0A. 2R. 11P. detached portion.

2 H 2

No. of Sheet of the Ordnance Survey Maps.	Townlands and Towns.	Area in Statute Acres.			County.	Barony.	Parish.	Poor Law Union in 1857.	Townland Census of 1851, Part I.	
		A.	R.	P.					Vol.	Page
9	Church Hill T.	—			Fermanagh	Magheraboy	Inishmacsaint	Ballyshannon	III.	213
126	Church Island	1	2	29	Galway	Longford	Lickmolassy	Portumna	IV.	61
25	Church Island	10	3	38	Leitrim	Carrigallen	Carrigallen	Bawnboy	IV.	90
42	Church Island	7	0	39	Londonderry	Loughinsholin	Ballyscullion	Magherafelt	III.	240
99	Church Island	7	3	36	Mayo	Carra	Ballintober	Castlebar	IV.	125
6	Church Island	4	1	28	Roscommon	Boyle	Boyle	Boyle	IV.	194
15	Church Island	41	2	10	Sligo	Carbury	Calry	Sligo	IV.	220
42	Church Island (Intake)	19	0	0	Londonderry	Loughinsholin	Ballyscullion	Magherafelt	III.	240
36, 39	Churchland	42	1	5	King's Co.	Ballybritt	Seirkieran	Parsonstown	I.	126
7	Churchland	445	0	17	Londonderry	Coleraine	Killowen	Coleraine	III.	232
38, 43	Churchland	81	0	8	Wicklow	Ballinacor South	Kilcommon	Shillelagh	I.	349
28	Churchland East	68	3	23	Kildare	Offaly East	Carn	Naas	I.	69
4, 11, 20	Churchland Quarters (Carrowtemple, Moneyshandoney, & Carrick)	5,187	1	15	Donegal	Inishowen East	Donagh	Inishowen	III.	118
47	Churchlands	116	3	21	Wexford	Forth	Mayglass	Wexford	I.	312
28	Churchland South	24	2	6	Kildare	Offaly East	Carn	Naas	I.	69
28	Churchland West	9	1	18	Kildare	Offaly East	Carn	Naas	I.	69
103	Churchpark	62	0	12	Mayo	Costello	Annagh	Claremorris	IV.	138
1	Church Quarter	51	0	17	Antrim	Cary	Rathlin Island	Ballycastle	III.	15
5	Church Quarter	123	0	12	Down	Castlereagh Lower	Dundonald	Belfast	III.	162
60	Churchquarter	99	3	11	Limerick	Coshlea	Kilbeheny	Mitchelstown	II.	239
10	Churchquarter	49	1	31	Longford	Granard	Granard	Granard	I.	156
26	Churchquarter	99	0	37	Roscommon	Castlereagh	Kiltullagh	Castlereagh	IV.	201
39	Churchquarter	280	0	20	Tipperary, N.R.	Kilnamanagh Upper	Templebeg	Thurles	II.	279
28, 33	Churchquarter	128	2	4	Waterford	Coshmore&Coshbride	Kilwatermoy	Lismore	II.	343
22	Churchquarter	103	3	39	Waterford	Decies without Drum	Modelligo	Lismore	II.	359
38	Churchquarter and Mill	72	2	25	Waterford	Decies within Drum	Lisgenan or Grange	Youghal	II.	352
26	Church Tamlaght	619	0	33a	Antrim	Kilconway	Rasharkin	Ballymoney	III.	27
76	Churchtown	105	1	1	Cork, E.R.	Barrymore	Inchinabacky	Middleton	II.	55
89	Churchtown	46	1	34	Cork, E.R.	Imokilly	Ballintemple	Middleton	II.	84
7, 16	Churchtown	164	2	26	Cork, E.R.	Orrery and Kilmore	Churchtown	Mallow	II.	107
44	Churchtown	525	3	2b	Donegal	Kilmacrenan	Gartan	Letterkenny	III.	127
79	Churchtown	216	1	33c	Donegal	Raphoe	Clonleigh	Strabane	III.	134
65	Churchtown	294	2	10	Kerry	Dunkerron North	Knockane	Killarney	II.	181
36	Churchtown	560	1	27	Limerick	Glenquin	Newcastle	Newcastle	II.	247
13	Churchtown	21	3	21	Louth	Ardee	Clonkeen	Ardee	I.	172
30, 31	Churchtown	750	0	39	Meath	Lower Navan	Churchtown	Navan	I.	214
16	Churchtown	150	2	32	Queen's Co.	Upperwoods	Offerlane	Abbeyleix	I.	251
16	Churchtown	290	2	14d	Tyrone	Omagh West	Urney	Castlederg	III.	318
2, 3	Churchtown	402	2	31e	Waterford	Upperthird	Dysert	Carrick on Suir	II.	369
10	Churchtown	473	1	25	Westmeath	Moygoish	Kilmacnevan	Mullingar	I.	280
25	Churchtown	218	1	12	Westmeath	Rathconrath	Churchtown	Mullingar	I.	282
47	Churchtown	75	3	24	Wexford	Bargy	Mulrankin	Wexford	I.	307
47	Churchtown	92	3	19	Wexford	Forth	Ballymore	Wexford	I.	308
53	Churchtown	132	1	29	Wexford	Forth	Carn	Wexford	I.	309
48	Churchtown	234	0	30	Wexford	Forth	Kilrane	Wexford	I.	311
42	Churchtown	62	0	25	Wexford	Forth	Rathaspick	Wexford	I.	312
48	Churchtown	191	1	30	Wexford	Forth	Rosslare	Wexford	I.	312
53	Churchtown	93	0	27	Wexford	Forth	Tacumshin	Wexford	I.	315
11	Churchtown	247	1	6	Wexford	Gorey	Liskinfere	Gorey	I.	320
54	Churchtown	221	1	24	Wexford	Shelburne	Hook	New Ross	I.	327
3	Churchtownhill	268	0	6	Waterford	Upperthird	Dysert	Carrick on Suir	II.	369
22	Churchtown Lower	180	3	0	Dublin	Rathdown	Taney	Rathdown	I.	38
34	Churchtown North	197	2	16	Kildare	Narragh&RebanWest	Churchtown	Athy	I.	67
34	Churchtown South	95	1	28	Kildare	Narragh&RebanWest	Churchtown	Athy	I.	67
89	Churchtown T.	—			Cork, E.R.	Imokilly	Ballintemple	Middleton	II.	84
7, 16	Churchtown T.	—			Cork, E.R.	Orrery and Kilmore	Churchtown	Mallow	II.	107
36	Churchtown T.	—			Limerick	Glenquin	Newcastle	Newcastle	II.	248
54	Churchtown T.	—			Wexford	Shelburne	Hook	New Ross	I.	327
22	Churchtown Upper	221	0	7	Dublin	Rathdown	Taney	Rathdown	I.	38
6	Clab	190	2	17	Clare	Burren	Carran	Ballyvaghan	II.	11
35, 38	Cladagh	282	0	12	Waterford	Decies within Drum	Clashmore	Youghal	II.	351
38	Claddagh	334	1	32	Cavan	Castlerahan	Castlerahan	Oldcastle	III.	67
36	Claddagh	550	3	29	Sligo	Leyny	Kilmacteige	Tobercurry	IV.	231
21, 22	Claddaghduff	416	2	10f	Galway	Ballynahinch	Omey	Clifden	IV.	14
30	Claddagh East	295	0	10	Galway	Ballymoe	Clonbern	Tuam	IV.	6
30	Claddagh West	352	0	7	Galway	Ballymoe	Clonbern	Tuam	IV.	6
93	Claddanure East	373	3	39	Kerry	Dunkerron South	Templenoe	Kenmare	II.	185
92, 93	Claddanure West	349	2	20	Kerry	Dunkerron South	Templenoe	Kenmare	II.	185
97,98,107,108	Claddy	1,038	1	33	Mayo	Murrisk	Aghagower	Westport	IV.	158
12	Cladowan	126	2	16g	Monaghan	Dartree	Clones	Clones	III.	264
15	Clady	165	2	31	Antrim	Lower Glenarm	Grange of Inispollan	Ballycastle	III.	21

(a) Including 6A. 2R. 19P. detached portion.
(b) Including 30A. 2R. 0P. water.
(c) Including 4A. 3R. 8P. water.
(d) Including 3A. 0R. 33P. water.
(e) Including 9A. 0R. 37P. water.
(f) Including 8A. 2R. 18P. water.
(g) Including 7A. 3R. 16P. water.

No. of Sheet of the Ordnance Survey Maps.	Townlands and Towns.	Area in Statute Acres.			County.	Barony.	Parish.	Poor Law Union in 1857.	Townland Census of 1851. Part I.	
		A.	R.	P.					Vol.	Page
29,30,34,35	Clady . . .	158	2	16	Antrim . .	Lower Glenarm .	Tickmacrevan .	Larne . .	III.	23
9	Clady . . .	173	2	22a	Tyrone . .	Strabane Lower .	Urney . . .	Strabane . .	III.	322
20, 21	Clady Beg . .	2,242	3	28	Armagh . .	Fews Lower . .	Kilclooney . .	Armagh . .	III.	46
10, 17	Clady Blair . .	89	1	20	Tyrone . .	Strabane Lower .	Ardstraw . .	Strabane . .	III.	318
9,10,16,17	Clady Haliday .	142	3	37	Tyrone . .	Strabane Lower .	Ardstraw . .	Strabane . .	III.	318
9, 10, 17	Clady Hood . .	151	0	31	Tyrone . .	Strabane Lower .	Ardstraw . .	Strabane . .	III.	318
10, 17	Clady Johnston .	118	3	22	Tyrone . .	Strabane Lower .	Ardstraw . .	Strabane . .	III.	318
20, 21	Clady More . .	1,787	1	16	Armagh . .	Fews Lower . .	Kilclooney . .	Armagh . .	III.	46
10	Clady-sproul or Lis-creevaghan . .	121	2	20b	Tyrone . .	Strabane Lower .	Ardstraw . .	Strabane . .	III.	319
9	CLADY T. . .	—			Tyrone . .	Strabane Lower .	Urney . . .	Strabane . .	III.	323
19	Clagan . . .	207	2	12	Londonderry .	Coleraine . .	Aghadowey . .	Coleraine . .	III.	229
5	Clagan . . .	128	1	6	Londonderry .	Keenaght . .	Magilligan . .	NewT⁰Limavady	III.	236
9, 16	Clagan . . .	236	2	38	Londonderry .	Keenaght . .	Tamlaght Finlagan .	NewT⁰Limavady	III.	237
45, 46	Clagan . . .	428	0	13	Londonderry .	Loughinsholin .	Lissan . . .	Magherafelt .	III.	242
23, 29	Clagan . . .	422	0	24	Londonderry .	Tirkeeran . .	Banagher now Learmount . .	Londonderry .	III.	247
22, 23	Clagernagh . .	833	2	36c	Tyrone . .	Omagh West .	Termonamongan .	Castlederg .	III.	317
12, 21	Claggan . . .	112	2	31	Donegal . .	Inishowen East .	Moville Upper .	Inishowen . .	III.	119
15	Claggan . . .	844	1	4	Donegal . .	Kilmacrenan . .	Clondahorky . .	Dunfanaghy .	III.	123
17, 18	Claggan . . .	112	1	21	Donegal . .	Kilmacrenan . .	Clondavaddog . .	Milford . .	III.	124
36	Claggan . . .	226	1	24d	Donegal . .	Kilmacrenan . .	Tullyfern . .	Milford . .	III.	133
39	Claggan . . .	412	3	13	Galway . .	Ross . . .	Cong . . .	Oughterard .	IV.	73
65	Claggan . . .	174	2	33	Mayo . . .	Burrishoole . .	Achill . . .	Newport . .	IV.	117
76	Claggan . . .	190	3	32	Mayo . . .	Burrishoole . .	Kilmeena . .	Westport . .	IV.	122
69	Claggan . . .	517	3	22e	Mayo . . .	Carra . . .	Islandeady . .	Castlebar . .	IV.	128
56	Claggan . . .	1,066	3	28	Mayo . . .	Erris . . .	Kilcommon . .	Newport . .	IV.	143
105	Claggan . . .	116	2	24	Mayo . . .	Murrisk . . .	Kilgeever . .	Westport . .	IV.	160
46	Claggan . . .	338	2	2	Tyrone . .	Dungannon Middle .	Pomeroy . .	Dungannon .	III.	304
39	Claggan . . .	83	3	8	Tyrone . .	Dungannon Upper .	Artrea . . .	Cookstown .	III.	305
29	Claggan . . .	179	3	19	Tyrone . .	Dungannon Upper .	Derryloran . .	Cookstown .	III.	306
43	Claggan Mountain .	237	1	27	Donegal . .	Kilmacrenan . .	Gartan . . .	Letterkenny .	III.	127
56	Clagganmountain .	1,848	0	30	Mayo . . .	Erris . . .	Kilcommon . .	Newport . .	IV.	143
43	Claggan Mountain North . . .	259	3	16	Donegal . .	Kilmacrenan . .	Gartan . . .	Dunfanaghy .	III.	127
43	Claggan Mountain South . . .	230	3	25	Donegal . .	Kilmacrenan . .	Gartan . . .	Letterkenny .	III.	127
44	Claggan North . .	136	1	10f	Donegal . .	Kilmacrenan . .	Gartan . . .	Letterkenny .	III.	127
3, 6	Claggan North . .	428	3	13	Tyrone . .	Strabane Lower .	Donaghedy . .	Strabane . .	III.	320
52	Claggan South . .	133	1	27g	Donegal . .	Kilmacrenan . .	Gartan . . .	Letterkenny .	III.	127
6	Claggan South . .	330	3	9	Tyrone . .	Strabane Lower .	Donaghedy . .	Gortin . .	III.	320
78	Claggarnagh East .	309	0	39h	Mayo . . .	Burrishoole . .	Islandeady . .	Westport . .	IV.	121
58, 68	Claggarnagh East .	998	3	33	Mayo . . .	Tirawley . . .	Addergoole . .	Castlebar . .	IV.	163
78, 89	Claggarnagh West .	372	1	15	Mayo . . .	Burrishoole . .	Islandeady . .	Westport . .	IV.	121
58, 68	Claggarnagh West .	963	1	12	Mayo . . .	Tirawley . . .	Addergoole . .	Castlebar . .	IV.	163
126	Claggernagh East .	237	3	27	Galway . .	Longford . .	Lickmolassy . .	Portumna . .	IV.	60
126	Claggernagh West .	28	3	0	Galway . .	Longford . .	Lickmolassy . .	Portumna . .	IV.	60
93	Clagnagh . . .	95	0	12	Mayo . . .	Costello . . .	Bekan . . .	Claremorris .	IV.	139
29, 38	Clahane . . .	2,170	2	21	Kerry . . .	Trughanacmy .	Annagh . . .	Tralee . .	II.	205
35	Clahernagh . .	68	0	22i	Fermanagh .	Clankelly . .	Clones . . .	Clones . .	III.	195
21	Clampernow . .	96	2	8	Londonderry .	Tirkeeran . .	Clondermot . .	Londonderry .	III.	247
96	Clamperpark . .	110	3	8	Galway . .	Athenry . .	Athenry . . .	Loughrea . .	IV.	3
42	Clanabogan Lower .	271	1	12	Tyrone . .	Omagh East .	Drumragh . .	Omagh . .	III.	312
34, 42	Clanabogan Upper .	233	3	16	Tyrone . .	Omagh East .	Drumragh . .	Omagh . .	III.	312
24	Clanagh . . .	33	0	34	Carlow . .	St. Mullins Lower .	St. Mullins . .	New Ross . .	I.	13
46	Clananeese Glebe .	162	1	29j	Tyrone . .	Dungannon Middle .	Donaghmore . .	Dungannon .	III.	301
93	Clanboorhin . .	254	0	20	Donegal . .	Banagh . . .	Killymard . .	Donegal . .	III.	111
110	Clancool Beg . .	536	0	31	Cork, W.R. .	Kinalmeaky . .	Ballymodan . .	Bandon . .	II.	151
110	Clancool More . .	374	1	20	Cork, W.R. .	Kinalmeaky . .	Ballymodan . .	Bandon . .	II.	151
14	Clane . . .	736	1	19	Kildare . .	Clane . . .	Clane . . .	Naas . .	I.	53
14	CLANE T. . .	—			Kildare . .	Clane . . .	Clane . . .	Naas . .	I.	54
11, 12	Clanhugh Demesne	291	3	16	Westmeath .	Corkaree . .	Leny . . .	Mullingar .	I.	262
11, 12	Clanhugh Demesne	76	1	18	Westmeath .	Corkaree . .	Portnashangan .	Mullingar .	I.	263
7	Clanickny . .	188	3	36	Monaghan .	Trough . . .	Donagh . . .	Monaghan .	III.	281
6	Clankilvoragh. .	162	1	34	Armagh . .	Oneilland East .	Magheralin . .	Lurgan . .	III.	49
42	Clanmaghery . .	365	0	31k	Down . .	Upper Iveagh, Lr.pt.	Drumgooland .	Banbridge .	III.	172
44	Clanmaghery . .	382	3	29	Down . .	Lecale Upper .	Tyrella . . .	Downpatrick .	III.	181
44	Clanmaghery, Commons of . .	33	3	32	Down . .	Lecale Upper .	Tyrella . . .	Downpatrick .	III.	181
6, 10	Clanrolla . .	132	1	37	Armagh . .	Oneilland East .	Seagoe . . .	Lurgan . .	III.	50
3, 6	Clanrolla . .	283	2	4	Armagh . .	Oneilland East .	Shankill . . .	Lurgan . .	III.	50
14	Clanterkee . .	42	0	11	Londonderry .	Tirkeeran . .	Faughanvale .	Londonderry .	III.	250
8	Clara . . .	503	2	27	King's Co. .	Kilcoursey . .	Kilbride . . .	Tullamore .	I.	141
24	Clarabeg North .	443	2	29	Wicklow . .	Ballinacor North .	Knockrath . .	Rathdrum .	I.	347

(a) Including 2A. 0R. 13P. water.
(b) Including 3A. 1R. 21P. water.
(c) Including 14A. 3R. 30P. water.
(d) Including 6A. 0R. 4P. water.

(e) Including 11A. 2R. 25P. water.
(f) Including 12A. 2R. 9P. water.
(g) Including 33A. 1R. 25P. water.
(h) Including 3A. 3R. 23P. water.

(i) Including 3A. 1R. 14P. water.
(j) Including 9A. 0R. 12P. water.
(k) Including 12A. 2R. 35P. water.

No. of Sheet of the Ordnance Survey Maps.	Townlands and Towns.	Area in Statute Acres.	County.	Barony.	Parish.	Poor Law Union in 1857.	Townland Census of 1851, Part I.	
		A. R. P.					Vol.	Page
24, 30	Clarabeg South	135 3 21	Wicklow	Ballinacor North	Knockrath	Rathdrum	I.	347
20	Clarabricken	567 3 18a	Kilkenny	Gowran	Clara	Kilkenny	I.	94
16	Claragh	300 2 0	Cavan	Tullygarvey	Annagh	Cootehill	III.	87
17	Claragh	246 1 38	Cavan	Tullygarvey	Kildrumsherdan	Cootehill	III.	89
14	Claragh	111 2 28	Cavan	Tullyhunco	Kildallan	Bawnboy	III.	96
45	Claragh	253 3 4	Donegal	Kilmacrenan	Tullyfern	Millford	III.	133
36	Claragh	579 1 15	Down	Kinelarty	Loughinisland	Downpatrick	III.	177
15	Claragh	99 2 31	Fermanagh	Magheraboy	Inishmacsaint	Enniskillen	III.	212
16	Claragh	107 2 16	King's Co.	Ballycowan	Lynally	Tullamore	I.	128
27	Claragh	673 3 36	Londonderry	Loughinsholin	Kilrea	Ballymoney	III.	241
39	Claraghatlea North	397 0 26	Cork, E.R.	Duhallow	Drishane	Millstreet	II.	71
39	Claraghatlea South	185 3 12	Cork, E.R.	Duhallow	Drishane	Millstreet	II.	71
38,39,47,48	Claragh Beg	328 2 35	Cork, W.R.	West Muskerry	Drishane	Millstreet	II.	156
32	Claragh Irish	321 3 18	Sligo	Leyny	Kilvarnet	Tobercurry	IV.	232
38, 39	Claragh More	462 0 36	Cork, E.R.	Duhallow	Drishane	Millstreet	II.	71
25, 34	Claraghmore	843 1 4b	Tyrone	Omagh West	Longfield East	Omagh	III.	315
14	Claraghpottle Glebe	41 0 36	Cavan	Tullyhunco	Kildallan	Bawnboy	III.	96
25, 32	Claragh Scotch	373 3 28	Sligo	Leyny	Kilvarnet	Tobercurry	IV.	232
24	Claraghy	105 1 11	Fermanagh	Magherastephana	Aghalurcher	Lisnaskea	III.	215
18, 23	Claraghy	123 2 27	Monaghan	Dartree	Ematris	Cootehill	III.	266
2, 3	Clarahill	301 1 38	Queen's Co.	Tinnahinch	Rearymore	Mountmellick	I.	249
24	Clara More	323 2 27	Wicklow	Ballinacor North	Knockrath	Rathdrum	I.	347
31	Claranagh	357 3 27	Armagh	Fews Upper	Creggan	Castleblayney	III.	48
17, 23	Claranagh	442 2 25	Fermanagh	Tirkennedy	Enniskillen	Enniskillen	III.	221
107	Clarary	152 1 15	Galway	Longford	Killimorbologue	Portumna	IV.	58
53	Clarary	181 0 26	Roscommon	Moycarn	Creagh	Ballinasloe	IV.	206
22, 25, 26	Claras	532 2 17	Longford	Rathcline	Cashel	Ballymahon	I.	163
32	Clarashinnagh	118 3 4c	Leitrim	Mohill	Mohill	Mohill	IV.	107
8	CLARA T.	—	King's Co.	Kilcoursey	Kilbride	Tullamore	I.	141
20	Clara Upper	559 0 33	Kilkenny	Gowran	Clara	Kilkenny	I.	94
9	Clarbally	145 2 34	Cavan	Tullyhaw	Templeport	Bawnboy	III.	94
27, 30	Clarbane	79 0 4	Armagh	Fews Upper	Creggan	Castleblayney	III.	48
24	Clarbarracum	299 3 26	Queen's Co.	Cullenagh	Dysartgallen	Abbeyleix	I.	239
94	Clarcam	245 2 9	Donegal	Tirhugh	Donegal	Donegal	III.	145
94	Clarcarricknagun	123 3 21d	Donegal	Tirhugh	Donegal	Donegal	III.	145
19	Clarderry	186 2 13	Monaghan	Cremorne	Clontibret	Monaghan	III.	260
94	Clardrumbarren	81 2 29	Donegal	Tirhugh	Donegal	Donegal	III.	145
94	Clardrumnagahan	39 0 26	Donegal	Tirhugh	Donegal	Donegal	III.	145
4, 8	Clare	202 3 32	Antrim	Cary	Ramoan	Ballycastle	III.	14
37	Clare	184 2 14	Antrim	Upper Toome	Drummaul	Ballymena	III.	34
13, 17	Clare	403 1 29	Armagh	Orior Lower	Ballymore	Banbridge	III.	55
32, 38	Clare	312 0 11	Cavan	Castlerahan	Crosserlough	Oldcastle	III.	67
21	Clare	957 3 9	Donegal	Inishowen East	Moville Upper	Inishowen	III.	119
13	Clare	147 3 10	Down	Lower Iveagh, Up.pt.	Moira	Lurgan	III.	170
19, 20, 26	Clare	1,334 2 20	Down	Lower Iveagh, Up. pt.	Tullylish	Lurgan	III.	171
54	Clare	78 2 10	Galway	Moycullen	Kilcummin	Oughterard	IV.	66
101	Clare	1,086 1 7e	Mayo	Clanmorris	Kilcolman	Claremorris	IV.	133
28, 29	Clare	197 0 33	Roscommon	Roscommon	Cloonfinlough	Strokestown	IV.	208
29, 30	Clare	154 1 28	Tyrone	Dungannon Upper	Derryloran	Cookstown	III.	306
29	Clare	312 3 7	Tyrone	Dungannon Upper	Kildress	Cookstown	III.	308
36	Clare	377 3 2	Tyrone	Omagh East	Termonmaguirk	Omagh	III.	314
24	Clare	847 2 17	Westmeath	Rathconrath	Killare	Mullingar	I.	283
33, 41	Clareabbey	231 3 28	Clare	Islands	Clareabbey	Ennis	II.	29
25	Clarebane	78 0 18	Cavan	Upper Loughtee	Kilmore	Cavan	III.	84
70, 71	Clare Beg	73 2 18	Tipperary, S.R.	Middlethird	Kiltinan	Clonmel	II.	328
31	Clareboy	101 1 9	Cavan	Upper Loughtee	Crosserlough	Cavan	III.	83
41	Clare Commons	43 0 1	Clare	Islands	Clareabbey	Ennis	II.	29
42	Clareen	156 0 23	King's Co.	Clonlisk	Kilmurryely	Roscrea	I.	131
111	Clareen	177 2 15	Mayo	Kilmaine	Kilcommon	Ballinrobe	IV.	154
40	Clareen	242 2 17	Tipperary, N.R.	Kilnamanagh Upper	Moyaliff	Thurles	II.	279
20	Clareen	169 3 26	Tipperary, N.R.	Owney and Arra	Burgesbeg	Nenagh	II.	294
52	Clareen	394 0 23	Tipperary, S.R.	Middlethird	Ardmayle	Cashel	II.	324
56, 66	Clarefield	432 2 38	Clare	Moyarta	Moyarta	Kilrush	II.	34
69, 70	Claregalway	585 2 38	Galway	Clare	Claregalway	Galway	IV.	18
41, 42	Clarehill	152 2 2	Clare	Islands	Clareabbey	Ennis	II.	29
11, 12	Clarehill	256 3 21	Londonderry	Coleraine	Aghadowey	Coleraine	III.	229
1	Clareisland or Derry-macegan	224 0 33	Westmeath	Fore	Foyran	Granard	I.	270
107	Claremadden	576 0 14	Galway	Longford	Kilquain	Portumna	IV.	60
14, 18	Claremont	114 1 20	Dublin	Coolock	Glasnevin	Dublin North	I.	27
70	Clare More	266 2 4	Tipperary, S.R.	Middlethird	Kiltinan	Clonmel	II.	328
51,52,58,59	Claremore	277 0 26	Tyrone	Clogher	Clogher	Clogher	III.	292
24	Claremore	170 0 17	Tyrone	Omagh West	Ardstraw	Castlederg	III.	315

(a) Including 3A. 2R. 37P. detached portion.   (c) Including 4A. 2R. 20P. water.   (e) Including 35A. 1R. 10P. water.
(b) Including 8A. 1R. 26P. water.   (d) Including 7A. 0R. 26P. detached portion.

No. of Sheet of the Ordnance Survey Maps.	Townlands and Towns.	Area in Statute Acres.	County.	Barony.	Parish.	Poor Law Union in 1857.	Townland Census of 1851. Part I.	
		A. R. P.					Vol.	Page
36	Claremount	175 0 24	Clare	Tulla Lower	Killuran	Tulla	II.	36
54	Claremount	569 2 33	Galway	Moycullen	Kilcummin	Oughterard	IV.	66
3	Claremount	200 2 39	Kildare	Carbury	Nurney	Edenderry	I.	53
29, 30	Claremount	75 3 36	King's Co.	Garrycastle	Reynagh	Parsonstown	I.	138
101	Claremount	313 0 30	Mayo	Clanmorris	Kilcolman	Claremorris	IV.	133
8, 9	Clare Mountain	184 0 13	Antrim	Cary	Ramoan	Ballycastle	III.	14
26,27,33,34	Claremount or Cummingstown	451 3 0	Westmeath	Fartullagh	Enniscoffey	Mullingar	I.	268
19, 24	Clare Oghill	132 2 33	Monaghan	Cremorne	Clontibret	Castleblayney	III.	260
23	Clare Rock Island	0 0 35	Dublin	Rathdown	Dalkey	Rathdown	I.	35
41, 42	CLARE T.	—	Clare	Islands	Clareabbey	Ennis	II.	29
101	CLARE T.		Mayo	Clanmorris	Kilcolman	Claremorris	IV.	134
4	Claretrock	299 0 9	Louth	Lower Dundalk	Ballymascanlan	Dundalk	I.	175
43	Claretuam	379 3 20	Galway	Clare	Belclare	Tuam	IV.	17
24	Clare Upper	379 2 35	Tyrone	Omagh West	Ardstraw	Castlederg	III.	315
5, 10	Clareview	202 2 22	Fermanagh	Lurg	Magheraculmoney	Lowtherstown	III.	207
31	Clarey	448 3 25	Kildare	Offaly West	Harristown	Athy	I.	72
95	CLARINBRIDGE T.	—	Galway	Dunkellin	Stradbally	Galway	IV.	32
28	Claristown	357 2 6	Meath	Upper Duleek	Moorechurch	Drogheda	I.	198
28	Clarkill	237 1 34	Armagh	Orior Upper	Forkill	Newry	III.	57
36, 43	Clarkill	1,718 3 14a	Down	Upper Iveagh, Lr. pt.	Kilmegan	Downpatrick	III.	173
7, 10	Clarkill	231 2 24	Tipperary, N.R.	Lower Ormond	Uskane	Borrisokane	II.	288
22	Clarkstown	81 3 26	Dublin	Rathdown	Whitechurch	Dublin South	I.	38
43, 49	Clarkstown	236 3 20	Meath	Upper Deece	Kilmore	Dunshaughlin	I.	193
11	Clarkville	10 2 23	King's Co.	Coolestown	Ballynakill	Edenderry	I.	132
11	Clarkville	81 2 9	King's Co.	Coolestown	Monasteroris	Edenderry	I.	133
94	Clarlougheask	204 2 3	Donegal	Tirhugh	Donegal	Donegal	III.	145
64	Clash	97 3 31	Cork, E.R.	Barrymore	Kilquane	Cork	II.	55
23	Clash	139 3 26	Cork, E.R.	Duhallow	Kilbrin	Kanturk	II.	72
94	Clash	91 2 33	Cork, W.R.	East Carbery (W.D.)	Kinneigh	Dunmanway	II.	134
138	Clash	96 1 35	Cork, W.R.	West Carbery (W.D.)	Kilcrohane	Bantry	II.	143
34	Clash	219 1 5	Kerry	Corkaguiny	Kilquane	Dingle	II.	179
67	Clash	225 0 22	Kerry	Magunihy	Killarney	Killarney	II.	203
11, 16	Clash	151 3 17	Queen's Co.	Upperwoods	Offerlane	Mountmellick	I.	251
22	Clash	440 2 29	Tipperary, N.R.	Upper Ormond	Ballymackey	Nenagh	II.	289
20	Clashabreeda	77 0 2	Tipperary, N.R.	Owney and Arra	Youghalarra	Nenagh	II.	297
26	Clashacollare	84 0 22	Kilkenny	Callan	Callan	Callan	I.	83
13	Clashacrow	560 3 28	Kilkenny	Crannagh	Clashacrow	Kilkenny	I.	85
117,130,131	Clashadoo	746 1 25	Cork, W.R.	West Carbery (W.D.)	Durrus	Bantry	II.	142
67	Clashadunna East	100 2 28	Cork, E.R.	Imokilly	Youghal	Youghal	II.	91
67	Clashadunna West	144 2 3	Cork, E.R.	Imokilly	Youghal	Youghal	II.	91
110	Clashafree	477 0 34	Cork, W.R.	East Carbery (E.D.)	Ballymodan	Bandon	II.	126
45	Clashagad Lower	262 2 26	King's Co.	Clonlisk	Dunkerrin	Roscrea	I.	130
45	Clashagad Upper	364 1 29	King's Co.	Clonlisk	Dunkerrin	Roscrea	I.	130
36, 45	Clashaganniv	423 0 32	Cork, E.R.	Kinnatalloon	Knockmourne	Fermoy	II.	98
97	Clashaganny	179 1 20	Galway	Athenry	Kiltullagh	Loughrea	IV.	5
16	Clashaganny	480 3 18	Galway	Dunmore	Liskeevy	Tuam	IV.	35
28	Clashaganny	59 2 4	Roscommon	Roscommon	Killukin	Strokestown	IV.	210
66, 67	Clashalaher	65 1 22	Tipperary, S.R.	Clanwilliam	Clonpet	Tipperary	II.	306
69	Clashalaher	139 0 18	Tipperary, S.R.	Middlethird	St. Patricksrock	Cahel	II.	330
84, 85	Clashanaffrin	297 0 36	Cork, E.R.	East Muskerry	Desertmore	Bandon	II.	102
38, 40	Clashanahy	136 3 23	Waterford	Decies within Drum	Lisgenan or Grange	Youghal	II.	352
33	Clashanea	90 1 39	Limerick	Coonagh	Oola	Tipperary	II.	235
96	Clashanimud	442 2 9	Cork, E.R.	Kinalea	Brinny	Bandon	II.	94
77	Clashaniska Lower	128 2 2	Tipperary, S.R.	Iffa and Offa East	Rathronan	Clonmel	II.	316
77	Clashaniska Upper	111 2 7	Tipperary, S.R.	Iffa and Offa East	Rathronan	Clonmel	II.	316
10, 15	Clashaniskera	159 2 23	Tipperary, N.R.	Lower Ormond	Modreeny	Borrisokane	II.	286
78	Clashanisky	119 1 4	Tipperary, S.R.	Iffa and Offa East	Kilcash	Clonmel	II.	313
72	Clashanure	574 0 23b	Cork, E.R.	East Muskerry	Athnowen	Cork	II.	101
29	Clashaphuca	85 0 33	Kerry	Trughanacmy	Clogherbrien	Tralee	II.	209
135	Clasharaggy	43 3 34	Cork, W.R.	Ibane and Barryroe	Kilkerranmore	Clonakilty	II.	149
58	Clashard	203 3 1	Galway	Tiaquin	Abbeyknockmoy	Tuam	IV.	75
77	Clasharinka	96 2 10	Cork, E.R.	Imokilly	Mogeely	Middleton	II.	89
42, 45	Clasharoe	56 2 6	Kilkenny	Iverk	Portnascully	Waterford	I.	106
121, 134	Clasharusheen	159 0 26	Cork, W.R.	Ibane and Barryroe	Castleventry	Clonakilty	II.	148
121, 134	Clashatarriff	274 1 38	Cork, W.R.	East Carbery (W.D.)	Castleventry	Clonakilty	II.	131
15	Clashateeaun	56 0 37	Tipperary, N.R.	Lower Ormond	Ardcrony	Nenagh	II.	281
38, 39	Clashatlea	335 3 35	Kerry	Trughanacmy	Ballymacelligott	Tralee	II.	207
76	Clashavaddra	42 0 9	Tipperary, S.R.	Iffa and Offa East	Inislilounaght	Clonmel	II.	313
26, 30	Clashavaha	148 2 34	Kilkenny	Kells	Coolaghmore	Callan	I.	107
67	Clashavickteery	71 0 29	Tipperary, S.R.	Clanwilliam	Kilshane	Tipperary	II.	309
75	CLASHAVODIG T.	—	Cork, E.R.	Barrymore	Little Island	Cork	II.	56
88, 91	Clashavougha	238 3 32	Tipperary, S.R.	Iffa and Offa West	Newcastle	Clogheen	II.	319

(a) Including 107A. 0R. 13P. water.   (b) Including 9A. 0R. 14P. water.

No. of Sheet of the Ordnance Survey Maps.	Townlands and Towns.	Area in Statute Acres.	County.	Barony.	Parish.	Poor Law Union in 1857.	Townland Census of 1851, Part I.	
		A. R. P.					Vol.	Page
23	Clashbane	210 3 26	Limerick	Clanwilliam	Caherconlish	Limerick	II.	222
55, 63	Clashbeg	199 0 20	Tipperary, S.R.	Slievardagh	Modeshil	Callan	II.	335
19, 25	Clashboy	163 1 32	Queen's Co.	Cullenagh	Fossy or Timahoe	Abbeyleix	I.	240
35	Clashbrack	226 1 17	Waterford	Decies within Drum	Ardmore	Dungarvan	II.	350
82, 94	Clashbredane	807 2 3	Cork, W.R.	West Muskerry	Kilmichael	Dunmanway	II.	158
106	Clashcame	673 0 37a	Mayo	Murrisk	Kilgeever	Westport	IV.	160
8, 14	Clashcarragh	97 2 25	Roscommon	Frenchpark	Tibohine	Castlereagh	IV.	204
66	Clashdermot East	44 3 13	Cork, E.R.	Imokilly	Killeagh	Youghal	II.	88
66	Clashdermot West	50 0 8	Cork, E.R.	Imokilly	Killeagh	Youghal	II.	88
65, 66	Clashdrumsmith	320 0 37	Tipperary, S.R.	Clanwilliam	Emly	Tipperary	II.	307
43	Clashduff	295 3 32	Clare	Tulla Lower	Clonlea	Tulla	II.	34
65, 76, 77	Clashduff	237 2 19	Cork, E.R.	Barrymore	Inchinabacky	Middleton	II.	55
74	Clashduff	52 2 0	Cork, E.R.	Cork	St. Finbars	Cork	II.	65
118	Clashduff	27 0 22	Cork, W.R.	Bantry	Kilmocomoge	Bantry	II.	120
103	Clashduff	1,066 0 9	Cork, W.R.	Bear	Kilcaskan	Castletown	II.	122
119,120,132	Clashduff	325 3 15	Cork, W.R.	West Carbery (E.D.)	Dromdaleague	Skibbereen	II.	140
5, 10	Clashduff	263 3 26	Kilkenny	Fassadinin	Dysart	Castlecomer	I.	39
49, 55	Clashduff	462 3 17	Tipperary, S.R.	Slievardagh	Ballingarry	Callan	II.	331
10	Clashduff Lower	39 2 24	Kilkenny	Fassadinin	Kilmacar	Castlecomer	I.	90
5, 10	Clashduff Upper	188 2 3	Kilkenny	Fassadinin	Kilmacar	Castlecomer	I.	90
64, 65	Clash East	49 2 10	Cork, E.R.	Barrymore	Ballycurrany	Middleton	II.	51
64, 65	Clash East	144 0 33	Cork, E.R.	Barrymore	Lisgoold	Middleton	II.	56
29	Clash East	170 2 21	Kerry	Trughanacmy	Ratass	Tralee	II.	213
38	Clashedmond	186 2 37	Kerry	Trughanacmy	Ballyseedy	Tralee	II.	208
67	Clasheel	162 3 24	Cork, E.R.	Imokilly	Clonpriest	Youghal	II.	84
67	Clasheen	244 0 31	Kerry	Magunihy	Killarney	Killarney	II.	203
16, 17	Clasheen	126 0 30	Wexford	Gorey	Monamolin	Gorey	I.	321
20	Clasheenanierin	94 0 37	Waterford	Coshmore&Coshbride	Lismore and Mocollop	Lismore	II.	345
16	Clashelane	175 0 26	Cork, E.R.	Orrery and Kilmore	Churchtown	Mallow	II.	107
66	Clasheleesha	50 0 34	Tipperary, S.R.	Clanwilliam	Emly	Tipperary	II.	308
19	Clashganniff	281 3 21	Limerick	Shanid	Kilmoylan	Glin	II.	256
19	Clashganniff	57 3 28	Limerick	Shanid	Shanagolden	Glin	II.	258
7	Clashganniv	276 1 6	Cork, E.R.	Orrery and Kilmore	Churchtown	Mallow	II.	107
2, 7	Clashganniv	107 3 32	Cork, E.R.	Orrery and Kilmore	Rathgoggan	Kilmallock	II.	109
39, 40	Clashganniv	512 1 25	Kerry	Trughanacmy	Dysart	Tralee	II.	210
17	Clashganny	176 0 33	Carlow	Idrone East	Myshall	Carlow	I.	8
4, 8	Clashganny	140 1 27	Waterford	Upperthird	Clonagam	Carrick on Suir	II.	369
88	Clashganny East	86 1 11b	Tipperary, S.R.	Iffa and Offa West	Newcastle	Clogheen	II.	319
37, 38	Clashganny or Kilmaloo	191 1 27	Waterford	Decies within Drum	Kinsalebeg	Youghal	II.	352
88, 91	Clashganny West	1,195 0 14c	Tipperary, S.R.	Iffa and Offa West	Newcastle	Clogheen	II.	319
38, 46	Clashgortmore	279 1 39	Limerick	Connello Upper	Corcomohide	Kilmallock	II.	232
56	Clash Island	3 0 21	Kerry	Trughanacmy	Killorglin	Killarney	II.	211
20, 21	Clashmagrath	143 0 13	Kilkenny	Gowran	Gowran	Kilkenny	I.	95
59	Clashmaguire	474 3 19	Cork, W.R.	West Muskerry	Clondrohid	Macroom	II.	155
31	Clashmalea	2 2 19	Waterford	Decies without Drum	Dungarvan	Dungarvan	II.	355
9	Clashmelcon	958 2 21	Kerry	Clanmaurice	Killury	Listowel	II.	171
28	Clashmore	50 0 3	Clare	Tulla Upper	Feakle	Scarriff	II.	39
112	Clashmore	74 2 3	Cork, E.R.	Kinsale	Clontead	Kinsale	II.	99
140	Clashmore	228 2 30	Cork, W.R.	West Carbery (W.D.)	Skull	Skull	II.	145
34, 37	Clashmore	541 1 16	Waterford	Decies within Drum	Clashmore	Youghal	II.	351
37	CLASHMORE T.	—	Waterford	Decies within Drum	Clashmore	Youghal	II.	351
41, 42	Clashmorgan	525 3 21	Cork, E.R.	Barretts	Mourneabbey	Mallow	II.	50
16	Clashnabuttry	38 1 1	Cork, E.R.	Orrery and Kilmore	Buttevant	Mallow	II.	107
120	Clashnacrona East	181 0 29d	Cork, W.R.	East Carbery (W.D.)	Fanlobbus	Dunmanway	II.	131
120	Clashnacrona West	286 0 17e	Cork, W.R.	East Carbery (W.D.)	Fanlobbus	Dunmanway	II.	131
51	Clashnacrony	125 2 21	Tipperary, S.R.	Kilnamanagh Lower	Donohill	Tipperary	II.	323
29, 30	Clashnadarriv	140 0 21	Waterford	Decies without Drum	Kilmolash	Lismore	II.	357
74	Clashnaganniff	35 3 27f	Cork, E.R.	Cork	St. Annes Shandon	Cork	II.	111
58, 59	Clashnagarrane	479 0 36	Kerry	Magunihy	Kilcummin	Killarney	II.	201
22, 30	Clashnagoneen	247 3 23	Waterford	Decies without Drum	Whitechurch	Lismore	II.	361
15	Clashnagraun	76 2 15	Tipperary, N.R.	Upper Ormond	Kilruane	Nenagh	II.	292
20	Clashnamonadee	125 1 32	Waterford	Coshmore&Coshbride	Lismore and Mocollop	Lismore	II.	345
29	Clashnamrock	61 3 9	Waterford	Coshmore&Coshbride	Lismore and Mocollop	Lismore	II.	345
16, 22	Clashnamuck	261 3 35	Queen's Co.	Upperwoods	Offerlane	Abbeyleix	II.	251
72, 79	Clashnasmut	437 0 0	Tipperary, S.R.	Slievardagh	Newtownlennan	Carrick on Suir	II.	335
21	Clashnevin	380 3 15	Tipperary, N.R.	Upper Ormond	Ballymackey	Nenagh	II.	289
35	Clash North	810 0 32	Limerick	Shanid	Rathronan	Newcastle	II.	257
67, 74	Clashoquirk	247 2 25	Tipperary, S.R.	Clanwilliam	Templeniry	Tipperary	II.	311
9	Clashrea	29 3 4g	Waterford	Middlethird	Trinity Without	Waterford	II.	369
124	Clashreagh	132 2 28	Cork, W.R.	East Carbery (E.D.)	Templetrine	Kinsale	II.	130
5, 14	Clashroe	191 1 7	Cork, E.R.	Duhallow	Clonfert	Kanturk	II.	68
112, 125	Clashroe	77 0 21	Cork, E.R.	Kinalea	Kinure	Kinsale	I.	95
39, 43	Clashroe	988 3 20	King's Co.	Ballybritt	Roscomroe	Parsonstown	I.	126

(a) Including 119A. 3R. 32P. water.
(b) Including 4A. 2R. 0P. water.
(c) Including 4A. 2R. 16P. water.
(d) Including 0A. 0R. 32P. water.
(e) Including 5A. 3R. 1P. water.
(f) Included in the parish of St. Annes Shandon.
(g) { Within the Municipal Boundary, 13A. 3R. 22P. / Without the Municipal Boundary, 15A. 3R. 22P.

No. of Sheet of the Ordnance Survey Maps.	Townlands and Towns.	Area in Statute Acres.			County.	Barony.	Parish.	Poor Law Union in 1857.	Townland Census of 1851, Part I.	
		A.	R.	P.					Vol.	Page
4	Clashroe . . .	212	3	30	Waterford	Upperthird	Clonagam	Carrick on Suir	II.	369
35	Clash South .	584	2	2	Limerick .	Shanid . .	Rathronan	Newcastle .	II.	257
64	Clash West .	27	2	6	Cork, E.R.	Barrymore	Ballycurrany	Middleton .	II.	51
64	Clash West .	101	3	39	Cork, E.R.	Barrymore	Lisgoold .	Middleton .	II.	56
29	Clash West .	64	1	34	Kerry .	Trughanacmy .	Ratass .	Tralee .	II.	213
20, 24	Clashwilliam .	220	0	33	Kilkenny .	Gowran .	Dunbell .	Kilkenny .	I.	94
20, 24	Clashwilliam .	282	1	6	Kilkenny .	Gowran .	Gowran .	Kilkenny .	I.	95
20, 24	Clashwilliam Upper	292	1	7	Kilkenny .	Gowran .	Gowran .	Kilkenny .	I.	95
54, 55, 63	Clashygowan . .	568	2	32	Donegal .	Raphoe .	Taughboyne .	Strabane .	III.	143
21, 22	Clashykinleen East	306	3	18	Cork, E.R.	Duhallow	Kilmeen .	Kanturk .	II.	72
13, 21	Clashykinleen West	449	2	25	Cork, E.R.	Duhallow	Kilmeen .	Kanturk .	II.	72
36, 37, 45	Classagh .	596	2	5	Clare .	Tulla Lower .	Killaloe .	Limerick .	II.	35
6	Classaghroe .	448	3	21	Galway .	Ballymoe .	Boyounagh .	Glennamaddy .	IV.	6
93	Classaghroe .	208	1	16	Mayo .	Costello . .	Annagh .	Claremorris .	IV.	138
73	Classes . . .	149	0	31a	Cork, E.R.	East Muskerry	Athnowen .	Cork .	II.	101
71	Classes . . .	152	2	15b	Cork, E.R.	East Muskerry	Cannaway .	Macroom .	II.	102
27, 33	Clatterstown .	216	1	33	Meath .	Upper Duleek .	Ardcath .	Drogheda .	I.	197
38	Clatteryknowes .	440	0	16	Antrim .	Lower Antrim	Glenwhirry .	Ballymena .	III.	4
23	Claudy . . .	1,154	1	26	Londonderry	Tirkeeran .	Cumber Upper	Londonderry .	III.	249
23	CLAUDY T. .	—			Londonderry	Tirkeeran .	Cumber Upper	Londonderry .	III.	249
17, 22	Claughey . .	353	1	5	Antrim .	Upper Dunluce	Ballymoney .	Ballymoney .	III.	18
33	Claureen . .	241	1	27	Clare .	Islands . .	Drumcliff .	Ennis .	II.	29
16, 29	Claureen . .	71	1	23	Galway .	Dunmore .	Kilbennan .	Tuam .	IV.	34
20	Clavass . . .	157	3	0	Wexford .	Scarawalsh .	St.MarysEnniscorthy	Enniscorthy .	I.	325
21	Clawinch .	39	0	15	Longford .	Rathcline .	Cashel .	Ballymahon .	I.	163
19, 20, 24	Clay . . .	1,405	0	38c	Armagh .	Armagh .	Keady .	Armagh .	III.	45
24	Clay . . .	518	3	37d	Down .	Dufferin .	Killyleagh .	Downpatrick .	III.	167
34	Clay . . .	371	2	23	Down .	Upper Iveagh, Up. pt.	Annaclone .	Banbridge .	III.	174
28	Clay . . .	128	1	30	Fermanagh .	Magherastephana .	Aghalurcher .	Lisnaskea .	III.	215
67	Claycastle .	61	3	19	Cork, E.R.	Imokilly . .	Youghal .	Youghal .	II.	91
34	Cleaboy . .	257	2	7	Roscommon	Castlereagh .	Ballintober .	Castlereagh .	IV.	198
9	Cleaboy . .	60	2	33	Waterford .	Middlethird .	Trinity Without .	Waterford .	II.	369
53	Cleaghbeg .	37	0	59e	Roscommon	Moycarn .	Creagh .	Ballinasloe .	IV.	206
53	Cleaghgarve .	57	3	17f	Roscommon	Moycarn .	Creagh .	Ballinasloe .	IV.	206
74, 87, 88	Cleaghmore .	138	0	23g	Galway .	Clonmacnowen .	Kilcloony .	Ballinasloe .	IV.	25
7	Cleaheen . .	681	3	28	Roscommon	Boyle .	Tumna .	Carn. on Shannon	IV.	197
24	Cleanagh . .	203	0	24	Queen's Co.	Cullenagh .	Dysartgallen .	Abbeyleix .	I.	239
52, 59	Cleanally .	254	0	31	Tyrone .	Clogher .	Errigal Keerogue .	Clogher .	III.	295
8, 14, 15	Cleanderry .	638	2	8	Kerry .	Clanmaurice .	Killury .	Listowel .	II.	171
43,44,52,53	Cleanglass North .	1,120	2	34	Limerick .	Glenquin .	Killeedy .	Newcastle .	II.	245
52, 53	Cleanglass South .	691	2	14	Limerick .	Glenquin .	Killeedy .	Newcastle .	II.	245
30	Cleanrath .	353	1	19	Cork, E.R.	Duhallow .	Cullen .	Millstreet .	II.	70
69	Cleanrath North .	564	3	39	Cork, W.R.	West Muskerry	Inchigeelagh .	Macroom .	II.	156
69, 81	Cleanrath South .	878	0	10	Cork, W.R.	West Muskerry	Inchigeelagh .	Macroom .	II.	156
83	Clearagh . .	461	2	1	Cork, W.R.	West Muskerry	Kilmurry .	Macroom .	II.	159
77	Clear's-land . .	12	2	0	Tipperary, S.R.	Iffa and Offa East .	Rathronan .	Clonmel .	II.	316
14, 15	Cleaveragh Demesne	276	1	0	Sligo .	Carbury .	St. John's .	Sligo .	IV.	223
34	Cleavry . .	255	0	39	Sligo .	Tirerrill .	Kilmacallan .	Sligo .	IV.	239
58	Cleedagh . .	60	1	3	Kerry .	Magunihy .	Kilcummin .	Killarney .	II.	201
24	Cleen . . .	175	1	37	Fermanagh .	Magherastephana .	Aghalurcher .	Lisnaskea .	III.	215
15	Cleen . . .	266	1	38	Leitrim .	Drumahaire .	Killanummery .	Manorhamilton .	IV.	97
3, 6, 7	Cleen . . .	426	0	13	Roscommon	Boyle .	Ardcarn .	Boyle .	IV.	192
43	Cleenagh . .	130	1	29	Fermanagh .	Coole .	Drummully .	Clones .	III.	199
29	Cleenagh . .	373	1	26	Donegal .	Inishowen West	Fahan Lower .	Inishowen .	III.	120
16	Cleenaghan .	212	2	10	Fermanagh .	Tirkennedy .	Magheracross .	Enniskillen .	III.	223
25	Cleenaghoo .	196	3	14h	Leitrim .	Carrigallen .	Oughteragh .	Bawnboy .	IV.	91
22, 25	Cleendargan .	211	3	32i	Leitrim .	Carrigallen .	Oughteragh .	Bawnboy .	IV.	91
56, 57	Cleenderry .	272	0	2j	Donegal .	Boylagh .	Templecrone .	Glenties .	III.	115
65	Cleengort . .	483	0	16	Donegal .	Boylagh .	Inishkeel .	Glenties .	III.	112
40	Cleenillaun .	9	1	20	Galway .	Ross .	Cong .	Oughterard .	IV.	73
27	Cleenish . .	565	0	33k	Fermanagh .	Clanawley .	Cleenish .	Enniskillen .	III.	190
10	Cleenishgarve Island	27	2	8	Fermanagh .	Lurg .	Magheraculmoney .	Lowtherstown .	III.	208
10	Cleenishmeen Island .	20	1	18	Fermanagh .	Lurg .	Magheraculmoney .	Lowtherstown .	III.	208
3, 6	Cleenrah . .	355	1	28l	Longford .	Granard .	Columbkille .	Granard .	I.	155
16	Cleenraugh .	207	1	31	Roscommon	Frenchpark .	Kilmacumsy .	Boyle .	IV.	203
34	Cleenriss . .	162	1	15	Fermanagh .	Magherastephana .	Aghalurcher .	Lisnaskea .	III.	215
21	Cleens New .	38	3	20	Fermanagh .	Magheraboy .	Devenish .	Enniskillen .	III.	210
21	Cleens Old .	54	1	10	Fermanagh .	Magheraboy .	Devenish .	Enniskillen .	III.	210
66	Cleeny . .	89	3	8	Kerry .	Magunihy .	Aghadoe .	Killarney .	II.	199
23	Cleffany . .	238	0	32m	Fermanagh .	Magherastephana .	Aghavea .	Lisnaskea .	III.	218
33	Cleffin . .	378	3	39	Cavan .	Castlerahan .	Killinkere .	Bailieborough .	III.	68
42, 48	Clegarrow . .	462	2	37	Meath .	Lower Moyfenrath .	Rathcore .	Trim .	I.	211
8, 9, 13, 14	Cleggan . .	252	1	13	Antrim .	Cary .	Armoy .	Ballycastle .	III.	11

(a) Including   1A. 0R. 22P. water.
(b) Including   6A. 0R. 12P. water.
(c) Including 109A. 0R. 18P. water.
(d) Including { 63A. 2R. 18P. detached portion. / 13A. 3R. 18P. Clay Lake North. / 11A. 3R. 15P. Clay Lake South.

(e) Including 4A. 2R. 16P. water.
(f) Including 5A. 2R. 32P. water.
(g) Including 15A. 0R. 24P. water.
(h) Including 2A. 3R. 26P. water.
(i) Including 3A. 3R. 22P. water.

(j) Including   6A. 2R. 32P. water.
(k) Including 126A. 1R. 5P. water.
(l) Including   6A. 2R. 12P. water.
(m) Including   9A. 1R. 37P. water.

No. of Sheet of the Ordnance Survey Maps.	Townlands and Towns.	Area in Statute Acres.			County.	Barony.	Parish.	Poor Law Union in 1857.	Townland Census of 1851, Part I.	
		A.	R.	P.					Vol.	Page
1	Cleggan .	202	3	12	Antrim .	Cary .	Rathlin Island .	Ballycastle .	III.	15
28, 29	Cleggan .	1,388	3	21	Antrim .	Lower Antrim .	Skerry .	Ballymena .	III.	4
33, 39	Cleggan .	95	0	19	Cavan .	Castlerahan .	Lurgan .	Oldcastle .	III.	69
26	Cleggan .	106	1	21	Fermanagh .	Clanawley .	Cleenish .	Enniskillen .	III.	190
9, 22	Cleggan .	889	1	1a	Galway .	Ballynahinch .	Ballynakill .	Clifden .	IV.	11
12, 13	Cleggan .	34	0	7	Leitrim .	Drumahaire .	Cloonclare .	Manorhamilton .	IV.	93
17	Cleggarnagh .	53	1	21	Westmeath .	Rathconrath .	Rathconrath .	Mullingar .	I.	284
8, 13	Cleggill .	240	0	38	Longford .	Longford .	Clongesh .	Longford .	I.	157
67	Cleghile .	155	3	19	Tipperary, S.R.	Clanwilliam .	Kilshane .	Tipperary .	II.	309
6, 7	Clegna .	326	1	29	Roscommon .	Boyle .	Ardcarn .	Carᵏ. on Shannon	IV.	192
4	Clegnagh .	250	3	23	Antrim .	Cary .	Ballintoy .	Ballycastle .	III.	12
7, 8	Clegnagh .	106	2	5	Antrim .	Cary .	Grange of Drumtullagh	Ballycastle .	III.	14
14, 15	Clegnagh .	81	0	8	Antrim .	Lower Glenarm .	Layd .	Ballycastle .	III.	22
10	Clehagh .	359	2	12	Donegal .	Inishowen East .	Clonmany .	Inishowen .	III.	117
34, 40	Clehile .	362	2	17	Tipperary, N.R.	Eliogarty .	Inch .	Thurles .	II.	270
3	Cleighragh .	560	1	25	Leitrim .	Rosclogher .	Rossinver .	Ballyshannon .	IV.	111
14	Cleighran .	246	1	31	Leitrim .	Drumahaire .	Killanummery .	Manorhamilton .	IV.	97
18, 20, 21	Cleighran Beg .	354	3	15	Leitrim .	Drumahaire .	Drumreilly .	Carᵏ. on Shannon	IV.	95
20, 21	Cleighran More .	368	1	14	Leitrim .	Drumahaire .	Drumreilly .	Carᵏ. on Shannon	IV.	95
45	Clementshill .	182	0	4	Antrim .	Lower Belfast .	Ballynure .	Larne .	III.	7
17	CLEMENTSTOWN T.	—			Cavan .	Tullygarvey .	Kildrumsherdan .	Cootehill .	III.	90
51	Clenagh .	713	0	15b	Clare .	Bunratty Lower .	Kilmaleery .	Ennis .	II.	5
11	Clenaghisle .	83	2	4	Fermanagh .	Lurg .	Derryvullan .	Lowtherstown .	III.	204
8	Clenlough .	86	0	4c	Monaghan .	Monaghan .	Drumsnat .	Monaghan .	III.	275
25	Clenor North .	306	1	3	Cork, E.R.	Fermoy .	Clenor .	Mallow .	II.	78
25	Clenor South .	220	3	7	Cork, E.R.	Fermoy .	Clenor .	Mallow .	II.	78
47, 48, 51	Cleomack .	1,153	0	9	Down .	Upper Iveagh, Lr. pt.	Clonduff .	Newry .	III.	171
25	Cleraun .	335	1	5	Longford .	Rathcline .	Cashel .	Ballymahon .	I.	163
41	Clerhaun .	593	0	30	Galway .	Clare .	Killursa .	Tuam .	IV.	21
88	Clerhaun .	115	0	10	Mayo .	Murrisk .	Oughaval .	Westport .	IV.	161
41, 42	Cleristown North .	241	0	22	Wexford .	Bargy .	Kilmannan .	Wexford .	I.	306
41, 42, 46	Cleristown South .	393	1	12	Wexford .	Bargy .	Kilmannan .	Wexford .	I.	306
66	Clerkstown .	11	1	31	Tipperary, S.R.	Clanwilliam .	Lattin .	Tipperary .	II.	309
15	Clermont .	159	3	6	Tipperary, N.R.	Upper Ormond .	Kilruane .	Borrisokane .	II.	292
3	Clerragh .	306	1	10	Roscommon .	Boyle .	Ardcarn .	Boyle .	IV.	192
20	Clerragh .	259	2	36	Roscommon .	Frenchpark .	Tibohine .	Castlereagh .	IV.	204
10, 14	Clerran .	237	1	24	Monaghan .	Cremorne .	Clontibret .	Monaghan .	III.	260
7	Clery .	118	1	29d	Monaghan .	Trough .	Donagh .	Monaghan .	III.	281
33	Cletty .	294	2	13	Sligo .	Corran .	Toomour .	Sligo .	IV.	228
34	Clevaghy .	58	2	28	Fermanagh .	Coole .	Galloon .	Lisnaskea .	III.	199
53	Cliddaun .	73	3	26	Kerry .	Corkaguiny .	Dingle .	Dingle .	II.	175
39	Cliddaun .	172	3	1	Kerry .	Trughanacmy .	Killeentierna .	Tralee .	II.	211
10	Clievragh .	331	1	13	Kerry .	Iraghticonnor .	Listowel .	Listowel .	II.	192
16, 17	Clifden .	477	2	20e	Clare .	Inchiquin .	Rath .	Corrofin .	II.	27
35	Clifden .	310	0	17f	Galway .	Ballynahinch .	Omey .	Clifden .	IV.	14
20	Clifden Commons .	114	0	26	Kilkenny .	Gowran .	Gowran .	Kilkenny .	I.	95
35	Clifden Demesne .	206	0	29	Galway .	Ballynahinch .	Omey .	Clifden .	IV.	14
20	Clifden or Rathgarvan	484	2	32	Kilkenny .	Gowran .	Clara .	Kilkenny .	I.	94
35	CLIFDEN T.	—			Galway .	Ballynahinch .	Omey .	Clifden .	IV.	15
26, 27	Clifferna .	872	1	11g	Cavan .	Tullygarvey .	Larah .	Cootehill .	III.	91
48	Cliff Island .	4	3	17	Mayo .	Tirawley .	Kilbelfad .	Ballina .	IV.	168
34	Clifford .	128	1	30h	Cork, E.R.	Fermoy .	Bridgetown .	Fermoy .	II.	77
14	Clifton .	82	2	11	Cavan .	Lower Loughtee .	Tomregan .	Bawnboy .	III.	81
31	Clincaun .	42	3	2	Kilkenny .	Kells .	Kilmaganny .	Callan .	I.	109
34	Clinstown .	388	1	23	Meath .	Upper Duleek .	Stamullin .	Drogheda .	I.	198
11	Clintagh .	371	2	0	Londonderry .	Coleraine .	Aghadowey .	Coleraine .	III.	229
9, 13	Clintstown .	232	1	26	Kilkenny .	Crannagh .	Freshford .	Kilkenny .	I.	85
10, 14	Clintstown .	447	3	38	Kilkenny .	Fassadinin .	Coolcraheen .	Kilkenny .	I.	89
32	Clinty .	236	0	2	Antrim .	Lower Toome .	Kirkinriola .	Ballymena .	III.	32
47	Clintycracken .	125	2	36	Tyrone .	Dungannon Middle .	Clonoe .	Dungannon .	III.	300
17, 18	Cliven .	239	2	37	Louth .	Ardee .	Mosstown .	Ardee .	I.	174
114	Cloan .	449	0	1	Cork, W.R.	Bear .	Kilnamanagh .	Castletown .	II.	125
35	Cloane .	1,036	2	4	Londonderry .	Loughinsholin .	Ballynascreen .	Magherafelt .	III.	238
114	CLOANMINES T.	—			Cork, W.R.	Bear .	Kilnamanagh .	Castletown .	II.	126
35, 41	Clobanna .	243	1	39	Tipperary, N.R.	Eliogarty .	Shyane .	Thurles .	II.	272
14, 15	Clobemon .	222	2	4i	Wexford .	Scarawalsh .	Ballycarney .	Enniscorthy .	I.	322
88	Clocully .	282	3	39j	Tipperary, S.R.	Iffa and Offa West .	Neddans .	Clogheen .	II.	319
107, 120	Clodagh .	1,046	3	28	Cork, W.R.	West Carbery (E.D.)	Dromdaleague .	Skibbereen .	II.	140
83	Clodah .	469	1	11	Cork, W.R.	West Muskerry .	Kilmurry .	Macroom .	II.	159
149, 153	Cloddagh .	232	0	31	Cork, W.R.	West Carbery (E.D.)	Tullagh .	Skibbereen .	II.	140
90	Clodragh .	276	0	20k	Kerry .	Iveragh .	Dromod .	Cahersiveen .	II.	194
19, 24	Clodrum .	95	1	39	Cavan .	Tullyhunco .	Killashandra .	Cavan .	III.	97
123	Clogagh North .	173	1	17	Cork, W.R.	East Carbery (E.D.)	Kilmaloda .	Clonakilty .	II.	129

(a) Including 20A. 0R. 19P. water.
(b) Including 13A. 0R. 2P. water.
(c) Including 14A. 3R. 8P. water.
(d) Including 0A. 3R. 24P. water.

(e) Including 41A. 0R. 35F. water.
(f) Including 2A. 2R. 19P. water.
(g) Including 17A. 2R. 2P. water.
(h) Including 5A. 2R. 8P. water.

(i) Including 4A. 2R. 32P. water.
(j) Including 12A. 2R. 32P. water.
(k) Including 2A. 3R. 25P. water.

No. of Sheet of the Ordnance Survey Maps	Townlands and Towns.	Area in Statute Acres.			County.	Barony.	Parish.	Poor Law Union in 1857.	Townland Census of 1851, Part I.	
		A.	R.	P.					Vol.	Page
123	Clogagh South	282	1	5	Cork, W.R.	East Carbery (E.D.)	Kilmaloda	Clonakilty	II.	129
33	Clogaralt	96	2	15	Kilkenny	Ida	The Rower	Thomastown	I.	104
52	Clogga	171	2	21	Clare	Bunratty Lower	Kilfinaghta	Limerick	II.	4
39, 42	Clogga	1,067	0	6	Kilkenny	Iverk	Pollrone	Carrick on Suir	I.	106
45	Clogga	110	2	11	Wicklow	Arklow	Arklow	Rathdrum	I.	341
38	Cloggagh	213	2	8	Cavan	Castlerahan	Castlerahan	Oldcastle	III.	67
14, 15	Cloggarnagh	407	0	7	Roscommon	Frenchpark	Tibohine	Castlereagh	IV.	204
29	Cloggernagh or Bellmount	50	0	3	Roscommon	Roscommon	Lissonuffy	Strokestown	IV.	211
24, 25	Cloggy	188	0	19	Cavan	Tullyhunco	Killashandra	Cavan	III.	97
72, 85	Clogh	1,638	3	36	Galway	Tiaquin	Clonkeen	Loughrea	IV.	76
2, 6	Clogh	506	2	22	Kilkenny	Fassadinin	Castlecomer	Castlecomer	I.	88
36, 37	Clogh	59	3	31	King's Co.	Ballybritt	Letterluna	Parsonstown	I.	126
10	Clogh	273	1	25	Longford	Granard	Abbeylara	Granard	I.	154
22	Clogh	185	2	8	Longford	Rathcline	Kilcommock	Ballymahon	I.	164
6	Clogh	778	1	1	Sligo	Carbury	Rossinver	Sligo	IV.	223
29, 30	Clogh	183	0	22	Waterford	Decies within Drum	Kilmolash	Dungarvan	II.	351
11	Clogh	301	1	18	Wexford	Gorey	Liskinfere	Gorey	I.	320
16	Cloghabrack	119	0	0	King's Co.	Ballycowan	Lynally	Tullamore	I.	128
75	Cloghabreedy	581	1	36	Tipperary, S.R.	Middlethird	Knockgraffon	Cashel	II.	328
28	Cloghabrody	375	0	20a	Kilkenny	Gowran	Thomastown	Thomastown	I.	99
13	Cloghacloka	339	2	31	Limerick	Pubblebrien	Mungret	Limerick	II.	254
24, 33	Cloghadalton	62	2	25	Limerick	Coonagh	Oola	Tipperary	II.	235
24	Cloghaderreen	402	1	22	Limerick	Coonagh	Grean	Tipperary	II.	235
70	Cloghadockan	146	0	7	Mayo	Carra	Turlough	Castlebar	IV.	130
22	Cloghadoolarty North	297	0	9	Limerick	Smallcounty	Fedamore	Croom	II.	259
22	Cloghadoolarty South	104	0	13	Limerick	Smallcounty	Fedamore	Croom	II.	259
35	Cloghagaddy	134	2	3	Fermanagh	Clankelly	Galloon	Lisnaskea	III.	198
87	Cloghagalla Eighter	350	2	36	Galway	Clonmacnowen	Aughrim	Ballinasloe	IV.	24
87	Cloghagalla Oughter	332	3	3	Galway	Clonmacnowen	Aughrim	Ballinasloe	IV.	24
24	Cloghala	577	1	32	Kilkenny	Gowran	Dungarvan	Thomastown	I.	94
24	Cloghala	35	3	8	Kilkenny	Gowran	Tullaherin	Thomastown	I.	100
95	Cloghalahard	300	1	36	Galway	Dunkellin	Stradbally	Galway	IV.	32
13, 14	Cloghal Beg	254	1	23	King's Co.	Garrycastle	Tisaran	Parsonstown	I.	138
13, 14	Cloghal More	292	3	39	King's Co.	Garrycastle	Tisaran	Parsonstown	I.	138
8, 9, 12, 13	Cloghan	358	1	10	Armagh	Oneilland West	Kilmore	Armagh	III.	53
80, 81	Cloghan	115	3	26	Donegal	Banagh	Glencolumbkille	Glenties	III.	105
38	Cloghan	117	3	23	Fermanagh	Knockninny	Kinawley	Lisnaskea	III.	201
38	Cloghan	420	3	1	King's Co.	Clonlisk	Ettagh	Roscrea	I.	130
22	Cloghan	158	0	25	King's Co.	Garrycastle	Gallen	Parsonstown	I.	136
2, 4	Cloghan	179	2	18	Leitrim	Rosclogher	Rossinver	Ballyshannon	IV.	111
17	Cloghan	583	1	38	Londonderry	Keenaght	Balteagh	NewTⁿLimavady	III.	234
19	Cloghan	384	2	7	Longford	Moydow	Moydow	Ballymahon	I.	162
23, 27	Cloghan	339	1	1b	Longford	Shrule	Forgney	Ballymahon	I.	166
87, 88	Cloghan	65	3	32	Mayo	Murrisk	Oughaval	Westport	IV.	161
33	Cloghan	397	1	16	Meath	Upper Duleek	Ardcath	Drogheda	I.	197
19	Cloghan	229	3	4c	Monaghan	Cremorne	Clontibret	Castleblayney	III.	260
44	Cloghan	376	1	30	Roscommon	Athlone	Taghboy	Athlone	IV.	184
82	Cloghanacody	281	1	26	Tipperary, S.R.	Iffa and Offa West	Ardfinnan	Clogheen	II.	316
82	Cloghanacody	84	3	10	Tipperary, S.R.	Iffa and Offa West	Derrygrath	Clogheen	II.	318
147	Cloghanaculleen	629	0	8	Cork, W.R.	West Carbery (W.D.)	Kilmoe	Skull	II.	144
21	Cloghanagh	109	1	28	Fermanagh	Magheraboy	Rossorry	Enniskillen	III.	214
147	Cloghanalehid	113	3	12	Cork, W.R.	West Carbery (W.D.)	Kilmoe	Skull	II.	144
1	Cloghanamina	96	3	38	King's Co.	Kilcoursey	Kilmanaghan	Tullamore	I.	141
20, 29	Cloghanarold	244	0	22	Limerick	Connello Lower	Doondonnell	Rathkeale	II.	228
31	Cloghanaskaw	204	1	26	Westmeath	Moycashel	Ardnurcher or Horseleap	Mullingar	I.	276
16, 24	Cloghanbane	113	1	17	King's Co.	Ballycowan	Lynally	Tullamore	I.	128
68	Cloghan Beg	256	2	17	Donegal	Raphoe	Kiltevogue	Stranorlar	III.	139
29	Cloghan Beg	95	3	8	King's Co.	Garrycastle	Lusmagh	Parsonstown	I.	137
29	Cloghanboy (Cooke)	7	3	2	Westmeath	Brawny	St. Mary's	Athlone	I.	259
29	Cloghanboy (Homan)	40	3	8	Westmeath	Brawny	St. Mary's	Athlone	I.	259
29	Cloghanboy (Strain)	13	2	0	Westmeath	Brawny	St. Mary's	Athlone	I.	259
29	Cloghanboy West	3	1	24	Westmeath	Brawny	St. Mary's	Athlone	I.	259
29	Cloghan Demesne	624	3	19	King's Co.	Garrycastle	Lusmagh	Parsonstown	I.	137
51	Cloghanduff	536	1	12	Antrim	Upper Belfast	Templepatrick	Antrim	III.	10
111	Cloghane	488	0	17	Cork, W.R.	East Carbery (E.D.)	Ballinadee	Bandon	II.	126
146, 152	Cloghane	392	3	10	Cork, W.R.	West Carbery (W.D.)	Kilmoe	Skull	II.	144
9	Cloghane	481	1	17	Kerry	Clanmaurice	Killury	Listowel	II.	171
34, 35	Cloghane	1,007	1	21d	Kerry	Corkaguiny	Cloghane	Dingle	II.	175
52	Cloghane	141	1	15	Kerry	Corkaguiny	Kildrum	Dingle	II.	177
69,70,79,80	Cloghane	143	2	15	Kerry	Iveragh	Killinane	Cahersiveen	II.	197
67	Cloghane	353	2	15	Kerry	Magunihy	Killaha	Killarney	II.	202

(a) Including 0A. 1R. 36P. River Nore.
(b) Including 8A. 0R. 26P. water.
(c) Including 5A. 3R. 27P. water.
(d) Including 8A. 3R. 20P. water.

No. of Sheet of the Ordnance Survey Maps.	Townlands and Towns.	Area in Statute Acres.	County.	Barony.	Parish.	Poor Law Union in 1857.	Townland Census of 1851, Part I.	
		A.　R.　P.					Vol.	Page
46, 47	Cloghane .	266　2　34	Tipperary, N.R.	Eliogarty	Holycross	Thurles .	II.	270
36	Cloghaneanode	535　0　16	Kerry	Corkaguiny .	Killiney .	Dingle .	II.	178
88, 97	Cloghaneanua .	566　1　31	Kerry	Iveragh .	Prior	Cahersiveen	II.	198
8	Cloghanebane .	171　2　23	Kerry	Clanmaurice .	Ballyheige	Tralee .	II.	167
132	Cloghane Beg .	134　2　11	Cork, W.R.	West Carbery (W.D.)	Caheragh .	Skibbereen	II.	142
87, 96	Cloghanecanuig	132　0　33	Kerry	Iveragh .	Killemlagh	Cahersiveen	II.	196
88, 89	Cloghanecarhan	1,039　2　6	Kerry	Iveragh .	Caher .	Cahersiveen	II.	194
33, 42	Cloghaneduff .	208　2　3	Kerry	Corkaguiny .	Kilmalkedar .	Dingle .	II.	178
8, 14	Cloghaneleesh .	300　0　32	Kerry	Clanmaurice .	Ballyheige	Tralee .	II.	167
22	Cloghaneleskirt	875　1　19	Kerry	Clanmaurice .	Kilflyn .	Tralee .	II.	170
69, 79	Cloghanelinaghan .	1,169　0　21	Kerry	Iveragh .	Caher .	Cahersiveen	II.	194
127	Cloghane Lower	84　2　16	Cork, W.R.	Bear .	Kilnamanagh .	Castletown	II.	125
132	Cloghane More	132　0　9	Cork, W.R.	West Carbery(W.D.)	Caheragh .	Skibbereen	II.	142
22	Cloghanenagleragh .	577　0　38	Kerry	Clanmaurice .	Kilfeighny .	Listowel .	II.	169
36	Cloghanesheskeen	165　3　37	Kerry	Corkaguiny .	Killiney .	Dingle .	II.	178
35	CLOGHANE T. .	—	Kerry	Corkaguiny .	Cloghane .	Dingle .	II.	175
127	Cloghane Upper	238　3　5	Cork, W.R.	Bear .	Kilnamanagh .	Castletown	II.	125
22	Cloghanhill or Coolreagh .	955　3　22	King's Co.	Garrycastle	Gallen .	Parsonstown	I.	136
90	Cloghanlucas North	266　0　39	Mayo	Carra .	Rosslee .	Castlebar .	IV.	130
68	Cloghan More .	472　2　11	Donegal .	Raphoe .	Kilteevoge .	Stranorlar	III.	139
36	Cloghanmore .	322　0　0	King's Co.	Eglish .	Drumcullen .	Parsonstown	I.	134
13	Cloghanmoyle .	116　0　30	Louth .	Ardee .	Clonkeen .	Ardee .	I.	172
8	Cloghanmurry .	283　2　36	Antrim .	Cary .	Ramoan .	Ballycastle	III.	14
15, 16, 23	Cloghannagarragh .	36　3　38	Westmeath	Kilkenny West	Noughaval .	Athlone .	I.	274
90	Cloghannageeragh .	283　0　1	Mayo	Carra .	Rosslee .	Castlebar .	IV.	130
55, 56	Cloghanower .	404　1　34	Galway .	Clare .	Killeany .	Tuam .	IV.	20
46, 47	Cloghanramer .	510　3　28	Down .	Lordship of Newry .	Newry .	Newry .	III.	182
39	Cloghans .	239　1　19	Mayo	Tirawley .	Kilbelfad .	Ballina .	IV.	167
119, 122	Cloghans Beg .	227　2　18	Mayo	Kilmaine .	Kilmainemore .	Ballinrobe	IV.	156
48	Cloghans Glebe .	89　0　30	Roscommon .	Athlone .	Kiltoom .	Athlone .	IV.	183
119	Cloghans More	165　1　15	Mayo	Kilmaine .	Kilmainemore .	Ballinrobe	IV.	156
20, 21	Cloghanstown .	109　2　18	Westmeath	Farbill .	Killucan .	Castletowndelvin	I.	266
22	CLOGHAN T. .	—	King's Co.	Garrycastle	Gallen .	Parsonstown	I.	136
2, 7	Cloghanughera .	366　3　29	Cork, E.R.	Orrery and Kilmore	Shandrum .	Kilmallock	II.	110
19, 20	Cloghanumera .	34　2　28	Westmeath	Moyashel and Magheradernon .	Rathconnell .	Mullingar .	I.	276
79	Cloghapistole .	112　2　38	Tipperary, S.R.	Iffa and Offa East .	Newtownlennan	Carrick on Suir	II.	315
35	Clogharaily Beg	264　1　34	Tipperary, N.R.	Eliogarty .	Loughmoe East	Thurles .	II.	271
35	Clogharaily More	605　0　13	Tipperary, N.R.	Eliogarty .	Loughmoe East	Thurles .	II.	271
79	Cloghard .	89　3　15	Donegal .	Raphoe .	Donaghmore .	Strabane .	III.	137
88	Cloghardeen .	31　1　35	Tipperary, S.R.	Iffa and Offa West .	Ardfinnan .	Clogheen .	II.	316
82, 88	Cloghardeen .	257　2　23a	Tipperary, S.R.	Iffa and Offa West .	Neddans .	Clogheen .	II.	319
57	Cloghaready .	287　2　20	Tipperary, S.R.	Clanwilliam .	Templebredon .	Tipperary .	II.	311
33	Cloghaready North .	14　3　8	Limerick .	Coonagh .	Templebredon .	Tipperary .	II.	236
33	Cloghaready South .	13　2　31	Limerick .	Coonagh .	Templebredon .	Tipperary .	II.	236
34,35,43,44	Clogharee .	1,026　2　29b	Kerry	Corkaguiny .	Cloghane .	Dingle .	II.	175
22, 26	Clogharevan .	300　3　7	Armagh .	Orior Upper .	Killevy .	Newry .	III.	58
85, 97	Clogharevaun .	286　2　7	Galway .	Athenry .	Kiltullagh .	Loughrea .	IV.	5
11	Clogharinka .	580　2　0	Kilkenny .	Fassadinin .	Muckalee .	Castlecomer	I.	90
106	Clogharoasty .	144　1　4	Galway .	Leitrim .	Kilmeen .	Loughrea .	IV.	54
49	Cloghast .	336　0　2	Limerick .	Coshlea .	Ballingarry .	Kilmallock	II.	237
105	Cloghastookeen	169　3　5	Galway .	Dunkellin .	Kilconickny .	Loughrea .	IV.	29
25, 29	Cloghasty North	137　3　4c	Kilkenny .	Gowran .	Ullard .	Thomastown	I.	100
25, 29	Cloghasty South	49　1　11d	Kilkenny .	Gowran .	Ullard .	Thomastown	I.	100
12	Cloghatacka .	190　3　38	Limerick .	Pubblebrien .	Kilkeedy .	Limerick .	II.	252
117	Cloghatanna .	124　2　15	Galway .	Longford .	Lickmolassy .	Portumna .	IV.	60
7, 8	Cloghatanny .	598　3　26	King's Co.	Kilcoursey .	Kilmanaghan .	Tullamore .	I.	141
55, 62, 63	Cloghateana .	364　2　32	Tipperary, S.R.	Middlethird .	Magowry .	Cashel .	II.	328
94	Cloghatisky .	33　1　13	Galway .	Galway .	Rahoon .	Galway .	IV.	37
20	Cloghatrida .	313　2　20	Limerick .	Connello Lower	Rathkeale .	Rathkeale .	II.	229
4, 8	Cloghaun .	331　2　0	Clare .	Corcomroe .	Killilagh .	Ennistimon .	II.	19
35	Cloghaun .	72　2　30	Clare .	Tulla Upper .	Tulla .	Tulla .	II.	41
70	Cloghaun .	11　1　39	Galway .	Clare .	Claregalway .	Galway .	IV.	18
70	Cloghaun .	96　2　16	Galway .	Clare .	Lackagh .	Galway .	IV.	22
114, 115	Cloghaun .	976　1　32	Galway .	Loughrea .	Killinan .	Loughrea .	IV.	64
20	Cloghaun .	353　3　9	Waterford .	Coshmore&Coshbride	Lismore and Mocollop	Lismore .	II.	345
35	Cloghaunard .	208　0　17e	Galway .	Ballynahinch .	Omey .	Clifden .	IV.	14
31	Cloghaun Beg	216　2　6	Clare .	Ibrickan .	Kilfarboy .	Ennistimon .	II.	22
71, 72	Cloghaunbeg .	101　1　10	Clare .	Moyarta .	Kilballyowen .	Kilrush .	II.	31
38,39,47,48	Cloghaun Beg (East)	467　1　25	Clare .	Moyarta .	Kilmacduane .	Kilrush .	II.	32
38, 47	Cloghaun Beg (West)	231　1　32	Clare .	Moyarta .	Kilmacduane .	Kilrush .	II.	32
14, 22	Cloghaundine .	244　3　8	Clare .	Corcomroe .	Kilmacrehy .	Ennistimon .	II.	20

(a) Including 3A. 0R. 26P. water.　　　(c) Including 1A. 2R. 22P. River Barrow.　　　(e) Including 4A. 3R. 12P. water.
(b) Including 29A. 1R. 30P. water.　　　(d) Including 5A. 3R. 26P. River Barrow.

No. of Sheet of the Ordnance Survey Maps	Townlands and Towns.	Area in Statute Acres.			County.	Barony.	Parish.	Poor Law Union in 1857.	Townland Census of 1851, Part I.	
		A.	R.	P.					Vol.	Page
38	Cloghauninchy	455	3	20a	Clare	Ibrickan	Kilmurry	Kilrush	II.	23
31	Cloghaun More	516	2	26	Clare	Ibrickan	Kilfarboy	Ennistimon	II.	22
38, 39, 47	Cloghaun More (East)	588	3	38	Clare	Moyarta	Kilmacduane	Kilrush	II.	32
38, 47	Cloghaun More (West)	559	0	34	Clare	Moyarta	Kilmacduane	Kilrush	II.	32
38	Cloghaunnatinny	271	3	25	Clare	Ibrickan	Kilmurry	Kilrush	II.	23
64, 71, 72	Cloghaunsavaun	573	0	7	Clare	Moyarta	Kilballyowen	Kilrush	II.	31
23, 32	Cloghaviller	345	0	7	Limerick	Smallcounty	Ballinard	Kilmallock	II.	259
30	Cloghavoola	130	2	1	Kerry	Trughanacmy	Ballymacelligott	Tralee	II.	207
16	Cloghbally	154	3	16	Fermanagh	Tirkennedy	Trory	Enniskillen	III.	223
40, 44	Cloghballybeg	545	2	3b	Cavan	Castlerahan	Mullagh	Kells	III.	70
40, 44	Cloghbally Lower	506	1	29	Cavan	Castlerahan	Mullagh	Oldcastle	III.	70
103	Cloghballymore	223	0	34c	Galway	Dunkellin	Killeenavarra	Gort	IV.	30
44	Cloghbally Upper	927	1	8	Cavan	Castlerahan	Mullagh	Oldcastle	III.	70
30, 31	Cloghbane	108	2	15d	Westmeath	Clonlonan	Kilmanaghan	Athlone	I.	262
29	Cloghbog	78	3	9	Waterford	Decies within Drum	Kilmolash	Dungarvan	II.	351
103, 113	Cloghboley	397	0	17e	Galway	Dunkellin	Killeenavarra	Gort	IV.	30
79	Cloghboley	154	0	37	Mayo	Carra	Kildacommoge	Castlebar	IV.	129
7	Cloghboley	183	2	11	Sligo	Carbury	Drumcliff	Sligo	IV.	221
57	Cloghbolie	1,634	0	0f	Donegal	Boylagh	Templecrone	Glenties	III.	115
103, 107	Cloghbolie	156	1	24	Donegal	Tirhugh	Kilbarron	Ballyshannon	III.	148
15	Cloghboola	411	0	33	Cork, E.R.	Duhallow	Kilbrin	Kanturk	II.	72
141	Cloghboola	143	3	6	Cork, W.R.	West Carbery (E.D.)	Abbeystrowry	Skibbereen	II.	136
92, 93	Cloghboola	743	1	2g	Cork, W.R.	West Muskerry	Inchigeelagh	Dunmanway	II.	156
23	Cloghboola	686	2	3	Kerry	Clanmaurice	Kilshenane	Listowel	II.	171
39, 48	Cloghboola Beg	1,213	2	0	Cork, W.R.	West Muskerry	Drishane	Millstreet	II.	156
48	Cloghboola More	524	1	22	Cork, W.R.	West Muskerry	Drishane	Millstreet	II.	156
73	Cloghboy	489	2	15	Donegal	Banagh	Inishkeel	Glenties	III.	106
1, 2	Cloghboy	204	1	23	Tyrone	Strabane Lower	Donaghedy	Strabane	III.	320
32	Cloghbrack	65	0	5	Galway	Killian	Killian	Mountbellew	IV.	44
106	Cloghbrack	64	2	26	Galway	Leitrim	Kilmeen	Loughrea	IV.	54
108	Cloghbrack and Budellagh	166	2	20	Galway	Longford	Donanaghta	Portumna	IV.	58
47, 59	Cloghbrack Far	1,042	3	14h	Mayo	Tirawley	Addergoole	Castlebar	IV.	163
26	Cloghbrack Lower	642	1	24	Galway	Ross	Ross	Oughterard	IV.	73
26	Cloghbrack Middle	110	0	15	Galway	Ross	Ross	Oughterard	IV.	74
47	Cloghbrack Near	798	0	15	Mayo	Tirawley	Addergoole	Castlebar	IV.	163
26	Cloghbrack Upper	1,041	0	0	Galway	Ross	Ross	Oughterard	IV.	74
23	Cloghbreen	125	3	36	Westmeath	Kilkenny West	Drumraney	Ballymahon	I.	273
84	Cloghcarrigeen East	2	2	33	Tipperary, S.R.	Iffa and Offa East	Kilsheelan	Clonmel	II.	314
78, 84	Cloghcarrigeen West	232	0	10i	Tipperary, S.R.	Iffa and Offa East	Kilsheelan	Clonmel	II.	314
27	Cloghcastle	229	3	35	Wicklow	Upper Talbotstown	Baltinglass	Baltinglass	I.	362
6, 7, 11	Cloghchurnel	563	0	23	Longford	Granard	Granard	Granard	I.	156
24, 25	Cloghcor	2,834	1	39j	Antrim	Lower Glenarm	Ardclinis	Larne	III.	21
48	Cloghcor	81	3	31	Donegal	Boylagh	Templecrone	Glenties	III.	115
27	Cloghcor	143	1	34	Fermanagh	Tirkennedy	Derryvullan	Enniskillen	III.	221
7	Cloghcor	89	3	13	Sligo	Carbury	Drumcliff	Sligo	IV.	221
2	Cloghcor	213	2	26	Tyrone	Strabane Lower	Leckpatrick	Strabane	III.	321
4, 8	Cloghcorr	608	1	28	Antrim	Cary	Ballintoy	Ballycastle	III.	12
84	Cloghduff	239	1	4	Cork, E.R.	East Muskerry	Kilbonane	Bandon	II.	104
20	Clogh East	233	0	4	Limerick	Connello Lower	Croagh	Rathkeale	II.	227
2, 5	Clogheder	62	0	39	Dublin	Balrothery East	Balrothery	Balrothery	I.	19
42	Clogheen	456	3	8	Cork, E.R.	Barretts	Mourneabbey	Mallow	II.	50
73, 74	Clogheen	490	1	22	Cork, E.R.	Cork	Currykippane	Cork	II.	64
25	Clogheen	442	0	12	Cork, E.R.	Fermoy	Caherduggan	Mallow	II.	77
111	Clogheen	249	0	7	Cork, E.R.	Kinalea	Leighmoney	Kinsale	II.	96
21	Clogheen	386	2	27	Kildare	Offaly West	Lackagh	Athy	I.	73
26	Clogheen	525	0	3	Kildare	Offaly West	Monasterevin	Athy	I.	73
5	Clogheen	291	1	11	Waterford	Glenahiry	Kilronan	Clonmel	II.	365
110	Clogheenavodig	70	2	38	Cork, W.R.	East Carbery (E.D.)	Ballymodan	Bandon	II.	126
97	Clogheenduane	447	2	8	Cork, E.R.	Kinalea	Timplemichael	Kinsale	II.	96
87	Clogheen Market	320	0	25	Tipperary, S.R.	Iffa and Offa West	Shanrahan	Clogheen	II.	319
62, 63	Clogheennilcon	581	2	21	Cork, E.R.	East Muskerry	Garrycloyne	Cork	II.	103
87	CLOGHEEN T.	—			Tipperary, S.R.	Iffa and Offa West	Shanrahan	Clogheen	II.	320
32	Clogher	595	0	1	Antrim	Lower Toome	Kirkinriola	Ballymena	III.	32
64	Clogher	231	3	12	Antrim	Upper Massereene	Derryaghy	Lisburn	III.	30
16	Clogher	495	0	29	Clare	Corcomroe	Kilfenora	Corrofin	II.	19
27, 35, 36	Clogher	1,068	2	11k	Clare	Tulla Upper	Kilnoe	Tulla	II.	40
18	Clogher	375	2	7	Cork, E.R.	Fermoy	Templeroan	Mallow	II.	82
102, 115	Clogher	961	3	37	Cork, W.R.	Bear	Kilcatherine	Castletown	II.	124
93	Clogher	442	1	10	Cork, W.R.	East Carbery (W.D.)	Inchigeelagh	Dunmanway	II.	132
147	Clogher	33	2	4	Cork, W.R.	West Carbery (W.D.)	Kilmoe	Skull	II.	144
94, 95	Clogher	1,281	2	35	Donegal	Tirhugh	Donegal	Donegal	III.	145
14, 15	Clogher	310	3	16	Down	Castlereagh Upper	Drumbo	Lisburn	III.	164

(a) Including 21A. 1R. 27P. water.
(b) Including 33A. 3R. 6P. water.
(c) Including 26A. 1R. 2P. water.
(d) Including 10A. 1R. 4P. water.

(e) Including 4A. 0R. 30P. water.
(f) Including 127A. 1R. 10P. water.
(g) Including 7A. 0R. 3P. water.
(h) Including 4A. 1R. 32P. water.

(i) Including 2A. 2R. 0P. water.
(j) Including 13A. 1R. 32P. water.
(k) Including 60A. 2R. 16P. water.

No. of Sheet of the Ordnance Survey Maps.	Townlands and Towns.	Area in Statute Acres.	County.	Barony.	Parish.	Poor Law Union in 1857.	Townland Census of 1851, Part I. Vol.	Page
		A. R. P.						
38	Clogher	376 2 21a	Down	Lecale Upper	Down	Downpatrick	III.	180
21	Clogher	531 2 13	Down	Lower Iveagh,Up. pt.	Hillsborough	Lisburn	III.	169
20	Clogher	145 0 35	Down	Lower Iveagh,Up. pt.	Magheralin	Lurgan	III.	170
43	Clogher	32 0 35	Fermanagh	Coole	Drummully	Clones	III.	199
27	Clogher	174 2 23	Galway	Ross	Cong	Oughterard	IV.	73
20	Clogher	156 0 13	Kerry	Clanmaurice	Kilmoyly	Tralee	II.	171
15, 16	Clogher	296 3 11	Kerry	Clanmaurice	Kiltomy	Listowel	II.	172
42	Clogher	368 3 30	Kerry	Corkaguiny	Dunurlin	Dingle	II.	176
30	Clogher	41 2 0	Kerry	Trughanacmy	Ballymacelligott	Tralee	II.	207
22	Clogher	299 3 7	Leitrim	Carrigallen	Oughteragh	Bawnboy	IV.	92
27, 31	Clogher	126 2 35	Leitrim	Leitrim	Kiltoghert	Cark. on Shannon	IV.	101
15	Clogher	88 2 12	Limerick	Coonagh	Doon	Tipperary	II.	234
22	Clogher	301 0 39	Louth	Ferrard	Clogher	Drogheda	I.	180
77	Clogher	197 3 15b	Mayo	Burrishoole	Islandeady	Westport	IV.	121
100	Clogher	303 0 23	Mayo	Carra	Burriscarra	Castlebar	IV.	127
70, 79	Clogher	297 3 32	Mayo	Carra	Turlough	Castlebar	IV.	130
24	Clogher	395 1 11	Mayo	Erris	Kilmore	Belmullet	IV.	145
111	Clogher	406 2 10	Mayo	Kilmaine	Kilcommon	Ballinrobe	IV.	154
19, 24	Clogher	286 1 6	Monaghan	Cremorne	Ballybay	Castleblayney	III.	259
11,12,17,18	Clogher	182 1 27	Roscommon	Ballintober North	Kilmore	Cark. on Shannon	IV.	187
35	Clogher	135 0 13	Roscommon	Ballymoe	Cloonygormican	Roscommon	IV.	191
10	Clogher	275 1 4c	Roscommon	Boyle	Estersnow	Boyle	IV.	195
44, 46	Clogher	1,025 0 38	Sligo	Coolavin	Kilcolman	Boyle	IV.	223
46	Clogher	455 1 0	Tipperary, S.R.	Kilnamanagh Lower	Clogher	Cashel	II.	322
16	Clogher	274 0 4d	Westmeath	Kilkenny West	Noughaval	Ballymahon	I.	274
53	Cloghera	278 0 30	Clare	Tulla Lower	O'Briensbridge	Limerick	II.	38
82	Cloghera Beg	885 1 33e	Kerry	Dunkerron North	Knockane	Cahersiveen	II.	181
58, 66	Clogherachullion	1,508 1 18	Donegal	Boylagh	Inishkeel	Glenties	III.	112
82	Cloghera More	794 3 14f	Kerry	Dunkerron North	Knockane	Kenmare	II.	181
3, 7	Clogher Anderson	47 1 9	Antrim	Cary	Billy	Coleraine	III.	12
108,109,111	Clogherane	699 3 37g	Kerry	Glanarought	Tuosist	Kenmare	II.	188
31	Clogherane	61 1 29	Waterford	Decies without Drum	Kilrush	Dungarvan	II.	358
83, 92	Clogheravaddy	251 3 24	Donegal	Banagh	Inver	Donegal	III.	107
101	Clogher Beg	126 3 26	Mayo	Clanmorris	Tagheen	Claremorris	IV.	135
16, 22	Clogher Beg	205 0 12	Roscommon	Roscommon	Elphin	Strokestown	IV.	209
15	Clogher Beg	108 0 23	Sligo	Carbury	Calry	Sligo	IV.	220
20	Clogherbog	315 2 34h	Fermanagh	Magheraboy	Boho	Enniskillen	III.	209
44	Clogherboy	587 0 38	Galway	Clare	Killererin	Tuam	IV.	21
25	Clogherboy	12 3 5	Meath	Lower Navan	Navan	Navan	I.	215
29	Clogherbrien	318 1 20	Kerry	Trughanacmy	Clogherbrien	Tralee	II.	209
29, 30	Clogherclemin	204 0 19	Kerry	Trughanacmy	Ballymacelligott	Tralee	II.	207
58, 65, 66	Cloghercor	2,914 2 19	Donegal	Boylagh	Inishkeel	Glenties	III.	112
18, 26	Clogher Demesne	108 1 24	Cork, E.R.	Fermoy	Templeroan	Mallow	II.	82
58,59,64,65	Clogher Demesne	566 3 22i	Tyrone	Clogher	Clogher	Clogher	III.	292
40,41,48,49	Clogherdillure	200 3 5j	Donegal	Boylagh	Templecrone	Glenties	III.	115
101	Clogherduff	52 1 24	Mayo	Clanmorris	Tagheen	Claremorris	IV.	136
66,67,75,76	Clogher East	1,444 3 12	Donegal	Boylagh	Inishkeel	Glenties	III.	112
39	Clogher East	695 3 38	Limerick	Coshma	Dromin	Kilmallock	II.	243
66, 74	Cloghereen Lower	256 0 28	Kerry	Magunihy	Killarney	Killarney	II.	203
74	Cloghereen Upper	270 3 28	Kerry	Magunihy	Killarney	Killarney	II.	203
39, 40	Cloghergoole	310 0 39	Cavan	Castlerahan	Mullagh	Oldcastle	III.	70
32	Clogher Lower	244 1 36	Roscommon	Castlereagh	Kiltullagh	Castlereagh	IV.	201
66	Cloghermore	1,958 0 25k	Galway	Moycullen	Kilcummin	Oughterard	IV.	66
30, 39	Cloghermore	62 3 22	Kerry	Trughanacmy	Ballymacelligott	Tralee	II.	207
101	Clogher More	244 3 36	Mayo	Clanmorris	Tagheen	Claremorris	IV.	136
16, 22	Clogher More	320 1 17	Roscommon	Roscommon	Elphin	Strokestown	IV.	209
15	Clogher More	292 0 14l	Sligo	Carbury	Calry	Sligo	IV.	220
15	Cloghernagh	272 0 31	Donegal	Kilmacrenan	Clondahorky	Dunfanaghy	III.	123
12	Cloghernagh	156 1 2	Monaghan	Dartree	Killeevan	Monaghan	III.	267
6	Cloghernagh	223 2 14m	Monaghan	Trough	Donagh	Monaghan	III.	281
58	Cloghernagore	1,619 2 38	Donegal	Boylagh	Inishkeel	Glenties	III.	112
79,80,91,92	Cloghernagun	2,324 1 16n	Galway	Moycullen	Killannin	Galway	IV.	69
80, 92	Cloghernalaura	716 3 21o	Galway	Moycullen	Killannin	Galway	IV.	69
73	Cloghernoosh	1,149 3 4p	Kerry	Dunkerron North	Knockane	Killarney	II.	181
3, 7	Clogher North	275 1 34	Antrim	Cary	Billy	Coleraine	III.	12
61	Clogherny	182 0 14q	Tyrone	Dungannon Middle	Clonfeacle	Dungannon	III.	299
6, 11	Clogherny	819 2 6	Tyrone	Strabane Lower	Donaghedy	Gortin	III.	320
12	Clogherny Glebe	973 0 21r	Tyrone	Strabane Upper	Bodoney Upper	Gortin	III.	324
43, 44	Clogherny Glebe Lower	159 3 12	Tyrone	Omagh East	Clogherny	Omagh	III.	310
44, 52	Clogherny Glebe Upper	766 3 4	Tyrone	Omagh East	Clogherny	Omagh	III.	310
79, 90	Clogherowan	145 0 26	Mayo	Carra	Drum	Castlebar	IV.	128

(a) Including 1A. 2R. 16P. water.
(b) Including 18A. 0R. 22P. water.
(c) Including 31A. 2R. 15P. water.
(d) Including 0A. 2R. 32P. water.
(e) Including 2A. 0R. 0P. water.
(f) Including 3A. 1R. 32P. water.
(g) Including 55A. 3R. 38P. water.
(h) Including 17A. 0R. 9P. water.
(i) Including 1A. 3R. 8P. water.
(j) Including 27A. 0R. 38P. water.
(k) Including 124A. 0R. 25P. water.
(l) Including 15A. 0R. 26P. water.
(m) Including 7A. 2R. 19P. water.
(n) Including 182A. 3R. 22P. water.
(o) Including 40A. 0R. 27P. water.
(p) Including 47A. 0R. 23P. water.
(q) Including 1A. 0R. 1P. water.
(r) Including 9A. 1R. 6P. water.

No. of Sheet of the Ordnance Survey Maps.	Townlands and Towns.	Area in Statute Acres.	County.	Barony.	Parish.	Poor Law Union in 1857.	Townland Census of 1851, Part I.	
		A. R. P.					Vol.	Page
15	Clogherrevagh	80 1 19	Sligo	Carbury	Calry	Sligo	IV.	220
13	Clogher and Rinn	261 0 23	Longford	Longford	Killashee	Longford	I.	158
29	Cloghers	192 1 11	Kerry	Trughanacmy	Annagh	Tralee	II.	205
3, 7	Clogher South	304 0 34	Antrim	Cary	Billy	Coleraine	III.	12
33	Clogherstown	43 2 8	Meath	Upper Duleek	Clonalvy	Drogheda	I.	197
58, 59, 64	Clogher Tenements	174 3 17	Tyrone	Clogher	Clogher	Clogher	III.	292
22	CLOGHER T.	—	Louth	Ferrard	Clogher	Drogheda	I.	180
58, 59	CLOGHER T.	—	Tyrone	Clogher	Clogher	Clogher	III.	293
32	Clogher Upper	452 3 32	Roscommon	Castlereagh	Kiltullagh	Castlereagh	IV.	201
76,77,85,86	Cloghervaddy	1,803 0 6	Donegal	Raphoe	Kilteevoge	Stranorlar	III.	139
64	Clogher West	241 3 24a	Donegal	Boylagh	Inishkeel	Glenties	III.	112
39	Clogher West	369 2 3	Limerick	Coshma	Dromin	Kilmallock	II.	243
47	Cloghfin	357 3 28	Antrim	Lower Belfast	Islandmagee	Larne	III.	8
8, 12	Cloghfin	190 3 30	Armagh	Armagh	Eglish	Armagh	III.	44
17	Cloghfin	253 2 16	Donegal	Kilmacrenan	Clondavaddog	Milford	III.	124
70	Cloghfin	162 3 28	Donegal	Raphoe	Clonleigh	Strabane	III.	134
55	Cloghfin	364 2 30	Donegal	Raphoe	Taughboyne	Londonderry	III.	143
79	Cloghfin	227 3 13b	Donegal	Raphoe	Urney	Strabane	III.	144
3, 6	Cloghfin	287 3 23	Monaghan	Trough	Errigal Trough	Clogher	III.	283
26, 27	Cloghfin	255 0 36	Sligo	Tirerrill	Kilmacallan	Sligo	IV.	239
38, 39	Cloghfin	97 0 27	Tyrone	Dungannon Middle	Donaghenry	Cookstown	III.	301
28, 37	Cloghfin	197 1 10	Tyrone	Dungannon Upper	Kildress	Cookstown	III.	308
44, 45	Cloghfin	1,815 0 20	Tyrone	Omagh East	Termonmaguirk	Omagh	III.	314
35	Cloghfin	811 2 33c	Tyrone	Strabane Upper	Cappagh	Omagh	III.	325
126, 127	Cloghfune	732 0 17	Cork, W.R.	Bear	Kilnamanagh	Castletown	II.	125
72, 82	Cloghfune	265 2 12	Kerry	Dunkerron North	Knockane	Cahersiveen	II.	181
74	Cloghfune	242 0 21	Kerry	Magunihy	Killarney	Killarney	II.	203
23, 27	Cloghgaldanagh	199 0 21	Antrim	Kilconway	Dunaghy	Ballymena	III.	25
22	Cloghgarret Glebe	62 2 20	Kildare	Offaly East	Kildare	Naas	I.	70
15, 20	Cloghglass	31 0 16	Antrim	Lower Glenarm	Layd	Ballycastle	III.	22
40	Cloghglass	129 0 21d	Donegal	Boylagh	Templecrone	Glenties	III.	115
19	Cloghglass or Retreat	406 3 23	Antrim	Lower Glenarm	Layd	Ballycastle	III.	23
61, 69	Cloghgore	64 3 11	Donegal	Raphoe	Convoy	Stranorlar	III.	136
135, 136	Cloghgriffin	286 1 24	Cork, W.R.	Ibane and Barryroe	Templequinlan	Clonakilty	II.	151
33	Cloghilawarreela	153 3 1	Limerick	Coonagh	Templebredon	Tipperary	II.	236
38	Cloghinarney	443 3 23	Antrim	Lower Antrim	Racavan	Ballymena	III.	4
27, 33	Cloghinch	29 3 26	Tipperary, N.R.	Kilnamanagh Upper	Glenkeen	Thurles	II.	278
27, 33	Cloghinch	446 3 29	Tipperary, N.R.	Upper Ormond	Templederry	Nenagh	II.	293
28,29,31,32	Cloghinny	327 1 34	Armagh	Orior Upper	Forkill	Newry	III.	57
22	Cloghinny	283 1 29	Armagh	Orior Upper	Killevy	Newry	III.	58
11, 16	Cloghjordanpark	432 1 3	Tipperary, N.R.	Lower Ormond	Modreeny	Borrisokane	II.	286
16	CLOGHJORDAN T.	—	Tipperary, N.R.	Lower Ormond	Modreeny	Borrisokane	II.	287
13	Cloghkeating	456 3 12	Limerick	Pubblebrien	Mungret	Limerick	II.	254
10	Cloghkeating	258 3 12	Tipperary, N.R.	Lower Ormond	Modreeny	Borrisokane	II.	286
52	Cloghlea	195 3 2	Clare	Bunratty Lower	Feenagh	Ennis	II.	4
18	Cloghlea	94 2 0	Louth	Ferrard	Rathdrumin	Drogheda	I.	182
19	Cloghleafin	520 1 23	Cork, E.R.	Condons&Clangibbon	Kilgullane	Mitchelstown	II.	61
19	Cloghleafin	161 1 24	Cork, E.R.	Condons&Clangibbon	Marshalstown	Mitchelstown	II.	63
33	Cloghleagh	118 3 24	Clare	Islands	Drumcliff	Ennis	II.	29
47	Cloghleagh	119 0 30	Kerry	Trughanacmy	Kiltallagh	Tralee	II.	212
2, 5, 6	Cloghleagh	700 3 17	Wicklow	Lower Talbotstown	Kilbride	Naas	I.	361
7	Cloghleigh	259 3 31	Tipperary, N.R.	Lower Ormond	Aglishcloghane	Borrisokane	II.	281
20, 26	Cloghleigh	62 2 11	Tipperary, N.R.	Owney and Arra	Burgesbeg	Nenagh	II.	294
60, 68	Cloghleigh	1,753 3 29	Tipperary, S.R.	Clanwilliam	Relickmurry & Athassel	Tipperary	II.	310
65	Cloghlin	76 0 2	Tyrone	Clogher	Clogher	Clogher	III.	292
30	Cloghlough	228 2 26	Leitrim	Carrigallen	Carrigallen	Mohill	IV.	89
27	Clogh Lower	294 2 26	Wicklow	Upper Talbotstown	Baltinglass	Baltinglass	I.	362
25	Cloghlucas North	292 0 27	Cork, E.R.	Fermoy	Mallow	Mallow	II.	81
25, 33	Cloghlucas South	269 0 22	Cork, E.R.	Fermoy	Mallow	Mallow	II.	81
21, 29	Cloghmackirkeam	251 0 0	Kerry	Trughanacmy	Clogherbrien	Tralee	II.	209
3, 6	Cloghmacoo	394 1 15	Meath	Morgallion	Nobber	Kells	I.	210
83	Cloghmacow	499 0 28	Cork, W.R.	West Muskerry	Kilmurry	Macroom	II.	159
110	Cloghmacsimon	258 1 18	Cork, W.R.	East Carbery (E.D.)	Ballymodan	Bandon	II.	126
47	Cloghmartin	391 3 39	Tipperary, N.R.	Eliogarty	Fertiana	Thurles	II.	269
4, 7	Cloghmeen	652 3 15	Leitrim	Rosclogher	Killasnet	Manorhamilton	IV.	109
23	Clogh Mills	115 2 9	Antrim	Kilconway	Killagan	Ballymoney	III.	27
23	CLOGHMILLS T.	—	Antrim	Kilconway {	Killagan	Ballymena {	III.	27
			Antrim	Kilconway {	Grange of Dundermot	Ballymoney }	III.	27
					Killagan	Ballymoney		
35, 41	Cloghmine	233 0 1	Sligo	Tirerrill	Kilmactranny	Boyle	IV.	240
36	Cloghmore	100 1 15	Fermanagh	Clankelly	Clones	Clones	III.	195
65	Cloghmore	168 1 4	Mayo	Burrishoole	Achill	Newport	IV.	117
91	Cloghmore North	1,091 3 1e	Galway	Moycullen	Killannin	Galway	IV.	69
91	Cloghmore South	284 0 27f	Galway	Moycullen	Killannin	Galway	IV.	69

(a) Including 6A. 2R. 12P. water.
(b) Including 10A. 1R. 34P. water.

(c) Including 5A. 2R. 35P. water.
(d) Including 6A. 1R. 38P. water.

(e) Including 37A. 2R. 15P. water.
(f) Including 14A. 1R. 38P. water.

No. of Sheet of the Ordnance Survey Maps.	Townlands and Towns.	Area in Statute Acres. A. R. P.	County.	Barony.	Parish.	Poor Law Union in 1857.	Townland Census of 1851, Part I. Vol.	Page
42	Cloghmoyle	233 0 1	King's Co.	Clonlisk	Shinrone	Roscrea	I.	131
123	Cloghmoyne	706 2 28	Mayo	Kilmaine	Shrule	Ballinrobe	IV.	158
7, 12	Cloghna	792 3 38a	Carlow	Carlow	Cloydagh	Carlow	I.	1
14	Cloghnadromin	554 0 34	Limerick	Clanwilliam	Abington	Limerick	II.	221
27	Cloghnagaune	144 1 12	Wicklow	Upper Talbotstown	Kilranelagh	Baltinglass	I.	364
123, 129	Cloghnakeava	184 2 7	Galway	Kiltartan	Beagh	Gort	IV.	46
123	Cloghnakeava	75 0 11	Galway	Kiltartan	Kilbeacanty	Gort	IV.	47
16	Cloghnamallaght	189 2 35	Wexford	Gorey	Monamolin	Gorey	I.	321
22, 31	Cloghnamanagh	94 3 30	Limerick	Smallcounty	Fedamore	Croom	II.	259
6	Cloghnart	96 1 26	Monaghan	Trough	Donagh	Monaghan	III.	281
44	Cloghnashade	249 2 33b	Roscommon	Athlone	Tisrara	Roscommon	IV.	185
43, 57	Clogh North	198 0 36	Galway	Clare	Cummer	Tuam	IV.	18
48	Cloghog	282 1 1	Londonderry	Loughinsholin	Derryloran	Magherafelt	III.	240
47	Cloghog	205 0 19	Tyrone	Dungannon Middle	Clonoe	Dungannon	III.	300
27,28,30,31	Cloghoge	929 1 6	Armagh	Fews Upper	Creggan	Castleblayney	III.	48
13,14,17,18	Cloghoge	229 2 29	Armagh	Orior Lower	Ballymore	Banbridge	III.	55
26, 29	Cloghoge	383 3 22c	Armagh	Orior Upper	Killevy	Newry	III.	58
7	Cloghoge	152 3 9	Cavan	Tullyhaw	Kinawley	Bawnboy	III.	93
17	Cloghoge	162 1 1	Fermanagh	Tirkennedy	Enniskillen	Enniskillen	III.	221
18, 19	Cloghoge	280 1 14	Kilkenny	Crannagh	Ballycallan	Kilkenny	I.	84
30	Cloghoge	189 2 10	Queen's Co.	Cullenagh	Dysartgallen	Abbeyleix	I.	239
36	Cloghoge	32 2 29	Wicklow	Arklow	Dunganstown	Rathdrum	I.	343
11,12,17,18	Cloghoge	6,583 0 38d	Wicklow	Ballinacor North	Derrylossary	Rathdrum	I.	346
34, 40	Cloghoge Lower	374 3 17	Sligo	Tirerrill	Aghanagh	Boyle	IV.	237
28	Cloghoge and Tievadinna	302 2 38e	Monaghan	Farney	Donaghmoyne	Carrickmacross	III.	269
34, 40	Cloghoge Upper	348 2 19	Sligo	Tirerrill	Aghanagh	Boyle	IV.	237
1, 2	Cloghogle	376 0 39	Tyrone	Strabane Lower	Donaghedy	Strabane	III.	320
17	Cloghogle or Glenknock	560 0 28f	Tyrone	Strabane Lower	Ardstraw	Gortin	III.	319
34	Cloghog Lower	238 0 28	Tyrone	Omagh East	Drumragh	Omagh	III.	312
37	Cloghogue	778 0 6	Antrim	Upper Toome	Drummaul	Ballymena	III.	34
42	Cloghogue	211 3 30	Antrim	Upper Toome	Duneane	Ballymena	III.	34
34	Cloghog Upper	162 2 17	Tyrone	Omagh East	Drumragh	Omagh	III.	312
14	Cloghole	186 3 5g	Londonderry	Tirkeeran	Faughanvale	Londonderry	III.	250
27, 33	Cloghonan	481 3 1	Tipperary, N.R.	Upper Ormond	Templederry	Nenagh	II.	293
43, 52	Cloghoolia	424 1 18h	Clare	Tulla Lower	Clonlea	Limerick	II.	34
107, 108	Cloghore	480 1 11i	Donegal	Tirhugh	Kilbarron	Ballyshannon	III.	148
20, 21	Cloghore or Greerstown	182 2 19	Londonderry	Tirkeeran	Clondermot	Londonderry	III.	247
62, 73	Cloghphilip	564 3 21	Cork, E.R.	East Muskerry	Matehy	Cork	II.	105
11, 15	Cloghpook	435 3 18	Kilkenny	Gowran	Kilmadum	Kilkenny	I.	97
9, 14	Cloghprior	270 3 28j	Tipperary, N.R.	Lower Ormond	Cloghprior	Borrisokane	II.	282
43, 44	Cloghram	756 0 32	Down	Kinelarty	Kilmegan	Downpatrick	III.	176
13, 14	Cloghran	95 3 22	Dublin	Castleknock	Cloghran	Dublin North	I.	24
11,12,14,15	Cloghran	604 2 12k	Dublin	Coolock	Cloghran	Balrothery	I.	26
35	Cloghraun	202 0 3	Waterford	Decies within Drum	Ardmore	Youghal	II.	350
26	Cloghreagh	225 0 5	Armagh	Orior Upper	Killevy	Newry	III.	58
3, 6	Cloghreagh	1,311 1 14	Meath	Morgallion	Ardagh	Kells	I.	209
12	Cloghristick	472 2 13l	Carlow	Carlow	Cloydagh	Carlow	I.	1
12	Cloghristick	28 0 23	Carlow	Carlow	Killerrig	Carlow	I.	2
104	Cloghroak	345 2 39	Galway	Dunkellin	Ardrahan	Loughrea	IV.	26
62, 73	Cloghroe	690 1 0	Cork, E.R.	East Muskerry	Matehy	Cork	II.	105
45	Cloghroe	276 2 1	Donegal	Kilmacrenan	Kilmacrenan	Letterkenny	III.	129
69	Cloghroe	524 2 2	Donegal	Raphoe	Convoy	Stranorlar	III.	136
19, 20	Cloghs	1,349 3 18	Antrim	Lower Glenarm	Layd	Ballycastle	III.	22
93	Cloghscoltia	204 1 28m	Galway	Galway	Rahoon	Galway	IV.	37
28, 29	Cloghscregg	1,032 2 34	Kilkenny	Gowran	Kilfane	Thomastown	I.	96
35	Cloghskelt	1,034 2 6	Down	Upper Iveagh, Lr. pt.	Drumgooland	Banbridge	III.	172
43, 57	Clogh South	243 2 6	Galway	Clare	Cummer	Tuam	IV.	18
17, 18	Cloghstuckagh	111 3 13	Cavan	Tullygarvey	Drumgoon	Cootehill	III.	88
22	Cloghtate	40 0 23	Fermanagh	Tirkennedy	Enniskillen	Enniskillen	III.	221
22, 23	Cloghtogle	355 0 15n	Fermanagh	Tirkennedy	Enniskillen	Enniskillen	III.	221
2	CLOGH T.		Kilkenny	Fassadinin	Castlecomer	Castlecomer	I.	89
36, 41	Cloghulatagh	273 2 37	Wexford	Shelmaliere West	Taghmon	Wexford	I.	334
26, 27	Clogh Upper	176 1 30	Wicklow	Upper Talbotstown	Baltinglass	Baltinglass	I.	362
28, 31	Cloghvally Lower	215 1 6	Monaghan	Farney	Magheross	Carrickmacross	III.	273
31	Cloghvally Upper	249 3 13	Monaghan	Farney	Magheross	Carrickmacross	III.	273
124, 125	Cloghvoley	900 1 25	Galway	Leitrim	Ballynakill	Loughrea	IV.	51
81	Cloghvoley	492 0 15o	Mayo	Costello	Aghamore	Swineford	IV.	137
98, 99	Cloghvoola	1,733 1 22p	Kerry	Iveragh	Dromod	Cahersiveen	II.	194
34	Cloghvoolia North	1,313 0 38	Cork, E.R.	Fermoy	Monanimy	Mallow	II.	81
34, 43	Cloghvoolia South	758 1 18	Cork, E.R.	Fermoy	Monanimy	Mallow	II.	81
4, 12, 13	Cloghvoula	1,249 0 24	Cork, E.R.	Duhallow	Kilmeen	Kanturk	II.	72

(a) Including 13A. 1R. 0P. River Barrow.
(b) Including 10A. 2R. 8P. water.
(c) Including 6A. 3R. 0P. water.
(d) {Including 38A. 1R. 29P. Lough Dan. / Including 54A. 2R. 29P. Lough Tay.}
(e) Including 11A. 0R. 16P. water.

(f) Including 0A. 2R. 39P. water.
(g) Including 9A. 1R. 33P. water.
(h) Including 1A. 1R. 6P. water.
(i) Including 30A. 2R. 22P. water.
(j) Including 7A. 1R. 8P. water.
(k) Including 12A. 1R. 30P. detached portion.

(l) Including 14A. 0R. 32P. River Barrow.
(m) Including 20A. 0R. 26P. water.
(n) Including 11A. 2R. 22P. water.
(o) Including 49A. 2R. 22P. water.
(p) Including 57A. 3R. 30P. water.

No. of Sheet of the Ordnance Survey Maps.	Townlands and Towns.	Area in Statute Acres. A. R. P.	County.	Barony.	Parish.	Poor Law Union in 1857.	Townland Census of 1851. Part I. Vol.	Page
20	Clogh West	298 3 6	Limerick	Connello Lower	Croagh	Rathkeale	II.	227
25	Cloghy	224 1 5	Down	Ards Upper	Castleboy	Downpatrick	III.	160
31, 32	Cloghy	222 3 31	Down	Lecale Lower	Kilclief	Downpatrick	III.	179
15	Cloghy East	34 1 29	Antrim	Lower Glenarm	Layd	Ballycastle	III.	22
14	Cloghy West	202 0 19	Antrim	Lower Glenarm	Layd	Ballycastle	III.	22
31, 35	Clogorrow	358 3 35	Kildare	Narragh&RebanWest	Kilberry	Athy	I.	67
6, 7	Clogrenan	1,485 1 34a	Carlow	Idrone West	Cloydagh	Carlow	I.	9
37	Clogrenan	788 0 28b	Queen's Co.	Slievemargy	Cloydagh	Carlow	I.	245
37	Clogrenan	81 2 35c	Queen's Co.	Slievemargy	Killeshin	Carlow	I.	245
9	Clohamon	350 3 29d	Wexford	Scarawalsh	Kilrush	Enniscorthy	I.	324
9	CLOHAMON T.	—	Wexford	Scarawalsh	Kilrush	Enniscorthy	I.	324
8	Clohaskin	254 3 25	Tipperary, N.R.	Lower Ormond	Loughkeen	Parsonstown	II.	286
25	Clohass	266 0 36	Wexford	Bantry	Templescoby	Enniscorthy	I.	303
19, 25	Cloheden	264 3 10	Wexford	Bantry	Rossdroit	Enniscorthy	I.	301
135	Cloheen	80 1 29	Cork, W.R.	East Carbery (E.D.)	Island	Clonakilty	II.	128
135	Cloheen	360 3 6	Cork, W.R.	East Carbery (E.D.)	Kilgarriff	Clonakilty	II.	128
69	Cloheena	648 3 14	Cork, W.R.	West Muskerry	Kilnamartry	Macroom	II.	159
74, 80, 81	Cloheenafishoge	2,077 0 6	Tipperary, S.R.	Iffa and Offa West	Tubbrid	Clogheen	II.	320
74	Clohernagh	505 2 4	Tipperary, S.R.	Clanwilliam	Templeneiry	Tipperary	II.	311
29	Clohernagh	940 2 10	Wicklow	Ballinacor South	Ballinacor	Rathdrum	I.	348
20	Clohoge	44 2 22	Kilkenny	Gowran	Clara	Kilkenny	I.	94
47	Clohoge	316 1 8	Tipperary, N.R.	Eliogarty	Fertiana	Cashel	II.	269
15, 16	Clologe	250 2 17	Wexford	Scarawalsh	Toome	Gorey	I.	326
16	Clologe Little	96 3 16	Wexford	Scarawalsh	Kilbride	Gorey	I.	323
15, 16	Clologe Lower	217 1 10	Wexford	Scarawalsh	Kilbride	Enniscorthy	I.	323
16	Clologe Upper	120 1 30	Wexford	Scarawalsh	Kilbride	Gorey	I.	323
20	Clolourish	21 1 21	Wexford	Scarawalsh	Clone	Enniscorthy	I.	322
20	Clolourish	17 3 13	Wexford	Scarawalsh	Templeshannon	Enniscorthy	I.	326
9, 12, 13	Clomantagh Lower	544 1 6	Kilkenny	Crannagh	Clomantagh	Urlingford	I.	85
8, 9, 12, 13	Clomantagh (Mt. Garret)	981 0 26	Kilkenny	Crannagh	Clomantagh	Urlingford	I.	85
12, 13	Clomantagh Upper	209 0 19	Kilkenny	Crannagh	Clomantagh	Urlingford	I.	85
19	Clomoney	233 3 21e	Carlow	Idrone East	Ballyellin	Carlow	I.	6
19	Clomoney	133 0 17	Carlow	Idrone East	Clonygoose	Carlow	I.	6
19	Clomoney	149 1 9f	Carlow	Idrone East	Lorum	Carlow	I.	8
5, 6	Clonaboy	272 1 18	Westmeath	Moygoish	Rathaspick	Mullingar	I.	280
15, 16	Clonabreany	627 0 9	Meath	Fore	Diamor	Oldcastle	I.	200
14	Clonachona or Broomville	236 2 39	Carlow	Forth	Ardoyne	Carlow	I.	3
48, 49	Clonachullion	2,698 1 26	Down	Upper Iveagh, Lr. pt.	Kilcoo	Kilkeel	III.	173
70, 77	Clonacody	266 0 30	Tipperary, S.R.	Middlethird	Baptistgrange	Cashel	II.	325
1	Clonacullan	73 3 22	Monaghan	Trough	Errigal Trough	Clogher	III.	283
23	Clonacullion	161 2 23	Monaghan	Cremorne	Aghnamullen	Cootehill	III.	257
16	Clonacur	70 0 16	Carlow	Idrone East	Dunleckny	Carlow	I.	6
19, 27	Clonad	896 1 33	King's Co.	Coolestown	Clonsast	Edenderry	I.	132
24, 25	Clonad	537 2 29	King's Co.	Geashill	Geashill	Tullamore	I.	140
18	Clonad	1,302 1 13	King's Co.	Lower Philipstown	Killaderry	Tullamore	I.	142
12, 17	Clonadacasey	649 2 15	Queen's Co.	Maryborough West	Clonenagh&Clonagheen	Abbeyleix	I.	242
17, 18	Clonaddadoran	1,893 3 15	Queen's Co.	Maryborough West	Clonenagh&Clonagheen	Abbeyleix	I.	242
6	Clonaderg	1,429 3 35	King's Co.	Garrycastle	Clonmacnoise	Parsonstown	I.	135
3, 4, 8	Clonagam	692 1 12	Waterford	Upperthird	Clonagam	Carrick on Suir	II.	369
45	Clonagannagh	549 0 37	King's Co.	Clonlisk	Dunkerrin	Roscrea	I.	130
11	Clonagara	147 2 10	Meath	Lower Kells	Newtown	Kells	I.	204
35	Clonageera	110 2 18	Queen's Co.	Clarmallagh	Durrow	Abbeyleix	I.	237
3	Clonagh	694 1 14	Kildare	Carbury	Cadamstown	Edenderry	I.	51
4, 9	Clonagh	461 0 29	Kildare	Carbury	Dunfierth	Edenderry	I.	52
10	Clonagh	251 0 21	Kildare	North Salt	Taghadoe	Celbridge	I.	76
10	Clonagh	463 0 2	King's Co.	Lower Philipstown	Kilclonfert	Tullamore	I.	142
28	Clonagh	353 3 39	Limerick	Connello Lower	Clonagh	Rathkeale	II.	227
12	Clonagh	364 3 22	Queen's Co.	Maryborough West	Clonenagh&Clonagheen	Mountmellick	I.	242
32	Clonagh	399 1 21	Queen's Co.	Slievemargy	Killabban	Carlow	I.	245
29	Clonagh	44 2 14	Westmeath	Brawny	St. Mary's	Athlone	I.	259
3	Clonaghadoo	240 1 24	Queen's Co.	Tinnahinch	Castlebrack	Mountmellick	I.	248
17, 24, 25	Clonagh East	379 2 23	King's Co.	Ballycowan	Lynally	Tullamore	I.	128
15	Clonaghlis	444 0 2g	Kildare	South Salt	Clonaghlis	Celbridge	I.	76
24, 25	Clonagh West	293 3 6	King's Co.	Ballycowan	Lynally	Tullamore	I.	128
38	Clonaglin	300 0 0	Westmeath	Moycashel	Kilbeggan	Tullamore	I.	278
25	Clonagonnell	258 0 11h	Cavan	Upper Loughtee	Kilmore	Cavan	III.	84
21	Clonagooden	316 2 36	Queen's Co.	Clandonagh	Skirk	Donaghmore	I.	235
63	Clonagoose	406 3 13	Tipperary, S.R.	Slievardagh	Kilvemnon	Callan	II.	334
40	Clonagun	279 3 33	Fermanagh	Clankelly	Clones	Clones	III.	195
7	Clonaheen	614 0 25	Queen's Co.	Tinnahinch	Rosenallis	Mountmellick	I.	250
29	Clonahenoge	535 1 14	King's Co.	Garrycastle	Lusmagh	Parsonstown	I.	137

(a) Including 3A. 3R. 24P. River Barrow.
(b) Including 245A. 3R. 33P. detached portion.
(c) Including 3A. 2R. 3P. River Barrow.
(d) Including 10A. 0R. 13P. water.
(e) Including 1A. 3R. 0P. River Barrow.
(f) Including 2A. 0R. 32P. River Barrow.
(g) Including 21A. 3R. 31P. detached portion.
(h) Including 17A. 0R. 32P. water.

2 K

No. of Sheet of the Ordnance Survey Maps.	Townlands and Towns.	Area in Statute Acres.	County.	Barony.	Parish.	Poor Law Union in 1857.	Townland Census of 1851, Part I.	
		A. R. P.					Vol.	Page
23	Clonakenny . .	811 2 37	Tipperary, N.R.	Ikerrin . . .	Bourney . . .	Roscrea . .	II.	274
135	CLONAKILTY T. .	—	Cork, W.R. .	East Carbery (E.D.)	Kilgarriff . .	Clonakilty . .	II.	129
5	Clonakle . .	89 2 18	Armagh . .	Oneilland West .	Tartaraghan .	Armagh . .	III.	54
21, 22	Clonalea . .	601 1 4	Tipperary, N.R.	Upper Ormond .	Ballymackey . .	Nenagh . .	II.	289
6	Clonaleenaghan .	311 2 18	Louth . .	Upper Dundalk .	Creggan . .	Dundalk . .	I.	177
30	Clonalig . .	613 1 15	Armagh . .	Fews Upper . .	Creggan . . .	Castleblayney .	III.	48
51, 54	Clonallan Glebe .	317 2 12	Down . .	Upper Iveagh, Up. pt.	Clonallan . .	Newry . .	III.	174
31	Clonalough . .	207 2 19	Tipperary, N.R.	Owney and Arra .	Killoscully . .	Nenagh . .	II.	295
36	Clonaltra (King) .	266 0 0	Westmeath .	Clonlonan . .	Kilcleagh . .	Athlone . .	I.	261
36	Clonaltra West .	78 2 16	Westmeath .	Clonlonan . .	Kilcleagh . .	Athlone . .	I.	261
33	Clonamery . .	554 0 28	Kilkenny . .	Ida . . .	Clonamery . .	Thomastown .	I.	101
43, 49	Clonamicklon . .	310 0 8	Tipperary, S.R.	Slievardagh . .	Buolick . .	Urlingford . .	II.	332
5	Clonamola . .	60 2 15	Armagh . .	Oneilland West .	Drumcree . .	Lurgan . .	III.	51
6	Clonamona Lower .	296 1 6	Wexford . .	Gorey . . .	Rossminoge . .	Gorey . .	I.	321
6	Clonamona Upper .	358 1 16	Wexford . .	Gorey . . .	Rossminoge . .	Gorey . .	I.	321
49	Clonamondra .	299 2 36	Tipperary, S.R.	Slievardagh . .	Buolick . .	Urlingford . .	II.	332
35	Clonamuckoge Beg	194 3 0	Tipperary, N.R.	Eliogarty . .	Loughmoe East .	Thurles . .	II.	271
35	Clonamuckoge More	367 2 11	Tipperary, N.R.	Eliogarty . .	Loughmoe East .	Thurles . .	II.	271
14	Clonamullig . .	156 3 37a	Cavan . .	Lower Loughtee .	Drumlane . .	Cavan . .	III.	79
26	Clonamullog .	106 0 34	Fermanagh .	Magheraboy . .	Rossorry . .	Enniskillen .	III.	214
8	Clonamully . .	109 1 3	Monaghan .	Monaghan . .	Tedavnet . .	Monaghan . .	III.	278
8	Clonamunsha . .	50 3 13	Monaghan .	Monaghan . .	Clones . .	Monaghan . .	III.	274
31	Clonanagh . .	10 0 6	Waterford .	Decies without Drum	Dungarvan . .	Dungarvan . .	II.	355
5	Clonanav . .	300 2 8	Waterford .	Glenahiry . .	Kilronan . .	Clonmel . .	II.	365
11, 12	Clonandra . .	345 0 26b	Cavan . .	Tullygarvey . .	Annagh . .	Cavan . .	III.	87
19	Clonaneor . .	174 2 12	Monaghan .	Cremorne . .	Clontibret . .	Castleblayney .	III.	260
5	Clonanny . .	418 1 28	Queen's Co. .	Portnahinch . .	Lea . . .	Mountmellick .	I.	244
22	Clonard . .	69 1 9	Kilkenny . .	Crannagh . .	Ballycallen . .	Kilkenny . .	I.	84
17, 23	Clonard or Cappaloughlin . .	1,592 0 19	Queen's Co. .	Maryborough West	Clonenagh&Clonagheen	Abbeyleix . .	I.	242
67, 78	Clonard East . .	196 0 12	Cork, E.R. .	Imokilly . .	Clonpriest . .	Youghal . .	II.	84
1, 2, 4, 5	Clonard or Folkstown Great . .	370 3 15	Dublin . .	Balrothery East .	Balrothery . .	Balrothery . .	I.	19
37, 42	Clonard Great . .	148 0 38	Wexford . .	Forth . .	St. Peters . .	Wexford . .	I.	314
37, 42	Clonard Little . .	147 2 4	Wexford . .	Forth . .	St. Peters . .	Wexford . .	I.	314
1	Clonard New . .	63 3 0	Kildare . .	Carbury . .	Kilrainy . .	Edenderry . .	I.	52
41, 47	Clonard Old or Anneville . .	1,256 3 5c	Meath . .	Upper Moyfenrath .	Clonard . .	Edenderry . .	I.	213
31, 32	Clonardran . .	352 3 28	Meath . .	Skreen . .	Templekeeran .	Navan . .	I.	222
67, 78	Clonard West . .	118 0 29	Cork, E.R. .	Imokilly . .	Clonpriest . .	Youghal . .	II.	84
40	Clonarney . .	198 2 0	Cavan . .	Castlerahan . .	Mullagh . .	Kells . .	III.	70
9	Clonarney . .	271 3 16	Westmeath .	Delvin . .	Clonarney . .	Castletowndelvin	I.	265
18, 19	Clonarrow or Riverlyons . .	1,897 3 14	King's Co. .	Lower Philipstown .	Kilclonfert . .	Tullamore . .	I.	142
6	Clonascra . .	1,055 3 15	King's Co. .	Garrycastle . .	Clonmacnoise . .	Parsonstown .	I.	135
10	Clonasillagh . .	318 0 35	Meath . .	Upper Kells . .	Kilskeer . .	Kells . .	I.	206
2	Clonaslee . .	77 1 30	Queen's Co. .	Tinnahinch . .	Kilmanman . .	Mountmellick .	I.	249
2	CLONASLEE T. .	—	Queen's Co. .	Tinnahinch . .	Kilmanman . .	Mountmellick .	I.	249
52	Clonaspoe . .	466 3 6	Tipperary, S.R.	Kilnamanagh Lower	Oughterleague .	Cashel . .	II.	324
40	Clonassy . .	720 3 27	Kilkenny . .	Iverk . .	Kilmacow . .	Waterford . .	I.	105
39, 40	Clonassy . .	341 2 35	Kilkenny . .	Iverk . .	Rathkieran . .	Waterford . .	I.	107
7	Clonatin Lower .	257 3 8	Wexford . .	Gorey . .	Kilmakilloge .	Gorey . .	I.	318
7	Clonatin Upper .	213 3 18	Wexford . .	Gorey . .	Kilmakilloge .	Gorey . .	I.	318
40	Clonatty . .	88 1 35	Fermanagh .	Clankelly . .	Clones . .	Clones . .	III.	195
2, 6	Clonava . .	1,125 0 1d	Westmeath .	Moygoish . .	Street . .	Mullingar .	I.	281
45, 53	Clonavaddy . .	590 2 11	Tyrone . .	Dungannon Middle .	Donaghmore . .	Dungannon .	III.	301
9, 13	Clonavarn . .	139 3 0	Monaghan .	Monaghan . .	Kilmore . .	Monaghan .	III.	276
12, 17	Clonavilla . .	100 3 0	Monaghan .	Dartree . .	Clones . .	Clones . .	III.	264
19, 27	Clonavoe . .	1,807 1 38	King's Co. .	Coolestown . .	Clonsast . .	Edenderry . .	I.	132
25	Clonavogy . .	125 0 10	Monaghan .	Cremorne . .	Clontibret . .	Castleblayney .	III.	260
25, 28	Clonavogy . .	128 0 16	Monaghan .	Farney . .	Donaghmoyne . .	Carrickmacross	III.	269
60	Clonavrick . .	313 3 39	Cork, W.R. .	East Muskerry .	Aghabulloge . .	Macroom . .	II.	153
5	Clonaweel . .	205 0 23	Fermanagh .	Lurg . .	Drumkeeran . .	Lowtherstown .	III.	205
17, 23	Clonawoolan . .	103 1 12	Queen's Co. .	Maryborough West	Clonenagh&Clonagheen	Abbeyleix . .	I.	242
17, 23	Clonbane . .	207 3 7	Queen's Co. .	Maryborough West	Clonenagh&Clonagheen	Abbeyleix . .	I.	242
25	Clonbara . .	312 3 24	Donegal . .	Kilmacrenan . .	Tullaghobegley .	Dunfanaghy .	III.	131
12, 17	Clonbarrow . .	186 2 9	Queen's Co. .	Maryborough West	Clonenagh&Clonagheen	Mountmellick .	I.	242
3	Clonbartan . .	706 0 38e	Meath . .	Lower Slane . .	Drumcondra .	Ardee . .	I.	222
30, 35	Clonbeale Beg Glebe	159 1 22	King's Co. .	Eglish . .	Drumcullen . .	Parsonstown .	I.	134
35	Clonbeale More .	647 2 5	King's Co. .	Eglish . .	Drumcullen . .	Parsonstown .	I.	134
31, 37	Clonbealy . .	130 1 23	Tipperary, N.R.	Owney and Arra .	Kilvellane . .	Nenagh . .	II.	296
55	Clonbeg . .	424 3 18	King's Co. .	Ballybritt . .	Kilcolman . .	Parsonstown .	I.	125
40	Clon Beg . .	101 3 10	Tipperary, N.R.	Eliogarty . .	Inch . .	Thurles . .	II.	270
62	Clonbeg . .	72 3 26	Tyrone . .	Dungannon Middle .	Clonfeacle . .	Dungannon .	III.	299

(a) Including 26A. 2R. 20P. water.   (c) Including 0A. 2R. 31P. detached portion.   (e) Including 12A. 2R. 31P. water.
(b) Including 18A. 1R. 17P. water.   (d) Including 85A. 2R. 25P. water.

No. of Sheet of the Ordnance Survey Maps.	Townlands and Towns.	Area in Statute Acres.			County.	Barony.	Parish.	Poor Law Union in 1857.	Townland Census of 1851, Part I.	
		A.	R.	P.					Vol.	Page
26	Clonbeg Glebe	103	3	28	Donegal	Kilmacrenan	Clondahorky	Dunfanaghy	III.	123
30, 31	Clonbern	937	1	38	Galway	Ballymoe	Clonbern	Tuam	IV.	6
29	Clonblosk and Bally-magan Upr. & Lwr.	481	0	17	Donegal	Inishowen West	Fahan Lower	Inishowen	III.	120
42	Clonbockoge	154	0	27	Cavan	Clanmahon	Kilbride	Oldcastle	III.	77
52, 60	Clonbonane	234	1	3	Tipperary, S.R.	Clanwilliam	Clonoulty	Tipperary	II.	306
14	Clonbonniff	1,039	1	7	King's Co.	Garrycastle	Tisaran	Parsonstown	I.	138
21	Clonbore	241	1	32	Westmeath	Farbill	Killucan	Castletowndelvin	I.	266
124	Clonbouig	219	3	5	Cork, W.R.	East Carbery (E.D.)	Ringrone	Kinsale	II.	130
124	Clonbouig	209	2	15	Cork, W.R.	East Carbery (E.D.)	Templetrine	Kinsale	II.	130
43, 49	Clonboy	405	0	29	Antrim	Upper Toome	Drummaul	Antrim	III.	34
44, 45, 54	Clonboy	270	0	12	Clare	Tulla Lower	O'Briensbridge	Limerick	II.	38
11	Clonboy	57	3	7	Monaghan	Dartree	Clones	Clones	III.	264
17, 24	Clonboy or Ballinacor	371	0	9	Westmeath	Rathconrath	Killare	Mullingar	I.	283
12,13,17,18	Clonboyne	747	3	13	Queen's Co.	Maryborough East	Clonenagh and Clon-agheen	Mountmellick	I.	241
34	Clonbrassil	53	3	30	Tipperary, N.R.	Eliogarty	Drom	Thurles	II.	269
42, 45	Clonbrennan	45	3	22	King's Co.	Clonlisk	Dunkerrin	Roscrea	I.	130
45	Clonbrennan	172	0	35	King's Co.	Clonlisk	Roscrea	Roscrea	I.	131
43	Clonbrick	145	2	6a	Clare	Tulla Lower	Clonlea	Tulla	II.	34
50, 58	Clonbrick	416	2	6	Tipperary, S.R.	Clanwilliam	Solloghodmore	Tipperary	II.	311
28	Clonbrin	920	0	6	King's Co.	Coolestown	Clonsast	Edenderry	I.	132
60	Clonbrock	97	2	33	Galway	Kilconnell	Ahascragh	Mountbellew	IV.	39
31	Clonbrock	914	2	12	Queen's Co.	Slievemargy	Killabban	Carlow	I.	245
60,61,73,74	Clonbrock Demesne	1,761	2	21	Galway	Kilconnell	Fohanagh	Mountbellew	IV.	39
27, 28	Clonbrock Lower	240	1	5	King's Co.	Coolestown	Clonsast	Edenderry	I.	132
27, 28	Clonbrock Upper	236	3	24	King's Co.	Coolestown	Clonsast	Edenderry	I.	132
62	Clonbrogan	301	3	12	Tipperary, S.R.	Middlethird	Magorban	Cashel	II.	328
35	Clonbrone	204	0	16	King's Co.	Ballybritt	Birr	Parsonstown	I.	125
35	Clonbrone	135	3	5	King's Co.	Eglish	Drumcullen	Parsonstown	I.	134
10	Clonbroney	333	0	36b	Longford	Granard	Clonbroney	Granard	I.	154
20	Clonbrown	1,103	0	30	King's Co.	Coolestown	Clonsast	Edenderry	I.	132
29	Clonbrusk	230	1	25	Westmeath	Brawny	St. Mary's	Athlone	I.	259
19, 20	Clonbulloge	522	0	35	King's Co.	Coolestown	Clonsast	Edenderry	I.	132
13, 17	Clonbulloge or Bally-callon	139	1	5	Carlow	Forth	Fennagh	Carlow	I.	4
19	CLONBULLOGE T.	—			King's Co.	Coolestown	Clonsast	Edenderry	I.	133
26, 27	Clonbunniagh	105	2	32	Fermanagh	Clanawley	Rossorry	Enniskillen	III.	194
37	Clonbunny	202	3	15	Tipperary, N.R.	Owney and Arra	Kilvellane	Nenagh	II.	296
24, 30	Clonbuogh	682	3	21	Tipperary, N.R.	Ikerrin	Killavinoge	Thurles	II.	275
24, 30	Clonbuogh	280	3	36	Tipperary, N.R.	Ikerrin	Templetouhy	Thurles	II.	277
28	Clonburren	37	2	1	Queen's Co.	Clandonagh	Donaghmore	Donaghmore	I.	233
33, 34	Clonburren (Moore)	452	1	9	Queen's Co.	Clandonagh	Rathdowney	Donaghmore	I.	234
28	Clonburren (White)	204	0	18	Queen's Co.	Clandonagh	Rathdowney	Donaghmore	I.	234
17	Clonburris Great	219	3	14	Dublin	Uppercross	Clondalkin	Dublin South	I.	39
17	Clonburris Little	48	1	34	Dublin	Uppercross	Clondalkin	Dublin South	I.	39
4, 5, 11, 12	Clonca	782	1	14	Donegal	Inishowen East	Clonca	Inishowen	III.	116
15	Clonca	297	2	4	Longford	Ardagh	Mostrim	Granard	I.	152
37	Cloncagh	306	2	2	Limerick	Connello Upper	Cloncagh	Newcastle	II.	231
5	Cloncah Rock	41	3	26	Fermanagh	Lurg	Drumkeeran	Lowtherstown	III.	205
43	Cloncallick	405	2	30	Fermanagh	Clankelly	Drummully	Clones	III.	197
16	Cloncallick	78	1	6	Monaghan	Dartree	Clones	Clones	III.	264
21, 22	Cloncallow or Cush-callow	197	3	14	King's Co.	Garrycastle	Reynagh	Parsonstown	I.	138
56	Cloncandra Glebe	213	0	17	Tyrone	Omagh East	Kilskeery	Enniskillen	III.	313
22	Cloncannon	1,194	3	17	Tipperary, N.R.	Ikerrin	Borrisnafarney	Roscrea	II.	274
12	Cloncanon	960	3	14	King's Co.	Coolestown	Monasteroris	Edenderry	I.	133
7	Cloncanon Lower	259	3	1	Queen's Co.	Tinnahinch	Rosenallis	Mountmellick	I.	250
7	Cloncanon Upper	207	2	14	Queen's Co.	Tinnahinch	Rosenallis	Mountmellick	I.	250
20	Cloncant	975	1	0	King's Co.	Coolestown	Clonsast	Edenderry	I.	132
30, 35	Cloncarban	458	0	39	King's Co.	Eglish	Drumcullen	Parsonstown	I.	134
26, 27	Cloncarlin or Globe-island	359	0	14	Kildare	Offaly West	Monasterevin	Athy	I.	73
40	Cloncarn	113	2	11	Fermanagh	Clankelly	Galloon	Clones	III.	198
35, 36	Cloncarneel	1,196	3	30	Meath	Lune	Kildalkey	Trim	I.	208
44	Cloncarney	832	3	37	Donegal	Kilmacrenan	Conwal	Letterkenny	III.	126
5	Cloncarrish	190	2	37	Armagh	Oneilland West	Tartaraghan	Lurgan	III.	54
27	Cloncassan	295	1	29	King's Co.	Coolestown	Clonsast	Edenderry	I.	132
23	Cloncat	450	2	11	Meath	Upper Kells	Girley	Kells	I.	205
7	Cloncaw	124	3	27	Monaghan	Trough	Donagh	Monaghan	III.	281
67, 68	Clonclayagh	255	0	0	Donegal	Raphoe	Kilteevoge	Stranorlar	III.	139
43	Cloncloghy	86	0	15	Fermanagh	Clankelly	Drummully	Clones	III.	197
70, 82	Clonclud	263	2	19	Cork, W.R.	West Muskerry	Kilnamartry	Macroom	II.	159
126, 132	Clonco	683	0	1	Galway	Leitrim	Ballynakill	Loughrea	IV.	51

(a) Including 12A. 0R. 6P. water.   (b) Including 12A. 1R. 30P. water.

No. of Sheet of the Ordnance Survey Maps.	Townlands and Towns.	Area in Statute Acres. A. R. P.	County.	Barony.	Parish.	Poor Law Union in 1857.	Townland Census of 1851, Part I. Vol.	Page
25, 26	Cloncoher	301 3 22	King's Co.	Geashill	Geashill	Tullamore	I.	140
17	Cloncollog	467 0 35	King's Co.	Ballycowan	Kilbride	Tullamore	I.	127
14	Cloncollow	139 1 38a	Cavan	Lower Loughtee	Tomregan	Bawnboy	III.	81
17, 25	Cloncon	555 2 35	King's Co.	Geashill	Geashill	Tullamore	I.	140
5	Clonconane	300 2 14	Limerick	Pubblebrien	St. Munchins	Limerick	II.	254
39, 42	Clonconey	406 0 5	Kilkenny	Iverk	Clonmore	Carrick on Suir	I.	105
2, 6	Clonconnell	190 0 33	Westmeath	Moygoish	Street	Granard	I.	281
21	Clonconor Glebe	57 2 38	Cavan	Upper Loughtee	Castleterra	Cavan	III.	82
74	Clonconwal	470 0 6b	Donegal	Banagh	Killybegs Lower	Glenties	III.	110
41	Cloncoohy	103 2 34	Fermanagh	Knockninny	Tomregan	Lisnaskea	III.	203
5	Cloncore	548 3 0	Armagh	Oneilland West	Tartaraghan	Lurgan	III.	54
43	Cloncorick	209 1 28	Fermanagh	Clankelly	Drummully	Clones	III.	197
5, 8	Cloncorig	195 1 38	Tipperary, N.R.	Lower Ormond	Loughkeen	Parsonstown	II.	286
40	Cloncorr	143 2 15	Fermanagh	Clankelly	Clones	Clones	III.	195
14, 19	Cloncose	86 0 21	Cavan	Tullyhunco	Kildallan	Cavan	III.	96
24	Cloncose	103 1 12	Cavan	Tullyhunco	Killashandra	Cavan	III.	97
31	Cloncoskoran	198 0 10	Waterford	Decies without Drum	Dungarvan	Dungarvan	II.	355
8	Cloncosney	141 0 19	Queen's Co.	Portnahinch	Ardea	Mountmellick	I.	243
23	Cloncough	246 1 2	Queen's Co.	Maryborough West	Clonenagh and Clonagheen	Abbeyleix	I.	242
15, 21	Cloncourse	405 0 14	Queen's Co.	Clandonagh	Kyle	Roscrea	I.	233
12, 17	Cloncourse	634 2 12	Queen's Co.	Maryborough West	Clonenagh and Clonagheen	Mountmellick	I.	242
111	Cloncouse	241 1 24	Cork, W.R.	East Carbery (E.D.)	Ballinadee	Bandon	II.	126
36, 37	Cloncovet	1,126 0 35	Cavan	Clanmahon	Drumlumman	Granard	III.	77
42	Cloncowan	338 0 2	Meath	Lower Moyfenrath	Rathmolyon	Trim	I.	211
2, 5	Cloncowley	361 1 17c	Longford	Longford	Killoe	Longford	I.	158
12, 17	Cloncracken	556 1 34	Tipperary, N.R.	Ikerrin	Corbally	Roscrea	II.	275
2	Cloncraff	157 3 15	King's Co.	Kilcoursey	Ardnurcher or Horse-leap	Tullamore	I.	140
6	Cloncraff or Bloomhill	1,626 3 30	King's Co.	Garrycastle	Clonmacnoise	Parsonstown	I.	135
27, 28	Cloncrave	819 1 3	Westmeath	Farbill	Killucan	Mullingar	I.	266
19	Cloncreen	1,829 0 34	King's Co.	Coolestown	Clonsast	Edenderry	I.	133
45, 54	Cloncrew	166 2 20	Limerick	Connello Upper	Cloncrew	Newcastle	II.	232
32,33,38,39	Cloncrow	489 1 32	Westmeath	Moycashel	Newtown	Mullingar	I.	278
24	Cloncullane	397 3 22	Queen's Co.	Cullenagh	Ballyroan	Abbeyleix	I.	239
30, 31	Cloncullen	401 2 24	Meath	Upper Navan	Bective	Navan	I.	216
12	Cloncullen	280 2 18	Queen's Co.	Maryborough West	Clonenagh and Clonagheen	Mountmellick	I.	242
20	Cloncullen	189 0 29	Westmeath	Farbill	Killucan	Mullingar	I.	266
32, 38	Cloncullen	210 2 30	Westmeath	Moycashel	Newtown	Mullingar	I.	278
16	Cloncullen	654 0 33	Westmeath	Rathconrath	Ballymore	Ballymahon	I.	281
15, 16	Cloncully	355 3 35	Queen's Co.	Upperwoods	Offerlane	Mountmellick	I.	251
12, 17	Cloncumber	466 1 3	Kildare	Connell	Kilmeage	Naas	I.	55
16	Cloncumber	97 3 6	Monaghan	Dartree	Clones	Clones	III.	264
9, 13	Cloncurkney	151 1 18d	Cavan	Tullyhaw	Templeport	Bawnboy	III.	94
16	Cloncurrin	129 3 34	Monaghan	Dartree	Clones	Clones	III.	264
4	Cloncurry	183 0 1	Kildare	Ikeathy & Oughterany	Cloncurry	Celbridge	I.	57
17	Cloncurry	182 0 36	Kildare	Offaly East	Cloncurry	Edenderry	I.	69
55	Cloncurry	45 2 5	Tipperary, S.R.	Slievardagh	Lismalin	Callan	II.	335
41	Clondalee Beg	496 1 35	Meath	Upper Moyfenrath	Killyon	Trim	I.	213
35, 41	Clondalee More	1,621 0 37	Meath	Upper Moyfenrath	Killyon	Trim	I.	213
8, 13	Clondalever	505 2 39	Westmeath	Fore	Kilpatrick	Castletowndelvin	I.	270
13	Clondalever	364 3 1	Westmeath	Moyashel and Magheradernon	Rathconnell	Mullingar	I.	276
17, 21	Clondalkin	507 0 21	Dublin	Uppercross	Clondalkin	Dublin South	I.	39
17	CLONDALKIN T.	—	Dublin	Uppercross	Clondalkin	Dublin South	I.	39
28	Clondallan	265 1 10	Donegal	Kilmacrenan	Killygarvan	Millford	III.	128
30, 35	Clondallow	508 2 36	King's Co.	Eglish	Eglish	Parsonstown	I.	134
18	Clondardis	11 1 4	Westmeath	Moyashel and Magheradernon	Mullingar	Mullingar	I.	275
18	Clondardis	210 1 7	Westmeath	Moygoish	Templeoran	Mullingar	I.	281
21	Clondargan	79 0 24	Cavan	Upper Loughtee	Larah	Cavan	III.	85
21	Clondargan Glebe	69 3 28	Cavan	Upper Loughtee	Larah	Cavan	III.	85
7	Clondarragh	78 1 26	Wexford	Gorey	Kilcavan	Gorey	I.	317
12	Clondarrig	381 0 28	Queen's Co.	Maryborough East	Clonenagh and Clonagheen	Mountmellick	I.	241
52	Clondavaddog	413 3 8	Donegal	Kilmacrenan	Gartan	Letterkenny	III.	127
33	Clondaval	90 0 0	Fermanagh	Clanawley	Kinawley	Enniskillen	III.	193
30, 36	Clondavan	32 0 38	Meath	Upper Navan	Moymet	Trim	I.	216
30, 36	Clondavan	103 2 0	Meath	Upper Navan	Trim	Trim	I.	216
20, 21	Clondaw	315 0 35	Wexford	Ballaghkeen	Kilcormick	Enniscorthy	I.	291
13	Clondelara	727 0 15	King's Co.	Garrycastle	Clonmacnoise	Parsonstown	I.	135
58, 68	Clonderalaw	463 2 39	Clare	Clonderalaw	Kilmurry	Killadysert	II.	17

(a) Including 4A. 2R. 30P. water.
(b) Including 9A. 2R. 2P. water.
(c) Including 21A. 1R. 4P. water.
(d) Including 10A. 3R. 23P. water.

No. of Sheet of the Ordnance Survey Maps.	Townlands and Towns.	Area in Statute Acres.	County.	Barony.	Parish.	Poor Law Union in 1857.	Townland Census of 1851, Part I.	
		A. R. P.					Vol.	Page
36	CLONDERALAW T.	—	Cork, E.R.	Condons&Clangibbon	Clondulane	Fermoy	II.	60
20	Clondermot	301 2 31	Londonderry	Tirkeeran	Clondermot	Londonderry	III.	247
17	Clondinnery	34 0 38	Monaghan	Dartree	Killeevan	Clones	III.	267
2, 6	Clondonnell	961 0 36	Waterford	Upperthird	Rathgormuck	Carrick on Suir	II.	371
24, 32	Clondonnell Glebe	138 3 8	King's Co.	Ballyboy	Killoughy	Tullamore	I.	124
42, 43	Clondoogan	836 0 5	Meath	Lower Moyfenrath	Laracor	Trim	I.	210
19	Clondoolagh	33 3 18a	Queen's Co.	Stradbally	Timogue	Athy	I.	248
34	Clondoolusk	322 3 20	King's Co.	Upper Philipstown	Clonyhurk	Mountmellick	I.	143
35	Clondoty	431 1 29	Tipperary, N.R.	Eliogarty	Loughmoe West	Thurles	II.	271
16	Clondouglas	292 0 0	Kerry	Clanmaurice	Kilfeighny	Listowel	II.	169
23	Clondouglas	119 3 21	Queen's Co.	Maryborough West	Clonenagh and Clonagheen	Abbeyleix	I.	242
12, 27	Clondouglas or Clonkeen	253 2 31	Queen's Co.	Maryborough West	Clonenagh and Clonagheen	Abbeyleix	I.	242
21, 22	Clondown	158 2 5	Kildare	Offaly West	Lackagh	Athy	I.	73
5	Clondrinagh	331 1 37	Limerick	Pubblebrien	Killeely	Limerick	II.	253
5, 10	Clonduff	206 0 30	Kildare	Ikeathy and Oughterany	Balraheen	Celbridge	I.	56
3	Clonduff	428 3 37b	Queen's Co.	Tinnahinch	Rearymore	Mountmellick	I.	249
36	Clondulane North	178 1 29c	Cork, E.R.	Condons&Clangibbon	Clondulane	Fermoy	II.	60
36	Clondulane South	129 1 6	Cork, E.R.	Condons&Clangibbon	Clondulane	Fermoy	II.	60
9	Clone	452 2 33	Kilkenny	Galmoy	Rathbeagh	Urlingford	I.	93
31	Clone	374 2 20	Kilkenny	Kells	Kilmaganny	Callan	I.	109
52	Clone	250 3 27	Tipperary, S.R.	Kilnamanagh Lower	Clonoulty	Cashel	II.	323
15, 20	Clone	1,009 0 5	Wexford	Scarawalsh	Clone	Enniscorthy	I.	322
39	Clone	647 1 34	Wicklow	Ballinacor South	Kilpipe	Rathdrum	I.	349
7	Clonea	416 2 25	Waterford	Upperthird	Mothel	Carrick on Suir	II.	370
31	Clonea Lower	227 1 12	Waterford	Decies without Drum	Clonea	Dungarvan	II.	354
31	Clonea Middle	155 3 7	Waterford	Decies without Drum	Clonea	Dungarvan	II.	354
10	Clonearl	91 1 2	King's Co.	Lower Philipstown	Killaderry	Tullamore	I.	142
10	Clonearl Demesne	716 0 11	King's Co.	Lower Philipstown	Kilclonfert	Tullamore	I.	142
13	Cloncary	142 0 9d	Cavan	Tullyhaw	Templeport	Bawnboy	III.	94
31	Clonea Upper	164 0 24	Waterford	Decies without Drum	Clonea	Dungarvan	II.	354
52, 58, 59	Cloneblaugh	308 2 16e	Tyrone	Clogher	Clogher	Clogher	III.	292
46, 52	Clonedarby	281 0 14	Tipperary, S.R.	Kilnamanagh Lower	Clonoulty	Cashel	II.	323
11	Clonedergole	84 3 34	Monaghan	Dartree	Clones	Clones	III.	264
6	Clonee	219 1 31	Fermanagh	Lurg	Drumkeeran	Lowtherstown	III.	205
50, 51, 53	Clonee	807 3 10	Meath	Dunboyne	Dunboyne	Dunshaughlin	I.	199
41	Clonee	468 3 26f	Meath	Lower Moyfenrath	Trim	Trim	I.	211
16, 21	Clone East	291 1 13	Wexford	Ballaghkeen	Monamolin	Gorey	I.	298
27,28,33,34	Cloneeb	215 1 28	Queen's Co.	Clandonagh	Rathdowney	Donaghmore	I.	234
17	Clonee East	112 2 15	Carlow	Forth	Myshall	Carlow	I.	5
10	Clonee Lower	433 0 18	Wexford	Scarawalsh	Kilcomb	Gorey	I.	323
12	Cloneen	276 2 25	Carlow	Idrone East	Agha	Carlow	I.	6
12	Cloneen	112 1 36	Carlow	Idrone East	Nurney	Carlow	I.	8
64	Cloneen	676 2 9	Cork, E.R.	Barrymore	Carrigtohill	Middleton	II.	52
2, 6	Cloneen	800 1 17	Kilkenny	Fassadinin	Castlecomer	Castlecomer	I.	88
10	Cloneen	292 3 28	King's Co.	Lower Philipstown	Kilclonfert	Tullamore	I.	142
17	Cloneen	495 3 11	Tipperary, N.R.	Ikerrin	Corbally	Roscrea	II.	275
34, 35	Cloneen	346 1 25	Wicklow	Ballinacor South	Ballykine	Rathdrum	I.	348
5, 9	Cloneen or Closeland	401 1 13	Queen's Co.	Portnahinch	Lea	Mountmellick	I.	244
41	Cloneen or Newtown	351 2 28	Meath	Upper Moyfenrath	Killyon	Trim	I.	213
36	Cloneens	15 1 24	Meath	Upper Navan	Trim	Trim	I.	216
51	CLONEE T.	—	Meath	Dunboyne	Dunboyne	Dunshaughlin	I.	200
31	Cloneety	10 3 7	Waterford	Decies without Drum	Dungarvan	Dungarvan	II.	355
10	Clonee Upper	549 3 34	Wexford	Scarawalsh	Kilcomb	Gorey	I.	323
17	Clonee West	39 3 33	Carlow	Idrone East	Myshall	Carlow	I.	8
16	Clonegah	397 0 3	Carlow	Idrone East	Fennagh	Carlow	I.	7
18	Clonegall	299 3 7	Carlow	St. Mullins Upper	Moyacomb	Shillelagh	I.	14
18	CLONEGALL T.	—	Carlow	St. Mullins Upper	Moyacomb	Carlow	I.	14
26, 27	Clonegath	596 0 8	Kildare	Offaly West	Monasterevin	Athy	I.	73
7	Clonehurk	697 0 26	Queen's Co.	Maryborough West	Clonenagh and Clonagheen	Mountmellick	I.	242
5	Clonelly	249 3 28	Fermanagh	Lurg	Drumkeeran	Lowtherstown	III.	205
40	Clonelty	192 3 3	Fermanagh	Coole	Galloon	Clones	III.	199
46	Clonely	188 0 17	Tipperary, S.R.	Kilnamanagh Lower	Clogher	Cashel	II.	322
12, 17	Clonenagh	513 3 35	Queen's Co.	Maryborough West	Clonenagh and Clonagheen	Mountmellick	I.	242
3, 7	Cloneranny	310 0 20	Wexford	Gorey	Kilgorman	Gorey	I.	318
29, 34	Clonerkin	355 0 17	Wicklow	Ballinacor South	Ballykine	Rathdrum	I.	348
21	Clonervy	414 3 8	Cavan	Upper Loughtee	Castleterra	Cavan	III.	82
4, 5, 7, 8	Cloneska	350 3 0	Tipperary, N.R.	Lower Ormond	Aglishcloghane	Borrisokane	II.	281
7	Clones Lower	113 3 25	Wexford	Gorey	Kilgorman	Gorey	I.	318
7	Clones Middle	175 1 14	Wexford	Gorey	Kilgorman	Gorey	I.	318

(a) Including 2A. 0R. 15P. detached portion.
(b) Including 4A. 2R. 13P. water.

(c) Including 2A. 3R. 4P. water.
(d) Including 3A. 1R. 26P. water.

(e) Including 2A. 0R. 0P. water.
(f) Including 13A. 1R. 0P. water.

No. of Sheet of the Ordnance Survey Maps.	Townlands and Towns.	Area in Statute Acres.	County.	Barony.	Parish.	Poor Law Union in 1857.	Townland Census of 1851, Part I.	
		A. R. P.					Vol.	Page
11	CLONES T. . .	—	Monaghan .	Dartree . .	Clones . .	Clones .	III.	265
7	Clones Upper .	203 1 8	Wexford .	Gorey . .	Kilgorman .	Gorey .	I.	318
17	Clonetoose .	108 1 6	Carlow .	Idrone East .	Fennagh .	Carlow .	I.	7
28	Clonetrace .	562 3 0	Antrim .	Lower Antrim .	Skerry . .	Ballymena .	III.	4
13	Clonever . .	334 0 23	King's Co. .	Garrycastle .	Clonmacnoise .	Parsonstown .	I.	135
22	Cloneveran .	121 2 22	Meath .	Fore . .	Killallon . .	Oldcastle .	I.	200
17, 22	Clonevin . .	206 1 19	Wexford .	Ballaghkeen .	Donaghmore .	Gorey .	I.	293
21	Clone West .	424 0 4	Wexford .	Ballaghkeen .	Monamolin .	Gorey .	I.	298
15	Cloney . .	44 2 2	Antrim .	Lower Glenarm .	Layd . .	Ballycastle .	III.	22
30, 31	Cloney . .	1,518 1 36a	Kildare .	Narragh&RebanWest	Kilberry . .	Athy .	I.	67
33	Cloney . .	225 0 21	Meath .	Upper Duleek .	Ardcath . .	Drogheda .	I.	197
31	Cloneybeg .	527 2 29	Kildare .	Offaly West .	Harristown .	Athy .	I.	72
19	Cloneybrien .	578 0 20	Tipperary, N.R.	Owney and Arra .	Castletownarra .	Nenagh .	II.	294
13,14 19,20	Cloneygowny .	115 3 17	Tipperary, N.R.	Owney and Arra .	Castletownarra .	Nenagh .	II.	294
40	Clonfad . .	231 3 15	Fermanagh .	Clankelly .	Clones . .	Clones .	III.	195
16	Clonfad . .	248 3 2	Monaghan .	Dartree . .	Drummully .	Clones .	III.	266
16, 21	Clonfad . .	127 2 15	Monaghan .	Dartree . .	Killeevan .	Clones .	III.	267
16, 22	Clonfad . .	229 1 18	Queen's Co. .	Upperwoods .	Offerlane .	Abbeyleix .	I.	251
27	Clonfad . .	443 0 19	Westmeath .	Farbill . .	Killucan .	Mullingar .	I.	266
32, 33	Clonfad . .	640 2 22	Westmeath .	Fartullagh .	Clonfad . .	Mullingar .	I.	268
70	Clonfadda .	242 0 10	Cork, W.R. .	West Muskerry .	Clondrohid .	Macroom .	II.	155
17, 26	Clonfadda .	176 1 22	Waterford .	Middlethird .	Reisk . .	Waterford .	II.	368
33	Clonfane . .	161 2 20	Fermanagh .	Knockninny .	Kinawley .	Lisnaskea .	III.	201
30, 36	Clonfane . .	366 0 32	Meath .	Upper Navan .	Moymet . .	Trim .	I.	216
43	Clonfard . .	79 2 20	Fermanagh .	Clankelly .	Drummully .	Clones .	III.	197
61	CLONFEACLE T. .	—	Tyrone .	Dungannon Middle .	Clonfeacle .	Dungannon .	III.	300
40	Clonfeile . .	98 0 18	Fermanagh .	Clankelly .	Clones . .	Clones .	III.	195
22	Clonfert . .	259 2 37	Cork, E.R. .	Duhallow .	Clonfert . .	Kanturk .	II.	68
101	Clonfert (Butson) .	1,605 3 7b	Galway .	Longford .	Clonfert . .	Ballinasloe .	IV.	57
100, 101	Clonfert Demesne .	526 0 19	Galway .	Longford .	Clonfert . .	Ballinasloe .	IV.	57
101	Clonfertdemesne Bog	270 3 16	Galway .	Longford .	Clonfert . .	Ballinasloe .	IV.	57
5, 10	Clonfert North .	212 0 4	Kildare .	Ikeathy and Ough-terany . .	Balraheen .	Celbridge .	I.	56
101	Clonfert (Seymour) North . .	171 2 32	Galway .	Longford .	Clonfert . .	Ballinasloe .	IV.	57
101	Clonfert (Seymour) South . .	16 0 33	Galway .	Longford .	Clonfert . .	Ballinasloe .	IV.	57
10	Clonfert South .	238 3 33	Kildare .	Ikeathy and Ough-terany . .	Balraheen .	Celbridge .	I.	56
5	Clonfinane .	446 2 6	Tipperary, N.R.	Lower Ormond .	Loughkeen .	Parsonstown .	II.	286
6, 13, 14	Clonfinlough .	2,457 0 33c	King's Co. .	Garrycastle .	Clonmacnoise .	Parsonstown .	I.	135
10	Clonfinnan .	102 2 27	Meath .	Upper Kells .	Dulane . .	Kells .	I.	205
8	Clonfree . .	174 3 10	Tipperary, N.R.	Lower Ormond .	Loughkeen .	Parsonstown .	II.	286
52	Clongaddy .	93 2 14	Wexford .	Bargy . .	Kilturk . .	Wexford .	I.	307
52	Clongall . .	458 1 31	Meath .	Upper Moyfenrath .	Castlejordan .	Edenderry .	I.	212
50, 51	Clonganhue .	454 2 39	Tipperary, S.R.	Clanwilliam .	Solloghodmore .	Tipperary .	II.	311
22	Clonganny .	39 0 36	Wexford .	Ballaghkeen .	Donaghmore .	Gorey .	I.	293
17, 22	Clonganny .	245 1 16	Wexford .	Gorey . .	Kiltrisk . .	Gorey .	I.	320
18	Clongarran .	205 2 39	Carlow .	St. Mullins Upper .	Moyacomb .	Shillelagh .	I.	14
19	Clongarret .	822 1 8	King's Co. .	Coolestown .	Clonsast . .	Edenderry .	I.	133
6	Clongawny .	833 0 6	King's Co. .	Garrycastle .	Clonmacnoise .	Parsonstown .	I.	135
19	Clongawny .	559 1 5	Westmeath .	Moyashel and Magh-eradernon .	Mullingar .	Mullingar .	I.	275
30	Clongawny Beg .	99 2 19	King's Co. .	Garrycastle .	Reynagh .	Parsonstown .	I.	138
30	Clongawny More .	805 2 13	King's Co. .	Garrycastle .	Reynagh .	Parsonstown .	I.	138
40	Clongeen . .	528 2 3	Wexford .	Shelmaliere West .	Clongeen .	New Ross .	I.	332
40	CLONGEEN T. .	—	Wexford .	Shelmaliere West .	Clongeen .	New Ross .	I.	333
17, 18	Clongill . .	1,207 0 27	Meath .	Morgallion .	Clongill . .	Navan .	I.	209
29	Clonglash and Bau-ville Keeloges	727 3 22	Donegal .	Inishowen West .	Fahan Lower .	Inishowen .	III.	120
114, 127	Clonglaskan .	600 2 30	Cork, W.R. .	Bear . .	Killaconenagh .	Castletown .	II.	124
18	Clongorey .	516 3 23	Kildare .	Connell . .	Feighcullen .	Naas .	I.	55
41	Clongower .	276 1 16	Tipperary, N.R.	Eliogarty .	Thurles . .	Thurles .	II.	273
10, 14	Clongowes or Castle-brown . .	704 0 36	Kildare .	Ikeathy and Ough-terany . .	Mainham .	Celbridge .	I.	58
38	Clongowly .	355 3 15	Westmeath .	Moycashel .	Ardnurcher or Horse-leap .	Tullamore .	I.	276
40, 43	Clongowna .	102 3 29	Fermanagh .	Clankelly .	Drummully .	Clones .	III.	197
2	Clongowna .	522 1 32	Tipperary N.R.	Lower Ormond .	Dorrha . .	Parsonstown .	II.	283
18	Clongownagh .	158 2 29d	Kildare .	Connell . .	Feighcullen .	Naas .	I.	55
22	Clongowny .	252 2 24	Meath .	Fore . .	Killallon . .	Oldcastle .	I.	200
47, 48	Clonguiffin .	762 0 35	Meath .	Lower Moyfenrath .	Rathcore .	Trim .	I.	211
57	Clongutery .	107 0 17	Meath .	Lower Deece .	Kiltale . .	Dunshaughlin .	I.	192
20	Clonhasten .	477 2 6e	Wexford .	Ballaghkeen .	Templeshannon .	Enniscorthy .	I.	298

(a) Including 9A. 3R. 35P. water.
(b) Including 8A. 0R. 20P. River Suck.
(c) Including 112A. 0R. 0P. water.
(d) Including　7A. 0R. 2P. detached portion.
(e) Including 8A. 2R. 16P. water.

No. of Sheet of the Ordnance Survey Maps.	Townlands and Towns.	Area in Statute Acres.	County.	Barony.	Parish.	Poor Law Union in 1857.	Townland Census of 1851, Part I.	
		A. R. P.					Vol.	Page
11	Clonhenret	205 2 33	Wexford	Scarawalsh	Toome	Gorey	I.	326
24	Clonickilroe	130 0 13	Westmeath	Rathconrath	Killare	Ballymahon	I.	283
20	Clonickilvant	1,164 0 8a	Westmeath	Moyashel and Magheradernon	Rathconnell	Mullingar	I.	276
13	Cloniff	445 0 6	King's Co.	Garrycastle	Clonmacnoise	Parsonstown	I.	135
13	Cloniffeen	587 0 32	King's Co.	Garrycastle	Clonmacnoise	Parsonstown	I.	135
4, 10, 11	Clonin	587 1 12b	King's Co.	Warrenstown	Ballyburly	Edenderry	I.	144
11, 16	Clonin	729 1·34	Queen's Co.	Upperwoods	Offerlane	Mountmellick	I.	251
11, 16	Clonincurragh	749 3 21	Queen's Co.	Upperwoods	Offerlane	Mountmellick	I.	251
1	Clonisboyle	59 0 8	Monaghan	Trough	Errigal Trough	Clogher	III.	283
34	Clonismullen	241 3 8	Tipperary, N.R.	Eliogarty	Drom	Thurles	II.	269
14, 19	Clonjordan	702 3 0	Wexford	Scarawalsh	Templeshanbo	Enniscorthy	I.	326
9	Clonkeady	107 2 21	Monaghan	Monaghan	Tedavnet	Monaghan	III.	278
40, 43	Clonkee	164 0 16	Fermanagh	Coole	Drummully	Clones	III.	199
14	Clonkeehan	133 0 34	Louth	Louth	Clonkeehan	Ardee	I.	183
16	Clonkeelan	230 2 36c	Monaghan	Dartree	Drummully	Clones	III.	266
42, 43	Clonkeen	471 0 24	Antrim	Upper Toome	Drummaul	Ballymena	III.	34
14	Clonkeen	193 3 35	Cavan	Tullyhunco	Kildallan	Bawnboy	III.	96
7, 8	Clonkeen	1,759 0 8	Kildare	Carbury	Carbury	Edenderry	I.	51
19	Clonkeen	107 2 15	King's Co.	Coolestown	Clonsast	Edenderry	I.	133
3	Clonkeen	181 3 37	Monaghan	Trough	Errigal Trough	Clogher	III.	283
29, 30	Clonkeen	551 1 28	Queen's Co.	Cullenagh	Abbeyleix	Abbeyleix	I.	238
12, 17, 18	Clonkeen	1,173 3 34	Queen's Co.	Maryborough West	Clonenagh and Clonagheen	Abbeyleix	I.	242
15, 16	Clonkeen	558 1 8d	Westmeath	Kilkenny West	Noughaval	Ballymahon	I.	274
6	Clonkeen	644 3 23e	Westmeath	Moygoish	Street	Granard	I.	281
22, 23	Clonkeen	427 2 23	Wicklow	Ballinacor South	Ballinacor	Rathdrum	I.	348
6, 14	Clonkeen (Barrington)	290 0 33	Limerick	Clanwilliam	Clonkeen	Limerick	II.	223
12, 17	Clonkeen or Clondouglas	253 2 31	Queen's Co.	Maryborough West	Clonenagh and Clonagheen	Abbeyleix	I.	242
11, 12	Clonkeen (Cole)	188 3 9	Monaghan	Dartree	Clones	Clones	III.	264
59, 72	Clonkeenkerrill	905 0 30	Galway	Tiaquin	Clonkeen	Loughrea	IV.	76
16, 17	Clonkeen (Lucas)	255 2 11f	Monaghan	Dartree	Clones	Clones	III.	264
6, 14	Clonkeen (Molyneux)	214 3 33	Limerick	Clanwilliam	Clonkeen	Limerick	II.	223
3, 8	Clonkeeran	577 1 0	Kildare	Carbury	Mylerstown	Edenderry	I.	52
38,39,42,43	Clonkeiffy	974 1 24	Cavan	Castlerahan	Castlerahan	Oldcastle	III.	67
38	Clonkelly	534 3 2	King's Co.	Ballybritt	Birr	Parsonstown	I.	125
52	Clonkelly	393 1 21	Tipperary, S.R.	Kilnamanagh Lower	Oughterleague	Cashel	II.	324
30	Clonkerdin	256 0 3	Waterford	Decies without Drum	Whitechurch	Dungarvan	II.	361
12, 13	Clonkill	797 1 6	Westmeath	Moyashel and Magheradernon	Rathconnell	Mullingar	I.	276
44, 45	Clonkilly Beg	249 2 31	Donegal	Kilmacrenan	Kilmacrenan	Millford	III.	129
44, 45	Clonkilly More	237 3 29	Donegal	Kilmacrenan	Kilmacrenan	Millford	III.	129
11, 12	Clonkirk	314 2 39	Monaghan	Dartree	Clones	Clones	III.	264
11	Clonlack	323 3 3	King's Co.	Coolestown	Castlejordan	Edenderry	I.	132
71	Clonlahy	237 0 16	Tipperary, S.R.	Slievardagh	Kilvemnon	Callan	II.	334
21	Clonlahy Corporation-land	41 0 19	Queen's Co.	Clandonagh	Skirk	Donaghmore	I.	235
44,45,49,50	Clonlard	274 0 1	Wexford	Shelburne	St. James & Dunbrody	New Ross	I.	328
43	Clonlea	188 3 10g	Clare	Tulla Lower	Clonlea	Tulla	II.	34
135	Clonlea	133 1 31	Cork, W.R.	Ibane and Barryroe	Kilkerranmore	Clonakilty	II.	149
14	Clonleame	527 3 7	Westmeath	Delvin	Castletowndelvin	Castletowndelvin	I.	264
23	Clonleasan	379 0 21	Meath	Upper Kells	Girley	Kells	I.	205
36, 39	Clonlee	896 2 21	King's Co.	Ballybritt	Kinnitty	Parsonstown	I.	125
7	Clonleek	63 2 1	Monaghan	Trough	Donagh	Monaghan	III.	281
112, 125	Clonleigh	159 3 37	Cork, E.R.	Kinsale	Ringcurran	Kinsale	II.	100
24, 30	Clonleigh	991 1 30	Wexford	Bantry	Clonleigh	New Ross	I.	300
33	Clonliff	142 3 21	Fermanagh	Clanawley	Kinawley	Enniskillen	III.	193
18	Clonliff East	135 2 12h	Dublin	Coolock	St. Georges	Dublin North	I.	29
18	Clonliff South	84 2 6i	Dublin	Dublin, Municipal Borough of	St. Georges	Dublin North	I.	44
18	Clonliff West	64 3 27j	Dublin	Coolock	St. Georges	Dublin North	I.	29
45	Clonlisk	466 2 21	King's Co.	Clonlisk	Kilcomin	Roscrea	I.	130
37	Clonloaghan	693 0 18	Cavan	Clanmahon	Drumlumman	Granard	III.	77
51	Clonloghan	401 1 26	Clare	Bunratty Lower	Clonloghan	Ennis	II.	3
10	Clonlonan	86 0 12	Monaghan	Monaghan	Tehallan	Monaghan	III.	280
36	Clonlonan	201 0 31	Westmeath	Clonlonan	Kilcleagh	Athlone	I.	261
5	Clonlong	36 3 26	Limerick	Clanwilliam	St. Nicholas	Limerick	II.	225
25	Clonloskan	137 0 31k	Cavan	Upper Loughtee	Kilmore	Cavan	III.	84
20	Clonlost	819 1 17	Westmeath	Moyashel and Magheradernon	Rathconnell	Mullingar	I.	276
6	Clonloughna	119 3 0	Limerick	Owneybeg	Abington	Limerick	II.	250
28, 29	Clonlum	692 1 13	Armagh	Orior Upper	Killevy	Newry	III.	58
16	Clonlura	136 3 34	Monaghan	Dartree	Drummully	Clones	III.	266

(a) Including 22A. 1R. 38P. water.
(b) Including 5A. 3R. 22P. water.
(c) Including 11A. 0R. 39P. water.
(d) Including 3A. 3R. 30P. water.
(e) Including 1A. 2R. 2P. water.

(f) Including 13A. 3R. 28P. water.
(g) Including 52A. 0R. 12P. water.
(h) { Within the Municipal Boundary, 24A. 3R. 17P. Without the Municipal Boundary, 110A. 2R. 35P.

(i) Included in the Parish of St. George.
(j) { Within the Municipal Boundary, 1A. 0R. 9P. Without the Municipal Boundary, 63A. 3R. 18P.
(k) Including 2A. 2R. 25P. water.

No. of Sheet of the Ordnance Survey Maps.	Townlands and Towns.	Area in Statute Acres.			County.	Barony.	Parish.	Poor Law Union in 1857.	Townland Census of 1851, Part I.	
		A.	R.	P.					Vol.	Page
27	Clonlusk . . .	55	3	20	Meath .	Lower Duleek .	Duleek . . .	Drogheda . .	I.	195
59	Clonlusk . . .	68	2	0	Tipperary, S.R.	Clanwilliam .	Rathlynin . .	Tipperary . .	II.	309
43, 49	Clonlyon . . .	386	1	36	Meath . .	Upper Deece .	Kilmore . . .	Dunshaughlin .	I.	193
2	Clonlyon . . .	533	1	30	Queen's Co. .	Tinnahinch .	Kilmanman . .	Mountmellick .	I.	249
6, 14	Clonlyon Castlequarter	659	3	21	King's Co. .	Garrycastle .	Clonmacnoise .	Parsonstown .	I.	135
14	Clonlyon (Gerald) .	530	0	38	King's Co. .	Garrycastle .	Clonmacnoise .	Parsonstown .	I.	135
6, 14	Clonlyon Glebe .	886	3	24	King's Co. .	Garrycastle .	Clonmacnoise .	Parsonstown .	I.	135
5	Clonmacash . .	196	0	9	Armagh .	Oneilland West .	Tartaraghan .	Armagh . .	III.	54
34	Clonmacfelimy .	67	2	34	Fermanagh .	Magherastephana .	Aghalurcher .	Lisnaskea .	III.	215
40	Clonmackan . .	135	3	29	Fermanagh .	Clankelly . .	Clones . .	Clones . .	III.	195
5	Clonmacken . .	227	2	19	Limerick . .	Pubblebrien .	St. Munchins .	Limerick . .	II.	254
40	Clonmacmara . .	192	0	27	Cavan . .	Castlerahan .	Mullagh . .	Bailieborough .	III.	70
5, 6	Clonmacnoise .	913	3	26	King's Co. .	Garrycastle .	Clonmacnoise .	Parsonstown .	I.	135
12, 13	Clonmacshane .	160	3	28	Carlow . .	Forth . .	Templepeter .	Carlow . .	I.	5
25	Clonmagaddan .	264	2	2	Meath . .	Lower Navan .	Donaghmore .	Navan . .	I.	214
42, 43	Clonmahon . .	487	0	21	Meath . .	Lower Moyfenrath .	Laracor . .	Trim . .	I	210
4, 8	Clonmain . .	380	1	20	Armagh . .	Oneilland West .	Loughgall . .	Armagh . .	III.	53
77	Clonmaine . .	348	0	21	Cork, E.R. .	Imokilly . .	Ightermurragh .	Middleton .	II.	87
59	Clonmaine . .	178	1	19	Tipperary, S.R.	Clanwilliam .	Rathlynin . .	Tipperary . .	II.	309
15, 23	Clonmakane . .	387	0	24	Londonderry .	Tirkeeran .	Cumber Lower .	Londonderry .	III.	248
2, 5	Clonmakate . .	302	0	20	Armagh . .	Oneilland West .	Tartaraghan .	Lurgan . .	III.	54
9	Clonmakilladuff .	259	2	32	Tipperary, N.R.	Lower Ormond .	Kilbarron . .	Borrisokane .	II.	284
31	Clonmalevin . .	99	3	30	Meath . .	Lower Navan .	Rataine . .	Navan . .	I.	215
19, 25	Clonmannan . .	688	2	15	Wicklow . .	Newcastle .	Rathnew . .	Rathdrum .	I.	354
5, 9	Clonmartin . .	97	2	2	Armagh . .	Oneilland West .	Drumcree . .	Lurgan . .	III.	51
9, 14	Clonmaskill . .	534	3	34	Westmeath .	Delvin . .	Castletowndelvin .	Castletowndelvin	I.	264
16, 26	Clonmass . .	337	2	28	Donegal . .	Kilmacrenan .	Clondahorky .	Dunfanaghy .	III.	123
16	Clonmass Isle .	21	0	11	Donegal . .	Kilmacrenan .	Clondahorky .	Dunfanaghy .	III.	123
40	Clonmaulin . .	166	3	37	Fermanagh .	Clankelly . .	Galloon . .	Clones . .	III.	198
11	Clonmeen . .	655	3	3	King's Co. .	Coolestown .	Castlejordan .	Edenderry .	I.	132
34	Clonmeenan . .	66	1	9	Monaghan .	Farney . .	Magheracloone .	Carrickmacross	III.	272
31	Clonmeen North .	142	3	20a	Cork, E.R. .	Duhallow .	Clonmeen . .	Kanturk .	II.	69
33	Clonmeen North .	866	1	25	Queen's Co. .	Clandonagh .	Rathdowney .	Donaghmore .	I.	234
31	Clonmeen South .	392	3	34	Cork, E.R. .	Duhallow .	Clonmeen . .	Kanturk .	II.	69
33	Clonmeen South .	539	3	10	Queen's Co. .	Clandonagh .	Rathdowney .	Donaghmore .	I.	234
33	Clonmeenwood .	116	3	20	Queen's Co. .	Clandonagh .	Rathdowney .	Donaghmore .	I.	234
14	Clonmel . .	90	3	36	Dublin . .	Coolock . .	Glasnevin . .	Dublin North .	I.	27
20	Clonmel . .	685	0	10	King's Co. .	Coolestown .	Clonsast . .	Edenderry .	I.	133
9	Clonmellon . .	343	0	15	Westmeath .	Delvin . .	Killua . .	Castletowndelvin	I.	265
9	CLONMELLON T. .	—			Westmeath .	Delvin . .	Killua . .	Castletowndelvin	I.	266
12	Clonmelsh . .	384	1	14	Carlow . .	Carlow . .	Clonmelsh . .	Carlow . .	I.	1
83	CLONMEL T. .	—			Tipperary, S.R.	Iffa and Offa East .	St. Marys, Clonmel .	Clonmel . .	II.	316
1	CLONMEL T. .	—			Waterford .	Upperthird .	St. Marys, Clonmel .	Clonmel . .	II.	372
7	Clonmethan . .	221	3	39b	Dublin . .	Balrothery West .	Clonmethan .	Balrothery .	I.	22
13	Clonminan . .	156	0	35	Queen's Co. .	Maryborough East .	Borris . .	Mountmellick .	I.	240
17, 25	Clonminch . .	717	1	30	King's Co. .	Ballycowan .	Kilbride . .	Tullamore .	I.	127
40, 45	Clonmines . .	1,251	2	29	Wexford . .	Shelburne .	Clonmines .	New Ross .	I.	327
39	Clonmin Glebe .	34	3	37c	Fermanagh .	Coole . .	Galloon . .	Lisnaskea .	III.	199
28	Clonmoher . .	474	0	23	Clare . .	Tulla Upper .	Kilnoe . .	Scarriff . .	II.	40
5	Clonmona . .	519	1	1	Tipperary, N.R.	Lower Ormond .	Dorrha . .	Parsonstown .	II.	283
51, 61	Clonmoney North .	359	2	5	Clare . .	Bunratty Lower .	Bunratty . .	Ennis . .	II.	3
51, 61	Clonmoney South .	391	0	14	Clare . .	Bunratty Lower .	Bunratty . .	Ennis . .	II.	3
51, 61	Clonmoney West .	737	2	14	Clare . .	Bunratty Lower .	Bunratty . .	Ennis . .	II.	3
19	Clonmoran . .	127	1	19	Kilkenny . .	Shillelogher .	St. Patrick's .	Kilkenny . .	I.	116
4	Clonmore . .	344	2	14	Armagh . .	Oneilland West .	Killyman . .	Armagh . .	III.	53
15	Clonmore . .	115	2	20	Carlow . .	Idrone West .	Oldleighlin .	Carlow . .	I.	9
9	Clonmore . .	169	1	11	Carlow . .	Rathvilly .	Clonmore . .	Shillelagh .	I.	10
26	Clonmore . .	237	2	33	Donegal . .	Kilmacrenan .	Clondahorky .	Dunfanaghy .	III.	123
42	Clonmore . .	923	0	22	Kilkenny . .	Iverk . .	Clonmore . .	Carrick on Suir	I.	105
39	Clonmore . .	60	2	24	King's Co. .	Ballybritt .	Seirkieran .	Parsonstown .	I.	126
27	Clonmore . .	427	3	17	King's Co. .	Coolestown .	Clonsast . .	Edenderry .	I.	133
17	Clonmore . .	708	1	22	King's Co. .	Geashill .	Geashill . .	Tullamore .	I.	140
4	Clonmore . .	1,741	2	2	King's Co. .	Warrenstown .	Castlejordan .	Edenderry .	I.	145
18, 19	Clonmore . .	726	1	7	Louth . .	Ferrard . .	Clonmore . .	Drogheda .	I.	180
29, 30	Clonmore . .	539	0	13	Meath . .	Lune . .	Kildalkey .	Trim . .	I.	208
16	Clonmore . .	132	2	1	Monaghan .	Dartree . .	Clones . .	Clones . .	III.	264
21, 27	Clonmore . .	633	2	32	Queen's Co. .	Clandonagh .	Rathdowney .	Donaghmore .	I.	234
32, 37	Clonmore . .	180	3	7	Queen's Co. .	Slievemargy .	Killeshin .	Carlow . .	I.	245
40	Clon More . .	179	1	23	Tipperary, N.R.	Eliogarty .	Inch . .	Thurles . .	II.	270
23, 29	Clonmore . .	1,235	1	26	Tipperary, N.R.	Ikerrin . .	Killavinoge .	Roscrea . .	II.	275
26, 27	Clonmore . .	70	1	18	Tipperary, N.R.	Upper Ormond .	Dolla . .	Nenagh . .	II.	290
76	Clonmore . .	95	2	20	Tipperary, S.R.	Iffa and Offa East .	Inishlounaght .	Clonmel . .	II.	313
61	Clonmore . .	65	0	15	Tipperary, S.R.	Middlethird .	St. Patricksrock .	Cashel . .	II.	330

(a) Including 10A. 0R. 24P. water.   (b) Including 12A. 1R. 3P. detached portions.   (c) Including 6A. 2R. 25P. water.

No. of Sheet of the Ordnance Survey Maps.	Townlands and Towns.	Area in Statute Acres.	County.	Barony.	Parish.	Poor Law Union in 1857.	Townland Census of 1851, Part I.	
		A. R. P.					Vol.	Page
62	Clonmore	114 2 18	Tyrone	Dungannon Middle	Clonfeacle	Dungannon	III	299
31	Clonmore	17 0 34	Waterford	Decies without Drum	Dungarvan	Dungarvan	II	355
36	Clonmore	257 1 6	Westmeath	Clonlonan	Kilcleagh	Athlone	I	261
19, 26	Clonmore	366 2 26	Westmeath	Moyashel and Magheradernon	Mullingar	Mullingar	I	275
2	Clonmore	326 1 27	Westmeath	Moygoish	Street	Granard	I	281
31	Clonmore	315 1 23	Wexford	Bantry	Clonmore	Enniscorthy	I	300
11, 16	Clonmore	207 3 28	Wexford	Gorey	Liskinfere	Gorey	I	320
11, 16	Clonmore	230 3 38	Wexford	Gorey	Toome	Gorey	I	321
26	Clonmore Lower	369 2 36	Wexford	Ballaghkeen	Ballyhuskard	Enniscorthy	I	291
75, 81	Clonmore North	396 3 26	Tipperary, S.R.	Iffa and Offa West	Caher	Clogheen	II	317
52	Clonmore North	332 0 29	Tipperary, S.R.	Middlethird	Ardmayle	Cashel	II	324
81	Clonmore South	614 1 31	Tipperary, S.R.	Iffa and Offa West	Caher	Clogheen	II	317
52, 60	Clonmore South	154 1 19	Tipperary, S.R.	Middlethird	Ardmayle	Cashel	II	324
26	Clonmore Upper	384 1 24	Wexford	Ballaghkeen	Ballyhuskard	Enniscorthy	I	291
59	Clonmorewalk	227 2 15	Tipperary, S.R.	Clanwilliam	Templenoe	Tipperary	II	311
14	Clonmorrill	193 1 4a	Westmeath	Delvin	Castletowndelvin	Castletowndelvin	I	264
41, 42	Clonmowley	213 1 12	Meath	Lower Moyfenrath	Rathmolyon	Trim	I	211
82	Clonmoyle	461 3 35	Cork, W.R.	West Muskerry	Kilmichael	Dunmanway	II	158
22	Clonmoyle	263 3 26	Kildare	Offaly East	Rathangan	Edenderry	I	71
7	Clonmoyle	202 3 13	Waterford	Upperthird	Mothel	Carrick on Suir	II	371
26	Clonmoyle	17 3 27	Westmeath	Fartullagh	Lynn	Mullingar	I	269
61	Clonmoyle East	756 0 8	Cork, W.R.	East Muskerry	Aghabulloge	Macroom	II	153
61	Clonmoyle West	774 0 10	Cork, W.R.	East Muskerry	Aghabulloge	Macroom	II	153
16, 21, 22	Clonmoyle West	572 3 0	Kildare	Offaly East	Rathangan	Edenderry	I	71
21	Clonmullen	291 1 34	Carlow	Forth	Barragh	Enniscorthy	I	4
35	Clonmullin	11 2 16	Kildare	Narragh & Reban West	St. Johns	Athy	I	68
35	Clonmullin	55 3 15	Kildare	Narragh & Reban West	St. Michaels	Athy	I	68
31	Clonmult	94 1 26	Cavan	Clanmahon	Crosserlough	Cavan	III	76
54, 55	Clonmult	466 1 28	Cork, E.R.	Barrymore	Clonmult	Middleton	II	53
55	CLONMULT T.	—	Cork, E.R.	Barrymore	{ Clonmult / Dungourney }	Middleton	II	{ 53 / 54 }
45	Clonmurragha	304 1 34	Tipperary, N.R.	Kilnamanagh Upper	Toem	Tipperary	II	280
8, 9, 13, 14	Clonnagapple	61 1 25	Westmeath	Delvin	Castletowndelvin	Castletowndelvin	I	264
3, 4	Clonnageeragh	675 3 0b	Westmeath	Fore	St. Feighins	Castletowndelvin	I	271
16	Clonnagore	165 0 38c	Monaghan	Dartree	Drummully	Clones	III	266
17	Clonnalynagh	103 1 19	Westmeath	Rathconrath	Killare	Ballymahon	I	283
24	Clonnamanagh	73 1 9	Westmeath	Rathconrath	Killare	Ballymahon	I	283
43	Clonnaroo	170 3 3d	Fermanagh	Coole	Drummully	Clones	III	199
32	Clonnasheeoge	163 0 19	Wexford	Ballaghkeen	Kilmallock	Enniscorthy	I	296
16	Clonnestin	170 3 15	Monaghan	Dartree	Drummully	Clones	III	266
18	Clonogan	543 1 23	Carlow	St. Mullins Upper	Moyacomb	Shillelagh	I	14
23, 29	Clonoghil	244 1 25	Queen's Co.	Cullenagh	Abbeyleix	Abbeyleix	I	238
15, 16	Clonoghil	527 1 6	Queen's Co.	Upperwoods	Offerlane	Mountmellick	I	251
35	Clonoghil Lower	578 0 38	King's Co.	Ballybritt	Birr	Parsonstown	I	125
35	Clonoghil Upper	541 2 6	King's Co.	Ballybritt	Birr	Parsonstown	I	125
95, 109	Clonomara	207 0 32	Cork, W.R.	East Carbery (W.D.)	Kinneigh	Dunmanway	II	134
21	Clononeen	327 2 25	Queen's Co.	Upperwoods	Offerlane	Donaghmore	I	251
21, 22	Clonony Beg	693 2 29	King's Co.	Garrycastle	Gallen	Parsonstown	I	136
22	Clonony More	732 1 32	King's Co.	Garrycastle	Gallen	Parsonstown	I	136
22	CLONONY T.	—	King's Co.	Garrycastle	Gallen	Parsonstown	I	136
15	Clonoonagh	346 3 13	Queen's Co.	Clandonagh	Kyle	Roscrea	I	233
16	Clonoony	213 1 27	Monaghan	Dartree	Drummully	Clones	III	266
37	Clonoose Big	376 2 11	Cavan	Clanmahon	Drumlumman	Granard	III	77
37	Clonoose Little	260 0 0	Cavan	Clanmahon	Drumlumman	Granard	III	77
11, 15	Clonosey	367 2 23e	Cavan	Lower Loughtee	Annagh	Cavan	III	78
3	Clonough	162 0 0	Wexford	Gorey	Kilgorman	Gorey	I	318
16	Clonoula	239 0 16	Monaghan	Dartree	Drummully	Clones	III	266
46, 52	Clonoulty Church-quarter	407 0 38	Tipperary, S.R.	Kilnamanagh Lower	Clonoulty	Cashel	II	323
46, 52	Clonoulty Curragh	204 3 33	Tipperary, S.R.	Kilnamanagh Lower	Clonoulty	Cashel	II	323
46	Clonoulty Hill	207 1 6	Tipperary, S.R.	Kilnamanagh Lower	Clonoulty	Cashel	II	323
48	Clonoura	1,596 1 28	Tipperary, S.R.	Slievardagh	Fennor	Urlingford	II	333
24	Clonownmore	184 1 13	Westmeath	Rathconrath	Conry	Mullingar	I	282
36	Clonpadden	94 1 16	Wicklow	Arklow	Ennereilly	Rathdrum	I	344
66, 67	Clonpet	387 0 1	Tipperary, S.R.	Clanwilliam	Clonpet	Tipperary	II	306
26	Clonpierce	540 1 5	Queen's Co.	Ballyadams	Killabban	Athy	I	231
78	Clonpriest East	114 0 38	Cork, E.R.	Imokilly	Clonpriest	Youghal	II	84
78	Clonpriest West	281 2 14	Cork, E.R.	Imokilly	Clonpriest	Youghal	II	84
29, 30, 35	Clonrah and Glaster	261 3 25	King's Co.	Garrycastle	Lusmagh	Parsonstown	I	137
5	Clonraskin	128 1 2	Tipperary, N.R.	Lower Ormond	Loughkeen	Parsonstown	II	286
22, 23	Clonvar	243 2 7	Cavan	Clankee	Drumgoon	Cootehill	III	72
20, 25	Clonreagh	191 3 26	Antrim	Lower Glenarm	Ardclinis	Larne	III	21

(a) Including 0A. 3R. 7P. water.
(b) Including 19A. 0R. 15P. water.
(c) Including 5A. 2R. 22P. water.
(d) Including 6A. 3R. 22P. water.
(e) Including 96A. 1R. 31P. water.

2 L

No. of Sheet of the Ordnance Survey Maps.	Townlands and Towns.	Area in Statute Acres.			County.	Barony.	Parish.	Poor Law Union in 1857.	Townland Census of 1851, Part I.	
		A.	R.	P.					Vol.	Page
20	Clonreagh . .	28	0	19	Westmeath .	Farbill . . .	Killucan . . .	Mullingar . .	I.	266
12, 13	Clonreher . .	567	1	0	Queen's Co. .	Maryborough East .	Borris . . .	Mountmellick .	I.	240
30	Clonrelick . .	144	1	8	Westmeath .	Clonlonan . .	Ballyloughloe .	Athlone . .	I.	260
33	Clonroad Beg .	274	0	28	Clare . .	Islands . . .	Drumcliff . .	Ennis . .	II.	29
33	Clonroad More .	654	1	11	Clare . .	Islands . . .	Drumcliff . .	Ennis . .	II.	30
3	Clonrobert . .	156	2	36	Westmeath .	Fore . . .	Lickbla . .	Granard . .	I.	270
23	Clonrobin . .	545	1	30	Cork, E.R. .	Duhallow . .	Kilbrin . . .	Kanturk . .	II.	72
25, 31	Clonroche . .	773	0	2	Wexford . .	Bantry . . .	Chapel . . .	Enniscorthy .	I.	299
25	CLONROCHE T. .	—			Wexford . .	Bantry . . .	Chapel . . .	Enniscorthy .	I.	299
2	Clonroe Lower .	225	1	35	Wexford . .	Gorey . . .	Kilnenor . .	Gorey . .	I.	319
2	Clonroe Upper .	230	2	0	Wexford . .	Gorey . . .	Kilnenor . .	Gorey . .	I.	319
13	Clonroosk . .	122	0	17	Queen's Co. .	Maryborough East .	Clonenagh and Clonagheen . .	Mountmellick .	I.	241
20, 28	Clonroosk Big .	158	0	19	King's Co. .	Coolestown . .	Clonsast . .	Edenderry .	I.	133
20	Clonroosk Little .	110	1	16	King's Co. .	Coolestown . .	Clonsast . .	Edenderry .	I.	133
13	Clonroosk Little .	111	3	33	Queen's Co. .	Maryborough East .	Clonenagh and Clonagheen . .	Mountmellick .	I.	241
9	Clonroot . .	404	0	32	Armagh . .	Oneilland West .	Kilmore . .	Armagh . .	III.	53
44	Clonross . .	230	3	20	Meath . .	Ratoath . . .	Dunshaughlin .	Dunshaughlin .	I.	218
17, 23	Clonrud . .	153	0	10	Queen's Co. .	Maryborough West .	Clonenagh and Clonagheen . .	Abbeyleix .	I.	242
135, 137	Clonrush . .	176	0	19	Galway . .	Leitrim . . .	Clonrush . .	Scarriff . .	IV.	52
16	Clonrye . .	77	1	19	Monaghan .	Dartree . . .	Drummully . .	Clones . .	III.	266
5	Clonsast . .	265	3	24	Kildare . .	Ikeathy & Oughterany	Kilcock . .	Celbridge . .	I.	57
27	Clonsast Lower .	1,077	2	18	King's Co. .	Coolestown . .	Clonsast . .	Edenderry .	I.	133
27	Clonsast Upper .	1,775	1	35	King's Co. .	Coolestown . .	Clonsast . .	Edenderry .	I.	133
31, 34	Clonsedy . .	297	2	1	Monaghan .	Farney . . .	Magheracloone .	Carrickmacross	III.	272
32	Clonseer . .	132	2	25	King's Co. .	Ballyboy . .	Killoughy . .	Tullamore .	I.	124
15	Clonshagh . .	16	0	10	Dublin . .	Coolock . . .	Cloghran . .	Balrothery .	I.	26
14, 15	Clonshagh . .	474	0	15	Dublin . .	Coolock . . .	Santry . . .	Dublin North .	I.	29
9, 10	Clonshanbo . .	444	1	13	Kildare . .	Ikeathy & Oughterany	Clonshanbo . .	Celbridge . .	I.	57
43	Clonshannagh .	180	1	7a	Fermanagh .	Coole . . .	Drummully . .	Clones . .	III.	199
32	Clonshannagh .	494	1	10	King's Co. .	Ballyboy . .	Killoughy . .	Tullamore .	I.	124
27	Clonshannon .	815	2	24	King's Co. .	Coolestown . .	Clonsast . .	Edenderry .	I.	133
22, 28	Clonshannon .	202	2	27	Wicklow . .	Upper Talbotstown .	Donaghmore .	Baltinglass .	I.	363
7, 8	Clonshanny . .	496	0	10	King's Co. .	Ballycowan . .	Rahan . . .	Tullamore .	I.	128
16	Clonshanvo . .	100	3	11	Monaghan .	Dartree . . .	Drummully . .	Clones . .	III.	266
44	Clonsharragh .	527	3	30	Wexford . .	Shelburne . .	St. James & Dunbrody	New Ross .	I.	328
6, 14	Clonshavoy .	24	1	28	Limerick . .	Owneybeg . .	Abington . .	Limerick . .	II.	250
19	Clonsheever .	401	0	29b	Westmeath .	Moyashel and Magheradernon .	Rathconnell .	Mullingar .	I.	276
21	Clonshire Beg .	270	3	10	Limerick . .	Connello Lower .	Clonshire . .	Rathkeale .	II.	227
20, 21	Clonshire More .	218	1	4	Limerick . .	Connello Lower .	Clonshire . .	Rathkeale .	II.	227
13	Clonsilla . .	382	3	9	Dublin . .	Castleknock . .	Clonsilla . .	Celbridge . .	I.	24
7	Clonsilla East .	300	3	23	Wexford . .	Gorey . . .	Kilcavan . .	Gorey . .	I.	317
7	Clonsilla West .	271	0	34	Wexford . .	Gorey . . .	Kilcavan . .	Gorey . .	I.	317
37	Clonsingle . .	287	3	2	Tipperary, N.R.	Owney and Arra .	Kilvellane . .	Nenagh . .	II.	296
32	Clonsingle . .	360	1	8	Westmeath .	Moycashel . .	Castletownkindalen	Mullingar .	I.	277
22	Clonskeagh . .	0	1	8	Dublin . .	Uppercross . .	Donnybrook .	Dublin South .	I.	40
18, 22	Clonskeagh . .	68	1	26	Dublin . .	Dublin . . .	Donnybrook .	Dublin South .	I.	30
22	CLONSKEAGH T. .	—			Dublin . .	Dublin . . .	Donnybrook .	Dublin South .	I.	30
7, 8, 12, 13	Clonsoghey . .	696	2	22	Queen's Co. .	Maryborough East .	Borris . . .	Mountmellick .	I.	240
1, 3	Clonsura . .	559	3	23c	Westmeath .	Fore . . .	Lickbla . .	Granard . .	I.	270
7	Clonswords . .	58	1	3	Dublin . .	Balrothery West .	Ballyboghil .	Balrothery .	I.	22
23	Clontaaffe . .	462	1	21	Tipperary, N.R.	Ikerrin . . .	Templemore .	Roscrea . .	II.	276
142	Clontaff . .	121	0	14	Cork, W.R. .	West Carbery (E.D.)	Myross . .	Skibbereen .	III.	141
51	Clonta Fleece .	436	1	39	Down . .	Upper Iveagh, Up. pt.	Clonallan . .	Newry . .	III.	174
23	Clontaghnaglar .	932	0	23	Down . .	Castlereagh Upper .	Kilmore . .	Downpatrick .	III.	165
31	Clontaglass . .	285	2	9	King's Co. .	Ballyboy . .	Ballyboy . .	Parsonstown .	I.	123
6, 12	Clontail . .	334	3	8	Meath . .	Lower Slane . .	Mitchelstown .	Ardee . .	I.	223
16	Clontallagh . .	230	2	15	Donegal . .	Kilmacrenan . .	Mevagh . .	Milford . .	III.	130
22, 29	Clontanagullion .	802	3	19d	Down . .	Kinelarty . .	Dromara . .	Lisburn . .	III.	176
18, 19	Clontarf East .	112	0	24	Dublin . .	Coolock . . .	Clontarf . .	Dublin North .	I.	26
19	CLONTARF SHEDS T. .	—			Dublin . .	Coolock . . .	Clontarf . .	Dublin North .	I.	26
19	CLONTARF T. .	—			Dublin . .	Coolock . . .	Clontarf . .	Dublin North .	I.	26
18	Clontarf West .	114	2	34	Dublin . .	Coolock . . .	Clontarf . .	Dublin North .	I.	26
16	Clontask . .	84	0	34	Monaghan .	Dartree . . .	Drummully . .	Clones . .	III.	266
72	Clontead Beg .	227	1	22	Cork, E.R. .	East Muskerry .	Magourney .	Macroom . .	II.	105
72	Clontead More .	339	1	9	Cork, E.R. .	East Muskerry .	Magourney .	Macroom . .	II.	105
7	Clonteens . .	67	2	0	Westmeath .	Fore . . .	Mayne . .	Granard . .	I.	271
55, 62	Clonteevy . .	155	0	7	Tyrone . .	Dungannon Middle .	Clonfeacle . .	Dungannon .	III.	299
21	Clonteige . .	65	2	25	Tipperary, N.R.	Upper Ormond .	Ballymackey .	Nenagh . .	II.	289
38	Clontelaghan .	106	0	12	Fermanagh .	Clanawley . .	Kinawley . .	Enniskillen .	III.	193
24	Clonterlough .	140	3	38	King's Co. .	Ballyboy . .	Killoughy . .	Tullamore .	I.	124

(a) Including 9A. 0R. 34P. water.
(b) Including 47A. 2R. 30P. water.
(c) Including 26A. 2R. 24P. water.
(d) Including 9A. 1R. 32P. water.

No. of Sheet of the Ordnance Survey Maps.	Townlands and Towns.	Area in Statute Acres. A. R. P.	County.	Barony.	Parish.	Poor Law Union in 1857.	Townland Census of 1851. Part I. Vol.	Page
4, 8	Clonterry	393 0 9	Queen's Co.	Portnahinch	Ardea	Mountmellick	I.	243
30	Clonthread	227 0 24	Westmeath	Clonlonan	Ballyloughloe	Athlone	I.	260
11,12,16,17	Clontibret	132 1 35a	Monaghan	Dartree	Clones	Clones	III.	264
25	Clontinteen	160 0 12	Westmeath	Rathconrath	Churchtown	Mullingar	I.	282
27	Clontinty	148 1 15	Cork, E.R.	Fermoy	Glanworth	Fermoy	II.	79
40	Clontivrin	228 3 26	Fermanagh	Clankelly	Clones	Clones	III.	195
9	Clontoe	86 0 36	Monaghan	Monaghan	Tedavnet	Monaghan	III.	278
9,10,15,16	Clontonakelly	621 0 23	Down	Castlereagh Upper	Comber	Lisburn	III.	164
9, 10	Clontonakelly	617 0 24	Down	Castlereagh Upper	Drumbo	Lisburn	III.	164
29, 30	Clontotan	123 0 3	King's Co.	Garrycastle	Reynagh	Parsonstown	I.	138
34	Clontrain	191 0 19	Monaghan	Farney	Magheracloone	Carrickmacross	III.	272
12, 17	Clontreat	91 0 13	Monaghan	Dartree	Clones	Clones	III.	264
9	Clontubbrid	386 1 35	Kilkenny	Crannagh	Sheffin	Urlingford	I.	86
9	Clontumpher	613 3 33	Longford	Longford	Killoe	Longford	I.	158
14, 18	Clonturk	235 2 37	Dublin	Coolock	Clonturk	Dublin North	I.	26
35	Clonturkan	173 1 17	Cavan	Clankee	Enniskeen	Bailieborough	III.	72
33, 38	Clonturkle	296 1 26	Fermanagh	Knockninny	Kinawley	Lisnaskea	III.	201
31, 34	Clonturk (Mason)	149 2 15	Monaghan	Farney	Killanny	Carrickmacross	III.	271
6	Clontybunnia	147 0 30	Monaghan	Monaghan	Tedavnet	Monaghan	III.	278
9	Clontycarnaghan	370 3 16	Cavan	Tullyhaw	Templeport	Bawnboy	III.	94
11	Clontycarty	178 0 12	Armagh	Tiranny	Tynan	Armagh	III.	60
6	Clontycasta	230 2 9	Monaghan	Monaghan	Tedavnet	Monaghan	III.	278
4	Clontyclay	328 0 2	Armagh	Oneilland West	Killyman	Armagh	III.	53
53	Clontyclevin	214 1 12	Tyrone	Dungannon Lower	Killeeshil	Dungannon	III.	298
24	Clontycoe	244 2 27	Queen's Co.	Cullenagh	Ballyroan	Abbeyleix	I.	239
24	Clontycoe	202 2 26	Queen's Co.	Cullenagh	Dysartgallen	Abbeyleix	I.	239
14	Clontycoo	94 0 22	Cavan	Lower Loughtee	Drumlane	Cavan	III.	79
33	Clontycoora	250 0 31b	Fermanagh	Tirkennedy	Cleenish	Enniskillen	III.	220
42	Clontyduffy (Hart)	131 3 35	Cavan	Clanmahon	Kilbride	Oldcastle	III.	77
42	Clontyduffy (Nugent)	200 3 20	Cavan	Clanmahon	Kilbride	Oldcastle	III.	77
53	Clontyfallow	109 1 5	Tyrone	Dungannon Lower	Killeeshil	Dungannon	III.	298
26	Clontyferagh	85 3 22	Fermanagh	Clanawley	Killesher	Enniskillen	III.	192
29	Clontyferagh	175 0 4	Tyrone	Dungannon Upper	Kildress	Cookstown	III.	308
13	Clontyfinnan East	340 0 13	Antrim	Upper Dunluce	Loughguile	Ballymoney	III.	20
13	Clontyfinnan West	415 3 12	Antrim	Upper Dunluce	Loughguile	Ballymoney	III.	20
7, 12	Clontyglass	331 2 30	Queen's Co.	Maryborough West	Clonenagh and Clonagheen	Mountmellick	I.	242
29, 32	Clontygora	1,205 1 11	Armagh	Orior Upper	Killevy	Newry	III.	58
14	Clontygrigny	379 2 7c	Cavan	Tullyhunco	Kildallan	Bawnboy	III.	96
5	Clontylew	147 2 27	Armagh	Oneilland West	Tartaraghan	Lurgan	III.	54
33	Clontymore	119 2 5d	Fermanagh	Clanawley	Kinawley	Enniskillen	III.	193
26,27,32,33	Clontymullan	587 1 31	Fermanagh	Clanawley	Killesher	Enniskillen	III.	192
20, 24	Clontymullan	654 0 1	Longford	Ardagh	Rathreagh	Ballymahon	I.	153
107, 110	Clontyseer	198 0 26	Donegal	Tirhugh	Kilbarron	Ballyshannon	III.	148
33	Clontytallon	121 1 34	Westmeath	Fartullagh	Castlelost	Mullingar	I.	268
3	Clonuff	553 3 29	Kildare	Carbury	Mylerstown	Edenderry	I.	52
40	Clonumphry	106 0 2	Fermanagh	Clankelly	Galloon	Clones	III.	198
33	Clonursan Glebe	228 1 28e	Fermanagh	Clanawley	Killesher	Enniskillen	III.	192
36, 43	Clonvaraghan	1,241 3 26	Down	Upper Iveagh, Lr. pt.	Kilmegan	Downpatrick	III.	173
77	Clonwalsh	263 2 30	Tipperary, S.R.	Iffa and Offa East	Kilgrant	Clonmel	II.	314
20	Clonwhelan	387 1 12	Longford	Ardagh	Mostrim	Granard	I.	152
40	Clonwilliam	356 2 38	Wicklow	Arklow	Killahurler	Rathdrum	I.	345
24	Clonybane	399 3 1	Westmeath	Rathconrath	Killare	Ballymahon	I.	283
26	Clonybecan	289 2 27	Queen's Co.	Slievemargy	Killabban	Carlow	I.	245
9	Clonyburn	204 2 30	Wexford	Scarawalsh	St. Marys Newtownbarry	Enniscorthy	I.	325
35, 41	Clonycavan	1,179 1 33	Meath	Lune	Killaconnigan	Trim	I.	208
42	Clonycurry	371 2 20	Meath	Lower Moyfenrath	Rathmolyon	Trim	I.	211
36	Clonydonnin	377 1 24	Westmeath	Clonlonan	Kilcleagh	Athlone	I.	261
30	Clonyegan	246 3 5	Westmeath	Clonlonan	Ballyloughloe	Athlone	I.	260
31, 32	Clonygaheen	189 3 9	Tipperary, N.R.	Owney and Arra	Killoscully	Nenagh	II.	295
1, 3	Clonygark or Rearyvalley	582 1 32	Queen's Co.	Tinnahinch	Rearymore	Mountmellick	I.	250
26	Clonygarra	120 0 27	Kilkenny	Kells	Coolaghmore	Callan	I.	107
22	Clonygoose	156 1 17	Carlow	Idrone East	Clonygoose	Carlow	I.	6
26, 33	Clonygowan	953 1 38	King's Co.	Upper Philipstown	Ballykean	Mountmellick	I.	143
7, 12	Clonygowan	1,276 3 25	Queen's Co.	Maryborough West	Clonenagh and Clonagheen	Mountmellick	I.	242
33	CLONYGOWAN T.	—	King's Co.	Upper Philipstown	Ballykean	Mountmellick	I.	143
35	Clonygrange	160 3 26	Meath	Lune	Killaconnigan	Trim	I.	208
32	Clonyhague	706 2 37	Westmeath	Moycashel	Newtown	Mullingar	I.	278
46	Clonyharp	42 1 16	Tipperary, N.R.	Kilnamanagh Upper	Moyaliff	Cashel	II.	279
46	Clonyharp	433 3 18	Tipperary, S.R.	Kilnamanagh Lower	Clogher	Cashel	II.	322
33	Clonyhurk	1,073 3 0	King's Co.	Upper Philipstown	Clonyhurk	Mountmellick	I.	143

(a) Including 10A. 1R. 21P. water.
(b) Including 12A. 3R. 31P. water.
(c) Including 29A. 1R. 16P. water.
(d) Including 8A. 1R. 8P. water.
(e) Including 10A. 3R. 36P. River Erne.

2 L 2

No. of Sheet of the Ordnance Survey Maps.	Townlands and Towns.	Area in Statute Acres.			County.	Barony.	Parish.	Poor Law Union in 1857.	Townland Census of 1851, Part I.	
		A.	R.	P.					Vol.	Page
35, 36	Clonylogan	450	3	22	Meath	Lune	Kildalkey	Trim	I.	208
43	Clonymeath	914	2	12	Meath	Lower Deece	Galtrim	Trim	I.	191
45	Clonymohan	480	1	29	King's Co.	Clonlisk	Castletownely	Roscrea	I.	129
24, 30	Clonymore	516	0	38	Meath	Lune	Rathmore	Trim	I.	208
17	Clonymurtagh	54	2	29	Westmeath	Rathconrath	Ballymorin	Mullingar	I.	282
13, 14	Clonyn	661	3	18	Westmeath	Delvin	Castletowndelvin	Castletowndelvin	I.	264
33, 34	Clonyquin	732	2	0	King's Co.	Upper Philipstown	Clonyhurk	Mountmellick	I.	143
78, 79	Clonyreel	224	2	3	Donegal	Raphoe	Donaghmore	Stranorlar	III.	137
24	Clonyrina	222	2	4	Westmeath	Rathconrath	Conry	Mullingar	I.	282
24	Clonyveey	212	2	5	Westmeath	Rathconrath	Killare	Ballymahon	I.	283
1	Cloodrevagh	27	3	26	Leitrim	Rosclogher	Rossinver	Ballyshannon	IV.	111
24, 28	Cloodrumman Beg	91	3	17a	Leitrim	Leitrim	Fenagh	Mohill	IV.	100
24, 28	Cloodrumman More	108	0	25b	Leitrim	Leitrim	Fenagh	Mohill	IV.	100
26, 34	Cloon	109	3	35	Cork, E.R.	Fermoy	Bridgetown	Fermoy	II.	77
55	Cloon	285	1	33	Donegal	Raphoe	Allsaints	Londonderry	III.	134
27	Cloon	48	3	17	Fermanagh	Tirkennedy	Cleenish	Enniskillen	III.	220
22	Cloon	342	2	31c	Galway	Ballynahinch	Ballynakill	Clifden	IV.	11
21	Cloon	94	2	5d	Galway	Ballynahinch	Omey	Clifden	IV.	15
82	Cloon	440	3	7	Galway	Dunkellin	Claregalway	Galway	IV.	27
123	Cloon	353	2	6	Galway	Kiltartan	Kilbeacanty	Gort	IV.	47
88, 97	Cloon	338	1	5	Kerry	Iveragh	Prior	Cahersiveen	II.	198
21	Cloon	35	3	29	Tipperary, N.R.	Upper Ormond	Templedowney	Nenagh	II.	293
52, 60	Cloon	35	0	14	Tipperary, S.R.	Middlethird	Ardmayle	Cashel	II.	324
47	Cloon	54	1	2	Wexford	Forth	Mayglass	Wexford	I.	312
3, 7	Cloon	693	0	39	Wicklow	Rathdown	Powerscourt	Rathdown	I.	356
25	Cloona	224	1	28	Clare	Inchiquin	Dysert	Ennis	II.	24
73	Cloonacalleen	158	0	36	Galway	Kilconnell	Kilconnell	Ballinasloe	IV.	40
73, 86	Cloonacalleen	118	2	18	Galway	Kilconnell	Killaan	Ballinasloe	IV.	41
48	Cloonacaltry	402	2	17	Roscommon	Athlone	Taghmaconnell	Athlone	IV.	185
39	Cloonacaltry	90	0	1	Sligo	Corran	Drumrat	Boyle	IV.	225
62	Cloonacannana	329	3	9e	Mayo	Gallen	Kilconduff	Swineford	IV.	147
33	Cloonacarn	53	1	32	Fermanagh	Magherastephana	Cleenish	Lisnaskea	III.	219
7	Cloonacarrow	109	1	15	Roscommon	Boyle	Tumna	Boyle	IV.	197
9	Cloonacarrow	230	3	23	Roscommon	Frenchpark	Kilnamanagh	Boyle	IV.	204
116	Cloonacastle	227	0	3	Galway	Leitrim	Duniry	Portumna	IV.	53
39	Cloonacauna	105	1	4	Mayo	Tirawley	Kilbelfad	Ballina	IV.	167
82	Cloonacauneen	29	0	16	Galway	Dunkellin	Claregalway	Galway	IV.	27
82	Cloonacauneen	449	2	32	Galway	Galway	Oranmore	Galway	IV.	37
32, 38	Cloonacleigha	145	3	30f	Sligo	Corran	Cloonoghil	Tobercurry	IV.	225
13	Cloonacolly	700	0	8g	Roscommon	Frenchpark	Tibohine	Castlereagh	IV.	204
24, 31	Cloonacool	4,291	1	0h	Sligo	Leyny	Achonry	Tobercurry	IV.	229
30	Cloonacullina	280	1	34	King's Co.	Garrycastle	Reynagh	Parsonstown	I.	138
26	Cloonacurra	471	1	9i	Sligo	Tirerrill	Ballysadare	Tobercurry	IV.	237
39	Cloonacurrig	153	1	22	Kerry	Trughanacmy	Dysert	Tralee	II.	210
92	Cloonacurry	194	3	20j	Mayo	Costello	Bekan	Claremorris	IV.	139
2	Cloonadarragh	328	3	31	Galway	Ballymoe	Drumatemple	Glennamaddy	IV.	7
34	Cloonadarragh East	104	1	18	Roscommon	Ballymoe	Drumatemple	Glennamaddy	IV.	191
36	Cloonaddra	613	0	9	Roscommon	Ballintober South	Cloontuskert	Roscommon	IV.	188
50, 53	Cloonaddron	732	1	4k	Roscommon	Athlone	Taghmaconnell	Ballinasloe	IV.	185
16	Cloonaderavally	129	2	13	Sligo	Tireragh	Kilglass	Dromore West	IV.	234
38	Cloonadrum	390	1	14	Clare	Ibrickan	Kilmurry	Kilrush	II.	23
12	Cloonaduff	50	0	14	Limerick	Pubblebrien	Croom	Limerick	II.	252
20	Cloonaff	345	2	7	Roscommon	Castlereagh	Kilkeevin	Castlereagh	IV.	200
32,33,38,39	Cloonagahaun	141	3	31l	Sligo	Corran	Cloonoghil	Tobercurry	IV.	225
61, 71	Cloonagalloon	155	3	12	Mayo	Gallen	Meelick	Swineford	IV.	150
33	Cloonagashel	248	0	31	Sligo	Corran	Kilmorgan	Sligo	IV.	226
30, 31	Cloonagawnagh	71	3	26	Galway	Ballymoe	Clonbern	Tuam	IV.	6
4, 8	Cloonageeher	707	0	29	Longford	Longford	Mohill	Longford	I.	159
36	Cloonageeragh	560	2	27	Roscommon	Ballintober South	Kilgiffin	Roscommon	IV.	189
31	Cloonagh	566	0	36	Galway	Ballymoe	Dunmore	Glennamaddy	IV.	7
57	Cloonagh	45	0	9	Galway	Clare	Annaghdown	Tuam	IV.	16
16, 17	Cloonagh	449	2	6	Galway	Dunmore	Dunmore	Tuam	IV.	33
15	Cloonagh	127	0	26	Leitrim	Drumahaire	Killarga	Manorhamilton	IV.	98
6	Cloonagh	463	2	6m	Longford	Granard	Columbkille	Granard	I.	155
4, 5, 8, 9	Cloonagh	676	0	39	Longford	Longford	Killoe	Longford	I.	158
19	Cloonagh	98	0	5	Longford	Moydow	Kilglass	Ballymahon	I.	161
78	Cloonagh	263	2	15	Mayo	Carra	Aglish	Castlebar	IV.	123
79	Cloonagh	111	0	28n	Mayo	Carra	Drum	Castlebar	IV.	128
101	Cloonagh	301	2	2	Mayo	Clanmorris	Tagheen	Claremorris	IV.	136
87	Cloonagh	169	3	14	Mayo	Murrisk	Aghagower	Westport	IV.	158
2	Cloonagh	44	3	38	Queen's Co.	Tinnahinch	Kilmanman	Mountmellick	I.	249
7	Cloonagh	161	0	7	Queen's Co.	Tinnahinch	Rosenallis	Mountmellick	I.	250
47	Cloonagh	360	3	0o	Roscommon	Athlone	Taghboy	Athlone	IV.	184

(a) Including 20A. 2R. 16P. water.
(b) Including 7A. 0R. 0P. water.
(c) Including 19A. 0R. 16P. water.
(d) Part of Omey Island, and includes 16A. 0R. 28P. water.
(e) Including 5A. 0R. 20P. water.

(f) Including 23A. 3R. 29P. water.
(g) Including 109A. 3R. 37P. water.
(h) Including 18A. 2R. 38P. water.
(i) Including 9A. 2R. 33P. water.
(j) Including 11A. 3R. 3P. water.

(k) Including 11A. 0R. 10P. water.
(l) Including 9A. 2R. 9P. water.
(m) Including 3A. 2R. 34P. water.
(n) Including 18A. 0R. 28P. water.
(o) Including 21A. 3R. 8P. water.

No. of Sheet of the Ordnance Survey Maps.	Townlands and Towns.	Area in Statute Acres.	County.	Barony.	Parish.	Poor Law Union in 1857.	Townland Census of 1851, Part I.	
		A. R. P.					Vol.	Page
13, 19	Cloonagh	488 2 19a	Roscommon	Frenchpark	Tibohine	Castlereagh	IV.	204
4	Cloonagh	315 3 34	Sligo	Carbury	Drumcliff	Sligo	IV.	221
39, 40	Cloonagh	171 2 38	Sligo	Corran	Toomour	Boyle	IV.	228
19	Cloonagh	948 1 36	Sligo	Tireragh	Dromard	Dromore West	IV.	233
27	Cloonagh	172 2 25b	Sligo	Tirerrill	Ballynakill	Sligo	IV.	237
12	Cloonagh	498 3 8	Tipperary, N.R.	Ikerrin	Roscrea	Roscrea	II.	276
32	Cloonagh	1,159 0 3	Westmeath	Moycashel	Castletownkindalen	Mullingar	I.	277
40	Cloonagh	326 2 31	Wexford	Shelburne	Owenduff	New Ross	I.	328
6	Cloonaghbaun	62 3 9	Roscommon	Boyle	Ardcarn	Boyle	IV.	192
2	Cloonagh Beg	200 0 30c	Queen's Co.	Tinnahinch	Kilmanman	Mountmellick	I.	249
30	Cloonagh Beg and Knockegan	178 0 21	Mayo	Tirawley	Ardagh	Ballina	IV.	164
62	Cloonaghboy	295 0 36	Mayo	Gallen	Kilconduff	Swineford	IV.	147
54, 56	Cloonaghbrack	80 1 39	Roscommon	Moycarn	Creagh	Ballinasloe	IV.	206
89, 90	Cloonaghduff	161 2 1	Mayo	Carra	Drum	Castlebar	IV.	128
91,92,101,102	Cloonaghduff	26 2 8	Mayo	Clanmorris	Kilcolman	Claremorris	IV.	133
16	Cloonaghgarve	191 2 18	Galway	Dunmore	Addergoole	Tuam	IV.	32
19, 23	Cloonagh & Kilglass	70 2 5	Longford	Ardagh	Kilglass	Ballymahon	I.	152
90	Cloonaghlin	1,428 1 5d	Kerry	Iveragh	Dromod	Cahersiveen	II.	194
128	Cloonaghlin Lower	78 0 20	Cork, W.R.	Bear	Killaconenagh	Castletown	II.	124
128	Cloonaghlin Upper	101 0 12	Cork, W.R.	Bear	Killaconenagh	Castletown	II.	124
128	Cloonaghlin West	175 0 39	Cork, W.R.	Bear	Killaconenagh	Castletown	II.	124
105	Cloonaghmanagh	56 1 7	Mayo	Murrisk	Kilgeever	Westport	IV.	160
107, 117	Cloonaghmore	45 3 19	Galway	Longford	Kilquain	Portumna	IV.	60
12	Cloonaghmore	534 3 5	Leitrim	Drumahaire	Cloonclare	Manorhamilton	IV.	93
11	Cloonaghmore	171 1 36	Longford	Granard	Abbeylara	Granard	I.	154
89	Cloonaghmore	176 2 3	Mayo	Carra	Ballyhean	Castlebar	IV.	125
78, 79	Cloonaghmore	143 1 30	Mayo	Carra	Breaghwy	Castlebar	IV.	127
30	Cloonagh More	384 2 17e	Mayo	Tirawley	Ardagh	Ballina	IV.	163
21	Cloonaghmore	137 0 35	Mayo	Tirawley	Moygawnagh	Killala	IV.	171
1, 2, 3	Cloonagh More	610 1 8	Queen's Co.	Tinnahinch	Kilmanman	Mountmellick	I.	249
11	Cloonagleavragh	391 0 38	Sligo	Tireragh	Easky	Dromore West	IV.	233
11	Cloonagleavragh Park	25 0 32	Sligo	Tireragh	Easky	Dromore West	IV.	233
26	Cloonagowan	75 3 26f	Clare	Bunratty Upper	Inchicronan	Ennis	II.	9
93	Cloonagower	33 0 13	Galway	Galway	Rahoon	Galway	IV.	37
34	Cloonagrassan	351 1 38	Roscommon	Ballymoe	Drumatemple	Castlereagh	IV.	191
10	Cloonagrouna	175 3 8	Meath	Upper Kells	Loughan or Castlekeeran	Kells	I.	206
39	Cloonagun	139 2 29	Sligo	Corran	Emlaghfad	Sligo	IV.	226
14	Cloonahard	366 0 23	Longford	Ardagh	Templemichael	Longford	I.	153
17	Cloonahee	317 0 15g	Roscommon	Roscommon	Clooncraff	Strokestown	IV.	208
38	Cloonaheen	614 1 29	King's Co.	Clonlisk	Kilmurryely	Roscrea	I.	131
35, 43	Cloonaherna	251 1 35	Clare	Bunratty Upper	Quin	Tulla	II.	10
73, 86	Cloonahinch	215 1 31	Galway	Kilconnell	Killaan	Ballinasloe	IV.	41
33, 39	Cloonahinshin	249 1 0h	Sligo	Corran	Cloonoghil	Tobercurry	IV.	225
14	Cloonahussey	153 2 33	Longford	Ardagh	Templemichael	Longford	I.	153
50	Cloonainra	532 3 19i	Mayo	Gallen	Killasser	Swineford	IV.	149
19	Cloonakeemoge	151 0 10	Sligo	Tireragh	Dromard	Dromore West	IV.	233
48, 51, 52	Cloonakille	274 0 0	Roscommon	Athlone	St. Peter's	Athlone	IV.	184
44	Cloonakilleg	609 1 33j	Roscommon	Athlone	Tisrara	Roscommon	IV.	185
52	Cloonakillina	279 0 18k	Mayo	Costello	Kilturra	Swineford	IV.	142
22, 23	Cloonakilly Beg	135 2 4l	Roscommon	Roscommon	Killukin	Strokestown	IV.	210
22, 23, 28	Cloonakilly More	206 3 11m	Roscommon	Roscommon	Killukin	Strokestown	IV.	210
14, 15	Cloonalaghan	235 3 15	Mayo	Tirawley	Lackan	Killala	IV.	170
47	Cloonalassan	154 1 11	Kerry	Trughanacmy	Kiltallagh	Tralee	II.	212
27, 35	Cloonaleary	162 0 38	Clare	Tulla Upper	Tulla	Tulla	II.	41
21	Cloonaleedin	56 2 28	Mayo	Tirawley	Kilfian	Killala	IV.	169
20, 26	Cloonalis	214 2 11	Roscommon	Castlereagh	Kilkeevin	Castlereagh	IV.	200
44	Cloonalisk	259 0 30	King's Co.	Clonlisk	Templeharry	Roscrea	I.	132
63, 73	Cloonalison	193 0 16	Mayo	Costello	Kilbeagh	Swineford	IV.	140
32, 37	Cloonaloo	198 3 4	Queen's Co.	Slievemargy	Killeshin	Carlow	I.	245
21	Cloonalough	74 3 17n	Mayo	Tirawley	Ballysakeery	Ballina	IV.	164
19, 25	Cloonalough	741 0 2	Roscommon	Castlereagh	Kiltullagh	Castlereagh	IV.	201
44	Cloonaloughan	271 1 37	King's Co.	Clonlisk	Templeharry	Roscrea	I.	132
29	Cloonalour	144 0 14	Kerry	Traghanacmy	Ratass	Tralee	II.	213
29	Cloonalour	85 1 11	Kerry	Trughanacmy	Tralee	Tralee	II.	213
26	Cloonamahan	331 1 38o	Sligo	Tirerrill	Ballysadare	Sligo	IV.	237
2	Cloonaman	819 1 36	Kerry	Iraghticonnor	Aghavallen	Listowel	II.	189
26, 33	Cloonamanagh	158 0 20p	Sligo	Corran	Emlaghfad	Sligo	IV.	226
39	Cloonameehan North	117 0 10	Sligo	Corran	Cloonoghil	Tobercurry	IV.	225
38, 39	Cloonameehan South	85 1 11	Sligo	Corran	Cloonoghil	Tobercurry	IV.	225
87	Cloonameragaun	101 1 16	Galway	Kilconnell	Aughrim	Ballinasloe	IV.	39
21	Cloonametagh	216 2 13	Kerry	Clanmaurice	O'Dorney	Tralee	II.	172

(a) Including 58A. 3R. 33P. water.
(b) Including 6A. 1R. 22P. water.
(c) Including 0A. 0R. 8P. water.
(d) Including 197A. 0R. 34P. water.
(e) Including 37A. 0R. 39P. water.
(f) Including 12A. 2R. 28P. water.

(g) Including 41A. 1R. 19P. water.
(h) Including 0A. 3R. 21P. water.
(i) Including 12A. 0R. 4P. water.
(j) Including 24A. 3R. 6P. water.
(k) Including 39A. 1R. 19P. water.

(l) Including 24A. 2R. 17P. water.
(m) Including 23A. 1R. 8P. of Loughs.
(n) Including 3A. 1R. 22P. water.
(o) Including 35A. 2R. 1P. water.
(p) Including 11A. 3R. 39P. water.

No. of Sheet of the Ordnance Survey Maps.	Townlands and Towns.	Area in Statute Acres.			County.	Barony.	Parish.	Poor Law Union in 1857.	Townland Census of 1851, Part I.	
		A.	R.	P.					Vol.	Page
134, 136	Cloonamirran .	397	3	19	Galway . .	Leitrim . . .	Inishcaltra . .	Scarriff . .	IV.	53
114	Cloonamore .	645	1	1a	Mayo . .	Murrisk . .	Inishbofin . .	Clifden . .	IV.	159
38	Cloonamuinia .	201	3	31b	Roscommon .	Ballymoe . .	Dunamon . .	Roscommon .	IV.	191
17, 18	Cloonamurgal .	128	0	36	Leitrim . .	Drumahaire . .	Inishmagrath . .	Manorhamilton	IV.	96
77, 78	Cloonan . .	239	1	20c	Mayo . .	Burrishoole . .	Islandeady . .	Westport . .	IV.	121
119	Cloonanaff .	297	2	39d	Mayo . .	Kilmaine . .	Kilcommon . .	Ballinrobe .	IV.	154
26	Cloonanagh .	220	2	2	Tipperary, N.R.	Upper Ormond .	Kilmore . .	Nenagh . .	II.	291
23, 31, 32	Cloonanaha .	629	0	33	Clare . .	Inchiquin . .	Inagh . .	Ennistimon .	II.	25
28	Cloonanart Beg .	93	1	19	Roscommon .	Roscommon . .	Kilcooley . .	Strokestown .	IV.	210
28	Cloonanart More .	122	1	9	Roscommon .	Roscommon . .	Kilcooley . .	Strokestown .	IV.	210
43, 52	Cloonanass .	113	2	24e	Clare . .	Bunratty Lower .	Kilfinaghta . .	Tulla . .	II.	4
14	Cloonanass .	126	0	22	Mayo . .	Tirawley . .	Lackan . .	Killala . .	IV.	170
123	Cloonanearla .	137	3	27	Galway . .	Kiltartan . .	Kiltartan . .	Gort . .	IV.	48
12, 21	Cloonanna .	661	3	11	Limerick . .	Pubblebrien .	Croom . .	Limerick . .	II.	252
18	Cloonanny .	175	1	12	Longford .	Moydow . .	Ballymacormick	Longford . .	I.	160
8, 9, 14	Cloonanny Glebe .	177	0	29	Longford .	Longford . .	Templemichael .	Longford . .	I.	160
29	Cloonanorig .	25	1	10	Kerry . .	Trughanacmy .	Tralee . .	Tralee . .	II.	213
44	Cloonanure .	240	0	28	Sligo . .	Coolavin . .	Kilfree . .	Boyle . .	IV.	224
30	Cloonapisha .	129	2	21	Mayo . .	Tirawley . .	Ardagh . .	Ballina . .	IV.	163
11	Cloonaquin .	1,044	0	18	Leitrim . .	Drumahaire . .	Cloonlogher .	Manorhamilton	IV.	94
39	Cloonaraher .	175	1	1	Sligo . .	Corran . .	Kilshalvy . .	Boyle . .	IV.	227
32	Cloonaraher .	240	3	27	Sligo . .	Leyny . .	Achonry . .	Tobercurry .	IV.	229
32	Cloonarara .	262	2	27	Sligo . .	Leyny . .	Achonry . .	Tobercurry .	IV.	229
58,59,68,69	Cloonarass .	293	0	18	Clare . .	Clonderalaw .	Killofin . .	Killadysert .	II.	16
12, 13	Cloonard . .	416	0	20	Longford .	Longford . .	Killashee . .	Longford . .	I.	158
23, 27	Cloonard . .	409	3	0f	Longford .	Rathcline . .	Taghshinny .	Ballymahon .	I.	165
20	Cloonard . .	355	0	11	Roscommon .	Frenchpark .	Tibohine . .	Castlereagh .	IV.	204
94, 108	Cloonareague .	182	1	24	Cork, W.R.	East Carbery (W.D.)	Kinneigh . .	Dunmanway .	II.	134
13	Cloonargid . .	563	3	5g	Roscommon .	Frenchpark .	Tibohine . .	Castlereagh .	IV.	204
110	Cloonark . .	79	2	0h	Mayo . .	Kilmaine . .	Ballinrobe .	Ballinrobe .	IV.	152
51,52,54,55	Cloonark . .	871	0	1	Roscommon .	Athlone . .	Drum . .	Athlone .	IV.	180
30	Cloonarkan .	356	0	6	Galway . .	Ballymoe . .	Clonbern . .	Tuam . .	IV.	6
36, 40	Cloonarragh .	508	3	11	Roscommon .	Ballintober South .	Kilbride . .	Roscommon .	IV.	188
20	Cloonarragh .	496	2	34	Roscommon .	Frenchpark .	Tibohine . .	Castlereagh .	IV.	204
4, 8	Cloonart North .	266	0	26	Longford .	Longford . .	Mohill . .	Longford . .	I.	159
4, 8	Cloonart South .	294	1	25	Longford .	Longford . .	Mohill . .	Longford . .	I.	159
32, 46	Cloonascarberry (Cheevers) .	190	0	4	Galway . .	Killian . .	Killian . .	Mountbellew .	IV.	44
32,33,46,47	Cloonascarberry Nth.	95	2	13	Galway . .	Killian . .	Killian . .	Mountbellew .	IV.	44
32, 46, 47	Cloonascarberry Sth.	206	0	32	Galway . .	Killian . .	Killian . .	Mountbellew .	IV.	44
12	Cloonascoffagh .	75	2	38	Sligo . .	Tireragh . .	Kilmacshalgan .	Dromore West .	IV.	234
43	Cloonascragh .	870	0	25	Galway . .	Clare . .	Tuam . .	Tuam . .	IV.	23
29	Cloonascragh .	224	3	26	Galway . .	Dunmore . .	Kilbennan .	Tuam . .	IV.	34
88, 100	Cloonascragh .	1,020	3	24i	Galway . .	Longford . .	Clontuskert .	Ballinasloe .	IV.	58
45	Cloonascragh .	405	0	24	Galway . .	Tiaquin . .	Moylough . .	Mountbellew .	IV.	79
28	Cloonastiallas .	245	3	7	Roscommon .	Roscommon . .	Killukin . .	Strokestown .	IV.	210
73	Cloonatleva Lower .	405	0	5	Galway . .	Kilconnell .	Fohanagh . .	Mountbellew .	IV.	40
73	Cloonatleva Upper .	61	0	2	Galway . .	Kilconnell .	Fohanagh . .	Mountbellew .	IV.	40
86	Cloonatloukaun .	113	0	8	Galway . .	Kilconnell .	Killaan . .	Ballinasloe .	IV.	41
26	Cloonatreane .	67	3	27	Fermanagh .	Clanawley . .	Killesher . .	Enniskillen .	III.	192
27	Cloonatrig .	198	0	23j	Fermanagh .	Clanawley . .	Cleenish . .	Enniskillen .	III.	190
26	Cloonatumpher .	86	2	0	Fermanagh .	Clanawley . .	Killesher . .	Enniskillen .	III.	192
24	Cloonaufill .	221	2	32	Roscommon .	Ballintober North .	Termonbarry .	Strokestown .	IV.	187
24	Cloonaufill Island .	2	0	20	Roscommon .	Ballintober North .	Termonbarry .	Strokestown .	IV.	188
14	Cloonavarry .	75	2	2	Mayo . .	Tirawley . .	Templemurry .	Killala . .	IV.	171
26	Cloonaveel .	166	3	37	Fermanagh .	Clanawley . .	Cleenish . .	Enniskillen .	III.	190
15	Cloonaveige .	90	3	10	Clare . .	Corcomroe . .	Kilmanaheen .	Ennistimon .	II.	21
11, 12	Cloonavery .	143	1	12	Roscommon .	Ballintober North .	Kilmore . .	Cark.on Shannon	IV.	187
46	Cloonavihony .	453	1	4	Galway . .	Killian . .	Killian . .	Mountbellew .	IV.	44
27	Cloonavindin .	232	1	18	Roscommon .	Castlereagh .	Kilkeevin . .	Castlereagh .	IV.	200
27	Cloonavoan .	48	0	30k	Fermanagh .	Tirkennedy .	Enniskillen .	Enniskillen .	III.	221
74	Cloonavullaun .	212	1	2	Mayo . .	Costello . .	Castlemore .	Castlereagh .	IV.	140
34	Cloonawee .	60	3	5	Clare . .	Bunratty Upper .	Doora . .	Ennis . .	II.	8
63	Cloonaweema .	225	1	2	Mayo . .	Costello . .	Kilbeagh . .	Swineford .	IV.	140
26	Cloonawillin .	162	2	13	Clare . .	Bunratty Upper .	Inchicronan .	Tulla . .	II.	9
1, 2	Cloonawillin .	138	0	1	Leitrim . .	Rosclogher . .	Rossinver . .	Ballyshannon	IV.	111
22	Cloonawillin .	134	2	16	Mayo . .	Tirawley . .	Ballysakeery .	Ballina . .	IV.	164
29, 38	Cloonawillin .	173	3	8	Mayo . .	Tirawley . .	Crossmolina .	Ballina . .	IV.	165
7	Cloonawillin .	209	2	33	Tipperary, N.R.	Lower Ormond .	Aglishcloghane .	Borrisokane .	II.	281
2, 5	Cloonback . .	320	0	0	Longford .	Granard . .	Columbkille .	Longford . .	I.	155
8, 13	Cloonbalt . .	269	3	25	Longford .	Longford . .	Templemichael .	Longford . .	I.	160
122	Cloonbanaun .	311	0	19	Mayo . .	Kilmaine . .	Shrule . .	Ballinrobe .	IV.	158
17	Cloonbane .	87	0	14	Cork, E.R.	Fermoy . .	Doneraile . .	Mallow . .	II.	78

(a) Including 10A. 1R. 39P. water.　　　　(e) Including 15A. 2R. 17P. water.　　　　(i) Including 40A. 0R. 32P. water.
(b) Including 4A. 1R. 8P. water.　　　　(f) Including 6A. 3R. 32P. Inny River.　　　　(j) Including 25A. 2R. 20P. water.
(c) Including 23A. 3R. 23P. water.　　　　(g) Including 2A. 3R. 13P. water.　　　　(k) Including 18A. 3R. 25P. water.
(d) Including 0A. 0R. 27P. water.　　　　(h) Including 6A. 1R. 19P. water.

No. of Sheet of the Ordnance Survey Maps.	Townlands and Towns.	Area in Statute Acres.			County.	Barony.	Parish.	Poor Law Union in 1857.	Townland Census of 1851, Part I.	
		A.	R.	P.					Vol.	Page
32	Cloonbaniff	371	2	32	Sligo	Leyny	Achonry	Tobercurry	IV.	229
39	Cloonbannan	43	3	34	Sligo	Corran	Drumrat	Boyle	IV.	225
30	Cloonbannin East	476	0	4	Cork, E.R.	Duhallow	Cullen	Millstreet	II.	70
30	Cloonbannin West	258	0	28	Cork, E.R.	Duhallow	Cullen	Millstreet	II.	70
61	Cloonbanniv	342	2	4a	Galway	Killian	Ahascragh	Ballinasloe	IV.	42
15, 17	Cloonbannive	415	3	27	Leitrim	Drumahaire	Killanummery	Manorhamilton	IV.	97
28	Cloonbar	858	3	38	Galway	Dunmore	Kilconla	Tuam	IV.	35
20, 21	Cloonbard	659	1	30	Roscommon	Castlereagh	Baslick	Castlereagh	IV.	199
36, 37	Cloonbarry	443	0	19	Sligo	Leyny	Kilmacteige	Tobercurry	IV.	231
91, 101	Cloonbaul	270	2	21	Mayo	Clanmorris	Mayo	Claremorris	IV.	135
12	Cloonbearla	693	1	38	Longford	Moydow	Killashee	Longford	I.	161
36,37,50,51	Cloonbeg	330	2	15b	Galway	Ballynahinch	Moyrus	Clifden	IV.	12
123	Cloonbeg	32	2	33	Galway	Kiltartan	Kilbeacanty	Gort	IV.	47
36	Cloonbeg	101	0	2	Kerry	Corkaguiny	Killiney	Dingle	II.	178
29	Cloon Beg	71	1	33	Kerry	Trughanacmy	Ratass	Tralee	II.	213
20	Cloonbeg	121	1	34c	Waterford	Coshmore&Coshbride	Lismore and Mocollop	Lismore	II.	345
54, 55	Cloonbeggaun	916	1	30	Roscommon	Moycarn	Moore	Ballinasloe	IV.	206
85, 86	Cloonbenes	420	1	7	Galway	Kilconnell	Grange	Loughrea	IV.	40
50	Cloonbigny	368	1	1	Roscommon	Athlone	Taghmaconnell	Ballinasloe	IV.	185
32	Cloonbo	156	0	10d	Leitrim	Mohill	Mohill	Mohill	IV.	107
51, 54	Cloonboley	440	3	4	Roscommon	Athlone	Drum	Athlone	IV.	180
35	Cloonboniagh North	165	2	20e	Leitrim	Mohill	Mohill	Mohill	IV.	107
35	Cloonboniagh South	471	0	23f	Leitrim	Mohill	Mohill	Mohill	IV.	107
111	Cloonbonniff	507	0	38	Mayo	Clanmorris	Crossboyne	Claremorris	IV.	132
20	Cloonbonniff	234	0	17	Roscommon	Castlereagh	Kilkeevin	Castlereagh	IV.	200
29, 35	Cloonbonny	1,441	1	17	Westmeath	Brawny	St. Mary's	Athlone	I.	259
30, 31	Cloonbonny	387	0	12	Clare	Ibrickan	Kilfarboy	Ennistimon	II.	22
12, 17	Cloonbony	540	1	5	Longford	Rathcline	Rathcline	Longford	I.	164
36	Cloonbony	472	1	1	Roscommon	Ballintober South	Kilbride	Roscommon	IV.	188
69	Cloonboo	425	0	15g	Galway	Clare	Annaghdown	Galway	IV.	16
30,31,44,45	Cloonboo Beg	134	2	21	Galway	Ballymoe	Dunmore	Glennamaddy	IV.	7
102	Cloonbookeighter	244	3	9	Mayo	Costello	Bekan	Claremorris	IV.	139
102	Cloonbookoughter	315	1	4	Mayo	Costello	Bekan	Claremorris	IV.	139
32	Cloonbooly	252	1	28	Clare	Islands	Kilmaley	Ennis	II.	31
31, 45	Cloonboo More	184	0	14	Galway	Ballymoe	Dunmore	Glennamaddy	IV.	7
100	Cloonboorhy	266	0	23h	Mayo	Carra	Burriscarra	Castlebar	IV.	127
72	Cloonbornia	314	3	25	Galway	Tiaquin	Clonkeen	Loughrea	IV.	76
91, 101	Cloonboy	445	0	14	Mayo	Clanmorris	Kilcolman	Claremorris	IV.	133
14, 15	Cloonboy	180	1	37	Mayo	Tirawley	Templemurry	Killala	IV.	171
25, 26, 30	Cloonboygher	398	3	20	Leitrim	Carrigallen	Carrigallen	Bawnboy	IV.	89
16, 22	Cloonboyoge	79	3	14i	Roscommon	Roscommon	Shankill	Strokestown	IV.	212
39	Cloonbrackna	94	0	37	Roscommon	Ballintober South	Roscommon	Roscommon	IV.	190
6	Cloonbrane	315	1	0	Kerry	Iraghticonnor	Murher	Listowel	II.	193
22	Cloonbreany	492	2	1	Longford	Rathcline	Kilcommock	Ballymahon	I.	164
39	Cloonbrien	398	2	21	Limerick	Coshma	Athlacca	Kilmallock	II.	241
23, 24	Cloonbrin	442	0	17j	Longford	Shrule	Abbeyshrule	Ballymahon	I.	165
12,13,17,18	Cloonbrock	383	2	30	Longford	Moydow	Killaslee	Longford	I.	161
40	Cloonbrone	280	1	32	Galway	Ross	Cong	Oughterard	IV.	73
30	Cloonbrone	51	1	0	Mayo	Tirawley	Ardagh	Ballina	IV.	163
4	Cloonbrusk	160	2	34	Galway	Dunmore	Addergoole	Tuam	IV.	32
84, 85	Cloonbrusk	321	1	16	Galway	Kilconnell	Monivea	Loughrea	IV.	42
102	Cloonbulban	242	2	37	Mayo	Costello	Bekan	Claremorris	IV.	139
103	Cloonbullig	115	1	39	Mayo	Costello	Annagh	Claremorris	IV.	138
20	Cloonbunny	631	2	29	Roscommon	Frenchpark	Tibohine	Castlereagh	IV.	204
27	Cloonbur	194	1	13	Galway	Ross	Ross	Oughterard	IV.	74
54, 56	Cloonburren	897	3	34	Roscommon	Moycarn	Moore	Ballinasloe	IV.	206
44	Cloonca	462	3	20	Roscommon	Athlone	Tisrara	Roscommon	IV.	185
31, 37	Cloonca	363	3	2	Sligo	Leyny	Kilmacteige	Tobercurry	IV.	231
7	Clooncah	364	0	29k	Galway	Ballymoe	Ballynakill	Glennamaddy	IV.	5
72, 85	Clooncah	765	3	20	Galway	Kilconnell	Killimordaly	Loughrea	IV.	42
81	Clooncah	145	1	3	Mayo	Costello	Aghamore	Swineford	IV.	137
40, 42	Clooncah	338	1	5	Roscommon	Ballintober South	Kilteevan	Roscommon	IV.	189
26	Clooncah	109	1	3	Roscommon	Castlereagh	Kilkeevin	Castlereagh	IV.	200
13, 19	Clooncah	270	0	23l	Roscommon	Frenchpark	Tibohine	Castlereagh	IV.	204
29, 36	Clooncah	566	3	5m	Roscommon	Roscommon	Cloonfinlough	Roscommon	IV.	208
32, 35	Clooncahir	381	0	18n	Leitrim	Mohill	Mohill	Mohill	IV.	107
25	Clooncalgy	86	0	3	Roscommon	Castlereagh	Kiltullagh	Castlereagh	IV.	201
25	Clooncalgy Beg	123	2	1	Roscommon	Castlereagh	Kiltullagh	Castlereagh	IV.	201
25, 32, 33	Clooncalgy More	419	2	10	Roscommon	Castlereagh	Kiltullagh	Castlereagh	IV.	201
123	Clooncalla Beg	219	0	12	Cork, W.R.	East Carbery (E.D.)	Rathclarin	Bandon	II.	129
45	Clooncallaga	571	0	10	Galway	Tiaquin	Moylough	Mountbellew	IV.	79
123	Clooncalla More	543	1	9	Cork, W.R.	East Carbery (E.D.)	Rathclarin	Bandon	II.	130
86	Clooncallis	30	0	11	Galway	Kilconnell	Killaan	Ballinasloe	IV.	41

(a) Including 10A. 0R. 0P. water.
(b) Including 18A. 3R. 3P. water.
(c) Including 4A. 2R. 32P. water.
(d) Including 46A. 1R. 7P. water.
(e) Including 23A. 1R. 29P. water.

(f) Including 21A. 2R. 16P. water.
(g) Including 19A. 1R. 24P. water.
(h) Including 38A. 0R. 9P. water.
(i) Including 2A. 2R. 10P. water.
(j) Including 16A. 3R. 19P. Inny River.

(k) Including 21A. 1R. 11P. water.
(l) Including 44A. 0R. 17P. water.
(m) Including 5A. 0R. 1P. water.
(n) Including 48A. 2R. 34P. water.

No of Sheet of the Ordnance Survey Maps.	Townlands and Towns.	Area in Statute Acres.			County.	Barony.	Parish.	Poor Law Union in 1857.	Townland Census of 1851, Part I.	
		A.	R.	P.					Vol.	Page
73, 86	Clooncallis	264	0	10	Galway	Kilconnell	Killallaghtan	Ballinasloe	IV.	41
27	Clooncallow	453	1	6a	Longford	Shrule	Forgney	Ballymahon	I.	166
100, 110	Clooncan	286	0	7	Mayo	Kilmaine	Robeen	Ballinrobe	IV.	157
19	Clooncan	1,203	2	33	Roscommon	Castlereagh	Kilkeevin	Castlereagh	IV.	200
77	Clooncanavan	117	0	39	Mayo	Burrishoole	Kilmaclasser	Westport	IV.	121
33	Clooncannon	277	1	2b	Galway	Killian	Athleague	Mountbellew	IV.	43
61	Clooncannon (*Dillon*)	284	1	28	Galway	Clonmacnowen	Ahascragh	Mountbellew	IV.	24
61	Clooncannon (*Kelly*)	392	1	18	Galway	Clonmacnowen	Ahascragh	Mountbellew	IV.	24
74	Clooncarha	204	3	14	Mayo	Costello	Kilmovee	Swineford	IV.	142
63	Clooncarhy	302	1	10	Clare	Tulla Lower	Kiltenanlea	Limerick	II.	37
86	Clooncarrabaun	123	3	2	Mayo	Murrisk	Kilgeever	Westport	IV.	160
35,36,37,38	Clooncarreen	835	0	22	Leitrim	Mohill	Mohill	Mohill	IV.	107
56	Clooncarrig	76	0	38	Kerry	Trughanacmy	Killorglin	Killarney	II.	211
36	Clooncashel Beg	346	2	28	Roscommon	Ballintober South	Kilgefin	Roscommon	IV.	189
36	Clooncashel More	276	0	22	Roscommon	Ballintober South	Kilgefin	Roscommon	IV.	189
14, 19	Clooncaulfield	368	1	26	Longford	Ardagh	Ardagh	Longford	I.	151
12	Clooncaura	51	1	19	Limerick	Kenry	Kildimo	Rathkeale	II.	249
32	Clooncaurha	157	0	25	Clare	Inchiquin	Kilnamona	Ennis	II.	27
20, 26	Cloonchambers	733	2	39	Roscommon	Castlereagh	Kilkeevin	Castlereagh	IV.	200
11	Cloonclare	11	1	25	Leitrim	Drumahaire	Cloonclare	Manorhamilton	IV.	93
42	Clooncleagh	589	2	20	Tipperary, N.R.	Eliogarty	Twomileborris	Thurles	II.	273
62	Clooncleevragh	142	1	6c	Mayo	Gallen	Killasser	Swineford	IV.	149
35	Cloonclivvy	241	0	30d	Leitrim	Mohill	Mohill	Mohill	IV.	107
48	Cloonclogh	244	2	19	Kerry	Trughanacmy	Killeentierna	Killarney	II.	211
35, 36	Clooncoe	672	1	38e	Leitrim	Mohill	Cloone	Mohill	IV.	105
13	Clooncogaile	511	2	1	Waterford	Decies without Drum	Seskinan	Dungarvan	II.	360
16	Clooncolla	168	2	25	Kerry	Clanmaurice	Dysert	Listowel	II.	169
4	Clooncolligan	196	2	39	Longford	Longford	Mohill	Longford	I.	159
49	Clooncolman	662	0	20	Clare	Islands	Clondagad	Killadysert	II.	29
35	Clooncolry	450	0	35	Leitrim	Mohill	Mohill	Mohill	IV.	107
18	Clooncommon Beg	116	2	12	Roscommon	Ballintober North	Kilmore	Cark. on Shannon	IV.	187
18	Clooncommon More	330	0	3	Roscommon	Ballintober North	Kilmore	Cark. on Shannon	IV.	187
1	Cloon and Commons	222	2	31	Limerick	Clanwilliam	Stradbally	Limerick	II.	226
44, 53	Clooncon	371	2	20	Limerick	Glenquin	Killeedy	Newcastle	II.	245
44	Clooncon	77	0	7	Limerick	Glenquin	Monagay	Newcastle	II.	247
107, 117	Clooncona	256	2	0	Galway	Longford	Killimorbologue	Portumna	IV.	58
117	Cloonconabeg	55	0	18	Galway	Longford	Killimorbologue	Portumna	IV.	58
6, 18, 19	Clooncon East	682	1	10	Galway	Ballymoe	Boyounagh	Glennamaddy	IV.	6
65, 72	Cloonconeen	318	0	22	Clare	Moyarta	Moyarta	Kilrush	II.	34
60, 70	Cloonconlan	464	3	39f	Mayo	Gallen	Templemore	Castlebar	IV.	151
121, 122	Cloonconneelaun	188	0	12	Mayo	Kilmaine	Kilmainemore	Ballinrobe	IV.	156
29	Cloonconny	92	0	27	Roscommon	Roscommon	Kilbride	Strokestown	IV.	210
101	Cloonconor	36	3	6	Mayo	Clanmorris	Kilcolman	Claremorris	IV.	133
31, 32, 46	Cloonconore	468	3	19	Galway	Tiaquin	Kilkerrin	Glennamaddy	IV.	76
30, 44	Clooncourra	228	3	14	Galway	Dunmore	Killererin	Tuam	IV.	35
100, 101	Clooncourra	233	0	19	Galway	Longford	Clonfert	Ballinasloe	IV.	57
60,61,70,71	Clooncourra	197	2	4	Mayo	Gallen	Templemore	Castlebar	IV.	151
40, 42	Clooncourra	221	0	17	Roscommon	Ballintober South	Kilteevan	Roscommon	IV.	189
26	Clooncourra	743	3	28	Roscommon	Castlereagh	Kilkeevin	Castlereagh	IV.	200
90	Clooncourragh East	147	2	13	Mayo	Carra	Ballyhean	Castlebar	IV.	125
89, 90	Clooncourragh West	281	2	9	Mayo	Carra	Ballyhean	Castlebar	IV.	125
21	Cloonconway	83	3	16	Mayo	Tirawley	Rathreagh	Killala	IV.	171
18	Clooncon West	744	0	35g	Galway	Ballymoe	Boyounagh	Glennamaddy	IV.	6
35	Clooncool	362	2	33	Clare	Tulla Lower	Killuran	Tulla	II.	36
37	Clooncooravane North	145	2	35	Limerick	Glenquin	Mahoonagh	Newcastle	II.	246
37	Clooncooravane South	141	0	29	Limerick	Glenquin	Mahoonagh	Newcastle	II.	246
10	Clooncoose	431	3	28	Clare	Burren	Carran	Ballyvaghan	II.	11
13, 14	Clooncoose	382	2	21	Longford	Ardagh	Templemichael	Longford	I.	153
9, 10	Clooncoose	107	0	10	Longford	Granard	Clonbroney	Granard	I.	154
17	Clooncoose	171	1	0h	Roscommon	Ballintober North	Kilmore	Cark. on Shannon	IV.	187
7	Clooncoose	86	1	26i	Roscommon	Boyle	Tumna	Cark. on Shannon	IV.	197
20	Clooncoose North	771	0	14j	Roscommon	Castlereagh	Kilkeevin	Castlereagh	IV.	200
26	Clooncoose South	118	3	22	Roscommon	Castlereagh	Kilkeevin	Castlereagh	IV.	200
22	Clooncor	174	0	21k	Roscommon	Roscommon	Kilcooley	Strokestown	IV.	210
50, 53	Clooncoran	540	3	0l	Roscommon	Athlone	Taghmaconnell	Ballinasloe	IV.	185
121, 122	Clooncorban	272	0	8	Cork, W.R.	East Carbery (W.D.)	Kilmeen	Clonakilty	II.	133
30	Clooncorick	372	1	6m	Leitrim	Carrigallen	Carrigallen	Mohill	III.	89
110, 118	Clooncormick	731	3	6n	Mayo	Kilmaine	Robeen	Ballinrobe	IV.	157
117	Clooncorraun	256	1	2o	Mayo	Kilmaine	Ballinrobe	Ballinrobe	IV.	152
26	Clooncose	341	2	17	Leitrim	Carrigallen	Carrigallen	Bawnboy	IV.	89
33, 36	Clooncose	406	3	34p	Leitrim	Mohill	Cloone	Mohill	IV.	105
32	Clooncose	361	1	36q	Sligo	Corran	Cloonoghil	Tobercurry	IV.	225
17	Clooncosker	165	2	23	Roscommon	Roscommon	Clooncraff	Strokestown	IV.	208

No. of Sheet of the Ordnance Survey Maps.	Townlands and Towns.	Area in Statute Acres. A. R. P.	County.	Barony.	Parish.	Poor Law Union in 1857.	Townland Census of 1851, Part I. Vol.	Page
15, 16	Clooncoul	441 3 9	Clare	Corcomroe	Kilmanaheen	Ennistimon	II.	21
63	Clooncous	153 2 7	Mayo	Costello	Kilbeagh	Swineford	IV.	140
40	Clooncraff	797 1 38	Roscommon	Ballintober South	Kilteevan	Roscommon	IV.	189
17	Clooncraff	327 3 35a	Roscommon	Roscommon	Clooncraff	Strokestown	IV.	208
20	Clooncraffield	291 0 8	Roscommon	Castlereagh	Kilkeevin	Castlereagh	IV.	200
26	Clooncran	115 0 38	Roscommon	Castlereagh	Kilkeevin	Castlereagh	IV.	200
22	Clooncree	79 2 33b	Galway	Ballynahinch	Ballynakill	Clifden	IV.	11
20	Clooncreestane	38 2 26	Kerry	Clanmaurice	Kilmoyly	Tralee	II.	171
19, 25	Clooncrim	825 3 3	Roscommon	Castlereagh	Kiltullagh	Castlereagh	IV.	201
45	Clooncrippa	593 1 33	Limerick	Connello Upper	Kilmeedy	Newcastle	II.	233
89	Clooncrooeel	147 0 29c	Mayo	Carra	Ballintober	Castlebar	IV.	124
3	Clooncruffer	140 1 20d	Roscommon	Boyle	Ardcarn	Boyle	IV.	192
132	Clooncugger	758 1 5	Cork, W.R.	West Carbery (W.D.)	Caheragh	Skibbereen	II.	142
22, 23	Clooncullaan	644 2 10e	Roscommon	Roscommon	Elphin	Strokestown	IV.	209
28	Clooncullaan	162 1 10	Roscommon	Roscommon	Kilcooley	Strokestown	IV.	210
19	Clooncullaun	691 1 14	Galway	Ballymoe	Ballynakill	Glennamaddy	IV.	5
27	Clooncullen	798 3 39	Longford	Shrule	Noughaval	Ballymahon	I.	166
58	Clooncullin	413 1 39	Clare	Moyarta	Kilmacduane	Kilrush	II.	32
37, 38	Clooncumber	442 2 23	Leitrim	Mohill	Cloone	Mohill	IV.	105
14	Clooncunna North	220 0 34	Limerick	Clanwilliam	Abington	Limerick	II.	221
14	Clooncunna South	29 0 9	Limerick	Clanwilliam	Abington	Limerick	II.	221
144	Clooncunnig	116 3 14	Cork, W.R.	Ibane and Barryroe	Ardfield	Clonakilty	II.	148
7, 8	Clooncunny	357 0 23f	Galway	Ballymoe	Ballynakill	Glennamaddy	IV.	5
22, 23	Clooncunny	394 2 36g	Roscommon	Roscommon	Elphin	Strokestown	IV.	209
46, 47	Clooncunny	153 2 21	Sligo	Coolavin	Killaraght	Boyle	IV.	224
39	Clooncunny	324 1 31	Sligo	Corran	Kilshalvy	Boyle	IV.	227
32	Clooncunny	166 1 7	Sligo	Leyny	Achonry	Tobercurry	IV.	229
43,44,53,54	Clooncurra	194 3 3	Kerry	Corkaguiny	Kinard	Dingle	II.	179
59	Clooncurreen	202 0 3	Galway	Tiaquin	Moylough	Mountbellew	IV.	79
26	Cloondacarra	283 0 35	Roscommon	Castlereagh	Kilkeevin	Castlereagh	IV.	200
26	Cloondacarra Beg	254 2 11	Roscommon	Castlereagh	Kilkeevin	Castlereagh	IV.	200
81, 92	Cloondace	354 0 8	Mayo	Costello	Knock	Claremorris	IV.	142
88	Cloondacon	247 2 35	Mayo	Burrishoole	Aghagower	Westport	IV.	118
132	Cloondadauv	151 3 23	Galway	Leitrim	Ballynakill	Portumna	IV.	51
58, 59, 68	Cloondaff	2,130 2 0	Mayo	Tirawley	Addergoole	Castlebar	IV.	163
30, 44, 45	Cloondahamper (Blake)	471 3 29	Galway	Ballymoe	Killererin	Tuam	IV.	9
30, 44	Cloondahamper (Brown)	202 3 13	Galway	Ballymoe	Killererin	Tuam	IV.	9
35	Cloondalin	118 1 36	Westmeath	Brawny	St. Mary's	Athlone	I.	259
27	Cloondanagh	329 3 39h	Clare	Tulla Upper	Tulla	Tulla	II.	41
8, 13	Cloondara	1,429 2 20i	Longford	Longford	Killashee	Longford	I.	158
41, 44	Cloondarah	280 3 35j	Roscommon	Athlone	Tisrara	Roscommon	IV.	185
13	CLOONDARA T.	—	Longford	Longford	Killashee	Longford	I.	158
43	Cloondarone	557 3 31k	Galway	Clare	Tuam	Tuam	IV.	23
19	Cloondart	194 0 3l	Roscommon	Frenchpark	Tibohine	Castlereagh	IV.	204
100, 110	Cloondaver	151 0 6	Mayo	Kilmaine	Robeen	Ballinrobe	IV.	157
78	Cloondeash	261 0 16m	Mayo	Carra	Ballyhean	Castlebar	IV.	125
4, 5	Cloondergan	709 2 4	Galway	Dunmore	Dunmore	Tuam	IV.	33
123	Cloonderreen	291 2 6	Cork, W.R.	East Carbery (E.D.)	Rathclarin	Bandon	II.	130
8, 9	Cloonderry	213 2 35	Sligo	Carbury	Drumcliff	Sligo	IV.	221
123	Cloondine	92 0 36	Galway	Kiltartan	Kilbeacanty	Gort	IV.	47
101	Cloondinnaire	185 2 4	Mayo	Clanmorris	Tagheen	Claremorris	IV.	136
80	Cloondoolough	230 0 38	Mayo	Gallen	Killedan	Swineford	IV.	150
27	Cloondoorney Beg	189 1 9n	Clare	Tulla Upper	Tulla	Tulla	II.	41
27	Cloondoorney More	399 2 4o	Clare	Tulla Upper	Tulla	Tulla	II.	41
32, 38	Cloondorragha	139 1 10	Sligo	Corran	Cloonoghil	Tobercurry	IV.	225
18	Cloondoyle Beg	188 2 33	Galway	Ballymoe	Boyounagh	Glennamaddy	IV.	6
18	Cloondoyle More	88 2 26	Galway	Ballymoe	Boyounagh	Glennamaddy	IV.	6
24, 25, 32	Cloondrihara	2,168 3 12	Sligo	Leyny	Achonry	Tobercurry	IV.	229
59	Cloondrinagh	923 3 32	Clare	Clonderalaw	Kilfiddane	Killadysert	II.	15
49, 50	Cloondrinagh	423 2 2	Clare	Islands	Clondagad	Killadysert	II.	29
4	Cloondroon	357 1 2p	Galway	Dunmore	Addergoole	Tuam	IV.	33
101	Cloondroon	243 0 2	Mayo	Clanmorris	Kilcolman	Claremorris	IV.	133
30, 36	Cloone	95 0 30	Cavan	Tullyhunco	Scrabby	Granard	III.	99
43	Cloone	171 1 38	Kilkenny	Ida	Dunkitt	Waterford	I.	101
33	Cloone	391 3 10q	Leitrim	Mohill	Cloone	Mohill	IV.	105
2	Cloone	331 0 39	Leitrim	Rosclogher	Rossinver	Ballyshannon	IV.	111
29	Cloone	267 2 17	Tipperary, N.R.	Eliogarty	Loughmoe East	Thurles	II.	271
9	Clooneagh	20 1 29	Kerry	Clanmaurice	Rattoo	Listowel	II.	173
35, 37	Clooneagh	360 2 32	Leitrim	Mohill	Mohill	Mohill	IV.	107
44	Clooneagh	306 2 19	Sligo	Coolavin	Kilfree	Boyle	IV.	224
21	Clooneally	112 2 30	Sligo	Tirerrill	Ballysumaghan	Sligo	IV.	238
82	Cloonean	257 3 3r	Mayo	Costello	Aghamore	Swineford	IV.	137
46	Clooneuragh	89 1 14	Kerry	Trughanacmy	Kilgarrylander	Tralee	II.	210

(a) Including 12A. 0R. 7P. water.
(b) Including 0A. 1R. 8P. water.
(c) Including 9A. 3R. 39P. water.
(d) Including 16A. 0R. 22P. water.
(e) Including 66A. 2R. 20P. water.
(f) Including 32A. 1R. 23P. water.

(g) Including 42A. 0R. 34P. water.
(h) Including 16A. 3R. 0P. water.
(i) Including Islands.
(j) Including 14A. 0R. 28P. water.
(k) Including 50A. 2R. 16P. water.
(l) Including 25A. 3R. 12P. water.

(m) Including 15A. 0R. 32P. water.
(n) Including 6A. 1R. 1P. water.
(o) Including 33A. 3R. 4P. water.
(p) Including 12A. 2R. 14P. water.
(q) Including 13A. 3R. 20P. water.
(r) Including 22A. 0R. 16P. water.

2 M

No. of Sheet of the Ordnance Survey Maps.	Townlands and Towns.	Area in Statute Acres.	County.	Barony.	Parish.	Poor Law Union in 1857.	Townland Census of 1851, Part I.	
		A. R. P.					Vol.	Page
29	Cloonearagh . .	339 0 24	Roscommon .	Roscommon . .	Cloonfinlough . .	Strokestown .	IV.	208
82	Cloon East . .	1,003 3 8a	Kerry . .	Dunkerron North .	Knockane . .	Cahersiveen .	II.	181
22	Cloonederowen .	100 2 23	Galway . .	Ballynahinch . .	Ballynakill . .	Clifden . .	IV.	11
6	Cloonee . . .	153 3 14	Cork, E.R. .	Orrery and Kilmore .	Kilbolane . .	Kanturk . .	II.	108
118, 131	Cloonee . . .	467 1 38	Cork, W.R. .	West Carbery (W.D.)	Durrus . . .	Bantry . .	II.	142
118, 131	Cloonee . . .	296 2 6	Cork, W.R. .	West Carbery (W.D.)	Kilmocomoge . .	Bantry . .	II.	144
2	Cloonee . . .	249 1 35	Galway . .	Ballymoe . .	Drumatemple . .	Glennamaddy .	IV.	7
42	Cloonee . . .	287 1 15	Galway . .	Clare . . .	Kilkilvery . .	Tuam . .	IV.	20
100, 101	Cloonee . . .	700 2 23b	Kerry . .	Glanarought . .	Tuosist . . .	Kenmare . .	II.	188
33, 36	Cloonee . . .	244 0 31	Leitrim . .	Mohill . . .	Cloone . . .	Mohill . .	IV.	105
46	Cloonee . . .	485 1 29	Limerick . .	Connello Upper .	Corcomohide . .	Croom . .	II.	232
9	Cloonee . . .	236 2 22	Longford . .	Longford . . .	Killoe . . .	Longford . .	I.	158
99	Cloonee . . .	455 3 7c	Mayo . .	Carra . . .	Ballyovey . .	Ballinrobe .	IV.	126
110	Cloonee . . .	459 3 16	Mayo . .	Kilmaine . .	Ballinrobe . .	Ballinrobe .	IV.	152
19	Clooneen . . .	157 1 11	Cavan . .	Tullyhunco . .	Kildallan . .	Cavan . .	III.	96
18	Clooneen . . .	363 1 26	Clare . .	Bunratty Upper .	Inchicronan . .	Ennis . .	II.	9
9, 16	Clooneen . . .	484 1 23	Clare . .	Corcomroe . .	Kilfenora . .	Corrofin . .	II.	19
42, 56	Clooneen . . .	142 0 22	Galway . .	Clare . . .	Killeany . .	Tuam . .	IV.	20
17	Clooneen . . .	65 0 29	Galway . .	Dunmore . .	Dunmore . .	Tuam . .	IV.	33
125	Clooneen . . .	44 1 33	Galway . .	Leitrim . .	Ballynakill . .	Loughrea .	IV.	51
123	Clooneen . . .	17 2 2	Galway . .	Loughrea . .	Kilthomas . .	Gort . .	IV.	65
15	Clooneen . . .	160 2 13	Kerry . .	Clanmaurice . .	Killahan . .	Listowel . .	II.	170
30	Clooneen . . .	487 1 33d	King's Co. .	Eglish . . .	Eglish . . .	Parsonstown .	I.	134
18	Clooneen . . .	163 3 12	Leitrim . .	Drumahaire . .	Inishmagrath . .	Manorhamilton .	IV.	96
7, 11	Clooneen . . .	229 0 24	Leitrim . .	Rosclogher . .	Killasnet . .	Manorhamilton .	IV.	109
6, 7	Clooneen . . .	429 3 24	Longford . .	Granard . .	Columbkille . .	Granard . .	I.	155
27	Clooneen . . .	378 0 3	Longford . .	Shrule . . .	Forgney . . .	Ballymahon .	I.	166
77	Clooneen . . .	169 3 2	Mayo . .	Burrishoole . .	Kilmeena . .	Westport . .	IV.	122
9, 10	Clooneen . . .	328 0 26	Mayo . .	Erris . . .	Kilmore . .	Belmullet .	IV.	145
71	Clooneen . . .	381 2 10	Mayo . .	Gallen . .	Meelick . .	Swineford .	IV.	150
111	Clooneen . . .	259 2 11	Mayo . .	Kilmaine . .	Kilcommon . .	Ballinrobe .	IV.	154
87, 88	Clooneen . . .	77 2 10	Mayo . .	Murrisk . .	Oughaval . .	Westport . .	IV.	161
41	Clooneen . . .	719 1 7e	Roscommon .	Athlone . .	Athleague . .	Roscommon .	IV.	179
45	Clooneen . . .	44 0 24	Roscommon .	Athlone . .	Rahara . .	Roscommon .	IV.	183
9	Clooneen . . .	217 2 16	Roscommon .	Frenchpark . .	Kilnamanagh . .	Boyle . .	IV.	204
54	Clooneen . . .	56 1 8	Roscommon .	Moycarn . .	Creagh . .	Ballinasloe .	IV.	206
8	Clooneen . . .	242 3 23	Sligo . .	Carbury . .	Drumcliff . .	Sligo . .	IV.	221
33	Clooneen . . .	109 1 30f	Sligo . .	Corran . .	Emlaghfad . .	Sligo . .	IV.	226
26, 33	Clooneen . . .	240 0 13g	Sligo . .	Corran . .	Kilmorgan . .	Sligo . .	IV.	226
11	Clooneen . . .	301 3 7	Sligo . .	Tireragh . .	Kilmacshalgan .	Dromore West .	IV.	234
48	Clooneenagh . .	294 2 12	Clare . .	Moyarta . .	Kilmacduane . .	Kilrush . .	II.	32
34, 35, 39	Clooneenbaun .	1,577 0 0h	Roscommon .	Athlone . .	Fuerty . .	Roscommon .	IV.	181
41	CLOONEENBEG T. .	—	Roscommon .	Athlone . .	Athleague . .	Roscommon .	IV.	179
4, 8	Clooneen (Beirne) .	114 0 34	Longford . .	Longford . .	Mohill . .	Longford . .	I.	159
23	Clooneen (Blakeny)	261 1 19i	Roscommon .	Ballintober North .	Kilglass . .	Strokestown .	IV.	186
38, 39	Clooneencapullagh .	83 0 23	King's Co. .	Ballybritt . .	Seirkieran . .	Roscrea . .	I.	126
100	Clooneencarra .	139 1 10j	Mayo . .	Carra . .	Touaghty . .	Ballinrobe .	IV.	130
8	Clooneen (Cox) .	149 1 16k	Longford . .	Longford . .	Mohill . .	Longford . .	I.	159
23	Clooneen (Hartland)	458 3 39	Roscommon .	Roscommon . .	Kilglass . .	Strokestown .	IV.	210
41	Clooneenhugh . .	70 2 10	Sligo . .	Tirerrill . .	Kilmactranny .	Boyle . .	IV.	240
8	Clooneen (Kennedy)	139 0 36	Longford . .	Longford . .	Mohill . .	Longford . .	I.	159
100	Clooneenkillew .	174 2 1l	Mayo . .	Carra . .	Touaghty . .	Ballinrobe .	IV.	130
36	Clooneen or Lettybrook	331 0 7	King's Co. .	Ballybritt . .	Letterluna . .	Parsonstown .	I.	126
15	Clooneen Lower .	78 1 36	Tipperary, N.R.	Lower Ormond .	Kilruane . .	Nenagh . .	II.	285
15	Clooneen Middle .	76 0 27	Tipperary, N.R.	Upper Ormond .	Kilruane . .	Nenagh . .	II.	292
26	Clooneenroe . .	102 0 27	Sligo . .	Tirerrill . .	Kilross . .	Sligo . .	IV.	241
4, 8	Clooneen (Shanly) .	123 3 28	Longford . .	Longford . .	Mohill . .	Longford . .	I.	159
15	Clooneen Upper .	242 2 25	Tipperary, N.R.	Upper Ormond .	Kilruane . .	Nenagh . .	II.	292
13	Clooneeny . .	413 1 17	Longford . .	Ardagh . .	Ballymacormick .	Longford . .	I.	152
30, 39	Clooneigh . .	115 3 35	Mayo . .	Tirawley . .	Ardagh . .	Ballina . .	IV.	163
40	Clooneigh . .	538 0 39	Roscommon .	Ballintober South .	Kilteevan . .	Roscommon .	IV.	190
7	Clooneigh . .	85 2 19	Roscommon .	Boyle . .	Tumna . .	Carn. on Shannon	IV.	197
22	Clooneigh . .	230 3 28m	Roscommon .	Roscommon . .	Kilcooley . .	Strokestown .	IV.	210
56	Clooneish . .	510 3 31	Roscommon .	Moycarn . .	Moore . .	Ballinasloe .	IV.	206
4, 8	Cloonellan . .	403 1 20	Longford . .	Longford . .	Clongesh . .	Longford . .	I.	157
2	Cloonelly . .	596 3 24n	Longford . .	Longford . .	Killoe . .	Longford . .	I.	158
28, 29	Cloonelly . .	82 0 6	Roscommon .	Roscommon . .	Kilbride . .	Strokestown .	IV.	210
5	Cloonelly . .	123 1 27	Sligo . .	Carbury . .	Drumcliff . .	Sligo . .	IV.	221
19, 20	Cloonelt . .	480 3 7	Roscommon .	Castlereagh . .	Kilkeevin . .	Castlereagh .	IV.	200
39, 44	Cloonena . .	173 3 38	Sligo . .	Corran . .	Kilshalvy . .	Boyle . .	IV.	227
117	Cloonenagh . .	261 0 6	Mayo . .	Kilmaine . .	Ballinrobe . .	Ballinrobe .	IV.	152
36, 41	Cloonerane . .	388 0 12	Wexford . .	Shelmaliere West .	Taghmon . .	Wexford . .	I.	334
2, 3, 5, 6	Cloonerco . .	353 1 1	Sligo . .	Carbury . .	Ahanlish . .	Sligo . .	IV.	219

(a) Including 92A. 0R. 3P. water.	(f) Including 6A. 1R. 22P. water.	(k) Including Islands.
(b) Including 134A. 0R. 18P. water.	(g) Including 1A. 2R. 14P. water.	(l) Including 0A. 3R. 13P. water.
(c) Including 5A. 3R. 19P. water.	(h) Including 32A. 0R. 20P. water.	(m) Including 16A. 0R. 15P. water.
(d) Including 13A. 0R. 25P. water.	(i) Including 7A. 2R. 6P. water.	(n) Including 17A. 1R. 17P. water.
(e) Including 12A. 3R. 10P. water.	(j) Including 4A. 1R. 10P. water.	

No. of Sheet of the Ordnance Survey Maps.	Townlands and Towns.	Area in Statute Acres. A. R. P.	County.	Barony.	Parish.	Poor Law Union in 1857.	Townland Census of 1851, Part I. Vol.	Page
36	Cloonerk	180 1 4	Roscommon	Ballintober South	Kilbride	Roscommon	IV.	189
32	Cloonerkaun	408 2 14	Roscommon	Castlereagh	Kiltullagh	Castlereagh	IV.	201
110, 118	Cloonerneen	441 2 8a	Mayo	Kilmaine	Ballinrobe	Ballinrobe	IV.	152
29	Cloonerra	129 0 11b	Roscommon	Roscommon	Cloonfinlough	Strokestown	IV.	209
68	Clooneshil	221 1 22c	Mayo	Burrishoole	Burrishoole	Newport	IV.	118
40, 42	Clooneskert	188 3 38	Roscommon	Ballintober South	Kilteevan	Roscommon	IV.	190
33	CLOONE T.	—	Leitrim	Mohill	Cloone	Mohill	IV.	106
18	Cloonevit	254 1 9	Longford	Moydow	Moydow	Longford	I.	162
2, 6	Clooney	45 1 34	Antrim	Lower Dunluce	Dunluce	Coleraine	III.	17
34	Clooney	604 3 37	Clare	Bunratty Upper	Clooney	Tulla	II.	7
64	Clooney	283 1 14d	Donegal	Boylagh	Inishkeel	Glenties	III.	112
36,37,45,46	Clooney	361 2 38e	Donegal	Kilmacrenan	Tullyfern	Millford	III.	133
28	Clooney	199 0 29f	Leitrim	Leitrim	Kiltubbrid	Car\(^k\). on Shannon	IV.	103
9	Clooney	65 1 21g	Londonderry	Keenaght	Aghanloo	NewT\(^n\)Limavady	III.	233
1, 2, 5, 6	Clooney	276 0 20	Londonderry	Keenaght	Magilligan	NewT\(^n\)Limavady	III.	236
36	Clooney	413 1 38	Londonderry	Loughinsholin	Kilcronaghan	Magherafelt	III.	241
20	Clooney	615 3 12	Londonderry	Tirkeeran	Clondermot	Londonderry	III.	247
11, 12	Clooney	472 3 15	Meath	Morgallion	Drakestown	Navan	I.	209
23	Clooneybreen	73 0 20	Clare	Corcomroe	Kilmanaheen	Ennistimon	II.	21
17	Clooney and Gortnamona	144 0 8h	Donegal	Kilmacrenan	Clondavaddog	Milford	III.	124
67	Clooneylissaun	513 0 7	Clare	Clonderalaw	Killimer	Kilrush	II.	16
36, 45	Clooney More	204 2 24i	Donegal	Kilmacrenan	Tullyfern	Milford	III.	133
16, 24	Clooney North	327 0 37	Clare	Corcomroe	Clooney	Ennistimon	II.	18
23	Clooneyogan North	250 3 7	Clare	Ibrickan	Kilfarboy	Ennistimon	II.	22
23	Clooneyogan South	358 0 17j	Clare	Ibrickan	Kilfarboy	Ennistimon	II.	22
16, 24	Clooney South	804 0 14	Clare	Corcomroe	Clooney	Ennistimon	II.	18
24	Cloonfad	550 0 2k	Roscommon	Ballintober North	Termonbarry	Strokestown	IV.	187
7	Cloonfad	315 2 30l	Roscommon	Boyle	Tumna	Car\(^k\). on Shannon	IV.	197
26, 33	Cloonfad	388 0 39	Roscommon	Castlereagh	Kilkeevin	Castlereagh	IV.	200
14	Cloonfad	637 1 9	Roscommon	Frenchpark	Tibohine	Castlereagh	IV.	204
56	Cloonfad	681 3 20	Roscommon	Moycarn	Moore	Ballinasloe	IV.	206
11	Cloonfadbeg	161 0 1	Roscommon	Roscommon	Aughrim	Car\(^k\). on Shannon	IV.	207
45	Cloonfadda	752 1 29	Clare	Tulla Lower	Killaloe	Scarriff	II.	35
21, 22	Cloonfadda	202 3 12	Mayo	Tirawley	Ballysakeery	Ballina	IV.	164
31, 32	Cloonfad East	1,090 3 33	Roscommon	Castlereagh	Kiltullagh	Castlereagh	IV.	201
11	Cloonfad More	370 0 34m	Roscommon	Roscommon	Aughrim	Car\(^k\). on Shannon	IV.	207
31, 32	Cloonfad West	334 2 34	Roscommon	Castlereagh	Kiltullagh	Castlereagh	IV.	201
7	Cloonfaghna	587 0 27n	Galway	Ballymoe	Ballynakill	Glennamaddy	IV.	5
4, 16	Cloonfane	492 2 31	Galway	Dunmore	Dunmore	Tuam	IV.	33
63	Cloonfane	265 2 6	Mayo	Costello	Kilbeagh	Swineford	IV.	140
92	Cloonfaughna	160 3 25o	Mayo	Costello	Knock	Claremorris	IV.	142
73	Cloonfaulus	605 2 28p	Mayo	Costello	Kilmovee	Swineford	IV.	142
31	Cloonfeacle	60 1 7	Leitrim	Leitrim	Kiltoghert	Car\(^k\). on Shannon	IV.	101
33	Cloonfeagh	272 3 2	Clare	Islands	Drumcliff	Ennis	II.	30
25	Cloonfeaghra	94 2 26	Clare	Inchiquin	Ruan	Corrofin	II.	28
82	Cloonfeaghra	444 2 2q	Mayo	Costello	Kilmovee	Swineford	IV.	142
52	Cloonfeightrin	627 0 29	Mayo	Costello	Kilturra	Swineford	IV.	142
26, 33	Cloonfelliv	471 2 31	Roscommon	Castlereagh	Kilkeevin	Castlereagh	IV.	200
78, 89	Cloonfert	206 3 12	Mayo	Carra	Ballyhean	Castlebar	IV.	125
23	Cloonfide	146 0 31	Longford	Moydow	Taghsheenod	Ballymahon	I.	162
10	Cloonfin	629 2 18r	Longford	Granard	Granard	Granard	I.	156
32	Cloonfincen	309 0 5	Roscommon	Castlereagh	Kiltullagh	Castlereagh	IV.	201
18	Cloonfinfy	341 2 4	Longford	Moydow	Killashee	Longford	I.	161
14,15,20,21	Cloonfinglas	809 3 3	Roscommon	Frenchpark	Tibohine	Castlereagh	IV.	205
67	Cloonfinglass	373 1 37	Tipperary, S.R.	Clanwilliam	Killardry	Tipperary	II.	308
50, 62	Cloonfinish	353 2 9	Mayo	Gallen	Killasser	Swineford	IV.	149
29	Cloonfinlough	401 1 13s	Roscommon	Roscommon	Cloonfinlough	Strokestown	IV.	209
32, 35	Cloonfinnan	226 0 27t	Leitrim	Mohill	Mohill	Mohill	IV.	107
61	Cloonfinnaun	469 1 1	Mayo	Gallen	Kilconduff	Swineford	IV.	147
32	Cloonfinnoge	99 0 2	Galway	Killian	Killian	Mountbellew	IV.	44
18	Cloonflugh	328 3 12	Longford	Moydow	Killashee	Longford	I.	161
90	Cloonflyn	298 2 39u	Mayo	Carra	Rosslee	Castlebar	IV.	130
67, 68	Cloonfoher	283 0 20	Mayo	Burrishoole	Burrishoole	Newport	IV.	119
17, 18	Cloonfore	999 3 10	Longford	Ratheline	Ratheline	Longford	I.	164
24	Cloonfower	255 0 23	Roscommon	Ballintober North	Termonbarry	Strokestown	IV.	187
19, 20	Cloonfower	1,215 2 11	Roscommon	Castlereagh	Kilkeevin	Castlereagh	IV.	200
23, 28, 29	Cloonfree	796 2 3v	Roscommon	Roscommon	Cloonfinlough	Strokestown	IV.	209
49, 50	Cloonfurrihis	224 1 30	Clare	Clonderalaw	Kilchreest	Killadysert	II.	15
29, 43	Cloonfush	398 1 1	Galway	Clare	Tuam	Tuam	IV.	23
34	Cloongad	153 1 13w	Sligo	Tirerrill	Tawnagh	Sligo	IV.	241
44	Cloongaheen East	330 1 1	Clare	Tulla Lower	Killokennedy	Limerick	II.	35
36, 44	Cloongaheen West	931 3 36	Clare	Tulla Lower	Killokennedy	Limerick	II.	35

(a) Including 6A. 0R. 36P. water.
(b) Including 5A. 1R. 23P. water.
(c) Including 10A. 1R. 38P. water.
(d) Including 7A. 1R. 4P. water.
(e) Including 5A. 0R. 5P. water.
(f) Including 42A. 1R. 39P. water.
(g) Including 1A. 3R. 36P. water.
(h) Including 4A. 3R. 8P. water.

(i) Including 28A. 2R. 4P. water.
(j) Including 4A. 0R. 16P. water.
(k) Including Islands.
(l) Including 19A. 0R. 10P. water.
(m) Including 8A. 0R. 24P. water.
(n) Including 20A. 1R. 27P. water.
(o) Including 7A. 2R. 0P. water.
(p) Including 1A. 3R. 13P. water.

(q) Including 105A. 2R. 23P. water.
(r) Including 14A. 3R. 38P. water.
(s) Including 59A. 1R. 10P. water.
(t) Including 30A. 2R. 36P. water.
(u) Including 5A. 2R. 36P. water.
(v) Including 104A. 1R. 8P. water.
(w) Including 5A. 0R. 1P. water.

No. of Sheet of the Ordnance Survey Maps.	Townlands and Towns.	Area in Statute Acres. A. R. P.	County.	Barony.	Parish.	Poor Law Union in 1857.	Vol.	Page
17	Cloongarvan	99 0 27a	Roscommon	Roscommon	Clooncraff	Strokestown	IV.	208
15	Cloongarve	120 1 38	Clare	Corcomroe	Kilshanny	Ennistimon	II.	21
73	Cloongawna	199 2 4	Galway	Tiaquin	Ballymacward	Ballinasloe	IV.	75
102	Cloongawnagh	328 3 29	Mayo	Clanmorris	Kilcolman	Claremorris	IV.	133
122	Cloongawnagh	234 1 26	Mayo	Kilmaine	Kilmainemore	Ballinrobe	IV.	156
82	Cloongawnagh(Burke)	838 1 2b	Mayo	Costello	Aghamore	Swineford	IV.	137
82	Cloongawnagh (Cosgrave)	586 3 21	Mayo	Costello	Aghamore	Swineford	IV.	137
60, 61	Cloongee	693 2 6c	Mayo	Gallen	Templemore	Swineford	IV.	151
22	Cloongeel	659 1 23	Cork, E.R.	Duhallow	Kilmeen	Kanturk	II.	72
30	Cloonglasney	188 0 18	Mayo	Tirawley	Ardagh	Ballina	IV.	163
17	Cloonglasny Beg	335 3 19d	Roscommon	Roscommon	Clooncraff	Strokestown	IV.	208
17	Cloonglasny More	163 1 6e	Roscommon	Roscommon	Clooncraff	Strokestown	IV.	208
20	Cloon Glebe	94 0 4	Kerry	Clanmaurice	Ardfert	Tralee	II.	167
37, 42	Cloongoonagh	880 0 12	Sligo	Leyny	Kilmacteige	Tobercurry	IV.	231
110, 118	Cloongowla	617 1 25f	Mayo	Kilmaine	Ballinrobe	Ballinrobe	IV.	152
6	Cloongown	238 1 24	Cork, E.R.	Duhallow	Tullylease	Kanturk	II.	76
32	Cloongowna	982 1 8g	Clare	Inchiquin	Kilnamona	Ennis	II.	27
48, 49, 52	Cloongowna	665 1 34	Roscommon	Athlone	Drum	Athlone	IV.	180
12	Cloongownagh	460 3 16	Limerick	Kenry	Adare	Croom	II.	248
7, 11	Cloongownagh	235 3 21	Roscommon	Boyle	Tumna	Cark. on Shannon	IV.	197
7	Cloongreaghan	326 0 12	Roscommon	Boyle	Ardcarn	Cark. on Shannon	IV.	192
61	Cloongullaun	452 1 5h	Mayo	Gallen	Kilconduff	Swineford	IV.	147
63, 73	Cloonierin	1,045 1 23	Mayo	Costello	Kilmovee	Swineford	IV.	142
81	Clooniff	1,131 3 19i	Galway	Moycullen	Moycullen	Galway	IV.	71
54, 56	Clooniff	715 1 6	Roscommon	Moycarn	Moore	Ballinasloe	IV.	206
73, 74	Cloonigny	1,024 2 10	Galway	Clonmacnowen	Kilgerrill	Ballinasloe	IV.	25
8	Clooniher	367 2 38	Longford	Longford	Mohill	Longford	I.	159
51, 54	Cloonillan	465 2 23	Roscommon	Athlone	Drum	Athlone	IV.	180
43, 44	Clooninagh	409 1 22	Galway	Clare	Cummer	Tuam	IV.	18
99, 107	Cloonineen	323 0 30	Galway	Longford	Kiltormer	Ballinasloe	IV.	60
37	Clooningan	468 1 31	Sligo	Leyny	Achonry	Tobercurry	IV.	229
6, 7	Clooninihy	572 0 26	Tipperary, N.R.	Lower Ormond	Terryglass	Borrisokane	II.	287
25, 26	Clooninisclin	550 2 20	Roscommon	Castlereagh	Kiltullagh	Castlereagh	IV.	201
61, 71	Clooninshin	144 2 16	Mayo	Gallen	Meelick	Swineford	IV.	150
56	Cloon Island	3 0 35	Kerry	Trughanacmy	Killorglin	Killarney	II.	211
51	Cloonisle	904 0 11	Galway	Ballynahinch	Moyrus	Clifden	IV.	12
101, 108, 109	Cloonkea	207 1 6	Galway	Longford	Clonfert	Ballinasloe	IV.	57
80	Cloonkedagh	110 3 29	Mayo	Gallen	Killedan	Swineford	IV.	150
29, 30	Cloonkee	469 2 37	Mayo	Tirawley	Kilfian	Ballina	IV.	169
101	Cloonkeeghan	83 0 34	Mayo	Clanmorris	Tagheen	Claremorris	IV.	136
118	Cloonkeeghan Commons	343 3 8j	Mayo	Kilmaine	Kilmainemore	Ballinrobe	IV.	156
25	Cloonkeehan East	156 2 15	Roscommon	Castlereagh	Kiltullagh	Castlereagh	IV.	201
25	Cloonkeehan West	164 0 38	Roscommon	Castlereagh	Kiltullagh	Castlereagh	IV.	201
12	Cloonkeel	313 3 4	Longford	Moydow	Killashee	Longford	I.	161
23	Cloonkeelaun	2,264 1 39	Sligo	Tireragh	Castleconor	Dromore West	IV.	232
41, 55	Cloonkeely	108 1 22	Galway	Clare	Kilursa	Tuam	IV.	21
7	Cloonkeen	406 1 31	Cork, E.R.	Orrery and Kilmore	Aglishdrinagh	Kilmallock	II.	106
133, 142	Cloonkeen	374 1 18	Cork, W.R.	West Carbery (E.D.)	Kilmacabea	Skibbereen	II.	140
5	Cloonkeen	971 0 34	Galway	Dunmore	Dunmore	Tuam	IV.	33
6	Cloonkeen	241 3 3	Galway	Tiaquin	Boyounagh	Glennamaddy	IV.	76
58, 59	Cloonkeen	525 3 29	Galway	Tiaquin	Moylough	Tuam	IV.	79
76, 86	Cloonkeen	707 0 34	Kerry	Magunihy	Killaha	Killarney	II.	202
18	Cloonkeen	142 2 4	Longford	Moydow	Ballymacormick	Longford	I.	160
19, 23	Cloonkeen	269 1 21	Longford	Moydow	Taghsheenod	Ballymahon	I.	162
23, 27	Cloonkeen	306 0 39k	Longford	Rathcline	Shrule	Ballymahon	I.	165
76	Cloonkeen	135 3 14l	Mayo	Burrishoole	Kilmeena	Westport	IV.	122
78, 89	Cloonkeen	560 0 5m	Mayo	Carra	Aglish	Castlebar	IV.	123
111	Cloonkeen	97 3 4	Mayo	Clanmorris	Tagheen	Claremorris	IV.	136
50	Cloonkeen	364 2 29n	Roscommon	Athlone	Taghmaconnell	Ballinasloe	IV.	185
7	Cloonkeen	132 0 39	Roscommon	Boyle	Tumna	Cark. on Shannon	IV.	197
26	Cloonkeen	1,181 3 29	Roscommon	Castlereagh	Kilkeevin	Castlereagh	IV.	200
72, 84, 85	Cloonkeenbeg	413 2 13	Galway	Tiaquin	Monivea	Loughrea	IV.	78
31	Cloonkeenclare	293 0 39	Galway	Tiaquin	Kilkerrin	Glennamaddy	IV.	76
32	Cloonkeen (Davies)	93 2 15	Galway	Killian	Killian	Mountbellew	IV.	44
133, 134	Cloonkeen East	151 0 34	Cork, W.R.	East Carbery (W.D.)	Kilmacabea	Skibbereen	II.	133
99	Cloonkeen East	217 3 17	Galway	Clonmacnowen	Killallaghtan	Ballinasloe	IV.	26
31	Cloonkeen Eighter	229 2 28	Galway	Tiaquin	Kilkerrin	Glennamaddy	IV.	76
32	Cloonkeen (Ffrench)	166 2 9	Galway	Killian	Killian	Mountbellew	IV.	44
32	Cloonkeen (Kelly)	122 3 23	Galway	Killian	Killian	Mountbellew	IV.	44
31	Cloonkeenleananode	348 2 10o	Galway	Tiaquin	Kilkerrin	Glennamaddy	IV.	76
85	Cloonkeenmore North	471 0 2	Galway	Tiaquin	Monivea	Loughrea	IV.	78
85	Cloonkeenmore South	504 2 6	Galway	Kilconnell	Monivea	Loughrea	IV.	42

(a) Including 2A. 2R. 20P. water.
(b) Including 26A. 1R. 2P. water.
(c) Including 28A. 1R. 19P. water.
(d) Including 29A. 2R. 36P. water.
(e) Including 22A. 3R. 10P. water.

(f) Including 19A. 2R. 12P. water.
(g) Including 35A. 1R. 30P. water.
(h) Including 11A. 0R. 32P. water.
(i) Including 67A. 1R. 29P. water.
(j) Including 23A. 1R. 12P. water.

(k) Including 4A. 3R. 32P. water.
(l) Including 6A. 1R. 9P. water.
(m) Including 15A. 1R. 0P. water.
(n) Including 3A. 2R. 19P. detached portion.
(o) Including 12A. 0R. 17P. water.

No. of Sheet of the Ordnance Survey Maps.	Townlands and Towns.	Area in Statute Acres.			County.	Barony.	Parish.	Poor Law Union in 1857.	Townland Census of 1851, Part I.	
		A.	R.	P.					Vol.	Page
31	Cloonkeennagran .	404	3	7	Galway . .	Tiaquin . . .	Kilkerrin . .	Glennamaddy .	IV.	76
32	Cloonkeen (*Netterville*)	95	2	36	Galway .	Killian . . .	Killian . . .	Mountbellew .	IV.	44
43	Cloonkeen North .	553	0	18*a*	Galway . .	Clare . .	Cummer . .	Tuam . .	IV.	18
31, 45	Cloonkeen Oughter .	453	3	30*b*	Galway . .	Tiaquin . .	Kilkerrin . .	Glennamaddy .	IV.	76
43	Cloonkeen South .	127	2	29*c*	Galway .	Clare . .	Cummer . .	Tuam . .	IV.	18
31	Cloonkeen (*Waldron*) .	206	3	21	Galway . .	Tiaquin . .	Kilkerrin .	Glennamaddy .	IV.	76
99	Cloonkeen West .	189	1	22	Galway . .	Clonmacnowen .	Killallaghtan . .	Ballinasloe .	IV.	26
33	Cloonkeevy . .	224	1	12	Sligo .	Corran . .	Emlaghfad . .	Tobercurry .	IV.	226
38	Cloonkelly . .	104	0	33	Mayo . .	Tirawley . .	Crossmolina . .	Ballina .	IV.	165
18	Cloonker . .	257	0	13	Longford .	Moydow . .	Moydow . .	Longford .	I.	162
15, 16	Cloonkerin . .	528	2	38*d*	Roscommon .	Frenchpark . .	Kilcolagh . .	Boyle .	IV.	203
26	Cloonkerry . .	171	3	33	Clare . .	Bunratty Upper .	Kilraghtis . .	Ennis .	II.	9
109, 110	Cloonkerry . .	400	1	20	Mayo . .	Kilmaine . .	Ballinrobe . .	Ballinrobe .	IV.	152
69	Cloonkerry East .	237	0	17	Clare . .	Clonderalaw .	Killofin . .	Killadysert .	II.	16
69	Cloonkerry West .	226	3	37	Clare . .	Clonderalaw .	Killofin . .	Killadysert .	II.	17
70	Cloonkesh . .	359	0	8*e*	Mayo . .	Carra . .	Turlough . .	Castlebar .	IV.	130
59	Cloonkett . .	630	3	3	Clare . .	Clonderalaw .	Killadysert . .	Killadysert .	II.	15
19	Cloonkilla . .	198	1	23	Cork, E.R. .	Condons&Clangibbon	Kilgullane . .	Mitchelstown .	II.	61
121	Cloonkirgeen . .	361	2	18	Cork, W.R. .	East Carbery (W.D.)	Kilmeen . .	Dunmanway .	II.	134
109, 110	Cloonlagheen .	404	1	26	Mayo . .	Carra . .	Ballyovey . .	Ballinrobe .	IV.	126
99	Cloonlahan (*Eyre*) .	302	3	24	Galway .	Longford . . .	Killoran . .	Ballinasloe .	IV.	59
99	Cloonlahan (*Geoghegan*)	173	3	23	Galway .	Longford . . .	Killoran . .	Ballinasloe .	IV.	59
18, 27	Cloonlahard East .	802	0	22	Limerick .	Shanid . .	Kilmoylan . .	Glin . .	II.	256
18, 27	Cloonlahard West .	728	0	19	Limerick .	Shanid . .	Kilmoylan . .	Glin . .	II.	256
32	Cloonlaheen . .	141	1	39	Clare .	Islands . .	Kilmaley . .	Ennis . .	II.	31
44	Cloonlaheen . .	346	0	33	Sligo . .	Coolavin . .	Kilfree . .	Boyle .	IV.	224
31,32,39 40	Cloonlaheen East .	955	2	19	Clare . .	Ibrickan . .	Kilmurry . .	Kilrush .	II.	23
31, 39	Cloonlaheen Middle .	1,129	1	13	Clare .	Ibrickan . .	Kilmurry . .	Kilrush .	II.	23
39	Cloonlaheen West .	721	3	7	Clare . .	Ibrickan . .	Kilmurry . .	Kilrush .	II.	23
53	Cloonlara . .	153	2	32	Clare . .	Tulla Lower . .	Kiltenanlea . .	Limerick .	II.	37
48	Cloonlara . .	174	2	28	Kerry . .	Magunihy . .	Molahiffe . .	Killarney .	II.	204
45	Cloonlara . .	180	3	6	Limerick .	Connello Upper .	Cloncrew . .	Newcastle .	II.	232
102	Cloonlara . .	345	3	19	Mayo . .	Costello . .	Bekan . .	Claremorris .	IV.	139
62	Cloonlara . .	488	3	35	Mayo . .	Gallen . .	Kilconduff . .	Swineford .	IV.	147
6	Cloonlara North .	215	2	26	Galway .	Ballymoe . .	Boyounagh . .	Glennamaddy .	IV.	6
18, 19	Cloonlara South .	508	3	34	Galway . .	Ballymoe . .	Boyounagh . .	Glennamaddy .	IV.	6
53	CLOONLARA T. .	—			Clare . .	Tulla Lower . .	Kiltenanlea . .	Limerick .	II.	37
40	Cloonlarge . .	330	3	10	Roscommon .	Ballintober South .	Kilteevan . .	Roscommon .	IV.	190
51, 52	Cloonlarhan . .	534	2	18	Mayo . .	Costello . .	Kilbeagh . .	Swineford .	IV.	140
26	Cloonlatieve . .	228	2	39	Roscommon .	Castlereagh . .	Kilkeevin . .	Castlereagh .	IV.	200
38	Cloonlaughil . .	559	1	12	Leitrim . .	Mohill . .	Cloone . .	Mohill .	IV.	105
33, 36	Cloonlaughil . .	125	0	0*f*	Leitrim . .	Mohill . .	Mohill . .	Mohill .	IV.	107
42	Cloonlaughil . .	1,197	0	0	Sligo . .	Leyny . .	Achonry . .	Tobercurry .	IV.	229
44	Cloonlaughnan .	829	1	12*g*	Roscommon .	Athlone . .	Tisrara . .	Roscommon .	IV.	185
95	Cloonlaur . .	84	2	18	Mayo . .	Murrisk . .	Kilgeever . .	Westport .	IV.	160
80, 91, 92	Cloonlavis Lower .	288	3	11	Mayo . .	Clanmorris . .	Knock . .	Claremorris .	IV.	135
91, 92	Cloonlavis Upper .	166	3	18	Mayo . .	Clanmorris . .	Knock . .	Claremorris .	IV.	135
2	Cloonleagh North .	305	3	1	Cork, E.R. .	Orrery and Kilmore	Shandrum . .	Kanturk .	II.	110
2	Cloonleagh South .	266	3	5	Cork, E.R. .	Orrery and Kilmore	Shandrum . .	Kanturk .	II.	110
116	Cloonlee . . .	551	3	27	Galway . .	Leitrim . .	Duniry . .	Loughrea .	IV.	53
81, 92	Cloonlee . .	463	2	2	Mayo . .	Costello . .	Knock . .	Claremorris .	IV.	142
25	Cloonlee . .	422	0	12	Roscommon .	Castlereagh . .	Kiltullagh . .	Castlereagh .	IV.	201
69	Cloonleenaun . .	220	2	26*h*	Galway . .	Clare . .	Annaghdown . .	Galway .	IV.	16
117	Cloonliffen . .	185	1	26	Mayo . .	Kilmaine . .	Ballinrobe . .	Ballinrobe .	IV.	152
26	Cloonlish or Robinhood	257	0	5	Roscommon .	Castlereagh . .	Kiltullagh . .	Castlereagh .	IV.	201
15	Cloonlogher . .	161	0	7	Kerry . .	Clanmaurice . .	Rattoo . .	Listowel .	II.	173
11	Cloonlogher . .	457	3	11	Leitrim . .	Drumahaire . .	Cloonlogher . .	Manorhamilton .	IV.	94
47	Cloonlogue . .	178	2	6	Limerick . .	Coshma . .	Kilbreedy Minor .	Kilmallock .	II.	243
9, 10	Cloonlooaun . .	832	3	16*i*	Galway . .	Ballynahinch . .	Ballynakill . .	Clifden .	IV.	11
45	Cloonloogh . .	431	0	37	Sligo . .	Coolavin . .	Killaraght . .	Boyle .	IV.	224
19	Cloonlough . .	327	0	25	Cork, E.R. .	Condons&Clangibbon	Brigown . . .	Mitchelstown .	II.	59
22	Cloonloughan or Dooyeaghny .	539	0	0	Sligo . .	Tireragh . .	Castleconor . .	Ballina .	IV.	232
35	Cloonloum Beg .	91	3	30	Clare . .	Tulla Lower . .	Clonlea . .	Tulla .	II.	34
35, 43	Cloonloum More .	841	3	21*j*	Clare . .	Tulla Lower . .	Clonlea . .	Tulla .	II.	34
63, 64	Cloonlumney . .	2,200	3	34	Mayo . .	Costello . .	Kilcolman . .	Castlereagh .	IV.	141
61, 62	Cloonlumney . .	324	1	5*k*	Mayo . .	Gallen . .	Kilconduff . .	Swineford .	IV.	147
33, 34	Cloonlurg . .	478	0	21	Sligo . .	Corran . .	Kilmorgan . .	Sligo .	IV.	227
44	Cloonlusk . .	339	0	36	Galway . .	Clare . .	Killererin . .	Tuam .	IV.	21
15,16,24,25	Cloonlusk . .	354	0	23	Limerick . .	Coonagh . .	Doon . .	Tipperary .	II.	234
79, 90	Cloonlynchaghaun .	106	1	37	Mayo . .	Carra . .	Drum . .	Castlebar .	IV.	128
32, 33	Cloonlyon . .	1,078	3	18	Galway . .	Killian . .	Killeroran . .	Mountbellew .	IV.	43

(*a*) Including 172A. 2R. 7P. water.   (*c*) Including 13A. 2R. 8P. water.   (*i*) Including 39A. 2R. 13P. water.
(*b*) Including 9A. 0R. 37P. water.   (*f*) Including 11A. 1R. 21P. water.   (*j*) Including 22A. 2R. 11P. water.
(*c*) Including 10A. 3R. 13P. water.   (*g*) Including 5A. 0R. 38P. water.   (*k*) Including 10A. 2R. 10P. water.
(*d*) Including 62A. 2R. 11P. water.   (*h*) Including 22A. 0R. 39P. water.

No. of Sheet of the Ordnance Survey Maps.	Townlands and Towns.	Area in Statute Acres.	County.	Barony.	Parish.	Poor Law Union in 1857.	Townland Census of 1851, Part I.	
		A. R. P.					Vol.	Page
62, 72	Cloonlyon	229 3 37	Mayo	Costello	Kilbeagh	Swineford	IV.	140
21, 22	Cloonmaan	41 3 21	Mayo	Tirawley	Ballysakeery	Ballina	IV.	164
7, 11	Cloonmaan	93 1 39	Roscommon	Boyle	Tumna	Carᵏ. on Shannon	IV.	197
5, 9	Cloonmacart	426 2 25	Longford	Longford	Killoe	Longford	I.	158
20, 26	Cloonmacduff	302 2 23a	Sligo	Tirerrill	Ballysadare	Sligo	IV.	237
32	Cloonmackan	161 2 13b	Clare	Inchiquin	Inagh	Ennistimon	II.	25
11	Cloonmackon	387 3 38	Kerry	Iraghticonnor	Listowel	Listowel	II.	192
9	Cloonmacmullan	166 2 35	Roscommon	Frenchpark	Kilnamanagh	Boyle	IV.	204
6	Cloonmaghaura	706 3 13c	Galway	Ballymoe	Templetogher	Glennamaddy	IV.	9
8	Cloonmagunnaun	587 1 38	Roscommon	Frenchpark	Kilnamanagh	Castlereagh	IV.	204
22	Cloonmahaan	179 1 24d	Roscommon	Roscommon	Elphin	Strokestown	IV.	209
98	Cloonmain	360 0 8	Galway	Leitrim	Killoran	Loughrea	IV.	54
59	Cloonmalonga	62 0 20	Tipperary, S.R.	Clanwilliam	Kilmucklin	Tipperary	II.	309
58	Cloonmanagh	51 3 20	Tipperary, S.R.	Clanwilliam	Cullen	Tipperary	II.	307
5	Cloonmartin	106 1 35	Clare	Burren	Rathborney	Ballyvaghan	II.	14
19	Cloonmaul	453 0 9	Roscommon	Frenchpark	Tibohine	Castlereagh	IV.	205
47, 48	Cloonmealane	264 1 28	Kerry	Magunihy	Kilnanare	Killarney	II.	204
17	Cloonmeane	125 2 9e	Roscommon	Ballintober North	Kilmore	Carᵏ. on Shannon	IV.	187
21	Cloonmee	397 3 17	Longford	Rathcline	Cashel	Ballymahon	I.	163
64	Cloonmeen	183 0 19	Mayo	Costello	Kilcolman	Castlereagh	IV.	141
64	Cloonmeen East	386 1 1	Mayo	Costello	Kilbeagh	Swineford	IV.	140
63	Cloonmeen West	263 1 3	Mayo	Costello	Kilbeagh	Swineford	IV.	140
18	Cloonmeone Lower	123 1 33	Leitrim	Drumahaire	Inishmagrath	Manorhamilton	IV.	96
18	Cloonmeone Upper	89 2 2	Leitrim	Drumahaire	Inishmagrath	Manorhamilton	IV.	96
6	Cloonminda	293 3 1	Galway	Ballymoe	Boyounagh	Glennamaddy	IV.	6
135	Cloonmohaun	83 0 9	Galway	Leitrim	Clonrush	Scarriff	IV.	52
88	Cloonmonad	159 0 0	Mayo	Murrisk	Oughaval	Westport	IV.	161
18, 26	Cloonmoney	73 3 39f	Clare	Bunratty Upper	Inchicronan	Ennis	II.	9
34, 42	Cloonmore	123 2 37	Clare	Bunratty Upper	Doora	Ennis	II.	8
38, 47	Cloonmore	1,154 1 26g	Clare	Ibrickan	Killard	Kilrush	II.	23
41, 50	Cloonmore	529 1 16	Clare	Islands	Clondagad	Killadysert	II.	29
2	Cloonmore	429 2 30	Cork, E.R.	Orrery and Kilmore	Shandrum	Kanturk	II.	110
17, 18	Cloonmore	959 0 17	Galway	Ballymoe	Dunmore	Glennamaddy	IV.	7
28, 29	Cloonmore	287 2 17h	Galway	Clare	Belclare	Tuam	IV.	17
43	Cloonmore	889 2 11i	Galway	Clare	Tuam	Tuam	IV.	23
55	Cloonmore	331 2 31	Galway	Moycullen	Killannin	Oughterard	IV.	69
47	Cloonmore	337 0 37	Kerry	Trughanacmy	Kilcolman	Killarney	II.	210
29	Cloon More	99 3 19	Kerry	Trughanacmy	Ratass	Tralee	II.	213
45	Cloonmore	731 0 36	Limerick	Glenquin	Mahoonagh	Newcastle	II.	246
13, 18	Cloonmore	670 3 35	Longford	Moydow	Killashee	Longford	I.	161
112	Cloonmore	273 0 15	Mayo	Clanmorris	Crossboyne	Claremorris	IV.	132
63	Cloonmore	161 1 32	Mayo	Costello	Kilbeagh	Swineford	IV.	140
30	Cloonmore	1,384 2 33	Roscommon	Ballintober North	Termonbarry	Strokestown	IV.	187
40	Cloonmore	349 0 37	Roscommon	Ballintober South	Kilteevan	Roscommon	IV.	190
21	Cloonmore	204 3 24	Tipperary, N.R.	Upper Ormond	Ballymackey	Nenagh	II.	289
80, 91	Cloonmore Lower	396 2 2	Mayo	Clanmorris	Kilcolman	Claremorris	IV.	133
91	Cloonmore Upper	356 0 7	Mayo	Clanmorris	Kilcolman	Claremorris	IV.	134
123	Cloonmorris	124 2 27	Galway	Kiltartan	Kilbeacanty	Gort	IV.	47
37	Cloonmorris	430 2 8	Leitrim	Mohill	Mohill	Mohill	IV.	107
126, 132	Cloonmoylan	1,141 0 38	Galway	Leitrim	Ballynakill	Portumna	IV.	51
126	Cloonmoylan	383 2 4	Galway	Leitrim	Tynagh	Portumna	IV.	55
16, 29	Cloonmoyle	192 0 20	Galway	Dunmore	Tuam	Tuam	IV.	36
18	Cloonmucker	138 1 26	Longford	Moydow	Moydow	Longford	I.	162
8	Cloonmull	218 1 15	Sligo	Carbury	Drumcliff	Sligo	IV.	221
34	Cloonmullenan	93 1 10	Roscommon	Ballymoe	Oran	Roscommon	IV.	192
27, 31	Cloonmulligan	71 2 39	Leitrim	Leitrim	Kiltoghert	Carᵏ. on Shannon	IV.	101
13,14,19,20	Cloonmullin	398 3 12	Roscommon	Frenchpark	Tibohine	Castlereagh	IV.	205
61	Cloonmung	382 3 19j	Mayo	Gallen	Toomore	Swineford	IV.	151
43	Cloonmunnia	208 0 13	Clare	Bunratty Lower	Kilmurry	Tulla	II.	6
40	Cloonmurly	327 1 6	Roscommon	Ballintober South	Kilteevan	Roscommon	IV.	190
28	Cloonmurray	273 0 23l	Roscommon	Roscommon	Killukin	Strokestown	IV.	210
37	Cloonmustra	168 1 5	Roscommon	Ballintober South	Cloontuskert	Roscommon	IV.	188
28, 29	Cloonweelaun	370 1 15	Galway	Dunmore	Kilconla	Tuam	IV.	35
59	Cloonweelaun	752 0 26	Galway	Tiaquin	Moylough	Mountbellew	IV.	79
68	Cloonnabinnia	440 2 7m	Galway	Moycullen	Moycullen	Galway	IV.	71
46	Cloonnabricka	404 1 9	Galway	Killian	Killeroran	Mountbellew	IV.	44
24, 37	Cloonnacartan	1,569 2 36n	Galway	Ballynahinch	Moyrus	Clifden	IV.	12
18	Cloonnacat	423 3 37	Galway	Ballymoe	Clonbern	Glennamaddy	IV.	6
16	Cloonnacorra	126 3 21	Galway	Dunmore	Liskeevy	Tuam	IV.	35
6, 7	Cloonnacross	245 3 11	Galway	Ballymoe	Boyounagh	Glennamaddy	IV.	6
4, 16	Cloonnacross	154 1 36	Galway	Dunmore	Addergoole	Tuam	IV.	33
117	Cloonnacusha	340 1 28	Galway	Longford	Tynagh	Portumna	IV.	62
22	Cloonnafinneela	745 1 18	Kerry	Clanmaurice	Kilflyn	Tralee	II.	170

(a) Including 2A. 0R. 9P. Ballysadare River.
(b) Including 7A. 2R. 21P. water.
(c) Including 9A. 1R. 26P. water.
(d) Including 7A. 0R. 13P. water.
(e) Including 3A. 1R. 15P. water.

(f) Including 2A. 0R. 36P. water.
(g) Including 24A. 3R. 22P. water.
(h) Including 0A. 1R. 12P. water.
(i) Including 102A. 2R. 6P. water.
(j) Including 6A. 2R. 38P. water.

(k) Including 4A. 2R. 34P. water.
(l) Including 40A. 0R. 20P. water.
(m) Including 20A. 3R. 17P. water.
(n) Including 194A. 2R. 21P. water.

No. of Sheet of the Ordnance Survey Maps.	Townlands and Towns.	Area in Statute Acres.			County.	Barony.	Parish.	Poor Law Union in 1857.	Townland Census of 1851, Part I.	
		A.	R.	P.					Vol.	Page
122, 128	Cloonnafunshin	225	1	34	Galway	Kiltartan	Kilmacduagh	Gort	IV.	48
11, 12	Cloonnagalleen	313	1	15	Limerick	Kenry	Kilcornan	Rathkeale	II.	24
117	Cloonnagark	99	1	30	Galway	Longford	Tynagh	Portumna	IV.	62
38	Cloonnagarnaun	702	0	0a	Clare	Ibrickan	Killard	Kilrush	II.	23
110	Cloonnagashel	486	3	11b	Mayo	Kilmaine	Ballinrobe	Ballinrobe	IV.	152
28, 29	Cloonnaglasha	1,027	3	35	Galway	Dunmore	Kilconla	Tuam	IV.	35
70	Cloonnagleragh	238	3	7	Mayo	Carra	Turlough	Castlebar	IV.	130
81	Cloonnagleragh	313	0	16c	Mayo	Costello	Knock	Claremorris	IV.	142
17, 25	Cloonnagloghaun	112	3	14	Clare	Inchiquin	Ruan	Corrofin	II.	28
100	Cloonnagoppoge	156	1	2	Mayo	Carra	Touaghty	Ballinrobe	IV.	130
19	Cloonnagro	290	0	29	Clare	Tulla Upper	Feakle	Tulla	II.	39
122,123,128	Cloonnahaha	339	3	10	Galway	Kiltartan	Beagh	Gort	IV.	46
81	Cloonnahulty	195	0	1	Mayo	Costello	Aghamore	Swineford	IV.	137
49,50,59,60	Cloonnakilla	246	1	34	Clare	Clonderalaw	Kilchreest	Killadysert	II.	15
48	Cloonnakilla	241	1	13	Clare	Clonderalaw	Kilmihil	Kilrush	II.	17
27	Cloonnamarve	68	1	30	Galway	Ross	Cong	Oughterard	IV.	73
107, 108	Cloonnamaskry	283	3	0	Galway	Longford	Kilquain	Portumna	IV.	60
122	Cloonnameeltoge and Caherrevagh	623	0	14	Mayo	Kilmaine	Kilmainemore	Ballinrobe	IV.	155
73	Cloonnamna	749	1	22	Mayo	Costello	Kilmovee	Swineford	IV.	142
113	Cloonnasee	478	0	20	Galway	Kiltartan	Kinvarradoorus	Gort	IV.	49
71	Cloonnavaddoge	596	3	4	Galway	Clare	Athenry	Galway	IV.	17
42	Cloonnavarnoge	158	1	7	Galway	Clare	Kilkilvery	Tuam	IV.	20
51	Cloonoghil	455	1	9	Roscommon	Athlone	Taghmaconnell	Athlone	IV.	185
15, 16	Cloonomra	341	3	9d	Clare	Corcomroe	Kilfenora	Ennistimon	II.	19
41, 55	Cloononaghaun	254	0	17e	Galway	Clare	Killursa	Tuam	IV.	21
105	Cloonoo East	220	2	32	Galway	Loughrea	Kilconickny	Loughrea	IV.	63
134	Cloonoolia North	130	0	8	Galway	Leitrim	Clonrush	Scarriff	IV.	52
134, 136	Cloonoolia South	287	1	23	Galway	Leitrim	Clonrush	Scarriff	IV.	52
107	Cloonoolish	316	3	29	Galway	Longford	Killimorbologue	Portumna	IV.	58
132	Cloonoon	375	2	5	Galway	Leitrim	Ballynakill	Portumna	IV.	51
28, 29	Cloonooragh	432	2	34f	Mayo	Tirawley	Crossmolina	Ballina	IV.	165
105	Cloonoo West	102	3	0	Galway	Loughrea	Kilconickny	Loughrea	IV.	63
45	Cloonoran	263	1	39	Galway	Tiaquin	Moylough	Mountbellew	IV.	79
45, 59	Cloonoranoughter	473	2	31	Galway	Tiaquin	Killoscobe	Mountbellew	IV.	77
63	Cloonoughter	129	0	12	Clare	Bunratty Lower	St. Patrick's	Limerick	II.	6
18	Cloonoughter	636	2	18	Limerick	Shanid	Kilfergus	Glin	II.	256
20	Cloonoul	181	3	28	Limerick	Connello Lower	Cappagh	Rathkeale	II.	227
52, 55	Cloonown	2,469	1	26	Roscommon	Athlone	St. Peter's	Athlone	IV.	184
45	Cloonpasteen	419	0	27	Limerick	Connello Upper	Kilmeedy	Newcastle	II.	233
60	Cloonpee	114	3	3	Galway	Tiaquin	Killosolan	Mountbellew	IV.	78
106, 107	Cloonprask	188	2	5	Galway	Longford	Duniry	Loughrea	IV.	58
6, 11	Cloonprohus	249	1	10	Kerry	Iraghticonnor	Murher	Listowel	II.	193
23	Cloonrabrackan	203	2	32	Roscommon	Roscommon	Bumlin	Strokestown	IV.	208
23, 29	Cloonradoon	461	0	11	Roscommon	Roscommon	Bumlin	Strokestown	IV.	208
8, 9, 13, 14	Cloonrallagh	400	1	25	Longford	Longford	Templemichael	Longford	I.	160
4	Cloonrane	476	2	8	Galway	Dunmore	Addergoole	Tuam	IV.	33
28, 29	Cloonrane	278	3	4g	Roscommon	Roscommon	Cloonfinlough	Strokestown	IV.	209
10, 11	Cloonreask	245	3	16	Limerick	Connello Lower	Askeaton	Rathkeale	II.	226
10	Cloonreask	128	0	5	Limerick	Connello Lower	Tomdeely	Rathkeale	II.	230
47, 48	Cloonreddan	709	2	36	Clare	Moyarta	Kilmacduane	Kilrush	II.	32
20	Cloonree	394	0	4	Roscommon	Castlereagh	Kilkeevin	Castlereagh	IV.	200
37	Cloonregan	119	3	30	Limerick	Connello Upper	Ballingarry	Croom	II.	230
45, 46	Cloonreleagh (Bellew)	360	3	11	Galway	Killian	Ballynakill	Mountbellew	IV.	43
46	Cloonreleagh East	9	1	18	Galway	Killian	Ballynakill	Mountbellew	IV.	43
45, 46	Cloonreleagh West	126	1	26	Galway	Killian	Ballynakill	Mountbellew	IV.	43
26, 33	Cloonreliagh	226	3	16	Roscommon	Castlereagh	Kiltullagh	Castlereagh	IV.	201
44	Cloonriddia	179	3	31	Galway	Clare	Killererin	Tuam	IV.	21
51	Cloonrollagh	223	3	35	Roscommon	Athlone	Drum	Athlone	IV.	180
45	Cloonroosk	287	2	28	Limerick	Connello Upper	Kilmeedy	Newcastle	II.	233
26	Cloonroughan	388	1	31	Roscommon	Castlereagh	Kilkeevin	Castlereagh	IV.	200
22	Cloonroughan	426	2	0h	Roscommon	Roscommon	Elphin	Strokestown	IV.	209
2, 7	Cloonruff	255	3	23i	Galway	Ballymoe	Kilcroan	Glennamaddy	IV.	8
33	Cloonruff	699	1	25j	Galway	Killian	Athleague	Mountbellew	IV.	43
19, 23	Cloonscott	369	1	20	Longford	Moydow	Taghsheenod	Ballymahon	I.	162
7, 11	Cloonselherny	749	2	30k	Clare	Inchiquin	Kilkeedy	Corrofin	II.	25
18	Cloonsellan	243	2	28	Longford	Moydow	Killashee	Longford	I.	161
40, 42	Cloonsellan	416	1	4	Roscommon	Ballintober South	Kiltceevan	Roscommon	IV.	190
10	Cloonshaghan	338	2	31l	Roscommon	Boyle	Estersnow	Boyle	IV.	195
39	Cloonshanbally	300	2	34	Sligo	Corran	Drumrat	Boyle	IV.	225
101	Cloonshanbo	181	1	30	Mayo	Clanmorris	Mayo	Claremorris	IV.	135
17	Cloonshannagh	64	1	30	Roscommon	Ballintober North	Kilmore	Car^{k.} on Shannon	IV.	187
24, 30	Cloonshannagh	665	1	39	Roscommon	Ballintober North	Termonbarry	Strokestown	IV.	187

(a) Including 40A. 0R. 11P. water.
(b) Including 14A. 3R. 9P. water.
(c) Including 3A. 3R. 21P. water.
(d) Including 16A. 0R. 0P. water.

(e) Including 2A. 3R. 13P. water.
(f) Including 6A. 0R. 11P. water.
(g) Including 83A. 0R. 19P. water.
(h) Including 47A. 0R. 35P. water.

(i) Including 6A. 2R. 22P. water.
(j) Including 24A. 3R. 20P. water.
(k) Including 3A. 2R. 7P. water.
(l) Including 55A. 3R. 31P. water.

No. of Sheet of the Ordnance Survey Maps.	Townlands and Towns.	Area in Statute Acres.	County.	Barony.	Parish.	Poor Law Union in 1857.	Townland Census of 1851, Part I.	
		A. R. P.					Vol.	Page
30	Cloonshannagh .	607 1 15a	Roscommon .	Roscommon .	Bumlin . .	Strokestown .	IV.	208
17	Cloonshannagh .	309 1 15b	Roscommon .	Roscommon .	Kiltrustan .	Strokestown .	IV.	211
15	Cloonshannagh or Cool- amberManor Demesne	590 3 8	Longford .	Ardagh .	Street . .	Granard .	I.	153
15	Cloonshanville .	929 3 8c	Roscommon .	Frenchpark .	Tibohine .	Castlereagh .	IV.	205
25,26,34,35	Cloonsharragh .	498 3 33	Kerry .	Corkaguiny .	Cloghane .	Dingle .	II.	175
56	Cloonshask .	324 1 37	Roscommon .	Moycarn .	Moore . .	Ballinasloe .	IV.	206
82	Cloonshear Beg .	182 0 13	Cork, W.R. .	West Muskerry .	Inchigeelagh .	Macroom .	II.	157
70, 81, 82	Cloonshear More .	448 2 7	Cork, W.R. .	West Muskerry .	Inchigeelagh .	Macroom .	II.	157
100	Cloonshease (Daly) .	76 1 34	Galway .	Longford .	Clonfert .	Ballinasloe .	IV.	57
100, 108	Cloonshease (Persse)	296 1 26	Galway .	Longford .	Clonfert .	Ballinasloe .	IV.	57
61	Cloonshee .	75 2 7	Galway .	Killian .	Ahascragh .	Mountbellew .	IV.	42
17, 23	Cloonshee .	233 1 28d	Roscommon .	Roscommon .	Clooncraff .	Strokestown .	IV.	208
27, 31	Cloonsheebane .	74 0 26	Leitrim .	Leitrim .	Kiltoghert .	Cark.on Shannon	IV.	101
85	Cloonsheecahill .	710 2 4	Galway .	Kilconnell .	Killimordaly .	Loughrea .	IV.	42
36	Cloonshee (Connor) .	122 2 7	Roscommon .	Ballintober South .	Kilgefin .	Roscommon .	IV.	189
61	Cloonshee (Dillon) .	209 3 34	Galway .	Killian .	Ahascragh .	Mountbellew .	IV.	42
36	Cloonshee (Hartland)	139 0 16	Roscommon .	Ballintober South .	Kilgefin .	Roscommon .	IV.	189
61	Cloonshee (Kelly) .	83 0 27	Galway .	Killian .	Ahascragh .	Mountbellew .	IV.	42
28	Cloonsheen .	581 3 22	Galway .	Dunmore .	Kinconla .	Tuam .	IV.	35
53	Cloonsheerea .	221 0 16	Clare .	Tulla Lower .	Kilseily .	Limerick .	II.	36
27	Cloonsheerevagh .	54 2 34	Leitrim .	Leitrim .	Kiltoghert .	Cark.on Shannon	IV.	101
18	Cloonsheerin .	212 0 35	Longford .	Moydow .	Killashee .	Longford .	I.	161
61	Cloonshee (Rochfort)	518 3 34	Galway .	Killian .	Ahascragh .	Mountbellew .	IV.	43
61	Cloonshee (Trench) .	226 3 24	Galway .	Killian .	Ahascragh .	Mountbellew .	IV.	43
20, 21	Cloonsheever .	879 3 9	Roscommon .	Frenchpark .	Tibohine .	Castlereagh .	IV.	205
44	Cloonsherick .	108 2 10	Limerick .	Glenquin .	Killeedy .	Newcastle .	II.	245
44	Cloonsherick .	166 3 39	Limerick .	Glenquin .	Mahoonagh .	Newcastle .	II.	246
78, 89	Cloonshinnagh .	170 1 4	Mayo .	Carra .	Ballyhean .	Castlebar .	IV.	125
22	Cloonshinnagh .	174 1 0	Mayo .	Tirawley .	Ballysakeery .	Ballina .	IV.	164
32	Cloonshivna .	274 0 0	Galway .	Killian .	Killian .	Mountbellew .	IV.	44
32	Cloonshivna (Kelly)	283 2 34	Galway .	Killian .	Killian .	Mountbellew .	IV.	44
6	Cloonsillagh .	405 1 14	Cork, E.R. .	Orrery and Kilmore	Tullylease .	Kanturk .	II.	110
15	Cloonsillagh .	69 2 29	Kerry .	Clanmaurice .	Kiltomy .	Listowel .	II.	172
17	Cloonsillagh .	230 0 24	Roscommon .	Ballintober North .	Kilmore .	Cark. on Shannon	IV.	187
44	Cloonsillagh .	631 0 5	Sligo .	Coolavin .	Kilfree .	Boyle .	IV.	224
21	Cloonskeagh .	196 0 36	Mayo .	Tirawley .	Kilfian .	Killala .	IV.	169
7, 11	Cloonskeeveen .	133 1 36	Roscommon .	Boyle .	Tumna .	Cark.on Shannon	IV.	197
98	Cloonskill .	333 3 30	Mayo .	Murrisk .	Aghagower .	Westport .	IV.	158
21	Cloonskirtaun .	43 3 36	Mayo .	Tirawley .	Killala .	Killala .	IV.	169
29	Cloonslanor .	392 0 23e	Roscommon .	Roscommon .	Cloonfinlough .	Strokestown .	IV.	209
29	Cloonslaun .	620 2 16f	Sligo .	Tireragh .	Kilmoremoy .	Ballina .	IV.	235
59	Cloonsnaghta .	389 0 13g	Clare .	Clonderalaw .	Killadysert .	Killadysert .	II.	15
21	Cloonsnaghta .	131 2 9	Mayo .	Tirawley .	Moygawnagh .	Killala .	IV.	171
23, 29	Cloonsreane .	212 2 15h	Roscommon .	Roscommon .	Killukin .	Strokestown .	IV.	210
19, 20, 26	Cloonsuck .	343 1 2	Roscommon .	Castlereagh .	Kilkeevin .	Castlereagh .	IV.	200
78, 89	Cloonsunna .	60 2 2	Mayo .	Carra .	Ballyhean .	Castlebar .	IV.	125
31	Cloonta .	491 3 23	Mayo .	Gallen .	Kilgarvan .	Ballina .	IV.	148
18, 22	Cloontabeg .	270 3 24	Longford .	Rathcline .	Rathcline .	Longford .	I.	164
32	Cloontabonniv .	764 2 12	Clare .	Islands .	Kilmaley .	Ennis .	II.	31
10, 19	Cloontagh .	1,930 1 32i	Donegal .	Inishowen East .	Clonmany .	Inishowen .	III.	117
4, 8	Cloontagh .	326 1 3	Longford .	Longford .	Clongesh .	Longford .	I.	157
18, 26	Cloontakilla .	1,178 3 10	Mayo .	Erris .	Kilcommon .	Belmullet .	IV.	143
21	Cloontakillew .	56 3 12	Mayo .	Tirawley .	Kilfian .	Killala .	IV.	169
39	Cloontally .	131 1 12	Mayo .	Tirawley .	Kilbelfad .	Ballina .	IV.	167
18, 22	Cloontamore .	566 3 1	Longford .	Moydow .	Killashee .	Longford .	I.	161
81	Cloontarriff .	97 3 38	Mayo .	Costello .	Aghamore .	Swineford .	IV.	137
92	Cloontarriff .	292 0 30j	Mayo .	Costello .	Knock .	Claremorris .	IV.	142
39	Cloontarriv .	361 2 9	Kerry .	Trughanacmy .	Nohaval .	Tralee .	II.	212
19, 25	Cloontarsna .	258 2 27	Roscommon .	Castlereagh .	Kilkeevin .	Castlereagh .	IV.	200
12	Cloonteem .	260 1 38	Roscommon .	Ballintober North .	Kilmore .	Cark.on Shannon	IV.	187
25	Cloonteen .	175 2 11k	Clare .	Bunratty Upper .	Templemaley .	Ennis .	II.	10
35	Cloonteen .	132 2 8	Clare .	Tulla Upper .	Tulla .	Tulla .	II.	41
28	Cloonteen .	775 0 13	Galway .	Dunmore .	Kilconla .	Tuam .	IV.	35
122	Cloonteen .	54 1 9	Galway .	Kiltartan .	Kilmacduagh .	Gort .	IV.	48
15, 16	Cloonteen .	357 1 36	Limerick .	Coonagh .	Doon .	Tipperary .	II.	234
31, 32	Cloonteens .	227 0 11	Cork, E.R. .	Duhallow .	Roskeen .	Kanturk .	II.	75
58	Cloonteens .	155 3 15	Kerry .	Magunihy .	Kilcummin .	Killarney .	II.	201
29, 37	Cloontemple .	72 0 24	Limerick .	Connello Upper .	Ballingarry .	Croom .	II.	230
133, 134,} 142, 143 }	Cloonties .	358 1 4l	Cork, W.R. .	East Carbery (W.D.) .	Kilfaughnabeg .	Skibbereen .	II.	132
49	Cloonties .	999 0 10	Kerry .	Corkaguiny .	Dunurlin .	Dingle .	II.	176
107	Cloonties East .	127 1 22	Cork, W.R. .	East Carbery (W.D.) .	Fanlobbus .	Dunmanway .	II.	131

(a) Including 3A. 1R. 5P. water.
(b) Including 39A. 3R. 6P. water.
(c) Including 17A. 2R. 9P. water.
(d) Including 21A. 0R. 22P. water.

(e) Including 29A. 2R. 1P. water.
(f) Including 8A. 2R. 36P. of River Moy.
(g) Including 3A. 3R. 24P. water.
(h) Including 12A. 0R. 24P. water.

(i) Including 14A. 2R. 8P. water.
(j) Including 7A. 1R. 32P. water.
(k) Including 4A. 1R. 16P. water.
(l) Including 4A. 3R. 9P. water.

No. of Sheet of the Ordnance Survey Maps.	Townlands and Towns.	Area in Statute Acres.			County.	Barony.	Parish.	Poor Law Union in 1857.	Townland Census of 1851, Part I.	
		A.	R.	P.					Vol.	Page
107, 120	Cloonties West	180	2	36	Cork, W.R.	East Carbery (W.D.)	Fanlobbus	Dunmanway	II.	131
40	Cloontimullan	224	2	7	Roscommon	Ballintober South	Kilteevan	Roscommon	IV.	190
107	Cloontiquirk	276	0	1	Cork, W.R.	East Carbery (W.D.)	Fanlobbus	Dunmanway	II.	131
13	Cloontirm	350	2	22	Longford	Ardagh	Ballymacormick	Longford	I.	152
40	Cloontogher	254	1	3	Roscommon	Ballintober South	Kilteevan	Roscommon	IV.	190
25	Cloontohil	181	1	16	Clare	Inchiquin	Dysert	Ennis	II.	24
43	Cloontooa	484	3	19	Galway	Clare	Tuam	Tuam	IV.	23
102	Cloontooa	510	3	7	Mayo	Clanmorris	Kilcolman	Claremorris	IV.	134
13, 19	Cloontowart	539	3	1a	Roscommon	Frenchpark	Tibohine	Castlereagh	IV.	205
43, 44, 53	Cloontra	681	1	1	Clare	Tulla Lower	Kilseily	Limerick	II.	36
44, 53	Cloontra East	588	2	29	Clare	Tulla Lower	Kilseily	Limerick	II.	36
26	Cloontrask	409	2	31	Roscommon	Castlereagh	Kilkeevin	Castlereagh	IV.	200
43,44,52,53	Cloontra West	456	0	6	Clare	Tulla Lower	Kilseily	Limerick	II.	36
115	Cloontreen	543	1	19	Cork, W.R.	Bear	Kilcatherine	Castletown	II.	124
60	Cloonts	466	0	20	Kerry	Magunihy	Nohavaldaly	Killarney	II.	205
38	Cloontubbrid	337	2	31	Leitrim	Mohill	Cloone	Mohill	IV.	105
70	Cloontubbrid	411	3	23b	Mayo	Carra	Turlough	Castlebar	IV.	130
62	Cloontubbrid	579	1	16	Mayo	Gallen	Killasser	Swineford	IV.	149
6, 11	Cloontubbrid North	250	2	30	Kerry	Iraghticonnor	Listowel	Listowel	II.	192
11	Cloontubbrid South	281	3	18	Kerry	Iraghticonnor	Listowel	Listowel	II.	192
92, 102, 103	Cloontumper	626	0	0	Mayo	Costello	Annagh	Claremorris	IV.	138
37	Cloontumpher	174	3	28	Leitrim	Mohill	Mohill	Mohill	IV.	107
35	Cloonturk	350	2	19c	Leitrim	Mohill	Mohill	Mohill	IV.	107
13	Cloonturk	275	1	11	Longford	Ardagh	Ballymacormick	Longford	I.	152
81	Cloonturk	323	2	2d	Mayo	Costello	Aghamore	Swineford	IV.	137
39	Cloonturk	164	0	2	Mayo	Tirawley	Ballynahaglish	Ballina	IV.	164
92	Cloonturnaun	155	2	12e	Mayo	Costello	Knock	Claremorris	IV.	142
36, 37	Cloontuskert	820	3	21	Roscommon	Ballintober South	Cloontuskert	Roscommon	IV.	188
37	CLOONTUSKERT T.	—			Roscommon	Ballintober South	Cloontuskert	Roscommon	IV.	188
7	Cloonty	491	3	22	Antrim	Lower Dunluce	Billy	Ballymoney	III.	16
1, 3	Cloonty	579	2	5f	Leitrim	Rosclogher	Rossinver	Ballyshannon	IV.	111
18, 19	Cloonty	401	1	10	Limerick	Shanid	Kilmoylan	Glin	II.	256
18	Cloonty	458	0	21	Limerick	Shanid	Shanagolden	Glin	II.	258
95, 105	Cloonty	179	0	16	Mayo	Murrisk	Kilgeever	Westport	IV.	160
25	Cloonty	324	3	18	Tyrone	Strabane Lower	Ardstraw	Strabane	III.	318
79	Cloontybaunan	122	1	17	Mayo	Carra	Breaghwy	Castlebar	IV.	127
44, 45	Cloontycarn	760	2	18	Sligo	Coolavin	Kilfree	Boyle	IV.	224
69	Cloontycarthy	541	3	29	Cork, W.R.	West Muskerry	Kilnamartry	Macroom	II.	159
22, 23	Cloontycommade	297	3	10	Cork, E.R.	Duhallow	Clonfert	Kanturk	II.	68
136	Cloontyconnaught	165	3	21	Galway	Leitrim	Inishcaltra	Scarriff	IV.	53
30	Cloontykillew	238	3	16	Mayo	Tirawley	Kilmoremoy	Ballina	IV.	170
26	Cloontymurphy	80	0	23	Clare	Bunratty Upper	Kilraghtis	Ennis	II.	9
29	Cloontymweenagh	228	3	24	Clare	Tulla Upper	Inishcaltra	Scarriff	II.	40
5	Cloontyprocklis	123	1	35	Sligo	Carbury	Ahamlish	Sligo	IV.	219
3	Cloontyprughlish	681	1	35	Leitrim	Rosclogher	Rossinver	Ballyshannon	IV.	111
23,24,31,32	Cloontysmarra	374	1	13	Clare	Inchiquin	Inagh	Ennistimon	II.	25
59	Cloonulla	594	3	28g	Clare	Clonderalaw	Killadysert	Killadysert	II.	15
54	Cloonulty	439	2	17	Roscommon	Moycarn	Moore	Ballinasloe	IV.	206
20, 28	Cloonusker	392	1	9	Clare	Tulla Upper	Tomgraney	Scarriff	II.	41
81,82,90,91	Cloon West	1,807	1	6h	Kerry	Dunkerron North	Knockane	Cahersiveen	II.	181
48	Cloonwhite North	257	1	32	Clare	Moyarta	Kilmacduane	Kilrush	II.	33
48	Cloonwhite South	270	1	31	Clare	Moyarta	Kilmacduane	Kilrush	II.	33
39	Cloonyarigaun	202	2	16	Mayo	Tirawley	Kilbelfad	Ballina	IV.	167
39, 40	Cloonybeirne	539	3	36	Roscommon	Ballintober South	Roscommon	Roscommon	IV.	190
28	Cloonybeirne	370	3	28i	Roscommon	Roscommon	Killukin	Strokestown	IV.	210
17, 23	Cloonybrennan	267	3	0	Roscommon	Roscommon	Elphin	Strokestown	IV.	209
6	Cloonybrien	83	3	4	Roscommon	Boyle	Ardcarn	Boyle	IV.	192
29	Cloonycarran Beg	13	3	37	Roscommon	Roscommon	Lissonuffy	Strokestown	IV.	211
29	Cloonycarran More	264	3	8	Roscommon	Roscommon	Lissonuffy	Strokestown	IV.	211
17	Cloonycattan	170	3	17j	Roscommon	Roscommon	Clooncraff	Car.on Shannon	IV.	208
18, 19	Cloonyclohassy	170	3	5	Limerick	Shanid	Kilmoylan	Glin	II.	256
34, 38	Cloonycolgan	188	2	5	Roscommon	Ballymoe	Oran	Roscommon	IV.	192
102	Cloonycollaran	101	2	22	Mayo	Clanmorris	Kilcolman	Claremorris	IV.	134
85, 86	Cloonyconaun	124	0	4	Galway	Kilconnell	Grange	Loughrea	IV.	40
44	Cloonyconry Beg	262	3	27	Clare	Tulla Lower	Killokennedy	Limerick	II.	35
44	Cloonyconry More	418	1	15	Clare	Tulla Lower	Killokennedy	Limerick	II.	35
65	Cloonycoppoge	203	0	0k	Tyrone	Clogher	Clogher	Clogher	III.	292
37	Cloonydiveen	135	0	30	Sligo	Leyny	Kilmacteige	Tobercurry	IV.	231
58	Cloonydonigan Lower	93	0	4	Kerry	Magunihy	Kilcredane	Killarney	II.	200
58	Cloonydonigan Upper	198	2	20	Kerry	Magunihy	Kilcredane	Killarney	II.	200
16	Cloonyeffer	166	0	8	Roscommon	Roscommon	Shankill	Strokestown	IV.	212
39	Cloonygarra	238	2	18	Limerick	Coshma	Dromin	Kilmallock	II.	243
106	Cloonygorman	273	1	2	Cork, W.R.	Bantry	Kilmocomoge	Bantry	II.	120

(a) Including 5A. 0R. 10P. water.
(b) Including 19A. 3R. 33P. water.
(c) Including 15A. 2R. 15P. water.
(d) Including 1A. 2R. 30P. water.

(e) Including 11A. 2R. 2P. water.
(f) Including 27A. 1R. 23P. water.
(g) Including 43A. 1R. 39P. water.
(h) Including 96A. 2R. 32P. water.

(i) Including 4A. 2R. 14P. water.
(j) Including 28A. 2R. 6P. water.
(k) Including 1A. 1R. 0P. water.

No. of Sheet of the Ordnance Survey Maps.	Townlands and Towns.	Area in Statute Acres.	County.	Barony.	Parish.	Poor Law Union in 1857.	Townland Census of 1851, Part I. Vol.	Page
		A. R. P.						
61	Cloonygowan .	208 1 7	Mayo .	Gallen .	Meelick .	Swineford .	IV.	150
39	Cloonygunnaun .	89 0 21	Mayo .	Tirawley .	Kilbelfad .	Ballina .	IV.	167
63	Cloonyhea .	213 2 2	Tipperary, S.R.	Middlethird .	Drangan .	Cashel .	II.	326
100, 108	Cloonykeevan .	147 2 19	Galway .	Longford .	Clonfert .	Ballinasloe .	IV.	57
41	Cloonykelly .	231 0 33a	Roscommon .	Athlone .	Athleague .	Roscommon .	IV.	179
26, 27	Cloonykerny .	309 1 7	Roscommon .	Castlereagh .	Ballintober .	Castlereagh .	IV.	198
29	Cloonylyon .	202 3 21	Roscommon .	Roscommon .	Cloonfinlough .	Strokestown .	IV.	209
34	Cloonymeenaghan .	123 0 20b	Sligo .	Tirerrill .	Tawnagh .	Sligo .	IV.	241
86	Cloonymorris .	110 2 13	Galway .	Kilconnell .	Killaan .	Ballinasloe .	IV.	41
31, 37, 38	Cloonymurrikin .	205 2 5	Westmeath .	Moycashel .	Ardnurcher or Horse-leap .	Tullamore .	I.	276
28	Cloonyogan .	139 3 29	Roscommon .	Roscommon .	Killukin .	Strokestown .	IV.	210
41	Cloonyourish .	264 0 12	Roscommon .	Athlone .	Fuerty .	Roscommon .	IV.	181
39	Cloonyquin .	258 2 37	Roscommon .	Athlone .	Fuerty .	Roscommon .	IV.	181
22	Cloonyquin .	528 2 9	Roscommon .	Roscommon .	Elphin .	Strokestown .	IV.	209
46	Cloonyross (Bolton)	166 2 38	Tipperary, S.R.	Kilnamanagh Lower	Clogher .	Cashel .	II.	322
46	Cloonyross (Percival)	446 2 35	Tipperary, S.R.	Kilnamanagh Lower	Clogher .	Cashel .	II.	322
36	Cloonyscrehane .	102 3 35	Limerick .	Glenquin .	Grange .	Newcastle .	II.	245
36	Cloonyscrehane .	196 3 7	Limerick .	Glenquin .	Monagay .	Newcastle .	II.	247
39	Cloonyvollow .	122 0 3c	Mayo .	Tirawley .	Kilbelfad .	Ballina .	IV.	167
17	Cloosecullen .	402 0 24	Queen's Co.	Maryborough West .	Clonenagh and Clonagheen .	Abbeyleix .	I.	242
27, 36	Cloosguire .	96 0 9	Kerry .	Corkaguiny .	Killiney .	Dingle .	II.	178
102, 112	Cloosh .	252 2 10	Galway .	Kiltartan .	Kinvarradoorus .	Gort .	IV.	49
54, 67	Clooshgereen .	913 1 11d	Galway .	Moycullen .	Kilcummin .	Oughterard .	IV.	66
27	Clooskirt .	335 2 33e	Sligo .	Tirerrill .	Ballynakill .	Sligo .	IV.	237
53	Cloosmore .	115 0 30	Kerry .	Corkaguiny .	Dingle .	Dingle .	II.	175
19	Clopook .	342 1 35	Queen's Co.	Stradbally .	Tullomoy .	Athy .	I.	248
18,19,24,25	Clora .	274 1 17	Wicklow .	Newcastle .	Killiskey .	Rathdrum .	I.	352
84, 96	Cloran .	431 0 35	Galway .	Athenry .	Athenry .	Loughrea .	IV.	3
9	Cloran & Corcullentry	906 3 5	Westmeath .	Delvin .	Killua .	Castletowndelvin .	I.	265
31	Clorane .	347 2 3	Limerick .	Coshma .	Croom .	Croom .	II.	242
71	Cloran New .	748 2 29	Tipperary, S.R.	Middlethird .	Cloneen .	Cashel .	II.	325
70, 71	Cloran Old .	735 0 26	Tipperary, S.R.	Middlethird .	Cloneen .	Cashel .	II.	325
13, 14, 19	Cloranshea .	353 3 34	Kilkenny .	Crannagh .	St. Canice .	Kilkenny .	I.	87
5, 13	Clorhane .	629 1 11	King's Co.	Garrycastle .	Clonmacnoise .	Parsonstown .	I.	135
12	Clorhane .	470 0 30	Limerick .	Kenry .	Adare .	Croom .	II.	248
29	Clorhaun .	209 1 34	Queen's Co.	Clarmallagh .	Rosconnell .	Abbeyleix .	I.	238
22	Clornagh .	119 1 29	Wicklow .	Upper Talbotstown .	Donaghmore .	Baltinglass .	I.	363
13, 14	Cloroge Beg .	1,195 0 14	Wexford .	Scarawalsh .	Templeshanbo .	Enniscorthy .	I.	326
13, 14	Cloroge More .	953 0 31	Wexford .	Scarawalsh .	Templeshanbo .	Enniscorthy .	I.	326
16	Clorusk Lower .	144 0 5	Carlow .	Idrone West .	Killinane .	Carlow .	I.	9
15, 16	Clorusk Upper .	246 1 21f	Carlow .	Idrone West .	Killinane .	Carlow .	I.	9
17	Closdaw .	185 2 8	Monaghan .	Dartree .	Aghabog .	Cootehill .	III.	263
118	Close .	86 1 6	Cork, W.R.	Bantry .	Kilmocomoge .	Bantry .	II.	120
33	Close .	115 3 8	Waterford .	Coshmore & Coshbride	Kilwatermoy .	Lismore .	II.	343
5, 9	Closeland or Clooneen	401 1 13	Queen's Co.	Portnahinch .	Lea .	Mountmellick .	I.	244
74	Closes .	31 1 38	Cork, E.R.	Cork .	St. Anne's Shandon	Cork .	II.	65
13, 17	Closh .	58 2 18	Carlow .	Forth .	Ballon .	Carlow .	I.	3
29	Closnabraddan or Taghart North	431 2 27g	Cavan .	Clankee .	Enniskeen .	Bailieborough .	III.	73
23	Clossagh Beg .	271 1 8h	Monaghan .	Cremorne .	Aghnamullen .	Cootehill .	III.	257
23	Clossagh More .	412 0 12i	Monaghan .	Cremorne .	Aghnamullen .	Cootehill .	III.	257
48, 60	Clossaghroe .	313 3 35	Mayo .	Tirawley .	Ballynahaglish .	Ballina .	IV.	164
15, 16	Closutton .	666 2 26	Carlow .	Idrone West .	Killinane .	Carlow .	I.	9
37	Clough .	396 1 12	Down .	Kinelarty .	Loughinisland .	Downpatrick .	III.	177
25	Clough .	25 3 7	Wexford .	Bantry .	Clonmore .	Enniscorthy .	I.	300
53	Clougheast .	106 3 8	Wexford .	Forth .	Carn .	Wexford .	I.	309
40	Cloughfin .	352 2 13	Londonderry .	Loughinsholin .	Ballynascreen .	Magherafelt .	III.	239
41	Cloughfin .	178 1 7	Londonderry .	Loughinsholin .	Kilcronaghan .	Magherafelt .	III.	241
13	Cloughglass .	87 0 13	Londonderry .	North West Liberties of Londonderry .	Templemore .	Londonderry .	III.	246
2, 6	Cloughorr .	378 2 31	Antrim .	Lower Dunluce .	Ballywillin .	Coleraine .	III.	15
37	CLOUGH T. .	—	Down .	Kinelarty .	Loughinisland .	Downpatrick .	III.	177
97	Clouracaun .	244 0 4	Cork, E.R.	Kinalea .	Inishannon .	Bandon .	II.	95
18	Cloustoge .	251 0 1	Cork, E.R.	Fermoy .	Doneraile .	Mallow .	II.	78
8	Cloven Eden .	323 0 30	Armagh .	Oneilland West .	Loughgall .	Armagh .	III.	54
20	Clover .	231 2 12	Kilkenny .	Gowran .	Gowran .	Kilkenny .	I.	95
45, 59	Cloverfield .	73 3 20	Galway .	Tiaquin .	Killoscobe .	Mountbellew .	IV.	77
23	Cloverfield .	171 3 19	Limerick .	Clanwilliam .	Aglishcormick .	Limerick .	II.	221
34	Cloverhill .	88 3 27j	Cavan .	Clankee .	Bailieborough .	Bailieborough .	III.	71
51	Cloverhill .	52 3 26	Clare .	Bunratty Lower .	Bunratty .	Ennis .	II.	5
22, 25	Cloverhill or Corglass	97 3 26	Leitrim .	Carrigallen .	Oughteragh .	Bawnboy .	IV.	92
15	Cloverhill Demesne .	297 1 30k	Cavan .	Tullygarvey .	Annagh .	Cavan .	III.	87

(a) Including 17A. 6R. 0P. water.
(b) Including 7A. 1R. 15P. water.
(c) Including 16A. 1R. 39P. water.
(d) Including 17A. 2R. 27P. water.

(e) Including 8A. 0R. 30P. water.
(f) Including 1A. 2R. 0P. River Barrow.
(g) Including 5A. 2R. 32P. water.
(h) Including 26A. 1R. 14P. water.

(i) Including 64A. 0R. 36P. water.
(j) Including 11A. 0R. 21P. water.
(k) Including 24A. 0R. 25P. water.

No. of Sheet of the Ordnance Survey Maps.	Townlands and Towns.	Area in Statute Acres.	County.	Barony.	Parish.	Poor Law Union in 1857.	Townland Census of 1851. Part I.	
		A. R. P.					Vol.	Page
92, 98	Cloverhill or Drumbeg	126 2 15	Donegal	Banagh	Inver	Donegal	III.	107
14, 20	Cloverhill or Knocknashammer	285 2 30a	Sligo	Carbury	Kilmacowen	Sligo	IV.	222
86	Cloverpark	22 0 12	Galway	Kilconnell	Killaan	Ballinasloe	IV.	41
56	Clovers	309 0 35	Limerick	Coshlea	Kilflyn	Kilmallock	II.	240
38	Clowanstown	340 3 32	Meath	Skreen	Killeen	Dunshaughlin	I.	221
38	Clowanstown	606 3 29	Meath	Skreen	Trevet	Dunshaughlin	I.	222
19	Clowater	106 1 23	Carlow	Idrone East	Ballyellin	Carlow	I.	6
19	Clowater	30 3 34	Carlow	Idrone East	Clonygoose	Carlow	I.	6
19	Clowater	97 3 2	Carlow	Idrone East	Lorum	Carlow	I.	8
9	Clownagh	295 2 22	Armagh	Oneilland West	Drumcree	Lurgan	III.	51
10, 14	Clowney	214 0 31b	Cavan	Lower Loughtee	Drumlane	Cavan	III.	79
23	Clownings	619 2 26	Kildare	Connell	Greatconnell	Naas	I.	55
14	Clownings	409 1 38	Kildare	Naas North	Whitechurch	Naas	I.	63
11	Clowninny	117 3 24c	Cavan	Lower Loughtee	Drumlane	Cavan	III.	79
26	Clownstown	249 2 22	Westmeath	Fartullagh	Mullingar	Mullingar	I.	269
6	Cloy	42 3 1	Fermanagh	Lurg	Magheraculmoney	Lowtherstown	III.	207
3, 4	Cloyfin North	158 3 21	Londonderry	North East Liberties of Coleraine	Ballywillin	Coleraine	III.	245
3, 4	Cloyfin South	139 3 13	Londonderry	North East Liberties of Coleraine	Ballyrashane	Coleraine	III.	245
87	Cloyne, Dean and Chapter Land of	30 0 18	Cork, E.R.	Barrymore	Clonmel	Cork	II.	53
88	CLOYNE T.	—	Cork, E.R.	Imokilly	Cloyne	Middleton	II.	86
5	Cloyragh	314 1 12	Sligo	Carbury	Ahamlish	Sligo	IV.	219
21	Cloyrawer	177 0 3	Mayo	Tirawley	Kilfian	Killala	IV.	169
2, 5	Cloysparra	202 3 33	Sligo	Carbury	Ahamlish	Sligo	IV.	219
41	Cloystuckera	110 1 23	Sligo	Tirerrill	Kilmactranny	Boyle	IV.	240
41, 42	Clucka North	180 1 34	King's Co.	Clonlisk	Kilcomin	Roscrea	I.	131
42	Clucka South	34 3 6	King's Co.	Clonlisk	Kilcomin	Roscrea	I.	131
13, 20	Cluddaun	1,772 0 14	Mayo	Tirawley	Kilfian	Killala	IV.	169
24	Cluggin	115 1 37	Limerick	Coonagh	Tuoghcluggin	Tipperary	II.	236
17, 18	Cluid	271 1 38	Galway	Ballymoe	Dunmore	Glennamaddy	IV.	7
33	Cluid	448 2 17d	Sligo	Corran	Emlaghfad	Sligo	IV.	226
17	Cluide	25 0 6	Louth	Ardee	Smarmore	Ardee	I.	174
18	Cluide	173 1 23	Louth	Ferrard	Dunleer	Ardee	I.	180
56	Cluidrevagh	678 1 4	Galway	Clare	Annaghdown	Tuam	IV.	16
33	Clunahill Glebe	404 0 9	Tyrone	Omagh West	Longfield West	Castlederg	III.	316
23,24,30,31	Cluntagh	1,072 3 33	Down	Dufferin	Killyleagh	Downpatrick	III.	167
21, 22	Cluntagh	1,010 3 1e	Down	Lower Iveagh, Lr. pt.	Annahilt	Lisburn	III.	167
63	Cluntirriff	315 2 29	Antrim	Upper Massereene	Ballinderry	Lisburn	III.	29
31, 40	Cluntoe (Quin)	197 2 21	Tyrone	Dungannon Upper	Arboe	Cookstown	III.	305
31, 40	Cluntoe (Richardson)	115 0 6	Tyrone	Dungannon Upper	Arboe	Cookstown	III.	305
29	Cluntydoon	304 2 30	Tyrone	Dungannon Upper	Derryloran	Cookstown	III.	306
29	Cluntyganny	264 0 22	Tyrone	Dungannon Upper	Lissan	Cookstown	III.	309
31, 35	Cluntygeeragh	3,722 1 26	Londonderry	Keenaght	Dungiven	NewTnLimavady	III.	236
21	Cluttahina	343 0 11	Waterford	Decies without Drum	Affane	Lismore	II.	353
17	Clutterland	12 0 15	Dublin	Newcastle	Kilmactalway	Celbridge	I.	33
17, 21	Clutterland	11 1 10	Dublin	Uppercross	Clondalkin	Dublin South	I.	39
121	Clyard	179 1 36f	Mayo	Kilmaine	Kilmainemore	Ballinrobe	IV.	156
12	Clybanane	312 3 12	Tipperary, N.R.	Ikerrin	Roscrea	Roscrea	II.	276
93, 94	Clybaun	221 2 14	Galway	Galway	Rahoon	Galway	IV.	37
32, 33	Clyda	62 2 12g	Cork, E.R.	Duhallow	Kilshannig	Mallow	II.	74
116	Clydagh	86 0 39	Cork, W.R.	Bear	Kilcaskan	Castletown	II.	122
55	Clydagh	290 2 37	Galway	Clare	Cargin	Tuam	IV.	18
81	Clydagh	306 2 17h	Galway	Moycullen	Moycullen	Galway	IV.	71
65	Clydagh	105 2 36	Kerry	Dunkerron North	Knockane	Killarney	II.	181
13, 14, 20	Clydagh	1,667 2 27	Mayo	Tirawley	Kilfian	Killala	IV.	169
25	Clydagh Lower	165 1 6	Roscommon	Castlereagh	Kiltullagh	Castlereagh	IV.	201
76, 77	Clydaghroe	1,286 2 32	Kerry	Magunihy	Killaha	Killarney	II.	202
55	Clydagh or Staunton's Island	2 0 28	Galway	Clare	Cargin	Tuam	IV.	18
25	Clydagh Upper	201 3 28	Roscommon	Castlereagh	Kiltullagh	Castlereagh	IV.	201
32, 33	Clydaville	66 2 23	Cork, E.R.	Duhallow	Kilshannig	Mallow	II.	74
2, 7	Clyderragh	292 3 9	Cork, E.R.	Orrery and Kilmore	Shandrum	Kilmallock	II.	110
76	Clyduff	111 2 32	Cork, E.R.	Barrymore	Carrigtohill	Middleton	II.	52
42, 45	Clyduff	668 2 29	King's Co.	Clonlisk	Dunkerrin	Roscrea	I.	130
10	Clyduff	349 2 22	King's Co.	Lower Philipstown	Kilclonfert	Tullamore	I.	142
6	Clyduff East	66 1 18	Limerick	Clanwilliam	Killeenagarriff	Limerick	II.	224
6	Clyduff West	32 2 27	Limerick	Clanwilliam	Killeenagarriff	Limerick	II.	224
20, 23, 24	Clygeen	102 1 0	Longford	Ardagh	Kilglass	Ballymahon	I.	152
24	Clyglass	72 0 31	Westmeath	Rathconrath	Killare	Mullingar	I.	283
25, 31	Clyhannagh	435 3 13	Fermanagh	Clanawley	Killesher	Enniskillen	III.	192
44, 45	Clykeel North	250 1 23	Cork, E.R.	Barrymore	Gortroe	Fermoy	II.	55

(a) Including 6A. 0R. 21P. water.
(b) Including 30A. 3R. 2P. water.
(c) Including 16A. 2R. 35P. water.
(d) Including 3A. 3R. 32P. water.
(e) Including 19A. 1R. 17P. water.
(f) Including 19A. 3R. 26P. water.
(g) Including 2A. 0R. 16P. water.
(h) Including 25A. 2R. 14P. water.

No. of Sheet of the Ordnance Survey Maps.	Townlands and Towns.	Area in Statute Acres. A. R. P.	County.	Barony.	Parish.	Poor Law Union in 1857.	Townland Census of 1851, Part I. Vol.	Page
44, 45	Clykeel South .	92 3 19	Cork, E.R. .	Barrymore .	Gortroe . .	Fermoy . .	II.	55
121	Clylea or Greyfield	92 2 19	Mayo .	Kilmaine .	Kilmainemore .	Ballinrobe .	IV.	156
33	Clynabroga .	26 3 20	Limerick .	Coonagh .	Templebredon .	Tipperary .	II.	236
78, 90	Clynagh .	837 2 22a	Galway .	Moycullen .	Killannin .	Oughterard .	IV.	69
65	Clynagh Island	102 3 36	Galway .	Moycullen .	Kilcummin .	Oughterard .	IV.	68
23, 27	Clynan . .	447 0 25b	Longford .	Shrule . .	Forgney . .	Ballymahon .	I.	166
76	Clynish . .	80 1 4	Mayo .	Burrishoole .	Kilmeena .	Westport .	IV.	122
46	Clynoe . .	214 3 13	King's Co. .	Clonlisk .	Cullenwaine .	Roscrea .	I.	129
21	Clyn's Island .	4 2 0	King's Co. .	Garrycastle .	Reynagh . .	Parsonstown .	I.	138
10	Clyroe . .	63 0 35	Cork, E.R. .	Condons and Clangibbon .	Marshalstown .	Mitchelstown .	II.	63
14	Clyttaghan .	447 3 5	Antrim .	Lower Glenarm .	Grange of Layd .	Ballycastle .	III.	22
16	Coa . .	401 3 33	Fermanagh .	Tirkennedy .	Magheracross .	Enniskillen .	III.	223
72	COACHFORD T. .	—	Cork, E.R. .	Muskerry East .	Magourney .	Macroom .	II.	105
17	Coad . .	423 3 10	Clare .	Inchiquin .	Killinaboy .	Corrofin .	II.	26
106	Coad . .	641 1 12	Kerry .	Dunkerron South .	Kilcrohane .	Cahersiveen .	II.	183
21, 22	Coagh . .	154 3 33	Fermanagh .	Magheraboy .	Devenish .	Enniskillen .	III.	210
39	Coagh . .	291 3 5c	Sligo .	Corran .	Kilshalvy .	Boyle .	IV.	227
30	Coagh . .	616 1 22	Tyrone .	Dungannon Upper .	Tamlaght .	Cookstown .	III.	309
32	Coaghan . .	170 3 3	Fermanagh .	Clanawley .	Killesher .	Enniskillen .	III.	192
12	Coaghen . .	100 3 11	Monaghan .	Dartree .	Killeevan .	Monaghan .	III.	267
31, 36	Coagh Lower .	259 0 27	King's Co. .	Eglish . .	Drumcullen .	Parsonstown .	I.	134
53, 61	Coaghmill .	46 1 23	Donegal .	Raphoe .	Leck . .	Letterkenny .	III.	140
30	COAGH T. .	—	Tyrone .	Dungannon Upper .	Tamlaght .	Cookstown .	III.	309
36	Coagh Upper .	271 1 1	King's Co. .	Eglish . .	Drumcullen .	Parsonstown .	I.	134
49	Coalbrook .	202 3 17	Tipperary, S.R. .	Slievardagh .	Ballingarry .	Callan .	II.	331
28, 34	Coalhill . .	189 0 14d	Fermanagh .	Magherastephana .	Aghalurcher .	Lisnaskea .	III.	215
47	COAL ISLAND T. .	—	Tyrone .	Dungannon Middle .	{ Donaghenry . } { Tullyniskan . }	{ Cookstown } { Dungannon }	III.	{ 301 } { 305 }
31, 35	Coalpitparks .	123 1 20	Kilkenny .	Knocktopher .	Aghaviller .	Thomastown .	I.	110
30, 39	Coalpits . .	132 2 11e	Cork, E.R. .	Duhallow .	Cullen .	Millstreet .	II.	70
19, 20	Coalpits . .	386 1 14	Galway .	Killian .	Athleague .	Mountbellew .	IV.	43
19	Coalpits . .	116 0 30	Meath .	Slane Upper .	Slane . .	Navan .	I.	225
23	Coalsfarm .	264 3 26	Kilkenny .	Shillelogher .	Burnchurch .	Callan .	I.	113
47	Coalspit . .	53 2 4	Wexford .	Forth .	Mayglass .	Wexford .	I.	312
22	Coan . .	370 0 1	Wicklow .	Upper Talbotstown .	Donaghmore .	Baltinglass .	I.	363
6, 11	Coan East .	1,720 1 17	Kilkenny .	Fassadinin .	Dysart . .	Castlecomer .	I.	89
6, 11	Coan West .	1,496 2 28	Kilkenny .	Fassadinin .	Dysart . .	Castlecomer .	I.	89
78, 87	Coarha Beg .	920 3 3	Kerry .	Iveragh .	Valencia .	Cahersiveen .	II.	198
78, 87	Coarha More .	832 1 2	Kerry .	Iveragh .	Valencia .	Cahersiveen .	II.	198
3	Coarliss . .	71 3 6	Cork, E.R. .	Orrery and Kilmore	Ballyhay .	Kilmallock .	II.	106
132	Coarliss . .	291 2 31	Cork, W.R. .	West Carbery (W.D.) .	Caheragh .	Skibbereen .	II.	142
80	Coars . .	543 3 32	Kerry .	Iveragh .	Killinane .	Cahersiveen .	II.	197
82	Coarsefield .	267 0 16	Galway .	Galway .	Oranmore .	Galway .	IV.	37
100, 101	Coarsefield .	204 1 31	Mayo .	Clanmorris .	Tagheen .	Claremorris .	IV.	136
68	Coarse Island .	4 0 38	Mayo .	Tirawley .	Addergoole .	Castlebar .	IV.	163
18	Coarse Island .	0 2 33	Roscommon .	Ballintober North .	Kilglass .	Strokestown .	IV.	186
69, 78	Coarsepark .	87 1 8	Mayo .	Carra .	Aglish . .	Castlebar .	IV.	123
41	Coarsepark or Parkgarve .	118 3 3	Galway .	Clare .	Killursa .	Tuam .	IV.	21
125	Coarseparks .	152 3 0	Galway .	Leitrim .	Ballynakill .	Loughrea .	IV.	51
20, 25	Coasan . .	206 0 38	Fermanagh .	Clanawley .	Cleenish .	Enniskillen .	III.	190
55	Coash . .	152 3 14	Tyrone .	Dungannon Middle .	Killyman .	Dungannon .	III.	303
29	Cobbs . .	350 1 23	Tipperary, N.R. .	Ikerrin .	Templeree .	Thurles .	II.	277
67	Cock-and-the-Bull .	24 0 30	Cork, E.R. .	Imokilly .	Youghal .	Youghal .	II.	91
3	Cockhill . .	172 3 32	Kerry .	Iraghticonnor .	Kilnaughtin .	Glin .	II.	191
48	Cock Mountain Common .	284 1 32	Down .	Iveagh Upper, Lr. pt.	Kilcoo .	Kilkeel .	III.	173
73, 83	Cockow . .	389 2 8f	Kerry .	Dunkerron North .	Knockane .	Killarney .	II.	181
14	Cockstown .	326 2 15	Westmeath .	Delvin .	Castletowndelvin .	Castletowndelvin .	I.	264
114	Cockstown East .	85 0 14	Galway .	Kiltartan .	Ardrahan .	Gort .	IV.	45
114	Cockstown West .	100 2 2	Galway .	Kiltartan .	Ardrahan .	Gort .	IV.	45
12, 20	Codd . .	764 2 18	King's Co. .	Coolestown .	Monasteroris .	Edenderry .	I.	133
48	Coddstown Great .	99 0 8	Wexford .	Forth .	Ballymore .	Wexford .	I.	308
48	Coddstown Little .	153 1 34	Wexford .	Forth .	Ballymore .	Wexford .	I.	308
70	Codrum . .	454 1 38	Cork, W.R. .	West Muskerry .	Macroom .	Macroom .	II.	160
18, 31	Cogaula . .	618 2 10g	Galway .	Ballymoe .	Dunmore .	Glennamaddy .	IV.	7
77, 88	Cogaula . .	400 0 34h	Mayo .	Burrishoole .	Islandeady .	Westport .	IV.	121
89, 90	Cogaula . .	477 3 31	Mayo .	Carra .	Ballintober .	Castlebar .	IV.	124
29	Coggalbeg .	276 1 4i	Roscommon .	Ballintober South .	Kilbride .	Strokestown .	IV.	189
29	Coggalfortyacres	165 3 20	Roscommon .	Roscommon .	Lissonuffy .	Strokestown .	IV.	211
29	Coggalkeenagh	94 2 23	Roscommon .	Roscommon .	Lissonuffy .	Strokestown .	IV.	211
29	Coggalmore .	86 3 5	Roscommon .	Roscommon .	Lissonuffy .	Strokestown .	IV.	211
29	Coggalstack .	100 2 25	Roscommon .	Roscommon .	Lissonuffy .	Strokestown .	IV.	211

(a) Including 32A. 0R. 12P. water.   (d) Including 6A. 0R. 26P. water.   (g) Including 20A. 1R. 24P. water.
(b) Including 6A. 2R. 21P. water.   (e) Including 1A. 1R. 6P. water.   (h) Including 20A. 3R. 15P. water.
(c) Including 4A. 0R. 10P. water.   (f) Including 28A. 2R. 37P. water.   (i) Including 2A. 3R. 0P. water.

No. of Sheet of the Ordnance Survey Maps.	Townlands and Towns.	Area in Statute Acres.			County.	Barony.	Parish.	Poor Law Union in 1857.	Townland Census of 1851, Part I.	
		A.	R.	P.					Vol.	Page
29	Coggaltonroe . .	119	1	39	Roscommon .	Roscommon .	Lissonuffy . .	Strokestown .	IV.	211
45	Coggrey . . .	652	2	16	Antrim . .	Antrim Upper .	Doagh Grange .	Antrim . .	III.	6
12, 18	Coghalstown . .	589	1	12	Meath . .	Upper Slane .	Rathkenny . .	Navan . .	I.	225
24, 29	Coghlanstown . .	367	2	18a	Kildare . .	Naas South .	Ballymore Eustace .	Naas . .	I.	64
24, 29	Coghlanstown . .	1,137	0	16b	Kildare . .	Naas South .	Coghlanstown .	Naas . .	I.	64
21, 29	Cogran . .	405	3	1	King's Co. .	Garrycastle .	Lusmagh . .	Parsonstown .	I.	137
90, 91	Coguish . .	1,087	3	39	Donegal . .	Banagh . .	Kilcar . .	Glenties . .	III.	108
55	Cohannan . .	366	1	12	Tyrone . .	Dungannon Middle .	Killyman .	Dungannon .	III.	303
9	Coharra . .	110	2	25	Armagh . .	Oneilland West .	Drumcree . .	Lurgan . .	III.	52
17, 18	Cohaw . .	258	3	12	Cavan . .	Tullygarvey .	Drumgoon . .	Cootehill . .	III.	88
9	Cohy . .	291	2	35	Clare . .	Corcomroe .	Kilfenora . .	Ennistimon .	II.	19
32, 36	Colbinstown .	251	0	14	Kildare . .	Narragh & Reban East	Davidstown .	Athy . .	I.	66
16, 17	Coldagh . .	277	0	26	Antrim . .	Upper Dunluce .	Ballymoney .	Ballymoney .	III.	18
17	Coldblow . .	279	1	29c	Dublin . .	Newcastle .	Leixlip . .	Celbridge .	I.	33
43	Coldblow . .	95	3	35	King's Co. .	Ballybritt .	Aghancon .	Roscrea . .	I.	124
41,42,44,45	Coldblow . .	164	2	1	King's Co. .	Clonlisk . .	Kilcomin . .	Roscrea . .	I.	131
48	Coldblow . .	37	3	29	Wexford . .	Forth . .	Ladyisland .	Wexford . .	I.	311
48	Coldblow . .	16	3	39	Wexford . .	Forth . .	Tacumshin .	Wexford . .	I.	315
17	Coldcut . .	63	1	12	Dublin . .	Uppercross .	Clondalkin .	Dublin South .	I.	39
17	Coldcut . .	38	2	38	Dublin . .	Uppercross .	Esker . .	Dublin South .	I.	40
41, 42	Coldfields .	321	2	7	Tipperary, N.R.	Eliogarty . .	Twomileborris .	Thurles . .	II.	273
12,13,17,18	Coldharbour .	222	0	0	Kilkenny .	Crannagh .	Killahy . .	Urlingford .	I.	86
16	Coldmanscurragh .	58	2	32	Queen's Co. .	Upperwoods .	Offerlane .	Mountmellick .	I.	251
28, 29	Coldrumman . .	86	0	22	Leitrim . .	Leitrim . .	Fenagh . .	Mohill . .	IV.	100
21	Coldwater Commons	8	2	16	Dublin . .	Newcastle .	Saggart . .	Celbridge .	I.	34
29	Coldwells . .	299	2	20	Kildare . .	Naas South .	Ballybought .	Naas . .	I.	64
8	Coldwinters . .	198	2	37d	Dublin . .	Balrothery East .	Lusk . .	Balrothery .	I.	21
14	Coldwinters . .	122	3	5	Dublin . .	Castleknock .	Finglas . .	Dublin North .	I.	24
95, 96	Coldwood or Foorkill	602	0	4	Galway . .	Dunkellin .	Athenry . .	Galway . .	IV.	27
57, 58	Cole . .	1,103	3	6	Tyrone . .	Clogher . .	Clogher . .	Clogher . .	III.	292
12	Colebreene Lower .	75	3	9	Londonderry .	North East Liberties of Coleraine .	Ballymoney .	Ballymoney .	III.	245
23, 24	Colebrook Demesne .	695	2	9	Fermanagh .	Magherastephana .	Aghalurcher .	Lisnaskea .	III.	215
7, 8	Colecot . .	101	3	26e	Dublin . .	Balrothery East .	Lusk . .	Balrothery .	I.	21
46, 47	Colehill . .	190	1	28	Donegal . .	Raphoe . .	Allsaints . .	Londonderry .	III.	134
17	Colehill . .	716	0	27	King's Co. .	Geashill . .	Geashill . .	Tullamore .	I.	140
23	Colehill . .	171	0	12	Longford . .	Shrule . .	Taghshinny .	Ballymahon .	I.	167
46	Colehill or Knocker-sally . .	1,761	2	0	Meath . .	Moyfenrath Upper .	Ballyboggan .	Edenderry .	I.	212
11, 16	Coleman . .	163	3	33f	Monaghan .	Dartree . .	Drummully .	Clones . .	III.	266
44	Coleman . .	551	3	12	Wexford . .	Shelburne .	St. James & Dunbrody	New Ross .	I.	328
8, 16	Coleraine . .	317	0	12	King's Co. .	Ballycowan .	Durrow . .	Tullamore .	I.	127
61	Coleraine . .	269	1	2	Tipperary, S.R.	Middlethird . .	Magorban .	Cashel . .	II.	328
7	Coleraine and Suburbs . .	413	2	6	Londonderry	North East Liberties of Coleraine .	Coleraine .	Coleraine . .	III.	246
7	COLERAINE T. .	—			Londonderry	Coleraine . .	Killowen .	Coleraine . .	III.	232
						North East Liberties of Coleraine .	Coleraine .			246
67	Colerenagh .	38	1	29	Cork, E.R. .	Imokilly . .	Clonpriest .	Youghal . .	II.	84
104	Colesgrove .	185	3	0	Galway . .	Dunkellin .	Killora . .	Loughrea .	IV.	31
22	Cole's Hill . .	167	1	17g	Fermanagh .	Magheraboy .	Rossorry .	Enniskillen .	III.	214
37, 42	Colestown . .	180	2	38	Wexford . .	Shelmaliere West .	Carrick . .	Wexford . .	I.	332
19	Colgagh . .	319	0	20	King's Co. .	Coolestown .	Clonsast . .	Edenderry .	I.	133
28, 29	Colgagh . .	180	0	1	Monaghan .	Farney . .	Donaghmoyne .	Carrickmacross	III.	269
15	Colgagh . .	490	2	32h	Sligo . .	Carbury . .	Calry . .	Sligo . .	IV.	220
20	Colganstown . .	198	3	26	Dublin . .	Newcastle .	Newcastle .	Celbridge .	I.	34
148	Colla . .	206	2	11	Cork, W.R. .	West Carbery (W.D.) .	Skull . .	Skull . .	II.	145
48	Colladussaun . .	163	1	10	Mayo . .	Tirawley . .	Kilbelfad .	Ballina . .	IV.	168
71	Collagh . .	299	0	11	Mayo . .	Gallen . .	Meelick . .	Swineford .	IV.	150
22	Collaghknock Glebe	143	1	31	Kildare . .	Offally East .	Kildare . .	Naas . .	I.	70
76	Collan Beg . .	16	3	2	Mayo . .	Burrishoole .	Kilmeena .	Westport . .	IV.	122
76	Collan More .	196	2	21	Mayo . .	Burrishoole .	Kilmeena .	Westport . .	IV.	122
149, 150	Collatrum Beg .	102	3	6	Cork, W.R. .	West Carbery (E.D.) .	Aghadown .	Skibbereen .	II.	136
149, 150	Collatrum More .	173	0	10	Cork, W.R. .	West Carbery (E.D.) .	Aghadown .	Skibbereen .	II.	136
5, 6	College . .	416	2	16	Meath . .	Morgallion .	Nobber . .	Kells . .	I.	210
37	College . .	112	3	4	Wexford . .	Shelmaliere West .	Carrick . .	Wexford . .	I.	332
20	Collegefield . .	25	2	28	Kerry . .	Clanmaurice .	Ardfert . .	Tralee . .	II.	167
11	College Hall or Marrassit . .	371	0	30	Armagh . .	Armagh . .	Tynan . .	Armagh . .	III.	46
21	Collegeland . .	571	3	4	Dublin . .	Newcastle .	Rathcoole .	Celbridge .	I.	34
5	Collegeland . :	136	3	35	Kildare . .	North Salt .	Laraghbryan .	Celbridge .	I.	75
43	Collegeland . .	75	2	36	Meath . .	Deece Upper .	Kilmore . .	Dunshaughlin	I.	193
67	Collegeland . .	110	3	33i	Tipperary, S.R.	Clanwilliam .	Cordangan .	Tipperary .	II.	306
29	Collegeland . .	28	0	10	Westmeath .	Brawny . .	St. Mary's .	Athlone . .	I.	259

(a) Including 11A. 0R. 14P. water.   (d) Including 0A. 3R. 25P. detached portion.   (g) Including 26A. 1R. 21P. water.
(b) Including 8A. 0R. 16P. water.   (e) Including 2A. 2R. 12P. detached portions.   (h) Including 33A. 2R. 4P. water.
(c) Including 9A. 2R. 8P. River Liffey.   (f) Including 9A. 3R. 16P. water.   (i) Including 5A. 3R. 36P. detached portions.

No. of Sheet of the Ordnance Survey Maps.	Townlands and Towns.	Area in Statute Acres.			County.	Barony.	Parish.	Poor Law Union in 1857.	Townland Census of 1851, Part I.	
		A.	R.	P.					Vol.	Page
19	Collegepark	9	3	32*a*	Kilkenny	Kilkenny, Municipal Borough of	St. John's	Kilkenny	I.	117
50	Colliersland North	74	2	14	Meath	Dunboyne	Dunboyne	Dunshaughlin	I.	199
50	Colliersland South	31	0	23	Meath	Dunboyne	Dunboyne	Dunshaughlin	I.	199
32, 38	Collierstown	309	0	1	Meath	Skreen	Skreen	Dunshaughlin	I.	221
27	Collierstown	625	3	24	Meath	Upper Duleek	Duleek	Drogheda	I.	197
22	Colliga	347	3	30	Wicklow	Upper Talbotstown	Donaghmore	Baltinglass	I.	363
22	Colligan Beg	232	0	10	Waterford	Decies without Drum	Colligan	Dungarvan	II.	354
22, 30	Colligan More	339	3	31	Waterford	Decies without Drum	Colligan	Dungarvan	II.	354
22, 30	Colliganmountain	116	0	23	Waterford	Decies without Drum	Colligan	Dungarvan	II.	354
30	Colliganwood	149	1	2	Waterford	Decies without Drum	Colligan	Dungarvan	II.	354
38	Collin	285	3	26	Kildare	Kilkea and Moone	Killelan	Baltinglass	I.	60
11	Collins	281	3	33	Londonderry	Coleraine	Aghadowey	Coleraine	III.	229
8, 9	Collinsford	244	2	34	Sligo	Carbury	Drumcliff	Sligo	IV.	221
5, 8	Collinstown	271	3	27	Dublin	Balrothery East	Lusk	Balrothery	I.	21
14	Collinstown	394	1	21	Dublin	Coolock	Santry	Dublin North	I.	29
17	Collinstown	155	1	20	Dublin	Uppercross	Clondalkin	Dublin South	I.	39
3, 8	Collinstown	505	2	35	Kildare	Carbury	Ardkill	Edenderry	I.	51
6, 11	Collinstown	197	2	9	Kildare	North Salt	Leixlip	Celbridge	I.	75
8	Collinstown	660	1	30	Westmeath	Fore	St. Feighins	Castletowndelvin	I.	271
33, 39	Collinstown and Kiltotan	328	1	36	Westmeath	Fartullagh	Castlelost	Mullingar	I.	268
56, 57	Collinward	449	3	26	Antrim	Lower Belfast	Carnmoney	Belfast	III.	7
49, 50	Collistown	310	2	33	Meath	Upper Deece	Kilclone	Dunshaughlin	I.	193
20, 21	Collon	4,348	0	37*b*	Louth	Ferrard	Collon	Ardee	I.	180
20	COLLON T.				Louth	Ferrard	Collon	Ardee	I.	180
20, 26	Collooney	257	3	11*c*	Sligo	Tirerrill	Ballysadare	Sligo	IV.	237
20, 26	COLLOONEY T.	—			Sligo	Tirerrill	Ballysadare	Sligo	IV.	238
28, 29, 35	Collops	531	2	21	Cavan	Clankee	Enniskeen	Bailieborough	III.	72
108	Collorus	474	2	1	Kerry	Glanarought	Tuosist	Kenmare	II.	188
33	Collow	221	3	20	Tyrone	Omagh West	Longfield West	Castlederg	III.	316
25	Collum	360	1	34	Longford	Rathcline	Cashel	Ballymahon	I.	163
69,70,76,77	Colman (*Cramptmore*)	970	2	39	Tipperary, S.R.	Middlethird	Colman	Cashel	II.	325
69, 70	Colman (*Hennessy*)	475	3	5	Tipperary, S.R.	Middlethird	Colman	Cashel	II.	325
68, 75	Colmanstown	638	1	28	Clare	Clonderalaw	Killofin	Killadysert	II.	17
20, 21	Colmanstown	191	1	8	Dublin	Newcastle	Newcastle	Celbridge	I.	34
59, 72	Colmanstown	1,456	2	25	Galway	Tiaquin	Clonkeen	Loughrea	IV.	76
59, 72	Colmanstown	79	2	12	Galway	Tiaquin	Monivea	Loughrea	IV.	78
31	Colmanstown	39	3	12	King's Co.	Eglish	Drumcullen	Parsonstown	I.	134
20, 21	Colp East	397	2	1	Meath	Lower Duleek	Colp	Drogheda	I.	194
20, 21	Colp West	309	0	19	Meath	Lower Duleek	Colp	Drogheda	I.	195
17,18,23,24	Colt	2,082	2	22	Queen's Co.	Maryborough West	Clonenagh&Clonagheen	Abbeyleix	I.	242
5	Colt Island	7	2	5	Dublin	Balrothery East	Holmpatrick	Balrothery	I.	20
76	Colt Island	4	0	0	Galway	Ballynahinch	Moyrus	Clifden	IV.	14
46, 48	Coltrim	461	3	24	Londonderry	Loughinsholin	Lissan	Magherafelt	III.	242
40	Coltstown	98	1	15	Kildare	Kilkea and Moone	Castledermot	Athy	I.	59
40	Coltstown	354	1	35	Kildare	Kilkea and Moone	Graney	Baltinglass	I.	60
28	Columbkille	989	3	37	Kilkenny	Gowran	Columbkille	Thomastown	I.	94
32, 38	Colvinstown	426	2	33	Meath	Skreen	Skreen	Dunshaughlin	I.	221
27	Colvinstown Lower	181	1	25	Wicklow	Upper Talbotstown	Kilranelagh	Baltinglass	I.	364
27	Colvinstown Upper	177	3	14	Wicklow	Upper Talbotstown	Kilranelagh	Baltinglass	I.	364
28	Com	106	2	27	Kilkenny	Gowran	Kilfane	Thomastown	I.	97
24	Comaghy	92	1	5	Fermanagh	Magherastephana	Aghalurcher	Lisnaskea	III.	215
15	Comaghy	247	1	10	Monaghan	Cremorne	Muckno	Castleblayney	III.	261
10	COMBER T.	—			Down	Castlereagh Lower	Comber	Newtownards	III.	162
14	Comeragh	364	2	7	Waterford	Decies without Drum	Kilrossanty	Kilmacthomas	II.	358
14, 15	Comeraghhouse	353	0	18	Waterford	Decies without Drum	Kilrossanty	Kilmacthomas	II.	358
14	Comeraghmountain	2,416	1	31	Waterford	Decies without Drum	Kilrossanty	Kilmacthomas	II.	358
60	Comerford's-lot	55	0	9	Tipperary, S.R.	Clanwilliam	Relickmurry & Athassel	Tipperary	II.	310
30	Comertagh	163	2	25*d*	Monaghan	Farney	Magheracloone	Carrickmacross	III.	272
153	Comillane	141	2	5	Cork, W.R.	West Carbery (E.D.)	Clear-island	Skibbereen	II.	138
37	Cominch	353	2	0	Mayo	Tirawley	Crossmolina	Ballina	IV.	165
44, 45	Commanealine	1,112	2	33	Tipperary, N.R.	Kilnamanagh Upper	Doon	Tipperary	II.	277
98	Commanes	544	0	34	Kerry	Iveragh	Dromod	Cahersiveen	II.	194
6, 7	Commas	2,564	0	9	Cavan	Tullyhaw	Kinawley	Bawnboy	III.	93
64	Commaun	561	1	39	Kerry	Iveragh	Glanbehy	Killarney	II.	195
33	Commaun Beg	425	1	4	Tipperary, N.R.	Upper Ormond	Templederry	Nenagh	II.	293
33	Commaun More	237	3	10	Tipperary, N.R.	Upper Ormond	Templederry	Nenagh	II.	293
59, 69	Commauns	515	3	33	Mayo	Carra	Turlough	Castlebar	IV.	130
99	Commeen	589	2	1	Cork, E.R.	Kerrycurrihy	Carrigaline	Kinsale	II.	92
50, 58	Commeen	3,743	1	19*e*	Donegal	Boylagh	Lettermacward	Glenties	III.	114
67, 76	Commeen	235	3	35	Donegal	Raphoe	Kilteevoge	Stranorlar	III.	139
47	Commeen	79	3	8	Roscommon	Athlone	Dysart	Athlone	IV.	181

(*a*) Contained in the parish of St. Johns, and including 2A. 0R. 0P. River Nore.

(*b*) Including 21A. 3R. 6P. water.
(*c*) Including 6A. 1R. 26P. water.

(*d*) Including 8A. 2R. 24P. water.
(*e*) Including 38A. 2R. 31P. water.

No. of Sheet of the Ordnance Survey Maps.	Townlands and Towns.	Area in Statute Acres.			County.	Barony.	Parish.	Poor Law Union in 1857.	Townland Census of 1851. Part I.	
		A.	R.	P.					Vol.	Page
17	Commeen	176	2	9a	Roscommon	Roscommon	Clooncraff	Strokestown	IV.	208
50	Commeenaplaw	415	0	22	Cork, E.R.	East Muskerry	Donaghmore	Macroom	II.	102
32, 38	Commeenlonagh or Aghanamanagh	59	3	13	Westmeath	Moycashel	Newtown	Mullingar	I.	279
18, 19	Commock	117	0	20	Longford	Moydow	Moydow	Longford	I.	162
112, 125	Commoge	42	0	6	Cork, E.R.	Kinsale	Kinsale	Kinsale	II.	100
26	Commoge	13	3	38	Kilkenny	Callan	Callan	Callan	I.	83
82	Common	155	3	23	Donegal	Banagh	Inishkeel	Glenties	III.	106
62, 70	Common	444	3	16	Donegal	Raphoe	Raphoe	Strabane	III.	140
11	Common	2	1	23	Dublin	Nethercross	Kilsallaghan	Balrothery	I.	31
19	Common	25	1	17	Galway	Ballymoe	Boyounagh	Glennamaddy	IV.	6
57	Common	77	1	28	Galway	Clare	Kilmoylan	Tuam	IV.	22
43	Common	36	3	14	Galway	Clare	Tuam	Tuam	IV.	23
23	Common	110	3	24b	Kildare	Connell	Morristownbiller	Naas	I.	56
14	Common	4	3	37	Kildare	Ikeathy&Oughterany	Mainham	Celbridge	I.	58
28	Common	26	1	26	Kildare	Kilcullen	Kilcullen	Naas	I.	58
31	Common	4	1	35	Kilkenny	Knocktopher	Knocktopher	Thomastown	I.	112
30, 37, 38	Common	653	3	26	Limerick	Connello Upper	Ballingarry	Croom	II.	230
15, 23	Common	98	3	26c	Tyrone	Omagh West	Termonamongan	Castlederg	III.	317
2	Common	1	0	23	Waterford	Upperthird	Dysert	Carrick on Suir	II.	369
47	Common	114	3	27	Wexford	Bargy	Mulrankin	Wexford	I.	307
47, 48	Common	15	2	7	Wexford	Forth	Killinick	Wexford	I.	310
16	Commonage	144	1	39	Clare	Corcomroe	Kilfenora	Ennistimon	II.	19
42	Commonage	13	2	39	Cork, E.R.	Fermoy	Rahan	Mallow	II.	82
27	Common or Kingsbog	663	1	28	Kildare	Offaly East	Kildare	Naas	I.	70
47	Common Moss (Reclaimed)	23	1	31	Tyrone	Dungannon Middle	Donaghenry	Cookstown	III.	301
82	Common Mountain	162	3	19	Donegal	Banagh	Inishkeel	Glenties	III.	106
28	Common North	112	3	14	Kildare	Offaly East	Carn	Naas	I.	69
45	Commonreagh	9	1	27	Down	Lecale Upper	Kilclief	Downpatrick	III.	181
46, 52	Commons	2,730	0	3	Antrim	Carrickfergus	Carrickfergus	Larne	III.	11
13	Commons	202	2	32	Carlow	Forth	Ballon	Carlow	I.	3
34, 42	Commons	9	2	23	Clare	Bunratty Upper	Quin	Tulla	II.	10
9, 10	Commons	414	2	25	Clare	Burren	Carran	Ballyvaghan	II.	11
19, 27	Commons	676	0	4d	Clare	Tulla Upper	Tulla	Tulla	II.	41
42, 51	Commons	575	0	34	Cork, E.R.	Barretts	Grenagh	Cork	II.	49
34, 43	Commons	389	3	4	Cork, E.R.	Barrymore	Ardnageehy	Fermoy	II.	50
54	Commons	9	3	16	Cork, E.R.	Barrymore	Gortroe	Fermoy	II.	55
19	Commons	11	2	4	Cork, E.R.	Condons&Clangibbon	Kilgullane	Mitchelstown	II.	61
74	Commons	268	3	1e	Cork, E.R.	Cork	St. Annes Shandon	Cork	II.	65
74	Commons	54	1	22	Cork, E.R.	Cork	St. Marys Shandon	Cork	II.	66
6, 15	Commons	185	1	11	Cork, E.R.	Duhallow	Knocktemple	Kanturk	II.	75
83, 95	Commons	74	1	23	Cork, E.R.	East Muskerry	Moviddy	Bandon	II.	105
19	Commons	25	3	28	Cork, E.R.	Fermoy	Ballydeloughy	Mitchelstown	II.	76
35	Commons	9	3	11	Cork, E.R.	Fermoy	Litter	Fermoy	II.	80
112	Commons	1	3	32	Cork, E.R.	Kinsale	Ringcurran	Kinsale	II.	100
83, 95, 96	Commons	270	1	34	Cork, W.R.	Kinalmeaky	Templemartin	Bandon	II.	152
81,82,93,94	Commons	114	3	34	Cork, W.R.	West Muskerry	Kilmichael	Dunmanway	II.	158
6	Commons	207	2	12f	Down	Castlereagh Lower	Newtownards	Newtownards	III.	163
31	Commons	74	1	29	Down	Dufferin	Killyleagh	Downpatrick	III.	167
46, 50, 51	Commons	581	1	5	Down	Lordship of Newry	Newry	Newry	III.	182
14	Commons	28	3	21	Dublin	Coolock	Santry	Dublin North	I.	29
20	Commons	156	0	27	Dublin	Newcastle	Newcastle	Celbridge	I.	34
21	Commons	26	3	35	Dublin	Newcastle	Rathcoole	Celbridge	I.	34
21	Commons	51	3	38g	Dublin	Uppercross	Clondalkin	Dublin South	I.	39
18, 22	Commons	94	0	7	Dublin	Uppercross	Crumlin	Dublin South	I.	39
8	Commons	254	3	12	Fermanagh	Lurg	Belleek	Ballyshannon	III.	203
115	Commons	191	1	24	Galway	Loughrea	Killeenadeema	Loughrea	IV.	64
115	Commons	367	0	18	Galway	Loughrea	Kilteskill	Loughrea	IV.	65
20	Commons	106	2	13h	Kerry	Clanmaurice	Kilmoyly	Tralee	II.	171
37	Commons	219	1	18	Kerry	Corkaguiny	Kilgobban	Tralee	II.	177
57	Commons	10	0	28	Kerry	Magunihy	Kilbonane	Killarney	II.	200
24	Commons	14	3	3	Kildare	Naas South	Tipperkevin	Naas	I.	65
11	Commons	93	1	35	Kildare	South Salt	Donaghcumper	Celbridge	I.	76
5	Commons	50	3	1	Kilkenny	Fassadinin	Kilmacar	Castlecomer	I.	90
20	Commons	116	3	35	Kilkenny	Gowran	Gowran	Kilkenny	I.	95
25, 29	Commons	95	0	12i	Leitrim	Leitrim	Fenagh	Mohill	IV.	100
30	Commons	17	2	17	Limerick	Connello Upper	Adare	Rathkeale	II.	230
30	Commons	16	0	25	Limerick	Connello Upper	Drehidtarsna	Rathkeale	II.	232
30	Commons	97	0	23	Limerick	Connello Upper	Kilfinny	Rathkeale	II.	233
47	Commons	15	1	20	Limerick	Coshma	Effin	Kilmallock	II.	243
28	Commons	89	0	21	Limerick	Shanid	Ardagh	Newcastle	II.	254
21	Commons	55	2	19	Longford	Rathcline	Cashel	Ballymahon	I.	163

(a) Including 3A. 3R. 35P. water.
(b) Including 4A. 0R. 2P. water.
(c) Including 2A. 2R. 9P. water.
(d) Including 12A. 1R. 2P. water.

(e) { Within the Municipal Boundary, 3A. 2R. 22P.
{ Without the Municipal Boundary, 265A. 0R. 19P.
(f) Including 10A. 2R. 10P. detached portion.

(g) Including 1A. 0R. 29P. detached portion.
(h) Including 0A. 3R. 38P. detached portion.
(i) Including 8A. 0R. 19P. water.

No. of Sheet of the Ordnance Survey Maps.	Townlands and Towns.	Area in Statute Acres.	County.	Barony.	Parish.	Poor Law Union in 1857.	Townland Census of 1851, Part I.	
		A.　R.　P.					Vol.	Page
24	Commons . .	200 3 23	Louth .	Drogheda .	St. Peter's . .	Drogheda .	I.	175
12	Commons . .	969 1 8	Louth .	Louth . .	Dromiskin . .	Dundalk .	I.	183
11	Commons . .	7 0 37	Louth .	Louth . .	Louth . .	Dundalk .	I.	184
5, 8	Commons . .	674 0 15	Louth .	Lower Dundalk .	Carlingford . .	Dundalk .	I.	176
111	Commons . .	11 3 24	Mayo .	Clanmorris .	Crossboyne . .	Claremorris .	IV.	132
123	Commons . .	4 3 26	Mayo .	Kilmaine .	Shrule . .	Ballinrobe .	IV.	158
30	Commons . .	37 2 3	Mayo .	Tirawley .	Kilmoremoy . .	Ballina .	IV.	170
27	Commons . .	1,050 3 14	Meath .	Lower Duleek .	Duleek . .	Drogheda .	I.	195
25	Commons . .	193 3 30	Meath .	Lower Navan .	Navan . .	Navan .	I.	215
44	Commons . .	299 2 6	Meath .	Ratoath . .	Ratoath . .	Dunshaughlin .	I.	219
38	Commons . .	124 2 3	Meath .	Skreen . .	Skreen . .	Dunshaughlin .	I.	221
19	Commons . .	234 1 38	Meath .	Upper Slane .	Slane . .	Navan .	I.	225
47	Commons . .	1 0 37	Roscommon .	Athlone .	Taghboy . .	Athlone .	IV.	184
25	Commons . .	89 1 25	Roscommon .	Castlereagh .	Kiltullagh . .	Castlereagh .	IV.	201
14	Commons . .	36 0 19	Sligo .	Carbury . .	St. John's .	Sligo .	IV.	223
41, 47	Commons . .	535 1 39	Tipperary, N.R.	Eliogarty .	Thurles . .	Thurles .	II.	273
88	Commons . .	17 2 32a	Tipperary, S.R.	Iffa and Offa West .	Ardfinnan . .	Clogheen .	II.	316
70	Commons . .	233 3 8	Tipperary, S.R.	Middlethird .	Fethard . .	Cashel .	II.	326
60	Commons . .	1 3 0	Tyrone .	Dungannon Lower .	Carnteel . .	Clogher .	III.	297
30	Commons . .	9 2 31	Waterford .	Decies without Drum	Dungarvan .	Dungarvan .	II.	355
27	Commons . .	29 1 8b	Waterford .	Gaultiere .	Killea . .	Waterford .	II.	363
6, 7	Commons . .	367 0 37	Waterford .	Upperthird .	Mothel . .	Carrick on Suir	II.	371
19	Commons . .	14 3 13	Westmeath .	Moyashel and Magh-eradernon .	Mullingar .	Mullingar .	I.	275
46	Commons . .	4 2 18	Wexford .	Bargy . .	Ambrosetown . .	Wexford .	I.	303
46	Commons . .	121 0 35	Wexford .	Bargy . .	Duncormick . .	Wexford .	I.	304
25	Commons . .	6 1 35	Wicklow .	Newcastle .	Rathnew . .	Rathdrum .	I.	354
1	Commons and Cloon	222 2 31	Limerick .	Clanwilliam .	Stradbally . .	Limerick .	II.	226
88, 89	Commons East .	317 1 38	Cork, E.R.	Imokilly . .	Cloyne . .	Middleton .	II.	85
102	Commons East .	881 1 25c	Cork, W.R.	Bear . .	Kilcatherine . .	Castletown .	II.	124
11, 12	Commons East .	15 0 34	Dublin .	Nethercross .	Swords . .	Balrothery .	I.	32
125	Commons East .	430 1 30	Galway .	Leitrim . .	Ballynakill .	Loughrea .	IV.	51
20, 21	Commons East .	176 3 8	Kerry .	Clanmaurice .	Ardfert . .	Tralee .	II.	167
5	Commons East .	16 1 26	Kildare .	Ikeathy&Oughterany	Kilcock . .	Celbridge .	I.	57
82	Commons-entire East	75 2 33	Tipperary, S.R.	Iffa and Offa West .	Derrygrath . .	Clogheen .	II.	318
82	Commons-entire West	7 3 20	Tipperary, S.R.	Iffa and Offa West .	Derrygrath . .	Clogheen .	II.	318
1	Commons (1st Division)	21 0 16	Dublin .	Balrothery East .	Balscaddan . .	Balrothery .	I.	20
36	Commons (1st Division)	23 1 26d	Meath .	Lower Moyfenrath .	Trim . .	Trim . .	I.	211
36	Commons (5th Division)	4 3 4e	Meath .	Lower Moyfenrath .	Trim . .	Trim . .	I.	211
36	Commons (5th Division)	15 2 35	Meath .	Upper Navan .	Trim . .	Trim . .	I.	216
36	Commons (4th Division)	1 2 18f	Meath .	Lower Moyfenrath .	Trim . .	Trim . .	I.	211
3	Commons or Laught	236 0 39	Queen's Co. .	Tinnahinch .	Castlebrack . .	Mountmellick .	I.	248
21	Commons Little .	52 1 18	Dublin .	Newcastle .	Newcastle . .	Celbridge .	I.	34
3, 4	Commons Lower .	608 1 17	Dublin .	Balrothery West .	Garristown . .	Dunshaughlin .	I.	22
11	Commons Lower .	115 3 16	Kildare .	South Salt .	Lyons . .	Celbridge .	I.	77
29	Commons or Newtown . .	698 3 38	Wexford .	Bantry . .	St. Mary's . .	New Ross .	I.	302
10, 17	Commons North .	425 3 22	Clare .	Inchiquin .	Killinaboy . .	Corrofin .	II.	26
5, 14	Commons North .	258 0 13	Cork, E.R.	Duhallow .	Clonfert . .	Kanturk .	II.	68
20	Commons North .	111 2 38	Kerry .	Clanmaurice .	Ardfert . .	Tralee .	II.	167
42, 52	Commons North .	359 0 19	Kerry .	Corkaguiny .	Dunquin . .	Dingle .	II.	176
20	Commons North .	73 2 13	Kilkenny .	Gowran . .	Gowran . .	Kilkenny .	I.	95
17	Commons North .	159 1 11	Longford .	Rathcline .	Rathcline . .	Longford .	I.	164
9, 10	Commons of Carney	280 2 32	Tipperary, N.R.	Lower Ormond .	Finnoe . .	Borrisokane .	II.	284
44	Commons of Clanmaghery .	33 3 32	Down .	Lecale Upper .	Tyrella . .	Downpatrick .	III.	181
43	Commons of Dingle .	876 2 21	Kerry .	Corkaguiny .	Dingle . .	Dingle .	II.	175
16, 17	Commons of Lloyd .	509 1 3	Meath .	Upper Kells .	Kells . .	Kells .	I.	206
43	Commons of Milltown	58 2 37	Kerry .	Corkaguiny .	Dingle . .	Dingle .	II.	175
1	Commons (2nd Division)	14 2 9	Dublin .	Balrothery East .	Balscaddan . .	Balrothery .	I.	20
36	Commons (2nd Division)	10 2 28	Meath .	Lower Moyfenrath .	Trim . .	Trim . .	I.	211
36	Commons (7th Division)	265 3 34	Meath .	Lower Moyfenrath .	Trim . .	Trim . .	I.	212
36	Commons (6th Division)	4 1 28g	Meath .	Lower Moyfenrath .	Trim . .	Trim . .	I.	212
17	Commons South .	635 3 6	Clare .	Inchiquin .	Killinaboy . .	Corrofin .	II.	26
14	Commons South .	1,131 3 23	Cork, E.R.	Duhallow .	Clonfert . .	Kanturk .	II.	68
52	Commons South .	281 0 2	Kerry .	Corkaguiny .	Dunquin . .	Dingle .	II.	176
5	Commons South .	48 2 39	Kildare .	Ikeathy&Oughterany	Kilcock . .	Celbridge .	I.	57
28	Commons South .	4 1 18	Kildare .	Offaly East .	Carn . .	Naas .	I.	69
20	Commons South .	9 2 16	Kilkenny .	Gowran . .	Gowran . .	Kilkenny .	I.	95
21	Commons South .	31 1 13	Longford .	Rathcline .	Rathcline . .	Longford .	I.	164
36	Commons (3rd Division)	11 2 37	Meath .	Lower Moyfenrath .	Trim . .	Trim . .	I	211
36, 38	Commonstown .	586 3 1	Kildare .	Kilkea and Moone .	Killelan . .	Baltinglass .	I.	60
43	Common or Turloughnaroyey .	93 3 4	Galway .	Clare . .	Belclare . .	Tuam .	IV.	17

(a) Including 2A. 3R. 32P. water.
(b) Including 8A. 3R. 38P. detached portions.
(c) Including 6A. 0R. 12P. Glenbeg Lough.

(d) Including 6A. 1R. 17P. water.
(e) Including 1A. 2R. 20P. water.

(f) Including 0A. 0R. 32P. water.
(g) Including 1A. 1R. 32P. water.

No. of Sheet of the Ordnance Survey Maps.	Townlands and Towns.	Area in Statute Acres.	County.	Barony.	Parish.	Poor Law Union in 1857.	Townland Census of 1851, Part I.	
		A. R. P.					Vol.	Page
3	Commons Upper	243 0 3	Dublin	Balrothery West	Garristown	Dunshaughlin	I.	22
11, 15	Commons Upper	243 0 30	Kildare	South Salt	Lyons	Celbridge	I.	77
88	Commons West	30 1 19	Cork, E.R.	Imokilly	Cloyne	Middleton	II.	85
114	Commons West	581 1 28	Cork, W.R.	Bear	Kilcatherine	Castletown	II.	124
11	Commons West	48 0 6	Dublin	Nethercross	Swords	Balrothery	I.	32
125	Commons West	380 2 12	Galway	Leitrim	Ballynakill	Loughrea	IV.	51
20	Commons West	61 0 4	Kerry	Clanmaurice	Ardfert	Tralee	II.	167
5	Commons West	41 1 14	Kildare	Ikeathy&Oughterany	Kilcock	Celbridge	I.	57
9	CommonThe,orSralahan	207 1 3	Cavan	Tullyhaw	Tomregan	Bawnboy	III.	96
32	Comraghs	207 0 12	Monaghan	Farney	Inishkeen	Dundalk	III.	271
13, 14	Conagher	1,385 1 16a	Fermanagh	Magheraboy	Inishmacsaint	Ballyshannon	III.	212
4	Conagher	813 3 21	Galway	Dunmore	Dunmore	Tuam	IV.	33
15	Conaghil	296 0 0	Leitrim	Drumahaire	Drumlease	Manorhamilton	IV.	94
16	Conaghoo	78 0 18	Cavan	Tullygarvey	Annagh	Cootehill	III.	87
6	Conaghra	461 3 4	Mayo	Tirawley	Doonfeeny	Killala	IV.	167
7	Conaghra	204 0 4	Mayo	Tirawley	Lackan	Killala	IV.	170
36, 37	Conaghrud	306 2 6	Donegal	Kilmacrenan	Tullyfern	Millford	III.	133
12	Conaghy	182 2 26	Monaghan	Dartree	Killeevan	Clones	III.	267
22	Conavalla	778 1 18b	Wicklow	Ballinacor North	Knockrath	Rathdrum	I.	347
15	Concaroe	61 0 37	Fermanagh	Magheraboy	Devenish	Enniskillen	III.	210
6	Concealment	87 1 29	Cork, E.R.	Orrery and Kilmore	Kilbolane	Kanturk	II.	108
22	Concealment	350 2 22	Kildare	Offaly West	Lackagh	Athy	I.	73
9	Concess	232 3 14	Tyrone	Strabane Lower	Ardstraw	Strabane	III.	318
40	Conckera	165 2 39c	Fermanagh	Clanawley	Galloon	Clones	III.	198
20, 25	Concra	319 2 32	Monaghan	Cremorne	Clontibret	Castleblayney	III.	260
64	Condonstown	71 0 12	Cork, E.R.	Barrymore	Ballycurrany	Middleton	II.	51
55	Condonstown	431 0 27	Cork, E.R.	Barrymore	Clonmult	Middleton	II.	53
35	Condonstown	322 1 25	Kilkenny	Knocktopher	Aghaviller	Thomastown	I.	110
53	Condonstown North	547 3 3	Cork, E.R.	Barrymore	Kilshanahan	Fermoy	II.	56
53	Condonstown South	512 1 9	Cork, E.R.	Barrymore	Kilshanahan	Fermoy	II.	56
19, 24	Condry	139 3 7d	Cavan	Tullyhunco	Killashandra	Cavan	III.	97
22	Conerick	222 1 17e	Fermanagh	Tirkennedy	Trory	Enniskillen	III.	223
6, 7	Cones	1,293 1 34	Queen's Co.	Tinnahinch	Rearymore	Mountmellick	I.	249
52,53,63,64	Coneybeg	449 0 4	Cork, E.R.	Barrymore	Templeusque	Cork	II.	59
71	Coneyburrow	130 1 14f	Donegal	Raphoe	Clonleigh	Strabane	III.	134
35	Coneyburrow	9 1 25	Kildare	Narragh&RebanWest	St. Johns	Athy	I.	68
35	Coneyburrow	85 1 36g	Kildare	Narragh&RebanWest	St. Michaels	Athy	I.	68
11	Coneyburrow	79 2 0h	Kildare	South Salt	Donaghcumper	Celbridge	I.	76
18	Coneyburrow	72 2 11	Louth	Ardee	Cappoge	Ardee	I.	171
12	CONEYBURROW T.	—	King's Co.	Coolestown	Monasteroris	Edenderry	I.	133
20	Coneygar	235 0 38	Kilkenny	Gowran	Clara	Kilkenny	I.	94
2	Coney Island	2 1 4	Armagh	Oneilland West	Tartaraghan	Lurgan	III.	55
50, 60	Coney Island	245 0 13	Clare	Clonderalaw	Killadysert	Killadysert	II.	16
148	Coney Island	6 1 14	Cork, W.R.	West Carbery (W.D.)	Skull	Skull	II.	146
46	Coney Island	13 1 34	Donegal	Raphoe	Allsaints	Londonderry	III.	134
45	Coney Island	48 0 24	Down	Lecale Lower	Ardglass	Downpatrick	III.	178
39	Coney Island	15 0 0	Fermanagh	Knockninny	Kinawley	Lisnaskea	III.	203
42	Coney Island	3 2 22	Londonderry	Loughinsholin	Ballyscullion	Magherafelt	III.	240
7, 8, 13, 14	Coney Island or Inishmulclohy	388 0 12	Sligo	Carbury	Killaspugbrone	Sligo	IV.	222
11, 12	Coneykeare	124 1 24	Carlow	Idrone West	Wells	Carlow	I.	10
87	Coney or Rat Island	0 0 39	Cork, E.R.	Barrymore	Templerobin	Cork	II.	59
6, 11	Confey	947 0 16	Kildare	North Salt	Confey	Celbridge	I.	74
120	Cong North	12 3 31i	Mayo	Kilmaine	Cong	Ballinrobe	IV.	153
28	Congo	42 0 37	Fermanagh	Magherastephana	Aghalurcher	Lisnaskea	III.	215
46	Congo	214 1 29j	Tyrone	Dungannon Middle	Drumglass	Dungannon	III.	302
120	Cong South	9 3 0k	Mayo	Kilmaine	Cong	Ballinrobe	IV.	153
120	CONG T.	—	Mayo	Kilmaine	Cong	Ballinrobe	IV.	154
37, 38, 44, 45	Coniamstown	424 2 15	Down	Lecale Upper	Bright	Downpatrick	III.	180
105	Conicar	117 1 29	Galway	Dunkellin	Kilconickny	Loughrea	IV.	29
116,117,126	Conicar	125 2 32	Galway	Leitrim	Ballynakill	Portumna	IV.	51
42	Conicker	185 1 33	King's Co.	Clonlisk	Ettagh	Roscrea	I.	130
19, 20	Conigar	267 1 34	Limerick	Connello Lower	Lismakeery	Rathkeale	II.	228
4, 5, 12, 13	Conigar	513 0 14	Limerick	Pubblebrien	Mungret	Limerick	II.	254
8	Coniker	161 2 3	King's Co.	Ballycowan	Durrow	Tullamore	I.	127
15	Conlans Hill	78 3 24	Wicklow	Lower Talbotstown	Hollywood	Baltinglass	I.	360
17	Conlanstown	262 1 18	Kildare	Offaly East	Cloncurry	Naas	I.	69
10	Conlanstown	549 0 2	Westmeath	Moygoish	Kilmacnevin	Mullingar	I.	280
38, 42	Conleen	103 1 9	Cavan	Clanmahon	Kilbride	Oldcastle	III.	77
2, 6	Conlig	637 1 4	Down	Ards Lower	Bangor	Newtownards	III.	157
2, 6	CONLIG T.	—	Down	Ards Lower	Bangor	Newtownards	III.	157
69	Conloon	280 2 19	Mayo	Carra	Turlough	Castlebar	IV.	130
17	Conly Island	64 3 34	Down	Dufferin	Killinchy	Downpatrick	III.	166

(a) Including 17A. 3R. 31P. water.
(b) Including 2A. 3R. 2P. water.
(c) Including 12A. 2R. 2P. water.
(d) Including 7A. 1R. 5P. water.

(e) Including 40A. 3R. 0P. water.
(f) Including 4A. 0R. 4P. water.
(g) Including 5A. 1R. 24P. water.
(h) Including 3A. 2R. 16P. water.

(i) Including 2A. 1R. 16P. water.
(j) Including 2A. 3R. 28P. water.
(k) Including 2A. 2R. 22P. water, and 1A. 2R. 31P. detached portion.

2 O

No. of Sheet of the Ordnance Survey Maps.	Townlands and Towns.	Area in Statute Acres.	County.	Barony.	Parish.	Poor Law Union in 1857.	Townland Census of 1851, Part I.	
		A. R. P.					Vol.	Page
37, 45, 46	Conna	466 2 34	Cork, E.R.	Kinnatalloon	Knockmourne	Fermoy	II.	98
26	Connaberry	106 3 16	Cork, E.R.	Fermoy	Castletownroche	Fermoy	II.	77
20, 25	Connabury	143 2 6	Monaghan	Cremorne	Muckno	Castleblayney	III.	261
94, 108	Connagh	309 3 16	Cork, W.R.	East Carbery (W.D.)	Kinneigh	Dunmanway	II.	134
50	Connagh	410 2 14	Wexford	Shelburne	Fethard	New Ross	I.	327
19, 29	Connaghkinnagoe	844 1 1	Donegal	Inishowen West	Fahan Lower	Inishowen	III.	120
2	Connahill	311 1 26	Wexford	Gorey	Kilnahue	Gorey	I.	319
10	Connahy	1,519 0 10	Kilkenny	Fassadinin	Grangemaccomb	Castlecomer	I.	89
35	Connary Lower	138 2 11	Wicklow	Arklow	Castlemacadam	Rathdrum	I.	342
35	Connary Upper	227 1 6	Wicklow	Arklow	Castlemacadam	Rathdrum	I.	342
45, 46	CONNA T.	—	Cork, E.R.	Kinnatalloon	Knockmourne	Fermoy	II.	98
48	Connellstown	306 1 20	Meath	Lower Moyfenrath	Rathcore	Trim	I.	211
117	Connet	68 3 18	Galway	Leitrim	Tynagh	Portumna	IV.	55
48	Connigar	238 3 23	Kerry	Magunihy	Molahiffe	Killarney	II.	204
38, 44	Connor	493 2 7a	Antrim	Lower Antrim	Connor	Antrim	III.	3
38	CONNOR T.	—	Antrim	Lower Antrim	Connor	Antrim	III.	4
12	Conogher	701 0 39	Antrim	Upper Dunluce	Ballymoney	Ballymoney	III.	18
27	Conor's Island	1 1 36	Galway	Ross	Cong	Oughterard	IV.	73
100	Conors Island	15 0 12	Mayo	Carra	Burriscarra	Ballinrobe	IV.	127
2, 5	Conors Island	111 0 30	Sligo	Carbury	Ahamlish	Sligo	IV.	219
107	Conorspark	49 3 17	Galway	Longford	Killimorbologue	Portumna	IV.	58
25	Conranstown	224 2 33	Westmeath	Moycashel	Castletownkindalen	Mullingar	I.	277
7, 11	Conray	340 3 22	Leitrim	Drumahaire	Drumlease	Manorhamilton	IV.	94
5	Conray	357 2 12	Leitrim	Rosclogher	Rossinver	Manorhamilton	IV.	111
77	Conrea	40 3 2	Mayo	Burrishoole	Kilmeena	Westport	IV.	122
30	Conspark	123 3 10	King's Co.	Garrycastle	Reynagh	Parsonstown	I.	138
4, 9	Constablehill	335 0 3	Carlow	Rathvilly	Hacketstown	Shillelagh	I.	11
31	Controversy	72 1 25	Tipperary, N.R.	Owney and Arra	Killoscully	Nenagh	II.	295
5	Controversyland or Ullard	223 3 24	Queen's Co.	Portnahinch	Lea	Mountmellick	I.	244
80, 81, 90	Contycro	335 3 36	Donegal	Banagh	Glencolumbkille	Glenties	III.	105
26, 34	Conva	714 1 26b	Cork, E.R.	Fermoy	Ballyhooly	Fermoy	II.	76
69	Convoy Demesne	312 0 18	Donegal	Raphoe	Convoy	Stranorlar	III.	136
69	CONVOY T.	—	Donegal	Raphoe	Convoy	Stranorlar	III.	136
69	Convoy Townparks	352 1 7	Donegal	Raphoe	Convoy	Stranorlar	III.	136
53	Conwal	180 0 34	Donegal	Kilmacrenan	Conwal	Letterkenny	III.	126
4	Conwal North	525 1 9	Leitrim	Rosclogher	Rossinver	Manorhamilton	IV.	111
4	Conwal South	292 1 27	Leitrim	Rosclogher	Rossinver	Manorhamilton	IV.	111
18	Conyngham Road	2 2 0	Dublin	Castleknock	St. James	Dublin North	I.	25
34, 35	Conywarren	229 0 9c	Tyrone	Strabane Upper	Cappagh	Omagh	III.	325
11	Cooey	169 0 27	Armagh	Tiranny	Tynan	Armagh	III.	60
50, 59, 60	Cooga	678 2 25	Clare	Clonderalaw	Killadysert	Killadysert	II.	15
17, 25	Cooga	289 0 37	Clare	Inchiquin	Ruan	Corrofin	II.	28
11, 17	Cooga	1,055 1 19	Sligo	Tireragh	Easky	Dromore West	IV.	233
39, 40	Cooga	165 2 29	Tipperary, N.R.	Kilnamanagh Upper	Upperchurch	Thurles	II.	280
15 16	Cooga Lower	541 0 27	Limerick	Coonagh	Doon	Tipperary	II.	234
34, 42	Coogaun	107 0 28	Clare	Bunratty Upper	Quin	Tulla	II.	10
15, 16	Cooga Upper	307 0 22	Limerick	Coonagh	Doon	Tipperary	II.	234
81, 92	Coogue Middle	282 3 11	Mayo	Costello	Aghamore	Claremorris	IV.	137
81, 92	Coogue North	329 1 34	Mayo	Costello	Aghamore	Claremorris	IV.	137
92	Coogue South	333 1 26	Mayo	Costello	Aghamore	Claremorris	IV.	137
29, 35	Coogulla	312 1 39	Tipperary, N.R.	Eliogarty	Loughmoe East	Thurles	II.	271
33	Cooguquid	86 2 29	Clare	Inchiquin	Kilnamona	Ennis	II.	27
29	Coogypark	74 3 25	Clare	Tulla Upper	Inishcaltra	Scarriff	II.	40
8	Coogyulla	151 0 37	Clare	Corcomroe	Killilagh	Ennistimon	II.	20
19	Coohey	229 0 4d	Monaghan	Monaghan	Tullycorbet	Monaghan	III.	281
22	Cookanamuck	3 3 26	Westmeath	Brawny	St. Mary's	Athlone	I.	259
16	Cookesfield	30 1 34	Queen's Co.	Upperwoods	Offerlane	Abbeyleix	I.	251
19, 20	Cooksborough	915 0 11e	Westmeath	Moyashel and Magh-eradernon	Rathconnell	Mullingar	I.	276
27	Cooksgrove	37 1 14	Meath	Upper Duleek	Duleek	Drogheda	I.	197
38, 44	Cooksland	223 0 38	Meath	Ratoath	Dunshaughlin	Dunshaughlin	I.	218
18, 21	Cookspark	143 0 12	Louth	Ardee	Mosstown	Ardee	I.	174
18, 25	Cookstown	291 3 38f	Down	Ards Upper	Ardkeen	Downpatrick	III.	159
7, 11	Cookstown	167 3 5	Dublin	Nethercross	Swords	Balrothery	I.	32
21	Cookstown	264 2 22	Dublin	Uppercross	Tallaght	Dublin South	I.	41
14	Cookstown	313 0 32	Louth	Ardee	Charlestown	Ardee	I.	171
44, 50	Cookstown	229 0 34	Meath	Ratoath	Ballymaglassan	Dunshaughlin	I.	217
39, 45	Cookstown	389 0 32	Meath	Ratoath	Cookstown	Dunshaughlin	I.	217
32, 38	Cookstown	558 2 26	Meath	Skreen	Skreen	Dunshaughlin	I.	221
29	Cookstown	217 2 18	Tyrone	Dungannon Upper	Derryloran	Cookstown	III.	306
1?	Cookstown	172 0 53	Wexford	Dallaghkeen	Donaghmore	Gorey	I.	290
7	Cookstown	300 2 34	Wicklow	Rathdown	Powerscourt	Rathdown	I.	356

(a) Including 0A. 2R. 17P. water.
(b) Including 9A. 2R. 27P. water.
(c) Including 10A. 0R. 16P. water.
(d) Including 41A. 2R. 31P. water.
(e) Including 1A. 0R. 32P. water.
(f) Including 11A. 3R. 26P. water.

No. of Sheet of the Ordnance Survey Maps.	Townlands and Towns.	Area in Statute Acres. A. R. P.	County.	Barony.	Parish.	Poor Law Union in 1857.	Townland Census of 1851, Part I. Vol.	Page
17	Cookstown Great	578 2 25	Meath	Upper Kells	Balrathboyne	Kells	I.	204
17, 24	Cookstown Little	36 3 2	Meath	Upper Kells	Balrathboyne	Kells	I.	204
29, 38	Cookstown T.	—	Tyrone	Dungannon Upper	Derryloran	Cookstown	III.	307
74	Cool	187 2 3	Galway	Clonmacnowen	Ahascragh	Ballinasloe	IV.	24
36, 37, 45	Cool	336 0 21	Kerry	Corkaguiny	Kilgobban	Tralee	II.	177
33	Cool	116 3 35	Limerick	Coonagh	Kilteely	Kilmallock	II.	235
29	Cool	162 3 21	Queen's Co.	Clarmallagh	Killermogh	Abbeyleix	I.	238
20	Cool	345 2 6	Waterford	Coshmore&Coshbride	Lismore & Mocollop	Lismore	II.	345
30	Cool	82 3 17	Waterford	Decies without Drum	Whitechurch	Dungarvan	II.	361
38	Coola	201 3 9	Westmeath	Moycashel	Kilbeggan	Tullamore	I.	278
108, 109	Coolabaun	107 3 37	Cork, W.R.	East Carbery (W.D.)	Kinneigh	Dunmanway	II.	134
32	Coolabaun	143 0 13	Leitrim	Mohill	Mohill	Mohill	IV.	107
2	Coolaboghlan	188 2 38	Queen's Co.	Tinnahinch	Kilmanman	Mountmellick	I.	249
54	Coolaboy	304 0 10	Limerick	Connello Upper	Dromcolliher	Newcastle	II.	232
71	Coolacareen	195 1 35	Cork, W.R.	East Muskerry	Aghinagh	Macroom	II.	153
31	Coolacheesker	117 3 6a	Cork, E.R.	Duhallow	Clonmeen	Kanturk	II.	69
75, 81	Coolaclamper	171 1 12	Tipperary, S.R.	Iffa and Offa West	Caher	Clogheen	II.	317
6, 11	Coolaclarig	665 3 8	Kerry	Iraghticonnor	Listowel	Listowel	II.	192
82, 94	Coolaclevane	615 3 0	Cork, W.R.	West Muskerry	Kilmichael	Dunmanway	II.	158
21, 22	Coolacloy	129 0 18	Galway	Ballynahinch	Omey	Clifden	IV.	14
28, 36	Coolacokery	440 0 29	Limerick	Shanid	Ardagh	Newcastle	II.	254
23	Coolacoosane	315 1 2	Cork, E.R.	Duhallow	Clonfert	Kanturk	II.	68
71	Coolacoosane	183 1 11b	Cork, W.R.	East Muskerry	Aghinagh	Macroom	II.	153
59, 60	Coolacoosane	242 3 8	Cork, W.R.	West Muskerry	Clondrohid	Macroom	II.	155
31	Coolacork	252 1 25	Wicklow	Arklow	Dunganstown	Rathdrum	I.	343
32, 37	Coolacrease	508 0 27	King's Co.	Ballybritt	Letterluna	Parsonstown	I.	126
59, 70	Coolacresig	159 1 32	Cork, W.R.	West Muskerry	Clondrohid	Macroom	II.	155
32	Coolacrim	103 0 19	Fermanagh	Clanawley	Killesher	Enniskillen	III.	192
35, 36	Coolaculla	378 3 24	Tipperary, N.R.	Eliogarty	Rahelty	Thurles	II.	272
72	Coolacullig	521 1 34	Cork, E.R.	East Muskerry	Magourney	Macroom	II.	105
101	Coolacurn North	36 0 35	Galway	Longford	Clonfert	Ballinasloe	IV.	57
100, 101	Coolacurn South	101 3 34	Galway	Longford	Clonfert	Ballinasloe	IV.	57
28	Coolacurragh	263 2 5	Queen's Co.	Clarmallagh	Coolkerry	Donaghmore	I.	237
51, 59	Coolacussane	541 1 8	Tipperary, S.R.	Kilnamanagh Lower	Kilpatrick	Cashel	II.	324
21	Cooladalane Lower	168 1 18	Waterford	Coshmore&Coshbride	Lismore and Mocollop	Lismore	II.	345
21	Cooladalane Upper	191 0 31	Waterford	Coshmore&Coshbride	Lismore and Mocollop	Lismore	II.	345
45	Cooladangan	204 2 10	Wicklow	Arklow	Arklow	Rathdrum	I.	341
78	Cooladawson	130 3 39	Donegal	Raphoe	Donaghmore	Stranorlar	III.	137
133, 134	Cooladerreen	157 2 15	Cork, W.R.	East Carbery (W.D.)	Kilmacabea	Skibbereen	II.	133
8	Cooladerry	129 1 34	Donegal	Kilmacrenan	Clondavaddog	Milford	III.	124
70	Cooladerry	255 3 16	Donegal	Raphoe	Raphoe	Strabane	III.	140
86	Cooladerry	434 1 32	Tipperary, S.R.	Iffa and Offa West	Templetenny	Clogheen	II.	320
8, 9	Cooladerry Mountain	186 3 12c	Donegal	Kilmacrenan	Clondavaddog	Milford	III.	124
20, 26	Cooladine	572 0 38	Wexford	Ballaghkeen	Ballyhuskard	Enniscorthy	I.	291
4, 16	Cooladooaun	151 3 39	Galway	Dunmore	Addergoole	Tuam	IV.	33
12, 13	Cooladoyle	68 2 30	Wicklow	Newcastle	Newcastle Upper	Rathdrum	I.	353
37, 46	Cooladurragh	185 3 32	Cork, E.R.	Kinnatalloon	Knockmourne	Fermoy	II.	98
7	Cooladye	177 1 31	Roscommon	Boyle	Tumna	Boyle	IV.	197
43, 44	Coolafancy	901 0 7	Wicklow	Shillelagh	Crosspatrick	Shillelagh	I.	357
14, 15	Coolafinny	167 0 26	Londonderry	Tirkeeran	Faughanvale	Londonderry	III.	250
35	Coolaflake	278 3 19	Wicklow	Ballinacor South	Ballykine	Rathdrum	I.	348
31	Coolafullaun	219 3 39	Wexford	Bantry	Ballyhoge	Enniscorthy	I.	299
38	Coolafunshoge	618 2 28	Wicklow	Ballinacor South	Kilcommon	Shillelagh	I.	349
8	Coolagad	285 3 30	Wicklow	Rathdown	Delgany	Rathdown	I.	355
16	Coolagadden	115 2 30	Waterford	Middlethird	Kilmeadan	Waterford	II.	368
80, 86	Coolagarranroe	3,493 1 22	Tipperary, S.R.	Iffa and Offa West	Templetenny	Clogheen	II.	320
99	Coolagarraun	57 3 16	Galway	Longford	Kiltormer	Ballinasloe	IV.	60
45, 48	Coolagarry	607 1 29d	Roscommon	Athlone	Cam	Athlone	IV.	179
20	Coolagarry	157 2 31	Roscommon	Frenchpark	Tibohine	Castlereagh	IV.	205
27	Coolagary	731 3 5	King's Co.	Upper Philipstown	Geashill	Tullamore	I.	144
15, 23	Coolageela East	473 2 11	Cork, E.R.	Duhallow	Kilbrin	Kanturk	II.	72
15, 23	Coolageela West	334 3 16	Cork, E.R.	Duhallow	Kilbrin	Kanturk	II.	72
52, 53	Coolageery	142 2 7e	Tyrone	Clogher	Errigal Keerogue	Clogher	III.	295
44	Coolagh	103 3 34	Clare	Tulla Lower	Kilseily	Limerick	II.	36
14, 22	Coolagh	335 0 1	Cork, E.R.	Duhallow	Clonfert	Kanturk	II.	68
82, 83	Coolagh	333 1 37	Galway	Dunkellin	Oranmore	Galway	IV.	32
82	Coolagh	365 2 25f	Galway	Galway	St. Nicholas	Galway	IV.	38
107	Coolagh	157 2 11	Galway	Longford	Abbeygormacan	Ballinasloe	IV.	56
68	Coolagh	67 0 18g	Galway	Moycullen	Moycullen	Galway	IV.	71
31	Coolagh	276 0 36	Kildare	Offaly West	Harristown	Athy	I.	72
9, 15, 16	Coolagh	324 0 11	Londonderry	Tirkeeran	Faughanvale	NewTⁿLimavady	III.	250
4	Coolagh	26 0 14	Queen's Co.	Portnahinch	Coolbanagher	Mountmellick	I.	244
2, 6	Coolagh	1,155 0 32	Queen's Co.	Tinnahinch	Kilmanman	Mountmellick	I.	249

(a) Including 0A. 0R. 16P. water.   (d) Including 27A. 2R. 37P. water.   (f) Including 29A. 3R. 37P. water.
(b) Including 8A. 1R. 18P. water.   (e) Including 3A. 1R. 10P. water.   (g) Including 14A. 1R. 19P. water.
(c) Including 4A. 3R. 28P. water.

No. of Sheet of the Ordnance Survey Maps.	Townlands and Towns.	Area in Statute Acres.			County.	Barony.	Parish.	Poor Law Union in 1857.	Townland Census of 1851, Part I.	
		A.	R.	P.					Vol.	Page
27	Coolagh . . .	117	1	17	Tipperary, N.R.	Upper Ormond .	Ballymaclogh . .	Nenagh . . .	II.	230
29, 30	Coolaghansglaster .	480	2	8	King's Co. .	Garrycastle . .	Lusmagh . . .	Parsonstown . .	I.	137
91	Coolaghbaun . .	112	1	18	Mayo . .	Clanmorris . .	Mayo . . .	Claremorris . .	IV.	135
110, 111, 118, 119 }	Coolaghbaun . .	132	2	16a	Mayo . .	Kilmaine . .	Kilcommon . .	Ballinrobe . .	IV.	154
140	Coolagh Beg . .	161	2	36	Cork, W.R. .	West Carbery (W.D.)	Skull . . .	Skull . . .	II.	146
1, 3, 4	Coolagh, Coolavoran and Derrymullen .	972	3	15	Queen's Co. .	Tinnahinch . .	Castlebrack . .	Mountmellick . .	I.	248
10	Coolagherty . .	322	2	30	Longford . .	Granard . .	Granard . .	Granard . .	I.	156
30	Coolaghflags . .	106	3	16	Kilkenny . .	Kells . . .	Coolaghmore . .	Callan . .	I.	107
140	Coolagh More . .	245	1	29	Cork, W.R. .	West Carbery (W.D.)	Skull . . .	Skull . .	II.	146
26, 30	Coolaghmore . .	430	2	0	Kilkenny . .	Kells . . .	Coolaghmore . .	Callan . .	I.	107
13, 18	Coolaght . . .	584	2	22	Kildare . .	Connell . .	Rathernan . .	Naas . .	I.	56
80, 91	Coolaght . . .	448	0	2b	Mayo . .	Clanmorris . .	Kilcolman . .	Claremorris . .	IV.	134
74	Coolaghtane . .	118	0	21	Mayo . .	Costello . .	Kilcolman . .	Castlereagh . .	IV.	141
2, 6	Coolaghty . .	228	2	23	Fermanagh . .	Lurg . . .	Drumkeeran . .	Lowtherstown . .	III.	205
70	Coolaghy . .	198	1	38	Donegal . .	Raphoe . .	Raphoe . .	Strabane . .	III.	140
17	Coolaghy . . .	133	3	4	Tyrone . .	Strabane Lower .	Ardstraw . .	Strabane . .	III.	318
4, 8	Coolaghy and Coolnavarnoge . .	1,316	2	7	Queen's Co. .	Portnahinch . .	Coolbanagher . .	Mountmellick . .	I.	244
70	Coolaghy Glebe .	129	1	39	Donegal . .	Raphoe . .	Raphoe . .	Strabane . .	III.	140
10	Coolagorane Lower .	110	0	16	Tipperary, N.R.	Lower Ormond .	Ardcrony . .	Borrisokane . .	II.	281
10, 15	Coolagorane Upper .	164	3	33	Tipperary, N.R.	Lower Ormond .	Ardcrony . .	Borrisokane . .	II.	281
12, 13, 21	Coolagortboy . .	424	1	10	Waterford .	Decies without Drum	Affane . .	Lismore . .	II.	353
10	Coolagowan . .	268	0	0	Kerry . .	Iraghticonnor .	Dysert . .	Listowel . .	II.	190
46	Coolagowan . .	323	1	28	Limerick . .	Connello Upper .	Corcomohide . .	Croom . .	II.	232
3, 6	Coolagraffy . .	331	3	14	Sligo . .	Carbury . .	Rossinver . .	Sligo . .	IV.	223
67	Coolaha . . .	71	3	16	Cork, E.R. .	Imokilly . .	Clonpriest . .	Youghal . .	II.	84
31	Coolaha . . .	109	2	1	Monaghan .	Farney . .	Killanny . .	Carrickmacross .	III.	271
29, 34	Coolahest . .	176	3	24	Waterford .	Decies within Drum	Aglish . . .	Dungarvan . .	II.	349
20	Coolahocka . .	119	2	13	Kildare . .	South Salt . .	Kilteel . .	Naas . .	I.	77
20	Coolaholloga . .	144	1	38	Tipperary, N.R.	Lower Ormond .	Nenagh . .	Nenagh . .	II.	287
39	Coolahullin . .	371	0	28	Wicklow . .	Arklow . .	Ballintemple . .	Rathdrum . .	I.	342
7	Coolakay . .	242	0	18	Wicklow . .	Rathdown . .	Kilmacanoge . .	Rathdown . .	I.	355
32	Coolakip . . .	227	0	34	Wexford . .	Ballaghkeen .	Ballynaslaney . .	Enniscorthy . .	I.	292
26, 32	Coolaknick . .	265	1	20	Wexford . .	Ballaghkeen .	Edermine . .	Enniscorthy . .	I.	294
26, 32	Coolaknickbeg . .	61	0	17	Wexford . .	Ballaghkeen .	Edermine . .	Enniscorthy . .	I.	294
9	Coolalaw . .	218	3	39	Carlow . .	Rathvilly . .	Clonmore . .	Shillelagh . .	I.	10
44, 53, 54	Coolaleen . . .	450	1	11	Limerick . .	Glenquin . .	Killeedy . .	Newcastle . .	II.	245
15, 22	Coolaleena . .	210	0	18	Westmeath .	Kilkenny West .	Noughaval . .	Athlone . .	I.	274
28, 36	Coolalisheen . .	269	1	27	Cork, E.R. .	Condons&Clangibbon	Leitrim . .	Fermoy . .	II.	62
26	Coolalong . .	79	0	15	Kilkenny . .	Callan . .	Callan . .	Callan . .	I.	83
32, 40, 41	Coolalough . .	454	0	10	Limerick . .	Smallcounty . .	Hospital . .	Kilmallock . .	II.	260
31, 37	Coolalough . .	422	2	27	Westmeath .	Moycashel .	Ardnurcher or Horse-leap . .	Tullamore . .	I.	276
71	Coolalta . . .	213	1	1c	Cork, W.R. .	East Muskerry .	Aghinagh . .	Macroom . .	II.	153
39	Coolalug . . .	529	2	12	Wicklow . .	Ballinacor South .	Kilpipe . .	Shillelagh . .	I.	349
21, 27	Coolamaddra . .	257	1	23	Wicklow . .	Upper Talbotstown .	Donaghmore . .	Baltinglass . .	I.	363
32	Coolamain . .	604	0	24	Wexford . .	Ballaghkeen .	Ballynaslaney . .	Enniscorthy . .	I.	292
15, 16	Coolamber . .	275	3	39	Longford . .	Ardagh . .	Street . . .	Granard . .	I.	153
2	Coolamber . .	182	0	31	Westmeath .	Moygoish . .	Street . . .	Granard . .	I.	281
15	{ Coolamber Manor) Demesne or Cloon- shannagh . . }	590	3	8	Longford . .	Ardagh . .	Street . . .	Granard . .	I.	153
25	Coolamurry . .	419	1	22	Wexford . .	Bantry . .	Rossdroit . .	Enniscorthy . .	I.	301
95	Coolanagh . .	633	2	37	Cork, W.R. .	Kinalmeaky . .	Murragh . .	Bandon . .	II.	152
26, 32	Coolanagh . .	221	1	0	Queen's Co. .	Slievemargy ? .	Killabban . .	Carlow . .	I.	245
38	Coolanarney . .	398	1	19d	Cork, W.R. .	West Muskerry .	Drishane . .	Millstreet . .	II.	156
24	Coolanarney . .	428	0	4	King's Co. .	Ballyboy . .	Killoughy . .	Tullamore . .	I.	124
102	Coolanarroo . .	155	1	2	Kerry . .	Glanarought .	Tuosist . .	Kenmare . .	II.	188
38	Coolane . .	240	1	34	Kildare . .	Kilkea and Moone .	Kilkea . .	Athy . .	I.	60
20, 28	Coolaneague . .	303	1	20	Cork, E.R. .	Condons&Clangibbon	Macroney . .	Fermoy . .	II.	63
35	Coolanearl . .	227	2	24	Wicklow . .	Arklow . .	Redcross . .	Rathdrum . .	I.	346
17, 18	Coolaneelig . .	405	2	2e	Kerry . .	Clanmaurice .	Duagh . .	Listowel . .	II.	168
10, 11	Coolaness . .	253	2	15	Fermanagh . .	Lurg . . .	Derryvullan . .	Lowtherstown . .	III.	204
25, 26	Coolaney . .	349	1	36	Sligo . .	Leyny . .	Killoran . .	Tobercurry . .	IV.	230
25	COOLANEY T. . .	—			Sligo . .	Leyny . .	Killoran . .	Tobercurry . .	IV.	231
46	Coolanga Lower .	127	3	19	Tipperary, S.R.	Kilnamanagh Lower	Clonoulty . .	Cashel . .	II.	323
46	Coolanga Upper .	242	0	21	Tipperary, S.R.	Kilnamanagh Lower	Clonoulty . .	Cashel . .	II.	323
21, 29, 30	Coolanheen . .	144	1	24	Waterford .	Decies without Drum	Affane . .	Lismore . .	II.	353
59, 60	Coolaniddane . .	625	3	12	Cork, W.R. .	West Muskerry .	Clondrohid . .	Macroom . .	II.	155
02	Coolanillaun . .	312	2	9f	Galway . .	Galway . .	Oranmore . .	Galway . .	IV.	37
36	Coolanimod North .	164	0	39	Kilkenny . .	Knocktopher .	Kilbeacon . .	Waterford . .	I.	112
36	Coolanimod South .	113	1	28	Kilkenny . .	Knocktopher .	Kilbeacon . .	Waterford . .	I.	112

(a) Including 2A. 1R. 38P. water.
(b) Including 27A. 0R. 5P. water.
(c) Including 2A. 2R. 15P. water.
(d) Including 3A. 3R. 0P. water.
(e) Including 4A. 3R. 31P. water.
(f) Including 38A. 0R. 27P. water.

No. of Sheet of the Ordnance Survey Maps.	Townlands and Towns.	Area in Statute Acres.	County.	Barony.	Parish.	Poor Law Union in 1857.	Townland Census of 1851, Part I.	
		A. R. P.					Vol.	Page
28, 36	Coolanoran	805 3 1	Limerick	Connello Lower	Kilscannell	Rathkeale	II.	228
26	Coolanowle	253 0 38	Queen's Co.	Slievemargy	Killabban	Carlow	I.	245
86	Coolantallagh	306 0 19	Tipperary, S.R.	Iffa and Offa West	Shanrahan	Clogheen	II.	319
43	Coolanure	209 1 8	King's Co.	Ballybritt	Roscrea	Roscrea	I.	126
62	Coolanure	374 0 30	Tipperary, S.R.	Middlethird	Rathcool	Cashel	II.	329
42	Coolaphubble	133 0 16	Roscommon	Athlone	Kilmeane	Roscommon	IV.	182
22, 23	Coolapoge	135 3 38	Kilkenny	Shillelogher	Tullaghanbrogue	Callan	I.	116
86, 89	Coolapreavan	772 1 34	Tipperary, S.R.	Iffa and Offa West	Templetenny	Clogheen	II.	320
34	Coolaran	101 1 27	Fermanagh	Magherastephana	Aghalurcher	Lisnaskea	III.	215
70	Coolaran	512 3 7	Galway	Clare	Athenry	Galway	IV.	17
5, 10	Coolard	363 1 1	Kerry	Iraghticonnor	Galey	Listowel	II.	190
20,21,25,26	Coolarkan	573 2 27	Fermanagh	Clanawley	Boho	Enniskillen	III.	189
72	Coolarkin	256 0 37	Tipperary, S.R.	Slievardagh	Templemichael	Carrick on Suir	II.	336
14	Coolartragh	334 0 9	Monaghan	Cremorne	Clontibret	Castleblayney	III.	260
15	Coolaruane	257 2 13	Kerry	Clanmaurice	Kiltomy	Listowel	II.	172
2	Coolasmuttane	705 2 27	Cork, E.R.	Orrery and Kilmore	Shandrum	Kanturk	II.	110
20	Coolasnaghta	1,240 3 9	Carlow	Idrone East	Fennagh	Carlow	I.	7
20, 23	Coolaspaddaun	166 2 0a	Galway	Killian	Athleague	Mountbellew	IV.	43
45	Coolastingan	83 3 37	Wicklow	Arklow	Arklow	Rathdrum	I.	341
45	Coolastingan	61 3 1	Wicklow	Arklow	Inch	Rathdrum	I.	344
34	Coolataggle	61 3 2	Tipperary, N.R.	Kilnamanagh Upper	Glenkeen	Thurles	II.	278
73	Coolatanavally	360 1 10	Cork, E.R.	East Muskerry	Carrigrohanebeg	Cork	II.	102
71	Coolatee	132 3 39	Donegal	Raphoe	Clonleigh	Strabane	III.	134
41	Coolateggart	165 0 33	Wexford	Shelmaliere West	Taghmon	Wexford	I.	334
25	Coolatinny	216 0 0	Roscommon	Castlereagh	Kiltullagh	Castlereagh	IV.	201
39	Coolatinny	32 0 11	Tyrone	Dungannon Middle	Donaghenry	Cookstown	III.	301
47	Coolatober	697 0 24	Roscommon	Athlone	Taghboy	Athlone	IV.	184
21	Coolatogher	180 1 9	Kildare	Offaly West	Lackagh	Athy	I.	73
25	Coolatogher	275 1 0	Kilkenny	Gowran	Powerstown	Thomastown	I.	97
85, 97	Coolatooder	426 2 2	Cork, E.R.	East Muskerry	Dunderrow	Cork	II.	103
30	Coolatoor	98 2 36	Waterford	Decies without Drum	Whitechurch	Dungarvan	II.	361
24, 31	Coolatoor	733 1 28	Westmeath	Moycashel	Kilcumreragh	Athlone	I.	278
24, 31	Coolatoor or Grouselodge	122 2 16	Westmeath	Moycashel	Kilcumreragh	Athlone	I.	278
11	Coolatoosane	252 3 22	Kerry	Iraghticonnor	Listowel	Listowel	II.	192
15	Coolatore	221 0 18	Wexford	Gorey	Ferns	Enniscorthy	I.	316
11	Coolatrath East	306 0 18	Dublin	Nethercross	Kilsallaghan	Balrothery	I.	31
11	Coolatrath West	35 1 29	Dublin	Nethercross	Kilsallaghan	Balrothery	I.	31
22	Coolatrindle	216 3 13	Wexford	Gorey	Kiltrisk	Gorey	I.	320
58	Coolattin	198 2 38	Limerick	Coshlea	Kilbeheny	Mitchelstown	II.	239
9	Coolattin	256 0 20b	Wexford	Scarawalsh	St. Marys, Newtownbarry	Enniscorthy	I.	325
43, 47	Coolattin	1,204 3 35	Wicklow	Shillelagh	Carnew	Shillelagh	I.	657
43	Coolattin Park	454 1 1	Wicklow	Shillelagh	Carnew	Shillelagh	I.	357
12	Coolatty	87 1 31	Monaghan	Monaghan	Clones	Monaghan	III.	274
73	Coolatubbrid	141 0 16	Cork, E.R.	East Muskerry	Carrigrohanebeg	Cork	II.	102
24, 25	Coolaught	444 3 12	Wexford	Bantry	Killegny	Enniscorthy	I.	301
34	Coolaun	221 2 39	Tipperary, N.R.	Kilnamanagh Upper	Glenkeen	Thurles	II.	278
8	Coolavacoose	187 0 19	Kildare	Carbury	Kilmore	Edenderry	I.	52
121, 123	Coolavally	242 3 14	Mayo	Kilmaine	Cong	Ballinrobe	IV.	153
33, 41	Coolavannagh	1,413 3 18	Tyrone	Omagh West	Longfield West	Castlederg	III.	316
40	Coolavanny	163 2 5	Kerry	Trughanacmy	Castleisland	Tralee	II.	208
9	Coolaveely	162 1 13	Antrim	Cary	Culfeightrin	Ballycastle	III.	13
56, 59	Coolavehy	569 2 23	Limerick	Coshlea	Kilfyn	Kilmallock	II.	240
58, 69	Coolavoher	165 3 23	Cork, W.R.	West Muskerry	Ballyvourney	Macroom	II.	154
59, 69, 70	Coolavokig	923 2 8	Cork, W.R.	West Muskerry	Ballyvourney	Macroom	II.	154
1, 3, 4	Coolavoran, Coolagh and Derrymullen	972 3 15	Queen's Co.	Tinnahinch	Castlebrack	Mountmellick	I.	248
57	Coolavorheen	107 2 25	Kerry	Magunihy	Kilbonane	Killarney	II.	200
41	Coolaw	301 0 30	Wexford	Shelmaliere West	Taghmon	Wexford	I.	334
23,24,31,32	Coolawaleen	291 1 1	Cork, E.R.	Duhallow	Castlemagner	Kanturk	II.	67
25	Coolawinnia	398 3 20	Wicklow	Newcastle	Rathnew	Rathdrum	I.	354
8	Coolback	132 1 8c	Donegal	Kilmacrenan	Clondavaddog	Millford	III.	124
49, 56	Coolback	124 3 34	Tyrone	Omagh East	Kilskeery	Lowtherstown	III.	313
23, 29	Coolback	204 3 17	Wexford	Bantry	Ballyanne	New Ross	I.	299
34	Coolbagh	726 2 34	Waterford	Decies within Drum	Clashmore	Youghal	II.	351
33, 34	Coolballintaggart	635 1 23	Wicklow	Ballinacor South	Moyne	Shillelagh	I.	350
39	Coolballintaggart or Coolbawn	1,137 0 38	Wicklow	Ballinacor South	Kilpipe	Shillelagh	I.	349
42	Coolballow	125 1 5	Wexford	Forth	Kerloge	Wexford	I.	310
22, 28	Coolbally	434 3 19	Queen's Co.	Clarmallagh	Aghaboe	Donaghmore	I.	235
17	Coolballyogan or Boston	144 1 29	Queen's Co.	Maryborough West	Abbeyleix	Abbeyleix	I.	242
20, 21	Coolballyshane	292 1 0	Limerick	Connello Lower	Clonshire	Rathkeale	II.	227

(a) Including 4A. 0R. 0P. water.   (b) Including 1A. 2R. 0P. water.   (c) Including 9A. 2R. 18P. water.

No. of Sheet of the Ordnance Survey Maps.	Townlands and Towns.	Area in Statute Acres.	County.	Barony.	Parish.	Poor Law Union in 1857.	Townland Census of 1851, Part I.	
		A. R. P.					Vol.	Page
8, 13	Coolbanagher .	947 1 36	Queen's Co.	Portnahinch .	Coolbanagher .	Mountmellick .	I.	244
24, 30, 31	Coolbane	199 1 33	Cavan .	Clanmahon .	Ballintemple .	Cavan .	III.	75
15, 16	Coolbane .	168 3 30	Cork, E.R.	Duhallow .	Knocktemple .	Mallow .	II.	75
6	Coolbane .	434 1 27	Cork, E.R.	Duhallow .	Tullylease .	Kanturk .	II.	76
15, 16	Coolbane .	288 2 12	Cork, E.R.	Orrery and Kilmore	Liscarroll .	Mallow .	II.	109
124	Coolbane .	355 3 9	Cork, W.R.	Courceys .	Ringrone .	Kinsale .	II.	147
132	Coolbane .	520 2 13	Cork, W.R.	West Carbery (W.D.)	Caheragh .	Skibbereen .	II.	142
58	Coolbane .	217 3 35	Kerry .	Magunihy .	Aglish .	Killarney .	II.	199
1	Coolbane .	94 0 23	Limerick .	Clanwilliam .	Stradbally .	Limerick .	II.	226
57	Coolbane East	12 1 5a	Kerry .	Magunihy .	Kilbonane .	Killarney .	II.	200
57	Coolbane East	262 1 8	Kerry .	Magunihy .	Killorglin .	Killarney .	II.	204
57	Coolbane West	15 0 21b	Kerry .	Magunihy .	Kilbonane .	Killarney .	II.	200
57	Coolbane West	129 2 28c	Kerry .	Magunihy .	Killorglin .	Killarney .	II.	204
76, 77	Coolbarreen .	212 1 24d	Mayo .	Burrishoole .	Kilmeena .	Westport .	IV.	122
11, 18	Coolbaun .	290 0 28	Clare .	Inchiquin .	Kilkeedy .	Corrofin .	II.	25
36	Coolbaun .	68 3 37	Cork, E.R.	Condons&Clangibbon	Knockmourne .	Fermoy .	II.	62
107	Coolbaun .	87 0 5	Galway .	Longford .	Killimorbologue .	Portumna .	IV.	58
58	Coolbaun .	109 2 13	Kerry .	Magunihy .	Kilcredane .	Killarney .	II.	200
58	Coolbaun .	173 1 31	Kerry .	Magunihy .	Kilcummin .	Killarney .	II.	201
6	Coolbaun .	683 2 6	Kilkenny .	Fassadinin .	Castlecomer .	Castlecomer .	I.	88
15,16,24,25	Coolbaun .	458 3 12	Limerick .	Coonagh .	Castletown .	Tipperary .	II.	234
21	Coolbaun .	61 1 30	Limerick .	Kenry .	Adare .	Croom .	II.	248
9	Coolbaun .	166 3 33	Tipperary, N.R.	Lower Ormond .	Kilbarron .	Borrisokane .	II.	284
19	Coolbaun .	243 2 26	Tipperary, N.R.	Owney and Arra .	Templeachally .	Nenagh .	II.	297
87	Coolbaun .	79 0 28	Tipperary, S.R.	Iffa and Offa West .	Tullaghorton .	Clogheen .	II.	321
51, 59	Coolbaun .	304 2 3	Tipperary, S.R.	Kilnamanagh Lower	Kilpatrick .	Cashel .	II.	324
62	Coolbaun .	343 2 26	Tipperary, S.R.	Middlethird .	Cooleagh .	Cashel .	II.	326
15	Coolbaun .	332 2 9	Wexford .	Scarawalsh .	Ferns .	Enniscorthy .	I.	323
107	Coolbaun West	79 2 5	Galway .	Longford .	Killimorbologue .	Portumna .	IV.	58
39	Coolbawn or Coolbal- lintaggart .	1,137 0 38	Wicklow .	Ballinacor South .	Kilpipe .	Shillelagh .	I.	349
24	Coolbawn Demesne.	599 1 20	Wexford .	Bantry .	Templeludigan .	New Ross .	I.	303
88	Coolbea .	222 2 30	Cork, E.R.	Imokilly .	Inch .	Middleton .	II.	87
103	Cool Beg .	286 2 25	Donegal .	Tirhugh .	Kilbarron .	Ballyshannon .	III.	148
33, 34	Coolbeg .	82 1 11	Fermanagh .	Magherastephana .	Aghalurcher .	Lisnaskea .	III.	215
99, 100	Coolbeg .	215 3 23	Galway .	Longford .	Clontuskert .	Ballinasloe .	IV.	58
12	Coolbeg .	181 3 23	Limerick .	Kenry .	Kildimo .	Rathkeale .	II.	249
8	Coolbeg .	242 1 0	Sligo .	Carbury .	Drumcliff .	Sligo .	IV.	221
31	Coolbeg .	371 2 21	Wicklow .	Arklow .	Glenealy .	Rathdrum .	I.	344
34	Coolbeggan East	791 1 26	Waterford .	Coshmore&Coshbride	Templemichael .	Youghal .	II.	348
33, 34	Coolbeggan West	1,002 3 10	Waterford .	Coshmore&Coshbride	Templemichael .	Youghal .	II.	348
5	Coolbeha .	187 0 33	Kerry .	Iraghticonnor .	Galey .	Listowel .	II.	190
3	Coolberrin .	172 0 11	Monaghan .	Trough .	Errigal Trough .	Clogher .	III.	283
26, 27	Coolbock .	253 3 9	Sligo .	Tirerrill .	Drumcolumb .	Sligo .	IV.	238
37, 38	Coolbooa .	216 0 34	Waterford .	Decies within Drum	Clashmore .	Youghal .	II.	351
31	Coolboreen .	206 2 38	Tipperary, N.R.	Owney and Arra .	Kilnarath .	Nenagh .	II.	295
132	Coolboy .	522 0 25	Cork, W.R.	West Carbery(W.D.)	Caheragh .	Skibbereen .	II.	142
58, 60	Coolboy .	650 2 14	Limerick .	Coshlea .	Kilbeheny .	Mitchelstown .	II.	239
39	Coolboy .	222 2 3	Limerick .	Coshma .	Athlacca .	Kilmallock .	II.	241
34	Coolboy .	206 3 7	Sligo .	Tirerrill .	Drumcolumb .	Sligo .	IV.	238
65, 66	Coolboy .	157 0 10	Tipperary, S.R.	Clanwilliam .	Emly .	Tipperary .	II.	308
35, 40	Coolboy .	417 2 20	Wexford .	Shelmaliere West .	Inch .	New Ross .	I.	333
40	Coolboy .	257 2 22	Wicklow .	Arklow .	Kilbride .	Rathdrum .	I.	344
43	Coolboy .	664 3 2	Wicklow .	Shillelagh .	Carnew .	Shillelagh .	I.	357
45	Coolboy Big .	350 2 9	Donegal .	Kilmacrenan .	Conwal .	Letterkenny .	III.	126
45, 53	Coolboy Little	238 0 33	Donegal .	Kilmacrenan .	Conwal .	Letterkenny .	III.	126
20	Coolboyoge .	119 1 25	Cavan .	Upper Loughtee .	Urney .	Cavan .	III.	86
6	Coolbreedeen .	258 3 34	Limerick .	Owneybeg .	Abington .	Limerick .	II.	250
14	Coolbricken .	119 2 25	Kilkenny .	Gowran .	Ratheoole .	Kilkenny .	I.	98
40, 41, 45	Coolbrock .	174 1 33	Wexford .	Bargy .	Kilcavan .	Wexford .	I.	305
22, 23, 28	Coolbuck .	491 1 35e	Fermanagh .	Tirkennedy .	Derryvullan .	Enniskillen .	III.	221
10	Coolbunnia .	353 0 2	Waterford .	Gaultiere .	Faithlegg .	Waterford .	II.	362
131, 140	Coolcaha .	257 3 22	Cork, W.R.	West Carbery(W.D.)	Skull .	Skull .	II.	145
27	Coolcahan .	107 1 31	Westmeath .	Farbill .	Killucan .	Mullingar .	II.	266
28	Coolcair .	157 0 9	Monaghan .	Farney .	Donaghmoyne .	Carrickmacross .	III.	269
32	Coolcam .	243 3 6f	Roscommon .	Castlereagh .	Kiltullagh .	Castlereagh .	IV.	201
53	Coolcam .	14 1 9	Wexford .	Forth .	Carn .	Wexford .	I.	309
16	Coolcanadas .	241 3 31	Cavan .	Tullygarvey .	Annagh .	Cootehill .	III.	87
66	Coolcap .	407 1 10	Cork, E.R.	Imokilly .	Mogeely .	Middleton .	II.	89
19, 28	Coolcappagh .	159 1 17	Limerick .	Connello Lower .	Clonagh .	Rathkeale .	II.	227
8, 9, 12, 13	Coolcarriga .	1,737 3 36	Kildare .	Clane .	Timahoe .	Naas .	I.	54
35	Coolcarron .	353 0 27	Cork, E.R.	Condons&Clangibbon	Fermoy .	Fermoy .	II.	60
98, 112	Coolcarron .	435 1 21	Cork, E.R.	Kinsale .	Ballymartle .	Kinsale .	II.	99

(a) Including 0A. 1R. 32P. water.   (c) Including 4A. 1R. 18P. water.   (e) Including 13A. 0R. 36P. water.
(b) Including 3A. 0R. 12P. water.   (d) Including 6A. 2R. 34P. water.   (f) Including 14A. 2R. 4P. Coolcam Lough.

No. of Sheet of the Ordnance Survey Maps.	Townlands and Towns.	Area in Statute Acres.			County.	Barony.	Parish.	Poor Law Union in 1857.	Townland Census of 1851, Part I.	
		A.	R.	P.					Vol.	Page
100, 101	Coolcarta East	647	3	6	Galway	Longford	Clonfert	Ballinasloe	IV.	57
100	Coolcarta West	684	1	0	Galway	Longford	Clonfert	Ballinasloe	IV.	57
9	Coolcashin	348	0	22	Kilkenny	Galmoy	Coolcashin	Urlingford	I.	92
49, 61	Coolcashla	193	0	0	Mayo	Gallen	Killasser	Swineford	IV.	149
67	Coolcaslagh	455	3	28	Kerry	Magunihy	Killarney	Killarney	II.	203
7	Coolcaum	406	0	33	Cork, E.R.	Orrery and Kilmore	Aglishdrinagh	Kilmallock	II.	106
93	Coolcaum	230	0	14	Cork, W.R.	East Carbery (W.D.)	Inchigeelagh	Dunmanway	II.	132
70, 82	Coolcaum	282	1	34	Cork, W.R.	West Muskerry	Kilnamartry	Macroom	II.	159
19	Coolcaw	277	2	11	Longford	Ardagh	Ardagh	Longford	I.	151
107	Coolcholly	819	1	1a	Donegal	Tirhugh	Kilbarron	Ballyshannon	III.	148
47	Coolclieve	174	3	19	Kerry	Magunihy	Molahiffe	Killarney	II.	205
40, 41	Coolcliffe	220	0	38	Wexford	Shelmaliere West	Ballymitty	Wexford	I.	332
31	Coolclogh	465	2	20	Cork, E.R.	Duhallow	Dromtarriff	Kanturk	II.	71
66	Coolclogher	119	0	8	Kerry	Magunihy	Killarney	Killarney	II.	203
30	Coolcloher East	215	2	17	Cork, E.R.	Duhallow	Cullen	Millstreet	II.	70
30	Coolcloher South	239	1	28	Cork, E.R.	Duhallow	Cullen	Millstreet	II.	70
30	Coolcloher West	214	0	22	Cork, E.R.	Duhallow	Cullen	Millstreet	II.	70
28	Coolcoghill	87	0	1	Fermanagh	Magherastephana	Aghavea	Lisnaskea	III.	218
7	Coolcollid	101	1	12	Monaghan	Trough	Donagh	Monaghan	III.	281
119	Coolcon	284	2	5	Mayo	Kilmaine	Kilcommon	Claremorris	IV.	154
8	Coolcor	353	3	35	Kildare	Carbury	Carbury	Edenderry	I.	51
3, 4, 10, 11	Coolcor	675	2	8b	King's Co.	Warrenstown	Ballyburly	Edenderry	I.	144
10	Coolcor	312	2	9c	Longford	Granard	Granard	Granard	I.	156
29	Coolcorberry	15	3	24	Queen's Co.	Clarmallagh	Abbeyleix	Abbeyleix	I.	235
29	Coolcorberry	52	3	7	Queen's Co.	Clarmallagh	Durrow	Abbeyleix	I.	237
58, 66	Coolcorcoran	289	0	21	Kerry	Magunihy	Aghadoe	Killarney	II.	199
34	Coolcormack	81	0	2	Tipperary, N.R.	Kilnamanagh Upper	Glenkeen	Thurles	II.	278
30	Coolcormuck	268	1	2	Waterford	Decies without Drum	Dungarvan	Dungarvan	III.	355
13	Coolcorragh	209	1	7	Monaghan	Monaghan	Drumsnat	Monaghan	III.	275
25,26,31,32	Coolcoscreaghan	1,808	2	16	Londonderry	Coleraine	Errigal	Coleraine	III.	232
37	Coolcots	459	0	23	Wexford	Shelmaliere West	Carrick	Wexford	I.	332
130, 131	Coolcoulaghta	1,145	3	13	Cork, W.R.	West Carbery (W.D.)	Durrus	Bantry	II.	142
71	Coolcour	416	0	31	Cork, W.R.	West Muskerry	Macroom	Macroom	II.	160
11, 16	Coolcraff	836	0	37d	Longford	Granard	Abbeylara	Granard	I.	154
134	Coolcraheen	265	2	30	Cork, W.R.	East Carbery (W.D.)	Castleventry	Clonakilty	II.	131
17	Coolcran	684	0	31	Fermanagh	Tirkennedy	Enniskillen	Enniskillen	III.	221
21, 22	Coolcran	36	2	35	Mayo	Tirawley	Ballysakeery	Ballina	IV.	164
39, 48	Coolcran	227	1	26e	Mayo	Tirawley	Kilbelfad	Ballina	IV.	168
30	Coolcran	199	3	5	Mayo	Tirawley	Kilmoremoy	Ballina	IV.	170
28	Coolcrannel	112	3	27	Fermanagh	Magherastephana	Aghalurcher	Lisnaskea	III.	215
23, 24	Coolcreaghy	282	3	33	Tyrone	Omagh West	Ardstraw	Castlederg	III.	315
11	Coolcreedan	352	3	2	Louth	Louth	Louth	Dundalk	I.	184
109, 111	Coolcreen	739	2	9f	Kerry	Glanarought	Tuosist	Kenmare	II.	188
37	Coolcreen	485	3	26	King's Co.	Ballybritt	Letterluna	Parsonstown	I.	126
27, 31	Coolcreeve	70	3	25	Leitrim	Leitrim	Annaduff	Cark. on Shannon	IV.	99
48	Coolcronaun	557	1	27g	Mayo	Tirawley	Ballynahaglish	Ballina	IV.	164
28	Coolcronoge	56	0	18	Limerick	Shanid	Ardagh	Newcastle	II.	254
42, 48	Coolcroo	191	3	39	Tipperary, N.R.	Eliogarty	Twomileborris	Thurles	II.	273
41	Coolcull Big	229	1	18	Wexford	Shelmaliere West	Taghmon	Wexford	I.	334
11, 15	Coolcullen	3,234	1	19	Kilkenny	Fassadinin	Mothell	Castlecomer	I.	90
97	Coolcullitha	357	0	4	Cork, E.R.	Kinalea	Templemichael	Kinsale	II.	96
41	Coolcull (Moylers)	132	1	4	Wexford	Shelmaliere West	Taghmon	Wexford	I.	334
41	Coolcull (Sheas)	119	1	18	Wexford	Shelmaliere West	Taghmon	Wexford	I.	335
65, 73	Coolcummisk	644	2	6	Kerry	Dunkerron North	Knockane	Killarney	II.	181
75, 76	Coolcurtoga	761	3	34	Kerry	Magunihy	Killaha	Killarney	II.	202
54	Coolcush	131	3	8	Tyrone	Dungannon Middle	Clonfeacle	Dungannon	III.	299
15	Coolcuttia	286	2	6	Kilkenny	Gowran	Shankill	Kilkenny	I.	99
70, 82	Cooldaniel	803	2	16	Cork, W.R.	West Muskerry	Kilmichael	Dunmanway	II.	158
9, 13	Cooldarragh	169	1	18	Monaghan	Monaghan	Drumsnat	Monaghan	III.	275
31	Cooldarragh	232	2	16	Armagh	Fews Upper	Creggan	Dundalk	III.	48
53	Coolderry	392	1	15	Clare	Tulla Lower	Killokennedy	Limerick	II.	35
38, 42	Coolderry	310	0	22	King's Co.	Clonlisk	Ettagh	Roscrea	I.	130
21,22,29,30	Coolderry	236	0	28	King's Co.	Garrycastle	Reynagh	Parsonstown	I.	138
42	Coolderry	468	2	2	Meath	Lower Moyfenrath	Rathmolyon	Trim	I.	211
32	Coolderry	223	3	18	Monaghan	Farney	Donaghmoyne	Carrickmacross	III.	269
34	Coolderry	263	3	23	Monaghan	Farney	Magheracloone	Carrickmacross	III.	272
31	Coolderry	152	1	6h	Monaghan	Farney	Magheross	Carrickmacross	III.	273
29	Coolderry	458	2	19	Queen's Co.	Clarmallagh	Killermogh	Abbeyleix	I.	238
44	Coolderry	424	1	35	Roscommon	Athlone	Tisrara	Roscommon	IV.	185
54, 56	Coolderry	220	0	8	Roscommon	Moycarn	Creagh	Ballinasloe	IV.	206
54, 56	Coolderry	139	0	29	Roscommon	Moycarn	Moore	Ballinasloe	IV.	206
34, 40	Coolderry	150	2	8	Tipperary, N.R.	Kilnamanagh Upper	Glenkeen	Thurles	II.	278
15	Coolderry	318	2	28	Tipperary, N.R.	Lower Ormond	Ardcrony	Nenagh	II.	281

(a) Including 8A. 0R. 23P. water.
(b) Including 5A. 0R. 24P. water.
(c) Including 1A. 3R. 2P. water.
(d) Including 14A. 3R. 23P. water.
(e) Including 61A. 2R. 0P. water.
(f) Including 19A. 2R. 28P. water.
(g) Including 16A. 3R. 32P. water.
(h) Including 10A. 2R. 13P. water.

No. of Sheet of the Ordnance Survey Maps.	Townlands and Towns.	Area in Statute Acres.	County.	Barony.	Parish.	Poor Law Union in 1857.	Townland Census of 1851, Part I.	
		A. R. P.					Vol.	Page
5, 8	Coolderry	108 1 28	Tipperary, N.R.	Lower Ormond	Loughkeen	Parsonstown	II.	286
10, 15	Coolderry	131 2 39	Tipperary, N.R.	Lower Ormond	Modreeny	Borrisokane	II.	286
31	Coolderry	52 3 6	Tipperary, N.R.	Lower Ormond	Modreeny	Borrisokane	II.	286
21	Coolderry	585 0 10	Tipperary, N.R.	Owney and Arra	Kilcomenty	Nenagh	II.	294
8	Coolderry North	234 3 29	Londonderry	North East Liberties of Coleraine	Kildollagh	Coleraine	III.	246
7, 8, 12	Coolderry South	269 1 21	Londonderry	North East Liberties of Coleraine	Kildollagh	Coleraine	III.	246
54	Cooldine	302 0 10	Tipperary, S.R.	Slievardagh	Killenaule	Cashel	II.	334
11, 16	Cooldoney	583 2 9	Longford	Granard	Abbeylara	Granard	I.	154
39	Cooldorragh	135 3 22	King's Co.	Ballybritt	Roscomroe	Roscrea	I.	126
7	Cooldorragh	885 1 9	King's Co.	Garrycastle	Lemanaghan	Parsonstown	I.	136
47	Cooldorragh	119 0 30	Roscommon	Athlone	Dysart	Athlone	IV.	181
29	Cooldorragha	89 1 23	Clare	Tulla Upper	Inishcaltra	Scarriff	II.	40
82	Cooldorragha	943 1 12	Cork, W.R.	West Muskerry	Kilmichael	Dunmanway	II.	158
44	Cooldorragha	198 0 0	Galway	Clare	Killererin	Tuam	IV.	21
117	Cooldorragha	166 2 16	Galway	Longford	Lickmolassy	Portumna	IV.	60
24	Cooldorragh Glebe	275 3 32	King's Co.	Ballyboy	Killoughy	Tullamore	I.	124
40	Cooldotia	29 2 29	Tipperary, N.R.	Kilnamanagh Upper	Ballycahill	Thurles	II.	277
21	Cooldown Commons	17 0 33	Dublin	Newcastle	Saggart	Celbridge	I.	34
17	Cooldrinagh	41 1 21a	Dublin	Newcastle	Aderrig	Celbridge	I.	32
17	Cooldrinagh	244 0 18	Dublin	Newcastle	Lucan	Celbridge	I.	33
21	Cooldrishoge	111 0 3	Waterford	Coshmore&Coshbride	Lismore andMocollop	Lismore	II.	345
37	Cooldrisla	43 1 4	Tipperary, N.R.	Owney and Arra	Kilvellane	Nenagh	II.	296
13	Cooldross Lower	205 0 8	Wicklow	Newcastle	Newcastle Lower	Rathdrum	I.	353
13	Cooldross Middle	76 0 1	Wicklow	Newcastle	Newcastle Lower	Rathdrum	I.	353
13	Cooldross Upper	49 3 34	Wicklow	Newcastle	Newcastle Lower	Rathdrum	I.	353
71	Cooldrum	189 2 33	Cork, E.R.	East Muskerry	Cannaway	Macroom	II.	102
5, 8	Cooldrumman Lower	240 2 29	Sligo	Carbury	Drumcliff	Sligo	IV.	221
5, 8	Cooldrumman Upper	211 1 36	Sligo	Carbury	Drumcliff	Sligo	IV.	221
83	Coolduff	674 2 17	Cork, W.R.	West Muskerry	Kilmurry	Macroom	II.	159
25	Cooldurragha	691 3 28	Cork, E.R.	Fermoy	Carrigleamleary	Mallow	II.	77
25	Cooldurragha	307 0 20	Cork, E.R.	Fermoy	Clenor	Mallow	II.	78
142	Cooldurragha	379 3 29b	Cork, W.R.	West Carbery (E.D.)	Myross	Skibbereen	II.	141
7, 12	Coole	234 0 10	Antrim	Lower Dunluce	Derrykeighan	Ballymoney	III.	16
4	Coole	289 3 8	Carlow	Rathvilly	Rathvilly	Baltinglass	I.	12
39	Coole	277 2 7	Cork, W.R.	West Muskerry	Drishane	Millstreet	II.	156
4, 5	Coole	203 0 26	Kilkenny	Fassadinin	Donaghmore	Castlecomer	I.	89
37	Coole	137 3 7	Kilkenny	Ida	The Rower	New Ross	I.	104
35	Coole	256 2 18	King's Co.	Eglish	Drumcullen	Parsonstown	I.	134
14, 15	Coole	539 0 30	King's Co.	Garrycastle	Wheery or Killagally	Parsonstown	I.	139
10, 11	Coole	777 1 23	King's Co.	Lower Philipstown	Ballyburly	Edenderry	I.	142
13, 14	Coole	482 0 0	Louth	Ardee	Charlestown	Ardee	I.	171
2, 5	Coole	256 0 29c	Meath	Lower Kells	Kilmainham	Kells	I.	203
17, 23	Coole	225 3 4	Queen's Co.	Maryborough West	Clonenagh&Clonagheen	Abbeyleix	I.	242
17, 23	Coole	360 2 28	Queen's Co.	Upperwoods	Offerlane	Abbeyleix	I.	251
13	Coole	42 0 32	Tipperary, N.R.	Owney and Arra	Castletownarra	Nenagh	II.	294
31	Coole	115 1 27	Tipperary, N.R.	Owney and Arra	Kilnarath	Nenagh	II.	296
22	Coole	137 1 33	Tipperary, N.R.	Upper Ormond	Aghnameadle	Nenagh	II.	288
82	Coole	147 0 9	Tipperary, S.R.	Iffa and Offa East	Inishlounaght	Clogheen	II.	313
48, 49	Coole	262 3 28	Tipperary, S.R.	Slievardagh	Buolick	Urlingford	II.	332
47	Coole	201 1 21	Tyrone	Dungannon Middle	Clonoe	Dungarvan	III.	300
2, 3	Coole	896 0 18d	Westmeath	Fore	Mayne	Granard	I.	271
32, 33	Coole	133 2 20	Wexford	Ballaghkeen	Kilmallock	Enniscorthy	I.	296
39	Coole	690 0 39	Wexford	Shelburne	Killesk	New Ross	I.	327
43, 44	Coolea	218 0 29	Cork, E.R.	Barrymore	Rathcormack	Fermoy	II.	57
58, 69	Coolea	584 3 23	Cork, W.R.	West Muskerry	Ballyvourney	Macroom	II.	154
4, 5	Cooleabeg	309 0 5	Clare	Burren	Kilmoon	Ballyvaghan	II.	13
62	Cooleagh	221 1 23	Tipperary, S.R.	Middlethird	Cooleagh	Cashel	II.	326
53	Cooleagh	533 1 31	Tipperary, S.R.	Slievardagh	Graystown	Cashel	II.	333
5	Cooleamore	205 1 23	Clare	Burren	Killeany	Ballyvaghan	II.	13
65	Cooleanig	461 0 37	Kerry	Dunkerron North	Knockane	Killarney	II.	181
13	Coolearagh East	300 2 1	Kildare	Clane	Timahoe	Naas	I.	54
13	Coolearagh West	608 2 22	Kildare	Clane	Timahoe	Naas	I.	54
78, 87	Cool East	364 1 26	Kerry	Iveragh	Valencia	Cahersiveen	II.	198
35	Cool East	713 2 31	Limerick	Shanid	Rathronan	Newcastle	II.	257
122	Coole Demesne	1,355 0 23e	Galway	Kiltartan	Kiltartan	Gort	IV.	48
63	Coole East	507 2 34	Cork, E.R.	Cork	Rathcooney	Cork	II.	65
2, 3, 8	Cooleen	328 0 17	Cork, E.R.	Fermoy	Ballyhay	Mallow	II.	76
70, 82	Cooleen	351 0 18	Cork, W.R.	West Muskerry	Inchigeelagh	Macroom	II.	157
37	Cooleen	317 3 13	Kilkenny	Ida	Dysartmoon	New Ross	I.	101
39	Cooleen	88 2 3	Limerick	Coshma	Bruree	Kilmallock	II.	240
119, 122	Cooleen	129 0 23	Mayo	Kilmaine	Kilmainemore	Ballinrobe	IV.	156

(a) Including 2A. 1R. 24P. water.
(b) Including 14A. 2R. 19P. water.
(c) Including 27A. 1R. 14P. water.
(d) Including 1CA. 1R. 32P. water.
(e) Including 36A. 2R. 2P. water.

No. of Sheet of the Ordnance Survey Maps.	Townlands and Towns.	Area in Statute Acres.			County.	Barony.	Parish.	Poor Law Union in 1857.	Townland Census of 1851, Part I.	
		A.	R.	P.					Vol.	Page
33, 34	Cooleen	381	0	32	Tipperary, N.R.	Kilnamanagh Upper	Glenkeen	Thurles	II.	278
31	Cooleen	376	1	30	Tipperary, N.R.	Owney and Arra	Kilcomenty	Nenagh	II.	294
26	Cooleen	542	3	5	Tipperary, N.R.	Upper Ormond	Kilmore	Nenagh	II.	291
30	Cooleen	345	3	34	Westmeath	Clonlonan	Ballyloughloe	Athlone	I.	260
94, 108	Cooleenagow	185	0	4	Cork, W.R.	East Carbery (W.D.)	Fanlobbus	Dunmanway	II.	131
39	Cooleenaree	183	0	30	Cork, W.R.	West Muskerry	Drishane	Millstreet	II.	156
91	Cooleenlemane	721	1	34	Cork, W.R.	Bantry	Kilmocomoge	Bantry	II.	120
74	Cooleen and Raheen	10	3	39	Cork, E.R.	Cork	St. Nicholas	Cork	II.	66
112	Cooleens	89	2	8	Cork, E.R.	Kinalea	Kinure	Kinsale	II.	95
83	Cooleens	69	0	34a	Tipperary, S.R.	Iffa and Offa East	St. Marys Clonmel	Clonmel	II.	316
98, 106	Cooleeny	340	3	21	Galway	Leitrim	Kilreckill	Loughrea	IV.	54
14	Cooleeny	687	2	20	Longford	Ardagh	Templemichael	Longford	I.	153
36	Cooleeny	1,285	3	37	Tipperary, N.R.	Eliogarty	Moyne	Thurles	II.	271
99	Cooleeny East	181	0	10	Galway	Longford	Kiltormer	Ballinasloe	IV.	60
99	Cooleeny West	104	0	23	Galway	Longford	Kiltormer	Ballinasloe	IV.	60
22	Cooleeshal	145	1	12	Kilkenny	Crannagh	Killaloe	Callan	I.	86
13	Cooleeshal Beg	97	1	10	Kilkenny	Crannagh	Odagh	Kilkenny	I.	86
13, 14	Cooleeshal More	182	3	25	Kilkenny	Crannagh	Odagh	Kilkenny	I.	86
43	Cooleeshill	194	3	12	King's Co.	Ballybritt	Corbally	Roscrea	I.	125
43	Cooleeshill	175	3	12	King's Co.	Ballybritt	Roscrea	Roscrea	I.	126
12	Cooleeshill	144	1	36	Tipperary, N.R.	Ikerrin	Corbally	Roscrea	II.	275
19	Cooleeshil or Richfort	289	2	38	Longford	Ardagh	Ardagh	Longford	I.	151
11, 12	Coole Glebe Lower	87	3	26	Londonderry	Coleraine	Macosquin	Coleraine	III.	233
11, 12	Coole Glebe Upper	212	3	22	Londonderry	Coleraine	Macosquin	Coleraine	III.	233
30, 34	Coolehill Lower	175	3	33	Kilkenny	Kells	Killamery	Callan	I.	108
30, 34	Coolehill Upper	402	0	7	Kilkenny	Kells	Killamery	Callan	I.	108
8	Cooleighter	195	3	16	Westmeath	Delvin	Kilcumny	Castletowndelvin	I.	265
16	Coolelan	289	3	19	Kildare	Offaly East	Rathangan	Edenderry	I.	71
24	Coole or Lisnagomman	63	0	1	Queen's Co.	Cullenagh	Dysartgallen	Abbeyleix	I.	239
36, 45	Coole Lower	606	0	24	Cork, E.R.	Barrymore	Coole	Fermoy	II.	53
39	Coolerin	117	1	10	Wexford	Shelburne	Kilmokea	New Ross	I.	327
39	Coolerin North	38	2	37	Wexford	Shelburne	Ballybrazil	New Ross	I.	327
39	Coolerin South	24	1	25	Wexford	Shelburne	Ballybrazil	New Ross	I.	327
2, 5	Coolermoney	307	0	1	Tyrone	Strabane Lower	Leckpatrick	Strabane	III.	321
6	Cooles	601	1	7	Cork, E.R.	Orrery and Kilmore	Tullylease	Kanturk	II.	110
43, 44	Coolesker	408	1	2	Tyrone	Omagh East	Clogherny	Omagh	III.	310
9	Coolessan	159	1	23d	Londonderry	Keenaght	Drumachose	New T^n Limavady	III.	235
3	Coole T.	—			Westmeath	Fore	Mayne	Granard	I.	271
36	Coole Upper	546	1	16	Cork, E.R.	Barrymore	Coole	Fermoy	II.	53
63	Coole West	550	0	21	Cork, E.R.	Cork	Rathcooney	Cork	II.	65
89	Cooley	74	3	56	Mayo	Carra	Ballyhean	Castlebar	IV.	125
44	Cooley	367	3	25f	Tyrone	Omagh East	Termonmaguirk	Omagh	III.	314
110	Coolfadda	380	0	19	Cork, W.R.	Kinalmeaky	Kilbrogan	Bandon	II.	152
29	Coolfarnamanagh	87	3	8	Kilkenny	Gowran	Graiguenamanagh	Thomastown	I.	95
113, 114	Coolfin	133	1	5	Galway	Kiltartan	Ardrahan	Gort	IV.	45
125, 126	Coolfin	451	2	24	Galway	Leitrim	Ballynakill	Portumna	IV.	51
22, 30	Coolfin	301	0	4	King's Co.	Garrycastle	Reynagh	Parsonstown	I.	138
28	Coolfin	3	2	11	Queen's Co.	Clandonagh	Rathdowney	Donaghmore	I.	234
22	Coolfin	56	1	38	Queen's Co.	Clarmallagh	Aghaboe	Abbeyleix	I.	235
28	Coolfin	271	3	0	Queen's Co.	Clarmallagh	Bordwell	Donaghmore	I.	237
31	Coolfin	162	1	5	Westmeath	Moycashel	Ardnurcher or Horse-leap	Mullingar	I.	276
31	Coolfin Glebe	671	3	16	King's Co.	Ballyboy	Ballyboy	Parsonstown	I.	123
8	Coolfinn	1,068	0	21	Waterford	Upperthird	Kilmeadan	Carrick on Suir	II.	370
11	Coolfitch	70	1	6	Kildare	South Salt	Donaghcumper	Celbridge	I.	76
62, 73	Coolflugh	415	2	21	Cork, E.R.	East Muskerry	Matehy	Cork	II.	105
21	Coolfore	556	0	7	Louth	Ferrard	Tullyallen	Drogheda	I.	183
39	Coolfore	196	1	9	Meath	Skreen	Kilmoon	Dunshaughlin	I.	221
33	Coolfore	134	0	14	Meath	Upper Duleek	Ardcath	Drogheda	I.	197
27, 28	Coolfore	183	2	14	Monaghan	Farney	Magheross	Carrickmacross	III.	273
1, 4	Coolfores	117	2	22	Dublin	Balrothery West	Naul	Balrothery	I.	23
58	Coolfowerbeg	113	2	30	Galway	Clare	Killererin	Tuam	IV.	21
56, 59	Coolfree	1,018	0	36	Limerick	Coshlea	Kilflyn	Kilmallock	II.	240
50, 51	Coolfree	472	2	0	Roscommon	Athlone	Taghmaconnell	Ballinasloe	IV.	185
31	Coolfune	144	0	38	Limerick	Smallcounty	Glenogra	Croom	II.	259
26	Coolgarragh	173	3	27	Queen's Co.	Ballyadams	Killabban	Athy	I.	231
16	Coolgarran	181	0	26	Fermanagh	Tirkennedy	Magheracross	Lowtherstown	III.	223
23	Coolgarran	41	3	1	Tipperary, N.R.	Ikerrin	Bourney	Roscrea	II.	274
35	Coolgarrane	77	3	3	Tipperary, N.R.	Eliogarty	Shyane	Thurles	II.	272
60	Coolgarriff	490	3	4	Cork, W.R.	East Muskerry	Aghinagh	Macroom	II.	153
58, 66	Coolgarriv	224	3	26	Kerry	Magunihy	Aghadoe	Killarney	II.	199
39	Coolgarriv	95	0	16	Kerry	Trughanacmy	Nohaval	Tralee	II.	212
20, 26	Coolgarrow	404	2	21	Wexford	Ballaghkeen	Templeshannon	Enniscorthy	I.	298

(a) { Within the Borough Boundary, 11A. 3R. 7P. / Without the Borough Boundary, 57A. 1R. 27P.
(b) Including 7A. 1R. 37P. water.
(c) Including 12A. 3R. 34P. water.
(d) Including 4A. 3R. 6P. water.
(e) Including 14A. 0R. 24P. water.
(f) Including 5A. 0R. 34P. water.

2 P

No. of Sheet of the Ordnance Survey Maps.	Townlands and Towns.	Area in Statute Acres.			County.	Barony.	Parish.	Poor Law Union in 1857.	Townland Census of 1851, Part I.	
		A.	R.	P.					Vol.	Page
14	Coolgarrow . .	265	1	26	Wexford . .	Scarawalsh . .	St. Marys, Newtown-barry . .	Enniscorthy .	I.	325
40	Coolgarrow . .	234	1	1	Wicklow . .	Arklow . . .	Ballintemple . .	Rathdrum .	I.	342
34	Coolgarrow . .	485	2	29	Wicklow . .	Ballinacor South .	Ballinacor . .	Rathdrum .	I.	348
25, 31	Coolglass . .	412	1	28	Queen's Co. .	Stradbally . .	Tullomoy . .	Athy . .	I.	248
28, 34	Coolgort . .	74	2	5	Tipperary, N.R. .	Eliogarty . .	Kilfithmone . .	Thurles . .	II.	270
74	Coolgort . .	108	3	6	Tipperary, S.R. .	Clanwilliam . .	Templeneiry . .	Tipperary .	II.	311
17	Coolgower . .	117	2	15	Waterford . .	Gaultiere . .	Kilbarry . .	Waterford .	II.	363
14, 19	Coolgrange . .	159	0	12	Kilkenny . .	Crannagh . .	St. Canice . .	Kilkenny . .	I.	87
20	Coolgrange . .	263	0	1	Kilkenny . .	Gowran . .	Tiscoffin . .	Kilkenny . .	I.	99
15	Coolgreany . .	366	0	39	Kilkenny . .	Gowran . .	Tiscoffin . .	Kilkenny . .	I.	99
3	Coolgreany . .	123	2	16	Wexford . .	Gorey . .	Inch . . .	Gorey . .	I.	316
3	Coolgreany Demesne	147	1	29	Wexford . .	Gorey . .	Inch . . .	Gorey . .	I.	316
3	COOLGREANY T. .	—			Wexford . .	Gorey . .	Inch . . .	Gorey . .	I.	316
52, 63	Coolgreen . .	481	0	23	Cork, E.R. .	Barrymore . .	Templeusque . .	Cork . .	II.	59
64	Coolguerisk . .	300	1	21	Cork, E.R. .	Barrymore . .	Kilquane . .	Cork . .	II.	55
21	Coolharbour . .	123	3	38	Wexford . .	Ballaghkeen . .	Kilnamanagh . .	Gorey . .	I.	297
21	Coolharbour Lower	45	1	39	Wicklow . .	Lower Talbotstown .	Donard . .	Baltinglass .	I.	359
15, 21	Coolharbour Upper	92	0	24	Wicklow . .	Lower Talbotstown .	Donard . .	Baltinglass .	I.	359
32	Coolhenry . .	149	2	38	Queen's Co. .	Slievemargy . .	Killeshin . .	Carlow . .	I.	245
33	Coolhill . . .	439	0	13	Kilkenny . .	Ida . . .	The Rower . .	Thomastown .	I.	104
19	Coolhill . . .	93	1	21	Londonderry .	Coleraine . .	Aghadowey . .	Ballymoney .	III.	229
53	Coolhill . . .	333	2	17	Tyrone . .	Dungannon Lower .	Killeeshil . .	Dungannon .	III.	298
54	Coolhill . . .	220	3	12	Tyrone . .	Dungannon Middle .	Drumglass . .	Dungannon .	III.	302
46	Coolhull . . .	292	3	16	Wexford . .	Bargy . .	Bannow . .	Wexford . .	I.	304
22	Coolier . . .	24	3	38	Kildare . .	Offaly West .	Lackagh . .	Athy . .	I.	73
104	Coolieragh . .	533	0	9	Cork, W.R. .	Bear . . .	Kilcaskan . .	Bantry . .	II.	122
58, 69	Coolierher . .	238	3	28	Cork, W.R. .	West Muskerry .	Ballyvourney . .	Macroom .	II.	154
25	Coolierin . .	127	1	27	Kilkenny . .	Gowran . .	Graiguenamanagh .	Thomastown .	I.	95
67, 74, 75	Coolies . . .	2,254	1	18a	Kerry . .	Magunihy . .	Killarney . .	Killarney .	II.	203
123	Cooligboy . .	89	2	37	Cork, W.R. .	Ibane and Barryroe	Timoleague . .	Clonakilty .	II.	151
149	*Coolim* . . .	2	0	16	Cork, W.R. .	West Carbery (E.D.)	Aghadown . .	Skibbereen .	II.	136
26	Coolin . . .	427	1	15b	Galway . .	Ross . . .	Ross . . .	Oughterard .	IV.	74
27	Coolinarrig Lower .	336	2	16	Wicklow . .	Upper Talbotstown .	Baltinglass . .	Baltinglass .	I.	362
27	Coolinarrig Upper .	186	3	12	Wicklow . .	Upper Talbotstown .	Baltinglass . .	Baltinglass .	I.	362
60, 61	Coolineagh . .	425	2	3	Cork, W.R. .	East Muskerry .	Aghabulloge . .	Macroom .	II.	153
7	Cooliney . . .	451	0	19	Cork, E.R. .	Orrery and Kilmore	Cooliney . .	Kilmallock .	II.	108
32	Coolinfin Glebe .	99	1	29	Fermanagh .	Clanawley . .	Kinawley . .	Enniskillen .	III.	193
35	Coolinny . .	177	0	29	Cork, E.R. .	Fermoy . .	Killathy . .	Fermoy . .	II.	80
6, 7	Coolintaggart . .	218	0	28	Wexford . .	Gorey . .	Kilcavan . .	Gorey . .	I.	317
6	Coolintaggarthill .	170	0	38	Wexford . .	Gorey . .	Kilcavan . .	Gorey . .	I.	317
14	Coolishal . .	61	1	7	Limerick . .	Clanwilliam . .	Carrigparson . .	Limerick . .	II.	223
20	Coolishal . .	131	3	3c	Waterford . .	Coshmore & Coshbride	Lismore and Mocollop	Lismore . .	II.	345
2	Coolishal . .	646	2	10	Waterford . .	Upperthird . .	Kilsheelan . .	Clonmel .	II.	370
46	Coolishal . .	295	0	32	Wexford . .	Bargy . .	Bannow . .	Wexford . .	I.	304
6, 11	Coolishal Lower	259	2	11	Wexford . .	Gorey . .	Kilnahue . .	Gorey . .	I.	319
11	Coolishal Upper	269	3	17	Wexford . .	Gorey . .	Kilnahue . .	Gorey . .	I.	319
10	Coolisk . . .	76	2	5	Fermanagh .	Lurg . . .	Derryvullan . .	Lowtherstown .	III.	204
37, 45	Cooliska . . .	287	3	8	Limerick . .	Glenquin . .	Mahoonagh . .	Newcastle .	II.	246
43	Coolistoonan . .	151	0	31d	Clare . .	Tulla Lower .	Clonlea . .	Tulla . .	II.	34
31, 37	Cooljohn . .	167	2	28	Meath . .	Lower Deece .	Balsoon . .	Trim . .	I.	191
38	Coolkeeghan . .	107	3	20	Tyrone . .	Dungannon Upper .	Derryloran . .	Cookstown .	III.	306
9	Coolkeenaght . .	76	0	32	Londonderry .	Tirkeeran . .	Faughanvale . .	New Tⁿ Limavady	III.	250
14	Coolkeeragh . .	555	1	39e	Londonderry .	Tirkeeran . .	Clondermot . .	Londonderry .	III.	247
34	Coolkeeragh . .	548	0	31	Tyrone . .	Omagh West .	Longfield East .	Omagh . .	III.	315
13, 18	Coolkeeran . .	260	1	39	Antrim . .	Upper Dunluce .	Loughguile . .	Ballymoney .	III.	20
47, 48	Coolkeeran . .	60	2	22	Wexford . .	Forth . . .	Killinick . .	Wexford . .	I.	310
107	Coolkellure . .	545	2	2	Cork, W.R. .	East Carbery (W.D.)	Fanlobbus . .	Dunmanway .	II.	131
42	Coolkenna . .	975	2	10	Wicklow . .	Shillelagh . .	Aghowle . .	Shillelagh .	I.	356
47	Coolkennedy . .	187	1	10	Tipperary, N.R. .	Eliogarty . .	Galbooly . .	Thurles . .	II.	270
8	Coolkenny . .	238	3	34	Antrim . .	Cary . . .	Ramoan . .	Ballycastle .	III.	14
5, 10	Coolkeragh . .	1,437	3	12	Kerry . .	Iraghticonnor .	Galey . .	Listowel .	II.	190
22	Coolkereen . .	145	1	8	Tipperary, N.R. .	Upper Ormond .	Aghnameadle .	Nenagh . .	II.	288
28	Coolkerry . .	480	0	23	Queen's Co. .	Clarmallagh . .	Coolkerry . .	Donaghmore .	I.	237
15	Coolkill . . .	232	2	23	Armagh . .	Tiranny . .	Tynan . .	Armagh . .	III.	60
38	Coolkill . . .	427	1	31f	Cavan . .	Castlerahan . .	Crosserlough . .	Cavan . .	III.	67
38	Coolkill . . .	57	2	11	Fermanagh .	Knockninny . .	Kinawley . .	Lisnaskea .	III.	201
40	Coolkill . . .	60	3	2	Tipperary, N.R. .	Kilnamanagh Upper	Ballycahill . .	Thurles . .	II.	277
40	Coolkill . . .	148	2	30	Tipperary, N.R. .	Kilnamanagh Upper	Moyaliff . .	Thurles . .	II.	279
54, 61	Coolkill . . .	135	1	8	Tyrone . .	Dungannon Middle .	Clonfeacle . .	Dungannon .	III.	299
18	Coolkill East . .	194	1	18	Monaghan .	Dartree . .	Ematris . .	Cootehill .	III.	266
9	Coolkill East . .	119	3	12g	Monaghan .	Monaghan . .	Tedavnet . .	Monaghan .	III.	278
18	Coolkill West . .	111	1	3h	Monaghan .	Dartree . .	Ematris . .	Cootehill .	III.	266

(a) Including 82A. 3R. 6P. water.
(b) Including 43A. 0R. 7P. water.
(c) Including 3A. 1R. 12P. water.
(d) Including 11A. 3R. 24P. Lough Avoher.
(e) Including 22A. 2R. 6P. water.
(f) Including 3A. 3R. 31P. Coolkill Lough.
(g) Including 4A. 2R. 32P. water.
(h) Including 9A. 0R. 16P. water.

No. of Sheet of the Ordnance Survey Maps.	Townlands and Towns.	Area in Statute Acres.			County.	Barony.	Parish.	Poor Law Union in 1857.	Townland Census of 1851, Part I.	
		A.	R.	P.					Vol.	Page
8, 9	Coolkill West	88	2	5	Monaghan	Monaghan	Tedavnet	Monaghan	III.	278
47	Coolkip	216	0	11	Tipperary, N.R.	Eliogarty	Moycarky	Thurles	II.	271
98	Coolkirky	526	0	34	Cork, E.R.	Kinalea	Ballymartle	Kinsale	II.	94
60, 71	Coolkisha	296	2	1	Cork, W.R.	East Muskerry	Aghinagh	Macroom	II.	153
45, 54	Coolknedane North	116	1	33	Cork, E.R.	Barrymore	Britway	Middleton	II.	51
45	Coolknedane South	67	1	18	Cork, E.R.	Barrymore	Britway	Middleton	II.	51
86, 95	Coolknoohil	1,128	2	24	Kerry	Glanarought	Kilgarvan	Kenmare	II.	187
49	Coollagagh	720	0	29	Mayo	Gallen	Killasser	Swineford	IV.	149
28	Coollane	88	1	19	Fermanagh	Magherastephana	Aghalurcher	Lisnaskea	III.	215
66	Coollegrean	56	3	6	Kerry	Magunihy	Killarney	Killarney	II.	203
32, 41	Coollegrean	1,246	3	19	Kerry	Trughanacmy	Ballincuslane	Tralee	II.	206
16	Coollegreane	654	3	25	Leitrim	Drumahaire	Inishmagrath	Manorhamilton	IV.	96
34	Coollemoneen	260	2	28a	Sligo	Tirerrill	Killadoon	Boyle	IV.	239
74	Coollena	104	3	18	Mayo	Costello	Kilcolman	Castlereagh	IV.	141
48, 58	Coollick	168	1	0	Kerry	Magunihy	Kilcredane	Killarney	II.	200
48, 58	Coollick	830	0	17	Kerry	Magunihy	Kilcummin	Killarney	II.	201
50, 61	Coollicka	517	1	14	Cork, E.R.	East Muskerry	Donaghmore	Macroom	II.	102
4, 16	Coollicknalea	313	3	30b	Galway	Dunmore	Addergoole	Tuam	IV.	33
118, 121	Coollisduff	101	0	33c	Mayo	Kilmaine	Kilmainemore	Ballinrobe	IV.	156
118, 121	Coollisduff	390	0	32	Mayo	Kilmaine	Kilmolara	Ballinrobe	IV.	156
53	Coollisteige	374	0	17	Clare	Tulla Lower	Kiltenanlea	Limerick	II.	37
89	Cool Lodge	107	2	34d	Mayo	Carra	Ballyhean	Castlebar	IV.	125
88	Coolloughra	56	3	12	Mayo	Burrishoole	Aghagower	Westport	IV.	118
93	Coolloughra	232	2	39	Mayo	Costello	Bekan	Claremorris	IV.	139
27, 36	Cool Lower	624	3	31	Donegal	Kilmacrenan	Kilmacrenan	Millford	III.	129
41	Coollusty	356	1	2	Roscommon	Athlone	Athleague	Roscommon	IV.	179
1, 2	Coolmaghery	469	2	7	Tyrone	Strabane Lower	Donaghedy	Strabane	III.	320
4	Coolmaghra	403	1	38	Antrim	Cary	Ballintoy	Ballycastle	III.	12
46	Coolmaghry	242	3	20	Tyrone	Dungannon Middle	Pomeroy	Dungannon	III.	304
65	Coolmagort	653	0	21e	Kerry	Dunkerron North	Knockane	Killarney	II.	181
15, 23	Coolmahane	197	0	11	Cork, E.R.	Duhallow	Kilbrin	Kanturk	II.	72
124, 137	Coolmain	450	1	39	Cork, W.R.	East Carbery (E.D.)	Ringrone	Kinsale	II.	130
9, 10	Coolmain	115	2	23	Monaghan	Monaghan	Monaghan	Monaghan	III.	276
101	Coolmakean	231	0	22	Mayo	Clanmorris	Crossboyne	Claremorris	IV.	132
4	Coolmanagh Lower	297	1	28	Carlow	Rathvilly	Haroldstown	Shillelagh	I.	11
4, 9	Coolmanagh Upper	543	1	24	Carlow	Rathvilly	Haroldstown	Shillelagh	I.	11
19	Coolmannan	158	2	10	Monaghan	Cremorne	Clontibret	Castleblayney	III.	260
15	Coolmarks	200	2	21	Kilkenny	Gowran	Tiscoffin	Kilkenny	I.	99
4	Coolmeen	186	0	39	Clare	Burren	Killonaghan	Ballyvaghan	II.	13
59, 69	Coolmeen	1,557	1	6	Clare	Clonderalaw	Kilfiddane	Killadysert	II.	15
31,32,35,36	Coolmeen	617	1	15	Kilkenny	Knocktopher	Derrynahinch	Thomastown	I.	111
39, 41	Coolmeen	145	0	22	Roscommon	Athlone	Fuerty	Roscommon	IV.	181
17	Coolmeen	247	2	19f	Roscommon	Roscommon	Clooncraff	Strokestown	IV.	208
35, 41	Coolmeen	172	0	31	Sligo	Tirerrill	Kilmactranny	Boyle	IV.	240
4, 5	Coolmela or Prospect	1,059	3	20	Wexford	Scarawalsh	Moyacomb	Shillelagh	I.	325
17	Coolmillish	334	1	0	Armagh	Fews Lower	Mullaghbrack	Armagh	III.	47
13	Coolmine	609	1	7	Dublin	Castleknock	Clonsilla	Celbridge	I.	24
21, 24	Coolmine	429	0	26	Dublin	Newcastle	Saggart	Celbridge	I.	34
50	Coolmona	802	2	19	Cork, E.R.	East Muskerry	Donaghmore	Macroom	II.	102
21	Coolmoney	95	3	15	Wicklow	Upper Talbotstown	Donaghmore	Baltinglass	I.	363
28	Coolmoohan	406	1	32	Cork, E.R.	Condons&Clangibbon	Macroney	Fermoy	II.	63
87, 99	Coolmore	558	2	21	Cork, E.R.	Kerrycurrihy	Carrigaline	Cork	II.	92
7	Coolmore	175	2	33	Cork, E.R.	Orrery and Kilmore	Churchtown	Mallow	II.	107
103	Cool More	115	3	14	Donegal	Tirhugh	Kilbarron	Ballyshannon	III.	148
31, 35	Coolmore	299	3	3	Kilkenny	Knocktopher	Knocktopher	Thomastown	I.	112
62	Coolmore	474	3	12	Tipperary, S.R.	Middlethird	Rathcool	Cashel	II.	329
36, 41	Coolmore	148	3	38	Wicklow	Arklow	Ennereilly	Rathdrum	I.	344
97, 111	Coolmoreen	391	2	32	Cork, E.R.	Kinalea	Inishannon	Bandon	II.	95
93	Coolmountain	963	1	3	Cork, W.R.	East Carbery (W.D.)	Inchigeelagh	Dunmanway	II.	132
61, 69	Coolmoyne	378	3	23	Tipperary, S.R.	Middlethird	Tullamain	Cashel	II.	331
61, 69	Coolmoyne (Fennell)	404	2	10	Tipperary, S.R.	Middlethird	Rathcool	Cashel	II.	329
61, 69	Coolmoyne (Taylor)	162	2	31	Tipperary, S.R.	Middlethird	Rathcool	Cashel	II.	329
9, 10	Coolmuckbane	42	3	25	Monaghan	Monaghan	Tehallan	Monaghan	III.	280
35	Coolmucky	303	1	35g	Cork, E.R.	Condons&Clangibbon	Fermoy	Fermoy	II.	61
35	Coolmucky	278	2	12	Cork, E.R.	Condons&Clangibbon	Litter	Fermoy	II.	62
84	Coolmucky	811	3	9	Cork, E.R.	East Muskerry	Moviddy	Bandon	II.	105
57, 58	Coolmuinga	357	1	26h	Clare	Moyarta	Kilrush	Kilrush	II.	33
35	Coolmurry	214	1	4	Sligo	Tirerrill	Kilmactranny	Boyle	IV.	240
18, 19	Coolnabacky	540	2	24	Queen's Co.	Cullenagh	Fossy or Timahoe	Abbeyleix	I.	240
2	Coolnabanch	134	0	38	Queen's Co.	Tinnahinch	Kilmanman	Mountmellick	I.	249
5, 13	Coolnabeasoon	248	3	37	Waterford	Glenahiry	Kilronan	Clonmel	II.	365
29	Coolnabehy	128	0	35	Queen's Co.	Clarmallagh	Durrow	Abbeyleix	I.	237
46, 58	Coolnabinnia	1,356	3	0	Mayo	Tirawley	Crossmolina	Ballina	IV.	165

(a) Including 12A. 3R. 22P. water.
(b) Including 5A. 0R. 31P. water.
(c) Including 3A. 0R. 1P. water.
(d) Including 5A. 1R. 28P. water.
(e) Including 3A. 1R. 32P. water.
(f) Including 34A. 0R. 35P. water.
(g) Including 4A. 2R. 24P. water.
(h) Including 8A. 3R. 3P. water.

No. of Sheet of the Ordnance Survey Maps.	Townlands and Towns.	Area in Statute Acres.	County.	Barony.	Parish.	Poor Law Union in 1857.	Townland Census of 1851, Part I.	
		A. R. P.					Vol.	Page
28	Coolnaboul East	4 2 12	Queen's Co.	Clandonagh	Coolkerry	Donaghmore	I.	233
28	Coolnaboul West	159 0 23	Queen's Co.	Clandonagh	Rathdowney	Donaghmore	I.	234
26, 32	Coolnaboy	507 1 29	Wexford	Ballaghkeen	Edermine	Enniscorthy	I.	294
25	Coolnabrone	163 0 30a	Kilkenny	Gowran	Powerstown	Thomastown	I.	97
22	Coolnabrone	103 1 28	Kilkenny	Shillelogher	Tullaghanbrogue	Callan	I.	116
64	Coolnacaha	132 3 24	Cork, E.R.	Barrymore	Killaspugmullane	Cork	II.	55
58,59,69,70	Coolnacaheragh	308 0 24	Cork, W.R.	West Muskerry	Ballyvourney	Macroom	II.	154
37	Coolnacalla	80 1 8	Tipperary, N.R.	Owney and Arra	Kilvellane	Nenagh	II.	296
39, 48	Coolnacalliagh	229 1 13	Kerry	Trughanacmy	Killeentierna	Killarney	II.	211
25	Coolnacarrick	148 2 36	Cavan	Clanmahon	Ballintemple	Cavan	III.	75
13, 18	Coolnacarrick	152 3 14	Queen's Co.	Maryborough East	Dysartenos	Mountmellick	I.	241
71	Coolnacarriga	190 2 27b	Cork, E.R.	East Muskerry	Cannaway	Macroom	II.	102
17	Coolnacartan	415 3 28	Queen's Co.	Maryborough West	Clonenagh&Clonagheen	Abbeyleix	I.	242
16	Coolnacarte	180 0 24	Monaghan	Dartree	Currin	Clones	III.	265
132, 141	Coolnaclehy	285 2 37	Cork, W.R.	West Carbery (W.D.)	Caheragh	Skibbereen	II.	142
67, 78	Coolnacloghafinna	221 1 24	Cork, E.R.	Imokilly	Clonpriest	Youghal	II.	85
33	Coolnacola	221 2 13	Cavan	Upper Loughtee	Killinkere	Bailieborough	III.	84
23, 24	Coolnacolpagh	604 0 7	Londonderry	Tirkeeran	Cumber Upper	NewTⁿLimavady	III.	249
24, 30	Coolnacon	360 3 6	Wexford	Bantry	Killegney	Enniscorthy	I.	301
121	Coolnaconarty	128 1 33	Cork, W.R.	East Carbery (W.D.)	Kilkerranmore	Dunmanway	II.	133
121	Coolnaconarty	268 0 17	Cork, W.R.	East Carbery (W.D.)	Kilmeen	Dunmanway	II.	134
10	Coolnacoppoge or Coolnambrisklaun	130 2 8	Kilkenny	Fassadinin	Kilmacar	Castlecomer	I.	90
33, 34	Coolnacran	402 2 0	Down	IveaghUpper, Up. pt.	Aghaderg	Banbridge	III.	174
82	Coolnacrannagh	121 3 17	Cork, W.R.	West Muskerry	Inchigeelagh	Macroom	II.	157
21	Coolnacreena	362 3 7	Waterford	Decies without Drum	Affane	Lismore	II.	353
24	Coolnacrunaght	404 3 3	Tyrone	Omagh West	Ardstraw	Castlederg	III.	315
3, 4, 8, 9	Coolnacrutta	888 3 0	Kilkenny	Galmoy	Glashare	Urlingford	I.	92
16, 19	Coolnacuppoge	242 1 26	Carlow	Idrone East	Sliguff	Carlow	I.	8
39	Coolnadead	124 3 21	Kerry	Trughanacmy	Ballymacelligott	Tralee	II.	207
25, 31	Coolnadornory	237 2 30	Tipperary, N.R.	Owney and Arra	Templeachally	Nenagh	II.	297
33	Coolnadown	145 0 21	Limerick	Coonagh	Templebreden	Tipperary	II.	236
93, 103	Coolnafarna	378 2 9	Mayo	Costello	Annagh	Claremorris	IV.	138
21, 26	Coolnafearagh	629 3 18	Kildare	Offaly West	Monasterevin	Athy	I.	73
19	Coolnafinnoge	28 3 32	Longford	Ardagh	Kilglass	Ballymahon	I.	152
29	Coolnafranky	89 0 33	Tyrone	Dungannon Upper	Derryloran	Cookstown	III.	306
35	Coolnagard Lower	21 3 14	Tyrone	Omagh East	Drumragh	Omagh	III.	312
35	Coolnagard Upper	130 0 23	Tyrone	Omagh East	Drumragh	Omagh	III.	312
58	Coolnagarrahy	53 1 5	Kerry	Magunihy	Kilcummin	Killarney	II.	201
141, 142	Coolnagarrane	310 3 16	Cork, W.R.	West Carbery (E.D.)	Abbeystrowry	Skibbereen	II.	136
112	Coolnagaug	56 1 31	Cork, E.R.	Kinalea	Kilmonoge	Kinsale	II.	95
134	Coolnagay	315 3 8	Cork, W.R.	East Carbery (W.D.)	Castleventry	Clonakilty	II.	131
71	Coolnagearagh	293 0 37c	Cork, W.R.	East Muskerry	Aghinagh	Macroom	II.	153
45, 48	Coolnageer	578 2 7	Roscommon	Athlone	Cam	Athlone	IV.	179
117	Coolnageeragh	204 3 13	Galway	Longford	Lickmolassy	Portumna	IV.	60
40, 49	Coolnageragh	556 2 34	Kerry	Trughanacmy	Castleisland	Tralee	II.	208
39	Coolnagillagh Lower	202 1 14	Cork, W.R.	West Muskerry	Drishane	Millstreet	II.	156
39	Coolnagillagh Upper	335 0 32	Cork, W.R.	West Muskerry	Drishane	Millstreet	II.	156
3	Coolnagloose	203 0 31	Wexford	Gorey	Kilcavan	Gorey	I.	317
9, 10	Coolnagoppoge	749 3 17	Antrim	Cary	Culfeightrin	Ballycastle	III.	13
44	Coolnagoppoge	434 2 16	Kerry	Corkaguiny	Ballynacourty	Dingle	II.	174
102, 103	Coolnagoppoge	757 3 13	Kerry	Glanarought	Kilcaskan	Kenmare	II.	186
94, 95	Coolnagoppoge	466 1 5	Kerry	Glanarought	Kilgarvan	Kenmare	II.	187
26	Coolnagoppoge	434 2 33	Waterford	Middlethird	Drumcannon	Waterford	II.	366
25	Coolnagor or Ricehill	128 1 18	Cavan	Upper Loughtee	Kilmore	Cavan	III.	84
1	Coolnagour	229 1 22	Cork, E.R.	Orrery and Kilmore	Kilbolane	Kanturk	II.	108
16	Coolnagour	168 1 29	Queen's Co.	Upperwoods	Offerlane	Mountmellick	I.	251
30, 35	Coolnagour	282 2 15	Waterford	Decies without Drum	Dungarvan	Dungarvan	II.	355
6	Coolnagraigue	292 1 38	Kerry	Iraghticonnor	Aghavallen	Listowel	II.	189
23	Coolnagrane	78 3 8	Fermanagh	Magherastephana	Aghavea	Lisnaskea	III.	218
5	Coolnagranshy	70 1 9	Roscommon	Boyle	Boyle	Boyle	IV.	194
29, 32	Coolnagrattan	154 1 37	Monaghan	Farney	Donaghmoyne	Carrickmacross	III.	269
31	Coolnagree	397 0 24	Wexford	Bantry	Doonooney	Wexford	I.	300
35, 38	Coolnagrower	344 0 10	King's Co.	Ballybritt	Birr	Parsonstown	I.	125
15	Coolnagrower	274 2 35	Tipperary, N.R.	Lower Ormond	Modreeny	Borrisokane	II.	286
59	Coolnagun	132 2 21	Tipperary, S.R.	Clanwilliam	Donohill	Tipperary	II.	307
59	Coolnagun	12 3 33	Tipperary, S.R.	Clanwilliam	Rathlynin	Tipperary	II.	309
59	Coolnagun	95 0 32	Tipperary, S.R.	Clanwilliam	Templenoe	Tipperary	II.	311
2, 6	Coolnagun	974 1 16d	Westmeath	Moygoish	Street	Granard	I.	281
31, 32	Coolnahane	484 1 5e	Cork, E.R.	Duhallow	Castlemagner	Kanturk	II.	67
82, 93	Coolnaha North	435 2 23	Mayo	Costello	Aghamore	Swineford	IV.	137
63	CoolnaharragillLower	137 3 36	Kerry	Iveragh	Glanbehy	Cahersiveen	II.	195
63	CoolnaharragillUpper	420 3 16	Kerry	Iveragh	Glanbehy	Cahersiveen	II.	195

(a) Including 2A. 3R. 32P. River Barrow.   (c) Including 4A. 3R. 18P. water.   (e) Including 16A. 0R. 32P. water.
(b) Including 4A. 2R. 28P. water.   (d) Including 5A. 3R. 18P. water.

No. of Sheet of the Ordnance Survey Maps.	Townlands and Towns.	Area in Statute Acres. A. R. P.	County.	Barony.	Parish.	Poor Law Union in 1857.	Townland Census of 1851, Part I. Vol.	Page
93	Coolnaha South	631 1 18a	Mayo	Costello	Aghamore	Swineford	IV.	137
36	Coolnahau	522 2 1	Kilkenny	Knocktopher	Jerpoint West	New Ross	I.	111
29, 38	Coolnahavil	42 2 25	Tyrone	Dungannon Upper	Derryloran	Cookstown	III.	306
18	Coolnahay	280 0 27	Westmeath	Moygoish	Templeoran	Mullingar	I.	281
36	Coolnahella	135 2 0	Clare	Tulla Lower	Killuran	Tulla	II.	36
8	Coolnahely	618 0 22	King's Co.	Ballycowan	Durrow	Tullamore	I.	127
67	Coolnaherin	59 0 2	Tipperary, S.R.	Clanwilliam	Clonpet	Tipperary	II.	306
67	Coolnaherin	99 0 28	Tipperary, S.R.	Clanwilliam	Cordangan	Tipperary	II.	306
24	Coolnaherin Park	81 0 27	Tyrone	Omagh West	Ardstraw	Castlederg	III.	315
6	Coolnahila (Palmer)	271 2 8	Limerick	Owneybeg	Abington	Limerick	II.	250
6	Coolnahila (Powell)	199 3 5	Limerick	Owneybeg	Abington	Limerick	II.	250
15, 16	Coolnahilla	135 1 30	Cork, E.R.	Duhallow	Kilbrin	Kanturk	II.	72
14	Coolnahinch	132 2 27	King's Co.	Garrycastle	Gallen	Parsonstown	I.	136
14	Coolnahinch	121 3 15	Longford	Ardagh	Templemichael	Longford	I.	153
18, 22	Coolnahinch	318 1 36b	Longford	Moydow	Kilcommock	Ballymahon	I.	161
4, 5	Coolnahinch	303 3 9	Meath	Lower Kells	Moynalty	Kells	I.	203
11, 12	Coolnahinch	165 2 11	Wexford	Ballaghkeen	Kilmakilloge	Gorey	I.	296
7	Coolnahorna	724 2 11	Waterford	Upperthird	Mothel	Carrick on Suir	II.	371
20	Coolnahorna	590 0 31c	Wexford	Scarawalsh	Monart	Enniscorthy	I.	324
11	Coolnakeeran	190 2 19	Carlow	Idrone West	Oldleighlin	Carlow	I.	9
35, 44	Coolnakilla	1,155 0 29	Cork, E.R.	Barrymore	Rathcormack	Fermoy	II.	57
24, 25	Coolnakilly	356 3 25	Wicklow	Newcastle	Glenealy	Rathdrum	I.	351
11, 12	Coolnakisha	1,307 1 11	Carlow	Idrone West	Tullowcreen	Carlow	I.	9
45, 54	Coolnaknockane	155 0 39	Limerick	Connello Upper	Cloncrew	Newcastle	II.	232
10	Coolnalaght	111 3 5	Kerry	Iraghticonnor	Listowel	Listowel	II.	192
2	Coolnaleen	430 1 1	Kilkenny	Fassadinin	Castlecomer	Castlecomer	I.	88
10, 11	Coolnaleen	547 3 5	Wexford	Scarawalsh	Kilcomb	Gorey	I.	323
10, 16	Coolnaleen Lower	229 2 33	Kerry	Clanmaurice	Kilshenane	Listowel	II.	171
10, 16, 17	Coolnaleen Upper	269 0 19	Kerry	Clanmaurice	Kilshenane	Listowel	II.	171
6, 7	Coolnalingady	367 1 19	Waterford	Upperthird	Mothel	Carrick on Suir	II.	371
53	Coolnalira	209 2 10	Clare	Tulla Lower	O'Briensbridge	Limerick	II.	38
15	Coolnalitteragh	93 2 14d	Cavan	Tullygarvey	Annagh	Cavan	III.	87
36	Coolnalong	53 0 29	Fermanagh	Clankelly	Clones	Clones	III.	195
16, 17	Coolnalong	179 2 2e	Monaghan	Dartree	Killevan	Clones	III.	267
32	Coolnamagh	156 0 9	Cork, E.R.	Duhallow	Ballyclogh	Mallow	II.	67
32	Coolnamagh	138 1 35	Cork, E.R.	Duhallow	Castlemagner	Kanturk	II.	67
24	Coolnamara	267 2 33	Carlow	St. Mullins Lower	Ullard	New Ross	I.	13
35	Coolnamarrow	71 3 38f	Fermanagh	Clankelly	Clones	Clones	III.	195
10	Coolnambrisklaun or Coolnacoppoge	130 2 8	Kilkenny	Fassadinin	Kilmacar	Castlecomer	I.	90
57	Coolnamohoge	517 3 10	Limerick	Coshlea	Kilbeheny	Mitchelstown	II.	239
25	Coolnamona	363 2 7	Limerick	Coonagh	Castletown	Tipperary	II.	234
12	Coolnanav	347 1 21	Queen's Co.	Maryborough East	Clonenagh&Clonagheen	Mountmellick	I.	241
30	Coolnamonan	372 3 4	Londonderry	Tirkeeran	Banagher	New T.Limavady	III.	247
40, 46	Coolnamoney	193 2 27	Tipperary, N.R.	Kilnamanagh Upper	Moyaliff	Thurles	II.	279
2	Coolnamony Lower	36 3 38	Queen's Co.	Tinnahinch	Rearymore	Mountmellick	I.	249
2, 6	Coolnamony Upper	562 1 26	Queen's Co.	Tinnahinch	Rearymore	Mountmellick	I.	249
33	Coolnamuck	493 3 11	Kilkenny	Ida	Clonamery	Thomastown	I.	101
3	Coolnamuck Demesne	319 3 12g	Waterford	Upperthird	Dysert	Carrick on Suir	II.	369
3	Coolnamuck East	322 2 21	Waterford	Upperthird	Dysert	Carrick on Suir	II.	369
3	Coolnamuck West	257 0 19	Waterford	Upperthird	Dysert	Carrick on Suir	II.	369
15	Coolnamunna	432 2 26	Tipperary, N.R.	Lower Ormond	Modreeny	Borrisokane	II.	286
30	Coolnanav	116 1 5	Waterford	Decies without Drum	Whitechurch	Dungarvan	II.	361
10, 11, 19	Coolnanave	403 1 15	Cork, E.R.	Condons&Clangibbon	Brigown	Mitchelstown	II.	59
20	Coolnaneagh	144 1 5	Waterford	Coshmore&Coshbride	Lismore and Mocollop	Lismore	II.	345
53	Coolnanoglagh	289 0 34	Limerick	Glenquin	Monagay	Newcastle	II.	247
3	Coolnanoonagh	178 1 1	Kerry	Iraghticonnor	Kilnaughtin	Glin	II.	191
16	Coolnapish	59 3 30	Carlow	Idrone East	Dunleckny	Carlow	I.	6
18	Coolnapisha	38 1 23	Kilkenny	Crannagh	Tullaroan	Kilkenny	I.	88
24	Coolnapisha	130 1 39	Limerick	Coonagh	Doon	Tipperary	II.	234
24	Coolnapisha	357 0 14	Limerick	Coonagh	Oola	Tipperary	II.	235
71, 83	Coolnashamroge	146 0 29	Cork, E.R.	East Muskerry	Cannaway	Macroom	II.	102
23	Coolnashamroge	196 3 22	Limerick	Clanwilliam	Aglishcormick	Limerick	II.	221
27	Coolnashanton	113 1 1h	Fermanagh	Tirkennedy	Derrybrusk	Enniskillen	III.	220
17	Coolnasheegan	108 0 17	Carlow	Forth	Myshall	Carlow	I.	5
49	Coolnashinnagh	85 1 33	Tipperary, S.R.	Slievardagh	Ballingarry	Callan	II.	331
19	Coolnashinny or Croaghan	132 2 2i	Cavan	Tullyhunco	Kildallan	Cavan	III.	96
35	Coolnasillagh	337 0 30	Fermanagh	Clankelly	Galloon	Clones	III.	198
17, 18	Coolnasillagh	1,168 2 7	Londonderry	Coleraine	Errigal	Coleraine	III.	232
35, 36	Coolnasillagh	754 0 17	Londonderry	Loughinsholin	Ballynascreen	Magherafelt	III.	239
8	Coolnaskeagh	125 1 30	Wicklow	Rathdown	Delgany	Rathdown	I.	355
22, 23	Coolnasmear Lower	323 2 32	Waterford	Decies without Drum	Kilgobnet	Dungarvan	II.	357

(a) Including 63A. 0R. 23P. water.
(b) Including 19A. 3R. 24P. water.
(c) Including 7A. 0R. 12P. water.
(d) Including 10A. 1R. 20P. water.

(e) Including 5A. 3R. 16P. water.
(f) Including 10A. 3R. 23P. water.
(g) { Including 8A. 1R. 4P. River Suir.
{ Including 7A. 1R. 18P. Lake.

(h) Including 20A. 1R. 15P. water.
(i) Including 9A. 2R. 27P. water.

No. of Sheet of the Ordnance Survey Maps.	Townlands and Towns.	Area in Statute Acres.	County.	Barony.	Parish.	Poor Law Union in 1857.	Townland Census of 1851, Part I.	
		A. R. P.					Vol.	Page
23	Coolnasmearmountain	492 1 26	Waterford	Decies without Drum	Kilgobnet	Dungarvan	II.	357
23	Coolnasmear Upper	390 3 1	Waterford	Decies without Drum	Kilgobnet	Dungarvan	II.	357
21	Coolnasmuttaun	109 3 36	Waterford	Coshmore&Coshbride	Lismore & Mocollop	Lismore	II.	345
71	Coolnasoon	125 1 12	Cork, E.R.	East Muskerry	Cannaway	Macroom	II.	102
11	Coolnastudd	243 3 37	Wexford	Gorey	Kilnahue	Gorey	I.	319
6	Coolnatullagh	368 0 12	Clare	Burren	Carran	Ballyvaghan	II.	11
6	Coolnatullagh	270 1 14	Clare	Burren	Oughtmama	Ballyvaghan	II.	14
4, 8	Coolnavarnoge and Coolaghy	1,316 2 7	Queen's Co.	Portnahinch	Coolbanagher	Mountmellick	I.	244
11, 12	Coolnaveagh	226 0 39	Wexford	Ballaghkeen	Kilmakilloge	Gorey	I.	296
15	Coolock	65 3 25	Dublin	Coolock	Coolock	Dublin North	I.	27
15	COOLOCK T.	—	Dublin	Coolock	Coolock	Dublin North	I.	27
5, 8	Coolodonnell	435 0 19	Leitrim	Rosclogher	Rossinver	Manorhamilton	IV.	111
13	Coologe	265 1 8a	Cavan	Tullyhaw	Templeport	Bawnboy	III.	94
26	Coologe	146 1 0	Kilkenny	Kells	Coolaghmore	Callan	I.	107
30	Coologe	248 3 33	King's Co.	Eglish	Eglish	Parsonstown	I.	134
24	Coologe	231 0 27	Limerick	Coonagh	Grean	Tipperary	II.	235
22	Coologe	23 2 0?	Limerick	Pubblebrien	Croom	Croom	II.	252
22, 28	Coologe	226 0 34	Tipperary, N.R.	Upper Ormond	Aghnameadle	Nenagh	II.	288
67, 74	Coologe	74 0 1	Tipperary, S.R.	Clanwilliam	Templeneiry	Tipperary	II.	311
85	Coologes	994 1 31	Kerry	Glanarought	Kilgarvan	Kenmare	II.	187
9	Coologmartin	661 0 16	Kildare	Clane	Timahoe	Naas	I.	54
20, 28	Coologory	895 0 18	Clare	Tulla Upper	Tomgraney	Scarriff	II.	41
87	Coololla	361 0 23c	Galway	Kilconnell	Aughrim	Ballinasloe	IV.	39
44, 45	Cooloo	984 3 35	Galway	Tiaquin	Moylough	Mountbellew	IV.	79
17	Coolook Beg	145 1 36	Wexford	Ballaghkeen	Killenagh	Gorey	I.	295
17	Coolook More	369 1 37	Wexford	Ballaghkeen	Killenagh	Gorey	I.	295
45	Cooloo Mountain	380 0 27	Galway	Tiaquin	Moylough	Mountbellew	IV.	79
10	Cooloorta	608 1 9d	Clare	Inchiquin	Killinaboy	Corrofin	II.	26
44, 58	Cooloorta	73 1 29	Galway	Tiaquin	Abbeyknockmoy	Tuam	IV.	75
77, 78	Cooloran	148 3 22	Tipperary, S.R.	Iffa and Offa East	Temple-etney	Clonmel	II.	316
26	Coolougher	258 1 5	Roscommon	Castlereagh	Kiltullagh	Castlereagh	IV.	201
47	Cooloughter	109 2 4	Wexford	Forth	Mayglass	Wexford	I.	312
3, 8	Cooloultha or Money-namuck	465 1 23	Kilkenny	Galmoy	Erke	Urlingford	I.	92
62, 63	Coolowen	1,033 2 33	Cork, E.R.	Cork	Whitechurch	Cork	II.	66
28	Coolowen	324 2 38	Waterford	Coshmore&Coshbride	Lismore and Mocollop	Lismore	II.	345
28	Coolowen Little	59 0 10	Waterford	Coshmore&Coshbride	Lismore and Mocollop	Lismore	II.	345
27	Coolowley (Mason)	317 3 23	Queen's Co.	Clandonagh	Rathdowney	Donaghmore	I.	234
27	Coolowley (Plott)	278 2 6	Queen's Co.	Clandonagh	Rathdowney	Donaghmore	I.	234
108	Coolownig	165 2 20	Kerry	Glanarought	Tuosist	Kenmare	II.	188
30, 44	Coolpark	195 3 18	Galway	Dunmore	Tuam	Tuam	IV.	36
42	Coolpeach	33 0 27	Wexford	Forth	Drinagh	Wexford	I.	309
8, 15, 16	Coolpeekaun	107 3 20	Clare	Corcomroe	Kilfenora	Ennistimon	II.	19
117	Coolpowra	362 1 8	Galway	Longford	Lickmolassy	Portumna	IV.	60
15	Coolpuck	217 3 32	Wexford	Scarawalsh	Ferns	Enniscorthy	I.	323
53	Coolquane	459 3 9	Cork, E.R.	Barrymore	Kilshanihan	Fermoy	II.	56
54	Coolquill	363 3 12	Tipperary, S.R.	Slievardagh	Crohane	Callan	II.	332
11	Coolquoy	91 0 24	Dublin	Nethercross	Kilsallaghan	Balrothery	I.	31
11	Coolquoy Common	159 1 28	Dublin	Nethercross	Kilsallaghan	Balrothery	I.	31
11	Coolraheen	188 2 6	Kilkenny	Fassadinin	Muckalee	Castlecomer	I.	90
41	Coolraheen	334 0 21	Wexford	Shelmaliere West	Taghmon	Wexford	I.	335
11	Coolraheen North	472 3 6	Kilkenny	Fassadinin	Mothel	Castlecomer	I.	90
11	Coolraheen South	660 2 38	Kilkenny	Fassadinin	Mothel	Castlecomer	I.	90
10, 11	Coolrahnee	208 2 15	Limerick	Connello Lower	Askeaton	Rathkeale	II.	226
32	Coolrain	63 0 6	Queen's Co.	Slievemargy	Killabban	Carlow	I.	245
32	Coolrain	133 0 35	Queen's Co.	Slievemargy	Killeshin	Carlow	I.	245
16	Coolrain	345 1 28	Queen's Co.	Upperwoods	Offerlane	Mountmellick	I.	251
5	Coolraine	216 1 14	Limerick	Pubblebrien	St. Munchins	Limerick	II.	254
33	Coolrainey	177 1 21	Wexford	Shelmaliere East	St. Margaret's	Wexford	I.	331
16	COOLRAIN T.	—	Queen's Co.	Upperwoods	Offerlane	Mountmellick	I.	252
32	Coolrainy	347 0 38	Kilkenny	Gowran	Inistioge	Thomastown	I.	96
33	Coolrainy	172 0 36	Kilkenny	Ida	The Rower	Thomastown	I.	104
38	Coolrake	299 1 8	Kildare	Kilkea and Moone	Killelan	Baltinglass	I.	60
23	Coolrakelly	236 1 37	Fermanagh	Magherastephana	Aghavea	Lisnaskea	III.	218
10	Coolranny	81 0 38	Antrim	Cary	Culfeightrin	Ballycastle	III.	13
11	Coolrath	33 2 11	Louth	Louth	Louth	Dundalk	I.	184
16	Coolrattin	72 3 18	Waterford	Middlethird	Dunhill	Waterford	II.	366
96	Coolraugh	252 3 22	Galway	Dunkellin	Lickerrig	Loughrea	IV.	31
42	Coolrawer	1,055 3 3	Sligo	Leyny	Achonry	Tobercurry	IV.	229
28, 36	Coolready	294 1 29e	Clare	Tulla Upper	Kilnoe	Scarriff	II.	40
1	Coolready	880 1 1	Limerick	Clanwilliam	Cuadbally	Limerick	II.	280
28	Coolreagh	615 1 24	Clare	Tulla Upper	Kilnoe	Scarriff	II.	40

(a) Including 50A. 0R. 15P. water.
(b) Including 2A. 0R. 32P. water.
(c) Including 8A. 1R. 1P. water.
(d) Including 17A. 1R. 27P. water.
(e) Including 7A. 1R. 11P. water.

No. of Sheet of the Ordnance Survey Maps.	Townlands and Towns.	Area in Statute Acres.			County.	Barony.	Parish.	Poor Law Union in 1857.	Townland Census of 1851, Part I.	
		A.	R.	P.					Vol.	Page
18, 23	Coolreagh .	151	0	23a	Kildare .	Connell .	Oldconnell .	Naas .	I.	56
14	Coolreagh .	60	2	35	Limerick .	Clanwilliam .	Cahernarry .	Limerick .	II.	222
46, 47	Coolreagh .	306	2	35	Limerick .	Connello Upper .	Bruree .	Kilmallock .	II.	231
31	Coolreagh .	138	0	7	Monaghan .	Farney .	Killanny .	Carrickmacross	III.	271
28	Coolreagh Beg	455	1	9b	Clare .	Tulla Upper .	Kilnoe .	Scarriff .	II.	40
22	Coolreagh or Cloghanhill .	955	3	22	King's Co.	Garrycastle .	Gallen .	Parsonstown .	I.	136
24, 31, 32	Coolreagh Glebe	123	3	10	King's Co.	Ballyboy .	Ballyboy .	Parsonstown .	I.	123
28	Coolreagh More	624	1	6c	Clare .	Tulla Upper .	Kilnoe .	Scarriff .	II.	40
29	Coolreaghs .	262	1	21	Tyrone .	Dungannon Upper .	Derryloran .	Cookstown .	III.	307
29	Coolreaghs .	42	3	6	Tyrone .	Dungannon Upper .	Lissan .	Cookstown .	III.	309
36, 37, 42	Coolrecuill .	1,321	0	27	Sligo .	Leyny .	Kilmacteige .	Tobercurry .	IV.	231
4	Coolree .	341	0	8	Kildare .	Carbury .	Dunfierth .	Edenderry .	I.	52
13	Coolree .	387	2	1d	Kildare .	Clane .	Downings .	Naas .	I.	54
37, 42	Coolree .	45	1	5	Wexford .	Forth .	St. Peters .	Wexford .	I.	314
14, 19	Coolree .	569	3	12	Wexford .	Scarawalsh .	Templeshanbo .	Enniscorthy .	I.	326
1	Coolreiry .	149	0	16	Limerick .	Clanwilliam .	Stradbally .	Limerick .	II.	226
31	Coolremony .	69	1	9	Monaghan .	Farney .	Killanny .	Carrickmacross	III.	271
44	Coolrevagh .	293	3	36	Galway .	Clare .	Killererin .	Tuam .	IV.	21
14, 18	Coolroe .	557	0	29	Carlow .	St. Mullins Upper .	Moyacomb .	Carlow .	I.	14
35	Coolroe .	389	1	8e	Cork, E.R.	Condons&Clangibbon	Litter .	Fermoy .	II.	62
73	Coolroe .	234	2	22f	Cork, E.R.	East Muskerry .	Carrigrohane .	Cork .	II.	102
36	Coolroe .	109	1	13	Kerry .	Corkaguiny .	Killiney .	Dingle .	II.	178
65, 73	Coolroe .	1,068	0	13	Kerry .	Dunkerron North .	Knockane .	Killarney .	II.	181
34, 35	Coolroe .	198	3	32	Kildare .	Narragh&RebanWest	Churchtown .	Athy .	I.	67
29	Coolroe .	910	1	32	Kilkenny .	Gowran .	Graiguenamanagh .	Thomastown .	I.	95
32	Coolroe .	428	3	35	Kilkenny .	Gowran .	Inistioge .	Thomastown .	I.	96
41, 44	Coolroe .	203	0	29	King's Co.	Clonlisk .	Dunkerrin .	Roscrea .	I.	130
42, 43	Coolroe .	320	3	35	King's Co.	Clonlisk .	Ettagh .	Roscrea .	I.	130
47, 48	Coolroe .	115	0	19	Limerick .	Kilmallock .	St. Peter's&St.Paul's	Kilmallock .	II.	250
111	Coolroe .	198	1	16	Mayo .	Clanmorris .	Crossboyne .	Claremorris .	IV.	132
9	Coolroe .	471	1	25	Queen's Co.	Portnahinch .	Lea .	Mountmellick .	I.	244
35, 36	Coolroe .	700	1	32	Waterford .	Decies within Drum	Ardmore .	Dungarvan .	II.	350
22	Coolroe .	125	2	39	Waterford .	Decies without Drum	Modelligo .	Lismore .	II.	359
8	Coolroe .	590	0	23	Waterford .	Upperthird .	Clonagam .	Carrick on Suir	II.	369
3	Coolroe .	217	1	15	Waterford .	Upperthird .	Mothel .	Carrick on Suir	II.	371
22	Coolroe .	334	2	21	Wexford .	Ballaghkeen .	Killincooly .	Gorey .	I.	295
25, 31	Coolroe .	336	3	2	Wexford .	Bantry .	Chapel .	Enniscorthy .	I.	299
15	Coolroe .	84	0	19	Wexford .	Scarawalsh .	Ferns .	Enniscorthy .	I.	323
40, 45	Coolroe .	433	3	9	Wexford .	Shelburne .	Tintern .	New Ross .	I.	329
43	Coolroe .	751	3	21	Wicklow .	Shillelagh .	Crosspatrick .	Shillelagh .	I.	357
31, 40	Coolroe Beg .	392	1	5	Cork, E.R.	Duhallow .	Clonmeen .	Kanturk .	II.	69
32	Coolroebeg .	320	2	23	Kilkenny .	Knocktopher .	Jerpointchurch .	Thomastown .	I.	111
82	Coolroe East .	287	1	0	Cork, W.R.	West Muskerry .	Inchigeelagh .	Dunmanway .	II.	157
58	Coolroe East .	323	1	13	Kerry .	Magunihy .	Aglish .	Killarney .	II.	199
3	Coolroe Great .	176	0	10	Wexford .	Gorey .	Kilgorman .	Gorey .	I.	318
3	Coolroe Little .	112	1	22	Wexford .	Gorey .	Kilgorman .	Gorey .	I.	318
63	Coolroe Lower .	242	3	29	Kerry .	Iveragh .	Glanbehy .	Cahersiveen .	II.	195
40	Coolroe More .	1,159	3	35	Cork, E.R.	Duhallow .	Clonmeen .	Kanturk .	II.	69
57	Coolroe North .	256	0	35	Kerry .	Magunihy .	Kilbonane .	Killarney .	II.	200
57	Coolroe South .	275	3	8g	Kerry .	Magunihy .	Kilbonane .	Killarney .	II.	200
63, 71	Coolroe Upper .	506	1	15	Kerry .	Iveragh .	Glanbehy .	Cahersiveen .	II.	195
81	Coolroe West .	104	1	33	Cork, W.R.	West Muskerry .	Inchigeelagh .	Dunmanway .	II.	157
58	Coolroe West .	110	1	6	Kerry .	Magunihy .	Aglish .	Killarney .	II.	199
20	Coolroghaun .	110	0	28	Galway .	Ballymoe .	Kilbegnet .	Roscommon .	IV.	8
29, 35	Coolronan .	2,684	3	14	Meath .	Lune .	Killaconnigan .	Trim .	I.	208
1, 2	Coolross .	1,251	2	12	Tipperary, N.R.	Lower Ormond .	Dorrha .	Parsonstown .	II.	283
31	Coolross .	153	2	16	Tipperary, N.R.	Owney and Arra .	Kilvellane .	Nenagh .	II.	296
38, 43	Coolross .	264	1	39	Wicklow .	Ballinacor South .	Kilcommon .	Shillelagh .	I.	349
42, 46	Coolross .	425	3	8	Wicklow .	Shillelagh .	Moyacomb .	Shillelagh .	I.	358
32	Coolruntha .	542	1	39	Tipperary, N.R.	Owney and Arra .	Killoscully .	Nenagh .	II.	295
38	Coolrus .	1,030	0	9	Limerick .	Connello Upper .	Ballingarry .	Croom .	II.	230
25	Coolrusk .	137	1	32	Queen's Co.	Stradbally .	Tullomoy .	Athy .	I.	248
70	Cools .	126	2	39	Cork, W.R.	West Muskerry .	Kilnamartry .	Macroom .	II.	159
88, 97	Cools .	726	0	4	Kerry .	Iveragh .	Prior .	Cahersiveen .	II.	198
67	Cools .	375	0	2	Kerry .	Magunihy .	Aghadoe .	Killarney .	II.	199
53	Cools .	22	3	31h	Wexford .	Forth .	Carn .	Wexford .	I.	309
36,37,41,42	Cools .	148	1	19	Wexford .	Shelmaliere West .	Coolstuff .	Wexford .	I.	333
36,37,41,42	Cools .	488	3	30	Wexford .	Shelmaliere West .	Kilbridcglynn .	Wexford .	I.	334
98	Coolsallagh .	273	2	9	Cork, E.R.	Kerrycurrihy .	Liscleary .	Kinsale .	II.	92
20	Coolsallagh .	671	3	27	Down .	Lower Iveagh, Lr.pt.	Dromore .	Banbridge .	III.	168
42	Coolsallagh .	186	1	26	Wexford .	Bargy .	Kilmannan .	Wexford .	I.	306
41 .	Coolsaragh .	526	0	16	Londonderry .	Loughinsholin .	Kilcronaghan .	Magherafelt .	III.	241

(a) Including 4A. 3R. 22P. water.
(b) Including 19A. 3R. 11P. water.
(c) Including 1A. 1R. 31P. water.
(d) Including 2A. 2R. 35P. Reservoir.
(e) Including 3A. 1R. 24P. water.
(f) Including 4A. 1R. 20P. water.
(g) Including 3A. 0R. 7P. water.
(h) Including 11A. 1R. 5P. detached portion.

No. of Sheet of the Ordnance Survey Maps	Townlands and Towns	Area in Statute Acres.	County.	Barony.	Parish.	Poor Law Union in 1857.	Townland Census of 1851, Part I.	
		A. R. P.					Vol.	Page
32, 40	Coolscart	175 0 18	Limerick .	Smallcounty .	Hospital .	Kilmallock	II.	260
17	Coolscuddan	163 3 19	Dublin	Newcastle	Kilmactalway .	Celbridge .	I.	33
46	Coolseskin	172 0 6	Wexford .	Bargy	Bannow .	Wexford .	I.	304
36, 40	Coolshaghtena	672 0 7	Roscommon	Ballintober South	Cloontuskert	Roscommon	IV.	188
34, 42	Coolshamroge	118 1 27	Clare	Bunratty Upper	Quin	Ennis	II.	10
92	Coolshangan .	142 2 39	Donegal .	Banagh .	Inver	Donegal .	III.	107
9	Coolshannagh .	132 1 31	Monaghan	Monaghan	Monaghan	Monaghan	III.	276
97	Coolsheskin	81 1 16	Cork, E.R.	Kinalea	Dunderrow	Kinsale	II.	94
110, 123	Coolshinagh .	181 0 7	Cork, W.R.	East Carbery (E.D.)	Kilbrittain	Bandon	II.	128
24	Coolshingaun .	260 2 25	Clare	Inchiquin	Inagh	Ennistimon	II.	25
41,42,46,47	Coolshinny	311 0 22	Londonderry	Loughinsholin	Magherafelt	Magherafelt	III.	243
21	Coolsickin or Quinsborough	617 2 16	Kildare .	Offaly West	Lackagh .	Athy	I.	73
32	Coolsillagh .	55 3 18	Kilkenny .	Gowran .	Inistioge .	Thomastown	I.	96
25	Coolskeagh	131 1 18a	Monaghan	Farney	Donaghmoyne	Castleblayney	III.	269
34	Coolskeagh	147 0 30	Sligo	Tirerrill .	Drumcolumb .	Sligo	IV.	238
93, 107	Coolsnaghtig .	613 2 36	Cork, W.R.	East Carbery (W.D.)	Fanlobbus	Dunmanway	II.	131
95	Coolsrahra .	172 1 20	Galway .	Dunkellin .	Ballynacourty	Galway .	IV.	27
95	Coolsrahra .	131 3 0	Galway .	Dunkellin .	Stradbally	Galway .	IV.	32
36, 41	Coolstuff	155 0 28	Wexford .	Shelmaliere West .	Coolstuff	Wexford .	I.	333
49, 50, 59	Coolsuppeen .	217 2 9	Clare	Clonderalaw .	Kilchreest	Killadysert	II.	15
43	Coolsythe .	310 3 20	Antrim .	Upper Toome .	Drummaul	Ballymena	III.	34
36	Cooltacker .	84 0 32	Roscommon	Ballintober South .	Kilgefin .	Roscommon	IV.	189
4, 5	Cooltedery .	764 0 17	Queen's Co.	Portnahinch .	Lea	Mountmellick .	I.	244
26	Coolteen .	125 0 9b	Sligo	Tirerrill .	Ballysadare	Sligo	IV.	237
36	Coolteen .	115 1 31	Wexford .	Shelmaliere West .	Kilbrideglynn .	Wexford .	I.	334
59	Coolteengowan .	246 1 19	Clare	Clonderalaw .	Killadysert	Killadysert	II.	15
18	Cooltegin .	118 0 25	Waterford .	Gaultiere .	Crooke .	Waterford .	II.	362
35, 36	Coolteige .	1,681 2 12	Roscommon	Ballintober South .	Kilbride .	Roscommon	IV.	189
25, 26	Coolteige .	242 2 39	Wexford .	Shelmaliere West .	Clonmore .	Enniscorthy	I.	333
6	Coolthawn .	109 2 15	Wexford .	Gorey .	Kilnahue .	Gorey .	I.	319
19	Cooltomin .	567 2 35	Limerick .	Shanid .	Kilbradran .	Rathkeale	II.	255
42	Cooltona .	116 3 26c	Roscommon	Athlone .	Kilmeane .	Roscommon	IV.	182
13	Cooltoran .	192 0 22	Queen's Co.	Maryborough East .	Borris .	Mountmellick .	I.	240
16, 22	Cooltrain .	161 0 19	Fermanagh	Tirkennedy .	Magheracross .	Enniskillen	III.	223
23, 24	Cooltrane .	73 1 33	Fermanagh	Magherastephana .	Aghalurcher .	Lisnaskea .	III.	215
24, 27	Cooltrim .	263 1 7	Monaghan	Cremorne .	Aghnamullen .	Castleblayney .	III.	257
24	Cooltrimegish .	251 0 39d	Monaghan	Cremorne .	Aghnamullen .	Castleblayney .	III.	257
9	Cooltrim North .	157 3 1	Kildare .	Ikeathy&Oughterany	Donadea .	Celbridge .	I.	57
9	Cooltrim South .	313 1 35	Kildare .	Ikeathy&Oughterany	Donadea .	Celbridge .	I.	57
15	Cooltubbrid East .	15 1 25	Waterford	Decies without Drum	Ballylaneen .	Kilmacthomas .	II.	354
15, 24	Cooltubbrid West .	178 2 17	Waterford	Decies without Drum	Ballylaneen	Kilmacthomas .	II.	354
28,29,37,38	Coolturk .	1,261 0 16e	Mayo .	Tirawley .	Crossmolina .	Ballina .	IV.	165
33	Cooltycanon .	725 0 16	King's Co.	Upper Philipstown .	Clonyhurk .	Mountmellick .	I.	143
99	Cooltymurraghy .	327 1 23	Galway .	Clonmacnowen .	Killallaghtan .	Ballinasloe	IV.	26
87	Cooltymurraghy .	429 0 7	Galway .	Kilconnell .	Aughrim .	Ballinasloe	IV.	39
27	Coolum .	155 0 8	Waterford .	Gaultiere .	Corbally .	Waterford .	II.	362
27	Coolum .	207 1 18	Waterford	Gaultiere .	Rathmoylan .	Waterford .	II.	364
55	Coolumber .	396 1 16	Roscommon	Moycarn .	Moore .	Ballinasloe	IV.	206
27, 36	Cool Upper .	530 2 7	Donegal .	Kilmacrenan .	Kilmacrenan .	Milford .	III.	129
7	Coolure Demesne .	325 3 29	Westmeath	Fore .	Mayne .	Granard .	I.	271
17	Coolvackagh .	57 1 14f	Kerry .	Clanmaurice .	Duagh .	Listowel .	II.	168
111, 112	Coolvallanane Beg .	173 0 29	Cork, E.R.	Kinsale .	Clontead .	Kinsale .	II.	99
4, 11	Coolville .	158 3 37	King's Co.	Warrenstown .	Ballyburly .	Edenderry	I.	144
16	Coolvin .	226 0 9	Westmeath	Kilkenny West .	Noughaval .	Ballymahon .	I.	274
58	Coolvoy .	754 3 4	Donegal .	Boylagh .	Inishkeel .	Glenties .	III.	112
22, 23, 29	Coolvuck Lower .	274 0 20	Westmeath	Clonlonan .	Ballyloughloe .	Athlone .	I.	260
22,23,29,30	Coolvuck Upper .	186 3 38g	Westmeath	Clonlonan .	Ballyloughloe .	Athlone .	I.	260
78, 87	Cool West .	272 2 28	Kerry .	Iveragh .	Valencia .	Cahersiveen .	II.	198
35	Cool West .	643 0 26	Limerick .	Shanid .	Rathronan .	Newcastle .	II.	257
45	Coolwoneen .	98 2 28	Galway .	Tiaquin .	Moylough .	Mountbellew .	IV.	79
12, 21	Cooly .	866 1 18	Donegal .	Inishowen East .	Moville Upper .	Inishowen .	III.	119
39	Cooly .	456 1 32h	Roscommon	Athlone .	Fuerty .	Roscommon .	IV.	181
28	Coolybrown .	177 2 2	Limerick .	Connello Lower .	Kilscannell .	Rathkeale .	II.	228
46	Coolycall .	139 3 36	Wexford .	Bargy .	Kilcowan .	Wexford .	I.	305
14, 19	Coolycarney .	522 0 31	Wexford .	Scarawalsh .	Templeshanbo .	Enniscorthy .	I.	326
43, 52	Coolycasey .	514 0 5i	Clare .	Bunratty Lower .	Kilfinaghta .	Limerick .	II.	4
28	Coolydoody .	233 3 29	Waterford .	Coshmore&Coshbride	Lismore & Mocollop	Lismore .	II.	345
20, 28	Coolydoody North .	252 3 5	Waterford .	Coshmore&Coshbride	Lismore & Mocollop	Lismore .	II.	345
28	Coolydoody South .	232 0 23	Waterford .	Coshmore&Coshbride	Lismore & Mocollop	Lismore .	II.	345
73	Coolyduff .	449 1 34j	Cork, E.R.	East Muskerry .	Carrigrohanebeg .	Cork .	II.	107
21, 26	Coolyermer .	244 2 33k	Fermanagh	Clanawley .	Cleenish .	Enniskillen	III.	190
20, 28	Coolygagan .	416 3 16	King's Co.	Coolestown .	Clonsast .	Edenderry	I.	133

(a) Including 8A. 2R. 0P. water.
(b) Including 0A. 2R. 30P. water.
(c) Including 0A. 2R. 34P. detached portion.
(d) Including 12A. 2R. 15P. water.

(e) Including 5A. 0R. 22P. Brackloon Lough.
(f) Including 1A. 3R. 24P. water.
(g) Including 2A. 3R. 20P. water.
(h) Including 11A. 2R. 13P. water.

(i) Including 2A. 0R. 14P. water.
(j) Including 12A. 2R. 13P. water.
(k) Including 25A. 0R. 6P. water.

No. of Sheet of the Ordnance Survey Maps.	Townlands and Towns.	Area in Statute Acres.	County.	Barony.	Parish.	Poor Law Union in 1857.	Townland Census of 1851. Part I.	
		A. R. P.					Vol.	Page
44, 45	Coolygorman .	227 3 12	Limerick .	Glenquin	Mahoonagh	Newcastle	II.	246
71	Coolyhanc	288 1 1	Cork, W.R.	West Muskerry	Macroom	Macroom .	II.	160
13, 14	Coolyhenan	347 3 21	Limerick .	Clanwilliam	Derrygalvin	Limerick .	II.	223
13	Coolyhill	80 0 29	Armagh .	Orior Lower	Ballymore	Banbridge	III.	55
24	Coolyhune	590 1 4	Carlow	St. Mullins Lower .	St. Mullins	New Ross	I.	13
38, 39	Coolykeerane .	623 3 26a	Cork, E.R.	Duhallow	Drishane .	Millstreet	II.	71
22, 23	Coolykereen .	200 1 39	Cork, E.R.	Duhallow	Clonfert .	Kanturk .	II.	68
110	Coolylaughnan	345 3 30	Mayo	Kilmaine	Robeen	Ballinrobe	IV.	157
73	Coolymurraghue .	658 0 32	Cork, E.R.	Cork	Currykippane .	Cork	II.	64
27, 31	Coolyphullagh	328 0 2	Kildare	Offaly West	Kilrush .	Athy	I.	72
124	Coolyrahilly .	190 3 34	Cork, W.R.	Courceys	Ringrone	Kinsale .	II.	147
10, 11	Coolyregan .	579 3 0	Cork, E.R.	Condons&Clangibbon	Brigown .	Mitchelstown	II.	59
45	Coolyroe .	168 2 38	Limerick .	Glenquin	Mahoonagh	Newcastle	II.	246
79	Coolyslin .	158 0 34b	Donegal .	Raphoe .	Urney .	Strabane	III.	144
11	Coolyvenny .	365 3 11	Londonderry	Coleraine	Macosquin	Coleraine	III.	233
43, 52	Coom	882 2 27	Cork, E.R.	Barrymore	Dunbulloge	Cork	II.	54
114	Coom	684 3 32	Cork, W.R.	Bear	Kilnamanagh .	Castletown	II.	125
107	Coom	455 0 38	Cork, W.R.	East Carbery (W.D.)	Fanlobbus	Dunmanway	II.	131
97	Coom	258 0 28	Kerry	Iveragh .	Prior	Cahersiveen	II.	198
60	Coom	954 2 4	Kerry	Magunihy	Kilcummin	Killarney .	II.	201
40, 41	Coom	1,799 1 2	Kerry	Trughanacmy .	Ballincuslane .	Tralee	II.	206
47	Coomacheo .	2,157 0 12	Cork, W.R.	West Muskerry	Drishane	Millstreet	II.	156
92	Coomacroobeg	461 3 31	Cork, W.R.	Bantry	Kilmocomoge .	Bantry	II.	120
76, 86	Coomacullen .	1,076 3 34	Kerry	Magunihy	Killaha .	Killarney .	II.	202
87, 88	Coomakeoge .	168 0 18	Kerry	Iveragh .	Killemlagh	Cahersiveen	II.	196
87	Coomanaspig .	256 1 37	Kerry	Iveragh .	Killemlagh	Cahersiveen	II.	196
106	Coomanore North	428 2 5	Cork, W.R.	Bantry	Kilmocomoge .	Bantry	II.	120
106,119	Coomanore South	377 1 32	Cork, W.R.	Bantry	Kilmocomoge .	Bantry	II.	120
104	Coomarkane .	2,034 0 29c	Cork, W.R.	Bear	Kilcaskan	Bantry	II.	122
71	Coomasaharn .	1,081 0 16d	Kerry	Iveragh .	Glanbehy	Cahersiveen	II.	195
71, 81	Coomaspeara .	1,212 3 6	Kerry	Iveragh .	Dromod .	Cahersiveen	II.	194
80, 89	Coomastow	701 3 16	Kerry	Iveragh .	Dromod .	Cahersiveen	II.	194
120,121,133	Coomatallin	609 3 21	Cork, W.R.	West Carbery (E.D.)	Drinagh .	Skibbereen	II.	139
105, 106	Coomatloukane	622 1 31	Kerry	Dunkerron South .	Kilcrohane	Cahersiveen	II.	183
90	Coomavanniha and Dughile .	1,195 1 16e	Kerry	Iveragh .	Dromod .	Cahersiveen	II.	195
150	Coomavarrodig	81 3 10	Cork, W.R.	West Carbery (E.D.)	Tullagh .	Skibbereen	II.	141
81, 90	Coomavoher .	1,476 1 27f	Kerry	Iveragh .	Dromod .	Cahersiveen	II.	194
63, 71	Coomavoon .	624 0 15	Kerry	Iveragh .	Glanbehy	Cahersiveen	II.	195
81	Coombaha .	838 2 8	Kerry	Iveragh .	Dromod .	Cahersiveen	II.	194
55, 56	Coombs .	780 2 34	Limerick .	Coshlea .	Ballingaddy .	Kilmallock	II.	237
73	Coomcallee	1,549 2 14g	Kerry	Dunkerron North .	Knockane	Killarney .	II.	182
92, 93	Coomclogh .	406 2 3	Cork, W.R.	Bantry	Kilmocomoge .	Bantry	II.	120
94, 103	Coomclogherane .	478 2 23h	Kerry	Glanarought	Kilgarvan	Kenmare .	II.	187
80	Coomdeeween .	258 2 10	Kerry	Iveragh .	Killinane	Cahersiveen	II.	197
80	Coomdorragha	109 2 23	Cork, W.R.	West Muskerry	Inchigeelagh .	Macroom .	II.	157
80	Coomduff .	81 0 27	Kerry	Iveragh .	Killinane	Cahersiveen	II.	197
43	Coom East	267 3 3	Cork, E.R.	Barrymore	Dunbulloge	Cork	II.	54
139	Coomfarna .	284 2 13	Cork, W.R.	West Carbery(W.D.)	Skull	Skull	II.	146
43	Coom (Fitzgerald)	385 1 35	Cork, E.R.	Barrymore	Dunbulloge	Cork	II.	54
103, 116	Coomgira .	953 2 26i	Cork, W.R.	Bear	Kilcaskan	Castletown	II.	122
42, 43	Coom (Hudson)	821 3 11	Cork, E.R.	Barrymore	Dunbulloge	Cork	II.	54
117,118,130,131	Coomkeen .	914 3 21	Cork, W.R.	West Carbery (W.D.)	Durrus .	Bantry	II.	142
80, 81	Coomleagh .	876 0 13	Kerry	Iveragh .	Dromod .	Cahersiveen	II.	194
106	Coomleagh East	848 1 12	Cork, W.R.	Bantry	Kilmocomoge .	Bantry	II.	120
106	Coomleagh West	534 2 4	Cork, W.R.	Bantry	Kilmocomoge .	Bantry	II.	120
64, 72	Coomlettra .	421 2 16j	Kerry	Dunkerron North .	Knockane	Cahersiveen	II.	182
69, 81	Coomlibane .	556 1 22	Cork, W.R.	West Muskerry	Inchigeelagh .	Macroom .	II.	157
39	Coomlogane .	615 3 11	Kerry	West Muskerry	Drishane	Millstreet	II.	156
82	Coomlumminy .	1,402 1 30	Kerry	Dunkerron South .	Templenoe	Kenmare .	II.	185
43	Coom (Midleton)	197 2 1	Cork, E.R.	Barrymore	Dunbulloge	Cork	II.	54
58	Coomnaclohy .	1,403 2 1	Cork, W.R.	West Muskerry	Ballyvourney	Macroom .	II.	154
64	Coomnafanida	364 2 10k	Kerry	Iveragh .	Killorglin	Killarney .	II.	197
141, 150	Coomnageehy .	75 0 19	Cork, W.R.	West Carbery (E.D.)	Abbeystrowry	Skibbereen	II.	136
58	Coomnagire .	854 3 9	Cork, W.R.	West Muskerry	Ballyvourney	Macroom .	II.	154
69	Coomnahincha	299 0 35	Kerry	Iveragh .	Killinane	Cahersiveen	II.	197
98, 106	Coomnahorna East .	710 2 8	Kerry	Dunkerron South .	Kilcrohane	Cahersiveen	II.	183
106	Coomnahorna West	326 2 19	Kerry	Dunkerron South .	Kilcrohane	Cahersiveen	II.	183
92	Coomnakilla North	492 2 9	Kerry	Dunkerron South .	Templenoe	Kenmare .	II.	185
92	Coomnakilla South	645 0 32	Kerry	Dunkerron South .	Templenoe	Kenmare .	II.	185
80	Coomroe .	953 3 10l	Cork, W.R.	West Muskerry	Inchigeelagh .	Dunmanway	II.	157
62, 70, 71	Coomshanna .	1,024 0 32	Kerry	Iveragh .	Killinane	Cahersiveen	II.	197
81, 90	Coomura .	356 3 18m	Kerry	Iveragh .	Dromod .	Cahersiveen	II.	194

(a) Including 5A. 1R. 4P. water.
(b) Including 4A. 2R. 8P. water.
(c) Including 50A. 3R. 37P. water.
(d) Including 121A. 2R. 21P. water.
(e) Including 8A. 0R. 13P. water.

(f) Including 75A. 0R. 34P. water.
(g) Including 66A. 0R. 0P. water.
(h) Including 16A. 1R. 3P. water.
(i) Including 24A. 1R. 22P. water.

(j) Including 1A. 1R. 22P. water.
(k) Including 1A. 1R. 38P. water.
(l) Including 5A. 0R. 36P. water.
(m) Including 6A. 0R. 32P. water.

2 Q

No. of Sheet of the Ordnance Survey Maps.	Townlands and Towns.	Area in Statute Acres.			County.	Barony.	Parish.	Poor Law Union in 1857.	Townland Census of 1851, Part I.	
		A.	R.	P.					Vol.	Page
43	Coom West	194	1	33	Cork, E.R.	Barrymore	Dunbulloge	Cork	II.	54
82, 91	Coomyanna	1,067	1	28	Kerry	Dunkerron South	Kilcrohane	Kenmare	II.	183
8	Coonagh	397	1	32	Kildare	Carbury	Ardkill	Edenderry	I.	51
4, 5	Coonagh East	270	3	28	Limerick	Pubblebrien	Killeely	Limerick	II.	253
4, 5	Coonagh West	548	3	34	Limerick	Pubblebrien	Killeely	Limerick	II.	253
90, 91	Coonane	715	3	36	Cork, W.R.	Bear	Kilcaskan	Bantry	II.	122
15, 21	Coonanstown	240	2	28	Wicklow	Upper Talbotstown	Rathsallagh	Baltinglass	I.	365
25, 26	Coonbeg	225	2	12	Queen's Co.	Slievemargy	Killabban	Carlow	I.	245
22, 30	Coonealcauraun	706	3	12a	Mayo	Tirawley	Ballysakeery	Ballina	IV.	165
22	Coonealmore	368	0	1b	Mayo	Tirawley	Ballysakeery	Ballina	IV.	165
24, 29	Cooneen	663	2	37	Fermanagh	Magherastephana	Aghalurcher	Lisnaskea	III.	215
19	Cooneen	66	0	39	Tipperary, N.R.	Owney and Arra	Castletownarra	Nenagh	II.	294
33	Cooneen	687	2	19	Tipperary, N.R.	Upper Ormond	Dolla	Nenagh	II.	290
34	Cooneen or Glenassy	93	1	29	Waterford	Decies within Drum	Aglish	Dungarvan	II.	349
33	Cooneen South	30	3	27	Tipperary, N.R.	Upper Ormond	Dolla	Nenagh	II.	290
20	Cooney	217	2	28	Sligo	Leyny	Ballysadare	Sligo	IV.	230
38, 39	Coonmore	697	1	38	Tipperary, N.R.	Owney and Arra	Abington	Nenagh	II.	293
16	Coonmore	158	1	21	Wicklow	Lower Talbotstown	Hollywood	Baltinglass	I.	360
30, 31	Coonoge	460	2	25	Wexford	Bantry	Adamstown	New Ross	I.	299
23	Coonogue	931	2	21	Carlow	Idrone East	Kiltennell	New Ross	I.	7
22, 23	Coontraght	23	2	39	Kilkenny	Shillelogher	Tullaghanbrogue	Callan	I.	116
4	Cooperhill	524	3	30	Limerick	Pubblebrien	Kilkeedy	Limerick	II.	252
27, 34	Cooperhill	466	3	36	Sligo	Tirerrill	Kilmacallan	Sligo	IV.	239
32	Cooperhill Demesne	396	2	20	Queen's Co.	Slievemargy	Killabban	Carlow	I.	245
26	Cooperhill or Gobbadagh	210	3	33	Sligo	Tirerrill	Drumcolumb	Sligo	IV.	238
61	Cooper's-lot	199	1	20	Tipperary, S.R.	Middlethird	St. John Baptist	Cashel	II.	330
17	Cooperstown	143	3	4	Wexford	Ballaghkeen	Donaghmore	Gorey	I.	293
33, 41	Coor	250	0	5	Clare	Islands	Drumcliff	Ennis	II.	30
57	COORACLARE T.	—			Clare	Moyarta	Kilmacduane	Kilrush	II.	33
82, 83	Cooracoosane	574	0	38c	Kerry	Dunkerron South	Templenoe	Kenmare	II.	185
98, 106	Cooracurkia	314	2	7	Galway	Leitrim	Abbeygormacan	Loughrea	IV.	50
139	Cooradarrigan	283	2	17	Cork, W.R.	West Carbery(W.D.)	Skull	Skull	II.	146
119	Cooradowny	163	1	16	Cork, W.R.	West Carbery (W.D.)	Caheragh	Skibbereen	II.	142
132	Cooragannive	347	0	16	Cork, W.R.	West Carbery (W.D.)	Caheragh	Skibbereen	II.	142
81	Cooragreenane	572	0	33d	Cork, W.R.	West Muskerry	Inchigeelagh	Dunmanway	II.	157
140	Cooragurteen	291	1	32	Cork, W.R.	West Carbery(W.D.)	Skull	Skull	II.	146
84, 93	Cooragweanish	238	1	14	Kerry	Glanarought	Kenmare	Kenmare	II.	186
93	Cooranig	652	1	31	Cork, W.R.	East Carbery (W.D.)	Fanlobbus	Dunmanway	II.	131
90, 104	Coorannel	543	2	24	Cork, W.R.	Bear	Kilcaskan	Bantry	II.	122
132, 141	Cooranuller	729	3	26	Cork, W.R.	West Carbery(W.D.)	Caheragh	Skibbereen	II.	142
26	Cooraun	158	1	27	Wexford	Ballaghkeen	Edermine	Enniscorthy	I.	294
97, 105	Coorbaun	81	3	26	Galway	Loughrea	Kilconickny	Loughrea	IV.	63
9	Coorduff	330	3	16	Wexford	Scarawalsh	St. Marys Newtownbarry	Enniscorthy	I.	325
31, 39	Coor East	273	3	13	Clare	Ibrickan	Kilmurry	Kilrush	II.	23
7	Coorevin	431	0	39	Tipperary, N.R.	Lower Ormond	Uskane	Borrisokane	II.	288
101	Coorinch	30	1	33	Galway	Longford	Clonfert	Ballinasloe	IV.	57
118	Coorinch	16	2	15	Galway	Longford	Meelick	Portumna	IV.	62
147	Coorlacka	309	2	4	Cork, W.R.	West Carbery(W.D.)	Kilmoe	Skull	II.	144
32, 37	Coorlaghan	398	3	5	Queen's Co.	Slievemargy	Killeshin	Carlow	I.	245
102, 103	Coorleagh	1,198	1	22	Kerry	Glanarought	Kilcaskan	Kenmare	II.	186
15, 16	Coorleagh	351	0	26	Kilkenny	Gowran	Shankill	Kilkenny	I.	99
134, 135	Coorleigh North	154	1	24	Cork, W.R.	Ibane and Barryroe	Kilkerranmore	Clonakilty	II.	149
135	Coorleigh South	131	2	13	Cork, W.R.	Ibane and Barryroe	Kilkerranmore	Clonakilty	II.	149
91, 105	Coorloum East	160	3	10	Cork, W.R.	Bantry	Kilmocomoge	Bantry	II.	120
91, 105	Coorloum North	514	1	37	Cork, W.R.	Bantry	Kilmocomoge	Bantry	II.	120
91, 105	Coorloum West	131	0	5	Cork, W.R.	Bantry	Kilmocomoge	Bantry	II.	120
101	Coornacaragh	326	3	28	Kerry	Glanarought	Tuosist	Kenmare	II.	188
101	Coornagillagh	213	0	23	Kerry	Glanarought	Tuosist	Kenmare	II.	188
64, 72	Coornagrena and Goulnacappy	816	1	27e	Kerry	Dunkerron North	Killorglin	Cahersiveen	II.	181
81	Coornahahilly	594	1	8f	Cork, W.R.	West Muskerry	Inchigeelagh	Dunmanway	II.	157
72	Coornameana	233	0	38g	Kerry	Dunkerron North	Killorglin	Cahersiveen	II.	181
32	Coornariska	221	1	6	Queen's Co.	Slievemargy	Killeshin	Carlow	I.	245
133	Coornishal	576	3	4	Cork, W.R.	West Carbery (E.D.)	Kilmacabea	Skibbereen	II.	140
81	Coorolagh	201	1	12	Cork, W.R.	West Muskerry	Inchigeelagh	Dunmanway	II.	157
39	Coor West	694	1	39h	Clare	Ibrickan	Kilmurry	Kilrush	II.	23
105	Coorycommane	618	2	38	Cork, W.R.	Bantry	Kilmocomoge	Bantry	II.	120
107	Coorycullane	202	0	36	Cork, W.R.	East Carbery (W.D.)	Fanlobbus	Dunmanway	II.	131
101	Cooryeen	629	3	31	Kerry	Glanarought	Tuosist	Kenmare	II.	188
105	Cooryleary	394	3	26	Cork, W.R.	Bantry	Kilmocomoge	Bantry	II.	120
68	Cooryvanaheen	97	3	0	Kerry	Iveragh	Dromod	Cahersiveen	II.	194
22, 29	Coosan	257	0	17	Westmeath	Brawny	St. Mary's	Athlone	I.	259

(a) Including 15A. 2R. 20P. water.	(d) Including 27A. 3R. 11P. water.	(g) Including 24A. 3R. 19P. water.
(b) Including 18A. 1R. 19P. water.	(e) Including 6A. 0R. 27P. water.	(h) Including 5A. 0R. 0P. water.
(c) Including 19A. 1R. 9P. water.	(f) Including 69A. 3R. 10P. water.	(i) Including 43A. 3R. 35P. water.

No. of Sheet of the Ordnance Survey Maps.	Townlands and Towns.	Area in Statute Acres.			County.	Barony.	Parish.	Poor Law Union in 1857.	Townland Census of 1851, Part I.	
		A.	R.	P.					Vol.	Page
44, 53	Coosane . .	331	1	0	Cork, E.R.	Barrymore . .	Kilshanahan .	Fermoy . .	II.	56
131	Coosane . .	270	0	19	Cork, W.R.	West Carbery(W.D.)	Skull . .	Skull . .	II.	146
39	Coosaun . .	71	3	5	Galway .	Moycullen .	Kilcummin .	Oughterard .	IV.	66
25, 32	Coosaun . .	133	2	30	Roscommon	Castlereagh .	Kiltullagh .	Castlereagh .	IV.	201
142	Cooscroneen .	121	1	35a	Cork, W.R.	West Carbery (E.D.)	Myross . . .	Skibbereen .	II.	141
26, 27	Coose . .	237	2	7	Down .	Lower Iveagh, Up.pt.	Tullylish .	Banbridge .	III.	171
24, 25	Coose . .	363	3	35b	Monaghan	Cremorne .	Aghnamullen .	Castleblayney .	III.	257
139, 140, 148, 149	Coosheen . .	329	2	1	Cork, W.R.	West Carbery(W.D.)	Skull . .	Skull . .	II.	146
120	Cooslughoga .	39	0	23	Mayo .	Kilmaine .	Cong . .	Ballinrobe .	IV.	153
131,132,135	Coos North .	1,200	0	23	Galway .	Leitrim . .	Ballynakill .	Portumna .	IV.	51
131, 132, 134, 135	Coos South .	973	3	30c	Galway .	Leitrim . .	Ballynakill .	Portumna .	IV.	51
7	Cootehall . .	225	0	26	Roscommon	Boyle . .	Tumna . .	Boyle . .	IV.	197
17	COOTEHILL T.	—			Cavan .	Tullygarvey .	Drumgoon .	Cootehill .	III.	88
6	Coothagh . .	95	1	36d	Galway .	Ballymoe .	Templetogher .	Glennamaddy .	IV.	9
94, 100	Copany . .	170	2	12	Donegal .	Tirhugh . .	Drumhome .	Donegal . .	III.	146
21	Copay . .	27	1	29	Limerick .	Kenry . .	Adare . .	Croom . .	II.	248
3	Copeland Island	295	0	13	Down .	Ards Lower .	Bangor . .	Newtownards .	III.	157
4	Copney . .	366	1	6	Armagh .	Oneilland West .	Clonfeacle .	Armagh . .	III.	51
27, 36	Copney . .	1,001	0	7	Tyrone .	Omagh East .	Termonmaguirk .	Omagh . .	III.	314
34	Coppanagh .	806	3	19	Cavan .	Clankee . .	Enniskeen .	Bailieborough .	III.	72
16	Coppanagh .	88	1	23	Cavan .	Tullygarvey .	Kildrumsherdan .	Cootehill .	III.	89
86	Coppanagh .	177	1	19	Galway .	Kilconnell .	Killaan . .	Ballinasloe .	IV.	41
115, 124	Coppanagh .	2,275	0	3	Galway .	Loughrea .	Killeenadeema .	Loughrea . .	IV.	64
25, 29	Coppanagh .	1,347	2	17	Kilkenny .	Gowran . .	Graiguenamanagh .	Thomastown .	I.	95
5	Coppanaghbane .	228	2	33	Cavan .	Tullyhaw .	Templeport .	Enniskillen .	III.	94
39	Coppanagh Glebe	227	1	15	Cavan .	Castlerahan .	Lurgan . .	Oldcastle .	III.	69
5	Coppanaghmore .	437	3	20	Cavan .	Tullyhaw .	Templeport .	Enniskillen .	III.	94
8	Coppenagh .	596	1	19	Carlow .	Rathvilly .	Tullowphelim .	Carlow . .	I.	12
67	Copperalley .	36	1	38	Cork, E.R.	Imokilly . .	Youghal . .	Youghal . .	II.	91
74	Coppingersacre .	5	0	7e	Cork, E.R.	Cork . .	St. Marys Shandon .	Cork . .	II.	66
74	Coppingersstang .	20	1	15	Cork, E.R.	Cork . .	St. Finbars .	Cork . .	II.	65
76	Coppingerstown .	247	1	9	Cork, E.R.	Imokilly . .	Middleton .	Middleton .	II.	89
5, 6	Copse . .	226	3	15	Roscommon	Boyle . .	Boyle . .	Boyle . .	IV.	194
30	Copse . .	258	3	36	Wicklow .	Ballinacor North .	Rathdrum .	Rathdrum .	I.	347
14, 15	Copsefield .	275	0	32	Cork, E.R.	Duhallow .	Clonfert . .	Kanturk . .	II.	68
24	Copsetown .	348	1	32	Cork, E.R.	Orrery and Kilmore	Buttevant .	Mallow . .	II.	107
9, 13	Cor . . .	153	1	7	Cavan .	Tullyhaw .	Templeport .	Bawnboy . .	III.	94
65	Cor . . .	85	2	9	Donegal .	Boylagh . .	Lettermacward .	Glenties . .	III.	114
67, 75	Coracow . .	106	3	26	Kerry .	Magunihy .	Killaha . .	Killarney .	II.	202
8	Coragh . .	304	2	29	Armagh .	Oneilland West .	Loughgall . .	Armagh . .	III.	54
32, 33	Coragh . . .	289	0	0f	Cavan .	Castlerahan .	Lurgan . .	Oldcastle .	III.	69
11	Coragh . . .	547	3	34g	Cavan .	Lower Loughtee .	Drumlane .	Cavan . .	III.	79
17	Coragh . . .	117	1	0h	Cavan .	Tullygarvey .	Drumgoon .	Cootehill .	III.	88
19	Coragh . . .	128	0	8	Cavan .	Tullyhunco .	Kildallan .	Cavan . .	III.	96
37	Coragh . . .	112	1	3	Fermanagh .	Clanawley .	Kinawley .	Enniskillen .	III.	193
38	Coragh . .	158	3	38	Fermanagh .	Knockninny .	Kinawley .	Lisnaskea . .	III.	201
22	Coragh . .	212	0	4	Leitrim .	Carrigallen .	Drumreilly .	Bawnboy . .	IV.	90
3	Coraghbrack .	166	1	0	Monaghan .	Trough . .	Errigal Trough .	Clogher . .	III.	283
32, 33	Coragh (Crawford).	112	0	31	Fermanagh .	Clanawley .	Kinawley .	Enniskillen .	III.	193
19	Coragh Glebe .	237	1	23i	Cavan .	Tullyhunco .	Killashandra .	Cavan . .	III.	97
32, 33	Coragh Glebe .	148	2	31	Fermanagh .	Clanawley .	Kinawley .	Enniskillen .	III.	193
14, 19	Coraghmuck or Greaghacholea .	281	0	25	Cavan .	Tullyhunco .	Kildallan .	Bawnboy . .	III.	97
12	Coraghy . .	205	0	36	Monaghan .	Dartree . .	Clones . .	Clones . .	III.	264
27	Coraghy . .	216	0	6j	Monaghan .	Farney . .	Magheross .	Carrickmacross	III.	273
15	Corah . . .	469	1	1k	Wexford .	Scarawalsh .	Ballycarney .	Enniscorthy .	I.	322
22	Coraknock Glebe .	32	0	19	King's Co. .	Garrycastle .	Gallen . .	Parsonstown .	I.	136
30, 34	Coranagh . .	208	2	14l	Leitrim .	Carrigallen .	Carrigallen .	Mohill . .	IV.	89
20	Coras Point .	41	0	33	Cavan .	Upper Loughtee .	Urney . .	Cavan . .	III.	86
31	Coraughrim .	120	1	14	Leitrim .	Leitrim . .	Kiltoghert .	Cark. on Shannon	IV.	101
14	Corballis . .	201	3	3	Dublin .	Coolock . .	Cloghran .	Balrothery .	I.	26
12	Corballis . . .	803	3	36	Dublin .	Nethercross .	Donabate .	Balrothery .	I.	30
38	Corballis . . .	373	0	12	Kildare .	Kilkea and Moone .	Kineagh . .	Baltinglass .	I.	61
26, 27	Corballis . . .	565	3	30	Meath .	Lower Duleek .	Duleek . .	Drogheda .	I.	195
42	Corballis . . .	252	2	27	Meath .	Lower Moyfenrath .	Rathmolyon .	Trim . .	I.	211
6, 7, 12, 13	Corballis . . .	430	3	35	Meath .	Lower Slane .	Siddan . .	Ardce . .	I.	223
35	Corballis . . .	678	1	22	Meath .	Lune . .	Kildalkey .	Trim . .	I.	208
31	Corballis . . .	284	2	27	Meath .	Skreen . .	Templekeeran .	Navan . .	I.	222
28	Corballis . . .	378	0	10	Meath .	Upper Duleek .	Ballygarth .	Drogheda .	I.	197
18	Corballis . . .	93	0	26	Meath .	Upper Slane .	Rathkenny .	Navan . .	I.	225
30	Corballis Lower .	363	0	18	Wicklow .	Ballinacor North .	Rathdrum .	Rathdrum .	I.	347

(a) Including 0A. 1R. 8P. water.
(b) Including 4A. 1R. 37P. water.
(c) Including 32A. 0R. 12P. water.
(d) Including 15A. 3R. 8P. water.

(e) { Within the Municipal Boundary, 3A. 2R. 20P.
    { Without the Municipal Boundary, 1A. 1R. 27P.
(f) Including 76A. 0R. 18P. water.
(g) Including 127A. 0R. 5P. water.
(h) Including 20A. 2R. 6P. water.

(i) Including 3A. 0R. 13P. water.
(j) Including 15A. 0R. 10P. water.
(k) Including 3A. 2R. 11P. water.
(l) Including 7A. 2R. 18P. water.

No. of Sheet of the Ordnance Survey Maps	Townlands and Towns.	Area in Statute Acres.	County.	Barony.	Parish.	Poor Law Union in 1857.	Townland Census of 1851, Part I.	
		A. R. P.					Vol.	Page
30	Corballis Upper	284 2 10	Wicklow . .	Ballinacor North .	Rathdrum . .	Rathdrum .	I.	347
6	Corbally . .	110 1 35	Antrim . .	Lower Dunluce .	Ballywillin .	Coleraine . .	III.	15
54, 55	Corbally . .	583 1 4	Antrim . .	Lower Massereene .	Killead . .	Antrim . .	III.	28
32, 37	Corbally . .	322 2 25	Antrim . .	Lower Toome . .	Ahoghill . .	Ballymena .	III.	32
34	Corbally . .	505 2 14	Clare . .	Bunratty Upper .	Clooney . .	Tulla . .	II.	7
46, 56	Corbally . .	778 3 35	Clare . .	Moyarta . .	Kilfearagh . .	Kilrush . .	II.	32
44, 53	Corbally . .	435 0 26a	Cork, E.R. .	Barrymore . .	Arduageehy .	Fermoy . .	II.	50
54, 55	Corbally . .	224 2 5	Cork, E.R. .	Barrymore . .	Dungourney .	Middleton . .	II.	54
23	Corbally . .	468 3 26	Cork, E.R. .	Duhallow . .	Kilbrin . .	Kanturk . .	II.	72
85	Corbally . .	344 0 35	Cork, E.R. .	East Muskerry .	Corbally . .	Cork . .	II.	102
26	Corbally . .	372 0 5	Cork, E.R. .	Fermoy . .	Glanworth . .	Fermoy . .	II.	79
55, 66	Corbally . .	176 2 37	Cork, E.R. .	Imokilly . .	Dangandonovan .	Youghal . .	II.	86
55, 66	Corbally . .	36 3 14b	Cork, E.R. .	Imokilly . .	Killeagh . .	Youghal . .	II.	88
31	Corbally . .	36 2 28	Down . .	Dufferin . .	Killyleagh .	Downpatrick .	III.	167
38	Corbally . .	331 1 34	Down . .	Lecale Lower .	Dunsfort . .	Downpatrick .	III.	179
37, 44	Corbally . .	338 3 10c	Down . .	Lecale Upper . .	Down . .	Downpatrick .	III.	180
28, 35	Corbally . .	837 1 28	Down . .	Upper Iveagh, Lr. pt.	Garvaghy . .	Banbridge .	III.	172
21, 24	Corbally . .	523 3 17	Dublin . .	Uppercross . .	Tallaght . .	Dublin South .	I.	41
57, 70	Corbally . .	222 1 30	Galway . .	Clare . .	Annaghdown .	Galway . .	IV.	16
68	Corbally . .	63 3 0d	Galway . .	Moycullen . .	Moycullen . .	Galway . .	IV.	71
9, 15	Corbally . .	170 2 28	Kerry . .	Clanmaurice . .	Rattoo . .	Listowel . .	II.	173
57	Corbally . .	400 1 15	Kerry . .	Magunihy . .	Killorglin .	Killarney . .	II.	204
48	Corbally . .	115 2 17	Kerry . .	Magunihy . .	Molahiffe . .	Killarney . .	II.	205
23, 24	Corbally . .	458 3 37	Kildare . .	Connell . .	Kildare . .	Naas . .	I.	55
10, 11	Corbally . .	176 1 6	Kildare . .	North Salt . .	Taghadoe . .	Celbridge .	I.	76
26	Corbally . .	61 0 33	Kilkenny . .	Callan . .	Callan . .	Callan . .	I.	83
35, 39	Corbally . .	824 3 39	Kilkenny . .	Iverk . .	Fiddown . .	Carrick on Suir	I.	105
31	Corbally . .	72 3 9	Leitrim . .	Leitrim . .	Kiltoghert .	Cark. on Shannon	IV.	101
41	Corbally . .	122 2 33	Limerick . .	Coshlea . .	Galbally . .	Mitchelstown .	II.	238
5	Corbally . .	321 0 7e	Limerick . .	Limerick, Municipal Borough of . .	St. Patricks . .	Limerick . .	II.	262
12	Corbally . .	39 2 17	Limerick . .	Pubblebrien . .	Kilkeedy . .	Limerick . .	II.	252
19	Corbally . .	156 3 6	Limerick . .	Shanid . .	Shanagolden .	Glin . .	II.	258
91, 92, 102	Corbally . .	198 1 14	Mayo . .	Clanmorris . .	Kilcolman .	Claremorris .	IV.	134
19, 25	Corbally . .	1,022 3 11	Queen's Co. .	Ballyadams . .	Tecolm . .	Athy . .	I.	232
23	Corbally . .	406 3 14	Queen's Co. .	Maryborough West .	Clonenagh and Clonagheen . .	Abbeyleix .	I.	242
2	Corbally . .	114 3 0	Queen's Co. .	Tinnahinch . .	Kilmanman .	Mountmellick .	I.	249
3, 7	Corbally . .	453 3 28	Queen's Co. .	Tinnahinch . .	Rosenallis . .	Mountmellick .	I.	250
28	Corbally . .	121 1 8	Roscommon .	Roscommon . .	Kilcooley . .	Strokestown .	IV.	210
22	Corbally . .	708 0 32	Sligo . .	Tireragh . .	Castleconor .	Dromore West .	IV.	232
41	Corbally . .	195 1 26	Tipperary, N.R.	Eliogarty . .	Rahelty . .	Thurles . .	II.	272
19	Corbally . .	334 2 34	Tipperary, N.R.	Owney and Arra .	Castletownarra .	Nenagh . .	II.	294
46	Corbally . .	106 3 13	Tipperary, S.R.	Kilnamanagh Lower	Clogher . .	Cashel . .	II.	322
62, 63	Corbally . .	530 0 15	Tipperary, S.R.	Middlethird . .	Drangan . .	Cashel . .	II.	326
50	Corbally . .	267 0 30	Tyrone . .	Clogher . .	Donacavey .	Omagh . .	III.	294
41, 49	Corbally . .	449 3 19	Tyrone . .	Omagh East . .	Dromore . .	Omagh . .	III.	311
20	Corbally . .	78 0 37	Westmeath .	Farbill . .	Killucan . .	Mullingar .	I.	266
26	Corbally . .	227 3 29	Westmeath .	Fartullagh . .	Lynn . .	Mullingar .	I.	269
3	Corbally . .	417 0 12f	Westmeath .	Fore . .	St. Feighins .	Castletowndelvin	I.	271
17, 22	Corbally . .	195 0 11	Wexford . .	Gorey . .	Kiltrisk . .	Gorey . .	I.	320
20	Corbally . .	292 1 18	Wexford . .	Scarawalsh . .	Templeshannon .	Enniscorthy .	I.	326
9, 10	Corbally or Bally-more East .	395 2 21	Roscommon .	Boyle . .	Boyle . .	Boyle . .	IV.	193
53,54,64,65	Corballybane . .	241 1 12	Cork, E.R. .	Barrymore . .	Lisgoold . .	Middleton . .	II.	56
107	Corbally Beg . .	112 0 39	Galway . .	Longford . .	Abbeygormacan .	Ballinasloe .	IV.	56
27	Corbally Beg . .	247 1 0	Waterford . .	Gaultiere . .	Corbally . .	Waterford . .	II.	262
11, 17	Corbally East . .	158 2 26g	Roscommon .	Frenchpark . .	Creeve . .	Cark. on Shannon	IV.	203
98, 99, 107	Corbally (Hogan) .	279 0 28	Galway . .	Longford . .	Abbeygormacan .	Ballinasloe .	IV.	56
11, 16, 17	Corbally Middle .	172 2 8h	Roscommon .	Frenchpark . .	Creeve . .	Cark. on Shannon	IV.	203
98	Corbally More . .	572 3 27	Galway . .	Longford . .	Abbeygormacan .	Ballinasloe .	IV.	56
27	Corbally More .	261 1 30	Waterford . .	Gaultiere . .	Corbally . .	Waterford . .	II.	362
100, 108	Corballymore and Camgort . .	140 0 23	Galway . .	Longford . .	Donanaghta .	Portumna .	IV.	58
64, 75	Corbally North .	69 2 21	Cork, E.R. .	Barrymore . .	Ballydeloher .	Cork . .	II.	51
54, 65	Corbally North .	338 1 7	Cork, E.R. .	Barrymore . .	Lisgoold . .	Middleton . .	II.	56
57	Corbally North .	162 1 9	Galway . .	Clare . .	Kilmoylan .	Tuam . .	IV.	22
17	Corballyquill . .	290 1 28	Cavan . .	Tullygarvey . .	Kildrumsherdan	Cootehill . .	III.	89
34, 38	Corbally and Slieve .	1,181 2 31i	Roscommon .	Ballymoe . .	Ballynakill .	Roscommon .	IV.	191
64, 75	Corbally South .	155 1 29	Cork, E.R. .	Barrymore . .	Ballydeloher .	Cork . .	II.	51
54, 65	Corbally South .	236 2 36	Cork, E.R. .	Barrymore . .	Lisgoold . .	Middleton . .	II.	56
57, 70	Corbally South .	795 0 30	Galway . .	Clare . .	Kilmoylan .	Tuam . .	IV.	22
·22	CORBALLY T. . .	—	Sligo . .	Tireragh . .	Castleconor .	Dromore West .	IV.	232
16	Corbally West .	223 3 16	Roscommon .	Frenchpark . .	Creeve . .	Cark. on Shannon	IV.	203

(a) Including 5A. 1R. 16P. detached portion.
(b) Including 2A. 0R. 20P. detached portion.
(c) Including 2A. 1R. 24P. water.
(d) Including 8A. 3R. 28P. water.
(e) Included in the parish of St. Patricks.
(f) Including 25A. 3R. 13P. water.
(g) Including 13A. 0R. 37P. water.
(h) Including 6A. 3R. 1P. water.
(i) Including 14A. 1R. 2P. water.

No. of Sheet of the Ordnance Survey Maps.	Townlands and Towns.	Area in Statute Acres.			County.	Barony.	Parish.	Poor Law Union in 1857.	Townland Census of 1851, Part I.	
		A.	R.	P.					Vol.	Page
35, 56	Corbane . . .	135	0	19	Fermanagh .	Clankelly . .	Clones . . .	Clones . .	III.	195
6, 7, 14, 15	Corbane . . .	268	1	31	King's Co. .	Garrycastle .	Lemanaghan .	Parsonstown .	I.	136
27	Corbane . . .	280	0	13	Monaghan .	Farney . . .	Magheross . .	Carrickmacross	III.	273
106	Corbaun . . .	271	1	35	Galway . .	Leitrim . .	Kilcooly . .	Loughrea . .	IV.	54
11, 17	Corbaun . . .	151	1	11	Roscommon .	Ballintober North .	Kilmore . .	Carᵏ.on Shannon	IV.	187
6, 7	Corbaun or Leitrim	466	1	15	Longford . .	Granard . .	Columbkille .	Granard . .	I.	155
32	Corbeagh . .	125	0	11	Cavan . .	Castlerahan .	Crosserlough .	Cavan . .	III.	68
23	Corbeagh . .	156	2	32	Cavan . .	Clankee . .	Shercock . .	Bailieborough .	III.	74
17	Corbeagh . .	392	0	27	Cavan . .	Tullygarvey .	Kildrumsherdan	Cootehill . .	III.	89
9, 14	Corbeagh . .	137	1	25a	Longford . .	Granard . .	Clonbroney .	Granard . .	I.	155
1	Corbeg . . .	79	3	5	Leitrim . .	Rosclogher .	Rossinver . .	Ballyshannon .	IV.	111
9, 10	Corbeg . . .	78	0	6	Monaghan .	Monaghan . .	Tehallan . .	Monaghan . .	III.	280
6, 7, 14, 15	Cor Beg and Cor More	611	2	6	King's Co. .	Garrycastle .	Lemanaghan .	Parsonstown .	I.	136
12, 19	Corbehagh . .	1,042	2	12	Clare . .	Tulla Upper .	Feakle . .	Tulla . .	II.	39
27, 34	Corbet . . .	618	1	2b	Down . .	Lower Iveagh, Lr. pt.	Magherally .	Banbridge .	III.	168
10, 14	Corbetstown .	502	0	33	Kilkenny .	Fassadinin .	Mothell . .	Castlecomer .	I.	90
4	Corbetstown .	1,188	3	30	King's Co. .	Warrenstown .	Castlejordan .	Edenderry .	I.	145
20	Corbetstown .	533	2	0	Westmeath .	Farbill . .	Killucan . .	Mullingar .	I.	266
16	Corbetstown .	58	0	16	Wexford . .	Scarawalsh .	Kilbride . .	Enniscorthy .	I.	323
5, 8	Corblonog .	49	2	31	Monaghan .	Monaghan . .	Tedavnet . .	Monaghan .	III.	278
36	Corbo . . .	370	1	0	Roscommon .	Ballintober South .	Kilbride . .	Roscommon .	IV.	189
51, 58	Corboe . . .	686	3	12	Tyrone . .	Clogher . .	Clogher . .	Clogher . .	III.	292
4	Corboggy . .	146	1	8	Meath . .	Kells Lower .	Moynalty . .	Kells . .	I.	203
32	Corboghil . .	169	1	19	Leitrim . .	Leitrim . .	Mohill . .	Mohill . .	IV.	104
29	Corboghil . .	139	0	6	Roscommon .	Roscommon .	Cloonfinlough .	Strokestown .	IV.	209
42	Corboley . .	366	2	9	Roscommon .	Athlone . .	Killinvoy . .	Roscommon .	IV.	181
81	Corboley (Lynch) .	247	1	4c	Galway . .	Galway . .	Rahoon . .	Galway . .	IV.	37
81, 93	Corboley (Morgan) .	660	0	24d	Galway . .	Galway . .	Rahoon . .	Galway . .	IV.	37
14	Corbollis . .	471	3	17e	Louth . .	Louth . .	Clonkeehan .	Ardee . .	I.	183
14	Corboy . . .	923	2	5	Longford . .	Longford . .	Killoe . .	Longford . .	I.	158
9, 13	Corboy Glebe .	144	3	17f	Cavan . .	Tullyhaw . .	Templeport .	Bawnboy . .	III.	94
19, 24	Corbrack . .	194	3	16	Monaghan .	Cremorne . .	Ballybay . .	Castleblayney .	III.	259
16	Corbrack . .	97	1	36	Westmeath .	Kilkenny West .	Noughaval .	Ballymahon .	I.	274
5	Corbracky . .	302	1	32	Armagh . .	Oneilland West .	Drumcree . .	Lurgan . .	III.	52
13	Corcaghan . .	270	1	5	Monaghan .	Monaghan . .	Kilmore . .	Monaghan . .	III.	276
78	Corcam . . .	60	3	34g	Donegal . .	Raphoe . .	Donaghmore .	Stranorlar .	III.	137
4, 12	Corcamore . .	1,346	3	14	Limerick . .	Pubblebrien .	Kilkeedy . .	Limerick . .	II.	252
15, 20	Corcanadas . .	97	0	28	Cavan . .	Lower Loughtee .	Drumlane . .	Cavan . .	III.	79
3, 7	Corcanon . .	306	3	15	Wexford . .	Gorey . .	Kilcavan . .	Gorey . .	I.	317
2, 5	Corcarra . .	207	1	34	Meath . .	Lower Kells .	Moybolgue .	Kells . .	I.	203
15, 16	Corcashel . .	326	3	18	Cavan . .	Tullygarvey .	Annagh . .	Cavan . .	III.	87
5	Corcashel . .	355	2	3	Cavan . .	Tullyhaw . .	Killinagh . .	Enniskillen .	III.	91
69	Corcashy . .	109	2	3	Donegal . .	Raphoe . .	Convoy . .	Stranorlar .	III.	136
14	Corcaskea . .	94	3	0	Monaghan .	Cremorne . .	Clontibret .	Monaghan . .	III.	260
1, 2	Corcas and Sandhills	125	3	10	Kerry . .	Iraghticonnor .	Kilconly . .	Listowel . .	II.	191
29	Corchoney . .	120	0	25	Tyrone . .	Dungannon Upper .	Kildress . .	Cookstown .	III.	308
18	Corchuill Lower .	111	1	27	Leitrim . .	Drumahaire .	Inishmagrath .	Manorhamilton	IV.	96
18	Corchuill Upper .	53	2	25	Leitrim . .	Drumahaire .	Inishmagrath .	Manorhamilton	IV.	96
15, 20	Corclaragh . .	431	3	33	Longford . .	Ardagh . .	Mostrim . .	Granard . .	I.	152
23	Corclare . .	62	1	38h	Cavan . .	Clankee . .	Shercock . .	Bailieborough .	III.	74
3	Corclare . .	110	0	6	Monaghan .	Trough . .	Errigal Trough .	Monaghan . .	III.	283
29	Corclogh . .	143	0	1	King's Co. .	Garrycastle .	Lusmagh . .	Parsonstown .	I.	137
10, 17	Corclogh . .	343	3	19	Mayo . .	Erris . .	Kilcommon .	Belmullet .	IV.	143
9	Corclogh . .	1,050	2	18	Mayo . .	Erris . .	Kilmore . .	Belmullet .	IV.	145
23	Corcloghan .	139	2	36i	Cavan . .	Clankee . .	Drumgoon .	Cootehill .	III.	72
16, 21	Corcloghan .	154	1	6	Cavan . .	Upper Loughtee .	Castleterra .	Cavan . .	III.	82
65	Corcloghy . .	1,150	2	5j	Tyrone . .	Clogher . .	Clogher . .	Clogher . .	III.	292
33	Corcloon . .	267	1	8	Westmeath .	Fartullagh .	Pass of Kilbride .	Mullingar .	I.	269
16, 17	Corconnelly . .	147	3	6k	Monaghan .	Dartree . .	Killeevan . .	Clones . .	III.	267
12	Corcoransacres .	36	3	27	Sligo . .	Tireragh . .	Templeboy .	Dromore West .	IV.	236
4	Corcoranstown .	441	2	35	Kildare . .	Ikeathy and Oughterany .	Cloncurry . .	Celbridge . .	I.	57
16, 18	Corcormick . .	157	0	0	Leitrim . .	Drumahaire .	Inishmagrath .	Manorhamilton	IV.	96
16, 21	Corcovety . .	182	3	4	Cavan . .	Tullygarvey .	Drung . .	Cootehill .	III.	88
16	Corcraff . .	160	3	25	Cavan . .	Tullygarvey .	Annagh . .	Cootehill .	III.	87
16	Corcraff . .	91	2	26	Cavan . .	Tullygarvey .	Drung . .	Cootehill .	III.	88
9	Corcrain . .	200	1	17l	Armagh . .	Oneilland West .	Drumcree . .	Lurgan . .	III.	52
55	Corcreaghan .	203	3	3	Down . .	Mourne . .	Kilkeel . .	Kilkeel . .	III.	183
17	Corcreeghagh .	122	2	24m	Cavan . .	Tullygarvey .	Drumgoon .	Cootehill .	III.	88
10	Corcreeghagh .	183	2	36	Louth . .	Ardee . .	Louth . .	Dundalk . .	I.	173
27, 30	Corcreeghagh .	402	2	14	Monaghan .	Farney . .	Magheross . .	Carrickmacross	III.	273
40, 41, 46	Corcreeghy .	439	3	24	Down . .	Lordship of Newry .	Newry . . .	Newry . .	III.	182
9, 13	Corcreeghy .	190	0	31	Monaghan .	Monaghan . .	Kilmore . .	Monaghan . .	III.	276

(a) Including 12A. 3R. 37P. water.
(b) Including 15A. 3R. 23P. water.
(c) Including 2A. 2R. 29P. water.
(d) Including 8A. 0R. 24P. water.
(e) Including 9A. 0R. 16P. water.

(f) Including 46A. 2R. 29P. water.
(g) Including 0A. 1R. 13P. water.
(h) Including 13A. 0R. 20P. water.
(i) Including 19A. 3R. 24P. water.

(j) Including 10A. 2R. 21P. water.
(k) Including 8A. 2R. 9P. water.
(l) Including 1A. 1R. 1P. water.
(m) Including 4A. 2R. 30P. water.

No. of Sheet of the Ordnance Survey Maps.	Townlands and Towns.	Area in Statute Acres.	County.	Barony.	Parish.	Poor Law Union in 1857.	Townland Census of 1851, Part I.	
		A. R. P.					Vol.	Page
19	Corcreeny	1,166 2 14	Down	Lower Iveagh, Up. pt.	Donaghcloney	Lurgan	III.	169
14, 21	Corcreeny	644 2 6	Down	Lower Iveagh, Up. pt.	Hillsborough	Lisburn	III.	169
9, 13	Corcreevy	230 2 18	Armagh	Oneilland West	Kilmore	Armagh	III.	53
63, 64	Corcreevy	179 2 17a	Tyrone	Clogher	Clogher	Clogher	III.	292
63	Corcreevy, (Part of)	8 1 2	Tyrone	Clogher	Clogher	Clogher	III.	292
63	Corcreevy Demesne	134 0 35	Tyrone	Clogher	Clogher	Clogher	III.	292
15, 25	Corcreggan	201 2 18	Donegal	Kilmacrenan	Clondahorky	Dunfanaghy	III.	123
31	Corcrin	223 2 0b	Monaghan	Farney	Magheross	Carrickmacross	III.	273
18	Corcrum	218 3 23	Armagh	Orior Lower	Ballymore	Newry	III.	55
31	Corcuilloge	244 3 14c	Monaghan	Farney	Magheross	Carrickmacross	III.	273
81	Corcullen	272 0 28d	Galway	Galway	Rahoon	Galway	IV.	37
81	Corcullen	10 2 29	Galway	Moycullen	Moycullen	Galway	IV.	71
9	Corcullentragh Beg	161 2 22	Armagh	Oneilland West	Drumcree	Lurgan	III.	52
9	Corcullentragh More	225 2 7	Armagh	Oneilland West	Drumcree	Lurgan	III.	52
9	Corcullentry and Cloran	906 3 5	Westmeath	Delvin	Killua	Castletowndelvin	I.	265
37	Corcullin	493 3 19e	Mayo	Tirawley	Crossmolina	Ballina	IV.	165
79	Corcullion	67 0 10	Donegal	Raphoe	Donaghmore	Strabane	III.	137
25, 28	Corcullioncrew	139 0 4	Monaghan	Farney	Donaghmoyne	Carrickmacross	III.	269
25, 28	Corcullionglish	114 3 20	Monaghan	Farney	Donaghmoyne	Carrickmacross	III.	269
16	Corcummins	118 3 10	Monaghan	Dartree	Killeevan	Clones	III.	267
15	Corcusconny	376 2 0	Leitrim	Drumahaire	Killanummery	Manorhamilton	IV.	97
16	Corcush	76 1 34	King's Co.	Ballycowan	Rahan	Tullamore	I.	128
19	Cordalea	128 1 6	Cavan	Upper Loughtee	Kilmore	Cavan	III.	84
40, 41, 49	Cordal East	1,886 3 22	Kerry	Trughanacmy	Ballincuslane	Tralee	II.	206
40	Cordal West	1,219 0 36	Kerry	Trughanacmy	Ballincuslane	Tralee	II.	206
67	Cordangan	680 2 21	Tipperary, S.R.	Clanwilliam	Cordangan	Tipperary	II.	306
26, 32	Cordarragh	75 0 34	Fermanagh	Clanawley	Killesher	Enniskillen	III.	192
41, 42	Cordarragh	413 0 5f	Galway	Clare	Killursa	Tuam	IV.	21
80	Cordarragh	379 2 20	Mayo	Gallen	Killedan	Swineford	IV.	150
98	Cordarragh North	448 2 11	Mayo	Murrisk	Aghagower	Westport	IV.	158
98	Cordarragh South	1,086 2 18	Mayo	Murrisk	Aghagower	Westport	IV.	158
34, 39	Corderraun	140 2 33	Wexford	Shelburne	Owenduff	New Ross	I.	328
52	Corderry	296 0 23g	Donegal	Kilmacrenan	Gartan	Letterkenny	III.	127
18	Corderry	130 3 5	Leitrim	Drumahaire	Inishmagrath	Manorhamilton	IV.	96
15	Corderry	208 3 25	Leitrim	Drumahaire	Killarga	Manorhamilton	IV.	98
11	Corderry	780 3 14	Louth	Louth	Louth	Dundalk	I.	184
3	Corderry	212 3 6h	Roscommon	Boyle	Ardcarn	Boyle	IV.	192
73	Corderry	546 0 31	Tipperary, S.R.	Clanwilliam	Clonbeg	Tipperary	II.	305
60	Corderry	166 3 13	Tyrone	Dungannon Lower	Carnteel	Clogher	III.	297
19, 24	Corderrybane	234 2 1	Monaghan	Cremorne	Clontibret	Castleblayney	III.	260
19, 24	Corderryduff	161 1 33	Monaghan	Cremorne	Clontibret	Castleblayney	III.	260
41	Corderryhugh	193 2 30i	Roscommon	Athlone	Fuerty	Roscommon	IV.	181
23, 24	Corderry (Morton)	178 0 34j	Leitrim	Leitrim	Kiltubbrid	Cark. on Shannon	IV.	103
28	Corderry (Peyton)	370 0 21	Leitrim	Leitrim	Kiltubbrid	Cark. on Shannon	IV.	103
21	Cordevlis	178 3 13	Cavan	Tullygarvey	Larah	Cootehill	III.	91
18, 23	Cordevlis	243 0 29k	Monaghan	Cremorne	Aghnamullen	Cootehill	III.	257
19	Cordevlis	138 3 39	Monaghan	Cremorne	Clontibret	Castleblayney	III.	260
10, 14	Cordevlis	71 0 37	Monaghan	Monaghan	Monaghan	Monaghan	III.	276
10	Cordevlis	82 2 39	Monaghan	Monaghan	Tehallan	Monaghan	III.	280
14	Cordevlis North	125 2 19	Monaghan	Monaghan	Tullycorbet	Monaghan	III.	281
18	Cordevlis South	143 1 6	Monaghan	Cremorne	Tullycorbet	Monaghan	III.	262
21, 26	Cordingin	270 0 12	Cavan	Tullygarvey	Larah	Cootehill	III.	91
2	Cordiver	273 2 9	Leitrim	Rosclogher	Rossinver	Ballyshannon	IV.	111
18, 19	Cordivin	135 2 33	Longford	Moydow	Ballymacormick	Longford	I.	160
35	Cordoagh	152 2 5	Cavan	Clankee	Enniskeen	Bailieborough	III.	72
27	Cordoagh	169 1 31	Cavan	Clankee	Knockbride	Bailieborough	III.	73
17	Cordoagh Glebe Upr.	101 1 14	Cavan	Tullygarvey	Kildrumsherdan	Cootehill	III.	89
17	Cordoagh Lower	89 3 12	Cavan	Tullygarvey	Kildrumsherdan	Cootehill	III.	89
30	Cordonaghy	239 3 11	Cavan	Tullyhunco	Scrabby	Cavan	III.	99
2, 5	Cordooey	104 3 1	Meath	Morgallion	Enniskeen	Kells	I.	209
21	Cordoogan	240 0 33	Louth	Ferrard	Monasterboice	Drogheda	I.	181
36	Cordoolagh	75 2 8	Fermanagh	Clankelly	Clones	Clones	III.	195
19	Cordoolough	304 0 5l	Monaghan	Monaghan	Tullycorbet	Monaghan	III.	281
13, 14	Cordrain	303 2 3	Armagh	Orior Lower	Kilmore	Banbridge	III.	56
11	Cordrehid	183 0 4	Roscommon	Boyle	Killukin	Cark. on Shannon	IV.	195
17	Cordressigo	108 1 17	Monaghan	Dartree	Ematris	Cootehill	III.	266
5	Cordressogagh	169 0 27m	Cavan	Tullyhaw	Killinagh	Enniskillen	III.	91
56	Cordromedy	206 1 25	Tyrone	Omagh East	Kilskeery	Lowtherstown	III.	313
121, 123	Cordroon	225 1 27	Mayo	Kilmaine	Cong	Ballinrobe	IV.	153
24, 30	Cordrumman	325 2 27	Roscommon	Roscommon	Bumlin	Strokestown	IV.	208
17, 23	Cordrumman	89 2 5n	Roscommon	Roscommon	Kiltrustan	Strokestown	IV.	211
28	Cordrummans Lower	69 1 38	Monaghan	Farney	Donaghmoyne	Carrickmacross	III.	269

(a) Including 4A. 3R. 34P. water.
(b) Including 12A. 0R. 35F. water.
(c) Including 9A. 2R. 33P. water.
(d) Including 2A. 1R. 39P. water.
(e) Including 22A. 3R. 17P. water.

(f) Including 4A. 2R. 30P. water.
(g) Including 33A. 0R. 37F. water.
(h) Including 67A. 2R. 39P. water.
(i) Including 5A. 0R. 25P. water.
(j) Including 29A. 3R. 39P. water.

(k) Including 18A. 2R. 5P. water.
(l) Including 21A. 2R. 0P. water.
(m) Including 12A. 3R. 0P. water.
(n) Including 13A. 1R. 30P. water.

No. of Sheet of the Ordnance Survey Maps.	Townlands and Towns.	Area in Statute Acres.			County.	Barony.	Parish.	Poor Law Union in 1857.	Townland Census of 1851, Part I.	
		A.	R.	P.					Vol.	Page
28	Cordrummans Middle	75	3	11	Monaghan	Farney	Donaghmoyne	Carrickmacross	III.	269
28	Cordrummans Upper	91	1	13	Monaghan	Farney	Donaghmoyne	Carrickmacross	III.	269
17	Cordrummond	194	2	36	Armagh	Fews Lower	Kilclooney	Armagh	III.	46
31	Corduff	778	3	20a	Cavan	Clanmahon	Ballintemple	Cavan	III.	75
31	Corduff	134	1	21	Cavan	Clanmahon	Crosserlough	Cavan	III.	76
8	Corduff	98	0	17b	Dublin	Balrothery East	Lusk	Balrothery	I.	21
13	Corduff	353	3	20	Dublin	Castleknock	Castleknock	Dublin North	I.	24
9, 13	Corduff	920	0	6	Kildare	Clane	Timahoe	Naas	I.	54
25	Corduff	52	2	23	Leitrim	Carrigallen	Drumreilly	Bawnboy	IV.	90
17, 18	Corduff	91	1	2	Leitrim	Drumahaire	Inishmagrath	Manorhamilton	IV.	96
32, 35	Corduff	234	1	24c	Leitrim	Mohill	Annaduff	Mohill	IV.	105
28	Corduff	94	1	36	Leitrim	Mohill	Mohill	Mohill	IV.	107
17	Corduff	253	2	39d	Monaghan	Dartree	Aghabog	Cootehill	III.	263
27	Corduff	267	2	20	Monaghan	Farney	Magheross	Carrickmacross	III.	273
8	Corduff Common	29	3	15	Dublin	Balrothery East	Lusk	Balrothery	I.	21
30	Corduff or Cormore	170	1	28	Cavan	Tullyhunco	Scrabby	Cavan	III.	99
8	Corduff (Hackett)	39	0	32	Dublin	Balrothery East	Lusk	Balrothery	I.	21
7, 8	Corduffhall	280	1	23	Dublin	Balrothery East	Lusk	Balrothery	I.	21
28	Corduffhill	23	1	7	Leitrim	Mohill	Mohill	Mohill	IV.	107
31	Corduff (Kelly)	245	1	9e	Monaghan	Farney	Magheross	Carrickmacross	III.	273
33	Corduff North	250	0	23	Leitrim	Carrigallen	Cloone	Mohill	IV.	90
33	Corduff South	428	0	13	Leitrim	Mohill	Cloone	Mohill	IV.	105
5	Cordwood	109	2	31	Fermanagh	Lurg	Drumkeeran	Lowtherstown	III.	205
28	Core	149	1	36	Clare	Tulla Upper	Feakle	Scarriff	II.	39
34	Corebeg	134	2	15	Clare	Bunratty Upper	Doora	Ennis	II.	8
24	Corelish East	169	0	7	Limerick	Coonagh	Grean	Tipperary	II.	235
24	Corelish West	266	2	26	Limerick	Clanwilliam	Grean	Tipperary	II.	224
18	Corernagh	235	0	1	Armagh	Orior Lower	Ballymore	Banbridge	III.	55
74, 84	Cores	1,434	2	31	Kerry	Magunihy	Killarney	Killarney	II.	203
39, 40	Corfad	653	2	18	Cavan	Castlerahan	Mullagh	Bailieborough	III.	70
22	Corfad	346	3	17	Cavan	Tullygarvey	Kildrumsherdan	Cootehill	III.	89
26	Corfad	266	2	35	Cavan	Upper Loughtee	Larah	Cavan	III.	85
23	Corfad	134	3	15f	Monaghan	Cremorne	Aghnamullen	Cootehill	III.	257
18, 19	Corfad	239	1	8	Monaghan	Cremorne	Ballybay	Castleblayney	III.	259
14	Corfad	108	2	39	Monaghan	Monaghan	Tullycorbet	Monaghan	III.	281
28	Corfannan	76	3	30	Fermanagh	Magherastephana	Aghalurcher	Lisnaskea	III.	215
21	Corfeehone	374	1	5g	Cavan	Tullygarvey	Larah	Cootehill	III.	91
15	Corfehan	252	1	26h	Armagh	Tiranny	Tynan	Armagh	III.	60
19	Corfinlough	195	3	14i	Monaghan	Monaghan	Tullycorbet	Monaghan	III.	281
35	Corflugh	89	3	2	Fermanagh	Clankelly	Clones	Clones	III.	195
30	Corfree	373	2	1	Cavan	Tullyhunco	Scrabby	Granard	III.	99
28	Corgallion	51	1	37	Leitrim	Mohill	Mohill	Mohill	IV.	107
15	Corgannive Glebe	189	1	1	Donegal	Kilmacrenan	Clondahorky	Dunfanaghy	III.	123
25	Corgar	159	3	17j	Leitrim	Carrigallen	Oughteragh	Bawnboy	IV.	92
28	Corgar	79	3	7	Leitrim	Mohill	Mohill	Mohill	IV.	107
25	Corgarran	62	0	17	Cavan	Upper Loughtee	Kilmore	Cavan	III.	84
73	Corgarriff	481	1	18	Mayo	Costello	Kilmovee	Swinford	IV.	142
17	Corgarrow	241	2	5k	Roscommon	Roscommon	Kiltrustan	Strokestown	IV.	211
35	Corgarry	122	0	3	Cavan	Clankee	Enniskeen	Bailieborough	III.	72
16, 21	Corgarve	331	1	11	Cavan	Upper Loughtee	Castleterra	Cavan	III.	82
7	Corgarve	120	2	15	Galway	Ballymoe	Ballynakill	Glennamaddy	IV.	5
121	Corgarve	69	1	36	Mayo	Kilmaine	Cong	Ballinrobe	IV.	153
42	Corgarve	131	3	17	Roscommon	Athlone	Kilmeane	Roscommon	IV.	182
16	Corgarve	279	1	2	Roscommon	Frenchpark	Creeve	Cark. on Shannon	IV.	203
31	Corgarve	316	0	17	Westmeath	Moycashel	Ardnurcher or Horseleap	Mullingar	I.	276
21	Corgarve or Creeve	73	3	0	Cavan	Upper Loughtee	Castleterra	Cavan	III.	82
29	Corgarve North	23	2	28	King's Co.	Garrycastle	Lusmagh	Parsonstown	I.	137
29	Corgarve South	24	2	7	King's Co.	Garrycastle	Lusmagh	Parsonstown	I.	137
78	Corgary	311	1	1	Donegal	Raphoe	Donaghmore	Stranorlar	III.	137
40, 46	Corgary	637	2	12	Down	Upper Iveagh, Up.pt.	Donaghmore	Newry	III.	175
8, 13	Corgary	273	3	21	Fermanagh	Magheraboy	Inishmacsaint	Ballyshannon	III.	212
14	Corgary Fifth or First Croagh	1,236	2	0l	Tyrone	Omagh West	Termonamongan	Castlederg	III.	317
15	Corgary First	131	2	25m	Tyrone	Omagh West	Termonamongan	Castlederg	III.	317
14, 15	Corgary Fourth or Meenablagh	766	1	27n	Tyrone	Omagh West	Termonamongan	Castlederg	III.	317
15	Corgary Second	176	2	15o	Tyrone	Omagh West	Termonamongan	Castlederg	III.	317
14	Corgary Sixth or Second Croagh	2,111	2	1p	Tyrone	Omagh West	Termonamongan	Castlederg	III.	317
14, 15	Corgary Third	360	0	17q	Tyrone	Omagh West	Termonamongan	Castlederg	III.	317
46, 59, 60	Corgerry Eighter	357	2	35	Galway	Tiaquin	Killoscobe	Mountbellew	IV.	78
59	Corgerry Oughter	413	3	34	Galway	Tiaquin	Killoscobe	Mountbellew	IV.	78
15, 17	Corglancey	517	1	10	Leitrim	Drumahaire	Killanummery	Manorhamilton	IV.	97

(a) Including 4A. 2R. 2P. water.
(b) Including 23A. 1R. 9P. detached portions.
(c) Including 3A. 3R. 6P. water.
(d) Including 20A. 3R. 9P. water.
(e) Including 44A. 0R. 39P. water.
(f) Including 5A. 1R. 5P. water.

(g) Including 10A. 2R. 4P. water.
(h) Including 13A. 2R. 24P. water.
(i) Including 32A. 3R. 24P. water.
(j) Including 36A. 0R. 34P. water.
(k) Including 25A. 1R. 32P. water.
(l) Including 2A. 0R. 38P. water.

(m) Including 1A. 3R. 37P. water.
(n) Including 4A. 0R. 20P. water.
(o) Including 2A. 1R. 34P. water.
(p) Including 5A. 3R. 38P. water.
(q) Including 2A. 1R. 20P. water.

No. of Sheet of the Ordnance Survey Maps.	Townlands and Towns.	Area in Statute Acres.			County.	Barony.	Parish.	Poor Law Union in 1857.	Townland Census of 1851, Part I.	
		A.	R.	P.					Vol.	Page
28	Corglass . . .	126	0	27a	Cavan . .	Clankee . . .	Bailieborough .	Bailieborough .	III.	71
29, 35	Corglass . . .	193	2	29	Cavan . .	Clankee . .	Enniskeen . .	Bailieborough .	III.	72
31	Corglass . . .	290	3	8b	Cavan . .	Clanmahon . .	Crosserlough .	Cavan . . .	III.	76
19, 20	Corglass . . .	221	3	9c	Cavan . .	Lower Loughtee .	Drumlane . .	Cavan . . .	III.	79
21, 22	Corglass . . .	58	2	24	Cavan . .	Tullygarvey . .	Drung . .	Cootehill . .	III.	88
25	Corglass . . .	74	0	3	Cavan . .	Upper Loughtee .	Annagelliff .	Cavan . .	III.	81
32	Corglass . . .	142	3	37	Cavan . .	Upper Loughtee .	Denn . .	Cavan . . .	III.	83
30	Corglass . . .	423	0	22d	Leitrim . .	Carrigallen .	Carrigallen .	Bawnboy . .	IV.	89
18	Corglass . . .	141	0	7e	Leitrim . .	Drumahaire .	Drumreilly .	Car\^k. on Shannon	IV.	95
20	Corglass . . .	36	3	29	Leitrim . .	Drumahaire .	Inishmagrath .	Manorhamilton	IV.	96
24	Corglass . . .	134	2	12f	Leitrim . .	Leitrim . . .	Kiltubbrid .	Car\^k. on Shannon	IV.	103
3, 6	Corglass . . .	1,034	0	2g	Leitrim . .	Rosclogher . .	Killasnet . .	Manorhamilton	IV.	109
2	Corglass . . .	750	0	0h	Longford .	Longford . .	Killoe . .	Longford . .	I.	158
18	Corglass . . .	87	2	35	Monaghan .	Dartree . . .	Ematris . .	Cootehill . .	III.	266
4	Corglass . . .	287	0	9	Roscommon .	Boyle . . .	Kilronan . .	Boyle . .	IV.	196
9	Corglass or Agha- nergill . .	93	0	1	Armagh . .	Oneilland West .	Drumcree . .	Lurgan . .	III.	51
22, 25	Corglass or Cloverhill	97	3	26	Leitrim . .	Carrigallen . .	Oughteragh .	Bawnboy . .	IV.	92
38	Corglass or Rassan .	96	0	35	Cavan . .	Castlerahan . .	Crosserlough .	Oldcastle . .	III.	68
25	Corgloghan . .	90	0	8	Leitrim . .	Carrigallen . .	Drumreilly .	Bawnboy . .	IV.	90
2	Corgorman . .	160	1	18	Roscommon .	Boyle . . .	Kilronan . .	Boyle . .	IV.	196
23	Corgowan . .	172	2	34	Roscommon .	Ballintober North .	Kilglass . .	Strokestown .	IV.	186
10, 11	Corgreagh . .	64	0	26i	Cavan . .	Lower Loughtee .	Drumlane . .	Cavan . . .	III.	79
22	Corgreagh . .	243	3	2	Cavan . .	Tullygarvey . .	Kildrumsherdan .	Cootehill . .	III.	90
21	Corgreagh . .	138	0	15	Cavan . .	Upper Loughtee .	Larah . .	Cavan . . .	III.	85
26, 27	Corgreagh . .	378	2	25	Monaghan .	Cremorne . .	Aghnamullen .	Carrickmacross	III.	257
1, 2	Corgreagh or Killagriff	412	3	17	Meath . .	Lower Kells . .	Moybolgue .	Kells . .	I.	203
1	Corgreenan . .	59	0	0	Monaghan .	Trough . . .	Errigal Trough .	Clogher . .	III.	283
10	Corgrig . . .	357	0	11	Limerick .	Shanid . . .	Robertstown .	Glin . . .	II.	257
11	Corgullion . .	227	2	19	Roscommon .	Ballintober North .	Kilmore . .	Car\^k. on Shannon	IV.	187
17	Corhammock . .	324	0	35	Armagh . .	Fews Lower . .	Kilclooney .	Armagh . .	II.	46
24	Corhanagh . .	359	0	38	Cavan . .	Tullyhunco .	Killashandra .	Cavan . .	III.	97
27	Corhawnagh . .	68	2	17	Leitrim . .	Leitrim . . .	Kiltoghert .	Car\^k. on Shannon	IV.	101
81	Corhawnagh . .	189	1	36	Mayo . .	Costello . .	Aghamore .	Swineford .	IV.	137
20	Corhawnagh . .	516	2	7	Sligo . .	Leyny . .	Ballysadare .	Sligo . . .	IV.	230
29	Corhawny . .	157	2	11	Roscommon .	Roscommon . .	Lissonuffy .	Strokestown .	IV.	211
27	Corhelshinagh .	297	0	0j	Monaghan .	Cremorne . .	Aghnamullen .	Carrickmacross	III.	257
33	Corhober . .	120	1	14	Sligo . .	Corran . .	Emlaghfad .	Sligo . . .	IV.	226
8, 12	Corhollan . .	125	3	7k	Monaghan .	Monaghan . .	Drumsnat . .	Monaghan .	III.	275
25, 26	Corhoogan . .	62	3	31	Cavan . .	Upper Loughtee .	Annagelliff .	Cavan . .	III.	81
17	Corick . . .	181	1	21	Cavan . .	Tullygarvey . .	Kildrumsherdan .	Cootehill . .	III.	90
31	Corick . . .	1,133	0	27	Londonderry .	Keenaght . .	Dungiven . .	NewT\^nLimavady	III.	236
40, 45	Corick . . .	1,181	1	36	Londonderry .	Loughinsholin . .	Ballynascreen .	Magherafelt .	III.	239
58, 59	Corick . . .	219	3	16	Tyrone . .	Clogher . .	Clogher . .	Clogher . .	III.	292
18	Corickmore . .	249	3	24l	Tyrone . .	Strabane Upper .	Bodoney Upper .	Gortin . .	III.	324
28	Corillaun . .	230	0	28m	Galway . .	Clare . . .	Donaghpatrick .	Tuam . .	IV.	19
22, 29	Corimla North .	333	0	23	Sligo . .	Tireragh . .	Kilmoremoy .	Ballina . .	IV.	235
22, 29	Corimla South .	967	0	34	Sligo . .	Tireragh . .	Kilmoremoy .	Ballina . .	IV.	235
46	Corkaboy . .	154	2	9	Kerry . .	Trughanacmy .	Kilgarrylander .	Tralee . .	II.	210
21	Corkagh . .	84	2	13	Dublin . .	Uppercross .	Clondalkin .	Dublin South .	I.	39
12, 13	Corkagh Beg .	253	1	20	Sligo . .	Tireragh . .	Templeboy .	Dromore West .	IV.	236
21	Corkagh Demesne .	219	3	1	Dublin . .	Uppercross .	Clondalkin .	Dublin South .	I.	39
12	Corkagh More .	300	3	10	Sligo . .	Tireragh . .	Templeboy .	Dromore West .	IV.	236
17	Corkan . .	352	1	37	Westmeath .	Rathconrath .	Rathconrath .	Mullingar .	I.	284
51	Corkanaknockaun .	61	1	3	Clare . .	Bunratty Lower .	Kilnasoolagh .	Ennis . .	II.	6
71	Corkan Isle .	101	0	14	Donegal . .	Raphoe . .	Clonleigh .	Strabane . .	III.	134
5	Corkanree . .	124	2	32	Limerick .	Pubblebrien .	St. Michaels .	Limerick . .	II.	254
27	Corkashybane .	258	1	15	Monaghan .	Farney . .	Magheross .	Carrickmacross	III.	273
27	Corkashyduff .	146	2	16	Monaghan .	Farney . .	Magheross .	Carrickmacross	III.	273
87, 88	Corkbeg . .	359	3	26	Cork, E.R. .	Imokilly . .	Corkbeg . .	Middleton .	II.	86
23	Corkeenagh .	71	2	29n	Roscommon .	Roscommon . .	Clooncraff .	Strokestown .	IV.	208
23	Corkeeran . .	214	2	18o	Monaghan .	Cremorne . .	Aghnamullen .	Cootehill . .	III.	257
19	Corkeeran . .	211	0	26	Monaghan .	Cremorne . .	Ballybay . .	Castleblayney .	III.	259
18, 23	Corkeeran . .	162	0	17	Monaghan .	Dartree . .	Ematris . .	Cootehill . .	III.	266
17	Corkeeran . .	117	0	30	Monaghan .	Dartree . .	Killeevan .	Clones . .	III.	267
31, 34	Corkeeran . .	147	1	1	Monaghan .	Farney . .	Magheracloone .	Carrickmacross	III.	272
113, 114, 122, 123	Corker . .	460	0	21	Galway . .	Kiltartan . .	Kiltartan .	Gort . .	IV.	43
28	Corker . .	141	2	5	Roscommon .	Roscommon . .	Kilcooley .	Strokestown .	IV.	210
9	Corkeragh . .	199	3	13	Kildare . .	Clane . .	Ballynafagh .	Naas . .	I.	53
92	Corker Beg .	201	0	25	Donegal . .	Banagh . .	Killaghtee .	Donegal . .	III.	109
35	Corkermain . .	382	1	2	Antrim . .	Upper Glenarm .	Carncastle .	Larne . .	III.	24
83, 92	Corker More .	759	1	31	Donegal . .	Banagh . .	Killaghtee .	Donegal . .	III.	109

(a) Including 5A. 0R. 1P. water.   (f) Including 26A. 2R. 8P. water.   (k) Including 6A. 1R. 8P. water.
(b) Including 45A. 0R. 12P. water.   (g) Including 17A. 1R. 8P. water.   (l) Including 7A. 0R. 18P. water.
(c) Including 79A. 3R. 22P. water.   (h) Including 40A. 2R. 0P. water.   (m) Including 27A. 3R. 29P. water.
(d) Including 8A. 0R. 30P. water.   (i) Including 1A. 2R. 21P. water.   (n) Including 3A. 2R. 0P. water.
(e) Including 5A. 1R. 0P. water.   (j) Including 62A. 2R. 28P. water.   (o) Including 19A. 0R. 31P. water.

No. of Sheet of the Ordnance Survey Maps.	Townlands and Towns.	Area in Statute Acres.			County.	Barony.	Parish.	Poor Law Union in 1857.	Townland Census of 1851, Part I.	
		A.	R.	P.					Vol.	Page
54, 61, 62	Corkey	342	3	35	Donegal	Raphoe	Raymoghy	Letterkenny	III.	141
18, 19	Corkey Middle	859	0	15	Antrim	Upper Dunluce	Loughguile	Ballymoney	III.	20
18, 19	Corkey North	768	0	18	Antrim	Upper Dunluce	Loughguile	Ballymoney	III.	20
18, 19, 23	Corkey South or Little	826	1	6	Antrim	Upper Dunluce	Loughguile	Ballymoney	III.	20
26	Cork Great	200	3	8	Dublin	Rathdown	Oldconnaught	Rathdown	I.	37
51	Corkhill	163	3	23	Tyrone	Clogher	Clogher	Clogher	III.	292
46	Corkhill	257	3	2	Tyrone	Dungannon Middle	Pomeroy	Dungannon	III.	304
29	Corkhill	224	1	5	Tyrone	Dungannon Upper	Kildress	Cookstown	III.	308
56	Corkhill	248	2	9	Tyrone	Omagh East	Kilskeery	Lowtherstown	III.	313
51	Corkhill Demesne	81	0	25	Tyrone	Clogher	Clogher	Clogher	III.	292
48, 51	Corkip	132	1	35a	Roscommon	Athlone	Taghmaconnell	Athlone	IV.	185
28, 34	Corkish	681	1	7	Cavan	Clankee	Bailieborough	Bailieborough	III.	71
17	Corkish	97	3	0	Monaghan	Dartree	Aghabog	Cootehill	III.	263
20, 24	Corkley	1,308	0	29	Armagh	Armagh	Keady	Armagh	III.	45
26	Cork Little	180	0	4	Dublin	Rathdown	Oldconnaught	Rathdown	I.	37
9	Corknock	55	3	38	Monaghan	Monaghan	Tedavnet	Monaghan	III.	278
56	Corkragh	94	2	8	Tyrone	Omagh East	Kilskeery	Lowtherstown	III.	313
51, 52	Corlack	108	0	35	Clare	Bunratty Lower	Bunratty	Ennis	II.	3
7, 19	Corlackan	376	2	12	Galway	Ballymoe	Kilbegnet	Glennamaddy	IV.	8
2	Corlackan	108	2	2	Galway	Ballymoe	Kilcroan	Glennamaddy	IV.	8
68, 77	Corlacky	587	2	32b	Donegal	Raphoe	Kilteevoge	Stranorlar	III.	139
24	Corlacky	290	0	39	Fermanagh	Magherastephana	Aghalurcher	Lisnaskea	III.	215
26, 32	Corlacky	1,315	0	10	Londonderry	Loughinsholin	Killelagh	Magherafelt	III.	241
18	Corlagan	112	2	12	Longford	Moydow	Ballymacormick	Longford	I.	160
14	Corlagan North	93	0	29	Monaghan	Cremorne	Clontibret	Monaghan	III.	260
19	Corlagan South	129	0	10	Monaghan	Cremorne	Clontibret	Castleblayney	III.	260
11	Corlaghaloo	162	3	36	Cavan	Tullygarvey	Annagh	Cavan	III.	87
35	Corlaghaloon	131	3	33	Fermanagh	Clankelly	Clones	Clones	III.	195
49	Corlaghdergan	531	0	16	Tyrone	Omagh East	Dromore	Omagh	III.	311
2	Corlaght East	358	0	16	Fermanagh	Lurg	Drumkeeran	Lowtherstown	III.	205
5	Corlaght West	78	0	25	Fermanagh	Lurg	Drumkeeran	Lowtherstown	III.	205
19	Corlane	40	0	22	Antrim	Lower Glenarm	Layd	Ballycastle	III.	22
28, 32	Corlaskagh	116	1	38	Leitrim	Leitrim	Mohill	Car^k. on Shannon	IV.	104
21	Corlat	223	2	7	Armagh	Fews Upper	Ballymyre	Newry	III.	48
40	Corlat	198	1	20	Cavan	Castlerahan	Mullagh	Kells	III.	70
27	Corlat	216	0	33	Monaghan	Cremorne	Aghnamullen	Carrickmacross	III.	257
12	Corlat	138	1	12	Monaghan	Dartree	Killeevan	Monaghan	III.	267
9	Corlat	66	2	38	Monaghan	Monaghan	Monaghan	Monaghan	III.	276
5	Corlat	87	2	25	Monaghan	Monaghan	Tedavnet	Monaghan	III.	278
32	Corlatcerin	154	1	21	Cavan	Castlerahan	Crosserlough	Cavan	III.	68
39	Corlatt	185	2	7c	Fermanagh	Coole	Galloon	Clones	III.	199
39	Corlatt	42	1	27	Fermanagh	Knockninny	Kinawley	Lisnaskea	III.	201
3, 6	Corlattallan	147	3	21d	Monaghan	Trough	Errigal Trough	Monaghan	III.	283
9, 13	Corlattan	100	0	34	Monaghan	Monaghan	Monaghan	Monaghan	III.	276
28	Corlattycarroll	113	3	1	Cavan	Clankee	Knockbride	Bailieborough	III.	73
23, 28	Corlattylannan	252	0	26e	Cavan	Clankee	Knockbride	Bailieborough	III.	73
1	Corlave	600	2	13	Fermanagh	Lurg	Drumkeeran	Lowtherstown	III.	205
29	Corlea	360	3	36	Cavan	Clankee	Enniskeen	Bailieborough	III.	72
3	Corlea	140	1	18	Cavan	Tullyhaw	Killinagh	Enniskillen	III.	91
52	Corlea	593	1	10f	Clare	Bunratty Lower	Kilfinaghta	Limerick	II.	4
13, 20	Corlea	294	2	24	Clare	Tulla Upper	Feakle	Scarriff	II.	39
87	Corlea	477	2	29	Donegal	Raphoe	Donaghmore	Stranorlar	III.	137
107, 108	Corlea	1,108	0	34g	Donegal	Tirhugh	Kilbarron	Ballyshannon	III.	148
105	Corlea	884	3	31h	Donegal	Tirhugh	Templecarn	Donegal	III.	149
28, 32	Corlea	148	3	18	Leitrim	Leitrim	Mohill	Car^k. on Shannon	IV.	104
4, 7	Corlea	614	0	31	Leitrim	Rosclogher	Rossinver	Manorhamilton	IV.	111
22	Corlea	659	0	39	Longford	Ratheline	Kilcommock	Ballymahon	I.	164
24, 27	Corlea	283	3	15i	Monaghan	Cremorne	Aghnamullen	Castleblayney	III.	257
28	Corlea	186	3	22	Monaghan	Farney	Donaghmoyne	Carrickmacross	III.	269
30	Corlea	252	3	17	Monaghan	Farney	Magheracloone	Carrickmacross	III.	272
30	Corlea	190	0	15	Monaghan	Farney	Magheross	Carrickmacross	III.	273
13, 14, 18, 19	Corlea	319	3	15	Monaghan	Monaghan	Tullycorbet	Monaghan	III.	281
34	Corlea	498	0	20	Tyrone	Omagh East	Drumragh	Omagh	III.	312
56	Corlea	158	1	18j	Tyrone	Omagh East	Kilskeery	Lowtherstown	III.	313
13, 20	Corlea Beg	159	2	4	Clare	Tulla Upper	Feakle	Scarriff	II.	39
13	Corleacommons North	465	1	27k	Clare	Tulla Upper	Feakle	Scarriff	II.	39
13	Corleacommons South	387	1	6l	Clare	Tulla Upper	Feakle	Scarriff	II.	39
19, 20	Corleadargan	314	0	20m	Monaghan	Cremorne	Clontibret	Castleblayney	III.	260
65	Corleaghan	872	0	2n	Tyrone	Clogher	Clogher	Clogher	III.	292
19	Corlealackagh	256	2	36	Monaghan	Cremorne	Clontibret	Castleblayney	III.	260
13, 20	Corlea More	905	0	30	Clare	Tulla Upper	Feakle	Scarriff	II.	39
19	Corleanamaddy	137	0	33	Monaghan	Cremorne	Clontibret	Castleblayney	III.	260
28	Corleck	202	3	18	Cavan	Clankee	Knockbride	Bailieborough	III.	73

(a) Including 40A. 2R. 16P. water.
(b) Including 3A. 1R. 19P. water.
(c) Including 8A. 2R. 7P. water.
(d) Including 4A. 0R. 36P. water.
(e) Including 6A. 3R. 37P. water.

(f) Including 0A. 1R. 39P. water.
(g) Including 24A. 2R. 28P. water.
(h) Including 7A. 1R. 24P. water.
(i) Including 15A. 0R. 21P. water.
(j) Including 9A. 0R. 32P. water.

(k) Including 32A. 1R. 22P. water.
(l) Including 11A. 0R. 21P. water.
(m) Including 22A. 0R. 5P. water.
(n) Including 3A. 0R. 0P. water.

2 R

No. of Sheet of the Ordnance Survey Maps.	Townlands and Towns.	Area in Statute Acres.			County.	Barony.	Parish.	Poor Law Union in 1857.	Townland Census of 1851. Part I.	
		A.	R.	P.					Vol.	Page
13, 18	Corleck . . .	305	2	26	Monaghan .	Dartree . .	Aghabog . .	Monaghan .	III.	263
28	Corleck . .	157	2	32	Monaghan .	Farney . . .	Donaghmoyne .	Carrickmacross	III.	269
5	Corleckagh Lower .	105	1	22	Cavan . .	Tullyhaw .	Killinagh . .	Enniskillen .	III.	91
5	Corleckagh Upper .	182	0	24	Cavan . .	Tullyhaw .	Killinagh . .	Enniskillen .	III.	91
23	Corleckduff . .	121	0	34	Cavan . .	Clankee . . .	Drumgoon . .	Cootehill . .	III.	72
49	Corlee . . .	476	3	30a	Mayo . .	Gallen . . .	Killasser . .	Swineford .	IV.	149
11	Corleggy . .	72	3	23b	Cavan . .	Lower Loughtee .	Annagh . . .	Cavan . .	III.	78
31, 32	Corlican . . .	729	2	23	Wexford . .	Bantry . . .	Whitechurchglynn .	Wexford . .	I.	303
24	Corlis . . .	30	0	20	Cavan . .	Tullyhunco .	Killashandra .	Cavan . .	III.	97
21, 27	Corlis . . .	537	3	19	Roscommon .	Castlereagh .	Baslick . . .	Castlereagh .	IV.	199
11, 17	Corlis . . .	151	1	35	Roscommon .	Roscommon .	Aughrim . .	Car^k.on Shannon	IV.	207
16	Corlis . . .	53	0	2	Westmeath .	Kilkenny West	Noughaval . .	Ballymahon .	I.	274
25	Corlisalee . .	135	2	11	Cavan . .	Upper Loughtee .	Annagelliff . .	Cavan . .	III.	81
20, 21	Corlisbane . .	170	0	36	Louth . .	Ferrard . .	Mullary . . .	Ardee . .	I.	181
5	Corlisbannan . .	258	2	23	Cavan . .	Tullyhaw .	Killinagh . .	Enniskillen .	III.	91
24	Corlisbrattan . .	453	3	30c	Cavan . .	Tullyhunco .	Killashandra .	Cavan . .	III.	97
28, 32	Corlisheen . .	159	0	39	Leitrim . .	Leitrim . . .	Annaduff . .	Car^k. on Shannon	IV.	99
34	Corlisheen . .	179	3	28	Sligo . .	Tirerrill . .	Kilmacallan .	Sligo . . .	IV.	239
2	Corliskea . . .	450	0	26	Galway . .	Ballymoe .	Drumatemple .	Glennamaddy .	IV.	7
90	Corlisland . .	4	1	26	Mayo . .	Clanmorris .	Mayo . . .	Claremorris .	IV.	135
31	Corlislea . . .	155	1	13	Cavan . .	Clanmahon .	Crosserlough .	Cavan . .	III.	76
25, 31	Corlismore . .	214	1	5	Cavan . .	Clanmahon .	Ballintemple .	Cavan . .	III.	75
27, 30	Corliss . . .	381	1	33d	Armagh . .	Fews Upper .	Creggan . .	Castleblayney .	III.	48
27, 28	Corlona . . .	79	0	32	Leitrim . .	Leitrim . .	Kiltoghert .	Car^k.on Shannon	IV.	101
14	Corlongford . .	120	0	32	Monaghan .	Monaghan .	Tullycorbet .	Monaghan .	III.	281
8, 9	Corlough . . .	209	2	38	Cavan . .	Tullyhaw .	Templeport .	Bawnboy . .	III.	94
24, 29	Corlough . .	313	1	18	Fermanagh .	Magherastephana	Aghalurcher .	Lisnaskea .	III.	215
24	Corlough . .	221	1	26e	Leitrim . .	Leitrim . .	Fenagh . . .	Mohill . .	IV.	100
23	Corlough . .	147	1	17	Leitrim . .	Leitrim . .	Kiltoghert .	Car^k. on Shannon	IV.	101
39, 42	Corloughan . .	356	2	26	Kilkenny .	Iverk . . .	Fiddown . .	Carrick on Suir	I.	105
17	Corlougharoe . .	135	2	22	Monaghan .	Dartree . .	Killeevan . .	Cootehill . .	III.	267
17	Corloughcahill .	175	2	9	Leitrim . .	Drumahaire .	Inishmagrath .	Manorhamilton .	IV.	96
23	Corloughlin . .	91	3	16	Leitrim . .	Leitrim . .	Kiltoghert .	Car^k. on Shannon	IV.	101
18	Corloughtomalty .	41	1	20	Leitrim . .	Drumahaire .	Inishmagrath .	Manorhamilton .	IV.	96
42, 45	Corluddy . .	331	1	25	Kilkenny .	Iverk . . .	Portnascully .	Waterford . .	I.	106
60	Corlummin . .	454	1	6f	Mayo . .	Tirawley . .	Ballynahaglish .	Ballina . .	IV.	164
34	Corlurgan . .	262	1	28	Cavan . .	Clankee . .	Bailieborough .	Bailieborough .	III.	71
25	Corlurgan . .	166	2	23	Cavan . .	Upper Loughtee .	Annagelliff . .	Cavan . .	III.	81
17, 18	Corlust . . .	349	2	30g	Armagh . .	Orior Lower .	Ballymore .	Banbridge .	III.	55
10, 14	Corlust . . .	101	0	35	Monaghan .	Monaghan .	Monaghan . .	Monaghan .	III.	276
28	Corlygorm . .	192	2	37	Monaghan .	Farney . . .	Donaghmoyne .	Carrickmacross	III.	269
40, 41, 47	Cormackstown .	1,002	0	33	Tipperary, N.R.	Eliogarty . .	Holycross . .	Thurles . .	II.	270
23	Cormaclew . .	196	0	31	Westmeath .	Kilkenny West	Drumraney .	Ballymahon .	I.	273
15	Cormacmullan .	61	3	35	Cavan . .	Lower Loughtee .	Annagh . .	Cavan . .	III.	78
72	Cormacuagh East .	215	0	16h	Galway . .	Tiaquin . .	Monivea . .	Loughrea .	IV.	78
72	Cormacuagh West .	411	1	39	Galway . .	Tiaquin . .	Monivea . .	Loughrea . .	IV.	79
39	Cormaddyduff .	565	3	21	Cavan . .	Castlerahan .	Castlerahan .	Oldcastle . .	III.	67
36, 37	Cormaddyduff .	84	1	12	Cavan . .	Clanmahon .	Drumlumman .	Granard . .	III.	77
22	Cormaglava . .	356	0	8	Longford .	Rathcline .	Cashel . .	Ballymahon .	I.	163
79	Cormakilly . .	192	0	10	Donegal .	Raphoe . .	Urney . . .	Strabane . .	III.	144
4	Cormeelick North .	105	1	21i	Galway . .	Dunmore .	Addergoole .	Tuam . . .	IV.	33
4	Cormeelick South .	87	1	39	Galway . .	Dunmore .	Addergoole .	Tuam . . .	IV.	33
23	Cormeeltan . .	78	1	18	Leitrim . .	Leitrim . .	Kiltoghert .	Car^k.on Shannon	IV.	101
11, 15	Cormeen . .	378	0	35	Armagh . .	Armagh . .	Derrynoose .	Armagh . .	III.	44
38, 39	Cormeen . .	417	3	34	Cavan . .	Castlerahan .	Castlerahan .	Oldcastle . .	III.	67
25, 31	Cormeen . .	123	1	25	Cavan . .	Clanmahon .	Kilmore . .	Cavan . .	III.	78
21, 26, 27	Cormeen . .	347	3	8	Cavan . .	Tullygarvey .	Larah . . .	Cootehill . .	III.	91
14	Cormeen . .	200	0	12j	Cavan . .	Tullyhunco .	Kildallan . .	Bawnboy . .	III.	96
32	Cormeen . .	155	0	37	King's Co. .	Ballyboy . .	Killoughy . .	Tullamore .	I.	124
5	Cormeen . .	253	1	38	Meath . .	Lower Kells .	Moybolgue .	Kells . . .	I.	203
1, 4	Cormeen . .	444	1	11	Meath . .	Lower Kells .	Moynalty . .	Kells . . .	I.	203
23	Cormeen . .	217	1	5	Monaghan .	Cremorne .	Aghnamullen .	Cootehill . .	III.	257
17, 22	Cormeen . .	228	1	29	Monaghan .	Dartree . .	Currin . . .	Cootehill . .	III.	265
13	Cormeen . .	181	2	5	Monaghan .	Monaghan .	Monaghan . .	Monaghan .	III.	276
21,22,26,27	Cormeen Glebe .	254	3	15	Cavan . .	Tullygarvey .	Larah . . .	Cootehill . .	III.	91
29, 35	Cormey . . .	333	3	23	Cavan . .	Clankee . . .	Enniskeen .	Bailieborough .	III.	72
106, 107	Cormick . . .	107	0	27	Galway . .	Longford .	Abbeygormacan .	Ballinasloe .	IV.	56
106, 107	Cormick . . .	110	1	30	Galway . .	Longford .	Duniry . .	Loughrea . .	IV.	58
5, 10	Cormickstown .	254	0	14	Kildare . .	North Salt .	Laraghbryan .	Celbridge . .	I.	75
34	Cormonalea . .	156	1	36	Fermanagh .	Clankelly .	Galloon . .	Lisnaskea .	III.	198
20	Cormongan . .	197	2	29	Leitrim . .	Leitrim . . .	Kiltoghert .	Car^k. on Shannon	IV.	101
28	Cormore . . .	78	1	31	Leitrim . .	Mohill . .	Mohill . .	Mohill . .	IV.	107
51, 58	Cormore . . .	492	2	18	Tyrone . .	Clogher . .	Clogher . .	Clogher . .	III.	292

(a) Including 2A. 2R. 21P. water.
(b) Including 8A. 0R. 4P. water.
(c) Including 13A. 0R. 25P. water.
(d) Including 7A. 0R. 0P. water.

(e) Including 35A. 2R. 30P. water.
(f) Including 3A. 0R. 27P. water.
(g) Including 6A. 0R. 34P. water.

(h) Including 2A. 2R. 24P. water.
(i) Including 6A. 0R. 16P. water.
(j) Including 9A. 2R. 0P. water.

No. of Sheet of the Ordnance Survey Maps.	Townlands and Towns.	Area in Statute Acres.	County.	Barony.	Parish.	Poor Law Union in 1857.	Townland Census of 1851, Part I.	
		A. R. P.					Vol.	Page
6, 7, 14, 15	Cor More and Cor Beg	611 2 6	King's Co.	Garrycastle	Lemanaghan	Parsonstown	I.	136
30	Cormore or Corduff	170 1 28	Cavan	Tullyhunco	Scrabby	Cavan	III.	99
12, 17	Cormoy	196 2 2	Monaghan	Dartree	Aghabog	Clones	III.	263
28	Cormoy	111 3 33a	Monaghan	Farney	Donaghmoyne	Carrickmacross	III.	269
28	Cormoy Lower	80 3 14	Monaghan	Farney	Donaghmoyne	Carrickmacross	III.	269
28	Cormoy Upper	74 0 31	Monaghan	Farney	Donaghmoyne	Carrickmacross	III.	269
54	Cormullagh	459 3 38b	Tyrone	Dungannon Middle	Clonfeacle	Dungannon	III.	299
100	Cormullin	519 1 21c	Donegal	Tirhugh	Drumhome	Donegal	III.	146
10, 14	Cormurphy	82 2 36	Monaghan	Monaghan	Monaghan	Monaghan	III.	277
32	Cornabanny	232 2 16	Roscommon	Castlereagh	Kiltullagh	Castlereagh	IV.	201
16, 21	Cornabaste	165 3 11	Cavan	Tullygarvey	Drung	Cootehill	III.	88
22	Cornabeagh	117 0 2	Cavan	Tullygarvey	Kildrumsherdan	Cootehill	III.	90
34	Cornabracken	39 2 33	Tyrone	Omagh East	Drumragh	Omagh	III.	312
17	Cornabraher	199 2 2	Cavan	Tullygarvey	Kildrumsherdan	Cootehill	III.	90
14	Cornabrandy	121 1 26	Monaghan	Cremorne	Clontibret	Monaghan	III.	260
39, 40	Cornabrass	200 2 34d	Fermanagh	Coole	Galloon	Clones	III.	199
87	Cornabrogue	131 3 0	Donegal	Raphoe	Donaghmore	Stranorlar	III.	137
21	Cornabroher	120 1 23	Leitrim	Carrigallen	Oughteragh	Bawnboy	IV.	92
24	Cornabrone	207 0 3e	Leitrim	Leitrim	Fenagh	Mohill	IV.	100
42, 43	Cornacaghan	177 2 37	Fermanagh	Coole	Drummully	Clones	III.	199
91	Cornacahan	135 2 39	Donegal	Banagh	Killybegs Upper	Glenties	III.	110
17	Cornacarrow	175 3 18	Cavan	Tullygarvey	Drumgoon	Cootehill	III.	88
21	Cornacarrow	122 0 38	Cavan	Tullygarvey	Drung	Cootehill	III.	88
2	Cornacarrow	104 0 39f	Meath	Lower Kells	Enniskeen	Kells	I.	202
24, 25, 27, 28	Cornacarrow	355 2 20g	Monaghan	Cremorne	Aghnamullen	Castleblayney	III.	257
31	Cornacarrow	50 2 18	Monaghan	Farney	Magheracloone	Carrickmacross	III.	272
22	Cornacarta	160 3 0	Longford	Rathcline	Kilcommock	Ballymahon	I.	164
102	Cornacarta	183 3 22	Mayo	Costello	Annagh	Claremorris	IV.	138
3	Cornacarta	332 1 33h	Roscommon	Boyle	Boyle	Boyle	IV.	194
30, 44	Cornacartan	209 3 38	Galway	Dunmore	Killererin	Tuam	IV.	35
121	Cornacartan	299 2 19	Mayo	Kilmaine	Kilmainebeg	Ballinrobe	IV.	155
20	Cornacask or Easterfield	484 3 19i	Galway	Killian	Athleague	Mountbellew	IV.	43
2	Cornacausk	334 2 28	Westmeath	Moygoish	Street	Granard	I.	281
40	Cornaclare or Johnstown	81 3 17	Fermanagh	Clankelly	Clones	Clones	III.	195
19	Cornaclea or Tawlagh	63 0 18j	Cavan	Tullyhunco	Kildallan	Cavan	III.	96
9	Cornacleigh	110 1 32	Cavan	Tullyhaw	Templeport	Bawnboy	III.	94
12	Cornacloy	239 0 18	Leitrim	Drumahaire	Cloonclare	Manorhamilton	IV.	93
17	Cornacloy	81 0 22	Leitrim	Drumahaire	Inishmagrath	Manorhamilton	IV.	96
31	Cornacorroo	109 2 36	Leitrim	Leitrim	Kiltoghert	Cark on Shannon	IV.	101
6	Cornacoyntia	131 2 2	Galway	Ballymoe	Boyounagh	Glennamaddy	IV.	6
27	Cornacranaghy	111 1 24	Leitrim	Leitrim	Kiltoghert	Cark on Shannon	IV.	101
25	Cornacrea	130 2 34	Cavan	Upper Loughtee	Kilmore	Cavan	III.	84
32	Cornacrea	114 0 28	Fermanagh	Clanawley	Kinawley	Enniskillen	III.	193
5	Cornacrea	50 3 21	Fermanagh	Lurg	Magheraculmoney	Lowtherstown	III.	207
25	Cornacreegh	126 2 30	Leitrim	Carrigallen	Oughteragh	Bawnboy	IV.	92
38, 39	Cornacreeve	156 2 34	Cavan	Castlerahan	Castlerahan	Oldcastle	III.	67
35	Cornacreeve	156 3 14	Fermanagh	Clankelly	Clones	Clones	III.	195
22	Cornacreeve	47 2 14	Leitrim	Carrigallen	Drumreilly	Bawnboy	IV.	90
22	Cornacreeve	71 1 8	Leitrim	Carrigallen	Oughteragh	Bawnboy	IV.	92
13, 14	Cornacreeve	120 2 33	Monaghan	Monaghan	Monaghan	Monaghan	III.	277
8	Cornacreeve	105 0 11	Monaghan	Monaghan	Tedavnet	Monaghan	III.	278
19	Cornacreeve	162 0 31	Monaghan	Monaghan	Tullycorbet	Monaghan	III.	281
6	Cornacreeve	225 3 27k	Monaghan	Trough	Donagh	Monaghan	III.	281
1	Cornacreevy	289 0 10l	Westmeath	Fore	Foyran	Granard	I.	270
13, 17	Cornacrew	149 2 24m	Armagh	Fews Lower	Mullaghbrack	Armagh	III.	47
28	Cornacrew	101 3 3	Monaghan	Farney	Donaghmoyne	Carrickmacross	III.	269
14	Cornacrum	246 3 29n	Cavan	Tullyhunco	Kildallan	Bawnboy	III.	97
2	Cornacullew	652 3 14o	Longford	Longford	Killoe	Longford	I.	159
19, 20	Cornacully	725 3 36	Fermanagh	Clanawley	Cleenish	Ballyshannon	III.	190
11	Cornadarragh	109 2 27p	Cavan	Lower Loughtee	Drumlane	Cavan	III.	79
15	Cornadarragh (Pleydell)	98 0 9q	Cavan	Lower Loughtee	Drumlane	Cavan	III.	79
13	Cornadarum	74 0 0	Fermanagh	Magheraboy	Inishmacsaint	Ballyshannon	III.	212
21	Cornadimpan Glebe	152 2 22	Cavan	Tullygarvey	Larah	Cootehill	III.	91
21, 22	Cornadowagh	515 2 33	Longford	Rathcline	Cashel	Ballymahon	I.	163
47	Cornadrum	65 3 20	Galway	Killian	Killeroran	Mountbellew	IV.	44
3	Cornadrung	402 3 5	Longford	Granard	Columbkille	Granard	I.	155
12	Cornafaghy	94 3 20	Monaghan	Dartree	Clones	Monaghan	III.	264
23, 28	Cornafannoge	276 3 26	Fermanagh	Magherastephana	Aghavea	Lisnaskea	III.	218
24	Cornafean	151 1 19	Cavan	Tullyhunco	Killashandra	Cavan	III.	97

(a) Including 5A. 1R. 7P. water.
(b) Including 7A. 2R. 20P. water.
(c) Including 8A. 0R. 24P. water.
(d) Including 28A. 1R. 19P. water.
(e) Including 13A. 1R. 29P. water.
(f) Including 5A. 0R. 16P. water.

(g) Including 42A. 1R. 13P. water.
(h) Including 22A. 1R. 1P. water.
(i) Including 32A. 2R. 0P. water.
(j) Including 7A. 1R. 12P. water.
(k) Including 5A. 1R. 11P. water.
(l) Including 14A. 2R. 0P. water.

(m) Including 3A. 3R. 11P. water.
(n) Including 23A. 2R. 3P. water.
(o) Including 16A. 3R. 8P. water.
(p) Including 7A. 0R. 5P. water.
(q) Including 5A. 3R. 6P. water.

No. of Sheet of the Ordnance Survey Maps.	Townlands and Towns.	Area in Statute Acres.	County.	Barony.	Parish.	Poor Law Union in 1857.	Townland Census of 1851, Part I.	
		A. R. P.					Vol.	Page
34	Cornaferst	323 0 12a	Leitrim	Carrigallen	Carrigallen	Mohill	IV.	89
29	Cornafostra	82 3 6	Leitrim	Leitrim	Fenagh	Mohill	IV.	100
51, 52, 55	Cornafulla	801 0 29	Roscommon	Athlone	Drum	Athlone	IV.	180
5, 9	Cornafunshin	262 3 14	Longford	Longford	Killoe	Longford	I.	159
7	Cornafurrish & Corrabeg	279 2 36	King's Co.	Garrycastle	Lemanaghan	Parsonstown	I.	136
21	Cornagall	243 2 10b	Cavan	Tullygarvey	Drung	Cootehill	III.	88
25	Cornagall	97 3 23	Monaghan	Farney	Donaghmoyne	Castleblayney	III.	269
31	Cornagark	181 1 32	King's Co.	Eglish	Drumcullen	Parsonstown	I.	134
16	Cornagarrow	251 3 19c	Cavan	Tullygarvey	Drung	Cootehill	III.	88
17	Cornagarrow	77 2 5d	Cavan	Tullygarvey	Kildrumsherdan	Cootehill	III.	90
32	Cornagarvoge	387 3 8	Monaghan	Farney	Inishkeen	Dundalk	III.	271
77	Cornagashlaun	475 0 14e	Mayo	Burrishoole	Islandeady	Westport	IV.	121
5	Cornagawna	258 2 2	Leitrim	Rosclogher	Rossinver	Ballyshannon	IV.	111
81, 82	Cornageaghta	84 0 27	Mayo	Costello	Aghamore	Swineford	IV.	137
35	Cornagee	93 0 12	Cavan	Clankee	Enniskeen	Bailieborough	III.	72
2, 4	Cornagee	430 3 28	Cavan	Tullyhaw	Killinagh	Enniskillen	III.	91
26	Cornagee	159 3 16	Fermanagh	Clanawley	Cleenish	Enniskillen	III.	190
2	Cornagee	172 3 1	Roscommon	Boyle	Kilronan	Boyle	IV.	196
18	Cornageeha	128 3 22	Leitrim	Drumahaire	Drumreilly	Car.on Shannon	IV.	95
32	Cornageeha	74 0 3	Leitrim	Leitrim	Mohill	Mohill	IV.	104
36	Cornageeha	304 2 30f	Leitrim	Mohill	Cloone	Mohill	IV.	105
1	Cornageeha	272 1 13	Leitrim	Rosclogher	Rossinver	Ballyshannon	IV.	111
50, 62	Cornageeha	215 3 21	Mayo	Gallon	Killasser	Swineford	IV.	149
48	Cornageeha	311 2 7g	Roscommon	Athlone	Cam	Athlone	IV.	179
14	Cornageeha	152 2 34	Sligo	Carbury	St. John's	Sligo	IV.	223
22, 25	Cornageeragh	146 1 27h	Leitrim	Carrigallen	Oughteragh	Bawnboy	IV.	92
29	Cornagher	567 0 2i	Leitrim	Mohill	Cloone	Mohill	IV.	105
30, 34	Cornaghy	182 1 20	Leitrim	Carrigallen	Carrigallen	Mohill	IV.	89
53	Cornagill	159 3 34	Donegal	Kilmacrenan	Aghanunshin	Letterkenny	III.	122
61, 69	Cornagillagh	289 0 16	Donegal	Raphoe	Convoy	Stranorlar	III.	136
27,28,31,32	Cornagillagh	90 1 27	Leitrim	Leitrim	Annaduff	Car.on Shannon	IV.	99
35, 37	Cornagillagh	287 0 3	Leitrim	Mohill	Mohill	Mohill	IV.	107
4, 7	Cornagillagh	618 1 23	Leitrim	Rosclogher	Killasnet	Manorhamilton	IV.	109
6	Cornagilty	117 0 30	Monaghan	Monaghan	Tedavnet	Monaghan	III.	278
2	Cornaglah	242 0 12	Leitrim	Rosclogher	Rossinver	Ballyshannon	IV.	111
22	Cornaglare	184 1 30	Monaghan	Dartree	Currin	Cootehill	III.	265
13	Cornaglare	210 2 14j	Monaghan	Monaghan	Kilmore	Monaghan	III.	276
40	Cornaglare or Palmira	389 3 2	Cavan	Castlerahan	Mullagh	Kells	III.	70
40	Cornaglea Lower	165 2 2	Cavan	Castlerahan	Mullagh	Bailieborough	III.	70
40	Cornaglea Upper	167 0 12	Cavan	Castlerahan	Mullagh	Bailieborough	III.	70
25	Cornagleragh or Oldtown	126 1 7	Cavan	Upper Loughtee	Annagelliff	Cavan	III.	81
5	Cornaglia	490 0 22	Roscommon	Boyle	Boyle	Boyle	IV.	194
28	Cornagon	108 2 1k	Leitrim	Mohill	Fenagh	Mohill	IV.	106
36	Cornagower East	194 1 28	Wicklow	Arklow	Dunganstown	Rathdrum	I.	343
36	Cornagower West	196 0 6	Wicklow	Arklow	Dunganstown	Rathdrum	I.	343
22	Cornagrade	184 3 38l	Fermanagh	Tirkennedy	Enniskillen	Enniskillen	III.	221
17, 21	Cornagrally	310 0 29	Armagh	Orior Lower	Loughgilly	Newry	III.	56
7	Cornagran	89 0 22	Cavan	Tullyhaw	Kinawley	Bawnboy	III.	93
30, 36	Cornagran	120 2 5m	Cavan	Tullyhunco	Scrabby	Granard	III.	99
3	Cornagrea	204 0 37n	Roscommon	Boyle	Ardcarn	Boyle	IV.	192
32	Cornagresha North	70 1 28	Leitrim	Mohill	Mohill	Mohill	IV.	107
32	Cornagresha South	69 1 1	Leitrim	Mohill	Mohill	Mohill	IV.	107
75	Cornagrillagh	515 2 14	Donegal	Boylagh	Inishkeel	Glenties	III.	112
14	Cornagrow	112 3 33	Cavan	Lower Loughtee	Drumlane	Cavan	III.	79
32	Cornagrow	247 1 36o	Cavan	Upper Loughtee	Denn	Cavan	III.	83
18	Cornaguillagh	121 3 36	Leitrim	Drumahaire	Drumreilly	Car.on Shannon	IV.	95
22	Cornaguillagh	101 0 37	Longford	Rathcline	Cashel	Ballymahon	I.	163
8	Cornaguillagh	109 1 27	Monaghan	Monaghan	Tedavnet	Monaghan	III.	278
51, 52	Cornaguillion	306 1 27	Donegal	Kilmacrenan	Gartan	Letterkenny	III.	127
32, 33	Cornagun	71 3 33	Fermanagh	Clanawley	Kinawley	Enniskillen	III.	193
13	Cornagunleog	182 3 18	Cavan	Tullyhaw	Templeport	Bawnboy	III.	94
13, 19	Cornahaia	139 0 5	Cavan	Tullyhunco	Kildallan	Bawnboy	III.	97
8, 13	Cornahaltie	357 1 32	Fermanagh	Magheraboy	Inishmacsaint	Ballyshannon	III.	212
90	Cornahavoley	68 1 4p	Mayo	Carra	Rosslee	Castlebar	IV.	130
3, 4	Cornahaw	425 2 23	Cavan	Tullyhaw	Killinagh	Enniskillen	III.	91
26	Cornahawla	183 3 18	Fermanagh	Clanawley	Cleenish	Enniskillen	III.	190
25	Cornahawla	138 0 14	Monaghan	Farney	Donaghmoyne	Castleblayney	III.	269
3	Cornaheive	85 2 20	Monaghan	Trough	Errigal Trough	Clogher	III.	283
38, 39	Cornaher	666 0 11	Westmeath	Moycashel	Newtown	Mullingar	I.	279
79	Cornahilt	100 2 4	Cavan	Castlerahan	Castlerahan	Oldcastle	III.	67
25	Cornahinch	161 1 10	Cork, E.R.	Fermoy	Caherduggan	Mallow	II.	77

(a) Including 72A. 3R. 28P. water.
(b) Including 11A. 1R. 8P. water.
(c) Including 20A. 0R. 37P. water.
(d) Including 4A. 1R. 29P. water.
(e) Including 44A. 1R. 15P. water.
(f) Including 16A. 1R. 16P. water.

(g) Including 14A. 1R. 21P. water.
(h) Including 17A. 1R. 12P. water.
(i) Including 30A. 0R. 24P. water.
(j) Including 15A. 3R. 8P. water.
(k) Including 6A. 2R. 6P. water.

(l) Including 1A. 1R. 19P. Cherry Island, and 59A. 2R. 23P. water.
(m) Including 3A. 0R. 26P. water.
(n) Including 4A. 0R. 19P. water.
(o) Including 19A. 3R. 13P. water.
(p) Including 14A. 0R. 11P. water.

No. of Sheet of the Ordnance Survey Maps.	Townlands and Towns.	Area in Statute Acres.			County.	Barony.	Parish.	Poor Law Union in 1857.	Townland Census of 1851, Part I.	
		A.	R.	P.					Vol.	Page
19, 24	Cornahoe	276	1	8	Monaghan	Cremorne	Ballybay	Castleblayney	III.	259
7	Cornahoe	71	1	23	Monaghan	Monaghan	Tehallan	Monaghan	III.	280
14, 19	Cornahoe	143	3	32	Monaghan	Monaghan	Tullycorbet	Monaghan	III.	281
10	Cornahoe Lower	161	1	8	Monaghan	Cremorne	Clontibret	Monaghan	III.	260
15	Cornahoe Upper	216	0	19	Monaghan	Cremorne	Clontibret	Castleblayney	III.	260
18, 22	Cornahoo	75	1	35	Longford	Moydow	Kilcommock	Ballymahon	I.	161
2	Cornahoova	369	0	18	Meath	Morgallion	Enniskeen	Kells	I.	209
38	Cornahoule	211	1	22	Fermanagh	Knockninny	Kinawley	Lisnaskea	III.	201
30	Cornahove	166	1	21a	Armagh	Fews Upper	Creggan	Castleblayney	III.	48
23,24,28,29	Cornakessagh	261	1	22	Fermanagh	Magherastephana	Aghalurcher	Lisnaskea	III.	215
40	Cornakill	531	3	34	Cavan	Castlerahan	Mullagh	Kells	III.	70
35	Cornakill	190	0	27	Cavan	Clankee	Enniskeen	Bailieborough	III.	72
21	Cornakill	260	3	31	Cavan	Tullygarvey	Drung	Cootehill	III.	88
39	Cornakill	126	0	0b	Fermanagh	Knockninny	Kinawley	Lisnaskea	III.	201
39	Cornakilly	216	1	19	Cavan	Castlerahan	Castlerahan	Oldcastle	III.	67
6	Cornakinnegar	306	1	15	Armagh	Oneilland East	Shankill	Lurgan	III.	50
5, 9	Cornalack	81	0	24	Armagh	Oneilland West	Drumcree	Lurgan	III.	52
6	Cornalack	70	3	11	Tipperary, N.R.	Lower Ormond	Terryglass	Borrisokane	II.	287
11	Cornalaghta	582	0	22	Leitrim	Drumahaire	Drumlease	Manorhamilton	IV.	94
28, 29	Cornalara	202	0	39c	Cavan	Clankee	Shercock	Bailieborough	III.	74
30	Cornalaragh	272	0	2	Monaghan	Farney	Magheracloone	Carrickmacross	III.	272
100	Cornalassan	185	1	13	Mayo	Kilmaine	Robeen	Ballinrobe	IV.	157
15, 16	Cornalaur	553	1	25	King's Co.	Ballycowan	Rahan	Tullamore	I.	128
11	Cornaleck	64	3	0	Cavan	Lower Loughtee	Drumlane	Cavan	III.	79
33	Cornaleck	175	0	12	Fermanagh	Knockninny	Kinawley	Lisnaskea	III.	201
24	Cornaleck	88	3	35d	Leitrim	Leitrim	Kiltubbrid	Car^k. on Shannon	IV.	103
44,45,47,48	Cornalee	617	1	38e	Roscommon	Athlone	Cam	Athlone	IV.	179
47	Cornalee	14	2	21f	Roscommon	Athlone	Dysart	Athlone	IV.	181
23, 29	Cornaleen	101	3	13	Cavan	Clankee	Shercock	Bailieborough	III.	74
7	Cornalon	104	2	31	Cavan	Tullyhaw	Kinawley	Bawnboy	III.	93
25	Cornalough	149	3	11	Monaghan	Cremorne	Clontibret	Castleblayney	III.	260
42	Cornamaddy	150	3	24	Roscommon	Athlone	Kilmeane	Roscommon	IV.	182
45	Cornamaddy	576	1	20	Tyrone	Dungannon Middle	Pomeroy	Dungannon	III.	304
29	Cornamaddy	128	3	0	Westmeath	Brawny	St. Mary's	Athlone	I.	259
28, 29, 35	Cornamagh	411	2	32	Cavan	Clankee	Enniskeen	Bailieborough	III.	72
29	Cornamagh	261	1	19	Westmeath	Brawny	St. Mary's	Athlone	I.	259
25	Cornamahan	97	1	16	Cavan	Clanmahon	Denn	Cavan	III.	76
35	Cornaman	114	1	2g	Cavan	Clankee	Enniskeen	Bailieborough	III.	72
12, 13	Cornaman	129	3	35	Leitrim	Drumahaire	Cloonclare	Manorhamilton	IV.	93
78, 89	Cornamarrow	264	0	6	Mayo	Carra	Ballyhean	Castlebar	IV.	125
42	Cornamart	180	2	4	Roscommon	Athlone	Killinvoy	Roscommon	IV.	181
15	Cornamarve	159	0	19	Leitrim	Drumahaire	Killarga	Manorhamilton	IV.	98
5	Cornameelta	725	2	25	Roscommon	Boyle	Boyle	Boyle	IV.	194
30, 31	Cornaminaun	53	3	23	Galway	Ballymoe	Clonbern	Glennamaddy	IV.	6
26, 39	Cornamona	333	3	13	Galway	Ross	Cong	Oughterard	IV.	73
22	Cornamona	214	3	24	King's Co.	Garrycastle	Gallen	Parsonstown	I.	136
90	Cornamonaster	178	0	18h	Mayo	Carra	Rosslee	Castlebar	IV.	130
35, 36	Cornamramurry	75	3	18	Fermanagh	Clankelly	Clones	Clones	III.	195
49	Cornamuck	318	2	0	Tyrone	Omagh East	Dromore	Omagh	III.	311
5, 9	Cornamucklagh	130	0	38	Armagh	Oneilland West	Drumcree	Lurgan	III.	52
38	Cornamucklagh	178	1	2	Cavan	Castlerahan	Castlerahan	Oldcastle	III.	67
25	Cornamucklagh	138	2	11i	Cavan	Clanmahon	Kilmore	Cavan	III.	78
22	Cornamucklagh	130	0	23	Cavan	Tullygarvey	Kildrumsherdan	Cootehill	III.	90
30, 36	Cornamucklagh	253	0	38j	Cavan	Tullyhunco	Scrabby	Granard	III.	99
35	Cornamucklagh	62	0	13	Fermanagh	Clankelly	Clones	Clones	III.	195
23, 28	Cornamucklagh	102	1	26	Fermanagh	Magherastephana	Aghavea	Lisnaskea	III.	218
2, 7	Cornamucklagh	376	3	11k	Galway	Ballymoe	Kilcroan	Glennamaddy	IV.	8
61	Cornamucklagh	401	2	2	Galway	Clonmacnowen	Ahascragh	Ballinasloe	IV.	24
3	Cornamucklagh	435	3	8	Kildare	Carbury	Kilrainy	Edenderry	I.	52
33, 34	Cornamucklagh	213	0	15	Leitrim	Carrigallen	Cloone	Mohill	IV.	90
27, 31	Cornamucklagh	68	2	39	Leitrim	Leitrim	Kiltoghert	Car^k. on Shannon	IV.	101
27	Cornamucklagh	404	1	8	Longford	Shrule	Forgney	Ballymahon	I.	166
1, 2	Cornamucklagh	749	1	36	Louth	Lower Dundalk	Carlingford	Dundalk	I.	176
3	Cornamucklagh	65	1	4	Roscommon	Boyle	Ardcarn	Boyle	IV.	192
34	Cornamucklagh	135	1	29l	Sligo	Tirerrill	Killadoon	Boyle	IV.	239
59	Cornamucklagh	197	0	14	Tyrone	Clogher	Clogher	Clogher	III.	292
54	Cornamucklagh	166	2	33m	Tyrone	Dungannon Middle	Drumglass	Dungannon	III.	302
50	Cornamucklagh	437	3	22	Tyrone	Omagh East	Dromore	Omagh	III.	311
15, 21	Cornamucklagh and Falmore	478	1	20	Roscommon	Castlereagh	Kilcorkey	Castlereagh	IV.	199
28	Cornamucklagh or Garranroe	193	3	4	Monaghan	Farney	Donaghmoyne	Carrickmacross	III.	270
18, 19	Cornamucklagh North	266	3	36	Leitrim	Drumahaire	Drumreilly	Car^k. on Shannon	IV.	95

(a) Including 36A. 2R. 24P. water.
(b) Including 32A. 0R. 18P. water.
(c) Including 12A. 0R. 14P. water.
(d) Including 3A. 2R. 33P. water.
(e) Including 49A. 2R. 11P. water.

(f) Including 5A. 3R. 0P. water.
(g) Including 1A. 2R. 1P. water.
(h) Including 9A. 1R. 8P. water.
(i) Including 4A. 0R. 22P. water.

(j) Including 16A. 0R. 26P. water.
(k) Including 2A. 2R. 25P. water.
(l) Including 5A. 2R. 2P. water.
(m) Including 5A. 2R. 35P. water.

No. of Sheet of the Ordnance Survey Maps.	Townlands and Towns.	Area in Statute Acres.			County.	Barony.	Parish.	Poor Law Union in 1857.	Townland Census of 1851, Part I.	
		A.	R.	P.					Vol.	Page
14, 19	CornamucklaghNorth	171	1	19	Monaghan	Cremorne	Clontibret	Monaghan	III.	260
20, 21	Cornamucklagh South	640	3	8	Leitrim	Drumahaire	Drumreilly	Carᵏ. on Shannon	IV.	95
19	Cornamucklagh South	185	0	7	Monaghan	Cremorne	Clontibret	Castleblayney	III.	260
7	CORNAMUCKLAGH T.	—			Galway	Ballymoe	Kilcroan	Glennamaddy	IV.	9
19	Cornamucklaglass	182	3	12a	Monaghan	Cremorne	Ballybay	Castleblayney	III.	259
19	Cornamucclagh	179	2	23	Londonderry	Coleraine	Aghadowey	Coleraine	III.	229
23	Cornamuddagh	96	3	13	Leitrim	Leitrim	Kiltoghert	Carᵏ. on Shannon	IV.	101
6	Cornamult	162	2	21	Tipperary, N.R.	Lower Ormond	Terryglass	Borrisokane	II.	287
9, 13	Cornamunady	123	1	27	Monaghan	Monaghan	Monaghan	Monaghan	III.	277
28, 34	Cornanaff	261	3	3b	Cavan	Clankee	Bailieborough	Bailieborough	III.	71
1, 6	Cornanaff	195	3	32	Galway	Ballymoe	Templetogher	Glennamaddy	IV.	9
70	Cornanaff	65	0	20	Mayo	Gallen	Kildacommoge	Castlebar	IV.	148
100	Cornanagh	342	1	22	Mayo	Kilmaine	Robeen	Ballinrobe	IV.	157
14, 19	Cornanagh	216	2	25c	Monaghan	Monaghan	Tullycorbet	Monaghan	III.	281
47	Cornananta Beg	267	1	20	Galway	Killian	Killeroran	Mountbellew	IV.	44
47	Cornananta More	227	1	21	Galway	Killian	Killeroran	Mountbellew	IV.	44
7	Cornaneane	144	0	34	Leitrim	Rosclogher	Killasnet	Manorhamilton	IV.	109
28	Cornan East	271	1	2	Wicklow	Upper Talbotstown	Kiltegan	Baltinglass	I.	364
28	Cornanerriff	93	3	4	Monaghan	Farney	Donaghmoyne	Carrickmacross	III.	269
33, 34	Cornanoe	193	3	1	Fermanagh	Knockninny	Kinawley	Lisnaskea	III.	201
78	Cornanool	132	1	19	Mayo	Carra	Islandeady	Castlebar	IV.	128
28	Cornanure	224	1	0	Monaghan	Farney	Donaghmoyne	Carrickmacross	III.	269
19	Cornanure	196	0	35	Monaghan	Monaghan	Tullycorbet	Monaghan	III.	281
6	Cornanure	63	1	30	Monaghan	Trough	Errigal Trough	Monaghan	III.	283
22	Cornanurney	238	3	28	Cavan	Tullygarvey	Kildrumsherdan	Cootehill	III.	90
28	Cornan West	121	2	20	Wicklow	Upper Talbotstown	Kiltegan	Baltinglass	I.	364
44	Cornapallis	116	3	8	Roscommon	Athlone	Tisrara	Roscommon	IV.	185
20	Cornapark	481	1	24d	Longford	Ardagh	Ardagh	Longford	I.	151
16, 21	Cornapaste	169	1	29e	Monaghan	Dartree	Currin	Clones	III.	265
91	Cornarona	1,568	3	4f	Galway	Moycullen	Killannin	Galway	IV.	69
24, 29	Cornarooslan	767	1	29g	Fermanagh	Magherastephana	Aghalurcher	Lisnaskea	III.	215
23, 27	Cornaroy	394	0	25h	Leitrim	Leitrim	Kiltoghert	Carᵏ. on Shannon	IV.	101
118	Cornaroya	361	3	33i	Mayo	Kilmaine	Ballinrobe	Ballinrobe	IV.	152
27	Cornasassonagh	284	2	21	Monaghan	Farney	Magheross	Carrickmacross	III.	273
34, 35	Cornasaus	215	2	9	Cavan	Clankee	Enniskeen	Bailieborough	III.	72
22	Cornasaus	327	1	6	Cavan	Tullygarvey	Kildrumsherdan	Cootehill	III.	90
10	Cornasaus	299	3	3	Meath	Upper Kells	Dulane	Kells	I.	205
13	Cornascreeb	651	3	7	Armagh	Orior Lower	Kilmore	Banbridge	III.	56
25	Cornaseer	223	3	10j	Cavan	Clanmahon	Denn	Cavan	III.	76
48, 49	Cornaseer	371	0	2	Roscommon	Athlone	Kiltoom	Athlone	IV.	183
20	Cornashamsoge	574	3	20	Leitrim	Leitrim	Kiltoghert	Carᵏ. on Shannon	IV.	101
28	Cornashannel	102	0	24	Fermanagh	Magherastephana	Aghalurcher	Lisnaskea	III.	215
34	Cornashee	93	2	26	Fermanagh	Magherastephana	Aghalurcher	Lisnaskea	III.	215
39	Cornashesk	533	1	37	Cavan	Castlerahan	Lurgan	Oldcastle	III.	69
33	Cornashesk	234	1	20	Tyrone	Omagh West	Longfield West	Castlederg	III.	316
32	Cornashesko	37	0	13	Fermanagh	Clanawley	Kinawley	Enniskillen	III.	193
29, 35, 36	Cornashinnagh	238	1	12	Roscommon	Ballintober South	Kilbride	Roscommon	IV.	189
32, 33	Cornaskeoge	184	3	6	Fermanagh	Clanawley	Kinawley	Enniskillen	III.	193
13	Cornasker	48	0	9	Cavan	Tullyhunco	Kildallan	Bawnboy	III.	97
11	Cornasleehan	157	1	38	Roscommon	Ballintober North	Kilmore	Carᵏ. on Shannon	IV.	187
28	Cornasleeve	120	1	15k	Monaghan	Farney	Donaghmoyne	Carrickmacross	III.	269
39	Cornaslieve	526	3	16l	Cavan	Castlerahan	Lurgan	Oldcastle	III.	69
31	Cornaslieve	36	3	2	Leitrim	Leitrim	Kiltoghert	Carᵏ. on Shannon	IV.	101
13	Cornasoo	129	0	17	Monaghan	Monaghan	Drumsnat	Monaghan	III.	275
13, 18	Cornasoo	158	0	5	Monaghan	Monaghan	Kilmore	Monaghan	III.	276
9	CornasoreorStraghan	124	2	11	Monaghan	Trough	Donagh	Monaghan	III.	283
7, 11	Cornastauk	460	1	1	Leitrim	Drumahaire	Cloonclare	Manorhamilton	IV.	93
28	Cornavad	210	1	3m	Leitrim	Mohill	Fenagh	Mohill	IV.	106
8, 12	Cornavannoge	77	1	15	Leitrim	Drumahaire	Cloonclare	Manorhamilton	IV.	93
34, 41, 42	Cornavarrow	1,429	1	29	Tyrone	Omagh West	Longfield East	Omagh	III.	315
27, 28	Cornaveagh	256	2	23n	Cavan	Clankee	Knockbride	Bailieborough	III.	73
85	Cornaveagh	155	0	10	Donegal	Tirhugh	Donegal	Donegal	III.	145
8, 20	Cornaveagh	655	3	31o	Galway	Ballymoe	Dunamon	Roscommon	IV.	7
89	Cornaveagh	200	3	12	Mayo	Carra	Ballyhean	Castlebar	IV.	125
72	Cornaveagh	124	2	30p	Mayo	Gallen	Kilconduff	Swineford	IV.	147
9	Cornaveagh	371	3	32	Roscommon	Boyle	Estersnow	Boyle	IV.	195
56	Cornaveagh	399	0	19	Roscommon	Moycarn	Moore	Ballinasloe	IV.	206
56, 67	Cornaveigh	161	0	28	Cork, E.R.	Imokilly	Ardagh	Youghal	II.	83
67	Cornaveigh	51	3	38	Cork, E.R.	Imokilly	Clonpriest	Youghal	II.	85
1, 4	Cornaville North	365	2	19	Meath	Lower Kells	Moynalty	Kells	I.	203
4	Cornaville South	17	2	12	Meath	Lower Kells	Moynalty	Kells	I.	203
39	Cornavray	200	2	17q	Fermanagh	Coole	Galloon	Lisnaskea	III.	199

(a) Including 23A. 25P. water.
(b) Including 2A. 2R. 5P. water.
(c) Including 4A. 1R. 24P. water.
(d) Including 89A. 3R. 16P. water.
(e) Including 7A. 2R. 32P. water.
(f) Including 40A. 3R. 29P. water.

(g) Including 12A. 0R. 0P. water.
(h) Including 14A. 2R. 39P. water.
(i) Including 2A. 2R. 27P. water.
(j) Including 7A. 3R. 1P. water.
(k) Including 4A. 1R. 1P. water.
(l) Including 9A. 1R. 21P. water.

(m) Including 11A. 1R. 0P. water.
(n) Including 6A. 0R. 8P. water.
(o) Including 14A. 3R. 18P. water.
(p) Including 13A. 3R. 1P. water.
(q) Including 1A. 3R. 19P. water.

No. of Sheet of the Ordnance Survey Maps.	Townlands and Towns.	Area in Statute Acres.	County.	Barony.	Parish.	Poor Law Union in 1857.	Townland Census of 1851, Part I.	
		A. R. P.					Vol.	Page
17	Cornawall	143 0 24	Monaghan	Dartree	Aghabog	Cootehill	III.	263
18	Cornawall	194 0 36	Monaghan	Dartree	Ematris	Cootehill	III.	266
12	Cornawall	205 0 11	Monaghan	Dartree	Killeevan	Monaghan	III.	268
55	Corncamble	324 1 27	Donegal	Raphoe	Allsaints	Londonderry	III.	134
9	Corndale Lower	76 3 6a	Londonderry	Keenaght	Tamlaght Finlagan	New Tn Limavady	III.	237
9	Corndale Upper	74 2 33b	Londonderry	Keenaght	Tamlaght Finlagan	New Tn Limavady	III.	237
17	Corndarragh	334 2 31	King's Co.	Ballycowan	Kilbride	Tullamore	I.	127
33, 38	Corndog	136 3 13	Wicklow	Ballinacor South	Moyne	Shillelagh	I.	350
9	Cornecassa Demesne	467 0 19	Monaghan	Monaghan	Monaghan	Monaghan	III.	277
5, 9	Corneddan	440 2 31	Longford	Longford	Killoe	Longford	I.	159
32	Cornee	231 3 26	Leitrim	Mohill	Mohill	Mohill	IV.	107
9	Corneen	205 2 22	Cavan	Tullyhaw	Templeport	Bawnboy	III.	94
4, 6	Corneenflynn	216 3 20c	Cavan	Tullyhaw	Templeport	Enniskillen	III.	94
123	Cornelian	2 2 3	Mayo	Kilmaine	Shrule	Ballinrobe	IV.	158
23, 26	Cornelscourt	111 1 31	Dublin	Rathdown	Kill	Rathdown	I.	35
23	Cornelscourt	233 2 39	Kildare	Connell	Morristownbiller	Naas	I.	56
50	Cornelstown	296 0 9	Meath	Dunboyne	Dunboyne	Dunshaughlin	I.	199
21	Cornerpark	178 2 38	Dublin	Newcastle	Newcastle	Celbridge	I.	34
47	Cornerstown	51 2 32	Wexford	Forth	Mayglass	Wexford	I.	312
93	Cornery	357 1 11d	Cork, W.R.	West Muskerry	Inchigeelagh	Dunmanway	II.	157
9, 13	Corness	99 3 19	Monaghan	Monaghan	Monaghan	Monaghan	III.	277
50	Cornfield	105 3 25	Clare	Clonderalaw	Kilchreest	Killadysert	II.	15
110	Cornfield	594 0 20e	Mayo	Kilmaine	Robeen	Ballinrobe	IV.	157
27	Cornhill	343 0 4	Cork, E.R.	Condons&Clangibbon	Glanworth	Fermoy	II.	61
5	Cornhill	58 0 37	Tipperary, N.R.	Lower Ormond	Loughkeen	Parsonstown	II.	286
13	Cornode	193 1 31	Tipperary, N.R.	Owney and Arra	Castletownarra	Nenagh	II.	294
13	Cornollen	169 2 32	Longford	Longford	Clongesh	Longford	I.	157
31	Cornoonagh	547 2 20	Armagh	Fews Upper	Creggan	Dundalk	III.	48
19	Cornreany	142 2 18	Down	Lower Iveagh, Up. pt.	Donaghcloney	Lurgan	III.	169
6	Cornstown	416 0 12	Dublin	Balrothery West	Ballymadun	Dunshaughlin	I.	22
29	Cornulla	410 2 4	Leitrim	Mohill	Cloone	Mohill	IV.	105
32	Cornwall	199 2 28	Wexford	Shelmaliere West	Killurin	Wexford	I.	334
26	Cornyeal	12 1 2	Kilkenny	Callan	Callan	Callan	I.	83
141	Coronea	582 2 16	Cork, W.R.	West Carbery (E.D.)	Abbeystrowry	Skibbereen	II.	136
12	Corporation	1,091 3 15	Armagh	Armagh	Armagh	Armagh	III.	43
91, 97	Corporation	358 3 16	Donegal	Banagh	Killybegs Upper	Glenties	III.	110
2	Corporation	1,388 1 15	Down	Ards Lower	Bangor	Newtownards	III.	157
24, 31	Corporation	1,482 2 5	Down	Dufferin	Killyleagh	Downpatrick	III.	167
36	Corporation-land	39 1 12	Meath	Upper Navan	Trim	Trim	I.	216
21	Corporationland (1st Division)	7 1 31	Queen's Co.	Clandonagh	Skirk	Donaghmore	I.	235
25	Corporation Land (1st Division)	3 0 2	Wicklow	Newcastle	Rathnew	Rathdrum	I.	354
30, 36	Corporationland North	45 3 20	Meath	Upper Navan	Trim	Trim	I.	216
30, 36	Corporationland Nth. (1st Division)	152 3 10	Meath	Upper Navan	Trim	Trim	I.	216
36	Corporationland Nth. (4th Division)	33 3 7	Meath	Upper Navan	Trim	Trim	I.	217
36	Corporationland Nth. (2nd Division)	72 1 23	Meath	Upper Navan	Trim	Trim	I.	216
11, 15	Corporation Lands	771 3 37f	Cavan	Lower Loughtee	Annagh	Cavan	III.	78
25	Corporation Lands	358 1 35	Wicklow	Arklow	Kilpoole	Rathdrum	I.	345
21	Corporation Land (2nd Division)	9 3 10	Queen's Co.	Clandonagh	Skirk	Donaghmore	I.	235
25	Corporation Land (2nd Division)	0 0 32	Wicklow	Newcastle	Rathnew	Rathdrum	I.	354
36	Corporationland (3rd Division)	118 0 3	Meath	Upper Navan	Trim	Trim	I.	216
21	Corporationland (3rd Division)	16 0 13	Queen's Co.	Clandonagh	Skirk	Donaghmore	I.	235
25	Corporation Murragh	67 0 8	Wicklow	Newcastle	Rathnew	Rathdrum	I.	354
6	Corporation North	398 1 8	Down	Ards Lower	Newtownards	Newtownards	III.	158
5, 6, 11	Corporation South	726 0 25	Down	Castlereagh Lower	Newtownards	Newtownards	III.	163
31	Corr	496 1 22	Cavan	Clanmahon	Ballintemple	Cavan	III.	75
24	Corr	374 0 30	Cavan	Tullyhunco	Killashandra	Cavan	III.	98
118	Corr	476 2 29	Galway	Longford	Kilmalinoge	Portumna	IV.	59
47, 55	Corr	374 3 33	Tyrone	Dungannon Middle	Killyman	Dungannon	III.	303
23	Corr	236 2 4	Westmeath	Kilkenny West	Drumraney	Ballymahon	I.	273
22, 23	Corr	140 1 28	Westmeath	Kilkenny West	Kilkenny West	Athlone	I.	273
17, 24	Corr	391 1 28	Westmeath	Rathconrath	Ballymorin	Mullingar	I.	282
11	Corraback	193 0 16a	Cavan	Lower Loughtee	Drumlane	Cavan	III.	79
135, 144	Corrabally	130 2 28	Cork, W.R.	Ibane and Barryroe	Ardfield	Clonakilty	II.	148
144	Corrabally	121 2 7	Cork, W.R.	Ibane and Barryroe	Kilkerranmore	Clonakilty	II.	149
28	Corrabarrack	266 3 34	Leitrim	Mohill	Fenagh	Mohill	IV.	106

No. of Sheet of the Ordnance Survey Maps.	Townlands and Towns.	Area in Statute Acres.			County.	Barony.	Parish.	Poor Law Union in 1857.	Townland Census of 1851, Part I.	
		A.	R.	P.					Vol.	Page
99	Corrabaun	94	0	1	Galway	Clonmacnowen	Clontuskert	Ballinasloe	IV.	24
86	Corrabaun	250	2	32	Galway	Kilconnell	Grange	Loughrea	IV.	40
46, 47	Corrabaun	226	0	0	Galway	Killian	Killeroran	Mountbellew	IV.	44
14	Corrabaun	74	1	34	Longford	Ardagh	Templemichael	Longford	I.	153
4, 5	Corrabaun	200	3	4	Longford	Longford	Killoe	Longford	I.	159
23	Corrabaun	135	1	8	Longford	Shrule	Taghshinny	Ballymahon	I.	167
90	Corrabaun	163	2	6a	Mayo	Carra	Drum	Castlebar	IV.	128
22	Corrabaun	312	1	13b	Roscommon	Roscommon	Elphin	Strokestown	IV.	209
71	Corrabaun or Nur-serypark	48	2	27	Galway	Tiaquin	Monivea	Tuam	IV.	79
24	Corrabeagh	190	2	33c	Leitrim	Leitrim	Fenagh	Mohill	IV.	100
28	Corrabeagh	246	0	5d	Leitrim	Mohill	Mohill	Mohill	IV.	107
24	Corrabeegher	147	0	14	Leitrim	Carrigallen	Oughteragh	Bawnboy	IV.	92
41	Corra Beg	396	3	37	Roscommon	Athlone	Athleague	Roscommon	IV.	179
28	Corrabeg	80	0	25	Roscommon	Roscommon	Kilcooley	Strokestown	IV.	210
7	Corrabeg and Corna-furrish	279	2	36	King's Co.	Garrycastle	Lemanaghan	Parsonstown	I.	136
88	Corrabella	125	0	18	Tipperary, S.R.	Iffa and Offa West	Neddans	Clogheen	II.	319
19	Corrabofin	181	0	13	Monaghan	Monaghan	Ballybay	Castleblayney	III.	274
20, 24	Corrabola	46	1	29	Longford	Ardagh	Rathreagh	Ballymahon	I.	153
23	Corrabola	282	2	24	Longford	Shrule	Taghshinny	Ballymahon	I.	167
21, 30, 31	Corrabul	139	3	19	Limerick	Pubblebrien	Croom	Croom	II.	252
21,22,30,31	Corrabulbeg	60	0	10	Limerick	Pubblebrien	Croom	Croom	II.	252
32	Corracaboon	33	1	3	Leitrim	Mohill	Mohill	Mohill	IV.	107
20	Corracanvy	162	3	27	Cavan	Upper Loughtee	Kilmore	Cavan	III.	84
26	Corracar	97	1	37	Leitrim	Carrigallen	Carrigallen	Bawnboy	IV.	89
32	Corracarrow	165	2	35e	Cavan	Upper Loughtee	Lavey	Cavan	III.	85
26, 27	Corracharra	329	2	9f	Monaghan	Cremorne	Aghnamullen	Carrickmacross	III.	257
25	Corrachole	93	1	8	Leitrim	Carrigallen	Oughteragh	Bawnboy	IV.	92
9	Corracholia Beg	83	1	17	Cavan	Tullyhaw	Templeport	Bawnboy	III.	94
9	Corracholia More	118	2	0	Cavan	Tullyhaw	Templeport	Bawnboy	III.	94
8	Corrachomera	336	1	8	Cavan	Tullyhaw	Templeport	Bawnboy	III.	94
24	Corrachoosaun	206	1	6g	Leitrim	Leitrim	Fenagh	Mohill	IV.	100
34	Corrachrow	151	3	11h	Fermanagh	Magherastephana	Aghalurcher	Lisnaskea	III.	215
23	Corrachuill	92	1	16	Leitrim	Leitrim	Kiltoghert	Carn. on Shannon	IV.	101
17	Corrachulter	111	1	34	Monaghan	Dartree	Aghabog	Cootehill	III.	263
16, 21	Corrackan	113	0	22	Monaghan	Dartree	Currin	Clones	III.	265
27, 28	Corraclare	116	0	6	Fermanagh	Magherastephana	Aghalurcher	Lisnaskea	III.	215
39	Corraclare Big	117	2	20	Fermanagh	Knockninny	Kinawley	Lisnaskea	III.	201
39	Corraclare Little	59	3	26	Fermanagh	Knockninny	Kinawley	Lisnaskea	III.	201
33, 38	Corraclare North	105	3	1	Fermanagh	Knockninny	Kinawley	Lisnaskea	III.	201
9	Corraclassy	56	0	17	Cavan	Tullyhaw	Templeport	Bawnboy	III.	94
6	Corracleigh	128	2	13	Cavan	Tullyhaw	Templeport	Enniskillen	III.	94
44, 45	Corraclevin	958	2	5	King's Co.	Clonlisk	Dunkerrin	Roscrea	I.	130
48, 49	Corraclogh	190	2	29	Roscommon	Athlone	Kiltoom	Athlone	IV.	183
20	Corracloghan	147	2	11i	Monaghan	Cremorne	Clontibret	Castleblayney	III.	260
20	Corracloon	491	0	30	Clare	Tulla Upper	Feakle	Scarriff	II.	39
10, 15	Corracloon	102	3	37	Fermanagh	Magheraboy	Inishmacsaint	Enniskillen	III.	212
8, 9	Corracloona	741	0	39	Leitrim	Rosclogher	Cloonclare	Manorhamilton	IV.	109
20	Corracloon Beg	102	1	34	Clare	Tulla Upper	Feakle	Scarriff	II.	39
20	Corracloon More	635	3	25	Clare	Tulla Upper	Feakle	Scarriff	II.	39
33	Corracoash	90	0	34j	Fermanagh	Clanawley	Kinawley	Enniskillen	III.	193
42	Corracoash	91	0	16k	Fermanagh	Knockninny	Kinawley	Lisnaskea	III.	201
13	Corracoggil North	523	0	27	Roscommon	Frenchpark	Tibohine	Castlereagh	IV.	205
13, 14, 20	Corracoggil South	354	2	27	Roscommon	Frenchpark	Tibohine	Castlereagh	IV.	205
13	Corracommeen	366	1	1l	Roscommon	Frenchpark	Tibohine	Castlereagh	IV.	205
47	Corracoolia	297	1	24	Galway	Killian	Taghboy	Mountbellew	IV.	45
85	Corracramph	168	3	5	Donegal	Tirhugh	Donegal	Donegal	III.	145
28	Corracramph North	44	3	11	Leitrim	Leitrim	Mohill	Carn. on Shannon	IV.	104
35	Corracramph South	413	2	23m	Leitrim	Mohill	Mohill	Mohill	IV.	107
15	Corracreeny	94	0	22	Cavan	Upper Loughtee	Castleterra	Cavan	III.	82
20	Corracreeny	71	0	3n	Cavan	Upper Loughtee	Urney	Cavan	III.	86
30	Corracreeny	93	0	15	Leitrim	Carrigallen	Carrigallen	Mohill	IV.	89
22	Corracreigh	396	1	13o	Roscommon	Roscommon	Elphin	Strokestown	IV.	209
6	Corracrin	45	1	26	Monaghan	Trough	Donagh	Monaghan	III.	281
111	Corracrow	538	2	2p	Mayo	Kilmaine	Kilcommon	Ballinrobe	IV.	154
19, 32	Corracullin	362	1	33	Galway	Tiaquin	Kilkerrin	Glennamaddy	IV.	76
7	Corracullin	777	1	38	King's Co.	Garrycastle	Lemanaghan	Parsonstown	I.	136
10, 11, 20	Corracunna	374	0	18	Cork, E.R.	Condons&Clangibbon	Brigown	Mitchelstown	II.	59
24	Corradarren	369	0	14q	Cavan	Tullyhunco	Killashandra	Cavan	III.	98
20	Corraderrybrock	297	0	12	Fermanagh	Clanawley	Cleenish	Enniskillen	III.	190
5	Corradoverrid	140	2	20	Cavan	Tullyhaw	Killinagh	Enniskillen	III.	91
39	Corradillar	112	3	34	Fermanagh	Magherastephana	Aghalurcher	Lisnaskea	III.	215

(a) Including 0A. 2R. 14P. water.
(b) Including 47A. 0R. 20P. water.
(c) Including 69A. 2R. 15P. water.
(d) Including 6A. 2R. 9P. water.
(e) Including 0A. 2R. 25P. water.
(f) Including 14A. 0R. 5P. water.

(g) Including 16A. 1R. 34P. water.
(h) Including 4A. 1R. 2P. water.
(i) Including 13A. 0R. 37P. water.
(j) Including 6A. 1R. 30P. water.
(k) Including 11A. 0R. 30P. water.
(l) Including 59A. 2R. 5P. water.

(m) Including 4A. 3R. 3P. water.
(n) Including 1A. 3R. 15P. water.
(o) Including 5A. 1R. 31P. water.
(p) Including 4A. 0R. 26P. water.
(q) Including 3A. 2R. 37P. water.

No. of Sheet of the Ordnance Survey Maps.	Townlands and Towns.	Area in Statute Acres.			County.	Barony.	Parish.	Poor Law Union in 1857.	Townland Census of 1851, Part I.	
		A.	R.	P.					Vol.	Page
34, 42	Corradinna	397	2	28	Tyrone	Omagh East	Drumragh	Omagh	III.	312
40, 45	Corradoo	161	3	39a	Sligo	Corran	Toomour	Boyle	IV.	228
33, 34	Corradooa	123	0	22	Cavan	Castlerahan	Killinkere	Bailieborough	III.	68
40, 45	Corradoo East	330	3	23	Sligo	Tirerrill	Aghanagh	Boyle	IV.	237
69	Corradooey	375	2	4	Donegal	Raphoe	Convoy	Stranorlar	III.	136
87	Corradooey	888	2	37	Donegal	Raphoe	Donaghmore	Stranorlar	III.	137
9, 14	Corradooey	176	2	12	Longford	Ardagh	Templemichael	Longford	I.	153
13	Corradoon	567	3	14	Waterford	Decies without Drum	Seskinan	Lismore	II.	360
40, 45	Corradoo West	304	0	21	Sligo	Tirerrill	Aghanagh	Boyle	IV.	237
10	Corradoran	109	3	14	Louth	Ardee	Killanny	Dundalk	I.	173
33, 38, 39	Corradovar	169	0	0b	Fermanagh	Knockninny	Kinawley	Lisnaskea	III.	201
24	Corradownan	281	3	21	Cavan	Tullyhunco	Killashandra	Cavan	III.	98
32	Corradreenan East	60	0	24	Fermanagh	Clanawley	Killesher	Enniskillen	III.	192
32	Corradreenan West	24	2	16	Fermanagh	Clanawley	Killesher	Enniskillen	III.	192
29, 36	Corradrehid	407	0	31	Roscommon	Ballintober South	Kilbride	Roscommon	IV.	189
29, 30	Corradrehid	139	1	36	Roscommon	Roscommon	Lissonuffy	Strokestown	IV.	211
69, 78	Corradrish	89	2	28c	Mayo	Carra	Aglish	Castlebar	IV.	123
48, 49	Corradrishy	818	0	36d	Mayo	Gallen	Attymass	Ballina	IV.	147
5	Corraduff	240	2	6	Tipperary, N.R.	Lower Ormond	Loughkeen	Parsonstown	II.	286
58, 71	Corrafaireen	516	3	12	Galway	Tiaquin	Monivea	Tuam	IV.	79
78, 87	Corraffrin	781	1	39	Donegal	Raphoe	Donaghmore	Stranorlar	III.	137
8, 9	Corragarrow	93	2	31	Longford	Longford	Templemichael	Longford	I.	160
13	Corragarrow	177	1	11	Longford	Moydow	Killashee	Longford	I.	161
22	Corragarry	328	3	23	Cavan	Clankee	Drumgoon	Cootehill	III.	72
17, 22	Corragarry	244	1	30	Monaghan	Dartree	Currin	Cootehill	III.	265
18	Corragarry	178	1	15	Monaghan	Dartree	Ematris	Cootehill	III.	266
25	Corragarry or Sruell	311	2	35e	Monaghan	Farney	Donaghmoyne	Castleblayney	III.	269
25	Corragarta	206	3	12	Monaghan	Cremorne	Clontibret	Castleblayney	III.	260
22, 28	Corragarve	136	1	36f	Roscommon	Roscommon	Kilcooley	Strokestown	IV.	210
76, 77	Corragaun	91	0	38	Mayo	Burrishoole	Burrishoole	Newport	IV.	119
105	Corragaun	184	2	1	Mayo	Murrisk	Kilgeever	Westport	IV.	160
34	Corragaun (Morris)	144	3	37	Kilkenny	Kells	Tullahought	Carrick on Suir	I.	110
34	Corragaun (Reade)	63	0	3	Kilkenny	Kells	Tullahought	Carrick on Suir	I.	110
24, 25	Corrageen	21	2	33	Dublin	Uppercross	Tallaght	Dublin South	I.	41
18	Corrageen	686	0	21	Wexford	Bantry	Killann	Enniscorthy	I.	300
4, 9	Corragh	752	3	37	Wexford	Scarawalsh	Moyacomb	Shillelagh	I.	325
16, 22	Corragh	1,579	3	1	Wicklow	Lower Talbotstown	Hollywood	Baltinglass	I.	360
6	Corraghbrack	70	1	14	Monaghan	Trough	Donagh	Monaghan	III.	281
7	Corraghdown	150	2	19	Monaghan	Trough	Donagh	Monaghan	III.	281
6	Corraghduff	126	0	32	Monaghan	Trough	Donagh	Monaghan	III.	281
40	*Corragh Island*	1	1	21	Donegal	Boylagh	Templecrone	Glenties	III.	116
6, 7, 9, 10	Corragh (Maxwell)	49	1	3	Monaghan	Trough	Donagh	Monaghan	III.	281
26	Corragho	331	1	14g	Cavan	Upper Loughtee	Lavey	Cavan	III.	85
34	Corraghy	240	0	20	Cavan	Clankee	Bailieborough	Bailieborough	III.	71
23	Corraghy	150	1	20h	Cavan	Clankee	Shercock	Bailieborough	III.	74
35	Corraghy	564	1	21	Fermanagh	Clankelly	Clones	Clones	III.	195
3	Corragina	56	1	21	Waterford	Upperthird	Dysert	Carrick on Suir	II.	369
26	Corraglass	249	3	17	Fermanagh	Clanawley	Cleenish	Enniskillen	III.	190
25	Corraglass West	91	3	6	Fermanagh	Clanawley	Cleenish	Enniskillen	III.	190
40	Corragloon	164	1	3	Cavan	Castlerahan	Mullagh	Bailieborough	III.	70
33, 38	Corragole	238	0	28	Fermanagh	Knockninny	Kinawley	Lisnaskea	III.	201
24	Corragoly	30	0	29	Leitrim	Mohill	Fenagh	Mohill	IV.	106
63	Corragooly	244	2	14	Mayo	Costello	Kilbeagh	Swineford	IV.	140
18	Corragore	161	3	19i	Monaghan	Dartree	Ematris	Cootehill	III.	266
29, 30	Corragunt	720	2	25j	Fermanagh	Clankelly	Clones	Clones	III.	195
42	Corraharra	84	0	11k	Fermanagh	Knockninny	Kinawley	Lisnaskea	III.	201
32, 33	Corraheen	39	3	6	Fermanagh	Clanawley	Kinawley	Enniskillen	III.	193
3	Corrahoash	140	3	28	Cavan	Tullyhaw	Killinagh	Enniskillen	III.	91
80	Corrahoor	198	1	4	Mayo	Gallen	Killedan	Swineford	IV.	150
48, 58	Corraige	481	3	34l	Clare	Clonderalaw	Kilmihil	Kilrush	II.	17
77	Corraine	1,411	2	28m	Donegal	Raphoe	Kilteevoge	Stranorlar	III.	139
46,47,54,55	Corrainy	230	1	0	Tyrone	Dungannon Middle	Killyman	Dungannon	III.	303
25	Corrakane	66	3	23	Cavan	Clanmahon	Denn	Cavan	III.	76
8	Corrakeel	221	3	12n	Fermanagh	Magheraboy	Inishmacsaint	Ballyshannon	III.	212
3	Corrakeeldrum	593	0	6o	Cavan	Tullyhaw	Killinagh	Enniskillen	III.	91
19	Corrakeen	133	0	22	Monaghan	Cremorne	Clontibret	Castleblayney	III.	260
28	Corrakeeran	233	2	2p	Cavan	Clankee	Knockbride	Bailieborough	III.	73
16	Corrakeeran	86	0	32	Cavan	Tullygarvey	Drung	Cootehill	III.	88
2	Corrakeeran	190	0	21	Meath	Lower Kells	Enniskeen	Kells	I.	202
33	Corrakelly	106	0	32	Fermanagh	Knockninny	Kinawley	Lisnaskea	III.	201
5	Corrakit	813	2	30	Louth	Lower Dundalk	Carlingford	Dundalk	I.	176
13, 20	Corrakyle	2,060	2	10	Clare	Tulla Upper	Tomgraney	Scarriff	II.	41
29, 30	Corrala	232	2	35q	Leitrim	Carrigallen	Drumreilly	Bawnboy	IV.	90

(a) Including 2A. 1R. 38P. water.
(b) Including 11A. 3R. 11P. water.
(c) Including 6A. 2R. 4P. water.
(d) Including 3A. 0R. 35P. water.
(e) Including 33A. 3R. 17P. water.
(f) Including 1A. 2R. 18P. water.

(g) Including 22A. 0R. 20P. water.
(h) Including 24A. 0R. 39P. water.
(i) Including 7A. 1R. 2P. water.
(j) Including 1A. 0R. 17P. water.
(k) Including 4A. 3R. 6P. water.
(l) Including 8A. 1R. 17P. water.

(m) Including 2A. 3R. 7P. water.
(n) Including 21A. 0R. 35P. water.
(o) Including 8A. 3R. 21P. water.
(p) Including 46A. 0R. 25P. water.
(q) Including 19A. 2R. 10P. water.

No. of Sheet of the Ordnance Survey Maps.	Townlands and Towns.	Area in Statute Acres.			County.	Barony.	Parish.	Poor Law Union in 1857.	Townland Census of 1851, Part I.	
		A.	R.	P.					Vol.	Page
25	Corralahan	36	1	23	Leitrim	Carrigallen	Drumreilly	Bawnboy	IV.	90
2	Corralanna	1,139	1	0a	Westmeath	Moygoish	Street	Granard	I.	281
11	Corralara	198	2	15	Roscommon	Ballintober North	Kilmore	Car. on Shannon	IV.	187
25	Corralea	181	3	35	Fermanagh	Clanawley	Cleenish	Enniskillen	III.	190
30	Corralea	185	3	13b	Galway	Ballymoe	Tuam	Tuam	IV.	10
44	Corralea	217	3	20	Galway	Tiaquin	Killererin	Tuam	IV.	77
71	Corralea	171	0	22	Galway	Tiaquin	Monivea	Tuam	IV.	79
45	Corralea	373	3	20	Roscommon	Athlone	Cam	Athlone	IV.	179
29	Corralea West	1	1	33	Galway	Clare	Tuam	Tuam	IV.	23
22	Corralcehan	152	0	15	Leitrim	Carrigallen	Drumreilly	Bawnboy	IV.	90
8	Corraleehanbeg	154	3	1	Cavan	Tullyhaw	Drumreilly	Bawnboy	III.	91
29, 30	Corraleek	511	2	37c	Fermanagh	Clankelly	Clones	Clones	III.	195
35	Corralena	314	1	21	Westmeath	Brawny	St. Mary's	Athlone	I.	259
5, 8	Corraleskin	314	0	9	Leitrim	Rosclogher	Rossinver	Manorhamilton	IV.	111
22	Corralinnen	67	1	30d	Fermanagh	Magheraboy	Rossorry	Enniskillen	III.	214
24	Corralongford	152	1	5e	Fermanagh	Magherastephana	Aghalurcher	Lisnaskea	III.	215
6	Corralough	529	0	15	Galway	Ballymoe	Templetogher	Glennamaddy	IV.	9
17, 18	Corralough	248	1	32	Longford	Rathcline	Rathcline	Longford	I.	164
61	Corralough	62	0	18	Tipperary, S.R.	Middlethird	St. John Baptist	Cashel	II.	330
6	Corralough South	74	3	36	Galway	Ballymoe	Templetogher	Glennamaddy	IV.	9
17	Corralustia	156	0	33	Leitrim	Drumahaire	Inishmagrath	Manorhamilton	IV.	96
42	Corramacorra	132	1	2	Wexford	Forth	Kildavin	Wexford	I.	310
19, 32	Corramaeeagh	591	2	20f	Galway	Tiaquin	Kilkerrin	Glennamaddy	IV.	76
30	Corramagrine	203	3	4	Roscommon	Ballintober North	Termonbarry	Strokestown	IV.	187
25	Corramahan	279	0	33	Leitrim	Carrigallen	Drumreilly	Bawnboy	IV.	90
24	Corramartin	56	2	24	Leitrim	Carrigallen	Oughteragh	Bawnboy	IV.	92
33, 38	Corrameen	165	3	32	Fermanagh	Clanawley	Kinawley	Enniskillen	III.	193
12, 17	Corramegan	152	3	29	Monaghan	Dartree	Aghabog	Monaghan	III.	263
38	Corramonaghan	108	2	32	Fermanagh	Knockninny	Kinawley	Lisnaskea	III.	201
13	Corramore	195	3	38	Fermanagh	Magheraboy	Inishmacsaint	Ballyshannon	III.	212
48, 49	Corramore	1,157	3	6	Roscommon	Athlone	Kiltoom	Athlone	IV.	183
12	Corramore	534	0	39g	Tyrone	Strabane Upper	Bodoney Upper	Gortin	III.	324
41	Corra More or Gorteenclough	682	2	6h	Roscommon	Athlone	Athleague	Roscommon	IV.	179
20	Corran	1,421	2	1	Armagh	Fews Upper	Lisnadill	Armagh	III.	49
13	Corran	145	2	4	Cavan	Tullyhaw	Templeport	Bawnboy	III.	94
24	Corran	394	3	4i	Cavan	Tullyhunco	Killashandra	Cavan	III.	98
85, 97	Corran	1,006	0	19	Cork, E.R.	East Muskerry	Dunderrow	Cork	II.	103
61	Corranagh	596	0	2	Donegal	Raphoe	Leck	Letterkenny	III.	140
32	Corranaheen	79	2	13	Fermanagh	Clanawley	Kinawley	Enniskillen	III.	193
2	Corrananagh	105	0	24	Meath	Lower Kells	Kilmainham	Kells	I.	203
26, 35	Corranarry	424	2	22	Tyrone	Strabane Upper	Cappagh	Omagh	III.	325
147, 152	Corran Beg	162	1	6	Cork, W.R.	West Carbery(W.D.)	Kilmoe	Skull	II.	144
72	Corrandoo	160	3	33	Galway	Tiaquin	Moylough	Tuam	IV.	79
57	Corrandrum	107	2	12	Galway	Clare	Annaghdown	Tuam	IV.	16
57	Corrandrum	432	0	19	Galway	Clare	Kilmoylan	Tuam	IV.	22
56, 69	Corrandulla	384	3	16	Galway	Clare	Annaghdown	Galway	IV.	16
24	Corranea Glebe	549	2	4	Cavan	Tullyhunco	Killashandra	Cavan	III.	98
7	Corranearty	90	3	19	Cavan	Tullyhaw	Kinawley	Bawnboy	III.	93
35	Corraneary	259	2	36	Cavan	Clankee	Enniskeen	Bailieborough	III.	72
23	Corraneary	342	2	34j	Cavan	Clankee	Knockbride	Cootehill	III.	73
24	Corraneary	335	3	25k	Cavan	Tullyhunco	Killashandra	Cavan	III.	98
26	Corraneary	104	0	35	Cavan	Upper Loughtee	Larah	Cavan	III.	85
29, 33	Corraneary	594	1	39	Leitrim	Carrigallen	Cloone	Mohill	IV.	90
33	Corraneden	174	1	8	Cavan	Castlerahan	Killinkere	Bailieborough	III.	68
86	Corraneena	418	3	35	Galway	Kilconnell	Kilconnell	Ballinasloe	IV.	40
55	Corranellistrum	234	0	22	Galway	Moycullen	Kilcummin	Oughterard	IV.	66
74, 83	Corraness Glebe	383	3	4	Donegal	Banagh	Killybegs Lower	Glenties	III.	110
28	Corranewy	100	1	15	Fermanagh	Magherastephana	Aghalurcher	Lisnaskea	III.	215
17, 18	Corranewy	211	3	2l	Monaghan	Dartree	Ematris	Cootehill	III.	266
9	Corranierna	60	0	39	Cavan	Tullyhaw	Templeport	Bawnboy	III.	94
10	Corranierna	176	1	3m	Cavan	Tullyhaw	Tomregan	Bawnboy	III.	96
133	Corran Middle	191	2	17	Cork, W.R.	East Carbery (W.D.)	Kilmacabea	Skibbereen	II.	133
147, 152	Corran More	172	3	37	Cork, W.R.	West Carbery(W.D.)	Kilmoe	Skull	II.	144
29, 34	Corrannaskeha	51	1	4	Waterford	Coshmore&Coshbride	Kilwatermoy	Lismore	II.	343
29, 34	Corrannaskeha North	62	1	7	Waterford	Coshmore&Coshbride	Kilwatermoy	Lismore	II.	343
34	Corrannaskeha South	103	0	8	Waterford	Coshmore&Coshbride	Kilwatermoy	Lismore	II.	343
120, 133	Corran North	473	0	26	Cork, W.R.	East Carbery (W.D.)	Kilmacabea	Skibbereen	II.	133
35	Corranny	136	3	3n	Fermanagh	Clankelly	Clones	Clones	III.	195
3	Corranroo	99	0	37	Clare	Burren	Abbey	Ballyvaghan	II.	11
133	Corran South	509	3	20o	Cork, W.R.	East Carbery (W.D.)	Kilmacabea	Skibbereen	II.	133
71	Corrantarramud	828	1	26	Galway	Tiaquin	Monivea	Loughrea	IV.	79
48	Corrantotan	171	2	33	Roscommon	Athlone	Kiltoom	Athlone	IV.	183

(a) Including 9A. 0R. 28P. water.
(b) Including 24A. 3R. 3P. water.
(c) Including 3A. 2R. 34P. water.
(d) Including 1A. 1R. 12P. water.
(e) Including 6A. 0R. 26P. water.

(f) Including 12A. 0R. 8P. water.
(g) Including 3A. 1R. 18P. water.
(h) Including 46A. 0R. 6P. water.
(i) Including 5A. 2R. 13P. water.
(j) Including 45A. 1R. 35P. water.

(k) Including 8A. 2R. 13P. water.
(l) Including 7A. 1R. 10P. water.
(m) Including 26A. 2R. 9P. water.
(n) Including 3A. 2R. 16P. water.
(o) Including 14A. 0R. 8P. water.

No. of Sheet of the Ordnance Survey Maps.	Townlands and Towns.	Area in Statute Acres. A. R. P.	County.	Barony.	Parish.	Poor Law Union in 1857.	Townland Census of 1851, Part I. Vol.	Page
20, 21	Corranure	231 2 11	Cavan	Upper Loughtee	Castleterra	Cavan	III.	82
24	Corraphort	153 1 0a	Leitrim	Leitrim	Fenagh	Mohill	IV.	100
3	Corraquigley	170 0 6	Cavan	Tullyhaw	Killinagh	Enniskillen	III.	91
10	Corraquill	244 0 23b	Cavan	Lower Loughtee	Drumlane	Bawnboy	III.	79
14	Corraquill	59 2 36	Tipperary, N.R.	Lower Ormond	Monsea	Nenagh	II.	287
5	Corrard	61 1 12	Cavan	Tullyhaw	Killinagh	Enniskillen	III.	91
28	Corrard	168 1 4	Fermanagh	Magherastephana	Aghalurcher	Lisnaskea	III.	215
33	Corrard	253 1 7	Fermanagh	Magherastephana	Cleenish	Lisnaskea	III.	219
35	Corrardaghy	184 1 18c	Fermanagh	Clankelly	Clones	Clones	III.	195
33, 38	Corrardreen	156 0 29	Fermanagh	Clanawley	Kinawley	Enniskillen	III.	193
51	Corraree and Ballygatta	525 0 33	Roscommon	Athlone	Taghmaconnell	Athlone	IV.	185
11, 15	Corrarod	260 0 3d	Cavan	Tullygarvey	Annagh	Cavan	III.	87
35	Corrascoffy	183 1 32e	Leitrim	Mohill	Mohill	Mohill	IV.	107
50, 57	Corrashesk	152 3 24	Tyrone	Clogher	Donacavey	Omagh	III.	294
42	Corrasheskin	299 3 19	Tyrone	Omagh East	Dromore	Omagh	III.	311
22, 23, 28, 29	Corrasillagh	944 0 24f	Wicklow	Ballinacor South	Ballinacor	Rathdrum	I.	348
18	Corraskea	260 2 23	Monaghan	Cremorne	Aghnamullen	Cootehill	III.	257
16	Corraskea	221 2 26	Monaghan	Dartree	Killeevan	Clones	III.	268
10	Corraskealy	77 2 31	Monaghan	Monaghan	Tehallan	Monaghan	III.	280
22, 23	Corraslira	365 1 16g	Roscommon	Roscommon	Ogulla	Strokestown	IV.	212
25	Corrasluastia	520 3 34	Roscommon	Castlereagh	Kiltullagh	Castlereagh	IV.	201
24	Corrasmaghooil	54 1 18	Leitrim	Leitrim	Kiltubbrid	Cark. on Shannon	IV.	103
9	Corrasmongan	116 3 15	Cavan	Tullyhaw	Templeport	Bawnboy	IV.	94
15	Corrasra	243 2 5h	Leitrim	Drumahaire	Killarga	Manorhamilton	IV.	98
34	Corrastoona Beg	201 1 4	Roscommon	Ballymoe	Drumatemple	Castlereagh	IV.	191
34	Corrastoona More	327 1 21	Roscommon	Ballymoe	Drumatemple	Castlereagh	IV.	191
13	Corrataghart	149 1 11	Monaghan	Monaghan	Drumsnat	Monaghan	III.	275
20	Corratanty	453 0 37i	Monaghan	Cremorne	Muckno	Castleblayney	III.	261
79	Corratanvally	224 0 12j	Mayo	Carra	Breaghwy	Castlebar	IV.	127
12, 13	Corratary	394 3 19	Tyrone	Strabane Upper	Bodoney Upper	Gortin	III.	324
3, 4	Corratawy	348 0 6	Cavan	Tullyhaw	Templeport	Enniskillen	III.	94
15	Corratawy	168 1 25	Leitrim	Drumahaire	Killarga	Manorhamilton	IV.	98
25	Corrateean	143 1 38	Monaghan	Farney	Donaghmoyne	Castleblayney	III.	269
28	Corrateemore	77 0 10	Monaghan	Farney	Donaghmoyne	Carrickmacross	III.	269
32	Corraterriff North	28 3 3	Leitrim	Mohill	Mohill	Mohill	IV.	107
32	Corraterriff South	80 1 30	Leitrim	Mohill	Mohill	Mohill	IV.	107
26	Corrateskin	105 3 34	Fermanagh	Clanawley	Cleenish	Enniskillen	III.	190
9	Corratillan	179 0 15	Cavan	Tullyhaw	Templeport	Bawnboy	III.	94
15, 17	Corratimore Glebe	583 2 1	Leitrim	Drumahaire	Killanummery	Manorhamilton	IV.	97
33	Corratinner	334 2 19k	Cavan	Castlerahan	Killinkere	Bailieborough	III.	68
2, 4	Corratirrim	198 0 2	Cavan	Tullyhaw	Killinagh	Enniskillen	III.	92
39	Corratistune	123 2 37	Fermanagh	Knockninny	Kinawley	Lisnaskea	III.	201
30	Corratober	394 0 28	Cavan	Tullyhunco	Scrabby	Granard	III.	99
21	Corratober	196 0 30l	Cavan	Upper Loughtee	Castleterra	Cavan	III.	82
20	Corratober	153 3 37m	Cavan	Upper Loughtee	Kilmore	Cavan	III.	84
2, 3	Corratober	551 1 9	Meath	Morgallion	Enniskeen	Kells	I.	209
5	Corratober Lower	172 1 22	Cavan	Tullyhaw	Killinagh	Enniskillen	III.	92
5	Corratober Upper	197 2 13	Cavan	Tullyhaw	Killinagh	Enniskillen	III.	92
77, 88	Corratowick	187 2 7	Mayo	Burrishoole	Kilmeena	Westport	IV.	122
38	Corratrasna	155 1 24	Fermanagh	Knockninny	Kinawley	Lisnaskea	III.	201
12	Corratrasna	46 3 20	Monaghan	Monaghan	Clones	Monaghan	III.	274
33	Corratrasna Glebe	84 2 18	Fermanagh	Knockninny	Kinawley	Lisnaskea	III.	201
3	Corratrench	88 0 10	Roscommon	Boyle	Ardcarn	Boyle	IV.	192
7	Corr and Aughantarragh	743 2 3	Armagh	Tiranny	Eglish	Armagh	III.	59
103	Corraun	573 0 0	Mayo	Costello	Annagh	Claremorris	IV.	138
70	Corraun	441 2 31	Mayo	Gallen	Kildacommoge	Castlebar	IV.	148
118	Corraun	136 0 34	Mayo	Kilmaine	Kilmainemore	Ballinrobe	IV.	156
22	Corraun	752 0 13	Queen's Co.	Clarmallagh	Aghaboe	Donaghmore	I.	235
30	Corraun	426 2 39	Roscommon	Ballintober North	Termonbarry	Strokestown	IV.	187
67	Corraunboy	76 3 17	Mayo	Burrishoole	Burrishoole	Newport	IV.	119
18	Corravacan	188 0 22	Monaghan	Dartree	Ematris	Cootehill	III.	266
61	Corravaddy	413 0 19	Donegal	Raphoe	Conwal	Letterkenny	III.	137
21	Corravahan	174 3 24	Cavan	Tullygarvey	Drung	Cootehill	III.	88
15	Corravally	222 1 18	Tipperary, N.R.	Lower Ormond	Ardcrony	Borrisokane	II.	281
21	Corravarry	140 1 15	Cavan	Upper Loughtee	Castleterra	Cavan	III.	82
25	Corraveaty	45 2 26	Cavan	Upper Loughtee	Kilmore	Cavan	III.	84
48	Corraveggaun East	140 2 17u	Mayo	Tirawley	Ballynahaglish	Ballina	IV.	164
39, 48	Corraveggaun West	274 0 14o	Mayo	Tirawley	Ballynahaglish	Ballina	IV.	164
33	Corravehy	122 2 11	Fermanagh	Knockninny	Kinawley	Lisnaskea	III.	201
23, 28	Corravilla	559 3 8p	Cavan	Clankee	Knockbride	Bailieborough	III.	73
23, 28	Corravilla	223 0 20q	Cavan	Clankee	Shercock	Bailieborough	III.	74

(a) Including 34A. 2R. 28P. water.
(b) Including 9A. 2R. 19P. water.
(c) Including 9A. 0R. 36P. water.
(d) Including 49A. 3R. 1P. water.
(e) Including 20A. 2R. 52P. water.
(f) Including 4A. 0R. 14P. Kelly's Lough.

(g) Including 41A. 0R. 27P. water.
(h) Including 96A. 3R. 16P. water.
(i) Including 12A. 0R. 38P. water.
(j) Including 14A. 2R. 4P. water.
(k) Including 32A. 2R. 14P. water.
(l) Including 4A. 1R. 3P. water.

(m) Including 4A. 0R. 33P. water.
(n) Including 2A. 2R. 22P. water.
(o) Including 3A. 1R. 15P. water.
(p) Including 6A. 1R. 3P. water.
(q) Including 50A. 1R. 27P. water.

No. of Sheet of the Ordnance Survey Maps.	Townlands and Towns.	Area in Statute Acres.			County.	Barony.	Parish.	Poor Law Union in 1857.	Townland Census of 1851, Part I.	
		A.	R.	P.					Vol.	Page
18	Corravilla	168	0	0	Monaghan	Dartree	Aghabog	Cootehill	III.	263
14	Corraviller	109	3	21	Monaghan	Monaghan	Tullycorbet	Monaghan	III.	281
17, 22	Corravoggy	272	0	32a	Cavan	Tullygarvey	Kildrumsherdan	Cootehill	III.	90
16, 21	Corravogy	199	2	12	Cavan	Tullygarvey	Drung	Cootehill	III.	88
21	Corravohy	80	0	31	Cavan	Tullygarvey	Drung	Cootehill	III.	88
28	Corravokeen	809	1	33	Mayo	Tirawley	Moygawnagh	Killala	II.	171
140	Corravoley	341	1	38	Cork, W.R.	West Carbery(W.D.)	Kilcoe	Skull	II.	143
25	Corravoo	269	2	29	Monaghan	Farney	Donaghmoyne	Castleblayney	III.	269
110	Corravreeda East	258	0	39	Cork, W.R.	East Carbery (E.D.)	Ballymodan	Bandon	II.	127
110	Corravreeda West	169	1	17	Cork, W.R.	East Carbery (E.D.)	Ballymodan	Bandon	II.	127
35	Corrawaddy	151	0	31b	Cavan	Clankee	Enniskeen	Bailieborough	III.	72
25, 29	Corrawaleen	358	1	17	Leitrim	Carrigallen	Drumreilly	Bawnboy	IV.	91
16, 18	Corraweehil Glebe	153	0	8	Leitrim	Drumahaire	Inishmagrath	Manorhamilton	IV.	96
34, 35	Corraweelis	481	3	5	Cavan	Clankee	Enniskeen	Bailieborough	III.	72
16	Corraweelis	52	3	12	Cavan	Tullygarvey	Drung	Cootehill	III.	88
26	Corraweelis	292	1	17c	Cavan	Upper Loughtee	Denn	Cavan	III.	83
26	Corrawillin	79	3	3	Cavan	Upper Loughtee	Lavey	Cavan	III.	85
10	Corrawillin	68	3	22	Monaghan	Monaghan	Tehallan	Monaghan	III.	280
32	Corrawully	85	3	29	Fermanagh	Clanawley	Killesher	Enniskillen	III.	192
37	Corray	240	0	38	Sligo	Leyny	Kilmacteige	Tobercurry	IV.	231
4, 8	Corr and Dunavally	453	1	30	Armagh	Armagh	Loughgall	Armagh	III.	45
22, 28	Correagh	55	0	8d	Roscommon	Roscommon	Kilcooley	Strokestown	IV.	210
21	Correagh	489	1	28	Sligo	Tirerrill	Killerry	Sligo	IV.	239
30	Correagh	122	0	6	Westmeath	Clonlonan	Ballyloughloe	Athlone	I.	260
37	Correagh	344	2	16	Westmeath	Moycashel	Ardnurcher or Horse-leap	Tullamore	I.	276
39	Correagh Glebe	279	1	25	Cavan	Castlerahan	Lurgan	Oldcastle	III.	69
39, 41	Correal	330	0	33	Roscommon	Athlone	Fuerty	Roscommon	IV.	181
44	Correal	342	2	17	Roscommon	Athlone	Tisrara	Roscommon	IV.	185
2, 6	Correaly	615	2	0	Westmeath	Moygoish	Street	Granard	I.	281
14	Correel	213	0	12	Queen's Co.	Stradbally	Curraclone	Athy	I.	246
14	Correel	0	3	3	Queen's Co.	Stradbally	Moyanna	Athy	I.	247
28, 33	Correen	673	3	22	Antrim	Lower Antrim	Skerry	Ballymena	III.	4
26	Correen	119	2	24	Fermanagh	Clanawley	Killesher	Enniskillen	III.	192
31	Correen	193	3	28	Leitrim	Leitrim	Kiltoghert	Cark. on Shannon	IV.	101
56	Correen	308	0	29e	Roscommon	Moycarn	Moore	Ballinasloe	IV.	206
56	Correenbeg	399	3	14f	Roscommon	Moycarn	Moore	Ballinasloe	IV.	206
32	Correenfeeradda	32	1	24	Limerick	Smallcounty	Knockainy	Kilmallock	II.	261
29	Correens	95	3	19	Mayo	Tirawley	Moygawnagh	Killala	II.	171
32	Correish	125	3	13g	Leitrim	Leitrim	Annaduff	Mohill	IV.	99
14	Correll	460	2	39h	Fermanagh	Magheraboy	Inishmacsaint	Ballyshannon	III.	212
27	Correllstown	598	0	13	Westmeath	Farbill	Killucan	Mullingar	I.	266
1	Correvan	303	1	8	Cavan	Tullyhaw	Killinagh	Enniskillen	III.	92
17	Correvan	211	2	20	Monaghan	Dartree	Aghabog	Cootehill	III.	263
19	Corries or Corrymore	646	2	32	Carlow	Idrone East	Lorum	Carlow	I.	8
19	Corries or Corry More	42	1	26i	Carlow	Idrone East	Sliguff	Carlow	I.	8
33, 34	Corriga	545	1	21	Leitrim	Carrigallen	Cloone	Mohill	IV.	90
17, 23	Corriga	278	2	0	Tipperary, N.R.	Ikerrin	Bourney	Roscrea	II.	274
22	Corrigeen	299	2	27	Queen's Co.	Upperwoods	Offerlane	Abbeyleix	I.	251
35, 44	Corrin	714	1	2	Cork, E.R.	Barrymore	Castlelyons	Fermoy	II.	53
2, 5	Corrinagh	449	2	2j	Longford	Granard	Columbkille	Longford	I.	155
17,18,21,22	Corrinare	167	0	38	Armagh	Orior Lower	Loughgilly	Newry	III.	56
17, 21, 22	Corrinary	188	3	6	Monaghan	Dartree	Currin	Cootehill	III.	265
25	Corrinary	105	1	33	Monaghan	Farney	Donaghmoyne	Castleblayney	III.	269
27	Corrineuty	344	2	37	Monaghan	Farney	Magheross	Carrickmacross	III.	273
25, 28	Corrinshigagh	183	2	7	Monaghan	Farney	Donaghmoyne	Carrickmacross	III.	269
31	Corrinshigagh	151	0	10	Monaghan	Farney	Magheross	Carrickmacross	III.	273
28	Corrinshigagh (Cope)	106	1	3	Monaghan	Farney	Donaghmoyne	Carrickmacross	III.	269
26	Corrinshigo	396	3	11	Armagh	Orior Upper	Killevy	Newry	III.	58
29, 35	Corrinshigo	189	3	34	Cavan	Clankee	Enniskeen	Bailieborough	III.	72
16	Corrinshigo	99	3	38	Cavan	Tullygarvey	Drung	Cootehill	III.	88
35, 36	Corrinshigo	76	3	38	Fermanagh	Clankelly	Clones	Clones	III.	195
19, 20	Corrinshigo	182	1	18	Monaghan	Cremorne	Clontibret	Castleblayney	III.	260
22	Corrinshigo	293	0	22	Monaghan	Dartree	Currin	Cootehill	III.	265
8	Corrinshigo	78	3	20	Monaghan	Monaghan	Clones	Monaghan	III.	274
14	Corrinshigo	75	1	34	Monaghan	Monaghan	Monaghan	Monaghan	III.	277
8	Corrinshigo	95	1	28	Monaghan	Monaghan	Tedavnet	Monaghan	III.	278
15, 20	Corrintra	456	0	11	Monaghan	Cremorne	Muckno	Castleblayney	III.	261
21	Corrinure	153	2	20	Armagh	Orior Lower	Loughgilly	Newry	III.	56
20	Corrody	192	2	24	Londonderry	Tirkeeran	Clondermot	Londonderry	III.	247
7	Corroe and Grogan	375	1	21	King's Co.	Garrycastle	Lemanaghan	Parsonstown	I.	136
43, 57	Corrofin	781	2	39k	Galway	Clare	Cummer	Tuam	IV.	18
17	Corrofin T.	—			Clare	Inchiquin	Killinaboy	Corrofin	II.	27

(a) Including 6A. 0R. 4P. water.
(b) Including 3A. 3R. 4P. water.
(c) Including 1A. 2R. 11P. water.
(d) Including 0A. 2R. 17P. water.

(e) Including 9A. 0R. 8P. water.
(f) Including 17A. 3R. 8P. water.
(g) Including 2A. 1R. 32P. water.
(h) Including 7A. 1R. 1P. water.

(i) Including 12A. 1R. 9P. detached portion.
(j) Including 8A. 0R. 12P. water.
(k) Including 154A. 0R. 30P. water.

No. of Sheet of the Ordnance Survey Maps.	Townlands and Towns.	Area in Statute Acres.			County.	Barony.	Parish.	Poor Law Union in 1857.	Townland Census of 1851, Part I.	
		A.	R.	P.					Vol.	Page
25, 32	Corrog	274	2	30	Down	Ards Upper	Ballytrustan	Downpatrick	III.	160
67	Corrogebeg	116	2	22	Tipperary, S.R.	Clanwilliam	Kilshane	Tipperary	II.	309
67	Corrogemore	327	1	6	Tipperary, S.R.	Clanwilliam	Corroge	Tipperary	II.	306
39, 43	Corronagh	369	0	6	Cavan	Castlerahan	Munterconnaught	Oldcastle	III.	71
21, 25, 26	Corrool (*Brennan*)	162	3	24	Longford	Rathcline	Cashel	Ballymahon	I.	163
26	Corrool (*Fox*)	204	3	10	Longford	Rathcline	Cashel	Ballymahon	I.	163
25, 26	Corrool (*Kenny*)	318	0	3	Longford	Rathcline	Cashel	Ballymahon	I.	163
40	Corrower	864	0	36a	Mayo	Gallen	Attymass	Ballina	IV.	147
10, 15	Corrowle	265	3	12	Tipperary, N.R.	Lower Ormond	Modreeny	Borrisokane	II.	286
39	Corroy	187	3	29b	Mayo	Tirawley	Ballynahaglish	Ballina	IV.	164
42	Corroy	201	0	28	Roscommon	Athlone	Kilmeane	Roscommon	IV.	182
16	Corroy	244	1	38	Roscommon	Frenchpark	Kilmacumsy	Boyle	IV.	203
7	Corrspark	191	1	18	Galway	Ballymoe	Ballynakill	Glennamaddy	IV.	5
11	Corrstown	367	2	19	Dublin	Nethercross	Kilsallaghan	Balrothery	I.	31
3	Corrstown	122	3	24	Londonderry	North East Liberties of Coleraine	Ballywillin	Coleraine	III.	245
11, 15	Corrudda	215	1	2c	Leitrim	Drumahaire	Drumlease	Manorhamilton	IV.	94
98	Corruragh	339	3	22	Cork, E.R.	Kinalea	Ballymartle	Kinsale	II.	94
13	Corry	254	3	8	Armagh	Fews Lower	Mullaghbrack	Armagh	III.	47
8, 9, 17, 18	Corry	334	0	34	Donegal	Kilmacrenan	Clondavaddog	Milford	III.	124
41, 42	Corry	174	3	28	Fermanagh	Knockninny	Kinawley	Lisnaskea	III.	201
8	Corry	427	1	24d	Fermanagh	Magheraboy	Inishmacsaint	Ballyshannon	III.	212
30	Corry	115	0	6	Galway	Ballymoe	Tuam	Tuam	IV.	10
107	Corry	133	2	13	Galway	Longford	Killimorbologue	Portumna	IV.	58
18	Corry	264	1	2	Leitrim	Drumahaire	Inishmagrath	Manorhamilton	IV.	96
8	Corry	315	3	28	Longford	Longford	Clongesh	Longford	I.	157
19, 23	Corry	208	0	9	Longford	Shrule	Kilglass	Ballymahon	I.	166
3	Corry	54	2	21	Monaghan	Trough	Errigal Trough	Clogher	III.	283
11, 12	Corry	101	3	5	Roscommon	Ballintober North	Kilmore	Car^k. on Shannon	IV.	187
36	Corry	319	2	22	Roscommon	Ballintober South	Kilgefin	Roscommon	IV.	189
11	Corry	804	3	38	Roscommon	Roscommon	Aughrim	Car^k.on Shannon	IV.	207
6, 11	Corry	362	0	12e	Westmeath	Moygoish	Rathaspick	Mullingar	I.	280
28	Corryagan	125	2	29	Monaghan	Farney	Donaghmoyne	Carrickmacross	III.	269
3	Corryarbeg	367	0	2	Monaghan	Trough	Errigal Trough	Clogher	III.	283
23	Corryard	55	2	27	Leitrim	Leitrim	Kiltoghert	Car^k.on Shannon	IV.	101
105, 106	Corryaughany	364	3	9	Mayo	Murrisk	Kilgeever	Westport	IV.	160
19	Corry Beg or Currenree	301	0	31	Carlow	Idrone East	Sliguff	Carlow	I.	8
30, 31	Corrybrackan	278	1	2f	Monaghan	Farney	Magheracloone	Carrickmacross	III.	272
19	Corrybrannan	228	3	2g	Monaghan	Cremorne	Ballybay	Castleblayney	III.	259
35	Corrycholman	158	3	11h	Cavan	Clankee	Enniskeen	Bailieborough	III.	72
19, 23	Corrycorka	152	1	24	Longford	Shrule	Kilglass	Ballymahon	I.	166
45, 46	Corrycroar	433	2	29	Tyrone	Dungannon Middle	Pomeroy	Cookstown	III.	304
11	Corrycullen	159	3	17i	Leitrim	Drumahaire	Drumlease	Manorhamilton	IV.	94
95,96,105,106	Corrydavit	493	2	1	Mayo	Murrisk	Kilgeever	Westport	IV.	160
6	Corrydonellan	358	3	20	Westmeath	Moygoish	Russagh	Granard	I.	280
16	Corry East	164	0	36	Roscommon	Roscommon	Shankill	Boyle	IV.	212
22	Corryena	140	1	3	Longford	Rathcline	Kilcommock	Ballymahon	I.	164
18, 23	Corryhagan	236	0	11j	Monaghan	Cremorne	Aghnamullen	Cootehill	III.	257
18	Corry Island	4	2	9	Leitrim	Drumahaire	Inishmagrath	Manorhamilton	IV.	97
19	Corryloan	162	0	21	Monaghan	Cremorne	Clontibert	Castleblayney	III.	260
105	Corrymailley	353	1	21	Mayo	Murrisk	Kilgeever	Westport	IV.	160
10, 15	Corrymellagh	84	2	13	Antrim	Cary	Culfeightrin	Ballycastle	III.	13
19	Corrymore or Corries	646	2	32	Carlow	Idrone East	'Lorum	Carlow	I.	8
19	Corry More or Corries	42	1	26k	Carlow	Idrone East	Sliguff	Carlow	I.	8
17, 18, 20	Corry Mountain or Seltannasaggart	131	3	36	Leitrim	Drumahaire	Inishmagrath	Manorhamilton	IV.	97
31	Corryolus	157	2	31	Leitrim	Leitrim	Kiltoghert	Car^k.on Shannon	IV.	101
40	Corryrourke	389	0	4	Cavan	Castlerahan	Mullagh	Bailieborough	III.	70
15, 16	Corry West	167	0	34	Roscommon	Roscommon	Shankill	Boyle	IV.	212
39	Corsale	98	3	30l	Fermanagh	Coole	Galloon	Lisnaskea	III.	199
31	Corsallagh	736	1	34	Sligo	Leyny	Achonry	Tobercurry	IV.	229
40	Corscreenagh	105	1	34	Fermanagh	Clankelly	Galloon	Clones	III.	198
39	Corsenshin	51	0	9m	Fermanagh	Coole	Galloon	Lisnaskea	III.	199
18, 19	Corsillagh	115	1	2	Wicklow	Newcastle	Newcastle Upper	Rathdrum	I.	353
23	Corsilloga	190	1	1n	Monaghan	Cremorne	Aghnamullen	Cootehill	III.	257
91	Corskeagh	83	0	7	Mayo	Clanmorris	Mayo	Claremorris	IV.	135
15	Corskeagh	314	2	38	Roscommon	Frenchpark	Tibohine	Castlereagh	IV.	205
23	Corskeagh	169	0	26	Roscommon	Roscommon	Kiltrustan	Strokestown	IV.	211
19	Corskeagh	166	0	38	Sligo	Tireragh	Dromard	Dromore West	IV.	233
44	Corskeagh Beg	117	2	3	Galway	Dunmore	Killererin	Tuam	IV.	35
72	Corskeagh (*Daly*)	736	2	38	Galway	Tiaquin	Ballymacward	Loughrea	IV.	75
44	Corskeagh More	253	2	8	Galway	Dunmore	Killererin	Tuam	IV.	35
72, 73	Corskeagh (*Trench*)	334	3	11	Galway	Tiaquin	Ballymacward	Ballinasloe	IV.	75

(*a*) Including 30A. 3R. 33P. water.
(*b*) Including 3A. 0R. 23P. water.
(*c*) Including 3A. 2R. 26P. water.
(*d*) Including 23A. 2R. 23P. water.
(*e*) Including 8A. 3R. 23P. water.

(*f*) Including 3A. 2R. 33P. water.
(*g*) Including 16A. 2R. 10P. water.
(*h*) Including 5A. 3R. 35P. water.
(*i*) Including 9A. 3R. 8P. water.
(*j*) Including 29A. 3R. 17P. water.

(*k*) Including 12A. 1R. 9P. detached portion.
(*l*) Including 27A. 0R. 26P. water.
(*m*) Including 1A. 1R. 36P. water.
(*n*) Including 24A. 2R. 29P. water.

No. of Sheet of the Ordnance Survey Maps.	Townlands and Towns.	Area in Statute Acres.			County.	Barony.	Parish.	Poor Law Union in 1857.	Townland Census of 1851, Part I.	
		A.	R.	P.					Vol.	Page
18	Corstown	312	0	17	Kilkenny	Crannagh	Ballycallan	Kilkenny	I.	84
18	Corstown	284	0	39	Louth	Ardee	Drumcar	Ardee	I.	172
16, 19	Corstown	226	3	6	Louth	Ferrard	Dunany	Ardee	I.	180
18	Corstown	64	2	35	Louth	Ferrard	Dunleer	Ardee	I.	180
9, 15	Corstown	385	3	29	Meath	Fore	Diamor	Oldcastle	I.	200
3, 6	Corstown	555	0	38a	Meath	Lower Slane	Drumcondra	Ardee	I.	222
25	Corstruce	88	0	20	Cavan	Clanmahon	Kilmore	Cavan	III.	78
24, 27	Cortaghart	335	2	3	Monaghan	Cremorne	Aghnamullen	Castleblayney	III.	257
35	Cortaher	19	0	4	Fermanagh	Clankelly	Clones	Clones	III.	195
24	Cortamlat	762	2	27	Armagh	Fews Upper	Newtownhamilton	Castleblayney	III.	49
23	Cortannel	64	0	23	Monaghan	Cremorne	Aghnamullen	Cootehill	III.	257
6	Cortial	437	3	26	Louth	Louth	Louth	Dundalk	I.	184
35	Cortober	469	1	33	Cavan	Clankee	Enniskeen	Bailieborough	III.	72
17	Cortober	397	1	11	Cavan	Tullygarvey	Kildrumsherdan	Cootehill	III.	90
18, 19	Cortober	558	3	22	Leitrim	Drumahaire	Drumreilly	Cark. on Shannon	IV.	95
26, 27	Cortober	205	2	21b	Monaghan	Cremorne	Aghnamullen	Carrickmacross	III.	257
22	Cortober	181	3	29c	Monaghan	Dartree	Currin	Cootehill	III.	265
18	Cortober	225	2	37	Monaghan	Dartree	Ematris	Cootehill	III.	266
31, 34	Cortober	61	1	32	Monaghan	Farney	Magheracloone	Carrickmacross	III.	272
11	Cortober	183	1	32	Roscommon	Boyle	Killukin	Cark. on Shannon	IV.	195
9, 13	Cortolvin	108	2	22	Monaghan	Monaghan	Monaghan	Monaghan	III.	277
17, 24	Cortown	454	0	19	Meath	Upper Kells	Balrathboyne	Kells	I.	204
37	Cortrasna	107	3	34	Cavan	Clanmahon	Drumlumman	Granard	III.	77
35, 36	Cortrasna	152	1	13	Fermanagh	Clankelly	Clones	Clones	III.	195
3	Cortrasna	85	0	36	Roscommon	Boyle	Ardcarn	Boyle	IV.	192
16	Cortrasna or Edergole	189	3	18	Cavan	Tullygarvey	Drung	Cootehill	III.	88
22	Cortreane	89	2	1	Monaghan	Dartree	Currin	Cootehill	III.	265
22	Cortullagh or Grove	192	2	12	King's Co.	Garrycastle	Gallen	Parsonstown	I.	136
11, 15	Cor Tynan	603	2	31d	Armagh	Tiranny	Tynan	Armagh	III.	60
26	Corvackan	304	2	17e	Monaghan	Cremorne	Aghnamullen	Cootehill	III.	257
16	Corvaghan	172	0	27	Monaghan	Dartree	Drummully	Clones	III.	266
8, 9, 14	Corvally	311	0	39	Antrim	Cary	Ramoan	Ballycastle	III.	14
27, 30	Corvally	356	1	37	Monaghan	Farney	Magheross	Carrickmacross	III.	273
9, 10	Corvally	164	2	5	Monaghan	Monaghan	Tehallan	Monaghan	III.	280
14	Corvally	236	2	17	Monaghan	Monaghan	Tullycorbet	Monaghan	III.	281
28, 29	Corvanaghan	712	3	38	Tyrone	Dungannon Upper	Kildress	Cookstown	III.	308
98	Corveagh Lower	299	2	29	Mayo	Murrisk	Aghagower	Westport	IV.	158
98	Corveagh Upper	988	2	22	Mayo	Murrisk	Aghagower	Westport	IV.	158
23, 24, 32, 33	Corveen	1,471	0	4f	Donegal	Kilmacrenan	Tullaghobegly	Dunfanaghy	III.	131
94	Corveen	231	2	31	Donegal	Tirhugh	Donegal	Donegal	III.	145
90	Corvickremon	71	3	37g	Mayo	Carra	Rosslee	Castlebar	IV.	130
12, 17, 18	Corville	568	2	36	Tipperary, N.R.	Ikerrin	Corbally	Roscrea	II.	275
13, 18	Corvoam	128	0	21	Monaghan	Monaghan	Kilmore	Monaghan	III.	276
28	Corvoderry	3,001	1	38h	Mayo	Tirawley	Moygawnagh	Killala	II.	171
20, 21	Corvoley	810	3	34	Mayo	Tirawley	Moygawnagh	Killala	II.	171
19	Corvoy	222	1	32	Monaghan	Monaghan	Tullycorbet	Monaghan	III.	281
28	Corweelis	130	0	1i	Cavan	Clankee	Knockbride	Bailieborough	III.	73
17	Corweelis	265	3	3j	Cavan	Tullygarvey	Kildrumsherdan	Cootehill	III.	90
18	Corweelis or Lisaderg	207	2	28	Cavan	Tullygarvey	Drumgoon	Cootehill	III.	88
2	Corwig	210	2	38	Kildare	Carbury	Carrick	Edenderry	I.	52
15	Corwillick	161	1	2	Sligo	Carbury	Calry	Sligo	IV.	220
18, 23, 24	Corwillin	229	2	5	Monaghan	Cremorne	Aghnamullen	Cootehill	III.	257
42	Corwin	99	2	9	Cavan	Clanmahon	Kilbride	Oldcastle	III.	77
15	Cosbystown	518	1	17k	Fermanagh	Magheraboy	Inishmacsaint	Enniskillen	III.	212
15	Cosbystown East or Rosspoint	117	1	1	Fermanagh	Magheraboy	Inishmacsaint	Enniskillen	III.	213
63, 64	Cosha North	213	0	12l	Kerry	Iveragh	Glanbehy	Killarney	II.	195
72	Cosha South	270	0	14	Kerry	Iveragh	Glanbehy	Cahersiveen	II.	195
89, 90	Coshcummeragh	347	0	31	Kerry	Iveragh	Dromod	Cahersiveen	II.	194
22	Cosher	47	3	4	Wexford	Ballaghkeen	Killincooly	Gorey	I.	295
15, 20	Coshkib	61	3	39	Antrim	Lower Glenarm	Layd	Ballycastle	III.	22
13, 20	Coshquin	833	1	31	Londonderry	North West Liberties of Londonderry	Templemore	Londonderry	III.	246
6	Coskeam	499	2	3	Clare	Burren	Carran	Ballyvaghan	II.	11
23	Coskemduff	280	2	39m	Cavan	Clankee	Drumgoon	Cootehill	III.	72
105	Cosmona	399	2	19	Galway	Loughrea	Loughrea	Loughrea	IV.	65
72	Coss	608	2	37n	Kerry	Dunkerron North	Knockane	Cahersiveen	II.	182
102	Cossallagh	204	1	13	Mayo	Costello	Annagh	Claremorris	IV.	138
71, 84	Cossaun	269	3	21	Galway	Clare	Athenry	Galway	IV.	17
116	Cossaunaclamper	74	0	2	Galway	Leitrim	Kilteskill	Loughrea	IV.	55
15	Cossycon	46	1	9	Fermanagh	Magheraboy	Devenish	Enniskillen	III.	210
101	Costello's Island	4	1	0	Galway	Longford	Clonfert	Ballinasloe	IV.	57
71	Costellospark	69	1	28	Galway	Tiaquin	Monivea	Tuam	IV.	79

(a) Including 13A. 2R. 14P. water.
(b) Including 31A. 0R. 30P. water.
(c) Including 6A. 2R. 28P. water.
(d) Including 7A. 3R. 30P. water.
(e) Including 11A. 1R. 26P. water.

(f) Including 13A. 0R. 20P. water.
(g) Including 3A. 0R. 9P. water.
(h) Including 99A. 2R. 12P. water.
(i) Including 4A. 2R. 39P. water.
(j) Including 11A. 1R. 26P. water.

(k) Including 4A. 2R. 27P. water.
(l) Including 2A. 2R. 8P. detached portion.
(m) Including 3A. 2R. 18P. water.
(n) Including 3A. 1R. 27P. water.

No. of Sheet of the Ordnance Survey Maps.	Townlands and Towns.	Area in Statute Acres. A. R. P.	County.	Barony.	Parish.	Poor Law Union in 1857.	Townland Census of 1851, Part I. Vol.	Page
25, 29	Costrea	221 3 33	Leitrim	Leitrim	Fenagh	Mohill	IV.	100
69	Coteeuty	358 3 27	Galway	Clare	Annaghdown	Galway	IV.	16
21	Cotlerstown	138 1 8	Louth	Ferrard	Ballymakenny	Drogheda	I.	179
13	Cott	212 0 6	Kildare	Clane	Killybegs	Naas	I.	54
53	Cottage	88 1 11	Clare	Tulla Lower	Kiltenanlea	Limerick	II.	37
54	Cottage	67 2 9	Donegal	Raphoe	Raymoghy	Londonderry	III.	141
44	Cottage	148 3 35	Galway	Clare	Killererin	Tuam	IV.	21
95	Cottage	164 1 33	Galway	Dunkellin	Ballynacourty	Galway	IV.	27
60	Cottage	331 0 28	Kerry	Magunihy	Nohavaldaly	Killarney	II.	205
39, 40	Cottage	137 2 10	Limerick	Smallcounty	Uregare	Kilmallock	II.	261
78, 79	Cottage	214 3 31	Mayo	Carra	Breaghwy	Castlebar	IV.	127
103	Cottage	241 1 11	Mayo	Costello	Annagh	Claremorris	IV.	138
40	Cottage	9 2 26	Tipperary, N.R.	Eliogarty	Inch	Thurles	II.	270
40	Cottage	39 2 23	Tipperary, N.R.	Kilnamanagh Upper	Glenkeen	Thurles	II.	278
48	Cottage	37 3 36	Wexford	Forth	Ballybrennan	Wexford	I.	308
8	Cottagefarm	199 2 9	Queen's Co.	Portnahinch	Coolbanagher	Mountmellick	I.	244
15, 21	*Cottage Island*	13 3 14	Sligo	Carbury	St. John's	Sligo	IV.	223
54	Cottagequinn	281 3 27a	Tyrone	Dungannon Middle	Donaghmore	Dungannon	III.	301
13	*Cotteenagh Island*	6 0 38	King's Co.	Garrycastle	Clonmacnoise	Parsonstown	I.	135
27, 28	Cotterellsbooly	781 0 27b	Kilkenny	Knocktopher	Jerpointchurch	Thomastown	I.	111
27	Cotterellsbooly	210 2 33	Kilkenny	Knocktopher	Stonecarthy	Thomastown	I.	113
23, 27	Cotterellsrath	421 0 37	Kilkenny	Shillelogher	Kells	Callan	I.	115
44, 45	Cottian	214 2 12	Donegal	Kilmacrenan	Kilmacrenan	Millford	III.	129
16, 22	Cottlestown	679 2 13	Sligo	Tireragh	Castleconor	Dromore West	IV.	232
2, 6	Cotton	1,266 0 29	Down	Ards Lower	Bangor	Newtownards	III.	157
70	Cottown	248 1 3	Donegal	Raphoe	Raphoe	Strabane	III.	140
31	Cottrellstown	129 3 0	Kilkenny	Kells	Kilmaganny	Callan	I.	109
7	Cottrelstown	229 1 28	Dublin	Balrothery West	Palmerstown	Balrothery	I.	23
48	Cotts	135 3 35	Wexford	Forth	Tacumshin	Wexford	I.	315
65	Cottstown	198 3 8	Cork, E.R.	Barrymore	Dungourney	Middleton	II.	54
114	Coulagh	362 3 22	Cork, W.R.	Bear	Kilcatherine	Castletown	II.	124
70, 71	Coulagh	1,000 0 38	Kerry	Iveragh	Killinane	Cahersiveen	II.	197
114	COULAGH T.	—	Cork, W.R.	Bear	Kilcatherine	Castletown	II.	124
14	Coultry	225 0 30	Dublin	Coolock	Santry	Dublin North	I.	29
91	Coumaclavlig	1,148 1 0	Cork, W.R.	Bantry	Kilmocomoge	Bantry	II.	120
57, 68	Coumaclovane	882 0 4	Cork, W.R.	West Muskerry	Ballyvourney	Macroom	II.	154
42, 52	Coumaleague	255 2 1	Kerry	Corkaguiny	Ventry	Dingle	II.	180
19, 20	Coum (Allen)	289 3 5	Tipperary, N.R.	Owney and Arra	Youghalarra	Nenagh	II.	297
35, 44	Coumanare	776 0 11c	Kerry	Corkaguiny	Ballyduff	Dingle	II.	174
14, 23	Coumaraglinmountain	2,474 3 27	Waterford	Decies without Drum	Kilgobnet	Dungarvan	II.	357
39	Coumbeg	22 3 3	Tipperary, N.R.	Kilnamanagh Upper	Upperchurch	Thurles	II.	280
19	Coumbeg	931 0 22	Tipperary, N.R.	Owney and Arra	Youghalarra	Nenagh	II.	297
43	Coumbowler	430 0 1	Kerry	Corkaguiny	Garfinny	Dingle	II.	176
36,37,44,45	Coumbrack	493 3 6	Clare	Tulla Lower	O'Briensbridge	Limerick	II.	38
35, 44	Coumduff	2,093 1 38d	Kerry	Corkaguiny	Ballynacourty	Dingle	II.	174
51, 52	Coumeenoole North	335 2 5	Kerry	Corkaguiny	Dunquin	Dingle	II.	176
52	Coumeenoole South	261 3 26	Kerry	Corkaguiny	Dunquin	Dingle	II.	176
43	Coumeenycorraun	375 1 29e	Kerry	Corkaguiny	Cloghane	Dingle	II.	175
42, 43	Coungagh	75 0 22	Kerry	Corkaguiny	Kilmalkedar	Dingle	II.	178
54	Coumlanders	49 3 8	Kerry	Corkaguiny	Kinard	Dingle	II.	179
14, 15	Coummahon	982 3 9	Waterford	Decies without Drum	Fews	Kilmacthomas	II.	356
14	Coumnagappul	303 3 22	Waterford	Decies without Drum	Seskinan	Dungarvan	II.	360
39	Coumnageeha	92 0 4	Tipperary, N.R.	Kilnamanagh Upper	Upperchurch	Thurles	II.	280
33, 38, 39	Coumnagillagh	632 1 16	Tipperary, N.R.	Upper Ormond	Dolla	Nenagh	II.	290
36, 37	Coumnagun	849 0 9	Clare	Tulla Lower	Killaloe	Scarriff	II.	35
19, 20	Coum (Parker)	69 3 29	Tipperary, N.R.	Owney and Arra	Youghalarra	Nenagh	II.	297
72, 73, 83	Coumreagh	265 0 38	Kerry	Dunkerrin North	Knockane	Killarney	II.	181
19	Coumroe	447 0 3	Tipperary, N.R.	Owney and Arra	Youghalarra	Nenagh	II.	297
135	Councambeg	127 1 6	Cork, W.R.	Ibane and Barryroe	Templeomalus	Clonakilty	II.	150
21	Countenan	232 3 23f	Cavan	Upper Loughtee	Larah	Cavan	III.	85
19	Countygate	154 1 35	Waterford	Coshmore&Coshbride	Leitrim	Lismore	II.	344
66	Couragh	236 1 0	Cork, E.R.	Imokilly	Dungourney	Middleton	II.	86
35, 36	Couravoughil	398 2 24	Galway	Ballynahinch	Omey	Clifden	IV.	14
22	Courhoor	531 3 33g	Galway	Ballynahinch	Omey	Clifden	IV.	14
123	Cournageeha	91 0 36	Galway	Kiltartan	Kilbeacanty	Gort	IV.	47
22, 24	Cournellan	446 2 27h	Carlow	St. Mullins Lower	Ullard	New Ross	I.	13
60	Course	279 2 21	Galway	Tiaquin	Killosolan	Mountbellew	IV.	78
29	Course	264 1 31	Queen's Co.	Clarmallagh	Durrow	Abbeyleix	I.	237
36	Court	412 0 24i	Donegal	Kilmacrenan	Kilmacrenan	Millford	III.	129
10	Court	34 0 20	Dublin	Castleknock	Mulhuddart	Dunshaughlin	I.	25
12	Court	697 0 18	Limerick	Kenry	Kildimo	Rathkeale	II.	249
17	Court	98 0 30	Limerick	Shanid	Kilfergus	Glin	II.	256
51	Court	48 3 2	Meath	Dunboyne	Kilbride	Dunshaughlin	I.	200

(a) Including 3A. 2R. 11P. water.
(b) Including 5A. 1R. 0P. River Nore.
(c) Including 42A. 2R. 11P. water.
(d) Including 28A. 2R. 5P. water.
(e) Including 40A. 0R. 36P. water.
(f) Including 11A. 2R. 0P. water.
(g) Including 15A. 0R. 35P. water.
(h) Including 13A. 0R. 19P. River Barrow.
(i) Including 59A. 2R. 11P. water.

No. of Sheet of the Ordnance Survey Maps.	Townlands and Towns.	Area in Statute Acres.	County.	Barony.	Parish.	Poor Law Union in 1857.	Townland Census of 1851, Part I.	
		A. R. P.					Vol.	Page
28	Court	149 2 38	Queen's Co.	Clarmallagh	Bordwell	Donaghmore	I.	237
124, 125	Courtaparteen	153 2 18	Cork, W.R.	Courceys	Kilroan	Kinsale	II.	147
16, 21	Courtballyedmond	312 3 21	Wexford	Ballaghkeen	Monamolin	Gorey	I.	298
3	Courtbane	421 2 0	Louth	Upper Dundalk	Creggan	Dundalk	I.	177
51, 62	Courtbrack	817 0 17	Cork, E.R.	East Muskerry	Matehy	Cork	II.	105
5	Courtbrack	264 2 21*a*	Limerick	Pubblebrien	St. Michaels	Limerick	II.	254
2,3,10,11	Courtbrown	596 3 11	Limerick	Connello Lower	Askeaton	Rathkeale	II.	226
27	Courtclogh Lower	289 1 1	Wexford	Ballaghkeen	Castle-ellis	Enniscorthy	I.	293
27	Courtclogh Upper	356 1 33	Wexford	Ballaghkeen	Castle-ellis	Enniscorthy	I.	293
7	Courteencurragh	337 3 23	Wexford	Gorey	Kilmakilloge	Gorey	I.	318
19	Courtfoyle	201 3 10	Wicklow	Newcastle	Killiskey	Rathdrum	I.	352
7, 10	Courthill	166 1 3	Tipperary, N.R.	Lower Ormond	Uskane	Borrisokane	II.	288
30, 35	Courthoyle New	466 2 35	Wexford	Bantry	Newbawn	New Ross	I.	301
35	Courthoyle Old	394 2 10	Wexford	Bantry	Newbawn	New Ross	I.	301
47	Courtlands East	80 0 14	Wexford	Forth	Mayglass	Wexford	I.	312
47	Courtlands West	79 3 17	Wexford	Forth	Mayglass	Wexford	I.	312
36	Courtland or View-mount	24 0 17	King's Co.	Ballybritt	Seirkieran	Parsonstown	I.	126
95	Courtleigh	284 0 0	Cork, W.R.	Kinalmeaky	Murragh	Bandon	II.	152
4, 5	Courtlough	876 0 15	Dublin	Balrothery East	Balrothery	Balrothery	I.	19
136	Courtmacsherry	215 1 29	Cork, W.R.	Ibane and Barryroe	Lislee	Clonakilty	II.	150
136	COURTMACSHERRY T.	—	Cork, W.R.	Ibane and Barryroe	Lislee	Clonakilty	II.	150
29	Courtmatrix	390 3 20	Limerick	Connello Lower	Rathkeale	Rathkeale	II.	229
25	Courtnaboghilla	425 0 4	Kilkenny	Gowran	Powerstown	Thomastown	I.	97
26	Courtnabooly	121 3 22	Kilkenny	Kells	Mallardstown	Callan	I.	110
26	Courtnabooly East	220 0 20	Kilkenny	Kells	Coolaghmore	Callan	I.	108
26	Courtnabooly West	227 0 26	Kilkenny	Kells	Coolaghmore	Callan	I.	108
19, 25	Courtnacuddy	1,078 0 16	Wexford	Bantry	Rossdroit	Enniscorthy	I.	301
12	Courtown	295 0 30	Wexford	Ballaghkeen	Kiltennell	Gorey	I.	297
5	Courtown Great	233 2 5	Kildare	Ikeathy and Oughterany	Kilcock	Celbridge	I.	57
12	COURTOWN HARBOUR T.	—	Wexford	Ballaghkeen	Ardamine	Gorey	I.	291
5	Courtown Little	124 1 29	Kildare	Ikeathy&Oughterany	Kilcock	Celbridge	I.	57
75	Courtstown	574 3 19	Cork, E.R.	Barrymore	Little Island	Cork	II.	56
18	Courtstown	429 3 18	Kilkenny	Crannagh	Tullaroan	Kilkenny	I.	88
34, 35	Courttown East	192 1 31	Kildare	Narragh&RebanWest	Churchtown	Athy	I.	67
34	Courttown West	124 3 0	Kildare	Narragh&RebanWest	Churchtown	Athy	I.	67
9, 14	Courtwood	1,740 1 37*b*	Queen's Co.	Portnahinch	Lea	Mountmellick	I.	244
92,93,106	Cousane	1,826 3 38	Cork, W.R.	Bantry	Kilmocomoge	Bantry	II.	120
17	Couse	111 2 39	Waterford	Gaultiere	Kill St. Lawrence	Waterford	II.	363
47	Cousinstown	230 3 20	Wexford	Bargy	Tomhaggard	Wexford	I.	307
53	Cousinstown	46 2 22	Wexford	Forth	St. Margaret's	Wexford	I.	314
148	Cove	283 0 8	Cork, W.R.	West Carbery (W.D.)	Skull	Skull	II.	146
9, 10	Cove	34 0 23	Waterford	Gaultiere	St. Johns Without	Waterford	II.	365
112	COVE T.	—	Cork, E.R.	Kinsale	Ringcurran	Kinsale	II.	100
10	Cowanstown	179 3 11	Kildare	North Salt	Taghadoe	Celbridge	I.	76
11	Cowbawn	246 3 23	Tipperary, N.R.	Lower Ormond	Modreeny	Borrisokane	II.	286
50	Cow Island	2 1 4	Clare	Islands	Clondagad	Killadysert	II.	29
89	Cow Island	3 1 16	Galway	Moycullen	Killannin	Oughterard	IV.	70
66	Cow Island	2 2 18	Kerry	Magunihy	Killarney	Killarney	II.	204
120	Cow Island	11 0 15	Mayo	Kilmaine	Cong	Ballinrobe	IV.	154
107	Cowpark	88 3 36	Donegal	Tirhugh	Kilbarron	Ballyshannon	III.	148
11	Cowpark	188 3 18	Limerick	Kenry	Kilcornan	Rathkeale	II.	249
21, 26	Cowpasture	179 3 0	Kildare	Offaly West	Monasterevin	Athy	I.	73
15	Cowpasture	229 0 4	Wicklow	Lower Talbotstown	Dunlavin	Baltinglass	I.	360
19	Cox's Fields	12 1 3	Kilkenny	Shillelogher	St. Patrick's	Kilkenny	I.	116
99	Coxtown	109 0 22	Donegal	Tirhugh	Drumhome	Donegal	III.	146
99	Coxtown	309 3 2	Galway	Longford	Kiltormer	Ballinasloe	IV.	60
27	Coxtown East	193 1 35	Waterford	Gaultiere	Killea	Waterford	II.	363
27	Coxtown West	224 0 25	Waterford	Gaultiere	Killea	Waterford	II.	363
42, 50	Coyagh	167 1 35	Tyrone	Omagh East	Dromore	Omagh	III.	311
50	Coyagh Glebe	146 1 9	Tyrone	Omagh East	Dromore	Omagh	III.	311
25	Coyne	215 1 20	Westmeath	Rathconrath	Churchtown	Mullingar	II.	282
7	Cozies	383 0 36	Antrim	Lower Dunluce	Billy	Coleraine	III.	16
18	Craan	51 0 31	Carlow	Forth	Aghade	Enniscorthy	I.	3
17, 18	Craan	477 1 25	Carlow	Forth	Barragh	Enniscorthy	I.	4
21, 22	Craan	184 3 20	Wexford	Ballaghkeen	Kilnamanagh	Gorey	I.	297
1, 2	Craan	276 2 17	Wexford	Gorey	Kilpipe	Gorey	I.	320
15	Craan	306 3 18	Wexford	Scarawalsh	Ferns	Enniscorthy	I.	323
8, 9	Craan	1,612 1 24	Wexford	Scarawalsh	St. Marys Newtownbarry	Enniscorthy	I.	325
37, 38	Craanagam	102 0 15	Wexford	Shelmaliere East	Ardcavan	Wexford	I.	329
17	Craanaha	188 2 37	Carlow	Forth	Fennagh	Carlow	I.	4

(*a*) { Within the Municipal Boundary, 156A. 1R. 35P.
{ Without the Municipal Boundary, 108A. 0R. 26P.

(*b*) Including 10A. 2R. 8P. River Barrow.

No. of Sheet of the Ordnance Survey Maps.	Townlands and Towns.	Area in Statute Acres.			County.	Barony.	Parish.	Poor Law Union in 1857.	Townland Census of 1851, Part I.	
		A.	R.	P.					Vol.	Page
38	Craanatore	9	1	30	Wexford	Shelmaliere East	Ardcolm	Wexford	I.	330
13, 18	Craane	90	0	26	Longford	Moydow	Ballymacormick	Longford	I.	160
25	Craane	187	0	24	Wexford	Bantry	Clonmore	Enniscorthy	I.	300
6	Craanhill	320	2	23	Wexford	Gorey	Kilnahue	Gorey	I.	319
6	Craan Lower	320	0	34	Wexford	Gorey	Kilnahue	Gorey	I.	319
6, 11, 12	Craanlusky	716	0	10	Carlow	Idrone West	Tullowcreen	Carlow	I.	9
13, 17	Craanpursheen	103	0	39	Carlow	Forth	Ballon	Carlow	I.	3
26	Craanroe	123	1	13	Wexford	Ballaghkeen	Edermine	Enniscorthy	I.	294
13, 14	Craans	777	0	2	Carlow	Forth	Ardoyne	Carlow	I.	3
6	Craan Upper	447	1	13	Wexford	Gorey	Kilnahue	Gorey	I.	319
43, 49	Crab	433	2	25	Tipperary, S.R.	Slievardagh	Buolick	Urlingford	II.	332
25, 31	Crabarkey	1,139	1	21	Londonderry	Keenaght	Dungiven	New Tʰ Limavady	III.	236
5	Crabb's-land	34	3	13	Limerick	Clanwilliam	St. Nicholas	Limerick	II.	225
14	Crab Island	1	0	25	Clare	Corcomroe	Killilagh	Ennistimon	II.	20
20, 21	Craddanstown	2,231	0	33	Westmeath	Farbill	Killucan	Castletowndelvin	I.	266
12	Craddockstown	249	1	39	Kilkenny	Crannagh	Tubbridbritain	Urlingford	I.	87
50	Cradockstown	92	1	36	Meath	Dunboyne	Dunboyne	Dunshaughlin	I.	199
19, 24	Cradockstown Demesne	379	3	28	Kildare	Naas North	Tipper	Naas	I.	63
19, 24	Cradockstown East	157	2	38	Kildare	Naas North	Tipper	Naas	I.	63
19, 24	Cradockstown North	121	2	32	Kildare	Naas North	Tipper	Naas	I.	63
19, 24	Cradockstown West	320	0	19	Kildare	Naas North	Tipper	Naas	I.	63
34	Craffield	537	1	25	Wicklow	Ballinacor South	Ballykine	Rathdrum	I.	348
48, 49	Crag	982	3	8	Clare	Clonderalaw	Kilfiddane	Kilrush	II.	15
48, 49	Crag	195	1	29	Clare	Clonderalaw	Kilmihil	Kilrush	II.	17
23	Crag	207	1	30	Clare	Corcomroe	Kilmanaheen	Ennistimon	II.	21
43	Crag	571	2	19	Clare	Tulla Lower	Kilseily	Limerick	II.	36
31, 40	Crag	282	0	21	Kerry	Trughanacmy	Castleisland	Tralee	II.	208
48	Crag	324	1	23	Kerry	Trughanacmy	Currans	Killarney	II.	209
30, 39	Crag	243	0	2	Kerry	Trughanacmy	Nohaval	Tralee	II.	212
30	Crag	156	2	19	Kerry	Trughanacmy	O'Brennan	Tralee	II.	212
52	Crag	672	3	5a	Limerick	Glenquin	Abbeyfeale	Newcastle	II.	244
63	Cragagh	86	0	15	Mayo	Costello	Kilbeagh	Swineford	IV.	140
26	Cragard	138	2	11	Clare	Bunratty Upper	Kilraghtis	Ennis	II.	9
25, 26	Cragaweelcross	82	1	20	Clare	Bunratty Upper	Templemaley	Ennis	II.	10
5, 6	Cragballyconoal	322	2	4	Clare	Burren	Oughtmama	Ballyvaghan	II.	14
12	Cragbeg	261	2	36	Limerick	Pubblebrien	Kilkeedy	Limerick	II.	252
41, 50	Cragbrien	559	0	6	Clare	Islands	Clondagad	Killadysert	II.	29
35, 43	Cragbwee	192	2	13	Clare	Bunratty Upper	Quin	Tulla	II.	10
27, 35	Cragg	316	2	16	Clare	Tulla Upper	Tulla	Tulla	II.	41
31	Cragg	396	1	5	Tipperary, N.R.	Owney and Arra	Kilcomenty	Nenagh	II.	295
4	Craggagh	209	3	23	Clare	Burren	Killonaghan	Ballyvaghan	II.	13
80	Craggagh	693	0	21	Mayo	Gallen	Killedan	Swineford	IV.	150
38, 47	Craggaknock East	371	3	32	Clare	Ibrickan	Kilmurry	Kilrush	II.	23
38, 47	Craggaknock West	389	1	27	Clare	Ibrickan	Kilmurry	Kilrush	II.	23
12	Cragganacree	129	1	19b	Limerick	Kenry	Kildimo	Rathkeale	II.	249
17	Craggane	233	0	19c	Kerry	Clanmaurice	Duagh	Listowel	II.	168
19	Craggard	180	1	19	Limerick	Shanid	Kilmoylan	Rathkeale	II.	256
34	Craggataska	210	0	15	Clare	Bunratty Upper	Quin	Tulla	II.	10
38	Craggaun	270	2	3	Clare	Ibrickan	Kilmurry	Kilrush	II.	23
16, 24	Craggaunboy	288	3	26	Clare	Inchiquin	Rath	Corrofin	II.	27
27	Craggaunkeel	159	0	36d	Clare	Tulla Upper	Tulla	Tulla	II.	41
40	Craggaunoonia	99	3	9	Kerry	Trughanacmy	Ballincuslane	Tralee	II.	206
43	Craggaunoween	96	3	8e	Clare	Bunratty Upper	Quin	Tulla	II.	10
40	Craggera	32	1	16	Mayo	Gallen	Kilgarvan	Ballina	IV.	148
10, 19	Craggs	383	2	34	Limerick	Shanid	Kilmoylan	Rathkeale	II.	256
10	Craggs	141	3	23	Limerick	Shanid	Robertstown	Rathkeale	II.	257
34, 35	Craggs	341	3	15	Waterford	Decies within Drum	Clashmore	Youghal	II.	351
94, 104	Craggy	172	2	28f	Mayo	Murrisk	Kilgeever	Westport	IV.	161
8	Craggycorradan East	207	0	5	Clare	Corcomroe	Killilagh	Ennistimon	II.	20
4, 8	Craggycorradan West	77	1	9	Clare	Corcomroe	Killilagh	Ennistimon	II.	20
41, 50	Craggykerrivan	232	2	2	Clare	Islands	Clondagad	Killadysert	II.	29
101	Craghalan Big	14	2	37	Galway	Longford	Clonfert	Ballinasloe	IV.	57
101	Craghalan Little	0	1	29	Galway	Longford	Clonfert	Ballinasloe	IV.	57
16	Craghan	184	2	2	Fermanagh	Tirkennedy	Magheracross	Lowtherstown	III.	223
49, 59	Craghera	616	0	33	Clare	Clonderalaw	Killadysert	Killadysert	II.	15
49	Craghy	1,409	3	32g	Donegal	Boylagh	Templecrone	Glenties	III.	115
51, 52, 60	Craghy	921	0	26	Donegal	Kilmacrenan	Conwal	Letterkenny	III.	126
37	Craglea	231	1	25	Clare	Tulla Lower	Killaloe	Scarriff	II.	35
33	Cragleagh	445	0	8	Clare	Islands	Drumcliff	Ennis	II.	30
11, 20	Cragmore	623	0	30	Limerick	Connello Lower	Askeaton	Rathkeale	II.	226
33	Cragnagower	84	1	36	Clare	Islands	Drumcliff	Ennis	II.	30
9	Cragnarooan	136	2	24	Clare	Burren	Noughaval	Ballyvaghan	II.	13
4, 5	Cragreagh	210	1	5	Clare	Burren	Kilmoon	Ballyvaghan	II.	13

(a) Including 5A. 0R. 0P. water.
(b) Including 7A. 0R. 38P. water.
(c) Including 3A. 1R. 10P. water.

(d) Including 13A. 1R. 9P. water.
(e) Including 6A. 1R. 14P. water.

(f) Including 30A. 3R. 12P. detached portion.
(g) Including 197A. 0R. 6P. water.

2 T

No. of Sheet of the Ordnance Survey Maps.	Townlands and Towns.	Area in Statute Acres.	County.	Barony.	Parish.	Poor Law Union in 1857.	Townland Census of 1851, Part I.	
		A. R. P.					Vol.	Page
11	Cragreagh . .	90 0 31	Limerick . .	Kenry . . .	Kilcornan . .	Rathkeale . .	II.	249
42, 43	Cragroe . .	220 3 39a	Clare . .	Bunratty Lower .	Kilmurry . .	Tulla . .	II.	6
27, 35	Cragroe . .	386 3 37	Clare . .	Tulla Upper .	Tulla . .	Tulla . .	II.	41
3	CRAG T. . .	—	Clare . .	Burren . .	Abbey . .	Ballyvaghan .	II.	11
15	Crahard . .	81 3 4	Cavan . .	Lower Loughtee .	Annagh . .	Cavan . .	III.	78
3	Craig . .	164 3 36	Antrim . .	Cary . . .	Ballintoy . .	Ballycastle .	III.	12
7	Craig . .	237 2 14	Antrim . .	Lower Dunluce .	Billy . . .	Coleraine . .	III.	16
39	Craig . .	483 2 15	Donegal . .	Inishowen West .	Muff . . .	Londonderry .	III.	121
26, 35	Craig . .	99 3 4b	Donegal . .	Kilmacrenan .	Clondahorky .	Dunfanaghy .	III.	123
2, 6	Craig . .	166 3 10	Londonderry .	Keenaght . .	Magilligan .	NewTⁿLimavady	III.	236
3, 7	Craigaboney .	136 3 27	Antrim . .	Lower Dunluce .	Dunluce . .	Coleraine . .	III.	17
36	Craigadick . .	337 0 29	Londonderry .	Loughinsholin .	Maghera . .	Magherafelt .	III.	242
6	Craigahulliar .	161 1 11	Antrim . .	Lower Dunluce .	Ballywillin .	Coleraine . .	III.	15
4, 8	Craigalappan .	376 1 17	Antrim . .	Cary . . .	Ballintoy . .	Ballycastle .	III.	12
19, 26, 27	Craigall . .	352 1 14	Londonderry .	Coleraine . .	Desertoghill .	Coleraine . .	III.	230
40, 41	Craiganboy . .	281 1 4	Antrim . .	Lower Belfast .	Glynn . . .	Larne . .	III.	8
4, 8	Craiganee . .	631 0 9	Antrim . .	Cary . . .	Ballintoy . .	Ballycastle .	III.	12
40,41,46,47	Craiganee . .	460 3 30	Antrim . .	Lower Belfast .	Glynn . . .	Larne . .	III.	8
32	Craigaroddan .	204 3 19	Down . .	Ards Upper .	Ballyphilip .	Downpatrick .	III.	160
51, 56	Craigarogan .	1,316 0 5	Antrim . .	Lower Belfast .	Templepatrick .	Antrim . .	III.	9
17	Craigarusky .	272 2 18	Down . .	Dufferin . .	Killinchy . .	Newtownards .	III.	166
17	Craigatempin .	331 0 4	Antrim . .	Upper Dunluce .	Ballymoney .	Ballymoney .	III.	18
11	Craigatuke . .	481 2 21	Tyrone . .	Strabane Upper .	Bodoney Upper .	Gortin . .	III.	324
1	Craigavad . .	264 1 6	Down . .	Castlereagh Lower .	Holywood . .	Belfast . .	III.	162
17	*Craigaveagh Rock* .	0 1 17	Down . .	Ards Upper .	Ardkeen . .	Newtownards .	III.	159
26	Craigavole . .	347 3 3	Londonderry .	Coleraine . .	Desertoghill .	Ballymoney .	III.	230
9	Craigban . .	184 0 27	Antrim . .	Cary . . .	Culfeightrin .	Ballycastle .	III.	13
6, 7	Craigboy . .	373 2 3	Down . .	Ards Lower .	Donaghadee .	Newtownards .	III.	158
15	Craigbrack . .	193 2 16	Londonderry .	Tirkeeran . .	Faughanvale .	Londonderry .	III.	250
69	Craigdoo . .	187 3 16	Donegal . .	Raphoe . .	Convoy . .	Stranorlar .	III.	136
24	Craigdunloof .	375 1 25	Antrim . .	Kilconway .	Dunaghy . .	Ballymena .	III.	25
5	Craigfad . .	111 0 3	Antrim . .	Cary . . .	Culfeightrin .	Ballycastle .	III.	13
27	Craigfad . .	363 0 16	Antrim . .	Kilconway .	Dunaghy . .	Ballymena .	III.	25
27	Craigfaddock .	52 3 12	Antrim . .	Kilconway .	Dunaghy . .	Ballymena .	III.	25
40	Craiginorne .	235 0 39	Antrim . .	Upper Glenarm .	Kilwaughter .	Larne . .	III.	25
11	Craiglea Glebe .	251 2 37	Londonderry .	Coleraine . .	Aghadowey .	Coleraine . .	III.	229
1	Craigmacagan .	153 2 25	Antrim . .	Cary . . .	Rathlin Island .	Ballycastle .	III.	15
37	Craigmaddyroe Far	139 1 9	Donegal . .	Kilmacrenan .	Killygarvan .	Milford . .	III.	128
37	Craigmaddyroe Near	126 3 20	Donegal . .	Kilmacrenan .	Killygarvan .	Milford . .	III.	128
16	Craigmonaghan(*Funston*)	101 0 33	Tyrone . .	Omagh West .	Urney . .	Castlederg .	III.	318
16	Craigmonaghan(*Nelson*)	192 0 0c	Tyrone . .	Omagh West .	Urney . .	Castlederg .	III.	318
43, 49	Craigmore . .	355 2 30	Antrim . .	Upper Toome .	Drummaul .	Antrim . .	III.	34
11	Craigmore . .	495 2 4	Londonderry .	Coleraine . .	Aghadowey .	Coleraine . .	III.	229
32, 36	Craigmore . .	414 0 24	Londonderry .	Loughinsholin .	Maghera . .	Magherafelt .	III.	242
3, 4	Craignacally or Carrowreagh .	497 0 23	Donegal . .	Inishowen East .	Clonmany .	Inishowen .	III.	117
5, 6, 10	Craignagapple .	781 1 10	Tyrone . .	Strabane Lower .	Leckpatrick .	Strabane . .	III.	322
25	Craignagat . .	150 2 29	Antrim . .	Lower Glenarm .	Ardclinis .	Larne . .	III.	21
31, 32, 37	Craignageeragh .	454 0 25	Antrim . .	Lower Toome .	Ahoghill . .	Ballymena .	III.	32
3	Craignahorn .	90 1 36	Londonderry .	North East Liberties of Coleraine .	Ballywillin .	Coleraine . .	III.	245
7, 8	Craignamaddy .	400 3 30	Antrim . .	Cary . . .	Billy . . .	Ballycastle .	III.	12
15, 16	Craignasasonagh .	599 3 2	Down . .	Castlereagh Upper .	Saintfield .	Lisburn . .	III.	166
5	Craigogantlet .	658 2 6	Down . .	Castlereagh Lower .	Newtownards .	Newtownards .	III.	163
94	Craigroe . .	112 3 25	Donegal . .	Tirhugh . .	Donegal . .	Donegal . .	III.	145
26,27,31,32	Craigs . .	2,801 2 21d	Antrim . .	Kilconway .	Ahoghill . .	Ballymena .	III.	25
22	Craigs . .	1,722 0 2	Antrim . .	Kilconway .	Finvoy . .	Ballymoney .	III.	26
62	Craigs . .	168 3 33	Donegal . .	Raphoe . .	Raphoe . .	Strabane .	III.	140
29	Craigs . .	256 0 3	Tyrone . .	Dungannon Upper .	Derryloran .	Cookstown .	III.	307
61, 69	Craigs or Tommyscroft	143 0 4	Donegal . .	Raphoe . .	Convoy . .	Stranorlar .	III.	136
38	Craigtown . .	219 1 18	Donegal . .	Inishowen West .	Fahan Upper .	Londonderry .	III.	121
24, 25	Craigtown . .	145 2 3	Donegal . .	Kilmacrenan .	Tullaghobegly .	Dunfanaghy .	III.	131
21	Craigtown . .	244 1 36	Londonderry .	Tirkeeran . .	Clondermot .	Londonderry .	III.	247
3	Craigtown Beg .	146 1 26	Londonderry .	North East Liberties of Coleraine .	Ballyaghran .	Coleraine . .	III.	244
3	Craigtown More .	154 1 35	Londonderry .	North East Liberties of Coleraine ·	Ballyaghran .	Coleraine . .	III.	244
38	Craigue . .	233 0 39	Kilkenny .	Iverk . . .	Whitechurch .	Carrick on Suir	I.	107
27, 33	Craigueavallagh .	303 3 1	Queen's Co. .	Clandonagh .	Rathsaran .	Donaghmore .	I.	234
35	Craigueavoice .	393 1 32	Queen's Co. .	Clarmallagh .	Aghmacart .	Abbeyleix .	I.	236
23, 29	Craiguedarg .	82 2 14	Tipperary, N.R. .	Ikerrin . .	Templemore .	Roscrea . .	II.	276
46	Craigue Little .	257 2 22	Wexford . .	Bargy . . .	Bannow . .	Wexford . .	I.	304
50	Craigy Hall .	101 0 2	Antrim . .	Upper Antrim .	Antrim . .	Antrim . .	III.	5
27,28,32,33	Craigywarren .	899 3 8	Antrim . .	Lower Toome .	Kirkinriola .	Ballymena .	III.	32

(a) Including 58A. 1R. 33P. water.   (c) Including 3A. 3R. 2P. water.
(b) Including 5A. 0R. 3P. water.   (d) Including 16A. 0R. 20P. water.

No. of Sheet of the Ordnance Survey Maps.	Townlands and Towns.	Area in Statute Acres.	County.	Barony.	Parish.	Poor Law Union in 1857.	Townland Census of 1851, Part I.	
		A. R. P.					Vol.	Page
38, 39	Crakenstown . .	89 2 24	Meath . .	Ratoath . . .	Crickstown . .	Dunshaughlin .	I.	217
38	Crakenstown . .	198 0 36	Meath . .	Ratoath . . .	Kilbrew . . .	Dunshaughlin .	I.	218
14	Cramersgrove or Grove	356 3 20	Kilkenny .	Gowran . . .	Kilkieran . .	Kilkenny . .	I.	97
29	Cramersvalley . .	35 1 4a	Kildare . .	Naas South .	Brannockstown .	Naas . .	I.	64
70	Crampscastle . .	539 1 18	Tipperary, S.R.	Middlethird . .	Peppardstown .	Cashel . .	II.	329
22	Cran . . .	218 1 6	Cavan . .	Clankee . . .	Drumgoon . .	Cootehill . .	III.	72
24	Cran . . .	193 0 10	Fermanagh .	Magherastephana .	Aghalurcher .	Lisnaskea . .	III.	215
11, 16	Cranacrower . .	146 1 5	Wexford . .	Gorey . . .	Ballycanew .	Gorey . .	I.	316
29,30,35,36	Cranagh . . .	664 0 37	Tipperary, N.R.	Ikerrin . . .	Templetouhy .	Thurles . .	II.	277
36	Cranagh . .	112 3 36	Wicklow . .	Arklow . . .	Dunganstown .	Rathdrum .	I.	343
10, 14	Cranaghan . .	494 2 6b	Cavan . .	Lower Loughtee .	Tomregan . .	Cavan . .	III.	81
26, 34	Cranagher . .	287 2 16	Clare . .	Bunratty Upper .	Clooney . .	Ennis . .	II.	8
4, 5, 9	Cranagill . .	284 2 31	Armagh . .	Oneilland West .	Tartaraghan .	Armagh . .	III.	54
26	Cranahurt . .	148 3 27	Tipperary, N.R.	Upper Ormond .	Kilmore . .	Nenagh . .	II.	291
15	Cranalagh Beg .	449 0 21	Longford . .	Ardagh . . .	Mostrim . .	Granard . .	I.	152
15	Cranalagh More .	834 1 6	Longford . .	Ardagh . . .	Mostrim . .	Granard . .	I.	152
6, 10	Cranally . .	269 1 32	Longford . .	Granard . . .	Abbeylara . .	Granard . .	I.	154
77	Cranareen . .	73 3 14	Mayo . .	Burrishoole . .	Kilmeena . .	Westport . .	IV.	122
28	Cranareen . .	179 3 27	Wicklow . .	Upper Talbotstown .	Kiltegan . .	Baltinglass .	I.	364
7	Cranasallagh . .	371 0 35	King's Co. .	Garrycastle . .	Lemanaghan .	Tullamore .	I.	136
37	Cranavaneen .	72 0 33	Tipperary, N.R.	Owney and Arra .	Kilvellane . .	Nenagh . .	II.	296
11, 12	Cranavonane . .	757 3 13	Carlow . .	Idrone West . .	Tullowcreen .	Carlow . .	I.	9
27	*Cranberry Island* .	1 0 28	Donegal . .	Kilmacrenan . .	Kilmacrenan .	Millford . .	III.	130
54	Cranberry Island .	386 2 16c	Roscommon .	Moycarn . . .	Moore . .	Ballinasloe .	IV.	206
52	Crancam . .	100 2 7	Roscommon .	Athlone . . .	Drum . .	Athlone . .	IV.	180
15, 16	Crancam or Kilfintan Lower . .	50 1 32	Longford . .	Ardagh . . .	Street . .	Granard . .	I.	153
22, 30	Crancreagh . .	280 3 3	King's Co. .	Garrycastle . .	Gallen . .	Parsonstown .	I.	136
22	Crandaniel . .	6 0 26	Wexford . .	Ballaghkeen . .	Donaghmore .	Gorey . .	I.	293
22	Crandaniel Great .	201 2 16	Wexford . .	Gorey . . .	Kiltrisk . .	Gorey . .	I.	320
22	Crandaniel Little .	170 1 11	Wexford . .	Gorey . . .	Kiltrisk . .	Gorey . .	I.	320
36, 37	Crandonnell . .	167 0 21	Wexford . .	Shelmaliere West .	Kilbrideglynn .	Wexford . .	I.	334
20	Crane . . .	425 2 29	Wexford . .	Scarawalsh . .	Clone . .	Enniscorthy .	I.	322
137	*Crane Island* . .	2 0 26	Galway . .	Leitrim . . .	Clonrush . .	Scarriff . .	IV.	53
26	*Crane Island* . .	0 1 11	Leitrim . .	Carrigallen . .	Carrigallen .	Bawnboy . .	IV.	90
20	*Crane Island* . .	1 0 1	Monaghan .	Cremorne . .	Clontibret . .	Castleblayney .	III.	261
25	*Crane Island* . .	1 1 8	Monaghan .	Cremorne . .	Muckno . .	Castleblayney .	III.	262
17, 20	Cranemore . .	1,417 1 5	Carlow . .	Forth . . .	Barragh . .	Enniscorthy .	I.	4
49	Cranfield . .	834 2 19	Antrim . .	Upper Toome .	Cranfield . .	Antrim . .	III.	33
57	Cranfield . .	474 1 33	Down . .	Mourne . .	Kilkeel . .	Kilkeel . .	III.	183
29, 30	Cranfield . .	96 3 21	Tyrone . .	Dungannon Upper .	Derryloran . .	Cookstown .	III.	307
27	Cranford . .	725 3 15d	Donegal . .	Kilmacrenan . .	Kilmacrenan .	Millford . .	III.	129
22	Crankey . . .	145 3 18	Armagh . .	Orior Lower . .	Killevy . .	Newry . .	III.	56
22	Crankey . .	138 3 25	Armagh . .	Orior Lower . .	Loughgilly . .	Newry . .	III.	56
27, 32	Crankill . .	553 0 8	Antrim . .	Lower Toome .	Ahoghill . .	Ballymena .	III.	32
45, 53	Cranlome . .	1,259 0 17	Tyrone . .	Dungannon Lower .	Killeeshil . .	Dungannon .	III.	298
99	Cranmore . .	97 1 37	Mayo . .	Carra . . .	Ballintober .	Castlebar .	IV.	124
63	Cranmore . .	149 2 17	Mayo . .	Costello . .	Kilbeagh . .	Swineford .	IV.	140
15,19	Crann . .	174 0 33	Armagh . .	Tiranny . .	Tynan . .	Armagh . .	III.	60
81	Cranna . .	310 2 0	Tipperary, S.R.	Iffa and Offa West .	Tubbrid . .	Clogheen . .	II.	320
39	Crannadillon .	280 0 4	Cavan . .	Castlerahan . .	Lurgan . .	Oldcastle .	III.	69
23	Crannagh . .	1,006 0 6	Carlow . .	Idrone East . .	Kiltennell . .	Carlow . .	I.	7
113, 122	Crannagh . .	407 2 31	Galway . .	Kiltartan . . .	Ardrahan . .	Gort . .	IV.	45
113, 122	Crannagh . .	546 0 11	Galway . .	Kiltartan . . .	Kilmacduagh .	Gort . .	IV.	48
117, 126	Crannagh . .	252 2 31	Galway . .	Leitrim . . .	Tynagh . .	Portumna .	IV.	55
60	Crannagh . .	104 2 37	Galway . .	Tiaquin . .	Killosolan . .	Mountbellew .	IV.	78
30, 39	Crannagh . .	233 1 16	Mayo . .	Tirawley . .	Ardagh . .	Ballina .	IV.	163
19	Crannagh . .	477 0 31	Queen's Co. .	Ballyadams . .	Ballyadams .	Athy . .	I.	231
16	Crannagh . .	464 1 7	Queen's Co. .	Upperwoods .	Offerlane . .	Mountmellick .	I.	251
52	Crannagh . .	327 2 24	Roscommon .	Athlone . .	Drum . .	Athlone . .	IV.	180
14, 20	Crannagh . .	271 3 5	Tipperary, N.R.	Lower Ormond .	Monsea . .	Nenagh . .	II.	287
86	Crannagh . .	144 0 17	Tipperary, S.R.	Iffa and Offa West .	Shanrahan . .	Clogheen . .	II.	319
52	Crannagh Beg .	204 3 38	Roscommon .	Athlone . .	Drum . .	Athlone . .	IV.	180
52	Crannagh More .	403 2 7	Roscommon .	Athlone . .	Drum . .	Athlone . .	IV.	180
23, 24	Crannaghtown .	192 1 14	Meath . .	Upper Kells .	Balrathboyne .	Kells . .	I.	204
81	Crannavone . .	239 0 23	Tipperary, S.R.	Iffa and Offa West .	Tubbrid . .	Clogheen . .	II.	321
73	Crannogeboy . .	393 1 19	Donegal . .	Banagh . . .	Inishkeel . .	Glenties . .	III.	106
9	*Crannoge Island* .	0 0 5	Leitrim . .	Drumahaire . .	Cloonclare .	Manorhamilton .	IV.	94
45	Crannogue . .	759 0 18	Tyrone . .	Dungannon Middle .	Pomeroy . .	Dungannon .	III.	304
41, 46	Cranny . . .	445 2 3	Londonderry .	Loughinsholin .	Desertmartin .	Magherafelt .	III.	240
42, 50	Cranny . . .	510 2 34	Tyrone . .	Omagh East . .	Donacavey .	Omagh . .	III.	310
42, 50	Cranny . . .	185 2 6	Tyrone . .	Omagh East . .	Dromore . .	Omagh . .	III.	311
35	Cranny . . .	416 0 10e	Tyrone . .	Strabane Upper .	Cappagh . .	Omagh . .	III.	325

(a) Including 2A. 2R. 34P. water.   (c) Including 14A. 2R. 13P. water.   (e) Including 8A. 2R. 17P. water.
(b) Including 101A. 1R. 13P. water.   (d) Including 2A. 0R. 7P. water.

2 T 2

No. of Sheet of the Ordnance Survey Maps.	Townlands and Towns.	Area in Statute Acres.			County.	Barony.	Parish.	Poor Law Union in 1857.	Townland Census of 1851, Part I.	
		A.	R.	P.					Vol.	Page
92, 98	Cranny Lower	280	1	27	Donegal	Banagh	Inver	Donegal	III.	107
92, 93	Cranny Upper	154	1	19	Donegal	Banagh	Inver	Donegal	III.	107
53, 60	Cranslough	286	1	27a	Tyrone	Dungannon Lower	Carnteel	Dungannon	III.	297
101, 102	Crantahar	119	1	19	Mayo	Clanmorris	Kilcolman	Claremorris	IV.	134
89	Crappagh	117	3	28	Galway	Moycullen	Kilcummin	Oughterard	IV.	68
17	Crappagh	174	3	16	Monaghan	Dartree	Aghabog	Cootehill	III.	263
35	Crataloe East	783	3	32	Limerick	Shanid	Rathronan	Newcastle	II.	257
34, 35	Crataloe West	777	1	9	Limerick	Shanid	Rathronan	Newcastle	II.	257
27, 36	Cratlagh	1,041	3	26b	Donegal	Kilmacrenan	Tullyfern	Millford	III.	133
39	Cratley	145	2	36	Tyrone	Dungannon Upper	Ballyclog	Cookstown	III.	306
52, 62	Cratloe	404	2	12	Clare	Bunratty Lower	Kilfintinan	Limerick	II.	5
62	Cratloe	445	3	35	Clare	Bunratty Lower	Killeely	Limerick	II.	5
52, 62	Cratloekeel	466	2	35	Clare	Bunratty Lower	Killeely	Limerick	II.	5
52, 62	Cratloemoyle	548	2	3	Clare	Bunratty Lower	Killeely	Limerick	II.	5
96	Craughwell	149	1	30	Galway	Dunkellin	Killora	Loughrea	IV.	31
100, 108	Craughwell	767	2	23	Galway	Longford	Kiltormer	Ballinasloe	IV.	60
96	CRAUGHWELL T.	—			Galway	Dunkellin	Killora	Loughrea	IV.	31
60	Cravenny Irish	146	0	21	Tyrone	Dungannon Lower	Carnteel	Clogher	III.	297
53, 60	Cravenny Scotch	175	2	33	Tyrone	Dungannon Lower	Carnteel	Clogher	III.	297
1	CRAWFORDSBURN T.	—			Down	Castlereagh Lower	Bangor	Newtownards	III.	161
21	Crawfords Hill	169	2	9	Fermanagh	Magheraboy	Devenish	Enniskillen	III.	210
45	Crawfordsland	252	0	9	Antrim	Upper Antrim	Kilbride	Antrim	III.	6
35	Crawhill	118	0	39	Sligo	Tirerrill	Kilmactranny	Boyle	IV.	240
28	Crawnglass	240	1	35	Kildare	Offaly West	Ballyshannon	Athy	I.	72
31	Craystown or Ennistown	68	2	20	Meath	Lower Deece	Balsoon	Trim	I.	191
29	Craywell	11	2	11	Wexford	Bantry	St. Mary's	New Ross	I.	302
27	Creadan	497	1	27	Waterford	Gaultiere	Killea	Waterford	II.	363
37	Creagh	253	2	33	Antrim	Upper Toome	Drummaul	Ballymena	III.	34
141, 150	Creagh	417	2	1	Cork, W.R.	West Carbery (E.D.)	Creagh	Skibbereen	II.	138
23	Creagh	161	1	14	Fermanagh	Magherastephana	Aghavea	Lisnaskea	III.	218
22	Creagh	238	3	21	Longford	Rathcline	Kilcommock	Ballymahon	I.	164
51	Creagh	191	2	31	Roscommon	Athlone	Drum	Athlone	IV.	180
53	Creagh	273	1	27c	Roscommon	Moycarn	Creagh	Ballinasloe	IV.	206
9	Creaghadoo	173	1	36	Sligo	Carbury	Drumcliff	Sligo	IV.	221
62, 63	Creaghadoos	562	1	6	Donegal	Raphoe	Taughboyne	Strabane	III.	143
34	Creaghamanone Island	3	3	29	Fermanagh	Magherastephana	Aghalurcher	Lisnaskea	III.	217
8	Creaghan	138	0	24	Armagh	Armagh	Clonfeacle	Armagh	III.	43
1	Creaghan	64	0	35	Monaghan	Trough	Errigal Trough	Clogher	III.	283
34	Creaghanameelta Island	3	3	11	Fermanagh	Magherastephana	Aghalurcher	Lisnaskea	III.	217
33	Creaghananure Island	0	3	16	Fermanagh	Knockninny	Kinawley	Lisnaskea	III.	203
34	Creaghanarourke Island	1	0	1	Fermanagh	Magherastephana	Aghalurcher	Lisnaskea	III.	217
79	Creaghanboy	155	1	19d	Mayo	Carra	Manulla	Castlebar	IV.	129
34, 39	Creaghanchreesty Island	1	0	20	Fermanagh	Magherastephana	Aghalurcher	Lisnaskea	III.	217
3	Creaghan Glebe	316	2	32e	Tyrone	Strabane Lower	Donaghedy	Strabane	III.	320
15, 20	Creaghanroe	195	0	35	Monaghan	Cremorne	Muckno	Castleblayney	III.	261
34	Creaghawaddy Island	9	1	30	Fermanagh	Magherastephana	Aghalurcher	Lisnaskea	III.	217
135	Creagh Beg	230	2	14	Cork, W.R.	Ibane and Barryroe	Kilkerranmore	Clonakilty	II.	149
1	Creaghcor	232	0	32	Tyrone	Strabane Lower	Donaghedy	Strabane	III.	320
109,117,118	Creagh Demesne	599	1	18f	Mayo	Kilmaine	Ballinrobe	Ballinrobe	IV.	152
6, 7	Creagh Demesne	298	3	34	Wexford	Gorey	Kilnahue	Gorey	I.	319
22	Creaghduff	318	0	17	Westmeath	Brawny	St. Mary's	Athlone	I.	259
22, 29	Creaghduff South	26	1	14	Westmeath	Brawny	St. Mary's	Athlone	I.	259
6	Creagh Lower	167	1	6	Wexford	Gorey	Kilnahue	Gorey	I.	319
33	Creaghmacwallen Island	4	1	38	Fermanagh	Tirkennedy	Cleenish	Lisnaskea	III.	220
135	Creagh More	257	1	28	Cork, W.R.	Ibane and Barryroe	Kilkerranmore	Clonakilty	II.	149
17	Creaghnakirka	72	1	29	Roscommon	Roscommon	Aughrim	Cark.on Shannon	IV.	207
33	Creaghnarourk Island	3	2	18	Fermanagh	Knockninny	Kinawley	Lisnaskea	III.	203
42, 43, 47	Creagh, The(Etre and Otre)	2,298	3	10	Londonderry	Loughinsholin	Artrea	Magherafelt	III.	238
42	Creagh, The(Etre and Otre) (Intake)	215	2	27	Londonderry	Loughinsholin	Artrea	Magherafelt	III.	238
42, 43, 47	Creagh, The(Etre and Otre) (Intake)	98	1	38	Londonderry	Loughinsholin	Artrea	Magherafelt	III.	238
6	Creagh Upper	296	1	19	Wexford	Gorey	Kilnahue	Gorey	I.	319
34	Creakan Lower	271	2	37	Wexford	Bantry	Oldross	New Ross	I.	301
34	Creakan Upper	220	3	1	Wexford	Bantry	Oldross	New Ross	I.	301
44	Crean	117	1	9	Clare	Tulla Lower	Killokennedy	Limerick	II.	35
36	Crean	202	3	25	Limerick	Glenquin	Monagay	Newcastle	II.	247
31	Crean	777	0	29	Limerick	Smallcounty	Glenogra	Croom	II.	259
31	Crean	619	2	0	Limerick	Smallcounty	Tullabracky	Croom	II.	261
11, 15	Crearum or Fellows Hall	261	1	35	Armagh	Armagh	Tynan	Armagh	III.	46
62, 63	Creatland	146	1	38	Donegal	Raphoe	Taughboyne	Strabane	III.	143
32, 33, 38	Crebilly	808	0	5	Antrim	Lower Antrim	Ballyclug	Ballymena	III.	3

(a) Including 9A. 2R. 35P. of Lake.
(b) Including 9A. 2R. 12P. water.
(c) Including 2A. 3R. 32P. water.
(d) Including 13A. 1R. 0P. water.
(e) Including 3A. 2R. 7P. water.
(f) Including 11A. 3R. 36P. water.

No. of Sheet of the Ordnance Survey Maps.	Townlands and Towns.	Area in Statute Acres.			County.	Barony.	Parish.	Poor Law Union in 1857.	Townland Census of 1851, Part I.	
		A.	R.	P.					Vol.	Page
144	Creboy	28	0	8	Cork, W.R.	Ibane and Barryroe	Ardfield	Clonakilty	II.	148
144	Creboy	50	0	22	Cork, W.R.	Ibane and Barryroe	Island	Clonakilty	II.	149
9	Crecrin	323	2	21	Carlow	Rathvilly	Crecrin	Shillelagh	I.	11
35, 38	Cree	282	2	6	King's Co.	Ballybritt	Birr	Parsonstown	I.	125
38	Cree	577	1	8	King's Co.	Ballybritt	Kilcolman	Parsonstown	I.	125
3, 4, 5, 6	Creea	318	2	1	Cavan	Tullyhaw	Templeport	Enniskillen	III.	94
23	Creeduff	574	2	28a	Tyrone	Omagh West	Termonamongan	Castlederg	III.	317
37	Creeghassaun	211	0	3	Sligo	Leyny	Kilmacteige	Tobercurry	IV.	231
37	Creeghduff	428	2	17	Down	Kinelarty	Loughinisland	Downpatrick	III.	177
47, 48	Creegh North	646	3	0	Clare	Moyarta	Kilmacduane	Kilrush	II.	33
47	Creegh South	488	0	2	Clare	Moyarta	Kilmacduane	Kilrush	II.	33
21	Creegooane	26	3	27	Kerry	Clanmaurice	Ardfert	Tralee	II.	167
44, 47	Creeharmore	355	1	19b	Roscommon	Athlone	Taghboy	Athlone	IV.	184
10, 17	Creehaun	663	3	0	Clare	Inchiquin	Killinaboy	Corrofin	II.	26
20, 30, 31	Creehennan	828	2	37	Donegal	Inishowen East	Moville Upper	Inishowen	III.	119
28, 34	Creelagh	108	0	16	Queen's Co.	Clandonagh	Rathdowney	Donaghmore	I.	234
2, 5	Creelaghta	432	0	29	Longford	Longford	Killoe	Longford	I.	159
89, 90	Creelogh	444	1	15c	Galway	Moycullen	Killannin	Oughterard	IV.	69
44	Creemore	193	3	36	Meath	Ratoath	Rathregan	Dunshaughlin	I.	219
21	Creemore	118	2	17	Wexford	Ballaghkeen	Kilmuckridge	Gorey	I.	296
21	Creemore	145	0	10	Wexford	Ballaghkeen	Meelnagh	Gorey	I.	298
38, 39, 41	Creemully and Aghagad Beg	940	2	38	Roscommon	Athlone	Fuerty	Roscommon	IV.	181
67	Creenagh	414	0	25	Antrim	Upper Massereene	Magheramesk	Lisburn	III.	31
8, 9	Creenagh	276	1	7	Armagh	Oneilland West	Kilmore	Armagh	III.	53
23	Creenagh	137	1	4d	Leitrim	Leitrim	Kiltoghert	Cark. on Shannon	IV.	101
32, 33	Creenagh	343	2	10	Leitrim	Mohill	Cloone	Mohill	IV.	105
8	Creenagh	316	1	33	Longford	Longford	Clongesh	Longford	I.	157
47, 55	Creenagh	465	1	9	Tyrone	Dungannon Middle	Tullyniskan	Dungannon	III.	304
19, 24	Creenagh Glebe	252	3	27e	Cavan	Tullyhunco	Killashandra	Cavan	III.	98
25, 26	Creenagho	132	0	13	Fermanagh	Clanawley	Cleenish	Enniskillen	III.	190
35	Creenary	548	3	32	Donegal	Kilmacrenan	Clondahorky	Dunfanaghy	III.	123
25,26,34,35	Creenasmear	872	2	10	Donegal	Kilmacrenan	Clondahorky	Dunfanaghy	III.	123
27, 30	Creenkill	319	3	26	Armagh	Fews Upper	Creggan	Castleblayney	III.	48
8	Creenkill Beg	113	3	3	Kilkenny	Galmoy	Balleen	Urlingford	I.	91
8, 9	Creenkill More	250	2	17	Kilkenny	Galmoy	Balleen	Urlingford	I.	91
31, 32	Creenow	105	2	36	Cavan	Castlerahan	Crosserlough	Cavan	III.	68
9	Creen or Tonroe	306	2	22	Roscommon	Frenchpark	Kilnamanagh	Boyle	IV.	204
89, 90	Creenveen	641	3	18f	Donegal	Banagh	Glencolumbkille	Glenties	III.	105
11	Creeny	297	1	4g	Cavan	Lower Loughtee	Annagh	Cavan	III.	79
14	Creeny	288	1	15	Cavan	Lower Loughtee	Drumlane	Cavan	III.	79
78	Creeragh	141	0	17	Mayo	Carra	Ballyhean	Castlebar	IV.	125
8, 11	Creeragh	92	2	39	Tipperary, N.R.	Lower Ormond	Ballingarry	Borrisokane	II.	282
7, 8, 10, 11	Creeragh	352	1	3	Tipperary, N.R.	Lower Ormond	Uskane	Borrisokane	II.	288
17	Creeran	169	1	10	Monaghan	Dartree	Currin	Cootehill	III.	265
72	Creeraun	244	2	20	Galway	Tiaquin	Ballymacward	Loughrea	IV.	75
9	Creesil	121	1	21	Monaghan	Monaghan	Tedavnet	Monaghan	III.	278
26	Creeslough	427	0	13h	Donegal	Kilmacrenan	Clondahorky	Dunfanaghy	III.	123
26	CREESLOUGH T.	—			Donegal	Kilmacrenan	Clondahorky	Dunfanaghy	III.	124
10	Creevagh	305	2	11	Clare	Burren	Carran	Ballyvaghan	II.	11
39	Creevagh	513	0	10i	Clare	Ibrickan	Kilmurry	Kilrush	II.	23
26	Creevagh	205	2	4	Donegal	Kilmacrenan	Mevagh	Millford	III.	130
85	Creevagh	168	3	10	Galway	Kilconnell	Killimordaly	Loughrea	IV.	42
5, 13	Creevagh	1,268	3	16	King's Co.	Garrycastle	Clonmacnoise	Parsonstown	I.	135
89	Creevagh	414	2	39	Mayo	Carra	Ballintober	Castlebar	IV.	124
7, 8	Creevagh	651	2	20	Mayo	Tirawley	Kilcummin	Killala	IV.	168
6, 7	Creevagh	421	3	37	Meath	Lower Slane	Siddan	Ardee	I.	223
16	Creevagh	153	0	36	Meath	Upper Kells	Kilskeer	Oldcastle	I.	206
18, 19	Creevagh	212	1	4	Monaghan	Cremorne	Tullycorbet	Monaghan	III.	262
35, 41	Creevagh	338	0	0j	Sligo	Tirerrill	Kilmactranny	Boyle	IV.	240
29	Creevagh	395	2	5	Tyrone	Dungannon Upper	Lissan	Cookstown	III.	309
67, 76, 77	Creevaghaun	39	2	19	Mayo	Burrishoole	Burrishoole	Newport	IV.	119
44	Creevaghbaun	150	2	22	Galway	Dunmore	Killererin	Tuam	IV.	35
34	Creevagh Beg	235	0	39	Clare	Bunratty Upper	Quin	Tulla	II.	10
27	Creevagh Beg	455	0	3k	Longford	Shrule	Noughaval	Ballymahon	I.	166
14	Creevagh Beg	255	3	3	Mayo	Tirawley	Rathreagh	Killala	II.	171
9	Creevaghern Island	0	0	4	Leitrim	Drumahaire	Cloonclare	Manorhamilton	IV.	94
20	Creevagh Lower	351	2	23	Londonderry	North West Liberties of Londonderry	Templemore	Londonderry	III.	246
46	Creevagh Lower	123	0	36	Tyrone	Dungannon Middle	Donaghmore	Dungannon	III.	301
120	Creevagh Middle	251	3	34	Mayo	Kilmaine	Cong	Ballinrobe	IV.	153
34, 42	Creevagh More	334	3	30	Clare	Bunratty Upper	Quin	Tulla	II.	10
27	Creevaghmore	384	2	25	Longford	Shrule	Forgney	Ballymahon	I.	166

(a) Including 8A. 1R. 2P. water.
(b) Including 22A. 1R. 20P. water.
(c) Including 31A. 2R. 14P. water.
(d) Including 1A. 3R. 3P. water.

(e) Including 11A. 2R. 5P. water.
(f) Including 8A. 2R. 5P. water.
(g) Including 16A. 3R. 31P. water.
(h) Including 25A. 3R. 24P. water.

(i) Including 4A. 3R. 24P. water.
(j) Including 59A. 1R. 37P. water.
(k) Including 8A. 2R. 4P. water.

No. of Sheet of the Ordnance Survey Maps.	Townlands and Towns.	Area in Statute Acres.	County.	Barony.	Parish.	Poor Law Union in 1857.	Townland Census of 1851, Part I.	
		A. R. P.					Vol.	Page
27	Creevaghmore	164 3 19*a*	Longford	Shrule	Noughaval	Ballymahon	I.	166
14, 21	Creevagh More	461 3 11	Mayo	Tirawley	Rathreagh	Killala	II.	171
120	Creevagh North	283 3 38	Mayo	Kilmaine	Cong	Ballinrobe	IV.	153
118	Creevagh North	247 2 19	Mayo	Kilmaine	Kilmolara	Ballinrobe	IV.	157
120	Creevagh South	414 3 10	Mayo	Kilmaine	Cong	Ballinrobe	IV.	153
118, 121	Creevagh South	404 0 39	Mayo	Kilmaine	Kilmolara	Ballinrobe	IV.	157
20	Creevagh Upper	371 3 30	Londonderry	North West Liberties of Londonderry	Templemore	Londonderry	III.	246
46	Creevagh Upper	109 2 28	Tyrone	Dungannon Middle	Drumglass	Dungannon	III.	302
12	Creevaghy	109 1 33	Monaghan	Dartree	Clones	Clones	III.	264
33	Creevamoy	586 3 3	Antrim	Lower Antrim	Racavan	Ballymena	III.	4
34, 42	Creevangar (*Alexander*)	138 0 6	Tyrone	Omagh East	Drumragh	Omagh	III.	312
42	Creevangar (*White*)	47 2 14	Tyrone	Omagh East	Drumragh	Omagh	III.	312
42	Creevanmore (*Crosby*)	37 3 33	Tyrone	Omagh East	Drumragh	Omagh	III.	312
42	Creevanmore (*Hunter*)	99 2 35	Tyrone	Omagh East	Drumragh	Omagh	III.	312
112	Creevard	222 3 25	Mayo	Clanmorris	Kilvine	Claremorris	IV.	134
121	Creevaroddaun	195 0 38	Mayo	Kilmaine	Kilmainemore	Ballinrobe	IV.	156
25	Creevaun	188 0 20	Sligo	Leyny	Killoran	Tobercurry	IV.	230
49	Creeve	214 0 8	Antrim	Upper Toome	Duneane	Antrim	III.	34
21	Creeve	131 2 3	Armagh	Orior Lower	Loughgilly	Newry	III.	56
55	Creeve	304 1 0	Donegal	Raphoe	Allsaints	Londonderry	III.	134
46, 47	Creeve	266 1 7	Down	Lordship of Newry	Newry	Newry	III.	182
14	Creeve	320 2 23	Longford	Longford	Killoe	Longford	I.	159
24	Creeve	684 3 32*b*	Monaghan	Cremorne	Aghnamullen	Castleblayney	III.	257
14	Creeve	184 1 0	Monaghan	Cremorne	Clontibret	Monaghan	III.	260
14	Creeve	158 1 23	Monaghan	Monaghan	Monaghan	Monaghan	III.	277
34	Creeve	192 3 10	Roscommon	Ballymoe	Oran	Roscommon	IV.	192
17	Creeve	324 0 14	Roscommon	Roscommon	Creeve	Strokestown	IV.	209
16, 22	Creeve	143 2 5	Roscommon	Roscommon	Shankill	Strokestown	IV.	212
46	Creeve	82 1 28*c*	Tyrone	Dungannon Middle	Pomeroy	Dungannon	III.	304
46	Creeve (*part of*)	36 2 34	Tyrone	Dungannon Middle	Pomeroy	Dungannon	III.	304
21, 29	Creeve	301 3 38	Tyrone	Dungannon Upper	Lissan	Cookstown	III.	309
23, 30	Creeve	980 1 31	Westmeath	Clonlonan	Ballyloughloe	Athlone	I.	260
24, 31	Creeve	442 2 36	Westmeath	Moycashel	Ardnurcher or Horseleap	Mullingar	I.	276
38	Creevebeg	81 0 7	Limerick	Coshma	Croom	Croom	II.	242
30	Creevebeg	60 2 6	Westmeath	Clonlonan	Ballyloughloe	Athlone	I.	260
21	Creeve or Corgarve	73 3 0	Cavan	Upper Loughtee	Castleterra	Cavan	III.	82
21	Creevedonnell	353 0 32	Londonderry	Tirkeeran	Clondermot	Londonderry	III.	247
108, 109	Creeveen	567 3 19	Kerry	Glanarought	Tuosist	Kenmare	II.	188
71	Creeveen	916 1 22	Kerry	Iveragh	Glanbehy	Cahersiveen	II.	195
112	Creeveeshel	188 0 39	Mayo	Clanmorris	Kilvine	Claremorris	IV.	134
53, 61	Creeve Glebe	295 2 6	Donegal	Raphoe	Leck	Letterkenny	III.	140
17,18,23,24	Creevehill	840 3 4	Fermanagh	Tirkennedy	Enniskillen	Lisnaskea	III.	221
39	Creeve Island	1 2 5	Mayo	Tirawley	Kilbelfad	Ballina	IV.	168
30	Creevekeeran	532 0 17*d*	Armagh	Fews Upper	Creggan	Castleblayney	III.	48
15	Creevekeeran	228 0 18*e*	Armagh	Tiranny	Tynan	Armagh	III.	60
14	Creevelea	57 2 20	Leitrim	Drumahaire	Killanummery	Manorhamilton	IV.	98
3, 4	Creevelea	206 2 31*f*	Leitrim	Rosclogher	Rossinver	Ballyshannon	IV.	111
12	Creevelea	213 3 22	Monaghan	Dartree	Clones	Clones	III.	264
6	Creevelea	109 2 31	Monaghan	Trough	Donagh	Monaghan	III.	281
28, 35	Creevelea	138 2 33	Roscommon	Ballymoe	Cloonygormican	Castlereagh	IV.	191
61, 67	Creevelough	889 3 37*g*	Tyrone	Dungannon Lower	Aghaloo	Dungannon	III.	296
35	Creevenagh	351 1 1*h*	Tyrone	Omagh East	Cappagh	Omagh	III.	310
16, 22, 23	Creevenamanagh	289 2 36*i*	Westmeath	Kilkenny West	Kilkenny West	Athlone	I.	273
28	Creeveoughter	846 1 36	Donegal	Kilmacrenan	Killygarvan	Millford	III.	128
12	Creeveroe	114 0 22	Armagh	Armagh	Eglish	Armagh	III.	44
45	Creeveroe	278 2 23	Clare	Tulla Lower	Killaloe	Scarriff	II.	35
32, 46	Creeveroe (*Davies*)	127 3 15	Galway	Killian	Killian	Mountbellew	IV.	44
32	Creeveroe (*Ffrench*)	272 1 21	Galway	Killian	Killian	Mountbellew	IV.	44
44	Creevery	515 3 13	Antrim	Upper Toome	Antrim	Antrim	III.	33
19	Creeves	259 1 29	Limerick	Connello Lower	Lismakeery	Rathkeale	II.	228
19	Creeves	241 0 14	Limerick	Shanid	Dunmoylan	Rathkeale	II.	255
53, 61	Creeve (*Smith*)	232 0 18	Donegal	Raphoe	Leck	Letterkenny	III.	140
98	Creevins	199 2 22	Donegal	Banagh	Inver	Donegal	III.	107
16	Creevolan	173 3 18	Roscommon	Frenchpark	Creeve	Car^k. on Shannon	IV.	203
103, 107	Creevy	815 2 2	Donegal	Tirhugh	Kilbarron	Ballyshannon	III.	148
15	Creevy	504 1 8*j*	Down	Castlereagh Upper	Drumbo	Lisburn	III.	164
34, 41	Creevy	471 2 21	Down	Upper Iveagh, Up. pt.	Aghaderg	Banbridge	III.	174
24, 25	Creevy	290 2 34	Leitrim	Carrigallen	Oughteragh	Bawnboy	IV.	92
11	Creevy	549 3 23	Longford	Granard	Granard	Granard	I.	156
90	Creevy	476 0 00	Mayo	Tirawley	Crossmolina	Ballina	IV.	105
13, 14	Creevy	644 1 21	Roscommon	Frenchpark	Tibohine	Castlereagh	IV.	205

(*a*) Including 3A. 1R. 15P. water.
(*b*) Including 30A. 2R. 11P. water.
(*c*) Exclusive of detached portion.
(*d*) Including 19A. 0R. 4P. water.

(*e*) Including 3A. 1R. 24P. water.
(*f*) Including 19A. 3R. 20P. water.
(*g*) Including 26A. 0R. 27P. water.

(*h*) Including 7A. 0R. 14P. water.
(*i*) Including 28A. 1R. 24P. water.
(*j*) Including 45A. 2R. 13P. detached portion.

No. of Sheet of the Ordnance Survey Maps.	Townlands and Towns.	Area in Statute Acres.	County.	Barony.	Parish.	Poor Law Union in 1857.	Townland Census of 1851, Part I.	
		A. R. P.					Vol.	Page
24	Creevy	408 0 8a	Tyrone	Strabane Lower	Ardstraw	Castlederg	III.	318
22, 23	Creevyargon	454 1 2	Down	Castlereagh Upper	Kilmore	Downpatrick	III.	165
23	Creevybeg	122 0 29	Down	Castlereagh Upper	Killinchy	Downpatrick	III.	165
23, 30	Creevycarnonan	825 0 0	Down	Castlereagh Upper	Kilmore	Downpatrick	III.	165
2, 3	Creevykeel	623 1 34b	Sligo	Carbury	Ahamlish	Sligo	IV.	219
23	Creevyloughgare	510 0 4c	Down	Castlereagh Upper	Saintfield	Downpatrick	III.	166
16	Creevy Lower	113 2 8	Tyrone	Omagh West	Urney	Castlederg	III.	318
2, 3	Creevymore	598 3 33d	Sligo	Carbury	Ahamlish	Sligo	IV.	219
28, 31	Creevy (Oliver)	102 2 11e	Monaghan	Farney	Donaghmoyne	Carrickmacross	III.	269
40	Creevyquin	229 2 28	Roscommon	Ballintober South	Kiltecvan	Roscommon	IV.	190
28, 31	Creevy (Swinburn)	68 2 3	Monaghan	Farney	Donaghmoyne	Carrickmacross	III.	269
22	Creevytenant	938 0 30f	Down	Kinelarty	Magheradrool	Lisburn	III.	177
16	Creevy Upper	237 2 20	Tyrone	Omagh West	Urney	Castlederg	III.	318
12, 13, 19	Creewood	785 2 0	Meath	Upper Slane	Grangegeeth	Ardee	I.	224
26	Crefoge	281 0 7	Wexford	Ballaghkeen	Templeshannon	Enniscorthy	I.	299
114	Cregaclare Demesne	531 3 13	Galway	Dunkellin	Ardrahan	Gort	IV.	26
4, 9	Cregagh	201 3 6	Down	Castlereagh Upper	Knockbreda	Belfast	III.	165
15	Cregan	151 3 28	Londonderry	Tirkeeran	Faughanvale	Londonderry	III.	250
120	Cregaree	217 0 35	Mayo	Kilmaine	Cong	Ballinrobe	IV.	153
5, 9	Cregavockoge	124 3 26	Clare	Burren	Rathborney	Ballyvaghan	II.	14
103	Cregballymore	150 1 12	Galway	Dunkellin	Killeenavarra	Gort	IV.	30
70, 82, 83	Cregboy	676 0 8	Galway	Dunkellin	Claregalway	Galway	IV.	27
128	Cregboy	335 2 38	Galway	Kiltartan	Beagh	Gort	IV.	46
102, 112	Cregboy	84 0 21	Galway	Kiltartan	Kinvarradoorus	Gort	IV.	49
70, 83	Cregcarragh	251 2 6	Galway	Clare	Lackagh	Galway	IV.	22
29	Cregcattan, part of Galdanagh	59 2 14	Antrim	Lower Glenarm	Tickmacrevan	Larne	III.	23
27	Cregdotia	45 2 36	Galway	Ross	Cong	Oughterard	IV.	73
69	Cregduff	640 3 30	Galway	Clare	Annaghdown	Galway	IV.	16
118	Cregduff	277 1 9	Mayo	Kilmaine	Ballinrobe	Ballinrobe	IV.	152
119	Cregduff	188 1 3	Mayo	Kilmaine	Kilcommon	Ballinrobe	IV.	154
121	Cregduff	248 1 16	Mayo	Kilmaine	Kilmainemore	Ballinrobe	IV.	156
143	Cregg	190 3 20	Cork, W.R.	East Carbery (W.D.)	Kilfaughnabeg	Clonakilty	II.	133
23, 36	Cregg	1,304 3 30g	Galway	Ballynahinch	Omey	Clifden	IV.	14
69, 70	Cregg	234 2 15	Galway	Clare	Annaghdown	Galway	IV.	16
96	Cregg	57 2 30	Galway	Dunkellin	Kilconierin	Loughrea	IV.	29
125	Cregg	162 3 36	Galway	Leitrim	Ballynakill	Loughrea	IV.	51
134, 135	Cregg	381 3 28h	Galway	Leitrim	Clonrush	Scarriff	IV.	52
54	Cregg	400 2 15i	Galway	Moycullen	Kilcummin	Oughterard	IV.	66
22, 23	Cregg	681 1 12	Londonderry	Tirkeeran	Cumber Upper	Londonderry	III.	249
79	Cregg	178 1 7	Mayo	Carra	Manulla	Castlebar	IV.	129
3, 5, 6	Cregg	911 0 22	Meath	Morgallion	Nobber	Kells	I.	210
8, 14	Cregg	433 3 37	Sligo	Carbury	Drumcliff	Sligo	IV.	221
79, 85	Cregg	707 1 33	Tipperary, S.R.	Iffa and Offa East	Newtownlennan	Carrick on Suir	II.	315
47	Cregg	88 1 16	Wexford	Forth	Mayglass	Wexford	I.	312
23	Cregga	480 1 30	Roscommon	Roscommon	Kiltrustan	Strokestown	IV.	211
61	Creggaballagh	255 1 4j	Mayo	Gallen	Killasser	Swineford	IV.	149
49, 61	Creggagh	475 1 33	Mayo	Gallen	Toomore	Swineford	IV.	151
26	Creggameen	571 1 15	Roscommon	Castlereagh	Kilkeevin	Castlereagh	IV.	200
24, 25	Creggan	792 1 15	Antrim	Lower Glenarm	Ardclinis	Larne	III.	21
49	Creggan	305 2 37	Antrim	Upper Toome	Duneane	Antrim	III.	34
61, 62, 70	Creggan	256 3 7	Donegal	Raphoe	Raphoe	Strabane	III.	140
68,69,77,78	Creggan	1,189 1 13k	Donegal	Raphoe	Stranorlar	Stranorlar	III.	142
14	Creggan	664 1 12	King's Co.	Garrycastle	Wheery or Killagally	Parsonstown	I.	139
13, 20	Creggan	342 3 36	Londonderry	North West Liberties of Londonderry	Templemore	Londonderry	III.	246
64, 74, 83	Creggan	682 1 15	Mayo	Costello	Kilcolman	Castlereagh	IV.	141
52, 55	Creggan	892 2 25	Roscommon	Athlone	Drum	Athlone	IV.	180
42	Creggan	115 0 21	Roscommon	Athlone	Killinvoy	Roscommon	IV.	181
56	Creggan	390 2 16l	Roscommon	Moycarn	Moore	Ballinasloe	IV.	206
27, 28, 36	Creggan	4,022 0 27m	Tyrone	Omagh East	Termonmaguirk	Omagh	III.	314
15	Creggan	251 0 22n	Westmeath	Kilkenny West	Noughaval	Athlone	I.	274
55	Cregganabeaka	242 0 36	Roscommon	Athlone	Drum	Athlone	IV.	180
32	Cregganagrogy or St. Brendan's	530 0 17	Galway	Killian	Killian	Mountbellew	IV.	45
95, 96	Creggananta	65 2 26	Galway	Dunkellin	Killeeneen	Gort	IV.	30
96, 106	Cregganawoddy	462 1 18o	Mayo	Murrisk	Kilgeever	Westport	IV.	160
30, 31	Creggan Bane Glebe	586 2 19	Armagh	Fews Upper	Creggan	Castleblayney	III.	48
96	Cregganbaun	368 3 24	Mayo	Murrisk	Kilgeever	Westport	IV.	160
5	Cregganbeg	631 0 4	Mayo	Tirawley	Doonfeeny	Killala	IV.	167
78, 89	Cregganbell	295 2 8	Mayo	Carra	Ballyhean	Castlebar	IV.	125
4	Cregganboy	185 0 30	Antrim	Cary	Ramoan	Ballycastle	III.	14
92	Cregganbrack	341 0 29	Mayo	Costello	Knock	Claremorris	IV.	142

(a) Including 33A. 3R. 3P. water.
(b) Including 4A. 0R. 4P. water.
(c) Including 8A. 1R. 14P. water.
(d) Including 18A. 2R. 31P. water.
(e) Including 2A. 1R. 36P. water.

(f) Including 42A. 1R. 38P. water.
(g) Including 31A. 1R. 18P. water.
(h) Including 11A. 0R. 32P. water.
(i) Including 6A. 0R. 24P. water.
(j) Including 11A. 3R. 9P. water.

(k) Including 5A. 0R. 4P. water.
(l) Including 21A. 1R. 8P. water.
(m) Including 6A. 1R. 7P. water.
(n) Including 57A. 0R. 0P. water.
(o) Including 2A. 2R. 22P. water.

No. of Sheet of the Ordnance Survey Maps.	Townlands and Towns.	Area in Statute Acres.			County.	Barony.	Parish.	Poor Law Union in 1857.	Townland Census of 1851, Part I.	
		A.	R.	P.					Vol.	Page
37	Cregganconroe	907	1	21a	Tyrone	Omagh East	Termonmaguirk	Omagh	III.	314
26	Creggancor	635	2	1	Roscommon	Castlereagh	Kilkeevin	Castlereagh	IV.	200
36, 37	Creggandevesky	1,458	1	6b	Tyrone	Omagh East	Termonmaguirk	Omagh	III.	314
28, 31	Creggan Duff	574	3	38	Armagh	Fews Upper	Creggan	Castleblayney	III.	48
31, 32	Creggane	218	0	29	Cork, E.R.	Duhallow	Kilshannig	Mallow	II.	74
16, 17	Creggane	278	3	0	Cork, E.R.	Orrery and Kilmore	Buttevant	Mallow	II.	107
143	Creggane	84	0	30	Cork, W.R.	East Carbery (W.D.)	Ross	Clonakilty	II.	135
123, 136	Creggane	310	0	38	Cork, W.R.	Ibane and Barryroe	Abbeymahon	Clonakilty	II.	148
46, 47	Creggane	972	0	20	Limerick	Coshma	Hackmys	Kilmallock	II.	243
20	Creggane	106	1	9	Tipperary, N.R.	Owney and Arra	Youghalarra	Nenagh	II.	297
5	Creggane	59	2	27	Waterford	Glenahiry	Kilronan	Clonmel	II.	365
22	Creggan & Glosterboy	158	3	39	King's Co.	Garrycastle	Gallen	Parsonstown	I.	136
21	Creggan Lower	220	0	5	Armagh	Orior Upper	Loughgilly	Newry	III.	58
29	Creggan Lower	161	3	8	Westmeath	Brawny	St. Mary's	Athlone	I.	259
36	Cregganmacar	104	3	31	Westmeath	Clonlonan	Kilcleagh	Athlone	I.	261
5, 12	Cregganmore	1,274	1	14c	Mayo	Erris	Kilcommon	Belmullet	IV.	143
95	Cregganna Beg	324	3	29	Galway	Dunkellin	Ballynacourty	Galway	IV.	27
16	Creggannacourty	255	0	2	Cork, E.R.	Orrery and Kilmore	Churchtown	Mallow	II.	107
96	Creggannagappul	71	1	31	Mayo	Murrisk	Kilgeever	Westport	IV.	160
95	Cregganna More	328	0	35	Galway	Dunkellin	Ballynacourty	Galway	IV.	27
88	Creggannaseer	18	2	35	Mayo	Burrishoole	Aghagower	Westport	IV.	118
79	Creggannavar	91	2	4	Mayo	Carra	Breaghwy	Castlebar	IV.	127
114	Cregganore	207	1	33	Galway	Loughrea	Killinan	Loughrea	IV.	64
96	Cregganroe	710	3	11	Mayo	Murrisk	Kilgeever	Westport	IV.	160
21	Creggan Upper	196	0	9	Armagh	Orior Upper	Loughgilly	Newry	III.	58
29	Creggan Upper	247	2	0	Westmeath	Brawny	St. Mary's	Athlone	I.	259
50	Cregganycarna	312	1	20d	Roscommon	Athlone	Taghmaconnell	Ballinasloe	IV.	185
27	Creggaree	90	2	19	Galway	Ross	Cong	Oughterard	IV.	73
100, 110	Creggarve	342	0	28	Mayo	Kilmaine	Robeen	Ballinrobe	IV.	157
26	Creggaslin	120	1	29	Roscommon	Castlereagh	Kilkeevin	Castlereagh	IV.	200
96	Creggaturlough	122	1	22	Galway	Dunkellin	Kilconierin	Loughrea	IV.	29
34	Creggaun	212	0	20	Clare	Bunratty Upper	Doora	Ennis	II.	8
9, 16	Creggaun	28	1	1	Clare	Corcomroe	Kilfenora	Ennistimon	II.	19
74	Creggaun	764	3	20e	Galway	Clonmacnowen	Ahascragh	Ballinasloe	IV.	24
96, 104	Creggaun	112	2	13	Galway	Dunkellin	Killora	Loughrea	IV.	31
61	Creggaun	70	2	5	Galway	Killian	Ahascragh	Mountbellew	IV.	43
60	Creggaun	318	1	3	Galway	Tiaquin	Ballymacward	Mountbellew	IV.	75
18	Creggaun	387	2	4f	Galway	Tiaquin	Kilkerrin	Glennamaddy	IV.	76
100, 101	Creggaun	187	3	12	Mayo	Clanmorris	Mayo	Claremorris	IV.	135
49, 50	Creggaun	382	1	15	Mayo	Gallen	Killasser	Swineford	IV.	149
30, 39	Creggaun	181	0	5	Mayo	Tirawley	Ballynahaglish	Ballina	IV.	164
61	Creggaun (Dillon)	40	3	31	Galway	Killian	Ahascragh	Mountbellew	IV.	43
61	Creggaun (Machugh)	72	2	26	Galway	Killian	Ahascragh	Mountbellew	IV.	43
60	Creggaunnagroagh	158	0	22	Galway	Tiaquin	Killosolan	Mountbellew	IV.	78
41	Creggaunnahilla	65	1	8	Clare	Islands	Clareabbey	Ennis	II.	29
77, 88	Creggaunnahorna	88	0	3	Mayo	Burrishoole	Kilmeena	Westport	IV.	122
20	Creggauns	226	2	11	Galway	Ballymoe	Kilbegnet	Glennamaddy	IV.	8
45	Creggauns	186	1	20g	Galway	Tiaquin	Moylough	Mountbellew	IV.	79
11, 18	Creggaunycahill	64	2	4	Clare	Inchiquin	Kilkeedy	Corrofin	II.	25
111	Creggawatta	128	0	39	Mayo	Kilmaine	Kilcommon	Ballinrobe	IV.	154
23	Cregg Barr	346	2	8	Londonderry	Tirkeeran	Cumber Upper	Londonderry	III.	249
133	Cregg Demesne	318	0	29h	Galway	Kiltartan	Beagh	Gort	IV.	46
117	Creggeen	151	2	23	Galway	Longford	Lickmolassy	Portumna	IV.	61
85	Creggeen	486	0	2	Kerry	Glanarought	Kilgarvan	Kenmare	II.	187
35	Cregg North	187	0	17i	Cork, E.R.	Fermoy	Litter	Fermoy	II.	81
48	Creggoduff	145	2	31j	Galway	Ballynahinch	Ballindoon	Clifden	IV.	10
27, 35	Creggolympry North	311	0	4k	Cork, E.R.	Fermoy	Litter	Fermoy	II.	81
35	Creggolympry South	191	3	26l	Cork, E.R.	Fermoy	Litter	Fermoy	II.	81
125	Creggpark	8	2	9	Leitrim	Ballymoe	Ballynakill	Loughrea	IV.	51
19, 20	Creggs	244	3	23	Galway	Ballymoe	Kilbegnet	Glennamaddy	IV.	8
35	Cregg South	238	3	19m	Cork, E.R.	Fermoy	Litter	Fermoy	II.	81
20	CREGGS T.	—			Galway	Ballymoe	Kilbegnet	Glennamaddy	IV.	8
20	Creggstown	208	2	21	Westmeath	Farbill	Killucan	Mullingar	I.	266
16	Creggy	370	1	17	Westmeath	Kilkenny West	Noughaval	Ballymahon	I.	274
8	Creggyconnell	233	1	36	Sligo	Carbury	Drumcliff	Sligo	IV.	221
104	Creggymulgreny	98	0	5	Galway	Dunkellin	Killogilleen	Loughrea	IV.	31
20, 26	Creglahan	447	3	6n	Roscommon	Castlereagh	Kilkeevin	Castlereagh	IV.	200
103	Creglucas	89	1	23	Galway	Dunkellin	Killeenavarra	Gort	IV.	30
128, 129	Cregmahon	228	3	11o	Galway	Kiltartan	Beagh	Gort	IV.	46
25	Cregmoher	336	3	31p	Clare	Inchiquin	Rath	Corrofin	II.	27
70, 83	Cregmore	374	2	15	Galway	Clare	Lackagh	Galway	IV.	22
103, 104	Cregmore	201	1	24	Galway	Dunkellin	Ardrahan	Gort	IV.	26
118	Cregmore (Browne)	174	1	38	Mayo	Kilmaine	Kilmainemore	Ballinrobe	IV.	156

(a) Including 11A. 1R. 34P. water.
(b) Including 7A. 1R. 21P. water.
(c) Including 67A. 0R. 10P. water.
(d) Including 12A. 0R. 27P. water.
(e) Including 19A. 2R. 15P. water.
(f) Including 87A. 0R. 0P. water.

(g) Including 4A. 0R. 1P. water.
(h) Including 8A. 3R. 28P. water.
(i) Including 2A. 3R. 12P. water.
(j) Including 2A. 0R. 1P. water.
(k) Including 5A. 0R. 16P. water.

(l) Including 6A. 2R. 8P. water.
(m) Including 6A. 3R. 8P. water.
(n) Including 4A. 0R. 17P. water.
(o) Including 13A. 0R. 31P. water.
(p) Including 37A. 2R. 36P. water.

No. of Sheet of the Ordnance Survey Maps.	Townlands and Towns.	Area in Statute Acres.			County.	Barony.	Parish.	Poor Law Union in 1857.	Townland Census of 1851. Part I.	
		A.	R.	P.					Vol.	Page
118	Cregmore (*Lynch*) .	124	0	0	Mayo . .	Kilmaine . .	Kilmainemore .	Ballinrobe .	IV.	156
61	Cregnafyla . .	161	2	37	Mayo . .	Gallen . .	Toomore . .	Swineford .	IV.	151
121	Cregnanagh . .	38	3	6	Mayo . .	Kilmaine . .	Kilmainebeg .	Ballinrobe .	IV.	155
121, 122	Cregnanagh . .	131	0	14	Mayo . .	Kilmaine . .	Moorgagagh .	Ballinrobe .	IV.	157
3	Crehanagh North .	88	0	1	Waterford .	Upperthird .	Fenoagh . .	Carrick on Suir	II.	369
3	Crehanagh South .	452	3	11	Waterford .	Upperthird .	Fenoagh . . .	Carrick on Suir	II.	369
39	Crehan Island . .	4	1	39	Fermanagh .	Coole . .	Galloon . . .	Lisnaskea .	III.	200
7, 8, 15	Crehaun . .	206	1	7	Limerick . .	Coonagh . .	Doon . . .	Tipperary .	II.	234
15	Crehelp . .	1,263	1	24	Wicklow . .	Lower Talbotstown	Crehelp . . .	Baltinglass .	I.	359
20, 25	Creighan . .	101	0	22*a*	Cavan . .	Upper Loughtee .	Urney . . .	Cavan .	III.	86
7, 10	Creighans . .	118	0	7	Monaghan .	Monaghan . .	Tehallan . .	Monaghan .	III.	280
67, 78	Creighmore . .	270	1	20*b*	Cork, E.R. .	Imokilly . .	Clonpriest . .	Youghal .	II.	85
19	Cremartin . .	212	1	22*c*	Monaghan .	Cremorne . .	Clontibret . .	Castleblayney .	III.	260
11	Cremona . . .	13	2	12	Dublin . .	Nethercross .	Swords . . .	Balrothery .	I.	32
18	Cremorgan . .	905	3	26	Queen's Co. .	Cullenagh . .	Kilcolmanbrack .	Abbeyleix .	I.	240
18	Cremoyle . .	208	2	37	Monaghan .	Dartree . .	Ematris . . .	Cootehill .	III.	266
25	Crenard . . .	120	1	27	Cavan . .	Clanmahon .	Kilmore . . .	Cavan .	III.	78
13	Creowen . . .	40	3	25*d*	Wicklow . .	Newcastle .	Newcastle Lower .	Rathdrum .	I.	353
37	Creroge . .	377	3	13	Meath . .	Lower Deece .	Scurlockstown .	Trim .	I.	192
5, 9	Cressy Crib . .	57	2	6*e*	Londonderry .	Keenaght . .	Aghanloo . .	NewT⁻Limavady	III.	233
23	Creta . . .	112	3	0	Roscommon .	Roscommon . .	Kiltrustan . .	Strokestown .	IV.	211
31, 36	Crettyard . .	204	0	32	Queen's Co. .	Slievemargy .	Killabban . .	Carlow .	I.	245
37	Crevary Lower .	157	3	34	Donegal . .	Kilmacrenan .	Killygarvan . .	Millford .	III.	128
37	Crevary Upper .	184	3	15*f*	Donegal . .	Kilmacrenan .	Killygarvan . .	Millford .	III.	128
34	Creveadornan . .	96	2	20	Monaghan .	Farney . .	Magheracloone .	Carrickmacross	III.	272
37	Crevilly-valley .	373	0	24	Antrim . .	Lower Antrim .	Connor . . .	Ballymena .	III.	3
5	Crevinish . .	95	2	9	Fermanagh .	Lurg . .	Magheraculmoney .	Lowtherstown .	III.	207
10	Crevinishaughy Island	122	3	16	Fermanagh .	Lurg . .	Magheraculmoney .	Lowtherstown .	III.	209
11	Crevolea . . .	309	3	32	Londonderry .	Coleraine . .	Aghadowey . .	Coleraine .	III.	229
59, 63	Crew . . .	610	2	21	Antrim . .	Upper Massereene .	Glenavy . . .	Lisburn .	III.	30
32, 36	Crew . .	492	1	25	Londonderry .	Loughinsholin .	Maghera . .	Magherafelt .	III.	242
52, 59	Crew . . .	189	1	25	Tyrone . .	Clogher . .	Errigal Keerogue .	Clogher .	III.	295
54, 61	Crew . . .	107	3	34	Tyrone . .	Dungannon Middle .	Clonfeacle . .	Dungannon .	III.	299
19	Crewbane . .	369	1	30*g*	Meath . .	Upper Slane .	Monknewtown .	Drogheda .	I.	224
17, 18	Crew Beg . .	257	3	0*h*	Armagh . .	Orior Lower .	Ballymore . .	Banbridge .	III.	55
9, 13	Crewcat . .	107	2	23	Armagh . .	Oneilland West .	Kilmore . . .	Armagh .	III.	53
5	Crewhill . .	215	1	29	Kildare . .	North Salt . .	Laraghbryan . .	Celbridge .	I.	75
16	Crew Lower . .	187	3	25*i*	Tyrone . .	Strabane Lower .	Ardstraw . .	Castlederg .	III.	318
13, 18	Crewmcige . .	154	3	29	Monaghan .	Monaghan . .	Kilmore . .	Monaghan .	III.	276
17, 18	Crew More . .	281	0	38	Armagh . .	Orior Lower .	Ballymore . .	Newry .	III.	55
59, 63	Crew Park . .	206	3	17	Antrim . .	Upper Massereene .	Ballinderry . .	Lisburn .	III.	29
16	Crew Upper . .	436	1	25*j*	Tyrone . .	Strabane Lower .	Ardstraw . .	Castlederg .	III.	318
23	Crey . . .	83	2	23	Leitrim . .	Leitrim . .	Kiltoghert . .	Carʳ. on Shannon	IV.	101
136	*Cribby Island* .	3	0	22	Galway . .	Leitrim . .	Inishcaltra . .	Scarriff .	IV.	54
42	Cribstown . .	43	3	5	Wexford . .	Forth . .	Rathaspick . .	Wexford .	I.	312
15, 21	Crickawn . .	47	2	14	Wicklow . .	Lower Talbotstown .	Donard . . .	Baltinglass .	I.	359
31	Crickeen . . .	38	0	3	Leitrim . .	Leitrim . .	Annaduff . .	Carʳ. on Shannon	IV.	99
38, 39	Crickstown . .	786	3	15	Meath . .	Ratoath . .	Crickstown . .	Dunshaughlin .	I.	217
22,23,31,32	Crighdenis . .	813	3	26*k*	Tyrone . .	Omagh West .	Termonamongan .	Castlederg .	III.	317
22	Crighshane . .	992	2	33*l*	Tyrone . .	Omagh West .	Termonamongan .	Castlederg .	III.	317
23	Crilea . . .	257	0	38*m*	Cavan . .	Clankee . .	Knockbride . .	Cootehill .	III.	73
5	Crillan . .	157	1	37	Fermanagh .	Lurg . .	Drumkeeran . .	Lowtherstown .	III.	205
60, 70	Crillaun . .	963	0	27*n*	Mayo . .	Carra . .	Turlough . .	Castlebar .	IV.	131
102	Crilly . .	681	1	35*o*	Donegal . .	Tirhugh . .	Templecarn . .	Donegal .	III.	149
66	Crilly . .	445	3	4	Tyrone . .	Dungannon Lower .	Aghaloo . . .	Dungannon .	III.	296
23	Crilly's Hill . .	226	0	1	Tyrone . .	Omagh West .	Termonamongan .	Castlederg .	III.	317
6	Crimlin . .	120	1	1	Fermanagh .	Lurg . .	Drumkeeran . .	Lowtherstown .	III.	205
102, 103	Crinagort . .	629	2	32	Kerry . .	Glanarought .	Kilcaskan . .	Kenmare .	II.	186
16, 25	Crinalisk . .	246	2	3	Waterford .	Middlethird .	Dunhill . .	Kilmacthomas .	II.	366
5, 9	Crindle . .	413	0	26*p*	Londonderry .	Keenaght . .	Tamlaght Finlagan .	NewTⁿLimavady	III.	237
50	Crininish . .	153	2	34	Clare . .	Clonderalaw .	Kilchreest . .	Killadysert .	II.	15
35, 38	Crinkill . .	948	2	36	King's Co. .	Ballybritt . .	Birr . . .	Parsonstown .	I.	125
19	Crinkill . .	127	3	22*q*	Monaghan .	Cremorne . .	Clontibret . .	Castleblayney .	III.	260
35	CRINKILL T. .	—			King's Co. .	Ballybritt . .	Birr . .	Parsonstown .	I.	125
96	Crinnage or Bally-wulash . .	401	0	10	Galway . .	Dunkellin . .	Killora . . .	Loughrea .	IV.	31
74	Crinnagh . .	571	1	9	Kerry . .	Magunihy . .	Killarney . .	Killarney .	II.	203
20, 28	Crinnaghtane . .	236	3	33	Cork, E.R. .	Condons&Clangibbon	Macroney . .	Fermoy .	II.	63
21	Crinnaghtaun East .	186	1	10	Waterford .	Decies without Drum	Affane . . .	Lismore .	II.	353
21	Crinnaghtaun West	190	0	26	Waterford .	Decies without Drum	Affane . . .	Lismore .	II.	353
40	Crinnaloo North .	535	3	33	Cork, W.R. .	West Muskerry .	Kilcorney . .	Millstreet .	II.	158
40, 49	Crinnaloo South .	1,203	2	9	Cork, W.R. .	West Muskerry .	Kilcorney . .	Millstreet .	II.	158
17, 18	Crinnish . .	459	2	10	Mayo . .	Erris . .	Kilcommon . .	Belmullet .	IV.	143

(*a*) Including 7A. 0R. 23P. water.
(*b*) Including 14A. 1R. 10P. detached portion.
(*c*) Including 9A. 2R. 1P. water.
(*d*) Including 3A. 0R. 23P. detached portion.
(*e*) Including 0A. 2R. 25P. water.
(*f*) Including 5A. 0R. 7P. water.

(*g*) Including 14A. 1R. 30P. water.
(*h*) Including 4A. 2R. 5P. water.
(*i*) Including 11A. 2R. 20P. water.
(*j*) Including 6A. 3R. 24P. water.
(*k*) Including 3A. 0R. 14P. water.
(*l*) Including 6A. 2R. 23P. water.

(*m*) Including 43A. 2R. 16P. water.
(*n*) Including 61A. 1R. 19P. water.
(*o*) Including 7A. 0R. 30P. water.
(*p*) Including 3A. 2R. 10P. water.
(*q*) Including 10A. 3R. 25P. water.

No. of Sheet of the Ordnance Survey Maps	Townlands and Towns.	Area in Statute Acres.			County.	Barony.	Parish.	Poor Law Union in 1857.	Townland Census of 1851, Part I.	
		A.	R.	P.					Vol.	Page
31	Crinny East	292	0	29	Kerry	Trughanacmy	Castleisland	Tralee	II.	208
31	Crinny West	284	1	25	Kerry	Trughanacmy	Castleisland	Tralee	II.	208
5, 10	Crinstown	226	1	17	Kildare	North Salt	Laraghbryan	Celbridge	I.	75
10, 11	Crippaun	146	1	7	Kildare	North Salt	Killadoon	Celbridge	I.	74
110	Cripplehill	125	1	13	Cork, W.R.	East Carbery (E.D.)	Ballymodan	Bandon	II.	127
110	Cripplehill	93	2	3	Cork, W.R.	East Carbery (E.D.)	Kilbrittain	Bandon	II.	128
38	Crislaghkeel	542	0	28	Donegal	Inishowen West	Fahan Upper	Londonderry	III.	121
38	Crislaghmore	515	0	19	Donegal	Inishowen West	Fahan Upper	Londonderry	III.	121
22	Crissadaun	311	3	5	Wicklow	Upper Talbotstown	Donaghmore	Baltinglass	I.	363
25	Crissard	733	1	9	Queen's Co.	Ballyadams	Rathaspick	Athy	I.	232
25	Crissaun	159	0	3	Westmeath	Rathconrath	Churchtown	Mullingar	I.	282
148	Croagh	167	3	30	Cork, W.R.	West Carbery (W.D.)	Skull	Skull	II.	146
83, 92	Croagh	1,238	0	7a	Donegal	Banagh	Killaghtee	Donegal	III.	109
101, 105	Croagh	357	2	4b	Donegal	Tirhugh	Templecarn	Donegal	III.	149
20	Croagh	684	1	36	Limerick	Connello Lower	Croagh	Rathkeale	II.	227
81	Croaghacullion	454	0	34c	Donegal	Banagh	Glencolumbkille	Glenties	III.	105
39, 43	Croaghan	442	1	6	Cavan	Castlerahan	Munterconnaught	Oldcastle	III.	71
46	Croaghan	380	3	20	Donegal	Kilmacrenan	Aughnish	Milford	III.	122
17	Croaghan	314	3	23	Donegal	Kilmacrenan	Clondavaddog	Milford	III.	124
70	Croaghan	106	2	7	Donegal	Raphoe	Clonleigh	Strabane	III.	134
15, 21	Croaghan	54	0	19	Fermanagh	Magheraboy	Devenish	Enniskillen	III.	210
34	Croaghan	97	3	37	Fermanagh	Magherastephana	Aghalurcher	Lisnaskea	III.	215
10, 11	Croaghan	1,140	1	14	Londonderry	Coleraine	Macosquin	Coleraine	III.	233
5, 6	Croaghan	95	2	39	Londonderry	Keenaght	Magilligan	NewtⁿLimavady	III.	236
14,15,19,20	Croaghan	509	2	1d	Monaghan	Cremorne	Clontibret	Castleblayney	III.	260
75, 84	Croaghanarget	1,368	0	5e	Donegal	Banagh	Killymard	Donegal	III.	111
19	Croaghan or Coolna-shinny	132	2	2f	Cavan	Tullyhunco	Kildallan	Cavan	III.	96
10	Croaghane	94	0	4	Limerick	Shanid	Robertstown	Glin	II.	257
10, 19	Croaghane	73	2	1	Limerick	Shanid	Shanagolden	Glin	II.	258
17	*Croaghan Island*	17	2	6	Donegal	Kilmacrenan	Clondavaddog	Milford	III.	125
33	Croaghaun	129	0	32	Clare	Inchiquin	Kilnamona	Ennis	II.	27
33	Croaghaun	48	3	18	Clare	Islands	Drumcliff	Ennis	II.	30
26, 35	Croaghaun	1,828	1	31	Mayo	Erris	Kilcommon	Belmullet	IV.	143
20	Croaghaun East	1,552	0	14	Mayo	Tirawley	Moygawnagh	Killala	II.	171
27, 28	Croaghaun West	1,409	1	19	Mayo	Tirawley	Moygawnagh	Killala	II.	171
3, 7	Croaghbeg	266	1	29	Antrim	Cary	Ballintoy	Ballycastle	III.	12
96, 97	Croaghbeg	208	3	3	Donegal	Banagh	Kilcar	Glenties	III.	108
95, 101	Croaghbrack	1,725	0	12g	Donegal	Tirhugh	Templecarn	Donegal	III.	149
108	Croaghbreesy	523	2	37h	Donegal	Tirhugh	Kilbarron	Ballyshannon	III.	148
20, 29	Croagh Commons	50	1	1	Limerick	Connello Lower	Croagh	Rathkeale	II.	227
50,51,58,59	Croagheen or Lough-barra	2,020	1	24i	Donegal	Kilmacrenan	Gartan	Letterkenny	III.	127
14	Croagh First or Cor-gary Fifth	1,236	2	0j	Tyrone	Omagh West	Termonamongan	Castlederg	III.	317
1, 6	Croaghill	456	2	29	Galway	Ballymoe	Templetogher	Glennamaddy	IV.	9
96	Croaghlin	281	0	33	Donegal	Banagh	Glencolumbkille	Glenties	III.	105
91, 97	Croaghlin	152	1	10	Donegal	Banagh	Killybegs Upper	Glenties	III.	110
3, 7, 8	Croaghmore	381	3	27	Antrim	Cary	Ballintoy	Ballycastle	III.	12
25	Croaghnacree	245	3	12	Cork, E.R.	Fermoy	Doneraile	Mallow	II.	78
76	Croaghnakeela Island	141	3	29	Galway	Ballynahinch	Moyrus	Clifden	IV.	14
95	Croaghnakern	942	1	7	Donegal	Tirhugh	Drumhome	Donegal	III.	146
56, 57	Croaghnamaddy	262	1	23k	Donegal	Boylagh	Templecrone	Glenties	III.	115
94,95,100,101	Croaghnameal	888	0	9l	Donegal	Tirhugh	Drumhome	Donegal	III.	146
49, 57	Croaghnashallog	1,250	1	29m	Donegal	Boylagh	Templecrone	Glenties	III.	115
5	Croagh North	274	3	20	Clare	Burren	Rathborney	Ballyvaghan	II.	14
77, 86	Croaghonagh	3,860	2	12n	Donegal	Raphoe	Donaghmore	Stranorlar	III.	137
26	Croaghrim	298	0	29	Fermanagh	Clanawley	Killesher	Enniskillen	III.	192
21	Croaghrim	70	2	13	Fermanagh	Magheraboy	Rossorry	Enniskillen	III.	214
27	Croaghrim	32	2	27	Galway	Ross	Cong	Oughterard	IV.	73
98, 108	Croaghrimbeg	875	1	17	Mayo	Carra	Ballintober	Ballinrobe	IV.	124
98, 108	Croaghrimcarra	1,147	2	0o	Mayo	Carra	Ballintober	Ballinrobe	IV.	124
18	Croaghross	312	1	0	Donegal	Kilmacrenan	Clondavaddog	Milford	III.	124
14	Croagh Second or Corgary Sixth	2,111	2	1p	Tyrone	Omagh West	Termonamongan	Castlederg	III.	317
5, 9	Croagh South	291	3	15	Clare	Burren	Rathborney	Ballyvaghan	II.	14
20	CROAGH T.	—			Limerick	Connello Lower	Croagh	Rathkeale	II.	228
75, 76	Croaghubbrid	556	1	20	Donegal	Boylagh	Inishkeel	Glenties	III.	112
47	Croan	216	3	2	Down	Upper Iveagh, Up. pt.	Clonallan	Newry	II.	174
31	Croan	277	2	32	Kilkenny	Knocktopher	Aghaviller	Thomastown	I.	110
23	Croan	410	1	29	Kilkenny	Shillelogher	Danesfort	Thomastown	I.	114
72	Croan	196	0	30	Tipperary, S.R.	Slievardagh	Templemichael	Carrick on Suir	II.	338
77	Croane	190	1	12	Tipperary, S.R.	Iffa and Offa East	Kilgrant	Clonmel	II.	314
75, 84	Croankeeran	681	1	19q	Donegal	Banagh	Killymard	Donegal	III.	111

(a) Including 43A. 1R. 36P. water.
(b) Including 5A. 2R. 11P. water.
(c) Including 9A. 0R. 36P. water.
(d) Including 10A. 1R. 20P. water.
(e) Including 22A. 0R. 24P. water.
(f) Including 9A. 2R. 27P. water.

(g) Including 11A. 0R. 22P. water.
(h) Including 9A. 3R. 22P. water.
(i) Including 56A. 0R. 18P. water.
(j) Including 2A. 0R. 38P. water.
(k) Including 18A. 0R. 10P. water.
(l) Including 14A. 1R. 9P. water.

(m) Including 39A. 3R. 5P. water.
(n) Including 122A. 0R. 20P. water.
(o) Including 10A. 0R. 15P. water.
(p) Including 5A. 3R. 28P. water.
(q) Including 4A. 0R. 35P. water.

No. of Sheet of the Ordnance Survey Maps	Townlands and Towns.	Area in Statute Acres.	County.	Barony.	Parish.	Poor Law Union in 1857.	Townland Census of 1851, Part I. Vol.	Page
		A. R. P.						
1	Croan Lower . .	77 0 25a	Waterford .	Upperthird . .	St. Marys, Clonmel	Clonmel . .	II.	371
13, 21	Croanrea . .	701 1 22	Cork, E.R. .	Duhallow . .	Kilmeen . . .	Kanturk . .	II.	72
17, 20	Croanruss . .	105 2 5	Carlow . .	Forth . . .	Myshall . .	Carlow . .	I.	5
1	Croan Upper . .	45 2 4	Waterford .	Upperthird . .	St. Marys, Clonmel	Clonmel . .	II.	371
41, 46	Croase . .	351 3 0	Wexford . .	Bargy . .	Ballyconnick . .	Wexford . .	I.	304
38, 39	Crobally Lower .	289 0 33	Waterford .	Decies within Drum	Ardmore . .	Dungarvan .	II.	350
26	Crobally Lower .	59 2 25	Waterford .	Middlethird .	Drumcannon .	Waterford . .	II.	366
38, 39	Crobally Upper .	468 3 10	Waterford .	Decies within Drum	Ardmore . .	Dungarvan .	II.	350
26	Crobally Upper .	461 2 21	Waterford .	Middlethird . .	Drumcannon .	Waterford . .	II.	366
47	Crobane . . .	581 1 9	Down . .	Lordship of Newry .	Newry . .	Newry . .	III.	182
40, 41	Croboy . . .	1,263 0 25b	Meath . .	Upper Moyfenrath .	Clonard . .	Edenderry .	I.	213
66	Crocam . . .	727 3 5c	Donegal . .	Boylagh . . .	Inishkeel . .	Glenties . .	III.	112
88	Crocane . . .	400 0 10	Cork, E.R. .	Imokilly . . .	Rostellan . .	Middleton .	II.	90
107	Crockacapple . .	125 0 2d	Donegal . .	Tirhugh . . .	Kilbarron . .	Ballyshannon .	III.	148
64, 68	Crockacleaven .	659 2 39e	Tyrone . .	Clogher . .	Aghalurcher .	Clogher . .	III.	291
19	Crockacullion . .	309 1 34	Sligo . .	Leyny . . .	Ballysadare . .	Sligo . .	IV.	230
30, 36	Crockada . . .	165 0 29	Fermanagh .	Clankelly . .	Clones . . .	Clones . .	III.	195
29	Crockadreen . .	156 3 37	Fermanagh .	Magherastephana .	Aghalurcher .	Lisnaskea .	III.	215
103	Crockahany or Ross-nowlagh Upper .	389 2 10	Donegal . .	Tirhugh . .	Drumhome . .	Ballyshannon .	III.	147
30	Crockahenny . .	857 0 13	Donegal . .	Inishowen East .	Moville Upper .	Inishowen .	III.	119
27	Crockaleen . .	73 2 28f	Fermanagh .	Tirkennedy .	Derryvullan .	Enniskillen .	III.	221
19, 27	Crockanboy . .	753 3 16	Tyrone . .	Strabane Upper .	Bodoney Lower .	Gortin . .	III.	323
34	Crockaness . .	30 2 38	Fermanagh .	Magherastephana .	Aghalurcher .	Lisnaskea .	III.	215
22	Crockanure Glebe .	59 2 13	Kildare . .	Offaly East .	Kildare . .	Naas . .	I.	70
27	Crockareddy . .	136 1 5g	Fermanagh .	Clanawley .	Cleenish . .	Enniskillen .	III.	190
35	Crockarevan . .	91 1 8	Fermanagh .	Clankelly . .	Clones . .	Clones . .	III.	195
51, 58, 59	Crockastoller . .	1,892 2 25h	Donegal . .	Kilmacrenan .	Gartan . .	Letterkenny .	III.	127
19	Crockatanty . .	479 2 33i	Tyrone . .	Strabane Upper .	Bodoney Lower .	Gortin . .	III.	323
5	Crockateggal . .	34 2 25	Fermanagh .	Lurg . . .	Drumkeeran .	Lowthertown .	III.	205
28	Crockaun . .	331 1 29j	Kildare . .	Offaly West .	Ballyshannon .	Athy . .	I.	72
13	Crockaun . .	84 2 9	Longford . .	Moydow . .	Ballymacormick .	Longford . .	I.	160
21, 24	Crockaunadreenagh	334 1 23	Dublin . .	Newcastle . .	Rathcoole . .	Celbridge .	I.	34
14	Crockaun Commons	42 1 3	Kildare . .	Clane . .	Clane . .	Naas . .	I.	53
92, 102	Crockaunrannell .	233 3 31	Mayo . .	Costello . .	Knock . . .	Claremorris .	IV.	142
22, 25	Crockawaddy . .	161 3 5	Leitrim . .	Carrigallen .	Drumreilly .	Bawnboy . .	IV.	91
35	Crockawaddy Glebe	142 0 26k	Fermanagh .	Clankelly .	Clones . .	Clones . .	III.	195
12	Crockcumberland .	78 3 30	Monaghan .	Dartree . .	Clones . . .	Monaghan .	III.	264
25, 26, 29, 30	Crockeen . .	141 0 36	Leitrim . .	Carrigallen .	Drumreilly .	Bawnboy . .	IV.	91
43	Crockerahoas . .	30 0 2	Fermanagh .	Coole . .	Galloon . .	Clones . .	III.	199
22	Crockets Town T.	—	Sligo . .	Tireragh . .	Kilmoremoy .	Ballina . .	IV.	235
30	Crockglass . .	358 0 19	Donegal . .	Inishowen East .	Moville Upper .	Inishowen .	III.	119
18	Crockindollagh .	285 0 0	Londonderry .	Coleraine . .	Errigal . .	Coleraine .	III.	232
28	Crocklusty . .	103 3 26	Cavan . .	Clankee . .	Shercock . .	Bailieborough .	III.	74
35	Crocknaboghil .	67 3 27	Fermanagh .	Clankelly .	Clones . .	Clones . .	III.	195
20	Crocknacally . .	1,099 0 2	Mayo . .	Tirawley . .	Kilfian . .	Killala . .	IV.	169
33	Crocknacreevy .	298 0 34l	Fermanagh .	Clanawley .	Kinawley . .	Enniskillen .	III.	193
101	Crocknacunny . .	1,726 3 38	Donegal . .	Tirhugh . .	Templecarn .	Donegal . .	III.	149
57	Crocknafarbrague .	231 1 31	Tyrone . .	Clogher . .	Donacavey .	Omagh . .	III.	294
91	Crocknafeola . .	167 2 27	Donegal . .	Banagh . .	Killybegs Upper .	Glenties . .	III.	110
83	Crocknagapple .	818 1 22	Donegal . .	Banagh . .	Killybegs Lower .	Glenties . .	III.	110
49	Crocknageeragh .	248 2 20m	Donegal . .	Boylagh . .	Templecrone .	Glenties . .	III.	115
24	Crocknagowan .	97 2 17n	Fermanagh .	Magherastephana .	Aghalurcher .	Lisnaskea .	III.	215
24	Crocknagrally .	339 1 3	Fermanagh .	Magherastephana .	Aghalurcher .	Lisnaskea .	III.	215
35, 36	Crocknagross . .	180 2·28	Fermanagh .	Clankelly . .	Clones . .	Clones . .	III.	195
28, 34	Crocknahattin .	585 2 4o	Cavan . .	Clankee . .	Bailieborough .	Bailieborough .	III.	71
64	Crocknahull . .	87 1 37	Tyrone . .	Clogher . .	Aghalurcher .	Clogher . .	III.	291
32	Crocknakeeragh .	24 0 8	Fermanagh .	Clanawley .	Killesher . .	Enniskillen .	III.	192
29	Crocknakelly Glebe	88 1 2p	Fermanagh .	Clankelly . .	Clones . .	Clones . .	III.	195
16	Crocknamurleog .	190 0 39	Donegal . .	Kilmacrenan .	Mevagh . .	Milford . .	III.	130
34	Crocknanane . .	68 1 2	Fermanagh .	Magherastephana .	Aghalurcher .	Lisnaskea .	III.	215
22	Crocknaraw . .	884 1 2q	Galway . .	Ballynahinch .	Ballynakill .	Clifden . .	IV.	11
52	Crockraw . .	147 2 27	Donegal . .	Kilmacrenan .	Gartan . .	Letterkenny .	III.	127
21	Crockshane . .	119 2 39	Dublin . .	Newcastle . .	Rathcoole . .	Celbridge .	I.	34
11	Crodaun . . .	78 2 11	Kildare . .	North Salt .	Kildrought .	Celbridge .	I.	74
30	Croftonpark . .	476 2 37	Mayo . .	Tirawley . .	Kilmoremoy .	Ballina . .	IV.	170
15	Croghan . . .	180 0 21	Mayo . .	Tirawley . .	Killala . .	Killala . .	IV.	169
10	Croghan . . .	387 1 20	Roscommon .	Boyle . .	Killukin . .	Boyle . .	IV.	195
5	Croghan . . .	475 0 7	Tipperary, N.R. .	Lower Ormond .	Loughkeen .	Parsonstown .	II.	286
10	Croghan Demesne .	305 0 11	King's Co. .	Lower Philipstown .	Ballyburly .	Edenderry .	I.	142
10	Croghan Demesne .	160 3 18	King's Co. .	Lower Philipstown .	Croghan . .	Edenderry .	I.	142
10	Croghanhill . .	70 3 17	King's Co. .	Lower Philipstown .	Ballyburly .	Edenderry .	I.	142
10	Croghanhill . .	86 0 38	King's Co. .	Lower Philipstown .	Croghan . .	Edenderry .	I.	142

(a) Including 6A. 2R. 22P. water.
(b) Including 10A. 2R. 2P. Croboy Lough.
(c) Including 77A. 0R. 18P. water.
(d) Including 1A. 0R. 20P. water.
(e) Including 10A. 3R. 9P. water.
(f) Including 12A. 2R. 32P. water.

(g) Including 29A. 1R. 18P. water.
(h) Including 36A. 1R. 32P. water.
(i) Including 0A. 3R. 10P. water.
(j) Including 46A. 0R. 20P. detached portion.
(k) Including 2A. 0R. 16P. water.
(l) Including 9A. 0R. 24P. water.

(m) Including 20A. 2R. 28P. water.
(n) Including 8A. 2R. 37P. water.
(o) Including 37A. 1R. 15P. water.
(p) Including 6A. 0R. 36P. water.
(q) Including 16A. 3R. 15P. water.

No. of Sheet of the Ordnance Survey Maps.	Townlands and Towns.	Area in Statute Acres.			County.	Barony.	Parish.	Poor Law Union in 1857.	Townland Census of 1851, Part I.	
		A.	R.	P.					Vol.	Page
2	Croghan Middle .	202	2	5	Wexford .	Gorey . . .	Kilnenor . . .	Gorey . .	I.	319
1, 2	Croghan Mountain .	653	3	31	Wexford .	Gorey . . .	Kilnenor . . .	Gorey . .	I.	319
2	Croghan Upper .	177	1	34	Wexford .	Gorey . . .	Kilnenor . . .	Gorey . .	I.	319
52, 57	Croghfern . .	542	0	3	Antrim .	Lower Belfast .	Carnmoney . .	Belfast . .	III.	8
64	*Croghnut* . .	15	2	14	Galway .	Ballynahinch .	Moyrus . . .	Clifden . .	IV.	14
30	Croghtabeg(*Bunbury*)	181	2	39	Kilkenny .	Kells . . .	Ballytobin . .	Callan . .	I.	107
30	Croghtabeg (*Courtown*)	189	3	37	Kilkenny .	Kells . . .	Ballytobin . .	Callan . .	I.	107
74	Croghtamore . .	88	3	13*a*	Cork, E.R.	Cork . . .	St. Finbars . .	Cork . .	II.	65
38, 46	Croghteen . .	257	3	5	Limerick .	Connello Upper .	Corcomohide . .	Croom . .	II.	232
6, 11	Croghtenclogh .	3,470	1	29	Kilkenny .	Fassadinin . .	Castlecomer . .	Castlecomer .	I.	88
153	Croha East . .	41	0	39	Cork, W.R.	West Carbery (E.D.)	Clearisland . .	Skibbereen .	II.	138
88, 91	Crohan . . .	1,860	2	3	Tipperary, S.R.	Iffa and Offa West .	Newcastle . .	Clogheen . .	II.	319
124	Crohane . . .	124	1	25	Cork, W.R.	Courceys . .	Kilroan . .	Kinsale . .	II.	147
122	Crohane . . .	21	3	25	Cork, W.R.	East Carbery (E.D.)	Kilnagross . .	Clonakilty .	II.	129
58, 66	Crohane . . .	466	2	34	Kerry .	Magunihy . .	Aghadoe . .	Killarney .	II.	199
75, 85	Crohane . . .	1,845	0	16	Kerry .	Magunihy . .	Killaha . .	Killarney .	II.	202
122	Crohane (*Bandon*) .	204	0	39	Cork, W.R.	East Carbery (E.D.)	Desertserges . .	Clonakilty .	II.	127
122	Crohane (*Bandon*) .	250	0	19	Cork, W.R.	East Carbery (E.D.)	Kilnagross . .	Clonakilty .	II.	129
122	Crohane East . .	108	0	8	Cork, W.R.	East Carbery (E.D.)	Desertserges . .	Clonakilty .	II.	127
54, 55	Crohane Lower .	1,530	3	39	Tipperary, S.R.	Slievardagh . .	Crohane . .	Callan . .	II.	332
54. 55, 63	Crohane Upper .	751	0	26	Tipperary, S.R.	Slievardagh . .	Crohane . . .	Callan . .	II.	332
122	Crohane West .	69	2	36	Cork, W.R.	East Carbery (E.D.)	Desertserges . .	Clonakilty .	II.	127
30, 34	Crohanree . .	295	0	26	Kildare .	Narragh&RebanWest	Churchtown . .	Athy . .	I.	67
153	Croha West . .	67	3	2	Cork, W.R.	West Carbery (E.D.)	Clearisland . .	Skibbereen .	II.	138
56	Crohy . . .	1,085	2	15*c*	Donegal .	Boylagh . .	Templecrone . .	Glenties .	III.	115
41, 49	Crohyboyle . .	1,607	3	0*d*	Donegal .	Boylagh . .	Templecrone . .	Glenties .	III.	115
19	Crokershill . .	25	3	30*e*	Kilkenny .	Crannagh . .	St. Canice . .	Kilkenny . .	I.	87
11	Crokerspark . .	205	1	38	Limerick .	Kenry . .	Kilcornan . .	Rathkeale .	II.	249
76	Crolack . . .	1,155	1	23	Donegal .	Raphoe . . .	Kilteevoge . .	Stranorlar .	III.	139
23, 28, 29	Croley . . .	222	2	15	Cavan .	Clankee . .	Shercock . .	Bailieborough .	III.	74
41, 42, 50	Crolly . . .	2,471	3	34*f*	Donegal .	Kilmacrenan .	Tullaghobegly .	Dunfanaghy .	III.	131
45	Crollys Quarter .	51	2	0	Down .	Lecale Upper .	Bright . . .	Downpatrick .	III.	180
13	Cromaghs . .	457	0	5	Antrim .	Cary . . .	Armoy . . .	Ballycastle .	III.	11
36	Cromaghy . .	181	1	8*g*	Fermanagh .	Clankelly . .	Clones . . .	Clones . .	III.	195
6	Cromagloun . .	76	0	39	Cork, E.R.	Orrery and Kilmore	Tullylease . .	Kanturk . .	II.	110
55, 56	Cromane Lower .	517	3	27	Kerry .	Trughanacmy .	Killorglin . .	Killarney .	II.	211
55, 56	Cromane Upper .	879	1	37	Kerry .	Trughanacmy .	Killorglin . .	Killarney .	II.	211
37	Cromkill . .	568	0	16	Antrim .	Lower Antrim .	Connor . .	Ballymena .	III.	3
20	Cromkill . .	108	3	0	Londonderry .	Tirkeeran . .	Clondermot . .	Londonderry .	III.	247
22	Cromlin . .	158	0	11	Leitrim .	Carrigallen .	Oughteragh . .	Bawnboy .	IV.	92
6, 7	Cromoge . .	559	2	37	Cork, E.R.	Orrery and Kilmore	Kilbolane . .	Kanturk . .	II.	108
17, 23	Cromoge . .	363	3	15	Queen's Co.	Maryborough West .	Clonenagh&Clonagheen	Abbeyleix .	I.	242
9, 14	Cromoge . .	591	1	35	Wexford .	Scarawalsh .	St. Marys Newtown-barry .	Enniscorthy .	I.	325
33	Cromwell . .	733	2	7	Limerick .	Smallcounty .	Ballinlough . .	Kilmallock .	II.	259
37	Cromwellsfort .	32	0	9	Wexford .	Forth . . .	Maudlintown .	Wexford . .	I.	312
109	*Cromwell's Island* .	5	0	7	Galway .	Longford . .	Meelick . .	Portumna .	IV.	62
20	Cromwellstown .	443	2	37	Kildare .	South Salt . .	Kilteel . .	Naas . .	I.	77
20	Cromwellstownhill .	320	3	3	Kildare .	South Salt . .	Kilteel . .	Naas . .	I.	77
50, 51	Cromy and Taggarts Land . .	185	3	23	Antrim .	Upper Antrim .	Donegore . .	Antrim . .	III.	6
75, 84	Cronacarkfree .	770	3	33*h*	Donegal .	Banagh . .	Inver . . .	Donegal .	III.	107
67	Cronadun . .	925	1	3	Donegal .	Raphoe . . .	Kilteevoge . .	Stranorlar .	III.	139
8, 15	Cronagort East .	252	0	18	Clare .	Corcomroe . .	Killilagh . .	Ennistimon .	II.	20
8, 15	Cronagort West .	237	1	21	Clare .	Corcomroe . .	Killilagh . .	Ennistimon .	II.	20
41, 42	Cronaguiggy . .	794	3	3*i*	Donegal .	Kilmacrenan .	Tullaghobegly .	Dunfanaghy .	III.	131
76, 85	Cronakerny . .	1,572	1	24*j*	Donegal .	Raphoe . . .	Kilteevoge . .	Stranorlar .	III.	139
36	Cronakip . .	138	2	31	Wicklow .	Arklow . .	Dunganstown .	Rathdrum .	I.	343
87	Cronalaghy . .	1,221	3	13	Donegal .	Raphoe . . .	Donaghmore . .	Stranorlar .	III.	137
17	Cronaliegh . .	180	3	14	Carlow .	Forth . . .	Barragh . .	Enniscorthy .	I.	4
76, 85	Cronamuck . .	814	1	36	Donegal .	Raphoe . . .	Kilteevoge . .	Stranorlar .	III.	139
83, 84	Cronaslieve . .	530	2	28	Donegal .	Banagh . .	Inver . . .	Donegal .	III.	107
53, 54	Cronavan . .	195	0	14	Cork, E.R.	Barrymore . .	Gortroe . .	Fermoy . .	II.	55
33. 34	Cronavone . .	463	3	15	Tipperary, N.R.	Kilnamanagh Upper	Glenkeen . .	Thurles .	II.	278
34	Cronawinnia . .	238	2	12	Wicklow .	Ballinacor South .	Ballykine . .	Rathdrum .	I.	348
7	Crone . . .	454	1	17	Wicklow .	Rathdown . .	Powerscourt . .	Rathdown .	I.	356
42, 43	Crone . . .	189	0	26	Wicklow .	Shillelagh . .	Aghowle . .	Shillelagh .	I.	356
35	Cronebane . .	155	0	38	Wicklow .	Arklow . .	Castlemacadam .	Rathdrum .	I.	342
34, 35	Crone Beg . .	210	1	16	Wicklow .	Ballinacor South .	Ballykine . .	Rathdrum .	I.	348
3, 7	Cronecribbin . .	144	1	39	Wexford .	Gorey . . .	Inch . . .	Gorey . .	I.	316
3, 7	Cronecribbin . .	90	0	26	Wexford .	Gorey . . .	Kilgorman . .	Gorey . .	I.	318
6	Croneen . .	149	0	7	Fermanagh .	Lurg . . .	Magheraculmoney .	Lowtherstown .	III.	207
6	Croneen Barr . .	165	2	4	Fermanagh .	Lurg . . .	Magheraculmoney .	Lowtherstown .	III.	207

(*a*) { Including 17A. 3R. 27P. water.
Within the Municipal Boundary, 0A. 0R. 39P.
Without the Municipal Boundary, 88A. 2R. 14P.
(*b*) Including 7A. 1R. 28P. water.
(*c*) Including 17A. 0R. 38P. water.

(*d*) Including 54A. 2R. 18P. water.
(*e*) { Within the Municipal Boundary, 20A. 1R. 28P.
Without the Municipal Boundary, 5A. 2R. 2P.
(*f*) Including 18A. 1R. 35P. water.

(*g*) Including 12A. 0R. 32P. water.
(*h*) Including 35A. 0R. 15P. water.
(*i*) Including 28A. 0R. 31P. water.
(*j*) Including 10A. 0R. 30P. water.

No. of Sheet of the Ordnance Survey Maps	Townlands and Towns.	Area in Statute Acres.	County.	Barony.	Parish.	Poor Law Union in 1857.	Townland Census of 1851, Part I. Vol.	Page
		A. R. P.						
31	Croneenlaun . .	61 0 18	Kilkenny . .	Kells . . .	Kilmaganny . .	Callan . .	I.	109
8	Cronekill . .	147 0 15	Tipperary, N.R.	Lower Ormond .	Loughkeen . .	Parsonstown .	II.	286
43	Cronelea . .	470 2 39	Wicklow . .	Shillelagh . .	Mullinacuff . .	Shillelagh . .	I.	358
7	Cronellard . .	121 3 6	Wexford . .	Ballaghkeen . .	Kilcavan . .	Gorey . .	I.	294
35, 36	Crone Lower .	191 1 11	Wicklow . .	Arklow . .	Redcross . .	Rathdrum .	I.	346
45	Cronelusk . .	131 0 17	Wicklow . .	Arklow . . .	Arklow . . .	Rathdrum . .	I.	341
35	Crone More . .	118 0 17	Wicklow . .	Ballinacor South .	Ballykine . .	Rathdrum . .	I.	348
9	Cronery . . .	188 3 22	Cavan . . .	Tullyhaw . .	Templeport . .	Bawnboy . .	III.	94
34, 35	Cronesallagh . .	197 0 26	Wicklow . .	Ballinacor South .	Ballykine . .	Rathdrum . .	I.	348
9, 10	Croneskagh Lower .	91 3 8	Carlow . .	Rathvilly . .	Clonmore . .	Shillelagh . .	I.	10
4, 9	Croneskagh Upper .	250 0 10	Carlow . . .	Rathvilly . .	Clonmore . .	Shillelagh . .	I.	10
35	Crone Upper . .	103 3 20	Wicklow . .	Arklow . . .	Redcross . .	Rathdrum . .	I.	346
60	Cronghill . . .	228 0 5	Tyrone . .	Dungannon Lower .	Aghaloo . .	Dungannon .	III.	296
47	Cronin . . .	202 0 21	Roscommon .	Athlone . . .	Taghboy . .	Athlone . .	IV.	184
83	Cronkceran . .	320 1 27	Donegal . .	Banagh . . .	Killybegs Lower .	Glenties . .	III.	110
1, 4	Cronkill . . .	144 2 37a	Armagh . .	Oneilland West .	Tartaraghan .	Armagh . .	III.	54
72	Cronody . . .	476 2 35b	Cork, E.R. .	East Muskerry .	Aglish . . .	Macroom . .	II.	101
27	Cronoge . . .	16 1 30	Kilkenny . .	Shillelogher . .	Earlstown . .	Callan . .	I.	114
28	Cronohill . .	725 1 2	Cork. E.R. .	Condons&Clangibbon	Leitrim . .	Fermoy . .	II.	62
24, 25	Cronroe . . .	566 3 0	Wicklow . .	Newcastle . .	Rathnew . .	Rathdrum .	I.	354
6	Cronstown . .	236 0 38	Down . . .	Ards Lower . .	Newtownards .	Newtownards .	III.	158
24, 30	Cronybyrne . .	244 2 31	Wicklow . .	Newcastle . .	Derrylossary .	Rathdrum . .	I.	351
24	Cronybyrne Demesne	152 3 21	Wicklow . .	Newcastle . .	Derrylossary .	Rathdrum . .	I.	351
15, 16	Cronyhorn . .	128 3 31	Wexford . .	Scarawalsh . .	Kilbride . .	Enniscorthy .	I.	323
47	Cronyhorn Lower .	648 1 4	Wicklow . .	Shillelagh . .	Carnew . .	Shillelagh . .	I.	357
47	Cronyhorn Upper .	894 0 39	Wicklow . .	Shillelagh . .	Carnew . .	Shillelagh . .	I.	357
19, 25	Cronykeery . .	232 0 39	Wicklow . .	Newcastle . .	Rathnew . .	Rathdrum . .	I.	354
3	Crooderry . .	113 1 30	Roscommon .	Boyle . . .	Ardcarn . .	Boyle . .	IV.	192
29	Croogorts . .	23 1 26	Kerry . . .	Trughanacmy .	Tralee . .	Tralee . .	II.	213
103, 116	Crooha East . .	293 3 9	Cork, W.R. .	Bear . . .	Kilcaskan . .	Castletown .	II.	122
103, 116	Crooha Middle .	183 1 11	Cork, W.R. .	Bear . . .	Kilcaskan . .	Castletown .	II.	122
103, 116	Crooha West .	205 0 29	Cork, W.R. .	Bear . . .	Kilcaskan . .	Castletown .	II.	122
18	Crooke . . .	425 2 22	Waterford . .	Gaultiere . .	Crooke . . .	Waterford . .	II.	362
55	Crookedstone . .	455 0 2	Antrim . .	Lower Massereene .	Killead . .	Antrim . .	III.	28
39	Crooket . . .	289 0 13	Kildare . .	Kilkea and Moone .	Killelan . .	Athy . .	I.	60
147, 152	Crookhaven . .	252 2 4	Cork, W.R. .	West Carbery (W.D.)	Kilmoe . .	Skull . .	II.	144
147	CROOKHAVEN T. .	—	Cork, W.R. .	WestCarbery (W.D.)	Kilmoe . .	Skull . .	II.	145
24, 28	Crooknahaya . .	421 2 37	Antrim . .	Lower Antrim .	Skerry . .	Ballymena .	III.	4
21, 24	Crooksling . .	545 2 15	Dublin . .	Newcastle . .	Saggart . .	Celbridge .	I.	34
36	Crookstown East .	40 1 8	Kildare . .	Narragh & RebanEast	Narraghmore .	Baltinglass .	I.	66
32, 36	Crookstown Lower .	296 2 23	Kildare . .	Narragh & RebanEast	Narraghmore .	Athy . .	I.	66
36	Crookstown Upper .	334 1 34	Kildare . .	Narragh & RebanEast	Narraghmore .	Baltinglass .	I.	66
30	Croom . . .	900 0 18c	Limerick . .	Coshma . . .	Croom . . .	Croom . .	II.	242
30	CROOM T. . .	—	Limerick . .	Coshma . .	Croom . . .	Croom . .	II.	242
71	Crooroe Park . .	49 0 34	Galway . .	Tiaquin . .	Monivea . .	Galway . .	IV.	79
38, 39	Croostan . .	74 2 28d	Fermanagh .	Knockninny . .	Kinawley . .	Lisnaskea .	III.	201
38, 40	Crophill . . .	151 1 9	Kildare . .	Kilkea and Moone .	Castledermot .	Athy . .	I.	59
47	Croreagh . .	303 0 36	Down . . .	Lordship of Newry .	Newry . .	Newry . .	III.	182
15	Crory . . .	416 1 26	Wexford . .	Scarawalsh . .	Ferns . .	Enniscorthy .	I.	323
32	Crory Lower . .	125 2 14	Wexford . .	Shelmaliere East .	Artramon . .	Wexford . .	I.	330
32	Crory Middle . .	174 1 10	Wexford . .	Shelmaliere East .	Artramon . .	Wexford . .	I.	330
32	Crory Upper . .	215 1 38	Wexford . .	Shelmaliere East .	Artramon . .	Wexford . .	I.	330
17	Crosh . . .	426 3 28e	Tyrone . .	Strabane Lower .	Ardstraw . .	Gortin . .	III.	318
26, 35	Crosh . . .	428 2 30	Tyrone . .	Strabane Upper .	Cappagh . .	Omagh . .	III.	325
17	Croshballinree .	79 0 2f	Tyrone . .	Strabane Lower .	Ardstraw . .	Gortin . .	III.	318
103	Crosheen . .	174 3 35	Galway . .	Dunkellin . .	Drumacoo . .	Gort . .	IV.	28
5	Cross . . .	784 3 16g	Antrim . .	Cary . . .	Culfeightrin .	Ballycastle .	III.	13
38	Cross . . .	1,529 2 34	Antrim . .	Lower Antrim .	Ballyclug . .	Ballymena .	III.	3
16	Cross . . .	207 3 12	Antrim . .	Upper Dunluce .	Ballymoney .	Ballymoney .	III.	18
26	Cross . . .	491 0 24	Armagh . .	Orior Upper . .	Killevy . .	Newry . .	III.	58
20, 21	Cross . . .	126 3 23	Cavan . .	Upper Loughtee .	Castleterra .	Cavan . .	III.	82
11	Cross . . .	110 2 29	Clare . .	Inchiquin . .	Kilkeedy . .	Corrofin . .	II.	25
65, 72	Cross . . .	543 1 35	Clare . .	Moyarta . .	Kilballyowen .	Kilrush . .	II.	31
30	Cross . . .	121 2 11	Donegal . .	Inishowen East .	Moville Upper .	Inishowen .	III.	119
54, 55	Cross . . .	237 0 24	Donegal . .	Raphoe . .	Taughboyne .	Londonderry .	III.	143
42,43,48,49	Cross . . .	627 1 31	Down . .	Upper Iveagh, Lr. pt.	Kilcoo . .	Kilkeel . .	III.	173
41,42,47,48	Cross . . .	404 3 26	Down . .	Upper Iveagh, Up.pt.	Drumgath . .	Newry . .	III.	175
22	Cross . . .	132 2 26	Fermanagh .	Tirkennedy . .	Enniskillen .	Enniskillen .	III.	221
85,86,97,98	Cross . . .	292 1 17	Galway . .	Kilconnell . .	Grange . .	Loughrea .	IV.	40
24	Cross . . .	353 0 1	Limerick . .	Coonagh . .	Tuoghcluggin .	Tipperary .	II.	236
28	Cross . . .	45 1 16	Limerick . .	Shanid . .	Ardagh . .	Newcastle .	II.	255
19	Cross . . .	204 2 1	Longford . .	Ardagh . .	Ardagh . .	Longford .	I.	151
21,22,25,26	Cross . . .	121 0 28	Longford . .	Ratheline . .	Cashel . .	Ballymahon .	I.	163

No. of Sheet of the Ordnance Survey Maps.	Townlands and Towns.	Area in Statute Acres.	County.	Barony.	Parish.	Poor Law Union in 1857.	Townland Census of 1851, Part I.	
		A. R. P.					Vol.	Page
76, 77	Cross	188 0 28a	Mayo	Burrishoole	Kilmeena	Westport	IV.	122
95	Cross	295 0 34b	Mayo	Murrisk	Kilgeever	Westport	IV.	160
22	Cross	209 3 11	Queen's Co.	Clarmallagh	Aghaboe	Donaghmore	I.	235
39	Cross	98 1 3	Sligo	Corran	Toomour	Boyle	IV.	228
18	Cross	229 0 5	Waterford	Gaultiere	Kill St. Nicholas	Waterford	II.	364
18	Cross	37 3 24	Waterford	Gaultiere	Kilmacomb	Waterford	II.	364
5	Cross	40 1 34	Westmeath	Moygoish	Rathaspick	Mullingar	I.	280
38	Cross	329 1 3	Wicklow	Ballinacor South	Kilcommon	Shillelagh	I.	349
6	Crossabegh	147 0 23	Louth	Louth	Louth	Dundalk	I.	184
32, 37	Crossabeg	57 1 3	Wexford	Shelmaliere East	Artramon	Wexford	I.	330
39, 43	Crossafehin	218 2 32	Cavan	Castlerahan	Munterconnaught	Oldcastle	III.	71
5, 13	Crossagalla	243 3 13	Limerick	Clanwilliam	St. Nicholas	Limerick	II.	225
51	Crossagh	247 0 26	Clare	Bunratty Lower	Drumline	Ennis	II.	3
14	Crossaghy	145 1 10	Monaghan	Cremorne	Clontibret	Monaghan	III.	260
16	Crossakeel	933 0 15	Meath	Upper Kells	Kilskeer	Oldcastle	I.	206
16	CROSSAKEEL T.	—	Meath	Upper Kells	Kilskeer	Oldcastle	I.	206
28	Crossalare	135 2 24c	Monaghan	Farney	Donaghmoyne	Carrickmacross	III.	269
14, 15	Crossan	416 0 24	Down	Castlereagh Upper	Drumbo	Lisburn	III.	164
49	Crossan	367 2 35	Tyrone	Omagh East	Kilskeery	Lowtherstown	III.	313
6, 7	Crossanagh	156 3 13	Tipperary, N.R.	Lower Ormond	Terryglass	Borrisokane	II.	287
13, 19	Crossane	167 2 37	Meath	Upper Slane	Grangegeeth	Ardee	I.	224
35	Crossanstown	502 2 32	Meath	Lune	Killaconnigan	Trim	I.	208
27	Crossanstown	329 1 15	Westmeath	Farbill	Killucan	Mullingar	I.	266
16, 17	Crossard	131 0 28	Clare	Inchiquin	Killinaboy	Corrofin	II.	26
82, 93	Crossard	569 3 13d	Mayo	Costello	Aghamore	Swineford	IV.	137
70	Crossard	54 3 35	Tipperary, S.R.	Middlethird	Barrettsgrange	Cashel	II.	325
41	Crossaun or Lettera	86 0 24	Galway	Clare	Killursa	Tuam	IV.	21
51	Crossayle	251 1 18	Tipperary, S.R.	Kilnamanagh Lower	Donohill	Tipperary	II.	323
22	Crossballycormick	327 0 7	Londonderry	Tirkeeran	Cumber Lower	Londonderry	III.	248
19, 23	Crossbane	466 1 15e	Armagh	Tiranny	Derrynoose	Armagh	III.	59
34, 40	Crossbane	359 1 22	Cavan	Castlerahan	Mullagh	Bailieborough	III.	70
17	Crossbane	239 1 33	Monaghan	Dartree	Killeevan	Clones	III.	268
58	Cross Beg	384 3 33	Clare	Clonderalaw	Kilmurry	Killadysert	II.	17
82, 93	Crossbeg	299 1 16f	Mayo	Costello	Aghamore	Swineford	IV.	137
21	Crossboy	438 1 18	Sligo	Tirerrill	Killerry	Sligo	IV.	239
59	Crossboy	95 3 17	Tyrone	Clogher	Errigal Keerogue	Clogher	III.	295
16	Cross (Boyd)	285 1 14g	Mayo	Erris	Kilmore	Belmullet	IV.	145
111	Crossboyne	112 0 9	Mayo	Clanmorris	Crossboyne	Claremorris	IV.	132
11	Crosscanley Glebe	151 1 39	Londonderry	Coleraine	Aghadowey	Coleraine	III.	229
54	Crosscannon	89 3 12	Tipperary, S.R.	Slievardagh	Killenaule	Cashel	II.	334
40	Crosscarn	71 0 4	Cavan	Castlerahan	Mullagh	Kells	III.	70
45	Crosscavanagh	268 1 12	Tyrone	Dungannon Middle	Pomeroy	Dungannon	III.	304
16	Cross Common	150 2 0h	Mayo	Erris	Kilmore	Belmullet	IV.	145
3, 10	Crossconnell	255 2 8	Donegal	Inishowen East	Clonmany	Inishowen	III.	117
99	Crossconnell Beg	32 3 24	Galway	Clonmacnowen	Clontuskert	Ballinasloe	IV.	24
99	Crossconnell More	178 2 30	Galway	Clonmacnowen	Clontuskert	Ballinasloe	IV.	24
25	Crosscoolharbour	110 1 23	Kildare	Naas North	Rathmore	Naas	I.	62
5	Crosscoolharbour	826 3 35	Wicklow	Lower Talbotstown	Blessington	Naas	I.	358
8	Crosscornaun	124 2 17	Clare	Corcomroe	Kilshanny	Ennistimon	II.	21
15, 19	Crossdall	487 0 31	Armagh	Tiranny	Tynan	Armagh	III.	60
20, 24	Crossdened	701 1 31i	Armagh	Armagh	Keady	Armagh	III.	45
46	Crossdernot	280 2 35	Tyrone	Dungannon Middle	Pomeroy	Dungannon	III.	304
59	Crossderry	531 2 39	Clare	Clonderalaw	Killadysert	Killadysert	II.	15
20	Crossderry	89 1 20	Clare	Tulla Upper	Feakle	Scarriff	II.	39
96, 104	Crossderry	80 3 23	Galway	Dunkellin	Lickerrig	Loughrea	IV.	31
83	Crossderry	830 3 1	Kerry	Dunkerron North	Knockane	Killarney	II.	182
25	Crossdoney	32 3 27	Cavan	Clanmahon	Kilmore	Cavan	III.	78
8, 9	Crossdrum Lower	964 2 10	Meath	Fore	Killeagh	Oldcastle	I.	201
28	Crossdrumman	114 1 26	Leitrim	Mohill	Mohill	Mohill	IV.	107
9, 15	Crossdrum Upper	331 2 6	Meath	Fore	Killeagh	Oldcastle	I.	201
24, 27	Crossduff	215 0 27j	Monaghan	Cremorne	Aghnamullen	Castleblayney	III.	257
19, 20	Crossea North	253 1 17	Longford	Ardagh	Ardagh	Longford	I.	151
20	Crossea South	300 3 12	Longford	Ardagh	Ardagh	Longford	I.	151
121	Cross East	465 1 35	Mayo	Kilmaine	Cong	Ballinrobe	IV.	153
59	Cross Eighter	252 2 5	Galway	Tiaquin	Killoscobe	Mountbellew	IV.	78
13	Crosserdree	258 3 4	Westmeath	Moyashel and Magheradernon	Rathconnell	Mullingar	I.	276
32, 38	Crosserlough	594 1 35	Cavan	Castlerahan	Crosserlough	Cavan	III.	68
38, 39	Crosserule	310 0 23	Cavan	Castlerahan	Castlerahan	Oldcastle	III.	67
34	Crossery	216 3 16	Waterford	Coshmore&Coshbride	Kilcockan	Lismore	II.	343
97	Crosses	143 1 12	Cork, E.R.	Kinalea	Inishannon	Bandon	II.	95
9, 10, 13, 14	Crosses	272 1 4	Monaghan	Monaghan	Monaghan	Monaghan	III.	277
9	Crosses	107 1 23	Monaghan	Monaghan	Tedavnet	Monaghan	III.	278

(a) Including 9A. 2R. 18P. water.
(b) Including 28A. 3R. 8P. water.
(c) Including 0A. 3R. 22P. water.
(d) Including 10A. 3R. 32P. water.

(e) Including 7A. 1R. 18P. water.
(f) Including 17A. 3R. 25P. water.
(g) Including 48A. 3R. 17P. water.

(h) Including 33A. 3R. 38P. water.
(i) Including 21A. 0R. 36P. water.
(j) Including 6A. 2R. 39P. water.

No. of Sheet of the Ordnance Survey Maps.	Townlands and Towns.	Area in Statute Acres.	County.	Barony.	Parish.	Poor Law Union in 1857.	Townland Census of 1851, Part I.	
		A. R. P.					Vol.	Page
51, 52	Crossfarnoge . .	59 3 18	Wexford . .	Bargy . . .	Kilmore . . .	Wexford . . .	I.	306
16	Crossfield . .	42 0 32	Queen's Co. .	Upperwoods . .	Offerlane . . .	Abbeyleix . .	I.	251
38	Crossford . .	130 0 29	Waterford . .	Decies within Drum	Ardmore . . .	Youghal . .	II.	350
38	Crossford . .	112 2 9	Waterford . .	Decies within Drum	Lisgenan or Grange	Youghal . .	II.	352
23, 30	Crossgar . . .	534 1 36	Down . . .	Castlereagh Upper .	Kilmore . . .	Downpatrick .	III.	165
28, 29	Crossgar . . .	1,216 2 24a	Down . . .	Upper Iveagh, Lr.pt.	Dromara . . .	Banbridge . .	III.	172
11	Crossgare . .	168 3 7	Londonderry .	Coleraine . . .	Macosquin . .	Coleraine . .	III.	233
30	CROSSGAR T. . .	—	Down . . .	Castlereagh Upper .	Kilmore . . .	Downpatrick .	III.	165
7	Cross Glebe . .	71 2 35	Londonderry .	North East Liberties of Coleraine . .	Coleraine . .	Coleraine . .	III.	246
38	Cross Glebe . .	109 3 20	Tyrone . . .	Dungannon Upper .	Desertcreat . .	Cookstown . .	III.	307
18	Crossguns . .	8 1 14b	Dublin . . .	Coolock . . .	Glasnevin . .	Dublin North .	I.	27
18	Crossguns North or Daneswell . .	78 3 22c	Dublin . . .	Coolock . . .	St. Georges . .	Dublin North .	I.	29
18	Crossguns South .	20 1 1d	Dublin . . .	Dublin, Municipal Borough of . .	St. Georges . .	Dublin North .	I.	44
99	Crosshaven . .	189 2 37	Cork, E.R. . .	Kerrycurrihy . .	Templebreedy .	Kinsale . .	II.	93
99	Crosshavenhill .	274 2 2	Cork, E.R. . .	Kerrycurrihy . .	Templebreedy .	Kinsale . .	II.	93
99	CROSSHAVEN T. .	—	Cork, E.R. . .	Kerrycurrihy . .	Templebreedy .	Kinsale . .	II.	93
38, 39	Crosshill . .	540 3 30	Antrim . . .	Lower Antrim . .	Glenwhirry . .	Ballymena . .	III.	4
55, 59	Crosshill . .	824 3 24	Antrim . . .	Lower Massereene .	Killead . . .	Antrim . .	III.	28
2, 4	Crosshill . .	261 0 3	Roscommon .	Boyle . . .	Kilronan . .	Boyle . .	IV.	196
27	Crosshue . .	291 0 23	Wexford . .	Ballaghkeen . .	Killila . . .	Enniscorthy .	I.	295
13, 14	Crosshugh . .	164 0 27	Monaghan . .	Monaghan . .	Monaghan . .	Monaghan . .	III.	277
17	Cross Island . .	12 3 29	Down . . .	Castlereagh Lower .	Tullynakill . .	Newtownards .	III.	163
44, 50	Crusskennan . .	409 2 21	Antrim . . .	Upper Antrim . .	Antrim . . .	Antrim . .	III.	5
26	Crossland . .	400 0 9	Londonderry .	Coleraine . . .	Desertoghill . .	Ballymoney .	III.	230
53	Crosslands . .	12 3 39	Wexford . .	Forth . . .	Carn . . .	Wexford . .	I.	309
151	Crosslea . . .	41 2 6	Cork, W.R. . .	West Carbery (E.D.) .	Castlehaven . .	Skibbereen .	II.	137
22	Crosslea . . .	134 2 21	Monaghan . .	Dartree . . .	Ematris . . .	Cootehill . .	III.	266
8, 13	Crosslow or Mount-wolseley . .	809 1 13	Carlow . . .	Rathvilly . . .	Tullowphelim . .	Carlow . .	I.	12
10	Crossmacahilly .	221 3 39	Armagh . . .	Oneilland East . .	Seagoe . . .	Lurgan . .	III.	50
85, 86	Crossmacrin . .	101 3 22	Galway . . .	Kilconnell . . .	Grange . . .	Loughrea . .	IV.	40
30	Crossmaglen . .	303 2 12	Armagh . . .	Fews Upper . .	Creggan . . .	Castleblayney .	III.	48
30	CROSSMAGLEN T. .	—	Armagh . . .	Fews Upper . .	Creggan . . .	Castleblayney .	III.	49
83	Crossmahon . .	209 2 4	Cork, W.R. . .	West Muskerry . .	Kilmurry . . .	Macroom . .	II.	159
28	Crossmakeelan .	265 3 26	Cavan . . .	Clankee . . .	Shercock . .	Bailieborough .	III.	74
11	Crossmakeever .	325 1 33	Londonderry .	Coleraine . . .	Aghadowey . .	Coleraine . .	III.	229
9,10,13,14	Crossmakelagher .	196 3 21	Cavan . . .	Tullyhaw . . .	Templeport . .	Bawnboy . .	III.	94
47, 53	Crossnary . .	207 0 14	Antrim . . .	Lower Belfast . .	Kilroot . . .	Larne . .	III.	9
29, 38	Crossmolina . .	126 3 32	Mayo . . .	Tirawley . . .	Crossmolina . .	Ballina . .	IV.	165
29, 38	CROSSMOLINA T. .	—	Mayo . . .	Tirawley . . .	Crossmolina . .	Ballina . .	IV.	167
20	Crossmore . .	358 3 20	Armagh . . .	Armagh . . .	Keady . . .	Armagh . .	III.	45
58	Cross More . .	653 2 5	Clare . . .	Clonderalaw . .	Kilmurry . . .	Killadysert .	II.	17
14	Crossmore . .	260 0 39	Monaghan . .	Cremorne . .	Clontibret . .	Monaghan . .	III.	260
22	Crossmorris . .	168 2 2	Kildare . .	Offaly West . .	Lackagh . . .	Athy . .	I.	73
11	Crossmoyle . .	82 3 1	Monaghan . .	Dartree . . .	Clones . . .	Clones . .	III.	264
31, 32	Crossmurrin . .	254 1 30	Fermanagh . .	Clanawley . .	Killesher . .	Enniskillen .	III.	192
3	Crossna . . .	203 2 37	Roscommon .	Boyle . . .	Ardcarn . . .	Boyle . .	IV.	192
2, 3, 5, 6	Crossnacaldoo . .	418 1 16	Monaghan . .	Trough . . .	Errigal Trough .	Clogher . .	III.	283
32	Crossnacole . .	312 2 39	Wicklow . .	Upper Talbotstown .	Kiltegan . . .	Baltinglass .	I.	364
9, 10	Crossnacreevy .	664 3 32	Down . . .	Castlereagh Upper .	Comber . . .	Newtownards .	III.	164
19	Crossnamoyle . .	298 0 9	Armagh . . .	Tiranny . . .	Keady . . .	Armagh . .	III.	60
6	Crossnamuckley .	258 0 22	Down . . .	Ards Lower . .	Newtownards . .	Newtownards .	III.	158
46, 48	Crossnarea . .	170 1 28	Londonderry .	Loughinsholin . .	Desertlyn . .	Magherafelt .	III.	240
37	Crossneen . .	520 3 20e	Queen's Co. .	Slievemargy . .	Killeshin . .	Carlow . .	I.	245
19, 23	Crossnenagh . .	338 2 23f	Armagh . . .	Tiranny . . .	Keady . . .	Armagh . .	III.	60
64	Cross North . .	16 2 10	Mayo . . .	Costello . . .	Kilcolman . .	Castlereagh .	IV.	141
105	Crossoge . .	45 1 24	Cork, W.R. . .	Bantry . . .	Kilmocomoge . .	Bantry . .	II.	120
26	Crossoge . .	3 1 32	Kilkenny . .	Callan . . .	Callan . . .	Callan . .	I.	83
40	Crossoge . .	92 2 9	Tipperary, N.R. .	Kilnamanagh Upper .	Ballycahill . .	Thurles . .	II.	277
14,15,20,21	Crossoge . .	241 1 20	Wicklow . .	Upper Talbotstown .	Rathsallagh . .	Baltinglass .	I.	365
43, 49	Crossoges . .	204 1 15	Tipperary, S.R. .	Slieveardagh . .	Kilcooly . .	Urlingford .	II.	333
52, 60	Crossogs . .	164 3 19	Donegal . .	Kilmacrenan . .	Conwal . . .	Letterkenny .	III.	126
112, 113	Crossooha . .	481 1 4	Galway . . .	Kiltartan . .	Kinvarradoorus .	Gort . .	IV.	49
59, 72	Cross Oughter .	442 2 4	Galway . . .	Tiaquin . . .	Killoscobe . .	Mountbellew .	IV.	78
59	Crossowen . .	37 3 32	Tyrone . . .	Clogher . . .	Clogher . . .	Clogher . .	III.	292
8	Crosspatrick . .	616 0 25	Kilkenny . .	Galmoy . . .	Erke . . .	Urlingford .	I.	92
22	Crosspatrick . .	166 3 10	Mayo . . .	Tirawley . . .	Killala . . .	Killala . .	IV.	169
48	Crosspatrick (alias) Ballydawley . .	257 3 39	Londonderry .	Loughinsholin . .	Artrea . . .	Magherafelt .	III.	238
42	Crossrah . . .	218 3 32	Cavan . . .	Clanmahon . .	Kilbride . . .	Oldcastle . .	III.	77
6	Crossreagh . .	19 2 31	Antrim . . .	Lower Dunluce . .	Ballywillin . .	Coleraine . .	III.	15
40	Crossreagh . .	219 1 2	Cavan . . .	Castlerahan . .	Mullagh . . .	Bailieborough .	III.	70

(a)   Including 18A. 2R. 1P. water.
(b) { Within the Municipal Boundary, 3A. 2R. 12P.
       { Without the Municipal Boundary, 4A. 3R. 2P.
(c) { Within the Municipal Boundary, 0A. 2R. 19P.
       { Without the Municipal Boundary, 78A. 1R. 3P.
(d)   Included in the Parish of St. George.
(e)   Including 13A. 2R. 26P. River Barrow.
(f)   Including 7A. 3R. 17P. water.

No. of Sheet of the Ordnance Survey Maps.	Townlands and Towns.	Area in Statute Acres.	County.	Barony.	Parish.	Poor Law Union in 1857.	Townland Census of 1851, Part I.	
		A. R. P.					Vol.	Page
20, 21	Crossreagh	97 2 15	Cavan	Upper Loughtee	Castleterra	Cavan	III.	82
3	Crossreagh	118 2 21	Londonderry	North East Liberties of Coleraine	Ballywillin	Coleraine	III.	245
17	Crossreagh	239 1 39	Monaghan	Dartree	Killeevan	Clones	III.	268
19, 23	Crossreagh or Doohat	203 2 3	Armagh	Tiranny	Derrynoose	Armagh	III.	59
3	Crossreagh East	425 3 22	Londonderry	North East Liberties of Coleraine	Ballyaghran	Coleraine	III.	244
3	Crossreagh West	158 3 16	Londonderry	North East Liberties of Coleraine	Ballyaghran	Coleraine	III.	244
25	CROSS ROADS T.	—	Donegal	Kilmacrenan	Raymunterdoney } Tullaghobegly	Dunfanaghy	III.	{131 132}
47, 52	Crossscales	155 0 12	Wexford	Bargy	Tomhaggard	Wexford	I.	307
64, 74	Cross South	264 0 8	Mayo	Costello	Kilcolman	Castlereagh	IV.	141
17	Crosstagherty	405 3 10	Antrim	Upper Dunluce	Kilraghts	Ballymoney	III.	19
54, 61	Crossteely	177 2 0a	Tyrone	Dungannon Middle	Clonfeacle	Dungannon	III.	299
90	Crossterry East	347 0 38	Cork, W.R.	Bear	Kilcaskan	Bantry	II.	122
90, 104	Crossterry West	1,050 2 4b	Cork, W.R.	Bear	Kilcaskan	Bantry	II.	122
65	Cross T.	—	Clare	Moyarta	Kilballyowen	Kilrush	II.	32
67	Crosstown	145 0 20	Kerry	Magunihy	Killaha	Killarney	II.	202
47	Crosstown	66 0 27	Wexford	Forth	Mayglass	Wexford	I.	312
37	Crosstown	348 1 18	Wexford	Shelmaliere East	Ardcavan	Wexford	I.	329
42	Crossursa	551 2 21	Galway	Clare	Kilcoona	Tuam	IV.	19
10	Cross or Valleymount	187 0 30	Wicklow	Lower Talbotstown	Boystown	Baltinglass	I.	359
16	Cross (Wallace) East	191 1 13c	Mayo	Erris	Kilmore	Belmullet	IV.	146
16	Cross (Wallace) West	224 2 27d	Mayo	Erris	Kilmore	Belmullet	IV.	146
121	Cross West	308 0 16	Mayo	Kilmaine	Cong	Ballinrobe	IV.	153
29	Crosswood	306 2 30	Westmeath	Brawny	St. Mary's	Athlone	I.	259
10	Crossybrennan	25 1 10	Kilkenny	Fassadinin	Muckalee	Castlecomer	I.	91
23	Crotanstown	150 0 31	Kildare	Connell	Morristownbiller	Naas	I.	56
21	Crott	244 1 37e	Fermanagh	Magheraboy	Devenish	Enniskillen	III.	210
3	Crott	780 1 36f	Longford	Granard	Killoe	Granard	I.	157
7	Crott	218 2 17	Mayo	Tirawley	Kilbride	Killala	IV.	168
15,16,21,22	Crotta	62 2 15	Kerry	Clanmaurice	Kilfeighny	Listowel	II.	170
15, 21, 22	Crotta	399 3 22	Kerry	Clanmaurice	Kilflyn	Listowel	II.	170
10	Crotta	311 1 14	Tipperary, N.R.	Lower Ormond	Borrisokane	Borrisokane	II.	282
25, 26	Crottan	195 2 28	Fermanagh	Clanawley	Cleenish	Enniskillen	III.	190
118, 131	Crottees	489 2 38	Cork, W.R.	West Carbery (W.D.)	Durrus	Bantry	II.	142
87, 97	Crott Mountain	1,329 1 16	Mayo	Murrisk	Oughaval	Westport	IV.	161
19, 20	Crouck	952 3 11	Tyrone	Strabane Upper	Bodoney Lower	Gortin	III.	323
14, 15	Crough	407 2 1	Waterford	Decies without Drum	Kilrossanty	Kilmacthomas	II.	358
16, 25	Crough	81 2 33	Waterford	Middlethird	Dunhill	Kilmacthomas	II.	366
24, 25	Croughal	666 2 18	Westmeath	Rathconrath	Churchtown	Mullingar	I.	282
44, 45	Croughil	99 1 1	King's Co.	Clonlisk	Dunkerrin	Roscrea	I.	130
24	Croughta	614 1 35	Cork, E.R.	Orrery and Kilmore	Ballyclogh	Mallow	II.	106
88	Croughta	114 1 15	Tipperary, S.R.	Iffa and Offa West	Ballybacon	Clogheen	II.	317
31	Croughtanaul(Marquis)	2 0 20	Waterford	Decies without Drum	Dungarvan	Dungarvan	II.	355
31	Croughtanaul(Stuart)	10 2 31	Waterford	Decies without Drum	Dungarvan	Dungarvan	II.	355
76	Croveenananta	777 2 14	Donegal	Boylagh	Inishkeel	Glenties	III.	112
49	Crovehy	1,334 1 32g	Donegal	Boylagh	Templecrone	Glenties	III.	115
38	Crover	389 2 14	Cavan	Clanmahon	Ballymachugh	Cavan	III.	76
17	Crover	128 0 15	Monaghan	Dartree	Aghabog	Cootehill	III.	263
25, 28	Crover	89 0 9	Monaghan	Farney	Donaghmoyne	Carrickmacross	III.	269
76	Crovinish	28 3 35	Mayo	Burrishoole	Kilmeena	Westport	IV.	122
60	Crovraghan	524 1 16	Clare	Clonderalaw	Killadysert	Killadysert	II.	15
17, 18, 24	Crowagh or Dunneill Mountain	3,150 1 1	Sligo	Tireragh	Kilmacshalgan	Dromore West	IV.	234
90, 91	Crowanrudda	1,040 0 39	Donegal	Banagh	Kilcar	Glenties	III.	108
90	Crowanrudda Beg	435 0 1	Donegal	Banagh	Kilcar	Glenties	III.	108
66	Crowbally	241 3 5	Cork, E.R.	Imokilly	Mogeely	Middleton	II.	89
24	Crowbally	144 3 31	Kilkenny	Gowran	Tullaherin	Thomastown	I.	100
36	Crowbally	520 0 10	Kilkenny	Knocktopher	Derrynahinch	Thomastown	I.	111
82, 91	Crowbane	1,359 0 2	Donegal	Banagh	Kilcar	Glenties	III.	108
82, 91	Crowdoo	1,112 0 32	Donegal	Banagh	Kilcar	Glenties	III.	108
5	Crowdrumman	294 0 19	Longford	Longford	Killoe	Longford	I.	159
81, 90, 91	Croweighter	1,236 3 13	Donegal	Banagh	Kilcar	Glenties	III.	108
9, 10	Crowey	66 2 36	Monaghan	Monaghan	Tehallan	Monaghan	III.	280
9, 13	Crowhill	216 2 17	Kilkenny	Crannagh	Freshford	Kilkenny	I.	85
88	Crowhill	32 3 9	Mayo	Burrishoole	Aghagower	Westport	IV.	118
9, 14	Crowinstown Great	721 3 24h	Westmeath	Delvin	Castletowndelvin	Castletowndelvin	I.	264
9	Crowinstown Little	180 3 17	Westmeath	Delvin	Castletowndelvin	Castletowndelvin	I.	264
42	Crow Island	0 3 24	Clare	Bunratty Lower	Kilnasoolagh	Ennis	II.	6
126	Crow Island	6 0 13	Cork, W.R.	Bear	Kilmocenogh	Castletown	II.	105
65	Crow Island	16 3 10	Galway	Moycullen	Kilcummin	Oughterard	IV.	68
44	Crow Island	0 2 16	Sligo	Coolavin	Kilcolman	Boyle	IV.	224
90, 91	Crowkeeragh	913 1 26	Donegal	Banagh	Kilcar	Glenties	III.	108

(a) Including 2A. 0R. 0P. water.
(b) Including 70A. 2R. 17P. water.
(c) Including 16A. 0R. 38P. water.
(d) Including 29A. 1R. 37P. water.
(e) Including 30A. 0R. 39P. water.
(f) Including 10A. 2R. 3P. water.
(g) Including 43A. 3R. 29P. water.
(h) Including 7A. 2R. 39P. water.

No. of Sheet of the Ordnance Survey Maps.	Townlands and Towns.	Area in Statute Acres.			County.	Barony.	Parish.	Poor Law Union in 1857.	Townland Census of 1851, Part I.	
		A.	R.	P.					Vol.	Page
105, 118	Crowkingle	99	0	30	Cork, W.R.	Bantry	Kilmocomoge	Bantry	II.	120
81,82,90,91	Crowlar	919	0	12	Donegal	Banagh	Kilcar	Glenties	III.	108
13	Crowmartin	478	0	14	Louth	Ardee	Clonkeen	Ardee	I.	172
91, 97	Crownasillagh	875	3	3	Donegal	Banagh	Kilcar	Glenties	III.	108
21, 26	Crownhall	130	2	17	Fermanagh	Magheraboy	Rossorry	Enniskillen	III.	214
36	Crowpark (1st Division)	227	2	25a	Meath	Upper Navan	Trim	Trim	I.	217
36	Crowpark (2nd Division)	27	2	33	Meath	Upper Navan	Trim	Trim	I.	217
11, 12	Crowscastle	106	1	22	Dublin	Nethercross	Swords	Balrothery	I.	32
42	Crowsgap	84	2	2	Roscommon	Athlone	Kilmeane	Roscommon	IV.	182
18	Crowsgrove	433	3	30	Carlow	St. Mullins Upper	Barragh	Shillelagh	I.	14
100	Crowsnest	463	3	12	Galway	Longford	Clontuskert	Ballinasloe	IV.	58
25	Cruagh	947	3	6	Dublin	Uppercross	Cruagh	Dublin South	I.	39
21	Cruagh	82	2	38	Galway	Ballynahinch	Omey	Clifden	IV.	15
30	Cruan	224	2	3	Kilkenny	Kells	Coolaghmore	Callan	I.	108
135, 136	Cruary East	188	0	4	Cork, W.R.	Ibane and Barryroe	Templeomalus	Clonakilty	II.	151
135	Cruary West	153	0	23	Cork, W.R.	Ibane and Barryroe	Templeomalus	Clonakilty	II.	151
25, 26	Crubany	359	0	28	Cavan	Upper Loughtee	Annagelliff	Cavan	III.	81
18, 24	Crubeen	600	1	12	Queen's Co.	Cullenagh	Ballyroan	Abbeyleix	I.	239
54, 61	Crubinagh	278	1	7	Tyrone	Dungannon Middle	Clonfeacle	Dungannon	III.	299
76	Cruboge	9	3	5	Tipperary, S.R.	Iffa and Offa East	Newchapel	Clonmel	II.	315
11	Cruckaclady	372	3	39	Tyrone	Strabane Upper	Bodoney Upper	Gortin	III.	324
25, 31	Cruckanim	760	2	4	Londonderry	Keenaght	Dungiven	New[T]n Limavady	III.	236
112	Cruckeen Island	1	2	12	Galway	Kiltartan	Kinvarradoorus	Gort	IV.	49
42	Crucknamona	60	0	11	Tyrone	Omagh East	Drumragh	Omagh	III.	312
23, 29	Cruell	199	2	13	Queen's Co.	Clarmallagh	Aghaboe	Abbeyleix	I.	235
27	Crufty	64	0	37	Meath	Lower Duleek	Kilsharvan	Drogheda	I.	196
10	Crughwill	183	3	0	Clare	Burren	Carran	Ballyvaghan	II.	11
20, 27	Cruicerath	417	2	3	Meath	Lower Duleek	Donore	Drogheda	I.	195
5, 11	Cruicetown	1,338	3	34b	Meath	Lower Kells	Cruicetown	Kells	I.	202
18, 19	Cruicetown	239	3	23c	Meath	Upper Slane	Stackallan	Navan	I.	225
49	Cruickaghmore	794	2	1d	Donegal	Boylagh	Templecrone	Glenties	III.	115
13	Cruiscrath	244	3	22	Dublin	Castleknock	Finglas	Dublin North	I.	25
19	Cruisetown	264	1	25	Louth	Ferrard	Parsonstown	Drogheda	I.	182
9, 10	Cruit	437	0	38	King's Co.	Lower Philipstown	Kilclonfert	Tullamore	I.	142
42	Cruit	49	2	18	Roscommon	Athlone	Kilmeane	Roscommon	IV.	182
40	Cruit Lower	432	3	15	Donegal	Boylagh	Templecrone	Glenties	III.	115
40, 41	Cruit Upper	308	2	13	Donegal	Boylagh	Templecrone	Glenties	III.	115
39	Crum	132	0	16e	Fermanagh	Coole	Galloon	Lisnaskea	III.	199
25, 26	Crumlin	142	0	4	Cavan	Upper Loughtee	Annagelliff	Cavan	III.	81
26	Crumlin	172	1	8	Cavan	Upper Loughtee	Denn	Cavan	III.	83
4	Crumlin	945	1	27	Clare	Burren	Killonaghan	Ballyvaghan	II.	13
73, 82	Crumlin	197	1	18	Donegal	Banagh	Inishkeel	Glenties	III.	106
92	Crumlin	256	1	0	Donegal	Banagh	Inver	Donegal	III.	107
18, 22	Crumlin	741	1	27f	Dublin	Uppercross	Crumlin	Dublin South	I.	39
58, 71	Crumlin	661	2	27	Galway	Tiaquin	Abbeyknockmoy	Tuam	IV.	75
7, 12	Crumlin	174	3	5	Louth	Upper Dundalk	Dundalk	Dundalk	I.	178
59,60,69,70	Crumlin	869	2	28	Mayo	Carra	Turlough	Castlebar	IV.	131
102, 112	Crumlin	439	2	23	Mayo	Clanmorris	Kilvine	Claremorris	IV.	134
33	Crumlin	266	1	2	Monaghan	Farney	Magheracloone	Carrickmacross	III.	272
13	Crumlin	116	2	13	Monaghan	Monaghan	Kilmore	Monaghan	III.	276
9	Crumlin	176	1	26	Monaghan	Monaghan	Tehallon	Monaghan	III.	280
22	Crumlin Big	704	0	32	Tipperary, N.R.	Ikerrin	Rathnaveoge	Roscrea	II.	276
26	Crumlin East	1,626	0	10	Galway	Ross	Ross	Oughterard	IV.	74
22, 23	Crumlin Little	423	3	22	Tipperary, N.R.	Ikerrin	Rathnaveoge	Roscrea	II.	276
5	Crumlin or Rockfield	297	1	9g	Westmeath	Moygoish	Rathaspick	Mullingar	I.	280
59	CRUMLIN T.	—			Antrim	Upper Massereene	Camlin	Antrim	III.	30
18	CRUMLIN T.	—			Dublin	Uppercross	Crumlin	Dublin South	I.	40
39, 40	Crumlin and Tulla	822	2	24	King's Co.	Ballybritt	Kinnitty	Parsonstown	I.	126
25, 26	Crumlin West	1,088	1	23	Galway	Ross	Ross	Oughterard	IV.	74
73, 86	Crummagh	81	0	25	Galway	Kilconnell	Kilconnell	Ballinasloe	IV.	40
32, 33	Crummer	239	2	29	Fermanagh	Clanawley	Kinawley	Enniskillen	III.	193
34	Crummy	40	2	4	Fermanagh	Magherastephana	Aghalurcher	Lisnaskea	III.	215
24	Crummy	525	3	11	Leitrim	Leitrim	Kiltubbrid	Car[k]. on Shannon	IV.	103
102, 115	Crumpane	1,088	0	11	Cork, W.R.	Bear	Kilcatherine	Castletown	II.	124
3	Crumpaun	282	1	9	Leitrim	Rosclogher	Rossinver	Ballyshannon	IV.	111
9	Crump Island	63	1	18	Galway	Ballynahinch	Ballynakill	Clifden	IV.	12
37	Crumpstown or Marshallstown	354	2	24	Meath	Lower Deece	Scurlockstown	Trim	I.	192
21	Crunagh	271	1	9h	Armagh	Fews Lower	Loughgilly	Armagh	III.	47
17	Crunaght	28	2	35	Armagh	Fews Lower	Mullaghbrack	Armagh	III.	47
74	Crunaun	446	2	31	Mayo	Costello	Castlemore	Castlereagh	IV.	140
5	Cruninish Island	27	0	0	Fermanagh	Lurg	Drumkeeran	Lowtherstown	III.	207

(a) Including 8A. 0R. 0P. water.
(b) Including 18A. 1R. 29P. water.
(c) Including 6A. 3R. 5P. water.

(d) Including 95A. 2R. 26P. water.
(e) Including 16A. 0R. 25P. water.
(f) Including 60A. 3R. 32P. detached portion.

(g) Including 52A. 1R. 39P. water.
(h) Including 9A. 2R. 9P. water.

2 X

No. of Sheet of the Ordnance Survey Maps.	Townlands and Towns.	Area in Statute Acres.			County.	Barony.	Parish.	Poor Law Union in 1857.	Townland Census of 1851, Part I.	
		A.	R.	P.					Vol.	Page
18	Crunkill . . .	105	2	5a	Roscommon .	Ballintober North .	Kilglass . . .	Strokestown .	IV.	186
2	Cruntully . .	150	0	7	Fermanagh .	Lurg . . .	Drumkeeran .	Lowtherstown .	III.	205
38	Crushea . . .	171	0	16	Waterford .	Decies within Drum	Ardmore . .	Youghal . .	II.	350
18, 26	Crusheen . .	86	1	16	Clare . .	Bunratty Upper .	Inchicronan .	Ennis . .	II.	9
28	Crusheenkeenoge .	39	3	7	Limerick .	Shanid . . .	Ardagh . .	Newcastle .	II.	255
18, 26	CRUSHEEN T. . .	—			Clare . .	Bunratty Upper .	Inchicronan .	Ennis . .	II.	9
70, 83	Crusheeny . .	141	2	30	Galway . .	Clare . . .	Lackagh . .	Galway . .	IV.	22
93	Crushterra . .	361	0	11	Cork, W.R. .	East Carbery (W.D.)	Kilmichael .	Dunmanway .	II.	134
26	Crushybracken .	973	3	3	Antrim . .	Kilconway . .	Rasharkin .	Ballymena .	III.	27
63, 64	Crushyriree . .	334	0	30	Cork, E.R. .	Barrymore . .	Templeusque .	Cork . .	II.	59
35	Crussera . . .	51	0	28	Waterford .	Decies without Drum	Dungarvan .	Dungarvan .	II.	355
1, 2, 5, 6	Crutt . . .	2,456	2	19	Kilkenny .	Fassadinin . .	Castlecomer .	Castlecomer .	I.	88
82	Crutta North .	20	3	2	Tipperary, S.R.	Iffa and Offa West .	Derrygrath .	Clogheen .	II.	318
82	Crutta South .	49	1	16	Tipperary, S.R.	Iffa and Offa West .	Derrygrath .	Clogheen .	II.	318
48	Crylough . .	56	1	10	Wexford .	Forth . . .	Ballymore .	Wexford .	I.	308
21, 29	Cuba . . .	104	0	28	King's Co. .	Garrycastle .	Reynagh .	Parsonstown .	I.	138
12	Cubbindall . .	327	0	13	Antrim . .	Upper Dunluce .	Ballymoney .	Ballymoney .	III.	18
47	Cubslough . .	32	3	11	Wexford .	Forth . . .	Mayglass .	Wexford .	I.	312
76, 82	Cuckoohill . .	140	3	4	Tipperary, S.R.	Iffa and Offa West .	Derrygrath .	Clogheen .	II.	318
16,17,22,23	Cuddagh . .	1,213	3	21	Queen's Co. .	Upperwoods .	Offerlane .	Abbeyleix .	I.	251
72	Cuddoo East .	276	3	18b	Galway . .	Tiaquin . .	Monivea .	Loughrea .	IV.	79
72	Cuddoo West .	470	3	5	Galway . .	Tiaquin . .	Monivea .	Loughrea .	IV.	79
22, 28, 29	Cuffsborough .	496	2	2	Queen's Co. .	Clarmallagh .	Aghaboe .	Abbeyleix .	I.	235
108, 111	Cuhig . . .	589	0	13	Kerry . .	Glanarought .	Tuosist .	Kenmare .	II.	188
4	Cuilbalkeen .	218	2	34c	Roscommon .	Boyle . . .	Kilronan .	Boyle .	IV.	196
26	Cuilbane . .	318	0	29	Londonderry .	Coleraine . .	Desertoghill .	Coleraine .	III.	230
30	Cuilbeg . .	86	0	32	Galway . .	Dunmore . .	Tuam . .	Tuam .	IV.	36
102	Cuilbeg . .	133	3	1	Mayo . .	Costello . .	Bekan . .	Claremorris .	IV.	139
24	Cuilbeg . .	332	3	32	Roscommon .	Ballintober North .	Termonbarry .	Strokestown .	IV.	187
14, 20	Cuilbeg . .	81	2	21	Sligo . .	Carbury . .	St. John's .	Sligo .	IV.	223
39, 40	Cuilcagh . .	250	3	10d	Cavan . .	Castlerahan .	Mullagh .	Bailieborough .	III.	70
61	Cuildoo . .	489	2	34	Mayo . .	Gallen . .	Killasser .	Swineford .	IV.	149
103	Cuildooish .	261	1	37e	Galway . .	Dunkellin .	Kilcolgan .	Gort .	IV.	28
51	Cuilfadda and Der-rinshin . .	530	3	6	Roscommon .	Athlone . .	Taghmaconnell .	Athlone .	IV.	185
81	Cuilgar . .	48	2	25f	Mayo . .	Gallen . .	Killedan .	Swineford .	IV.	150
51, 52	Cuilglass . .	42	2	6	Roscommon .	Athlone . .	Drum . .	Athlone .	IV.	180
4	Cuilkeel . .	106	3	39	Roscommon .	Boyle . . .	Kilronan .	Boyle .	IV.	196
47	Cuilkillew .	677	1	21	Mayo . .	Tirawley . .	Addergoole .	Castlebar .	IV.	163
24,25,28,29	Cuillagh . .	215	2	3g	Leitrim .	Leitrim . .	Fenagh .	Mohill .	IV.	100
10	Cuillaghan . .	405	2	26h	Cavan . .	Lower Loughtee .	Drumlane .	Bawnboy .	III.	79
80	Cuillalea . .	708	3	17	Mayo . .	Gallen . .	Killedan .	Swineford .	IV.	150
66	Cuillaloughaun .	1,432	3	14i	Mayo . .	Burrishoole .	Achill .	Newport .	IV.	117
4	Cuillard . .	144	1	15j	Roscommon .	Boyle . . .	Kilronan .	Boyle .	IV.	196
90	Cuillare . .	95	3	36	Mayo . .	Carra . .	Drum . .	Castlebar .	IV.	128
92	Cuillatinny .	158	2	21	Mayo . .	Costello . .	Knock . .	Claremorris .	IV.	142
102, 112	Cuillaun . .	813	1	5	Mayo . .	Clanmorris .	Kilvine .	Claremorris .	IV.	134
62	Cuillaun . .	659	2	9	Mayo . .	Gallen . .	Kilconduff .	Swineford .	IV.	147
110	Cuillaun . .	224	1	39	Mayo . .	Kilmaine .	Robeen . .	Ballinrobe .	IV.	157
44	Cuillawinnia .	282	3	17	Roscommon .	Athlone . .	Tisrara .	Roscommon .	IV.	185
63,64,76,77	Cuilleen . .	676	2	30k	Galway . .	Ballynahinch .	Moyrus .	Clifden .	IV.	12
41,42,55,56	Cuillcen . .	208	0	10	Galway . .	Clare . . .	Cargin . .	Tuam .	IV.	18
125	Cuilleen . .	102	2	36	Galway . .	Leitrim . .	Ballynakill .	Loughrea .	IV.	51
86,87,96,97	Cuilleen . .	885	1	14	Mayo . .	Murrisk . .	Oughaval .	Westport .	IV.	161
52	Cuilleen . .	49	0	10	Roscommon .	Athlone . .	Drum . .	Athlone .	IV.	180
53, 54	Cuilleen . .	1,115	3	14l	Roscommon .	Moycarn . .	Creagh .	Ballinasloe .	IV.	206
125	Cuilleendaeagh .	81	1	20	Galway . .	Leitrim . .	Ballynakill .	Loughrea .	IV.	51
47, 48	Cuilleenirwan .	400	0	3m	Roscommon .	Athlone . .	Dysart .	Athlone .	IV.	181
47, 48	Cuilleenoolagh .	526	0	32	Roscommon .	Athlone . .	Dysart .	Athlone .	IV.	181
11, 12	Cuillenstown .	379	1	37	Louth . .	Louth . .	Darver .	Dundalk .	I.	183
49, 61	Cuillonaghtan .	1,144	1	29n	Mayo . .	Gallen . .	Killasser .	Swineford .	IV.	149
100	Cuilly . .	253	2	17	Donegal .	Tirhugh . .	Drumhome .	Donegal .	III.	146
114, 123	Cuilmore . .	140	1	11	Galway . .	Loughrea .	Kilthomas .	Loughrea .	IV.	65
31, 45	Cuilmore . .	309	3	11	Galway . .	Tiaquin . .	Kilkerrin .	Glennamaddy .	IV.	76
25	Cuilmore . .	302	2	9o	Leitrim .	Carrigallen .	Drumreilly .	Bawnboy .	IV.	91
32, 35	Cuilmore . .	97	3	33	Leitrim .	Mohill . .	Annaduff .	Mohill .	IV.	105
68, 77	Cuilmore . .	402	3	21p	Mayo . .	Burrishoole .	Burrishoole .	Newport .	IV.	119
102	Cuilmore . .	999	0	38	Mayo . .	Clanmorris .	Kilcolman .	Claremorris .	IV.	134
62	Cuilmore . .	983	1	21	Mayo . .	Gallen . .	Kilconduff .	Swineford .	IV.	147
107	Cuilmore . .	765	3	38	Mayo . .	Murrisk . .	Oughaval .	Westport .	IV.	161
51	Cuilmore . .	516	1	10	Roscommon .	Athlone . .	Taghmaconnell .	Athlone .	IV.	185
6, 7	Cuilmore . .	26	1	1	Roscommon .	Boyle . . .	Ardcarn .	Boyle .	IV.	192
17, 23	Cuilmore . .	243	1	12q	Roscommon .	Roscommon .	Clooncraff .	Strokestown .	IV.	208

(a) Including 1A. 0R. 7P. water.
(b) Including 5A. 2R. 0P. water.
(c) Including 4A. 1R. 11P. water.
(d) Including 18A. 0R. 32P. water.
(e) Including 3A. 0R. 13P. water.
(f) Including 2A. 1R. 0P. water.

(g) Including 42A. 1R. 31P. water.
(h) Including 38A. 3R. 35P. water.
(i) Including 0A. 2R. 10P. water.
(j) Including 6A. 3R. 8P. water.
(k) Including 44A. 1R. 2½P. water.
(l) Including 2A. 3R. 4P. water.

(m) Including 38A. 1R. 0P. water.
(n) Including 112A. 1R. 34P. water.
(o) Including 7A. 0R. 32P. water.
(p) Including 21A. 1R. 1P. water.
(q) Including 6A. 1R. 7P. water.

No. of Sheet of the Ordnance Survey Maps.	Townlands and Towns.	Area in Statute Acres.	County.	Barony.	Parish.	Poor Law Union in 1857.	Townland Census of 1851, Part I.	
		A. R. P.					Vol.	Page
23	Cuilmore	165 2 0a	Roscommon	Roscommon	Kiltrustan	Strokestown	IV.	211
39, 43, 44	Cuilmore	1,934 3 6	Sligo	Coolavin	Kilfree	Boyle	IV.	224
59	Cuilmullagh	1,107 0 9	Mayo	Tirawley	Addergoole	Castlebar	IV.	163
19, 20	Cuilnacappy	184 1 10	Galway	Ballymoe	Kilbegnet	Glennamaddy	IV.	8
41	Cuilnagleragh	158 2 32	Sligo	Tirerrill	Kilmactranny	Boyle	IV.	240
44	Cuilnakeava	126 2 8	Roscommon	Athlone	Taghboy	Roscommon	IV.	184
44	Cuilprughlish	183 2 28	Sligo	Coolavin	Kilfree	Boyle	IV.	224
23	Cuilrevagh	418 1 14	Roscommon	Roscommon	Kiltrustan	Strokestown	IV.	211
19, 32	Cuilsallagh	247 3 8	Galway	Tiaquin	Kilkerrin	Glennamaddy	IV.	76
40	Cuilsheeghary Beg	108 2 6	Sligo	Tirerrill	Aghanagh	Boyle	IV.	237
40	Cuilsheeghary Mòre	242 1 26	Sligo	Tirerrill	Aghanagh	Boyle	IV.	237
3	Cuiltaboolia	144 3 15	Roscommon	Boyle	Ardcarn	Boyle	IV.	192
18	Cuiltia	85 1 24	Leitrim	Drumahaire	Drumreilly	Carᴷ. on Shannon	IV.	95
12, 13	Cuilties	47 0 37	Leitrim	Drumahaire	Cloonclare	Manorhamilton	IV.	93
80, 81	Cuiltrasna	267 3 13b	Mayo	Gallen	Killedan	Swineford	IV.	150
77	Cuiltrean	227 2 11	Mayo	Burrishoole	Kilmaclasser	Westport	IV.	121
80, 91	Cuiltybo	670 2 33c	Mayo	Clanmorris	Kilcolman	Claremorris	IV.	134
72, 81	Cuiltybo	298 1 14d	Mayo	Gallen	Kilconduff	Swineford	IV.	147
20	Cuiltyboe	227 0 25	Roscommon	Frenchpark	Tibohine	Castlereagh	IV.	205
7, 11	Cuiltyconeen	137 2 25	Roscommon	Boyle	Tumna	Carᴷ. on Shannon	IV.	197
11	Cuiltyconway	163 3 15	Roscommon	Ballintober North	Kilmore	Carᴷ. on Shannon	IV.	187
102	Cuiltycreaghan	407 0 9	Mayo	Costello	Bekan	Claremorris	IV.	139
27	Cuiltydangan	252 1 21	Sligo	Tirerrill	Ballynakill	Sligo	IV.	237
1	Cuiltygower	170 3 18	Roscommon	Boyle	Kilronan	Boyle	IV.	196
27, 34	Cuiltylough	146 1 27e	Sligo	Tirerrill	Drumcolumb	Sligo	IV.	238
17	Cuiltyshinnoge	234 3 5	Roscommon	Ballintober North	Kilmore	Carᴷ. on Shannon	IV.	187
2, 3, 5, 6	Cuingareen	265 2 24	Longford	Granard	Columbkille	Longford	I.	155
48	Cuing Beg	337 2 18	Mayo	Tirawley	Kilbelfad	Ballina	IV.	168
48, 60	Cuing More	189 3 10	Mayo	Tirawley	Kilbelfad	Ballina	IV.	168
13, 18	Culbane	626 2 26	Antrim	Upper Dunluce	Loughguile	Ballymoney	III.	20
20	Culbidag	26 1 22	Antrim	Lower Glenarm	Layd	Ballycastle	III.	22
16	Culbrim Lower	37 2 12	Antrim	Upper Dunluce	Ballymoney	Ballymoney	III.	18
16	Culbrim Upper	86 3 31	Antrim	Upper Dunluce	Ballymoney	Ballymoney	III.	18
34	Culbuck	179 2 21	Tyrone	Omagh East	Drumragh	Omagh	III.	312
14	Culcavy	758 0 1f	Down	Lower Iveagh, Up. pt.	Blaris	Lisburn	III.	169
44, 50	Culcommon	156 1 27	Meath	Ratoath	Culmullin	Dunshaughlin	I.	218
49	Culcor	246 3 16	Meath	Upper Deece	Gallow	Trim	I.	193
12	Culcrow	196 1 7	Londonderry	Coleraine	Agivey	Coleraine	III.	230
23	Culcrum	115 3 32	Antrim	Kilconway	Killagan	Ballymoney	III.	27
5	Culdaff	245 1 12	Donegal	Inishowen East	Culdaff	Inishowen	III.	118
5	Culdaff Glebe	158 1 21	Donegal	Inishowen East	Culdaff	Inishowen	III.	118
5	CULDAFF T.	—	Donegal	Inishowen East	Culdaff	Inishowen	III.	118
10	Culdaloo	54 0 34	Monaghan	Monaghan	Tehallan	Monaghan	III.	280
36	Culdaly	1,827 1 15g	Sligo	Leyny	Kilmacteige	Tobercurry	IV.	231
17	Culdoo Lower	173 0 23	Antrim	Upper Dunluce	Ballymoney	Ballymoney	III.	18
17	Culdoo Upper	357 2 20	Antrim	Upper Dunluce	Ballymoney	Ballymoney	III.	18
11	Culdrum	42 2 35	Londonderry	Coleraine	Aghadowey	Coleraine	III.	229
11	Culdrum	253 0 13	Londonderry	Coleraine	Macosquin	Coleraine	III.	233
10, 11	Cules Long	164 1 38	Fermanagh	Lurg	Derryvullan	Lowtherstown	III.	204
10,11,15,16	Cules Short	127 0 8	Fermanagh	Lurg	Derryvullan	Lowtherstown	III.	204
10	Culfin	324 0 25	Galway	Ballynahinch	Ballynakill	Clifden	IV.	11
4	Culfore	84 1 36	Louth	Lower Dundalk	Ballymascanlan	Dundalk	I.	175
21, 31	Culineen	300 2 17	Donegal	Inishowen East	Moville Upper	Inishowen	III.	119
31, 32	Culkeen	354 0 28	Roscommon	Castlereagh	Kiltullagh	Castlereagh	IV.	201
7, 11	Culkeeran	243 2 30	Armagh	Tiranny	Eglish	Armagh	III.	59
61, 62	Culkeeran	134 1 36	Tyrone	Dungannon Middle	Clonfeacle	Dungannon	III.	299
27	Culky	260 0 1h	Fermanagh	Clanawley	Rossorry	Enniskillen	III.	194
46, 51	Cull	280 1 21	Wexford	Bargy	Killag	Wexford	I.	306
41	Cullaboy Lower	190 1 12	Cavan	Clanmahon	Drumlumman	Granard	III.	77
41	Cullaboy Upper	226 1 11	Cavan	Clanmahon	Drumlumman	Granard	III.	77
122	Cullagh	107 0 26	Mayo	Kilmaine	Shrule	Ballinrobe	IV.	158
4, 5	Cullagh	431 0 0	Tipperary, N.R.	Lower Ormond	Dorrha	Parsonstown	II.	283
8	Cullagh Beg	204 0 34	Sligo	Carbury	Drumcliff	Sligo	IV.	221
10, 11	Cullaghmore	154 0 9	Fermanagh	Lurg	Derryvullan	Lowtherstown	III.	204
8	Cullagh More	329 3 7	Sligo	Carbury	Drumcliff	Sligo	IV.	221
6	Cullaghreeva	32 2 2	Kildare	North Salt	Confey	Celbridge	I.	74
23, 24	Cullahill	1,052 2 10	Tipperary, N.R.	Ikerrin	Bourney	Roscrea	II.	274
34	Cullahill	267 3 30	Tipperary, N.R.	Kilnamanagh Upper	Glenkeen	Thurles	II.	278
35	Cullahill Mountain	570 2 14	Queen's Co.	Clarmallagh	Aghmacart	Abbeyleix	I.	236
84	Cullairbaun	186 1 32	Galway	Athenry	Athenry	Loughrea	IV.	4
65	Cullamore	517 1 30i	Tyrone	Clogher	Errigal Trough	Clogher	III.	296
39	Cullamus	85 2 34	Limerick	Kilmallock	St. Peter's & St. Paul's	Kilmallock	II.	250
133, 134	Cullane East	288 0 39	Cork, W.R.	East Carbery (W.D.)	Kilmacabea	Skibbereen	II.	133

(a) Including 12ᴀ. 1ʀ. 11ᴘ. water.
(b) Including 2ᴀ. 0ʀ. 10ᴘ. water.
(c) Including 30ᴀ. 0ʀ. 4ᴘ. water.

(d) Including 6ᴀ. 0ʀ. 0ᴘ. water.
(e) Including 9ᴀ. 1ʀ. 4ᴘ. water.
(f) Including 4ᴀ. 1ʀ. 0ᴘ. water.

(g) Including 9ᴀ. 3ʀ. 23ᴘ. water.
(h) Including 13ᴀ. 1ʀ. 23ᴘ. water.
(i) Including 23ᴀ. 1ʀ. 34ᴘ. water.

2 X 2

No. of Sheet of the Ordnance Survey Maps.	Townlands and Towns.	Area in Statute Acres.	County.	Barony.	Parish.	Poor Law Union in 1857.	Townland Census of 1851, Part I.	
		A. R. P.					Vol.	Page
57	Cullane Middle	491 3 37	Limerick	Coshlea	Ballylanders	Mitchelstown	II.	237
57	Cullane North	638 0 15	Limerick	Coshlea	Ballylanders	Mitchelstown	II.	237
57	Cullane South	747 2 9	Limerick	Coshlea	Ballylanders	Mitchelstown	II.	237
133	Cullane West	165 1 15	Cork, W.R.	East Carbery (W.D.)	Kilmacabea	Skibbereen	II.	133
32	Cullatagh	150 3 13	Fermanagh	Clanawley	Kinawley	Enniskillen	III.	193
35, 43	Cullaun	419 2 12a	Clare	Bunratty Upper	Quin	Tulla	II.	10
5	Cullaun	269 1 35	Clare	Burren	Rathborney	Ballyvaghan	II.	14
33	Cullaun	486 3 24	Kilkenny	Ida	The Rower	Thomastown	I.	104
18	Cullaun	414 2 6	Tipperary, N.R.	Ikerrin	Corbally	Roscrea	II.	275
30	Cullaville	145 2 25	Armagh	Fews Upper	Creggan	Castleblayney	III.	48
51	Culleen	233 0 24	Clare	Bunratty Lower	Drumline	Ennis	II.	3
11	Culleen	219 2 4b	Clare	Inchiquin	Kilkeedy	Corrofin	II.	25
32	Culleen	168 0 13c	Clare	Islands	Kilmaley	Ennis	II.	31
38	Culleen	144 1 35	Fermanagh	Knockninny	Kinawley	Lisnaskea	III.	201
43, 57	Culleen	360 1 38	Galway	Clare	Belclare	Tuam	IV.	17
8, 9, 17	Culleen	344 1 34	King's Co.	Ballycowan	Durrow	Tullamore	I.	127
1, 4	Culleen	167 1 17	Tipperary, N.R.	Lower Ormond	Dorrha	Parsonstown	II.	283
12	Culleenabohoge	287 2 28	Westmeath	Corkaree	Leny	Mullingar	I.	262
29	Culleenagh	162 2 30	Tipperary, N.R.	Eliogarty	Templemore	Thurles	II.	272
24, 30	Culleenaghamore	662 1 8	Roscommon	Ballintober North	Kilglass	Strokestown	IV.	186
36	Culleenagower	177 1 4	Westmeath	Clonlonan	Kilmanaghan	Athlone	I.	262
27	Culleenalena	97 0 7	Galway	Ross	Cong	Oughterard	IV.	73
13, 14	Culleenamore	122 1 21	Sligo	Carbury	Killaspugbrone	Sligo	IV.	222
29, 36	Culleenanory	167 0 32	Roscommon	Roscommon	Lissonuffy	Strokestown	IV.	212
11	Culleenatreen or Flagford	185 1 12	Roscommon	Boyle	Killummod	Carᵏ.on Shannon	IV.	196
19	Culleen Beg	809 1 13d	Westmeath	Moyashel & Magheradernon	Mullingar	Mullingar	I.	275
11, 12	Culleendarragh	210 3 23	Westmeath	Corkaree	Leny	Mullingar	I.	262
14	Culleenduff	107 2 30	Sligo	Carbury	Killaspugbrone	Sligo	IV.	222
6, 7	Culleenmore	459 1 34e	Longford	Granard	Columbkille	Granard	I.	155
12, 19	Culleen More	835 0 21	Westmeath	Moyashel & Magheradernon	Mullingar	Mullingar	I.	275
17	Culleenrevagh	212 0 5	Roscommon	Roscommon	Aughrim	Carᵏ.on Shannon	IV.	207
30	Culleens	530 0 36	Mayo	Tirawley	Kilmoremoy	Ballina	IV.	170
17	Culleens	2,505 0 10f	Sligo	Tireragh	Kilglass	Dromore West	IV.	234
57	Culleeny Beg	116 2 0	Kerry	Magunihy	Kilbonane	Killarney	II.	200
57	Culleeny More	348 2 3	Kerry	Magunihy	Kilbonane	Killarney	II.	200
98	Cullen	480 1 30	Cork, E.R.	Kinalea	Cullen	Kinsale	II.	94
15	Cullen	278 1 4	Fermanagh	Magheraboy	Devenish	Enniskillen	III.	210
19, 26	Cullen	525 3 26	Meath	Lower Duleek	Knockcommon	Navan	I.	196
58	Cullen	62 2 9	Tipperary, S.R.	Clanwilliam	Cullen	Tipperary	II.	307
18, 26	Cullenagh	86 1 37	Clare	Bunratty Upper	Kilraghtis	Ennis	II.	9
42	Cullenagh	119 3 18	Clare	Bunratty Upper	Quin	Tulla	II.	10
68, 69	Cullenagh	393 2 23	Clare	Clonderalaw	Killofin	Killadysert	II.	17
23, 24	Cullenagh	406 3 36	Clare	Corcomroe	Clooney	Ennistimon	II.	18
35	Cullenagh	316 2 37	Cork, E.R.	Condons&Clangibbon	Fermoy	Fermoy	II.	61
9, 18	Cullenagh	56 0 30	Cork, E.R.	Condons&Clangibbon	Kildorrery	Mitchelstown	II.	61
9, 18	Cullenagh	308 1 31	Cork, E.R.	Condons&Clangibbon	Templemolaga	Mitchelstown	II.	63
45, 46	Cullenagh	367 1 16	Cork, E.R.	Kinnatalloon	Ballynoe	Fermoy	II.	97
80, 92	Cullenagh	356 3 28	Cork, W.R.	Bantry	Kilmocomoge	Bantry	II.	120
106, 107	Cullenagh	821 2 16g	Cork, W.R.	East Carbery (W.D.)	Fanlobbus	Dunmanway	II.	131
136	Cullenagh	363 1 18h	Cork, W.R.	Ibane and Barryroe	Lislee	Clonakilty	II.	150
133, 142	Cullenagh	860 0 6	Cork, W.R.	West Carbery (E.D.)	Castlehaven	Skibbereen	II.	137
115, 116, 124, 125	Cullenagh	663 3 35	Galway	Leitrim	Ballynakill	Loughrea	IV.	51
43	Cullenagh	177 2 17	Kerry	Corkaguiny	Dingle	Dingle	II.	175
36	Cullenagh	267 0 33	Limerick	Glenquin	Monagay	Newcastle	II.	247
15	Cullenagh	330 2 15	Limerick	Owneybeg	Doon	Limerick	II.	251
26	Cullenagh	269 3 30	Queen's Co.	Ballyadams	Killabban	Athy	I.	231
26	Cullenagh	128 0 28	Queen's Co.	Ballyadams	Tankardstown	Athy	I.	232
18, 24	Cullenagh	1,531 0 11	Queen's Co.	Cullenagh	Ballyroan	Abbeyleix	I.	239
25	Cullenagh	227 1 27	Tipperary, N.R.	Owney and Arra	Templeachally	Nenagh	II.	297
80	Cullenagh	2,740 0 23	Tipperary, S.R.	Iffa and Offa West	Shanrahan	Clogheen	II.	319
8, 16	Cullenagh	365 2 35	Waterford	Middlethird	Kilmeadan	Waterford	II.	368
113	Cullenagh Beg	176 2 1	Galway	Dunkellin	Ardrahan	Gort	IV.	26
65	Cullenagh Lower	175 0 7i	Kerry	Dunkerron North	Knockane	Killarney	II.	182
113	Cullenagh More	381 2 5	Galway	Dunkellin	Ardrahan	Gort	IV.	26
80, 86	Cullenagh South	333 2 33	Tipperary, S.R.	Iffa and Offa West	Shanrahan	Clogheen	II.	319
65	Cullenagh Upper	513 3 36	Kerry	Dunkerron North	Knockane	Killarney	II.	182
59	Cullenbrone	324 1 15	Tyrone	Clogher	Errigal Keerogue	Clogher	III.	295
30	Cullen and Brownhill	212 2 18j	Leitrim	Carrigallen	Carrigallen	Bawnboy	IV.	89
17, 26	Cullencastle	390 3 4	Waterford	Middlethird	Kilbride	Waterford	II.	367

(a) Including 33ᴀ. 3ʀ. 14ᴘ. water.
(b) Including 46ᴀ. 3ʀ. 18ᴘ. water.
(c) Including 3ᴀ. 1ʀ. 37ᴘ. water.
(d) Including 81ᴀ. 2ʀ. 0ᴘ. water.

(e) Including 3ᴀ. 0ʀ. 28ᴘ. water.
(f) Including 8ᴀ. 0ʀ. 11ᴘ. Lough Scorrew.
(g) Including 5ᴀ. 2ʀ. 8ᴘ. water.

(h) Including 33ᴀ. 1ʀ. 11ᴘ. detached portion.
(i) Including 3ᴀ. 1ʀ. 5ᴘ. water.
(j) Including 2ᴀ. 2ʀ. 22ᴘ. water.

No. of Sheet of the Ordnance Survey Maps.	Townlands and Towns.	Area in Statute Acres.			County.	Barony.	Parish.	Poor Law Union in 1857.	Townland Census of 1851, Part I.	
		A.	R.	P.					Vol.	Page
8	Cullendragh	405	2	8	Meath	Fore	Killeagh	Oldcastle	I.	201
44, 50	Cullendragh	280	3	19	Meath	Upper Deece	Culmullin	Dunshaughlin	I.	193
54	Cullenfad	250	3	22	Tyrone	Dungannon Middle	Donaghmore	Dungannon	III.	301
5	Cullenhill	63	0	28	Dublin	Balrothery East	Balrothery	Balrothery	I.	19
6, 11	Cullenhugh	389	3	9a	Westmeath	Corkaree	Leny	Mullingar	I.	262
31	Cullen Lower	287	3	3	Wicklow	Arklow	Dunganstown	Rathdrum	I.	343
19	Cullenmore	54	2	20	Wicklow	Newcastle	Killiskey	Rathdrum	I.	352
7	Cullenoge	305	1	11	Wexford	Gorey	Kilcavan	Gorey	I.	317
54	Cullenramer	233	0	12	Tyrone	Dungannon Middle	Donaghmore	Dungannon	III.	301
46	Cullenstown	339	1	39	Wexford	Bargy	Bannow	Wexford	I.	304
35, 36	Cullenstown	545	3	8	Wexford	Shelmaliere West	Horetown	New Ross	I.	333
18, 22	Cullenswood	118	1	17	Dublin	Uppercross	St. Peters	Dublin South	I.	41
58	CULLEN T.	—			Tipperary, S.R.	Clanwilliam	Cullen	Tipperary	II.	307
64	Cullentra	242	0	17b	Tyrone	Clogher	Aghalurcher	Clogher	III.	291
53	Cullentra	188	0	1	Tyrone	Dungannon Lower	Killeeshil	Dungannon	III.	298
22	Cullentra	177	2	28	Wexford	Ballaghkeen	Donaghmore	Gorey	I.	293
16,17,21,22	Cullentra	575	0	21	Wexford	Gorey	Monamolin	Gorey	I.	321
37	Cullentra	111	1	19	Wexford	Shelmaliere West	Carrick	Wexford	I.	332
11	Cullentragh	243	2	3	Armagh	Armagh	Eglish	Armagh	III.	44
22	Cullentragh	244	0	10	Armagh	Orior Lower	Ballymore	Newry	III.	55
21	Cullentragh	232	0	30	Cavan	Tullygarvey	Drung	Cootehill	III.	88
21	Cullentragh	192	1	14	Cavan	Upper Loughtee	Castleterra	Cavan	III.	82
25, 31	Cullentragh	120	0	11	Fermanagh	Clanawley	Killesher	Enniskillen	III.	192
33	Cullentragh	565	3	1	Kilkenny	Ida	The Rower	Thomastown	I.	104
8, 12	Cullentragh	375	1	5	Leitrim	Drumahaire	Cloonclare	Manorhamilton	IV.	93
21	Cullentragh	143	0	33	Longford	Ratheline	Cashel	Ballymahon	I.	163
21	Cullentragh	504	1	32	Longford	Ratheline	Ratheline	Ballymahon	I.	164
68, 77	Cullentragh	106	3	5	Mayo	Burrishoole	Burrishoole	Newport	IV.	119
89, 99	Cullentragh	540	2	35c	Mayo	Carra	Ballintober	Castlebar	IV.	124
90, 100	Cullentragh	152	2	10	Mayo	Clanmorris	Mayo	Claremorris	IV.	135
92	Cullentragh	260	2	7d	Mayo	Costello	Bekan	Claremorris	IV.	139
13	Cullentragh	734	0	2	Wexford	Scarawalsh	Templeshanbo	Enniscorthy	I.	326
28	Cullentraghbane	103	0	18	Monaghan	Farney	Donaghmoyne	Carrickmacross	III.	269
23	Cullentragh Big	933	3	2	Wicklow	Ballinacor North	Knockrath	Rathdrum	I.	347
28	Cullentraghduff	124	1	0e	Monaghan	Farney	Donaghmoyne	Carrickmacross	III.	269
23	Cullentragh Little	304	0	30	Wicklow	Ballinacor North	Knockrath	Rathdrum	I.	347
23	Cullentragh Park	537	2	5	Wicklow	Ballinacor North	Knockrath	Rathdrum	I.	347
41,42,47,48	Cullentry	916	0	22	Meath	Lower Moyfenrath	Rathmolyon	Trim	I.	211
31	Cullen Upper	269	1	22	Wicklow	Arklow	Dunganstown	Rathdrum	I.	343
44, 46	Cullenwaine	742	3	14	King's Co.	Clonlisk	Cullenwaine	Roscrea	I.	129
9	Culliagh	267	1	28	Cavan	Tullyhaw	Templeport	Bawnboy	III.	94
60, 68	Culliagh	421	3	32	Donegal	Raphoe	Kilteevoge	Stranorlar	III.	139
21, 26	Culliagh	304	0	34	Fermanagh	Clanawley	Cleenish	Enniskillen	III.	190
73	Culliagh	581	1	38	Mayo	Costello	Kilmovee	Swinford	IV.	142
53	Culliagharny	579	2	27	Roscommon	Moycarn	Creagh	Ballinasloe	IV.	206
12	Culliagh Beg	342	1	20	Galway	Ross	Ross	Oughterard	IV.	74
56	Culliaghbeg	525	0	23f	Roscommon	Moycarn	Creagh	Ballinasloe	IV.	206
29, 30	Culliagh Lower	238	0	24g	Roscommon	Roscommon	Bumlin	Strokestown	IV.	208
12	Culliagh More	649	3	29	Galway	Ross	Ross	Oughterard	IV.	74
53, 54, 56	Culliaghmore	1,651	3	14h	Roscommon	Moycarn	Moore	Ballinasloe	IV.	206
58	Culliagh North	361	1	33	Galway	Tiaquin	Abbeyknockmoy	Tuam	IV.	75
58	Culliagh South	440	3	37	Galway	Tiaquin	Abbeyknockmoy	Tuam	IV.	75
29	Culliagh Upper	180	1	33	Roscommon	Roscommon	Bumlin	Strokestown	IV.	208
36, 37	Culliaghy	45	2	0	Roscommon	Ballintober South	Cloontuskert	Roscommon	IV.	188
23	Cullies	342	2	29i	Cavan	Clankee	Knockbride	Cootehill	III.	73
20	Cullies	279	2	7	Cavan	Upper Loughtee	Annagelliff	Cavan	III.	81
30	Cullies	270	1	0j	Leitrim	Carrigallen	Carrigallen	Mohill	IV.	89
7	Cullig	277	1	31	Cork, E.R.	Orrery and Kilmore	Churchtown	Mallow	II.	107
67	Culligan	98	2	37	Tyrone	Dungannon Lower	Aghaloo	Armagh	III.	296
17, 22	Cullin	77	3	32	Cavan	Tullygarvey	Kildrumsherdan	Cootehill	III.	90
49	Cullin	505	2	23	Mayo	Gallen	Killasser	Swinford	IV.	149
66, 74	Cullinagh	598	0	39	Kerry	Dunkerron North	Aghadoe	Killarney	II.	181
10, 11	Cullintraw	160	0	39k	Down	Castlereagh Lower	Comber	Newtownards	III.	162
7, 9	Cullion	372	3	29	Cavan	Tullyhaw	Kinawley	Bawnboy	III.	93
91	Cullion	210	3	24	Donegal	Banagh	Killybegs Upper	Glenties	III.	110
65	Cullion	83	0	5	Donegal	Boylagh	Lettermacward	Glenties	III.	114
53, 61	Cullion	145	1	7	Donegal	Raphoe	Leck	Letterkenny	III.	140
101,102,105	Cullion	872	3	30	Donegal	Tirhugh	Templecarn	Donegal	III.	149
47	Cullion	415	2	12	Down	Upper Iveagh Up. pt.	Clonallan	Newry	III.	174
39, 40	Cullion	288	2	23l	Fermanagh	Coole	Galloon	Clones	III.	199
17, 23	Cullion	160	1	33	Fermanagh	Tirkennedy	Enniskillen	Enniskillen	III.	221
41, 46	Cullion	846	1	37	Londonderry	Loughinsholin	Desertmartin	Magherafelt	III.	298
46	Cullion	183	2	24m	Tyrone	Dungannon Middle	Tullyniskan	Dungannon	III.	304

(a) Including 4A. 2R. 22P. water.
(b) Including 4A. 3R. 6P. water.
(c) Including 18A. 1R. 19P. water.
(d) Including 51A. 3R. 10P. water.
(e) Including 18A. 2R. 10P. water.

(f) Including 3A. 0R. 16P. water.
(g) Including 0A. 1R. 8P. water.
(h) Including 30A. 3R. 8P. water.
(i) Including 32A. 1R. 39P. water.

(j) Including 22A. 2R. 18P. water.
(k) Including 6A. 3R. 18P. water.
(l) Including 20A. 0R. 27P. water.
(m) Including 9A. 3R. 35P. Lough.

No. of Sheet of the Ordnance Survey Maps.	Townlands and Towns.	Area in Statute Acres.	County.	Barony.	Parish.	Poor Law Union in 1857.	Townland Census of 1851, Part I.	
		A. R. P.					Vol.	Page
2	Cullion	435 0 7	Tyrone	Strabane Lower	Donaghedy	Strabane	III.	320
26	Cullion	1,117 2 39	Tyrone	Strabane Upper	Cappagh	Omagh	III.	325
94, 95	Cullion Boy	1,650 2 18a	Donegal	Tirhugh	Donegal	Donegal	III.	145
4, 7	Cullionboy	435 3 34	Leitrim	Rosclogher	Killasnet	Manorhamilton	IV.	109
39	Culliondoo	148 0 26b	Fermanagh	Coole	Galloon	Lisnaskea	III.	199
51	*Cull Island*	4 1 18	Wexford	Bargy	Killag	Wexford	I.	306
15	Culloge	111 2 17	Longford	Ardagh	Mostrim	Granard	I.	152
118, 119	Cullomane East	755 2 39	Cork, W.R.	West Carbery(W.D.)	Caheragh	Skibbereen	II.	142
118	Cullomane West	364 3 5	Cork, W.R.	West Carbery(W.D.)	Caheragh	Skibbereen	II.	142
32	Cullow	111 3 25	Cavan	Castlerahan	Crosserlough	Cavan	III.	68
16, 24	Cully	417 0 29	King's Co.	Ballyboy	Killoughy	Tullamore	I.	124
25, 26	Cully	138 2 35	Leitrim	Carrigallen	Drumreilly	Bawnboy	IV.	91
42	Cully	869 1 7	Sligo	Leyny	Achonry	Tobercurry	IV.	229
32	Cullybackey	531 1 16	Antrim	Lower Toome	Ahoghill	Ballymena	III.	32
32	CULLYBACKEY T.	—	Antrim	Lower Toome	Ahoghill	Ballymena	III.	32
18, 19	Cullycapple	167 3 25	Londonderry	Coleraine	Aghadowey	Coleraine	III.	229
27	Cullyhanna Big	656 2 14	Armagh	Fews Upper	Creggan	Castleblayney	III.	48
27	Cullyhanna Little	330 3 18c	Armagh	Fews Upper	Creggan	Castleblayney	III.	48
27	CULLYHANNA T.	—	Armagh	Fews Upper	Creggan	Castleblayney	III.	49
10	Cullyleenan	76 2 24d	Cavan	Tullyhaw	Tomregan	Bawnboy	III.	96
64	Cullynane	128 2 24	Tyrone	Clogher	Aghalurcher	Clogher	III.	291
18, 19	Cullyramer	212 2 3	Londonderry	Coleraine	Aghadowey	Coleraine	III.	229
18, 19	Cullyramer	149 3 23	Londonderry	Coleraine	Desertoghill	Coleraine	III.	230
14,15,19,20	Cullyvore and Ballin-dagny	291 2 12	Longford	Ardagh	Mostrim	Granard	I.	152
26	Culmore	537 1 18	Antrim	Kilconway	Rasharkin	Ballymoney	III.	27
13, 14	Culmore	708 1 12	Londonderry	North West Liberties of Londonderry	Templemore	Londonderry	III.	246
34, 35	Culmore	160 3 19	Tyrone	Omagh East	Drumragh	Omagh	III.	312
14	Culmore Level (*Intake*)	108 0 36	Londonderry	Nth. West Liberties of Londonderry	Templemore	Londonderry	III.	246
9	Culmore Lower	275 1 33e	Londonderry	Keenaght	Tamlaght Finlagan	New T⁹Limavady	III.	237
16	Culmore Upper	141 3 32	Londonderry	Keenaght	Tamlaght Finlagan	New T⁹Limavady	III.	237
43, 44	Culmullin	1,266 2 24	Meath	Upper Deece	Culmullin	Dunshaughlin	I.	193
102,103,113	Culnacleha	395 3 10	Mayo	Costello	Annagh	Claremorris	IV.	138
32,33,36,37	Culnady	489 2 18	Londonderry	Loughinsholin	Maghera	Magherafelt	III.	242
36	Culnafay	362 1 4	Antrim	Upper Toome	Ballyscullion Grange	Ballymena	III.	33
54, 55	Culnagor	88 2 9	Tyrone	Dungannon Middle	Killyman	Dungannon	III.	303
99	Culnagore	129 3 32	Galway	Longford	Killoran	Ballinasloe	IV.	59
21, 25	Culnagore	184 0 9f	Longford	Rathcline	Cashel	Ballymahon	I.	163
26, 32	Culnagrew	593 0 37	Londonderry	Loughinsholin	Maghera now Kille-lagh	Magherafelt	III.	242
54, 55	Culnagrew	123 2 15	Tyrone	Dungannon Middle	Killyman	Dungannon	III.	303
59	Culnaha	171 0 36	Tyrone	Clogher	Errigal Keerogue	Clogher	III.	295
19, 27	Culnaman	534 1 25	Londonderry	Coleraine	Desertoghill	Coleraine	III.	230
1, 2, 3, 4	Culoort	987 1 5	Donegal	Inishowen East	Clonca	Inishowen	III.	116
12, 17	Culramoney	233 1 5	Antrim	Upper Dunluce	Ballymoney	Ballymoney	III.	18
6	Culray	658 3 15	Longford	Granard	Abbeylara	Granard	I.	154
61, 62	Culrevog	385 2 12	Tyrone	Dungannon Middle	Clonfeacle	Dungannon	III.	299
6	Cultiafadda	346 0 1	Galway	Ballymoe	Boyounagh	Glennamaddy	IV.	6
27	Cultiagh	151 2 37	Fermanagh	Tirkennedy	Derryvullan	Enniskillen	III.	221
44	Cultromer	333 3 24	Meath	Upper Deece	Culmullin	Dunshaughlin	I.	193
11, 18	Culvacullion	1,102 3 21g	Tyrone	Strabane Upper	Bodoney Lower	Gortin	III.	323
6	Culvin	395 0 30	Westmeath	Moygoish	Street	Granard	I.	281
38, 47	Cum	297 3 15	Mayo	Tirawley	Addergoole	Castlebar	IV.	163
52	Cumask	64 2 36	Tipperary, S.R.	Kilnamanagh Lower	Oughterleague	Cashel	II.	324
29, 30	Cumber	659 3 7	Down	Kinelarty	Magheradrool	Downpatrick	III.	177
23	Cumber	346 3 19	Londonderry	Tirkeeran	Cumber Upper	Londonderry	III.	249
50	Cumber	189 0 20	Tyrone	Clogher	Donacavey	Omagh	III.	294
60, 66	Cumber	599 0 24	Tyrone	Dungannon Lower	Aghaloo	Dungannon	III.	296
36, 39	Cumber Lower	532 0 33	King's Co.	Ballybritt	Kinnitty	Parsonstown	I.	125
36, 39, 40	Cumber Upper	590 0 31	King's Co.	Ballybritt	Kinnitty	Parsonstown	I.	125
106, 107	Cummeen	438 2 3	Cork, W.R.	West Carbery (E.D.)	Dromdaleague	Skibbereen	II.	140
101, 102	Cummeen	433 0 3h	Kerry	Glanarought	Tuosist	Kenmare	II.	188
21, 22	Cummeen	53 0 6	King's Co.	Garrycastle	Reynagh	Parsonstown	I.	138
21	Cummeen	109 2 32	Limerick	Coshma	Adare	Croom	II.	241
14	Cummeen	290 0 23	Sligo	Carbury	Killaspugbrone	Sligo	IV.	222
15	Cummeen	418 3 4	Waterford	Decies without Drum	Fews	Kilmacthomas	II.	356
76	Cummeenavrick	1,151 1 11	Kerry	Magunihy	Killaha	Killarney	II.	202
84	Cummeenboy	765 1 9	Kerry	Glanarought	Kenmare	Kenmare	II.	186
84	Cummeenduvasig	931 1 27	Kerry	Glanarought	Kilgarvan	Kenmare	II.	187
111	Cummeengeera	466 0 16	Kerry	Glanarought	Tuosist	Kenmare	II.	188
94	Cummeen Lower	183 0 9	Kerry	Glanarought	Kilgarvan	Kenmare	II.	187
77	Cummeennabuddoge	1,499 1 28	Kerry	Magunihy	Killaha	Killarney	II.	202

(a) Including 42A. 0R. 32P. water.
(b) Including 4A. 0R. 18P. water.
(c) Including 7A. 3R. 37P. water.
(d) Including 2A. 2R. 30P. water.
(e) Including 7A. 1R. 31P. water.
(f) Including 3A. 1R. 24P. water.
(g) Including 3A. 0R. 30P. water.
(h) Including 6A. 0R. 8P. water.

No. of Sheet of the Ordnance Survey Maps.	Townlands and Towns.	Area in Statute Acres.			County.	Barony.	Parish.	Poor Law Union in 1857.	Townland Census of 1851, Part I.	
		A.	R.	P.					Vol.	Page
102,103,110	Cummeenshrule	718	1	5	Kerry	Glanarought	Kilcaskan	Kenmare	II.	186
94	Cummeen Upper	899	1	3	Kerry	Glanarought	Kilgarvan	Kenmare	II.	187
43, 57	Cummer	559	0	15a	Galway	Clare	Cummer	Tuam	IV.	18
13	Cummer	534	0	18	Galway	Ross	Ross	Ballinrobe	IV.	74
68,69,77,78	Cummer	414	1	9	Mayo	Carra	Islandeady	Westport	IV.	128
82	Cummer	353	2	20b	Mayo	Costello	Aghamore	Swineford	IV.	137
10, 11	Cummer	769	1	39	Queen's Co.	Upperwoods	Offerlane	Mountmellick	I.	251
33	Cummer	518	2	36	Tipperary, N.R.	Upper Ormond	Templederry	Nenagh	II.	293
2	Cummer	352	1	8	Wexford	Gorey	Kilnahue	Gorey	I.	319
39, 45	Cummer Beg	493	0	5	Tipperary, N.R.	Kilnamanagh Upper	Toem	Tipperary	II.	280
14	Cummerduff	216	3	10	Cork, E.R.	Duhallow	Clonfert	Kanturk	II.	68
2	Cummerduff	644	1	23	Wexford	Gorey	Crosspatrick	Gorey	I.	316
39, 45	Cummer More	773	3	0	Tipperary, N.R.	Kilnamanagh Upper	Toem	Tipperary	II.	280
33, 39	Cummer (Mulloghney)	320	1	28	Tipperary, N.R.	Kilnamanagh Upper	Upperchurch	Thurles	II.	280
33, 39	Cummer (Quinlan)	171	3	7	Tipperary, N.R.	Kilnamanagh Upper	Upperchurch	Thurles	II.	280
109	Cummers East	389	3	30	Kerry	Glanarought	Tuosist	Kenmare	II.	188
8	Cummerstown	1,192	1	22c	Westmeath	Fore	St. Mary's	Castletowndelvin	I.	272
108, 109	Cummers West	229	2	2	Kerry	Glanarought	Tuosist	Kenmare	II.	188
5	Cummery Connell (North)	813	2	22	Cork, E.R.	Duhallow	Clonfert	Kanturk	II.	68
4, 5	Cummery Connell (South)	1,536	3	26	Cork, E.R.	Duhallow	Clonfert	Kanturk	II.	68
17	Cummingstown or Ballynamenagh Nth.	151	0	28	Antrim	Upper Dunluce	Ballymoney	Ballymoney	III.	18
26,27,33,34	Cummingstown or Claremount	451	3	0	Westmeath	Fartullagh	Enniscoffey	Mullingar	I.	268
38	Cumminstown	382	2	19	Westmeath	Moycashel	Newtown	Mullingar	I.	279
10, 11	Cumminstown	428	0	29d	Westmeath	Moygoish	Kilbixy	Mullingar	I.	279
59	Cummirk	942	0	30	Donegal	Kilmacrenan	Conwal	Stranorlar	III.	126
37	Cumran	154	1	12	Down	Kinelarty	Loughinisland	Downpatrick	III.	177
18, 23	Cumry	194	1	36e	Monaghan	Cremorne	Aghnamullen	Cootehill	III.	257
48	Cumshinstown	100	3	10	Wexford	Forth	Tacumshin	Wexford	I.	315
13	Cunaberry	324	2	26	Carlow	Forth	Ballon	Carlow	I.	3
25	Cunard	257	1	8	Dublin	Uppercross	Tallaght	Dublin South	I.	41
32	Cunghill	225	0	26	Sligo	Leyny	Achonry	Tobercurry	IV.	229
101	Cunlaghfadda	330	0	30f	Mayo	Clanmaurice	Tagheen	Claremorris	IV.	136
91	Cunlin	276	3	12	Donegal	Banagh	Killybegs Upper	Glenties	III.	110
15	Cunnagare	205	1	5	Kerry	Clanmaurice	Kilcaragh	Listowel	II.	169
15, 24	Cunnagavale	235	0	23	Limerick	Owneybeg	Tuogh	Limerick	II.	251
60, 70	Cunnagher North	682	3	10	Mayo	Carra	Turlough	Castlebar	IV.	131
70	Cunnagher South	229	2	32	Mayo	Carra	Turlough	Castlebar	IV.	131
21	Cunnahurt East	67	1	22	Tipperary, N.R.	Upper Ormond	Lisbunny	Nenagh	II.	292
21	Cunnahurt West	105	2	8	Tipperary, N.R.	Upper Ormond	Lisbunny	Nenagh	II.	292
89	Cunnaker	97	3	1	Mayo	Carra	Ballyhean	Castlebar	IV.	125
149	Cunnamore	134	1	35	Cork, W.R.	West Carbery (E.D.)	Aghadown	Skibbereen	II.	137
47	Cunnavoola	131	0	8	Kerry	Trughanacmy	Kiltallagh	Tralee	II.	212
30	Cunniamstown Big	410	1	11	Wicklow	Arklow	Dunganstown	Rathdrum	I.	343
30	Cunniamstown Little	90	0	38	Wicklow	Arklow	Dunganstown	Rathdrum	I.	343
6	Cunnicar	133	0	28	Louth	Upper Dundalk	Barronstown	Dundalk	I.	177
31, 36	Cunnigar	44	0	8	Waterford	Decies within Drum	Ringagonagh	Dungarvan	II.	353
14	Cunnihee	132	2	36	Limerick	Clanwilliam	Carrigparson	Limerick	II.	223
6, 11	Cunningburn	396	0	24	Down	Ards Lower	Newtownards	Newtownards	III.	158
70, 79	Cunninghamstown or Legnabraid	100	0	20	Donegal	Raphoe	Clonleigh	Strabane	III.	135
15	Cunnion	124	0	9	Leitrim	Drumahaire	Killarga	Manorhamilton	IV.	98
20	Cupidstown	240	2	15	Kildare	South Salt	Kilteel	Naas	I.	77
20	Cupidstownhill	301	2	39	Kildare	South Salt	Kilteel	Naas	I.	77
27	Cuppage	227	1	6	Cork, E.R.	Fermoy	Dunmahon	Fermoy	II.	79
45, 47	Cuppanagh	356	2	7	Sligo	Coolavin	Killaraght	Boyle	IV.	224
25, 38	Cur	1,069	0	10	Galway	Ross	Ross	Oughterard	IV.	74
27	Curclogh	304	2	32	Wexford	Ballaghkeen	Killisk	Enniscorthy	I.	296
39	Curglassan	214	1	3	Tyrone	Dungannon Upper	Ballyclog	Cookstown	III.	306
105	Curheen	259	1	22	Galway	Loughrea	Killeenadeema	Loughrea	IV.	64
115	Curhoor	692	0	4	Galway	Loughrea	Killeenadeema	Loughrea	IV.	64
35	Curhownagh	91	1	4	Galway	Ballynahinch	Ballindoon	Clifden	IV.	10
26	Curkacrone	45	1	8	Kilkenny	Callan	Callan	Callan	I.	83
44	Curkeen	140	1	5	Meath	Ratoath	Ratoath	Dunshaughlin	I.	219
3	Curkin	67	1	7	Monaghan	Trough	Errigal Trough	Monaghan	III.	283
66	Curlagh	365	0	13	Tyrone	Dungannon Lower	Aghaloo	Armagh	III.	296
41	Curley	382	3	28	Down	Lordship of Newry	Newry	Newry	III.	182
23, 24, 29	Curleyland and Mill Land	173	0	1	Meath	Lune	Athboy	Trim	I.	207
38, 46	Curlonan	143	0	14	Tyrone	Dungannon Middle	Pomeroy	Dungannon	III.	304
42, 50	Curly	221	0	9	Tyrone	Omagh East	Dromore	Omagh	III.	311

(a) Including 31A. 2R. 32P. water.
(b) Including 39A. 1R. 38P. water.
(c) Including 23A. 0R. 18P. water.
(d) Including 10A. 1R. 20P. water.
(e) Including 5A. 3R. 4P. water.
(f) Including 28A. 0R. 28P. water.

No. of Sheet of the Ordnance Survey Maps	Townlands and Towns.	Area in Statute Acres.			County.	Barony.	Parish.	Poor Law Union in 1857.	Townland Census of 1851. Part I.	
		A.	R.	P.					Vol.	Page
10	*Curmweela*	1	1	12	Limerick . .	Connello Lower .	Morgans . . .	Rathkeale .	II.	228
91	Curneen . .	290	2	18a	Mayo . .	Clanmorris .	Kilcolman .	Claremorris .	IV.	134
18	Curniaghanstown	180	1	38	Meath . .	Upper Slane .	Stackallan .	Navan . .	I.	225
41	Curr . . .	210	3	12	Londonderry .	Loughinsholin .	Desertmartin .	Magherafelt .	III.	240
43, 51, 52	Curr . . .	711	1	34	Tyrone . .	Omagh East .	Clogherny .	Omagh .	III.	310
98	Curra . . .	143	1	19	Cork, E.R. .	Kinalea . .	Ballymartle .	Kinsale .	II.	94
97	Curra . . .	253	2	22	Cork, E.R. .	Kinalea . .	Inishannon .	Bandon .	II.	95
112	Curra . . .	290	1	7	Cork, E.R. .	Kinalea . .	Kinure .	Kinsale .	II.	95
6	Curra . . .	187	2	3	Cork, E.R. .	Orrery and Kilmore	Kilbolane .	Kanturk .	II.	108
70	Curra . . .	163	3	9	Cork, W.R. .	West Muskerry .	Clondrohid .	Macroom .	II.	155
68	Curra . . .	174	3	3	Galway . .	Moycullen .	Moycullen .	Galway .	IV.	71
63	Curra . . .	257	0	32	Kerry . .	Iveragh . .	Glanbehy .	Cahersiveen .	II.	195
27, 28, 34	Currabaha . .	580	0	32	Tipperary, N.R.	Kilnamanagh Upper	Glenkeen .	Thurles .	II.	278
22, 23	Currabaha . .	457	3	7	Waterford .	Decies without Drum	Kilgobnet .	Dungarvan .	II.	357
15	Currabaha East .	299	2	38	Waterford .	Decies without Drum	Ballylaneen .	Kilmacthomas .	II.	354
15	Currabaha West .	354	1	35	Waterford .	Decies without Drum	Ballylaneen .	Kilmacthomas .	II.	354
75, 76, 87	Currabally . .	210	2	23b	Cork, E.R. .	Barrymore . .	Templerobin .	Cork .	II.	58
48, 49	Currabanefield .	201	1	2	Kerry . .	Trughanacmy .	Killeentierna .	Killarney .	II.	211
108	Currabeg . .	173	1	19	Cork, W.R. .	East Carbery (E.D.)	Ballymoney .	Dunmanway .	II.	127
149	Currabeg . .	59	2	38	Cork, W.R. .	West Carbery (E.D.)	Aghadown .	Skibbereen .	II.	137
142	Currabeg . .	245	2	24	Cork, W.R. .	West Carbery (E.D.)	Castlehaven .	Skibbereen .	II.	138
93	Currabeg . .	452	0	8	Kerry . .	Glanarought .	Kenmare .	Kenmare .	II.	186
31, 36	Currabeg . .	556	2	0	King's Co. .	Ballybritt .	Letterluna .	Parsonstown .	I.	126
18	Curra Beg . .	133	3	9	Limerick . .	Shanid . .	Loghill .	Glin .	II.	256
36	Currabeha . .	434	1	22	Cork, E.R. .	Condons&Clangibbon	Castlelyons .	Fermoy .	II.	60
36	Currabeha . .	168	2	15	Cork, E.R. .	Condons&Clangibbon	Knockmourne .	Fermoy .	II.	62
73	Currabeha . .	326	2	0	Cork, E.R. .	East Muskerry .	Inishcarra .	Cork .	II.	103
83	Currabeha . .	648	0	26	Cork, W.R. .	West Muskerry .	Kilmurry .	Macroom .	II.	159
110	Curraboy . .	689	2	29c	Mayo . .	Kilmaine . .	Robeen .	Ballinrobe .	IV.	157
118	Curraboy (*Kilmaine*)	117	1	8	Mayo . .	Kilmaine . .	Ballinrobe .	Ballinrobe .	IV.	152
118	Curraboy (*Knox*)	237	3	37	Mayo . .	Kilmaine . .	Ballinrobe .	Ballinrobe .	IV.	152
120, 121	Currabwee . .	469	0	33d	Cork, W.R. .	East Carbery (W.D.)	Drinagh .	Dunmanway .	II.	131
47, 48	Curracahill . .	691	3	24	Cork, W.R. .	West Muskerry .	Drishane .	Millstreet .	II.	156
48	Curracitty . .	310	2	28	Kerry . .	Trughanacmy .	Killeentierna .	Killarney .	II.	211
33, 38	Curracloe . .	192	0	15	Wexford . .	Shelmaliere East .	St. Margaret's .	Wexford .	I.	331
83	Curraclogh . .	905	1	20	Cork, W.R. .	West Muskerry .	Kilmurry .	Macroom .	II.	159
39	Curracloghan .	204	2	15	Cavan . .	Castlerahan .	Lurgan .	Oldcastle .	III.	69
14	Curraclone . .	24	0	12	Queen's Co. .	Stradbally . .	Curraclone .	Athy .	I.	246
37	Curracullenagh	866	2	31	Kerry . .	Corkaguiny .	Kilgobban .	Tralee .	II.	177
34, 35	Curradarra . .	207	0	10	Waterford .	Decies within Drum	Aglish .	Dungarvan .	II.	349
26	Curraderra . .	500	2	34e	Clare . .	Bunratty Upper .	Kilraghtis .	Ennis .	II.	9
115	Curradonohoe .	181	1	10	Cork, W.R. .	Bear . .	Killaconenagh .	Castletown .	II.	124
94	Curradrinagh .	598	1	25	Cork, W.R. .	East Carbery (W.D.)	Kilmichael .	Dunmanway .	II.	134
14, 22	Curraduff . .	565	0	10	Cork, E.R. .	Duhallow .	Clonfert .	Kanturk .	II.	68
104	Curraduff . .	218	3	33	Cork, W.R. .	Bear . .	Kilcaskan .	Castletown .	II.	122
115	Curraduff . .	122	3	12	Cork, W.R. .	Bear . .	Killaconenagh .	Castletown .	II.	124
37	Curraduff . .	160	2	16	Kerry . .	Corkaguiny .	Kilgobban .	Tralee .	II.	177
23, 29	Curraduff . .	175	1	25	Tipperary, N.R.	Ikerrin . .	Templemore .	Roscrea .	II.	276
10	Curraduff . .	394	2	28	Wexford . .	Scarawalsh .	Kilrush .	Enniscorthy .	I.	324
13, 14	Curraduff . .	386	0	10	Wexford . .	Scarawalsh .	Templeshanbo .	Enniscorthy .	I.	326
46, 47	Currafarry . .	310	1	7	Galway . .	Kilconnell .	Killosolan .	Mountbellew .	IV.	42
64, 72	Curraflugh . .	144	1	20	Kerry . .	Dunkerron North .	Knockane .	Cahersiveen .	II.	182
15	Curragh . .	93	3	13	Antrim . .	Cary . .	Culfeightrin .	Ballycastle .	III.	13
4	Curragh . .	109	0	26	Carlow . .	Rathvilly .	Hacketstown .	Shillelagh .	I.	11
27, 28	Curragh . .	278	0	20	Clare . .	Tulla Upper .	Feakle .	Scariff .	II.	39
50	Curragh . .	307	3	37	Cork, E.R. .	Barretts . .	Donaghmore .	Cork .	II.	49
65	Curragh . .	585	3	4	Cork, E.R. .	Barrymore .	Carrigtohill .	Middleton .	II.	52
23	Curragh . .	687	1	32	Cork, E.R. .	Duhallow .	Clonfert .	Kanturk .	II.	68
23, 24	Curragh . .	259	0	7	Cork, E.R. .	Duhallow .	Kilbrin .	Kanturk .	II.	72
23	Curragh . .	120	1	7	Cork, E.R. .	Duhallow .	Kilmeen .	Kanturk .	II.	72
88	Curragh . .	123	2	15	Cork, E.R. .	Imokilly .	Aghada .	Middleton .	II.	83
116	Curragh . .	27	3	2	Cork, W.R. .	Bear . .	Killaconenagh .	Castletown .	II.	124
134, 135	Curragh . .	313	0	23	Cork, W.R. .	Ibane and Barryroe	Kilkerranmore .	Clonakilty .	II.	149
141	Curragh . .	296	1	39	Cork, W.R. .	West Carbery (E.D.)	Abbeystrowry .	Skibbereen .	II.	136
47, 48	Curragh . .	996	0	36	Cork, W.R. .	West Muskerry .	Drishane .	Millstreet .	II.	156
71, 83	Curragh . .	273	2	29	Cork, W.R. .	West Muskerry .	Kilmurry .	Macroom .	II.	159
61	Curragh . .	125	0	31	Donegal . .	Raphoe . .	Leck .	Letterkenny .	III.	140
26	Curragh . .	205	3	27	Fermanagh .	Clanawley .	Killesher .	Enniskillen .	III.	192
34	Curragh . .	143	1	13f	Fermanagh .	Magherastephana .	Aghalurcher .	Lisnaskea .	III.	215
9	Curragh . .	103	1	25	Galway . .	Ballynahinch .	Ballynakill .	Clifden .	IV.	11
87	Curragh . .	971	1	16	Galway . .	Clonmacnowen .	Kilcloony .	Ballinasloe .	IV.	26
116	Curragh . .	159	2	39	Galway . .	Leitrim . .	Ballynakill .	Loughrea .	IV.	51
58, 66	Curragh . .	305	3	31	Kerry . .	Magunihy .	Aghadoe .	Killarney .	II.	199

No. of Sheet of the Ordnance Survey Maps.	Townlands and Towns.	Area in Statute Acres.	County.	Barony.	Parish.	Poor Law Union in 1857.	Townland Census of 1851, Part I.	
		A. R. P.					Vol.	Page
23, 28	Curragh	2,141 1 30	Kildare	Offaly East	Ballysax	Naas	I.	69
22, 23, 28	Curragh	2,744 0 13	Kildare	Offaly East	Kildare	Naas	I.	70
22	Curragh	188 2 17	Kilkenny	Crannagh	Ballycallan	Kilkenny	I.	84
30	Curragh	60 0 27	Kilkenny	Kells	Coolaghmore	Callan	I.	108
38, 42	Curragh	295 0 32	King's Co.	Clonlisk	Ettagh	Roscrea	I.	130
18, 26	Curragh	227 3 27	King's Co.	Geashill	Geashill	Tullamore	I.	140
6, 14	Curragh	97 0 12	Limerick	Clanwilliam	Killeenagarriff	Limerick	II.	224
36,37,44,45	Curragh	566 2 13	Limerick	Glenquin	Mahoonagh	Newcastle	II.	246
11, 12	Curragh	395 1 18	Londonderry	Coleraine	Macosquin	Coleraine	III.	233
36, 37	Curragh	411 2 21	Londonderry	Loughinsholin	Maghera	Magherafelt	III.	242
78	Curragh	114 0 3a	Mayo	Carra	Aglish	Castlebar	IV.	123
48	Curragh	220 3 2b	Mayo	Tirawley	Ballynahaglish	Ballina	IV.	164
10	Curragh	578 0 15	Meath	Upper Kells	Dulane	Kells	I.	205
28	Curragh	190 2 26	Queen's Co.	Clarmallagh	Bordwell	Donaghmore	I.	237
32	Curragh	185 0 7	Queen's Co.	Slievemargy	Killeshin	Carlow	I.	245
32	Curragh	109 2 10	Roscommon	Castlereagh	Kiltullagh	Castlereagh	IV.	201
10	Curragh	128 3 20	Tipperary, N.R.	Lower Ormond	Uskane	Borrisokane	II.	288
19	Curragh	476 2 30	Tipperary, N.R.	Owney and Arra	Castletownarra	Nenagh	II.	294
27	Curragh	104 0 30	Tipperary, N.R.	Upper Ormond	Latteragh	Nenagh	II.	292
88, 91	Curragh	1,684 0 24	Tipperary, S.R.	Iffa and Offa West	Ballybacon	Clogheen	II.	317
11	Curragh	157 0 4	Waterford	Coshmore&Coshbride	Lismore and Mocollop	Lismore	II.	345
38	Curragh	291 0 35	Waterford	Decies within Drum	Ardmore	Youghal	II.	350
29	Curragh	63 3 12	Westmeath	Brawny	St. Mary's	Athlone	I.	259
24, 31	Curragh	451 1 3	Westmeath	Moycashel	Kilcumreragh	Athlone	I.	278
3, 7	Curragh	124 0 11	Wexford	Gorey	Kilcavan	Gorey	I.	317
23, 24	Curragha	180 3 3	Leitrim	Leitrim	Kiltubbrid	Cark. on Shannon	IV.	103
32	Curragha	167 2 32	Leitrim	Mohill	Mohill	Mohill	IV.	107
30	Curraghaboy	174 3 6c	Leitrim	Carrigallen	Carrigallen	Bawnboy	IV.	89
38	Curraghabreedin	139 3 12	Cavan	Castlerahan	Crosserlough	Cavan	III.	68
9	Curraghabweehan	54 2 8	Cavan	Tullyhaw	Templeport	Bawnboy	III.	94
20	Curraghacnav	298 0 36	Waterford	Coshmore&Coshbride	Lismore and Mocollop	Lismore	II.	345
29	Curraghacronacon	131 3 32	Queen's Co.	Cullenagh	Abbeyleix	Abbeyleix	I.	238
16	Curraghacruit	251 3 13	Carlow	Idrone East	Dunleckny	Carlow	I.	7
4, 16	Curraghaderry	272 1 30d	Galway	Dunmore	Liskeevy	Tuam	IV.	35
110, 111	Curraghaderry	65 0 28	Mayo	Clanmorris	Tagheen	Claremorris	IV.	136
79	Curraghadobbin	682 0 15	Tipperary, S.R.	Iffa and Offa East	Kilmurry	Carrick on Suir	II.	314
15	Curraghadoo	132 3 0	Clare	Corcomroe	Killaspuglonane	Ennistimon	II.	19
111	Curraghadooey	721 0 37	Mayo	Clanmorris	Crossboyne	Claremorris	IV.	132
44	Curraghadoon	256 2 24	Roscommon	Athlone	Taghboy	Athlone	IV.	184
92	Curraghafeaghan	196 3 2	Donegal	Banagh	Killaghtee	Glenties	III.	109
8	Curraghafoil	947 3 2	Limerick	Coonagh	Doon	Tipperary	II.	234
19, 27	Curraghagalla North	282 0 39	Cork, E.R.	Fermoy	Glanworth	Fermoy	II.	79
27	Curraghagalla South	140 2 12	Cork, E.R.	Fermoy	Glanworth	Fermoy	II.	79
56	Curraghagower	358 0 17	Roscommon	Moycarn	Moore	Ballinasloe	IV.	206
25	Curraghakerry	193 1 1	Cork, E.R.	Fermoy	Caherduggan	Mallow	II.	77
8, 16	Curraghakimikeen	563 1 30	Limerick	Coonagh	Doon	Tipperary	II.	234
45	Curraghalaher	97 1 18	Roscommon	Athlone	St. Johns	Athlone	IV.	183
70, 71, 79	Curraghalane	152 2 23e	Donegal	Raphoe	Clonleigh	Strabane	III.	134
15	Curraghalassa	323 2 21	King's Co.	Garrycastle	Wheery or Killagally	Parsonstown	I.	139
51	Curraghaleen	439 0 29	Roscommon	Athlone	Drum	Athlone	IV.	!80
24, 32	Curraghalehane	132 2 8	Cork, E.R.	Orrery and Kilmore	Ballyclogh	Mallow	II.	106
120	Curraghalicky	317 3 5f	Cork, W.R.	West Carbery (E.D.)	Drinagh	Skibbereen	II.	139
33, 41	Curraghamulkin	1,150 0 14	Tyrone	Omagh West	Longfield West	Castlederg	III.	316
10, 11	Curraghan	275 0 17	Leitrim	Drumahaire	Drumlease	Manorhamilton	IV.	94
28	Curraghanall	56 0 18	Fermanagh	Magherastephana	Aghavea	Lisnaskea	III.	218
18, 26	Curraghanaltig	404 1 3	Cork, E.R.	Fermoy	Wallstown	Mallow	II.	83
2	Curraghanana	95 3 9	King's Co.	Kilcoursey	Kilcumreragh	Tullamore	I.	141
25, 33	Curraghanearla	153 2 27	Cork, E.R.	Fermoy	Mallow	Mallow	II.	81
71	Curraghanearla	437 3 1	Cork, W.R.	East Muskerry	Aghinagh	Macroom	II.	153
8	Curraghane or Carn	740 0 27	Queen's Co.	Portnahinch	Coolbanagher	Mountmellick	I.	244
22	Curraghaneety	106 0 38	Tipperary, N.R.	Upper Ormond	Aghnameadle	Nenagh	II.	288
26	Curraghaniron or Halfquarter	166 0 18	Sligo	Leyny	Killoran	Tobercurry	IV.	230
15	Curraghanoe	140 0 9g	Cavan	Upper Loughtee	Castleterra	Cavan	III.	82
20, 28	Curraghanolomer	367 3 35	Cork, E.R.	Condons&Clangibbon	Macroney	Fermoy	II.	63
27	Curraghanuddy	367 3 8	Tipperary, N.R.	Upper Ormond	Kilnaneave	Nenagh	II.	291
45, 54	Curraghard	106 1 13	Cork, E.R.	Barrymore	Gortroe	Fermoy	II.	55
13	Curraghard	319 1 19	Roscommon	Frenchpark	Tibohine	Castlereagh	IV.	205
26, 27	Curragharneen	394 3 15	Tipperary, N.R.	Upper Ormond	Kilmore	Nenagh	II.	291
25	Curraghashillaun	76 2 34h	Leitrim	Carrigallen	Oughteragh	Bawnboy	IV.	92
7, 8	Curraghataggart	407 2 9	Waterford	Upperthird	Guilcagh	Carrick on Suir	II.	370
25, 29	Curraghatawy	253 0 26	Leitrim	Carrigallen	Drumreilly	Bawnboy	IV.	91
5, 13	Curraghateskin	594 0 33	Waterford	Glenahiry	Kilronan	Clonmel	II.	365

(a) Including 25A. 3R. 36P. water.
(b) Including 15A. 3R. 16P. water.
(c) Including 20A. 1R. 20P. water.

(d) Including 8A. 2R. 23P. water.
(e) Including 3A. 0R. 27P. water.
(f) Including 0A. 2R. 24P. water.

(g) Including 5A. 2R. 2P. water.
(h) Including 6A. 2R. 30P. water.

No. of Sheet of the Ordnance Survey Maps.	Townlands and Towns.	Area in Statute Acres. A. R. P.	County.	Barony.	Parish.	Poor Law Union in 1857.	Townland Census of 1851, Part I. Vol.	Page
81, 87	Curraghatoor	340 3 11	Tipperary, S.R.	Iffa and Offa West	Tubbrid	Clogheen	II.	321
10	Curraghatoosane	296 2 15a	Kerry	Iraghticonnor	Listowel	Listowel	II.	192
18	Curraghatouk	153 0 16b	Kerry	Clanmaurice	Duagh	Listowel	II.	168
4, 16	Curraghaun	589 2 19	Galway	Dunmore	Dunmore	Tuam	IV.	33
16, 29	Curraghaun	426 0 21	Galway	Dunmore	Tuam	Tuam	IV.	36
118	Curraghavaddra	194 0 12	Cork, W.R.	Bantry	Durrus	Bantry	II.	119
21, 29	Curraghavarna and Portavrolla	235 1 11	King's Co.	Garrycastle	Reynagh	Parsonstown	I.	138
23	Curraghaveara	67 1 12	Limerick	Clanwilliam	Grean	Limerick	II.	224
19, 25	Curraghaviller	254 1 15	Tipperary, N.R.	Owney and Arra	Templeachally	Nenagh	II.	297
20	Curraghavoe	941 0 12	Cork, E.R.	Condons&Clangibbon	Brigown	Mitchelstown	II.	59
52	Curraghavogy	274 2 13c	Donegal	Kilmacrenan	Gartan	Letterkenny	III.	127
74, 80	Curraghavoke	631 2 23	Tipperary, S.R.	Clanwilliam	Templeneiry	Tipperary	II.	311
33, 34	Curraghawaddra	105 2 23	Cork, E.R.	Fermoy	Monanimy	Mallow	II.	81
60	Curraghawaddra	396 2 9	Cork, W.R.	East Muskerry	Aghinagh	Macroom	II.	153
20, 33	Curraghbaghla	178 1 26d	Galway	Killian	Athleague	Mountbellew	IV.	43
3, 4	Curraghballintlea	568 0 32	Waterford	Upperthird	Fenoagh	Carrick on Suir	II.	369
23	Curraghbane	78 1 0	Westmeath	Kilkenny West	Drumraney	Ballymahon	I.	273
121	Curraghbaun	37 2 2	Mayo	Kilmaine	Kilmainebeg	Ballinrobe	IV.	155
19	Curraghbaun	96 1 26	Tipperary, N.R.	Owney and Arra	Youghalarra	Nenagh	II.	297
73	Curraghbeg	1,078 1 12e	Cork, E.R.	East Muskerry	Athnowen	Cork	II.	101
96, 97	Curragh Beg	33 3 39	Galway	Athenry	Kiltullagh	Loughrea	IV.	5
32	Curragh Beg	126 2 15	Galway	Tiaquin	Kilkerrin	Glennamaddy	IV.	76
72	Curragh Beg	356 0 2	Kerry	Dunkerron North	Knockane	Cahersiveen	II.	182
21	Curraghbeg	121 2 1	Limerick	Kenry	Adare	Croom	II.	248
17	Curraghbeg	232 1 10	Louth	Ardee	Ardee	Ardee	I.	171
35	Curraghbeg	41 3 16	Westmeath	Clonlonan	Kilcleagh	Athlone	I.	261
39, 40	Curraghbehy	298 2 23	Kilkenny	Knocktopher	Killahy	Waterford	I.	112
87, 99	Curraghbinny	586 1 11	Cork, E.R.	Kerrycurrihy	Carrigaline	Cork	II.	92
19	Curraghbog	123 2 15	Galway	Ballymoe	Kilbegnet	Glennamaddy	IV.	8
37, 42	Curraghbonaun	848 3 5	Sligo	Leyny	Achonry	Tobercurry	IV.	229
19	Curraghbowen	138 2 22	Cork, E.R.	Condons&Clangibbon	Kilgullane	Mitchelstown	II.	61
32, 41	Curraghbower	220 3 26	Cork, E.R.	Duhallow	Kilshannig	Mallow	II.	74
67	Curraghboy	226 3 12	Cork, E.R.	Imokilly	Youghal	Youghal	II.	91
47	Curraghboy	167 1 21	Galway	Killian	Killeroran	Mountbellew	IV.	44
16	Curraghboy	141 1 20	Mayo	Erris	Kilmore	Belmullet	IV.	146
45, 48	Curraghboy	743 1 12	Roscommon	Athlone	Cam	Athlone	IV.	179
37	Curraghboy	306 1 20	Sligo	Leyny	Kilmacteige	Tobercurry	IV.	231
7	Curraghboy	88 2 11	Westmeath	Fore	Rathgarve	Castletowndelvin	I.	271
17	Curraghboy	264 2 15	Westmeath	Rathconrath	Piercetown	Mullingar	I.	283
48	CURRAGHBOY T.	—	Roscommon	Athlone	Cam	Athlone	IV.	180
2	Curraghboy or Woodfield	624 3 23	King's Co.	Kilcoursey	Kilbride	Tullamore	I.	141
19	Curraghbrack	123 1 39	Westmeath	Moyashel and Magheradernon	Rathconnell	Mullingar	I.	276
21	Curraghbridge	435 0 29	Limerick	Kenry	Adare	Croom	II.	248
34	Curraghcarroll	68 2 25	Tipperary, N.R.	Kilnamanagh Upper	Glenkeen	Thurles	II.	278
88, 91	Curraghcloney	316 2 31	Tipperary, S.R.	Iffa and Offa West	Newcastle	Clogheen	II.	319
81, 87	Curraghcloney	218 0 5	Tipperary, S.R.	Iffa and Offa West	Tubbrid	Clogheen	II.	321
2, 7	Curraghcloonabro East	452 2 23	Cork, E.R.	Orrery and Kilmore	Shandrum	Kanturk	II.	110
2, 7	Curraghcloonabro West	464 1 16	Cork, E.R.	Orrery and Kilmore	Shandrum	Kanturk	II.	110
65	Curraghcondon	158 0 39	Cork, E.R.	Barrymore	Templenacarriga	Middleton	II.	58
74, 86	Curraghconway	527 0 29	Cork, E.R.	Cork	St. Finbars	Cork	II.	65
24, 32	Curraghcreen	181 1 25	Cork, E.R.	Duhallow	Ballyclogh	Mallow	II.	67
30	Curraghcreen	354 2 24f	Galway	Ballymoe	Tuam	Tuam	IV.	10
29	Curraghcreen	36 1 15	Galway	Dunmore	Tuam	Tuam	IV.	36
10, 16	Curraghcroneen	480 1 33	Kerry	Clanmaurice	Dysert	Listowel	II.	169
109	Curraghcrowly East	327 3 36	Cork, W.R.	East Carbery (E.D.)	Ballymoney	Dunmanway	II.	127
108, 109	Curraghcrowly West	242 0 38	Cork, W.R.	East Carbery (E.D.)	Ballymoney	Dunmanway	II.	127
45, 54	Curraghdermot	719 2 31	Cork, E.R.	Barrymore	Britway	Middleton	II.	52
2	Curraghderrig	523 0 0	Kerry	Iraghticonnor	Aghavallen	Listowel	II.	189
43	Curraghdoo	98 2 14	Meath	Upper Deece	Kilmore	Dunshaughlin	I.	193
13	Curraghduff	77 2 37	Kilkenny	Crannagh	Freshford	Kilkenny	I.	85
40	Curraghduff	655 3 11	Tipperary, N.R.	Kilnamanagh Upper	Upperchurch	Thurles	II.	280
31, 32	Curraghduff	206 2 17	Tipperary, N.R.	Owney and Arra	Killoscully	Nenagh	II.	295
3, 7	Curraghduff	394 2 7	Waterford	Upperthird	Mothel	Carrick on Suir	II.	371
6, 14	Curraghduff	1,706 3 11	Waterford	Upperthird	Rathgormuck	Carrick on Suir	II.	371
17	Curraghduff	106 2 24	Wexford	Gorey	Monamolin	Gorey	I.	321
34, 39	Curraghduff	187 1 34	Wexford	Shelburne	Ballybrazil	New Ross	I.	327
39, 40	Curraghduff East	147 1 22	Galway	Moycullen	Kilcummin	Oughterard	IV.	66
39, 40	Curraghduff Middle	106 2 20	Galway	Moycullen	Kilcummin	Oughterard	IV.	67
80	Curraghduff West	050 0 27	Galway	Moycullen	Kilcummin	Oughterard	IV.	67
29	Curraghduffy	80 0 26	Roscommon	Roscommon	Lissonuffy	Strokestown	IV.	212

(a) Including 3A. 0R. 9P. water.
(b) Including 21A. 0R. 16P. water.
(c) Including 37A. 1R. 24P. water.
(d) Including 0A. 3R. 0P. water.
(e) Including 21A. 0R. 35P. water.
(f) Including 14A. 0R. 16P. water.

No. of Sheet of the Ordnance Survey Maps	Townlands and Towns.	Area in Statute Acres.			County.	Barony.	Parish.	Poor Law Union in 1857.	Townland Census of 1851, Part I.	
		A.	R.	P.					Vol.	Page
104, 117	Curragh East . .	369	0	9	Cork, W.R. .	Bear . .	Kilcaskan . .	Castletown .	II.	122
4	Curragh East . .	111	0	37	Dublin . .	Balrothery West	Hollywood . .	Balrothery .	I.	23
6	Curragh East . .	49	2	26	Galway . .	Ballymoe . .	Templetogher .	Glennamaddy .	IV.	9
84	Curragheenbrien .	209	1	29	Cork, E.R. .	East Muskerry .	Kilbonane . .	Bandon . .	II.	104
29	Curraghfad . .	166	1	8	Fermanagh .	Magherastephana .	Aghalurcher .	Lisnaskea .	III.	215
22, 23	Curraghfarm . .	206	1	3	Kildare . .	Offaly East .	Kildare . . .	Naas . .	I.	70
7	Curraghfore . .	53	2	2	Leitrim . .	Drumahaire .	Cloonclare . .	Manorhamilton	IV.	93
7	Curraghfore . .	203	1	29	Leitrim . .	Rosclogher .	Killasnet . .	Manorhamilton	IV.	109
34	Curraghfurnisha .	46	3	28	Tipperary, N.R.	Kilnamanagh Upper	Glenkeen . .	Thurles . .	II.	278
6	Curraghglass . .	175	3	8	Cavan . .	Tullyhaw .	Templeport .	Enniskillen .	III.	94
28, 34	Curraghglass . .	232	1	13	Tipperary, N.R.	Kilnamanagh Upper	Glenkeen . .	Thurles . .	II.	278
4	Curraghglass . .	1,222	0	18	Tipperary, N.R.	Lower Ormond .	Lorrha . .	Borrisokane .	II.	285
33	Curragh Glebe .	105	0	2	Tyrone . .	Omagh West .	Longfield West .	Castlederg .	III.	316
10, 19	Curraghgorm . .	721	2	23	Cork, E.R. .	Condons&Clangibbon	Marshalstown .	Mitchelstown .	II.	63
34	Curraghgraigue .	165	3	14	Tipperary, N.R.	Kilnamanagh Upper	Glenkeen . .	Thurles . .	II.	278
19	Curraghgraigue .	655	3	26	Wexford . .	Scarawalsh .	Templeshanbo .	Enniscorthy .	I.	326
27	Curraghgraigue Lower	106	3	23	Tipperary, N.R.	Upper Ormond .	Kilnaneave .	Nenagh . .	II.	291
27	Curraghgraigue Upper	184	1	25	Tipperary, N.R.	Upper Ormond .	Kilnaneave .	Nenagh . .	II.	291
135	Curraghgrane Beg .	72	1	6	Cork, W.R. .	Ibane and Barryroe	Desert . .	Clonakilty .	II.	148
135	Curraghgrane More	110	2	4	Cork, W.R. .	East Carbery (E.D.)	Desert . .	Clonakilty .	II.	127
19	Curraghinalt . .	526	3	3a	Tyrone . .	Strabane Upper .	Bodoney Lower .	Gortin . .	III.	323
66	Curraghishal . .	232	2	6	Cork, E.R. .	Imokilly . .	Killeagh . .	Youghal . .	II.	88
34	Curraghkeal . .	156	0	14	Tipperary, N.R.	Kilnamanagh Upper	Glenkeen . .	Thurles . .	II.	278
39	Curraghkeel . .	67	2	1	Cavan . .	Castlerahan .	Lurgan . .	Oldcastle .	III.	69
17, 25	Curraghkeel . .	107	1	9	Clare . .	Inchiquin . .	Rath . .	Corrofin . .	II.	27
18	Curraghkehoe . .	261	3	22	Kilkenny . .	Crannagh .	Ballycallan .	Kilkenny . .	I.	84
2, 6	Curraghkiely . .	848	3	3	Waterford .	Upperthird .	Rathgormuck .	Clonmel . .	II.	371
49	Curraghkilbran .	282	3	16	Limerick . .	Coshlea . .	Galbally . .	Mitchelstown .	II.	238
43	Curraghkilleen .	74	3	6	Clare . .	Bunratty Lower .	Kilfinaghta .	Tulla . .	II.	4
22	Curraghlahan . .	126	0	5	King's Co. .	Garrycastle .	Reynagh . .	Parsonstown .	I.	138
7, 8, 15, 16	Curraghlahan . .	516	0	0	Limerick . .	Coonagh . .	Doon . .	Tipperary .	II.	234
102	Curraghlahan . .	282	1	24	Mayo . .	Costello . .	Knock . .	Claremorris .	IV.	142
36, 37	Curraghlane . .	343	2	7	Kilkenny . .	Ida . . .	Dysartmoon .	New Ross .	I.	101
25	Curraghlane . .	645	3	33	Londonderry .	Keenaght . .	Dungiven . .	Newᵀ Limavady	III.	236
25	Curraghlane Lower	306	0	22	Kilkenny . .	Gowran . .	Powerstown .	Thomastown .	I.	97
25	Curraghlane Upper	262	2	34	Kilkenny . .	Gowran . .	Powerstown .	Thomastown .	I.	97
22	Curraghlare . .	28	2	1	Fermanagh .	Tirkennedy .	Derryvullan .	Enniskillen .	III.	221
39, 44	Curraghlawn . .	346	2	4	Wicklow . .	Ballinacor South .	Kilpipe . .	Shillelagh .	I.	349
53	Curraghlea . .	310	2	28	Donegal . .	Kilmacrenan .	Conwal . .	Letterkenny .	III.	126
78	Curraghleagh . .	95	3	9	Cork, E.R. .	Imokilly . .	Kilmacdonagh .	Youghal . .	II.	88
29, 38	Curraghleha East .	56	0	31	Kerry . .	Trughanacmy .	Ratass . .	Tralee . .	II.	213
31, 32	Curraghlehanagh .	407	3	38	Galway . .	Tiaquin . .	Kilkerrin . .	Glennamaddy .	IV.	76
29, 38	Curraghleha West .	74	2	22	Kerry . .	Trughanacmy .	Ratass . .	Tralee . .	II.	213
34	Curraghleigh . .	146	3	16	Tipperary, N.R.	Kilnamanagh Upper	Glenkeen . .	Thurles . .	II.	278
27	Curraghleigh . .	140	2	33	Tipperary, N.R.	Upper Ormond .	Dolla . .	Nenagh . .	II.	290
36	Curragh Lower .	120	3	11b	Cork, E.R. .	Condons&Clangibbon	Clondulane .	Fermoy . .	II.	60
31	Curragh Lower .	182	2	5	King's Co. .	Eglish . . .	Drumcullen .	Parsonstown .	I.	134
32, 33	Curraghmacall .	1,088	1	15c	Tyrone . .	Omagh West .	Longfield West .	Castlederg .	III.	316
29	Curraghmacdonagh	25	3	29	Kerry . .	Trughanacmy .	Ballymacelligott .	Tralee . .	II.	207
29, 38	Curraghmacdonagh	102	3	33	Kerry . .	Trughanacmy .	Ballyseedy .	Tralee . .	II.	208
44, 45	Curraghmarky .	1,112	0	13	Tipperary, N.R.	Kilnamanagh Upper	Doon . . .	Tipperary .	II.	277
43, 46	Curraghmartin .	153	3	1	Kilkenny . .	Iverk . . .	Aglish . .	Waterford .	I.	105
31, 32	Curraghmartin .	123	2	34	Leitrim . .	Leitrim . .	Annaduff . .	Carʳ. on Shannon	IV.	99
29	Curragh (Mechum) .	7	3	28	Westmeath .	Brawny . .	St. Mary's .	Athlone . .	I.	259
24	Curraghmeelagh .	271	2	29	King's Co. .	Ballyboy . .	Killoughy .	Tullamore .	I.	124
34	Curraghmoghaun .	112	3	12	Clare . .	Bunratty Upper .	Clooney . .	Ennis . .	II.	8
39	Curraghmore . .	208	3	35	Cavan . .	Castlerahan .	Lurgan . .	Oldcastle .	III.	69
11, 20	Curragh More . .	523	3	17	Cork, E.R. .	Condons&Clangibbon	Brigown . .	Mitchelstown .	II.	59
5	Curraghmore . .	318	1	5	Fermanagh .	Lurg . . .	Drumkeeran .	Lowtherstown .	III.	206
96, 97	Curragh More . .	95	0	25	Galway . .	Athenry . .	Kiltullagh .	Loughrea . .	IV.	5
69, 82	Curraghmore . .	792	3	11	Galway . .	Clare . .	Claregalway .	Galway . .	IV.	18
41, 55	Curraghmore . .	365	2	15d	Galway . .	Clare . .	Killursa . .	Tuam . .	IV.	21
117, 118	Curraghmore . .	139	3	38	Galway . .	Longford .	Lickmolassy .	Portumna .	IV.	61
31, 32	Curragh More . .	273	0	21	Galway . .	Tiaquin . .	Kilkerrin . .	Glennamaddy .	IV.	77
72, 73	Curragh More . .	1,282	2	27e	Kerry . .	Dunkerron North .	Knockane . .	Killarney .	II.	182
32,33,36,37	Curraghmore . .	467	2	10	Kilkenny . .	Ida . . .	Jerpoint West .	New Ross .	I.	102
44	Curraghmore . .	239	2	0	Kilkenny . .	Ida . . .	Kilcolumb .	Waterford .	I.	102
35	Curraghmore . .	576	2	3	Kilkenny . .	Iverk . . .	Owning . .	Carrick on Suir	I.	106
31	Curraghmore . .	696	0	9	King's Co. .	Eglish . . .	Drumcullen .	Parsonstown .	I.	134
13	Curraghmore . .	592	3	26	King's Co. .	Garrycastle .	Clonmacnoise .	Parsonstown .	I.	135
18, 19	Curraghmore . .	204	1	1	Longford .	Moydow . .	Moydow . .	Ballymahon .	I.	162
90	Curraghmore . .	160	2	30	Mayo . .	Carra . .	Drum . .	Castlebar .	IV.	128
47, 59	Curraghmore . .	1,068	2	18f	Mayo . .	Tirawley . .	Addergoole .	Castlebar .	IV.	163

(a) Including 4A. 2R. 19P. water.
(b) Including 8A. 2R. 10P. water.
(c) Including 18A. 2R. 22P. water.
(d) Including 9A. 1R. 24P. water.
(e) Including 31A. 0R. 23P. water.
(f) Including 128A. 3R. 32P. water.

No. of Sheet of the Ordnance Survey Maps.	Townlands and Towns.	Area in Statute Acres.			County.	Barony.	Parish.	Poor Law Union in 1857.	Townland Census of 1851, Part I.	
		A.	R.	P.					Vol.	Page
21	Curraghmore . .	325	1	25	Queen's Co. .	Clandonagh . .	Skirk . . .	Donaghmore .	I.	235
6	Curraghmore . .	402	0	1	Sligo . .	Carbury . .	Rossinver . .	Sligo . .	IV.	223
35	Curraghmore . .	268	2	23	Tipperary, N.R.	Eliogarty . .	Loughmoe East .	Thurles . .	II.	271
10	Curraghmore . .	321	2	13	Tipperary, N.R.	Lower Ormond .	Finnoe . . .	Borrisokane .	II.	284
9	Curraghmore . .	320	2	10	Tipperary, N.R.	Lower Ormond .	Kilbarron . .	Borrisokane .	II.	284
19, 25	Curraghmore . .	1,055	0	19	Tipperary, N.R.	Owney and Arra .	Kilmastulla .	Nenagh . .	II.	295
3, 4, 7, 8	Curraghmore . .	1,186	0	37	Waterford . .	Upperthird . .	Clonagam . .	Carrick on Suir	II.	369
19	Curraghmore . .	399	2	26	Westmeath .	Moyashel & Maghera-dernon . .	Rathconnell .	Mullingar .	I.	276
44	Curraghmore . .	320	3	4	Wexford . .	Shelburne . .	Rathroe . .	New Ross .	I.	328
45	Curraghmore . .	461	0	1	Wexford . .	Shelburne . .	Tintern . .	New Ross .	I.	329
38,39,47,48	Curraghmore East .	340	3	29	Kerry . .	Trughanacmy .	Currans . .	Killarney .	II.	209
29	Curraghmoreen .	152	0	38	Waterford . .	Decies without Drum	Kilmolash .	Dungarvan .	II.	357
38, 47, 48	Curraghmore West .	784	0	0	Kerry . .	Trughanacmy .	Currans . .	Killarney .	II.	209
6, 7, 18, 19	Curraghmulmurry .	512	0	16	Galway . .	Ballymoe . .	Ballynakill .	Glennamaddy .	IV.	5
21, 22	Curraghnabania .	620	3	28	Leitrim . .	Carrigallen . .	Oughteragh .	Bawnboy . .	IV.	92
31	Curraghnabola .	269	2	1	Wexford . .	Bantry . . .	Kilcowanmore .	Enniscorthy .	I.	300
2, 4	Curraghnaboley .	71	3	30	Roscommon .	Boyle . . .	Kilronan . .	Boyle . .	IV.	196
55	Curraghnaboll .	410	2	20	Roscommon .	Athlone . .	Drum . . .	Athlone . .	IV.	180
34	Curraghnaboola .	152	0	27	Tipperary, N.R.	Kilnamanagh Upper	Glenkeen . .	Thurles . .	II.	278
14,15,23,24	Curraghnaboul .	83	0	33	Limerick . .	Clanwilliam .	Drumkeen .	Limerick .	II.	223
20	Curraghnadeely .	48	0	37	Limerick . .	Connello Lower .	Nantinan . .	Rathkeale .	II.	229
2	Curraghnadeige .	57	3	32	Queen's Co. .	Tinnahinch . .	Kilmanman .	Mountmellick .	I.	249
34, 35	Curraghnadimpaun .	168	0	13	Kilkenny . .	Kells . . .	Tullahought .	Carrick on Suir	I.	110
11	Curraghnagap .	117	3	26	Sligo . .	Tireragh . .	Easky . . .	Dromore West .	IV.	233
3, 4	Curraghnagarraha .	223	3	8	Waterford .	Upperthird . .	Fenoagh . .	Carrick on Suir	II.	370
5	Curraghnagree .	172	1	29	Waterford . .	Glenahiry . .	Kilronan . .	Clonmel . .	II.	365
62	Curraghnalaght .	430	1	25	Cork, E.R. .	East Muskerry .	Garrycloyne .	Cork . .	II.	103
120	Curraghnaloughra .	356	0	28	Cork, W.R. .	East Carbery(W.D.)	Drinagh . .	Skibbereen .	II.	131
22	Curraghnamaddree .	210	1	39	Waterford .	Decies without Drum	Colligan . .	Dungarvan .	II.	354
33	Curraghnamoe .	9	2	27	Tipperary, N.R.	Kilnamanagh Upper	Upperchurch .	Thurles . .	II.	280
88, 97	Curraghnanav .	281	3	14	Kerry . .	Iveragh . .	Prior . . .	Cahersiveen .	II.	198
39, 40	Curraghnatinny .	158	2	22	Tipperary, N.R.	Kilnamanagh Upper	Moyaliff . .	Thurles . .	II.	279
45	Curraghnaveen .	123	0	36	Roscommon .	Athlone . .	Rahara . .	Roscommon .	IV.	183
22	Curraghnawall .	235	2	38	Leitrim . .	Carrigallen . .	Oughteragh .	Bawnboy . .	IV.	92
20	Curragho . .	118	3	20a	Cavan . .	Upper Loughtee .	Annagelliff .	Cavan . .	III.	81
28, 32	Curraghoaghry .	97	3	30	Leitrim . .	Leitrim . .	Mohill . .	Mohill . .	IV.	104
23, 31	Curraghodea . .	698	0	17	Clare . .	Inchiquin . .	Inagh . . .	Ennistimon .	II.	25
68, 77	Curraghomongan .	1,417	3	28b	Donegal . .	Raphoe . .	Stranorlar .	Stranorlar .	III.	142
19, 27	Curraghoo Beg .	291	2	2	Cork, E.R. .	Fermoy . .	Glanworth .	Mitchelstown .	II.	79
27	Curraghoo More .	198	0	39	Cork, E.R. .	Fermoy . .	Glanworth .	Fermoy . .	II.	79
25	Curraghphadeen .	143	0	39	Cork, E.R. .	Fermoy . .	Mallow . .	Mallow . .	II.	81
7	Curraghphilipeen .	224	0	11	Waterford .	Upperthird . .	Mothel . .	Carrick on Suir	II.	371
45	Curraghphlibbode .	98	2	12	Cork, E.R. .	Barrymore . .	Gortroe . .	Fermoy . .	II.	55
59	Curraghpoor . .	337	0	31	Tipperary, S.R.	Clanwilliam .	Rathlynin .	Tipperary .	II.	309
44	Curraghprevin .	503	2	15	Cork, E.R. .	Barrymore . .	Rathcormack .	Fermoy . .	II.	57
28	Curraghreigh North	331	2	14	Waterford .	Coshmore&Coshbride	Lismore & Mocollop	Lismore .	II.	345
28	Curraghreigh South	274	0	3	Waterford .	Coshmore&Coshbride	Lismore & Mocollop	Lismore .	II.	345
19	Curraghrevagh .	429	1	38	Galway . .	Ballymoe . .	Kilbegnet .	Glennamaddy .	IV.	8
49	Curraghroche .	396	2	38	Limerick . .	Coshlea . .	Galbally . .	Mitchelstown .	II.	238
29	Curraghroche .	514	2	28	Waterford .	Decies without Drum	Affane . . .	Dungarvan .	II.	353
97, 105	Curraghroe . .	99	2	35	Galway . .	Loughrea . .	Kilconickny .	Loughrea .	IV.	63
29, 30, 36	Curraghroe . .	146	0	21	Roscommon .	Roscommon . .	Lissonuffy .	Strokestown .	IV.	212
23	Curraghroodle .	46	1	3	Westmeath .	Kilkenny West .	Drumraney .	Ballymahon .	I.	273
31	Curraghrour East .	572	3	2c	Cork, E.R. .	Duhallow . .	Clonmeen .	Kanturk . .	II.	69
31	Curraghrour West .	480	3	11d	Cork, E.R. .	Duhallow . .	Clonmeen .	Kanturk . .	II.	69
15	Curraghs . .	513	3	24	Cork, E.R. .	Duhallow . .	Kilbrin . .	Kanturk . .	II.	72
105	Curraghs . .	55	1	23	Galway . .	Loughrea . .	Loughrea . .	Loughrea .	IV.	65
13	Curraghsallagh .	1,099	3	6	Roscommon .	Frenchpark . .	Tibohine . .	Swineford .	IV.	205
18	Curraghscarteen .	116	1	9	Kilkenny . .	Crannagh . .	Tullaroan .	Kilkenny .	I.	88
62	Curraghscarteen .	405	3	29	Tipperary, S.R.	Middlethird .	Rathcool . .	Cashel . .	II.	329
87	Curraghslagh .	79	0	10	Tipperary, S.R.	Iffa and Offa West .	Shanrahan . .	Clogheen .	II.	319
18	Curraghs North .	87	3	38	Leitrim . .	Drumahaire .	Inishmagrath .	Manorhamilton	IV.	96
20	Curraghs South .	75	3	20	Leitrim . .	Drumahaire .	Inishmagrath .	Manorhamilton	IV.	96
61	Curraghtarsna .	371	3	22	Tipperary, S.R.	Middlethird .	Magorban . .	Cashel . .	II.	328
44	Curraghteemore .	120	3	6	Cork, E.R. .	Barrymore . .	Rathcormack .	Fermoy . .	II.	57
80,81,91,92	Curraghteemore .	193	2	4	Mayo . .	Costello . .	Knock . . .	Claremorris .	IV.	142
20	Curraghtemple .	121	1	23	Tipperary, N.R.	Owney and Arra .	Youghalarra .	Nenagh . .	II.	297
43	Curraghtown .	94	2	3	Meath . .	Lower Deece .	Galtrim . .	Trim . .	I.	191
26	Curraghtown .	351	3	10	Meath . .	Lower Duleek .	Kentstown .	Navan . .	I.	196
11	Curraghtown .	232	0	28	Meath . .	Lower Kells .	Moynalty .	Kells . .	I.	203
31	Curraghtown .	329	2	6	Meath . .	Lower Navan .	Ardbraccan .	Navan . .	I.	214
33, 39	Curraghtown .	287	3	14	Meath . .	Skreen . . .	Cushinstown .	Dunshaughlin .	I.	220

(a) Including 4A. 1R. 26P. Beaghy Lough.
(b) Including 9A. 2R. 13P. water.
(c) Including 11A. 2R. 17P. water.
(d) Including 8A. 3R. 20P. water.

No. of Sheet of the Ordnance Survey Maps.	Townlands and Towns.	Area in Statute Acres.			County.	Barony.	Parish.	Poor Law Union in 1857.	Townland Census of 1851, Part I.	
		A.	R.	P.					Vol.	Page
43, 44	Curraghtown .	492	2	35	Meath . .	Upper Deece . .	Culmullin . .	Dunshaughlin .	I.	193
49, 57	Curraghturk .	794	3	10	Limerick . .	Coshlea . .	Ballylanders .	Mitchelstown .	II.	237
36	Curragh Upper	312	3	18	Cork, E.R. .	Condons&Clangibbon	Clondulane .	Fermoy . .	II.	60
31	Curragh Upper	101	3	11	King's Co. .	Eglish . .	Drumcullen .	Parsonstown .	I.	134
5, 6	Curraghvah .	398	3	32	Cavan . .	Tullyhaw . .	Templeport .	Enniskillen .	III.	94
33	Curraghwalls .	185	3	24	Meath . .	Upper Duleek .	Ardcath . .	Drogheda .	I.	197
4, 5	Curraghweesha	196	2	0	Kerry . .	Iraghticonnor .	Lisselton .	Listowel .	II.	192
104, 117	Curragh West	22	3	25	Cork, W.R. .	Bear . .	Kilcaskan .	Castletown .	II.	122
4	Curragh West	388	3	35	Dublin . .	Balrothery West .	Hollywood .	Balrothery .	I.	23
5, 6	Curragh West	485	1	7a	Galway . .	Ballymoe . .	Templetogher .	Glennamaddy .	IV.	9
15	Curraghwheery	87	3	4	King's Co. .	Garrycastle . .	Wheery or Killagally	Parsonstown .	I.	139
3	Curraghwood .	63	2	27	Wexford . .	Gorey . .	Kilcavan .	Gorey .	I.	317
16, 24	Curraglass .	320	3	22	Cork, E.R. .	Orrery and Kilmore	Buttevant .	Mallow .	II.	107
80, 92	Curraglass .	1,417	3	20	Cork, W.R. .	Bantry . .	Kilmocomoge .	Bantry .	II.	120
67, 75	Curraglass .	513	1	0	Kerry . .	Magunihy . .	Killaha .	Killarney .	II.	202
46	Curraglass East	68	2	32	Cork, E.R. .	Kinnatalloon .	Mogeely . .	Fermoy .	II.	98
85	Curraglass North	177	2	23	Kerry . .	Glanarought .	Kilgarvan .	Kenmare .	II.	187
85	Curraglass South	211	1	31	Kerry . .	Glanarought .	Kilgarvan .	Kenmare .	II.	187
46	CURRAGLASS T. .	—			Cork, E.R. .	Kinnatalloon .	Mogeely . .	Fermoy .	II.	99
46	Curraglass West	97	2	30	Cork, E.R. .	Kinnatalloon .	Mogeely . .	Fermoy .	II.	98
29	Curragraig .	165	3	0	Waterford .	Coshmore&Coshbride	Lismore and Mocollop	Lismore .	II.	345
33	Curragraigue .	140	3	37	Kerry . .	Corkaguiny . .	Kilquane .	Dingle .	II.	179
102	Curragraigue .	160	0	1	Kerry . .	Glanarought .	Kilcaskan .	Kenmare .	II.	186
29, 38	Curragraigue .	704	3	15	Kerry . .	Trughanacmy .	Annagh . .	Tralee .	II.	205
94, 95	Curragrean .	249	0	9	Galway . .	Galway . .	Oranmore .	Galway .	IV.	37
77	Curragrine .	140	0	38	Cork, E.R. .	Imokilly . .	Ballyoughtera .	Middleton .	II.	84
72, 84	Currahaly .	1,036	0	25	Cork, E.R. .	East Muskerry .	Aglish . .	Macroom .	II.	101
11, 20	Currahchase .	512	3	36b	Limerick . .	Kenry . .	Adare . .	Rathkeale .	II.	248
11, 20	Currahchase .	593	1	37c	Limerick . .	Kenry . .	Kilcornan .	Rathkeale .	II.	249
11	Currahchase North .	283	3	23d	Limerick . .	Kenry . .	Kilcornan .	Rathkeale .	II.	249
19	Curraheen .	199	3	10	Cork, E.R. .	Condons&Clangibbon	Kilgullane .	Mitchelstown .	II.	61
73	Curraheen .	61	3	4	Cork, E.R. .	Cork . .	Carrigrohane .	Cork .	II.	64
73	Curraheen .	196	0	18	Cork, E.R. .	Cork . .	Inishkenny .	Cork .	II.	64
15	Curraheen .	606	3	29	Cork, E.R. .	Duhallow . .	Kilbrin .	Kanturk .	II.	72
78	Curraheen .	191	3	39	Cork, E.R. .	Imokilly . .	Kilmacdonogh .	Youghal .	II.	88
37, 46	Curraheen .	602	0	24	Cork, E.R. .	Kinnatalloon .	Knockmourne .	Fermoy .	II.	98
143	Curraheen .	86	1	18	Cork, W.R. .	East Carbery (W.D.)	Ross . .	Clonakilty .	II.	135
136	Curraheen .	236	1	22	Cork, W.R. .	Ibane and Barryroe	Lislee . .	Clonakilty .	II.	150
81	Curraheen .	255	3	13e	Cork, W.R. .	West Muskerry .	Inchigeelagh .	Dunmanway .	II.	157
70	Curraheen .	71	0	15	Cork, W.R. .	West Muskerry .	Kilnamartry .	Macroom .	II.	159
63, 64	Curraheen .	657	0	39	Kerry . .	Iveragh . .	Glanbehy .	Cahersiveen .	II.	195
37	Curraheen .	2,302	0	22	Kerry . .	Trughanacmy .	Annagh . .	Tralee .	II.	205
11, 12	Curraheen .	158	2	20f	Limerick . .	Kenry . .	Kildimo .	Rathkeale .	II.	249
47,48,53,54	Curraheen .	895	3	6	Tipperary, N.R.	Eliogarty . .	Ballymurreen .	Thurles .	II.	269
45	Curraheen .	636	3	23	Tipperary, N.R.	Kilnamanagh Upper	Toem . .	Tipperary .	II.	280
25, 26	Curraheen .	163	1	23	Tipperary, N.R.	Owney and Arra .	Killoscully .	Nenagh .	II.	295
28	Curraheen .	333	2	36	Tipperary, N.R.	Upper Ormond .	Aghnameadle .	Nenagh .	II.	288
21	Curraheen .	110	1	37	Tipperary, N.R.	Upper Ormond .	Lisbunny .	Nenagh .	II.	292
88	Curraheen .	46	0	16	Tipperary, S.R.	Iffa and Offa West .	Ballybacon .	Clogheen .	II.	317
62, 63	Curraheen .	325	3	18	Tipperary, S.R.	Middlethird . .	Peppardstown .	Cashel .	II.	329
72, 79	Curraheen .	576	0	7	Tipperary, S.R.	Slievardagh . .	Newtownlennan	Carrick on Suir	II.	335
29, 34, 35	Curraheen .	355	3	11	Waterford .	Decies within Drum	Aglish . .	Dungarvan .	II.	349
23	Curraheen .	341	2	19	Waterford .	Decies without Drum	Kilrossanty .	Kilmacthomas .	II.	358
24	Curraheen .	282	2	4	Waterford .	Decies without Drum	Stradbally .	Kilmacthomas .	II.	360
2, 6	Curraheen .	1,766	2	17	Waterford .	Upperthird . .	Rathgormuck .	Carrick on Suir	II.	371
31	Curraheenaris .	4	2	27	Waterford .	Decies without Drum	Dungarvan .	Dungarvan .	II.	355
1, 5	Curraheenavoher .	411	3	0	Waterford .	Glenahiry . .	Kilronan .	Clonmel .	II.	365
31	Curraheen Commons .	29	0	31	Waterford .	Decies without Drum	Kilrush .	Dungarvan .	II.	358
49	Curraheenduff .	321	3	36	Tipperary, S.R.	Slievardagh . .	Ballingarry .	Callan .	II.	331
63	Curraheen Little .	60	0	28	Kerry . .	Iveragh . .	Glanbehy .	Cahersiveen .	II.	195
20	Curraheen North .	166	1	15	Limerick . .	Connello Lower .	Nantinan .	Rathkeale .	II.	229
28	Curraheen North .	300	3	24	Waterford .	Coshmore&Coshbride	Lismore and Mocollop	Lismore .	II.	345
20	Curraheen South .	100	1	31	Limerick . .	Connello Lower .	Nantinan .	Rathkeale .	II.	229
28	Curraheen South .	316	1	7	Waterford .	Coshmore&Coshbride	Lismore and Mocollop	Lismore .	II.	345
136	Currahevern East .	233	0	23	Cork, W.R. .	Ibane and Barryroe	Abbeymahon .	Clonakilty .	II.	148
136	Currahevern West .	164	3	15	Cork, W.R. .	Ibane and Barryroe .	Abbeymahon .	Clonakilty .	II.	148
30, 31	Currahill Lower .	234	2	25	Kilkenny .	Kells . .	Kilmaganny .	Callan .	I.	109
30, 31	Currahill Upper .	250	1	17	Kilkenny .	Kells . .	Kilmaganny .	Callan .	I.	109
124	Currahoo .	273	0	32	Cork, W.R. .	Courceys . .	Ringrone .	Kinsale .	II.	147
136	Currahy . .	192	0	34	Cork, W.R. .	Ibane and Barryroe .	Abbeymahon .	Clonakilty .	II.	148
81	Currahy . .	1,075	0	34g	Cork, W.R. .	West Muskerry .	Inchigeelagh .	Macroom .	II.	157
80, 92	Currakeal .	872	2	33	Cork, W.R. .	Bantry . .	Kilmocomoge .	Bantry .	II.	120
90	Currakeal .	124	0	26	Cork, W.R. .	Bear . .	Kilcaskan .	Bantry .	II.	122

(a) Including 4A. 3R. 10P. water.
(b) Including 33A. 3R. 28P. water.
(c) Including 7A. 2R. 4P. water.

(d) Including 7A. 0R. 35P. water.
(e) Including 6A. 2R. 37P. water.

(f) Including 3A. 2R. 8P. water.
(g) Including 142A. 0R. 1P. water.

No. of Sheet of the Ordnance Survey Maps.	Townlands and Towns.	Area in Statute Acres.	County.	Barony.	Parish.	Poor Law Union in 1857.	Townland Census of 1851, Part I.	
		A. R. P.					Vol.	Page
90	Currakillane	381 1 11	Cork, W.R.	Bear	Kilcaskan	Bantry	II.	122
48, 49	Curraknockaun	102 2 32	Kerry	Trughanacmy	Killeentierna	Killarney	II.	211
10	Curralane	372 1 36	Wexford	Scarawalsh	Kilrush	Enniscorthy	I.	324
10	Curralane Oldtown	145 1 35	Wexford	Scarawalsh	Kilrush	Enniscorthy	I.	324
38, 42	Curralanty	539 1 12	King's Co.	Clonlisk	Kilmurryely	Roscrea	I.	131
6	Curraleagh	157 0 25	Cork, E.R.	Duhallow	Tullylease	Kanturk	II.	76
73	Curraleigh	372 0 39a	Cork, E.R.	East Muskerry	Inishcarra	Cork	II.	103
59	Curraleigh	559 1 3	Cork, W.R.	West Muskerry	Clondrohid	Macroom	II.	155
86, 89	Curraleigh East	411 0 28	Tipperary, S.R.	Iffa and Offa West	Templetenny	Clogheen	II.	320
86, 89	Curraleigh West	322 1 3	Tipperary, S.R.	Iffa and Offa West	Templetenny	Clogheen	II.	320
8	Curramoney	185 0 25	Antrim	Cary	Ballintoy	Ballycastle	III.	12
7	Curramoney or Billy	358 2 2	Antrim	Lower Dunluce	Billy	Coleraine	III.	16
91	Curramore	1,523 3 3b	Cork, W.R.	Bantry	Kilmocomoge	Bantry	II.	120
18	Curra More	332 1 22	Limerick	Shanid	Loghill	Glin	II.	257
117	Curramore	200 1 22	Mayo	Kilmaine	Ballinrobe	Ballinrobe	IV.	152
36,37,41,42	Curran	541 0 14	Londonderry	Loughinsholin	Maghera	Magherafelt	III.	242
61	Curran	105 0 30c	Tyrone	Dungannon Middle	Clonfeacle	Dungannon	III.	299
46	Curran	180 1 0	Tyrone	Dungannon Middle	Tullyniskan	Dungannon	III.	304
120	Curranashingane	309 0 10	Cork, W.R.	West Carbery (E.D.)	Drinagh	Skibbereen	II.	139
35, 40	Curran and Drumaliss	224 0 19	Antrim	Upper Glenarm	Larne	Larne	III.	25
19	Currane	365 3 1	Carlow	Idrone East	Clonygoose	Carlow	I.	6
109, 122	Currane	156 1 12	Cork, W.R.	East Carbery (E.D.)	Desertserges	Clonakilty	II.	127
31	Currane	12 2 28	Waterford	Decies without Drum	Dungarvan	Dungarvan	II.	355
79, 90	Curranny	85 0 12	Mayo	Carra	Drum	Castlebar	IV.	128
39, 48	CURRANS T.	—	Kerry	Trughanacmy	Currans	Killarney	II.	209
45	Curranstown Lower	221 2 25	Wicklow	Arklow	Arklow	Rathdrum	I.	341
45	Curranstown Upper	209 0 17	Wicklow	Arklow	Arklow	Rathdrum	I.	341
101, 111	Currantawy	59 3 16	Mayo	Clanmorris	Tagheen	Claremorris	IV.	136
42	CURRAN T.	—	Londonderry	Loughinsholin	Maghera	Magherafelt	III.	243
96, 110	Curranure	362 1 27	Cork, W.R.	East Carbery (E.D.)	Inishannon	Bandon	II.	128
124	Currarane	271 2 1	Cork, W.R.	East Carbery (E.D.)	Ringrone	Kinsale	II.	130
124	Currarane	100 2 21	Cork, W.R.	East Carbery (E.D.)	Templetrine	Kinsale	II.	130
40	Currarevagh	179 0 37	Galway	Moycullen	Kilcummin	Oughterard	IV.	67
12, 25	Currarevagh	813 2 34	Galway	Ross	Ross	Oughterard	IV.	74
49, 59	Curraross	496 1 19	Kerry	Trughanacmy	Killeentierna	Killarney	II.	211
72	Currasilla Lower	235 2 13	Tipperary, S.R.	Slieveardagh	Templemichael	Carrick on Suir	II.	336
71, 72	Currasilla Upper	394 2 38	Tipperary, S.R.	Slieveardagh	Templemichael	Carrick on Suir	II.	336
134, 136	Curratober	34 1 32	Galway	Leitrim	Inishcaltra	Scarriff	IV.	53
16, 17	Curratubbin Lower	138 0 9	Wexford	Gorey	Monamolin	Gorey	I.	321
16	Curratubbin Upper	183 3 32	Wexford	Gorey	Monamolin	Gorey	I.	321
34, 43	Currauly	193 1 5	Kerry	Corkaguiny	Kilmalkedar	Dingle	II.	178
29, 32, 33	Curraun	475 3 37	Leitrim	Mohill	Mohill	Mohill	IV.	107
14, 23	Curraun	601 0 24	Waterford	Decies without Drum	Kilrossanty	Kilmacthomas	II.	358
23, 24	Curraun	296 0 4	Wexford	Bantry	St. Mullin's	New Ross	I.	303
39	Curraun Beg	147 3 14	Galway	Moycullen	Kilcummin	Oughterard	IV.	67
4	Curraun Boy	2,755 0 23	Mayo	Erris	Kilcommon	Belmullet	IV.	143
39	Curraun Hill	233 0 15	Galway	Moycullen	Kilcummin	Oughterard	IV.	67
39	Curraun More	93 3 20	Galway	Moycullen	Kilcummin	Oughterard	IV.	67
81, 82	Curravaha	1,263 0 28	Kerry	Iveragh	Glanbehy	Cahersiveen	II.	195
150	Curravally	111 1 27d	Cork, W.R.	West Carbery (E.D.)	Creagh	Skibbereen	II.	138
38	Curravanish	129 3 0	Wicklow	Ballinacor South	Kilcommon	Shillelagh	I.	349
110	Curravarahane	327 3 17	Cork, W.R.	Kinalmeaky	Ballymodan	Bandon	II.	151
54, 55	Curraveha or Birch-hall	116 2 8	Galway	Moycullen	Kilcummin	Oughterard	IV.	67
21, 29	Curravogh North	257 0 2	Kerry	Trughanacmy	Tralee	Tralee	II.	213
29	Curravogh South	262 0 3	Kerry	Trughanacmy	Tralee	Tralee	II.	213
112	Curravohill	127 3 14	Cork, E.R.	Kinalea	Nohaval	Kinsale	II.	96
81, 90	Curravoola	1,732 2 20	Kerry	Iveragh	Dromod	Cahersiveen	II.	194
95, 96	Curravordy	751 2 21	Cork, W.R.	Kinalmeaky	Templemartin	Bandon	II.	153
68	Currawatia	122 3 14	Galway	Moycullen	Moycullen	Galway	IV.	71
67, 75	Curreal	484 3 0	Kerry	Magunihy	Killaha	Killarney	II.	202
17	Curreen	61 2 37	Longford	Ratheline	Ratheline	Longford	I.	164
80,81,89,90	Curreen and Gannew	332 0 24	Donegal	Banagh	Glencolumbkille	Glenties	III.	105
14, 20	Curreentorpan	347 1 14	Roscommon	Frenchpark	Tibohine	Castlereagh	IV.	205
33, 39	Curreeny	1,558 3 17	Tipperary, N.R.	Upper Ormond	Templederry	Nenagh	II.	293
32, 33	Curreeny Commons	1,864 3 16	Tipperary, N.R.	Upper Ormond	Dolla	Nenagh	II.	290
19	Currenree or Corry Beg	301 0 31	Carlow	Idrone East	Sliguff	Carlow	I.	8
76	Currenstown	211 1 36	Tipperary, S.R.	Iffa and Offa East	Inishlounaght	Clonmel	II.	313
13	Curriersbog	73 2 36	Queen's Co.	Maryborough East	Borris	Mountmellick	I.	240
2, 7	Curries	186 0 35	Galway	Ballymoe	Kilcroan	Glennamaddy	IV	9
105	Curries	306 0 32	Mayo	Costello	Annagh	Claremorris	IV.	138
36	Curries	204 2 22	Westmeath	Clonlonan	Kilcleagh	Athlone	I.	261

(a) Including 10A. 0R. 39P. water.
(b) Including 3A. 1R. 4P. Curramore Lough.
(c) Including 1A. 1R. 28P. water.
(d) Including 1A. 1R. 6P. detached portion.

No. of Sheet of the Ordnance Survey Maps.	Townlands and Towns.	Area in Statute Acres.	County.	Barony.	Parish.	Poor Law Union in 1857.	Townland Census of 1851, Part I.	
		A. R. P.					Vol.	Page
35, 44	Currin	360 0 3	Donegal	Kilmacrenan	Kilmacrenan	Millford	III.	129
23, 28	Currin	243 2 4	Fermanagh	Magherastephana	Aghavea	Lisnaskea	III.	218
16	Currin	328 3 11	Fermanagh	Tirkennedy	Magheracross	Enniskillen	III.	223
63, 64, 74	Currinah	456 2 8	Mayo	Costello	Kilbeagh	Castlereagh	IV.	140
5, 10	Curristeen	267 0 26a	Westmeath	Moygoish	Rathaspick	Mullingar	I.	280
20, 27	Curristown	191 1 7	Westmeath	Farbill	Killucan	Mullingar	I.	266
18, 25	Curristown or Bell-mount	195 2 29	Westmeath	Moyashel and Magheradernon	Mullingar	Mullingar	I.	275
34	Currogs	65 3 12	Fermanagh	Magherastephana	Aghalurcher	Lisnaskea	III.	215
31, 32	Currudda	1,013 2 8	Londonderry	Keenaght	Dungiven	NewTⁿLimavady	III.	236
61	Curry	106 2 25b	Galway	Killian	Ahascragh	Ballinasloe	IV.	43
15	Curry	157 3 12	Leitrim	Drumahaire	Killarga	Manorhamilton	IV.	98
15	Curry	148 0 22	Longford	Ardagh	Mostrim	Granard	I.	152
15	Curry	167 3 4	Longford	Ardagh	Street	Granard	I.	153
18	Curry	359 2 20	Longford	Moydow	Ballymacormick	Longford	I.	160
18	Curry	187 1 17	Longford	Moydow	Kilcommock	Ballymahon	I.	161
78	Curry	236 0 34	Mayo	Carra	Breaghwy	Castlebar	IV.	127
90	Curry	115 1 22	Mayo	Carra	Drum	Castlebar	IV.	128
47, 48	Curry	861 2 18c	Roscommon	Athlone	Cam	Athlone	IV.	179
42	Curry	280 0 27	Roscommon	Athlone	Kilmeane	Roscommon	IV.	182
17	Curry	136 2 4d	Roscommon	Roscommon	Clooncraff	Strokestown	IV.	208
29	Curry	102 0 3	Roscommon	Roscommon	Cloonfinlough	Strokestown	IV.	209
23	Curry	219 0 36	Roscommon	Roscommon	Kiltrustan	Strokestown	IV.	211
42, 43	Curry	956 0 17	Sligo	Leyny	Achonry	Tobercurry	IV.	229
3	Curry	550 1 33	Westmeath	Fore	Lickbla	Granard	I.	270
28	Curryann	73 2 5	Fermanagh	Magherastephana	Aghalurcher	Lisnaskea	III.	215
72	Curryaun	588 2 16e	Mayo	Gallen	Kilconduff	Swineford	IV.	147
9	Curryeahill	105 2 3f	Longford	Granard	Clonbroney	Granard	I.	155
96, 110	Curryclogh	365 0 1	Cork. W.R.	Kinalmeaky	Kilbrogan	Bandon	II.	152
23	Currycreaghan	306 0 4	Longford	Moydow	Taghsheenod	Ballymahon	I.	162
79, 90	Curryeallaun	123 1 18g	Mayo	Carra	Drum	Castlebar	IV.	128
43, 57	Curry Eighter	116 2 14h	Galway	Clare	Cummer	Tuam	IV.	19
21	Curryfree	622 0 12	Londonderry	Tirkeeran	Clondermot	Londonderry	III.	248
1, 2, 6, 7	Curryglass	488 3 6	Cork, E.R.	Orrery and Kilmore	Shandrum	Kanturk	II.	110
115	Curryglass	145 3 32	Cork, W.R.	Bear	Killaconenagh	Castletown	II.	124
9, 14	Currygrane	600 1 25i	Longford	Granard	Clonbroney	Granard	I.	155
4, 8	Currygranny	427 0 36	Longford	Longford	Clongesh	Longford	I.	157
24	Currygurry	108 2 32	King's Co.	Ballycowan	Rahan	Tullamore	I.	128
13	Curryhills	817 0 6	Kildare	Clane	Killybegs	Naas	I.	54
100	Curry (Kirwan)	558 0 10	Mayo	Kilmaine	Mayo	Ballinrobe	IV.	157
57	Currylaur	32 3 8	Galway	Clare	Cummer	Tuam	IV.	19
90, 100	Curry (Macmanus)	202 3 14	Mayo	Clanmorris	Mayo	Ballinrobe	IV.	135
100	Curry (Macmanus)	167 3 17	Mayo	Kilmaine	Mayo	Ballinrobe	IV.	157
16	Currymount	259 1 35	Cork, E.R.	Orrery and Kilmore	Bregoge	Mallow	II.	106
66	Currynanerriagh	951 1 2j	Donegal	Boylagh	Inishkeel	Glenties	III.	112
20, 22	Currynierin	188 3 10	Londonderry	Tirkeeran	Clondermot	Londonderry	III.	248
57	Curry Oughter	65 1 22	Galway	Clare	Cummer	Tuam	IV.	19
27, 32, 33	Curryquin	890 1 19	Tipperary, N.R.	Upper Ormond	Kilmore	Nenagh	II.	291
51	Curryroe	195 3 1	Roscommon	Athlone	Drum	Athlone	IV.	180
3	Currysheskin	337 3 16	Antrim	Cary	Ballintoy	Ballycastle	III.	12
16	Currysheskin	156 0 28	Antrim	Upper Dunluce	Ballymoney	Ballymoney	III.	15
42	CURRY T.	—	Sligo	Leyny	Achonry	Tobercurry	IV.	230
10, 23	Currywongaun	644 3 36k	Galway	Ballynahinch	Ballynakill	Clifden	IV.	11
22	Curstown	215 1 30	Louth	Ferrard	Termonfeckin	Drogheda	I.	182
128	Curtaun	284 2 13l	Galway	Kiltartan	Beah	Gort	IV.	46
77	Curtistown	52 2 2	Tipperary, S.R.	Iffa and Offa East	Kilsheelan	Clonmel	II.	314
37	Curtistown Lower or Baldoyle	174 1 38	Meath	Lower Deece	Kilmessan	Dunshaughlin	I.	192
37	Curtistown Upper	193 2 34	Meath	Lower Deece	Kilmessan	Dunshaughlin	I.	192
5	Curtiswood	203 2 3	Waterford	Glenahiry	Kilronan	Clonmel	II.	365
7	Curtlestown Lower	133 0 5	Wicklow	Rathdown	Powerscourt	Rathdown	I.	356
3, 7	Curtlestown Upper	198 1 2	Wicklow	Rathdown	Powerscourt	Rathdown	I.	356
32	Cusackstown	213 0 0	Meath	Skreen	Monktown	Navan	I.	221
105	Cuscarrick	256 0 0	Galway	Loughrea	Loughrea	Loughrea	IV.	65
82	Cusduff	264 0 13	Cork, W.R.	West Muskerry	Kilmichael	Dunmanway	II.	158
30, 31	Cush	172 3 26	Kildare	Offaly West	Ballybrackan	Athy	I.	71
30	Cush	270 0 25	King's Co.	Eglish	Eglish	Parsonstown	I.	134
22	Cush	125 2 21	King's Co.	Garrycastle	Gallen	Parsonstown	I.	136
48	Cush	795 0 25	Limerick	Coshlea	Emlygrennan	Kilmallock	II.	238
6, 7	Cushacorra	41 3 14	Clare	Inchiquin	Kilkeedy	Corrofin	II.	25
11, 12, 16	Cushaling	843 3 36	Kildare	Offaly East	Rathangan	Edenderry	I.	71
20	Cushaling	1,286 3 13	King's Co.	Coolestown	Monasteroris	Edenderry	I.	133
76, 77	Cushalogurt	158 0 27	Mayo	Burrishoole	Kilmeena	Westport	IV.	122

(a) Including 3A. 3R. 4P. Inny River.
(b) Including 15A. 2R. 0P. water.
(c) Including 30A. 3R. 20P. water.
(d) Including 3A. 1R. 36P. water.
(e) Including 6A. 1R. 5P. water.
(f) Including 0A. 3R. 37P. water.
(g) Including 8A. 2R. 30P. water.
(h) Including 0A. 2R. 16P. water.
(i) Including 59A. 3R. 30P. water.
(j) Including 85A. 2R. 3P. water.
(k) Including 4A. 2R. 28P. water.
(l) Including 7A. 3R. 31P. water.

No. of Sheet of the Ordnance Survey Maps.	Townlands and Towns.	Area in Statute Acres.			County.	Barony.	Parish.	Poor Law Union in 1857.	Townland Census of 1851, Part I.	
		A.	R.	P.					Vol.	Page
22	Cushatrough . .	501	1	7	Galway . .	Ballynahinch . .	Omey . . .	Clifden . .	IV.	14
50	Cushatrower . .	1,028	0	37a	Galway . .	Ballynahinch . .	Moyrus . . .	Clifden . .	IV.	12
21, 22	Cushcallow or Cloncallow . .	197	3	14	King's Co. .	Garrycastle . .	Reynagh . . .	Parsonstown .	I.	138
31	Cushcam . .	46	1	20	Waterford .	Decies without Drum	Dungarven . .	Dungarvan . .	II.	355
14, 22	Cush East . .	339	1	36	King's Co. .	Garrycastle . .	Gallen . . .	Parsonstown .	I.	136
113	*Cusheen Island* .	9	0	39	Galway . .	Kiltartan . .	Kinvarradoorus .	Gort . . .	IV.	49
20	Cushendall . .	153	1	27	Antrim . .	Lower Glenarm .	Layd . . .	Ballycastle .	III.	22
20	CUSHENDALL T. .	—			Antrim . .	Lower Glenarm .	Layd . . .	Ballycastle .	III.	23
15	Cushendun . .	247	2	14	Antrim . .	Cary . . .	Culfeightrin .	Ballycastle .	III.	13
20	Cushenilt . .	65	2	7	Antrim . .	Lower Glenarm .	Ardclinis . .	Larne . .	III.	21
9	Cushenny . .	83	2	35	Armagh . .	Oneilland West .	Drumcree . .	Lurgan . .	III.	52
30, 35	Cushenstown . .	1,352	1	39	Wexford . .	Bantry . . .	Carnagh . .	New Ross .	I.	299
27, 34	Cushina . . .	755	2	31	King's Co. .	Coolestown . .	Clonsast . .	Edenderry .	I.	133
27, 34	Cushina . . .	1,787	2	5	King's Co. .	Upper Philipstown .	Ballykean . .	Mountmellick .	I.	143
88	Cushinkeel . .	217	0	28	Mayo . .	Burrishoole . .	Aghagower . .	Westport . .	IV.	118
88	Cushinsheeaun .	280	3	0b	Mayo . .	Burrishoole . .	Aghagower . .	Westport . .	IV.	118
50	Cushinstown . .	216	3	14c	Meath . .	Dunboyne . .	Dunboyne . .	Dunshaughlin .	I.	199
32,33,38,39	Cushinstown . .	690	0	11	Meath . .	Skreen . . .	Cushinstown .	Dunshaughlin .	I.	220
32,33,38,39	Cushinstown . .	105	2	22	Meath . .	Skreen . . .	Kilmoon . .	Dunshaughlin .	I.	221
27	Cushinstown . .	376	1	37	Westmeath .	Farbill . . .	Killucan . .	Mullingar .	I.	266
106	Cushinyen . .	247	2	1	Mayo . .	Murrisk . .	Kilgeever . .	Westport . .	IV.	160
9, 10	Cushleake Mountain Middle . .	1,103	1	21	Antrim . .	Cary . . .	Culfeightrin .	Ballycastle .	III.	13
9, 10	Cushleake Mountain North . .	995	2	27	Antrim . .	Cary . . .	Culfeightrin .	Ballycastle .	III.	13
9, 10, 15	Cushleake Mountain South . .	1,103	2	10	Antrim . .	Cary . . .	Culfeightrin .	Ballycastle .	III.	13
66	Cushlecka . .	587	3	33	Mayo . .	Burrishoole . .	Burrishoole . .	Newport . .	IV.	119
1, 2, 3	Cush Lower . .	397	2	2	Queen's Co. .	Tinnahinch . .	Kilmanman .	Mountmellick .	I.	249
93	Cushmaigmore .	241	3	9	Galway . .	Moycullen . .	Rahoon . .	Galway . .	IV.	72
14	Cushmona . .	143	2	36	Tipperary, N.R.	Lower Ormond .	Dromineer . .	Nenagh . .	II.	283
38	Cush of Grange .	244	3	33	Waterford .	Decies within Drum	Lisgenan or Grange	Youghal . .	II.	352
26	*Cushrush Island* .	35	2	35	Fermanagh .	Clanawley . .	Killesher . .	Enniskillen .	III.	193
2	Cush Upper . .	242	3	12d	Queen's Co. .	Tinnahinch . .	Kilmanman .	Mountmellick .	I.	249
34	Cushwash . .	69	0	19	Fermanagh .	Magherastephana .	Aghalurcher .	Lisnaskea .	III.	215
11, 17	Cuskernagh . .	78	2	19	Sligo . .	Tireragh . .	Kilmacshalgan .	Dromore West .	IV.	234
87	Cuskinny . .	91	1	28	Cork, E.R. .	Barrymore . .	Templerobin .	Cork . .	II.	58
90, 96	Cuskry Glebe . .	203	3	5	Donegal . .	Banagh . .	Kilcar . .	Glenties . .	III.	108
40	Cuslea . . .	55	1	7	Fermanagh .	Clankelly . .	Galloon . .	Clones . .	III.	198
117	Cuslough Demesne .	278	3	31e	Mayo . .	Kilmaine . .	Ballinrobe . .	Ballinrobe .	IV.	152
48, 59	Cusloura . . .	1,443	2	18	Cork, W.R. .	West Muskerry .	Macroom . .	Macroom . .	II.	160
140	Cusovinna . .	190	1	35	Cork, W.R. .	West Carbery (W.D.)	Skull . . .	Skull . .	II.	146
6	Cuss . . .	148	3	29	Kerry . .	Iraghticonnor .	Murher . .	Listowel . .	II.	193
47	Cuss . . .	130	0	4	Monaghan .	Trughanacmy .	Kiltallagh . .	Tralee . .	II.	212
14	Cussaboy . .	64	1	3	Monaghan .	Monaghan . .	Tullycorbet .	Monaghan .	III.	281
54	*Cussafoor Island* .	1	0	39	Galway . .	Moycullen . .	Kilcummin .	Oughterard .	IV.	68
34	Cussan . . .	288	2	7	Kilkenny . .	Kells . . .	Tullahought .	Callan . .	I.	110
45, 46	Cussana . .	58	1	12	Kilkenny . .	Iverk . . .	Aglish . .	Waterford .	I.	105
45, 46	Cussana . .	124	2	2	Kilkenny . .	Iverk . . .	Portnascully .	Waterford .	I.	106
9	Cussee . .	73	2	7	Monaghan .	Monaghan . .	Tedavnet . .	Monaghan .	III.	278
2	Custodium . .	144	3	13	Wexford . .	Gorey . . .	Kilnenor . .	Gorey . .	I.	319
31	Custorum . .	39	0	24	Westmeath .	Moycashel . .	Kilcumreragh .	Athlone . .	I.	278
19	Cutteanta . .	36	1	19	Sligo . .	Tireragh . .	Dromard . .	Dromore West .	IV.	233
42, 43	Cutteen . .	207	1	28	Clare . .	Bunratty Upper .	Quin . . .	Tulla . .	II.	10
26, 27	Cutteen . .	46	1	33	Kerry . .	Corkaguiny .	Stradbally . .	Dingle . .	II.	180
35	Cutteen Beg . .	107	0	1	Clare . .	Tulla Upper . .	Tulla . . .	Tulla . .	II.	41
35	Cutteen More . .	176	3	32	Clare . .	Tulla Upper . .	Tulla . . .	Tulla . .	II.	41
14	Cutteen North .	1,283	3	31	Waterford .	Decies without Drum	Kilrossanty .	Kilmacthomas .	II.	358
14, 23	Cutteen South .	1,024	2	16	Waterford .	Decies without Drum	Kilrossanty .	Kilmacthomas .	II.	358
26	Cuttragh . .	179	0	26f	Cavan . .	Upper Loughtee .	Lavey . . .	Cavan . .	III.	85
63	Cuttymanhill . .	97	2	34	Donegal . .	Raphoe . .	Taughboyne .	Strabane .	III.	143
14	Daars North . .	242	0	35	Kildare . .	Naas North . .	Bodenstown . .	Naas . .	I.	62
14	Daars South . .	426	1	14	Kildare . .	Naas North . .	Bodenstown . .	Naas . .	I.	62
17	Dabrian . .	72	1	24	Clare . .	Inchiquin . .	Killinaboy . .	Corrofin . .	II.	26
11	Dacklin . .	191	1	13g	Roscommon .	Boyle . . .	Killummod . .	Cark. on Shannon	IV.	196
155, 106	Dadreen . .	861	1	17	Mayo . .	Murrisk . .	Kilgeever . .	Westport . .	IV.	160
20	Daggan . .	169	0	18	Cavan . .	Upper Loughtee .	Castleterra , .	Cavan . .	III.	88
39, 40	Daghboonagh . .	366	2	21	Sligo . .	Corran . . .	Drumrat . .	Boyle . .	IV.	225
144	Dairies . .	8	1	3	Cork, W.R. .	Ibane and Barryroe	Ardfield . .	Clonakilty .	II.	148
15, 21	Dairies Big . .	138	3	31	Fermanagh .	Magheraboy . .	Devenish . .	Enniskillen .	III.	210

(a) Including 35A. 1R. 12P. water.
(b) Including 9A. 3R. 7P. water.
(c) Including 23A. 1R. 19P. detached portions.

(d) Including 3A. 2R. 0P. water.
(e) Including 2A. 2R. 31P. water.

(f) Including 6A. 1R. 4P. water.
(g) Including 22A. 1R. 18P. water.

No. of Sheet of the Ordnance Survey Maps.	Townlands and Towns.	Area in Statute Acres.	County.	Barony.	Parish.	Poor Law Union in 1857.	Townland Census of 1851, Part I.	
		A. R. P.					Vol.	Page
15	Dairies Little . .	73　0　10	Fermanagh .	Magheraboy . .	Devenish . .	Enniskillen .	III.	210
40	Dairyfarm . .	85　2　24	Kildare . .	Kilkea and Moone .	Castledermot . .	Athy . .	I.	59
22	Dairyhill . .	98　2　12	Kilkenny . .	Shillelogher . .	Killaloe . .	Callan . .	I.	115
23, 28, 29	Dairyhill . .	426　3　2	Queen's Co. .	Clarmallagh . .	Aghaboe . .	Abbeyleix .	I.	235
22	Dales . . .	239　0　26	Louth . .	Ferrard . .	Mayne . .	Drogheda .	I.	181
18, 26	Dalgan . .	271　1　14	King's Co. .	Geashill . . .	Geashill . . .	Tullamore .	I.	140
122	Dalgan Demesne .	916　0　14a	Mayo . .	Kilmaine . .	Shrule . .	Ballinrobe .	IV.	158
4, 16	Dalgin . . .	202　0　20	Galway . .	Dunmore . .	Addergoole . .	Tuam . .	IV.	33
23	Dalkey . .	247　1　4	Dublin . .	Rathdown . .	Dalkey . .	Rathdown .	I.	35
23	Dalkey Commons .	196　1　25	Dublin . .	Rathdown . .	Dalkey . .	Rathdown .	I.	35
23	*Dalkey Island* .	21　2　27	Dublin . .	Rathdown . .	Dalkey . .	Rathdown .	I.	35
23	DALKEY T. . .	—	Dublin . .	Rathdown . .	Dalkey . .	Rathdown .	I.	35
32	Dalkinstown . .	256　2　30	Kildare . .	Kilcullen . .	Kilcullen . .	Naas . .	I.	58
66	Dalraghan Beg .	546　2　38b	Donegal .	Boylagh . .	Inishkeel . .	Glenties . .	III.	112
66	Dalraghan More .	850　0　19	Donegal .	Boylagh . .	Inishkeel . .	Glenties . .	III.	112
91, 92	Dalteen . . .	399　2　14	Mayo . .	Clanmorris . .	Kilcolman . .	Claremorris .	IV.	134
61	Dalysgrove . .	408　0　16c	Galway .	Killian . .	Ahascragh . .	Ballinasloe .	IV.	43
6, 10	Dalystown . .	444　0　34	Longford .	Granard . .	Abbeylara . .	Granard . .	I.	154
41, 42	Dalystown . .	524　2　27	Meath . .	Lower Moyfenrath .	Trim . .	Trim . .	I.	212
32, 33	Dalystown . .	878　1　37	Westmeath .	Fartullagh . .	Clonfad . .	Mullingar .	I.	268
17	Dalystown . .	354　1　33	Westmeath .	Rathconrath . .	Ballymorin . .	Mullingar .	I.	282
116	Dalystown Demesne	509　1　34	Galway . .	Leitrim . .	Leitrim . .	Loughrea . .	IV.	55
4, 7	Damastown . .	890　3　22	Dublin . .	Balrothery West .	Hollywood . .	Balrothery .	I.	23
13	Damastown . .	351　3　31	Dublin . .	Castleknock .	Mulhuddart . .	Dublin North .	I.	25
10, 11	Damerstown East .	532　0　31	Kilkenny . .	Fassadinin . .	Dysart . .	Castlecomer .	I.	89
10	Damerstown West .	338　3　17	Kilkenny . .	Fassadinin . .	Dysart . .	Castlecomer .	I.	89
8	Dam Head . .	263　1　21	Londonderry .	North East Liberties of Coleraine . .	Kildollagh . .	Coleraine .	III.	246
18, 19	Damma Lower .	589　1　32	Kilkenny . .	Crannagh . .	Ballycallan . .	Kilkenny . .	I.	84
18, 19	Damma Upper .	164　0　33	Kilkenny . .	Crannagh . .	Ballycallan . .	Kilkenny . .	I.	84
16, 17	Damoily . .	644　0　27	Armagh . .	Fews Lower . .	Kilclooney . .	Armagh . .	III.	46
46, 47	Damolly . .	508　2　36	Down . .	Lordship of Newry .	Newry . .	Newry . .	III.	182
47	Damptown . .	46　0　19	Wexford . .	Forth . .	Mayglass . .	Wexford . .	I.	312
33, 34	Damselstown . .	263　0　16	Meath . .	Upper Duleek . .	Stamullin . .	Drogheda .	I.	198
16	Dandlestown or Springville . .	462　0　34	Meath . .	Upper Kells . .	Burry . .	Kells . .	I.	205
45, 46	Danescastle . .	456　1　26	Wexford . .	Bargy . .	Bannow . .	Wexford . .	I.	304
23	Danesfort . .	771　3　2	Kilkenny . .	Shillelogher . .	Danesfort . .	Thomastown .	I.	114
11	Danesfort . .	385　3　29	Roscommon .	Boyle . .	Killummod . .	Cark on Shannon	IV.	196
20, 25	Danesfort Demesne or Togher . .	202　1　18d	Cavan . .	Upper Loughtee .	Kilmore . .	Cavan . .	III.	85
27, 28	Danesfort Lower .	160　1　8	Wicklow . .	Upper Talbotstown .	Kiltegan . .	Baltinglass .	I.	364
27, 28	Danesfort Upper .	244　3　8	Wicklow . .	Upper Talbotstown .	Kiltegan . .	Baltinglass .	I.	364
3	Danes Hill . .	72　0　20	Londonderry .	North East Liberties of Coleraine . .	Coleraine .	Coleraine .	III.	246
27,28,31,32	Danesrath . .	335　1　3	Kilkenny . .	Knocktopher . .	Knocktopher .	Thomastown .	I.	112
32	Danestown . .	1,197　2　35	Meath . .	Skreen . .	Danestown . .	Navan . .	I.	220
18	Daneswell . .	9　0　4	Dublin . .	Coolock . .	St. Georges .	Dublin North .	I.	29
18	Daneswell or Crossguns North .	78　3　22e	Dublin . .	Coolock . .	St. Georges .	Dublin North .	I.	29
34, 35	Dangan . .	756　1　17	Clare . .	Bunratty Upper .	Quin . .	Tulla . .	II.	10
2, 5	Dangan . .	813　2　20	Clare . .	Burren . .	Drumcreehy .	Ballyvaghan .	II.	12
11, 15	Dangan . .	171　0　15	Kildare . .	South Salt . .	Lyons . .	Celbridge . .	I.	77
28	Dangan . .	409　3　7f	Kilkenny . .	Gowran . .	Columbkille .	Thomastown .	I.	94
40, 43	Dangan . .	592　2　20	Kilkenny . .	Iverk . .	Kilmacow . .	Waterford .	I.	105
42, 43	Dangan . .	907　0　25	Meath . .	Lower Moyfenrath .	Laracor . .	Trim . .	I.	210
86	Dangan . .	562　3　24	Tipperary, S.R.	Iffa and Offa West .	Templetenny .	Clogheen . .	II.	320
47, 57	Dangananella East .	678　1　30	Clare . .	Moyarta . .	Kilmacduane .	Kilrush . .	II.	33
47, 57	Dangananella West .	490　1　4	Clare . .	Moyarta . .	Kilmacduane .	Kilrush . .	II.	33
110	Dangan Beg . .	181　0　11	Cork, W.R.	Kinalmeaky . .	Ballymodan .	Bandon . .	II.	151
44, 58	Danganbeg . .	233　2　38	Galway . .	Tiaquin . .	Killererin . .	Tuam . .	IV.	77
27, 31	Danganbeg . .	370　2　6	Kilkenny . .	Kells . .	Kilree . .	Callan . .	I.	109
25	Danganbeg . .	178　0　36	King's Co. .	Geashill . .	Geashill . .	Tullamore .	I.	140
36, 44	Danganbeg . .	211　0　37	Limerick . .	Glenquin . .	Mahoonagh .	Newcastle .	II.	246
34, 42	Danganbrack .	186　2　16	Clare . .	Bunratty Upper .	Quin . .	Tulla . .	II.	10
60, 68	Dangandargan .	422　3　20	Tipperary, S.R.	Clanwilliam . .	Dangandargan .	Tipperary .	II.	307
44	Dangan Eighter .	431　0　21	Galway . .	Tiaquin . .	Killererin . .	Tuam . .	IV.	77
11, 17	Dangan (*King*) .	170　2　12	Roscommon .	Ballintober North .	Kilmore . .	Cark on Shannon	IV.	187
82	Dangan Lower .	260　2　25g	Galway . .	Galway . .	Rahoon . .	Galway . .	IV.	37
110	Dangan More . .	365　0　24	Cork, W.R.	Kinalmeaky . .	Desertserges .	Bandon . .	II.	152
31	Danganmore .	375　2　24	Kilkenny . .	Kells . .	Dunnamaggan .	Callan . .	I.	108
70, 79	Danganmore . .	389　3　29	Mayo . .	Gallen . .	Kildacommoge .	Castlebar .	IV.	148
11, 12	Dangan (*Nugent*) .	308　3　16h	Roscommon .	Ballintober North .	Kilmore . .	Cark on Shannon	IV.	187
44, 58	Dangan Oughter .	357　1　3	Galway . .	Tiaquin . .	Killererin . .	Tuam . .	IV.	77

(a) Including 6A. 0R. 0P. water.
(b) Including 18A. 1R. 12P. water.
(c) Including 8A. 0R. 0P. water.

(d) Including 2A. 3R. 36P. water.
(e) { Within the Municipal Boundary, 0A. 2R. 19P.
{ Without the Municipal Boundary, 78A. 1R. 3P.

(f) Including 15A. 0R. 39P. River Nore.
(g) Including 31A. 0R. 21P. water.
(h) Including 9A. 3R. 28P. water.

No. of Sheet of the Ordnance Survey Maps.	Townlands and Towns.	Area in Statute Acres.			County.	Barony.	Parish.	Poor Law Union in 1857.	Townland Census of 1851, Part I.	
		A.	R.	P.					Vol.	Page
43	Danganreagh . .	87	1	5	King's Co. .	Ballybritt . .	Aghancon . .	Roscrea . .	I.	124
16	Danganroe . .	170	1	23	Queen's Co. .	Upperwoods .	Offerlane . .	Abbeyleix .	I.	251
8	Dangans . .	439	0	16	Queen's Co. .	Portnahinch .	Ardea . .	Mountmellick .	I.	243
58, 59	Dangansallagh .	708	3	5	Cork, W.R. .	West Muskerry .	Ballyvourney .	Macroom . .	II.	154
17	Dangansallagh .	330	3	1	Tipperary, N.R.	Ikerrin . .	Bourney . .	Roscrea . .	II.	274
43	DANGAN T. .	—			Kilkenny . .	Iverk . .	Kilmacow . .	Waterford .	I.	106
82, 94	Dangan Upper .	280	2	6	Galway . .	Galway . .	Rahoon . .	Galway . .	IV.	37
10	Danielstown . .	136	2	12	Kildare . .	Ikeathy&Oughterany	Mainham . .	Celbridge . .	I.	58
18, 26	Dannanstown . .	145	1	0	Cork, E.R. .	Fermoy . .	Templeroan .	Mallow . .	II.	82
19	Danville . .	143	2	5	Kilkenny . .	Shillelogher .	St. Patrick's .	Kilkenny . .	I.	116
19	Daphney . .	37	0	6	Wexford . .	Scarawalsh .	Monart . .	Enniscorthy .	I.	·324
12	Darbyshill . .	76	0	20	Kilkenny . .	Crannagh . .	Clomantagh .	Urlingford .	I.	85
36, 40	Darbystown . .	273	1	17	Kilkenny . .	Knocktopher .	Listerlin . .	New Ross . .	I.	113
5	Darcystown . .	542	0	17a	Dublin . .	Balrothery East .	Balrothery . .	Balrothery . .	I.	19
22	Dardisrath . .	281	0	29	Louth . .	Ferrard . .	Termonfeckin .	Drogheda . .	I.	182
14	Dardistown . .	69	1	30	Dublin . .	Coolock . .	Santry . .	Dublin North .	I.	29
45	Dardistown . .	129	1	25	Meath . .	Dunboyne . .	Kilbride . .	Dunshaughlin .	I.	200
27, 28	Dardistown . .	691	0	10	Meath . .	Upper Duleek .	Moorechurch .	Drogheda . .	I.	198
13, 20	Dardistown . .	406	0	1	Westmeath .	Delvin . .	Killagh . .	Castletowndelvin	I.	265
17	Dargan . .	134	1	31	Donegal . .	Kilmacrenan .	Clondavaddog .	Milford . .	III.	124
62	Darhanagh . .	124	1	26b	Mayo . .	Gallen . .	Killasser . .	Swineford .	IV.	149
15	Darkisland . .	70	1	10	Limerick . .	Coonagh . .	Doon . .	Tipperary .	II.	234
20	Darkley . .	845	0	35	Armagh . .	Armagh . .	Keady . .	Armagh . .	III.	45
23	Darkley . .	447	0	12c	Cavan . .	Clankee . .	Shercock . .	Bailieborough .	III.	74
15	Darkvalley . .	81	1	11	Leitrim . .	Drumahaire .	Killarga . .	Manorhamilton .	IV.	98
107	Darkwood . .	70	0	22	Cork, W.R. .	East Carbery (W.D.)	Fanlobbus . .	Dunmanway .	II.	131
15	Darndale . .	87	2	1	Dublin . .	Coolock . .	Coolock . .	Dublin North .	I.	27
92, 98	Darney . .	402	3	23	Donegal . .	Banagh . .	Killaghtee . .	Donegal . .	III.	109
26	Daroge . .	412	2	4d	Longford . .	Rathcline . .	Shrule . .	Ballymahon .	I.	165
57, 59	Darragh Beg . .	336	2	28	Limerick . .	Coshlea . .	Darragh . .	Kilmallock .	II.	238
17	*Darragh Island* .	18	0	26	Down . .	Dufferin . .	Killinchy . .	Downpatrick .	III.	166
13	Darraghlan . .	193	3	4	Monaghan . .	Monaghan . .	Kilmore . .	Monaghan . .	III.	276
56, 57, 59	Darragh More .	485	3	24	Limerick . .	Coshlea . .	Darragh . .	Kilmallock .	II.	238
41	Darragh North .	362	0	7	Clare . .	Islands . .	Killone . .	Ennis . .	II.	30
41	Darragh South .	151	2	4	Clare . .	Islands . .	Killone . .	Ennis . .	II.	30
40, 48	Darranstown . .	733	0	33	Limerick . .	Coshlea . .	Emlygrennan .	Kilmallock .	II.	238
26	Darraragh . .	329	2	9e	Mayo . .	Erris . .	Kilcommon .	Belmullet . .	IV.	143
135	Darrary . .	356	1	23	Cork, W.R. .	Ibane and Barryroe	Templeomalus .	Clonakilty .	II.	151
4, 16, 17	Darrary North .	160	0	7	Galway . .	Dunmore . .	Dunmore . .	Tuam . .	IV.	33
16, 17	Darrary South .	168	2	22	Galway . .	Dunmore . .	Dunmore . .	Tuam . .	IV.	33
44, 53	Darrery . .	426	3	14	Limerick . .	Glenquin . .	Killeedy . .	Newcastle .	II.	245
8	Darrigal . .	795	2	9	Waterford .	Middlethird .	Kilmeadan .	Waterford .	II.	368
106	Darrynane Beg .	609	2	17	Kerry . .	Dunkerron South .	Kilcrohane .	Cahersiveen .	II.	183
106	Darrynane More .	404	1	10	Kerry . .	Dunkerron South .	Kilcrohane .	Cahersiveen .	II.	183
15, 16	Dartans . .	367	2	27f	Tyrone . .	Omagh West .	Urney . .	Castlederg .	III.	318
98, 106	Dartfield . .	367	2	35	Galway . .	Leitrim . .	Kilreekill . .	Loughrea . .	IV.	54
11	Darton . .	232	0	27	Armagh . .	Armagh . .	Tynan . .	Armagh . .	III.	46
3, 6, 7	Dartress . .	425	3	17	Londonderry .	Coleraine . .	Dunboe . .	Coleraine . .	III.	231
11, 12	Darver . .	296	3	20	Louth . .	Louth . .	Darver . .	Dundalk . .	I.	183
4, 7	Dary . .	291	0	20	Tipperary, N.R.	Lower Ormond .	Aglishcloghane .	Borrisokane .	II.	281
17	Davagh . .	32	0	14	Monaghan . .	Dartree . .	Killeevan . .	Clones . .	III.	268
3, 6	Davagh Etra . .	140	2	6	Monaghan . .	Trough . .	Errigal Trough .	Monaghan . .	III.	283
20	Davagh Lower .	974	0	22	Tyrone . .	Dungannon Upper .	Lissan . .	Cookstown .	III.	309
6	Davagh Otra . .	137	0	34	Monaghan . .	Trough . .	Errigal Trough .	Monaghan . .	III.	283
20	Davagh Upper .	464	3	14	Tyrone . .	Dungannon Upper .	Lissan . .	Cookstown .	III.	309
38	Davidstown . .	223	2	18	Kildare . .	Kilkea and Moone .	Killelan . .	Baltinglass .	I.	60
32	Davidstown . .	267	3	13	Kildare . .	Narragh & RebanEast	Davidstown .	Athy . .	I.	66
43, 44	Davidstown . .	428	3	19	Kilkenny . .	Ida . .	Kilcolumb .	Waterford .	I.	102
33	Davidstown . .	125	0	13	Meath . .	Upper Duleek .	Clonalvy . .	Drogheda . .	I.	197
19	Davidstown . .	203	2	37	Meath . .	Upper Slane .	Slane . .	Navan . .	I.	225
17, 18	Davidstown . .	572	0	5	Westmeath .	Rathconrath .	Rathconrath .	Mullingar .	I.	284
25	Davidstown . .	292	3	6	Wexford . .	Bantry . .	Rossdroit . .	Enniscorthy .	I.	301
36	Davidstown . .	455	0	32	Wexford . .	Bantry . .	Whitechurchglynn .	Wexford . .	I.	303
37	Davidstown . .	219	3	33	Wexford . .	Shelmaliere West .	Kilbrideglynn .	Wexford . .	I.	334
21	Davidstown . .	264	3	17	Wicklow . .	Upper Talbotstown .	Donaghmore .	Baltinglass .	I.	363
19	Davidstown or Bal-lydaw . .	328	2	18	Wexford . .	Scarawalsh .	Monart . .	Enniscorthy .	I.	324
38	Davidstown Demesne	279	2	12	Kildare . .	Kilkea and Moone .	Killelan . .	Baltinglass .	I.	60
32, 33	Davidstown or Guil-ford . .	179	2	3	Westmeath .	Fartullagh . .	Clonfad . .	Mullingar .	I.	268
40	Davidstown Lower .	271	2	8	Kildare . .	Kilkea and Moone .	Graney . .	Athy . .	I.	60
78, 40	Davidstown (Pillsworth)	387	1	28	Kildare . .	Kilkea and Moone .	Graney . .	Baltinglass .	I.	60
40	Davidstown Upper .	295	3	15	Kildare . .	Kilkea and Moone .	Graney . .	Athy . .	I.	60

(a) Including 2A. 0R. 29P. detached portion.
(b) Including 5A. 1R. 23P. water.
(c) Including 39A. 2R. 13P. water.
(d) Including 0A. 2R. 38P. water.
(e) Including 12A. 0R. 39P. water.
(f) Including 9A. 3R. 14P. water.

No. of Sheet of the Ordnance Survey Maps.	Townlands and Towns.	Area in Statute Acres.	County.	Barony.	Parish.	Poor Law Union in 1857.	Townland Census of 1851, Part I.	
		A. R. P.					Vol.	Page
104, 114	Davillaun	60 0 5	Mayo	Murrisk	Inishbofin	Clifden	IV.	159
9	Davisshill	202 2 13	Carlow	Rathvilly	Clonmore	Shillelagh	I.	10
7	Davis's Island	38 3 23	Roscommon	Boyle	Tumna	Boyle	IV.	198
31	Davistown	210 0 18	King's Co.	Eglish	Drumcullen	Parsonstown	I.	134
119	Davros	663 2 21a	Mayo	Kilmaine	Kilcommon	Ballinrobe	IV.	154
10	Davy's Island	12 1 37	Fermanagh	Lurg	Magheraculmoney	Lowtherstown	III.	208
33	Daw	87 3 22	Meath	Upper Duleek	Duleek Abbey	Drogheda	I.	198
64	Dawros	468 1 15b	Donegal	Boylagh	Inishkeel	Glenties	III.	112
57	Dawros	188 1 29	Galway	Clare	Kilmoylan	Tuam	IV.	22
92,101,102	Dawros	415 2 19	Kerry	Glanarought	Tuosist	Kenmare	II.	186
37, 42	Dawros	628 3 25	Sligo	Leyny	Kilmacteige	Tobercurry	IV.	231
22, 23	Dawros Beg	170 1 27	Galway	Ballynahinch	Ballynakill	Clifden	IV.	11
64	Dawros Island	9 0 23	Donegal	Boylagh	Inishkeel	Glenties	III.	114
16	Dawros Lower	102 3 8	Galway	Dunmore	Addergoole	Tuam	IV.	33
10, 23	Dawros More	612 2 4	Galway	Ballynahinch	Ballynakill	Clifden	IV.	11
16	Dawros Upper	185 3 5	Galway	Dunmore	Addergoole	Tuam	IV.	33
22, 23	Dawson Grove Demesne	597 1 22c	Monaghan	Dartree	Ematris	Cootehill	III.	266
33	Dawsonsbog	159 3 1	Tipperary, N.R.	Upper Ormond	Templederry	Nenagh	II.	293
17	Dawsonsdemesne	148 1 9	Louth	Ardee	Ardee	Ardee	I.	171
62	Dawstown	502 0 33	Cork, E.R.	East Muskerry	Garrycloyne	Cork	II.	103
62	Dawstown	341 2 36	Cork, E.R.	East Muskerry	Matehy	Cork	II.	105
33	Deal Island	7 3 39	Fermanagh	Tirkennedy	Cleenish	Lisnaskea	III.	220
87	Dean and Chapter Land of Cloyne	30 0 18	Cork, E.R.	Barrymore	Clonmel	Cork	II.	53
16	Deanery	92 1 27	Roscommon	Roscommon	Elphin	Strokestown	IV.	209
5	Deanery-land	16 1 13d	Limerick	Limerick, Municipal Borough of	St. Nicholas	Limerick	II.	262
7, 8	Deanestown	61 0 34e	Dublin	Balrothery East	Lusk	Balrothery	I.	21
13, 14	Deanestown	173 0 2	Dublin	Castleknock	Castleknock	Dublin North	I.	24
7	Deanestown	222 3 21	Dublin	Nethercross	Swords	Balrothery	I.	32
74	Deanrock	90 3 2	Cork, E.R.	Cork	St. Finbars	Cork	II.	65
13	Deanscurragh	75 0 33	Longford	Ardagh	Templemichael	Longford	I.	153
23	Deansgrange	377 2 8	Dublin	Rathdown	Kill	Rathdown	I.	35
23	DEANSGRANGE T.	—	Dublin	Rathdown	Kill	Rathdown	I.	36
19	Deansground	35 0 13f	Kilkenny	Kilkenny, Municipal Borough of	St. Patrick's	Kilkenny	I.	117
61	Deansgrove	252 2 8	Tipperary, S.R.	Middlethird	St. Patricksrock	Cashel	II.	330
17, 21	Deansrath	216 1 39	Dublin	Uppercross	Clondalkin	Dublin South	I.	39
20	Deanstown	116 1 10	Limerick	Connello Lower	Cappagh	Rathkeale	II.	227
8	Debicot	126 3 21	Queen's Co.	Portnahinch	Ardea	Mountmellick	I.	243
76	Decoy	70 1 0	Tipperary, S.R.	Iffa and Offa East	Inishlounaght	Clonmel	III.	313
15, 21	Decoy	209 2 19	Wicklow	Lower Talbotstown	Dunlavin	Baltinglass	I.	360
47, 48	Deebert	129 0 24	Limerick	Kilmallock	St. Peter's & St. Paul's	Kilmallock	II.	250
39	Deechomade	216 3 8	Sligo	Corran	Cloonoghil	Tobercurry	IV.	225
11	Deegerty	215 0 2	Limerick	Kenry	Kilcornan	Rathkeale	II.	249
35	Deehommed	1,525 1 28	Down	Upper Iveagh, Lr. pt.	Drumgooland	Banbridge	III.	172
29,30,38,39	Deelcastle	615 2 29	Mayo	Tirawley	Ardagh	Ballina	IV.	163
6	Declin Beg	320 2 24	Clare	Burren	Oughtmama	Ballyvaghan	II.	14
5, 6	Declin More	630 1 1	Clare	Burren	Oughtmama	Ballyvaghan	II.	14
36	Declis	244 0 11	Kerry	Corkaguiny	Killiney	Dingle	II.	178
102	Declis	230 2 20	Kerry	Glanarought	Kilcaskan	Kenmare	II.	186
108, 111	Declis	477 0 24	Kerry	Glanarought	Tuosist	Kenmare	II.	188
70, 80	Declis	190 2 1	Kerry	Iveragh	Killinane	Cahersiveen	II.	197
60	Deelish	341 0 15	Cork, W.R.	East Muskerry	Aghabulloge	Macroom	II.	153
141	Deelish	70 2 27	Cork, W.R.	West Carbery (E.D.)	Abbeystrowry	Skibbereen	II.	136
119	Deelish	788 0 5	Cork, W.R.	West Carbery (E.D.)	Dromdaleague	Skibbereen	II.	140
28	Deelish	49 2 20	Limerick	Connello Lower	Clonagh	Rathkeale	II.	227
19	Deelish	140 2 14	Limerick	Shanid	Kilmoylan	Rathkeale	II.	256
23, 31	Deelish	332 1 19	Waterford	Decies without Drum	Kilgobnet	Dungarvan	II.	357
23, 31	Deelishmountain	444 0 18	Waterford	Decies without Drum	Kilgobnet	Dungarvan	II.	357
27, 33	Deenes	367 2 1	Meath	Lower Duleek	Duleek	Drogheda	I.	195
105	Deenish	122 1 20	Kerry	Dunkerron South	Kilcrohane	Cahersiveen	II.	183
50, 51	Deenish Island	43 2 31	Clare	Bunratty Lower	Kilmaleery	Ennis	II.	5
25, 32	Deenodes	292 0 38	Sligo	Leyny	Killoran	Tobercurry	IV.	230
53	Deenystown	31 0 19	Donegal	Kilmacrenan	Aghanunshin	Letterkenny	III.	122
32, 37	Deeps	236 1 18	Wexford	Shelmaliere East	Tikillin	Wexford	I.	331
12	Deepstown	99 1 0	Antrim	Lower Dunluce	Derrykeighan	Ballymoney	III.	16
68	Deerfield or Gortnavea	57 0 20g	Galway	Moycullen	Moycullen	Galway	IV.	71
33, 38	Deerfin	788 0 19	Antrim	Lower Antrim	Ballyclug	Ballymena	III.	3
24	Deer Island	4 3 8	Galway	Ballynahinch	Moyrus	Clifden	IV.	14
100	Deer Island	0 1 18	Mayo	Carra	Burriscarra	Ballinrobe	IV.	127
50	Decrisland or Inishmore	443 3 24	Clare	Clonderalaw	Kilchreest	Killadysert	II.	15

(a) Including 17A. 2R. 36P. water.
(b) Including 17A. 3R. 35P. water.
(c) Including 101A. 2R. 8P. water.

(d) Included in the Parish of St. Nicholas.
(e) Including 0A. 3R. 6P. detached portion.

(f) Included in the Parish of St. Patrick.
(g) Including 4A. 1R. 36P. water.

No. of Sheet of the Ordnance Survey Maps.	Townlands and Towns.	Area in Statute Acres. A. R. P.	County.	Barony.	Parish.	Poor Law Union in 1857.	Townland Census of 1851, Part I. Vol.	Page
49,50,54,55	Deer Park	605 3 11	Antrim	Lower Massereene	Muckamore (Grange of)	Antrim	III.	28
62	Deer Park	1,260 0 26a	Antrim	Upper Massereene	Glenavy	Lurgan	III.	30
39	Deerpark	354 3 26	Cavan	Castlerahan	Lurgan	Oldcastle	III.	69
51, 52	Deerpark	65 1 26	Clare	Bunratty Lower	Bunratty	Ennis	II.	3
51, 52	Deerpark	116 1 1	Clare	Bunratty Lower	Feenagh	Ennis	II.	4
34, 42	Deerpark	178 1 5	Clare	Bunratty Upper	Doora	Ennis	II.	8
9, 16	Deerpark	165 1 24	Clare	Burren	Noughaval	Corrofin	II.	13
45	Deerpark	336 0 7	Cork, E.R.	Barrymore	Castlelyons	Fermoy	II.	53
35	Deer Park	242 3 6b	Cork, E.R.	Condons&Clangibbon	Litter	Fermoy	II.	62
66	Deer Park	391 1 14	Cork, E.R.	Imokilly	Mogeely	Middleton	II.	89
61, 62, 69	Deerpark	240 1 7	Donegal	Raphoe	Raphoe	Strabane	III.	140
32	Deer Park	170 2 3	Fermanagh	Clanawley	Killesher	Enniskillen	III.	192
36	Deer Park	184 1 21	Fermanagh	Clankelly	Clones	Clones	III.	195
28	Deer Park	285 0 22	Fermanagh	Magherastephana	Aghavea	Lisnaskea	III.	218
84, 96	Deerpark	468 1 22	Galway	Athenry	Kilconierin	Loughrea	IV.	4
83, 84	Deerpark	121 3 29	Galway	Clare	Athenry	Galway	IV.	17
42	Deerpark	108 2 30	Galway	Clare	Kilkilvery	Tuam	IV.	20
42	Deerpark	298 1 6	Galway	Clare	Killeany	Tuam	IV.	20
74, 87	Deerpark	191 3 20	Galway	Clonmacnowen	Kilcloony	Ballinasloe	IV.	25
104, 114	Deerpark	117 0 29	Galway	Dunkellin	Kilchreest	Loughrea	IV.	28
104	Deerpark	153 2 37	Galway	Dunkellin	Killeely	Gort	IV.	29
83, 95	Deerpark	65 2 29	Galway	Dunkellin	Oranmore	Galway	IV.	32
30	Deerpark	147 1 19	Galway	Dunmore	Tuam	Tuam	IV.	36
123	Deerpark	50 1 20	Galway	Kiltartan	Kiltartan	Gort	IV.	48
108, 118	Deerpark	214 0 14	Galway	Longford	Kilquain	Portumna	IV.	60
117,118,126	Deerpark	110 3 11	Galway	Longford	Lickmolassy	Portumna	IV.	61
27	Deerpark	97 1 35	Galway	Ross	Cong	Oughterard	IV.	73
15	Deerpark	277 0 7	Kerry	Clanmaurice	Kilcaragh	Listowel	II.	169
44	Deerpark	138 2 7	Kerry	Corkaguiny	Kinard	Dingle	II.	179
44	Deerpark	47 3 18	Kerry	Corkaguiny	Minard	Dingle	II.	179
66	Deer Park	420 0 29	Kerry	Magunihy	Killarney	Killarney	II.	203
40	Deerpark	158 3 1	Kildare	Kilkea and Moone	Castledermot	Carlow	I.	59
19	Deerpark	530 0 10	Kilkenny	Crannagh	St. Canice	Kilkenny	I.	87
29	Deerpark	229 2 10	Kilkenny	Gowran	Graiguenamanagh	Thomastown	I.	95
40	Deerpark	198 1 29	Kilkenny	Knocktopher	Rossinan	Waterford	I.	113
22	Deerpark	102 0 20	Kilkenny	Shillelogher	Killaloe	Callan	I.	115
32, 37	Deerpark	422 0 16	King's Co.	Ballybritt	Letterluna	Parsonstown	I.	126
7, 8, 15, 16	Deerpark	321 0 23	King's Co.	Ballycowan	Rahan	Tullamore	I.	128
14, 22	Deerpark	301 0 24	King's Co.	Garrycastle	Tisaran	Parsonstown	I.	138
7	Deerpark	286 0 14	Leitrim	Rosclogher	Killasnet	Manorhamilton	IV.	109
24	Deerpark	75 0 20	Limerick	Clanwilliam	Dromkeen	Limerick	II.	223
24	Deerpark	44 3 19	Limerick	Clanwilliam	Grean	Limerick	II.	224
49	Deerpark	317 1 8	Limerick	Coshlea	Galbally	Mitchelstown	II.	238
9, 16	Deer Park	212 3 25c	Londonderry	Keenaght	Drumachose	NewTⁿLimavady	III.	235
9, 16	Deer Park	58 3 12d	Londonderry	Keenaght	Tamlaght Finlagan	NewTⁿLimavady	III.	237
14, 19	Deerpark	45 3 22	Longford	Ardagh	Ardagh	Longford	I.	151
8	Deerpark	191 3 27	Longford	Longford	Clongesh	Longford	I.	157
23	Deerpark	271 2 4	Longford	Shrule	Agharra	Ballymahon	I.	166
6	Deerpark	79 3 21	Louth	Upper Dundalk	Philipstown	Dundalk	I.	179
88	Deerpark	329 0 22e	Mayo	Burrishoole	Aghagower	Westport	IV.	118
100	Deerpark	211 1 29	Mayo	Carra	Burriscarra	Ballinrobe	IV.	127
100	Deerpark	131 0 6	Mayo	Carra	Toughty	Ballinrobe	IV.	130
11	Deerpark	78 0 12	Meath	Lower Kells	Newtown	Kells	I.	204
7, 12	Deerpark	741 0 9	Queen's Co.	Maryborough West	Clonenagh&Clonagheen	Mountmellick	I.	242
11, 12	Deerpark	667 1 11	Queen's Co.	Upperwoods	Offerlane	Mountmellick	I.	251
6	Deerpark	794 0 17	Roscommon	Boyle	Boyle	Boyle	IV.	194
11	Deerpark	69 0 5	Roscommon	Boyle	Killukin	Carᵏ. on Shannon	IV.	195
11	Deerpark	31 2 36	Roscommon	Boyle	Killummod	Carᵏ. on Shannon	IV.	196
21	Deerpark	103 1 10	Roscommon	Castlereagh	Kilcorkey	Castlereagh	IV.	199
33	Deerpark	123 1 24	Sligo	Corran	Kilmorgan	Sligo	IV.	227
26	Deerpark	201 1 27	Tipperary, N.R.	Upper Ormond	Kilmore	Nenagh	II.	291
67	Deerpark	133 3 5	Tipperary, S.R.	Clanwilliam	Kilfeakle	Tipperary	II.	308
66	Deerpark	345 0 2	Tipperary, S.R.	Clanwilliam	Shronell	Tipperary	II.	310
85	Deerpark	634 2 18f	Tipperary, S.R.	Iffa and Offa East	Carrick	Carrick on Suir	II.	312
82	Deerpark	54 2 22g	Tipperary, S.R.	Iffa and Offa East	Inishlounaght	Clogheen	II.	313
60, 61	Deerpark	152 3 9	Tipperary, S.R.	Middlethird	Horeabbey	Cashel	II.	327
43, 49	Deerpark	164 0 10	Tipperary, S.R.	Slievardagh	Kilcooly	Urlingford	II.	333
20	Deerpark	288 0 35	Waterford	Coshmore&Coshbride	Lismore & Mocollop	Lismore	II.	345
5	Deerpark	326 3 11	Waterford	Glenahiry	Kilronan	Clonmel	II.	365
7	Deerpark	13 0 5	Westmeath	Fore	Rathgarve	Castletowndelvin	I.	271
7	Deerpark	220 2 28	Westmeath	Fore	St. Feighins	Castletowndelvin	I.	271
22	Deerpark	70 0 30	Westmeath	Kilkenny West	Kilkenny West	Athlone	I.	273

(a) Including 156A. 3R. 21P. Portmore Lough.   (d) Including 3A. 1R. 29P. water.   (f) Including 4A. 3R. 20P. water.
(b) Including 5A. 3R. 38P. water.   (e) Including 37A. 3R. 14P. water.   (g) Including 3A. 2R. 20P. water.
(c) Including 4A. 1R. 1P. water.

No. of Sheet of the Ordnance Survey Maps.	Townlands and Towns.	Area in Statute Acres.			County.	Barony.	Parish.	Poor Law Union in 1857.	Townland Census of 1851, Part I.	
		A.	R.	P.					Vol.	Page
10, 11	Deerpark	109	3	30	Westmeath	Moygoish	Kilmacnevan	Mullingar	I.	280
2, 6	Deerpark	247	3	20	Wexford	Gorey	Kilnahue	Gorey	I.	319
36	Deerpark	132	2	24	Wexford	Shelmaliere West	Horetown	New Ross	I.	333
5	Deerpark	341	1	26	Wicklow	Lower Talbotstown	Blessington	Naas	I.	358
7, 12	Deerpark	990	3	25	Wicklow	Rathdown	Powerscourt	Rathdown	I.	356
43, 47	Deerpark	505	2	27	Wicklow	Shillelagh	Carnew	Shillelagh	I.	357
27	Deerpark	333	1	8	Wicklow	Upper Talbotstown	Baltinglass	Baltinglass	I.	362
21	Deerpark	198	3	30	Wicklow	Upper Talbotstown	Donaghmore	Baltinglass	I.	363
28, 33	Deerpark	118	0	29	Wicklow	Upper Talbotstown	Kiltegan	Baltinglass	I.	364
34	Deer Park (*Clarke*)	165	2	17	Tyrone	Omagh East	Drumragh	Omagh	III.	312
88	Deerpark East	169	3	39	Mayo	Murrisk	Oughaval	Westport	IV.	161
29	Deerpark East	267	0	27	Waterford	Coshmore&Coshbride	Lismore and Mocollop	Lismore	II.	345
29, 34, 35	Deer Park Farms	2,180	0	4	Antrim	Lower Glenarm	Tickmacrevan	Larne	III.	23
29	Deer Park Great	832	3	11	Antrim	Lower Glenarm	Tickmacrevan	Larne	III.	23
29	Deerparkhill	357	3	4	Waterford	Coshmore&Coshbride	Lismore and Mocollop	Lismore	II.	345
30	Deer Park Little	217	1	32	Antrim	Lower Glenarm	Tickmacrevan	Larne	III.	23
85	Deerparklodge	91	1	1	Tipperary, S.R.	Iffa and Offa East	Carrick	Carrick on Suir	II.	312
15	Deerpark Lower	33	2	38	Clare	Corcomroe	Kilmanaheen	Ennistimon	II.	21
79, 90	Deerpark Lower	69	1	2	Mayo	Carra	Drum	Castlebar	IV.	128
17	Deer Park Lower or Old	170	3	27	Tyrone	Strabane Lower	Ardstraw	Strabane	III.	319
15	Deer Park or Magheraghanrush	270	2	37	Sligo	Carbury	Calry	Sligo	IV.	220
34	Deer Park (*McCormick*)	118	3	27	Tyrone	Omagh East	Drumragh	Omagh	III.	312
15	Deerpark Middle	31	2	9	Clare	Corcomroe	Kilmanaheen	Ennistimon	II.	21
17	Deer Park Middle	81	1	8	Tyrone	Strabane Lower	Ardstraw	Strabane	III.	318
5	Deerpark Mountain	131	1	5	Waterford	Glenahiry	Kilronan	Clonmel	II.	365
20, 21	Deerpark New	757	0	9	Carlow	Forth	Barragh	Enniscorthy	I.	4
43	Deerpark North	126	3	31*a*	Clare	Bunratty Upper	Quin	Tulla	II.	10
21, 29	Deerpark North	552	2	20	Waterford	Coshmore&Coshbride	Lismore and Mocollop	Lismore	II.	345
20, 21	Deerpark Old	727	1	38	Carlow	Forth	Barragh	Enniscorthy	I.	4
43	Deerpark South	12	0	13	Clare	Bunratty Upper	Quin	Tulla	II.	10
15	Deerpark Upper	74	1	37	Clare	Corcomroe	Kilmanaheen	Ennistimon	II.	21
90	Deerpark Upper	106	3	31	Mayo	Carra	Drum	Castlebar	IV.	128
17	Deer Park Upper or New	229	1	15	Tyrone	Strabane Lower	Ardstraw	Strabane	III.	319
15, 23	Deerpark West	184	0	10	Clare	Corcomroe	Kilmanaheen	Ennistimon	II.	21
87	Deerpark West	288	1	22	Mayo	Murrisk	Oughaval	Westport	IV.	161
94	Deesert	250	0	8	Kerry	Glanarought	Kilgarvan	Kenmare	II.	187
61, 72	Deeshart	101	1	3	Cork, E.R.	East Muskerry	Magourney	Macroom	II.	105
23, 27	Deffier	569	1	28*b*	Leitrim	Leitrim	Kiltoghert	Cark. on Shannon	IV.	101
7, 12	Deffrick	355	0	38	Antrim	Lower Dunluce	Billy	Ballymoney	III.	16
40, 49	Dehomad	1,920	2	15	Clare	Islands	Clondagad	Killadysert	II.	29
24, 29	Delamain	171	1	16	Kildare	Naas South	Carnalway	Naas	I.	64
8, 13	Delgany	259	3	26	Wicklow	Rathdown	Delgany	Rathdown	I.	355
13	DELGANY T.	—			Wicklow	Rathdown	Delgany	Rathdown	I.	355
5	Dellabrown	28	2	38	Dublin	Balrothery East	Holmpatrick	Balrothery	I.	20
1, 6	Delliga	182	0	30	Cork, E.R.	Orrery and Kilmore	Kilbolane	Kanturk	II.	108
22	Delligabaun	166	2	38	Queen's Co.	Clarmallagh	Aghaboe	Donaghmore	I.	236
12	Dellin	112	0	36	Louth	Louth	Darver	Dundalk	I.	183
14	DELVIN T.	—			Westmeath	Delvin	Castletowndelvin	Castletowndelvin	I.	264
18	Demailestown	715	0	35	Meath	Morgallion	Kilberry	Navan	I.	209
1	Demesne	67	2	27	Antrim	Cary	Rathlin Island	Ballycastle	III.	15
40	Demesne	245	2	39*c*	Antrim	Upper Glenarm	Kilwaughter	Larne	III.	25
6	Demesne	259	0	1*d*	Armagh	Oneilland East	Shankill	Lurgan	III.	50
11	Demesne	108	3	5	Carlow	Idrone West	Oldleighlin	Carlow	I.	9
22	Demesne	203	1	31	Cork, E.R.	Duhallow	Clonfert	Kanturk	II.	68
17, 25	Demesne	413	0	33	Cork, E.R.	Fermoy	Doneraile	Mallow	II.	78
77, 88, 89	Demesne	368	2	36	Cork, E.R.	Imokilly	Cloyne	Middleton	II.	85
107, 108	Demesne	279	0	4	Cork, W.R.	East Carbery (W.D.)	Fanlobbus	Dunmanway	II.	131
79	Demesne	130	1	9*e*	Donegal	Raphoe	Donaghmore	Strabane	III.	137
24, 25	Demesne	211	2	32	Down	Ards Upper	Arduin	Downpatrick	III.	159
17, 23	Demesne	177	2	8*f*	Fermanagh	Tirkennedy	Enniskillen	Enniskillen	III.	221
29	Demesne	374	0	13	Galway	Dunmore	Tuam	Tuam	IV.	36
66	Demesne	174	2	39	Kerry	Magunihy	Killarney	Killarney	II.	203
8	Demesne	79	3	6*g*	Kildare	Carbury	Ardkill	Edenderry	I.	51
8	Demesne	360	3	11*h*	Kildare	Carbury	Carbury	Edenderry	I.	51
13	Demesne	146	1	11	Longford	Longford	Templemichael	Longford	I.	160
7	Demesne	373	3	23	Louth	Upper Dundalk	Dundalk	Dundalk	I.	178
79	Demesne	182	0	20	Mayo	Carra	Breaghwy	Castlebar	IV.	127
6	Demesne	1,499	0	3*i*	Roscommon	Boyle	Ardcarn	Boyle	IV.	193
6	Demesne	103	3	11	Roscommon	Boyle	Boyle	Boyle	IV.	194
6	Demesne	436	1	38	Roscommon	Boyle	Kilbryan	Boyle	IV.	195

(a) Including 0A. 1R. 0P. water.
(b) Including Islands.
(c) Including 5A. 1R. 16P. water.
(d) Including 59A. 0R. 36P. water.
(e) Including 2A. 2R. 7P. water.
(f) Including 11A. 1R. 30P. water.
(g) Including 3A. 0R. 10P. water.
(h) Including 19A. 1R. 8P. water.
(i) Including 58A. 2R. 32P. water.

No. of Sheet of the Ordnance Survey Maps.	Townlands and Towns.	Area in Statute Acres.	County.	Barony.	Parish.	Poor Law Union in 1857.	Townland Census of 1851, Part I.	
		A. R. P.					Vol.	Page
20, 26	Demesne	557 1 33a	Roscommon	Castlereagh	Kilkeevin	Castlereagh	IV.	200
12	Demesne	71 0 27	Tipperary, N.R.	Ikerrin	Roscrea	Roscrea	II.	276
67	Demesne	594 2 8	Tyrone	Dungannon Lower	Aghaloo	Armagh	III.	296
38	Demesne or Mears-parkfarm	238 2 0	Westmeath	Moycashel	Kilbeggan	Tullamore	I.	278
30,31,37,38	Demesne of Down	1,486 3 34b	Down	Lecale Upper	Down	Downpatrick	III.	180
12	Demesne or Parkmore	222 1 10	Armagh	Armagh	Armagh	Armagh	III.	43
29	Demesne Upper	121 0 25	Antrim	Lower Glenarm	Tickmacrevan	Larne	III.	23
18, 22	Demoan	341 1 39	Armagh	Orior Lower	Ballymore	Newry	III.	55
52	Demone	183 1 30	Tipperary, S.R.	Kilnamanagh Lower	Clonoulty	Cashel	II.	323
33	Denhamstown	215 0 15	Meath	Upper Duleek	Ardcath	Drogheda	I.	197
26, 32	Dennbane	323 1 23	Cavan	Upper Loughtee	Denn	Cavan	III.	83
26	Denn Glebe	48 2 23	Cavan	Upper Loughtee	Denn	Cavan	III.	83
5	Dennis' Fields	14 0 2	Dublin	Balrothery East	Balrothery	Balrothery	I.	19
42	Dennistown	144 0 33	Wexford	Forth	Kildavin	Wexford	I.	310
25, 26, 32	Dennmore or Leggandenn	445 1 5	Cavan	Upper Loughtee	Denn	Cavan	III.	83
14, 19	Deralk	128 3 12c	Cavan	Lower Loughtee	Drumlane	Cavan	III.	79
19, 20	Deramfield	234 3 7d	Cavan	Lower Loughtee	Drumlane	Cavan	III.	79
5	Derawley	649 3 20	Longford	Longford	Killoe	Longford	I.	159
19	Derdimus	129 3 4	Kilkenny	Shillelogher	Castleinch or Inchyolaghan	Kilkenny	I.	114
15, 20	Deredis Lower	279 0 23e	Cavan	Upper Loughtee	Urney	Cavan	III.	86
20	Deredis Upper	298 1 28f	Cavan	Upper Loughtee	Urney	Cavan	III.	86
5	Dergalt	488 1 35	Tyrone	Strabane Lower	Camus	Strabane	III.	320
36, 37	Derganagh	339 3 36	Londonderry	Loughinsholin	Termoneeny	Magherafelt	III.	244
49	Dergany (Maguire)	153 3 37	Tyrone	Omagh East	Dromore	Omagh	III.	311
49	Dergany (Neville)	161 0 0	Tyrone	Omagh East	Dromore	Lowtherstown	III.	311
101	Derg Beg Island	2 2 3	Donegal	Tirhugh	Templecarn	Donegal	III.	149
11, 18	Dergbrough	674 1 13g	Tyrone	Strabane Upper	Bodoney Upper	Gortin	III.	324
53, 60	Dergenagh	437 0 38	Tyrone	Dungannon Lower	Killeeshil	Dungannon	III.	298
35	Dergmoney Lower	234 2 36h	Tyrone	Omagh East	Drumragh	Omagh	III.	312
35	Dergmoney Upper	88 3 10i	Tyrone	Omagh East	Drumragh	Omagh	III.	312
101	Derg More Island	5 1 20	Donegal	Tirhugh	Templecarn	Donegal	III.	149
7	Dergraw	285 3 17	Roscommon	Boyle	Ardcarn	Cark. on Shannon	IV.	192
76	Dergroagh	253 1 30	Donegal	Raphoe	Kilteevoge	Stranorlar	III.	139
12, 16	Dergvone	1,515 2 35j	Leitrim	Drumahaire	Killarga	Manorhamilton	IV.	98
19, 20	Derinch Island	81 0 21	Sligo	Tireragh	Dromard	Dromore West	IV.	233
20	Derinish Beg	51 3 27	Cavan	Upper Loughtee	Kilmore	Cavan	III.	84
20	Derinish More	82 1 29	Cavan	Upper Loughtee	Kilmore	Cavan	III.	84
17, 23	Derk	408 2 27	Kerry	Clanmaurice	Duagh	Listowel	II.	168
24, 33	Derk	372 2 32	Limerick	Coonagh	Grean	Tipperary	II.	235
65	Derk Beg	486 0 26k	Donegal	Boylagh	Inishkeel	Glenties	III.	112
13	Derk Beg	54 3 21	Sligo	Tireragh	Skreen	Dromore West	IV.	235
65	Derk More	239 3 18l	Donegal	Boylagh	Inishkeel	Glenties	III.	112
13	Derk More	71 0 29	Sligo	Tireragh	Skreen	Dromore West	IV.	236
30	Derlangan	482 1 4	Meath	Lune	Athboy	Trim	I.	207
17, 21	Derlett	215 3 34	Armagh	Fews Lower	Loughgilly	Armagh	III.	47
4	Dermotstown	186 1 13	Dublin	Balrothery East	Balscaddan	Balrothery	I.	20
35	Dernabacky	159 1 6	Fermanagh	Clankelly	Clones	Clones	III.	195
60	Dernabane	372 1 9	Tyrone	Dungannon Lower	Carnteel	Clogher	III.	297
53, 60	Dernaborey	228 1 6	Tyrone	Dungannon Lower	Carnteel	Dungannon	III.	297
55	Dernacally	252 3 3	Donegal	Raphoe	Taughboyne	Londonderry	III.	143
6	Dernacapplekeagh	63 3 38	Fermanagh	Lurg	Drumkeeran	Lowtherstown	III.	206
3	Dernacart	154 0 19	Queen's Co.	Tinnahinch	Castlebrack	Mountmellick	I.	248
3	Dernacoo	56 3 31	Monaghan	Trough	Errigal Trough	Monaghan	III.	283
3	Dernadarriff	164 1 22	Monaghan	Trough	Errigal Trough	Clogher	III.	283
22	Dernafanny	139 2 17	King's Co.	Garrycastle	Reynagh	Parsonstown	I.	138
36	Dernaferst	193 2 19	Cavan	Tullyhunco	Scrabby	Granard	III.	99
47	Dernagh	271 3 9	Tyrone	Dungannon Middle	Clonoe	Dungannon	III.	300
56	Dernagilly	130 3 30	Tyrone	Omagh East	Kilskeery	Lowtherstown	III.	313
19	Dernaglug	147 0 26m	Monaghan	Cremorne	Clontibret	Castleblayney	III.	260
35	Dernaglug & Drumaa	180 3 9n	Fermanagh	Clankelly	Clones	Clones	III.	195
11	Dernaglush	192 1 22o	Cavan	Lower Loughtee	Annagh	Cavan	III.	79
3	Dernagola	149 3 28	Monaghan	Trough	Errigal Trough	Clogher	III.	283
41	Dernagore	120 2 20p	Fermanagh	Knockninny	Kinawley	Lisnaskea	III	201
30	Dernagree	147 1 1	Cork, E.R.	Duhallow	Dromtarriff	Millstreet	II.	71
30	DERNAGREE T.	—	Cork, E.R.	Duhallow	Dromtarriff	Millstreet	II.	71
18	Dernagross	118 2 34	Londonderry	Coleraine	Aghadowey	Coleraine	III.	229
8	Dernahamsha	29 1 36	Monaghan	Monaghan	Clones	Monaghan	III.	274
3, 4	Dernamatten	115 0 19	Monaghan	Trough	Errigal Trough	Monaghan	III.	283
21	Dernahelty Beg	70 1 30	Leitrim	Carrigallen	Oughteragh	Bawnboy	IV.	92
21, 22	Dernahelty More	464 1 26	Leitrim	Carrigallen	Oughteragh	Bawnboy	IV.	92

(a) Including 11A. 2R. 22P. water.　　(g) Including 7A. 1R. 10P. water.　　(l) Including 16A. 1R. 19P. water.
(b) Including 34A. 3R. 0P. water.　　(h) Including 4A. 1R. 29P. water.　　(m) Including 6A. 2R. 36P. water.
(c) Including 18A. 0R. 23P. water.　　(i) Including 0A. 3R. 25P. water.　　(n) Including 20A. 0R. 13P. water.
(d) Including 50A. 2R. 6P. water.　　(j) Including 2A. 1R. 35P. water.　　(o) Including 23A. 1R. 19P. water.
(e) Including 47A. 0R. 5P. water.　　(k) Including 27A. 3R. 36P. water.　　(p) Including 7A. 2R. 30P. water.
(f) Including 111A. 1R. 8P. water.

No. of Sheet of the Ordnance Survey Maps.	Townlands and Towns.	Area in Statute Acres.	County.	Barony.	Parish.	Poor Law Union in 1857.	Townland Census of 1851. Part I.	
		A. R. P.					Vol.	Page
3	Dernahinch	106 2 8	Monaghan	Trough	Errigal Trough	Monaghan	III.	283
22	Dernakesh	248 1 7	Cavan	Clankee	Drumgoon	Cootehill	III.	72
15	Dernalea	333 0 35	Armagh	Armagh	Derrynoose	Armagh	III.	44
10	Dernalebe	419 1 22	Tyrone	Strabane Lower	Camus	Strabane	III.	320
3	Dernalosset	246 2 22	Monaghan	Trough	Errigal Trough	Monaghan	III.	283
11	Dernamanagh	117 0 2	Queen's Co.	Upperwoods	Offerlane	Mountmellick	I.	251
17, 22	Dernamoyle	276 3 39	Monaghan	Dartree	Ematris	Cootehill	III.	266
3	Dernamuck	48 2 31	Monaghan	Trough	Errigal Trough	Monaghan	III.	283
45	Dernanaught	325 0 9	Tyrone	Dungannon Middle	Pomeroy	Dungannon	III.	304
17, 18	Dernaroy	84 3 16	Monaghan	Dartree	Aghabog	Cootehill	III.	263
45, 53	Dernascer	319 1 10	Tyrone	Dungannon Middle	Donaghmore	Dungannon	III.	301
59, 65	Dernasell	141 1 30a	Tyrone	Clogher	Errigal Trough	Clogher	III.	296
21	Dernashesk	66 0 0	Fermanagh	Magheraboy	Rossory	Enniskillen	III.	214
11	Dernasigh	151 3 38	Armagh	Tiranny	Eglish	Armagh	III.	59
16, 17	Dernaskeagh	192 0 28	Cavan	Tullygarvey	Kildrumsherdan	Cootehill	III.	90
40, 45	Dernaskeagh	696 2 6b	Sligo	Corran	Toomour	Boyle	IV.	228
21, 22	Dernasmallan	231 0 9	Leitrim	Carrigallen	Oughteragh	Bawnboy	IV.	92
32	Dernaveagh	227 0 23	Antrim	Lower Toome	Kirkinriola	Ballymena	III.	32
1, 3	Dernaved	208 0 8	Monaghan	Trough	Errigal Trough	Clogher	III.	283
24	Dernaweel	296 0 19c	Cavan	Tullyhunco	Killashandra	Cavan	III.	98
61	*Dernish Island*	7 3 14	Clare	Bunratty Lower	Kilconry	Ennis	II.	4
39	Dernish Island	101 0 8	Fermanagh	Coole	Galloon	Lisnaskea	III.	200
2	Dernish Island	103 1 16	Sligo	Carbury	Ahamlish	Sligo	IV.	220
35	Deroran	500 2 5d	Tyrone	Omagh East	Termonmaguirk	Omagh	III.	314
1, 2, 4, 5	Derra	496 0 14	Kerry	Iraghticonnor	Kilconly	Listowel	II.	191
24	Derra	347 2 1e	Kerry	Trughanacmy	Brosna	Tralee	II.	208
6	Derradd	288 1 17f	Westmeath	Moygoish	Street	Granard	I.	281
87	Derradda	225 3 16	Galway	Clonmacnowen	Kilcloony	Ballinasloe	IV.	25
107, 117	Derradda	230 0 37	Galway	Longford	Killimorbologue	Portumna	IV.	58
53,54,66,67	Derradda	1,506 0 17g	Galway	Moycullen	Kilcummin	Oughterard	IV.	67
22	Derradda	258 0 21	Leitrim	Carrigallen	Drumreilly	Bawnboy	IV.	91
67	Derradda	193 2 13h	Mayo	Burrishoole	Burrishoole	Newport	IV.	119
109	Derradda	228 2 30	Mayo	Carra	Ballyovey	Ballinrobe	IV.	126
102	Derradda	147 1 21	Mayo	Costello	Knock	Claremorris	IV.	142
117	Derradda South	107 2 28	Galway	Longford	Killimorbologue	Portumna	IV.	58
10	Derra East	243 0 26	Kerry	Iraghticonnor	Galey	Listowel	II.	190
29, 30	Derragh	317 0 15	Cork, E.R.	Duhallow	Cullen	Millstreet	II.	70
93, 107	Derragh	781 3 10	Cork, W.R.	East Carbery (W.D.)	Fanlobbus	Dunmanway	II.	131
69	Derragh	439 2 13	Cork, W.R.	West Muskerry	Kilnamartry	Macroom	II.	159
11, 16	Derragh	1,115 0 37i	Longford	Granard	Abbeylara	Granard	I.	154
72	Derragh	156 0 30	Mayo	Costello	Kilmovee	Swineford	IV.	142
92	Derragh	43 1 27	Mayo	Costello	Knock	Claremorris	IV.	142
46, 54	Derraghadoan	210 1 23	Tyrone	Dungannon Middle	Drumglass	Dungannon	III.	303
22	Derraghan Beg	387 2 6	Longford	Ratheline	Cashel	Ballymahon	I.	163
18, 22	Derraghan More	723 2 16	Longford	Ratheline	Cashel	Ballymahon	I.	163
134, 135	Derrainy	615 2 26j	Galway	Leitrim	Clonrush	Scarriff	IV.	53
97, 107	Derrakillew	563 1 6	Mayo	Murrisk	Aghagower	Westport	IV.	158
35,36,39,40	Derrane	818 0 36	Roscommon	Ballintober South	Kilbride	Roscommon	IV.	189
77	Derrartan	160 0 17	Mayo	Burrishoole	Islandeady	Westport	IV.	121
98,99,108,109	Derrassa	1,299 3 25	Mayo	Carra	Ballyovey	Ballinrobe	IV.	126
99	Derrassa Commons	238 1 21	Mayo	Carra	Ballyovey	Ballinrobe	IV.	126
17	Derraugh	329 2 39	Queen's Co.	Maryborough West	Clonenagh and Clonagheen	Mountmellick	I.	242
38	Derraulin	597 1 8	Limerick	Connello Upper	Corcomohide	Croom	II.	232
11	Derraun	157 3 13	Roscommon	Boyle	Killummod	Carr. on Shannon	IV.	196
81	Derravoher	416 1 33	Tipperary, S.R.	Iffa and Offa West	Tubbrid	Clogheen	II.	321
81	Derravoher Lower	16 3 27	Tipperary, S.R.	Iffa and Offa West	Tubbrid	Clogheen	II.	321
52,53,65,66	Derravonniff	1,102 2 37k	Galway	Moycullen	Kilcummin	Oughterard	IV.	67
10	Derra West	503 3 27	Kerry	Iraghticonnor	Galey	Listowel	II.	190
11	Derreary	149 0 20l	Cavan	Lower Loughtee	Annagh	Cavan	III.	79
69	Derree	360 1 26	Cork, W.R.	West Muskerry	Ballyvourney	Macroom	II.	154
58	Derreen	375 2 13	Clare	Clonderalaw	Kilmurry	Kilrush	II.	17
14	Derreen	186 1 7	Clare	Corcomroe	Kilmacrehy	Ennistimon	II.	20
15	Derreen	169 3 5	Clare	Corcomroe	Kilshanny	Ennistimon	II.	21
38, 39	Derreen	217 1 19	Clare	Ibrickan	Kilmurry	Kilrush	II.	23
42	Derreen	181 3 28	Clare	Islands	Clareabbey	Ennis	II.	29
72	Derreen	378 1 39	Cork, E.R.	East Muskerry	Magourney	Macroom	II.	105
121	Derreen	252 2 36	Cork, W.R.	East Carbery (W.D.)	Kilmeen	Dunmanway	II.	134
38	Derreen	111 1 23	Cork, W.R.	West Muskerry	Drishane	Millstreet	II.	156
81	Derreen	355 0 32	Cork, W.R.	West Muskerry	Inchigeelagh	Macroom	II.	157
7	Derreen	211 2 30m	Galway	Ballymoe	Ballynakill	Glennamaddy	IV.	5
35	Derreen	198 1 28	Galway	Ballynahinch	Omey	Clifden	IV.	14
47	Derreen	559 2 10n	Galway	Killian	Taghboy	Mountbellew	IV.	45

(a) Including 0A. 1R. 8P. water.
(b) Including 5A. 1R. 15P. water.
(c) Including 5A. 0R. 4P. water.
(d) Including 11A. 1R. 5P. water.
(e) Including 7A. 0R. 32P. water.

(f) Including 3A. 2R. 20P. water.
(g) Including 19A. 2R. 24P. water.
(h) Including 2A. 1R. 24P. water.
(i) Including 25A. 3R. 11P. water.
(j) Including 17A. 0R. 24P. water.

(k) Including 52A. 1R. 36P. water.
(l) Including 6A. 2R. 10P. water.
(m) Including 15A. 2R. 12P. water.
(n) Including 30A. 0R. 0P. water.

No. of Sheet of the Ordnance Survey Maps.	Townlands and Towns.	Area in Statute Acres.	County.	Barony.	Parish.	Poor Law Union in 1857.	Townland Census of 1851, Part I.	
		A. R. P.					Vol.	Page
129	Derreen . . .	597 0 8	Galway .	Kiltartan .	Kilbeacanty . .	Gort . .	IV.	47
99	Derreen . . .	379 3 39	Galway .	Longford .	Kiltormer . .	Ballinasloe .	IV.	60
25	Derreen . . .	708 3 2	Galway .	Ross . .	Ross . . .	Oughterard .	IV.	74
58	Derreen . . .	186 3 29	Galway .	Tiaquin . .	Abbeyknockmoy .	Tuam . .	IV.	75
108, 109	Derreen . . .	282 1 36	Kerry .	Glanarought .	Tuosist . .	Kenmare . .	II.	188
88	Derreen . . .	592 0 32	Kerry .	Iveragh . .	Caher . .	Cahersiveen .	II.	194
81, 90	Derreen . . .	642 3 12	Kerry .	Iveragh . .	Dromod . .	Cahersiveen .	II.	194
66	Derreen . . .	70 0 29	Kerry .	Magunihy .	Killarney . .	Killarney . .	II.	203
49, 50	Derreen . . .	1,033 1 18	Kerry .	Trughanacmy .	Ballincuslane .	Tralee . .	II.	206
22	Derreen . . .	205 3 31	Kilkenny .	Shillelogher .	Killaloe . .	Callan . .	I.	115
26, 33	Derreen . . .	343 0 34	King's Co. .	Upper Philipstown .	Ballykean . .	Mountmellick .	I.	143
32	Derreen . . .	119 1 14	Leitrim .	Leitrim . .	Annaduff . .	Cark. on Shannon	IV.	99
24	Derreen . . .	139 2 16	Leitrim .	Leitrim . .	Fenagh . .	Mohill . .	IV.	100
35	Derreen . . .	223 2 28	Leitrim .	Mohill . .	Mohill . .	Mohill . .	IV.	107
1	Derreen . . .	82 0 18	Limerick .	Clanwilliam .	Stradbally . .	Limerick . .	II.	226
11, 12	Derreen . . .	184 0 11	Limerick .	Kenry . .	Kilcornan . .	Rathkeale .	II.	249
26, 34	Derreen . . .	1,339 0 3	Limerick .	Shanid . .	Nantinan . .	Glin . .	II.	257
65	Derreen . . .	1,770 2 1	Mayo .	Burrishoole .	Achill . .	Newport . .	IV.	117
79	Derreen . . .	117 1 8	Mayo .	Carra . .	Drum . .	Castlebar .	IV.	128
79	Derreen . . .	105 1 23a	Mayo .	Carra . .	Manulla . .	Castlebar .	IV.	129
30	Derreen . . .	186 1 6	Mayo .	Tirawley .	Ardagh . .	Ballina . .	IV.	163
46,47,58,59	Derreen . . .	641 0 29	Mayo .	Tirawley .	Crossmolina .	Ballina . .	IV.	165
4, 7	Derreen . . .	149 2 22	Roscommon	Boyle . .	Tumna . .	Cark. on Shannon	IV.	197
15	Derreen . . .	250 2 15	Roscommon	Castlereagh .	Kilcorkey . .	Castlereagh .	IV.	199
20	Derreen . . .	129 1 9	Roscommon	Castlereagh .	Kilkeevin . .	Castlereagh .	IV.	200
29, 36	Derreen . . .	196 2 7b	Roscommon	Roscommon .	Cloonfinlough .	Strokestown .	IV.	209
11	Derreen . . .	88 0 23	Tipperary, N.R.	Lower Ormond .	Ballingarry . .	Borrisokane .	II.	282
80	Derreenabourky .	2-0 2 1	Cork, W.R.	West Muskerry .	Inchigeelagh .	Macroom . .	II.	157
84, 93	Derreenacahill .	447 1 36	Kerry .	Glanarought .	Kenmare . .	Kenmare . .	II.	186
101	Derreenacallaha .	287 1 6	Kerry .	Glanarought .	Tuosist . .	Kenmare . .	II.	188
104, 117	Derreenacarrin .	940 1 0	Cork, W.R.	Bear . .	Kilcaskan . .	Castletown .	II.	122
100	Derreenaclaurig .	496 0 32	Kerry .	Dunkerron South .	Kilcrohane .	Kenmare . .	II.	183
3, 4	Derreenacoosan .	110 3 38	Roscommon	Boyle . .	Ardcarn . .	Boyle . .	IV.	192
106	Derreenacrinnig East	504 3 21	Cork, W.R.	West Carbery (E.D.)	Dromdaleague .	Skibbereen .	II.	140
106	Derreenacrinnig West	530 3 33	Cork, W.R.	West Carbery (E.D.)	Dromdaleague .	Skibbereen .	II.	140
75, 76, 85	Derreenacullig .	415 0 9	Kerry .	Magunihy .	Killaha . .	Killarney .	II.	202
69	Derreenaculling .	467 2 39	Cork, W.R.	West Muskerry .	Ballyvourney .	Macroom . .	II.	154
3, 4	Derreenadouglas .	406 0 38	Roscommon	Boyle . .	Ardcarn . .	Boyle . .	IV.	193
91,92,100,101	Derreenafoyle .	874 2 2	Kerry .	Dunkerron South .	Kilcrohane .	Kenmare . .	II.	183
3	Derreenagan .	146 3 17c	Roscommon	Boyle . .	Kilbryan . .	Boyle . .	IV.	195
90	Derreenagarig .	144 2 17	Cork, W.R.	Bear . .	Kilcaskan . .	Bantry . .	II.	122
18, 19	Derreenageer .	144 0 13	Leitrim .	Drumahaire .	Drumreilly .	Cark. on Shannon	IV.	95
3	Derreenahinch .	84 3 28d	Roscommon	Boyle . .	Ardcarn . .	Boyle . .	IV.	193
57, 58	Derreenaling . .	1,670 2 26	Cork, W.R.	West Muskerry .	Ballyvourney .	Macroom . .	II.	154
19	Derreenamackaun .	244 2 16e	Roscommon	Frenchpark .	Tibohine . .	Castlereagh .	IV.	205
3	Derreenanarry .	127 0 15	Roscommon	Boyle . .	Ardcarn . .	Boyle . .	IV.	193
71, 72	Derreenanaryagh .	1,228 1 16	Kerry .	Iveragh . .	Glanbehy . .	Cahersiveen .	II.	195
7	Derreenannagh .	197 3 10f	Roscommon	Boyle . .	Ardcarn . .	Cark. on Shannon	IV.	193
131, 140	Derreenard . .	294 0 31	Cork, W.R.	West Carbery (W.D.)	Skull . .	Skull . .	II.	146
4	Derreenargan . .	451 2 39	Roscommon	Boyle . .	Ardcarn . .	Boyle . .	IV.	193
3	Derreenasalt . .	93 0 23	Roscommon	Boyle . .	Ardcarn . .	Boyle . .	IV.	193
3	Derreenasecr . .	190 2 15	Roscommon	Boyle . .	Ardcarn . .	Boyle . .	IV.	193
4	Derreenasoo . .	325 1 28g	Roscommon	Boyle . .	Tumna . .	Cark. on Shannon	IV.	197
120	Derreenaspeeg .	338 0 35h	Cork, W.R.	West Carbery (E.D.)	Drinagh . .	Skibbereen .	II.	139
114, 115	Derreenataggart Commons . .	318 3 39	Cork, W.R.	Bear . .	Killaconenagh .	Castletown .	II.	124
115	Derreenataggart East	175 1 6	Cork, W.R.	Bear . .	Killaconenagh .	Castletown .	II.	124
115	Derreenataggart Middle . .	103 1 26i	Cork, W.R.	Bear . .	Killaconenagh .	Castletown .	II.	124
115	Derreenataggart West . .	146 0 12	Cork, W.R.	Bear . .	Killaconenagh .	Castletown .	II.	124
3	Derreenatawy .	83 3 21	Roscommon	Boyle . .	Ardcarn . .	Boyle . .	IV.	193
91, 105	Derreenathirigy .	58 1 13	Cork, W.R.	Bantry . .	Kilmocomoge .	Bantry . .	II.	120
7	Derreenatloghtan .	336 3 26	Clare .	Inchiquin .	Kilkeedy . .	Corrofin . .	II.	25
108	Derreenatlooig .	208 0 4	Kerry .	Glanarought .	Tuosist . .	Kenmare . .	II.	188
99, 107	Derreenauliff .	926 0 29	Kerry .	Dunkerron South .	Kilcrohane .	Kenmare . .	II.	183
119, 132	Derreenavarrihy .	282 0 38	Cork, W.R.	West Carbery (W.D.)	Caheragh . .	Skibbereen .	II.	142
4	Derreenavicara .	149 2 37	Roscommon	Boyle . .	Kilronan . .	Boyle . .	IV.	196
5, 6	Derreenavoggy .	187 2 29	Longford .	Granard . .	Columbkille .	Granard .	I.	155
2	Derreenavoggy .	389 1 38	Roscommon	Boyle . .	Kilronan . .	Boyle . .	IV.	196
90	Derreenavroonig .	150 3 21	Cork, W.R.	Bear . .	Kilcaskan . .	Bantry . .	II.	122
99, 100	Derreenavurrig .	1,269 0 24	Kerry .	Dunkerron South .	Kilcrohane .	Kenmare . .	II.	183
99	Derreenboy . .	145 2 29	Galway .	Longford .	Killoran . .	Ballinasloe .	IV.	59

(a) Including 36A. 0R. 31P. water.
(b) Including 4A. 1R. 14P. water.
(c) Including 10A. 2R. 12P. water.

(d) Including 39A. 1R. 38P. water.
(e) Including 85A. 0R. 29P. water.
(f) Including 1A. 2R. 36P. water.

(g) Including Island.
(h) Including 4A. 2R. 37P. water.
(i) Including 16A. 1R. 38P. detached portions.

No. of Sheet of the Ordnance Survey Maps	Townlands and Towns	Area in Statute Acres (A. R. P.)	County	Barony	Parish	Poor Law Union in 1857	Townland Census of 1851, Part I. (Vol. / Page)
90, 104	Derreenboy Lower	374 2 28	Cork, W.R.	Bear	Kilcaskan	Bantry	II. 122
90, 104	Derreenboy Upper	432 0 26c	Cork, W.R.	Bear	Kilcaskan	Bantry	II. 122
29, 35	Derreen and Carrow-reagh	524 0 3	Queen's Co.	Clarmallagh	Aghmacart	Abbeyleix	I. 236
68, 80	Derreenclodig	204 1 3	Cork, W.R.	West Muskerry	Inchigeelagh	Macroom	II. 157
79, 80	Derreencollig	1,396 2 16	Cork. W.R.	Bantry	Kilmocomoge	Bantry	II. 120
141	Derreendangan	212 3 17	Cork, W.R.	West Carbery(E.D.)	Abbeystrowry	Skibbereen	II. 136
92	Derreendarragh	225 3 13	Kerry	Dunkerron South	Templenoe	Kenmare	II. 185
80	Derreendonee	438 1 8	Cork, W.R.	West Muskerry	Inchigeelagh	Dunmanway	II. 157
12, 13	Derreendooagh	105 1 36	Clare	Tulla Upper	Feakle	Tulla	II. 39
3	Derreendooey	163 2 21	Roscommon	Boyle	Ardcarn	Boyle	IV. 192
26	Derreendorragh	109 3 23	Roscommon	Castlereagh	Kiltullagh	Castlereagh	IV. 201
99, 107	Derreendrislagh	712 1 17	Kerry	Dunkerron South	Kilcrohane	Kenmare	II. 183
4	Derreen East	191 1 11	Clare	Burren	Killonaghan	Ballyvaghan	II. 13
83, 92	Derreenfinlehid	843 3 28	Kerry	Dunkerron South	Templenoe	Kenmare	II. 185
101, 102	Derreengarrinshagh	203 1 12	Kerry	Glanarought	Tuosist	Kenmare	II. 188
80	Derreenglass	454 0 31	Cork, W.R.	West Muskerry	Inchigeelagh	Dunmanway	II. 157
118	Derreengreanagh	273 1 27	Cork, W.R.	West Carbery(W.D.)	Kilmocomoge	Bantry	II. 144
3, 4	Derreenine	368 1 38	Roscommon	Boyle	Ardcarn	Boyle	IV. 193
18	Derreen Island	0 1 22	Roscommon	Roscommon	Clooncraff	Strokestown	IV. 208
21, 24	Derreen (Johnston)	740 1 1	Leitrim	Leitrim	Kiltubbrid	Car^s. on Shannon	IV. 103
105,106,119	Derreenkealig	281 1 32	Cork, W.R.	Bantry	Kilmocomoge	Bantry	II. 120
28	Derreen (Lloyd)	100 3 2c	Leitrim	Leitrim	Kiltubbrid	Car^s. on Shannon	IV. 103
103, 116	Derreen Lower	560 1 29d	Cork, W.R.	Bear	Kilcaskan	Castletown	II. 122
18, 31	Derreen Lower	181 2 14	Galway	Tiaquin	Kilkerrin	Glennamaddy	IV. 77
80	Derreenlunnig	542 2 13	Cork, W.R.	West Muskerry	Inchigeelagh	Macroom	II. 157
69	Derreenmanus	257 1 18e	Mayo	Carra	Aglish	Castlebar	IV. 123
40, 54	Derreenmeel	426 3 1	Galway	Moycullen	Kilcummin	Oughterard	IV. 67
70, 80	Derreenmoria	100 0 4	Kerry	Iveragh	Killinane	Cahersiveen	II. 197
3, 7	Derreen or Mullagh-anard	188 0 12	Queen's Co.	Tinnahinch	Rosenallis	Mountmellick	I. 250
78	Derreenmalroy	45 2 29	Mayo	Carra	Ballyhean	Castlebar	IV. 125
69	Derreenmacarton	102 0 18	Cork, W.R.	West Muskerry	Kilnamartry	Macroom	II. 159
131	Derreenaclogh	276 2 14	Cork, W.R.	West Carbery(W.D.)	Skull	Skull	II. 146
119, 132	Derreenaeno	201 1 5	Cork, W.R.	West Carbery(W.D.)	Caheragh	Skibbereen	II. 142
80	Derreenacusha	327 3 37f	Cork, W.R.	West Muskerry	Inchigeelagh	Dunmanway	II. 157
81	Derreenagecha	880 0 19	Kerry	Iveragh	Dromod	Cahersiveen	II. 194
90, 91	Derreenagough	368 2 5	Cork, W.R.	Bear	Kilcaskan	Bantry	II. 122
82, 91	Derreenagrcer	585 2 22	Kerry	Dunkerron South	Kilcrohane	Kenmare	II. 183
39, 53	Derreenagusfoor	762 0 21g	Galway	Moycullen	Kilcummin	Oughterard	IV. 67
130,131, 139,140	Derreennalomane	943 3 31	Cork, W.R.	West Carbery(W.D.)	Skull	Skull	II. 146
124,125,130	Derreennamucka	767 2 18	Galway	Leitrim	Ballynakill	Loughrea	IV. 51
100	Derreennamucklagh	541 3 27h	Kerry	Dunkerron South	Kilcrohane	Kenmare	II. 183
115	Derreennanalbanagh	264 2 17	Mayo	Murrisk	Kilgeever	Westport	IV. 160
99	Derreennascooba	590 2 33i	Mayo	Carra	Ballintober	Castlebar	IV. 124
140, 149	Derreennatra	497 1 39	Cork. W.R.	West Carbery(W.D.)	Skull	Skull	II. 146
115	Derreennawinshin	391 2 16	Mayo	Murrisk	Kilgeever	Westport	IV. 160
107, 108	Derreens	361 3 33	Cork, W.R.	East Carbery (W.D.)	Fanlobbus	Dunmanway	II. 131
18	Derreens	425 0 11	Kildare	Clane	Carragh	Naas	I. 53
17, 18	Derreens	149 1 33	Leitrim	Drumahaire	Inishmagrath	Manorhamilton	IV. 96
60	Derreens	260 2 22j	Mayo	Carra	Turlough	Castlebar	IV. 131
103	Derreens	178 2 38	Mayo	Costello	Annagh	Claremorris	IV. 138
18	Derreens	537 3 20	Mayo	Erris	Kilcommon	Belmullet	IV. 143
22	Derreens	246 1 31	Mayo	Tirawley	Ballysakeery	Ballina	IV. 165
24, 31	Derreens	842 2 19	Sligo	Leyny	Achonry	Tobercurry	IV. 229
26	Derreens East	356 1 2	Fermanagh	Clanawley	Cleenish	Enniskillen	III. 190
107	Derreensillagh	191 3 13	Kerry	Dunkerron South	Kilcrohane	Kenmare	II. 183
18	Derreens Island	16 2 8	Mayo	Erris	Kilcommon	Belmullet	IV. 145
4	Derreen South	210 1 13	Clare	Burren	Killonaghan	Ballyvaghan	II. 13
24	Derreen (Southwell)	20 0 13	Leitrim	Leitrim	Kiltubbrid	Car^s. on Shannon	IV. 103
26	Derreens West	71 1 33	Fermanagh	Clanawley	Cleenish	Enniskillen	III. 190
26, 33	Derreenteige	244 1 24	Roscommon	Castlereagh	Kiltullagh	Castlereagh	IV. 201
3	Derreentunny	100 1 25k	Roscommon	Boyle	Kilbryan	Boyle	IV. 195
103, 116	Derreen Upper	588 3 1	Cork, W.R.	Bear	Kilcaskan	Castletown	II. 122
31	Derreen Upper	351 2 36l	Galway	Tiaquin	Kilkerrin	Glennamaddy	IV. 77
4	Derreen West	347 3 29	Clare	Burren	Killonaghan	Ballyvaghan	II. 13
116	Derreeny	406 2 9	Cork, W.R.	Bear	Kilcaskan	Castletown	II. 122
132	Derreeny	306 1 23	Cork, W.R.	West Carbery(W.D.)	Caheragh	Skibbereen	II. 142
82	Derreeny	501 3 20	Kerry	Dunkerron South	Templenoe	Kenmare	II. 185
60, 70	Derreenyanimna	281 1 5	Mayo	Gallen	Templemore	Castlebar	IV. 151
53	Derreighter	877 2 19m	Galway	Moycullen	Kilcummin	Oughterard	IV. 67
19	Derreskit	332 3 22n	Cavan	Tullyhunco	Killashandra	Cavan	III. 98
107	Derrew	150 3 32	Galway	Longford	Killimorbologue	Portumna	IV. 58

(a) Including 33A. 2R. 11P. water.
(b) Including 24A. 2R. 0P. water.
(c) Including 5A. 0R. 32P. water.
(d) Including 13A. 3R. 11P. water.
(e) Including 3A. 2R. 5P. water.

(f) Including 28A. 3R. 19P. water.
(g) Including 74A. 0R. 15P. water.
(h) Including 15A. 3R. 16P. water.
(i) Including 8A. 1R. 38P. water.
(j) Including 4A. 1R. 12P. water.

(k) Including 4A. 1R. 13P. water.
(l) Including 0A. 1R. 8P. water.
(m) Including 30A. 1R. 7P. water.
(n) Including 48A. 1R. 35P. water.

No. of Sheet of the Ordnance Survey Maps.	Townlands and Towns.	Area in Statute Acres.	County.	Barony.	Parish.	Poor Law Union in 1857.	Townland Census of 1851, Part I.	
		A. R. P.					Vol.	Page
117, 118	Derrew	357 2 32	Galway	Longford	Kilquain	Portumna	IV.	60
89	Derrew	198 2 23a	Mayo	Carra	Ballintober	Castlebar	IV.	124
99	Derrew	444 0 3b	Mayo	Carra	Ballyovey	Ballinrobe	IV.	126
89	Derrew Old	138 1 21	Mayo	Carra	Ballintober	Castlebar	IV.	124
90	Derriana	327 3 27	Kerry	Iveragh	Dromod	Cahersiveen	II.	194
15	Derrica Beg	74 2 30	King's Co.	Garrycastle	Wheery or Killagally	Parsonstown	I.	139
15	Derrica More	303 3 36	King's Co.	Garrycastle	Wheery or Killagally	Parsonstown	I.	139
54	Derricknew	643 2 30	Tipperary, S.R.	Slievardagh	Graystown	Cashel	II.	333
36	Derries	179 1 23	Cavan	Clanmahon	Drumlumman	Granard	III.	77
74	Derries	398 2 24	Donegal	Boylagh	Killybegs Lower	Glenties	III.	114
104	Derries	733 0 7c	Donegal	Tirhugh	Drumhome	Ballyshannon	III.	146
32	Derries	294 3 22	King's Co.	Ballyboy	Killoughy	Tullamore	I.	124
8, 16	Derries	559 0 11	King's Co.	Ballycowan	Rahan	Tullamore	I.	128
12, 20	Derries	1,693 1 12	King's Co.	Coolestown	Monasteroris	Edenderry	I.	133
15, 23	Derries	720 2 23	King's Co.	Garrycastle	Wheery or Killagally	Parsonstown	I.	139
9, 10	Derries	170 3 17	King's Co.	Lower Philipstown	Kilclonfert	Tullamore	I.	142
10	Derries	161 1 9	Tipperary, N.R.	Lower Ormond	Finnoe	Borrisokane	II.	284
59	Derries	105 2 22	Tyrone	Clogher	Clogher	Clogher	III.	292
29	Derries	220 0 29	Westmeath	Brawny	St. Mary's	Athlone	I.	259
8, 13	Derries and Ballymacahil	428 3 15	Westmeath	Delvin	Kilcumny	Castletowndelvin	I.	265
19	Derries Lower	246 1 35d	Cavan	Upper Loughtee	Kilmore	Cavan	III.	84
9	Derries, The, or Ballyshaneduff	618 3 16	Queen's Co.	Portnahinch	Lea	Mountmellick	I.	244
19, 24, 25	Derries Upper	273 3 3	Cavan	Upper Loughtee	Kilmore	Cavan	III.	84
35, 49	Derrigimlagh	2,636 1 6e	Galway	Ballynahinch	Ballindoon	Clifden	IV.	10
109	Derrigra	177 2 4	Cork, W.R.	East Carbery (E.D.)	Ballymoney	Dunmanway	II.	127
109	Derrigra	231 0 5	Cork, W.R.	East Carbery (W.D.)	Kinneigh	Bandon	II.	134
108, 109	Derrigra West	320 0 30	Cork, W.R.	East Carbery (E.D.)	Ballymoney	Dunmanway	II.	127
6	Derrilla	244 3 1	Monaghan	Trough	Donagh	Monaghan	III.	281
4	Derrin	154 2 15	Fermanagh	Lurg	Templecarn	Lowtherstown	III.	209
17, 23	Derrin	184 1 31	Fermanagh	Tirkennedy	Enniskillen	Enniskillen	III.	221
22	Derrin	485 3 20	Queen's Co.	Clandonagh	Aghaboe	Donaghmore	I.	232
15	Derrinaher	151 1 2	Leitrim	Drumahaire	Killanummery	Manorhamilton	IV.	98
46	Derrinatallan Island	2 0 9	Sligo	Coolavin	Killaraght	Boyle	IV.	225
31	Derrinboy	460 3 8	King's Co.	Ballyboy	Ballyboy	Parsonstown	I.	123
41	Derrinclare	377 0 10	King's Co.	Clonlisk	Kilcomin	Roscrea	I.	131
85	Derrincullig	495 1 19	Kerry	Glanarought	Kilgarvan	Kenmare	II.	187
17	Derrindaff	763 3 7	Kerry	Clanmaurice	Duagh	Listowel	I.	168
99	Derrindaffderg	1,366 1 5f	Mayo	Carra	Ballintober	Castlebar	IV.	124
99	Derrindaffderg Commons	187 3 5	Mayo	Carra	Ballintober	Castlebar	IV.	124
18	Derrindangan	91 3 36	Leitrim	Drumahaire	Inishmagrath	Manorhamilton	IV.	96
22	Derrindiff	329 0 8	Longford	Rathcline	Cashel	Ballymahon	I.	163
19	Derrindrehid	134 2 2g	Cavan	Tullyhunco	Killashandra	Cavan	III.	98
29	Derrindrehid	287 3 0h	Leitrim	Carrigallen	Cloone	Mohill	IV.	90
35	Derrinduff	224 0 23	King's Co.	Ballybritt	Birr	Parsonstown	I.	125
16	Derrinduff	54 2 18	Queen's Co.	Upperwoods	Offerlane	Mountmellick	I.	251
13	Derrinea	282 0 36	Roscommon	Frenchpark	Tibohine	Castlereagh	IV.	205
69, 81	Derrineanig	743 3 24	Cork, W.R.	West Muskerry	Inchigeelagh	Macroom	II.	157
89	Derrineden	1,150 1 17	Kerry	Iveragh	Dromod	Cahersiveen	II.	194
41	Derrineel	214 0 23	Roscommon	Athlone	Athleague	Roscommon	IV.	179
54, 55	Derrineel	543 3 28	Roscommon	Moycarn	Moore	Ballinasloe	IV.	206
58	Derriniddane	344 3 5	Clare	Clonderalaw	Kilfiddane	Killadysert	II.	15
76	Derrinish	29 3 38	Mayo	Burrishoole	Kilmeena	Westport	IV.	122
2	Derrinisky	146 1 33	Roscommon	Boyle	Kilronan	Boyle	IV.	196
22	Derrinivver	147 3 0	Leitrim	Carrigallen	Drumreilly	Bawnboy	IV.	91
98, 108	Derrinkee	2,211 0 28i	Mayo	Murrisk	Aghagower	Westport	IV.	158
22	Derrinkeher (Brady)	120 0 6	Leitrim	Carrigallen	Oughteragh	Bawnboy	IV.	92
21,22,24,25	Derrinkeher (McDonnell)	233 0 10j	Leitrim	Carrigallen	Oughteragh	Bawnboy	IV.	92
24	Derrinkeher (Raycroft)	310 2 15	Leitrim	Carrigallen	Oughteragh	Bawnboy	IV.	92
24	Derrinkip	105 1 17h	Leitrim	Leitrim	Fenagh	Mohill	IV.	100
101	Derrinknow	157 1 5l	Kerry	Glanarought	Tuosist	Kenmare	II.	188
2	Derrinlaur Lower	225 1 16m	Waterford	Upperthird	Killaloan	Clonmel	II.	370
2	Derrinlaur Upper	433 1 27	Waterford	Upperthird	Killaloan	Clonmel	II.	370
29	Derrinleagh	199 3 24	Tyrone	Dungannon Upper	Kildress	Cookstown	III.	308
10	Derrinlee	149 1 12	Tipperary, N.R.	Lower Ormond	Modreeny	Borrisokane	III.	286
19	Derrinlester	115 2 13	Cavan	Tullyhunco	Kildallan	Bawnboy	III.	97
78	Derrinlevaun	116 2 6n	Mayo	Carra	Ballyhean	Castlebar	IV.	125
5	Derrinlieragh	91 2 19	Tipperary, N.R.	Lower Ormond	Loughkeen	Parsonstown	II.	286
41	Derrinlig	191 0 11	Meath	Upper Moyfenrath	Castlerickard	Trim	I.	213
41	Derrinlig	18 1 20	Meath	Upper Moyfenrath	Clonard	Trim	I.	213
31	Derrinlough	236 3 34o	Galway	Tiaquin	Kilkerrin	Glennamaddy	IV.	77

(a) Including 12A. 3R. 26P. water.
(b) Including 74A. 1R. 11P. water.
(c) Including 67A. 2R. 22P. water.
(d) Including 8A. 1R. 24P. water.
(e) Including 353A. 2R. 9P. water.

(f) Including 49A. 2R. 24P. water.
(g) Including 15A. 0R. 38P. water.
(h) Including 38A. 2R. 20P. water.
(i) Including 4A. 2R. 31P. water.
(j) Including 2A. 3R. 24P. water.

(k) Including 6A. 1R. 26P. water.
(l) Including 16A. 3R. 4P. water.
(m) Including 4A. 2R. 17P. water.
(n) Including 6A. 1R. 0P. water.
(o) Including 19A. 0R. 32P. water.

No. of Sheet of the Ordnance Survey Maps.	Townlands and Towns.	Area in Statute Acres.	County.	Barony.	Parish.	Poor Law Union in 1857.	Townland Census of 1851, Part I.	
		A. R. P.					Vol.	Page
22, 30	Derrinlough	1,514 1 27a	King's Co.	Eglish	Eglish	Parsonstown	I.	134
1	Derrinloughan	736 1 12	Leitrim	Roselogher	Rossinver	Ballyshannon	IV.	111
31	Derrin Lower	115 1 22	Cavan	Clanmahon	Crosserlough	Cavan	III.	76
44	Derrinlurg	218 1 22	Roscommon	Athlone	Tisrara	Roscommon	IV.	185
45	Derrinoghran	765 1 16	Sligo	Coolavin	Killaraght	Boyle	IV.	224
22	Derrinoliver	75 2 20	Queen's Co.	Clandonagh	Aghaboe	Donaghmore	I.	232
2, 5	Derrinraw	907 2 26	Armagh	Oneilland West	Tartaraghan	Lurgan	III.	54
17	Derrins	192 2 16	Monaghan	Dartree	Currin	Cootehill	III.	265
21, 22	Derrinsallagh	424 0 38	Queen's Co.	Clandonagh	Aghaboe	Donaghmore	I.	232
2, 5	Derrinsallow	217 1 9	Tipperary, N.R.	Lower Ormond	Dorrha	Parsonstown	II.	283
51	Derrinshin and Cuilfadda	530 3 6	Roscommon	Athlone	Taghmaconnell	Athlone	IV.	185
10	Derrinstown	133 3 23	Kildare	North Salt	Taghadoe	Celbridge	I.	76
68	Derrintaggart	154 0 18c	Mayo	Burrishoole	Burrishoole	Newport	IV.	119
15	Derrintawny	200 1 17d	Leitrim	Drumahaire	Killarga	Manorhamilton	IV.	98
18	Derrintawy Glebe	126 2 22	Leitrim	Drumahaire	Inishmagrath	Manorhamilton	IV.	96
107, 116	Derrintin	1,995 0 35e	Mayo	Murrisk	Aghagower	Westport	IV.	158
14, 19	Derrintinny	133 1 29f	Cavan	Lower Loughtee	Drumlane	Cavan	III.	79
68, 77	Derrintloura	219 3 34	Mayo	Burrishoole	Islandeady	Westport	IV.	121
20, 23	Derrintober	192 2 2	Leitrim	Leitrim	Kiltoghert	Cark. on Shannon	IV.	101
70	Derrintogher	187 0 24	Cork, W.R.	West Muskerry	Kilnamartry	Macroom	II.	159
103	Derrintogher	163 1 15	Mayo	Costello	Annagh	Claremorris	IV.	138
23	Derrintonny	159 0 4	Leitrim	Leitrim	Kiltoghert	Cark. on Shannon	IV.	101
8	Derrintonny	88 0 6	Monaghan	Monaghan	Clones	Monaghan	III.	274
38, 41	Derrintony	146 2 13	Fermanagh	Knockninny	Tomregan	Lisnaskea	III.	203
24	Derrintony	123 1 24	Fermanagh	Magherastephana	Aghadurcher	Lisnaskea	III.	215
2	Derrintray Glebe	284 0 8g	Queen's Co.	Tinnahinch	Kilmanman	Mountmellick	I.	249
40	Derrinturk	125 2 28	Roscommon	Ballintober South	Kilteevan	Roscommon	IV.	190
8	Derrinturn	340 2 14	Kildare	Carbury	Ardkill	Edenderry	I.	51
68, 77	Derrinumera	701 3 38	Mayo	Burrishoole	Kilmaclasser	Westport	IV.	121
31	Derrin Upper	67 1 4	Cavan	Clanmahon	Crosserlough	Cavan	III.	76
17	Derrinurn	121 2 8	Leitrim	Drumahaire	Inishmagrath	Manorhamilton	IV.	96
18	Derrinvoher	95 3 1	Leitrim	Drumahaire	Inishmagrath	Manorhamilton	IV.	96
7	Derrinvohil	477 0 34	Tipperary, N.R.	Lower Ormond	Uskane	Borrisokane	II.	288
18	Derrinvoney Lower	128 1 32	Leitrim	Drumahaire	Inishmagrath	Manorhamilton	IV.	96
18	Derrinvoney Upper	126 0 5	Leitrim	Drumahaire	Inishmagrath	Manorhamilton	IV.	96
15, 16, 24	Derrinvullig	596 3 0	King's Co.	Ballycowan	Rahan	Tullamore	I.	128
17, 18	Derrinweer	115 2 34	Leitrim	Drumahaire	Inishmagrath	Manorhamilton	IV.	96
18	Derrinwillin	154 1 6	Leitrim	Drumahaire	Drumreilly	Cark. on Shannon	IV.	95
18	Derriawillin Glebe	123 1 19h	Leitrim	Drumahaire	Inishmagrath	Manorhamilton	IV.	96
36	Derrinydaly	642 3 18i	Meath	Lower Moyfenrath	Trim	Trim	I.	212
35	Derriscligh	1,546 3 12j	Donegal	Kilmacrenan	Kilmacrenan	Milford	III.	129
22, 30	Derrishal	321 2 19	Cork, E.R.	Duhallow	Kilmeen	Kanturk	II.	72
43, 44	Derroar	710 0 28k	Tyrone	Omagh East	Termonmaguirk	Omagh	III.	314
44	Derrockstown	389 3 25	Meath	Ratoath	Dunshaughlin	Dunshaughlin	I.	218
72	Derroogh	391 1 31l	Galway	Tiaquin	Monivea	Loughrea	IV.	79
52, 53	Derroogh North	1,232 1 16m	Galway	Moycullen	Kilcummin	Oughterard	IV.	67
19, 32	Derrooghs	650 2 9	Galway	Tiaquin	Kilkerrin	Glennamaddy	IV.	77
79, 91	Derroogh South	1,679 3 18n	Galway	Moycullen	Kilcummin	Galway	IV.	67
91	Derroograne	593 3 21	Cork, W.R.	Bantry	Kilmocomoge	Bantry	II.	120
25	Derroolagh	143 0 38	Clare	Inchiquin	Kilnamona	Ennis	II.	27
15, 16	Derrooly	483 2 22	King's Co.	Ballycowan	Rahan	Tullamore	I.	128
33	Derroon	158 1 5	Sligo	Corran	Emlaghfad	Sligo	IV.	226
52	Derrora	1,143 2 14	Donegal	Kilmacrenan	Conwal	Letterkenny	III.	126
131, 134	Derroran East	887 0 7	Galway	Leitrim	Inishcaltra	Scarriff	IV.	53
134	Derroran West	993 3 16	Galway	Leitrim	Inishcaltra	Scarriff	IV.	53
39	Derroura	646 3 38	Galway	Moycullen	Kilcummin	Oughterard	IV.	67
91	Derrowel Beg	63 0 3	Mayo	Clanmorris	Mayo	Castlebar	IV.	135
91	Derrowel More	215 2 7	Mayo	Clanmorris	Mayo	Claremorris	IV.	135
6	Derry	152 3 39	Armagh	Oneilland East	Shankill	Lurgan	III.	51
32	Derry	288 0 29	Cavan	Castlerahan	Crosserlough	Cavan	III.	68
28, 29	Derry	371 2 37o	Cavan	Clankee	Shercock	Bailieborough	III.	74
19	Derry	144 1 19p	Cavan	Tullyhunco	Killa-handra	Cavan	III.	98
25, 26	Derry	190 2 23	Clare	Bunratty Upper	Templemaley	Ennis	II.	10
24	Derry	376 2 1	Clare	Inchiquin	Inagh	Ennistimon	II.	25
44	Derry	110 2 27	Clare	Tulla Lower	Kilseily	Limerick	II.	36
31, 40	Derry	776 1 6	Cork, E.R.	Duhallow	Clonmeen	Kanturk	II.	69
61	Derry	611 1 8	Cork, E.R.	East Muskerry	Donaghmore	Macroom	II.	102
109	Derry	140 2 21	Cork, W.R.	East Carbery (E.D.)	Desertserges	Clonakilty	II.	128
134, 143	Derry	471 1 30	Cork, W.R.	East Carbery (W.D.)	Ross	Clonakilty	II.	135
25, 32	Derry	267 3 18	Down	Ards Upper	Ballyphilip	Downpatrick	III.	160
22, 28, 29	Derry	631 0 14	Down	Lower Iveagh, Lr. pt.	Dromara	Lisburn	III.	167
33	Derry	114 1 3	Fermanagh	Clanawley	Kinawley	Enniskillen	III.	193

(a) Including 48A. 0R. 8P. water.
(b) Including 21A. 2R. 11P. water.
(c) Including 3A. 3R. 3P. water.
(d) Including 47A. 3R. 24P. water.
(e) Including 69A. 1R. 18P. water.
(f) Including 26A. 2R. 8P. water.

(g) Including 31A. 0R. 26P. water.
(h) Including 1A. 1R. 11P. water.
(i) Including 13A. 2R. 0P. water.
(j) Including 82A. 0R. 22P. water.
(k) Including 5A. 0R. 20P. water.

(l) Including 10A. 0R. 0P. water.
(m) Including 88A. 1R. 30P. water.
(n) Including 26A. 3R. 32P. water.
(o) Including 2A. 0R. 16P. water.
(p) Including 5A. 2R. 36P. water.

No. of Sheet of the Ordnance Survey Maps.	Townlands and Towns.	Area in Statute Acres.			County.	Barony.	Parish.	Poor Law Union in 1857.	Townland Census of 1851, Part I.	
		A.	R.	P.					Vol.	Page
95	Derry	208	2	21	Galway	Dunkellin	Ballynacourty	Galway	IV.	27
128	Derry	353	1	31	Galway	Kiltartan	Beagh	Gort	IV.	46
108	Derry	879	2	26	Galway	Longford	Meelick	Portumna	IV.	61
12, 13	Derry	2,101	0	34	Galway	Ross	Ballinchalla	Ballinrobe	IV.	72
6, 11	Derry	459	1	33	Kerry	Iraghticonnor	Listowel	Listowel	II.	192
20	Derry	147	3	20	Limerick	Connello Lower	Nantinan	Rathkeale	II.	229
111	Derry	162	1	6	Mayo	Clanmorris	Crossboyne	Claremorris	IV.	132
92	Derry	273	1	22a	Mayo	Clanmorris	Knock	Claremorris	IV.	135
121, 123	Derry	109	0	13	Mayo	Kilmaine	Cong	Ballinrobe	IV.	153
115	Derry	344	1	5	Mayo	Murrisk	Kilgeever	Westport	IV.	160
23	Derry	138	2	1	Monaghan	Cremorne	Aghnamullen	Cootehill	III.	257
34	Derry	244	1	2b	Monaghan	Farney	Magheracloone	Carrickmacross	III.	272
10	Derry	97	2	35	Monaghan	Monaghan	Tehallan	Monaghan	III.	280
13	Derry	140	2	38	Queen's Co.	Maryborough East	Dysartenos	Mountmellick	I.	241
13	Derry	286	2	17	Queen's Co.	Maryborough East	Straboe	Mountmellick	I.	241
2	Derry	326	3	4c	Queen's Co.	Tinnahinch	Kilmanman	Mountmellick	I.	249
3	Derry	638	2	6	Queen's Co.	Tinnahinch	Rearymore	Mountmellick	I.	249
13, 19	Derry	170	0	10d	Roscommon	Frenchpark	Tibohine	Castlereagh	IV.	205
5	Derry	176	2	28	Sligo	Carbury	Ahamlish	Sligo	IV.	219
35	Derry	82	0	38	Tipperary, N.R.	Eliogarty	Loughmoe East	Thurles	II.	271
1, 2, 4, 5	Derry	904	2	33	Tipperary, N.R.	Lower Ormond	Dorrha	Parsonstown	II.	283
46, 47	Derry	263	2	7	Tyrone	Dungannon Middle	Tullyniskan	Dungannon	III.	304
56	Derry	187	3	23	Tyrone	Omagh East	Kilskeery	Enniskillen	III.	313
33	Derry	243	3	12	Westmeath	Fartullagh	Castllost	Mullingar	I.	268
20,21,26,27	Derry	295	0	26	Wexford	Ballaghkeen	Ballyhuskard	Enniscorthy	I.	291
6, 7	Derrya	592	2	36e	Westmeath	Fore	Mayne	Granard	I.	271
27	Derryabbert	77	0	35	Clare	Tulla Upper	Feakle	Scarriff	ii.	39
34, 39	Derryad	488	0	3	Fermanagh	Coole	Galloon	Lisnaskea	III.	199
30	Derryad	260	1	26	King's Co.	Eglish	Eglish	Parsonstown	I.	134
25	Derryad	131	3	27	King's Co.	Geashill	Geashill	Tullamore	I.	140
18	Derryad	639	2	33	Longford	Moydow	Killashee	Longford	I.	161
22	Derryad	457	1	9	Longford	Ratheline	Kilcommock	Ballymahon	I.	164
2, 3, 5, 6	Derryadd	702	1	22	Armagh	Oneilland East	Montiaghs	Lurgan	III.	49
4, 5	Derryadd	453	1	9f	Armagh	Oneilland West	Tartaraghan	Armagh	III.	54
89	Derryadda	86	0	9g	Mayo	Carra	Ballyhean	Castlebar	IV.	125
37, 51	Derryadd East	421	3	27h	Galway	Ballynahinch	Moyrus	Clifden	IV.	12
36, 50, 51	Derryadd West	1,414	3	16i	Galway	Ballynahinch	Moyrus	Clifden	IV.	12
26	Derryaghna	136	1	29	Fermanagh	Clanawley	Cleenish	Enniskillen	III.	190
64	Derryaghy	538	0	4	Antrim	Upper Belfast	Derryaghy	Lisburn	III.	10
5	Derryall	363	1	0j	Armagh	Oneilland West	Drumcree	Lurgan	III.	52
5, 8	Derryallaghan	175	1	3	Monaghan	Monaghan	Tedavnet	Monaghan	III.	278
13, 14	Derryallen	382	2	15	Armagh	Orior Lower	Ballymore	Banbridge	III.	55
56	Derryallen	156	0	13	Tyrone	Omagh East	Kilskeery	Enniskillen	III.	313
56	Derryallen Glebe	25	0	29	Tyrone	Omagh East	Kilskeery	Enniskillen	III.	313
45, 46	Derryalskea	147	0	6	Tyrone	Dungannon Middle	Donaghmore	Dungannon	III.	301
1, 2, 4, 5	Derryane	556	3	31k	Armagh	Oneilland West	Tartaraghan	Armagh	III.	54
5	Derryanvil	217	1	0l	Armagh	Oneilland West	Drumcree	Lurgan	III.	52
39	Derryany	85	0	7	Fermanagh	Coole	Galloon	Lisnaskea	III.	199
36	Derryard	190	2	14	Fermanagh	Clankelly	Clones	Clones	III.	195
73, 83	Derryard	639	2	39	Kerry	Dunkerron North	Knockane	Killarney	II.	182
24, 25	Derryard	255	3	15	Londonderry	Keenaght	Bovevagh	NewT"Limavady	III.	235
22	Derryargon	146	1	33m	Fermanagh	Tirkennedy	Trory	Enniskillen	III.	223
106	Derryarkane	216	3	13	Cork, W.R.	Bantry	Kilmocomoge	Bantry	II.	120
3	Derryarkin	982	2	12	King's Co.	Lower Phillipstown	Croghan	Edenderry	I.	142
14, 15	Derryarkin Lower	101	1	38	Londonderry	Tirkeeran	Faughanvale	Londonderry	III.	250
14, 15	Derryarkin Upper	313	3	11	Londonderry	Tirkeeran	Faughanvale	Londonderry	III.	250
11	Derryarmush	180	2	25n	Cavan	Lower Loughtee	Annagh	Cavan	III.	79
12, 17	Derryaroge	382	3	12	Longford	Moydow	Killashee	Longford	I.	161
14, 19	Derryarrilly	251	2	37o	Monaghan	Cremorne	Clontibret	Monaghan	III.	260
5, 8	Derryarrit	260	0	24	Monaghan	Monaghan	Clones	Monaghan	III.	274
16	Derryarrow	184	1	32	Queen's Co.	Upperwoods	Offerlane	Abbeyleix	I.	251
26	Derryart	193	2	12	Donegal	Kilmacrenan	Clondahorky	Dunfanaghy	III.	123
38, 41	Derryart	113	3	1	Fermanagh	Knockninny	Tomregan	Lisnaskea	III.	203
3	Derryart	43	2	4	Kildare	Carbury	Nurney	Edenderry	I.	53
18	Derryart	270	2	2	Longford	Moydow	Killashee	Ballymahon	I.	161
8	Derryartry	69	1	14	Monaghan	Monaghan	Clones	Monaghan	III.	274
34	Derryasna	73	0	8p	Fermanagh	Magherastephana	Aghalurcher	Lisnaskea	III.	215
2	Derryaugh	174	2	24	Armagh	Oneilland West	Tartaraghan	Lurgan	III.	54
97, 107	Derryaun	164	0	0	Mayo	Murrisk	Oughaval	Westport	IV.	161
75, 85	Derrybanane	719	0	30q	Kerry	Magunihy	Killaha	Killarney	II.	202
91	Derrybane	113	2	8	Tipperary, N.R.	Upper Ormond	Ballymackey	Nenagh	II.	289
51	Derrybard	319	3	30	Tyrone	Clogher	Donacavey	Omagh	III.	294
134	Derrybaun	80	1	21	Cork, W.R.	East Carbery(W.D.)	Castleventry	Clonakilty	II.	131

(a) Including 33A. 0R. 2P. water.
(b) Including 14A. 0R. 2P. water.
(c) Including 30A. 2R. 34P. water.
(d) Including 3A. 3R. 23P. water.
(e) Including 8A. 0R. 37P. water.
(f) Including 53A. 0R. 26P. water.

(g) Including 12A. 3R. 36P. water.
(h) Including 13A. 2R. 0P. water.
(i) Including 23A. 2R. 4P. water.
(j) Including 7A. 2R. 26P. water.
(k) Including 46A. 2R. 0P. water.
(l) Including 3A. 2R. 15P. water.

(m) Including 11A. 1R. 12P. water.
(n) Including 12A. 1R. 35P. water.
(o) Including 8A. 0R. 36P. water.
(p) Including 8A. 2R. 2P. water.
(q) Including 8A. 2R. 0P. water.

No. of Sheet of the Ordnance Survey Maps.	Townlands and Towns.	Area in Statute Acres.			County.	Barony.	Parish.	Poor Law Union in 1857.	Townland Census of 1851, Part I.	
		A.	R.	P.					Vol.	Page
44	Derrybaun	175	2	17	Galway	Clare	Killererin	Tuam	IV.	21
23	Derrybawn	1,711	3	15a	Wicklow	Ballinacor North	Derrylossary	Rathdrum	I.	346
26	Derry Beg	369	3	35	Armagh	Orior Upper	Newry	Newry	III.	58
9	Derry Beg	113	3	36	Cavan	Tullyhaw	Templeport	Bawnboy	III.	94
62	Derrybeg	47	2	28	Clare	Bunratty Lower	Killeely	Limerick	II.	5
43	Derrybeg	167	3	27c	Donegal	Kilmacrenan	Gartan	Letterkenny	III.	127
32	Derrybeg	112	2	8	Donegal	Kilmacrenan	Tullaghobegly	Dunfanaghy	III.	131
5, 6	Derry Beg	83	2	36	Fermanagh	Lurg	Drumkeeran	Lowtherstown	III.	206
27	Derrybeg	218	2	30d	Fermanagh	Tirkennedy	Derryvullan	Enniskillen	III.	224
116, 117	Derrybeg	151	2	13	Galway	Leitrim	Tynagh	Portumna	IV.	55
39	Derrybeg	214	0	3	Galway	Moycullen	Kilcummin	Oughterard	IV.	67
36, 39	Derrybeg	221	1	5	King's Co.	Ballybritt	Seirkieran	Parsonstown	I.	127
17, 25	Derrybeg	423	3	4	King's Co.	Geashill	Geashill	Tullamore	I.	140
13	Derrybeg	152	2	16	Limerick	Pubblebrien	Knocknagaul	Limerick	II.	253
9, 10	Derry Beg	224	2	24	Londonderry	Keenaght	Drumachose	New T^le Limavady	III.	235
16	Derrybeg	53	2	8	Monaghan	Dartree	Drummully	Clones	III.	266
17	Derry Beg	140	2	29	Queen's Co.	Maryborough West	Clonenagh and Clonagheen	Mountmellick	I.	242
47	Derrybeg	77	2	9	Sligo	Coolavin	Killaraght	Boyle	IV.	224
34	Derry Beg	117	1	37	Sligo	Tirerrill	Killadoon	Boyle	IV.	239
19	Derrybeg	168	1	37	Tipperary, N.R.	Owney and Arra	Templeachally	Nenagh	II.	297
42, 43	Derrybeg East	64	1	22c	Fermanagh	Coole	Galloon	Clones	III.	199
39	Derrybeg West	113	3	37f	Fermanagh	Coole	Galloon	Lisnaskea	III.	199
27, 28	Derrybehagh	65	3	8	Clare	Tulla Upper	Feakle	Scarriff	II.	39
17, 18	Derrybofin	91	0	14	Leitrim	Drumahaire	Inishmagrath	Manorhamilton	IV.	96
23, 24	Derryboy	1,032	1	19	Down	Dufferin	Killyleagh	Downpatrick	III.	167
46	Derryboy	304	2	31	Down	Lordship of Newry	Newry	Newry	III.	182
27	Derryboy	251	1	6	Westmeath	Farbill	Killucan	Mullingar	I.	266
40	Derrybrack	37	3	31	Fermanagh	Clankelly	Drummully	Clones	III.	197
35	Derrybrack	195	3	32	Leitrim	Leitrim	Annaduff	Car^k on Shannon	IV.	99
81	Derrybrack	73	1	16o	Mayo	Costello	Aghamore	Swinford	IV.	137
4, 5	Derrybreen	334	3	6	Tipperary, N.R.	Lower Ormond	Lorrha	Borrisokane	II.	285
12	Derrybrennan	273	3	17	Kildare	Carbury	Kilpatrick	Edenderry	I.	52
14, 15	Derrybrick	143	1	29h	Cavan	Lower Loughtee	Drunlane	Cavan	III.	80
58	Derrybrick	320	0	36	Clare	Clonderalaw	Kilmurry	Killadysert	II.	17
38, 39	Derrybrick	132	2	7	Fermanagh	Knockninny	Kinawley	Lisnaskea	III.	201
5	Derrybrick	87	1	23	Fermanagh	Lurg	Drumkeeran	Lowtherstown	III.	206
124, 130	Derrybrien East	2,692	2	21c	Galway	Loughrea	Killeenadeema	Loughrea	IV.	64
124	Derrybrien North	2,846	2	21	Galway	Loughrea	Killeenadeema	Loughrea	IV.	64
124, 130	Derrybrien South	2,473	2	29	Galway	Loughrea	Killeenadeema	Loughrea	IV.	64
124	Derrybrien West	2,145	2	5	Galway	Loughrea	Killeenadeema	Loughrea	IV.	64
14	Derrybrisk	175	0	4	Leitrim	Drumahaire	Killanummery	Manorhamilton	IV.	98
57, 58	Derrybrock	1,309	1	11	Mayo	Burrishoole	Burrishoole	Newport	IV.	119
14	Derrybrock	141	0	2	Queen's Co.	Stradbally	Moyanna	Athy	I.	247
5	Derrybrughas	252	2	6j	Armagh	Oneilland West	Drumcree	Lurgan	III.	52
27	Derrybrusk	204	1	27k	Fermanagh	Tirkennedy	Derrybrusk	Enniskillen	III.	220
47, 50	Derrycahill	501	3	18l	Roscommon	Athlone	Dysart	Athlone	IV.	181
33	Derrycallaghan	81	1	24m	Fermanagh	Magherastephana	Cleenish	Lisnaskea	III.	219
22	Derrycallaghan	324	2	4	Tipperary, N.R.	Ikerrin	Cullenwaine	Roscrea	II.	275
129, 133	Derrycallan Commons	269	1	6n	Galway	Kiltartan	Beagh	Gort	IV.	46
128, 129	Derrycallan North	327	1	20o	Galway	Kiltartan	Beagh	Gort	IV.	46
129	Derrycallan South	265	0	33	Galway	Kiltartan	Beagh	Gort	IV.	46
18, 26, 27	Derrycalliff	1,196	3	29	Clare	Bunratty Upper	Clooney	Tulla	II.	8
14, 15	Derrycammagh	540	0	24p	Louth	Louth	Man-fieldstown	Ardee	I.	185
35, 36	Derrycanan	436	1	6	Roscommon	Ballintober South	Kilbride	Roscommon	IV.	189
34, 39	Derrycanon	204	1	38q	Fermanagh	Coole	Galloon	Lisnaskea	III.	199
39	Derrycanon	217	0	38r	Fermanagh	Knockninny	Kinawley	Lisnaskea	III.	201
16	Derrycanton	364	1	33	Queen's Co.	Upperwoods	Offerlane	Mountmellick	I.	251
40	Derrycarbry	279	1	21	Roscommon	Ballintober South	Kilteevan	Roscommon	IV.	190
131	Derrycarhoon	445	1	38	Cork, W.R.	West Carbery (W.D.)	Skull	Skull	II.	146
11	Derrycark	166	2	34s	Cavan	Lower Loughtee	Annagh	Cavan	III.	79
73	Derrycarna	1,436	3	9t	Kerry	Dunkerron North	Knockane	Killarney	II.	182
35	Derrycarne Demesne	365	1	17	Leitrim	Mohill	Annaduff	Mohill	IV.	105
15, 23	Derrycarney	364	0	38	King's Co.	Garrycastle	Gallen	Parsonstown	I.	136
21	Derrycarney	85	1	31	Tipperary, N.R.	Upper Ormond	Ballymackey	Nenagh	II.	289
12	Derrycarran	99	1	1	Clare	Tulla Upper	Feakle	Tulla	II.	39
11, 16	Derrycarrow	522	0	25	Queen's Co.	Upperwoods	Offerlane	Mountmellick	I.	251
72, 81	Derrycashel	375	2	23u	Mayo	Costello	Aghamore	Swinford	IV.	137
3	Derrycashel	256	2	37v	Roscommon	Boyle	Ardcarn	Boyle	IV.	193
30	Derrycashel	849	2	17	Roscommon	Roscommon	Lissonuffy	Strokestown	IV.	212
3	Derrycashel or Bridgecartron	362	1	33	Roscommon	Boyle	Ardcarn	Boyle	IV.	192
13	Derrycassan	497	3	9w	Cavan	Tullyhaw	Templeport	Bawnboy	III.	94

(a) Including 7A. 0R. 24P. water.
(b) Including 0A. 2R. 15P. Brackley Lough.
(c) Including 18A. 3R. 24P. water.
(d) Including 60A. 2R. 25P. water.
(e) Including 5A. 2R. 32P. water.
(f) Including 15A. 3R. 11P. water.
(g) Including 4A. 0R. 32P. water.
(h) Including 60A. 3R. 25P. water.

(i) Including 15A. 1R. 24P. water.
(j) Including 14A. 2R. 5P. water.
(k) Including 26A. 1R. 28P. water.
(l) Including 39A. 0R. 6P. water.
(m) Including 14A. 2R. 35P. water.
(n) Including 14A. 0R. 5P. water.
(o) Including 46A. 2R. 16P. water.
(p) Including 8A. 2R. 21P. water.

(q) Including 9A. 3R. 0P. water.
(r) Including 13A. 0R. 24P. water.
(s) Including 14A. 2R. 10P. water.
(t) Including 12A. 1R. 24P. water.
(u) Including 4A. 0R. 9P. water.
(v) Including 13A. 1R. 0P. water.
(w) Including 37A. 1R. 36P. water.

No. of Sheet of the Ordnance Survey Maps	Townlands and Towns	Area in Statute Acres.			County	Barony	Parish	Poor Law Union in 1857.	Townland Census of 1851, Part I.	
		A.	R.	P.					Vol.	Page
16	Derrycassan	632	3	38	Donegal	Kilmacrenan	Mevagh	Millford	III.	130
6	Derrycassan	944	2	38a	Longford	Granard	Columbkille	Granard	I.	155
4	Derrycaw	286	3	14	Armagh	Oneilland West	Clonfeacle	Armagh	III.	51
5	Derrycaw	172	2	17	Armagh	Oneilland West	Drumcree	Lurgan	III.	52
5	Derrycaw	269	2	16	Armagh	Oneilland West	Tartaraghan	Lurgan	III.	54
34	Derrychaan	60	0	1	Fermanagh	Magherastephana	Aghalurcher	Lisnaskea	III.	215
22	Derrychara	270	1	39b	Fermanagh	Tirkennedy	Enniskillen	Enniskillen	III.	221
38, 39, 41	Derrychorran	140	1	10	Fermanagh	Knockninny	Kinawley	Lisnaskea	III.	201
39	Derrychree	215	2	24c	Fermanagh	Knockninny	Kinawley	Lisnaskea	III.	201
24, 30	Derrychrier	680	0	14	Londonderry	Keenaght	Banagher	NewTⁿLimavady	III.	234
34	Derrychulla	139	3	10d	Fermanagh	Magherastephana	Aghalurcher	Lisnaskea	III.	215
3, 4	Derrychulloo	402	0	12e	Fermanagh	Lurg	Belleek	Pallyshannon	III.	203
26	Derrychurra	104	3	2	Fermanagh	Clanawley	Cleenish	Enniskillen	III.	190
81	Derryclaha	242	3	5	Mayo	Costello	Aghamore	Swineford	IV.	137
43	Derryclare	203	2	24	Meath	Lower Deece	Galtrim	Trim	I.	191
24, 37	Derryclare	2,531	1	21f	Galway	Ballynahinch	Moyrus	Clifden	IV.	12
22, 27	Derryclawan	248	2	13	Fermanagh	Tirkennedy	Derryvullan	Enniskillen	III.	221
59	Derryclay	152	0	6	Tyrone	Clogher	Errigal Trough	Clogher	III.	296
68	Derrycleetagh	97	1	27	Mayo	Burrishoole	Burrishoole	Newport	IV.	119
32,33,37,38	Derryclegna	138	1	3	Fermanagh	Clanawley	Kinawley	Enniskillen	III.	193
79,80,91,92	Derryclogher	2,204	2	10	Cork, W.R.	Bantry	Kilmocomoge	Bantry	II.	120
120, 133	Derryclogh Lower	400	3	9	Cork, W.R.	West Carbery (E.D.)	Drinagh	Skibbereen	II.	139
120, 133	Derryclogh Upper	605	3	25	Cork, W.R.	West Carbery (E.D.)	Drinagh	Skibbereen	II.	139
62, 66	Derryclone	414	2	16	Antrim	Upper Massereene	Aghagallon	Lurgan	III.	29
7, 8	Derrycloney	625	0	2	Queen's Co.	Portnahinch	Ardea	Mountmellick	I.	243
68, 75	Derrycloney	512	2	29	Tipperary, S.R.	Clanwilliam	Relickmurry & Athassel	Tipperary	II.	310
59, 65	Derrycloony	297	2	16g	Tyrone	Clogher	Errigal Trough	Clogher	III.	296
25	Derryclure	196	3	19	King's Co.	Geashill	Geashill	Tullamore	I.	140
129	Derrycluvane	371	0	24	Cork, W.R.	West Carbery (W.D.)	Kilcrohane	Bantry	II.	143
13, 20	Derrycnaw	595	2	2	Clare	Tulla Upper	Feakle	Scarriff	II.	39
9	Derryco	174	2	35	Kerry	Clanmaurice	Rattoo	Listowel	II.	173
9	Derrycoagh	114	3	17h	Roscommon	Frenchpark	Kilnamanagh	Boyle	IV.	204
3, 10	Derrycoffey	898	3	4	King's Co.	Lower Philipstown	Croghan	Edenderry	I.	142
22, 26	Derrycolumb	409	3	26i	Longford	Rathcline	Cashel	Ballymahon	I.	163
11	Derrycon	393	1	6	Queen's Co.	Upperwoods	Offerlane	Mountmellick	I.	251
134	Derrycon Lower	273	3	4	Galway	Leitrim	Inishcaltra	Scarriff	IV.	53
140	Derryconnell	535	1	21	Cork, W.R.	West Carbery(W.D.)	Skull	Skull	II.	146
104	Derryconnery	528	1	3	Cork, W.R.	Bear	Kilcaskan	Bantry	II.	122
108, 109	Derryconnery	401	2	18	Kerry	Glanarought	Tuosist	Kenmare	II.	188
9	Derryconnessy	113	1	15	Cavan	Tullyhaw	Templeport	Bawnboy	III.	94
40	Derryconny	64	2	9	Roscommon	Ballintober South	Kilbride	Roscommon	IV.	189
24, 33	Derryconor	1,224	1	23j	Donegal	Kilmacrenan	Tullaghobegly	Dunfanaghy	III.	131
35, 41	Derryconor	436	0	13	Meath	Lune	Killaconnigan	Trim	I.	208
68	Derrycontoort East	183	0	30	Mayo	Burrishoole	Burrishoole	Newport	IV.	119
68	Derrycontoort West	66	0	7	Mayo	Burrishoole	Burrishoole	Newport	IV.	119
134	Derrycon Upper	788	1	7	Galway	Leitrim	Inishcaltra	Scarriff	IV.	53
42	Derrycoogh	444	2	19	Tipperary, S.R.	Slievardagh	Buolick	Urlingford	II.	332
95, 109	Derrycool	408	3	19	Cork, W.R.	Kinalmeaky	Kilbrogan	Bandon	II.	152
67	Derrycooldrim	519	3	21k	Mayo	Burrishoole	Burrishoole	Newport	IV.	119
15, 16	Derrycooly	1,707	0	25	King's Co.	Ballycowan	Rahan	Tullamore	I.	128
77, 78	Derrycooraun	341	1	2l	Mayo	Burrishoole	Islandeady	Westport	IV.	121
4, 5	Derrycoose	386	1	3	Armagh	Oneilland West	Loughgall	Armagh	III.	54
78, 89	Derrycoosh	224	3	4m	Mayo	Carra	Aglish	Castlebar	IV.	123
78	Derrycoosh	513	3	7	Mayo	Carra	Islandeady	Westport	IV.	128
81	Derrycoosh	60	3	24	Mayo	Costello	Aghamore	Swineford	IV.	137
5, 6	Derrycor	319	2	15n	Armagh	Oneilland East	Montiaghs	Lurgan	III.	49
4, 5	Derrycor	395	1	6	Armagh	Oneilland West	Tartaraghan	Armagh	III.	54
34	Derrycorban	141	2	37	Fermanagh	Magherastephana	Aghalurcher	Lisnaskea	III.	215
39	Derrycorby	159	1	15o	Fermanagh	Coole	Galloon	Clones	III.	199
26	Derrycormick	172	1	36	Fermanagh	Clanawley	Cleenish	Enniskillen	III.	190
17	Derrycorrib	692	3	32	Mayo	Erris	Kilcommon	Belmullet	IV.	143
4	Derrycorry North	365	3	18	Armagh	Oneilland West	Killyman	Armagh	III.	53
4	Derrycorry South	295	1	32	Armagh	Oneilland West	Killyman	Armagh	III.	53
5	Derrycory	196	2	2p	Armagh	Oneilland West	Drumcree	Lurgan	III.	52
66	Derrycourtney	101	2	10	Tyrone	Dungaunon Lower	Aghaloo	Armagh	III.	296
98, 108	Derrycraff	1,300	3	21	Mayo	Murrisk	Aghagower	Westport	IV.	158
131, 132	Derrycrag	283	0	32	Galway	Leitrim	Ballynakill	Loughrea	IV.	51
20, 25	Derrycramph	169	3	12	Cavan	Upper Loughtee	Urney	Cavan	III.	86
1	Derrycrave	748	0	33q	Westmeath	Fore	Lickbla	Granard	I.	270
40	Derrycraw	384	2	37	Down	Upper Iveagh, Up. pt.	Donaghmore	Newry	III.	175
40	Derrycree	43	1	21	Fermanagh	Clankelly	Clones	Clones	III.	195
77, 78	Derrycreeve	186	0	28	Mayo	Burrishoole	Islandeady	Westport	IV.	121
115, 128	Derrycreeveen	1,085	1	12	Cork, W.R.	Bear	Killaconenagh	Castletown	II.	124

(a) Including 13A. 0R. 34P. water.
(b) { Including 1A. 3R. 32P. Holly Island, Including 90A. 2R. 2P. water.
(c) Including 36A. 2R. 15P. water.
(d) Including 33A. 0R. 15P. water.
(e) Including 3A. 2R. 2P. water.

(f) Including 147A. 3R. 0P. water.
(g) Including 2A. 2R. 3P. water.
(h) Including 3A. 1R. 30P. water.
(i) Including 39A. 3R. 20P. water.
(j) Including 16A. 3R. 17P. water.
(k) Including 21A. 2R. 16P. water.

(l) Including 4A. 2R. 10P. water.
(m) Including 7A. 3R. 36P. water.
(n) Including 122A. 2R. 13P. Lough Gullion.
(o) Including 17A. 2R. 15P. water.
(p) Including 5A. 3R. 3P. water.
(q) Including 31A. 1R. 26P. water.

No. of Sheet of the Ordnance Survey Maps.	Townlands and Towns.	Area in Statute Acres.	County.	Barony.	Parish.	Poor Law Union in 1857.	Townland Census of 1851, Part I.	
		A. R. P.					Vol.	Page
20	Derrycreevy	148 1 32a	Monaghan	Cremorne	Muckno	Castleblayney	III.	261
60	Derrycreevy	328 3 18	Tyrone	Dungannon Lower	Carnteel	Clogher	III.	297
61	Derrycreevy	306 2 27	Tyrone	Dungannon Middle	Clonfeacle	Dungannon	III.	299
54	Derrycreevy (Knox)	118 2 12	Tyrone	Dungannon Middle	Clonfeacle	Dungannon	III.	299
105	Derrycreigh	435 3 5	Cork, W.R.	Bantry	Kilmocomoge	Bantry	II.	120
4, 8	Derrycrew	444 0 14	Armagh	Oneilland West	Loughgall	Armagh	III.	54
9	Derrycrib	624 0 22	Kildare	Clane	Ballynafagh	Naas	I.	53
19	Derrycricket	747 2 35	King's Co.	Upper Philipstown	Geashill	Edenderry	I.	144
81, 93	Derrycrib	445 3 22b	Galway	Moycullen	Rahoon	Galway	IV.	72
30, 31	Derrycrin (Conyngham)	513 2 24	Tyrone	Dungannon Upper	Ballinderry	Cookstown	III.	306
30, 31	Derrycrin (Eglish)	444 3 29	Tyrone	Dungannon Upper	Ballinderry	Cookstown	III.	306
5	Derrycrossan	168 2 34	Monaghan	Monaghan	Tedavnet	Monaghan	III.	278
29	Derrycrum	166 0 28	Fermanagh	Magherastephana	Aghalurcher	Lisnaskea	III.	215
48	Derrycrummy	215 1 20	Londonderry	Loughinsholin	Derryloran	Magherafelt	III.	240
17	Derrycughan	199 0 3	Armagh	Orior Lower	Kilclooney	Armagh	III.	56
17	Derrycullinan	150 0 10	Leitrim	Drumahaire	Inishmagrath	Manorhamilton	IV.	96
17	Derrycullinan Beg	18 3 0	Leitrim	Drumahaire	Inishmagrath	Manorhamilton	IV.	96
24, 29	Derrycullion	276 1 33	Fermanagh	Magherastephana	Aghalurcher	Lisnaskea	III.	215
74, 84	Derrycunnihy	524 3 38	Kerry	Magunihy	Killarney	Killarney	II.	203
35, 36, 50	Derrycunlagh	2,128 1 37c	Galway	Ballynahinch	Moyrus	Clifden	IV.	13
60	Derrycush	229 0 7	Tyrone	Dungannon Lower	Carnteel	Clogher	III.	297
28	Derrydamph	253 1 5d	Cavan	Clankee	Knockbride	Bailieborough	III.	73
25	Derrydarragh	239 3 4	Longford	Rathcline	Cashel	Ballymahon	I.	163
14	Derrydarragh or Oakfield	344 3 0	Sligo	Carbury	St. John's	Sligo	IV.	223
8	Derrydavy	250 0 34	Queen's Co.	Portnahinch	Ardea	Mountmellick	I.	243
19	Derry Demesne	421 1 3	Tipperary, N.R.	Owney and Arra	Templeachally	Nenagh	II.	297
23, 31	Derrydolney	1,427 3 29	King's Co.	Ballyboy	Killoughy	Tullamore	I.	124
39,40,41,42	Derrydonnell	207 1 20	Roscommon	Ballintober South	Roscommon	Roscommon	IV.	190
95	Derrydonnell Beg	296 2 29	Galway	Dunkellin	Athenry	Galway	IV.	27
83,84,95,96	Derrydonnell More	523 3 25	Galway	Athenry	Athenry	Loughrea	IV.	4
83, 95	Derrydonnell North	317 1 33	Galway	Dunkellin	Athenry	Galway	IV.	27
5	Derrydooan Lower	447 1 0	Westmeath	Moygoish	Rathaspick	Granard	I.	280
5	Derrydooan Middle	299 0 38e	Westmeath	Moygoish	Rathaspick	Granard	I.	280
5, 6	Derrydooan Upper	155 0 25	Westmeath	Moygoish	Rathaspick	Granard	I.	280
39, 42	Derrydoon	107 1 13f	Fermanagh	Coole	Galloon	Clones	III.	199
63	Derrydorneen	226 1 32	Mayo	Costello	Kilbeagh	Swineford	IV.	140
11	Derrydorragh	161 0 18	Armagh	Tiranny	Eglish	Armagh	III.	59
11	Derrydorragh	271 2 26	Londonderry	Coleraine	Macosquin	Coleraine	III.	233
78	Derrydorragh	27 1 31	Mayo	Carra	Ballyhean	Castlebar	IV.	125
6	Derrydorraghy	124 0 8g	Monaghan	Monaghan	Tedavnet	Monaghan	III.	278
57	Derrydruel Lower	580 1 1h	Donegal	Boylagh	Templecrone	Glenties	III.	115
57	Derrydruel Upper	447 1 34	Donegal	Boylagh	Templecrone	Glenties	III.	115
65	Derrydrummond	155 2 8	Tyrone	Clogher	Clogher	Clogher	III.	292
34	Derrydrummuck	729 2 8	Down	Upper Iveagh, Up. pt	Aghaderg	Banbridge	III.	174
13	Derrydrummult	130 2 8	Down	Lower Iveagh, Up. pt.	Moira	Lurgan	III.	170
107	Derryduff	519 3 34	Cork, W.R.	East Carbery (W.D.)	Fanlobbus	Dunmanway	II.	131
134	Derryduff	427 3 16	Cork, W.R.	Ibane and Barryroe	Ross	Clonakilty	II.	150
132	Derryduff	187 3 22	Cork, W.R.	West Carbery (E.D.)	Dromdaleague	Skibbereen	II.	140
1	Derryduff	155 3 31	Leitrim	Rosclogher	Rossinver	Ballyshannon	IV.	111
25	Derryduff	153 2 18	Londonderry	Keenaght	Dungiven	NewTnLimavady	III.	236
16	Derryduff	348 1 18	Queen's Co.	Upperwoods	Offerlane	Mountmellick	I.	251
91	Derryduff Beg	438 1 24	Cork, W.R.	Bantry	Kilmocomoge	Bantry	II.	120
91	Derryduff More	1,610 1 28i	Cork, W.R.	Bantry	Kilmocomoge	Bantry	II.	120
27	Derryeaghra	80 1 20	Clare	Tulla Upper	Feakle	Scarriff	II.	39
99	Derry East	556 2 14	Kerry	Dunkerron South	Kilcrohane	Kenmare	II.	183
35	Derryeighter	116 2 15j	Galway	Ballynahinch	Ballindoon	Clifden	IV.	10
43	Derryelvin	118 0 0k	Fermanagh	Coole	Drummully	Clones	III.	199
53	Derryerglinna	661 2 19l	Galway	Moycullen	Kilcummin	Oughterard	IV.	67
16	Derryesker	265 3 14	King's Co.	Ballyowan	Rahan	Tullamore	I.	128
32	Derryevin	67 3 31m	Cavan	Castlerahan	Lurgan	Oldcastle	III.	69
35	Derryfad	645 0 35n	Donegal	Kilmacrenan	Clondahorky	Dunfanaghy	III.	123
63	Derryfadda	461 2 30	Clare	Tulla Lower	Kiltananlea	Limerick	II.	37
12	Derryfadda	237 3 35	Clare	Tulla Upper	Feakle	Tulla	II.	39
92	Derryfadda	366 0 27	Cork, W.R.	Bantry	Kilmocomoge	Bantry	II.	120
47, 61	Derryfadda	1,688 0 8o	Galway	Killian	Taghboy	Mountbellew	IV.	45
59	Derryfadda	578 1 5	Mayo	Tirawley	Addergoole	Castlebar	IV.	163
36	Derryfadda	901 2 25	Tipperary, N.R.	Eliogarty	Moyne	Thurles	II.	271
100,101,110	Derryfadda Lower	307 0 2p	Mayo	Clanmorris	Tagheen	Claremorris	IV.	136
100, 101, 110, 111	Derryfadda Upper	256 0 14q	Mayo	Clanmorris	Tagheen	Claremorris	IV.	136
6	Derryfalone	159 1 14	Louth	Upper Dundalk	Barronstown	Dundalk	I.	177
18	Derryfeacle	134 0 8	Roscommon	Ballintober North	Kilglass	Strokestown	IV.	186

(a) Including 8A. 1R. 27P. water.
(b) Including 2A. 0R. 7P. water.
(c) Including 430A. 1R. 39P. water.
(d) Including 15A. 1R. 39P. water.
(e) Including 5A. 0R. 0P. water.
(f) Including 4A. 3R. 15P. water.

(g) Including 5A. 1R. 28P. water.
(h) Including 45A. 3R. 6P. water.
(i) Including 11A. 2R. 18P. Curramore Lough.
(j) Including 6A. 3R. 38P. water.
(k) Including 11A. 3R. 15P. water.
(l) Including 43A. 2R. 37P. water.

(m) Including 5A. 3R. 39P. water.
(n) Including 16A. 3R. 30P. water.
(o) Including 49A. 1R. 16P. water.
(p) Including 5A. 0R. 22P. water.
(q) Including 6A. 3R. 18P. water.

No. of Sheet of the Ordnance Survey Maps.	Townlands and Towns.	Area in Statute Acres.	County.	Barony.	Parish.	Poor Law Union in 1857.	Townland Census of 1851. Part I.	
		A. R. P.					Vol.	Page
69	Derryfineen	480 1 29	Cork, W.R.	West Muskerry	Kilnamartry	Macroom	II.	159
24	Derryfore	269 3 15	Queen's Co.	Cullenagh	Ballyroan	Abbeyleix	I.	239
106, 107, 116, 117	Derryfrench	676 3 1	Galway	Leitrim	Tynagh	Loughrea	IV.	55
61	Derryfubble	118 1 8	Tyrone	Dungannon Middle	Clonfeacle	Dungannon	III.	299
130, 139	Derryfunshion	242 2 19	Cork, W.R.	West Carbery(W.D.)	Skull	Skull	II.	146
55	Derrygally	180 2 14a	Tyrone	Dungannon Middle	Killyman	Dungannon	III.	303
55	Derrygally Demesne	77 1 19b	Tyrone	Dungannon Middle	Killyman	Dungannon	III.	303
22, 23, 30	Derrygalun	397 1 24	Cork, E.R.	Duhallow	Kilmeen	Kanturk	II.	72
45, 46	Derryganard	826 3 30	Londonderry	Loughinsholin	Lissan	Magherafelt	III.	242
30	Derrygannon	149 3 13	Fermanagh	Clankelly	Clones	Clones	III.	195
37	Derrygareen	194 2 33	Tipperary. N.R.	Owney and Arra	Kilvellane	Nenagh	II.	296
15, 20	Derrygarra Lower	79 3 33c	Cavan	Upper Loughtee	Castleterra	Cavan	III.	82
27, 28	Derrygarran	351 3 37	King's Co.	Coolestown	Clonsast	Edenderry	I.	133
13	Derrygarran	358 2 0	Queen's Co.	Maryborough East	Straboe	Mountmellick	I.	241
82, 83	Derrygarrane North	386 0 26d	Kerry	Dunkerron South	Templenoe	Kenmare	II.	185
82,83,91,92	Derrygarrane South	861 3 14e	Kerry	Dunkerron South	Templenoe	Kenmare	II.	185
15, 20	Derrygarra Upper	90 2 25f	Cavan	Upper Loughtee	Castleterra	Cavan	III.	82
18	Derrygarriff	347 2 11	Clare	Bunratty Upper	Inchicronan	Ennis	II.	9
116	Derrygarriff	66 0 5	Galway	Leitrim	Ballynakill	Loughrea	IV.	51
73, 83	Derrygarriv	544 3 36	Kerry	Dunkerron North	Knockane	Killarney	II.	182
93, 102	Derrygarriv	365 0 36	Kerry	Glanarought	Kenmare	Kenmare	II.	186
42	Derrygarve	856 1 35	Londonderry	Loughinsholin	Artrea	Magherafelt	III.	238
88	Derrygarve	170 1 4	Mayo	Burrishoole	Aghagower	Westport	IV.	118
68	Derrygarve	265 3 39g	Mayo	Burrishoole	Burrishoole	Newport	IV.	119
96, 106	Derrygarve Beg	304 2 9h	Mayo	Murrisk	Kilgeever	Westport	IV.	160
89	Derrygarve East	24 2 9	Mayo	Carra	Ballyhean	Castlebar	IV.	125
95, 96	Derrygarve More	304 3 0i	Mayo	Murrisk	Kilgeever	Westport	IV.	160
78, 89	Derrygarve West	42 0 15	Mayo	Carra	Ballyhean	Castlebar	IV.	125
6	Derrygassan Lower	114 0 9j	Monaghan	Trough	Donagh	Monaghan	III.	281
6	Derrygassan Upper	117 0 20	Monaghan	Trough	Donagh	Monaghan	III.	281
60	Derrygaury	251 0 2k	Mayo	Tirawley	Ballynahaglish	Ballina	IV.	164
81	Derrygay	191 3 8	Mayo	Costello	Aghamore	Swineford	IV.	137
58, 59	Derrygeeha	437 0 28l	Clare	Clonderalaw	Kilfiddane	Killadysert	II.	15
17, 18	Derrygeel	321 1 36	Longford	Rathcline	Rathcline	Longford	I.	164
14, 15	Derrygeeraghan	238 2 12m	Cavan	Lower Loughtee	Drumlane	Cavan	III.	80
30	Derrygelly	162 0 30	Fermanagh	Clankelly	Clones	Clones	III.	195
39	Derrygennedy	111 0 17	Fermanagh	Coole	Galloon	Clones	III.	199
141	Derrygereen	293 3 26	Cork, W.R.	West Carbery (E.D.)	Creagh	Skibbereen	III.	139
19	Derrygid	190 2 33	Cavan	Tullyhunco	Killashandra	Cavan	III.	98
20	Derrygid	175 2 24n	Cavan	Upper Loughtee	Urney	Cavan	III.	86
26	Derrygiff	217 0 0	Fermanagh	Clanawley	Cleenish	Enniskillen	III.	190
8	Derrygile	795 1 16	Queen's Co.	Portnahinch	Ardea	Mountmellick	I.	243
131, 132	Derrygill	544 3 18	Galway	Leitrim	Ballynakill	Portumna	IV.	51
118, 119	Derryginagh East	280 0 30o	Cork, W.R.	Bantry	Kilmocomoge	Bantry	II.	120
118	Derryginagh Middle	153 3 18	Cork, W.R.	Bantry	Kilmocomoge	Bantry	II.	120
118	Derryginagh West	87 1 4	Cork, W.R.	Bantry	Kilmocomoge	Bantry	II.	120
10	Derryginny	125 3 15p	Cavan	Tullyhaw	Tomregan	Bawnboy	III.	96
4, 7	Derrygirraun	392 2 17q	Roscommon	Boyle	Ardcarn	Car[t]. on Shannon	IV.	193
48	Derryglad	228 0 6	Roscommon	Athlone	Cam	Athlone	IV.	179
21, 22	Derryglash	211 1 23	Longford	Rathcline	Cashel	Ballymahon	I.	163
59	Derryglassaun	873 1 0	Galway	Tiaquin	Moylough	Mountbellew	IV.	79
26	Derryglen	216 0 22	Cavan	Upper Loughtee	Lavey	Cavan	III.	85
18, 22	Derryglogher	326 2 7	Longford	Moydow	Kilcommock	Ballymahon	I.	161
25	Derrygoan	230 0 17r	Leitrim	Carrigallen	Drumreilly	Bawnboy	IV.	91
40	Derrygoas	110 2 21	Fermanagh	Clankelly	Drummully	Clones	III.	197
3, 6	Derrygola	273 3 25	Monaghan	Trough	Errigal Trough	Monaghan	III.	284
40, 45	Derrygolagh	940 2 5	Sligo	Corran	Toomour	Boyle	IV.	223
17, 25	Derrygolan	436 1 18	King's Co.	Geashill	Geashill	Tullamore	I.	140
40	Derrygolan	378 1 23	Westmeath	Moycashel	Durrow	Tullamore	I.	277
30, 39	Derrygonigan	214 3 12	Tyrone	Dungannon Upper	Artrea	Cookstown	III.	305
15	Derrygonnelly	84 1 27	Fermanagh	Magheraboy	Inishmacsaint	Enniskillen	III.	212
15	DERRYGONNELLY T.	—	Fermanagh	Magheraboy	Inishmacsaint	Enniskillen	III.	213
141	Derrygool	114 2 36	Cork, W.R.	West Carbery (E.D.)	Abbeystrowry	Skibbereen	II.	136
131, 134	Derrygoolin North	2,202 0 24	Galway	Leitrim	Ballynakill	Portumna	IV.	51
131, 134	Derrygoolin South	2,079 1 35	Galway	Leitrim	Ballynakill	Portumna	IV.	51
67	Derrygooly	108 0 13	Tyrone	Dungannon Lower	Aghaloo	Armagh	III.	296
24	Derrygoon	498 3 8	Tyrone	Strabane Lower	Ardstraw	Castlederg	III.	319
61	Derrygoonan	178 0 33	Tyrone	Dungannon Middle	Clonfeacle	Dungannon	III.	299
26	Derrygoony	283 2 20s	Monaghan	Cremorne	Aghnamullen	Cootehill	III.	257
22	Derrygore	148 1 16t	Fermanagh	Tirkennedy	Trory	Enniskillen	III.	223
44, 45	Derrygorman	395 0 32	Kerry	Corkaguiny	Ballinvoher	Dingle	II.	174
88	Derrygorman	324 1 27	Mayo	Murrisk	Aghagower	Westport	IV.	158

(a) Including 5A. 1R. 26P. water.
(b) Including 1A. 3R. 3P. water.
(c) Including 4A. 3R. 0P. water.
(d) Including 8A. 2R. 21P. water.
(e) Including 20A. 1R. 27P. water.
(f) Including 5A. 0R. 37P. water.
(g) Including 2A 0R. 5P. water.

(h) Including 9A. 1R. 16P. water.
(i) Including 12A. 3R. 12P. water.
(j) Including 5A. 3R. 14P. water.
(k) Including 7A. 1R. 34P. water.
(l) Including 10A. 2R. 16P. water.
(m) Including 19A. 0R. 21P. water.
(n) Including 53A. 3R. 15P. water.

(o) Including 20A. 1R. 27P. water.
(p) Including 2A. 2R. 4P. water.
(q) Including 8A. 3R. 5P. water.
(r) Including 50A. 1R. 8P. water.
(s) Including 51A. 0R. 39P. water.
(t) Including 32A. 3R. 8P. water.

No. of Sheet of the Ordnance Survey Maps.	Townlands and Towns.	Area in Statute Acres.	County.	Barony.	Parish.	Poor Law Union in 1857.	Townland Census of 1851, Part I. Vol.	Page
		A. R. P.					Vol.	Page
1	Derrygorry	184 1 22	Monaghan	Trough	Errigal Trough	Clogher	III.	284
37, 38, 46	Derrygortanea	252 1 33	Tyrone	Dungannon Upper	Desertcreat	Cookstown	III.	307
81, 82	Derrygortnacloghy	173 3 0	Cork, W.R.	West Muskerry	Inchigeelagh	Dunmanway	II.	157
54, 61	Derrygortrevy	250 2 35	Tyrone	Dungannon Middle	Clonfeacle	Dungannon	III.	299
15, 20	Derrygoss	147 0 15a	Cavan	Upper Loughtee	Urney	Cavan	III.	86
49	Derrygowan	145 2 27	Antrim	Upper Toome	Duneane	Antrim	III.	34
77	Derrygowla	81 2 18	Mayo	Burrishoole	Islandeady	Westport	IV.	121
40, 41	Derrygowna	418 0 23	Cork, E.R.	Duhallow	Kilshannig	Mallow	II.	74
21, 22	Derrygowna	902 1 7	Longford	Rathcline	Cashel	Ballymahon	I.	163
76, 82	Derrygrath Lower	508 3 14	Tipperary, S.R.	Iffa and Offa West	Derrygrath	Clogheen	II.	318
76, 82	Derrygrath Upper	109 0 17	Tipperary, S.R.	Iffa and Offa West	Derrygrath	Clogheen	II.	318
27, 28	Derrygravaun	54 1 5	Clare	Tulla Upper	Feakle	Scarriff	II.	39
3	Derrygreenagh	1,115 2 30	King's Co.	Warrenstown	Castlejordan	Edenderry	I.	145
108	Derrygreenia	472 0 24	Kerry	Glanarought	Tuosist	Kenmare	II.	188
9, 17	Derrygrogan Big	240 0 20	King's Co.	Lower Philipstown	Ballycommon	Tullamore	I.	142
9, 10	Derrygrogan Little	217 0 3	King's Co.	Lower Philipstown	Ballycommon	Tullamore	I.	142
39	Derrygullinaun	160 3 25b	Mayo	Tirawley	Kilbelfad	Ballina	IV.	168
25	Derrygunnigan	202 2 19	King's Co.	Geashill	Geashill	Tullamore	I.	140
38	Derrygurdry	115 3 1	Fermanagh	Knockninny	Kinawley	Lisnaskea	III.	201
9, 13	Derryhale	834 0 0	Armagh	Oneilland West	Kilmore	Armagh	III.	53
31	Derryhall	225 3 21	Westmeath	Moycashel	Kilcumreragh	Athlone	I.	278
23	Derryhallagh	211 3 19c	Leitrim	Leitrim	Kiltoghert	Cark. on Shannon	IV.	101
14, 19	Derryhallagh	298 0 20d	Monaghan	Monaghan	Tullycorbet	Monaghan	III.	281
6	Derryhallagh	152 0 38	Monaghan	Trough	Donagh	Monaghan	III.	282
30, 37	Derryhanee	348 0 33	Roscommon	Roscommon	Lissonuffy	Strokestown	IV.	212
13, 21	Derryharan and Timolin or Derryholmes	533 2 18	King's Co.	Garrycastle	Tisaran	Parsonstown	I.	138
27	Derryharney	220 2 32e	Fermanagh	Magherastephana	Cleenish	Lisnaskea	III.	219
6, 14	Derryharney	456 3 21	King's Co.	Garrycastle	Clonmacnoise	Parsonstown	I.	135
26	Derryharraun East	130 1 26	Roscommon	Castlereagh	Kiltullagh	Castlereagh	IV.	202
25, 26	Derryharraun West	259 3 33	Roscommon	Castlereagh	Kiltullagh	Castlereagh	IV.	202
26	Derryharriff Glebe	467 2 34	Donegal	Kilmacrenan	Raymunterdoney	Dunfanaghy	III.	131
69	Derryharriff North	498 0 5f	Mayo	Carra	Islandeady	Castlebar	IV.	128
69, 78	Derryharriff South	429 1 8g	Mayo	Carra	Islandeady	Castlebar	IV.	128
32	Derryharriv	255 2 8h	Clare	Inchiquin	Inagh	Ennistimon	II.	25
8, 9	Derryharrow	275 0 14	Longford	Longford	Templemichael	Longford	I.	160
37	Derryhash	104 3 17	Tyrone	Dungannon Upper	Desertcreat	Cookstown	III.	307
6, 14	Derryhask	487 1 0	King's Co.	Garrycastle	Clonmacnoise	Parsonstown	I.	135
1	Derryhasna	204 3 8	Limerick	Clanwilliam	Stradbally	Limerick	II.	226
15	Derryhaw	699 1 11	Armagh	Armagh	Tynan	Armagh	III.	46
27, 33	Derryhawlagh	134 3 15	Fermanagh	Clanawley	Killesher	Enniskillen	III.	192
97, 107	Derryhawna	349 1 13	Mayo	Murrisk	Oughaval	Westport	IV.	161
17	Derryhay	42 0 25	Queen's Co.	Upperwoods	Offerlane	Mountmellick	I.	251
36	Derryheanlish	232 1 26	Fermanagh	Clankelly	Clones	Clones	III.	195
6	Derryhee	87 0 29	Monaghan	Trough	Donagh	Monaghan	III.	282
96, 106	Derryhecagh	312 0 34	Mayo	Murrisk	Kilgeever	Westport	IV.	160
5	Derryheelan	250 1 5	Longford	Longford	Killoe	Longford	I.	159
28	Derryheely	358 3 9	Fermanagh	Magherastephana	Aghavea	Lisnaskea	III.	218
20	Derryheen	327 0 18i	Cavan	Upper Loughtee	Urney	Cavan	III.	86
3	Derryhellan	100 3 7	Monaghan	Trough	Errigal Trough	Monaghan	III.	284
15, 19	Derryhennet	364 3 37	Armagh	Armagh	Derrynoose	Armagh	III.	44
33	Derryhenny	107 0 10j	Fermanagh	Clanawley	Kinawley	Enniskillen	III.	193
10	Derryherbert	552 1 15k	Galway	Ballynahinch	Ballynakill	Clifden	IV.	11
39	Derryherbert	157 1 16	Galway	Moycullen	Kilcummin	Oughterard	IV.	67
107, 108	Derryherbert	1,059 3 18	Mayo	Murrisk	Aghagower	Westport	IV.	158
2	Derryherk	495 3 26	Leitrim	Rosclogher	Rossinver	Ballyshannon	IV.	111
3	Derryherk	365 1 16	Roscommon	Boyle	Ardcarn	Boyle	IV.	193
32	Derryhevlin Glebe	26 3 31	Fermanagh	Clanawley	Kinawley	Enniskillen	III.	193
60, 70	Derryhick	211 0 35l	Mayo	Carra	Turlough	Castlebar	IV.	131
22	Derryhillagh	204 1 27	Fermanagh	Tirkennedy	Derryvullan	Enniskillen	III.	221
68	Derryhillagh	211 2 37m	Mayo	Burrishoole	Burrishoole	Newport	IV.	119
37,38,46,47	Derryhillagh	1,832 0 12	Mayo	Tirawley	Crossmolina	Ballina	IV.	165
46	Derryhinch	300 0 35	Meath	Upper Moyfenrath	Castlejordan	Edenderry	I.	212
20	Derryhippoo	565 3 17	Galway	Ballymoe	Kilbegnet	Roscommon	IV.	8
62, 66	Derryhirk	228 3 29	Antrim	Upper Massereene	Aghagallon	Lurgan	III.	29
4	Derryhirk	186 3 28	Armagh	Oneilland West	Killyman	Armagh	III.	53
92, 93	Derryhirk	101 1 9	Donegal	Banagh	Inver	Donegal	III.	107
118	Derryhiveny North	751 3 16	Galway	Longford	Kilmalinoge	Portumna	IV.	59
118	Derryhiveny South	570 0 0	Galway	Longford	Kilmalinoge	Portumna	IV.	59
53,54,60,61	Derryhoar	171 3 6	Tyrone	Dungannon Middle	Donaghmore	Dungannon	III.	302
48	Derryhogan	970 3 35	Tipperary, N.R.	Eliogarty	Twomileborris	Thurles	II.	273
43, 49	Derryhollagh	482 0 20n	Antrim	Upper Toome	Duneane	Antrim	III.	34

(a) Including 16A. 1R. 4P. water.
(b) Including 3A. 3R. 0P. water.
(c) Including 20A. 3R. 2P. water.
(d) Including 13A. 3R. 38P. water.
(e) Including 36A. 1R. 28P. water.

(f) Including 7A. 0R. 0P. water.
(g) Including 8A. 3R. 36P. water.
(h) Including 5A. 0R. 0P. water.
(i) Including 64A. 1R. 11P. water.
(j) Including 7A. 3R. 38P. water.

(k) Including 8A. 3R. 35P. water.
(l) Including 48A. 2R. 6P. water.
(m) Including 17A. 2R. 35P. water.
(n) Including 2A. 1R. 18P. water.

3 B

No. of Sheet of the Ordnance Survey Maps.	Townlands and Towns.	Area in Statute Acres.	County.	Barony.	Parish.	Poor Law Union in 1857.	Townland Census of 1851, Part I.	
		A. R. P.					Vol.	Page
13, 21	Derryholmes or Ti-molin & Derryharan	533 2 18	King's Co.	Garrycastle	Tisaran	Parsonstown	I.	138
23, 28	Derryhoney	161 3 28a	Fermanagh	Tirkennedy	Cleenish	Enniskillen	III.	220
15	Derryhoo	246 3 17b	Cavan	Lower Loughtee	Drumlane	Cavan	III.	80
11	Derryhoo	221 3 20c	Cavan	Tullygarvey	Annagh	Cavan	III.	87
41, 42	Derryhooly	217 1 13d	Fermanagh	Knockninny	Kinawley	Lisnaskea	III.	201
7	Derryhoosh	101 1 5	Monaghan	Trough	Donagh	Monaghan	III.	282
27, 33	Derryhowlaght East	189 2 22e	Fermanagh	Magherastephana	Cleenish	Lisnaskea	III.	219
26	Derryhowlaght West	355 2 6	Fermanagh	Clanawley	Cleenish	Enniskillen	III.	190
96, 104	Derryhoyle Beg	197 2 22	Galway	Dunkellin	Lickerrig	Loughrea	IV.	31
96, 104	Derryhoyle More	250 2 19	Galway	Dunkellin	Lickerrig	Loughrea	IV.	31
4	Derryhubbert East	572 2 6f	Armagh	Oneilland West	Killyman	Armagh	III.	53
4	Derryhubbert North	289 3 39	Armagh	Oneilland West	Killyman	Armagh	III.	53
4	Derryhubbert South	168 3 6	Armagh	Oneilland West	Killyman	Armagh	III.	53
33	Derryhum	430 2 21	Cavan	Upper Loughtee	Killinkere	Bailieborough	III.	84
34	Derryhurdin	94 3 37	Fermanagh	Magherastephana	Aghalurcher	Lisnaskea	III.	216
25, 28	Derryilan or Knock-namullagh	212 1 18	Monaghan	Farney	Donaghmoyne	Carrickmacross	III.	269
107, 108	Derryilra	433 0 10	Mayo	Murrisk	Aghagower	Westport	IV.	159
27	Derryinch	215 2 39g	Fermanagh	Clanawley	Cleenish	Enniskillen	III.	190
22	Derryinch	226 3 10h	Fermanagh	Tirkennedy	Trory	Enniskillen	III.	223
2	Derryinver	837 0 9i	Armagh	Oneilland East	Montiaghs	Lurgan	III.	49
9, 10	Derryinver	867 2 37j	Galway	Ballynahinch	Ballynakill	Clifden	IV.	11
3, 4	Derryiron	983 2 31	King's Co.	Warrenstown	Ballyburly	Edenderry	I.	144
118, 119	Derryishal	278 0 31	Cork, W.R.	West Carbery(W.D.)	Caheragh	Skibbereen	II.	142
19, 24, 25	Derryisland	194 1 27	Monaghan	Cremorne	Clontibret	Castleblayney	III.	260
27	Derrykeadgran	80 2 39	Clare	Tulla Upper	Tulla	Tulla	II.	41
23	Derrykearn	1,044 3 5	Queen's Co.	Maryborough West	Clonenagh and Clon-agheen	Abbeyleix	I.	242
22	Derrykeeghan	144 1 34	Fermanagh	Tirkennedy	Enniskillen	Enniskillen	III.	221
123, 129	Derrykeel	590 0 21	Galway	Kiltartan	Kilbeacanty	Gort	IV.	47
36, 39	Derrykeel	540 2 19	King's Co.	Ballybritt	Kinnitty	Parsonstown	I.	125
53	Derrykeel and Gort-lenaghan	401 1 7	Tyrone	Dungannon Middle	Donaghmore	Dungannon	III.	302
5	Derrykeeran	382 2 18	Armagh	Oneilland West	Tartaraghan	Lurgan	III.	54
5	Derrykeevan	277 0 22	Armagh	Oneilland West	Tartaraghan	Lurgan	III.	54
12	Derrykeighan	161 2 13	Antrim	Lower Dunluce	Derrykeighan	Ballymoney	III.	16
39,40,42,43	Derrykeny	150 3 35k	Fermanagh	Coole	Galloon	Clones	III.	199
5	Derrykerran	251 2 10	Armagh	Oneilland West	Drumcree	Lurgan	III.	52
42, 43	Derrykerrib	446 0 11	Fermanagh	Coole	Drummully	Clones	III.	199
68	Derrykill East	251 0 27	Mayo	Burrishoole	Burrishoole	Newport	IV.	119
108	Derrykillew	1,051 3 12l	Donegal	Tirhugh	Kilbarron	Ballyshannon	III.	148
63	Derrykillultagh	683 3 16	Antrim	Upper Massereene	Ballinderry	Lisburn	III.	29
68	Derrykill West	203 3 11	Mayo	Burrishoole	Burrishoole	Newport	IV.	119
18	Derrykinard	114 0 31	Monaghan	Dartree	Ematris	Cootehill	III.	266
3	Derrykinard	73 1 3	Monaghan	Trough	Errigal Trough	Monaghan	III.	284
52	Derrykinlough	560 3 29m	Mayo	Costello	Kilbeagh	Swineford	IV.	140
80, 81	Derrykinlough	504 0 35n	Mayo	Gallen	Killedan	Swineford	IV.	150
3, 6	Derrykinnigh Beg	183 1 32	Monaghan	Trough	Errigal Trough	Clogher	III.	284
3, 6	Derrykinnigh More	194 1 16	Monaghan	Trough	Errigal Trough	Clogher	III.	284
67	Derrykintone	48 1 14	Tyrone	Dungannon Lower	Aghaloo	Armagh	III.	296
13	Derryknockane	349 3 12	Limerick	Pubblebrien	Knocknagaul	Limerick	II.	253
79	Derrykyle	1,428 0 24o	Galway	Moycullen	Killannin	Galway	IV.	69
36	Derrylacky	826 0 22	Kilkenny	Knocktopher	Derrynahinch	Thomastown	I.	111
32	Derrylahan	417 3 13p	Cavan	Castlerahan	Crosserlough	Cavan	III.	68
3, 4	Derrylahan	910 1 28	Cavan	Tullyhaw	Templeport	Enniskillen	III.	94
10	Derrylahan	333 1 26	Cork, E.R.	Condons&Clangibbon	Marshalstown	Mitchelstown	II.	63
93,107,108	Derrylahan	509 0 22	Cork, W.R.	East Carbery (W.D.)	Fanlobbus	Dunmanway	II.	131
68	Derrylahan	645 3 4	Cork, W.R.	West Muskerry	Ballyvourney	Macroom	II.	154
90, 96	Derrylahan	640 2 0	Donegal	Banagh	Kilcar	Glenties	III.	108
34,35,43,44	Derrylahan	2,309 2 19q	Donegal	Kilmacrenan	Gartan	Dunfanaghy	III.	127
9, 22	Derrylahan	67 2 5	Galway	Ballynahinch	Ballynakill	Clifden	IV.	11
126	Derrylahan	118 1 9	Galway	Leitrim	Ballynakill	Loughrea	IV.	51
83	Derrylahan	253 3 0	Kerry	Dunkerron North	Knockane	Killarney	II.	182
93, 94	Derrylahan	560 0 30	Kerry	Glanarought	Kenmare	Kenmare	II.	186
24	Derrylahan	157 0 21	King's Co.	Ballyboy	Killoughy	Tullamore	I.	124
14	Derrylahan	449 3 33	King's Co.	Garrycastle	Clonmacnoise	Parsonstown	I.	135
25	Derrylahan	85 3 23	Leitrim	Carrigallen	Carrigallen	Bawnboy	IV.	89
69	Derrylahan	267 1 8	Mayo	Carra	Turlough	Castlebar	IV.	131
93	Derrylahan	278 0 8r	Mayo	Costello	Bekan	Claremorris	IV.	139
86	Derrylahan	100 0 29	Mayo	Murrisk	Kilgeever	Westport	IV.	160
29	Derrylahan	196 0 27	Queen's Co.	Cullenagh	Abbeyleix	Abbeyleix	I.	238
15, 16	Derrylahan	610 0 7	Queen's Co.	Upperwoods	Offerlane	Mountmellick	I.	251
32	Derrylahan	256 2 20	Roscommon	Castlereagh	Kiltullagh	Castlereagh	IV.	202

No. of Sheet of the Ordnance Survey Maps.	Townlands and Towns.	Area in Statute Acres.	County.	Barony.	Parish.	Poor Law Union in 1857.	Townland Census of 1851, Part I.	
		A. R. P.					Vol.	Page
19	Derrylahan	250 1 3	Roscommon	Frenchpark	Tibohine	Castlereagh	IV.	205
54, 55	Derrylahan	897 1 31	Roscommon	Moycarn	Moore	Ballinasloe	IV.	206
23	Derrylahan	100 3 22	Tipperary, N.R.	Ikerrin	Bourney	Roscrea	II.	274
131	Derrylahard	311 0 28	Cork, W.R.	West Carbery (W.D.)	Skull	Skull	II.	146
31	Derrylane	57 3 35	Cavan	Clanmahon	Ballintemple	Cavan	III.	75
24	Derrylane	178 1 9a	Cavan	Tullyhunco	Killashandra	Cavan	III	98
24	Derrylane	459 1 11	Londonderry	Keenaght	Bovevagh	Newᵗ.ᵃLimavady	III.	235
41	Derrylaney	124 0 25	Fermanagh	Knockninny	Kinawley	Lisnaskea	III.	201
61	Derrylappen	220 3 14b	Tyrone	Dungannon Lower	Aghaloo	Dungannon	III.	296
2, 5	Derrylard	595 3 5c	Armagh	Oneilland West	Tartaraghan	Lurgan	III.	54
61	Derrylattinee	391 0 11d	Tyrone	Dungannon Middle	Clonfeacle	Dungannon	III.	299
30	Derrylaughta	166 1 26	Tipperary, N.R.	Ikerrin	Templetouhy	Thurles	II.	277
32, 35	Derrylaur	93 3 29e	Leitrim	Leitrim	Annaghduff	Carᵏ.on Shannon	IV.	99
54	Derrylaura	86 0 6	Galway	Moycullen	Kilcummin	Oughterard	IV.	67
31	Derrylavan	218 0 13f	Monaghan	Farney	Magheross	Carrickmacross	III.	273
38	Derrylea	287 3 24	Cavan	Castlerahan	Crosserlough	Oldcastle	III.	68
59, 60	Derrylea	352 2 18	Clare	Clonderalaw	Killadysert	Killadysert	II.	16
32, 37	Derrylea	109 1 14	Fermanagh	Clanawley	Kinawley	Enniskillen	III.	193
39	Derrylea	511 3 37g	Fermanagh	Coole	Galloon	Lisnaskea	III.	199
38	Derrylea	129 1 17	Fermanagh	Knockninny	Kinawley	Lisnaskea	III.	201
36	Derrylea	1,634 1 1h	Galway	Ballynahinch	Moyrus	Clifden	IV.	13
83	Derrylea	262 0 0	Kerry	Dunkerron North	Knockane	Killarney	II.	182
21	Derrylea	1,205 2 15	Kildare	Offaly West	Lackagh	Athy	I.	73
77	Derrylea	118 1 21	Mayo	Burrishoole	Kilmeena	Westport	IV.	122
78	Derrylea	195 1 24	Mayo	Carra	Aglish	Castlebar	IV.	123
103	Derrylea	172 2 18	Mayo	Costello	Annagh	Claremorris	IV.	138
107	Derrylea	480 1 32	Mayo	Murrisk	Oughaval	Westport	IV.	161
8	Derrylea	146 0 23	Monaghan	Monaghan	Clones	Monaghan	III.	274
3, 4, 6, 7	Derrylea	126 1 38	Monaghan	Trough	Donagh	Monaghan	III.	282
40, 41	Derrylea	189 0 38i	Sligo	Tirerrill	Kilmactranny	Boyle	IV.	240
56, 57	Derrylea	170 0 33	Tyrone	Omagh East	Kilskeery	Enniskillen	III.	313
3	Derrylea Beg	105 3 2	Monaghan	Trough	Errigal Trough	Clogher	III.	284
30	Derryleagh	315 0 2	Cork, E.R.	Duhallow	Kilmeen	Millstreet	II.	72
82, 90, 91	Derryleagh	1,916 0 0j	Kerry	Dunkerron South	Kilcrohane	Kenmare	II.	183
15	Derryleague	125 2 23k	Cavan	Upper Loughtee	Urney	Cavan	III.	86
33	Derryleague	61 1 28l	Fermanagh	Clanawley	Kinawley	Enniskillen	III.	193
3	Derrylea More	112 0 23	Monaghan	Trough	Errigal Trough	Clogher	III.	284
148	Derryleary	183 1 9	Cork, W.R.	West Carbery(W.D.)	Skull	Skull	II.	146
26	Derryleck	99 2 7	Fermanagh	Clanawley	Cleenish	Enniskillen	III.	190
47, 51	Derryleckagh	631 2 38m	Down	Lordship of Newry	Newry	Newry	III.	182
57, 58	Derryleconnell Far	1,227 3 13n	Donegal	Boylagh	Lettermacward	Glenties	III.	114
57, 58	Derryleconnell Near	1,368 1 10o	Donegal	Boylagh	Lettermacward	Glenties	III.	114
1, 4	Derrylee	486 2 4p	Armagh	Oneilland West	Tartaraghan	Armagh	III.	54
8	Derryleedigan	160 1 38	Monaghan	Monaghan	Clones	Monaghan	III.	274
8	Derryleedigan(Jackson)	93 0 0	Monaghan	Monaghan	Clones	Monaghan	III.	274
34	Derryleeg	149 0 6q	Monaghan	Farney	Magheracloone	Carrickmacross	III.	272
12	Derryleggan	16 1 32	Monaghan	Dartree	Killeevan	Clones	III.	268
5, 6	Derrylehan	593 1 29	Sligo	Carbury	Ahamlish	Sligo	IV.	219
142	Derryleigh	264 3 39r	Cork, W.R.	West Carbery (E.D.)	Castlehaven	Skibbereen	II.	138
59	Derryleigh	465 1 15	Cork, W.R.	West Muskerry	Clondrohid	Macroom	II.	155
81, 93	Derryleigh	400 3 25	Cork, W.R.	West Muskerry	Inchigeelagh	Dunmanway	II.	157
37	Derryleigh	404 3 4	Tipperary, N.R.	Owney and Arra	Kilvellane	Nenagh	II.	296
7	Derrylemoge	583 0 10	Queen's Co.	Tinnahinch	Rosenallis	Mountmellick	I.	250
32	Derrylester	44 3 3	Fermanagh	Clanawley	Killesher	Enniskillen	III.	192
5	Derrylettiff	182 0 17	Armagh	Oneilland West	Drumcree	Lurgan	III.	52
1	Derrylevick	95 3 23	Monaghan	Trough	Errigal Trough	Clogher	III.	284
82, 83	Derrylicka	574 1 39	Kerry	Dunkerron South	Templenoe	Kenmare	II.	185
2, 5	Derrylileagh	419 3 14s	Armagh	Oneilland West	Tartaraghan	Lurgan	III.	54
38	Derrylin	149 2 29	Fermanagh	Knockninny	Kinawley	Lisnaskea	III.	201
15	Derrylina	99 3 7t	Cavan	Upper Loughtee	Urney	Cavan	III.	86
2	Derrylinneen	55 3 23	Queen's Co.	Tinnahinch	Kilmanman	Mountmellick	I.	249
6	Derrylisnahavil	149 1 26	Armagh	Oneilland East	Magheralin	Lurgan	III.	49
65, 66	Derryloaghan	841 3 17	Donegal	Boylagh	Inishkeel	Glenties	III.	112
23, 24, 29	Derryloman	239 1 10	Fermanagh	Magherastephana	Aghalurcher	Lisnaskea	III.	216
93	Derryloney	43 0 23	Galway	Galway	Rahoon	Galway	IV.	37
20	Derryloo	104 2 28	Fermanagh	Clankelly	Clones	Clones	III.	195
73, 83	Derrylooscaunagh	619 2 23	Kerry	Dunkerron North	Knockane	Killarney	II.	182
29, 38	Derryloran (alias) Kirktown	174 0 1	Tyrone	Dungannon Upper	Derryloran	Cookstown	III.	307
18	Derrylosset	170 0 13	Monaghan	Dartree	Ematris	Cootehill	III.	267
2, 5	Derryloste	555 3 23u	Armagh	Oneilland East	Montiaghs	Lurgan	III.	50
57,58,67,68	Derrylough	236 3 4	Clare	Clonderalaw	Killimer	Kilrush	II.	16
117	Derrylough	295 2 23	Cork, W.R.	Bear	Kilcaskan	Castletown	II.	122

(a) Including 4A. 0R. 22P. water.
(b) Including 1A. 0R. 16P. water.
(c) Including 5A. 1R. 15P. River Bann.
(d) Including 14A. 1R. 37P. water.
(e) Including 0A. 1R. 15P. water.
(f) Including 3A. 2R. 16P. water.
(g) Including 46A. 2R. 23P. water.

(h) Including 143A. 1A. 35P. water.
(i) Including 3A. 2R. 34P. water.
(j) Including 17A. 2R. 37P. water.
(k) Including 3A. 2R. 35P. water.
(l) Including 3A. 2R. 32P. water.
(m) Including 44A. 0R. 8P. water.
(n) Including 24A. 2R. 2P. water.

(o) Including 55A. 3R. 23P. water.
(p) Including 39A. 2R. 0P. water.
(q) Including 3A. 2R. 35P. water.
(r) including 4A. 1R. 16P. water.
(s) Including 22A. 2R. 31P. water.
(t) Including 10A. 0R. 36P. water.
(u) Including 27A. 2R. 22P. River Bann.

No. of Sheet of the Ordnance Survey Maps.	Townlands and Towns.	Area in Statute Acres. A. R. P.	County.	Barony.	Parish.	Poor Law Union in 1857.	Townland Census of 1851, Part I. Vol.	Page
34	Derrylough	222 0 3	Down	Upper Iveagh, Up. pt.	Annaclone	Banbridge	III.	174
101	Derrylough	855 0 25a	Kerry	Glanarought	Tuosist	Kenmare	II.	188
22	Derrylough	517 0 13b	Longford	Ratheline	Kilcommock	Ballymahon	I.	164
9	Derryloughan	259 2 35	Armagh	Oneilland West	Kilmore	Armagh	III.	53
47, 55	Derryloughan	1,751 0 11c	Tyrone	Dungannon Middle	Clonoe	Dungannon	III.	300
68	Derryloughan Beg	57 1 37d	Mayo	Burrishoole	Burrishoole	Newport	IV.	119
68	Derryloughan East	916 3 33e	Mayo	Burrishoole	Burrishoole	Newport	IV.	119
68	Derryloughan More	231 0 38f	Mayo	Burrishoole	Burrishoole	Newport	IV.	119
68	Derryloughan North	241 2 35	Mayo	Burrishoole	Burrishoole	Newport	IV.	119
68	Derryloughan South	301 3 20	Mayo	Burrishoole	Burrishoole	Newport	IV.	119
93	Derryloughaun East	378 3 23	Galway	Moycullen	Moycullen	Galway	IV.	71
93	Derryloughaun West	300 0 1	Galway	Moycullen	Moycullen	Galway	IV.	71
17	Derryloughbannow	161 3 19g	Longford	Ratheline	Ratheline	Longford	I.	164
4	Derrylougher	194 1 22h	Fermanagh	Lurg	Templecarn	Lowtherstown	III.	209
10	Derrylow	424 0 34	Roscommon	Boyle	Killukin	Boyle	IV.	195
31	Derry Lower	184 3 31	King's Co.	Eglish	Drumcullen	Parsonstown	I.	134
27,28,36,37	Derry Lower	1,471 0 1	Mayo	Tirawley	Crossmolina	Ballina	IV.	165
22	Derry Lower	157 2 12	Waterford	Decies without Drum	Modelligo	Lismore	II.	359
132, 133	Derrylugga	524 2 2	Cork, W.R.	West Carbery (E.D.)	Abbeystrowry	Skibbereen	II.	136
11, 18	Derrylumman	92 1 18i	Clare	Inchiquin	Kilkeedy	Corrofin	II.	25
32, 38	Derrylurgan	480 3 23j	Cavan	Castlerahan	Denn	Oldcastle	III.	68
.1	Derrylusk	114 2 16	Limerick	Clanwilliam	Stradbally	Limerick	II.	226
8	Derrylusk	134 1 2	Monaghan	Monaghan	Clones	Monaghan	III.	274
14, 19	Derrylusk	181 3 27	Monaghan	Monaghan	Tullycorbet	Monaghan	III.	281
12, 17	Derrylusk	339 2 17	Queen's Co.	Maryborough West	Clonenagh&Clonagheen	Mountmellick	I.	242
62, 69, 70	Derryluskan	835 2 25	Tipperary, S.R.	Middlethird	Rathcool	Cashel	II.	329
16, 17, 18	Derrylustia	168 0 2	Leitrim	Drumahaire	Inishmagrath	Manorhamilton	IV.	96
49	Derrymacanna	147 3 11	Tyrone	Omagh East	Kilskeery	Lowtherstown	III.	313
22, 23	Derrymacar	426 3 4k	Longford	Ratheline	Cashel	Ballymahon	I.	163
6	Derrymacash	803 3 19l	Armagh	Oneilland East	Montiaghs	Lurgan	III.	50
39	Derrymacausey	93 2 33	Fermanagh	Knockninny	Kinawley	Lisnaskea	III.	201
42	Derrymacedmond	167 3 2	King's Co.	Clonlisk	Kilmurryely	Roscrea	I.	131
1	Derrymacegan or Clareisland	224 0 33	Westmeath	Fore	Foyran	Granard	I.	270
5	Derrymacfall	431 3 38m	Armagh	Oneilland West	Drumcree	Lurgan	III.	52
70	Derrymaclaughna	207 1 16	Galway	Clare	Athenry	Galway	IV.	17
76	Derrymaclavlode	988 0 14	Kerry	Magunihy	Killaha	Killarney	II.	202
24	Derrymacoffin	119 2 13n	Leitrim	Leitrim	Fenagh	Mohill	IV.	100
39	Derrymacrow	292 2 2o	Fermanagh	Coole	Galloon	Lisnaskea	III.	199
18	Derrymacstur	143 0 7p	Roscommon	Ballintober North	Kilglass	Strokestown	IV.	186
4	Derrymagowan	250 3 0	Armagh	Oneilland West	Clonfeacle	Armagh	III.	51
22, 27	Derrymakeen	33 1 2	Fermanagh	Tirkennedy	Enniskillen	Enniskillen	III.	221
39, 48	Derrymannin	173 2 38q	Mayo	Tirawley	Ballynahaglish	Ballina	IV.	164
22	Derrymany	311 3 0	Longford	Ratheline	Cashel	Ballymahon	I.	163
5	Derrymaquirk	281 1 35	Roscommon	Boyle	Boyle	Boyle	IV.	194
47, 59	Derrymartin	821 0 26	Mayo	Tirawley	Addergoole	Castlebar	IV.	163
5	Derrymattry	118 3 18	Armagh	Oneilland West	Drumcree	Lurgan	III.	52
109	Derrymeeleen	441 3 29	Cork, W.R.	East Carbery (E.D.)	Desertserges	Clonakilty	II.	128
40	Derrymeen	151 2 6	Fermanagh	Clankelly	Clones	Clones	III.	195
59	Derrymeen	203 2 6	Tyrone	Clogher	Errigal Keerogue	Clogher	III.	295
55	Derrymeen	205 3 30	Tyrone	Dungannon Middle	Killyman	Dungannon	III.	303
115	Derrymihin East	521 0 7	Cork, W.R.	Bear	Killaconenagh	Castletown	II.	124
115	Derrymihin West	606 0 14	Cork, W.R.	Bear	Killaconenagh	Castletown	II.	124
9	Derrymony	254 0 16r	Cavan	Tullyhaw	Templeport	Bawnboy	III.	94
62	Derrymore	457 0 19	Antrim	Upper Massereene	Aghagallon	Lurgan	III.	29
26	Derry More	325 3 21	Armagh	Orior Upper	Newry	Newry	III.	58
9	Derry More	126 1 12s	Cavan	Tullyhaw	Templeport	Bawnboy	III.	94
52, 62	Derry More	489 1 28	Clare	Bunratty Lower	Killeely	Limerick	II.	5
26	Derrymore	395 0 10t	Clare	Bunratty Upper	Inchicronan	Tulla	II.	9
24	Derrymore	128 1 28u	Clare	Corcomroe	Clooney	Ennistimon	II.	18
55	Derrymore	139 0 15	Donegal	Raphoe	Taughboyne	Londonderry	III.	143
5, 6	Derry More	142 0 15	Fermanagh	Lurg	Drumkeeran	Lowtherstown	III.	206
28	Derrymore	360 0 30	Galway	Clare	Donaghpatrick	Tuam	IV.	19
5, 17	Derrymore	176 1 36	Galway	Dunmore	Dunmore	Tuam	IV.	33
61	Derrymore	238 0 13	Galway	Kilconnell	Fohanagh	Mountbellew	IV.	40
46	Derrymore	370 2 12	Galway	Tiaquin	Killosolan	Mountbellew	IV.	78
80	Derrymore	586 1 22	Kerry	Iveragh	Killinane	Cahersiveen	II.	197
15,16,23,24	Derrymore	726 2 18	King's Co.	Ballyboy	Killoughy	Tullamore	I.	124
19,20,27,28	Derrymore	293 0 30	King's Co.	Coolestown	Clonsast	Edenderry	I.	133
10	Derry More	199 0 22	Londonderry	Keenaght	Drumachose	NewTnLimavady	III.	235
14, 19	Derrymore	357 2 33	Longford	Moydow	Ardagh	Longford	I.	160
99, 109	Derrymore	216 2 1w	Mayo	Carra	Ballyovey	Ballinrobe	IV.	126
92, 93	Derrymore	165 2 28x	Mayo	Costello	Bekan	Claremorris	IV.	139

(a) Including 64A. 0R. 9P. water.
(b) Including 30A. 0R. 24P. water.
(c) Including 18A. 3R. 12P. water.
(d) Including 2A. 1R. 7P. water.
(e) Including 50A. 3R. 20P. water.
(f) Including 8A. 1R. 26P. water.
(g) Including 20A. 1R. 24P. water.
(h) Including 2A. 3R. 20P. water.

(i) Including 0A. 1R. 7P. water.
(j) Including 9A. 3R. 7P. water.
(k) Including 45A. 3R. 20P. water.
(l) Including 3A. 1R. 32P. Rathlin Island.
(m) Including 9A. 3R. 24P. water.
(n) Including 67A. 3R. 37P. water.
(o) Including 95A. 2R. 27P. water.
(p) Including 1A. 3R. 17P. water.

(q) Including 55A. 3R. 13P. water.
(r) Including 97A. 2R. 22P. Brackley Lough.
(s) Including 30A. 3R. 15P. Brackley Lough.
(t) Including 2A. 3R. 2P. water.
(u) Including 4A. 0R. 21P. water.
(v) Including 21A. 1R. 28P. water.
(w) Including 7A. 0R. 36P. water.
(x) Including 8A. 1R. 28P. water.

No. of Sheet of the Ordnance Survey Maps.	Townlands and Towns.	Area in Statute Acres. A. R. P.			County.	Barony.	Parish.	Poor Law Union in 1857.	Townland Census of 1851, Part I. Vol.	Page
111	Derrymore	329	0	38	Mayo	Kilmaine	Kilcommon	Ballinrobe	IV.	154
97	Derrymore	604	0	32a	Mayo	Murrisk	Oughaval	Westport	IV.	161
17	Derry More	152	3	10	Queen's Co.	Maryborough West	Clonenagh and Clonagheen	Mountmellick	I.	242
34	Derry More	79	0	31	Sligo	Tirerrill	Killadoon	Boyle	IV.	239
17, 18	Derrymore	1,096	3	16	Tipperary, N.R.	Ikerrin	Corbally	Roscrea	II.	275
46	Derrymore	115	3	29	Tipperary, S.R.	Kilnamanagh Lower	Clogher	Cashel	II.	322
21, 27, 28	Derrymore	886	3	37b	Westmeath	Farbill	Killucan	Mullingar	I.	266
35, 43	Derrymore East	535	0	7c	Clare	Tulla Upper	Tulla	Tulla	II.	41
37	Derrymore East	2,708	3	5	Kerry	Corkaguiny	Annagh	Tralee	II.	173
47	Derrymore Island	33	0	27	Sligo	Coolavin	Killaraght	Boyle	IV.	225
35	Derrymore West	615	3	26	Clare	Tulla Upper	Tulla	Tulla	II.	41
28, 37	Derrymore West	1,371	2	34	Kerry	Corkaguiny	Annagh	Tralee	II.	173
32	Derrymoyle	141	3	2d	Queen's Co.	Slievemargy	Killeshin	Carlow	I.	245
24	Derrymoylin	476	2	14	Roscommon	Ballintober North	Termonbarry	Strokestown	IV.	187
74	Derrymullan	225	3	36e	Galway	Clonmacnowen	Kilcloony	Ballinasloe	IV.	25
13	Derrymullen	533	0	3	Kildare	Connell	Kilmeage	Naas	I.	55
1, 3, 4	Derrymullen,Coolagh, and Coolavoran	972	3	15	Queen's Co.	Tinnahinch	Castlebrack	Mountmellick	I.	248
30	Derrymullin and Loughderry	369	1	5f	King's Co.	Eglish	Eglish	Parsonstown	I.	134
20	Derryna	133	1	6	Cavan	Upper Loughtee	Kilmore	Cavan	III.	84
40, 40	Derrynabaunshy	502	1	18	Mayo	Gallen	Attymas	Ballina	IV.	147
82	Derrynablaha	985	1	18	Kerry	Dunkerron South	Templenoe	Kenmare	II.	185
74, 84	Derrynablunnaga	75	1	5	Kerry	Dunkerron South	Knockane	Killarney	II.	184
101	Derrynabrack	390	0	36g	Kerry	Glanarought	Tuosist	Kenmare	II.	188
32	Derrynabrin	318	1	32	Galway	Tiaquin	Kilkerrin	Glennamaddy	IV.	77
63, 64	Derrynabrock	1,478	3	29	Mayo	Costello	Kilbeagh	Swineford	IV.	140
26	Derrynabuntale	526	0	15h	Longford	Rathcline	Shrule	Ballymahon	I.	165
93, 107	Derrynacaheragh	423	3	29	Cork, W.R.	East Carbery (W.D.)	Fanlobbus	Dunmanway	II.	131
102	Derrynacaheragh	684	0	30	Kerry	Glanarought	Kenmare	Kenmare	II.	186
89, 99	Derrynacannana	268	0	24	Mayo	Carra	Ballintober	Castlebar	IV.	124
32	Derrynacarragh	206	2	16	Clare	Islands	Kilmaley	Ennis	II.	31
58	Derrynacarrow	718	2	37i	Donegal	Boylagh	Lettermacward	Glenties	III.	114
58	Derrynacarrow East or Bellanaboy	99	0	23	Donegal	Boylagh	Lettermacward	Glenties	III.	114
11	Derrynacleigh	1,058	3	30	Galway	Ballynahinch	Ballynakill	Clifden	IV.	11
35	Derrynacloy	212	1	19	Fermanagh	Clankelly	Clones	Clones	III.	195
93	Derrynacong	332	1	12	Mayo	Costello	Annagh	Claremorris	IV.	138
102	Derrynacoulagh	730	3	8	Kerry	Glanarought	Kenmare	Kenmare	II.	186
3, 8	Derrynacrannog Glebe	1,051	1	18j	Fermanagh	Lurg	Belleek	Ballyshannon	III.	203
7, 9	Derrynacreeve	122	2	4	Cavan	Tullyhaw	Templeport	Bawnboy	III.	94
4	Derrynacrit	115	0	19	Longford	Longford	Clongesh	Longford	I.	157
19	Derrynacross	169	2	33k	Cavan	Tullyhunco	Killashandra	Cavan	III.	98
7, 8	Derrynacross	385	0	21	Fermanagh	Magheraboy	Inishmacsaint	Ballyshannon	III.	212
5, 9	Derrynacross	328	1	32	Longford	Longford	Killoe	Longford	I.	159
79	Derrynacross	63	0	28	Mayo	Carra	Turlough	Castlebar	IV.	131
74	Derrynacross	98	0	17	Mayo	Costello	Kilcolman	Castlereagh	IV.	141
27, 34	Derrynadarragh or Chevychase	349	2	19	King's Co.	Coolestown	Clonsast	Edenderry	I.	132
69	Derrynadivva	889	2	11l	Mayo	Carra	Aglish	Castlebar	IV.	123
2, 4	Derrynadooey	147	0	8m	Roscommon	Boyle	Kilronan	Boyle	IV.	197
14	Derrynafaugher	107	3	36	Fermanagh	Magheraboy	Devenish	Enniskillen	III.	210
72, 73	Derrynafeana	986	0	15	Kerry	Dunkerron North	Killorglin	Cahersiveen	II.	181
72, 73	Derrynafeana	1,174	2	4n	Kerry	Dunkerron North	Knockane	Cahersiveen	II.	182
91, 92	Derrynafinchin	792	1	20	Cork, W.R.	Bantry	Kilmocomoge	Bantry	II.	120
76	Derrynafinnia	839	2	6	Kerry	Magunihy	Killaha	Killarney	II.	202
24	Derrynaflaw	612	3	0	Londonderry	Keenaght	Bovevagh	NewTnLimavady	III.	235
104	Derrynafulla	768	1	26	Cork, W.R.	Bear	Kilcaskan	Bantry	II.	122
83	Derrynafunsha	338	3	24o	Kerry	Dunkerron South	Templenoe	Kenmare	II.	185
5	Derrynafunshion	210	0	13	Queen's Co.	Portnahinch	Lea	Mountmellick	I.	244
5	Derrynagad	108	2	25	Monaghan	Monaghan	Tedavnet	Monaghan	III.	278
17	Derrynagall or Ballydaly	464	2	33	King's Co.	Ballycowan	Kilbride	Tullamore	I.	127
26	Derrynagalliagh	348	3	23	Longford	Rathcline	Cashel	Ballymahon	I.	163
2	Derrynagallion	46	3	5	Roscommon	Boyle	Kilronan	Boyle	IV.	197
20	Derrynagan	83	2	14	Cavan	Upper Loughtee	Kilmore	Cavan	III.	84
7, 8, 13	Derrynagarragh	1,163	1	32p	Westmeath	Fore	Faughalstown	Castletowndelvin	I.	269
97, 111	Derrynagasha	426	3	7	Cork, E.R.	Kinalea	Leighmoney	Kinsale	II.	96
58	Derrynageeha	259	1	36	Clare	Clonderalaw	Kilfiddane	Killadysert	II.	15
20	Derrynagittagh (Naughton)	115	3	14	Clare	Tulla Upper	Feakle	Scarriff	II.	39
20	Derrynagittagh (Purcell)	153	3	19	Clare	Tulla Upper	Feakle	Scarriff	II.	39

(a) Including 4A. 1R. 0P. water.
(b) Including 2A. 3R. 8P. Croboy Lough.
(c) Including 2A. 2R. 28P. water.
(d) Including 11A. 1R. 19P. detached portion.
(e) Including 7A. 3R. 16P. water.
(f) Including 42A. 0R. 14P. water.

(g) Including 59A. 0R. 38P. water.
(h) Including 3A. 0R. 22P. water.
(i) Including 62A. 2R. 12P. water.
(j) Including 51A. 0R. 2P. water.
(k) Including 2A. 2R. 13P. water.

(l) Including 11A. 0R. 34P. water.
(m) Including Islands.
(n) Including 63A. 1R. 0P. water.
(o) Including 16A. 3R. 15P. water.
(p) Including 25A. 0R. 2P. water.

No. of Sheet of the Ordnance Survey Maps.	Townlands and Towns.	Area in Statute Acres.			County.	Barony.	Parish.	Poor Law Union in 1857.	Townland Census of 1851, Part I.	
		A.	R.	P.					Vol.	Page
34	Derrynaglah . .	278	1	29a	Monaghan .	Farney . . .	Magheracloone .	Carrickmacross	III.	272
18	Derrynagleragh .	73	0	16	Clare . .	Bunratty Upper .	Inchicronan . .	Ennis . .	II.	9
78, 89	Derrynagooley .	74	3	25	Mayo . .	Carra . . .	Ballyhean . .	Castlebar . .	IV.	125
91	Derrynagower .	211	0	34	Mayo . .	Clanmorris . .	Mayo . . .	Claremorris .	IV.	135
31, 45	Derrynagran . .	302	2	3	Galway .	Tiaquin . . .	Kilkerrin . .	Glennamaddy .	IV.	77
22	Derrynagran . .	293	0	17	Longford .	Ratheline . .	Cashel . .	Ballymahon .	I.	163
48, 60	Derrynagran . .	178	2	30	Mayo . .	Tirawley . .	Ballynahaglish .	Ballina . .	IV.	164
44	Derrynagraug .	183	0	32	Sligo . .	Corran . . .	Kilshalvy . .	Boyle . .	IV.	227
80,81,92,93	Derrynagree .	320	1	16	Cork, W.R.	West Muskerry .	Inchigeelagh .	Dunmanway .	II.	157
90	Derrynagree . .	1,155	0	29b	Kerry . .	Dunkerron South .	Kilcrohane .	Kenmare . .	II.	183
120	Derrynagree East .	303	1	12	Cork, W.R.	West Carbery (E.D.)	Dromdaleague .	Skibbereen .	II.	140
119, 120	Derrynagree West .	355	1	15	Cork, W.R.	West Carbery (E.D.)	Dromdaleague .	Skibbereen .	II.	140
9	Derrynagrew . .	108	3	0c	Monaghan	Monaghan . .	Tedavnet . .	Monaghan .	III.	278
50, 58	Derrynagrial . .	1,437	2	11d	Donegal .	Boylagh . . .	Lettermacward .	Glenties . .	III.	114
7, 15	Derrynagun . .	409	0	0	King's Co.	Garrycastle . .	Lemanaghan .	Parsonstown .	I.	136
74	Derrynagur . .	76	3	27	Mayo . .	Costello . .	Kilcolman . .	Castlereagh .	IV.	141
28	Derrynaheila . .	264	0	37	Clare . .	Tulla Upper . .	Feakle . . .	Scarriff . .	II.	39
16	Derrynaheilla .	108	1	28	Clare . .	Corcomroe . .	Kiltoraght . .	Corrofin . .	II.	22
5, 8	Derrynahesco .	496	2	31	Monaghan .	Monaghan . .	Tedavnet . .	Monaghan .	III.	278
5	Derrynahimmirk .	450	3	29	Leitrim .	Rosclogher . .	Rossinver . .	Manorhamilton	IV.	111
31, 32	Derrynahinch . .	993	0	39	Kilkenny .	Knocktopher .	Derrynahinch .	Thomastown .	I.	111
18	Derrynahinch .	78	2	31	Leitrim . .	Drumahaire . .	Inishmagrath .	Manorhamilton	IV.	96
18	Derrynahona . .	129	3	3	Leitrim .	Drumahaire . .	Drumreilly . .	Cark. on Shannon	IV.	95
91	Derrynakilla . .	340	2	35	Cork, W.R.	Bantry . . .	Kilmocomoge .	Bantry . .	II.	120
72	Derrynaleck . .	285	3	16	Mayo . .	Costello . .	Kilmovee . .	Swineford .	IV.	142
58	Derrynalecka . .	354	1	34	Clare . .	Clonderalaw . .	Kilfiddane . .	Killadysert .	II.	15
58	Derrynalecka . .	392	0	30	Clare . .	Clonderalaw . .	Kilmurry . .	Killadysert .	II.	17
3, 5	Derrynalester . .	125	3	3	Cavan . .	Tullyhaw . .	Killinagh . .	Enniskillen .	III.	92
19	Derrynaloobinagh .	197	0	2e	Monaghan	Cremorne . .	Ballybay . .	Castleblayney .	III.	259
18, 20	Derrynalurgan .	43	3	1	Leitrim .	Drumahaire . .	Inishmagrath .	Manorhamilton	IV.	96
85	Derrynamanagh .	705	2	4	Galway .	Kilconnell . .	Grange . . .	Loughrea . .	IV.	40
41	Derrynamansher .	349	3	1f	Donegal .	Boylagh . .	Templecrone .	Glenties . .	III.	115
10, 17	Derrynameel . .	488	1	31	Mayo . .	Erris . . .	Kilcommon . .	Belmullet .	IV.	143
8, 13	Derrynameeo . .	300	2	13	Fermanagh .	Magheraboy . .	Inishmacsaint .	Ballyshannon .	III.	212
30	Derrynamona . .	111	2	5	Cork, E.R.	Duhallow . .	Kilmeen . .	Kanturk . .	II.	72
79	Derrynamrahe r .	52	2	6	Mayo . .	Carra . . .	Breaghwy . .	Castlebar . .	IV.	127
69, 70	Derrynamuck . .	119	3	0	Mayo . .	Carra . . .	Turlough . .	Castlebar . .	IV.	131
113	Derrynamuck . .	254	2	8	Mayo . .	Costello . .	Annagh . . .	Claremorris .	IV.	138
39	Derrynamuck . .	276	1	13g	Mayo . .	Tirawley . .	Ballynahaglish .	Ballina . .	IV.	164
22, 28	Derrynamuck . .	278	3	11	Wicklow . .	Upper Talbotstown .	Donaghmore .	Baltinglass .	I.	363
101	Derrynamucklagh .	453	1	11h	Kerry . .	Glanarought .	Tuosist . .	Kenmare . .	II.	188
77	Derrynanaff . .	59	2	12	Mayo . .	Burrishoole . .	Kilmeena . .	Westport . .	IV.	122
63, 64	Derrynanaff . .	112	0	26	Mayo . .	Costello . .	Kilbeagh . .	Castlereagh .	IV.	140
8, 16	Derrynanagh . .	122	1	23	King's Co.	Ballycowan . .	Rahan . . .	Tullamore .	I.	128
8, 16	Derrynanagh or Tullymorerahan	119	0	4	King's Co.	Ballycowan . .	Rahan . . .	Tullamore .	I.	129
5	Derrynanamph .	233	3	38	Monaghan .	Monaghan . .	Tedavnet . .	Monaghan .	III.	278
6, 8	Derrynananta Lower	789	0	9	Cavan . .	Tullyhaw . .	Templeport . .	Enniskillen .	III.	94
6, 8	Derrynananta Upper	1,059	3	18	Cavan . .	Tullyhaw . .	Templeport . .	Enniskillen .	III.	94
50, 58	Derrynanaspol .	2,667	0	22i	Donegal .	Boylagh . . .	Lettermacward .	Glenties . .	III.	114
27, 28	Derrynaneal . .	182	3	27j	Clare . .	Tulla Upper . .	Feakle . . .	Scarriff . .	II.	39
41	Derrynancane .	50	2	8	Sligo . .	Tirerrill . .	Kilmactranny .	Boyle . .	IV.	240
81	Derrynaned . .	79	3	13	Mayo . .	Costello . .	Aghamore . .	Swineford .	IV.	137
11, 16	Derrynanny . .	328	2	21	Fermanagh .	Lurg . . .	Derryvullan .	Lowtherstown .	III.	204
10, 19	Derrynanool . .	458	1	7	Cork, E.R.	Condons&Clangibbon	Marshalstown .	Mitchelstown .	II.	63
77	Derrynaraw . .	142	1	7h	Mayo . .	Burrishoole . .	Kilmeena . .	Westport . .	IV.	122
3	Derrynarget . .	50	1	36	Monaghan .	Trough . . .	Errigal Trough .	Clogher . .	III.	284
72, 81	Derrynarud . .	24	2	33	Mayo . .	Costello . .	Aghamore . .	Swineford .	IV.	137
107	Derrynasafagh .	416	1	3	Cork, W.R.	East Carbery (W.D.)	Fanlobbus . .	Dunmanway .	II.	131
58	Derrynasaggart .	1,812	0	15	Cork, W.R.	West Muskerry .	Ballyvourney .	Macroom . .	II.	154
31, 34	Derrynascobe .	164	2	1	Monaghan .	Farney . . .	Magheracloone .	Carrickmacross	III.	272
59	Derrynascobe .	139	1	15	Tyrone . .	Clogher . .	Clogher . .	Clogher . .	III.	292
48	Derrynasce . .	205	0	1	Roscommon .	Athlone . .	Kiltoom . .	Athlone . .	IV.	183
66	Derrynaseer . .	244	0	32	Antrim .	Upper Massereene .	Aghagallon .	Lurgan . .	III.	29
1	Derrynaseer . .	155	0	5	Cavan . .	Tullyhaw . .	Killinagh . .	Enniskillen .	III.	92
23	Derrynaseer . .	35	2	36	Leitrim . .	Leitrim . .	Kiltoghert . .	Cark. on Shannon	IV.	101
2	Derrynaseer . .	550	0	7	Leitrim . .	Rosclogher . .	Rossinver . .	Ballyshannon .	IV.	111
41, 42	Derrynaseer . .	280	1	26	Tyrone . .	Omagh East . .	Dromore . .	Omagh . .	III.	311
16	Derrynaseera . .	682	0	18	Queen's Co.	Upperwoods . .	Offerlane . .	Mountmellick .	I.	251
5, 6	Derrynasell East .	263	0	35	Monaghan .	Monaghan . .	Tedavnet . .	Monaghan .	III.	278
5	Derrynasell West .	406	3	0	Monaghan .	Monaghan . .	Tedavnet . .	Monaghan .	III.	278
6	Derrynashallog .	168	0	31	Monaghan .	Trough . . .	Donagh . .	Monaghan .	III.	282
78	Derrynashask . .	36	3	38l	Mayo . .	Carra . . .	Ballyhean . .	Castlebar . .	IV.	125

(a) Including 6A. 1R. 2P. water.
(b) Including 27A. 0R. 26P. water.
(c) Including 2A. 1R. 24P. water.
(d) Including 4A. 3R. 35P. water.

(e) Including 22A. 2R. 33P. water.
(f) Including 27A. 1R. 37P. water.
(g) Including 25A. 3R. 12P. water.
(h) Including 30A. 2R. 10P. water.

(i) Including 25A. 3R. 33P. water.
(j) Including 7A. 0R. 25P. water.
(k) Including 1A. 2R. 35P. water.
(l) Including 6A. 0R. 29P. water.

No. of Sheet of the Ordnance Survey Maps.	Townlands and Towns.	Area in Statute Acres.			County.	Barony.	Parish.	Poor Law Union in 1857.	Townland Census of 1851, Part I.	
		A.	R.	P.					Vol.	Page
1	Derrynashesk	108	3	20	Fermanagh	Lurg	Drumkeeran	Lowtherstown	III.	206
18, 22	Derrynaskea	531	2	0	Longford	Moydow	Kilcommock	Ballymahon	I.	161
78	Derrynaskeagh	74	1	15a	Mayo	Carra	Ballyhean	Castlebar	IV.	125
6	Derrynaskineen	46	3	37b	Roscommon	Boyle	Ardcarn	Boyle	IV.	193
9	Derrynaslieve	94	1	10	Cavan	Tullyhaw	Templeport	Bawnboy	III.	94
41	Derrynaslieve	193	1	21c	Sligo	Tirerrill	Kilmactranny	Boyle	IV.	240
10, 15	Derrynasling	198	3	8	Tipperary, N.R.	Lower Ormond	Ardcrony	Borrisokane	II.	281
3	Derrynatuan	185	1	1	Cavan	Tullyhaw	Templeport	Enniskillen	III.	94
22, 30	Derrynatubbrid	375	0	22	Cork, E.R.	Duhallow	Kilmeen	Millstreet	II.	72
13, 17	Derrynaught	265	0	25	Armagh	Fews Lower	Mullaghbrack	Armagh	III.	47
5	Derrynavahagh	570	0	17	Clare	Burren	Kilmoon	Ballyvaghan	II.	13
52, 53	Derrynaveagh	876	3	36d	Clare	Tulla Lower	Clonlea	Limerick	II.	34
12	Derrynaveagh	50	1	7	Clare	Tulla Upper	Feakle	Tulla	II.	39
36, 37	Derrynavglaun	1,362	0	23e	Galway	Ballynahinch	Moyrus	Clifden	IV.	13
24	Derrynavogy	274	2	8	Fermanagh	Magherastephana	Aghalurcher	Lisnaskea	III.	216
21, 24	Derrynawana	211	3	4	Leitrim	Carrigallen	Oughteragh	Bawnboy	IV.	92
36	Derrynawilt East	147	2	17	Fermanagh	Clankelly	Clones	Clones	III.	195
35	Derrynawilt West	194	1	31	Fermanagh	Clankelly	Clones	Clones	III.	195
78, 79, 91	Derrynea	1,122	1	23f	Galway	Moycullen	Killannin	Oughterard	IV.	69
9, 10	Derryneel	72	2	35	Longford	Granard	Clonbroney	Granard	I.	155
38	Derryneen	221	3	4g	Galway	Ballynahinch	Moyrus	Clifden	IV.	13
30, 36	Derryneese	128	3	25	Fermanagh	Clankelly	Clones	Clones	III.	195
1, 5	Derryneeve	132	1	16	Fermanagh	Lurg	Drumkeeran	Lowtherstown	III.	206
35, 42	Derryneill	1,049	3	13	Down	Upper Iveagh, Lower part	Drumgooland	Banbridge	III.	172
5	Derryneskan	214	2	18	Armagh	Oneilland West	Drumcree	Lurgan	III.	52
73	Derryness	374	0	22	Donegal	Boylagh	Inishkeel	Glenties	III.	112
73	*Derryness Island*	6	2	29	Donegal	Boylagh	Inishkeel	Glenties	III.	114
101	Derrynid	231	1	28	Kerry	Glanarought	Tuosist	Kenmare	II.	188
26	Derryniggin	206	1	16h	Leitrim	Carrigallen	Carrigallen	Bawnboy	IV.	89
26	Derrynim	57	1	17	Fermanagh	Clanawley	Cleenish	Enniskillen	III.	190
31	Derrynine	263	2	8	Kildare	Offaly West	Fontstown	Athy	I.	72
67	Derrynisk	119	0	0	Antrim	Upper Massereene	Magheramesk	Lisburn	III.	31
35, 40	Derrynoyd	1,039	0	23	Londonderry	Loughinsholin	Ballynascreen	Magherafelt	III.	239
28	Derrynure	245	1	6	Cavan	Clankee	Bailieborough	Bailieborough	III.	71
43	Derrynure	43	1	26	Fermanagh	Clankelly	Drummully	Clones	III.	197
55, 57	Derryoge	659	0	24	Down	Mourne	Kilkeel	Kilkeel	III.	183
18	Derryoghil	642	3	34	Longford	Moydow	Kilcommock	Ballymahon	I.	161
62	Derryoghill	349	3	37	Tyrone	Dungannon Middle	Clonfeacle	Dungannon	III.	299
15	Derryola	89	2	31i	Cavan	Tullygarvey	Annagh	Cavan	III.	87
31	Derryolam	190	0	4	Monaghan	Farney	Magheross	Carrickmacross	III.	273
18, 24	Derryonogh	157	0	17	Roscommon	Ballintober North	Termonbarry	Strokestown	IV.	188
131, 132	Derryoober East	477	3	21	Galway	Leitrim	Ballynakill	Portumna	IV.	51
131	Derryoober West	1,198	1	31	Galway	Leitrim	Ballynakill	Portumna	IV.	51
78	Derryool	111	3	6	Mayo	Carra	Ballyhean	Castlebar	IV.	125
81	Derryool	156	2	36	Mayo	Costello	Aghamore	Swineford	IV.	137
92	Derryool	67	0	14j	Mayo	Costello	Knock	Claremorris	IV.	142
89	Derryoran	131	2	22	Mayo	Carra	Ballintober	Castlebar	IV.	124
24	Derryorgan	286	1	11	Cork, E.R.	Orrery and Kilmore	Bailyclogh	Mallow	II.	106
25	Derryork	34	3	22	Londonderry	Keenaght	Bovevagh	NewT⁰Limavady	III.	235
25	Derryork	609	0	26	Londonderry	Keenaght	Dungiven	NewT⁰Limavady	III.	236
93	Derryoughter	74	1	39	Galway	Moycullen	Rahoon	Galway	IV.	72
32	Derryoughter	189	3	1k	Leitrim	Leitrim	Annaghduff	Car⁰·on Shannon	IV.	99
26,27,30,31	Derryoughter East	600	3	28	Kildare	Offaly West	Ballybrackan	Athy	I.	71
26, 30	Derryoughter West	654	2	29l	Kildare	Offaly West	Ballybrackan	Athy	I.	71
34	Derryounce	171	0	38	King's Co.	Upper Philipstown	Ballykean	Mountmellick	I.	143
11	Derryowen	263	2	24	Clare	Inchiquin	Kilkeedy	Corrofin	II.	25
13	Derrypark	279	1	21	Galway	Ross	Ballinchalla	Ballinrobe	IV.	72
37, 43	Derrypatrick	967	3	35	Meath	Lower Deece	Derrypatrick	Dunshaughlin	I.	191
37, 43	Derrypatrick Grange	505	1	26	Meath	Lower Deece	Derrypatrick	Dunshaughlin	I.	191
28	Derryphatten	151	3	27	Roscommon	Roscommon	Kilukin	Strokestown	IV.	211
100	Derryquin	692	0	14	Kerry	Dunkerron South	Kilcrohane	Kenmare	II.	183
22	Derryquirk	227	0	35m	Roscommon	Roscommon	Kilcooley	Strokestown	IV.	210
9	Derryra Beg	34	3	8	Kerry	Clanmaurice	Killury	Listowel	II.	171
13	Derryragh	207	2	18n	Cavan	Tullyhaw	Templeport	Bawnboy	III.	94
16, 22	Derryraghan	156	1	8	Fermanagh	Tirkennedy	Magheracross	Enniskillen	III.	223
38, 46	Derryraghan	170	2	20	Tyrone	Dungannon Upper	Desertcreat	Cookstown	III.	307
13, 17	Derryraine	182	3	17	Armagh	Fews Lower	Mullaghbrack	Armagh	III.	47
9	Derryra More	23	0	8	Kerry	Clanmaurice	Killury	Listowel	II.	171
76, 86	Derryreag	1,138	1	16	Kerry	Magunihy	Killaha	Killarney	II.	202
7	Derryrealt	250	0	4	Cavan	Tullyhaw	Kinawley	Bawnboy	III.	93
34	Derryree	58	0	7	Fermanagh	Magherastephana	Aghalurcher	Lisnaskea	III.	216
25	Derryreel	786	0	37o	Donegal	Kilmacrenan	Clondahorky	Dunfanaghy	III.	123

(a) Including 2A. 2R. 25P. water.
(b) Including 13A. 1R. 39P. water.
(c) Including 3A. 3R. 35P. water.
(d) Including 2A. 1R. 37P. water.
(e) Including 88A. 1R. 32P. water.

(f) Including 72A. 0R. 23P. water.
(g) Including 21A. 0R. 31P. water.
(h) Including 55A. 1R. 10P. water.
(i) Including 3A. 1R. 20P. water.
(j) Including 12A. 1R. 15P. water.

(k) Including 45A. 2R. 31P. water.
(l) Including 8A. 2R. 14P. water.
(m) Including 8A. 2R. 13P. water.
(n) Including 10A. 2R. 9P. water.
(o) Including 5A. 3R. 26P. water.

No. of Sheet of the Ordnance Survey Maps.	Townlands and Towns.	Area in Statute Acres.			County.	Barony.	Parish.	Poor Law Union in 1857.	Townland Census of 1851, Part I.	
		A.	R.	P.					Vol.	Page
25	Derryreel	738	1	16a	Donegal	Kilmacrenan	Raymunterdoney	Dunfanaghy	III.	131
3	Derryrellan	163	2	23	Monaghan	Trough	Errigal Trough	Clogher	III.	284
68, 77	Derryribbeen	599	2	25	Mayo	Burrishoole	Kilmaclasser	Westport	IV.	121
92	Derryriordane North	205	2	12	Cork, W.R.	West Muskerry	Inchigeelagh	Dunmanway	II.	157
92, 93	Derryriordane South	332	0	6	Cork, W.R.	West Muskerry	Inchigeelagh	Dunmanway	II.	157
60, 71	Derryroe	505	0	10	Cork, W.R.	East Muskerry	Aghabulloge	Macroom	II.	153
17, 23	Derryroe	58	3	36	Queen's Co.	Maryborough West	Clonenagh and Clonagheen	Abbeyleix	I.	242
32	Derryroe and Benalbit	407	3	17	Westmeath	Moycashel	Castletownkindalen	Mullingar	I.	277
3, 8	Derryrona Glebe	833	1	23b	Fermanagh	Lurg	Belleek	Ballyshannon	III.	203
62, 72	Derryronan	993	2	17	Mayo	Gallen	Kilconduff	Swineford	IV.	147
23	Derryroosk	141	0	38c	Monaghan	Cremorne	Aghnamullen	Cootehill	III.	258
52, 64, 65	Derryrush	1,634	0	30d	Galway	Ballynahinch	Moyrus	Clifden	IV.	13
108	Derryrush	230	0	16	Kerry	Glanarought	Tuosist	Kenmare	II.	188
101, 102	Derrysallagh	483	2	20e	Kerry	Glanarought	Tuosist	Kenmare	II.	188
35	Derrysallagh	499	0	33	Sligo	Tirerrill	Kilmactranny	Boyle	IV.	240
26	Derryscobe	172	1	18	Fermanagh	Clanawley	Cleenish	Enniskillen	III.	190
4, 8	Derryscollop	365	3	18	Armagh	Oneilland West	Clonfeacle	Armagh	III.	51
4, 8	DERRYSCOLLOP T.	—			Armagh	Oneilland West	Clonfeacle	Armagh	III.	51
58, 59	Derryshaan	338	2	31	Clare	Clonderalaw	Kilfiddane	Killadysert	II.	15
26	Derryshandra	28	0	36	Fermanagh	Clanawley	Cleenish	Enniskillen	III.	190
17,18,21,22	Derryshannoge	538	3	33	Longford	Rathcline	Cashel	Longford	I.	163
8	Derrysheridan	101	3	0	Meath	Fore	Killeagh	Oldcastle	I.	201
50, 51	Derrysillagh	137	0	12	Galway	Ballynahinch	Moyrus	Clifden	IV.	13
107	Derrysiskal	177	3	13	Galway	Longford	Killimorbologue	Portumna	IV.	58
42	Derrysteaton	187	2	8f	Fermanagh	Coole	Galloon	Clones	III.	199
2, 5	Derrytagh North	266	0	5g	Armagh	Oneilland East	Montiaghs	Lurgan	III.	50
5	Derrytagh South	541	0	22h	Armagh	Oneilland East	Montiaghs	Lurgan	III.	50
20, 23	Derryteigeroe	98	0	29	Leitrim	Leitrim	Kiltoghert	Carⁿ. on Shannon	IV.	101
2, 5	Derrytrasna	811	1	1i	Armagh	Oneilland East	Montiaghs	Lurgan	III.	50
18	Derrytrasna	119	0	19	Queen's Co.	Stradbally	Fossy or Timahoe	Athy	I.	247
47, 55	Derrytresk	1,020	0	35j	Tyrone	Dungannon Middle	Clonoe	Dungannon	III.	300
28	Derryulk	90	1	38k	Clare	Tulla Upper	Feakle	Scarriff	II.	39
27	Derryulk Lower	103	0	13	Clare	Tulla Upper	Tulla	Tulla	II.	41
27	Derryulk Middle	193	1	2	Clare	Tulla Upper	Tulla	Tulla	II.	41
19, 27	Derryulk Upper	421	0	19	Clare	Tulla Upper	Tulla	Tulla	II.	41
31	Derry Upper	66	3	33	King's Co.	Eglish	Drumcullen	Parsonstown	I.	134
36, 37	Derry Upper	1,725	1	38	Mayo	Tirawley	Crossmolina	Ballina	IV.	165
22	Derry Upper	157	0	22	Waterford	Decies without Drum	Modelligo	Lismore	II.	359
20	Derryvackny	213	1	25l	Cavan	Lower Loughtee	Drumlane	Cavan	III.	80
80, 81	Derryvacorneen	439	2	1	Cork, W.R.	West Muskerry	Inchigeelagh	Dunmanway	II.	157
118, 131	Derryvahalla	554	0	33	Cork, W.R.	West Carbery (W.D.)	Kilmocomoge	Bantry	II.	144
7, 9	Derryvahan	105	3	32	Cavan	Tullyhaw	Templeport	Bawnboy	III.	94
14	Derryvahon	177	3	35	Fermanagh	Magheraboy	Inishmacsaint	Ballyshannon	III.	212
16, 18	Derryvalannagher Glebe	131	3	23	Leitrim	Drumahaire	Inishmagrath	Manorhamilton	IV.	96
12	Derryvale	43	3	7	Tipperary, N.R.	Ikerrin	Corbally	Roscrea	II.	275
81	Derryvaleen	198	3	5	Cork, W.R.	West Muskerry	Inchigeelagh	Macroom	II.	157
18, 19	Derryvally	234	3	19m	Monaghan	Cremorne	Ballybay	Castleblayney	III.	259
5	Derryvane	190	1	33	Armagh	Oneilland West	Drumcree	Lurgan	III.	52
81	Derryvane	353	3	16	Cork, W.R.	West Muskerry	Inchigeelagh	Macroom	II.	157
39	Derryvane	929	3	6	Donegal	Inishowen West	Muff	Londonderry	III.	121
9	Derryvarroge	1,115	0	15	Kildare	Clane	Timahoe	Naas	I.	54
15	Derryvary Beg	202	0	12	Fermanagh	Magheraboy	Devenish	Enniskillen	III.	210
15	Derryvary More	207	3	21	Fermanagh	Magheraboy	Devenish	Enniskillen	III.	210
22	Derryveagh	295	1	26	Longford	Rathcline	Kilcommock	Ballymahon	I.	164
3	Derryveagh	241	3	2	Monaghan	Trough	Errigal Trough	Monaghan	III.	284
25, 38	Derryvealawauma	1,434	3	28	Galway	Ballynahinch	Moyrus	Clifden	IV.	13
6	Derryveen	195	2	15	Monaghan	Trough	Donagh	Monaghan	III.	282
54	Derryveen	202	2	7	Tyrone	Dungannon Middle	Donaghmore	Dungannon	III.	302
108,109,117	Derryveeny	1,302	2	27	Mayo	Carra	Ballyovey	Ballinrobe	IV.	126
15	Derryvehil	140	1	8n	Cavan	Lower Loughtee	Drumlane	Cavan	III.	80
9	Derryvella	112	3	15	Cavan	Tullyhaw	Templeport	Bawnboy	III.	94
48	Derryvella	857	2	3	Tipperary, S.R.	Slievardagh	Kilcooly	Urlingford	II.	334
11	Derryveone	71	3	29	Fermanagh	Lurg	Derryvullan	Lowtherstown	III.	204
26	Derryvet	657	2	0	Clare	Bunratty Upper	Inchicronan	Tulla	II.	9
36, 50	Derryvickrune	852	1	8o	Galway	Ballynahinch	Moyrus	Clifden	IV.	13
49	Derryvicneill	161	2	23	Mayo	Gallen	Attymass	Ballina	IV.	147
34	Derryvilla	509	2	15	King's Co.	Upper Philipstown	Clonyhurk	Mountmellick	I.	143
18, 19, 27	Derryvillane	540	2	19	Cork, E.R.	Fermoy	Derryvillane	Mitchelstown	II.	78
30, 36	Derryville	1,226	2	5	Tipperary, N.R.	Eliogarty	Templetouhy	Thurles	II.	273
27	Derryvinna	52	0	4	Clare	Tulla Upper	Feakle	Scarriff	II.	39
53	Derryvinnaan	271	2	13	Clare	Tulla Lower	Kilseily	Limerick	II.	36

(a) Including 17A. 1R. 4P. water.
(b) Including 60A. 3R. 2P. water.
(c) Including 14A. 3R. 14P. water.
(d) Including 96A. 1R. 8P. water.
(e) Including 21A. 2R. 36P. water.
(f) Including 24A. 0R. 19P. water.

(g) Including 27A. 1R. 19P. Lough Gullion.
(h) { Including 92A. 0R. 6P. Lough Gullion. Including 22A. 1R. 16P. River Bann.
(i) { Including 52A. 0R. 19P. Lough Gullion. Including 9A. 1R. 2P. River Bann.
(j) Including 10A. 2R. 8P. water.

(k) Including 5A. 2R. 38P. water.
(l) Including 70A. 2R. 27P. water.
(m) Including 15A. 2R. 10P. water.
(n) Including 42A. 3R. 0P. water.
(o) Including 70A. 2R. 20P. water.

No. of Sheet of the Ordnance Survey Maps.	Townlands and Towns.	Area in Statute Acres.	County.	Barony.	Parish.	Poor Law Union in 1857.	Townland Census of 1851, Part I.	
		A. R. P.					Vol.	Page
21	Derryvinnane . .	163 3 37	Limerick . .	Coshma . . .	Adare . . .	Croom . .	II.	241
67	Derryvoghil . .	579 0 0	Galway . .	Moycullen . .	Killannin . .	Oughterard .	IV.	69
21	Derryvogue . .	74 0 13	Fermanagh .	Clanawley . .	Cleenish . .	Enniskillen .	III.	190
80, 91	Derryvohy . .	280 2 33	Mayo . .	Gallen . .	Killedan . .	Swineford .	IV.	150
114, 115	Derryvokeel . .	457 2 35	Galway . .	Loughrea . .	Ardrahan . .	Gort . .	IV.	62
30, 36	Derryvolan . .	284 3 7	Fermanagh .	Clankelly . .	Clones . .	Clones . .	III.	195
11	Derryvony . .	407 0 11	Cavan . .	Lower Loughtee .	Drumlane . .	Cavan . .	III.	80
101, 102	Derryvorahig .	277 0 36a	Kerry . .	Glanarought .	Tuosist . .	Kenmare . .	II.	188
5	Derryvore . .	177 3 15b	Armagh . .	Oneilland East .	Seagoe . .	Lurgan . .	III.	50
39, 42	Derryvore . .	512 0 4c	Fermanagh .	Knockninny . .	Kinawley . .	Lisnaskea .	III.	201
27	Derryvore . .	135 2 1d	Fermanagh .	Tirkennedy . .	Enniskillen .	Enniskillen .	III.	221
24,25,37,38	Derryvoreada .	740 1 37e	Galway . .	Ballynahinch .	Moyrus . .	Clifden . .	IV.	13
22	Derryvorrigan .	238 1 38	Queen's Co. .	Clandonagh .	Aghaboe . .	Donaghmore .	I.	232
33	Derryvrane . .	137 2 22	Fermanagh .	Knockninny . .	Kinawley . .	Lisnaskea .	III.	201
28	Derryvree . .	151 2 30	Fermanagh .	Magherastephana .	Aghavea . .	Lisnaskea .	III.	218
121, 122	Derryvreen . .	76 3 5	Cork, W.R. .	Ibane and Barryroe	Castleventry .	Clonakilty .	II.	148
121, 122	Derryvreen . .	316 0 14	Cork, W.R. .	Ibane and Barryroe	Kilmeen . .	Clonakilty .	II.	149
15	Derryvrin . .	365 3 4	Kerry . .	Clanmaurice .	Kilcaragh . .	Listowel . .	II.	169
66	Derryvrisk . .	973 0 10f	Galway . .	Moycullen . .	Kilcummin . .	Oughterard .	IV.	67
60, 70	Derryvulcaun .	421 0 8	Mayo . .	Carra . .	Turlough . .	Castlebar .	IV.	131
27	Derryvullan . .	296 3 22g	Fermanagh .	Tirkennedy . .	Derryvullan . .	Enniskillen .	III.	221
25, 32	Derryvung . .	309 2 35	Roscommon .	Castlereagh .	Kiltullagh . .	Castlereagh .	IV.	202
125, 126	Derryvunlam . .	1,146 0 37	Galway . .	Leitrim . .	Ballynakill . .	Portumna .	IV.	51
3	Derryvunny . .	184 2 3h	Roscommon .	Boyle . .	Kilbryan . .	Boyle . .	IV.	195
3	Derrywanna . .	95 0 26i	Roscommon .	Boyle . .	Kilbryan . .	Boyle . .	IV.	195
25	Derryware . .	201 3 25	Londonderry .	Keenaght . .	Dungiven . .	NewTⁿLimavady	III.	236
123, 124, 129, 130	Derrywee East .	560 1 30	Galway . .	Kiltartan . .	Kilthomas . .	Gort . .	IV.	49
26	Derryweelan . .	143 0 33	King's Co. .	Geashill . .	Geashill . .	Tullamore .	I.	140
123,129,130	Derrywee West .	761 1 39	Galway . .	Kiltartan . .	Kilthomas . .	Gort . .	IV.	49
99	Derry West . .	719 0 15	Kerry . .	Dunkerron South .	Kilcrohane . .	Kenmare . .	II.	183
22, 26	Derrywilligan .	314 0 15	Armagh . .	Orior Upper . .	Killevy . .	Newry . .	III.	58
28	Derrywillin . .	75 3 7	Clare . .	Tulla Upper . .	Feakle . .	Scarriff . .	II.	39
35	Derrywillow . .	307 2 15	Leitrim . .	Mohill . .	Annaduff . .	Mohill . .	IV.	105
46, 47	Derrywinnin Glebe .	115 2 18	Tyrone . .	Dungannon Middle .	Tullyniskan .	Dungannon .	III.	304
20	Derrywinny . .	104 1 34	Cavan . .	Upper Loughtee .	Kilmore . .	Cavan . .	III.	84
1, 6	Derrywode . .	482 1 24	Galway . .	Ballymoe . .	Templetogher .	Glennamaddy .	IV.	9
43	Dervaghroy . .	591 3 36	Tyrone . .	Omagh East . .	Clogherny . .	Omagh . .	III.	310
10	Derver . . .	528 2 35	Meath . .	Upper Kells . .	LoughanorCastlekeeran	Kells . .	I.	207
38, 47	Dervin . . .	281 3 2	Mayo . .	Tirawley . .	Addergoole . .	Ballina . .	IV.	163
12	Dervock . . .	132 2 4	Antrim . .	Lower Dunluce .	Derrykeighan .	Ballymoney .	III.	16
12	DERVOCK T. . .	—	Antrim . .	Lower Dunluce .	Derrykeighan .	Ballymoney .	III.	17
9	Dervotstown . .	285 0 33	Westmeath .	Delvin . .	Killua . .	Castletowndelvin	I.	265
22, 23	Desart Demesne .	500 1 8	Kilkenny . .	Shillelogher .	Tullaghanbrogue .	Callan . .	I.	116
18	Descart . . .	136 0 36	Monaghan .	Dartree . .	Aghabog . .	Cootehill . .	III.	263
34	Descart . . .	226 2 12j	Monaghan .	Farney . .	Magheracloone .	Carrickmacross .	III.	272
45, 54	Desert . . .	296 0 3	Cork, E.R. .	Barrymore . .	Gortroe . .	Fermoy . .	II.	55
135	Desert . . .	339 3 8	Cork, W.R. .	East Carbery (E.D.)	Desert . . .	Clonakilty .	II.	127
47	Desert . . .	685 0 20	Down . .	Lordship of Newry .	Newry . .	Newry . .	III.	182
6, 7	Desert . . .	105 0 32	Monaghan .	Trough . .	Donagh . .	Monaghan .	III.	282
2, 5	Desert . . .	377 0 24k	Tyrone . .	Strabane Lower .	Leckpatrick .	Strabane . .	III.	322
38	Desertcreat . .	123 2 5	Tyrone . .	Dungannon Upper .	Desertcreat . .	Cookstown .	III.	307
22	Desertderrin . .	88 0 20	Antrim . .	Kilconway . .	Finvoy . .	Ballymoney .	III.	26
41	DESERTMARTIN T. . .	—	Londonderry .	Loughinsholin .	Desertmartin .	Magherafelt .	III.	241
82	Deshure . . .	715 2 13	Cork, W.R. .	West Muskerry .	Kilmichael . .	Dunmanway .	II.	158
16	Destinrath . .	200 3 21	Meath . .	Upper Kells . .	Kells . .	Kells . .	I.	206
16	Devally . . .	69 1 31	Cavan . .	Tullygarvey . .	Drung . .	Cootehill . .	III.	88
22	Devenish . . .	123 0 8	Fermanagh .	Magheraboy . .	Devenish . .	Enniskillen .	III.	212
117	Devenish Island	7 2 5	Mayo . .	Kilmaine . .	Ballinrobe . .	Ballinrobe .	IV.	153
56	Devenish Island	20 2 3	Roscommon .	Moycarn . .	Moore . .	Ballinasloe .	IV.	207
55	Devinish Island	9 2 12	Galway . .	Moycullen . .	Kilcummin . .	Oughterard .	IV.	68
12	Devinstown . .	223 0 18	Meath . .	Lower Slane . .	Killary . .	Ardee . .	I.	223
81	Devleash . . .	125 3 1	Mayo . .	Gallen . .	Killedan . .	Swineford .	IV.	150
89, 99	Devleash East .	193 1 30	Mayo . .	Carra . .	Ballintober . .	Castlebar .	IV.	124
89, 98, 99	Devleash West .	548 0 36l	Mayo . .	Carra . .	Ballintober . .	Castlebar .	IV.	124
34, 43	Devlin . . .	2,203 1 3	Donegal . .	Kilmacrenan .	Gartan . .	Dunfanaghy .	III.	127
101	Devlin . . .	100 1 10	Mayo . .	Clanmorris . .	Tagheen . .	Claremorris .	IV.	136
19	Devlin . . .	136 3 32	Monaghan .	Cremorne . .	Clontibret . .	Castleblayney .	III.	260
34	Devlin or Barr of Ballyconnell .	1,129 3 30	Donegal . .	Kilmacrenan .	Raymunterdoney .	Dunfanaghy .	III.	131
17, 27	Devlinmore . .	617 0 18m	Donegal . .	Kilmacrenan .	Mevagh . .	Milford . .	III.	130
95, 105	Devlin North . .	273 3 25n	Mayo . .	Murrisk . .	Kilgeever . .	Westport .	IV.	160
17, 27	Devlinreagh . .	382 1 10	Donegal . .	Kilmacrenan .	Mevagh . .	Milford . .	III.	130

(a) Including 8A. 3R. 27P. water.
(b) Including 10A. 2R. 38P. water.
(c) Including 4A. 1R. 20P. water.
(d) Including 18A. 1R. 10P. water.
(e) Including 24A. 3R. 0P. water.

(f) Including 76A. 3R. 32P. water.
(g) Including 112A. 0R. 39P. water.
(h) Including 3A. 0R. 21P. water.
(i) Including 13A. 3R. 23P. water.
(j) Including 21A. 2R. 23P. water.

(k) { Including 17A. 0R. 36P. Yew Island. / Including 10A. 2R. 18P. water.
(l) Including 3A. 0R. 5P. water.
(m) Including 5A. 3R. 32P. water.
(n) Including 13A. 2R. 19P. water.

3 C

No. of Sheet of the Ordnance Survey Maps.	Townlands and Towns.	Area in Statute Acres.			County.	Barony.	Parish.	Poor Law Union in 1857.	Townland Census of 1851, Part I.	
		A.	R.	P.					Vol.	Page
105	Devlin South . .	267	2	15	Mayo . .	Murrisk . . .	Kilgeever . .	Westport . .	IV.	160
93, 103	Devlis . . .	133	1	6	Mayo . .	Costello . . .	Bekan . . .	Claremorris .	IV.	139
14, 19	Diamondhill or Drumcartagh . .	69	1	11	Cavan . .	Tullyhunco . .	Kildallan . .	Bawnboy . .	III.	97
15	Diamor . . .	1,322	3	11	Meath . .	Fore . . .	Diamor . .	Oldcastle . .	I.	200
28	Dian . . .	115	1	1	Monaghan .	Farney . . .	Donaghmoyne .	Carrickmacross	III.	269
29, 30	Dickey's Town .	388	2	18	Antrim . .	Lower Glenarm .	Tickmacrevan .	Larne . .	III.	23
19	Dicksborough . .	136	0	29	Kilkenny . .	Shillelogher . .	St. Patrick's .	Kilkenny . .	I.	116
48	Dicksgrove . .	196	3	25	Kerry . .	Trughanacmy .	Dysert . .	Killarney . .	II.	210
148	Dick's Island . .	2	0	27	Cork, W.R. .	West Carbery (W.D.)	Skull . .	Skull . .	II.	147
29, 30	Diffin . . .	155	1	28	Leitrim . .	Carrigallen . .	Cloone . .	Mohill . .	IV.	90
70	Difflin . . .	33	2	9	Donegal . .	Raphoe . . .	Raphoe . .	Strabane . .	III.	140
6, 10	Diffreen . . .	715	1	24	Leitrim . .	Rosclogher . .	Killasnet . .	Manorhamilton	IV.	109
31	Dillagh . . .	254	2	30a	Cavan . .	Clanmahon . .	Ballintemple .	Cavan . .	III.	75
11, 15	Dillay . . .	156	1	24	Armagh . .	Tiranny . . .	Tynan . .	Armagh . .	III.	60
38	Dillin . . .	266	3	26	Down . .	Lecale Lower . .	Ballee . .	Downpatrick .	III.	178
5	Dillonsdown . .	159	3	9	Wicklow . .	Lower Talbotstown .	Blessington .	Naas . .	I.	358
25	Dillonsland . .	77	2	13b	Meath . .	Lower Navan . .	Navan . .	Navan . .	I.	215
15	Dillonstown . .	460	0	17c	Louth . .	Ardee . . .	Drumcar . .	Ardee . .	I.	172
28	Dimanistown East .	148	3	7	Meath . .	Upper Duleek . .	Julianstown .	Drogheda .	I.	198
28	Dimanistown West .	133	2	13	Meath . .	Upper Duleek . .	Julianstown .	Drogheda .	I.	198
35	Dingin . . .	112	0	38d	Cavan . .	Clankee . . .	Enniskeen . .	Bailieborough .	III.	72
17, 22	Dinginavanty . .	226	2	19	Cavan . .	Tullygarvey . .	Kildrumsherdan .	Cootehill . .	III.	90
30	Dingins . . .	306	1	3e	Cavan . .	Tullyhunco . .	Scrabby . .	Cavan . .	III.	99
43	Dingle . . .	15	2	3	Kerry . .	Corkaguiny . .	Dingle . .	Dingle . .	II.	175
43	Dingle Commons of	876	2	21	Kerry . .	Corkaguiny . .	Dingle . .	Dingle . .	II.	175
43, 53	DINGLE T. . .	—			Kerry . .	Corkaguiny . .	Dingle . .	Dingle . .	II.	176
89	Dinish . . .	95	3	3	Galway . .	Moycullen . .	Kilcummin . .	Oughterard .	IV.	68
115	Dinish Island . .	45	0	22	Cork, W.R. .	Bear . . .	Killaconenagh .	Castletown .	II.	124
101	Dinish Island . .	25	2	23	Kerry . .	Glanarought . .	Tuosist . .	Kenmare . .	II.	188
74	Dinish Island . .	34	2	1	Kerry . .	Magunihy . .	Killarney . .	Killarney . .	II.	203
17	Dinnahorra . .	275	1	11	Armagh . .	Oneilland West .	Mullaghbrack .	Banbridge .	III.	54
20	Dinneens . .	199	3	10	Kerry . .	Clanmaurice . .	Kilmoyly . .	Tralee . .	II.	171
21	Dinnydoon . .	59	1	15	Fermanagh .	Magheraboy . .	Rossorry . .	Enniskillen .	III.	214
4	Diralagh . .	299	1	23	Meath . .	Lower Kells . .	Moynalty . .	Kells . .	I.	203
14	Dira or Upper Broghindrummin . .	186	0	37	Antrim . .	Lower Glenarm .	Grange of Layd .	Ballycastle .	III.	22
3, 12, 13	Dirkbeg . . .	1,519	0	26f	Galway . .	Ross . . .	Ballinchalla .	Ballinrobe .	IV.	72
45, 46	Dirnan . . .	637	1	3	Londonderry .	Loughinsholin .	Lissan . .	Magherafelt .	III.	242
22	Dirraw . . .	649	2	13	Antrim . .	Kilconway . .	Finvoy . .	Ballymoney .	III.	26
6, 10	Dirtagh . . .	320	2	13	Londonderry .	Keenaght . .	Aghanloo . .	New Tn Limavady	III.	233
14	Dirtane . . .	277	1	7	Kerry . .	Clanmaurice . .	Ballyheige . .	Tralee . .	II.	168
26	Dirtystep . . .	31	0	14	Kilkenny . .	Callan . . .	Callan . .	Callan . .	I.	83
19	Disert . . .	105	2	26g	Cavan . .	Tullyhunco . .	Kildallan . .	Cavan . .	III.	97
127, 128	Disert . . .	352	0	2	Cork, W.R. .	Bear . . .	Kilaconenagh .	Castletown .	II.	124
84	Disert . . .	1,190	2	31	Donegal . .	Banagh . . .	Inver . .	Donegal . .	III.	107
40	Disert . . .	412	3	10	Londonderry .	Loughinsholin .	Ballynascreen .	Magherafelt .	III.	239
21	Disertowen . .	193	2	6	Londonderry .	Tirkeeran . .	Clondermot .	Londonderry .	III.	248
24, 25	Diskirt . . .	190	0	23	Antrim . .	Lower Glenarm .	Ardclinis . .	Larne . .	III.	21
13, 17	Diswellstown . .	418	3	29	Dublin . .	Castleknock . .	Castleknock .	Dublin North .	I.	24
59	Divinagh . .	94	2	26	Tyrone . .	Clogher . .	Clogher . .	Clogher . .	III.	292
9	Diviny . . .	157	1	13	Armagh . .	Oneilland West .	Drumcree . .	Lurgan . .	III.	52
6	Diviny . . .	47	1	12	Fermanagh .	Lurg . . .	Magheraculmoney .	Lowtherstown .	III.	207
60	Divis . . .	946	1	30	Antrim . .	Upper Belfast .	Shankill . .	Belfast . .	III.	10
24	Divish . . .	60	1	36	Mayo . .	Erris . . .	Kilmore . .	Belmullet .	IV.	146
37	D'Loughtane . .	471	1	1	Waterford .	Decies within Drum	Kinsalebeg .	Youghal . .	II.	351
45, 51	Doagh . . .	631	1	19h	Antrim . .	Upper Antrim .	Doagh Grange .	Antrim . .	III.	6
7, 16	Doagh . . .	372	3	24	Donegal . .	Kilmacrenan .	Mevagh . .	Millford . .	III.	130
30	Doagh . . .	322	1	35	Monaghan .	Farney . . .	Magheracloone .	Carrickmacross	III.	272
9	Doagh Beg . .	564	1	1	Donegal . .	Kilmacrenan .	Clondavaddog .	Millford . .	III.	124
9	DOAGHBEG T. . .	—			Donegal . .	Kilmacrenan .	Clondavaddog .	Millford . .	III.	125
9	Doaghcrabbin . .	198	3	18	Donegal . .	Kilmacrenan .	Clondavaddog .	Millford . .	III.	124
7	Doagheys . .	96	1	15	Monaghan .	Trough . . .	Donagh . .	Monaghan .	III.	282
14	Doagh Glebe . .	590	2	2i	Fermanagh .	Magheraboy . .	Devenish . .	Enniskillen .	III.	210
8, 17	Doagh More . .	800	2	30j	Donegal . .	Kilmacrenan .	Clondavaddog .	Millford . .	III.	124
1	Doaghs Lower . .	427	0	1	Londonderry .	Keenaght . .	Magilligan .	New Tn Limavady	III.	236
1	Doaghs Lower Middle	413	2	25	Londonderry .	Keenaght . .	Magilligan .	New Tn Limavady	III.	236
1, 2	Doaghs Upper . .	354	2	10	Londonderry .	Keenaght . .	Magilligan .	New Tn Limavady	III.	236
1, 2	Doaghs Upper Middle	357	0	30	Londonderry .	Keenaght . .	Magilligan .	New Tn Limavady	III.	236
51	DOAGH T. . .	—			Antrim . .	Upper Antrim .	Doagh Grange .	Antrim . .	III.	6
47, 53	Dobbsland . .	794	2	9	Antrim . .	Lower Belfast .	Kilroot . .	Larne . .	III.	9
9	Dobbynsparks . .	45	2	18	Waterford .	Middlethird . .	Trinity Without .	Waterford .	II.	369
18	Dockery's Island .	0	3	14	Roscommon .	Ballintober North .	Kilglass . .	Strokestown .	IV.	186

(a) Including 4A. 3R. 38P. water.
(b) Including 1A. 2R. 32P. water.
(c) Including 3A. 2R. 29P. water.
(d) Including 2A. 1R. 22P. water.

(e) Including 5A. 2R. 0P. water.
(f) Including 32A. 3R. 31P. water.
(g) Including 18A. 2R. 9P. water.

(h) Including 6A. 3R. 16P. water.
(i) Including 4A. 1R. 14P. water.
(j) Including 9A. 0R. 30P. water.

No. of Sheet of the Ordnance Survey Maps.	Townlands and Towns.	Area in Statute Acres. A. R. P.	County.	Barony.	Parish.	Poor Law Union in 1857.	Townland Census of 1851, Part I. Vol.	Page
28	Doctor's Quarter	83 2 32	Armagh	Orior Upper	Forkill	Newry	III.	57
17	Doddsborough	271 3 6	Dublin	Newcastle	Lucan	Celbridge	I.	33
24	Dodds Island	1 1 17	Down	Dufferin	Killyleagh	Downpatrick	III.	167
13, 14, 20	Dog Big	867 0 24a	Fermanagh	Magheraboy	Devenish	Ballyshannon	III.	210
38,39,44,45	Doghtog	219 0 6	Meath	Ratoath	Ratoath	Dunshaughlin	I.	219
101	Dog Island	0 1 10	Galway	Longford	Clonfert	Ballinasloe	IV.	57
65	Dog Island	4 3 37	Galway	Moycullen	Kilcummin	Oughterard	IV.	68
13, 14	Dog Little	355 1 35	Fermanagh	Magheraboy	Devenish	Ballyshannon	III.	210
42	Dogs Island	0 0 38	Roscommon	Athlone	Kilmeane	Roscommon	IV.	182
15	Dogstown	20 1 39	Meath	Fore	Diamor	Oldcastle	I.	200
15, 16	Dogstown	225 0 8	Meath	Upper Kells	Kilskeer	Oldcastle	I.	206
40	Dogstown	21 1 8	Tipperary, N.R.	Kilnamanagh Upper	Glenkeen	Thurles	II.	278
68	Dogstown	406 1 30	Tipperary, S.R.	Middlethird	Dogstown	Cashel	II.	326
36	Dogstown 1st Division	33 1 24	Meath	Lower Moyfenrath	Trim	Trim	I.	212
36	Dogstown 2nd Division	63 0 7	Meath	Lower Moyfenrath	Trim	Trim	I.	212
36	Dogstown 3rd Division	170 1 29	Meath	Lower Moyfenrath	Trim	Trim	I.	212
78	Dohilla	221 2 6	Kerry	Iveragh	Valencia	Cahersiveen	II.	198
30	Dohora	236 1 9	Limerick	Coshma	Anhid	Croom	II.	241
30, 38	Dohora	538 2 39	Limerick	Coshma	Croom	Croom	II.	242
49, 50, 62	Dolan	1,084 0 37c	Galway	Ballynahinch	Ballindoon	Clifden	IV.	10
49	Dolanstown	474 2 16	Meath	Upper Deece	Rodanstown	Celbridge	I.	194
54	Dolanstown Kilcashel	199 2 4	Roscommon	Moycarn	Moore	Ballinasloe	IV.	206
7, 11	Dollards	61 1 30	Dublin	Nethercross	Swords	Balrothery	I.	32
37	Dollardstown	189 3 13	Kildare	Killea and Moone	Tankardstown	Athy	I.	61
19, 25, 26	Dollardstown	715 3 17d	Meath	Lower Duleck	Painstown	Navan	I.	196
30	Dollas	126 2 13	Limerick	Connello Upper	Ballingarry	Croom	II.	230
30	Dollas Lower	245 1 39	Limerick	Coshma	Croom	Croom	II.	242
30	Dollas Upper	466 1 34	Limerick	Coshma	Croom	Croom	II.	242
20	DOLLINGSTOWN T.	—	Down	Lower Iveagh, Up. pt.	Magheralin	Lurgan	III.	170
19	DOLLYMOUNT T.	—	Dublin	Coolock	Clontarf	Dublin North	I.	26
18	Dolphinsbarn	169 0 29e	Dublin	Uppercross	St. James	Dublin South	I.	41
18	Dolphinsbarn North	5 1 6f	Dublin	Uppercross	St. James	Dublin South	I.	41
46, 48	Dolu-key	128 3 36	Londonderry	Loughinsholin	Artrea	Magherafelt	III.	238
12	Donabate	53 1 15	Dublin	Nethercross	Donabate	Balrothery	I.	30
12	DONABATE T.	—	Dublin	Nethercross	{ Donabate / Portraine }	Balrothery	I. {	30 / 31 }
21	Donacarney Great	335 2 20	Meath	Lower Duleck	Colp	Drogheda	I.	195
21	Donacarney Little	199 2 12	Meath	Lower Duleck	Colp	Drogheda	I.	195
21	DONACARNEY T.	—	Meath	Lower Duleck	Colp	Drogheda	I.	195
51	Donacavey	38 0 8	Tyrone	Clogher	Donacavey	Omagh	III.	294
9, 10	Donadea North	450 0 31	Kildare	Ikeathy&Oughterany	Donadea	Celbridge	I.	57
9	Donadea South	379 3 25	Kildare	Ikeathy&Oughterany	Donadea	Celbridge	I.	57
34, 39	Donagh	263 0 23g	Fermanagh	Clankelly	Galloon	Lisnaskea	III.	198
6,7	Donagh	131 3 25	Monaghan	Trough	Donagh	Monaghan	III.	282
3	DONAGHADEE T.	—	Down	Ards Lower	Donaghadee	Newtownards	III.	158
51, 54	Donaghaguy	400 0 29	Down	Upper Iveagh, Up. pt.	Clonallen	Newry	III.	174
35, 43	Donaghanie	1,217 2 26h	Tyrone	Omagh East	Clogherny	Omagh	III.	310
7, 11, 12	Donagh Beg	169 3 5	Leitrim	Drumahaire	Cloonclare	Manorhamilton	IV.	93
20	Donaghcloney	300 2 28	Down	Lower Iveagh, Up. pt.	Donaghcloney	Lurgan	III.	169
20	DONAGHCLONEY T.	—	Down	Lower Iveagh, Up. pt.	Donaghcloney	Lurgan	III.	169
11	Donaghcumper	357 1 28i	Kildare	South Salt	Donaghcumper	Celbridge	I.	76
39	Donaghenry	152 0 38	Tyrone	Dungannon Middle	Donaghenry	Cookstown	III.	301
38	Donaghey	258 0 11	Tyrone	Dungannon Middle	Donaghenry	Cookstown	III.	301
12	Donaghintraine	325 3 13	Sligo	Tireragh	Templeboy	Dromore West	IV.	236
136	Donaghmore	312 0 28	Cork, W.R.	Ibane and Barryroe	Donaghmore	Clonakilty	II.	148
6, 11	Donaghmore	92 2 22	Kildare	North Salt	Donaghmore	Celbridge	I.	74
10	Donaghmore	867 0 24	Kilkenny	Fassadinin	Donaghmore	Castlecomer	I.	89
19	Donaghmore	53 3 18	Kilkenny	Shillelogher	St. Patrick's	Kilkenny	I.	116
11, 12	Donagh More	197 0 30	Leitrim	Drumahaire	Cloonclare	Manorhamilton	IV.	93
6,7	Donaghmore	540 1 31	Louth	Upper Dundalk	Dunbin	Dundalk	I.	178
25	Donaghmore	352 1 5	Meath	Lower Navan	Donaghmore	Navan	I.	214
45	Donaghmore	432 0 4	Meath	Ratoath	Donaghmore	Dunshaughlin	I.	218
28	Donaghmore	191 1 12	Queen's Co.	Clandonagh	Donaghmore	Donaghmore	I.	233
28	Donaghmore	174 3 9	Queen's Co.	Clandonagh	Rathdowney	Donaghmore	I.	234
77	Donaghmore	652 2 4	Tipperary, S.R.	Iffa and Offa East	Donaghmore	Clonmel	II.	313
46	Donaghmore	91 3 13	Tyrone	Dungannon Middle	Donaghmore	Dungannon	III.	302
17	Donaghmore	76 2 28	Wexford	Ballaghkeen	Donaghmore	Gorey	I.	293
21	Donaghmore	236 0 37	Wicklow	Upper Talbotstown	Donaghmore	Baltinglass	I.	363
79	Donaghmore Glebe	221 0 12j	Donegal	Raphoe	Donaghmore	Strabane	III.	137
8, 12	Donaghmore Lower	527 2 37	Kilkenny	Galmoy	Fertagh	Urlingford	I.	92
28	DONAGHMORE T.	—	Queen's Co.	Clandonogh	{ Donaghmore / Rathdowney }	Donaghmore	I. {	233 / 234 }
46	DONAGHMORE T.	—	Tyrone	Dungannon Middle	Donaghmore	Dungannon	III.	302

(a) Including 10A. 2R. 6P. water.
(b) Including 14A. 0R. 15P. water.
(c) Including 10¼A. 3R. 14P. water.
(d) Including 7A. 0R. 13P. water.

(e) { Within the Municipal Boundary, 49A. 0R. 37P. / Without the Municipal Boundary, 120A. 3R. 38P.
(f) { Within the Municipal Boundary, 5A. 0R. 17P. / Without the Municipal Boundary, 0A. 0R. 29P.

(g) Including 6A. 2R. 11P. water.
(h) Including 12A. 2R. 9P. water.
(i) Including 5A. 2R. 0P. water.
(j) Including 3A. 0R. 19P. water.

No. of Sheet of the Ordnance Survey Maps.	Townlands and Towns.	Area in Statute Acres.	County.	Barony.	Parish.	Poor Law Union in 1857.	Townland Census of 1851, Part I.	
		A. R. P.					Vol.	Page
8	Donaghmore Upper	148 2 19	Kilkenny	Galmoy	Fertagh	Urlingford	I.	92
28, 31	Donaghmoyne	569 0 24	Monaghan	Farney	Donaghmoyne	Carrickmacross	III.	269
58, 64	Donaghmoyne	174 2 9a	Tyrone	Clogher	Clogher	Clogher	III.	292
42	Donaghpatrick	693 2 12b	Galway	Clare	Donaghpatrick	Tuam	IV.	19
17, 18	Donaghpatrick	178 2 29	Meath	Upper Kells	Donaghpatrick	Navan	I.	205
38	Donaghrisk	239 0 18	Tyrone	Dungannon Upper	Desertcreat	Cookstown	III.	307
10	Donaghstown	300 1 6	Kildare	North Salt	Laraghbryan	Celbridge	I.	75
6	Donagreagh	174 2 2	Armagh	Oneilland East	Magheralin	Lurgan	III.	49
5	Donaguile	784 3 9	Kilkenny	Fassadinin	Castlecomer	Castlecomer	I.	88
24	Donard	525 0 22	Wexford	Bantry	Clonleigh	New Ross	I.	300
15, 21	Donard Demesne East	203 0 2	Wicklow	Lower Talbotstown	Donard	Baltinglass	I.	359
15, 21	Donard Demesne West	53 3 0	Wicklow	Lower Talbotstown	Donard	Baltinglass	I.	359
21	Donard Lower	187 0 39	Wicklow	Lower Talbotstown	Donard	Baltinglass	I.	359
21	Donard Mountain	85 0 19	Wicklow	Lower Talbotstown	Donard	Baltinglass	I.	359
15, 21	DONARD T.	—	Wicklow	Lower Talbotstown	Donard	Baltinglass	I.	360
21	Donard Upper	102 0 9	Wicklow	Lower Talbotstown	Donard	Baltinglass	I.	359
59	Donaskeagh	701 3 4	Tipperary, S.R.	Clanwilliam	Rathlynin	Tipperary	II.	309
75, 87	Donegal	127 2 21	Cork, E.R.	Barrymore	Clonmel	Cork	II.	53
93, 94	Donegal	133 1 33	Donegal	Tirhugh	Donegal	Donegal	III.	145
76	Donegal	462 1 27	Tipperary, S.R.	Middlethird	Knockgraffon	Cashel	II.	328
21	Donegall	41 0 19	Fermanagh	Magheraboy	Devenish	Enniskillen	III.	210
150	Donegall East	101 0 3	Cork, W.R.	West Carbery (E.D.)	Creagh	Skibbereen	II.	139
150	Donegall Middle	75 1 24	Cork, W.R.	West Carbery (E.D.)	Creagh	Skibbereen	II.	139
150	Donegall West	110 1 11	Cork, W.R.	West Carbery (E.D.)	Creagh	Skibbereen	II.	139
93, 94	DONEGAL T.	—	Donegal	{ Banagh / Tirhugh	{ Killymard / Donegal	Donegal	III.	{ 112 / 145
50	Donegore	416 2 5	Antrim	Upper Antrim	Donegore	Antrim	III.	6
50	Donegore	154 0 0	Antrim	Upper Antrim	Nilteen Grange	Antrim	III.	6
17, 25	Doneraile	105 3 13	Cork, E.R.	Fermoy	Doneraile	Mallow	II.	78
17, 25	DONERAILE T.	—	Cork, E.R.	Fermoy	Doneraile	Mallow	II.	79
55, 66	Donickmore	694 1 6	Cork, E.R.	Imokilly	Clonmult	Middleton	II.	84
110	Donnageaga or Brownstown	343 3 13	Mayo	Kilmaine	Robeen	Ballinrobe	IV.	157
21	Donnellystown	77 3 37	Louth	Ferrard	Drumshallon	Drogheda	I.	180
14, 15	Donnybrewer	744 1 36	Londonderry	Tirkeeran	Faughanvale	Londonderry	III.	250
14, 15	Donnybrewer Level (Intake)	1,077 2 32	Londonderry	Tirkeeran	Faughanvale	Londonderry	III.	250
51, 52	Donnybrook	71 1 32	Clare	Bunratty Lower	Feenagh	Ennis	II.	4
15, 21	Donnybrook	139 0 20	Tipperary, N.R.	Upper Ormond	Ballymackey	Nenagh	II.	289
18, 22	Donnybrook East	53 3 33	Dublin	Dublin	Donnybrook	Dublin South	I.	30
18, 22	Donnybrook West	100 2 22	Dublin	Dublin	Donnybrook	Dublin South	I.	30
14, 18	Donnycarney	128 2 26	Dublin	Coolock	Clonturk	Dublin North	I.	26
18	DONNYCARNEY T.	—	Dublin	Coolock	Clonturk	Dublin North	I.	27
54	Donnydeade	163 1 36	Tyrone	Dungannon Middle	Clonfeacle	Dungannon	III.	299
9	Donnygowen	53 3 21c	Tyrone	Strabane Lower	Urney	Strabane	III.	322
24	Donode	49 0 23	Kildare	Naas South	Ballymore Eustace	Naas	I.	64
24	Donode	378 1 6	Kildare	Naas South	Coghlanstown	Naas	I.	64
59	Donohill Lands	57 2 11	Tipperary, S.R.	Clanwilliam	Donohill	Tipperary	II.	307
16	Donore	236 2 35	Carlow	Idrone East	Lorum	Carlow	I.	8
16, 19	Donore	463 3 14	Carlow	Idrone East	Sliguff	Carlow	I.	8
13, 18, 19	Donore	896 2 18	Kildare	Clane	Carragh	Naas	I.	53
20	Donore	478 3 16	Meath	Lower Duleek	Donore	Drogheda	I.	195
10, 11	Donore	463 3 36	Meath	Lower Kells	Moynalty	Kells	I.	203
41	Donore	119 1 19d	Meath	Lune	Castlerickard	Trim	I.	207
41	Donore	703 2 37e	Meath	Lune	Killaconnigan	Trim	I.	208
23	Donore	110 0 25	Queen's Co.	Upperwoods	Offerlane	Abbeyleix	I.	251
6, 7	Donore	552 2 3	Westmeath	Corkaree	Multyfarnham	Mullingar	I.	263
21	Donore Demesne	82 1 30	Westmeath	Moycashel	Ardnurcher or Horseleap	Mullingar	I.	276
144	Donoure	416 3 36f	Cork, W.R.	Ibane and Barryroe	Rathbarry	Clonakilty	II.	150
40	Donoure East	173 3 11	Cork, W.R.	West Muskerry	Kilcorney	Millstreet	II.	158
40	Donoure Middle	111 3 20	Cork, W.R.	West Muskerry	Kilcorney	Millstreet	II.	158
40	Donoure West	174 2 36	Cork, W.R.	West Muskerry	Kilcorney	Millstreet	II.	158
55, 63	Dooaghs	557 0 39	Kerry	Iveragh	Killorglin	Killarney	II.	197
55,56,63,64	Dooaghs Commons	383 0 16g	Kerry	Iveragh	Killorglin	Killarney	II.	197
105	Dooaghtry	274 2 37	Mayo	Murrisk	Kilgeever	Westport	IV.	160
36	Dooily	399 3 38	Limerick	Glenquin	Newcastle	Newcastle	II.	247
24	Dooan	66 3 3	Roscommon	Ballintober North	Kilglass	Strokestown	IV.	186
5	Dooard	140 0 2	Leitrim	Rosclogher	Rossinver	Ballyshannon	IV.	111
24	Dooary	977 1 16	Queen's Co.	Cullenagh	Ballyroan	Abbeyleix	I.	239
61	Dooballagh	1,234 0 14	Donegal	Raphoe	Leck	Letterkenny	III.	140
107	Doobally	504 1 9	Donegal	Tirhugh	Kilbarron	Ballyshannon	III.	148
1	Doobally	387 2 5	Leitrim	Rosclogher	Rossinver	Ballyshannon	IV.	111
33	Doo Beg	65 3 35	Sligo	Corran	Kilmorgan	Sligo	IV.	227

(a) Including 0A. 0R. 16P. water.
(b) Including 35A. 3R. 31P. water.
(c) Including 2A. 3R. 18P. water.

(d) Including 7A. 1R. 32P. water.
(e) Including 9A. 3R. 13P. water.

(f) Including 15A. 0R. 34P. water.
(g) Including 35A. 3R. 4P. water.

No. of Sheet of the Ordnance Survey Maps.	Townlands and Towns.	Area in Statute Acres.			County.	Barony.	Parish.	Poor Law Union in 1857.	Townland Census of 1851, Part I.	
		A.	R.	P.					Vol.	Page
38	Doobeg . . .	742	2	7	Sligo . .	Corran . . .	Kilturra . . .	Tobercurry .	IV.	227
20, 28	Doobehy . . .	1,254	0	37	Mayo . .	Tirawley . .	Moygawnagh .	Killala . .	IV.	171
74,75,83,84	Doobin . . .	2,166	1	2a	Donegal . .	Boylagh . .	Inishkeel . .	Glenties . .	III.	112
17	Doocarrick . .	332	2	36	Cavan . .	Tullygarvey .	Kildrumsherdan .	Cootehill . .	III.	90
17	Doocarrick . .	97	3	37	Donegal . .	Kilmacrenan .	Clondavaddog .	Milford . .	III.	124
68	Doocarrig Beg .	542	3	1	Kerry . .	Magunihy . .	Kilcummin .	Killarney . .	II.	201
68, 76	Doocarrig More .	685	0	21	Kerry . .	Magunihy . .	Kilcummin .	Killarney . .	II.	201
26	Doocashel Glebe .	273	3	18	Donegal . .	Kilmacrenan .	Clondahorky .	Dunfanaghy .	III.	123
16, 21	Doocassan . .	186	2	34	Cavan . .	Tullygarvey .	Drung . .	Cootehill . .	III.	89
51, 52	Doocastle or Ballindoo	1,956	1	32c	Mayo . .	Costello . .	Kilturra . .	Swineford . .	IV.	142
28, 36	Doocatteen . .	200	3	17	Limerick . .	Glenquin . .	Newcastle .	Newcastle . .	II.	247
28, 34	Doocharn . .	188	1	23	Fermanagh .	Magherastephana .	Aghalurcher .	Lisnaskea . .	III.	216
15	Doocharn . .	210	0	22	Monaghan .	Cremorne . .	Muckno . .	Castleblayney .	III.	261
33	*Doocharn Island* .	6	0	5	Fermanagh .	Knockninny .	Kinawley . .	Lisnaskea . .	III.	203
74, 83	Doohill North .	448	0	4	Donegal . .	Banagh . .	Killybegs Lower .	Glenties . .	III.	110
74, 83	Doohill South .	152	2	0	Donegal . .	Banagh . .	Killybegs Lower .	Glenties . .	III.	110
30	Doochorran . .	245	3	37	Leitrim . .	Carrigallen .	Drumreilly .	Bawnboy . .	IV.	91
2	Doochrock . .	377	1	31	Fermanagh .	Lurg . . .	Drumkeeran .	Lowterstown .	III.	206
87, 99	Doocreggaun . .	195	0	4	Galway . .	Clonmacnowen .	Aughrim . .	Ballinasloe .	IV.	24
49	Doocrock . .	426	1	39d	Tyrone . .	Omagh East .	Dromore . .	Lowterstown .	III.	311
75,76,84,85	Doocrow . . .	2,412	1	37e	Donegal . .	Banagh . .	Killymard .	Donegal . .	III.	111
15, 21	Doodys Bottoms .	59	2	22	Wicklow . .	Lower Talbotstown .	Donard . .	Baltinglass .	I.	359
26	Dooederny . .	71	2	33	Fermanagh .	Clanawley . .	Rossorry .	Enniskillen .	III.	194
24	Dooederny . .	185	2	10	Fermanagh .	Magherastephana .	Aghalurcher .	Lisnaskea . .	III.	216
54, 55, 65	Dooega . . .	3,761	1	7	Mayo . .	Burrishoole .	Achill . .	Newport . .	IV.	117
3	Dooey . . .	208	1	19	Antrim . .	Cary . . .	Billy . . .	Coleraine . .	III.	12
80, 89	Dooey . . .	149	2	19f	Donegal . .	Banagh . .	Glencolumbkille .	Glenties . .	III.	105
57, 65	Dooey . . .	1,804	3	25g	Donegal . .	Boylagh . .	Lettermacward .	Glenties . .	III.	114
25, 32	Dooey . . .	166	2	16	Down . .	Ards Upper .	Slanes . .	Downpatrick .	III.	161
3	Dooey Beg . .	53	3	4	Londonderry .	North East Liberties of Coleraine .	Ballyaghran .	Coleraine . .	III.	244
43, 48	Doogans Warren .	64	0	38	Wexford . .	Forth . . .	Rosslare . .	Wexford . .	I.	313
97, 105	Doogarraun . .	272	0	6	Galway . .	Dunkellin .	Kilconickny .	Loughrea . .	IV.	29
15	Doogary . .	291	2	17h	Armagh . .	Tiranny . .	Tynan . .	Armagh . .	III.	60
13, 14, 19	Doogary . .	318	0	5	Cavan . .	Tullyhunco .	Kildallan . .	Bawnboy . .	III.	97
24	Doogary . .	80	3	6	Fermanagh .	Magherastephana .	Aghalurcher .	Lisnaskea . .	III.	216
73, 74	Doogary . . .	1,804	2	14	Kerry . .	Dunkerron North .	Knockane . .	Killarney . .	II.	182
68	Doogary . . .	440	3	23i	Mayo . .	Burrishoole .	Burrishoole .	Newport . .	IV.	119
78, 79	Doogary . . .	126	2	1	Mayo . .	Carra . . .	Breaghwy . .	Castlebar . .	IV.	127
59, 69	Doogary . . .	906	0	16j	Mayo . .	Carra . . .	Islandeady .	Castlebar . .	IV.	128
81	Doogary . . .	439	1	4	Mayo . .	Costello . .	Aghamore . .	Swineford . .	IV.	137
74	Doogary . . .	100	2	25	Mayo . .	Costello . .	Castlemore .	Castlereagh .	IV.	140
74	Doogary . . .	74	2	8	Mayo . .	Costello . .	Kilcolman .	Castlereagh .	IV.	141
6	Doogary . . .	228	1	10	Monaghan .	Monaghan . .	Tedavnet . .	Monaghan . .	III.	278
4	Doogary . . .	306	1	12	Roscommon .	Boyle . . .	Ardcarn . .	Boyle . .	IV.	193
35, 43	Doogary . . .	303	1	2k	Tyrone . .	Omagh East .	Drumragh .	Omagh . .	III.	312
49	Doogary . . .	295	2	14	Tyrone . .	Omagh East .	Kilskeery .	Lowterstown .	III.	313
40	Doogarymore . .	260	1	27	Roscommon .	Ballintober South .	Kilteevan .	Roscommon .	IV.	190
70, 79	Dooghan . ' .	119	2	7	Donegal . .	Raphoe . .	Donaghmore .	Strabane . .	III.	137
51, 54	Dooghan . .	557	2	31	Roscommon .	Athlone . .	Drum . .	Athlone . .	IV.	180
34	Dooghary . .	436	2	31	Down . .	Upper Iveagh, Up.pt.	Seapatrick .	Banbridge .	III.	176
65, 66	Dooghbeg . .	1,791	2	3	Mayo . .	Burrishoole .	Burrishoole .	Newport . .	IV.	119
72, 85, 86	Dooghcloon . .	728	1	1	Galway . .	Kilconnell .	Killimordaly .	Loughrea . .	IV.	42
56, 66	Dooghill . .	448	2	27	Mayo . .	Burrishoole .	Burrishoole .	Newport . .	IV.	119
85, 95	Dooghmakeon . .	1,213	3	8l	Mayo . .	Murrisk . .	Kilgeever . .	Westport . .	IV.	160
26, 39	Dooghta . .	1,567	2	2	Galway . .	Ross . . .	Cong . . .	Oughterard .	IV.	73
19	Dooglaun . .	342	3	17	Clare . .	Tulla Upper .	Feakle . .	Tulla . .	II.	39
29, 36	Dooglen . .	572	2	28	Down . .	Kinelarty . .	Dromara . .	Downpatrick .	III.	176
42	Doogort . .	226	1	15	Mayo . .	Burrishoole .	Achill . .	Newport . .	IV.	117
42, 43	Doogort East .	2,034	2	25	Mayo . .	Burrishoole .	Achill . .	Newport . .	IV.	117
42	Doogort West .	1,659	0	30	Mayo . .	Burrishoole .	Achill . .	Newport . .	IV.	117
23	Doohallat . .	188	2	2m	Cavan . .	Clankee . .	Drumgoon .	Cootehill . .	III.	72
19	Doohamlat . .	138	2	11	Monaghan .	Cremorne . .	Clontibret .	Castleblayney .	III.	260
39	Doohat . .	215	0	27n	Fermanagh .	Coole . . .	Galloon . .	Clones . .	III.	199
17	Doohat . .	249	1	20o	Monaghan .	Dartree . .	Aghabog . .	Cootehill . .	III.	263
19, 23	Doohat or Crossreagh	203	2	3	Armagh . .	Tiranny . .	Derrynoose .	Armagh . .	III.	59
31	Doohatty . .	458	0	17p	Monaghan .	Farney . .	Magheracloone .	Carrickmacross	III.	272
32	Doohatty Glebe .	468	3	11	Fermanagh .	Clanawley . .	Killesher .	Enniskillen .	III.	192
35	Dooherty . .	310	1	19	Roscommon .	Ballintober South .	Kilbride . .	Roscommon .	IV.	189
34	Doohooma . .	1,102	0	14q	Mayo . .	Erris . . .	Kilcommon .	Belmullet . .	IV.	143
49	Doohulla . .	887	2	39r	Galway . .	Ballynahinch .	Ballindoon .	Clifden . .	IV.	10
20	Doohyle Beg .	188	2	14s	Limerick . .	Connello Lower .	Nantinan .	Rathkeale .	II.	229
20	Doohyle More .	159	1	16	Limerick . .	Connello Lower .	Nantinan .	Rathkeale .	II.	229

(a) Including 16A. 2R. 12P. water.
(b) Including 11A. 2R. 27P. water.
(c) Including 7A. 2R. 35P. Cloonakillina Lough.
(d) Including 1A. 2R. 6P. water.
(e) Including 11A. 0R. 6P. water.
(f) Including 4A. 2R. 28P. detached portion.
(g) Including 11A. 1R. 17P. water.

(h) Including 17A. 2R. 16P. water.
(i) Including 5A. 3R. 33P. water.
(j) Including 8A. 3R. 10P. water.
(k) Including 4A. 1R. 5P. water.
(l) Including 25A. 2R. water.
(m) Including 37A. 1R. 10P. water.

(n) Including 14A. 3R. 34P. water.
(o) Including 29A. 0R. 24P. water.
(p) Including 27A. 0R. 12P. water.
(q) Including 12A. 3R. 11P. water.
(r) Including 94A. 3R. 23P. water.
(s) Including 14A. 1R. 8P. water.

No. of Sheet of the Ordnance Survey Maps	Townlands and Towns.	Area in Statute Acres.	County.	Barony.	Parish.	Poor Law Union in 1857.	Townland Census of 1851, Part I. Vol.	Page
		A. R. P.						
54	Dooish . . .	998 1 25	Donegal . .	Raphoe . . .	Raymoghy . .	Strabane . .	III.	141
77	Dooish . . .	1,089 3 19a	Donegal . .	Raphoe . . .	Stranorlar . .	Stranorlar . .	III.	142
33, 41	Dooish . . .	845 0 7	Tyrone . .	Omagh West . .	Longfield West .	Castlederg . .	III.	316
42,43,54,55	Dookinelly (Calvy) .	1,935 1 0b	Mayo . .	Burrishoole . .	Achill . . .	Newport . .	IV.	117
42	Dookinelly (Calvy) Bal of . . .	189 2 22	Mayo . .	Burrishoole . .	Achill . . .	Newport . .	IV.	117
54	Dookinelly (Thulis)	793 3 17	Mayo . .	Burrishoole . .	Achill . . .	Newport . .	IV.	117
1, 4	Doolagh . .	65 3 31	Dublin . .	Balrothery West .	Naul . . .	Balrothery . .	I.	23
63	Doolahig . .	129 2 39	Kerry . .	Iveragh . . .	Killorglin . .	Killarney . .	II.	197
30, 39	Doolaig North .	531 0 7	Kerry . .	Trughanacmy . .	Castleisland . .	Tralee . .	II.	208
30, 39	Doolaig South .	210 0 12	Kerry . .	Trughanacmy . .	Castleisland . .	Tralee . .	II.	208
4, 5	Doolargy . .	1,222 0 4	Louth . .	Lower Dundalk .	Ballymascanlan .	Dundalk . .	I.	175
60	Doolargy . .	313 1 31	Tyrone . .	Dungannon Lower .	Carnteel . .	Clogher . .	III.	297
18	Doolargy Glebe .	136 0 5c	Leitrim . .	Drumahaire . .	Inishmagrath . .	Manorhamilton .	IV.	96
77,78,88,89	Dooleague . .	249 1 18	Mayo . .	Burrishoole . .	Islandeady . .	Westport . .	IV.	121
28, 37	Dooleeg Beg . .	682 1 36	Mayo . .	Tirawley . .	Crossmolina . .	Ballina . .	IV.	166
28, 37	Dooleeg More . .	1,472 3 29d	Mayo . .	Tirawley . .	Crossmolina . .	Ballina . .	IV.	166
20, 25, 26	Dooletter . .	512 2 34e	Fermanagh . .	Clanawley . .	Boho . . .	Enniskillen . .	III.	189
12, 13	Dooletter . .	904 1 38	Galway . .	Ross . . .	Ross . . .	Ballinrobe . .	IV.	74
64, 77	Dooletter East .	739 1 0f	Galway . .	Ballynahinch . .	Moyrus . .	Clifden . .	IV.	13
64, 77	Dooletter West .	527 3 31g	Galway . .	Ballynahinch . .	Moyrus . .	Clifden . .	IV.	13
8, 14	Doolin . . .	238 0 2	Clare . .	Corcomroe . .	Killilagh . .	Ennistimon . .	II.	20
86	Doolis . . .	228 1 2	Tipperary, S.R. .	Iffa and Offa West .	Templetenny . .	Clogheen . .	II.	320
39	Doolough . .	1,925 2 35	Clare . .	Ibrickan . .	Kilmurry . .	Kilrush . .	II.	23
25	Doolough . .	2,499 3 7	Mayo . .	Erris . . .	Kilcommon . .	Belmullet . .	IV.	143
4, 5, 8, 9	Doolough . .	206 1 5	Queen's Co. .	Portnahinch . .	Lea . . .	Mountmellick .	I.	244
36, 42	Doolystown . .	418 0 27h	Meath . .	Lower Moyfenrath .	Trim . . .	Trim . .	I.	212
33	Doomore . .	163 3 5	Sligo . .	Corran . .	Kilmorgan . .	Sligo . .	IV.	227
31, 32	Doomore . .	664 3 18	Sligo . .	Leyny . .	Achonry . .	Tobercurry . .	IV.	229
33, 39	Doon . . .	339 0 37	Cavan . .	Castlerahan . .	Mullagh . .	Bailieborough .	III.	70
8	Doon . . .	1,189 1 36	Cavan . .	Tullyhaw . .	Drumreilly . .	Bawnboy . .	III.	91
10	Doon . . .	110 3 31i	Cavan . .	Tullyhaw . .	Tomregan . .	Bawnboy . .	III.	96
18, 19	Doon . . .	694 0 19j	Clare . .	Bunratty Upper .	Inchicronan . .	Gort . .	II.	9
15, 16	Doon . . .	253 1 38	Clare . .	Corcomroe . .	Kilfenora . .	Ennistimon . .	II.	19
43, 44	Doon . . .	97 3 28	Clare . .	Tulla Lower .	Killuran . .	Tulla . .	II.	36
44	Doon . . .	118 3 17	Clare . .	Tulla Lower .	Kilseily . .	Limerick . .	II.	36
44	Doon . . .	344 1 33	Donegal . .	Kilmacrenan . .	Kilmacrenan . .	Milford . .	III.	129
38	Doon . . .	1,003 0 16	Fermanagh . .	Knockninny . .	Kinawley . .	Lisnaskea . .	III.	201
23	Doon . . .	459 1 21	Fermanagh . .	Tirkennedy . .	Enniskillen . .	Enniskillen . .	III.	222
22	Doon . . .	554 0 0	Galway . .	Ballynahinch . .	Omey . .	Clifden . .	IV.	15
98	Doon . . .	855 2 15	Galway . .	Leitrim . .	Kilreckill . .	Loughrea . .	IV.	54
67, 68	Doon . . .	957 1 16	Galway . .	Moycullen . .	Killannin . .	Oughterard . .	IV.	69
91, 100	Doon . . .	863 2 39	Kerry . .	Dunkerron South .	Kilcrohane . .	Kenmare . .	II.	183
12	Doon . . .	41 3 22	Limerick . .	Pubblebrien . .	Killkeedy . .	Limerick . .	II.	252
40	Doon . . .	645 0 34	Londonderry . .	Loughinsholin . .	Ballynaskreen . .	Magherafelt . .	III.	239
88	Doon . . .	247 3 18	Mayo . .	Burrishoole . .	Aghagower . .	Westport . .	IV.	118
1, 2, 5	Doon . . .	365 1 21k	Meath . .	Lower Kells . .	Moybolgue . .	Kells . .	I.	203
22	Doon . . .	315 0 33	Queen's Co. .	Clandonagh . .	Aghaboe . .	Donaghmore . .	I.	232
17	Doon . . .	539 2 21	Queen's Co. .	Maryborough West.	Clonenagh&Clonagheen	Abbeyleix . .	I.	243
3, 6	Doon . . .	761 1 1	Roscommon . .	Boyle . .	Boyle . . .	Boyle . .	IV.	194
23	Doon . . .	242 1 11l	Roscommon . .	Roscommon . .	Killukin . .	Strokestown .	IV.	211
44, 46	Doon . . .	986 2 35	Sligo . .	Coolavin . .	Kilfree . .	Boyle . .	IV.	224
77	Doon . . .	193 0 24	Tipperary, S.R. .	Iffa and Offa East .	Kilgrant . .	Clonmel . .	II.	314
89, 90	Doon . . .	2,165 2 14	Tipperary, S.R. .	Iffa and Offa West .	Shanrahan . .	Clogheen . .	II.	319
13	Doon . . .	453 0 8	Waterford . .	Decies without Drum	Seskinan . .	Lismore . .	II.	360
1, 3	Doon . . .	302 0 38m	Westmeath . .	Fore . . .	Lickbla . .	Granard . .	I.	270
34, 35, 43	Doona . . .	1,212 2 23n	Mayo . .	Erris . . .	Kilcommon . .	Newport . .	IV.	143
22	Doonacurry . .	58 1 37	Longford . .	Rathcline . .	Kilcommock . .	Ballymahon . .	I.	164
22	Doonacurry . .	26 1 16	Longford . .	Rathcline . .	Shrule . .	Ballymahon . .	I.	165
7	Doonadoba . .	661 3 32	Mayo . .	Tirawley . .	Kilcummin . .	Killala . .	IV.	168
55, 56	Doonaghboy or Bal-lyonan . .	775 3 6	Clare . .	Moyarta . .	Kilfearagh . .	Kilrush . .	II.	32
66	Doonaha East .	450 2 5	Clare . .	Moyarta . .	Moyarta . .	Kilrush . .	II.	34
29	Doonahaha . .	45 2 1	Roscommon . .	Roscommon . .	Lissonuffy . .	Strokestown .	IV.	212
66	DOONAHA T. . .	—	Clare . .	Moyarta . .	Moyarta . .	Kilrush . .	II.	34
66	Doonaha West .	747 2 7	Clare . .	Moyarta . .	Moyarta . .	Kilrush . .	II.	34
35, 43	Doonakenna . .	418 1 10	Limerick . .	Glenquin . .	Monagay . .	Newcastle . .	II.	247
9, 14, 15	Doonally . .	204 3 12	Sligo . .	Carbury . .	Calry . .	Sligo . .	IV.	220
8, 9, 14, 15	Doonally . .	181 2 20	Sligo . .	Carbury . .	Drumcliff . .	Sligo . .	IV.	221
21, 27	Doonally . .	178 1 35	Sligo . .	Tirerrill . .	Ballysumaghan .	Sligo . .	IV.	238
123	Doonally East .	380 2 6	Galway . .	Loughrea . .	Kilthomas . .	Gort . .	IV.	65
123	Doonally West .	113 2 13	Galway . .	Loughrea . .	Kilthomas . .	Gort . .	IV.	65
80, 89	Doonalt . . .	268 3 5	Donegal . .	Banagh . . .	Glencolumbkille .	Glenties . .	III.	105

(a) Including 11A. 3R. 20P. water.
(b) Including 29A. 3R. 32P. water.
(c) Including 8A. 1R. 14P. water.
(d) Including 46A. 3R. 38R. Lough Dahybaun.
(e) Including 2A. 0R. 25P. water.
(f) Including 90A. 3R. 20P. water.
(g) Including 38A. 1R. 0P. water.
(h) Including 2A. 1R. 0P. water.
(i) Including 2A. 2R. 0P. water.
(j) Including 73A. 1R. 6P. water.
(k) Including 12A. 2R. 29P. water.
(l) Including 4A. 1R. 2 P. water.
(m) Including 1A. 2R. 32P. water.
(n) Including 34A. 1R. 3P. water.

No. of Sheet of the Ordnance Survey Maps.	Townlands and Towns.	Area in Statute Acres.			County.	Barony.	Parish.	Poor Law Union in 1857.	Townland Census of 1851. Part I.	
		A.	R.	P.					Vol.	Page
11, 12	Doonaltan	384	3	33	Sligo	Tireragh	Templeboy	Dromore West	IV.	236
18	Doonameran	75	1	8	Longford	Moydow	Ballymacormick	Longford	I.	160
14	Doonamona	146	3	2	Mayo	Tirawley	Templemurry	Killala	IV.	172
16, 23	Doonamona	108	2	23	Westmeath	Kilkenny West	Noughaval	Ballymahon	I.	274
14	Doonamontane	265	0	25	Kerry	Clanmaurice	Ballyheige	Tralee	II.	168
21	Doonamurray	121	2	13	Sligo	Tirerrill	Kilross	Sligo	IV.	241
29	Doonan	465	2	33	Antrim	Lower Glenarm	Tickmacrevan	Larne	III.	23
93	Doonan	183	2	18	Donegal	Banagh	Killymard	Donegal	III.	111
10	Doonan	187	3	13	Fermanagh	Lurg	Derryvullan	Lowtherstown	III.	204
21	Doonanarroo Lower	283	3	15	Mayo	Tirawley	Kilfian	Killala	IV.	169
21	Doonanarroo Upper	199	0	33	Mayo	Tirawley	Kilfian	Killala	IV.	169
31	Doonane	1,685	0	22	Queen's Co.	Slievemargy	Rathaspick	Carlow	I.	246
31, 32	Doonane	341	1	22	Tipperary, N.R.	Owney and Arra	Killoscully	Nenagh	II.	295
14	Doonanpatrick	0	1	10	Sligo	Carbury	Killaspugbrone	Sligo	IV.	222
13	Doonans	79	0	19	Antrim	Cary	Armoy	Ballycastle	III.	11
28	Doonarah	157	1	27a	Leitrim	Mohill	Mohill	Mohill	IV.	107
96	Doonard	42	3	14	Galway	Dunkellin	Kilora	Loughrea	IV.	31
23	Doonard Beg	140	3	34b	Roscommon	Roscommon	Kiltrustan	Strokestown	IV.	211
3	Doonard Lower	166	3	34	Kerry	Iraghticonnor	Kilnaughtin	Glin	II.	191
23	Doonard More	275	2	15c	Roscommon	Roscommon	Kiltrustan	Strokestown	IV.	211
3	Doonard Upper	401	1	11	Kerry	Iraghticonnor	Kilnaughtin	Glin	II.	191
98	Doonaree	217	1	36	Galway	Kilconnell	Killallaghtan	Ballinasloe	IV.	41
46, 47	Doonaroya	737	1	2	Mayo	Tirawley	Addergoole	Castlebar	IV.	163
29	Doonasleen East	196	3	20	Cork, E.R.	Duhallow	Kilmeen	Millstreet	II.	72
21, 29	Doonasleen North	526	1	6	Cork, E.R.	Duhallow	Kilmeen	Millstreet	II.	72
29	Doonasleen South	600	0	24	Cork, E.R.	Duhallow	Kilmeen	Millstreet	II.	72
53, 54	Doonass	424	0	26	Clare	Tulla Lower	Kiltenanlea	Limerick	II.	37
53, 54	Doonass Demesne	263	1	11	Clare	Tulla Lower	Kiltenanlea	Limerick	II.	37
27, 35	Doonaun	145	2	12	Clare	Tulla Upper	Tulla	Tulla	II.	41
72	Doonaun	144	3	37	Galway	Tiaquin	Moylough	Mountbellew	IV.	80
99, 113	Doonavanig	495	0	19	Cork, E.R.	Kinalea	Tracton	Kinsale	II.	97
40	Doonaveeragh	196	3	23	Sligo	Tirerrill	Aghanagh	Boyle	IV.	237
26	Doonawanly	235	2	39	Cork, E.R.	Fermoy	Wallstown	Mallow	II.	83
18	Doonbeakin	562	1	32	Sligo	Tireragh	Kilmacshalgan	Dromore West	IV.	234
46, 47	Doon Beg	1,310	2	25	Clare	Ibrickan	Killard	Kilrush	II.	23
43,44,57,58	Doonbeg	249	0	5	Galway	Clare	Kilmoylan	Tuam	IV.	22
47	DOONBEG T.	—			Clare	Ibrickan	Killard	Kilrush	II.	23
29, 37	Doonbeirne	217	0	26	Limerick	Connello Lower	Rathkeale	Croom	II.	229
27	Doonbought	237	3	25	Antrim	Kilconway	Dunaghy	Ballymena	III.	25
38, 47	Doonbreedia	366	3	29	Mayo	Tirawley	Addergoole	Castlebar	IV.	163
47	Doonbreedia Mountain	278	0	6	Mayo	Tirawley	Addergoole	Castlebar	IV.	163
7	Doonbristy	0	2	21	Mayo	Tirawley	Kilbride	Killala	IV.	168
3, 6	Dooncaha	1,097	3	6	Kerry	Iraghticonnor	Kilnaughtin	Glin	II.	191
19	Dooncaha	611	1	20	Limerick	Shanid	Dunmoylan	Glin	II.	255
3, 4, 10, 11	Dooncarton or Glengad	830	2	23	Mayo	Erris	Kilcommon	Belmullet	IV.	143
88	Dooncastle	338	0	11	Mayo	Burrishoole	Aghagower	Westport	IV.	118
6	Doon Demesne	981	2	33	King's Co.	Garrycastle	Lemanaghan	Parsonstown	I.	136
4	Doon East	416	3	13	Kerry	Iraghticonnor	Killehenny	Listowel	II.	191
34	Dooneen	49	0	1	Clare	Bunratty Upper	Doorra	Ennis	II.	8
3	Dooneen	313	1	16	Clare	Burren	Abbey	Ballyvaghan	II.	11
64	Dooneen	185	1	17	Cork, E.R.	Barrymore	Ballycurrany	Middleton	II.	51
151	Dooneen	271	1	8	Cork, W.R.	West Carbery (E.D.)	Castlehaven	Skibbereen	II.	138
138	Dooneen	164	3	26	Cork, W.R.	West Carbery (W.D.)	Kilcrohane	Bantry	II.	143
32	Dooneen	421	3	32	Fermanagh	Clanawley	Killesher	Enniskillen	III.	192
17	Dooneen	257	2	8	Fermanagh	Tirkennedy	Enniskillen	Enniskillen	III.	222
22	Dooneen	24	0	29d	Galway	Ballynahinch	Ballynakill	Clifden	IV.	11
70	Dooneen	525	2	32	Kerry	Iveragh	Killinane	Cahersiveen	II.	197
58,59,66,67	Dooneen	262	0	22	Kerry	Magunihy	Aghadoe	Killarney	II.	199
58	Dooneen	171	1	13	Kerry	Magunihy	Kilcummin	Killarney	II.	201
31, 40	Dooneen	881	0	39	Kerry	Trughanacmy	Castleisland	Tralee	II.	208
13, 22	Dooneen	376	2	34	Limerick	Pubblebrien	Crecora	Croom	II.	252
115	Dooneen	2	0	9	Mayo	Murrisk	Kilgeever	Westport	IV.	161
28	Dooneen	79	1	0	Roscommon	Ballymoe	Cloonygormican	Castlereagh	IV.	191
9, 10, 15, 16	Dooneen	861	2	0	Roscommon	Frenchpark	Kilcolagh	Boyle	IV.	203
17	Dooneen	393	2	2e	Roscommon	Roscommon	Clooncraff	Carr. on Shannon	IV.	208
16, 22	Dooneen	343	2	30	Sligo	Tireragh	Castleconor	Dromore West	IV.	232
17	Dooneen	72	1	35	Waterford	Middlethird	Kilmeadan	Waterford	II.	368
17	Dooneen	55	2	20	Waterford	Middlethird	Lisnakill	Waterford	II.	368
26	Dooneen Island	4	1	9	Galway	Ross	Ross	Oughterard	IV.	74
124	Dooneen Lower	161	0	18	Cork, W.R.	Courceys	Kilroan	Kinsale	II.	147
89	Dooneenmacotter	134	1	26	Cork, E.R.	Imokilly	Kilmahon	Middleton	II.	89
98	Dooneen North	102	2	37	Cork, E.R.	Kinalea	Ballymartle	Kinsale	II.	94

(a) Including 14A. 0R. 6P. water.
(b) Including 24A. 1R. 16P. water.
(c) Including 7A. 1R. 25P. water.
(d) Including 7A. 2R. 6P. water.
(e) Including 45A. 0R. 35P. water.

No. of Sheet of the Ordnance Survey Maps	Townlands and Towns	Area in Statute Acres.			County	Barony	Parish	Poor Law Union in 1857.	Townland Census of 1851. Part I.	
		A.	R.	P.					Vol.	Page
49, 60	Dooneens	780	1	39	Cork, W.R.	East Muskerry	Aghabulloge	Macroom	II.	153
39	Dooneens	594	1	11a	Cork, W.R.	West Muskerry	Drishane	Millstreet	II.	156
80, 92	Dooneens	751	2	13	Cork, W.R.	West Muskerry	Inchigeelagh	Dunmanway	II.	157
98, 112	Dooneen South	149	2	17	Cork, E.R.	Kinalea	Ballymartle	Kinsale	II.	94
124	Dooneen Upper	117	0	21	Cork, W.R.	Courceys	Kilroan	Kinsale	II.	147
13, 22	Dooneen Upper	60	2	12	Limerick	Pubblebrien	Crecora	Croom	II.	252
29, 35	Doon and Esheleagh	645	3	10b	Fermanagh	Clankelly	Clones	Clones	III.	195
6	Doonfeeny Lower	51	3	14	Mayo	Tirawley	Doonfeeny	Killala	IV.	167
6, 7	Doonfeeny Upper	635	0	5	Mayo	Tirawley	Doonfeeny	Killala	IV.	16
14	Doonfin	203	2	30	Antrim	Cary	Ramoan	Ballycastle	III.	14
12, 18	Doonflin Lower	137	0	31	Sligo	Tireragh	Skreen	Dromore West	IV.	236
18	Doonflin Upper	780	1	35	Sligo	Tireragh	Skreen	Dromore West	IV.	236
4, 5, 7, 8	Doonfore	656	3	20	Sligo	Carbury	Drumcliff	Sligo	IV.	221
34	Doongelagh	411	2	10c	Sligo	Tirerrill	Kilmacallan	Boyle	IV.	239
52, 60, 61	Doon Glebe	913	0	0	Donegal	Kilmacrenan	Conwal	Letterkenny	III.	126
8	Doonierin	42	1	7	Sligo	Carbury	Drumcliff	Sligo	IV.	221
39	Doonimlaghbeg	158	3	37	Kerry	Trughanacmy	Ballymacelligott	Tralee	II.	207
15 .	Doonis	866	0	28d	Westmeath	Kilkenny West	Noughaval	Ballymahon	I.	274
60	*Doon Island*	2	1	36	Clare	Clonderalaw	Killadysert	Killadysert	II.	16
43	Dooniver	767	3	25e	Mayo	Burrishoole	Achill	Newport	IV.	117
10	Doonkelly	334	3	5f	Leitrim	Drumahaire	Drumlease	Manorhamilton	IV.	94
58	Doonkinane	276	2	15	Kerry	Magunihy	Aglish	Killarney	II.	200
48	Doonloughan	186	2	26g	Galway	Ballynahinch	Ballindoon	Clifden	IV.	10
73, 74	Doon Lower	116	0	19	Galway	Kilconnell	Fohanagh	Mountbellew	IV.	40
8, 14	Doonmacfelim	186	2	27	Clare	Corcomroe	Killilagh	Ennistimon	II.	20
112	Doonmacreena	138	1	29	Mayo	Clanmorris	Kilvine	Claremorris	IV.	134
12	Doonmadden	226	2	10	Sligo	Tireragh	Templeboy	Dromore West	IV.	236
54	Doonmanagh	285	1	34	Kerry	Corkaguiny	Minard	Dingle	II.	179
49,50,61,62	Doonmaynor	431	1	35	Mayo	Gallen	Killasser	Swineford	IV.	149
33, 34	Doonmeegin	286	1	39	Sligo	Corran	Kilmorgan	Sligo	IV.	227
40	Doonmoon	205	2	11	Limerick	Coshlea	Knocklong	Kilmallock	II.	240
46, 47	Doonmore	1,545	3	11	Clare	Ibrickan	Killard	Kilrush	II.	23
10, 11	Doonmorgan	92	0	32	Leitrim	Drumahaire	Drumlease	Manorhamilton	IV.	94
8, 14, 15	Doonnagore	619	0	6	Clare	Corcomroe	Killilagh	Ennistimon	II.	20
67, 68	Doonnagurroge	695	3	34h	Clare	Clonderalaw	Killimer	Kilrush	II.	16
114	*Doonnahinneena*	2	1	24	Mayo	Murrisk	Inishbofin	Clifden	IV.	159
90	Doonnamona	76	0	29	Mayo	Carra	Drum	Castlebar	IV.	128
21, 29	Doon North	342	0	16	Kerry	Trughanacmy	Tralee	Tralee	II.	213
16	Doon North	888	3	36	Limerick	Coonagh	Doon	Tipperary	II.	234
38, 39	Doonogan	1,043	1	2i	Clare	Ibrickan	Kilmurry	Kilrush	II.	23
31	Doonooney	684	0	15	Wexford	Bantry	Doonooney	Wexford	I.	300
59	Doonoor	39	1	7	Tipperary, S.R.	Clanwilliam	Donohill	Tipperary	II.	307
59	Doonoor	50	1	18	Tipperary, S.R.	Clanwilliam	Templenoe	Tipperary	II.	311
36	Doonore North	216	3	9	Kerry	Corkaguiny	Kilgobban	Tralee	II.	177
36, 45	Doonore South	207	1	39	Kerry	Corkaguiny	Kilgobban	Tralee	II.	177
129, 130	Doonour	240	3	10	Cork, W.R.	West Carbery(W.D.)	Kilcrohane	Bantry	II.	143
122	Doonowen	279	1	20j	Galway	Kiltartan	Kilmacduagh	Gort	IV.	48
5, 8	Doonowney	569	3	6	Sligo	Carbury	Drumcliff	Sligo	IV.	221
43	Doonpeter	556	2	32	Cork, E.R.	Barrymore	Dunbulloge	Cork	II.	54
51	Doonreaghan	158	3	39	Galway	Ballynahinch	Moyrus	Clifden	IV.	13
58	Doonryan	135	2	18	Kerry	Magunihy	Kilcummin	Killarney	II.	201
28, 29	Doons	262	1	4	Tyrone	Dungannon Upper	Kildress	Cookstown	III.	308
31	Doonsallagh East	919	0	15	Clare	Ibrickan	Kilmurry	Ennistimon	II.	23
31	Doonsallagh West	454	0	15	Clare	Ibrickan	Kilmurry	Ennistimon	II.	23
4, 5	Doonshaskin	190	3	20	Sligo	Carbury	Ahamlish	Sligo	IV.	219
53	Doonsheane	417	2	12	Kerry	Corkaguiny	Dingle	Dingle	II.	175
34	Doonsheheen	264	1	3	Sligo	Tirerrill	Kilmacallan	Sligo	IV.	240
9, 10, 18	Doonskerdeen	125	3	6	Limerick	Shanid	Robertstown	Glin	II.	257
29	Doon South	174	3	11	Kerry	Trughanacmy	Tralee	Tralee	II.	213
16	Doon South	873	3	9	Limerick	Coonagh	Doon	Tipperary	II.	234
53, 54	Doonties Commons	129	2	22	Kerry	Corkaguiny	Minard	Dingle	II.	180
54	Doonties East	37	2	38	Kerry	Corkaguiny	Minard	Dingle	II.	179
53, 54	Doonties West	414	2	33	Kerry	Corkaguiny	Minard	Dingle	II.	180
16	Doon T.	—			Limerick	Coonagh	Doon	Tipperary	II.	234
67	Doontrusk	471	3	20k	Mayo	Burrishoole	Burrishoole	Newport	IV.	119
49	Doonty	356	2	22	Mayo	Gallen	Killasser	Swineford	IV.	149
73, 74	Doon Upper	1,126	3	20	Galway	Kilconnell	Fohanagh	Mountbellew	IV.	40
1	*Doonvinalla*	6	2	0	Mayo	Erris	Kilcommon	Belmullet	IV.	145
23	Doonvullen Lower	256	2	6	Limerick	Clanwilliam	Ballybrood	Limerick	II.	221
23	Doonvullen Upper	350	0	38	Limerick	Clanwilliam	Ballybrood	Limerick	II.	221
4	Doon West	242	0	18	Kerry	Iraghticonnor	Killehenny	Listowel	II.	191
45, 59	Doonwood	323	3	14	Galway	Tiaquin	Killoscobe	Mountbellew	IV.	78
1, 6	Doony	302	2	1	Cork, E.R.	Orrery and Kilmore	Kilbolane	Kanturk	II.	108

(a) Including 13A. 0R. 16P. water.
(b) Including 2A. 1R. 15P. water.
(c) Including 11A. 0R. 17P. water.
(d) Including 63A. 2R. 16P. water.

(e) Including 74A. 2R. 26P. water.
(f) Including 14A. 3R. 38P. water.
(g) Including 18A. 1R. 11P. water.
(h) Including 17A. 1R. 1P. water.

(i) Including 1A. 0R. 0P. water.
(j) Including 43A. 2R. 12P. water.
(k) Including 59A. 3R. 34P. water.

No. of Sheet of the Ordnance Survey Maps.	Townlands and Towns.	Area in Statute Acres.			County.	Barony.	Parish.	Poor Law Union in 1857.	Townland Census of 1851, Part I.	
		A.	R.	P.					Vol.	Page
12	Doonycoy	176	0	28	Sligo	Tireragh	Templeboy	Dromore West	IV.	236
5	Doonyvardan	344	3	17	Clare	Burren	Rathborney	Ballyvaghan	II.	14
35	Doora	86	1	7	Leitrim	Mohill	Annaduff	Mohill	IV.	105
24, 27	Dooraa	265	0	2	Monaghan	Cremorne	Aghnamullen	Castleblayney	III.	258
28	Dooraa	172	1	25	Monaghan	Farney	Donaghmoyne	Carrickmacross	III.	269
5	Dooraa North	239	1	2	Fermanagh	Lurg	Drumkeeran	Lowtherstown	III.	206
5	Dooraa South	173	1	15	Fermanagh	Lurg	Drumkeeran	Lowtherstown	III.	206
62	Doorabble	134	1	30	Donegal	Raphoe	Raphoe	Letterkenny	III.	141
13	Dooradoyle	467	2	7	Limerick	Pubblebrien	Mungret	Limerick	II.	254
39	Dooragh	107	0	13	Tyrone	Dungannon Middle	Donaghenry	Cookstown	III.	301
44, 54	Doorah	217	3	2	Kerry	Corkaguiny	Ballinvoher	Dingle	II.	174
32	Dooraheen	139	2	24	Westmeath	Moycashel	Castletownkindalen	Mullingar	I.	277
6, 11	Doorat	929	2	33	Tyrone	Strabane Lower	Donaghedy	Gortin	III.	320
18, 22	Doorath	494	2	24	Kilkenny	Crannagh	Ballycallan	Kilkenny	I.	84
119, 122	Doorath	216	0	35	Mayo	Kilmaine	Kilmainemore	Ballinrobe	IV.	156
22	Dooreagh	533	3	28	Cavan	Clankee	Drumgoon	Cootehill	III.	72
39, 40	Dooree Commons	444	3	20	Tipperary, N.R.	Kilnamanagh Upper	Moyaliff	Thurles	II.	279
43	Dooreel	1,177	2	8*a*	Mayo	Erris	Kilcommon	Newport	IV.	143
74, 75	Doorian	296	0	35	Donegal	Boylagh	Inishkeel	Glenties	III.	112
45, 46, 52	Doorish	516	0	24	Tipperary, S.R.	Kilnamanagh Lower	Clonoulty	Cashel	II.	323
39	Doorless	106	3	39	Tyrone	Dungannon Upper	Derryloran	Cookstown	III.	307
30, 38	Doorlus	172	1	7	Limerick	Connello Upper	Ballingarry	Croom	II.	230
26	Doorly	273	2	0	Sligo	Corran	Kilmorgan	Sligo	IV.	227
42	Doornane	417	1	15	Kilkenny	Iverk	Pollrone	Waterford	I.	106
42	DOORNANE T.	—			Kilkenny	Iverk	Pollrone	Waterford	I.	106
5, 9	Dooroc	376	2	23	Longford	Longford	Killoe	Longford	I.	159
7	Dooroge	203	0	17	Dublin	Balrothery West	Ballyboghil	Balrothery	I.	22
70, 79	Dooros	85	3	7	Donegal	Raphoe	Clonleigh	Strabane	III.	135
132	Dooros	1,057	3	25	Galway	Leitrim	Ballynakill	Portumna	IV.	51
136	Dooros	66	2	38	Galway	Leitrim	Inishcaltra	Scarriff	IV.	53
100, 108	Dooros	266	0	16	Galway	Longford	Clonfert	Ballinasloe	IV.	57
26, 39, 40	Dooros	535	1	10	Galway	Ross	Cong	Oughterard	IV.	73
79	Dooros	78	2	8*b*	Mayo	Clanmorris	Balla	Castlebar	IV.	132
30	Doorosheath	50	2	3	King's Co.	Eglish	Eglish	Parsonstown	I.	134
34	Dooross	162	0	26	Fermanagh	Magherastephana	Aghalurcher	Lisnaskea	III.	216
27	Dooroy	409	1	21	Galway	Ross	Cong	Oughterard	IV.	73
35, 36, 43	Doorus	141	1	8*c*	Clare	Tulla Lower	Killuran	Tulla	II.	36
90	Doorus	184	0	18	Cork, W.R.	Bear	Kilcaskan	Bantry	II.	122
102, 112	Doorus	261	2	25	Galway	Kiltartan	Kinvarradoorus	Gort	IV.	49
112	Doorus Demesne	90	0	26	Galway	Kiltartan	Kinvarradoorus	Gort	IV.	49
19, 20	Doorus East	259	2	20	Clare	Tulla Upper	Feakle	Tulla	II.	39
112	Dooruspark	136	2	25	Galway	Kiltartan	Kinvarradoorus	Gort	IV.	49
19	Doorus West	165	3	19	Clare	Tulla Upper	Feakle	Tulla	II.	39
20, 25	Doory	89	0	2	Antrim	Lower Glenarm	Layd	Ballycastle	III.	22
89	Doory	794	2	0	Kerry	Iveragh	Dromod	Cahersiveen	II.	194
82	Doory	284	3	12	Kerry	Iveragh	Glanbehy	Cahersiveen	II.	195
87	Doory	584	2	33	Kerry	Iveragh	Killemlagh	Cahersiveen	II.	196
8	Doory	609	2	29	King's Co.	Ballycowan	Durrow	Tullamore	I.	127
23	Doory	606	1	25	Longford	Shrule	Taghshinny	Ballymahon	I.	167
14	Doosky	196	2	1	Monaghan	Cremorne	Clontibret	Monaghan	III.	260
13	Doosky	233	0	0	Monaghan	Dartree	Killeevan	Monaghan	III.	268
24	Dooslattagh	485	2	38	Roscommon	Ballintober North	Kilglass	Strokestown	IV.	186
3	Doostroke	89	2	34	Leitrim	Rosclogher	Rossinver	Ballyshannon	IV.	111
105, 115	Doovilra	118	0	4	Mayo	Murrisk	Kilgeever	Westport	IV.	160
52	Doovoge	182	1	29	Roscommon	Athlone	St. Peter's	Athlone	IV.	184
22	Dooycaghny or Cloonloughan	539	0	0	Sligo	Tireragh	Castleconor	Ballina	IV.	232
63, 76	Dooyeher	347	2	2*d*	Galway	Ballynahinch	Moyrus	Clifden	IV.	13
25, 34	Dooyork	1,164	0	30	Mayo	Erris	Kilcommon	Belmullet	IV.	143
117	Dorans Island	5	1	24	Mayo	Kilmaine	Ballinchalla	Ballinrobe	IV.	152
46	Doras	9	0	20	Tyrone	Dungannon Middle	Tullyniskan	Dungannon	III.	304
32, 33, 41, 42	Dore	964	3	25	Donegal	Kilmacrenan	Tullaghobegly	Dunfanaghy	III.	131
87	Dorinishbeg	5	2	3	Mayo	Burrishoole	Kilmeena	Westport	IV.	122
76, 87	Dorinishmore	9	2	21	Mayo	Burrishoole	Kilmeena	Westport	IV.	122
82	Dorneyswell	64	2	18	Tipperary, S.R.	Iffa and Offa West	Tullaghmelan	Clogheen	II.	321
25, 26	Dornogagh	50	3	11	Fermanagh	Clanawley	Cleenish	Enniskillen	III.	190
11	Dorrary	192	2	38	Roscommon	Boyle	Tumna	Car^k. on Shannon	IV.	197
23	Dorrusawillin	92	3	5	Leitrim	Leitrim	Kiltoghert	Car^k. on Shannon	IV.	101
28	Dorsy	1,423	2	15	Armagh	Fews Upper	Creggan	Castleblayney	III.	48
28	Dorsy (*Cavan O'Hanlon*) or Roxborough	147	0	31	Armagh	Fews Upper	Newtownhamilton	Castleblayney	III.	49
25, 28	Dorsy (*Hearty*)	249	0	26	Armagh	Fews Upper	Newtownhamilton	Castleblayney	III.	49
25, 28	Dorsy (*Macdonald*) or Carrickrovaddy	570	1	20	Armagh	Fews Upper	Newtownhamilton	Castleblayney	III.	49

(a) { Including 267A. 1R. 31P. detached portions. / Including 73A. 0R. 6P. water.

(b) Including 10A. 3R. 22P. water.
(c) Including 4A. 3R. 4P. water.

(d) Including 12A. 2R. 13P. water.

3 D

No. of Sheet of the Ordnance Survey Maps	Townlands and Towns.	Area in Statute Acres.	County.	Barony.	Parish.	Poor Law Union in 1857.	Townland Census of 1851, Part I.	
		A.　R.　P.					Vol.	Page
25, 28	Dorsy (Mullaghglass)	224　0　35	Armagh . .	Fews Upper . .	Newtownhamilton .	Castleblayney .	III.	49
15, 23	Dough . . .	702　0　22	Clare . .	Corcomroe . .	Kilmacrehy . .	Ennistimon .	II.	20
30	Dough . . .	248　3　11	Clare . .	Ibrickan . . .	Kilfarboy . .	Ennistimon .	II.	22
56	Dough . . .	958　0　25	Clare . .	Moyarta . .	Kilfearagh . .	Kilrush . .	II.	32
147, 152	Dough . . .	244　1　0	Cork, W.R. .	West Carbery (W.D.)	Kilmoe . . .	Skull . .	II.	144
12	Doughal . . .	118　2　11	Wexford . .	Ballaghkeen . .	Ardamine . .	Gorey . .	I.	291
74, 86	Doughcloyne . .	381　1　22	Cork, E.R. .	Cork . . .	St. Finbars . .	Cork . .	II.	65
6	Dougher . . .	176　3　29	Armagh . .	Oneilland East .	Shankill . .	Lurgan . .	III.	51
29, 36	Doughil . .	666　0　34	Roscommon .	Roscommon . .	Cloonfinlough .	Strokestown .	IV.	209
93, 94	Doughill . . .	423　1　36	Kerry . .	Glanarought . .	Kenmare . .	Kenmare . .	II.	186
87	Doughill . . .	90　2　1	Tipperary, S.R.	Iffa and Offa West .	Tullaghorton .	Clogheen . .	II.	321
82, 94	Doughiska . .	615　1　18	Galway . .	Galway . . .	Oranmore . .	Galway . .	IV.	37
5, 8	Doughkill . .	189　1　17	Tipperary, N.R.	Lower Ormond .	Loughkeen . .	Parsonstown .	II.	286
23	Doughloon . .	60　3　35	Roscommon .	Roscommon . .	Kiltrustan . .	Strokestown .	IV.	211
34, 38, 39	Douglas . . .	671　1　9	Antrim . .	Lower Antrim .	Glenwhirry . .	Ballymena .	III.	4
33,34,38,39	Douglas . . .	679　0　1	Antrim . .	Lower Antrim .	Racavan . .	Ballymena .	III.	4
74, 86	Douglas . . .	254　0　30	Cork, E.R. .	Cork . . .	Carrigaline . .	Cork . .	II.	64
56	Douglas . . .	308　3　33	Kerry . .	Trughanacmy .	Killorglin . .	Killarney . .	II.	211
45	Douglasland . .	204　2　21	Antrim . .	Upper Antrim .	Kilbride . . .	Antrim . .	III.	6
5, 10, 11	Douglas or Ligfordrum	3,883　1　37	Tyrone . .	Strabane Lower .	Ardstraw . .	Strabane . .	III.	319
74	DOUGLAS T. . .	—	Cork, E.R. .	Cork . . .	Carrigaline . .	Cork . .	II.	64
34, 35	Dovea Lower . .	674　2　39	Tipperary, N.R.	Eliogarty . .	Inch . . .	Thurles . .	II.	270
34, 35, 41	Dovea Upper . .	400　0　0	Tipperary, N.R.	Eliogarty . .	Inch . . .	Thurles . .	II.	270
35	Dovegrove . .	459　2　10	King's Co. .	Eglish . .	Eglish . . .	Parsonstown .	I.	134
31	Dove Hill . .	500　0　39	King's Co. .	Eglish . .	Drumcullen . .	Parsonstown .	I.	134
68	Dovepark . .	46　3　27	Galway . .	Moycullen . .	Moycullen . .	Galway . .	IV.	71
121	Dowagh East . .	70　3　12	Mayo . .	Kilmaine . .	Cong . . .	Ballinrobe .	IV.	153
121	Dowagh West . .	165　3　22	Mayo . .	Kilmaine . .	Cong . . .	Ballinrobe .	IV.	153
7	Dowdallshill . .	442　1　38	Louth . .	Upper Dundalk .	Dundalk . .	Dundalk . .	I.	178
24	Dowdenstown Great	334　2　2	Kildare . .	Naas South . .	Tipperkevin . .	Naas . .	I.	65
24	Dowdenstown Little	109　1　21	Kildare . .	Naas South . .	Tipperkevin . .	Naas . .	I.	65
24	Dowdingstown . .	235　3　32	Kildare . .	Connell . .	Ladytown . .	Naas . .	I.	55
10	Dowdstown . .	199　0　28	Kildare . .	North Salt . .	Laraghbryan .	Celbridge . .	I.	75
14	Dowdstown . .	218　0　15	Louth . .	Ardee . . .	Mapastown . .	Ardee . .	I.	173
11,12,17,18	Dowdstown . .	251　0　38	Meath . .	Morgallion . .	Kilshine . .	Navan . .	I.	210
31	Dowdstown . .	546　0　2a	Meath . .	Skreen . . .	Dowdstown . .	Navan . .	I.	220
31	Dowdstown . .	22　2　3	Meath . .	Skreen . . .	Tara . . .	Navan . .	I.	222
77	Dower . . .	30　1　4	Cork, E.R. .	Imokilly . .	Ightermurragh .	Middleton .	II.	87
77	Dower . . .	270　3　38	Cork, E.R. .	Imokilly . .	Mogeely . .	Middleton .	II.	90
9	Dower . . .	106　1　15	Roscommon .	Frenchpark . .	Kilnamanagh .	Castlereagh .	IV.	204
23, 27	Dowgry . . .	245　3　11	Antrim . .	Kilconway . .	Grange of Dundermot	Ballymena .	III.	26
9	Dowland . .	170　0　39	Londonderry .	Keenaght . .	Aghanloo . .	New T^n Limavady	III.	233
39	Dowling . . .	440　1　20	Kilkenny . .	Iverk . . .	Fiddown . .	Carrick on Suir	I.	105
10	Down . . .	445　1　38	King's Co. .	Lower Philipstown .	Killaderry . .	Tullamore .	I.	143
26	Down . . .	196　2　22	King's Co. .	Upper Philipstown .	Ballykean . .	Mountmellick .	I.	143
12	Down . . .	181　1　6	Westmeath .	Corkaree . .	Tyfarnham . .	Mullingar .	I.	264
20, 26	Downamona . .	174　2　39	Tipperary, N.R.	Upper Ormond .	Kilmore . .	Nenagh . .	II.	291
30,31,37,38	Down, Demesne of .	1,486　3　34b	Down . .	Lecale Upper .	Down . . .	Downpatrick .	III.	180
143	Downeen . . .	885　0　34	Cork, W.R. .	East Carbery (W.D.)	Ross . . .	Clonakilty .	II.	135
26, 27	Downestown . .	373　2　22	Meath . .	Lower Duleek .	Duleek . .	Drogheda .	I.	195
2	Downhill . .	204　2　18	Londonderry .	Coleraine . .	Dunboe . .	Coleraine .	III.	231
29	Downhill or Knocknalyre . .	60　0　37	Sligo . .	Tireragh . .	Kilmoremoy .	Ballina . .	IV.	235
16	Downies . . .	311　2　9	Donegal . .	Kilmacrenan .	Mevagh . .	Milford . .	III.	130
27	Downies Barr . .	183　3　2	Donegal . .	Kilmacrenan .	Mevagh . .	Milford . .	III.	130
27	Downing North .	329　0　36	Cork, E.R. .	Fermoy . .	Kilcrumper . .	Fermoy . .	II.	80
3, 8	Downings . .	691　0　6	Carlow . .	Rathvilly . .	Tullowphelim .	Carlow . .	I.	12
27	Downings . .	127　1　5	Wicklow . .	Upper Talbotstown .	Kilranelagh . .	Baltinglass .	I.	364
13	Downings North .	878　1　39	Kildare . .	Clane . . .	Downings . .	Naas . .	I.	54
27	Downing South .	293　1　17	Cork, E.R. .	Fermoy . .	Kilcrumper . .	Fermoy . .	II.	80
13	Downings South .	475　2　32	Kildare . .	Clane . . .	Downings . .	Naas . .	I.	54
37	Downkillybegs .	468　1　8c	Antrim . .	Upper Toome .	Drummaul . .	Ballymena .	III.	34
137	Downmacpatrick or Oldhead . .	202　1　10	Cork, W.R. .	Courceys . .	Ringrone . .	Kinsale . .	II.	147
37	DOWNPATRICK T. .	—	Down . .	Lecale Upper .	Down . . .	Downpatrick .	III.	181
37	Downs . . .	174　1　13	Limerick . .	Connello Upper .	Ballingarry . .	Croom . .	II.	230
14	Downs . . .	90　2　6	Monaghan .	Cremorne . .	Clontibret . .	Monaghan .	III.	260
13	Downs . . .	71　3　25	Queen's Co. .	Maryborough East .	Borris . .	Mountmellick .	I.	240
38	Downs . . .	156　2　14	Tyrone . .	Dungannon Upper .	Desertcreat . .	Cookstown .	III.	307
12	Downs . . .	175　1　12	Westmeath .	Corkaree . .	Taghmon . .	Mullingar .	I.	264
10	Downs . . .	110　0　00	Wicklow . .	Newcastle . .	Kilcoole . .	Rathdrum .	I.	351
12	Downs or Drumarg	171　0　32	Armagh . .	Armagh . .	Armagh . .	Armagh . .	III.	43
12, 13	Downshill . .	839　2　10	Wicklow . .	Newcastle . .	Calary . .	Rathdrum .	I.	350

(a) Including 5A. 1R. 26P. River Boyne.　　　　(b) Including 34A. 3R. 0P. water.　　　　(c) Including 12A. 3R. 0P. water.

No. of Sheet of the Ordnance Survey Maps.	Townlands and Towns.	Area in Statute Acres.	County.	Barony.	Parish.	Poor Law Union in 1857.	Townland Census of 1851, Part I.	
		A. R. P.					Vol.	Page
5	Dowra	311 1 23	Cavan	Tullyhaw	Killinagh	Enniskillen	III.	92
27	Dowrea	193 2 29	Sligo	Tirerrill	Kilross	Sligo	IV.	241
19, 20	Dowth	1,221 3 17a	Meath	Upper Slane	Dowth	Drogheda	I.	224
18	Dowthstown	63 2 22	Meath	Morgallion	Clongill	Navan	I.	209
38	Dragh	116 3 22	Fermanagh	Knockninny	Kinawley	Lisnaskea	III.	201
16, 19	Draghanstown	319 1 21	Louth	Ferrard	Dunany	Ardee	I.	180
9, 15	Dragoonhill	226 2 11	Wicklow	Lower Talbotstown	Hollywood	Baltinglass	I.	360
61	Drain	125 1 16	Tyrone	Dungannon Middle	Clonfeacle	Dungannon	III.	299
3, 6	Drain	459 1 6	Tyrone	Strabane Lower	Donaghedy	Strabane	III.	320
35	Drains	395 0 37	Antrim	Upper Glenarm	Grange of Killyglen	Larne	III.	24
35	Drains Bog	316 1 2	Antrim	Upper Glenarm	Carncastle	Larne	III.	24
19	Drakeland Lower	104 0 7	Kilkenny	Shillelogher	St. Patrick's	Kilkenny	I.	116
19	Drakeland Middle	230 0 11	Kilkenny	Shillelogher	St. Patrick's	Kilkenny	I.	116
19	Drakeland Upper	40 0 35	Kilkenny	Shillelogher	St. Patrick's	Kilkenny	I.	116
11	Drakerath	925 0 12	Meath	Lower Kells	Staholmog	Kells	I.	204
17, 20	Drakestown	364 1 25	Louth	Ardee	Kildemock	Ardee	I.	172
11, 12	Drakestown	793 3 28	Meath	Morgallion	Drakestown	Navan	I.	209
24, 26	Dranagh	1,074 2 14	Carlow	St. Mullins Lower	St. Mullins	New Ross	I.	13
21	Dranagh	568 3 9	Wexford	Ballaghkeen	Kilcormick	Enniscorthy	I.	294
19, 25	Dranagh	403 2 2	Wexford	Bantry	Rossdroit	Enniscorthy	I.	302
68, 75	Drangan Beg	440 1 17	Tipperary, S.R.	Clanwilliam	Killardry	Tipperary	II.	308
68, 75	Drangan More	430 2 32	Tipperary, S.R.	Clanwilliam	Killardry	Tipperary	II.	308
5	Drangan or Mountedward	307 0 26	Sligo	Carbury	Ahamlish	Sligo	IV.	219
63	DRANGAN T.	—	Tipperary, S.R.	Middlethird	Drangan	Cashel	II.	326
40	DRAPERSTOWN T.	—	Londonderry	Loughinsholin	Ballynascreen	Magherafelt	III.	239
51	Draughton	286 2 16	Tyrone	Clogher	Donacavey	Omagh	III.	294
54	Drean	200 3 30	Donegal	Raphoe	Raymoghy	Letterkenny	III.	141
53, 54	Dredolt & Dristernan	293 2 23	Tyrone	Dungannon Middle	Donaghmore	Dungannon	III.	302
28,29,35,36	Dree	1,342 1 16	Down	Upper Iveagh, Lr. pt.	Dromara	Banbridge	III.	172
18	Dreelingstown	289 2 15	Kilkenny	Crannagh	Ballycallan	Kilkenny	I.	84
54, 55	Dreemore	248 0 26	Tyrone	Dungannon Middle	Killyman	Dungannon	III.	303
26	Dreen	394 3 10	Antrim	Kilconway	Rasharkin	Ballymoney	III.	27
32	Dreen	365 2 36	Antrim	Lower Toome	Ahoghill	Ballymena	III.	32
29, 30, 34	Dreen	2,128 1 26	Londonderry	Tirkeeran	Banagher	Londonderry	III.	247
38, 46	Dreenan	64 2 22	Limerick	Connello Upper	Corcomohide	Croom	II.	232
8, 13, 14	Dreenagh	903 1 5	Kerry	Clanmaurice	Ballyheige	Tralee	II.	168
71, 72	Dreenagh	595 3 25	Kerry	Iveragh	Glanbehy	Cahersiveen	II.	195
16, 24	Dreenagh East	230 3 31	Cork, E.R.	Orrery and Kilmore	Buttevant	Mallow	II.	107
16, 24	Dreenagh West	196 1 32	Cork, E.R.	Orrery and Kilmore	Buttevant	Mallow	II.	107
25	Dreenan	88 0 20	Cavan	Upper Loughtee	Kilmore	Cavan	III.	84
78	Dreenan	295 1 17b	Donegal	Raphoe	Donaghmore	Stranorlar	III.	137
4	Dreenan	188 0 29	Fermanagh	Lurg	Templecarn	Lowtherstown	III.	209
8	Dreenan	371 1 6	Kildare	Carbury	Ardkill	Edenderry	I.	51
33, 37	Dreenan	1,425 1 36	Londonderry	Loughinsholin	Maghera	Magherafelt	III.	242
15	Dreenan	459 3 22c	Tyrone	Omagh West	Termonamongan	Castlederg	III.	317
8, 9	Drehid	2,161 2 11	Kildare	Carbury	Ardkill	Edenderry	I.	51
21	Drehidtarsna	244 1 27	Limerick	Coshna	Drehidtarsna	Rathkeale	II.	242
56	Dreigh	243 1 35	Tyrone	Omagh East	Kilskeery	Enniskillen	III.	313
12, 18	Dreminstown	200 1 13	Meath	Upper Slane	Rathkenny	Navan	I.	225
15	Drennan	305 3 19	Down	Castlereagh Upper	Drumbo	Lisburn	III.	164
79	Dresnagh	124 0 39	Donegal	Raphoe	Urney	Strabane	III.	144
5, 9	Dressogagh	80 1 8	Armagh	Oneilland West	Tartaraghan	Armagh	III.	54
11	Dressogagh	63 2 12	Armagh	Tiranny	Eglish	Armagh	III.	59
28	Dressoge	91 1 38	Fermanagh	Magherastephana	Aghavea	Lisnaskea	III.	218
41, 42	Dressoge	202 1 8	Tyrone	Omagh East	Dromore	Omagh	III.	311
34	Dressoge	844 1 8	Tyrone	Omagh West	Longfield East	Omagh	III.	315
16	Dresternagh	312 1 28	Cavan	Tullygarvey	Annagh	Cootehill	III.	87
36	Dresternan	139 1 20	Fermanagh	Clankelly	Clones	Clones	III.	186
38, 39	Dresternan	274 0 23	Fermanagh	Knockninny	Kinawley	Lisnaskea	III.	201
14	Dresternan	184 3 36d	Fermanagh	Magheraboy	Inishmacsaint	Ballyshannon	III.	212
28	Drewsborough	518 3 31e	Clare	Tulla Upper	Tomgraney	Scarriff	II.	41
46	Drewscourt East	991 3 8	Limerick	Connello Upper	Corcomohide	Croom	II.	232
46	Drewscourt West	627 2 35	Limerick	Connello Upper	Corcomohide	Croom	II.	232
23	Drewstown Great	557 1 27f	Meath	Upper Kells	Girley	Kells	I.	205
23	Drewstown Little	478 2 34	Meath	Upper Kells	Girley	Castletowndelvin	I.	205
39	Drillistown	156 1 25	Wexford	Shelburne	Killesk	New Ross	I.	327
34	Drim	217 1 32	Clare	Bunratty Upper	Doora	Ennis	II.	8
11	Drim	572 3 13	Queen's Co.	Upperwoods	Offerlane	Mountmellick	I.	251
28	Drim	272 0 17	Wicklow	Upper Talbotstown	Kiltegan	Baltinglass	I.	364
48	Drimagh	11 3 29	Wexford	Forth	Rosslare	Wexford	I.	313
30	Drimaterril	330 1 35	Queen's Co.	Cullenagh	Dysartgallen	Abbeyleix	I.	239
68	Drimcong	117 2 22g	Galway	Moycullen	Moycullen	Galway	IV.	71

(a) Including 24A. 3R. 3P. water.
(b) Including 6A. 2R. 15P. water.
(c) Including 2A. 1R. 27P. water.

(d) Including 45A. 1R. 8P. water.
(e) Including 17A. 2R. 13P. water.

(f) Including 10A. 1R. 0P. water.
(g) Including 12A. 2R. 21P. water.

No. of Sheet of the Ordnance Survey Maps.	Townlands and Towns.	Area in Statute Acres.	County.	Barony.	Parish.	Poor Law Union in 1857.	Townland Census of 1851, Part I.	
		A. R. P.					Vol.	Page
26	Drimeen . .	59 1 3	Kilkenny . .	Callan . . .	Callan . . .	Callan . .	I.	83
26	Drimeen North .	26 2 4	Kilkenny . .	Callan . . .	Callan . . .	Callan . .	I.	83
26	Drimeen South .	5 1 32	Kilkenny . .	Callan . . .	Callan . . .	Callan . .	I.	83
11	Drimhill or Quarry-farm . . .	71 2 35	Queen's Co. .	Upperwoods . .	Offerlane . .	Mountmellick .	I.	251
31, 37	Drimina . .	635 1 17	Sligo . .	Leyny . . .	Kilmacteige .	Tobercurry .	IV.	231
133	Driminidy North .	262 1 20	Cork, W.R.	West Carbery (E.D.)	Drinagh . .	Skibbereen .	II.	139
133	Driminidy South .	548 3 33	Cork, W.R.	West Carbery (E.D.)	Drinagh . .	Skibbereen .	II.	139
68, 81	Drimmavohaun .	497 0 26a	Galway . .	Moycullen . .	Moycullen . .	Galway . .	IV.	71
36	Drimmeen . .	248 2 33	Clare . .	Tulla Lower .	Killuran . .	Tulla . .	II.	36
35	Drimmeen . .	257 1 15	Galway . .	Ballynahinch .	Ballindoon . .	Clifden . .	IV.	10
36, 44	Drimmeennagun .	162 2 12	Clare . .	Tulla Lower .	Killuran . .	Tulla . .	II.	36
11	Drimmo . . .	142 3 4	Queen's Co. .	Upperwoods . .	Offerlane . .	Mountmellick .	I.	251
67	Drimna . . .	68 2 0	Clare . .	Moyarta . .	Kilrush . .	Kilrush . .	II.	33
28	Drimna . . .	113 1 12	Leitrim . .	Mohill . .	Mohill . .	Mohill . .	IV.	107
99, 100	Drimna Beg . .	349 3 27	Kerry . .	Dunkerron South .	Kilcrohane .	Kenmare . .	II.	183
126	Drimna East . .	76 2 0	Galway . .	Leitrim . .	Tynagh . .	Portumna .	IV.	55
18, 22	Drimnagh . .	274 3 36	Dublin . .	Uppercross . .	Drimnagh . .	Dublin South .	I.	40
22	Drimnagh . .	230 1 31	Roscommon .	Roscommon . .	Ogulla . .	Strokestown .	IV.	212
54, 67	Drimnahoon . .	88 0 24	Galway . .	Moycullen . .	Killannin . .	Oughterard .	IV.	69
100	Drimna More . .	785 0 17	Kerry . .	Dunkerron South .	Kilcrohane .	Kenmare . .	II.	183
126	Drimna West . .	77 1 14	Galway . .	Leitrim . .	Tynagh . .	Portumna .	IV.	55
54, 67	Drimneen . .	39 1 34	Galway . .	Moycullen . .	Kilcummin . .	Oughterard .	IV.	67
68	Drimneen . .	59 3 14b	Galway . .	Moycullen . .	Moycullen . .	Galway . .	IV.	71
28, 29, 36	Drin . . .	1,176 3 11	Down . .	Upper Iveagh, Lr. pt.	Dromara . .	Banbridge .	III.	172
13, 26	Drin . . .	697 3 2	Galway . .	Ross . .	Ross . .	Oughterard .	IV.	74
24	Drinagh . . .	484 3 12	Clare . .	Inchiquin . .	Rath . .	Ennistimon .	II.	27
35	Drinagh . . .	393 2 0c	Galway . .	Ballynahinch .	Ballindoon . .	Clifden . .	IV.	10
22,23,30,31	Drinagh . . .	1,683 1 10	King's Co. .	Eglish . .	Eglish . .	Parsonstown .	I.	135
7	Drinagh . . .	178 0 29	Queen's Co. .	Tinnahinch .	Rosenallis .	Mountmellick .	I.	250
30	Drinagh . . .	1,323 0 2d	Roscommon .	Roscommon . .	Lissonuffy .	Strokestown .	IV.	212
48, 53	Drinagh . . .	31 3 1	Wexford . .	Forth . .	St. Margaret's .	Wexford . .	I.	314
21	Drinaghan . .	108 2 29	Mayo . .	Tirawley . .	Kilfian . .	Killala . .	IV.	169
14	Drinaghan . .	371 0 14	Sligo . .	Carbury . .	Killaspugbrone .	Sligo . .	IV.	222
3, 6	Drinaghan . .	565 1 1	Sligo . .	Carbury . .	Rossinver .	Sligo . .	IV.	223
16, 17	Drinaghan Beg .	161 3 7	Sligo . .	Tireragh . .	Kilglass . .	Dromore West .	IV.	234
17	Drinaghan More .	206 2 11	Sligo . .	Tireragh . .	Kilglass . .	Dromore West .	IV.	234
121	Drinagh East . .	448 3 28e	Cork, W.R.	East Carbery (W.D.)	Drinagh . .	Dunmanway .	II.	131
31	Drinagh and Knockhill . . .	436 1 10	King's Co. .	Ballyboy . .	Ballyboy . .	Parsonstown .	I.	123
42, 43	Drinagh North .	109 0 15	Wexford . .	Forth . .	Drinagh . .	Wexford . .	I.	309
42, 43	Drinagh South .	74 2 32	Wexford . .	Forth . .	Drinagh . .	Wexford . .	I.	309
120	Drinagh West . .	270 3 11f	Cork, W.R.	East Carbery (W.D.)	Drinagh . .	Dunmanway .	II.	131
11, 12	Drinan . . .	441 2 33	Dublin . .	Coolock . .	Kinsaley . .	Balrothery .	I.	28
22,23,26,27	Drinan . . .	391 0 0	Longford . .	Ratheline .	Shrule . .	Ballymahon .	I.	165
148	Drinane . . .	156 1 21	Cork, W.R.	West Carbery(W.D.)	Skull . .	Skull . .	II.	146
29	Drinaun . . .	37 3 15	Galway . .	Dunmore . .	Tuam . .	Tuam . .	IV.	36
33, 47	Drinaun . . .	873 1 31	Galway . .	Killian . .	Killeroran .	Mountbellew .	IV.	44
22, 23	Drinaun . . .	470 3 29g	Roscommon .	Roscommon . .	Elphin . .	Strokestown .	IV.	209
38	Drinaun . . .	121 1 26	Sligo . .	Corran . .	Cloonoghil .	Tobercurry .	IV.	225
32, 38	Drinaun Bog . .	10 2 10	Sligo . .	Corran . .	Cloonoghil .	Tobercurry .	IV.	225
14, 20	Drincy . . .	520 1 0	Roscommon .	Frenchpark .	Tibohine . .	Castlereagh .	IV.	205
14	Dring . . .	182 1 5h	Cavan . .	Tullyhunco .	Kildallan .	Bawnboy .	III.	97
16	Dring . . .	133 0 7	Fermanagh .	Lurg . .	Derryvullan .	Lowtherstown .	III.	204
6	Dring . . .	241 2 0	Longford . .	Granard . .	Columbkille .	Granard . .	I.	156
120	Dringeen Eighter .	211 3 10i	Mayo . .	Kilmaine .	Cong . .	Ballinrobe .	IV.	153
120	Dringeen Middle .	180 3 23	Mayo . .	Kilmaine .	Cong . .	Ballinrobe .	IV.	153
120	Dringeen Oughter .	329 0 18	Mayo . .	Kilmaine .	Cong . .	Ballinrobe .	IV.	153
19	Drinmore . .	109 2 26j	Westmeath .	Moyashel and Magheradernon .	Rathconnell .	Mullingar .	I.	276
17	Drinnanstown North	404 0 21	Kildare . .	Offaly East .	Cloncurry .	Edenderry .	I.	69
17	Drinnanstown South	404 0 23	Kildare . .	Offaly East .	Cloncurry .	Edenderry .	I.	69
24	Driny . . .	293 2 36k	Leitrim . .	Leitrim . .	Kiltubbrid .	Car'k. on Shannon	IV.	103
72	Dripsey Lower T.	—	Cork, E.R.	East Muskerry .	Inishcarra .	Cork . .	II.	104
72	Dripsey Upper T.	—	Cork, E.R.	East Muskerry .	Inishcarra .	Cork . .	II.	104
41	Drish . . .	160 0 38	Tipperary, N.R.	Eliogarty .	Rahelty . .	Thurles . .	II.	272
16, 22	Drishaghan or Cherryfield . .	174 0 2	Roscommon .	Roscommon . .	Shankill . .	Strokestown .	IV.	212
26	Drishaghaun . .	512 0 19	Galway . .	Ross . .	Ross . .	Oughterard .	IV.	74
100	Drishaghaun . .	239 0 3	Mayo . .	Kilmaine .	Mayo . .	Ballinrobe .	IV.	157
9, 15	Drishaghaun . .	375 0 26	Roscommon .	Frenchpark .	Kilcolagh .	Boyle . .	IV.	200
2	Drishaghaun East .	176 2 3	Roscommon .	Castlereagh .	Baslick . .	Castlereagh .	IV.	199
21, 27	Drishaghaun West .	166 3 34	Roscommon .	Castlereagh .	Baslick . .	Castlereagh .	IV.	199
142, 151	Drishane . .	77 2 38	Cork, W.R.	West Carbery (E.D.)	Castlehaven .	Skibbereen .	II.	138

(a) Including 8A. 1R. 27P. water.　　(e) Including 1A. 0R. 24P. water.　　(i) Including 7A. 1R. 8P. water.
(b) Including 3A. 3R. 14P. water.　　(f) Including 2A. 0R. 27P. water.　　(j) Including 13A. 2R. 20P. water.
(c) Including 14A. 1R. 17P. water.　　(g) Including 97A. 3R. 0P. water.　　(k) Including 90A. 0R. 20P. water.
(d) Including 1A. 0R. 0P. water.　　(h) Including 14A. 0R. 23P. water.

No. of Sheet of the Ordnance Survey Maps.	Townlands and Towns.	Area in Statute Acres.	County.	Barony.	Parish.	Poor Law Union in 1857.	Townland Census of 1851. Part I.	
		A. R. P.					Vol.	Page
130, 139	Drishane	324 3 2	Cork, W.R.	West Carbery(W.D.)	Skull	Skull	II.	146
59	Drishane	249 0 21	Tipperary, S.R.	Clanwilliam	Rathlynin	Tipperary	II.	309
66, 67	Drishane Beg	168 0 13	Cork, E.R.	Imokilly	Ardagh	Youghal	II.	83
141, 150	Drishanebeg	336 1 9a	Cork, W.R.	West Carbery (E.D.)	Abbeystrowry	Skibbereen	II.	136
39	Drishane Beg	383 0 35b	Cork, W.R.	West Muskerry	Drishane	Millstreet	II.	156
66, 67	Drishane More	213 1 12	Cork, E.R.	Imokilly	Killeagh	Youghal	II.	88
150	Drishanemore	300 1 26	Cork, W.R.	West Carbery (E.D.)	Creagh	Skibbereen	II.	139
39	Drishane More	278 1 5	Cork, W.R.	West Muskerry	Drishane	Millstreet	II.	156
141	Drisheen	239 0 12	Cork, W.R.	West Carbery (E.D.)	Aghadown	Skibbereen	II.	137
7	Drishoge	306 1 6	Dublin	Balrothery West	Ballyboghil	Balrothery	I.	22
14, 18	Drishoge	188 1 16	Dublin	Coolock	Clonturk	Dublin North	I.	27
18	Drishoge	18 0 38	Dublin	Coolock	St. Georges	Dublin North	I.	29
7	Drishoge	100 3 25	Dublin	Nethercross	Killossery	Balrothery	I.	31
31	Drishoge	38 3 28	Leitrim	Leitrim	Annaduff	Cark.on Shannon	IV.	99
11	Drishoge	79 2 38	Roscommon	Boyle	Killukin	Cark.on Shannon	IV.	195
76	Drishoge	105 1 22	Tipperary, S.R.	Iffa and Offa East	Newchapel	Clonmel	II.	315
22	Drishoge or Strawberry hill	182 1 12	King's Co.	Garrycastle	Gallen	Parsonstown	I.	136
13	Drisoge	55 2 23	Carlow	Forth	Ballon	Carlow	I.	3
30	Drissoge	441 1 24	Meath	Lune	Athboy	Trim	I.	207
12	Dristernan	508 2 21	Donegal	Inishowen East	Culdaff	Inishowen	III.	118
32	Dristernan	135 1 20c	Leitrim	Leitrim	Annaduff	Cark.on Shannon	IV.	99
53, 54	Dristernan and Dredolt	293 2 23	Tyrone	Dungannon Middle	Donaghmore	Dungannon	III.	302
23	Dristernaun	66 0 28	Leitrim	Leitrim	Kiltoghert	Cark. on Shannon	IV.	101
35	Droagh	146 2 13	Antrim	Upper Glenarm	Carncastle	Larne	III.	24
10, 15	Drogan	102 0 22	Fermanagh	Lurg	Derryvullan	Lowtherstown	III.	204
19	Droghed	150 0 24	Londonderry	Coleraine	Aghadowey	Coleraine	III.	229
10	Droghill	138 2 6	Cavan	Lower Loughtee	Drumlane	Cavan	III.	80
18	Droit	768 2 35d	Tyrone	Strabane Upper	Bodoney Lower	Gortin	III.	323
23	Drokaghbane	198 3 9e	Cavan	Clankee	Drumgoon	Cootehill	III.	72
27, 28	Droles	107 3 32	Fermanagh	Magherastephana	Aghalurcher	Lisnaskea	III.	216
15, 20	Drollagh	308 1 16	Monaghan	Cremorne	Muckno	Castleblayney	III.	261
17, 18	Drollagh	180 2 38	Monaghan	Dartree	Aghabog	Cootehill	III.	263
133, 142	Drom	211 3 20	Cork, W.R.	East Carbery (W.D.)	Kilfaughnabeg	Skibbereen	II.	133
1, 4	Drom	87 2 0	Kerry	Iraghticonnor	Kilconly	Listowel	II.	191
63	Drom	491 2 0	Kerry	Iveragh	Glanbehy	Cahersiveen	II.	196
67, 68	Drom	529 0 7	Kerry	Magunihy	Kilcummin	Killarney	II.	201
28,29,34,35	Drom	816 2 36	Tipperary, N.R.	Eliogarty	Drom	Thurles	II.	269
105	Dromacappul	90 1 22	Cork, W.R.	Bantry	Kilmocomoge	Bantry	II.	120
105	Dromaclarig	95 2 14	Cork, W.R.	Bantry	Kilmocomoge	Bantry	II.	120
111	Dromaclaurig	746 1 17	Kerry	Glanarought	Tuosist	Kenmare	II.	188
118	Dromacoosane	71 3 21	Cork, W.R.	Bantry	Kilmocomoge	Bantry	II.	120
85	Dromacoosh	596 1 12	Kerry	Glanarought	Kilgarvan	Kenmare	II.	187
60	Dromacullen	206 3 25	Cork, W.R.	East Muskerry	Aghinagh	Macroom	II.	154
39	Dromacummer East	220 2 16	Limerick	Coshma	Bruree	Kilmallock	II.	242
39	Dromacummer West	193 1 38	Limerick	Coshma	Bruree	Kilmallock	II.	242
35	Dromada	185 3 10	Limerick	Shanid	Rathronan	Newcastle	II.	257
50, 62	Dromada (Duke)	567 0 12f	Mayo	Gallen	Killasser	Swineford	IV.	149
50, 62	Dromada (Gore)	287 1 34g	Mayo	Gallen	Killasser	Swineford	IV.	149
62	Dromada (Joyce)	165 3 18h	Mayo	Gallen	Killasser	Swineford	IV.	149
77	Dromadda Beg	219 1 7	Cork, E.R.	Imokilly	Ightermurragh	Middleton	II.	87
22, 23	Dromadda Beg	855 1 24	Kerry	Clanmaurice	Kilshenane	Listowel	II.	172
77	Dromadda East	8 3 30	Cork, E.R.	Imokilly	Ightermurragh	Middleton	II.	87
77	Dromadda More	195 0 35	Cork, E.R.	Imokilly	Ballyoughtera	Middleton	II.	84
22,23,30,31	Dromadda More	2,000 3 27	Kerry	Clanmaurice	Kilshenane	Listowel	II.	172
58	Dromadeesirt	283 0 5	Kerry	Magunihy	Kilcummin	Killarney	II.	201
150	Dromadoon	137 1 35i	Cork, W.R.	West Carbery (E.D.)	Creagh	Skibbereen	II.	139
18	Dromagarraun	281 3 16	Limerick	Shanid	Kilmoylan	Glin	II.	256
70	Dromagarry	221 1 13	Cork, W.R.	West Muskerry	Clondrohid	Macroom	II.	155
30, 31	Dromagh	446 2 33	Cork, E.R.	Duhallow	Dromtarriff	Kanturk	II.	71
102	Dromagorteen	297 1 14	Kerry	Glanarought	Kilcaskan	Kenmare	II.	186
116, 117	Dromagowlane	240 2 0	Cork, W.R.	Bear	Kilcaskan	Castletown	II.	122
30	Dromahoe	568 2 10j	Cork, E.R.	Duhallow	Dromtarriff	Kanturk	II.	71
35	Dromain	223 2 9	Antrim	Upper Glenarm	Grange of Killyglen	Larne	III.	24
6	Dromalivaun	364 2 38	Kerry	Iraghticonnor	Aghavallen	Listowel	II.	189
71,72,81,82	Dromalonhurt	1,805 3 28	Kerry	Iveragh	Glanbehy	Cahersiveen	II.	196
65	Dromaloughane	166 1 39	Kerry	Dunkerron North	Knockane	Killarney	II.	182
23, 31	Dromalour	412 2 29	Cork, E.R.	Duhallow	Dromtarriff	Kanturk	II.	71
15, 24	Dromalta	322 2 33	Limerick	Owneybeg	Tuogh	Limerick	II.	251
10	Dromalught	607 2 11	Kerry	Iraghticonnor	Galey	Listowel	II.	190
29	Dromana	343 2 38	Waterford	Decies within Drum	Aglish	Dungarvan	II.	349
29	Dromana	759 1 26	Waterford	Decies without Drum	Affane	Dungarvan	II.	353

(a) Including 0A. 0R. 6P. water.
(b) Including 10A. 1R. 24P. water.
(c) Including 11A. 3R. 6P. water.
(d) Including 13A. 1R. 22P. water.

(e) Including 42A. 2R. 28P. water.
(f) Including 2A. 3R. 23P. water.
(g) Including 3A. 3R. 39P. water.

(h) Including 5A. 2R. 13P. water.
(i) Including 4A. 1R. 7P. water.
(j) Including 6A. 0R. 32P. water.

No. of Sheet of the Ordnance Survey Maps.	Townlands and Towns.	Area in Statute Acres.			County.	Barony.	Parish.	Poor Law Union in 1857.	Townland Census of 1851, Part I.	
		A.	R.	P.					Vol.	Page
21, 29	*Dromana Island*	2	1	8	Waterford	Decies without Drum	Affane	Lismore	II.	353
80, 81	Dromanallig	328	0	20	Cork, W.R.	West Muskerry	Inchigeelagh	Macroom	II.	157
22	Dromanarrigle	467	1	3	Cork, E.R.	Duhallow	Kilmeen	Kanturk	II.	72
105	Dromanassa	82	1	10a	Cork, W.R.	Bantry	Kilmocomoge	Bantry	II.	120
93, 102	Dromanassig	466	3	31	Kerry	Glanarought	Kenmare	Kenmare	II.	186
32	Dromaneen	790	2	7b	Cork, E.R.	Duhallow	Kilshannig	Mallow	II.	74
6	Dromanig	297	2	25	Cork, E.R.	Duhallow	Tullylease	Kanturk	II.	76
28	Dromara	242	0	13	Down	Lower Iveagh, Lr. pt.	Dromara	Lisburn	III.	167
89	Dromaragh	528	1	27	Kerry	Iveragh	Dromod	Cahersiveen	II.	194
28	DROMARA T.	—			Down	Lower Iveagh, Lr. pt. } Upper Iveagh, Lr. pt. }	Dromara	Lisburn } Banbridge }	III.	168 172
19	Dromard	346	1	6	Sligo	Tireragh	Dromard	Dromore West	IV.	233
23, 24	Dromard Beg	842	1	13	Tipperary, N.R.	Ikerrin	Killavinoge	Roscrea	II.	275
29	Dromard Demesne	713	2	7	Limerick	Connello Lower	Rathkeale	Rathkeale	II.	229
23, 24	Dromard More	1,085	0	23	Tipperary, N.R.	Ikerrin	Killavinoge	Roscrea	II.	275
73	Dromasmole	217	3	8	Cork, E.R.	East Muskerry	Carrigrohanebeg	Cork	II.	102
119	Dromasta	449	1	39	Cork, W.R.	West Carbery (E.D.)	Dromdaleague	Skibbereen	II.	140
131	Dromataniheen	98	0	22	Cork, W.R.	West Carbery (W.D.)	Durrus	Bantry	II.	142
104	Dromateebara	171	1	14	Cork, W.R.	Bear	Kilcaskan	Castletown	II.	123
61	Dromatimore	429	3	39	Cork, W.R.	East Muskerry	Aghabulloge	Macroom	II.	153
14	Dromatoor	438	0	15	Kerry	Clanmaurice	Ballyheige	Tralee	II.	168
93	Dromatouk	485	2	35	Kerry	Glanarought	Kenmare	Kenmare	II.	186
44, 45	Dromavally	884	2	38c	Kerry	Corkaguiny	Ballinvoher	Dingle	II.	174
38	Dromavally	358	2	23	Kerry	Trughanacmy	Ballyseedy	Tralee	II.	208
56	Dromavally	144	0	5	Kerry	Trughanacmy	Killorglin	Killarney	II.	211
109	Dromavane	491	1	13	Cork, W.R.	East Carbery (W.D.)	Murragh	Bandon	II.	135
76	Dromavrauka	191	1	1	Kerry	Magunihy	Killaha	Killarney	II.	202
102	Drombane	229	0	3d	Kerry	Glanarought	Tuosist	Kenmare	II.	188
15, 24	Drombane	279	2	28	Limerick	Clanwilliam	Grean	Limerick	II.	224
13	Drombanny	560	1	18	Limerick	Clanwilliam	Caheravally	Limerick	II.	221
13	Drombanny	483	2	16e	Limerick	Clanwilliam	Cahernarry	Limerick	II.	222
13	Drombanny	355	3	35	Limerick	Clanwilliam	Donaghmore	Limerick	II.	223
143	Drombeg	180	3	20	Cork, W.R.	East Carbery (W.D.)	Kilfaughnabeg	Skibbereen	II.	133
71	Drombeg	371	2	28	Cork, W.R.	East Muskerry	Aghinagh	Macroom	II.	154
135	Drombeg	81	2	35	Cork, W.R.	Ibane and Barryroe	Island	Clonakilty	II.	149
39	Drombeg	58	2	26	Cork, W.R.	West Muskerry	Kilcorney	Millstreet	II.	158
5, 6, 10, 11	Drombeg	215	1	15	Kerry	Iraghticonnor	Galey	Listowel	II.	190
31, 39	Drombeg	574	3	28	Limerick	Smallcounty	Glenogra	Croom	II.	260
109	Drombofinny	86	1	18	Cork, W.R.	East Carbery (E.D.)	Desertserges	Bandon	II.	128
100, 101, } 108, 109 }	Drombohilly Lower	814	0	25	Kerry	Glanarought	Tuosist	Kenmare	II.	188
101, 109	Drombohilly Upper	777	1	34	Kerry	Glanarought	Tuosist	Kenmare	II.	188
51, 52	Dromboy North	197	3	10	Cork, E.R.	Barrymore	Dunbulloge	Cork	II.	54
51, 52	Dromboy South	544	3	5	Cork, E.R.	Barrymore	Dunbulloge	Cork	II.	54
71, 72	Drombrane	621	2	29	Kerry	Iveragh	Glanbehy	Cahersiveen	II.	196
57	Drombrick	97	3	6	Kerry	Magunihy	Kilbonane	Killarney	II.	200
105, 118	Drombrow	320	2	17f	Cork, W.R.	Bantry	Kilmocomoge	Bantry	II.	120
93	Dromcahan East	303	1	27	Kerry	Glanarought	Kenmare	Kenmare	II.	186
84, 93	Dromcahan West	366	3	27	Kerry	Glanarought	Kenmare	Kenmare	II.	186
64, 75	Dromcarban	290	3	39	Kerry	Magunihy	Killaha	Killarney	II.	202
82	Dromcarra North	230	2	21	Cork, W.R.	West Muskerry	Inchigeelagh	Macroom	II.	157
82	Dromcarra South	276	1	11	Cork, W.R.	West Muskerry	Inchigeelagh	Macroom	II.	157
118	Dromclogh	117	2	1	Cork, W.R.	Bantry	Kilmocomoge	Bantry	II.	120
16	Dromclogh	370	3	34	Kerry	Clanmaurice	Kilshenane	Listowel	II.	172
106	Dromclogh East	268	0	39	Cork, W.R.	Bantry	Kilmocomoge	Bantry	II.	120
106	Dromclogh West	179	3	11	Cork, W.R.	Bantry	Kilmocomoge	Bantry	II.	120
15	Dromcluher	292	1	7	Limerick	Owneybeg	Tuogh	Limerick	II.	251
54	DROMCOLLIHER T.	—			Limerick	Connello Upper	Dromcolliher	Newcastle	II.	233
132	Dromcorragh	584	0	9	Cork, W.R.	West Carbery (W.D.)	Caheragh	Skibbereen	II.	142
31	Dromcummer Beg	249	2	25g	Cork, E.R.	Duhallow	Clonmeen	Kanturk	II.	69
31	Dromcummer More	373	1	35h	Cork, E.R.	Duhallow	Clonmeen	Kanturk	II.	69
92	Dromcunnia	103	0	1	Kerry	Dunkerron South	Templenoe	Kenmare	II.	185
21	Dromcunnig	703	0	30	Kerry	Clanmaurice	O'Dorney	Tralee	II.	172
119, 120	Dromdaleague	557	1	30	Cork, W.R.	West Carbery (E.D.)	Dromdaleague	Skibbereen	II.	140
105	Dromdaniel	105	1	20	Cork, W.R.	Bantry	Kilmocomoge	Bantry	II.	120
72, 82	Dromdarragh	421	3	28	Kerry	Dunkerron North	Knockane	Cahersiveen	II.	182
13	Dromdarrig	146	2	8	Limerick	Pubblebrien	Mungret	Limerick	II.	254
93	Dromdeegy	385	3	24	Cork, W.R.	East Carbery (W.D.)	Fanlobbus	Dunmanway	II.	131
25, 26	Dromdeer	208	2	9	Cork, E.R.	Fermoy	Clenor	Mallow	II.	78
25, 26	Dromdeer East	352	0	38	Cork, E.R.	Fermoy	Doneraile	Mallow	II.	78
25	Dromdeer West	101	3	7	Cork, E.R.	Fermoy	Doneraile	Mallow	II.	70
52	Dromdeeveen	982	2	36	Limerick	Glenquin	Monagay	Newcastle	II.	247
90, 91	Dromderaown	86	3	6	Cork, W.R.	Bear	Kilcaskan	Bantry	II.	123

(a) Including 6A. 1R. 4P. water.　　(d) Including 4A. 1R. 26P. water.　　(g) Including 15A. 3R. 31P. River Blackwater.
(b) Including 12A. 3R. 12P. water.　(e) Including 17A. 3R. 32P. detached portion.　(h) Including 12A. 1R. 32P. water.
(c) Including 39A. 1R. 4P. water.　　(f) Including 17A. 3R. 14P. water.

No. of Sheet of the Ordnance Survey Maps.	Townlands and Towns.	Area in Statute Acres.			County.	Barony.	Parish.	Poor Law Union in 1857.	Townland Census of 1851, Part I.	
		A.	R.	P.					Vol.	Page
112, 125	Dromderrig	136	2	33	Cork, E.R.	Kinsale	Kinsale	Kinsale	II.	100
66	Dromdihy	141	0	20	Cork, E.R.	Imokilly	Killeagh	Youghal	II.	88
75	Dromdiralough	225	1	28a	Kerry	Magunihy	Killaha	Killarney	II.	202
109	Dromdiraowen	105	3	1	Kerry	Glanarought	Tuosist	Kenmare	II.	188
105, 118	Dromdoneen	60	2	30	Cork, W.R.	Bantry	Kilmocomoge	Bantry	II.	120
105	Dromdoneen East	46	3	25	Cork, W.R.	Bantry	Kilmocomoge	Bantry	II.	120
105, 118	Dromdoneen West	53	1	9	Cork, W.R.	Bantry	Kilmocomoge	Bantry	II.	120
58	Dromdoohig Beg	114	0	27	Kerry	Magunihy	Aglish	Killarney	II.	200
58	Dromdoohig More	367	1	32	Kerry	Magunihy	Aghadoe	Killarney	II.	199
72	Dromdoory	164	1	16	Kerry	Dunkerron North	Knockane	Cahersiveen	II.	182
124	Dromdough	332	3	4	Cork, W.R.	Courceys	Ringrone	Kinsale	II.	147
90, 104	Dromdour	133	3	7	Cork, W.R.	Bear	Kilcaskan	Bantry	II.	123
24	Dromdowney	56	1	32	Cork, E.R.	Orrery and Kilmore	Drumdowney	Mallow	II.	108
24	Dromdowney Lower	183	1	22	Cork, E.R.	Orrery and Kilmore	Drumdowney	Mallow	II.	108
24, 32	Dromdowney Upper	419	2	10	Cork, E.R.	Orrery and Kilmore	Drumdowney	Mallow	II.	108
107	Dromdrasdil	1,161	3	12b	Cork, W.R.	East Carbery (W.D.)	Fanlobbus	Dunmanway	II.	131
60, 71	Dromduff	392	2	24	Cork, W.R.	West Muskerry	Macroom	Macroom	II.	160
105	Dromduff East	222	2	34	Cork, W.R.	Bantry	Kilmocomoge	Bantry	II.	120
105	Dromduff West	216	2	6	Cork, W.R.	Bantry	Kilmocomoge	Bantry	II.	120
120, 133	Dromduvane	192	3	23	Cork, W.R.	West Carbery (E.D.)	Dromdalcague	Skibbereen	II.	140
35	Drom East	355	2	9	Kerry	Corkaguiny	Cloghane	Dingle	II.	175
71, 72	Drom East	135	2	29	Kerry	Iveragh	Glanbehy	Cahersiveen	II.	196
18	Dromeen	159	2	2c	Clare	Inchiquin	Ruan	Corrofin	II.	28
24	Dromeenboy	152	0	22	Limerick	Coonagh	Grean	Tipperary	II.	235
14, 15	Dromeliagh	671	1	29	Limerick	Owneybeg	Abington	Limerick	II.	251
108	Dromerk	279	0	8	Cork, W.R.	East Carbery (W.D.)	Fanlobbus	Dunmanway	II.	131
108, 109	Dromerkeen	226	1	35	Kerry	Glanarought	Tuosist	Kenmare	II.	188
94	Dromfeagh	399	0	9	Cork, W.R.	East Carbery (W.D.)	Kinneigh	Dunmanway	II.	134
116	Dromgare	44	3	5	Cork, W.R.	Bear	Killaconenagh	Castletown	II.	125
91,104,105	Dromgarriff	965	3	39	Cork, W.R.	Bantry	Kilmocomoge	Bantry	II.	120
122	Dromgarriff	335	2	4	Cork, W.R.	East Carbery (E.D.)	Kilmaloda	Clonakilty	II.	129
122	Dromgarriff East	385	0	20	Cork, W.R.	East Carbery (E.D.)	Kilnagross	Clonakilty	II.	129
51, 52	Dromgarriff North	348	2	31	Cork, E.R.	Barretts	Whitechurch	Cork	II.	50
51, 52, 62	Dromgarriff South	218	3	22	Cork, E.R.	Barretts	Whitechurch	Cork	II.	50
122	Dromgarriff West	138	2	1	Cork, W.R.	East Carbery (E.D.)	Kilnagross	Clonakilty	II.	129
103, 116	Dromgarvan	230	1	6	Cork, W.R.	Bear	Kilcaskan	Castletown	II.	123
14, 15, 18	Dromgoolestown	247	0	32	Louth	Ardee	Stabannan	Ardee	I.	174
14	Dromgower	216	1	26	Kerry	Clanmaurice	Ballyheige	Tralee	II.	168
72	Dromgownagh	200	2	30	Cork, E.R.	East Muskerry	Inishcarra	Cork	II.	103
66	Dromhale	103	0	30	Kerry	Magunihy	Killarney	Killarney	II.	203
66, 67	Dromhumper	158	1	39	Kerry	Magunihy	Killarney	Killarney	II.	203
67, 75	Dromickbane	202	0	7	Kerry	Magunihy	Killarney	Killarney	II.	203
108	Dromidiclogh	293	0	1	Cork, W.R.	East Carbery (W.D.)	Kinneigh	Dunmanway	II.	134
108	Dromidiclogh West	312	1	12	Cork, W.R.	East Carbery (W.D.)	Kinneigh	Dunmanway	II.	134
133,134,143	Dromillihy	423	1	32	Cork, W.R.	East Carbery (W.D.)	Kilmacabea	Skibbereen	II.	133
24	Dromin	90	1	17	Cork, E.R.	Duhallow	Kilbrin	Kanturk	II.	72
62, 73	Dromin	263	0	37	Cork, E.R.	East Muskerry	Matehy	Cork	II.	105
7	Dromin	106	2	12	Cork, E.R.	Fermoy	Imphrick	Mallow	II.	80
4	Dromin	239	0	33	Kerry	Iraghticonnor	Killehenny	Listowel	II.	191
10, 11	Dromin	272	1	2	Kerry	Iraghticonnor	Listowel	Listowel	II.	192
58, 66	Dromin	239	0	8	Kerry	Magunihy	Aghadoe	Killarney	II.	199
57	Dromin	254	1	35	Kerry	Magunihy	Killorglin	Killarney	II.	204
36	Dromin	378	1	26	Limerick	Glenquin	Grange	Newcastle	II.	245
18	Dromin	605	2	19	Louth	Ardee	Dromin	Ardee	I.	172
26	Dromin	405	0	10	Tipperary, N.R.	Owney and Arra	Burgesbeg	Nenagh	II.	294
6,7	Dromina	721	2	26	Cork, E.R.	Orrery and Kilmore	Shandrum	Kanturk	II.	110
18	Dromina	373	0	0	Waterford	Gaultiere	Crooke	Waterford	II.	362
11	Dromanaclara	106	2	5	Limerick	Kenry	Kilcornan	Rathkeale	II.	249
45	Dromanacreen	425	0	13	Limerick	Connello Upper	Kilmeedy	Newcastle	II.	233
6	Drominagh	136	3	39	Tipperary, N.R.	Lower Ormond	Terryglass	Borrisokane	II.	287
6	Drominagh Demesne	369	2	24	Tipperary, N.R.	Lower Ormond	Terryglass	Borrisokane	II.	287
30	Drominagh North	575	1	31	Cork, E.R.	Duhallow	Dromtarriff	Millstreet	II	71
30	Drominagh South	463	0	31	Cork, E.R.	Duhallow	Dromtarriff	Millstreet	II	71
6	Drominagh Wood	137	1	35	Tipperary, N.R.	Lower Ormond	Terryglass	Borrisokane	II.	287
15, 23	Drominagore	405	1	8	Cork, E.R.	Duhallow	Kilbrin	Kanturk	II.	72
75	Drominaharee	280	2	29	Kerry	Magunihy	Killaha	Killarney	II.	202
39	Drominahilla	139	0	27	Cork, W.R.	West Muskerry	Drishane	Millstreet	II.	156
66	Drominane	385	3	15	Cork, E.R.	Imokilly	Mogeely	Middleton	II.	90
7	DROMINA T.	—			Cork, E.R.	Orrery and Kilmore	Shandrum	Kanturk	II.	110
36	Dromin (Beesom)	303	2	10	Limerick	Glenquin	Newcastle	Newcastle	II.	247
6	Drominboy	91	3	26	Limerick	Clanwilliam	Stradbally	Limerick	II.	226
6	Drominboy Lower	162	1	18	Limerick	Clanwilliam	Killeenagarriff	Limerick	II.	224
6	Drominboy Upper	90	1	25	Limerick	Clanwilliam	Killeenagarriff	Limerick	II.	224

(a) Including 7A. 2R. 9P. water.   (b) Including 13A. 3R. 37P. water.   (c) Including 5A. 2R. 23P. water.

No. of Sheet of the Ordnance Survey Maps.	Townlands and Towns.	Area in Statute Acres.	County.	Barony.	Parish.	Poor Law Union in 1857.	Townland Census of 1851, Part I.	
		A. R. P.					Vol.	Page
57	Dromin East . .	261 0 15	Kerry . .	Magunihy . .	Killorglin . .	Killarney . .	II.	204
14	Dromineer . .	267 3 18	Tipperary, N.R.	Lower Ormond .	Dromineer . .	Nenagh . .	II.	283
11	Dromin Lower .	105 3 11a	Kerry . .	Iraghticonnor .	Listowel . .	Listowel . .	II.	193
36	Dromin (Macturlogh)	369 2 32	Limerick . .	Glenquin . .	Newcastle . .	Newcastle . .	II.	247
39	Dromin North .	175 0 5	Limerick . .	Coshma . .	Dromin . .	Kilmallock .	II.	243
11	Drominoona . .	109 1 7	Limerick . .	Kenry . .	Iveruss . .	Rathkeale .	II.	248
39	Dromin South .	247 2 11	Limerick . .	Coshma . .	Dromin . .	Kilmallock .	II.	243
53	Dromintobin North	118 0 20	Clare . .	Tulla Lower .	Kiltenanlea .	Limerick . .	II.	37
53	Dromintobin South	75 1 25	Clare . .	Tulla Lower .	Kiltenanlea .	Limerick . .	II.	37
18	DROMIN T. .	—	Louth . .	Ardee . .	Dromin . .	Ardee . .	I.	172
11	Dromin Upper .	199 2 29	Kerry . .	Iraghticonnor .	Listowel . .	Listowel . .	II.	193
57	Dromin West .	274 1 20	Kerry . .	Magunihy . .	Killorglin . .	Killarney . .	II.	204
22	Drominycarra .	201 1 13	Limerick . .	Smallcounty .	Fedamore . .	Croom . .	II.	259
11	Drominycullane .	51 0 23	Limerick . .	Kenry . .	Iveruss . .	Rathkeale .	II.	249
12, 15	Dromiskin . .	1,093 1 8	Louth . .	Louth . .	Dromiskin . .	Dundalk . .	I.	183
12	DROMISKIN T. .	—	Louth . .	Louth . .	Dromiskin . .	Dundalk . .	I.	183
105	Dromkeal . .	194 2 35	Cork, W.R. .	Bantry . .	Kilmocomoge .	Bantry . .	II.	120
131	Dromkeal . .	171 0 24	Cork, W.R. .	West Carbery (W.D.)	Skull . .	Skull . .	II.	146
89, 98	Dromkeare . .	255 0 1	Kerry . .	Iveragh . .	Dromod . .	Cahersiveen .	II.	194
96,97,110,111	Dromkeen . .	673 0 37	Cork, W.R. .	East Carbery (E.D.)	Inishannon .	Bandon . .	II.	128
70, 82	Dromkeen . .	344 2 11	Cork, W.R. .	West Muskerry .	Kilmichael .	Dunmanway .	II.	159
23, 24	Dromkeen . .	112 1 9	Limerick . .	Clanwilliam .	Grean . .	Limerick . .	II.	224
9, 15	Dromkeen East .	684 0 22	Kerry . .	Clanmaurice .	Killury . .	Listowel . .	II.	171
23, 24	Dromkeen North .	164 3 21	Limerick . .	Clanwilliam .	Dromkeen . .	Limerick . .	II.	223
23, 24	Dromkeen South .	152 1 17	Limerick . .	Clanwilliam .	Dromkeen . .	Limerick . .	II.	223
15	Dromkeen West .	729 1 15	Kerry . .	Clanmaurice .	Killury . .	Listowel . .	II.	171
57, 58, 66	Dromkerry . .	312 0 21	Kerry . .	Magunihy . .	Kilbonane .	Killarney . .	II.	200
24	Dromlara . .	352 0 34	Limerick . .	Coonagh . .	Grean . .	Tipperary .	II.	235
64, 72	Dromleagh . .	312 2 20b	Kerry . .	Dunkerron North .	Killorglin .	Cahersiveen .	II.	181
107	Dromleena . .	692 3 10	Cork, W.R. .	East Carbery (W.D.)	Fanlobbus .	Dunmanway .	II.	131
18	Dromlegagh . .	92 1 25c	Kerry . .	Clanmaurice .	Duagh . .	Listowel . .	II.	168
17, 18	Dromlegagh Demesne	73 0 28d	Kerry . .	Clanmaurice .	Duagh . .	Listowel . .	II.	168
19	Dromleigh . .	318 1 14	Cork, E.R. .	Condons & Clangibbon	Kilgullane .	Mitchelstown .	II.	61
82	Dromleigh . .	87 0 18	Cork, W.R. .	West Muskerry .	Kilmichael .	Dunmanway .	II.	159
118	Dromleigh North .	102 0 7	Cork, W.R. .	Bantry . .	Kilmocomoge .	Bantry . .	II.	120
118	Dromleigh South .	399 3 34	Cork, W.R. .	Bantry . .	Kilmocomoge .	Bantry . .	II.	120
105, 106	Dromlickacrue .	242 3 11	Cork, W.R. .	Bantry . .	Kilmocomoge .	Bantry . .	II.	120
67	Dromline . .	540 3 17	Tipperary, S.R.	Clanwilliam .	Kilfeacle .	Tipperary .	II.	308
11	Dromlohan . .	375 0 17	Limerick . .	Kenry . .	Kilcornan .	Rathkeale .	II.	249
93	Dromlough . .	248 2 38	Cork, W.R. .	East Carbery (W.D.)	Kilmichael .	Dunmanway .	II.	134
22	Dromloughan North	142 3 14	Limerick . .	Pubblebrien .	Killeenoghty .	Croom . .	II.	253
22	Dromloughan South	68 1 31e	Limerick . .	Pubblebrien .	Killeenoghty .	Croom . .	II.	253
105	Dromloughlin . .	62 1 6	Cork, W.R. .	Bantry . .	Kilmocomoge .	Bantry . .	II.	120
10	Dromloughra . .	291 0 24f	Kerry . .	Iraghticonnor .	Dysert . .	Listowel . .	II.	190
91, 92	Dromlusk . .	1,559 3 16	Kerry . .	Dunkerron South .	Kilcrohane .	Kenmare . .	II.	183
73	Dromluska . .	320 1 15g	Kerry . .	Dunkerron North .	Knockane .	Killarney . .	II.	182
32, 41	Drommahane . .	531 2 0	Cork, E.R. .	Duhallow . .	Kilshannig .	Mallow . .	II.	74
32	DROMMAHANE T. .	—	Cork, E.R. .	Duhallow . .	Kilshannig .	Mallow . .	II.	74
21	Drommakee . .	311 1 34	Kerry . .	Clanmaurice .	Kiltomy . .	Listowel . .	II.	172
9, 15	Drommartin . .	382 0 32	Kerry . .	Clanmaurice .	Rattoo . .	Listowel . .	II.	173
9	DROMMARTIN T. .	—	Kerry . .	Clanmaurice .	Rattoo . .	Listowel . .	II.	173
3	Drommoher . .	129 2 5	Limerick . .	Kenry . .	Kilcornan .	Rathkeale .	II.	249
6, 11	Drommurher . .	197 2 35	Kerry . .	Iraghticonnor .	Murher . .	Listowel . .	II.	193
10	Drommurrin . .	491 0 27	Kerry . .	Iraghticonnor .	Galey . .	Listowel . .	II.	190
141, 150	Dromnacaheragh .	108 3 8	Cork, W.R. .	West Carbery (E.D.)	Aghadown .	Skibbereen .	II.	137
8, 9	Dromnacarra . .	673 0 33	Kerry . .	Clanmaurice .	Killury . .	Listowel . .	II.	171
105, 118	Dromnafinshin .	69 1 22	Cork, W.R. .	Bantry . .	Kilmocomoge .	Bantry . .	II.	120
81, 82	Dromnagapple .	135 3 12	Cork, W.R. .	West Muskerry .	Inchigeelagh .	Dunmanway .	II.	157
81, 90	Dromnakilly . .	564 2 26	Kerry . .	Iveragh . .	Dromod . .	Cahersiveen .	II.	194
129,130,138	Dromnea . .	371 2 2	Cork, W.R. .	West Carbery (W.D.)	Kilcrohane .	Bantry . .	II.	143
93	Dromneavane . .	330 2 33	Kerry . .	Glanarought .	Kenmare . .	Kenmare . .	II.	186
115	Drom North . .	170 2 13h	Cork, W.R. .	Bear . .	Killaconenagh .	Castletown .	II.	124
94	Dromnycolman .	379 1 23	Kerry . .	Glanarought .	Kilgarvan .	Kenmare . .	II.	187
89	Dromod . .	429 2 28	Kerry . .	Iveragh . .	Dromod . .	Cahersiveen .	II.	195
42	Dromoland . .	812 1 39i	Clare . .	Bunratty Lower .	Kilnasoolagh .	Ennis . .	II.	6
74	Dromomarka . .	353 3 31	Tipperary, S.R.	Clanwilliam .	Cordangan .	Tipperary .	II.	306
74	Dromomarka (College)	139 3 32	Tipperary, S.R.	Clanwilliam .	Cordangan .	Tipperary .	II.	306
70	Dromonig . .	303 3 28	Cork, W.R. .	West Muskerry .	Clondrohid .	Macroom .	II.	155
27	Dromore . .	547 2 4	Antrim . .	Kilconway .	Rasharkin .	Ballymena .	III.	27
15	Dromore . .	119 1 0	Antrim . .	Lower Glenarm .	Layd . .	Ballycastle .	III.	22
22, 21	Dromore . .	443 0 10j	Cavan . .	Clankee . .	Bailieborough .	Bailieborough .	III.	71
17,18,25,26	Dromore . .	1,018 2 31k	Clare . .	Inchiquin .	Ruan . .	Corrofin . .	II.	28
28	Dromore . .	105 2 23l	Clare . .	Tulla Upper .	Feakle . .	Scarriff . .	II.	39

(a) Including 5A. 0R. 15P. water.
(b) Including 1A. 1R. 37P. water.
(c) Including 6A. 3R. 24P. water.
(d) Including 4A. 3R. 19P. water.
(e) Including 1A. 2R. 0P. water.

(f) Including 0A. 3R. 32P. water.
(g) Including 12A. 0R. 37P. water.
(h) Including 51A. 0R. 10P. detached portion.
(i) Including 33A. 0R. 33P. water.
(j) Including 5A. 1R. 27P. water.

(k) { Including 182A. 1R. 25P. water. Including 15A. 0R. 29P. Rabbit Island. Including 6A. 2R. 14P. Holly Island.
(l) Including 4A. 1R. 25P. water.

No. of Sheet of the Ordnance Survey Maps.	Townlands and Towns.	Area in Statute Acres. A. R. P.	County.	Barony.	Parish.	Poor Law Union in 1857.	Townland Census of 1851, Part I. Vol.	Page
32,33,41,42	Dromore	760 2 10	Cork, E.R.	Duhallow	Kilshannig	Mallow	II.	74
119	Dromore	621 0 21	Cork, W.R.	West Carbery (W.D.)	Caheragh	Skibbereen	II.	142
99	Dromore	389 1 33	Donegal	Banagh	Inver	Donegal	III.	107
93, 99	Dromore	526 3 14	Donegal	Banagh	Killymard	Donegal	III.	111
44	Dromore	662 3 19	Donegal	Kilmacrenan	Conwal	Letterkenny	III.	126
70, 71	Dromore	134 3 38	Donegal	Raphoe	Clonleigh	Strabane	III.	135
78	Dromore	144 2 28a	Donegal	Raphoe	Donaghmore	Stranorlar	III.	137
53, 61	Dromore	381 1 14	Donegal	Raphoe	Leck	Letterkenny	III.	140
103	Dromore	349 3 14b	Donegal	Tirhugh	Drumhome	Ballyshannon	III.	146
51, 54	Dromore	392 0 11	Down	Upper Iveagh Up. pt.	Warrenspoint	Newry	III.	176
11	Dromore	102 1 34	Fermanagh	Lurg	Derryvullan	Lowtherstown	III.	204
21	Dromore	125 0 35	Fermanagh	Magheraboy	Devenish	Enniskillen	III.	210
14	Dromore	165 3 11	Fermanagh	Magheraboy	Inishmacsaint	Enniskillen	III.	212
92, 101	Dromore	518 1 9	Kerry	Dunkerron South	Templenoe	Kenmare	II.	185
48	Dromore	612 0 9	Kerry	Magunihy	Molahiffe	Killarney	II.	205
29	Dromore	154 0 38	Leitrim	Carrigallen	Cloone	Mohill	IV.	90
25	Dromore	164 2 25c	Leitrim	Carrigallen	Oughteragh	Bawnboy	IV.	92
14, 15	Dromore	159 3 11	Leitrim	Drumahaire	Killanummery	Manorhamilton	IV.	98
31	Dromore	125 2 23	Leitrim	Leitrim	Kiltoghert	Cark. on Shannon	IV.	101
6, 7	Dromore	64 1 22	Leitrim	Rosclogher	Killasnet	Manorhamilton	IV.	109
12	Dromore	48 2 5d	Limerick	Kenry	Kildimo	Rathkeale	II.	249
11	Dromore	277 2 33	Londonderry	Coleraine	Macosquin	Coleraine	III.	233
9, 16	Dromore	198 2 33	Londonderry	Keenaght	Tamlaght Finlagan	New Tn Limavady	III.	237
41	Dromore	327 2 17	Londonderry	Loughinsholin	Desertmartin	Magherafelt	III.	240
7, 8	Dromore	44 3 33	Londonderry	North East Liberties of Coleraine	Kildollagh	Coleraine	III.	246
89, 99, 100	Dromore	236 2 2	Mayo	Carra	Ballintober	Castlebar	IV.	124
14	Dromore	147 2 16	Monaghan	Cremorne	Clontibret	Monaghan	III.	260
20, 25	Dromore	360 2 7e	Monaghan	Cremorne	Muckno	Castleblayney	III.	261
18	Dromore	325 3 4	Monaghan	Cremorne	Tullycorbet	Monaghan	III.	262
32	Dromore	84 2 14	Monaghan	Farney	Inishkeen	Dundalk	III.	271
10	Dromore	117 0 2	Monaghan	Monaghan	Tehallan	Monaghan	III.	280
1	Dromore	113 0 13	Monaghan	Trough	Errigal Trough	Clogher	III.	284
4	Dromore	126 0 21	Roscommon	Boyle	Kilronan	Boyle	IV.	197
4	Dromore	176 2 29	Roscommon	Boyle	Tumna	Cark. on Shannon	IV.	197
11, 12, 18	Dromore	219 2 19	Sligo	Tireragh	Kilmacshalgan	Dromore West	IV.	234
21	Dromore	388 0 21	Sligo	Tirerrill	Killerry	Sligo	IV.	239
35	Dromore	181 1 20	Sligo	Tirerrill	Kilmactranny	Boyle	IV.	240
66	Dromore	349 3 19	Tyrone	Dungannon Lower	Aghaloo	Armagh	III.	296
39	Dromore	354 2 2	Tyrone	Dungannon Upper	Arboe	Cookstown	III.	305
42, 50	Dromore	157 0 20	Tyrone	Omagh East	Dromore	Omagh	III.	311
29, 34	Dromore	1,454 3 34	Waterford	Decies within Drum	Aglish	Dungarvan	II.	349
32	Dromore	196 1 7	Westmeath	Moycashel	Castletownkindalen	Mullingar	I.	277
62	Dromore Big	258 1 0	Donegal	Raphoe	Taughboyne	Strabane	III.	143
1	Dromore Big	364 3 24	Fermanagh	Lurg	Drumkeeran	Lowtherstown	III.	206
34	Dromorebrague	411 2 21	Down	Upper Iveagh, Up.pt.	Aghaderg	Banbridge	III.	174
18	Dromore East	162 0 10	Monaghan	Dartree	Ematris	Cootehill	III.	267
114, 123	Dromorehill	53 1 11	Galway	Kiltartan	Kiltartan	Gort	IV.	48
114, 123	Dromorehill	144 1 1f	Galway	Kiltartan	Kilthomas	Gort	IV.	49
62, 70	Dromore Little	73 2 29	Donegal	Raphoe	Taughboyne	Strabane	III.	143
1	Dromore Little	266 0 9	Fermanagh	Lurg	Drumkeeran	Lowtherstown	III.	206
58	Dromore Lower	262 2 13	Tyrone	Clogher	Clogher	Clogher	III.	292
58	Dromore Middle	409 3 32	Tyrone	Clogher	Clogher	Clogher	III.	292
33, 41, 42	Dromore North	697 2 27	Cork, E.R.	Duhallow	Kilshannig	Mallow	II.	74
92	Dromore Old	492 2 15	Kerry	Dunkerron South	Templenoe	Kenmare	II.	185
41, 42	Dromore South	566 1 30	Cork, E R.	Duhallow	Kilshannig	Mallow	II.	74
21	Dromore T.	—	Down	Lower Iveagh, Lr. pt.	Dromore	Banbridge	III.	168
50	Dromore T.	—	Tyrone	Omagh East	Dromore	Omagh	III.	311
58	Dromore Upper	226 1 12	Tyrone	Clogher	Clogher	Clogher	III.	292
22	Dromore West	52 3 33	Monaghan	Dartree	Ematris	Cootehill	III.	267
118, 119, 131, 132	Dromourneen	1,107 3 13	Cork, W.R.	West Carbery (W.D.)	Caheragh	Skibbereen	II.	142
38, 39	Dromoyle	820 2 23	King's Co.	Ballybritt	Kilcolman	Parsonstown	I.	125
32, 41	Drompeesh	292 2 32	Cork, E.R.	Duhallow	Kilshannig	Mallow	II.	74
33	Dromrahan	225 1 20g	Cork, E.R.	Fermoy	Rahan	Mallow	II.	82
28	Dromrahnee	105 1 19	Limerick	Shanid	Ardagh	Newcastle	II.	255
32	Dromrastill	238 1 30	Cork, E.R.	Duhallow	Ballyclogh	Mallow	II.	67
47	Dromreag	215 3 38	Kerry	Magunihy	Kilnanare	Killarney	II.	204
131	Dromreagh	841 2 4	Cork, W.R.	West Carbery (W.D.)	Durrus	Bantry	II.	142
118	Dromreague	91 3 34	Cork, W.R.	Bantry	Durrus	Bantry	II.	119
70	Dromreague	434 0 30	Cork, W.R.	West Muskerry	Kilnamartry	Macroom	II.	159
26	Dromreask	775 1 0	Limerick	Shanid	Kilfergus	Glin	II.	256
59,60,70,71	Dromree	348 3 15	Cork, W.R.	West Muskerry	Clondrohid	Macroom	II.	155

(a) Including 4A. 3R. 8P. water.
(b) Including 5A. 2R. 18P. water.
(c) Including 6A. 3R. 36P. water.

(d) Including 8A. 1R. 14P. water.
(e) Including 7A. 3R. 30P. water.

(f) Including 8A. 2R. 16P. water.
(g) Including 4A. 1R. 0P. water.

3 E

No. of Sheet of the Ordnance Survey Maps.	Townlands and Towns.	Area in Statute Acres. A. R. P.	County.	Barony.	Parish.	Poor Law Union in 1857.	Townland Census of 1851. Part I. Vol.	Page
15	Dromroe	101 1 20	Kerry	Clanmaurice	Rattoo	Listowel	II.	173
101, 102	Dromroe	393 0 8	Kerry	Glanarought	Tuosist	Kenmare	II.	188
48	Dromroe	152 2 12	Kerry	Trughanacmy	Dysert	Killarney	II.	210
5	Dromroe	151 3 12	Limerick	Clanwilliam	Kilmurry	Limerick	II.	224
44	Dromroe	729 3 38	Limerick	Glenquin	Monagay	Newcastle	II.	247
25	Dromroe Commons	84 2 9	Cork, E.R.	Fermoy	Caherduggan	Mallow	II.	77
44	Dromruagh	26 3 39	Cork, E.R.	Barrymore	Rathcormack	Fermoy	II.	57
15	Dromsallagh	851 1 22	Limerick	Owneybeg	Tuogh	Limerick	II.	251
77	Dromsarane	185 3 36	Cork, E.R.	Imokilly	Ballyoughtera	Middleton	II.	84
39	Dromsicane	397 3 14a	Cork, E.R.	Duhallow	Cullen	Millstreet	II.	70
25	Dromsiveen	82 3 35	Cork, E.R.	Fermoy	Carrigleamleary	Mallow	II.	77
21	Dromskarragh Beg	167 0 38	Cork, E.R.	Duhallow	Kilmeen	Kanturk	II.	72
21, 29	Dromskarragh More	282 0 37	Cork, E.R.	Duhallow	Kilmeen	Kanturk	II.	72
30	Dromskehy	422 0 39	Cork, E.R.	Duhallow	Dromtarriff	Kanturk	II.	71
24,25,32,33	Dromsligo	455 2 28	Cork, E.R.	Fermoy	Mallow	Mallow	II.	81
115	Drom South	117 3 19b	Cork, W.R.	Bear	Killaconenagh	Castletown	II.	124
72	Dromstabla	61 1 23	Kerry	Dunkerron North	Knockane	Cahersiveen	II.	182
105, 106	Dromsullivan North	151 1 21	Cork, W.R.	Bantry	Kilmocomoge	Bantry	II.	120
105, 106	Dromsullivan South	149 2 18	Cork, W.R.	Bantry	Kilmocomoge	Bantry	II.	120
30, 31	Dromtarriff	122 0 9	Cork, E.R.	Duhallow	Dromtarriff	Kanturk	II.	71
70	Dromtea	236 0 37	Kerry	Iveragh	Killinane	Cahersiveen	II.	197
72, 82	Dromteewakeen	804 1 17c	Kerry	Dunkerron North	Knockane	Kenmare	II.	182
29	Dromthacker	242 2 4	Kerry	Trughanacmy	Ratass	Tralee	II.	213
90	Dromtine	917 0 6d	Kerry	Dunkerron South	Kilcrohane	Kenmare	II.	183
42, 43	Dromtrasna (Collins)	1,610 3 13	Limerick	Glenquin	Abbeyfeale	Newcastle	II.	244
43	Dromtrasna (Hartnett)	865 1 11	Limerick	Glenquin	Abbeyfeale	Newcastle	II.	244
43	Dromtrasna North	656 0 6	Limerick	Glenquin	Abbeyfeale	Newcastle	II.	244
43, 52	Dromtrasna South	967 0 22	Limerick	Glenquin	Abbeyfeale	Newcastle	II.	244
28	Dromturk	72 0 26	Limerick	Connello Lower	Kilbradran	Rathkeale	II.	228
49	Dromultan	679 1 33	Kerry	Trughanacmy	Castleisland	Tralee	II.	208
40, 49	Dromultan	840 1 7	Kerry	Trughanacmy	Killentierna	Killarney	II.	211
115	Drom West	118 2 17e	Cork, W.R.	Bear	Killaconenagh	Castletown	II.	124
35	Drom West	244 2 6	Kerry	Corkaguiny	Cloghane	Dingle	II.	175
63	Drom West	474 3 7	Kerry	Iveragh	Glanbehy	Cahersiveen	II.	196
66, 74	Dromyrourk	266 3 3	Kerry	Magunihy	Killarney	Killarney	II.	203
60	Drone	104 2 28	Tyrone	Dungannon Lower	Carnteel	Clogher	III.	297
10, 19	Drough	239 2 13	Cork, E.R.	Condons&Clangibbon	Marshalstown	Mitchelstown	II.	63
5	Droughill	286 0 22	Queen's Co.	Portnahinch	Lea	Mountmellick	I.	244
98, 106	Drought	482 0 28	Galway	Leitrim	Kilreekill	Loughrea	IV.	54
36	Droughtville	287 1 18	King's Co.	Eglish	Drumcullen	Parsonstown	I.	134
42	Drudgeon	168 1 2f	Tyrone	Omagh East	Drumragh	Omagh	III.	312
11, 15	Drum	240 3 11	Armagh	Armagh	Tynan	Armagh	III.	46
80, 81	Drum	176 3 20	Donegal	Banagh	Glencolumbkille	Glenties	III.	105
99	Drum	108 0 35	Galway	Clonmacnowen	Clontuskert	Ballinasloe	IV.	24
4, 16	Drum	279 3 30g	Galway	Dunmore	Addergoole	Tuam	IV.	33
29,30,43,44	Drum	256 1 38	Galway	Dunmore	Tuam	Tuam	IV.	36
124, 125	Drum	688 2 15	Galway	Leitrim	Ballynakill	Loughrea	IV.	51
24	Drum	2,540 3 2	Londonderry	Keenaght	Bovevagh	Newt[n]Limavady	III.	235
102	Drum	75 2 17	Mayo	Costello	Bekan	Claremorris	IV.	139
92	Drum	430 1 14h	Mayo	Costello	Knock	Claremorris	IV.	142
16	Drum	302 3 14	Mayo	Erris	Kilmore	Belmullet	IV.	146
22	Drum	144 2 35i	Monaghan	Dartree	Currin	Cootehill	III.	265
51	Drum	20 1 28	Roscommon	Athlone	Drum	Athlone	IV.	180
7	Drum	97 3 16	Tipperary, N.R.	Lower Ormond	Aglishcloghane	Borrisokane	II.	281
19	Drum	142 3 5	Tipperary, N.R.	Owney and Arra	Castletownarra	Nenagh	II.	294
46	Drum	167 2 15	Tipperary, S.R.	Kilnamanagh Lower	Clonoulty	Cashel	II.	323
29	Drum	237 3 37j	Tyrone	Dungannon Upper	Kildress	Cookstown	III.	308
43	Drum	361 2 0k	Tyrone	Omagh East	Drumragh	Omagh	III.	312
21	Drumaa	187 0 23l	Fermanagh	Magheraboy	Boho	Enniskillen	III.	209
35	Drumaa & Dernaglug	180 3 9m	Fermanagh	Clankelly	Clones	Clones	III.	195
45	Drumabodan	329 0 22	Donegal	Kilmacrenan	Kilmacrenan	Milford	III.	129
15	Drumacanver	408 0 12	Armagh	Armagh	Derrynoose	Armagh	III.	44
33	Drumacappul Island	3 0 39	Mayo	Erris	Kilmore	Belmullet	IV.	146
9, 16	Drumacarney	225 2 0	Londonderry	Keenaght	Tamlaght Finlagan	Newt[n]Limavady	III.	237
33, 34	Drumacarrow	516 3 22n	Cavan	Clankee	Bailieborough	Bailieborough	III.	71
9	Drumacaslan	118 1 27	Monaghan	Monaghan	Kilmore	Monaghan	III.	276
16, 17	Drumachee	450 1 5	Armagh	Fews Lower	Mullaghbrack	Armagh	III.	47
16	Drumachon	168 3 5o	Cavan	Tullygarvey	Drung	Cootehill	III.	89
26	Drumack	1,236 0 10	Antrim	Kilconway	Rasharkin	Ballymoney	III.	27
13	Drumaclan	177 1 31	Monaghan	Monaghan	Kilmore	Monaghan	III.	276
90, 104	Drumaclarig	117 0 20	Cork, W.R.	Bear	Kilcaskan	Bantry	II.	123
16	Drumcleeskin	138 2 33	Cavan	Tullygarvey	Drung	Cootehill	III.	89
36, 37	Drumacloghan	210 1 35	Donegal	Kilmacrenan	Tullyfern	Milford	III.	133

(a) Including 12A. 3R. 28P. water.
(b) Including 22A. 3R. 35P. detached portions.
(c) Including 4A. 2R. 20P. water.
(d) Including 15A. 1R. 32P. water.
(e) Including 13A. 1R. 10P. detached portions.

(f) Including 2A. 2R. 14P. water.
(g) Including 14A. 2R. 21P. water.
(h) Including 6A. 2R. 16P. water.
(i) Including 19A. 2R. 4P. water.
(j) Including 1A. 2R. 38P. detached portion.

(k) Including 1A. 3R. 11P. water.
(l) Including 14A. 0R. 3P. water.
(m) Including 20A. 0R. 13P. water.
(n) Including 2A. 1R. 13P. water.
(o) Including 5A. 3R. 12P. water.

No. of Sheet of the Ordnance Survey Maps.	Townlands and Towns.	Area in Statute Acres. A. R. P.	County.	Barony.	Parish.	Poor Law Union in 1857.	Townland Census of 1851, Part I. Vol.	Page
3	Drumacolla	72 0 7	Leitrim	Rosclogher	Rossinver	Ballyshannon	IV.	111
10, 11, 14, 15	Drumacon	266 0 14	Cavan	Lower Loughtee	Drumlane	Cavan	III.	80
20, 25	Drumacon	511 0 20a	Monaghan	Cremorne	Muckno	Castleblayney	III.	261
23	Drumaconnell East	119 1 11	Down	Castlereagh Upper	Saintfield	Lisburn	III.	166
16, 23	Drumaconnell West	149 3 12	Down	Castlereagh Upper	Saintfield	Lisburn	III.	166
28	Drumaconvern	163 3 4	Monaghan	Farney	Donaghmoyne	Carrickmacross	III.	269
9	Drumacony	71 0 4	Londonderry	Keenaght	Tamlaght Finlagan	NewTⁿLimavady	III.	237
103	Drumacoo	246 1 11	Galway	Dunkellin	Drimacoo	Gort	IV.	28
64	Drumacoo	621 0 17	Mayo	Costello	Kilcolman	Castlereagh	IV.	141
12, 17	Drumacoon	97 0 1	Monaghan	Dartree	Killeevan	Clones	III.	268
17	Drumacreeve	137 3 20	Monaghan	Dartree	Aghabog	Cootehill	III.	263
18	Drumacreeve	144 0 4	Monaghan	Dartree	Ematris	Cootehill	III.	267
20	Drumacrib	237 0 32b	Monaghan	Cremorne	Muckno	Castleblayney	III.	261
106, 107	Drumacrin	450 1 0	Donegal	Tirhugh	Inishmacsaint	Ballyshannon	III.	147
36	Drumacrittin	100 1 39c	Fermanagh	Clankelly	Clones	Clones	III.	196
18	Drumacrow	158 3 7	Londonderry	Coleraine	Aghadowey	Coleraine	III.	229
13	Drumacruttan	146 2 6	Monaghan	Monaghan	Monaghan	Monaghan	III.	277
9	Drumacruttan	37 3 13	Monaghan	Monaghan	Tehallan	Monaghan	III.	280
9, 14	Drumacullin	1,173 3 12	Antrim	Cary	Culfeightrin	Ballycastle	III.	13
27	Drumacullion	156 2 10	Cavan	Clankee	Knockbride	Cootehill	III.	73
28	Drumad	359 0 24	Cavan	Clankee	Shercock	Bailieborough	III.	74
27, 28	Drumad	403 3 0	Fermanagh	Tirkennedy	Cleenish	Enniskillen	III.	220
1, 4	Drumad	308 2 17d	Louth	Lower Dundalk	Ballymascanlan	Dundalk	I.	175
39	Drumad	421 1 11	Tyrone	Dungannon Upper	Tamlaght	Cookstown	III.	309
28	Drumadagarve	243 2 0	Fermanagh	Magherastephana	Aghavea	Lisnaskea	III.	218
44, 45	Drumadarragh	1,145 0 11e	Antrim	Upper Antrim	Kilbride	Antrim	III.	6
18, 23	Drumadarragh	252 0 27	Antrim	Upper Dunluce	Killagan	Ballymoney	III.	19
59	Drumadarragh	148 0 18	Tyrone	Clogher	Errigal Trough	Clogher	III.	296
92	Drumadart	121 3 38	Donegal	Banagh	Inver	Donegal	III.	107
24	Drumad (Beirne)	112 0 30	Leitrim	Leitrim	Kiltubbrid	Carᵏ. on Shannon	IV.	103
12	Drumadd	179 2 13	Armagh	Armagh	Armagh	Armagh	III.	43
12	Drumaddagorry	109 0 14	Monaghan	Dartree	Clones	Clones	III.	264
12	Drumaddarainy	144 3 9	Monaghan	Dartree	Clones	Clones	III.	264
9, 10	Drumaderry	235 1 24	Londonderry	Keenaght	Aghanloo	NewTⁿLimavady	III.	233
102, 103	Drumaderry	358 0 31	Mayo	Costello	Annagh	Claremorris	IV.	138
15	Drumadillar	190 1 27	Fermanagh	Magheraboy	Devenish	Enniskillen	III.	210
24	Drumad (Moran)	129 3 25	Leitrim	Leitrim	Kiltubbrid	Carᵏ. on Shannon	IV.	103
94	Drumadoney	102 0 7	Donegal	Tirhugh	Donegal	Donegal	III.	145
21, 28	Drumadoney	854 2 9	Down	Lower Iveagh, Lr. pt.	Dromara	Lisburn	III.	167
35, 42	Drumadonnell	1,034 3 15	Down	Upper Iveagh, Lr. pt.	Drumgooland	Banbridge	III.	172
38	Drumadoocy	227 1 38	Donegal	Inishowen West	Fahan Upper	Londonderry	III.	121
9	Drumadoon	173 2 26	Antrim	Cary	Culfeightrin	Ballycastle	III.	13
23	Drumadoon	428 1 3	Antrim	Kilconway	Killagan	Ballymoney	III.	27
78	Drumadoon	206 2 1f	Mayo	Carra	Islandeady	Castlebar	IV.	128
79, 90	Drumadoon	209 3 16	Mayo	Clanmorris	Balla	Castlebar	IV.	132
33, 36	Drumadorn	311 3 25	Leitrim	Mohill	Cloone	Mohill	IV.	105
15	Drumadown	156 1 16	Fermanagh	Magheraboy	Devenish	Enniskillen	III.	210
3	Drumadragh	74 2 38	Londonderry	North East Liberties of Coleraine	Coleraine	Coleraine	III.	246
5	Drumadraghy	142 0 3	Fermanagh	Lurg	Magheraculmoney	Lowtherstown	III.	207
10, 11	Drumadravy	146 0 30	Fermanagh	Lurg	Derryvullan	Lowtherstown	III.	204
16, 17, 24, 25	Drumadreen	1,011 1 30	Londonderry	Keenaght	Bovevagh	NewTⁿLimavady	III.	235
41	Drumadrehid	255 3 19	Clare	Islands	Killone	Ennis	II.	30
20	Drumadried	29 3 13	Antrim	Lower Glenarm	Ardclinis	Larne	III.	21
11	Drumaduan	22 2 18	Antrim	Upper Dunluce	Kildollagh	Coleraine	III.	19
8	Drumaduan	201 3 15	Londonderry	North East Liberties of Coleraine	Kildollagh	Coleraine	III.	246
40	Drumady	68 3 11	Fermanagh	Clankelly	Clones	Clones	III.	196
101	Drumady	517 1 15g	Mayo	Clanmorris	Crossboyne	Claremorris	IV.	132
24	Drumadykey	57 2 34	Leitrim	Leitrim	Kiltubbrid	Carᵏ. on Shannon	IV.	103
27	Drumagarner	596 0 19	Londonderry	Loughinsholin	Tamlaght O'Crilly	Ballymoney	III.	243
26	Drumageever	154 0 39	Fermanagh	Clanawley	Cleenish	Enniskillen	III.	190
20	Drumagelvin	237 1 11	Monaghan	Cremorne	Muckno	Castleblayney	III.	261
7, 10	Drumagelvin	201 0 32	Monaghan	Monaghan	Tehallan	Monaghan	III.	280
91, 101	Drumagh	36 3 30	Mayo	Clanmorris	Kilcolman	Claremorris	IV.	134
50	Drumagh	177 3 18	Mayo	Gallen	Killasser	Swineford	IV.	149
31	Drumagh	384 3 5	Queen's Co.	Slievemargy	Killabban	Carlow	I.	245
27, 28	Drumaghadone	314 1 16	Down	Lower Iveagh, Lr. pt.	Dromore	Banbridge	III.	168
17	Drumaghakeel	116 1 35	Monaghan	Dartree	Aghabog	Cootehill	III.	263
23, 30	Drumaghlis	695 3 38	Down	Kinelarty	Kilmore	Downpatrick	III.	177
73, 82	Drumaghy	116 0 38	Donegal	Banagh	Inishkeel	Glenties	III.	106
91, 92	Drumaghy	168 1 21	Donegal	Banagh	Killaghtee	Glenties	III.	109
23	Drumagissaun	197 1 34	Roscommon	Ballintober North	Kilglass	Strokestown	IV.	186

(a) Including 17A. 1R. 26P. water.
(b) Including 1A. 2R. 5P. water.
(c) Including 10A. 2R. 27P. water.

(d) Including 6A. 1R. 2P. water.
(e) Including 5A. 3R. 16P. water.

(f) Including 0A. 0R. 30P. water.
(g) Including 25A. 0R. 28P. water.

3 E 2

No. of Sheet of the Ordnance Survey Maps.	Townlands and Towns.	Area in Statute Acres.	County.	Barony.	Parish.	Poor Law Union in 1857.	Townland Census of 1851. Part I.	
		A.　R.　P.					Vol.	Page
33, 39	Drumagolan	518 0 28	Cavan	Castlerahan	Killinkere	Oldcastle	III.	68
21	Drumagore	218 1 5	Londonderry	Tirkeeran	Clondermot	Londonderry	III.	248
50	Drumagorgan	141 2 1	Antrim	Upper Antrim	Donegore	Antrim	III.	6
17	Drumagosker	176 0 19	Londonderry	Keenaght	Balteagh	NewTⁿLimavady	III.	234
84, 93	Drumagraa	525 0 33a	Donegal	Banagh	Inver	Donegal	III.	107
27	Drumagrove	251 0 4	Antrim	Kilconway	Dunaghy	Ballymena	III.	25
39, 47	Drumagullion	256 3 4	Tyrone	Dungannon Middle	Donaghenry	Cookstown	III.	301
2	Drumagully	223 2 5	Londonderry	Coleraine	Dunboe	Coleraine	III.	231
14, 15	Drumahaire	123 3 13	Leitrim	Drumahaire	Drumlease	Manorhamilton	IV.	94
14	DRUMAHAIRE T.	—	Leitrim	Drumahaire	Drumlease	Manorhamilton	IV.	95
9	Drumahaman	88 3 22	Antrim	Cary	Culfeightrin	Ballycastle	III.	13
15, 19	Drumahean	124 3 38	Armagh	Tiranny	Tynan	Armagh	III.	60
16	Drumaheglis	245 2 5	Antrim	Upper Dunluce	Ballymoney	Ballymoney	III.	18
22	Drumahira	71 1 24	Leitrim	Carrigallen	Drumreilly	Bawnboy	IV.	91
16, 17	Drumahiskey	185 1 9	Antrim	Upper Dunluce	Ballymoney	Ballymoney	III.	18
9	Drumahitt	140 2 34	Antrim	Cary	Culfeightrin	Ballycastle	III.	13
14, 20, 22	Drumahoe	286 1 1	Londonderry	Tirkeeran	Clondermot	Londonderry	III.	248
1, 2	Drumahorgan	268 2 12	Londonderry	Keenaght	Magilligan	NewTⁿLimavady	III.	236
20	Drumahurk	69 3 3	Cavan	Upper Loughtee	Castleterra	Cavan	III.	82
27	Drumakeely	153 1 36	Antrim	Kilconway	Grange of Dundermot	Ballymena	III.	26
15, 16	Drumakeenan	132 3 25	Cavan	Tullygarvey	Annagh	Cavan	III.	87
42	Drumakeenan	327 0 9	King's Co.	Clonlisk	Ettagh	Roscrea	I.	130
42	Drumakeenan	412 3 27	King's Co.	Clonlisk	Roscrea	Roscrea	I.	131
20, 25	Drumakill	322 0 25	Monaghan	Cremorne	Muckno	Castleblayney	III.	261
31	Drumakinneo	201 0 25	Cavan	Clanmahon	Crosserlough	Cavan	III.	76
21	Drumaknockan	480 2 23	Down	Lower Iveagh, Lr. pt.	Dromore	Lisburn	III.	168
54, 56	Drumalagagh	832 3 25	Roscommon	Moycarn	Moore	Ballinasloe	IV.	206
26, 29	Drumalane	299 3 26b	Armagh	Orior Upper	Newry	Newry	III.	59
17	Drumalaragh	214 3 23	Armagh	Orior Lower	Kilclooney	Armagh	III.	56
24, 28	Drumaleague	153 3 20c	Leitrim	Leitrim	Kiltubbrid	Carᵏ. on Shannon	IV.	103
10	Drumalee	98 1 17	Cavan	Lower Loughtee	Drumlane	Cavan	III.	80
11, 15	Drumalee	280 1 22d	Cavan	Tullygarvey	Annagh	Cavan	III.	87
20	Drumalee	85 3 35	Cavan	Upper Loughtee	Annagelliff	Cavan	III.	81
20	Drumalee	192 3 11	Cavan	Upper Loughtee	Urney	Cavan	III.	86
62, 66	Drumaleet	351 3 3	Antrim	Upper Massereene	Aghagallon	Lurgan	III.	29
78, 79	Drumaleheen	68 1 19	Mayo	Carra	Breaghwy	Castlebar	IV.	127
10	Drumalief	191 2 1	Londonderry	Keenaght	Aghanloo	NewTⁿLimavady	III.	234
15	Drumalig	879 0 5	Down	Castlereagh Upper	Saintfield	Lisburn	III.	166
5	Drumalis	88 1 9	Armagh	Oneilland West	Drumcree	Lurgan	III.	52
20	Drumaliss	329 0 29e	Monaghan	Cremorne	Muckno	Castleblayney	III.	261
35, 40	Drumaliss and Curran	224 0 19	Antrim	Upper Glenarm	Larne	Larne	III.	25
14	Drumalla or Feugh (Bishops)	272 0 36	Cavan	Lower Loughtee	Drumlane	Cavan	III.	80
62	Drumalooaun	160 0 5f	Mayo	Gallen	Killasser	Swineford	IV.	149
20	Drumalough	424 0 36g	Roscommon	Castlereagh	Kilkeevin	Castlereagh	IV.	200
73	Drumalough or Lough Hill	166 3 33h	Donegal	Banagh	Inishkeel	Glenties	III.	106
24, 30	Drumalt	251 3 22i	Cavan	Tullyhunco	Killashandra	Cavan	III.	98
13, 18	Drumalt	137 1 30	Monaghan	Monaghan	Kilmore	Monaghan	III.	276
28	Drumaltnamuck	64 0 11	Armagh	Fews Upper	Newtownhamilton	Castleblayney	III.	49
15	Drumalure Beg	95 1 35j	Cavan	Lower Loughtee	Annagh	Cavan	III.	79
15	Drumalure More	205 0 5	Cavan	Lower Loughtee	Annagh	Cavan	III.	79
17	Drumamoodan	135 3 30	Roscommon	Roscommon	Aughrim	Carᵏ. on Shannon	IV.	207
24	Drumamry	116 1 35	Cavan	Tullyhunco	Killashandra	Cavan	III.	98
23, 28	Drumamuck Glebe	243 1 30k	Cavan	Clankee	Knockbride	Bailieborough	III.	73
18, 26	Drumanaffrin	1,194 3 17l	Mayo	Erris	Kilcommon	Belmullet	IV.	144
8	Drumanagh	46 1 29	Dublin	Balrothery East	Lusk	Balrothery	I.	21
36	Drumanaghan or Drumulcaw	447 3 19	Down	Kinelarty	Loughinisland	Downpatrick	III.	177
29, 36	Drumanakelly	250 2 3	Down	Kinelarty	Loughinisland	Downpatrick	III.	177
32	Drumanalaragh	160 1 8	Cavan	Upper Loughtee	Crosserlough	Cavan	III.	83
17	Drumanan	1 14	Monaghan	Dartree	Aghabog	Cootehill	III.	263
36	Drumanaquoile	1,036 2 37	Down	Kinelarty	Kilmegan	Downpatrick	III.	176
39	Drumanaraher	78 2 11m	Sligo	Corran	Kilshalvy	Boyle	IV.	227
52, 60	Drumanaught	1,294 1 33	Donegal	Raphoe	Conwal	Letterkenny	III.	137
43	Drumanaway	237 0 33	Antrim	Upper Toome	Drummaul	Ballymena	III.	34
12, 19	Drumandoora	854 0 30n	Clare	Tulla Upper	Feakle	Tulla	II.	39
63	Drumanduff	121 2 10	Antrim	Upper Massereene	Ballinderry	Lisburn	III.	29
10	Drumane	147 1 30	Cavan	Tullyhaw	Templeport	Bawnboy	III.	94
27	Drumane	135 0 23	Fermanagh	Clanawley	Cleenish	Enniskillen	III.	190
21	Drumane	508 1 26	Londonderry	Loughinsholin	Tamlaght O'Crilly	Ballymoney	III.	243
58	Drumaneany	1,074 3 20	Donegal	Boylagh	Inishkeel	Glenties	III.	112
99	Drumaneary	250 1 17	Donegal	Banagh	Inver	Donegal	III.	107

(a) Including 9A. 2R. 36P. water.
(b) Including 6A. 2R. 24P. water.
(c) Including 23A. 1R. 25P. water.
(d) Including 25A. 1R. 33P. water.
(e) Including 24A. 1R. 36P. water.

(f) Including 11A. 2R. 6P. water.
(g) Including 32A. 3R. 11P. water.
(h) Including 9A. 0R. 25P. water.
(i) Including 67A. 3R. 22P. water.
(j) Including 10A. 2R. 23P. water.

(k) Including 18A. 0R. 26P. water.
(l) Including 5A. 2R. 11P. water.
(m) Including 0A. 2R. 35P. water.
(n) Including 8A. 0R. 23P. water.

No. of Sheet of the Ordnance Survey Maps.	Townlands and Towns.	Area in Statute Acres.			County.	Barony.	Parish.	Poor Law Union in 1857.	Townland Census of 1851, Part I.	
		A.	R.	P.					Vol.	Page
4	Drumaneber	70	1	10	Meath	Lower Kells	Moynalty	Kells	I.	203
99, 100, 103	Drumaneel	113	3	32	Donegal	Tirhugh	Drumhome	Donegal	III.	146
39	Drumaneel	204	3	24	Sligo	Corran	Drumrat	Boyle	IV.	226
37, 42	Drumanee Lower	205	3	25	Londonderry	Loughinsholin	Ballyscullion	Magherafelt	III.	239
37	Drumanee Upper	121	3	25	Londonderry	Loughinsholin	Ballyscullion	Magherafelt	III.	239
27, 33	Drumanespick	777	2	7	Cavan	Clankee	Bailieborough	Bailieborough	III.	71
29, 30	Drumaness	761	0	35	Down	Kinelarty	Magheradrool	Downpatrick	III.	177
3	Drumanilra or Annagh	166	3	39	Roscommon	Boyle	Kilbryan	Boyle	IV.	195
7	Drumanilra or Mounteagle	312	1	33a	Roscommon	Boyle	Tumna	Cark.on Shannon	IV.	198
63, 64	Drumankelly	302	1	36	Antrim	Upper Massereene	Derryaghy	Lisburn	III.	30
22	Drumanny	221	2	15	Monaghan	Dartree	Ematris	Cootehill	III.	267
5	Drumanone	155	0	31	Roscommon	Boyle	Boyle	Boyle	IV.	194
97	Drumanoo	689	3	11	Donegal	Banagh	Killybegs Upper	Glenties	III.	110
5	Drumanphy	118	0	5	Armagh	Oneilland West	Tartaraghan	Armagh	III.	54
40	Drumantine	597	3	13b	Down	Upper Iveagh, Up.pt.	Donaghmore	Newry	III.	175
55, 62	Drumanuey	132	3	37	Tyrone	Dungannon Middle	Clonfeacle	Dungannon	III.	299
24	Drumanure	224	1	36c	Clare	Inchiquin	Inagh	Ennistimon	II.	25
32	Drumanure	320	1	38d	Clare	Islands	Kilmaley	Ennis	I.	31
14, 15	Drumanure	384	0	5	Fermanagh	Magheraboy	Devenish	Enniskillen	III.	210
30	Drumanure	206	3	7	Leitrim	Carrigallen	Carrigallen	Bawnboy	IV.	89
5	Drumanure	169	1	10	Leitrim	Rosclogher	Rossinver	Ballyshannon	IV.	111
23	Drumanure	414	3	8e	Longford	Shrule	Abbeyshrule	Ballymahon	I.	165
18	Drumany	85	1	25	Donegal	Kilmacrenan	Clondavaddog	Milliord	III.	124
53, 61	Drumany	271	1	30	Donegal	Raphoe	Leck	Letterkenny	III.	140
33	Drumany	131	3	39	Fermanagh	Clanawley	Kinawley	Enniskillen	III.	193
34	Drumany	298	3	7f	Fermanagh	Magherastephana	Aghalurcher	Lisnaskea	III.	216
24, 25	Drumany	98	2	39	Leitrim	Carrigallen	Oughteragh	Bawnboy	IV.	92
15	Drumany	104	0	33	Leitrim	Drumahaire	Killanummery	Manorhamilton	IV.	98
24	Drumany	111	0	27	Leitrim	Leitrim	Kiltubbrid	Cark. on Shannon	IV.	103
39	Drumany Beg	71	1	4	Fermanagh	Knockninny	Kinawley	Lisnaskea	III.	201
29	Drumany (Beirne)	122	0	22	Leitrim	Carrigallen	Fenagh	Bawnboy	IV.	91
15	Drumany Glebe	158	2	7	Leitrim	Drumahaire	Killarga	Manorhamilton	IV.	98
38	Drumany More	198	3	31	Fermanagh	Knockninny	Kinawley	Lisnaskea	III.	201
24	Drumany (O'Brien)	126	0	4g	Leitrim	Mohill	Fenagh	Mohill	IV.	106
24	Drumany (Tenants)	106	3	22	Leitrim	Mohill	Fenagh	Mohill	IV.	106
17	Drumaqueran	133	0	25	Antrim	Upper Dunluce	Kilraghts	Ballymoney	III.	19
7	Drumaquill	194	3	24	Londonderry	Coleraine	Killowen	Coleraine	III.	232
19	Drumar	181	2	8	Monaghan	Cremorne	Ballybay	Castleblayney	III.	259
28	Drumaragh	181	1	14	Leitrim	Leitrim	Kiltubbrid	Cark. on Shannon	IV.	103
26	Drumaran	837	2	0h	Down	Lower Iveagh, Up.pt.	Tullylish	Banbridge	III.	171
26	Drumaran	199	2	14	Fermanagh	Clanawley	Cleenish	Enniskillen	III.	190
10	Drumaran	55	0	6	Fermanagh	Lurg	Derryvullan	Lowtherstown	III.	204
16	Drumaraw	149	2	21i	Cavan	Upper Loughtee	Castleterra	Cavan	III.	82
21	Drumaraw	93	3	6	Fermanagh	Magheraboy	Devenish	Enniskillen	III.	210
12, 17	Drumard	255	0	19	Antrim	Upper Dunluce	Ballymoney	Ballymoney	III.	18
31	Drumard	98	0	22	Cavan	Clanmahon	Ballintemple	Cavan	III.	75
20	Drumard	292	1	13	Cavan	Upper Loughtee	Kilmore	Cavan	III.	84
93	Drumard	254	2	38	Donegal	Banagh	Inver	Donegal	III.	107
5, 10	Drumard	219	3	1	Fermanagh	Lurg	Magheraculmoney	Lowtherstown	III.	207
27	Drumard	94	2	34j	Fermanagh	Tirkennedy	Enniskillen	Enniskillen	III.	222
40, 41	Drumard	890	0	31	Londonderry	Loughinsholin	Ballynascreen	Magherafelt	III.	239
46, 48	Drumard	504	1	2	Londonderry	Loughinsholin	Lissan	Magherafelt	III.	242
37	Drumard	979	0	7	Londonderry	Loughinsholin	Maghera	Magherafelt	III.	242
33	Drumard	655	2	14	Londonderry	Loughinsholin	Tamlaght O'Crilly	Ballymoney	III.	243
1, 2	Drumard	544	1	15k	Longford	Longford	Killoe	Granard	I.	159
10	Drumard	355	3	28	Louth	Ardee	Killanny	Dundalk	I.	173
77	Drumard	146	1	3l	Mayo	Burrishoole	Kilmeena	Westport	IV.	122
43	Drumard	127	2	11	Meath	Lower Deece	Galtrim	Trim	I.	191
11	Drumard	82	0	20m	Monaghan	Dartree	Clones	Clones	III.	264
46	Drumard	108	3	16	Tyrone	Dungannon Middle	Tullyniskan	Dungannon	III.	304
39, 47	Drumard	196	1	18	Tyrone	Dungannon Upper	Arboe	Cookstown	III.	305
29, 38	Drumard	337	1	30	Tyrone	Dungannon Upper	Derryloran	Cookstown	III.	307
53, 54	Drumardagh	332	2	25	Donegal	Raphoe	Leck	Letterkenny	III.	140
25	Drumardan	147	3	26	Down	Ards Upper	Castleboy	Downpatrick	III.	160
25	Drumardan Quarter	67	2	22	Down	Ards Upper	Castleboy	Downpatrick	III.	160
55	Drumard Cross	50	1	9	Tyrone	Dungannon Middle	Killyman	Dungannon	III.	303
55	Drumard Glebe	67	0	27	Tyrone	Dungannon Middle	Killyman	Dungannon	III.	303
9	Drumard (Jones)	221	2	30n	Armagh	Oneilland West	Kilmore	Armagh	IV.	53
32, 35	Drumard (Jones)	393	2	33o	Leitrim	Mohill	Mohill	Mohill	IV.	107
35, 37	Drumard (Magerraun)	452	2	12	Leitrim	Mohill	Mohill	Mohill	IV.	107
49	Drumardnagross	326	1	19	Tyrone	Omagh East	Kilskeery	Lowtherstown	III.	313

(a) Including 12A. 1R. 39P. water.
(b) Including 12A. 2R. 1P. water.
(c) Including 4A. 0R. 24P. water.
(d) Including 0A. 1R. 8P. water.
(e) Including 14A. 1R. 20P. Inny River.

(f) Including 88A. 1R. 0P. Loughs.
(g) Including 10A. 2R. 13P. water.
(h) Including 9A. 1R. 11P. Drumaran Lake.
(i) Including 7A. 2R. 25P. water.
(j) Including 3A. 2R. 5P. water.

(k) Including 24A. 2R. 4P. water.
(l) Including 17A. 2R. 24P. water.
(m) Including 8A. 2R. 39P. water.
(n) Including 14A. 0R. 9P. detached portion.
(o) Including 0A. 2R. 7P. water.

No. of Sheet of the Ordnance Survey Maps.	Townlands and Towns.	Area in Statute Acres.			County.	Barony.	Parish.	Poor Law Union in 1857.	Townland Census of 1851, Part I.	
		A.	R.	P.					Vol.	Page
9	Drumard (*Primate*)	248	1	8	Armagh	Oneilland West	Kilmore	Armagh	III.	53
12	Drumarg or Downs	171	0	32	Armagh	Armagh	Armagh	Armagh	III.	43
9	Drumaridly	41	1	22	Antrim	Cary	Culfeightrin	Ballycastle	III.	13
22, 25	Drumarigna	123	2	24a	Leitrim	Carrigallen	Drumreilly	Bawnboy	IV.	91
93	Drumark	156	0	35	Donegal	Banagh	Killymard	Donegal	III.	111
42	Drumarkin	201	0	3	Down	Upper Iveagh, Lr. pt.	Drumballyroney	Newry	III.	172
10	Drumarky	172	3	21	Fermanagh	Lurg	Derryvullan	Lowtherstown	III.	204
8	Drumarn	81	1	24	Armagh	Armagh	Clonfeacle	Armagh	III.	43
36	Drumaroad	803	1	0	Down	Kinelarty	Loughinisland	Downpatrick	III.	177
5, 9	Drumaroan	109	1	17	Antrim	Cary	Culfeightrin	Ballycastle	III.	13
28	Drumarraght	127	0	34	Fermanagh	Magherastephana	Aghavea	Lisnaskea	III.	218
3	Drumarrell	94	1	12	Monaghan	Trough	Errigal Trough	Monaghan	III.	284
8	Drumart	88	2	13	Armagh	Oneilland West	Grange	Armagh	III.	52
8	Drumart	92	3	11	Armagh	Oneilland West	Loughgall	Armagh	III.	54
13	Drumart	353	2	33	Armagh	Oneilland West	Mullaghbrack	Banbridge	III.	54
1	Drumartigan	96	1	22	Monaghan	Trough	Errigal Trough	Clogher	III.	284
14, 15	Drumary	165	2	36	Fermanagh	Magheraboy	Devenish	Enniskillen	III.	210
14	Drumary	115	3	4	Fermanagh	Magheraboy	Inishmacsaint	Ballyshannon	III.	212
17	Drumary	161	1	31	Monaghan	Dartree	Aghabog	Cootehill	III.	263
56	Drumash	141	2	17b	Tyrone	Omagh East	Kilskeery	Enniskillen	III.	313
24	Drumashellig	324	3	38	Queen's Co.	Cullenagh	Ballyroan	Abbeyleix	I.	239
69, 78	Drumask	80	3	30	Mayo	Carra	Aglish	Castlebar	IV.	123
8	Drumask or Ballycullen	86	1	15	Armagh	Armagh	Clonfeacle	Armagh	III.	43
20	Drumaskibbole	656	0	18	Sligo	Carbury	St. John's	Sligo	IV.	223
30	Drumaskin	25	0	22	Galway	Dunmore	Dunmore	Tuam	IV.	33
30	Drumaskin	178	3	6	Galway	Dunmore	Tuam	Tuam	IV.	36
14	Drumasladdy	193	1	20c	Cavan	Lower Loughtee	Drumlane	Cavan	III.	80
59, 60	Drumaslaghy	200	3	39	Tyrone	Dungannon Lower	Carnteel	Clogher	III.	297
55	Drumaspil	177	2	26	Tyrone	Dungannon Middle	Killyman	Dungannon	III.	303
29	Drumass	401	2	19	Monaghan	Farney	Inishkeen	Dundalk	III.	271
8	Drumataffan	134	3	28	Fermanagh	Magheraboy	Inishmacsaint	Ballyshannon	III.	212
17	Drumate	176	3	8d	Monaghan	Dartree	Aghabog	Cootehill	III.	263
17	Drumatee	288	1	34	Armagh	Fews Lower	Mullaghbrack	Armagh	III.	47
32	Drumatehy	193	1	6	Clare	Islands	Kilmaley	Ennis	II.	31
34	Drumatemple	264	1	34	Roscommon	Ballymoe	Drumatemple	Castlereagh	IV.	191
14	Drumatihugh	34	3	19	Down	Lower Iveagh,Up.pt.	Blaris	Lisburn	III.	169
14, 21	Drumatihugh	262	3	25	Down	Lower Iveagh,Up.pt.	Hillsborough	Lisburn	III.	169
106, 107	Drumatober	310	2	1	Galway	Longford	Abbeygormacan	Ballinasloe	IV.	56
62	Drumatoland	487	2	34	Donegal	Raphoe	Raymoghy	Strabane	III.	141
27, 28	Drumatrumman	390	0	38	Donegal	Kilmacrenan	Tullyfern	Milford	III.	133
92, 93	Drumatumpher	202	2	26	Donegal	Banagh	Inver	Donegal	III.	107
7	Drumatybonniff	110	1	20	Roscommon	Boyle	Tumna	Cark. on Shannon	IV.	198
16, 21	Drumauna	227	2	3	Cavan	Tullygarvey	Drung	Cootehill	III.	89
18, 23	Drumavaddy	144	0	14	Antrim	Kilconway	Killagan	Ballymoney	III.	27
25, 31	Drumavaddy	336	2	2	Cavan	Clanmahon	Denn	Cavan	III.	76
15	Drumavaddy	114	1	35e	Cavan	Lower Loughtee	Annagh	Cavan	III.	79
15, 16	Drumavaddy	160	1	8	Cavan	Tullygarvey	Annagh	Cavan	III.	87
22	Drumavaddy	122	1	4	Monaghan	Dartree	Currin	Cootehill	III.	265
25	Drumavaddy	145	2	30	Monaghan	Farney	Donaghmoyne	Castleblayney	III.	269
1, 5	Drumavally	171	0	0	Londonderry	Keenaght	Magilligan	New Tn. Limavady	III.	236
21	Drumavan	163	3	3	Monaghan	Dartree	Currin	Clones	III.	265
20	Drumavanagh	84	3	0	Cavan	Upper Loughtee	Urney	Cavan	III.	86
16	Drumavcale	93	2	28	Monaghan	Dartree	Currin	Clones	III.	265
15, 21	Drumaveel	110	2	27	Fermanagh	Magheraboy	Devenish	Enniskillen	III.	210
17	Drumaveel North	72	3	32	Cavan	Tullygarvey	Drumgoon	Cootehill	III.	88
23	Drumaveel South	276	1	10f	Cavan	Clankee	Drumgoon	Cootehill	III.	72
4, 11	Drumaville	1,298	2	4	Donegal	Inishowen East	Clonca	Inishowen	III.	116
12	Drumaville	369	1	12	Donegal	Inishowen East	Culdaff	Inishowen	III.	118
4	Drumavohy	187	3	22	Donegal	Inishowen East	Clonca	Inishowen	III.	116
9, 18	Drumavohy and Ballybolagan	350	3	17	Donegal	Kilmacrenan	Clondavaddog	Milford	III.	124
9	Drumavoley	214	1	7	Antrim	Cary	Ramoan	Ballycastle	III.	14
16	Drumavrack	172	1	6	Cavan	Tullygarvey	Annagh	Cootehill	III.	87
101,102,105	Drumawark	502	1	15	Donegal	Tirhugh	Templecarn	Donegal	III.	149
24	Drumaweel Glebe	163	0	35	Leitrim	Leitrim	Kiltubbrid	Cark. on Shannon	IV.	103
13, 22	Drumaweer	608	3	37	Donegal	Inishowen East	Moville Lower	Inishowen	III.	119
6	Drumawhy	1,127	2	20	Down	Ards Lower	Newtownards	Newtownards	III.	158
22, 27	Drumawill	76	2	8	Fermanagh	Magheraboy	Rossorry	Enniskillen	III.	214
8	Drumawillin	227	1	13	Antrim	Cary	Ramoan	Ballycastle	III.	14
26	Drumawillin	55	3	34	Fermanagh	Clanawley	Cleenish	Enniskillen	III.	190
61	Drumay	919	0	20	Tyrone	Dungannon Middle	Clonfeacle	Dungannon	III.	299
28	Drumbad	80	0	26	Fermanagh	Magherastephana	Aghavea	Lisnaskea	III.	218

(a) Including 7A. 2R. 28P. water.
(b) Including 2A. 3R. 35P. water.
(c) Including 7A. 3R. 6P. water.
(d) Including 13A. 1R. 28P. water.
(e) Including 8A. 0R. 36P. water.
(f) Including 5A. 2R. 30P. water.

No. of Sheet of the Ordnance Survey Maps.	Townlands and Towns.	Area in Statute Acres.			County.	Barony.	Parish.	Poor Law Union in 1857.	Townland Census of 1851, Part I.	
		A.	R.	P.					Vol.	Page
22, 25	Drumbad . .	170	0	5a	Leitrim . .	Carrigallen . .	Oughteragh . .	Bawnboy . .	IV.	92
36	Drumbad . .	159	3	10b	Leitrim . .	Mohill . .	Cloone . .	Mohill . .	IV.	105
5	Drumbad . .	234	1	9	Longford . .	Longford . .	Killoe . .	Longford . .	I.	159
28, 34	Drumbad Beg .	75	2	3	Fermanagh .	Magherastephana .	Aghalurcher .	Lisnaskea .	III.	216
9	Drumbadmeen .	171	1	35	Fermanagh .	Magheraboy . .	Inishmacsaint .	Ballyshannon .	III.	212
8, 9, 13, 14	Drumbadmeen, Barr of	514	1	14c	Fermanagh .	Magheraboy . .	Inishmacsaint	Ballyshannon .	III.	212
34	Drumbad More .	151	1	4	Fermanagh .	Magherastephana .	Aghalurcher .	Lisnaskea .	III.	216
8	Drumbadreevagh .	324	2	29d	Fermanagh .	Magheraboy . .	Inishmacsaint .	Ballyshannon .	III.	212
14, 19	Drumbagh . .	48	3	4	Cavan . .	Tullyhunco .	Kildallan . .	Cavan . .	III.	97
28	Drumbaghlin .	106	1	16	Fermanagh .	Magherastephana .	Aghalurcher .	Lisnaskea .	III.	216
31	Drumbally . .	256	0	37	Armagh . .	Fews Upper .	Creggan . . .	Castleblayney .	III.	48
11	Drumballycaslan .	53	2	33	Donegal . .	Inishowen East .	Clonca . .	Inishowen .	III.	117
9	Drumballydonaghy	202	0	18e	Londonderry .	Keenaght . .	Tamlaght Finlagan	New TLimavady	III.	237
36	Drumballyhagan .	320	3	4	Londonderry .	Loughinsholin .	Kilcronaghan .	Magherafelt .	III.	241
36	Drumballyhagan Clark	117	1	34	Londonderry .	Loughinsholin .	Kilcronaghan .	Magherafelt .	III.	241
38	Drumballyhugh .	217	2	15	Tyrone . .	Dungannon Upper .	Desertcreat .	Cookstown .	III.	307
18	Drum & Ballynawall	108	2	35	Donegal . .	Kilmacrenan .	Clondavaddog .	Millford . .	III.	124
22	Drumbanagher .	291	2	1	Armagh . .	Orior Lower .	Killevy . .	Newry . .	III.	56
7	Drumbanagher .	172	3	19	Monaghan .	Trough . .	Donagh . .	Monaghan .	III.	282
39	Drumbanaway .	193	2	31	Tyrone . .	Dungannon Upper .	Ballyclog . .	Cookstown .	III.	306
79	Drumbane . .	98	0	10f	Donegal . .	Raphoe . .	Urney . . .	Strabane . .	III.	144
13	Drumbane . .	182	3	16g	Down . .	Lower Iveagh, Up.pt.	Moira . . .	Lurgan . .	III.	170
5, 10	Drumbane . .	114	3	17	Fermanagh .	Lurg . .	Magheraculmoney .	Lowtherstown .	III.	207
5	Drumbane . .	402	2	16	Galway . .	Dunmore . .	Dunmore . .	Tuam . .	IV.	34
35	Drumbane . .	103	0	26	King's Co. .	Ballybritt . .	Birr . . .	Parsonstown .	I.	125
26	Drumbane . .	424	2	18	Londonderry .	Coleraine . .	Errigal . .	Coleraine . .	III.	232
5, 9	Drumbane . .	184	3	9	Londonderry .	Keenaght . .	Aghanloo . .	New TLimavady	III.	234
40, 46	Drumbane . .	1,748	2	25	Tipperary, N.R.	Kilnamanagh Upper	Moyaliff . .	Thurles . .	II.	279
25	Drumbane . .	100	0	16	Tipperary, N.R.	Owney and Arra .	Templeachally .	Nenagh . .	II.	297
28, 34	Drumbannan .	452	1	21h	Cavan . .	Clankee . .	Bailieborough .	Bailieborough .	III.	71
31, 37	Drumbannow .	111	1	17i	Cavan . .	Clanmahon .	Drumlumman .	Granard . .	III.	77
34, 35	Drumbar . .	131	1	15	Cavan . .	Clankee . .	Enniskeen .	Bailieborough .	III.	72
27, 28	Drumbar . .	120	0	19	Cavan . .	Clankee . .	Knockbride .	Bailieborough .	III.	73
25	Drumbar . .	44	2	0	Cavan . .	Clanmahon .	Kilmore . .	Cavan . .	III.	78
7	Drumbar . .	306	1	2	Cavan . .	Tullyhaw .	Kinawley . .	Bawnboy . .	III.	93
20	Drumbar . .	43	0	25	Cavan . .	Upper Loughtee .	Urney . . .	Cavan . .	III.	86
100	Drumbar . .	144	2	10	Donegal . .	Tirhugh . .	Donegal . .	Donegal . .	III.	145
16	Drumbaragh .	862	3	17	Meath . .	Upper Kells .	Kells . . .	Kells . .	I.	206
12, 17	Drumbaragh .	179	3	15	Monaghan .	Dartree . .	Aghabog . .	Clones . .	III.	263
93	Drumbaran .	209	0	35	Donegal . .	Banagh . .	Inver . . .	Donegal . .	III.	107
73, 82	Drumbaran .	92	2	9	Donegal . .	Banagh . .	Killybegs Lower .	Glenties . .	III.	110
2, 5, 6	Drumbaran .	227	1	6	Fermanagh .	Lurg . .	Drumkeeran . .	Lowtherstown .	III.	206
23	Drumbare . .	310	2	33	Antrim . .	Kilconway .	Grange of Dundermot	Ballymena .	III.	26
27	Drumbargy .	110	2	19	Fermanagh .	Clanawley . .	Cleenish . .	Enniskillen .	III.	190
91, 97	Drumbarity .	67	2	1	Donegal . .	Banagh . .	Killybegs Upper .	Glenties . .	III.	110
17	Drumbarkey .	139	3	13	Cavan . .	Tullygarvey .	Drumgoon . .	Cootehill . .	III.	88
34	Drumbarley .	228	3	31	Tyrone . .	Omagh West .	Longfield East .	Omagh . .	III.	315
11	Drumbarlom .	204	2	7j	Cavan . .	Lower Loughtee .	Drumlane . .	Cavan . .	III.	80
10	Drumbarna .	126	1	21	Fermanagh .	Lurg . .	Magheraculmoney .	Lowtherstown .	III.	207
47	Drumbarnet .	255	2	29	Donegal . .	Raphoe . .	Allsaints . .	Londonderry .	III.	134
9	Drumbarnet .	87	2	34	Monaghan .	Monaghan . .	Tedavnet . .	Monaghan .	III.	278
54	Drumbarnet Lower	184	3	39	Donegal . .	Raphoe . .	Raymoghy . .	Londonderry .	III.	141
54	Drumbarnet Middle	112	3	11	Donegal . .	Raphoe . .	Raymoghy . .	Londonderry .	III.	141
54	Drumbarnet Upper	175	2	22	Donegal . .	Raphoe . .	Raymoghy . .	Londonderry .	III.	141
94	Drumbarren .	66	2	31	Donegal . .	Tirhugh . .	Donegal . .	Donegal . .	III.	145
32	Drumbarry .	286	2	7	Cavan . .	Upper Loughtee .	Denn . . .	Cavan . .	III.	83
40	Drumbarry .	102	3	18	Fermanagh .	Clankelly .	Galloon . .	Clones . .	III.	198
16	Drumbartagh .	127	3	17	Cavan . .	Tullygarvey .	Annagh . .	Cootehill . .	III.	87
23, 31	Drumbaun .	241	3	10k	Clare . .	Ibrickan . .	Kilfarboy . .	Ennistimon .	II.	22
70	Drumbaun .	35	2	29	Galway . .	Clare . .	Annaghdown .	Galway . .	IV.	16
14, 19	Drumbaun . .	294	2	19	Longford . .	Ardagh . .	Ardagh . .	Longford . .	I.	151
103	Drumbaun .	306	3	32	Mayo . .	Costello . .	Annagh . .	Claremorris .	IV.	138
37, 42, 43	Drumbaun .	1,490	3	28	Sligo . .	Leyny . .	Achonry . .	Tobercurry .	IV.	229
22	Drumbaun .	128	2	1	Tipperary, N.R.	Ikerrin . .	Cullenwaine .	Roscrea . .	II.	275
31	Drumbaun .	251	3	27	Tipperary, N.R.	Owney and Arra .	Killoscully .	Nenagh . .	II.	295
12	Drumbawn .	417	3	16	Wicklow . .	Newcastle . .	Calary . .	Rathdrum .	I.	350
7, 9	Drumbeagh .	188	1	26	Cavan . .	Tullyhaw .	Templeport . .	Bawnboy . .	III.	94
93	Drumbeagh .	391	2	37	Donegal . .	Banagh . .	Inver . . .	Donegal . .	III.	107
97	Drumbeagh .	75	1	23	Donegal . .	Banagh . .	Killybegs Upper .	Glenties . .	III.	110
35, 40	Drumbealimy .	90	2	36	Fermanagh .	Clankelly .	Clones . .	Clones . .	III.	196
9, 13	Drumbear . .	143	3	2	Monaghan .	Monaghan . .	Monaghan . .	Monaghan .	III.	277
46	Drumbearn .	169	1	37l	Tyrone . .	Dungannon Middle .	Donaghmore .	Dungannon .	III.	302
12	Drumbee . .	161	3	26	Armagh . .	Armagh . .	Eglish . . .	Armagh . .	II.	44

(a) Including 17A. 1R. 30P. water.   (e) Including 3A. 3R. 38P. water.   (i) Including 2A. 6R. 2P. water.
(b) Including 17A. 0R. 2P. water.   (f) Including 1A. 1R. 9P. water.   (j) Including 2A. 2R. 23P. water.
(c) Including 43A. 0R. 6P. water.   (g) Including 6A. 2R. 16P. water.   (k) Including 2A. 0R. 23P. water.
(d) Including 12A. 3R. 29P. water.   (h) Including 18A. 2R. 11P. water.   (l) Including 12A. 3R. 19P. water.

No. of Sheet of the Ordnance Survey Maps.	Townlands and Towns.	Area in Statute Acres.	County.	Barony.	Parish.	Poor Law Union in 1857.	Townland Census of 1851, Part I.	
		A. R. P.					Vol.	Page
31, 32, 37	Drumbee	274 2 39	Cavan	Castlerahan	Crosserlough	Cavan	III.	68
12	Drumbee Beg	207 2 18a	Armagh	Fews Lower	Lisnadill	Armagh	III.	46
17	Drumbeecross	120 3 19	Armagh	Fews Lower	Mullaghbrack	Armagh	III.	47
12	Drumbee More	180 2 21	Armagh	Fews Lower	Lisnadill	Armagh	III.	46
62, 70	Drumbeg	93 2 13	Donegal	Raphoe	Taughboyne	Strabane	III.	143
9	Drumbeg	376 2 20	Down	Castlereagh Upper	Drumbeg	Lisburn	III.	164
92, 98	Drumbeg or Cloverhill	126 2 15	Donegal	Banagh	Inver	Donegal	III.	107
15, 21	Drumbeggan	299 2 5	Fermanagh	Magheraboy	Devenish	Enniskillen	III.	210
14, 20, 21	Drumbegger	150 0 38	Fermanagh	Magheraboy	Boho	Enniskillen	III.	209
35	Drumbeg North	61 3 27	Sligo	Tirerrill	Kilmactranny	Boyle	IV.	240
35	Drumbeg South	98 1 23	Sligo	Tirerrill	Kilmactranny	Boyle	IV.	240
35	Drumbeg West	81 0 31	Sligo	Tirerrill	Kilmactranny	Boyle	IV.	240
29, 33	Drumbeighra	160 0 3	Leitrim	Mohill	Mohill	Mohill	IV.	107
9	Drumbenagh	138 1 38	Monaghan	Monaghan	Tedavnet	Monaghan	III.	278
10	Drumbeo	188 3 5	Monaghan	Cremorne	Clontibret	Monaghan	III.	260
27, 28	Drumberagh	340 1 17	Monaghan	Farney	Donaghmoyne	Carrickmacross	III.	269
36	Drumbern	171 3 13	Donegal	Kilmacrenan	Tullyfern	Milford	III.	133
21	Drumberny	84 1 39	Fermanagh	Magheraboy	Devenish	Enniskillen	III.	210
24	Drumberry	105 0 16	Cavan	Tullyhunco	Killashandra	Cavan	III.	98
24	Drumbess	584 2 30	Cavan	Tullyhunco	Killashandra	Cavan	III.	98
17, 18	Drumbest	228 1 6b	Antrim	Upper Dunluce	Kilraghts	Ballymoney	III.	19
21, 24	Drumbibe	196 1 23	Leitrim	Carrigallen	Oughteragh	Bawnboy	IV.	92
9	Drumbier	166 3 20	Monaghan	Monaghan	Tedavnet	Monaghan	III.	278
33	Drumbiggil	204 1 31	Clare	Islands	Drumcliff	Ennis	II.	30
3	Drumbilla	532 2 13	Louth	Upper Dundalk	Roche	Dundalk	I.	179
9	Drumbin	153 0 3c	Monaghan	Monaghan	Tedavnet	Monaghan	III.	278
49	Drumbinnion	258 1 0	Tyrone	Omagh East	Kilskeery	Lowtherstown	III.	313
22, 23	Drumbinnis	369 3 6d	Cavan	Clankee	Knockbride	Cootehill	III.	73
19	Drumbinnis	90 3 38	Cavan	Tullyhunco	Kildallan	Bawnboy	III.	97
33	Drumbinnis	149 0 32	Fermanagh	Clanawley	Kinawley	Enniskillen	III.	194
33	Drumbinnis	106 3 15	Leitrim	Carrigallen	Cloone	Mohill	IV.	90
40	Drumbinnisk	73 0 21	Fermanagh	Clankelly	Clones	Clones	III.	196
1, 3	Drumbirn	121 2 38	Monaghan	Trough	Errigal Trough	Clogher	III.	284
16	Drumbo	94 0 31	Cavan	Tullygarvey	Annagh	Cootehill	III.	87
14, 19	Drumbo	156 1 7	Cavan	Tullyhunco	Kildallan	Cavan	III.	97
20, 21	Drumbo	290 0 14	Cavan	Upper Loughtee	Annagelliff	Cavan	III.	81
9, 15	Drumbo	1,274 0 7e	Down	Castlereagh Upper	Drumbo	Lisburn	III.	164
10, 11	Drumbo	206 1 30	Fermanagh	Lurg	Derryvullan	Lowtherstown	III.	204
34	Drumbo	191 2 3f	Monaghan	Farney	Magheracloone	Carrickmacross	III.	272
84, 93	Drumboarty	470 1 5	Donegal	Banagh	Inver	Donegal	III.	107
6	Drumboarty	152 0 9	Fermanagh	Lurg	Drumkeeran	Lowtherstown	III.	206
29	Drumboat	486 2 23	Monaghan	Farney	Inishkeen	Dundalk	III.	271
10, 15	Drumbockany	115 1 11	Fermanagh	Magheraboy	Inishmacsaint	Enniskillen	III.	212
49	Drumboe	79 3 35	Antrim	Upper Toome	Duneane	Antrim	III.	35
78	Drumboe Lower	331 0 30g	Donegal	Raphoe	Stranorlar	Stranorlar	III.	142
78	Drumboe Upper	167 2 36	Donegal	Raphoe	Stranorlar	Stranorlar	III.	142
43	Drumboghanagh Glebe	177 1 31h	Fermanagh	Coole	Drummully	Clones	III.	199
64, 73	Drumboghill	980 3 25i	Donegal	Boylagh	Inishkeel	Glenties	III.	112
29, 33	Drumboher	286 0 27	Leitrim	Mohill	Cloone	Mohill	IV.	105
52	Drumbologe	76 3 20	Donegal	Kilmacrenan	Conwal	Letterkenny	III.	126
39	Drumbominy	82 0 31j	Fermanagh	Knockninny	Kinawley	Lisnaskea	III.	201
42, 48	Drumbonniff	523 1 21	Down	Upper Iveagh, Lr. pt.	Clonduff	Newry	III.	171
26	Drumbonniv	336 1 3	Clare	Bunratty Upper	Inchicronan	Tulla	II.	9
7	Drumboory	177 2 37	Cavan	Tullyhaw	Kinawley	Bawnboy	III.	93
39	Drumboory	66 1 31k	Fermanagh	Knockninny	Kinawley	Lisnaskea	III.	201
21	Drumboory	95 0 24	Fermanagh	Magheraboy	Devenish	Enniskillen	III.	210
31, 34	Drumboory	556 1 23l	Monaghan	Farney	Magheracloone	Carrickmacross	III.	272
17, 22	Drumborisk	238 2 38m	Monaghan	Dartree	Currin	Cootehill	III.	265
30	Drumboy	273 3 1	Armagh	Fews Upper	Creggan	Castleblayney	III.	48
46	Drumboy	325 3 11	Donegal	Raphoe	Allsaints	Londonderry	III.	134
70, 71	Drumboy	143 1 9	Donegal	Raphoe	Clonleigh	Strabane	III.	135
21	Drumboy	166 0 17	Fermanagh	Clanawley	Boho	Enniskillen	III.	189
32	Drumboy	254 2 19	Leitrim	Mohill	Mohill	Mohill	IV.	107
4, 7	Drumboylan	207 3 12n	Roscommon	Boyle	Tumna	Carᵏ. on Shannon	IV.	198
30, 33	Drumbrackan	219 3 15	Monaghan	Farney	Magheracloone	Carrickmacross	III.	272
31	Drumbrade	149 0 39	Cavan	Clanmahon	Ballintemple	Cavan	III.	75
18	Drumbrade	244 2 4	Cavan	Tullygarvey	Drumgoon	Cootehill	III.	88
16, 18	Drumbrahade	120 1 12	Leitrim	Drumahaire	Inishmagrath	Manorhamilton	IV.	96
27, 28	Drumbranned	145 0 20	Leitrim	Leitrim	Kiltubbrid	Carᵏ. on Shannon	IV.	119
67, 68	Drumbrastle East	97 3 21	Mayo	Burrishoole	Burrishoole	Newport	IV.	119
67	Drumbrastle West	89 3 32	Mayo	Burrishoole	Burrishoole	Newport	IV.	119
15	Drumbrawn	452 0 36	Cavan	Tullygarvey	Annagh	Cavan	III.	87
18	Drumbrean	268 0 20	Monaghan	Dartree	Aghabog	Cootehill	III.	263

(a) Including 6A. 2R. 16P. water.
(b) Including 1A. 3R. 24P. water.
(c) Including 6A. 2R. 0P. water.
(d) Including 5A. 3R. 31P. water.
(e) Including 1A. 0R. 12P. water.

(f) Including 26A. 0R. 36P. water.
(g) Including 7A. 3R. 18P. water.
(h) Including 24A. 0R. 23P. water.
(i) Including 70A. 0R. 12P. water.
(j) Including 6A. 1R. 14P. water.

(k) Including 5A. 1R. 33P. water.
(l) Including 15A. 1R. 27P. water.
(m) Including 8A. 1R. 37P. water.
(n) Including Island.

No. of Sheet of the Ordnance Survey Maps.	Townlands and Towns.	Area in Statute Acres.	County.	Barony.	Parish.	Poor Law Union in 1857.	Townland Census of 1851, Part I. Vol.	Page
		A. R. P.						
30, 34	Drumbreanlis . .	497 0 1a	Leitrim . .	Carrigallen . .	Carrigallen . .	Mohill . .	IV.	89
44	Drumbrick . .	214 2 34	Donegal . .	Kilmacrenan . .	Kilmacrenan . .	Millford . .	III.	129
2, 6	Drumbrick . .	179 2 32	Fermanagh .	Lurg . .	Drumkeeran . .	Lowterstown .	III.	206
26, 30	Drumbrick . .	377 0 8	Leitrim . .	Carrigallen . .	Carrigallen . .	Bawnboy . .	IV.	89
22	Drumbrick . .	73 3 15	Leitrim . .	Carrigallen . .	Drumreilly . .	Bawnboy . .	IV.	91
4, 7	Drumbrick . .	185 2 9	Roscommon .	Boyle . .	Ardcarn . .	Cark. on Shannon	IV.	193
5	Drumbrickaun .	59 0 35	Clare . .	Burren . .	Rathborney . .	Ballyvaghan .	II.	14
3	Drumbride . .	88 0 0	Meath . .	Lower Slane . .	Drumcondra . .	Ardee . .	I.	222
30	Drumbriskan . .	177 1 4	Cavan . .	Tullyhunco . .	Scrabby . .	Granard . .	III.	99
4	Drumbrisny . .	175 2 4b	Roscommon .	Boyle . .	Tumna . .	Cark. on Shannon	IV.	198
2	Drumbristan . .	176 3 34	Fermanagh .	Lurg . .	Drumkeeran . .	Lowterstown .	III.	206
3	Drumbristan . .	324 1 8	Monaghan .	Trough . .	Errigal Trough .	Clogher . .	III.	284
99	Drumbristan Glebe .	99 3 5	Donegal . .	Tirhugh . .	Drumhome . .	Donegal . .	III.	146
28, 31	Drumbroagh . .	187 1 10	Monaghan .	Farney . .	Magheross . .	Carrickmacross .	III.	273
16	Drumbrollisk . .	198 1 36	Cavan . .	Tullygarvey . .	Drung . .	Cootehill . .	III.	89
30	Drumbrone . .	126 0 35	Monaghan .	Farney . .	Magheracloone .	Carrickmacross .	III.	272
20,21,27,28	Drumbroneth . .	747 1 16	Down . .	Lower Iveagh, Lr. pt.	Dromore . .	Banbridge . .	III.	168
31, 37	Drumbrucklis . .	309 0 31	Cavan . .	Clanmahon . .	Ballintemple . .	Cavan . .	III.	75
30, 31	Drumbrucklis . .	134 3 15c	Cavan . .	Clanmahon . .	Drumlumman . .	Granard . .	III.	77
10, 14	Drumbrughas . .	249 3 22d	Cavan . .	Lower Loughtee .	Drumlane . .	Cavan . .	III.	80
7	Drumbrughas . .	195 0 12	Cavan . .	Tullyhaw . .	Kinawley . .	Bawnboy . .	III.	93
33	Drumbrughas . .	216 0 15	Fermanagh .	Clanawley . .	Killesher . .	Enniskillen . .	III.	192
35	Drumbrughas . .	133 0 39	Fermanagh .	Clankelly . .	Clones . .	Clones . .	III.	196
33	Drumbrughas . .	94 0 22	Fermanagh .	Knockninny . .	Kinawley . .	Lisnaskea . .	III.	201
28	Drumbrughas . .	147 2 8	Fermanagh .	Maghera-tephana .	Aghavea . .	Lisnaskea . .	III.	218
39	Drumbrughas East .	106 0 37e	Fermanagh .	Coole . .	Galloon . .	Clones . .	III.	199
34	Drumbrughas North .	182 1 39	Fermanagh .	Magherastephana .	Aghalurcher . .	Lisnaskea . .	III.	216
34, 39	Drumbrughas South	82 2 15f	Fermanagh .	Magherastephana .	Aghalurcher . .	Lisnaskea . .	III.	216
39	Drumbrughas West	140 0 16g	Fermanagh .	Coole . .	Galloon . .	Lisnaskea . .	III.	199
11	Drumbulcan . .	479 3 25	Fermanagh .	Lurg . .	Derryvullan . .	Lowterstown .	III.	204
16	Drumbulcan . .	302 0 3	Fermanagh .	Tirkennedy . .	Magheracross . .	Lowterstown .	III.	223
30	Drumbulcaun . .	228 3 29	Galway . .	Dunmore . .	Tuam . .	Tuam . .	IV.	36
39	Drumbulgan . .	54 0 12	Tyrone . .	Dungannon Upper .	Ballyclog . .	Cookstown . .	III.	306
19, 24	Drumbullion . .	241 1 17h	Cavan . .	Tullyhunco . .	Killashandra . .	Cavan . .	III.	98
40	Drumbullog . .	95 2 32	Fermanagh .	Clankelly . .	Galloon . .	Clones . .	III.	198
23, 24, 28	Drumbullog . .	153 2 9i	Leitrim . .	Leitrim . .	Kiltubbrid . .	Cark. on Shannon	IV.	103
5	Drumbulrisk . .	118 3 19	Meath . .	Lower Kells . .	Moybolgue . .	Kells . .	I.	203
16	Drumbure . .	100 0 34	Monaghan .	Dartree . .	Currin . .	Clones . .	III.	265
6	Drumcah . .	253 0 23j	Louth . .	Louth . .	Louth . .	Dundalk . .	I.	184
32	Drumcah . .	185 3 22	Monaghan .	Farney . .	Inishkeen . .	Dundalk . .	III.	271
6	Drumcahy . .	173 2 28	Fermanagh .	Lurg . .	Magheraculmoney .	Lowterstown .	III.	208
17, 22	Drumcall . .	233 0 22k	Monaghan .	Dartree . .	Ematris . .	Cootehill . .	III.	267
15	Drumcalpin . .	170 0 33l	Cavan . .	Lower Loughtee .	Annagh . .	Cavan . .	III.	79
22	Drumcalpin . .	332 3 4	Cavan . .	Tullygarvey . .	Larah . .	Cootehill . .	III.	91
20	Drumcalpin . .	215 1 21	Cavan . .	Upper Loughtee .	Castleterra . .	Cavan . .	III	82
6, 11	Drumcamill . .	86 1 3	Louth . .	Louth . .	Inishkeen . .	Dundalk . .	I.	184
78	Drumcannon . .	160 0 33	Donegal . .	Raphoe . .	Donaghmore . .	Stranorlar . .	III.	137
17, 26	Drumcannon . .	293 2 17	Waterford .	Middlethird . .	Drumcannon . .	Waterford . .	II.	366
7	Drumcanon . .	73 2 37	Cavan . .	Tullyhaw . .	Kinawley . .	Bawnboy . .	III.	93
14, 19	Drumcanon . .	81 0 32	Cavan . .	Tullyhunco . .	Kildallan . .	Bawnboy . .	III.	97
26, 32	Drumcanon . .	104 0 39	Cavan . .	Upper Loughtee .	Denn . .	Cavan . .	III.	83
32	Drumcanon . .	220 2 20	Fermanagh .	Clanawley . .	Killesher . .	Enniskillen . .	III.	192
30	Drumcanon . .	160 1 31m	Leitrim . .	Carrigallen . .	Carrigallen . .	Mohill . .	IV.	89
23, 26	Drumcanon . .	323 1 1n	Monaghan .	Cremorne . .	Aghnamullen . .	Cootehill . .	III.	258
7, 9	Drumcar . .	74 1 3	Cavan . .	Tullyhaw . .	Kinawley . .	Bawnboy . .	III.	93
15, 18	Drumcar . .	1,045 2 5	Louth . .	Ardee . .	Drumcar . .	Ardee . .	I.	172
33	Drumcaran Beg .	91 0 12	Clare . .	Islands . .	Drumcliff . .	Ennis . .	II.	30
33	Drumcaran More .	180 0 3	Clare . .	Islands . .	Drumcliff . .	Ennis . .	II.	30
25	Drumcarban . .	358 1 4o	Cavan . .	Clanmahon . .	Kilmore . .	Cavan . .	III.	78
4	Drumcarbit . .	742 3 19p	Donegal . .	Inishowen East .	Clonca . .	Inishowen . .	III.	117
32	Drumcard . .	53 2 17	Fermanagh .	Clanawley . .	Killesher . .	Enniskillen . .	III.	192
30	Drumcarey . .	244 1 27	Cavan . .	Tullyhunco . .	Killashandra . .	Cavan . .	III.	98
31, 34	Drumcargy . .	160 1 24q	Monaghan .	Farney . .	Magheracloone .	Carrickmacross .	III.	272
12	Drumcarn . .	245 0 11	Armagh . .	Armagh . .	Grange . .	Armagh . .	III.	45
16	Drumcarn . .	284 0 23	Cavan . .	Tullygarvey . .	Drung . .	Cootehill . .	III.	87
54, 62	Drumcarn . .	353 0 5	Donegal . .	Raphoe . .	Raymoghy . .	Letterkenny . .	III.	141
24	Drumcarna . .	171 1 39	Clare . .	Inchiquin . .	Inagh . .	Ennistimon . .	II.	25
24	Drumcarra . .	180 2 30r	Leitrim . .	Leitrim . .	Fenagh . .	Mohill . .	IV.	100
30	Drumcarrow . .	232 1 36	Monaghan .	Farney . .	Magheracloone .	Carrickmacross .	III.	272
55, 62	Drumcart . .	203 3 15	Tyrone . .	Dungannon Middle .	Clonfeacle . .	Dungannon . .	III.	299
14, 19	Drumcartagh or Diamondhill . .	69 1 11	Cavan . .	Tullyhunco . .	Kildallan . .	Bawnboy . .	III.	97
14, 19	Drumcase . .	84 3 37	Cavan . .	Tullyhunco . .	Kildallan . .	Cavan . .	III.	97

(a) Including 29A. 0R. 18P. water.
(b) Including Island.
(c) Including 6A. 1R. 8P. water.
(d) Including 12A. 3R. 19P. water.
(e) Including 13A. 3R. 0P. water.
(f) Including 1A. 3R. 37P. water.

(g) Including 1A. 1R. 33P. water.
(h) Including 9A. 2R. 12P. water.
(i) Including 12A. 0R. 39P. water.
(j) Including 5A. 3R. 38P. water.
(k) Including 10A. 0R. 36P. water.
(l) Including 23A. 2R. 26P. water.

(m) Including 2A. 2R. 26P. water.
(n) Including 46A. 1R. 8P. water.
(o) Including 10A. 0R. 25P. water.
(p) Including 21A. 1R. 21P. water.
(q) Including 3A. 2R. 10P. water.
(r) Including 4A. 2R. 30P. water.

No. of Sheet of the Ordnance Survey Maps	Townlands and Towns.	Area in Statute Acres.	County.	Barony.	Parish.	Poor Law Union in 1857.	Townland Census of 1851, Part I.	
		A. R. P.					Vol.	Page
3	Drumcashel	477 3 29	Leitrim	Rosclogher	Rossinver	Ballyshannon	IV.	111
14, 15	Drumcashel	1,060 3 24	Louth	Ardee	Stabannan	Ardee	I.	174
46	Drumcashellone	300 0 17	Down	Lordship of Newry	Newry	Newry	III.	182
15, 17	Drumcashlagh	135 3 33	Leitrim	Drumahaire	Killarga	Manorhamilton	IV.	98
7	Drumcask	298 3 4	Cavan	Tullyhaw	Kinawley	Bawnboy	III.	93
31, 32	Drumcassidy	162 3 14	Cavan	Castlerahan	Crosserlough	Cavan	III.	68
29	Drumcattan	206 1 37a	Leitrim	Leitrim	Fenagh	Mohill	III.	100
28, 29	Drumcattan	129 2 34	Monaghan	Farney	Donaghmoyne	Carrickmacross	III.	270
25	Drumcavan	230 0 19b	Clare	Inchiquin	Ruan	Corrofin	II.	28
52	Drumcavany	309 2 17	Donegal	Kilmacrenan	Conwal	Letterkenny	III.	126
36, 37, 43	Drumcaw	856 2 20	Down	Kinelarty	Loughinisland	Downpatrick	III.	177
34, 39	Drumcaw	124 1 11	Fermanagh	Coole	Galloon	Lisnaskea	III.	199
10, 15	Drumcaw	203 3 11	Fermanagh	Lurg	Derryvullan	Lowtherstown	III.	204
12	Drumcaw	153 1 20	Monaghan	Dartree	Killeevan	Clones	III.	268
6	Drumcaw	264 2 27	Monaghan	Trough	Donagh	Monaghan	III.	282
11, 18, 19	Drumcaw or Mountlucas	1,250 1 4	King's Co.	Coolestown	Ballynakill	Edenderry	I.	132
27	Drumcharley	183 0 24	Clare	Tulla Upper	Tulla	Tulla	II.	41
21, 22	Drumchoe	266 2 33	Cavan	Tullygarvey	Drung	Cootehill	III.	89
1, 2, 5, 6	Drumchorick	216 0 4	Fermanagh	Lurg	Drumkeeran	Lowtherstown	III.	206
99	Drumchory Glebe	115 2 31	Donegal	Tirhugh	Drumhome	Donegal	III.	146
105	Drumchrin	146 3 28	Donegal	Tirhugh	Templecarn	Donegal	III.	149
16, 24	Drumclamph	458 1 18c	Tyrone	Strabane Lower	Ardstraw	Castlederg	III.	319
39, 40	Drumclay	127 3 32	Fermanagh	Coole	Galloon	Clones	III.	199
22	Drumclay	219 0 21d	Fermanagh	Tirkennedy	Enniskillen	Enniskillen	III.	222
11, 12	Drumcleavry	140 0 8	Roscommon	Ballintober North	Kilmore	Cark. on Shannon	IV.	187
59	Drumclieve	394 0 2	Tipperary, S.R.	Clanwilliam	Templenoe	Tipperary	II.	311
25, 33	Drumcliff	1,105 3 33e	Clare	Islands	Drumcliff	Ennis	II.	30
93	Drumcliff	59 0 16	Donegal	Banagh	Killymard	Donegal	III.	111
8	Drumcliff Glebe	70 0 8	Sligo	Carbury	Drumcliff	Sligo	IV.	221
8	Drumcliff North	216 3 17	Sligo	Carbury	Drumcliff	Sligo	IV.	221
8	Drumcliff South	421 1 31	Sligo	Carbury	Drumcliff	Sligo	IV.	221
8	Drumcliff West	13 1 16	Sligo	Carbury	Drumcliff	Sligo	IV.	221
5	Drumcloona	102 3 24	Fermanagh	Lurg	Drumkeeran	Lowtherstown	III.	206
32	Drumclounish	39 1 27	Fermanagh	Clanawley	Killesher	Enniskillen	III.	192
98, 99	Drumcoe	454 3 20	Donegal	Banagh	Inver	Donegal	III.	107
108, 109	Drumcoggy Mountain	875 2 22	Mayo	Carra	Ballyovey	Ballinrobe	IV.	126
24	Drumcoghill Lower	126 3 21	Cavan	Tullyhunco	Killashandra	Cavan	III.	98
24, 25	Drumcoghill Upper	124 0 33	Cavan	Tullyhunco	Killashandra	Cavan	III.	98
10, 11	Drumcole	225 3 12	Cavan	Lower Loughtee	Drumlane	Cavan	III.	80
26	Drumcolgny	192 2 20	Fermanagh	Clanawley	Cleenish	Enniskillen	III.	190
32	Drumcollagan	261 1 3	Leitrim	Mohill	Mohill	Mohill	IV.	107
28	Drumcollop	185 2 4f	Leitrim	Mohill	Fenagh	Mohill	IV.	106
27, 34	Drumcolumb	248 2 21	Sligo	Tirerrill	Drumcolumb	Sligo	IV.	238
65	Drumcomoge	260 1 19	Tipperary, S.R.	Clanwilliam	Emly	Tipperary	II.	308
26, 31	Drumcon	1,056 0 18	Antrim	Kilconway	Rasharkin	Ballymoney	III.	27
24	Drumcon	102 3 22	Cavan	Tullyhunco	Killashandra	Cavan	III.	98
25	Drumcon	61 2 38	Cavan	Upper Loughtee	Kilmore	Cavan	III.	84
34	Drumcon	82 1 34	Fermanagh	Magherastephana	Aghalurcher	Lisnaskea	III.	216
20, 21	Drumconan	157 1 10	Londonderry	Tirkeeran	Clondermot	Londonderry	III.	248
75	Drumconcoose	393 2 27	Donegal	Boylagh	Inishkeel	Glenties	III.	112
23	Drumcondra	195 3 38	Cavan	Clankee	Drumgoon	Cootehill	III.	72
14, 18	Drumcondra	109 3 19	Dublin	Coolock	Clonturk	Dublin North	I.	27
6	Drumcondra	188 2 22	Meath	Lower Slane	Drumcondra	Ardee	I.	222
3	Drumcondra	82 0 10	Monaghan	Trough	Errigal Trough	Monaghan	III.	284
21	Drumcondra	217 2 16	Sligo	Tirerrill	Killerry	Sligo	IV.	239
18	DRUMCONDRA T.	—	Dublin	Coolock	Clonturk	Dublin North	I.	27
6	DRUMCONDRA T.		Meath	Lower Slane	Drumcondra	Ardee	I.	223
24	Drumcong	142 1 17g	Leitrim	Leitrim	Kiltubbrid	Cark. on Shannon	IV.	103
78	Drumconlan	92 2 35	Mayo	Carra	Aglish	Castlebar	IV.	123
26	Drumconlan East	129 0 33	Fermanagh	Clanawley	Cleenish	Enniskillen	III.	190
26	Drumconlan West	48 1 9	Fermanagh	Clanawley	Cleenish	Enniskillen	III.	190
19	Drumconlester	97 1 20h	Cavan	Tullyhunco	Killashandra	Cavan	III.	98
30	Drumconlevan	107 1 24	Leitrim	Carrigallen	Drumreilly	Bawnboy	IV.	91
6	Drumconnelly	150 1 14	Monaghan	Trough	Errigal Trough	Monaghan	III.	284
43	Drumconnelly	357 1 1	Tyrone	Omagh East	Drumragh	Omagh	III.	312
20, 25	Drumconnick	227 0 7i	Cavan	Upper Loughtee	Urney	Cavan	III.	86
16	Drumconnis	158 3 23	Fermanagh	Tirkennedy	Magheracross	Enniskillen	III.	223
42, 50	Drumconnis	108 3 2	Tyrone	Omagh East	Dromore	Omagh	III.	311
33, 36	Drumconny	477 1 35	Leitrim	Mohill	Cloone	Mohill	IV.	105
93, 98, 99	Drumconor	445 0 38	Donegal	Banagh	Inver	Donegal	III.	107
21	Drumconor	127 1 13	Fermanagh	Clanawley	Cleenish	Enniskillen	III.	190
39	Drumconor	53 2 33	Fermanagh	Knockninny	Kinawley	Lisnaskea	III.	201

(a) Including 38A. 1R. 8P. water.
(b) Including 21A. 2R. 10P. water.
(c) Including 2A. 1R. 8P. water.
(d) Including 33A. 3R. 7P. water.
(e) Including 96A. 1R. 9P. water.
(f) Including 6A. 3R. 28P. water.
(g) Including 34A. 0R. 24P. water.
(h) Including 12A. 2R. 25P. water.
(i) Including 4A. 3R. 33P. water.

No. of Sheet of the Ordnance Survey Maps.	Townlands and Towns.	Area in Statute Acres. A. R. P.	County.	Barony.	Parish.	Poor Law Union in 1857.	Townland Census of 1851, Part I. Vol.	Page
15	Drumconor	349 2 6	Leitrim	Drumahaire	Killanummery	Manorhamilton	IV.	98
46	Drumconor	278 0 14	Tyrone	Dungannon Middle	Pomeroy	Dungannon	III.	304
16	Drumconra	116 2 35	Cavan	Tullygarvey	Annagh	Cootehill	III.	87
7	Drumconra or Lowforge	189 2 36	Cavan	Tullyhaw	Kinawley	Bawnboy	III.	93
36	Drumconready	490 0 8	Londonderry	Loughinsholin	Maghera	Magherafelt	III.	242
30, 39	Drumconway	539 1 33	Tyrone	Dungannon Upper	Tamlaght	Cookstown	III.	309
16	Drumconwell	254 1 38	Armagh	Fews Lower	Lisnadill	Armagh	III.	47
25	Drumcoo	67 3 16	Fermanagh	Clanawley	Cleenish	Enniskillen	III.	190
33, 34	Drumcoo	72 3 34	Fermanagh	Magherastephana	Aghalurcher	Lisnaskea	III.	216
22	Drumcoo	113 0 23a	Fermanagh	Tirkennedy	Trory	Enniskillen	III.	223
54	Drumcoo	509 0 11	Tyrone	Dungannon Middle	Drumglass	Dungannon	III.	303
27	Drumcoo or Belview	161 2 32b	Fermanagh	Tirkennedy	Enniskillen	Enniskillen	III.	222
6	Drumcoo (Brady)	220 2 6	Monaghan	Monaghan	Tedavnet	Monaghan	III.	278
5	Drumcoo (Foster)	175 0 8	Monaghan	Monaghan	Tedavnet	Monaghan	III.	278
6, 9	Drumcoo (Jackson)	138 0 8	Monaghan	Monaghan	Tedavnet	Monaghan	III.	278
11, 12	Drumcooly	1,096 2 1	King's Co.	Coolestown	Monasteroris	Edenderry	I.	133
23	Drumcoora	97 2 39	Leitrim	Leitrim	Kiltoghert	Cark. on Shannon	IV.	101
32	Drumcoora	86 3 33	Leitrim	Mohill	Annaduff	Mohill	IV.	105
12	Drumcoote	85 1 33	Armagh	Armagh	Armagh	Armagh	III.	43
6	Drumcoo (Woods)	74 1 0	Monaghan	Monaghan	Tedavnet	Monaghan	III.	278
31	Drumcor	374 3 21c	Cavan	Clanmahon	Drumlumman	Cavan	III.	77
12, 16	Drumcor	316 2 2d	Cavan	Tullygarvey	Drung	Cootehill	III.	89
20, 25	Drumcor	108 0 17e	Cavan	Upper Loughtee	Kilmore	Cavan	III.	84
17	Drumcor	264 1 37f	Fermanagh	Tirkennedy	Enniskillen	Enniskillen	III.	222
15	Drumcorban	112 3 38	Fermanagh	Magheraboy	Devenish	Enniskillen	III	210
18	Drumcore	259 2 35g	Clare	Bunratty Upper	Inchicronan	Gort	II.	9
59	Drumcorke	87 0 21	Tyrone	Clogher	Errigal Keerogue	Clogher	III.	295
3, 6	Drumcormick	117 1 5	Roscommon	Boyle	Ardcarn	Boyle	IV.	193
34	Drumcormick	222 2 39	Sligo	Corran	Kilmorgan	Sligo	IV.	227
79	Drumcorrabaun	175 0 12	Mayo	Carra	Breaghwy	Castlebar	IV.	127
90	Drumcorrabaun	133 0 39	Mayo	Carra	Drum	Castlebar	IV.	128
6	Drumcose	102 2 14	Fermanagh	Lurg	Magheraculmoney	Lowtherstown	III.	208
15	Drumcose	119 0 19	Fermanagh	Magheraboy	Devenish	Enniskillen	III.	210
25, 29	Drumcoura	706 0 16h	Leitrim	Carrigallen	Drumreilly	Bawnboy	IV.	91
30	Drumcovit	428 1 27	Londonderry	Tirkeeran	Banagher	NewTnLimavady	III.	247
28	Drumcramph	96 2 34	Fermanagh	Magherastephana	Aghalurcher	Lisnaskea	III.	216
27	Drumcramph	61 3 37i	Fermanagh	Tirkennedy	Cleenish	Enniskillen	III.	220
20	Drumcrauve	197 1 27j	Cavan	Upper Loughtee	Annagelliff	Cavan	III.	81
30	Drumcraw	159 0 25	Tyrone	Dungannon Upper	Derryloran	Cookstown	III.	307
5, 9	Drumcree	162 0 17	Armagh	Oneilland West	Drumcree	Lurgan	III.	52
32	Drumcree	185 1 15k	Leitrim	Mohill	Annaduff	Cark. on Shannon	IV.	105
8	Drumcree	314 2 9	Westmeath	Delvin	Kilcumny	Castletowndelvin	I.	265
23, 24	Drumcreeghan	205 3 22	Monaghan	Cremorne	Aghnamullen	Castleblayney	III.	258
16	Drumcreen	125 2 4	Fermanagh	Tirkennedy	Magheracross	Lowtherstown	III.	223
8	DRUMCREE T.	—	Westmeath	Delvin	Kilcumny	Castletowndelvin	I.	265
25	Drumcrew	222 0 4	Monaghan	Cremorne	Clontibret	Castleblayney	III.	260
34, 35	Drumcrin	158 1 20	Cavan	Clankee	Enniskeen	Bailieborough	III.	72
43	Drumcrin	72 3 24l	Fermanagh	Coole	Drummully	Clones	III.	199
11	Drumcrin	153 3 7	Fermanagh	Lurg	Derryvullan	Lowtherstown	III.	204
1, 5	Drumcrin	193 3 17	Fermanagh	Lurg	Drumkeeran	Lowtherstown	III.	206
5	Drumcrin	75 3 33	Fermanagh	Lurg	Magheraculmoney	Lowtherstown	III.	208
34	Drumcrin	67 2 0	Fermanagh	Magherastephana	Aghalurcher	Lisnaskea	III.	216
22, 27	Drumcrin	113 1 28m	Fermanagh	Tirkennedy	Enniskillen	Enniskillen	III.	222
55	Drumcro	339 0 36	Down	Mourne	Kilkeel	Kilkeel	III.	183
94, 100	Drumcroagh	148 3 0n	Donegal	Tirhugh	Donegal	Donegal	III.	145
13, 20	Drumcro and Drumo	427 0 2	Down	Lower Iveagh, Up. pt.	Magheralin	Lurgan	III.	170
22	Drumcroman	313 3 5	Leitrim	Carrigallen	Oughteragh	Bawnboy	IV.	92
23, 24	Drumcroman	145 1 34	Leitrim	Leitrim	Kiltoghert	Cark. on Shannon	IV.	101
28	Drumcromaun	96 2 10	Leitrim	Leitrim	Kiltubbrid	Cark. on Shannon	IV.	103
15	Drumcroohen	130 0 21	Fermanagh	Magheraboy	Devenish	Enniskillen	III.	210
27	Drumcrooil	58 0 31o	Fermanagh	Tirkennedy	Derryvullan	Enniskillen	III.	221
11	Drumcroon	427 1 8	Londonderry	Coleraine	Macosquin	Coleraine	III.	233
12, 13	Drumcrottagh	252 1 30	Antrim	Lower Dunluce	Derrykeighan	Ballymoney	III.	16
34	Drumcrow	815 0 23	Antrim	Lower Glenarm	Tickmacrevan	Larne	III.	23
21	Drumcrow	310 3 36	Armagh	Orior Lower	Loughgilly	Newry	III.	56
25, 31	Drumcrow	141 3 34	Cavan	Clanmahon	Denn	Cavan	III.	76
25, 31	Drumcrow	548 0 23p	Cavan	Clanmahon	Kilmore	Cavan	III.	78
15	Drumcrow	499 2 23	Cavan	Lower Loughtee	Annagh	Cavan	III.	79
16	Drumcrow	97 0 19q	Cavan	Upper Loughtee	Castleterra	Cavan	III.	82
21	Drumcrow	176 2 17	Cavan	Upper Loughtee	Larah	Cavan	III.	85
62, 70	Drumcrow	236 2 0	Donegal	Raphoe	Taughboyne	Strabane	III.	143
22, 27	Drumcrow	41 1 34	Fermanagh	Tirkennedy	Derrybrusk	Enniskillen	III.	220
36	Drumcrow	108 0 23	Londonderry	Loughinsholin	Kilcronaghan	Magherafelt	III.	241

(a) Including 7A. 2R. 4P. water.
(b) Including 24A. 3R. 9P. water.
(c) Including 8A 3R. 16P. water.
(d) Including 6A. 0R. 3P. water.
(e) Including 1A. 0R 14P. water.
(f) Including 10A. 1R. 10P. water.

(g) Including 23A. 0R. 0P. water.
(h) Including 96A. 0R. 12P. water.
(i) Including 3A. 2R. 32P. water.
(j) Including 6A. 2R. 7P. Beaghy Lough.
(k) Including 6A. 2R. 29P. water.
(l) Including 3A. 0R. 1P. water.

(m) Including 10A. 0R. 3P. water.
(n) Including 4A. 0R. 2P. water.
(o) Including 4A. 1R. 1P. water.
(p) Including 32A. 3R. 18P. water.
(q) Including 6A. 0R. water.

3 F 2

No. of Sheet of the Ordnance Survey Maps.	Townlands and Towns.	Area in Statute Acres.	County.	Barony.	Parish.	Poor Law Union in 1857.	Townland Census of 1851, Part I.	
		A. R. P.					Vol.	Page
17	Drumcrow . .	122 1 37	Monaghan .	Dartree . . .	Killeevan . .	Cootehill . .	III.	268
55	Drumcrow . .	343 3 13	Tyrone .	Dungannon Middle .	Killyman . .	Dungannon .	III.	303
10, 15	Drumcrow East .	188 3 7	Fermanagh .	Magheraboy .	Inishmacsaint .	Enniskillen .	III.	212
19	Drumcrow North .	125 3 36	Cavan .	Tullyhunco .	Killashandra .	Cavan . .	III.	98
24	Drumcrow South .	292 0 12a	Cavan .	Tullyhunco .	Killashandra .	Cavan . .	III.	98
9	Drumcrow West .	164 0 19	Fermanagh .	Magheraboy .	Inishmacsaint .	Ballyshannon .	III.	212
32	Drumcroy . .	109 3 39	Leitrim .	Mohill . .	Mohill . .	Mohill . .	IV.	107
40	Drumcru . .	116 1 27	Fermanagh .	Clankelly .	Clones . .	Clones . .	III.	196
39, 40	Drumcru . .	110 2 37	Fermanagh .	Coole . .	Galloon . .	Clones . .	III.	199
28, 34	Drumcru . .	59 2 22	Fermanagh .	Magherastephana .	Aghalurcher .	Lisnaskea .	III.	216
12, 17	Drumcru (*Dickson*)	88 0 37	Monaghan .	Dartree . . .	Clones . .	Clones . .	III.	264
12	Drumcru (*Renwick*)	93 1 3	Monaghan .	Dartree . . .	Clones . .	Clones . .	III.	264
15	Drumcudree .	49 2 32	Antrim .	Lower Glenarm .	Layd . .	Ballycastle .	III.	22
24	Drumcullaun .	347 2 24b	Clare .	Inchiquin .	Inagh . .	Ennistimon .	II.	25
42, 48	Drumcullen .	238 3 37	Antrim .	Upper Toome .	Duneane . .	Antrim .	III.	35
8	Drumcullen .	230 2 22	Armagh .	Armagh . .	Clonfeacle .	Armagh . .	III.	43
7	Drumcullion .	86 1 2	Cavan .	Tullyhaw .	Kinawley .	Bawnboy . .	III.	93
24	Drumcullion .	166 0 12	Cavan .	Tullyhunco .	Killashandra .	Cavan . .	III.	98
37	Drumcullion .	135 2 29	Fermanagh .	Clanawley .	Kinawley .	Enniskillen .	III.	194
5	Drumcullion .	200 3 2	Fermanagh .	Lurg . .	Drumkeeran .	Lowtherstown .	III.	206
27	Drumcullion .	103 3 12c	Fermanagh .	Tirkennedy .	Derrybrusk .	Enniskillen .	III.	220
16	Drumcullion .	433 2 18	Fermanagh .	Tirkennedy .	Magheracross .	Enniskillen .	III.	223
25	Drumcullion .	202 3 11d	Leitrim .	Carrigallen .	Drumreilly .	Bawnboy . .	IV.	91
59	Drumcullion .	183 2 39	Tyrone .	Clogher .	Errigal Keerogue .	Clogher . .	III.	295
19	Drumcully .	301 3 0e	Fermanagh .	Clanawley .	Cleenish . .	Ballyshannon .	III.	190
26, 27	Drumcunnion .	439 0 8f	Monaghan .	Cremorne .	Aghnamullen .	Carrickmacross .	III.	258
28, 34	Drumcunny .	34 2 39	Fermanagh .	Magherastephana .	Aghalurcher .	Lisnaskea .	III.	216
24, 25	Drumcurreen .	195 1 4g	Clare .	Inchiquin .	Dysert . .	Ennis . .	II.	24
5	Drumcurren .	212 1 2	Fermanagh .	Lurg . .	Drumkeeran .	Lowtherstown .	III.	206
70	Drumdaff .	151 2 10	Mayo .	Carra . .	Turlough .	Castlebar .	IV.	131
36	Drumdaff .	276 2 17	Roscommon .	Ballintober South .	Kilbride . .	Roscommon .	IV.	189
2, 4	Drumdaff .	73 0 31	Roscommon .	Boyle . .	Kilronan .	Boyle . .	IV.	197
13, 18	Drumdallagh .	514 2 13	Antrim .	Upper Dunluce .	Loughguile .	Ballymoney .	III.	20
30	Drumdangan .	426 1 8	Wicklow .	Newcastle .	Kilcommon .	Rathdrum .	I.	351
29, 33	Drumdarkan .	278 3 0h	Leitrim .	Mohill . .	Cloone . .	Mohill . .	IV.	105
32	Drumdart .	134 2 24i	Leitrim .	Leitrim . .	Mohill . .	Mohill . .	IV.	104
6	Drumdart .	155 0 26	Monaghan .	Monaghan .	Tedavnet .	Monaghan .	III.	278
21, 24	Drumdartan Glebe .	147 3 8	Leitrim .	Carrigallen .	Oughteragh .	Bawnboy . .	IV.	92
70	Drumdeel .	292 3 8	Tipperary, S.R.	Middlethird .	Baptistgrange .	Clonmel . .	II.	325
35, 44	Drumdeevin .	401 2 25	Donegal .	Kilmacrenan .	Kilmacrenan .	Milford . .	III.	129
42, 48	Drumderg .	344 2 1	Antrim .	Upper Toome .	Duneane . .	Ballymena .	III.	34
16, 20	Drumderg .	361 3 8	Armagh .	Armagh . .	Keady . .	Armagh . .	III.	45
39	Drumderg .	73 2 32	Cavan .	Castlerahan .	Lurgan . .	Oldcastle .	III.	69
26	Drumderg .	223 2 0	Fermanagh .	Clanawley .	Cleenish .	Enniskillen .	III.	190
41	Drumderg .	123 1 30	Fermanagh .	Knockninny .	Kinawley .	Lisnaskea .	III.	201
23	Drumderg .	390 1 14	Fermanagh .	Tirkennedy .	Enniskillen .	Enniskillen .	III.	222
22	Drumderg .	200 1 22	Leitrim .	Carrigallen .	Drumreilly .	Bawnboy . .	IV.	91
15	Drumderg .	127 2 2j	Leitrim .	Drumahaire .	Killarga .	Manorhamilton .	IV.	98
23	Drumderg .	141 0 34	Leitrim .	Leitrim . .	Kiltoghert .	Carⁿ. on Shannon	IV.	101
35, 40	Drumderg .	998 0 23	Londonderry .	Loughinsholin .	Ballynascreen .	Magherafelt .	III.	239
5, 9	Drumderg .	401 3 34	Longford .	Granard . .	Clonbroney .	Granard . .	I.	155
61, 62	Drumderg .	105 2 27	Tyrone .	Dungannon Middle .	Clonfeacle .	Dungannon .	III.	299
39	Drumderg Glebe .	43 3 5	Cavan .	Castlerahan .	Lurgan . .	Oldcastle .	III.	69
42, 50	Drumderg Glebe .	365 3 26k	Tyrone .	Omagh East .	Dromore .	Omagh . .	III.	311
30, 34	Drumderglin .	393 3 1l	Leitrim .	Carrigallen .	Carrigallen .	Mohill .	IV.	89
34	Drumderry .	135 2 21	Sligo .	Tirerrill .	Kilmacallan .	Sligo . .	IV.	240
4, 9	Drumderry .	592 3 3m	Wexford .	Scarawalsh .	Moyacomb .	Shillelagh .	I.	325
67, 76	Drumderrydonan .	1,080 1 13	Donegal .	Raphoe . .	Kilteevoge .	Stranorlar .	III.	139
6, 9	Drumdesco .	136 0 4n	Monaghan .	Monaghan .	Tedavnet .	Monaghan .	III.	278
25, 29	Drumdiffer .	407 3 38	Leitrim .	Carrigallen .	Drumreilly .	Bawnboy . .	IV.	91
58	Drumdigus .	791 2 18	Clare .	Clonderalaw .	Kilmurry .	Killadysert .	II.	17
46	Drumdiha .	189 2 31	Tipperary, N.R.	Kilnamanagh Upper .	Moyaliff .	Thurles .	II.	279
7	Drumdillure .	67 1 30	Leitrim .	Rosclogher .	Killasnet .	Manorhamilton .	IV.	109
39	Drumdiveen .	101 0 24	Sligo .	Corran . .	Kilshalvy .	Boyle . .	IV.	227
3	Drumdoe .	449 3 40	Roscommon .	Boyle . .	Boyle . .	Boyle . .	IV.	194
79, 88	Drumdoit .	397 1 1	Donegal .	Raphoe . .	Urney . .	Strabane .	III.	144
38	Drumdoney .	112 0 24	Fermanagh .	Knockninny .	Kinawley .	Lisnaskea .	III.	202
34, 40	Drumdoney .	90 2 12	Sligo .	Tirerrill .	Aghanagh .	Boyle . .	IV.	237
34	Drumdoney .	205 0 39	Sligo .	Tirerrill .	Kilmacallan .	Boyle . .	IV.	240
32	Drumdoo .	239 2 10	Leitrim .	Mohill . .	Mohill . .	Mohill . .	IV.	107
79	Drumdoogh .	156 2 34	Mayo .	Carra . .	Breaghwy .	Castlebar .	IV.	127
34	Drumdoolaghty .	71 3 0	Clare .	Bunratty Upper .	Doora . .	Ennis . .	II.	8
44	Drumdowney Lower .	178 2 13	Kilkenny .	Ida . . .	Rathpatrick .	Waterford .	I.	103

(a) Including 8A. 2R. 7P. water.
(b) Including 44A. 3R. 30P. water.
(c) Including 23A. 0R. 35P. water.
(d) Including 20A. 0R. 20P. water.
(e) Including 9A. 1R. 27P. water.

(f) Including 46A. 1R. 34P. water.
(g) Including 6A. 1R. 15P. water.
(h) Including 5A. 1R. 10P. water.
(i) Including 32A. 0R. 21P. water.
(j) Including 2A. 1R. 24P. water.

(k) Including 1A. 1R. 3P. water.
(l) Including 6A. 1R. 28P. water.
(m) Including 14A. 1R. 0P. water.
(n) Including 4A. 2R. 30P. water.
(o) Including 11A. 0R. 32P. water.

No. of Sheet of the Ordnance Survey Maps	Townlands and Towns.	Area in Statute Acres.	County.	Barony.	Parish.	Poor Law Union in 1857.	Townland Census of 1851, Part I. Vol.	Page
		A. R. P.					Vol.	Page
44, 47	Drumdowney Upper	952 0 11	Kilkenny	Ida	Rathpatrick	Waterford	I.	103
28	Drumdran	65 0 39	Fermanagh	Tirkennedy	Cleenish	Enniskillen	III.	220
56	Drumdran	223 2 8	Tyrone	Omagh East	Kilskeery	Enniskillen	III.	313
42	Drumdreenagh	388 1 21	Down	Upper Iveagh, Lr. pt.	Drumballyroney	Banbridge	III.	172
28	Drumdreeny	114 3 27	Monaghan	Farney	Donaghmoyne	Carrickmacross	III.	270
90	Drumdrishaghaun	149 0 36	Mayo	Carra	Drum	Castlebar	IV.	128
7, 8	Drumduff	177 1 30	Armagh	Tiranny	Eglish	Armagh	III.	59
24	Drumduff	206 3 17	Clare	Inchiquin	Inagh	Ennistimon	II.	25
92, 93	Drumduff	146 0 38	Donegal	Banagh	Inver	Donegal	III.	107
32	Drumduff	195 3 32	Fermanagh	Clanawley	Killesher	Enniskillen	III.	192
11	Drumduff	226 2 34	Fermanagh	Lurg	Derryvullan	Lowtherstown	III.	204
1, 5	Drumduff	188 3 30	Fermanagh	Lurg	Drumkeeran	Lowtherstown	III.	206
14	Drumduff	203 2 6	Leitrim	Drumahaire	Killanummery	Manorhamilton	IV.	98
23	Drumduff	115 1 37a	Leitrim	Leitrim	Kiltoghert	Car^k. on Shannon	IV.	101
27	Drumduff	39 3 38	Leitrim	Leitrim	Kiltoghert	Car^k. on Shannon	IV.	101
35, 36, 44	Drumduff	1,046 2 27b	Tyrone	Omagh East	Termonmaguirk	Omagh	III.	314
15	Drumduffy	184 1 18c	Leitrim	Drumahaire	Killarga	Manorhamilton	IV.	98
26	Drumdutton	454 2 9d	Donegal	Kilmacrenan	Mevagh	Millford	III.	130
9	Drumeagle	145 2 34	Tyrone	Strabane Lower	Urney	Strabane	III.	322
28	Drumeague	419 1 7e	Cavan	Clankee	Knockbride	Bailieborough	III.	73
24	Drumeanan Beg	67 3 20	Leitrim	Leitrim	Fenagh	Mohill	IV.	100
24	Drumeanan More	95 3 4	Leitrim	Leitrim	Fenagh	Mohill	IV.	100
63	Drumearn	116 2 0	Donegal	Raphoe	Taughboyne	Strabane	III.	143
60, 66	Drumearn	342 1 35	Tyrone	Dungannon Lower	Aghaloo	Clogher	III.	296
29	Drumearn	247 0 35	Tyrone	Dungannon Upper	Derryloran	Cookstown	III.	307
26, 35	Drumeasan	441 3 33f	Donegal	Kilmacrenan	Kilmacrenan	Dunfanaghy	III.	129
81	Drum East	197 0 38	Galway	Galway	Rahoon	Galway	IV.	37
8, 9	Drum East	155 1 36	Sligo	Carbury	Drumcliff	Sligo	IV.	221
27	Drumederalena	201 2 36	Sligo	Tirerrill	Ballynakill	Sligo	IV.	237
33	Drumederglass	96 3 25	Cavan	Castlerahan	Killinkere	Bailieborough	III.	69
43	Drumee	636 3 28	Down	Upper Iveagh, Lr. pt.	Maghera	Kilkeel	III.	173
28	Drumee	51 1 7	Fermanagh	Magherastephana	Aghavea	Lisnaskea	III.	218
17	Drumee	122 0 23	Monaghan	Dartree	Killeevan	Clones	III.	268
27	Drumee	359 3 9	Sligo	Tirerrill	Ballysumaghan	Sligo	IV.	238
26, 30	Drumeela	154 1 27	Leitrim	Carrigallen	Carrigallen	Bawnboy	IV.	89
16	Drumeena	251 1 29	Cavan	Tullygarvey	Annagh	Cootehill	III.	87
9	Drumeeny	193 3 3	Antrim	Cary	Ramoan	Ballycastle	III.	14
37	Drumeeny	56 2 35	Cavan	Clanmahon	Ballymachugh	Cavan	III.	76
38	Drumeeshil	44 1 20	Fermanagh	Knockninny	Kinawley	Lisnaskea	III.	202
16	Drumeevin	522 2 9	Clare	Corcomroe	Kiltoraght	Corrofin	II.	22
32	Drumegil	206 0 36	Cavan	Castlerahan	Crosserlough	Cavan	III.	68
19	Drumeil	263 0 4	Londonderry	Coleraine	Aghadowey	Coleraine	III.	229
20	Drumelis	266 3 37	Cavan	Upper Loughtee	Urney	Cavan	III.	86
47	Drumellihy (Cunningham)	921 1 3	Clare	Moyarta	Kilmacduane	Kilrush	II.	33
47	Drumellihy (MacDonnell)	479 3 28	Clare	Moyarta	Kilmacduane	Kilrush	II.	33
47	Drumellihy (Westby)	853 2 35	Clare	Moyarta	Kilmacduane	Kilrush	II	33
47	Drumellihy (Westropp)	599 1 4	Clare	Moyarta	Kilmacduane	Kilrush	II.	33
15	Drumellis	123 3 29	Cavan	Lower Loughtee	Annagh	Cavan	III.	79
25	Drumelly	149 2 0	Fermanagh	Clanawley	Cleenish	Enniskillen	III.	190
121	Drumelly	256 0 13	Mayo	Kilmaine	Cong	Ballinrobe	IV.	153
22	Drumeltan	242 3 20	Cavan	Tullygarvey	Kildrumsherdan	Cootehill	III.	90
42, 43	Drumena	550 2 26h	Down	Upper Iveagh, Lr. pt.	Kilcoo	Kilkeel	III.	173
47	Drumenagh	602 2 22	Londonderry	Loughinsholin	Artrea	Magherafelt	III.	238
55	Drumenagh	162 3 4	Tyrone	Dungannon Middle	Killyman	Dungannon	III.	303
52, 60	Drumenan	1,012 2 14	Donegal	Kilmacrenan	Conwal	Letterkenny	III.	126
63	Drumenan	232 1 27	Donegal	Raphoe	Taughboyne	Strabane	III.	143
12, 13	Drumennis	155 3 18	Armagh	Fews Lower	Mullaghbrack	Armagh	III.	47
2	Drumenny Big	307 1 4i	Tyrone	Strabane Lower	Donaghedy	Strabane	III.	320
31, 40	Drumenny (Conyngham)	482 2 26	Tyrone	Dungannon Upper	Arboe	Cookstown	III.	305
2	Drumenny Little	132 1 30	Tyrone	Strabane Lower	Donaghedy	Strabane	III.	320
31, 39, 40	Drumenny (Stewart)	170 1 3	Tyrone	Dungannon Upper	Arboe	Cookstown	III.	305
11	Drumercool	163 1 29	Roscommon	Boyle	Killukin	Car^k. on Shannon	IV.	195
26, 30	Drumercross	98 2 12	Leitrim	Carrigallen	Carrigallen	Bawnboy	IV	89
19	Drumerdannan	142 3 34j	Cavan	Tullyhunco	Kildallan	Cavan	III.	97
30	Drumergoole	249 3 25k	Leitrim	Carrigallen	Carrigallen	Bawnboy	IV.	89
36	Drumerheeve	211 1 13	Fermanagh	Clankelly	Clones	Clones	III.	196
10,11,14,15	Drumerhin	387 3 14	Kilkenny	Fassadinin	Kilmadum	Kilkenny	I.	90
29,30,33,34	Drumerkeane	528 2 11l	Leitrim	Carrigallen	Cloone	Mohill	IV.	90
22	Drumerkillew	563 3 15	Cavan	Tullygarvey	Kildrumsherdan	Cootehill	III.	90
30, 33	Drumerlough Beg	141 3 37	Monaghan	Farney	Magheracloone	Carrickmacross	III.	272
30	Drumerlough More	134 1 7	Monaghan	Farney	Magheracloone	Carrickmacross	III.	272

(a) Including 5A. 3R. 6P. water.
(b) Including 11A. 0R. 32P. water.
(c) Including 19A. 3R. 8P. water.
(d) Including 5A. 3R. 8P. water.
(e) Including 14A. 3R. 1P. water.

(f) Including 4A. 0R. 33P. water.
(g) Including 22A. 2R. 10P. water.
(h) Including 39A. 1R. 30P. water.
(i) Including 7A. 3R. 19P. water. Including 7A. 1R. 33P. Salt Marsh.

(j) Including 2A. 2R. 12P. water.
(k) Including 50A. 2R. 34P. water.
(l) Including 8A. 1R. 24P. water.

No. of Sheet of the Ordnance Survey Maps.	Townlands and Towns.	Area in Statute Acres.			County.	Barony.	Parish.	Poor Law Union in 1857.	Townland Census of 1851, Part I.	
		A.	R.	P.					Vol.	Page
11	Drumerr . . .	187	2	20	Roscommon .	Boyle . . .	Killummod . .	Car*. on Shannon	IV.	196
7	Drumersee . .	317	2	15	Cavan . .	Tullyhaw . .	Kinawley . .	Bawnboy . .	III.	93
30, 36	Drumersnaw . .	101	2	31a	Cavan . .	Clanmahon . .	Drumlumman .	Granard . .	III.	77
35, 36	Drumerwinter . .	131	0	10	Fermanagh .	Clankelly . .	Clones . .	Clones . .	III.	196
67	Drumess . . .	128	1	1	Tyrone . .	Dungannon Lower .	Aghaloo . .	Armagh . .	III.	296
27, 33	Drumestagh . .	182	0	2	Cavan . .	Upper Loughtee .	Lavey . . .	Cavan . .	III.	85
42	Drumettagh . .	227	0	34b	Fermanagh .	Knockninny . .	Kinawley . .	Lisnaskea . .	III.	202
31	Drumever . .	193	1	32	Monaghan .	Farney . .	Killanny . .	Carrickmacross	III.	271
78	Drumevish . .	392	0	7	Donegal . .	Raphoe . .	Donaghmore .	Stranorlar .	III.	137
39, 47	Drumey . . .	67	2	39	Tyrone . .	Dungannon Middle .	Donaghenry .	Cookstown .	III.	301
46	Drumey . . .	90	0	13	Tyrone . .	Dungannon Middle .	Tullyniskan .	Dungannon .	III.	304
106, 107	Drumeyre . .	275	2	11	Galway . .	Longford . .	Abbeygormacan	Ballinasloe .	IV.	56
18, 28	Drumfad . .	282	0	17	Donegal . .	Kilmacrenan .	Clondavaddog .	Milford . .	III.	124
62, 70	Drumfad . .	164	1	4	Donegal . .	Raphoe . .	Taughboyne .	Strabane . .	III.	143
7	Drumfad . .	256	2	16	Down . .	Ards Lower . .	Donaghadee .	Newtownards .	III.	158
2, 3, 5, 6	Drumfad . .	640	3	25	Sligo . .	Carbury . .	Ahamlish . .	Sligo . .	IV.	219
53	Drumfad . .	335	3	0	Tyrone . .	Dungannon Lower .	Killeeshil . .	Dungannon .	III.	298
18	Drumfad Lower .	170	2	13	Donegal . .	Kilmacrenan .	Clondavaddog .	Milford . .	III.	124
18, 28	Drumfad Upper .	166	2	33	Donegal . .	Kilmacrenan .	Clondavaddog .	Milford . .	III.	124
23	Drumfaldra . .	81	1	31	Monaghan .	Cremorne . .	Aghnamullen .	Cootehill . .	III.	258
32, 33	Drumfane . .	338	2	0	Antrim . .	Lower Toome .	Kirkinriola .	Ballymena .	III.	32
39	Drumfarnoght .	138	0	9	Sligo . .	Corran . .	Cloonoghil .	Tobercurry .	IV.	225
19, 20	Drumfea . .	433	1	0	Carlow . .	Idrone East .	Fennagh . .	Carlow . .	I.	7
13, 17	Drumfergus . .	82	2	24	Armagh . .	Fews Lower .	Mullaghbrack .	Armagh . .	III.	47
78	Drumfergus . .	154	0	6	Donegal . .	Raphoe . .	Donaghmore .	Stranorlar .	III.	137
3	Drumfernasky .	139	3	22	Monaghan .	Trough . .	Errigal Trough .	Clogher . .	III.	284
27	Drumfin . .	352	3	18	Antrim . .	Lower Toome .	Kirkinriola .	Ballymena .	III.	32
92	Drumfin . .	214	2	18	Donegal . .	Banagh . .	Inver . .	Donegal . .	III.	107
26,27,33,34	Drumfin . .	561	2	39c	Sligo . .	Corran . .	Kilmorgan .	Sligo . .	IV.	227
27	Drumfin or Islandroy Barr . .	159	0	26	Donegal . .	Kilmacrenan .	Mevagh . .	Milford . .	III.	130
61	Drumflugh . .	306	2	18	Tyrone . .	Dungannon Middle .	Clonfeacle .	Dungannon .	III.	299
33	Drumfomina .	267	0	32	Cavan . .	Castlerahan .	Killinkere .	Bailieborough .	III.	69
14	Drumfresky . .	493	3	35	Antrim . .	Lower Glenarm .	Grange of Layd .	Ballycastle .	III.	22
67	Drumfurban .	46	3	23	Mayo . .	Burrishoole .	Burrishoole .	Newport . .	IV.	119
2	Drumfurrer . .	540	0	16	Monaghan .	Trough . .	Errigal Trough .	Clogher . .	III.	284
6	Drumgaghan .	132	2	35	Monaghan .	Trough . .	Donagh . .	Monaghan .	III.	282
32, 33	Drumgague . .	108	2	2	Fermanagh .	Clanawley . .	Killesher . .	Enniskillen .	III.	192
34,35,39,40	Drumgallan .	177	1	29d	Fermanagh .	Clankelly . .	Galloon . .	Lisnaskea .	III.	198
22, 27	Drumgallan .	176	1	0	Fermanagh .	Magheraboy .	Rossorry . .	Enniskillen .	III.	214
15	Drumgallan .	186	1	12	Monaghan .	Cremorne . .	Clontibret .	Castleblayney .	III.	260
24	Drumgallan .	459	3	31	Tyrone . .	Omagh West .	Longfield West .	Castlederg .	III.	316
21	Drumgallon .	173	0	35	Cavan . .	Tullygarvey .	Drung . .	Cootehill . .	III.	89
21	Drumgamph .	99	1	31	Fermanagh .	Clanawley . .	Boho . .	Enniskillen .	III.	189
17, 21	Drumgane . .	259	2	26	Armagh . .	Fews Lower .	Loughgilly .	Armagh . .	III.	47
5	Drumgane . .	113	3	37	Leitrim . .	Rosclogher .	Rossinver . .	Manorhamilton .	IV.	111
28	Drumganny . .	153	1	28	Monaghan .	Farney . .	Donaghmoyne .	Carrickmacross	III.	270
25	Drumganus Lower .	163	1	8	Monaghan .	Farney . .	Donaghmoyne .	Castleblayney .	III.	270
25	Drumganus Upper .	156	0	5	Monaghan .	Farney . .	Donaghmoyne .	Castleblayney .	III.	270
11	Drumgar . .	334	1	26	Armagh . .	Armagh . .	Derrynoose .	Armagh . .	III.	44
77	Drumgar . .	146	0	31	Mayo . .	Burrishoole .	Kilmaclasser .	Westport . .	IV.	121
22	Drumgarkin .	155	2	38	Monaghan .	Dartree . .	Ematris . .	Cootehill . .	III.	267
12, 17	Drumgarly . .	184	1	19	Monaghan .	Dartree . .	Aghabog . .	Clones . .	III.	263
28	Drumgarn .	101	1	11	Leitrim . .	Mohill . .	Mohill . .	Mohill . .	IV.	107
9	Drumgarn .	50	0	19	Monaghan .	Trough . .	Donagh . .	Monaghan .	III.	282
24	Drumgarra . .	345	3	6	Monaghan .	Cremorne . .	Ballybay . .	Castleblayney .	III.	259
15	Drumgarran .	100	2	15	Armagh . .	Tiranny . .	Tynan . .	Armagh . .	III.	60
16	Drumgarran .	68	3	6	Monaghan .	Dartree . .	Currin . .	Clones . .	III.	265
9	Drumgarran .	84	2	37	Monaghan .	Monaghan .	Tedavnet . .	Monaghan .	III.	278
30	Drumgarrell .	289	0	20	Tyrone . .	Dungannon Upper .	Derryloran .	Cookstown .	III.	307
22	Drumgarrow .	60	0	32	Fermanagh .	Tirkennedy .	Enniskillen .	Enniskillen .	III.	222
16	Drumgarrow .	106	3	37	Fermanagh .	Tirkennedy .	Trory . .	Lowtherstown .	III.	223
10	Drumgart . .	136	0	1e	Cavan . .	Lower Loughtee .	Drumlane .	Cavan . .	III.	80
76	Drumgarve . .	168	2	11	Mayo . .	Burrishoole .	Kilmeena . .	Westport . .	IV.	122
13	Drumgarve . .	120	3	13	Monaghan .	Monaghan .	Drumsnat . .	Monaghan .	III.	275
6, 10	Drumgask . .	171	0	10	Armagh . .	Oneilland East .	Seagoe . .	Lurgan . .	III.	50
47	Drumgath . .	375	2	12	Down . .	Upper Iveagh, Up. pt.	Drumgath . .	Newry . .	III.	175
2	Drumgauty . .	246	2	3f	Tyrone . .	Strabane Lower .	Donaghedy .	Strabane . .	III.	320
17	Drumgavenny Lower	233	2	39	Londonderry .	Keenaght .	Balteagh . .	NewᵀᵒLimavady	III.	234
17	Drumgavenny Upper	229	0	4	Londonderry .	Keenaght .	Balteagh . .	NewᵀᵒLimavady	III.	234
29	Drumgavlin . .	546	3	32g	Down . .	Kinelarty . .	Dromara . .	Downpatrick .	III.	176
18	Drumgavny . .	211	2	33	Monaghan .	Cremorne . .	Tullycorbet .	Monaghan .	III.	262
12, 16	Drumgaw . .	360	1	32	Armagh . .	Fews Lower .	Lisnadill . .	Armagh . .	III.	47

No. of Sheet of the Ordnance Survey Maps.	Townlands and Towns.	Area in Statute Acres.			County.	Barony.	Parish.	Poor Law Union in 1857.	Townland Census of 1851, Part I.	
		A.	R.	P.					Vol.	Page
22	Drumgay	175	0	37a	Fermanagh	Tirkennedy	Enniskillen	Enniskillen	III.	222
21, 22	Drumgaze	133	0	27	Monaghan	Dartree	Currin	Cootehill	III.	265
27	Drumgeaglom	157	2	4	Leitrim	Leitrim	Kiltoghert	Car^k. on Shannon	IV.	101
51, 61	Drumgeely	216	0	16	Clare	Bunratty Lower	Clonloghan	Ennis	II.	3
34	Drumgeeny	255	1	8	Monaghan	Farney	Killanny	Carrickmacross	III.	271
6	Drumgeeny	186	1	32	Monaghan	Trough	Donagh	Monaghan	III.	282
19, 24	Drumgerd	83	3	8	Cavan	Tullyhunco	Killashandra	Cavan	III.	98
14	Drumgesh	172	1	19	Cavan	Lower Loughtee	Drumlane	Cavan	III.	80
10, 17	Drumgesh	214	3	20	Londonderry	Keenaght	Balteagh	New T^n Limavady	III.	234
22	Drumgill	192	3	11	Cavan	Tullygarvey	Kildrumsherdan	Cootehill	III.	90
6	Drumgill	209	3	23	Meath	Lower Slane	Loughbrackan	Ardee	I.	223
2	Drumgill	456	2	10	Meath	Morgallion	Erniskeen	Kells	I.	209
34	Drumgill	175	2	19	Tipperary, N.R.	Kilnamanagh Upper	Glenkeen	Thurles	II.	278
3, 6	Drumgill Lower	332	2	34	Meath	Lower Slane	Drumcondra	Ardee	I.	222
3, 6	Drumgill Upper	99	3	7	Meath	Lower Slane	Drumcondra	Ardee	I.	222
32	Drumgilra	116	3	20b	Leitrim	Leitrim	Annaduff	Car^k. on Shannon	IV.	99
36	Drumgilra	372	3	19	Leitrim	Mohill	Cloone	Mohill	IV.	105
23	Drumgiven	410	1	12	Down	Castlereagh Upper	Kilmore	Downpatrick	III.	165
6	Drumgivery	280	3	17	Fermanagh	Lurg	Magheraculmoney	Lowtherstown	III.	208
26	Drumgloon	208	3	17	Clare	Bunratty Upper	Kilraghtis	Ennis	II.	9
19	Drumgoa	125	0	21	Cavan	Tullyhunco	Killashandra	Cavan	III.	98
31	Drumgoan	119	3	27	Monaghan	Farney	Magheross	Carrickmacross	III.	273
9	Drumgoask	142	0	31	Monaghan	Monaghan	Tedavnet	Monaghan	III.	278
36	Drumgoast	143	2	17	Fermanagh	Clankelly	Clones	Clones	III.	196
8	Drumgoast	136	2	11	Monaghan	Monaghan	Clones	Monaghan	III.	274
29	Drumgoff	1,016	1	1	Wicklow	Ballinacor South	Knockrath	Rathdrum	I.	350
20	Drumgola	156	2	35c	Cavan	Upper Loughtee	Urney	Cavan	III.	86
39, 40	Drumgoland	140	3	8	Fermanagh	Coole	Galloon	Clones	III.	199
10	Drumgolat	148	1	29	Monaghan	Cremorne	Clontibret	Monaghan	III.	260
54,55,61,62	Drumgold	153	0	39	Tyrone	Dungannon Middle	Clonfeacle	Dungannon	III.	299
20, 26	Drumgold	702	3	6	Wexford	Ballaghkeen	Templeshannon	Enniscorthy	I.	299
34, 39	Drumgole	68	2	5d	Fermanagh	Coole	Galloon	Lisnaskea	III.	199
17, 22	Drumgole	167	0	27e	Monaghan	Dartree	Ematris	Cootehill	III.	267
44, 56	Drumgollagh	550	1	19	Mayo	Erris	Kilcommon	Newport	IV.	144
11	Drumgolliff	164	1	1	Armagh	Tiranny	Tynan	Armagh	III.	60
21	Drumgoney	182	0	4	Cavan	Tullygarvey	Larah	Cootehill	III.	91
77	Drumgoney	142	3	33	Mayo	Burrishoole	Kilmaclasser	Westport	IV.	121
6	Drumgonnelly	261	2	18	Louth	Louth	Louth	Dundalk	I.	184
128, 133	Drumgooaun	135	3	13	Galway	Kiltartan	Beagh	Gort	IV.	46
19	Drumgoohy	104	3	1	Cavan	Tullyhunco	Kildallan	Bawnboy	III.	97
11	Drumgoolan	265	3	27	Louth	Louth	Louth	Dundalk	I.	184
37	Drumgooland	455	0	20f	Down	Kinelarty	Loughinisland	Downpatrick	III.	177
5, 6	Drumgoole	295	0	31	Kilkenny	Fassadinin	Castlecomer	Castlecomer	I.	88
10	Drumgoole	90	2	35	Monaghan	Monaghan	Tehallan	Monaghan	III.	280
17, 22	Drumgoon	210	1	19	Cavan	Clankee	Drumgoon	Cootehill	III.	72
19, 24	Drumgoon	286	3	1	Cavan	Tullyhunco	Killashandra	Cavan	III.	98
28	Drumgoon	362	2	33	Fermanagh	Magherastephana	Aghalurcher	Lisnaskea	III.	216
30, 31	Drumgoosat	196	2	11	Monaghan	Farney	Magheracloone	Carrickmacross	III.	272
5, 9	Drumgoose	95	2	37	Armagh	Oneilland West	Drumcree	Lurgan	III.	52
25	Drumgoose	267	1	39g	Monaghan	Farney	Donaghmoyne	Castleblayney	III.	270
18, 19	Drumgooter	88	1	34	Louth	Ferrard	Rathdrumin	Drogheda	I.	182
6, 10	Drumgor	328	3	5	Armagh	Oneilland East	Seagoe	Lurgan	III.	50
25	Drumgor	38	1	35	Cavan	Upper Loughtee	Kilmore	Cavan	III.	84
23,24,26,27	Drumgor	327	1	4	Monaghan	Cremorne	Aghnamullen	Castleblayney	III.	258
33, 39	Drumgora	278	2	26	Cavan	Castlerahan	Lurgan	Oldcastle	III.	69
26	Drumgora	177	0	15	Cavan	Upper Loughtee	Lavey	Cavan	III.	85
30	Drumgore	341	3	14h	Cavan	Clanmahon	Drumlumman	Granard	III.	77
13	Drumgorey	263	1	11	Waterford	Glenahiry	Kilronan	Clonmel	II.	365
54	Drumgormal	153	2	20	Tyrone	Dungannon Middle	Clonfeacle	Dungannon	III.	299
47	Drumgormal	235	3	4	Tyrone	Dungannon Middle	Donaghenry	Cookstown	III.	301
98, 99	Drumgorman	313	2	30	Donegal	Banagh	Inver	Donegal	III.	107
23, 27	Drumgorman	224	1	26i	Leitrim	Leitrim	Kiltoghert	Car^k. on Shannon	IV.	101
93, 99	Drumgorman Barr	79	2	11	Donegal	Banagh	Inver	Donegal	III.	107
14	Drumgormly	276	3	14	Fermanagh	Magheraboy	Devenish	Enniskillen	III.	210
13,14,19,20	Drumgormly, Barr of	196	2	35	Fermanagh	Magheraboy	Devenish	Ballyshannon	III.	210
93	Drumgorran	377	3	21	Donegal	Banagh	Killymard	Donegal	III.	111
28	Drumgorran	67	2	35	Fermanagh	Magherastephana	Aghavea	Lisnaskea	III.	218
11, 15	Drumgorry	152	0	35j	Cavan	Tullygarvey	Annagh	Cavan	III.	87
30	Drumgose	166	1	19k	Armagh	Fews Upper	Creggan	Castleblayney	III.	48
15, 19	Drumgose	246	1	4	Armagh	Tiranny	Tynan	Armagh	III.	60
61	Drumgose	137	1	7	Tyrone	Dungannon Middle	Clonfeacle	Dungannon	III.	299
99, 100	Drumgowan	269	1	15	Donegal	Tirhugh	Donegal	Donegal	III.	145
47	Drumgower	113	1	37	Tipperary, N.R.	Eliogarty	Moycarky	Thurles	II.	271

(a) Including 29A. 2R. 30P. water.
(b) Including 1A. 0R. 0P. water.
(c) Including 5A. 0R. 0P. water.
(d) Including 10A. 1R. 36P. water.

(e) Including 6A. 1R. 4P. water.
(f) Including 10A. 1R. 31P. Lake.
(g) Including 17A. 0R. 1P. water.
(h) Including 25A. 3R. 25P. water.

(i) Including 8A. 3R. 33P. water.
(j) Including 13A. 0R. 39P. water.
(k) Including 85A. 1R. 17P. water.

No. of Sheet of the Ordnance Survey Maps.	Townlands and Towns.	Area in Statute Acres.			County.	Barony.	Parish.	Poor Law Union in 1857.	Townland Census of 1851. Part I.	
		A.	R.	P.					Vol.	Page
28	Drumgowla	245	1	5	Leitrim	Leitrim	Kiltoghert	Car^k.on Shannon	IV.	101
29, 33	Drumgowla	454	3	17	Leitrim	Mohill	Cloone	Mohill	IV.	105
28	Drumgowna	86	1	33	Fermanagh	Magherastephana	Aghavea	Lisnaskea	III.	218
10, 11	Drumgowna	276	1	14	Louth	Louth	Louth	Dundalk	I.	184
27, 28	Drumgowna	346	2	27	Monaghan	Farney	Magheross	Carrickmacross	III.	273
2	Drumgowna East	182	1	35	Fermanagh	Lurg	Drumkeeran	Lowtherstown	III.	206
22	Drumgownagh	191	1	27	Leitrim	Carrigallen	Oughteragh	Bawnboy	IV.	92
27, 28	Drumgownagh	190	1	0	Leitrim	Leitrim	Kiltoghert	Car^k.on Shannon	IV.	101
28	Drumgownagh	258	0	3	Leitrim	Leitrim	Mohill	Mohill	IV.	104
33, 36	Drumgownagh	462	0	34	Leitrim	Mohill	Cloone	Mohill	IV.	105
1, 5	Drumgowna West	312	0	14	Fermanagh	Lurg	Drumkeeran	Lowtherstown	III.	206
43	Drumgramph	87	3	28	Fermanagh	Coole	Drummully	Clones	III.	199
17	Drumgramph	121	3	15	Monaghan	Dartree	Aghabog	Cootehill	III.	263
22	Drumgramph	87	3	29a	Monaghan	Dartree	Currin	Cootehill	III.	265
34	Drumgranagh	89	0	22b	Clare	Bunratty Upper	Kilraghtis	Ennis	II.	9
36	Drumgrania	335	0	7	Leitrim	Mohill	Cloone	Mohill	IV.	105
62	Drumgrannon	186	1	3	Tyrone	Dungannon Middle	Clonfeacle	Dungannon	III.	299
29	Drumgrass	148	3	25	Tyrone	Dungannon Upper	Lissan	Cookstown	III.	309
17	Drumgreen	48	1	9	Cavan	Tullygarvey	Drumgoon	Cootehill	III.	88
15, 19	Drumgreenagh	436	2	34	Armagh	Armagh	Derrynoose	Armagh	III.	44
41, 47	Drumgreenagh	439	2	14	Down	Upper Iveagh, Up.pt.	Drumgath	Newry	III.	175
13, 18	Drumgreeny	146	0	23	Monaghan	Monaghan	Kilmore	Monaghan	III.	276
53	Drumgreggan	83	0	36	Donegal	Raphoe	Leck	Letterkenny	III.	140
5	Drumgrenaghan	137	1	10	Fermanagh	Lurg	Drumkeeran	Lowtherstown	III.	206
69	Drumgriffin	233	0	7	Galway	Clare	Annaghdown	Galway	IV.	16
19	Drumgristin	158	2	13c	Monaghan	Cremorne	Clontibret	Castleblayney	III.	260
17	Drumgristin	88	2	22	Monaghan	Dartree	Aghabog	Cootehill	III.	263
25	Drumgristin Lower	128	2	24	Monaghan	Farney	Donaghmoyne	Castleblayney	III.	270
31, 32	Drumgristin Upper	198	1	4	Monaghan	Farney	Donaghmoyne	Carrickmacross	III.	270
19	Drumgrole	288	2	20	Monaghan	Cremorne	Ballybay	Castleblayney	III.	259
22	Drumgrone	205	0	8	Monaghan	Dartree	Currin	Cootehill	III.	265
24	Drumgud	79	2	28	Leitrim	Leitrim	Kiltubbrid	Car^k. on Shannon	IV.	103
17	Drumguff	37	0	21	Monaghan	Dartree	Killeevan	Clones	III.	268
36	Drumguff	118	1	13	Fermanagh	Clankelly	Clones	Clones	III.	196
34, 39	Drumguiff	97	1	9d	Fermanagh	Magherastephana	Aghalurcher	Lisnaskea	III.	216
13	Drumguill	174	0	6	Monaghan	Monaghan	Drumsnat	Monaghan	III.	275
40	Drumguillagh	79	1	9	Fermanagh	Coole	Galloon	Clones	III.	199
19, 24	Drumguillew Lower	147	0	7	Monaghan	Cremorne	Ballybay	Castleblayney	III.	259
24	Drumguillew Upper	150	0	14	Monaghan	Cremorne	Ballybay	Castleblayney	III.	259
12	Drumguilly	111	2	2	Monaghan	Dartree	Killeevan	Monaghan	III.	268
4	Drumguin	255	3	24	Carlow	Rathvilly	Hacketstown	Shillelagh	I.	11
38	Drumgullane East	220	3	9	Waterford	Decies within Drum	Kinsalebeg	Youghal	II.	352
38	Drumgullane West	167	0	16	Waterford	Decies within Drum	Kinsalebeg	Youghal	II.	352
69	Drumgumberland	241	3	27	Donegal	Raphoe	Convoy	Stranorlar	III.	136
93, 99	Drumgun	83	1	15	Donegal	Banagh	Killymard	Donegal	III.	111
105	Drumgun	193	2	26e	Donegal	Tirhugh	Templecarn	Donegal	III.	149
29	Drumgunny	218	0	8	Leitrim	Carrigallen	Cloone	Mohill	IV.	90
21	Drumgur	98	1	28	Cavan	Tullygarvey	Larah	Cootehill	III.	91
10	Drumgur	88	0	29	Louth	Ardee	Louth	Dundalk	I.	173
41	Drumgurland	199	2	8	Antrim	Lower Belfast	Islandmagee	Larne	III.	8
30	Drumgurra	417	2	1	Monaghan	Farney	Magheross	Carrickmacross	III.	273
32, 33	Drumhack	141	1	37	Fermanagh	Clanawley	Killesher	Enniskillen	III.	192
34	Drumhack	92	1	30	Fermanagh	Magherastephana	Aghalurcher	Lisnaskea	III.	216
38, 39	Drumhaggart	490	2	16	Donegal	Inishowen West	Burt	Londonderry	III.	119
32	Drumhallagh	63	1	35	Cavan	Castlerahan	Crosserlough	Cavan	III.	68
21	Drumhallagh	159	0	34	Cavan	Tullygarvey	Larah	Cootehill	III.	91
29, 33	Drumhallagh	419	1	39f	Leitrim	Mohill	Cloone	Mohill	IV.	105
28	Drumhallagh Lower	149	3	10	Donegal	Kilmacrenan	Killygarvan	Millford	III.	128
28	Drumhallagh Upper	590	3	18	Donegal	Kilmacrenan	Killygarvan	Millford	III.	128
30	Drumhalry	194	2	3	Leitrim	Carrigallen	Carrigallen	Bawnboy	IV.	89
1, 3	Drumhalry	895	1	11g	Longford	Granard	Killoe	Granard	I.	157
23	Drumhalwy	31	2	28h	Leitrim	Leitrim	Kiltoghert	Car^k.on Shannon	IV.	101
25, 28	Drumhaman	127	0	1	Monaghan	Farney	Donaghmoyne	Carrickmacross	III.	270
32	Drumhany	77	3	24	Leitrim	Mohill	Mohill	Mohill	IV.	107
32	Drumhany North	109	2	13	Leitrim	Mohill	Mohill	Mohill	IV.	107
32	Drumhany South	201	1	39	Leitrim	Mohill	Mohill	Mohill	IV.	107
15	Drumharid	231	3	7	Cavan	Upper Loughtee	Castleterra	Cavan	III.	82
29	Drumharkan	162	0	13i	Leitrim	Leitrim	Fenagh	Mohill	IV.	100
33	Drumharkan Glebe	569	2	36	Leitrim	Mohill	Cloone	Mohill	IV.	106
7	Drumharlow	144	1	16	Roscommon	Boyle	Tumna	Boyle	IV.	198
5, 9	Drumharriff	196	1	29	Armagh	Oneilland West	Drumcree	Lurgan	III.	52
8, 9	Drumharriff	217	2	6	Armagh	Oneilland West	Loughgall	Armagh	III.	54
21, 25	Drumharriff	600	1	39	Armagh	Orior Upper	Loughgilly	Newry	III.	58

(a) Including 3A. 0R. 9P. water.
(b) Including 0A. 0R. 24P. water.
(c) Including 14A. 2R. 17P. water.

(d) Including 7A. 0R. 36P. water.
(e) Including 21A. 0R. 20P. water.
(f) Including 23A. 0R. 32P. water.

(g) Including 12A. 1R. 10P. water.
(h) Including 1A. 3R. 6P. water.
(i) Including 14A. 1R. 25P. water.

No. of Sheet of the Ordnance Survey Maps.	Townlands and Towns.	Area in Statute Acres.			County.	Barony.	Parish.	Poor Law Union in 1857.	Townland Census of 1851, Part I.	
		A.	R.	P.					Vol.	Page
105	Drumharriff	250	2	9	Donegal	Tirhugh	Templecarn	Donegal	III.	149
26	Drumharriff	95	0	12	Fermanagh	Clanawley	Cleenish	Enniskillen	III.	190
32	Drumharriff	71	1	23	Fermanagh	Clanawley	Kinawley	Enniskillen	III.	194
40	Drumharriff	100	3	0	Fermanagh	Clankelly	Clones	Clones	III.	196
27,28,33,34	Drumharriff	178	1	28	Fermanagh	Magherastephana	Aghalurcher	Lisnaskea	III.	216
28	Drumharriff	171	3	19	Monaghan	Farney	Donaghmoyne	Carrickmacross	III.	270
54	Drumharriff	35	2	22	Tyrone	Dungannon Middle	Drumglass	Dungannon	III.	303
25	Drumharriff North	173	2	13	Monaghan	Farney	Donaghmoyne	Castleblayney	III.	270
113	Drumharsna North	127	1	1	Galway	Dunkellin	Ardrahan	Gort	IV.	26
113	Drumharsna South	689	1	37	Galway	Dunkellin	Ardrahan	Gort	IV.	26
24	Drumhart	253	3	23a	Cavan	Tullyhunco	Killashandra	Cavan	III.	98
49	Drumharvey	707	0	1	Tyrone	Omagh East	Kilskeery	Lowtherstown	III.	313
31	Drumhasket	74	2	16	Monaghan	Farney	Killanny	Carrickmacross	III.	271
36	Drumhass	257	3	19b	Leitrim	Mohill	Cloone	Mohill	IV.	106
9	Drumhaughly	190	1	18	Longford	Longford	Killoe	Longford	I.	159
23	Drumhauver	89	2	22	Leitrim	Leitrim	Kiltoghert	Car^k. on Shannon	IV.	101
34	Drumhaw	99	0	2	Fermanagh	Magherastephana	Aghalurcher	Lisnaskea	III.	216
24	Drumhawan	327	0	26	Monaghan	Cremorne	Ballybay	Castleblayney	III.	259
30, 31, 37	Drumhawnagh	431	2	0	Cavan	Clanmahon	Drumlumman	Granard	III.	77
30, 31	Drumhawragh	573	3	1c	Cavan	Clanmahon	Drumlumman	Granard	III.	77
17, 22	Drumhay	160	2	12d	Monaghan	Dartree	Aghabog	Cootehill	III.	263
27	Drumheckil	91	1	14e	Leitrim	Leitrim	Kiltoghert	Car^k. on Shannon	IV.	101
25	Drumhecknagh	142	1	29	Cavan	Upper Loughtee	Kilmore	Cavan	III.	84
39,40,43,44	Drumheel	184	3	8	Cavan	Castlerahan	Lurgan	Oldcastle	III.	69
20	Drumheel	57	0	1	Cavan	Lower Loughtee	Drumlane	Cavan	III.	80
25	Drumheel	246	3	27	Cavan	Upper Loughtee	Kilmore	Cavan	III.	84
23	Drumherney	256	1	17	Armagh	Tiranny	Derrynoose	Armagh	III.	59
14	Drumherriff	175	0	37	Cavan	Lower Loughtee	Drumlane	Cavan	III.	80
23	Drumherriff	212	1	32f	Leitrim	Leitrim	Kiltoghert	Car^k. on Shannon	IV.	101
16	Drumherriff North	48	0	30	Cavan	Tullygarvey	Drung	Cootehill	III.	89
17,21,22	Drumherriff South	169	1	19g	Cavan	Tullygarvey	Drung	Cootehill	III.	89
20	Drumherrish	36	2	4	Cavan	Upper Loughtee	Castleterra	Cavan	III.	82
37	Drumherrive	273	1	3	Donegal	Kilmacrenan	Aughnish	Millford	III.	122
33	Drumhervin	135	0	27	Fermanagh	Knockninny	Kinawley	Lisnaskea	III.	202
27	Drumhierny	216	0	28	Leitrim	Leitrim	Kiltoghert	Car^k. on Shannon	IV.	101
27	Drumhillagh	187	0	26	Cavan	Clankee	Knockbride	Cootehill	III.	73
31	Drumhillagh	140	0	12	Cavan	Clanmahon	Ballintemple	Cavan	III.	75
21	Drumhillagh	203	0	19	Cavan	Tullygarvey	Drung	Cootehill	III.	89
19	Drumhillagh	136	0	25	Cavan	Tullyhunco	Killashandra	Cavan	III.	98
30	Drumhillagh	176	2	11	Cavan	Tullyhunco	Scrabby	Cavan	III.	99
21, 26	Drumhillagh	181	1	28	Cavan	Upper Loughtee	Lavey	Cavan	III.	85
23	Drumhillagh	132	1	9	Monaghan	Cremorne	Aghnamullen	Castleblayney	III.	258
18,19,23,24	Drumhillagh	232	2	4	Monaghan	Cremorne	Ballybay	Castleblayney	III.	259
16, 21	Drumhillagh	97	3	14	Monaghan	Dartree	Currin	Clones	III.	265
13	Drumhillagh	276	3	38	Monaghan	Dartree	Killeevan	Monaghan	III.	268
28, 31	Drumhillagh	142	1	34	Monaghan	Farney	Donaghmoyne	Carrickmacross	III.	270
6, 9	Drumhillagh	229	0	33	Monaghan	Monaghan	Tedavnet	Monaghan	III.	278
23	Drumhillagh North	371	0	4h	Cavan	Clankee	Knockbride	Bailieborough	III.	73
28	Drumhillagh South	291	1	20i	Cavan	Clankee	Knockbride	Bailieborough	III.	73
15, 19	Drumhillcry	152	3	31	Armagh	Tiranny	Tynan	Armagh	III.	60
16	Drumhirk	346	0	12	Armagh	Armagh	Derrynoose	Armagh	III.	44
17	Drumhirk	161	2	10	Cavan	Tullygarvey	Kildrumsherdan	Cootehill	III.	90
32	Drumhirk	129	1	39	Cavan	Upper Loughtee	Denn	Cavan	III.	83
26	Drumhirk	370	3	10j	Cavan	Upper Loughtee	Lavey	Cavan	III.	85
2, 6	Drumhirk	869	0	6	Down	Ards Lower	Newtownards	Newtownards	III.	158
10	Drumhirk	514	3	21k	Down	Castlereagh Lower	Kilmood	Newtownards	III.	163
21	Drumhirk	129	3	33	Fermanagh	Clanawley	Cleenish	Enniskillen	III.	190
2	Drumhirk	102	1	33	Fermanagh	Lurg	Drumkeeran	Lowtherstown	III.	206
27	Drumhirk	117	2	32l	Fermanagh	Tirkennedy	Derryvullan	Enniskillen	III.	221
17, 18	Drumhirk	152	3	2m	Fermanagh	Tirkennedy	Enniskillen	Enniskillen	III.	222
36	Drumhirk	348	0	30	Leitrim	Mohill	Cloone	Mohill	IV.	106
29	Drumhirk	90	3	4n	Leitrim	Mohill	Mohill	Mohill	IV.	107
12,13,17,18	Drumhirk	280	1	9	Monaghan	Dartree	Aghabog	Monaghan	III.	263
9	Drumhirk	107	3	7	Monaghan	Monaghan	Monaghan	Monaghan	III.	277
58, 59	Drumhirk	159	1	4	Tyrone	Clogher	Clogher	Clogher	III.	292
54	Drumhirk	209	2	6o	Tyrone	Dungannon Middle	Donaghmore	Dungannon	III.	302
59	Drumhirk Glebe	81	2	22	Tyrone	Clogher	Clogher	Clogher	III.	292
21	Drumhirk Lower	77	2	31	Fermanagh	Clanawley	Boho	Enniskillen	III.	189
21	Drumhirk Upper	70	3	27	Fermanagh	Clanawley	Boho	Enniskillen	III.	189
107	Drumhogan	108	0	28	Galway	Longford	Abbeygormacan	Ballinasloe	IV.	56
15, 16	Drumhome	74	0	35p	Cavan	Upper Loughtee	Castleterra	Cavan	III.	82
103	Drumhome	303	0	4q	Donegal	Tirhugh	Drumhome	Ballyshannon	III.	146
10	Drumhoney	206	1	31	Fermanagh	Lurg	Derryvullan	Lowtherstown	III.	204

(a) Including 6A. 2R. 6P. water.   (g) Including 5A. 0R. 26P. water.   (m) Including 3A. 3R. 0P. water.
(b) Including 59A. 3R. 8P. water.   (h) Including 14A. 1R. 2P. water.   (n) Including 4A. 3R. 34P. water.
(c) Including 21A. 3R. 19P. water.   (i) Including 58A. 0R. 20P. water.   (o) Including 1A. 1R. 27P. water.
(d) Including 19A. 3R. 29P. water.   (j) Including 3A. 3R. 22P. water.   (p) Including 6A. 0R. 26P. water.
(e) Including 13A. 1R. 14P. water.   (k) Including 4A. 1R. 1P. water.   (q) Including 8A. 2R. 18P. water.
(f) Including Islands.   (l) Including 4A. 2R. 38P. water.

3 G

No. of Sheet of the Ordnance Survey Maps.	Townlands and Towns.	Area in Statute Acres.	County.	Barony.	Parish.	Poor Law Union in 1857.	Townland Census of 1851, Part I.	
		A. R. P.					Vol.	Page
5, 10	Drumhoney	168 2 9	Fermanagh	Lurg	Magheraculmoney	Lowtherstown	III.	208
33, 34	Drumhonish	151 0 0	Tyrone	Omagh West	Longfield East	Omagh	III.	315
26	Drumhorc	114 3 29	Down	Lower Iveagh, Up. pt.	Tullylish	Banbridge	III.	171
55	Drumhorrik	132 1 21	Tyrone	Dungannon Middle	Killyman	Dungannon	III.	303
17	Drumhose	162 3 10	Cavan	Tullygarvey	Kildrumsherdan	Cootehill	III.	90
34, 39	Drumhose	151 0 4	Fermanagh	Coole	Galloon	Lisnaskea	III.	199
23	Drumhoy	85 2 15	Fermanagh	Magherastephana	Aghavea	Lisnaskea	III.	218
47	Drumhubbert	100 0 25	Tyrone	Dungannon Upper	Arboe	Cookstown	III.	305
24	Drumhubbrid	157 0 20	Leitrim	Leitrim	Kiltubbrid	Car^k. on Shannon	IV.	103
3, 4, 5	Drumhurrin	373 0 31	Cavan	Tullyhaw	Templeport	Enniskillen	III.	94
17, 22	Drumhurt	245 3 24a	Cavan	Tullygarvey	Kildrumsherdan	Cootehill	III.	90
77	Drumhuskert	107 1 20	Mayo	Burrishoole	Kilmeena	Westport	IV.	122
5, 6	Drumierna	137 1 26	Fermanagh	Lurg	Drumkeeran	Lowtherstown	III.	206
17	Drumilkin	84 0 26	Monaghan	Dartree	Aghabog	Cootehill	III.	263
24, 27	Drumillard	267 2 21b	Monaghan	Cremorne	Aghnamullen	Castleblayney	III.	258
28	Drumillard	122 0 28	Monaghan	Farney	Donaghmoyne	Carrickmacross	III.	270
20	Drumillard Big	221 0 2c	Monaghan	Cremorne	Muckno	Castleblayney	III.	262
20	Drumillard Little	108 1 6	Monaghan	Cremorne	Muckno	Castleblayney	III.	262
29	Drumiller	215 3 37	Cavan	Clankee	Enniskeen	Bailieborough	III.	72
15	Drumillion	71 2 17	Leitrim	Drumahaire	Killarga	Manorhamilton	IV.	98
8	Drumilly	261 3 8d	Armagh	Oneilland West	Loughgall	Armagh	III.	54
25	Drumilly	681 1 17	Armagh	Orior Upper	Killevy	Newry	III.	58
68, 77	Drumilra	894 0 18e	Mayo	Burrishoole	Kilmaclasser	Westport	IV.	121
18	Drumin	93 1 10	Louth	Ferrard	Dunleer	Ardee	I.	181
18	Drumin	155 2 19	Louth	Ferrard	Dysart	Drogheda	I.	181
7	Druminacrehir	353 1 29	Longford	Granard	Columbkille	Granard	I.	156
25, 29	Druminagh	71 1 34	Antrim	Lower Glenarm	Tickmacrevan	Larne	III.	23
20	Druminagh	172 2 35	Roscommon	Frenchpark	Tibohine	Castlereagh	IV.	205
18	Druminalass	133 3 5	Leitrim	Drumahaire	Drumreilly	Car^k. on Shannon	IV.	95
5, 9	Druminallyduff	96 3 15	Armagh	Oneilland West	Drumcree	Lurgan	III.	52
5, 6, 8	Druminane	289 2 23	Monaghan	Monaghan	Tedavnet	Monaghan	III.	278
49	Druminard	489 2 14	Londonderry	Loughinsholin	Tamlaght	Magherafelt	III.	243
94, 100	Druminardagh	242 1 37	Donegal	Tirhugh	Donegal	Donegal	III.	145
18	Druminargal	389 1 8f	Armagh	Orior Lower	Ballymore	Banbridge	III.	55
5	Druminargid	164 1 11	Leitrim	Rosclogher	Rossinver	Manorhamilton	IV.	111
71	Druminaw	97 3 39	Donegal	Raphoe	Clonleigh	Strabane	III.	135
51	Druminda	130 0 34	Tipperary, N.R.	Kilnamanagh Upper	Toem	Tipperary	II.	280
29	Druminderry Upper and Lower	585 2 3	Donegal	Inishowen West	Fahan Lower	Inishowen	III.	120
55	Drumindoney	143 1 19	Down	Mourne	Kilkeel	Kilkeel	III.	183
41, 42	Druminduff	70 1 11	King's Co.	Clonlisk	Shinrone	Roscrea	I.	131
24	Drumineigh Glebe	150 1 34	Leitrim	Leitrim	Kiltubbrid	Car^k. on Shannon	IV.	103
70	Drumineney	93 1 18	Donegal	Raphoe	Raphoe	Strabane	III.	141
19	Druming	597 1 32	Longford	Moydow	Kilglass	Ballymahon	I.	161
28	Drumingna	205 2 11	Leitrim	Leitrim	Kiltubbrid	Car^k. on Shannon	IV.	103
8	Druminillar	351 0 37g	Fermanagh	Lurg	Belleek	Ballyshannon	III.	203
92, 98	Druminiscal	56 3 15	Donegal	Banagh	Killaghtee	Donegal	III.	109
32	Druminisclin	162 3 31	Cavan	Castlerahan	Crosserlough	Cavan	III.	68
11	Druminisclin	153 1 10h	Cavan	Tullygarvey	Annagh	Cavan	III.	87
19	Druminiskill	152 2 3	Cavan	Tullyhunco	Kildallan	Bawnboy	III.	97
27, 32, 33	Druminiskill	355 3 21	Fermanagh	Clanawley	Killesher	Enniskillen	III.	192
38, 39	Druminiskill	246 0 17	Fermanagh	Knockninny	Kinawley	Lisnaskea	III.	202
4	Druminiskin	306 3 37	Meath	Lower Kells	Moynalty	Kells	I.	204
23	Druminnick	77 1 26i	Cavan	Clankee	Knockbride	Cootehill	III.	73
94	Druminnin	308 3 1	Donegal	Tirhugh	Donegal	Donegal	III.	145
24, 25	Druminshin	137 1 29	Clare	Inchiquin	Dysart	Ennis	II.	24
12, 13	Druminshin	32 2 11	Leitrim	Drumahaire	Cloonclare	Manorhamilton	IV.	93
6	Druminshin	152 3 7	Meath	Lower Slane	Loughbrackan	Ardee	I.	223
10	Druminshinardagh	110 1 32	Fermanagh	Lurg	Derryvullan	Lowtherstown	III.	204
16	Druminshin Beg	85 0 26	Fermanagh	Lurg	Derryvullan	Lowtherstown	III.	204
30	Druminshin Glebe	667 3 1	Leitrim	Carrigallen	Carrigallen	Mohill	IV.	89
26	Druminshingore	408 3 30j	Leitrim	Carrigallen	Carrigallen	Bawnboy	IV.	89
16	Druminshin More	101 1 5	Fermanagh	Lurg	Derryvullan	Lowtherstown	III.	204
28, 29, 32	Drumintee	1,061 1 2	Armagh	Orior Upper	Killevy	Newry	III.	58
17,18,22,23	Drumintin	263 1 0	Monaghan	Dartree	Ematris	Cootehill	III.	267
30	Druminuff	113 1 20k	Leitrim	Carrigallen	Carrigallen	Bawnboy	IV.	89
13, 14	Druminure	213 3 10	Armagh	Orior Lower	Ballymore	Banbridge	III.	55
7, 10	Druminure	323 2 21	Tipperary, N.R.	Lower Ormond	Uskane	Borrisokane	II.	288
32	Drumirril	279 3 7	Monaghan	Farney	Inishkeen	Dundalk	III.	271
73	Drumirrin	565 0 25	Donegal	Banagh	Inishkeel	Glenties	III.	106
78	Drumkeaghta	96 0 32	Mayo	Carra	Ballyhean	Castlebar	IV.	195
116, 125	Drumkeary East	242 0 19	Galway	Leitrim	Ballynakill	Loughrea	IV.	51
116, 125	Drumkeary West	484 3 19	Galway	Leitrim	Ballynakill	Loughrea	IV.	51

(a) Including 4A. 3R. 21P. water.
(b) Including 4A. 0R. 20P. water.
(c) Including 11A. 1R. 30P. water.
(d) Including 20A. 1R. 32P. water.

(e) Including 7A. 2R. 0P. water.
(f) Including 32A. 3R. 0P. Lough Shark.
(g) Including 24A. 3R. 36P. water.
(h) Including 12A. 2R. 9P. water.

(i) Including 5A. 2R. 4P. water.
(j) Including 6A. 0R. 24P. water.
(k) Including 10A. 2R. 36P. water.

No. of Sheet of the Ordnance Survey Maps.	Townlands and Towns.	Area in Statute Acres. A. R. P.	County.	Barony.	Parish.	Poor Law Union in 1857.	Townland Census of 1851, Part I. Vol.	Page
55	Drumkee .	285 3 32	Tyrone .	Dungannon Middle .	Killyman .	Dungannon .	III.	303
93	Drumkeeghan .	334 3 17	Donegal .	Banagh .	Killymard .	Donegal .	III.	111
15	Drumkeel .	155 1 21	Leitrim .	Drumahaire .	Killarga .	Manorhamilton .	IV.	98
93	Drumkeelan .	611 0 23a	Donegal .	Banagh .	Inver .	Donegal .	III.	107
23	Drumkeelan .	200 2 38	Leitrim .	Leitrim .	Kiltubbrid .	Carᵏ. on Shannon	IV.	103
23, 27	Drumkeelan Beg .	120 3 1	Leitrim .	Leitrim .	Kiltoghert .	Carᵏ. on Shannon	IV.	101
23	Drumkeelan More .	123 2 0b	Leitrim .	Leitrim .	Kiltoghert .	Carᵏ. on Shannon	IV.	101
30, 34	Drumkeelwick .	157 0 18	Leitrim .	Carrigallen .	Carrigallen .	Mohill .	IV.	89
15	Drumkeen .	40 0 38	Cavan .	Lower Loughtee .	Drumlane .	Cavan .	III.	80
20	Drumkeen .	79 1 8	Cavan .	Upper Loughtee .	Annagelliff .	Cavan .	III.	81
61, 69	Drumkeen .	558 2 21	Donegal .	Raphoe .	Convoy .	Stranorlar .	III.	136
27	Drumkeen .	220 2 26	Fermanagh .	Clanawley .	Rossorry .	Enniskillen .	III.	194
6	Drumkeen .	134 1 6	Fermanagh .	Lurg .	Magheraculmoney .	Lowtherstown .	III.	208
16	Drumkeen .	144 2 33	Fermanagh .	Tirkennedy .	Magheracross .	Enniskillen .	III.	223
24	Drumkeen .	242 0 14	Leitrim .	Carrigallen .	Oughteragh .	Bawnboy .	IV.	92
101, 102	Drumkeen .	178 0 37	Mayo .	Clanmorris .	Kilcolman .	Claremorris .	IV.	134
19, 20	Drumkeenagh .	104 1 19	Fermanagh .	Clanawley .	Cleenish .	Enniskillen .	III.	190
23	Drumkeenragh .	162 2 31	Fermanagh .	Tirkennedy .	Enniskillen .	Enniskillen .	III.	222
29	Drumkeeragh .	724 0 35c	Down .	Kinelarty .	Dromara .	Downpatrick .	III.	176
43, 44	Drumkeeran .	556 3 39	Antrim .	Upper Toome .	Shilvodan Grange .	Antrim .	III.	35
15, 20	Drumkeeran .	86 3 17	Cavan .	Upper Loughtee .	Castleterra .	Cavan .	III.	82
5	Drumkeeran .	232 0 7	Fermanagh .	Lurg .	Drumkeeran .	Lowtherstown .	III.	206
17, 18	Drumkeeran .	43 0 32	Leitrim .	Drumahaire .	Inishmagrath .	Manorhamilton .	IV.	96
32	Drumkeeran .	113 1 18	Leitrim .	Leitrim .	Annaduff .	Mohill .	IV.	99
31	Drumkeeran .	149 2 9	Leitrim .	Leitrim .	Kiltoghert .	Carᵏ. on Shannon	IV.	101
24	Drumkeeran Beg .	106 0 9	Cavan .	Tullyhunco .	Killashandra .	Cavan .	III.	98
24	Drumkeeran Black .	139 0 4	Cavan .	Tullyhunco .	Killashandra .	Cavan .	III.	98
24	Drumkeeran More .	138 1 22	Cavan .	Tullyhunco .	Killashandra .	Cavan .	III.	98
18	DRUMKEERAN T.	—	Leitrim .	Drumahaire .	Inishmagrath .	Manorhamilton .	IV.	97
28	Drumkeery .	176 0 39d	Cavan .	Clankee .	Bailieborough .	Bailieborough .	III.	71
33	Drumkeilvy .	462 3 23	Leitrim .	Mohill .	Cloone .	Mohill .	IV.	106
39, 47	Drumkern .	295 1 28	Tyrone .	Dungannon Upper .	Ballyclog .	Cookstown .	III.	306
14	Drumkerril .	67 0 13	Cavan .	Lower Loughtee .	Drumlane .	Cavan .	III.	80
32	Drumkilla .	112 1 3	Leitrim .	Mohill .	Mohill .	Mohill .	IV.	107
28	Drumkilleen .	100 2 37	Leitrim .	Mohill .	Mohill .	Mohill .	IV.	108
39	Drumkillen .	108 0 11e	Fermanagh .	Knockninny .	Kinawley .	Lisnaskea .	III.	202
31	Drumkilly .	230 2 24	Cavan .	Clanmahon .	Crosserlough .	Cavan .	III.	76
24	Drumkilroosk .	288 0 8	Cavan .	Tullyhunco .	Killashandra .	Cavan .	III.	98
9	Drumkilsellagh .	239 2 12	Sligo .	Carbury .	Drumcliff .	Sligo .	IV.	221
28	Drumkirwan .	129 1 9f	Leitrim .	Leitrim .	Fenagh .	Mohill .	IV.	100
90	Drum or Knockatemple	208 0 9g	Mayo .	Carra .	Drum .	Castlebar .	IV.	128
17	Drumlack .	82 0 14	Armagh .	Fews Lower .	Mullaghbrack .	Armagh .	III.	47
26	Drumlackagh .	759 3 19h	Donegal .	Kilmacrenan .	Mevagh .	Millford .	III.	130
33	Drumlaggagh .	197 0 38i	Leitrim .	Mohill .	Cloone .	Mohill .	IV.	106
57	Drumlaghdrid .	1,076 2 17	Donegal .	Boylagh .	Templecrone .	Glenties .	III.	115
50	Drumlagher .	161 2 33	Tyrone .	Clogher .	Donacavey .	Omagh .	III.	294
94	Drumlaght .	91 0 10	Donegal .	Tirhugh .	Donegal .	Donegal .	III.	145
92	Drumlaghtafin .	271 3 32	Donegal .	Banagh .	Inver .	Donegal .	III.	107
26	Drumlaghy .	142 1 21	Fermanagh .	Clanawley .	Cleenish .	Enniskillen .	III.	190
32	Drumlaghy .	96 0 19	Fermanagh .	Clanawley .	Killesher .	Enniskillen .	III.	192
4, 7	Drumlahard .	236 0 5	Roscommon .	Boyle .	Tumna .	Carᵏ. on Shannon	IV.	168
24, 28	Drumlaheen .	402 3 23j	Leitrim .	Leitrim .	Fenagh .	Mohill .	IV.	100
37, 42	Drumlamph .	1,147 1 29	Londonderry .	Loughinsholin .	Maghera .	Magherafelt .	III.	242
25	Drumlandrick .	124 0 26	Monaghan .	Farney .	Donaghmoyne .	Castleblayney .	III.	270
14, 15	Drumlane .	212 2 18k	Cavan .	Lower Loughtee .	Drumlane .	Cavan .	III.	80
21	Drumlane .	306 0 39	Cavan .	Tullygarvey .	Larah .	Cootehill .	III.	91
33	Drumlane .	658 2 27	Londonderry .	Loughinsholin .	Tamlaght O'Crilly .	Ballymoney .	III.	243
24	Drumlane .	248 0 14	Monaghan .	Cremorne .	Ballybay .	Castleblayney .	III.	259
32	Drumlara .	177 3 36l	Leitrim .	Mohill .	Mohill .	Mohill .	IV.	108
6, 9	Drumlara .	63 1 34	Monaghan .	Monaghan .	Tedavnet .	Monaghan .	III.	278
14, 19	Drumlarah .	193 3 32	Cavan .	Tullyhunco .	Kildallan .	Bawnboy .	III.	97
43, 49	Drumlargan .	1,276 0 31	Meath .	Upper Deece .	Drumlargan .	Trim .	I.	193
20	Drumlark .	145 2 0	Cavan .	Upper Loughtee .	Annagelliff .	Cavan .	III.	81
24	Drumlarney .	138 2 19m	Cavan .	Tullyhunco .	Killashandra .	Cavan .	III.	98
100	Drumlask .	171 0 18	Donegal .	Tirhugh .	Drumhome .	Donegal .	III.	146
5	Drumlattery .	64 3 19	Dublin .	Balrothery East .	Lusk .	Balrothery .	I.	21
21, 26	Drumlaunaght .	89 0 5	Cavan .	Upper Loughtee .	Larah .	Cavan .	III.	85
20	Drumlaunaght .	38 2 22	Cavan .	Upper Loughtee .	Urney .	Cavan .	III.	86
116	Drumlave .	384 0 2	Cork, W.R. .	Bear .	Kilcaskan .	Castletown .	II.	123
9, 13	Drumlaydan .	123 1 4	Cavan .	Tullyhaw .	Templeport .	Bawnboy .	III.	94
5	Drumlayne .	190 0 23	Meath .	Lower Kells .	Moybolgue .	Kells .	I.	203
25, 29	Drumlea .	340 2 5n	Leitrim .	Carrigallen .	Drumreilly .	Bawnboy .	IV.	91
18, 19	Drumlea .	670 3 29o	Tyrone .	Strabane Upper .	Bodoncy Lower .	Gortin .	III.	323

No. of Sheet of the Ordnance Survey Maps.	Townlands and Towns.	Area in Statute Acres.	County.	Barony.	Parish.	Poor Law Union in 1857.	Townland Census of 1851, Part I.	
		A. R. P.					Vol.	Page
73, 74, 80	Drumleagh	1,344 1 24a	Tipperary, S.R.	Clanwilliam	Clonbeg	Tipperary	II.	305
17, 22	Drumleague	223 3 13	Cavan	Tullygarvey	Kildrumsherdan	Cootehill	III.	90
23, 27	Drumleague	295 1 15	Leitrim	Leitrim	Kiltoghert	Cark. on Shannon	IV.	102
28, 34	Drumleagues Big	170 0 11	Fermanagh	Magherastephana	Aghalurcher	Lisnaskea	III.	216
28	Drumleagues Little	41 3 22	Fermanagh	Magherastephana	Aghalurcher	Lisnaskea	III.	216
14, 15	Drumlease	221 3 33	Leitrim	Drumahaire	Drumlease	Manorhamilton	IV.	94
35	Drumleavalliagh	67 3 10	Donegal	Kilmacrenan	Clondahorky	Dunfanaghy	III.	123
15	Drumleck	17 3 32	Louth	Ardee	Gernonstown	Ardee	I.	172
15	Drumleck	313 3 25	Louth	Louth	Dromiskin	Dundalk	I.	183
33	Drumleckney	150 2 6	Antrim	Lower Antrim	Racavan	Ballymena	III.	4
22	Drumlee	654 0 38	Antrim	Kilconway	Finvoy	Ballymoney	III.	26
12	Drumlee	630 2 29	Donegal	Inishowen East	Culdaff	Inishowen	III.	118
42	Drumlee	541 2 19b	Down	Upper Iveagh, Lr. pt.	Drumgooland	Banbridge	III.	172
61, 62	Drumlee	218 0 1	Tyrone	Dungannon Middle	Clonfeacle	Dungannon	III.	299
20	Drumleek North	264 0 23c	Monaghan	Cremorne	Muckno	Castleblayney	III.	262
20	Drumleek South	334 1 28	Monaghan	Cremorne	Muckno	Castleblayney	III.	262
62,63,70,71	Drumleene	337 1 10	Donegal	Raphoe	Clonleigh	Strabane	III.	135
26, 30	Drumleevan	209 2 14	Leitrim	Carrigallen	Carrigallen	Bawnboy	IV.	89
24, 25	Drumlegagh	847 0 1d	Tyrone	Strabane Lower	Ardstraw	Strabane	III.	319
5	Drumlellum	231 0 38	Armagh	Oneilland West	Drumcree	Lurgan	III.	52
25	Drumleny	137 1 38	Cavan	Upper Loughtee	Kilmore	Cavan	III.	84
13	Drumleny	220 3 31	Monaghan	Dartree	Killeevan	Monaghan	III.	268
9	Drumlerry	783 0 28	Meath	Fore	Oldcastle	Oldcastle	I.	202
24	Drumlesh	243 2 39e	Clare	Inchiquin	Inagh	Ennistimon	II.	25
3	Drumlester	118 2 21	Monaghan	Trough	Errigal Trough	Clogher	III.	284
36, 44	Drumlester	719 1 13	Tyrone	Omagh East	Termonmaguirk	Omagh	III.	314
15, 16	Drumliff	456 1 25f	Cavan	Upper Loughtee	Castleterra	Cavan	III.	82
26, 32	Drumliff	122 3 10	Cavan	Upper Loughtee	Denn	Cavan	III.	83
28	Drumliff	136 1 0	Fermanagh	Magherastephana	Aghalurcher	Lisnaskea	III.	216
27, 28	Drumliffin Glebe	182 0 27	Leitrim	Leitrim	Kiltoghert	Cark. on Shannon	IV.	102
20	Drumlin	251 0 15	Down	Lower Iveagh, Up. pt.	Magheralin	Lurgan	III.	170
17	Drumlina	119 3 23	Monaghan	Dartree	Killeevan	Cootehill	III.	268
51	Drumline	879 0 10	Clare	Bunratty Lower	Drumline	Ennis	II.	3
13, 18	Drumlinny	230 2 35	Monaghan	Dartree	Aghabog	Monaghan	III.	263
13, 18	Drumlinny	80 3 26	Monaghan	Monaghan	Kilmore	Monaghan	III.	276
25, 31	Drumlion	169 1 19	Cavan	Clanmahon	Ballintemple	Cavan	III.	75
20, 25	Drumlion	88 3 32	Cavan	Upper Loughtee	Kilmore	Cavan	III.	84
11	Drumlion	241 3 23	Roscommon	Boyle	Killukin	Cark. on Shannon	IV.	195
8	Drumlisaleen	278 2 26	Fermanagh	Magheraboy	Inishmacsaint	Ballyshannon	III.	212
33	Drumlish	110 3 31	Fermanagh	Clanawley	Kinawley	Enniskillen	III.	194
15, 21	Drumlish	163 3 22	Fermanagh	Magheraboy	Devenish	Enniskillen	III.	210
5	Drumlish	557 3 24	Longford	Longford	Killoe	Longford	I.	159
6	Drumlish	80 1 37	Monaghan	Monaghan	Tedavnet	Monaghan	III.	278
17	Drumlish	347 0 12g	Roscommon	Roscommon	Clooncraff	Strokestown	IV.	208
42	Drumlish	375 3 8	Tyrone	Omagh East	Dromore	Omagh	III.	311
5	DRUMLISH T.	—	Longford	Longford	Killoe	Longford	I.	159
10	Drumlisnagrilly	70 0 1	Armagh	Oneilland East	Seagoe	Lurgan	III.	50
24	Drumlitten(Besborough)	48 2 30	Leitrim	Leitrim	Fenagh	Mohill	IV.	100
24	Drum tten (King)	57 3 12h	Leitrim	Leitrim	Fenagh	Mohill	IV.	100
17	Drumloaghan	102 1 12	Cavan	Tullygarvey	Kildrumsherdan	Cootehill	III.	90
24	Drumlohan	296 3 0	Waterford	Decies without Drum	Stradbally	Kilmacthomas	II.	360
23, 28	Drumlom	208 0 34i	Cavan	Clankee	Shercock	Bailieborough	III.	74
35	Drumlom	166 0 31	Leitrim	Mohill	Annaduff	Mohill	IV.	105
31	Drumloman	300 3 5	Cavan	Castlerahan	Crosserlough	Cavan	III.	68
28	Drumlon	205 3 23	Cavan	Clankee	Bailieborough	Bailieborough	III.	71
23	Drumlona	105 1 37	Monaghan	Dartree	Ematris	Cootehill	III.	267
94	Drumlonagher	136 1 21	Donegal	Tirhugh	Donegal	Donegal	III.	145
25	Drumlonan	131 3 16j	Leitrim	Carrigallen	Oughteragh	Bawnboy	IV.	92
39	Drumlone	184 1 34k	Fermanagh	Coole	Galloon	Lisnaskea	III.	199
23, 28	Drumlone	339 3 32	Fermanagh	Magherastephana	Aghavea	Lisnaskea	III.	218
68	Drumlong	68 3 27l	Mayo	Burrishoole	Burrishoole	Newport	IV.	119
1, 5	Drumlongfield	95 2 13	Fermanagh	Lurg	Templecarn	Lowtherstown	III.	209
19	Drumlongfield	214 3 23	Monaghan	Monaghan	Tullycorbet	Monaghan	III.	281
8	Drumloo	137 0 7	Monaghan	Monaghan	Clones	Monaghan	III.	274
23	Drumlood	225 2 31	Monaghan	Cremorne	Aghnamullen	Cootehill	III.	258
26, 30	Drumloona	133 2 21	Leitrim	Carrigallen	Carrigallen	Bawnboy	IV.	89
17	Drumloo North	25 0 33	Monaghan	Dartree	Killeevan	Clones	III.	268
18	Drumloose	233 3 15	Westmeath	Moyashel and Magheradernon	Mullingar	Mullingar	I.	275
17	Drumloo South	27 0 18	Monaghan	Dartree	Killeevan	Clones	III.	268
55	Drumlosh	1,493 0 1	Roscommon	Athlone	Drum	Athlone	IV.	199
19	Drumlough	318 2 38m	Donegal	Inishowen West	Fahan Lower	Inishowen	III.	126
21	Drumlough	1,092 1 36	Down	Lower Iveagh, Lr. pt.	Dromore	Lisburn	III.	168

(a) Including 9A. 2R. 34P. water.
(b) Including 1A. 1R. 5P. water.
(c) Including 25A. 0R. 5P. water.
(d) Including 2A. 0R. 31P. water.
(e) Including 13A. 3R. 24P. water.

(f) Including 3A. 0R. 1P. water.
(g) Including 34A. 2R. 19P. water.
(h) Including 7A. 3R. 12P. water.
(i) Including 5A. 1R. 38P. water.

(j) Including 19A. 0R. 3P. water.
(k) Including 10A. 0R. 0P. water.
(l) Including 6A. 0R. 5P. water.
(m) Including 8A. 3R. 8P. water.

No. of Sheet of the Ordnance Survey Maps.	Townlands and Towns.	Area in Statute Acres.	County.	Barony.	Parish.	Poor Law Union in 1857.	Townland Census of 1851, Part I.	
		A. R. P.					Vol.	Page
41, 47	Drumlough	695 3 5	Down	Upper Iveagh, Up. pt.	Drumgath	Newry	III.	175
27	Drumlougher	554 0 14a	Armagh	Fews Upper	Creggan	Castleblayney	III.	48
15	Drumlougher	51 0 8b	Cavan	Lower Loughtee	Drumlane	Cavan	III.	80
9, 13	Drumlougher	338 2 35c	Cavan	Tullyhaw	Templeport	Bawnboy	III.	94
54, 55	Drumlougher	308 0 0	Donegal	Raphoe	Allsaints	Londonderry	III.	134
19	Drumlougher	75 3 23	Longford	Ardagh	Ardagh	Longford	I.	151
18	Drumloughlin	142 0 3d	Monaghan	Dartree	Ematris	Cootehill	III.	267
78, 89	Drumloughra	42 3 30	Mayo	Carra	Ballyhean	Castlebar	IV.	125
79	Drumloughra	181 2 10	Mayo	Carra	Manulla	Castlebar	IV.	129
28	Drumlowan	138 2 34	Leitrim	Mohill	Mohill	Mohill	IV.	108
38	Drumlught	106 3 2	Fermanagh	Knockninny	Kinawley	Lisnaskea	III.	202
34	Drumlught	197 1 23	Fermanagh	Magherastephana	Aghalurcher	Lisnaskea	III.	216
23	Drumlumman	158 1 21e	Cavan	Clankee	Drumgoon	Cootehill	III.	72
27, 31	Drumlumman	135 2 38	Leitrim	Leitrim	Kiltoghert	Carᴷ. on Shannon	IV.	102
15	Drumlumman Glebe	68 2 17	Leitrim	Drumahaire	Killarga	Manorhamilton	IV.	98
87	Drumlummin	502 2 13	Tipperary, S.R.	Iffa and Offa West	Tubbrid	Clogheen	II.	321
28	Drumlurg	230 2 38	Monaghan	Farney	Donaghmoyne	Carrickmacross	III.	270
44	Drumlurgagh	156 3 29	Donegal	Kilmacrenan	Kilmacrenan	Millford	III.	129
28, 31	Drumlusty	181 0 25	Monaghan	Farney	Donaghmoyne	Carrickmacross	III.	270
22	Drumlyon	124 3 28f	Fermanagh	Magheraboy	Rossorry	Enniskillen	III.	214
135	Drummaanadeevan	32 1 27	Galway	Leitrim	Clonrush	Scarriff	IV.	53
135	Drummaan East	359 0 16	Galway	Leitrim	Clonrush	Scarriff	IV.	53
135	Drummaan South	199 0 22	Galway	Leitrim	Clonrush	Scarriff	IV.	53
135	Drummaan West	189 2 5	Galway	Leitrim	Clonrush	Scarriff	IV.	53
26, 32	Drummacabranagher	134 0 8	Fermanagh	Clanawley	Killesher	Enniskillen	III.	192
92	Drummacachapple	111 3 26	Donegal	Banagh	Inver	Donegal	III.	107
92	Drummacacullen	306 2 6	Donegal	Banagh	Inver	Donegal	III.	107
5, 6	Drummacahan	80 2 37	Fermanagh	Lurg	Drumkeeran	Lowtherstown	III.	206
27	Drummacaladdery	271 1 21	Donegal	Kilmacrenan	Kilmacrenan	Millford	III.	129
5, 6	Drummacalara	144 3 16	Fermanagh	Lurg	Magheraculmoney	Lowtherstown	III.	208
52	Drummacanoo	189 1 27	Donegal	Kilmacrenan	Conwal	Letterkenny	III.	126
31	Drummacavoy	171 0 11	Monaghan	Farney	Donaghmoyne	Carrickmacross	III.	270
28, 34	Drummack	213 2 11	Fermanagh	Magherastephana	Aghalurcher	Lisnaskea	III.	216
17	Drummackan	362 0 19	Fermanagh	Tirkennedy	Enniskillen	Enniskillen	III.	222
16	Drummackilowney	248 2 36	Fermanagh	Lurg	Trory	Lowtherstown	III.	209
9	Drummaconor	132 2 7	Monaghan	Monaghan	Kilmore	Monaghan	III.	276
27, 34	Drummacool	138 3 36	Sligo	Tirerrill	Kilmacallan	Sligo	IV.	240
21	Drummacoorin	126 0 10	Fermanagh	Clanawley	Boho	Enniskillen	III.	189
19	Drummad	548 0 38	Roscommon	Frenchpark	Tibohine	Castlereagh	IV.	205
31	Drummagh	80 0 1	Leitrim	Leitrim	Kiltoghert	Carᴷ. on Shannon	IV.	102
27, 35	Drummaghmartin	156 2 26	Clare	Tulla Upper	Tulla	Tulla	II.	41
6, 7	Drummahan	244 1 18	Leitrim	Roselogher	Killasnet	Manorhamilton	IV.	109
23, 32, 33	Drummahon	510 0 5	Tyrone	Omagh West	Termonamongan	Castlederg	III.	317
10	Drummal	202 2 34	Fermanagh	Lurg	Derryvullan	Lowtherstown	III.	204
32, 33	Drummallaght	737 3 34g	Cavan	Castlerahan	Killinkere	Bailieborough	III.	69
50	Drummallard	212 2 16h	Tyrone	Omagh East	Dromore	Omagh	III.	311
13	Drumman	214 0 7	Armagh	Fews Lower	Mullaghbrack	Armagh	III.	47
17	Drumman	111 1 12	Cavan	Tullygarvey	Drumgoon	Cootehill	III.	88
45	Drumman	107 2 12	Donegal	Kilmacrenan	Tullyfern	Millford	III.	133
25	Drumman	288 2 31	Fermanagh	Clanawley	Cleenish	Enniskillen	III.	190
15	Drumman	71 2 29	Longford	Ardagh	Street	Granard	I.	153
26	Drumman	289 0 34	Meath	Lower Duleek	Duleek	Drogheda	I.	195
22, 23	Drumman	117 0 34i	Roscommon	Roscommon	Elphin	Strokestown	IV.	209
2, 3, 5, 6	Drumman	330 1 13j	Tyrone	Strabane Lower	Donaghedy	Strabane	III.	320
33, 34	Drumman	2,606 3 0	Westmeath	Fartullagh	Castlelost	Mullingar	I.	268
53	Drumman	6 1 31	Westmeath	Fartullagh	Pass of Kilbride	Mullingar	I.	269
7	Drumman	87 2 25	Westmeath	Fore	Rathgarve	Castletowndelvin	I.	271
17, 18	Drummanacappul	61 0 0	Leitrim	Drumahaire	Inishmagrath	Manorhamilton	IV.	96
18, 20	Drummanasooan	85 1 18	Leitrim	Drumahaire	Inishmagrath	Manorhamilton	IV.	96
32	Drummanbane	247 1 4	Cavan	Upper Loughtee	Lavey	Cavan	III.	85
33, 34	Drummanbane	168 2 3	Leitrim	Carrigallen	Cloone	Mohill	IV.	90
12	Drumman Beg	138 3 16	Armagh	Oneilland West	Grange	Armagh	III.	52
18	Drumman Beg	204 2 37k	Roscommon	Ballintober North	Kilglass	Strokestown	IV.	186
32, 33	Drummandutf	406 3 25	Cavan	Upper Loughtee	Lavey	Cavan	III.	86
15	Drummaneny	212 1 21	Londonderry	Tirkeeran	Faughanvale	Londonderry	III.	250
18	Drummanfaughnan	159 2 36	Leitrim	Drumahaire	Inishmagrath	Manorhamilton	IV.	96
18	Drummangarvagh	48 0 21	Leitrim	Drumahaire	Inishmagrath	Manorhamilton	IV.	96
55	Drummanlane	86 0 1	Down	Mourne	Kilkeel	Kilkeel	III.	183
12	Drumman More	403 2 30	Armagh	Oneilland West	Grange	Armagh	III.	52
55, 57	Drummanmore	324 3 5	Down	Mourne	Kilkeel	Kilkeel	III.	183
18, 24	Drumman More	548 2 20	Roscommon	Ballintober North	Kilglass	Strokestown	IV.	186
38	Drummannagapple	65 2 9	Fermanagh	Knockninny	Kinawley	Lisnaskea	III.	202
68	Drummannaglieve	94 1 24l	Mayo	Burrishoole	Burrishoole	Newport	IV.	119

No. of Sheet of the Ordnance Survey Maps.	Townlands and Towns.	Area in Statute Acres.			County.	Barony.	Parish.	Poor Law Union in 1857.	Townland Census of 1851, Part I.	
		A.	R.	P.					Vol.	Page
18, 26	Drummanneen . .	253	1	27a	Clare . .	Bunratty Upper .	Inchicronan . .	Ennis . .	II.	9
5, 9	Drummannon . .	326	0	34	Armagh . .	Oneilland West .	Tartaraghan . .	Armagh . .	III.	54
28	Drummanreagh .	139	3	29	Monaghan .	Farney . . .	Donaghmoyne . .	Carrickmacross	III.	270
8	Drummans . .	331	3	10	Antrim . .	Cary . . .	Ramoan . . .	Ballycastle .	III.	14
1	Drummans . .	94	1	27	Dublin . .	Balrothery East .	Balscaddan . .	Balrothery .	I.	20
7	Drummans . .	197	2	13	Leitrim . .	Rosclogher . .	Killasnet . .	Manorhamilton	IV.	109
3	Drummans . .	210	1	26	Leitrim . .	Rosclogher . .	Rossinver . .	Ballyshannon .	IV.	111
8	Drummans . .	264	2	16	Monaghan .	Monaghan . .	Clones . . .	Monaghan .	III.	274
35	Drummans Glebe .	118	0	15	Fermanagh .	Clankelly . .	Clones . . .	Clones . .	III.	196
18	*Drummans Island* .	1	1	23	Leitrim . .	Drumahaire . .	Inishmagrath . .	Manorhamilton	IV.	97
6	*Drummans Island* .	37	2	24	Roscommon .	Boyle . . .	Kilbryan . .	Boyle . .	IV.	195
18	Drummans Lower .	185	1	17	Leitrim . .	Drumahaire . .	Inishmagrath . .	Manorhamilton	IV.	96
1	Drummans Lower .	183	3	25	Londonderry .	Keenaght . .	Magilligan . .	NewTⁿLimavady	III.	236
1	Drummans Middle .	163	1	28	Londonderry .	Keenaght . .	Magilligan . .	NewTⁿLimavady	III.	236
18	Drummans Upper .	124	3	28	Leitrim . .	Drumahaire . .	Inishmagrath . .	Manorhamilton	IV.	96
1, 2	Drummans Upper .	201	0	30	Londonderry .	Keenaght . .	Magilligan . .	NewTⁿLimavady	III.	236
99	Drummanus Glebe .	94	3	3	Donegal . .	Tirhugh . . .	Drumhome . .	Donegal . .	III.	146
11	Drummany . .	107	2	32	Cavan . .	Tullygarvey . .	Annagh . .	Cavan . .	III.	87
19	Drummany . .	177	0	38	Cavan . .	Tullyhunco . .	Kildallan . .	Bawnboy . .	III.	97
19	Drummany . .	194	2	25	Cavan . .	Tullyhunco . .	Killashandra .	Cavan . .	III.	98
15, 20	Drummany . .	105	0	18b	Cavan . .	Upper Loughtee .	Castleterra . .	Cavan . .	III.	82
20	Drummany Beg .	43	1	6	Cavan . .	Lower Loughtee .	Drumlane . .	Cavan . .	III.	80
14	Drummany Glebe .	125	1	19c	Cavan . .	Lower Loughtee .	Drumlane . .	Cavan . .	III.	80
10	Drummany Montiaghs	116	1	29d	Cavan . .	Lower Loughtee .	Drumlane . .	Cavan . .	III.	80
15	Drummany (*Pleydell*)	184	1	3e	Cavan . .	Lower Loughtee .	Drumlane . .	Cavan . .	III.	80
20	Drummany Rahan .	135	0	23f	Cavan . .	Lower Loughtee .	Drumlane . .	Cavan . .	III.	80
22	Drummartin . .	148	1	6	Cavan . .	Tullygarvey . .	Kildrumsherdan .	Cootehill .	III.	90
22	Drummartin . .	188	1	0	Dublin . .	Rathdown . .	Taney . . .	Rathdown .	I.	38
31, 37	Drummartin . .	569	1	24	Sligo . .	Leyny . . .	Kilmacteige . .	Tobercurry .	IV.	231
43	Drummaul . .	339	2	4	Antrim . .	Upper Toome .	Drummaul . .	Ballymena .	III.	34
31	Drummaunroe . .	77	3	35	Leitrim . .	Leitrim . . .	Kiltoghert . .	Carᵏ. on Shannon	IV.	102
68, 81	Drummaveg . .	272	1	39	Galway . .	Moycullen . .	Moycullen . .	Galway . .	IV.	71
40	Drummaw . .	101	3	8	Fermanagh .	Clankelly . .	Galloon . .	Clones . .	III.	198
54, 55	Drummay . .	262	0	20	Donegal . .	Raphoe . . .	Allsaints . .	Londonderry .	III.	134
21, 22	Drummee . .	156	0	32	Fermanagh .	Magheraboy . .	Rossorry . .	Enniskillen .	III.	214
27	Drummee . .	177	1	29g	Fermanagh .	Tirkennedy . .	Derryvullan . .	Enniskillen .	III.	221
9, 10, 14, 15	Drummeel . .	737	3	15h	Longford .	Granard . . .	Clonbroney . .	Granard . .	I.	155
54	Drummeen . .	110	0	6	Clare . .	Tulla Lower .	Kiltenanlea . .	Limerick . .	II.	37
33	Drummeen . .	219	3	21	Leitrim . .	Mohill . . .	Cloone . . .	Mohill . .	IV.	106
48	Drummeen . .	84	0	38	Londonderry .	Loughinsholin .	Lissan . . .	Magherafelt .	III.	242
46, 48	Drummeen . .	160	3	39i	Londonderry .	Loughinsholin .	Lissan . . .	Magherafelt .	III.	242
15	Drummeenagh . .	56	1	35	Louth . .	Ardee . . .	Gernonstown . .	Ardee . .	I.	172
92	Drummeenanagh .	168	0	14	Donegal . .	Banagh . . .	Inver . . .	Donegal . .	III.	107
94	Drummeenanagh .	265	3	28	Donegal . .	Banagh . . .	Killymard . .	Donegal . .	III.	111
41	Drummeen East .	104	3	8	Clare . .	Islands . . .	Killone . .	Ennis . .	II.	30
90	Drummeennavaddoge	50	1	3	Mayo . .	Carra . . .	Drum . . .	Castlebar .	IV.	128
41	Drummeen West .	106	2	31	Clare . .	Islands . . .	Killone . .	Ennis . .	II.	30
25	Drummeer . .	191	2	12	Clare . .	Inchiquin . .	Dysert . .	Ennis . .	II.	24
28	Drummeer . .	185	0	5	Fermanagh .	Magherastephana .	Aghalurcher . .	Lisnaskea .	III.	216
19	Drummeland . .	269	1	2	Armagh . .	Tiranny . . .	Derrynoose . .	Armagh . .	III.	59
5	Drummenagh . .	160	2	16	Armagh . .	Oneilland West .	Drumcree . .	Lurgan . .	III.	52
33	Drummenagh . .	238	3	38	Tyrone . .	Omagh West .	Longfield West .	Castlederg .	III.	316
9, 10	Drummenagh Beg .	164	0	32	Fermanagh .	Magheraboy . .	Inishmacsaint .	Ballyshannon .	III.	212
9, 10	Drummenagh More	140	1	32	Fermanagh .	Magheraboy . .	Inishmacsaint .	Ballyshannon .	III.	212
94, 100	Drummenny Lower	162	3	12	Donegal . .	Tirhugh . . .	Donegal . .	Donegal . .	III.	145
94	Drummenny Middle	152	1	37	Donegal . .	Tirhugh . . .	Donegal . .	Donegal . .	III.	145
94	Drummenny Upper	196	0	12	Donegal . .	Tirhugh . . .	Donegal . .	Donegal . .	III.	145
27	Drummeva . .	225	3	12	Cavan . .	Clankee . . .	Knockbride . .	Bailieborough .	III.	73
132, 141	Drummig . .	473	3	3	Cork, W.R. .	West Carbery (E.D.)	Abbeystrowry .	Skibbereen .	II.	136
38	Drummillard . .	176	0	25	Tyrone . .	Dungannon Upper .	Desertcreat . .	Cookstown .	III.	307
26, 33	Drummiller . .	325	3	38	Down . .	Lower Iveagh, Lr. pt.	Aghaderg . .	Banbridge .	III.	167
21, 28	Drummiller . .	637	2	8	Down . .	Lower Iveagh, Lr.pt.	Dromore . .	Banbridge .	III.	168
26	Drummiller . .	179	0	34	Down . .	Lower Iveagh, Up.pt.	Tullylish . .	Banbridge .	III.	171
40, 46	Drummiller . .	389	3	31	Down . .	Upper Iveagh, Up. pt.	Donaghmore . .	Newry . .	III.	175
17, 21	Drummilt . .	236	1	30	Armagh . .	Orior Lower . .	Loughgilly . .	Newry . .	III.	56
26	Drummin . .	797	3	0	Carlow . .	St. Mullins Lower .	St. Mullins . .	New Ross .	I.	13
53	Drummin . .	196	3	9	Clare . .	Bunratty Lower .	St. Patricks . .	Limerick . .	II.	6
22, 23, 30	Drummin . .	330	1	21	Clare . .	Ibrickan . . .	Kilfarboy . .	Ennistimon .	II.	22
39	Drummin . .	1,016	1	32	Clare . .	Ibrickan . . .	Kilmurry . .	Kilrush . .	II.	23
36, 44	Drummin . .	297	1	0	Clare . .	Tulla Lower .	Killuran . .	Limerick . .	II.	36
80, 44	Drummin . .	114	0	16	Clare . .	Tulla Lower .	Kilselly . .	Limerick . .	II.	36
13	Drummin . .	571	2	21	Clare . .	Tulla Upper .	Feakle . . .	Scarriff . .	II.	39
123, 129	Drummin . .	816	1	14	Galway . .	Kiltartan . .	Kilbeacanty .	Gort . .	IV.	47

(a) Including 3A. 1R. 9P. water.
(b) Including 12A. 2R. 19P. water.
(c) Including 22A. 0R. 33P. water.

(d) Including 5A. 1R. 16P. water.
(e) Including 38A. 3R. 9P. water.
(f) Including 24A. 0R. 36P. water.

(g) Including 29A. 0R. 32P. water.
(h) Including 7A. 2R. 4P. water.
(i) Property of the Drapers' Company.

No. of Sheet of the Ordnance Survey Maps.	Townlands and Towns.	Area in Statute Acres.			County.	Barony.	Parish.	Poor Law Union in 1857.	Townland Census of 1851, Part I.	
		A.	R.	P.					Vol.	Page
132	Drummin	210	0	11	Galway	Leitrim	Ballynakill	Portumna	IV.	51
115, 124	Drummin	108	3	36	Galway	Loughrea	Killeenadeema	Loughrea	IV.	64
115	Drummin	381	1	35	Galway	Loughrea	Kilteskill	Loughrea	IV.	65
36	Drummin	40	0	22	King's Co.	Ballybritt	Letterluna	Parsonstown	I.	126
48, 60	Drummin	245	1	37	Mayo	Tirawley	Ballynahaglish	Ballina	IV.	164
15, 21	Drummin	265	2	34	Roscommon	Castlereagh	Kilcorkey	Castlereagh	IV.	199
20	Drummin	180	1	21	Tipperary, N.R.	Lower Ormond	Nenagh	Nenagh	II.	287
11, 17, 18	Drummin	3,889	1	2	Wicklow	Ballinacor North	Derrylossary	Rathdrum	I.	346
39	Drummin	303	1	33	Wicklow	Ballinacor South	Preban	Shillelagh	I.	350
46, 47	Drummin	351	2	35	Wicklow	Shillelagh	Moyacomb	Shillelagh	I.	358
25	Drummina	189	0	15	Clare	Inchiquin	Dysert	Ennis	II.	24
77	Drumminabo	287	0	16	Mayo	Burrishoole	Kilmeena	Westport	IV.	122
18	Drumminacknew	260	1	17	Clare	Bunratty Upper	Inchicronan	Ennis	II.	9
122	Drumminacloghaun	218	0	5	Galway	Kiltartan	Kilmacduagh	Gort	IV.	48
123	Drumminacoosaun	156	2	33	Galway	Loughrea	Kilthomas	Gort	IV.	65
51	Drumminacroahy	113	1	7	Tipperary, S.R.	Kilnamanagh Lower	Kilpatrick	Cashel	II.	324
51	Drumminacunna	168	1	22	Tipperary, S.R.	Kilnamanagh Lower	Aghacrew	Tipperary	II.	322
40	Drumminagower	14	3	39	Tipperary, N.R.	Kilnamanagh Upper	Moyaliff	Thurles	II.	279
69	Drumminaguncan	472	3	10a	Mayo	Carra	Islandeady	Castlebar	IV.	128
77, 78	Drumminahaha	231	3	31b	Mayo	Burrishoole	Islandeady	Westport	IV.	121
43	Drumminakela	154	0	20	Clare	Tulla Lower	Kilseily	Limerick	I.	36
123	Drumminalough	216	3	16c	Galway	Kiltartan	Kilbeacanty	Gort	IV.	47
14, 15	Drumminascart	221	1	26d	Tipperary, N.R.	Lower Ormond	Knigh	Nenagh	II.	285
87	Drumminaweelaun	36	3	34	Mayo	Murrisk	Oughaval	Westport	IV.	161
77, 88	Drummindoo	323	1	1	Mayo	Murrisk	Aghagower	Westport	IV.	159
30	Drummindoo	63	1	1	Mayo	Tirawley	Ardagh	Ballina	IV.	163
111	Drummin East	84	2	9	Mayo	Clanmorris	Crossboyne	Claremorris	IV.	132
97, 107	Drummin East	242	0	32	Mayo	Murrisk	Oughaval	Westport	IV.	161
13	Drummin East	261	3	1	Wicklow	Newcastle	Kilcoole	Rathdrum	I.	351
26	Drumminick	163	1	29	Cavan	Tullygarvey	Larah	Cavan	III.	91
30	Drummin and Lisdalleen	596	2	36	Tipperary, N.R.	Ikerrin	Templetouhy	Thurles	II.	277
40	Drumminnagleagh	106	2	31	Tipperary, N.R.	Kilnamanagh Upper	Ballycahill	Thurles	II.	277
15	Drumminnagran	102	2	37	Clare	Corcomroe	Kilshanny	Ennistimon	II.	21
40	Drumminnakill	50	0	19	Galway	Moycullen	Kilcummin	Oughterard	IV.	67
125	Drumminnamuckla North	299	0	23	Galway	Leitrim	Ballynakill	Loughrea	IV.	51
125, 126	Drumminnamuckla South	524	3	2	Galway	Leitrim	Ballynakill	Loughrea	IV.	51
28	Drumminnanav	202	1	21e	Clare	Tulla Upper	Feakle	Scarriff	II.	39
14	Drumminnion	123	3	22	Cavan	Tullyhunco	Kildallan	Bawnboy	III.	97
111	Drummin North	55	0	38	Mayo	Clanmorris	Crossboyne	Claremorris	IV.	132
40	Drumminphilip	72	1	9	Tipperary, N.R.	Kilnamanagh Upper	Moyaliff	Thurles	II.	279
78, 79	Drumminracahill	146	0	18	Mayo	Carra	Ballyhean	Castlebar	IV.	125
78	Drumminracahill	1	1	2	Mayo	Carra	Breaghwy	Castlebar	IV.	127
89, 99	Drumminroe East	145	3	9	Mayo	Carra	Ballintober	Castlebar	IV.	124
99	Drumminroe West	1,104	3	14f	Mayo	Carra	Ballintober	Castlebar	IV.	124
111	Drummin South	48	3	0	Mayo	Clanmorris	Crossboyne	Claremorris	IV.	132
111	Drummin West	86	0	14	Mayo	Clanmorris	Crossboyne	Claremorris	IV.	132
97, 107	Drummin West	583	1	0	Mayo	Murrisk	Oughaval	Westport	IV.	161
13	Drummin West	51	3	5	Wicklow	Newcastle	Kilcoole	Rathdrum	I.	351
77	Drumminwonagh	319	1	11	Mayo	Burrishoole	Islandeady	Westport	IV.	121
26, 32	Drummoan or Newtate	210	2	23	Fermanagh	Clanawley	Killesher	Enniskillen	III.	192
28, 36	Drummod	1,013	3	9	Clare	Tulla Upper	Kilnoe	Scarriff	II.	40
17, 23	Drummod	239	3	21g	Roscommon	Roscommon	Clooncraff	Strokestown	IV.	208
15, 21	Drummoghan	45	0	38	Fermanagh	Magheraboy	Devenish	Enniskillen	III.	210
16	Drummoher	465	2	15	Clare	Inchiquin	Killinaboy	Corrofin	II.	26
21	Drummole	197	2	24	Cavan	Tullygarvey	Larah	Cootehill	III.	91
52	Drummonaclara	145	3	29	Tipperary, S.R.	Kilnamanagh Lower	Clonoulty	Cashel	II.	323
10	Drummonaghan	95	0	38	Fermanagh	Lurg	Derryvullan	Lowthertown	III.	204
45	Drummonaghan or Bridge End	229	0	19	Donegal	Kilmacrenan	Tullyfern	Millford	III.	132
15, 19	Drummond	298	0	29	Armagh	Armagh	Tynan	Armagh	III.	46
21, 22	Drummond	211	3	22	Armagh	Orior Lower	Loughgilly	Newry	III.	56
8, 12	Drummond	733	3	37	Kildare	Carbury	Kilpatrick	Edenderry	I.	52
10	Drummond	358	0	20	Londonderry	Keenaght	Drumachose	New^{Tn}Limavady	III.	235
9	Drummond	117	2	23	Londonderry	Keenaght	Tamlaght Finlagan	New^{Tn}Limavady	III.	237
41	Drummond	283	1	30h	Meath	Upper Moyfenrath	Killyon	Trim	I.	213
29	Drummond	198	0	37	Monaghan	Farney	Inishkeen	Dundalk	III.	271
30,31,33,34	Drummond	344	3	22	Monaghan	Farney	Magheracloone	Carrickmacross	III.	272
3	Drummond	922	0	38	Queen's Co.	Tinnahinch	Rearymore	Mountmellick	I.	249
9	Drummond	140	2	10	Tipperary, N.R.	Lower Ormond	Cloghprior	Borrisokane	II.	283
50	Drummond	234	0	20	Tyrone	Clogher	Donacavey	Omagh	III.	294

(a) Including 6A. 0R. 7P. water.
(b) Including 29A. 0R. 33P. water.
(c) Including 3A. 1R. 25P. water.

(d) Including 2A. 0R. 12P. water.
(e) Including 4A. 3R. 32P. water.
(f) Including 51A. 2R. 21P. water.

(g) Including 17A. 2R. 7P. water.
(h) Including 4A. 3R. 0P. water.

No. of Sheet of the Ordnance Survey Maps.	Townlands and Towns.	Area in Statute Acres. A. R. P.	County.	Barony.	Parish.	Poor Law Union in 1857.	Townland Census of 1851, Part I. Vol.	Page
60, 66	Drummond	266 3 25	Tyrone	Dungannon Lower	Aghaloo	Clogher	III.	296
54, 61	Drummond	566 1 18	Tyrone	Dungannon Middle	Clonfeacle	Dungannon	III.	299
38, 46	Drummond	321 2 11	Tyrone	Dungannon Middle	Pomeroy	Dungannon	III.	304
39	Drummond	15 0 29	Tyrone	Dungannon Upper	Derryloran	Cookstown	III.	307
5, 6	Drummond	298 1 15	Wexford	Scarawalsh	Carnew	Gorey	I.	322
31	Drummond Etra	66 3 8	Monaghan	Farney	Magheross	Carrickmacross	III.	273
17	*Drummond Island*	11 0 5	Down	Ards Upper	Ardkeen	Downpatrick	III.	159
31	Drummond Otra	298 2 21a	Monaghan	Farney	Magheross	Carrickmacross	III.	273
39	Drummoney	264 1 11	Cavan	Castlerahan	Lurgan	Oldcastle	III.	69
1, 5	Drummoney	255 0 37	Fermanagh	Lurg	Drumkeeran	Lowtherstown	III.	206
20	Drummonum	296 2 16b	Cavan	Upper Loughtee	Urney	Cavan	III.	86
25	Drummora Great	279 0 21c	Cavan	Upper Loughtee	Kilmore	Cavan	III.	84
25	Drummora Little	127 3 14d	Cavan	Upper Loughtee	Kilmore	Cavan	III.	84
11	Drummoy	106 1 14	Cavan	Tullygarvey	Annagh	Cavan	III.	87
10	Drummoyagh	112 2 23	Fermanagh	Lurg	Magheraculmoney	Lowtherstown	III.	208
33	Drummuek	295 0 33	Antrim	Lower Antrim	Racavan	Ballymena	III.	4
30, 31	Drummuck	138 1 23	Armagh	Fews Upper	Creggan	Castleblayney	III.	48
26	Drummuck	235 3 7	Cavan	Upper Loughtee	Larah	Cavan	III.	85
32	Drummuck	143 1 3	Fermanagh	Clanawley	Killesher	Enniskillen	III.	192
33, 37	Drummuck	827 2 4	Londonderry	Loughinsholin	Maghera	Magherafelt	III.	242
18	Drummuck	168 3 24	Monaghan	Cremorne	Ballybay	Castleblayney	III.	259
10	Drummuck	84 1 23	Monaghan	Cremorne	Tehallan	Monaghan	III.	262
13	Drummuck	149 3 31	Monaghan	Monaghan	Kilmore	Monaghan	III.	276
54, 55	Drummuck	83 1 23	Tyrone	Dungannon Middle	Killyman	Dungannon	III.	303
30, 31	Drummuckavall	286 3 1	Armagh	Fews Upper	Creggan	Castleblayney	III.	48
26, 30	Drummucker	149 3 35	Leitrim	Carrigallen	Carrigallen	Bawnboy	IV.	89
62	Drummucklagh	179 3 4	Donegal	Raphoe	Taughboyne	Strabane	III.	143
18	Drummulla	172 2 15	Monaghan	Dartree	Ematris	Cootehill	III.	267
14	Drummullagh	124 3 33	Cavan	Lower Loughtee	Drumlane	Cavan	III.	80
2, 5	Drummullagh	453 0 29	Louth	Lower Dundalk	Carlingford	Dundalk	I.	176
20	Drummullan	103 3 32	Cavan	Upper Loughtee	Kilmore	Cavan	III.	84
48	Drummullan	551 1 16	Londonderry	Loughinsholin	Arboe	Magherafelt	III.	238
12	Drummullan	121 0 30	Monaghan	Dartree	Aghabog	Clones	III.	263
20	Drummullig	119 0 7e	Cavan	Upper Loughtee	Urney	Cavan	III.	86
17	Drummullin	94 1 4	Roscommon	Roscommon	Clooncraff	Strokestown	IV.	208
43	Drummully	101 0 18	Fermanagh	Coole	Drummully	Clones	III.	199
38, 39	Drummully	142 1 6f	Fermanagh	Knockninny	Kinawley	Lisnaskea	III.	202
12	Drummully	90 3 26g	Monaghan	Dartree	Clones	Clones	III.	264
6	Drummully	144 3 39	Monaghan	Trough	Donagh	Monaghan	III.	282
19	Drummully East	215 3 31h	Cavan	Tullyhunco	Kildallan	Cavan	III.	97
15, 20	Drummully or Oakwood	182 3 2	Cavan	Upper Loughtee	Castleterra	Cavan	III.	83
19	Drummully West	113 0 2	Cavan	Tullyhunco	Kildallan	Cavan	III.	97
39	Drummurl Glebe	110 1 6i	Fermanagh	Coole	Galloon	Lisnaskea	III.	199
79	Drummurphy	383 3 35j	Donegal	Raphoe	Donaghmore	Strabane	III.	137
47	Drummurrer	288 0 28	Tyrone	Dungannon Middle	Clonoe	Dungannon	III.	300
20, 25	Drummurry	158 1 30	Cavan	Upper Loughtee	Kilmore	Cavan	III.	84
16	Drummurry	172 2 35	Fermanagh	Tirkennedy	Magheracross	Enniskillen	III.	223
17	Drummury	221 2 17	Cavan	Tullygarvey	Kildrumsherdan	Cootehill	III.	90
15	Drummury	160 3 14	Leitrim	Drumahaire	Killanummery	Manorhamilton	IV.	98
40	Drummusky	69 1 22	Fermanagh	Clankelly	Galloon	Clones	III.	198
29	Drumna	243 1 6	Leitrim	Mohill	Cloone	Mohill	IV.	106
3	Drumnabehy	267 2 11	Queen's Co.	Tinnahinch	Rearymore	Mountmellick	I.	249
16	Drumnabey	413 1 14k	Tyrone	Omagh West	Ardstraw	Castlederg	III.	315
5, 10	Drumnaboy	327 1 26l	Tyrone	Strabane Lower	Camus	Strabane	III.	320
70	Drumnabratty	86 3 12	Donegal	Raphoe	Raphoe	Strabane	III.	141
13, 20	Drumnabreeze	321 3 30	Down	Lower Iveagh, Up. pt.	Magheralin	Lurgan	II.	170
33	Drumnacanon	747 0 19	Londonderry	Loughinsholin	Tamlaght O'Crilly	Ballymoney	III.	243
10	Drumnacanvy	111 2 37	Armagh	Oneilland East	Seagoe	Lurgan	III.	50
4	Drumnacarra	201 3 8	Louth	Lower Dundalk	Ballymascanlan	Dundalk	I.	175
92	Drumnacarry	120 2 16	Donegal	Banagh	Inver	Donegal	III.	107
94	Drumnacarry	203 3 30	Donegal	Banagh	Killymard	Donegal	III.	111
35	Drumnacarry	286 3 16	Donegal	Kilmacrenan	Clondahorky	Dunfanaghy	III.	123
41	Drumnacart	29 3 10	Donegal	Boylagh	Templecrone	Glenties	III.	115
78	Drumnacarta	53 0 26m	Mayo	Carra	Aglish	Castlebar	IV.	123
41	Drumnacart Mountain Pasture	856 3 8n	Donegal	Boylagh	Templecrone	Glenties	III.	115
25	Drumnacole	99 0 6	Antrim	Lower Glenarm	Tickmacrevan	Larne	III.	23
23, 30	Drumnaconagher	904 0 15o	Down	Kinelarty	Kilmore	Downpatrick	III.	177
9	Drumnacooha	243 1 19	Longford	Longford	Killoe	Longford	I.	159
26	Drumnacor	237 3 39p	Longford	Rathcline	Shrule	Ballymahon	I.	165
51, 52	Drumnacoit	109 1 37	Leitrim	Leitrim	Annaduff	Cark. on Shannon	IV.	99
9	Drumnacraig	199 3 6	Donegal	Kilmacrenan	Clondavaddog	Millford	III.	124

No. of Sheet of the Ordnance Survey Maps.	Townlands and Towns.	Area in Statute Acres.	County.	Barony.	Parish.	Poor Law Union in 1857.	Townland Census of 1851, Part I.	
		A. R. P.					Vol.	Page
99, 103	Drumnacroil .	154 2 13	Donegal . .	Tirhugh . . .	Drumhome . .	Donegal . .	III.	146
25	Drumnacross .	77 3 20	Antrim . .	Lower Glenarm	Ardclinis . .	Larne . .	II.	21
74	Drumnacross .	318 1 33	Donegal . .	Boylagh . .	Killybegs Lower	Glenties . .	III.	114
69	Drumnacross .	133 0 27	Donegal . .	Raphoe . .	Convoy . .	Stranorlar .	III.	136
5	Drumnacross .	138 3 5	Fermanagh .	Lurg . . .	Magheraculmoney .	Lowtherstown .	III.	208
7	Drumnacross .	105 0 25	Leitrim . .	Rosclogher . .	Killasnet . .	Manorhamilton	IV.	109
9, 14	Drumnacross .	467 2 16	Longford . .	Granard . .	Clonbroney .	Granard . .	I.	155
29, 38	Drumnacross Lower	190 2 31	Tyrone . .	Dungannon Upper .	Kildress . .	Cookstown .	III.	308
29, 38	Drumnacross Upper	69 2 32	Tyrone . .	Dungannon Upper .	Kildress . .	Cookstown .	III.	308
20	Drumnacur .	188 3 23	Antrim . .	Lower Glenarm	Ardclinis . .	Larne . .	III.	21
15	Drumnacur .	127 3 34	Antrim . .	Lower Glenarm .	Layd . . .	Ballycastle .	III.	22
11	Drumnadeevna .	242 1 1	Clare . .	Inchiquin . .	Kilkeedy . .	Corrofin . .	II.	25
27, 31	Drumnadober .	228 1 26	Leitrim . .	Leitrim . .	Kiltoghert . .	Car^k. on Shannon	IV.	102
40	Drumnadonaghy .	89 0 12	Antrim . .	Upper Glenarm .	Kilwaughter .	Larne . .	III.	25
41, 47	Drumnadreagh .	223 1 28	Antrim . .	Lower Belfast .	Glynn . . .	Larne . .	II.	8
56, 57	Drumnadrough .	436 2 38	Antrim . .	Lower Belfast . .	Carnmoney .	Belfast . .	III.	8
54	Drumnafern .	306 0 37	Tyrone . .	Dungannon Middle	Donaghmore .	Dungannon .	III.	302
20	Drumnaferry .	140 0 28	Down . .	Lower Iveagh, Up.pt.	Magheralin .	Lurgan . .	III.	170
96	Drumnafinnagle .	178 3 5	Donegal . .	Banagh . .	Kilcar . .	Glenties . .	III.	108
18, 19	Drumnafinnila .	141 0 7	Leitrim . .	Drumahaire . .	Drumreilly . .	Car^k. on Shannon	IV.	95
19	Drumnafinnila Barr	251 1 10	Leitrim . .	Drumahaire . .	Drumreilly . .	Car^k. on Shannon	IV.	95
12, 13, 18	Drumnafivey .	358 0 1	Antrim . .	Upper Dunluce .	Loughguile .	Ballymoney .	III.	20
33, 34	Drumnaforbe .	288 0 28a	Tyrone . .	Omagh West .	Longfield East	Omagh . .	III.	315
24	Drumnagah .	195 2 30	Clare . .	Inchiquin . .	Inagh . . .	Ennistimon .	II.	25
94	Drumnagahan .	66 2 13	Donegal . .	Tirhugh . . .	Donegal . .	Donegal . .	III.	145
1, 5	Drumnagalliagh .	349 0 7	Fermanagh .	Lurg . . .	Drumkeeran .	Lowtherstown .	III.	206
26, 27	Drumnagally .	316 0 9	Down . .	Lower Iveagh, Lr. pt.	Seapatrick .	Banbridge .	III.	169
21, 22	Drumnagar .	208 2 32	Cavan . .	Tullygarvey .	Larah . . .	Cootehill . .	III.	91
8, 12	Drumnagavlin .	47 1 16	Monaghan .	Monaghan . .	Clones . .	Monaghan .	III.	274
3	Drumnagee .	229 2 1	Antrim . .	Cary . . .	Ballintoy . .	Ballycastle .	III.	12
3	Drumnagessan .	349 0 6	Antrim . .	Cary . . .	Ballintoy . .	Ballycastle .	III.	12
23	Drumnaglea .	278 1 7	Antrim . .	Kilconway . .	Grange of Dundermot	Ballymena .	III.	27
29	Drumnaglogh .	257 3 2	Tyrone . .	Dungannon Upper .	Kildress . .	Cookstown .	III.	308
13, 14	Drumnaglontagh .	72 3 36	Armagh . .	Orior Lower .	Ballymore .	Banbridge .	III.	55
13	Drumnagloy .	50 2 16	Armagh . .	Fews Lower .	Mullaghbrack .	Armagh . .	III.	47
19	Drumnagoal .	717 0 29	Sligo . .	Tireragh . . .	Skreen . .	Dromore West	IV.	236
6	Drumnagoon .	254 2 22	Armagh . .	Oneilland East	Seagoe . .	Lurgan . .	III.	50
17, 22	Drumnagran .	356 2 16	Cavan . .	Tullygarvey .	Kildrumsherdan .	Cootehill . .	III.	90
33, 39, 40	Drumnagranshy .	384 3 7	Sligo . .	Corran . . .	Toomour . .	Sligo . .	IV.	228
29, 30	Drumnagreagh and Slievebane .	1,127 3 20	Antrim . .	Upper Glenarm .	Carncastle .	Larne . .	III.	24
32	Drumnagrella .	212 3 9	Monaghan .	Farney . . .	Inishkeen .	Dundalk . .	III.	271
1, 5	Drumnagreshial .	145 3 4	Fermanagh .	Lurg . . .	Drumkeeran .	Lowtherstown .	III.	206
17, 22	Drumnagress .	264 1 38	Cavan . .	Tullygarvey .	Kildrumsherdan .	Cootehill . .	III.	90
107	Drumnagroagh .	162 1 18	Donegal . .	Tirhugh . . .	Kilbarron .	Ballyshannon	III.	148
58	Drumnaha .	816 1 31b	Donegal . .	Boylagh . .	Inishkeel . .	Glenties . .	III.	112
70	Drumnaha .	87 1 38	Donegal . .	Raphoe . .	Clonleigh . .	Strabane . .	III.	135
79	Drumnaha .	82 1 5	Donegal . .	Raphoe . .	Urney . . .	Strabane . .	III.	144
9, 10	Drumnahara .	183 3 35	Longford . .	Granard . .	Clonbroney .	Granard . .	I.	155
34	Drumnahare .	720 3 7c	Down . .	Upper Iveagh, Up.pt.	Aghaderg . .	Banbridge .	III.	174
19, 23	Drumnahavil .	671 3 9d	Armagh . .	Tiranny . . .	Derrynoose .	Armagh . .	III.	59
5	Drumnahay .	263 0 31	Londonderry .	Keenaght . .	Magilligan .	New T^nLimavady	III.	236
93	Drumnaheark East .	297 2 1	Donegal . .	Banagh . .	Inver . . .	Donegal . .	III.	107
93	Drumnaheark West	94 1 10	Donegal . .	Banagh . .	Inver . . .	Donegal . .	III.	107
8	Drumnaheigh .	219 0 4	Antrim . .	Cary . . .	Grange of Drumtullagh	Ballycastle .	III.	14
53	Drumnahoagh .	260 1 29	Donegal . .	Raphoe . .	Leck . . .	Letterkenny .	III.	140
40	Drumnahoe .	192 3 0	Antrim . .	Upper Glenarm .	Kilwaughter .	Larne . .	III.	25
10	Drumnahoe .	315 1 7	Tyrone . .	Strabane Lower .	Ardstraw . .	Strabane . .	III.	319
21, 25	Drumnahoney .	343 3 36	Armagh . .	Orior Upper .	Loughgilly .	Newry . .	III.	58
52, 60	Drumnahough .	58 2 27	Donegal . .	Raphoe . .	Conwal . .	Stranorlar .	III.	137
60	Drumnahough Mountain or Meenadaura .	491 1 27	Donegal . .	Raphoe . .	Conwal . .	Stranorlar .	III.	137
94	Drumnahoul .	141 0 6	Donegal . .	Tirhugh . . .	Donegal . .	Donegal . .	III.	145
9	Drumnahunshin .	361 1 29	Armagh . .	Oneilland West	Kilmore . .	Armagh . .	III.	53
21, 25	Drumnahunshin .	185 3 16	Armagh . .	Orior Upper .	Loughgilly .	Newry . .	III.	58
10	Drumnahunshin .	88 2 19	Monaghan .	Cremorne . .	Tehallan . .	Monaghan .	III.	262
9	Drumnakeel .	208 2 7	Antrim . .	Cary . . .	Culfeightrin .	Ballycastle .	III.	13
6	Drumnakelly .	199 2 11	Armagh . .	Oneilland East	Seagoe . .	Lurgan . .	III.	50
9, 13	Drumnakelly .	484 2 23	Armagh . .	Oneilland West	Drumcree .	Lurgan . .	III.	52
26, 35	Drumnakillew .	289 3 35	Donegal . .	Kilmacrenan .	Clondahorky .	Dunfanaghy .	III.	123
92, 98	Drumnakilly .	91 3 9	Donegal . .	Banagh . .	Inver . . .	Donegal . .	III.	107
35, 36	Drumnakilly .	1,352 3 6e	Tyrone . .	Strabane Upper .	Termonmaguirk .	Omagh . .	III.	326
31	Drumnalaragh .	246 3 16f	Cavan . .	Clanmahon .	Crosserlough .	Cavan . .	III.	76

(a) Including 3A. 0R. 31P. water.   (c) Including 23A. 0R. 32P. Lough Brickland.   (e) Including 3A. 1R. 19P. water.
(b) Including 10A. 2R. 14P. water.   (d) Including 9A. 0R. 11P. water.   (f) Including 6A. 2R. 27P. water.

3 H

No. of Sheet of the Ordnance Survey Maps	Townlands and Towns.	Area in Statute Acres.	County.	Barony.	Parish.	Poor Law Union in 1857.	Townland Census of 1851, Part I. Vol.	Page
		A. R. P.					Vol.	
74	Drumnalassan	518 3 38	Mayo	Costello	Castlemore	Castlereagh	IV.	140
14	Drumnaleg	213 0 24	Armagh	Orior Lower	Ballymore	Banbridge	III.	55
51, 52	Drumnalifferny	226 2 10a	Donegal	Kilmacrenan	Gartan	Letterkenny	III.	127
43, 50, 51	Drumnaliffeny Mountain	2,353 0 24	Donegal	Kilmacrenan	Gartan	Dunfanaghy	III.	127
93	Drumnalost	400 2 27	Donegal	Banagh	Inver	Donegal	III.	107
75	Drumnalough	612 0 38b	Donegal	Boylagh	Inishkeel	Glenties	III.	112
10	Drumnamahane	451 0 28	Tipperary, N.R.	Lower Ormond	Uskane	Borrisokane	II.	288
10	Drumnamahaneisland	350 3 22	Tipperary, N.R.	Lower Ormond	Uskane	Borrisokane	II.	288
17	Drumnamallaght	76 0 0	Antrim	Upper Dunluce	Ballymoney	Ballymoney	III.	18
33	Drumnamalra	266 2 4	Tyrone	Omagh West	Longfield West	Castlederg	III.	316
26	Drumnamalragh	128 2 30	Fermanagh	Clanawley	Cleenish	Enniskillen	III.	190
52, 59	Drumnamalta	112 1 1	Tyrone	Clogher	Errigal Keerogue	Clogher	III.	295
29	Drumnamalta	107 0 27	Tyrone	Dungannon Upper	Kildress	Cookstown	III.	308
18, 24	Drumnameel	276 2 28	Fermanagh	Tirkennedy	Enniskillen	Lisnaskea	III.	222
13, 17	Drumnamether	385 3 13c	Armagh	Oneilland West	Mullaghbrack	Banbridge	III.	54
6	Drumnamoe	71 3 33d	Armagh	Oneilland East	Shankill	Lurgan	III.	51
61	Drumnamoless	197 1 32e	Tyrone	Dungannon Middle	Clonfeacle	Dungannon	III.	299
29	Drumnanaliv	133 0 26	Monaghan	Farney	Donaghmoyne	Carrickmacross	III.	270
14	Drumnanane	94 3 29	Fermanagh	Magheraboy	Devenish	Enniskillen	III.	210
21	Drumnanangle	179 0 31	Mayo	Tirawley	Moygawnagh	Killala	IV.	171
21	Drumnanarragh	220 2 4	Cavan	Upper Loughtee	Larah	Cavan	III.	85
35	Drumnaraw	206 3 1	Donegal	Kilmacrenan	Clondahorky	Dunfanaghy	III.	123
14	Drumnart	106 3 15	Monaghan	Cremorne	Clontibret	Monaghan	III.	260
5	Drumnarullagh	82 3 22	Fermanagh	Lurg	Magheraculmoney	Lowtherstown	III.	208
26, 27	Drumnascamph	394 3 8	Down	Lower Iveagh, Up. pt.	Tullylish	Banbridge	III.	171
42, 48	Drumnascamph	411 0 8	Down	Upper Iveagh, Lr.pt.	Clonduff	Newry	III.	171
54, 61	Drumnashaloge	123 1 8	Tyrone	Dungannon Middle	Clonfeacle	Dungannon	III.	299
52	Drumnashammar	203 3 25	Donegal	Kilmacrenan	Conwal	Letterkenny	III.	126
51	Drumnasharragh	2,029 3 34	Donegal	Kilmacrenan	Gartan	Letterkenny	III.	127
55	Drumnashear	84 2 36	Donegal	Raphoe	Killea	Londonderry	III.	138
100	Drumnashinnagh	228 0 28	Mayo	Carra	Burriscarra	Ballinrobe	IV.	127
74, 75	Drumnasillagh	764 0 36	Donegal	Boylagh	Inishkeel	Glenties	III.	112
4	Drumnasillagh	173 0 34	Louth	Lower Dundalk	Ballymascanlan	Dundalk	I.	176
2, 4	Drumnaskea	314 2 17	Donegal	Inishowen East	Clonca	Inishowen	III.	117
45, 53	Drumnaskea	272 2 15	Donegal	Kilmacrenan	Aghanunshin	Letterkenny	III.	122
105	Drumnaskea	108 3 34	Donegal	Tirhugh	Templecarn	Donegal	III.	149
79	Drumnaslooeen	186 3 21f	Mayo	Carra	Manulla	Castlebar	IV.	129
15	Drumnasmear	78 0 20g	Antrim	Lower Glenarm	Layd	Ballycastle	III.	22
20, 25	Drumnasole	1,454 1 30h	Antrim	Lower Glenarm	Ardclinis	Larne	III.	21
9	Drumnasoo	221 0 39	Armagh	Oneilland West	Drumcree	Lurgan	III.	52
8, 12, 13	Drumnasoo	332 3 13	Armagh	Oneilland West	Loughgall	Armagh	III.	54
27, 28	Drumnasoohy	399 0 8	Sligo	Tirerrill	Kilmacallan	Sligo	IV.	240
92	Drumnasorn	67 1 38	Donegal	Banagh	Killaghtee	Donegal	III.	109
11	Drumnaspar Lower	591 1 18i	Tyrone	Strabane Upper	Bodoney Upper	Gortin	III.	324
11, 12	Drumnaspar Upper	282 2 28j	Tyrone	Strabane Upper	Bodoney Upper	Gortin	III.	324
21	Drumnasreane	61 1 26k	Cavan	Tullygarvey	Drung	Cootehill	III.	89
7, 8, 12, 13	Drumnasreane	521 3 19	Fermanagh	Magheraboy	Inishmacsaint	Ballyshannon	III.	212
54, 61	Drumnastrade	192 3 4	Tyrone	Dungannon Middle	Clonfeacle	Dungannon	III.	299
24, 25	Drumnatinny	650 3 26	Donegal	Kilmacrenan	Raymunterdoney	Dunfanaghy	III.	131
34	Drumnatinny Barr	697 3 37	Donegal	Kilmacrenan	Raymunterdoney	Dunfanaghy	III.	131
22	Drumnatread	449 3 30	Cavan	Tullygarvey	Kildrumsherdan	Cootehill	III.	90
20, 27	Drumnavaddy	353 2 35l	Down	Lower Iveagh, Lr.pt.	Seapatrick	Banbridge	III.	169
2, 6	Drumnavahan	107 2 34	Fermanagh	Lurg	Drumkeeran	Lowtherstown	III.	206
26, 27, 32, 33	Drumnaveagh	399 0 2	Cavan	Upper Loughtee	Lavey	Cavan	III.	86
37	Drumnavrick	120 1 30	Cavan	Clanmahon	Ballymachugh	Cavan	III.	76
24, 30	Drumnawall	159 0 24m	Cavan	Tullyhunco	Killashandra	Cavan	III.	98
51, 52	Drumnawooa	60 2 27	Donegal	Kilmacrenan	Gartan	Letterkenny	III.	127
22, 26	Drumnee	565 1 39n	Longford	Rathcline	Cashel	Ballymahon	I.	163
17, 24, 25	Drumneechy	313 1 9	Londonderry	Keenaght	Bovevagh	New Tn Limavady	III.	235
77, 88	Drumneen	310 3 27o	Mayo	Burrishoole	Islandeady	Westport	IV.	121
78	Drumneen	105 0 15p	Mayo	Carra	Aglish	Castlebar	IV.	123
89, 99	Drumneen	325 0 17q	Mayo	Carra	Ballintober	Castlebar	IV.	124
91, 101	Drumneen	505 0 6r	Mayo	Clanmorris	Kilcolman	Claremorris	IV.	134
19	Drumneen	395 1 1	Queen's Co.	Stradbally	Ballyadams	Athy	I.	246
89	Drumneen Beg	67 0 17	Mayo	Carra	Ballintober	Castlebar	IV.	124
89	Drumneen More	99 1 17	Mayo	Carra	Ballintober	Castlebar	IV.	124
101	Drumneen (Prendergast)	144 3 0	Mayo	Clanmaurice	Kilcolman	Claremorris	IV.	134
101	Drumneen South	104 2 3s	Mayo	Clanmaurice	Kilcolman	Claremorris	IV.	134
10	Drumneill	205 1 32	Monaghan	Cremorne	Clontibret	Monaghan	III.	260
28	Drumneill	133 0 22	Monaghan	Farney	Donaghmoyne	Carrickmacross	III.	270
27	Drumneth	101 2 02	Down	Lower Iveagh, Lr. pt.	Magherally	Banbridge	III.	168
5	Drumnevan	70 1 20	Armagh	Oneilland West	Drumcree	Lurgan	III.	52
28, 32	Drumnid	159 3 7	Leitrim	Mohill	Mohill	Mohill	IV.	108

(a) Including 18A. 3R. 32P. water.
(b) Including 13A. 0R. 6P. water.
(c) Including 2A. 3R. 0P. water.
(d) Including 14A. 0R. 38P. detached portion.
(e) Including 3A. 2R. 1P. water.
(f) Including 6A. 1R. 30P. water.
(g) Including 4A. 3R. 18P. detached portions.

(h) Including 6A. 1R. 26P. water.
(i) Including 4A. 2R. 29P. water.
(j) Including 3A. 1R. 12P. water.
(k) Including 6A. 2R. 22P. water.
(l) Including 5A. 2R. 9P. water.
(m) Including 23A. 2R. 2P. water.

(n) Including 27A. 2R. 20P. water.
(o) Including 47A. 1R. 4P. water.
(p) Including 3A. 2R. 10P. water.
(q) Including 17A. 0R. 19P. water.
(r) Including 5A. 2R. 24P. water.
(s) Including 3A. 0R. 22P. water.

No. of Sheet of the Ordnance Survey Maps.	Townlands and Towns.	Area in Statute Acres.			County.	Barony.	Parish.	Poor Law Union in 1857.	Townland Census of 1851, Part I.	
		A.	R.	P.					Vol.	Page
15	Drumnigh	107	2	15	Dublin	Coolock	Kinsaley	Balrothery	I.	28
7	Drumnolan	120	3	22	Monaghan	Trough	Donagh	Monaghan	III.	282
14	Drumnoose	199	1	11	Cavan	Lower Loughtee	Drumlane	Cavan	III.	80
28	Drumny	88	2	28	Monaghan	Farney	Donaghmoyne	Carrickmacross	III.	270
6	Drumnykerne	213	3	29	Armagh	Oneilland East	Shankill	Lurgan	III.	51
23, 26	Drumod	424	0	1a	Monaghan	Cremorne	Aghnamullen	Cootehill	III.	258
35	Drumod Beg	245	3	14b	Leitrim	Mohill	Annaduff	Mohill	IV.	105
7	Drumod Glebe	77	0	25	Cavan	Tullyhaw	Kinawley	Bawnboy	III.	93
35, 37	Drumod More	248	3	10	Leitrim	Mohill	Annaduff	Mohill	IV.	105
13, 20	Drumo and Drumcro	427	0	2	Down	Lower Iveagh, Up. pt.	Magheralin	Lurgan	III.	170
35	DRUMOD T.	—			Leitrim	Mohill	Annaduff	Mohill	IV.	105
8, 12	Drumogher	191	2	29c	Armagh	Oneilland West	Grange	Armagh	III.	52
35, 44	Drumoghill	340	1	2	Donegal	Kilmacrenan	Kilmacrenan	Millford	III.	129
54, 62	Drumoghill	272	2	20	Donegal	Raphoe	Raymoghy	Letterkenny	III.	141
26, 32	Drumoghill	78	1	28	Fermanagh	Clanawley	Killesher	Enniskillen	III.	192
21	Drumoghra	84	1	3	Cavan	Upper Loughtee	Annagelliff	Cavan	III.	81
28, 32	Drumoghty Beg	104	0	20	Leitrim	Mohill	Mohill	Mohill	IV.	108
28	Drumoghty More	93	2	13	Leitrim	Mohill	Mohill	Mohill	IV.	108
21	Drumohan	103	0	34	Cavan	Upper Loughtee	Castleterra	Cavan	III.	82
15	Drumone	64	2	13	Meath	Fore	Loughcrew	Oldcastle	I.	201
15	Drumone	135	2	2	Meath	Fore	Moylagh	Oldcastle	I.	201
33	Drumoolish	487	0	20	Londonderry	Loughinsholin	Tamlaght O'Crilly	Ballymoney	III.	243
27, 28	Drumoosclin	322	0	29	Cavan	Clankee	Bailieborough	Bailieborough	III.	71
13	Drumorgan	274	2	8	Armagh	Fews Lower	Mullaghbrack	Armagh	III.	47
28	Drumoris	52	0	32	Fermanagh	Magherastephana	Aghavea	Lisnaskea	III.	218
103	Drumoske	112	3	17d	Donegal	Tirhugh	Drumhome	Ballyshannon	III.	146
32	Drumoula	106	3	36	Leitrim	Leitrim	Mohill	Mohill	IV.	104
25, 29	Drumourne	723	1	33	Antrim	Lower Glenarm	Tickmacrevan	Larne	III.	23
33	Drumowen	302	2	34e	Tyrone	Omagh West	Longfield West	Castlederg	III.	316
28	Drumparsons	54	3	20	Leitrim	Leitrim	Kiltubbrid	Cark. on Shannon	IV.	103
29, 35	Drumpeak	251	0	36	Cavan	Clankee	Enniskeen	Bailieborough	III.	72
10	Drumpeen	88	0	0	Fermanagh	Lurg	Derryvullan	Lowtherstown	III.	204
14	Drumquill	54	2	0	Cavan	Lower Loughtee	Drumlane	Cavan	III.	80
19, 20	Drumquill	227	0	31	Monaghan	Cremorne	Clontibret	Castleblayney	III.	260
40	Drumquillia	109	0	8	Fermanagh	Coole	Galloon	Clones	III.	199
26	Drumquin	243	0	30	Clare	Bunratty Upper	Kilraghtis	Ennis	II.	9
41, 50	Drumquin	257	2	1	Clare	Islands	Clondagad	Killadysert	II.	29
33	Drumquin	398	1	34f	Tyrone	Omagh West	Longfield West	Castlederg	III.	316
33	DRUMQUIN T.	—			Tyrone	Omagh West	{ Longfield West / Longfield East	{ Castlederg / Omagh }	III.	316
15	Drumra	136	2	3	Down	Castlereagh Upper	Drumbo	Lisburn	III.	164
21, 24	Drumrackan	278	1	27	Leitrim	Carrigallen	Oughteragh	Bawnboy	IV.	92
43	Drumragh (Caldwell)	370	3	3g	Tyrone	Omagh East	Drumragh	Omagh	III.	312
43	Drumragh (J. M'Causland)	45	1	16h	Tyrone	Omagh East	Drumragh	Omagh	III.	312
32	Drumraghool North	207	0	16	Leitrim	Mohill	Mohill	Mohill	IV.	108
32	Drumraghool South	221	2	15	Leitrim	Mohill	Mohill	Mohill	IV.	108
43	Drumragh (P. M'Causland)	207	3	0	Tyrone	Omagh East	Drumragh	Omagh	III.	312
32	Drumrahan	191	3	8	Leitrim	Leitrim	Mohill	Mohill	IV.	104
16	Drumraighland	805	2	18	Londonderry	Keenaght	Tamlaght Finlagan	NewTⁿLimavady	III.	237
39	Drumrainbane	117	1	1i	Fermanagh	Coole	Galloon	Lisnaskea	III.	199
39, 40	Drumrainduff	69	3	27	Fermanagh	Coole	Galloon	Clones	III.	199
32, 33	Drumraine	203	3	34j	Sligo	Corran	Cloonoghil	Tobercurry	IV.	225
34	Drumraine	257	0	32	Sligo	Tirerrill	Kilmacallan	Sligo	IV.	240
25	Drumraine Glebe	222	0	11	Leitrim	Carrigallen	Oughteragh	Mohill	IV.	92
41, 42	Drumrainey	267	0	2	Londonderry	Loughinsholin	Magherafelt	Magherafelt	III.	243
92	Drumrainy	231	3	31	Donegal	Banagh	Inver	Donegal	III.	107
26	Drumrainy	115	2	35	Fermanagh	Clanawley	Cleenish	Enniskillen	III.	190
40	Drumrainy	133	2	1k	Fermanagh	Clankelly	Clones	Clones	III.	196
27	Drumrainy	56	3	16	Fermanagh	Tirkennedy	Derrybrusk	Enniskillen	III.	220
16	Drumrainy	141	1	14	Fermanagh	Tirkennedy	Magheracross	Enniskillen	III.	222
40	Drumralla	223	0	28	Fermanagh	Coole	Galloon	Clones	III.	200
37	Drumramer	295	1	2	Antrim	Upper Toome	Ahoghill	Ballymena	III.	33
10	Drumramer	772	0	21	Londonderry	Keenaght	Drumachose	NewTⁿLimavady	III.	235
16, 21	Drumrane	185	3	16	Cavan	Tullygarvey	Drung	Cootehill	III.	89
14	Drumrane	286	3	31	Leitrim	Drumahaire	Killanummery	Manorhamilton	IV.	98
9, 16	Drumrane	120	2	30l	Londonderry	Keenaght	Tamlaght Finlagan	NewTⁿLimavady	III.	237
23	Drumraney	631	3	13	Westmeath	Kilkenny West	Drumraney	Ballymahon	I.	273
18, 23	Drumrankin	300	2	36	Antrim	Kilconway	Loughguile	Ballymoney	III.	27
32	Drumrankin	596	2	18	Antrim	Lower Toome	Ahoghill	Ballymena	III.	32
39, 40	Drumrat	142	1	15	Cavan	Castlerahan	Mullagh	Bailieborough	III.	70
21	Drumrat	152	3	2	Cavan	Tullygarvey	Larah	Cootehill	III.	91

(a) Including 16A. 3R. 36P. water.
(b) Including 9A. 2R. 13P. water.
(c) Including 10A. 3R. 8P. water.
(d) Including 4A. 2R. 2P. water.

(e) Including 1A. 0R. 17P. water.
(f) Including 11A. 3R. 6P. water.
(g) Including 7A. 1R. 24P. water.
(h) Including 0A. 1R. 35P. water.

(i) Including 1A. 3R. 0P. water.
(j) Including 30A. 0R. 16P. water.
(k) Including 6A. 0R. 17P. water.
(l) Including 0A. 2R. 26P. water.

No. of Sheet of the Ordnance Survey Maps.	Townlands and Towns.	Area in Statute Acres.	County.	Barony.	Parish.	Poor Law Union in 1857.	Townland Census of 1851, Part I.	
		A. R. P.					Vol.	Page
94	Drumrat	149 2 15	Donegal	Tirhugh	Donegal	Donegal	III.	145
31, 37	Drumrath	207 1 37a	Cavan	Clanmahon	Crosserlough	Cavan	III.	76
31	Drumraw	283 0 14	Antrim	Lower Toome	Ahoghill	Ballymena	III.	32
38	Drumraw	146 1 21	Tyrone	Dungannon Upper	Desertcreat	Cookstown	III.	307
33, 34	Drumrawn	494 0 15b	Tyrone	Omagh West	Longfield East	Omagh	III.	315
42	Drumraymond	296 0 34c	Antrim	Upper Toome	Duneane	Ballymena	III.	34
16, 17	Drumreagh	266 1 1	Antrim	Upper Dunluce	Ballymoney	Ballymoney	III.	18
90, 96	Drumreagh	189 2 31	Donegal	Banagh	Kilcar	Glenties	III.	108
16	Drumreagh	1,096 0 27	Down	Castlereagh Lower	Killinchy	Newtownards	III.	163
51, 54	Drumreagh	487 3 4	Down	Upper Iveagh, Up. pt.	Kilbroney	Kilkeel	III.	175
16	Drumreagh	757 3 28d	Mayo	Erris	Kilmore	Belmullet	IV.	146
15	Drumreagh	251 2 12	Wicklow	Lower Talbotstown	Hollywood	Baltinglass	I.	360
21	Drumreagh	147 0 29	Wicklow	Upper Talbotstown	Donaghmore	Baltinglass	I.	363
46, 47	Drumreagh Etra	179 3 26	Tyrone	Dungannon Middle	Tullyniskan	Dungannon	III.	304
46	Drumreagh Otra	186 2 3	Tyrone	Dungannon Middle	Tullyniskan	Dungannon	III.	304
51	Drumreagh Upper	522 1 17	Down	Upper Iveagh, Up. pt.	Kilbroney	Kilkeel	III.	175
10	Drumreane	141 0 9e	Fermanagh	Lurg	Magheraculmoney	Lowtherstown	III.	208
54	Drumreany	183 3 0f	Tyrone	Dungannon Middle	Donaghmore	Dungannon	III.	302
39	Drumrearty	74 2 22	Fermanagh	Coole	Galloon	Lisnaskea	III.	200
9, 10	Drumreask	154 1 32	Fermanagh	Magheraboy	Inishmacsaint	Ballyshannon	III.	212
28	Drumreask	93 3 10	Leitrim	Mohill	Mohill	Mohill	IV.	108
9	Drumreask	119 0 2	Monaghan	Monaghan	Tedavnet	Monaghan	III.	278
44	Drumree	72 1 3	Meath	Lower Deece	Knockmark	Dunshaughlin	I.	192
17	Drumreenagh	132 3 7	Monaghan	Dartree	Currin	Clones	III.	265
17	Drumreenagh	172 1 12	Monaghan	Dartree	Killeevan	Clones	III.	268
32	Drumregan	140 1 29	Leitrim	Mohill	Mohill	Mohill	IV.	108
25, 26	Drumreilly	253 0 25g	Leitrim	Carrigallen	Drumreilly	Bawnboy	IV.	91
39	Drumrevagh	473 0 30h	Mayo	Tirawley	Ballynahaglish	Ballina	IV.	164
18	Drumrewy	149 2 19	Leitrim	Drumahaire	Inishmagrath	Manorhamilton	IV.	96
18,19,20,21	Drumristin	419 3 1	Leitrim	Drumahaire	Drumreilly	Carᵏ. on Shannon	IV.	95
8, 13	Drumroan	132 2 6	Antrim	Cary	Grange of Drumtullagh	Ballycastle	III.	14
24	Drumrockady	177 3 2	Cavan	Tullyhunco	Killashandra	Cavan	III.	98
24	Drumroe	174 0 6	Cavan	Tullyhunco	Killashandra	Cavan	III.	98
80, 81	Drumroe	52 3 25	Donegal	Banagh	Glencolumbkille	Glenties	III.	105
47	Drumroe	296 2 29	King's Co.	Clonlisk	Castletownely	Roscrea	I.	129
14, 19	Drumroe	207 1 13	Longford	Ardagh	Ardagh	Longford	I.	151
20, 26	Drumroe	170 3 15	Queen's Co.	Ballyadams	Ballyadams	Athy	I.	231
10	Drumroe	315 0 20	Tipperary, N.R.	Lower Ormond	Modreeny	Borrisokane	II.	286
86	Drumroe	141 2 35	Tipperary, S.R.	Iffa and Offa West	Templetenny	Clogheen	II.	320
29, 30	Drumroe	242 1 23	Waterford	Decies without Drum	Affane	Lismore	II.	353
21, 29	Drumroe Lower	194 1 3	Waterford	Coshmore&Coshbride	Lismore and Mocollop	Lismore	II.	345
21, 29	Drumroe Upper	190 1 14	Waterford	Coshmore&Coshbride	Lismore and Mocollop	Lismore	II.	345
44	Drumrolla	99 0 16	Sligo	Corran	Kilshalvy	Boyle	IV.	227
93	Drumrone	264 1 23	Donegal	Banagh	Inver	Donegal	III.	107
28	Drumroo	106 2 33	Fermanagh	Magherastephana	Aghalurcher	Lisnaskea	III.	216
17, 18	Drumrooghill	224 0 31	Cavan	Tullygarvey	Drumgoon	Cootehill	III.	88
18	Drumrooghill	247 1 15i	Monaghan	Dartree	Ematris	Cootehill	III.	267
31	Drumroosk	290 3 9j	Cavan	Clanmahon	Ballintemple	Cavan	III.	75
19	Drumroosk	105 3 25k	Cavan	Tullyhunco	Killashandra	Cavan	III.	98
93	Drumroosk	126 2 36	Donegal	Banagh	Killymard	Donegal	III.	111
33, 38	Drumroosk	150 3 1	Fermanagh	Knockninny	Kinawley	Lisnaskea	III.	202
34	Drumroosk	55 1 3l	Fermanagh	Magherastephana	Aghalurcher	Lisnaskea	III.	216
19	Drumroosk	191 0 18	Monaghan	Monaghan	Tullycorbet	Monaghan	III.	281
94	Drumroosk East	103 1 9	Donegal	Banagh	Killymard	Donegal	III.	111
93, 94	Drumroosk Middle	100 2 19	Donegal	Banagh	Killymard	Donegal	III.	111
24	Drumroosk North	201 2 36m	Leitrim	Leitrim	Fenagh	Mohill	IV.	100
29	Drumroosk South	177 3 11n	Leitrim	Leitrim	Fenagh	Mohill	IV.	100
25	Drumroosk or Thomascourt	59 2 7	Cavan	Upper Loughtee	Kilmore	Cavan	III.	85
93	Drumroosk West	100 3 9	Donegal	Banagh	Killymard	Donegal	III.	111
38	Drumroragh	609 3 10	Cavan	Castlerahan	Crosserlough	Cavan	III.	68
48	Drumrot	51 0 17	Londonderry	Loughinsholin	Derryloran	Magherafelt	III.	240
48	Drumrot	348 2 21	Londonderry	Loughinsholin	Lissan	Magherafelt	III.	242
100	Drumrud	150 0 0	Mayo	Carra	Touaghty	Ballinrobe	IV.	130
23, 27, 28	Drumruekill	194 2 19o	Leitrim	Leitrim	Kiltubbrid	Carᵏ. on Shannon	IV.	103
10	Drumrush	159 3 26p	Cavan	Lower Loughtee	Drumlane	Cavan	III.	80
5	Drumrush	233 1 20	Fermanagh	Lurg	Drumkeeran	Lowtherstown	III.	206
7	Drumrusk	229 0 25	Armagh	Tiranny	Eglish	Armagh	III.	59
18	Drumrusk	306 1 39	Waterford	Gaultiere	Kill St. Nicholas	Waterford	II.	364
9	Drumrutagh	203 2 30	Monaghan	Monaghan	Tehallan	Monaghan	III.	280
21	Drumryan	52 3 22	Cavan	Upper Loughtee	Castleterra	Cavan	III.	82
29, 35	Drumsallagh	149 1 11	Cavan	Clankee	Enniskeen	Bailieborough	III.	72
18, 26	Drumsallagh	97 1 31	Clare	Bunratty Upper	Inchicronan	Ennis	II.	9

(a) Including 9A. 2R. 22P. water.
(b) Including 0A. 0R. 30P. water.
(c) Including 1A. 3R. 12P. Island.
(d) Including 85A. 0R. 38P. water.
(e) Including 1A. 0R. 28P. water.
(f) Including 2A. 1R. 22P. water.

(g) Including 2A. 0R. 6P. water.
(h) Including 12A. 3R. 36P. water.
(i) Including 3A. 1R. 17P. water.
(j) Including 7A. 3R. 32P. water.
(k) Including 4A. 0R. 15P. water.

(l) Including 9A. 0R. 16P. water.
(m) Including 32A. 3R. 34P. water.
(n) Including 4A. 3R. 27P. water.
(o) Including 2A. 3R. 16P. water.
(p) Including 8A. 3R. 38P. water.

No. of Sheet of the Ordnance Survey Maps.	Townlands and Towns.	Area in Statute Acres. A. R. P.	County.	Barony.	Parish.	Poor Law Union in 1857.	Townland Census of 1851, Part I. Vol.	Page
51	Drumsallagh . .	136 3 12	Donegal . .	Kilmacrenan . .	Gartan . . .	Letterkenny .	III.	127
33	Drumsallagh . .	690 3 8	Down . .	Upper Iveagh, Up.pt.	Aghaderg . .	Banbridge .	III.	174
7, 11	Drumsallan Lower .	211 0 1	Armagh . .	Tiranny . . .	Eglish . . .	Armagh . .	III.	59
11	Drumsallan Upper .	157 1 9	Armagh . .	Tiranny . . .	Eglish . . .	Armagh . .	III.	59
41	Drumsamney . .	233 3 4	Londonderry .	Loughinsholin .	Kilcronaghan . .	Magherafelt .	III.	241
11	Drumsara . .	132 0 4	Fermanagh .	Lurg . . .	Derryvullan . .	Lowtherstown .	III.	204
27	Drumsaragh . .	426 0 14	Londonderry .	Coleraine . .	Tamlaght O'Crilly .	Ballymoney .	III.	233
39	Drumsastry . .	156 3 27	Fermanagh .	Coole . . .	Galloon . . .	Lisnaskea .	III.	200
18	Drumsaul . .	75 2 12a	Monaghan .	Dartree . . .	Ematris . . .	Cootehill . .	III.	267
12, 13	Drumsavage . .	182 3 5	Armagh . .	Fews Lower .	Mullaghbrack . .	Armagh . .	III.	47
6	Drumsawna Beg .	136 2 37	Fermanagh .	Lurg . . .	Magheraculmoney .	Lowtherstown .	III.	208
6	Drumsawna More .	224 2 28	Fermanagh .	Lurg . . .	Magheraculmoney .	Lowtherstown .	III.	208
9, 15	Drumsawry or Summerbank . .	809 1 38	Meath . .	Fore . . .	Loughcrew . .	Oldcastle . .	I.	201
117, 126	Drumscar . .	353 3 35	Galway . .	Longford . .	Lickmolassy . .	Portumna . .	IV.	61
48, 49	Drumscoba . .	208 1 23b	Mayo . .	Gallen . . .	Attymass . .	Ballina . .	IV.	147
15, 21	Drumscollop . .	289 3 17c	Fermanagh .	Magheraboy . .	Devenish . .	Enniskillen .	III.	210
5	Drumscor . .	149 3 7	Monaghan .	Monaghan . .	Tedavnet . .	Monaghan . .	III.	278
33	Drumscra . .	248 2 33d	Tyrone . .	Omagh West .	Longfield West .	Castlederg .	III.	316
32, 38	Drumscruddan .	375 1 10	Cavan . .	Castlerahan . .	Crosserlough .	Cavan . .	III.	68
51, 54	Drumsesk . .	248 0 11	Down . .	Upper Iveagh, Up.pt.	Kilbroney . .	Kilkeel . .	III.	175
13, 17	Drumshallan . .	127 0 25	Armagh . .	Fews Lower .	Mullaghbrack . .	Armagh . .	III.	47
21	Drumshallon . .	511 1 30	Louth . .	Ferrard . . .	Drumshallon . .	Drogheda .	I.	180
23	Drumshanbo . .	127 1 38	Leitrim . .	Leitrim . . .	Kiltoghert . .	Carᵏ. on Shannon	IV.	102
28, 29	Drumshanbo Glebe .	871 1 12	Tyrone . .	Dungannon Upper .	Kildress . . .	Cookstown .	III.	308
29, 33	Drumshanbo North	395 0 10	Leitrim . .	Mohill . . .	Cloone . . .	Mohill . .	IV.	106
36, 38	Drumshanbo South	955 2 1e	Leitrim . .	Mohill . . .	Cloone . . .	Mohill . .	IV.	106
23	DRUMSHANBO T. .	—	Leitrim . .	Leitrim . . .	Kiltoghert . .	Carᵏ. on Shannon	IV.	103
36	Drumshancorick .	225 1 7	Fermanagh .	Clankelly . .	Clones . . .	Clones . .	III.	196
10	Drumshane . .	192 3 34	Fermanagh .	Lurg . . .	Derryvullan . .	Lowtherstown .	III.	204
26, 30	Drumshangore .	186 3 35	Leitrim . .	Carrigallen . .	Carrigallen . .	Bawnboy . .	IV.	89
43	Drumshanly . .	202 2 2f	Tyrone . .	Omagh East .	Drumragh . .	Omagh . .	III.	312
5	Drumshannagh .	153 1 37	Roscommon .	Boyle . . .	Boyle . . .	Boyle . .	IV.	194
17	Drumshannon . .	149 1 38	Monaghan .	Dartree . . .	Aghabog . .	Clones . .	III.	263
6, 9	Drumshanny . .	164 3 29	Monaghan .	Monaghan . .	Tedavnet . .	Monaghan . .	III.	279
65	Drumshantony .	16 0 12	Donegal . .	Boylagh . .	Inishkeel . .	Glenties . .	III.	112
6, 9	Drumsheaver . .	309 0 17	Monaghan .	Monaghan . .	Tedavnet . .	Monaghan . .	III.	279
120	Drumsheel Lower .	235 3 33	Mayo . .	Kilmaine . .	Cong . . .	Ballinrobe .	IV.	153
120	Drumsheel Upper .	120 2 10	Mayo . .	Kilmaine . .	Cong . . .	Ballinrobe .	IV.	153
31, 40	Drumsheen . .	1,513 0 13	Mayo . .	Gallen . . .	Kilgarvan . .	Ballina . .	IV.	148
13	Drumsheeny . .	238 2 24	Monaghan .	Monaghan . .	Drumsnat . .	Monaghan . .	III.	275
6, 7	Drumsheeny . .	58 0 15	Monaghan .	Trough . . .	Donagh . . .	Monaghan . .	III.	282
17	Drumsheil . .	208 2 16g	Cavan . .	Tullygarvey . .	Kildrumsherdan .	Cootehill .	III.	90
42	Drumsheil . .	251 3 12	Tyrone . .	Omagh East .	Dromore . .	Omagh . .	III.	311
38	Drumshimuck . .	216 3 0	Fermanagh .	Knockninny . .	Kinawley . .	Lisnaskea .	III.	202
78	Drumshinnagh .	77 2 28h	Mayo . .	Carra . . .	Aglish . . .	Castlebar . .	IV.	123
101	Drumshinnagh .	173 0 13	Mayo . .	Clanmorris . .	Tagheen . .	Claremorris .	IV.	136
62	Drumshinnagh .	270 0 9	Mayo . .	Gallen . . .	Kilconduff . .	Swineford .	IV.	147
34	Drumshinnagh .	130 1 29	Sligo . .	Tirerrill . .	Kilmacallan . .	Sligo . .	IV.	240
101	Drumshinnagh (Lynch)	64 1 26	Mayo . .	Clanmorris . .	Tagheen . .	Claremorris .	IV.	136
24, 30	Drumshinny . .	194 1 22	Cavan . .	Tullyhunco .	Killashandra .	Cavan . .	III.	98
67	Drumsill . .	340 0 38	Antrim . .	Upper Massereene .	Magheragall . .	Lisburn . .	III.	31
12	Drumsill . .	162 3 12	Armagh . .	Armagh . .	Grange . . .	Armagh . .	III.	45
22	Drumsillagh . .	171 0 13	Cavan . .	Tullygarvey . .	Kildrumsherdan .	Cootehill .	III.	90
15	Drumsillagh . .	242 0 15i	Cavan . .	Upper Loughtee .	Castleterra . .	Cavan . .	III.	82
26	Drumsillagh . .	185 0 34	Fermanagh .	Clanawley . .	Cleenish . .	Enniskillen .	III.	190
32	Drumsillagh . .	72 2 0	Fermanagh .	Clanawley . .	Killesher . .	Enniskillen .	III.	192
21	Drumsillagh . .	228 0 30	Fermanagh .	Magheraboy . .	Rossorry . .	Enniskillen .	III.	214
30	Drumsillagh . .	264 2 21j	Leitrim . .	Carrigallen . .	Carrigallen . .	Mohill . .	IV.	89
4	Drumsillagh . .	86 2 9	Meath . .	Lower Slane .	Drumcondra . .	Ardee . .	I.	222
3, 4, 6, 7	Drumsillagh . .	278 1 10	Roscommon .	Boyle . . .	Ardcarn . .	Carᵏ. on Shannon	IV.	193
7	Drumsillagh . .	140 2 36	Roscommon .	Boyle . . .	Tumna . . .	Boyle . .	IV.	198
44, 53	Drumsillagh or Sallybank (Merritt) .	523 2 1	Clare . .	Tulla Lower .	Kilseily . .	Limerick . .	II.	36
44, 53	Drumsillagh or Sallybank (Parker) .	588 3 28	Clare . .	Tulla Lower .	Kilseily . .	Limerick . .	II.	36
6	Drumsinnot . .	96 0 20	Louth . .	Upper Dundalk .	Inishkeen . .	Dundalk . .	I.	179
17	Drumsivney . .	68 2 14	Cavan . .	Tullygarvey . .	Kildrumsherdan .	Cootehill .	III.	90
17	Drumskea . .	131 0 19	Antrim . .	Upper Dunluce .	Ballymoney . .	Ballymoney .	III.	18
10	Drumskea . .	142 0 37	Fermanagh .	Lurg . . .	Derryvullan . .	Lowtherstown .	III.	204
25	Drumskeagh . .	50 3 39	Cavan . .	Upper Loughtee .	Kilmore . .	Cavan . .	III.	84
20, 27	Drumskee . .	248 0 25	Down . .	Lower Iveagh, Lr. pt.	Dromore . .	Banbridge .	III.	168
30, 39	Drumskellan . .	1,254 2 39	Donegal . .	Inishowen West .	Muff . . .	Londonderry .	III.	121

(a) Including 9A. 0R. 23P. water.
(b) Including 2A. 0R. 22P. water.
(c) Including 22A. 3R. 20P. water.
(d) Including 1A. 1R. 32P. water.
(e) Including 39A. 2R. 0P. water.
(f) Including 5A. 1R. 29P. water.
(g) Including 7A. 2R. 29P. water.
(h) Including 10A. 2R. 1P. water.
(i) Including 35A. 2R. 35P. water.
(j) Including 11A. 1R. 8P. water.

No. of Sheet of the Ordnance Survey Maps	Townlands and Towns.	Area in Statute Acres.			County.	Barony.	Parish.	Poor Law Union in 1857.	Townland Census of 1851, Part I.	
		A.	R.	P.					Vol.	Page
16	Drumskelt . .	148	2	9	Cavan . .	Tullygarvey . .	Drung . . .	Cootehill . .	III.	89
18	Drumskelt . .	261	3	23a	Monaghan .	Cremorne . .	Aghnamullen .	Cootehill . .	III.	258
17	Drumskelt . .	195	3	35	Monaghan .	Dartree . . .	Killeevan . .	Cootehill . .	III.	268
29	Drumskerry . .	133	1	8	Cavan . .	Clankee . .	Enniskeen . .	Bailieborough .	III.	72
21, 22	Drumskew . .	70	2	8	Fermanagh .	Magheraboy . .	Rossorry . .	Enniskillen .	III.	214
15	Drumskimly . .	177	2	25	Fermanagh .	Magheraboy . .	Inishmacsaint .	Enniskillen .	III.	212
1	Drumskinny . .	289	1	39	Fermanagh .	Lurg . . .	Drumkeeran .	Lowtherstown .	III.	206
61	Drumskinny . .	64	1	17	Tyrone . .	Dungannon Middle .	Clonfeacle .	Dungannon .	III.	299
49, 50	Drumskinny . .	793	0	35b	Tyrone . .	Omagh East . .	Dromore . .	Omagh . .	III.	311
10, 11	Drumskool . .	168	2	5c	Fermanagh .	Lurg . . .	Derryvullan .	Lowtherstown .	III.	204
3	Drumslade . .	164	1	21	Londonderry .	North East Liberties of Coleraine .	Ballyaghran .	Coleraine . .	III.	244
8	Drumslavog . .	78	1	9	Monaghan .	Monaghan . .	Tedavnet . .	Monaghan . .	III.	279
34,35,43,44	Drumsleed . .	1,061	0	27d	Mayo . .	Erris . . .	Kilcommon . .	Newport . .	IV.	144
35	Drumslig . .	529	3	1	Waterford .	Decies within Drum	Ardmore . .	Dungarvan .	II.	350
16	Drumsloe . .	238	1	37e	Fermanagh .	Tirkennedy . .	Magheracross .	Enniskillen .	III.	223
16	Drumsloe . .	120	0	37	Monaghan .	Dartree . . .	Drummully . .	Clones . .	III.	266
16	Drumsluice . .	158	1	9	Fermanagh .	Lurg . . .	Derryvullan .	Lowtherstown .	III.	204
22, 27	Drumsna . .	89	3	25f	Fermanagh .	Clanawley . .	Rossorry . .	Enniskillen .	III.	194
31, 32	Drumsna . .	271	1	0g	Leitrim . .	Leitrim . . .	Annaduff . .	Carᵏ. on Shannon	IV.	99
29, 36	Drumsnade . .	561	3	7	Down . .	Kinelarty . .	Magheradrool .	Downpatrick .	III.	177
31	Drumsna T. . .	—			Leitrim . .	Leitrim . . .	Annaduff . .	Carᵏ. on Shannon	IV.	100
39	Drumsnauv . .	486	0	25	Galway . .	Ross . . .	Cong . . .	Oughterard .	IV.	73
41	Drumsoghla . .	121	1	39	Sligo . .	Tirerrill . .	Kilmactranny .	Boyle . .	IV.	240
56	Drumsonnus . .	391	0	36	Tyrone . .	Omagh East . .	Kilskeery . .	Lowtherstown .	III.	313
35	Drumsoo . .	113	3	22	Fermanagh .	Clankelly . .	Clones . .	Clones . .	III.	196
43, 44, 49	Drumsough . .	728	0	23	Antrim . .	Upper Toome .	Drummaul . .	Antrim . .	III.	34
26	Drumsroohil . .	73	2	21	Fermanagh .	Clanawley . .	Cleenish . .	Enniskillen .	III.	190
26, 32	Drumsroohil . .	121	2	33	Fermanagh .	Clanawley . .	Killesher . .	Enniskillen .	III.	192
12, 17	Drumsru . .	674	3	39	Kildare . .	Connell . .	Kilmeage . .	Naas . .	I.	55
17	Drumsru . .	348	2	38h	Kildare . .	Offaly East . .	Feighcullen .	Edenderry .	I.	70
11, 12	Drumsteeple . .	163	3	19	Londonderry .	Coleraine . .	Aghadowey . .	Coleraine . .	III.	229
93	Drumstevlin . .	153	0	39	Donegal . .	Banagh . .	Killymard . .	Donegal . .	III.	111
17	Drumsurn Lower .	258	1	10	Londonderry .	Keenaght . .	Balteagh . .	NewTⁿLimavady	III.	234
17	Drumsurn T. . .	—			Londonderry .	Keenaght . .	Balteagh . .	NewTⁿLimavady	III.	234
17	Drumsurn Upper .	690	2	12	Londonderry .	Keenaght . .	Balteagh . .	NewTⁿLimavady	III.	234
35	Drumswords . .	81	1	8	Fermanagh .	Clankelly . .	Clones . .	Clones . .	III.	196
17	Drumswords . .	117	2	21	Monaghan .	Dartree . . .	Killeevan . .	Clones . .	III.	268
34	Drumtarsna . .	139	0	22	Tipperary, N.R.	Kilnamanagh Upper	Glenkeen . .	Thurles . .	II.	278
22	Drum T. . .	—			Monaghan .	Dartree . . .	Currin . .	Cootehill . .	III.	266
31, 34	Drumturk . .	158	1	15	Monaghan .	Farney . . .	Killanny . .	Carrickmacross	III.	271
3, 4	Drumturk . .	139	0	23	Monaghan .	Trough . . .	Errigal Trough .	Monaghan . .	III.	284
36	Drumulcaw or Drumanaghan .	447	3	19	Down . .	Kinelarty . .	Loughinisland .	Downpatrick .	III.	177
43	Drumullan . .	366	2	21i	Clare . .	Bunratty Lower .	Kilmurry . .	Tulla . .	II.	6
27	Drumullan . .	93	3	27	Clare . .	Tulla Upper .	Tulla . . .	Tulla . .	II.	41
8	Drumummery . .	106	3	33j	Monaghan .	Monaghan . .	Clones . .	Monaghan . .	III.	274
18	Drumumna . .	494	0	35k	Clare . .	Bunratty Upper .	Inchicronan .	Ennis . .	II.	9
22	Drumurcher . .	172	1	26	Monaghan .	Dartree . . .	Currin . .	Cootehill . .	III.	265
9	Drumure . .	351	1	15	Longford .	Longford . .	Clongesh . .	Longford . .	I.	157
30, 31	Drumury . .	169	1	15	Cavan . .	Clanmahon . .	Ballintemple .	Cavan . .	III.	75
1	Drumury . .	283	2	21l	Longford .	Granard . .	Killoe . .	Granard . .	I.	157
6	Drum or Warren .	581	0	3	Roscommon .	Boyle . . .	Boyle . . .	Boyle . .	IV.	194
81	Drum West . .	226	0	24m	Galway . .	Galway . .	Rahoon . .	Galway . .	IV.	37
8	Drum West . .	168	3	25	Sligo . .	Carbury . .	Drumcliff . .	Sligo . .	IV.	221
5	Drumwhinny . .	142	1	20	Fermanagh .	Lurg . . .	Magheraculmoney .	Lowtherstown .	III.	208
43, 51	Drumwhisker . .	175	0	29	Tyrone . .	Clogher . .	Clogher . .	Omagh . .	III.	294
50,51,58,59	Drumwood . .	354	1	18	Tipperary, S.R.	Clanwilliam . .	Solloghodmore .	Tipperary .	II.	311
46	Drumwood . .	296	1	4	Tipperary, S.R.	Kilnamanagh Lower	Clogher . .	Cashel . .	II.	322
36	Drumyarkin . .	83	1	19	Fermanagh .	Clankelly . .	Clones . .	Clones . .	III.	196
24	Drumyouth . .	201	0	15n	Cavan . .	Tullyhunco . .	Killashandra .	Cavan . .	III.	98
21	Drung . . .	231	1	12	Cavan . .	Tullygarvey . .	Drung . . .	Cootehill . .	III.	89
4	Drung . . .	197	2	30	Donegal . .	Inishowen East .	Clonca . .	Inishowen .	III.	117
20,21,30,31	Drung . . .	1,757	0	34o	Donegal . .	Inishowen East .	Moville Upper .	Inishowen .	III.	119
4, 5	Drungan . . .	164	3	19	Leitrim . .	Rosclogher . .	Rossinver . .	Ballyshannon .	IV.	111
79	Druganagh East .	241	3	16	Mayo . .	Carra . . .	Kildacommoge .	Castlebar .	IV.	129
79	Druganagh West .	200	3	25	Mayo . .	Carra . . .	Kildacommoge .	Castlebar .	IV.	129
12, 17	Drunkendult East .	223	2	8	Antrim . .	Upper Dunluce .	Ballymoney .	Ballymoney .	III.	18
12, 17	Drunkendult West .	327	0	38	Antrim . .	Upper Dunluce .	Ballymoney .	Ballymoney .	III.	19
22	Drutamon . .	239	3	25	Cavan . .	Clankee . .	Drumgoon . .	Cootehill . .	III.	72
34	Drutamy . .	217	0	13	Cavan . .	Castlerahan .	Killinkere . .	Bailieborough .	III.	69
12	Dryderstown . .	254	1	33p	Westmeath .	Delvin . . .	Killulagh . .	Castletowndelvin	I.	266
17	Duagh . . .	236	0	6q	Kerry . .	Clanmaurice .	Duagh . . .	Listowel . .	II.	168
36	Duagh . . .	303	3	5	Kerry . .	Corkaguiny .	Killiney . .	Dingle . .	II.	178

(a) Including 25A. 3R. 34P. water.
(b) Including 2A. 2R. 30P. water.
(c) Including 0A. 3R. 8P. water.
(d) Including 71A. 0R. 20P. water.
(e) Including 4A. 1R. 5P. water.
(f) Including 28A. 0R. 16P. water.

(g) Including 7A. 1R. 4P. water.
(h) Including 28A. 3R. 0P. detached portion.
(i) Including 38A. 3R. 11P. water.
(j) Including 5A. 0R. 29P. water.
(k) Including 7A. 3R. 39P. water.
(l) Including 39A. 0R. 11P. water.

(m) Including 8A. 1R. 31P. water.
(n) Including 13A. 3R. 10P. water.
(o) Including 2A. 0R. 30P. water.
(p) Including 17A. 0R. 3P. water.
(q) Including 14A. 2R. 24P. water.

No. of Sheet of the Ordnance Survey Maps.	Townlands and Towns.	Area in Statute Acres.	County.	Barony.	Parish.	Poor Law Union in 1857.	Townland Census of 1851, Part I.	
							Vol.	Page
		A. R. P.						
17	Duagh . . .	404 3 15	Waterford .	Middlethird . .	Drumcannon . .	Waterford .	II.	366
17	DUAGH T. . .	—	Kerry . .	Clanmaurice . .	Duagh . .	Listowel .	II.	169
53, 61	Dually . .	319 2 27	Tipperary, S.R. .	Middlethird .	Ballysheehan . .	Cashel .	II.	325
14,15,22,23	Duarrigle . .	520 0 15	Cork, E.R. .	Duhallow . .	Clonfert . .	Kanturk .	II.	68
30, 39	Duarrigle . .	147 2 11a	Cork, E.R. .	Duhallow .	Cullen . .	Millstreet .	II.	70
14	Dubber . .	239 3 38	Dublin . .	Coolock . .	Santry . . .	Dublin North .	I.	29
14	Dubber . .	8 1 23	Dublin . .	Coolock . .	St. Margarets . .	Dublin North .	I.	29
18	DUBLIN CITY . .	—	—	—	—	Dublin North } Dublin South }	I. {	44 / 45
25	Duburren . .	530 1 5	Armagh . .	Orior Upper . .	Killevy . .	Newry .	III.	58
96, 97, 104	Ducalla . .	411 2 39	Kerry . .	Iveragh . .	Killemlagh . .	Cahersiveen .	II.	196
11, 20	Ducarrig . .	227 3 10	Waterford .	Coshmore&Coshbride	Lismore and Mocollop	Lismore .	II.	345
3	Ducavan . .	99 0 16	Louth . .	Upper Dundalk .	Roche . .	Dundalk .	I.	179
4	Duckfield . .	295 2 13	Cavan . .	Tullyhaw . .	Killinagh . .	Enniskillen .	III.	92
48	Duck Island .	3 1 31	Donegal .	Boylagh . .	Templecrone . .	Glenties .	III.	116
48	Duck Island .	13 3 16	Galway . .	Ballynahinch . .	Ballindoon . .	Clifden .	IV.	10
31	Duckspool . .	166 0 1	Waterford .	Decies without Drum	Dungarvan . .	Dungarvan .	II.	355
29, 37	Duckstown . .	788 0 4	Limerick . .	Connello Lower .	Rathkeale . .	Rathkeale .	II.	229
30, 31	Ducleagh . .	323 3 9b	Cork, E.R. .	Duhallow . .	Dromtarriff . .	Kanturk .	II.	71
38, 40	Duffcarrick .	178 2 10	Waterford .	Decies within Drum	Ardmore . .	Youghal .	II.	350
7, 12	Duffcarrick .	81 1 4	Wexford . .	Ballaghkeen . .	Kiltennell . .	Gorey .	I.	297
32	Duffcastle . .	182 1 18	Cavan . .	Castlerahan . .	Crosserlough . .	Cavan .	III.	68
4, 9	Duffery . .	326 0 3	Carlow . .	Rathvilly . .	Haroldstown . .	Shillelagh .	I.	11
22	Duffsfarm . .	378 2 10	Louth . .	Ferrard . .	Termonfeckin . .	Drogheda .	I.	182
25	Duffsland .	46 2 19c	Meath . .	Lower Navan . .	Navan . .	Navan .	I.	215
39	Dufless . .	169 1 31	Tyrone . .	Dungannon Upper .	Artrea . .	Cookstown .	III.	306
90	Dughile and Cooma-vanniha . .	1,195 1 16d	Kerry . .	Iveragh . .	Dromod . .	Cahersiveen .	II.	195
21	Dughlone . .	146 3 5	Wexford . .	Ballaghkeen . .	Kilmuckridge . .	Gorey .	I.	296
31	Duinch . .	690 0 26	Cork, E.R. .	Duhallow . .	Clonmeen . .	Kanturk .	II.	69
19	Dukesmeadows .	8 0 11	Kilkenny . .	Shillelogher .	St. Canice . .	Kilkenny .	I.	115
19	Dukesmeadows .	69 3 4e	Kilkenny . .	Shillelogher .	St. John's . .	Kilkenny .	I.	115
19	Dukesmeadows .	37 0 32f	Kilkenny . .	Shillelogher .	St. Patrick's .	Kilkenny .	I.	116
17, 18	Dukespark or Sher-wood . . .	334 1 7	Carlow . .	Forth . .	Barragh . .	Enniscorthy .	I.	4
11, 17	Dulane . .	231 0 12	Meath . .	Upper Kells .	Dulane . .	Kells .	I.	205
27	DULEEK T. . .	—	Meath . .	Lower Duleek .	Duleek . .	Drogheda .	I.	195
33	Dulick . .	232 2 19g	Clare . .	Bunratty Upper .	Templemaley . .	Ennis .	II.	10
41	Dullaghan . .	697 3 0	Tyrone . .	Omagh East . .	Dromore . .	Omagh .	III.	311
26, 27	Dullaghy . .	519 2 13	Londonderry .	Coleraine . .	Desertoghill . .	Ballymoney .	III.	230
2	Dullerton . .	185 2 4	Tyrone . .	Strabane Lower .	Donaghedy . .	Strabane .	III.	320
8	Dulrush . .	80 2 33	Fermanagh .	Lurg . .	Belleck . .	Ballyshannon .	III.	203
25	Dunabrattin .	422 3 30	Waterford .	Drum . .	Kilbarrymeaden .	Kilmacthomas .	II.	356
28	Dunacleggan .	126 0 8	Queen's Co. .	Clandonagh . .	Rathdowney . .	Donaghmore .	I.	234
50	Dunadry . .	657 3 3	Antrim . .	Upper Antrim .	Nilteen Grange .	Antrim .	III.	6
29	Dunady . .	220 0 30	Londonderry .	Tirkeeran . .	Cumber Upper .	Londonderry .	III.	249
2, 3, 9, 10	Dunaff . .	1,174 3 5	Donegal . .	Inishowen East .	Clonmany . .	Inishowen .	III.	117
2	Dunagard . .	289 0 20	Donegal . .	Inishowen East .	Clonca . .	Inishowen .	III.	117
17	Dunaghy . .	160 1 13	Antrim . .	Upper Dunluce .	Ballymoney . .	Ballymoney .	III.	19
33	Dunaird . .	445 1 9	Antrim . .	Lower Antrim .	Racavan . .	Ballymena .	III.	4
9, 13	Dunaldron . .	77 1 10	Monaghan .	Monaghan . .	Monaghan . .	Monaghan .	III.	277
7	Dunalis Lower .	153 2 19	Londonderry .	Coleraine . .	Dunboe . .	Coleraine .	III.	231
7	Dunalis Upper .	184 3 30	Londonderry .	Coleraine . .	Dunboe . .	Coleraine .	III.	231
13	Dunamase or Park	338 2 0	Queen's Co. .	Maryborough East .	Dysartenos . .	Mountmellick .	I.	241
8	Dunamon . .	348 1 23h	Galway . .	Ballymoe . .	Dunamon . .	Roscommon .	IV.	7
2, 6	Dunamon . .	180 0 18	Westmeath .	Moygoish . .	Street . .	Granard .	I.	281
42, 47	Dunamoney . .	341 1 7	Londonderry .	Loughinsholin .	Magherafelt . .	Magherafelt .	III.	243
54, 61	Dunamony . .	351 2 22	Tyrone . .	Dungannon Middle .	Clonfeacle . .	Dungannon .	III.	299
45	Dunamoy . .	584 3 5	Antrim . .	Upper Antrim .	Rashee . .	Antrim .	III.	7
44,45,50,51	Dunamuggy . .	172 3 18	Antrim . .	Upper Antrim .	Donegore . .	Antrim .	III.	6
39	Dunancory . .	288 2 13	Cavan . .	Castlerahan . .	Lurgan . .	Oldcastle .	III.	69
57	Dunanney . .	367 0 16	Antrim . .	Lower Belfast .	Carnmoney . .	Belfast .	III.	8
28	Dunanny . .	145 2 21	Monaghan .	Farney . .	Donaghmoyne .	Carrickmacross .	III.	270
25, 26	Dunanore . .	326 0 33	Wexford . .	Bantry . .	Clonmore . .	Enniscorthy .	I.	300
30	Dunanore or Golden-town . . .	432 0 33	Wexford . .	Bantry . .	Oldross . .	New Ross .	I.	301
16, 19	Dunany . .	619 3 16i	Louth . .	Ferrard . .	Dunany . .	Ardee .	I.	180
2	Dunard . .	61 1 1	King's Co. .	Kilcoursey .	Ardnurcher or Horse-leap . .	Tullamore .	I.	140
35	Dunaree . .	348 0 5	Cavan . .	Clankee . .	Enniskeen . .	Bailieborough .	III.	73
27, 28	Dunaree . .	299 0 15	Monaghan .	Farney . .	Donaghmoyne .	Carrickmacross .	III.	270
27, 28	Dunaree Latin .	340 1 24j	Monaghan .	Farney . .	Donaghmoyne .	Carrickmacross .	III.	270
41, 42, 46	Dunarnon . .	263 2 5	Londonderry .	Loughinsholin .	Magherafelt . .	Magherafelt .	III.	243
29	Dunarragan . .	110 0 11	Antrim . .	Lower Glenarm .	Tickmacrevan .	Larne .	III.	23
4, 8	Dunavally and Corr	453 1 30	Armagh . .	Armagh . .	Loughgall . .	Armagh .	III.	45

(a) Including 0A. 1R. 16P. water.
(b) Including 5A. 1R. 16P. water.
(c) Including 26A. 3R. 21P. detached portions.
(d) Including 8A. 0R. 13P. water.

(e) { Including 5A. 2R. 16P. River Nore.
Within the Municipal Boundary, 60A. 3R. 0P.
Without the Municipal Boundary, 9A. 0R. 4P.

(f) { Including 3A. 3R. 0P. River Nore.
Within the Municipal Boundary, 0A. 1R. 10P.
Without the Municipal Boundary, 36A. 3R. 22P.

(g) Including 15A. 0R. 30P. water.
(h) Including 23A. 2R. 1P. water.
(i) Including 9A. 2R. 25P. detached portion.
(j) Including 16A. 2R. 5P. water.

No. of Sheet of the Ordnance Survey Maps.	Townlands and Towns.	Area in Statute Acres.	County.	Barony.	Parish.	Poor Law Union in 1857.	Townland Census of 1851, Part I.	
		A. R. P.					Vol.	Page
12	Dunaverney	306 0 9	Antrim	Upper Dunluce	Ballymoney	Ballymoney	III.	19
29	Dunavinally	361 0 7a	Leitrim	Mohill	Cloone	Mohill	IV.	106
19	Dunaweel	651 1 27b	Cavan	Tullyhunco	Killashandra	Cavan	III.	98
16	Dunbarry	40 2 0	Cork, E.R.	Orrery and Kilmore	Bregoge	Mallow	II.	106
16	Dunbarry	108 1 8	Cork, E.R.	Orrery and Kilmore	Churchtown	Mallow	II.	107
130, 139	Dunbeacon	1,459 0 32	Cork, W.R.	West Carbery(W.D.)	Skull	Skull	II.	146
10	Dunbeg	1,142 3 26	Londonderry	Keenaght	Drumachose	NewT⁻Limavady	III.	235
6	Dunbeggan	324 3 33c	Longford	Granard	Columbkille	Granard	I.	156
13, 18	Dunbeggan	284 1 28	Longford	Moydow	Ballymacormick	Longford	I.	160
29	Dunbeg Lower	289 3 35d	Down	Kinelarty	Dromara	Downpatrick	III.	176
29	Dunbeg Upper	385 2 1e	Down	Kinelarty	Dromara	Downpatrick	III.	176
20, 24	Dunbell Big	1,298 0 13f	Kilkenny	Gowran	Dunbell	Kilkenny	I.	94
24	Dunbell Little	36 1 4g	Kilkenny	Gowran	Dunbell	Kilkenny	I.	94
20	DUNBELL T.	—	Kilkenny	Gowran	Dunbell	Kilkenny	I.	94
51	Dunbiggan	295 0 9	Tyrone	Clogher	Clogher	Clogher	III.	292
6, 7, 11	Dunbin Big	423 3 10	Louth	Upper Dundalk	Dunbin	Dundalk	I.	178
6	Dunbin Little	148 0 8	Louth	Upper Dundalk	Dunbin	Dundalk	I.	178
118	Dunbittern East	76 1 31	Cork, W.R.	Bantry	Kilmocomoge	Bantry	II.	120
118	Dunbittern West	73 1 22	Cork, W.R.	Bantry	Kilmocomoge	Bantry	II.	120
17, 30	Dunblaney	450 3 0h	Galway	Ballymoe	Dunmore	Tuam	IV.	7
26, 33	Dunboden Demesne	148 1 9	Westmeath	Fartullagh	Moylisker	Mullingar	I.	269
112, 113	Dunbogey	464 3 30	Cork, E.R.	Kinalea	Nohaval	Kinsale	II.	96
115, 128	Dunboy	203 2 29	Cork, W.R.	Bear	Killaconenagh	Castletown	II.	125
15	Dunboyke	187 2 21	Wicklow	Lower Talbotstown	Hollywood	Baltinglass	I.	360
50	Dunboyne	946 3 31i	Meath	Dunboyne	Dunboyne	Dunshaughlin	I.	199
50	DUNBOYNE T.	—	Meath	Dunboyne	Dunboyne	Dunshaughlin	I.	200
26	Dunbreen	484 3 11	Tyrone	Strabane Upper	Cappagh	Omagh	III.	325
20	Dunbrin Lower	186 0 24j	Queen's Co.	Ballyadams	Ballyadams	Athy	I.	231
20	Dunbrin Upper	167 2 36k	Queen's Co.	Ballyadams	Ballyadams	Athy	I.	231
11, 14	Dunbro	206 1 12	Dublin	Coolock	St. Margarets	Dublin North	I.	29
16	Dunbrock	1,071 2 7	Londonderry	Keenaght	Tamlaght Finlagan	NewT⁻Limavady	III.	237
39	Dunbrody	325 1 26	Wexford	Shelburne	St.James & Dunbrody	New Ross	I.	328
14	Dunbro Great	10 2 2	Dublin	Coolock	Santry	Dublin North	I.	29
14	Dunbro Little	18 3 35	Dublin	Coolock	Santry	Dublin North	I.	29
52, 63	Dunbulloge	518 3 10	Cork, E.R.	Barrymore	Dunbulloge	Cork	II.	54
18	Dunbunrawer	942 2 26	Tyrone	Strabane Upper	Bodoney Lower	Gortin	III.	323
25, 31	Dunbur Head	251 0 7	Wicklow	Arklow	Kilpoole	Rathdrum	I.	345
25, 31	Dunbur Lower	250 1 8	Wicklow	Arklow	Kilpoole	Rathdrum	I.	345
31	Dunbur Upper	393 3 9	Wicklow	Arklow	Kilpoole	Rathdrum	I.	345
18	Dunbyrne	490 1 12	Kildare	Connell	Rathernan	Naas	I.	56
44	Duncannon	243 2 1	Wexford	Shelburne	St.James & Dunbrody	New Ross	I.	328
44	DUNCANNON T.	—	Wexford	Shelburne	St.James & Dunbrody	New Ross	I.	328
45	Duncansland	205 3 2	Antrim	Upper Antrim	Kilbride	Antrim	III.	6
25	Duncansland	24 3 17l	Meath	Lower Navan	Navan	Navan	I.	215
9, 14	Duncarbit	832 2 0	Antrim	Cary	Culfeightrin	Ballycastle	III.	13
1	Duncarbry	166 0 11	Leitrim	Rosclogher	Rossinver	Ballyshannon	IV.	111
32	Dunclug	216 3 27	Antrim	Lower Toome	Kirkinriola	Ballymena	III.	32
16	Duncollog	138 3 34	Cavan	Tullygarvey	Drung	Cootehill	III.	89
46	Duncormick	202 2 17	Wexford	Bargy	Duncormick	Wexford	I.	304
46	Duncormick Hill	166 3 16	Wexford	Bargy	Duncormick	Wexford	I.	304
46	DUNCORMICK T.	—	Wexford	Bargy	Duncormick	Wexford	I.	305
5	Duncreevan	131 3 32	Kildare	Ikeathy&Oughterany	Kilcock	Celbridge	I.	57
5, 6	Dunerun	584 2 28	Londonderry	Keenaght	Magilligan	NewT⁻Limavady	III.	236
57, 65	Duncummin	551 0 26	Tipperary, S.R.	Clanwilliam	Emly	Tipperary	II.	308
7	DUNDALK T.	—	Louth	Upper Dundalk	Dundalk	Dundalk	I.	178
74	Dundanion	198 2 37	Cork, E.R.	Cork	St. Finbars	Cork	II.	65
70	Dundareirke	310 1 12	Cork, W.R.	West Muskerry	Kilnamartry	Macroom	II.	159
23	Dundaryark	546 1 39	Kilkenny	Shillelogher	Danesfort	Thomastown	I.	114
37	Dundavan	216 3 31	Cavan	Clanmahon	Drumlumman	Granard	III.	77
96	*Dundawoona Point*	9 0 28	Donegal	Banagh	Kilcar	Glenties	III.	109
144	Dundeady	354 2 11	Cork, W.R.	Ibane and Barryroe	Rathbarry	Clonakilty	II.	150
55, 63	Dundee	138 3 25	Donegal	Raphoe	Taughboyne	Strabane	III.	143
7	Dunderg	251 3 38	Londonderry	Coleraine	Macosquin	Coleraine	III.	233
18	Dunderk	112 3 1	Meath	Upper Slane	Rathkenny	Navan	I.	225
27	Dundermot	105 2 30	Antrim	Kilconway	Grange of Dundermot	Ballymena	III.	27
34	Dundermot	224 0 28	Roscommon	Ballymoe	Drumatemple	Castlereagh	IV.	191
111	Dunderrow	227 0 28	Cork, E.R.	Kinsale	Dunderrow	Kinsale	II.	99
111	DUNDERROW T.	—	Cork, E.R.	Kinalea	Dunderrow	Kinsale	II.	95
30	Dunderry	246 3 18	Meath	Lower Navan	Churchtown	Navan	I.	214
55, 59	Dundesert	456 2 6	Antrim	Lower Massereene	Killead	Antrim	III.	28
3	Dundillin	145 2 5	Monaghan	Trough	Errigal Trough	Monaghan	III.	284
51, 57, 58	Dundivin Glebe	486 3 15	Tyrone	Clogher	Donacavey	Omagh	III.	294
6	Dundonagh	173 2 11	Monaghan	Trough	Donagh	Monaghan	III.	282

(a) Including 19A. 2R. 20P. water.
(b) Including 146A. 1R. 12P. water.
(c) Including 6A. 3R. 17P. water.
(d) Including 4A. 3R. 36P. water.

(e) Including 1A. 1R. 17P. water.
(f) Including 12A. 3R. 2P. River Nore.
(g) Including 1A. 1R. 32P. River Nore.
(h) Including 14A. 3R. 8P. water.

(i) Including 7A. 0R. 12P. detached portion.
(j) Including 5A. 0R. 15P. River Barrow.
(k) Including 3A. 3R. 0P. River Barrow.
(l) Including 5A. 1R. 1P. detached portion.

No. of Sheet of the Ordnance Survey Maps.	Townlands and Towns.	Area in Statute Acres.			County.	Barony.	Parish.	Poor Law Union in 1857.	Townland Census of 1851, Part I.	
		A.	R.	P.					Vol.	Page
5	DUNDONALD T. . .	—			Down . .	Castlereagh Lower .	Dundonald . .	Belfast . .	III.	162
50, 51	Dundonnell . .	393	0	18	Roscommon .	Athlone . . .	Taghmaconnell .	Ballinasloe .	IV.	185
18, 25	Dundonnell . .	411	3	32	Westmeath .	Rathconrath . .	Churchtown . .	Mullingar .	I.	282
3	Dundooan . .	37	1	6	Londonderry .	North East Liberties of Coleraine . .	Ballyaghran .	Coleraine .	III.	244
3	Dundooan . .	3	2	34	Londonderry .	North East Liberties of Coleraine . .	Ballywillin .	Coleraine .	III.	245
3	Dundooan . .	624	1	8	Londonderry .	North East Liberties of Coleraine. .	Coleraine . .	Coleraine .	III.	246
7, 8, 16, 17	Dundooan Lower .	655	3	19	Donegal .	Kilmacrenan .	Mevagh . .	Millford . .	III.	130
16	Dundooan Upper .	141	2	5	Donegal .	Kilmacrenan .	Mevagh . .	Millford . .	III.	130
73,74,86,87	Dundoogan .	205	3	38	Galway .	Clonmacnowen .	Kilgerrill . .	Ballinasloe .	IV.	25
28, 34	Dundragon .	114	0	3	Cavan .	Clankee . . .	Bailieborough .	Bailieborough .	III.	71
18	Dundrannan .	167	2	11	Monaghan .	Dartree . . .	Ematris . .	Cootehill . .	III.	267
38, 39, 47	Dundrean .	602	2	9	Donegal .	Inishowen West .	Burt . . .	Londonderry .	III.	119
41	Dundressan .	255	2	35	Antrim .	Lower Belfast .	Islandmagee .	Larne . .	III.	8
43	Dundrinne .	368	0	18	Down .	Upper Iveagh,Lr. pt.	Kilmegan . .	Downpatrick .	III.	173
28	Dundrockan .	138	1	39	Monaghan .	Farney . .	Donaghmoyne .	Carrickmacross	III.	270
59, 60	Dundrod .	1,214	1	39	Antrim .	Upper Massereene .	Tullyrusk . .	Lisburn . .	III.	31
16	Dundrudian .	60	1	6	Donegal .	Kilmacrenan .	Clondahorky .	Dunfanaghy .	III.	123
20	Dundrum .	453	2	21	Armagh .	Armagh . .	Keady . .	Armagh . .	III.	45
43, 44	Dundrum .	279	2	12	Down .	Lecale Upper .	Kilmegan . .	Downpatrick .	III.	181
22	Dundrum .	317	2	38	Dublin .	Rathdown .	Taney . . .	Rathdown .	I.	38
51,52,59.60	Dundrum .	1,666	0	15	Tipperary, S.R.	Kilnamanagh Lower	Ballintemple .	Cashel . .	III.	322
22	Dundrum .	273	0	13	Wexford .	Ballaghkeen . .	Kilmuckridge .	Gorey . .	I.	296
5, 8	Dundrumman .	219	2	9	Monaghan .	Monaghan . .	Clones . .	Monaghan .	III.	274
44	DUNDRUM T. . .	—			Down .	Lecale Upper .	Kilmegan . .	Downpatrick .	III.	181
22	DUNDRUM T. . .	—			Dublin .	Rathdown .	Taney . . .	Rathdown .	I.	38
54	Dunduffsfort .	299	2	19	Donegal .	Raphoe . .	Raymoghy . .	Londonderry .	III.	141
53, 54	Dundullerick East .	390	3	16	Cork, E.R. .	Barrymore . .	Templebodan .	Middleton .	II.	58
53, 54	Dundullerick West	146	0	30	Cork, E.R. .	Barrymore . .	Templebodan .	Middleton .	II.	58
23, 26, 27	Duneany .	1,061	1	20	Antrim .	Kilconway . .	Rasharkin . .	Ballymena .	III.	27
27	Duneany .	1,092	3	0	Kildare .	Offaly West .	Duneany . .	Athy . .	I.	72
17, 24	Duneel . .	433	0	30	Westmeath .	Rathconrath . .	Killare . .	Ballymahon .	I.	283
144	Duneen . .	22	2	29	Cork, W.R. .	Ibane and Barryroe	Ardfield . .	Clonakilty .	II.	148
135, 144	Duneen . .	185	3	9	Cork, W.R. .	Ibane and Barryroe	Island . .	Clonakilty .	II.	149
28	Duneena . .	176	2	4	Cavan .	Clankee . . .	Bailieborough .	Bailieborough .	III.	71
30	Dunegan . .	197	0	17	Westmeath .	Clonlonan .	Ballyloughloe .	Athlone .	I.	260
14	Duneight .	416	0	26	Down .	Castlereagh Upper .	Blaris . . .	Lisburn . .	III.	164
31, 32	Dunelty . .	173	1	4a	Monaghan .	Farney . .	Killanny . .	Carrickmacross	III.	271
17	Dunesmullan .	146	0	7	Armagh .	Fews Lower .	Mullaghbrack .	Armagh . .	III.	47
25	Dunevly . .	261	3	32b	Down .	Ards Upper .	Ardkeen . .	Downpatrick .	III.	159
15	Dunfanaghy .	147	3	2	Donegal .	Kilmacrenan .	Clondahorky .	Dunfanaghy .	III.	123
15	DUNFANAGHY T.	—			Donegal .	Kilmacrenan .	Clondahorky .	Dunfanaghy .	III.	124
19	Dunfelimy .	235	1	23	Monaghan .	Cremorne . .	Clontibret . .	Castleblayney .	III.	260
4, 9	Dunferris .	146	3	10	Kerry . .	Iraghticonnor .	Lisselton . .	Listowel . .	II.	192
4	Dunfierth .	651	1	28	Kildare .	Carbury . .	Dunfierth . .	Edenderry .	I.	52
17	Dung . .	186	2	8c	Cavan .	Tullygarvey .	Drumgoon . .	Cootehill . .	III.	88
24	Dungaghy .	207	3	37	Westmeath .	Rathconrath . .	Killare . .	Mullingar .	I.	283
27	Dungall . .	289	3	8	Antrim .	Lower Toome .	Kirkinriola . .	Ballymena .	III.	32
134	Dungannon .	97	3	39	Cork, W.R. .	East Carbery (W.D.)	Kilmacabea . .	Skibbereen .	II.	133
54	DUNGANNON T.	—			Tyrone .	Dungannon Middle .	Drumglass . .	Dungannon .	III.	303
30, 31, 37	Dunganny .	342	2	21	Meath .	Upper Navan .	Kilcooly . .	Trim . .	I.	216
8	Dunganstown .	30	3	9	Dublin .	Balrothery East .	Lusk . . .	Balrothery .	I.	21
13	Dunganstown .	81	0	0	Westmeath .	Delvin . . .	Castletowndelvin	Castletowndelvin	I.	264
8, 9, 13	Dunganstown .	205	1	36	Westmeath .	Delvin . . .	Castletowndelvin	Castletowndelvin	I.	264
34	Dunganstown .	771	1	37	Wexford .	Shelburne . .	Whitechurch .	New Ross . .	I.	329
2	Dunganstown or Bestfield .	55	2	37d	Carlow . .	Carlow . .	Carlow . .	Carlow . .	I.	1
2	Dunganstown or Bestfield .	101	2	33e	Carlow . .	Carlow . .	Painestown .	Carlow . .	I.	2
31	Dunganstown East .	287	1	16	Wicklow . .	Arklow . .	Dunganstown .	Rathdrum .	I.	343
31	Dunganstown West	352	3	23	Wicklow . .	Arklow . .	Dunganstown .	Rathdrum .	I.	343
28	Dunganville Lower	137	1	2	Limerick . .	Glenquin . .	Newcastle . .	Newcastle .	II.	247
28	Dunganville Upper	241	0	30	Limerick . .	Glenquin . .	Newcastle . .	Newcastle .	II.	247
43	Dungar . .	223	2	3	King's Co. .	Ballybritt . .	Corbally . .	Roscrea . .	I.	125
43	Dungar . .	368	1	4	King's Co. .	Ballybritt . .	Roscrea . .	Roscrea . .	I.	126
15	Dungar . .	36	2	26	Roscommon .	Frenchpark . .	Tibohine . .	Castlereagh .	IV.	205
24	Dungarvan .	464	3	35	Kilkenny . .	Gowran . .	Dungarvan .	Thomastown .	I.	94
24	Dungarvan .	41	0	29	Kilkenny . .	Gowran . .	Tullaherin . .	Thomastown .	I.	100
31	Dungarvan .	95	0	32	Waterford .	Decies without Drum	Dungarvan .	Dungarvan .	II.	355
24	Dungarvan Glebe .	48	3	10	Kilkenny . .	Gowran . .	Dungarvan .	Thomastown .	I.	94
24	DUNGARVAN T. .	—			Kilkenny . .	Gowran . .	Dungarvan .	Thomastown .	I.	94
31	DUNGARVAN T. .	---			Waterford .	Decies without Drum	Dungarvan .	Dungarvan .	II.	356

3 I

No. of Sheet of the Ordnance Survey Maps.	Townlands and Towns.	Area in Statute Acres.	County.	Barony.	Parish.	Poor Law Union in 1857.	Townland Census of 1851, Part I.	
		A. R. P.					Vol.	Page
28	Dungate . . .	346 1 29	Tyrone . .	Dungannon Upper .	Kildress . . .	Cookstown .	III.	308
97	Dungeagan . .	207 0 9	Kerry . .	Iveragh . . .	Prior . . .	Cahersiveen .	II.	198
36	Dungeeha . .	130 3 17	Limerick . .	Glenquin . .	Grange . . .	Newcastle .	II.	245
36	Dungeeha . .	173 0 26	Limerick . .	Glenquin . .	Newcastle . .	Newcastle .	II.	247
57	Dungeel . . .	326 2 6a	Kerry . .	Magunihy . .	Killorglin . .	Killarney . .	II.	204
36	Dungeer . . .	411 3 8	Wexford . .	Shelmaliere West .	Taghmon . .	Wexford . .	I.	335
36	Dungeer . . .	22 0 24	Wexford . .	Shelmaliere West .	Whitechurchglynn .	Wexford . .	I.	335
3, 6	Dungillick . .	158 2 35	Monaghan . .	Trough . . .	Errigal Trough .	Monaghan .	III.	284
24,25,30,31	Dungiven . .	738 2 17	Londonderry .	Keenaght . .	Dungiven . .	NewT\nLimavady	III.	236
24, 25	DUNGIVEN T. . .	—	Londonderry .	Keenaght . .	Dungiven . .	NewT\nLimavady	III.	236
33	Dunglady . .	520 3 38	Londonderry .	Loughinsholin .	Maghera . .	Magherafelt .	III.	242
7	Dunglave . .	143 2 2	Cavan . .	Tullyhaw . .	Kinawley . .	Bawnboy . .	III.	93
49	Dunglow . .	406 1 16b	Donegal . .	Boylagh . .	Templecrone .	Glenties . .	III.	115
49	DUNGLOW T. .	—	Donegal . .	Boylagh . .	Templecrone .	Glenties . .	III.	116
23	Dungoghy . .	42 1 28	Fermanagh .	Magherastephana .	Aghavea . .	Lisnaskea .	III.	218
23	Dungolman . .	110 0 21	Westmeath .	Rathconrath .	Ballymore . .	Ballymahon .	I.	281
16	Dungonnan . .	132 0 11	Cavan . .	Tullygarvey .	Drung . . .	Cootehill . .	III.	89
16, 21	Dungonnan . .	51 0 17	Monaghan . .	Dartree . .	Currin . .	Clones . .	III.	265
24	Dungonnell . .	536 3 12	Antrim . .	Kilconway . .	Dunaghy . .	Ballymena .	III.	25
54, 55	Dungonnell . .	771 2 36	Antrim . .	Lower Massereene .	Killead . .	Antrim . .	III.	28
42, 43	Dungooly . .	352 1 10	Kilkenny . .	Iverk . . .	Rathkieran .	Waterford .	I.	107
3, 4	Dungooly . .	609 2 33	Louth . .	Upper Dundalk .	Faughart . .	Dundalk . .	I.	178
50,51,57,58	Dungoran . .	305 2 23	Tyrone . .	Clogher . . .	Donacavey .	Omagh . .	III.	294
17	Dungorbery . .	159 3 24	Antrim . .	Upper Dunluce .	Kilraghts . .	Ballymoney .	III.	19
23	Dungorkin . .	308 3 20	Londonderry .	Tirkeeran . .	Cumber Upper .	NewT\nLimavady	III.	249
79	Dungorman . .	254 2 26c	Donegal . .	Raphoe . .	Donaghmore .	Strabane .	III.	138
55	Dungorman . .	162 2 28	Tyrone . .	Dungannon Middle .	Killyman . .	Dungannon .	III.	303
45, 46	Dungororan . .	262 0 38	Tyrone . .	Dungannon Middle .	Pomeroy . .	Dungannon .	III.	304
113	Dungory East .	132 1 29	Galway . .	Kiltartan . .	Kinvarradoorus .	Gort . .	IV.	49
113	Dungory West .	76 3 2	Galway . .	Kiltartan . .	Kinvarradoorus .	Gort . .	IV.	49
66	Dungourney . .	303 3 2	Cork, E.R. .	Barrymore . .	Dungourney .	Middleton .	II.	54
66	DUNGOURNEY T. .	—	Cork, E.R. .	Barrymore . .	Dungourney .	Middleton .	II.	54
54	Dunguib . . .	195 2 2	Tipperary, S.R. .	Slievardagh .	Graystown . .	Cashel . .	II.	333
54	Dunguib . . .	127 1 1	Tipperary, S.R. .	Slievardagh .	Killenaule . .	Cashel . .	II.	334
15	Dungullion . .	276 2 15	Londonderry .	Tirkeeran . .	Faughanvale .	NewT\nLimavady	III.	250
45, 50	Dungulph . .	271 0 31	Wexford . .	Shelburne . .	Fethard . .	New Ross .	I.	327
42	Dungummin Lower	297 3 26	Cavan . .	Clanmahon . .	Kilbride . .	Oldcastle .	III.	77
42	Dungummin Upper	704 0 13	Cavan . .	Clanmahon . .	Kilbride . .	Oldcastle .	III.	77
2, 3	Dunheeda . .	202 2 37	Meath . .	Morgallion . .	Enniskeen .	Kells . .	I.	209
25	Dunhill . . .	469 0 31	Waterford .	Middlethird .	Dunhill . .	Kilmacthomas .	II.	366
25	Dunhilllodge . .	62 0 30	Waterford .	Middlethird .	Islandikane .	Waterford .	II.	367
20	Dunhugh . .	138 2 35	Londonderry .	Tirkeeran . .	Clondermot .	Londonderry .	III.	248
21	Duninga . . .	1,255 1 17d	Kilkenny . .	Gowran . .	Grangesilvia .	Kilkenny .	I.	95
116	Duniry . . .	117 3 27	Galway . .	Leitrim . .	Duniry . .	Portumna .	IV.	53
5	Dunishal . .	442 0 36	Wexford . .	Scarawalsh .	Carnew . .	Gorey . .	I.	322
71, 83	Dunisky . . .	1,186 2 20e	Cork, W.R. .	West Muskerry .	Dunisky . .	Macroom .	II.	156
103	Dunkellin . .	101 1 7	Galway . .	Dunkellin . .	Kilacely . .	Gort . .	IV.	29
138, 147	Dunkelly East .	290 2 39	Cork, W.R. .	West Carbery(W.D.)	Kilmoe . .	Skull . .	II.	144
138, 147	Dunkelly Middle .	124 2 36	Cork, W.R. .	West Carbery(W.D.)	Kilmoe . .	Skull . .	II.	144
138, 147	Dunkelly West .	380 1 15	Cork, W.R. .	West Carbery(W.D.)	Kilmoe . .	Skull . .	II.	145
97	Dunkereen . .	454 0 20	Cork, E.R. .	Kinalea . .	Inishannon .	Bandon . .	II.	95
45	DUNKERRIN T. .	—	King's Co. .	Clonlisk . .	Dunkerrin .	Roscrea . .	I.	130
92, 93	Dunkerron . .	713 0 28	Kerry . .	Dunkerron South .	Templenoe .	Kenmare .	II.	185
92	Dunkerron Island East	22 0 0	Kerry . .	Dunkerron South .	Templenoe .	Kenmare .	II.	185
92	Dunkerron Island West	30 1 2	Kerry . .	Dunkerron South .	Templenoe .	Kenmare .	II.	185
74, 75	Dunkettle . .	413 3 7	Cork, E.R. .	Barrymore . .	Caherlag . .	Cork . .	II.	52
98	Dunkineely . .	136 1 29	Donegal . .	Banagh . .	Killaghtee .	Donegal .	III.	109
98	DUNKINEELY T. .	—	Donegal . .	Banagh . .	Killaghtee .	Donegal .	III.	110
31	Dunkip . . .	574 3 16	Limerick . .	Coshma . .	Croom . .	Croom . .	II.	242
43	Dunkitt . . .	530 1 4	Kilkenny . .	Ida . . .	Dunkitt . .	Waterford .	I.	101
15	Dunlade Glebe .	349 1 31	Londonderry .	Tirkeeran . .	Faughanvale .	NewT\nLimavady	III.	250
5	Dunlady . . .	544 3 13	Down . .	Castlereagh Lower .	Dundonald .	Belfast .	III.	162
16, 20	Dunlarg . . .	468 0 20	Armagh . .	Armagh . .	Keady . .	Armagh . .	III.	45
14, 15	Dunlavin Lower .	392 3 30	Wicklow . .	Lower Talbotstown .	Dunlavin .	Baltinglass .	I.	360
15	DUNLAVIN T. . .	—	Wicklow . .	Lower Talbotstown .	Dunlavin .	Baltinglass .	I.	360
15	Dunlavin Upper .	452 2 23	Wicklow . .	Lower Talbotstown .	Dunlavin .	Baltinglass .	I.	360
23	Dunleary . .	387 1 12	Dublin . .	Rathdown . .	Monkstown .	Rathdown .	I.	36
16	Dunleckny . .	481 1 29f	Carlow . .	Idrone East .	Dunleckny .	Carlow . .	I.	7
18	Dunleer . . .	99 3 3	Louth . .	Ferrard . .	Dunleer . .	Ardee . .	I.	181
18	DUNLEER T. . .	—	Louth . .	Ferrard . .	Dunleer . .	Ardee . .	I.	181
36	Dunleever Glebe .	305 1 7g	Meath . .	Upper Navan .	Trim . . .	Trim . .	I.	217
42,43,50,51	Dunlewy Far .	4,033 2 24h	Donegal . .	Kilmacrenan .	Tullaghobegly .	Dunfanaghy .	III.	131
42, 43	Dunlewy Near .	1,547 1 0i	Donegal . .	Kilmacrenan .	Tullaghobegly .	Dunfanaghy .	III.	131

(a) Including 14A. 2R. 18P. water.
(b) Including 22A. 2R. 9P. water.
(c) Including 7A. 0R. 7P. water.

(d) Including 16A. 0R. 3P. River Barrow.
(e) Including 4A. 0R. 39P. water.
(f) Including 9A. 1R. 24P. River Barrow.

(g) Including 5A. 1R. 26P. water.
(h) Including 195A. 3R. 34P. water.
(i) Including 9A. 0R. 28P. water.

No. of Sheet of the Ordnance Survey Maps.	Townlands and Towns.	Area in Statute Acres.	County.	Barony.	Parish.	Poor Law Union in 1857.	Townland Census of 1851. Part I.	
		A. R. P.					Vol.	Page
87, 88	Dunlo	346 0 11a	Galway	Clonmacnowen	Kilcloony	Ballinasloe	IV.	25
65, 66	Dunloe Lower	157 2 16b	Kerry	Dunkerron North	Knockane	Killarney	II.	182
65,66,73,74	Dunloe Upper	4,089 1 17c	Kerry	Dunkerron North	Knockane	Killarney	II.	182
35	Dunlogan	1,677 3 2	Londonderry	Loughinsholin	Ballynascreen	Magherafelt	III.	239
30	Dunlom East	137 1 5	Westmeath	Clonlonan	Ballyloughloe	Athlone	I.	260
30	Dunlom West	112 1 34	Westmeath	Clonlonan	Ballyloughloe	Athlone	I.	260
146	Dunlough	319 2 11d	Cork, W.R.	West Carbery (W.D.)	Kilmoe	Skull	II.	145
30, 31	Dunlough	401 0 35	Meath	Upper Navan	Bective	Navan	I.	216
22, 23	Dunloy	833 1 20	Antrim	Kilconway	Finvoy	Ballymoney	III.	26
2, 6	Dunluce	183 3 38	Antrim	Lower Dunluce	Dunluce	Coleraine	III.	17
66	Dunmacmay	305 2 11	Tyrone	Dungannon Lower	Aghaloo	Armagh	III.	296
3, 6	Dunmadigan	64 0 22	Monaghan	Trough	Errigal Trough	Monaghan	III.	284
27	Dunmahon	599 2 37	Cork, E.R.	Fermoy	Dunmahon	Fermoy	II.	79
12	Dunmahon	421 1 14	Louth	Upper Dundalk	Haynestown	Dundalk	I.	178
34,35,39,40	Dunmain	688 3 37	Wexford	Shelburne	Owenduff	New Ross	I.	328
6	Dunmakeever	1,233 2 4	Cavan	Tullyhaw	Kinawley	Enniskillen	III.	93
5, 9	Dunmakelter	257 1 37	Antrim	Cary	Culfeightrin	Ballycastle	III.	13
23	Dunmakenna	201 1 22	Monaghan	Cremorne	Aghnamullen	Cootehill	III.	258
20	Dunmall	85 0 6	Antrim	Lower Glenarm	Ardclinis	Larne	III.	21
48	Dunman	117 1 26	Londonderry	Loughinsholin	Derryloran	Magherafelt	III.	240
56, 57	Dunmaniheen	131 3 10	Kerry	Magunihy	Killorglin	Killarney	II.	204
39	Dunmanoge	318 3 27	Kildare	Kilkea and Moone	Dunmanoge	Athy	I.	59
138, 139	Dunmanus East	543 1 17	Cork, W.R.	West Carbery (W.D.)	Skull	Skull	II.	146
138, 139	Dunmanus West	576 3 26	Cork, W.R.	West Carbery (W.D.)	Skull	Skull	II.	146
107, 108	Dunmanway North	336 2 34e	Cork, W.R.	East Carbery (W.D.)	Fanlobbus	Dunmanway	II.	131
107	Dunmanway South	83 2 8	Cork, W.R.	East Carbery (W.D.)	Fanlobbus	Dunmanway	II.	131
107	DUNMANWAY T.	—	Cork, W.R.	East Carbery (W.D.)	Fanlobbus	Dunmanway	II.	132
83	Dunmarklun	476 1 24	Cork, W.R.	West Muskerry	Kilmurry	Macroom	II.	159
19	Dunmaurice	258 3 17f	Monaghan	Cremorne	Ballybay	Castleblayney	III.	259
27	Dunminning	697 3 6	Antrim	Kilconway	Rasharkin	Ballymena	III.	27
36, 37, 45	Dunmisk	235 1 7	Tyrone	Omagh East	Termonmaguirk	Omagh	III.	314
18, 25	Dunmoe	975 2 26g	Meath	Lower Navan	Dunmoe	Navan	I.	215
33, 34	Dunmoon	264 3 11	Waterford	Coshmore&Coshbride	Kilwatermoy	Lismore	II.	343
33, 34	Dunmoon North	342 0 33	Waterford	Coshmore&Coshbride	Kilwatermoy	Lismore	II.	343
33, 34	Dunmoon South	211 1 27	Waterford	Coshmore&Coshbride	Kilwatermoy	Lismore	II.	343
13	Dunmoran	119 3 30	Sligo	Tireragh	Skeen	Dromore West	IV.	236
135, 144	Dunmore	226 2 20	Cork, W.R.	Ibane and Barryroe	Island	Clonakilty	II.	149
32	Dunmore	141 3 4	Donegal	Boylagh	Templecrone	Glenties	III.	115
26, 27	Dunmore	371 2 22	Donegal	Kilmacrenan	Mevagh	Millford	III.	130
25, 34	Dunmore	1,730 2 35	Donegal	Kilmacrenan	Raymunterdoney	Dunfanaghy	III.	131
27, 28	Dunmore	496 1 6	Donegal	Kilmacrenan	Tullyfern	Millford	III.	133
55	Dunmore	383 3 7	Donegal	Raphoe	Killea	Londonderry	III.	138
29, 36	Dunmore	725 0 35	Down	Kinelarty	Dromara	Downpatrick	III.	176
17	Dunmore	142 2 37	Galway	Dunmore	Dunmore	Tuam	IV.	34
14	Dunmore	242 2 24h	Kilkenny	Fassadinin	Dunmore	Kilkenny	I.	89
14, 19	Dunmore	105 1 32i	Kilkenny	Gowran	St. John's	Kilkenny	I.	98
6, 10	Dunmore	1,122 3 20	Londonderry	Keenaght	Drumachose	New T.Limavady	III.	235
29	Dunmore	286 3 6	Queen's Co.	Clarmallagh	Abbeyleix	Abbeyleix	I.	235
29	Dunmore	446 3 39	Queen's Co.	Clarmallagh	Durrow	Abbeyleix	I.	237
21	Dunmore	999 0 39j	Tyrone	Dungannon Upper	Lissan	Cookstown	III.	309
27	Dunmore	401 0 26	Waterford	Gaultiere	Killea	Waterford	II.	363
17	Dunmore Demesne	121 0 24	Galway	Dunmore	Dunmore	Tuam	IV.	34
14	Dunmore East	479 2 19	Kilkenny	Fassadinin	Dunmore	Kilkenny	I.	89
14	Dunmore Park	399 3 11	Kilkenny	Fassadinin	Dunmore	Kilkenny	I.	89
14	Dunmorepark	111 2 9	Kilkenny	Gowran	St. John's	Kilkenny	I.	98
17	DUNMORE T.	—	Galway	{ Ballymoe } { Dunmore }	Dunmore	Tuam	IV.	{ 8 } { 34 }
27	DUNMORE T.	—	Waterford	Gaultiere	Killea	Waterford	II.	363
14	Dunmore West	825 3 30k	Kilkenny	Fassadinin	Dunmore	Kilkenny	I.	89
19	Dunmoylan	433 1 6	Limerick	Shanid	Dunmoylan	Glin	II.	255
19	Dunmoylan	180 2 20	Limerick	Shanid	Kilmoylan	Glin	II.	256
44	Dunmoyle	587 0 27	Tyrone	Clogher	Errigal Keerogue	Clogher	III.	295
107, 110	Dunmuckrum	823 3 37	Donegal	Tirhugh	Inishmacsaint	Ballyshannon	III.	147
11	Dunmucky	68 3 35	Dublin	Nethercross	Kilsallaghan	Balrothery	I.	31
26	Dunmullan	261 1 2	Tyrone	Strabane Upper	Cappagh	Omagh	III.	325
9	Dunmurraghill	501 3 30	Kildare	Ikeathy&Oughterany	Dunmurraghill	Celbridge	I.	57
23	Dunmurraghoe	75 0 15l	Roscommon	Roscommon	Elphin	Strokestown	IV.	209
64	Dunmurry	460 1 7	Antrim	Upper Belfast	Drumbeg	Lisburn	III.	10
64	Dunmurry	362 0 9m	Antrim	Upper Belfast	Shankill	Lisburn	III.	10
16	Dunmurry	79 2 34	Cavan	Tullygarvey	Drung	Cootehill	III.	89
35	Dunmurry	818 0 9	Londonderry	Loughinsholin	Ballynascreen	Magherafelt	III.	239
22	Dunmurry East	301 1 11	Kildare	Offaly East	Dunmurry	Naas	I.	69

(a) Including 6A. 0R. 20P. water.
(b) Including 6A. 0R. 34P. water.
(c) Including 51A. 1R. 33P. water.
(d) Including 7A. 1R. 5P. water.
(e) Including 8A. 0R. 26P. Dunmanway Lake.

(f) Including 23A. 3R. 9P. water.
(g) Including 17A. 3R. 21P. water.
(h) Including 1A. 3R. 4P. River Nore.
(i) Including 0A. 1R. 4P. River Nore.

(j) Including 18A. 2R. 26P. Lough Fea.
(k) Including 13A. 2R. 0P. River Nore.
(l) Including 1A. 1R. 29P. water.
(m) Including 72A. 2R. 1P. detached portions.

No. of Sheet of the Ordnance Survey Maps.	Townlands and Towns.	Area in Statute Acres.			County.	Barony.	Parish.	Poor Law Union in 1857.	Townland Census of 1851, Part I.	
		A.	R.	P.					Vol.	Page
64	DUNMURRY T. . .	—			Antrim . .	Upper Belfast . .	Drumbeg . .	Lisburn . .	III.	10
22	Dunmurry West .	495	3	38	Kildare . .	Offaly East . .	Dunmurry . .	Naas . .	I.	69
48	Dunnabraggy . .	342	1	4	Londonderry .	Loughinsholin .	Lissan . .	Magherafelt .	III.	242
15, 22	Dunnagorran . .	283	0	8	Meath . .	Fore . . .	Killallon . .	Oldcastle . .	I.	200
1	Dunnalong . .	29	2	31	Tyrone . .	Strabane Lower .	Donaghedy . .	Strabane . .	III.	320
79	Dunnaloob . .	36	1	22a	Donegal . .	Raphoe . .	Urney . . .	Strabane . .	III.	144
17, 22	Dunnaluck . .	175	1	18b	Monaghan . .	Dartree . .	Currin . . .	Cootehill . .	III.	265
27, 31	Dunnamaggan East	212	0	23	Kilkenny . .	Kells . . .	Dunnamaggan .	Callan . .	I.	108
31	DUNNAMAGGAN T. .	—			Kilkenny . .	Kells . . .	Dunnamaggan .	Callan . .	I.	108
27, 31	Dunnamaggan West	293	1	9	Kilkenny . .	Kells . . .	Dunnamaggan .	Callan . .	I.	108
55	Dunnaman . .	328	3	14	Down . .	Mourne . .	Kilkeel . .	Kilkeel . .	III.	183
21, 30	Dunnaman . .	1,521	2	33	Limerick . .	Coshma . .	Croom . .	Croom . .	II.	242
3	Dunnamanagh .	130	3	32	Tyrone . .	Strabane Lower .	Donaghedy . .	Strabane . .	III.	321
3	DUNNAMANAGH T. .	—			Tyrone . .	Strabane Lower .	Donaghedy . .	Strabane . .	III.	321
105, 118	Dunnamark . .	99	0	37	Cork, W.R. .	Bantry . . .	Kilmocomoge .	Bantry . .	II.	120
118	Dunnamark Mill-lot	9	2	37	Cork, W.R. .	Bantry . . .	Kilmocomoge .	Bantry . .	II.	120
23	Dunnamona . .	523	1	38	Tyrone . .	Omagh East .	Donacavey . .	Omagh . .	III.	310
42	Dunnamona . .	450	2	2	Westmeath . .	Kilkenny West	Drumraney . .	Ballymahon .	I.	273
51	Dunnamona Glebe .	216	3	36	Tyrone . .	Clogher . .	Donacavey . .	Omagh . .	III.	294
28	Dunnamore . .	876	2	23	Tyrone . .	Dungannon Upper .	Kildress . .	Cookstown .	III.	309
30	Dunnanelly . .	719	0	14	Down . .	Lecale Lower .	Inch . . .	Downpatrick .	III.	179
37	Dunnanew . .	383	0	5	Down . .	Kinelarty . .	Loughinisland .	Downpatrick .	III.	177
33	Dunnaree . .	239	1	20	Tyrone . .	Omagh West .	Longfield West .	Castlederg .	III.	316
55, 57	Dunnaval . .	273	0	36	Down . .	Mourne . .	Kilkeel . .	Kilkeel . .	III.	183
26	Dunnavenny . .	744	2	34	Londonderry .	Coleraine . .	Errigal . .	Coleraine .	III.	232
67, 68	Dunneill . . .	416	2	19c	Clare . .	Clonderalaw .	Killimer . .	Kilrush . .	II.	16
12, 18	Dunneill . . .	451	3	28	Sligo . .	Tireragh . .	Kilmacshalgan .	Dromore West .	IV.	234
17, 18, 24	Dunneill Mountain or Crowagh . .	3,150	1	1	Sligo . .	Tireragh . .	Kilmacshalgan .	Dromore West .	IV.	234
14, 19	Dunningstown .	467	3	38	Kilkenny . .	Crannagh . .	St. Canice .	Kilkenny . .	I.	87
24, 29	Dunnstown . .	522	1	17	Kildare . .	Naas South .	Carnalway . .	Naas . .	I.	64
6	Dunnyboe . .	519	1	34d	Tyrone . .	Strabane Lower .	Donaghedy . .	Strabane . .	III.	321
144	Dunnycove . .	121	1	14	Cork, W.R. .	Ibane and Barryroe	Ardfield . .	Clonakilty .	II.	148
32	Dunnygarran . .	289	3	4	Antrim . .	Lower Toome .	Ahoghill . .	Ballymena .	III.	32
24	*Dunnyneill Islands* .	2	1	15	Down . .	Dufferin . .	Killyleagh . .	Downpatrick .	III.	167
38	Dunnyvadden .	766	0	15	Antrim . .	Lower Antrim .	Ballyclug . .	Ballymena .	III.	3
31	Dunoge . . .	165	0	12	Monaghan . .	Farney . .	Magheross . .	Carrickmacross	III.	273
15	Dunouragan . .	121	0	24	Antrim . .	Lower Glenarm .	Layd . . .	Ballycastle .	III.	22
12	Dunover . .	480	0	37	Down . .	Ards Upper .	Ballywalter . .	Newtownards .	III.	160
144	Dunowen . .	559	0	10	Cork, W.R. .	Ibane and Barryroe .	Ardfield . .	Clonakilty .	II.	148
144	Dunowen . .	56	3	11	Cork, W.R. .	Ibane and Barryroe .	Island . .	Clonakilty .	II.	149
18, 24	Dunowla . .	3,181	1	11	Sligo . .	Tireragh . .	Kimacshalgan .	Dromore West .	IV.	234
19	Dunran Demesne .	266	2	34	Wicklow . .	Newcastle . .	Killiskey . .	Rathdrum .	I.	352
19	Dunran Demesne .	37	2	23	Wicklow . .	Newcastle . .	Newcastle Upper .	Rathdrum .	I.	353
19	Dunranhill . .	267	1	4	Wicklow . .	Newcastle . .	Newcastle Upper .	Rathdrum .	I.	353
18	Dunraymond . .	120	1	9	Monaghan . .	Monaghan . .	Kilmore . .	Monaghan .	III.	276
39, 45	Dunreagh . .	166	2	4	Meath . .	Ratoath . .	Donaghmore . .	Dunshaughlin .	I.	218
18	Dunree . .	212	1	18	Donegal . .	Inishowen West .	Desertegny . .	Inishowen .	III.	120
16	Dunrevan . .	260	1	36e	Tyrone . .	Strabane Lower .	Ardstraw . .	Castlederg .	III.	319
19	Dunroe . .	700	3	0	Carlow . .	Idrone East .	Sliguff . .	Carlow . .	I.	8
46	Dunronan . .	415	2	23	Londonderry .	Loughinsholin .	Desertlynn . .	Magherafelt .	III.	240
12, 16	Dunrora . .	44	2	31	Cavan . .	Tullygarvey .	Annagh . .	Cavan . .	III.	87
4, 5, 11, 12	Dunross . .	604	2	16	Donegal . .	Inishowen East .	Clonca . .	Inishowen .	III.	117
31	Dunsallagh . .	30	2	2	Waterford . .	Decies without Drum	Clonea . .	Dungarvan .	II.	354
97	Dunsandle . .	651	2	23	Galway . .	Loughrea . .	Lickerrig . .	Loughrea .	IV.	65
37, 38	Dunsany . .	964	0	26	Meath . .	Skreen . .	Dunsany . .	Dunshaughlin .	I.	220
134	Dunscullib . .	168	3	28	Cork, W.R. .	East Carbery (W.D.)	Kilmacabea . .	Skibbereen .	II.	133
17	Dunseark . .	145	2	20	Monaghan . .	Dartree . .	Killeevan . .	Clones . .	III.	268
54	Dunseark . .	181	0	34	Tyrone . .	Dungannon Middle .	Clonfeacle . .	Dungannon .	III.	299
3	Dunseverick (*alias*) Feigh . .	247	0	21	Antrim . .	Cary . . .	Billy . .	Ballycastle .	III.	12
76	Dunsfort . .	141	2	16	Cork, E.R. .	Imokilly . .	Middleton . .	Middleton .	II.	89
38	Dunsfort . .	384	0	5	Down . .	Lecale Lower .	Dunsfort . .	Downpatrick .	III.	179
38, 44	Dunshaughlin .	673	0	38	Meath . .	Ratoath . .	Dunshaughlin .	Dunshaughlin .	I.	218
44	DUNSHAUGHLIN T. .	—			Meath . .	Ratoath . .	Dunshaughlin .	Dunshaughlin .	I.	218
44, 50	Dunsilly . .	941	3	29	Antrim . .	Upper Toome .	Antrim . .	Antrim . .	III.	33
19, 20, 25	Dunsinane . .	222	0	11	Wexford . .	Bantry . .	Templescoby .	Enniscorthy .	I.	303
9, 13	Dunsinare . .	136	2	15	Monaghan . .	Monaghan . .	Monaghan . .	Monaghan .	III.	277
13, 14	Dunsink . .	423	2	15	Dublin . .	Castleknock .	Castleknock . .	Dublin North .	I.	24
14	Dunsoghly . .	265	1	25	Dublin . .	Coolock . .	St. Margarets .	Dublin North .	I.	29
16, 21	Dunsrim . .	197	2	25	Monaghan . .	Dartree . .	Currin . .	Clones . .	III.	266
17, 21	*Dunsy Island* .	33	1	37	Down . .	Dufferin . .	Killinchy . .	Downpatrick .	III.	166
24	*Dunsy Rock* . .	0	2	22	Down . .	Dufferin . .	Killinchy . .	Downpatrick .	III.	166

(a) Including 1A. 2R. 24P. water.
(b) Including 5A. 1R. 31P. water.
(c) Including 1A. 0R. 34P. water.
(d) Including 30A. 2R. 12P. Moor Lough.
(e) Including 2A. 1R. 7P. water.

No. of Sheet of the Ordnance Survey Maps.	Townlands and Towns.	Area in Statute Acres.			County.	Barony.	Parish.	Poor Law Union in 1857.	Townland Census of 1851, Part I.	
		A.	R.	P.					Vol.	Page
35	Duntahane	459	3	11a	Cork, E.R.	Condons&Clangibbon	Fermoy	Fermoy	II.	61
34, 35	Dunteige	447	2	26	Antrim	Lower Glenarm	Tickmacrevan	Larne	III.	23
25	Dunteige	644	2	2	Tyrone	Strabane Lower	Ardstraw	Omagh	III.	319
36, 41	Duntibryan	210	1	2	Londonderry	Loughinsholin	Ballynascreen	Magherafelt	III.	239
17, 18	Duntinny	135	3	29	Donegal	Kilmacrenan	Clondavaddog	Miliford	III.	124
41, 49	Duntryleague	764	0	26	Limerick	Coshlea	Galbally	Mitchelstown	II.	238
36	Dunturk	561	2	29	Down	Kinelarty	Loughinisland	Downpatrick	III.	177
45, 46	Dunturky	502	2	2	Antrim	Lower Belfast	Ballynure	Larne	III.	7
4, 11	Dunville	198	0	13	King's Co.	Warrenstown	Ballyburly	Edenderry	I.	144
69, 78	Dunwiley	490	3	33	Donegal	Raphoe	Stranorlar	Stranorlar	III.	142
34	Dunwish	256	1	25b	Tyrone	Omagh East	Drumragh	Omagh	III.	312
136, 145	Dunworly	328	2	31	Cork, W.R.	Ibane and Barryroe	Lislee	Clonakilty	II.	150
97, 98, 112	Durah	144	2	7	Cork, E.R.	Kinalea	Ballymartle	Kinsale	II.	94
57	Durha	235	1	33	Clare	Moyarta	Kilrush	Kilrush	II.	33
50, 51	Durhams Land	175	1	16	Antrim	Upper Antrim	Donegore	Antrim	III.	6
24	Durhamstown	1,027	0	12	Meath	Lower Navan	Ardbraccan	Navan	I.	214
96, 97	Durless	1,092	0	23c	Mayo	Murrisk	Oughaval	Westport	IV.	161
59, 65	Durless Black	197	0	31	Tyrone	Clogher	Errigal Trough	Clogher	III.	296
59, 65	Durless White	143	0	34	Tyrone	Clogher	Errigal Trough	Clogher	III.	296
41	Durnascallon	499	0	24	Londonderry	Loughinsholin	Desertmartin	Magherafelt	III.	240
103	Durnesh	239	1	24	Donegal	Tirhugh	Drumhome	Ballyshannon	III.	146
10	Durnish	181	0	1	Limerick	Shanid	Robertstown	Glin	II.	257
10	Duross	184	1	20	Fermanagh	Lurg	Derryvullan	Lowtherstown	III.	204
26	Durra	29	2	22d	Clare	Bunratty Upper	Inchicronan	Tulla	II.	9
41, 42	Durra Big	139	0	25	Wexford	Shelmaliere West	Taghmon	Wexford	I.	335
37, 38	Durraclogh	443	3	34	Limerick	Connello Upper	Ballingarry	Croom	II.	230
41	Durra Little	86	0	13	Wexford	Shelmaliere West	Taghmon	Wexford	I.	335
2	Durrow	229	2	27	Galway	Ballymoe	Drumatemple	Glennamaddy	IV.	7
23, 24	Durrow	273	1	6	Waterford	Decies without Drum	Stradbally	Kilmacthomas	II.	360
8, 9	Durrow Demesne	605	3	16	King's Co.	Ballycowan	Durrow	Tullamore	I.	127
29	DURROW T.	—			Queen's Co.	Clarmallagh	Durrow	Abbeyleix	I.	237
29, 35	Durrow Townparks	721	3	36	Queen's Co.	Clarmallagh	Durrow	Abbeyleix	I.	237
16, 18, 21	Duryhole	11	2	37	Louth	Ardee	Mosstown	Ardee	I.	174
21,22,25,26	Duvernagh	754	0	15	Armagh	Orior Upper	Killevy	Newry	III.	58
33	Duvillaun-beg	24	2	19	Mayo	Erris	Kilmore	Belmullet	IV.	146
33	Duvillaun More	155	1	4	Mayo	Erris	Kilmore	Belmullet	IV.	146
22	Dyan	32	1	7	Monaghan	Dartree	Ematris	Cootehill	III.	267
12	Dyan	57	1	18	Monaghan	Dartree	Killeevan	Monaghan	III.	268
67	Dyan	149	3	5	Tyrone	Dungannon Lower	Aghaloo	Armagh	III.	296
13	Dyrick	244	1	18	Waterford	Decies without Drum	Lickoran	Lismore	II.	358
12, 21	Dyrick Lower	841	2	4	Waterford	Coshmore&Coshbride	Lismore and Mocollop	Lismore	II.	345
12	Dyrick Upper	232	0	5	Waterford	Coshmore&Coshbride	Lismore and Mocollop	Lismore	II.	345
67	Dysart	29	1	31	Cork, E.R.	Imokilly	Youghal	Youghal	II.	91
4	Dysart	632	2	4	Kildare	Carbury	Dunfierth	Edenderry	I.	52
28, 32	Dysart	239	0	1e	Kilkenny	Gowran	Pleberstown	Thomastown	I.	97
18	Dysart	200	1	26	Louth	Ferrard	Dysart	Drogheda	I.	181
13, 18	Dysart	773	0	17	Queen's Co.	Maryborough East	Dysartenos	Mountmellick	I.	241
13	Dysart	167	0	7f	Westmeath	Delvin	Killulagh	Castletowndelvin	I.	266
25	Dysart	1,827	0	15	Westmeath	Moyashel & Magheradernon	Dysart	Mullingar	I.	274
16, 17	Dysartbeagh	438	0	15	Queen's Co.	Maryborough West	Clonenagh and Clonagheen	Mountmellick	I.	243
10	Dysart Glebe	144	2	36	Kilkenny	Fassadinin	Dysart	Castlecomer	I.	89
67	Dysert	327	0	39	Clare	Clonderalaw	Killimer	Kilrush	II.	16
25	Dysert	80	0	38	Clare	Inchiquin	Dysert	Ennis	II.	24
31	Dysert	639	2	37g	Cork, E.R.	Duhallow	Dromtarriff	Kanturk	II.	71
9, 10	Dysert	337	3	3	Kerry	Clanmaurice	Dysert	Listowel	II.	169
10	Dysert	84	3	1	Limerick	Shanid	Robertstown	Rathkeale	II.	257
40	Dysert	224	3	17	Waterford	Decies within Drum	Ardmore	Youghal	II.	350
9, 10	Dysert Marshes	298	0	0	Kerry	Clanmaurice	Dysert	Listowel	II.	169
19,20.24,25	Eadestown	461	2	11	Kildare	Naas North	Rathmore	Naas	I.	62
21, 27	Eadestown Hill	124	2	11	Wicklow	Upper Talbotstown	Donaghmore	Baltinglass	I.	363
21	Eadestown Middle	248	1	35	Wicklow	Upper Talbotstown	Donaghmore	Baltinglass	I.	363
21	Eadestown North	151	2	25	Wicklow	Upper Talbotstown	Donaghmore	Baltinglass	I.	363
21, 27	Eadestown South	175	1	20	Wicklow	Upper Talbotstown	Donaghmore	Baltinglass	I.	363
4, 5, 9, 10	Eaglehill	303	2	8	Carlow	Rathvilly	Clonmore	Shillelagh	I.	10
4, 5	Eaglehill	154	1	10	Carlow	Rathvilly	Hacketstown	Shillelagh	I.	11
9	Eaglehill	101	2	8	Cavan	Tullyhaw	Templeport	Bawnboy	III.	94
116, 125	Eaglehill	160	1	25	Galway	Leitrim	Ballynakill	Loughrea	IV.	51
27, 28	Eaglehill	337	3	34	Kildare	Offaly West	Kilrush	Athy	I.	73

(a) Including 12A. 1R. 39P. water.
(b) Including 5A. 2R. 2P. water.
(c) Including 4A. 3R. 4P. water.

(d) Including 0A. 3R. 5P. water.
(e) Including 9A. 2R. 2r. River Nore.

(f) Including 4A. 1R. 17P. water.
(g) Including 10A. 0R. 16P. water.

No. of Sheet of the Ordnance Survey Maps.	Townlands and Towns.	Area in Statute Acres.			County.	Barony.	Parish.	Poor Law Union in 1857.	Townland Census of 1851. Part I.	
		A.	R.	P.					Vol.	Page
22	Eaglehill . .	215	2	29	Waterford .	Decies without Drum	Modelligo . .	Dungarvan .	II.	359
5, 9, 10	Eaglehill (*Newton*) .	161	2	1	Carlow . .	Rathvilly . .	Clonmore . .	Shillelagh . .	I.	10
14, 19, 24	Eagle Hill or Ouna .	2,888	2	31	Antrim . .	Lower Glenarm .	Layd . .	Ballycastle .	III.	23
9	*Eagle Island* . .	1	2	3	Fermanagh .	Lurg . .	Belleek . .	Ballyshannon .	III.	204
2	*Eagle Island* . .	14	1	35	Mayo . .	Erris . .	Kilmore . .	Belmullet .	IV.	146
44	*Eagle Island* . .	0	2	1	Sligo . .	Coolavin . .	Kilfree . .	Boyle . .	IV.	224
20	Eagleshill . .	67	1	21	Kilkenny .	Gowran . .	Clara . .	Kilkenny . .	I.	94
98	*Eagle's Nest* . .	0	0	16	Donegal .	Banagh . .	Inver . .	Donegal . .	III.	108
8	Eagralougher . .	234	0	3	Armagh .	Oneilland West	Loughgall .	Armagh . .	III.	54
7	Eagry . . .	169	3	33	Antrim . .	Lower Dunluce .	Billy . .	Coleraine .	III.	16
5, 9	Eantybeg North .	113	0	19	Clare . .	Burren . .	Kilcorney .	Ballyvaghan .	II.	12
9	Eantybeg South .	117	0	25	Clare . .	Burren . .	Kilcorney .	Ballyvaghan .	II.	12
5, 6, 9, 10	Eantymore . .	467	3	32	Clare . .	Burren . .	Kilcorney .	Ballyvaghan .	II.	12
48, 53	Eardownes Great .	161	0	17	Wexford .	Forth . .	Ladysisland .	Wexford .	I.	311
48	Eardownes Little .	25	0	4	Wexford .	Forth . .	Ladysisland .	Wexford .	I.	311
53	Earlhill . . .	99	3	12	Clare . .	Tulla Lower .	O'Briensbridge .	Limerick .	II.	38
13	Earlsbog . . .	195	2	25	Kilkenny .	Crannagh .	Odagh . .	Kilkenny .	I.	86
20, 24	Earlsbog Commons .	77	3	4	Kilkenny .	Gowran . .	Gowran . .	Kilkenny .	I.	95
2	Earlscarrron . .	32	2	21	King's Co. .	Kilcoursey .	Kilcumreragh .	Tullamore .	I.	141
33	Earlsfield or Carrow- cauly . .	115	0	20	Sligo . .	Corran . .	Emlaghfad .	Sligo . .	IV.	226
6	Earlsfields . .	47	1	0	Cork, E.R. .	Orrery and Kilmore	Shandrum .	Kanturk .	II.	110
4, 5	Earlsgarden . .	208	0	18	Kilkenny .	Fassadinin .	Attanagh .	Castlecomer .	I.	88
5	Earlsgarden . .	47	1	12	Kilkenny .	Fassadinin .	Rosconnell .	Castlecomer .	I.	91
32	Earlsgrove . .	108	0	2	Kilkenny .	Knocktopher .	Knocktopher .	Thomastown .	I.	112
48,49,54,55	Earlshill . .	277	2	18	Tipperary, S.R.	Slievardagh .	Ballingarry .	Callan . .	II.	331
26	*Earls Island* . .	6	3	13	Galway . .	Ross . .	Ross . .	Oughterard .	IV.	74
26	Earlsland . .	61	1	22	Kilkenny .	Callan . .	Callan . .	Callan . .	I.	83
14	Earlsmeadow or Lis- clogher Little .	199	0	18	Westmeath .	Delvin . .	Castletowndelvin .	Castletowndelvin	I.	264
105	Earlspark . .	587	2	10	Galway . .	Loughrea .	Killeenadeema .	Loughrea .	IV.	64
105	Earlspark . .	326	0	6	Galway . .	Loughrea .	Loughrea .	Loughrea .	IV.	65
24	Earlsquarter . .	126	2	1	Kilkenny .	Gowran . .	Tullaherin .	Thomastown .	I.	100
8	Earls Quarter . .	117	1	3	Louth . .	Lower Dundalk .	Carlingford .	Dundalk .	I.	176
36, 40	Earlsrath . .	144	0	25	Kilkenny .	Knocktopher .	Kilbeacon .	Waterford .	I.	112
39	Eary Lower . .	120	0	19	Tyrone .	Dungannon Upper .	Arboe . .	Cookstown .	III.	305
39	Eary Upper . .	133	0	6	Tyrone .	Dungannon Upper .	Ballyclog .	Cookstown .	III.	306
11	Easky T. . .	—			Sligo . .	Tireragh . .	Easky . .	Dromore West .	IV.	234
126	Easterfield . .	251	2	24	Galway . .	Leitrim . .	Ballynakill .	Portumna .	IV.	51
20	Easterfield or Corna- cask . .	484	3	19a	Galway . .	Killian . .	Athleague .	Mountbellew .	IV.	43
121	*Easter Island* . .	0	2	33	Mayo . .	Kilmaine .	Cong . .	Ballinrobe .	IV.	154
121	*Easter Rock Island* .	0	0	29	Mayo . .	Kilmaine .	Cong . .	Ballinrobe .	IV.	154
12, 13	Easthill . . .	72	2	0	Wicklow .	Newcastle .	Newcastle Upper .	Rathdrum .	I.	353
60, 61	Eastlone . . .	87	1	22	Tipperary, S.R.	Middlethird .	St. Patricksrock .	Cashel . .	II.	330
11	Easton . . .	134	3	9	Kildare . .	North Salt .	Leixlip . .	Celbridge . .	I.	75
6	East Park . .	181	0	25	Antrim . .	Lower Dunluce .	Dunluce . .	Coleraine .	III.	17
9, 10	East Torr . .	612	1	4	Antrim . .	Cary . .	Culfeightrin .	Ballycastle .	III.	13
98	Eastwell . .	597	0	1	Galway . .	Kilconnell .	Killallaghtan .	Ballinasloe .	IV.	41
29	Eastwood . .	225	1	15	Tipperary, N.R.	Eliogarty .	Templemore .	Thurles . .	II.	272
45	Ecawn . .	129	0	3	Wicklow .	Arklow . .	Arklow . .	Rathdrum .	I.	341
53	Ecclestown . .	79	2	17	Wexford .	Forth . .	Tacumshin .	Wexford .	I.	315
50, 51	Ecclesville Demesne	229	0	4	Tyrone .	Clogher . .	Donacavey .	Omagh . .	III.	294
18	Echlinville . .	481	2	16	Down . .	Ards Upper .	St. Andrews (*alias*) Ballyhalbert .	Newtownards .	III.	161
93	Eddrim Glebe . .	641	1	27b	Donegal .	Banagh . .	Killymard .	Donegal .	III.	111
16,17,21,22	Eden . . .	693	0	39	Antrim . .	Kilconway .	Finvoy . .	Ballymoney .	III.	26
64	Eden . . .	248	3	39c	Donegal .	Boylagh .	Inishkcel .	Glenties . .	III.	112
18	Eden . . .	187	3	37	Leitrim .	Drumahaire .	Drumreilly .	Cark. on Shannon	IV.	95
5	Eden . . .	211	0	8	Leitrim .	Rosclogher .	Rossinver .	Ballyshannon .	IV.	111
25, 31, 32	Eden . . .	1,960	2	36	Londonderry .	Keenaght .	Dungiven .	NewᵀᵉLimavady	III.	236
33, 37	Eden . . .	755	0	18	Londonderry .	Loughinsholin .	Tamlaght O'Crilly .	Magherafelt .	III.	243
30	Eden . . .	191	3	36	Londonderry .	Tirkeeran .	Banagher .	Londonderry .	III.	247
81, 92	Eden . . .	327	2	14	Mayo . .	Costello .	Knock . .	Claremorris .	IV.	143
5	Eden . . .	240	0	17	Meath . .	Lower Kells .	Kilmainham .	Kells . .	I.	203
14, 20	Eden . . .	422	2	7	Roscommon .	Frenchpark .	Tibohine . .	Castlereagh .	IV.	205
2	Eden . . .	250	3	7	Tyrone .	Strabane Lower	Donaghedy .	Strabane .	III.	321
45, 53	Edenacarnan North .	211	2	19	Donegal .	Kilmacrenan .	Kilmacrenan .	Letterkenny .	III.	129
45, 53	Edenacarnan South .	230	1	4	Donegal .	Kilmacrenan .	Kilmacrenan .	Letterkenny .	III.	129
6	Edenaclogh . .	129	1	12	Fermanagh .	Lurg . .	Magheraculmoney .	Lowtherstown .	III.	208
53, 54	Edenacrannon .	270	3	11	Tyrone .	Dungannon Middle .	Donaghmore .	Dungannon .	III.	302
18	Edenafelklu . .	192	3	19	Monaghan .	Cremorne .	Tullycorbet .	Monaghan .	III.	263
42	Edenafogry . .	213	2	20	Tyrone .	Omagh East .	Donacavey .	Omagh . .	III.	310
12	Edenaforan . .	127	2	12	Monaghan .	Dartree . .	Clones . .	Clones . .	III.	264

No. of Sheet of the Ordnance Survey Maps	Townlands and Towns	Area in Statute Acres.			County.	Barony.	Parish.	Poor Law Union in 1857.	Townland Census of 1851, Part I.	
		A.	R.	P.					Vol.	Page
41	Edenagarry	561	1	38	Down	Upper Iveagh, Lr. pt.	Drumballyroney	Banbridge	III.	172
6	Edenagee	58	2	13	Fermanagh	Lurg	Magheraculmoney	Lowtherstown	III.	208
60	Edenageeragh	334	0	22a	Tyrone	Dungannon Lower	Aghaloo	Dungannon	III.	296
23	Edenagilhorn	302	0	3	Fermanagh	Magherastephana	Aghavea	Lisnaskea	III.	218
12	Edenagoash	122	1	18	Monaghan	Dartree	Killeevan	Monaghan	III.	268
49, 50	Edenagon	223	2	25	Tyrone	Omagh East	Dromore	Lowtherstown	III.	311
107	Edenagor	117	2	15b	Donegal	Tirhugh	Kilbarron	Ballyshannon	III.	148
6	Edenagrena	163	0	39c	Louth	Upper Dundalk	Inishkeen	Dundalk	I.	179
3	Edenakill	284	2	20	Louth	Upper Dundalk	Roche	Dundalk	I.	179
29	Edenamo	86	2	24	Monaghan	Farney	Inishkeen	Dundalk	I.	271
78, 87	Edenamoghil	269	2	23	Donegal	Raphoe	Donaghmore	Stranorlar	III.	138
6	Edenamohill Black	144	0	10	Fermanagh	Lurg	Magheraculmoney	Lowtherstown	III.	208
6	Edenamohill Under	108	3	7	Fermanagh	Lurg	Magheraculmoney	Lowtherstown	III.	208
93	Edenamuck	165	2	13	Donegal	Banagh	Inver	Donegal	III.	107
16	Edenan	42	0	19	Roscommon	Roscommon	Shankill	Strokestown	IV.	213
24	Edenanay	125	0	5	Monaghan	Cremorne	Ballybay	Castleblayney	III.	259
18	Edenaneane	246	1	13	Monaghan	Cremorne	Ballybay	Castleblayney	III.	259
15, 16	Edenan and Kinclare	624	1	10	Roscommon	Roscommon	Shankill	Boyle	IV.	213
32	Edenappa	504	0	38	Armagh	Orior Upper	Jonesborough	Newry	III.	57
10	Edenaquin	152	3	13	Louth	Ardee	Louth	Dundalk	I.	173
23	Edenasop	274	0	6	Tyrone	Omagh West	Termonamongan	Castlederg	III.	317
51	Edenasop East	23	2	38	Tyrone	Clogher	Donacavey	Omagh	III.	294
51	Edenasop West	25	0	33	Tyrone	Clogher	Donacavey	Omagh	III.	294
51, 58	Edenatoodry	288	3	28	Tyrone	Clogher	Donacavey	Omagh	III.	294
6	Edenaveagh	105	0	13	Fermanagh	Lurg	Drumkeeran	Lowtherstown	III.	206
12	Edenaveys	231	3	11	Armagh	Fews Lower	Lisnadill	Armagh	III.	47
24	Edenavow	90	1	2	Leitrim	Leitrim	Kiltubbrid	Cark. on Shannon	IV.	103
11	Eden Back	563	0	14d	Tyrone	Strabane Upper	Bodoney Upper	Gortin	III.	324
20	Edenballycoggill	255	1	39	Down	Lower Iveagh, Up.pt.	Magheralin	Lurgan	III.	170
13, 20	Edenballymore	567	1	33	Londonderry	North West Liberties of Londonderry	Templemore	Londonderry	III.	246
23	Edenbane	82	0	17	Fermanagh	Tirkennedy	Enniskillen	Lisnaskea	III.	222
26	Edenbane	153	2	2	Londonderry	Coleraine	Desertoghill	Coleraine	III.	230
33	Edenbaun	313	1	32e	Leitrim	Mohill	Cloone	Mohill	IV.	106
9	Edenbaun	319	3	21	Sligo	Carbury	Calry	Sligo	IV.	220
23	Edenbrone	129	1	39	Monaghan	Cremorne	Aghnamullen	Cootehill	III.	258
10	Edenbrone	36	3	10	Monaghan	Monaghan	Monaghan	Monaghan	III.	277
9	Edenbrone	67	1	17	Monaghan	Monaghan	Tedavnet	Monaghan	III.	279
43, 44	Edenburt	1,096	1	9	Cavan	Castlerahan	Loughan or Castlekeeran	Oldcastle	III.	69
6	Edenclaw Great	204	3	26	Fermanagh	Lurg	Magheraculmoney	Lowtherstown	III.	208
6	Edenclaw Little	73	2	19	Fermanagh	Lurg	Magheraculmoney	Lowtherstown	III.	208
6	Edencullentragh or Hollyfield	81	2	32	Sligo	Carbury	Rossinver	Sligo	IV.	223
108, 121	Edencurra	516	1	25f	Cork, W.R.	East Carbery (E.D.)	Ballymoney	Dunmanway	II.	127
29, 36	Edendarriff	551	3	30g	Down	Kinelarty	Dromara	Downpatrick	III.	176
60, 61	Edenderry	505	2	23	Antrim	Upper Belfast	Shankill	Belfast	III.	35
9, 10	Edenderry	247	1	19h	Armagh	Oneilland East	Seagoe	Lurgan	III.	50
7, 8	Edenderry	170	3	26i	Armagh	Tiranny	Eglish	Armagh	III.	59
9	Edenderry	126	0	14j	Down	Castlereagh Upper	Drumbo	Lisburn	III.	164
33	Edenderry	261	3	29	Down	Upper Iveagh, Up.pt.	Aghaderg	Banbridge	III.	174
26, 27	Edenderry	490	1	11	Down	Upper Iveagh, Up.pt.	Seapatrick	Banbridge	III.	176
11, 12	Edenderry	2,003	2	10	King's Co.	Coolestown	Monasteroris	Edenderry	I.	133
35, 43	Edenderry	326	3	8k	Tyrone	Omagh East	Cappagh	Omagh	III.	310
60	EDENDERRY T.	—			Antrim	Upper Belfast	Shankill	Belfast	III.	35
12	EDENDERRY T.	—			King's Co.	Coolestown	Monasteroris	Edenderry	I.	133
37	Edendoit	350	1	8l	Tyrone	Dungannon Upper	Desertcreat	Cookstown	III.	307
46	Edendork	111	0	13	Tyrone	Dungannon Middle	Tullyniskan	Dungannon	III.	304
75	Edenfinfreagh	393	3	39m	Donegal	Boylagh	Inishkeel	Glenties	III.	112
23, 24	Edenforan	209	0	20	Monaghan	Cremorne	Aghnamullen	Cootehill	III.	258
11	Eden Fore	414	3	0n	Tyrone	Strabane Upper	Bodoney Upper	Gortin	III.	324
28	Edengilrevy	181	0	22o	Monaghan	Farney	Donaghmoyne	Carrickmacross	III.	270
2	Edengora	230	0	10	Meath	Lower Kells	Kilmainham	Kells	I.	203
104	Edenhill	73	2	11	Galway	Loughrea	Killogilleen	Loughrea	IV.	64
9	Eden Island	118	0	10	Monaghan	Trough	Donagh	Monaghan	III.	282
12, 16, 17	Edenknappagh	341	2	9	Armagh	Fews Lower	Lisnadill	Armagh	III.	47
11	Eden Mill	30	2	20p	Tyrone	Strabane Upper	Bodoney Upper	Gortin	III.	324
4	Edenmore	716	2	29	Cavan	Tullyhaw	Killinagh	Enniskillen	III.	92
71	Edenmore	200	2	29	Donegal	Raphoe	Clonleigh	Strabane	III.	135
78	Edenmore	258	3	13q	Donegal	Raphoe	Donaghmore	Stranorlar	III.	138
47, 51	Edenmore	396	1	16	Down	Lordship of Newry	Newry	Newry	III.	182
13, 20	Edenmore	251	2	16	Down	Lower Iveagh, Up.pt.	Magheralin	Lurgan	III.	170
15	Edenmore	123	2	33	Dublin	Coolock	Raheny	Dublin North	I.	28

(a) Including 6A. 1R. 22P. Lake.
(b) Including 3A. 1R. 38P. water.
(c) Including 0A. 3R. 34P. water.
(d) Including 2A. 0R. 6P. water.
(e) Including 17A. 0R. 20P. water.
(f) Including 12A. 1R. 24P. Ballynacarriga Lough.

(g) Including 6A. 2R. 15P. water.
(h) Including 12A. 1R. 31P. water.
(i) Including 4A. 1R. 15P. water.
(j) Including 2A. 0R. 25P. water.
(k) Including 9A. 3R. 0P. water.
(l) Including 5A. 2R. 36P. Lough Bracken.

(m) Including 15A. 3R. 11P. water.
(n) Including 2A. 2R. 21P. water.
(o) Including 10A. 2R. 4P. water.
(p) Including 0A. 0R. 35P. water.
(q) Including 5A. 3R. 0P. water.

No. of Sheet of the Ordnance Survey Maps.	Townlands and Towns.	Area in Statute Acres.			County.	Barony.	Parish.	Poor Law Union in 1857.	Townland Census of 1851, Part I.	
		A.	R.	P.					Vol.	Page
26, 32	Edenmore	139	3	2	Fermanagh	Clanawley	Killesher	Enniskillen	III.	192
17, 23	Edenmore	538	3	35	Fermanagh	Tirkennedy	Enniskillen	Enniskillen	III.	222
28	Edenmore	71	2	25	Leitrim	Leitrim	Kiltubbrid	Car^t. on Shannon	IV.	103
10, 17	Edenmore	236	3	25	Londonderry	Keenaght	Balteagh	New Tⁿ Limavady	III.	234
5	Edenmore	898	1	21	Longford	Longford	Killoe	Longford	I.	159
6	Edenmore	110	2	11	Monaghan	Trough	Donagh	Monaghan	III.	282
3	Edenmore	69	3	34	Monaghan	Trough	Errigal Trough	Clogher	III.	284
76	Edenmore	78	2	4	Tipperary, S.R.	Iffa and Offa West	Caher	Clogheen	II.	317
59	Edenmore	30	3	8	Tyrone	Clogher	Errigal Trough	Clogher	III.	296
34	Edennagully	321	1	14	Cavan	Clankee	Enniskeen	Bailieborough	III.	73
27	Edenordinary	452	1	26	Down	Lower Iveagh, Lr. pt.	Dromore	Banbridge	III.	168
42	Edenreagh	165	0	7	Londonderry	Loughinsholin	Ballyscullion	Magherafelt	III.	239
2	Edenreagh	246	2	27	Sligo	Carbury	Ahamlish	Sligo	IV.	219
23	Edenreagh	630	0	30	Tyrone	Omagh West	Termonamongan	Castlederg	III.	317
14	Edenreagh Beg	217	0	4	Londonderry	Tirkeeran	Clondermot	Londonderry	III.	248
14	Edenreagh More	270	0	28	Londonderry	Tirkeeran	Clondermot	Londonderry	III.	248
10, 16	Edenslate	122	2	33a	Down	Castlereagh Lower	Comber	Newtownards	III.	162
11	Edenterriff	116	2	18b	Cavan	Lower Loughtee	Annagh	Cavan	III.	79
21, 26	Edenticlare	305	0	26	Cavan	Upper Loughtee	Annagelliff	Cavan	III.	81
5	Edenticromman	173	0	4	Fermanagh	Lurg	Drumkeeran	Lowtherstown	III.	206
14, 21	Edenticullo	347	1	12c	Down	Lower Iveagh, Up. pt.	Hillsborough	Lisburn	III.	169
60	Edentiloan	243	3	5d	Tyrone	Dungannon Lower	Carnteel	Dungannon	III.	297
20, 27	Edentiroory	257	2	32	Down	Lower Iveagh, Lr. pt.	Dromore	Banbridge	III.	168
1	Edentober	458	1	16	Louth	Lower Dundalk	Ballymascanlan	Dundalk	I.	176
53	EDEN T.	—			Antrim	Carrickfergus	Carrickfergus	Larne	III.	11
21	Edentrillick	917	1	37	Down	Lower Iveagh, Lr. pt.	Dromore	Lisburn	III.	168
47, 51	Edentrumly	445	0	30	Down	Upper Iveagh, Up. pt.	Clonallan	Newry	III.	174
59	Edenturcher	144	0	22	Antrim	Upper Massereene	Glenavy	Lisburn	III.	30
44	Edenvale	516	2	20	Antrim	Upper Toome	Shilvodan Grange	Antrim	III.	35
33, 41	Edenvale	148	3	22e	Clare	Islands	Killone	Ennis	II.	30
2	Edenvella	454	0	36	Leitrim	Rosclogher	Rossinver	Ballyshannon	IV.	111
17	Edenykennedy	304	1	18	Armagh	Fews Lower	Kilclooney	Armagh	III.	46
22, 26	Edera	303	3	10	Longford	Rathcline	Shrule	Ballymahon	I.	165
4	Edercloon	201	1	16	Longford	Longford	Mohill	Longford	I.	160
28	Ederdacurragh	165	1	6f	Fermanagh	Magherastephana	Aghalurcher	Lisnaskea	III.	216
27	Ederdaglass or Hollybank	50	0	3	Fermanagh	Tirkennedy	Cleenish	Enniskillen	III.	220
27	Ederdaglass or Hollybank	4	3	34	Fermanagh	Tirkennedy	Derryvullan	Enniskillen	III.	221
18	Ederglen	861	3	5	Mayo	Erris	Kilcommon	Belmullet	IV.	144
21	Edergole	173	1	33	Cavan	Upper Loughtee	Larah	Cavan	III.	85
82	Edergole	196	1	34	Donegal	Banagh	Inishkeel	Glenties	III.	106
76, 85	Edergole	4,370	1	18g	Donegal	Banagh	Killymard	Donegal	III.	111
28	Edergole	38	2	14	Fermanagh	Magherastephana	Aghalurcher	Lisnaskea	III.	216
14, 15	Edergole	249	3	5	Leitrim	Drumahaire	Killanummery	Manorhamilton	IV.	98
29, 33	Edergole	279	3	39	Leitrim	Mohill	Cloone	Mohill	IV.	106
18	Edergole	156	3	30	Monaghan	Dartree	Ematris	Cootehill	III.	267
57, 58	Edergole	1,094	3	11	Tyrone	Clogher	Clogher	Clogher	III.	292
16	Edergole or Cortrasna	189	3	18	Cavan	Tullygarvey	Drung	Cootehill	III.	88
34	*Edergole Island*	17	1	27	Fermanagh	Magherastephana	Aghalurcher	Lisnaskea	III.	217
43	Edergool	159	2	26	Fermanagh	Coole	Drummully	Clones	III.	199
43	Edergoole Lower	268	1	14h	Tyrone	Omagh East	Drumragh	Omagh	III.	312
42, 43	Edergoole Upper	329	1	25i	Tyrone	Omagh East	Drumragh	Omagh	III.	312
9	Ederland	67	1	28	Longford	Granard	Clonbroney	Granard	I.	155
20	Edermin	77	3	23	Cavan	Upper Loughtee	Urney	Cavan	III.	86
26	Edermine	99	2	2	Wexford	Ballaghkeen	Edermine	Enniscorthy	I.	294
39	Edernagh	168	2	19	Tyrone	Dungannon Upper	Artrea	Cookstown	III.	306
40, 48	*Edernishfree Island*	28	3	1	Donegal	Boylagh	Templecrone	Glenties	III.	116
48	*Edernish Island*	10	3	28	Donegal	Boylagh	Templecrone	Glenties	III.	116
48	*Edernish Island*	7	0	25	Donegal	Boylagh	Templecrone	Glenties	III.	116
6	Ederny	133	2	21	Fermanagh	Lurg	Magheraculmoney	Lowtherstown	III.	208
6	EDERNY T.	—			Fermanagh	Lurg	Magheraculmoney	Lowtherstown	III.	209
15, 20	Edgeworthstown	283	2	18	Longford	Ardagh	Mostrim	Granard	I.	152
15	EDGEWORTHSTOWN T.	—			Longford	Ardagh	Mostrim	Granard	I.	153
22	Edmondstown	226	0	36	Dublin	Rathdown	Whitechurch	Dublin South	I.	38
13	Edmondstown	486	1	14	Louth	Ardee	Philipstown	Ardee	I.	174
20	Edmondstown	524	3	3	Westmeath	Farbill	Killucan	Mullingar	I.	266
13	Edmondstown	197	2	6	Westmeath	Moyashel and Magheradernon	Rathconnell	Mullingar	I.	276
5	Edmondstown	24	0	3	Wicklow	Lower Talbotstown	Blessington	Naas	I.	358
64, 74	Edmondstown Demesne or Tullaghanmore	440	2	12	Mayo	Costello	Kilcolman	Castlereagh	IV.	141
22	EDMONDSTOWN T.	—			Dublin	Rathdown	Whitechurch	Dublin South	I.	38
24	Ednashanlaght	93	0	22	Tyrone	Omagh West	Longfield West	Castlederg	III.	316

(a) Including 1A. 2R. 32P. water.
(b) Including 25A. 0R. 22P. water.
(c) Including 100A. 1R. 27P. detached portion.
(d) Including 2A. 3R. 31P. Lake.
(e) Including 13A. 3R. 24P. water.
(f) Including 7A. 2R. 19P. Lough Corban.
(g) Including 88A. 1R. 26P. water.
(h) Including 7A. 3R. 20P. water.
(i) Including 3A. 1R. 36P. water.

No. of Sheet of the Ordnance Survey Maps.	Townlands and Towns.	Area in Statute Acres.			County.	Barony.	Parish.	Poor Law Union in 1857.	Townland Census of 1851, Part I.	
		A.	R.	P.					Vol.	Page
27, 28	Ednego	516	0	17	Down	Lower Iveagh, Lr. pt.	Dromore	Banbridge	III.	168
32	Edoxtown	311	1	20	Meath	Skreen	Rathfeigh	Dunshaughlin	I.	221
22	Edrans	213	2	39	Cavan	Tullygarvey	Drung	Cootehill	III.	89
13	Edwardstown	103	2	15	Limerick	Clanwilliam	Cahernarry	Limerick	II.	222
41, 46	Edwardstown	294	0	18	Wexford	Bargy	Ballyconnick	Wexford	I.	304
5, 10	Edymore	951	1	36	Tyrone	Strabane Lower	Camus	Strabane	III.	320
21, 34	Eeshal Island	12	2	8	Galway	Ballynahinch	Omey	Clifden	IV.	15
8	Effelstown	83	3	6	Dublin	Balrothery East	Lusk	Balrothery	I.	21
17	Effernagh	140	0	28	Monaghan	Dartree	Aghabog	Clones	III.	263
59, 69	Effernan	638	2	25a	Clare	Clonderalaw	Kilfiddane	Killadysert	II.	15
56	Effernan Glebe	521	0	34	Tyrone	Omagh East	Kilskeery	Enniskillen	III.	313
15, 20	Effernoge	1,099	2	2	Wexford	Scarawalsh	Ferns	Enniscorthy	I.	323
47, 55	Effin	737	3	16	Limerick	Coshma	Effin	Kilmallock	II.	243
27, 28	Efirinagh	330	1	35b	Leitrim	Leitrim	Kiltoghert	Cark. on Shannon	IV.	102
87, 88	Egglybane	385	3	19	Donegal	Raphoe	Donaghmore	Strabane	III.	138
9	Eglish	204	1	20	Antrim	Cary	Culfeightrin	Ballycastle	III.	13
27	Eglish	83	3	28	Antrim	Kilconway	Dunaghy	Ballymena	III.	25
27,28,32,33	Eglish	503	1	22	Antrim	Lower Antrim	Skerry	Ballymena	III.	4
5	Eglish	308	0	16	Armagh	Oneilland West	Tartaraghan	Armagh	III.	55
7	Eglish	180	1	2	Armagh	Tiranny	Eglish	Armagh	III.	59
84, 85	Eglish	2,554	3	17c	Donegal	Banagh	Killymard	Donegal	III.	111
61, 74	Eglish	567	1	17	Galway	Killian	Ahascragh	Ballinasloe	IV.	43
30	Eglish	729	0	30	King's Co.	Eglish	Eglish	Parsonstown	I.	135
27	Eglish	118	2	26	Queen's Co.	Clandonagh	Rathsaran	Donaghmore	I.	234
31	Eglish(alias)The Gort	74	1	8	Tyrone	Dungannon Upper	Ballinderry	Cookstown	III.	306
16	Egmont	612	3	12	Cork, E.R.	Orrery and Kilmore	Churchtown	Mallow	II.	107
15, 20	Egramush	200	2	33d	Cavan	Upper Loughtee	Castleterra	Cavan	III.	82
39, 43	Eighter	718	2	31	Cavan	Castlerahan	Munterconnaught	Oldcastle	III.	71
54	Eighterard	116	2	1	Galway	Moycullen	Kilcummin	Oughterard	IV.	67
98	Eightercua	503	1	2	Kerry	Dunkerron South	Kilcrohane	Cahersiveen	II.	183
40, 48	Eighter Island	60	0	30	Donegal	Boylagh	Templecrone	Glenties	III.	116
53, 54	Eighterross	195	3	36	Donegal	Kilmacrenan	Aghanunshin	Letterkenny	III.	122
29, 30	Eightyeight Acres	156	1	8	Meath	Lune	Athboy	Trim	I.	207
56, 57	Einagh	1,085	2	26	Clare	Ibrickan	Killard	Kilrush	II.	23
100	Einaun Island	7	2	1	Kerry	Dunkerron South	Kilcrohane	Kenmare	II.	184
83	Eirk	787	0	10e	Kerry	Dunkerron South	Templenoe	Kenmare	II.	185
39	Elagh	329	0	4	Tyrone	Dungannon Upper	Ardboe	Cookstown	III.	305
10	Elagh	578	2	30	Tyrone	Strabane Lower	Camus	Strabane	III.	320
38, 47	Elaghbeg	482	3	31	Donegal	Inishowen West	Burt	Londonderry	III.	119
13	Elagh More	512	0	34	Londonderry	North West Liberties of Londonderry	Templemore	Londonderry	III.	246
16	Elderfield	40	0	39	Queen's Co.	Upperwoods	Offerlane	Abbeyleix	I.	251
8, 12	Eldron	58	0	15	Monaghan	Monaghan	Drumsnat	Monaghan	III.	275
48	Elevenacre	23	0	19	Wexford	Forth	Killinick	Wexford	I.	310
22	Eleven Ballyboes	408	0	16	Donegal	Inishowen East	Moville Lower	Inishowen	III.	119
21	Elfeet (Adamson)	188	2	11	Longford	Ratheline	Cashel	Ballymahon	I.	163
21	Elfeet (Burke)	87	0	1f	Longford	Ratheline	Cashel	Ballymahon	I.	163
65	Elfordstown	218	3	4	Cork, E.R.	Barrymore	Ballyspillane	Middleton	II.	51
44	Elgarstown	206	2	20	Meath	Ratoath	Ratoath	Dunshaughlin	I.	219
28, 33	Elginny	936	3	36	Antrim	Lower Antrim	Skerry	Ballymena	III.	5
41	Ellagh	128	0	18	Galway	Clare	Killursa	Tuam	IV.	21
73, 86, 87	Ellagh	359	3	6	Galway	Kilconnell	Kilconnell	Ballinasloe	IV.	40
40	Ellagh-Beg	955	2	37g	Mayo	Gallen	Kilgarvan	Ballina	IV.	148
40	Ellagh-More	896	2	33h	Mayo	Gallen	Kilgarvan	Ballina	IV.	148
21	Ellaghs	282	2	5	Mayo	Tirawley	Kilfian	Killala	IV.	169
19	Ellaha	100	0	14	Limerick	Shanid	Robertstown	Rathkeale	II.	258
20	Ellanabough	28	3	33	Antrim	Lower Glenarm	Layd	Ballycastle	III.	22
14	Ellenstown	58	0	35	Westmeath	Delvin	Castletowndelvin	Castletowndelvin	I.	264
50, 53	Ellickstown	219	0	33	Meath	Dunboyne	Dunboyne	Dunshaughlin	I.	199
17	Ellinure	129	0	10	Monaghan	Dartree	Killeevan	Clones	III.	268
29	Ellisholding	294	1	12	Armagh	Orior Upper	Killevy	Newry	III.	58
7	Ellistown	217	1	30	Dublin	Balrothery West	Ballyboghil	Balrothery	I.	22
22	Ellistown	467	0	0	Kildare	Offaly East	Rathangan	Edenderry	I.	71
45	Ellistrin Big	241	0	21	Donegal	Kilmacrenan	Conwal	Letterkenny	III.	126
45, 53	Ellistrin Little	192	3	17	Donegal	Kilmacrenan	Conwal	Letterkenny	III.	126
118	Ellistronbeg	343	3	4	Mayo	Kilmaine	Kilmainemore	Ballinrobe	IV.	156
118	Ellistronparks	76	2	32	Mayo	Kilmaine	Kilmainemore	Ballinrobe	IV.	156
28	Elly	488	0	13	Donegal	Kilmacrenan	Killygarvan	Millford	III.	128
16, 24	Elly	703	1	32	Mayo	Erris	Kilmore	Belmullet	IV.	146
11	Elmhall	124	2	11	Kildare	South Salt	Donaghcumper	Celbridge	I.	76
11	Elmhall	12	1	2	Kildare	South Salt	Stacumny	Celbridge	I.	78
79, 90	Elmhall	202	2	0	Mayo	Carra	Drum	Castlebar	IV.	128
36	Elmhill	69	2	4	Clare	Tulla Lower	Killuran	Tulla	II.	36

(a) Including 13A. 1R. 29P. water. (d) Including 0A. 2R. 37P. water. (g) Including 8A. 2R. 9P. water.
(b) Including 37A. 1R. 27P. water. (e) Including 6A. 0R. 25P. water. (h) Including 5A. 1R. 10P. water.
(c) Including 17A. 0R. 8P. water. (f) Including 2A. 0R. 32P. water.

3 K

No. of Sheet of the Ordnance Survey Maps.	Townlands and Towns.	Area in Statute Acres.	County.	Barony.	Parish.	Poor Law Union in 1857.	Townland Census of 1851, Part I.	
		A. R. P.					Vol.	Page
45	Elmhill . . .	308 3 7	Galway . .	Tiaquin . .	Moylough . .	Mountbellew .	IV.	80
15	Elmhill . . .	138 3 24	Tipperary, N.R.	Upper Ormond .	Ballymackey .	Nenagh . .	II.	289
19	Elm Park . .	107 0 33	Dublin . .	Coolock . .	Clontarf . .	Dublin North .	I.	26
12	Elmpark Demesne .	318 0 34	Limerick . .	Pubblebrien .	Kilkeedy . .	Limerick . .	II.	252
11	Elm Park or Mullagh-atinny .	197 2 29	Armagh . .	Tiranny . .	Eglish . .	Armagh . .	III.	59
16, 17	Elmvale . . .	105 1 16	Clare . .	Inchiquin .	Killinaboy .	Corrofin . .	II.	26
31, 32	Elone . . .	213 2 19	Kildare . .	Offaly West .	Kilrush . .	Athy . .	I.	73
16	Elphin . . .	787 1 31	Roscommon .	Roscommon .	Elphin . .	Strokestown .	IV.	209
16	ELPHIN T. . .	—	Roscommon .	Roscommon .	Elphin . .	Strokestown .	IV.	210
15, 16	Elteen . . .	103 3 24a	Cavan . .	Upper Loughtee .	Castleterra .	Cavan . .	III.	82
40	Elton . . .	739 2 18	Limerick . .	Smallcounty .	Knockainy .	Kilmallock .	II.	261
24, 25	Elverstown Great .	248 0 38	Kildare . .	Naas South .	Tipperkevin .	Naas . .	I.	65
24, 25	Elverstown Little .	161 1 0	Kildare . .	Naas South .	Tipperkevin .	Naas . .	I.	65
3	Elvey . . .	96 3 2	Monaghan .	Trough . .	Errigal Trough .	Monaghan .	III.	284
15	Ely Island . .	176 3 17	Fermanagh .	Magheraboy .	Devenish . .	Enniskillen .	III.	212
10	Eminiska . .	283 0 11	Tipperary, N.R.	Lower Ormond .	Modreeny .	Borrisokane .	II.	286
10	Eminiska . .	68 0 6	Tipperary, N.R.	Lower Ormond .	Uskane . .	Borrisokane .	II.	288
30	Emlagh . . .	154 3 15	Clare . .	Ibrickan . .	Kilmurry . .	Kilrush . .	II.	23
56	Emlagh . . .	285 1 0	Clare . .	Moyarta . .	Kilfearaght .	Kilrush . .	II.	32
21, 22	Emlagh . . .	313 1 12	Galway . .	Ballynahinch .	Omey . .	Clifden . .	IV.	15
104	Emlagh . . .	213 1 17	Galway . .	Dunkellin .	Killogilleen .	Loughrea . .	IV.	31
98	Emlagh . . .	236 0 16	Galway . .	Leitrim . .	Kilreekill .	Loughrea . .	IV.	54
45	Emlagh . . .	929 1 20	Kerry . .	Corkaguiny .	Ballinvoher .	Dingle . .	II.	174
43, 44, 53	Emlagh . . .	120 2 17	Kerry . .	Corkaguiny .	Cloghane . .	Dingle . .	II.	175
42	Emlagh . . .	65 1 13	Kerry . .	Corkaguiny .	Kilmalkedar .	Dingle . .	II.	178
69, 79	Emlagh . . .	162 2 21	Kerry . .	Iveragh . .	Caher . .	Cahersiveen .	II.	194
11	Emlagh . . .	66 3 11	Louth . .	Louth . .	Louth . .	Dundalk . .	I.	184
85, 95	Emlagh . . .	375 2 16b	Mayo . .	Murrisk . .	Kilgeever .	Westport . .	IV.	160
11, 17	Emlagh . . .	493 3 9	Meath . .	Lower Kells .	Emlagh . .	Kells . .	I.	202
10	Emlagh . . .	134 1 36	Roscommon .	Boyle . .	Tumna . .	Boyle . .	IV.	198
27	Emlagh . . .	458 3 11	Roscommon .	Castlereagh .	Baslick . .	Castlereagh .	IV.	199
26, 27	Emlagh . . .	231 0 12	Roscommon .	Castlereagh .	Kilkeevin .	Castlereagh .	IV.	200
9	Emlagh . . .	261 3 12c	Roscommon .	Frenchpark .	Kilnamanagh .	Boyle . .	IV.	204
16, 22	Emlagh . . .	182 0 35	Roscommon .	Roscommon .	Elphin . .	Strokestown .	IV.	209
45, 47	Emlagh . . .	85 1 1	Sligo . .	Coolavin . .	Killaraght .	Boyle . .	IV.	224
39	Emlagh . . .	109 0 37	Sligo . .	Corran . .	Emlaghfad .	Boyle . .	IV.	226
39	Emlagh . . .	117 1 29	Sligo . .	Corran . .	Kilshalvy .	Boyle . .	IV.	227
27, 34	Emlagh . . .	327 1 38	Sligo . .	Tirerrill . .	Kilmacallan .	Sligo . .	IV.	240
27, 34	Emlagh . . .	196 2 23	Sligo . .	Tirerrill . .	Tawnagh . .	Sligo . .	IV.	241
59	Emlagh . . .	76 3 5	Tipperary, S.R.	Clanwilliam .	Kilmucklin .	Tipperary .	II.	309
48, 49	Emlagharan .	398 1 14d	Galway . .	Ballynahinch .	Ballindoon .	Clifden . .	IV.	10
38, 39	Emlagh Beg .	231 3 30	Roscommon .	Ballymoe .	Oran . .	Roscommon .	IV.	192
36	Emlaghdauroe .	750 2 7e	Galway . .	Ballynahinch .	Moyrus . .	Clifden . .	IV.	13
88, 97	Emlaghdreenagh .	217 0 8	Kerry . .	Iveragh . .	Prior . .	Cahersiveen .	II.	198
53	Emlagh East .	137 3 27	Kerry . .	Corkaguiny .	Dingle . .	Dingle . .	II.	175
42	Emlagh East .	265 0 27	Kerry . .	Corkaguiny .	Marhin . .	Dingle . .	II.	179
28	Emlagher . .	82 1 10	Kildare . .	Offaly East .	Carn . .	Naas . .	I.	69
33, 39	Emlaghfad . .	154 0 1	Sligo . .	Corran . .	Emlaghfad .	Boyle . .	IV.	226
33, 39	Emlaghgissan .	87 2 15	Sligo . .	Corran . .	Emlaghfad .	Sligo . .	IV.	226
34	Emlaghglasny .	363 2 10	Roscommon .	Ballymoe .	Ballynakill .	Castlereagh .	IV.	191
39	Emlaghkeadew .	548 3 31f	Roscommon .	Athlone . .	Fuerty . .	Roscommon .	IV.	181
88	Emlaghlea . .	173 0 23	Kerry . .	Iveragh . .	Prior . .	Cahersiveen .	II.	198
49, 50	Emlaghmore .	1,178 2 11g	Galway . .	Ballynahinch .	Ballindoon .	Clifden . .	IV.	10
36, 50	Emlaghmore .	1,736 0 3h	Galway . .	Ballynahinch .	Moyrus . .	Clifden . .	IV.	13
34,35,38,39	Emlagh More .	664 3 19	Roscommon .	Ballymoe .	Oran . .	Roscommon .	IV.	192
88, 97	Emlaghmore East .	332 1 21	Kerry . .	Iveragh . .	Prior . .	Cahersiveen .	II.	198
88, 97	Emlaghmore West .	178 3 14	Kerry . .	Iveragh . .	Prior . .	Cahersiveen .	II.	198
33	Emlaghnaghtan .	430 2 33i	Sligo . .	Corran . .	Emlaghfad .	Tobercurry .	IV.	226
39	Emlaghnagree .	267 3 18	Roscommon .	Ballymoe .	Oran . .	Roscommon .	IV.	192
88, 97	Emlaghnamuck .	381 1 19	Kerry . .	Iveragh . .	Prior . .	Cahersiveen .	II.	198
88	Emlaghpeastia .	562 1 21	Kerry . .	Iveragh . .	Killemlagh .	Cahersiveen .	II.	196
42	Emlaghreagh .	142 2 19	Kerry . .	Corkaguiny .	Marhin . .	Dingle . .	II.	179
52	Emlaghslat . .	204 2 4	Kerry . .	Corkaguiny .	Ventry . .	Dingle . .	II.	180
53	Emlagh West .	41 3 16	Kerry . .	Corkaguiny .	Dingle . .	Dingle . .	II.	175
42	Emlagh West .	209 3 39	Kerry . .	Corkaguiny .	Marhin . .	Dingle . .	II.	179
38	Emlaghyroyin .	417 2 16j	Roscommon .	Ballymoe .	Dunamon .	Roscommon .	IV.	191
13	Emlicon . .	80 0 28	Carlow . .	Forth . .	Kellistown .	Carlow . .	I.	4
65	Emly . . .	201 3 28	Tipperary, S.R.	Clanwilliam .	Emly . .	Tipperary .	II.	308
9, 16	Emlybeg (Kyle) .	68 0 2	Mayo . .	Erris . .	Kilmore . .	Belmullet .	IV.	146
9, 10, 16	Emlybeg North .	496 0 3	Mayo . .	Erris . .	Kilmore . .	Belmullet .	IV.	146
9, 16	Emlybeg South .	465 1 12k	Mayo . .	Erris . .	Kilmore . .	Belmullet .	IV.	146
9	Emlycass . .	214 0 36l	Mayo . .	Erris . .	Kilmore . .	Belmullet .	IV.	146

(a) Including 4A. 2R. 36P. water.
(b) Including 54A. 3R. 11P. water.
(c) Including 13A. 0R. 39P. water.
(d) Including 35A. 1R. 31P. water.

(e) Including 0A. 0R. 32P. water.
(f) Including 8A. 1R. 18P. water.
(g) Including 275A. 1R. 7P. water.
(h) Including 183A. 2R. 34P. water.

(i) Including 3A. 1R. 3P. water.
(j) Including 15A. 0R. 21P. water.
(k) Including 91A. 2R. 38P. detached portion.
(l) Including 6A. 6R. 4P. water

No. of Sheet of the Ordnance Survey Maps.	Townlands and Towns.	Area in Statute Acres.			County.	Barony.	Parish.	Poor Law Union in 1857.	Townland Census of 1851, Part I.	
		A.	R.	P.					Vol.	Page
22, 23	Emlymoran	573	1	38	Sligo	Tireragh	Castleconor	Dromore West	IV.	232
65	EMLY T.	—			Tipperary, S.R.	Clanwilliam	Emly	Tipperary	II.	308
44	Emmel	385	1	9	King's Co.	Clonlisk	Templeharry	Roscrea	I.	132
44	Emmel East	206	2	5	King's Co.	Clonlisk	Templeharry	Roscrea	I.	132
44	Emmel West	308	0	23	King's Co.	Clonlisk	Templeharry	Roscrea	I.	132
40	Emmoo	247	1	22	Roscommon	Ballintober South	Roscommon	Roscommon	IV.	190
8, 9	Emo Park	1,945	3	19a	Queen's Co.	Portnahinch	Coolbanagher	Mountmellick	I.	244
10	Emper	1,625	1	26b	Westmeath	Moygoish	Kilmacnevin	Mullingar	I.	280
3, 6	Emy	252	2	30c	Monaghan	Trough	Donagh	Monaghan	III.	282
6	Emyvale or Scarna-geeragh	119	2	4	Monaghan	Trough	Donagh	Monaghan	III.	282
6	EMYVALE T.	—			Monaghan	Trough	Donagh	Monaghan	III.	283
12, 16	Enagh	217	0	34	Armagh	Armagh	Lisnadill	Armagh	III.	45
16,17,20,21	Enagh	537	1	10	Armagh	Fews Lower	Kilclooney	Armagh	III.	46
22	Enagh	167	2	16	Armagh	Orior Lower	Killevy	Newry	III.	56
11, 15	Enagh	75	2	8	Armagh	Tiranny	Tynan	Armagh	III.	60
39	Enagh	346	1	23	Cavan	Castlerahan	Castlerahan	Oldcastle	III.	67
44	Enagh	359	2	21	Cavan	Castlerahan	Loughan or Castle-keeran	Oldcastle	III.	69
39	Enagh	179	0	34	Cavan	Castlerahan	Mullagh	Bailieborough	III.	70
27, 28	Enagh	159	2	18d	Cavan	Clankee	Knockbride	Bailieborough	III.	73
42	Enagh	198	3	27	Cavan	Clanmahon	Kilbride	Oldcastle	III.	77
16	Enagh	88	1	39e	Cavan	Tullygarvey	Kildrumsherdan	Cootehill	III.	90
28	Enagh	738	1	30	Down	Lower Iveagh, Lr. pt.	Garvaghy	Banbridge	III.	168
9, 10	Enagh	170	2	23	Londonderry	Keenaght	Drumachose	New Tn Limavady	III.	235
13, 14	Enagh	184	2	33f	Londonderry	Tirkeeran	Clondermot	Londonderry	III.	248
18	Enagh	171	1	9	Monaghan	Dartree	Ematris	Cootehill	III.	267
34	Enagh	253	1	5	Monaghan	Farney	Magheracloone	Carrickmacross	III.	272
6, 9	Enagh	131	3	1	Monaghan	Trough	Donagh	Monaghan	III.	282
10	Enagh	277	3	14	Roscommon	Boyle	Killukin	Boyle	IV.	195
67	Enagh	194	3	15g	Tyrone	Dungannon Lower	Aghaloo	Armagh	III.	296
15	Enaghan	131	1	26	Fermanagh	Magheraboy	Devenish	Enniskillen	III.	210
26, 27	Enaghan	1,278	2	18	King's Co.	Upper Philipstown	Ballykean	Tullamore	I.	143
3	Enaghan	760	2	6h	Longford	Granard	Killoe	Granard	I.	157
29, 38	Enagh Beg	400	0	6	Mayo	Tirawley	Crossmolina	Ballina	IV.	166
43	Enagh East	152	1	18	Clare	Tulla Lower	Clonlea	Tulla	II.	34
28	Enaghgare	96	3	18	Limerick	Shanid	Ardagh	Newcastle	II.	255
16, 17	Enagh Lower	142	1	10	Antrim	Upper Dunluce	Ballymoney	Ballymoney	III.	19
29, 38	Enagh More	410	2	24	Mayo	Tirawley	Crossmolina	Ballina	IV.	166
43	Enagh North	120	2	18i	Clare	Tulla Lower	Clonlea	Tulla	II.	34
147	Enaghoughter East	260	3	15	Cork, W.R.	West Carbery (W.D.)	Kilmoe	Skull	II.	145
147	Enaghoughter West	166	2	13	Cork, W.R.	West Carbery (W.D.)	Kilmoe	Skull	II.	145
22	Enaghroe	223	1	37	Limerick	Smallcounty	Fedamore	Croom	II.	259
17	Enagh Upper	174	2	29	Antrim	Upper Dunluce	Ballymoney	Ballymoney	III.	19
43	Enagh West	300	2	39j	Clare	Tulla Lower	Clonlea	Tulla	II.	34
6, 14	Endrim	1,642	0	10	King's Co.	Garrycastle	Wheery or Killagally	Parsonstown	I.	139
27, 34	Enfield	413	2	8	Roscommon	Castlereagh	Ballintober	Castlereagh	IV.	198
70	Englishgarden	33	1	34	Cork, W.R.	West Muskerry	Clondrohid	Macroom	II.	155
143	English Island	7	2	17	Cork, W.R.	East Carbery (W.D.)	Ross	Clonakilty	II.	135
29	Englishtenements	81	0	3	Limerick	Connello Lower	Rathkeale	Rathkeale	II.	229
60, 64	Englishtown	345	3	14	Antrim	Upper Belfast	Shankill	Belfast	III.	10
99	Englishtown	222	3	38	Galway	Longford	Killoran	Ballinasloe	IV.	59
5	Englishtown	34	1	30	Limerick	Borough of Limerick	St. Mary's	Limerick	II.	262
11	Englishtown	222	0	10	Londonderry	Coleraine	Macosquin	Coleraine	III.	233
19	Englishtown	49	0	22	Tipperary, N.R.	Owney and Arra	Templeachally	Nenagh	II.	297
23, 31	Englishtown	151	3	29	Waterford	Decies without Drum	Kilrossanty	Kilmacthomas	II.	358
27	Englishtown	282	0	38	Wicklow	Upper Talbotstown	Kilranelagh	Baltinglass	I.	364
41	Ennereilly	132	3	20	Wicklow	Arklow	Ennereilly	Rathdrum	I.	344
10, 14	Ennis	78	0	11	Monaghan	Cremorne	Clontibret	Monaghan	III.	260
31	Ennisboyne	142	0	9	Wicklow	Arklow	Dunganstown	Rathdrum	I.	343
26, 27	Enniscoffey or Caran	1,421	2	4	Westmeath	Fartullagh	Enniscoffey	Mullingar	I.	268
20, 26	Enniscorthy	934	2	17k	Wexford	Scarawalsh	St. Marys, Enniscorthy	Enniscorthy	I.	325
20	ENNISCORTHY T.	—			Wexford	{ Ballaghkeen, Scarawalsh	{ Templeshannon, St. Marys, Enniscorthy	Enniscorthy	I.	{ 299, 325
29	Enniscoush	57	0	20	Limerick	Connello Lower	Nantinan	Rathkeale	II.	229
29	Enniscoush	344	2	21	Limerick	Connello Lower	Rathkeale	Rathkeale	II.	229
53	Ennish	174	0	0	Tyrone	Dungannon Lower	Killeeshil	Dungannon	III.	298
35	Enniskeen	271	1	20	Cavan	Clankee	Enniskeen	Bailieborough	III.	73
109	ENNISKEEN T.	—			Cork, W.R.	East Carbery (W.D.)	Kinneigh	Bandon	II.	135
7	Enniskerry	5	2	25	Wicklow	Rathdown	Powerscourt	Rathdown	I.	356
7	ENNISKERRY T.	—			Wicklow	Rathdown	Powerscourt	Rathdown	I.	356
22	Enniskillen	53	1	34l	Fermanagh	Magheraboy	Enniskillen	Enniskillen	III.	212

3 K 2

No. of Sheet of the Ordnance Survey Maps.	Townlands and Towns.	Area in Statute Acres. A. R. P.	County.	Barony.	Parish.	Poor Law Union in 1857.	Townland Census of 1851, Part I. Vol.	Page
22	Enniskillen	45 1 16a	Fermanagh	Tirkennedy	Enniskillen	Enniskillen	III.	222
39	Enniskillen	243 1 32	Tyrone	Dungannon Upper	Artrea	Cookstown	III.	306
22	ENNISKILLEN T.	—	Fermanagh	{ Magheraboy	Rossorry	} Enniskillen	III. {	214
				Tirkennedy	Enniskillen			223
				Magheraboy	Enniskillen			212
16	Ennislare	262 2 7	Armagh	Fews Lower	Lisnadill	Armagh	III.	47
10, 16	Ennismore	432 3 4	Kerry	Iraghticonnor	Dysert	Listowel	II.	190
23, 27	Ennisnag	1,240 1 24	Kilkenny	Shillelogher	Ennisnag	Thomastown	I.	114
15	Ennistimon	79 2 16	Clare	Corcomroe	Kilmanaheen	Ennistimon	II.	21
15	ENNISTIMON T.	—	Clare	Corcomroe	Kilmanaheen	Ennistimon	II.	21
33	ENNIS T.	—	Clare	Islands	Drumcliff	Ennis	II.	30
31, 37	Ennistown	32 2 25	Meath	Lower Deece	Balsoon	Trim	I.	191
44	Ennistown	132 0 35	Meath	Ratoath	Rathbeggan	Dunshaughlin	I.	219
31	Ennistown or Craystown	68 2 20	Meath	Lower Deece	Balsoon	Trim	I.	191
24, 25	Envagh	1,147 0 35b	Tyrone	Strabane Lower	Ardstraw	Strabane	III.	319
9	Enybegs	832 2 4	Longford	Longford	Killoe	Longford	I.	159
19, 20	Eonish	245 1 6	Cavan	Upper Loughtee	Kilmore	Cavan	III.	84
90	Eragh Island South	10 3 31	Galway	Moycullen	Kilcummin	Oughterard	IV.	68
24	Erdinagh	167 3 32	Fermanagh	Magherastephana	Aghalurcher	Lisnaskea	III.	216
37	Erenagh	369 3 29	Down	Lecale Upper	Bright	Downpatrick	III.	180
36, 37	Erenagh	154 1 7	Roscommon	Ballintober South	Cloontuskert	Roscommon	IV.	188
27	Erganagh	317 3 25	Londonderry	Loughinsholin	Kilrea	Ballymoney	III.	241
16	Erganagh	498 2 30c	Tyrone	Strabane Lower	Ardstraw	Castlederg	III.	319
26	Erganagh Glebe	573 1 18	Tyrone	Strabane Upper	Cappagh	Omagh	III.	325
26	Erinagh	413 0 29	Tipperary, N.R.	Upper Ormond	Kilmore	Nenagh	II.	291
33	Erinagh Beg	144 2 2	Clare	Inchiquin	Dysert	Ennis	II.	24
25, 33	Erinagh More	257 3 27	Clare	Inchiquin	Dysert	Ennis	II.	24
102, 103	Erneen	1,713 3 1	Kerry	Glanarought	Kilcaskan	Kenmare	II.	186
30, 37	Erra	854 2 36	Roscommon	Roscommon	Lissonuffy	Strokestown	IV.	212
9	Erraran	155 1 12d	Cavan	Tullyhaw	Templeport	Bawnboy	III.	94
25	Errarooey Beg	195 0 12	Donegal	Kilmacrenan	Raymunterdoney	Dunfanaghy	III.	131
15, 25	Errarooey More	542 2 33	Donegal	Kilmacrenan	Raymunterdoney	Dunfanaghy	III.	131
29, 35	Errasallagh	455 0 20e	Fermanagh	Clankelly	Clones	Clones	III.	196
30, 34	Errew	314 2 0f	Leitrim	Carrigallen	Carrigallen	Mohill	IV.	89
36	Errew	268 3 17g	Leitrim	Mohill	Cloone	Mohill	IV.	106
89	Errew	200 0 30h	Mayo	Carra	Ballyhean	Castlebar	IV.	125
38, 47	Errew	497 3 2	Mayo	Tirawley	Crossmolina	Ballina	IV.	166
16	Erriblagh	177 2 11	Roscommon	Frenchpark	Creeve	Car.on Shannon	IV.	203
69	Erribul	860 3 1	Clare	Clonderalaw	Kilfiddane	Killadysert	II.	15
44	Errick Beg	47 3 35	Roscommon	Athlone	Tisrara	Roscommon	IV.	185
44	Errick More	129 1 13	Roscommon	Athlone	Tisrara	Roscommon	IV.	185
4	Erriff	891 3 4	Leitrim	Rosclogher	Rossinver	Ballyshannon	IV.	111
70, 79	Erriff	278 3 27	Mayo	Carra	Turlough	Castlebar	IV.	131
92, 93	Erriff	305 0 4i	Mayo	Costello	Bekan	Claremorris	IV.	139
108, 116	Erriff	2,438 2 25j	Mayo	Murrisk	Aghagower	Westport	IV.	159
17	Errigal	170 0 30	Cavan	Tullygarvey	Kildrumsherdan	Cootehill	III.	90
52, 59	Errigal	570 1 6	Tyrone	Clogher	Errigal Keerogue	Clogher	III.	295
27	Errill	390 0 18	Queen's Co.	Clandonagh	Rathdowney	Donaghmore	I.	234
27	ERRILL T.	—	Queen's Co.	Clandonagh	Rathdowney	Donaghmore	I.	234
54	Errina	334 3 32	Clare	Tulla Lower	Kiltenanlea	Limerick	II.	37
27, 28	Errinagh	228 0 31k	Clare	Tulla Upper	Feakle	Scarriff	II.	39
6	Errironagh	367 2 31l	Roscommon	Boyle	Ardcarn	Boyle	IV.	193
6	Erris	323 0 39	Roscommon	Boyle	Boyle	Boyle	IV.	194
50, 63	Errisbeg East	1,471 1 6m	Galway	Ballynahinch	Moyrus	Clifden	IV.	13
50, 63	Errisbeg West	1,120 2 19n	Galway	Ballynahinch	Moyrus	Clifden	IV.	13
21	Erris or Skirk Glebe	105 0 8	Queen's Co.	Clandonagh	Skirk	Donaghmore	I.	235
13, 19	Errit	1,203 0 38o	Roscommon	Frenchpark	Tibohine	Castlereagh	IV.	205
54	Errity	293 1 13	Donegal	Raphoe	Raymoghy	Letterkenny	III.	142
54	Errity Churchland	44 0 6	Donegal	Raphoe	Raymoghy	Letterkenny	III.	142
53	Erry	1,034 3 38	Tipperary, S.R.	Middlethird	Erry	Cashel	II.	326
8	Erry (Armstrong)	832 2 25	King's Co.	Kilcoursey	Kilbride	Tullamore	I.	141
20	Errybane	135 2 14p	Monaghan	Cremorne	Muckno	Castleblayney	III.	262
8	Erry (Maryborough)	1,844 0 24	King's Co.	Kilcoursey	Kilbride	Tullamore	I.	141
20	Erryroe	294 0 39	Monaghan	Cremorne	Muckno	Castleblayney	III.	262
63	Ervallagh	353 1 8q	Galway	Ballynahinch	Moyrus	Clifden	IV.	13
61, 74	Ervallagh Eighter	110 1 23	Galway	Clonmacnowen	Ahascragh	Ballinasloe	IV.	24
74	Ervallagh Oughter	536 0 24	Galway	Clonmacnowen	Ahascragh	Ballinasloe	IV.	24
32	Erveny	55 0 35	Fermanagh	Clanawley	Killesher	Enniskillen	III.	192
29, 35	Ervey	338 3 33	Fermanagh	Clankelly	Clones	Clones	III.	196
29	Ervey	123 0 10	Fermanagh	Magherastephana	Aghavea	Lisnaskea	III.	218
??	Ervey	590 2 1r	Londonderry	Tirkeeran	Cumber Lower	Londonderry	III.	248
2	Ervey	392 1 14r	Meath	Lower Kells	Enniskeen	Kells	I.	202
28, 29	Eshacorran	294 3 35	Fermanagh	Magherastephana	Aghavea	Lisnaskea	III.	218

(a) { Including 0A. 0R. 13P. Enniskillen Island.
    { Including 15A. 3R. 31P. water.
(b) Including 12A. 0R. 0P. water.
(c) Including 6A. 0R. 2P. water.
(d) Including 12A. 3R. 15P. Brackley Lough.
(e) Including 10A. 1R. 21P. water.
(f) Including 42A. 3R. 28P. water.

(g) Including 22A. 3R. 34P. water.
(h) Including 9A. 0R. 2P. water.
(i) Including 1A. 3R. 25P. water.
(j) Including 185A. 2R. 5P. water.
(k) Including 9A. 1R. 37P. water.
(l) Including 16A. 3R. 28P. water.

(m) Including 74A. 2R. 18P. water.
(n) Including 5A. 1R. 18P. water.
(o) Including 148A. 1R. 19P. water.
(p) Including 0A. 3R. 29P. water.
(q) Including 16A. 1R. 23P. water.
(r) Including 22A. 3R. 34P. water.

No. of Sheet of the Ordnance Survey Maps.	Townlands and Towns.	Area in Statute Acres.	County.	Barony.	Parish.	Poor Law Union in 1857.	Townland Census of 1851, Part I.	
							Vol.	Page
		A. R. P.						
5	Eshacrin	141 0 30	Monaghan	Monaghan	Tedavnet	Monaghan	III.	279
34	Eshanummer	51 1 32	Fermanagh	Magherastephana	Aghalurcher	Lisnaskea	III.	216
29, 35	Eshbane	224 3 24	Fermanagh	Magherastephana	Aghalurcher	Lisnaskea	III.	216
34, 35	Eshbralley	261 2 12	Fermanagh	Magherastephana	Aghalurcher	Lisnaskea	III.	216
29, 35	Eshcarcoge	124 3 15	Fermanagh	Magherastephana	Aghalurcher	Lisnaskea	III.	216
29, 35	Eshcleagh and Doon	645 3 10a	Fermanagh	Clankelly	Clones	Clones	III.	195
5	Eshcloghfin	309 2 11	Monaghan	Monaghan	Tedavnet	Monaghan	III.	279
29, 35	Eshekerin	357 0 31	Fermanagh	Clankelly	Clones	Clones	III.	196
14, 19	Eshcry	1,005 2 10	Antrim	Lower Glenarm	Layd	Ballycastle	III.	22
35	Eshmeen	236 3 0	Fermanagh	Magherastephana	Aghalurcher	Lisnaskea	III.	216
29, 30	Eshnadarragh	820 0 12b	Fermanagh	Clankelly	Clones	Clones	III.	196
29	Eshnadarragh	137 1 32	Fermanagh	Magherastephana	Aghavea	Lisnaskea	III.	218
29, 35	Eshnadeelada	209 0 18	Fermanagh	Clankelly	Clones	Clones	III.	196
5	Eshnaglogh	1,341 0 9	Monaghan	Monaghan	Tedavnet	Monaghan	III.	279
34	Eshnagorr	66 2 19	Fermanagh	Magherastephana	Aghalurcher	Lisnaskea	III.	216
29	Eshnanumera	207 3 16	Fermanagh	Magherastephana	Aghavea	Lisnaskea	III.	218
34	Eshnascreen	63 1 17	Fermanagh	Magherastephana	Aghalurcher	Lisnaskea	III.	216
29	Eshnasillog Beg	149 0 3	Fermanagh	Magherastephana	Aghalurcher	Lisnaskea	III.	216
29	Eshnasillog More	288 0 32	Fermanagh	Magherastephana	Aghalurcher	Lisnaskea	III.	216
34, 35	Eshthomas	61 0 24	Fermanagh	Magherastephana	Aghalurcher	Lisnaskea	III.	216
4, 6	Eshveagh	439 1 35	Cavan	Tullyhaw	Kinawley	Enniskillen	III.	93
25, 26	Eshwary	512 2 29	Armagh	Orior Upper	Killevy	Newry	III.	58
29	Eshywulligan	200 1 35c	Fermanagh	Clankelly	Clones	Clones	III.	196
22, 20	Esk	294 1 19	Kerry	Trughanacmy	O'Brennan	Tralee	II.	212
108	Eskadawer	371 2 25	Kerry	Glanarought	Tuosist	Kenmare	II.	188
30, 39	Eskaheen	1,347 0 37	Donegal	Inishowen West	Muff	Londonderry	III.	121
102, 110	Esk East	994 2 19	Kerry	Glanarought	Kilcaskan	Kenmare	II.	186
115	Eskenacartan	17 3 35	Cork, W.R.	Bear	Killaconenagh	Castletown	II.	125
84, 96	Esker	262 0 22	Galway	Athenry	Kiltullagh	Loughrea	IV.	5
109	Esker	1,633 1 19	Galway	Longford	Clonfert	Ballinasloe	IV.	57
60, 73	Esker	811 0 14	Galway	Tiaquin	Ballymacward	Mountbellew	IV.	75
59	Esker	79 3 2	Galway	Tiaquin	Moylough	Mountbellew	IV.	80
10	Esker	451 1 33	Kilkenny	Fassadinin	Mothell	Castlecomer	I.	90
6, 7	Esker	599 2 18	King's Co.	Garrycastle	Lemanaghan	Parsonstown	I.	136
33	Esker	61 1 27	Leitrim	Mohill	Cloone	Mohill	IV.	106
92	Esker	71 3 13	Mayo	Clanmorris	Knock	Claremorris	IV.	135
62	Esker	149 3 15	Mayo	Gallen	Kilconduff	Swineford	IV.	148
61	Esker	134 0 28	Mayo	Gallen	Meelick	Swineford	IV.	150
1, 3	Esker	105 3 9	Monaghan	Trough	Errigal Trough	Clogher	III.	284
18, 19	Esker	368 1 25	Queen's Co.	Cullenagh	Fossy or Timahoe	Abbeyleix	I.	240
7	Esker	272 0 18	Queen's Co.	Maryborough West	Clonenagh and Clonagheen	Mountmellick	I.	243
51	Esker	260 0 30	Roscommon	Athlone	Taghmaconnell	Athlone	IV.	185
20	Esker	109 0 35	Tipperary, N.R.	Owney and Arra	Youghalarra	Nenagh	II.	297
49, 50	Esker	515 0 11d	Tyrone	Omagh East	Dromore	Omagh	III.	311
18, 26	Esker	563 1 19	Tyrone	Strabane Upper	Cappagh	Omagh	III.	325
23, 24	Eskeragh	93 2 7	Fermanagh	Magherastephana	Aghalurcher	Lisnaskea	III.	216
28, 37	Eskeragh	944 2 35	Mayo	Tirawley	Crossmolina	Ballina	IV.	166
60	Eskerballycahill	363 3 5	Galway	Kilconnell	Killosolan	Mountbellew	IV.	42
48	Eskerbaun	490 3 1	Roscommon	Athlone	Cam	Athlone	IV.	180
19	Esker Beg	49 3 21	King's Co.	Coolestown	Ballynakill	Edenderry	I.	132
18, 19	Esker Beg	46 3 25	King's Co.	Coolestown	Monasteroris	Edenderry	I.	133
51	Esker Beg	176 0 17	Roscommon	Athlone	Taghmaconnell	Athlone	IV.	185
107	Eskerboy	743 3 36	Galway	Longford	Abbeygormacan	Ballinasloe	IV.	56
44	Eskerboy	231 0 5	Tyrone	Omagh East	Termonmaguirk	Omagh	III.	314
111	Esker East	140 1 11	Mayo	Clanmorris	Crossboyne	Claremorris	IV.	132
27, 31	Eskerhill	137 0 39	Kildare	Offaly West	Harristown	Athy	I.	72
109	Esker Island	9 0 32	Galway	Longford	Clonfert	Ballinasloe	IV.	57
87, 99	Eskerkeel	34 3 3	Galway	Clonmacnowen	Clontuskert	Ballinasloe	IV.	24
101	Eskerlevally	236 1 28c	Mayo	Clanmorris	Kilcolman	Claremorris	IV.	134
61	Eskermore	222 1 34	Galway	Killian	Ahascragh	Mountbellew	IV.	43
11, 19	Esker More	1,455 1 5	King's Co.	Coolestown	Ballynakill	Edenderry	I.	132
11, 19	Esker More	930 0 3	King's Co.	Coolestown	Monasteroris	Edenderry	I.	133
59	Eskermore	347 3 27	Tyrone	Clogher	Clogher	Clogher	III.	292
43	Eskermore	318 0 12	Tyrone	Omagh East	Clogherny	Omagh	III.	310
46	Eskermurry	51 3 31	Galway	Killian	Killeroran	Mountbellew	IV.	44
58	Eskernabrogue	269 0 24	Tyrone	Clogher	Clogher	Clogher	III.	292
17	Esker North	74 3 7	Dublin	Newcastle	Esker	Celbridge	I.	33
32, 35	Esker North	153 2 32f	Leitrim	Mohill	Mohill	Mohill	IV.	108
5	Esker North	315 2 24	Longford	Longford	Killoe	Longford	I.	159
111	Esker North	103 3 11	Mayo	Clanmorris	Crossboyne	Claremorris	IV.	132
6, 18	Eskeromullacaun	864 3 20	Galway	Tiaquin	Boyounagh	Glennamaddy	IV.	76
87	Eskerroe	19 1 31	Galway	Clonmacnowen	Kilcloony	Ballinasloe	IV.	25

(a) Including 2A. 1R. 15P. water.
(b) Including 3A. 3R. 33P. water.

(c) Including 1A. 1R. 39P. water.
(d) Including 5A. 1R. 10P. water.

(e) Including 10A. 2R. 15P. water.
(f) Including 21A. 3R. 0P. water.

No. of Sheet of the Ordnance Survey Maps.	Townlands and Towns.	Area in Statute Acres.	County.	Barony.	Parish.	Poor Law Union in 1857.	Townland Census of 1851, Part I.	
		A. R. P.					Vol.	Page
45, 59	Eskerroe	321 1 39	Galway	Tiaquin	Killoscobe	Mountbellew	IV.	78
104, 105	Eskershanore	203 0 31	Galway	Loughrea	Kilchreest	Loughrea	IV.	63
17	Esker South	460 1 1	Dublin	Newcastle	Esker	Celbridge	I.	33
32, 35	Esker South	129 3 6a	Leitrim	Mohill	Mohill	Mohill	IV.	108
9	Esker South	747 2 12	Longford	Longford	Killoe	Longford	I.	159
111	Esker South	182 2 14	Mayo	Clanmorris	Crossboyne	Claremorris	IV.	132
92	Eskerymorilly	204 3 29	Mayo	Clanmorris	Knock	Claremorris	IV.	135
91	Eskine	483 3 3	Kerry	Dunkerron South	Kilcrohane	Kenmare	II.	183
90, 104	Esknamucky	153 2 28	Cork, W.R.	Bear	Kilcaskan	Bantry	II.	123
41	Esk North	277 2 0	Cork, E.R.	Duhallow	Kilshannig	Mallow	II.	74
37	Eskragh	564 0 21	Sligo	Leyny	Kilmacteige	Tobercurry	IV.	231
51	Eskragh	532 1 25	Tyrone	Clogher	Clogher	Clogher	III.	292
53	Eskragh	270 0 36	Tyrone	Dungannon Lower	Killeeshil	Dungannon	III.	298
54	Eskragh	292 1 33b	Tyrone	Dungannon Middle	Donaghmore	Dungannon	III.	302
138	Eskraha	317 3 20	Cork, W.R.	West Carbery (W.D.)	Kilcrohane	Bantry	II.	143
40, 41	Esk South	471 3 26	Cork, E.R.	Duhallow	Kilshannig	Mallow	II.	74
73, 83	Eskwacruttia	263 1 13e	Kerry	Dunkerron North	Knockane	Killarney	II.	182
102, 110	Esk West	534 3 25	Kerry	Glanarought	Kilcaskan	Kenmare	II.	187
44	Eskylane	485 2 1	Antrim	Upper Toome	Shilvodan Grange	Antrim	III.	35
8, 9, 14	Essan	218 3 21	Antrim	Cary	Armoy	Ballycastle	III.	11
22	Essan	630 3 15d	Tyrone	Omagh West	Termonamongan	Castlederg	III	317
56, 57	Essaun	727 0 24	Mayo	Erris	Kilcommon	Newport	IV.	144
10	Essexford	167 3 0	Louth	Ardee	Killanny	Dundalk	I.	173
5	Estea Island	4 1 24	Fermanagh	Lurg	Drumkeeran	Lowtherstown	III.	207
10	Estersnow	216 2 20e	Roscommon	Boyle	Estersnow	Boyle	IV.	195
16, 23	Ethelstown	408 3 0	Meath	Upper Kells	Burry	Kells	I.	205
29	Euglaune	137 3 21	Cork, E.R.	Duhallow	Cullen	Millstreet	II.	70
78	Eustaceland	40 2 18	Tipperary, S.R.	Iffa and Offa East	Kilsheelan	Clonmel	II.	314
28, 36	Evegallahoo	211 3 30	Limerick	Glenquin	Grange	Newcastle	II.	245
142	Eve Island	0 0 22	Cork, W.R.	East Carbery (W.D.)	Kilfaughnabeg	Skibbereen	II.	133
70	Everardsgrange	169 2 14	Tipperary, S.R.	Middlethird	Peppardstown	Cashel	II.	329
38, 39	Everlaun	202 3 29	Sligo	Corran	Kilturra	Tobercurry	IV.	227
5	Evikeens	198 3 37	Roscommon	Boyle	Boyle	Boyle	IV.	194
5, 10	Evish	870 2 25	Tyrone	Strabane Lower	Camus	Strabane	III.	320
28	Evishacrancussy	629 0 10	Tyrone	Dungannon Upper	Kildress	Cookstown	III.	309
19, 24	Evishacrow	837 2 10	Antrim	Kilconway	Dunaghy	Ballymena	III.	25
25	Evishagaran	813 1 12	Londonderry	Keenaght	Dungiven	NewT^rLimavady	III.	236
28, 37	Evishanoran	743 3 24f	Tyrone	Dungannon Upper	Kildress	Cookstown	III.	309
20, 28	Evishbrack	426 0 17	Tyrone	Dungannon Upper	Kildress	Cookstown	III.	309
20	Evishbreedy	1,059 2 32	Donegal	Inishowen West	Fahan Lower	Inishowen	III.	120
24, 28	Evishnablay	488 1 17	Antrim	Lower Antrim	Skerry	Ballymena	III.	5
14, 19	Evlagh Beg	166 1 5	Cavan	Tullyhunco	Kildallan	Bawnboy	III.	97
14, 19	Evlagh More	140 1 39	Cavan	Tullyhunco	Kildallan	Bawnboy	III.	97
78	Evneenmore Island	24 3 36	Galway	Moycullen	Kilcummin	Oughterard	IV.	68
2	Exorna	91 2 10	Londonderry	Coleraine	Dunboe	Coleraine	III.	231
101,102,114	Eyeries	604 0 12	Cork, W.R.	Bear	Kilcatherine	Castletown	II.	124
101	Eyeries Island	2 1 24	Cork, W.R.	Bear	Kilcatherine	Castletown	II.	124
101	EYERIES T.	—	Cork, W.R.	Bear	Kilcatherine	Castletown	II.	124
8	Eyne	692 3 29	Queen's Co.	Maryborough East	Straboe	Mountmellick	I.	241
14, 15	Eyon	542 2 21	Limerick	Clanwilliam	Abington	Limerick	II.	221
108	Eyrecourt Demesne	61 0 4	Galway	Longford	Clonfert	Portumna	IV.	57
100, 108	Eyrecourt Demesne	723 0 9	Galway	Longford	Donanaghta	Portumna	IV.	58
108	EYRECOURT T.	—	Galway	Longford	Donanaghta	Portumna	IV.	58
27	Eyrehill	100 2 6	Clare	Tulla Upper	Tulla	Tulla	II.	41
21, 22, 35	Eyrephort	142 3 39	Galway	Ballynahinch	Omey	Clifden	IV.	15
19	Faartan	519 0 33	Galway	Ballymoe	Ballynakill	Glennamaddy	IV.	5
26,27,35,36	Faccary	1,766 3 33	Tyrone	Strabane Upper	Cappagh	Omagh	III.	325
91	Facefield	468 2 38	Mayo	Clanmorris	Mayo	Claremorris	IV.	135
25	FACTORY T.	—	Meath	Skreen	Athlumney	Navan	I.	220
14	Faddan Beg	549 3 22	King's Co.	Garrycastle	Tisaran	Parsonstown	I.	138
5, 8	Faddan Beg	116 2 9	Tipperary, N.R.	Lower Ormond	Loughkeen	Parsonstown	II.	286
14	Faddan More	258 2 13	King's Co.	Garrycastle	Tisaran	Parsonstown	I.	138
5, 8	Faddan More	820 1 11	Tipperary, N.R.	Lower Ormond	Loughkeen	Parsonstown	II.	286
21	Fadduaga	187 0 4	Waterford	Coshmore&Coshbride	Lismore & Mocollop	Lismore	II.	345
18	Faganstown	144 0 30	Meath	Upper Slane	Gernonstown	Navan	I.	224
67	Faghbane	109 0 15	Kerry	Magunihy	Killarney	Killarney	II.	203
67, 75	Faghcullia	358 2 27	Kerry	Magunihy	Killarney	Killarney	II.	203
8	Faghey	131 1 9	Longford	Longford	Clongesh	Longford	I.	158
72, 73	Faha	443 0 10g	Cork, E.R.	East Muskerry	Inishcarra	Cork	II.	103
34, 35	Faha	1,079 2 39	Kerry	Corkaguiny	Cloghane	Dingle	II.	175

(a) Including 5A. 1R. 24P. water.
(b) Including 26A. 2R. 19P. water.
(c) Including 13A. 3R. 10P. water.
(d) Including 5A. 1R. 10P. water.
(e) Including 11A. 2R. 32P. water.
(f) Including 14A. 1R. 14P. Cam Lough.
(g) Including 5A. 2R. 23P. water.

No. of Sheet of the Ordnance Survey Maps.	Townlands and Towns.	Area in Statute Acres.	County.	Barony.	Parish.	Poor Law Union in 1857.	Townland Census of 1851, Part I.	
		A. R. P.					Vol.	Page
1	Faha	252 3 34	Kerry	Iraghticonnor	Kilconly	Listowel	II.	191
63	Faha	281 0 9	Kerry	Iveragh	Glanbehy #	Cahersiveen	II.	196
12	Faha	228 0 12	Limerick	Kenry	Kildimo	Rathkeale	II.	249
19	Faha	63 0 23	Tipperary, N.R.	Owney and Arra	Castletownarra	Nenagh	II.	294
36	Faha	211 0 12	Waterford	Decies within Drum	Ardmore	Dungarvan	II.	350
15, 24	Faha	685 2 19	Waterford	Decies without Drum	Stradbally	Kilmacthomas	II.	360
12	Faha Demesne	428 2 22	Limerick	Pubblebrien	Kilkeedy	Limerick	II.	252
31	Fahaduff	718 1 18	Kerry	Trughanacmy	Castleisland	Tralee	II.	208
116	Faha East	126 3 16	Cork, W.R.	Bear	Kilcaskan	Castletown	II.	123
57	Faha East	229 1 8	Kerry	Magunihy	Kilbonane	Killarney	II.	200
15, 24	Fahafeelagh	546 1 2	Waterford	Decies without Drum	Ballylaneen	Kilmacthomas	II.	354
94	Fahalea	285 0 1	Cork, E.R.	Kerrycurrihy	Carrigaline	Kinsale	II.	92
27	Fahamore	244 0 12	Kerry	Corkaguiny	Stradbally	Dingle	II.	180
52	Fahan	490 0 22	Kerry	Corkaguiny	Ballinvoher	Dingle	II.	174
98	Fahanalooscane	536 3 21	Cork, E.R.	Kinalea	Ballymartle	Kinsale	II.	94
57	Fahanasoodry	411 0 12	Limerick	Coshlea	Ballylanders	Mitchelstown	II.	237
117, 130	Fahane	144 0 6	Cork, W.R.	West Carbery(W.D.)	Kilcrohane	Bantry	II.	143
38	Fahan Level (*Intake*)	390 0 0a	Donegal	Inishowen West	Fahan Upper	Londonderry	III.	121
23	Fahanlunaghta Beg	257 2 11	Clare	Corcomroe	Kilmanaheen	Ennistimon	II.	21
23, 31	Fahanlunaghta More	205 2 34	Clare	Corcomroe	Kilmanaheen	Ennistimon	II.	21
11	Faharlagh	94 2 29b	Cavan	Lower Loughtee	Annagh	Cavan	III.	79
21, 22	Fahavane	359 3 38	Kerry	Clanmaurice	Kilflyn	Tralee	II.	170
116	Faha West	250 3 15	Cork, W.R.	Bear	Kilcaskan	Castletown	II.	123
57	Faha West	187 3 6	Kerry	Magunihy	Kilbonane	Killarney	II.	200
87, 97	Fahburren	696 2 17c	Mayo	Murrisk	Oughaval	Westport	IV.	161
6, 10	Fahee North	856 3 26	Clare	Burren	Carran	Ballyvaghan	II.	11
72	Faheens	464 2 38	Mayo	Gallen	Kilconduff	Swineford	IV.	148
2	Faheeran	484 3 38	King's Co.	Kilcoursey	Kilcumreragh	Tullamore	I.	141
10	Fahee South	539 3 4	Clare	Burren	Carran	Ballyvaghan	II.	11
5, 9	Faherlaghroe	72 1 11	Clare	Burren	Kilcorney	Ballyvaghan	II.	12
142, 151	Fahouragh	114 3 29	Cork, W.R.	West Carbery (E.D.)	Castlehaven	Skibbereen	II.	138
12, 19	Fahy	1,638 1 7d	Clare	Tulla Upper	Feakle	Tulla	II.	39
35	Fahy	204 1 35	Galway	Ballynahinch	Omey	Clifden	IV.	15
86	Fahy	208 1 39	Galway	Kilconnell	Killallaghtan	Ballinasloe	IV.	41
108, 118	Fahy	808 3 11	Galway	Longford	Fahy	Portumna	IV.	58
54, 67	Fahy	110 2 36e	Galway	Moycullen	Killannin	Oughterard	IV.	69
27	Fahy	105 2 36	Galway	Ross	Ross	Oughterard	IV.	74
72	Fahy	208 3 1	Galway	Tiaquin	Clonkeen	Loughrea	IV.	76
40, 43	Fahy	355 0 28	Kilkenny	Ida	Gaulskill	Waterford	I.	102
11	Fahy	138 2 6	King's Co.	Warrenstown	Ballyburly	Edenderry	I.	144
18	Fahy	215 2 21f	Leitrim	Drumahaire	Drumreilly	Cark.on Shannon	IV.	95
34, 43	Fahy	269 2 14g	Mayo	Erris	Kilcommon	Newport	IV.	144
21	Fahy	157 0 19	Mayo	Tirawley	Kilfian	Killala	IV.	169
44, 45, 53	Fahy Beg	623 2 27	Clare	Tulla Lower	O'Briensbridge	Limerick	II.	38
77	Fahy Beg	120 2 21	Mayo	Burrishoole	Kilmaclasser	Westport	IV.	121
90, 100	Fahybeg	12 0 35	Mayo	Clanmorris	Mayo	Claremorris	IV.	135
64, 75	Fahydorgan	147 2 2	Cork, E.R.	Barrymore	Carrigtohill	Middleton	II.	52
52	Fahykeen	105 0 37	Donegal	Kilmacrenan	Conwal	Letterkenny	III.	126
95,96,103,104	Fahymactibbot	233 3 19	Galway	Dunkellin	Killeeneen	Gort	IV.	30
27	Fahymore	22 1 11	Leitrim	Leitrim	Kiltoghert	Cark.on Shannon	IV.	102
77	Fahy More	92 1 20	Mayo	Burrishoole	Kilmaclasser	Westport	IV.	121
44	Fahy More North	244 0 33	Clare	Tulla Lower	O'Briensbridge	Limerick	II.	38
44, 53	Fahy More South	472 1 38	Clare	Tulla Lower	O'Briensbridge	Limerick	II.	38
84	Fahysvillage	89 0 23	Galway	Athenry	Athenry	Galway	IV.	4
91	Faiafannan	204 2 11	Donegal	Banagh	Killybegs Upper	Glenties	III.	110
15	Fairfield	73 1 19	Dublin	Coolock	Coolock	Dublin North	I.	27
18	Fairfield	7 2 1	Dublin	Coolock	St. Georges	Dublin North	I.	29
19	Fairfield	422 1 10	Galway	Ballymoe	Kilbegnet	Glennamaddy	IV.	8
74	Fairfield	936 0 34	Galway	Clonmacnowen	Kilgerrill	Ballinasloe	IV.	25
105	Fairfield	145 0 38	Galway	Loughrea	Loughrea	Loughrea	IV.	65
9	Fairfield	161 2 37	King's Co.	Lower Philipstown	Ballycommon	Tullamore	I.	142
23, 30	Fairfield	403 2 22	Westmeath	Kilkenny West	Drumraney	Athlone	I.	273
42	Fairfield	27 0 34	Wexford	Forth	Rathaspick	Wexford	I.	312
23	Fairfield Demesne	642 1 31h	Monaghan	Dartree	Ematris	Cootehill	III.	267
19	Fairfield or Forge-lands	124 0 18	Wexford	Scarawalsh	Monart	Enniscorthy	I.	324
117, 118	Fairfield or Gortrea	279 1 5	Galway	Longford	Kilmalinoge	Portumna	IV.	59
29	Fairfield Lower	502 2 39	Mayo	Tirawley	Kilfian	Ballina	IV.	169
29	Fairfield Upper	281 1 37	Mayo	Tirawley	Kilfian	Ballina	IV.	169
20	Fairhill	143 3 10	Clare	Tulla Upper	Feakle	Scarriff	II.	39
59	Fairhill	401 0 13	Galway	Tiaquin	Killoscobe	Mountbellew	IV.	78
7	Fairhill	233 2 30	Louth	Upper Dundalk	Dundalk	Dundalk	I.	178
89	Fairhill	109 1 22	Mayo	Burrishoole	Islandeady	Westport	IV.	121

(a) The area of this Intake does not appear on the Ordnance Maps; that here given is from the "Tenement Valuation."
(b) Including 12A. 0R. 26P. water.
(c) Including 1A. 2R. 35P. water.
(d) Including 3A. 0R. 28P. water.
(e) Including 3A. 0R. 0P. water.
(f) Including 8A. 2R. 38P. water.
(g) Including 115A. 0R. 24P. water.
(h) Including 161A. 0R. 13P. water.

No. of Sheet of the Ordnance Survey Maps.	Townlands and Towns.	Area in Statute Acres.	County.	Barony.	Parish.	Poor Law Union in 1857.	Townland Census of 1851, Part I.	
		A. R. P.					Vol.	Page
31	Fairlane . . .	24 0 16	Waterford .	Decies without Drum	Dungarvan . .	Dungarvan . .	II.	355
31	Fairlane . . .	2 3 10	Waterford .	Decies without Drum	Kilrush . . .	Dungarvan . .	II.	358
27	Fairtahy . .	308 3 18a	Monaghan .	Cremorne . .	Aghnamullen . .	Carrickmacross	III.	258
17, 21	Fairview . .	86 0 2	Dublin . .	Uppercross . .	Clondalkin . .	Dublin South .	I.	39
11, 15	Fairview or Mucklagh	235 3 13b	Armagh . .	Tiranny . . .	Tynan . . .	Armagh . .	III.	60
48	Fairyfield Glebe	55 1 34	Limerick . .	Kilmallock . .	St. Peters & St. Pauls	Kilmallock . .	II.	250
1	Fairyhall . .	105 2 21	Limerick . .	Clanwilliam . .	Stradbally . .	Limerick . .	II.	226
63	Fairyhill . .	9 3 29	Clare . .	Bunratty Lower .	St. Patricks . .	Limerick . .	II.	6
127	Fairyhill . .	350 1 34	Galway . .	Longford . .	Lickmolassy . .	Portumna . .	IV.	61
32, 37	Fairyhill or Ballyregan	133 2 28	Wexford . .	Shelmaliere East .	Artramon . .	Wexford . .	I.	330
15	Fairy Island . .	1 2 5	Sligo . .	Carbury . . .	Calry . . .	Sligo . . .	IV.	220
36	Fairymount . .	676 1 5	Roscommon .	Ballintober South .	Kilgefin . .	Roscommon . .	IV.	189
10	Faithlegg . .	635 1 31	Waterford .	Gaultiere . .	Faithlegg . .	Waterford . .	II.	362
35	Fakeeragh . .	137 1 4c	Galway . .	Ballynahinch . .	Omey . . .	Clifden . .	IV.	15
52	Falbane . . .	163 2 7	Donegal . .	Kilmacrenan . .	Gartan . . .	Letterkenny . .	III.	127
25	Falcarragh . .	186 2 0	Donegal . .	Kilmacrenan . .	Tullaghobegly . .	Dunfanaghy . .	III.	131
56, 57	Falchorrib . .	977 0 8d	Donegal . .	Boylagh . .	Templecrone . .	Glenties . .	III.	115
37	Falduff or Ballyara .	239 0 25	Sligo . .	Leyny . . .	Achonry . .	Tobercurry . .	IV.	228
13	Falfin . . .	31 1 35	Sligo . .	Tireragh . .	Skreen . . .	Dromore West .	IV.	236
67, 76	Falgarrow . .	388 3 13	Donegal . .	Raphoe . .	Kilteevoge . .	Stranorlar . .	III.	139
36	Falgortrevy . .	312 0 28	Londonderry .	Loughinsholin .	Maghera . .	Magherafelt . .	III.	242
4, 7	Fallacarra . .	877 0 30e	Leitrim . .	Rosclogher . .	Killasnet . .	Manorhamilton .	IV.	109
7, 15	Fallagh . . .	342 3 11	Waterford .	Upperthird . .	Mothel . . .	Carrick on Suir	II.	371
44, 52	Fallaghearn . .	1,628 2 22	Tyrone . .	Clogher . .	Errigal Keerogue	Clogher . .	III.	295
42	Fallaghearn . .	168 3 17	Tyrone . .	Omagh East . .	Donacavey . .	Omagh . .	III.	310
18, 19	Fallagh Lower .	487 3 10f	Tyrone . .	Strabane Upper .	Bodoney Lower .	Gortin . .	III.	323
18,19,26,27	Fallagh Middle .	439 1 39g	Tyrone . .	Strabane Upper .	Bodoney Lower .	Gortin . .	III.	323
19, 25	Fallaghmore . .	229 3 35	Queen's Co. .	Ballyadams . .	Ballyadams . .	Athy . . .	I.	231
19, 27	Fallagh Upper .	192 1 0	Tyrone . .	Strabane Upper .	Bodoney Lower .	Gortin . .	III.	323
31,32,35,36	Fallagloon . .	1,642 3 8	Londonderry .	Loughinsholin .	Maghera . .	Magherafelt . .	III.	242
48	Fallagowan . .	132 2 17	Donegal . .	Boylagh . .	Templecrone . .	Glenties . .	III.	115
27, 33	Fallahogy . .	388 3 21	Londonderry .	Loughinsholin .	Kilrea . . .	Ballymoney . .	III.	241
112	Fallakeeran . .	213 1 19	Mayo . .	Clanmorris . .	Kilvine . .	Claremorris . .	IV.	134
8	Fallaneas . .	124 0 9h	Donegal . .	Kilmacrenan . .	Clondavaddog . .	Millford . .	III.	124
45, 53	Fallard or Calhame .	269 2 16	Donegal . .	Kilmacrenan . .	Conwal . .	Letterkenny . .	III.	126
25	Fallarees Commons .	7 3 25i	Kildare . .	Naas South . .	Ballymore Eustace .	Naas . . .	I.	64
19	Fallask . . .	1,009 3 13	Donegal . .	Inishowen West .	Fahan Lower . .	Inishowen . .	III.	120
15	Fallataggart . .	4 1 30	Mayo . .	Tirawley . .	Templemurry . .	Killala . .	IV.	172
13	Fallathurteen . .	105 3 22	Sligo . .	Tireragh . .	Skreen . . .	Dromore West .	IV.	236
86	Fallduff . .	543 3 31	Mayo . .	Murrisk . .	Kilgeever . .	Westport . .	IV.	160
25	Falledeen . .	104 2 11	Roscommon .	Castlereagh . .	Kiltullagh . .	Castlereagh . .	IV.	202
21, 22	Falleen . . .	393 0 20	Tipperary, N.R.	Upper Ormond .	Ballymackey . .	Nenagh . .	II.	289
7, 8	Falleenadatha .	332 2 18	Limerick . .	Owneybeg . .	Doon . . .	Limerick . .	II.	251
44, 46	Falleens . . .	433 0 1	Sligo . .	Coolavin . .	Kilcolman . .	Boyle . . .	IV.	223
27	Falleeny . .	189 2 17	Tipperary, N.R.	Upper Ormond .	Templederry . .	Nenagh . .	II.	293
81, 82	Falleighter . .	819 2 26j	Mayo . .	Costello . .	Aghamore . .	Swineford . .	IV.	137
21	Fallgarve . .	74 1 1	Mayo . .	Tirawley . .	Moygawnagh . .	Killala . .	IV.	171
15	Fallinerlea . .	54 1 35	Antrim . .	Lower Glenarm .	Layd . . .	Ballycastle . .	III.	22
24, 33	Fallmore . .	680 2 4	Mayo . .	Erris . . .	Kilmore . .	Belmullet . .	IV.	146
39, 40	Fallougher . .	68 2 11	Sligo . .	Corran . .	Toomour . .	Boyle . . .	IV.	228
14	Falloward . .	228 0 20	Londonderry .	Tirkeeran . .	Faughanvale . .	Londonderry . .	III.	250
19, 25	Fallowbeg Lower .	292 2 18	Queen's Co. .	Stradbally . .	Tullomoy . .	Athy . . .	I.	248
19, 25	Fallowbeg Middle .	117 0 9	Queen's Co. .	Stradbally . .	Tullomoy . .	Athy . . .	I.	248
25	Fallowbeg Upper .	411 2 30	Queen's Co. .	Stradbally . .	Tullomoy . .	Athy . . .	I.	248
14	Fallowlea . .	116 3 38	Londonderry .	Tirkeeran . .	Faughanvale . .	Londonderry . .	III.	250
20	Fallowvee . .	75 3 9	Antrim . .	Lower Glenarm .	Ardclinis . .	Larne . . .	III.	21
23	Falls . . .	235 1 33	Fermanagh .	Tirkennedy . .	Enniskillen . .	Enniskillen . .	III.	222
64	Fallsollus . .	149 1 21	Mayo . .	Costello . .	Kilcolman . .	Castlereagh . .	IV.	141
32, 36	Fallylea . .	977 0 25	Londonderry .	Loughinsholin .	Killelagh . .	Magherafelt . .	III.	241
20	Falmacbreed . .	31 0 7	Antrim . .	Lower Glenarm .	Ardclinis . .	Larne . . .	III.	21
14, 19	Falmacrilly . .	444 2 4	Antrim . .	Lower Glenarm .	Layd . . .	Ballycastle . .	III.	22
3, 4, 7	Falmore . . .	286 2 30	Louth . .	Upper Dundalk .	Roche . . .	Dundalk . .	I.	179
15, 21	Falmore and Corna-mucklagh .	478 1 20	Roscommon .	Castlereagh . .	Kilcorkey . .	Castlereagh . .	IV.	199
15	Falnaglass . .	122 0 12	Antrim . .	Lower Glenarm .	Layd . . .	Ballycastle . .	III.	22
21, 27	Falnashammer .	73 1 31	Sligo . .	Tirerrill . .	Ballysumaghan .	Sligo . . .	IV.	238
25, 32, 33	Falnasoogaun or Rope-field .	384 0 38	Sligo . .	Leyny . . .	Kilvarnet . .	Tobercurry . .	IV.	232
20, 25	Falrusklin . .	159 0 26	Antrim . .	Lower Glenarm .	Ardclinis . .	Larne . . .	III.	21
14,15,22,23	Falsk . . .	1,107 1 37	King's Co. .	Garrycastle . .	Gallen . . .	Parsonstown .	I.	136
22, 23, 29	Falsk . . .	198 1 15k	Roscommon .	Roscommon . .	Killukin . .	Strokestown .	IV.	211
18	Faltagh . .	201 2 18	Monaghan .	Dartree . .	Aghabog . .	Cootehill . .	III.	203
54, 56	Faltia . . .	432 2 27	Roscommon .	Moycarn . .	Moore . . .	Ballinasloe . .	IV.	207

(a) Including 12A. 3R. 36P. water.
(b) Including 2A. 0R. 37P. water.
(c) Including 2A. 1R. 13P. water.
(d) Including 17A. 2R. 33P. water.

(e) Including 9A. 2R. 1P. water.
(f) Including 5A. 0R. 10P. water.
(g) Including 0A. 2R. 22P. water.
(h) Including 10A. 1R. 2P. water.

(i) Including 1A. 0R. 10P. water.
(j) Including 21A. 0R. 6P. water.
(k) Including 12A. 0R. 25P. water.

No. of Sheet of the Ordnance Survey Maps.	Townlands and Towns.	Area in Statute Acres.			County.	Barony.	Parish.	Poor Law Union in 1857.	Townland Census of 1851. Part I.	
		A.	R.	P.					Vol.	Page
20	Falty	127	1	32	Leitrim	Drumahaire	Inishmagrath	Manorhamilton	IV.	96
17	Faltybanes	100	3	27	Donegal	Kilmacrenan	Clondavaddog	Milford	III.	124
46	Fana	96	1	2	Tipperary, S.R.	Kilnamanagh Lower	Clogher	Cashel	II.	322
92, 98	Fanaghans	168	1	8	Donegal	Banagh	Inver	Donegal	III.	107
4, 9	Fanaghs	409	3	17	Kildare	Ikeathy&Oughterany	Cloncurry	Celbridge	I.	57
114, 115, 127, 128	Fanahy	976	2	11	Cork, W.R.	Bear	Ki'laconenagh	Castletown	II.	125
15	Fanaleen	16	2	19	Clare	Corcomroe	Kilshanny	Ennistimon	II.	21
29	Fananierin	1,526	1	14	Wicklow	Ballinacor South	Ballinacor	Rathdrum	I.	348
8	Fanavolty	216	3	18a	Donegal	Kilmacrenan	Clondavaddog	Milford	III.	124
28	Fanbeg	26	2	1	King's Co.	Coolestown	Clonsast	Edenderry	I.	133
43	Fancroft	490	1	1	King's Co.	Ballybritt	Seirkieran	Roscrea	I.	127
75, 87	Fanick	86	3	3	Cork, E.R.	Barrymore	Templerobin	Cork	II.	58
37, 38	Fanit	315	0	31	Tipperary, N.R.	Owney and Arra	Kilvellane	Nenagh	II.	296
55	Fanningsbog	112	1	27	Tipperary, S.R.	Slievardagh	Lismalin	Callan	II.	335
38, 39	Fanningstown	421	3	19	Kilkenny	Iverk	Owning	Carrick on Suir	I.	106
56	Fanningstown	604	3	35	Limerick	Coshlea	Particles	Kilmallock	II.	240
21	Fanningstown	544	0	34	Limerick	Coshma	Adare	Croom	II.	241
13, 22	Fanningstown	1,049	0	25	Limerick	Smallcounty	Fedamore	Croom	II.	259
46	Fannystown	153	3	29	Wexford	Bargy	Duncormick	Wexford	I.	304
1, 4	Fanore Beg	49	1	7	Clare	Burren	Killonaghan	Ballyvaghan	II.	13
1, 4	Fanore More	1,175	3	15	Clare	Burren	Killonaghan	Ballyvaghan	II.	13
8, 9	Fanta Glebe	375	3	34	Clare	Corcomroe	Kilfenora	Ennistimon	II.	19
28, 34	Fantane North	164	1	4	Tipperary, N.R.	Kilnamanagh Upper	Glenkeen	Thurles	II.	278
34	Fantane South	184	3	5	Tipperary, N.R.	Kilnamanagh Upper	Glenkeen	Thurles	II.	278
48	Fantstown	366	3	23	Limerick	Coshlea	Kilbreedy Major	Kilmallock	II.	239
9, 10	Fanygalvan	245	3	34	Clare	Burren	Carran	Ballyvaghan	II.	11
27	Faraghy	199	1	24b	Monaghan	Farney	Magheross	Carrickmacross	III.	273
18	Farahy	1,127	1	37	Cork, E.R.	Fermoy	Farahy	Mitchelstown	II.	79
28	Farbreaga	441	2	15	Wicklow	Ballinacor South	Moyne	Shillelagh	I.	350
41, 42	Farbreagues	222	2	8	Roscommon	Athlone	Kilmeane	Roscommon	IV.	182
64	Fardross Demesne	173	0	17	Tyrone	Clogher	Clogher	Clogher	III.	292
64, 68	Fardross Mountain	985	2	32	Tyrone	Clogher	Clogher	Clogher	III.	292
15	Fardrum	266	0	37	Fermanagh	Magheraboy	Devenish	Enniskillen	III.	210
29, 35	Fardrum	178	1	33	Westmeath	Clonlonan	Kilcleagh	Athlone	I.	261
2, 5	Fardrumman	823	0	17c	Longford	Longford	Killoe	Longford	I.	159
42, 47	Fardystown	326	3	26	Wexford	Forth	Kildavin	Wexford	I.	310
40	Fargrim	68	1	5	Fermanagh	Clankelly	Galloon	Clones	III.	198
5	Fargrim	72	1	1	Fermanagh	Lurg	Magheraculmoney	Lowtherstown	III.	208
31, 32	Fargrim	173	1	36d	Leitrim	Leitrim	Annaduff	Cark. on Shannon	IV.	99
23, 24	Farkland	917	3	37	Londonderry	Keenaght	Bovevagh	NewTnLimavady	III.	235
121	Farlehanes	213	3	7	Cork, W.R.	East Carbery (W.D.)	Kilkerranmore	Dunmanway	II.	133
121	Farlehanes	352	2	39	Cork, W.R.	East Carbery (W.D.)	Kilmeen	Dunmanway	II.	134
97	Farlistown	35	0	9	Cork, E.R.	Kinalea	Ballymartle	Kinsale	II.	94
97	Farlistown	708	2	31	Cork, E.R.	Kinalea	Templemichael	Kinsale	II.	96
43	Farlough	268	1	27e	Antrim	Upper Toome	Drummaul	Antrim	III.	34
46	Farlough	369	0	16f	Tyrone	Dungannon Middle	Tullyniskan	Dungannon	III.	304
9	Farlow	268	0	6	Londonderry	Keenaght	Tamlaght Finlagan	NewTnLimavady	III.	237
40, 43	Farm	114	2	2g	Fermanagh	Coole	Galloon	Clones	III.	200
1, 2	Farm	503	3	16	Galway	Ballymoe	Templetogher	Glennamaddy	IV.	9
12, 16	Farmacaffly	304	2	10	Armagh	Armagh	Lisnadill	Armagh	III.	45
24	Farmersvale	127	2	14	Dublin	Newcastle	Rathcoole	Celbridge	I.	34
58	Farmhill	181	1	26	Galway	Tiaquin	Abbeyknockmoy	Tuam	IV.	75
101, 111	Farmhill	167	2	38	Mayo	Clanmorris	Crossboyne	Claremorris	IV.	132
14, 21	Farmhill	297	0	39	Mayo	Tirawley	Rathreagh	Killala	IV.	171
32	Farmhill or Barratober	131	0	24	Wexford	Shelmaliere East	Artramon	Wexford	I.	330
23	Farmley	255	2	28	Kilkenny	Shillelogher	Burnchurch	Callan	I.	113
15	Farmley or Skeahanagh	330	0	3h	Wexford	Scarawalsh	Ballycarney	Enniscorthy	I.	322
1, 2	Farmullagh	586	1	18i	Longford	Longford	Killoe	Granard	I.	159
38, 47	Farna	1,500	3	32	Kerry	Trughanacmy	Kilgarrylander	Tralee	II.	210
21	Farnaconnell	185	3	5j	Fermanagh	Magheraboy	Boho	Enniskillen	III.	209
46	Farnagh	146	3	12	Donegal	Kilmacrenan	Aughnish	Milford	III.	122
27	Farnagh	210	3	14k	Leitrim	Leitrim	Kiltoghert	Cark. on Shannon	IV.	102
13, 14	Farnagh	213	0	15	Longford	Ardagh	Ballymacormick	Longford	I.	152
30, 36	Farnagh	269	2	16	Westmeath	Clonlonan	Kilcleagh	Athlone	I.	261
27	Farnaght	42	1	10	Fermanagh	Tirkennedy	Derryvullan	Enniskillen	III.	221
39	Farnaght	257	0	8	Galway	Ross	Cong	Oughterard	IV.	73
36	Farnaght	480	3	9l	Leitrim	Mohill	Cloone	Mohill	IV.	106
88	Farnaght	389	3	15m	Mayo	Murrisk	Oughaval	Westport	IV.	162
97	Farnahoe	398	1	6	Cork, E.R.	Kinalea	Inishannon	Bandon	II.	95
15, 16	Farnaloy	556	1	28	Armagh	Armagh	Derrynoose	Armagh	III.	44

(a) Including 9A. 1R. 1P. water.
(b) Including 10A. 0R. 14P. water.
(c) Including 68A. 2R. 4P. water.
(d) Including 4A. 0R. 31P. water.
(e) Including 6A. 1R. 29P. water.

(f) Including 13A. 3R. 30P. Lough.
(g) Including 22A. 0R. 15P. water.
(h) Including 6A. 2R. 1P. water.
(i) Including 18A. 0R. 39P. water.

(j) Including 2A. 0R. 32P. water.
(k) Including 20A. 0R. 4P. water.
(l) Including 25A. 2R. 18P. water.
(m) Including 3A. 3R. 13P. water.

No. of Sheet of the Ordnance Survey Maps.	Townlands and Towns.	Area in Statute Acres.			County.	Barony.	Parish.	Poor Law Union in 1857.	Townland Census of 1851, Part I.	
		A.	R.	P.					Vol.	Page
27	Farnamullan . .	453	3	28	Fermanagh .	Tirkennedy . .	Cleenish . . .	Enniskillen .	III.	220
20, 21	Farnamurry . .	31	2	32	Tipperary, N.R.	Upper Ormond .	Nenagh . . .	Nenagh . .	II.	292
6, 7, 14, 15	Farnane . . .	431	2	31	Limerick . .	Owneybeg . .	Abington . .	Limerick . .	II.	251
15	Farnanefranklin .	605	2	30	Limerick . .	Owneybeg . .	Doon . . .	Limerick . .	II.	251
22	Farnane Lower .	222	3	38	Waterford .	Decies without Drum	Lickoran . .	Lismore . .	II.	358
72, 83, 84	Farnanes . .	580	0	5	Cork, E.R. .	East Muskerry .	Moviddy . .	Bandon . .	II.	105
107	Farnanes . .	374	3	32	Cork, W.R. .	East Carbery (W.D.)	Fanlobbus . .	Dunmanway .	II.	131
22	Farnane Upper .	233	2	10	Waterford .	Decies without Drum	Lickoran . .	Lismore . .	II.	358
25, 26, 31	Farnans . . .	1,596	3	11	Queen's Co. .	Slievemargy . .	Killabban . .	Carlow . .	I.	245
26	Farnatrane . .	59	0	2	Wexford . .	Ballaghkeen .	Ballyhuskard .	Enniscorthy .	I.	291
123 102, 103, 112, 113	Farnaun . . .	112	2	38	Galway . .	Loughrea . .	Kilthomas . .	Gort . .	IV.	65
	Farnaun . . .	317	3	27	Mayo . .	Costello . . .	Annagh . .	Claremorris .	IV.	138
23, 29	Farnbeg . . .	189	3	10	Roscommon .	Roscommon . .	Bumlin . .	Strokestown .	IV.	208
38	Farnees . . .	450	2	4	Wicklow . .	Ballinacor South .	Kilcommon . .	Shillelagh .	I.	349
31	Farneigh . .	473	2	34	Tipperary, N.R.	Owney and Arra .	Killoscully . .	Nenagh . .	II.	295
40, 41	Farneybridge . .	248	0	37	Tipperary, N.R.	Eliogarty . .	Holycross . .	Thurles . .	II.	270
40	Farneybridgehill .	57	0	14	Tipperary, N.R.	Kilnamanagh Upper	Ballycahill . .	Thurles . .	II.	277
20	Farnham . .	418	2	10a	Cavan . .	Upper Loughtee .	Urney . . .	Cavan . .	III.	86
29	Farnmore . .	173	0	36	Roscommon, .	Roscommon . .	Cloonfinlough .	Strokestown .	IV.	209
40	Farnoge . . .	117	2	27	Kilkenny . .	Ida . . .	Dunkitt . .	Waterford .	I.	101
40	Farnoge East . .	210	2	36	Kilkenny . .	Ida	Rossinan . .	Waterford .	I.	104
40	Farnoge West . .	621	0	31	Kilkenny . .	Ida	Rossinan . .	Waterford .	I.	104
5, 9	Farra . . .	84	3	26	Armagh . .	Oneilland West .	Drumcree . .	Lurgan . .	III.	52
65	Farragans . .	374	2	23	Donegal . .	Boylagh . . .	Lettermacward .	Glenties . .	III.	114
61, 69	Farragans . .	505	0	39	Donegal . .	Raphoe . . .	Convoy . .	Stranorlar .	III.	136
32	Farragh . . .	99	1	9	Cavan . .	Castlerahan . .	Denn . . .	Oldcastle .	III.	68
25	Farragh . . .	118	2	33	Cavan . .	Upper Loughtee .	Kilmore . . .	Cavan . .	III.	84
21, 22	Farragh . . .	186	2	18	Mayo . .	Tirawley . .	Ballysakeery .	Ballina . .	IV.	165
9, 14	Farraghroe . .	463	2	24	Longford . .	Longford . .	Killoe . . .	Longford . .	I.	159
50, 51	Farran . . .	527	3	15	Cork, E.R. .	Barretts . . .	Mourneabbey .	Mallow . .	II.	50
72, 84	Farran . . .	1,072	1	30b	Cork, E.R. .	East Muskerry .	Aglish . . .	Macroom . .	II.	101
8	Farran . . .	102	0	8	Cork, E.R. .	Orrery and Kilmore	Ballyhay . .	Kilmallock .	II.	106
110, 123	Farran . . .	502	2	12	Cork, W.R. .	East Carbery (E.D.)	Kilmaloda . .	Clonakilty .	II.	129
144	Farran . . .	89	3	9	Cork, W.R. .	Ibane and Barryroe .	Ardfield . .	Clonakilty .	II.	148
135	Farran . . .	77	0	9	Cork, W.R. .	Ibane and Barryroe .	Templeomalus .	Clonakilty .	II.	151
15	Farran . . .	189	2	3	Kerry . .	Clanmaurice .	Killury . .	Listowel . .	II.	171
21	Farran . . .	187	0	21	Kerry . .	Clanmaurice .	O'Dorney . .	Tralee . .	II.	172
26	Farran . . .	18	2	15	Kerry . .	Corkaguiny .	Cloghane . .	Dingle . .	II.	175
43, 53	Farran . . .	91	2	27	Kerry . .	Corkaguiny .	Dingle . .	Dingle . .	II.	175
39	Farran . . .	122	1	13	Kerry . .	Trughanacmy .	Dysert . .	Tralee . .	II.	210
65	Farran . . .	56	3	17	Tipperary, S.R.	Clanwilliam .	Emly . . .	Tipperary .	II.	308
84, 96	Farranablake East .	148	2	21	Galway . .	Athenry . .	Athenry . .	Loughrea . .	IV.	4
84, 96	Farranablake West .	51	1	37	Galway . .	Athenry . .	Athenry . .	Loughrea . .	IV.	4
23	Farranacahill . .	79	2	23	Tipperary, N.R.	Eliogarty . .	Templemore .	Roscrea . .	II.	272
14, 15	Farranacardy . .	66	1	4	Sligo . .	Carbury . .	Calry . . .	Sligo . .	IV.	220
59	Farranaclara . .	133	3	22	Tipperary, S.R.	Clanwilliam .	Kilmucklin . .	Tipperary .	II.	309
66	Farranacliff . .	277	2	13	Tipperary, S.R.	Clanwilliam .	Bruis . . .	Tipperary .	II.	305
34	Farranaconaghy .	73	2	8	Fermanagh .	Magherastephana .	Aghalurcher .	Lisnaskea .	III.	216
134	Farranacounter .	94	1	12	Cork, W.R. .	East Carbery (W.D.)	Ross . . .	Clonakilty .	II.	135
149	Farranacoush . .	377	3	17	Cork, W.R. .	West Carbery (E.D.)	Tullagh . .	Skibbereen .	II.	141
34	Farranacurky . .	131	0	7	Fermanagh .	Magherastephana .	Aghalurcher .	Lisnaskea .	III.	216
11	Farranacurragh .	37	0	21	Carlow . .	Idrone West . .	Oldleighlin .	Carlow . .	I.	9
27	Farranacushog .	127	3	20	Antrim . .	Kilconway . .	Dunaghy . .	Ballymena .	III.	26
29	Farranaderry . .	172	3	38	Tipperary, N.R.	Eliogarty . .	Templemore .	Thurles . .	II.	272
10	Farranadoony . .	128	2	0	Meath . .	Lower Kells . .	Moynalty . .	Kells . .	I.	204
10	Farranadum . .	259	3	2	Kildare . .	Ikeathy & Oughterany	Clonshanbo .	Celbridge .	I.	57
24, 33	Farranafina . .	74	0	12	Limerick . .	Coonagh . .	Oola . . .	Tipperary .	II.	235
15, 16	Farranafreney . .	136	3	25	Carlow . .	Idrone West . .	Killinane . .	Carlow . .	I.	9
10	Farranagalliagh .	98	3	18	Roscommon .	Boyle . . .	Estersnow . .	Boyle . .	IV.	195
6	Farranagalliagh East	49	1	17	Roscommon .	Boyle . . .	Ardcarn . .	Boyle . .	IV.	193
6	Farranagalliagh West	42	3	17	Roscommon .	Boyle . . .	Ardcarn . .	Boyle . .	IV.	193
142, 151	Farranagilla . .	61	3	33	Cork, W.R. .	West Carbery (E.D.)	Abbeystrowry .	Skibbereen .	II.	136
142, 151	Farranagilla . .	102	2	19c	Cork, W.R. .	West Carbery (E.D.)	Castlehaven .	Skibbereen .	II.	138
8, 9	Farranaglogh . .	258	1	20	Meath . .	Fore . . .	Kilbride . .	Oldcastle .	I.	200
111	Farranagow . .	99	1	12	Cork, W.R. .	East Carbery (E.D.)	Inishannon .	Bandon . .	II.	128
23	Farranakill . .	20	2	38	Longford . .	Shrule . . .	Taghsheenod .	Ballymahon .	I.	166
25	Farranalahesery .	274	2	6	Waterford .	Decies without Drum	Kilbarrymeaden	Kilmacthomas .	I.	356
11	Farranalcock . .	180	0	12	Meath . .	Lower Kells . .	Kilbeg . .	Kells . .	I.	202
62	Farranaleen . .	115	2	38	Tipperary, S.R.	Middlethird . .	Rathcool . .	Cashel . .	II.	329
12, 17	Farranalessary .	288	0	17	Antrim . .	Upper Dunluce .	Ballymoney . .	Ballymoney .	III.	13
45	Farranalickeen .	52	3	28	Kerry . .	Corkaguiny .	Ballinvoher .	Dingle . .	II.	174
95, 96	Farranalough . .	1,262	0	6	Cork, W.R. .	Kinalmeaky . .	Murragh . .	Bandon . .	II.	152

(a) Including 39A. 0R. 2P. water.   (b) Including 11A. 3R. 11P. water.   (c) Including 4A. 1R. 22P. water.

No. of Sheet of the Ordnance Survey Maps.	Townlands and Towns.	Area in Statute Acres.	County.	Barony.	Parish.	Poor Law Union in 1857.	Townland Census of 1851, Part I.	
		A. R. P.					Vol.	Page
39	Farranalounty	87 2 9	Waterford	Decies within Drum	Ardmore	Dungarvan	II.	350
105	Farranalynch	40 3 10	Loughrea	Loughrea	Loughrea	Loughrea	IV.	65
129, 138	Farranamanagh	313 3 17	Cork, W.R.	West Carbery (W.D.)	Kilcrohane	Bantry	II.	143
60	Farranamanagh	655 3 10	Tipperary, S.R.	Middlethird	Horeabbey	Cashel	II.	327
112	Farranamoy	94 1 19	Cork, E.R.	Kinsale	Clontead	Kinsale	II.	99
39, 48	Farranamranagh	260 0 0	Kerry	Trughanacmy	Currans	Killarney	II.	209
16, 20	Farranamucklagh	478 2 34	Armagh	Fews Upper	Lisnadill	Armagh	III.	49
8	Farranaphlure	207 3 34	Carlow	Carlow	Grangeford	Carlow	I.	2
59	Farranaraheen	48 1 30	Tipperary, S.R.	Clanwilliam	Rathlynin	Tipperary	II.	309
30	Farranaree	73 2 38	Kilkenny	Kells	Killamery	Callan	I.	108
112	Farranarouga North	23 0 30	Cork, E.R.	Kinsale	Ringcurran	Kinsale	II.	100
112	Farranarouga South	9 1 2	Cork, E.R.	Kinsale	Ringcurran	Kinsale	II.	100
65, 66	Farranasa	171 1 35	Tipperary, S.R.	Clanwilliam	Emly	Tipperary	II.	308
34	Farranasculloge	195 0 37	Fermanagh	Magherastephana	Aghalurcher	Lisnaskea	III.	216
66	Farranaspig	70 0 32	Kerry	Magunihy	Aghadoe	Killarney	II.	199
5	Farranastack	368 0 23	Kerry	Iraghticonnor	Lisselton	Listowel	II.	192
51,52,62,63	Farranastig	1,799 1 31	Cork, E.R.	Cork	Whitechurch	Cork	II.	66
28	Farranatlaba	197 2 18	Limerick	Shanid	Ardagh	Newcastle	II.	255
112	Farranatouke	35 2 0	Cork, E.R.	Kinsale	Ringcurran	Kinsale	II.	100
72	Farranavarra	60 2 14	Cork, E.R.	East Muskerry	Aglish	Macroom	II.	101
53	Farranavarra	395 1 28	Tipperary, S.R.	Middlethird	Ballysheehan	Cashel	II.	325
71	Farranavarrigane	171 2 13	Cork, W.R.	West Muskerry	Macloneigh	Macroom	II.	160
51	Farranavulla	127 1 39	Tipperary, S.R.	Kilnamanagh Lower	Ballintemple	Cashel	II.	322
3	Farranawana	213 2 38	Kerry	Iraghticonnor	Kilnaughtin	Glin	II.	191
27, 28	Farranawillin	100 2 26	Roscommon	Castlereagh	Baslick	Castlereagh	IV.	199
22	Farranboley	150 2 7	Dublin	Rathdown	Taney	Rathdown	I.	38
99, 113	Farranbrien East	649 3 32	Cork, E.R.	Kinalea	Tracton	Kinsale	II.	97
98,99,112,113	Farranbrien West	659 3 34	Cork, E.R.	Kinalea	Tracton	Kinsale	II.	97
30	Farranbullen	13 3 35	Waterford	Decies without Drum	Whitechurch	Dungarvan	II.	361
12	Farrancallin	227 2 21	Westmeath	Corkaree	Taghmon	Mullingar	I.	264
8	Farrancassidy	325 0 11	Fermanagh	Magheraboy	Inishmacsaint	Ballyshannon	III.	212
74	Farrancleary	15 1 17a	Cork, E.R.	Cork, Municipal Borough of	St. Annes Shandon	Cork	II.	111
151	Farranconnor	114 1 30	Cork, W.R.	West Carbery (E.D.)	Castlehaven	Skibbereen	II.	138
16, 24	Farrancotter	165 2 10	Cork, E.R.	Orrery and Kilmore	Buttevant	Mallow	II.	107
74	Farrandahadore Beg	34 2 36	Cork, E.R.	Cork	St. Finbar's	Cork	II.	66
74	Farrandahadore More	137 1 10	Cork, E.R.	Cork	St. Finbar's	Cork	II.	66
35	Farrandalouge	219 0 24	Kerry	Corkaguiny	Stradbally	Dingle	II.	180
142, 151	Farrandau	117 0 21	Cork, W.R.	West Carbery (E.D.)	Castlehaven	Skibbereen	II.	138
30, 39	Farrandeelion	238 1 29	Mayo	Tirawley	Ballynahaglish	Ballina	IV.	164
16	Farrandeen	47 2 26	Kerry	Clanmaurice	Kilcaragh	Listowel	II.	169
151	Farrandeligeen	101 3 10	Cork, W.R.	West Carbery (E.D.)	Castlehaven	Skibbereen	II.	138
31	Farranderry	16 1 3	Meath	Lower Navan	Ardsallagh	Navan	I.	214
39	Farrandoctor	193 0 26	Kerry	Trughanacmy	Currans	Killarney	II.	209
7	Farrandreg	134 1 1	Louth	Upper Dundalk	Castletown	Dundalk	I.	177
83, 84	Farranduff	15 1 5	Cork, E.R.	East Muskerry	Moviddy	Bandon	II.	105
9	Farranedmond	10 0 32	Kerry	Clanmaurice	Rattoo	Listowel	II.	173
112	Farraneen	50 2 17	Cork, E.R.	Kinalea	Tracton	Kinsale	II.	97
53	Farraneesteenig	57 2 26	Kerry	Corkaguiny	Garfinny	Dingle	II.	176
22, 23	Farraneglish Glebe	177 1 20	Queen's Co.	Clarmallagh	Aghaboe	Abbeyleix	I.	236
88	Farraneshagh	48 1 16	Tipperary, S.R.	Iffa and Offa West	Ardfinnan	Clogheen	II.	316
59	Farranetra	129 1 5c	Tyrone	Clogher	Clogher	Clogher	III.	292
37	Farranfad	643 3 32	Down	Kinelarty	Loughinisland	Downpatrick	III.	177
91, 105	Farranfadda	557 1 8	Cork, W.R.	Bantry	Kilmocomoge	Bantry	II.	121
74	Farranferris	93 2 21d	Cork, E.R.	Cork and Municipal Borough	St. Annes Shandon	Cork	II.	65
43	Farranflaherty	66 1 4	Kerry	Corkaguiny	Dingle	Dingle	II.	175
19, 26	Farranfolliot	136 0 33	Westmeath	Moyashel and Magheradernon	Mullingar	Mullingar	I.	275
48	Farranfore	210 3 5	Kerry	Magunihy	Molahiffe	Killarney	II.	205
111, 112	Farrangalway	211 1 32	Cork, E.R.	Kinsale	Ringcurran	Kinsale	II.	100
22	Farrangarode	349 2 4	Sligo	Tireragh	Castleconor	Ballina	IV.	232
40	Farrangarret	81 1 2e	Waterford	Decies within Drum	Ardmore	Youghal	II.	350
30	Farrangarve	435 0 0	Cavan	Tullyhunco	Killashandra	Cavan	III.	98
55	Farrangavnagh	57 0 23	Galway	Clare	Cargin	Tuam	IV.	18
22, 30	Farrangeel	391 2 20	Cork, E.R.	Duhallow	Kilmeen	Kanturk	II.	72
96	Farranhavane	496 1 25	Cork, W.R.	Kinalmeaky	Templemartin	Bandon	II.	153
106	Farraniaragh	408 0 30	Kerry	Dunkerron South	Kilcrohane	Cahersiveen	II.	183
22, 23	Farranimrish	150 1 36	Sligo	Tireragh	Castleconor	Dromore West	IV.	232
19	Farranistick	87 3 19	Westmeath	Moyashel and Magheradernon	Mullingar	Mullingar	I.	275
83	Farranjordan	52 1 9	Tipperary, S.R.	Iffa and Offa East	Kilaloan	Clonmel	II.	314
29	Farrankeal	408 2 10	Cork, E.R.	Duhallow	Nohavaldaly	Millstreet	II.	75
48, 49, 59	Farrankeal	246 3 0	Kerry	Trughanacmy	Killeentierna	Killarney	II.	211

(a) Included in the Parish of St. Annes Shandon.
(b) Including 5A. 2R. 32P. water.
(c) Including 0A. 3R. 0P. water.
(d) { Within the Municipal Boundary, 25A. 0R. 35P.
{ Without the Municipal Boundary, 68A. 1R. 26P.
(e) Including 0A. 1R. 35P. detached portions.

No. of Sheet of the Ordnance Survey Maps.	Townlands and Towns.	Area in Statute Acres.			County.	Barony.	Parish.	Poor Law Union in 1857.	Townland Census of 1851, Part I.	
		A.	R.	P.					Vol.	Page
13	Farrankelly .	126	1	17	Wicklow . .	Newcastle . .	Kilcoole . .	Rathdrum .	I.	351
69	Farrankindry .	197	0	37	Tipperary, S.R.	Middlethird .	Knockgraffon .	Cashel .	II.	328
75	Farranlahassery .	105	2	9a	Tipperary, S.R.	Iffa and Offa West .	Caher . .	Clogheen .	II.	317
27	Farranlaheshery East	37	1	15	Cork, E.R. .	Condons&Clangibbon	Dunmahon .	Fermoy .	II.	60
27	FarranlahesheryWest	169	2	24	Cork, E.R. .	Fermoy . .	Dunmahon .	Fermoy .	II.	79
33, 42	Farranlateeve .	374	1	0	Kerry . .	Corkaguiny .	Dunurlin .	Dingle .	II.	176
3, 7	Farranlester . .	213	3	38	Londonderry .	Coleraine .	Dunboe . .	Coleraine .	III.	231
7	Farranlester . .	191	3	17	Londonderry .	Coleraine .	Macosquin .	Coleraine .	III.	233
68, 69	Farranliney .	156	1	25	Tipperary, S.R.	Middlethird .	Knockgraffon .	Cashel .	II.	328
10	Farranmacallan .	160	3	36	Antrim . .	Cary . .	Culfeightrin .	Ballycastle .	III.	13
9	Farranmacarter .	117	1	0	Antrim . .	Cary . .	Culfeightrin .	Ballycastle .	III.	13
80	Farranmacbride .	56	0	38	Donegal . .	Banagh . .	Glencolumbkille .	Glenties .	III.	105
15	Farranmacbrien .	168	1	16	Tipperary, N.R.	Lower Ormond .	Modreeny .	Borrisokane .	II.	286
42	Farranmacedmond .	140	0	0	Kilkenny . .	Iverk . .	Rathkieran .	Waterford .	I.	107
12, 18	Farranmacfarrell .	518	0	21	Sligo . .	Tireragh . .	Kilmacshalgan .	Dromore West .	IV.	235
14	Farranmacshane .	43	1	35	King's Co. .	Garrycastle .	Tisaran . .	Parsonstown .	I.	138
74	Farranmacteige .	135	1	16b	Cork, E.R. .	Cork . .	St. Finbars .	Cork .	II.	66
47, 57	Farranmanagh .	741	3	18	Kerry . .	Magunihy .	Kilcolman .	Killarney .	II.	200
36	Farranmanny North	20	1	4	Westmeath .	Clonlonan .	Kilcleagh .	Athlone .	I.	261
35, 36	Farranmanny South	18	1	31	Westmeath .	Clonlonan .	Kilcleagh .	Athlone .	I.	261
95	Farranmareen .	493	2	2	Cork, W.R. .	East Carbery (W.D.)	Kinneagh .	Bandon .	II.	134
32	Farranmaurice .	140	2	18	Sligo . .	Corran . .	Cloonoghil .	Tobercurry .	IV.	225
17	Farranmiller . .	106	3	37	Limerick .	Shanid . .	Kilfergus .	Glin . .	II.	256
22	Farranmorgan .	206	0	21	Sligo . .	Tireragh . .	Kilmoremoy .	Ballina .	IV.	235
43	Farrannabox .	25	1	5	Galway . .	Clare . .	Tuam . .	Tuam .	IV.	23
39	Farrannabrack .	144	1	18	Kerry . .	Trughanacmy .	Castleisland .	Tralee .	II.	208
44	Farrannacarriga .	202	3	18	Kerry . .	Corkaguiny .	Ballynacourty .	Dingle .	II.	174
123	Farrannagark .	290	1	6	Cork, W.R. .	East Carbery (E.D.)	Rathclarin .	Bandon .	II.	130
81	Farrannagark .	57	3	27c	Tipperary, S.R.	Iffa and Offa West .	Caher . .	Clogheen .	II.	317
93	Farrannahineeny .	230	1	32	Cork, W.R. .	East Carbery (W.D.)	Kilmichael .	Dunmanway .	II.	134
89	Farrannahow .	245	0	28	Kerry . .	Iveragh . .	Dromod .	Cahersiveen .	II.	195
43	Farrannakilla .	49	2	18	Kerry . .	Corkaguiny .	Dingle . .	Dingle .	II.	175
35	Farrannakilla .	92	2	17	Kerry . .	Corkaguiny .	Stradbally .	Dingle .	II.	180
88	Farrannamanagh .	84	1	10	Cork, E.R. .	Imokilly . .	Cloyne . .	Middleton .	II.	85
43	Farrannamartin .	93	3	38	Galway . .	Clare . .	Tuam . .	Tuam .	IV.	23
22	Farrannamoreen .	379	2	31	Westmeath .	Kilkenny West .	Kilkenny West .	Athlone .	I.	273
22, 30	Farrannaculloge .	657	0	21	Mayo . .	Tirawley .	Ardagh .	Ballina .	IV.	163
109	Farrannasheshery .	304	3	11	Cork, W.R. .	East Carbery (E.D.)	Desertserges .	Bandon .	II.	128
30	Farrannoo .	316	0	20	Mayo . .	Tirawley .	Kilmoremoy .	Ballina .	IV.	170
35	Farran North .	80	3	27	Cork, E.R. .	Barrymore .	Castlelyons .	Fermoy .	II.	53
4, 5	Farranpierce . .	509	1	38	Kerry . .	Iraghticonnor .	Killehenny .	Listowel .	II.	191
79	Farranreagh .	430	3	24	Kerry . .	Iveragh . .	Valencia .	Cahersiveen .	II.	198
43	Farranredmond .	30	2	8	Kerry . .	Corkaguiny .	Dingle . .	Dingle .	II.	175
41	Farranreigh .	152	3	8	Tipperary, N.R.	Eliogarty .	Thurles .	Thurles .	II.	273
49, 55	Farranrory Lower .	888	3	5	Tipperary, S.R.	Slievardagh .	Ballingarry .	Callan .	II.	331
49	Farranrory Upper .	395	2	2	Tipperary, S.R.	Slievardagh .	Ballingarry .	Callan .	II.	331
24, 25	Farranseer . .	336	1	7	Cavan . .	Tullyhunco .	Killashandra .	Cavan .	III.	98
7	Farranseer . .	97	1	14	Londonderry .	Coleraine .	Macosquin .	Coleraine .	III.	233
50	Farranshane .	115	2	32	Antrim . .	Upper Antrim .	Antrim . .	Antrim .	III.	5
70	Farranshea .	277	2	16	Tipperary, S.R.	Middlethird .	Peppardstown .	Cashel .	II.	329
19	Farranshock or Rathgowan . . }	85	3	38	Westmeath .	Moyashel & Magheradernon . }	Mullingar .	Mullingar .	I.	275
5	Farranshone Beg .	34	3	35d	Limerick . .	Pubblebrien & Municipal Borough .	St. Nicholas .	Limerick .	II.	254
9, 10, 17, 18	Farranshoneen .	174	2	1	Waterford .	Gaultiere .	Ballynakill .	Waterford .	II.	362
5	Farranshone More .	232	3	35e	Limerick . .	Pubblebrien & Municipal Borough .	St. Nicholas .	Limerick .	II.	254
7	Farranshonikeen .	84	0	21	Cork, E.R. .	Orrery and Kilmore .	Rathgoggan .	Kilmallock .	II.	109
35, 44	Farran South .	127	2	26	Cork, E.R. .	Barrymore .	Castlelyons .	Fermoy .	II.	53
29	Farranstephen .	45	0	20	Kerry . .	Trughanacmy .	Tralee . .	Tralee .	II.	213
36	Farrantaun .	22	3	13	Kerry . .	Corkaguiny .	Killiney .	Dingle .	II.	178
33	Farrantemple .	151	0	32	Kilkenny . .	Ida . .	The Rower .	New Ross .	I.	104
26	Farrantemple Glebe	396	2	35	Londonderry .	Coleraine .	Errigal . .	Coleraine .	III.	232
95	Farranthomas .	546	1	12	Cork, W.R. .	Kinalmeaky .	Murragh .	Bandon .	II.	152
35	Farrantooleen .	219	3	14	Kerry . .	Corkaguiny .	Stradbally .	Dingle .	II.	180
56	Farrantoreen .	336	3	34f	Kerry . .	Trughanacmy .	Killorglin .	Killarney .	II.	211
77	Farrantrenchard .	129	0	39g	Cork, E.R. .	Imokilly . .	Ballyoughtera .	Middleton .	II.	34
28	Farranville .	108	1	36	Queen's Co. .	Clandonagh .	Bordwell .	Donaghmore .	I.	233
20	Farranwilliam .	22	1	16	Kerry . .	Clanmaurice .	Ardfert . .	Tralee .	II.	167
25	Farranydaly .	237	2	34	Cavan . .	Upper Loughtee .	Kilmore .	Cavan .	III.	84
12, 13, 18, 19, 24, 25 }	Farranyharpy .	2,200	1	9	Sligo . .	Tireragh . .	Skreen . .	Dromore West	IV	236
38, 41	Farranykelly .	419	2	26h	Roscommon .	Athlone . .	Fuerty . .	Roscommon .	IV.	181
13	Farranyoogan .	202	2	12	Longford . .	Ardagh . .	Ballymacormick .	Longford .	I.	152

(a) Including 1A. 3R. 8P. water.
(b) Including 6A. 1R. 28P. water.
(c) Including 1A. 0R. 20P. water.

(d) { Within the Municipal Boundary, 34A. 2R. 18P.
{ Without the Municipal Boundary, 0A. 1R. 17P.
(e) { Within the Municipal Boundary, 173A. 3R. 30P.
{ Without the Municipal Boundary, 59A. 0R. 5P.

(f) Including 28A. 1R. 6P. water.
(g) Including 17A. 1R. 20P. Lough Aderry.
(h) Including 1A. 0R. 8P. water.

No. of Sheet of the Ordnance Survey Maps.	Townlands and Towns.	Area in Statute Acres. A. R. P.	County.	Barony.	Parish.	Poor Law Union in 1857.	Townland Census of 1851, Part I. Vol.	Page
71	Farravaun . .	1,125 3 34	Galway . .	Clare . . .	Monivea . . .	Galway . .	IV.	23
40	Farravaun . .	232 0 14	Galway . .	Moycullen . .	Kilcummin . .	Oughterard .	IV.	67
26	Farrest . . .	181 2 31	Tyrone . .	Strabane Upper .	Cappagh . . .	Omagh . .	III.	325
46	Farrihy . . .	584 2 10a	Clare . .	Moyarta . .	Kilfearagh . .	Kilrush . .	II.	32
54	Farrihy . . .	1,030 0 33	Limerick . .	Glenquin . .	Killagholehane .	Newcastle .	II.	245
53	Farriter . . .	271 0 33	Tyrone . .	Dungannon Lower .	Killeeshil . .	Dungannon .	III.	298
11	Farrow . . .	365 0 30	Westmeath .	Corkaree . .	Leny . . .	Mullingar .	I.	262
12	Farrow, Barr of .	844 3 26b	Leitrim . .	Drumahaire . .	Cloonclare . .	Manorhamilton .	IV.	93
53	Farsetmore . .	125 2 28	Donegal . .	Raphoe . .	Leck . . .	Letterkenny .	III.	140
88	FARSID T. . .	—	Cork, E.R. .	Imokilly . .	Aghada . . .	Middleton .	II.	83
40	Farsnagh . . .	199 3 29	Tyrone . .	Dungannon Upper .	Arboe . . .	Cookstown .	III.	305
97	Farta . . .	133 1 29	Galway . .	Athenry . .	Kiltullagh . .	Loughrea .	IV.	5
34	Fartadreen . .	244 1 19	Cavan . .	Castlerahan . .	Killinkere . .	Bailieborough .	III.	69
29	Fartagar . . .	196 1 7	Galway . .	Dunmore . .	Kilbennan . .	Tuam . .	IV.	34
44	Fartagh . . .	604 3 31	Cavan . .	Castlerahan . .	Loughan or Castle-keeran . .	Oldcastle . .	III.	69
27	Fartagh . . .	141 3 35c	Cavan . .	Clankee . .	Knockbride . .	Cootehill . .	III.	73
2	Fartagh . . .	60 2 39	Fermanagh .	Lurg . . .	Drumkeeran . .	Lowtherstown .	III.	206
21	Fartagh . . .	91 0 37	Fermanagh .	Magheraboy . .	Devenish . .	Enniskillen .	III.	210
27, 30	Fartagorman . .	124 1 28	Monaghan .	Farney . .	Magheross . .	Carrickmacross	III.	273
16, 29	Fartamore . .	563 3 31d	Galway . .	Dunmore . .	Kilbennan . .	Tuam . .	IV.	34
21	Fartan Lower .	147 3 27	Cavan . .	Upper Loughtee .	Castleterra . .	Cavan . .	III.	82
17	Fartannan . .	593 3 15	Sligo . .	Tireragh . .	Kilmacshalgan .	Dromore West .	IV.	235
21	Fartan Upper .	84 1 19	Cavan . .	Upper Loughtee .	Castleterra . .	Cavan . .	III.	82
98, 112	Fartha . . .	524 2 1	Cork, E.R. .	Kinalea . .	Ballyfeard . .	Kinsale . .	II.	93
33, 39	Farthingstown .	1,804 3 37	Westmeath .	Fartullagh . .	Castlelost . .	Mullingar .	I.	268
17	Farthingstown .	281 1 3	Westmeath .	Rathconrath .	Rathconrath . .	Mullingar .	I.	284
7	Farthingville East .	482 3 10	Cork, E.R. .	Orrery and Kilmore	Shandrum . .	Kanturk . .	II.	110
1, 6, 7	Farthingville West .	430 3 13	Cork. E.R. .	Orrery and Kilmore	Shandrum . .	Kanturk . .	II.	110
14	Fartrin . . .	281 1 34e	Cavan . .	Lower Loughtee .	Tomregan . .	Bawnboy . .	III.	81
35	Fary . . .	94 0 28	Wexford . .	Shelmaliere West .	Clongeen . .	New Ross .	I.	332
149	Fasagh . . .	133 3 34	Cork, W.R. .	West Carbery (E.D.)	Aghadown . .	Skibbereen .	II.	137
26, 27	Fasagh . . .	199 3 26	Kildare . .	Offaly West . .	Ballybrackan . .	Athy . .	I.	71
48	Fasagh . . .	16 1 16	Wexford . .	Forth . . .	Kilrane . .	Wexford . .	I.	311
53	Fasglashagh . .	501 1 37	Tyrone . .	Dungannon Lower .	Killeeshil . .	Dungannon .	III.	298
10	Faslowart . .	125 3 33	Leitrim . .	Drumahaire . .	Drumlease . .	Manorhamilton .	IV.	94
7, 8	Fassagh . . .	863 2 32	Fermanagh .	Magheraboy . .	Inishmacsaint .	Ballyshannon .	III.	213
29, 30	Fassagh . . .	204 3 17	Westmeath .	Clonlonan . .	Ballyloughloe .	Athlone . .	I.	260
3, 4, 7, 8	Fassaroe . . .	568 1 35	Wicklow . .	Rathdown . .	Kilmacanoge . .	Rathdown .	I.	355
153	Fastness Rock .	—	Cork, W.R. .	West Carbery(W.D.)	Kilmoe . .	Skull . .	II.	145
16	Fastry . . .	144 0 19	Monaghan .	Dartree . .	Currin . . .	Clones . .	III.	266
22	Fastry or Racreeghan	284 0 10f	Monaghan .	Dartree . .	Ematris . . .	Cootehill . .	III.	267
17	Fatharnagh . .	134 0 2	Queen's Co. .	Maryborough West .	Clonenagh&Clonagheen	Abbeyleix .	I.	243
29	Fathom Lower .	730 2 7g	Armagh . .	Orior Upper . .	Newry . . .	Newry . .	III.	59
29	Fathom Upper .	813 3 16	Armagh . .	Orior Upper . .	Newry . . .	Newry . .	III.	59
20	Fatthen . . .	54 3 37	Tipperary, N.R. .	Owney and Arra .	Monsea . . .	Nenagh . .	II.	296
7	Faughalstown .	995 0 25	Westmeath .	Fore . . .	Faughalstown .	Castletowndelvin	I.	269
24	Faughanhill . .	159 2 25	Meath . .	Lower Navan .	Martry . .	Kells . .	I.	215
15	Faughanvale . .	218 0 28	Londonderry .	Tirkeeran . .	Faughanvale .	NewTnLimavady	III.	250
27, 28	Faughard . .	124 2 17	Fermanagh .	Tirkennedy . .	Cleenish . .	Enniskillen .	III.	220
4, 7	Faughart Lower .	331 1 11	Louth . .	Lower Dundalk .	Ballymascanlan .	Dundalk . .	I.	176
4	Faughart Upper .	452 0 18	Louth . .	Lower Dundalk .	Ballymascanlan .	Dundalk . .	I.	176
7, 8	Faughary . .	1,162 2 8	Leitrim . .	Rosclogher . .	Killasnet . .	Manorhamilton .	IV.	109
80, 81	Faugher . . .	46 3 35	Donegal . .	Banagh . .	Glencolumbkille .	Glenties . .	III.	105
16, 26	Faugher . . .	329 1 36	Donegal . .	Kilmacrenan .	Clondahorky . .	Dunfanaghy .	III.	123
21	Faugher . . .	54 0 6	Fermanagh .	Magheraboy . .	Boho . .	Enniskillen .	III.	209
21	Faugher . . .	54 2 13	Fermanagh .	Magheraboy . .	Devenish . .	Enniskillen .	III.	210
80, 81	Faugher Mountain .	436 0 0	Donegal . .	Banagh . .	Glencolumbkille .	Glenties . .	III.	105
20	Faughil . . .	88 1 9	Antrim . .	Lower Glenarm .	Layd . . .	Ballycastle .	III.	22
80, 81	Faughil . . .	189 3 28	Mayo . .	Costello . .	Knock . .	Claremorris .	IV.	143
15	Faughts . . .	196 3 22	Sligo . .	Carbury . .	Calry . . .	Sligo . .	IV.	220
35	Faul . . .	185 2 24	Galway . .	Ballynahinch .	Moyrus . .	Clifden . .	IV.	13
11	Faulagh . . .	946 1 0	Mayo . .	Erris . . .	Kilcommon . .	Belmullet .	IV.	144
67, 68	Fauleens . . .	140 1 19h	Mayo . .	Burrishoole .	Burrishoole . .	Newport . .	IV.	119
63	Fauleens . . .	543 2 27	Mayo . .	Costello . .	Kilbeagh . .	Swineford .	IV.	140
17, 18	Fauleens . . .	600 2 33	Mayo . .	Erris . . .	Kilcommon . .	Belmullet .	IV.	144
6, 9, 10	Faulkland . .	226 1 33	Monaghan .	Trough . .	Donagh . .	Monaghan .	III.	282
127	Faulkner's Island	0 1 13	Galway . .	Longford . .	Lickmolassy . .	Portumna .	IV.	61
35	Faulties . . .	99 3 6i	Leitrim . .	Mohill . .	Annaduff . .	Mohill . .	IV.	105
21	Fauna . . .	235 2 24	Wicklow . .	Upper Talbotstown .	Donaghmore . .	Baltinglass .	I.	363
4	Faunarooska . .	232 0 26	Clare . .	Burren . .	Killonaghan . .	Ballyvaghan .	II.	13
5	Faunarooska . .	536 0 29	Clare . .	Burren . . .	Rathborney . .	Ballyvaghan .	II.	14

(a) Including 29A. 0R. 15P. water.
(b) Including 3A. 2R. 16P. water.
(c) Including 5A. 2R. 1P. water.
(d) Including 23A. 1R. 28P. water.

(e) Including 9A. 2R. 13P. water.
(f) Including 22A. 1R. 31P. water.
(g) { Including 23A. 1R. 15P. detached portion.
      { Including 3A. 2R. 39P. water.

(h) Including 6A. 0R. 29P. water.
(i) Including 4A. 1R. 1P. water.

No. of Sheet of the Ordnance Survey Maps.	Townlands and Towns.	Area in Statute Acres.	County.	Barony.	Parish.	Poor Law Union in 1857.	Townland Census of 1851, Part I.	
		A. R. P.					Vol.	Page
122	Faunin	90 1 19	Galway	Kiltartan	Kilmacduagh	Gort	IV.	48
101, 102	Faunkill-and-the-Woods	370 0 5	Cork, W.R.	Bear	Kilcatherine	Castletown	II.	124
129	Faunmore	262 0 8	Cork, W.R.	West Carbery(W.D.)	Kilcrohane	Bantry	II.	143
25, 26	Faunrusk	115 0 28a	Clare	Bunratty Upper	Templemaley	Ennis	II.	11
33	Faurkagh	113 2 35	Fermanagh	Knockninny	Kinawley	Lisnaskea	III.	202
10	Faus	574 0 9	Roscommon	Boyle	Estersnow	Boyle	IV.	195
59	Favor Royal Demesne	670 3 20b	Tyrone	Clogher	Errigal Trough	Clogher	III.	296
35	Fawans	385 3 15	Donegal	Kilmacrenan	Kilmacrenan	Milford	III.	129
10,11,14,15	Fawn	615 1 20c	Leitrim	Drumahaire	Drumlease	Manorhamilton	IV.	94
27	Fawn	146 0 24	Leitrim	Leitrim	Kiltoghert	Car.k on Shannon	IV.	102
33, 42	Fawnaboy	1,824 1 9d	Donegal	Kilmacrenan	Tullaghobegly	Dunfanaghy	III.	131
67	Fawnagowan	253 1 24	Tipperary, S.R.	Clanwilliam	Cordangan	Tipperary	II.	306
10	Fawnamore	209 2 2	Limerick	Shanid	Robertstown	Rathkeale	II.	258
6, 10	Fawnanierin	146 3 27	Roscommon	Boyle	Kilbryan	Boyle	IV.	195
104	Fawnarevagh	284 2 5	Galway	Dunkellin	Kilcolgan	Gort	IV.	28
11	Fawnarry	221 2 22	Leitrim	Drumahaire	Drumlease	Manorhamilton	IV.	94
22	Fawney	297 2 10	Londonderry	Tirkeeran	Cumber Lower	Londonderry	III.	248
3	Fawney	357 2 5e	Tyrone	Strabane Lower	Donaghedy	Strabane	III.	321
85	Fawnglass	146 1 13	Mayo	Murrisk	Kilgeever	Westport	IV.	161
36	Fawninoughan	373 0 24f	Donegal	Kilmacrenan	Tullyfern	Milford	III.	133
36, 44	Fawnlehane	464 1 16	Limerick	Glenquin	Mahoonagh	Newcastle	II.	246
6, 10	Fawnlion	719 1 15	Leitrim	Drumahaire	Drumlease	Manorhamilton	IV.	94
20,21,26,27	Fawnlough	380 2 16	Tipperary, N.R.	Upp.r Ormond	Nenagh	Nenagh	II.	292
25	Fawnmore	352 3 6	Donegal	Kilmacrenan	Clondahorky	Dunfanaghy	III.	123
114	Fawnmore	194 1 14g	Mayo	Murrisk	Inishbofin	Clifden	IV.	159
25, 26	Faymore	873 0 4	Donegal	Kilmacrenan	Clondahorky	Dunfanaghy	III.	123
48, 53	Faythe	60 3 27	Wexford	Forth	Tacumshin	Wexford	I.	315
48, 51	Feacle	459 2 31	Roscommon	Athlone	Taghmaconnell	Athlone	IV.	185
11, 20	Feagarrid	350 3 20	Waterford	Coshmore&Coshbride	Lismore and Mocollop	Lismore	II.	345
67	Feagarroge	298 2 36	Clare	Moyarta	Kilrush	Kilrush	II.	33
41	Feagh	132 1 14h	Clare	Islands	Clareabbey	Ennis	II.	29
35, 36	Feagh	82 1 21	Fermanagh	Clankelly	Clones	Clones	III.	196
116	Feagh	332 3 36	Galway	Leitrim	Duniry	Portumna	IV.	53
99, 100, 107, 108	Feagh	97 2 25	Galway	Longford	Kiltormer	Ballinasloe	IV.	60
4, 5	Feagh	559 0 18	Meath	Lower Kells	Moynalty	Kells	I.	204
17	Feagh	240 2 19i	Monaghan	Dartree	Aghabog	Cootehill	III.	263
39	Feagh	58 2 31	Tyrone	Dungannon Upper	Arboe	Cookstown	III.	305
108	Feaghbeg	746 2 20	Galway	Longford	Fahy	Portumna	IV.	58
44, 58	Feagh East	206 0 39	Galway	Tiaquin	Abbeyknockmoy	Tuam	IV.	75
78, 79, 87	Feaghmaan East	158 1 16	Kerry	Iveragh	Valencia	Cahersiveen	II.	198
78, 87	Feaghmaan West	387 0 10	Kerry	Iveragh	Valencia	Cahersiveen	II.	198
108	Feaghmore Eighter	221 3 6	Galway	Longford	Fahy	Portumna	IV.	58
108	Feaghmore Oughter	164 1 4	Galway	Longford	Fahy	Portumna	IV.	58
42	Feaghquin	187 3 13	Clare	Bunratty Upper	Quin	Tulla	II.	10
44, 58	Feagh West	498 1 3	Galway	Tiaquin	Abbeyknockmoy	Tuam	IV.	75
23	Feagreen	324 2 19	Clare	Corcomroe	Clooney	Ennistimon	II.	18
34	Feahoe	284 0 16j	Monaghan	Farney	Magheracloone	Carrickmacross	III.	272
20, 28	Feakle	1,151 1 9	Clare	Tulla Upper	Feakle	Scarriff	II.	39
28	FEAKLE T.	— —	Clare	Tulla Upper	Feakle	Scarriff	II.	40
11, 15	Feamore	221 2 2	Carlow	Idrone West	Oldleighlin	Carlow	I.	9
112, 113	Feamore	910 0 21	Mayo	Costello	Annagh	Claremorris	IV.	138
48	Feamore	123 1 16	Roscommon	Athlone	Kiltoom	Athlone	IV.	183
29	Fearagh	81 1 15	Queen's Co.	Clarmallagh	Aghaboe	Abbeyleix	I.	236
40, 42	Fearagh	901 3 7	Roscommon	Athlone	Kilmeane	Roscommon	IV.	182
42, 56	Fearagha	762 0 18	Galway	Clare	Kilcoona	Tuam	IV.	19
54	Fearaghafin	88 0 25	Roscommon	Ballymoe	Oran	Roscommon	IV.	192
14, 22	Fearaghalee	92 2 5	King's Co.	Garrycastle	Tisaran	Parsonstown	I.	138
17	Fearagh (Caddell)	227 0 13k	Roscommon	Ballintober North	Kilmore	Car.k on Shannon	IV.	187
17	Fearagh (Mahon)	264 3 15l	Roscommon	Ballintober North	Kilmore	Car.k on Shannon	IV.	187
31, 32	Fearaun	207 0 19	Kildare	Offaly West	Kilrush	Athy	I.	73
3	Fearavolla	74 3 8	Kildare	Carbury	Nurney	Edenderry	I.	53
30	Fear Beg	37 3 30	Galway	Dunmore	Dunmore	Tuam	IV.	34
2	Fearboy	184 2 10	King's Co.	Kilcoursey	Kilcumreragh	Tullamore	I.	141
7, 12	Fearbranagh or Multyfarnham	142 2 34	Westmeath	Corkaree	Stonehall	Mullingar	I.	263
7, 12	Fearbranagh or Multyfarnham	116 3 23	Westmeath	Corkaree	Tyfarnham	Mullingar	I.	264
2	Feargarrow	114 0 13	King's Co.	Kilcoursey	Kilcumreragh	Tullamore	I.	141
36	Fearglass North	340 0 16m	Leitrim	Mohill	Cloone	Mohill	IV.	106
38	Fearglass South	233 3 1	Leitrim	Mohill	Cloone	Mohill	IV.	106
36	Fear More	79 1 0	Galway	Dunmore	Dunmore	Tuam	IV.	34
108	Fearmore	178 0 34	Galway	Longford	Clonfert	Portumna	IV.	57

(a) Including 3A. 2R. 0P. water.
(b) Including 2A. 1R. 18P. water.
(c) Including 15A. 0R. 24P. water.
(d) Including 23A. 1R. 3P. water.
(e) Including 3A. 2R. 7P. water.

(f) Including 6A. 2R. 2P. water.
(g) Including 12A. 1R. 2P. water.
(h) Including 6A. 3R. 24P. water.
(i) Including 9A. 1R. 11P. water.

(j) Including 31A. 1R. 37P. water.
(k) Including 13A. 0R. 7P. water.
(l) Including 7A. 1R. 31P. water.
(m) Including 14A. 2R. 16P. water.

No. of Sheet of the Ordnance Survey Maps	Townlands and Towns.	Area in Statute Acres. A. R. P.	County.	Barony.	Parish.	Poor Law Union in 1857.	Townland Census of 1851, Part I. Vol.	Page
108	Fearmore	82 2 18	Galway	Longford	Meelick	Portumna	IV.	61
26	Fearmore	65 1 3	Kildare	Offaly West	Ballybrackan	Athy	I.	71
42	Fearmore	449 0 23	Meath	Lower Moyfenrath	Trim	Trim	I.	212
40	Fearmore	50 1 8	Roscommon	Ballintober South	Kilbride	Roscommon	IV.	189
30, 36	Fearmore	137 1 27	Westmeath	Clonlonan	Kilcleagh	Athlone	I.	261
33	Fearmore	151 2 20	Westmeath	Fartullagh	Kilbride	Mullingar	I.	268
3	Fearmore	78 3 35	Westmeath	Fore	Mayne	Granard	I.	271
23	Fearmore	158 0 1	Westmeath	Kilkenny West	Drumraney	Athlone	I.	273
23, 30	Fearmore	83 2 38	Westmeath	Kilkenny West	Drumraney	Athlone	I.	273
2, 6	Fearmore	311 3 6	Westmeath	Moygoish	Street	Granard	I.	281
88	Fearn	904 2 27	Donegal	Raphoe	Urney	Strabane	III.	144
35	Fearnaght	387 0 3a	Leitrim	Mohill	Annaduff	Mohill	IV.	105
26, 36	Fearnamona	115 2 28	King's Co.	Upper Philipstown	Ballykean	Mountmellick	I.	143
22	Fearoe	146 1 30	Limerick	Pubblebrien	Killeenoghty	Croom	II.	253
15	Feathallagh	295 1 14	Kilkenny	Gowran	Kilderry	Kilkenny	I.	96
26	Feaugh	179 1 26	Cavan	Upper Loughtee	Lavey	Cavan	III.	86
23	Feavautia	412 3 1	Kerry	Trughanacmy	Castleisland	Tralee	II.	208
17	Febog	98 2 15	Meath	Upper Kells	Kells	Kells	I.	206
22	Fedamore	188 2 17	Limerick	Smallcounty	Fedamore	Croom	II.	259
22	FEDAMORE T.	—	Limerick	Smallcounty	Fedamore	Croom	II.	259
28	Fedany	723 2 34	Down	Lower Iveagh, Lr. pt.	Garvaghy	Banbridge	III.	168
32	Fedaro	44 2 8	Leitrim	Mohill	Annaduff	Mohill	IV.	105
22	Feddan	385 1 16b	Fermanagh	Tirkennedy	Derryvullan	Enniskillen	III.	221
59	Feddan	119 3 22	Tyrone	Clogher	Errigal Keerogue	Clogher	III.	295
5	Feddans	285 0 16	Fermanagh	Lurg	Drumkeeran	Lowtherstown	III.	206
10	Feddans	127 0 11	Monaghan	Cremorne	Clontibret	Monaghan	III.	260
3, 7	Feddans	722 2 37	Waterford	Upperthird	Mothel	Carrick on Suir	II.	371
12, 21	Feddaun	173 0 16	Waterford	Coshmore&Coshbride	Lismore and Mocollop	Lismore	II.	345
62, 70	Feddyglass	385 3 13	Donegal	Raphoe	Taughboyne	Strabane	III.	143
18	Federnagh	234 2 7	Armagh	Orior Lower	Ballymore	Newry	III.	55
15	Fedian	124 0 32	Fermanagh	Magheraboy	Devenish	Enniskillen	III.	211
10	Fedoo	165 2 25	Monaghan	Monaghan	Tehallan	Monaghan	III.	280
20	Feeagh	103 0 13	Limerick	Connello Lower	Nantinan	Rathkeale	II.	229
8, 9, 14, 15	Feeans	510 2 28	Kerry	Clanmaurice	Killury	Listowel	II.	171
64,65,71,72	Feeard	653 3 11	Clare	Moyarta	Kilballyowen	Kilrush	II.	31
5, 6	Feebaghbane	218 1 39	Monaghan	Monaghan	Tedavnet	Monaghan	III.	279
6	Feebaghduff	143 3 4	Monaghan	Monaghan	Tedavnet	Monaghan	III.	279
10	Feebane	86 3 29	Monaghan	Monaghan	Monaghan	Monaghan	III.	277
7, 10	Fee Beg	48 3 7	Tipperary, N.R.	Lower Ormond	Borrisokane	Borrisokane	II.	282
117	Feebrack or Nutgrove	264 3 36	Galway	Longford	Tynagh	Portumna	IV.	62
10, 11	Feedarragh	104 1 33	Cavan	Lower Loughtee	Drumlane	Cavan	III.	80
4	Feede	445 0 30	Louth	Lower Dundalk	Ballymascanlan	Dundalk	I.	176
29	Feegarran	289 1 17	Tyrone	Dungannon Upper	Derryloran	Cookstown	III.	307
29	Feegarran	166 2 3	Tyrone	Dungannon Upper	Lissan	Cookstown	III.	309
10	Feegat	353 0 38	Meath	Upper Kells	Loughan or Castlekeeran	Kells	I.	207
28	Feegavla	263 3 36c	Monaghan	Farney	Donaghmoyne	Carrickmacross	III.	270
29	Feeghroe or Mountcarteret	52 3 9	King's Co.	Garrycastle	Reynagh	Parsonstown	I.	138
21, 29	Feeghs	191 0 24	King's Co.	Garrycastle	Reynagh	Parsonstown	I.	138
17	Feehary Island	10 0 34	Down	Dufferin	Killinchy	Downpatrick	III.	166
43	Feehogue	179 1 23	Antrim	Upper Toome	Drummaul	Antrim	III.	34
10	Fee More	204 3 20	Tipperary, N.R.	Lower Ormond	Borrisokane	Borrisokane	II.	282
82	Feemore	63 3 22	Tipperary, S.R.	Iffa and Offa West	Ardfinnan	Clogheen	II.	316
34	Feenagh	51 3 36	Clare	Bunratty Upper	Clooney	Tulla	II.	8
2, 5	Feenagh	367 2 5	Clare	Burren	Rathborney	Ballyvaghan	II.	14
45	Feenagh	455 3 9	Limerick	Connello Upper	Kilmeedy	Newcastle	II.	233
51, 52	Feenagh (Moloney)	258 0 38	Clare	Bunratty Lower	Feenagh	Ennis	II.	4
39	Feenaghmore	106 1 24d	Sligo	Corran	Toomour	Boyle	IV.	228
39	Feenaghroe	103 0 0e	Sligo	Corran	Toomour	Boyle	IV.	228
9	Feenagh or Tonroe	217 3 35	Roscommon	Frenchpark	Kilnamanagh	Boyle	IV.	204
45	FEENAGH T.	—	Limerick	Connello Upper	Kilmeedy	Newcastle	II.	233
51, 52	Feenagh (Wilson)	254 0 17	Clare	Bunratty Lower	Feenagh	Ennis	II.	4
50	Feenan	154 2 24	Tyrone	Clogher	Donacavey	Omagh	III.	294
46	Feenan Beg	31 2 2	Londonderry	Loughinsholin	Desertlyn	Magherafelt	III.	240
46	Feenan More	112 0 28	Londonderry	Loughinsholin	Desertlyn	Magherafelt	III.	240
50, 60	Feenish	177 0 10	Clare	Bunratty Lower	Kilconry	Ennis	II.	4
37, 45	Feenlea	486 0 13	Clare	Tulla Lower	Killaloe	Scarriff	II.	35
95, 96	Feenune	899 1 28	Mayo	Murrisk	Kilgeever	Westport	IV.	160
30	Feeny	651 1 21	Londonderry	Tirkeeran	Banagher	New T.n Limavady	III.	247
30	FEENY T.	—	Londonderry	Tirkeeran	Banagher	New T.n Limavady	III.	247
47, 50	Feevagh	120 3 17f	Roscommon	Athlone	Dysart	Athlone	IV.	181
47, 50	Feevagh Beg	244 2 32g	Roscommon	Athlone	Dysart	Athlone	IV.	181

(a) Including 4A. 2R. 20P. water.
(b) Including 6A. 1R. 25P. water.
(c) Including 8A. 0R. 8P. water.

(d) Including 7A. 1R. 35P. water.
(e) Including 2A. 3R. 22P. water.

(f) Including 14A. 2R. 3P. water.
(g) Including 20A. 0R. 29P. water.

No. of Sheet of the Ordnance Survey Maps.	Townlands and Towns.	Area in Statute Acres.	County.	Barony.	Parish.	Poor Law Union in 1857.	Townland Census of 1851, Part I.	
		A. R. P.					Vol.	Page
47, 50	Feevagh More . .	954 0 22a	Roscommon . .	Athlone . . .	Dysart . . .	Athlone . .	IV.	181
4	Fegart . . .	308 1 6	Donegal . .	Inishowen East .	Clonmany . .	Inishowen . .	III.	117
49	Feglish . . .	366 3 31	Tyrone . .	Omagh East .	Kilskeery . .	Lowtherstown . .	III.	313
109	Fehanagh . .	529 0 15	Kerry . .	Glanarought .	Tuosist . . .	Kenmare . .	II.	188
62	Fehoonree . .	23 1 11	Tipperary, S.R.	Middlethird . .	Rathcool . .	Cashel . .	II.	329
7	Feigh . . .	424 1 13	Tipperary, N.R.	Lower Ormond .	Uskane . . .	Borrisokane . .	II.	288
17	Feighcullen . .	720 2 15	Kildare . .	Offaly East .	Feighcullen . .	Edenderry . .	I.	70
3	Feigh (alias) Dunseverick . .	247 0 21	Antrim . . .	Cary . . .	Billy . . .	Ballycastle . .	III.	12
7	Feigh East . .	86 0 39	Tipperary, N.R.	Lower Ormond .	Aglishcloghane .	Borrisokane . .	II.	281
3	Feigh Mountain .	119 0 27	Antrim . .	Cary . . .	Billy . . .	Ballycastle . .	III.	12
32	Feighroe . . .	505 1 39b	Clare . .	Islands . . .	Kilmaley . .	Ennis . .	II.	31
7	Feigh West . .	46 0 7	Tipperary, N.R.	Lower Ormond .	Aglishcloghane .	Borrisokane . .	II.	281
115	Felane East . .	109 3 16	Cork, W.R.	Bear . . .	Killaconenagh .	Castletown . .	II.	125
115	Felane Middle .	195 3 29	Cork, W.R.	Bear . . .	Killaconenagh .	Castletown . .	II.	125
115	Felane West .	202 1 26	Cork, W.R.	Bear . . .	Killaconenagh .	Castletown . .	II.	125
6	Felimspark . .	45 0 16	Galway . .	Ballymoe . .	Boyounagh . .	Glennamaddy . .	IV.	6
11, 15	Fellows Hall or Crearum . . .	261 1 35	Armagh . .	Armagh . . .	Tynan . . .	Armagh . .	III.	46
23, 24	Feloree . . .	70 2 13	Limerick . .	Clanwilliam .	Aglishcormick .	Limerick . .	II.	221
12, 15	Feltrim . . .	177 1 36	Dublin . .	Coolock . .	Kinsaley . .	Balrothery . .	I.	28
32	Fenagh . . .	652 0 18	Antrim . .	Lower Toome . .	Ahoghill . .	Ballymena . .	III.	32
15	Fenagh . . .	120 2 27	Leitrim . .	Drumahaire .	Killarga . .	Manorhamilton . .	IV.	98
7	Fenagh . . .	395 2 12	Leitrim . .	Rosclogher . .	Killasnet . .	Manorhamilton . .	IV.	109
24, 25	Fenagh Beg . .	299 1 7c	Leitrim . .	Leitrim . . .	Fenagh . . .	Mohill . .	IV.	100
32, 37	Fenaghy . . .	73 2 9	Antrim . .	Lower Toome .	Ahoghill . .	Ballymena . .	III.	32
63	Fenane . . .	184 1 18	Tipperary, S.R.	Slievardagh .	Kilvemnon . .	Callan . .	II.	334
48, 53	Fence . . .	48 0 24	Wexford . .	Forth . . .	Tacumshin . .	Wexford . .	I.	315
13	Fency . . .	202 3 25	Down . .	Lower Iveagh, Up. pt.	Magheralin . .	Lurgan . .	III.	170
28	Fenit Within . .	438 2 18	Kerry . .	Trughanacmy .	Fenit . . .	Tralee . .	II.	210
28	Fenit Without .	243 3 31	Kerry . .	Trughanacmy .	Fenit . . .	Tralee . .	II.	210
16, 17	Fennagh . . .	29 1 0	Carlow . .	Idrone East .	Fennagh . .	Carlow . .	I.	7
15, 16	Fenniscourt . .	793 0 37d	Carlow . .	Idrone West .	Wells . . .	Carlow . .	I.	10
27	Fennor . . .	308 1 39	Kildare . .	Offaly West .	Duneany . .	Athy . .	I.	72
19	Fennor . . .	1,047 1 30e	Meath . .	Lower Duleek .	Fennor . . .	Navan . .	I.	196
33	Fennor . . .	240 3 5	Meath . .	Upper Duleek .	Ardcath . .	Drogheda . .	I.	197
42, 43	Fennor . . .	1,126 0 35	Tipperary, S.R.	Slievardagh . .	Fennor . . .	Urlingford . .	II.	333
13	Fennor . . .	683 0 14	Westmeath . .	Moyashel and Magheradernon . .	Rathconnell . .	Mullingar . .	I.	276
9	Fennor Lower . .	750 3 29	Meath . .	Fore . . .	Oldcastle . .	Oldcastle . .	I.	202
25, 26	Fennor North . .	239 2 27	Waterford .	Middlethird . .	Islandikane . .	Waterford . .	II.	367
25, 26	Fennor South .	172 3 36	Waterford .	Middlethird . .	Islandikane . .	Waterford . .	II.	367
9	Fennor Upper .	624 3 14	Meath . .	Fore . . .	Oldcastle . .	Oldcastle . .	I.	202
33	Feohanagh . .	205 3 7	Kerry . .	Corkaguiny . .	Kilquane . .	Dingle . .	II.	179
45	Feohanagh . .	1,196 3 15	Limerick . .	Glenquin . .	Mahoonagh . .	Newcastle . .	II.	246
101	Feoramore . .	591 2 14	Kerry . .	Glanarought .	Tuosist . .	Kenmare . .	II.	188
101	Feorus East . .	233 0 20	Kerry . .	Glanarought .	Tuosist . .	Kenmare . .	II.	188
101	Feorus West .	295 1 21	Kerry . .	Glanarought .	Tuosist . .	Kenmare . .	II.	188
13	Feragh . . .	275 2 23	Monaghan . .	Monaghan . .	Monaghan . .	Monaghan . .	III.	277
14	Feraghfad . .	722 0 37	Longford . .	Ardagh . .	Ballymacormick .	Longford . .	I.	152
11	Feraghs . . .	181 1 9	Louth . .	Louth . . .	Louth . . .	Dundalk . .	I.	184
14	Ferbane . . .	356 2 14	King's Co. .	Garrycastle .	Wheery or Killagally	Parsonstown . .	I.	139
14	FERBANE T. . .	—	King's Co. .	Garrycastle .	{ Gallen . . . . } { Wheery or Killagally }	Parsonstown . .	I.	{ 136 } { 139 }
25	Ferganstown and Ballymacon .	695 3 0f	Meath . .	Skreen . .	Athlumney . .	Navan . .	I.	220
19	Fergort . . .	360 3 27	Armagh . .	Tiranny . .	Derrynoose . .	Armagh . .	III.	59
72	Fergus . . .	407 3 37g	Cork, E.R.	East Muskerry .	Aglish . . .	Macroom . .	II.	101
72	Fergus . . .	557 1 11h	Cork, E.R.	East Muskerry .	Magourney . .	Macroom . .	II.	105
61	Fergus Island . .	0 0 29	Clare . .	Bunratty Lower .	Drumline . .	Ennis . .	II.	3
51	Ferguson's Land .	121 0 21	Antrim . .	Upper Antrim .	Donegore . .	Antrim . .	III.	6
38	Ferm . . .	106 1 25	Cork, W.R.	West Muskerry .	Drishane . .	Millstreet . .	II.	156
35	Fermoy . . .	709 1 34i	Cork, E.R.	Condons&Clangibbon	Fermoy . . .	Fermoy . .	II.	61
31, 40	•Fermoyle . .	380 2 0	Cork, E.R.	Duhallow . .	Clonmeen . .	Kanturk . .	II.	69
35	Fermoyle . .	172 1 21j	Kerry . .	Corkaguiny . .	Cloghane . .	Dingle . .	II.	175
90, 91	Fermoyle . .	1,397 0 24	Kerry . .	Dunkerron South .	Kilcrohane . .	Kenmare . .	II.	183
88	Fermoyle . .	1,921 2 38	Kerry . .	Iveragh . .	Prior . . .	Cahersiveen . .	II.	198
29	Fermoyle . .	131 0 0	Queen's Co. .	Clarmallagh .	Durrow . .	Abbeyleix . .	I.	237
29	Fermoyle . .	198 1 5	Queen's Co. .	Clarmallagh .	Rosconnell . .	Abbeyleix . .	I.	238
35	FERMOY T. . .	—	Cork, E.R.	Condons&Clangibbon	Fermoy . . .	Fermoy . .	II.	61
26	Fernagh . . .	194 0 17	Antrim . .	Kilconway .	Rasharkin . ,	Ballymoney . .	III.	97
35	Fernagh . . .	916 0 0	Tyrone .	Strabane Upper .	Cappagh . .	Omagh . .	III.	325
51	Fernaghaudrum .	537 1 21	Tyrone . .	Clogher . .	Clogher . .	Clogher . .	III.	292
4, 5, 8, 9	Fernagreevagh .	290 3 34	Armagh . .	Oneilland West .	Loughgall . .	Armagh . .	III.	54

(a) Including 14A. 2R. 23P. water.
(b) Including 13A. 0R. 27P. water.
(c) Including 15A. 2R. 25P. water.
(d) Including 16A. 3R. 3P. River Barrow.

(e) Including 36A. 2R. 12P. water.
(f) Including 12A. 3R. 27P. water.
(g) Including 9A. 3R. 6P. water.

(h) Including 9A. 2R. 26P. water.
(i) Including 12A. 0R. 0P. water.
(j) Including 18A. 0R. 4P. Island.

No. of Sheet of the Ordnance Survey Maps.	Townlands and Towns.	Area in Statute Acres. A. R. P.	County.	Barony.	Parish.	Poor Law Union in 1857.	Townland Census of 1851, Part I. Vol.	Page
52, 59	Fernamenagh .	103 1 15	Tyrone .	Clogher .	Errigal Keerogue .	Clogher .	III.	295
16	Ferney .	92 1 30	Fermanagh .	Tirkennedy .	Magheracross .	Enniskillen .	III.	223
49	Ferney .	404 1 16	Tyrone .	Omagh East .	Kilskeery .	Lowtherstown .	III.	313
44	Fernisky .	527 1 20	Antrim .	Lower Antrim .	Connor .	Ballymena .	III.	3
15	Ferns .	5 2 39	Wexford .	Scarawalsh .	Kilbride .	Enniscorthy .	I.	323
15	Ferns Demesne .	381 1 27	Wexford .	Scarawalsh .	Ferns .	Enniscorthy .	I.	323
15	Ferns Demesne .	13 3 32	Wexford .	Scarawalsh .	Kilbride .	Enniscorthy .	I.	323
15	Ferns Lower .	235 1 29	Wexford .	Scarawalsh .	Ferns .	Enniscorthy .	I.	323
15	FERNS T. .	—	Wexford .	Scarawalsh .	Ferns .	Enniscorthy .	I.	323
15	Ferns Upper .	174 0 3	Wexford .	Scarawalsh .	Ferns .	Enniscorthy .	I.	323
25	Fernyhill .	86 1 39	Queen's Co. .	Stradbally .	Tullomoy .	Athy .	I.	248
47, 48	Fernyhill .	54 3 34	Wexford .	Forth .	Killinick .	Wexford .	I.	310
8	Ferny Island .	1 3 35	Fermanagh .	Lurg .	Belleek .	Ballyshannon .	III.	204
15, 16	Ferny Island .	13 2 20	Fermanagh .	Tirkennedy .	Trory .	Enniskillen .	III.	224
46	Feroy .	162 1 10	Tyrone .	Dungannon Middle .	Donaghmore .	Dungannon .	III.	302
49	Ferrans .	412 2 4	Meath .	Upper Deece .	Gallow .	Trim .	I.	193
49	Ferrestown .	89 3 38	Meath .	Upper Deece .	Rodanstown .	Celbridge .	I.	194
40	Ferrinch Island .	3 3 13	Roscommon .	Ballintober South .	Cloontuskert .	Roscommon .	IV.	188
42, 52	Ferritersquarter .	498 3 26	Kerry .	Corkaguiny .	Dunquin .	Dingle .	II.	176
40	Ferrybank .	190 2 29a	Wicklow .	Arklow .	Kilbride .	Rathdrum .	I.	344
37	Ferrybank North .	4 2 31	Wexford .	Shelmaliere East .	Ardcavan .	Wexford .	I.	329
37	Ferrybank South .	3 2 1	Wexford .	Shelmaliere East .	Ardcavan .	Wexford .	I.	329
37	Ferrycarrig .	23 3 6	Wexford .	Shelmaliere East .	Kilpatrick .	Wexford .	I.	330
37	Ferrycarrig .	78 0 16	Wexford .	Shelmaliere West .	Tikillin .	Wexford .	I.	331
6	Ferryfort .	179 3 6	Cork, E.R. .	Orrery and Kilmore .	Shandrum .	Kanturk .	II.	110
83	Ferryhouse .	47 2 37b	Tipperary, S.R. .	Iffa and Offa East .	Kilgrant .	Clonmel .	II.	314
32	Ferryquarter .	70 0 23	Down .	Lecale Lower .	Ballyculter .	Downpatrick .	III.	178
10, 15	Ferskill .	532 2 19	Longford .	Granard .	Granard .	Granard .	I.	156
74	Ferta .	938 3 8c	Kerry .	Magunihy .	Killarney .	Killarney .	II.	203
1, 2, 3, 4	Fertagh .	285 2 16	Leitrim .	Rosclogher .	Rossinver .	Ballyshannon .	IV.	111
1, 4	Fertagh .	157 2 19	Meath .	Lower Kells .	Moynalty .	Kells .	I.	204
16	Fertaun .	62 2 18	King's Co. .	Ballycowan .	Lynally .	Tullamore .	I.	128
47	Fertiana .	556 1 20	Tipperary, N.R. .	Eliogarty .	Fertiana .	Thurles .	II.	269
70	Fethard .	533 2 35	Tipperary, S.R. .	Middlethird .	Fethard .	Cashel .	II.	326
50	Fethard .	336 3 35	Wexford .	Shelburne .	Fethard .	New Ross .	I.	327
70	FETHARD T. .	—	Tipperary, S.R. .	Middlethird .	Fethard .	Cashel .	II.	327
50	FETHARD T. .	—	Wexford .	Shelburne .	Fethard .	New Ross .	I.	327
25, 26	Fetherneen .	154 3 34	Sligo .	Leyny .	Kilvarnet .	Tobercurry .	IV.	232
40	Feugh .	131 0 39	Fermanagh .	Coole .	Galloon .	Clones .	III.	200
14	Feugh (Bishops) or Drumalla .	272 0 36	Cavan .	Lower Loughtee .	Drumlane .	Cavan .	III.	80
15	Feugh (Maxwell) .	166 3 26d	Cavan .	Lower Loughtee .	Drumlane .	Cavan .	III.	80
58, 62	Feumore .	513 3 7e	Antrim .	Upper Massereene .	Glenavy .	Lurgan .	III.	30
60	Ffrenchpark .	14 1 25	Galway .	Kilconnell .	Killosolan .	Mountbellew .	IV.	42
47	Ffrench's Acres .	20 0 25	Galway .	Killian .	Killian .	Mountbellew .	IV.	44
27	Fiddan .	191 1 5	Wicklow .	Upper Talbotstown .	Kiltegan .	Baltinglass .	I.	364
27,28,32,33	Fiddancoyle .	219 3 11	Wicklow .	Upper Talbotstown .	Kiltegan .	Baltinglass .	I.	364
23, 30	Fiddandarry .	1,929 1 31f	Sligo .	Tireragh .	Kilmacshalgan .	Dromore West .	IV.	235
7	Fiddane .	244 2 1	Cork, E.R. .	Orrery and Kilmore .	Aglishdrinagh .	Kilmallock .	II.	106
39	Fiddane .	156 2 1	Kerry .	Trughanacmy .	Nohaval .	Tralee .	II.	212
31, 32	Fiddane .	592 2 23	Tipperary, N.R. .	Owney and Arra .	Kilnarath .	Nenagh .	II.	296
33, 42	Fiddane North .	915 0 39	Cork, E.R. .	Fermoy .	Rahan .	Mallow .	II.	82
33, 42	Fiddane South .	560 1 37	Cork, E.R. .	Fermoy .	Rahan .	Mallow .	II.	82
104, 114	Fiddaun .	296 0 6	Galway .	Dunkellin .	Ardrahan .	Loughrea .	IV.	26
128	Fiddaun .	757 2 27g	Galway .	Kiltartan .	Beagh .	Gort .	IV.	46
31	Fiddaun .	225 0 15	Galway .	Tiaquin .	Kilkerrin .	Glennamaddy .	IV.	77
31	Fiddaun .	180 0 17	Roscommon .	Castlereagh .	Kiltullagh .	Castlereagh .	IV.	202
22	Fiddaun .	177 2 31	Sligo .	Tireragh .	Castleconor .	Dromore West .	IV.	232
102	Fiddaun Island .	4 3 9	Galway .	Dunkellin .	Drumacoo .	Galway .	IV.	28
29	Fiddaun Lower .	127 3 29	Kilkenny .	Gowran .	Inistioge .	Thomastown .	I.	96
36,37,45,46	Fiddaunnageeroge .	1,798 3 25h	Mayo .	Tirawley .	Cross-molina .	Ballina .	IV.	166
29	Fiddaun Upper .	257 3 11	Kilkenny .	Gowran .	Inistioge .	Thomastown .	I.	96
39, 42	Fiddown .	466 1 31	Kilkenny .	Iverk .	Fiddown .	Carrick on Suir .	I.	105
42	Fiddown Island .	40 2 14	Kilkenny .	Iverk .	Fiddown .	Carrick on Suir .	I.	105
42	FIDDOWN T. .	—	Kilkenny .	Iverk .	Fiddown .	Carrick on Suir .	I.	105
46, 51	Fidorfe .	241 3 23	Meath .	Ratoath .	Ratoath .	Dunshaughlin .	I.	219
34	Fidwog .	92 2 8	Sligo .	Tirerrill .	Kilmacallan .	Sligo .	IV.	240
7, 11	Fieldstown .	787 0 36	Dublin .	Balrothery West .	Clonmethan .	Balrothery .	I.	22
21	Fieldstown .	279 3 37	Louth .	Ferrard .	Drumshallon .	Drogheda .	I.	180
19	Fieldstown .	54 3 31	Meath .	Upper Slane .	Slane .	Navan .	I.	225
48	Fieries .	254 3 9	Kerry .	Magunihy .	Kilnanare .	Killarney .	II.	204
40	Fieries .	407 3 11	Kerry .	Trughanacmy .	Ballincuslane .	Tralee .	II.	206

(a) Including Islands.
(b) Including 6A. 1R. 8P. water.
(c) Including 12A. 3R. 3P. water.
(d) Including 12A. 2R. 20P. water.
(e) Including 144A. 2R. 0P. Portmore Lough.
(f) Including 6A. 0R. 5P. water.
(g) Including 17A. 1R. 25P. water.
(h) Including 6A. 1R. 43P. water.

3 M

No. of Sheet of the Ordnance Survey Maps	Townlands and Towns.	Area in Statute Acres. A. R. P.	County.	Barony.	Parish.	Poor Law Union in 1857.	Townland Census of 1851, Part I. Vol.	Page
14	Fifth Corgary or First Croagh	1,236 2 0a	Tyrone	Omagh West	Termonamongan	Castlederg	III.	317
51	Fifty Acres	91 0 1	Antrim	Upper Antrim	Kilbride	Antrim	III.	6
4	Figanny	103 1 38	Monaghan	Trough	Errigal Trough	Monaghan	III.	284
15	Figart	134 0 38	Donegal	Kilmacrenan	Clondahorky	Dunfanaghy	III.	123
70	Figart	273 1 35	Donegal	Raphoe	Raphoe	Strabane	III.	141
38	Figary	183 2 39	Donegal	Inishowen West	Fahan Upper	Londonderry	III.	121
13, 14	Figh	734 0 37b	Roscommon	Frenchpark	Tibohine	Castlereagh	IV.	205
79, 85	Figlash	763 1 22	Tipperary, S.R.	Iffa and Offa East	Kilmurry	Carrick on Suir	II.	314
3, 4	Figullar	264 3 11	Monaghan	Trough	Errigal Trough	Monaghan	III.	284
67	Fihertagh	146 0 7	Tipperary, S.R.	Clanwilliam	Templeneiry	Tipperary	II.	311
29, 30	Fihidy	368 2 29	Limerick	Connello Lower	Croagh	Rathkeale	II.	227
13	Fihoges	99 2 37	Longford	Longford	Clongesh	Longford	I.	158
1, 3	Fihoragh	789 1 30c	Longford	Granard	Killoe	Granard	I.	157
42	Filbuckstown	159 2 35	Kilkenny	Iverk	Rathkieran	Waterford	I.	107
9	Finaghoo	285 0 1	Cavan	Tullyhaw	Kinawley	Bawnboy	III.	93
34	Finanagh	175 0 31	Clare	Bunratty Upper	Doora	Ennis	II.	8
3	Finavarra Demesne	86 2 10	Clare	Burren	Oughtmama	Ballyvaghan	II.	14
2, 3	FINAVARRA T.	—	Clare	Burren	Oughtmama	Ballyvaghan	II.	14
38	Finaway	347 3 22	Cavan	Castlerahan	Crosserlough	Cavan	III.	68
30	Fincarn	771 2 7	Londonderry	Keenaght	Banagher	NewTⁿLimavady	III.	234
14, 22	Fincarn	273 0 9	Londonderry	Tirkeeran	Clondermot	Londonderry	III.	248
25	Fincarn	229 0 5	Monaghan	Farney	Donaghmoyne	Castleblayney	III.	270
105	Fincashel	500 0 9d	Donegal	Tirhugh	Templecarn	Donegal	III.	149
58, 64	Findermore	195 2 29e	Tyrone	Clogher	Clogher	Clogher	III.	292
69	Findrum	381 0 38	Donegal	Raphoe	Convoy	Stranorlar	III.	136
52	Findrum	221 3 3	Tyrone	Clogher	Errigal Keerogue	Clogher	III.	295
61	Finelly	159 2 14	Tyrone	Dungannon Middle	Clonfeacle	Dungannon	III.	299
14	Finglas East	327 2 32	Dublin	Castleknock	Finglas	Dublin North	I.	25
14	FINGLAS T.	—	Dublin	Castleknock	Finglas	Dublin North	I.	25
14	Finglas West	111 2 3	Dublin	Castleknock	Finglas	Dublin North	I.	25
14, 18	Finglas Wood	84 2 3	Dublin	Castleknock	Finglas	Dublin North	I.	25
30, 34	Finglen	1,649 0 36	Londonderry	Keenaght	Banagher	NewTⁿLimavady	III.	234
35, 40	Finglen	502 0 27	Londonderry	Loughinsholin	Ballynascreen	Magherafelt	III.	239
66	Finglush	123 3 27	Tyrone	Dungannon Lower	Aghaloo	Armagh	III.	296
18	Fingreagh Lower	52 3 35	Leitrim	Drumahaire	Inishmagrath	Manorhamilton	IV.	96
16, 18	Fingreagh Upper	269 3 11	Leitrim	Drumahaire	Inishmagrath	Manorhamilton	IV.	96
9, 15	Finisclin	527 3 16	Roscommon	Boyle	Estersnow	Boyle	IV.	195
77	Finish Island	153 2 12	Galway	Ballynahinch	Moyrus	Clifden	IV.	14
66, 67	Finisk	263 0 18	Cork, E.R.	Imokilly	Clonpriest	Youghal	II.	85
66,67,77,78	Finisk	143 0 15	Cork, E.R.	Imokilly	Kilmacdonogh	Youghal	II.	88
28, 32	Finiskil	232 0 10	Leitrim	Mohill	Mohill	Mohill	IV.	108
80, 81	Finisklin	558 1 29f	Galway	Moycullen	Moycullen	Galway	IV.	71
27, 28	Finisklin	296 1 22g	Leitrim	Leitrim	Kiltoghert	Carˢ. on Shannon	IV.	102
14	Finisklin	218 1 25	Sligo	Carbury	St. John's	Sligo	IV.	223
39	Finisklin	123 1 21	Sligo	Corran	Drumrat	Boyle	IV.	226
31	Finkiltagh	537 3 32	Antrim	Lower Toome	Ahoghill	Ballymena	III.	32
37	Finlaghtown Great	195 3 8h	Meath	Lower Deece	Scurlockstown	Trim	I.	192
37	Finlaghtown Little	127 0 39	Meath	Lower Deece	Scurlockstown	Trim	I.	192
32	Finlane	148 3 25	Fermanagh	Clanawley	Killesher	Enniskillen	III.	192
42	Finlough	409 2 13i	Clare	Bunratty Lower	Tomfinlough	Ennis	II.	7
25, 32	Finlough	247 3 38j	Sligo	Leyny	Kilvarnet	Tobercurry	IV.	232
94	Finnabanes	188 0 39	Donegal	Tirhugh	Donegal	Donegal	III.	145
30, 31	Finnabrogue	530 1 39k	Down	Lecale Lower	Inch	Downpatrick	III.	179
94	Finnadoos	236 2 35	Donegal	Tirhugh	Donegal	Donegal	III.	145
61, 69	Finnadork Glebe	223 3 30	Donegal	Raphoe	Convoy	Stranorlar	III.	136
34, 40	Finnahy	827 2 17	Tipperary, N.R.	Kilnamanagh Upper	Upperchurch	Thurles	II.	280
35	Finnalaghta	248 1 20	Leitrim	Mohill	Annaduff	Mohill	IV.	105
5, 10	Finnan	567 1 23	Kilkenny	Fassadinin	Donaghmore	Castlecomer	I.	89
39,40,48,49	Finnanfield	361 1 11	Cork, W.R.	West Muskerry	Kilcorney	Millstreet	II.	158
19	Finnaragh	183 1 14	Longford	Ardagh	Ardagh	Longford	I.	151
41, 47	Finnard	607 0 17	Down	Lordship of Newry	Newry	Newry	III.	182
66,67,79,80	Finnaun	7,555 0 16l	Galway	Moycullen	Kilannin	Galway	IV.	69
1	Finnea	495 3 28m	Westmeath	Fore	Foyran	Granard	I.	270
1	FINNEA T.	—	Westmeath	Fore	Foyran	Granard	I.	270
8	Finned	183 0 18	Sligo	Carbury	Drumcliff	Sligo	IV.	221
11	Finned	665 2 29	Sligo	Tireragh	Easky	Dromore West	IV.	233
106, 107	Finner	1,582 0 38	Donegal	Tirhugh	Inishmacsaint	Ballyshannon	III.	147
8	Finner	92 2 8	Fermanagh	Lurg	Belleek	Ballyshannon	III.	203
96	Finnis	642 1 9	Cork, W.R.	Kinalmeaky	Brinny	Bandon	II.	151
28, 35	Finnis	1,353 1 18	Down	Upper Iveagh, Lr. pt.	Dromara	Banbridge	III.	172
24, 37	Finnisglin	1,086 0 29	Galway	Ballynahinch	Ballynakill	Clifden	IV.	11

(a) Including 2A. 0R. 38P. water.
(b) Including 19A. 3R. 33P. water.
(c) Including 42A. 1R. 14P. water.
(d) Including 26A. 2R. 4P. water.
(e) Including 0A. 2R. 16P. water.
(f) Including 21A. 1R. 32P. water.
(g) Including 27A. 3R. 36P. water.
(h) Including 1A. 1R. 8P. water.
(i) Including 69A. 1R. 34P. water.
(j) Including 7A. 1R. 12P. water.
(k) Including 28A. 3R. 28P. water.
(l) Including 247A. 0R. 23P. water.
(m) Including 10A. 0R. 10P. water.

No. of Sheet of the Ordnance Survey Maps.	Townlands and Towns.	Area in Statute Acres.	County.	Barony.	Parish.	Poor Law Union in 1857.	Townland Census of 1851, Part I.	
		A. R. P.					Vol.	Page
21, 30	Finniterstown . .	536 3 17	Limerick . .	Connello Upper .	Adare . . .	Rathkeale .	II.	230
21, 30	Finniterstown . .	438 3 31	Limerick . .	Connello Upper .	Drehidtarsna . .	Rathkeale .	II.	232
18	Finnoo . .	671 0 18	Limerick . .	Shanid . . .	Kilmoylan . .	Glin . .	II.	256
10, 11	Finnor . .	365 0 11a	Roscommon .	Boyle . . .	Killummod . .	Cark. on Shannon	IV.	196
38	Finnor Beg .	306 2 34	Clare . .	Ibrickan . .	Kilmurry . .	Kilrush .	II.	23
38	Finnor More . .	421 1 14	Clare . .	Ibrickan . .	Kilmurry . .	Kilrush .	II.	23
23	Finns . . .	87 0 30	Longford . .	Moydow . .	Taghsheenod . .	Ballymahon .	I.	162
17	Finnstown . .	416 2 26	Dublin . .	Newcastle . .	Esker . . .	Celbridge .	I.	33
98, 106	Finnure . .	317 3 27	Galway . .	Leitrim . .	Abbeygormacan .	Loughrea .	IV.	50
13	Finnure . . .	195 0 33	Sligo . .	Tireragh . .	Skreen . . .	Dromore West .	IV.	236
13, 26	Finny . . .	278 3 23	Galway . .	Ross . . .	Ross . . .	Ballinrobe .	IV.	74
34	Finshoge . .	139 1 14	Wexford . .	Bantry . .	Oldross . .	New Ross .	I.	301
33	Fintawan . .	258 1 4b	Cavan . .	Castlerahan .	Lurgan . .	Oldcastle .	III.	69
25	Finter . . .	598 3 39	King's Co. .	Geashill . .	Ballykean . .	Tullamore .	I.	139
34, 40	Finternagh .	295 1 7c	Cavan . .	Castlerahan .	Killinkere . .	Bailieborough .	III.	69
51	Fintona . .	17 0 33	Tyrone . .	Clogher . .	Donacavey . .	Omagh . .	III.	294
21, 22	Fintonagh . .	42 3 4	Fermanagh .	Magheraboy . .	Devenish . .	Enniskillen .	III.	211
50, 51	FINTONA T. .	—	Tyrone . .	Clogher . .	Donacavey . .	Omagh . .	III.	295
58, 66, 67	Fintown . .	846 1 37d	Donegal . .	Boylagh . .	Inishkeel . .	Glenties . .	III.	112
22, 30	Fintra Beg . .	387 3 29	Clare . .	Ibrickan . .	Kilfarboy . .	Ennistimon .	II.	22
91, 97	Fintragh . .	3,145 1 12	Donegal . .	Banagh . .	Killybegs Upper .	Glenties . .	III.	110
30	Fintra More . .	389 0 29	Clare . .	Ibrickan . .	Kilfarboy . .	Ennistimon .	II.	22
14	Fintully . .	139 3 34	Monaghan .	Cremorne . .	Clontibret . .	Monaghan .	III.	260
10, 16	Finuge . .	883 0 19e	Kerry . .	Clanmaurice .	Finuge . .	Listowel .	II.	169
16	FINUGE T. .	—	Kerry . .	Clanmaurice .	Finuge . .	Listowel .	II.	169
45,46,53,54	Finulagh . .	162 1 24	Tyrone . .	Dungannon Middle .	Donaghmore . .	Dungannon .	III.	302
100	Finure . .	396 0 34	Cork, E.R. .	Imokilly . . .	Corkbeg . .	Middleton .	II.	36
16, 26	Finver . .	127 0 6	Donegal . .	Kilmacrenan .	Mevagh . .	Milford .	III.	130
38	Finvey . .	94 1 11	Tyrone . .	Dungannon Upper .	Desertcreat . .	Cookstown .	III.	307
18	Finvoy . .	134 2 12	Louth . .	Ardee . . .	Drumcar . .	Ardee .	I.	172
34, 42	Fireagh (Cochrane) .	91 1 0	Tyrone . .	Omagh East .	Drumragh . .	Omagh . .	III.	312
34, 42	Fireagh (Gardiner) .	82 2 14	Tyrone . .	Omagh East .	Drumragh . .	Omagh . .	III.	312
34, 42	Fireagh (Thompson)	137 3 35	Tyrone . .	Omagh East .	Drumragh . .	Omagh . .	III.	312
51	Firgrove . .	158 2 6	Clare . .	Bunratty Lower .	Drumline . .	Ennis .	II.	3
32	Firgrove . .	157 2 3	Kilkenny .	Gowran . .	Inistioge . .	Thomastown .	I.	96
9	Firgrove . .	184 3 38	Tipperary, N.R.	Lower Ormond .	Kilbarron . .	Borrisokane .	II.	284
126	FIRKEEL T. .	—	Cork, W.R. .	Bear . . .	Kilnamanagh . .	Castletown .	II.	126
50, 51, 61	Firmount . .	268 2 20	Cork, E.R. .	Barretts . .	Donaghmore . .	Cork . .	II.	49
15	Firmount . .	160 3 38	Longford . .	Granard . .	Clonbroney . .	Granard .	I.	155
4, 7	Firmount . .	472 1 17	Tipperary, N.R.	Lower Ormond .	Terryglass . .	Borrisokane .	II.	287
14	Firmount Demesne .	169 2 27	Kildare . .	Clane . .	Clane . . .	Naas .	I.	53
14	Firmount East .	163 1 8f	Kildare . .	Clane . .	Clane . .	Naas .	I.	53
14	Firmount West .	220 3 27	Kildare . .	Clane . .	Clane . .	Naas .	I.	53
5	Firoda Lower or Glenmagoo .	1,049 0 29	Kilkenny .	Fassadinin .	Castlecomer . .	Castlecomer .	I.	88
1, 5	Firoda Upper .	1,184 2 28	Kilkenny .	Fassadinin .	Castlecomer . .	Castlecomer .	I.	88
44, 58, 59	Firpark . .	91 2 1	Galway . .	Tiaquin . .	Abbeyknockmoy .	Tuam .	IV.	75
15, 16	Firpark . .	157 1 12	Meath . .	Fore . .	Diamor . . .	Oldcastle .	I.	200
5	Firs . . .	34 2 20	Fermanagh .	Lurg . .	Drumkeeran . .	Lowtherstown .	III.	206
14	First Croagh or Fifth Corgary . .	1,236 2 0g	Tyrone . .	Omagh West .	Termonamongan .	Castlederg .	III.	317
32	Firville East .	8 1 2	Cork, E.R. .	Fermoy . .	Mallow . . .	Mallow .	II.	81
32	Firville West .	350 0 5h	Cork, E.R. .	Duhallow .	Mallow . .	Mallow .	II.	75
60	Fisherhill . .	335 1 15	Mayo . .	Carra . .	Turlough . .	Castlebar .	IV.	131
29	Fishersgraigue .	64 0 11i	Kilkenny .	Gowran . .	Graiguenamanagh .	Thomastown .	I.	95
9	Fisherstown .	594 2 29j	Queen's Co. .	Portnahinch .	Lea . . .	Mountmellick .	I.	244
39	Fisherstown .	379 3 17	Wexford . .	Shelburne .	Kilmokea . .	New Ross .	I.	327
8	FISHERSTREET T. .	—	Clare . .	Corcomroe .	Killilagh . .	Ennistimon .	II.	20
7, 8	Fishloughan .	148 0 28k	Londonderry .	North East Liberties of Coleraine .	Kildollagh . .	Coleraine .	III.	246
34	Fishmoyne . .	699 1 33	Tipperary, N.R.	Eliogarty . .	Kilfithmone . .	Thurles .	II.	270
18	Fish Quarter .	263 3 18	Down . .	Ards Upper .	Inishargy . .	Newtownards .	III.	160
48	Fiveacre . . .	10 1 10	Wexford . .	Forth . .	Rosslare . .	Wexford .	I.	313
12	Five Acres . .	38 2 28	Antrim . .	Lower Dunluce .	Billy . . .	Ballymoney .	III.	16
17	Fiveacres . .	70 1 24	Westmeath .	Rathconrath .	Piercetown . .	Ballymahon .	I.	283
63, 64	Fivemiletown .	231 2 22l	Tyrone . .	Clogher . .	Clogher . .	Clogher .	III.	292
64	FIVEMILETOWN .	—	Tyrone . .	Clogher . .	Clogher . .	Clogher .	III.	293
7	Fivepoundland .	46 1 5	Leitrim . .	Rosclogher .	Killasnet . .	Manorhamilton .	IV.	109
4	Flacketstown . .	112 0 15	Dublin . .	Balrothery West .	Naul . . .	Balrothery .	I.	23
11	Flagford or Cullean-atreen .	185 1 12	Roscommon .	Boyle . .	Killummod . .	Cark. on Shannon	IV.	196
117	Flag Island . .	1 1 9	Mayo . .	Kilmaine .	Ballinchalla .	Ballinrobe .	IV.	152
20	Flagmount . .	201 3 39	Clare . .	Tulla Upper .	Feakle . .	Scarriff .	II.	39
20	Flagmount North .	418 3 39	Kilkenny .	Gowran . .	Gowran . . .	Kilkenny .	I.	95

3 M 2

No. of Sheet of the Ordnance Survey Maps.	Townlands and Towns.	Area in Statute Acres.			County.	Barony.	Parish.	Poor Law Union in 1857.	Townland Census of 1851, Part I.	
		A.	R.	P.					Vol.	Page
20	Flagmount South .	24	2	17a	Kilkenny . .	Gowran . . .	Gowran . . .	Kilkenny . . .	I.	95
18	Flanafreeson or Goat Island . . .	0	0	7	Roscommon .	Roscommon . .	Clooncraff . .	Strokestown .	IV.	208
24	Flanders . . .	394	2	13	Londonderry .	Keenaght . .	Bovevagh . .	Newt⁰Limavady	III.	235
5	Flankerhouse . .	14	1	4	Limerick . .	Clanwilliam . .	St. Nicholas .	Limerick . .	II.	225
5	Flaskagh Beg . .	509	3	38	Galway . .	Ballymoe . .	Dunmore . .	Glennamaddy .	IV.	7
22	Flaskagh Beg . .	87	0	7	Roscommon .	Roscommon . .	Elphin . .	Strokestown .	IV.	209
5, 6	Flaskagh More . .	649	3	20	Galway . .	Ballymoe . .	Dunmore . .	Glennamaddy .	IV.	7
22	Flaskagh More .	191	0	18	Roscommon .	Roscommon . .	Elphin . .	Strokestown .	IV.	209
35	Flat Island . .	1	1	8	Galway . .	Ballynahinch . .	Moyrus . .	Clifden . .	IV.	14
21	Flat Island . .	4	0	37	Sligo . .	Carbury . . .	St. John's .	Sligo . .	IV.	223
58	Flats . . .	141	2	4	Cork, W.R. .	West Muskerry .	Ballyvourney .	Macroom .	II.	154
18	Flean Beg . .	112	1	2	Limerick . .	Shanid . . .	Kilfergus . .	Glin . .	II.	256
18	Flean More . .	1,031	3	30	Limerick . .	Shanid . . .	Kilfergus . .	Glin . .	II.	256
45	Fleenstown Great .	411	0	34	Meath . .	Ratoath . .	Donaghmore .	Dunshaughlin .	I.	218
45	Fleenstown Little .	273	1	15	Meath . .	Ratoath . .	Donaghmore .	Dunshaughlin .	I.	218
45	Flegans . . .	32	2	17	Roscommon .	Athlone . .	Kiltoom . .	Athlone . .	IV.	183
39	Flemby . . .	518	0	21	Kerry . .	Trughanacmy .	Ballymacelligott	Tralee . .	II.	207
19	Flemingstown . .	535	2	20	Cork, E.R. .	Condons&Clangibbon	Kilgullane .	Mitchelstown .	II.	61
19	Flemingstown . .	9	0	23	Cork, E.R. .	Condons&Clangibbon	Kilphelan .	Mitchelstown .	II.	62
61, 69	Flemingstown . .	129	3	2	Donegal . .	Raphoe . . .	Raphoe . .	Strabane . .	III.	141
45	Flemingstown . .	383	1	25	Kerry . .	Corkaguiny . .	Ballinvoher .	Dingle . .	II.	174
43, 53	Flemingstown . .	177	2	1	Kerry . .	Corkaguiny . .	Garfinny . .	Dingle . .	II.	176
41	Flemingstown . .	195	3	4	Kilkenny . .	Ida . . .	Kilcoan . .	Waterford .	I.	102
42, 43	Flemingstown . .	156	0	11	Kilkenny . .	Iverk . . .	Kilmacow . .	Waterford .	I.	106
48	Flemingstown . .	284	3	21	Limerick . .	Coshlea . .	Ballingaddy .	Kilmallock .	II.	237
26, 32	Flemingstown . .	876	2	29	Meath . .	Lower Duleek .	Kentstown .	Navan . .	I.	196
88	Flemingstown . .	95	1	39	Tipperary, S.R.	Iffa and Offa West .	Molough . .	Clogheen .	II.	318
86, 87, 90	Flemingstown . .	1,347	1	29	Tipperary, S.R.	Iffa and Offa West .	Shanrahan .	Clogheen .	II.	319
88	Flemingstown . .	106	0	36	Tipperary, S.R.	Iffa and Offa West .	Tullaghmelan .	Clogheen .	II.	321
1, 2	Flemingtown . .	393	2	15	Dublin . .	Balrothery East .	Balrothery .	Balrothery .	I.	19
38	Flemingtown . .	172	3	16	Meath . .	Ratoath . .	Ratoath . .	Dunshaughlin .	I.	219
33	Flemingtown . .	272	2	39	Meath . .	Upper Duleek .	Clonalvy . .	Drogheda . .	I.	197
24	Flemingtown North	137	1	25	Kildare . .	Naas South . .	Killashee .	Naas . .	I.	65
24	Flemingtown South or Tonaphuca .	448	0	1	Kildare . .	Naas South . .	Killashee .	Naas . .	I.	65
14	Fleshtown . .	341	2	22	Kildare . .	Clane . . .	Killybegs .	Naas . .	I.	54
11, 17, 18	Fletcherstown . .	601	3	35	Meath . .	Morgallion . .	Clongill . .	Navan . .	I.	209
57, 58	Flintfield . .	147	3	32	Kerry . .	Magunihy . .	Aglish . .	Killarney .	II.	200
27, 31	Floodhall or Rathtooterny . .	394	1	11	Kilkenny . .	Knocktopher . .	Jerpointchurch .	Thomastown .	I.	111
32	Florence Court Demesne . .	768	0	5	Fermanagh .	Clanawley . .	Killesher .	Enniskillen .	III.	192
7	Flower Hill . .	194	0	23	Antrim . .	Lower Dunluce .	Dunluce . .	Coleraine .	III.	17
38	Flowerhill . .	130	0	38	Sligo . .	Corran . .	Cloonoghil .	Tobercurry .	IV.	225
20	Flowerhill . .	128	3	30b	Waterford .	Coshmore&Coshbride	Lismore and Mocollop	Lismore . .	II.	345
117	Flowerhill or Bouluskeagh . . .	321	3	8	Galway . .	Longford . .	Tynagh . .	Portumna .	IV.	62
15	Flughanagh . .	367	3	3	Leitrim . .	Drumahaire . .	Killanummery .	Manorhamilton	IV.	98
52	Flughany . .	782	1	24	Mayo . .	Costello . .	Kilturra . .	Swineford .	IV.	142
30	Flughland . .	170	3	36	Donegal . .	Inishowen East .	Moville Upper .	Inishowen .	III.	119
4, 9	Flushtown . .	116	2	18c	Tyrone . .	Strabane Lower .	Urney . .	Strabane .	III.	322
11	Foalies . .	46	2	28	Cavan . .	Lower Loughtee .	Drumlane .	Cavan . .	III.	80
83, 84	Foardal . .	758	2	8d	Kerry . .	Dunkerron South .	Knockane .	Killarney .	II.	184
87	Foats or Levallynearl . .	224	1	38	Galway . .	Kilconnell . .	Aughrim .	Ballinasloe .	IV.	39
75	Foaty . . .	221	2	26	Cork, E.R. .	Barrymore . .	Carrigtohill .	Cork . .	II.	52
75	Foaty . . .	544	3	33	Cork, E.R. .	Barrymore . .	Clonmel . .	Cork . .	II.	53
22	Fodagh . . .	109	2	13	Wexford . .	Ballaghkeen . .	Donaghmore .	Gorey . .	I.	293
31	Fodeen . . .	5	3	29	Meath . .	Skreen . .	Tara . .	Navan . .	I.	222
20	Fodeens . . .	241	1	31	Kildare . .	South Salt . .	Kill . .	Naas . .	I.	77
71	Fodry . . .	453	1	28	Clare . .	Moyarta . .	Kilballyowen .	Kilrush . .	II.	31
42, 48, 52	Fofannybane . .	940	1	38	Down . .	Upper Iveagh, Lr. pt.	Kilcoo . .	Kilkeel . .	III.	173
42, 48	Fofannyreagh . .	1,199	1	25	Down . .	Upper Iveagh, Lr. pt.	Kilcoo . .	Kilkeel . .	III.	173
19, 29	Foffanagh . .	462	2	3	Donegal . .	Inishowen West .	Fahan Lower .	Inishowen .	III.	120
58	Fogart . . .	281	0	31	Tyrone . .	Clogher . .	Clogher . .	Clogher . .	III.	292
34	Foghanagh Beg .	148	1	27	Roscommon .	Ballymoe . .	Drumatemple .	Castlereagh .	IV.	191
34	Foghanagh More .	268	1	26	Roscommon .	Ballymoe . .	Drumatemple .	Castlereagh .	IV.	191
36	Fogher . . .	442	3	27	Donegal . .	Kilmacrenan .	Tullyfern .	Millford . .	III.	133
14, 15	Foghill . . .	439	2	25	Mayo . .	Tirawley . .	Kilcummin .	Killala . .	IV.	168
24	Foglish . .	381	0	13	Fermanagh .	Magherastephana .	Aghalurcher .	Lisnaskea .	III.	216
60, 73	Fohanagh . .	633	0	3	Galway . .	Kilconnell . .	Fohanagh . .	Mountbellew .	IV.	40
10, 11	Foher . . .	623	3	6	Galway . .	Ballynahinch . .	Ballynakill .	Clifden . .	IV.	11
25	Fohera . . .	107	1	37	Leitrim . .	Carrigallen . .	Oughteragh .	Bawnboy .	IV.	92

(a) Including 7A. 1R. 26P. detached portion.　　　(c) Including 3A. 2R. 26P. water.
(b) Including 1A. 1R. 0P. water.　　　　　　　　　(d) Including 42A. 3R. 25P. water.

No. of Sheet of the Ordnance Survey Maps.	Townlands and Towns.	Area in Statute Acres.			County.	Barony.	Parish.	Poor Law Union in 1857.	Townland Census of 1851, Part I.	
		A.	R.	P.					Vol.	Page
53, 54	Foheraghmore	276	0	9	Kerry	Corkaguiny	Kinard	Dingle	II.	179
141	Foherlagh	214	0	16	Cork, W.R.	West Carbery (E.D.)	Aghadown	Skibbereen	II.	137
17, 18, 23	Foil	76	2	38a	Kerry	Clanmaurice	Duagh	Listowel	II.	168
49	Foilacamin	372	0	33	Tipperary, S.R.	Slievardagh	Buolick	Urlingford	II.	332
45, 51	Foilaclug	563	1	16	Tipperary, N.R.	Kilnamanagh Upper	Toem	Tipperary	II.	280
13	Foiladaun	287	2	3	Cork, E.R.	Duhallow	Clonfert	Kanturk	II.	68
75, 76	Foiladuane	703	3	23	Kerry	Magunihy	Killaha	Killarney	II.	202
39, 40	Foilagoule	228	3	30	Tipperary, N.R.	Kilnamanagh Upper	Moyaliff	Thurles	II.	279
130	Foilakilly	361	0	28	Cork, W.R.	West Carbery (W.D.)	Kilcrohane	Bantry	II.	143
36	Foilatrisnig	207	3	29	Kerry	Corkaguiny	Kilgobban	Tralee	II.	177
45	Foildarg	685	0	12	Tipperary, N.R.	Kilnamanagh Upper	Doon	Tipperary	II.	277
38, 39	Foildarragh	511	2	15	Tipperary, N.R.	Owney and Arra	Abington	Nenagh	II.	293
115	Foildarrig	472	1	0	Cork, W.R.	Bear	Killaconenagh	Castletown	II.	125
17	Foildarrig	264	3	8b	Kerry	Clanmaurice	Duagh	Listowel	II.	168
31	Foildarrig	121	0	37	Tipperary, N.R.	Owney and Arra	Kilnarath	Nenagh	II.	296
89	Foildrenagh	392	3	33	Kerry	Iveragh	Dromod	Cahersiveen	II.	195
70	Foilduff	290	2	1	Kerry	Iveragh	Killinane	Cahersiveen	II.	197
32, 33, 38	Foilduff	2,506	0	1	Tipperary, N.R.	Owney and Arra	Abington	Nenagh	II.	293
32,33,38,39	Foilduff (Jackson)	1,149	3	27	Tipperary, N.R.	Owney and Arra	Abington	Nenagh	II.	293
45	Foilmacduff	591	3	36	Tipperary, S.R.	Kilnamanagh Lower	Donohill	Tipperary	II.	323
38,39,44,45	Foilmahonmore	401	1	27	Tipperary, N.R.	Kilnamanagh Upper	Doon	Tipperary	II.	277
55	Foilmarnell Lower	110	2	37	Tipperary, S.R.	Slievardagh	Ballingarry	Callan	II.	331
49, 55	Foilmarnell Upper	261	3	27	Tipperary, S.R.	Slievardagh	Ballingarry	Callan	II.	331
70	Foilmore	147	2	30	Kerry	Iveragh	Killinane	Cahersiveen	II.	197
39	Foilnacanony	176	2	16	Tipperary, N.R.	Kilnamanagh Upper	Upperchurch	Nenagh	II.	280
87	Foilnageragh	172	2	35	Kerry	Iveragh	Killemlagh	Cahersiveen	II.	196
33, 39	Foilnaman	347	1	39	Tipperary, N.R.	Kilnamanagh Upper	Upperchurch	Thurles	II.	280
140	Foilnamuck	378	2	19	Cork, W.R.	West Carbery (W.D.)	Skull	Skull	II.	146
27, 33	Foilnamuck	389	3	4	Tipperary, N.R.	Upper Ormond	Dolla	Nenagh	II.	290
13, 21	Foilogohig	735	2	5	Cork, E.R.	Duhallow	Kilmeen	Kanturk	II.	73
17, 18	Foilrim	143	1	5	Clare	Inchiquin	Ruan	Corrofin	II.	28
8, 16	Foilycleara	408	0	34	Limerick	Coonagh	Doon	Tipperary	II.	234
44, 45	Foilycleary	341	3	19	Tipperary, N.R.	Kilnamanagh Upper	Doon	Tipperary	II.	277
16, 20	Foley	382	1	21	Armagh	Fews Lower	Lisnadill	Armagh	III.	47
44, 50	Folistown	196	2	2	Meath	Dunboyne	Dunboyne	Dunshaughlin	I.	199
1, 2, 4, 5	Folkstown Great or Clonard	370	3	15	Dublin	Balrothery East	Balrothery	Balrothery	I.	19
4, 5	Folkstown Little	124	2	12	Dublin	Balrothery East	Balrothery	Balrothery	I.	19
25,26,31,32	Follistown	653	0	33	Meath	Skreen	Follistown	Navan	I.	220
36	Follum Big	155	3	36	Fermanagh	Clankelly	Clones	Clones	III.	196
35	Follum Little	109	2	22	Fermanagh	Clankelly	Clones	Clones	III.	195
6, 7	Folly	228	2	25	Dublin	Balrothery West	Palmerston	Balrothery	I.	23
34, 35	Fomerla	308	0	3	Clare	Tulla Upper	Tulla	Tulla	II.	41
7, 12	Fonthill	156	1	31	Carlow	Idrone West	Cloydagh	Carlow	I.	9
17	Fonthill	99	1	13c	Dublin	Uppercross	Palmerston	Dublin South	I.	40
31	Fontstown Lower	352	2	16	Kildare	Narragh & Reban East	Fontstown	Athy	I.	66
31	Fontstown Upper	326	0	25	Kildare	Narragh & Reban East	Fontstown	Athy	I.	66
55, 56	Foohagh	305	0	26	Clare	Moyarta	Kilfearagh	Kilrush	II.	32
117	Foolagh	106	2	26	Galway	Longford	Tynagh	Portumna	IV.	62
40	Fooranagh	3	2	27	Galway	Moycullen	Kilcummin	Oughterard	IV.	68
49	Foorglass	222	2	7d	Galway	Ballynahinch	Ballindoon	Clifden	IV.	10
95, 96	Foorkill or Coldwood	602	0	4	Galway	Dunkellin	Athenry	Galway	IV.	27
6, 12	Footstown Great	279	3	20	Meath	Lower Slane	Siddan	Ardee	I.	223
6, 12	Footstown Little	186	3	17	Meath	Lower Slane	Siddan	Ardee	I.	223
48	Ford of Ling	18	1	28	Wexford	Forth	Ballybrennan	Wexford	I.	308
48	Ford of Ling	45	3	34	Wexford	Forth	Kilscoran	Wexford	I.	311
29, 30	Fordrath	200	1	13	Meath	Lune	Athboy	Trim	I.	207
42	Fordstown	278	3	16	Meath	Lower Moyfenrath	Rathmolyon	Trim	I.	211
23, 24	Fordstown	633	0	19	Meath	Upper Kells	Girley	Kells	I.	205
16, 23	Fordstown or Ballash-boy	72	3	3	Meath	Upper Kells	Balrathboyne	Kells	I.	204
22	Foad T.	—			Wexford	Ballaghkeen	} Killincooly Kilmuckridge {	Gorey	I.	} 295 297
4, 8	Fore	135	3	37	Westmeath	Fore	St. Feighins	Castletowndelvin	I.	271
12	Forekill	167	1	24	Kilkenny	Crannagh	Clomantagh	Urlingford	I.	89
36,37,39,40	Forelacka	1,415	1	23	King's Co.	Ballybritt	Kinnitty	Parsonstown	I.	125
34	Foremass	25	1	31	Fermanagh	Coole	Galloon	Lisnaskea	III.	200
8	Foremass	106	1	0	Monaghan	Monaghan	Tedavnet	Monaghan	III.	279
44	Foremass Lower	360	2	26	Tyrone	Clogher	Errigal Keerogue	Clogher	III.	295
44	Foremass Upper	729	3	13	Tyrone	Clogher	Errigal Keerogue	Clogher	III.	295
142	Forenaght	683	3	4e	Cork, W.R.	West Carbery (E.D.)	Castlehaven	Skibbereen	II.	138
19	Forenaghts Great	252	0	7	Kildare	South Salt	Forenaghts	Naas	I.	77
19	Forenaghts Little	210	0	23	Kildare	South Salt	Forenaghts	Naas	I.	77

(a) Including 1A. 1R. 32P. water.
(b) Including 5A. 0R. 24P. water.
(c) Including 2A. 1R. 8P. water.
(d) Including 30A. 0R. 8P. water.
(e) Including 1A. 2R. 5P. water.

No. of Sheet of the Ordnance Survey Maps.	Townlands and Towns.	Area in Statute Acres.	County.	Barony.	Parish.	Poor Law Union in 1857.	Townland Census of 1851, Part I.	
		A.　R.　P.					Vol.	Page
35	Forest . . .	315 1 8	Kildare . .	Narragh and Reban West . . .	Kilberry . . .	Athy . . .	I.	67
17	Forest . . .	184 0 27	Queen's Co. .	Maryborough West	Clonenagh and Clon-agheen . . .	Abbeyleix .	I.	243
29	Forest . . .	199 2 5	Tipperary, N.R.	Eliogarty . .	Templemore . .	Thurles . .	II.	272
36	Forest . . .	251 1 32	Wexford . .	Shelmaliere West .	Taghmon . .	Wexford . .	I.	335
41	Forestalstown . .	318 1 20	Kilkenny . .	Ida	Ballygurrim . .	New Ross .	I.	101
4	Forest Lower . .	856 3 30	Queen's Co. .	Tinnahinch . .	Castlebrack . .	Mountmellick .	I.	248
64, 75	Forest-town . .	124 2 23	Cork, E.R. .	Ballymore . .	Carrigtohill . .	Middleton . .	II.	52
3, 4, 8	Forest Upper . .	1,274 0 31	Queen's Co. .	Tinnahinch . .	Castlebrack . .	Mountmellick .	I.	248
30	Forestwood . .	195 0 21	Wexford . .	Bantry . . .	Killegney . .	Enniscorthy .	I.	301
34	Forfey . . .	230 1 14	Fermanagh .	Magherastephana .	Aghalurcher . .	Lisnaskea . .	III.	216
17	Forgeland . .	151 1 2	Queen's Co. .	Maryborough West	Clonenagh and Clon-agheen . . .	Mountmellick .	I.	243
19	Forgelands or Fair-field . . .	124 0 18	Wexford . .	Scarawalsh . .	Monart . . .	Enniscorthy .	I.	324
47	Forgestown . .	291 2 34	Tipperary, N.R.	Eliogarty . .	Moycarky . .	Thurles . .	II.	271
27	Forgney . . .	687 2 24	Longford . .	Shrule . . .	Forgney . . .	Ballymahon .	I.	166
20	Foriff . . .	435 3 12	Antrim . .	Lower Glenarm .	Layd . . .	Ballycastle .	III.	22
7	Forkeala . . .	1,090 2 33	Limerick . .	Owneybeg . .	Abington . .	Limerick . .	II.	251
88, 89	Forkfield or Gowel .	156 1 36a	Mayo . . .	Burrishoole . .	Aghagower . .	Westport . .	IV.	118
9, 15	Forkill . . .	172 1 26	Meath . .	Fore . . .	Loughcrew . .	Oldcastle . .	I.	201
31	FORKILL T. . .	—	Armagh . .	Orior Upper . .	Forkill . . .	Newry . . .	III.	57
42	Formal . . .	188 3 22	Meath . .	Lower Moyfenrath .	Rathmolyon . .	Trim . . .	I.	211
42	Formil . . .	124 1 32	Fermanagh .	Knockninny . .	Kinawley . .	Lisnaskea . .	III.	202
1, 5	Formil . . .	494 1 7	Fermanagh .	Lurg . . .	Drumkeeran . .	Lowtherstown .	III.	206
25	Formil . . .	1,039 3 19	Londonderry .	Keenaght . .	Bovevagh . .	Newtn Limavady	III.	235
24, 27	Formil . . .	308 3 39	Monaghan .	Cremorne . .	Aghnamullen . .	Castleblayney .	III.	258
25	Formil . . .	187 1 29	Monaghan .	Cremorne . .	Clontibret . .	Castleblayney .	III.	260
20	Formil . . .	133 2 11	Monaghan .	Cremorne . .	Muckno . . .	Castleblayney .	III.	262
19,20,27,28	Formil . . .	2,691 2 32	Tyrone . .	Strabane Upper .	Bodoney Lower .	Gortin . . .	III.	323
6	Formoyle . .	152 3 22	Leitrim . .	Rosclogher . .	Killasnet . .	Manorhamilton .	IV.	109
6, 10	Formoyle . .	609 0 37	Londonderry .	Coleraine . .	Dunboe . . .	Coleraine . .	III.	231
95, 96	Formoyle . .	1,795 1 21	Mayo . . .	Murrisk . . .	Kilgeever . .	Westport . .	IV.	160
28	Formoyle . .	454 1 28	Mayo . . .	Tirawley . .	Moygawnagh . .	Killala . .	IV.	171
8	Formoyle . .	146 3 36b	Monaghan .	Monaghan . .	Tedavnet . .	Monaghan . .	III.	279
9, 15	Formoyle . .	1,205 2 24	Sligo . . .	Carbury . .	Calry . . .	Sligo . . .	IV.	220
44	Formoyle Beg . .	254 2 3	Clare . .	Tulla Lower .	Killokennedy . .	Limerick . .	II.	35
1, 2, 5	Formoyle East .	847 3 33	Clare . .	Burren . .	Killonaghan . .	Ballyvaghan .	II.	13
32	Formoyle Eighteragh (East) . . .	465 3 4c	Clare . .	Inchiquin . .	Inagh . . .	Ennistimon .	II.	25
32	Formoyle Eighteragh (West) . . .	562 0 17	Clare . .	Inchiquin . .	Inagh . . .	Ennistimon .	II.	25
21	Formoyle (Farrell) .	226 1 18	Longford . .	Ratheline . .	Ratheline . .	Longford . .	I.	164
44	Formoyle More . .	340 0 13	Clare . .	Tulla Lower .	Killokennedy . .	Limerick . .	II.	35
21	Formoyle (Newcomen)	214 1 17	Longford . .	Ratheline . .	Ratheline . .	Longford . .	I.	164
32	Formoyle Oughter-agh (East) . .	554 2 28	Clare . .	Inchiquin . .	Inagh . . .	Ennistimon .	II.	25
32	Formoyle Oughter-agh (West) . .	621 1 7	Clare . .	Inchiquin . .	Inagh . . .	Ennistimon .	II.	25
1, 2, 4, 5	Formoyle West .	700 0 39	Clare . .	Burren . .	Killonaghan . .	Ballyvaghan .	II.	13
6, 7	Formullen . .	109 0 13	Londonderry .	Coleraine . .	Dunboe . . .	Coleraine . .	III.	231
66, 79	Formweel . .	1,246 2 5d	Galway . .	Moycullen . .	Kilcummin . .	Galway . .	IV.	67
50, 61	Fornaght . .	662 3 6	Cork, E.R. .	East Muskerry .	Donaghmore . .	Macroom . .	II.	103
27	Fornaght . .	384 2 2	Waterford .	Gaultiere . .	Kiliea . . .	Waterford . .	II.	363
93	Forramoyle East .	255 2 24	Galway . .	Galway . .	Rahoon . . .	Galway . .	IV.	37
93	Forramoyle West .	221 2 32	Galway . .	Galway . .	Rahoon . . .	Galway . .	IV.	37
24	Forrestalstown . .	772 1 12	Wexford . .	Bantry . . .	Killegney . .	Enniscorthy .	I.	301
11	Forrestfields . .	92 3 17	Dublin . .	Nethercross . .	Swords . . .	Balrothery .	I.	32
11, 14	Forrest Great . .	524 0 16	Dublin . .	Nethercross . .	Swords . . .	Balrothery .	I.	32
11, 14	Forrest Little . .	255 0 16	Dublin . .	Nethercross . .	Swords . . .	Balrothery .	I.	32
20,21,28,29	Forrew . . .	710 0 31e	Mayo . . .	Tirawley . .	Moygawnagh . .	Killala . .	IV.	171
15	Forristeen . .	197 3 37	Wicklow . .	Lower Talbotstown .	Dunlavin . .	Baltinglass .	I.	360
35	Fortane Beg . .	467 1 17	Clare . .	Tulla Upper .	Tulla . . .	Tulla . . .	II.	41
27, 35	Fortane More . .	292 2 38f	Clare . .	Tulla Upper .	Tulla . . .	Tulla . . .	II.	41
26	Fortaugustus . .	83 0 23	Roscommon .	Castlereagh . .	Kiltullagh . .	Castlereagh .	IV.	202
30, 31	Fortbrown . .	270 2 23	Galway . .	Ballymoe . .	Clonbern . .	Glennamaddy .	IV.	6
3	Fortchester Lower .	295 2 18	Wexford . .	Gorey . . .	Inch . . .	Gorey . . .	I.	316
3	Fortchester Upper .	183 2 25	Wexford . .	Gorey . . .	Inch . . .	Gorey . . .	I.	316
46	Fort East . .	570 0 22	Limerick . .	Connello Upper .	Colmanswell . .	Kilmallock .	II.	232
35, 36	Fortel . . .	1,182 0 23	King's Co. .	Ballybritt . .	Birr . . .	Parsonstown .	I.	125
19, 91	Fortetna . .	175 0 30	Limerick . .	Pubblebrian . .	Killonahan . .	Croom . .	II.	258
50	Fortfergus . .	178 2 29	Clare . .	Clonderalaw .	Kilchreest . .	Killadysert .	II.	15

(a) Including 2A. 3R. 26P. water.
(b) Including 7A. 3R. 14P. water.

(c) Including 17A. 2R. 10P. water.
(d) Including 116A. 2R. 33P. water.

(e) Including 1A. 3R. 9P. water.
(f) Including 2A. 1R. 0P. water.

No. of Sheet of the Ordnance Survey Maps.	Townlands and Towns.	Area in Statute Acres. A. R. P.	County.	Barony.	Parish.	Poor Law Union in 1857.	Townland Census of 1851, Part I. Vol.	Page
31	Fortgrady	506 2 29a	Cork, E.R.	Duhallow	Dromtarriff	Kanturk	II.	71
27, 32	Fortgranite	121 0 4	Wicklow	Upper Talbotstown	Kilranelagh	Baltinglass	I.	364
42	Forth Commons	835 3 7b	Wexford	Forth	Kildavin	Wexford	I.	310
42	Forth Commons	331 3 19	Wexford	Forth	Rathaspick	Wexford	I.	312
42	Forth Commons	122 2 9	Wexford	Forth	St. Peters	Wexford	I.	314
16, 17	Forthenry or Largy	346 3 29	Cavan	Tullygarvey	Kildrumsherdan	Cootehill	III.	90
44	Forthill	307 1 25	Antrim	Lower Antrim	Connor	Antrim	III.	3
47	Forthill	417 2 39	Antrim	Lower Belfast	Templecorran	Larne	III.	9
30	Forthill	212 0 17	Cavan	Tullyhunco	Scrabby	Cavan	III.	99
112, 125	Forthill	77 0 1	Cork, E.R.	Kinsale	Ringcurran	Kinsale	II.	100
11	Forthill	74 1 11	Fermanagh	Lurg	Derryvullan	Lowtherstown	III.	204
22, 26	Forthill	565 1 0c	Longford	Ratheline	Cashel	Ballymahon	I.	163
93	Forthill	159 2 34	Mayo	Costello	Bekan	Claremorris	IV.	139
15	Forties	203 2 12	Wexford	Scarawalsh	Kilbride	Enniscorthy	I.	323
37, 38	Fortland	350 3 23	Cavan	Clanmahon	Ballymachugh	Cavan	III.	76
29	Fortland	189 1 10	Mayo	Tirawley	Kilfian	Ballina	IV.	169
11	Fortland	546 2 22	Sligo	Tireragh	Easky	Dromore West	IV.	233
2	Fortlands	121 0 15	Cork, E.R.	Orrery and Kilmore	Rathgoggan	Kilmallock	II.	109
90	Fortlawn	46 0 30	Mayo	Carra	Drum	Castlebar	IV.	128
46	Fort Middle	836 1 33	Limerick	Connello Upper	Colmanswell	Kilmallock	II.	232
19	Fortmill and Moyra	168 0 2	Longford	Ardagh	Ardagh	Longford	I.	151
7	Fortmoy	222 3 18	Tipperary, N.R.	Lower Ormond	Aglishcloghane	Borrisokane	II.	281
30	Fortpark	35 1 12	Galway	Dunmore	Dunmore	Tuam	IV.	34
46	Fortstewart	138 3 35	Donegal	Kilmacrenan	Aughnish	Milford	III.	122
11, 12	Fort Town	304 3 4	Antrim	Upper Dunluce	Ballymoney	Ballymoney	III.	19
9	Fort-town	57 3 1	Tyrone	Strabane Lower	Urney	Strabane	III.	322
21	Fortunestown	261 2 31	Dublin	Newcastle	Saggart	Celbridge	I.	34
46	Fort West	474 3 36	Limerick	Connello Upper	Colmanswell	Kilmallock	II.	232
52	Fortwilliam	76 0 36	Clare	Bunratty Lower	Kilfinaghta	Limerick	II.	4
52	Fortwilliam	103 3 18	Clare	Bunratty Lower	Kilfintinan	Limerick	II.	5
21	Fortwilliam	288 0 7	Kerry	Clanmaurice	O'Dorney	Tralee	II.	172
42, 43	Fortwilliam	44 1 13	King's Co.	Clonlisk	Aghancon	Roscrea	I.	129
21	Fortwilliam	195 3 39	Longford	Ratheline	Cashel	Ballymahon	I.	163
20, 28	Fortwilliam	110 2 11d	Waterford	Coshmore and Coshbride	Lismore and Mocollop	Lismore	II.	345
66, 77	Fortyacres	51 3 33	Cork, E.R.	Imokilly	Killeagh	Middleton	II.	88
1, 4	Fortyacres	60 1 7	Dublin	Balrothery West	Naul	Balrothery	I.	23
18	Fortyacres	83 1 10	Dublin	Dublin	Donnybrook	Dublin South	I.	30
1	Fortyacres	161 1 37	Galway	Ballymoe	Templetogher	Glennamaddy	IV.	9
44	Fortyacres	72 2 25	Galway	Clare	Killererin	Tuam	IV.	21
29	Fortyacres	185 2 33	Galway	Dunmore	Tuam	Tuam	IV.	36
10	Fortyacres	77 2 37	King's Co.	Lower Philipstown	Kilclonfert	Tullamore	I.	142
10, 18	Fortyacres	109 1 16	King's Co.	Lower Philipstown	Killadurry	Tullamore	I.	143
39	Fortyacres	66 0 31	Limerick	Connello Upper	Bruree	Kilmallock	II.	231
58	Fortyacres	65 0 7	Tipperary, S.R.	Clanwilliam	Cullen	Tipperary	II.	307
16, 23	Fortyacres	45 2 30	Westmeath	Kilkenny West	Kilkenny West	Athlone	I.	273
42	Fortyacres	72 2 11	Wexford	Forth	Rathaspick	Wexford	I.	312
66	Fossa	177 2 18	Kerry	Magunihy	Aghadoe	Killarney	II.	199
28	Fossa Beg	573 2 15	Clare	Tulla Upper	Tomgraney	Scarriff	II.	41
28	Fossa More	810 3 3c	Clare	Tulla Upper	Tomgraney	Scarriff	II.	41
18,19,24,25	Fossy Lower	245 1 32	Queen's Co.	Cullenagh	Fossy or Timahoe	Abbeyleix	I.	240
24, 25	Fossy Upper	933 0 37	Queen's Co.	Cullenagh	Fossy or Timahoe	Abbeyleix	I.	240
23, 29	Fostersfields	223 3 13	Meath	Lune	Athboy	Trim	I.	207
36	Fostersholding	14 3 25	Meath	Upper Navan	Trim	Trim	I.	217
36	Fosterstown	91 1 9	Meath	Lower Moyfenrath	Trim	Trim	I.	212
11	Fosterstown North	107 1 18	Dublin	Nethercross	Swords	Balrothery	I.	32
11	Fosterstown South	123 0 14	Dublin	Nethercross	Swords	Balrothery	I.	32
5, 6	Fostragh	617 2 27	Longford	Longford	Killoe	Longford	I.	159
3, 4	Fostragh	320 1 28f	Roscommon	Boyle	Ardcarn	Boyle	IV.	193
29, 38	Fotish	274 1 24	Mayo	Tirawley	Crossmolina	Ballina	IV.	166
54	Fough East	43 0 22	Galway	Moycullen	Kilcummin	Oughterard	IV.	67
26	Foughil	527 0 9	Roscommon	Castlereagh	Kilkeevin	Castlereagh	IV.	200
79	*Foughil Island*	15 0 35	Kerry	Iveragh	Caher	Cahersiveen	II.	194
29, 32	Foughill Etra	719 0 28	Armagh	Orior Upper	Jonesborough	Newry	III.	57
29, 32	Foughill Otra	962 1 28	Armagh	Orior Upper	Jonesborough	Newry	III.	57
54	Fough West	20 2 4	Galway	Moycullen	Kilcummin	Oughterard	IV.	67
40	FOULKESMILL T.	—	Wexford	Shelmaliere West	{ Ballylannan / Clongeen&Horetown }	New Ross	I. {	332 / 333 }
8	Foulkscourt	113 3 23	Kilkenny	Galmoy	Erke	Urlingford	I.	92
8	Foulkscourt	868 0 15	Kilkenny	Galmoy	Fertagh	Urlingford	I.	92
26	Foulksrath	162 0 7	Kilkenny	Callan	Callan	Callan	I.	83
10	Foulksrath	355 3 20	Kilkenny	Fassadinin	Cooleraheen	Kilkenny	I.	89
19, 23	Foulkstown	131 3 10g	Kilkenny	Shillelogher	Outrath	Kilkenny	I.	115

(a) Including 6A. 2R. 32P. water.
(b) Including 7A. 3R. 7P. detached portion.
(c) Including 19A. 1R. 12P. water.
(d) Including 2A. 2R. 24P. water.
(e) Including 152A. 2R. 23P. water.
(f) Including 6A. 1R. 18P. water.
(g) Including 13A. 1R. 37P. detached portion.

No. of Sheet of the Ordnance Survey Maps.	Townlands and Towns.	Area in Statute Acres. (A. R. P.)	County.	Barony.	Parish.	Poor Law Union in 1857.	Townland Census of 1851, Part I. (Vol. | Page)
61, 62	Foulkstown . .	378 1 17	Tipperary, S.R.	Middlethird . .	Magorban . .	Cashel . .	II. 328
33	Fountain . .	211 1 25	Clare . .	Islands . . .	Drumcliff . .	Ennis . .	II. 30
29	Fountain . .	303 2 21	Waterford . .	Coshmore&Coshbride	Kilwatermoy . .	Lismore . .	II. 343
121	Fountainhill .	207 2 13	Mayo . .	Kilmaine . .	Kilmainebeg . .	Ballinrobe . .	IV. 155
21, 22	Fountainhill or Knockavilra	143 0 11	Galway . .	Ballynahinch . .	Omey . . ˙ .	Clifden . .	IV. 15
99	Fountainstown .	669 3 25	Cork, E.R.	Kinalea . .	Kilpatrick . .	Kinsale . .	II. 95
99	Fountainstown North	80 1 21	Cork, E.R.	Kerrycurrihy . .	Kilpatrick . .	Kinsale . .	II. 92
122	Fourcuil . .	125 0 26	Cork, W.R.	East Carbery (E.D.)	Kilgarriff . .	Clonakilty . .	II. 129
122	Fourcuil . .	244 3 2	Cork, W R.	East Carbery (E.D.)	Templebryan . .	Clonakilty . .	II. 130
33	Fourknocks . .	86 3 34	Meath . .	Upper Duleck .	Stamullin . .	Drogheda . .	I. 198
35	Four Score Acre .	150 5 17	Antrim . .	Upper Glenarm .	Carncastle . .	Larne . .	III. 24
14, 15	Fourth Corgary or Meenablagh .	766 1 27a	Tyrone . .	Omagh West . .	Termonamongan .	Castlederg . .	III. 317
33	Fowlerstown .	257 2 27	Meath . .	Upper Duleck . .	Duleck Abbey . .	Drogheda . .	I. 198
35	Foxandgeese .	113 2 21b	Clare . .	Tulla Lower . .	Killuran . .	Tulla . .	II. 36
17,18,21,22	Fox-and-geese .	183 2 12c	Dublin . .	Uppercross . .	Clondalkin . .	Dublin South .	I. 39
17, 18	Fox-and-geese Common .	105 1 10	Dublin . .	Uppercross . .	Clondalkin . .	Dublin South .	I. 39
31	Foxborough .	61 2 17	Leitrim . .	Leitrim . .	Annaduff . .	Cark. on Shannon	IV. 99
26, 32, 33	Foxborough .	403 3 28	Roscommon . .	Castlereagh . .	Kiltullagh . .	Castlereagh . .	IV. 202
22	Foxborough .	330 1 25d	Roscommon . .	Roscommon . .	Elphin . .	Strokestown . .	IV. 209
44, 45	Foxburrow . .	248 0 19	King's Co. .	Clonlisk . .	Templeharry . .	Roscrea . .	I. 132
17, 23	Foxburrow . .	161 1 32	Queen's Co. .	Maryborough West .	Clonenagh and Clonagheen	Abbeyleix . .	I. 243
12	Foxburrow . .	63 3 31	Westmeath . .	Corkaree . .	Taghmon . .	Mullingar . .	I. 264
22	Foxcover . .	237 2 9	Kilkenny . .	Shillelogher . .	Killaloe . .	Callan . .	I. 115
2, 6	Foxcover . .	269 2 34	Wexford . .	Gorey . .	Kilnahue . .	Gorey . .	I. 319
48,49,60,61	Foxford . .	1,019 1 37e	Mayo . .	Gallen . .	Toomore . .	Swineford . .	IV. 151
60, 61	FOXFORD T. . .	—	Mayo . .	Gallen . .	Toomore . .	Swineford . .	IV. 151
67, 74	Foxfort . .	435 0 30	Tipperary, S.R.	Clanwilliam . .	Templeneiry . .	Tipperary . .	II. 311
24	Foxglen or Garbally	45 1 7	King's Co. .	Ballyboy . .	Killoughy . .	Tullamore . .	I. 124
134	Foxhall . .	390 0 29	Cork, W.R.	East Carbery (W.D.)	Castleventry . .	Clonakilty . .	II. 131
52	Foxhall . .	171 3 33	Donegal . .	Kilmacrenan . .	Conwal . .	Letterkenny . .	III. 126
106	Foxhall . .	304 1 18	Galway . .	Longford . .	Abbeygormacan .	Loughrea . .	IV. 56
24	Foxhall . .	297 0 3	Longford . .	Ardagh . . .	Rathreagh . .	Ballymahon . .	I. 153
37	Foxhall . .	299 1 35	Tipperary, N.R.	Owney and Arra .	Kilvellane . .	Nenagh . .	II. 296
46, 47	Foxhall East .	289 1 35	Limerick . .	Connello Upper .	Colmanswell . .	Kilmallock . .	II. 232
24	Foxhall Glebe .	32 3 32	Longford . .	Ardagh . .	Rathreagh . .	Ballymahon . .	I. 153
106, 107	Foxhall Little .	389 1 14	Galway . .	Longford . .	Abbeygormacan .	Loughrea . .	IV. 56
46	Foxhall West .	316 1 39	Limerick . .	Connello Upper .	Colmanswell . .	Kilmallock . .	II. 232
35	Foxhill . .	578 2 33	Kildare . .	Narragh and Reban East . .	Moone . . .	Athy . .	I. 66
7	Foxhill . .	147 3 27	Roscommon . .	Boyle . .	Tumna . .	Cark. on Shannon	IV. 198
67	Foxhole . .	94 2 23	Cork, E.R.	Imokilly . .	Youghal . .	Youghal . .	II. 91
6	Foxhole . .	34 1 10	Monaghan . .	Trough . . .	Donagh . .	Monaghan . .	III. 282
49	Fox Island . .	3 2 10	Galway . .	Ballynahinch . .	Ballindoon . .	Clifden . .	IV. 10
15, 19	Foxlands . .	85 0 8	Dublin . .	Coolock . .	Raheny . .	Dublin North .	I. 28
23, 26	Foxrock . .	204 1 7	Dublin . .	Rathdown . .	Kill . .	Rathdown . .	I. 35
24	Fox's Castle .	245 0 17	Waterford . .	Decies without Drum	Stradbally . .	Kilmacthomas .	II. 361
37	Foxtown . .	153 3 30	Meath . .	Lower Deece . .	Galtrim . .	Trim . .	I. 191
16	Foy . .	19 1 5	Kildare . .	Offaly East . .	Rathangan . .	Edenderry . .	I. 71
103	Foyagh . .	133 3 58	Donegal . .	Tirhugh . .	Drumhome . .	Ballyshannon .	III. 146
11	Foyarr . .	147 0 20	Armagh . .	Tiranny . .	Tynan . .	Armagh . .	III. 60
5	Foy Beg . .	214 0 4	Armagh . .	Oneilland West .	Drumcree . .	Lurgan . .	III. 52
23	Foydragh . .	264 2 38	Fermanagh . .	Magherastephana .	Aghavea . .	Lisnaskea . .	III. 219
15	Foyduff . .	254 2 15	Armagh . .	Tiranny . .	Tynan . .	Armagh . .	III. 60
79	Foyfin . .	213 1 21f	Donegal . .	Raphoe . .	Urney . .	Strabane . .	III. 144
22	Foygh . .	401 3 3	Longford . .	Ratheline . .	Kilcommock . .	Ballymahon . .	I. 164
46	Foygh . .	156 3 32g	Tyrone . .	Dungannon Middle .	Donaghmore . .	Dungannon . .	III. 302
18	Foylatalure .	357 3 26	Kilkenny . .	Crannagh . .	Tullaroan . .	Kilkenny . .	I. 88
6	Foyle . .	115 1 3	Limerick . .	Clanwilliam . .	Killeenagarriff .	Limerick . .	II. 224
9	Foyle North .	117 1 16	Kilkenny . .	Galmoy . .	Balleen . .	Urlingford . .	I. 91
9	Foyle South .	351 3 1	Kilkenny . .	Galmoy . .	Balleen . .	Urlingford . .	I. 91
5	Foy More . .	216 0 31	Armagh . .	Oneilland West .	Drumcree . .	Lurgan . .	III. 52
10	Foynes Island .	293 2 3	Limerick . .	Shanid . . .	Robertstown . .	Glin . .	II. 258
10	FOYNES T. . .	—	Limerick . .	Shanid . . .	Robertstown . .	Glin . .	II. 258
35	Foyoges . .	276 1 14	Sligo . .	Tirerrill . .	Kilmactranny . .	Boyle . .	IV. 240
1	Foyran . .	272 0 5	Westmeath . .	Fore . .	Foyran . .	Granard . .	I. 270
29	Fraine . .	936 0 15	Meath . .	Lune . .	Athboy . .	Trim . .	I. 207
9	France . .	126 3 25h	Longford . .	Granard . . ,	Clonbroney . .	Granard . .	I. 166
45	Frankfort . .	1,315 1 7	King's Co. .	Clonlisk . .	Dunkerrin . .	Roscrea . .	I. 130
31	Frankford . .	214 3 15	King's Co. .	Ballyboy . .	Ballyboy . .	Parsonstown . .	II. 123
16	Frankford . .	565 0 19	Sligo . .	Tireragh . .	Kilglass . .	Dromore West .	IV. 234

(a) Including 4A. 0R. 20P. water.
(b) Including 6A. 0R. 11P. water.
(c) Including 14A. 1R. 4P. detached portion.
(d) Including 30A. 2R. 26P. water.
(e) Including 22A. 3R. 1P. water.
(f) Including 4A. 2R. 29P. water.
(g) Including 6A. 1R. 30P. water.
(h) Including 5A. 2R. 38P. water.

No. of Sheet of the Ordnance Survey Maps.	Townlands and Towns.	Area in Statute Acres.	County.	Barony.	Parish.	Poor Law Union in 1857.	Townland Census of 1851, Part I.	
		A. R. P.					Vol.	Page
8, 9	Frankford or Bally-kieran	457 2 34	Kilkenny	Galmoy	Balleen	Urlingford	I.	91
31	FRANKFORD T.	—	King's Co.	Ballyboy	Ballyboy	Parsonstown	I.	123
46	Frankfort	20 0 30	Cork, E.R.	Kinnatalloon	Mogeely	Fermoy	II.	98
37	Frankfort	518 2 9	Limerick	Connello Upper	Ballingarry	Newcastle	II.	230
11	Frankfort	188 0 30	Wexford	Gorey	Liskinfere	Gorey	I.	320
30	Frankfort East	282 0 1	Kilkenny	Kells	Killamery	Callan	I.	109
30	Frankfort West	278 3 17	Kilkenny	Kells	Killamery	Callan	I.	109
38	Frankstown	139 0 30	Meath	Ratoath	Kilbrew	Dunshaughlin	I.	218
64	Frasnadeffa	121 2 8	Mayo	Costello	Kilcolman	Castlereagh	IV.	141
19	Frass	285 0 29	Galway	Ballymoe	Boyounagh	Glennamaddy	IV.	6
3, 8	Freagh	223 0 29	Kildare	Carbury	Kilmore	Edenderry	I.	52
31	Freagh	238 3 10	King's Co.	Ballyboy	Ballyboy	Parsonstown	I.	123
41	Freagh	262 0 20	Meath	Upper Moyfenrath	Castlerickard	Trim	I.	213
31	Freagh	117 2 3	Tipperary, N.R.	Owney and Arra	Kilnarath	Nenagh	II.	296
85	Freaghanagh	446 3 20	Kerry	Magunihy	Killaha	Killarney	II.	202
22, 23	Freaghavaleen	331 2 27	Clare	Ibrickan	Kilfarboy	Ennistimon	II.	22
22, 30	Freaghcastle	389 2 25	Clare	Ibrickan	Kilfarboy	Ennistimon	II.	22
52,53,60,61	Freaghduff	539 2 29	Tipperary, S.R.	Middlethird	St. Patricksrock	Cashel	II.	330
76	Freaghillan	19 2 39	Mayo	Burrishoole	Kilmeena	Westport	IV.	122
48	*Freaghillan*	6 2 5	Mayo	Carra	Turlough	Castlebar	IV.	131
22	*Freaghillan*	4 1 36	Mayo	Tirawley	Ballysakeery	Ballina	IV.	165
67	*Freaghillanluggagh,*	3 3 25	Mayo	Burrishoole	Burrishoole	Newport	IV.	120
67	*Freaghillan West,*	3 0 2	Mayo	Burrishoole	Burrishoole	Newport	IV.	120
63	*Freaghillaun,*	39 0 17	Galway	Ballynahinch	Moyrus	Clifden	IV.	14
89	*Freaghillaun-beg,*	26 1 9	Galway	Moycullen	Kilcummin	Oughterard	IV.	68
78	*Freaghillaun-more,*	8 2 34	Galway	Moycullen	Kilcummin	Oughterard	IV.	68
89	*Freaghillaun-more,*	22 2 18	Galway	Moycullen	Kilcummin	Oughterard	IV.	68
9	*Freaghillaun North,*	9 3 10	Galway	Ballynahinch	Ballynakill	Clifden	IV.	12
9	Freaghillaun South	57 0 4a	Galway	Ballynahinch	Ballynakill	Clifden	IV.	12
30	*Freagh Island,*	0 2 37	Clare	Ibrickan	Kilfarboy	Ennistimon	II.	22
15, 16	Freaghmeen	137 3 27	Longford	Ardagh	Street	Granard	I.	153
3	Freaghmore	371 2 4	Westmeath	Fore	Rathgarve	Castletowndelvin	I.	271
74	Freagh and Vicars-acre	22 2 29	Cork, E.R.	Cork	St. Finbars	Cork	II.	66
134	Freahanes	454 1 2	Cork, W.R.	East Carbery (W.D.)	Ross	Clonakilty	II.	135
22	Freame Mount De-mesne	199 0 3	Monaghan	Dartree	Ematris	Cootehill	III.	267
27, 28	Freeduff	303 2 14	Armagh	Fews Upper	Creggan	Castleblayney	III.	48
37, 41	Freeduff	310 3 8	Cavan	Clanmahon	Drumlumman	Granard	III.	77
2	Freehall, Dunlop	125 3 34	Londonderry	Coleraine	Dunboe	Coleraine	III.	231
6, 10	Freehall or Money-vennon	209 1 15	Londonderry	Keenaght	Aghanloo	NewTⁿLimavady	III.	234
2	Freehall, Watson	121 3 21	Londonderry	Coleraine	Dunboe	Coleraine	III.	231
14	Freehalman	119 3 27	Longford	Ardagh	Templemichael	Longford	I.	153
90	Freeheen	172 2 37	Mayo	Clanmorris	Mayo	Ballinrobe	IV.	135
29, 38	Freeheen	135 3 37	Mayo	Tirawley	Crossmolina	Ballina	IV.	166
55	*Freeheen Island,*	1 3 1	Galway	Moycullen	Kilcummin	Oughterard	IV.	68
12	Freehold	218 1 30	Donegal	Inishowen East	Culdaff	Inishowen	III.	118
50, 51	Freemanstown	200 1 36	Antrim	Upper Antrim	Donegore	Antrim	III.	6
6, 15	Freemount	382 2 1	Cork, E.R.	Duhallow	Knocktemple	Kanturk	II.	75
60, 68	Freemount	185 2 34	Kerry	Magunihy	Kilcummin	Killarney	II.	201
6	FREEMOUNT T.	—	Cork, E.R.	Duhallow	Knocktemple	Kanturk	II.	75
93	Freeport	40 0 38	Galway	Galway	Rahoon	Galway	IV.	37
41	Freeschool Land	1 2 4	Sligo	Tirerrill	Kilmactranny	Boyle	IV.	240
36, 37	Freffans Great	345 2 23	Meath	Lower Moyfenrath	Laracor	Trim	I.	210
36, 37	Freffans Little	616 2 19	Meath	Lower Moyfenrath	Laracor	Trim	I.	210
88	Frehans	346 1 27	Tipperary, S.R.	Iffa and Offa West	Ballybacon	Clogheen	II.	317
16, 17	Fremagh	54 0 18	Monaghan	Dartree	Killevan	Clones	III.	268
121	Frenchbrook North	221 1 8b	Mayo	Kilmaine	Kilmainemore	Ballinrobe	IV.	156
121	Frenchbrook South	575 1 7	Mayo	Kilmaine	Kilmainemore	Ballinrobe	IV.	156
83, 95	Frenchfort	1,379 0 31	Galway	Dunkellin	Oranmore	Galway	IV.	32
83, 95	FRENCHFORT T.	—	Galway	Dunkellin	Oranmore	Galway	IV.	32
99	Frenchfurze	490 2 8	Cork, E.R.	Kerrycurrihy	Carrigaline	Kinsale	II.	92
119	Frenchgrove	668 1 11	Mayo	Kilmaine	Kilcommon	Ballinrobe	IV.	154
27, 34	Frenchlawn	413 2 10	Roscommon	Castlereagh	Ballintober	Castlereagh	IV.	198
103	Frenchpark	163 0 35c	Galway	Dunkellin	Kilcolgan	Gort	IV.	28
9, 15	Frenchpark Demesne	1,134 1 28	Roscommon	Frenchpark	Tibohine	Castlereagh	IV.	205
15	FRENCHPARK T.	—	Roscommon	Frenchpark	Tibohine	Castlereagh	IV.	205
15, 20	Freneystown	876 1 6	Kilkenny	Gowran	Tiscoffin	Kilkenny	I.	99
13	Freshford	97 0 14	Kilkenny	Crannagh	Freshford	Kilkenny	I.	85
9, 13	Freshford Lots	66 1 26	Kilkenny	Crannagh	Freshford	Kilkenny	I.	85
13	FRESHFORD T.	—	Kilkenny	Crannagh	Freshford	Kilkenny	I.	85

(a) Including 7A. 3R. 20P. detached portion.   (b) Including 28A. 0R. 9P. water.   (c) Including 10A. 3R. 24P. water.

3 N

No. of Sheet of the Ordnance Survey Maps	Townlands and Towns.	Area in Statute Acres.	County.	Barony.	Parish.	Poor Law Union in 1857.	Townland Census of 1851, Part I. Vol.	Page
		A. R. P.						
17, 18	Freugh . . .	1,113 0 3	Londonderry .	Coleraine . .	Errigal . . .	Coleraine . .	III.	232
16	Freughlough . .	592 2 10	Tyrone . .	Omagh West .	Urney . . .	Castlederg . .	III.	318
58, 64	Freughmore . .	244 3 14a	Tyrone . .	Clogher . .	Clogher . . .	Clogher . .	III.	292
51	Freughmore . .	339 2 25	Tyrone . .	Clogher . .	Donacavey . .	Omagh . .	III.	294
43	Freughmore . .	466 3 27	Tyrone . .	Omagh East .	Drumragh . .	Omagh . .	III.	312
19	Frevagh . .	352 3 36b	Fermanagh .	Magheraboy .	Devenish . .	Ballyshannon .	III.	211
38, 40	Frevanagh . .	309 1 3	Westmeath .	Moycashel .	Durrow . . .	Tullamore .	I.	277
21	Freynestownhill .	180 3 27	Wicklow . .	Upper Talbotstown	Freynestown .	Baltinglass .	I.	364
21	Freynestown Lower .	186 0 26	Wicklow . .	Upper Talbotstown	Freynestown .	Baltinglass .	I.	364
21	Freynestown Upper	223 1 11	Wicklow . .	Upper Talbotstown	Freynestown .	Baltinglass .	I.	364
15	Friarhill . . .	229 1 35	Wicklow . .	Lower Talbotstown	Tober . . .	Baltinglass .	I.	361
21	Friar Island . .	24 3 20	Galway . .	Ballynahinch .	Omey . . .	Clifden . .	IV.	15
22	Friarland . .	39 2 9	Dublin . .	Rathdown . .	Taney . . .	Rathdown .	I.	38
85	Friarsbush . .	33 2 5	Donegal . .	Tirhugh . .	Donegal . .	Donegal . .	III.	145
59	Friarsfield . .	331 0 6	Tipperary, S.R.	Clanwilliam .	Templenoe . .	Tipperary .	II.	311
70	Friarsgrange . .	253 2 9	Tipperary, S.R.	Middlethird .	Coolmundry .	Cashel . .	II.	326
93	Friarsground . .	16 3 25	Mayo . .	Costello . .	Annagh . .	Claremorris .	IV.	138
74	Friarshill . .	26 0 24	Mayo . .	Costello . .	Castlemore .	Castlereagh .	IV.	140
25	Friarshill . .	10 1 16	Wicklow . .	Newcastle . .	Rathnew . .	Rathdrum .	I.	354
19	Friarsinch . .	43 1 17c	Kilkenny . .	Gowran and Municipal Borough	St. John's . .	Kilkenny . .	I.	98
34	*Friar's Island* . .	2 0 16	Fermanagh .	Magherastephana	Aghalurcher .	Lisnaskea .	III.	218
108, 109, 118	Friarsisland . .	127 3 36	Galway . .	Longford . .	Meelick . .	Portumna .	IV.	62
81	Friars Island . .	29 2 21d	Galway . .	Moycullen . .	Moycullen . .	Galway . .	IV.	71
22	Friars Island . .	112 1 32	Westmeath .	Brawny . .	St. Mary's .	Athlone . .	I.	259
108, 109	Friarsland . .	32 2 13	Galway . .	Longford . .	Meelick . .	Portumna .	IV.	61
22	Friarsland . .	144 1 9	Queen's Co. .	Clarmallagh .	Aghaboe . .	Donaghmore .	I.	236
30	Friarspark . .	11 2 12	Meath . .	Upper Navan .	Trim . . .	Trim . .	I.	217
36	Friarspark 5th Division . . .	4 3 10	Meath . .	Lower Moyfenrath .	Trim . . .	Trim . .	I.	212
36	Friarspark 1st Division . . .	23 0 4e	Meath . .	Lower Moyfenrath .	Trim . . .	Trim . .	I.	212
36	Friarspark 4th Division . . .	6 3 19	Meath . .	Lower Moyfenrath .	Trim . . .	Trim . .	I.	212
36	Friarspark 2nd Division . . .	4 3 21	Meath . .	Lower Moyfenrath .	Trim . . .	Trim . .	I.	212
36	Friarspark 6th Division . . .	148 3 5	Meath . .	Lower Moyfenrath .	Trim . . .	Trim . .	I.	212
118	Friarsquarter East .	220 3 0f	Mayo . .	Kilmaine . .	Ballinrobe .	Ballinrobe .	IV.	152
118	Friarsquarter West .	241 0 37g	Mayo . .	Kilmaine . .	Ballinrobe .	Ballinrobe .	IV.	152
3, 8	Friarstown . .	891 1 5	Carlow . .	Carlow . .	Killerrig . .	Carlow . .	I.	2
22	Friarstown . .	478 2 15	Kildare . .	Offaly East .	Tully . .	Naas . .	I.	71
11, 14, 15	Friarstown . .	170 2 38h	Kildare . .	South Salt .	Castledillon .	Celbridge .	I.	76
14	Friarstown . .	233 3 16	Leitrim . .	Drumahaire .	Killanummery .	Manorhamilton	IV.	98
13	Friarstown . .	415 2 15	Limerick . .	Clanwilliam .	Caheravally .	Limerick .	II.	221
23	Friarstown . .	166 1 9	Limerick . .	Clanwilliam .	Caherelly .	Limerick .	II.	222
23	Friarstown . .	70 3 22	Limerick . .	Clanwilliam .	Fedamore .	Limerick .	II.	223
23	Friarstown . .	512 1 35	Limerick . .	Clanwilliam .	Rochestown .	Limerick .	II.	225
39	Friarstown . .	257 1 35	Mayo . .	Tirawley . .	Kilbelfad .	Ballina .	IV.	168
32	Friarstown . .	459 3 24	Westmeath .	Fartullagh .	Clonfad . .	Mullingar .	I.	268
24, 25	Friarstown Lower .	54 0 4	Dublin . .	Uppercross .	Tallaght . .	Dublin South .	I.	41
13, 22	Friarstown North .	314 2 14	Limerick . .	Smallcounty .	Fedamore .	Croom . .	II.	259
23	Friarstown South .	65 1 22	Limerick . .	Smallcounty .	Fedamore .	Limerick .	II.	259
21, 24, 25	Friarstown Upper .	179 1 16	Dublin . .	Uppercross .	Tallaght . .	Dublin South .	I.	41
13, 18	Friary . . .	527 1 32	Antrim . .	Upper Dunluce .	Loughguile .	Ballymoney .	III.	20
85, 94	Friary . . .	349 2 32	Donegal . .	Banagh . .	Killymard .	Donegal . .	III.	111
125	Friary . . .	12 2 25	Galway . .	Leitrim . .	Ballynakill .	Portumna .	IV.	51
36	Friaryland 3rd Division . . .	5 1 3i	Meath . .	Lower Moyfenrath .	Trim . . .	Trim . .	I.	212
12	Fringestown . .	403 2 8	Meath . .	Morgallion .	Castletown .	Navan . .	I.	209
134	Froe . . .	743 1 16	Cork, W.R. .	East Carbery (W.D.)	Ross . . .	Clonakilty .	II.	135
15	Froghan . . .	188 0 39	Longford . .	Ardagh . .	Street . .	Granard .	I.	153
7	Froghanstown .	100 2 1	Westmeath .	Corkaree . .	Multyfarnham .	Mullingar .	I.	263
7	Froghanstown .	162 3 5j	Westmeath .	Fore . .	Faughalstown .	Castletowndelvin	I.	269
9	Frolick . . .	190 3 23	Tipperary, N.R.	Lower Ormond .	Cloghprior .	Borrisokane .	II.	283
23, 27	Frosses . . .	821 0 15	Antrim . .	Kilconway .	Grange of Dundermot	Ballymena .	III.	27
9, 10	Fruithill . . .	291 0 16	Londonderry .	Keenaght . .	Drumachose .	NewTnLimavady	III.	235
47	Fuddletown . .	99 0 16	Wexford . .	Forth . .	Mayglass . .	Wexford .	I.	312
39	Fuerty . . .	216 3 17	Roscommon .	Athlone . .	Fuerty . .	Roscommon .	IV.	181
39	FUERTY T. . .	—	Roscommon .	Athlone . .	Fuerty . .	Roscommon .	IV.	181
68, 69	Fuhiry . . .	1,034 1 20	Cork, W.R. .	West Muskerry .	Ballyvourney .	Macroom .	II.	154
127, 128	Fuhur . . .	460 3 21	Cork, W.R. .	Bear . . .	Killaconenagh .	Castletown .	II.	125
6, 11	Fulmort . . .	365 2 28	Westmeath .	Corkaree . .	Lackan . . .	Mullingar .	I.	262

(a) Including 0A. 3R. 8P. water.
(b) Including 7A. 0R. 38P. water.
(c) { Including 8A. 2R. 19P. River Nore.
Within the Municipal Boundary, 13A. 3R. 33P.
Without the Municipal Boundary, 29A. 1R. 24P.
(d) Including 6A. 2R. 9P. water.
(e) Including 0A. 0R. 26P. water.
(f) Including 7A. 2R. 35P. water.
(g) Including 8A. 1R. 7P. water.
(h) Including 7A. 1R. 4P. water.
(i) Including 1A. 0R. 12F. water.
(j) Including 5A. 2R. 11P. water.

No. of Sheet of the Ordnance Survey Maps.	Townlands and Towns.	Area in Statute Acres.			County.	Barony.	Parish.	Poor Law Union in 1857.	Townland Census of 1851, Part I.	
		A.	R.	P.					Vol.	Page
29	Fulough or Macnahanny	438	3	12	King's Co.	Garrycastle	Lusmagh	Parsonstown	I.	137
115, 124	Funshadaun	583	2	25	Galway	Loughrea	Killeenadeema	Loughrea	IV.	64
19	Funshin	532	0	13	Galway	Ballymoe	Kilbegnet	Glennamaddy	IV.	8
28	Funshinagh	264	3	33a	Leitrim	Leitrim	Kiltubbrid	Cark. on Shannon	IV.	103
44, 45	Funshinagh	218	3	20	Roscommon	Athlone	Tisrara	Roscommon	IV.	185
44	Funshinagh (Madden)	241	0	28	Roscommon	Athlone	Tisrara	Roscommon	IV.	185
44	Funshinagh (Trench)	309	2	26	Roscommon	Athlone	Tisrara	Roscommon	IV.	185
121, 123	Funshinaugh	361	3	33	Mayo	Kilmaine	Cong	Ballinrobe	IV.	153
112, 121	Funshin Beg	549	1	9	Galway	Kiltartan	Kinvarradoorus	Gort	IV.	49
112, 121	Funshin More	832	3	32	Galway	Kiltartan	Kinvarradoorus	Gort	IV.	49
17, 20	Funshog	906	1	36	Louth	Ferrard	Collon	Ardee	I.	180
21	Funshoge	114	2	8	Wexford	Ballaghkeen	Killincooly	Gorey	I.	295
93	Furboghgarve	125	3	36	Galway	Moycullen	Rahoon	Galway	IV.	72
96	Furgill	439	3	15	Mayo	Murrisk	Oughaval	Westport	IV.	162
16, 17	Furhane	412	2	36	Kerry	Clanmaurice	Kilshenane	Listowel	II.	172
35	Furhee	66	0	37	Clare	Tulla Upper	Tulla	Tulla	II.	41
104	Furkeal	444	2	10	Cork, W.R.	Bear	Kilcaskan	Bantry	II.	123
36, 41	Furlongstown	278	0	18	Wexford	Shelmaliere West	Coolstuff	Wexford	I.	333
134, 135	Furnace	144	1	30b	Galway	Leitrim	Clonrush	Scarriff	IV.	53
89	Furnace	218	3	31	Galway	Moycullen	Kilcummin	Oughterard	IV.	68
57,58,67,68	Furnace	242	0	28	Mayo	Burrishoole	Burrishoole	Newport	IV.	119
99	Furnace	220	1	33c	Mayo	Carra	Ballyovey	Ballinrobe	IV.	126
35	Furnace or Bleankillew	177	1	19d	Leitrim	Mohill	Annaduff	Mohill	IV.	105
7	Furnaceland	364	0	23	Cavan	Tullyhaw	Kinawley	Bawnboy	III.	93
18, 24	Furnish	367	0	17	Fermanagh	Tirkennedy	Enniskillen	Lisnaskea	III.	222
23	Furraglaun	241	0	0e	Clare	Corcomroe	Kilmanaheen	Ennistimon	II.	21
15	Furraleigh	433	3	4	Waterford	Decies without Drum	Fews	Kilmacthomas	II.	356
40, 48, 49	Furroor	2,786	3	12f	Clare	Islands	Clondagad	Killadysert	II.	29
40	Furroor	851	1	35g	Clare	Islands	Kilmaley	Ennis	II.	31
56, 66	Furroor Lower	307	1	33	Clare	Moyarta	Moyarta	Kilrush	II.	34
55, 56, 66	Furroor Upper	223	1	25	Clare	Moyarta	Moyarta	Kilrush	II.	34
11	Furrow	425	1	10	Cork, E.R.	Condons&Clangibbon	Brigown	Mitchelstown	II.	59
20	Furryhill	673	0	0	Kildare	Naas North	Rathmore	Naas	I.	62
19	Furry Park	43	3	11	Dublin	Coolock	Clontarf	Dublin North	I.	26
24	Furze	81	1	13	Longford	Ardagh	Rathreagh	Ballymahon	I.	153
41	Furze	137	0	32	Tipperary, N.R.	Eliogarty	Thurles	Thurles	II.	273
31	Furzeditch East	95	3	24	Wicklow	Arklow	Dunganstown	Rathdrum	I.	343
31	Furzeditch West	135	2	18	Wicklow	Arklow	Dunganstown	Rathdrum	I.	343
19, 23	Furzehouse	296	3	3	Kilkenny	Shillelogher	Outrath	Kilkenny	I.	115
139	Furze Island	15	2	29	Cork, W.R.	West Carbery(W.D.)	Skull	Skull	II.	146
53	Furziestown	128	1	9	Wexford	Forth	Tacumshin	Wexford	I.	315
19	Furzyhill	136	1	21	Meath	Upper Slane	Slane	Navan	I.	225
84	Furzypark	42	1	35	Galway	Athenry	Athenry	Loughrea	IV.	4
104, 114	Furzypark	201	3	34	Galway	Dunkellin	Ardrahan	Gort	IV.	26
114	Furzypark	58	2	7	Galway	Loughrea	Isertkelly	Loughrea	IV.	63
94	Fussa	239	0	5	Kerry	Glanarought	Kilgarvan	Kenmare	II.	187
53, 61	Fussough	108	2	21	Tipperary, S.R.	Middlethird	Ballyshechan	Cashel	II.	325
84, 93	Fustane Lower	471	0	39	Kerry	Glanarought	Kenmare	Kenmare	II.	186
84	Fustane Upper	236	3	2	Kerry	Glanarought	Kenmare	Kenmare	II.	186
27	Fyagh	122	0	2h	Fermanagh	Tirkennedy	Derrybrusk	Enniskillen	III.	220
17	Fyanstown	53	2	18	Meath	Upper Kells	Donaghpatrick	Kells	I.	205
17	Fyanstown	427	3	31	Meath	Upper Kells	Kells	Kells	I.	206
37, 46	Fybagh	933	2	33	Kerry	Trughanacmy	Kilgarrylander	Tralee	II.	210
61	Fycorranagh	88	0	7	Donegal	Raphoe	Leck	Letterkenny	III.	140
16	Fyfin	282	2	18	Tyrone	Strabane Lower	Ardstraw	Castlederg	III.	319
5	Fyfin	222	3	2	Tyrone	Strabane Lower	Leckpatrick	Strabane	III.	322
59	Fymore Mourtray	118	1	20i	Tyrone	Clogher	Errigal Trough	Clogher	III.	296
59	Fymore Todd	113	3	0j	Tyrone	Clogher	Errigal Trough	Clogher	III.	296
100	Fynagh	274	3	7	Galway	Longford	Clonfert	Ballinasloe	IV.	57
3, 8	Gadalough Glebe	333	0	4k	Fermanagh	Lurg	Belleek	Ballyshannon	III.	203
25, 32	Gaddaghanstown	91	3	13	Westmeath	Fartullagh	Carrick	Mullingar	I.	267
32	Gaddaghanstown	176	0	0	Westmeath	Fartullagh	Clonfad	Mullingar	I.	268
27	Gaddan	179	0	0	Sligo	Tirerrill	Ballysumaghan	Sligo	IV.	238
27	Gaddanbeg	62	1	15	Sligo	Tirerrill	Ballysumaghan	Sligo	IV.	238
18	Gaddrystown	290	1	25	Westmeath	Moygoish	Templeoran	Mullingar	I.	281
10	Gaddyduff	165	2	32	Donegal	Inishowen East	Clonmany	Inishowen	III.	117
10	Gaffer Island	6	0	36	Fermanagh	Lurg	Derryvullan	Lowtherstown	III.	205
27	Gainey	168	3	8	Meath	Lower Duleek	Duleek	Drogheda	I.	195

(a) Including 5A. 0R. 7P. water.
(b) Including 16A. 1R. 8P. water.
(c) Including 3A. 1R. 20P. water.
(d) Including 6A. 2R. 18P. water.

(e) Including 5A. 2R. 22P. water.
(f) Including 9A. 0R. 11P. water.
(g) Including 9A. 3R. 23P. water.
(h) Including 26A. 0R. 3P. water.

(i) Including 0A. 1R. 24P. water.
(j) Including 6A. 2R. 16P. water.
(k) Including 20A. 0R. 28P. water.

3 N 2

No. of Sheet of the Ordnance Survey Maps.	Townlands and Towns.	Area in Statute Acres.			County.	Barony.	Parish.	Poor Law Union in 1857.	Townland Census of 1851, Part I.	
		A.	R.	P.					Vol.	Page
27	Gafney . . .	120	3	23	Meath . .	Lower Duleek .	Kilsharvan . .	Drogheda . .	I.	196
27	Gafney Little . .	77	1	13	Meath . .	Upper Duleek .	Duleek . . .	Drogheda . .	I.	197
29	Gaganstown . .	512	3	22a	Kildare . .	Naas South . .	Jago . . .	Naas . . .	I.	65
109, 110	Gaggan . . .	599	2	11	Cork, W.R. .	Kinalmeaky . .	Ballymodan . .	Bandon . .	II.	151
33	Gaghta Island .	4	1	19	Mayo . . .	Erris . . .	Kilmore . . .	Belmullet . .	IV.	146
5	Gaigue . . .	952	3	4	Longford . .	Longford . .	Killoe . . .	Longford . .	I.	159
47, 53	Gaile . . .	1,110	3	36	Tipperary, S.R.	Middlethird . .	Gaile . . .	Cashel . .	II.	327
26	Gainestown . .	171	0	6	Westmeath .	Fartullagh . .	Lynn . . .	Mullingar . .	I.	269
25, 31	Gainstown . .	373	0	16	Meath . .	Lower Navan .	Ardbraccan . .	Navan . .	I.	214
14	Gainstown Upper .	110	0	14	Louth . .	Louth . . .	Mansfieldstown .	Ardee . .	I.	185
20	Gairha . . .	120	3	15b	Waterford . .	Coshmore&Coshbride	Lismore & Mocollop	Lismore . .	II.	345
35, 40	Galbally . . .	55	3	26	Fermanagh .	Clankelly . .	Clones . . .	Clones . .	III.	196
42	Galbally . . .	132	1	35	King's Co. .	Clonlisk . .	Kilmurryely . .	Roscrea . .	I.	131
49	Galbally . . .	240	0	31	Limerick . .	Coshlea . .	Galbally . . .	Mitchelstown .	II.	238
45	Galbally . . .	258	2	9	Tyrone . .	Dungannon Middle .	Pomeroy . .	Dungannon .	III.	304
35	Galbally . . .	140	0	1c	Tyrone . .	Omagh East . .	Cappagh . .	Omagh . .	III.	310
49, 50	Galbally . . .	390	0	9d	Tyrone . .	Omagh East . .	Dromore . .	Lowtherstown .	III.	311
31	Galbally . . .	805	1	11	Wexford . .	Bantry . .	Ballyhoge . .	Enniscorthy .	I.	299
33	Galbally . . .	242	1	33	Wexford . .	Shelmaliere East .	Ardcolm . .	Wexford . .	I.	330
37	Galbally . . .	65	3	21	Wexford . .	Shelmaliere East .	Artramon . .	Wexford . .	I.	330
33	Galballybeg . .	81	2	7	Wexford . .	Shelmaliere East .	Skreen . . .	Wexford . .	I.	331
37	Galbally East . .	32	2	32	Wexford . .	Shelmaliere East .	Kilpatrick . .	Wexford . .	I.	330
37	Galbally North .	12	3	36	Wexford . .	Shelmaliere East .	Kilpatrick . .	Wexford . .	I.	331
49	GALBALLY T. . .	—			Limerick . .	Coshlea . . .	Galbally . .	Mitchelstown .	II.	239
37	Galbally West . .	25	3	33	Wexford . .	Shelmaliere East .	Kilpatrick . .	Wexford . .	I.	331
47	Galbertstown Lower	594	3	38	Tipperary, N.R.	Eliogarty . .	Fertiana . .	Thurles . .	II.	269
47	Galbertstown Upper	367	3	4	Tipperary, N.R.	Eliogarty . .	Fertiana . .	Thurles . .	II.	269
97	Galboley . . .	104	3	24	Galway . .	Athenry . .	Killimordaly . .	Loughrea . .	IV.	4
97	Galboley . . .	451	3	22	Galway . .	Athenry . .	Kiltullagh . .	Loughrea . .	IV.	5
28, 34	Galbolie . . .	433	3	22e	Cavan . .	Clankee . .	Bailieborough .	Bailieborough .	III.	71
20	Galboly Lower .	66	0	30	Antrim . .	Lower Glenarm .	Ardclinis . .	Larne . .	III.	21
20	Galboly Mountain North . .	187	2	33f	Antrim . .	Lower Glenarm .	Ardclinis . .	Larne . .	III.	21
20	Galboly Mountain South . .	250	0	7	Antrim . .	Lower Glenarm .	Ardclinis . .	Larne . .	III.	21
20	Galboly Upper .	69	1	11	Antrim . .	Lower Glenarm .	Ardclinis . .	Larne . .	III.	21
23	Galboola . . .	250	2	18	Limerick . .	Clanwilliam .	Rathgordan . .	Limerick . .	II.	225
41, 47, 48	Galbooly . . .	433	3	22	Tipperary, N.R.	Eliogarty . .	Galbooly . .	Thurles . .	II.	270
47, 48	Galbooly Little .	245	3	31	Tipperary, N.R.	Eliogarty . .	Galbooly . .	Thurles . .	II.	270
22, 23	Galboystown . .	642	0	34g	Meath . .	Fore . . .	Killallon . .	Oldcastle . .	I.	200
38	Galcussagh . .	234	1	10	Tyrone . .	Dungannon Upper .	Desertcreat . .	Cookstown . .	III.	307
25, 29	Galdanagh . .	109	3	37	Antrim . .	Lower Glenarm .	Tickmacrevan .	Larne . .	III.	24
54	Galdonagh . .	537	0	31	Donegal . .	Raphoe . .	Raymoghy . .	Strabane . .	III.	142
54, 62	Galdonagh Glebe .	342	0	22	Donegal . .	Raphoe . .	Raymoghy . .	Strabane . .	III.	142
35	Galesquarter . .	203	0	25	Queen's Co. .	Clarmallagh . .	Aghmacart . .	Abbeyleix .	I.	236
42	Galey . . .	439	3	31	Roscommon .	Athlone . .	Killinvoy . .	Roscommon .	IV.	182
42, 45	Galey Beg . .	295	1	24	Roscommon .	Athlone . .	St. John's . .	Athlone . .	IV.	183
32, 37	Galgorm . . .	446	2	21	Antrim . .	Lower Toome .	Ahoghill . .	Ballymena . .	III.	32
32, 37	Galgorm Parks .	1,224	0	37	Antrim . .	Lower Toome .	Ahoghill . .	Ballymena . .	III.	32
37	GALGORM T. . .	—			Antrim . .	Lower Toome .	Ahoghill . .	Ballymena . .	III.	32
49, 54	Galgystown . .	122	1	13	Wexford . .	Shelburne . .	Hook . . .	New Ross . .	I.	327
48	Gallagh . . .	270	3	38	Antrim . .	Upper Toome .	Duneane . .	Antrim . .	III.	35
32	Gallagh . . .	57	3	37	Fermanagh .	Clanawley . .	Killesher . .	Enniskillen .	III.	192
60	Gallagh . . .	425	3	29	Galway . .	Tiaquin . .	Killosolan . .	Mountbellew .	IV.	78
18	Gallagh . . .	262	2	34	Louth . .	Ferrard . .	Dysart . .	Drogheda . .	I.	181
99	Gallagh . . .	178	1	29h	Mayo . . .	Carra . . .	Ballyovey . .	Ballinrobe .	IV.	126
14	Gallagh . . .	184	2	4	Monaghan .	Cremorne . .	Clontibret . .	Monaghan . .	III.	260
40	Gallagh . . .	230	0	32	Roscommon .	Ballintober South .	Cloontuskert . .	Roscommon .	IV.	188
59	Gallagh . . .	144	3	26	Tyrone . .	Clogher . .	Errigal Trough .	Clogher . .	III.	296
47, 52	Gallagh . . .	179	0	19	Wexford . .	Bargy . . .	Kilturk . . .	Wexford . .	I.	307
21	Gallaghers Island .	2	0	6	King's Co. .	Garrycastle . .	Tisaran . .	Parsonstown .	I.	138
20	Gallanagh . .	42	0	20	Antrim . .	Lower Glenarm .	Ardclinis . .	Larne . .	III.	21
44	Gallanagh . .	270	1	23	Antrim . .	Upper Toome .	Shilvodan Grange .	Antrim . .	III.	35
9	Gallanagh . .	129	1	18	Monaghan .	Monaghan . .	Monaghan . .	Monaghan . .	III.	277
38	Gallanagh . .	65	2	23	Tyrone . .	Dungannon Upper .	Derryloran . .	Cookstown . .	III.	307
143	Gallane . . .	243	1	22	Cork, W.R. .	East Carbery (W.D.)	Ross . . .	Clonakilty . .	II.	135
122, 135	Gallanes . . .	353	0	33	Cork, W.R. .	East Carbery (E.D.)	Kilnagross . .	Clonakilty . .	II.	129
10, 17	Gallan Lower .	343	1	21	Tyrone . .	Strabane Lower .	Ardstraw . .	Gortin . .	III.	319
10, 13	Gallanstown . .	192	2	3	Dublin . .	Castleknock . .	Mulhuddart . .	Dublin North .	I.	25
17, 18	Gallanstown . .	395	2	17	Dublin . .	Uppercross . .	Ballyfermot . .	Dublin South .	I.	39
10, 17	Gallan Upper . .	904	1	0	Tyrone . .	Strabane Lower .	Ardstraw . .	Gortin . .	III.	319
30	Gallany . . .	372	3	20	Londonderry .	Keenaght . .	Banagher . .	NewTⁿLimavady	III.	234
9	Gallany . . .	296	2	2	Tyrone . .	Strabane Lower .	Urney . . .	Strabane . .	III.	322

No. of Sheet of the Ordnance Survey Maps.	Townlands and Towns.	Area in Statute Acres.			County.	Barony.	Parish.	Poor Law Union in 1857.	Townland Census of 1851. Part I.	
		A.	R.	P.					Vol.	Page
42	Gallarus . . .	492	0	16	Kerry . .	Corkaguiny . .	Kilmalkedar . .	Dingle . .	II.	178
73, 83	Gallavally . .	118	1	30	Kerry . .	Dunkerron North .	Knockane . .	Killarney . .	II.	182
73, 74, 83	Gallavally . .	210	1	33	Kerry . .	Dunkerron South .	Knockane . .	Killarney . .	II.	184
15	Galleastown . .	427	3	23	Meath . .	Fore . . .	Loughcrew . .	Oldcastle . .	I.	201
14, 22	Gallen . . .	625	2	29	King's Co. .	Garrycastle . .	Gallen . .	Parsonstown .	I.	136
100	Gallgort . . .	74	1	38a	Mayo . .	Carra . . .	Burriscarra .	Ballinrobe .	IV.	127
10	Gallid . . .	252	1	5	Longford . .	Granard . .	Granard . .	Granard . .	I.	156
15	Gall Island .	12	3	39	Fermanagh .	Magheraboy . .	Devenish . .	Enniskillen .	III.	212
33	Gallon . . .	193	2	10b	Cavan . .	Castlerahan . .	Killinkere . .	Bailieborough .	III.	69
38	Gallonbane . .	128	3	10	Cavan . .	Clanmahon . .	Kilbride . .	Cavan . .	III.	77
35	Gallonboy . .	89	3	5	Cavan . .	Clankee . .	Enniskeen . .	Bailieborough .	III.	73
26	Gallonbulloge or Black Bull . .	45	0	5	Cavan . .	Upper Loughtee .	Denn . .	Cavan . .	III.	83
33	Galloncurra . .	107	3	21c	Cavan . .	Castlerahan . .	Killinkere .	Bailieborough .	III.	69
22	Gallon Etra . .	200	2	20	Cavan . .	Clankee . .	Knockbride . .	Cootehill . .	III.	73
26	Gallon Glebe .	61	0	33	Cavan . .	Upper Loughtee .	Denn . .	Cavan . .	III.	83
39	Gallonnambraher .	274	3	37	Cavan . .	Castlerahan . .	Lurgan . .	Oldcastle .	III.	70
23	Gallonreagh . .	101	0	2	Cavan . .	Clankee . .	Drumgoon . .	Cootehill . .	III.	72
38	Gallonreagh . .	146	3	31	Cavan . .	Clanmahon . .	Kilbride . .	Cavan . .	III.	77
42	Galloon . . .	186	0	27d	Fermanagh .	Coole . . .	Galloon . .	Clones . .	III.	200
23	Galloping Green North	112	0	18	Dublin . .	Rathdown . .	Kill . .	Rathdown . .	I.	36
23	Galloping Green South	264	1	4	Dublin . .	Rathdown . .	Kill . .	Rathdown . .	I.	36
23	GALLOPING GREEN T.	—			Dublin . .	Rathdown . .	Kill . .	Rathdown . .	I.	36
49	Gallow . . .	846	2	3	Meath . .	Upper Deece .	Gallow . .	Trim . .	I.	193
29	Gallowsfields . .	89	0	31	Kerry . .	Trughanacmy .	Tralee . .	Tralee . .	II.	213
52	Gallowshill . .	267	2	34	Clare . .	Bunratty Lower .	Kilfintinan .	Limerick . .	II.	5
35	Gallowshill . .	306	1	13	Kildare . .	Narragh&Reban West	St. Michael's .	Athy . .	I.	68
20	Gallowshill . .	106	3	26	Kilkenny . .	Gowran . .	Gowran . .	Kilkenny . .	I.	95
19	Gallowshill . .	86	0	11e	Kilkenny . .	Shillelogher .	St. Patrick's .	Kilkenny . .	I.	116
31	Gallowshill . .	7	1	26	Waterford .	Decies without Drum	Dungarvan .	Dungarvan .	II.	355
31	Gallowshill . .	25	0	32	Waterford .	Decies without Drum	Kilrush . .	Dungarvan .	II.	358
11	Gallowstown or Bally-nacroghy . .	358	0	0	Westmeath .	Moygoish . .	Kilbixy . .	Mullingar .	I.	279
39	Gallowstown or Lis-nacroghy . .	229	0	10	Roscommon .	Ballintober South .	Roscommon .	Roscommon .	IV.	190
5	Gallrock . . .	244	3	34	Armagh .	Oneilland West .	Tartaraghan .	Armagh . .	III.	55
18, 21	Gallstown . .	221	0	27	Louth . .	Ferrard . .	Marlestown .	Drogheda . .	I.	181
33	Gallstown . .	243	1	38	Westmeath .	Fartullagh . .	Castlelost . .	Mullingar .	I.	268
33	Gallstown . .	643	1	29f	Westmeath .	Fartullagh . .	Pass of Kilbride .	Mullingar .	I.	269
50	Gallyhill . . .	132	2	27	Antrim . .	Upper Antrim .	Antrim . .	Antrim . .	III.	5
12	Galmoylestown Lower	254	1	6	Westmeath .	Corkaree . .	Stonehall . .	Mullingar .	I.	263
12	Galmoylestown Upper	387	2	35	Westmeath .	Corkaree . .	Stonehall . .	Mullingar .	I.	263
15, 22	Galmoystown . .	686	3	17	Meath . .	Fore . . .	Loughcrew . .	Oldcastle . .	I.	201
21, 22	Galroostown . .	388	1	36	Louth . .	Ferrard . .	Termonfeckin .	Drogheda . .	I.	182
22	Galros . . .	667	1	26	King's Co. .	Garrycastle .	Gallen . .	Parsonstown .	I.	136
30	Galros East . .	411	1	39	King's Co. .	Eglish . .	Eglish . .	Parsonstown .	I.	135
30	Galros West .	362	3	0	King's Co. .	Eglish . .	Eglish . .	Parsonstown .	I.	135
37, 43	Galtrim . . .	274	3	6g	Meath . .	Lower Deece .	Galtrim . .	Trim . .	I.	191
8	Galtrimsland . .	147	1	19	Louth . .	Lower Dundalk .	Carlingford .	Dundalk . .	I.	176
3	Galvally . . .	97	0	32	Londonderry .	North East Liberties of Coleraine .	Ballyaghran .	Coleraine .	III.	244
5	Galvone . . .	48	1	31	Limerick . .	Clanwilliam . .	St. Nicholas .	Limerick . .	II.	225
9	Galwally . . .	224	3	34h	Down . .	Castlereagh Upper .	Knockbreda .	Lisburn . .	III.	165
11	Galway . . .	183	1	28	Limerick . .	Connello Lower .	Askeaton . .	Rathkeale .	II.	226
82, 94	GALWAY T. . .	—			Galway . .	Borough of Galway { Rahoon . . } { St. Nicholas . }		Galway . .	IV.	81
57,58,65,66	Galwolie . . .	1,467	0	32i	Donegal . .	Boylagh . .	Lettermacward .	Glenties .	III.	114
67, 68	Galwolie . . .	361	1	22	Donegal . .	Raphoe . .	Kilteevoge .	Stranorlar .	III.	139
78, 84	Gammonsfield .	22	0	15	Tipperary, S.R.	Iffa and Offa East .	Kilsheelan .	Clonmel . .	II.	314
42, 43	Gammy . . .	138	2	39j	Tyrone . .	Omagh East . .	Drumragh . .	Omagh . .	III.	312
17	Ganaby . . .	197	0	9	Antrim . .	Upper Dunluce .	Kilraghts . .	Ballymoney .	III.	20
45	Ganaveens . .	59	3	32	Roscommon .	Athlone . .	Rahara . .	Roscommon .	IV.	183
7	Ganaway . . .	184	3	18	Down . .	Ards Lower .	Donaghadee .	Newtownards .	III.	158
7, 12	Ganaway . . .	360	0	31	Down . .	Ards Upper .	Ballywalter .	Newtownards .	III.	160
22	Ganderstown .	167	3	22	Louth . .	Ferrard . .	Termonfeckin .	Drogheda . .	I.	182
2	Gannavagh . .	31	3	5	Leitrim . .	Rosclogher . .	Rossinver . .	Ballyshannon .	IV.	111
7, 8	Gannavane . .	378	3	4	Limerick . .	Coonagh . .	Doon . .	Tipperary .	II.	234
7, 8	Gannavane Upper .	528	3	39	Limerick . .	Owneybeg . .	Doon . .	Limerick . .	II.	251
100	Gannaveen . .	407	2	33	Galway . .	Longford . .	Clontuskert .	Ballinasloe .	IV.	58
80,81,89,90	Gannew and Curreen	332	0	24	Donegal . .	Banagh . .	Glencolumbkille .	Glenties .	III.	105
144	Ganniv Beg . .	155	2	25	Cork, W.R. .	Ibane and Barryroe .	Rathbarry . .	Clonakilty .	II.	150
144	Ganniv More . .	146	1	28	Cork, W.R. .	Ibane and Barryroe .	Rathbarry . .	Clonakilty .	II.	150
21	Gannoughs . .	233	3	32k	Galway . .	Ballynahinch .	Omey . .	Clifden . .	IV.	15
85	Gannow . . .	94	0	5	Galway . .	Kilconnell . .	Grange . .	Loughrea .	IV.	40

(a) Including 4A. 3R. 18P. water.
(b) Including 10A. 1R. 0P. water.
(c) Including 6A. 0R. 28P. water.
(d) Including 24A. 0R. 1P. water.

(e) Including 0A. 1R. 20P. River Nore.
(f) Including 21A. 0R. 12P. water.
(g) Including 7A. 1R. 10P. detached portion.
(h) Including 1A. 3R. 18P. River Lagan.

(i) Including 43A. 1R. 33P. water.
(j) Including 3A. 1R. 8P. water.
(k) Including 10A. 0R. 39P. water.

No. of Sheet of the Ordnance Survey Maps.	Townlands and Towns.	Area in Statute Acres.	County.	Barony.	Parish.	Poor Law Union in 1857.	Townland Census of 1851. Part I.	
		A. R. P.					Vol.	Page
96	Ganty . . .	135 1 16	Galway . .	Dunkellin . .	Kilconierin . .	Loughrea . .	IV.	29
15, 23, 24	Ganvaghan Hemphill	446 1 26	Tyrone . .	Omagh West . .	Urney . . .	Castlederg .	III.	318
15, 23	Ganvaghan Kyle .	54 3 8d	Tyrone . .	Omagh West . .	Urney . . .	Castlederg .	III.	318
15,16,23,24	Ganvaghan Semple .	272 0 35b	Tyrone . .	Omagh West . .	Urney . . .	Castlederg .	III.	318
25	Garadice . .	250 3 37	Leitrim . .	Carrigallen . .	Drumreilly . .	Bawnboy . .	IV.	91
28	Garadice . .	221 0 33c	Leitrim . .	Mohill . . .	Fenagh . .	Mohill . .	IV.	106
49	Garadice . .	941 3 15	Meath . .	Upper Deece . .	Gallow . .	Trim . .	I.	193
26, 27	Garballagh . .	665 2 21	Meath . .	Lower Duleek .	Duleek . .	Drogheda .	I.	195
59	Garbally . .	74 1 27	Galway . .	Tiaquin . .	Moylough . .	Mountbellew .	IV.	80
23, 24	Garbally . .	524 1 13	King's Co. .	Ballyboy . .	Killoughy . .	Tullamore .	I.	124
30	Garbally . .	462 2 19	King's Co. .	Garrycastle . .	Reynagh . .	Parsonstown .	I.	138
37, 45	Garbally . .	429 0 19	Limerick . .	Connello Upper .	Kilmeedy . .	Newcastle .	II.	233
31	Garbally . .	46 0 23	Limerick . .	Coshma . .	Bruff . . .	Kilmallock .	II.	242
31, 39	Garbally . .	171 1 8	Limerick . .	Coshma . .	Dromin . .	Kilmallock .	II.	243
45	Garbally . .	73 2 15	Limerick . .	Glenquin . .	Mahoonagh . .	Newcastle .	II.	246
51	Garbally and Carrowduff . .	924 1 32	Roscommon .	Athlone . . .	Taghmaconnell .	Athlone . .	IV.	185
87	Garbally Demesne .	1,042 0 28d	Galway . .	Clonmacnowen .	Kilcloony . .	Ballinasloe .	IV.	25
24	Garbally or Foxglen	45 1 7	King's Co. .	Ballyboy . .	Killoughy . .	Tullamore .	I.	124
3	Garborgle . .	96 0 5	Londonderry .	North East Liberties of Coleraine . .	Ballyaghran .	Coleraine .	III.	244
47	Gardamus Great .	207 3 12	Wexford . .	Forth . . .	Mayglass . .	Wexford . .	I.	312
47	Gardamus Little .	116 0 26	Wexford . .	Forth . . .	Mayglass . .	Wexford . .	I.	312
15	Gardeen . . .	178 1 15	Cork, E.R. .	Duhallow . .	Clonfert . .	Kanturk .	II.	68
15, 23	Gardeen . .	117 2 39	Cork, E.R. .	Duhallow . .	Kilcorcoran .	Kanturk .	II.	72
114, 123	Gardenblake . .	303 3 19	Galway . .	Loughrea . .	Kilthomas . .	Gort . .	IV.	65
123	Gardenblake Commons	537 0 18	Galway . .	Loughrea . .	Kilthomas . .	Gort . .	IV.	65
5	Gardenershill . .	13 1 28	Dublin . .	Balrothery East .	Balrothery . .	Balrothery .	I.	19
29	Gardenfield . .	314 0 25	Galway . .	Dunmore . .	Tuam . . .	Tuam . .	IV.	36
36, 44	Gardenfield . .	429 2 29	Limerick . .	Glenquin . .	Monagay . .	Newcastle .	II.	247
45, 54	Gardenfield East .	157 0 21	Limerick . .	Connello Upper .	Dromcolliher .	Newcastle .	II.	232
45, 54	Gardenfield South .	329 3 7	Limerick . .	Connello Upper .	Dromcolliher .	Newcastle .	II.	232
45, 54	Gardenfield West .	159 2 12	Limerick . .	Connello Upper .	Dromcolliher .	Newcastle .	II.	232
69, 70	Gardenham or Garrymore . .	145 2 26	Galway . .	Clare . . .	Annaghdown .	Galway . .	IV.	16
69, 70	Gardenham or Garrymore . .	65 0 26	Galway . .	Clare . . .	Lackagh . .	Galway . .	IV.	22
20, 25	Gardenhill . .	456 2 3	Fermanagh .	Clanawley . .	Cleenish . .	Enniskillen .	III.	190
6	Gardenhill . .	5 1 17e	Limerick . .	Clanwilliam .	Killeenagarriff .	Limerick . .	II.	224
1, 6	Gardenhill . .	538 1 23	Limerick . .	Clanwilliam .	Stradbally .	Limerick . .	II.	226
25	Gardenmorris . .	262 3 10	Waterford .	Decies without Drum	Kilbarrymeaden .	Kilmacthomas .	II.	356
17	Gardenrath . .	190 1 12	Meath . .	Upper Kells . .	Kells . . .	Kells . .	I.	206
19	Gardens . . .	81 1 0f	Kilkenny . .	Kilkenny, Municipal Borough of . .	St. Canice . .	Kilkenny . .	I.	117
19	Gardens . . .	55 0 24g	Kilkenny . .	Kilkenny, Municipal Borough of . .	St. John's . .	Kilkenny . .	I.	117
19	Gardens . . .	30 1 7	Kilkenny . .	Kilkenny, Municipal Borough of . .	St. Patrick's .	Kilkenny . .	I.	117
11	Gardenstown or Legvoy	176 1 10	Roscommon .	Boyle . . .	Killukin . .	Cark. on Shannon	IV.	195
40	Gardentown . .	207 2 13	Roscommon .	Ballintober South .	Clountuskert .	Roscommon .	IV.	188
26	Gardrum . .	114 3 34	Fermanagh .	Clanawley . .	Cleenish . .	Enniskillen .	III.	190
42, 50	Gardrum . .	247 1 24	Tyrone . .	Omagh East . .	Dromore . .	Omagh . .	III.	311
43, 53	Garfinny . .	556 0 21	Kerry . .	Corkaguiny . .	Garfinny . .	Dingle . .	II.	177
14, 15, 20	Garfiny . .	182 3 37h	Cavan . .	Lower Loughtee .	Drumlane . .	Cavan . .	III.	80
49, 56	Gargadis . .	252 0 21	Tyrone . .	Omagh East . .	Kilskeery . .	Lowtherstown .	III.	313
42	Gargarry . .	682 2 13i	Down . .	Upper Iveagh, Lr.pt.	Drumgooland .	Banbridge .	III.	172
92, 93	Gargrim . .	258 1 39	Donegal . .	Banagh . .	Inver . . .	Donegal . .	III.	107
6	Gargrim . .	36 3 18	Fermanagh .	Lurg . . .	Magheraculmoney .	Lowtherstown .	III.	208
1	Gargrim . .	99 1 28	Leitrim . .	Rosclogher . .	Rossinver . .	Ballyshannon .	IV.	111
51	Gargrim . .	217 1 22	Tyrone . .	Clogher . .	Donacavey . .	Omagh . .	III.	294
90, 91	Garhawnagh . .	181 2 15	Mayo . .	Clanmorris . .	Balla . . .	Castlebar .	IV.	132
24,25,31,32	Garhy . .	655 0 8	Westmeath .	Moycashel . .	Castletown Kindalen	Mullingar .	I.	277
104	*Garinish* . .	36 1 38	Cork, W.R. .	Bear . . .	Kilcaskan . .	Bantry . .	II.	123
126	Garinish . .	110 1 3	Cork, W.R. .	Bear . . .	Kilnamanagh .	Castletown .	II.	125
99, 100	Garinish . .	57 3 22	Kerry . .	Dunkerron South .	Kilcrohane . .	Kenmare .	II.	183
126	*Garinish Island*	4 3 18	Cork, W.R. .	Bear . . .	Kilnamanagh .	Castletown .	II.	125
104, 117	*Garinish West*	5 2 24	Cork, W.R. .	Bear . . .	Kilcaskan . .	Castletown .	II.	123
16, 23	Garistown . .	210 3 38	Meath . .	Upper Kells . .	Burry . . .	Kells . .	I.	205
94, 95	Garland . .	189 1 3	Cork, W.R. .	East Carbery (W.D.)	Kinneigh . .	Dunmanway .	II.	134
58, 64	Garlaw . .	177 3 18	Tyrone . .	Clogher . .	Clogher . .	Clogher . .	III.	292
31	Garlegobban . .	90 2 9	Monaghan .	Farney . .	Killanny . .	Carrickmacross .	III.	271
5	Garmanagh . .	418 3 20	Meath . .	Morgallion . .	Nobber . .	Kells . .	I.	210
12	Garnagale . .	244 0 27	Kilkenny . .	Crannagh . .	Tubbridbritain .	Urlingford .	I.	87
22	*Garnagh Island*	6 1 33	Westmeath .	Kilkenny West .	Bunown . .	Athlone . .	I.	272

(a) Including 5A. 0R. 20P. water.
(b) Including 4A. 1R. 22P. water.
(c) Including 39A. 2R. 22P. water.

(d) Including 11A. 3R. 11P. water.
(e) Including 1A. 0R. 5P. detached portion.
(f) Including 2A. 0R. 11P. River Nore.

(g) Including 3A. 0R. 16P. River Nore.
(h) Including 74A. 3R. 19P. water.
(i) Including 24A. 3R. 29P. water.

No. of Sheet of the Ordnance Survey Maps.	Townlands and Towns.	Area in Statute Acres.			County.	Barony.	Parish.	Poor Law Union in 1857.	Townland Census of 1851, Part I.	
		A.	R.	P.					Vol.	Page
40	Garnagowlan .	222	2	10	Wicklow . .	Arklow . . .	Castlemacadam .	Rathdrum .	I.	342
17	Garnakill .	87	0	27	Wexford . .	Ballaghkeen . .	Killenagh .	Gorey . .	I.	295
81, 82	Garnavilla .	849	2	13a	Tipperary, S.R.	Iffa and Offa West .	Caher . .	Clogheen .	II.	318
82	Garnavilla .	30	2	7	Tipperary, S.R.	Iffa and Offa West .	Derrygrath .	Clogheen .	II.	318
34, 35	Garoke . . .	152	1	9	Sligo . .	Tirerrill . .	Shancough .	Boyle .	IV.	241
4	Garr . . .	1,531	2	30	King's Co. .	Warrenstown . .	Castlejordan .	Edenderry .	I.	145
25	Garr . . .	116	2	3	Wexford . .	Bantry . . .	Clonmore . .	Enniscorthy .	I.	300
44	Garra . . .	124	2	29	Galway . .	Clare . . .	Killererin .	Tuam . .	IV.	21
21, 27	Garra . . .	110	0	15	Wexford . .	Ballaghkeen . .	Meelnagh . .	Enniscorthy .	I.	298
5	Garracloon .	99	0	22	Clare . .	Burren . . .	Rathborney .	Ballyvaghan .	II.	14
29	Garracloon .	74	1	35	Galway . .	Dunmore . .	Tuam . . .	Tuam . .	IV.	36
121	Garracloon .	133	2	3	Mayo . .	Kilmaine . .	Cong . . .	Ballinrobe .	IV.	153
96	Garracloon North	87	3	25	Galway . .	Dunkellin . .	Kilconierin .	Loughrea .	IV.	29
96	Garracloon South .	93	3	15	Galway . .	Dunkellin . .	Kilconierin .	Loughrea .	IV.	29
39, 45	Garracummer .	958	0	29	Tipperary, N.R.	Kilnamanagh Upper	Doon . . .	Tipperary .	II.	277
19	Garradevlin .	118	3	37	Monaghan .	Cremorne . .	Clontibret . .	Castleblayney .	III.	260
41	Garradreen .	163	2	5	Wexford . .	Shelmaliere West .	Coolstuff . .	Wexford . .	I.	333
20	Garra East .	77	1	3b	Waterford .	Coshmore&Coshbride	Lismore & Mocollop	Lismore . .	II.	345
11, 16	Garrafin . .	296	1	37	Queen's Co. .	Upperwoods . .	Offerlane . .	Mountmellick .	I.	251
60	Garrafine .	242	0	34	Galway . .	Kilconnell . .	Ballymacward .	Mountbellew .	IV.	39
60	Garrafine (Trench) .	229	0	11	Galway . .	Kilconnell . .	Ballymacward .	Mountbellew .	IV.	39
60, 73	Garrafine (Ussher) .	561	2	5	Galway . .	Kilconnell . .	Ballymacward .	Mountbellew .	IV.	39
4,5,16,17	Garrafrauns .	201	2	30	Galway . .	Dunmore . .	Dunmore . .	Tuam . .	IV.	34
70	Garraghill .	517	3	28c	Mayo . .	Carra . . .	Turlough . .	Castlebar .	IV.	131
31, 32	Garragh or Woodland	209	1	5	Queen's Co. .	Slievemargy . .	Killabban .	Carlow . .	I.	245
15, 16	Garragort .	223	1	19	Cork, E.R. .	Duhallow . .	Knocktemple .	Mallow . .	II.	75
112	Garraha . .	143	3	18	Cork, E.R. .	Kinsale . .	Ringcurran .	Kinsale . .	II.	100
56	Garrahadoo .	140	2	11	Kerry . .	Trughanacmy .	Killorglin .	Killarney .	II.	211
36, 37	Garrahies .	86	2	27	Kerry . .	Corkaguiny . .	Kilgobban .	Tralee . .	II.	177
24	Garrahylish .	194	1	39	Waterford .	Decies without Drum	Stradbally .	Kilmacthomas .	I.	361
135	Garralacka .	230	0	12	Cork, W.R. .	Ibane and Barryroe	Kilkerranmore .	Clonakilty .	II.	149
12	Garran . .	218	1	33	Monaghan .	Dartree . .	Aghabog . .	Monaghan .	III.	263
12	Garran . .	166	0	35	Monaghan .	Dartree . .	Clones . .	Clones . .	III.	264
74	Garranabraher .	316	0	32	Cork, E.R. .	Cork . . .	St Mary's Shandon .	Cork . .	II.	66
59, 67	Garranacanty .	444	2	19	Tipperary, S.R.	Clanwilliam .	Corroge . .	Tipperary .	II.	306
26	Garranachole .	124	1	18	Cork, E.R. .	Fermoy . . .	Castletownroche .	Mallow . .	II.	77
26	Garranachole .	296	3	28	Cork, E.R. .	Fermoy . . .	Clenor . .	Mallow . .	II.	78
9	Garranacleary .	80	0	38	Tipperary, N.R.	Lower Ormond .	Cloghprior .	Borrisokane .	II.	283
49, 55	Garranacool .	630	1	24	Tipperary, S.R.	Slievardagh . .	Ballingarry .	Callan . .	II.	331
3	Garranagerra .	1,342	1	2	Galway . .	Ross . . .	Ballinrobe .	Ballinrobe .	IV.	72
135	Garranagoleen	266	2	21	Cork, W.R. .	Ibane and Barryroe	Kilkerranmore .	Clonakilty .	II.	149
14, 20	Garranakeevin	52	3	3	Tipperary, N.R.	Owney and Arra .	Youghalarra .	Nenagh . .	II.	297
33	Garranakilka .	294	0	36	Tipperary, N.R.	Kilnamanagh Upper	Upperchurch .	Thurles . .	II.	280
9	Garranamanagh	357	3	39	Kilkenny .	Crannagh . .	Garranamanagh .	Urlingford .	I.	86
37	Garrananaspick	184	3	23	Waterford .	Decies within Drum	Ardmore . .	Youghal . .	II.	350
77	Garrananassig	145	3	23	Cork, E.R. .	Imokilly . . .	Bohillane . .	Middleton .	II.	84
11, 20	Garranard .	167	0	33	Limerick . .	Kenry . . .	Kilcornan .	Rathkeale .	II.	249
21	Garranard .	230	3	33	Mayo . .	Tirawley . .	Moygawnagh .	Killala . .	IV.	171
13, 14	Garranashingaun	51	0	17	Tipperary, N.R.	Owney and Arra .	Castletownarra .	Nenagh . .	II.	294
7	Garranbane .	927	1	4	Limerick . .	Owneybeg . .	Abington . .	Limerick .	II.	251
22, 30	Garranbaun .	93	3	16	Cork, E.R. .	Duhallow . .	Kilmeen . .	Kanturk . .	II.	73
10, 15	Garranbaun .	1,238	0	30	Queen's Co. .	Upperwoods . .	Offerlane . .	Mountmellick .	I.	251
31	Garranbaun .	522	0	12	Waterford .	Decies without Drum	Kilgobnet .	Dungarvan .	II.	357
110	Garranbeg .	170	1	37	Cork, W.R. .	East Carbery (E.D.)	Ballymodan .	Bandon . .	II.	127
71,72,78,79	Garranbeg .	174	2	34	Tipperary, S.R.	Slievardagh . .	Garrangibbon .	Carrick on Suir	II.	333
37	Garranbehy Big	189	1	15	Kilkenny .	Ida . . .	Rosbercon .	New Ross .	I.	103
37	Garranbehy Little .	24	1	11	Kilkenny .	Ida . . .	Rosbercon .	New Ross .	I.	103
19	Garranboy .	65	0	19	Longford .	Moydow . .	Moydow . .	Longford .	I.	162
104	Garranboy Island .	1	2	17	Cork, W.R. .	Bantry . . .	Kilmocomoge .	Bantry . .	II.	121
88	Garrancasey .	118	0	36d	Tipperary, S.R.	Iffa and Offa West .	Molough . .	Clogheen .	II.	318
64, 75	Garrancloyne .	170	1	0	Cork, E.R. .	Barrymore . .	Carrigtohill .	Middleton .	II.	52
12	Garranconnell .	155	1	36	Kilkenny .	Crannagh . .	Tubbridbritain .	Urlingford .	I.	87
32, 36	Garrandarragh .	699	2	28	Kilkenny .	Ida . . .	Jerpoint West .	New Ross .	I.	102
40	Garrandarragh .	376	1	8	Kilkenny .	Knocktopher .	Kilbeacon .	Waterford .	I.	112
68	Garrandee .	152	0	21	Tipperary, S.R.	Middlethird .	Knockgraffon .	Tipperary .	II.	328
86, 87	Garrandillon .	477	2	14	Tipperary, S.R.	Iffa and Offa West .	Shanrahan .	Clogheen .	II.	319
10	Garrane . .	487	1	26	Cork, E.R. .	Condons &Clangibbon	Brigown . .	Mitchelstown .	II.	59
31	Garrane . .	244	1	34e	Cork, E.R. .	Duhallow . .	Clonmeen .	Kanturk . .	II.	69
41	Garrane . .	599	0	17	Cork, E.R. .	Duhallow . .	Kilshannig .	Mallow . .	II.	74
8	Garrane . .	1,211	0	0	Cork, E.R. .	Fermoy . . .	Ardskeagh .	Mallow . .	II.	76
134	Garrane . .	133	2	35	Cork, W.R. .	East Carbery (W.D.)	Ross . . .	Clonakilty .	II.	135
136	Garrane . .	296	2	12	Cork, W.R. .	Ibane and Barryroe	Abbeymahon .	Clonakilty .	II.	148
132	Garrane . .	969	0	17	Cork, W.R. .	West Carbery(W.D.)	Caheragh . .	Skibbereen .	II.	142

(a) Including 8A. 1R. 31P. water.
(b) Including 2A. 0R. 32P. water.
(c) Including 15A. 0R. 28P. water.
(d) Including 2A. 1R. 32P. water.
(e) Including 2A. 2R. 2P. water.

No. of Sheet of the Ordnance Survey Maps.	Townlands and Towns.	Area in Statute Acres.			County.	Barony.	Parish.	Poor Law Union in 1857.	Townland Census of 1851, Part I.	
		A.	R.	P.					Vol.	Page
42, 43	Garrane . . .	556	3	22	Kerry . .	Corkaguiny . .	Kilmalkedar . .	Dingle . .	II.	178
72, 82	Garrane . . .	369	2	22	Kerry . .	Dunkerron North .	Knockane . .	Cahersiveen . .	II.	182
88	Garrane . . .	399	1	4	Kerry . .	Iveragh . . .	Killemlagh . .	Cahersiveen . .	II.	196
29	Garrane . . .	327	3	4	Kerry . .	Trughanacmy . .	Tralee . . .	Tralee . . .	II.	213
47	Garrane . . .	506	2	6	Limerick . .	Connello Upper .	Bruree . . .	Kilmallock . .	II.	231
37, 45	Garrane . . .	504	3	33	Limerick . .	Glenquin . .	Mahoonagh . .	Newcastle . .	II.	246
22, 31	Garrane . . .	657	0	4a	Limerick . .	Pubblebrien . .	Monasteranenagh .	Croom . .	II.	253
34	Garrane . . .	160	2	36	Tipperary, N.R.	Kilnamanagh Upper	Glenkeen . .	Thurles . .	II.	278
8	Garrane . . .	98	1	16	Tipperary, N.R.	Lower Ormond .	Ballingarry . .	Borrisokane . .	II.	282
6	Garrane . . .	158	1	9	Tipperary, N.R.	Lower Ormond .	Kilbarron . .	Borrisokane . .	II.	284
27, 28	Garrane . . .	293	2	38	Tipperary, N.R.	Upper Ormond .	Aghnameadle . .	Nenagh . .	II.	288
27, 28	Garrane . . .	171	1	19	Tipperary, N.R.	Upper Ormond .	Latteragh . .	Nenagh . .	II.	292
27	Garrane . . .	51	1	16	Tipperary, N.R.	Upper Ormond .	Templederry . .	Nenagh . .	II.	293
21, 22	Garrane . . .	495	3	31	Tipperary, N.R.	Upper Ormond .	Templedowney . .	Nenagh . .	II.	293
52, 60	Garrane . . .	363	1	2	Tipperary, S.R.	Clanwilliam . .	Ballygriffin . .	Tipperary . .	II.	305
54	Garrane . . .	73	.3	32	Tipperary, S.R.	Slievardagh . .	Killenaule . .	Cashel . .	II.	334
33, 39	Garrane . . .	120	3	30	Westmeath . .	Fartullagh . .	Castlelost . .	Mullingar . .	I.	268
124, 137	Garraneanasig .	270	3	31	Cork, W.R. .	East Carbery (E.D.)	Ringrone . .	Kinsale . .	II.	130
79	Garranearagh .	414	3	4	Kerry . .	Iveragh . . .	Caher . . .	Cahersiveen . .	II.	194
122	Garraneard .	276	0	30	Cork, W.R. .	East Carbery (E.D.)	Kilnagross . .	Clonakilty . .	II.	129
79	Garranebane .	506	1	5	Kerry . .	Iveragh . . .	Caher . . .	Cahersiveen . .	II.	194
24	Garrane Beg .	32	1	1	Limerick . .	Coonagh . .	Grean . . .	Tipperary . .	II.	235
63	Garraneboy .	200	0	33	Cork, E.R. .	Cork . . .	Rathcooney . .	Cork . . .	II.	65
122	Garranecore .	186	0	7	Cork, W.R. .	East Carbery (E.D.)	Kilgarriff . .	Clonakilty . .	II.	129
122	Garranecore .	144	1	10b	Cork, W.R. .	East Carbery (E.D.)	Templebryan . .	Clonakilty . .	II.	130
134, 143	Garranecore .	189	2	4	Cork, W.R. .	East Carbery (W.D.)	Ross . . .	Clonakilty . .	II.	135
74, 86	Garranedarragh .	169	0	5	Cork, E.R. .	Cork . . .	St. Finbars . .	Cork . . .	II.	66
39	Garraneduff .	335	2	8	Cork, W.R. .	West Muskerry .	Drishane . .	Millstreet . .	II.	156
56	Garrane East .	465	0	12	Kerry . .	Trughanacmy . .	Killorglin . .	Killarney . .	II.	211
123, 124	Garranefeen .	478	1	3	Cork, W.R. .	East Carbery (E.D.)	Rathclarin . .	Bandon . .	II.	130
122	Garraneishal .	121	3	4	Cork, W.R. .	East Carbery (E.D.)	Kilnagross . .	Clonakilty . .	II.	129
66	Garranejames .	392	0	15	Cork, E.R. .	Imokilly . .	Mogeely . .	Middleton . .	II.	90
47, 55	Garranekeagh .	270	2	19	Limerick . .	Coshma . .	Effin . . .	Kilmallock . .	II.	243
28, 36	Garranekeevan .	180	1	34	Limerick . .	Glenquin . .	Newcastle . .	Newcastle . .	II.	248
76, 88	Garranekinnefeake .	642	3	13	Cork, E.R. .	Imokilly . .	Garranekinnefeake .	Middleton . .	II.	86
109	Garranelahan .	126	0	39	Cork, W.R. .	East Carbery (E.D.)	Desertserges . .	Bandon . .	II.	128
71,72,83,84	Garraneleigh .	249	1	27	Cork, E.R. .	East Muskerry .	Moviddy . .	Bandon . .	II.	105
24	Garrane More .	198	0	10	Limerick . .	Coonagh . .	Grean . . .	Tipperary . .	II.	235
59, 70	Garranenagappul .	592	0	6	Cork, W.R. .	West Muskerry .	Clondrohid . .	Macroom . .	II.	155
24	Garranenageevoge .	227	0	27	Cork, E.R. .	Orrery and Kilmore	Buttevant . .	Mallow . .	II.	107
83, 84	Garranenamuddagh .	289	2	29	Cork, E.R. .	East Muskerry .	Moviddy . .	Bandon . .	II.	105
30	Garrane North .	175	3	37	Cork, E.R. .	Duhallow . .	Dromtarriff . .	Millstreet . .	II.	71
80	Garrane North .	360	3	0	Kerry . .	Iveragh . . .	Killinane . .	Cahersiveen . .	II.	197
124	Garranereagh .	398	1	6	Cork, W.R. .	East Carbery (E.D.)	Ringrone . .	Kinsale . .	II.	130
83, 95	Garranereagh .	1,135	2	34	Cork, W.R. .	West Muskerry .	Kilmichael . .	Macroom . .	II.	159
55	Garraneribbeen .	343	1	11	Cork, E.R. .	Kinnatalloon .	Ballynoe . .	Fermoy . .	II.	97
64, 65	Garranes . .	295	0	4	Cork, E.R. .	Barrymore . .	Carrigtohill . .	Middleton . .	II.	52
127	Garranes . .	606	0	34	Cork, W.R. .	Bear . . .	Kilnamanagh . .	Castletown . .	II.	125
109, 122	Garranes . .	416	2	26	Cork, W.R. .	East Carbery (E.D.)	Desertserges . .	Clonakilty . .	II.	128
120	Garranes . .	452	1	27c	Cork, W.R. .	East Carbery (W.D.)	Fanlobbus . .	Dunmanway . .	II.	131
84, 96	Garranes . .	1,215	2	1	Cork, W.R. .	Kinalmeaky . .	Templemartin .	Bandon . .	II.	153
148	Garranes . .	112	2	8	Cork, W.R. .	West Carbery (W.D.)	Skull . . .	Skull . . .	II.	146
102	Garranes . .	203	2	18	Kerry . .	Glanarought . .	Kilcaskan . .	Kenmare . .	II.	187
109	Garranes . .	944	3	29	Kerry . .	Glanarought . .	Tuosist . .	Kenmare . .	II.	188
106, 119	Garranes North	552	2	8	Cork, W.R. .	West Carbery (E.D.)	Dromdaleague . .	Skibbereen . .	II.	140
30, 39	Garrane South .	201	3	3d	Cork, E.R. .	Duhallow . .	Dromtarriff . .	Millstreet . .	II.	71
80	Garrane South .	776	1	22	Kerry . .	Iveragh . . .	Killinane . .	Cahersiveen . .	II.	197
119	Garranes South .	430	2	0	Cork, W.R. .	West Carbery (E.D.)	Dromdaleague . .	Skibbereen . .	II.	140
85	Garranewaterig .	483	2	0	Cork, E.R. .	East Muskerry .	Knockavilly . .	Bandon . .	II.	104
30, 39	Garrane West .	194	0	5	Cork, E.R. .	Duhallow . .	Dromtarriff . .	Millstreet . .	II.	71
56	Garrane West .	334	0	3	Kerry . .	Trughanacmy . .	Killorglin . .	Killarney . .	II.	211
47, 48, 59	Garraneycarney .	1,182	1	16	Cork, W.R. .	West Muskerry .	Clondrohid . .	Macroom . .	II.	155
78	Garrangibbon .	132	1	20	Tipperary, S.R.	Slievardagh . .	Garrangibbon . .	Carrick on Suir	II.	333
28, 34	Garrangrena Lower	412	3	24	Tipperary, N.R.	Kilnamanagh Upper	Glenkeen . .	Thurles . .	II.	278
28	Garrangrena Upper	202	2	29	Tipperary, N.R.	Kilnamanagh Upper	Glenkeen . .	Thurles . .	II.	278
30, 34	Garranhalloo .	194	2	20	Kilkenny . .	Kells . . .	Tullahought . .	Callan . .	I.	110
10	Garran Itra .	175	2	9	Monaghan . .	Monaghan . .	Tehallan . .	Monaghan . .	III.	280
30	Garrankeel .	135	2	31	Mayo . .	Tirawley . .	Kilmoremoy . .	Ballina . .	IV.	170
29	Garrankesh .	37	1	19	Westmeath . .	Brawny . .	St. Marys . .	Athlone . .	II.	259
62,63,70,71	Garrankyle .	210	1	7	Tipperary, S.R.	Middlethird . .	Cloneen . .	Cashel . .	II.	325
96	Garrankyle East	49	1	19	Galway . .	Dunkellin . .	Kilconierin . .	Loughrea . .	IV.	29
96	Garrankyle West	77	3	12	Galway . .	Dunkellin . .	Kilconierin . .	Loughrea . .	IV.	29
32	Garranlahan Beg .	128	3	31	Roscommon .	Castlereagh . .	Kiltullagh . .	Castlereagh . .	IV.	202

(a) Including 3A. 3R. 8P. water.　　　　(c) Including 11A. 3R. 19P. water.　　　　(d) Including 7A. 0R. 0P. water.
(b) Including 21A. 0R. 2P. detached portion.

No. of Sheet of the Ordnance Survey Maps.	Townlands and Towns.	Area in Statute Acres.			County.	Barony.	Parish.	Poor Law Union in 1857.	Townland Census of 1851, Part I.	
		A.	R.	P.					Vol.	Page
32	Garranlahan More .	171	1	27	Roscommon	Castlereagh	Kiltullagh	Castlereagh	IV.	202
68	Garranlea . .	594	0	30	Tipperary, S.R.	Middlethird	Knockgraffon	Cashel	II.	328
15, 23	Garranmacgarrett .	323	3	37	Cork, E.R.	Duhallow	Kilbrin	Kanturk	II.	72
30	Garranmachenry .	433	2	0	Kilkenny .	Kells	Killamery	Callan	I.	109
27	Garranmaconly .	298	2	21	Queen's Co.	Clandonagh	Rathdowney	Donaghmore	I.	234
21, 27	Garranmaconly .	789	0	25	Queen's Co.	Clandonagh	Skirk	Donaghmore	I.	235
15, 24	Garranmillon Lower	537	0	26	Waterford	Decies without Drum	Kilrossanty	Kilmacthomas	II.	358
15, 24	Garranmillon Upper	311	0	7	Waterford	Decies without Drum	Kilrossanty	Kilmacthomas	II.	358
13, 14	Garranmore . .	225	3	23	Tipperary, N.R.	Owney and Arra	Youghalarra	Nenagh	II.	297
46	Garranmore . .	264	1	20	Tipperary, S.R.	Kilnamanagh Lower	Clogher	Cashel	II.	322
53, 61	Garranmore . .	368	3	22	Tipperary, S.R.	Middlethird	St. Patricksrock	Cashel	II.	330
89	Garrannafulla .	312	0	11	Kerry	Iveragh	Dromod .	Cahersiveen	II.	195
5	Garrannaguilly .	386	0	8	Kilkenny .	Fassadinin	Donaghmore	Castlecomer	I.	89
10	Garran Otra or Gibraltar . .	131	2	24	Monaghan	Monaghan	Tehallan .	Monaghan	III.	280
30	Garranrobin .	116	2	21	Kilkenny .	Kells	Kilmaganny .	Callan	I.	109
21	Garranroe . .	370	1	24	Limerick .	Coshma .	Killonahan	Croom	II.	243
13	Garranroe . .	70	2	39	Monaghan	Monaghan	Kilmore .	Monaghan	III.	276
36, 42	Garranroe . .	415	1	19	Tipperary, N.R.	Eliogarty	Rahelty .	Thurles .	II.	272
28	Garranroe or Cornamucklagh .	193	3	4	Monaghan	Farney	Donaghmoyne	Carrickmacross	III.	270
14	Garrans . .	469	2	29	Queen's Co.	Stradbally	Curraclone	Athy	I.	246
49	Garransilly .	321	2	0	Tipperary, S.R.	Slievardagh	Kilcooly .	Urlingford	II.	334
31, 32	Garranstackle .	640	2	0	Wexford .	Bantry .	Ballyhoge	Enniscorthy	I.	299
23, 27	Garranstan .	211	0	29	Kilkenny .	Kells	Kells	Callan	I.	108
21	Garranstown or Kingswood .	122	3	1	Dublin	Uppercross	Tallaght .	Dublin South .	I.	41
21	Garranthurles .	51	0	19	Tipperary, N.R.	Upper Ormond	Ballymackey .	Nenagh	II.	289
20, 26	Garrantrowlan .	175	3	24	Wexford .	Ballaghkeen	Ballyhuskard .	Enniscorthy	I.	292
24	Garranturton .	1,063	3	7	Waterford	Decies without Drum	Stradbally	Kilmacthomas	II.	361
94	Garranty . .	301	2	13	Mayo	Murrisk .	Kilgeever	Westport .	IV.	161
108, 121	Garranure . .	436	3	21	Cork, W.R.	East Carbery (E.D.)	Ballymoney	Dunmanway	II.	127
33, 37	Garranvabby .	151	1	5	Kilkenny .	Ida .	The Rower	New Ross	I.	104
12	Garraree . .	79	0	5	Westmeath	Corkaree .	Tyfarnham	Mullingar	I.	264
39	Garraroosky .	110	1	22	Fermanagh	Coole	Galloon .	Lisnaskea	III.	200
26	Garrarus . .	324	1	23	Waterford	Middlethird	Drumcannon	Waterford	II.	366
63	Garraun . .	37	3	21	Clare	Bunratty Lower	St. Patricks	Limerick .	II.	7
23	Garraun . .	277	1	13	Clare	Corcomroe .	Clooney .	Ennistimon	II.	18
56	Garraun . .	230	2	32	Clare	Moyarta .	Kilfearagh	Kilrush .	II.	22
63	Garraun . .	264	0	19	Clare	Tulla Lower	Kiltenanlea .	Limerick .	II.	37
20, 28	Garraun . .	299	0	26	Clare	Tulla Upper .	Feakle .	Scarriff	II.	39
44	Garraun . .	33	3	15	Galway	Clare	Killererin	Tuam	IV.	21
70	Garraun . .	168	0	6	Galway	Clare	Lackagh .	Galway	IV.	22
103, 104	Garraun . .	96	3	2	Galway	Dunkellin	Killeely .	Gort	IV.	29
116	Garraun . .	64	1	30	Galway	Leitrim .	Ballynakill .	Loughrea .	IV.	51
135	Garraun . .	48	2	30	Galway	Leitrim .	Clonrush	Scarriff .	IV.	53
117	Garraun . .	251	0	21	Galway	Leitrim .	Tynagh .	Portumna .	IV.	55
38, 47	Garraun . .	653	3	8	Kerry	Magunihy	Molahiffe	Killarney .	II.	205
30	Garraun . .	165	3	6	Kilkenny .	Kells	Coolaghmore .	Callan	I.	108
19, 23	Garraun . .	181	2	27	Kilkenny .	Shillelogher .	Castleinch or Inchyolaghan	Kilkenny .	I.	114
6	Garraun . .	67	1	5	Limerick .	Clanwilliam	Killeenagarriff	Limerick .	II.	224
103	Garraun . .	237	3	30	Mayo	Costello .	Annagh .	Claremorris	IV.	138
121, 122	Garraun . .	82	3	5	Mayo	Kilmaine .	Moorgagagh .	Ballinrobe	IV.	157
29	Garraun . .	216	1	13	Mayo	Tirawley .	Crossmolina .	Ballina	IV.	166
42	Garraun . .	564	0	26	Tipperary, N.R.	Eliogarty	Twomileborris	Thurles .	II.	273
11, 16	Garraun . .	298	2	4	Tipperary, N.R.	Lower Ormond	Modreeny	Borrisokane	II.	286
25, 31	Garraun . .	675	0	13	Tipperary, N.R.	Owney and Arra	Kilnarath .	Nenagh	II.	296
53, 61	Garraun . .	673	2	34	Tipperary, S.R.	Middlethird	Ballysheehan .	Cashel	II.	325
69, 70	Garraun . .	343	3	18	Tipperary, S.R.	Middlethird	Mora .	Cashel	II.	329
60, 68	Garraun . .	183	0	8	Tipperary, S.R.	Middlethird	St. Patricksrock	Cashel	II.	330
30	Garraun . .	141	3	30	Waterford	Decies without Drum	Modelligo	Lismore .	II.	359
27	Garraun . .	66	0	35	Wexford .	Ballaghkeen	Ballyvaldon .	Enniscorthy	I.	292
27	Garraun . .	275	0	18	Wexford .	Ballaghkeen	Meelnagh .	Enniscorthy	I.	298
20, 21	Garraunanearla .	84	0	0	Tipperary, N.R.	Lower Ormond	Knigh .	Nenagh	II.	285
71	Garraunard .	167	2	4	Galway	Tiaquin .	Monivea .	Tuam	IV.	79
29	Garraunard .	169	3	38	Mayo	Tirawley .	Crossmolina .	Ballina	IV.	166
22, 23	Garraunawarrig Lower	484	2	14	Cork, E.R.	Duhallow	Clonfert .	Kanturk .	II.	68
14, 22	Garraunawarrig Upper	391	2	9	Cork, E.R.	Duhallow	Clonfert .	Kanturk .	II.	68
30	Garraunbaun .	293	3	29	Galway	Ballymoe .	Clonbern	Tuam	IV.	6
22	Garraunbaun .	171	3	10a	Galway	Ballynahinch .	Ballynakill	Clifden .	IV.	11
44	Garraun Beg .	102	2	14	Galway	Clare	Killererin	Tuam	IV.	21
30	Garraun Beg .	87	3	4	Kerry	Trughanacmy .	Ballymacelligott	Tralee	II.	207
31, 32	Garraunbeg .	406	0	10	Tipperary, N.R.	Owney and Arra	Killoscully .	Nenagh	II.	295

(o) Including 17A. 2R. 10P. water.

3 O

No. of Sheet of the Ordnance Survey Maps.	Townlands and Towns.	Area in Statute Acres.	County.	Barony.	Parish.	Poor Law Union in 1857.	Townland Census of 1851, Part I.	
		A. R. P.					Vol.	Page
45	Garraunboy . .	312 1 34	Clare . .	Tulla Lower . .	Killaloe . . .	Scarriff . .	II.	35
21	Garraunboy . .	258 0 0	Limerick . .	Connello Lower .	Clonshire . .	Rathkeale . .	II.	227
44	Garraun (Coyle) .	222 3 0	Galway . .	Clare . . .	Killererin . .	Tuam . . .	IV.	21
57,58,70,71	Garrauncreen . .	213 0 32	Galway . .	Clare . . .	Kilmoylan . .	Tuam . . .	IV.	22
39	Garraundarragh .	316 0 35	Kerry . .	Trughanacmy . .	Currans . . .	Killarney . .	II.	209
14	Garraunfadda . .	324 0 3	Tipperary, N.R.	Lower Ormond .	Monsea . . .	Nenagh . .	II.	287
22, 30	Garraunfadda . .	224 3 13	Waterford . .	Decies without Drum	Whitechurch . .	Dungarvan . .	II.	361
27, 35	Garraunigerinagh .	677 1 29	Cork, E.R. .	Condons&Clangibbon	Litter . . .	Fermoy . .	II.	62
94, 95	Garraun Lower .	214 1 26	Galway . .	Dunkellin . .	Ballynacourty .	Galway . .	IV.	27
18,19,24,25	Garraun Lower .	450 2 18	Wexford . .	Bantry . . .	Killann . . .	Enniscorthy .	I.	300
19	Garraunmore . .	245 3 19a	Galway . .	Ballymoe . .	Kilbegnet . .	Glennamaddy .	IV.	8
44	Garraun More .	172 0 24	Galway . .	Clare . . .	Killererin . .	Tuam . . .	IV.	21
30	Garraun More .	232 3 35	Kerry . .	Trughanacmy . .	Ballymacelligott .	Tralee . .	II.	207
106,107,117	Garraunnameetagh .	303 3 35	Galway . .	Longford . .	Tynagh . .	Portumna . .	IV.	62
57	Garraunnatooha .	286 0 17	Clare . .	Moyarta . . .	Kilmacduane . .	Kilrush . .	II.	33
50, 51, 62	Garraun North .	746 2 17	Cork, E.R. .	Barretts . . .	Donaghmore . .	Cork . . .	II.	49
19, 20	Garraun North .	225 2 26	Galway . .	Ballymoe . .	Kilbegnet . .	Roscommon .	IV.	8
43	Garraun North .	280 1 26	Galway . .	Clare . . .	Belclare . .	Tuam . . .	IV.	17
83, 95	Garraun North .	500 1 26	Galway . .	Dunkellin . .	Oranmore . .	Galway . .	IV.	32
10, 11, 15	Garraunorish . .	125 3 2	Tipperary, N.R.	Lower Ormond .	Modreeny . .	Borrisokane .	II.	286
125	Garraunphaudeen .	46 2 23	Galway . .	Leitrim . . .	Ballynakill . .	Loughrea . .	IV.	51
50	Garraunredmond .	492 3 25	Cork, E.R. .	East Muskerry .	Donaghmore . .	Macroom . .	II.	103
30	Garrauns . .	177 2 25	Galway . .	Ballymoe . .	Clonbern . .	Tuam . . .	IV.	6
29, 30	Garrauns . .	165 2 30	Galway . .	Dunmore . .	Dunmore . .	Tuam . . .	IV.	34
29	Garrauns . .	150 0 2	Galway . .	Dunmore . .	Tuam . . .	Tuam . . .	IV.	36
51, 62	Garraun South .	512 0 0	Cork, E.R. .	Barretts . . .	Donaghmore . .	Cork . . .	II.	49
19	Garraun South .	154 2 2	Galway . .	Ballymoe . .	Kilbegnet . .	Roscommon .	IV.	8
43, 57	Garraun South .	347 0 4	Galway . .	Clare . . .	Belclare . .	Tuam . . .	IV.	17
83, 95	Garraun South .	248 0 28	Galway . .	Dunkellin . .	Oranmore . .	Galway . .	IV.	32
23	Garraunteefineen .	137 0 21	Cork, E.R. .	Duhallow . .	Castlemagner .	Kanturk . .	II.	67
95	Garraun Upper .	174 1 35	Galway . .	Dunkellin . .	Ballynacourty .	Galway . .	IV.	27
22	Garraun Upper .	68 1 20	Waterford . .	Decies without Drum	Modelligo . .	Lismore . .	II.	359
18, 24	Garraun Upper .	496 3 31	Wexford . .	Bantry . . .	Killann . . .	Enniscorthy .	I.	300
6	Garraunykee . .	90 2 18	Limerick . .	Clanwilliam . .	Killeenagarriff .	Limerick . .	II.	224
6	Garraunykee . .	88 3 17	Limerick . .	Clanwilliam . .	Stradbally . .	Limerick . .	II.	226
73	Garravagh . .	469 0 25b	Cork, E.R. .	East Muskerry .	Inishcarra . .	Cork . . .	II.	103
21	Garravally . .	108 3 26	Tipperary, N.R.	Upper Ormond .	Ballymackey .	Nenagh . .	II.	289
23, 31	Garraveasoge . .	407 3 14	Cork, E.R. .	Duhallow . .	Dromtarriff . .	Kanturk . .	II.	71
112	Garravesoge . .	327 0 1	Cork, E.R. .	Kinalea . . .	Ballymartle . .	Kinsale . .	II.	94
24	Garravin . .	268 0 16	Limerick . .	Coonagh . .	Tuoghcluggin .	Tipperary . .	II.	236
101, 111	Garravlagh . .	299 0 39	Mayo . .	Clanmorris . .	Tagheen . .	Claremorris .	IV.	136
3	Garravoone . .	371 3 28	Waterford . .	Upperthird . .	Kilmoleran . .	Carrick on Suir .	II.	370
20	Garra West . .	77 2 24c	Waterford . .	Coshmore&Coshbride	Lismore and Mocollop	Lismore . .	II.	345
13	Garreenleen . .	329 1 6	Carlow . .	Forth . . .	Gilbertstown . .	Carlow . .	I.	4
111	Garreens . .	202 0 25	Mayo . .	Kilmaine . .	Kilcommon . .	Ballinrobe .	IV.	154
33	Garreer . . .	176 3 7d	Galway . .	Killian . . .	Athleague . .	Mountbellew .	IV.	43
89,90,98,99	Garreiny . . .	785 0 6e	Kerry . .	Iveragh . . .	Dromod . .	Cahersiveen .	II.	195
31, 36	Garrendenny . .	620 3 35	Queen's Co. .	Slievemargy . .	Killabban . .	Carlow . .	I.	245
38	Garretstown . .	662 1 31	Meath . .	Skreen . . .	Trevet . . .	Dunshaughlin .	I.	222
1, 3	Garrettstown . .	494 3 35	Carlow . .	Rathvilly . .	Rahill . . .	Baltinglass .	I.	12
124, 137	Garrettstown . .	967 0 39	Cork, W.R. .	Courceys . .	Templetrine . .	Kinsale . .	II.	147
75	Garries . . .	618 2 37	Kerry . .	Magunihy . .	Killaha . . .	Killarney . .	II.	202
48, 49	Garriffgeery . .	118 2 23	Antrim . .	Upper Toome .	Duneane . .	Antrim . .	III.	35
32	Garrifly . . .	142 1 34	Fermanagh . .	Clanawley . .	Killesher . .	Enniskillen .	III.	192
28	Garrifly . . .	77 0 18f	Monaghan . .	Farney . . .	Donaghmoyne .	Carrickmacross .	III.	270
70	Garrinch . .	152 2 32	Tipperary, S.R.	Middlethird . .	Fethard . .	Cashel . .	II.	326
19	Garrincreen . .	116 3 32	Kilkenny . .	Gowran . .	St. John's . .	Kilkenny . .	I.	98
24	Garrintaggart . .	289 2 1	Queen's Co. .	Cullenagh . .	Dysartgallen .	Abbeyleix .	I.	239
3	Garrisker . .	855 2 21	Kildare . .	Carbury . .	Ballynadrumny .	Edenderry .	I.	51
6	Garriskil . .	431 2 17g	Westmeath . .	Moygoish . .	Street . . .	Granard . .	I.	281
37	Garrison . .	84 2 22	Cavan . .	Clanmahon . .	Ballymachugh .	Cavan . .	III.	76
15, 23	Garrison . .	471 0 25	Cork, E.R. .	Duhallow . .	Kilbrin . .	Kanturk . .	II.	72
13	Garrison . .	328 3 8	Fermanagh . .	Magheraboy . .	Devenish . .	Ballyshannon .	III.	211
107, 108	Garrison . .	107 2 35	Galway . .	Longford . .	Kiltormer . .	Ballinasloe .	IV.	60
24	Garrison . .	147 2 30	Limerick . .	Coonagh . .	Grean . . .	Tipperary . .	II.	235
27	Garrison . .	85 2 23	Queen's Co. .	Clandonagh . .	Rathdowney . .	Donaghmore .	I.	234
20	Garrison . .	196 2 4h	Waterford . .	Coshmore&Coshbride	Lismoreand Mocollop	Lismore . .	II.	345
41	Garrison . .	164 3 26	Wexford . .	Bargy . . .	Duncormick .	Wexford . .	I.	304
33, 41	Garrison Glebe .	262 2 38i	Tyrone . .	Omagh West . .	Longfield West .	Castlederg .	III.	316
78	Garrisonhill . .	195 0 23j	Donegal . .	Raphoe . .	Donaghmore .	Stranorlar .	III.	138
2, 4	Garristown . .	1,050 1 11	Dublin . .	Balrothery West .	Garristown . .	Dunshaughlin .	I.	22
3	GARRISTOWN T. .	—	Dublin . .	Balrothery West .	Garristown . .	Dunshaughlin .	I.	22
65, 78	Garrivinnagh . .	360 0 27	Galway . .	Moycullen . .	Kilcummin . .	Oughterard .	IV.	67

(a) Including 10A. 2R. 34P. water.
(b) Including 19A. 0R. 11P. water.
(c) Including 2A. 1R. 2P. water.
(d) Including 11A. 3R. 23P. water.

(e) Including 39A. 1R. 29P. water.
(f) Including 4A. 0R. 3P. water.
(g) Including 6A. 2R. 1P. water.

(h) Including 6A. 0R. 32P. water.
(i) Including 4A. 2R. 24P. water.
(j) Including 5A. 0R. 0P. water.

No. of Sheet of the Ordnance Survey Maps.	Townlands and Towns.	Area in Statute Acres.			County.	Barony.	Parish.	Poor Law Union in 1857.	Townland Census of 1851, Part I.	
		A.	R.	P.					Vol.	Page
22	Garrolagh	61	2	1	Louth	Ferrard	Mayne	Drogheda	I.	181
22	Garrolagh	188	3	23	Louth	Ferrard	Rathdrumin	Drogheda	I.	182
37, 51	Garroman	1,966	2	11a	Galway	Ballynahinch	Moyrus	Clifden	IV.	13
20	Garroonagh	130	1	31	Queen's Co.	Ballyadams	Ballyadams	Athy	I.	231
7	Garroon or Summergrove	239	1	4	Queen's Co.	Tinnahinch	Rosenallis	Mountmellick	I.	250
39, 47	Garroose	773	2	36	Limerick	Connello Upper	Bruree	Kilmallock	II.	231
106	Garrough	480	0	32	Kerry	Dunkerron South	Kilcrohane	Cahersiveen	II.	183
32	Garrough	151	3	1	Queen's Co.	Slievemargy	Killeshin	Carlow	I.	246
88	Garrow	92	1	30b	Mayo	Burrishoole	Aghagower	Westport	IV.	118
5, 6	Garrow	689	2	23	Roscommon	Boyle	Boyle	Boyle	IV.	194
25	Garrow or Buck Islands	5	2	25	Fermanagh	Clanawley	Cleenish	Enniskillen	III.	191
52, 53	Garrowcarry	758	1	26	Donegal	Kilmacrenan	Kilmacrenan	Letterkenny	III.	129
82	Garrowchuill	151	2	34	Donegal	Banagh	Inishkeel	Glenties	III.	106
8, 9	Garrowhill	260	3	28	Longford	Longford	Clongesh	Longford	I.	158
6, 7, 10, 11	Garrowlougher	121	2	23	Roscommon	Boyle	Tumna	Boyle	IV.	198
27, 35	Garruragh	838	3	28	Clare	Tulla Upper	Tulla	Tulla	II.	41
51	Garryadeen	264	3	14	Cork, E.R.	Barretts	Grenagh	Cork	II.	49
107, 117	Garryad & Garryduff	346	0	4	Galway	Longford	Killimorbologue	Portumna	IV.	58
15, 20	Garryandrew	148	3	0	Longford	Ardagh	Mostrim	Granard	I.	152
69	Garryandrew North	76	0	15	Tipperary, S.R.	Middlethird	St. Patricksrock	Cashel	II.	331
69	Garryandrew South	23	0	1	Tipperary, S.R.	Middlethird	St. Patricksrock	Cashel	II.	331
44, 53	Garryantaggart	106	2	30	Cork, E.R.	Barrymore	Gortroe	Fermoy	II.	55
45	Garryantaggart	312	2	12c	Cork, E.R.	Kinnatalloon	Aghern	Fermoy	II.	97
10, 16, 17	Garryantanvally	703	1	19d	Kerry	Clanmaurice	Finuge	Listowel	II.	169
81, 93	Garryantornora	264	0	37e	Cork, W.R.	West Muskerry	Inchigeelagh	Dunmanway	II.	157
10	Garryard	232	0	23	Kerry	Iraghticonnor	Galey	Listowel	II.	190
7	Garryard	325	0	6	Tipperary, N.R.	Lower Ormond	Terryglass	Borrisokane	II.	287
53	Garryard	89	1	31	Tipperary, S.R.	Middlethird	St. Patricksrock	Cashel	II.	331
26	Garryard East	102	0	19	Tipperary, N.R.	Upper Ormond	Kilmore	Nenagh	II.	291
26	Garryard West	333	1	18	Tipperary, N.R.	Upper Ormond	Kilmore	Nenagh	II.	291
56, 59	Garryarthur	625	2	15	Limerick	Coshlea	Kilflyn	Kilmallock	II.	240
23, 24	Garrybane	158	1	16	Monaghan	Cremorne	Aghnamullen	Castleblayney	III.	258
107, 120	Garrybaun	90	0	37	Cork, W.R.	East Carbery (W.D.)	Fanlobbus	Dunmanway	II.	131
7	Garrybaun	57	2	1	Tipperary, N.R.	Lower Ormond	Aglishcloghane	Borrisokane	II.	281
98	Garryboghala	125	3	1	Galway	Leitrim	Abbeygormacan	Loughrea	IV.	50
21	Garrybran	244	1	5	Wexford	Ballaghkeen	Meelnagh	Enniscorthy	I.	298
21	Garrybrit Lower	256	3	31	Wexford	Gorey	Kilcormick	Enniscorthy	I.	317
28	Garrybrittas	165	3	38	Waterford	Coshmore&Coshbride	Lismore and Mocollop	Lismore	I.	345
20, 21	Garrybrit Upper	103	2	2	Wexford	Gorey	Kilcormick	Enniscorthy	I.	317
45	Garrycaheragh	383	2	29	Cork, E.R.	Kinnatalloon	Aghern	Fermoy	II.	97
19	Garrycam	331	0	25	Longford	Moydow	Kilglass	Ballymahon	I.	161
29, 30	Garrycastle	900	0	22	King's Co.	Garrycastle	Reynagh	Parsonstown	I.	138
29	Garrycastle	252	1	25	Westmeath	Brawny	St. Mary's	Athlone	I.	259
32	Garrycleary	205	2	9	Wexford	Shelmaliere East	Kilpatrick	Wexford	I.	331
42, 43	Garryclogh	323	1	38	Tipperary, S.R.	Slievardagh	Fennor	Urlingford	II.	333
26	Garryclogher	89	2	38	Tipperary, N.R.	Upper Ormond	Kilmore	Nenagh	II.	291
81	Garrycloher	238	3	1	Tipperary, S.R.	Iffa and Offa West	Caher	Clogheen	II.	318
4, 7	Garryclohy	114	2	38	Tipperary, N.R.	Lower Ormond	Terryglass	Borrisokane	II.	287
22	Garryclone	327	1	3	Waterford	Decies without Drum	Colligan	Dungarvan	II.	354
39	Garrycloonagh	173	1	30	Mayo	Tirawley	Kilbelfad	Ballina	IV.	168
62	Garrycloyne	426	3	37	Cork, E.R.	Barretts	Garrycloyne	Cork	II.	49
20, 28	Garrycloyne	234	1	37	Waterford	Coshmore&Coshbride	Lismore and Mocollop	Lismore	II.	345
20	Garryconnell	138	3	9	Longford	Ardagh	Ardagh	Longford	I.	151
45	Garrycullen	383	3	39	Wexford	Shelburne	Tintern	New Ross	I.	329
9	Garrydague	157	2	9	Kilkenny	Galmoy	Coolcashin	Urlingford	I.	92
16, 21	Garrydaniel	420	0	19	Wexford	Ballaghkeen	Monamolin	Gorey	I.	298
70	Garrydine	305	0	38	Kerry	Iveragh	Killinane	Cahersiveen	II.	197
33	Garrydoolis	355	0	2	Limerick	Coonagh	Templebredon	Tipperary	II.	236
17, 22	Garryduff	753	0	38	Antrim	Kilconway	Ballymoney	Ballymoney	III.	25
76	Garryduff	233	1	20	Cork, E.R.	Barrymore	Mogeesha	Middleton	II.	57
54, 55	Garryduff	578	2	1	Cork, E.R.	Kinnatalloon	Clonmult	Fermoy	II.	98
24	Garryduff	390	1	2	Cork, E.R.	Orrery and Kilmore	Ballyclogh	Mallow	II.	106
87, 99	Garryduff	70	2	7	Galway	Clonmacnowen	Clontuskert	Ballinasloe	IV.	24
100, 101	Garryduff	406	3	32f	Galway	Longford	Clonfert	Ballinasloe	IV.	57
60	Garryduff	166	0	12	Galway	Tiaquin	Killosolan	Mountbellew	IV.	78
20, 21	Garryduff	866	2	33	Kilkenny	Gowran	Kilmacahill	Kilkenny	I.	97
35	Garryduff	515	2	19	Kilkenny	Iverk	Owning	Carrick on Suir	I.	106
23	Garryduff	59	3	10	Limerick	Clanwilliam	Caherconlish	Limerick	II.	222
24, 25	Garryduff	133	1	5	Limerick	Coonagh	Oola	Tipperary	II.	235
36, 44	Garryduff	93	3	7	Limerick	Glenquin	Mahoonagh	Newcastle	II.	246
35, 36	Garryduff	1,083	0	30	Limerick	Glenquin	Monagay	Newcastle	II.	247

(a) Including 307A. 0R. 6P. water.
(b) Including 1A. 0R. 6P. water.
(c) Including 7A. 1R. 39P. detached portion.
(d) Including 19A. 2R. 23P. water.
(e) Including 6A. 0R. 7P. detached portion.
(f) Including 13A. 1R. 24P. River Suck.

No. of Sheet of the Ordnance Survey Maps.	Townlands and Towns.	Area in Statute Acres. A. R. P.	County.	Barony.	Parish.	Poor Law Union in 1857.	Townland Census of 1851, Part I. Vol.	Page
78	Garryduff	182 3 8*a*	Mayo	Carra	Aglish	Castlebar	IV.	123
23, 24	Garryduff	242 1 27	Monaghan	Cremorne	Aghnamullen	Castleblayney	III.	258
27	Garryduff	815 2 38	Queen's Co.	Clandonagh	Rathdowney	Donaghmore	I.	234
22, 28	Garryduff	295 3 24	Queen's Co.	Clarmallagh	Aghaboe	Donaghmore	I.	236
28	Garryduff	143 0 34	Queen's Co.	Clarmallagh	Kildellig	Donaghmore	I.	238
13, 14	Garryduff	26 2 32	Queen's Co.	Stradbally	Killenny	Mountmellick	I.	247
12	Garryduff	81 1 0	Sligo	Tireragh	Templeboy	Dromore West	IV.	236
14	Garryduff	73 2 28	Tipperary, N.R.	Lower Ormond	Dromineer	Nenagh	II.	283
66, 67	Garryduff	268 1 4	Tipperary, S.R.	Clanwilliam	Clonpet	Tipperary	II.	306
79	Garryduff	536 0 8	Tipperary, S.R.	Iffa and Offa East	Garrangibbon	Carrick on Suir	II.	313
87, 88	Garryduff	231 3 30	Tipperary, S.R.	Iffa and Offa West	Ballybacon	Clogheen	II.	317
88, 91	Garryduff	999 2 0*b*	Tipperary, S.R.	Iffa and Offa West	Newcastle	Clogheen	II.	319
37	Garryduff	273 3 37	Waterford	Coshmore&Coshbride	Templemichael	Youghal	II.	348
22	Garryduff	400 0 27	Waterford	Decies without Drum	Colligan	Dungarvan	II.	354
38	Garryduff	290 0 22	Westmeath	Moycashel	Newtown	Mullingar	I.	279
38, 39	Garryduff	338 0 19	Westmeath	Moycashel	Rahugh	Mullingar	I.	279
20, 21	Garryduff	321 1 0	Wexford	Ballaghkeen	Kilcormick	Enniscorthy	I.	294
39	Garryduff	412 2 21	Wexford	Shelburne	Owenduff	New Ross	I.	328
24, 30	Garryduff	300 3 27	Wicklow	Newcastle	Kilcommon	Rathdrum	I.	351
51, 52	Garryduff East	186 0 28	Tipperary, S.R.	Kilnamanagh Lower	Ballintemple	Cashel	II.	322
107, 117	Garryduff and Garryad	346 0 4	Galway	Longford	Killimorbologue	Portumna	IV.	58
1, 2, 7, 8	Garryduff or Greenville	185 0 23	King's Co.	Kilcoursey	Kilmanaghan	Tullamore	I.	141
112	Garryduff Middle	75 1 34	Mayo	Clanmorris	Crossboyne	Claremorris	IV.	132
101, 102 } 111, 112	Garryduff North	87 2 36	Mayo	Clanmorris	Crossboyne	Claremorris	IV.	132
112	Garryduff South	124 1 35	Mayo	Clanmorris	Crossboyne	Claremorris	IV.	132
111, 112	Garryduff West	175 0 32	Mayo	Clanmorris	Crossboyne	Claremorris	IV.	132
51	Garryduff West	56 0 31	Tipperary, S.R.	Kilnamanagh Lower	Ballintemple	Cashel	II.	322
135	Garryeighter	289 0 36*c*	Galway	Leitrim	Clonrush	Scarriff	IV.	53
22	Garryellen	304 0 0	Limerick	Smallcounty	Fedamore	Croom	II.	259
38,46	Garryfine	1,024 0 4	Limerick	Connello Upper	Bruree	Kilmallock	II.	231
8	Garryfliugh	305 1 6	Cavan	Tullyhaw	Drumreilly	Bawnboy	III.	91
24	Garryfrask	151 2 0	Limerick	Coonagh	Tuoghcluggin	Tipperary	II.	236
35, 39	Garrygaug	495 1 9	Kilkenny	Iverk	Muckalee	Carrick on Suir	I.	106
38	Garrygibbon	115 2 13	Wexford	Shelmaliere East	Ardcolm	Wexford	I.	330
120,121	Garryglass	488 0 5	Cork, W.R.	West Carbery (E.D.)	Drinagh	Skibbereen	II.	139
88, 89	Garryglass	130 3 39	Kerry	Iveragh	Dromod	Cahersiveen	II.	195
5, 13	Garryglass	120 3 33	Limerick	Clanwilliam	Derrygalvin	Limerick	II.	223
24	Garryglass	1,210 0 32	Queen's Co.	Cullenagh	Fossy or Timahoe	Abbeyleix	I.	240
24, 30	Garryglass	92 3 4	Roscommon	Roscommon	Bumlin	Strokestown	IV.	208
33	Garryglass	774 0 28	Tipperary, N.R.	Upper Ormond	Kilnaneave	Nenagh	II.	291
27, 36, 37	Garrygort	606 3 5*d*	Donegal	Kilmacrenan	Tullyfern	Millford	III.	133
47	Garryhack	126 3 34	Wexford	Forth	Ballymore	Wexford	I.	308
96, 97	Garryhankard	325 2 24	Cork, E.R.	Kinalea	Knockavilly	Bandon	II.	96
4	Garryhasten	904 2 9	Wexford	Scarawalsh	Moyacomb	Shillelagh	I.	325
33	Garryheakin	222 3 29	Limerick	Coonagh	Oola	Tipperary	II.	235
58	Garryheakin	147 3 10	Tipperary, S.R.	Clanwilliam	Cullen	Tipperary	II.	307
2, 6	Garryhedder	611 1 16	Queen's Co.	Tinnahinch	Kilmanman	Mountmellick	I.	249
72, 84, 85	Garryhesty	839 0 39	Cork, E.R.	East Muskerry	Desertmore	Bandon	II.	102
12	Garryhiggin	132 0 38	Kilkenny	Crannagh	Tubbridbritain	Urlingford	I.	87
16,17,19,20	Garryhill	392 1 19	Carlow	Idrone East	Dunleckny	Carlow	I.	7
17	Garryhill	16 3 12	Carlow	Idrone East	Myshall	Carlow	I.	8
33	Garryhinch	1,376 0 19	King's Co.	Upper Philipstown	Clonyhurk	Mountmellick	I.	143
17, 18	Garryhintoge	330 0 20	Cork, E.R.	Fermoy	Doneraile	Mallow	II.	78
38, 39	Garryhoe	335 2 37	Wicklow	Ballinacor South	Kilcommon	Shillelagh	I.	349
33	Garryhubbock	210 0 38	Wexford	Ballaghkeen	St. Nicholas	Enniscorthy	I.	298
116	Garryhubert	110 2 34	Galway	Leitrim	Duniry	Loughrea	IV.	53
12	Garryhundon	786 2 1	Carlow	Carlow	Clonmelsh	Carlow	I.	1
13, 19	Garrykennedy	598 2 7	Tipperary, N.R.	Owney and Arra	Castletownarra	Nenagh	II.	294
10, 16	Garryknock	1,263 2 35	Wicklow	Lower Talbotstown	Boystown	Naas	I.	359
3	Garrylaban	59 3 36	Londonderry	North East Liberties of Coleraine	Ballyaghran	Coleraine	III.	244
122	Garryland	350 2 14*e*	Galway	Kiltartan	Kilmacduagh	Gort	IV.	48
3, 8	Garrylaun	245 2 38	Kilkenny	Galmoy	Erke	Urlingford	I.	92
54, 55	Garrylaurence	800 0 25	Cork, E.R.	Barrymore	Clonmult	Middleton	II.	53
99	Garrylawrence	42 1 20	Galway	Clonmacnowen	Clontuskert	Ballinasloe	IV.	24
11	Garryleagh	185 1 27	Cork, E.R.	Condons&Clangibbon	Brigown	Mitchelstown	II.	59
25	Garryleesha	60 1 1	Kilkenny	Gowran	Powerstown	Thomastown	I.	97
102	Garryletter	329 1 30	Kerry	Glanarought	Kilcaskan	Kenmare	II.	187
33	Garrylough Lower	394 3 9	Wexford	Ballaghkeen	St. Nicholas	Enniscorthy	I.	298
33	Garrylough Upper	126 3 27	Wexford	Ballaghkeen	St. Nicholas	Enniscorthy	I.	298
12	Garry Lower	314 0 19	Antrim	Upper Dunluce	Ballymoney	Ballymoney	III.	19

(*a*) Including 2A. 3R. 18P. water.   (*c*) Including 27A. 3R. 0P. water.   (*e*) Including 4A. 2R. 20P. water.
(*b*) Including 3A. 1R. 15P. River Suir.   (*d*) Including 6A. 3R. 13P. water.

No. of Sheet of the Ordnance Survey Maps.	Townlands and Towns.	Area in Statute Acres.			County.	Barony.	Parish.	Poor Law Union in 1857.	Townland Census of 1851, Part I.	
		A.	R.	P.					Vol.	Page
124	Garrylucas . .	151	3	25	Cork, W.R. .	Courceys . .	Ringrone . .	Kinsale . .	II.	147
19	Garrymacteige .	48	2	15	Tipperary, N.R. .	Owney and Arra .	Castletownarra .	Nenagh . .	II.	294
9, 14	Garrymaddock .	382	1	8	Queen's Co. .	Stradbally . .	Moyanna . .	Athy . .	I.	247
20, 26	Garrymile . .	383	1	28	Wexford . .	Ballaghkeen .	Ballyhuskard .	Enniscorthy .	I.	292
26, 27	Garrymona . .	318	0	28	King's Co. .	Upper Philipstown .	Geashill . .	Tullamore .	I.	144
17, 18	*Garrymona Island* .	9	0	0	Roscommon .	Ballintober North .	Kilmore . .	Car^k. on Shannon	IV.	187
25, 31	Garrymore . .	580	2	23	Cavan . .	Clanmahon .	Ballintemple .	Cavan . .	III.	75
77	Garrymore . .	266	1	8	Cork, E.R. .	Imokilly . .	Ightermurragh .	Middleton .	II.	87
135, 144	Garrymore . .	65	0	2	Cork, W.R. .	Ibane and Barryroe	Ardfield . .	Clonakilty .	II.	148
27,28,36,37	Garrymore . .	158	0	8	Donegal . .	Kilmacrenan .	Tullyfern . .	Milford . .	III.	133
30	Garrymore . .	7	0	4	Galway . .	Dunmore . .	Tuam . .	Tuam . .	IV.	36
87	Garrymore . .	273	3	1	Galway . .	Kilconnell .	Aughrim . .	Ballinasloe .	IV.	39
72, 73	Garrymore . .	446	2	7	Galway . .	Kilconnell .	Ballymacward .	Ballinasloe .	IV.	39
102	Garrymore . .	161	3	9	Kerry . .	Glanarought .	Kilcaskan .	Kenmare . .	II.	187
13	Garrymore . .	277	0	21	King's Co. .	Garrycastle .	Clonmacnoise .	Parsonstown .	I.	135
6, 14	Garrymore . .	163	1	38	Limerick . .	Clanwilliam .	Killeenagarriff .	Limerick . .	II.	224
119	Garrymore . .	663	0	16	Mayo . .	Kilmaine . .	Kilcommon .	Claremorris .	IV.	154
3, 4	Garrymore . .	1,198	2	16	Queen's Co. .	Tinnahinch .	Castlebrack .	Mountmellick .	I.	248
26	Garrymore . .	58	3	9	Tipperary, N.R. .	Upper Ormond .	Kilmore . .	Nenagh . .	II.	291
87	Garrymore . .	331	3	1	Tipperary, S.R. .	Iffa and Offa West .	Tullaghorton .	Clogheen .	II.	321
27	Garrymore . .	81	1	16	Wexford . .	Ballaghkeen .	Castle-ellis .	Enniscorthy .	I.	293
69, 70	Garrymore or Gardenham . .	145	2	26	Galway . .	Clare . . .	Annaghdown .	Galway . .	IV.	16
69, 70	Garrymore or Gardenham . .	65	0	26	Galway . .	Clare . . .	Lackagh . .	Galway . .	IV.	22
29, 30	Garrymore Lower .	270	1	20	Wicklow . .	Ballinacor North .	Rathdrum . .	Rathdrum .	I.	347
30	Garrymore Upper .	177	0	14	Wicklow . .	Ballinacor North .	Rathdrum .	Rathdrum .	I.	347
79	Garrymorris . .	210	2	19	Tipperary, S.R. .	Slievardagh .	Garrangibbon .	Carrick on Suir	II.	333
27	Garrymoyle . .	63	0	20	Wexford . .	Ballaghkeen .	Ballyvaldon .	Enniscorthy .	I.	292
101	Garrynabba . .	78	1	27	Mayo . .	Clanmorris .	Kilcolman .	Claremorris .	IV.	134
15	Garrynabolie . .	252	2	31	Meath . .	Fore . . .	Moylagh . .	Oldcastle .	I.	201
44	Garrynacole . .	116	1	38	Cork, E.R. .	Barrymore . .	Rathcormack .	Fermoy . .	II.	57
44, 54	Garrynadur . .	207	0	37	Kerry . .	Corkaguiny .	Minard . .	Dingle . .	II.	180
21	Garrynafana . .	363	0	1	Tipperary, N.R. .	Upper Ormond .	Ballymackey .	Nenagh . .	II.	289
22, 29	Garrynafela . .	145	3	38*a*	Westmeath .	Brawny . . .	St. Mary's .	Athlone . .	I.	259
52	Garrynagawna .	427	0	2	Roscommon .	Athlone . . .	Drum . . .	Athlone . .	IV.	180
52	Garrynagawna Bog & Carrickynaghtan .	973	2	18	Roscommon .	Athlone . . .	Drum . . .	Athlone . .	IV.	180
42	Garrynagearagh .	576	2	3	Cork, E.R. .	Barretts . . .	Mourneabbey .	Mallow . .	II.	50
31	Garrynageragh East	161	1	17	Waterford .	Decies without Drum	Dungarvan .	Dungarvan .	II.	355
31	Garrynageragh West	74	0	28	Waterford .	Decies without Drum	Dungarvan .	Dungarvan .	II.	355
26	Garrynagh . .	94	3	31*b*	Longford . .	Shrule . . .	Noughaval .	Ballymahon .	I.	166
116, 117, 125, 126	Garrynaglogh . .	98	3	30	Galway . .	Leitrim . . .	Ballynakill .	Portumna .	IV.	51
23, 24	Garrynagoord . .	90	0	18	Limerick . .	Clanwilliam .	Aglishcormick .	Limerick . .	II.	221
15, 21	Garrynagore . .	361	0	38	Kerry . .	Clanmaurice .	Kiltomy . .	Listowel . .	II.	172
37	Garrynagoul . .	266	3	18	Cork, E.R. .	Condons&Clangibbon	Lismore and Mocollop	Fermoy . .	II.	62
21	Garrynagran . .	251	2	19	Mayo . .	Tirawley . .	Moygawnagh .	Killala . .	IV.	171
47	Garrynagran . .	336	0	4*c*	Roscommon .	Athlone . . .	Taghboy . .	Athlone . .	IV.	184
2, 7	Garrynagranoge .	355	3	3	Cork, E.R. .	Orrery and Kilmore	Rathgoggan .	Kilmallock .	II.	109
49	Garrynagree . .	273	2	39	Tipperary, S.R. .	Slievardagh .	Ballingarry .	Callan . .	II.	331
35	Garrynagree . .	308	3	12	Waterford .	Decies within Drum	Ardmore . .	Dungarvan .	II.	350
32, 33	Garrynagry . .	398	2	18*d*	Clare . . .	Islands . . .	Kilmaley . .	Ennis . .	II.	31
55, 68	Garrynagry . .	168	1	30	Galway . .	Moycullen . .	Killannin .	Oughterard .	IV.	69
49	Garrynalyna . .	284	3	17	Limerick . .	Coshlea . . .	Galbally . .	Mitchelstown .	II.	238
27	Garrynamann Lower	189	0	14	Kilkenny . .	Kells . . .	Kells . . .	Callan . .	I.	108
23, 27	Garrynamann Upper	345	2	1	Kilkenny . .	Kells . . .	Kells . . .	Callan . .	I.	108
87	Garrynamishaun or Aughrim Plots .	125	2	37	Galway . .	Kilconnell .	Aughrim . .	Ballinasloe .	IV.	39
61	Garrynamona .	176	3	29	Clare . . .	Bunratty Lower .	Kilconry . .	Ennis . .	II.	4
40, 41	Garrynamona . .	579	3	18	Tipperary, N.R. .	Eliogarty . .	Ballycahill .	Thurles . .	II.	269
14, 20	Garrynaneaskagh .	503	1	8	Kerry . .	Clanmaurice .	Kilmoyly . .	Tralee . .	II.	171
80	Garrynapeaka . .	188	0	35	Cork, W.R. .	West Muskerry .	Inchigeelagh .	Dunmanway .	II.	157
38, 39	Garrynarea . .	510	3	3	Kilkenny . .	Iverk . . .	Owning . .	Carrick on Suir	I.	106
107, 117	Garrynasillagh .	51	3	6	Galway . .	Longford . .	Killimorbologue .	Portumna .	IV.	59
25	Garrynatineel . .	392	3	14	Tipperary, N.R. .	Owney and Arra .	Templeachally .	Nenagh . .	II.	297
33	Garryncahera . .	334	3	21	Limerick . .	Smallcounty .	Ballinlough .	Kilmallock .	II.	259
17	Garryncallaha . .	108	2	20*e*	Clare . . .	Inchiquin . .	Kilkeedy . .	Corrofin . .	II.	25
47, 55	Garryncoonagh North	612	1	2	Limerick . .	Coshlea . . .	Effin . . .	Kilmallock .	II.	238
55	Garryncoonagh South	155	2	1	Limerick . .	Coshlea . . .	Effin . . .	Kilmallock .	II.	238
62	Garryncurra . .	259	3	13	Clare . . .	Bunratty Lower .	Kilfintinan .	Limerick . .	II.	5
9	Garryncurry . .	176	1	35	Tipperary, N.R. .	Lower Ormond .	Kilbarron .	Borrisokane .	III.	284
47	Garrynderk North .	501	0	4	Limerick . .	Coshma . . .	Effin . . .	Kilmallock .	II.	243
47, 55	Garrynderk South .	358	0	13	Limerick . .	Coshma . . .	Effin . . .	Kilmallock .	II.	243

(*a*) Including 59A. 33P. detached portion.   (*c*) Including 1A. 2R. 36P. water.   (*e*) Including 3A. 0R. 7P. water.
(*b*) Including 7A. 0R. 0P. water.   (*d*) Including 8A. 0R. 11P. water.

No. of Sheet of the Ordnance Survey Maps.	Townlands and Towns.	Area in Statute Acres.	County.	Barony.	Parish.	Poor Law Union in 1857.	Townland Census of 1851, Part I.	
		A. R. P.					Vol.	Page
76	Garryndrihid . .	12 2 26	Tipperary, S.R.	Iffa and Offa East .	Newchapel . .	Clonmel . .	II.	315
123	Garryndruig .	856 1 28	Cork, W.R. .	East Carbery (E.D.)	Rathclarin . .	Bandon . .	II.	130
12, 17	Garrynew . .	376 1 26	Wexford . .	Ballaghkeen . .	Ardamine . .	Gorey . .	I.	291
27	Garrynisk . .	263 1 19	Wexford . .	Ballaghkeen . .	Castle-ellis . .	Enniscorthy .	I.	293
26	Garrynisk . .	148 0 3	Wexford . .	Ballaghkeen . .	Edermine . .	Enniscorthy .	I.	294
28	Garryniska . .	44 0 30	Queen's Co. .	Clarmallagh . .	Bordwell . .	Donaghmore .	I.	237
27	Garryniskbeg .	71 3 17	Wexford . .	Ballaghkeen . .	Castle-ellis . .	Enniscorthy .	I.	293
48	Garrynlease . .	124 1 1	Limerick . .	Coshlea . .	Kilfinnane . .	Kilmallock .	II.	240
36	Garrynoe . .	169 3 10	Cork, E.R. .	Condons & Clangibbon	Clondulane . .	Fermoy . .	II.	60
39, 47	Garrynoe . .	109 3 5	Limerick . .	Kilmallock . .	St. Peters & St. Pauls	Kilmallock .	II.	250
55	Garrynoe . .	365 2 36	Tipperary, S.R.	Slievardagh . .	Mowney . .	Callan . .	II.	335
20	Garrynoe . .	97 3 15	Waterford .	Coshmore&Coshbride	Lismore and Mocollop	Lismore . .	II.	346
38	Garrynogher .	143 2 4	Cavan . .	Castlerahan . .	Crosserlough .	Oldcastle . .	III.	68
44, 47	Garrynphort . .	388 3 13a	Roscommon .	Athlone . .	Cam . .	Athlone . .	IV.	180
44, 47	Garrynphort . .	116 2 19b	Roscommon .	Athlone . .	Taghboy . .	Athlone . .	IV.	184
15, 21	Garrynphort . .	188 2 32	Roscommon .	Roscommon . .	Shankill . .	Castlereagh .	IV.	213
82	Garryntemple .	294 2 6	Tipperary, S.R.	Iffa and Offa East .	Inishlounaght .	Clonmel . .	II.	313
27, 33	Garryntinodagh .	133 2 39	Wexford . .	Ballaghkeen . .	Killisk . .	Enniscorthy .	I.	296
66	Garryoughtragh North	143 2 1	Cork, E.R. .	Imokilly . .	Mogeely . .	Middleton . .	II.	90
66	Garryoughtragh South	27 3 10	Cork, E.R. .	Imokilly . .	Mogeely . .	Middleton . .	II.	90
20	Garryphelim . .	184 1 4	Wexford . .	Scarawalsh . .	Clone . .	Enniscorthy .	I.	322
102	Garryredmond .	624 2 15	Mayo . .	Clanmorris . .	Kilcolman . .	Claremorris .	IV.	134
35, 40	Garryrichard . .	265 3 25	Wexford . .	Shelmaliere West .	Clongeen . .	New Ross . .	I.	333
26, 30	Garryrickin . .	1,067 3 8	Kilkenny . .	Kells . .	Killamery . .	Callan . .	I.	109
81	Garryroan . .	448 1 33	Tipperary, S.R.	Iffa and Offa West .	Whitechurch .	Clogheen . .	II.	321
80	Garryroe . .	92 0 39	Mayo . .	Gallen . .	Killedan . .	Swineford . .	IV.	150
77, 83	Garryroe . .	61 3 3	Tipperary, S.R.	Iffa and Offa East .	Kiltegan . .	Clonmel . .	II.	315
87	Garryroe . .	185 3 35	Tipperary, S.R.	Iffa and Offa West .	Ballybacon . .	Clogheen . .	II.	317
82	Garryroe . .	112 3 19	Tipperary, S.R.	Iffa and Offa West .	Derrygrath . .	Clogheen . .	II.	318
39, 43	Garryross . .	333 0 10	Cavan . .	Castlerahan . .	Castlerahan . .	Oldcastle . .	III.	67
55	Garrysallagh .	101 2 25	Tipperary, S.R.	Slievardagh . .	Crohane . .	Callan . .	II.	332
12	Garrysallagh . .	238 0 26	Westmeath .	Corkaree . .	Stonehall . .	Mullingar . .	I.	263
38, 42	Garrysallagh (D'Arcy)	151 2 10	Cavan . .	Clanmahon . .	Kilbride . .	Oldcastle . .	III.	78
36	Garrysallagh Glebe	80 3 15	King's Co. .	Eglish . .	Drumcullen . .	Parsonstown .	I.	134
38, 42	Garrysallagh (O'Reilly)	169 1 25	Cavan . .	Clanmahon . .	Kilbride . .	Oldcastle . .	III.	78
59	Garryshane . .	145 3 34	Tipperary, S.R.	Clanwilliam . .	Donohill . .	Tipperary . .	II.	307
83	Garryshane . .	52 0 20	Tipperary, S.R.	Iffa and Offa East .	Inishlounaght .	Clonmel . .	II.	313
67	Garryskillane .	25 2 6	Tipperary, S.R.	Clanwilliam . .	Cordangan . .	Tipperary . .	II.	306
49	GARRYSPELLANE T.	—	Limerick . .	Coshlea . .	Ballyscaddan .	Kilmallock .	II.	238
37	Garryteige . .	229 2 1	Tipperary, N.R.	Owney and Arra .	Kilvellane . .	Nenagh . .	II.	296
30	Garrythomas .	151 0 24	Kilkenny . .	Kells . .	Killamery . .	Callan . .	I.	109
12, 17	Garry Upper . .	154 1 12	Antrim . .	Upper Dunluce .	Ballymoney . .	Ballymoney .	III.	19
9	Garryvacum . .	417 0 1	Queen's Co. .	Portnahinch . .	Lea . .	Mountmellick .	I.	244
27	Garryvadden . .	268 1 17	Wexford . .	Ballaghkeen . .	Castle-ellis . .	Enniscorthy .	I.	293
27	Garryvaddenbeg .	57 2 2	Wexford . .	Ballaghkeen . .	Castle-ellis . .	Enniscorthy .	I.	293
27, 33	Garryvadden Lower	271 3 25	Wexford . .	Ballaghkeen . .	Castle-ellis . .	Enniscorthy .	I.	293
27, 33	Garryvadden Upper	279 1 26	Wexford . .	Ballaghkeen . .	Castle-ellis . .	Enniscorthy .	I.	293
40	Garryvanus . .	167 2 32	Tipperary, N.R.	Kilnamanagh Upper	Ballycahill . .	Thurles . .	II.	277
32	Garryvarren . .	370 0 20	Wexford . .	Ballaghkeen . .	Kilmallock . .	Enniscorthy .	I.	296
41	Garryvicleheen .	117 2 21	Tipperary, N.R.	Eliogarty . .	Thurles . .	Thurles . .	II.	273
77, 89	Garryvoe Lower .	514 0 14	Cork, E.R. .	Imokilly . .	Garryvoe . .	Middleton . .	II.	86
77	Garryvoe Upper .	241 1 35	Cork, E.R. .	Imokilly . .	Garryvoe . .	Middleton . .	II.	87
58, 60	Garryvurragha .	272 2 35	Limerick . .	Coshlea . .	Kilbeheny . .	Mitchelstown .	II.	239
91, 101	Garrywadreen .	287 0 32	Mayo . .	Clanmorris . .	Kilcolman . .	Claremorris .	IV.	134
26, 27	Garrywilliam . .	75 0 1	Kerry . .	Corkaguiny . .	Stradbally . .	Dingle . .	II.	180
32, 37	Garrywilliam . .	176 0 8	Wexford . .	Shelmaliere East .	Kilpatrick . .	Wexford . .	I.	331
55	Garshooey . .	375 3 1	Donegal . .	Raphoe . .	Allsaints . .	Londonderry .	III.	134
14	Gartacara . .	98 3 3c	Cavan . .	Lower Loughtee .	Drumlane . .	Cavan . .	III.	80
33	Gartagher . .	51 3 18d	Tyrone . .	Omagh West . .	Longfield East .	Omagh . .	III.	315
44, 52	Gartan or Bellville .	174 0 19e	Donegal . .	Kilmacrenan . .	Gartan . .	Letterkenny .	III.	127
35, 43, 44	Gartan Mountain .	4,124 3 31f	Donegal . .	Kilmacrenan . .	Gartan . .	Letterkenny .	III.	127
14	Gartaquill . .	363 3 38g	Cavan . .	Lower Loughtee .	Drumlane . .	Cavan . .	III.	80
15	Gartbrattan . .	106 3 4h	Cavan . .	Lower Loughtee .	Drumlane . .	Cavan . .	III.	80
20	Gartbrattan . .	264 1 18i	Cavan . .	Upper Loughtee .	Kilmore . .	Cavan . .	III.	84
38, 40	Garterfarm . .	124 0 28	Kildare . .	Kilkea and Moone .	Castledermot .	Athy . .	I.	59
4	Garterhill . .	671 1 0	Mayo . .	Erris . .	Kilcommon . .	Belmullet . .	IV.	144
25	Gartford . .	74 0 12	Antrim . .	Lower Glenarm .	Tickmacrevan .	Larne . .	III.	24
24	Gartinardress .	324 1 29j	Cavan . .	Tullyhunco . .	Killashandra .	Cavan . .	III.	98
7, 12	Gartlandstown .	1,005 0 6	Westmeath .	Fore . .	Faughalstown .	Castletowndelvin	I.	269
28	Gartnaneane . .	701 2 24k	Cavan . .	Clankee . .	Bailieborough .	Bailieborough .	III.	71
19, 20	Gartnanoul . .	246 1 16	Cavan . .	Upper Loughtee .	Kilmore . .	Cavan . .	III.	84
25	Gartnasillagh . .	173 2 16	Cavan . .	Upper Loughtee .	Urney . .	Cavan . .	III.	86
58	Gartree . .	569 1 8	Antrim . .	Lower Massereene .	Killead . .	Antrim . .	III.	28

(a) Including 44A. 0R. 28P. water.   (e) Including 87A. 3R. 0P. water.   (i) Including 22A. 0R. 18P. water.
(b) Including 4A. 2R. 18P. water.   (f) Including 304A. 2R. 17P. water.   (j) Including 4A. 3R. 39P. water,
(c) Including 15A. 0R. 23P. water.   (g) Including 3A. 0R. 30P. water.   (k) Including 10A. 2R. 29P. water.
(d) Including 0A. 2R. 16P. water.   (h) Including 8A. 1R. 30P. water.

No. of Sheet of the Ordnance Survey Maps.	Townlands and Towns.	Area in Statute Acres.			County.	Barony.	Parish.	Poor Law Union in 1857.	Townland Census of 1851, Part I.	
		A.	R.	P.					Vol.	Page
13, 20	Gartross . . .	209	3	8	Down . .	Lower Iveagh,Up.pt.	Magheralin . .	Lurgan . .	III.	170
24, 30	Gartylough . .	260	3	38a	Cavan . .	Tullyhunco .	Killashandra . .	Cavan . .	III.	98
13, 17	Garvagh . .	141	0	35	Armagh . .	Fews Lower . .	Mullaghbrack .	Armagh . .	III.	47
4	Garvagh . .	757	0	39b	Cavan . .	Tullyhaw . .	Killinagh . .	Enniskillen .	III.	92
85, 94	Garvagh . .	183	3	4	Donegal . .	Tirhugh . . .	Donegal . .	Donegal . .	III.	145
15, 17	Garvagh . .	563	2	27	Leitrim . .	Drumahaire . .	Killanummery .	Manorhamilton	IV.	98
28	Garvagh . .	67	3	7	Leitrim . .	Leitrim . . .	Kiltubbrid . .	Carᵏ.on Shannon	IV.	103
28, 29	Garvagh . .	274	3	14c	Leitrim . .	Mohill . . .	Mohill . .	Mohill . .	IV.	108
18	Garvagh . .	786	1	17	Londonderry .	Coleraine . .	Errigal . .	Coleraine .	III.	232
13	Garvagh . .	145	2	15	Longford . .	Ardagh . .	Ballymacormick .	Longford . .	I.	152
9	Garvagh . .	368	3	10	Longford . .	Granard . . .	Clonbroney . .	Granard . .	I.	155
46	Garvagh . .	265	1	36	Tyrone . .	Dungannon Middle .	Donaghmore . .	Dungannon .	III.	302
42	Garvagh . .	303	1	30d	Tyrone . .	Omagh East .	Drumragh . .	Omagh . .	III.	312
15	Garvagh · . .	957	1	3e	Tyrone . .	Omagh West .	Termonamongan .	Castlederg .	III.	317
11,12,18,19	Garvagh . .	1,213	2	22f	Tyrone . .	Strabane Upper .	Bodoney Lower .	Gortin . .	III.	323
7, 12	Garvagh . .	859	2	10g	Tyrone . .	Strabane Upper .	Bodoney Upper .	Gortin . .	III.	324
15	Garvagh Blane .	357	3	38	Tyrone . .	Omagh West .	Termonamongan .	Castlederg .	III.	317
15, 17	Garvagh Glebe .	1,221	2	36	Leitrim . .	Drumahaire . .	Killanummery .	Manorhamilton	IV.	98
15	Garvagh Pullans .	214	1	10	Tyrone . .	Omagh West .	Termonamongan .	Castlederg .	III.	317
18	GARVAGH T: . .	—			Londonderry .	Coleraine . .	Errigal . .	Coleraine .	III.	232
25, 34	Garvaghullion .	640	0	12h	Tyrone . .	Omagh West .	Longfield East .	Omagh . .	III.	315
31	Garvaghy . .	853	2	1	Antrim . .	Lower Toome .	Ahoghill . . .	Ballymena .	III.	32
9	Garvaghy . .	135	2	3i	Armagh . .	Oneilland West .	Drumcree . .	Lurgan . .	III.	52
11, 12	Garvaghy . .	86	0	1	Armagh . .	Tiranny . . .	Eglish . .	Armagh . .	III.	59
28	Garvaghy . .	722	1	25	Down . .	Lower Iveagh, Lr. pt.	Garvaghy . .	Banbridge .	III.	168
34	Garvaghy . .	63	2	27	Fermanagh .	Magherastephana .	Aghalurcher .	Lisnaskea .	III.	216
52	Garvaghy . .	1,523	3	35	Tyrone . .	Clogher . . .	Errigal Keerogue .	Clogher . .	III.	295
61	Garvaghy . .	140	1	12	Tyrone . .	Dungannon Middle .	Clonfeacle . .	Dungannon .	III.	299
35	Garvaghy . .	312	3	26j	Tyrone . .	Omagh East .	Cappagh . .	Omagh . .	III.	310
49	Garvaghy . .	199	0	31	Tyrone . .	Omagh East .	Kilskeery . .	Lowtherstown .	III.	313
51	Garvallagh , .	507	3	24	Tyrone . .	Clogher . . .	Donacavey . .	Omagh . .	III.	294
6	Garvalt Lower .	238	3	18	Cavan . .	Tullyhaw . .	Templeport . .	Enniskillen .	III.	94
6	Garvalt Upper or Gub	201	2	0	Cavan . .	Tullyhaw . .	Templeport . .	Enniskillen .	III.	95
67	Garvan . . .	516	1	13	Donegal . .	Raphoe . .	Kilteevoge . .	Stranorlar .	III.	139
103, 104	Garvanagh . .	827	0	16k	Donegal . .	Tirhugh . . .	Kilbarron . .	Ballyshannon .	III.	148
9	Garvary . . .	109	0	36	Cavan . .	Tullyhaw . .	Templeport . .	Bawnboy . .	III.	94
38	Garvary . . .	710	2	30	Donegal . .	Inishowen West .	Fahan Upper .	Londonderry .	III.	121
35	Garvary . . .	143	1	14	Donegal . .	Kilmacrenan .	Clondahorky .	Dunfanaghy .	III.	123
26	Garvary . . .	52	2	22	Fermanagh .	Clanawley . .	Rossorry . .	Enniskillen .	III.	194
41	Garvary . . .	249	1	16l	Fermanagh .	Knockninny .	Tomregan . .	Lisnaskea .	III.	203
3, 4, 8	Garvary . . .	413	0	10	Fermanagh .	Lurg . . .	Belleek . .	Ballyshannon .	III.	203
22	Garvary . . .	330	0	37	Fermanagh .	Tirkennedy .	Enniskillen .	Enniskillen .	III.	222
2	Garvary . . .	231	3	8m	Longford . .	Longford . .	Killoe . .	Longford . .	I.	159
35	Garvary Mounⁱaiⁿ .	767	0	35	Donegal . .	Kilmacrenan .	Clondahorky .	Dunfanaghy .	III.	123
74	Garvegort Glebe .	411	3	5	Donegal . .	Banagh . .	Killybegs Lower .	Glenties . .	III.	110
80	Garveross . .	125	3	24	Donegal . .	Banagh . .	Glencolumbkille .	Glenties . .	III.	105
80	Garveross Mountain and Beefan .	228	0	5	Donegal . .	Banagh . .	Glencolumbkille .	Glenties . .	III.	105
5	Garvesk . . .	286	1	5	Cavan . .	Tullyhaw . .	Killinagh . .	Enniskillen .	III.	92
24	Garvetagh Lower .	308	1	13	Tyrone . .	Omagh West .	Ardstraw . .	Castlederg .	III.	315
24	Garvetagh Upper .	367	3	26	Tyrone . .	Omagh West .	Ardstraw . .	Castlederg .	III.	315
59, 60	Garvey . . .	310	2	31	Tyrone . .	Dungannon Lower .	Carnteel . .	Clogher . .	III.	297
24	Garvillaun . .	412	0	24n	Clare . .	Inchiquin . .	Inagh . . .	Ennistimon .	II.	25
17, 18	Garvillaun . .	281	3	16o	Clare . .	Inchiquin . .	Ruan . . .	Corrofin . .	II.	28
31	Garvlough . .	235	0	12	Leitrim . .	Leitrim . .	Kiltoghert . .	Carᵏ.on Shannon	IV.	102
9, 13	Garvoge . . .	618	2	13p	Kildare . .	Clane . . .	Ballynafagh . .	Naas . .	I.	53
24	Garvoghil . .	242	1	22	Clare . .	Inchiquin . .	Inagh . . .	Ennistimon .	II.	25
28	Garvoghill . .	42	1	12	Fermanagh .	Magherastephana .	Aghalurcher .	Lisnaskea .	III.	216
13	Garvros . . .	91	0	34	Fermanagh .	Magheraboy .	Inishmacsaint .	Ballyshannon .	III.	213
16, 17	Gash . . .	182	2	33	Queen's Co. .	Upperwoods .	Offerlane . .	Abbeyleix .	I.	251
26, 27	Gaskinstown .	316	1	28	Meath . .	Lower Duleek .	Duleek . .	Drogheda .	I.	195
17	Gaterstreet . .	1	3	8	Galway . .	Ballymoe . .	Dunmore . .	Tuam . .	IV.	7
39	Gates . . .	97	3	25	Waterford .	Decies within Drum	Ardmore . .	Dungarvan .	II.	350
3	Gateside . . .	145	0	37	Londonderry .	North East Liberties of Coleraine	Coleraine . .	Coleraine . .	III.	246
52	Gatterstown .	214	3	18	Tipperary, S.R.	Kilnamanagh Lower	Clogher . .	Cashel . .	II.	322
10	Gaulross . . .	362	0	16	Tipperary, N.R.	Lower Ormond .	Borrisokane . .	Borrisokane .	II.	282
10, 11	Gaulstown . .	485	2	11	Kilkenny . .	Fassadinin .	Muckalee . .	Castlecomer .	I.	91
43	Gaulstown . .	251	2	21q	Kilkenny . .	Ida . . .	Gaulskill . .	Waterford .	I.	102
41, 44	Gaulstown . .	143	0	5	Kilkenny . .	Ida . . .	Kilcolumb . .	Waterford .	I.	102
26, 32	Gaulstown . .	245	1	33	Meath . .	Lower Duleek .	Duleek . .	Drogheda .	I.	195
38	Gaulstown . .	135	2	7	Meath . .	Ratoath . .	Dunshaughlin .	Dunshaughlin .	I.	218
26, 32, 33	Gaulstown . .	69	3	6	Meath . .	Skreen . . .	Timoole . . .	Dunshaghlin .	I.	222

(a) Including 43A. 0R. 28P. water.
(b) Including 12A. 1R. 10P. water.
(c) Including 5A. 1R. 18P. water.
(d) Including 2A. 2R. 12P. water.
(e) Including 3A. 2R. 5P. water.
(f) Including 7A. 0R. 18P. water.

(g) Including 2A. 3R. 39P. water.
(h) Including 5A. 2R. 16P. water.
(i) Including 4A. 3R. 32P. water.
(j) Including 4A. 3R. 16P. water.
(k) Including 58A. 3R. 3P. water.
(l) Including 23A. 3R. 23P. water.

(m) Including 26A. 2R. 0P. water.
(n) Including 3A. 2R. 4P. water.
(o) Including 49A. 0R. 19P. water.
(p) Including 22A. 3R. 32P. water.
(q) Including 1A. 3R. 36P. water.

No. of Sheet of the Ordnance Survey Maps.	Townlands and Towns.	Area in Statute Acres.	County.	Barony.	Parish.	Poor Law Union in 1857.	Townland Census of 1851, Part I.	
		A. R. P.					Page	Vol.
44	Gaulstown . .	429 1 3	Meath . .	Upper Deece . .	Culmullin . .	Dunshaughlin .	I.	193
17	Gaulstown . .	270 1 20	Waterford .	Middlethird . .	Lisnakill . .	Waterford .	II.	368
13, 18	Gaulstown Lower .	330 2 22	Kilkenny .	Crannagh . .	Ballinamara .	Kilkenny . .	I.	84
13, 18	Gaulstown Upper .	373 3 15	Kilkenny .	Crannagh . .	Ballinamara .	Kilkenny . .	I.	84
34	Gaurus . . .	167 1 22	Clare . .	Bunratty Upper .	Doora . . .	Ennis . .	II.	8
31	Gawny . . .	31 2 13	Westmeath .	Moycashel . .	Ardnurcher or Horse-leap . .	Mullingar .	I.	276
26	Gaybrook Demesne	845 2 33a	Westmeath .	Fartullagh . .	Enniscoffey .	Mullingar .	I.	276
17	Gayfield . . .	75 3 12	King's Co. .	Ballycowan .	Kilbride . .	Tullamore .	I.	268
10	Gay Island . .	1 1 6	Fermanagh .	Lurg . . .	Magheraculmoney .	Lowtherstown .	III.	127
42	Gaynestown . .	177 0 5	Wexford .	Bargy . . .	Kilmannan . .	Wexford . .	I.	306
16	Geaglom . .	333 2 31	Leitrim . .	Drumahaire . .	Inishmagrath .	Manorhamilton	IV.	96
39	Geaglum . .	137 2 19b	Fermanagh .	Knockninny .	Kinawley . .	Lisnaskea .	III.	202
44	Gearagh . .	167 3 0	Cork, E.R. .	Barrymore . .	Rathcormack .	Fermoy . .	II.	57
35, 36	Gearagh . .	159 1 21c	Cork, E.R. .	Condons and Clan-gibbon .	Clondulane .	Fermoy . .	II.	60
76	Gearagh . .	258 2 28	Cork, E.R. .	Imokilly . . .	Middleton . .	Middleton .	II.	89
105, 106	Gearagh . .	100 2 34	Cork, W.R. .	Bantry . . .	Kilmocomoge .	Bantry . .	II.	121
121, 122	Gearagh . .	498 3 17	Cork, W.R. .	Ibane and Barryroe	Kilmeen . . .	Clonakilty .	II.	149
70, 71	Gearagh East .	68 1 1	Cork, W.R. .	West Muskerry .	Macloneigh .	Macroom .	II.	160
70	Gearagh West .	37 0 21	Cork, W.R. .	West Muskerry .	Macloneigh .	Macroom .	II.	160
32	Gearanaskagh .	280 3 17d	Cork, E.R. .	Duhallow . .	Ballyclogh .	Mallow . .	II.	67
39, 48	Geararoe . .	76 0 15	Cork, W.R. .	West Muskerry .	Drishane . .	Millstreet .	II.	156
65	Gearha . .	337 0 25	Kerry . .	Dunkerron North .	Knockane . .	Killarney .	II.	182
91, 100	Gearha . .	491 2 7	Kerry . .	Dunkerron South .	Kilcrohane .	Kenmare .	II.	183
102	Gearha . .	331 0 0	Kerry . .	Glanarought .	Kilcaskan .	Kenmare .	II.	187
48	Gearha . .	457 3 35	Kerry . .	Magunihy . .	Molahiffe .	Killarney .	II.	205
93	Gearhadiveen .	403 2 25	Kerry . .	Glanarought .	Kenmare . .	Kenmare .	II.	186
117, 130	Gearhameen .	645 2 18	Cork, W.R. .	West Carbery (W.D.)	Durrus . .	Bantry . .	II.	142
73, 74	Gearhameen .	983 2 33	Kerry . .	Dunkerron North .	Knockane . .	Killarney .	II.	182
73, 74	Gearhameen .	48 2 25	Kerry . .	Dunkerron South .	Knockane . .	Killarney .	II.	184
102, 103	Gearhanagoul .	806 1 5	Kerry . .	Glanarought .	Kilcaskan .	Kenmare .	II.	187
82, 91, 92	Gearha North .	431 1 26	Kerry . .	Dunkerron South .	Templenoe .	Kenmare .	II.	185
83	Gearhasallagh .	984 2 30	Kerry . .	Dunkerron South .	Templenoe .	Kenmare .	II.	185
91, 92	Gearha South .	519 0 29	Kerry . .	Dunkerron South .	Templenoe .	Kenmare .	II.	185
26	Geashill . .	29 1 17	King's Co. .	Geashill . .	Geashill . .	Tullamore .	I.	140
26	GEASHILL T. .	—	King's Co. .	Geashill . .	Geashill . .	Tullamore .	I.	140
22	Geehanstown .	535 3 21	Meath . .	Fore . . .	Killallon . .	Oldcastle .	I.	200
102, 112	Geehy North .	68 1 35	Galway . .	Kiltartan . .	Kinvarradoorus .	Gort . .	IV.	49
112	Geehy South .	134 2 34	Galway . .	Kiltartan . .	Kinvarradoorus .	Gort . .	IV.	49
57, 58, 60	Geeragh . .	423 3 7	Limerick . .	Coshlea . .	Kilbeheny .	Mitchelstown .	II.	239
5, 6	Geevraun . .	762 0 35	Mayo . .	Tirawley . .	Doonfeeny .	Killala . .	IV.	167
5, 6, 10	Gelshagh . .	539 0 6	Longford . .	Granard . .	Columbkille .	Granard . .	I.	156
17	Genagh . .	196 0 35	Monaghan .	Dartree . .	Aghabog . .	Clones . .	III.	263
52	Genstown . .	148 2 7	Wexford .	Bargy . . .	Tomhaggard .	Wexford . .	I.	308
61	George's Land .	104 2 5	Tipperary, S.R. .	Middlethird .	St. Patricksrock .	Cashel . .	II.	331
16, 25	Georgestown .	450 1 31	Waterford .	Decies without Drum	Kilbarrymeaden .	Kilmacthomas .	II.	356
37	Georgia or Gorteen-oran . .	56 0 20	Leitrim . .	Mohill . . .	Mohill . .	Mohill . .	IV.	108
117, 130	Gerahies . . .	325 3 16	Cork, W.R. .	West Carbery (W.D.)	Kilcrohane .	Bantry . .	II.	143
35	Geraldine . .	356 0 39	Kildare . .	Narragh and Reban West .	Kilberry . .	Athy . .	I.	68
18, 19	Gernonstown .	674 1 39	Meath . .	Upper Slane . .	Gernonstown .	Navan . .	I.	224
7	Gerrardstown .	235 3 14	Dublin . .	Balrothery West .	Ballyboghil .	Balrothery .	I.	22
31, 32	Gerrardstown .	369 1 14	Meath . .	Skreen . . .	Kilcarn . .	Navan . .	I.	220
13, 19	Gerrib Big .	208 0 28	Sligo . .	Tireragh . .	Skreen . .	Dromore West .	IV.	236
13	Gerrib Little .	126 1 6	Sligo . .	Tireragh . .	Skreen . .	Dromore West .	IV.	236
17	Gerry . . .	92 0 17	Wexford .	Ballaghkeen .	Donaghmore .	Gorey . .	I.	293
15	Geskanagh Glebe	79 1 23	Leitrim . .	Drumahaire . .	Killarga . .	Manorhamilton	IV.	98
77	Giantsgrave . .	256 0 21	Tipperary, S.R. .	Iffa and Offa East .	Rathronan . .	Clonmel . .	II.	316
46	Gibberpatrick .	202 0 28e	Wexford .	Bargy . . .	Duncormick .	Wexford . .	I.	304
46	Gibberwell .	196 2 15	Wexford .	Bargy . . .	Duncormick .	Wexford . .	I.	304
9	Gibbethill .	197 1 9f	Waterford .	Middlethird and Mu-nicipal Borough .	Trinity Without .	Waterford .	II.	369
34	Gibblockstown .	205 2 13	Meath . .	Upper Duleek .	Stamullin .	Drogheda .	I.	198
47	Gibboghstown .	37 2 21	Wexford .	Forth . . .	Ballymore .	Wexford . .	I.	308
21	Gibbons . .	247 3 21	Dublin . .	Uppercross . .	Tallaght . .	Dublin South .	I.	41
5	Gibbonsmoor .	9 0 35	Dublin . .	Balrothery East .	Balrothery .	Balrothery .	I.	19
40, 48	Gibbonstown .	91 0 5	Limerick . .	Coshlea . .	Athneasy .	Kilmallock .	II.	237
40, 48	Gibbonstown .	465 0 2	Limerick . .	Coshlea . .	Kilbreedy Major .	Kilmallock .	II.	239
15, 16	Gibbonstown .	313 0 36	Meath . .	Fore . . .	Killallon . .	Oldcastle .	I.	200
26, 30	Gibbonstown .	448 3 23	Westmeath .	Fartullagh . .	Kilbride . .	Mullingar .	I.	268
31	Gibb's Island .	12 2 8	Down . .	Dufferin . .	Killyleagh .	Downpatrick .	III.	167
46	Gibletstown .	110 0 30	Wexford .	Bargy . . .	Ambrosetown .	Wexford . .	I.	303

(a) Including 12A. 2R. 32P. water.
(b) Including 17A. 1R. 30P. water.
(c) Including 4A. 3R. 17P. water.
(d) Including 3A. 3R. 16P. water.
(e) Including 8A. 1R. 29P. detached portion.
(f) { Within the Municipal Boundary, 21A. 1R. 38P.
{ Without the Municipal Boundary 175A. 3R. 11P.

No. of Sheet of the Ordnance Survey Maps.	Townlands and Towns.	Area in Statute Acres.	County.	Barony.	Parish.	Poor Law Union in 1857.	Townland Census of 1851, Part I.	
		A. R. P.					Vol.	Page
21	Gibraltar	22 1 35	Dublin	Uppercross	Clondalkin	Dublin South	I.	39
37	Gibraltar	20 1 32	Meath	Lower Deece	Kiltale	Dunshaughlin	I.	192
21	Gibraltar	239 3 11	Wicklow	Upper Talbotstown	Rathbran	Baltinglass	I.	365
10	Gibraltar or Garran Otra	131 2 24	Monaghan	Monaghan	Tehallan	Monaghan	III.	280
7, 12	Gibstown	212 2 32	Louth	Upper Dundalk	Louth	Dundalk	I.	179
18	Gibstown	320 2 13	Meath	Upper Kells	Donaghpatrick	Navan	I.	205
24	Gibstown	93 0 34	Westmeath	Rathconrath	Killare	Mullingar	I.	283
21	Gibstown	313 1 19	Wicklow	Upper Talbotstown	Donaghmore	Baltinglass	I.	363
17, 18	Gibstown Demesne	1,043 0 14	Meath	Upper Kells	Donaghpatrick	Navan	I.	205
2	Giddaun	55 1 34	Roscommon	Boyle	Kilronan	Boyle	IV.	197
13	Gigginstown	568 1 1	Westmeath	Delvin	Killulagh	Castletowndelvin	I.	266
13	Gilbertstown	142 1 30	Carlow	Forth	Gilbertstown	Carlow	I.	4
92	Gilbertstown	562 3 18d	Donegal	Banagh	Killaghtee	Donegal	III.	109
14	Gilbertstown	39 2 6	Louth	Ardee	Clonkeen	Ardee	I.	172
14	Gilbertstown	237 0 38	Louth	Louth	Mansfieldstown	Ardee	I.	185
41, 42	Gilbertstown	394 0 26	Meath	Lower Moyfenrath	Rathmolyon	Trim	I.	211
3	Gilbertstown	186 3 2	Westmeath	Fore	Lickbla	Castletowndelvin	I.	270
32, 33	Gilbinstown	374 2 21	Kildare	Kilcullen	Kilcullen	Naas	I.	58
62	Gilcagh	541 2 14	Cork, E.R.	East Muskerry	Matehy	Cork	II.	105
6	Gilford	92 0 1	Monaghan	Monaghan	Tedavnet	Monaghan	III.	279
26	GILFORD T.	—	Down	Lower Iveagh, Up. pt.	Tullylish	Banbridge	III.	171
58, 59	Gilkagh	553 3 5	Galway	Tiaquin	Moylough	Mountbellew	IV.	80
2	Gilkagh East	106 3 26	Galway	Ballymoe	Kilcroan	Glennamaddy	IV.	9
2	Gilkagh West	141 1 23	Galway	Ballymoe	Kilcroan	Glennamaddy	IV.	9
23, 29	Gilky Hill	126 1 7	Londonderry	Tirkeeran	Cumber Upper	Londonderry	III.	249
74	Gillabbey	83 0 0b	Cork, E.R.	Cork and Municipal Borough	St. Finbars	Cork	II.	66
7, 8	Gillardstown	933 1 27	Westmeath	Fore	St. Feighins	Castletowndelvin	I.	272
32, 33	Gilliamstown	175 0 27	Meath	Skreen	Timoole	Dunshaughlin	I.	222
26, 27	Gillinstown	324 1 27	Meath	Lower Duleek	Duleek	Drogheda	I.	195
36,37,42,43	Gillistown	554 0 29	Antrim	Upper Toome	Ballyscullion Grange	Ballymena	III.	33
63	Gilloge	163 3 2	Clare	Tulla Lower	Kiltenanlea	Limerick	II.	37
11, 12	Gills	287 3 25	Londonderry	Coleraine	Macosquin	Coleraine	III.	233
63	Gillstown	79 3 0	Donegal	Raphoe	Taughboyne	Strabane	III.	143
31, 32	Gillstown	266 3 31	Meath	Skreen	Templekeeran	Navan	I.	222
31	Gillstown	223 0 19c	Meath	Upper Navan	Bective	Navan	I.	216
23	Gillstown	193 0 12	Roscommon	Ballintober North	Kilglass	Strokestown	IV.	186
23, 24	Gillstown Great	390 1 10	Meath	Lune	Rathmore	Trim	I.	208
23, 24	Gillstown Little	513 0 33	Meath	Lune	Rathmore	Trim	I.	208
9	Gilltown	932 1 1	Kildare	Clane	Balinyafagh	Naas	I.	53
28, 29	Gilltown	1,195 3 8	Kildare	Naas South	Gilltown	Naas	I.	65
26	Gilltown	485 0 31d	Meath	Lower Duleek	Knockcommon	Navan	I.	196
28	Gilltown Common	5 2 2	Kildare	Kilcullen	Kilcullen	Naas	I.	58
34	Gillygooly	434 1 8e	Tyrone	Omagh East	Drumragh	Omagh	III.	312
21	Gillyholme (Ely)	114 0 32	Fermanagh	Magheraboy	Devenish	Enniskillen	III.	211
15, 21	Gillyholme(L'Estrange)	122 3 29	Fermanagh	Magheraboy	Devenish	Enniskillen	III.	211
5, 10	Gilnahirk	499 3 5	Down	Castlereagh Lower	Knockbreda	Belfast	III.	163
129, 133	Gilroe	340 3 24f	Galway	Kiltartan	Beagh	Gort	IV.	46
15	Giltagh	108 3 19	Fermanagh	Magheraboy	Devenish	Enniskillen	III.	211
23, 28	Giltagh	202 2 3	Fermanagh	Magherastephana	Aghavea	Lisnaskea	III.	219
8	Giltspur	206 0 31	Wicklow	Rathdown	Bray	Rathdown	I.	354
18, 19	Gingerstown	195 3 20g	Kildare	Clane	Carragh	Naas	I.	53
30, 44	Ginnaun	172 0 7	Galway	Ballymoe	Tuam	Tuam	IV.	10
37, 43	Ginnets Great	694 2 38	Meath	Lower Deece	Agher	Trim	I.	191
43	Ginnets Little	74 0 6	Meath	Lower Deece	Agher	Trim	I.	191
3	Girfin	25 2 14	Monaghan	Trough	Errigal Trough	Clogher	III.	284
23	Girley	1,123 3 32	Meath	Upper Kells	Girley	Kells	I.	205
34, 35	Glack	377 0 4	Donegal	Kilmacrenan	Clondahorky	Dunfanaghy	III.	123
2, 4	Glack	313 3 11	Leitrim	Rosclogher	Rossinver	Ballyshannon	IV.	111
16, 24	Glack	1,373 3 27	Londonderry	Keenaght	Tamlaght Finlagan	New Tn Limavady	III.	237
13, 14	Glack	107 1 9	Longford	Ardagh	Templemichael	Longford	I.	154
13, 14	Glack	332 3 33	Louth	Ardee	Clonkeen	Ardee	I.	172
35, 41	Glack	402 1 27	Meath	Lune	Killaconnigan	Trim	I.	208
60	Glack	411 3 5	Tyrone	Dungannon Lower	Carnteel	Clogher	III.	297
5, 12	Glackadrumman	576 0 26	Donegal	Inishowen East	Clonca	Inishowen	III.	117
17, 20	Glackaunadarragh	1,070 1 0	Leitrim	Drumahaire	Inishmagrath	Manorhamilton	IV.	96
9	Glackbaun	228 2 27	Sligo	Carbury	Calry	Sligo	IV.	220
37, 38	Glack or Bohullion	296 0 20	Donegal	Inishowen West	Inch	Londonderry	III.	121
13	Glackstown	658 1 11h	Westmeath	Delvin	Killulagh	Castletowndelvin	I.	266
9	Gladree	554 0 35	Mayo	Erris	Kilmore	Belmullet	IV.	146
48	Glaglig	27 0 13	Wexford	Forth	St. Iberius	Wexford	I.	314
121	Glan	194 1 3	Cork, W.R.	East Carbery (E.D.)	Ballymoney	Dunmanway	II.	127

(a) Including 9A. 3R. 12P. water.
(b) { Including 16A. 3R. 15P. water.
{ Within the Municipal Boundary, 45A. 2R. 2P.
{ Without the Municipal Boundary, 67A. 1R. 38P.

(c) Including 0A. 3R. 16P. water.
(d) Including 0A. 3R. 24P. water.
(e) Including 0A. 1R. 30P. water.

(f) Including 5A. 2R. 11P. water.
(g) Including 2A. 0R. 0P. water.
(h) Including 6A. 3R. 28P. water.

3 P

No. of Sheet of the Ordnance Survey Maps.	Townlands and Towns.	Area in Statute Acres.	County.	Barony.	Parish.	Poor Law Union in 1857.	Townland Census of 1851, Part I.	
		A. R. P.					Vol.	Page
94	Glan . .	395 0 24	Cork, W.R.	East Carbery (W.D.)	Fanlobbus . .	Dunmanway .	II.	131
139	Glan . .	1,046 3 16	Cork, W.R.	West Carbery (W.D.)	Skull . .	Skull . .	II.	146
106, 119	Glanaclogha .	587 1 33	Cork, W.R.	West Carbery(E.D.)	Dromdaleague .	Skibbereen .	II.	140
16, 17, 22	Glanaderhig .	499 3 21	Kerry .	Clanmaurice .	Kilshenane .	Listowel .	II.	172
30	Glanageenty .	421 3 30	Kerry .	Trughanacmy .	Ballymacelligott .	Tralee .	II.	207
88, 99, 100	Glanagow .	138 1 7	Cork, E.R.	Imokilly . .	Corkbeg . . .	Middleton .	II.	86
35, 44	Glanakip .	678 2 8	Cork, E.R.	Barrymore .	Rathcormack .	Fermoy .	II.	57
129	Glanalin .	96 1 23	Cork, W.R.	West Carbery(W.D.)	Kilcrohane .	Bantry .	II.	143
70	Glananarig .	393 0 18	Cork, W.R.	West Muskerry .	Clondrohid .	Macroom .	II.	155
132	Glanaphuca .	629 0 36	Cork, W.R.	West Carbery(W.D.)	Caheragh .	Skibbereen .	II.	142
67	Glanaradotia .	27 3 21	Cork, E.R.	Imokilly . .	Youghal . .	Youghal .	II.	91
106	Glanareagh .	743 0 8	Cork, W.R.	Bantry . .	Kilmocomoge .	Bantry .	II.	121
126	Glanarough .	215 2 14	Cork, W.R.	Bear . .	Kilmanagh .	Castletown .	II.	125
119	Glanatnaw .	690 1 30	Cork, W.R.	West Carbery (W.D.)	Caheragh .	Skibbereen .	II.	142
124	Glanavaud .	98 1 14	Cork, W.R.	East Carbery (E.D.)	Ringrone .	Kinsale .	II.	130
124, 137	Glanavirane .	91 3 37	Cork, W.R.	East Carbery (E.D.)	Ringrone .	Kinsale .	II.	130
124, 137	Glanavirane .	107 1 34	Cork, W.R.	East Carbery (E.D.)	Templetrine .	Kinsale .	II.	130
41, 50	Glanawaddra .	1,415 2 11	Kerry .	Trughanacmy .	Ballincuslane .	Tralee .	II.	206
2	Glanawillin .	224 1 29	Kerry .	Iraghticonnor .	Aghavallen .	Listowel .	II.	189
22	Glanballyma .	397 0 6	Kerry .	Clanmaurice .	Kilflyn . .	Tralee .	II.	170
39	Glanbane .	448 0 13	Kerry .	Trughanacmy .	Currans . .	Killarney .	II.	209
106, 119	Glanbannoo Lower .	196 1 30	Cork, W.R.	Bantry . .	Kilmocomoge .	Bantry .	II.	121
106, 119	Glanbannoo Upper .	512 3 8	Cork, W.R.	Bantry . .	Kilmocomoge .	Bantry .	II.	121
112	Glanbeg . .	21 0 28	Cork, E.R.	Kinsale . .	Ringcurran .	Kinsale .	II.	100
106	Glanbeg . .	144 1 20	Kerry .	Dunkerron South .	Kilcrohane .	Cahersiveen .	II.	183
98	Glanbeg . .	362 2 14	Kerry .	Iveragh . .	Dromod . .	Cahersiveen .	II.	195
121, 134	Glanbrack .	534 1 0	Cork, W.R.	East Carbery (W.D.)	Ross . .	Clonakilty .	II.	135
51	Glancam . .	527 1 19	Cork, E.R.	Barretts . .	Grenagh . .	Cork .	II.	49
3	Glancullare North .	117 1 14	Kerry .	Iraghticonnor .	Kilnaughtin .	Glin . .	II.	191
3, 6	Glancullare South .	389 3 26	Kerry .	Iraghticonnor .	Kilnaughtin .	Glin . .	II.	191
64, 65	Glancuttaun Lower	1,124 2 33	Kerry .	Dunkerron North .	Killorglin .	Cahersiveen .	II.	181
64, 72, 73	Glancuttaun Upper	897 2 25	Kerry .	Dunkerron North .	Killorglin .	Cahersiveen .	II.	181
49, 59	Glandaeagh .	633 1 1	Kerry .	Trughanacmy .	Killeentierna .	Killarney .	II.	211
8, 14	Glandahalin East .	611 3 14	Kerry .	Clanmaurice .	Ballyheige .	Tralee .	II.	168
8, 14	Glandahalin West .	236 1 34	Kerry .	Clanmaurice .	Ballyheige .	Tralee .	II.	168
106, 119	Glandart .	385 2 26	Cork, W.R.	West Carbery (E.D.)	Dromdaleague .	Skibbereen .	II.	140
119	Glandarta .	471 0 29	Cork, W.R.	West Carbery (W.D.)	Caheragh .	Skibbereen .	II.	142
41, 50	Glandine . .	755 3 1	Cork, E.R.	Duhallow .	Kilshannig .	Mallow .	II.	74
37	Glandine . .	152 1 13	Kerry .	Corkaguiny .	Kilgobban .	Tralee .	II.	177
34, 43	Glandonohoe .	1,227 3 34	Cork, E.R.	Fermoy . .	Bridgetown .	Fermoy .	II.	77
6, 11	Glandoran Lower .	153 3 8	Wexford .	Gorey . .	Kilnahue .	Gorey .	I.	319
6	Glandoran Upper .	75 2 15	Wexford .	Gorey . .	Kilnahue .	Gorey .	I.	319
142	GLANDORE T. .	—	Cork, W.R.	East Carbery (W.D.)	Kilfaughnabeg .	Skibbereen .	II.	133
123, 124	Glanduff .	464 2 28	Cork, W.R.	East Carbery (E.D.)	Rathclarin .	Bandon .	II.	130
87, 96	Glanearagh .	234 0 6	Kerry .	Iveragh . .	Killemlagh .	Cahersiveen .	II.	196
37	Glane Great .	168 3 35	Meath .	Lower Deece .	Knockmark .	Dunshaughlin .	I.	192
37	Glane Little .	74 0 36	Meath .	Lower Deece .	Knockmark .	Dunshaughlin .	I.	192
9, 15	Glanerdalliv .	258 2 29	Kerry .	Clanmaurice .	Rattoo . .	Listowel .	II.	173
52	Glanfahan .	513 3 8	Kerry .	Corkaguiny .	Ballinvoher .	Dingle .	II.	174
60	Glangristeen .	289 2 21	Kerry .	Magunihy .	Kilcummin .	Killarney .	II.	201
21	Glankeagh .	155 0 17	Kerry .	Clanmaurice .	O'Dorney .	Tralee .	II.	172
74	Glankittane .	60 3 16	Cork, E.R.	Cork,MunicipalBor.of	St. Annes Shandon .	Cork .	II.	111
31, 40	Glanlarehan .	549 0 16	Kerry .	Trughanacmy .	Ballincuslane .	Tralee .	II.	206
49, 59	Glanlea . .	851 2 36	Kerry .	Trughanacmy .	Dysert . .	Tralee .	II.	210
79	Glanleam .	257 1 7	Kerry .	Iveragh . .	Valencia . .	Cahersiveen .	II.	198
52	Glanlick . .	74 1 25	Kerry .	Corkaguiny .	Dunquin .	Dingle .	II.	176
117, 130	Glanlough .	1,183 1 30a	Cork, W.R.	West Carbery (W.D.)	Kilcrohane .	Bantry .	II.	143
131	Glanlough .	341 2 10	Cork, W.R.	West Carbery (W.D.)	Kilmocomoge .	Bantry .	II.	144
99, 107	Glanlough Lower .	284 2 21	Kerry .	Dunkerron South .	Kilcrohane .	Kenmare .	II.	183
36	Glanlough North .	120 3 31	Kerry .	Corkaguiny .	Killiney .	Dingle .	II.	178
36, 45	Glanlough South .	735 1 35b	Kerry .	Corkaguiny .	Killiney .	Dingle .	II.	178
99, 107	Glanlough Upper .	306 2 1c	Kerry .	Dunkerron South .	Kilcrohane .	Kenmare .	II.	183
36, 45	Glanlough West .	344 3 28	Kerry .	Corkaguiny .	Killiney .	Dingle .	II.	178
72, 82	Glanmakee .	761 1 37	Kerry .	Dunkerron North .	Knockane .	Cahersiveen .	II.	182
36, 45	Glanmane .	352 3 38	Kerry .	Corkaguiny .	Killiney .	Dingle .	II.	178
54	Glanminard .	374 0 30	Kerry .	Corkaguiny .	Minard . .	Dingle .	II.	180
41	Glanminnane .	541 0 9	Cork, E.R.	Duhallow .	Kilshannig .	Mallow .	II.	74
74	GLANMIRE T. .	—	Cork, E.R.	Cork . .	Rathcooney .	Cork .	II.	65
42	Glanmore .	126 1 19	Kerry .	Corkaguiny .	Dunquin .	Dingle .	II.	176
45	Glanmore .	554 2 27	Kerry .	Corkaguiny .	Kilgobban .	Tralee .	II.	177
111	Glanmore .	2,915 1 05	Kerry .	Glanarought .	Tuosist . .	Kenmare .	II.	188
150	Glannafeen .	259 0 12	Cork, W.R.	West Carbery (E.D.)	Tullagh . .	Skibbereen .	II.	141
36, 45	Glannagalt .	370 2 30	Kerry .	Corkaguiny .	Kilgobban .	Tralee .	II.	177

(a) Including 10A. 3R. 15P. water.   (b) Including 15A. 3R. 28P. water.   (c) Including 6A. 0R. 1P. water.

No. of Sheet of the Ordnance Survey Maps.	Townlands and Towns.	Area in Statute Acres.			County.	Barony.	Parish.	Poor Law Union in 1857.	Townland Census of 1851, Part I.	
		A.	R.	P.					Vol.	Page
44	Glannagaul	1,320	1	36	Cork, E.R.	Barrymore	Rathcormack	Fermoy	II.	57
33, 34	Glannagear	423	2	26	Cork, E.R.	Fermoy	Monanimy	Mallow	II.	81
150	Glannageel	110	2	26	Cork, W.R.	West Carbery (E.D.)	Castlehaven	Skibbereen	II.	138
14	Glannagh	243	0	27	Longford	Granard	Killoe	Granard	I.	157
56, 64	Glannagilliagh	977	3	9	Kerry	Iveragh	Killorglin	Killarney	II.	197
41, 50	Glannaharee East	1,081	2	10	Cork, E.R.	Duhallow	Kilshannig	Mallow	II.	74
40, 41, 50	Glannaharee West	533	2	30	Cork, E.R.	Duhallow	Kilshannig	Mallow	II.	74
19	Glannahary	251	0	8	Carlow	Idrone East	Lorum	Carlow	I.	8
16, 19	Glannahary	109	0	21	Carlow	Idrone East	Sliguff	Carlow	I.	8
45	Glannaheera	393	3	15	Kerry	Corkaguiny	Ballinvoher	Dingle	II.	174
131, 140	Glannakilleenagh	286	2	30	Cork, W.R.	West Carbery(W.D.)	Kilcoe	Skull	II.	143
6, 7	Glannalappa East	729	0	30	Kerry	Iraghticonnor	Murher	Glin	II.	193
6, 7	Glannalappa Middle	188	0	22	Kerry	Iraghticonnor	Murher	Glin	II.	193
6	Glannalappa West	201	0	8	Kerry	Iraghticonnor	Murher	Glin	II.	193
7	Glannan	46	0	11	Monaghan	Trough	Donagh	Monaghan	III.	282
83	Glannarouge East	102	3	33	Cork, W.R.	West Muskerry	Kilmurry	Macroom	II.	159
83, 95	Glannarouge West	158	2	28	Cork, W.R.	West Muskerry	Kilmurry	Macroom	II.	159
43	Glannasack	485	0	20	Cork, E.R.	Barrymore	Ardnagechy	Fermoy	II.	50
41	Glannoge	411	2	39	Cork, E.R.	Duhallow	Kilshannig	Mallow	II.	74
16, 22	Glanoe	423	2	36	Kerry	Clanmaurice	Kilfeighny	Listowel	II.	170
41	Glanowen	1,718	2	21	Kerry	Trughanacmy	Ballincuslane	Tralee	II.	206
109	Glanrastel	2,629	0	17	Kerry	Glanarought	Tuosist	Kenmare	II.	188
44	Glanreagh	23	0	8	Cork, E.R.	Barrymore	Rathcormack	Fermoy	II.	57
129	Glanroon	144	2	2	Cork, W.R.	West Carbery(W.D.)	Kilcrohane	Bantry	II.	143
131	Glansallagh	137	1	16	Cork, W.R.	West Carbery(W.D.)	Skull	Skull	II.	146
34, 35, 43	Glanshanacuirp	2,339	2	13a	Kerry	Corkaguiny	Cloghane	Dingle	II.	175
40	Glanshearoon	324	0	1	Kerry	Trughanacmy	Castleisland	Tralee	II.	208
28	Glansheskin	217	1	23	Cork, E.R.	Condons&Clangibbon	Kilworth	Fermoy	II.	62
3	Glansillagh	247	1	4	Kerry	Iraghticonnor	Kilnaughtin	Glin	II.	191
32, 41	Glantane	482	3	37	Cork, E.R.	Duhallow	Kilshannig	Mallow	II.	74
45	Glantane	310	0	2	Kerry	Corkaguiny	Ballinvoher	Dingle	II.	174
29	Glantane Beg	222	0	36	Cork, E.R.	Duhallow	Cullen	Millstreet	II.	70
48	Glantane East	651	1	1	Cork, W.R.	West Muskerry	Clondrohid	Macroom	II.	155
29	Glantane More	311	2	5	Cork, E.R.	Duhallow	Cullen	Millstreet	II.	70
32	Glantane T.	—			Cork, E.R.	Duhallow	Kilshannig	Mallow	II.	74
48	Glantane West	601	1	1	Cork, W.R.	West Muskerry	Clondrohid	Macroom	II.	155
32	Glantaunluskaha	282	1	38	Kerry	Trughanacmy	Brosna	Tralee	II.	208
22	Glantaunmacarthy	135	1	22	Cork, E.R.	Duhallow	Kilmeen	Kanturk	II.	73
22, 23	Glantaunyalkeen	643	0	30	Kerry	Clanmaurice	Kilshenane	Listowel	II.	172
35,36,44,45	Glanteenassig	3,187	0	4b	Kerry	Corkaguiny	Killiney	Dingle	II.	178
109	Glantrasna	2,105	3	37	Kerry	Glanarought	Tuosist	Kenmare	II.	188
100	Glanturkin	385	2	8c	Cork, E.R.	Imokilly	Corkbeg	Middleton	II.	86
27	Glanworth	435	0	5	Cork, E.R.	Fermoy	Glanworth	Fermoy	II.	79
27	Glanworth T.	—			Cork, E.R.	Fermoy	Glanworth	Fermoy	II.	79
92, 93, 106, 107	Glanycarney	1,206	2	7	Cork, W.R.	East Carbery (W.D.)	Kilmocomoge	Bantry	II.	134
6, 15	Glanycummane Lower	265	3	15	Cork, E.R.	Duhallow	Tullylease	Kanturk	II.	76
6, 15	Glanycummane Upper	329	0	33	Cork, E.R.	Duhallow	Tullylease	Kanturk	II.	76
46	Glar	113	0	9	Donegal	Raphoe	Allsaints	Londonderry	III.	134
15, 23	Glasakeeran	594	0	12	Londonderry	Tirkeeran	Faughanvale	New T. Limavady	III.	250
11, 19, 20	Glasalt or Treanfasy	1,448	3	10	Donegal	Inishowen East	Donagh	Inishowen	III.	118
103	Glasbolie	716	2	13	Donegal	Tirhugh	Drumhome	Ballyshannon	III.	146
44, 45	Glascarn	299	2	28	Meath	Ratoath	Ratoath	Dunshaughlin	I.	219
18	Glascarn	863	3	27	Westmeath	Moyashel and Magheradernon	Mullingar	Mullingar	I.	275
37	Glascarrick	294	1	13d	Cavan	Clanmahon	Drumlumman	Granard	III.	77
17	Glascarrig North	189	3	9	Wexford	Ballagheen	Donaghmore	Gorey	I.	293
17	Glascarrig South	352	3	27	Wexford	Ballaghkeen	Donaghmore	Gorey	I.	293
46	Glascloon	702	1	19	Clare	Ibrickan	Killard	Kilrush	II.	23
43	Glascloon	171	0	36	King's Co.	Ballybritt	Aghancon	Roscrea	I.	124
43	Glascloon	48	1	25	King's Co.	Ballybritt	Seirkieran	Roscrea	I.	127
45	Glascloon	236	2	2	King's Co.	Clonlisk	Dunkerrin	Roscrea	I.	130
53	Glascloyne	21	3	36	Tipperary, S.R.	Middlethird	Ballysheehan	Cashel	II.	325
12	Glascurram	213	3	37	Limerick	Pubblebrien	Kilkeedy	Limerick	II.	252
42	Glasderry Beg	212	1	7	King's Co.	Clonlisk	Ettagh	Roscrea	I.	130
38, 42	Glasderry More	754	1	18	King's Co.	Clonlisk	Ettagh	Roscrea	I.	130
31	Glasdrumman	1,137	1	9e	Armagh	Fews Upper	Creggan	Dundalk	III.	48
18	Glasdrumman	97	0	34	Armagh	Orior Lower	Ballymore	Newry	III.	55
22, 23	Glasdrumman	412	1	16	Cavan	Clankee	Knockbride	Cootehill	III.	73
16	Glasdrumman	158	2	5	Cavan	Tullygarvey	Annagh	Cootehill	III.	87
21, 26	Glasdrumman	195	2	11	Cavan	Upper Loughtee	Annagelliff	Cavan	III.	81
16	Glasdrumman	695	1	22f	Down	Castlereagh Upper	Saintfield	Lisburn	III.	166
22	Glasdrumman	1,110	1	16g	Down	Kinelarty	Magheradrool	Lisburn	III.	177

(a) Including 73A. 1R. 23P. water.
(b) Including 54A. 3R. 7P. water.
(c) Including 1A. 0R. 29P. detached portion.
(d) Including 11A. 2R. 24P. water.
(e) Including 19A. 0R. 35P. water.
(f) Including 4A. 3R. 23P. water.
(g) Including 42A. 3R. 15P. water.

3 P 2

No. of Sheet of the Ordnance Survey Maps	Townlands and Towns	Area in Statute Acres.			County.	Barony.	Parish.	Poor Law Union in 1857.	Townland Census of 1851, Part I.	
		A.	R.	P.					Vol.	Page
53	Glasdrumman	1,170	1	19	Down	Mourne	Kilkeel	Kilkeel	III.	183
38	Glasdrumman	282	1	9	Fermanagh	Knockninny	Kinawley	Lisnaskea	III.	202
1	Glasdrumman	130	2	7	Fermanagh	Lurg	Drumkeeran	Lowtherstown	III.	206
34	Glasdrumman	251	1	36	Fermanagh	Magherastephana	Aghalurcher	Lisnaskea	III.	216
22, 23	Glasdrumman	107	3	31	Fermanagh	Tirkennedy	Derrybrusk	Enniskillen	III.	220
28	Glasdrumman	180	1	0	Leitrim	Leitrim	Fenagh	Mohill	IV.	100
28	Glasdrumman	115	3	18	Leitrim	Mohill	Mohill	Mohill	IV.	108
3, 6	Glasdrumman	592	2	37	Leitrim	Rosclogher	Killasnet	Manorhamilton	IV.	110
9	Glasdrumman	168	3	26	Monaghan	Monaghan	Tedavnet	Monaghan	III.	279
2	Glasdrumman	111	1	33	Roscommon	Boyle	Kilronan	Boyle	IV.	197
30	Glasdrummanaghy	191	2	28	Armagh	Fews Upper	Creggan	Castleblayney	III.	48
15, 16, 17, 18	Glasdrumman Beg	140	1	9	Leitrim	Drumahaire	Inishmagrath	Manorhamilton	IV.	96
14	Glasdrumman East	174	1	34	Monaghan	Cremorne	Clontibret	Castleblayney	III.	260
15, 17	Glasdrumman More	284	1	8	Leitrim	Drumahaire	Inishmagrath	Manorhamilton	IV.	96
49, 53	Glasdrumman Upper	1,890	2	17	Down	Mourne	Kilkeel	Kilkeel	III.	183
14	Glasdrumman West	100	2	35	Monaghan	Cremorne	Clontibret	Monaghan	III.	260
17	Glasdrummond	287	1	1	Armagh	Fews Lower	Kilclooney	Armagh	III.	46
26	Glasdrummond	242	0	23	Armagh	Orior Upper	Killevy	Newry	III.	58
15, 19	Glasdrummond	133	1	21	Armagh	Tiranny	Tynan	Armagh	III.	60
12, 13	Glasdrummond	223	1	28	Monaghan	Dartree	Killeevan	Monaghan	III.	268
60	Glasdrummond	357	0	3	Tyrone	Dungannon Lower	Aghaloo	Dungannon	III.	296
32, 33	Glasganny	226	1	30	Wexford	Shelmaliere East	Ardcavan	Wexford	I.	329
12, 19	Glasgort	181	1	9	Londonderry	Coleraine	Agivey	Coleraine	III.	230
89, 99	Glasgort	307	3	35	Mayo	Carra	Ballintober	Castlebar	IV.	124
34	Glasha	154	1	20	Queen's Co.	Clandonagh	Rathdowney	Donaghmore	I.	234
5	Glasha	350	2	26	Waterford	Glenahiry	Kilronan	Clonmel	II.	365
8	Glasha Beg	281	1	19	Clare	Corcomroe	Killilagh	Ennistimon	II.	20
33	Glashabeg	98	3	21	Kerry	Corkaguiny	Kilmalkedar	Dingle	II.	178
43, 52	Glashaboy East	832	0	12	Cork, E.R.	Barrymore	Dunbulloge	Cork	II.	54
41, 50	Glashaboy East	567	3	9	Cork, E.R.	Duhallow	Kilshannig	Mallow	II.	74
42, 43, 51, 52	Glashaboy North	1,660	2	37	Cork, E.R.	Barrymore	Dunbulloge	Cork	II.	54
42, 51, 52	Glashaboy South	693	1	5	Cork, E.R.	Barrymore	Dunbulloge	Cork	II.	54
41, 50	Glashaboy West	633	2	36	Cork, E.R.	Duhallow	Kilshannig	Mallow	II.	74
76	Glashacormick	1,980	3	4	Kerry	Magunihy	Killaha	Killarney	II.	202
23, 24, 33	Glashagh	1,919	2	12a	Donegal	Kilmacrenan	Tullaghobegly	Dunfanaghy	III.	131
67	Glashagh Beg	867	3	13	Donegal	Raphoe	Kilteevoge	Stranorlar	III.	139
67	Glashagh More	1,123	0	4	Donegal	Raphoe	Kilteevoge	Stranorlar	III.	139
8	Glasha More	252	0	4	Clare	Corcomroe	Killilagh	Ennistimon	II.	20
22, 23	Glashanacree	742	2	33	Kerry	Clanmaurice	Kilshenane	Listowel	II.	172
23	Glashananoon	436	3	5	Kerry	Clanmaurice	Kilshenane	Listowel	II.	172
26, 27	Glashapullagh	490	0	34	Limerick	Shanid	Kilmoylan	Glin	II.	256
3, 8	Glashare	872	0	15	Kilkenny	Galmoy	Glashare	Urlingford	I.	92
48, 49	Glashbeggan	144	0	20b	Donegal	Boylagh	Templecrone	Glenties	III.	115
3	Glashedy Island	7	2	28	Donegal	Inishowen East	Clonmany	Inishowen	III.	117
111, 112	Glasheen	20	0	20	Cork, E.R.	Kinsale	Clontead	Kinsale	II.	99
70, 82	Glasheen	130	0	1	Cork, W.R.	West Muskerry	Inchigeelagh	Macroom	II.	157
13	Glasheenanargid	354	2	28	Cork, E.R.	Duhallow	Clonfert	Kanturk	II.	68
151	Glasheenaulin	133	1	8	Cork, W.R.	West Carbery (E.D.)	Castlehaven	Skibbereen	II.	138
37, 46	Glasheens	781	0	0	Mayo	Tirawley	Crossmolina	Ballina	IV.	166
5	Glashina	218	1	17	Wicklow	Lower Talbotstown	Burgage	Naas	I.	359
67, 76	Glashydevet	784	0	30	Donegal	Raphoe	Kilteevoge	Stranorlar	III.	139
11	Glashygolgan	516	0	29c	Tyrone	Strabane Upper	Bodoney Upper	Gortin	III.	324
104	Glaskeeragh	1,054	2	6d	Donegal	Tirhugh	Templecarn	Donegal	III.	149
7	Glaskenny	199	0	4	Wicklow	Rathdown	Powerscourt	Rathdown	I.	356
41	Glaskerbeg East	282	3	19	Down	Upper Iveagh, Up. pt.	Aghaderg	Banbridge	III.	174
41	Glaskerbeg West	249	0	10	Down	Upper Iveagh, Up. pt.	Aghaderg	Banbridge	III.	174
41	Glaskermore	578	1	22	Down	Upper Iveagh, Up. pt.	Aghaderg	Banbridge	III.	174
16	Glaskill	547	0	25	King's Co.	Ballycowan	Lynally	Tullamore	I.	128
46	Glaskill	56	3	26	King's Co.	Clonlisk	Borrisnafarney	Roscrea	I.	129
9	Glaslacken	237	1	8	Wexford	Scarawalsh	St. Marys Newtown-barry	Enniscorthy	I.	325
28	Glasleck	691	2	6e	Cavan	Clankee	Shercock	Bailieborough	III.	74
7	Glaslough	190	1	20f	Monaghan	Trough	Donagh	Monaghan	III.	282
7	GLASLOUGH T.	—			Monaghan	Trough	Donagh	Monaghan	III.	283
69	Glasly	176	3	1	Donegal	Raphoe	Convoy	Stranorlar	III.	136
100	Glasmansally	28	3	10	Mayo	Carra	Burriscarra	Castlebar	IV.	127
21, 26	Glasmullagh	157	0	5	Fermanagh	Clanawley	Cleenish	Enniskillen	III.	190
42	Glasmullagh	221	0	1	Fermanagh	Knockninny	Kinawley	Lisnaskea	III.	202
2, 6	Glasmullagh	186	2	12	Fermanagh	Lurg	Drumkeeran	Lowtherstown	III.	206
6	Glasmullagh	27	3	35	Fermanagh	Lurg	Magheraculmoney	Lowtherstown	III.	208
27	Glasmullagh	82	0	12	Fermanagh	Tirkennedy	Derrybrusk	Enniskillen	III	990
3	Glasmullagh	167	0	27	Monaghan	Trough	Errigal Trough	Monaghan	III.	284
54	Glasmullagh	255	2	9g	Tyrone	Dungannon Middle	Donaghmore	Dungannon	III.	302

(a) Including 26A. 2R. 5P. water.
(b) Including 24A. 1R. 30P. water.
(c) Including 4A. 3R. 29P. water.
(d) Including 102A. 1R. 32P. water.
(e) Including 66A. 1R. 14P. water.
(f) Including 27A. 3R. 30P. water.
(g) Including 16A. 3R. 25P. water.

No. of Sheet of the Ordnance Survey Maps.	Townlands and Towns.	Area in Statute Acres. A. R. P.	County.	Barony.	Parish.	Poor Law Union in 1857.	Townland Census of 1851, Part I. Vol.	Page
38	Glasmullagh	69 2 22	Tyrone	Dungannon Upper	Kildress	Cookstown	III.	309
25	Glasmullagh	713 3 22	Tyrone	Strabane Lower	Ardstraw	Omagh	III.	319
49,50,56,57	Glasmullagh North	195 0 19	Tyrone	Omagh East	Kilskeery	Lowtherstown	III.	313
56	Glasmullagh South	111 3 36	Tyrone	Omagh East	Kilskeery	Enniskillen	III.	313
19	Glasmullan	1,073 0 34a	Donegal	Inishowen West	Mintiaghs or Barr of Inch	Inishowen	III.	121
55	Glasmullan	40 2 39	Donegal	Raphoe	Killea	Londonderry	III.	139
19,20,24,25	Glasmullen	1,167 0 15	Antrim	Lower Glenarm	Layd	Ballycastle	III.	22
12	Glasnamullen	1,828 3 29	Wicklow	Ballinacor North	Calary	Rathdrum	I.	346
36	Glasnant	83 0 25	Donegal	Kilmacrenan	Kilmacrenan	Milford	III.	129
30	Glasnarget North	200 3 4	Wicklow	Newcastle	Kilcommon	Rathdrum	I.	351
30	Glasnarget South	149 0 10	Wicklow	Arklow	Kilcommon	Rathdrum	I.	345
14, 18	Glasnevin	53 1 4	Dublin	Coolock	Glasnevin	Dublin North	I.	27
14, 18	Glasnevin Demesne	3 0 6	Dublin	Castleknock	Finglas	Dublin North	I.	25
14, 18	Glasnevin Demesne	42 1 25	Dublin	Coolock	Glasnevin	Dublin North	I.	27
18	GLASNEVIN T.	—	Dublin	Coolock	Glasnevin	Dublin North	I.	27
87	Glaspatrick	823 2 29	Mayo	Murrisk	Oughaval	Westport	IV.	162
22	Glaspistol	501 2 17	Louth	Ferrard	Clogher	Drogheda	I.	180
13	Glassallen	339 1 18	Meath	Upper Slane	Collon	Ardee	I.	224
17	Glassalt	79 2 4	Leitrim	Drumahaire	Inishmagrath	Manorhamilton	IV.	96
24, 25	Glassamucky	422 0 0	Dublin	Uppercross	Tallaght	Dublin South	I.	41
25, 27	Glassamucky Brakes	1,115 2 21	Dublin	Uppercross	Tallaght	Dublin South	I.	41
25	Glassamucky Mountain	176 0 5	Dublin	Uppercross	Tallaght	Dublin South	I.	41
34, 35	Glassan	642 0 21b	Donegal	Kilmacrenan	Clondahorky	Dunfanaghy	III.	123
22	Glassan	149 0 10	Westmeath	Kilkenny West	Bunown	Athlone	I.	272
22	Glassan	47 3 16	Westmeath	Kilkenny West	Kilkenny West	Athlone	I.	273
7	Glassaneeran Lower	287 0 15	Antrim	Lower Dunluce	Billy	Ballymoney	III.	16
7	Glassaneeran Upper	218 2 18c	Antrim	Lower Dunluce	Billy	Ballymoney	III.	16
22	GLASSAN T.	—	Westmeath	Kilkenny West	Kilkenny West	Athlone	I.	274
24, 25, 27	Glassavullaun	1,090 2 19	Dublin	Uppercross	Tallaght	Dublin South	I.	41
51	Glassdrum	593 3 30	Tipperary, S.R.	Kilnamanagh Lower	Donohill	Tipperary	II.	323
31,32,35,36	Glassely	660 3 17	Kildare	Narragh & RebanEast	Narraghmore	Athy	I.	66
24	Glasserchoo	547 3 34d	Donegal	Kilmacrenan	Tullaghobegly	Dunfanaghy	III.	131
46	Glasshouse	245 3 6	Cork, E.R.	Kinnatalloon	Mogeely	Fermoy	II.	98
16, 24	Glasshouse	134 3 16	King's Co.	Ballycowan	Rahan	Tullamore	I.	128
42, 44, 45	Glasshouse	838 2 38	King's Co.	Clonlisk	Kilcomin	Roscrea	I.	131
43	Glassillan	25 2 0	Mayo	Erris	Kilcommon	Newport	IV.	145
43	Glassillan Island	0 1 11	Mayo	Erris	Kilcommon	Newport	IV.	145
10	Glassillaun	322 0 9	Galway	Ballynahinch	Ballynakill	Clifden	IV.	11
9	Glassillaun	2 0 35	Galway	Ballynahinch	Ballynakill	Clifden	IV.	12
78	Glassillaun	4 0 2	Galway	Moycullen	Kilcummin	Oughterard	IV.	68
48	Glassillaun Islands	1 3 11	Galway	Ballynahinch	Ballindoon	Clifden	IV.	10
49	Glassillaunvealancurra	6 2 29	Galway	Ballynahinch	Ballindoon	Clifden	IV.	11
32	Glass Island or Illancarragh	4 2 32	Donegal	Kilmacrenan	Tullaghobegly	Dunfanaghy	III.	132
10	Glassmoss	38 0 33	Down	Castlereagh Lower	Comber	Newtownards	III.	162
14, 19	Glasstown or Port	118 2 30	Cavan	Tullyhunco	Kildallan	Cavan	III.	97
29	Glaster	606 1 0	King's Co.	Garrycastle	Lusmagh	Parsonstown	I.	137
29, 30, 35	Glaster and Clonrah	261 3 25	King's Co.	Garrycastle	Lusmagh	Parsonstown	I.	137
23	Glasthule	66 1 4	Dublin	Rathdown	Monkstown	Rathdown	I.	36
23	GLASTHULE T.	—	Dublin	Rathdown	Monkstown	Rathdown	I.	37
63, 73	Glastrasna	390 2 33	Mayo	Costello	Kilbeagh	Swineford	IV.	140
33, 39	Glastrigan	525 3 1	Tipperary, N.R.	Upper Ormond	Templederry	Nenagh	II.	293
18	Glastry	897 0 3	Down	Ards Upper	Inishargy	Newtownards	III.	160
123	Glasvally	143 3 25	Mayo	Kilmaine	Shrule	Ballinrobe	IV.	158
18	Glasvaunta	91 1 35	Cork, E.R.	Condons&Clangibbon	Kildorrery	Mitchelstown	II.	61
9	Glasvey	128 1 18	Londonderry	Keenaght	Tamlaght Finlagan	NewT.Limavady	III.	237
12	Glear	125 3 35e	Monaghan	Dartree	Clones	Clones	III.	264
13	Glebe	37 2 5	Antrim	Cary	Armoy	Ballycastle	III.	11
8	Glebe	44 3 34	Antrim	Cary	Ramoan	Ballycastle	III.	14
1	Glebe	24 1 22	Antrim	Cary	Rathlin Island	Ballycastle	III.	15
27	Glebe	41 1 32	Antrim	Kilconway	Dunaghy	Ballymena	III.	26
22	Glebe	12 3 36	Antrim	Kilconway	Finvoy	Ballymoney	III.	26
26	Glebe	54 1 15	Antrim	Kilconway	Rasharkin	Ballymoney	III.	27
6	Glebe	8 2 27	Antrim	Lower Dunluce	Ballywillin	Coleraine	III.	15
7	Glebe	39 0 22	Antrim	Lower Dunluce	Billy	Coleraine	III.	16
12	Glebe	38 1 32	Antrim	Lower Dunluce	Derrykeighan	Ballymoney	III.	16
7	Glebe	29 3 37	Antrim	Lower Dunluce	Dunluce	Coleraine	III.	17
15	Glebe	9 1 28	Antrim	Lower Glenarm	Layd	Ballycastle	III.	22
29	Glebe	39 0 20	Antrim	Lower Glenarm	Tickmacrevan	Larne	III.	24
17	Glebe	33 2 15	Antrim	Upper Dunluce	Ballymoney	Ballymoney	III.	19
40	Glebe	8 2 13	Antrim	Upper Glenarm	Kilwaughter	Larne	III.	25
40	Glebe	9 1 26	Antrim	Upper Glenarm	Larne	Larne	III.	25

(a) Including 24A. 2R. 14P. water.
(b) Including 15A. 1R. 32P. water.
(c) Including 12A. 1R. 35P. water.
(d) Including 9A. 1R. 26P. water.
(e) Including 9A. 2R. 36P. water.

No. of Sheet of the Ordnance Survey Maps.	Townlands and Towns.	Area in Statute Acres.			County.	Barony.	Parish.	Poor Law Union in 1857.	Townland Census of 1851, Part I.	
		A.	R.	P.					Vol.	Page
37	Glebe	178	2	33	Antrim	Upper Toome	Ahoghill	Ballymena	III.	33
28	Glebe	93	1	25	Armagh	Orior Upper	Forkill	Newry	III.	57
21	Glebe	48	1	8	Carlow	Forth	Barragh	Enniscorthy	I.	4
12, 13, 16	Glebe	26	3	4	Carlow	Idrone East	Fennagh	Carlow	I.	7
12	Glebe	26	2	38	Carlow	Idrone West	Tullowcreen	Carlow	I.	9
9	Glebe	16	3	5	Carlow	Rathvilly	Clonmore	Shillelagh	I.	10
26	Glebe	33	3	28a	Carlow	St. Mullins Lower	St. Mullins	New Ross	I.	13
40, 44	Glebe	53	1	17b	Cavan	Castlerahan	Mullagh	Kells	III.	70
44	Glebe	3	0	39	Cavan	Castlerahan	Mullagh	Kells	III.	70
37	Glebe	20	1	0	Cavan	Clanmahon	Ballymachugh	Cavan	III.	76
17	Glebe	39	1	39	Cavan	Tullygarvey	Drumgoon	Cootehill	III.	88
15	Glebe	63	2	37	Clare	Corcomroe	Kilmanaheen	Ennistimon	II.	21
66	Glebe	14	2	0	Cork, E.R.	Barrymore	Dungourney	Middleton	II.	54
72	Glebe	69	3	21	Cork, E.R.	East Muskerry	Magourney	Macroom	II.	105
89	Glebe	10	2	15c	Cork, E.R.	Imokilly	Ballintemple	Middleton	II.	84
78	Glebe	10	3	26	Cork, E.R.	Imokilly	Clonpriest	Youghal	II.	85
76	Glebe	14	1	31	Cork, E.R.	Imokilly	Middleton	Middleton	II.	89
45	Glebe	4	1	2	Cork, E.R.	Kinnatalloon	Knockmourne	Fermoy	II.	98
121	Glebe	26	3	20	Cork, W.R.	East Carbery (W.D.)	Kilmeen	Clonakilty	II.	134
141	Glebe	43	3	33	Cork, W.R.	West Carbery (E.D.)	Aghadown	Skibbereen	II.	137
58	Glebe	63	0	25	Cork, W.R.	West Muskerry	Ballyvourney	Macroom	II.	154
70	Glebe	76	2	7	Cork, W.R.	West Muskerry	Clondrohid	Macroom	II.	155
81, 82	Glebe	249	3	8	Cork, W.R.	West Muskerry	Inchigeelagh	Macroom	II.	157
39	Glebe	13	2	29	Cork, W.R.	West Muskerry	Kilcorney	Millstreet	II.	158
70	Glebe	40	3	30	Cork, W.R.	West Muskerry	Kilnamartry	Macroom	II.	159
97	Glebe	101	3	21	Donegal	Banagh	Killybegs Upper	Glenties	III.	110
64	Glebe	81	2	0d	Donegal	Boylagh	Inishkeel	Glenties	III.	112
65	Glebe	66	0	5	Donegal	Boylagh	Lettermacward	Glenties	III.	114
11	Glebe	267	3	38	Donegal	Inishowen East	Donagh	Inishowen	III.	118
21	Glebe	99	1	35	Donegal	Inishowen East	Moville Upper	Inishowen	III.	119
18	Glebe	193	2	10	Donegal	Inishowen West	Desertegny	Inishowen	III.	120
38	Glebe	8	2	22	Donegal	Inishowen West	Fahan Upper	Londonderry	III.	121
53	Glebe	388	3	17e	Donegal	Kilmacrenan	Aghanunshin	Letterkenny	III.	122
44	Glebe	94	1	0f	Donegal	Kilmacrenan	Gartan	Letterkenny	III.	127
28	Glebe	6	2	14	Donegal	Kilmacrenan	Killygarvan	Millford	III.	128
16	Glebe	184	0	19	Donegal	Kilmacrenan	Mevagh	Millford	III.	130
24	Glebe	69	3	19	Donegal	Kilmacrenan	Tullaghobegly	Dunfanaghy	III.	131
70, 71	Glebe	38	0	1	Donegal	Raphoe	Clonleigh	Strabane	III.	135
68	Glebe	35	1	16g	Donegal	Raphoe	Kilteevoge	Stranorlar	III.	139
54	Glebe	7	1	25	Donegal	Raphoe	Raymoghy	Letterkenny	III.	142
78	Glebe	77	1	23	Donegal	Raphoe	Stranorlar	Stranorlar	III.	142
55	Glebe	8	1	33	Donegal	Raphoe	Taughboyne	Londonderry	III.	143
93, 99	Glebe	76	0	24	Donegal	Tirhugh	Donegal	Donegal	III.	145
31,32,38,39	Glebe	400	2	29	Down	Lecale Lower	Kilclief	Downpatrick	III.	179
44	Glebe	8	0	14	Down	Lecale Upper	Rathmullan	Downpatrick	III.	181
22	Glebe	91	0	14	Down	Lower Iveagh, Lr. pt.	Annahilt	Lisburn	III.	167
40, 41	Glebe	58	2	19	Down	Upper Iveagh, Up. pt.	Donaghmore	Newry	III.	175
6	Glebe	32	0	29	Dublin	Balrothery West	Ballymadun	Dunshaughlin	I.	22
7	Glebe	62	2	30	Dublin	Balrothery West	Clonmethan	Balrothery	I.	22
14	Glebe	6	3	0	Dublin	Castleknock	Finglas	Dublin North	I.	25
14, 15	Glebe	16	1	13	Dublin	Coolock	Portmarnock	Balrothery	I.	28
15, 19	Glebe	41	1	26	Dublin	Coolock	Raheny	Dublin North	I.	28
11	Glebe	5	3	29	Dublin	Coolock	Swords	Balrothery	I.	29
11	Glebe	52	0	28	Dublin	Nethercross	Kilsallaghan	Balrothery	I.	31
11	Glebe	31	0	9	Dublin	Nethercross	Swords	Balrothery	I.	32
17	Glebe	46	1	38	Dublin	Newcastle	Esker	Celbridge	I.	33
20, 21	Glebe	30	2	15	Dublin	Newcastle	Newcastle	Celbridge	I.	34
21	Glebe	6	1	22	Dublin	Newcastle	Rathcoole	Celbridge	I.	34
26	Glebe	23	0	21	Dublin	Rathdown	Kiltiernan	Rathdown	I.	36
26	Glebe	32	3	3	Dublin	Rathdown	Rathmichael	Rathdown	I.	37
23	Glebe	7	0	4	Dublin	Rathdown	Stillorgan	Rathdown	I.	37
70	Glebe	33	0	8	Galway	Clare	Annaghdown	Galway	IV.	16
43	Glebe	14	3	31	Galway	Clare	Cummer	Tuam	IV.	19
42	Glebe	55	0	27	Galway	Clare	Kilkilvery	Tuam	IV.	20
29, 43	Glebe	23	3	22	Galway	Clare	Tuam	Tuam	IV.	23
96	Glebe	53	3	25	Galway	Dunkellin	Kilconierin	Loughrea	IV.	29
86	Glebe	45	0	8	Galway	Kilconnell	Kilconnell	Ballinasloe	IV.	40
60	Glebe	132	1	10	Galway	Kilconnell	Kilosolan	Mountbellew	IV.	42
101	Glebe	66	2	4h	Galway	Longford	Clonfert	Ballinasloe	IV.	57
54	Glebe	37	2	9	Galway	Moycullen	Kilcummin	Oughterard	IV.	67
31	Glebe	65	1	6	Galway	Tiaquin	Kilkerrin	Glennamaddy	IV.	77
52	Glebe	44	1	18	Kerry	Corkaguiny	Dunquin	Dingle	II.	176
80	Glebe	100	3	27	Kerry	Iveragh	Killinane	Cahersiveen	II.	197

(a) Including 9A. 2R. 24P. detached portion.　　(d) Including 12A. 2R. 4P. water.　　(g) Including 1A. 2R. 4P. water.
(b) Including 19A. 3R. 7P. water.　　(e) Including 3A. 2R. 16P. detached portion.　　(h) Including 1A. 1R. 0P. detached portion.
(c) Including 4A. 1R. 16P. detached portion.　　(f) Including 45A. 3R. 25P. water.

No. of Sheet of the Ordnance Survey Maps.	Townlands and Towns.	Area in Statute Acres.			County.	Barony.	Parish.	Poor Law Union in 1857.	Townland Census of 1851, Part I.	
		A.	R.	P.					Vol.	Page
58	Glebe	49	2	10	Kerry	Magunihy	Kilcredane	Killarney	II.	200
58	Glebe	75	2	39	Kerry	Magunihy	Kilcummin	Killarney	II.	201
28	Glebe	34	0	29	Kerry	Trughanacmy	Ballynahaglish	Tralee	II.	207
36	Glebe	34	3	8	Kildare	Narragh & RebanEast	Timolin	Baltinglass	I.	67
10, 14	Glebe	81	1	13	Kildare	North Salt	Straffan	Celbridge	I.	76
5	Glebe	19	2	23	Kilkenny	Fassadinin	Castlecomer	Castlecomer	I.	88
8	Glebe	27	0	13	Kilkenny	Galmoy	Fertagh	Urlingford	I.	92
28	Glebe	75	3	1	Kilkenny	Gowran	Kilfane	Thomastown	I.	97
27	Glebe	34	1	13	Kilkenny	Kells	Kells	Callan	I.	108
31	Glebe	24	3	30	Kilkenny	Knocktopher	Knocktopher	Thomastown	I.	112
23	Glebe	51	2	18	Kilkenny	Shillelogher	Castleinch or Inchyolaghan	Kilkenny	I.	114
39	Glebe	22	1	23	King's Co.	Ballybritt	Aghancon	Roscrea	I.	124
36	Glebe	19	3	1	King's Co.	Ballybritt	Seirkieran	Parsonstown	I.	127
42	Glebe	60	0	27	King's Co.	Clonlisk	Ettagh	Roscrea	I.	130
42	Glebe	52	0	2	King's Co.	Clonlisk	Kilmurryely	Roscrea	I.	131
6	Glebe	128	2	23	King's Co.	Garrycastle	Clonmacnoise	Parsonstown	I.	135
6, 7	Glebe	127	2	5	King's Co.	Garrycastle	Lemanaghan	Parsonstown	I.	136
15	Glebe	35	0	37	King's Co.	Garrycastle	Wheery or Killagally	Parsonstown	I.	139
22, 25	Glebe	410	2	33a	Leitrim	Carrigallen	Drumreilly	Bawnboy	IV.	91
29	Glebe	44	3	8b	Leitrim	Leitrim	Fenagh	Mohill	IV.	100
7	Glebe	514	0	32	Leitrim	Rosclogher	Killasnet	Manorhamilton	IV.	110
24, 25	Glebe	41	0	14	Limerick	Coonagh	Oola	Tipperary	II.	235
21	Glebe	30	1	8	Limerick	Coshma	Drehidtarsna	Croom	II.	242
44	Glebe	44	1	2	Limerick	Glenquin	Killeedy	Newcastle	II.	245
36	Glebe	86	0	25	Limerick	Glenquin	Monagay	Newcastle	II.	247
5	Glebe	20	1	5	Limerick	Limerick, Municipal Borough of	Killeeny	Limerick	II.	262
22	Glebe	29	3	18	Limerick	Pubblebrien	Crecora	Croom	II.	252
12	Glebe	70	1	23	Limerick	Pubblebrien	Kilkeedy	Limerick	II.	252
5, 9	Glebe	32	1	19	Londonderry	Keenaght	Aghanloo	NewTⁿLimavady	III.	234
10, 17	Glebe	135	0	33	Londonderry	Keenaght	Balteagh	NewTⁿLimavady	III.	234
24	Glebe	79	2	19	Londonderry	Keenaght	Bovevagh	NewTⁿLimavady	III.	235
10	Glebe	113	2	15	Londonderry	Keenaght	Drumachose	NewTⁿLimavady	III.	235
5	Glebe	32	3	9	Londonderry	Keenaght	Magilligan	NewTⁿLimavady	III.	236
9	Glebe	249	3	11	Londonderry	Keenaght	Tamlaght Finlagan	NewTⁿLimavady	III.	237
36, 41	Glebe	161	3	12	Londonderry	Loughinsholin	Ballynascreen	Magherafelt	III.	239
32	Glebe	272	2	10	Londonderry	Loughinsholin	Killelagh	Magherafelt	III.	241
48	Glebe	92	3	27	Londonderry	Loughinsholin	Lissan	Magherafelt	III.	242
42	Glebe	10	2	29	Londonderry	Loughinsholin	Magherafelt	Magherafelt	III.	243
3	Glebe	32	3	32	Londonderry	North East Liberties of Coleraine	Ballyaghran	Coleraine	III.	244
8	Glebe	33	1	14	Londonderry	North East Liberties of Coleraine	Ballyrashane	Coleraine	III.	245
3	Glebe	22	2	22	Londonderry	North East Liberties of Coleraine	Ballywillin	Coleraine	III.	245
15	Glebe	409	1	30	Londonderry	Tirkeeran	Faughanvale	NewTⁿLimavady	III.	250
13	Glebe	24	3	2	Longford	Ardagh	Ballymacormick	Longford	I.	152
19, 23	Glebe	80	1	14	Longford	Ardagh	Kilglass	Ballymahon	I.	152
13	Glebe	42	0	13	Longford	Longford	Killashee	Longford	I.	158
21	Glebe	54	3	26	Longford	Rathcline	Cashel	Ballymahon	I.	163
17	Glebe	52	0	23	Longford	Rathcline	Rathcline	Longford	I.	164
26	Glebe	57	2	17c	Longford	Rathcline	Shrule	Ballymahon	I.	165
23	Glebe	46	3	32	Longford	Shrule	Taghshinny	Ballymahon	I.	167
14	Glebe	135	0	11	Louth	Ardee	Ardee	Ardee	I.	171
18	Glebe	17	3	13	Louth	Ferrard	Rathdrumin	Drogheda	I.	182
24	Glebe	17	3	13	Louth	Ferrard	Tullyallen	Drogheda	I.	183
6	Glebe	16	0	11	Louth	Upper Dundalk	Barronstown	Dundalk	I.	177
7	Glebe	30	3	1	Louth	Upper Dundalk	Dundalk	Dundalk	I.	178
90	Glebe	36	2	36	Mayo	Carra	Drum	Castlebar	IV.	128
74	Glebe	62	2	19	Mayo	Costello	Castlemore	Castlereagh	IV.	140
9	Glebe	67	1	5	Mayo	Erris	Kilmore	Belmullett	IV.	146
120	Glebe	41	3	15	Mayo	Kilmaine	Cong	Ballinrobe	IV.	153
86	Glebe	47	2	4	Mayo	Murrisk	Kilgeever	Westport	IV.	160
29, 38	Glebe	61	2	37	Mayo	Tirawley	Crossmolina	Ballina	IV.	166
39	Glebe	31	2	13	Mayo	Tirawley	Kilbelfad	Ballina	IV.	168
7, 14	Glebe	47	3	16	Mayo	Tirawley	Lackan	Killala	IV.	170
8	Glebe	35	0	37	Meath	Fore	Kilbride	Oldcastle	I.	200
22, 23	Glebe	51	3	26	Meath	Fore	Killallon	Oldcastle	I.	200
8, 9	Glebe	33	0	3	Meath	Fore	Killeagh	Oldcastle	I.	201
9, 15	Glebe	71	1	38	Meath	Fore	Loughcrew	Oldcastle	I.	201
28	Glebe	16	1	35	Meath	Lower Duleek	Julianstown	Drogheda	I.	196
11	Glebe	32	2	34	Meath	Lower Kells	Kilbeg	Kells	I.	202
11	Glebe	21	2	37	Meath	Lower Kells	Moynalty	Kells	I.	204

(a) Including 4A. 1R. 20P. water.   (b) Including 15A. 2R. 37P. water.   (c) Including 8A. 2R. 26P. detached portion.

No. of Sheet of the Ordnance Survey Maps.	Townlands and Towns.	Area in Statute Acres.			County.	Barony.	Parish.	Poor Law Union in 1857.	Townland Census of 1851, Part I.	
		A.	R.	P.					Vol.	Page
42	Glebe	151	3	18	Meath	Lower Moyfenrath	Rathmolyon	Trim	I.	211
41	Glebe	20	2	20	Meath	Lower Moyfenrath	Trim	Trim	I.	212
25	Glebe	61	1	4	Meath	Lower Navan	Ardbraccan	Navan	I.	214
6	Glebe	33	0	35	Meath	Lower Slane	Siddan	Ardee	I.	223
35	Glebe	34	3	4	Meath	Lune	Killaconnigan	Trim	I.	208
17, 18	Glebe	31	1	15	Meath	Morgallion	Clongill	Navan	I.	209
44	Glebe	40	3	5	Meath	Ratoath	Rathregan	Dunshaughlin	I.	219
38	Glebe	93	0	28	Meath	Skreen	Killeen	Dunshaughlin	I.	221
20	Glebe	33	0	2a	Meath	Upper Slane	Dowth	Drogheda	I.	224
3	Glebe	68	3	7	Monaghan	Trough	Errigal Trough	Monaghan	III.	284
35	Glebe	71	3	34	Queen's Co.	Clarmallagh	Attanagh	Abbeyleix	I.	237
29	Glebe	31	0	35	Queen's Co.	Clarmallagh	Durrow	Abbeyleix	I.	237
30	Glebe	49	1	17	Queen's Co.	Cullenagh	Dysartgallen	Abbeyleix	I.	239
2	Glebe	27	2	18	Queen's Co.	Tinnahinch	Kilmanman	Mountmellick	I.	249
2	Glebe	165	2	30	Queen's Co.	Tinnahinch	Rearymore	Mountmellick	I.	249
16	Glebe	421	0	22	Queen's Co.	Upperwoods	Offerlane	Mountmellick	I.	251
41	Glebe	37	0	1b	Roscommon	Athlone	Athleague	Roscommon	IV.	179
39	Glebe	32	3	3	Roscommon	Athlone	Fuerty	Roscommon	IV.	181
42	Glebe	56	3	33	Roscommon	Athlone	Killinvoy	Roscommon	IV.	182
23, 24	Glebe	23	2	28	Roscommon	Ballintober North	Kilglass	Strokestown	IV.	186
24	Glebe	26	2	6	Roscommon	Ballintober North	Termonbarry	Strokestown	IV.	188
6	Glebe	33	0	12	Roscommon	Boyle	Ardcarn	Boyle	IV.	193
5	Glebe	35	3	17	Roscommon	Boyle	Boyle	Boyle	IV.	194
11	Glebe	21	0	38	Roscommon	Boyle	Killukin	Cark. on Shannon	IV.	195
3, 4	Glebe	81	1	20c	Roscommon	Boyle	Kilronan	Boyle	IV.	197
17	Glebe	30	2	8	Roscommon	Roscommon	Aughrim	Cark. on Shannon	IV.	207
32	Glebe	33	1	32	Sligo	Leyny	Kilvarnet	Tobercurry	IV.	232
29	Glebe	40	1	12d	Sligo	Tireragh	Kilmoremoy	Ballina	IV.	235
13, 19	Glebe	34	0	34	Sligo	Tireragh	Skreen	Dromore West	IV.	236
41	Glebe	65	0	31	Tipperary, N.R.	Eliogarty	Thurles	Thurles	II.	273
23, 24	Glebe	73	0	19	Tipperary, N.R.	Ikerrin	Killavinoge	Roscrea	II.	275
12	Glebe	7	3	16e	Tipperary, N.R.	Ikerrin	Roscrea	Roscrea	II.	276
40, 46	Glebe	64	3	7	Tipperary, N.R.	Kilnamanagh Upper	Moyaliff	Thurles	II.	279
14	Glebe	36	3	2	Tipperary, N.R.	Lower Ormond	Killodiernan	Nenagh	II.	284
75	Glebe	27	3	20	Tipperary, S.R.	Clanwilliam	Killardry	Tipperary	II.	308
59	Glebe	33	1	22	Tipperary, S.R.	Clanwilliam	Kilmucklin	Tipperary	II.	309
51	Glebe	57	3	36	Tipperary, S.R.	Kilnamanagh Lower	Aghacrew	Tipperary	II.	322
39	Glebe	49	1	14	Tyrone	Dungannon Middle	Donaghenry	Cookstown	III.	301
39	Glebe	45	2	8	Tyrone	Dungannon Upper	Artrea	Cookstown	III.	306
39	Glebe	92	0	31	Tyrone	Dungannon Upper	Ballyclog	Cookstown	III.	306
38	Glebe	74	1	4	Tyrone	Dungannon Upper	Derryloran	Cookstown	III.	307
34	Glebe	41	3	6	Tyrone	Omagh West	Longfield East	Omagh	III.	315
23	Glebe	33	1	16f	Tyrone	Omagh West	Termonamongan	Castlederg	III.	317
2, 5	Glebe	196	0	36	Tyrone	Strabane Lower	Leckpatrick	Strabane	III.	322
9	Glebe	281	0	24	Tyrone	Strabane Lower	Urney	Strabane	III.	322
40	Glebe	7	0	13	Waterford	Decies within Drum	Kinsalebeg	Youghal	II.	352
31	Glebe	21	1	35	Waterford	Decies without Drum	Kilrush	Dungarvan	II.	358
27	Glebe	15	0	2	Waterford	Gaultiere	Killea	Waterford	II.	363
18	Glebe	37	1	24	Waterford	Gaultiere	Kill St. Nicholas	Waterford	II.	364
1	Glebe	13	3	7	Waterford	Glenahiry	Kilronan	Clonmel	II.	365
1	Glebe	5	3	38	Waterford	Upperthird	St. Marys Clonmel	Clonmel	II.	371
30	Glebe	55	1	2	Westmeath	Clonlonan	Ballyloughloe	Athlone	I.	260
6, 11	Glebe	35	1	29	Westmeath	Corkaree	Leny	Mullingar	I.	262
12	Glebe	65	2	10	Westmeath	Corkaree	Taghmon	Mullingar	I.	264
20	Glebe	68	3	20	Westmeath	Farbill	Killucan	Mullingar	I.	266
22	Glebe	30	1	11	Westmeath	Kilkenny West	Bunown	Athlone	I.	272
24	Glebe	69	3	24	Westmeath	Rathconrath	Ballymore	Ballymahon	I.	281
17	Glebe	18	1	11	Westmeath	Rathconrath	Piercetown	Ballymahon	I.	283
26	Glebe	33	0	29	Wexford	Ballaghkeen	Edermine	Enniscorthy	I.	294
27	Glebe	31	3	1	Wexford	Ballaghkeen	Killila	Enniscorthy	I.	295
27	Glebe	33	1	4	Wexford	Ballaghkeen	Killisk	Enniscorthy	I.	296
21, 27	Glebe	48	0	33	Wexford	Ballaghkeen	Mcelnagh	Enniscorthy	I.	298
16, 21	Glebe	43	1	24	Wexford	Ballaghkeen	Monamolin	Gorey	I.	298
32, 33	Glebe	5	0	26	Wexford	Ballaghkeen	St. Nicholas	Enniscorthy	I.	298
33	Glebe	33	2	33	Wexford	Ballaghkeen	Skreen	Wexford	I.	298
46	Glebe	15	2	24	Wexford	Bargy	Duncormick	Wexford	I.	304
42	Glebe	9	2	6	Wexford	Bargy	Kilmannan	Wexford	I.	306
52	Glebe	26	2	29	Wexford	Bargy	Kilturk	Wexford	I.	307
47	Glebe	14	0	8g	Wexford	Forth	Mayglass	Wexford	I.	312
2, 3	Glebe	29	2	27	Wexford	Gorey	Kilnenor	Gorey	I.	319
22	Glebe	96	3	36	Wexford	Gorey	Kiltrisk	Gorey	I.	320
32,33,37,38	Glebe	52	1	26	Wexford	Shelmaliere East	Ardcolm	Wexford	I.	330
18, 24	Glebe	99	2	33	Wicklow	Ballinacor North	Derrylossary	Rathdrum	I.	346

(a) Including 1A. 3R. 26P. water.
(b) Including 1A. 2R. 36F. water.
(c) Including 31A. 1R. 4P. water.

(d) Including 2A. 2R. 30P. River Moy.
(e) Including 1A. 3R. 3P. detached portion.

(f) Including 5A. 3R. 33P. detached portion.
(g) Including 2A. 1R. 18P. detached portion.

No. of Sheet of the Ordnance Survey Maps.	Townlands and Towns.	Area in Statute Acres.	County.	Barony.	Parish.	Poor Law Union in 1857.	Townland Census of 1851, Part I.	
		A. R. P.					Vol.	Page
9	Glebe	42 3 10	Wicklow	Lower Talbotstown	Hollywood	Baltinglass	I.	360
25	Glebe	7 1 34	Wicklow	Newcastle	Drumkay	Rathdrum	I.	351
25	Glebe	63 1 26a	Wicklow	Newcastle	Rathnew	Rathdrum	I.	354
7	Glebe	5 1 16	Wicklow	Rathdown	Kilmacanoge	Rathdown	I.	355
2, 6	Glebe Big	165 2 5	Londonderry	Coleraine	Dunboe	Coleraine	III.	231
6	Glebe Bog	2 3 17	Louth	Upper Dundalk	Barronstown	Dundalk	I.	177
4	Glebe East	9 3 36	Dublin	Balrothery West	Garristown	Dunshaughlin	I.	22
25	Glebe East	124 0 20b	Kildare	Naas South	Tipperkevin	Naas	I.	65
26	Glebe East	195 3 16	King's Co.	Geashill	Geashill	Tullamore	I.	140
37	Glebe East	16 3 28	Londonderry	Loughinsholin	Ballyscullion	Magherafelt	III.	239
19, 22	Glebe East	4 3 27	Louth	Ferrard	Mayne	Drogheda	I.	181
14	Glebe East	34 1 20	Roscommon	Frenchpark	Tibohine	Castlereagh	IV.	205
36	Glebe East	36 0 7	Westmeath	Clonlonan	Kilcleagh	Athlone	I.	261
47	Glebe Farm	11 2 25	Tyrone	Dungannon Middle	Clonoe	Dungannon	III.	300
44	Glebehill	10 0 35	Donegal	Kilmacrenan	Gartan	Letterkenny	III.	127
45	Glebe or Kilconnell	197 3 22	Donegal	Kilmacrenan	Kilmacrenan	Milford	III.	129
38	Glebe Large	59 3 5	Donegal	Inishowen West	Fahan Upper	Londonderry	III.	121
141	Glebe Marsh	46 3 23	Cork, W.R.	West Carbery (E.D.)	Aghadown	Skibbereen	II.	137
5	Glebe North	14 0 31	Dublin	Balrothery East	Balrothery	Balrothery	I.	19
28	Glebe North	143 1 17	Kildare	Kilcullen	Kilcullen	Naas	I.	58
9	Glebe (Old)	189 1 30	Tyrone	Strabane Lower	Urney	Strabane	III.	322
5	Glebe South	31 1 24	Dublin	Balrothery East	Balrothery	Balrothery	I.	19
28	Glebe South	80 1 21	Kildare	Kilcullen	Kilcullen	Naas	I.	58
22	Glebe South	1 3 14	Louth	Ferrard	Mayne	Drogheda	I.	181
80	Glebe or Straid	83 0 32	Donegal	Banagh	Glencolumbkille	Glenties	III.	106
3	Glebe West	20 0 12	Dublin	Balrothery West	Garristown	Dunshaughlin	I.	22
24	Glebe West	127 3 6c	Kildare	Naas South	Tipperkevin	Naas	I.	65
37	Glebe West	54 0 31	Londonderry	Loughinsholin	Ballyscullion	Magherafelt	III.	239
19, 22	Glebe West	4 1 19	Louth	Ferrard	Mayne	Drogheda	I.	181
20	Glebe West	35 1 16	Roscommon	Frenchpark	Tibohine	Castlereagh	IV.	205
30, 36	Glebe West	59 3 1	Westmeath	Clonlonan	Kilcleagh	Athlone	I.	261
62,63,70,71	Gleensk	1,031 3 37	Kerry	Iveragh	Killinane	Cahersiveen	II.	197
99	Gleesk	532 1 18	Kerry	Dunkerron South	Kilcrohane	Kenmare	II.	183
10	Glen	102 1 31d	Cavan	Lower Loughtee	Drumlane	Cavan	III.	80
93, 99	Glen	68 0 21	Donegal	Banagh	Killymard	Donegal	III.	111
17	Glen	938 3 28	Fermanagh	Tirkennedy	Enniskillen	Enniskillen	III.	222
22	Glen	291 2 32	Galway	Ballynahinch	Omey	Clifden	IV.	15
29	Glen	175 2 38	Galway	Dunmore	Dunmore	Tuam	IV.	34
18, 31	Glen	167 1 20	Galway	Tiaquin	Kilkerrin	Glennamaddy	IV.	77
75, 76	Glen	237 2 12	Kerry	Magunihy	Killaha	Killarney	II.	202
31	Glen	71 2 38	Kilkenny	Kells	Kilmaganny	Callan	I.	109
13,14,22,23	Glen	249 1 20	Limerick	Clanwilliam	Cahernarry	Limerick	II.	223
24	Glen	128 1 1	Limerick	Coonagh	Grean	Tipperary	II.	235
20	Glen	510 1 26	Longford	Ardagh	Ardagh	Longford	I.	151
85	Glen	491 1 29	Mayo	Murrisk	Kilgeever	Westport	IV.	161
17	Glen	100 2 15	Monaghan	Dartree	Aghabog	Cootehill	III.	263
18, 23	Glen	288 2 2e	Monaghan	Dartree	Ematris	Cootehill	III.	267
23	Glen	40 2 5	Roscommon	Ballintober North	Kilglass	Strokestown	IV.	186
14	Glen	13 1 8	Sligo	Carbury	Killaspugbrone	Sligo	IV.	222
20, 26	Glen	518 2 32	Sligo	Leyny	Ballysadare	Sligo	IV.	230
27	Glen	474 0 26	Sligo	Tirerrill	Ballynakill	Sligo	IV.	237
35	Glen	681 1 30	Sligo	Tirerrill	Kilmactranny	Boyle	IV.	240
31, 32	Glen	211 2 39	Waterford	Decies without Drum	Clonea	Dungarvan	II.	354
29	Glen	706 0 39	Westmeath	Clonlonan	Ballyloughloe	Athlone	I.	260
3	Glen	61 1 26	Westmeath	Fore	Rathgarve	Castletowndelvin	I.	271
66, 74	Glena	2,062 2 28	Kerry	Magunihy	Killarney	Killarney	II.	203
14, 19	Glenaan	813 1 38	Antrim	Lower Glenarm	Layd	Ballycastle	III.	22
1	Glenabbey	84 0 10	Waterford	Glenahiry	Inishlounaght	Clonmel	II.	365
58, 59, 66	Glenaboghil	469 2 27	Donegal	Boylagh	Inishkeel	Glenties	III.	112
28	Glenaboy	224 3 39	Waterford	Coshmore & Coshbride	Tallow	Lismore	II.	348
4, 13	Glenacarney	897 1 1	Cork, E.R.	Duhallow	Clonfert	Kanturk	II.	68
105, 115	Glenaclara East	173 0 35	Galway	Loughrea	Killeenadeema	Loughrea	IV.	64
105	Glenaclara West	128 3 15	Galway	Loughrea	Killeenadeema	Loughrea	IV.	64
25	Glenacre	66 3 7	Tipperary, N.R.	Owney and Arra	Templeachally	Nenagh	II.	297
55	Glenacroghery	308 2 11	Cork, E.R.	Kinnatalloon	Mogeely	Youghal	II.	98
86, 89	Glenacunna	1,393 3 25	Tipperary, S.R.	Iffa and Offa West	Templetenny	Clogheen	II.	320
71, 78	Glenacunna	165 1 11	Tipperary, S.R.	Slievardagh	Garrangibbon	Carrick on Suir	III.	333
38	Glenacurragh	349 1 4	King's Co.	Ballybritt	Ettagh	Roscrea	I.	125
57, 58, 60	Glenacurrane	422 2 17	Limerick	Coshlea	Kilbeheny	Mitchelstown	II.	239
54	Glenadush	239 2 18f	Tyrone	Dungannon Middle	Donaghmore	Dungannon	III.	302
39, 40	Glenafelly	755 3 0	King's Co.	Ballybritt	Kinnitty	Parsonstown	I.	125
23	Glenagarey	182 2 4	Dublin	Rathdown	Monkstown	Rathdown	I.	36
23	GLENAGARERY or SALLY NOGGINS T.	—	Dublin	Rathdown	Monkstown	Rathdown	I.	37

(a) Including 14A. 1R. 22P. detached portion.
(b) Including 20A. 0R. 7P. detached portion.
(c) Including 16A. 1R. 1P. detached portion.
(d) Including 6A. 0R. 32P. water.
(e) Including 12A. 3R. 1P. water.
(f) Including 5A. 2R. 19P. water.

3 Q

No. of Sheet of the Ordnance Survey Maps.	Townlands and Towns.	Area in Statute Acres.			County.	Barony.	Parish.	Poor Law Union in 1857.	Townland Census of 1851, Part I.	
		A.	R.	P.					Vol.	Page
12, 13	Glenagh . . .	1,200	1	24	Mayo . . .	Tirawley . . .	Doonfeeny . .	Killala . .	IV.	167
49, 60	Glenaglogh North .	618	0	18	Cork, W.R. . .	East Muskerry .	Aghabulloge . .	Macroom . .	II.	153
49, 60	Glenaglogh South .	667	1	36	Cork, W.R. . .	East Muskerry .	Aghabulloge . .	Macroom . .	II.	153
46	Glenagort . .	645	1	4	Mayo . . .	Tirawley . . .	Crossmolina . .	Ballina . .	IV.	166
27, 35	Glenagower . .	809	0	9	Limerick . .	Shanid . . .	Rathronan . .	Newcastle .	II.	257
26, 27	Glenagragara . .	1,125	0	26	Limerick . .	Shanid . . .	Kilfergus . .	Glin . . .	II.	256
28	Glenaguile . .	522	1	29	Tipperary, N.R. .	Upper Ormond .	Aghnameadle . .	Nenagh . .	II.	288
28	Glenaguile . .	322	0	20	Tipperary, N.R. .	Upper Ormond .	Latteragh . .	Nenagh . .	II.	292
36, 37	Glenagurteen . .	156	2	20	Cork, E.R. . .	Condons&Clangibbon	Lismore and Mocollop	Fermoy . .	II.	62
15	Glenahilty . .	527	1	27	Tipperary, N.R. .	Upper Ormond .	Ballygibbon . .	Nenagh . .	II.	289
40,41,49,50	Glenaknockane . .	915	0	20	Cork, E.R. . .	Duhallow . . .	Kilshannig . .	Mallow . .	II.	74
12	Glenaknockaun East	254	2	39	Waterford . .	Coshmore&Coshbride	Lismore and Mocollop	Lismore . .	II.	346
11, 12	Glenaknockaun West	226	1	6	Waterford . .	Coshmore&Coshbride	Lismore and Mocollop	Lismore . .	II.	346
36	Glenaleeriska . .	84	2	34	Waterford . .	Decies within Drum	Ardmore . . .	Dungarvan .	II.	350
83	Glenalemy . .	48	0	4	Tipperary, S.R. .	Iffa and Offa East .	Kilgrant . .	Clonmel . .	II.	314
11	Glenall . . .	152	3	8	Fermanagh . .	Lurg . . .	Derryvullan . .	Lowtherstown .	III.	204
10, 11	Glenall . . .	357	1	6	Queen's Co. . .	Upperwoods . .	Offerlane . .	Mountmellick .	I.	251
28, 37	Glenalla . . .	1,302	0	6	Donegal . . .	Kilmacrenan . .	Aughnish . .	Millford . .	III.	122
21	Glenalougha . .	335	1	16	Cork. E.R. . .	Duhallow . . .	Kilmeen . .	Kanturk . .	II.	73
30, 31	Glenamony Glebe .	333	0	17	King's Co. . .	Eglish . . .	Eglish . . .	Parsonstown .	I.	135
10, 11	Glenamoon . .	311	1	4	Queen's Co. . .	Upperwoods . .	Offerlane . .	Mountmellick .	I.	251
26	Glenamuck North .	111	0	39	Dublin . . .	Rathdown . .	Tully . . .	Rathdown .	I.	38
26	Glenamuck South .	260	1	3	Dublin . . .	Rathdown . .	Tully . . .	Rathdown .	I.	38
82	Glenanail . . .	178	0	9	Galway . . .	Galway . . .	St. Nicholas . .	Galway . .	IV.	38
56, 59	Glenanair East . .	1,322	0	8	Limerick . .	Coshlea . . .	Particles . .	Kilmallock .	II.	240
55, 56, 59	Glenanair West .	1,151	3	4	Limerick . .	Coshlea . . .	Particles . .	Kilmallock .	II.	240
66	Glenane Beg . .	219	2	23	Cork, E.R. . .	Imokilly . . .	Killeagh . .	Youghal . .	II.	88
66	Glenane More . .	373	1	22	Cork, E.R. . .	Imokilly . . .	Mogeely . .	Middleton .	II.	90
66	Glenane Wood . .	24	2	19	Cork, E.R. . .	Imokilly . . .	Mogeely . .	Middleton .	II.	90
66	Glenaphuca . .	282	0	31	Cork, E.R. . .	Imokilly . . .	Dungourney . .	Middleton .	II.	86
24	Glenaraneen . .	292	3	18	Dublin . . .	Newcastle . .	Saggart . .	Celbridge . .	I.	34
67	Glenarb . . .	191	2	0	Tyrone . . .	Dungannon Lower .	Aghaloo . .	Armagh . .	III.	296
30	Glenard . . .	1,147	0	31	Donegal . . .	Inishowen West .	Muff . . .	Londonderry .	III.	121
17	Glenaree . . .	282	0	25	Kildare . . .	Offaly East . .	Cloncurry . .	Edenderry .	I.	69
49	Glenaree . . .	360	2	7	Limerick . .	Coshlea . . .	Ballingarry . .	Kilmallock .	II.	237
20, 25	Glenariff Mountain Lower . . .	600	2	31a	Antrim . . .	Lower Glenarm .	Ardclinis . .	Larne . .	III.	21
20, 25	Glenariff Mountain Upper East . .	986	2	15b	Antrim . . .	Lower Glenarm .	Ardclinis . .	Larne . .	III.	21
25	Glenariff Mountain Upper West . .	313	1	16c	Antrim . . .	Lower Glenarm .	Ardclinis . .	Larne . .	III.	21
29	Glenarm Demesne .	401	0	16	Antrim . . .	Lower Glenarm .	Tickmacrevan .	Larne . .	III.	23
29	GLENARM T. . .	—			Antrim . . .	Lower Glenarm .	Tickmacrevan .	Larne . .	III.	24
2, 6	Glenarn . . .	1,092	2	14	Fermanagh . .	Lurg . . .	Magheraculmoney .	Lowtherstown .	III.	208
38	Glenarny . .	179	2	20	Tyrone . . .	Dungannon Upper .	Kildress . .	Cookstown .	III.	309
35, 36	Glenarousk . .	1,059	2	15	Cork, E.R. . .	Barrymore . .	Castlelyons . .	Fermoy . .	II.	53
40	Glenart . . .	258	0	13	Wicklow . .	Arklow . . .	Arklow . .	Rathdrum .	I.	341
64, 77	Glenaruid . .	550	3	13d	Galway . . .	Ballynahinch . .	Moyrus . .	Clifden . .	IV.	13
1, 2	Glenary . . .	2,502	0	8	Waterford . .	Upperthird . .	St. Marys Clonmel .	Clonmel . .	II.	371
29	Glenasaggart . .	93	3	2	Waterford . .	Coshmore&Coshbride	Lismore and Mocollop	Lismore . .	II.	346
34	Glenassy or Cooneen	93	1	29	Waterford . .	Decies within Drum	Aglish . . .	Dungarvan .	II.	349
27, 28	Glenastar . .	788	2	13	Limerick . .	Glenquin . .	Newcastle . .	Newcastle .	II.	248
105	Glenatallan . .	119	3	16	Galway . . .	Dunkellin . .	Kilconickny . .	Loughrea .	IV.	29
65	Glenathonacash .	307	3	1	Cork, E.R. . .	Barrymore . .	Ballyspillane . .	Middleton .	II.	51
19, 20	Glenatlucky . .	454	2	25	Cork, E.R. . .	Condons&Clangibbon	Brigown . . .	Mitchelstown .	II.	59
37	Glenatore Lower .	139	2	33	Cork, E.R. . .	Kinnatalloon .	Knockmourne . .	Fermoy . .	II.	98
37	Glenatore Upper .	173	0	30	Cork, E.R. . .	Kinnatalloon .	Knockmourne . .	Fermoy . .	II.	98
87,88,99,100	Glenaun . .	104	0	34	Galway . . .	Clonmacnowen .	Clontuskert . .	Ballinasloe .	IV.	24
22, 30	Glenavaddra . .	204	1	21	Waterford . .	Decies without Drum	Whitechurch . .	Dungarvan .	II.	361
20	Glenaveha . .	274	0	10	Waterford . .	Coshmore&Coshbride	Lismore and Mocollop	Lismore . .	II.	346
38, 47	Glenavenew . .	137	3	31	Mayo . . .	Tirawley . . .	Addergoole . .	Castlebar .	IV.	163
9	Glenaviegh . .	61	3	37	Tipperary, N.R. .	Lower Ormond .	Kilbarron . .	Borrisokane .	II.	284
59	Glenavy . .	372	3	34	Antrim . . .	Upper Massereene .	Glenavy . .	Lisburn . .	III.	30
59	GLENAVY T. . .	—			Antrim . . .	Upper Massereene .	{ Camlin . . . / Glenavy . . .	{ Antrim . . / Lisburn . . }	III.	30
14, 15	Glenaward . .	132	3	11	Meath . . .	Fore . . .	Moylagh . .	Oldcastle .	I.	201
65	Glenawillin . .	114	1	23	Cork, E.R. . .	Barrymore . .	Templenacarriga .	Middleton .	II.	58
78	Glenawilling . .	403	1	2	Cork, E.R. . .	Imokilly . . .	Kilmacdonogh .	Youghal . .	II.	88
22, 28	Glenawinna . .	126	2	32	Tipperary, N.R. .	Upper Ormond .	Aghnameadle . .	Nenagh . .	II.	289
12	Glenback . .	88	0	37	Londonderry . .	Coleraine . .	Aghadowey . .	Coleraine . .	III.	229
21, 22	Glenballythomas .	835	3	35	Roscommon . .	Roscommon . .	Ogulla . . .	Strokestown .	IV.	212
37	Glenballyvally . .	440	0	00	Kilkenny . .	Ida . . .	Dysartmoon . .	New Ross .	I.	101
58, 66	Glenbane . .	943	1	5	Tipperary, S.R. .	Clanwilliam . .	Glenbane . .	Tipperary .	II.	308
10	Glenbane East .	260	3	26	Limerick . .	Shanid . . .	Shanagolden . .	Rathkeale .	II.	258

No. of Sheet of the Ordnance Survey Maps.	Townlands and Towns.	Area in Statute Acres.	County.	Barony.	Parish.	Poor Law Union in 1857.	Townland Census of 1851, Part I. Vol.	Page
		A.　R.　P.						
46, 47, 52, 53	Glenbane Lower	832 1 36	Tipperary, S.R.	Middlethird	Holycross	Cashel	II.	327
47	Glenbane Upper	395 1 6	Tipperary, S.R.	Middlethird	Holycross	Cashel	II.	327
10	Glenbane West	73 2 24	Shanid	Shanagolden	Rathkeale	II.	258
3, 7	Glenbarrow	347 2 39	Queen's Co.	Tinnahinch	Rearymore	Mountmellick	I.	250
27	Glenbaun	1,424 1 21	Limerick	Shanid	Kilmoylan	Glin	II.	256
87, 96, 97	Glenbaun	338 1 16	Mayo	Murrisk	Oughaval	Westport	IV.	162
15, 16	Glenbaun	124 0 1	Wexford	Gorey	Kilcormick	Enniscorthy	I.	317
43, 51	Glenbeagh	751 2 32a	Donegal	Kilmacrenan	Gartan	Letterkenny	III.	127
65	Glenbeg	442 3 23	Cork, E.R.	Barrymore	Dungourney	Middleton	II.	54
102	Glenbeg	1,203 1 16b	Cork, W.R.	Bear	Kilcatherine	Castletown	II.	124
2, 3	Glen Beg	191 3 17	Monaghan	Trough	Errigal Trough	Clogher	III.	284
39, 40	Glenbeg	181 1 20	Tipperary, N.R.	Kilnamanagh Upper	Upperchurch	Thurles	II.	280
45	Glenbeg	322 2 21	Tyrone	Dungannon Middle	Pomeroy	Dungannon	III.	304
20	Glen Beg	175 1 21c	Waterford	Coshmore and Coshbride	Lismore and Mocollop	Lismore	II.	346
30, 35	Glen Beg	283 1 4	Waterford	Decies without Drum	Dungarvan	Dungarvan	II.	355
13	Glenbeg East	244 1 11	Galway	Ross	Ross	Ballinrobe	IV.	74
13	Glenbeg West	511 2 29	Galway	Ross	Ross	Ballinrobe	IV.	74
17	Glenbeha	188 2 19	Tipperary, N.R.	Ikerrin	Corbally	Roscrea	II.	275
31	Glenbevan	173 3 23	Limerick	Coshma	Croom	Croom	II.	242
19, 20, 28	Glenbonniv	436 0 11	Clare	Tulla Upper	Feakle	Scarriff	II.	39
33	Glenbough	213 3 20	Wexford	Shelmaliere East	St. Margarets	Wexford	I.	331
35, 39	Glenbower	244 0 39	Kilkenny	Iverk	Fiddown	Carrick on Suir	I.	105
11, 16	Glenbower	389 0 26	Queen's Co.	Upperwoods	Offerlane	Mountmellick	I.	251
9	Glenbower	139 2 12	Tipperary, N.R.	Lower Ormond	Kilbarron	Borrisokane	II.	284
12	Glenboy	621 2 39	Leitrim	Drumahaire	Cloonclare	Manorhamilton	IV.	93
8, 9	Glenboy	273 3 17	Meath	Fore	Kilbride	Oldcastle	I.	200
122, 123	Glenbrack	631 2 12	Galway	Kiltartan	Kiltartan	Gort	IV.	48
88	Glenbradagh	113 0 11	Cork, E.R.	Imokilly	Aghada	Middleton	II.	83
28	Glenbreedy	577 1 27	Tipperary, N.R.	Kilnamanagh Upper	Glenkeen	Thurles	II.	278
22	Glenbrickeen	567 2 19d	Galway	Ballynahinch	Omey	Clifden	IV.	15
10, 11, 16, 17	Glenbride	2,770 1 38	Wicklow	Lower Talbotstown	Boystown	Naas	I.	359
49	Glenbrohane	230 3 27	Limerick	Coshlea	Ballingarry	Kilmallock	III.	237
22, 23, 26, 27	Glenbuck	1,736 0 36e	Antrim	Kilconway	Rasharkin	Ballymena	III.	27
42	Glenbullock	34 0 10	Wexford	Bargy	Kilmannan	Wexford	I.	306
45	Glenburrisk	186 1 31	Tyrone	Dungannon Middle	Pomeroy	Dungannon	III.	304
20, 28	Glencairn	542 2 28f	Waterford	Coshmore & Coshbride	Lismore and Mocollop	Lismore	II.	346
86	Glencallaghan	131 1 10	Tipperary, S.R.	Iffa and Offa West	Shanrahan	Clogheen	II.	319
87, 97	Glencally	511 2 17	Mayo	Murrisk	Oughaval	Westport	IV.	162
12, 13	Glencalry Lower	784 3 36	Mayo	Tirawley	Doonfeeny	Killala	IV.	167
12	Glencalry Upper	1,151 3 35	Mayo	Tirawley	Doonfeeny	Killala	IV.	167
7	Glencap Commons North	190 1 9	Wicklow	Rathdown	Kilmacanoge	Rathdown	I.	355
7, 8	Glencap Commons South	526 0 5	Wicklow	Rathdown	Kilmacanoge	Rathdown	I.	355
7	Glencap Commons Upper	354 1 11	Wicklow	Rathdown	Kilmacanoge	Rathdown	I.	355
45	Glencarbry	223 0 7	Tipperary, S.R.	Kilnamanagh Lower	Donohill	Tipperary	II.	323
6, 9	Glencarbury	443 1 30	Sligo	Carbury	Drumcliff	Sligo	IV.	221
53	Glencar Irish	254 2 32	Donegal	Kilmacrenan	Conwal	Letterkenny	III.	126
53	Glencar Scotch	357 2 17	Donegal	Kilmacrenan	Conwal	Letterkenny	III.	126
70, 71	Glencash	119 3 33	Donegal	Raphoe	Clonleigh	Strabane	III.	135
17, 18	Glencastle	2,336 1 13	Mayo	Erris	Kilcommon	Belmullet	IV.	144
20, 30, 31	Glencaw	528 0 19	Donegal	Inishowen East	Moville Upper	Inishowen	III.	119
12	Glenchiel	1,514 0 25g	Tyrone	Strabane Upper	Bodoney Upper	Gortin	III.	324
52, 59	Glenchuil	662 1 4	Tyrone	Clogher	Errigal Keerogue	Clogher	III.	295
37	Glencloghlea	128 2 36	Kilkenny	Ida	Shanbogh	New Ross	I.	104
93	Glencoagh	344 0 1h	Donegal	Banagh	Inver	Donegal	III.	107
93	Glencoagh	115 0 23	Donegal	Banagh	Killymard	Donegal	III.	111
24, 36, 37	Glencoaghan	3,139 1 27i	Galway	Ballynahinch	Moyrus	Clifden	IV.	13
65	Glencoh	626 1 2	Galway	Moycullen	Kilcummin	Oughterard	IV.	67
21	Glencollins Lower	393 1 29	Cork, E.R.	Duhallow	Nohavaldaly	Kanturk	II.	75
21	Glencollins Upper	966 2 4	Cork, E.R.	Duhallow	Nohavaldaly	Kanturk	II.	75
6, 10	Glencolumbkille North	595 3 4	Clare	Burren	Carran	Ballyvaghan	II.	11
10	Glencolumbkille South	396 2 26	Clare	Burren	Carran	Ballyvaghan	II.	11
34, 35	Glencommaun	227 1 28	Kilkenny	Kells	Tullahought	Carrick on Suir	I.	110
46	Glencon	323 2 7	Tyrone	Dungannon Middle	Tullyniskan	Dungannon	III.	304
59	Glenconaun Beg	152 1 19	Clare	Clonderalaw	Killadysert	Killadysert	II.	16
59	Glenconaun More	782 2 32j	Clare	Clonderalaw	Killadysert	Killadysert	II.	16
106, 115	Glenconnelly	1,672 0 21k	Mayo	Murrisk	Kilgeever	Westport	IV.	160
83	Glenconnor	148 2 13	Tipperary, S.R.	Iffa and Offa East	Kiltegan	Clonmel	II.	315
10, 15	Glenconra	838 0 21	Queen's Co.	Upperwoods	Offerlane	Mountmellick	I.	251
16, 24	Glenconway	1,410 2 22	Londonderry	Keenaght	Bovevagh	Newt Limavady	III.	235
16	Glencoonra	165 1 28	Fermanagh	Tirkennedy	Magheracross	Lowtherstown	III.	223

(a) Including 23a. 1r. 16p. water.
(b) Including 149a. 0r. 18p. Glenbeg Lough.
(c) Including 2a. 1r. 24p. water.
(d) Including 9a. 3r. 13p. water.
(e) Including 2a. 2r. 16p. water.
(f) Including 11a. 2a. 36p. water.
(g) Including 4a. 3r. 5p. water.
(h) Including 29a. 0r. 33p. water.
(i) Including 131a. 3r. 16p. water.
(j) Including 31a. 3r. 34p. water.
(k) Including 8a. 0r. 37p. water.

3 Q 2

No. of Sheet of the Ordnance Survey Maps.	Townlands and Towns.	Area in Statute Acres.	County.	Barony.	Parish.	Poor Law Union in 1857.	Townland Census of 1851, Part I.	
		A. R. P.					Vol.	Page
11	Glencoppogagh . .	1,079 0 1a	Tyrone . .	Strabane Upper .	Bodoney Upper .	Gortin . .	III.	324
26, 35	Glencordial . .	1,340 3 36	Tyrone . .	Strabane Upper .	Cappagh . .	Omagh . .	III.	325
18	Glencorick . .	140 3 21	Monaghan .	Dartree . .	Ematris . .	Cootehill .	III.	267
7	Glencormick North .	42 2 17	Wicklow . .	Rathdown . .	Kilmacanoge .	Rathdown .	I.	355
7	Glencormick South .	129 3 13b	Wicklow . .	Rathdown . .	Kilmacanoge .	Rathdown .	I.	355
25, 26	Glencorran . .	450 0 34	Cavan . .	Upper Loughtee .	Kilmore . .	Cavan . .	III.	84
2	Glencosh . .	354 2 10c	Tyrone . .	Strabane Lower .	Donaghedy . .	Strabane .	III.	321
74, 80	Glencoshabinnia .	1,552 1 13d	Tipperary, S.R.	Clanwilliam .	Clonbeg . .	Tipperary .	II.	305
25, 29	Glencoum . .	604 3 35	Kilkenny . .	Gowran . .	Graiguenamanagh .	Thomastown .	I.	95
78	Glencovet . .	169 2 0	Donegal . .	Raphoe . .	Donaghmore .	Stranorlar .	III.	138
18	Glencovet Glebe .	79 1 7	Fermanagh .	Tirkennedy .	Enniskillen .	Enniskillen .	III.	222
11, 24	Glencraff . .	1,562 3 24	Galway . .	Ballynahinch .	Ballynakill .	Clifden . .	IV.	11
51	Glencrees . .	95 2 6	Galway . .	Ballynahinch .	Moyrus . .	Clifden . .	IV.	13
60	Glencrew . .	150 2 23	Tyrone . .	Dungannon Lower .	Aghaloo . .	Clogher . .	III.	297
32	Glencroe . .	251 2 34	Tipperary, N.R.	Owney and Arra .	Kilnarath . .	Nenagh . .	II.	296
28, 37	Glencross . .	395 1 1	Donegal . .	Kilmacrenan .	Killygarvan .	Millford . .	III.	128
21	Glencrow . .	268 3 15	Donegal . .	Inishowen East .	Moville Upper .	Inishowen .	III.	119
13, 19	Glencrue . .	64 1 12	Tipperary, N.R.	Owney and Arra .	Castletownarra .	Nenagh . .	II.	294
60	Glencull . .	241 1 13	Tyrone . .	Dungannon Lower .	Killeeshil .	Clogher . .	III.	298
25, 26	Glencullen . .	523 1 1	Dublin . .	Rathdown . .	Kiltiernan .	Rathdown .	I.	36
11, 19, 20	Glencullen . .	409 2 10	Waterford .	Coshmore&Coshbride	Lismore and Mocollop	Lismore . .	II.	346
25, 27	Glencullen Mountain	639 0 3	Dublin . .	Rathdown . .	Kiltiernan .	Rathdown .	I.	36
106, 115	Glencullin . .	2,086 1 36e	Mayo . .	Murrisk . .	Kilgeever . .	Westport .	IV.	160
6, 13	Glencullin . .	1,000 1 1	Mayo . .	Tirawley . .	Doonfeeny .	Killala . .	IV.	167
18, 19	Glencullin Lower .	2,068 1 2f	Mayo . .	Erris . .	Kilcommon .	Belmullet .	IV.	144
19, 27	Glencullin Upper .	2,780 3 18	Mayo . .	Erris . .	Kilcommon .	Belmullet .	IV.	144
26	Glencunny . .	220 3 0	Fermanagh .	Magheraboy .	Rossorry . .	Enniskillen .	III.	214
11	Glencurb . .	213 1 13	Londonderry .	Coleraine .	Aghadowey .	Coleraine .	III.	229
49	Glendaduff . .	747 1 32g	Mayo . .	Gallen . .	Attymass . .	Ballina . .	IV.	147
57, 67	Glendahurk . .	1,455 0 37	Mayo . .	Burrishoole .	Burrishoole .	Newport .	IV.	119
23	Glendalligan . .	1,304 2 29	Waterford .	Decies without Drum	Kilrossanty .	Kilmacthomas .	II.	358
1, 2, 5, 6	Glendalough . .	2,902 0 6	Waterford .	Upperthird .	St. Marys, Clonmel	Clonmel . .	II.	371
35, 36	Glendarragh . .	1,042 0 6	Limerick . .	Glenquin . .	Monagay . .	Newcastle .	II.	247
12, 13	Glendarragh . .	322 3 33	Wicklow . .	Newcastle .	Newcastle Upper .	Rathdrum .	I.	353
47,48,58,59	Glendav . .	1,387 2 9	Cork, W.R.	West Muskerry .	Clondrohid .	Macroom .	II.	155
60, 66	Glendavagh . .	588 2 23	Tyrone . .	Dungannon Lower .	Aghaloo . .	Dungannon .	III.	297
107,115,116	Glendavock . .	1,743 1 29h	Mayo . .	Murrisk . .	Aghagower .	Westport .	IV.	159
46, 58	Glendavoolagh .	2,024 2 8	Mayo . .	Tirawley . .	Crossmolina .	Ballina . .	IV.	166
2	Glendaw . .	142 1 5	Waterford .	Upperthird .	Killaloan . .	Clonmel .	II.	370
11,12,20,21	Glendeish East .	475 0 15	Waterford .	Coshmore&Coshbride	Lismore and Mocollop	Lismore . .	II.	346
11, 20	Glendeish West .	614 1 27	Waterford .	Coshmore&Coshbride	Lismore and Mocollop	Lismore . .	II.	346
20, 21	Glenderowen . .	132 1 28	Londonderry .	Tirkeeran .	Clondermot .	Londonderry .	III.	248
13, 14	Glenderry . .	1,075 3 33	Kerry . .	Clanmaurice .	Ballyheige .	Tralee . .	II.	168
26	Glendevine . .	152 2 32	Westmeath .	Fartullagh .	Lynn . .	Mullingar .	I.	269
28	Glendiheen . .	199 3 25	Limerick . .	Shanid . .	Rathronan .	Glin . .	II.	257
19	Glendine . .	123 1 31i	Kilkenny . .	Gowran and Municipal Borough .	St. John's .	Kilkenny .	I.	98
39, 40	Glendine . .	1,221 2 37	King's Co. .	Ballybritt .	Kinnitty . .	Parsonstown .	I.	125
46	Glendine . .	50 2 28	King's Co. .	Clonlisk . .	Borrisnafarney .	Roscrea . .	I.	129
6	Glendine . .	751 3 18	Queen's Co. .	Tinnahinch .	Kilmanman .	Mountmellick .	I.	249
10, 11	Glendine . .	819 0 2	Queen's Co. .	Upperwoods .	Offerlane . .	Mountmellick .	I.	251
31	Glendine North .	492 1 39	Clare . .	Ibrickan . .	Kilfarboy .	Ennistimon .	II.	22
6	Glendineoregan .	858 1 19	Queen's Co. .	Tinnahinch .	Rearymore .	Mountmellick .	I.	250
31	Glendine South .	320 1 29	Clare . .	Ibrickan . .	Kilfarboy .	Ennistimon .	II.	22
40	Glendonnell . .	358 3 4	Kilkenny . .	Knocktopher .	Rossinan .	Waterford .	I.	113
25	Glendoo . .	933 1 1	Dublin . .	Uppercross .	Cruagh . .	Dublin South .	I.	39
46, 58	Glendorragha .	1,874 0 33	Mayo . .	Tirawley . .	Addergoole .	Castlebar .	IV.	163
36, 37, 40	Glendossaun . .	698 2 20	King's Co. .	Ballybritt .	Kinnitty . .	Parsonstown .	I.	125
51	Glendowanbeg .	188 1 38	Donegal . .	Kilmacrenan .	Gartan . .	Letterkenny .	III.	127
17	Glen (Doyne) . .	162 3 20	Wexford .	Ballaghkeen .	Ardamine .	Gorey . .	I.	291
19, 27	Glendree . .	2,564 1 34j	Clare . .	Tulla Upper .	Tulla . .	Tulla . .	II.	41
42	Glendrislagh . .	15 0 21	Wexford .	Bargy . .	Kilmanman .	Wexford .	I.	306
20	Glenduff . .	1,132 2 26	Cork, E.R.	Condons&Clangibbon	Brigown . .	Mitchelstown .	II.	59
29	Glenduff . .	103 2 27	King's Co. .	Garrycastle .	Lusmagh .	Parsonstown .	I.	137
53	Glenduff . .	879 2 26	Limerick . .	Glenquin . .	Monagay . .	Newcastle .	II.	247
33	Glenduff . .	162 1 19	Tipperary, N.R.	Upper Ormond .	Dolla . .	Nenagh . .	II.	290
37	Glenduff . .	65 0 21	Wexford .	Shelmaliere West .	Kilbrideglynn .	Wexford .	I.	334
24, 30	GLENEALY T. . .	—	Wicklow . .	Newcastle .	Glencaly . .	Rathdrum .	I.	351
153	Glen East . .	108 0 8	Cork, W.R.	West Carbery (E.D.)	Clear-island .	Skibbereen .	II.	138
13	Glen East . .	877 2 34	Fermanagh .	Magheraboy .	Inishmacsaint .	Ballyshannon .	III.	213
24	Glen East . .	172 0 24	Waterford .	Decies without Drum	Stradbally .	Kilmacthomas .	II.	361
13,14,20,21	Glenedagh Eighter .	433 0 20	Mayo . .	Tirawley . .	Kilfian . .	Killala . .	IV.	169
13,14,20,21	Glenedagh Oughter .	1,071 2 6	Mayo . .	Tirawley . .	Kilfian . .	Killala . .	IV.	169

(a) { Including 11A. 1R. 11P. detached portion. / Including 6A. 1R. 6P. water.
(b) Including 1A. 2R. 24P. detached portion.
(c) Including 3A. 0R. 10P. water.
(d) Including 6A. 0R. 22P. water.
(e) Including 272A. 2R. 30P. water.
(f) Including 7A. 3R. 35P. water.
(g) Including 18A. 1R. 26P. water.
(h) Including 54A. 1R. 16P. water.
(i) { Within the Municipal Boundary, 8A. 3R. 24P. / Without the Municipal Boundary, 114A. 2R. 7P.
(j) Including 22A. 1R. 17P. water.
(k) Including 9A. 2R. 4P. water.

No. of Sheet of the Ordnance Survey Maps.	Townlands and Towns.	Area in Statute Acres.			County.	Barony.	Parish.	Poor Law Union in 1857.	Townland Census of 1851. Part I.	
		A.	R.	P.					Vol.	Page
34, 35	Glenedra	2,150	1	18	Londonderry	Keenaght	Banagher	NewT⁰Limavady	III.	234
78, 87	Gleneely	292	0	24	Donegal	Raphoe	Donaghmore	Stranorlar	III.	138
44, 45	Gleneeny	586	1	19	Tyrone	Omagh East	Termonmaguirk	Omagh	III.	314
6, 10	Glencige	514	3	6	Leitrim	Drumahaire	Drumlease	Manorhamilton	IV.	94
8, 13	Glenerin	2,014	2	11	Tyrone	Strabane Upper	Bodoney Upper	Gortin	III.	324
71	Glenfad	265	2	10	Donegal	Raphoe	Clonleigh	Strabane	III.	135
47	Glenfield	428	2	39	Limerick	Kilmallock	St. Peter's & St.Paul's	Kilmallock	II.	250
6, 7	Glenfield North	136	1	23	Cork, E.R.	Duhallow	Knocktemple	Kanturk	II.	75
6, 7, 15, 16	Glenfield South	343	3	1	Cork, E.R.	Duhallow	Knocktemple	Kanturk	II.	75
42, 45	Glenfin	43	2	32	Roscommon	Athlone	Rahara	Roscommon	IV.	183
34	Glenfinshinagh	94	3	36	Tipperary, N.R.	Kilnamanagh Upper	Upperchurch	Thurles	II.	280
20	Glenfooran	119	1	20	Waterford	Coshmore & Coshbride	Lismore and Mocollop	Lismore	II.	346
11	Glenga	579	0	31	Tyrone	Strabane Upper	Bodoney Upper	Gortin	III.	324
21	Glengad	105	3	19	Antrim	Kilconway	Finvoy	Ballymoney	III.	26
2, 4, 5	Glengad	2,569	0	33	Donegal	Inishowen East	Culdaff	Inishowen	III.	118
3, 4, 10, 11	Glengad or Dooncarton	830	2	23	Mayo	Erris	Kilcommon	Belmullet	IV.	143
70	Glengaddy	128	0	12	Tipperary, S.R.	Middlethird	Barrettsgrange	Cashel	II.	325
55	Glengall	661	1	28	Tipperary, S.R.	Slievardagh	Ballingarry	Callan	II.	331
44, 45	Glengar	788	1	29	Tipperary, N.R.	Kilnamanagh Upper	Doon	Tipperary	II.	277
74, 80	Glengarra	1,029	2	11	Tipperary, S.R.	Iffa and Offa West	Shanrahan	Clogheen	II.	319
12, 20, 21	Glengarra	234	0	7	Waterford	Coshmore & Coshbride	Lismore and Mocollop	Lismore	II.	346
2	Glengarriff	279	3	14	Cork, E.R.	Orrery and Kilmore	Shandrum	Kilmallock	II.	110
90, 104	Glengarriff	74	0	21	Cork, W.R.	Bear	Kilcaskan	Bantry	II.	123
41	Glengarriff	114	3	33	Tipperary, N.R.	Eliogarty	Thurles	Thurles	II.	273
53, 64	Glengarriff Beg	180	1	35	Cork, E.R.	Barrymore	Lisgoold	Middleton	II.	56
64	Glengarriff More	184	2	29	Cork, E.R.	Barrymore	Lisgoold	Middleton	II.	56
6, 7, 11	Glengarrow	996	1	7	Tyrone	Strabane Lower	Donaghedy	Gortin	III.	321
26	Glengawna	850	2	2	Tyrone	Strabane Upper	Cappagh	Omagh	III.	325
50, 57	Glengeen	1,044	3	20	Tyrone	Omagh East	Dromore	Omagh	III.	311
82	Glengesh	1,626	2	29	Donegal	Banagh	Killybegs Lower	Glenties	III.	110
17	Glengesh	547	2	32	Fermanagh	Tirkennedy	Enniskillen	Enniskillen	III.	222
26, 27	Glengillagrana High	480	0	4	Donegal	Kilmacrenan	Mevagh	Milford	III.	130
18, 19	Glenglass	440	2	14	Wexford	Bantry	Killann	Enniscorthy	I.	300
6, 13	Glenglassera	1,191	2	31	Mayo	Tirawley	Doonfeeny	Killala	IV.	167
16	Glenglush	373	3	4	Tyrone	Strabane Lower	Ardstraw	Castlederg	III.	319
34	Glengoagh	181	1	35	Waterford	Coshmore & Coshbride	Kilcockan	Lismore	II.	343
35, 40	Glengomna	1,702	3	13	Londonderry	Loughinsholin	Ballynascreen	Magherafelt	III.	239
48, 54	Glengoole North	809	3	10	Tipperary, S.R.	Slievardagh	Kilcooly	Urlingford	II.	334
48, 54	Glengoole South	714	0	14	Tipperary, S.R.	Slievardagh	Kilcooly	Urlingford	II.	334
32	Glengorm	169	0	0	Westmeath	Moycashel	Castletownkindalen	Mullingar	I.	277
56	Glengormly	215	1	4	Antrim	Lower Belfast	Carnmoney	Belfast	III.	8
43	Glengort North	697	3	2	Limerick	Glenquin	Killeedy	Newcastle	II.	245
43, 52	Glengort South	1,507	0	6	Limerick	Glenquin	Killeedy	Newcastle	II.	246
46	Glengoura Lower	184	1	21	Cork, E.R.	Kinnatalloon	Mogeely	Fermoy	II.	98
46	Glengoura Upper	324	2	21	Cork, E.R.	Kinnatalloon	Mogeely	Fermoy	II.	98
54	Glengowla East	366	2	0a	Galway	Moycullen	Kilcummin	Oughterard	IV.	67
53, 54	Glengowla West	597	0	25b	Galway	Moycullen	Kilcummin	Oughterard	IV.	67
45	Glengrant	72	3	18	Kilkenny	Iverk	Portnascully	Waterford	I.	106
11	Glenhall	112	2	2	Londonderry	Coleraine	Macosquin	Coleraine	III.	233
34, 39	Glenhead	1,397	0	34	Antrim	Lower Antrim	Glenwhirry	Ballymena	III.	4
8	Glenhouse	647	0	21	Waterford	Upperthird	Kilmeadan	Carrick on Suir	II.	370
59	Glenhoy	152	2	28	Tyrone	Clogher	Clogher	Clogher	III.	292
32	Glenhugh	377	2	19	Antrim	Lower Toome	Aghoghill	Ballymena	III.	32
79	Glenicmurrin	2,482	3	26c	Galway	Moycullen	Kilcummin	Galway	IV.	67
4, 8	Glenidan	1,139	1	9	Westmeath	Fore	St. Mary's	Castletowndelvin	I.	272
26, 35	Glenieraragh	1,166	1	14d	Donegal	Kilmacrenan	Mevagh	Milford	III.	130
6	Gleniff	767	2	34	Sligo	Carbury	Rossinver	Sligo	IV.	223
24	Gleninagh	657	2	25	Galway	Ballynahinch	Ballynakill	Clifden	IV.	11
24, 37	Gleninagh	2,654	1	24	Galway	Ballynahinch	Moyrus	Clifden	IV.	13
2	Gleninagh North	486	0	4	Clare	Burren	Gleninagh	Ballyvaghan	II.	12
2	Gleninagh South	635	3	5	Clare	Burren	Gleninagh	Ballyvaghan	II.	12
39	Gleninchnaveigh	113	0	13	Tipperary, N.R.	Kilnamanagh Upper	Upperchurch	Thurles	II.	280
26	Glenineeny	77	1	33e	Donegal	Kilmacrenan	Mevagh	Milford	III.	130
5	Gleninsheen	595	2	22	Clare	Burren	Rathborney	Ballyvaghan	II.	14
13, 14, 18	Glenish	143	0	8	Monaghan	Monaghan	Kilmore	Monaghan	III.	276
55	Glenkeal	76	2	10	Cork, E.R.	Kinnatalloon	Mogeely	Youghal	II.	98
20	Glenkeel	661	0	2f	Fermanagh	Magheraboy	Boho	Enniskillen	III.	209
8	Glenkeel	316	2	25	Leitrim	Rosclogher	Cloonclare	Manorhamilton	IV.	109
36	Glenkeen	157	0	32g	Donegal	Kilmacrenan	Tullyfern	Milford	III.	133
10	Glenkeen	181	3	21h	Fermanagh	Lurg	Derryvullan	Lowtherstown	III.	204
11,12,18,19	Glenkeen	220	3	27	Londonderry	Coleraine	Aghadowey	Coleraine	III.	229
18	Glenkeen	336	1	14	Londonderry	Coleraine	Errigal	Coleraine	III.	232

(a) Including 6A. 1R. 11P. water.
(b) Including 24A. 3R. 11P. water.
(c) Including 319A. 1R. 29P. water.
(d) Including 160A. 0R. 34P. water.
(e) Including 9A. 0R. 32P. water.
(f) Including 2A. 1R. 27P. water.
(g) Including 1A. 3R. 11P. water.
(h) Including 22A. 1R. 26P. water.

No. of Sheet of the Ordnance Survey Maps.	Townlands and Towns.	Area in Statute Acres. A. R. P.	County.	Barony.	Parish.	Poor Law Union in 1857.	Townland Census of 1851, Part I. Vol.	Page
10	Glenkeen	236 1 32	Londonderry	Keenaght	Drumachose	NewT.Limavady	III.	235
20, 21, 22	Glenkeen	369 3 30	Londonderry	Tirkeeran	Clondermot	Londonderry	III.	248
96, 106	Glenkeen	3,667 2 19	Mayo	Murrisk	Kilgeever	Westport	IV.	160
34	Glenkeen	266 1 36	Tipperary, N.R.	Kilnamanagh Upper	Glenkeen	Thurles	II.	278
66	Glenkeen	468 0 22	Tyrone	Dungannon Lower	Aghaloo	Dungannon	III.	297
2	Glenkeen Lower	228 1 35	Queen's Co.	Tinnahinch	Kilmanman	Mountmellick	I.	249
2, 6	Glenkeen Upper	1,331 2 0	Queen's Co.	Tinnahinch	Kilmanman	Mountmellick	I.	249
52	Glenkeeragh	555 2 36	Donegal	Kilmacrenan	Conwal	Letterkenny	III.	126
61	Glenkeeran	422 0 29	Donegal	Raphoe	Raphoe	Letterkenny	III.	141
52, 53	Glenkeo	215 3 12	Donegal	Kilmacrenan	Kilmacrenan	Letterkenny	III.	129
27	Glenkeo	1,157 1 32a	Donegal	Kilmacrenan	Mevagh	Millford	III.	130
10	Glenkitt	706 2 10	Queen's Co.	Upperwoods	Offerlane	Mountmellick	I.	251
17	Glenknock or Cloghogle	560 0 28b	Tyrone	Strabane Lower	Ardstraw	Gortin	III.	319
12, 13	Glenlahan	1,457 1 6	Cork, E.R.	Duhallow	Kilmeen	Kanturk	II.	73
14, 22	Glenlara	951 3 3	Cork, E.R.	Duhallow	Clonfert	Kanturk	II.	68
58	Glenlara	1,302 0 33	Mayo	Burrishoole	Burrishoole	Newport	IV.	119
2, 3, 10	Glenlara	1,822 1 7c	Mayo	Erris	Kilmore	Belmullet	IV.	146
12, 19	Glenlark	3,140 0 37	Tyrone	Strabane Upper	Bodoney Lower	Gortin	III.	323
48, 49	Glenlary	813 0 14	Limerick	Coshlea	Ballingarry	Kilmallock	II.	237
107	Glenlaur	1,138 1 13	Mayo	Murrisk	Oughaval	Westport	IV.	162
8, 14	Glenlea	309 0 27	Kerry	Clanmaurice	Ballyheige	Tralee	II.	168
45, 46	Glenleary	332 0 16	Donegal	Kilmacrenan	Aughnish	Millford	III.	122
7, 11	Glenleary	681 2 26	Londonderry	Coleraine	Macosquin	Coleraine	III.	233
97	Glenlee	144 0 33	Donegal	Banagh	Killybegs Upper	Glenties	III.	110
39	Glenleigh	638 2 28	Cork, W.R.	West Muskerry	Kilcorney	Millstreet	II.	158
23, 27	Glenleslie	611 2 30	Antrim	Kilconway	Dunaghy	Ballymena	III.	26
37	Glenletter	1,138 0 37	King's Co.	Ballybritt	Letterluna	Parsonstown	I.	126
31, 32, 39, 40	Glenletternafinny	387 2 27	Clare	Islands	Kilmaley	Ennis	II.	31
15	Glenlevan	146 3 11	Fermanagh	Magheraboy	Inishmacsaint	Enniskillen	III.	213
35, 38	Glenlicky	309 3 29	Waterford	Decies within Drum	Ardmore	Youghal	II.	350
23	Glenlohane	63 0 31	Cork, E.R.	Duhallow	Castlemagner	Kanturk	II.	67
53	Glenlon North	175 0 8	Clare	Tulla Lower	O'Briensbridge	Limerick	II.	38
53	Glenlon South	172 2 27	Clare	Tulla Lower	O'Briensbridge	Limerick	II.	38
17	Glenlough	429 2 36	Antrim	Upper Dunluce	Ballymoney	Ballymoney	III.	19
103, 104	Glenlough	1,726 2 28d	Cork, W.R.	Bear	Kilcaskan	Castletown	II.	123
72, 81	Glenlough	2,231 2 2e	Donegal	Banagh	Glencolumbkille	Glenties	III.	105
22, 28	Glenlough	664 0 12	Londonderry	Tirkeeran	Cumber Upper	Londonderry	III.	249
55	Glenloughan	355 1 0	Down	Mourne	Kilkeel	Kilkeel	III.	183
26, 33	Glenloughan	261 3 5	Down	Upper Iveagh, Up. pt.	Aghaderg	Banbridge	III.	174
55	Glenloughan Upper	330 0 32	Down	Mourne	Kilkeel	Kilkeel	III.	183
87	Glenloughaun	299 2 19	Galway	Clonmacnowen	Clontuskert	Ballinasloe	IV.	24
36, 45	Glen Lower	356 3 27	Donegal	Kilmacrenan	Tullyfern	Millford	III.	133
9	Glen Lower	129 3 31	Sligo	Carbury	Drumcliff	Sligo	IV.	221
22	Glen Lower	125 0 14	Waterford	Decies without Drum	Modeligo	Dungarvan	II.	359
2, 3	Glen Lower	620 3 36	Waterford	Upperthird	Dysert	Carrick on Suir	II.	369
26, 39	Glenlusk	401 0 17	Galway	Ross	Cong	Oughterard	IV.	73
39	Glenma	154 2 25	Limerick	Coshma	Athlacca	Kilmallock	II	241
74, 75	Glenmacannive	480 2 24	Donegal	Boylagh	Inishkeel	Glenties	III.	112
18, 19, 26	Glenmacoffer	2,703 3 3	Tyrone	Strabane Upper	Bodoney Lower	Gortin	III.	323
34, 35	Glenmacolla & Scrub	391 3 36	Queen's Co.	Clarmallagh	Aghmacart	Abbeyleix	I.	236
5	Glenmageo or Firoda Lower	1,049 0 29	Kilkenny	Fassadinin	Castlecomer	Castlecomer	I.	88
11	Glenmakee	716 2 8	Donegal	Inishowen East	Donagh	Inishowen	III.	118
9, 14	Glenmakeeran	2,818 1 29	Antrim	Cary	Culfeightrin	Ballycastle	III.	13
3	Glenmanus	148 0 9	Londonderry	North East Liberties of Coleraine	Ballywillin	Coleraine	III.	245
41, 42	Glenmaquill	157 1 7	Londonderry	Loughinsholin	Magherafelt	Magherafelt	III.	243
61, 62	Glenmaquin Lower	793 2 27	Donegal	Raphoe	Raphoe	Letterkenny	III.	141
61, 62	Glenmaquin Upper	404 3 6	Donegal	Raphoe	Raphoe	Letterkenny	III.	141
108	Glenmask	1,872 0 14	Mayo	Carra	Ballyovey	Ballinrobe	IV.	126
98, 106	Glenmeen	220 0 36	Galway	Leitrim	Kilreckill	Loughrea	IV.	54
26, 27	Glenmenagh	658 2 31	Donegal	Kilmacrenan	Mevagh	Millford	III.	130
153	Glen Middle	52 2 18	Cork, W.R.	West Carbery (E.D.)	Clear-island	Skibbereen	II.	138
39, 40, 48	Glenmore	2,054 3 25	Clare	Clonderalaw	Kilmihil	Kilrush	II.	17
71	Glenmore	224 3 11	Galway	Clare	Lackagh	Galway	IV.	22
24, 25	Glenmore	351 1 30	Kildare	Naas South	Tipperkevin	Naas	I.	65
27, 28	Glenmore	160 3 17	Kilkenny	Knocktopher	Jerpointchurch	Thomastown	I.	111
44	Glenmore	86 3 17	Limerick	Glenquin	Monagay	Newcastle	II.	247
5, 6	Glenmore	689 2 19	Longford	Longford	Killoe	Longford	I.	159
22, 26	Glenmore	494 0 10	Longford	Moydow	Kilcommock	Ballymahon	I.	161
5, 8	Glenmore	2,206 2 11	Louth	Lower Dundalk	Carlingford	Dundalk	I.	176
2, 3	Glen More	212 2 0	Monaghan	Trough	Errigal Trough	Clogher	III.	284

(a) Including 12A. 3R. 29P. water.
(b) Including 0A. 2R. 39P. water.
(c) Including 9A. 2R. 5P. water.
(d) Including 92A. 2R. 4P. water.
(e) Including 38A. 0R. 34P. water.

No. of Sheet of the Ordnance Survey Maps.	Townlands and Towns.	Area in Statute Acres.			County.	Barony.	Parish.	Poor Law Union in 1857.	Townland Census of 1851, Part I.	
		A.	R.	P.					Vol.	Page
50	Glenmore	316	1	24	Roscommon	Athlone	Taghmaconnell	Ballinasloe	IV.	185
32	Glenmore	35	0	32	Roscommon	Castlereagh	Kiltullagh	Castlereagh	IV.	202
20	Glen More	309	2	20a	Waterford	Coshmore&Coshbride	Lismore and Mocollop	Lismore	II.	346
35	Glen More	325	2	9	Waterford	Decies without Drum	Dungarvan	Dungarvan	II.	355
43, 44	Glenmore East	731	0	8	Limerick	Glenquin	Killeedy	Newcastle	II.	246
28	Glenmore Lower	188	3	5	Tipperary, N.R.	Upper Ormond	Latteragh	Nenagh	II.	292
41	GLENMORE T.	—			Kilkenny	Ida	Kilcoan / Kilmakeevoge	Waterford	I.	102 / 103
28	Glenmore Upper	426	2	28	Tipperary, N.R.	Upper Ormond	Latteragh	Nenagh	II.	292
43, 44	Glenmore West	320	3	20	Limerick	Glenquin	Killeedy	Newcastle	II.	246
20, 28	Glenmorrishmeen	257	3	20b	Waterford	Coshmore&Coshbride	Lismore and Mocollop	Lismore	II.	346
50	Glenmullion	75	1	1	Antrim	Upper Antrim	Antrim	Antrim	III.	5
63, 73	Glenmullynaha East	871	3	30	Mayo	Costello	Kilbeagh	Swineford	IV.	140
63, 73	Glenmullynaha West	945	2	29	Mayo	Costello	Kilbeagh	Swineford	IV.	140
107, 116	Glennacally	5,247	1	4	Mayo	Murrisk	Aghagower	Westport	IV.	159
26	Glennacanon	269	2	25	Wicklow	Upper Talbotstown	Ballynure	Baltinglass	I.	361
82	Glennaclohalea	62	0	3	Tipperary, S.R.	Iffa and Offa West	Ardfinnan	Clogheen	II.	316
12	Glennafallia	586	1	9	Waterford	Coshmore&Coshbride	Lismore and Mocollop	Lismore	II.	346
43	Glennafosha	481	0	32	Galway	Clare	Belclare	Tuam	IV.	17
28	Glennafunshoge or Ashglen	68	0	19	Kilkenny	Gowran	Woolengrange	Thomastown	I.	100
1	Glennagad	160	3	11	Waterford	Upperthird	St. Mary's, Clonmel	Clonmel	II.	372
21, 27	Glennagark	260	3	28	Wexford	Ballaghkeen	Kilcormick	Enniscorthy	I.	294
1, 5	Glennagarran	113	0	28	Fermanagh	Lurg	Drumkeeran	Lowtherstown	III.	206
42	Glennagarraun	109	3	20	Galway	Clare	Kilkilvery	Tuam	IV.	20
108	Glennagashleeny	969	1	21	Mayo	Carra	Ballyovey	Ballinrobe	IV.	126
76	Glennagat	351	1	36	Tipperary, S.R.	Middlethird	Knockgraffon	Cashel	II.	328
77	Glennageare East	270	1	6	Cork, E.R.	Imokilly	Ballyoughtera	Middleton	II.	84
77	Glennageare West	296	1	36	Cork, E.R.	Imokilly	Ballyoughtera	Middleton	II.	84
31, 32	Glennageer	844	3	32	Clare	Inchiquin	Inagh	Ennistimon	II.	25
52, 59	Glennageeragh	359	0	4	Tyrone	Clogher	Clogher	Clogher	III.	292
12	Glennagevlagh	1,203	2	5	Galway	Ross	Ross	Oughterard	IV.	74
13	Glennagiveny	1,697	1	0	Donegal	Inishowen East	Moville Lower	Inishowen	III.	119
11	Glennaglass	229	2	34	Queen's Co.	Upperwoods	Offerlane	Mountmellick	I.	251
33	Glennaglogh	247	1	27	Waterford	Coshmore&Coshbride	Tallow	Lismore	II.	348
12	Glennaglogh	122	3	14	Wexford	Ballaghkeen	Kiltennell	Gorey	I.	297
84, 85	Glennagloghaun	53	3	1	Galway	Tiaquin	Monivea	Loughrea	IV.	79
71	Glennagloghaun North	418	0	25	Galway	Tiaquin	Monivea	Tuam	IV.	79
71	Glennagloghaun South	365	1	33	Galway	Tiaquin	Monivea	Tuam	IV.	79
20	Glennagoolagh	233	0	20	Sligo	Tirerrill	Ballysadare	Sligo	IV.	237
3	Glennagoorland Glebe	691	0	11	Tyrone	Strabane Lower	Donaghedy	Strabane	III.	321
35, 36	Glennagowan	271	0	25	Limerick	Glenquin	Newcastle	Newcastle	II.	248
52, 53	Glennagross	928	0	13	Clare	Bunratty Lower	St. Munchins	Limerick	II.	6
49, 57	Glennahaglish	427	2	25	Limerick	Coshlea	Ballylanders	Mitchelstown	II.	237
40, 48	Glennahilt	79	0	10c	Donegal	Boylagh	Templecrone	Glenties	III.	115
35	Glennahoo	458	3	14	Kerry	Corkaguiny	Ballyduff	Dingle	II.	174
35	Glennahoo	88	3	24	Kerry	Corkaguiny	Stradbally	Dingle	II.	180
19	Glennahulla	250	3	3	Cork, E.R.	Condons&Clangibbon	Marshalstown	Mitchelstown	II.	63
19	Glennahulla	365	1	7	Cork, E.R.	Fermoy	Ballydeloughy	Mitchelstown	II.	76
4, 13	Glennakeel North	307	0	2	Cork, E.R.	Duhallow	Clonfert	Kanturk	II.	68
13	Glennakeel South	1,540	1	39	Cork, E.R.	Duhallow	Clonfert	Kanturk	II.	68
13	Glennakeel West	791	3	9	Cork, E.R.	Duhallow	Clonfert	Kanturk	II.	68
13	Glennaknockane	646	2	11	Cork, E.R.	Duhallow	Clonfert	Kanturk	II.	68
56, 66, 67	Glennamaddoo	2,045	2	26	Mayo	Burrishoole	Burrishoole	Newport	IV.	119
18	Glennamaddy	299	2	15	Galway	Ballymoe	Boyounagh	Glennamaddy	IV.	6
18	GLENNAMADDY T.	—			Galway	Ballymoe	Boyounagh	Glennamaddy	IV.	6
11, 12	Glennameade	483	0	30d	Limerick	Kenry	Kildimo	Rathkeale	II.	250
29	Glennameeltoge or Midgefield	90	2	5	Roscommon	Roscommon	Cloonfinlough	Strokestown	IV.	209
14	Glennameenagh or Springvale	283	1	24	Wexford	Scarawalsh	Ballycarney	Enniscorthy	I.	322
45, 57	Glennamong	4,453	2	30	Mayo	Burrishoole	Burrishoole	Newport	IV.	119
72	Glennamucka	347	0	19	Galway	Tiaquin	Ballymacward	Loughrea	IV.	75
13,14,21,22	Glennamucklagh East	843	2	35	Cork, E.R.	Duhallow	Clonfert	Kanturk	II.	68
13, 21	Glennamucklagh West	1,320	1	8	Cork, E.R.	Duhallow	Clonfert	Kanturk	II.	68
42	Glennan	217	2	32	Tyrone	Omagh East	Donacavey	Omagh	III.	310
41	Glennanammer	177	3	37	Roscommon	Athlone	Athleague	Roscommon	IV.	179
25	Glennanbeg	48	0	1e	Leitrim	Carrigallen	Drumreilly	Bawnboy	IV.	91
25	Glennan Beg	68	1	35f	Leitrim	Carrigallen	Oughteragh	Bawnboy	IV.	92
51	Glennanea	262	0	33	Roscommon	Athlone	Taghmaconnell	Athlone	IV.	185
13, 14	Glennaneane	170	1	28	Waterford	Decies without Drum	Seskinan	Dungarvan	II.	360
13, 14	Glennaneanemountain	216	0	4	Waterford	Decies without Drum	Seskinan	Dungarvan	II.	360
56, 57	Glennaneeny	180	2	10	Galway	Clare	Cummer	Tuam	IV.	19
25	Glennan More	82	2	23g	Leitrim	Carrigallen	Oughteragh	Bawnboy	IV.	92

(a) Including 5A. 1R. 7P. water.
(b) Including 4A. 3R. 4P. water.
(c) Including 7A. 1R. 6P. water.
(d) Including 6A. 1R. 0P. Feereagh Lough.
(e) Including 3A. 2R. 3P. water.
(f) Including 2A. 2R. 28P. water.
(g) Including 1A. 2R. 14P. water.

No. of Sheet of the Ordnance Survey Maps	Townlands and Towns.	Area in Statute Acres.			County.	Barony.	Parish.	Poor Law Union in 1857.	Townland Census of 1851, Part I.	
		A.	R.	P.					Vol.	Page
34	Glennanoge	104	0	2	Tipperary, N.R.	Kilnamanagh Upper	Glenkeen	Thurles	II.	278
6	Glennanore	1,293	3	35	Waterford	Upperthird	Rathgormuck	Clonmel	II.	371
2	Glennanummer or Burrow	97	1	22	King's Co.	Kilcoursey	Kilcumreragh	Tullamore	I.	141
7	Glennaphuca	560	0	29	Waterford	Upperthird	Mothel	Carrick on Suir	II.	371
28, 34	Glennariesk	55	2	31	Tipperary, N.R.	Kilnamanagh Upper	Glenkeen	Thurles	II.	278
83	Glennascaul	947	2	2	Galway	Dunkellin	Oranmore	Galway	IV.	32
14	Glennasheevar	900	2	21	Fermanagh	Magheraboy	Inishmacsaint	Ballyshannon	III.	213
46	Glennashouk	423	1	3	Wicklow	Shillelagh	Carnew	Shillelagh	I.	357
71	Glennaskagh	1,218	0	12	Tipperary, S.R.	Slievardagh	Grangemockler	Carrick on Suir	II.	333
98	Glennaskehy	422	2	22	Galway	Leitrim	Kilreekill	Loughrea	IV.	54
106	Glennaslat	168	0	39	Galway	Leitrim	Kilteskill	Loughrea	IV.	55
71	Glennaslat	168	3	16	Galway	Tiaquin	Monivea	Tuam	IV.	79
69	Glennaslaud	62	3	15	Tipperary, S.R.	Middlethird	Kilbragh	Cashel	II.	327
64	Glennaun	397	0	26a	Galway	Ballynahinch	Moyrus	Clifden	IV.	13
79, 91	Glennaun	1,228	0	37b	Galway	Moycullen	Killannin	Galway	IV.	69
87	Glennavaddoge	111	0	15	Galway	Clonmacnowen	Kilcloony	Ballinasloe	IV.	25
108	Glennavaddoge	68	0	20	Galway	Longford	Meelick	Portumna	IV.	61
58	Glennaveel	274	0	4	Galway	Tiaquin	Abbeyknockmoy	Tuam	IV.	75
28, 29	Glennawillin	73	0	37	Waterford	Coshmore&Coshbride	Kilwatermoy	Lismore	II.	343
30, 36, 37	Glennawoo	2,005	0	0c	Sligo	Leyny	Kilmacteige	Tobercurry	IV.	231
64, 68	Glennoo	1,713	1	27d	Tyrone	Clogher	Clogher	Clogher	III.	292
15, 23	Glen North	132	0	35	Clare	Corcomroe	Clooney	Ennistimon	II.	18
31, 40	Glen North	541	1	35	Cork, E.R.	Duhallow	Clonmeen	Kanturk	II.	69
30, 35	Glenns	145	1	7	King's Co.	Eglish	Eglish	Parsonstown	I.	135
14	Glennyhorn	117	1	39	Monaghan	Cremorne	Clontibret	Monaghan	III.	260
7	Gleno	760	1	13	Limerick	Owneybeg	Abington	Limerick	II.	251
28	Glenocum	636	1	23	Antrim	Lower Antrim	Skerry	Ballymena	III.	5
8	Glenoge	131	1	18	Carlow	Carlow	Grangeford	Carlow	I.	2
2, 3	Glenoge	257	3	20	Wexford	Gorey	Inch	Gorey	I.	316
2, 3	Glenoge	234	2	35	Wexford	Gorey	Kilnenor	Gorey	I.	319
9, 14	Glenoghil	520	1	6	Longford	Granard	Clonbroney	Granard	I.	155
22, 31	Glenogra	409	3	11	Limerick	Smallcounty	Glenogra	Croom	II.	260
7	GlenoKnocklatteragh	144	0	34	Limerick	Owneybeg	Abington	Limerick	II.	251
33, 37	Glenone	825	0	27	Londonderry	Loughinsholin	Tamlaght O'Crilly	Magherafelt	III.	243
7	Gleno Newtown	194	1	32	Limerick	Owneybeg	Abington	Limerick	II.	251
7, 16	Glenoory	277	2	7	Donegal	Kilmacrenan	Mevagh	Millford	III.	120
13	Glenora	781	0	7	Mayo	Tirawley	Doonfeeny	Killala	IV.	167
56, 59	Glenosheen	773	2	5	Limerick	Coshlea	Particles	Kilmallock	II.	240
45, 46	Glenough Lower	2,354	1	27	Tipperary, S.R.	Kilnamanagh Lower	Clonoulty	Cashel	II.	323
61	Glenoughty	297	3	25	Donegal	Raphoe	Leck	Letterkenny	III.	140
45	Glenough Upper	722	1	22	Tipperary, S.R.	Kilnamanagh Lower	Clonoulty	Cashel	II.	323
31, 36	Glenour	273	3	12	Wexford	Shelmalier West	Kilgarvan	New Ross	I.	334
2, 6	Glenpatrick	1,905	3	21	Waterford	Upperthird	Rathgormuck	Clonmel	II.	371
45, 51	Glenpaudeen	845	2	32	Tipperary, S.R.	Kilnamanagh Lower	Donohill	Tipperary	II.	323
38	Glenphilipeen	235	3	30	Wicklow	Ballinacor South	Kilcommon	Shillelagh	I.	349
36	Glenpipe	1,157	3	36	Kilkenny	Knocktopher	Jerpoint West	New Ross	I.	111
10	Glenquin	1,004	3	30	Clare	Inchiquin	Killinaboy	Corrofin	II.	26
43, 44	Glenquin	712	3	19	Limerick	Glenquin	Killeedy	Newcastle	II.	246
44	Glenquin	203	1	31	Limerick	Glenquin	Monagay	Newcastle	II.	247
43, 44	Glenquin South	332	2	11	Limerick	Glenquin	Monagay	Newcastle	II.	247
21	Glenranny	374	0	23	Wexford	Ballaghkeen	Kilcormick	Gorey	I.	294
11	Glenrath	44	3	26	Meath	Lower Kells	Kilbeg	Kells	I.	202
65	Glenreagh	71	1	4	Cork, E.R.	Barrymore	Templenacarriga	Middleton	II.	58
21	Glenreagh	788	3	20	Cork, E.R.	Duhallow	Kilmeen	Kanturk	II.	73
46	Glenreagh	343	1	39	Cork, E.R.	Kinnatalloon	Ballynoe	Fermoy	II.	97
12	Glenreagh	157	1	17	Kilkenny	Crannagh	Tubbridbritain	Urlingford	I.	87
28, 29	Glenreagh	208	3	10	Tipperary, N.R.	Ikerrin	Killea	Roscrea	II.	275
47	Glenreagh Beg	227	2	28	Tipperary, N.R.	Eliogarty	Holycross	Thurles	II.	270
46, 47	Glenreagh More	241	1	17	Tipperary, N.R.	Eliogarty	Holycross	Thurles	II.	270
26	Glenree	449	3	30e	Donegal	Kilmacrenan	Mevagh	Millford	III.	130
37, 40	Glenregan	1,798	3	2	King's Co.	Ballybritt	Kinnitty	Parsonstown	I.	125
56	Glenrevagh	553	3	26	Galway	Clare	Annaghdown	Tuam	IV.	16
82, 83	Glenrevagh	133	3	35	Galway	Dunkellin	Oranmore	Galway	IV.	32
42	Glenrevagh	170	0	34	Roscommon	Athlone	Kilmeane	Roscommon	IV.	182
47	Glenrevagh	165	2	13	Roscommon	Athlone	Taghboy	Athlone	IV.	184
21	Glenribbeen	179	1	9	Waterford	Coshmore and Coshbride	Lismore and Mocollop	Lismore	II.	346
12, 17	Glen (Richards)	297	3	4	Wexford	Ballaghkeen	Ardamine	Gorey	I.	291
11, 12	Glenroan	2,153	2	8f	Tyrone	Strabane Upper	Bodoney Upper	Gortin	III.	324
60	Glenroe	93	3	11	Tyrone	Dungannon Lower	Carnteel	Clogher	III.	207
35, 40	Glenross	167	3	0	Wexford	Shelmaliere West	Clongeen	New Ross	I.	333
10	Glenross	153	2	6	Fermanagh	Lurg	Derryvullan	Lowtherstown	III.	204

(a) Including 14A. 3R. 24P. water.
(b) Including 51A. 0R. 0P. water.
(c) Including 120A. 3R. 35P. water.
(d) Including 3A. 2R. 38P. water.
(e) Including 9A. 1R. 38P. water.
(f) Including 9A. 0R. 19P. water.

No. of Sheet of the Ordnance Survey Maps	Townlands and Towns.	Area in Statute Acres.			County.	Barony.	Parish.	Poor Law Union in 1857.	Townland Census of 1851, Part I.	
		A.	R.	P.					Vol.	Page
37	Glensansaw	137	1	32	Kilkenny	Ida	Rosbercon	New Ross	I.	103
31, 35	Glenshane	2,569	0	34	Londonderry	Keenaght	Dungiven	New^TLimavady	III.	236
18, 27, 28	Glensharrold	996	3	36	Limerick	Shanid	Kilcolman	Newcastle	II.	255
27, 28	Glensharrold	1,220	3	14	Limerick	Shanid	Rathronan	Newcastle	II.	257
20	Glenshask Beg	107	2	7	Waterford	Coshmore&Coshbride	Lismore and Mocollop	Lismore	II.	346
20, 21	Glenshask More	278	0	36	Waterford	Coshmore&Coshbride	Lismore and Mocollop	Lismore	II.	346
5, 9	Glensleade	212	2	22	Clare	Burren	Kilcorney	Ballyvaghan	II.	12
70, 79	Glensmoil	213	3	7	Donegal	Raphoe	Clonleigh	Strabane	III.	135
15, 23	Glen South	94	1	16	Clare	Corcomroe	Clooney	Ennistimon	II.	18
40	Glen South	1,023	2	33	Cork, E.R.	Duhallow	Clonmeen	Kanturk	II.	69
4	Glenstaghey	475	2	38	Antrim	Cary	Ballintoy	Ballycastle	III.	12
7	Glenstal	1,084	0	6	Limerick	Owneybeg	Abington	Limerick	II.	251
16	Glenstall	194	0	7	Antrim	Upper Dunluce	Ballymoney	Ballymoney	III	19
7	Glenstown	343	0	0	Waterford	Upperthird	Mothel	Carrick on Suir	II.	371
54	Glentane	274	0	20	Cork, E.R.	Kinnatalloon	Ballynoe	Fermoy	II.	97
27,28,33,34	Glentane	372	0	36	Tipperary, N.R.	Kilnamanagh Upper	Glenkeen	Thurles	II.	278
40	Glentaneatnagh North	513	1	37	Cork, E.R.	Duhallow	Clonmeen	Kanturk	II.	69
40, 49	Glentaneatnagh South	448	3	23	Cork, E.R.	Duhallow	Clonmeen	Kanturk	II.	69
21	Glentanedowney	363	3	9	Cork, E.R.	Duhallow	Kilmeen	Kanturk	II.	73
13, 21	Glentanefinnane	1,621	1	38	Cork, E.R.	Duhallow	Kilmeen	Kantu.k	II.	73
13	Glentanemacelligot	585	3	8	Cork, E.R.	Duhallow	Clonfert	Kanturk	II.	68
12	Glentara	57	0	20	Tipperary, N.R.	Ikerrin	Roscrea	Roscrea	II.	276
2, 6	Glentask	149	1	7	Antrim	Lower Dunluce	Dunluce	Coleraine	III.	17
53	Glentaun	224	1	13	Roscommon	Moycarn	Creagh	Ballinasloe	IV.	206
11	Glentaunatinagh	274	2	16	Waterford	Coshmore&Coshbride	Lismore and Mocollop	Lismore	II.	346
21	Glentaun East	127	1	27	Waterford	Coshmore&Coshbride	Lismore and Mocollop	Lismore	II.	346
11, 12	Glentaunemon	184	3	32	Waterford	Coshmore&Coshbride	Lismore and Mocollop	Lismore	II.	346
21	Glentaun West	120	1	11	Waterford	Coshmore&Coshbride	Lismore and Mocollop	Lismore	II.	346
72, 73	Glentavraun	1,578	0	33	Mayo	Costello	Kilmovee	Swineford	IV.	142
26	Glenteige	71	3	22	Wexford	Ballaghkeen	Edermine	Enniscorthy	I.	294
33, 40	Glenteige	203	0	15	Wicklow	Arklow	Kilbride	Rathdrum	I	344
56, 57	Glenthomas	1,129	2	10	Mayo	Burrishoole	Burrishoole	Newport	IV.	119
37	Glentidaly	416	0	9	Donegal	Kilmacrenan	Tullyfern	Millford	III.	133
36, 37	Glentidaly Glebe	255	3	20	Donegal	Kilmacrenan	Tullyfern	Millford	III	133
32	Glenties	83	3	39	Roscommon	Castlereagh	Kiltullagh	Castlereagh	IV.	202
74	GLENTIES T.	—			Donegal	Boylagh	Inishkeel	Glenties	III.	114
61	Glentillid	309	2	25	Donegal	Raphoe	Leck	Letterkenny	III.	140
9, 10	Glentimon	317	2	6	Tyrone	Strabane Lower	Urney	Strabane	III.	322
27	Glentire	116	3	22	Wexford	Ballaghkeen	Killisk	Enniscorthy	I.	296
57	Glentiroe	189	0	32	Kilkenny	Ida	Dysartmoon	New Ross	I.	101
20, 30	Glentogher or Carrowmore	5,784	3	38	Donegal	Inishowen East	Donagh	Inishowen	III.	118
14, 19	Glentop or Ardaghmore	1,508	0	28	Antrim	Cary	Culfeightrin	Ballycastle	III.	13
42	Glentornan	2,731	0	34d	Donegal	Kilmacrenan	Tullaghobegly	Dunfanaghy	III.	131
54, 62	Glentown	241	3	31	Donegal	Raphoe	Taughboyne	Strabane	III.	143
9	Glentown	230	0	27	Tyrone	Strabane Lower	Urney	Strabane	III.	322
45, 54	Glentrasna	284	2	14	Cork, E.R.	Kinnatalloon	Aghern	Fermoy	II.	97
53, 66	Glentrasna	1,850	0	25b	Galway	Moycullen	Kilcummin	Oughterard	IV.	67
45	Glentrasna North	219	1	1	Cork, E.R.	Kinnatalloon	Aghern	Fermoy	II.	97
54	Glentrasna South	220	3	30	Cork, E.R.	Kinnatalloon	Aghern	Fermoy	II.	97
18, 19	Glenturk Beg	1,823	0	36	Mayo	Erris	Kilcommon	Belmullet	IV.	144
18, 19	Glenturk More	1,547	2	29	Mayo	Erris	Kilcommon	Belmullet	IV.	144
6	Glenulra	2,164	3	10	Mayo	Tirawley	Doonfeeny	Killala	IV.	167
106, 107, 115, 116	Glenummera	2,866	0	9	Mayo	Murrisk	Aghagower	Westport	IV.	159
105	Glenummera	524	1	15c	Mayo	Murrisk	Kilgeever	Westport	IV.	160
36, 45	Glen Upper	274	1	25d	Donegal	Kilmacrenan	Tullyfern	Millford	III.	133
6, 9	Glen Upper	452	2	5e	Sligo	Carbury	Drumcliff	Sligo	IV.	221
27, 36	Glen Upper	320	1	11	Tyrone	Omagh East	Termonmaguirk	Omagh	III.	314
22	Glen Upper	96	1	36	Waterford	Decies without Drum	Modelligo	Dungarvan	II.	359
2	Glen Upper	805	1	27	Waterford	Upperthird	Dysert	Clonmel	II.	369
1	Glenvannan	267	1	0	Fermanagh	Lurg	Drumkeeran	Lowtherstown	III.	206
21, 27	Glenvela	266	2	33	Roscommon	Castlereagh	Baslick	Castlereagh	IV.	199
39,40,44,45	Glenviggan	1,716	0	15	Londonderry	Loughinsholin	Ballynascreen	Magherafelt	III.	239
43, 52	Glenville	941	1	2	Cork, E.R.	Barrymore	Ardnageehy	Cork	II.	50
28	Glenville	235	3	33	Limerick	Shanid	Rathronan	Newcastle	II	257
15, 20	Glenville or Leamore	83	3	9	Antrim	Lower Glenarm	Layd	Ballycastle	III.	22
43, 52	GLENVILLE T.				Cork, E.R.	Barrymore	Ardnageehy	Cork	II.	51
134	Glenwanish	490	1	1	Galway	Letrim	In shealtra	Scarriff	IV.	53
153	Glen West	65	2	26	Cork. W.R.	West Carbery (E.D.)	Clear-island	Skibbereen	III.	138
13	Glen West	1,225	2	14f	Fermanagh	Magheraboy	Inish macsaint	Bally-hannon	III.	213
24	Glen West	208	0	33	Waterford	Decies without Drum	Stradbally	Kilmacthomas	II.	361

(a) Including 257A. 1R. 23P. water.   (c) Including 52A. 1R. 32P. water.   (e) Including 5A. 1R. 27P. water.
(b) Including 85A. 3R. 3P. water.   (d) Including 3A. 0R. 20P. water.   (f) Including 19A. 1R. 0P. water.

3 R

No. of Sheet of the Ordnance Survey Maps.	Townlands and Towns.	Area in Statute Acres.	County.	Barony.	Parish.	Poor Law Union in 1857.	Townland Census of 1851, Part I.	
		A. R. P.					Vol.	Page
39	Glenwhirry . .	1,243 1 0	Antrim . .	Lower Antrim .	Glenwhirry . .	Ballymena .	III.	4
37	Glenwilliam . .	552 0 1	Limerick . .	Connello Upper .	Ballingarry . .	Croom . .	II.	230
38	Glenwilliam . .	431 3 39	Waterford .	Decies within Drum	Lisgenan or Grange	Youghal . .	II.	352
15	Glenwinny . .	149 0 9	Fermanagh .	Magheraboy . .	Inishmacsaint .	Enniskillen .	III.	213
43	Glenwood . .	61 1 29	Clare . .	Tulla Lower .	Clonlea . .	Limerick . .	II.	34
27	Glenwood . .	36 1 11	Cork, E.R. .	Fermoy . .	Kilcrumper .	Fermoy . .	II.	80
24	Glenwood . .	252 3 23	Wicklow . .	Newcastle . .	Derrylossary .	Rathdrum .	I.	351
31	Gliddane Beg .	92 1 4	Waterford .	Decies without Drum	Kilgobnet . .	Dungarvan .	II.	357
31	Gliddane More .	125 2 4	Waterford .	Decies without Drum	Kilgobnet . .	Dungarvan .	II.	357
17	Glinch . .	116 0 1	Monaghan .	Dartree . .	Aghabog . .	Clones . .	III.	263
17	Glin Demesne .	406 2 18	Limerick . .	Shanid . .	Kilfergus . .	Glin . .	II.	256
37	Glinn . .	77 3 21	Kilkenny .	Ida . .	Rosbercon .	New Ross .	I.	103
34, 43	Glin North . .	1,264 3 35	Kerry . .	Corkaguiny .	Dingle . .	Dingle . .	II.	175
98	Glinny . .	860 2 12	Cork, E.R. .	Kinalea . .	Cullen . .	Kinsale . .	II.	94
8, 17	Glinsk . .	684 1 5a	Donegal .	Kilmacrenan .	Clondavaddog .	Milford . .	III.	125
7	Glinsk . .	871 0 39b	Galway .	Ballymoe . .	Ballynakill .	Glennamaddy .	IV.	5
63, 64	Glinsk . .	1,161 2 25c	Galway .	Ballynahinch .	Moyrus . .	Clifden . .	IV.	13
5	Glinsk . .	2,054 1 0	Mayo . .	Erris . .	Kilcommon .	Belmullet .	IV.	144
97, 98	Glinsk . .	505 2 19d	Mayo . .	Murrisk . .	Aghagower .	Westport .	IV.	159
36, 37	Glinsk and Castletown . .	900 2 32	King's Co. .	Ballybritt .	Kinnitty . .	Parsonstown .	I.	125
43	Glin South . .	407 1 3	Kerry . .	Corkaguiny .	Dingle . .	Dingle . .	II.	175
17	GLIN T. . .	—	Limerick . .	Shanid . .	Kilfergus . .	Glin . .	II.	256
37, 38	Glistinane . .	167 3 12	Waterford .	Decies within Drum	Kinsalebeg .	Youghal . .	II.	352
26, 27	Globe Island or Cloncarlin . .	359 0 14	Kildare .	Offaly West .	Monasterevin .	Athy . .	I.	73
25	Glomerstown .	198 1 16	Westmeath .	Rathconrath .	Churchtown .	Mullingar .	I.	282
37	Gloonan . .	370 1 2	Antrim . .	Lower Toome .	Ahoghill . .	Ballymena .	III.	32
7	Glooria . .	199 3 29	Roscommon .	Boyle . .	Ardcarn . .	Cark. on Shannon	IV.	193
10	Glooria . .	177 3 24e	Roscommon .	Boyle . .	Estersnow .	Boyle . .	IV.	195
90	Gloragh . .	982 3 24	Kerry . .	Dunkerron South	Kilcrohane .	Kenmare . .	II.	183
29	Glore . .	92 2 30	Antrim . .	Lower Glenarm .	Tickmacrevan .	Larne . .	III.	24
22	Glosterboy and Creggan . .	158 3 39	King's Co. .	Garrycastle .	Gallen . .	Parsonstown .	I.	136
2	Gloudstown . .	131 0 16f	Tyrone . .	Strabane Lower .	Donaghedy .	Strabane .	III.	321
5, 10	Glouria . .	645 2 13	Kerry . .	Iraghticonnor .	Galey . .	Listowel . .	II.	190
84, 85	Gloves East .	265 3 33	Galway .	Athenry . .	Kiltullagh .	Loughrea .	IV.	5
84	Gloves Middle .	216 2 34	Galway .	Athenry . .	Athenry . .	Loughrea .	IV.	4
84, 85	Gloves Middle .	370 0 7	Galway .	Athenry . .	Kiltullagh .	Loughrea .	IV.	5
84, 85	Gloves South .	326 0 18	Galway .	Athenry . .	Kiltullagh .	Loughrea .	IV.	5
84	Gloves West .	155 0 19	Galway .	Athenry . .	Athenry . .	Loughrea .	IV.	4
84	Gloves West .	105 1 26	Galway .	Athenry . .	Kiltullagh .	Loughrea .	IV.	5
44	Glovet . .	436 0 24	Down . .	Lecale Upper .	Tyrella . .	Downpatrick .	III.	181
38	Glowens . .	273 1 26	Kildare .	Kilkea and Moone .	Kineagh . .	Baltinglass .	I.	61
11, 14	Glydefarm . .	477 3 32	Louth . .	Louth . .	Louth . .	Ardee . .	I.	184
14	Glyn . .	136 2 32	King's Co. .	Garrycastle .	Gallen . .	Parsonstown .	I.	136
40	Glynn . .	308 2 19	Antrim . .	Lower Belfast .	Glynn . .	Larne . .	III.	8
42, 51	Glynn . .	592 3 6	Cork, E.R. .	Barretts . .	Mourneabbey .	Mallow . .	II.	50
40	GLYNN T. . .	—	Antrim . .	Lower Belfast .	Glynn . .	Larne . .	III.	8
42	Gneeve . .	222 3 29	Cavan . .	Clanmahon .	Kilbride . .	Oldcastle .	III.	78
20	Gneeve . .	166 0 24	Longford .	Ardagh . .	Mostrim . .	Granard .	I.	152
79	Gneeve . .	274 3 12	Mayo . .	Carra . .	Kildaconmoge .	Castlebar .	IV.	129
33, 39	Gneevebane . .	327 2 32	Westmeath .	Fartullagh .	Castlelost .	Mullingar .	I.	268
32	Gneevebeg . .	301 1 22	Westmeath .	Moycashel .	Castletownkindalen	Mullingar .	I.	277
31, 32	Gneevebrack .	111 1 7	Westmeath .	Moycashel .	Castletownkindalen	Mullingar .	I.	277
31	Gneevekeel .	72 2 11	Westmeath .	Moycashel .	Ardnurcher or Horseleap	Mullingar .	I.	276
44	Gneeves . .	70 3 18	Cork, E.R. .	Barrymore .	Rathcormack .	Fermoy . .	II.	57
24, 32	Gneeves . .	170 2 17	Cork, E.R. .	Duhallow .	Castlemagner .	Kanturk .	II.	67
22, 30	Gneeves . .	425 3 12	Cork, E.R. .	Duhallow .	Kilmeen . .	Kanturk .	II.	73
41	Gneeves . .	620 0 8	Cork, E.R. .	Duhallow .	Kilshannig .	Mallow . .	II.	74
141	Gneeves . .	38 0 23	Cork, W.R. .	West Carbery (E.D.)	Aghadown .	Skibbereen .	II.	137
149	Gneeves . .	89 0 0	Cork, W.R. .	West Carbery (E.D.)	Tullagh . .	Skibbereen .	II.	141
47, 48	Gneeves . .	467 3 8	Cork, W.R. .	West Muskerry .	Drishane .	Millstreet .	II.	156
57, 65	Gneeves . .	131 3 23g	Kerry . .	Magunihy .	Kilbonane .	Killarney .	II.	200
32	Gneeves . .	857 3 4	Kerry . .	Trughanacmy .	Brosna . .	Tralee . .	II.	208
32	GNEEVES T. . .	—	Cork, E.R. .	Duhallow .	Castlemagner . Roskeen .	Kanturk .	II.	{ 67 75
24, 25	Gneevestown .	74 3 28	Westmeath .	Rathconrath .	Conry . .	Mullingar .	I.	282
60	Gneevgullia .	347 2 0	Kerry . .	Magunihy .	Kilcummin .	Killarney .	II.	201
74	Goat Island . .	3 2 16	Cork, E.R. .	Cork . .	Carrigaline .	Cork . .	II.	64
148	Goat Island . .	24 0 26	Cork, W.R. .	West Carbery (W.D.)	Skull . .	Skull . .	II.	146
15	Goat Island . .	2 2 28	Fermanagh .	Magheraboy . .	Inishmacsaint .	Enniskillen .	III.	213
40	Goat Island .	161 1 3	Limerick . .	Coshma . .	Uregare . .	Kilmallock .	II.	244

(a) Including 19A. 0R. 31P. water.
(b) Including 1A. 3R. 0P. water.
(c) Including 37A. 0R. 39P. water.
(d) Including 39A. 1R. 8P. water.
(e) Including 53A. 1R. 31P. water.
(f) Including 1A. 1R. 35P. water.
(g) Including 1A. 3R. 18P. water.

No. of Sheet of the Ordnance Survey Maps.	Townlands and Towns.	Area in Statute Acres. A. R. P.	County.	Barony.	Parish.	Poor Law Union in 1857.	Townland Census of 1851, Part I. Vol.	Page
9	Goat Island	1 0 28	Tipperary, N.R.	Lower Ormond	Kilbarron	Borrisokane	II.	284
18	Goat Island or Fianafreeson	0 0 7	Roscommon	Roscommon	Clooncraff	Strokestown	IV.	208
148	Goat Island Little	4 0 31	Cork, W.R.	West Carbery (W.D.)	Skull	Skull	II.	147
108	Goatland	24 0 33	Galway	Longford	Clonfert	Ballinasloe	IV.	57
21	Goats Island	3 2 0	Longford	Rathcline	Rathcline	Longford	I.	164
13	Goatstown	339 2 18	Kildare	Clane	Downings	Naas	I.	54
7	GOATSTOWN T.	—	Tipperary, N.R.	Lower Ormond	Borrisokane	Borrisokane	II.	282
26	Gobbadagh or Cooperhill	210 3 33	Sligo	Tirerrill	Drumcolumb	Sligo	IV.	228
24, 30	Gobbinstown	649 0 0	Wexford	Bantry	Ballyanne	New Ross	I.	299
69	Gobnascale	120 2 35	Donegal	Raphoe	Convoy	Stranorlar	III.	136
20	Gobnascale	179 2 22	Londonderry	Tirkeeran	Clondermot	Londonderry	III.	248
2, 5	Gobnascale	208 2 23	Tyrone	Strabane Lower	Donaghedy	Strabane	III.	321
59	Gobrana	388 0 23	Antrim	Upper Massereene	Camlin	Antrim	III.	30
13	Goddamendy	83 3 13	Dublin	Castleknock	Mulhuddart	Dublin North	I.	25
85, 97	Gogganshill	913 1 23	Cork, E.R.	East Muskerry	Ballinaboy	Cork	II.	101
64	Gogganstown	278 0 36	Cork, E.R.	Barrymore	Kilquane	Cork	II.	55
24, 32	Go Island	9 0 16	Donegal	Kilmacrenan	Tullaghobegly	Dunfanaghy	III.	132
150	Gokane	167 3 34	Cork, W.R.	West Carbery (E.D.)	Castlehaven	Skibbereen	II.	138
27, 33	Gola	271 0 6	Cavan	Castlerahan	Killinkere	Bailieborough	III.	69
32	Gola	424 0 3a	Donegal	Kilmacrenan	Tullaghobegly	Dunfanaghy	III.	132
28	Gola	62 3 35	Fermanagh	Magherastephana	Aghavea	Lisnaskea	III.	219
27	Gola	183 0 32b	Fermanagh	Magherastephana	Derrybrusk	Lisnaskea	III.	219
8	Gola	36 1 27	Monaghan	Monaghan	Clones	Monaghan	III.	274
85	Goladoo	217 3 3	Donegal	Tirhugh	Donegal	Donegal	III.	145
6	Goladoo	70 1 20	Fermanagh	Lurg	Magheraculmoney	Lowtherstown	III.	208
42	Goladuff	103 0 27	Fermanagh	Coole	Drummully	Clones	III.	199
8	Gola English	268 0 38	Monaghan	Monaghan	Tedavnet	Monaghan	III.	279
8	Gola Irish	228 3 34	Monaghan	Monaghan	Tedavnet	Monaghan	III.	279
32	Gola Island	424 0 3c	Donegal	Kilmacrenan	Tullaghobegly	Dunfanaghy	III.	132
89	Golam	34 1 1	Galway	Moycullen	Kilcummin	Oughterard	IV.	68
17	Golamore & beg Islands	1 2 2	Donegal	Kilmacrenan	Clondavaddog	Milford	III.	125
36	Golan	1,185 1 25d	Donegal	Kilmacrenan	Kilmacrenan	Milford	III.	129
35	Golan	78 0 12	Fermanagh	Clankelly	Clones	Clones	III.	196
3, 5, 6	Golan	523 0 13	Monaghan	Trough	Donagh	Monaghan	III.	282
53, 60	Golan	682 0 17	Tyrone	Dungannon Lower	Carnteel	Clogher	III.	297
42	Golan	280 3 33	Tyrone	Omagh East	Dromore	Omagh	III.	311
26	Golan	245 2 32	Tyrone	Strabane Upper	Cappagh	Omagh	III.	325
16	Golan Adams	87 0 34	Tyrone	Omagh West	Ardstraw	Castlederg	III.	315
77	Goland	762 2 31	Donegal	Raphoe	Donaghmore	Stranorlar	III.	138
16, 17	Golanduff	64 3 31	Monaghan	Dartree	Killeevan	Clones	III.	268
23, 32	Golandun Dolan	447 2 21	Tyrone	Omagh West	Termonamongan	Castlederg	III	317
23, 32	Golandun M'Hugh	538 3 4e	Tyrone	Omagh West	Termonamongan	Castlederg	III.	317
56, 57	Golan Glebe	463 2 18	Tyrone	Omagh East	Kilskeery	Enniskillen	III.	313
16	Golan Hunter	77 0 30	Tyrone	Omagh West	Ardstraw	Castlederg	III.	315
12, 13	Golanmurphy	94 0 33	Monaghan	Dartree	Killeevan	Monaghan	III.	268
16, 24	Golan Sproul	180 1 5f	Tyrone	Omagh West	Ardstraw	Castlederg	III.	315
100	Golard	517 3 9	Donegal	Tirhugh	Drumhome	Donegal	III.	146
1, 4	Golashane	287 3 14	Meath	Lower Kells	Moynalty	Kells	I.	204
18	Goldenbridge North	162 2 21g	Dublin	Uppercross and Municipal Borough	St. James	Dublin South	I.	41
18	Goldenbridge South	222 3 28h	Dublin	Uppercross and Municipal Borough	St. James	Dublin South	I.	41
18	GOLDENBRIDGE T.	—	Dublin	Uppercross	St. James	Dublin South	I.	41
18	Goldenfield	224 2 26	Kilkenny	Crannagh	Ballycallan	Kilkenny	I.	84
20, 21	Goldenfort	365 2 18	Wicklow	Upper Talbotstown	Rathbran	Baltinglass	I.	365
51, 59	Goldengarden	330 0 12	Tipperary, S.R.	Kilnamanagh Lower	Kilpatrick	Cashel	II.	324
40	Goldengrove	101 3 17	Tipperary, N.R.	Eliogarty	Inch	Thurles	II.	270
42, 43	Goldengrove or Knocknamase	580 0 29	King's Co.	Clonlisk	Ettagh	Roscrea	I.	130
1, 5	Goldenhill	181 0 38	Wicklow	Lower Talbotstown	Kilbride	Naas	I.	361
60	Goldenhills	108 3 26	Tipperary, S.R.	Clanwilliam	Relickmurry and Athassel	Tipperary	II.	310
29	Goldenisland	157 2 6	Westmeath	Brawny	St. Mary's	Athlone	I.	259
29	Goldenisland (Kilmaine)	72 0 20	Westmeath	Brawny	St. Mary's	Athlone	I.	259
29	Goldenisland (St. George)	21 1 29	Westmeath	Brawny	St. Mary's	Athlone	I.	259
43	Goldenpark	134 1 8	Galway	Clare	Killower	Tuam	IV.	21
60	GOLDEN T.	—	Tipperary, S.R.	Clanwilliam	Relickmurry and Athassel	Tipperary	II.	310
30	Goldentown or Dunanore	432 0 33	Wexford	Bantry	Oldross	New Ross	I.	301
35,36,44,45	Goldrum	451 1 10i	Donegal	Kilmacrenan	Kilmacrenan	Milford	III.	129
16	Goldsmithslot	148 0 11	King's Co.	Ballycowan	Rahan	Tullamore	I.	128
39	Gole	153 0 31j	Fermanagh	Knockninny	Kinawley	Lisnaskea	III.	202

(a) Including 4A. 3R. 20P. water.
(b) Including 17A. 0R. 22P. water.
(c) Including 4A. 3R. 20P. water.
(d) Including 0P. 2R. 25P. Lough Nacreaght.
(e) Including 0A. 2R. 15P. water.
(f) Including 1A. 2R. 24P. water.
(g) { Within the Municipal Boundary, 23A. 3R. 8P. / Without the Municipal Boundary, 136A. 3R. 12P.
(h) { Within the Municipal Boundary, 25A. 3R. 0P. / Without the Municipal Boundary, 197A. 1R. 28P.
(i) Including 6A. 2R. 16P. water.
(j) Including 23A. 2R. 9P. water.

3 R 2

No. of Sheet of the Ordnance Survey Maps	Townlands and Towns.	Area in Statute Acres. A. R. P.	County.	Barony.	Parish.	Poor Law Union in 1857.	Townland Census of 1851. Part I. Vol.	Page
147	Goleen	58 1 15	Cork, W.R.	West Carbery(W.D.)	Kilmoe	Skull	II.	145
141	Goleenmarsh	69 2 12	Cork, W.R.	West Carbery (E.D.)	Aghadown	Skibbereen	II.	137
8, 13	Goles	4,255 1 3	Tyrone	Strabane Upper	Bodoney Upper	Gortin	III.	324
17	Gollierstown	431 3 33	Dublin	Newcastle	Kilmactalway	Celbridge	I.	33
10	Golree	46 2 38	Monaghan	Monaghan	Tehallen	Monaghan	III.	280
5, 9	Goodland	422 2 26	Antrim	Cary	Culfeightrin	Ballycastle	III.	13
27	Goodwinsgarden	684 3 18	Kilkenny	Kells	Kells	Callan	I.	108
1	Gooig	573 2 12	Limerick	Clanwilliam	Stradbally	Limerick	II.	226
26	Goolamore	254 3 32a	Mayo	Erris	Kilcommon	Belmullet	IV.	144
33	Gooldshill	285 3 6	Cork, E.R.	Fermoy	Mallow	Mallow	II.	81
21	Gooreen	145 2 17b	Galway	Ballynahinch	Omey	Clifden	IV.	15
21	Gooreenatinny	117 0 28c	Galway	Ballynahinch	Omey	Clifden	IV.	15
4	Goorey	203 2 39	Donegal	Inishowen East	Clonca	Inishowen	III.	117
18	Gooseacre	3 2 2	Dublin	Coolock	St. Georges	Dublin North	I.	29
5, 14, 15	Gooseberryhill	1,361 0 11	Cork, E.R.	Duhallow	Clonfert	Kanturk	II.	68
14, 18	Goosegreen	140 0 36	Dublin	Coolock	Clonturk	Dublin North	I.	27
54	Goose Island	0 0 3	Clare	Tulla Lower	O Briensbridge	Limerick	II.	38
102	Goose Island	3 1 9	Galway	Dunkellin	Ballynacourty	Galway	IV.	27
126	Goose Island	0 1 2	Galway	Longford	Lickmolassy	Portumna	IV.	61
22	Goose Island	9 3 30	Mayo	Tirawley	Ballysakeery	Ballina	IV.	165
22, 26	Goragh	428 0 33	Armagh	Orior Upper	Killevy	Newry	III.	58
11	Gordonall	112 0 5	Down	Ards Lower	Greyabbey	Newtownards	III.	158
21	GORESBRIDGE T.	—	Kilkenny	Gowran	Grangesilvia	Thomastown	I.	96
31	Gores Island	98 3 5	Down	Lecale Lower	Saul	Downpatrick	III.	180
61, 62	Gorestown	315 0 21	Tyrone	Dungannon Middle	Clonfeacle	Dungannon	III.	299
53	Gorey	280 3 14	Tyrone	Dungannon Middle	Donaghmore	Dungannon	III.	302
7	Goreybridge	118 3 2	Wexford	Gorey	Kilmakilloge	Gorey	I.	318
6, 7	Gorey Corporation Lands	402 2 14	Wexford	Gorey	Kilmakilloge	Gorey	I.	318
6	Goreyhill	200 2 18	Wexford	Gorey	Kilmakilloge	Gorey	I.	318
6, 7	GOREY T.	—	Wexford	{ Ballaghkeen Gorey }	Kilmakilloge	Gorey	I.	296 318
38	Gorgesh	227 2 12	Fermanagh	Knockninny	Kinawley	Lisnaskea	III.	202
9, 17	Gormagh	319 1 20	King's Co.	Ballycowan	Durrow	Tullamore	I.	127
28, 34	Gormanston	916 1 38	Meath	Upper Duleek	Stamullin	Drogheda	I.	198
1	Gormanston Demesne	132 3 29	Dublin	Balrothery East	Balscaddan	Balrothery	I.	20
28,29,32,33	Gormanstown	919 2 30	Kildare	Kilcullen	Kilcullen	Naas	I.	58
44	Gormanstown	208 2 16	Meath	Ratoath	Rathbeggan	Dunshaughlin	I.	219
30, 36	Gormanstown	158 1 12	Meath	Upper Navan	Trim	Trim	I.	217
40	Gormanstown	51 3 22	Limerick	Smallcounty	Knockainy	Kilmallock	II.	261
40	Gormanstown	48 2 22	Limerick	Smallcounty	Uregare	Kilmallock	II.	261
87	Gormanstown	334 2 6	Tipperary, S.R.	Iffa and Offa West	Ballybacon	Clogheen	II.	317
8	Gormanstown	95 1 6	Westmeath	Delvin	Kilcumny	Castletowndelvin	I.	265
31	Gormanstown	212 3 3	Wicklow	Arklow	Dunganstown	Rathdrum	I.	343
40	Gormanstown (Grady)	238 0 38	Limerick	Smallcounty	Athneasy	Kilmallock	II.	258
40	Gormanstown (Phillips)	292 3 29	Limerick	Smallcounty	Athneasy	Kilmallock	II.	258
28	GORMANSTOWN T.	—	Meath	Upper Duleek	Stamullin	Drogheda	I.	199
12, 13	Gorminish	11 2 23	Fermanagh	Magheraboy	Inishmacsaint	Ballyshannon	III.	213
52	Gormlee	551 2 8	Cork, E.R.	Barrymore	Dunbulloge	Cork	II.	54
16	Gormona	261 2 28	Carlow	Idrone East	Dunleckny	Carlow	I.	7
16, 19	Gormona	96 1 26	Carlow	Idrone East	Lorum	Carlow	I.	8
2, 6	Gorragh Lower	234 2 39	Queen's Co.	Tinnahinch	Kilmanman	Mountmellick	I.	249
2, 6	Gorragh Upper	568 0 6	Queen's Co.	Tinnahinch	Kilmanman	Mountmellick	I.	249
11	Gorran	320 2 37	Londonderry	Coleraine	Aghadowey	Coleraine	III.	229
43	Gorraun	874 3 17	King's Co.	Ballybritt	Aghancon	Roscrea	I.	124
44	Gorraun	255 3 28	King's Co.	Clonlisk	Templeharry	Roscrea	I.	132
25	Gorreelagh	171 2 22	Queen's Co.	Stradbally	Tullomoy	Athy	I.	248
5	Gort	4 0 37	Donegal	Inishowen East	Clonca	Inishowen	III.	117
12	Gort	1 0 0	Donegal	Inishowen East	Clonca	Inishowen	III.	117
5	Gort	1 3 19	Donegal	Inishowen East	Culdaff	Inishowen	III.	118
71	Gort	2 3 18	Donegal	Raphoe	Clonleigh	Strabane	III.	135
122, 123	Gort	170 3 8	Galway	Kiltartan	Kiltartan	Gort	IV.	48
31	Gort	161 0 19	Leitrim	Leitrim	Kiltoghert	Cark. on Shannon	IV.	102
26	Gort	7 0 4	Londonderry	Coleraine	Desertoghill	Coleraine	III.	230
5	Gort	5 0 4d	Londonderry	Keenaght	Magilligan	New Tn Limavady	III.	237
59, 60	Gort	463 2 22	Mayo	Carra	Turlough	Castlebar	IV.	131
52, 59	Gort	297 0 39	Tyrone	Clogher	Errigal Keerogue	Clogher	III.	295
61	Gort	463 0 11e	Tyrone	Dungannon Middle	Clonfeacle	Dungannon	III.	299
113	Gortaboy	163 0 18	Galway	Dunkellin	Killeenavarra	Gort	IV.	30
82	Gortacallow or Anglisham	269 1 35	Galway	Galway	Oranmore	Galway	IV.	37
49	Gortacappul	285 2 30	Kerry	Trughanacmy	Ballincuslane	Tralee	II.	206
5	Gortacar	910 2 05	Fermanagh	Lurg	Drumkeeran	Lowtherstown	III.	206
38	Gortacar (Doris)	227 0 14	Tyrone	Dungannon Upper	Desertcreat	Cookstown	III.	307

(a) Including 1A. 3R. 1P. water. (c) Including 10A. 2R. 31P. water. (e) Including 35A. 1R. 15P. water.
(b) Including 13A. 3R. 11P. water. (d) Part of Glebe, 32A. 3R. 9P. Magilligan Parish.

No. of Sheet of the Ordnance Survey Maps.	Townlands and Towns.	Area in Statute Acres.			County.	Barony.	Parish.	Poor Law Union in 1857.	Townland Census of 1851, Part I.	
		A.	R.	P.					Vol.	Page
68, 76	Gortacareen	614	2	10a	Kerry	Magunihy	Kilcummin	Killarney	II.	201
38	Gortacar (Glassy)	62	0	23	Tyrone	Dungannon Upper	Desertcreat	Cookstown	III.	307
32	Gortacarn	62	3	34	Fermanagh	Clanawley	Kinawley	Enniskillen	III.	194
45	Gortacarnan	49	2	29	Roscommon	Athlone	Rahara	Roscommon	IV.	183
129	Gortacarnaun	1,611	1	27b	Galway	Kiltartan	Kilbeacanty	Gort	IV.	47
67	Gortacarnaun	446	1	34c	Galway	Moycullen	Killannin	Oughterard	IV.	69
7	Gortacashel	90	0	11	Cavan	Tullyhaw	Kinawley	Bawnboy	III.	93
68	Gortachalla	452	0	12d	Galway	Moycullen	Moycullen	Galway	IV.	71
21, 29	Gortachallow	28	1	3	King's Co.	Garrycastle	Lusmagh	Parsonstown	I.	137
34	Gortacharn	43	1	36	Fermanagh	Magherastephana	Aghalurcher	Lisnaskea	III	216
25, 29	Gortachoosh	237	2	17e	Leitrim	Carrigallen	Drumreilly	Bawnboy	IV.	91
25	Gortachurk	37	3	36	Cavan	Clanmahon	Crosserlough	Cavan	III.	76
25	Gortachurk	105	1	30	Cavan	Clanmahon	Kilmore	Cavan	III.	78
8, 16	Gortaclade	500	3	16	Waterford	Middlethird	Kilmeadan	Waterford	II.	368
28, 37	Gortaclady	302	2	19	Tyrone	Dungannon Upper	Kildress	Cookstown	III.	309
6	Gortaclare	722	0	26	Clare	Burren	Oughtmama	Ballyvaghan	II.	14
24, 25	Gortaclare	336	1	33	Londonderry	Keenaght	Bovevagh	New Tn Limavady	III.	235
43	Gortaclare	151	2	22	Tyrone	Omagh East	Clogherny	Omagh	III.	310
3, 6	Gortaclare	365	3	15	Tyrone	Strabane Lower	Donaghedy	Strabane	III.	321
24, 33	Gortaclareen	173	0	15	Limerick	Coonagh	Oola	Tipperary	II.	235
20	Gortaclee	38	0	2	Antrim	Lower Glenarm	Layd	Ballycastle	III.	22
73	Gortaclivore	49	0	6	Tipperary, S.R.	Clanwilliam	Clonbeg	Tipperary	II.	305
8	Gortaclob	174	0	13	Clare	Corcomroe	Killilagh	Ennistimon	II.	20
26	Gortacloghan	326	1	27	Londonderry	Coleraine	Desertoghill	Coleraine	III.	230
39	Gortacloghan	60	3	20	Tyrone	Dungannon Middle	Donaghenry	Cookstown	III.	301
17, 23	Gortacloghane	649	1	3	Kerry	Clanmaurice	Kilshenane	Listowel	II.	172
82, 91	Gortacloghane	553	1	30	Kerry	Dunkerron South	Templenoe	Kenmare	II.	185
13	Gortaclogher	253	1	29f	Cavan	Tullyhaw	Templeport	Bawnboy	III.	94
118	Gortacloona	169	3	15	Cork, W.R.	West Carbery (W.D.)	Kilmocomoge	Bantry	II.	144
32	Gortacloona	374	3	3	Limerick	Smallcounty	Knockainy	Kilmallock	II.	261
112	Gortacluggy	13	2	19	Cork, E.R.	Kinalea	Kilmonoge	Kinsale	II.	95
58, 65, 66	Gortacollopa	229	2	3	Kerry	Magunihy	Aghadoe	Killarney	II.	199
48	Gortacoosan	138	3	39	Roscommon	Athlone	Kiltoom	Athlone	IV.	183
47	Gortacoosaun	186	1	17	Galway	Killian	Killeroran	Mount Bellew	IV.	44
15, 16	Gortacorka	160	1	4	Leitrim	Drumahaire	Inishmagrath	Manorhamilton	IV.	96
31	Gortacoula	128	3	20	Tipperary, N.R.	Owney and Arra	Kilnarath	Nenagh	II.	296
47	Gortacrank	27	1	13	Limerick	Coshma	Effin	Kilmallock	II.	243
94, 103	Gortacreenteen	984	3	22	Kerry	Glanarought	Kilgarvan	Kenmare	II.	187
60	Gortacroghig	190	2	13	Cork, W.R.	East Muskerry	Aghabulloge	Macroom	II.	153
10	Gortacrossane	390	0	9	Kerry	Iraghticonnor	Listowel	Listowel	II.	193
151	Gortacrossig	204	3	30	Cork, W.R.	West Carbery (E.D.)	Castlehaven	Skibbereen	II.	138
65	Gortacrue	454	3	28	Cork, E.R.	Barrymore	Ballyspillane	Middleton	II.	51
44	Gortacullin	515	2	30	Clare	Tulla Lower	Kilseily	Limerick	II.	36
87, 90	Gortacullin	1,551	0	10	Tipperary, S.R.	Iffa and Offa West	Ballybacon	Clogheen	II.	317
46	Gortaculrush	189	2	13	Tipperary, S.R.	Kilnamanagh Lower	Clogher	Cashel	II.	322
24, 32	Gortacur	463	2	10	King's Co.	Ballyboy	Killoughy	Tullamore	I.	124
121	Gortacurra	253	0	18	Mayo	Kilmaine	Cong	Ballinrobe	IV.	153
29	Gortacurra	287	3	33	Tipperary, N.R.	Ikerrin	Killea	Roscrea	II.	275
44	Gortacurraun	366	2	31	Kerry	Corkaguiny	Ballynacourty	Dingle	II.	174
9	Gortacurrig	321	3	39	Cork, E.R.	Condons&Clangibbon	Kildorrery	Mitchelstown	II.	61
82	Gortacurrig	150	2	23	Cork, W.R.	West Muskerry	Kilmichael	Dunmanway	II.	159
15	Gortadalaun	244	2	27	Tipperary, N.R.	Lower Ormond	Ardcrony	Nenagh	II.	281
86	Gortadeegan	31	0	3	Galway	Kilconnell	Kilconnell	Ballinasloe	IV.	40
20	Gortaderry	1,718	0	38	Clare	Tulla Upper	Tomgraney	Scariff	II.	41
5	Gortaderry	170	0	21	Sligo	Carbury	Ahamlish	Sligo	IV.	219
50	Gortaderry	75	1	14	Tipperary, N.R.	Kilnamanagh Upper	Toem	Tipperary	II.	280
66, 74	Gortadirra	1,527	2	33	Kerry	Dunkerron North	Aghadoe	Killarney	II.	181
42	Gortadoo	418	3	31	Kerry	Corkaguiny	Dunurlin	Dingle	II.	176
69, 70	Gortadooey	229	2	26	Galway	Clare	Claregalway	Galway	IV.	18
114,123,124	Gortadragaun	724	1	19	Galway	Loughrea	Kilthomas	Gort	IV.	65
61, 69	Gortadragon	134	3	36	Donegal	Raphoe	Convoy	Stranorlar	III.	136
21	Gortadrehid	99	0	21	Fermanagh	Clanawley	Cleenish	Enniskillen	III.	190
22, 27	Gortadrehid Big	157	0	2g	Fermanagh	Clanawley	Rossorry	Enniskillen	III.	194
22, 27	Gortadrehid Little	66	0	7	Fermanagh	Magheraboy	Rossorry	Enniskillen	III.	214
15	Gortadrislig	173	1	13	Kerry	Clanmaurice	Kilcaragh	Listowel	II.	169
149,150	Gortadrohid	86	1	38	Cork, W.R.	West Carbery (E.D.)	Creagh	Skibbereen	II.	139
43	Gortadroma	135	0	20	Clare	Tulla Lower	Clonlea	Tulla	II.	34
18	Gortadroma	385	1	6	Limerick	Shanid	Dunmoylan	Glin	II.	255
118	Gortadullisk	172	3	7	Galway	Longford	Tiranascragh	Portumna	IV.	62
18	Gortaficka	301	0	9	Clare	Bunratty Upper	Inchicronan	Ennis	II.	9
80	Gortafludig	644	1	34	Cork, W.R.	West Muskerry	Inchigeelagh	Macroom	II.	157
62, 70	Gortaforia	380	2	34	Kerry	Iveragh	Killinane	Cahersiveen	II.	197
38, 39	Gortagammon	120	0	18	Tyrone	Dungannon Middle	Donaghenry	Cookstown	III.	301

(a) Including 1A. 1R. 37P. water.
(b) Including 1A. 0R. 17P. water.
(c) Including 17A. 1R. 3P. water.

(d) Including 47A. 3R. 4P. water.
(e) Including 3A. 1R. 22P. water.

(f) Including 14A. 3R. 13P. water.
(g) Including 24A. 3R. 18P. water.

No. of Sheet of the Ordnance Survey Maps.	Townlands and Towns.	Area in Statute Acres.	County.	Barony.	Parish.	Poor Law Union in 1857.	Townland Census of 1851, Part I.	
		A. R. P.					Vol.	Page
21	Gortaganniff, .	62 1 29	Limerick .	Coshma . . .	Adare . . .	Croom . .	II.	241
32, 33	Gortaganniv .	354 0 33	Clare .	Islands . . .	Kilmaley . .	Ennis . .	II.	31
6, 18	Gortaganny .	296 3 10	Galway .	Tiaquin . . .	Boyounagh . .	Glennamaddy .	IV.	76
45	Gortaganny .	97 0 24	Galway .	Tiaquin . . .	Moylough . .	Mountbellew .	IV.	80
44	Gortaganny .	82 2 3	Roscommon .	Athlone . . .	Kahara . . .	Roscommon .	IV.	183
19	Gortaganny .	443 1 16a	Roscommon .	Frenchpark . .	Tibohine . .	Castlereagh .	IV.	205
30	Gortagarraun .	479 0 2b	Galway .	Ballymoe . .	Clonbern . .	Tuam . .	IV.	6
105	Gortagarry .	112 1 34	Cork, W.R. .	Bantry . . .	Kilmocomoge .	Bantry . .	II.	121
28	Gortagarry .	671 1 12	Tipperary, N.R.	Upper Ormond .	Aghnameadle .	Nenagh . .	II.	289
93	Gortagass .	357 3 28	Kerry .	Glanarought .	Kenmare . .	Kenmare . .	II.	186
70	Gortagea . .	16 2 4	Tipperary, S.R.	Middlethird .	Fethard . .	Cashel . .	II.	327
39	Gortageen .	569 2 16c	Cork, E.R. .	Duhallow . .	Cullen . .	Millstreet .	II.	70
115	Gortagenerick .	65 1 25	Cork, W.R. .	Bear . . .	Killaconenagh .	Castletown .	II.	125
32	Gortaggle .	52 3 1d	Leitrim .	Leitrim . .	Annaduff .	Carⁿ. on Shannon	IV.	99
49	Gortaghurn .	318 2 26	Antrim .	Upper Toome .	Drummaul . .	Antrim . .	III.	34
14	Gortagherty Lower	135 1 0	Londonderry .	Tirkeeran . .	Faughanvale .	Londonderry .	III.	250
14	Gortagherty Upper	163 0 5	Londonderry .	Tirkeeran . .	Faughanvale .	Londonderry .	III.	250
68	Gortaghokera .	229 1 21	Galway .	Moycullen . .	Moycullen . .	Galway . .	IV.	71
15	Gortaghragan .	82 3 32	Antrim .	Lower Glenarm .	Layd . . .	Ballycastle .	III.	22
46	Gortagilly .	368 1 14	Londonderry .	Loughinsholin .	Desertlyn . .	Magherafelt .	III.	240
86	Gortagoulane .	401 2 34	Cork, E.R. .	Cork . . .	St. Finbars .	Cork . .	II.	66
115	Gortagoulane .	20 2 16	Cork, W.R. .	Bear . . .	Killaconenagh .	Castletown .	II.	125
76	Gortagousta .	23 1 33	Cork. E.R. .	Barrymore . .	Carrigtohill .	Middleton .	II.	52
96	Gortagowan .	76 1 21	Galway .	Dunkellin . .	Kilconieran .	Loughrea .	IV.	29
91, 100	Gortagowan .	2,043 0 18	Kerry .	Dunkerron South .	Kilcrohane .	Kenmare .	II.	183
38	Gortagowan .	99 0 17	Tyrone .	Dungannon Upper .	Desertcreat .	Cookstown .	III.	308
66	Gortagowlane .	43 1 0	Tipperary, S.R.	Clanwilliam .	Clonpet . .	Tipperary .	II.	306
115	Gortagraffer .	61 0 4	Cork, W.R. .	Bear . . .	Killaconenagh .	Castletown .	II.	125
64	Gortagreenane .	167 3 1	Kerry .	Dunkerron North .	Killorglin . .	Cahersiveen .	II.	181
143	Gortagrenane .	129 1 39	Cork, W.R. .	Ibane and Barryroe	Rathbarry . .	Clonakilty .	II.	150
67, 74, 75	Gortagullane .	870 1 28	Kerry .	Magunihy . .	Killarney . .	Killarney .	II.	203
39	Gortagullane .	68 1 31	Kerry .	Trughanacmy .	Ballymacelligott	Tralee . .	II.	207
10	Gortagurrane East .	89 3 31	Kerry .	Iraghticonnor .	Ballyconry . .	Listowel . .	II.	190
5, 9, 10	Gortagurrane West	125 0 5	Kerry .	Iraghticonnor .	Ballyconry . .	Listowel . .	II.	190
118, 127	Gortaha . .	368 2 14	Galway .	Longford . .	Lickmolassy .	Portumna .	IV.	61
26	Gortahar .	267 2 26	Antrim .	Kilconway . .	Rasharkin . .	Ballymoney .	III.	27
1	Gortaheeda .	28 2 4	Cork, E.R. .	Orrery and Kilmore	Kilbolane . .	Kanturk . .	II.	108
26, 31	Gortaheran .	482 2 10	Antrim .	Lower Toome .	Ahoghill . .	Ballymena .	III.	32
36, 37	Gortahile .	869 0 18	Queen's Co. .	Slievemargy .	Killabban . .	Carlow . .	I.	245
27	Gortahilly .	155 3 23	Waterford .	Gaultiere . .	Rathmoylan .	Waterford .	II.	364
40, 46	Gortahoola .	258 1 27	Tipperary, N.R.	Kilnamanagh Upper	Moyaliff . .	Thurles . .	II.	279
66, 67	Gortahoonig .	115 3 39e	Kerry .	Magunihy . .	Killarney . .	Killarney .	II.	203
67, 75	Gortahoosh .	305 2 27	Kerry .	Magunihy . .	Killaha . .	Killarney . .	II.	202
24	Gortahork .	160 0 32	Donegal .	Kilmacrenan .	Tullaghobegly .	Dunfanaghy .	III.	132
78, 87	Gortahork .	286 2 0	Donegal .	Raphoe . . .	Donaghmore .	Stranorlar .	III.	188
15	Gortahork .	130 1 36	Leitrim .	Drumahaire .	Killarga . .	Manorhamilton	IV.	98
33	Gortahumma .	615 0 35	Tipperary, N.R.	Upper Ormond .	Kilnaneave . .	Nenagh . .	II.	291
38, 41	Gortahurk .	389 2 39	Fermanagh .	Knockninny .	Tomregan . .	Lisnaskea .	III.	203
40, 41	Gortahurk .	878 2 22	Londonderry .	Loughinsholin .	Kilcronaghan .	Magherafelt .	III.	241
26	Gortahurk East .	81 1 31	Fermanagh .	Clanawley . .	Cleenish . .	Enniskillen .	III.	190
26	Gortahurk West .	345 0 36	Fermanagh .	Clanawley . .	Cleenish . .	Enniskillen .	III.	190
9	Gortakeeghan .	149 1 16	Monaghan .	Monaghan . .	Monaghan . .	Monaghan .	III.	277
85	Gortakeeran .	219 2 13	Galway .	Athenry . .	Kiltullagh . .	Loughrea .	IV.	5
19, 25	Gortakeeran .	905 1 31f	Sligo .	Leyny . . .	Killoran . .	Tobercurry .	IV.	230
25, 33	Gortakilleen .	127 3 26	Limerick .	Coonagh . .	Oola . . .	Tipperary .	II.	235
58	Gortakilleen .	96 3 27	Tipperary, S.R.	Clanwilliam .	Cullen . .	Tipperary .	II.	307
81	Gortaknockane .	191 1 36g	Cork, W.R. .	West Muskerry .	Inchigeelagh .	Dunmanway .	II.	157
67	Gortaknockeare .	527 2 15	Tipperary, S.R.	Clanwilliam .	Cordangan . .	Tipperary .	II.	306
45, 53	Gortalaban .	99 2 1	Donegal .	Kilmacrenan .	Kilmacrenan .	Letterkenny .	III.	129
20	Gortalassa .	116 3 14	Clare .	Tulla Upper .	Feakle . . .	Scarriff . .	II.	39
117, 130	Gortalassa .	264 0 39	Cork, W.R. .	West Carbery (W.D.)	Kilcrohane .	Bantry . .	II.	143
84, 93	Gortalassa .	103 0 32	Kerry .	Glanarought .	Kenmare . .	Kenmare .	II.	186
48	Gortalassa .	165 2 7	Kerry .	Magunihy . .	Molahiffe . .	Killarney .	II.	205
45	Gortalassa .	282 3 17	Limerick .	Connello Upper .	Kilmeedy . .	Newcastle .	II.	233
100, 101	Gortalavaun .	39 1 21	Mayo .	Clanmorris .	Tagheen . .	Claremorris .	IV.	136
5	Gortaleam .	343 1 19	Galway .	Ballymoe . .	Dunmore . .	Glennamaddy .	IV.	7
75,76,85,86	Gortalee . .	1,237 0 18	Kerry .	Magunihy . .	Killaha . .	Killarney . .	II.	202
94	Gortaleen .	185 3 13	Cork, W.R. .	East Carbery (W.D.)	Kinneigh . .	Dunmanway .	II.	134
46	Gortaleen .	250 0 11	Kerry .	Trughanacmy .	Kilgarrylander .	Tralee . .	II.	210
37, 46	Gortaleen-mountain	977 1 18	Kerry .	Trughanacmy .	Kilgarrylander .	Tralee . .	II.	210
90	Gortalia . .	133 0 39	Donegal .	Banagh . . .	Kilcar . . .	Glenties . .	III.	108
76, 86	Gortalicka .	616 2 20	Kerry .	Magunihy . .	Killaha . .	Killarney . .	II.	202
93	Gortalinny North .	395 1 11	Kerry .	Glanarought .	Kenmare . .	Kenmare .	II.	186

(a) Including 32A. 2R. 24P. water.   (d) Including 9A. 3R. 20P. water.   (f) Including 13A. 3R. 26P. water.
(b) Including 49A. 3R. 2P. water.   (e) Including 2A. 1R. 24P. water.   (g) Including 9A. 0R. 9P. water.
(c) Including 12A. 1R. 3P. water.

No. of Sheet of the Ordnance Survey Maps.	Townlands and Towns.	Area in Statute Acres.			County.	Barony.	Parish.	Poor Law Union in 1857.	Townland Census of 1851, Part I.	
		A.	R.	P.					Vol.	Page
93	Gortalinny South	258	1	10	Kerry	Glanarought	Kenmare	Kenmare	II.	186
150	Gortaliscaw	81	1	11	Cork, W.R.	West Carbery (E.D.)	Creagh	Skibbereen	II.	139
114, 123	Gortaloman	78	2	29	Galway	Loughrea	Kilthomas	Loughrea	IV.	65
99, 107	Gortalough	115	1	26	Galway	Longford	Abbeygormacan	Ballinasloe	IV.	56
40	Gortalough	59	0	2	Sligo	Tirerrill	Aghanagh	Boyle	IV.	237
28, 34	Gortalough	150	0	7	Tipperary, N.R.	Kilnamanagh Upper	Glenkeen	Thurles	II	278
31, 32	Gortalougha	6	6	2a	Clare	Inchiquin	Inagh	Ennistimon	II	25
16, 22	Gortaloughan	262	3	5b	Fermanagh	Tirkennedy	Magheracross	Enniskillen	III.	223
108	Gortaloughane	22	1	26	Galway	Longford	Clonfert	Ballinasloe	IV.	57
75, 86	Gortaloughane	1,241	2	25c	Kerry	Glanarought	Kilgarvan	Killarney	II.	187
29, 35	Gortalowry	281	0	15	Tyrone	Dungannon Upper	Derryloran	Cookstown	III.	307
32	Gortalughany	45	3	29	Fermanagh	Clanawley	Killesher	Enniskillen	III.	192
32, 37	Gortalughany	270	3	19	Fermanagh	Clanawley	Kinawley	Enniskillen	III.	194
8	Gortamaddy or White Hall	82	3	8	Antrim	Cary	Ramoan	Ballycastle	III.	14
32	Gortamarle	101	2	5	Roscommon	Castlereagh	Kiltullagh	Castlereagh	IV.	202
36, 41	Gortamney	372	1	12	Londonderry	Loughinsholin	Kilcronaghan	Magherafelt	III.	241
93	Gortamullin	783	0	0	Kerry	Dunkerron South	Templenoe	Kenmare	II.	185
50, 51, 53	Gortanabla	406	0	17	Roscommon	Athlone	Taghmaconnell	Ballinasloe	IV.	185
58, 69	Gortanacra	233	1	34	Cork, W.R.	West Muskerry	Ballyvourney	Macroom	II.	154
69	Gortanaddan	192	2	10	Cork, W.R.	West Muskerry	Kilnamartry	Macroom	II.	159
68	Gortanahaneboy East	699	3	38	Kerry	Magunihy	Kilcummin	Killarney	II.	201
68	Gortanahaneboy West	443	1	22	Kerry	Magunihy	Kilcummin	Killarney	II.	201
47	Gortananny	152	0	12d	Galway	Kilian	Taghboy	Mountbellew	IV.	45
55	Gortanassy East	62	2	33	Tipperary, S.R.	Slievardagh	Crohane	Callan	II.	332
54, 55	Gortanassy West	160	3	13	Tipperary, S.R.	Slievardagh	Crohane	Callan	II.	332
81, 82	Gortaneadin	308	1	20	Cork, W.R.	West Muskerry	Inchigeelagh	Dunmanway	II.	157
2	Gortanear	234	1	22	Westmeath	Moygoish	Street	Granard	I	281
106	Gortaneare	59	0	22	Galway	Longford	Duniry	Loughrea	IV.	58
15	Gortaneare	124	1	15	Kerry	Clanmaurice	Kilcaragh	Listowel	II.	169
15	Gortaneare	37	2	10	Kerry	Clanmaurice	Kiltomey	Listowel	II.	172
37, 46	Gortaneden	888	1	8	Kerry	Trughanacmy	Kilgarrylander	Tralee	II.	210
2, 3, 10	Gortaneden	789	3	7	Mayo	Erris	Kilmore	Belmullet	IV.	146
38	Gortaneden	189	3	20	Mayo	Tirawley	Crossmolina	Ballina	IV.	166
42	Gortanecelig	221	1	29	Cork, E.R.	Fermoy	Rahan	Mallow	II.	82
59	Gortanerrig	181	0	19	Tipperary, S.R.	Clanwilliam	Solloghodbeg	Tipperary	II.	310
46	Gortanewry	331	2	29	Londonderry	Loughinsholin	Desertmartin	Magherafelt	III.	240
34	Gortaniddan	143	0	10	Tipperary, N.R.	Kilnamanagh Upper	Glenkeen	Thurles	II.	278
111	Gortanierin	108	1	14	Mayo	Clanmorris	Crossboyne	Claremorris	IV.	132
11, 17	Gortanimerisk	61	1	6	Kerry	Clanmaurice	Duagh	Listowel	II.	168
69	Gortanimill	593	2	21	Cork, W.R.	West Muskerry	Kilnamartry	Macroom	II.	159
18	Gortaniska	305	1	14e	Clare	Bunratty Upper	Inchicronan	Ennis	II.	9
29	Gortanisky	83	2	10	King's Co.	Garrycastle	Lusmagh	Parsonstown	I.	137
30	Gortanny	125	2	32	Donegal	Inishowen East	Moville Upper	Inishowen	III.	119
14	Gortanoura	82	1	1	Tipperary, N.R.	Lower Ormond	Monsea	Nenagh	II.	287
117	Gortanummera	199	2	21	Galway	Longford	Lickmolassy	Portumna	IV.	61
93, 94, 107, 108	Gortanure	302	0	20	Cork, W.R.	East Carbery (W.D.)	Fanlobbus	Dunmanway	II.	132
63, 64	Gortanure	564	0	29	Mayo	Costello	Kilbengh	Castlereagh	IV.	140
28	Gortanure North	178	1	32	Leitrim	Leitrim	Mohill	Mohill	IV.	104
35	Gortanure South	194	3	12f	Leitrim	Mohill	Mohill	Mohill	IV.	108
90	Gortaphuill	230	2	1	Mayo	Carra	Rosslee	Castlebar	IV.	130
47	Gortaphuill	40	2	3	Roscommon	Athlone	Cam	Athlone	IV.	180
47	Gortaphuill	255	0	6	Roscommon	Athlone	Taghboy	Athlone	IV.	184
90, 91, 100, 101	Gortaphuntaun	149	3	32	Mayo	Clanmorris	Mayo	Claremorris	IV.	135
70	Gortaquigley	149	1	11	Donegal	Raphoe	Raphoe	Strabane	III.	141
1	Gortaquill	109	2	11	Cavan	Tullyhaw	Killinagh	Enniskillen	III.	92
95	Gortard	378	3	11	Galway	Dunkellin	Stradbally	Galway	IV.	32
114	Gortard	88	0	14	Galway	Loughrea	Isortkelly	Loughrea	IV.	63
2	Gortard	135	0	24	Kerry	Iraghticonnor	Aghavallen	Listowel	II.	189
51	Gortard	204	0	32	Tipperary, S.R.	Kilnamanagh Lower	Donohill	Cashel	II.	323
31	Gortaree	178	3	9g	Fermanagh	Clanawley	Killesher	Enniskillen	III.	192
38, 41	Gortaree	280	0	7	Fermanagh	Knockninny	Tomregan	Lisnaskea	III.	203
58, 66	Gortaree	137	3	27	Kerry	Magunihy	Aghadoe	Killarney	II.	199
29	Gortarevan	160	3	10	King's Co.	Garrycastle	Lusmagh	Parsonstown	I.	137
42	Gortarica	176	2	19	Galway	Clare	Kilkilvery	Tuam	IV.	20
103	Gortaroe	100	0	36	Galway	Dunkellin	Kilcolgan	Gort	IV.	28
120	Gortaroe	59	1	24	Mayo	Kilmaine	Cong	Ballinrobe	IV	154
77, 88	Gortaroe	114	3	20	Mayo	Murrisk	Oughaval	Westport	IV.	162
67	Gortaroo	302	3	35	Cork, E.R.	Imokilly	Clonpriest	Youghal	II.	85
5, 8	Gortarowey	506	1	25	Sligo	Carbury	Drumcliff	Sligo	IV.	221
90	Gortaruaun	56	0	20	Mayo	Carra	Drum	Castlebar	IV.	128

(a) Including 4A. 3R. 35P. water.
(b) Including 9A. 3R. 32P. water.
(c) Including 2A. 0R. 1P. water.
(d) Including 7A. 0R. 0P. water.
(e) Including 4A. 2R. 10P. water.
(f) Including 6A. 3R. 6P. water.
(g) Including 2A. 1R. 30P. water.

No. of Sheet of the Ordnance Survey Maps	Townlands and Towns.	Area in Statute Acres.			County.	Barony.	Parish.	Poor Law Union in 1857.	Townland Census of 1851, Part I.	
		A.	R.	P.					Vol.	Page
51, 52	Gortarush Lower	836	1	27	Tipperary, S.R.	Kilnamanagh Lower	Ballintemple	Cashel	II.	322
51	Gortarush Upper	158	2	27	Tipperary, S.R.	Kilnamanagh Lower	Ballintemple	Cashel	II.	322
39, 48	Gortaskibbole	464	0	35a	Mayo	Tirawley	Ballynahaglish	Ballina	IV.	164
20	Gortaspiddale	22	0	27	Kerry	Clanmaurice	Ardfert	Tralee	II.	167
34	Gortataggart	24	0	15	Clare	Bunratty Upper	Doora	Ennis	II.	8
41	Gortataggart	108	2	20	Tipperary, N.R.	Eliogarty	Thurles	Thurles	II.	273
81, 93	Gortatanavally	218	3	4	Cork, W.R.	West Muskerry	Inchigeelagh	Duamanway	II.	157
19, 20	Gortateean	135	3	16	Antrim	Lower Glenarm	Layd	Ballycastle	III.	22
22	Gortateeboy	177	3	39	Cork, E.R.	Duhallow	Kilmeen	Kanturk	II.	73
65	Gortatemple	28	3	9	Tipperary, S.R.	Clanwilliam	Emly	Tipperary	II.	308
81, 90	Gortatlea	458	2	7	Kerry	Iveragh	Dromod	Cahersiveen	II.	195
39	Gortatlea	699	3	8	Kerry	Trughanacmy	Ballymacelligott	Tralee	II.	207
70, 83	Gortatleva	336	2	37	Galway	Dunkellin	Claregalway	Galway	IV.	27
81, 82	Gortatleva	218	2	13	Galway	Galway	Rahoon	Galway	IV.	37
123	Gortatober	171	1	7	Mayo	Kilmaine	Shrule	Ballinrobe	IV.	158
63	Gortatogher	148	3	13	Clare	Bunratty Lower	St. Patricks	Limerick	II.	7
30, 39	Gortatogher	324	0	25	Mayo	Tirawley	Ardagh	Ballina	IV.	163
26	Gortatoue	69	1	21	Fermanagh	Clanawley	Cleenish	Enniskillen	III.	190
25, 26	Gortatole	329	0	9	Fermanagh	Clanawley	Killesher	Enniskillen	III.	192
40	Gortatooda	126	2	24	Tipperary, N.R.	Kilnamanagh Upper	Upperchurch	Thurles	II.	280
7, 14	Gortatoor	191	3	22	Mayo	Tirawley	Lackan	Killala	IV.	170
102, 115	Gortatornora	17	0	5	Cork, W.R.	Bear	Kilcatherine	Castletown	II.	124
36	Gortatrassa	484	1	2	Clare	Tulla Lower	Killuran	Limerick	II.	36
61	Gortatray	147	1	33	Cork, E.R.	East Muskerry	Inishcarra	Cork	II.	103
39, 47	Gortatray	169	2	39	Tyrone	Dungannon Middle	Donaghenry	Cookstown	III.	301
47	Gortatray Bog	8	2	32	Tyrone	Dungannon Middle	Donaghenry	Cookstown	III.	301
15	Gortatresk	123	2	18	Leitrim	Drumahaire	Killarga	Manorhamilton	IV.	98
32	Gortavacan	100	3	25	Leitrim	Leitrim	Mohill	Mohill	IV.	104
7, 15	Gortavacoosh	127	1	38	Limerick	Owneybeg	Abington	Limerick	II.	251
78	Gortavadda	136	2	36	Cork, E.R.	Imokilly	Kilmacdonogh	Youghal	II.	88
38, 46	Gortavale	354	3	5	Tyrone	Dungannon Upper	Desertcreat	Cookstown	III.	308
11	Gortavalla	183	1	24	Tipperary, N.R.	Lower Ormond	Modreeny	Borrisokane	II.	286
67	Gortavalla	11	3	20	Tipperary, S.R.	Clanwilliam	Cordangan	Tipperary	II.	306
15, 16, 24	Gortavalla East	318	1	10	Limerick	Coonagh	Doon	Tipperary	II.	234
15	Gortavalla North	310	3	17	Limerick	Coonagh	Doon	Tipperary	II.	234
15, 24	Gortavalla South	561	3	6	Limerick	Coonagh	Doon	Tipperary	II.	234
129, 138	Gortavallig	296	1	26	Cork, W.R.	West Carbery(W.D.)	Kilcrohane	Bantry	II.	143
108, 111	Gortavallig	283	3	18b	Kerry	Glanarought	Tuosist	Kenmare	II.	188
60	Gortavally	32	2	4	Galway	Tiaquin	Killosolan	Mountbellew	IV.	78
38, 42	Gortavally	145	1	39	King's Co.	Clonlisk	Kilmurryely	Roscrea	I.	131
71	Gortavaura	55	3	17	Galway	Clare	Abbeyknockmoy	Galway	IV.	16
1, 2	Gortavea	256	0	34c	Tyrone	Strabane Lower	Donaghedy	Strabane	III.	321
81, 82	Gortaveer	436	3	0	Cork, W.R.	West Muskerry	Inchigeelagh	Macroom	II.	157
12, 13	Gortaveha	1,072	3	16	Clare	Tulla Upper	Feakle	Tulla	II.	39
38, 47	Gortavehy East	512	0	28	Cork, W.R.	West Muskerry	Drishane	Millstreet	II.	156
38, 47	Gortavehy West	536	1	29	Cork, W.R.	West Muskerry	Drishane	Millstreet	II.	156
78	Gortavella	92	0	26	Cork, E.R.	Imokilly	Kilmacdonogh	Youghal	II.	88
23	Gortavicary	294	1	36	Waterford	Decies without Drum	Kilrossanty	Kilmacthomas	III.	358
38	Gortavilly	152	1	22	Tyrone	Dungannon Upper	Desertcreat	Cookstown	III.	308
16	Gortavoata	3	2	31	Queen's Co.	Upperwoods	Offerlane	Abbeyleix	I.	252
32	Gortavoher	181	1	28d	Cork, E.R.	Duhallow	Kilshannig	Mallow	II.	74
133	Gortavoher	270	2	13	Galway	Kiltartan	Beagh	Gort	IV.	46
99, 107	Gortavoher	167	1	23	Galway	Longford	Killoran	Ballinasloe	IV.	59
67, 74	Gortavoher East	510	1	15	Tipperary, S.R.	Clanwilliam	Clonbeg	Tipperary	II.	305
67, 74	Gortavoher West	805	0	38	Tipperary, S.R.	Clanwilliam	Clonbeg	Tipperary	II.	305
45	Gortavoy	105	3	5	Tyrone	Dungannon Middle	Pomeroy	Dungannon	III.	304
59	Gortavranner	289	3	16	Cork, W.R.	West Muskerry	Clondrohid	Macroom	II.	155
20	Gortavrulla	520	2	28	Clare	Tulla Upper	Feakle	Scarriff	II.	39
48	Gortavullin	106	2	28	Kerry	Magunihy	Molahiffe	Killarney	II.	205
92,93,98,99	Gortaward	229	3	0	Donegal	Banagh	Inver	Donegal	III.	107
77	Gortawarla	196	3	23	Mayo	Burrishoole	Kilmeena	Newport	IV.	122
46	Gortaway	182	2	26	Donegal	Kilmacrenan	Aughnish	Milford	III.	122
10	Gortawee or Scotchtown	137	1	28e	Cavan	Tullyhaw	Tomregan	Bawnboy	III.	96
15	Gortawoer	12	1	32	Tipperary, N.R.	Lower Ormond	Ardcrony	Nenagh	II.	281
105	Gortawullaun	112	3	29	Galway	Dunkellin	Kilconickny	Loughrea	IV.	29
118	Gortawullaun	183	3	7	Galway	Longford	Kilmalinoge	Portumna	IV.	59
89	Gortbaun	380	2	38f	Mayo	Carra	Ballintober	Castlebar	IV.	124
44, 58	Gortbeg	223	3	20	Galway	Clare	Killererin	Tuam	IV.	21
44, 58	Gortbeg	260	3	7	Galway	Clare	Kilmoylan	Tuam	IV.	22
24	Gortbofarna	467	3	29g	Clare	Inchiquin	Inagh	Ennistimon	II.	25
32	Gortbofinna	255	3	20	Cork, E.R.	Duhallow	Ballyclogh	Mallow	II.	67
65	Gortboy	546	1	21	Kerry	Dunkerron North	Knockane	Killarney	II.	182

(a) Including 3A. 1R. 5P. water.
(b) Including 44A. 3R. 24P. water.
(c) Including 14A. 1R. 31P. Salt Marsh.
(d) Including 5A. 3R. 21P. water.
(e) Including 2A. 0R. 30P. water.
(f) Including 0A. 3R. 30P. water.
(g) Including 3A. 1R. 16P. water.

No. of Sheet of the Ordnance Survey Maps.	Townlands and Towns.	Area in Statute Acres.			County.	Barony.	Parish.	Poor Law Union in 1857.	Townland Census of 1851, Part I.	
		A.	R.	P.					Vol.	Page
23	Gortboy	114	0	17	Limerick	Clanwilliam	Caherelly	Limerick	II.	222
36	Gortboy	87	3	12	Limerick	Glenquin	Grange	Newcastle	II.	245
36	Gortboy	229	1	37	Limerick	Glenquin	Newcastle	Newcastle	II.	248
47	Gortboy	163	0	18	Limerick	Kilmallock	St.Peter's & St. Paul's	Kilmallock	II.	250
34	Gortboy	41	1	31	Roscommon	Castlereagh	Ballintober	Castlereagh	IV.	198
6	Gortboyheen	215	2	20	Clare	Burren	Oughtmama	Ballyvaghan	II.	14
142, 151	Gortbrack	222	1	22	Cork, W.R.	West Carbery (E.D.)	Castlehaven	Skibbereen	II.	138
147	Gortbrack	105	1	14	Cork, W.R.	West Carbery (W.D.)	Kilmoe	Skull	II.	145
72	Gortbrack	199	0	22	Galway	Tiaquin	Ballymacward	Loughrea	IV.	75
91	Gortbrack	431	2	30	Kerry	Dunkerron South	Templenoe	Kenmare	II.	185
2, 3, 9, 10	Gortbrack	294	0	31	Mayo	Erris	Kilmore	Belmullet	IV.	146
123	Gortbrack	332	3	8	Mayo	Kilmaine	Shrule	Ballinrobe	IV.	158
78	Gortbrack	46	0	32	Tipperary, S.R.	Iffa and Offa East	Kilsheelan	Clonmel	II.	314
38, 39	Gortbrack East	178	2	26	Kerry	Trughanacmy	Ballyseedy	Tralee	II.	208
74	Gortbrackmoor	135	0	20	Galway	Clonmacnowen	Ahascragh	Ballinasloe	IV.	24
10, 11	Gortbrack North	1,070	0	8	Mayo	Erris	Kilcommon	Belmullet	IV.	144
35, 44	Gortbrack South	1,114	2	23	Mayo	Erris	Kilcommon	Newport	IV.	144
38	Gortbrack West	178	2	21	Kerry	Trughanacmy	Ballyseedy	Tralee	II.	208
40	Gortbrannan	116	3	15	Fermanagh	Clankelly	Galloon	Clones	III.	198
45	Gortbreagoge	233	2	6	Kerry	Corkaguiny	Ballinvoher	Dingle	II.	174
23	Gortbrien	85	1	3	Limerick	Clanwilliam	Caherconlish	Limerick	II.	222
108, 109	Gortbunacullin	1,204	2	20	Mayo	Carra	Ballyovey	Ballinrobe	IV.	126
45	Gortcallyroe	263	2	28	Clare	Tulla Lower	Killaloe	Scarriff	II.	35
27, 28	Gortcalvy	798	0	30	Donegal	Kilmacrenan	Tullyfern	Millford	III.	133
97	Gortcam	110	0	39	Galway	Loughrea	Bullaun	Loughrea	IV.	63
25, 29	Gortcarney	94	0	11	Antrim	Lower Glenarm	Tickmacrevan	Larne	III.	24
22	Gortclohy	795	3	16	Kerry	Clanmaurice	Kilflyn	Tralee	II.	170
35	Gortcloonagh	199	2	19	Roscommon	Ballymoe	Cloonygormican	Roscommon	IV.	191
69	Gortcloonmore	517	2	39	Galway	Clare	Claregalway	Galway	IV.	18
31, 32	Gortconnellan	115	0	1a	Leitrim	Leitrim	Annaduff	Carᵏ. on Shannon	IV.	99
4, 8	Gortconny	738	2	15	Antrim	Cary	Ramoan	Ballycastle	III.	14
24, 25	Gortcooldurrin	88	3	23b	Clare	Inchiquin	Rath	Corrofin	II.	27
10	Gortcorbies	1,062	0	11	Londonderry	Keenaght	Drumachose	Newᵀⁿ Limavady	III.	235
77, 78	Gortcorcoran	348	1	1	Cork, E.R.	Imokilly	Kilmacdonogh	Youghal	II.	88
38, 39	Gortcormacan	594	2	22	Donegal	Inishowen West	Burt	Londonderry	III.	120
42	Gortcreen	175	2	39	King's Co.	Clonlisk	Shinrone	Roscrea	I.	131
28, 37	Gortcross	66	2	23	Donegal	Kilmacrenan	Killygarvan	Millford	III.	128
25	Gortcurka	344	2	25	Clare	Inchiquin	Dysert	Ennis	II.	24
10	Gortcurreen	406	1	31c	Kerry	Iraghticonnor	Listowel	Listowel	II.	193
74	Gortderraree	389	1	34	Kerry	Magunihy	Killarney	Killarney	II.	203
68, 76	Gortderrig	1,201	1	33d	Kerry	Magunihy	Kilcummin	Killarney	II.	201
23	Gortderryboy	242	2	16	Tipperary, N.R.	Ikerrin	Bourney	Roscrea	II.	274
63, 71	Gortdirragh	367	3	21	Kerry	Iveragh	Glanbehy	Cahersiveen	II.	196
62	Gortdonaghmore	595	0	25	Cork, E.R.	East Muskerry	Matehy	Cork	II.	105
27	Gortdonaghy	245	2	18	Fermanagh	Clanawley	Cleenish	Enniskillen	III.	190
51	Gortdotia North	130	3	17	Cork, E.R.	Barretts	Whitechurch	Cork	II.	50
51	Gortdotia South	136	1	8	Cork, E.R.	Barretts	Whitechurch	Cork	II.	50
6	Gortdrishagh	54	3	5	Galway	Ballymoe	Templetogher	Glennamaddy	IV.	9
106	Gortdrishagh	80	1	0	Galway	Leitrim	Abbeygormacan	Loughrea	IV.	50
40	Gortdrishagh	88	1	35	Galway	Moycullen	Kilcummin	Oughterard	IV.	67
119, 132	Gortdromagh	335	0	36	Cork, W.R.	West Carbery (W.D.)	Caheragh	Skibbereen	II.	142
99	Gortdromagh	988	0	36e	Kerry	Dunkerron South	Kilcrohane	Kenmare	II.	183
11	Gortdromagownagh	1,186	3	14	Kerry	Iraghticonnor	Knockanure	Listowel	II.	192
75, 85	Gortdromakiery	3,022	2	9f	Kerry	Magunihy	Killarney	Killarney	II.	203
6, 7, 11	Gortdromasillahy	705	0	18	Kerry	Iraghticonnor	Murher	Listowel	II.	193
48	Gortdromerillagh	409	1	28	Kerry	Magunihy	Kilnanare	Killarney	II.	204
58, 59	Gortdrum	198	3	28	Tipperary, S.R.	Clanwilliam	Solloghodmore	Tipperary	II.	311
138, 147	Gortduff	221	0	24	Cork, W.R.	West Carbery (W.D.)	Kilmoe	Skull	II.	145
6	Gortduff	143	1	35	Galway	Ballymoe	Templetogher	Glennamaddy	IV.	9
32, 33	Gorteade	487	0	21	Londonderry	Loughinsholin	Maghera	Magherafelt	III.	242
130	Gorteanish	345	2	28	Cork, W.R.	West Carbery (W.D.)	Kilcrohane	Bantry	II.	143
22	Gortearagh	356	0	3	Cork, E.R.	Duhallow	Kilmeen	Kanturk	II.	73
7	Gorteen	137	0	18	Cavan	Tullyhaw	Kinawley	Bawnboy	III.	93
13	Gorteen	104	1	33	Cavan	Tullyhaw	Templeport	Bawnboy	III.	94
34	Gorteen	256	1	10	Clare	Bunratty Upper	Doora	Ennis	II.	8
35	Gorteen	445	0	26	Clare	Bunratty Upper	Quin	Tulla	II.	10
18	Gorteen	43	0	33g	Clare	Inchiquin	Ruan	Corrofin	II.	28
25	Gorteen	62	3	24	Fermanagh	Clanawley	Cleenish	Enniskillen	III.	190
26, 32	Gorteen	193	2	34	Fermanagh	Clanawley	Killesher	Enniskillen	III.	192
35	Gorteen	168	0	28	Fermanagh	Clankelly	Clones	Clones	III.	196
38	Gorteen	214	1	35	Fermanagh	Knockninny	Kinawley	Lisnaskea	III.	202
5, 10	Gorteen	80	3	23	Fermanagh	Lurg	Magheraculmoney	Lowtherstown	III.	208
13	Gorteen	917	0	24h	Fermanagh	Magheraboy	Devenish	Ballyshannon	III.	211

(a) Including 17A. 3R. 36P. water.
(b) Including 4A. 3R. 32P. water.
(c) Including 2A. 0R. 22P. water.

(d) Including 5A. 2R. 32P. water.
(e) Including 6A. 3R. 14P. water.
(f) Including 64A. 0R. 19P. water.

(g) Including 4A. 2R. 16P. water.
(h) Including 4A. 3R. 15P. water.

3 S

No. of Sheet of the Ordnance Survey Maps.	Townlands and Towns.	Area in Statute Acres.			County.	Barony.	Parish.	Poor Law Union in 1857.	Townland Census of 1851. Part I.	
		A.	R.	P.					Vol.	Page
23	Gorteen . . .	470	3	14	Fermanagh .	Magherastephana .	Aghavea . .	Lisnaskea .	III.	219
17	Gorteen . . .	900	3	25	Galway . .	Ballymoe . .	Dunmore . .	Glennamaddy .	IV.	7
6	Gorteen . . .	299	1	24	Galway . .	Ballymoe . .	Templetogher .	Glennamaddy .	IV.	9
87	Gorteen . . .	96	3	25a	Galway . .	Clonmacnowen .	Kilcloony . .	Ballinasloe .	IV.	25
46	Gorteen . . .	150	1	23	Galway . .	Killian . .	Ballynakill . .	Mountbellew .	IV.	43
72	Gorteen . . .	428	3	24	Galway . .	Tiaquin . .	Ballymacward .	Loughrea . .	IV.	75
4	Gorteen . . .	353	0	12	Kildare . .	Carbury . .	Dunfierth . .	Edenderry . .	I.	52
26	Gorteen . . .	87	2	28	Kildare . .	Offaly West .	Ballybrackan .	Athy . .	I.	71
6	Gorteen . . .	682	2	36	Kilkenny . .	Fassadinin .	Castlecomer .	Castlecomer .	I.	88
25	Gorteen . . .	421	2	1	Kilkenny . .	Gowran . .	Powerstown .	Thomastown .	I.	97
39, 43	Gorteen . . .	644	3	35	King's Co. .	Ballybritt . .	Roscomroe . .	Roscrea . .	I.	126
43	Gorteen . . .	1,058	2	34	King's Co. .	Ballybritt . .	Roscrea . .	Roscrea . .	I.	126
24, 25	Gorteen . . .	1,513	3	20	King's Co. .	Geashill . .	Geashill . .	Tullamore .	I.	140
2, 8	Gorteen . . .	763	2	13	King's Co. .	Kilcoursey . .	Kilmanaghan .	Tullamore .	I.	141
10	Gorteen . . .	249	1	29	King's Co. .	Lower Philipstown .	Killaderry . .	Tullamore .	I.	143
33, 34	Gorteen . . .	194	3	24	Leitrim . .	Carrigallen .	Cloone . .	Mohill . .	IV.	90
15	Gorteen . . .	78	0	22	Leitrim . .	Drumahaire .	Killarga . .	Manorhamilton .	IV.	98
37	Gorteen . . .	82	0	28	Limerick . .	Connello Upper .	Ballingarry .	Croom . .	II.	230
45, 46	Gorteen . . .	533	0	25	Limerick . .	Connello Upper .	Kilmeedy . .	Newcastle .	II.	233
44	Gorteen . . .	85	0	4	Limerick . .	Glenquin . .	Killeedy . .	Newcastle .	II.	246
44	Gorteen . . .	111	1	36	Limerick . .	Glenquin . .	Mahoonagh .	Newcastle .	II.	246
21	Gorteen . . .	27	1	9	Limerick . .	Pubblebrien .	Croom . .	Limerick . .	II.	252
9	Gorteen . . .	108	0	6b	Longford . .	Granard . .	Clonbroney .	Granard . .	I.	155
6	Gorteen . . .	263	1	0	Louth . .	Upper Dundalk .	Inishkeen . .	Dundalk . .	I.	179
88	Gorteen . . .	121	2	22	Mayo . .	Burrishoole .	Aghagower .	Westport . .	IV.	118
77	Gorteen . . .	145	1	36c	Mayo . .	Burrishoole .	Kilmaclasser .	Westport . .	IV.	121
93, 103	Gorteen . . .	335	0	8	Mayo . .	Costello . .	Annagh . .	Claremorris .	IV.	138
61, 71	Gorteen . . .	241	3	9d	Mayo . .	Gallen . .	Templemore .	Castlebar . .	IV.	151
30	Gorteen . . .	314	2	39	Mayo . .	Tirawley . .	Kilmoremoy .	Ballina . .	IV.	170
28,29,34,35	Gorteen . . .	435	3	26	Queen's Co. .	Clarmallagh .	Aghmacart . .	Abbeyleix .	I.	236
13	Gorteen . . .	43	1	25	Queen's Co. .	Maryborough East .	Borris . .	Mountmellick .	I.	240
12, 17	Gorteen . . .	321	0	13	Queen's Co. .	Maryborough West .	Clonenagh and Clonagheen .	Mountmellick .	I.	243
3, 7	Gorteen . . .	410	0	31	Queen's Co. .	Tinnahinch .	Rosenallis .	Mountmellick .	I.	250
3, 6	Gorteen . . .	249	0	8	Sligo . .	Carbury . .	Rossinver . .	Sligo . .	IV.	223
44	Gorteen . . .	380	3	20	Sligo . .	Coolavin . .	Kilfree . .	Boyle . .	IV.	224
23	Gorteen . . .	386	3	24	Tipperary, N.R.	Ikerrin . .	Bourney . .	Roscrea . .	II.	274
6, 9	Gorteen . . .	267	2	16e	Tipperary, N.R.	Lower Ormond .	Finnoe . .	Borrisokane .	II.	284
65	Gorteen . . .	234	0	11	Tipperary, S.R.	Clanwilliam .	Emly . .	Tipperary .	II.	308
59	Gorteen . . .	139	0	0	Tipperary, S.R.	Clanwilliam .	Rathlynin .	Tipperary .	II.	309
36	Gorteen . . .	242	0	13	Waterford . .	Decies within Drum	Ardmore . .	Dungarvan .	II.	350
31	Gorteen . . .	30	3	4	Waterford . .	Decies without Drum	Dungarvan .	Dungarvan .	II.	355
36	Gorteen . . .	76	1	5	Westmeath .	Clonlonan .	Kilcleagh . .	Athlone . .	I.	261
26	Gorteen . . .	585	1	22f	Westmeath .	Fartullagh .	Lynn . .	Mullingar .	I.	269
9	Gorteen . . .	414	3	23	Wexford . .	Scarawalsh .	Kilrush . .	Enniscorthy .	I.	324
14	Gorteen . . .	880	1	16	Wexford . .	Scarawalsh .	Templeshanbo .	Enniscorthy .	I.	326
43	Gorteen . . .	221	2	35	Wicklow . .	Shillelagh .	Crosspatrick .	Shillelagh .	I.	357
31, 32	Gorteenacammadil .	480	3	19	Roscommon .	Castlereagh .	Kiltullagh .	Castlereagh .	IV.	202
4	Gorteenachurry .	559	2	37g	Leitrim . .	Rosclogher .	Rossinver . .	Manorhamilton .	IV.	111
84	Gorteenacra . .	60	0	12	Galway . .	Athenry . .	Athenry . .	Loughrea . .	IV.	4
40	Gorteenadiha . .	30	2	3	Tipperary, N.R.	Kilnamanagh Upper	Templebeg .	Thurles . .	II.	279
26	Gorteenadiha . .	406	3	13	Tipperary, N.R.	Upper Ormond .	Kilmore . .	Nenagh . .	II.	291
82	Gorteenadrolane .	125	2	32	Cork, W.R. .	West Muskerry .	Inchigeelagh .	Dunmanway .	II.	157
38	Gorteenafoly or Newhall . .	125	0	39	King's Co. .	Clonlisk . .	Ettagh . .	Roscrea . .	I.	130
14, 19	Gorteenagarry or Gorteen . .	153	1	39	Cavan . .	Tullyhunco .	Kildallan . .	Cavan . .	III.	97
18, 19	Gorteenagloon .	148	3	29	Longford . .	Moydow . .	Ballymacormick .	Longford . .	I.	160
6, 7	Gorteenaguinnell .	537	0	11	Leitrim . .	Rosclogher .	Killasnet . .	Manorhamilton .	IV.	110
150	Gorteenalomane .	190	1	0	Cork, W.R. .	West Carbery (E.D.)	Creagh . .	Skibbereen .	II.	139
27	Gorteenaneelig .	158	1	31	Clare . .	Tulla Upper .	Tulla . .	Tulla . .	II.	41
115	Gorteenanillaun .	231	0	35	Galway . .	Loughrea . .	Kilchreest .	Loughrea . .	IV.	63
114, 123	Gorteenaniska .	148	1	3	Galway . .	Loughrea . .	Kilthomas .	Gort . .	IV.	65
105	Gorteenaphcebera .	154	3	38	Galway . .	Loughrea . .	Loughrea . .	Loughrea . .	IV.	65
51, 59	Gorteenaphooka .	50	3	10	Tipperary, S.R.	Clanwilliam .	Donohill . .	Tipperary .	II.	307
40, 46	Gorteenaphoria .	167	2	39	Tipperary, N.R.	Kilnamanagh Upper	Moyaliff . .	Thurles . .	II.	279
5	Gorteenara . .	83	0	24	Kilkenny . .	Fassadinin .	Kilmenan . .	Castlecomer .	I.	90
26	Gorteenard . .	199	2	1	King's Co. .	Upper Philipstown .	Geashill . .	Mountmellick .	I.	144
22, 23	Gorteenashingaun .	458	3	4	Tipperary, N.R.	Ikerrin . .	Rathnaveoge .	Roscrea . .	II.	276
10	Gorteenatarriff .	417	3	27	Cork, E.R. .	Condons & Clangibbon	Marshalstown .	Mitchelstown .	II.	63
30	Gorteenaterriff or Gorteen . .	315	1	9	Cavan . .	Tullyhunco .	Killashandra .	Cavan . .	III.	98
33	Gorteenavalla . .	163	1	6	Tipperary, N.R.	Upper Ormond .	Templederry .	Nenagh . .	II.	293
99	Gorteenavecla . .	229	3	16	Galway . .	Clonmacnowen .	Clontuskert .	Ballinasloe .	IV.	24

(a) Including 4A. 2R. 35P. water.
(b) Including 12A. 2R. 16P. water.
(c) Including 7A. 3R. 21P. water.

(d) Including 2A. 2R. 19P. water.
(e) Including 0A. 2R. 20P. water.

(f) Including 0A. 1R. 20P. detached portion.
(g) Including 7A. 3R. 32P. water.

No. of Sheet of the Ordnance Survey Maps.	Townlands and Towns.	Area in Statute Acres.			County.	Barony.	Parish.	Poor Law Union in 1857.	Townland Census of 1851, Part I.	
		A.	R.	P.					Vol.	Page
98, 99	Gorteenawillin	218	0	12	Galway	Kilconnell	Killallaghtan	Ballinasloe	IV.	41
125	Gorteenayanka	214	2	31	Galway	Leitrim	Ballynakill	Loughrea	IV.	51
93	Gorteen Beg	83	0	19	Mayo	Costello	Bekan	Claremorris	IV.	139
123	Gorteenboy	420	0	10	Galway	Kiltartan	Kilbeacanty	Gort	IV.	47
18	Gorteenboy	163	0	12	Longford	Moydow	Ballymacormick	Longford	I.	160
39, 41	Gorteenbrack	94	0	16	Roscommon	Athlone	Fuerty	Roscommon	IV.	181
87, 88	Gorteencahill	88	2	26	Galway	Clonmacnowen	Clontuskert	Ballinasloe	IV.	24
26	Gorteenclareen	644	2	15	Longford	Rathcline	Shrule	Ballymahon	I.	165
41	Gorteencloogh or Corra More	682	2	6a	Roscommon	Athlone	Athleague	Roscommon	IV.	179
48	Gorteencrin	19	1	21	Wexford	Forth	Kilscoran	Wexford	I.	311
29	Gorteendangan	173	1	12	Tipperary, N.R.	Ikerrin	Templeree	Thurles	II.	277
2, 4	Gorteendarragh	438	3	10	Leitrim	Rosclogher	Rossinver	Ballyshannon	IV.	111
97	Gorteendarragh	12	3	9	Mayo	Murrisk	Oughaval	Westport	IV.	162
59	Gorteendrishagh	118	1	15	Galway	Tiaquin	Moylough	Mountbellew	IV.	80
78	Gorteendrunagh	243	1	25	Mayo	Carra	Aglish	Castlebar	IV.	123
51	Gorteenduvane	138	2	14	Tipperary, S.R.	Clanwilliam	Donohill	Tipperary	II.	307
37	Gorteen East	178	2	15	Limerick	Connello Upper	Cloncagh	Newcastle	II.	231
19	Gorteenfadda	238	2	24	Galway	Ballymoe	Kilbegnet	Glennamaddy	IV.	8
17	Gorteengar	246	2	9	Longford	Rathcline	Rathcline	Longford	I.	164
14, 19	Gorteen or Gorteenagarry	153	1	39	Cavan	Tullyhunco	Kildallan	Cavan	III.	97
30	Gorteen or Gorteenaterriff	345	1	9	Cavan	Tullyhunco	Killashandra	Cavan	III.	98
2	Gorteengrone	88	0	29	Carlow	Carlow	Urglin	Carlow	I.	3
18	Gorteenkeel	334	1	28	King's Co.	Upper Philipstown	Geashill	Tullamore	I.	144
45	Gorteenlahard	128	1	20	Galway	Tiaquin	Moylough	Mountbellew	IV.	80
31	Gorteen Lower	129	1	12	Kildare	Offaly West	Fontstown	Athy	I.	72
48, 49	Gorteen Lower	218	2	30	Tipperary, S.R.	Slievardagh	Buolick	Urlingford	II.	332
3	Gorteen Lower	244	2	37	Wexford	Gorey	Inch	Gorey	I.	316
118	Gorteenlynagh	126	2	19b	Mayo	Kilmaine	Ballinrobe	Ballinrobe	IV.	153
16	Gorteenmacnamara	309	0	27c	Clare	Corcomroe	Clooney	Ennistimon	II.	18
29	Gorteenmagher	222	2	24	Tipperary, N.R.	Ikerrin	Templeree	Thurles	II.	277
42	Gorteenminoge Lower	236	3	5	Wexford	Forth	Kildavin	Wexford	I.	310
42	Gorteenminoge Upper	238	0	32	Wexford	Forth	Kildavin	Wexford	I.	310
109	Gorteenmore	140	2	19	Mayo	Carra	Ballyovey	Ballinrobe	IV.	126
91	Gorteenmore	291	0	38	Mayo	Clanmorris	Kilcolman	Claremorris	IV.	134
93	Gorteen More	159	1	34d	Mayo	Costello	Bekan	Claremorris	IV.	139
34	Gorteennabarna	155	1	22	Tipperary, N.R.	Kilnamanagh Upper	Glenkeen	Thurles	II.	278
105	Gorteennabohogy	118	1	2	Galway	Loughrea	Loughrea	Loughrea	IV.	65
32, 40	Gorteennacreeagh	68	2	11	Limerick	Smallcounty	Knockainy	Kilmallock	II.	261
30, 39	Gorteennafinnoge	446	3	33e	Cork, E.R.	Duhallow	Cullen	Millstreet	II.	70
7	Gorteennaglogh	115	3	33	Cavan	Tullyhaw	Kinawley	Bawnboy	III.	93
10	Gorteennaglogh	283	0	28	Galway	Ballynahinch	Ballynakill	Clifden	IV.	11
27	Gorteennaguppoge	107	0	18	Clare	Tulla Upper	Tulla	Tulla	II.	41
34, 35	Gorteennahilla	432	1	27	Queen's Co.	Clarmallagh	Glashare	Abbeyleix	I.	238
68,69,80,81	Gorteennakilla	423	3	25	Cork, W.R.	West Muskerry	Inchigeelagh	Macroom	II.	157
20	Gorteennakilla	312	0	5	Tipperary, N.R.	Owney and Arra	Monsea	Nenagh	II.	296
22	Gorteennalee	64	2	17	Kilkenny	Shillelogher	Killaloe	Callan	I.	115
6, 11	Gorteennameale	1,610	0	37	Queen's Co.	Upperwoods	Offerlane	Mountmellick	I.	252
46, 52	Gorteennamona	430	3	25	Tipperary, S.R.	Kilnamanagh Lower	Clonoulty	Cashel	II.	323
20	Gorteennamrock	85	1	9	Limerick	Connello Lower	Nantinan	Rathkeale	II.	229
8, 9	Gorteennamuck	513	1	7	Kilkenny	Galmoy	Coolcashin	Urlingford	I.	92
48	Gorteennamuck	201	0	12	Mayo	Tirawley	Ballynahaglish	Ballina	IV.	164
14	Gorteennaskagh	296	2	19	Limerick	Clanwilliam	Caherconlish	Limerick	II.	222
51	Gorteen North	26	0	22	Tipperary, S.R.	Clanwilliam	Donohill	Tipperary	II.	307
26	Gorteenoona	69	1	9	Kildare	Offaly West	Monasterevin	Athy	I.	73
29	Gorteenoran	100	2	36f	Leitrim	Mohill	Cloone	Mohill	IV.	106
37	Gorteenoran or Georgia	56	0	20	Leitrim	Mohill	Mohill	Mohill	IV.	108
8, 9	Gorteenorna	278	0	35	Longford	Longford	Clongesh	Longford	I.	158
117, 126	Gorteenphadder	264	2	2	Galway	Longford	Lickmolassy	Portumna	IV.	61
43, 49	Gorteenrainee	149	3	22	Tipperary, S.R.	Slievardagh	Buolick	Urlingford	II.	332
27	Gorteenreagh	207	3	36	Clare	Tulla Upper	Feakle	Scarriff	II	39
9	Gorteenrevagh	55	0	24g	Longford	Granard	Clonbroney	Granard	I.	155
36, 44	Gorteenreynard	130	0	33	Limerick	Glenquin	Monagay	Newcastle	II.	247
120	Gorteenroe	101	1	22	Mayo	Kilmaine	Cong	Ballinrobe	IV.	154
19,20,32,33	Gorteenruckaun	228	2	22	Galway	Killian	Athleague	Mountbellew	IV.	43
43,44,46,47	Gorteens	1,002	2	13	Kilkenny	Ida	Rathpatrick	Waterford	I.	103
54	Gorteens	129	2	28	Limerick	Connello Upper	Kilbolane	Newcastle	II.	233
122	Gorteens	372	0	16h	Mayo	Kilmaine	Moorgagagh	Ballinrobe	IV.	157
25	Gorteens	119	3	13	Monaghan	Farney	Donaghmoyne	Castleblayney	III.	270
45	Gorteens	283	0	33	Wexford	Shelburne	Fethard	New Ross	I.	327
62	Gorteenshamrogue	99	3	23	Tipperary, S.R.	Middlethird	Rathcool	Cashel	II.	329

(a) Including 46A. 0R. 6P. water.
(b) Including 2A. 2R. 6P. water.
(c) Including 0A. 1R. 22P. water.

(d) Including 1A. 1R. 28P. water.
(e) Including 1A. 3R. 14P. water.
(f) Including 0A. 1R. 30P. water.

(g) Including 1A. 1R. 7P. water.
(h) Including 4A. 1R. 8P. water.

3 S 2

No. of Sheet of the Ordnance Survey Maps.	Townlands and Towns.	Area in Statute Acres. A. R. P.	County.	Barony.	Parish.	Poor Law Union in 1857.	Townland Census of 1851, Part I. Vol.	Page
59	Gorteen South	10 2 13	Tipperary, S.R.	Clanwilliam	Donohill	Tipperary	II.	307
18	Gorteenteen	198 1 34	Kilkenny	Crannagh	Ballycallan	Kilkenny	I.	84
44	GORTEEN T.	—	Sligo	Coolavin	Kilfree	Boyle	IV.	224
31	Gorteen Upper	341 3 3	Kildare	Offaly West	Fontstown	Athy	I.	72
49	Gorteen Upper	242 0 8	Tipperary, S.R.	Slievardagh	Buolick	Urlingford	II.	332
3	Gorteen Upper	330 0 19	Wexford	Gorey	Inch	Gorey	I.	316
39, 40	Gorteenvacan	283 1 35	Kildare	Kilkea and Moone	Castledermot	Athy	I.	59
37	Gorteen West	119 2 35	Limerick	Connello Upper	Cloncagh	Newcastle	II.	231
131, 132	Gorteeny	1,111 3 22	Galway	Leitrim	Ballynakill	Portumna	IV.	51
34	Gorteeny	199 0 37	Tipperary, N.R.	Kilnamanagh Upper	Glenkeen	Thurles	II.	278
86, 89	Gorteeshal	1,176 2 14	Tipperary, S.R.	Iffa and Offa West	Templetenny	Clogheen	II.	320
14, 15	Gortenny	133 0 38	Londonderry	Tirkeeran	Faughanvale	Londonderry	III.	250
26	Gortereghy	828 2 18	Antrim	Kilconway	Rasharkin	Ballymoney	III.	27
26	Gortermoan	85 2 7	Fermanagh	Clanawley	Killesher	Enniskillen	III.	192
34	Gortermone	644 2 27a	Leitrim	Carrigallen	Carrigallen	Mohill	IV.	89
11, 15, 16	Gortermone	487 0 11	Leitrim	Drumahaire	Killarga	Manorhamilton	IV.	98
37	Gortermone	593 3 18	Sligo	Leyny	Kilmacteige	Tobercurry	IV.	231
30,31,36,37	Gortersluin	1,385 3 17b	Sligo	Leyny	Kilmacteige	Tobercurry	IV.	231
40	Gorterwulla	200 3 15	Galway	Moycullen	Kilcummin	Oughterard	IV.	67
31	Gortfad .	573 3 36	Antrim	Lower Toome	Ahoghill	Ballymena	III.	32
79	Gortfad .	262 1 31	Donegal	Raphoe	Donaghmore	Strabane	III.	138
18, 26	Gortfad .	446 0 9	Londonderry	Coleraine	Errigal	Coleraine	III.	232
38	Gortfad .	139 1 22	Tyrone	Dungannon Upper	Desertcreat	Cookstown	III.	308
86	Gortfadda	142 3 20	Galway	Kilconnell	Killaan	Ballinasloe	IV.	41
91	Gortfadda	379 3 38	Kerry	Dunkerron South	Kilcrohane	Kenmare	II.	183
32	Gortfadda	162 2 27	Leitrim	Mohill	Mohill	Mohill	IV.	108
30	Gortfadda	186 1 22	Limerick	Connello Upper	Kilfinny	Croom	II.	233
101	Gortfadda	52 3 32	Mayo	Clanmorris	Kilcolman	Claremorris	IV.	134
38, 46	Gortfad Glebe	185 3 7	Tyrone	Dungannon Upper	Desertcreat	Cookstown	III.	308
67	Gortfahy	164 2 19	Mayo	Burrishoole	Burrishoole	Newport	IV.	119
44	Gortfin .	197 3 26	Tyrone	Omagh East	Termonmaguirk	Omagh	III.	314
44, 45	Gortfinbar	1,028 3 3	Tyrone	Omagh East	Termonmaguirk	Omagh	III.	314
28	Gortflugh	221 0 6	Donegal	Kilmacrenan	Killygarvan	Millford	III.	128
109	Gortfree .	284 1 23	Mayo	Carra	Ballyovey	Ballinrobe	IV.	126
49	Gortfree .	299 3 13	Tipperary, S.R.	Slievardagh	Ballingarry	Callan	II.	331
45	Gortfree and Inchiroe	263 1 24c	Roscommon	Athlone	Cam	Athlone	IV.	180
21, 26	Gortgall .	620 3 33	Fermanagh	Clanawley	Boho	Enniskillen	III.	189
36, 37	Gortgallan	482 0 13	Roscommon	Ballintober South	Cloontuskert	Roscommon	IV.	188
15	Gortgare	279 0 19	Londonderry	Tirkeeran	Faughanvale	NewTⁿLimavady	III.	250
42, 48	Gortgarn	180 1 25	Antrim	Upper Toome	Duneane	Antrim	III.	35
10	Gortgarn	52 2 37	Londonderry	Keenaght	Drumachose	NewTⁿLimavady	III.	235
25	Gortgarn	642 1 15	Londonderry	Keenaght	Dungiven	NewTⁿLimavady	III.	236
40, 48	Gortgarra	177 2 39	Donegal	Boylagh	Templecrone	Glenties	III.	115
22	Gortgarralt	241 2 39	Limerick	Smallcounty	Fedamore	Croom	II.	259
34	Gortgarran	55 2 6	Fermanagh	Magherastephana	Aghalurcher	Lisnaskea	III.	216
63	Gortgarraun	267 3 12	Clare	Bunratty Lower	St. Munchins	Limerick	II.	6
101	Gortgarriff	255 2 33	Cork, W.R.	Bear	Kilcatherine	Castletown	II.	124
11	Gortgarrigan	286 0 13	Leitrim	Drumahaire	Cloonlogher	Manorhamilton	IV.	94
18	Gortgarrow	395 3 15	Galway	Ballymoe	Clonbern	Glennamaddy	IV.	6
40	Gortgarvan	129 2 23	Fermanagh	Clankelly	Galloon	Clones	III.	198
101	Gortgarve	24 1 35	Mayo	Clanmorris	Crossboyne	Claremorris	IV.	132
80	Gortgarve	154 3 16	Mayo	Gallen	Killedan	Swineford	IV.	150
5	Gortgeran	136 0 30	Fermanagh	Lurg	Drumkeeran	Lowtherstown	III.	206
42	Gortgill .	171 1 24	Antrim	Upper Toome	Duneane	Ballymena	III.	35
40, 49	Gortglass	829 1 20	Kerry	Trughanacmy	Ballincuslane	Tralee	II.	206
11	Gort Glebe	5 0 22	Donegal	Inishowen East	Donagh	Inishowen	III.	118
70	Gort Glebe	12 3 3	Donegal	Raphoe	Raphoe	Strabane	III.	141
70	Gort Glebe (Cooladerry)	11 0 31	Donegal	Raphoe	Raphoe	Strabane	III.	141
31	Gortgole .	735 3 36	Antrim	Lower Toome	Ahoghill	Ballymena	III.	32
40	Gortgommon .	112 1 26	Fermanagh	Coole	Galloon	Clones	III.	200
47	Gortgonis	363 0 19	Tyrone	Dungannon Middle	Tullyniskan	Dungannon	III.	305
22	Gortgonnell	43 3 10	Fermanagh	Tirkennedy	Enniskillen	Enniskillen	III.	222
14	Gortgor .	72 2 13	Fermanagh	Magheraboy	Devenish	Enniskillen	III.	211
39	Gortgorgan	284 1 30d	Fermanagh	Knockninny	Kinawley	Lisnaskea	III.	202
78, 79	Gortgower	53 1 3	Kerry	Iveragh	Valencia	Cahersiveen	II.	198
3, 7	Gortgran	152 1 29	Londonderry	Coleraine	Dunboe	Coleraine	III.	231
71	Gortgranagh	69 2 39	Donegal	Raphoe	Clonleigh	Strabane	III.	135
34, 39	Gortgranagh	225 2 4e	Fermanagh	Coole	Galloon	Lisnaskea	III.	200
20, 21	Gortgranagh	349 1 0	Londonderry	Tirkeeran	Clondermot	Londonderry	III.	248
17, 25	Gortgranagh	222 3 6	Tyrone	Strabane Upper	Cappagh	Omagh	III.	325
17	Gortgranard	146 2 2	Monaghan	Dartree	Killeevan	Clones	III.	268
5	Gortgrib	71 2 11	Down	Castlereagh Lower	Knockbreda	Belfast	III.	163
32	Gortgullenan	71 2 32	Fermanagh	Clanawley	Killesher	Enniskillen	III.	192

(a) Including 25A. 1R. 10P. water.
(b) Including 103A. 0R. 39P. water.
(c) Including 157A. 3R. 10P. water.
(d) Including 1A. 2R. 2P. water.
(e) Including 1A. 1R. 6P. water.

No. of Sheet of the Ordnance Survey Maps.	Townlands and Towns.	Area in Statute Acres.			County.	Barony.	Parish.	Poor Law Union in 1857.	Townland Census of 1851, Part I.	
		A.	R.	P.					Vol.	Page
14, 22	Gortica . . .	264	1	6	Londonderry .	Tirkeeran . .	Clondermot . .	Londonderry .	III.	248
12, 19	Gorticashel Lower .	1,009	2	7a	Tyrone . .	Strabane Upper .	Bodoney Lower .	Gortin . .	III.	323
12, 19	Gorticashel Upper .	723	1	29b	Tyrone . .	Strabane Upper .	Bodoney Lower .	Gortin . .	III.	323
3	Gorticleave . .	70	0	18	Monaghan .	Trough . . .	Errigal Trough .	Monaghan .	III.	284
4, 8	Gorticloghan . .	209	1	23	Londonderry .	North East Liberties of Coleraine .	Ballyrashane .	Coleraine . .	III.	245
34	Gorticmeelra . .	14	3	28	Roscommon .	Ballymoe . .	Oran . . .	Roscommon .	IV.	192
14	Gorticross . .	470	0	18	Londonderry .	Tirkeeran . .	Clondermot . .	Londonderry .	III.	248
5	Gorticrum Irish .	126	1	32	Tyrone . .	Strabane Lower .	Leckpatrick . .	Strabane . .	III.	322
5	Gorticrum Scotch .	191	1	38	Tyrone . .	Strabane Lower .	Leckpatrick . .	Strabane . .	III.	322
39	Gortigal . . .	217	3	10	Tyrone . .	Dungannon Upper .	Arboe . . .	Cookstown .	III.	305
99	Gortigrenane . .	466	3	34	Cork, E.R. .	Kinalea . . .	Kilpatrick . .	Kinsale . .	II.	95
23	Gortilea . . .	1,080	1	33	Londonderry .	Tirkeeran . .	Cumber Upper .	NewTⁿLimavady	III.	249
5	Gortileck . .	427	2	5	Tyrone . .	Strabane Lower .	Donaghedy . .	Strabane . .	III.	321
24, 25	Gortin . . .	631	2	21	Antrim . .	Lower Glenarm .	Ardclinis . .	Larne . .	III.	21
17, 22	Gortin . . .	206	0	21	Cavan . .	Tullygarvey .	Kildrumsherdan .	Cootehill . .	III.	90
45	Gortin . . .	39	1	38	Donegal . .	Kilmacrenan .	Tullyfern . .	Millford . .	III.	133
20, 21	Gortin . . .	244	2	13	Londonderry .	Tirkeeran . .	Clondermot . .	Londonderry .	III.	248
46, 47	Gortin . . .	202	0	25	Tyrone . .	Dungannon Middle .	Tullyniskan . .	Dungannon .	III.	305
29	Gortin . . .	62	0	0	Tyrone . .	Dungannon Upper .	Derryloran . .	Cookstown .	III.	307
18	Gortin . . .	706	0	27c	Tyrone . .	Strabane Upper .	Bodoney Lower .	Gortin . .	III.	323
25	Gortinagin . .	586	2	36d	Tyrone . .	Strabane Upper .	Cappagh . .	Omagh . .	III.	325
7	Gortinar . .	776	0	1	Leitrim . .	Rosclogher . .	Killasnet . .	Manorhamilton	IV.	110
8	Gortinarable . .	208	3	15	Tipperary, N.R.	Lower Ormond .	Ballingarry . .	Borrisokane .	II.	282
19	Gortincoolhill .	127	2	25	Londonderry .	Coleraine . .	Aghadowey . .	Ballymoney .	III.	229
35, 36	Gortindarragh .	140	3	18	Fermanagh .	Clankelly . .	Clones . .	Clones . .	III.	196
45	Gortindarragh .	297	1	29	Tyrone . .	Dungannon Middle .	Pomeroy . .	Dungannon .	III.	304
37	Gortindarragh .	233	0	2e	Tyrone . .	Dungannon Upper .	Desertcreat . .	Cookstown .	III.	308
41	Gortineddan . .	255	1	30	Fermanagh .	Knockninny . .	Tomregan . .	Lisnaskea .	III.	203
35	Gortinee . .	236	2	37	Leitrim . .	Mohill . .	Annaduff . .	Mohill . .	IV.	105
68	Gortiness . .	101	2	9f	Donegal . .	Raphoe . .	Kilteevoge . .	Stranorlar .	III.	139
105	Gortinessy . .	275	0	12	Donegal . .	Tirhugh . .	Templecarn . .	Donegal . .	III.	149
47	Gortinlieve . .	306	0	14	Donegal . .	Raphoe . .	Allsaints . .	Londonderry .	III.	134
18	Gortin Mayoghill .	232	1	26	Londonderry .	Coleraine . .	Aghadowey . .	Coleraine . .	III.	229
70	Gortin North . .	227	0	24	Donegal . .	Raphoe . .	Clonleigh . .	Strabane . .	III.	135
70	Gortinreagh . .	110	2	23	Donegal . .	Raphoe . .	Clonleigh . .	Strabane . .	III.	135
14, 15	Gortinreid . .	136	3	36	Londonderry .	Tirkeeran . .	Cumber Lower .	Londonderry .	III.	248
46	Gortins . .	79	2	10	Wexford . .	Bargy . .	Duncormick . .	Wexford . .	I.	304
42, 47	Gortins Great .	143	1	34	Wexford . .	Bargy . .	Kilmannan . .	Wexford . .	I.	306
42, 47	Gortins Little .	143	2	10	Wexford . .	Bargy . .	Kilmannan . .	Wexford . .	I.	306
70, 79	Gortin South .	183	2	12	Donegal . .	Raphoe . .	Clonleigh . .	Strabane . .	III.	135
18	GORTIN T. . .	—			Tyrone . .	Strabane Upper .	Bodoney Lower .	Gortin . .	III.	324
32	Gortinty . .	217	1	2g	Leitrim . .	Leitrim . .	Annaduff . .	Carᵏ. on Shannon	IV.	99
40	Gortinure . .	122	1	32	Fermanagh .	Clankelly . .	Clones . .	Clones . .	III.	196
33	Gortinure . .	137	1	11	Leitrim . .	Mohill . .	Cloone . .	Mohill . .	IV.	106
32	Gortinure . .	279	0	5	Londonderry .	Loughinsholin .	Killelagh . .	Magherafelt .	III.	241
20, 21	Gortinure . .	179	3	25	Londonderry .	Tirkeeran . .	Clondermot . .	Londonderry .	III.	248
121	Gortjordan . .	124	1	3	Mayo . .	Kilmaine . .	Kilmainebeg . .	Ballinrobe .	IV.	155
24	Gortkeel . .	40	0	13	Clare . .	Corcomroe . .	Clooney . .	Corrofin . .	II.	18
40	Gortkelly . .	438	2	24	Tipperary, N.R.	Kilnamanagh Upper	Upperchurch . .	Thurles . .	II.	280
45	Gort and Killiaghan	764	1	14	Roscommon .	Athlone . .	St. Johns . .	Athlone . .	IV.	183
79, 88	Gortkilly . .	142	3	29	Donegal . .	Raphoe . .	Urney . . .	Strabane . .	III.	144
107	Gortknappagh .	127	3	39	Galway . .	Longford . .	Abbeygormacan .	Ballinasloe .	IV.	56
72	Gortknock . .	55	3	23	Tipperary. S.R.	Slievardagh . .	Templemichael .	Carrick on Suir	II.	336
22, 23	Gortknockaneroe .	290	1	27	Cork, E.R. .	Duhallow . .	Clonfert . .	Kanturk . .	II.	68
70	Gortlahan . .	248	1	8	Mayo . .	Carra . .	Kildacommoge .	Castlebar .	IV.	129
93,94,102,103	Gortlahard . .	784	0	32	Kerry . .	Glanarought .	Kenmare . .	Kenmare . .	II.	186
85,86,94,95	Gortlahard . .	649	0	33	Kerry . .	Glanarought .	Kilgarvan . .	Kenmare . .	II.	187
20	Gortlandroe . .	218	1	13	Tipperary, N.R.	Lower Ormond .	Nenagh . .	Nenagh . .	II.	287
19, 20	Gortlane . .	188	0	19	Antrim . .	Lower Glenarm .	Layd . . .	Ballycastle .	III.	22
23	Gortlanna . .	92	1	36	Monaghan .	Cremorne . .	Aghnamullen .	Cootehill . .	III.	258
19, 25	Gortlassabrien .	992	3	34	Tipperary, N.R.	Owney and Arra .	Templeachally .	Nenagh . .	II.	297
7	Gortlaunaght . .	107	1	16h	Cavan . .	Tullyhaw . .	Kinawley . .	Bawnboy .	III.	93
5, 12	Gortleatilla . .	2,023	3	30	Mayo . .	Erris . .	Kilcommon . .	Belmullet .	IV.	144
10, 18, 19	Gortleck . .	1,356	3	32	Donegal . .	Inishowen West .	Desertegny . .	Inishowen .	III.	120
7	Gortleck . .	96	2	16	Roscommon .	Boyle . .	Tumna . .	Carᵏ. on Shannon	IV.	198
10, 17	Gortlecka . .	895	1	4	Clare . .	Inchiquin . .	Killinaboy . .	Corrofin . .	II.	26
53	Gortlee . . .	213	2	23	Donegal . .	Kilmacrenan .	Conwal . .	Letterkenny .	III.	126
35, 40	Gortleet . .	13	3	28	Fermanagh .	Coole . .	Galloon . .	Clones . .	III.	200
86	Gortlemon . .	78	0	17	Galway . .	Kilconnell . .	Killaan . .	Ballinasloe .	IV.	41
53	Gortlenaghan and Derrykeel .	401	1	7	Tyrone . .	Dungannon Middle .	Donaghmore . .	Dungannon .	III.	302
69, 78	Gortletteragh .	261	3	19	Donegal . .	Raphoe . .	Stranorlar . .	Stranorlar .	III.	142

(a) Including 5A. 0R. 7P. water.   (d) Including 3A. 2R. 10P. water.   (g) Including 32A. 3R. 17P. water.
(b) Including 4A. 1R. 27P. water.   (e) Including 13A. 0R. 16P. detached portion.   (h) Including 19A. 1R. 18P. detached portion.
(c) Including 9A. 2R. 29P. water.   (f) Including 3A. 2R. 17P. water.

No. of Sheet of the Ordnance Survey Maps.	Townlands and Towns.	Area in Statute Acres.			County.	Barony.	Parish.	Poor Law Union in 1857.	Townland Census of 1851, Part I.	
		A.	R.	P.					Vol.	Page
36	Gortletteragh . .	268	3	12	Leitrim . .	Mohill . . .	Cloone . . .	Mohill . .	IV.	106
102	Gortlicka . .	459	2	14	Kerry . .	Glanarought .	Tuosist . .	Kenmare . .	II.	188
9	Gortlogher . .	309	1	23	Tyrone . .	Strabane Lower	Urney . .	Strabane . .	III.	322
15	Gortloney . .	545	1	31a	Meath . .	Fore . . .	Moylagh . .	Oldcastle . .	I.	201
93, 94	Gortlosky . .	88	3	24	Donegal . .	Banagh . .	Killymard .	Donegal . .	III.	111
37	Gortlough . .	138	0	4b	Donegal . .	Kilmacrenan .	Killygarvan .	Millford . .	III.	128
94	Gortloughera . .	391	0	29	Kerry . .	Glanarought .	Kilgarvan .	Kenmare . .	II.	187
92, 93	Gortloughra . .	1,443	0	0	Cork, W.R. .	Bantry . .	Kilmocomoge .	Bantry . .	II.	121
64	Gortloughra . .	936	3	27c	Kerry . .	Dunkerron North .	Killorglin .	Killarney .	II.	181
21	Gortlownan .	180	3	33	Sligo . .	Tirerrill . .	Killerry . .	Sligo . .	IV.	239
24	Gortlum . . .	342	1	24	Dublin . .	Uppercross .	Tallaght . .	Dublin South .	I.	41
26	Gortlumman or Bare-field . . .	170	1	12	Clare . .	Bunratty Upper .	Templemaley .	Ennis . .	II.	10
18, 26	Gortlurkaun .	89	1	3	Clare . .	Bunratty Upper .	Inchicronan .	Ennis . .	II.	9
47	Gortlush . .	112	3	18d	Donegal . .	Raphoe . .	Allsaints . .	Londonderry .	III.	134
117	Gortlusky . .	107	2	9	Galway . .	Longford . .	Lickmolassy .	Portumna .	IV.	61
15	Gortlusky . .	198	0	18	Queen's Co. .	Upperwoods .	Offerlane . .	Mountmellick .	I.	252
29	Gortlustia . .	118	1	38	Roscommon .	Roscommon .	Bumlin . .	Strokestown .	IV.	208
36	Gortmacall Beg .	340	1	20	Donegal . .	Kilmacrenan .	Kilmacrenan .	Millford . .	III.	129
36	Gortmacall More .	388	1	27e	Donegal . .	Kilmacrenan .	Kilmacrenan .	Millford . .	III.	129
32, 37	Gortmaconnell .	844	3	8	Fermanagh .	Clanawley .	Killesher .	Enniskillen .	III.	192
27	Gortmacrane .	768	0	10	Londonderry .	Loughinsholin .	Tamlaght O'Crilly .	Ballymoney .	III.	243
37, 45	Gortmagy . .	706	2	31	Clare . .	Tulla Lower .	Killaloe . .	Scarriff . .	II.	35
39	Gortmahonoge .	427	3	7	Tipperary, N.R.	Kilnamanagh Upper	Toem . .	Tipperary .	II.	280
53, 61	Gortmakellis .	357	1	18	Tipperary, S.R.	Middlethird .	St. Patricksrock .	Cashel . .	II.	331
11	Gortmalegg .	68	3	31	Armagh . .	Tiranny . .	Tynan . .	Armagh . .	III.	60
83	Gortmaloge . .	67	2	9	Tipperary, S.R.	Iffa and Offa East .	St. Mary's, Clonmel	Clonmel . .	II.	316
72	Gortmaloon East .	571	3	24f	Kerry . .	Dunkerron North .	Knockane .	Cahersiveen .	II.	182
72	Gortmaloon West .	563	2	18	Kerry . .	Dunkerron North .	Knockane .	Cahersiveen .	II.	182
15	Gortmanna . .	37	3	18	Limerick . .	Coonagh . .	Doon . .	Tipperary .	II.	234
85, 94	Gortmarrahafineen .	733	0	33	Kerry . .	Glanarought .	Kilgarvan .	Kenmare . .	II.	187
2	Gortmellan . .	574	1	12	Tyrone . .	Strabane Lower .	Donaghedy .	Strabane . .	III.	321
10, 11	Gortmellia . .	1,236	2	34	Mayo . .	Erris . .	Kilcommon .	Belmullet .	IV.	144
61	Gortmerron . .	303	3	31	Tyrone . .	DungannonMiddle .	Clonfeacle .	Dungannon .	III.	299
54	Gortmerron . .	140	3	3	Tyrone . .	DungannonMiddle .	Drumglass .	Dungannon .	III.	303
22	Gortmessan . .	157	0	20	Fermanagh .	Tirkennedy .	Derryvullan .	Enniskillen .	III.	221
2	Gortmessan . .	175	1	14g	Tyrone . .	Strabane Lower .	Donaghedy .	Strabane . .	III.	321
8, 13	Gortmillish . .	416	3	2	Antrim . .	Cary . .	Armoy . .	Ballycastle .	III.	11
32	Gortmolire . .	211	0	24	Cork, E.R. .	Duhallow .	Kilshannig .	Mallow . .	II.	74
6	Gortmoney . .	21	0	6	Monaghan .	Trough . .	Donagh . .	Monaghan .	III.	282
1, 2	Gortmonly . .	255	0	0	Tyrone . .	Strabane Lower .	Donaghedy .	Strabane . .	III.	321
7, 9	Gortmore . .	112	2	32	Cavan . .	Tullyhaw .	Templeport .	Bawnboy .	III.	94
33	Gortmore . .	426	2	12	Clare . .	Islands . .	Drumcliff .	Ennis . .	II.	30
31, 32	Gortmore . .	1,684	0	38h	Cork, E.R. .	Duhallow .	Clonmeen .	Kanturk . .	II.	69
99	Gortmore . .	127	3	30	Galway . .	Clonmacnowen .	Clontuskert .	Ballinasloe .	IV.	24
86	Gortmore . .	173	0	29	Galway . .	Kilconnell .	Killaan . .	Ballinasloe .	IV.	41
107	Gortmore . .	136	1	24	Galway . .	Longford . .	Abbeygormacan .	Ballinasloe .	IV.	56
52, 65	Gortmore . .	543	0	39i	Galway . .	Moycullen .	Kilcummin .	Oughterard .	IV.	67
55, 68	Gortmore . .	408	3	32	Galway . .	Moycullen .	Killannin .	Oughterard .	IV.	69
13	Gortmore . .	526	3	33j	Galway . .	Ross . .	Ballinrobe .	Ballinrobe .	IV.	72
42	Gortmore . .	26	1	31	Kerry . .	Corkaguiny .	Dunurlin .	Dingle . .	II.	176
70	Gortmore . .	84	1	33	Kerry . .	Iveragh . .	Killinane .	Cahersiveen .	II.	197
45	Gortmore . .	178	0	30	Limerick . .	Connello Upper .	Kilmeedy .	Newcastle .	II.	233
44, 45	Gortmore . .	133	2	33	Limerick . .	Glenquin .	Mahoonagh .	Newcastle .	II.	246
2, 6	Gortmore . .	583	1	23	Londonderry .	Keenaght .	Magilligan .	Newt͟n͟Limavady .	III.	237
18	Gortmore . .	769	3	31	Mayo . .	Erris . .	Kilcommon .	Belmullet .	IV.	144
39, 41	Gortmore . .	54	3	15	Roscommon .	Athlone . .	Fuerty . .	Roscommon .	IV.	181
6	Gortmore . .	222	1	12	Tipperary, N.R.	Lower Ormond .	Terryglass .	Borrisokane .	II.	288
26	Gortmore . .	891	1	17	Tipperary, N.R.	Owney and Arra .	Burgesbeg .	Nenagh . .	II.	294
83	Gortmore . .	43	3	37	Tipperary, S.R.	Iffa and Offa East .	Inishlounaght .	Clonmel .	II.	313
64	Gortmore . .	216	3	15k	Tyrone . .	Clogher . .	Clogher . .	Clogher . .	III.	292
34, 35	Gortmore . .	219	1	38l	Tyrone . .	Omagh East .	Drumragh .	Omagh . .	III.	312
16, 23	Gortmore . .	487	2	29	Westmeath .	Kilkenny West .	Noughaval .	Ballymahon .	I.	274
8	Gortmore North .	136	0	15	Monaghan .	Monaghan .	Drumsnat .	Monaghan .	III.	275
12, 13	Gortmore South .	95	3	2	Monaghan .	Monaghan .	Drumsnat .	Monaghan .	III.	275
7	Gortmorris . .	215	3	30	Galway . .	Ballymoe .	Kilbeguet .	Glennamaddy .	IV.	8
41	Gortmullan . .	315	0	10	Fermanagh .	Knockninny .	Tomregan .	Lisnaskea .	III.	203
17	Gortmullin . .	304	1	27	Tipperary, N.R.	Ikerrin . .	Corbaliy . .	Roscrea . .	II.	275
9	Gortmunga . .	94	1	22m	Tipperary, N.R.	Lower Ormond .	Kilbarron .	Borrisokane .	II.	284
105	Gortnabarnaboy .	14	3	8	Galway . .	Dunkellin .	Kilconickny .	Loughrea .	IV.	29
58	Gortnabarnan .	141	3	26	Tipperary, S.R.	Clanwilliam .	Cullen . .	Tipperary .	II.	307
69	Gortnabinna . .	780	0	25	Cork, W.R. .	West Muskerry .	Kilnamartry .	Macroom . .	II.	159
102	Gortnabinny . .	415	2	10	Kerry . .	Glanarought .	Kilcaskan .	Kenmare . .	II.	187

(a) Including 16A. 0R. 17P. water.
(b) Including 5A. 0R. 37P. water.
(c) Including 11A. 3R. 12P. water.
(d) Including 1A. 2R. 26P. water.
(e) Including 7A. 1R. 36P. water.

(f) Including 61A. 2R. 24P. water.
(g) Including 23A. 2R. 27P. Salt Marsh.
(h) Including 22A. 0R. 23P. water.
(i) Including 20A. 1R. 7P. water.

(j) Including 4A. 0R. 26P. water.
(k) Including 1A. 0R. 32P. water.
(l) Including 7A. 0R. 12P. water.
(m) Including 31A. 2R. 25P. detached portion.

No. of Sheet of the Ordnance Survey Maps.	Townlands and Towns.	Area in Statute Acres.			County.	Barony.	Parish.	Poor Law Union in 1857.	Townland Census of 1851, Part I.	
		A.	R.	P.					Vol.	Page
85, 86	Gortnaboha	172	0	2	Galway	Kilconnell	Killimordaly	Loughrea	IV.	42
28, 34	Gortnaboley	80	2	38	Tipperary, N.R.	Kilnamanagh Upper	Glenkeen	Thurles	II.	278
33	Gortnaboola	8	0	13	Limerick	Coonagh	Oola	Tipperary	II.	236
33	Gortnaboola	18	3	22	Limerick	Coonagh	Tuoghcluggin	Tipperary	II.	236
15	Gortnaboul	270	1	36	Clare	Corcomroe	Kilshanny	Ennistimon	II.	21
85, 94	Gortnaboul	254	3	23	Kerry	Glanarought	Kilgarvan	Kenmare	II.	187
84	Gortnaboul Lower	203	1	37	Kerry	Glanarought	Kenmare	Kenmare	II.	186
84	Gortnaboul Upper	126	3	7	Kerry	Glanarought	Kenmare	Kenmare	II.	186
17, 27	Gortnabrade	425	1	26a	Donegal	Kilmacrenan	Mevagh	Millford	III.	130
32	Gortnacally	187	3	6	Fermanagh	Clanawley	Killesher	Enniskillen	III.	192
18	Gortnacally	135	1	23	Tipperary, N.R.	Ikerrin	Bourney	Roscrea	II.	274
18	Gortnacally	44	1	15	Tipperary, N.R.	Ikerrin	Corbally	Roscrea	II.	275
33	Gortnacamdarragh	768	3	39	Leitrim	Carrigallen	Cloone	Mohill	IV.	90
3, 6, 7	Gortnacapple	130	3	11	Antrim	Lower Dunluce	Dunluce	Coleraine	III.	17
9	Gortnacargy	155	3	18b	Cavan	Tullyhaw	Templeport	Bawnboy	III.	94
147	Gortnacarriga	273	1	9	Cork, W.R.	West Carbery (W.D.)	Kilmoe	Skull	II.	145
81, 93	Gortnacarriga	595	0	25	Cork, W.R.	West Muskerry	Inchigeelagh	Dunmanway	II.	157
58	Gortnacarriga	258	2	34	Kerry	Magunihy	Aghadoe	Killarney	II.	199
43	Gortnacarrow	231	3	33c	Fermanagh	Coole	Drummully	Clones	III.	199
74, 83	Gortnacart Glebe	681	1	30d	Donegal	Banagh	Killybegs Lower	Glenties	III.	110
123	Gortnaclassagh	25	0	3	Galway	Kiltartan	Kilbeacanty	Gort	IV.	47
27	Gortnaclassagh	78	2	31	Galway	Ross	Cong	Oughterard	IV.	73
77	Gortnaclassagh	499	0	24	Mayo	Burrishoole	Kilmaclasser	Westport	IV.	121
23	Gortnaclea	372	2	38	Queen's Co.	Clarmallagh	Aghaboe	Abbeyleix	I.	236
26	Gortnacleha	132	1	31	Tipperary, N.R.	Upper Ormond	Kilmore	Nenagh	II.	291
14, 19	Gortnacleigh	98	2	28	Cavan	Tullyhunco	Kildallan	Cavan	III.	97
85, 97	Gortnaclogh	574	3	21	Cork, E.R.	East Muskerry	Dunderrow	Cork	II.	103
40	Gortnaclogh	246	1	8	Cork, W.R.	West Muskerry	Kilcorney	Millstreet	II.	158
52	Gortnaclogh	34	2	8	Tipperary, S.R.	Middlethird	Ardmayle	Cashel	II.	324
117, 118, 126, 127	Gortnacloghy	153	2	39	Galway	Longford	Lickmolassy	Portumna	IV.	61
23	Gortnaclohy	193	3	11	Clare	Corcomroe	Kilmanaheen	Ennistimon	II.	21
141, 142	Gortnaclohy	1,035	1	24	Cork, W.R.	West Carbery (E.D.)	Creagh	Skibbereen	II.	139
44, 53	Gortnaclohy	752	3	2	Limerick	Glenquin	Killeedy	Newcastle	II.	246
16	Gortnacloy	435	3	19	Roscommon	Frenchpark	Kilmacumsy	Boyle	IV.	203
117	Gortnacooheen	132	0	19	Galway	Longford	Lickmolassy	Portumna	IV.	61
24	Gortnacoolagh	44	3	8	Limerick	Coonagh	Grean	Tipperary	II.	235
51, 59	Gortnacoolagh	179	3	39	Tipperary, S.R.	Clanwilliam	Donohill	Tipperary	II.	307
67	Gortnacor	95	3	25e	Antrim	Upper Massereene	Blaris	Lisburn	III.	30
17, 18	Gortnacor	119	1	14	Donegal	Kilmacrenan	Clondavaddog	Millford	III.	125
15	Gortnacorkoge	254	3	34	Leitrim	Drumahaire	Killarga	Manorhamilton	IV.	98
67	Gortnacor Lower	46	3	32	Antrim	Upper Massereene	Magheramesk	Lisburn	III.	31
43	Gortnacorragh	84	0	9f	Clare	Tulla Lower	Conlea	Tulla	II.	34
53	Gortnacorrib	289	3	19	Donegal	Kilmacrenan	Kilmacrenan	Letterkenny	III.	129
67	Gortnacor Upper	97	0	36	Antrim	Upper Massereene	Magheramesk	Lisburn	III.	31
106	Gortnacowly	466	0	18	Cork, W.R.	Bantry	Kilmocomoge	Bantry	II.	121
34	Gortnacran Beg	36	2	18	Tipperary, N.R.	Kilnamanagh Upper	Glenkeen	Thurles	II.	278
34	Gortnacran More	170	0	23	Tipperary, N.R.	Kilnamanagh Upper	Glenkeen	Thurles	II.	278
29	Gortnacrannagh	160	1	12	King's Co.	Garrycastle	Lusmagh	Parsonstown	I.	137
22	Gortnacrannagh	324	0	30	Roscommon	Roscommon	Shankill	Strokestown	IV.	213
25	Gortnacreagh	451	1	39	Tyrone	Strabane Upper	Cappagh	Omagh	III.	325
29	Gortnacreha	225	0	14	Cork, E.R.	Duhallow	Cullen	Millstreet	II.	70
37	Gortnacreha Lower	509	2	33	Limerick	Connello Upper	Cloncagh	Newcastle	II.	231
37	Gortnacreha Upper	445	1	30	Limerick	Connello Upper	Cloncagh	Newcastle	II.	231
4, 5, 7, 8	Gortnacrieve	537	0	24	Leitrim	Rosclogher	Rossinver	Manorhamilton	IV.	111
72	Gortnacross	36	2	20	Galway	Tiaquin	Clonkeen	Loughrea	IV.	76
124	Gortnacrusha North	279	0	9	Cork, W.R.	Courceys	Templetrine	Kinsale	II.	147
124	Gortnacrusha South	257	1	25	Cork, W.R.	Courceys	Templetrine	Kinsale	II.	147
128	Gortnacullia	268	3	38g	Galway	Kiltartan	Kilmacduagh	Gort	IV.	48
59	Gortnacurra	149	2	39	Clare	Clonderalaw	Killadysert	Killadysert	II.	16
84, 93	Gortnacurra	355	1	16	Kerry	Glanarought	Kenmare	Kenmare	II.	186
26	Gortnacurragh	15	0	23	Kilkenny	Shillelogher	Killaloe	Callan	I.	115
40	Gortnada	67	1	31	Tipperary, N.R.	Kilnamanagh Upper	Upperchurch	Thurles	II.	280
45	Gortnadarra	63	2	22	Roscommon	Athlone	Rahara	Roscommon	IV.	183
19	Gortnadeeve East	201	2	2	Galway	Ballymoe	Ballynakill	Glennamaddy	IV.	5
19	Gortnadeeve West	717	3	4	Galway	Ballymoe	Ballynakill	Glennamaddy	IV.	5
25	Gortnaderg	91	1	5	Fermanagh	Clanawley	Cleenish	Enniskillen	III.	190
5, 8	Gortnaderrary	577	1	12	Leitrim	Rosclogher	Rossinver	Manorhamilton	IV.	111
7	Gortnaderrylea	43	3	34	Cavan	Tullyhaw	Kinawley	Bawnboy	III.	93
36	Gortnadiha Lower	222	2	0	Waterford	Decies within Drum	Ringagonagh	Dungarvan	II.	353
36	Gortnadiha Upper	287	2	28	Waterford	Decies within Drum	Ringagonagh	Dungarvan	II.	353
121	Gortnadihy	145	0	38	Cork, W.R.	East Carbery (W.D.)	Kilmeen	Dunmanway	II.	134
142	Gortnadihy	111	1	20h	Cork, W.R.	West Carbery (E.D.)	Kilmacabea	Skibbereen	II.	140

(a) Including 14A. 0R. 0P. water.
(b) { Including 39A. 0R. 18P. Bunerky Lough.
{ Including 5A. 1R. 19P. Lakefield Lough.
(c) Including 13A. 1R. 7P. water.
(d) Including 12A. 1R. 8P. water.
(e) Including 0A. 3R. 3P. water.
(f) Including 0A. 2R. 0P. water.
(g) Including 9A. 0R. 20P. water.
(h) Including 5A. 0R. 33P. water.

No. of Sheet of the Ordnance Survey Maps.	Townlands and Towns.	Area in Statute Acres.	County.	Barony.	Parish.	Poor Law Union in 1857.	Townland Census of 1851, Part I.	
		A. R. P.					Vol.	Page
25, 32	Gortnadrass	434 0 18	Sligo	Leyny	Achonry	Tobercurry	IV.	229
48	Gortnadrehy	294 0 6	Mayo	Tirawley	Ballynahaglish	Ballina	IV.	164
15, 24	Gortnadromin	119 0 37	Limerick	Clanwilliam	Dromkeen	Limerick	II.	223
21	Gortnadrumman	164 3 21	Tipperary, N.R.	Upper Ormond	Ballymackey	Nenagh	II.	289
6	Gortnadrung	568 1 2	Sligo	Carbury	Rossinver	Sligo	IV.	223
93	Gortnadullagh	205 0 19	Kerry	Glanarought	Kenmare	Kenmare	II.	186
17, 23	Gortnadumagh	186 3 23	Tipperary, N.R.	Ikerrin	Bourney	Roscrea	II.	274
46	Gortnafira	78 3 14	Cork, E.R.	Kinnatalloon	Mogeely	Fermoy	II.	98
70	Gortnafolla	426 1 12	Mayo	Carra	Turlough	Castlebar	IV.	131
58, 69	Gortnafunshion	103 1 1	Cork, W.R.	West Muskerry	Ballyvourney	Macroom	II.	154
74	Gortnafurra	171 2 18	Tipperary, S.R.	Clanwilliam	Clonbeg	Tipperary	II.	305
54, 58	Gortnagallon	430 3 0	Antrim	Lower Massereene	Killead	Antrim	III.	28
64	Gortnagan Beg	159 0 9	Kerry	Dunkerron North	Knockane	Cahersiveen	II.	182
68, 76	Gortnagane	643 0 31d	Kerry	Magunihy	Kilcummin	Killarney	II.	201
64	Gortnagan More	145 3 36	Kerry	Dunkerron North	Knockane	Cahersiveen	II.	182
17, 18	Gortnagap	654 2 20	Kilkenny	Crannagh	Tullaroan	Kilkenny	I.	88
66	Gortnagappul	449 1 12	Cork, E.R.	Imokilly	Killeagh	Youghal	II.	88
102	Gortnagappul	154 1 29	Kerry	Glanarought	Kilcaskan	Kenmare	II.	187
15	Gortnagarde	153 1 24	Limerick	Coonagh	Doon	Tipperary	II.	234
6	Gortnagark	93 3 18	Cork, E.R.	Duhallow	Tullylease	Kanturk	II.	76
67, 78	Gortnagark	46 2 35	Cork, E.R.	Imokilly	Clonpriest	Youghal	II.	85
3, 6	Gortnagarn	729 1 5	Leitrim	Rosclogher	Killasnet	Manorhamilton	IV.	110
37	Gortnagarn	844 0 1	Tyrone	Dungannon Middle	Pomeroy	Cookstown	III.	304
147	Gortnagashel	80 0 15	Cork, W.R.	West Carbery (W.D.)	Kilmoe	Skull	II.	145
135	Gortnagearagh	77 2 24	Cork, W.R.	Ibane and Barryroe	Kilkerranmore	Clonakilty	II.	149
28	Gortnageeragh	291 1 13	Antrim	Lower Antrim	Skerry	Ballymena	III.	5
103	Gortnageeragh	190 3 38	Mayo	Costello	Annagh	Claremorris	IV.	138
18	Gortnagier East	233 2 30	Galway	Ballymoe	Boyounagh	Glennamaddy	IV.	6
18	Gortnagier West	99 2 38	Galway	Ballymoe	Boyounagh	Glennamaddy	IV.	6
59	Gortnagishagh	391 2 2	Cork, W.R.	West Muskerry	Clondrohid	Macroom	II.	155
43	Gortnaglearagh	8 3 5	Clare	Tulla Lower	Clonlea	Tulla	II.	34
114, 115	Gortnagleav	686 0 5	Galway	Loughrea	Killinan	Loughrea	IV.	64
16	Gortnaglogh	112 3 19	Clare	Inchiquin	Rath	Corrofin	II.	27
44	Gortnaglogh	186 1 22	Clare	Tulla Lower	Kilseily	Limerick	II.	37
14, 22	Gortnaglogh	99 0 16	Cork, E.R.	Duhallow	Clonfert	Kanturk	II.	68
74	Gortnaglogh	262 3 26	Galway	Clonmacnowen	Kilgerrill	Ballinasloe	IV.	25
112, 121	Gortnaglogh	666 2 7	Galway	Kiltartan	Killinny	Gort	IV.	47
59	Gortnaglogh	81 1 14	Galway	Tiaquin	Moylough	Tuam	IV.	80
48	Gortnaglogh	198 3 33	Kerry	Magunihy	Kilnanare	Killarney	II.	204
30, 34	Gortnaglogh	189 0 27	Kilkenny	Kells	Tullahought	Callan	I.	110
28	Gortnaglogh	6 3 29	Limerick	Shanid	Newcastle	Newcastle	II.	257
10, 15	Gortnaglogh	103 3 39	Queen's Co.	Upperwoods	Offerlane	Mountmellick	I.	252
41	Gortnaglogh	225 2 35	Tipperary, N.R.	Eliogarty	Thurles	Thurles	II.	273
47	Gortnaglogh	182 1 27	Tyrone	Dungannon Middle	Clonoe	Dungannon	III.	300
45	Gortnagluggin	235 1 13	Limerick	Connello Upper	Kilmeedy	Newcastle	II.	233
46	Gortnaglush	129 3 17	Tyrone	Dungannon Middle	Donaghmore	Dungannon	III.	302
45, 46	Gortnagola	187 1 8	Tyrone	Dungannon Middle	Pomeroy	Dungannon	III.	304
70, 79	Gortnagole	165 1 17	Donegal	Raphoe	Clonleigh	Strabane	III.	135
44	Gortnagonnella	156 2 6	Clare	Tulla Lower	Kilseily	Limerick	II.	37
25	Gortnagory	103 2 36	Antrim	Lower Glenarm	Ardclinis	Larne	III.	21
1, 2, 6	Gortnagoul	338 3 29	Cork, E.R.	Orrery and Kilmore	Kilbolane	Kanturk	II.	108
23	Gortnagowna	881 2 1	Tipperary, N.R.	Ikerrin	Killavinoge	Roscrea	II.	275
33	Gortnagowna	581 0 23	Tipperary, N.R.	Upper Ormond	Templederry	Nenagh	II.	293
5, 16, 17	Gortnagoyne	689 3 28	Galway	Dunmore	Dunmore	Tuam	IV.	34
21	Gortnagoyne	250 3 30	Roscommon	Castlereagh	Kilcorkey	Castlereagh	IV.	199
79, 88	Gortnagrace	417 2 27	Donegal	Raphoe	Urney	Strabane	III.	144
33	Gortnagraiga	393 0 3	Cork, E.R.	Fermoy	Mourneabbey	Mallow	II.	82
101	Gortnagranagher	31 3 31	Mayo	Clanmorris	Tagheen	Claremorris	IV.	136
7	Gortnagrann	335 0 16	Tipperary, N.R.	Lower Ormond	Aglishcloghane	Borrisokane	II.	281
52	Gortnagranna	76 3 19	Tipperary, S.R.	Kilnamanagh Lower	Clonoulty	Cashel	II.	323
70	Gortnagree	780 2 36	Kerry	Iveragh	Killinane	Cahersiveen	II.	197
9	Gortnagrelly	783 1 2b	Sligo	Carbury	Drumcliff	Sligo	IV.	221
32	Gortnagriffin	45 1 24	Fermanagh	Clanawley	Killesher	Enniskillen	III.	192
54,55,67,68	Gortnagroagh	128 1 18c	Galway	Moycullen	Killannin	Oughterard	IV.	69
22, 23	Gortnagroagh	61 2 11	Queen's Co.	Clarmallagh	Aghaboe	Abbeyleix	I.	236
6	Gortnagrogerny	304 3 21	Leitrim	Rosclogher	Killasnet	Manorhamilton	IV.	110
24, 32	Gortnagross	962 3 29d	Cork, E.R.	Duhallow	Ballyclogh	Mallow	II.	67
32	Gortnagross	55 3 33e	Cork, E.R.	Duhallow	Mallow	Mallow	II.	75
58, 69	Gortnagross	151 3 26	Cork, W.R.	West Muskerry	Ballyvourney	Macroom	II.	154
34, 35	Gortnagross	870 0 23	Limerick	Shanid	Rathronan	Newcastle	II.	257
25	Gortnagross	879 1 15	Londonderry	Keenaght	Dungiven	New T Limavady	III.	236
29	Gortnagross	150 2 31	Tyrone	Dungannon Upper	Kildress	Cookstown	III.	309
23	Gortnagross	442 1 39f	Tyrone	Omagh West	Termonamongan	Castlederg	III.	317

(a) Including 2A. 2R. 16P. water.
(b) Including 50A. 1R. 16P. water.
(c) Including 3A. 2R. 34P. water.
(d) Including 7A. 2R. 16P. water.
(e) Including 0A. 1R. 24P. water.
(f) Including 4A. 3R. 13P. water.

No. of Sheet of the Ordnance Survey Maps.	Townlands and Towns.	Area in Statute Acres.			County.	Barony.	Parish.	Poor Law Union in 1857.	Townland Census of 1851, Part I.	
		A.	R.	P.					Vol.	Page
19, 20	Gortnagross Lower or Murroo	67	1	27	Antrim	Lower Glenarm	Layd	Ballycastle	III.	22
19	Gortnagross Middle	33	2	25	Antrim	Lower Glenarm	Layd	Ballycastle	III.	22
19	Gortnagross Upper or Issbawn	244	0	9	Antrim	Lower Glenarm	Layd	Ballycastle	III.	22
131	Gortnagrough	455	3	28	Cork, W.R.	West Carbery(W.D.)	Skull	Skull	II.	146
20, 21	Gortnagrour	100	0	28	Limerick	Connello Lower	Clonshire	Rathkeale	II.	227
70, 71	Gortnagulla	475	3	20	Kerry	Iveragh	Killinane	Cahersiveen	II.	197
44, 54	Gortnagullanagh	96	3	28	Kerry	Corkaguiny	Minard	Dingle	II.	180
1, 5	Gortnagullion	378	0	25	Fermanagh	Lurg	Drumkeeran	Lowtherstown	III.	206
28	Gortnagullion	402	0	22	Leitrim	Leitrim	Kiltubbrid	Car^k. on Shannon	IV.	104
4	Gortnagunned	217	3	19a	Galway	Dunmore	Addergoole	Tuam	IV.	33
90, 100	Gortnagusetaul	32	1	2	Mayo	Clanmorris	Mayo	Claremorris	IV.	135
47	Gortnagwyg	128	0	14	Tyrone	Dungannon Upper	Arboe	Cookstown	III.	305
59	Gortnahaha	445	2	3	Clare	Clonderalaw	Killadysert	Killadysert	II.	16
35	Gortnahaha	72	1	6	Tipperary, N.R.	Eliogarty	Loughmoe East	Thurles	II.	271
59	Gortnahahaboy	19	1	0	Tipperary, S.R.	Clanwilliam	Donohill	Tipperary	II.	307
34, 40	Gortnahalla	354	0	5	Tipperary, N.R.	Kilnamanagh Upper	Upperchurch	Thurles	II.	280
31	Gortnahaskany	67	0	13	Galway	Tiaquin	Kilkerrin	Glennamaddy	IV.	77
58, 68	Gortnabeltia	1,423	2	9	Mayo	Tirawley	Addergoole	Castlebar	IV.	163
24	Gortnahey Beg	167	1	10	Londonderry	Keenaght	Bovevagh	New T^n Limavady	III.	235
24	Gortnahey More	98	0	25	Londonderry	Keenaght	Bovevagh	New T^n Limavady	III.	235
86, 98	Gortnahimrissan	58	2	18	Galway	Kilconnell	Killallaghtan	Ballinasloe	IV.	41
77	Gortnahomna Beg	30	2	16	Cork, E.R.	Imokilly	Ightermurragh	Middleton	II.	87
77	Gortnahomna More	96	1	38	Cork, E.R.	Imokilly	Ightermurragh	Middleton	II.	87
42, 43	Gortnahoo	652	2	7	Tipperary, S.R.	Slievardagh	Buolick	Urlingford	II.	332
86, 98	Gortnahoon	249	0	28	Galway	Kilconnell	Killallaghtan	Ballinasloe	IV.	41
55, 68	Gortnahoon	217	2	18	Galway	Moycullen	Killannin	Oughterard	IV.	69
43	GORTNAHOO T.	—			Tipperary, S.R.	Slievardagh	Buolick	Urlingford	II.	332
46	Gortnahorna	168	0	10	Meath	Upper Moyfenrath	Castlejordan	Edenderry	I.	212
87	Gortnahorna (Clancarty)	240	3	38	Galway	Clonmacnowen	Clontuskert	Ballinasloe	IV.	24
87, 99	Gortnahorna (Clanricarde)	448	2	24	Galway	Clonmacnowen	Clontuskert	Ballinasloe	IV.	24
81, 93	Gortnahoughtee	735	3	11	Cork, W.R.	West Muskerry	Inchigeelagh	Dunmanway	II.	157
3, 6	Gortnahoula	463	0	14	Sligo	Carbury	Rossinver	Sligo	IV.	223
19	Gortnahown	574	1	1	Cork, E.R.	Condons&Clangibbon	Glanworth	Mitchelstown	II.	61
84	Gortnahown	60	0	2	Galway	Athenry	Athenry	Loughrea	IV.	4
46	Gortnahulla	64	0	20	Kerry	Trughanacmy	Kilgarrylander	Tralee	II.	210
7	Gortnahulla	51	3	9	Tipperary, N.R.	Lower Ormond	Aglishcloghane	Borrisokane	II.	281
72	Gortnahultra	370	0	18	Galway	Tiaquin	Ballymacward	Loughrea	IV.	75
28, 29	Gortnahurra Lower	1,901	1	14	Mayo	Tirawley	Crossmolina	Ballina	IV.	166
29	Gortnahurra Upper	585	3	6	Mayo	Tirawley	Crossmolina	Ballina	IV.	166
25	Gortnakesh	25	0	24	Cavan	Upper Loughtee	Annagelliff	Cavan	III.	82
125	Gortnakilla	142	2	30	Galway	Leitrim	Ballynakill	Loughrea	IV.	51
108	Gortnakilla	195	1	0	Galway	Longford	Donanaghta	Portumna	IV.	58
76, 86	Gortnakilla	640	0	27	Kerry	Magunihy	Killaha	Killarney	II.	202
26	Gortnakillew	212	3	19b	Cavan	Upper Loughtee	Lavey	Cavan	III.	86
129	Gortnakilly	478	3	35	Cork, W.R.	West Carbery(W.D.)	Kilcrohane	Bantry	II.	143
106	Gortnakilly	62	0	6	Kerry	Dunkerron South	Kilcrohane	Cahersiveen	II.	183
24, 25	Gortnakistin	227	3	37	Limerick	Coonagh	Doon	Tipperary	II.	234
14,15,23,24	Gortnalaght	636	0	29	Waterford	Decies without Drum	Kilrossanty	Kilmacthomas	II.	358
6	Gortnalahagh	24	2	39	Limerick	Clanwilliam	Stradbally	Limerick	II.	226
52	Gortnalahee	309	2	27	Cork, E.R.	Barrymore	Dunbulloge	Cork	II.	54
32, 35	Gortnalamph	289	1	2c	Leitrim	Mohill	Mohill	Mohill	IV.	108
33	Gortnalara	160	0	10	Tipperary, N.R.	Upper Ormond	Templederry	Nenagh	II.	293
44	Gortnalaragh	223	3	24	Donegal	Kilmacrenan	Kilmacrenan	Millford	III.	129
20	Gortnalavey	155	3	29	Galway	Ballymoe	Kilbegnet	Glennamaddy	IV.	8
5	Gortnalea	473	2	17	Galway	Dunmore	Dunmore	Tuam	IV.	34
30	Gortnaleaha	107	1	7	Kerry	Trughanacmy	Ballymacelligott	Tralee	II.	207
30	Gortnaleaha	58	0	38	Kerry	Trughanacmy	O'Brennan	Tralee	II.	212
13	Gortnaleck	94	3	32d	Cavan	Tullyhaw	Templeport	Bawnboy	III.	95
25,26,34,35	Gortnaleck	1,586	0	1	Donegal	Kilmacrenan	Clondahorky	Dunfanaghy	III.	123
5, 6, 8	Gortnaleck	1,182	2	11	Sligo	Carbury	Ahamlish	Sligo	IV.	219
93	Gortnalecka	14	0	5	Galway	Galway	Rahoon	Galway	IV.	37
8	Gortnalee	495	1	30	Fermanagh	Magheraboy	Inishmacsaint	Ballyshannon	III.	213
27, 28	Gortnalee	399	0	20	Queen's Co.	Clandonagh	Donaghmore	Donaghmore	I.	233
2, 4	Gortnaleg	262	3	30	Cavan	Tullyhaw	Killinagh	Enniskillen	III.	92
7	Gortnaleg	172	2	26	Cavan	Tullyhaw	Kinawley	Bawnboy	III.	93
11, 12	Gortnalibbert	1,125	0	25	Leitrim	Drumahaire	Cloonclare	Manorhamilton	IV.	93
112	Gortnalicky	17	3	6	Cork, E.R.	Kinsale	Clontead	Kinsale	II.	99
150	Gortnalicky	149	3	4	Cork, W.R.	West Carbery (E.D.)	Creagh	Skibbereen	III.	139
59, 70	Gortnalicky	319	2	23	Cork, W.R.	West Muskerry	Clondrohid	Macroom	II.	155
72, 85	Gortnalone North	337	1	28	Galway	Tiaquin	Clonkeen	Loughrea	IV.	76

(a) Including 9A. 3R. 17P. water.
(b) Including 4A. 1R. 13P. water.
(c) Including 8A. 0R. 11P. water.
(d) Including 4A. 0R. 28P. water.

No. of Sheet of the Ordnance Survey Maps.	Townlands and Towns.	Area in Statute Acres.	County.	Barony.	Parish.	Poor Law Union in 1857.	Townland Census of 1851, Part I.	
		A. R. P.					Vol.	Page
85	Gortnalone South	277 0 1	Galway	Tiaquin	Clonkeen	Loughrea	IV.	76
33	Gortnalougher	278 2 22	Leitrim	Mohill	Cloone	Mohill	IV.	106
80	Gortnaloughra	224 0 28	Cork, W.R.	West Muskerry	Inchigeelagh	Macroom	II.	157
153	Gortnalour	49 2 19	Cork, W.R.	West Carbery (E.D.)	Clear-island	Skibbereen	II.	138
81, 82	Gortnalour	487 0 18	Cork, W.R.	West Muskerry	Inchigeelagh	Dunmanway	II.	157
16	Gortnaloura	67 0 12	Galway	Dunmore	Addergoole	Tuam	IV.	33
88	Gortnalower	12 3 24	Tipperary, S.R.	Iffa and Offa West	Ardfinnan	Clogheen	II.	317
99, 100	Gortnalug	24 3 30	Galway	Longford	Kiltormer	Ballinasloe	IV.	60
32, 33	Gortnalug	70 2 24	Leitrim	Mohill	Mohill	Mohill	IV.	108
7, 8	Gortnalughoge	187 3 15a	Donegal	Kilmacrenan	Mevagh	Millford	III.	130
112	Gortnalusheen	57 2 11	Cork, E.R.	Kinsale	Clontead	Kinsale	II.	99
29	Gortnalyer	43 2 23	Mayo	Tirawley	Crossmolina	Ballina	IV.	166
105	Gortnamackan	153 0 17	Galway	Dunkellin	Kilchreest	Loughrea	IV.	28
98	Gortnamackanee	699 2 5b	Kerry	Dunkerron South	Kilcrohane	Cahersiveen	II.	183
115	Gortnamannagh East	413 2 11	Galway	Loughrea	Kilchreest	Loughrea	IV.	63
115	Gortnamannagh West	426 2 7	Galway	Loughrea	Kilchreest	Loughrea	IV.	63
18, 19	Gortnamearacaun	802 0 39	Clare	Bunratty Upper	Inchicronan	Tulla	II.	9
10	Gortnaminna	189 3 28	Cork, E.R.	Condons&Clangibbon	Marshalstown	Mitchelstown	II.	63
10	Gortnaminsha	301 3 10c	Kerry	Iraghticonnor	Dysert	Listowel	II.	190
140	Gortnamona	232 0 0	Cork, W.R.	West Carbery(W.D.)	Skull	Skull	II.	146
81	Gortnamona	136 0 24	Cork, W.R.	West Muskerry	Inchigeelagh	Macroom	II.	157
42	Gortnamona	58 1 35	Galway	Clare	Kilkilvery	Tuam	IV.	20
99	Gortnamona	184 2 37	Galway	Clonmacnowen	Clontuskert	Ballinasloe	IV.	24
116, 125	Gortnamona	169 0 34	Galway	Leitrim	Ballynakill	Loughrea	IV.	51
17	Gortnamona and Clooney	144 0 8d	Donegal	Kilmacrenan	Clondavaddog	Millford	III.	124
68	Gortnamona East	85 0 14	Galway	Moycullen	Moycullen	Galway	IV.	71
108	Gortnamona or Moorfield	109 2 20	Galway	Longford	Fahy	Portumna	IV.	58
108	Gortnamona or Moorfield	460 2 10	Galway	Longford	Kilquain	Portumna	IV.	60
68	Gortnamona West	95 0 13	Galway	Moycullen	Moycullen	Galway	IV.	71
55	Gortnamoney	19 0 14	Donegal	Raphoe	Taughboyne	Strabane	III.	143
9	Gortnamoney	66 3 29	Londonderry	Keenaght	Aghanloo	NewTnLimavady	III.	234
13	Gortnamony	199 1 1	Down	Lower Iveagh, Up.pt.	Moira	Lurgan	III.	170
17, 18, 26	Gortnamoyagh	1,104 1 21	Londonderry	Coleraine	Errigal	Coleraine	III.	232
50	Gortnamuck	135 3 39	Clare	Islands	Clondagad	Killadysert	II.	29
79	Gortnamuck	582 0 15	Donegal	Raphoe	Donaghmore	Strabane	III.	138
31	Gortnamuck	349 1 4	King's Co.	Ballyboy	Ballyboy	Parsonstown	I.	123
29	Gortnamuckaly	66 0 23	Kerry	Trughanacmy	Clogherbrien	Tralee	II.	209
108	Gortnamucklagh	693 3 23	Cork, W.R.	East Carbery (W.D.)	Fanlobbus	Dunmanway	II.	132
132, 141	Gortnamucklagh	332 0 19	Cork, W.R.	West Carbery (E.D.)	Abbeystrowry	Skibbereen	II.	136
74	Gortnamucklagh	432 1 36	Donegal	Boylagh	Inishkeel	Glenties	III.	112
64,65,75,76	Gortnamucky	239 2 34	Cork, E.R.	Barrymore	Carrigtohill	Middleton	II.	52
13	Gortnamuinga	216 0 19	Clare	Tulla Upper	Feakle	Tulla	II.	39
16, 17	Gortnana	114 0 10c	Monaghan	Dartree	Killeevan	Clones	III.	268
13	Gortnana	141 0 18	Monaghan	Monaghan	Kilmore	Monaghan	III.	276
114	Gortnanark	70 2 12	Galway	Loughrea	Kilthomas	Gort	IV.	65
55	Gortnandarragh or Oakfield	259 0 19	Galway	Moycullen	Killannin	Oughterard	IV.	70
52	Gortnanool	75 2 19	Clare	Bunratty Lower	Kilfintinan	Limerick	II.	5
99	Gortnanoon	203 1 9	Cork, E.R.	Kerrycurrihy	Templebreedy	Kinsale	II.	93
44, 45, 55	Gortnanooran	197 2 22	Kerry	Corkaguiny	Ballinvoher	Dingle	II.	174
24	Gortnanuv	67 2 20	Limerick	Coonagh	Ballynaclogh	Tipperary	II.	233
20	Gortnapeaky	304 3 1	Waterford	Coshmore&Coshbride	Lismore and Mocollop	Lismore	II.	346
59, 70	Gortnapeasty	190 0 33	Cork, W.R.	West Muskerry	Clondrohid	Macroom	II.	155
42, 56	Gortnaporia	253 2 36	Galway	Clare	Kilcoona	Tuam	IV.	19
60	Gortnaprocess	334 1 14	Kerry	Magunihy	Kileummin	Killarncy	II.	201
29, 38	Gortnaraby	212 3 15	Mayo	Tirawley	Crossmolina	Ballina	IV.	166
33	Gortnarah	213 0 39	Leitrim	Mohill	Cloone	Mohill	IV.	106
91	Gortnaraha	455 2 33	Mayo	Clanmorris	Kilcolman	Claremorris	IV.	134
99	Gortnaraheen	148 3 1	Galway	Longford	Kiltormer	Ballinasloe	IV.	60
22, 23	Gortnaran	268 3 36	Londonderry	Tirkeeran	Cumber Upper	Londonderry	III.	249
81	Gortnarea	282 1 7f	Cork, W.R.	West Muskerry	Inchigeelagh	Dunmanway	II.	157
1	Gortnaree	161 3 8	Fermanagh	Lurg	Drumkeeran	Lowtherstown	III.	206
17	Gortnarne	561 2 15	Londonderry	Keenaght	Balteagh	NewTnLimavady	III.	234
26, 27	Gortnarup	187 0 30	Galway	Ross	Cong	Oughterard	IV.	73
41	Gortnasate	75 0 37	Donegal	Boylagh	Templecrone	Glenties	III.	115
15	Gortnascarry	197 2 21	Limerick	Coonagh	Doon	Limerick	II.	234
135	Gortnascarty	91 2 38	Cork, W.R.	Ibane and Barryroe	Kilkerranmore	Clonakilty	II.	149
69	Gortnascarty	255 0 0	Cork, W.R.	West Muskerry	Ballyvourney	Macroom	II.	154
119	Gortnascreeny	712 0 10	Cork, W.R.	West Carbery (W.D.)	Caheragh	Skibbereen	II.	142
134, 135	Gortnascreeny	301 0 15g	Galway	Leitrim	Clonrush	Scarriff	IV.	53
15	Gortnascregga	336 0 0	Cork, E.R.	Duhallow	Clonfert	Kanturk	II.	68

(a) Including 3A. 2R. 10P. water.
(b) Including 41A. 0R. 24P. water.
(c) Including 8A. 2R. 18P. water.

(d) Including 4A. 3R. 8P. water.
(e) Including 10A. 0R. 17P. water.

(f) Including 9A. 2R. 6P. water.
(g) Including 4A. 3R. 12P. water.

No. of Sheet of the Ordnance Survey Maps.	Townlands and Towns.	Area in Statute Acres.			County.	Barony.	Parish.	Poor Law Union in 1857.	Townland Census of 1851, Part I.	
		A.	R.	P.					Vol.	Page
28, 42	Gortnasculloge	85	2	39	Galway	Clare	Donaghpatrick	Tuam	IV.	19
49	Gortnasculloge	178	1	10	Tipperary, S.R.	Slievardagh	Ballingarry	Callan	II.	331
110, 111	Gortnashammer	128	1	10	Mayo	Kilmaine	Kilcommon	Ballinrobe	IV.	154
25	Gortnashangan Lower or Bingfield	123	1	14	Cavan	Clanmahon	Kilmore	Cavan	III.	78
25	Gortnashangan Upper or Hermitage	163	0	12	Cavan	Clanmahon	Kilmore	Cavan	III.	78
54, 56	Gortnasharvoge	194	1	30	Roscommon	Moycarn	Creagh	Ballinasloe	IV.	206
39, 40	Gortnashingaun	69	1	8	Galway	Moycullen	Kilcummin	Oughterard	IV.	67
65	Gortnasillagh	601	2	6a	Donegal	Boylagh	Inishkeel	Glenties	III.	112
117	Gortnasillagh	171	3	2	Galway	Leitrim	Tynagh	Portumna	IV.	55
2, 4	Gortnasillagh	181	1	22	Leitrim	Rosclogher	Rossinver	Ballyshannon	IV.	111
71	Gortnasillagh	196	2	32	Mayo	Gallen	Bohola	Swineford	IV.	147
21, 27	Gortnasillagh	426	1	3	Roscommon	Castlereagh	Baslick	Castlereagh	IV.	199
16, 18	Gortnasillagh East	313	3	2	Leitrim	Drumahaire	Inishmagrath	Manorhamilton	IV.	96
17	Gortnasillagh West	106	0	21	Leitrim	Drumahaire	Inishmagrath	Manorhamilton	IV.	96
57, 58	Gortnaskagh	163	1	32b	Clare	Moyarta	Kilrush	Kilrush	II.	33
32	Gortnaskagh	72	3	16	Limerick	Smallcounty	Kilcullane	Kilmallock	II.	260
57	Gortnaskarry	322	1	38c	Kerry	Dunkerron North	Knockane	Killarney	II.	182
28, 38, 39	Gortnaskea	1,922	3	4	Donegal	Inishowen West	Fahan Upper	Londonderry	III.	121
47	Gortnaskea	46	2	7	Tyrone	Dungannon Middle	Tullyniskan	Dungannon	III.	305
39	Gortnaskea	159	2	32	Tyrone	Dungannon Upper	Ballyclog	Cookstown	III.	306
36, 45	Gortnaskeagh	433	2	25	Donegal	Kilmacrenan	Kilmacrenan	Millford	III.	129
94, 103	Gortnaskeagh	395	2	27	Kerry	Glanarought	Kilgarvan	Kenmare	II.	187
11	Gortnaskeagh	646	0	25	Leitrim	Drumahaire	Drumlease	Manorhamilton	IV.	94
4	Gortnaskeha	718	0	37	Kerry	Iraghticonnor	Killehenny	Listowel	II.	191
4	Gortnaskeha Commons	150	3	12	Kerry	Iraghticonnor	Killehenny	Listowel	II.	191
20, 28	Gortnaskehy	935	1	29	Cork, E.R.	Condons and Clangibbon	Macroney	Fermoy	II.	63
78	Gortnaskehy	153	2	28	Cork, E.R.	Imokilly	Kilmacdonogh	Youghal	II.	88
43, 44	Gortnaskehy	262	3	32	Limerick	Glenquin	Killeedy	Newcastle	II.	246
23	Gortnaskehy	288	1	8	Tipperary, N.R.	Ikerrin	Bourney	Roscrea	II.	274
40	Gortnaskehy	225	1	19	Tipperary, N.R.	Kilnamanagh Upper	Upperchurch	Thurles	II.	280
25, 26	Gortnaskehy	416	3	10	Tipperary, N.R.	Owney and Arra	Kilmastulla	Nenagh	II.	295
31, 32	Gortnaskehy	257	3	8	Tipperary, N.R.	Owney and Arra	Kilnarath	Nenagh	II.	296
46	Gortnaskehy	298	0	22	Tipperary, S.R.	Kilnamanagh Lower	Clogher	Cashel	II.	322
36, 41	Gortnaskey	427	3	13	Londonderry	Loughinsholin	Ballynascreen	Magherafelt	III.	239
22, 28	Gortnaskey	532	0	37	Londonderry	Tirkeeran	Cumber Upper	Londonderry	III.	249
121	Gortnaskohoge	103	0	11	Mayo	Kilmaine	Kilmainebeg	Ballinrobe	IV.	155
78, 79	Gortnasmuttaun	155	2	26	Mayo	Carra	Ballyhean	Castlebar	IV.	125
49	Gortnasmuttaun	104	2	2	Tipperary, S.R.	Slievardagh	Ballingarry	Callan	II.	332
10	Gortnasna	117	0	37	Cork, E.R.	Condons&Clangibbon	Marshalstown	Mitchelstown	II.	63
32, 33, 41	Gortnasoal Glebe	298	1	39	Tyrone	Omagh West	Longfield West	Castlederg	III.	316
45	Gortnasoolboy	119	3	33	Roscommon	Athlone	Cam	Athlone	IV.	180
26	Gortnasragh	19	0	9	Kilkenny	Callan	Killaloe	Callan	I.	84
118,121,122	Gortnastang	65	3	19	Mayo	Kilmaine	Kilmainemore	Ballinrobe	IV.	156
122	Gortnasteal	142	2	12	Galway	Kiltartan	Kilmacduagh	Gort	IV.	48
48	Gortnasythe	219	3	36	Roscommon	Athlone	Cam	Athlone	IV.	180
58	Gortnatona	162	3	4	Kerry	Magunihy	Kilcummin	Killarney	II.	201
8	Gortnatraw North	282	1	37	Donegal	Kilmacrenan	Clondavaddog	Millford	III.	125
27, 28	Gortnatraw South	807	3	32	Donegal	Kilmacrenan	Clondavaddog	Millford	III.	125
58	Gortnatubbrid	513	2	18	Cork, W.R.	West Muskerry	Ballyvourney	Macroom	II.	154
31	Gortnavarnoge	141	0	38	Tipperary, N.R.	Owney and Arra	Kilcomenty	Nenagh	II.	295
68	Gortnavea or Deerfield	57	0	20d	Galway	Moycullen	Moycullen	Galway	IV.	71
20	Gortnaveigh	60	2	5	Tipperary, N.R.	Owney and Arra	Youghalarra	Nenagh	II.	297
45	Gortnavern	656	3	17	Donegal	Kilmacrenan	Conwal	Letterkenny	III.	126
27, 28, 37	Gortnavern	740	0	21	Donegal	Kilmacrenan	Tullyfern	Millford	III.	133
79	Gortnavilly	76	1	27	Donegal	Raphoe	Clonleigh	Strabane	III.	135
59	Gortnavreaghaun	180	1	13	Clare	Clonderalaw	Killadysert	Killadysert	II.	16
9	Gortnavreeghan	383	0	9	Cavan	Tullyhaw	Templeport	Bawnboy	III.	95
21, 24	Gortnawaun	505	0	27	Leitrim	Leitrim	Kiltubbrid	Cark. on Shannon	IV.	104
11, 12	Gortnawinny	185	2	24e	Monaghan	Dartree	Clones	Clones	III.	264
2, 3, 6, 7	Gortnee	157	3	36	Antrim	Lower Dunluce	Dunluce	Coleraine	III.	17
70	Gortnesk	68	0	2	Donegal	Raphoe	Raphoe	Strabane	III.	141
14	Gortnessy	723	3	22	Londonderry	Tirkeeran	Clondermot	Londonderry	III.	248
21	Gort North	2	0	6	Donegal	Inishowen East	Moville Upper	Inishowen	III.	119
31	Gortolee	27	2	6	Tipperary, N.R.	Owney and Arra	Killoscully	Nenagh	II.	295
43, 53	Gortonora	85	1	26	Kerry	Corkaguiny	Dingle	Dingle	II.	175
10	Gortoorlan	208	3	37	Cavan	Tullyhaw	Tomregan	Bawnboy	III.	96
37, 38	Gortoral	301	3	36	Fermanagh	Knockninny	Kinawley	Enniskillen	III.	202
27	Gortore	198	3	34	Cork, E.R.	Fermoy	Kilcrumper	Fermoy	II.	80
5	Gort part of Glebe	5	0	4	Londonderry	Keenaght	Magilligan	Newt". Limavady	III.	237
26	Gortphaudeen	11	2	7	Kilkenny	Kells	Coolaghmore	Callan	I.	108

(a) Including 15A. 0R. 35P. water.
(b) Including 3A. 2R. 1P. water.
(c) Including 16A. 3R. 19P. water.
(d) Including 4A. 1R. 36P. water.
(e) Including 15A. 0R. 3P. water.

No. of Sheet of the Ordnance Survey Maps.	Townlands and Towns.	Area in Statute Acres.	County.	Barony.	Parish.	Poor Law Union in 1857.	Townland Census of 1851, Part I. Vol.	Page
		A. R. P.					Vol.	Page
74	Gortracussane	408 0 25	Kerry	Magunihy	Killarney	Killarney	II.	203
62, 63	Gortrany	230 3 16	Antrim	Upper Massereene	Ballinderry	Lurgan	III.	29
40	Gortraw	98 1 28	Fermanagh	Clankelly	Galloon	Clones	III.	198
55	Gortrea	125 0 15	Tyrone	Dungannon Middle	Killyman	Dungannon	III.	303
117, 118	Gortrea or Fairfield	279 1 5	Galway	Longford	Kilmalinoge	Portumna	IV.	59
87	Gortreagh	77 2 1	Kerry	Iveragh	Killemlagh	Cahersiveen	II.	196
65, 66	Gortreagh	98 1 25a	Kerry	Magunihy	Aghadoe	Killarney	II.	199
20, 29	Gortreagh	109 1 34	Limerick	Connello Lower	Croagh	Rathkeale	II.	228
35	Gortreagh	205 1 29	Tipperary, N.R.	Eliogarty	Loughmoe East	Thurles	II.	271
29	Gortreagh	133 0 32	Tyrone	Dungannon Upper	Derryloran	Cookstown	III.	307
37, 38	Gortreagh	776 0 39	Tyrone	Dungannon Upper	Kildress	Cookstown	III.	309
54	Gortree	378 2 24	Donegal	Raphoe	Allsaints	Londonderry	III.	134
14	Gortree	328 2 33	Londonderry	Tirkeeran	Clondermot	Londonderry	III.	248
64, 72	Gortrelig	240 0 11b	Kerry	Dunkerron North	Knockane	Cahersiveen	II.	182
54	Gortrevagh	222 0 8	Galway	Moycullen	Kilcummin	Oughterard	IV.	67
34, 35	Gortroche	1,259 3 31	Cork, E.R.	Fermoy	Ballyhooly	Fermoy	II.	76
10	Gortroe	482 3 5	Cork, E.R.	Condons&Clangibbon	Marshalstown	Mitchelstown	II.	63
32	Gortroe	376 1 12c	Cork, E.R.	Duhallow	Kilshannig	Mallow	II.	74
105	Gortroe	251 3 9	Cork, W.R.	Bantry	Kilmocomoge	Bantry	II.	121
134	Gortroe	155 1 8	Cork, W.R.	East Carbery (W.D.)	Kilmacabea	Skibbereen	II.	133
94	Gortroe	516 2 30	Cork, W.R.	East Carbery(W.D.)	Kilmichael	Dunmanway	II.	134
84, 96	Gortroe	109 3 23	Galway	Athenry	Athenry	Loughrea	IV.	4
56, 69	Gortroe	312 3 4	Galway	Clare	Annaghdown	Galway	IV.	16
104	Gortroe	124 2 22	Galway	Dunkellin	Kilcolgan	Gort	IV.	28
66	Gortroe	382 2 12	Kerry	Magunihy	Aghadoe	Killarney	II.	199
74, 84	Gortroe	1,353 2 7	Kerry	Magunihy	Killarney	Killarney	II.	203
23	Gortroe	630 3 10	Kerry	Trughanacmy	Castleisland	Tralee	II.	208
19	Gortroe	133 3 5	Limerick	Connello Lower	Clonagh	Rathkeale	II.	227
46	Gortroe	323 2 30	Limerick	Connello Upper	Colmanswell	Kilmallock	II.	232
37, 38, 45	Gortroe	565 3 20	Limerick	Connello Upper	Corcomohide	Croom	II.	232
36	Gortroe	174 3 26	Limerick	Glenquin	Grange	Newcastle	II.	245
90, 91	Gortroe Lower	96 1 18	Cork, W.R.	Bear	Kilcaskan	Bantry	II.	123
91	Gortroe Upper	77 0 31	Cork, W.R.	Bear	Kilcaskan	Bantry	II.	123
72	Gortronnagh	184 1 25	Galway	Tiaquin	Clonkeen	Loughrea	IV.	76
93, 102	Gortrooskagh	323 2 5	Kerry	Glanarought	Kenmare	Kenmare	II.	186
42, 56	Gortrory or Rogersfield	52 3 32	Galway	Clare	Killeany	Tuam	IV.	20
35	Gortrummagh	283 3 22	Galway	Ballynahinch	Omey	Clifden	IV.	15
39	Gortrush	396 1 35	Kilkenny	Iverk	Fiddown	Carrick on Suir	I.	105
34, 35	Gortrush	106 1 21	Tyrone	Omagh East	Drumragh	Omagh	III.	312
115	Gortsallagh	24 0 23	Cork, W.R.	Bear	Killaconenagh	Castletown	II.	125
29	Gortscreagan	316 0 11	Londonderry	Tirkeeran	Cumber Upper	Londonderry	III.	249
54, 55	Gortshalgan	217 3 6d	Tyrone	Dungannon Middle	Killyman	Dungannon	III.	303
48	Gortshanavogh	486 2 25	Kerry	Magunihy	Killeentierna	Killarney	II.	204
141, 150	Gortshanecrone	134 0 24	Cork, W.R.	West Carbery (E.D.)	Creagh	Skibbereen	II.	139
31	Gortshane East	183 3 26	Tipperary, N.R.	Owney and Arra	Kilnarath	Nenagh	II.	296
31	Gortshane Middle	230 1 0	Tipperary, N.R.	Owney and Arra	Kilnarath	Nenagh	II.	296
26	Gortshaneroe	537 2 25	Tipperary, N.R.	Upper Ormond	Kilmore	Nenagh	II.	291
31	Gortshane West	192 3 32	Tipperary, N.R.	Owney and Arra	Kilnarath	Nenagh	II.	296
30, 39	Gortshanvally	82 0 7	Kerry	Trughanacmy	Ballymacelligott	Tralee	II.	207
105	Gortsheela	19 0 15	Galway	Loughrea	Kilconickny	Loughrea	IV.	63
2	Gortskagh	185 3 14	Cork, E.R.	Orrery and Kilmore	Shandrum	Kilmallock	II.	110
37	Gortskagh	347 0 13	Limerick	Glenquin	Mahoonagh	Newcastle	II.	246
16, 21	Gortskeagh	246 1 14	Cavan	Tullygarvey	Drung	Cootehill	III.	89
112,113,122	Gortskeagh	139 2 5	Galway	Kiltartan	Killinny	Gort	IV.	47
29	Gortskeddia	230 0 4	Mayo	Tirawley	Crossmolina	Ballina	IV.	166
29	Gortskeha	268 2 9	King's Co.	Garrycastle	Lusmagh	Parsonstown	I.	137
111, 119	Gortskehy	226 1 6	Mayo	Kilmaine	Kilcommon	Claremorris	IV.	154
82	Gortsmoorane	186 0 32	Cork, W.R.	West Muskerry	Inchigeelagh	Macroom	II.	157
21	Gort South	3 1 25	Donegal	Inishowen East	Moville Upper	Inishowen	III.	119
77	Gortstoke	190 1 29	Cork, E.R.	Imokilly	Ballyoughtera	Middleton	II.	84
123	Gortstuckanagh	84 1 13	Galway	Kiltartan	Kilbeacanty	Gort	IV.	47
29, 30	Gorttoose	253 3 23	Roscommon	Roscommon	Bumlin	Strokestown	IV.	208
122, 123	GORT T.	—	Galway	Kiltartan	Beagh, Kiltartan, and Kilmacduagh	Gort	IV.	46 48
139	Gorttyowen	257 0 21	Cork, W.R.	West Carbery(W.D.)	Skull	Skull	II.	146
7, 9	Gortullaghan	171 0 38	Cavan	Tullyhaw	Templeport	Bawnboy	III.	95
33	Gortumly	618 3 34	Westmeath	Fartullagh	Castlelost	Mullingar	I.	268
51	Gortussa	554 1 13	Tipperary, S.R.	Kilnamanagh Lower	Ballintemple	Cashel	II.	322
51	Gortussa	323 0 5	Tipperary, S.R.	Kilnamanagh Lower	Kilpatrick	Cashel	II.	324
65	Gortvunatrime	87 0 30	Tipperary, S.R.	Clanwilliam	Emly	Tipperary	II.	308
10, 20	Gortyarrigan	602 1 58	Donegal	Inishowen West	Desertegny	Inishowen	III.	120
25, 31	Gortybrigane	298 0 34	Tipperary, N.R.	Owney and Arra	Kilcomenty	Nenagh	II.	295

(a) Including 2A. 2R. 16P. water.
(b) Including 4A. 1R. 32P. water.
(c) Including 3A. 2R. 26P. water.
(d) Including 13A. 1R. 7P. water.

No. of Sheet of the Ordnance Survey Maps.	Townlands and Towns.	Area in Statute Acres.			County.	Barony.	Parish.	Poor Law Union in 1857.	Townland Census of 1851, Part I.	
		A.	R.	P.					Vol.	Page
7	Gortycavan	385	0	38	Londonderry	Coleraine	Dunboe	Coleraine	III.	231
32	Gortyclery	120	3	24	Leitrim	Mohill	Mohill	Mohill	IV.	108
20, 26	Gortycullane	138	3	27	Tipperary, N.R.	Owney and Arra	Burgesbeg	Nenagh	II.	294
39, 44	Gortygara	347	2	38	Sligo	Coolavin	Kilfree	Boyle	IV.	224
49	Gortygeeheen	1,717	1	35a	Clare	Islands	Clondagad	Killadysert	II.	29
36	Gortyknaveen	70	2	31	Limerick	Glenquin	Monagay	Newcastle	II.	247
70	Gortyleahy	136	3	21	Cork, W.R.	West Muskerry	Macroom	Macroom	II.	160
36	Gortyleane	107	3	38	Roscommon	Ballintober South	Kilgefin	Roscommon	IV.	189
68, 81	Gortyloughlin	332	2	35	Galway	Moycullen	Moycullen	Galway	IV.	71
106	Gortymadden	449	0	21	Galway	Longford	Abbeygormacan	Ballinasloe	IV.	56
118	Gortyneill	102	3	8	Galway	Longford	Kilmalinoge	Portumna	IV.	59
14	Gortyogan	92	1	36	Tipperary, N.R.	Lower Ormond	Monsea	Nenagh	II.	287
142, 143	Gortyowen	84	1	33	Cork, W.R.	East Carbery (W.D.)	Kilfaughnabeg	Skibbereen	II.	133
69	Gortyrahilly	1,054	2	33	Cork, W.R.	West Muskerry	Ballyvourney	Macroom	II.	154
73	Gortyroyan East	119	1	16	Galway	Kilconnell	Ballymacward	Ballinasloe	IV.	39
73	Gortyroyan West	98	0	30	Galway	Kilconnell	Ballymacward	Ballinasloe	IV.	39
25	Gortyvahane	181	3	5	Limerick	Coonagh	Oola	Tipperary	II.	236
17	Gosford Demesne	644	2	38	Armagh	Fews Lower	Mullaghbrack	Armagh	III.	47
22	Gosheden	572	2	34	Londonderry	Tirkeeran	Cumber Lower	Londonderry	III.	249
19, 23	Goslingstown	311	3	11	Kilkenny	Shillelogher	Castleinch or Inchyolaghan	Kilkenny	I.	114
16	Gossbrook	55	1	33	Queen's Co.	Upperwoods	Offerlane	Mountmellick	I.	252
39	Gotham	221	2	2	Kildare	Kilkea and Moone	Ballaghmoon	Athy	I.	59
58	Gotinstown	527	0	11	Tipperary, S.R.	Clanwilliam	Solloghodmore	Tipperary	II.	311
47	Gotoon	84	3	24	Limerick	Coshlea	Ballingaddy	Kilmallock	II.	237
40	Gotoon	279	1	2	Limerick	Smallcounty	Hospital	Kilmallock	II.	260
31	Gougane	561	1	27	Cork, E.R.	Duhallow	Clonmeen	Kanturk	II.	69
106, 107	Goulacullin	1,426	2	8	Cork, W.R.	East Carbery (W.D.)	Fanlobbus	Dunmanway	II.	132
129, 130	Gouladoo	288	2	37	Cork, W.R.	West Carbery (W.D.)	Kilcrohane	Bantry	II.	143
45, 46	Goulaun	661	2	31b	Mayo	Tirawley	Crossmolina	Ballina	IV.	166
13	Gouldavoher	211	0	7	Limerick	Pubblebrien	Mungret	Limerick	II.	254
38	Goulmore	538	0	13	Tipperary, N.R.	Owney and Arra	Abington	Nenagh	II.	293
64, 72	Goulnacappy and Coornagrena	816	1	27c	Kerry	Dunkerron North	Killorglin	Cahersiveen	II.	181
26	Goulreagh	241	2	39	Tipperary, N.R.	Owney and Arra	Killoscully	Nenagh	II.	295
34, 35	Goulyduff	375	2	36	Kildare	Narragh & Reban West	Churchtown	Athy	I.	67
114, 127	Gour	739	3	30	Cork, W.R.	Bear	Killaconenagh	Castletown	II.	125
105	Gouree Beg	75	3	11	Cork, W.R.	Bantry	Kilmocomoge	Bantry	II.	121
105	Gouree More	124	2	2	Cork, W.R.	Bantry	Kilmocomoge	Bantry	II.	121
48, 52	Goward	1,533	0	38	Down	Upper Iveagh, Lr. pt.	Clonduff	Newry	III.	171
27, 28	Gowel	355	1	15d	Leitrim	Leitrim	Kiltoghert	Carᵏ. on Shannon	IV.	102
100	Gowel	206	2	28	Mayo	Clanmorris	Mayo	Claremorris	IV.	135
63	Gowel	322	1	1	Mayo	Costello	Kilbeagh	Swineford	IV.	140
80	Gowelboy	210	3	34	Mayo	Gallen	Killedan	Swineford	IV.	150
88, 89	Gowel or Forkfield	156	1	36e	Mayo	Burrishoole	Aghagower	Westport	IV.	118
57	Gowerhass	933	0	33	Clare	Moyarta	Kilrush	Kilrush	II.	33
57	Gower North	320	1	24	Clare	Moyarta	Kilmacduane	Kilrush	II.	33
57	Gower South	525	1	30f	Clare	Moyarta	Kilmacduane	Kilrush	II.	33
118, 127	Gowil	120	0	8	Galway	Longford	Lickmolassy	Portumna	IV.	61
29, 30	Gowkstown (alias) Ault	367	2	14	Antrim	Lower Glenarm	Tickmacrevan	Larne	III.	23
51, 64	Gowla	3,167	2	26g	Galway	Ballynahinch	Moyrus	Clifden	IV.	13
47, 61	Gowla	1,107	0	33	Galway	Killian	Ahascragh	Mountbellew	IV.	43
9	Gowlagh North	140	0	35	Cavan	Tullyhaw	Templeport	Bawnboy	III.	95
9, 13	Gowlagh South	165	0	2	Cavan	Tullyhaw	Templeport	Bawnboy	III.	95
4	Gowlan	260	0	13	Cavan	Tullyhaw	Killinagh	Enniskillen	III.	92
8	Gowlan	937	3	30	Cavan	Tullyhaw	Templeport	Bawnboy	III.	95
13, 18	Gowlan	532	1	29	Longford	Moydow	Ballymacormick	Longford	I.	160
102, 115	Gowlane	1,171	0	16	Cork, W.R.	Bear	Kilcatherine	Castletown	II.	124
35	Gowlane	875	0	6h	Kerry	Corkaguiny	Stradbally	Dingle	II.	180
92	Gowlane	399	1	38	Kerry	Dunkerron South	Templenoe	Kenmare	II.	185
84	Gowlane	651	3	25	Kerry	Glanarought	Kenmare	Kenmare	II.	186
63	Gowlane	412	1	17	Kerry	Iveragh	Glanbehy	Cahersiveen	II.	196
48, 58	Gowlane	332	1	0	Kerry	Magunihy	Molahiffe	Killarney	II.	205
44	Gowlaneard	479	3	33i	Kerry	Corkaguiny	Kinard	Dingle	II.	179
51,52,64,65	Gowlan East	3,042	2	22j	Galway	Ballynahinch	Moyrus	Clifden	IV.	13
44	Gowlane Beg	669	3	9k	Kerry	Corkaguiny	Kinard	Dingle	II.	179
44	Gowlane East	537	3	20l	Kerry	Corkaguiny	Kinard	Dingle	II.	179
50	Gowlane North	1,184	0	23	Cork, E.R.	East Muskerry	Donaghmore	Macroom	II.	103
98,99,106,107	Gowlanes	827	0	20	Kerry	Dunkerron South	Kilcrohane	Kenmare	II.	183
90, 99	Gowlanes East	731	2	9	Kerry	Dunkerron South	Kilcrohane	Kenmare	II.	183
50	Gowlane South	531	0	4	Cork, E.R.	East Muskerry	Donaghmore	Macroom	II.	103
36	Gowlan West	768	0	39m	Galway	Ballynahinch	Moyrus	Clifden	IV.	13

(a) Including 28A. 1R. 10P. water.
(b) Including 31A. 0R. 10P. water.
(c) Including 6A. 0R. 27P. water.
(d) Including 18A. 2R. 31P. water.
(e) Including 2A. 3R. 26P. water.

(f) Including 16A. 0R. 20P. water.
(g) Including 85A. 1R. 18P. water.
(h) Including 7A. 3R. 30P. water.
(i) Including 1A. 2R. 11P. water.

(j) Including 99A. 0R. 28P. water.
(k) Including 9A. 1R. 27P. water.
(l) Including 15A. 1R. 8P. water.
(m) Including 12A. 3R. 24P. water.

No. of Sheet of the Ordnance Survey Maps.	Townlands and Towns.	Area in Statute Acres.	County.	Barony.	Parish.	Poor Law Union in 1857.	Townland Census of 1851, Part I.	
		A. R. P.					Vol.	Page
5	Gowlat . . .	301 0 27	Cavan . .	Tullyhaw . .	Templeport . .	Enniskillen .	III.	95
8	Gowlaun . .	180 1 20	Clare . .	Burren . .	Kilmoon . .	Ballyvaghan .	II.	13
39, 40	Gowlaun . .	275 0 25	Galway . .	Moycullen . .	Kilcummin . .	Oughterard .	IV.	67
12, 25	Gowlaun . .	1,370 3 9	Galway . .	Ross . .	Ross . .	Oughterard .	IV.	74
16	Gowlaun . .	461 2 9	Leitrim . .	Drumahaire . .	Killarga . .	Manorhamilton .	IV.	98
51,52,63,64	Gowlaun . .	957 2 34	Mayo . .	Costello . . .	Kilbeagh . .	Swineford .	IV.	140
72, 81	Gowlaun . .	607 1 32a	Mayo . .	Costello . . .	Kilmovee . .	Swineford .	IV.	142
35,36,38,39	Gowlaun . .	600 1 27	Waterford . .	Decies within Drum	Ballymacart . .	Dungarvan .	II.	351
24, 25	Gowlaunlee . .	1,734 0 28	Galway . .	Ross . .	Ross . .	Oughterard .	IV.	74
35, 36, 38	Gowlaun Mountain .	74 3 11	Waterford . .	Decies within Drum	Ardmore . .	Dungarvan .	II.	350
17	Gowlaunrevagh .	256 0 3	Leitrim . .	Drumahaire . .	Inishmagrath . .	Manorhamilton .	IV.	96
37	Gowle . . .	597 2 21	Wicklow . .	Shillelagh . .	Crecrin . .	Shillelagh .	I.	357
24, 25	Gowlin . . .	685 3 5	Carlow . .	St. Mullins Lower .	St. Mullins . .	New Ross .	I.	13
44	Gowlin . . .	614 0 4	Kerry . .	Corkaguiny . .	Kinard . .	Dingle .	II.	179
24, 28	Gowly . . .	210 1 6b	Leitrim . .	Leitrim . .	Kiltubbrid . .	Carr. on Shannon	IV.	104
40	Gowny . . .	107 3 23	Fermanagh . .	Clankelly . .	Clones . .	Clones .	III.	196
20	Gowran . . .	259 1 21	Kilkenny . .	Gowran . . .	Gowran . . .	Kilkenny .	I.	95
20,21,24,25	Gowran Demesne .	846 2 10	Kilkenny . .	Gowran . . .	Gowran . . .	Kilkenny .	I.	95
20	GOWRAN T. .	—	Kilkenny . .	Gowran . . .	Gowran . . .	Kilkenny .	I.	95
39	Gowshill . .	85 3 7	Tyrone . .	Dungannon Middle .	Donaghenry . .	Cookstown .	III.	301
21	Graan . . .	158 1 18	Fermanagh . .	Magheraboy . .	Devenish . .	Enniskillen .	III.	211
7	Gracedieu . .	224 0 30	Dublin . .	Balrothery East .	Lusk . .	Balrothery .	I.	21
9	Gracedieu East .	229 2 31	Waterford . .	Middlethird . .	Killoteran . .	Waterford .	II.	367
9	Gracedieu West .	394 0 25	Waterford . .	Middlethird . .	Killoteran . .	Waterford .	II.	367
25	Gracefield . .	74 3 37	Queen's Co. .	Ballyadams . .	Rathaspick . .	Athy .	I.	232
13	Gracehill . .	167 3 24	Antrim . .	Lower Dunluce .	Derrykeighan . .	Ballymoney .	III.	16
37	GRACEHILL T. .	—	Antrim . .	Lower Toome .	Ahoghill . .	Ballymena .	III.	32
40	Graceland . .	27 2 35	Tipperary, N.R. .	Kilnamanagh Upper	Templebeg . .	Thurles .	II.	279
29	Graceswood . .	180 3 36	Queen's Co. .	Clarmallagh . .	Abbeyleix . .	Abbeyleix .	I.	235
44	Graddoge . .	119 3 30	Galway . .	Clare . .	Killererin . .	Tuam .	IV.	21
90, 100	Graddoge . .	131 1 36	Mayo . .	Carra . .	Rosslee . .	Ballinrobe .	IV.	130
32	Graddum . .	363 1 5c	Cavan . .	Castlerahan . .	Crosserlough . .	Cavan .	III.	68
33, 34	Gradoge . .	121 3 36	Leitrim . .	Carrigallen . .	Cloone . .	Mohill .	IV.	90
78	Graffa Beg .	135 1 29d	Mayo . .	Carra . .	Islandeady . .	Castlebar .	IV.	128
8	Graffagh . .	125 0 15	Monaghan . .	Monaghan . .	Tedavnet . .	Monaghan .	III.	279
69, 78	Graffa More . .	478 3 24	Mayo . .	Carra . .	Islandeady . .	Castlebar .	IV.	128
44	Graffan . .	135 3 27	King's Co. .	Clonlisk . .	Templeharry . .	Roscrea .	II.	132
13	Graffanstown . .	223 0 30	Westmeath . .	Delvin . .	Killagh . .	Castletowndelvin	I.	265
33, 34	Graffee . .	175 1 14	Kerry . .	Corkaguiny . .	Kilquane . .	Dingle .	II.	179
48	Graffeens . .	54 0 14	Kerry . .	Magunihy . .	Molahiffe . .	Killarney .	II.	205
23	Graffin . .	818 1 35	Tipperary, N.R. .	Ikerrin . .	Killavinoge . .	Roscrea .	II.	275
51	Graffin . .	104 3 25	Tipperary, S.R. .	Kilnamanagh Lower	Donohill . .	Cashel .	II.	323
51	Graffin . .	119 3 2	Tipperary, S.R. .	Kilnamanagh Lower	Kilpatrick . .	Cashel .	II.	324
10	Graffoge . .	124 0 8	Longford . .	Granard . .	Granard . .	Granard .	I.	156
19	Graffoge . .	152 3 7	Longford . .	Moydow . .	Ardagh . .	Longford .	I.	160
29, 30	Graffoge . .	483 3 21	Roscommon . .	Roscommon . .	Bumlin . .	Strokestown .	IV.	208
66, 75	Graffy . .	406 3 28	Donegal . .	Boylagh . .	Inishkeel . .	Glenties .	III.	112
79	Graffy . .	136 2 0	Donegal . .	Raphoe . .	Urney . .	Strabane .	III.	144
33	Graffy . .	71 0 7	Fermanagh . .	Clanawley . .	Kinawley . .	Enniskillen .	III.	194
8	Graffy . .	186 1 6e	Fermanagh . .	Lurg . .	Belleek . .	Ballyshannon .	III.	203
68	Graffy . .	297 0 5	Mayo . .	Burrishoole .	Burrishoole . .	Newport .	IV.	119
79	Graffy . .	175 1 6f	Mayo . .	Carra . .	Kildacommoge . .	Castlebar .	IV.	129
40, 49	Graffy . .	1,293 3 36g	Mayo . .	Gallen . .	Kilgarvan . .	Ballina .	IV.	148
49, 61	Graffy . .	358 2 28	Mayo . .	Gallen . .	Killasser . .	Swineford .	IV.	149
5	Gragadder . .	175 3 12	Kildare . .	Ikeathy&Oughterany	Kilcock . .	Celbridge .	I.	57
14, 23	Gragane . .	372 0 1	Limerick . .	Clanwilliam . .	Caherconlish . .	Limerick .	II.	222
5	Gragan East .	698 1 3	Clare . .	Burren . .	Rathborney . .	Ballyvaghan .	II.	14
5	Gragan West .	958 3 21	Clare . .	Burren . .	Rathborney . .	Ballyvaghan .	II.	14
10, 14	Gragara . .	594 3 31	Kilkenny . .	Fassadinin . .	Mayne . .	Kilkenny .	I.	90
24	Gragarnagh . .	214 3 21	Monaghan . .	Cremorne . .	Aghnamullen . .	Castleblayney .	III.	258
55	Gragaugh . .	754 0 33	Tipperary, S.R. .	Slievardagh . .	Lismalin . .	Callan .	II.	335
47	Grageelagh . .	129 1 32	Wexford . .	Forth . .	Ballymore . .	Wexford .	I.	308
47	Grageen . .	56 1 31	Wexford . .	Forth . .	Ballymore . .	Wexford .	I.	308
47	Grageen Little .	22 0 8	Wexford . .	Forth . .	Ballymore . .	Wexford .	I.	308
13, 18	Gragh . .	104 2 19	Longford . .	Moydow . .	Ballymacormick .	Longford .	I.	161
3, 4, 10, 11	Graghil . .	468 3 26	Mayo . .	Erris . .	Kilcommon . .	Belmullet .	IV.	144
17	Gragullagh . .	72 2 3	Roscommon . .	Roscommon . .	Aughrim . .	Carr. on Shannon	IV.	207
79	Grahamsland . .	284 3 3h	Donegal . .	Raphoe . .	Donaghmore . .	Strabane .	III.	138
103	Grahamstown . .	65 3 21	Donegal . .	Tirhugh . .	Drumhome . .	Ballyshannon .	III.	146
47, 48	Graheeroge . .	150 3 25	Wexford . .	Forth . .	Ballymore . .	Wexford .	I.	308
48	Grahormack .	114 1 9½	Wexford . .	Forth . .	Rosslare . .	Wexford .	I.	315
47	Grahormick . .	199 1 36	Wexford . .	Forth . .	Ballymore . .	Wexford .	I.	308
18	Graig . .	381 2 29	Cork, E.R. .	Fermoy . .	Templeroan . .	Mallow .	II.	82

(a) Including 6A. 0R. 29P. water.
(b) Including 81A. 1R. 28P. water.
(c) Including 11A. 2R. 39P. water.
(d) Including 12A. 1R. 22P. water.
(e) { Including 1A. 0R. 0P. Sally Island.
      { Including 31A. 1R. 12P. water.
(f) Including 50A. 0R. 32P. water.
(g) Including 4A. 0R. 4P. water.
(h) Including 2A. 2R. 25P. water.

No. of Sheet of the Ordnance Survey Maps.	Townlands and Towns.	Area in Statute Acres.	County.	Barony.	Parish.	Poor Law Union in 1857.	Townland Census of 1851, Part I.	
		A. R. P.					Vol.	Page
38	Graig	487 1 15	Limerick	Connello Upper	Corcomohide	Croom	II.	232
84	Graigabbey	4 1 8	Galway	Tiaquin	Monivea	Loughrea	IV.	79
84	Graigabbey South	346 1 32	Galway	Kilconnell	Monivea	Loughrea	IV.	42
30, 38	Graigacurragh	609 0 1	Limerick	Connello Upper	Ballingarry	Croom	II.	230
43	Graigaheesha	496 3 13	Tipperary, S.R.	Slievardagh	Kilcooly	Urlingford	II.	334
49	Graigaman	480 1 17	Tipperary, S.R.	Slievardagh	Buolick	Urlingford	II.	332
47	Graiganster	89 0 31	Limerick	Coshma	Effin	Kilmallock	II.	243
47	Graiganster	191 2 32	Limerick	Kilmallock	St.Peter's & St.Paul's	Kilmallock	II.	250
27	Graigariddy	166 2 30	Waterford	Gaultiere	Killea	Waterford	II.	363
6, 7	Graigavalla	1,217 2 5	Waterford	Upperthird	Rathgormuck	Carrick on Suir	II.	371
9	Graigavern	185 1 11	Queen's Co.	Portnahinch	Lea	Mountmellick	I.	244
42	Graigavine	268 3 38	Kilkenny	Iverk	Clonmore	Carrick on Suir	I.	105
38	Graigbeg	219 0 34	Limerick	Connello Upper	Ballingarry	Croom	II.	230
20	Graigeen	122 1 19	Limerick	Connello Lower	Nantinan	Rathkeale	II.	229
9, 10	Graigillane	104 3 26	Tipperary, N.R.	Lower Ormond	Finnoe	Borrisokane	II.	284
83	Graignagower	788 1 9a	Kerry	Dunkerron South	Templenoe	Kenmare	II.	185
5	Graignagower	983 1 19	Waterford	Glenahiry	Kilronan	Clonmel	II.	365
83	Graignagreana	698 1 5	Kerry	Dunkerron North	Templenoe	Kenmare	II.	182
19	Graigoor	178 0 38	Limerick	Shanid	Kilbradran	Rathkeale	II.	255
9	Graigrooth	41 2 33	Kildare	Ikeathy&Oughterany	Cloncurry	Celbridge	I.	57
18, 25	Graigs	446 2 8	Meath	Lower Navan	Donaghmore	Navan	I.	214
19, 27, 28	Graigue	727 3 22	Cork, E.R.	Condons&Clangibbon	Kilworth	Fermoy	II.	62
9, 18	Graigue	561 0 10	Cork, E.R.	Condons&Clangibbon	Templemolaga	Mitchelstown	II.	63
81	Graigue	594 0 10b	Cork, W.R.	West Muskerry	Inchigeelagh	Macroom	II.	157
17, 30	Graigue	196 3 26	Galway	Dunmore	Tuam	Tuam	IV.	36
97, 105	Graigue	275 3 16	Galway	Loughrea	Loughrea	Loughrea	IV.	65
45, 59	Graigue	136 3 34	Galway	Tiaquin	Killoscobe	Mountbellew	IV.	78
42	Graigue	363 3 37	Kerry	Corkaguiny	Dunurlin	Dingle	II.	176
44, 54	Graigue	266 1 35	Kerry	Corkaguiny	Minard	Dingle	II.	180
30	Graigue	338 3 8	Kilkenny	Kells	Coolaghmore	Callan	I.	108
25	Graigue	703 1 10	King's Co.	Geashill	Geashill	Tullamore	I.	140
20	Graigue	54 2 25	Limerick	Connello Lower	Cappagh	Rathkeale	II.	227
20	Graigue	71 3 37	Limerick	Connello Lower	Clonshire	Rathkeale	II.	227
29	Graigue	118 3 21	Limerick	Connello Lower	Rathkeale	Rathkeale	II.	229
21	Graigue	296 0 33	Limerick	Coshma	Adare	Croom	II.	241
20, 26	Graigue	167 2 34	Queen's Co.	Ballyadams	Tankardstown	Athy	I.	232
24, 30	Graigue	309 3 14	Queen's Co.	Cullenagh	Dysartgallen	Abbeyleix	I.	239
32, 37	Graigue	622 3 11c	Queen's Co.	Slievemargy	Killeshin	Carlow	I.	246
2	Graigue	39 3 27	Queen's Co.	Tinnahinch	Kilmanman	Mountmellick	I.	249
3, 4, 7, 8	Graigue	646 1 37	Queen's Co.	Tinnahinch	Rosenallis	Mountmellick	I.	250
14, 20	Graigue	282 1 28	Sligo	Carbury	Kilmacowen	Sligo	IV.	222
35	Graigue	221 3 12	Tipperary, N.R.	Eliogarty	Drom	Thurles	II.	269
47	Graigue	970 1 14	Tipperary, N.R.	Eliogarty	Moycarky	Thurles	II.	271
5	Graigue	242 0 11	Tipperary, N.R.	Lower Ormond	Dorrha	Parsonstown	II.	283
15	Graigue	145 0 12	Tipperary, N.R.	Lower Ormond	Kilruane	Borrisokane	II.	285
19	Graigue	375 0 26	Tipperary, N.R.	Upper Ormond	Ballygibbon	Borrisokane	II.	289
76	Graigue	402 0 31	Tipperary, S.R.	Iffa and Offa East	Newchapel	Clonmel	II.	315
78	Graigue	648 1 35	Tipperary, S.R.	Iffa and Offa East	Temple-etney	Clonmel	II.	316
87	Graigue	455 2 21	Tipperary, S.R.	Iffa and Offa West	Ballybacon	Clogheen	II.	317
87, 90	Graigue	881 1 23	Tipperary, S.R.	Iffa and Offa West	Tullaghorton	Clogheen	II.	321
68,69,75,76	Graigue	408 1 22	Tipperary, S.R.	Middlethird	Knockgraffon	Cashel	II.	328
69	Graigue	577 1 6	Tipperary, S.R.	Middlethird	Mora	Cashel	II.	329
63, 64	Graigue	224 1 26	Tipperary, S.R.	Slievardagh	Modeshil	Callan	II.	335
34, 35	Graigue	418 2 39	Waterford	Decies within Drum	Aglish	Dungarvan	II.	349
27	Graigue	95 0 2	Waterford	Gaultiere	Rathmoylan	Waterford	II.	364
45	Graigue	197 2 22	Wexford	Bargy	Bannow	Wexford	I.	304
46	Graigue	230 3 24	Wexford	Bargy	Kilcavan	Wexford	I.	305
27	Graigue	279 1 17	Wicklow	Upper Talbotstown	Kiltegan	Baltinglass	I.	364
16, 17	Graigueachullaire	593 2 14	Galway	Dunmore	Dunmore	Tuam	IV.	34
33, 34	Graigueadrisly	815 3 30	Queen's Co.	Clandonagh	Erke	Donaghmore	I.	233
1, 2, 3	Graigueafulla	975 0 32	Queen's Co.	Tinnahinch	Kilmanman	Mountmellick	I.	249
34	Graigueagarran	313 0 30	Queen's Co.	Clarmallagh	Erke	Donaghmore	I.	237
117	Graigueagowan	293 2 4	Galway	Longford	Lickmolassy	Portumna	IV.	61
117, 126	Graigueakilleen	243 3 11	Galway	Longford	Lickmolassy	Portumna	IV.	61
12	Graiguealug	142 3 3	Carlow	Forth	Nurney	Carlow	I.	5
12	Graiguealug	37 3 32	Carlow	Forth	Templepeter	Carlow	I.	5
12	Graiguealug	267 2 20	Carlow	Forth	Tullowmagimma	Carlow	I.	5
28, 34	Graigueanossy	182 1 32	Queen's Co.	Clarmallagh	Coolkerry	Abbeyleix	I.	237
34	Graigueard	397 0 1	Queen's Co.	Clarmallagh	Erke	Donaghmore	I.	237
15	Graiguearush	322 0 13	Waterford	Decies without Drum	Fews	Kilmacthomas	II.	356
33	Graigueavallagh	134 3 11	Queen's Co.	Clandonagh	Rathdowney	Donaghmore	I.	234
22	Graigueavurra	203 0 31	Waterford	Decies without Drum	Modelligo	Lismore	II.	359
87, 88	Graigueawoneen	311 1 2	Galway	Clonmacnowen	Clontuskert	Ballinasloe	IV.	24

(a) Including 16A. 2R. 25P. water.   (b) Including 45A. 0R. 8P. water.   (c) Including 14A. 3R. 0P. River Barrow.

No. of Sheet of the Ordnance Survey Maps.	Townlands and Towns.	Area in Statute Acres.	County.	Barony.	Parish.	Poor Law Union in 1857.	Townland Census of 1851, Part I.	
		A. R. P.					Vol.	Page
58	Graiguebaun . .	350 1 2	Galway . .	Tiaquin . . .	Monivea . .	Tuam . .	IV.	79
29	Graiguebeg . .	37 0 31	Tipperary, N.R.	Ikerrin . . .	Templemore . .	Roscrea . .	II.	276
22	Graigue Beg .	99 2 24	Waterford . .	Decies without Drum	Modelligo . .	Lismore . .	II.	359
9	Graigue Beg . .	645 0 17	Wexford . .	Scarawalsh . .	Kilrush . .	Enniscorthy .	I.	324
52	Graigue East . .	192 0 34	Cork, E.R. .	Barrymore . .	Ardnageehy . .	Cork . .	II.	50
35	Graiguefrahane .	497 0 9	Tipperary, N.R.	Eliogarty . .	Loughmoe East .	Thurles . .	II.	271
20, 28	Graigue Glebe .	184 1 35	Kerry . . .	Clanmaurice . .	Ardfert . .	Tralee . .	II.	167
50	Graigue Great .	343 0 4	Wexford . .	Shelburne . .	Templetown . .	New Ross .	I.	328
22	Graigue (Hartford) .	160 0 28	Kilkenny . .	Crannagh . .	Kilmanagh . .	Callan . .	I.	86
22	Graigue (Hayden) .	243 1 21	Kilkenny . .	Crannagh . .	Kilmanagh . .	Callan . .	I.	86
62	Graigue Island .	3 1 19	Clare . . .	Bunratty Lower .	Kilfintinan . .	Limerick . .	II.	5
10	Graiguelin . .	204 1 9	Kildare . .	North Salt . .	Taghadoe . .	Celbridge . .	I.	76
68, 69	Graigue Little .	28 3 10	Tipperary, S.R.	Middlethird . .	Knockgraffon .	Cashel . .	II.	328
49, 50	Graigue Little .	284 1 8	Wexford . .	Shelburne . .	Templetown . .	New Ross .	I.	328
23	Graigue Lower .	129 0 33	Kilkenny . .	Shillelogher . .	Burnchurch . .	Callan . .	I.	113
15	Graigue Lower .	255 0 35	Tipperary, N.R.	Lower Ormond .	Ardcrony . .	Borrisokane .	II.	281
54	Graigue Lower .	586 0 33	Tipperary, S.R.	Slievardagh . .	Killenaule . .	Cashel . .	II.	334
22	Graigue More .	195 3 28	Waterford . .	Decies without Drum	Modelligo . .	Lismore . .	II.	359
4, 5, 9, 10	Graigue More .	960 2 7	Wexford . .	Scarawalsh . .	Kilrush . .	Enniscorthy .	I.	324
15	Graiguenageeha .	182 0 31	Waterford . .	Decies without Drum	Rossmire . .	Kilmacthomas .	II.	360
24	Graiguenageeha .	177 2 14	Waterford . .	Decies without Drum	Stradbally . .	Kilmacthomas .	II.	361
24, 30	Graiguenahown .	1,061 1 24	Queen's Co. .	Cullenagh . .	Dysartgallen . .	Abbeyleix .	I.	239
41	Graiguenakill . .	156 3 4	Kilkenny . .	Ida . . .	Kilmakevoge . .	Waterford . .	I.	103
29	Graiguenamanagh .	356 2 7a	Kilkenny . .	Gowran . . .	Graiguenamanagh .	Thomastown .	I.	95
29	GRAIGUENAMANAGH T.	—	Kilkenny . .	Gowran . . .	Graiguenamanagh .	Thomastown .	I.	95
24	Graiguenasmuttan .	845 0 3	Queen's Co. .	Cullenagh . .	Dysartgallen . .	Abbeyleix .	I.	239
12	Graiguenaspiddoge .	287 2 32	Carlow . .	Forth . . .	Tullowmagimma .	Carlow . .	I.	5
46, 60	Graiguenavaddoge .	245 1 34	Galway . .	Tiaquin . . .	Killosolan . .	Mountbellew .	IV.	78
47	Graiguenoe . .	588 1 31	Tipperary, S.R.	Middlethird . .	Holycross . .	Cashel . .	II.	327
22	Graigueooly . .	221 0 35	Kilkenny . .	Shillelogher . .	Killaloe . .	Callan . .	I.	115
36, 42, 43	Graiguepadeen .	1,115 2 4	Tipperary, S.R.	Slievardagh . .	Fennor . . .	Urlingford .	II.	533
10	Graiguepottle .	240 2 2	Kildare . .	Ikeathy&Oughterany	Balraheen . .	Celbridge . .	I.	56
98, 99	Graigues . .	336 0 2b	Kerry . . .	Dunkerron South .	Kilcrohane . .	Cahersiveen .	II.	183
13	Graigues . .	330 1 8	Kildare . .	Clane . . .	Downings . .	Naas . .	I.	54
20	Graigues . .	232 2 15	Limerick . .	Connello Lower .	Nantinan . .	Rathkeale .	II.	229
11	Graigues . .	69 2 19	Limerick . .	Kenry . . .	Kilcornan . .	Rathkeale .	I.	249
10	Graiguesallagh .	393 2 2	Kildare . .	North Salt . .	Taghadoe . .	Celbridge . .	I.	76
46	Graiguesallagh .	142 1 10	Wexford . .	Bargy . . .	Duncormick . .	Wexford . .	I.	305
15	Graigueshoneen .	553 3 36	Waterford . .	Decies without Drum	Ballylaneen . .	Kilmacthomas .	II.	354
26	Graiguesmeadow .	8 3 28	Kilkenny . .	Callan . . .	Callan . . .	Callan . .	I.	83
21	Graiguesparling .	137 2 35	Limerick . .	Coshma . . .	Adare . . .	Croom . .	II.	241
9	Graigueswood .	254 0 37	Kilkenny . .	Crannagh . .	Sheffin . .	Urlingford .	I.	86
37	GRAIGUE T. . .	—	Queen's Co. .	Slievemargy . .	Killeshin . .	Carlow . .	I.	246
23	Graigue Upper .	241 2 9	Kilkenny . .	Shillelogher . .	Burnchurch . .	Callan . .	I.	113
15	Graigue Upper .	169 3 6	Tipperary, N.R.	Lower Ormond .	Ardcrony . .	Borrisokane .	II.	281
54	Graigue Upper .	200 1 25	Tipperary, S.R.	Slievardagh . .	Killenaule . .	Cashel . .	II.	334
43, 52	Graigue West .	969 2 20	Cork, E.R. .	Barrymore . .	Ardnageehy . .	Cork . .	II.	50
9, 18	Graig Upper . .	600 2 24	Cork, E.R. .	Fermoy . . .	Templeroan . .	Mallow . .	II.	82
4, 7	Grallagh . .	791 3 31	Dublin . .	Balrothery West .	Grallagh . .	Balrothery .	I.	22
21, 22	Grallagh . .	160 0 35c	Galway . .	Ballynahinch . .	Omey . . .	Clifden . .	IV.	15
106, 116	Grallagh . .	248 1 26	Galway . .	Leitrim . . .	Leitrim . .	Loughrea . .	IV.	55
101	Grallagh . .	24 3 21	Mayo . . .	Clanmorris . .	Tagheen . .	Claremorris .	IV.	136
103	Grallagh . .	612 3 14	Mayo . . .	Costello . . .	Annagh . .	Claremorris .	IV.	138
70, 71	Grallagh . .	460 2 21	Mayo . . .	Gallen . . .	Kildacommoge .	Castlebar .	IV.	148
14, 15	Grallagh . .	392 2 17	Roscommon .	Frenchpark . .	Tibohine . .	Castlereagh .	IV.	205
22	Grallagh . .	295 0 11	Roscommon .	Roscommon . .	Elphin . . .	Strokestown .	IV.	209
20	Grallagh . .	313 1 37	Tipperary, N.R.	Lower Ormond .	Monsea . . .	Nenagh . .	II.	287
27	Grallagh . .	77 2 20	Tipperary, N.R.	Upper Ormond .	Dolla . . .	Nenagh . .	II.	290
68	Grallagh . .	135 3 34	Tipperary, S.R.	Clanwilliam . .	Clonbulloge . .	Tipperary .	II.	306
47, 53	Grallagh . .	908 2 30	Tipperary, S.R.	Middlethird . .	Graystown . .	Cashel . .	II.	327
38	Grallagh . .	189 3 10	Waterford . .	Decies within Drum	Ardmore . .	Dungarvan .	II.	350
6, 10	Grallagh Beg .	120 0 19	Roscommon .	Boyle . . .	Boyle . . .	Boyle . .	IV.	194
93	Grallaghgarden .	29 2 13	Mayo . . .	Costello . . .	Bekan . . .	Claremorris .	IV.	139
41	Grallaghgreenan .	443 2 38d	Down . . .	Upper Iveagh, Lr. pt.	Drumballyroney .	Banbridge .	III.	172
38	Grallagh Lower .	239 0 3	Waterford . .	Decies within Drum	Lisgenan or Grange	Youghal . .	II.	352
6, 10	Grallagh More .	240 1 30	Roscommon .	Boyle . . .	Boyle . . .	Boyle . .	IV.	194
38	Grallagh Upper .	282 0 37	Waterford . .	Decies within Drum	Lisgenan or Grange	Youghal . .	II.	352
16	Granabeg Lower .	270 1 11	Wicklow . .	Lower Talbotstown .	Boystown . .	Baltinglass .	I.	359
16	Granabeg Upper .	242 0 9	Wicklow . .	Lower Talbotstown .	Boystown . .	Baltinglass .	I.	359
29	Granafallow . .	170 2 5	Queen's Co. .	Cullenagh . .	Abbeyleix . .	Abbeyleix .	I.	238
22, 26	Granagh . .	046 2 5	Antrim . .	Kilconway . .	Rasharkin . .	Ballymoney .	III.	28
32	Granagh . .	155 1 36	Down . . .	Ards Upper . .	Ballyphilip . .	Downpatrick .	III.	160
38	Granagh . .	366 3 15	Limerick . .	Connello Upper .	Ballingarry . .	Croom . .	II.	230

(a) Including 8A. 1R. 37P. River Barrow.
(b) Including 0A. 3R. 24P. water.
(c) Including 3A. 3R. 3P. water.
(d) Including 0A. 3R. 15P. Lough.

No. of Sheet of the Ordnance Survey Maps.	Townlands and Towns.	Area in Statute Acres.			County.	Barony.	Parish.	Poor Law Union in 1857.	Townland Census of 1851, Part I.	
		A.	R.	P.					Vol.	Page
27, 36	Granagh . . .	771	1	14	Tyrone . .	Omagh East . .	Termonmaguirk .	Omagh . .	III.	314
42	Granaghan . .	128	3	35a	Clare . .	Bunratty Lower .	Tomfinlough . .	Ennis . .	II.	7
32	Granaghan . .	619	3	32	Londonderry .	Loughinsholin .	Killelagh . .	Magherafelt .	III.	241
42	Granaghan Beg .	157	3	11b	Clare . .	Bunratty Lower .	Tomfinlough . .	Ennis . .	II.	7
29, 30	Granaghan (Dillon)	477	0	14	Roscommon .	Roscommon . .	Lissonuffy . .	Strokestown .	IV.	212
29, 30	Granaghan (Martin)	356	0	9	Roscommon .	Roscommon . .	Lissonuffy . .	Strokestown .	IV.	212
42	Granaghan More .	339	0	25c	Clare . .	Bunratty Lower .	Tomfinlough . .	Ennis . .	II.	7
16, 22	Granamore . .	1,735	3	29	Wicklow . .	Lower Talbotstown .	Hollywood . .	Baltinglass .	I.	360
21, 30	Granard . . .	140	1	26	Limerick . .	Connello Upper .	Croom . . .	Croom . .	II.	232
10	Granard . . .	65	0	39	Longford . .	Granard . . .	Granard . . .	Granard . .	I.	156
10	Granardkill . .	409	3	22	Longford . .	Granard . . .	Granard . . .	Granard . .	I.	156
10	GRANARD T. . . .	—			Longford . .	Granard . . .	Granard . . .	Granard . .	I.	157
25	Grandy . . .	189	3	10	Cork, E.R. .	Fermoy . . .	Clenor . . .	Mallow . .	II.	78
20	Granemore . .	785	2	24	Armagh . .	Armagh . . .	Keady . . .	Armagh . .	III.	45
40	Graney East .	175	3	19	Kildare . .	Kilkea and Moone .	Graney . . .	Baltinglass .	I.	60
40	Graney West .	233	0	12	Kildare . .	Kilkea and Moone .	Graney . . .	Baltinglass .	I.	60
45	Grange . . .	337	3	4	Cork, E.R. .	Barrymore . .	Castlelyons . .	Fermoy . .	II.	53
74, 86	Grange . . .	156	1	26	Cork, E.R. .	Cork . . .	Carrigaline . .	Cork . .	II.	64
74, 86	Grange . . .	238	0	20	Cork, E.R. .	Cork . . .	St. Finbars . .	Cork . .	II.	66
73, 85	Grange . . .	647	3	37	Cork, E.R. .	East Muskerry .	Athnowen . .	Bandon . .	II.	101
24	Grange . . .	357	1	3d	Cork, E.R. .	Fermoy . . .	Bridgetown . .	Fermoy . .	II.	77
77	Grange . . .	96	2	27	Cork, E.R. .	Imokilly . . .	Mogeely . . .	Middleton .	II.	90
46, 47	Grange . . .	403	2	33	Donegal . .	Inishowen West .	Burt . . .	Londonderry .	III.	120
37, 38	Grange . . .	588	2	28	Donegal . .	Inishowen West .	Inch . . .	Londonderry .	III.	121
57	Grange . . .	175	3	16	Down . .	Mourne . . .	Kilkeel . . .	Kilkeel . .	III.	183
1, 4	Grange . . .	284	3	2	Dublin . .	Balrothery East .	Balscaddan . .	Balrothery .	I.	20
5	Grange . . .	132	1	8	Dublin . .	Balrothery East .	Holmpatrick . .	Balrothery .	I.	20
7	Grange . . .	428	3	32	Dublin . .	Balrothery West .	Ballyboghill . .	Balrothery .	I.	22
14	Grange . . .	171	0	34	Dublin . .	Castleknock . .	Cloghran . .	Dublin North .	I.	24
15	Grange . . .	457	2	16	Dublin . .	Coolock . . .	Baldoyle . .	Dublin North .	I.	26
12, 15	Grange . . .	68	0	8	Dublin . .	Coolock . . .	Portmarnock . .	Balrothery .	I.	28
17	Grange . . .	345	1	22	Dublin . .	Newcastle . .	Kilmactalway . .	Celbridge .	I.	33
56	Grange . . .	262	3	33	Galway . .	Clare . . .	Annaghdown . .	Galway . .	IV.	16
44	Grange . . .	254	3	0	Galway . .	Clare . . .	Killererin . .	Tuam . .	IV.	21
87	Grange . . .	210	2	9e	Galway . .	Clonmacnowen .	Kilcloony . .	Ballinasloe .	IV.	25
17	Grange . . .	188	2	38	Galway . .	Dunmore . .	Dunmore . .	Tuam . .	IV.	34
16	Grange . . .	260	1	27	Galway . .	Dunmore . .	Tuam . . .	Tuam . .	IV.	36
86	Grange . . .	127	3	38	Galway . .	Kilconnell . .	Grange . . .	Loughrea .	IV.	40
108	Grange . . .	243	2	21	Galway . .	Longford . .	Fahy . . .	Portumna .	IV	58
105	Grange . . .	220	3	35	Galway . .	Loughrea . .	Killeenadeema .	Loughrea .	IV.	64
4, 5	Grange . . .	541	2	4	Kildare . .	Ikeathy&Oughterany	Cloncurry . .	Celbridge .	I.	57
9, 10	Grange . . .	674	1	29	Kilkenny . .	Fassadinin . .	Grangemaccomb .	Urlingford .	I.	89
37	Grange . . .	414	2	12	Kilkenny . .	Ida . . .	The Rower . .	New Ross .	I.	104
42	Grange . . .	643	0	10	Kilkenny . .	Iverk . . .	Pollrone . . .	Waterford .	I.	106
23	Grange . . .	25	1	34	Kilkenny . .	Shillelogher . .	Castleinch or Inchyolaghan .	Kilkenny .	I.	114
23	Grange . . .	287	1	35	Kilkenny . .	Shillelogher . .	Grange . . .	Kilkenny .	I.	114
39	Grange . . .	389	2	23	King's Co. .	Ballybritt . .	Seirkieran . .	Parsonstown .	I.	127
27	Grange . . .	131	2	27f	Leitrim . .	Leitrim . . .	Kiltoghert . .	Carᵏon Shannon	IV.	102
22, 23	Grange . . .	111	0	8	Limerick . .	Clanwilliam . .	Fedamore . .	Limerick . .	II.	223
41	Grange . . .	331	3	22	Limerick . .	Coshlea . . .	Knocklong . .	Kilmallock .	II.	240
22,23,31,32	Grange . . .	1,097	0	30g	Limerick . .	Smallcounty . .	Monasteranenagh .	Croom . .	II.	261
31, 32	Grange . . .	296	0	30	Limerick . .	Smallcounty . .	Tullabracky . .	Croom . .	II.	261
41	Grange . . .	648	0	6	Londonderry .	Loughinsholin .	Desertmartin . .	Magherafelt .	III.	240
11	Grange . . .	766	3	38	Louth . .	Louth . . .	Louth . . .	Dundalk .	I.	184
29, 30, 38	Grange . . .	608	2	14	Mayo . .	Tirawley . . .	Crossmolina . .	Ballina . .	IV.	166
50, 53	Grange . . .	273	1	39	Meath . .	Dunboyne . .	Dunboyne . .	Dunshaughlin .	I.	199
37	Grange . . .	500	1	18h	Meath . .	Lower Deece .	Scurlockstown .	Trim . .	I.	192
24	Grange . . .	493	1	20	Meath . .	Lower Navan .	Ardbraccan . .	Navan . .	I.	214
12	Grange . . .	180	2	38	Meath . .	Morgallion . .	Kilshine . .	Navan . .	I.	210
45	Grange . . .	100	3	30	Meath . .	Ratoath . . .	Ratoath . . .	Dunshaughlin .	I.	219
33	Grange . . .	182	2	23	Meath . .	Upper Duleek .	Clonalvy . .	Drogheda .	I.	197
31	Grange . . .	829	1	18i	Meath . .	Upper Navan . .	Bective . . .	Navan . .	I.	216
26, 32	Grange . . .	863	2	2j	Queen's Co. .	Ballyadams . .	Monksgrange . .	Athy . .	I.	231
1, 3	Grange . . .	321	2	13	Queen's Co. .	Tinnahinch . .	Castlebrack . .	Mountmellick .	I.	248
44, 45	Grange . . .	1,018	3	25k	Roscommon .	Athlone . . .	Cam . . .	Athlone . .	IV.	180
28, 35	Grange . . .	1,578	2	13l	Roscommon .	Ballintober South .	Kilbride . .	Roscommon .	IV.	189
25, 32	Grange . . .	390	0	4	Roscommon .	Castlereagh . .	Kiltullagh . .	Castlereagh .	IV.	202
11	Grange . . .	271	3	17	Roscommon .	Roscommon . .	Aughrim . .	Carᵏon Shannon	IV.	207
23	Grange . . .	246	1	12m	Roscommon .	Roscommon . .	Kiltrustan . .	Strokestown .	IV.	211
22	Grange . . .	102	2	12	Roscommon .	Roscommon . .	Ogulla . . .	Strokestown .	IV.	212
5	Grange . . .	550	1	36	Sligo . .	Carbury . . .	Ahamlish . .	Sligo . .	IV.	219
46, 47	Grange . . .	371	2	34	Tipperary, N.R.	Eliogarty . . .	Holycross . .	Thurles . .	II.	270

No. of Sheet of the Ordnance Survey Maps	Townlands and Towns.	Area in Statute Acres.	County.	Barony.	Parish.	Poor Law Union in 1857.	Townland Census of 1851. Part I.	
		A. R. P.					Vol.	Page
41	Grange	248 1 2	Tipperary, N.R.	Eliogarty	Thurles	Thurles	II.	273
17	Grange	164 2 5	Tipperary, N.R.	Ikerrin	Corbally	Roscrea	II.	275
1, 4	Grange	493 2 32	Tipperary, N.R.	Lower Ormond	Lorrha	Borrisokane	II.	285
19, 25	Grange	360 2 14	Tipperary, N.R.	Owney and Arra	Templeachally	Nenagh	II.	297
59	Grange	199 0 2	Tipperary, S.R.	Clanwilliam	Donohill	Tipperary	II.	307
64, 65	Grange	102 0 24	Tyrone	Clogher	Clogher	Clogher	III.	292
53, 59, 60	Grange	338 1 36a	Tyrone	Clogher	Errigal Keerogue	Clogher	III.	295
54, 55, 62	Grange	518 0 33	Tyrone	Dungannon Middle	Clonfeacle	Dungannon	III.	299
38, 39	Grange	298 2 27	Tyrone	Dungannon Upper	Desertcreat	Cookstown	III.	308
17	Grange	802 2 19b	Tyrone	Strabane Lower	Ardstraw	Strabane	III.	319
38	Grange	184 2 36	Waterford	Decies within Drum	Lisgenan or Grange	Youghal	II.	352
6	Grange	208 2 37c	Westmeath	Corkaree	Lackan	Mullingar	I.	262
31	Grange	191 0 2	Westmeath	Moycashel	Kilcumreragh	Athlone	I.	278
11	Grange	330 1 15	Westmeath	Moygoish	Kilbixy	Mullingar	I.	279
20, 21	Grange	322 3 12	Wexford	Ballaghkeen	Kilcormick	Enniscorthy	I.	294
45, 46	Grange	579 3 1	Wexford	Bargy	Bannow	Wexford	I.	304
52	Grange	189 2 25	Wexford	Bargy	Kilmore	Wexford	I.	306
47, 52	Grange	162 0 0	Wexford	Forth	Ishartmon	Wexford	I.	309
42, 43	Grange	167 0 11	Wexford	Forth	Kilmacree	Wexford	I.	311
48	Grange	101 0 8	Wexford	Forth	St. Iberius	Wexford	I.	314
45, 50	Grange	869 2 39	Wexford	Shelburne	Fethard	New Ross	I.	327
39, 44	Grange	497 3 38	Wexford	Shelburne	St James &Dunbrody	New Ross	I.	328
62	Grangebarry	161 3 33	Tipperary, S.R.	Middlethird	Cooleagh	Cashel	II.	326
136	Grange Beg	264 1 13	Cork, W.R.	Ibane and Barryroe	Abbeymahon	Clonakilty	II.	148
106, 116	Grange Beg	111 3 19	Galway	Leitrim	Duniry	Loughrea	IV.	53
29, 33	Grange Beg	1,832 1 6	Kildare	Naas South	Gilltown	Naas	I.	65
22, 27	Grangebeg	389 1 23	Kildare	Offaly West	Monasterevin	Athy	I.	73
3	Grange Beg	120 3 28	Londonderry	Coleraine	Dunboe	Coleraine	III.	231
22	Grange Beg	250 0 4	Queen's Co.	Clandonagh	Aghaboe	Donaghmore	I.	232
5, 6, 9, 10	Grange Beg	545 0 19	Roscommon	Boyle	Boyle	Boyle	IV.	194
12, 18	Grange Beg	487 3 32	Sligo	Tireragh	Templeboy	Dromore West	IV.	236
81	Grange Beg	61 0 8d	Tipperary, S.R.	Iffa and Offa West	Caher	Clogheen	II.	318
53	Grange Beg	166 2 20	Tipperary, S.R.	Middlethird	Erry	Cashel	II.	326
70, 77	Grangebeg	469 0 38	Tipperary, S.R.	Middlethird	Kiltinan	Clonmel	II.	328
21, 28	Grange Beg	667 3 14	Westmeath	Farbill	Killucan	Castletowndelvin	I.	266
18, 24	Grangebeg Barr	536 0 36	Sligo	Tireragh	Templeboy	Dromore West	IV.	236
18	Grangebellew	144 2 38	Louth	Ferrard	Dysart	Drogheda	I.	181
43	Grange Big	111 2 27	Wexford	Forth	Rosslare	Wexford	I.	313
8	Grange Blundel	550 0 11	Armagh	Armagh	Grange	Armagh	III.	45
43, 49	Grangecastle	214 3 26	Tipperary, S.R.	Slievardagh	Kilcooly	Urlingford	II.	334
22	Grangeclare	162 0 34	Kildare	Offaly East	Grangeclare	Edenderry	I.	70
13, 18	Grangeclare East	308 3 20	Kildare	Connell	Kilmeage	Naas	I.	55
13	Grangeclare Little	7 0 16	Kildare	Connell	Kilmeage	Naas	I.	55
13, 18	Grangeclare West	369 0 31	Kildare	Connell	Kilmeage	Naas	I.	55
17	Grangecommon	24 0 19	Kildare	Connell	Feighcullen	Naas	I.	55
17	Grangecommon	23 2 15	Kildare	Offaly East	Cloncurry	Naas	I.	69
17	Grangecommon	1 2 18	Kildare	Offaly East	Dunmurry	Naas	I.	69
20	Grangecon Demesne	190 2 36	Wicklow	Upper Talbotstown	Ballynure	Baltinglass	I.	361
20, 21	Grangecon Hill	298 0 19	Wicklow	Upper Talbotstown	Ballynure	Baltinglass	I.	361
20, 21	Grangecon Lower	157 3 0	Wicklow	Upper Talbotstown	Ballynure	Baltinglass	I.	361
20	Grangecon Parks	132 2 16	Wicklow	Upper Talbotstown	Ballynure	Baltinglass	I.	361
20	Grangecon Rocks	159 0 9	Wicklow	Upper Talbotstown	Ballynure	Baltinglass	I.	361
20	Grangecon Upper	173 3 28	Wicklow	Upper Talbotstown	Ballynure	Baltinglass	I.	361
26	Grangecoor	243 3 25	Kildare	Offaly West	Monasterevin	Athy	I.	73
43	Grangecrag	138 2 28	Tipperary, S.R.	Slievardagh	Kilcooly	Urlingford	II.	334
23	Grangecuffe	324 2 30	Kilkenny	Shillelogher	Grange	Kilkenny	I.	114
38	Grange, Cush of	244 3 33	Waterford	Decies within Drum	Lisgenan or Grange	Youghal	II.	352
18	Grange Demesne	253 3 20	Wexford	Bantry	Killann	Enniscorthy	I.	300
70	Grangeduff	37 1 35	Tipperary, S.R.	Middlethird	Rathcool	Cashel	II.	329
6, 7	Grangee	558 0 35	Down	Ards Lower	Donaghadee	Newtownards	III.	158
35	Grange East	243 3 19e	Cork, E.R.	Condons &Clangibbon	Fermoy	Fermoy	II.	61
16,17,24,25	Grange East	513 1 4	Cork, E.R.	Orrery and Kilmore	Buttevant	Mallow	II.	107
70, 83, 84	Grange East	1,831 3 27	Galway	Clare	Lackagh	Galway	IV.	23
2	Grange East	107 1 23f	Kildare	Carbury	Carrick	Edenderry	I.	52
14	Grange East	200 1 7	Limerick	Clanwilliam	Caherconlish	Limerick	II.	222
14, 20	Grange East	315 2 18	Sligo	Carbury	Killaspugbrone	Sligo	IV.	222
8	Grangefertagh	920 1 11	Kilkenny	Galmoy	Fertagh	Urlingford	I.	92
8	Grangeford	353 2 0	Carlow	Carlow	Grangeford	Carlow	I.	2
38	Grangeford	124 2 17	Kildare	Kilkea and Moone	Killelan	Baltinglass	I.	60
8	Grangeford Old	475 3 39	Carlow	Carlow	Grangeford	Carlow	I.	2
9	Grange Foyle	593 2 24g	Tyrone	Strabane Lower	Donaghedy	Strabane	III.	321
13, 19	Grangegeeth	1,598 3 8	Meath	Upper Slane	Grangegeeth	Ardee	I.	224
11	Grangegeeth	150 2 38	Westmeath	Corkaree	Portloman	Mullingar	I.	263

(a) Including 2A. 2R. 25P. Martray Lough.
(b) Including 23A. 2R. 8P. water.
(c) Including 2A. 3R. 7P. water.

(d) Including 3A. 2R. 15P. water.
(e) Including 2A. 0R. 32P. water.

(f) Including 7A. 3R. 10P. detached portion.
(g) Including 68A. 1R. 38P. Salt Marsh.

No. of Sheet of the Ordnance Survey Maps.	Townlands and Towns.	Area in Statute Acres.	County.	Barony.	Parish.	Poor Law Union in 1857.	Townland Census of 1851, Part I.	
		A. R. P.					Vol.	Page
38	Grangegibbon .	141 2 23	Westmeath	Moycashel . .	Kilbeggan . .	Tullamore . .	I.	278
11, 17	Grange Glebe . .	422 2 14	Meath . .	Upper Kells . .	Kells . . .	Kells . .	I.	206
17	Grangegoddan Glebe	232 2 4	Meath . .	Upper Kells . .	Kells . . .	Kells . .	I.	206
18	Grangegorman East	169 2 29a	Dublin . .	Dublin, Municipal Borough of . .	Grangegorman .	Dublin North .	I.	44
18	Grangegorman Middle	365 2 33b	Dublin . .	Coolock and Municipal Borough	Grangegorman .	Dublin North .	I.	27
18	Grangegorman North	71 1 17	Dublin . .	Coolock . . .	Grangegorman .	Dublin North .	I.	27
18	Grangegorman South	120 3 28	Dublin . .	Coolock . . .	Grangegorman .	Dublin North .	I.	27
18	Grangegorman West	126 0 35c	Dublin . .	Dublin, Municipal Borough of . .	Grangegorman .	Dublin North .	I.	44
18	Grangehiggin . .	888 2 30	Kildare . .	Connell . . .	Rathernan . .	Naas . .	I.	56
20	Grangehill . .	378 3 8	Kilkenny . .	Gowran . . .	Tiscoffin . .	Kilkenny . .	I.	99
43, 49	Grangehill . .	208 1 26	Tipperary, S.R.	Slievardagh . .	Kilcooly . .	Urlingford . .	II.	334
8	Grange Irish . .	503 1 39	Louth . .	Lower Dundalk .	Carlingford . .	Dundalk . .	I.	176
38	Grange and Kiltober	296 3 29	Westmeath .	Moycashel . .	Kilbeggan . .	Tullamore . .	I.	278
43, 48	Grange Little . .	90 1 22	Wexford . .	Forth . . .	Rosslare . .	Wexford . .	I.	313
25	Grange or Lockclose	166 0 31	King's Co. .	Geashill . . .	Geashill . .	Tullamore . .	I.	140
28, 34	Grangelough . .	105 2 2	Tipperary, N.R.	Kilnamanagh Upper	Glenkeen . .	Thurles . .	II	278
9	Grange Lower .	903 3 19	Armagh . .	Oneilland West .	Newry . . .	Armagh . .	III.	54
21, 25	Grange Lower .	1,962 1 5d	Kilkenny . .	Gowran . . .	Grangesilvia . .	Thomastown .	I.	96
6	Grange Lower .	126 2 12	Limerick . .	Clanwilliam . .	Killeenagarriff .	Limerick . .	II.	224
28, 36	Grange Lower .	311 1 39	Limerick . .	Glenquin . . .	Grange . .	Newcastle .	II.	245
14	Grange Lower .	225 1 1	Queen's Co. .	Stradbally . .	Dysartenos . .	Athy . .	I.	247
14,15,20,21	Grange Lower .	166 0 28	Tipperary, N.R.	Lower Ormond .	Knigh . . .	Nenagh . .	II.	285
9, 17	Grange Lower .	158 2 22e	Waterford .	Gaultiere and Municipal Borough .	St. Johns Without .	Waterford . .	II.	365
18	Grange Lower .	444 0 2	Wexford . .	Bantry . . .	Killann . .	Enniscorthy .	I.	300
9	GRANGE LOWER T. .	—	Waterford .	Gaultiere . .	St. Johns Without .	Waterford . .	II.	365
37	Grangemellon .	924 3 9f	Kildare . .	Kilkea and Moone .	Tankardstown .	Athy . .	I.	61
71, 72	Grangemockler .	899 3 31	Tipperary, S.R.	Slievardagh . .	Grangemockler .	Carrick on Suir .	II.	333
12	Grangemore .	366 2 5	Armagh . .	Armagh . . .	Grange . .	Armagh . .	III.	45
136	Grange More .	503 3 4	Cork, W.R.	Ibane and Barryroe	Abbeymahon .	Clonakilty .	II.	148
106, 116	Grange More .	367 2 18	Galway . .	Leitrim . .	Duniry . .	Loughrea . .	IV.	53
29	Grangemore .	148 3 17	Kildare . .	Naas South . .	Brannockstown .	Naas . .	I.	64
28, 29	Grange More .	645 3 8	Kildare . .	Naas South . .	Gilltown . .	Naas . .	I.	65
3	Grange More .	332 0 25	Londonderry .	Coleraine . .	Dunboe . .	Coleraine . .	III.	231
22	Grange More .	468 0 32	Queen's Co. .	Clandonagh . .	Aghaboe . .	Donaghmore .	I.	232
9	Grange More .	509 0 1	Roscommon .	Boyle . . .	Boyle . .	Boyle . .	IV.	194
18	Grange More .	365 1 21	Sligo . . .	Tireragh . .	Templeboy . .	Dromore West .	IV.	236
81	Grange More .	105 1 12	Tipperary, S.R.	Iffa and Offa West .	Caher . . .	Clogheen . .	II.	318
53	Grange More .	342 0 1	Tipperary, S.R.	Middlethird .	Erry . . .	Cashel . .	II.	326
20, 21	Grange More .	2,154 1 35	Westmeath .	Farbill . . .	Killucan . .	Castletowndelvin	I.	266
3, 7	Grange More Upper	48 2 22	Londonderry .	Coleraine . .	Dunboe . .	Coleraine . .	III.	231
64, 65, 68	Grange Mountain Bar	1,026 0 6g	Tyrone . .	Clogher . .	Clogher . .	Clogher . .	III.	292
38, 44	Grangend . .	9 3 27	Meath . .	Ratoath . .	Dunshaughlin .	Dunshaughlin .	I.	218
38, 44	Grangend Common	63 3 12	Meath . .	Ratoath . .	Dunshaughlin .	Dunshaughlin .	I.	218
14	Grange North .	170 1 16	Sligo . . .	Carbury . .	Killaspugbrone .	Sligo . .	IV.	222
68	Grange North .	107 1 33	Tipperary, S.R.	Clanwilliam .	Relickmurry & Athassel	Tipperary .	II.	310
19	Grange North .	99 3 27	Westmeath .	Moyashel and Magheradernon .	Mullingar . .	Mullingar . .	I.	275
19	Grange North .	295 0 5	Wicklow . .	Newcastle . .	Killiskey . .	Rathdrum . .	I.	352
51	Grange of Ballyrobert	883 2 17	Antrim . .	Lower Belfast .	Templepatrick .	Antrim . .	III.	9
51	Grange of Ballywalter	320 1 37	Antrim . .	Lower Belfast .	Ballylinny . .	Antrim . .	III.	7
10, 14, 15	Grange of Inispollan Mountain . .	477 0 18	Antrim . .	Lower Glenarm .	Grange of Inispollan	Ballycastle .	III.	21
56	Grange of Umgall .	753 2 19	Antrim . .	Upper Belfast .	Templepatrick .	Antrim . .	III.	10
8, 9	Grange Old . .	83 3 20	Louth . .	Lower Dundalk .	Carlingford . .	Dundalk . .	I.	176
42	Grange Park .	271 0 17	Antrim . .	Upper Toome .	Ballyscullion Grange	Ballymena .	III.	33
105	Grangepark . .	65 3 0	Galway . .	Loughrea . .	Killeenadeema .	Loughrea . .	IV.	64
6	Grange Park .	1,076 0 27	Londonderry .	Keenaght . .	Aghanloo . .	NewTnLimavady	III.	234
28	Grangeroe . .	109 3 38	Tipperary, N.R.	Kilnamanagh Upper	Glenkeen . .	Thurles . .	II.	278
37	Grangerosnolvan .	153 2 25	Kildare . .	Kilkea and Moone .	Grangerosnolvan .	Athy . .	I.	60
35,36,37,38	Grangerosnolvan Lower	719 2 37	Kildare . .	Kilkea and Moone .	Grangerosnolvan .	Athy . .	I.	60
37, 38	Grangerosnolvan Upper	519 1 8	Kildare . .	Kilkea and Moone .	Grangerosnolvan .	Athy . .	I.	60
68	Grange South .	154 1 2	Tipperary, S.R.	Clanwilliam .	Relickmurry & Athassel	Tipperary .	II.	310
19	Grange South .	177 1 7	Westmeath .	Moyashel and Magheradernon .	Mullingar . .	Mullingar . .	I.	275
19	Grange South .	266 2 36	Wicklow . .	Newcastle . .	Killiskey . .	Rathdrum . .	I.	352
8	Grangestown .	113 2 12	Westmeath .	Delvin . . .	Castletowndelvin .	Castletowndelvin	I.	264
8	Grangestown .	68 2 28	Westmeath .	Delvin . . .	Kilcumny . .	Castletowndelvin	I.	265
7	Grangestown .	142 0 2	Westmeath .	Fore . . .	Faughalstown .	Castletowndelvin	I.	270
42	GRANGE T. . .	—	Kilkenny . .	Iverk . . .	Pollrone . .	Waterford .	I.	106
5	GRANGE T. .	—	Sligo . . .	Carbury . .	Ahamlish . .	Sligo . .	IV.	220
39	GRANGE T. .	—	Tyrone . .	Dungannon Upper .	Desertcreat . .	Cookstown .	III.	308

(a) Included in Grangegorman parish.
(b) { Within the Municipal Boundary, 30A. 0R. 24P.
    { Without the Municipal Boundary, 335A. 2R. 9P.
(c) Included in Grangegorman parish.
(d) Including 9A. 1R. 23P. River Barrow.
(e) { Within the Municipal Boundary, 10A. 3R. 2P.
    { Without the Municipal Boundary, 147A. 3R. 20P.
(f) Including 21A. 0R. 0P. River Barrow.
(g) Including 18A. 3R. 18P. water.

No. of Sheet of the Ordnance Survey Maps.	Townlands and Towns.	Area in Statute Acres.	County.	Barony.	Parish.	Poor Law Union in 1857.	Townland Census of 1851, Part I.	
		A. R. P.					Vol.	Page
9	Grange Upper .	64 2 14	Armagh . .	Oneilland West .	Newry . . .	Armagh . .	III.	54
21, 25	Grange Upper .	864 2 3	Kilkenny .	Gowran . .	Grangesilvia .	Thomastown .	I.	96
6	Grange Upper .	288 0 32	Limerick .	Clanwilliam .	Killeenagarriff .	Limerick . .	II.	224
36	Grange Upper .	260 1 24	Limerick . .	Glenquin .	Grange . .	Newcastle .	II.	245
13, 14, 18, 19	Grange Upper .	417 3 6	Queen's Co. .	Stradbally .	Dysartenos .	Athy . .	I.	247
14, 20, 21	Grange Upper .	202 0 3	Tipperary, N.R.	Lower Ormond .	Knigh . .	Nenagh .	II.	285
9, 10, 17	Grange Upper .	173 2 7	Waterford .	Gaultiere . .	St. Johns Without .	Waterford .	II.	365
18, 24	Grange Upper .	571 0 2	Wexford .	Bantry . .	Killann . .	Enniscorthy .	I.	300
38, 45	Grangewalls . .	527 1 11	Down . .	Lecale Upper .	Bright . .	Downpatrick .	III.	180
8	Grangewat . .	76 3 9	Carlow . .	Carlow . .	Killerrig . .	Carlow . .	I.	2
35	Grange West . .	270 2 24a	Cork, E.R. .	Condons&Clangibbon	Fermoy .	Fermoy . .	II.	61
16, 24	Grange West . .	425 0 20	Cork, E.R. .	Orrery and Kilmore	Buttevant .	Mallow . .	II.	107
83	Grange West . .	5 1 16	Galway .	Clare . .	Lackagh . .	Galway . .	IV.	23
2	Grange West . .	200 0 28	Kildare . .	Carbury . .	Carrick . .	Edenderry .	I.	52
14	Grange West .	157 1 14	Limerick . .	Clanwilliam .	Caherconlish .	Limerick . .	II.	222
14	Grange West .	103 1 32	Sligo . .	Carbury . .	Killaspugbrone .	Sligo . .	IV.	222
37, 38	Grangicam .	375 0 30	Down . .	Lecale Upper .	Down . .	Downpatrick .	III.	180
33, 34	Graniamore .	83 3 29	Sligo . .	Corran . .	Toomour . .	Sligo . .	IV.	228
34	Graniaroe .	81 3 13	Sligo . .	Corran . .	Toomour . .	Sligo . .	IV.	228
39	Graniera . .	688 2 23	Tipperary, N.R.	Kilnamanagh Upper	Upperchurch .	Thurles . .	II.	280
98, 99	Granig . . .	744 1 1	Cork, E.R. .	Kinalea . .	Tracton . .	Kinsale . .	II.	97
47	Granisk . .	120 2 13	Wexford .	Forth . .	Mayglass . .	Wexford .	I.	312
114	Grannagh . .	162 3 21	Galway . .	Kiltartan .	Kilthomas . .	Loughrea .	IV.	49
114	Grannagh . .	501 2 17	Galway . .	Loughrea .	Ardrahan . .	Loughrea . .	IV.	62
9	Grannagh .	125 1 17b	Londonderry .	Keenaght .	Aghanloo . .	New Tn Limavady	III.	234
114	Grannagh Beg .	78 0 4	Galway . .	Loughrea .	Ardrahan .	Loughrea . .	IV.	62
43	Granny . .	1,137 1 8	Kilkenny .	Iverk . .	Kilmacow .	Waterford .	I.	106
36, 41	Granny . .	158 0 34	Londonderry .	Loughinsholin .	Kilcronaghan .	Magherafelt .	III.	241
9, 10	Granny . .	504 2 34	Roscommon .	Boyle . .	Estersnow .	Boyle . .	IV.	195
41, 49	Gransha . .	638 3 22	Antrim . .	Lower Belfast .	Islandmagee .	Larne . .	III.	8
29, 38	Gransha . .	446 1 16	Donegal . .	Inishowen West .	Fahan Lower .	Inishowen .	III.	120
2, 6	Gransha . .	1,418 3 17	Down . .	Ards Lower .	Bangor . .	Newtownards .	III.	157
18, 25	Gransha . .	494 3 37	Down . .	Ards Upper .	Inishargy . .	Newtownards .	III.	160
10	Gransha . .	673 2 15c	Down . .	Castlereagh Lower .	Comber . .	Newtownards .	III.	162
41	Gransha . .	588 3 18	Down . .	Lordship of Newry .	Newry . .	Newry . .	III.	182
28, 35	Gransha . .	1,293 1 13	Down . .	Upper Iveagh, Lr. pt.	Dromara .	Banbridge .	III.	172
13, 14	Gransha . .	299 0 23d	Londonderry .	Tirkeeran . .	Clondermot .	Londonderry .	III.	248
12	Gransha Beg .	250 2 37	Monaghan .	Dartree . .	Clones . .	Clones . .	III.	264
15	Granshagh . .	201 2 37	Kerry . .	Clanmaurice .	Kilcaragh . .	Listowel . .	II.	169
26, 27	Granshagh Big .	97 0 38	Fermanagh .	Clanawley .	Rossorry . .	Enniskillen .	III.	194
26, 27	Granshagh Little .	92 0 25e	Fermanagh .	Clanawley .	Rossorry . .	Enniskillen .	III.	194
13, 20	Gransha (Intake) .	44 3 4	Londonderry .	Tirkeeran . .	Clondermot .	Londonderry .	III.	248
47	Gransha Lower .	147 2 20	Kerry . .	Trughanacmy .	Kiltallagh . .	Tralee . .	II.	212
12	Gransha More .	220 2 26	Monaghan .	Dartree . .	Clones . .	Clones . .	III.	264
38, 47	Gransha Upper .	257 0 5	Kerry . .	Trughanacmy .	Kiltallagh . .	Tralee . .	II.	212
21	Grant's Island .	11 2 9	King's Co. .	Garrycastle .	Reynagh . .	Parsonstown .	I.	138
28	Grantstown .	23 2 26	Queen's Co. .	Clarmallagh .	Aghaboe . .	Donaghmore .	I.	236
28	Grantstown .	472 2 32f	Queen's Co. .	Clarmallagh .	Bordwell . .	Donaghmore .	I.	237
59, 60	Grantstown .	784 3 35	Tipperary, S.R.	Clanwilliam .	Kilfeacle . .	Tipperary .	II.	308
10, 18	Grantstown .	276 2 33	Waterford .	Gaultiere . .	Ballynakill .	Waterford .	II.	362
47	Grascur Great .	80 2 15	Wexford . .	Bargy . .	Kilcowen . .	Wexford . .	I.	305
47	Grascur Little .	38 0 34	Wexford . .	Bargy . .	Kilcowen . .	Wexford . .	I.	305
4	Grass Island . .	2 1 10	Limerick . .	Kenry . .	Ardcanny . .	Rathkeale .	II.	248
10, 11	Grassyard . .	192 0 13	Longford . .	Granard . .	Granard . .	Granard . .	I.	156
38	Grattan . .	63 2 27	Fermanagh .	Knockninny .	Kinawley . .	Lisnaskea .	III.	202
18	Grattanstown .	135 0 5	Louth . .	Ferrard . .	Dysart . .	Drogheda .	I.	181
11	Gravelstown . .	1,007 3 17	Meath . .	Lower Kells .	Emlagh . .	Kells . .	I.	202
99, 100	Graveshill . .	228 2 4	Galway . .	Longford .	Kiltormer . .	Ballinasloe .	IV.	60
54	Grawky . .	330 1 0	Donegal . .	Raphoe . .	Raymoghy .	Letterkenny .	III.	142
54	Grawky Glebe .	70 0 10	Donegal . .	Raphoe . .	Raymoghy .	Letterkenny .	III.	142
47, 52	Grayrobin . .	241 2 33	Wexford . .	Bargy . .	Tomhaggard .	Wexford . .	I.	308
35	Graysland . .	2 0 11	Kildare . .	Narragh & Reban West	St. Johns .	Athy . .	I.	68
35	Graysland . .	53 3 30	Kildare . .	Narragh & Reban West	St. Michaels .	Athy . .	I.	68
54	Graystown . .	588 2 10	Tipperary, S.R.	Slievardagh .	Graystown .	Cashel . .	II.	333
27	Greagh . .	275 3 21	Cavan . .	Clankee . .	Knockbride .	Cootehill .	III.	73
13	Greagh . .	141 2 25	Cavan . .	Tullyhaw .	Templeport .	Bawnboy .	III.	95
28	Greagh . .	91 2 25	Fermanagh .	Magherastephana .	Aghavea . .	Lisnaskea .	III.	219
15, 17	Greagh . .	50 2 32	Leitrim . .	Drumahaire .	Killarga . .	Manorhamilton	IV.	98
25, 28, 29	Greagh . .	228 0 34g	Leitrim . .	Leitrim . .	Fenagh . .	Mohill . .	IV.	100
31	Greagh . .	25 1 15	Leitrim . .	Leitrim . .	Kiltoghert .	Cark. on Shannon	IV.	102
3	Greagh . .	107 0 1	Longford . .	Longford .	Killoe . .	Longford .	I.	159
24	Greagh . .	386 1 3	Monaghan .	Cremorne .	Ballybay . .	Castleblayney .	III.	259
13	Greagh . .	241 3 5	Monaghan .	Monaghan .	Drumsnat . .	Monaghan .	III.	275

(a) Including 8A. 0R. 14P. water.
(b) Including 3A. 1R. 29P. water.
(c) Including 0A. 2R. 24P. water.
(d) Including 6A. 0R. 16P. water.
(e) Including 9A. 0R. 25P. water.
(f) Including 27A. 1R. 20P. water.
(g) Including 48A. 2R. 15P. water.

No. of Sheet of the Ordnance Survey Maps.	Townlands and Towns.	Area in Statute Acres.			County.	Barony.	Parish.	Poor Law Union in 1857.	Townland Census of 1851, Part I.	
		A.	R.	P.					Vol.	Page
5, 6	Greagh . . .	147	3	39	Monaghan	Monaghan	Tedavnet	Monaghan	III.	279
2, 3	Greagh . . .	345	2	35a	Monaghan	Trough	Errigal Trough	Clogher	III.	284
2	Greagh . . .	192	0	4	Roscommon	Boyle	Kilronan	Boyle	IV.	197
35	Greaghacapple	39	2	8	Fermanagh	Clankelly	Clones	Clones	III.	196
35	Greaghacholea	167	1	20	Fermanagh	Clankelly	Clones	Clones	III.	196
14, 19	Greaghacholea or Coraghmuck	281	0	25	Cavan	Tullyhunco	Kildallan	Bawnboy	III.	97
2	Greaghacorra .	94	3	24	Roscommon	Boyle	Kilronan	Boyle	IV.	197
33	Greaghadoo .	183	2	19	Cavan	Castlerahan	Killinkere	Bailieborough	III.	69
33	Greaghadossan	556	3	19	Cavan	Castlerahan	Killinkere	Bailieborough	III.	69
27	Greaghagarran	157	2	30b	Cavan	Clankee	Knockbride	Cootehill	III.	73
27	Greaghagibney	524	3	18c	Cavan	Tullygarvey	Larah	Cootehill	III.	91
119	Greaghans .	281	1	25	Mayo	Kilmaine	Kilcommon	Ballinrobe	IV.	154
20, 25	Greaghaphort .	127	3	21	Fermanagh	Clanawley	Cleenish	Enniskillen	III.	191
34	Greagharue .	138	1	32	Cavan	Clankee	Bailieborough	Bailieborough	III.	71
34, 35	Greaghatirrive	94	1	36	Fermanagh	Clankelly	Galloon	Lisnaskea	III.	198
29,30,35,36	Greaghaverrin	137	2	29	Fermanagh	Clankelly	Clones	Clones	III.	196
37	Greaghavockan	77	1	29	Fermanagh	Clanawley	Kinawley	Enniskillen	III.	194
30, 36	Greaghawarren	98	0	32	Fermanagh	Clankelly	Clones	Clones	III.	196
30	Greaghawillin (Jackson)	117	2	4	Monaghan	Farney	Magheracloone	Carrickmacross	III.	272
30	Greaghawillin (Richey)	135	1	6	Monaghan	Farney	Magheracloone	Carrickmacross	III.	272
35	Greaghcashel .	231	3	17	Fermanagh	Clankelly	Galloon	Lisnaskea	III.	198
33	Greaghclaugh	221	0	9d	Cavan	Castlerahan	Killinkere	Bailieborough	III.	69
34, 40	Greaghclogh .	513	1	22	Cavan	Castlerahan	Mullagh	Bailieborough	III.	70
27	Greaghcrottagh	193	3	2	Cavan	Clankee	Knockbride	Bailieborough	III.	73
22	Greaghcrottagh	225	3	10	Cavan	Tullygarvey	Drung	Cootehill	III.	89
30, 31	Greaghdrumit	174	3	3	Monaghan	Farney	Magheross	Carrickmacross	III.	273
28	Greaghdrumneesk .	141	3	2	Monaghan	Farney	Magheross	Carrickmacross	III.	273
33	Greaghduff .	40	3	10	Cavan	Castlerahan	Bailieborough	Bailieborough	III.	67
33, 34	Greaghduff .	140	3	2	Cavan	Castlerahan	Killinkere	Bailieborough	III.	69
27	Greaghettiagh	425	0	28e	Cavan	Clankee	Knockbride	Cootehill	III.	73
20, 23	Greaghfarnagh	179	0	36	Leitrim	Leitrim	Kiltoghert	Cark. on Shannon	IV.	102
21, 24	Greaghglass .	237	2	4	Leitrim	Carrigallen	Oughteragh	Bawnboy	IV.	92
13, 14	Greaghglass .	186	0	25	Monaghan	Monaghan	Monaghan	Monaghan	III.	277
27	Greaghlane .	266	1	13	Monaghan	Farney	Magheross	Carrickmacross	III.	273
27	Greaghlatacapple	350	1	16	Monaghan	Farney	Magheross	Carrickmacross	III.	273
30	Greaghlone .	449	1	32f	Monaghan	Farney	Magheracloone	Carrickmacross	III.	272
38	Greaghmore .	59	3	2	Fermanagh	Knockninny	Kinawley	Lisnaskea	III.	202
1	Greaghmore .	229	2	20	Fermanagh	Lurg	Drumkeeran	Lowtherstown	III.	206
14	Greaghmore .	70	2	32	Fermanagh	Magheraboy	Devenish	Enniskillen	III.	211
22	Greaghnacross	394	0	22	Cavan	Tullygarvey	Kildrumsherdan	Cootehill	III.	90
33	Greaghnacunnia	203	2	11	Cavan	Castlerahan	Killinkere	Bailieborough	III.	69
40	Greaghnadarragh	174	2	34	Cavan	Castlerahan	Mullagh	Kells	III.	70
34	Greaghnadarragh	268	1	0	Cavan	Clankee	Moybolgue	Bailieborough	III.	74
17	Greaghnadarragh	132	2	9	Leitrim	Drumahaire	Inishmagrath	Manorhamilton	IV.	96
8	Greaghnadoony	88	1	11	Cavan	Tullyhaw	Templeport	Bawnboy	III.	95
27, 33	Greaghnafarna	530	2	5	Cavan	Upper Loughtee	Killinkere	Cavan	III.	84
18, 19	Greaghnafarna	409	0	8	Leitrim	Drumahaire	Drumreilly	Cark. on Shannon	IV.	95
14, 17	Greaghnafarna	1,122	2	10	Leitrim	Drumahaire	Killanummery	Manorhamilton	IV.	98
2	Greaghnafarna	298	2	35	Roscommon	Boyle	Kilronan	Boyle	IV.	197
37, 38	Greaghnafine .	212	1	28	Fermanagh	Knockninny	Kinawley	Enniskillen	III.	202
32	Greaghnagee .	114	1	2	Cavan	Upper Loughtee	Lavey	Cavan	III.	86
1, 2	Greaghnageeragh	316	3	34	Roscommon	Boyle	Kilronan	Boyle	IV.	197
20, 25	Greaghnagleragh	224	1	37	Fermanagh	Clanawley	Cleenish	Enniskillen	III.	191
16	Greaghnaglogh	693	3	6	Leitrim	Drumahaire	Inishmagrath	Manorhamilton	IV.	96
2	Greaghnaglogh	318	3	7	Roscommon	Boyle	Kilronan	Boyle	IV.	197
15, 16	Greaghnagon .	47	1	30	Leitrim	Drumahaire	Killarga	Manorhamilton	IV.	98
29, 35	Greaghnagore .	59	2	7	Fermanagh	Clankelly	Clones	Clones	III.	196
20, 21	Greaghnaguillaun	1,325	3	19	Leitrim	Leitrim	Kiltoghert	Cark. on Shannon	IV.	102
2	Greaghnaleava Beg	75	1	23	Roscommon	Boyle	Kilronan	Boyle	IV.	197
2	Greaghnaleava More	83	1	34	Roscommon	Boyle	Kilronan	Boyle	IV.	197
22	Greaghnaloughry	100	1	15	Leitrim	Carrigallen	Drumreilly	Bawnboy	IV.	91
34	Greaghnamale	213	3	21	Cavan	Clankee	Bailieborough	Bailieborough	III.	71
36	Greaghnamoyle	59	3	25	Fermanagh	Clankelly	Clones	Clones	III.	196
27,28,30,31	Greaghnaroog	232	0	14	Monaghan	Farney	Magheross	Carrickmacross	III.	273
18, 20	Greaghnaslieve	447	3	12	Leitrim	Drumahaire	Inishmagrath	Manorhamilton	IV.	96
14	Greaghrahan .	284	2	22g	Cavan	Lower Loughtee	Drumlane	Cavan	III.	80
23	Greaghrawer .	137	0	9h	Fermanagh	Tirkennedy	Enniskillen	Enniskillen	III.	222
21	Greaghrevagh Beg .	96	0	7	Leitrim	Carrigallen	Oughteragh	Bawnboy	IV.	92
21, 24	Greaghrevagh More Glebe . .	192	1	10	Leitrim	Carrigallen	Oughteragh	Bawnboy	IV.	92
100	Greaghs . .	301	2	31	Donegal	Tirhugh	Drumhome	Donegal	III.	146
100	Greaghs Barr or Meen-avanaghan . .	232	1	5	Donegal	Tirhugh	Drumhome	Donegal	III.	146

(a) Including 39A. 3R. 22P. water.
(b) Including 3A. 3R. 34P. water.
(c) Including 14A. 1R. 36P. water.

(d) Including 7A. 1R. 35P. water.
(e) Including 10A. 3R. 31P. water.
(f) Including 37A. 1R. 10P. water.

(g) Including 26A. 2R. 6P. water.
(h) Including 3A. 3R. 26P. water.

No. of Sheet of the Ordnance Survey Maps.	Townlands and Towns.	Area in Statute Acres.	County.	Barony.	Parish.	Poor Law Union in 1857.	Townland Census of 1851. Part I.	
		A. R. P.					Vol.	Page
51, 61	Great Blasket Island	1,020 3 12	Kerry . .	Corkaguiny . .	Dunquin . .	Dingle . .	II.	176
8	Greatcommon . .	197 0 3	Dublin . .	Balrothery East .	Lusk . .	Balrothery .	I.	21
23	Greatconnell . .	1,312 0 23a	Kildare . .	Connell . .	Greatconnell .	Naas . .	I.	55
19,20,26,27	Greatdown . .	633 0 3	Westmeath .	Farbill . .	Killucan . .	Mullingar .	I.	267
30, 36	Greatfurze . .	153 2 7	Meath . .	Upper Navan . .	Trim . .	Trim . .	I.	217
13	Greatheath . .	274 2 21	Queen's Co. .	Maryborough East .	Kilteale . .	Mountmellick .	I.	241
13	Greatheath . .	150 3 38	Queen's Co. .	Portnahinch . .	Coolbanagher .	Mountmellick .	I.	244
11	Greathill . .	111 0 5b	Cavan . .	Lower Loughtee .	Drumlane . .	Cavan . .	III.	80
73	Great Island . .	72 1 5c	Cork, E.R. .	East Muskerry .	Carrigrohane .	Cork . .	II.	102
101	Great Island .	49 0 33	Galway . .	Longford . .	Clonfert . .	Ballinasloe .	IV.	57
39	Greatisland . .	799 0 23	Wexford . .	Shelburne . .	Kilmokea . .	New Ross .	I.	327
6	Greatmeadow . .	105 0 9	Roscommon .	Boyle . .	Boyle . .	Boyle . .	IV.	194
17	Great Minnis's Island	3 3 28	Down . .	Ards Upper . .	Ardkeen . .	Downpatrick .	III.	159
22	Greatoak . .	197 3 37	Kilkenny . .	Shillelogher . .	Killaloe . .	Callan . .	I.	115
32	Greatrath . .	230 3 26	Kildare . .	Offaly West . .	Kilrush . .	Athy . .	I.	73
22	Greatwood . .	218 2 28	Kilkenny . .	Shillelogher . .	Killaloe . .	Callan . .	I.	115
13	Greatwood . .	284 3 26	Louth . .	Ardee . .	Clonkeen . .	Ardee . .	I.	172
16, 24	Greatwood or Mough	132 3 20	King's Co. .	Ballyboy . .	Killoughy . .	Tullamore .	I.	124
61	Green . .	19 3 10	Tipperary, S.R.	Middlethird . .	St. John Baptist .	Cashel . .	II.	330
20, 25	Greenaghan . .	233 2 10	Antrim . .	Lower Glenarm .	Ardclinis . .	Larne . .	III.	21
9, 14	Greenan . .	965 3 26	Antrim . .	Cary . .	Culfeightrin .	Ballycastle .	III.	13
49	Greenan . .	255 0 13	Antrim . .	Upper Toome . .	Duneane . .	Antrim . .	III.	35
8	Greenan . .	194 0 12	Armagh . .	Oneilland West .	Grange . .	Armagh . .	III.	52
85, 94	Greenan . .	1,477 3 4d	Donegal . .	Banagh . .	Killymard . .	Donegal . .	III.	111
50, 51	Greenan . .	838 3 27e	Down . .	Lordship of Newry .	Newry . .	Newry . .	III.	182
20	Greenan . .	515 2 0	Down . .	Lower Iveagh, Lr. pt.	Dromore . .	Banbridge .	III.	168
33, 34	Greenan . .	195 0 25f	Down . .	Upper Iveagh, Up.pt.	Aghaderg . .	Banbridge .	III.	174
32, 37	Greenan . .	698 2 26	Fermanagh .	Clanawley . .	Kinawley . .	Enniskillen .	III.	194
14	Greenan . .	149 2 0	Londonderry .	Tirkeeran . .	Faughanvale .	Londonderry .	III.	250
101	Greenan . .	58 0 12	Mayo . .	Clanmorris . .	Crossboyne .	Claremorris .	IV.	132
14, 15	Greenan . .	668 3 1	Meath . .	Fore . .	Moylagh . .	Oldcastle .	I.	201
6	Greenan . .	312 2 10	Meath . .	Lower Slane . .	Drumcondra .	Ardee . .	I.	222
40	Greenan . .	152 2 13	Sligo . .	Corran . .	Toomour . .	Boyle . .	IV.	228
33	Greenan . .	305 3 32	Tipperary, N.R.	Upper Ormond .	Templederry .	Nenagh . .	II.	293
41	Greenan . .	1,306 2 0	Tyrone . .	Omagh East . .	Dromore . .	Omagh . .	III.	311
57	Greenan . .	337 0 34g	Tyrone . .	Omagh East . .	Kilskeery . .	Enniskillen .	III.	313
19	Greenan . .	310 0 10h	Tyrone . .	Strabane Upper .	Bodoney Lower .	Gortin . .	III.	323
16	Greenan . .	898 1 35	Waterford .	Decies without Drum	Rossmire . .	Kilmacthomas .	II.	360
1	Greenan . .	245 2 19i	Waterford .	Glenahiry . .	Inishlounaght .	Clonmel . .	II.	365
20	Greenan . .	4 1 25	Westmeath .	Delvin . .	Killucan . .	Castletowndelvin	I.	266
32, 38	Greenan . .	318 0 33	Westmeath .	Moycashel . .	Kilbeggan . .	Tullamore .	I.	278
19	Greenan . .	316 2 17	Wexford . .	Bantry . .	Killann . .	Enniscorthy .	I.	300
29	Greenan Beg . .	31 2 2	Wicklow . .	Ballinacor North .	Knockrath . .	Rathdrum .	I.	347
3	Greenane . .	67 3 21	Carlow . .	Carlow . .	Killerrig . .	Carlow . .	I.	2
23	Greenane . .	283 3 6	Cork, E.R. .	Duhallow . .	Kilroe . .	Kanturk . .	II.	73
128	Greenane . .	809 1 16	Cork, W.R. .	Bear . .	Killaconenagh .	Castletown .	II.	125
147	Greenane . .	57 3 17	Cork, W.R. .	West Carbery(W.D.)	Kilmoe . .	Skull . .	II.	145
92	Greenane . .	697 2 5	Kerry . .	Dunkerron South .	Templenoe .	Kenmare .	II.	185
14, 23	Greenane . .	236 1 34	Limerick . .	Clanwilliam . .	Caherconlish .	Limerick .	II.	222
59	Greenane . .	233 3 33	Tipperary, S.R.	Clanwilliam . .	Templenoe .	Tipperary .	II.	312
22, 30	Greenane . .	51 0 2	Waterford .	Decies without Drum	Colligan . .	Dungarvan .	II.	354
92	Greenane Islands .	24 0 34	Kerry . .	Dunkerron South .	Templenoe .	Kenmare .	II.	185
144	Greenanes . .	15 1 25	Cork, W.R. .	Ibane and Barryroe	Ardfield . .	Clonakilty .	II.	148
29, 30	Greenan More . .	344 0 13	Wicklow . .	Ballinacor North .	Knockrath . .	Rathdrum .	I.	347
75	Greenans . .	208 3 24	Donegal . .	Boylagh . .	Inishkeel . .	Glenties .	III.	112
59, 60	Greenans . .	1,002 1 31	Mayo . .	Carra . .	Turlough . .	Castlebar .	IV.	131
33	Greenanstown . .	174 0 0	Meath . .	Upper Duleek .	Stamullin . .	Drogheda .	I.	198
3, 13	Greenaun . .	548 3 24	Galway . .	Ross . .	Ballinrobe .	Ballinrobe .	IV.	72
28, 32	Greenaun . .	200 3 0	Leitrim . .	Leitrim . .	Mohill . .	Mohill . .	IV.	104
56	Greenaun . .	2,240 2 37	Mayo . .	Erris . .	Kilcommon .	Newport . .	IV.	144
30	Greenaun . .	287 0 17j	Mayo . .	Tirawley . .	Ardagh . .	Ballina . .	IV.	163
10, 14	Greenaun North .	192 3 28	Leitrim . .	Drumahaire .	Drumlease .	Manorhamilton .	IV.	94
10, 14	Greenaun South .	147 2 6	Leitrim . .	Drumahaire .	Drumlease .	Manorhamilton .	IV.	94
24	Greenbatter . .	116 0 2	Louth . .	Drogheda . .	St. Peter's .	Drogheda .	I.	175
5	Greenbrae . .	110 0 4k	Tyrone . .	Strabane Lower .	Leckpatrick .	Strabane .	III.	322
56, 57	Green Castle . .	430 3 36	Antrim . .	Upper Belfast .	Shankill . .	Belfast . .	III.	10
57	Greencastle . .	626 2 21l	Down . .	Mourne . .	Kilkeel . .	Kilkeel . .	III.	183
67	Greencloyne . .	33 3 38	Cork, E.R. .	Imokilly . .	Youghal . .	Youghal . .	II.	91
105	Greeneenagh . .	71 3 9	Galway . .	Loughrea . .	Loughrea . .	Loughrea .	IV.	65
23	Greenfield . .	249 3 22m	Cork, E.R. .	Duhallow . .	Clonfert . .	Kanturk . .	II.	68
73	Greenfield . .	130 0 28	Cork, E.R. .	East Muskerry .	Kilnaglory . .	Cork . .	II.	104
144	Greenfield . .	44 2 26	Cork, W.R. .	Ibane and Barryroe	Kilkerranmore .	Clonakilty .	II.	149
69	Greenfield . .	55 2 10	Donegal . .	Raphoe . .	Convoy . .	Stranorlar .	III.	136

(a) Including 29A. 3R. 10P. water.
(b) Including 1A. 1R. 8P. water.
(c) Including 5A. 3R. 18P. water.
(d) Including 10A. 3R. 20P. water.
(e) Including 14A. 2R. 27P. water.
(f) Including 1A. 1R. 28P. Lough Brickland.
(g) Including 0A. 3R. 30P. water.
(h) Including 2A. 3R. 0P. water.
(i) Including 14A. 1R. 10P. water.
(j) Including 21A. 1R. 26P. water.
(k) Including 2A. 2R. 7P. water.
(l) Including 1A. 2R. 32P. Thompson's Island.
Including 1A. 0R. 8P. Island, south of Thompson's Island.
Including 0A. 3R. 8P. Green Island.
Including 0A. 0R. 4P. Block House Island.
(m) Including 3A. 1R. 1P. detached portion.

No. of Sheet of the Ordnance Survey Maps.	Townlands and Towns.	Area in Statute Acres.	County.	Barony.	Parish.	Poor Law Union in 1857.	Townland Census of 1851, Part I.	
		A. R. P.					Vol.	Page
5, 10	Greenfield	197 0 30	Kildare	North Salt	Laraghbryan	Celbridge	I.	75
51	Greenfield	382 2 0	Tipperary, S.R.	Kilnamanagh Lower	Donohill	Tipperary	II.	323
48	Greenfield	66 1 10	Wexford	Forth	Ballymore	Wexford	I.	308
12	Greenfields	55 1 9	Dublin	Nethercross	Swords	Balrothery	I.	32
41	Greenfield or Shanbally	199 0 28	Galway	Clare	Killursa	Tuam	IV.	21
18	Greenfort Demesne	145 3 37	Donegal	Kilmacrenan	Clondavaddog	Millford	III.	125
18	*Greenfort Island*	2 0 15	Donegal	Kilmacrenan	Clondavaddog	Millford	III.	125
5	Greengraves	727 0 39	Down	Castlereagh Lower	Newtownards	Newtownards	III.	163
25, 26	Greenhall	271 0 8	Tipperary, N.R.	Owney and Arra	Killoscully	Nenagh	II.	295
21	Greenhall	80 2 5	Wexford	Ballaghkeen	Kilnamanagh	Gorey	I.	297
43	Greenhall	176 3 28	Wicklow	Shillelagh	Crosspatrick	Shillelagh	I.	357
24	Greenhall Lower	100 3 20	Kildare	Naas South	Tipperkevin	Naas	I.	65
21	Greenhall Lower	102 3 22	Longford	Rathcline	Cashel	Ballymahon	I.	163
24	Greenhall Upper	77 0 22	Kildare	Naas South	Tipperkevin	Naas	I.	65
21	Greenhall Upper	231 2 33	Longford	Rathcline	Cashel	Ballymahon	I.	163
38	Greenhill	852 1 4	Antrim	Lower Antrim	Glenwhirry	Ballymena	III.	4
42	Greenhill	657 0 17	Cork, E.R.	Barretts	Mourneabbey	Mallow	II.	50
53	Greenhill	100 2 9	Donegal	Kilmacrenan	Aghanunshin	Letterkenny	III.	122
25	Greenhill	166 3 37a	Donegal	Kilmacrenan	Clondahorky	Dunfanaghy	III.	123
23	Greenhill	130 2 31	Fermanagh	Magherastephana	Aghavea	Lisnaskea	III.	219
13	Greenhill	258 3 34	Kilkenny	Crannagh	Killahy	Urlingford	I.	86
52	Green Hill Demesne	254 0 24	Tyrone	Clogher	Errigal Keerogue	Clogher	III.	295
78	Greenhills	8 2 15	Donegal	Raphoe	Stranorlar	Stranorlar	III.	142
22	Greenhills	188 0 11	Dublin	Uppercross	Crumlin	Dublin South	I.	39
73, 86	Greenhills	392 2 22	Galway	Kilconnell	Ballymacward	Ballinasloe	IV.	39
23, 28	Greenhills	419 0 3b	Kildare	Connell	Kildare	Naas	I.	55
19	Greenhills	199 3 30	Kildare	South Salt	Kill	Naas	I.	77
4	Greenhills	399 1 17	King's Co.	Warrenstown	Ballyburly	Edenderry	I.	144
13, 22	Greenhills	574 3 21	Limerick	Pubblebrien	Knocknagaul	Limerick	II.	253
6	Greenhills	148 1 24	Meath	Lower Slane	Siddan	Ardee	I.	223
16, 22	Greenhills	204 0 17	Tipperary, N.R.	Ikerrin	Cullenwaine	Roscrea	II.	275
25	Greenhills	197 0 16	Tipperary, N.R.	Owney and Arra	Kilmastulla	Nenagh	II.	295
22	GREEN HILLS T.	—	Dublin	Uppercross	Tallaght	Dublin South	I.	42
10	*Greenish Island*	46 1 19	Limerick	Connello Lower	Tomdeely	Rathkeale	II.	230
62	*Green Island*	14 3 30	Clare	Bunratty Lower	Kilfintinan	Limerick	II.	5
2	*Green Island*	0 3 35	Clare	Burren	Drumcreehy	Ballyvaghan	II.	12
20	*Green Island*	5 2 10	Clare	Tulla Upper	Feakle	Scarriff	II.	39
98	*Green Island*	2 2 2	Donegal	Banagh	Killaghtee	Donegal	III.	110
17	*Green Island*	1 1 36	Donegal	Kilmacrenan	Clondavaddog	Millford	III.	125
25	*Green Island*	2 1 10	Down	Ards Upper	St. Andrews (*alias*) Ballyhalbert	Newtownards	III.	161
17	*Green Island*	7 2 2	Down	Dufferin	Killinchy	Downpatrick	III.	166
31	*Green Island*	12 3 6	Down	Lecale Lower	Saul	Downpatrick	III.	180
112	*Green Island*	0 0 28	Galway	Kiltartan	Kinvarradoorus	Gort	IV.	50
120, 123	*Green Island*	2 0 26	Mayo	Kilmaine	Cong	Ballinrobe	IV.	154
6	*Green Island*	1 2 11	Roscommon	Boyle	Ardcarn	Boyle	IV.	193
35, 40	Greenland	88 1 29	Antrim	Upper Glenarm	Larne	Larne	III.	25
14	Greenlane	150 2 36	Louth	Ardee	Charlestown	Ardee	I.	171
10	Greenlane	259 3 8	Tipperary, N.R.	Lower Ormond	Finnoe	Borrisokane	II	284
19	Greenlanes	358 0 30	Dublin	Coolock	Clontarf	Dublin North	I.	26
2, 5	Greenlaw	158 3 17c	Tyrone	Strabane Lower	Leckpatrick	Strabane	III.	322
140	Greenmount	355 1 24	Cork, W.R.	West Carbery (W.D.)	Kilcoe	Skull	II.	143
18	Greenmount	8 2 20	Dublin	Coolock	St. Georges	Dublin North	I.	29
20, 25	Greenmount	122 0 18	Kildare	Naas North	Rathmore	Naas	I.	62
12, 13	Greenmount	301 2 31	Limerick	Pubblebrien	Crecora	Croom	II.	252
15	Greenmount	533 3 12	Louth	Ardee	Kilsaran	Ardee	I.	173
10	Greenmount	97 0 17	Monaghan	Cremorne	Clontibret	Monaghan	II.	260
88	Greenmount	268 0 17d	Tipperary, S.R.	Iffa and Offa West	Molough	Clogheen	II.	318
15	GREENMOUNT T.	—	Louth	Ardee	Kilsaran	Ardee	I.	173
20, 21	Greenoge	376 3 4	Down	Lower Iveagh, Lr. pt.	Dromore	Banbridge	III.	168
21	Greenoge	217 0 2	Dublin	Newcastle	Rathcoole	Celbridge	I.	34
45	Greenoge	687 3 17	Meath	Ratoath	Greenoge	Dunshaughlin	I.	218
45	GREENOGE T.	—	Meath	Ratoath	Greenoge	Dunshaughlin	I.	218
9	Greenore	257 2 4	Louth	Lower Dundalk	Carlingford	Dundalk	I.	176
59	Greenrath	196 2 39	Tipperary, S.R.	Clanwilliam	Tipperary	Tipperary	II.	312
14, 15, 19	Greenridge	163 0 0	Kilkenny	Gowran	St. John's	Kilkenny	I.	98
17	Greenshields Lower	196 1 31	Antrim	Upper Dunluce	Ballymoney	Ballymoney	III.	19
17	Greenshields Upper	145 3 37	Antrim	Upper Dunluce	Ballymoney	Ballymoney	III.	19
78	Greensland	37 1 32	Tipperary, S.R.	Iffa and Offa East	Kilsheelan	Clonmel	II.	314
32	Greentown or Knocknabrattoge	209 1 24	Fermanagh	Clanawley	Killesher	Enniskillen	III.	193
17	Greenville	121 1 31	Antrim	Upper Dunluce	Ballymoney	Ballymoney	III.	19

(a) Including 19A. 0R. 27P. water.
(b) Including 7A. 3R. 0P. water.
(c) { Including 4A. 2R. 19P. water. / Including 0A. 3R. 2P. Island.
(d) Including 7A. 0R. 25P. water.

No. of Sheet of the Ordnance Survey Maps.	Townlands and Towns.	Area in Statute Acres.	County.	Barony.	Parish.	Poor Law Union in 1857.	Townland Census of 1851, Part I.	
		A. R. P.					Vol.	Page
83	Greenville	454 2 22a	Cork, W.R.	West Muskerry	Kilmichael	Macroom	II.	159
46, 60	Greenville	410 3 19	Galway	Tiaquin	Killosolan	Mountbellew	IV.	78
43	Greenville	273 0 32	Kilkenny	Ida	Dunkitt	Waterford	I.	101
20	Greenville	92 0 14	Wexford	Scarawalsh	St. MarysEnniscorthy	Enniscorthy	I.	325
1, 2, 7, 8	Greenville or Garryduff	185 0 23	King's Co.	Kilcoursey	Kilmanaghan	Tullamore	I.	141
15	Greenwood	111 3 36	Dublin	Coolock	Kinsaley	Balrothery	I.	28
92	Greenwood	278 2 39b	Mayo	Costello	Bekan	Claremorris	IV.	139
29	Greenwood	40 3 38	Tipperary, N.R.	Eliogarty	Templemore	Thurles	II.	272
26	Greenwoodhill	79 3 35	Fermanagh	Clanawley	Cleenish	Enniskillen	III.	191
29	Greenwoodpark	270 2 22	Mayo	Tirawley	Kilfian	Ballina	IV.	169
20, 21	Greerstown or Cloghore	182 2 19	Londonderry	Tirkeeran	Clondermot	Londonderry	III.	247
96	Greethill	248 3 27	Galway	Athenry	Athenry	Loughrea	IV.	4
24	Greetiagh	226 0 9	Meath	Lower Navan	Martry	Kells	I.	215
78	Greeve Island	1 3 8	Galway	Ballynahinch	Moyrus	Clifden	IV.	14
25	Gregmoher	16 0 39c	Clare	Inchiquin	Ruan	Corrofin	II.	28
20	Gregorlough	246 3 28	Down	Lower Iveagh,Up.pt.	Magheralin	Lurgan	III.	170
42	Gregorystown	31 0 22	Wexford	Forth	Rathmacknee	Wexford	I.	313
100	Gregstown	86 0 17	Donegal	Tirhugh	Donegal	Donegal	III.	145
6	Gregstown	129 1 37	Down	Ards Lower	Newtownards	Newtownards	III.	158
27	Grehanstown	282 0 9	Westmeath	Farbill	Killucan	Mullingar	I.	267
26	Grellagh	344 2 17	Cavan	Upper Loughtee	Lavey	Cavan	III.	86
3	Grellagh	418 0 13	Sligo	Carbury	Ahamlish	Sligo	IV.	219
65, 66	Grenagh	299 1 23d	Kerry	Magunihy	Aghadoe	Killarney	II.	199
51	Grenagh North	476 1 17	Cork, E.R.	Barretts	Grenagh	Cork	II.	49
51	Grenagh South	390 3 6	Cork, E.R.	Barretts	Grenagh	Cork	II.	49
28, 32	Grenan	653 0 12e	Kilkenny	Gowran	Thomastown	Thomastown	I.	99
29, 35	Grenan	519 2 36	Queen's Co.	Clarmallagh	Attanagh	Abbeyleix	I.	237
29, 35	Grenan	494 3 24f	Queen's Co.	Clarmallagh	Durrow	Abbeyleix	I.	237
29, 35	Grenan	139 1 36	Queen's Co.	Clarmallagh	Rosconnell	Abbeyleix	I.	238
21, 27	Grenanstown	655 0 3	Tipperary, N.R.	Upper Ormond	Ballymackey	Nenagh	II.	289
21, 27	Grenanstown	284 3 10	Tipperary, N.R.	Upper Ormond	Kilkeary	Nenagh	II.	290
23, 29	Grennanstown	704 2 7	Meath	Lune	Athboy	Trim	I.	207
54	GRENVILLE T.		Tyrone	Dungannon Middle {	Clonfeacle Donaghmore }	Dungannon	III.	{300 }302
15	Gresteel Beg	351 1 32	Londonderry	Tirkeeran	Faughanvale	NewT⁰Limavady	III.	250
15	Gresteel More	192 0 36	Londonderry	Tirkeeran	Faughanvale	NewT⁰Limavady	III.	250
10, 11	Greville	32 2 39	Longford	Granard	Granard	Granard	I.	156
23	Grevine East	385 0 23	Kilkenny	Shillelogher	Outrath	Kilkenny	I.	115
23	Grevine West	130 2 36	Kilkenny	Shillelogher	Outrath	Kilkenny	I.	115
6	Grevisk	146 3 1	Roscommon	Boyle	Ardcarn	Boyle	IV.	193
11, 12	Grey Abbey	208 0 34	Down	Ards Lower	Greyabbey	Newtownards	III.	158
22	Greyabbey	169 2 27	Kildare	Offaly East	Kildare	Naas	I.	70
11, 12	GREYABBEY T.		Down	Ards Lower	Greyabbey	Newtownards	III.	158
18	Greyfield	88 0 31	Leitrim	Drumahaire	Inishmagrath	Manorhamilton	IV.	96
4	Greyfield	189 1 24g	Roscommon	Boyle	Kilronan	Boyle	IV.	197
44	Greyfield	264 0 8	Sligo	Coolavin	Kilfree	Boyle	IV.	224
39	Greyfield	101 2 24	Sligo	Corran	Kilshalvy	Boyle	IV.	227
39	Greyfield	100 1 24h	Sligo	Corran	Toomour	Boyle	IV.	228
121	Greyfield or Clylea	92 2 19	Mayo	Kilmaine	Kilmainemore	Ballinrobe	IV.	156
85, 96, 97	Greyford	365 0 38	Galway	Athenry	Kiltullagh	Loughrea	IV.	5
10	Greyfort	234 0 29	Tipperary, N.R.	Lower Ormond	Borrisokane	Borrisokane	II.	282
48	Greygrove	667 0 22	Clare	Clonderalaw	Kilmihil	Kilrush	II.	17
21	Greyhillan	205 1 23	Armagh	Orior Upper	Loughgilly	Newry	III.	58
21	Greystone	76 3 36	Fermanagh	Magheraboy	Rossorry	Enniskillen	III.	214
8	GREYSTONES T.		Wicklow	Rathdown	Delgany	Rathdown	I.	355
11	Griffinrath	472 3 26	Kildare	North Salt	Laraghbryan	Celbridge	I.	75
60	Griffins Island	0 0 19	Mayo	Tirawley	Ballynahaglish	Ballina	IV.	164
25	Griffinstown	250 3 22	Kilkenny	Gowran	Ullard	Thomastown	I.	100
27	Griffinstown	1,676 2 28	Westmeath	Farbill	Killucan	Mullingar	I.	267
14, 20	Griffinstown Glen	111 1 12	Wicklow	Upper Talbotstown	Ballynure	Baltinglass	I.	361
20	Griffinstown Hill	267 1 27	Wicklow	Upper Talbotstown	Ballynure	Baltinglass	I.	361
20, 21	Griffinstown Lower	203 1 25	Wicklow	Upper Talbotstown	Ballynure	Baltinglass	I.	362
20, 21	Griffinstown Upper	252 0 30	Wicklow	Upper Talbotstown	Ballynure	Baltinglass	I.	362
19, 20	Grig	191 0 23	Monaghan	Cremorne	Clontibret	Castleblayney	III.	260
12, 25	Griggins	1,513 2 32	Galway	Ross	Ross	Oughterard	IV.	74
6, 9	Griggy	133 0 5	Monaghan	Trough	Donagh	Monaghan	III.	282
108	Grillagh	316 2 0	Cork, W.R.	East Carbery (E.D.)	Ballymoney	Dunmanway	II.	127
122, 135	Grillagh	136 0 29	Cork. W.R.	East Carbery (E.D.)	Kilnagross	Clonakilty	II.	129
32	Grillagh	281 2 2	Limerick	Coshma	Tullabracky	Kilmallock	II.	244
39	Grillagh	254 1 38	Londonderry	Loughinsholin	Maghera	Magherafelt	III.	242
19	Grillagh	135 0 12	Longford	Ardagh	Ardagh	Longford	I.	151

(a) Including 11A. 1R. 14P. water.
(b) Including 27A. 0R. 24P. water.
(c) Including 3A. 0R. 11P. water.

(d) Including 6A. 2R. 32P. water.
(e) Including 23A. 1R. 11P. River Nore.
(f) Including 2A. 0R. 19P. detached portion.

(g) Including 3A. 2R. 7P. water.
(h) Including 3A. 0R. 28P. water.

No. of Sheet of the Ordnance Survey Maps.	Townlands and Towns.	Area in Statute Acres.	County.	Barony.	Parish.	Poor Law Union in 1857.	Townland Census of 1851, Part I.	
		A. R. P.					Vol.	Page
18	Grillagh . . .	192 3 33	Longford . .	Moydow . . .	Killashee . .	Longford . .	I.	161
15	Grillough . .	356 1 1	Cork, E.R. .	Duhallow . .	Clonfert . .	Kanturk . .	II.	68
15	Grillough . .	7 0 33a	Cork, E.R. .	Duhallow . .	Kilcorcoran .	Kanturk . .	II.	72
11	Grilly . . .	171 3 21b	Cavan . .	Lower Loughtee .	Annagh . . .	Cavan . . .	III.	79
49	Griston East .	233 1 25	Limerick . .	Coshlea . . .	Ballingarry . .	Kilmallock . .	II.	237
49, 57	Griston West .	197 2 13	Limerick . .	Coshlea . .	Ballingarry . .	Kilmallock . .	II.	237
26, 35	Grogagh . . .	126 1 30	Donegal . .	Kilmacrenan .	Clondahorky .	Dunfanaghy .	III.	123
5	Grogagh . .	192 1 10	Sligo . . .	Carbury . .	Ahamlish . .	Sligo . . .	IV.	219
40, 43, 44	Grogan . . .	407 2 9	Kilkenny . .	Ida . . .	Kilcolumb . .	Waterford . .	I.	102
27, 28	Grogan . .	156 2 21	Queen's Co. .	Clandonagh . .	Rathsaran . .	Donaghmore .	I.	234
53	Grogan . . .	78 3 1	Wexford . .	Forth . . .	Tacumshin . .	Wexford . .	I.	315
52, 53	Grogan Burrow .	134 3 38	Wexford . .	Forth . . .	Tacumshin . .	Wexford . .	I.	315
7	Grogan and Corroe .	375 1 21	King's Co. .	Garrycastle . .	Lemanaghan .	Parsonstown .	I.	136
11	Grogeen . . .	95 1 8	Kerry . . .	Clanmaurice . .	Finuge . . .	Listowel . .	II.	169
24, 29	Grogey . . .	1,014 2 38	Fermanagh .	Magherastephana .	Aghalurcher .	Lisnaskea . .	III.	216
43	Groggan . . .	620 3 28	Antrim . .	Upper Toome . .	Drummaul . .	Ballymena . .	III.	34
56, 57	Groin . . .	177 2 8	Kerry . .	Dunkerron North .	Killorglin . .	Killarney . .	II.	181
66	Groin . . .	67 3 30	Kerry . .	Magunihy . .	Aghadoe . .	Killarney . .	II.	199
21	Groom . . .	33 0 20	Louth . .	Ferrard . . .	Mullary . .	Drogheda . .	I.	181
2	Groomsport . .	316 0 32	Down . . .	Ards Lower . .	Bangor . .	Newtownards .	III.	157
2	GROOMSPORT T. .	—	Down . .	Ards Lower . .	Bangor . .	Newtownards .	III.	157
37	Grousehall . .	288 3 7	Cavan . .	Clanmahon . .	Drumlumman .	Granard . .	III.	77
102	Grousehall . .	2,037 3 36	Donegal . .	Tirhugh . . .	Templecarn . .	Donegal . .	III.	149
33, 39	Grousehall . .	468 1 21	Tipperary, N.R. .	Kilnamanagh Upper .	Upperchurch .	Thurles . .	II.	280
19, 28	Grouselodge . .	363 2 3	Limerick . .	Shanid . .	Kilcolman . .	Glin . . .	II.	255
24, 31	Grouselodge or Coola-toor . . .	122 2 16	Westmeath .	Moycashel . .	Kilcumreragh .	Athlone . .	I.	278
94, 95, 103	Grousemount . .	1,609 1 15	Kerry . . .	Glanarought . .	Kilgarvan . .	Kenmare . .	II.	187
43	Grove . . .	72 3 15	Kerry . .	Corkaguiny . .	Dingle . . .	Dingle . .	II.	175
20	Grove . . .	101 2 27	Kilkenny . .	Gowran . .	Blanchvilleskill .	Kilkenny . .	I.	93
25	Grove . . .	169 3 7	Kilkenny . .	Gowran . . .	Powerstown . .	Thomastown .	I.	97
23	Grove . . .	324 0 17	Kilkenny . .	Shillelogher . .	Tullaghanbrogue .	Callan . .	I.	116
31	Grove . . .	9 1 13	Leitrim . .	Leitrim . . .	Kiltoghert . .	Cark. on Shannon	IV.	102
70	Grove . . .	219 3 27	Tipperary, S.R. .	Middlethird . .	Fethard . . .	Cashel . .	II.	327
27	Grovebeg . .	233 2 4	Kilkenny . .	Kells . . .	Kilree . . .	Callan . .	I.	109
22	Grove or Cortullagh	192 2 12	King's Co. .	Garrycastle . .	Gallen . . .	Parsonstown .	I.	136
14	Grove or Cramers-grove . . .	356 3 20	Kilkenny . .	Gowran . . .	Kilkieran . .	Kilkenny . .	I.	97
6	Grove Great . .	184 3 4	Wexford . .	Gorey . . .	Kilnahue . .	Gorey . . .	I.	319
45	Grovehall or New-towngrove . .	196 3 6	Donegal . .	Kilmacrenan . .	Kilmacrenan . .	Millford . .	III.	129
5	Grove Island . .	3 0 29c	Limerick . .	Limerick, Municipal Borough of .	St. Patrick . .	Limerick . .	II.	262
20	Grove Island . .	5 3 34	Meath . . .	Lower Duleek . .	Donore . .	Drogheda . .	I.	195
6	Grove Little . .	99 0 11	Wexford . .	Gorey . . .	Kilnahue . .	Gorey . .	I.	319
6	Grovemill . .	49 2 33	Wexford . .	Gorey . . .	Kilnahue . .	Gorey . .	I.	319
10	Grovesend . .	38 2 1	King's Co. .	Lower Philipstown .	Ballyburly . .	Edenderry . .	I.	142
4, 11	Grovesend or Mooneys-land . . .	92 2 25	King's Co. .	Warrenstown . .	Ballyburly . .	Edenderry . .	I.	144
10	Groves Lower . .	117 1 15	Monaghan .	Cremorne . .	Tehallan . .	Monaghan . .	III.	262
10	Groves Upper . .	122 1 36	Monaghan .	Cremorne . . .	Tehallan . .	Monaghan . .	III.	262
21	Growell . . .	467 1 11d	Down . .	Lower Iveagh, Lr. pt.	Dromore . .	Lisburn . .	III.	168
44, 50	Growtown . .	222 3 31	Meath . .	Ratoath . . .	Ballymaglassan .	Dunshaughlin .	I.	217
44	Growtown . .	307 3 30	Meath . .	Ratoath . . .	Rathbeggan . .	Dunshaughlin .	I.	219
36	Growtown Lower .	233 0 14	Wexford . .	Shelmaliere West .	Coolstuff . .	Wexford . .	I.	333
36	Growtown Upper .	335 2 8	Wexford . .	Shelmaliere West .	Coolstuff . .	Wexford . .	I.	333
23	Gruig . . .	223 2 11	Antrim . .	Kilconway . .	Loughguile . .	Ballymoney .	III.	27
14, 15	Gruig . . .	180 2 26	Antrim . .	Lower Glenarm .	Layd . . .	Ballycastle .	III.	22
17	Guardhill . .	105 1 14	Monaghan .	Dartree . . .	Killeevan . .	Clones . .	III.	268
111	Guardhousepark .	66 3 17	Mayo . . .	Clanmorris . .	Crossboyne . .	Claremorris .	IV.	132
7, 9	Gub . . .	158 2 20	Cavan . .	Tullyhaw . .	Kinawley . .	Bawnboy . .	III.	93
1, 2	Gubacreeny . .	566 2 17	Leitrim . .	Rosclogher . .	Rossinver . .	Ballyshannon .	IV.	111
15	Gubaderry . .	141 0 21	Leitrim . .	Drumahaire . .	Killarga . .	Manorhamilton .	IV.	98
38	Gubadorris . .	447 1 8	Leitrim . .	Mohill . . .	Cloone . . .	Mohill . .	IV.	106
28, 29	Gubadruish . .	129 0 39	Leitrim . .	Mohill . . .	Mohill . . .	Mohill . .	IV.	108
35	Gubagraffy . .	129 1 24e	Leitrim . .	Mohill . . .	Mohill . . .	Mohill . .	IV.	108
5	Gubalaun . .	210 0 31	Leitrim . .	Rosclogher . .	Rossinver . .	Ballyshannon .	IV.	111
54	Gubalennaun-beg .	2 2 31	Mayo . .	Burrishoole . .	Achill . . .	Newport . .	IV.	117
2	Gubanummera .	64 3 13	Leitrim . .	Rosclogher . .	Rossinver . .	Ballyshannon .	IV.	111
3	Gubaveeny . .	1,372 2 1	Cavan . .	Tullyhaw . .	Killinagh . .	Enniskillen .	III.	92
39	Gubb . . .	183 1 4f	Fermanagh .	Coole . . .	Galloon . .	Clones . .	III.	200
18	Gubb . . .	43 2 12	Leitrim . .	Drumahaire . .	Inishmagrath .	Manorhamilton .	IV.	96
26, 32	Gubbacrock . .	121 1 33	Fermanagh .	Clanawley . .	Killesher . .	Enniskillen .	III.	192
5	Gubbakip . .	64 3 0	Fermanagh .	Lurg . . .	Drumkeeran .	Lowtherstown .	III.	206

(a) Including 1A. 2R. 31P. detached portion.   (c) Included in the Parish of St. Patrick.   (e) Including 4A. 2R. 5P. water.
(b) Including 10A. 2R. 16P. water.   (d) Including 51A. 3R. 2P. water.   (f) Including 7A. 3R. 13P. water.

3 X

No. of Sheet of the Ordnance Survey Maps.	Townlands and Towns.	Area in Statute Acres. A. R. P.	County.	Barony.	Parish.	Poor Law Union in 1857.	Townland Census of 1851, Part I. Vol.	Page
5, 10	Gubbaroe	254 1 30	Fermanagh	Lurg	Magheraculmoney	Lowtherstown	III.	208
1, 2	Gubbarudda	357 0 18	Roscommon	Boyle	Kilronan	Boyle	IV.	197
139, 148	Gubbeen	828 3 28	Cork, W.R.	West Carbery (W.D.)	Skull	Skull	II.	146
43	Gubdoo	92 0 16a	Fermanagh	Coole	Drummully	Clones	III.	199
6	Gub or Garvalt Upper	201 2 0	Cavan	Tullyhaw	Templeport	Enniskillen	III.	95
4, 7	Gubinea	496 2 26b	Leitrim	Rosclogher	Killasnet	Manorhamilton	IV.	110
15, 16	Gublusk	162 0 0	Fermanagh	Lurg	Trory	Lowtherstown	III.	209
5	Gubmanus	110 0 8	Leitrim	Rosclogher	Rossinver	Manorhamilton	IV.	111
12	Gubnacurrafore	327 0 29	Leitrim	Drumahaire	Cloonclare	Manorhamilton	IV.	93
7	Gubnafarna	250 3 4	Cavan	Tullyhaw	Kinawley	Bawnboy	III.	93
5	Gubnageer	228 2 21	Leitrim	Rosclogher	Rossinver	Manorhamilton	IV.	111
9	Gubnagree	125 1 15	Cavan	Tullyhaw	Templeport	Bawnboy	III.	95
4	Gubnaguinie	83 1 21	Fermanagh	Lurg	Templecarn	Lowtherstown	III.	209
65	Gubnahardia	159 0 21c	Mayo	Burrishoole	Achill	Newport	IV.	117
21	Gubnaveagh	784 2 38	Leitrim	Carrigallen	Oughteragh	Bawnboy	IV.	92
7, 9	Gubrawully	303 0 23	Cavan	Tullyhaw	Kinawley	Bawnboy	III.	93
7	Gubrimmaddera	65 1 28	Cavan	Tullyhaw	Kinawley	Bawnboy	III.	93
24	Gubroe	118 2 23d	Leitrim	Mohill	Fenagh	Mohill	IV.	106
33	Gubrusdinna	110 0 8e	Fermanagh	Tirkennedy	Cleenish	Enniskillen	III.	220
25, 29	Gubs	333 3 29	Leitrim	Carrigallen	Drumreilly	Bawnboy	IV.	91
14	Gudderstown	296 1 24	Louth	Ardee	Ardee	Ardee	I.	171
22, 30	Guernal	282 3 26	King's Co.	Garrycastle	Gallen	Parsonstown	I.	136
5	Guhard North	315 1 39	Kerry	Iraghticonnor	Lisselton	Listowel	II.	192
5	Guhard South	413 1 24	Kerry	Iraghticonnor	Lisselton	Listowel	II.	192
17, 22	Guidenstown North	182 1 14	Kildare	Offaly East	Rathangan	Naas	I.	71
17, 22, 23	Guidenstown South	273 0 17	Kildare	Offaly East	Rathangan	Naas	I.	71
38	Guigginstown	235 0 34	Westmeath	Moycashel	Kilbeggan	Tullamore	I.	278
8	Guilcagh	780 2 13	Waterford	Upperthird	Guilcagh	Carrick on Suir	II.	370
19	Guileen	36 1 3	Queen's Co.	Stradbally	Timogue	Athy	I.	248
19	Guileen	365 2 5	Queen's Co.	Stradbally	Tullomoy	Athy	I.	248
32, 33	Guilford or Davids-town	179 2 3	Westmeath	Fartullagh	Clonfad	Mullingar	I.	268
36,37,40,41	Guilkagh Beg	68 2 8	Kilkenny	Ida	Listerlin	New Ross	I.	103
36,37,40,41	Guilkagh More	134 1 19	Kilkenny	Ida	Listerlin	New Ross	I.	103
29, 36	Guiness	860 0 34	Down	Kinelarty	Dromara	Downpatrick	III.	176
67	Guiness	145 1 1	Tyrone	Dungannon Lower	Aghaloe	Armagh	III.	297
55	Guineways	65 2 32	Down	Mourne	Kilkeel	Kilkeel	III.	183
55	Guineways Upper	31 3 29	Down	Mourne	Kilkeel	Kilkeel	III.	183
94, 103	Gullaba	765 3 36f	Kerry	Glanarought	Kilgarvan	Kenmare	II.	187
12, 21	Gulladoo	1,086 1 21	Donegal	Inishowen East	Moville Lower	Inishowen	III.	119
34	Gulladoo	630 0 30g	Leitrim	Carrigallen	Carrigallen	Mohill	IV.	89
50	Gulladoo	197 0 22	Tyrone	Omagh East	Donacavey	Omagh	III.	310
37	Gulladuff	383 0 27	Londonderry	Loughinsholin	Maghera	Magherafelt	III.	242
1, 2	Gullane East	402 1 1	Kerry	Iraghticonnor	Kilconly	Listowel	II.	191
1	Gullane Middle	146 1 19	Kerry	Iraghticonnor	Kilconly	Listowel	II.	191
1	Gullane West	150 2 4	Kerry	Iraghticonnor	Kilconly	Listowel	II.	191
60	Gullaun East	328 1 20	Kerry	Magunihy	Kilcummin	Killarney	II.	201
60	Gullaun West	405 2 26	Kerry	Magunihy	Kilcummin	Killarney	II.	201
72	Gull Island	3 2 19	Donegal	Banagh	Glencolumbkille	Glenties	III.	106
27	Gull Island	3 2 21	Donegal	Kilmacrenan	Kilmacrenan	Milford	III.	130
17	Gull Rock	0 1 34	Down	Castlereagh Lower	Tullynakill	Newtownards	III.	163
10	Gull Rock	0 1 33	Fermanagh	Lurg	Derryvullan	Lowtherstown	III.	205
110	Gully	228 2 17	Cork, W.R.	Kinalmeaky	Ballymodan	Bandon	II.	151
64	Gunnell	88 2 29h	Tyrone	Clogher	Clogher	Clogher	III.	293
50, 51	Gunnocks	517 3 9i	Meath	Dunboyne	Dunboyne	Dunshaughlin	I.	199
32, 46	Gunnode	632 0 30	Galway	Killian	Killian	Mountbellew	IV.	44
148	Gunpoint	135 0 17	Cork, W.R.	West Carbery (W.D.)	Skull	Skull	II.	146
39	Guns Island	53 3 1	Down	Lecale Lower	Dunsfort	Downpatrick	III.	179
18, 21	Gunstown	155 1 3	Louth	Ardee	Mosstown	Ardee	I.	174
45	Gunstown	43 1 11	Meath	Ratoath	Ratoath	Dunshaughlin	I.	219
68	Gurlaun Island	1 2 16	Galway	Moycullen	Killannin	Oughterard	IV.	70
46	Gurlins	125 2 34	Wexford	Bargy	Duncormick	Wexford	I.	305
105, 118	Gurraghy	113 0 35	Cork, W.R.	Bantry	Kilmocomoge	Bantry	II.	121
142	Gurranes	163 1 3	Cork, W.R.	West Carbery (E.D.)	Castlehaven	Skibbereen	II.	138
29, 30	Gurraun	240 1 15	Queen's Co.	Clarmallagh	Rosconnell	Abbeyleix	I.	238
70	Gurraunard	162 3 25j	Mayo	Gallen	Templemore	Castlebar	IV.	151
13, 14	Gurrawirra	788 2 3	King's Co.	Garrycastle	Clonmacnoise	Parsonstown	I.	135
19	Gurrig Island	8 2 16	Kerry	Corkaguiny	Killiney	Dingle	II.	178
54, 55	Gurteen	724 2 6	Cork, E.R.	Barrymore	Clonmult	Middleton	II.	53
31	Gurteen	536 3 5k	Cork, E.R.	Duhallow	Drumtarriff	Kanturk	II.	71
73	Gurteen	176 3 12	Cork, E.R.	East Muskerry	Inishcarra	Cork	II.	103
35	Gurteen	256 3 0l	Cork, E.R.	Fermoy	Killathy	Fermoy	II.	80
118	Gurteen	126 1 17	Cork, W.R.	Bantry	Durrus	Bantry	II.	119

(a) Including 13A. 2R. 15P. water.
(b) Including 33A. 1R. 37P. water.
(c) Including 18A. 3R. 7P. detached portion.
(d) Including 25A. 1R. 32P. water.

(e) Including 24A. 3R. 10P. water.
(f) Including 14A. 0R. 3P. water.
(g) Including 84A. 0R. 4P. water.
(h) Including 3A. 1R. 32P. water.

(i) Including 20A. 2R. 7P. detached portions.
(j) Including 8A. 2R. 37P. water.
(k) Including 6A. 0R. 8P. water.
(l) Including 5A. 2R. 35P. water.

No. of Sheet of the Ordnance Survey Maps.	Townlands and Towns.	Area in Statute Acres.	County.	Barony.	Parish.	Poor Law Union in 1857.	Townland Census of 1851, Part I.	
		A. R. P.					Vol.	Page
93	Gurteen . . .	177 2 5	Cork, W.R.	East Carbery (W.D.)	Kilmichael . .	Dunmanway .	II.	134
109, 110	Gurteen . . .	256 1 30	Cork, W.R.	Kinalmeaky . .	Ballymodan .	Bandon . .	II.	151
96	Gurteen . . .	578 0 21	Cork, W.R.	Kinalmeaky . .	Kilbrogan . .	Bandon . .	II.	152
44, 54	Gurteen . . .	533 0 35	Kerry . .	Corkaguiny . .	Ballinvoher .	Dingle . .	II.	174
44	Gurteen . . .	30 3 39	Kerry . .	Corkaguiny . .	Ballynacourty .	Dingle . .	II.	174
94	Gurteen . . .	445 2 37	Kerry . .	Glanarought . .	Kilgarvan . .	Kenmare . .	II.	187
79, 80	Gurteen . . .	343 3 28	Kerry . .	Iveragh . .	Caher . . .	Cahersiveen .	II.	194
26	Gurteen . . .	303 0 6	Queen's Co. .	Slievemargy .	Killabban . .	Carlow . .	I.	245
8	Gurteen . . .	312 3 17	Tipperary, N.R.	Lower Ormond .	Ballingarry .	Borrisokane .	II.	282
2, 5	Gurteen . . .	549 3 21	Tipperary, N.R.	Lower Ormond .	Dorrha . . .	Parsonstown .	II.	283
8	Gurteen . . .	414 3 23	Tipperary, N.R.	Lower Ormond .	Loughkeen .	Borrisokane .	II.	286
27, 28	Gurteen . . .	71 3 17	Tipperary, N.R.	Upper Ormond .	Latteragh . .	Nenagh . .	II.	292
133	Gurteenaduige .	290 0 9	Cork, W.R.	East Carbery (W.D.)	Kilmacabea . .	Skibbereen .	II.	133
23	Gurteenard . .	329 3 33	Cork, E.R.	Duhallow . .	Clonmeen .	Kanturk . .	II.	69
74	Gurteenaspig .	45 3 31a	Cork, E.R.	Cork, and Municipal Borough . .	St. Finbars .	Cork . .	II.	66
3	Gurteenavallig .	277 1 2	Kerry . .	Iraghticonnor .	Kilnaughtin .	Glin . . .	II.	191
31	Gurteenbeha .	296 2 13b	Cork, E.R.	Duhallow . .	Castlemagner .	Kanturk . .	II.	67
71	Gurteen (Bryan) .	207 3 15	Tipperary, S.R.	Slievardagh . .	Kilvemnon .	Callan . .	II.	335
68	Gurteenflugh . .	235 3 31	Cork, W.R.	West Muskerry .	Inchigeelagh .	Macroom .	II.	157
119	Gurteeniher . .	362 3 25	Cork, W.R.	West Carbery (E.D.)	Dromdaleague .	Skibbereen .	II.	140
76, 77	Gurteenina .	124 1 26	Cork, E.R.	Imokilly . .	Ballyoughtera .	Middleton .	II.	84
76, 77	Gurteenina . .	42 1 9	Cork, E.R.	Imokilly . .	Cloyne . .	Middleton .	II.	85
2	Gurteen Lower .	408 1 29c	Waterford .	Upperthird . .	Kilsheelan .	Clonmel . .	II.	370
11, 20	Gurteennaboul .	223 1 6	Cork, E.R.	Condons&Clangibbon	Brigown . .	Mitchelstown .	II.	59
32	Gurteennacloona .	189 1 30	Cork, E.R.	Duhallow . .	Roskeen . .	Kanturk . .	II.	75
6	Gurteennacloona .	402 3 9	Kerry . .	Iraghticonnor .	Aghavallen .	Listowel . .	II.	189
131, 140	Gurteennakilla .	520 3 7	Cork, W.R.	West Carbery(W.D.)	Skull . .	Skull . . .	II.	146
108	Gurteennasowna .	508 3 39	Cork, W.R.	East Carbery (W.D.)	Fanlobbus .	Dunmanway .	II.	132
44	Gurteen North .	63 2 16	Kerry . .	Corkaguiny . .	Ballynacourty .	Dingle . .	II.	174
68, 80	Gurteenowen . .	142 1 38	Cork, W.R.	West Muskerry .	Inchigeelagh .	Macroom . .	II.	157
63, 64	Gurteen(Pennefather)	459 3 13	Tipperary, S.R.	Slievardagh . .	Kilvemnon .	Callan . .	II.	335
16	Gurteenroe . .	433 2 0	Cork, E.R.	Orrery and Kilmore	Churchtown .	Mallow . .	II.	107
105, 118	Gurteenroe . .	260 3 5d	Cork, W.R.	Bantry . . .	Kilmocomoge .	Bantry . .	II.	121
108, 109	Gurteenroe . .	291 2 29	Cork, W.R.	East Carbery (W.D.)	Kinneigh . .	Dunmanway .	II.	134
141	Gurteenroe . .	128 1 37	Cork, W.R.	West Carbery (E.D.)	Aghadown .	Skibbereen .	II.	137
140	Gurteenroe . .	234 3 26	Cork, W.R.	West Carbery(W.D.)	Skull . .	Skull . . .	II.	146
70, 71	Gurteenroe . .	447 2 26	Cork, W.R.	West Muskerry .	Macroom . .	Macroom . .	II.	160
48	Gurteenroe . .	288 1 37	Kerry . .	Magunihy . .	Molahiffe .	Killarney . .	II.	205
16	Gurteenroe Commons	51 1 20	Cork, E.R.	Orrery and Kilmore	Churchtown .	Mallow . .	II.	107
131, 140	Gurteenulla . .	151 3 28	Cork, W.R.	West Carbery(W.D.)	Kilcoe . .	Skull . . .	II.	143
2	Gurteen Upper .	1,531 3 38	Waterford .	Upperthird . .	Kilsheelan .	Clonmel . .	II.	370
83	Gurtnafleur . .	71 3 2	Tipperary, S.R.	Iffa and Offa East .	Kilgrant . .	Clonmel . .	II.	314
71	Gurtnapisha . .	667 1 4	Tipperary, S.R.	Middlethird . .	Cloneen . .	Cashel . .	II.	325
1, 2	Gushedy Beg . .	144 2 11	Fermanagh .	Lurg . . .	Drumkeeran .	Lowtherstown .	III.	206
1, 2	Gushedy More .	273 2 19	Fermanagh .	Lurg . . .	Drumkeeran .	Lowtherstown .	III.	206
132	Gut Island . .	2 0 13	Galway . .	Leitrim . . .	Ballynakill .	Portumna .	IV.	52
70	Guystown . .	113 1 15	Donegal . .	Raphoe . .	Clonleigh .	Strabane . .	III.	135
135	Gweeneeny . .	92 0 5	Galway . .	Leitrim . .	Clonrush .	Scarriff . .	IV.	53
25	Gweesalia . .	997 0 11	Mayo . .	Erris . . .	Kilcommon .	Belmullet .	IV.	144
90	Gweeshadan . .	214 1 26	Mayo . .	Carra . . .	Drum . . .	Castlebar . .	IV.	128
100	GYLEEN T. . .	—	Cork, E.R.	Imokilly . . .	Corkbeg . . .	Middleton .	II.	86
62, 70	Habbitstown . .	73 2 38	Donegal . .	Raphoe . .	Raphoe . .	Strabane . .	III.	141
18, 25	Habsborough . .	216 3 38	Westmeath .	Moyashel and Magheradernon . .	Mullingar .	Mullingar .	I.	275
15	Hackelty . .	35 0 22e	Cavan . .	Lower Loughtee .	Annagh . .	Cavan . .	III.	79
124	Hacketstown . .	182 0 25	Cork, W.R.	East Carbery (E.D.)	Templetrine .	Kinsale . .	II.	130
5	Hacketstown . .	170 0 36	Dublin . .	Balrothery East .	Lusk . . .	Balrothery .	I.	21
39	Hacketstown . .	193 3 31	Waterford .	Decies within Drum	Ardmore .	Dungarvan .	II.	350
8, 16	Hacketstown . .	304 3 28	Waterford .	Middlethird .	Newcastle .	Waterford .	II.	368
4, 5	Hacketstown Lower	191 2 10	Carlow . .	Rathvilly . .	Hacketstown .	Shillelagh .	I.	11
4	HACKETSTOWN T. .	—	Carlow . .	Rathvilly . .	Hacketstown .	Shillelagh .	I.	11
4, 5	Hacketstown Upper	76 2 7	Carlow . .	Rathvilly . .	Hacketstown .	Shillelagh .	I.	11
26	Hackettsland . .	44 3 27	Dublin . .	Rathdown . .	Killiney . .	Rathdown .	I.	36
49, 56	Hackincon . .	173 1 26	Tyrone . .	Omagh East . .	Kilskeery .	Lowtherstown .	III.	313
17	Hacklim . . .	183 1 30	Louth . .	Ardee . . .	Kildemock .	Ardee . .	I.	173
10	Hacknahay . .	100 2 7f	Armagh . .	Oneilland East .	Seagoe . .	Lurgan . .	III.	50
62, 63	Hagfield or Treanacally	860 0 5	Mayo . .	Costello . .	Kilbeagh . .	Swineford .	IV.	141
3, 8	Haggard . . .	536 2 1	Kildare . .	Carbury . .	Carbury . .	Edenderry .	I.	51
40	Haggard . . .	543 3 7	Kilkenny . .	Ida . . .	Kilmakevoge .	Waterford .	I.	103
27	Haggard . . .	172 2 29	Kilkenny . .	Kells . . .	Kilree . . .	Callan . .	I.	109
45, 50	Haggard . . .	240 0 22	Wexford . .	Bargy . . .	Bannow . .	Wexford . .	I.	304

(a) { Within the Municipal Boundary, 11A. 1R. 18P. / Without the Municipal Boundary, 34A. 2R. 13P.   (c) Including 18A. 3R. 22P. water.   (e) Including 9A. 3R. 0P. water.
(b) Including 12A. 1R. 20P. water.   (d) Including 30A. 1R. 7P. water.   (f) Including 47A. 3R. 16P. detached portion.

No. of Sheet of the Ordnance Survey Maps.	Townlands and Towns.	Area in Statute Acres.			County.	Barony.	Parish.	Poor Law Union in 1857.	Townland Census of 1851, Part I.	
		A.	R.	P.					Vol.	Page
44	Haggard . . .	620	3	0	Wexford . .	Shelburne . .	Rathroe . . .	New Ross . .	I.	328
49, 50	Haggard . . .	294	3	10	Wexford . .	Shelburne . .	Templetown . .	New Ross . .	I.	328
7, 12	Haggardstown .	1,400	0	21	Louth . .	Upper Dundalk .	Haggardstown .	Dundalk . .	I.	178
47	Haggardtown . .	59	1	3	Wexford . .	Forth . . .	Mayglass . .	Wexford . .	I.	312
26	Haggartsgreen .	109	1	34	Kilkenny . .	Callan . . .	Callan . . .	Callan . .	I.	83
8	Halfcarton . .	298	2	24	Meath . .	Fore . . .	Killeagh . .	Oldcastle . .	I.	201
52	Halfcartron . .	339	1	27a	Galway . .	Moycullen . .	Kilcummin . .	Oughterard .	IV.	67
10	Halfcartron . .	48	0	39	Longford . .	Granard . .	Granard . .	Granard . .	I.	156
32	Halfgayne . .	257	2	36	Londonderry .	Loughinsholin .	Killelagh . .	Magherafelt .	III.	241
76	Halfmace . .	119	0	27b	Galway . .	Ballynahinch . .	Moyrus . .	Clifden . .	IV.	13
40	Halfmiletown . .	22	3	12	Kildare . .	Kilkea and Moone .	Castledermot .	Athy . . .	I.	59
20	Halfquarter . .	99	0	34	Sligo . .	Leyny . . .	Ballysadare .	Sligo . .	IV.	230
13, 19	Halfquarter . .	78	0	17	Sligo . .	Tireragh . .	Skreen . .	Dromore West .	IV.	236
26	Halfquarter or Curraghaniron . .	166	0	18	Sligo . .	Leyny . . .	Killoran . .	Tobercurry .	IV.	230
29	Halfstraddle . .	81	3	6	Galway . .	Dunmore . .	Tuam . . .	Tuam . .	IV.	36
11	Halftate . . .	61	0	23	Louth . .	Louth . . .	Louth . . .	Dundalk . .	I.	184
34	Halftate . . .	73	0	10	Monaghan .	Farney . . .	Magheracloone .	Carrickmacross	III.	272
44, 45	Halftown . .	432	1	16	Antrim . .	Upper Antrim .	Donegore . .	Antrim . .	III.	6
79	Halftown . .	106	0	28	Donegal . .	Raphoe . . .	Urney . . .	Strabane . .	III.	144
59	Halftown . .	76	1	7	Tyrone . .	Clogher . .	Errigal Keerogue .	Clogher . .	III.	295
50	Half Umry . .	94	2	16	Antrim . .	Upper Toome . .	Antrim . . .	Antrim . .	III.	33
36	Hall . . .	1,113	0	20	Westmeath . .	Clonlonan . .	Kilcleagh . .	Athlone . .	I.	261
37, 38, 39	Hallahoise . .	895	0	29	Kildare . .	Kilkea and Moone .	Killelan . .	Athy . .	I.	60
99	Hall Demesne .	360	0	15	Donegal . .	Banagh . . .	Inver . . .	Donegal . .	III.	107
29	Halls . . .	436	1	37	Leitrim . .	Mohill . . .	Cloone . . .	Mohill . .	IV.	106
38	Hallsfarm . .	189	3	4	Westmeath . .	Moycashel . .	Kilbeggan . .	Tullamore . .	I.	278
38	Hallstown . .	286	2	31	Meath . .	Ratoath . .	Trevet . . .	Dunshaughlin .	I.	220
30	Halltown . .	339	1	12	Meath . .	Lower Navan .	Churchtown . .	Navan . .	I.	214
46	Halscyrath . .	131	0	24	Wexford . .	Bargy . . .	Ambrosetown .	Wexford . .	I.	303
19	Halverstown . .	363	0	2c	Kildare . .	Clane . . .	Carragh . .	Naas . .	I.	53
28	Halverstown . .	340	1	32	Kildare . .	Kilcullen . .	Kilcullen . .	Naas . .	I.	58
13	Hamiltonsbawn .	293	1	20	Armagh . .	Fews Lower .	Mullaghbrack .	Armagh . .	III.	47
13	HAMILTONS BAWN T.	—			Armagh . .	Fews Lower .	Mullaghbrack .	Armagh . .	III.	47
21	Hamlinstown . .	232	3	25	Louth . .	Ferrard . .	Drumshallon .	Drogheda . .	I.	180
15	Hamlinstown .	171	0	25	Meath . .	Fore . . .	Diamor . .	Oldcastle . .	I.	200
40	Hammondstown .	69	0	28	Limerick . .	Coshlea . .	Knocklong . .	Kilmallock .	II.	240
18	Hammondstown .	81	0	37	Louth . .	Ardee . . .	Cappoge . .	Ardee . .	I.	171
18	Hammondstown .	320	2	36	Louth . .	Ardee . .	Mosstown . .	Ardee . .	I.	174
33	Hammondstown .	82	1	7	Meath . .	Upper Duleek .	Clonalvy . .	Drogheda . .	I.	197
1, 3, 4	Hammondstown and Tonaghmore . .	546	0	36	Westmeath . .	Fore . . .	St. Feighins . .	Castletowndelvin .	I.	272
39	Hammondtown .	99	3	37	Meath . .	Ratoath . .	Cookstown . .	Dunshaughlin .	I.	217
60, 72, 73	Hampstead . .	547	0	23	Galway . .	Kilconnell . .	Ballymacward .	Ballinasloe .	IV.	39
14, 18	Hampsteadhill .	33	0	39	Dublin . .	Coolock . .	Glasnevin . .	Dublin North .	I.	27
14	Hampstead North .	52	1	5	Dublin . .	Coolock . .	Glasnevin . .	Dublin North .	I.	27
14	Hampstead South .	58	0	27	Dublin . .	Coolock . .	Glasnevin . .	Dublin North .	I.	27
5	Hampton Demesne .	365	0	8	Dublin . .	Balrothery East .	Balrothery . .	Balrothery .	I.	19
50	Hamwood . .	321	2	13	Meath . .	Dunboyne . .	Dunboyne . .	Dunshaughlin .	I.	199
25, 31	Hanlonstown . .	324	0	13	Meath . .	Lower Navan .	Ardbraccan .	Navan . .	I.	214
60	Hannahstown . .	319	0	3	Antrim . .	Upper Belfast .	Shankill . .	Belfast . .	III.	10
13	Hansfield or Phibblestown . .	223	1	36	Dublin . .	Castleknock . .	Clonsilla . .	Celbridge . .	I.	24
15	Hanslough . .	164	2	9d	Armagh . .	Tiranny . .	Tynan . . .	Armagh . .	III.	60
25	Hanstown . .	361	2	13	Westmeath . .	Moyashel & Magheradernon . .	Mullingar . .	Mullingar . .	I.	275
149	Harboursmouth .	41	2	2	Cork, W.R. .	West Carbery (E.D.) .	Tullagh . .	Skibbereen .	II.	141
72	Hardbog . .	205	3	18	Tipperary, S.R. .	Slievardagh . .	Templemichael .	Carrick on Suir	II.	336
38, 39	Harding Grove .	354	1	28	Limerick . .	Coshma . .	Bruree . .	Kilmallock .	II.	242
87, 99	Hardwood . .	139	0	21	Galway . .	Clonmacnowen .	Aughrim . .	Ballinasloe .	IV.	24
40, 46	Hardwood . .	714	2	19	Meath . .	Upper Moyfenrath .	Clonard . .	Edenderry .	I.	213
48	Hardyglass . .	49	0	6	Wexford . .	Forth . . .	Tacumshin . .	Wexford . .	I.	315
47	Hardygregan .	44	1	11	Wexford . .	Forth . . .	Mayglass . .	Wexford . .	I.	312
91, 101	Harefield . .	217	0	31e	Mayo . .	Clanmorris . .	Mayo . . .	Claremorris .	IV.	135
31	*Hare Island* . .	10	2	34	Down . .	Lecale Lower .	Saul . . .	Downpatrick .	III.	180
5	Hare Island . .	56	1	4	Fermanagh .	Lurg . . .	Drumkeeran .	Lowtherstown .	III.	207
94	*Hare Island* . .	5	3	4	Galway . .	Galway . . .	St. Nicholas .	Galway . .	IV.	38
22	Hareisland . .	110	3	13	Westmeath . .	Kilkenny West .	Bunown . .	Athlone . .	I.	272
149	Hare Island or Inishodriscol . .	380	3	32	Cork, W.R. .	West Carbery (E.D.) .	Aghadown . .	Skibbereen .	II.	137
82, 94	Haremount . .	646	3	1	Cork, W.R. .	West Muskerry .	Kilmichael .	Dunmanway .	II.	159
10	Harepark . .	69	1	4	Roscommon .	Boyle . . .	Boyle . .	Boyle . .	IV.	104
40, 41	Haresmead . .	302	3	3	Wexford . .	Shelmaliere West .	Horetown . .	New Ross .	I.	333
55, 56	Harley Park . .	317	1	20	Tipperary, S.R. .	Slievardagh . .	Ballingarry .	Callan . .	II.	332

(a) Including 8A. 3R. 26P. water.
(b) Including 2A. 0R. 16P. water.
(c) Including 7A. 0R. 32P. water.
(d) Including 8A. 0R. 36P. water.
(e) Including 0A. 1R. 10P. water.

No. of Sheet of the Ordnance Survey Maps.	Townlands and Towns.	Area in Statute Acres.	County.	Barony.	Parish.	Poor Law Union in 1857.	Townland Census of 1851, Part I.	
		A.　R.　P.					Vol.	Page
55	Harleypark . .	57 1 15	Tipperary, S.R.	Slievardagh . .	Lismalin . .	Callan . .	II.	335
19	Harlinstown . .	4 1 24	Meath . .	Upper Slane . .	Gernonstown . .	Navan . .	I.	224
19	Harlinstown . .	178 1 37	Meath . .	Upper Slane . .	Slane . .	Navan . .	I.	225
50	Harlockstown . .	197 1 17	Meath . .	Ratoath . .	Ballymaglassan .	Dunshaughlin .	I.	217
45	Harlockstown . .	375 3 22	Meath . .	Ratoath . .	Ratoath . .	Dunshaughlin .	I.	219
18, 25	Harmanstown .	243 1 36	Meath . .	Upper Slane . .	Stackallan . .	Navan . .	I.	225
15, 19	Harmonstown .	90 3 5	Dublin . .	Coolock . .	Clontarf . .	Dublin North .	I.	26
18	Haroldscross .	87 0 35a	Dublin . .	Uppercross, and Municipal Borough .	St. Catherines .	Dublin South .	I.	40
18	Haroldscross East .	103 0 7	Dublin . .	Uppercross . .	St. Peters . .	Dublin South .	I.	41
18	Haroldscross T. .	—	Dublin . .	Uppercross . .	St. Catherines .	Dublin South .	I.	40
18, 22	Haroldscross West .	148 1 22	Dublin . .	Uppercross . .	St. Peters . .	Dublin South .	I.	41
22	Haroldsgrange .	341 2 27	Dublin . .	Rathdown . .	Whitechurch . .	Dublin South .	I.	38
4, 9	Haroldstown . .	364 1 10	Carlow . .	Rathvilly . .	Haroldstown . .	Shillelagh . .	I.	11
75	Harpers Island .	69 2 23	Cork, E.R. .	Barrymore . .	Little Island . .	Cork . .	II.	56
41	Harperstown .	370 3 9	Wexford . .	Bargy . . .	Taghmon . .	Wexford . .	I.	307
25, 29	Harphall . .	1,675 2 6	Antrim . .	Lower Glenarm .	Tickmacrevan .	Larne . .	III.	24
47	Harpoonstown .	182 2 6	Wexford . .	Bargy . . .	Mulrankin . .	Wexford . .	I.	307
7	Harpur'shill . .	78 2 37	Londonderry .	North East Liberties of Coleraine . .	Coleraine . .	Coleraine . .	III.	246
65	Harrisgrove . .	38 2 6	Cork, E.R. .	Barrymore . .	Inchinabacky . .	Middleton . .	II.	55
24	Harristown . .	327 3 32b	Carlow . .	St. Mullins Lower .	St. Mullins . .	New Ross . .	I.	13
14	Harristown . .	289 2 4	Dublin . .	Coolock . .	St. Margarets .	Dublin North .	I.	29
24, 29	Harristown . .	618 0 12c	Kildare . .	Naas South . .	Carnalway . .	Naas . .	I.	64
35	Harristown . .	630 3 13	Kilkenny . .	Knocktopher . .	Muckalee . .	Carrick on Suir	I.	113
14	Harristown . .	70 2 9	Louth . .	Ardee . . .	Charlestown . .	Ardee . .	I.	171
14, 17	Harristown . .	282 0 31	Louth . .	Ardee . . .	Stickillin . .	Ardee . .	I.	175
25, 26	Harristown . .	859 0 20	Meath . .	Skreen . . .	Ardmulchan . .	Navan . .	I.	220
50	Harristown . .	216 1 37	Meath . .	Upper Deece . .	Moyglare . .	Celbridge . .	I.	194
46, 52	Harristown . .	835 3 9	Meath . .	Upper Moyfenrath .	Ballyboggan . .	Edenderry . .	I.	212
28, 34	Harristown . .	478 0 19	Queen's Co. .	Clandonagh . .	Rathdowney . .	Donaghmore .	I.	234
32	Harristown . .	180 2 26	Queen's Co. .	Slievemargy . .	Killeshin . .	Carlow . .	I.	246
26	Harristown . .	394 0 36	Roscommon .	Castlereagh . .	Kilkeevin . .	Castlereagh . .	IV.	200
27	Harristown . .	229 0 14	Waterford . .	Gaultiere . .	Kilmacomb . .	Waterford . .	II.	364
41, 46	Harristown . .	273 1 20	Wexford . .	Bargy . . .	Kilcavan . .	Wexford . .	I.	305
48	Harristown . .	101 2 23	Wexford . .	Forth . . .	Kilrane . .	Wexford . .	I.	311
10	Harristown . .	142 0 36	Wicklow . .	Lower Talbotstown .	Hollywood . .	Baltinglass . .	I.	360
39	Harristown or Ballonaghan . .	75 1 30	Sligo . .	Corran . . .	Kilshalvy . .	Boyle . .	IV.	227
36	Harristown Big .	307 3 15	Wexford . .	Shelmaliere West .	Kilbrideglynn . .	Wexford . .	I.	334
24	Harristown Common	181 1 0	Kildare . .	Naas South . .	Carnalway . .	Naas . .	I.	64
36	Harristown Little .	276 1 26	Wexford . .	Shelmaliere West .	Kilbrideglynn . .	Wexford . .	I.	334
27	Harristown Lower .	258 1 11	Kildare . .	Offaly West . .	Harristown . .	Athy . .	I.	72
41, 46	Harristown (Reask)	116 0 18	Wexford . .	Bargy . . .	Kilcavan . .	Wexford . .	I.	305
27	Harristown Upper .	203 3 12	Kildare . .	Offaly West . .	Harristown . .	Athy . .	I.	72
34	Harrowhill . .	451 0 16	Waterford . .	Coshmore&Coshbride	Templemichael .	Youghal . .	II.	349
23	Harrystown . .	168 0 13	Westmeath .	Rathconrath . .	Ballymore . .	Ballymahon .	I.	282
32	Harryville T. .	—	Antrim . .	Lower Antrim . .	Ballyclug . .	Ballymena . .	III.	3
27, 31	Hartley . . .	253 0 7	Leitrim . .	Leitrim . . .	Kiltoghert . .	Cark.on Shannon	IV.	102
13	Hartstown . .	181 2 2	Dublin . .	Castleknock . .	Clonsilla . .	Celbridge . .	I.	24
16, 23	Hartstown . .	855 0 19	Meath . .	Fore . . .	Killallon . .	Oldcastle . .	I.	200
20, 26	Hartstown . .	217 2 2	Wicklow . .	Upper Talbotstown .	Ballynure . .	Baltinglass . .	I.	362
19, 20	Hartwell Lower .	261 0 20	Kildare . .	South Salt . .	Kill . . .	Naas . .	I.	77
19, 20	Hartwell Upper .	230 3 22	Kildare . .	South Salt . .	Kill . . .	Naas . .	I.	77
47, 48	Harveystown . .	62 3 11	Wexford . .	Forth . . .	Ballymore . .	Wexford . .	I.	308
41	Harveystown . .	217 2 21	Wexford . .	Shelmaliere West .	Coolstuff . .	Wexford . .	I.	333
17	Hasley . . .	80 1 30	Louth . .	Ardee . . .	Ardee . .	Ardee . .	I.	171
25	Hass . . .	242 3 34	Londonderry .	Keenaght . .	Dungiven . .	NewTnLimavady	III.	236
93, 94	Haugh . . .	202 2 9	Donegal . .	Banagh . .	Killymard . .	Donegal . .	III.	111
54	Haughey's Isle . .	6 3 18	Donegal . .	Raphoe . .	Leck . . .	Letterkenny .	III.	140
21	Haughtons Island .	13 1 4	King's Co. .	Garrycastle . .	Reynagh . .	Parsonstown .	I.	138
87	Haulbowline Island .	27 3 35	Cork, E.R. .	Barrymore . .	Templerobin . .	Cork . .	II.	58
70, 79	Haw . . .	131 3 23d	Donegal . .	Raphoe . .	Clonleigh . .	Strabane . .	III.	135
55	Haw . . .	128 0 17	Donegal . .	Raphoe . .	Taughboyne . .	Londonderry .	III.	143
18, 23	Hawkfield . .	723 0 17	Kildare . .	Connell . .	Morristownbiller .	Naas . .	I.	56
33	Hawkinstown . .	3 1 11	Meath . .	Upper Duleek . .	Ardcath . .	Dunshaughlin .	I.	197
33	Hawkinstown . .	259 2 39	Meath . .	Upper Duleek . .	Piercetown . .	Dunshaughlin .	I.	198
64	Hawksford . .	456 0 19	Mayo . .	Costello . .	Kilcolman . .	Castlereagh . .	IV.	141
25	Hawkstown Lower .	198 3 18	Wicklow . .	Arklow . .	Drumkay . .	Rathdrum . .	I.	342
25, 31	Hawkstown Upper .	248 3 21	Wicklow . .	Arklow . .	Drumkay . .	Rathdrum . .	I.	342
7	Hawkswood . .	180 1 28	Cavan . .	Tullyhaw . .	Kinawley . .	Bawnboy . .	III.	93
25	Hawkswood . .	485 0 30	King's Co. .	Geashill . .	Geashill . .	Tullamore . .	I.	140
129	Hawthorn Island .	0 2 3	Galway . .	Kiltartan . .	Kilbeacanty . .	Gort . .	IV.	47
78	Hawthornlodge .	143 1 15	Mayo . .	Carra . .	Breaghwy . .	Castlebar . .	IV.	127

(a) { Within the Municipal Boundary, 23A. 2R. 37P.　　(b) Including 7A. 2R. 35P. River Barrow.　　(d) Including 2A. 3R. 17P. water.
{ Without the Municipal Boundary, 63A. 1R. 38P.　　(c) Including 5A. 3R. 21P. water.

No. of Sheet of the Ordnance Survey Maps.	Townlands and Towns.	Area in Statute Acres.			County.	Barony.	Parish.	Poor Law Union in 1857.	Townland Census of 1851, Part I.	
		A.	R.	P.					Vol.	Page
3	*Hayes' Island* .	9	2	10	Tipperary, N.R.	Lower Ormond .	Lorrha .	Borrisokane .	II.	285
48	Hayesland .	157	0	18	Wexford .	Forth .	Kilrane .	Wexford .	I.	311
44	Hayestown .	124	1	39	Meath .	Upper Deece .	Culmullin .	Dunshaughlin .	I.	193
42	Hayestown Great .	502	3	5	Wexford .	Forth .	Rathaspick .	Wexford .	I.	312
42	Hayestown Little .	156	1	30	Wexford .	Forth .	Rathaspick .	Wexford .	I.	312
15	*Hay Island* .	16	2	28	Fermanagh .	Lurg .	Trory .	Lowtherstown .	III.	209
5	Haylands .	142	0	31	Wicklow .	Lower Talbotstown .	Blessington .	Naas .	I.	358
19, 20	Haynestown .	255	3	1	Kildare .	South Salt .	Haynestown .	Naas .	I.	77
12	Haynestown .	1,292	3	27	Louth .	Upper Dundalk .	Haynestown .	Dundalk .	I.	178
4	Haystown .	253	0	35	Dublin .	Balrothery East .	Balscaddan .	Balrothery .	I.	20
8	Haystown .	133	3	31	Dublin .	Balrothery East .	Lusk .	Balrothery .	I.	21
31, 36	Haystown .	421	2	9	Wexford .	Bantry .	Whitechurchglynn .	Wexford .	I.	303
25, 26	Haystown and Carnuff Little .	1,005	1	0	Meath .	Skreen .	Ardmulchan .	Navan .	I.	220
49, 50	Haytown .	127	0	1	Wexford .	Shelburne .	Templetown .	New Ross .	I.	328
83	Haywood .	13	0	25	Tipperary, S.R.	Iffa and Offa East .	Rathronan .	Clonmel .	II.	316
83	Haywood .	68	2	18	Tipperary, S.R.	Iffa and Offa East .	St. Marys, Clonmel .	Clonmel .	II.	316
30	Haywood Demesne .	304	2	30*a*	Queen's Co. .	Cullenagh .	Dysartgallen .	Abbeyleix .	I.	239
4	Hazardstown .	157	2	15	Dublin .	Balrothery West .	Naul .	Balrothery .	I.	23
15	Hazelbrook .	38	3	23	Dublin .	Coolock .	Portmarnock .	Balrothery .	I.	28
10	Hazelfield .	150	2	9	Limerick .	Shanid .	Robertstown .	Rathkeale .	II.	258
86	Hazelfort .	452	0	15	Galway .	Kilconnell .	Killallaghtan .	Ballinasloe .	IV.	41
20	Hazelhatch .	118	0	34	Dublin .	Newcastle .	Newcastle .	Celbridge .	I.	34
93, 103	Hazelhill .	449	3	3	Mayo .	Costello .	Annagh .	Claremorris .	IV.	138
14, 15	Hazelwood Demesne .	886	1	28	Sligo .	Carbury .	Calry .	Sligo .	IV.	220
29, 34	Headborough .	536	0	25	Waterford .	Coshmore&Coshbride .	Kilwatermoy .	Lismore .	II.	343
41, 42	Headford .	142	2	11	Galway .	Clare .	Killursa .	Tuam .	IV.	21
32	Headford .	276	1	35*b*	Leitrim .	Leitrim .	Annaduff .	Car*k*. on Shannon .	IV.	99
41, 42	HEADFORD T. .	—			Galway .	Clare .	{ Cargin . } Kilkilvery . } Killursa . }	Tuam .	IV.	{18 {20 {22
67, 68	Headfort .	385	0	1	Kerry .	Magunihy .	Aghadoe .	Killarney .	II.	199
11, 17	Headfort Demesne .	946	0	10*c*	Meath .	Upper Kells .	Kells .	Kells .	I.	206
12	Headstown .	307	2	26	Meath .	Morgallion .	Castletown .	Navan .	I.	209
40, 46	Headwood .	492	2	25	Antrim .	Upper Glenarm .	Kilwaughter .	Larne .	III.	25
11	Heagles .	263	2	24	Antrim .	Upper Dunluce .	Ballymoney .	Ballymoney .	III.	19
8	Heagles .	192	0	34	Londonderry .	North East Liberties of Coleraine .	Ballymoney .	Ballymoney .	III.	245
37	Healthfield .	79	0	20	Wexford .	Shelmaliere West .	Killurin .	Wexford .	I.	334
29	Healysland .	21	1	30	Wexford .	Bantry .	St. Mary's .	New Ross .	I.	302
34	Heapstown .	204	3	3	Sligo .	Tirerrill .	Kilmacallan .	Sligo .	IV.	240
107, 117	Hearnesbrooke Demesne .	83	0	12	Galway .	Longford .	Killimorbologue .	Portumna .	IV.	59
19	Heath .	193	1	31	Carlow .	Idrone East .	Lorum .	Carlow .	I.	8
35, 37	Heath .	197	2	25	Kildare .	Kilkea and Moone .	Tankardstown .	Athy .	I.	61
16, 24	Heath .	143	2	30	King's Co. .	Ballycowan .	Lynally .	Tullamore .	I.	128
42, 43	Heath .	141	0	2	King's Co. .	Clonlisk .	Aghancon .	Roscrea .	I.	129
111, 119	Heath .	554	3	22	Mayo .	Clanmorris .	Crossboyne .	Claremorris .	IV.	133
27	Heath or Castlefleming .	329	3	20	Queen's Co. .	Clandonagh .	Rathdowney .	Donaghmore .	I.	234
27	Heathfield .	263	2	18	Roscommon .	Castlereagh .	Baslick .	Castlereagh .	IV.	199
56	*Heath Island* .	1	1	11	Mayo .	Burrishoole .	Achill ● .	Newport .	IV.	117
11	Heathland .	257	0	32	Westmeath .	Corkaree .	Lackan .	Mullingar .	I.	262
117	Heathlawn .	718	1	32	Galway .	Longford .	Killimorbologue .	Portumna .	IV.	59
91	Heathlawn .	182	1	3	Mayo .	Clanmorris .	Mayo .	Castlebar .	IV.	135
13	Heathlodge .	182	0	30	Queen's Co. .	Maryborough East .	Kilteale .	Mountmellick .	I.	241
52	Heathmount .	237	2	34	Clare .	Bunratty Lower .	Kilfintinan .	Limerick .	II.	5
30, 35	Heathpark .	324	3	6	Wexford .	Bantry .	Oldross .	New Ross .	I.	301
48	Heaths .	19	2	2	Wexford .	Forth .	Tacumshin .	Wexford .	I.	315
9, 14	Heathstown .	508	1	7	Westmeath .	Delvin .	Killua .	Castletowndelvin .	I.	265
27	Heathstown .	864	1	36	Westmeath .	Farbill .	Killucan .	Mullingar .	I.	267
5, 8	Heathtown .	85	1	10	Dublin .	Balrothery East .	Lusk .	Balrothery .	I.	21
33	Heathtown .	372	3	7	Meath .	Upper Duleek .	Clonalvy .	Drogheda .	I.	197
78	Heathview .	244	3	22	Tipperary, S.R.	Slievardagh .	Garrangibbon .	Carrick on Suir .	II.	333
47	Heavenstown .	124	3	18	Wexford .	Bargy .	Kilmannan .	Wexford .	I.	306
4, 5	Hedgestown .	128	1	21*d*	Dublin .	Balrothery East .	Lusk .	Balrothery .	I.	21
14	Heirhill .	395	2	29	Kerry .	Clanmaurice .	Ballyheige .	Tralee .	II.	168
36	Helvick .	231	0	28	Waterford .	Decies within Drum .	Ringagonagh .	Dungarvan .	II.	353
1, 5	Hempstown .	279	3	16	Wicklow .	Lower Talbotstown .	Blessington .	Naas .	I.	358
20, 25	Hempstown Commons .	238	2	26	Kildare .	Naas North .	Rathmore .	Naas .	I.	62
21	Heney .	91	0	32*e*	Cavan .	Upper Loughtee .	Castleterra .	Cavan .	III.	82
94	Heneys .	334	3	36	Donegal .	Banagh .	Killymard .	Donegal .	III.	111
5	Henfield .	10	0	10	Westmeath .	Moygoish .	Rathaspick .	Mullingar .	I.	280
6	Hennigan .	152	1	36	Meath .	Morgallion .	Nobber .	Kells .	I.	210
28, 34	Henrystughan .	109	3	27	Fermanagh .	Magherastephana .	Aghalurcher .	Lisnaskea .	III.	216

(*a*) Including 13A. 2R. 26P. water.
(*b*) Including 12A. 1R. 37P. water.
(*c*) Including 44A. 1R. 32P. water.
(*d*) Including 1A. 1R. 36P. detached portion.
(*e*) Including 2A. 0R. 18P. water.

No. of Sheet of the Ordnance Survey Maps.	Townlands and Towns.	Area in Statute Acres.			County.	Barony.	Parish.	Poor Law Union in 1857.	Townland Census of 1851, Part I.	
		A.	R.	P.					Vol.	Page
23, 24	Herbertstown .	493	3	20	Kildare . .	Connell . .	Greatconnell .	Naas . .	I.	55
44,45,50,51	Herbertstown .	308	3	8	Meath . .	Dunboyne . .	Dunboyne . .	Dunshaughlin .	I.	199
15, 22	Herbertstown .	452	3	20	Meath . .	Fore . .	Killallon . .	Oldcastle . .	I.	200
24	Herbertstown .	572	2	8	Meath . .	Lower Navan .	Martry . .	Kells . .	I.	215
33, 34	Herbertstown .	595	3	3	Meath . .	Upper Duleek .	Stamullin . .	Drogheda . .	I.	198
32	Herbertstown(O'Grady)	163	1	36	Limerick . .	Smallcounty .	Kilcullane .	Kilmallock .	II.	260
32	Herbertstown (Powell)	163	0	11	Limerick . .	Smallcounty .	Kilcullane .	Kilmallock .	II.	260
32	HERBERTSTOWN T. .	—			Limerick . .	Smallcounty .	{ Ballinard } { Kilcullane }	Kilmallock .	II.	{ 259 } { 260 }
2, 6	Herdstown . .	240	2	23	Down . .	Ards Lower .	Donaghadee .	Newtownards .	III.	158
64	Hermitage . .	100	3	8	Cork, E.R. .	Barrymore . .	Templeusque .	Cork . .	II.	59
88	Hermitage . .	155	3	18	Cork, E.R. .	Imokilly . .	Aghada . .	Middleton .	II.	83
17	Hermitage . .	139	3	6a	Dublin . .	Newcastle . .	Esker . .	Celbridge .	I.	33
43	Hermitage . .	118	0	4	Fermanagh .	Clankelly . .	Currin . .	Clones . .	III.	197
33	Hermitage . .	287	2	33	Galway . .	Killian . .	Killeroran .	Mountbellew .	IV.	44
37	Hermitage . .	104	2	29	Kilkenny . .	Ida . .	The Rower .	New Ross .	I.	104
1, 6	Hermitage . .	167	2	14	Limerick . .	Clanwilliam .	Stradbally .	Limerick . .	II.	226
5	Hermitage or Agh-naneane .	198	1	35	Meath . .	Lower Kells .	Moynalty .	Kells . .	I.	203
25	Hermitage or Gort-nashangan Upper	163	0	12	Cavan . .	Clanmahon .	Kilmore . .	Cavan . .	III.	78
42, 43	Hermitage or Whites-town Lower	37	3	7	Wexford . .	Forth . .	Drinagh . .	Wexford . .	I.	309
6	Hermit Island .	0	2	17	Roscommon .	Boyle . .	Kilbryan .	Boyle . .	IV.	195
44, 53	Hernsbrook . .	167	0	27	Limerick . .	Glenquin . .	Killeedy . .	Newcastle .	II.	246
19	Heronstown . .	108	0	20	Dublin . .	Coolock . .	Clontarf . .	Dublin North .	I.	26
12	Heronstown . .	599	3	27	Meath . .	Lower Slane .	Killary . .	Ardee . .	I.	223
127	Herringback Island .	0	0	1	Galway . .	Longford . .	Kilmalinoge .	Portumna .	IV.	59
29	Hewitsland . .	52	1	35	Wexford . .	Bantry . .	St. Mary's .	New Ross .	I.	302
15, 20	Higginstown . .	629	1	20	Kilkenny . .	Gowran . .	Blackrath .	Kilkenny . .	I.	93
10, 11	Higginstown . .	144	1	26	Longford . .	Granard . .	Granard . .	Granard . .	I.	156
29	Higginstown . .	470	3	20	Meath . .	Lune . .	Athboy . .	Trim . .	I.	207
19	Higginstown . .	197	2	22	Meath . .	Upper Slane .	Slane . .	Navan . .	I.	225
62	Higginstown . .	294	2	8	Tipperary, S.R.	Middlethird .	Peppardstown .	Cashel . .	II.	329
20	Higginstown . .	309	0	26	Westmeath .	Farbill . .	Killucan .	Mullingar .	I.	267
32, 33	Higginstown . .	247	0	23	Westmeath .	Fartullagh .	Carrick .	Mullingar .	I.	267
32, 38	Higginstown . .	693	1	39	Westmeath .	Moycashel .	Newtown .	Mullingar .	I.	279
54	Highbank . .	66	2	19	Donegal . .	Raphoe . .	Raymoghy .	Letterkenny .	III.	142
45	Highbog . .	141	1	35	Roscommon .	Athlone . .	Rahara . .	Roscommon .	IV.	183
38	High Cross . .	181	0	33	Tyrone . .	Dungannon Middle .	Donaghenry .	Cookstown .	III.	301
20, 21	Highdownhill . .	153	0	24	Dublin . .	Newcastle . .	Newcastle .	Celbridge .	I.	34
141, 150	Highfield . .	576	2	3	Cork, W.R. .	West Carbery (E.D.)	Creagh . .	Skibbereen .	II.	139
86, 87	Highfield . .	164	0	3	Galway . .	Kilconnell .	Aughrim .	Ballinasloe .	IV.	39
87	Highfield . .	51	3	35	Galway . .	Kilconnell .	Kilgerrill .	Ballinasloe .	IV.	40
27, 36	Highglen . .	800	2	4	Donegal . .	Kilmacrenan .	Mevagh . .	Milford .	III.	130
19	Highhays . .	10	0	16b	Kilkenny .	Kilkenny, Municipal Borough of .	St. John's .	Kilkenny . .	I.	117
151	High Island . .	3	1	5	Cork, W.R. .	West Carbery (E.D.)	Myross . .	Skibbereen .	II.	141
21	High Island . .	82	3	21	Galway . .	Ballynahinch .	Omey . .	Clifden . .	IV.	15
34, 35	Highlake or Ard-lagheen More .	528	0	2	Roscommon .	Ballymoe . .	Cloonygormican .	Castlereagh .	IV.	191
25	Highlandtown .	122	1	27	Antrim . .	Lower Glenarm .	Ardclinis .	Larne . .	III.	21
14,15,22,23	Highmoor . .	618	3	16	Londonderry .	Tirkeeran .	Cumber Lower .	Londonderry .	III.	249
45, 54	Highmount . .	284	1	17	Limerick . .	Connello Upper .	Cloncrew .	Newcastle .	II.	232
45	Highmount . .	638	3	16	Limerick . .	Connello Upper .	Kilmeedy .	Newcastle .	II.	233
86, 98	Highpark . .	189	0	24	Galway . .	Kilconnell .	Killaan .	Loughrea .	IV.	41
14	Highpark . .	519	3	21	Limerick . .	Clanwilliam .	Caherconlish .	Limerick . .	II.	222
32, 33	Highpark Lower .	213	2	33	Wicklow . .	Upper Talbotstown .	Kiltegan .	Baltinglass .	I.	364
32, 33	Highpark Upper .	203	1	38	Wicklow . .	Upper Talbotstown .	Kiltegan .	Baltinglass .	I.	364
20	Highrath . .	223	3	6c	Kilkenny . .	Gowran . .	Blackrath .	Kilkenny . .	I.	93
20	Highrath . .	51	2	36d	Kilkenny . .	Gowran . .	St. Martins .	Kilkenny . .	I.	98
31	Highstreet . .	79	2	11	Galway . .	Tiaquin . .	Kilkerrin .	Glennamaddy .	IV.	77
39, 40	Hightown . .	1,395	1	11	Antrim . .	Upper Glenarm .	Kilwaughter .	Larne . .	III.	25
44, 53	Hightown . .	404	1	3	Cork, E.R. .	Barrymore . .	Gortroe . .	Fermoy . .	II.	55
41	Hightown . .	76	3	32	Wexford . .	Bargy . .	Duncormick .	Wexford . .	I.	305
26, 27	Hightown or Bal-loughter .	1,283	1	16	Westmeath .	Farbill . .	Killucan .	Mullingar .	I.	267
35, 41	Highwood . .	246	2	15	Sligo . .	Tirerrill . .	Kilmactranny .	Boyle . .	IV.	240
47, 52	Hill . .	158	0	31	Wexford . .	Bargy . .	Kilturk . .	Wexford . .	I.	307
43	Hillbrook Lower .	566	0	30	Wicklow . .	Shillelagh .	Carnew .	Shillelagh .	I.	357
43, 47	Hillbrook Upper .	570	0	13	Wicklow . .	Shillelagh .	Carnew .	Shillelagh .	I.	357
36, 41	Hillburn . .	117	0	7	Wexford . .	Shelmaliere West .	Taghmon .	New Ross .	I.	335
48	Hillcastle . .	145	0	6	Wexford . .	Forth . .	Kilscoran .	Wexford . .	I.	311
13, 18	Hillend . .	139	0	33	Kilkenny . .	Crannagh . .	Killahy . .	Urlingford .	I.	86

(a) Including 4A. 2R. 0P. water.
(b) Included in the Parish of St. John.
(c) Including 0A. 2R. 19P. River Nore.
(d) Including 0A. 3R. 16P. River Nore.

No. of Sheet of the Ordnance Survey Maps.	Townlands and Towns.	Area in Statute Acres.	County.	Barony.	Parish.	Poor Law Union in 1857.	Townland Census of 1851, Part I.	
		A. R. P.					Vol.	Page
32	Hillfarm .	238 3 30	Kildare	Offaly West	Kilrush	Athy	I.	73
79	Hillgrove	99 0 14	Kerry	Iveragh	Caher	Cahersiveen	II.	194
9, 15	Hillhall .	307 1 15	Down	Castlereagh Upper	Drumbeg	Lisburn	III.	164
9, 15	Hillhall .	262 2 32	Down	Castlereagh Upper	Drumboe	Lisburn	III.	164
6, 7	Hillhall .	146 2 32	Monaghan	Trough	Donagh	Monaghan	III.	282
33	Hill Head	48 2 10a	Tyrone	Omagh West	Longfield West	Castlederg	III.	316
21, 24	Hill of Rath .	230 2 9	Louth	Ferrard	Tullyallen	Drogheda	I.	183
48	Hill of Sea	89 0 12	Wexford	Forth	Rosslare .	Wexford	I.	313
95	Hillpark .	54 0 26	Galway	Dunkellin	Stradbally	Galway	IV.	32
22, 29	Hillquarter	392 1 20	Westmeath	Brawny	St. Mary's	Athlone	I.	259
14, 21	Hillsborough .	642 2 33	Down	Lower Iveagh, Up.pt.	Hillsborough	Lisburn	III.	169
23	Hillsborough .	251 3 25	Kildare	Connell	Greatconnell .	Naas	I.	55
14	HILLSBOROUGH T. .	—	Down	Lower Iveagh, Up. pt.	Hillsborough	Lisburn	III.	170
44	Hillsbrook Demesne	415 0 24	Galway	Clare	Killererin	Tuam	IV.	21
54, 56	Hillsend .	74 3 25	Roscommon	Moycarn	Moore	Ballinasloe	IV.	207
69	Hill's-lot .	401 2 16	Tipperary, S.R.	Middlethird	St. John Baptist	Cashel	II.	330
17	HILLSTREET T.	—	Roscommon	{ Ballintober North .	Kilmore .	} Cark. on Shannon	IV. {	187
				Roscommon .	Aughrim			207
73, 86	Hillswood .	457 2 8	Galway	Kilconnell	Kilconnell	Ballinasloe	IV.	40
30, 44	Hillswood East	481 0 4	Galway	Dunmore	Tuam	Tuam	IV.	36
30	Hillswood West	44 2 28	Galway	Dunmore	Tuam	Tuam	IV.	36
87	Hilltown .	140 0 33	Cork, E.R.	Kerrycurrihy	Carrigaline	Cork	II.	92
11	Hilltown .	221 2 28	Dublin	Nethercross	Swords	Balrothery	I.	32
53	Hilltown .	196 1 20	Meath	Dunboyne	Dunboyne	Dunshaughlin	I.	199
33, 39	Hilltown .	137 1 7	Meath	Upper Duleek	Piercetown	Dunshaughlin	I.	198
3, 4	Hilltown .	682 3 2	Westmeath	Fore	St. Feighins	Castletowndelvin	I.	272
47	Hilltown .	126 3 28	Wexford	Forth	Ballymore	Wexford	I.	308
53	Hilltown .	15 0 4b	Wexford	Forth	Carn	Wexford	I.	309
48	Hilltown .	117 0 29	Wexford	Forth	Kilrane	Wexford	I.	311
48	Hilltown .	12 1 22	Wexford	Forth	Ladysisland	Wexford	I.	311
53	Hilltown .	70 1 15	Wexford	Forth	Tacumshin	Wexford	I.	315
41	Hilltown .	277 2 39	Wexford	Shelmaliere West	Ballymitty	Wexford	I.	332
27	Hilltown Great	441 3 35	Meath	Upper Duleek	Duleek	Drogheda .	I.	197
27	Hilltown Little	184 3 20	Meath	Upper Duleek	Duleek	Drogheda	I.	197
48	HILLTOWN T.	—	Down	Upper Iveagh, Lr. pt.	Clonduff .	Newry	III.	171
10, 15	Hilton .	125 2 6	Tipperary, N.R.	Lower Ormond	Modreeny	Borrisokane	II.	286
16	Hilton Demesne	542 1 5c	Monaghan	Dartree	Currin	Clones	III.	266
13	Hiskinstown .	305 2 38	Westmeath	Delvin	Killulagh	Castletowndelvin	I.	266
18	Hitchestown .	117 1 23	Louth	Ferrard	Dysart	Drogheda .	I.	181
13	Hoardstown .	264 0 7	Meath	Lower Slane	Killary	Ardee	I.	223
11	Hoarstone .	138 2 35	Louth	Louth	Louth	Dundalk	I.	184
17	Hoathstown .	348 3 30	Louth	Ardee	Stickillin	Ardee	I.	175
38	Hobartstown East	287 0 7	Kildare	Kilkea and Moone	Castledermot	Athy	I.	59
38	Hobartstown West .	422 3 11	Kildare	Kilkea and Moone	Castledermot	Athy	I.	59
47	Hobbinstown .	62 2 20	Wexford	Forth	Rathmacknee	Wexford	I.	313
99	Hoddersfield .	535 0 31	Cork, E.R.	Kerrycurrihy	Templebreedy	Kinsale	II.	93
42	Hodgesmill .	48 3 3	Wexford	Forth	Rathmacknee .	Wexford	I.	313
9, 13	Hodgestown .	628 0 21	Kildare	Clane	Timahoe .	Naas	I.	54
10	Hodgestown .	239 1 34	Kildare	Ikeathy&Oughterany	Clonshanbo	Celbridge .	I.	57
5	Hodgestown .	151 0 4	Kildare	Ikeathy&Oughterany	Kilcock .	Celbridge .	I.	57
34	Hodgestown .	112 1 31	Meath	Upper Duleek	Stamullin	Drogheda .	I.	198
20	Hodgestown .	272 2 0	Westmeath	Farbill	Killucan .	Mullingar	I.	267
14	Hoganswood .	95 3 3	Kildare	Clane	Clane	Naas	I.	53
14	Hoganswood East	6 3 30	Kildare	Clane	Clane	Naas	I.	53
118	Hog Island	0 3 0	Cork, W.R.	Bantry	Kilmocomoge .	Bantry	II.	121
21, 22	Hog Island	9 0 28	Galway	Ballynahinch .	Omey	Clifden	IV.	15
110	Hog Island .	2 2 33	Mayo	Carra	Burriscarra	Ballinrobe	IV.	127
67	Hog Island or Inishbig.	43 1 14	Clare	Moyarta	Kilrush .	Kilrush .	II.	33
105	Hogs Head Island .	9 0 13	Kerry	Dunkerron South	Kilcrohane	Cahersiveen	II.	184
6	Hogs Island .	10 2 11	Roscommon	Boyle	Boyle	Boyle	IV.	194
2	Hogstown .	137 2 30	Down	Ards Lower	Donaghadee	Newtownards .	III.	158
19	Holdensrath .	320 2 0	Kilkenny .	Shillelogher	St. Patrick's	Kilkenny .	I.	116
24	Holdenstown .	276 1 13	Kilkenny .	Gowran	Dunbell .	Kilkenny .	I.	94
27	Holdenstown Lower	214 3 23	Wicklow .	Upper Talbotstown .	Baltinglass	Baltinglass	I.	362
27, 32	Holdenstown Upper	240 1 25	Wicklow .	Upper Talbotstown.	Baltinglass	Baltinglass	I.	362
45, 51	Holestone .	872 1 23	Antrim .	Upper Antrim	Kilbride .	Antrim .	III.	6
70	Hollands .	109 1 32	Donegal .	Raphoe	Clonleigh	Strabane .	III.	135
24	Hollimshill .	408 2 29d	King's Co.	Ballyboy .	Killoughy	Tullamore	I.	124
90	Hollowpark .	167 0 39	Mayo	Carra	Rosslee .	Castlebar .	IV.	130
27	Hollybank or Ederdaglass .	50 0 3	Fermanagh	Tirkennedy	Cloonish	Enniskillen	III.	220
27	Hollybank or Ederdaglass .	4 3 34	Fermanagh	Tirkennedy	Derryvullan .	Enniskillen	III.	221

(a) Including 0A. 2R. 31P. water.
(b) Including 1A. 2R. 26P. detached portion.

(c) Including 19A. 2R. 32P. water.
(d) Including 22A. 0R. 24P. water.

No. of Sheet of the Ordnance Survey Maps.	Townlands and Towns.	Area in Statute Acres.	County.	Barony.	Parish.	Poor Law Union in 1857.	Townland Census of 1851, Part I.	
		A. R. P.					Vol.	Page
34	Hollybrook	78 3 36	Fermanagh	Magherastephana	Aghalurcher	Lisnaskea	III.	216
7, 8	Hollybrook	108 2 24	Wicklow	Rathdown	Kilmacanoge	Rathdown	I.	355
40	Hollybrook Demesne or Ballyhealy	285 2 6	Sligo	Tirerrill	Aghanagh	Boyle	IV.	237
6	Hollyfield or Edencullentragh	81 2 32	Sligo	Carbury	Rossinver	Sligo	IV.	223
3	Hollyfort	43 2 32	Wexford	Gorey	Kilgorman	Gorey	I.	318
6	Hollyfort	118 2 20	Wexford	Gorey	Kilnahue	Gorey	I.	319
19	Hollyfort	115 1 0	Wexford	Scarawalsh	Monart	Enniscorthy	I.	324
20, 33	Hollygrove	273 3 8a	Galway	Killian	Athleague	Mountbellew	IV.	43
44	Hollyhill	111 0 6	Cork, E.R.	Barrymore	Gortroe	Fermoy	II.	55
111, 124	Hollyhill	388 0 29	Cork, E.R.	Kinsale	Tisaxon	Kinsale	II.	101
118	Hollyhill	105 2 16	Cork, W.R.	Bantry	Kilmocomoge	Bantry	II.	121
140, 141	Hollyhill	357 3 7	Cork, W.R.	West Carbery (E.D.)	Aghadown	Skibbereen	II.	137
5	Holly-hill	629 0 19	Tyrone	Strabane Lower	Leckpatrick	Strabane	III.	322
129	Holly Island	0 0 13	Galway	Kiltartan	Kilbeacanty	Gort	IV.	47
10	Holly Island	2 1 10	Limerick	Connello Lower	Tomdeely	Rathkeale	II.	230
37	Hollymount	884 1 13b	Down	Lecale Upper	Down	Downpatrick	III.	180
28	Hollymount	61 2 24	Fermanagh	Magherastephana	Aghavea	Lisnaskea	III.	219
133	Hollymount	59 3 1c	Galway	Kiltartan	Beagh	Gort	IV.	46
123	Hollymount	603 3 25	Galway	Loughrea	Kilthomas	Gort	IV.	65
27	Hollymount	123 2 12	Meath	Upper Duleek	Moorechurch	Drogheda	I.	198
32	Hollymount	47 0 19	Queen's Co.	Slievemargy	Killabban	Carlow	I.	245
32	Hollymount	380 0 35	Queen's Co.	Slievemargy	Shrule	Carlow	I.	246
110, 111	Hollymount Demesne	403 1 30	Mayo	Kilmaine	Kilcommon	Ballinrobe	IV.	154
6, 10	Hollymount or Knockaculleen	540 0 18	Roscommon	Boyle	Ardcarn	Boyle	IV.	193
110	Hollymount T.	—	Mayo	Kilmaine	Kilcommon	Ballinrobe	IV.	155
96	Hollypark	133 1 1	Galway	Dunkellin	Kilconierin	Loughrea	IV.	29
13	Hollystown	196 3 20	Dublin	Castleknock	Mulhuddart	Dublin North	I.	25
13	Hollywood	58 2 5	Dublin	Castleknock	Mulhuddart	Dublin North	I.	25
9	Hollywood Demesne	198 3 28	Wicklow	Lower Talbotstown	Hollywood	Baltinglass	I.	360
4	Hollywood Great	340 2 14	Dublin	Balrothery West	Hollywood	Balrothery	I.	23
4, 7	Hollywood Little	302 0 14	Dublin	Balrothery West	Hollywood	Balrothery	I.	23
9	Hollywood Lower	123 3 22	Wicklow	Lower Talbotstown	Hollywood	Baltinglass	I.	360
13	Hollywoodrath	218 1 28	Dublin	Castleknock	Mulhuddart	Dublin North	I.	25
9	Hollywood Upper	93 0 34	Wicklow	Lower Talbotstown	Hollywood	Baltinglass	I.	360
46	Holmanhill	69 1 8	Wexford	Bargy	Ambrosetown	Wexford	I.	303
93, 99	Holmes	51 2 33	Donegal	Banagh	Killymard	Donegal	III.	111
37	Holmestown Great	170 1 39	Wexford	Shelmaliere West	Kilbrideglynn	Wexford	I.	334
37	Holmestown Little	172 2 23	Wexford	Shelmaliere West	Kilbrideglynn	Wexford	I.	334
5	Holmpatrick	238 3 5	Dublin	Balrothery East	Holmpatrick	Balrothery	I.	20
11	Holybanks	17 0 30	Dublin	Nethercross	Swords	Balrothery	I.	32
47	Holycross	641 2 1	Tipperary, N.R.	Eliogarty	Holycross	Thurles	II.	270
47	Holycross T.	—	Tipperary, S.R. { Middlethird	Holycross	Cashel	} II.	{327
			Eliogarty	Holycross	Thurles	}	{270
120, 123	Holy Island or Camillaun	4 1 11	Mayo	Kilmaine	Cong	Ballinrobe	IV.	154
136	Holy Island or Inishcaltra	45 1 11	Galway	Leitrim	Inishcaltra	Scarriff	IV.	54
5	Holyvalley	59 0 2	Wicklow	Lower Talbotstown	Blessington	Naas	I.	358
50	Holy Well	98 0 2	Antrim	Upper Antrim	Antrim	Antrim	III.	5
13	Holywell	23 2 19	Wicklow	Newcastle	Kilcoole	Rathdrum	I.	351
103	Holywell Lower	233 1 24	Mayo	Costello	Annagh	Claremorris	IV.	138
102, 103	Holywell Upper	150 1 28	Mayo	Costello	Annagh	Claremorris	IV.	138
1, 5	Holywood	755 2 17	Down	Castlereagh Lower	Holywood	Belfast	III.	162
1	Holywood T.	—	Down	Castlereagh Lower	Holywood	Belfast	III.	163
17, 23	Honeymount	281 1 22	Tipperary, N.R.	Ikerrin	Rathnaveoge	Roscrea	II.	276
23	Honeypark	62 2 11	Dublin	Rathdown	Monkstown	Rathdown	I.	36
21, 30	Honeypound	86 3 15	Limerick	Pubblebrien	Croom	Croom	II.	252
37	Hoodsgrove	295 0 33	Kilkenny	Ida	Rosbercon	New Ross	I.	103
46	Hooks	113 3 0	Wexford	Bargy	Kilcowan	Wexford	I.	305
60	Hoops-lot	45 1 18	Tipperary, S.R.	Clanwilliam	Relickmurry & Athassel	Tipperary	II	310
36	Hopefield	119 0 29	Wexford	Shelmaliere West	Horetown	New Ross	I.	333
43	Hopeland	214 0 16	Wexford	Forth	Rosslare	Wexford	I.	313
18	Hopestown	330 1 12	Westmeath	Moyashel and Magheradernon	Mullingar	Mullingar	I.	275
18	Hophall	325 1 14	Queen's Co.	Maryborough East	Dysartenos	Mountmellick	I.	241
75	Hop-island	12 1 2	Cork, E.R.	Cork	Carrigaline	Cork	II.	64
80	Hopkinsrea	460 3 0	Tipperary, S.R.	Iffa and Offa West	Shanrahan	Clogheen	II.	319
13	Hopkinstown	300 3 18	Meath	Lower Slane	Killary	Ardee	II.	223
5, 11	Horath	419 2 38	Meath	Lower Kells	Kilbeg	Kells	I.	202
60, 61	Horeabbey	379 0 38	Tipperary, S.R.	Middlethird	Horeabbey	Cashel	II.	327
46	Horesland	191 2 13	Wexford	Bargy	Duncormick	Wexford	I.	305

(a) Including 17A. 3R. 32P. water.   (b) Including 17A. 2R. 29P. water.   (c) Including 6A. 0R. 3P. water.

No. of Sheet of the Ordnance Survey Maps.	Townlands and Towns.	Area in Statute Acres.	County.	Barony.	Parish.	Poor Law Union in 1857.	Townland Census of 1851, Part I.	
		A. R. P.					Vol.	Page
8	Horestown	81 1 27	Dublin	Balrothery East	Lusk	Balrothery	I.	21
39	Horeswood	266 3 38	Wexford	Shelburne	Kilmokea	New Ross	I.	327
47, 48	Horetown	84 3 22	Wexford	Forth	Killinick	Wexford	I.	310
35,36,40,41	Horetown North	860 1 26	Wexford	Shelmaliere West	Horetown	New Ross	I.	333
36, 41	Horetown South	301 1 15	Wexford	Shelmaliere West	Horetown	New Ross	I.	333
12, 18	Horistown	560 2 9	Meath	Upper Slane	Rathkenny	Navan	I.	225
17	Horseclose	77 0 12	Cork, E.R.	Fermoy	Doneraile	Mallow	II.	78
111	Horsehill Beg	26 2 17	Cork, E.R.	Kinalea	Dunderrow	Kinsale	II.	94
111	Horsehill More (North)	347 3 37	Cork, E.R.	Kinalea	Dunderrow	Kinsale	II.	94
111	Horsehill More (South)	19 3 7	Cork, E.R.	Kinalea	Dunderrow	Kinsale	II.	94
50	Horse Island	34 0 9	Clare	Islands	Clondagad	Killadysert	II.	29
105	Horse Island	1 0 19	Cork, W.R.	Bantry	Kilmocomoge	Bantry	II.	121
151	Horse Island	26 2 4	Cork, W.R.	West Carbery (E.D.)	Castlehaven	Skibbereen	II.	138
149	Horse Island	154 1 15	Cork, W.R.	West Carbery(W.D.)	Skull	Skull	II.	146
18	Horse Island	23 1 11	Down	Ards Upper	Inishargy	Newtownards	III.	160
15	Horse Island	46 0 0	Fermanagh	Lurg	Derryvullan	Lowtherstown	III.	205
48	Horse Island	13 3 5	Galway	Ballynahinch	Ballindoon	Clifden	IV.	10
87	Horse Island	6 3 28	Kerry	Iveragh	Killemlagh	Cahersiveen	II.	196
97	Horse Island	34 1 4	Kerry	Iveragh	Prior	Cahersiveen	II.	198
25	Horse Island	1 3 36	Longford	Rathcline	Cashel	Ballymahon	I.	163
110	Horse Island	3 0 6	Mayo	Carra	Burriscarra	Ballinrobe	IV.	127
5	Horse Island	8 3 6	Mayo	Tirawley	Doonfeeny	Killala	IV.	167
49	Horse Island	1 1 5	Roscommon	Athlone	Kiltoom	Athlone	IV.	183
7	Horse Island	2 1 0	Sligo	Carbury	Drumcliff	Sligo	IV.	222
40, 49	Horsemountmountain	631 3 22	Cork, W.R.	West Muskerry	Kilcorney	Millstreet	II.	158
39, 40	Horsemount North	495 1 7	Cork, W.R.	West Muskerry	Kilcorney	Millstreet	II.	158
39, 40, 49	Horsemount South	315 0 19	Cork, W.R.	West Muskerry	Kilcorney	Millstreet	II.	158
25, 29	Horsepasstown	77 3 5a	Kildare	Naas South	Ballymore Eustace	Naas	I.	64
77	Horsepasture	129 1 24	Tipperary, S.R.	Iffa and Offa East	Kilgrant	Clonmel	II.	314
137	Horse Rock Little	0 0 37	Cork, W.R.	Ibane and Barryroe	Lislee	Clonakilty	II.	150
4, 9	Hortland	1,409 2 10	Kildare	Ikeathy&Oughterany	Scullogestown	Celbridge	I.	58
6	Hospitalbank	67 1 35b	Westmeath	Moygoish	Street	Granard	I.	281
23	Hospital Land	68 3 38	Meath	Lune	Athboy	Trim	I.	207
32	HOSPITAL T.	—	Limerick	Smallcounty	Hospital	Kilmallock	II.	260
56, 59	Houndscourt	250 0 38	Limerick	Coshlea	Kilfyn	Kilmallock	II.	240
121, 123	Houndswood Middle	426 3 38	Mayo	Kilmaine	Cong	Ballinrobe	IV.	154
121, 123	Houndswood North	377 0 22	Mayo	Kilmaine	Cong	Ballinrobe	IV.	154
121, 123	Houndswood South	316 1 12	Mayo	Kilmaine	Cong	Ballinrobe	IV.	154
49, 50	Houseland	289 3 35	Wexford	Shelburne	Templetown	New Ross	I.	328
39	Howardstown North	64 1 34	Limerick	Coshma	Bruree	Kilmallock	II.	242
39	Howardstown South	327 2 18	Limerick	Coshma	Bruree	Kilmallock	II.	242
15, 16, 19	Howth	1,188 0 32	Dublin	Coolock	Howth	Dublin North	I.	28
15, 16, 19	Howth Demesne	563 3 34	Dublin	Coolock	Howth	Dublin North	I.	28
6	Howthstown	299 2 33	Meath	Lower Slane	Siddan	Ardee	I.	28
15, 16	HOWTH T.	—	Dublin	Coolock	Howth	Dublin North	I.	224
								28
74	Huggarts-land	76 1 16	Cork, E.R.	Cork	St. Finbars	Cork	II.	66
31, 35	Hugginstown	327 3 0	Kilkenny	Knocktopher	Aghaviller	Thomastown	I.	110
31	HUGGINSTOWN T.	—	Kilkenny	Knocktopher	Aghaviller	Thomastown	I.	111
61	Hughes'-lot East	413 0 9	Tipperary, S.R.	Middlethird	St. John Baptist	Cashel	II.	330
60	Hughes'-lot West	40 1 15	Tipperary, S.R.	Middlethird	St. John Baptist	Cashel	II.	330
6, 7	Hugheston	106 3 14	Roscommon	Boyle	Tumna	Boyle	IV.	198
38	Hughstown	752 2 32	Kildare	Kilkea and Moone	Killelan	Baltinglass	I.	60
27, 32	Humewood	289 1 10	Wicklow	Upper Talbotstown	Kiltegan	Baltinglass	I.	364
10	Humphrystown	664 1 14	Wicklow	Lower Talbotstown	Boystown	Naas	I.	359
60	Hundredacres	202 2 38	Galway	Tiaquin	Ballymacward	Mountbellew	IV.	75
71	Hundredacres	120 0 11	Galway	Tiaquin	Monivea	Tuam	IV.	79
39	Hundredacres	279 1 12	King's Co.	Ballybritt	Letterluna	Parsonstown	I.	126
121, 122	Hundred Acres	186 3 26	Mayo	Kilmaine	Kilmainebeg	Ballinrobe	IV.	155
32	Hundredacres	230 3 28	Roscommon	Castlereagh	Kiltuliagh	Castlereagh	IV.	202
14	Hundredacres East	161 0 36	Limerick	Clanwilliam	Caherconlish	Limerick	II.	222
14	Hundredacres West	163 3 17	Limerick	Clanwilliam	Caherconlish	Limerick	II.	222
54	Hungersmother	154 1 7	Donegal	Raphoe	Raymoghy	Londonderry	III.	142
50	Hungry Hall	69 3 30	Antrim	Upper Antrim	Antrim	Antrim	III.	5
2, 6	Hunter's Glebe	196 2 29	Londonderry	Coleraine	Dunboe	Coleraine	III.	231
17	Hunterstown	166 3 26	Louth	Ardee	Kildemock	Ardee	I.	173
9	Hunterstown	37 2 24	Tyrone	Strabane Lower	Urney	Strabane	III.	322
28	Hunthill	89 2 14	Waterford	Coshmore&Coshbride	Tallow	Lismore	II.	348
20	Huntingdon	135 3 39	Westmeath	Farbill	Killucan	Mullingar	I.	267
1, 6	Huntingstown	27 3 35	Limerick	Clanwilliam	Stradbally	Limerick	II.	226
18	Huntington	156 0 6	Carlow	St. Mullins Upper	Moyacomb	Shillelagh	I.	14
24	Huntingtown	287 1 2	Kilkenny	Gowran	Dungarvan	Thomastown	I.	94
11	Huntingtown	278 2 29	Wexford	Gorey	Liskinfere	Gorey	I.	320
36, 37	Huntspark or Ardough	647 0 31	Queen's Co.	Slievemargy	Killabban	Carlow	I.	245

(a) Including 5A. 0R. 35P. water.   (b) Including 5A. 3R. 9P. water.

No. of Sheet of the Ordnance Survey Maps.	Townlands and Towns.	Area in Statute Acres.	County.	Barony.	Parish.	Poor Law Union in 1857.	Townland Census of 1851, Part I.	
		A. R. P.					Vol.	Page
14, 22	Huntston	170 3 7	King's Co.	Garrycastle	Tisaran	Parsonstown	I.	138
14	Huntstown	299 3 38	Dublin	Castleknock	Castleknock	Dublin North	I.	24
13	Huntstown	304 0 13a	Dublin	Castleknock	Mulhuddart	Dublin North	I.	25
14	Huntstown	193 3 39	Dublin	Coolock	Santry	Dublin North	I.	29
18	Huntstown	568 3 0	Kilkenny	Crannagh	Tullaroan	Kilkenny	I.	88
13, 19	Hurcle	489 2 5	Meath	Upper Slane	Tullyallen	Drogheda	I.	225
44	Hurdleston	559 3 32	Clare	Tulla Lower	Kilseily	Limerick	II.	37
17	Hurdlestown	458 0 31	Meath	Upper Kells	Teltown	Kells	I.	207
17	Hurlstone	274 0 13	Louth	Ardee	Smarmore	Ardee	I.	174
50	Hurtletoot	163 2 25	Antrim	Upper Antrim	Antrim	Antrim	III.	5
76	Husseystown	188 3 34	Tipperary, S.R.	Iffa and Offa West	Caher	Clogheen	II.	318
15, 20	Huttonread	233 3 7	Kildare	South Salt	Oughterard	Naas	I.	78
21,22,26,27	Hybla or Ballyneage	641 2 30	Kildare	Offaly West	Duneany	Athy	I.	72
27, 28	Hydepark	701 0 22	Westmeath	Farbill	Killucan	Mullingar	I.	267
3, 7	Hydepark	182 2 39	Wexford	Gorey	Kilgorman	Gorey	I.	318
68	Hymenstown	498 0 30	Tipperary, S.R.	Clanwilliam	Relickmurry and Athassel	Tipperary	II.	310
5	Hynespark	13 2 20	Dublin	Balrothery East	Balrothery	Balrothery	I.	19
4	Hynestown	274 2 1	Dublin	Balrothery West	Naul	Balrothery	I.	23
20, 21	Hynestown	291 1 16	Dublin	Newcastle	Newcastle	Celbridge	I.	34
22	Iceford or Bellanira	81 1 4	Sligo	Tireragh	Castleconor	Ballina	IV.	232
8, 12, 13	Iderown	314 3 34	Antrim	Cary	Grange of Drumtullagh	Ballycastle	III.	14
52	Ieverstown	60 2 27	Clare	Bunratty Lower	Kilfinaghta	Limerick	II.	4
36	Iffernock	489 2 15b	Meath	Lower Moyfenrath	Laracor	Trim	I.	210
77	Ightermurragh	356 2 27	Cork, E.R.	Imokilly	Ightermurragh	Middleton	II.	87
18	*Illanamoe*	0 1 26	Roscommon	Ballintober North	Kilglass	Strokestown	IV.	186
103	*Illananirey*	1 2 16	Galway	Dunkellin	Killeenavarra	Gort	IV.	30
34	Illananummera	31 1 37	Tipperary, N.R.	Eliogarty	Inch	Thurles	II.	270
48	*Illanaran Island*	13 2 18	Donegal	Boylagh	Templecrone	Glenties	III.	116
76	*Illanataggart*	29 3 0	Mayo	Burrishoole	Kilmeena	Westport	IV.	122
110	*Illanatrim*	1 0 37	Mayo	Kilmaine	Robeen	Ballinrobe	IV.	158
120	*Illan Boebeg*	3 1 0	Mayo	Kilmaine	Ballinchalla	Ballinrobe	IV.	152
120	*Illan Boemore*	8 0 28	Mayo	Kilmaine	Ballinchalla	Ballinrobe	IV.	152
32	*Illancarragh or Glass Island*	4 2 32	Donegal	Kilmacrenan	Tullaghobegly	Dunfanaghy	III.	132
109	*Illan Columbkille*	1 3 31	Mayo	Carra	Ballyovey	Ballinrobe	IV.	126
21, 29	*Illancoogan*	1 1 12	King's Co.	Garrycastle	Lusmagh	Parsonstown	I.	137
56	*Illancroagh*	5 1 18	Mayo	Erris	Kilcommon	Newport	IV.	145
48	*Illancrone Island*	6 1 12	Donegal	Boylagh	Templecrone	Glenties	III.	116
3	*Illandavuck*	6 3 4	Mayo	Erris	Kilmore	Belmullet	IV.	146
109	*Illandawaur*	3 3 8	Mayo	Carra	Ballyovey	Ballinrobe	IV.	126
91, 92	Illane	334 1 6	Cork, W.R.	Bantry	Kilmocomoge	Bantry	II.	121
126	*Illanebeg*	7 2 3	Cork, W.R.	Bear	Kilnamanagh	Castletown	II.	125
60	*Illanee*	0 0 36	Mayo	Carra	Turlough	Castlebar	IV.	131
64, 65	*Illanfad*	1 2 30	Donegal	Boylagh	Inishkeel	Glenties	III.	114
23	*Illangarve*	3 0 0	Roscommon	Ballintober North	Kilglass	Strokestown	IV.	186
17	*Illangarve*	1 1 4	Roscommon	Roscommon	Clooncraff	Strokestown	IV.	208
60	*Illangub*	0 2 11	Mayo	Carra	Turlough	Castlebar	IV.	131
5	*Illanmaster*	6 3 14	Mayo	Erris	Kilcommon	Belmullet	IV.	145
76	*Illanmaw*	1 1 39	Mayo	Burrishoole	Kilmeena	Westport	IV.	122
121	Illanmore	211 2 3	Mayo	Kilmaine	Kilmainebeg	Ballinrobe	IV.	155
17	*Illannachurry South*	5 3 2	Donegal	Kilmacrenan	Mevagh	Milford	III.	130
76	*Illannaconney*	2 1 15	Mayo	Burrishoole	Kilmeena	Westport	IV.	122
48	Illannaglashy	81 2 22	Mayo	Tirawley	Kilbeifad	Ballina	IV.	168
67	*Illannambraher East*	14 0 7	Mayo	Burrishoole	Burrishoole	Newport	IV.	120
67	*Illannambraher West*	11 2 13	Mayo	Burrishoole	Burrishoole	Newport	IV.	120
76	*Illannamona*	4 2 13	Mayo	Burrishoole	Kilmeena	Westport	IV.	122
60	*Illanneill*	0 2 36	Mayo	Carra	Turlough	Castlebar	IV.	131
66	*Illanoona*	2 2 24	Mayo	Burrishoole	Burrishoole	Newport	IV.	120
101	*Illan Philipboy*	7 0 26	Donegal	Tirhugh	Templecarn	Donegal	III.	149
67	*Illanroe*	2 2 30	Mayo	Burrishoole	Burrishoole	Newport	IV.	120
44	*Illanroe*	2 3 32	Mayo	Erris	Kilcommon	Newport	IV.	145
87	*Illanroe*	2 1 21	Mayo	Murrisk	Oughaval	Westport	IV.	162
78	*Illanteige East*	38 2 32	Mayo	Burrishoole	Islandeady	Westport	IV.	121
78	*Illanteige West*	21 2 21	Mayo	Burrishoole	Islandeady	Westport	IV.	121
60	*Illanulque*	0 2 18	Mayo	Carra	Turlough	Castlebar	IV.	131
36, 31	Illaun	413 0 28	Clare	Ibrickan	Kilfarboy	Ennistimon	II.	22
4	Illaun	302 1 4c	Galway	Dunmore	Addergoole	Tuam	IV.	33
56	*Illaunaclaggin*	0 1 8	Clare	Moyarta	Kilrush	Kilrush	II.	33
54	*Illaunaconaun*	26 1 9	Galway	Moycullen	Kilcummin	Oughterard	IV.	68
3	*Illaunacoran*	2 1 21	Clare	Burren	Abbey	Ballyvaghan	II.	11

(a) Including 13A. 3R. 20P. detached portion.   (b) Including 8A. 2R. 32P. water.   (c) Including 19A. 0R. 0P. water.

3 Y 2

No. of Sheet of the Ordnance Survey Maps.	Townlands and Towns.	Area in Statute Acres.			County.	Barony.	Parish.	Poor Law Union in 1857.	Townland Census of 1851, Part I.	
		A.	R.	P.					Vol.	Page
51, 64	*Illaunacroghnut*	23	3	26	Galway	Ballynahinch	Moyrus	Clifden	IV.	14
103	*Illaunacrusha*	0	2	27	Galway	Dunkellin	Drumacoo	Gort	IV.	28
99, 107	*Illaunacummig*	7	0	15	Kerry	Dunkerron South	Kilcrohane	Kenmare	II.	184
109	*Illaunadroughearla*	0	1	2	Galway	Longford	Meelick	Portumna	IV.	62
40	*Illaunagawna*	1	2	4	Galway	Ross	Cong	Oughterard	IV.	73
109	*Illaunaglee*	0	1	14	Galway	Longford	Meelick	Portumna	IV.	62
109	*Illaunagoughal*	1	2	7	Galway	Longford	Meelick	Portumna	IV.	62
78	*Illaunagreasy*	3	3	29	Galway	Moycullen	Killannin	Oughterard	IV.	70
26, 27	*Illaunaknick*	0	3	23	Galway	Ross	Cong	Oughterard	IV.	73
64	*Illaunaknock*	3	3	26	Galway	Ballynahinch	Moyrus	Clifden	IV.	14
56	*Illaunalea*	1	0	5	Clare	Moyarta	Kilrush	Kilrush	II.	33
48	*Illaunaleama*	20	3	5	Galway	Ballynahinch	Ballindoon	Clifden	IV.	11
48	*Illaunamenara*	5	1	32	Galway	Ballynahinch	Ballindoon	Clifden	IV.	11
48	*Illaunamid*	29	0	15	Galway	Ballynahinch	Ballindoon	Clifden	IV.	11
100, 108	*Illaunanadan*	16	0	32	Kerry	Dunkerron South	Kilcrohane	Kenmare	II.	184
45	*Illaunanadderha*	3	2	31	Clare	Tulla Lower	Killaloe	Scarriff	II.	35
40	*Illaunanarrew*	2	1	39	Galway	Ross	Cong	Oughterard	IV.	73
103	*Illaunanarroor*	2	0	13	Galway	Dunkellin	Kilcolgan	Gort	IV.	28
109	*Illaunanbissan*	1	0	38	Galway	Longford	Meelick	Portumna	IV.	62
48	*Illaunane*	11	2	13	Galway	Ballynahinch	Ballindoon	Clifden	IV.	11
69	*Illaunaneel*	13	3	11	Galway	Clare	Annaghdown	Galway	IV.	17
69	*Illaunaneel West*	2	1	39	Galway	Clare	Annaghdown	Galway	IV.	17
127	*Illaunard*	0	0	6	Cork, W.R.	Bear	Kilnamanagh	Castletown	II.	126
78	*Illaunard*	12	3	33	Galway	Ballynahinch	Moyrus	Clifden	IV.	14
63	*Illaunaroan*	0	3	19	Clare	Bunratty Lower	St. Patricks	Limerick	II.	7
40, 48, 49	Illaunatoo or Sorrel-island	276	1	20	Clare	Clonderalaw	Kilmihil	Ennis	II.	17
78	*Illaunatraghta*	5	3	23	Galway	Moycullen	Killannin	Oughterard	IV.	70
55	*Illaunaveel*	5	0	34	Galway	Moycullen	Killannin	Oughterard	IV.	70
56	*Illaunaveetry*	1	3	20	Galway	Clare	Annaghdown	Galway	IV.	17
23, 24	Illaunbaun	436	2	17	Clare	Corcomroe	Clooney	Ennistimon	II.	18
23, 31	Illaunbaun	418	2	1*a*	Clare	Ibrickan	Kilfarboy	Ennistimon	II.	22
60	*Illaunbeg or O'Don-nell's Island*	8	0	36	Clare	Clonderalaw	Killadysert	Killadysert	II.	16
19	*Illaunboe*	4	3	17	Kerry	Corkaguiny	Killiney	Dingle	II.	178
108, 109	*Illaunboy*	2	2	13	Galway	Longford	Meelick	Portumna	IV.	62
51	*Illaunboy*	3	2	38	Kerry	Corkaguiny	Dunquin	Dingle	II.	176
153	*Illaunbrock*	3	0	2	Cork, W.R.	West Carbery (E.D.)	Tullagh	Skibbereen	II.	141
102	*Illaunbweeheen*	2	1	35	Cork, W.R.	Bear	Kilcatherine	Castletown	II.	124
55	*Illauncarbry*	2	0	36	Galway	Clare	Cargin	Tuam	IV.	18
54	*Illauncarbry*	4	3	7	Galway	Moycullen	Kilcummin	Oughterard	IV.	68
36	Illauncaum	161	0	26	Kerry	Corkaguiny	Killiney	Dingle	II.	178
127	*Illauncohid*	0	2	8	Cork, W.R.	Bear	Kilnamanagh	Castletown	II.	126
89	*Illauncosheen*	16	0	37	Galway	Moycullen	Kilcummin	Oughterard	IV.	68
3	*Illauncraggagh*	2	3	27	Clare	Burren	Drumcreehy	Ballyvaghan	II.	12
116	*Illauncreagh*	0	0	9	Cork, W.R.	Bear	Kilcaskan	Castletown	II.	123
105	*Illauncreeveen*	3	2	6	Cork, W.R.	Bantry	Kilmocomoge	Bantry	II.	121
78	*Illauncurragilka*	1	1	15	Galway	Moycullen	Killannin	Oughterard	IV.	70
27	*I'laundarragh*	2	1	28	Galway	Ross	Cong	Oughterard	IV.	73
40	*Illaundaulaur*	3	3	24	Galway	Ross	Cong	Oughterard	IV.	73
40	*Illaundavrack*	1	2	26	Galway	Moycullen	Kilcummin	Oughterard	IV.	68
40	*Illaundonoghrevy*	3	1	12	Galway	Ross	Cong	Oughterard	IV.	73
107	*Illaundrane*	26	1	38	Kerry	Dunkerron South	Kilcrohane	Kenmare	II.	184
77, 89	Illauneeragh	89	2	7	Galway	Moycullen	Killannin	Oughterard	IV.	70
65	Illauneeragh West	77	3	29	Galway	Moycullen	Kilcummin	Oughterard	IV.	68
64	*Illaunfadda*	2	0	16	Galway	Ballynahinch	Moyrus	Clifden	IV.	14
68	*Illaunfadda*	5	1	30	Galway	Moycullen	Killannin	Oughterard	IV.	70
55	*Illaunfadda Beg*	5	0	33	Galway	Moycullen	Kilcummin	Oughterard	IV.	68
55	*Illaunfadda More*	10	3	24	Galway	Moycullen	Kilcummin	Oughterard	IV.	68
149	*Illaungawna*	8	0	1	Cork, W.R.	West Carbery (E.D.)	Aghadown	Skibbereen	II.	137
51, 64	*Illaungorm North*	33	0	19	Galway	Ballynahinch	Moyrus	Clifden	IV.	14
64	*Illaungorm South*	12	1	11	Galway	Ballynahinch	Moyrus	Clifden	IV.	14
78	*Illaungurraig*	3	0	0	Galway	Ballynahinch	Moyrus	Clifden	IV.	14
137	*Illaunhobert*	5	1	19	Galway	Leitrim	Clonrush	Scarriff	IV.	53
19	*Illaunimmil*	29	1	23	Kerry	Corkaguiny	Killiney	Dingle	II.	178
81	Illauninagh East	186	2	39*b*	Cork, W.R.	West Muskerry	Inchigeelagh	Dunmanway	II.	157
81	Illauninagh West	456	0	37*c*	Cork, W.R.	West Muskerry	Inchigeelagh	Dunmanway	II.	157
149	*Illaunkearagh*	1	3	23	Cork, W.R.	West Carbery (E.D.)	Aghadown	Skibbereen	II.	137
21	Illaunknocknanagh	233	2	11	Cork, E.R.	Duhallow	Kilmeen	Kanturk	II.	73
109	*Illaunkyle*	2	2	26	Galway	Longford	Meelick	Portumna	IV.	62
99, 107	*Illaunleagh*	9	3	25	Kerry	Dunkerron South	Kilcrohane	Kenmare	II.	184
40, 41	*Illaunleenagh*	1	3	0	Galway	Moycullen	Killannin	Oughterard	IV	70
77	*Illaunmaan*	1	1	24	Galway	Ballynahinch	Moyrus	Clifden	IV.	14

(*a*) Including 4A. 0R. 32P. water. (*b*) Including 20A. 2R. 30P. water. (*c*) Including 12A. 1R. 16P. water.

No. of Sheet of the Ordnance Survey Maps.	Townlands and Towns.	Area in Statute Acres.	County.	Barony.	Parish.	Poor Law Union in 1857.	Townland Census of 1851, Part I.	
		A. R. P.					Vol.	Page
68	Illaunmahon	1 3 29	Galway	Moycullen	Moycullen	Galway	IV.	71
58	Illaunmeen	142 0 15	Tipperary, S.R.	Clanwilliam	Cullen	Tipperary	II.	307
143	Illaunmore	0 2 27	Cork, W.R.	East Carbery (W.D.)	Kilfaughnabeg	Skibbereen	II.	133
135	Illaunmore	212 2 10	Galway	Leitrim	Kilbarron	Scarriff	IV.	54
65	Illaunmore	95 2 22	Galway	Moycullen	Kilcummin	Oughterard	IV.	68
68	Illaunaboolia	4 2 0	Galway	Moycullen	Killannin	Oughterard	IV.	70
21, 29	Illaunnacalliagh	7 2 28	King's Co.	Garrycastle	Lusmagh	Parsonstown	I.	137
63	Illaunnacroughbeg	2 3 3	Galway	Ballynahinch	Moyrus	Clifden	IV.	14
63	Illaunnacroaghmore	12 1 38	Galway	Ballynahinch	Moyrus	Clifden	IV.	14
68	Illaunnafinnoge	0 2 35	Galway	Moycullen	Moycullen	Galway	IV.	71
65	Illaunnagappul	17 0 3	Galway	Moycullen	Kilcummin	Oughterard	IV.	68
54, 55	Illaunnagappul	4 0 20	Galway	Moycullen	Kilcummin	Oughterard	IV.	68
65	Illaunnaginga	1 3 10	Galway	Moycullen	Kilcummin	Oughterard	IV.	68
55	Illaunnagower	3 1 25	Galway	Moycullen	Kilcummin	Oughterard	IV.	68
112	Illaunnaguroge	1 1 8	Galway	Kiltartan	Kinvarradoorus	Gort	IV.	50
100	Illaunnakilla	7 0 5	Kerry	Dunkerron South	Kilcrohane	Kenmare	II.	184
77	Illaunnakirka	8 3 6	Galway	Ballynahinch	Moyrus	Clifden	IV.	14
101	Illaunnameanla	2 1 18	Cork, W.R.	Bear	Kilcatherine	Castletown	II.	124
126	Illaunnamoe	0 2 38	Longford	Longford	Lickmolassy	Portumna	IV.	61
89	Illaunnanownim	24 3 14	Galway	Moycullen	Killannin	Oughterard	IV.	70
29	Illaunnarank	1 3 34	King's Co.	Garrycastle	Lusmagh	Parsonstown	I.	137
150	Illaunnaseer	2 1 2	Cork, W.R.	West Carbery (E.D.)	Creagh	Skibbereen	II.	139
69	Illaunnashinnagh	10 1 24	Galway	Moycullen	Moycullen	Galway	IV.	72
68	Illaunnaskeagh	6 1 2	Galway	Moycullen	Moycullen	Galway	IV.	72
106	Illaunnaweelaun	6 1 22	Kerry	Dunkerron South	Kilcrohane	Cahersiveen	II.	184
55	Illaunonearaun	9 0 0	Clare	Moyarta	Moyarta	Kilrush	II.	34
109	Illaunord	0 3 13	Galway	Longford	Meelick	Portumna	IV.	62
27	Illaunree	2 3 30	Galway	Ross	Cong	Oughterard	IV.	73
40	Illaunribbeen	15 0 8	Galway	Ross	Cong	Oughterard	IV.	73
148	Illaunricmonia	1 0 5	Cork, W.R.	West Carbery (W.D.)	Skull	Skull	II.	147
140	Illaunroe	6 0 6	Cork, W.R.	West Carbery (W.D.)	Skull	Skull	II.	146
43	Illaunroe	104 1 28a	Galway	Clare	Cummer	Tuam	IV.	19
78	Illaunroe	8 3 33	Galway	Moycullen	Kilcummin	Oughterard	IV.	68
89	Illaunroe	1 1 35	Galway	Moycullen	Killannin	Oughterard	IV.	70
77	Illaunroe	9 2 2	Galway	Moycullen	Killannin	Oughterard	IV.	70
140	Illaunroemore	15 1 4	Cork, W.R.	West Carbery (W.D.)	Kilcoe	Skull	II.	143
65	Illaunrossalough	2 1 13	Galway	Moycullen	Kilcummin	Oughterard	IV.	68
35	Illaunrush	2 2 38	Galway	Ballynahinch	Ballindoon	Clifden	IV.	11
107	Illaunsillagh	9 2 19	Kerry	Dunkerron South	Kilcrohane	Kenmare	II.	184
100	Illaunslea	18 1 0	Kerry	Dunkerron South	Kilcrohane	Kenmare	II.	184
55, 56	Illaunstookagh	311 1 7b	Kerry	Iveragh	Killorglin	Killarney	II.	198
19	Illauntannig	32 1 2	Kerry	Corkaguiny	Killiney	Dingle	II.	178
49	Illaunurra	21 2 39	Galway	Ballynahinch	Ballindoon	Clifden	IV.	11
53, 63	Illaunyregan	351 3 2	Clare	Tulla Lower	Kiltenanlea	Limerick	II.	37
52, 53	Illeny	1,341 3 39c	Galway	Moycullen	Kilcummin	Oughterard	IV.	67
20, 29, 30	Illies	2,293 1 32	Donegal	Inishowen West	Fahan Lower	Inishowen	III.	120
40, 48	Illion	639 1 27	Donegal	Boylagh	Templecrone	Glenties	III.	115
24, 37	Illion	477 3 10	Galway	Ballynahinch	Ballynakill	Clifden	IV.	11
38	Illion East	1,531 0 2d	Galway	Ballynahinch	Moyrus	Clifden	IV.	13
24, 25, 37	Illion West	662 0 4e	Galway	Ballynahinch	Moyrus	Clifden	IV.	13
41	Imdel	746 2 5f	Down	Upper Iveagh, Lr. pt.	Drumballyroney	Banbridge	III.	172
17	Imeroo	560 3 10	Fermanagh	Tirkennedy	Enniskillen	Enniskillen	III.	222
55	Imlick	169 1 34	Donegal	Raphoe	Killea	Londonderry	III.	139
16	Imogane	278 2 7	Cork, E.R.	Orrery and Kilmore	Churchtown	Mallow	II.	107
78	Imokishy	89 2 2	Cork, E.R.	Imokilly	Ightermurragh	Middleton	II.	87
7, 8	Imphrick	181 3 38	Cork, E.R.	Fermoy	Imphrick	Mallow	II.	80
13	Inagh	1,235 1 2	Mayo	Tirawley	Doonfeeny	Killala	IV.	167
40, 41	Inan	405 0 33	Meath	Upper Moyfenrath	Killyon	Trim	I.	213
151	Inane	79 0 25	Cork, W.R.	West Carbery (E.D.)	Castlehaven	Skibbereen	II.	138
149, 150	Inane	188 0 9	Cork, W.R.	West Carbery (E.D.)	Creagh	Skibbereen	II.	139
12, 17	Inane	507 0 37	Tipperary, N.R.	Ikerrin	Roscrea	Roscrea	II.	276
100	Inch	387 3 34	Cork, E.R.	Imokilly	Inch	Middleton	II.	87
30, 37	Inch	561 1 10g	Down	Lecale Lower	Inch	Downpatrick	III.	179
5	Inch	175 2 3h	Dublin	Balrothery East	Balrothery	Balrothery	I.	19
45, 55	Inch	1,003 2 14	Kerry	Corkaguiny	Ballinvoher	Dingle	II.	174
75, 76	Inch	193 0 2	Kerry	Magunihy	Killaha	Killarney	II.	202
66	Inch	77 2 33	Kerry	Magunihy	Killarney	Killarney	II.	203
35	Inch	598 2 5	Kildare	Narragh & RebanEast	Moone	Athy	I.	66
25	Inch	195 0 28	Queen's Co.	Ballyadams	Rathaspick	Athy	I.	232
14	Inch	397 2 16	Queen's Co.	Stradbally	Curraclone	Athy	I.	246
34, 40	Inch	199 3 27	Tipperary, N.R.	Eliogarty	Inch	Thurles	II.	270
27, 33	Inch	770 3 25	Wexford	Ballaghkeen	Killila	Enniscorthy	I.	295
3	Inch	117 3 6	Wexford	Gorey	Inch	Gorey	I.	316

(a) Including 78A. 0R. 8P. water.
(b) Including 35A. 1R. 20P. water.
(c) Including 153A. 1R. 30P. water.

(d) Including 17A. 0R. 37P. water.
(e) Including 28A. 0R. 39P. water.
(f) Including 1A. 0R. 30P. water.

(g) Including 23A. 0R. 23P. water.
(h) Including 57A. 3R. 26P. detached portions.

No. of Sheet of the Ordnance Survey Maps.	Townlands and Towns.	Area in Statute Acres.	County.	Barony.	Parish.	Poor Law Union in 1857.	Townland Census of 1851, Part I.	
		A. R. P.					Vol.	Page
46	Incha . . .	208 0 36	Limerick . .	Connello Upper .	Corcomohide . .	Croom . .	II.	232
25	Incha Beg . .	126 1 21	Tipperary, N.R.	Owney and Arra .	Templeachally .	Nenagh . .	II.	297
123	Inchaboy North .	48 0 30	Galway . .	Kiltartan . .	Kilbeacanty .	Gort . .	IV.	47
129	Inchaboy South .	575 0 5a	Galway . .	Kiltartan . .	Kilbeacanty .	Gort . .	IV.	47
10, 14	Inchabride . .	40 1 14	Kilkenny . .	Fassadinin . .	Mothell . .	Castlecomer .	I.	90
40	Inchacarran . .	118 1 18	Kilkenny . .	Knocktopher .	Killahy . .	Waterford . .	I.	112
68	Inchacommaun Islands	6 0 12	Galway . .	Moycullen . .	Moycullen . .	Galway . .	IV.	72
5	Inchacooly . .	1,271 1 35	Queen's Co. .	Portnahinch .	Lea . . .	Mountmellick .	I.	244
49, 57, 58	Inchacoomb . .	544 3 0	Limerick . .	Coshlea . .	Galbally . .	Mitchelstown .	II.	238
12, 19	Inchadoghill . .	98 3 34	Londonderry .	Coleraine . .	Aghadowey .	Coleraine . .	III.	229
37	Inchadrinagh . .	305 2 39	Tipperary, N.R.	Owney and Arra .	Kilvellane . .	Nenagh . .	II.	296
25	Inchadrinagh . .	282 3 15	Tipperary, N.R.	Owney and Arra .	Templeachally .	Nenagh . .	II.	297
108, 121	Inchafune . .	871 3 5b	Cork, W.R. .	East Carbery (E.D.)	Ballymoney .	Dunmanway .	II.	127
77	Inchaghaun . .	28 1 16	Galway . .	Moycullen . .	Killannin . .	Oughterard .	IV.	70
40	Inchagoill . .	80 3 1	Galway . .	Ross . . .	Cong . . .	Oughterard .	IV.	73
67	Inchagreana . .	6 0 8	Tipperary, S.R.	Clanwilliam .	Kilfeakle . .	Tipperary . .	II.	308
10, 19	Inchagreenoge .	37 1 39	Limerick . .	Shanid . .	Robertstown .	Rathkeale . .	II.	258
17, 18	Inchakevin . .	85 0 22	Cork, E.R. .	Fermoy . .	Wallstown .	Mallow . .	II.	83
10, 14	Inchakill Glebe .	168 1 21	Kilkenny . .	Fassadinin . .	Mayne . .	Kilkenny . .	I.	90
60, 71	Inchaleagh . .	292 2 0	Cork, W.R. .	East Muskerry .	Aghinagh . .	Macroom . .	II.	154
36	Inchaloughra . .	50 2 6	Kerry . .	Corkaguiny .	Killiney . .	Dingle . .	II.	178
36	Inchalughoge .	387 2 13	Clare . .	Tulla Upper .	Kilnoe . .	Scarriff . .	II.	40
78, 90	Inchamakinna . .	108 3 21	Galway . .	Moycullen . .	Kilcummin .	Oughterard .	IV.	68
90	Inchamakinna . .	1 0 1	Galway . .	Moycullen . .	Kilcummin .	Oughterard .	IV.	68
40, 49	Inchamay North .	895 0 34	Cork, E.R. .	Duhallow . .	Clonmeen .	Kanturk . .	II.	69
40, 49	Inchamay South .	1,083 1 6	Cork, E.R. .	Duhallow . .	Clonmeen .	Kanturk . .	II.	69
57	Inchamore . .	1,635 2 29	Cork, W.R. .	West Muskerry .	Ballyvourney .	Macroom . .	II.	154
130	Inchamore . .	208 2 0	Galway . .	Kiltartan . .	Kilthomas .	Gort . .	IV.	49
25	Incha More . .	439 0 39	Tipperary, N.R.	Owney and Arra .	Templeachally .	Nenagh . .	II.	297
83	Inchanabraher .	30 0 23c	Tipperary, S.R.	Iffa and Offa East .	Killaloan . .	Clonmel . .	II.	314
21, 29	Inchanaclea . .	14 3 30	King's Co. .	Garrycastle .	Lusmagh . .	Parsonstown .	I.	137
107	Inchanadreen . .	236 2 19	Cork, W.R. .	East Carbery (W.D.)	Fanlobbus .	Dunmanway .	II.	132
34	Inchanaglogh . .	133 1 25	Kilkenny . .	Kells . .	Tullahought .	Callan . .	I.	110
66	Inchanapisha . .	42 3 16	Cork, E.R. .	Imokilly . .	Killeagh . .	Youghal . .	II.	88
19, 25	Inchanappa North .	62 2 30	Wicklow . .	Newcastle . .	Killiskey . .	Rathdrum . .	I.	352
25	Inchanappa South .	183 0 9	Wicklow . .	Newcastle . .	Killiskey . .	Rathdrum . .	I.	352
17	Inchancarl . .	67 2 38	Kildare . .	Offaly East .	Rathangan .	Edenderry .	I.	71
11	Inchamisky . .	271 0 25	Queen's Co. .	Upperwoods .	Offerlane .	Mountmellick .	I.	252
13, 14	Inchantotane . .	531 0 31	Cork, E.R. .	Duhallow . .	Clonfert . .	Kanturk . .	II.	68
22, 24	Inchaphuca or Inch	83 1 7	Carlow . .	St. Mullins Lower .	St. Mullins .	New Ross .	I.	13
32, 36	Inchaquire . .	686 3 1	Kildare . .	Narragh & Reban East	Narraghmore .	Athy . .	I.	66
17	Incharmedermot .	12 0 6	Longford . .	Rathcline . .	Rathcline .	Longford . .	I.	164
33, 41	Inchbeg . .	203 0 19	Clare . .	Islands . .	Drumcliff .	Ennis . .	II.	30
9, 10	Inchbeg . .	252 3 5	Kilkenny . .	Crannagh . .	Coolcraheen .	Kilkenny . .	I.	85
47	Inchbeg Island .	15 2 32	Sligo . .	Coolavin . .	Killaraght .	Boyle . .	IV.	225
15	Inchbofin . .	65 3 11	Westmeath .	Kilkenny West .	Noughaval .	Athlone . .	I.	274
21	Inchcleraun . .	100 1 16	Longford . .	Rathcline . .	Cashel . .	Ballymahon .	I.	163
67	Inchcorly . .	1 3 18	Mayo . .	Burrishoole .	Burrishoole .	Newport . .	IV.	120
107	Inch East . .	587 3 21	Cork, W.R. .	East Carbery(W.D.)	Fanlobbus .	Dunmanway .	II.	132
45	Inch East . .	251 0 16	Kerry . .	Corkaguiny .	Bailinvoher .	Dingle . .	II.	174
10	Inch East . .	312 0 15	Kerry . .	Iraghticonnor .	Galey . .	Listowel . .	II.	190
85,86,94,95	Inchee . .	1,772 0 4	Kerry . .	Glanarought .	Kilgarvan .	Kenmare . .	II.	187
98, 106	Inchee East . .	601 3 4	Kerry . .	Dunkerron South .	Kilcrohane .	Cahersiveen .	II.	183
84	Incheens . .	580 2 3	Kerry . .	Magunihy . .	Killarney .	Killarney . .	II.	203
98, 106	Inchee West . .	798 1 25	Kerry . .	Dunkerron South .	Kilcrohane .	Cahersiveen .	II.	183
21	Inchenagh . .	69 0 32	Longford . .	Rathcline . .	Rathcline .	Longford . .	I.	164
4, 9	Inchenny . .	174 1 8	Tyrone . .	Strabane Lower .	Urney . .	Strabane . .	III.	322
9	Inchenny Upper .	169 0 21	Tyrone . .	Strabane Lower .	Urney . .	Strabane . .	III.	322
75	Inchera . .	84 1 21	Cork, E.R. .	Barrymore .	Little Island .	Cork . .	II.	56
21, 29	Incherky . .	191 2 32	King's Co. .	Garrycastle .	Lusmagh . .	Parsonstown .	I.	137
101, 102, 114, 115	Inches . .	850 3 28	Cork, W.R. .	Bear . . .	Kilcatherine .	Castletown .	II.	124
38	Inches . .	400 2 11d	Cork, W.R. .	West Muskerry .	Drishane .	Millstreet .	II.	156
98	Inchfarrannaglcragh Glebe . .	828 1 23e	Kerry . .	Dunkerron South .	Kilcrohane .	Cahersiveen .	II.	183
80	Inchi Beg . .	447 1 13	Cork, W.R. .	West Muskerry .	Inchigeelagh .	Dunmanway .	II.	157
89	Inchiboy . .	775 0 19	Kerry . .	Iveragh . .	Dromod . .	Cahersiveen .	II.	195
70	Inchibrackane .	93 2 31	Cork, W.R. .	West Muskerry .	Kilnamartry .	Macroom . .	II.	159
105	Inchiclogh . .	111 1 35	Cork, W.R. .	Bantry . .	Kilmocomoge .	Bantry . .	II.	121
79, 80	Inchiclogh . .	227 2 17	Kerry . .	Iveragh . .	Caher . .	Cahersiveen .	II.	194
102	Inchicleon . .	301 1 27f	Kerry . .	Glanarought .	Tuosist . .	Kenmare . .	II.	189
10	Inchicore North .	210 0 30g	Dublin . .	Uppercross .	St. James .	Dublin South .	I.	41
18	Inchicore South .	154 3 34	Dublin . .	Uppercross .	St. James .	Dublin South .	I.	41

(a) Including 7A. 1R. 2P. water.
(b) Including 7A. 3R. 8P. Ballynacarriga Lough.
(c) Including 1A. 3R. 26P. water.

(d) Including 8A. 0R. 38P. water.
(e) Including 13A. 1R. 7P. water.

(f) Including 6A. 3R. 27P. water.
(g) Including 14A. 2R. 19P. water.

No. of Sheet of the Ordnance Survey Maps.	Townlands and Towns.	Area in Statute Acres.			County.	Barony.	Parish.	Poor Law Union in 1857.	Townland Census of 1851, Part I.	
		A.	R.	P.					Vol.	Page
59	Inchicorrigane East	463	0	2	Kerry	Magunihy	Kilcummin	Killarney	II.	201
59	Inchicorrigane West	545	0	6	Kerry	Magunihy	Kilcummin	Killarney	II.	201
26	Inchicronan Island	184	1	31a	Clare	Bunratty Upper	Inchicronan	Ennis	II.	9
31	Inchidaly	208	1	4b	Cork, E.R.	Duhallow	Clonmeen	Kanturk	II.	69
81	Inchideraille	277	1	20	Cork, W.R.	West Muskerry	Inchigeelagh	Dunmanway	II.	157
73, 74	Inchigaggin	250	2	8c	Cork, E.R.	Cork	St. Finbars	Cork	II.	66
99	Inchigeelagh	13	3	13	Cork, E.R.	Kerricurrihy	Templebreedy	Kinsale	II.	93
81	Inchigeelagh	105	0	7	Cork, W.R.	West Muskerry	Inchigeelagh	Macroom	II.	157
81	INCHIGEELAGH T.	—			Cork, W.R.	West Muskerry	Inchigeelagh	Macroom	II.	158
82	Inchigrady	458	1	35	Cork, W.R.	West Muskerry	Inchigeelagh	Dunmanway	II.	157
39	Inchileigh	262	3	37	Cork, W.R.	West Muskerry	Drishane	Millstreet	II.	156
80	Inchimacteige	252	0	27	Kerry	Iveragh	Caher	Cahersiveen	II.	194
80	Inchi More	602	2	13	Cork, W.R.	West Muskerry	Inchigeelagh	Dunmanway	II.	157
84, 93	Inchimore	311	1	18	Kerry	Glanarought	Kenmare	Kenmare	II.	186
94, 103	Inchimore	1,014	0	26d	Kerry	Glanarought	Kilgarvan	Kenmare	II.	187
132, 133	Inchinagotagh	303	2	26	Cork, W.R.	West Carbery (E.D.)	Abbeystrowry	Skibbereen	II.	136
91	Inchinagoum	359	1	8	Cork, W.R.	Bantry	Kilmocomoge	Bantry	II.	121
70	Inchinahoury	158	2	0	Cork, W.R.	West Muskerry	Clondrohid	Macroom	II.	155
55	Inchinalee	18	3	29	Roscommon	Athlone	Drum	Athlone	IV.	180
99, 100	Inchinaleega East	83	1	16	Kerry	Dunkerron South	Kilcrohane	Kenmare	II.	183
99, 100	Inchinaleega West	115	2	3	Kerry	Dunkerron South	Kilcrohane	Kenmare	II.	184
43	Inchinanagh	230	3	7	Cork, E.R.	Barrymore	Ardnageehy	Fermoy	II.	50
103	Inchinanagh	1,736	2	15	Kerry	Glanarought	Kilgarvan	Kenmare	II.	187
82	Inchinaneave	353	3	3	Cork, W.R.	West Muskerry	Inchigeelagh	Macroom	II.	157
27, 35	Inchinapallas	335	2	21e	Cork, E.R.	Fermoy	Killathy	Fermoy	II.	80
24	Inchinapoagh	711	1	1f	Kerry	Trughanacmy	Brosna	Tralee	II.	208
91, 92	Inchinarihen	360	3	33	Cork, W.R.	Bantry	Kilmocomoge	Bantry	II.	121
80, 81	Inchinascarty	368	1	10	Kerry	Iveragh	Dromod	Cahersiveen	II.	195
71	Inchinashingane	505	1	1	Cork, W.R.	West Muskerry	Macloneigh	Macroom	II.	160
101, 109	Inchinaskeagh	9	3	16	Galway	Longtord	Clonfert	Ballinasloe	IV.	57
89	Inchinatinny	334	2	26	Kerry	Iveragh	Dromod	Cahersiveen	II.	195
121	Inchinattin	399	2	20	Cork, W.R.	East Carbery (W.D.)	Castleventry	Clonakilty	II.	131
22, 24	Inch or Inchaphuca	83	1	7	Carlow	St. Mullins Lower	St. Mullins	New Ross	I.	13
39	Inchinclare	240	0	11	Limerick	Coshma	Athlacca	Croom	II.	241
31, 39	Inchinclare	257	2	31	Limerick	Coshma	Croom	Croom	II.	242
85, 86	Inchincoosh	911	3	14	Kerry	Glanarought	Kilgarvan	Kenmare	II.	187
49	Inchincummer	368	0	27	Kerry	Trughanacmy	Killeentierna	Killarney	II.	211
93, 94	Inchincurka	668	3	21	Cork. W.R.	East Carbery (W.D.)	Kilmichael	Dunmanway	II.	134
30, 31	Inchindrisla	473	0	21	Waterford	Decies without Drum	Kilgobnet	Dungarvan	II.	357
30	Inchindrisla Wood	110	3	21	Waterford	Decies without Drum	Kilgobnet	Dungarvan	II.	357
82	Inchineill	311	3	33	Cork, W.R.	West Muskerry	Inchigeelagh	Macroom	II.	157
119	Inchingerig	390	0	30	Cork, W.R.	West Carbery (W.D.)	Caheragh	Skibbereen	II.	142
82, 83	Inchinglanna	740	1	25g	Kerry	Dunkerron South	Templenoe	Kenmare	II.	185
19	Inchinleama East	161	2	32h	Waterford	Coshmore and Coshbride	Leitrim	Lismore	II.	344
19	Inchinleama West	332	2	0i	Waterford	Coshmore and Coshbride	Leitrim	Lismore	II.	344
70	Inchinlinane	226	1	16	Cork, W.R.	West Muskerry	Clondrohid	Macroom	II.	155
101, 109	Inchin Lough	335	2	25j	Kerry	Glanarought	Tuosist	Kenmare	II.	189
80, 81	Inchinossig	331	1	20	Cork, W.R.	West Muskerry	Inchigeelagh	Dunmanway	II.	157
45, 51	Inchinsquillib	707	1	6	Tipperary, N.R.	Kilnamanagh Upper	Toem	Tipperary	II.	280
104	Inchintaggart	145	3	12	Cork. W.R.	Bear	Kilcaskan	Bantry	II.	123
103	Inchintaglin	1,140	0	2	Cork, W.R.	Bear	Kilcaskan	Castletown	II.	123
114	Inchinteskin	86	3	10	Cork, W.R.	Bear	Kilcatherine	Castletown	II.	124
70, 80	Inchintrea	190	0	26	Kerry	Iveragh	Killinane	Cahersiveen	II.	197
48	Inchinveema	195	2	21	Kerry	Magunihy	Molahiffe	Killarney	II.	205
17	Inchiquin	290	1	21k	Clare	Inchiquin	Killinaboy	Corrofin	II.	26
67, 78	Inchiquin	409	3	21	Cork, E.R.	Imokilly	Clonpriest	Youghal	II.	85
41	Inchiquin	229	2	25	Galway	Clare	Killursa	Tuam	IV.	22
83, 84	Inchirahilly	70	3	1	Cork, E.R.	East Muskerry	Kilmurry	Bandon	II.	104
83, 84	Inchirahilly	474	0	16	Cork, E.R.	East Muskerry	Moviddy	Bandon	II.	105
93, 107	Inchireagh	301	1	37	Cork, W.R.	East Carbery (W.D.)	Fanlobbus	Dunmanway	II.	132
92	Inchiroe	975	0	31	Cork, W.R.	Bantry	Kilmocomoge	Bantry	II.	121
45	Inchiroe and Gortfree	263	1	24l	Roscommon	Athlone	Cam	Athlone	IV.	180
36, 42, 43	Inchirourke	1,492	2	32	Tipperary, S.R.	Slievardagh	Fennor	Thurles	II.	333
74	Inchisarsfield	60	0	35	Cork, E.R.	Cork	St. Finbars	Cork	II.	66
70, 82	Inchisine	380	2	36	Cork, W.R.	West Muskerry	Macloneigh	Macroom	II.	160
19	Inch Island	87	1	4	Cavan	Upper Loughtee	Kilmore	Cavan	III.	84
47	Inch Island	13	0	21	Sligo	Coolavin	Killaraght	Boyle	IV.	225
8	Inchisland or Moatalusha	233	0	35	Carlow	Carlow	Grangeford	Carlow	I.	2
39	Inchivara	271	1	20	Tipperary, N.R.	Kilnamanagh Upper	Toem	Tipperary	II.	280
38, 47	Inch Level (Intake)	292	0	0m	Donegal	Inishowen West	Inch	Londonderry	III.	121

(a) Including 105A. 3R. 5P. water.
(b) Including 12A. 0R. 4P. River Blackwater.
(c) Including 12A. 2R. 7P. water.
(d) Including 10A. 0R. 38P. water.
(e) Including 5A. 0R. 30P. water.
(f) Including 7A. 0R. 3P. water.
(g) Including 15A. 0R. 36P. water.
(h) Including 3A. 3R. 18P. water.
(i) Including 11A. 0R. 32P. water.
(j) Including 48A. 3R. 10P. water.
(k) Including 126A. 0R. 21P. water.
(l) Including 157A. 3R. 10P. water.
(m) The area of this Intake does not appear on the Ordnance Maps; that here given is from the "Tenement Valuation."

No. of Sheet of the Ordnance Survey Maps	Townlands and Towns.	Area in Statute Acres.	County.	Barony.	Parish.	Poor Law Union in 1857.	Townland Census of 1851. Part I.	
		A. R. P.					Vol.	Page
3	Inchmearing . .	94 1 29	Londonderry .	North East Liberties of Coleraine . .	Ballywillin . .	Coleraine . .	III.	245
10	Inch Moor . .	340 1 15	Kerry . .	Iraghticonnor . .	Galey . . .	Listowel . .	II.	190
33, 41	Inch More . .	191 1 36	Clare . .	Islands . . .	Drumcliff . .	Ennis . .	II.	30
9, 13, 14	Inch More . .	352 0 24	Kilkenny . .	Crannagh . .	Coolcraheen . .	Kilkenny . .	I.	85
13	Inchmore . .	21 3 6	Kilkenny . .	Crannagh . .	Freshford . .	Kilkenny . .	I.	85
13	Inchmore . .	70 1 5	Limerick . .	Clanwilliam . .	St. Nicholas . .	Limerick . .	II.	225
6	Inchmore . .	17 2 27	Longford . .	Granard . .	Abbeylara . .	Granard . .	I.	154
6	Inchmore . .	14 2 7	Longford . .	Granard . .	Columbkille . .	Granard . .	I.	156
46	Inchmore . .	21 0 27	Sligo . .	Coolavin . .	Killaraght . .	Boyle . .	IV.	225
15, 22	Inchmore . .	132 0 32	Westmeath .	Kilkenny West .	Bunown . . .	Athlone . .	I.	272
15, 22	Inchmore (Tiernan)	65 0 18	Westmeath .	Kilkenny West .	Bunown . . .	Athlone . .	I.	272
35	Inchmurrin or Rabbit Island . .	27 1 2	Leitrim . .	Mohill . . .	Annaduff . .	Mohill . .	IV.	105
17	Inchnagree . .	262 1 5	Cork, E.R. .	Fermoy . . .	Doneraile . .	Mallow . .	II.	78
86, 87	Inchnamuck . .	274 0 35	Tipperary, S.R. .	Iffa and Offa West .	Shanrahan . .	Clogheen . .	II.	319
134	Inchnanoon . .	127 2 4	Cork, W.R. .	East Carbery (W.D.)	Kilmacabea . .	Skibbereen . .	II.	133
14	Inch St. Lawrence	135 1 17	Limerick . .	Clanwilliam . .	Ludden . . .	Limerick . .	II.	225
14, 23	Inch St. Lawrence North . .	344 3 15	Limerick . .	Clanwilliam . .	Inch St. Lawrence .	Limerick . .	II.	224
14, 25	Inch St. Lawrence South . .	128 1 19	Limerick . .	Clanwilliam . .	Inch St. Lawrence .	Limerick . .	II.	224
15	Inchturk . .	50 1 6	Westmeath .	Kilkenny West .	Noughaval . .	Athlone . .	I.	274
107	Inch West . .	295 0 8	Cork, W.R. .	East Carbery (W.D.)	Fanlobbus . .	Dunmanway . .	II.	132
45	Inch West . .	360 0 22	Kerry . .	Corkaguiny . .	Ballinvoher . .	Dingle . .	II.	174
10	Inch West . .	207 0 17	Kerry . .	Iraghticonnor . .	Galey . . .	Listowel . .	II.	190
116	Inchy . . .	161 3 10	Galway . .	Leitrim . . .	Ballynakill . .	Loughrea . .	IV.	51
37	Inchyallagh . .	8 0 14	Cork, E.R. .	Kinnatalloon . .	Mogeely . .	Fermoy . .	II.	98
118, 119	Inchybegga . .	264 1 11	Cork, W.R. .	West Carbery(W.D.)	Caheragh . .	Skibbereen . .	II.	142
58, 66	Inchycullane . .	229 2 33	Kerry . .	Magunihy . .	Kileummin . .	Killarney . .	II.	201
135	Inchydoney Island .	474 3 1	Cork, W.R. .	East Carbery (E.D.)	Island . . .	Clonakilty . .	II.	128
11	Inchymagilleragh East	28 1 22a	Kerry . .	Clanmaurice . .	Duagh . . .	Listowel . .	II.	168
11	Inchymagilleragh West	92 2 11b	Kerry . .	Clanmaurice . .	Duagh . . .	Listowel . .	II.	168
19, 23	Inchyolaghan or Castleinch . .	447 2 27	Kilkenny . .	Shillelogher . .	Castleinch or Inchyolaghan . .	Kilkenny . .	I.	114
50, 51	Ing . . .	222 0 30	Clare . .	Bunratty Lower .	Kilmaleery . .	Ennis . .	II.	5
107	Inga or Nail . .	200 2 21	Galway . .	Longford . .	Killimorbologue .	Portumna . .	IV.	59
50, 51	Ing East . . .	101 1 30	Clare . .	Bunratty Lower .	Kilnasoolagh . .	Ennis . .	II.	6
42, 50, 51	Ing West . . .	241 3 9	Clare . .	Bunratty Lower .	Kilnasoolagh . .	Ennis . .	II.	6
41, 46	Iniscarn . . .	719 3 1	Londonderry .	Loughinsholin . .	Desertmartin . .	Magherafelt . .	III.	240
9, 16	Inisclan . . .	363 3 28	Tyrone . .	Strabane Lower .	Urney . . .	Strabane . .	III.	322
27	Inisclan . . .	449 2 17	Tyrone . .	Strabane Upper .	Cappagh . .	Omagh . .	III.	325
1	Inisclin . . .	403 3 18	Fermanagh .	Lurg . . .	Drumkeeran . .	Lowtherstown . .	III.	206
24, 25	Inisconagher . .	216 1 6	Londonderry .	Keenaght . .	Bovevagh . .	New Tⁿ Limavady	III.	235
56	Inish . . .	69 1 6	Galway . .	Clare . . .	Kilcoona . .	Tuam . .	IV.	19
51	Inish . . .	114 3 20	Wexford . .	Bargy . . .	Killag . . .	Wexford . .	I.	306
53	Inish . . .	4 1 1	Wexford . .	Forth . . .	Carn . . .	Wexford . .	I.	309
53	Inish . . .	19 2 1	Wexford . .	Forth . . .	Ladysisland . .	Wexford . .	I.	311
67	Inishacrick . .	5 3 0	Mayo . .	Burrishoole . .	Burrishoole . .	Newport . .	IV.	120
50	Inishaellaun . .	37 0 13	Clare . .	Islands . . .	Clondagad . .	Killadysert . .	II.	29
43	Inishaghoo . .	14 0 11	Mayo . .	Erris . . .	Kilcommon . .	Newport . .	IV.	145
48	Inishal . . .	70 2 3	Donegal . .	Boylagh . .	Templecrone . .	Glenties . .	III.	116
8, 12	Inishammon . .	142 0 26c	Monaghan .	Monaghan . .	Clones . . .	Monaghan . .	III.	274
117	Inishangan or Shangorman . .	16 3 38	Mayo . .	Kilmaine . .	Ballinrobe . .	Ballinrobe . .	IV.	153
17	Inishanier Island .	5 2 3	Down . .	Ards Upper . .	Ardkeen . .	Downpatrick . .	III.	159
40	Inishannagh . .	9 3 9	Galway . .	Ross . . .	Cong . . .	Oughterard . .	IV.	73
97	INISHANNON T. .	—	Cork, E.R. .	Kinalea . . .	Inishannon . .	Bandon . .	II.	95
117, 120	Inishard . . .	209 2 12	Mayo . .	Kilmaine . .	Ballinchalla . .	Ballinrobe . .	IV.	152
12, 18	Inishargy . . .	1,050 0 37	Down . .	Ards Upper . .	Inishargy . .	Newtownards . .	III.	160
17	Inisharoan Island .	5 1 38	Down . .	Ards Upper . .	Ardkeen . .	Downpatrick . .	III.	159
7	Inishatirra . .	19 1 34	Roscommon .	Boyle . . .	Tumna . . .	Carᵏ. on Shannon	IV.	198
36,37,44,45	Inishative . .	1,466 3 16d	Tyrone . .	Omagh East . .	Termonmaguirk .	Omagh . .	III.	314
10	Inishbarna . .	19 3 28	Galway . .	Ballynahinch . .	Ballynakill . .	Clifden . .	IV.	12
72, 73	Inishbarnog Island .	12 0 1	Donegal . .	Boylagh . .	Inishkeel . .	Glenties . .	III.	114
77, 89	Inishbarra . .	262 1 25	Galway . .	Moycullen . .	Killannin . .	Oughterard . .	IV.	70
40	Inishbeagh . .	3 3 27	Galway . .	Moycullen . .	Kilcummin . .	Oughterard . .	IV.	68
76	Inishbee . . .	38 0 19	Mayo . .	Burrishoole . .	Kilmeena . .	Westport . .	IV.	122
15	Inishbeg . . .	192 1 5a	Cavan . .	Upper Loughtee .	Castleterra . .	Cavan . .	III.	82
141, 150	Inishbeg . . .	370 0 37	Cork, W.R. .	West Carbery (E.D.)	Aghadown . .	Skibbereen . .	II.	137
14	Inishbeg . . .	23 0 34	Donegal . .	Kilmacrenan . .	Tullaghobegly .	Dunfanaghy . .	III.	132
40	Inishbey . . .	19 3 4	Sligo . .	Tberrill . . .	Kilmactranny . .	Boyle . .	IV.	241
40, 41	Inishbiana . .	8 0 12	Galway . .	Moycullen . .	Killannin . .	Oughterard . .	IV.	70

(a) Including 6A. 0R. 8P. water.
(b) Including 7A. 1R. 6P. water.

(c) Including 3A. 0R. 8P. water.
(d) Including 2A. 0R. 38P. water.

(e) Including 10A. 3R. 17P. water.

No. of Sheet of the Ordnance Survey Maps.	Townlands and Towns.	Area in Statute Acres.			County.	Barony.	Parish.	Poor Law Union in 1857.	Townland Census of 1851, Part I.	
		A.	R.	P.					Vol.	Page
63	Inishbigger	8	2	3	Galway	Ballynahinch	Moyrus	Clifden	IV.	14
43, 55	Inishbiggle	637	0	34	Mayo	Erris	Kilcommon	Newport	IV.	145
67	Inishbig or Hog Island	43	1	14	Clare	Moyarta	Kilrush	Kilrush	II.	33
67	Inishbobunnan	24	1	14	Mayo	Burrishoole	Burrishoole	Newport	IV.	120
14	Inishbofin	297	2	1	Donegal	Kilmacrenan	Tullaghobegly	Dunfanaghy	III.	132
76	Inishbollog	3	1	16	Mayo	Burrishoole	Kilmeena	Newport	IV.	122
9	Inishbroon	12	0	4	Galway	Ballynahinch	Ballynakill	Clifden	IV.	12
136	Inishcaltra or Holy Island	45	1	11	Galway	Leitrim	Inishcaltra	Scarriff	IV.	54
67	Inishcannon	3	1	33	Mayo	Burrishoole	Burrishoole	Newport	IV.	120
54	Inishcash	8	2	36	Galway	Moycullen	Kilcummin	Oughterard	IV.	68
38	Inishcoe	115	0	5	Mayo	Tirawley	Crossmolina	Ballina	IV.	167
34	Inishcollan	78	1	5	Fermanagh	Magherastephana	Aghalurcher	Lisnaskea	III.	216
27	Inishconga	1	3	36	Galway	Ross	Cong	Oughterard	IV.	73
20	Inishconnell	154	1	23	Cavan	Upper Loughtee	Kilmore	Cavan	III.	84
10	Inish Conra	6	1	25	Fermanagh	Lurg	Derryvullan	Lowtherstown	III.	205
40, 48	Inishcoo	109	1	1	Donegal	Boylagh	Templecrone	Glenties	III.	116
66	Inishcooa	20	3	2	Mayo	Burrishoole	Burrishoole	Newport	IV.	120
117	Inishcoog	64	2	27	Mayo	Kilmaine	Ballinchalla	Ballinrobe	IV.	152
67	Inishcoragh	8	1	29	Mayo	Burrishoole	Burrishoole	Newport	IV.	120
60	Inishcorker	207	0	27	Clare	Clonderalaw	Killadysert	Killadysert	II.	16
34	Inishcorkish	45	3	22	Fermanagh	Magherastephana	Aghalurcher	Lisnaskea	III.	218
102	Inishcorra	42	3	25	Galway	Dunkellin	Ballynacourty	Galway	IV.	27
76	Inishcottle	23	2	29	Mayo	Burrishoole	Kilmeena	Westport	IV.	122
33	Inishcreagh	15	0	15	Fermanagh	Tirkennedy	Cleenish	Lisnaskea	III.	220
33	Inishcreenry	133	0	27	Fermanagh	Magherastephana	Aghalurcher	Lisnaskea	III.	218
34, 39	Inishcrevan	60	3	13	Fermanagh	Knockninny	Kinawley	Lisnaskea	III.	203
16	INISHCRONE T.	—			Sligo	Tireragh	Kilglass	Dromore West	IV.	234
67, 76	Inishcuill East	14	0	17	Mayo	Burrishoole	Kilmeena	Newport	IV.	122
76	Inishcuill West	2	0	10	Mayo	Burrishoole	Kilmeena	Newport	IV.	122
15	Inish Dacharne	12	3	25	Fermanagh	Lurg	Derryvullan	Lowtherstown	III.	205
60	Inishdadroum	4	3	25	Clare	Clonderalaw	Killadysert	Killadysert	II.	16
76	Inishdaff	32	2	3	Mayo	Burrishoole	Kilmeena	Newport	IV.	123
132	Inishdala	4	1	31	Galway	Leitrim	Ballynakill	Portumna	IV.	52
132	Inishdala	2	0	17	Galway	Leitrim	Ballynakill	Portumna	IV.	52
132	Inishdala	13	0	2	Galway	Leitrim	Ballynakill	Portumna	IV.	52
104	Inishdalla	15	1	7	Mayo	Murrisk	Kilgeever	Westport	IV.	161
67	Inishdasky	15	3	23	Mayo	Burrishoole	Burrishoole	Newport	IV.	120
87	Inishdaugh	6	0	8	Mayo	Murrisk	Oughaval	Westport	IV.	162
54	Inishdauwee	9	2	13	Galway	Moycullen	Kilcummin	Oughterard	IV.	68
27, 40	Inishdauwee	26	0	3	Galway	Ross	Cong	Oughterard	IV.	73
15	Inish Davar	17	0	34	Fermanagh	Lurg	Derryvullan	Lowtherstown	III.	205
67	Inishdaweel	15	0	34	Mayo	Burrishoole	Burrishoole	Newport	IV.	120
49	Inishdawros	22	1	19	Galway	Ballynahinch	Ballindoon	Clifden	IV.	11
50	Inishdea	600	2	11	Clare	Clonderalaw	Kilchreest	Killadysert	II.	15
67	Inishdeashmore	6	0	24	Mayo	Burrishoole	Burrishoole	Newport	IV.	120
105	Inishdegilbeg	1	0	30	Mayo	Murrisk	Kilgeever	Westport	IV.	161
105	Inishdegilmore	32	0	3	Mayo	Murrisk	Kilgeever	Westport	IV.	161
10	Inishderry	3	0	0	Mayo	Erris	Kilcommon	Belmullet	IV.	145
6	Inishdevlin	90	3	24	Monaghan	Trough	Donagh	Monaghan	III.	282
15	Inish Divann	18	2	9	Fermanagh	Lurg	Derryvullan	Lowtherstown	III.	205
15	Inish Doney	40	1	10	Fermanagh	Lurg	Derryvullan	Lowtherstown	III.	205
14	Inishdooey	87	0	12	Donegal	Kilmacrenan	Tullaghobegly	Dunfanaghy	III.	132
67	Inishdoonver	12	3	13	Mayo	Burrishoole	Burrishoole	Newport	IV.	120
40	Inishdoorus	142	1	38	Galway	Ross	Cong	Oughterard	IV.	73
97	Inishduff	3	3	3	Donegal	Banagh	Kilcar	Glenties	III.	109
48	Inishdugga	42	1	20	Galway	Ballynahinch	Ballindoon	Clifden	IV.	10
22	Inishdugh	8	2	2	Mayo	Tirawley	Ballysakeery	Ballina	IV.	165
117	Inishdurra	12	1	31	Mayo	Kilmaine	Ballinrobe	Ballinrobe	IV.	153
49	Inisheane	19	3	1	Donegal	Boylagh	Templecrone	Glenties	III.	116
25	Inishee	1	3	1	Fermanagh	Clanawley	Killesher	Enniskillen	III.	193
109	Inishee	70	0	37	Galway	Longford	Clonfert	Ballinasloe	IV.	57
87	Inisheeny	25	2	28	Mayo	Murrisk	Oughaval	Westport	IV.	162
119, 120	Inisheer	1,400	0	12a	Galway	Aran	Inisheer	Galway	IV.	3
2	Inisheher	18	1	34	Leitrim	Rosclogher	Rossinver	Ballyshannon	IV.	112
65	Inisheltia	66	3	24	Galway	Moycullen	Kilcummin	Oughterard	IV.	68
39	Inisherk	91	0	16	Fermanagh	Knockninny	Kinawley	Lisnaskea	III.	203
89	Inisherk	64	2	19	Galway	Moycullen	Kilcummin	Oughterard	IV.	68
66, 67	Inisherkin	30	2	30	Mayo	Burrishoole	Burrishoole	Newport	IV.	120
103	Inishfad	180	2	7	Donegal	Tirhugh	Drumhome	Ballyshannon	III.	146
19	Inishfall	3	2	2	Sligo	Tireragh	Dromard	Dromore West	IV.	233
101	Inishfarnard	64	1	12	Cork, W.R.	Bear	Kilcatherine	Castletown	II.	124
17	Inishfaugh	2	3	35	Donegal	Kilmacrenan	Mevagh	Millford	III.	130

(a) Including 16A. 2R. 27P. water.

No. of Sheet of the Ordnance Survey Maps.	Townlands and Towns.	Area in Statute Acres.			County.	Barony.	Parish.	Poor Law Union in 1857.	Townland Census of 1851, Part I.	
		A.	R.	P.					Vol.	Page
33	Inishfausy	5	3	22	Fermanagh	Magherastephana	Aghalurcher	Lisnaskea	III.	218
39, 42	Inishfendra	243	2	2	Fermanagh	Knockninny	Galloon	Lisnaskea	III.	201
76	Inishfesh	12	3	33	Mayo	Burrishoole	Kilmeena	Newport	IV.	123
55	Inishflynn	2	1	21	Galway	Moycullen	Kilcummin	Oughterard	IV.	68
15	Inish Fovar	40	1	1	Fermanagh	Magheraboy	Devenish	Enniskillen	III.	212
102, 110	Inishfoyle	753	0	22	Kerry	Glanarought	Kilcaskan	Kenmare	II.	187
15	Inish Free	9	0	8	Fermanagh	Lurg	Trory	Lowtherstown	III.	209
15	Inishfree	0	3	29	Sligo	Tirerrill	Killerry	Sligo	IV.	239
32	Inishfree Lower	45	0	25	Donegal	Boylagh	Templecrone	Glenties	III.	116
48	Inishfree Upper	341	0	18	Donegal	Boylagh	Templecrone	Glenties	III.	116
54	Inishgalloon	13	3	11	Mayo	Burrishoole	Achill	Newport	IV.	117
55	Inishgarraunbeg	3	2	33	Galway	Moycullen	Kilcummin	Oughterard	IV.	69
55	Inishgarraunmore	12	2	17	Galway	Moycullen	Kilcummin	Oughterard	IV.	69
15	Inish Garve	9	2	4	Fermanagh	Lurg	Derryvullan	Lowtherstown	III.	205
120	Inishgleasty	15	0	4	Mayo	Kilmaine	Cong	Ballinrobe	IV.	154
9, 16	Inishglora	37	0	28	Mayo	Erris	Kilmore	Belmullet	IV.	146
101	Inishgoosk	13	2	24	Donegal	Tirhugh	Templecarn	Donegal	III.	149
76	Inishgort	27	3	22	Mayo	Burrishoole	Kilmeena	Westport	IV.	123
114	Inishgort	34	2	10	Mayo	Murrisk	Inishbofin	Clifden	IV.	159
67	Inishgowla	31	2	20	Mayo	Burrishoole	Burrishoole	Newport	IV.	120
76	Inishgowla	32	1	24	Mayo	Burrishoole	Kilmeena	Westport	IV.	123
76, 87	Inishgowla South	28	1	33	Mayo	Burrishoole	Kilmeena	Westport	IV.	123
40, 41	Inishillintry	12	3	8	Donegal	Boylagh	Templecrone	Glenties	III.	116
67	Inishilra	8	1	31	Mayo	Burrishoole	Burrishoole	Newport	IV.	120
87	Inishimmel	3	2	28	Mayo	Burrishoole	Kilmeena	Westport	IV.	123
40	Inishinny	39	2	26	Donegal	Boylagh	Templecrone	Glenties	III.	116
48	Inishinny	8	0	12	Donegal	Boylagh	Templecrone	Glenties	III.	116
32	Inishinny	62	1	29	Donegal	Kilmacrenan	Tullaghobegly	Dunfanaghy	III.	132
103	Inishinny	17	1	38	Donegal	Tirhugh	Drumhome	Ballyshannon	III.	147
23	Inishkea North	464	1	32	Mayo	Erris	Kilmore	Belmullet	IV.	146
23	Inishkea South	344	3	19	Mayo	Erris	Kilmore	Belmullet	IV.	146
67	Inishkee	12	0	5	Mayo	Burrishoole	Burrishoole	Newport	IV.	120
64	Inishkeel	80	2	12	Donegal	Boylagh	Inishkeel	Glenties	III.	114
66, 67	Inishkeel	30	2	33	Mayo	Burrishoole	Burrishoole	Newport	IV.	120
25	Inishkeen	32	0	20	Fermanagh	Clanawley	Cleenish	Enniskillen	III.	191
27	Inishkeen	260	1	15a	Fermanagh	Tirkennedy	Enniskillen	Enniskillen	III.	222
2	Inishkeen	33	1	35	Leitrim	Rosclogher	Rossinver	Ballyshannon	IV.	112
44	Inishkeen	162	0	3	Limerick	Glenquin	Mahoonagh	Newcastle	II.	246
29	Inishkeen Glebe	69	2	3	Monaghan	Farney	Inishkeen	Dundalk	III.	271
48	Inishkeeragh	46	2	3	Donegal	Boylagh	Templecrone	Glenties	III.	116
4	Inishkeeragh	14	2	21	Fermanagh	Lurg	Templecarn	Lowtherstown	III.	209
48	Inishkeeragh	24	3	39	Galway	Ballynahinch	Ballindoon	Clifden	IV.	11
16	Inishkeeragh North	8	2	0	Mayo	Erris	Kilmore	Belmullet	IV.	146
16	Inishkeeragh South	16	1	16	Mayo	Erris	Kilmore	Belmullet	IV.	146
85	Inishkenny	212	1	33	Cork, E.R.	Cork	Inishkenny	Cork	II.	64
100	Inishkeragh	12	1	7	Kerry	Dunkerron South	Kilcrohane	Kenmare	II.	184
63	Inishlackan	129	1	36	Galway	Ballynahinch	Moyrus	Clifden	IV.	14
76, 87	Inishlaghan	1	3	8	Mayo	Burrishoole	Kilmeena	Westport	IV.	123
40	Inishlannaun	9	0	24	Galway	Moycullen	Kilcummin	Oughterard	IV.	69
76	Inishlaughil	28	0	35	Mayo	Burrishoole	Kilmeena	Westport	IV.	123
78	Inishlay	21	1	52	Galway	Moycullen	Killannin	Oughterard	IV.	70
33	Inishleague	125	0	39	Fermanagh	Magherastephana	Aghalurcher	Lisnaskea	III.	218
87	Inishleague	13	0	35	Mayo	Burrishoole	Kilmeena	Westport	IV.	123
39	Inishlee	1	1	23	Mayo	Tirawley	Kilbelfad	Ballina	IV.	168
72	Inishleena	60	0	35b	Cork, E.R.	East Muskerry	Inishcarra	Cork	II.	104
149	Inishleigh	13	0	15	Cork. W.R.	West Carbery (E.D.)	Aghadown	Skibbereen	II.	137
67	Inishlim	6	3	20	Mayo	Burrishoole	Burrishoole	Newport	IV.	120
33	Inishlirroo	13	3	13	Fermanagh	Knockninny	Kinawley	Lisnaskea	III.	203
60	Inishloe	131	1	3	Clare	Clonderalaw	Killadysert	Killadysert	II.	16
54	Inishlosky	21	2	16	Clare	Tulla Lower	O'Briensbridge	Limerick	II.	38
15	Inish Lougher	36	3	23	Fermanagh	Magheraboy	Devenish	Enniskillen	III.	212
83	Inishlounaght	348	1	2c	Tipperary, S.R.	Iffa and Offa East	Inishlounaght	Clonmel	II.	313
76	Inishloy	21	0	20	Mayo	Burrishoole	Kilmeena	Newport	IV.	123
33, 34	Inishlught	49	1	22	Fermanagh	Knockninny	Kinawley	Lisnaskea	III.	203
78	Inishlusk	12	3	34	Galway	Moycullen	Killannin	Oughterard	IV.	70
114	Inishlyon	74	3	21	Mayo	Murrisk	Inishbofin	Clifden	IV.	159
76	Inishlyre	52	1	39	Mayo	Burrishoole	Kilmeena	Westport	IV.	123
48	Inishmacadurn or Rutland Island	312	3	9	Donegal	Boylagh	Templecrone	Glenties	III.	116
50,51,60,61	Inishmacnaghtan	284	3	29	Clare	Bunratty Lower	Kilconry	Ennis	II.	4
60	Inishmacowney	225	0	5	Clare	Clonderalaw	Killadysert	Killadysert	II.	16
15	Inishmacsaint	55	3	39	Fermanagh	Magheraboy	Inishmacsaint	Enniskillen	III.	213
53	Inishmagh	289	2	5	Tyrone	Dungannon Lower	Carnteel	Dungannon	III.	297

(a) Including 75A. 1R. 39P. water.   (b) Including 4A. 2R. 12P. water.   (c) Including 6A. 1R. 12P. water.

No. of Sheet of the Ordnance Survey Maps.	Townlands and Towns.	Area in Statute Acres.	County.	Barony.	Parish.	Poor Law Union in 1857.	Townland Census of 1851, Part I.	
		A. R. P.					Vol.	Page
18	Inishmagrath . .	6 1 28	Leitrim . .	Drumahaire . .	Drumreilly . .	Car^k. on Shannon	IV.	95
117	Inishmaine . .	165 2 6	Mayo . .	Kilmaine . .	Ballinchalla . .	Ballinrobe .	IV.	152
10	Inishmakill . .	69 2 30	Fermanagh .	Lurg . . .	Magheraculmoney .	Lowtherstown .	III.	208
48	Inishmeal . .	18 3 24	Donegal . .	Boylagh . .	Templecrone . .	Glenties . .	III.	116
2	Inishmean . .	20 1 24	Leitrim . .	Rosclogher . .	Rossinver . .	Ballyshannon .	IV.	112
23, 32	Inishmeane . .	117 0 6	Donegal . .	Kilmacrenan . .	Tullaghobegly .	Dunfanaghy .	III.	132
4	Inishmeely . .	6 3 26	Fermanagh .	Lurg . . .	Templecarn . .	Lowtherstown .	III.	209
40, 41	Inishmicatreer .	203 1 27	Galway . .	Moycullen . .	Killannin . .	Oughterard .	IV.	70
76	Inishmolt . .	4 3 17	Mayo . .	Burrishoole . .	Kilmeena . .	Newport . .	IV.	123
15, 20	Inishmore . .	491 0 9a	Cavan . .	Upper Loughtee .	Urney . .	Cavan . .	III.	86
25	Inishmore . .	105 2 6b	Clare . .	Bunratty Upper .	Templemaley . .	Corrofin . .	II.	11
34, 40	Inishmore . .	44 2 28	Sligo . .	Tirerrill . . .	Killadoon . .	Boyle . .	IV.	239
50	Inishmore or Deer-island . . .	443 3 24	Clare . .	Clonderalaw . . `	Kilchreest . .	Killadysert .	II.	15
18	Inishmoylin . .	7 3 18	Roscommon .	Ballintober North .	Kilglass . .	Strokestown .	IV.	186
15	Inishmuck . .	128 2 32	Cavan . .	Upper Loughtee .	Urney . .	Cavan . .	III.	86
31	Inishmucker . .	13 0 9	Leitrim . .	Leitrim . . .	Kiltoghert . .	Car^k. on Shannon	IV.	103
7, 8, 13, 14	Inishmulclohy or Coney Island .	388 0 12	Sligo . .	Carbury . . .	Killaspugbrone .	Sligo . .	IV.	222
1	Inishmurray . .	209 0 5	Sligo . .	Carbury . . .	Ahamlish . .	Sligo . .	IV.	220
59	Inishmurry . .	9 1 10	Clare . .	Clonderalaw . .	Killadysert . .	Killadysert .	II.	16
89	Inishmuskerry . .	18 2 18	Galway . .	Ballynahinch . .	Moyrus . .	Clifden . .	IV.	14
99	Inishnabo . .	4 3 17	Donegal . .	Tirhugh . . .	Drumhome . .	Donegal . .	III.	147
61	Inishnabro . .	102 1 10	Kerry . .	Corkaguiny . .	Dunquin . .	Dingle . .	II.	176
67	Inishnacross . .	25 2 25	Mayo . .	Burrishoole . .	Burrishoole . .	Newport . .	IV.	120
99	Inishnagor . .	4 3 6	Donegal . .	Tirhugh . .	Drumhome . .	Donegal . .	III.	147
5	Inishnagor . .	5 0 16	Sligo . .	Carbury . . .	Ahamlish . .	Sligo . .	IV.	220
76	Inishnakillew . .	58 3 13	Mayo . .	Burrishoole . .	Kilmeena . .	Westport . .	IV.	123
40	Inishnawean . .	4 1 1	Galway . .	Ross . . .	Cong . .	Oughterard .	IV.	73
50, 63	Inishnee . . .	856 1 7	Galway . .	Ballynahinch . .	Moyrus . .	Clifden . .	IV.	14
149	Inishodriscol or Hare Island . .	380 3 32	Cork, W.R. .	West Carbery (E.D.)	Aghadown . .	Skibbereen .	II.	137
117, 120	Inishoght . .	13 3 0	Mayo . .	Kilmaine . .	Ballinchalla .	Ballinrobe .	IV.	152
76	Inishoo . .	17 3 33	Mayo . .	Burrishoole . .	Kilmeena . .	Westport . .	IV.	123
54	Inishool . .	10 2 7	Galway . .	Moycullen . .	Kilcummin . .	Oughterard .	IV.	69
34	Inishore . . .	9 1 19	Fermanagh .	Magherastephana .	Aghalurcher . .	Lisnaskea .	III.	218
60	Inishoul or O'Grady's Island . .	1 1 35	Clare . .	Clonderalaw . .	Killadysert .	Killadysert .	II.	16
117	Inishowel . .	5 0 17	Mayo . .	Kilmaine . .	Ballinchalla .	Ballinrobe .	IV.	152
117	Inishowen . .	29 0 25	Mayo . .	Kilmaine . .	Ballinchalla .	Ballinrobe .	IV.	152
64	Inishowen Island .	1 0 20	Donegal . .	Boylagh . .	Inishkeel . .	Glenties . .	III.	114
67	Inishower . .	36 0 5	Mayo . .	Burrishoole . .	Burrishoole . .	Newport . .	IV.	120
99	Inishpat . .	17 0 27	Donegal . .	Tirhugh . .	Drumhome . .	Donegal . .	III.	147
67	Inishquirk . .	28 0 14	Mayo . .	Burrishoole . .	Burrishoole . .	Newport . .	IV.	120
87	Inishraher . .	26 3 21	Mayo . .	Burrishoole . .	Kilmeena . .	Westport . .	IV.	123
117	Inishrobe . .	21 3 12	Mayo . .	Kilmaine . .	Ballinrobe . .	Ballinrobe .	IV.	153
112	Inishroo . .	185 2 34	Galway . .	Kiltartan . .	Kinvarradoorus .	Gort . .	IV.	49
33, 34	Inishroosk . .	269 3 30	Fermanagh .	Magherastephana .	Aghalurcher . .	Lisnaskea .	III.	216
33	Inishrush . .	692 2 23	Londonderry .	Loughinsholin .	Tamlaght O'Crilly .	Magherafelt .	III.	243
33	INISHRUSH T. .	—	Londonderry .	Loughinsholin .	Tamlaght O'Crilly .	Magherafelt .	III.	244
54	Inishskanboc .	16 2 33	Galway . .	Moycullen . .	Kilcummin . .	Oughterard .	IV.	69
114	Inishshark . .	581 1 30	Mayo . .	Murrisk . .	Inishbofin . .	Clifden . .	IV.	159
23	Inishsirrer . .	108 3 16c	Donegal . .	Kilmacrenan . .	Tullaghobegly .	Dunfanaghy .	III.	132
41	Inishskehan . .	3 1 33	Galway . .	Clare . .	Killursa . .	Tuam . .	IV.	22
114	Inishskinnybeg . .	4 0 33	Mayo . .	Murrisk . .	Inishbofin . .	Clifden . .	IV.	159
114	Inishskinnymore .	12 2 37	Mayo . .	Murrisk . .	Inishbofin . .	Clifden . .	IV.	159
20, 25	Inishteige . .	12 3 5	Fermanagh .	Clanawley . .	Cleenish . .	Enniskillen .	III.	191
2	Inishtemple . .	32 2 30	Leitrim . .	Rosclogher . .	Rossinver . .	Ballyshannon .	IV.	112
40	Inishthee . .	7 3 2	Galway . .	Ross . .	Cong . .	Oughterard .	IV.	73
51	Inishtooskert . .	186 2 30	Kerry . .	Corkaguiny . .	Dunquin . .	Dingle . .	II.	176
19	Inishtooskert . .	12 2 9	Kerry . .	Corkaguiny . .	Killiney . .	Dingle . .	II.	178
2	Inishtrahull . .	113 3 37	Donegal . .	Inishowen East .	Clonca . .	Inishowen .	III.	117
78	Inishtravin . .	190 1 21	Galway . .	Ballynahinch . .	Moyrus . .	Clifden . .	IV.	14
63	Inishtreh . .	10 1 21	Galway . .	Ballynahinch . .	Moyrus . .	Clifden . .	IV.	14
76	Inishtroghenmore .	11 3 32	Galway . .	Ballynahinch . .	Moyrus . .	Clifden . .	IV.	14
60	Inishtubbrid . .	85 1 21	Clare . .	Clonderalaw . .	Killadysert . .	Killadysert .	II.	16
67	Inishtubbrid . .	37 0 12	Mayo . .	Burrishoole . .	Burrishoole . .	Newport . .	IV.	120
4	Inishturk . .	2 1 36	Fermanagh .	Lurg . .	Templecarn . .	Lowtherstown .	III.	209
34	Inishturk . .	37 2 0	Fermanagh .	Magherastephana .	Aghalurcher . .	Lisnaskea .	III.	218
21, 34	Inishturk . .	132 2 1	Galway . .	Ballynahinch . .	Omey . .	Clifden . .	IV.	15
76	Inishturk . .	59 0 9	Mayo . .	Burrishoole . .	Kilmeena . .	Westport . .	IV.	123
67	Inishturlin . .	20 2 20	Mayo . .	Burrishoole . .	Burrishoole . .	Newport . .	IV.	120
49	Inishule . .	6 3 20	Galway . .	Ballynahinch . .	Ballindoon . .	Clifden . .	IV.	11
61	Inishvickillane . .	171 3 23	Kerry . .	Corkaguiny . .	Dunquin . .	Dingle . .	II.	176

(a) Including 8A. 0R. 8P. water.   (b) Including 17A. 2R. 33P. water.   (c) Including 6A. 1R. 4P. water.

No. of Sheet of the Ordnance Survey Maps.	Townlands and Towns.	Area in Statute Acres.			County.	Barony.	Parish.	Poor Law Union in 1857.	Townland Census of 1851, Part I.	
		A.	R.	P.					Vol.	Page
40	Inishvinlush	2	3	24	Galway	Ross	Cong	Oughterard	IV.	73
27	Inishyweel	2	1	28	Donegal	Kilmacrenan	Kilmacrenan	Millford	III.	130
67	Inisloughlin	363	1	38	Antrim	Upper Massereene	Magheramesk	Lisburn	III.	31
15	Inispollan	51	1	35	Antrim	Lower Glenarm	Grange of Inispollan	Ballycastle	III.	21
10, 14, 15	Inispollan Mountain, Grange of	477	0	18	Antrim	Lower Glenarm	Grange of Inispollan	Ballycastle	III.	21
32, 33	Inistioge	1,739	0	8a	Kilkenny	Gowran	Inistioge	Thomastown	I.	96
32	INISTIOGE T.	—			Kilkenny	Gowran	Inistioge	Thomastown	I.	96
15	Inisway	114	0	13	Fermanagh	Magheraboy	Inishmacsaint	Enniskillen	III.	213
39	Innevall	191	1	13	Tyrone	Dungannon Middle	Donaghenry	Cookstown	III.	301
48	INNFIELD T.	—			Meath	Lower Moyfenrath	Rathcore	Trim	I.	211
66	Innisfallen	21	1	34	Kerry	Magunihy	Aghadoe	Killarney	II.	199
51, 52	Inniskil	471	3	11	Donegal	Kilmacrenan	Gartan	Letterkenny	III.	127
28	Inniskil	95	3	0	Donegal	Kilmacrenan	Kilygarvan	Millford	III.	128
95	Innplot	18	3	6	Galway	Dunkellin	Oranmore	Galway	IV.	32
76	Innygraga	222	1	17	Cork, E.R.	Imokilly	Middleton	Middleton	II.	89
18	Inshaleen	482	0	18	Londonderry	Coleraine	Errigal	Coleraine	III.	232
27	Inshamph	141	2	30	Antrim	Kilconway	Dunaghy	Ballymena	III.	26
17	Inshinagh	141	0	36	Antrim	Upper Dunluce	Ballymoney	Ballymoney	III.	19
15	Intack	80	2	37	Wicklow	Lower Talbotstown	Donard	Baltinglass	I.	359
23	Intake	70	0	35	Dublin	Dublin	Booterstown	Rathdown	I.	30
76	Intake	55	3	0b	Mayo	Burrishoole	Kilmeena	Westport	IV.	122
40	Inver	290	0	14	Antrim	Lower Belfast	Inver	Larne	III.	8
36	Inver	77	3	21c	Fermanagh	Clankelly	Clones	Clones	III.	196
10, 11	Inver	662	3	17	Mayo	Erris	Kilcommon	Belmullet	IV.	144
91	Inveran	673	2	10d	Galway	Moycullen	Killannin	Galway	IV.	69
92, 98	Inver Glebe	164	0	10	Donegal	Banagh	Inver	Donegal	III.	107
33, 34	Invyarroge	216	3	9	Cavan	Castlerahan	Killinkere	Bailieborough	III.	69
35, 36	Iragh	317	0	13	Clare	Tulla Lower	Killuran	Tulla	II.	36
12, 17	Irby	116	2	18	Tipperary, N.R.	Ikerrin	Roscrea	Roscrea	II.	276
15, 16	Ireland's Eye	53	0	24	Dublin	Coolock	Howth	Dublin North	I.	28
23, 24	Irishomerbane	526	1	4	Antrim	Kilconway	Dunaghy	Ballymena	III.	26
50	Irishtown	149	3	12	Antrim	Upper Antrim	Antrim	Antrim	III.	5
7	Irishtown	172	3	12	Dublin	Balrothery East	Lusk	Balrothery	I.	21
10, 13	Irishtown	187	2	3	Dublin	Castleknock	Ward	Dublin North	I.	25
18	Irishtown	56	3	6	Dublin	Dublin	Donnybrook	Dublin South	I.	30
17	Irishtown	260	1	6	Dublin	Uppercross	Palmerston	Dublin South	I.	40
35, 36	Irishtown	517	2	19	Kildare	Kilkea and Moone	Moone	Athy	I.	61
38	Irishtown	314	0	29	King's Co.	Ballybritt	Kilcolman	Parsonstown	I.	125
45	Irishtown	93	3	38	King's Co.	Clonlisk	Dunkerrin	Roscrea	I.	130
5	Irishtown	61	2	23e	Limerick	Limerick, Municipal Borough of	St. Johns	Limerick	II.	262
14	Irishtown	287	3	23	Louth	Ardee	Mapastown	Ardee	I.	173
45, 51	Irishtown	158	1	31	Meath	Dunboyne	Kilbride	Dunshaughlin	I.	200
24, 30	Irishtown	162	1	11	Meath	Lower Navan	Ardbraccan	Navan	I.	214
38	Irishtown	228	3	26	Meath	Skreen	Kilmoon	Dunshaughlin	I.	221
32	Irishtown	252	1	5	Meath	Skreen	Timoole	Dunshaughlin	I.	222
33	Irishtown	96	3	21	Meath	Upper Duleek	Ardcath	Drogheda	I.	197
28	Irishtown	586	3	18	Meath	Upper Duleek	Moorechurch	Drogheda	I.	198
16	Irishtown	106	0	1	Meath	Upper Kells	Burry	Kells	I.	205
19	Irishtown	785	2	13	Westmeath	Moyashel and Magheradernon	Mullingar	Mullingar	I.	275
10, 17	Irishtown	767	2	23	Westmeath	Rathconrath	Rathconrath	Mullingar	I.	284
29	Irishtown	41	1	15	Wexford	Bantry	St. Mary's	New Ross	I.	302
8	Irishtown	105	0	19	Wicklow	Rathdown	Bray	Rathdown	I.	354
15, 21	Irishtown East	86	1	9	Wicklow	Lower Talbotstown	Donard	Baltinglass	I.	359
14	Irishtown Lower	229	1	6f	Kildare	North Salt	Straffan	Celbridge	I.	76
15, 21	Irishtown Park	95	0	21	Wicklow	Lower Talbotstown	Donard	Baltinglass	I.	359
18	IRISHTOWN T.	—			Dublin	Dublin	Donnybrook	Dublin South	I.	30
14	Irishtown Upper	274	1	25g	Kildare	North Salt	Straffan	Celbridge	I.	76
21	Irishtown West	66	2	16	Wicklow	Lower Talbotstown	Donard	Baltinglass	I.	359
26	Irongrange Lower	181	1	22	Wicklow	Upper Talbotstown	Baltinglass	Baltinglass	I.	362
26, 27	Irongrange Upper	280	0	19	Wicklow	Upper Talbotstown	Baltinglass	Baltinglass	I.	362
27	Ironhills	720	0	20	Kildare	Offaly West	Kilrush	Athy	I.	73
30	Ironmills or Kilrush	1,548	3	13	Queen's Co.	Cullenagh	Abbeyleix	Abbeyleix	I.	238
15, 28	Ironpool	450	0	27	Galway	Dunmore	Kilconla	Tuam	IV.	35
77, 78	Ironworks	80	1	32h	Donegal	Raphoe	Stranorlar	Stranorlar	III.	142
15, 16	Irrabeg	269	1	35	Kerry	Clanmaurice	Kiltomy	Listowel	II.	172
14, 15	Irragh	320	1	27	Antrim	Lower Glenarm	Grange of Layd	Ballycastle	III.	22
16	Irramore	596	3	6	Kerry	Clanmaurice	Kilfeighney	Listowel	II.	170
12	Iry	1,137	1	27	Queen's Co.	Maryborough West	Clonenagh and Clonagheen	Mountmellick	I.	243
42	Isaacstown	820	1	1	Meath	Lower Moyfenrath	Rathmolyon	Trim	I.	211
104, 114	Isertkelly North	365	2	19	Galway	Loughrea	Isertkelly	Loughrea	IV.	63

(a) { Including 130A. 3R. 10P. detached portion.
{ Including 1A. 0R. 0P. River Nore.
(b) The area of this Intake does not appear on the Ordnance Maps; that here given is from the "Tenement Valuation."

(c) Including 11A. 0R. 15P. water.
(d) Including 3A. 0R. 8P. water.
(e) Included in the Parish of St. John.

(f) Including 3A. 1R. 10P. water.
(g) Including 6A. 0R. 30P. water.
(h) Including 4A. 3R. 10P. water.

No. of Sheet of the Ordnance Survey Maps.	Townlands and Towns.	Area in Statute Acres.	County.	Barony.	Parish.	Poor Law Union in 1857.	Townland Census of 1851, Part I.	
							Vol.	Page
		A. R. P.						
114	Isertkelly South	350 0 19	Galway	Loughrea	Isertkelly	Loughrea	IV.	63
74	Ishlaun	368 3 5	Mayo	Costello	Castlemore	Castlereagh	IV.	140
104, 105	Iskanafeelna	237 1 21	Cork, W.R.	Bantry	Kilmocomoge	Bantry	II.	121
116	Iskanamucky	9 1 2	Cork, W.R.	Bear	Killaconenagh	Castletown	II.	125
9	Iskancullin	220 0 39	Clare	Burren	Carran	Ballyvaghan	II.	11
30	Iskaroon	274 2 9	Meath	Upper Navan	Moymet	Trim	I.	216
30	Iskaroon Little	14 1 25	Meath	Upper Navan	Moymet	Trim	I.	216
16, 20	Iskymeadow	270 2 35	Armagh	Armagh	Keady	Armagh	III.	45
37	Islafalcon	84 3 15	Wexford	Shelmaliere East	Artramon	Wexford	I.	330
9	Island	75 2 13	Carlow	Rathvilly	Clonmore	Shillelagh	I.	10
43	Island	369 1 25	Cavan	Castlerahan	Munterconnaught	Oldcastle	III.	71
52	Island	52 3 29	Clare	Bunratty Lower	Kilfintinan	Limerick	II.	5
8	Island	76 1 39	Clare	Corcomroe	Killilagh	Ennistimon	II.	20
52	Island	236 2 1	Cork, E.R.	Barrymore	Dunbulloge	Cork	II.	54
22	Island	534 3 7	Cork, E.R.	Duhallow	Clonfert	Kanturk	II.	68
42	Island	679 2 7	Cork, E.R.	Fermoy	Rahan	Mallow	II.	82
70	Island	124 2 8	Galway	Clare	Lackagh	Galway	IV.	23
85	Island	53 1 35	Galway	Kilconnell	Killimordaly	Loughrea	IV.	42
38	Island	135 1 34	King's Co.	Ballybritt	Kilcolman	Parsonstown	I.	125
44	Island	182 1 6	King's Co.	Clonlisk	Cullenwaine	Roscrea	I.	129
18	Island	687 2 6	King's Co.	Lower Philipstown	Killaderry	Tullamore	I.	143
22	Island	238 2 35	Longford	Rathcline	Kilcommock	Ballymahon	I.	164
92, 93	Island	842 1 30a	Mayo	Costello	Bekan	Claremorris	IV.	139
23, 24	Island	145 0 32	Queen's Co.	Cullenagh	Abbeyleix	Abbeyleix	I.	238
10	Island	430 3 32	Queen's Co.	Upperwoods	Offerlane	Mountmellick	I.	252
33	*Island*	14 1 21b	Sligo	Corran	Cloonoghil	Tobercurry	IV.	225
32	Island	164 2 23	Waterford	Decies without Drum	Stradbally	Kilmacthomas	II.	361
26, 32	Island	38 3 9	Wexford	Ballaghkeen	Kilmallock	Enniscorthy	I.	296
21	Island	123 2 18	Wexford	Ballaghkeen	Kilmuckridge	Gorey	I.	296
21, 27	Island	137 0 38	Wexford	Ballaghkeen	Meelnagh	Gorey	I.	298
43	Island	10 1 5	Wexford	Forth	Rosslare	Wexford	I.	313
132	*Islandaqu*	2 2 0	Galway	Leitrim	Ballynakill	Portumna	IV.	52
7, 12	Islandahoe	250 3 14	Antrim	Lower Dunluce	Derrykeighan	Ballymoney	III.	17
21, 22, 30	Islandav	351 3 10	Cork, E.R.	Duhallow	Kilmeen	Kanturk	II.	73
41	*Islandavanna*	29 0 7	Clare	Islands	Clareabbey	Ennis	II.	29
50	Islandbane	267 3 25	Antrim	Lower Massereene	Muckamore (Grange of)	Antrim	III.	28
24	Islandbane	41 0 16	Down	Dufferin	Killinchy	Downpatrick	III.	166
37	Islandbane	56 2 12	Down	Lecale Upper	Rathmullan	Downpatrick	III.	181
21	Islandbawn	140 3 30	Tipperary, N.R.	Upper Ormond	Lisbunny	Nenagh	II.	292
71	*Island Beg*	5 0 14	Donegal	Raphoe	Clonleigh	Strabane	III.	135
26	*Islandbeg*	3 0 13	Galway	Ross	Ross	Oughterard	IV.	74
8	Islandboy	296 3 33	Antrim	Cary	Grange of Drumtullagh	Ballycastle	III.	14
11, 17	Islandboy	137 0 26c	Kerry	Clanmaurice	Duagh	Listowel	II.	168
80, 81	Islandboy	985 1 29	Kerry	Iveragh	Dromod	Cahersiveen	II.	195
28, 29	Islandboy	104 1 6	Limerick	Connello Lower	Rathkeale	Rathkeale	II.	229
17, 18	Islandboy East	81 1 26d	Kerry	Clanmaurice	Duagh	Listowel	I.	168
17	Islandboy West	9 1 12e	Kerry	Clanmaurice	Duagh	Listowel	I.	168
29, 30	Islandbrack	370 0 15	Cork, E.R.	Duhallow	Kilmeen	Milstreet	II.	73
18	ISLANDBRIDGE T.	—	Dublin	Uppercross	St. James	Dublin South	I.	41
7	Island Carragh North	199 1 33	Antrim	Lower Dunluce	Dunluce	Coleraine	III.	17
7	Island Carragh South	137 0 3	Antrim	Lower Dunluce	Dunluce	Coleraine	III.	17
27, 37	Islandcosgry	333 3 3	Clare	Tulla Lower	Ogonnelloe	Scarriff	II.	38
30	Island-dahill	439 2 0	Cork, E.R.	Duhallow	Dromtarriff	Millstreet	II.	71
20	Islandderry	426 3 27f	Down	Lower Iveagh, Lr. pt.	Dromore	Banbridge	III.	168
40, 48	Island Dromagh	109 0 39	Limerick	Coshlea	Knocklong	Kilmallock	II.	240
12, 13	Islandduane	222 2 5	Limerick	Pubblebrien	Mungret	Limerick	II.	254
21	Islandea	207 1 20	Limerick	Coshma	Adare	Croom	II.	241
78	Islandeady	20 1 8	Mayo	Burrishoole	Islandeady	Westport	IV.	121
60	Islandearagh	425 0 13	Kerry	Magunihy	Nohavaldaly	Killarney	II.	205
1	Island East	298 2 10	Galway	Ballymoe	Templetogher	Glennamaddy	IV.	9
102	Island Eddy	137 3 3	Galway	Dunkellin	Drumacoo	Galway	IV.	28
7	Island Effrick North	163 1 39	Londonderry	North East Liberties of Coleraine	Ballyrashane	Coleraine	III.	245
7, 8	Island Effrick South	85 1 14	Londonderry	North East Liberties of Coleraine	Ballyrashane	Coleraine	III.	245
3	Island Flackey	102 3 4	Londonderry	North East Liberties of Coleraine	Ballywillin	Coleraine	III.	245
10	Islandganniv North	135 2 37g	Kerry	Iraghticonnor	Listowel	Listowel	II.	193
10	Islandganniv South	21 2 0h	Kerry	Clanmaurice	Listowel	Listowel	II.	172
33	Islandgar	84 3 27i	Clare	Inchiquin	Kilnamona	Ennis	II.	27
7	Island Heaghey	92 1 21	Londonderry	North East Liberties of Coleraine	Coleraine	Coleraine	III.	246
45	Island Henry	17 3 24	Down	Lecale Upper	Bright	Downpatrick	III.	180
6	Islandhill	142 2 10	Down	Ards Lower	Donaghadee	Newtownards	III.	158

(a) Including 147A. 1R. 8P. water.
(b) Island in Templehouse Lake.
(c) Including 1A. 2R. 18P. water.
(d) Including 8A. 2R. 26P. water.
(e) Including 1A. 2R. 36P. water.
(f) Including 10A. 0R. 7P. water.
(g) Including 7A. 2R. 35P. water.
(h) Including 5A. 0R. 2P. water.
(i) Including 8A. 3R. 18P. water.

No. of Sheet of the Ordnance Survey Maps.	Townlands and Towns.	Area in Statute Acres. A. R. P.	County.	Barony.	Parish.	Poor Law Union in 1857.	Townland Census of 1851, Part I. Vol.	Page
32	Islandhubbock	235 1 34	Waterford	Decies without Drum	Stradbally	Kilmacthomas	II.	361
26	Islandikane East	218 0 22	Waterford	Middlethird	Islandikane	Waterford	II.	367
25, 26	Islandikane North	201 1 12	Waterford	Middlethird	Islandikane	Waterford	II.	367
25, 26	Islandikane South	194 2 7	Waterford	Middlethird	Islandikane	Waterford	II.	367
25	*Island in Broad Lough*	9 1 36	Wicklow	Newcastle	Rathnew	Rathdrum	I.	354
59, 63	Islandkelly	351 1 6	Antrim	Upper Massereene	Derryaghy	Lisburn	III.	30
38	Island Lower	205 3 10a	Roscommon	Ballymoe	Oran	Roscommon	IV.	192
11	Island Lower	222 2 39	Wexford	Gorey	Rossminoge	Gorey	I.	321
8	Island Macallan	326 0 15	Antrim	Cary	Ballintoy	Ballycastle	III.	12
10	Islandmacloughry	153 2 29b	Kerry	Clanmaurice	Finuge	Listowel	II.	169
51	Islandmacnevin	58 0 4	Clare	Bunratty Lower	Kilmaleery	Ennis	II.	5
10	Island MacTeige	47 0 4	Limerick	Shanid	Robertstown	Rathkeale	II.	258
41, 42	Islandmagrath	537 3 29	Clare	Islands	Clareabbey	Ennis	II.	29
105	*Island M'Coo*	0 0 18	Galway	Loughrea	Killeenadeema	Loughrea	IV.	64
6, 11	Island Middle	133 3 12	Wexford	Gorey	Rossminoge	Gorey	I.	321
12, 17	Islandmore	169 2 6	Antrim	Upper Dunluce	Kilraghts	Ballymoney	III.	20
17	Islandmore	146 1 35c	Clare	Inchiquin	Killinaboy	Corrofin	II.	26
13	Islandmore	33 0 0	Clare	Tulla Upper	Feakle	Tulla	II.	39
71	Island More	149 0 12	Donegal	Raphoe	Clonleigh	Strabane	III.	135
24	Islandmore	122 1 34	Down	Dufferin	Killinchy	Downpatrick	III.	166
70, 83	Islandmore	223 3 24	Galway	Clare	Lackagh	Galway	IV.	23
123	Islandmore	119 1 6	Galway	Kiltartan	Kilbeacanty	Gort	IV.	47
26	*Islandmore*	7 0 9	Galway	Ross	Ross	Oughterard	IV.	74
75, 76	Islandmore	125 3 21	Kerry	Magunihy	Killaha	Killarney	II.	202
76	Island More	77 1 20	Mayo	Burrishoole	Kilmeena	Westport	IV.	123
64	Islandmore	264 1 35	Mayo	Costello	Kilcolman	Castlereagh	IV.	141
38, 47	Islandmore	187 1 35	Mayo	Tirawley	Addergoole	Castlebar	IV.	163
68	*Islandmore*	5 3 31	Mayo	Tirawley	Addergoole	Castlebar	IV.	163
3	Islandmore Lower	100 0 3	Londonderry	North East Liberties of Coleraine	Ballywillin	Coleraine	III.	245
3	Islandmore Upper	109 1 10	Londonderry	North East Liberties of Coleraine	Ballywillin	Coleraine	III.	245
123	*Island Morris*	6 0 11	Mayo	Kilmaine	Cong	Ballinrobe	IV.	154
42	Islandmoyle	642 3 16d	Down	Upper Iveagh, Lr. pt.	Clonduff	Newry	III.	171
28	Islandnabracky	110 2 3	Antrim	Lower Antrim	Skerry	Ballymena	III.	5
50	Islandreagh	392 3 13	Antrim	Upper Antrim	Nilteen Grange	Antrim	III.	6
17	*Island Reagh*	11 0 38	Donegal	Kilmacrenan	Mevagh	Millford	III.	130
7	Islandrose	357 3 14	Antrim	Lower Dunluce	Billy	Ballymoney	III.	16
17	Island Roy	91 1 33	Donegal	Kilmacrenan	Mevagh	Millford	III.	131
27	Islandroy Barr or Drumfin	159 0 26	Donegal	Kilmacrenan	Mevagh	Millford	III.	130
46	Islands	665 0 21	Galway	Killian	Killian	Mountbellew	IV.	44
60	Islands	95 3 30	Galway	Tiaquin	Killosolan	Mountbellew	IV.	78
9, 10, 13, 14	Islands	138 3 37	Kilkenny	Crannagh	Coolcraheen	Kilkenny	I.	85
8, 12	Islands	1,719 1 32	Kilkenny	Galmoy	Urlingford	Urlingford	I.	93
5	Islands	148 3 13	Monaghan	Monaghan	Tedavnet	Monaghan	III.	279
55	Islands	344 0 10	Tipperary, S.R.	Slievardagh	Lismalin	Callan	II.	335
9	*Island Sack*	25 1 12	Kerry	Iraghticonnor	Ballyconry	Listowel	II.	190
9	*Island Sack Little*	8 0 14	Kerry	Iraghticonnor	Lisselton	Listowel	II.	192
7	Islands of Carnmoon	594 0 14	Antrim	Lower Dunluce	Billy	Ballymoney	III.	16
11	*Island South*	20 2 30	Down	Ards Lower	Greyabbey	Newtownards	III.	158
15	Island Spa	10 2 39	Armagh	Tiranny	Tynan	Armagh	III.	61
85	*Islands, The*	28 1 7e	Tipperary, S.R.	Iffa and Offa East	Carrick	Carrick on Suir	II.	313
28	Islandstown	194 0 28	Antrim	Lower Antrim	Skerry	Ballymena	III.	5
24	Island Taggart	76 3 25	Down	Dufferin	Killyleagh	Downpatrick	III.	167
26	Islandtarsney North	246 2 29	Waterford	Middlethird	Islandikane	Waterford	II.	367
26	Islandtarsney South	246 0 8	Waterford	Middlethird	Islandikane	Waterford	II.	367
3	Islandtasserty	57 3 6	Londonderry	North East Liberties of Coleraine	Ballyaghran	Coleraine	III.	244
38	Island Upper	113 3 36f	Roscommon	Ballymoe	Oran	Roscommon	IV.	192
6, 11	Island Upper	368 3 14	Wexford	Gorey	Rossminoge	Gorey	I.	321
3	Island Vardin	64 0 32	Londonderry	North East Liberties of Coleraine	Ballyaghran	Coleraine	III.	244
1	Island West	222 3 38	Galway	Ballymoe	Templetogher	Glennamaddy	IV.	9
11, 16	Islandwood	260 3 16	Tipperary, N.R.	Lower Ormond	Modreeny	Borrisokane	II.	286
38	Isle M'Cricket	8 0 37	Down	Lecale Lower	Kilclief	Downpatrick	III.	179
10	*Isle Namanfin*	1 1 5	Fermanagh	Lurg	Derryvullan	Lowtherstown	III.	205
3, 11	Issane	125 0 1	Limerick	Kenry	Iveruss	Rathkeale	II.	249
19	Issbawn or Upper Gortnagross	244 0 9	Antrim	Lower Glenarm	Layd	Ballycastle	III.	22
84	Istalea Lower	151 3 3	Kerry	Glanarought	Kenmare	Kenmare	II.	186
84	Istalea Upper	349 0 32	Kerry	Glanarought	Kenmare	Kenmare	II.	186
8, 9	Ittereery	123 2 8	Monaghan	Monaghan	Tedavnet	Monaghan	III.	279
29	Ivyhall	74 2 18	Tipperary, N.R.	Eliogarty	Templemore	Thurles	II.	272
3	Ivy Hill	92 3 36	Monaghan	Trough	Errigal Trough	Clogher	III.	284

(a) Including 3A. 3R. 30P. water.
(b) Including 15A. 2R. 29P. water.
(c) Including 55A. 3R. 17P. water.
(d) Including 6A. 1R. 2P. water.
(e) Nine Islands in the River Suir.
(f) Including 6A. 1R. 25P. water.

No. of Sheet of the Ordnance Survey Maps.	Townlands and Towns.	Area in Statute Acres.	County.	Barony.	Parish.	Poor Law Union in 1857.	Townland Census of 1851, Part I.	
		A. R. P.					Vol.	Page
31	*Jackdaw Island*	5 0 29	Down	Lecale Lower	Ballyculter	Downpatrick	III.	178
42, 43	Jacketstown	112 1 34	Wexford	Forth	Drinagh	Wexford	I.	309
28	Jackstown	120 2 6	Kilkenny	Gowran	Columbkille	Thomastown	I.	94
88	Jamesbrook	247 1 15	Cork, E.R.	Imokilly	Garranekinnefeake	Middleton	II.	86
19	Jamesgreen	33 1 24a	Kilkenny	Kilkenny, Municipal Borough of	St. Canice	Kilkenny	I.	117
19	Jamespark	40 3 36b	Kilkenny	Crannagh, and Municipal Borough	St. Canice	Kilkenny	I.	87
11	Jamestown	40 0 30	Dublin	Nethercross	Swords	Balrothery	I.	32
25, 26	Jamestown	405 1 7	Dublin	Rathdown	Kilgobbin	Rathdown	I.	35
26	Jamestown	64 0 18	Dublin	Rathdown	Tully	Rathdown	I.	38
25	Jamestown	92 1 36	Dublin	Uppercross	Cruagh	Dublin South	I.	39
18	Jamestown	117 3 13	Dublin	Uppercross	Drimnagh	Dublin South	I.	40
41	Jamestown	294 0 18	Kilkenny	Ida	Ballygurrim	New Ross	I.	101
39	Jamestown	255 1 7	Kilkenny	Iverk	Fiddown	Carrick on Suir	I.	105
31	Jamestown	209 1 35c	Leitrim	Leitrim	Kiltoghert	Cark. on Shannon	IV.	102
55	Jamestown	836 2 28	Limerick	Coshlea	Kilquane	Kilmallock	II.	240
24	Jamestown	535 2 5	Meath	Lune	Rathmore	Trim	I.	208
44, 45	Jamestown	235 2 26	Meath	Ratoath	Ratoath	Dunshaughlin	I.	219
44	Jamestown	363 3 11	Roscommon	Athlone	Taghboy	Athlone	IV.	184
76	Jamestown	310 3 1	Tipperary, S.R.	Iffa and Offa East	Rathronan	Clonmel	II.	316
63, 64	Jamestown	318 0 29	Tipperary, S.R.	Slievardagh	Modeshil	Callan	II.	335
25	Jamestown	189 1 3	Westmeath	Rathconrath	Churchtown	Mullingar	I.	282
24, 25, 31	Jamestown	610 3 3	Westmeath	Rathconrath	Conry	Mullingar	I.	282
32	Jamestown	294 1 11	Wexford	Ballaghkeen	Edermine	Enniscorthy	I.	294
19, 25	Jamestown	153 3 20	Wexford	Bantry	Templescoby	Enniscorthy	I.	303
9	Jamestown or Ballyteigeduff	699 1 4	Queen's Co.	Portnahinch	Lea	Mountmellick	I.	244
14	Jamestown Great	180 3 7	Dublin	Castleknock	Finglas	Dublin North	I.	25
14	Jamestown Little	86 0 34	Dublin	Castleknock	Finglas	Dublin North	I.	25
31	JAMESTOWN T.	—	Leitrim	Leitrim	Kiltoghert	Cark. on Shannon	IV.	103
28	Janeville	250 1 26	Waterford	Coshmore & Coshbride	Kilwatermoy	Lismore	II.	343
12, 16	Janeville or Kilgarron	232 3 10	Carlow	Idrone East	Fennagh	Carlow	I.	7
6	Jarretstown	47 2 32	Kildare	North Salt	Confey	Celbridge	I.	74
53	Jarretstown	250 3 31	Meath	Dunboyne	Dunboyne	Dunshaughlin	I.	199
6	*Jasper Island*	0 3 3	Longford	Granard	Columbkille	Granard	I.	156
38	Jealoustown	383 2 2	Meath	Ratoath	Trevet	Dunshaughlin	I.	220
13	Jeffrystown	327 3 28	Westmeath	Moyashel and Magheradernon	Rathconnell	Mullingar	I.	276
10, 14	Jenkinstown	610 1 39	Kilkenny	Fassadinin	Mayne	Kilkenny	I.	90
5, 7, 8	Jenkinstown	976 1 0	Louth	Lower Dundalk	Ballymascanlan	Dundalk	I.	176
49	Jenkinstown	97 3 34	Meath	Upper Deece	Kilclone	Dunshaughlin	I.	193
43, 49	Jenkinstown	302 1 38	Meath	Upper Deece	Kilmore	Dunshaughlin	I.	193
149	*Jeremiah's Island*	1 1 17	Cork, W.R.	West Carbery (E.D.)	Creagh	Skibbereen	II.	139
28, 32	Jerpointabbey	764 2 0d	Kilkenny	Gowran	Jerpointabbey	Thomastown	I.	96
28, 32	Jerpointchurch	635 3 23e	Kilkenny	Knocktopher	Jerpointchurch	Thomastown	I.	111
28, 32	Jerpointhill	518 2 9	Kilkenny	Knocktopher	Jerpointchurch	Thomastown	I.	111
28	Jerpoint West	399 3 27f	Kilkenny	Gowran	Jerpoint West	Thomastown	I.	96
39	Jerusalem	288 1 15g	Kildare	Kilkea and Moone	Painestown	Athy	I.	61
49, 55	Jessfield	388 3 28	Tipperary, S.R.	Slievardagh	Ballingarry	Callan	II.	332
19, 24	Jigginstown	1,038 0 10	Kildare	Naas North	Naas	Naas	I.	62
3	Joanstown	506 3 6	Waterford	Upperthird	Mothel	Carrick on Suir	II.	371
6, 11	Joanstown	1,386 3 36h	Westmeath	Moygoish	Rathaspick	Mullingar	I.	280
21	Jobstown	420 2 4	Dublin	Uppercross	Tallagh	Dublin South	I.	41
28	Jockeyhall	50 3 18	Kilkenny	Gowran	Jerpointabbey	Thomastown	I.	96
21, 22	Jockeyhall	265 0 36	Limerick	Pubblebrien	Crecora	Croom	II.	252
29	Jockeyhall	42 3 5	Tipperary, N.R.	Eliogarty	Templemore	Thurles	II.	272
34, 39	Jockeysquarter	1,202 3 6	Antrim	Lower Antrim	Glenwhirry	Ballymena	III.	4
11	Johndutfswood	431 1 18	Carlow	Idrone West	Oldleighlin	Carlow	I.	9
20	John Gillins	25 0 0	Antrim	Lower Glenarm	Ardclinis	Larne	III.	21
10	Johninstown	224 0 8	Kildare	North Salt	Taghadoe	Celbridge	I.	76
11	Johnsborough	443 2 28i	Queen's Co.	Upperwoods	Offerlane	Mountmellick	I.	252
23	Johnsbrook	172 2 5	Meath	Upper Kells	Girley	Kells	I.	205
71, 72	Johnsfort	158 0 15	Mayo	Gallen	Kilconduff	Swineford	IV.	148
13	Johnstown	44 2 15	Armagh	Fews Lower	Mullaghbrack	Armagh	III.	47
7, 8	Johnstown	766 1 16	Carlow	Carlow	Urglin	Carlow	I.	3
75	Johnstown	175 0 17	Cork, E.R.	Barrymore	Carrigtohill	Middleton	II.	52
19	Johnstown	192 1 29	Cork, E.R.	Condons & Clangibbon	Kilgullane	Mitchelstown	II.	61
82, 94	Johnstown	643 2 11	Cork, W.R.	West Muskerry	Kilmichael	Dunmanway	II.	159
7	Johnstown	258 2 8	Dublin	Balrothery East	Lusk	Balrothery	I.	21
14	Johnstown	67 1 37	Dublin	Castleknock	Castleknock	Dublin North	I.	24
14	Johnstown	96 1 35	Dublin	Castleknock	Finglas	Dublin North	I.	25
20, 21, 24	Johnstown	316 0 25	Dublin	Newcastle	Rathcoole	Celbridge	I.	34
23	Johnstown	70 0 13	Dublin	Rathdown	Kill	Rathdown	I.	36

(a) Included in the Parish of St. Canice.
(b) { Within the Municipal Boundary, 25A. 2R. 3P. / Without the Municipal Boundary, 15A. 1R. 33P.
(c) Including Islands.
(d) Including 4A. 1R. 8P. River Nore.
(e) Including 6A. 0R. 20P. River Nore.
(f) Including 15A. 1R. 35P. River Nore.
(g) Including 8A. 0R. 0P. water.
(h) Including 5A. 3R. 4P. water.
(i) Including 22A. 3R. 27P. detached portion.

No. of Sheet of the Ordnance Survey Maps.	Townlands and Towns.	Area in Statute Acres.	County.	Barony.	Parish.	Poor Law Union in 1857.	Townland Census of 1851, Part I.	
		A. R. P.					Vol.	Page
26	Johnstown	20 1 27	Dublin	Rathdown	Rathmichael	Rathdown	I.	37
17, 18	Johnstown	89 2 35	Dublin	Uppercross	Palmerston	Dublin South	I.	40
43	Johnstown	119 3 4	Galway	Clare	Killower	Tuam	IV.	21
3, 4	Johnstown	409 1 2	Kildare	Carbury	Cadamstown	Edenderry	I.	51
19	Johnstown	145 0 34	Kildare	Naas North	Johnstown	Naas	I.	62
24	Johnstown	178 0 19	Kildare	Naas South	Carnalway	Naas	I.	64
16, 19	Johnstown	345 1 37	Louth	Ferrard	Dunany	Ardee	I.	180
19, 26	Johnstown	79 2 24	Meath	Lower Duleek	Fennor	Navan	I.	196
48	Johnstown	806 0 8	Meath	Lower Moyfenrath	Rathcore	Trim	I.	211
42	Johnstown	265 2 39	Meath	Lower Moyfenrath	Rathmolyon	Trim	I.	211
39, 45	Johnstown	180 2 24	Meath	Ratoath	Donaghmore	Dunshaughlin	I.	218
44	Johnstown	457 1 4	Meath	Ratoath	Dunshaughlin	Dunshaughlin	I.	218
25	Johnstown	123 2 2	Meath	Skreen	Athlumney	Navan	I.	220
33	Johnstown	128 0 12	Meath	Upper Duleek	Duleek	Drogheda	I.	197
23	Johnstown	418 2 21	Meath	Upper Kells	Kilskeer	Kells	I.	206
9, 14	Johnstown	802 2 8a	Tipperary, N.R.	Lower Ormond	Killodiernan	Borrisokane	II.	284
16	Johnstown	226 2 19	Waterford	Middlethird	Dunhill	Waterford	II.	366
8	Johnstown	426 1 26b	Westmeath	Delvin	Kilcumny	Castletowndelvin	I.	265
13	Johnstown	458 1 22c	Westmeath	Delvin	Killulagh	Castletowndelvin	I.	266
11, 18	Johnstown	936 3 31	Westmeath	Moygoish	Templeoran	Mullingar	I.	281
46	Johnstown	528 1 2	Wexford	Bargy	Duncormick	Wexford	I.	305
47	Johnstown	57 2 7	Wexford	Bargy	Mulrankin	Wexford	I.	307
42	Johnstown	152 3 33	Wexford	Forth	Rathaspick	Wexford	I.	312
4	Johnstown	444 0 33	Wexford	Scarawalsh	Moyacomb	Shillelagh	I.	325
38	Johnstown	342 3 20	Wexford	Shelmaliere East	Ardcolm	Wexford	I.	330
9, 10, 16	Johnstown	435 0 13	Wicklow	Lower Talbotstown	Hollywood	Baltinglass	I.	360
13	Johnstown	79 1 21	Wicklow	Newcastle	Kilcoole	Rathdrum	I.	352
40	Johnstown or Cornaclare	81 3 17	Fermanagh	Clankelly	Clones	Clones	III.	195
51,52,54,55	Johnstown Demesne	745 1 37	Roscommon	Athlone	Drum	Athlone	IV.	180
27	Johnstown East	521 3 14	Cork, E.R.	Fermoy	Dunmahon	Fermoy	II.	79
28	Johnstown Glebe	435 2 30	Queen's Co.	Clandonagh	Rathdowney	Donaghmore	I.	234
45	Johnstown Hill	216 2 28	Wicklow	Arklow	Inch	Rathdrum	I.	344
45	Johnstown Lower	171 2 27	Wicklow	Arklow	Inch	Rathdrum	I.	344
37, 39	Johnstown North	424 1 8	Kildare	Kilkea and Moone	Castledermot	Athy	I.	59
41	Johnstown North	212 1 2	Wicklow	Arklow	Kilbride	Rathdrum	I.	344
11, 18	Johnstown (Nugent) or Monroe	113 3 34	Westmeath	Moygoish	Templeoran	Mullingar	I.	281
39, 40	Johnstown South	319 0 10	Kildare	Kilkea and Moone	Castledermot	Athy	I.	59
40, 41	Johnstown South	215 3 10	Wicklow	Arklow	Kilbride	Rathdrum	I.	344
4	JOHNSTOWN T.	—	Kildare	Carbury	Cadamstown	Edenderry	I.	51
8	JOHNSTOWN T.	—	Kilkenny	Galmoy	Fertagh	Urlingford	I.	92
45	Johnstown Upper	146 1 38	Wicklow	Arklow	Inch	Rathdrum	I.	344
27, 35	Johnstown West	462 1 11	Cork, E.R.	Fermoy	Dunmahon	Fermoy	II.	79
15	Johnswell	445 3 1	Kilkenny	Gowran	Rathcoole	Kilkenny	I.	98
19	Joinersfolly	116 1 20	Kilkenny	Shillelogher	St. Patrick's	Kilkenny	I.	116
47	Jonastown	73 3 1	Wexford	Forth	Ballymore	Wexford	I.	308
10, 16	Jonesborough or Killaconin	252 3 0	Meath	Upper Kells	Loughan or Castle-keeran	Kells	I.	207
32	JONESBOROUGH T.	—	Armagh	Orior Upper	Jonesborough	Newry	III.	57
11, 12	Jonestown	158 1 26	King's Co.	Warrenstown	Ballymacwilliam	Edenderry	I.	144
38	Jordans Acre	6 0 19	Down	Lecale Upper	Down	Downpatrick	III.	180
45	Jordans Crew	290 2 35	Down	Lecale Lower	Ballee	Downpatrick	III.	178
27	Jordansquarter	85 3 22	Tipperary, N.R.	Upper Ormond	Kilnaneave	Nenagh	II.	291
52, 57	Jordanstown	964 3 28	Antrim	Lower Belfast	Carnmoney	Belfast	III.	8
16	Jordanstown	142 3 25	Cork, E.R.	Orrery and Kilmore	Kilbroney	Mallow	II.	109
4, 5, 7, 8	Jordanstown	493 3 37d	Dublin	Balrothery East	Lusk	Balrothery	I.	21
7	Jordanstown	92 3 23e	Dublin	Balrothery West	Clonmethan	Balrothery	I.	22
7	Jordanstown	317 2 24	Dublin	Balrothery West	Palmerston	Balrothery	I.	23
21	Jordanstown	73 3 12	Dublin	Newcastle	Kilmactalway	Celbridge	I.	33
16, 21	Jordanstown	95 3 6	Kilkenny	Gowran	Kilmacahill	Kilkenny	I.	97
16	Jordanstown	52 0 35	Kilkenny	Gowran	Shankill	Kilkenny	I.	99
48	Jordanstown	472 0 33	Meath	Lower Moyfenrath	Rathcore	Trim	I.	211
24	Jordanstown	148 1 18	Meath	Lower Navan	Martry	Kells	I.	215
31, 32	Jordanstown	184 0 36	Meath	Skreen	Tara	Navan	I.	222
17	Jordanstown	95 2 8	Westmeath	Rathconrath	Rathconrath	Ballymahon	I.	284
20	Joristown Lower	289 1 4	Westmeath	Farbill	Killucan	Mullingar	I.	267
20	Joristown Upper	267 1 14	Westmeath	Farbill	Killucan	Mullingar	I.	267
70, 77	Jossestown	671 0 14	Tipperary, S.R.	Middlethird	Donaghmore	Cashel	II.	326
31	Joulterspark	1 0 30	Waterford	Decies without Drum	Dungarvan	Dungarvan	II.	355
17, 30	Joycegrove	154 0 31	Galway	Dunmore	Tuam	Tuam	IV.	36
76	Joyces Island	1 2 0	Galway	Ballynahinch	Moyrus	Clifden	IV.	14
28, 42	Joyces Park	70 3 31	Galway	Clare	Donaghpatrick	Tuam	IV.	19
10	Julianstown	97 0 16	Kilkenny	Fassadinin	Dysart	Castlecomer	I.	89

(a) Including 33A. 2R. 34P. water.
(b) Including 9A. 1R. 29P. water.
(c) Including 18A. 2R. 21P. water.
(d) Including 23A. 2R. 16P. detached portions.
(e) Including 24A. 3R. 2P. detached portion.

No. of Sheet of the Ordnance Survey Maps	Townlands and Towns.	Area in Statute Acres. A. R. P.	County.	Barony.	Parish.	Poor Law Union in 1857.	Townland Census of 1851, Part I. Vol.	Page
6, 12	Julianstown	177 2 35	Meath	Morgallion	Castletown	Navan	I.	209
6	Julianstown	776 1 24a	Meath	Morgallion [1]	Nobber	Kells	I.	210
21, 28	Julianstown East	204 1 8	Meath	Lower Duleek	Julianstown	Drogheda	I.	196
28	Julianstown South	59 1 6	Meath	Lower Duleek	Julianstown	Drogheda	I.	196
28	JULIANSTOWN T.	—	Meath	Lower Duleek	Julianstown	Drogheda	I.	196
21, 28	Julianstown West	266 2 0	Meath	Lower Duleek	Julianstown	Drogheda	I.	196
26	Juniper Island	1 0 12	Donegal	Kilmacrenan	Clondahorky	Dunfanaghy	III.	124
97	Kanargad	6 1 24	Galway	Loughrea	Kilconickny	Loughrea	IV.	63
3	Kane	109 0 2	Louth	Upper Dundalk	Kane	Dundalk	I.	179
21	Kanefield	159 3 34	Roscommon	Castlereagh	Baslick	Castlereagh	IV.	199
9	Kanrawer	70 1 12	Galway	Ballynahinch	Ballynakill	Clifden	IV.	11
23	Kanturk	325 0 38	Cork, E.R.	Duhallow	Clonfert	Kanturk	II.	68
23	KANTURK T.	—	Cork, E.R.	Duhallow	Castlemagner / Clonfert / Kilroe	Kanturk	II.	67 / 69 / 74
37	Kavanaghspark	77 2 28	Wexford	Shelmaliere East	Kilpatrick	Wexford	I.	331
40	Kayle	440 1 24	Wexford	Shelmaliere West	Inch	New Ross	I.	333
31	Kead	450 1 26	Galway	Ballymoe	Clonbern	Glennamaddy	IV.	6
48	Keadagh	40 1 34	Roscommon	Athlone	Kiltoom	Athlone	IV.	183
27	Keadeen	361 1 32	Wicklow	Upper Talbotstown	Kilranelagh	Baltinglass	I.	364
21	Keadew	177 3 16	Cavan	Upper Loughtee	Castleterra	Cavan	III.	82
20	Keadew	233 0 1	Cavan	Upper Loughtee	Urney	Cavan	III.	86
40, 41, 49	Keadew	983 2 22b	Donegal	Boylagh	Templecrone	Glenties	III.	115
14	Keadew	117 0 4	Fermanagh	Magheraboy	Devenish	Enniskillen	III.	211
4	Keadew East	318 0 6	Roscommon	Boyle	Kilronan	Boyle	IV.	197
94	Keadew Lower	119 1 20	Donegal	Tirhugh	Donegal	Donegal	III.	145
11	Keadews	14 2 14	Sligo	Tireragh	Easky	Dromore West	IV.	233
4	KEADEW T.	—	Roscommon	Boyle	Kilronan	Boyle	IV.	197
85,86,94,95	Keadew Upper	2,342 3 25c	Donegal	Tirhugh	Donegal	Donegal	III.	145
4	Keadew West	273 1 8d	Roscommon	Boyle	Kilronan	Boyle	IV.	197
34	Keady	91 3 10	Fermanagh	Coole	Galloon	Lisnaskea	III.	200
10	Keady	167 1 15	Londonderry	Keenaght	Drumachose	New Tn Limavady	III.	235
32	Keady	405 2 13	Londonderry	Loughinsholin	Maghera	Magherafelt	III.	242
59	Keady	212 2 32	Tyrone	Clogher	Errigal Keerogue	Clogher	III.	295
21	Keady Beg	321 3 29	Armagh	Orior Lower	Loughgilly	Newry	III.	56
13	Keadycam	588 1 14	Tyrone	Strabane Upper	Bodoney Upper	Gortin	III.	324
21	Keady More	366 1 9	Armagh	Orior Lower	Loughgilly	Newry	III.	56
20	KEADY T.	—	Armagh	Armagh	Keady	Armagh	III.	45
129	Keaghery Island	0 1 16	Galway	Kiltartan	Beagh	Gort	IV.	46
88	Keal	52 0 14	Tipperary, S.R.	Iffa and Offa West	Neddans	Clogheen	II.	319
80, 89	Kealafreaghane East	933 0 15	Kerry	Iveragh	Dromod	Cahersiveen	II.	195
80, 89	Kealafreaghane West	602 1 17	Kerry	Iveragh	Dromod	Cahersiveen	II.	195
104	Kealagowlane	787 1 35	Cork, W.R.	Bear	Kilcaskan	Castletown	II.	123
91, 105	Kealanine	628 3 27	Cork, W.R.	Bantry	Kilmocomoge	Bantry	II.	121
119	Kealanine	779 2 32	Cork, W.R.	West Carbery (W.D.)	Caheragh	Skibbereen	II.	142
91	Kealariddig	463 1 24	Kerry	Dunkerron South	Kilcrohane	Kenmare	II.	184
105	Kealcoum	49 3 5	Cork, W.R.	Bantry	Kilmocomoge	Bantry	II.	121
63, 71	Kealduff Lower	279 3 25	Kerry	Iveragh	Glanbehy	Cahersiveen	II.	196
71	Kealduff Upper	815 0 10e	Kerry	Iveragh	Glanbehy	Cahersiveen	II.	196
56	Keale	652 2 31	Limerick	Coshlea	Kilflyn	Kilmallock	II.	240
35	Keale	1,606 1 31	Limerick	Shanid	Rathronan	Newcastle	II.	257
30	Keale North	258 2 31	Cork, E.R.	Duhallow	Cullen	Millstreet	II.	70
39	Keale South	240 3 17f	Cork, E.R.	Duhallow	Cullen	Millstreet	II.	70
138, 147	Kealfadda	477 2 17	Cork, W.R.	West Carbery (W.D.)	Kilmoe	Skull	II.	145
15	Kealfoun	902 1 0	Waterford	Decies without Drum	Fews	Kilmacthomas	II.	356
39, 40	Kealgorm	109 0 7	Kerry	Trughanacmy	Castleisland	Tralee	II.	208
11	Kealid	865 1 10	Kerry	Iraghticonnor	Knockanure	Listowel	II.	192
92, 106	Kealkill	772 2 24	Cork, W.R.	Bantry	Kilmocomoge	Bantry	II.	121
30, 39	Kealmanagh	265 2 10	Cork, E.R.	Duhallow	Cullen	Millstreet	II.	70
114, 127	Kealoge	327 0 5	Cork, W.R.	Bear	Kilnamanagh	Castletown	II.	126
31	Kealroe	46 3 8	Waterford	Decies without Drum	Kilgobnet	Dungarvan	II.	357
10	Kealstown	326 1 0	Kildare	North Salt	Taghadoe	Celbridge	I.	76
130	Kealties	614 2 14	Cork, W.R.	West Carbery (W.D.)	Durrus	Bantry	II.	142
81	Kealvaugh Beg	229 3 4g	Cork, W.R.	West Muskerry	Inchigeelagh	Dunmanway	II.	157
80, 81	Kealvaugh More	390 3 31	Cork, W.R.	West Muskerry	Inchigeelagh	Dunmanway	II.	157
30	Keam	120 1 5	Kerry	Trughanacmy	O'Brennan	Tralee	II.	212
80, 81	Keamcorravooly	415 0 2	Cork, W.R.	West Muskerry	Inchigeelagh	Macroom	II.	157
134	Keamnabricka	89 0 23	Cork, W.R.	East Carbery (W.D.)	Ross	Clonakilty	II.	135
116	Keamnalicky	7 3 21h	Cork, W.R.	Bear	Killaconenagh	Castletown	II.	125
133, 142	Keamore	469 3 33	Cork, W.R.	West Carbery (E.D.)	Kilmacabea	Skibbereen	II.	140
103	Keamsellagh East	217 1 5	Galway	Dunkellin	Killeenavarra	Gort	IV.	30
103	Keamsellagh West	233 0 3i	Galway	Dunkellin	Killeenavarra	Gort	IV.	30

(a) Including 6A. 2R. 33P. water.
(b) Including 74A. 2R. 35P. water.
(c) Including 54A. 2R. 33P. water.

(d) Including 8A. 3R. 15P. water.
(e) Including 57A. 1R. 10P. water.
(f) Including 5A. 2R. 32P. water.

(g) Including 13A. 3R. 30P. water.
(h) Including 2A. 2R. 39P. detached portion.
(i) Including 1A. 2R. 16P. water.

No. of Sheet of the Ordnance Survey Maps.	Townlands and Towns.	Area in Statute Acres. A. R. P.	County.	Barony.	Parish.	Poor Law Union in 1857.	Townland Census of 1851, Part I. Vol.	Page
32	Kearney	236 0 39	Down	Ards Upper	Ballytrustan	Downpatrick	III.	160
41, 44	Kearneysbay	141 0 5	Kilkenny	Ida	Kilcolumb	Waterford	I.	102
21	Kearneystown	115 3 17	Louth	Ferrard	Mullary	Drogheda	I.	182
15	Kearneystown Lower	72 3 22	Kildare	South Salt	Lyons	Celbridge	I.	77
15	Kearneystown Upper	79 2 11	Kildare	South Salt	Lyons	Celbridge	I.	77
3, 6	Kearntown	324 2 19	Meath	Lower Slane	Drumcondra	Ardee	I.	222
21	Keatingspark	194 0 34	Dublin	Newcastle	Rathcoole	Celbridge	I.	34
14, 19	Keatingstown	733 0 4	Kilkenny	Crannagh	St. Canice	Kilkenny	I.	87
35	Keatingstown	110 1 28	Kilkenny	Knocktopher	Lismateige	Thomastown	I.	113
33	Keatleysclose	72 2 35	Cork, E.R.	Fermoy	Mallow	Mallow	II.	81
61	Keave	94 2 2	Galway	Kilconnell	Ahascragh	Mountbellew	IV.	39
1	Kebble	269 2 18	Antrim	Cary	Rathlin Island	Ballycastle	III.	15
67	Kedew	250 2 32	Tyrone	Dungannon Lower	Aghaloo	Armagh	III.	297
150	*Kedge Island*	7 1 32	Cork, W.R.	West Carbery (E.D.)	Tullagh	Skibbereen	II.	141
25	Kednagullion	171 3 33	Monaghan	Farney	Donaghmoyne	Castleblayney	III.	270
32	Kednaminsha	201 2 3	Monaghan	Farney	Donaghmoyne	Carrickmacross	III.	270
75, 76	Kedrah	751 0 0	Tipperary, S.R.	Iffa and Offa West	Mortlestown	Clogheen	II.	318
81	Keeagh	599 1 10	Galway	Moycullen	Moycullen	Galway	IV.	71
72	Keeas	459 0 39	Kerry	Dunkerron North	Knockane	Cahersiveen	II.	182
102	Keebagh	84 0 12	Mayo	Costello	Bekan	Claremorris	IV.	139
17	Keeghan	117 3 20	Cavan	Tullygarvey	Kildrumsherdan	Cootehill	III.	90
55, 56	Keekill	435 3 12	Galway	Clare	Killeany	Tuam	IV.	20
22	Keel	206 0 39	Cork, E.R.	Duhallow	Kilmeen	Kanturk	II.	73
71, 72	Keel	581 3 7	Kerry	Iveragh	Glanbehy	Cahersiveen	II.	196
46	Keel	263 3 12	Kerry	Trughanacmy	Kilgarrylander	Tralee	II.	210
19, 23	Keel	740 2 9	Longford	Moydow	Kilglass	Ballymahon	I.	161
27	Keel	524 2 37	Longford	Shrule	Noughaval	Ballymahon	I.	166
16	Keelagh	247 1 14a	Cavan	Tullygarvey	Annagh	Cootehill	III.	87
19	Keelagh	335 3 25b	Cavan	Tullyhunco	Killashandra	Cavan	III.	98
35	Keelagh	163 1 11c	Leitrim	Mohill	Mohill	Mohill	IV.	108
24, 30	Keelagh	267 3 10	Queen's Co.	Cullenagh	Dysartgallen	Abbeyleix	I.	239
15, 21	Keelaghan	153 3 34	Fermanagh	Magheraboy	Devenish	Enniskillen	III.	211
39	Keelagh Glebe	19 0 26	Cavan	Castlerahan	Lurgan	Oldcastle	III.	70
25, 26	Keelagho	44 0 9	Fermanagh	Clanawley	Cleenish	Enniskillen	III.	191
43	Keelaghy	114 0 13	Fermanagh	Clankelly	Drummully	Clones	III.	197
93, 107	Keelaraheen	413 1 13	Cork, W.R.	East Carbery (W.D.)	Fanlobbus	Dunmanway	II.	132
{ 74, 83 } Mayo Co.	Keelbanada	1,047 3 31	Roscommon	Frenchpark	Kilcolman	Castlereagh	IV.	203
27	Keelbaun	68 3 20	Longford	Shrule	Noughaval	Ballymahon	I.	166
32	Keelbeg	118 2 8	Westmeath	Moycashel	Castletownkindalen	Mullingar	I.	277
36	Keelcurragh or Carrowreagh	53 0 14	Roscommon	Ballintober South	Kilgefin	Roscommon	IV.	189
31, 37	Keelderry	274 0 39d	Cavan	Clanmahon	Crosserlough	Cavan	III.	76
36	Keelderry	368 3 31e	Clare	Tulla Lower	Killuran	Tulla	II.	36
123, 124	Keelderry	1,088 2 0	Galway	Loughrea	Kilthomas	Gort	IV.	65
33	Keeldra	284 0 6f	Leitrim	Mohill	Cloone	Mohill	IV.	106
94	Keeldrum	110 1 21	Donegal	Tirhugh	Donegal	Donegal	III.	145
24	Keeldrum Lower	215 0 23	Donegal	Kilmacrenan	Tullaghobegly	Dunfanaghy	III.	132
33, 42	Keeldrum Upper	3,634 0 7g	Donegal	Kilmacrenan	Tullaghobegly	Dunfanaghy	III.	132
42, 54	Keel East	1,644 1 8h	Mayo	Burrishoole	Achill	Newport	IV.	117
6	Keelhilla	1,035 3 31	Clare	Burren	Carran	Ballyvaghan	II.	11
79	Keelkill	169 2 32	Mayo	Carra	Breaghwy	Castlebar	IV.	127
98	Keelkill	644 1 19	Mayo	Murrisk	Aghagower	Westport	IV.	159
23, 24	Keelkyle	226 3 17	Clare	Corcomroe	Clooney	Ennistimon	II.	18
23	Keelkyle	1,006 3 23	Galway	Ballynahinch	Ballynakill	Clifden	IV.	11
80	Keelnagore	351 1 26	Kerry	Iveragh	Killinane	Cahersiveen	II.	197
18, 19	Keelogalabaun	82 2 23	Longford	Moydow	Moydow	Longford	I.	162
108, 109	Keeloge	236 2 32	Galway	Longford	Meelick	Portumna	IV.	61
17	Keeloge	137 1 36	Kildare	Offaly East	Rathangan	Naas	I.	71
43	Keeloge	168 0 17	King's Co.	Ballybritt	Roscrea	Roscrea	I.	126
42	Keeloge	510 3 37	King's Co.	Clonlisk	Shinrone	Roscrea	I.	131
15	Keeloge	51 1 37	King's Co.	Garrycastle	Wheery or Killagally	Parsonstown	I.	139
32	Keeloge	55 3 39	Leitrim	Leitrim	Mohill	Mohill	IV.	104
18, 19	Keeloge	150 0 13	Longford	Moydow	Moydow	Ballymahon	I.	162
32, 37	Keeloge	495 1 36	Queen's Co.	Slievemargy	Killeshin	Carlow	I.	246
37, 38, 40	Keeloge	142 3 17	Westmeath	Moycashel	Durrow	Tullamore	I.	277
40	Keeloge	82 0 15	Wicklow	Arklow	Kilbride	Rathdrum	I.	344
19	Keeloge Lower	146 3 1	Wicklow	Newcastle	Newcastle Upper	Rathdrum	I.	353
15	Keelogenasause	124 3 20	Longford	Ardagh	Mostrim	Granard	I.	152
15	Keeloge North	400 0 31	Queen's Co.	Upperwoods	Offerlane	Mountmellick	I.	252
92	Keeloges	440 2 24	Donegal	Banagh	Inver	Donegal	III.	107
44, 52	Keeloges	553 2 9	Donegal	Kilmacrenan	Conwal	Letterkenny	III.	100
70, 79	Keeloges	109 0 34	Donegal	Raphoe	Clonleigh	Strabane	III.	135
21	Keeloges	217 1 8	Dublin	Newcastle	Newcastle	Celbridge	I.	34

(a) Including 15A. 0R. 33P. water.
(b) Including 55A. 1R. 14P. water.
(c) Including 2A. 3R. 2P. water.
(d) Including 33A. 2R. 35P. water.
(e) Including 4A. 3R. 19P. water.
(f) Including 28A. 1R. 22P. water.
(g) Including 135A. 2R. 17P. water.
(h) Including 145A. 3R. 32P. water.

No. of Sheet of the Ordnance Survey Maps.	Townlands and Towns.	Area in Statute Acres.	County.	Barony.	Parish.	Poor Law Union in 1857.	Townland Census of 1851, Part I.	
		A. R. P.					Vol.	Page
29	Keeloges	98 2 31	Galway	Dunmore	Tuam	Tuam	IV.	36
60, 61	Keeloges	83 3 3	Galway	Kilconnell	Ahascragh	Mountbellew	IV.	39
14, 15	Keeloges	133 3 34	Kildare	Naas North	Whitechurch	Naas	I.	63
3, 4	Keeloges	517 3 30	Leitrim	Rosclogher	Rossinver	Ballyshannon	IV.	111
25	Keeloges	254 1 32	Limerick	Coonagh	Oola	Tipperary	II.	236
49, 50	Keeloges	961 2 1	Limerick	Coshlea	Galbally	Mitchelstown	II.	238
14, 19	Keeloges	170 0 36	Longford	Ardagh	Ardagh	Longford	I.	151
67	Keeloges	122 2 19	Mayo	Burrishoole	Burrishoole	Newport	IV.	119
77, 88, 89	Keeloges	292 1 32	Mayo	Burrishoole	Islandeady	Westport	IV.	121
52	Keeloges	45 3 26	Roscommon	Athlone	Drum	Athlone	IV.	180
6	Keeloges	164 0 5	Roscommon	Boyle	Kilbryan	Boyle	IV.	195
6	Keeloges	258 3 21	Sligo	Carbury	Rossinver	Sligo	IV.	223
37	Keeloges	97 0 26	Wexford	Shelmaliere West	Kilbrideglynn	Wexford	I.	334
30	Keeloges	67 3 34	Wicklow	Arklow	Kilcommon	Rathdrum	I.	345
29	Keeloges, Bauville, and Clonglash	727 3 22	Donegal	Inishowen West	Fahan Lower	Inishowen	III.	120
7	Keelogesbeg	185 3 27	Galway	Ballymoe	Ballynakill	Glennamaddy	IV.	5
7, 19	Keeloges East	941 1 21	Galway	Ballymoe	Ballynakill	Glennamaddy	IV.	5
7, 14	Keeloges Lower	29 3 13	Mayo	Tirawley	Lackan	Killala	IV.	170
70, 79	Keeloges New	297 0 30	Mayo	Carra	Kildacommoge	Castlebar	IV.	129
70, 79	Keeloges Old	337 1 22	Mayo	Carra	Kildacommoge	Castlebar	IV.	129
15,16,21,22	Keelogue South	221 2 4	Queen's Co.	Upperwoods	Offerlane	Donaghmore	I.	252
79	KEELOGES T.	—	Mayo	Carra	Kildacommoge	Castlebar	IV.	129
7	Keeloges Upper	32 1 4	Mayo	Tirawley	Lackan	Killala	IV.	170
19	Keeloges West	525 2 17	Galway	Ballymoe	Ballynakill	Glennamaddy	IV.	5
18, 19	Keeloge Upper	146 2 12	Wicklow	Newcastle	Newcastle Upper	Rathdrum	I.	353
9, 15	Keelogyboy	704 2 36a	Sligo	Carbury	Calry	Sligo	IV.	220
22	Keelough Glebe	220 1 10	Queen's Co.	Clarmallagh	Aghaboe	Donaghmore	I.	236
33	Keelpark Glebe	101 2 31	Fermanagh	Clanawley	Kinawley	Enniskillen	III.	194
26	Keelrin	13 2 11	Leitrim	Carrigallen	Carrigallen	Bawnboy	IV.	89
25, 26	Keelrin	412 3 4	Leitrim	Carrigallen	Drumreilly	Bawnboy	IV.	91
6	Keeltane	537 0 22	Cork, E.R.	Duhallow	Tullylease	Kanturk	II.	76
47, 57	Keelties	406 2 35	Kerry	Magunihy	Kilnanare	Killarney	II.	204
103, 104, 116, 117	Keeltrasna	156 3 12	Cork, W.R.	Bear	Kilcaskan	Castletown	II.	123
33	Keelty	51 3 30	Clare	Islands	Drumcliff	Ennis	II.	30
52	Keelty	196 3 14	Roscommon	Athlone	Drum	Athlone	IV.	180
27, 34	Keelty	102 0 9	Roscommon	Castlereagh	Ballintober	Castlereagh	IV.	198
8	Keelty	304 0 4	Sligo	Carbury	Drumcliff	Sligo	IV.	221
41,42,53,54	Keel West	4,071 0 11b	Mayo	Burrishoole	Achill	Newport	IV.	117
11	Keely	148 0 39	Londonderry	Coleraine	Aghadowey	Coleraine	III.	229
38	Keenagh	247 1 13	Cavan	Castlerahan	Crosserlough	Oldcastle	III.	68
9	Keenagh	61 3 21	Cavan	Tullyhaw	Templeport	Bawnboy	III.	95
2, 4	Keenagh	226 2 10	Donegal	Inishowen East	Clonca	Inishowen	III.	117
22	Keenagh	216 1 15	Longford	Ratheline	Kilcommock	Ballymahon	I.	164
4, 8	Keenaghan	401 2 11	Armagh	Armagh	Loughgall	Armagh	III.	45
10, 14	Keenaghan	127 3 17c	Cavan	Lower Loughtee	Drumlane	Cavan	III.	80
96	Keenaghan	194 1 21	Donegal	Banagh	Kilcar	Glenties	III.	108
45	Keenaghan	355 0 38	Donegal	Kilmacrenan	Kilmacrenan	Letterkenny	III.	129
32	Keenaghan	110 1 5	Fermanagh	Clanawley	Kinawley	Enniskillen	III.	194
8	Keenaghan	171 0 6d	Fermanagh	Lurg	Belleek	Ballyshannon	III.	203
108	Keenaghan	143 0 35	Galway	Longford	Clonfert	Portumna	IV.	57
31	Keenaghan	114 3 14	Leitrim	Leitrim	Kiltoghert	Cark. on Shannon	IV.	102
22	Keenaghan	294 3 29	Meath	Fore	Killallon	Oldcastle	I.	200
2, 5	Keenaghan	296 0 1	Meath	Lower Kells	Enniskeen	Kells	I.	202
33	Keenaghan	113 3 30	Sligo	Corran	Emlaghfad	Sligo	IV.	226
54, 55	Keenaghan	180 0 0	Tyrone	Dungannon Middle	Killyman	Dungannon	III.	303
37, 38	Keenaghan	731 3 14	Tyrone	Dungannon Upper	Kildress	Cookstown	III.	309
5, 10	Keenaghan	1,377 2 33	Tyrone	Strabane Lower	Leckpatrick	Strabane	III.	322
37, 46	Keenagh Beg	1,778 1 29e	Mayo	Tirawley	Crossmolina	Ballina	IV.	166
41	Keenagh (Clanrickard)	184 2 9	Roscommon	Athlone	Athleague	Roscommon	IV.	179
41	Keenagh (Donnellan East)	80 0 18	Roscommon	Athlone	Athleague	Roscommon	IV.	179
41	Keenagh (Donnellan West)	117 2 31	Roscommon	Athlone	Athleague	Roscommon	IV.	179
37, 46	Keenagh More	1,922 2 31	Mayo	Tirawley	Crossmolina	Ballina	IV.	166
41	Keenaght	311 0 10	Londonderry	Loughinsholin	Kilcronaghan	Magherafelt	III.	241
22	KEENAGH T.	—	Longford	Ratheline	Kilcommock	Ballymahon	I.	164
34	Keenaghy	87 1 18	Fermanagh	Magherastephana	Aghalurcher	Lisnaskea	III.	216
25, 28	Keeneraboy	165 3 9	Monaghan	Farney	Donaghmoyne	Carrickmacross	III.	270
29	Keenheen	628 2 2f	Leitrim	Carrigallen	Drumreilly	Bawnboy	IV.	91
153	Keenleen	86 0 37	Cork, W.R.	West Carbery (E.D.)	Clear-island	Skibbereen	II.	138
8, 12	Keenog	111 0 30g	Monaghan	Monaghan	Drumsnat	Monaghan	III.	275
18, 23	Keenogbane	139 3 16h	Monaghan	Cremorne	Aghnamullen	Cootehill	III.	258

(a) Including 7A. 1R. 6P. Keelogyboy Lough.
(b) Including 57A. 1R. 25P. water.
(c) Including 16A. 2R. 21P. water.
(d) Including 11A. 2R. 16P. water.
(e) Including 11A. 3R. 5P. water.
(f) Including 41A. 3R. 0P. water.
(g) Including 8A. 2R. 32P. water.
(h) Including 9A. 3R. 32P. water.

No. of Sheet of the Ordnance Survey Maps.	Townlands and Towns.	Area in Statute Acres.	County.	Barony.	Parish.	Poor Law Union in 1857.	Townland Census of 1851, Part I.	
		A. R. P.					Vol.	Page
18, 23	Keenogduff	172 3 31a	Monaghan	Cremorne	Aghnamullen	Cootehill	III.	258
27	Keenoge	185 1 2	Meath	Upper Duleek	Duleek	Drogheda	I.	197
28	Keenoge	134 2 15	Meath	Upper Duleek	Moorechurch	Drogheda	I.	198
29	Keenoge	295 1 30	Monaghan	Farney	Inishkeen	Dundalk	III.	271
17	Keenoge	89 1 38	Westmeath	Rathconrath	Killare	Ballymahon	I.	283
49, 56	Keenogue	268 0 33	Tyrone	Omagh East	Kilskeery	Lowtherstown	III.	313
93, 107	Keenrath	424 3 31	Cork, W.R.	East Carbery (W.D.)	Fanlobbus	Dunmanway	II.	132
32	Keentagh	138 1 32	Down	Ards Upper	Witter	Downpatrick	III.	161
15	Keeny	220 2 20	Cavan	Lower Loughtee	Annagh	Cavan	III.	79
6, 11	Keeran	418 2 24	Fermanagh	Lurg	Derryvullan	Lowtherstown	III.	204
6	Keeran	71 3 9	Fermanagh	Lurg	Drumkeeran	Lowtherstown	III.	206
7	Keeran	106 3 3	Meath	Lower Slane	Siddan	Ardee	I.	224
20, 21	Keeranbane	479 0 38b	Donegal	Inishowen East	Moville Upper	Inishowen	III.	119
35	Keeran Beg	81 3 11	Fermanagh	Clankelly	Galloon	Lisnaskea	III.	198
35	Keeran More	160 1 21	Fermanagh	Clankelly	Galloon	Lisnaskea	III.	198
81, 93	Keeraun	134 0 34c	Galway	Galway	Rahoon	Galway	IV.	37
90	Keeraunbeg	708 1 5d	Galway	Moycullen	Killannin	Oughterard	IV.	69
79	KeeraunnagarkNorth	918 2 7e	Galway	Moycullen	Killannin	Galway	IV.	69
90, 91	KeeraunnagarkSouth	702 2 4f	Galway	Moycullen	Killannin	Galway	IV.	69
29, 30	Keereen Lower	170 2 2	Waterford	Decies within Drum	Kilmolash	Dungarvan	II.	351
30	Keereen Upper	261 3 26	Waterford	Decies within Drum	Kilmolash	Dungarvan	II.	351
13, 14, 20	Keerglen	1,768 1 16	Mayo	Tirawley	Kilfian	Killala	IV.	169
23	Keerhan	114 3 38	Louth	Ferrard	Tullyallen	Drogheda	I.	183
48	Keerhaunmore	163 3 25	Galway	Ballynahinch	Ballindoon	Clifden	IV.	10
35	Keerhaun North	100 0 3	Galway	Ballynahinch	Ballindoon	Clifden	IV.	10
48, 49	Keerhaun South	185 3 22g	Galway	Ballynahinch	Ballindoon	Clifden	IV.	10
19, 20	Keerin	430 0 30	Tyrone	Strabane Upper	Bodoney Lower	Gortin	III.	323
56	Keernaun	486 3 13	Galway	Clare	Killeany	Tuam	IV.	20
34	Keevagh	218 0 21	Clare	Bunratty Upper	Quin	Ennis	II.	10
18, 21	Keeverstown	223 1 8	Louth	Ferrard	Mullary	Drogheda	I.	182
26	Keggall	478 3 0h	Armagh	Orior Upper	Killevy	Newry	III.	58
14, 19	Keilagh	171 0 5	Cavan	Tullyhunco	Kildallan	Bawnboy	III.	97
118	Keilnascarta	317 0 4	Cork, W.R.	West Carbery (W.D.)	Kilmocomoge	Bantry	II.	144
18	Keiloge	555 0 19	Waterford	Gaultiere	Kilmacleague	Waterford	II.	364
8, 13	Kellistown East	868 3 9	Carlow	Carlow	Kellistown	Carlow	I.	2
7, 8, 12, 13	Kellistown West	983 0 22	Carlow	Carlow	Kellistown	Carlow	I.	2
38, 44	Kells	463 3 16	Antrim	Lower Antrim	Connor	Ballymena	III.	3
17	Kells	745 0 28i	Clare	Inchiquin	Kilkeedy	Corrofin	II.	25
62, 70	Kells	864 3 1j	Kerry	Iveragh	Killinane	Cahersiveen	II.	197
27	Kells	629 3 16	Kilkenny	Kells	Kells	Callan	I.	108
54	Kells	372 2 36	Limerick	Connello Upper	Dromcolliher	Newcastle	II.	232
27	Kellsborough	62 0 37	Kilkenny	Kells	Kells	Callan	I.	108
23, 27	Kellsgrange	478 2 3	Kilkenny	Kells	Kells	Callan	I.	108
38	KELLS T.	—	Antrim	Lower Antrim	Connor	Ballymena	III.	4
27	KELLS T.		Kilkenny	Kells	Kells	Callan	I.	108
17	KELLS T.	—	Meath	Upper Kells	Kells	Kells	I.	206
42, 45	Kellybrook	422 2 32	Roscommon	Athlone	Killinvoy	Roscommon	IV.	182
42, 45	Kellybrook	51 1 7	Roscommon	Athlone	St. Johns	Roscommon	IV.	183
24	Kellybrook	111 3 38	Westmeath	Rathconrath	Conry	Mullingar	I.	282
15,16,20,21	Kellymount	1,094 3 31	Kilkenny	Gowran	Shankill	Kilkenny	I.	99
87, 88	Kellysgrove	1,753 0 33k	Galway	Clonmacnowen	Clontuskert	Ballinasloe	IV.	24
40	Kelly's Island	2 0 17	Galway	Ross	Cong	Oughterard	IV.	73
79	Kellysmeadow	3 1 19	Donegal	Raphoe	Urney	Strabane	III.	144
13, 17	Kellystown	174 0 32	Dublin	Castleknock	Clonsilla	Celbridge	I.	24
6	Kellystown	212 3 31	Kildare	North Salt	Laraghbryan	Celbridge	I.	75
21	Kellystown	124 0 12	Louth	Ferrard	Drumshallon	Drogheda	I.	180
26	Kellystown	119 1 30	Meath	Lower Duleek	Duleek	Drogheda	I.	195
3	Kellystown	340 2 23	Meath	Lower Slane	Drumcondra	Ardee	I.	222
13, 19	Kellystown	531 0 0	Meath	Upper Slane	Monknewtown	Drogheda	I.	224
25	Kellystown	194 0 35	Queen's Co.	Ballyadams	Rathaspick	Athy	I.	232
31	Kellystown	917 3 16	Wexford	Bantry	Adamstown	New Ross	I.	299
42	Kellystown	92 2 38	Wexford	Forth	Drinagh	Wexford	I.	309
42	Kellystown	93 3 14	Wexford	Forth	Rathaspick	Wexford	I.	312
19	Kellystown	128 1 5	Wicklow	Newcastle	Killiskey	Rathdrum	I.	352
19	Kellyville	409 1 10l	Queen's Co.	Ballyadams	Ballyadams	Athy	I.	231
27	Kelsha	279 1 12	Wicklow	Upper Talbotstown	Kiltegan	Baltinglass	I.	365
27	Kelshabeg	245 2 18	Wicklow	Upper Talbotstown	Kiltegan	Baltinglass	I.	365
21	Kelshamore	330 0 9	Wicklow	Upper Talbotstown	Donaghmore	Baltinglass	I.	363
49	Kemmins Mill	81 2 34	Meath	Upper Deece	Kilclone	Dunshaughlin	I.	193
93	Kenmare	268 1 2	Kerry	Glanarought	Kenmare	Kenmare	II.	186
93	Kenmare Old	253 2 35	Kerry	Glanarought	Kenmare	Kenmare	II.	186
93	KENMARE T.	—	Kerry	Glanarought	Kenmare	Kenmare	II.	186
53	Kennaghstown	79 2 19	Meath	Dunboyne	Dunboyne	Dunshaughlin	I.	199

(a) Including 39A. 2R. 22P. water.
(b) Including 16A. 1R. 8P. water.
(c) Including 4A. 3R. 30P. water.
(d) Including 26A. 1R. 25P. water.

(e) Including 11A. 1R. 30P. water.
(f) Including 32A. 2R. 21P. water.
(g) Including 5A. 3R. 35P. water.
(h) Including 39A. 1R. 16P. water.

(i) Including 173A. 2R. 8P. water.
(j) Including 11A. 0R. 11P. water.
(k) Including 9A. 3R. 12P. water.
(l) Including 14A. 3R. 26P. water.

No. of Sheet of the Ordnance Survey Maps.	Townlands and Towns.	Area in Statute Acres. A. R. P.	County.	Barony.	Parish.	Poor Law Union in 1857.	Townland Census of 1851, Part I. Vol.	Page
36	Kennastown . .	360 1 17	Meath . .	Lower Moyfenrath .	Trim . . .	Trim . . .	I.	212
31	Kennastown . .	359 3 4	Meath . .	Lower Navan . .	Ardsallagh . .	Navan . .	I.	214
12	Kennedies . .	203 2 10	Armagh . .	Armagh . .	Lisnadill . .	Armagh . .	III.	45
11	Kennedies . .	191 2 12	Armagh . .	Armagh . .	Tynan . .	Armagh . .	III.	46
67	Kennel . .	159 1 12	Cork, E.R. .	Imokilly . .	Youghal . .	Youghal . .	II.	91
27	Kennetstown .	257 3 34	Meath . .	Upper Duleek .	Moorechurch .	Drogheda .	I.	198
27	Kennyborough .	46 1 10	Roscommon .	Castlereagh .	Ballintober .	Castlereagh .	IV.	198
29	Kennycourt . .	733 2 21	Kildare . .	Naas South .	Gilltown . .	Naas . .	I.	65
9	Kennystown .	102 2 17	Tyrone . .	Strabane Lower	Urney . .	Strabane .	III.	322
47	Kennystown .	201 0 29	Wicklow . .	Shillelagh . .	Carnew . .	Shillelagh .	I.	357
82	Kentfield . .	144 0 32a	Galway . .	Galway . .	Rahoon . .	Galway . .	IV.	37
32	Kentstown . .	98 3 7	Galway .	Killian . .	Killian . .	Mountbellew .	IV.	44
26, 32	Kentstown . .	459 3 26	Meath . .	Lower Duleek .	Kentstown .	Navan . .	I.	196
25	Keoltown . .	494 0 29	Westmeath .	Moyashel and Magheradernon .	Mullingar . .	Mullingar .	I.	275
27	Keonbrook . .	148 2 34	Leitrim . .	Leitrim . .	Kiltoghert .	Cark. on Shannon	IV.	102
26, 27	Kerane . .	93 2 8	Tipperary, N.R.	Upper Ormond .	Dolla . .	Nenagh . .	II.	290
28	Keranstown .	60 3 24	Donegal . .	Kilmacrenan .	Killygarvan .	Milford . .	III.	128
43	Keraun . .	154 2 31	King's Co. .	Ballybritt . .	Aghancon .	Roscrea .	I.	124
14, 19	Kerdiffstown .	703 0 27	Kildare . .	Naas North .	Kerdiffstown .	Naas . .	I.	62
31, 32	Kereight . .	840 2 30	Wexford . .	Bantry . .	Ballyhoge .	Enniscorthy .	I.	299
37	Kereight . .	185 3 37	Wexford . .	Shelmaliere East	Kilpatrick .	Wexford . .	I.	331
37	Kereight . .	60 0 19	Wexford . .	Shelmaliere East	Tikillin . .	Wexford . .	I.	331
20, 27	Kerinstown and Balrowan (Rowley) .	747 0 14	Westmeath .	Farbill . .	Killucan . .	Mullingar .	I.	267
24	Kerlagh . .	59 2 5	Roscommon .	Ballintober North	Kilglass . .	Strokestown .	IV.	186
42	Kerloge . .	84 3 35	Wexford . .	Forth . .	Kerloge . .	Wexford . .	I.	310
6, 10	Kernan . .	170 0 12	Armagh . .	Oneilland East .	Seagoe . .	Lurgan . .	III.	50
26	Kernan . .	749 1 27b	Down . .	Lower Iveagh, Up. pt.	Tullylish . .	Banbridge .	III.	171
7	Kernanstown .	267 1 20c	Carlow . .	Carlow . .	Carlow . .	Carlow . .	I.	1
7	Kernanstown .	178 0 8	Carlow . .	Carlow . .	Urglin . .	Carlow . .	I.	3
38	Kernyhill . .	300 0 12	Antrim . .	Lower Antrim .	Glenwhirry .	Ballymena .	III.	4
45, 46	Kerrib . .	435 3 30	Tyrone . .	Dungannon Middle .	Pomeroy . .	Dungannon .	III.	304
29	Kerries East .	309 2 21	Kerry . .	Trughanacmy .	Clogherbrien .	Tralee . .	II.	209
28, 29	Kerries West .	268 3 6	Kerry . .	Trughanacmy .	Clogherbrien .	Tralee . .	II.	209
28	Kerrikyle . .	397 0 4	Limerick . .	Shanid . .	Rathronan .	Newcastle .	II.	257
74	Kerryhall . .	6 3 1d	Cork, E.R. .	Cork and Municipal Borough	St. Annes Shandon .	Cork . .	II.	65
23, 26	Kerrymount .	143 1 13	Dublin . .	Rathdown . .	Tully . .	Rathdown .	I.	38
24, 28	Keshcarrigan .	272 3 25e	Leitrim . .	Leitrim . .	Kiltubbrid .	Cark. on Shannon	IV.	104
24, 28	KESHCARRIGAN T.	—	Leitrim . .	Leitrim . .	Kiltubbrid .	Cark. on Shannon	IV.	104
47	Keshends . .	70 0 14f	Donegal . .	Raphoe . .	Allsaints .	Londonderry .	III.	134
5	KESH T. . .	—	Fermanagh .	Lurg . .	Magheraculmoney .	Lowtherstown .	III.	209
6, 9	Kevanstown North .	163 1 38	Tipperary, N.R.	Lower Ormond .	Kilbarron .	Borrisokane .	II.	284
9	Kevanstown South .	44 2 1	Tipperary, N.R.	Lower Ormond .	Kilbarron .	Borrisokane .	II.	284
39, 42	Kevenagh . .	235 2 18g	Fermanagh .	Coole . .	Galloon . .	Clones . .	III.	200
25	Kevit Lower .	134 2 18	Cavan . .	Clanmahon .	Kilmore . .	Cavan . .	III.	78
25	Kevit Upper or Castlecosby .	136 1 33	Cavan . .	Clanmahon .	Kilmore . .	Cavan . .	III.	78
6, 14	Keyanna . .	228 0 34	Limerick . .	Clanwilliam .	Derrygalvin .	Limerick .	II.	223
25,26,32,33	Keyfield . .	206 3 23	Roscommon .	Castlereagh .	Kiltullagh .	Castlereagh .	IV.	202
75, 76	Keylong . .	84 0 30	Tipperary, S.R.	Iffa and Offa West .	Caher . .	Clogheen .	II.	318
8, 9	Kibberidog . .	103 1 11	Monaghan .	Monaghan .	Tedavnet .	Monaghan .	III.	279
109	Kid Island .	4 1 25	Mayo . .	Carra . .	Ballyovey .	Ballinrobe .	IV.	126
3	Kid Island .	25 1 26	Mayo . .	Erris . .	Kilcommon .	Belmullet .	IV.	145
9	Kiernans Hill .	152 1 14	Wicklow . .	Lower Talbotstown .	Hollywood .	Baltinglass .	I.	360
32, 38	Kiffagh . .	400 3 37	Cavan . .	Castlerahan .	Crosserlough .	Cavan . .	III.	68
24	Kihaska . .	359 0 30	Clare . .	Inchiquin .	Rath . .	Corrofin .	II.	27
80, 89	Kilaned . .	128 0 7h	Donegal . .	Banagh . .	Glencolumbkille .	Glenties .	III.	105
11, 12	Kilbaha Middle .	238 2 39	Kerry . .	Iraghticonnor .	Murher . .	Listowel .	II.	193
71	Kilbaha North .	756 1 32	Clare . .	Moyarta . .	Kilballyowen .	Kilrush . .	II.	31
6, 7, 11, 12	Kilbaha North .	441 0 6	Kerry . .	Iraghticonnor .	Murher . .	Listowel .	II.	193
71	Kilbaha South .	1,044 3 27	Clare . .	Moyarta . .	Kilballyowen .	Kilrush . .	II.	31
11, 12	Kilbaha South .	258 0 24	Kerry . .	Iraghticonnor .	Murher . .	Listowel .	II.	193
71	KILBAHA T. . .	—	Clare . .	Moyarta . .	Kilballyowen .	Kilrush . .	II.	32
6, 11	Kilbaha West .	155 3 33	Kerry . .	Iraghticonnor .	Murher . .	Listowel .	I.	193
35	Kilballivor .	225 0 20	Meath . .	Lune . .	Killaconnigan .	Trim . .	I.	208
87, 90	Kilballyboy .	1,419 2 27	Tipperary, S.R.	Iffa and Offa West .	Tullaghorton .	Clogheen .	II.	321
76, 77	Kilballycurrane .	112 3 38	Cork, E.R. .	Imokilly . .	Cloyne . .	Middleton .	II.	85
87, 88	Kilballygorman .	354 1 10	Tipperary, S.R.	Iffa and Offa West .	Ballybacon .	Clogheen .	II.	317
23	Kilballyhemikin .	446 2 39	Tipperary, N.R.	Ikerrin . .	Killea . .	Roscrea .	II.	275
53, 61	Kilballyherberry .	745 0 18	Tipperary, S.R.	Middlethird .	Ballysheehan .	Cashel .	II.	325
7, 12	Kilballyhue .	385 3 4	Carlow . .	Carlow . .	Tullowmagimma .	Carlow . .	I.	2
22	Kilballykeefe .	158 0 19	Kilkenny . .	Crannagh .	Ballycallan .	Callan . .	I.	84

(a) Including 16A. 3R. 18P. water.
(b) { Including 8A. 2R. 16P. Drumaran Lake. Including 25A. 1R. 5P. Kernan Lake.
(c) Including 76A. 0R. 20P. detached portion.
(d) { Within the Municipal Boundary, 5A. 3R. 15P. Without the Municipal Boundary, 0A. 3R. 26P.
(e) Including 59A. 2R. 32P. water.
(f) Including 2A. 1R. 24P. water.
(g) Including 28A. 1R. 8P. water.
(h) Including 1A. 1R. 3P. detached portion.

No. of Sheet of the Ordnance Survey Maps.	Townlands and Towns.	Area in Statute Acres.			County.	Barony.	Parish.	Poor Law Union in 1857.	Townland Census of 1851, Part I.	
		A.	R.	P.					Vol.	Page
22	Kilballykeefe . .	236	1	22	Kilkenny . .	Crannagh . .	Tullaghanbrogue .	Callan . .	I.	87
36	Kilballylahiff . .	712	1	9a	Kerry . .	Corkaguiny .	Killiney . .	Dingle . .	II.	178
65, 72	Kilballyowen . .	1,012	2	14	Clare . .	Moyarta . .	Kilballyowen .	Kilrush . .	II.	31
32, 40	Kilballyowen . .	1,079	3	13	Limerick . .	Smallcounty .	Knockainy .	Kilmallock .	II.	261
34, 39	Kilballyowen . .	1,339	2	15	Wicklow . .	Ballinacor South .	Preban . .	Shillelagh .	I.	350
42	Kilballyporter .	434	0	14	Meath . .	Lower Moyfenrath .	Rathmolyon .	Trim . .	I.	211
3	Kilballyquilty .	601	2	39	Waterford .	Upperthird . .	Rathgormuck .	Carrick on Suir	II.	371
42	Kilballyskea . .	725	1	28	King's Co. .	Clonlisk . .	Shinrone . .	Roscrea . .	I.	131
32	Kilbalraherd . .	231	3	35	Westmeath .	Moycashel . .	Castletownkindalen	Mullingar .	I.	277
36, 44	Kilbane . . .	794	3	28	Clare . .	Tulla Lower .	Killokennedy . .	Limerick . .	II.	35
84	Kilbane . . .	281	2	2	Cork, E.R. .	East Muskerry .	Desertmore .	Bandon . .	II.	102
30	Kilbane . . .	291	3	33	Kerry . .	Trughanacmy .	Ballymacelligott .	Tralee . .	II.	207
5, 6	Kilbane . . .	210	3	3	Limerick . .	Clanwilliam .	Kilmurry . .	Limerick . .	II.	224
40	Kilbannivane . .	550	0	13	Kerry . .	Trughanacmy .	Castleisland .	Tralee . .	II.	208
15	Kilbarrack Lower .	259	3	26	Dublin . .	Coolock . .	Kilbarrack .	Dublin North .	I.	28
15	Kilbarrack Upper .	390	2	30	Dublin . .	Coolock . .	Kilbarrack .	Dublin North .	I.	28
32	Kilbarrahan .	126	0	19	Cork, E.R. .	Duhallow . .	Roskeen . .	Kanturk . .	II.	75
89	Kilbarraree .	141	0	33	Cork, E.R. .	Imokilly . .	Cloyne . .	Middleton .	II.	85
28	Kilbarron . .	428	1	32	Clare . .	Tulla Upper .	Feakle . .	Scarriff . .	II.	39
103, 107	Kilbarron . .	384	1	12	Donegal . .	Tirhugh . .	Kilbarron .	Ballyshannon .	III.	148
9	Kilbarron . .	108	2	36	Tipperary, N.R.	Lower Ormond .	Kilbarron .	Borrisokane .	II.	284
36	Kilbarry . .	877	1	22b	Cork, E.R. .	Condons&Clangibbon	Castlelyons .	Fermoy . .	II.	60
63, 74	Kilbarry . .	311	2	17c	Cork, E.R. .	Cork and Municipal Borough . .	St. Annes Shandon .	Cork . .	II.	65
16, 24	Kilbarry . .	498	1	26	Cork, E.R. .	Duhallow . .	Kilbrin . .	Kanturk . .	II.	72
107, 120	Kilbarry . .	1,230	3	17	Cork, W.R. .	East Carbery (West Division) . .	Fanlobbus .	Dunmanway .	II.	132
96	Kilbarry . .	275	0	13	Cork, W.R. .	Kinalmeaky .	Templemartin .	Bandon . .	II.	153
147	Kilbarry . .	79	0	10	Cork, W.R. .	West Carbery (West Division) . .	Kilmoe . .	Skull . .	II.	145
83	Kilbarry . .	697	1	20d	Cork, W.R. .	West Muskerry .	Ballinadee .	Macroom . .	II.	154
82	Kilbarry . .	166	0	17	Cork, W.R. .	West Muskerry .	Inchigeelagh .	Macroom . .	II.	157
24, 30	Kilbarry . .	861	1	15e	Roscommon .	Ballintober North .	Termonbarry .	Strokestown .	IV.	188
9, 17	Kilbarry .	458	0	24	Waterford .	Gaultiere . .	Kilbarry . .	Waterford .	II.	363
25	Kilbarrymeaden .	412	3	39	Waterford .	Decies without Drum	Kilbarrymeaden .	Kilmacthomas .	II.	356
15	Kilbaylet Lower .	235	1	20	Wicklow . .	Lower Talbotstown	Donard . .	Baltinglass .	I.	360
15	Kilbaylet Upper .	482	2	4	Wicklow . .	Lower Talbotstown	Donard . .	Baltinglass .	I.	360
123	Kilbeacanty .	223	2	1	Galway . .	Kiltartan . .	Kilbeacanty .	Gort . .	IV.	47
77	Kilbeg . . .	189	2	20	Cork, E.R. .	Imokilly . .	Ightermurragh .	Middleton .	II.	87
99, 113	Kilbeg . . .	175	3	37	Cork, E.R. .	Kinalea . .	Tracton . .	Kinsale . .	II.	97
134,142,143	Kilbeg . . .	200	1	11	Cork, W.R. .	East Carbery (W.D.)	Kilfaughnabeg .	Skibbereen .	II.	133
96	Kilbeg . . .	244	1	36	Donegal . .	Banagh . .	Kilcar . .	Glenties . .	III.	108
1	Kilbeg . . .	752	1	4f	Galway . .	Ballymoe . .	Templetogher .	Glennamaddy .	IV.	9
55	Kilbeg . . .	217	0	18	Galway . .	Clare . .	Cargin . .	Tuam . .	IV.	18
107	Kilbeg . . .	348	2	16	Galway . .	Longford . .	Abbeygormacan .	Ballinasloe .	IV.	56
115, 124	Kilbeg . . .	995	3	19	Galway . .	Loughrea . .	Killinan . .	Loughrea . .	IV.	64
59, 72	Kilbeg . . .	266	2	18	Galway . .	Tiaquin . .	Moylough .	Tuam . .	IV.	80
26, 27	Kilbeg . . .	83	1	3	Kildare . .	Offaly West .	Ballybrackan .	Athy . .	I.	71
26, 27	Kilbeg . . .	535	1	0	King's Co. .	Upper Philipstown .	Geashill . .	Tullamore .	I.	144
22	Kilbeg . . .	182	1	19	Queen's Co. .	Clandonagh .	Aghaboe . .	Donaghmore .	I.	232
24	Kilbeg . . .	90	3	39	Roscommon .	Ballintober North .	Kilglass . .	Strokestown .	IV.	186
50, 51	Kilbeg . . .	208	3	36	Tipperary, N.R.	Kilnamanagh Upper	Toem . .	Tipperary .	II.	280
9	Kilbeg . . .	188	2	0	Tipperary, N.R.	Lower Ormond .	Finnoe . .	Borrisokane .	II.	284
81, 87	Kilbeg . . .	230	3	27	Tipperary, S.R.	Iffa and Offa West .	Shanrahan .	Clogheen .	II.	320
31	Kilbeg . . .	116	2	36	Waterford .	Decies without Drum	Clonea . .	Dungarvan .	II.	354
25	Kilbeg . . .	186	1	34	Waterford .	Decies without Drum	Kilbarrymeaden .	Kilmacthomas .	II.	356
31, 37	Kilbeg . . .	603	3	13	Westmeath .	Moycashel .	Ardnurcher or Horse-leap .	Tullamore .	I.	276
5, 10	Kilbeg . . .	2,107	3	9	Wicklow . .	Lower Talbotstown	Boystown . .	Naas . .	I.	359
79	Kilbeg East . .	99	3	34	Kerry . .	Iveragh . .	Valencia . .	Cahersiveen .	II.	198
30	Kilbeg East . .	41	2	33	Limerick . .	Connello Upper .	Ballingarry .	Croom . .	II.	230
38	Kilbeggan . .	306	3	13	Westmeath .	Moycashel .	Kilbeggan .	Tullamore .	I.	278
38	Kilbeggan North .	84	1	0	Westmeath .	Moycashel .	Kilbeggan .	Tullamore .	I.	278
38	Kilbeggan South .	196	3	3	Westmeath .	Moycashel .	Kilbeggan .	Tullamore .	I.	278
38	KILBEGGAN T.	—			Westmeath .	Moycashel .	Kilbeggan .	Tullamore .	I.	278
27	Kilbeg Lower .	148	1	0	Galway . .	Ross . .	Ross . .	Oughterard .	IV.	74
11	Kilbeg Lower .	344	3	8	Meath . .	Lower Kells .	Kilbeg . .	Kells . .	I.	202
33	Kilbeg Lower .	167	2	37	Waterford .	Coshmore&Coshbride	Tallow . .	Lismore . .	II.	348
54, 56	Kilbegly . .	395	0	2	Roscommon .	Moycarn . .	Moore . .	Ballinasloe .	IV.	207
101, 102	Kilbeg (Malone) .	203	1	36	Mayo . .	Clanmorris .	Kilcolman .	Claremorris .	IV.	134
7, 19, 20	Kilbegnet . .	29	3	18	Galway . .	Ballymoe . .	Dunamon .	Roscommon .	IV.	7
7, 19, 20	Kilbegnet . .	400	3	14	Galway . .	Ballymoe . .	Kilbegnet .	Roscommon .	IV.	8
7	Kilbegnet . .	105	0	20	Wexford . .	Gorey . .	Kilgorman .	Gorey . .	I.	318
96, 110	Kilbeg North . .	216	3	14	Cork, W.R. .	Kinalmeaky .	Kilbrogan .	Bandon . .	II.	152

(a) Including 17A. 1R. 25P. water.
(b) Including 15A. 2R. 27P. water.
(c) { Within the Municipal Boundary, 15A. 3R. 18P.
{ Without the Municipal Boundary, 295A. 2R. 39P.
(d) Including 46A. 2R. 34P. water.
(e) { Including 1A. 2R. 25P. Islands.
{ Including 11A. 3R. 23P. water.
(f) Including 9A. 2R. 30P. water.

No. of Sheet of the Ordnance Survey Maps.	Townlands and Towns.	Area in Statute Acres.	County.	Barony.	Parish.	Poor Law Union in 1857.	Townland Census of 1851, Part I.	
		A. R. P.					Vol.	Page
49, 50	Kilbegs . . .	478 1 29	Antrim . .	Upper Toome . .	Antrim . . .	Antrim . .	III.	33
96, 110	Kilbeg South .	182 0 20	Cork, W.R. .	Kinalmeaky . .	Kilbrogan . .	Bandon . .	II.	152
26, 27	Kilbeg Upper .	328 0 1a	Galway . .	Ross . . .	Ross . . .	Oughterard .	IV.	74
11	Kilbeg Upper .	311 3 5	Meath . .	Lower Kells .	Kilbeg . . .	Kells . .	I.	202
33	Kilbeg Upper .	484 0 33	Waterford .	Coshmore&Coshbride	Tallow . . .	Lismore . .	II.	348
79	Kilbeg West .	97 1 19	Kerry . .	Iveragh . . .	Valencia . .	Cahersiveen .	II.	198
30	Kilbeg West .	164 2 26	Limerick . .	Connello Upper .	Ballingarry .	Croom . .	II.	230
11, 20	Kilbehy . .	247 1 24	Limerick . .	Connello Lower .	Nantinan . .	Rathkeale .	II.	229
23	Kilbelin . .	288 2 25b	Kildare . .	Connell . . .	Greatconnell .	Naas . .	I.	55
121	Kilbeloge . .	216 3 31	Cork, W.R. .	East Carbery (E.D.)	Desertserges .	Clonakilty .	II.	128
40	Kilberehert .	63 3 35	Kerry . .	Trughanacmy .	Ballincuslane .	Tralee . .	II.	206
15	Kilberrihert .	905 0 37	Cork, E.R. .	Duhallow . .	Knocktemple .	Kanturk . .	II.	75
60	Kilberrihert .	942 1 16	Cork, W.R. .	East Muskerry .	Aghabulloge .	Macroom . .	II.	153
30, 31, 34	Kilberry . .	1,497 0 16c	Kildare . .	Narragh&RebanWest	Kilberry . .	Athy . .	I.	68
18	Kilberry . .	566 3 34	Meath . .	Morgallion . .	Kilberry . .	Navan . .	I.	209
18	KILBERRY T. .	—	Meath . .	Morgallion . .	Kilberry . .	Navan . .	I.	209
35	Kilbillaghan .	246 1 29	Westmeath .	Clonlonan . .	Kilcleagh . .	Athlone . .	I.	261
9	Kilbiller . .	280 1 1d	Tipperary, N.R.	Lower Ormond .	Kilbarron . .	Borrisokane .	II.	284
11	Kilbixy . .	67 0 30	Westmeath .	Moygoish . .	Kilbixy . .	Mullingar .	I.	279
61, 72	Kilblaffer . .	566 3 31	Cork, E.R. .	East Muskerry .	Inishcarra .	Cork . .	II.	104
24, 28	Kilbline . .	690 1 14	Kilkenny . .	Gowran . . .	Tullaherin .	Thomastown .	I.	100
31	Kilboderry .	69 0 14	Leitrim . .	Leitrim . . .	Kiltoghert .	Cark. on Shannon	IV.	102
31	Kilboggan .	171 2 9	Kildare . .	Offaly West .	Kilrush . .	Athy . .	I.	73
23, 26	Kilbogget . .	331 3 33	Dublin . .	Rathdown . .	Killiney . .	Rathdown .	I.	36
35	Kilboggoon .	157 3 21	Clare . .	Tulla Upper .	Tulla . . .	Tulla . .	II.	41
98, 106	Kilboght . .	218 3 22	Galway . .	Leitrim . . .	Kilreekill .	Loughrea .	IV.	54
20	Kilboglashy .	290 3 20e	Sligo . .	Leyny . . .	Ballysadare .	Sligo . .	IV.	230
1	Kilbolane . .	420 1 20	Cork, E.R. .	Orrery and Kilmore	Kilbolane . .	Kanturk . .	II.	108
84	Kilbonane . .	185 2 24	Cork, E.R. .	East Muskerry .	Kilbonane . .	Bandon . .	II.	104
57, 65	Kilbonane . .	228 0 3f	Kerry . .	Magunihy . .	Kilbonane . .	Killarney . .	II.	200
10, 15	Kilbora . .	647 2 3	Wexford . .	Scarawalsh . .	Ferns . . .	Enniscorthy .	I.	323
59, 70	Kilboultragh .	583 0 3	Cork, W.R. .	West Muskerry .	Clondrohid .	Macroom . .	II.	155
88	Kilboy . .	168 1 34	Cork, E.R. .	Imokilly . .	Cloyne . .	Middleton .	II.	85
98	Kilboy . .	182 1 22	Cork, E.R. .	Kinalea . .	Ballyfeard .	Kinsale . .	II.	93
26	Kilboy . .	578 2 3	Tipperary, N.R.	Upper Ormond .	Kilmore . .	Nenagh . .	II.	291
54	Kilboy . .	67 0 31	Tipperary, S.R.	Slievardagh .	Graystown .	Cashel . .	II.	333
31	Kilboy . .	96 2 19	Wicklow . .	Arklow . .	Dunganstown .	Rathdrum .	I.	343
2	Kilboyne . .	161 3 8g	Meath . .	Lower Kells .	Moybolgue .	Kells . .	I.	203
17, 18, 25	Kilbrack . .	369 2 17	Cork, E.R. .	Fermoy . .	Doneraile . .	Mallow . .	II.	78
2, 3, 6, 7	Kilbrack . .	596 3 38	Waterford .	Upperthird .	Rathgormuck .	Carrick on Suir	II.	371
30	Kilbrackan .	229 0 19h	Leitrim . .	Carrigallen .	Carrigallen .	Mohill . .	IV.	89
9	Kilbrackan .	256 1 5	Queen's Co. .	Portnahinch .	Lea . . .	Mountmellick .	I.	244
17	Kilbracks . .	427 1 15	Armagh . .	Fews Lower .	Kilclooney .	Armagh . .	III.	46
19	Kilbradran .	413 3 27	Limerick . .	Shanid . .	Kilbradran .	Rathkeale .	II.	255
61, 69	Kilbragh . .	324 3 19	Tipperary, S.R.	Middlethird .	Kilbragh . .	Cashel . .	II.	327
61, 69	Kilbragh . .	131 2 39	Tipperary, S.R.	Middlethird .	Railstown . .	Cashel . .	II.	329
22	Kilbraghan .	411 0 16	Kilkenny . .	Crannagh . .	Kilmanagh .	Callan . .	I.	86
37	Kilbraghan .	288 2 4	Kilkenny . .	Ida . . .	Dysartmoon .	New Ross .	I.	101
35, 40	Kilbraney . .	974 3 12	Wexford . .	Shelmaliere West .	Clongeen . .	New Ross .	I.	333
54	Kilbrannel .	293 3 13	Tipperary, S.R.	Slievardagh .	Kilcooly . .	Cashel . .	II.	334
20	Kilbrannish North .	837 3 15	Carlow . .	Forth . . .	Barragh . .	Enniscorthy .	I.	4
20, 23	Kilbrannish South .	1,822 2 13	Carlow . .	Forth . . .	Barragh . .	Enniscorthy .	I.	4
33	Kilbrattan .	217 0 23i	Sligo . .	Corran . .	Emlaghfad .	Tobercurry .	IV.	226
49	Kilbraugh . .	651 1 32	Tipperary, S.R.	Slievardagh .	Buolick . .	Urlingford .	II.	332
59, 67	Kilbreanbeg .	198 2 18	Kerry . .	Magunihy . .	Aghadoe . .	Killarney . .	II.	199
59	Kilbrean Beg .	167 0 32	Kerry . .	Magunihy . .	Kilcummin .	Killarney . .	II.	201
59, 67	Kilbrean More .	301 2 35j	Kerry . .	Magunihy . .	Killarney . .	Killarney . .	II.	203
34	Kilbreckan .	576 0 11	Clare . .	Bunratty Upper .	Doora . . .	Ennis . .	II.	8
28, 34	Kilbreckstown .	147 2 8	Meath . .	Upper Duleek .	Stamullin . .	Drogheda .	I.	198
77	Kilbree . .	252 2 34	Cork, E.R. .	Imokilly . .	Ballyoughtera .	Middleton .	II.	84
122, 135	Kilbree . . .	284 1 32	Cork, W.R. .	East Carbery (E.D.)	Island . . .	Clonakilty .	II.	128
38, 39	Kilbreedy . .	428 0 39	Limerick . .	Coshma . .	Bruree . . .	Kilmallock .	II.	242
47	Kilbreedy . .	370 3 14	Limerick . .	Coshma . .	Kilbreedy Minor .	Kilmallock .	II.	243
11,12,20,21	Kilbreedy . .	720 3 19k	Limerick . .	Kenry . .	Kilcornan . .	Rathkeale .	II.	249
28	Kilbreedy . .	421 0 33	Queen's Co. .	Clarmallagh .	Bordwell . .	Donaghmore .	I.	237
52	Kilbreedy . .	320 0 11	Tipperary, S.R.	Middlethird .	Ardmayle . .	Cashel . .	II.	324
54, 62	Kilbreedy . .	174 3 13	Tipperary, S.R.	Middlethird .	Cooleagh . .	Cashel . .	II.	326
48	Kilbreedy East	139 0 29	Limerick . .	Coshlea . .	Kilbreedy Major .	Kilmallock .	II.	239
48	Kilbreedy West	132 0 11	Limerick . .	Coshlea . .	Kilbreedy Major .	Kilmallock .	II.	239
21	Kilbree East .	385 2 23	Waterford .	Coshmore&Coshbride	Lismore and Mocollop	Lismore . .	II.	346
77, 88	Kilbree Lower .	404 2 25	Mayo . .	Burrishoole .	Ballintober .	Westport . .	IV.	118
88	Kilbree Upper .	325 2 34	Mayo . .	Burrishoole .	Ballintober .	Westport . .	IV.	118
21	Kilbree West .	266 3 0	Waterford .	Coshmore&Coshbride	Lismore and Mocollop	Lismore . .	II.	346

(a) Including 3A. 0R. 19P. water.   (e) Including 3A. 2R. 17P. water.   (i) Including 17A. 3R. 17P. water.
(b) Including 10A. 1R. 2P. water.   (f) Including 5A. 3R. 37P. water.   (j) Including 10A. 3R. 8P. water.
(c) Including 13A. 0R. 10P. water.   (g) Including 6A. 3R. 0P. water.   (k) Including 1A. 0R. 11P. water.
(d) Including 3A. 3R. 8P. water.   (h) Including 4A. 2R. 38P. water.

No. of Sheet of the Ordnance Survey Maps.	Townlands and Towns.	Area in Statute Acres.			County.	Barony.	Parish.	Poor Law Union in 1857.	Townland Census of 1851, Part I.	
		A.	R.	P.					Vol.	Page
21	Kilbreffy . .	183	3	15	Wicklow . .	Upper Talbotstown .	Donaghmore . .	Baltinglass .	I.	363
84	Kilbrenan . .	461	0	1	Cork, E.R. .	East Muskerry .	Moviddy . . .	Bandon . .	II.	105
90	Kilbrenan . .	90	0	10	Mayo . .	Carra . . .	Drum . . .	Castlebar . .	IV.	128
33	Kilbrennan . .	620	1	21	Westmeath .	Fartullagh . .	Castlelost . .	Mullingar . .	I.	268
38, 39	Kilbrew . . .	799	0	30	Meath . .	Ratoath . . .	Kilbrew . .	Dunshaughlin .	I.	218
38, 39	Kilbrew . . .	160	3	31	Meath . .	Skreen . . .	Kilmoon . . .	Dunshaughlin .	I.	221
13	Kilbrickan . .	191	1	36	Carlow . .	Forth . . .	Fennagh . . .	Carlow . .	I.	4
13	Kilbrickan . .	28	3	17	Carlow . .	Forth . . .	Templepeter . .	Carlow . .	I.	5
65	Kilbrickan . .	520	2	10	Galway . .	Moycullen . .	Kilcummin . .	Oughterard .	IV.	67
26, 27	Kilbrickan . .	538	0	30	Kilkenny . .	Shillelogher . .	Earlstown . .	Callan . .	I.	114
17, 23	Kilbrickan . .	161	1	29	Queen's Co. .	Upperwoods . .	Offerlane . .	Abbeyleix . .	I.	252
15, 21	Kilbrickane . .	135	3	3	Kerry . .	Clanmaurice . .	Killahan . . .	Tralee . .	II.	170
35	Kilbrickane . .	78	1	35	Tipperary, N.R.	Eliogarty . .	Loughmoe East .	Thurles . .	II.	271
45	Kilbride . . .	7	0	13	Antrim . .	Upper Antrim .	Doagh Grange .	Antrim . .	III.	6
45, 51	Kilbride . . .	480	3	21	Antrim . .	Upper Antrim .	Kilbride . . .	Antrim . .	III.	6
17, 18	Kilbride . . .	255	1	18	Carlow . .	Forth . . .	Aghade . . .	Carlow . .	I.	3
17, 18	Kilbride . . .	594	2	39	Carlow . .	Forth . . .	Barragh . . .	Carlow . .	I.	4
38	Kilbride . . .	496	3	11	Cavan . .	Clanmahon . .	Kilbride . . .	Oldcastle . .	III.	78
45	Kilbride . . .	321	2	4	Down . .	Lecale Upper .	Bright . . .	Downpatrick .	III.	180
21	Kilbride . . .	266	3	20	Dublin . .	Newcastle . .	Kilbride . . .	Celbridge . .	I.	33
106	Kilbride . . .	236	1	22	Galway . .	Leitrim . . .	Abbeygormacan .	Loughrea . .	IV.	50
13, 26	Kilbride . . .	1,963	3	0	Galway . .	Ross . . .	Ross . . .	Ballinrobe .	IV.	74
4	Kilbride . . .	206	1	25	Kildare . .	Ikeathy&Oughterany	Cloncurry . .	Celbridge . .	I.	57
26	Kilbride . . .	2	0	22	Kilkenny . .	Callan . . .	Callan . . .	Callan . .	I.	83
40, 41	Kilbride . . .	378	0	3	Kilkenny . .	Ida	Kilbride . . .	Waterford .	I.	102
16	Kilbride . . .	192	2	26	King's Co. .	Ballycowan . .	Kilbride . . .	Tullamore .	I.	127
8	Kilbride . . .	147	0	27	King's Co. .	Kilcoursey . .	Kilbride . . .	Tullamore .	I.	141
11	Kilbride . . .	255	3	12	Longford . .	Granard . . .	Abbeylara . .	Granard . .	I.	154
11	Kilbride . . .	22	1	34	Louth . .	Louth . . .	Louth . . .	Dundalk . .	I.	184
68	Kilbride . . .	225	2	15a	Mayo . .	Burrishoole . .	Burrishoole . .	Newport . .	IV.	119
90, 91, 101	Kilbride . . .	250	2	0	Mayo . .	Clanmorris . .	Mayo . . .	Claremorris .	IV.	135
62, 72	Kilbride . . .	631	3	8	Mayo . .	Gallen . . .	Kilconduff . .	Swineford .	IV.	148
7	Kilbride . . .	817	0	10	Mayo . .	Tirawley . .	Kilbride . . .	Killala . .	IV.	168
6, 12	Kilbride . . .	493	1	9	Meath . .	Morgallion . .	Nobber . . .	Kells . .	I.	210
30	Kilbride . . .	1,102	0	2	Meath . .	Upper Navan .	Moymet . . .	Trim . .	I.	216
4, 5, 8, 9	Kilbride . . .	625	2	11	Queen's Co. .	Portnahinch . .	Lea	Mountmellick .	I.	244
11	Kilbride . . .	76	0	7	Roscommon .	Ballintober North .	Kilmore . . .	Carᵏ. on Shannon	IV.	187
33	Kilbride . . .	470	1	23	Westmeath .	Fartullagh . .	Kilbride . . .	Mullingar .	I.	268
26, 27	Kilbride . . .	417	2	32	Wexford .	Ballaghkeen . .	Ballyhuskard . .	Enniscorthy .	I.	292
12	Kilbride . . .	204	2	21	Wexford .	Ballaghkeen . .	Kiltennell . .	Gorey . .	I.	297
44	Kilbride . . .	456	0	15	Wexford .	Shelburne . .	St.James&Dunbrody	New Ross . .	I.	328
31	Kilbride . . .	189	3	33	Wicklow . .	Arklow . . .	Dunganstown .	Rathdrum .	I.	343
40	Kilbride . . .	317	2	35	Wicklow . .	Arklow . . .	Kilbride . . .	Rathdrum .	I.	344
1, 5	Kilbride . . .	938	2	7	Wicklow . .	Lower Talbotstown	Kilbride . . .	Naas . .	I.	361
4, 7, 8	Kilbride . . .	139	3	28	Wicklow . .	Rathdown . .	Bray . . .	Rathdown .	I.	354
26	Kilbride Glebe .	39	3	10	Kilkenny . .	Callan . . .	Callan . . .	Callan . .	I.	83
17	Kilbride North .	231	2	23	Waterford .	Middlethird . .	Kilbride . . .	Waterford .	II.	367
17, 26	Kilbride South .	231	1	26	Waterford .	Middlethird . .	Kilbride . . .	Waterford .	II.	367
44	Kilbrien . . .	217	0	5	Cork, E.R. .	Barrymore . .	Rathcormack .	Fermoy . .	II.	57
7, 12	Kilbright . . .	232	0	3	Down . .	Ards Lower . .	Donaghadee . .	Newtownards .	III.	158
123, 124	Kilbrittain . .	483	0	9	Cork, W.R. .	East Carbery (E.D.)	Kilbrittain . .	Bandon . .	II.	128
123, 124	Kilbrittain T. .	—			Cork, W.R. .	East Carbery (E.D.)	Rathclarin . .	Bandon . .	II.	130
96, 110	Kilbrogan . .	371	2	9	Cork, W.R. .	Kinalmeaky . .	Kilbrogan . .	Bandon . .	II.	152
16, 17	Kilbroney . .	144	1	11	Cork, E.R. .	Orrery and Kilmore	Kilbroney . .	Mallow . .	II.	109
51, 54	Kilbroney . .	575	3	37	Down . .	Upper Iveagh, Up. pt.	Kilbroney . .	Kilkeel . .	III.	175
51, 52	Kilbroney Upper .	1,068	0	9	Down . .	Upper Iveagh, Up. pt.	Kilbroney . .	Kilkeel . .	III.	175
140, 149	Kilbronoge . .	645	1	27	Cork, W.R. .	West Carbery (W.D.)	Skull . . .	Skull . .	II.	146
4	Kilbrook . . .	406	3	17	Kildare . .	Ikeathy&Oughterany	Cloncurry . .	Celbridge . .	I.	57
147	Kilbrown . .	191	2	16	Cork, W.R. .	West Carbery(W.D.)	Kilmoe . . .	Skull . .	II.	145
6	Kilbryan . .	64	0	9	Roscommon .	Boyle . . .	Kilbryan . .	Boyle . .	IV.	195
13, 14, 22, 23	Kilbryan Lower .	272	1	31	Waterford .	Decies without Drum	Kilgobnet . .	Dungarvan .	II.	357
14, 23	Kilbryan Upper .	461	3	19	Waterford .	Decies without Drum	Kilgobnet . .	Dungarvan .	II.	357
94	Kilbunow . .	513	3	39	Kerry . .	Glanarought . .	Kilgarvan . .	Kenmare . .	II.	187
17, 25	Kilburn . . .	204	2	10	Cork, E.R. .	Fermoy . . .	Caherduggan .	Mallow . .	II.	77
47	Kilburn . . .	133	2	33	Kerry . .	Trughanacmy .	Kilcolman . .	Killarney .	II.	210
71	Kilburry East .	272	0	0	Tipperary, S.R.	Slievardagh . .	Cloneen . . .	Callan . .	II.	332
71	Kilburry West .	143	0	36	Tipperary, S.R.	Middlethird . .	Cloneen . . .	Callan . .	II.	325
78	Kilcaddan . .	193	1	31b	Donegal . .	Raphoe . . .	Donaghmore .	Stranorlar .	III.	138
57	Kilcahill . . .	429	0	32	Galway . .	Clare . . .	Annaghdown .	Tuam . .	IV.	16
95	Kilcaimin . .	36	0	26	Galway . .	Dunkellin . .	Ballynacourty .	Galway . .	IV.	27
33	Kilcalf East . .	204	3	15	Waterford .	Coshmore&Coshbride	Tallow . . .	Lismore . .	II.	348
33	Kilcalfmountain .	442	2	13	Waterford .	Coshmore&Coshbride	Tallow . . .	Lismore . .	II.	348
28, 33	Kilcalf West . .	347	3	15	Waterford .	Coshmore&Coshbride	Tallow . . .	Lismore . .	II.	348

(a) Including 3A. 1R. 1P. water.　　　　　(b) Including 3A. 2R. 32P. water.

No. of Sheet of the Ordnance Survey Maps.	Townlands and Towns.	Area in Statute Acres.			County.	Barony.	Parish.	Poor Law Union in 1857.	Townland Census of 1851. Part I.	
		A.	R.	P.					Vol.	Page
22, 23	Kilealtan	310	1	3	Londonderry	Tirkeeran	Cumber Upper	Londonderry	III.	249
19,20,23,24	Kileam	354	0	24a	Armagh	Tiranny	Keady	Armagh	III.	60
44	Kileam	203	0	21	Tyrone	Omagh East	Clogherny	Omagh	III.	310
22	Kileamin	398	0	39	King's Co.	Garrycastle	Gallen	Parsonstown	I.	136
7, 15	Kileanavee	852	3	16	Waterford	Upperthird	Mothel	Carrick on Suir	II.	371
30	Kileandra	183	2	2	Wicklow	Arklow	Dunganstown	Rathdrum	I.	343
30, 31	Kileandra	457	1	28	Wicklow	Arklow	Glenealy	Rathdrum	I.	344
25	Kileannon	240	0	1	Waterford	Middlethird	Dunhill	Kilmacthomas	II.	366
20	Kileannon	528	3	8b	Wexford	Scarawalsh	St. Marys Enniscorthy	Enniscorthy	I.	325
30	Kileannon (Hely)	62	0	25	Waterford	Decies without Drum	Whitechurch	Dungarvan	II.	361
22, 30	Kileannon (Osborne)	151	1	10	Waterford	Decies without Drum	Whitechurch	Dungarvan	II.	361
11, 17	Kileanoran	113	3	6	Roscommon	Roscommon	Aughrim	Car^k. on Shannon	IV.	207
25,26,33,34	Kileanway	670	2	35c	Cork, E.R.	Fermoy	Carrigleamleary	Mallow	II.	77
26,27,33,34	Kileappagh	628	3	37	King's Co.	Upper Philipstown	Ballykean	Mountmellick	I.	143
96	Kilear	233	3	22	Donegal	Banagh	Kilear	Glenties	III.	108
48	Kilear	776	0	17	Roscommon	Athlone	Cam	Athlone	IV.	180
18	Kilearagh	333	2	4	Waterford	Gaultiere	Kilearagh	Waterford	II.	363
21	Kilearbery	153	3	37	Dublin	Newcastle	Kilbride	Celbridge	I.	33
26	Kilearbry	17	0	23	Wexford	Bantry	Clonmore	Enniscorthy	I.	300
7	Kilearn	201	3	22	Armagh	Tiranny	Eglish	Armagh	III.	59
25, 31	Kilearn	985	1	11d	Meath	Skreen	Kilearn	Navan	I.	220
33	Kilearney Lower	407	3	21	Wicklow	Ballinacor South	Hacketstown	Baltinglass	I.	348
28, 33	Kilearney Upper	432	0	7	Wicklow	Ballinacor South	Hacketstown	Baltinglass	I.	348
17	Kilearra Beg	241	1	10e	Kerry	Clanmaurice	Duagh	Listowel	II.	168
40	Kilearra East	197	2	20	Wicklow	Arklow	Arklow	Rathdrum	I.	341
16	Kilearragh	209	1	37	Clare	Corcomroe	Kilfenora	Ennistimon	II.	19
17	Kilearra More	308	2	0f	Kerry	Clanmaurice	Duagh	Listowel	II.	168
40	Kilearra West	480	3	34	Wicklow	Arklow	Arklow	Rathdrum	I.	341
4	Kilearren	382	0	19	Tipperary, N.R.	Lower Ormond	Lorrha	Borrisokane	II.	285
16	Kilearrig	909	3	35g	Carlow	Idrone East	Dunleckny	Carlow	I.	7
57, 67	Kilearroll	712	0	1	Clare	Moyarta	Kilrush	Kilrush	II.	33
86, 89	Kilearroon	1,634	0	17	Tipperary, S.R.	Iffa and Offa West	Shanrahan	Clogheen	II.	320
114	Kilearrooraun	294	2	28	Galway	Loughrea	Kilthomas	Gort	IV.	65
18	Kilearry	926	3	34	Carlow	St. Mullins Upper	Moyacomb	Shillelagh	I.	14
26	Kilearton	165	0	9h	Waterford	Middlethird	Reisk	Waterford	II.	368
96	KILCAR T.	—			Donegal	Banagh	Kilear	Glenties	III.	109
37	Kilearty	710	1	26	Meath	Lower Deece	Kilmessan	Dunshaughlin	I.	192
90, 96	Kileasey	452	0	11	Donegal	Banagh	Kilear	Glenties	III.	108
16	Kileasey Lower	148	1	24	Wexford	Scarawalsh	Kilbride	Enniscorthy	I.	323
16	Kileasey Upper	175	2	18	Wexford	Scarawalsh	Kilbride	Enniscorthy	I.	323
41, 42	Kileash	683	2	21	Roscommon	Athlone	Kilmeane	Roscommon	IV.	182
78	Kileash	1,115	3	22	Tipperary, S.R.	Iffa and Offa East	Kileash	Clonmel	II.	313
55,56,65,66	Kileasheen	189	0	1	Clare	Moyarta	Moyarta	Kilrush	II.	34
73	Kileashel	121	3	10	Donegal	Banagh	Inishkeel	Glenties	III.	106
73	Kileashel	265	0	19	Mayo	Costello	Kilmovee	Swineford	IV.	142
35	Kileashel	336	1	32	Wicklow	Arklow	Castlemacadam	Rathdrum	I.	342
54	Kileashel Dolanstown	199	2	4	Roscommon	Moycarn	Moore	Ballinasloe	IV.	206
78	KILCASH T.	—			Tipperary, S.R.	Iffa and Offa East	Kileash	Clonmel	II.	313
103	Kileaskan	942	2	20	Cork, W.R.	Bear	Kileaskan	Castletown	II.	123
108	Kileaskan	221	2	35i	Cork, W.R.	East Carbery (E.D.)	Ballymoney	Dunmanway	II.	127
23, 31	Kileaskan North	333	0	5	Cork, E.R.	Duhallow	Clonmeen	Kanturk	II.	70
31	Kileaskan South	261	2	22	Cork, E.R.	Duhallow	Clonmeen	Kanturk	II.	70
22	Kileaskin	261	2	3	Limerick	Smallcounty	Fedamore	Croom	II.	259
5	Kileat	249	1	29	Sligo	Carbury	Ahamlish	Sligo	IV.	219
31	Kileatherina	229	3	32	Westmeath	Clonlonan	Kilcumreragh	Athlone	I.	262
101, 102	Kileatherine	2,097	0	34j	Cork, W.R.	Bear	Kileatherine	Castletown	II.	124
1, 3	Kileavan	561	2	25	Queen's Co.	Tinnahinch	Castlebrack	Mountmellick	I.	248
41, 46	Kileavan	179	3	12	Wexford	Bargy	Kileavan	Wexford	I.	305
7	Kileavan Lower	220	3	0	Wexford	Gorey	Kileavan	Gorey	I.	317
47	Kileavan Lower	423	3	38	Wicklow	Shillelagh	Carnew	Shillelagh	I.	357
41, 46	Kileavan (Old Mill)	265	0	17	Wexford	Bargy	Kileavan	Wexford	I.	305
46	Kileavan (Retrenched)	141	2	0	Wexford	Bargy	Kileavan	Wexford	I.	305
41	Kileavan (Tree)	75	2	1	Wexford	Bargy	Kileavan	Wexford	I.	305
7	Kileavan Upper	279	0	8	Wexford	Gorey	Kileavan	Gorey	I.	317
43, 47	Kileavan Upper	341	1	19	Wicklow	Shillelagh	Carnew	Shillelagh	I.	357
112	Kileawha	135	2	8	Cork, E.R.	Kinsale	Ringcurran	Kinsale	II.	100
16	Kileaysan	47	3	19	Wexford	Scarawalsh	Kilbride	Enniscorthy	I.	323
105	Kilchreest	267	1	2	Galway	Dunkellin	Kilchreest	Loughrea	IV.	28
105	KILCHREEST T.	—			Galway	Dunkellin	Kilchreest	Loughrea	IV.	28
34	Kilclammon	147	1	11	Wexford	Bantry	Oldross	New Ross	I.	301
20	Kilclaran	17	1	37	Clare	Tulla Upper	Feakle	Scarriff	II.	39
8	Kilclare	237	3	18	King's Co.	Ballycowan	Durrow	Tullamore	I.	127
27	Kilclare Beg	189	1	32	Leitrim	Leitrim	Kiltubbrid	Car^k. on Shannon	IV.	104

(a) Including 10A. 3R. 8P. water.
(b) Including 10A. 3R. 10P. water.
(c) Including 8A. 0R. 24P. water.
(d) Including 12A. 2R. 8P. water.

(e) Including 8A. 3R. 0P. water.
(f) Including 2A. 3R. 32P. water.
(g) Including 0A. 0R. 24P. River Barrow.

(h) Including 7A. 3R. 14P. water.
(i) Including 3A. 3R. 13P. detached portion.
(j) Including 42A. 3R. 17P. water.

No. of Sheet of the Ordnance Survey Maps.	Townlands and Towns.	Area in Statute Acres. A. R. P.	County.	Barony.	Parish.	Poor Law Union in 1857.	Townland Census of 1851. Part I. Vol.	Page
23	Kilclareen .	156 3 38	Tipperary, N.R.	Eliogarty	Templemore	Thurles	II.	272
45	Kilclare Lower	109 0 7	Cork, E.R.	Kinnatalloon	Knockmourne	Fermoy	II.	98
27, 28	Kilclare More .	206 2 9a	Leitrim	Leitrim	Kiltubbrid	Car^k. on Shannon	IV.	104
45	Kilclare Upper	493 1 28	Cork, E.R.	Kinnatalloon	Knockmourne	Fermoy	II.	98
59	Kilclay .	215 1 1	Tyrone	Clogher	Clogher	Clogher	III.	293
36	Kilcleagh	385 0 3	Westmeath	Clonlonan	Kilcleagh	Athlone	I.	261
15, 16	Kilclean .	907 1 18	Tyrone	Omagh West	Urney	Castlederg	III.	318
38	Kilclehaun	391 2 3	Clare	Ibrickan	Kilmurry	Kilrush	II.	23
32, 38, 39	Kilclief .	623 3 6	Down	Lecale Lower	Kilclief	Downpatrick	III.	179
49	Kilcloggan	326 1 14	Wexford	Shelburne	Templetown	New Ross	I.	328
68	Kilcloggaun	189 0 29	Galway	Moycullen	Moycullen	Galway	IV.	71
28	Kilclogh .	517 0 6	Cork, E.R.	Condons&Clangibbon	Macroney	Fermoy	II.	63
61, 62	Kilclogh .	754 1 1	Cork, E.R.	East Muskerry	Matehy	Cork	III.	105
32	Kilclogh .	422 3 21	Galway	Killian	Killian	Mountbellew	IV.	44
18, 23	Kilclogha	185 1 28b	Cavan	Clankee	Drumgoon	Cootehill	III.	72
17	Kilcloghan	206 1 12c	Roscommon	Roscommon	Kiltrustan	Strokestown	IV.	211
38	Kilcloghan	191 0 15	Westmeath	Moycashel	Newtown	Mullingar	I.	279
29	Kilcloghans	367 3 14	Galway	Dunmore	Tuam	Tuam	IV.	36
57, 68	Kilclogherane .	257 2 17	Kerry	Magunihy	Kilbonane	Killarney	II.	200
17, 23	Kilclogherna .	89 1 37	Roscommon	Roscommon	Kiltrustan	Strokestown	IV.	211
40, 41	Kilcloher	552 0 4	Clare	Islands	Kilmaley	Ennis	II.	31
71, 72	Kilcloher	678 3 3	Clare	Moyarta	Kilballyowen	Kilrush	II.	31
30	Kilcloher	222 2 18	Waterford	Decies without Drum	Whitechurch	Lismore	II.	361
35, 36	Kilclonagh	758 3 37	Tipperary, N.R.	Eliogarty	Kilclonagh	Thurles	II.	270
28	Kilcloncorkry .	244 1 33	King's Co.	Coolestown	Clonsast	Edenderry	I.	133
49, 50	Kilclone .	599 3 4	Meath	Upper Deece	Kilclone	Dunshaughlin	I.	193
19, 22	Kilcloney	415 3 31	Carlow	Idrone East	Clonygoose	Carlow	I.	6
10	Kilclonfert	546 3 20	King's Co.	Lower Philipstown	Kilclonfert	Tullamore	I.	142
9, 10	Kilclooney	777 3 30	Cork, E.R.	Condons&Clangibbon	Templemolaga	Mitchelstown	II.	63
6, 7, 14, 15	Kilclooney	3,218 0 2d	Waterford	Upperthird	Mothel	Carrick on Suir	II.	371
64, 73	Kilclooney Beg	257 1 11e	Donegal	Boylagh	Inishkeel	Glenties	III.	112
64, 73	Kilclooney More	592 0 13	Donegal	Boylagh	Inishkeel	Glenties	III.	113
74, 87	Kilcloony	1,259 2 3	Galway	Clonmacnowen	Kilcloony	Ballinasloe	IV.	25
16	Kilcloony	302 1 38	Galway	Dunmore	Liskeevy	Tuam	IV.	35
16	Kilcloony	61 1 24	Galway	Dunmore	Tuam	Tuam	IV.	36
10, 11, 16	Kilcloran	430 1 9	Wexford	Scarawalsh	Kilcomb	Gorey	I.	323
15, 16, 21	Kilcoagh East	1,128 3 5	Wicklow	Lower Talbotstown	Donard	Baltinglass	I.	360
15	Kilcoagh West	114 2 26	Wicklow	Lower Talbotstown	Donard	Baltinglass	I.	360
41	Kilcoan Beg	164 2 23	Antrim	Lower Belfast	Islandmagee	Larne	III.	8
41	Kilcoan More .	339 3 6f	Antrim	Lower Belfast	Islandmagee	Larne	III.	8
5	Kilcock .	378 1 39	Kildare	Ikeathy&Oughterany	Kilcock	Celbridge	I.	57
18	Kilcock .	92 1 37g	Roscommon	Ballintober North	Kilmore	Car^k. on Shannon	IV.	187
34	Kilcockan	249 2 15	Waterford	Coshmore&Coshbride	Kilcockan	Lismore	II.	343
5	Kilcock Lower	242 1 8	Kerry	Iraghticonnor	Lisselton	Listowel	II.	192
5	KILCOCK T. .	—	Kildare	Ikeathy&Oughterany	Kilcock	Celbridge	I.	57
49	KILCOCK T. .	--	Meath	Upper Deece	Rodanstown	Celbridge	I.	194
5	Kilcock Upper	291 3 12	Kerry	Iraghticonnor	Lisselton	Listowel	II.	192
140	Kilcoe .	586 3 18	Cork, W.R.	West Carbery (W.D.)	Kilcoe	Skull	II.	143
37	Kilcogy .	831 2 25	Cavan	Clanmahon	Drumlumman	Granard	III.	77
17	Kilcohan .	228 1 27	Waterford	Gaultiere	Ballynakill	Waterford	II.	362
16	Kilcoilshy	172 2 5	Wexford	Gorey	Kilcormick	Enniscorthy	I.	317
22, 28	Kilcoke .	639 2 14	Queen's Co.	Clandonagh	Rathdowney	Donaghmore	I.	234
35	Kilcoke .	180 3 23	Tipperary, N.R.	Eliogarty	Loughmoe East	Thurles	II.	271
10	Kilcolagh	248 0 25	Roscommon	Frenchpark	Kilcolagh	Boyle	IV.	203
103	Kilcolgan	231 0 28	Galway	Dunkellin	Kilcolgan	Gort	IV.	28
15	Kilcolgan Beg	377 3 6	King's Co.	Garrycastle	Wheery or Killagally	Parsonstown	I.	139
3	Kilcolgan Lower	388 3 7	Kerry	Iraghticonnor	Kilnaughtin	Glin	II.	191
15	Kilcolgan More	260 3 9	King's Co.	Garrycastle	Wheery or Killagally	Parsonstown	I.	139
3	Kilcolgan Upper	249 3 15	Kerry	Iraghticonnor	Kilnaughtin	Glin	II.	191
10	Kilcollan .	408 1 15	Kilkenny	Fassadinin	Mothel	Castlecomer	I.	90
8	Kilcollin .	54 3 38	King's Co.	Kilcoursey	Kilbride	Tullamore	I.	141
31	Kilcolman .	213 0 25	Cork, E.R.	Duhallow	Dromtarriff	Kanturk	II.	71
41.	Kilcolman .	410 1 27	Cork, E.R.	Duhallow	Kilshannig	Mallow	II.	74
61	Kilcolman .	90 2 29	Cork, E.R.	East Muskerry	Magourney	Macroom	II.	105
124	Kilcolman .	305 1 35	Cork, W.R.	Courceys	Ringrone	Kinsale	II.	147
109	Kilcolman .	556 1 11	Cork, W.R.	Kinalmeaky	Desertserges	Bandon	II.	152
42	Kilcolman .	77 2 33	Kerry	Corkaguiny	Marhin	Dingle	II.	179
2	Kilcolman .	366 2 25	Kerry	Iraghticonnor	Aghavallen	Listowel	II.	189
47, 57	Kilcolman .	224 3 39	Kerry	Trughanacmy	Kilcolman	Killarney	II.	210
38	Kilcolman .	176 2 0	King's Co.	Ballybritt	Kilcolman	Parsonstown	I.	125
45, 46	Kilcolman .	201 0 1	Limerick	Connello Upper	Kilmeedy	Newcastle	II.	233
12	Kilcolman .	220 0 0	Limerick	Pubblebrien	Kilkeedy	Limerick	II.	252
19	Kilcolman .	137 1 14	Limerick	Shanid	Kilcolman	Glin	II.	255

(a) Including 1A. 1R. 2P. water.
(b) Including 17A. 2R. 1P. water.
(c) Including 15A. 3R. 0P. water.
(d) Including 36A. 2R. 16P. Coumshingaun Lough.
(e) Including 3A. 0R. 20P. water.
(f) Including 1A. 0R. 30P. water.
(g) Including 0A. 1R. 13P. water.

No. of Sheet of the Ordnance Survey Maps.	Townlands and Towns.	Area in Statute Acres. A. R. P.	County.	Barony.	Parish.	Poor Law Union in 1857.	Vol.	Page
91, 101	Kilcolman	354 0 38	Mayo	Clanmorris	Kilcolman	Claremorris	IV.	134
74	Kilcolman	171 0 9	Mayo	Costello	Kilcolman	Castlereagh	IV.	141
20	Kilcolman	152 2 39	Tipperary, N.R.	Owney and Arra	Burgesbeg	Nenagh	II.	294
20	Kilcolman	190 3 5	Tipperary, N.R.	Owney and Arra	Youghalarra	Nenagh	II.	297
38	Kilcolman	325 0 10	Waterford	Decies within Drum	Ardmore	Dungarvan	II.	350
13, 18	Kilcolmanbane	401 1 15	Queen's Co.	Maryborough East	Kilcolmanbane	Mountmellick	I.	241
17	Kilcolman East	209 1 1	Cork, E.R.	Fermoy	Doneraile	Mallow	II.	78
29, 37	Kilcolman East	449 0 18	Limerick	Connello Lower	Rathkeale	Rathkeale	II.	229
17	Kilcolman Middle	233 3 8	Cork, E.R.	Fermoy	Doneraile	Mallow	II.	78
109	Kilcolmanpark	244 3 26	Cork, W.R.	Kinalmeaky	Desertserges	Bandon	II.	152
124	KILCOLMAN T.	—	Cork, W.R.	Courceys	Ringrone	Kinsale	II.	147
17	Kilcolman West	751 0 21	Cork, E.R.	Fermoy	Doneraile	Mallow	II.	78
29, 37	Kilcolman West	248 3 11	Limerick	Connello Lower	Rathkeale	Rathkeale	II.	229
99	Kilcolta	140 3 6	Cork, E.R.	Kerrycurrihy	Templebreedy	Kinsale	II.	93
22	Kilcoltrim	934 3 9	Carlow	Idrone East	Kiltennell	Carlow	I.	7
32, 40	Kilcolumb	667 2 18a	Clare	Islands	Kilmaley	Ennis	II.	31
7, 19	Kilcolumb	427 0 25	Galway	Ballymoe	Ballynakill	Glennamaddy	IV.	5
88	Kilcoman	505 1 19	Kerry	Iveragh	Caher	Cahersiveen	II.	194
139	Kilcomane	424 3 35	Cork, W.R.	West Carbery (W.D.)	Skull	Skull	II.	146
15	Kilcomeragh	124 2 2	Waterford	Decies without Drum	Kilrossanty	Kilmacthomas	II.	358
41, 42	Kilcomin	111 1 23	King's Co.	Clonlisk	Kilcomin	Roscrea	I.	131
87	Kilcommadan	448 3 5	Galway	Clonmacnowen	Aughrim	Ballinasloe	IV.	24
22	Kilcommock Glebe	352 1 6	Longford	Rathcline	Kilcommock	Ballymahon	I.	164
111, 119	Kilcommon	115 1 19	Mayo	Kilmaine	Kilcommon	Ballinrobe	IV.	154
39	Kilcommon	297 2 10	Tipperary, N.R.	Kilnamanagh Upper	Templebeg	Thurles	II.	279
7	Kilcommon	202 3 29	Tipperary, N.R.	Lower Ormond	Aglishcloghane	Borrisokane	II.	281
81	Kilcommon Beg	337 2 29b	Tipperary, S.R.	Iffa and Offa West	Caher	Clogheen	II.	318
81	Kilcommon More (North)	572 3 30c	Tipperary, S.R.	Iffa and Offa West	Caher	Clogheen	II.	318
81	Kilcommon More (South)	604 1 7	Tipperary, S.R.	Iffa and Offa West	Caher	Clogheen	II.	318
11	Kilcommon or Pollatomish	672 2 30	Mayo	Erris	Kilcommon	Belmullet	IV.	144
21	Kilcon	180 1 20	Armagh	Orior Lower	Loughgilly	Newry	III.	56
21	Kilconane	293 3 30	Tipperary, N.R.	Upper Ormond	Lisbunny	Nenagh	II.	292
83	Kilcondy	88 2 29	Cork, E.R.	East Muskerry	Kilmurry	Bandon	II.	104
83	Kilcondy	165 1 8	Cork, E.R.	East Muskerry	Moviddy	Bandon	II.	105
96	Kilconierin	91 2 37	Galway	Dunkellin	Kilconierin	Loughrea	IV.	29
1	Kilconly North	130 0 5	Kerry	Iraghticonnor	Kilconly	Listowel	II.	191
1	Kilconly South	212 0 27	Kerry	Iraghticonnor	Kilconly	Listowel	II.	191
4	Kilconnaught	135 3 3	Carlow	Rathvilly	Hacketstown	Shillelagh	I.	11
14	Kilconnell	228 3 31	Clare	Corcomroe	Kilmacrehy	Ennistimon	II.	20
61	Kilconnell	587 3 14	Tipperary, S.R.	Middlethird	Kilconnell	Cashel	II.	327
45	Kilconnell or Glebe	197 3 22	Donegal	Kilmacrenan	Kilmacrenan	Millford	III.	129
86	KILCONNELL T.	—	Galway	Kilconnell	Kilconnell	Ballinasloe	IV.	40
33	Kilconnelly	177 2 0	Kilkenny	Ida	The Rower	Thomastown	I.	104
17	Kilconner	354 2 39	Carlow	Idrone East	Fennagh	Carlow	I.	7
20	Kilconnib	435 2 18	Wexford	Ballaghkeen	Kilcormick	Enniscorthy	I.	294
18	Kilconnor	215 1 14	Cork, E.R.	Fermoy	Doneraile	Mallow	II.	78
11, 15	Kilconny	375 1 15d	Cavan	Lower Loughtee	Drumlane	Cavan	III.	80
11	KILCONNY T.	—	Cavan	Lower Loughtee	Drumlane	Cavan	III.	81
34	Kilcoo	287 3 17	Kildare	Narragh and Reban West	Churchtown	Athy	I.	67
3	Kilcoobin	117 2 19	Antrim	Cary	Billy	Coleraine	III.	12
20	Kilcool	147 1 8	Limerick	Connello Lower	Doondonnell	Rathkeale	II.	228
66	Kilcoolaght	43 0 30	Kerry	Magunihy	Killarney	Killarney	II.	203
65	Kilcoolaght East	182 1 18	Kerry	Dunkerron North	Killorglin	Killarney	II.	181
64, 65	Kilcoolaght West	413 3 32	Kerry	Dunkerron North	Killorglin	Killarney	II.	181
12, 13	Kilcoole	295 1 39	Carlow	Forth	Gilbertstown	Carlow	I.	4
13	Kilcoole	233 3 11	Wicklow	Newcastle	Kilcoole	Rathdrum	I.	352
13	KILCOOLE T.	—	Wicklow	Newcastle	Kilcoole	Rathdrum	I.	352
7	Kilcooley	376 2 3	Galway	Ballymoe	Kilcroan	Glennamaddy	IV.	9
28	Kilcooley	106 0 12	Roscommon	Roscommon	Kilcooley	Strokestown	IV.	210
75	Kilcoolishal	442 1 39	Cork, E.R.	Barrymore	Caherlag	Cork	II.	52
106	Kilcooly	414 3 10	Galway	Leitrim	Kilcooly	Loughrea	IV.	54
33, 42	Kilcooly	393 2 23	Kerry	Corkaguiny	Kilmalkedar	Dingle	II.	178
44	Kilcooly	82 1 3	Meath	Lower Deece	Knockmark	Dunshaughlin	I.	192
30,31,36,37	Kilcooly	419 3 38	Meath	Upper Navan	Kilcooly	Trim	I.	216
43	Kilcoolyabbey	1,455 1 15e	Tipperary, S.R.	Slievardagh	Kilcooly	Urlingford	II.	334
15	Kilcooly North	229 1 10	Kerry	Clanmaurice	Kilmoyly	Tralee	II.	171
15	Kilcooly South	187 2 39	Kerry	Clanmaurice	Kilmoyly	Tralee	II.	171
15	Kilcoon	64 3 26	Leitrim	Drumahaire	Killanummery	Manorhamilton	IV.	98
56	Kilcoona	169 0 32	Galway	Clare	Kilcoona	Tuam	IV.	20
135	Kilcooney	131 2 21	Galway	Leitrim	Clonrush	Scarriff	IV.	53

(a) Including 2A. 2R. 37P. water.
(b) Including 8A. 1R. 1P. water.
(c) Including 4A. 0R. 25P. water.
(d) Including 27A. 3R. 18P. water.
(e) Including 10A. 2R. 19P. water.

No. of Sheet of the Ordnance Survey Maps.	Townlands and Towns.	Area in Statute Acres.			County.	Barony.	Parish.	Poor Law Union in 1857.	Townland Census of 1851, Part I.	
		A.	R.	P.					Vol.	Page
26	Kilcooney	1,198	1	1	King's Co.	Upper Philipstown	Ballykean	Mountmellick	I.	143
13, 22	Kilcooney	582	2	21	Waterford	Decies without Drum	Seskinan	Dungarvan	II.	360
39, 47	Kilcoony	80	0	28	Tyrone	Dungannon Upper	Ballyclog	Cookstown	III.	306
44	Kilcoorha	360	3	35	Limerick	Glenquin	Killeedy	Newcastle	II.	246
32	Kilcoosh	381	3	8	Galway	Killian	Killian	Mountbellew	IV.	44
11, 15	Kilcoosy	498	2	19a	Leitrim	Drumahaire	Drumlease	Manorhamilton	IV.	94
51	Kilcootry	274	0	27	Tyrone	Clogher	Donacavey	Omagh	III.	294
18	Kilcop Lower	96	3	26	Waterford	Gaultiere	Kilcop	Waterford	II.	363
18	Kilcop Upper	291	3	21	Waterford	Gaultiere	Kilcop	Waterford	II.	363
28, 34	Kilcoran	298	1	1	Queen's Co.	Clandonagh	Rathdowney	Donaghmore	I.	234
74,75,80,81	Kilcoran	953	1	8	Tipperary, S.R.	Iffa and Offa West	Tubbrid	Clogheen	II.	321
37	Kilcoran North	83	0	8	Cork, E.R.	Condons&Clangibbon	Knockmourne	Fermoy	II.	62
37	Kilcoran South	474	1	35	Cork, E.R.	Condons&Clangibbon	Knockmourne	Fermoy	II.	62
117	Kilcorban	208	0	8	Galway	Leitrim	Tynagh	Portumna	IV.	55
10	Kilcorbry	199	2	7	King's Co.	Lower Philipstown	Croghan	Edenderry	I.	142
10	Kilcorby	212	1	7b	Cavan	Lower Loughtee	Drumlane	Cavan	III.	80
31	Kilcorcoran	406	2	13	Clare	Ibrickan	Kilfarboy	Ennistimon	II.	22
63	Kilcorig	494	1	36	Antrim	Upper Massereene	Magheragall	Lisburn	III.	31
11	Kilcorkan	285	0	13	Clare	Inchiquin	Kilkeedy	Corrofin	II.	26
94	Kilcorkey	31	0	17	Galway	Galway	Rahoon	Galway	IV.	37
21	Kilcorkey	215	0	3	Roscommon	Castlereagh	Kilcorkey	Castlereagh	IV.	199
16	Kilcorkey	430	2	17	Wexford	Gorey	Monamolin	Gorey	I.	321
21	Kilcormick	389	1	16	Wexford	Ballaghkeen	Kilcormick	Enniscorthy	I.	294
43	Kilcornan	419	0	21c	Clare	Bunratty Lower	Kilmurry	Tulla	II.	6
15	Kilcornan	345	2	7	Clare	Corcomroe	Kilmanaheen	Ennistimon	II.	21
95, 103	Kilcornan	814	2	29	Galway	Dunkellin	Stradbally	Galway	IV.	32
84	Kilcornan	414	2	28	Galway	Kilconnell	Monivea	Loughrea	IV.	42
31	Kilcornan	187	2	16	Galway	Tiaquin	Kilkerrin	Glennamaddy	IV.	77
58	Kilcornan	376	1	16	Tipperary, S.R.	Cianwilliam	Kilcornan	Tipperary	II.	308
23	Kilcornan	21	2	29	Westmeath	Kilkenny West	Drumraney	Ballymahon	I.	273
16, 23	Kilcornan	404	0	18	Westmeath	Kilkenny West	Noughaval	Ballymahon	I.	274
9	Kilcorney	248	1	32	Clare	Burren	Kilcorney	Ballyvaghan	II.	12
39	Kilcorney	101	0	24	Cork, W.R.	West Muskerry	Kilcorney	Millstreet	II.	158
48	Kilcorney	454	2	26	Meath	Lower Moyfenrath	Rathcore	Trim	I.	211
9	Kilcorney Glebe	28	1	32	Clare	Burren	Kilcorney	Ballyvaghan	II.	12
45	Kilcor North	538	0	11	Cork, E.R.	Barrymore	Castlelyons	Fermoy	II.	53
32, 33	Kilcorral	365	2	39	Wexford	Shelmaliere East	Ardcavan	Wexford	I.	329
8	Kilcorran	268	2	15d	Monaghan	Monaghan	Clones	Monaghan	III.	274
45	Kilcor South	889	0	11	Cork, E.R.	Barrymore	Castlelyons	Fermoy	II.	53
19	Kilcosgrave	134	2	4	Limerick	Shanid	Kilmoylan	Glin	II.	256
19	Kilcosgrave	42	3	0	Limerick	Shanid	Shanagolden	Glin	II.	258
11	Kilcoskan	298	3	20	Dublin	Nethercross	Kilsallaghan	Balrothery	I.	31
22	Kilcotton	382	3	7	Queen's Co.	Clandonagh	Aghaboe	Donaghmore	I.	232
26	Kilcotty Beg	216	1	33	Wexford	Ballaghkeen	Ballyhuskard	Enniscorthy	I.	292
26	Kilcotty More	303	1	33	Wexford	Ballaghkeen	Ballyhuskard	Enniscorthy	I.	292
55, 66	Kilcounty	936	2	26	Cork, E.R.	Imokilly	Dangandonovan	Middleton	II.	86
15	Kilcourcey	216	2	2	Longford	Ardagh	Mostrim	Granard	I.	152
8	Kilcoursey	394	0	8	King's Co.	Kilcoursey	Kilbride	Tullamore	I.	141
39	Kilcow	736	2	8	Kerry	Trughanacmy	Dysert	Tralee	II.	210
46	Kilcowan Lower	79	2	1	Wexford	Bargy	Kilcowan	Wexford	I.	305
46, 47	Kilcowan Upper	96	3	34	Wexford	Bargy	Kilcowan	Wexford	I.	305
9	Kilcowran	176	2	29e	Tipperary, N.R.	Lower Ormond	Finnoe	Borrisokane	II.	284
42	Kilcraggan	369	2	21	Kilkenny	Iverk	Ballytarsney	Waterford	I.	105
77, 78	Kilcraheen	317	3	4	Cork, E.R.	Imokilly	Ightermurragh	Middleton	II.	87
7	Kilcran	39	3	26	Monaghan	Trough	Donagh	Monaghan	III.	282
24, 32	Kilcranathan	409	1	9	Cork, E.R.	Duhallow	Ballyclogh	Mallow	II.	67
84	Kilcrea	965	1	27	Cork, E.R.	East Muskerry	Desertmore	Bandon	II.	102
12	Kilcrea	277	0	32	Dublin	Nethercross	Donabate	Balrothery	I.	30
77, 78	Kilcredan	502	1	30	Cork, E.R.	Imokilly	Kilcredan	Middleton	II.	87
65, 72	Kilcredaun	275	2	34	Clare	Moyarta	Moyarta	Kilrush	II.	34
45	Kilcredaun	275	2	17	Clare	Tulla Lower	O'Briensbridge	Limerick	II.	38
46	Kilcreen	208	1	24	Donegal	Kilmacrenan	Aughnish	Millford	III.	122
10	Kilcreen	47	2	13f	Kerry	Clanmaurice	Finuge	Listowel	II.	169
19	Kilcreen	42	2	21g	Kilkenny	Crannagh and Municipal Borough	St. Canice	Kilkenny	I.	87
19	Kilcreen	118	1	29	Kilkenny	Shillelogher	St. Patrick's	Kilkenny	I.	116
30, 34	Kilcreen	384	0	10	Londonderry	Tirkeeran	Banagher	Londonderry	III.	247
8	Kilcreen	153	0	31	Monaghan	Monaghan	Clones	Monaghan	III.	274
63	Kilcreeny	237	3	29	Antrim	Upper Massereene	Ballinderry	Lisburn	III.	29
16, 29	Kilcreevanty	1,581	1	21	Galway	Dunmore	Kilbennan	Tuam	IV.	34
33	Kilcreevin	316	2	34	Sligo	Corran	Kilmorgan	Sligo	IV.	227
33	Kilcreevin (Phibbs)	223	3	11	Sligo	Corran	Kilmorgan	Sligo	IV.	227
15, 16	Kilcreevy Etra	411	3	25	Armagh	Armagh	Derrynoose	Armagh	III.	44

(a) Including 65A. 3R. 4P. water.
(b) Including 4A. 0R. 11P. water.
(c) Including 72A. 2R. 6P. water.

(d) Including 32A. 1R. 7P. water.
(e) Including 6A. 3R. 24P. water.
(f) Including 4A. 3R. 26P. water.

(g) { Within the Municipal Boundary, 6A. 2R. 2P.
{ Without the Municipal Boundary, 36A. 0R. 19P.

No. of Sheet of the Ordnance Survey Maps.	Townlands and Towns.	Area in Statute Acres.	County.	Barony.	Parish.	Poor Law Union in 1857.	Townland Census of 1851, Part I.	
		A. R. P.					Vol.	Page
16	Kilcreevy Otra	377 1 27	Armagh	Armagh	Derrynoose	Armagh	III.	44
8, 9	Kilcreg	158 1 2	Antrim	Cary	Ramoan	Ballycastle	III.	14
5	Kilcreggane	106 3 10	Waterford	Glenahiry	Kilronan	Clonmel	II.	365
43	Kilcreman	225 2 4	King's Co.	Ballybritt	Roscrea	Roscrea	I.	126
123, 129	Kilcrimple	340 0 7a	Galway	Kiltartan	Kilbeacanty	Gort	IV.	47
61	Kilcrin	129 3 26	Galway	Killian	Ahascragh	Ballinasloe	IV.	43
13	Kilcroagh	342 0 34	Antrim	Cary	Armoy	Ballycastle	III.	11
16	Kilcroagh	351 3 35b	Tyrone	Omagh West	Urney	Castlederg	III.	318
46	Kilcroe	71 1 1	Tipperary, S.R.	Kilnamanagh Lower	Clogher	Cashel	II.	322
129, 138	Kilcrohane	287 1 5	Cork, W.R.	West Carbery (W.D.)	Kilcrohane	Bantry	II.	143
38	Kilcronagh	184 0 13	Tyrone	Dungannon Upper	Derryloran	Cookstown	III.	307
63	Kilcronan	376 2 20	Cork, E.R.	Cork	Whitechurch	Cork	II.	66
30	Kilcronan	170 3 3	Queen's Co.	Cullenagh	Dysartgallen	Abbeyleix	I.	239
46, 55	Kilcronat	516 3 26	Cork, E.R.	Kinnatalloon	Mogeely	Youghal	II.	98
55	Kilcronatmountain	385 2 3	Cork, E.R.	Kinnatalloon	Mogeely	Youghal	II.	98
88, 89	Kilcrone	62 1 19	Cork, E.R.	Imokilly	Cloyne	Middleton	II.	85
11, 14	Kilcroney	1,068 3 14	Louth	Louth	Louth	Dundalk	I.	184
7	Kilcroney	218 1 1	Wicklow	Rathdown	Kilmacanoge	Rathdown	I.	355
55, 56	Kilcross	642 0 10	Antrim	Lower Massereene	Killead	Antrim	III.	28
32, 33	Kilcross	894 3 2	Kilkenny	Gowran	Inistioge	Thomastown	I.	96
28	Kilcrossbeg	171 0 11c	Cavan	Clankee	Shercock	Bailieborough	III.	74
28, 29	Kilcrossduff	442 0 29	Cavan	Clankee	Shercock	Bailieborough	III.	74
107	Kilcrow	215 3 28	Galway	Longford	Killimorbologue	Portumna	IV.	59
34	Kilcrow	357 3 26	Kildare	Narragh&RebanWest	Churchtown	Athy	I.	67
14	Kilcrow	196 2 32	Monaghan	Cremorne	Clontibret	Monaghan	III.	260
22	Kilcrow	124 2 16	Monaghan	Dartree	Ematris	Cootehill	III.	267
11, 17	Kilcroy	128 1 2	Roscommon	Roscommon	Aughrim	Carton Shannon	IV.	207
56, 59	Kilcruaig	565 2 2	Limerick	Coshlea	Kiltyn	Kilmallock	II.	240
25, 26, 31	Kilcruise	656 3 1	Queen's Co.	Slievemargy	Killabban	Carlow	I.	245
19	Kilcruit	188 2 27	Carlow	Idrone East	Lorum	Carlow	I.	8
17	Kilcruttin	83 3 17	King's Co.	Ballycowan	Kilbride	Tullamore	I.	127
32	Kilcullane	724 3 33	Limerick	Smallcounty	Kilcullane	Kilmallock	II.	260
14	Kilculleen	527 2 21	Limerick	Clanwilliam	Ludden	Limerick	II.	225
28, 32	Kilcullen	662 0 6d	Kilkenny	Gowran	Columbkille	Thomastown	I.	94
14	Kilcullen	521 0 39	Wexford	Scarawalsh	Templeshanbo	Enniscorthy	I.	326
23, 28	Kilcullenbridge	201 3 15e	Kildare	Kilcullen	Kilcullen	Naas	I.	58
28	Kilcullenbridge	136 3 11f	Kildare	Naas South	Carnalway	Naas	I.	64
10, 18	Kilcullen Lower	113 1 1	Waterford	Gaultiere	Faithlegg	Waterford	II.	362
49, 50	Kilcullen North	790 1 31	Cork, E.R.	East Muskerry	Donaghmore	Macroom	II.	103
49,50,60,61	Kilcullen South	926 3 37	Cork, E.R.	East Muskerry	Donaghmore	Macroom	II.	103
28	KILCULLEN T.	—	Kildare	Kilcullen / Naas South	Kilcullen / Carnalway	Naas	I.	58 / 64
10, 18	Kilcullen Upper	193 0 20	Waterford	Gaultiere	Faithlegg	Waterford	II.	362
63	Kilcully	324 3 26	Cork, E R.	Cork	Kilcully	Cork	II.	64
23, 24, 30	Kilculmagrandal	481 0 28	Londonderry	Tirkeeran	Cumber Upper	New Tª Limavady	III.	249
19, 20	Kilcumber	280 0 19	King's Co.	Coolestown	Clonsast	Edenderry	I.	133
16	Kilcumber	55 3 32g	Monaghan	Dartree	Killeevan	Clones	III.	268
26, 34	Kilcummer Lower	188 3 16h	Cork, E R.	Fermoy	Kilcummer	Fermoy	II.	80
26, 34	Kilcummer Upper	655 1 31	Cork, E.R.	Fermoy	Kilcummer	Fermoy	II.	80
14	Kilcummin	872 1 15	King's Co.	Garrycastle	Tisaran	Parsonstown	I.	138
8	Kilcummin	186 2 0	Mayo	Tirawley	Kilcummin	Killala	IV.	168
24, 31	Kilcummin	807 2 26	Sligo	Leyny	Achonry	Tobercurry	IV.	229
35	Kilcummin Beg	637 3 27	Kerry	Corkaguiny	Killiney	Dingle	II.	178
35	Kilcummin More	290 3 31	Kerry	Corkaguiny	Killiney	Dingle	II.	178
19	Kilcumney	133 2 12	Carlow	Idrone East	Ballyellin	Carlow	I.	6
19	Kilcumney	299 1 31	Carlow	Idrone East	Clonygoose	Carlow	I.	6
8, 13	Kilcumny	271 1 10	Westmeath	Delvin	Kilcumny	Castletowndelvin	I.	265
31	Kilcumreragh	478 3 37	Westmeath	Moycashel	Kilcumreragh	Athlone	I.	278
8, 11	Kilcunnahin Beg	281 1 37i	Tipperary, N.R.	Lower Ormond	Ballingarry	Borrisokane	II.	282
8, 11	Kilcunnahin More	389 0 30	Tipperary, N.R.	Lower Ormond	Ballingarry	Borrisokane	II.	282
75	Kilcurfin Glebe	10 0 35	Cork, E.R.	Barrymore	Carrigtohill	Middleton	II.	52
29, 35	Kilcurkree	456 0 21	Tipperary, N.R.	Eliogarty	Loughmoe East	Thurles	II.	271
31	Kilcurl (Anglesey)	113 0 36j	Kilkenny	Knocktopher	Knocktopher	Thomastown	I.	112
1, 2	Kilcurley	185 3 4	King's Co.	Kilcoursey	Kilmanaghan	Tullamore	I.	141
31	Kilcurl (Feronsby)	141 2 4	Kilkenny	Knocktopher	Knocktopher	Thomastown	I.	112
12, 21	Kilcurly	334 0 14	Limerick	Kenry	Adare	Croom	II.	248
22	Kilcurly	239 3 3	Limerick	Pubblebrien	Monasteranenagh	Croom	II.	253
6, 7	Kilcurly	437 3 30	Louth	Upper Dundalk	Dunbin	Dundalk	I.	178
84	Kilcurrane East	665 1 2	Kerry	Glanarought	Kenmare	Kenmare	II.	186
84	Kilcurrane West	160 2 10	Kerry	Glanarought	Kenmare	Kenmare	II.	186
25, 33	Kilcurrish	262 1 22	Clare	Inchiquin	Dysert	Ennis	II.	24
57	Kilcurrivard	610 1 36	Galway	Clare	Cummer	Tuam	IV.	19
56, 57	Kilcurriv Eighter	409 2 2	Galway	Clare	Cummer	Tuam	IV.	19

(a) Including 10A. 2R. 21P. water.
(b) Including 1A. 0R. 36P. water.
(c) Including 13A. 3R. 17P. water.
(d) Including 3A. 2R. 7P. River Nore.
(e) Including 9A. 2R. 32P. water.
(f) { Including 13A. 1R. 37P. detached portions. / Including 3A. 0R. 32P. water. }
(g) Including 4A. 1R. 30P. water.
(h) Including 5A. 2R. 27P. water.
(i) Including 1A. 0R. 0P. water.
(j) Including 26A. 2R. 9P. detached portion.

No. of Sheet of the Ordnance Survey Maps.	Townlands and Towns.	Area in Statute Acres.	County.	Barony.	Parish.	Poor Law Union in 1857.	Townland Census of 1851, Part I.	
		A. R. P.					Vol.	Page
36, 37	Kilcurry	784 2 35	Antrim	Lower Toome	Ahoghill	Ballymena	III.	32
23	Kilcurry	578 1 37a	Longford	Shrule	Taghshinny	Ballymahon	I.	167
4	Kilcurry	177 1 11	Louth	Upper Dundalk	Ballymascanlan	Dundalk	I.	177
31, 40	Kilcusnaun	739 1 21	Kerry	Trughanacmy	Ballincuslane	Tralee	II.	206
29,30,35,36	Kildalkey	1,314 0 23	Meath	Lune	Kildalkey	Trim	I.	208
35	KILDALKEY T.	—	Meath	Lune	Kildalkey	Trim	I.	208
14	Kildallan	397 0 18	Cavan	Tullyhunco	Kildallan	Bawnboy	III.	97
18	Kildallan	248 0 27	Westmeath	Moygoish	Templeoran	Mullingar	I.	281
11, 18	Kildallan North	257 0 32	Westmeath	Moygoish	Templeoran	Mullingar	I.	281
23	Kildalloge	205 2 18	Roscommon	Roscommon	Kiltrustan	Strokestown	IV.	211
10, 15	Kildalloo	206 2 22	Wexford	Scarawalsh	Ballycarney	Enniscorthy	I.	322
39	Kildalton	799 3 25	Kilkenny	Iverk	Fiddown	Carrick on Suir	I.	105
27	Kildangan	988 3 11	Kildare	Offaly West	Kildangan	Athy	I.	72
8, 9, 16, 17	Kildangan	441 0 32	King's Co.	Ballycowan	Durrow	Tullamore	I.	127
46, 52	Kildangan	529 1 35	Meath	Upper Moyfenrath	Castlejordan	Edenderry	I.	212
87,88,90,91	Kildanoge	2,676 3 31	Tipperary, S.R.	Iffa and Offa West	Ballybacon	Clogheen	II.	317
22	Kildare	761 2 9	Kildare	Offaly East	Kildare	Naas	I.	70
1, 6	Kildaree	370 1 11	Galway	Ballymoe	Templetogher	Glennamaddy	IV.	9
41	Kildaree	161 3 12	Galway	Clare	Killursa	Tuam	IV.	21
38	Kildaree	117 1 24	Mayo	Tirawley	Crossmolina	Ballina	IV.	166
45	Kildares Crew	211 0 30b	Down	Lecale Lower	Ballee	Downpatrick	III.	178
22	KILDARE T.	—	Kildare	Offaly East	Kildare	Naas	I.	70
39	Kildarganmore	96 3 11	Sligo	Corran	Kilshalvy	Boyle	IV.	227
111	Kildarra	463 0 39	Cork, W.R.	East Carbery (E.D.)	Ballinadee	Bandon	II.	126
102	Kildarra	104 3 21	Mayo	Costello	Annagh	Claremorris	IV.	138
25, 26	Kildarragh	1,019 3 21c	Donegal	Kilmacrenan	Clondahorky	Dunfanaghy	III.	123
38	Kildavaroge	246 3 26	Mayo	Tirawley	Crossmolina	Ballina	IV.	166
18, 21	Kildavin	321 1 14d	Carlow	St. Mullins Upper	Barragh	Shillelagh	I.	14
20, 28	Kildavin	265 0 31	Clare	Tulla Upper	Feakle	Scariff	II.	39
42	Kildavin Lower	182 0 8	Wexford	Forth	Kildavin	Wexford	I.	310
42	Kildavin Upper	106 1 14	Wexford	Forth	Kildavin	Wexford	I.	310
18, 19	Kilday	234 1 28	Wicklow	Newcastle	Newcastle Upper	Rathdrum	I.	353
121	Kildee	550 2 5	Cork, W.R.	East Carbery (W.D.)	Kilmeen	Dunmanway	II.	134
56	Kildeema	274 1 27	Clare	Moyarta	Kilfearagh	Kilrush	II.	32
30, 31	Kildeema North	202 0 24	Clare	Ibrickan	Kilfarboy	Ennistimon	II.	22
30, 31	Kildeema South	468 3 23	Clare	Ibrickan	Kilfarboy	Ennistimon	II.	22
22	Kildellig	51 0 38	Queen's Co.	Clarmallagh	Aghaboe	Donaghmore	I.	236
22, 28	Kildellig	1,054 1 1	Queen's Co.	Clarmallagh	Kildellig	Donaghmore	I.	238
16	Kildermody	227 2 39	Waterford	Middlethird	Newcastle	Waterford	II.	368
40	Kildermot	139 1 26e	Mayo	Gallen	Attymass	Ballina	IV.	147
7	Kildermot	223 2 1	Wexford	Ballaghkeen	Kilcavan	Gorey	I.	294
7	Kildermot	410 2 7	Wexford	Ballaghkeen	Kiltennell	Gorey	I.	297
15	Kilderreen	74 3 7	Longford	Granard	Clonbroney	Granard	I.	155
89	Kilderrig	207 1 19	Cork, E.R.	Imokilly	Ballintemple	Middleton	II.	84
21	Kilderriheen	144 2 25	Waterford	Decies without Drum	Affane	Lismore	II.	353
15, 20	Kilderry	419 0 11	Kilkenny	Gowran	Kilderry	Kilkenny	I.	96
22	Kilderry	121 0 20	Limerick	Pubblebrien	Monasteranenagh	Croom	II.	253
22	Kilderry	508 1 31	Limerick	Smallcounty	Ballycahane	Croom	II.	259
41	Kilderry	154 3 21	Wexford	Bargy	Kilcavan	Wexford	I.	305
47, 57	Kilderry North	268 2 6	Kerry	Trughanacmy	Kilcolman	Killarney	II.	210
57	Kilderry South	170 3 30	Kerry	Trughanacmy	Kilcolman	Killarney	II.	210
12	Kildimo	340 3 2	Limerick	Kenry	Kildimo	Rathkeale	II.	250
12	KILDIMO T.	—	Limerick	Kenry	Kildimo	Rathkeale	II.	250
44	Kildinan	748 2 33	Cork, E.R.	Barrymore	Rathcormack	Fermoy	II.	57
22	Kildoag	705 1 17	Londonderry	Tirkeeran	Cumber Lower	Londonderry	III.	249
9, 13	Kildoagh	179 0 13f	Cavan	Tullyhaw	Templeport	Bawnboy	III.	95
10	Kildoagh	94 0 37	Monaghan	Monaghan	Tehallan	Monaghan	III.	280
14	Kildonan	163 0 16	Dublin	Castleknock	Finglas	Dublin North	I.	25
106, 107	Kildoney Glebe	508 2 34	Donegal	Tirhugh	Kilbarron	Ballyshannon	III.	148
22	Kildonnell	122 0 0	Limerick	Pubblebrien	Ballycahane	Croom	II.	251
32	Kildoo	40 1 39	Leitrim	Mohill	Mohill	Mohill	IV.	108
27, 31	Kildoon	410 2 6	Kildare	Offaly West	Nurney	Athy	I.	74
53, 54	Kildoorus	331 2 37	Clare	Tulla Lower	Kiltenanlea	Limerick	II.	37
27	Kildordan	121 3 26	Longford	Shrule	Forgney	Ballymahon	I.	166
25	Kildorragh	161 2 7	Leitrim	Carrigallen	Oughteragh	Bawnboy	IV.	92
31	Kildorragh	99 3 7	Leitrim	Leitrim	Kiltoghert	Cark. on Shannon	IV.	102
38	Kildorragh Glebe	607 1 16	Cavan	Castlerahan	Castlerahan	Oldcastle	III.	67
18	Kildorrery	111 0 38	Cork, E.R.	Condons&Clangibbon	Kildorrery	Mitchelstown	II.	61
18	KILDORRERY T.	—	Cork, E.R.	Condons&Clangibbon	Kildorrery	Mitchelstown	II.	61
121	Kildotia	93 2 33	Mayo	Kilmaine	Kilmolara	Ballinrobe	IV.	157
97	Kildowney	615 0 80	Antrim	Lower Toome	Ahoghill	Ballymena	III.	32
97, 105	Kildreelig	420 2 10	Kerry	Iveragh	Prior	Cahersiveen	II.	198
16	Kildreenagh	555 1 22	Carlow	Idrone East	Dunleckny	Carlow	I.	7

(a) Including 7A. 0R. 4P. Inny River.
(b) Including 40A. 0R. 35P. detached portion.
(c) Including 19A. 2R. 28P. water.
(d) Including 8A. 1R. 14P. River Slaney.
(e) Including 50A. 0R. 0P. water.
(f) Including 34A. 1R. 28P. water.

No. of Sheet of the Ordnance Survey Maps.	Townlands and Towns.	Area in Statute Acres.	County.	Barony.	Parish.	Poor Law Union in 1857.	Townland Census of 1851, Part I.	
		A. R. P.					Vol.	Page
29	Kildress Lower	198 3 31	Tyrone	Dungannon Upper	Kildress	Cookstown	III.	309
29	Kildress Upper	82 0 25	Tyrone	Dungannon Upper	Kildress	Cookstown	III.	309
16	Kildrimeen	98 0 2	Wexford	Gorey	Monamolin	Gorey	I.	321
12, 13, 17	Kildrinagh	474 1 27	Kilkenny	Crannagh	Tubbridbritain	Urlingford	I.	87
16	Kildrinagh	69 3 17	Queen's Co.	Upperwoods	Offerlane	Abbeyleix	I.	252
103, 116	Kildromalive	425 3 37	Cork, W.R.	Bear	Kilcaskan	Castletown	II.	123
23,24,32,33	Kildromin	750 3 22	Limerick	Smallcounty	Kilteely	Kilmallock	II.	260
3	Kildroughtaun	188 0 20a	Waterford	Upperthird	Dysert	Carrick on Suir	II.	369
37, 38, 44	Kildrum	273 0 23	Antrim	Lower Antrim	Connor	Ballymena	III.	3
42	Kildrum	94 2 0	Clare	Bunratty Upper	Quin	Tulla	II.	10
11, 20	Kildrum	411 0 7	Cork, E.R.	Condons and Clangibbon	Brigown	Mitchelstown	II.	59
42	Kildrum	193 0 14	Galway	Clare	Donaghpatrick	Tuam	IV.	19
42, 50	Kildrum	405 3 22	Tyrone	Omagh East	Dromore	Omagh	III.	311
55	Kildrum Lower	246 3 39	Donegal	Raphoe	Allsaints	Londonderry	III.	134
27	Kildrumman	117 2 16	King's Co.	Coolestown	Clonsast	Edenderry	I.	133
30	Kildrummy	325 1 22	Kilkenny	Kells	Kilmaganny	Callan	I.	109
55	Kildrum Upper	306 1 27	Donegal	Raphoe	Allsaints	Londonderry	III.	134
25	Kilduane	285 0 38	Waterford	Decies without Drum	Monksland	Kilmacthomas	II.	359
15	Kilduff	177 2 30b	Cavan	Lower Loughtee	Annagh	Cavan	III.	79
15, 16	Kilduff	174 0 11	Cavan	Tullygarvey	Annagh	Cavan	III.	87
14	Kilduff	100 2 12	Fermanagh	Magheraboy	Devenish	Enniskillen	III.	211
45	Kilduff	539 2 36	Kerry	Corkaguiny	Ballinvoher	Dingle	II.	174
30	Kilduff	229 0 39	Kerry	Trughanacmy	O'Brennan	Tralee	II.	212
10	Kilduff	612 3 22	King's Co.	Lower Philipstown	Kilconfert	Tullamore	I.	142
24	Kilduff	252 0 0	Limerick	Coonagh	Ballynaclogh	Tipperary	II.	233
24	Kilduff	167 2 39	Limerick	Coonagh	Grean	Tipperary	II.	235
22,23,28,29	Kilduff	629 2 23	Tipperary, N.R.	Ikerrin	Killea	Roscrea	II.	275
7, 15	Kilduffahoo	862 1 23	Limerick	Owneybeg	Doon	Limerick	II.	251
5	Kilduff Lower	127 2 26	Cavan	Tullyhaw	Killinagh	Enniskillen	III.	92
27	Kilduff Lower	119 0 11	Clare	Tulla Upper	Tulla	Tulla	II.	41
5	Kilduff Middle	140 0 21	Cavan	Tullyhaw	Killinagh	Enniskillen	III.	92
27	Kilduff Middle	111 1 34	Clare	Tulla Upper	Tulla	Tulla	II.	41
5	Kilduff Upper	96 2 8c	Cavan	Tullyhaw	Killinagh	Enniskillen	III.	92
27	Kilduff Upper	206 0 39	Clare	Tulla Upper	Tulla	Tulla	II.	41
44, 56	Kildun	308 0 14	Mayo	Erris	Kilcommon	Newport	IV.	144
121	Kildun Beg	285 3 9	Mayo	Kilmaine	Cong	Ballinrobe	IV.	154
121	Kildun More	289 2 0	Mayo	Kilmaine	Cong	Ballinrobe	IV.	154
45	Kildurney	241 3 24	Roscommon	Athlone	Cam	Athlone	IV.	180
52	Kildurrihy East	237 1 13d	Kerry	Corkaguiny	Ventry	Dingle	II.	180
52	Kildurrihy West	269 2 11	Kerry	Corkaguiny	Ventry	Dingle	II.	180
40	Kileroe	109 0 22	Tipperary, N.R.	Kilnamanagh Upper	Glenkeen	Thurles	II.	278
4, 7	Kilfadda	744 3 17	Tipperary, N.R.	Lower Ormond	Aglishcloghane	Borrisokane	II.	281
94	Kilfadda Beg	213 1 5	Kerry	Glanarought	Kilgarvan	Kenmare	II.	187
85, 94	Kilfadda More	429 3 10	Kerry	Glanarought	Kilgarvan	Kenmare	II.	187
142	Kilfadeen	147 3 6e	Cork, W.R.	West Carbery (E.D.)	Kilmacabea	Skibbereen	II.	140
3	Kilfahavon	199 1 28	Monaghan	Trough	Errigal Trough	Monaghan	III.	284
39	Kilfallinga	633 1 23	Kerry	Trughanacmy	Currans	Killarney	II.	209
28	Kilfane Demesne	514 2 8	Kilkenny	Gowran	Kilfane	Thomastown	I.	97
28	Kilfane East	95 0 0	Kilkenny	Gowran	Kilfane	Thomastown	I.	97
24, 28	Kilfane West	91 0 12	Kilkenny	Gowran	Kilfane	Thomastown	I.	97
5	Kilfannan	184 2 3	Meath	Lower Kells	Moybolgue	Kells	I.	203
23, 31	Kilfarboy	430 1 32	Clare	Ibrickan	Kilfarboy	Ennistimon	II.	22
52	Kilfarnoge	247 2 2	Kerry	Corkaguiny	Ventry	Dingle	II.	180
25	Kilfarrasy	258 1 31	Waterford	Middlethird	Islandikane	Waterford	II.	367
3, 6	Kilfaughna	164 3 0	Roscommon	Boyle	Ardcarn	Boyle	IV.	193
15, 22	Kilfaughny	145 0 31	Westmeath	Kilkenny West	Kilkenny West	Athlone	I.	273
99	Kilfaul	379 0 32	Mayo	Carra	Ballyovey	Ballinrobe	IV.	126
78	Kilfea	181 3 18f	Mayo	Burrishoole	Islandeady	Westport	IV.	121
25	Kilfeacle	231 2 18	Queen's Co.	Ballyadams	Rathaspick	Athy	I.	232
55	Kilfeaghan	298 0 19	Down	Upper Iveagh,Up. pt.	Kilbroney	Kilkeel	III.	175
55	Kilfeaghan Upper	517 2 29	Down	Upper Iveagh,Up. pt.	Kilbroney	Kilkeel	III.	175
59, 67	Kilfeakle	1,208 0 4	Tipperary, S.R.	Clanwilliam	Kilfeacle	Tipperary	II.	308
59	Kilfeakle Church-quarter	286 3 14	Tipperary, S.R.	Clanwilliam	Kilfeacle	Tipperary	II.	308
56, 66	Kilfearagh	1,290 1 32	Clare	Moyarta	Kilfearagh	Kilrush	II.	32
16	Kilfeighny North	306 0 17	Kerry	Clanmaurice	Kilfeighny	Listowel	II.	170
16, 22	Kilfeighny South	445 3 26	Kerry	Clanmaurice	Kilfeighny	Listowel	II.	170
34	Kilfeilim	94 0 4	Clare	Bunratty Upper	Doora	Ennis	II.	8
39, 48	Kilfelim	179 1 16	Kerry	Trughanacmy	Killeentierna	Killarney	II.	211
59	Kilfelligy	83 0 22	Galway	Tiaquin	Killoscobe	Mountbellew	IV.	78
9, 16	Kilfenora	629 3 10	Clare	Corcomroe	Kilfenora	Ennistimon	II.	19
28	Kilfenora	123 3 34	Kerry	Trughanacmy	Ardfert	Tralee	II.	205

(a) Including 8A. 2R. 33P. water.
(b) Including 9A. 2R. 11P. water.
(c) Including 8A. 3R. 13P. water.
(d) Including 5A. 0R. 33P. water.
(e) Including 2A. 3R. 36P. water.
(f) Including 34A. 3R. 17P. water.

No. of Sheet of the Ordnance Survey Maps.	Townlands and Towns.	Area in Statute Acres.			County.	Barony.	Parish.	Poor Law Union in 1857.	Townland Census of 1851, Part I.	
		A.	R.	P.					Vol.	Page
16	KILFENORA T.	—			Clare	Corcomroe	Kilfenora	Ennistimon	II.	19
19, 20, 23	Kilferagh	365	0	0a	Kilkenny	Shillelogher	Kilferagh	Kilkenny	I.	115
17, 18	Kilfergus	109	3	37	Limerick	Shanid	Loghill	Glin	II.	257
142, 143	Kilfinnan	386	2	7	Cork, W.R.	East Carbery (W.D.)	Kilfaughnabeg	Skibbereen	II.	133
14, 20	Kilfinnan	287	0	29	Londonderry	Tirkeeran	Clondermot	Londonderry	III.	248
48, 56	Kilfinnane	667	1	14	Limerick	Coshlea	Kilfinnane	Kilmallock	II.	240
48, 56	KILFINNANE T.	—			Limerick	Coshlea	Kilfinnane	Kilmallock	II.	240
30	Kilfinny	717	3	0	Limerick	Connello Upper	Kilfinny	Croom	II.	233
16	Kilfintan	323	0	35	Longford	Ardagh	Street	Granard	I.	153
15, 16	Kilfintan Lower or Crancam	50	1	32	Longford	Ardagh	Street	Granard	I.	153
34	Kilfithmone	200	1	32	Tipperary, N.R.	Eliogarty	Kilfithmone	Thurles	II.	270
34	Kilfithmone	27	3	2	Tipperary, N.R.	Kilnamanagh Upper	Glenkeen	Thurles	II.	278
21	KILFLYN T.	—			Kerry	Clanmaurice	Kilflyn	Listowel	II.	170
43	Kilfountan	359	2	36	Kerry	Corkaguiny	Kildrum	Dingle	II.	177
1, 2, 7	Kilfoylan	672	2	15	King's Co.	Kilcoursey	Kilmanaghan	Tullamore	I.	141
42	Kilfrancis	167	1	27	King's Co.	Clonlisk	Shinrone	Roscrea	I.	131
44	Kilfree	835	0	0	Sligo	Coolavin	Kilfree	Boyle	IV.	224
40, 41	Kilfrush	797	1	1	Limerick	Smallcounty	Kilfrush	Kilmallock	II.	260
20	Kilfullert	131	3	33	Down	Lower Iveagh, Up. pt.	Magheralin	Lurgan	III.	170
37, 38	Kilgabriel	601	3	4	Waterford	Decies within Drum	Kinsalebeg	Youghal	II.	352
38	Kilgad	606	1	24	Antrim	Lower Antrim	Connor	Ballymena	III.	3
1	Kilgainy Lower	50	0	1b	Waterford	Upperthird	St. Marys Clonmel	Clonmel	II.	372
1	Kilgainy Upper	93	2	19	Waterford	Upperthird	St. Marys Clonmel	Clonmel	II.	372
3, 4	Kilgalligan	852	2	7	Mayo	Erris	Kilcommon	Belmullet	IV.	144
4, 8	Kilgar	475	2	35	Westmeath	Delvin	Castletowndelvin	Castletowndelvin	I.	264
37, 38	Kilgaroan	345	0	20	Westmeath	Moycashel	Ardnurcher or Horse-leap	Tullamore	I.	276
7	Kilgarran	22	3	38	Wicklow	Rathdown	Powerscourt	Rathdown	I.	356
40	Kilgarrett	145	0	2	Fermanagh	Coole	Galloon	Clones	III.	200
122, 135	Kilgarriff	835	0	9	Cork, W.R.	East Carbery (E.D.)	Kilgarriff	Clonakilty	II.	129
56	Kilgarriff	283	0	18	Galway	Clare	Kilcoona	Tuam	IV.	20
18	Kilgarriff	200	0	22	Leitrim	Drumahaire	Drumreilly	Car^k.on Shannon	IV.	95
57	Kilgarriff	662	3	2	Limerick	Coshlea	Ballingarry	Kilmallock	II.	237
92	Kilgarriff	403	0	11	Mayo	Costello	Aghamore	Claremorris	IV.	137
52, 64	Kilgarriff	788	3	35c	Mayo	Costello	Kilbeagh	Swineford	IV.	140
30	Kilgarriff North	214	2	14d	Galway	Ballymoe	Tuam	Tuam	IV.	10
30	Kilgarriff South	77	0	33e	Galway	Ballymoe	Tuam	Tuam	IV.	10
72, 73	Kilgarriff West	1,139	2	33	Mayo	Costello	Kilbeagh	Swineford	IV.	140
85	Kilgarriv	529	0	2	Kerry	Glanarought	Kilgarvan	Kenmare	II.	187
12, 16	Kilgarron or Janeville	232	3	10	Carlow	Idrone East	Fennagh	Carlow	I.	7
43	Kilgarrow	143	2	25f	Fermanagh	Coole	Drummully	Clones	III.	199
14	Kilgarrow	145	2	21	Fermanagh	Magheraboy	Devenish	Enniskillen	III.	211
32	Kilgarrow Glebe	86	1	4	Fermanagh	Clanawley	Kinawley	Enniskillen	III.	194
87	Kilgarvan	83	2	31	Cork, E.R.	Barrymore	Templerobin	Cork	II.	58
5	Kilgarvan	1,176	3	14	Kerry	Iraghticonnor	Lisselton	Listowel	II.	192
40	Kilgarvan	820	3	5	Mayo	Gallen	Kilgarvan	Ballina	IV.	148
6, 9	Kilgarvan	182	3	11	Tipperary, N.R.	Lower Ormond	Kilbarron	Borrisokane	II.	284
35	Kilgarvan	228	3	23	Westmeath	Clonlonan	Kilcleagh	Athlone	I.	261
36	Kilgarvan	316	2	21	Wexford	Shelmaliere West	Kilgarvan	New Ross	I.	334
35	Kilgarvan Glebe	1,363	1	2	Westmeath	Clonlonan	Kilcleagh	Athlone	I.	261
94	KILGARVAN T.	—			Kerry	Glanarought	Kilgarvan	Kenmare	II.	188
30	Kilgarve	103	0	37	Cavan	Tullyhunco	Killashandra	Cavan	III.	98
59, 68, 69	Kilgarve	714	3	30	Mayo	Carra	Islandeady	Castlebar	IV.	129
18	Kilgarve	324	0	19	Roscommon	Ballintober North	Kilglass	Strokestown	IV.	186
4	Kilgarve	179	0	7	Roscommon	Boyle	Kilronan	Boyle	IV.	197
20	Kilgarve	715	0	15	Roscommon	Frenchpark	Tibohine	Castlereagh	IV.	205
53	Kilgarve	224	1	21	Roscommon	Moycarn	Creagh	Ballinasloe	IV.	206
58	Kilgarve North	315	2	29	Galway	Tiaquin	Abbeyknockmoy	Tuam	IV.	75
58	Kilgarve South	57	3	27	Galway	Tiaquin	Abbeyknockmoy	Tuam	IV.	75
4, 7	Kilgask	663	0	0	Tipperary, N.R.	Lower Ormond	Lorrha	Borrisokane	II.	285
44	Kilgavanagh	215	1	29	Antrim	Upper Toome	Antrim	Antrim	III.	33
17	Kilgawny	533	0	25	Westmeath	Rathconrath	Piercetown	Mullingar	I.	283
86, 96	Kilgeever	546	0	39	Mayo	Murrisk	Kilgeever	Westport	IV.	160
40, 49	Kilgellia	518	0	3g	Mayo	Gallen	Attymass	Ballina	IV.	147
74	Kilgerrill	186	0	33	Galway	Clonmacnowen	Kilgerrill	Ballinasloe	IV.	25
16	Kilgevrin	767	0	31	Galway	Dunmore	Liskeevy	Tuam	IV.	35
26, 32	Kilgibbon	480	2	3	Wexford	Shelmaliere West	Clonmore	Enniscorthy	I.	333
24	Kilgilky North	173	2	14	Cork, E.R.	Duhallow	Castlemagner	Kanturk	II	67
24	Kilgilky South	378	3	18	Cork, E.R.	Duhallow	Castlemagner	Kanturk	II.	67
57, 70	Kilgill	311	3	19	Galway	Clare	Annaghdown	Tuam	IV.	16
61	Kilglass	465	1	0	Galway	Clonmacnowen	Ahascragh	Mountbellew	IV.	24
3	Kilglass	443	0	14	Kildare	Carbury	Kilrainy	Edenderry	I.	52

(a) Including 5A. 0R. 36P. River Nore.
(b) Including 5A. 2R. 38P. water.
(c) Including 2A. 2R. 12P. water.

(d) Including 1A. 3R. 15P. water.
(e) Including 18A. 2R. 29P. water.

(f) Including 16A. 3R. 20P. water.
(g) Including 36A. 2R. 35P. water.

No. of Sheet of the Ordnance Survey Maps.	Townlands and Towns.	Area in Statute Acres.	County.	Barony.	Parish.	Poor Law Union in 1857.	Townland Census of 1851, Part I.	
		A. R. P.					Vol.	Page
57, 60	Kilglass . . .	671 1 18	Limerick .	Coshlea . . .	Kilbeheny . .	Mitchelstown .	II.	239
42	Kilglass . . .	161 0 30	Roscommon .	Athlone . . .	Kilmeane . .	Roscommon .	IV.	182
16	Kilglass . . .	308 1 19	Sligo . .	Tireragh . .	Kilglass . .	Dromore West .	IV.	234
119	Kilglassan . .	281 3 4	Mayo . .	Kilmaine . .	Kilcommon .	Ballinrobe .	IV.	154
19, 23	Kilglass & Cloonagh	70 2 5	Longford . .	Ardagh . . .	Kilglass . .	Ballymahon .	I.	152
41	Kilglassy . .	92 0 7	Clare . .	Islands . . .	Killone . .	Ennis . .	II.	30
49	Kilglin . . .	336 3 37	Meath . .	Upper Deece .	Balfeaghan .	Celbridge .	I.	193
34	Kilgobban . .	156 2 10	Clare . .	Bunratty Upper .	Clooney . .	Tulla . .	II.	8
32	Kilgobban . .	152 3 10	Cork, E.R. .	Duhallow . .	Ballyclogh .	Mallow . .	II.	67
15	Kilgobban . .	73 1 37	Mayo . .	Tirawley . .	Killala . .	Killala .	IV.	169
111, 124	Kilgobbin . .	1,263 0 37	Cork, W.R. .	East Carbery (E.D.)	Ballinadee .	Bandon .	II.	126
22,23,25,26	Kilgobbin . .	440 2 24	Dublin . .	Rathdown . .	Kilgobbin .	Rathdown .	I.	35
12, 21	Kilgobbin . .	439 3 14	Limerick .	Coshma . .	Adare . .	Croom .	II.	241
41	Kilgobnet . .	111 2 33	Cork, E.R. .	Duhallow . .	Kilshannig .	Mallow . .	II.	74
72	Kilgobnet . .	310 3 34	Cork, E.R. .	East Muskerry .	Magourney .	Macroom .	II.	105
59	Kilgobnet . .	318 3 20	Cork, W.R. .	West Muskerry .	Clondrohid .	Macroom .	II.	155
65	Kilgobnet . .	271 3 28	Kerry . .	Dunkerron North .	Knockane .	Killarney .	II.	182
23, 31	Kilgobnet . .	300 1 2	Waterford .	Decies without Drum	Kilgobnet .	Dungarvan .	II.	357
41	Kilgolagh . .	399 1 32a	Cavan . .	Clanmahon .	Drumlumman .	Granard .	III.	77
31	Kilgolan Lower .	175 0 3	King's Co. .	Ballyboy . .	Ballyboy . .	Parsonstown .	I.	123
31	Kilgolan Upper .	144 1 13	King's Co. .	Ballyboy . .	Ballyboy . .	Parsonstown .	I.	123
37	Kilgolban . .	414 3 34	Limerick . .	Glenquin . .	Clonelty . .	Newcastle .	II.	245
99	Kilgole . . .	132 3 20	Donegal . .	Tirhugh . .	Drumhome .	Donegal .	III.	146
81	Kilgoly . . .	64 3 3	Donegal . .	Banagh . .	Glencolumbkille .	Glenties .	III.	105
7	Kilgorman . .	53 0 4	Wexford . .	Gorey . .	Kilgorman .	Gorey .	I.	318
12	Kilgormly . .	100 0 5	Monaghan .	Dartree . .	Clones . . .	Clones .	III.	264
54, 55	Kilgort . . .	147 0 24	Donegal . .	Raphoe . .	Taughboyne .	Londonderry .	III.	143
29	Kilgort . . .	1,029 2 16	Londonderry .	Tirkeeran .	Cumber Upper .	Londonderry .	III.	249
43, 51	Kilgort . . .	295 0 16	Tyrone . .	Clogher . .	Donacavey .	Omagh .	III.	294
93	Kilgortaree . .	412 3 22	Kerry . .	Glanarought .	Kenmare .	Kenmare .	II.	186
21, 22	Kilgorteen . .	201 0 36	Tipperary, N.R.	Upper Ormond .	Ballymackey .	Nenagh .	II.	289
16	Kilgortin . .	123 3 13	King's Co. .	Ballycowan .	Kilbride . .	Tullamore .	I.	127
16	Kilgortin . .	201 1 29	King's Co. .	Ballycowan .	Rahan . .	Tullamore .	I.	128
16	Kilgortnaleague .	200 1 29	Fermanagh .	Tirkennedy .	Magheracross .	Enniskillen .	III.	223
35	Kilgory . . .	324 1 14b	Clare . .	Tulla Upper .	Kilnoe . .	Tulla . .	II.	40
36	Kilgory . . .	363 0 32	Queen's Co. .	Slievemargy .	Killabban .	Carlow .	I.	245
28, 32	Kilgowan . .	696 0 1	Kildare . .	Kilcullen .	Kilcullen .	Naas .	I.	58
67	Kilgowney . .	113 0 25	Tyrone . .	Dungannon Lower .	Aghaloo . .	Armagh .	III.	297
23,24,29,30	Kilgraffy . .	84 1 33	Roscommon .	Ballintober North .	Kilglass .	Strokestown .	IV.	186
50	Kilgraigue . .	385 3 0	Meath . .	Upper Deece .	Moyglare .	Celbridge .	I.	194
18	Kilgraney . .	78 2 9	Carlow . .	Forth . .	Aghade . .	Carlow .	I.	3
17, 18	Kilgraney . .	246 0 19	Carlow . .	Forth . .	Barragh . .	Carlow .	I.	4
19	Kilgraney . .	890 0 18c	Carlow . .	Idrone East .	Lorum . .	Carlow .	I.	8
49	Kilgreana . .	81 1 28	Limerick . .	Coshlea . .	Galbally . .	Mitchelstown .	II.	238
100	Kilgreana . .	244 2 28d	Mayo . .	Kilmaine . .	Mayo . .	Ballinrobe .	IV.	157
30	Kilgreany . .	186 1 0	Waterford .	Decies without Drum	Whitechurch .	Dungarvan .	II.	361
5	Kilgreany . .	256 0 36	Waterford .	Glenahiry . .	Kilronan .	Clonmel .	II.	365
51, 56	Kilgreel . . .	1,000 1 8	Antrim . .	Lower Belfast .	Templepatrick .	Antrim .	III.	9
52, 59	Kilgreen Lower .	88 0 23	Tyrone . .	Clogher . .	Errigal Keerogue .	Clogher .	III.	295
52, 59	Kilgreen Upper .	73 2 15	Tyrone . .	Clogher . .	Errigal Keerogue .	Clogher .	III.	295
76, 88	Kilgrellane . .	89 2 24	Cork, E.R. .	Imokilly . .	Cloyne . .	Middleton .	II.	85
7	Kilgrogan . .	231 1 21	Cork, E.R. .	Orrery and Kilmore	Kilgrogan .	Mallow . .	II.	109
20, 21	Kilgrogan . .	237 0 31	Limerick . .	Kenry . .	Adare . .	Croom .	II.	248
87	Kilgrogy Beg .	17 0 26	Tipperary, S.R.	Iffa and Offa West .	Ballybacon .	Clogheen .	II.	317
87, 88	Kilgrogy More .	191 2 22	Tipperary, S.R.	Iffa and Offa West .	Ballybacon .	Clogheen .	II.	317
31	Kilgrovan . .	68 2 15	Waterford .	Decies without Drum	Clonea . .	Dungarvan .	II.	354
21	Kilgulbin East .	555 3 20	Kerry . .	Clanmaurice .	O'Dorney .	Tralee .	II.	172
21	Kilgulbin West .	456 2 11	Kerry . .	Clanmaurice .	O'Dorney .	Tralee .	II.	172
19	Kilgullane . .	256 1 25	Cork, E.R. .	Condons&Clangibbon	Kilgullane .	Mitchelstown .	II.	61
69	Kilhale . . .	830 3 8	Mayo . .	Carra . .	Islandeady .	Castlebar .	IV.	129
78, 83, 84	Kilheffernan . .	209 0 3e	Tipperary, S.R.	Iffa and Offa East .	Killaloan .	Clonmel .	II.	314
44	Kilhile . . .	446 1 37	Wexford . .	Shelburne .	St.James&Dunbrody	New Ross .	I.	328
109	Kilhonerush or Wood-lands . . .	116 3 35	Galway . .	Longford . .	Meelick . .	Portumna .	IV.	61
17	Kilhoyle . . .	813 0 16	Londonderry .	Keenaght .	Balteagh . .	NewᵀⁿLimavady	III.	234
32	Kilhugh . . .	404 1 6	Westmeath .	Moycashel .	Castletownkindalen	Mullingar .	I.	277
28	Kiljames Lower .	222 2 39	Kilkenny . .	Gowran . .	Columbkille .	Thomastown .	I.	94
28	Kiljames Upper .	248 2 39	Kilkenny . .	Gowran . .	Columbkille .	Thomastown .	I.	94
37, 38	Kilkea Lower .	438 2 19	Kildare . .	Kilkea and Moone .	Kilkea . .	Athy .	I.	60
84, 93	Kilkeana . .	645 1 15f	Kerry . .	Glanarought .	Kenmare .	Kenmare .	II.	186
5	Kilkeany . .	243 3 24	Waterford .	Decies without Drum	Seskinan . .	Dungarvan .	II.	360
5, 13	Kilkeanymountain .	236 1 30	Waterford .	Decies without Drum	Seskinan . .	Dungarvan .	II.	360
21, 27	Kilkeary . .	366 1 9	Tipperary, N.R.	Upper Ormond .	Kilkeary . .	Nenagh .	II.	290

(a) Including 21A. 3R. 3P. water.　　(c) Including 3A. 0R. 24P. River Barrow.　　(e) Including 4A. 1R. 13P. water.
(b) Including 51A. 3R. 32P. water.　　(d) Including 1A. 2R. 32P. water.　　(f) Including 11A. 0R. 35P. water.

4 C

No. of Sheet of the Ordnance Survey Maps.	Townlands and Towns.	Area in Statute Acres.	County.	Barony.	Parish.	Poor Law Union in 1857.	Townland Census of 1851, Part I.	
		A. R. P.					Vol.	Page
8	Kilkeaskin	990 1 6	Kildare	Carbury	Kilpatrick	Edenderry	I.	52
31, 35, 36	Kilkeasy	1,508 1 24	Kilkenny	Knocktopher	Kilkeasy	Thomastown	I.	112
37	Kilkea Upper	532 1 11	Kildare	Kilkea and Moone	Kilkea	Athy	I.	60
87, 88	Kilkeaveragh	231 1 22	Kerry	Iveragh	Killemlagh	Cahersiveen	II.	196
25	Kilkee East	211 1 18	Clare	Inchiquin	Ruan	Corrofin	II.	28
63	Kilkeehagh	653 2 34	Kerry	Iveragh	Glanbehy	Cahersiveen	II.	196
55, 56	Kilkeel	554 1 19	Down	Mourne	Kilkeel	Kilkeel	III.	183
23	Kilkeelan	681 2 16	Meath	Lune	Athboy	Trim	I.	207
56	Kilkee Lower	100 1 27	Clare	Moyarta	Kilfearagh	Kilrush	II.	32
55, 56	KILKEEL T.	—	Down	Mourne	Kilkeel	Kilkeel	III.	183
33	Kilkeeran	502 3 13	King's Co.	Upper Philipstown	Clonyhurk	Mountmellick	I.	143
99,109,110	Kilkeeran	373 2 24	Mayo	Carra	Ballyovey	Ballinrobe	IV.	126
74	Kilkeeran	241 2 19	Mayo	Costello	Castlemore	Castlereagh	IV.	140
117, 118	Kilkeeran	246 2 0a	Mayo	Kilmaine	Ballinrobe	Ballinrobe	IV.	153
121	Kilkeeran	309 3 6	Mayo	Kilmaine	Kilmainebeg	Ballinrobe	IV.	155
46	Kilkeeran	151 1 12	Meath	Upper Moyfenrath	Castlejordan	Edenderry	I.	212
56	KILKEE T.	—	Clare	Moyarta	Kilfearagh	Kilrush	II.	32
56	Kilkee Upper	129 1 21	Clare	Moyarta	Kilfearagh	Kilrush	II.	32
25	Kilkee West	138 3 10	Clare	Inchiquin	Ruan	Corrofin	II.	28
72, 81	Kilkelly	46 0 18	Mayo	Costello	Kilmovee	Swineford	IV.	142
72, 81	KILKELLY T.	—	Mayo	Costello	Kilmovee	Swineford	IV.	142
65	Kilkenny	143 3 33	Donegal	Boylagh	Inishkeel	Glenties	III.	113
78	Kilkenny	91 3 12	Mayo	Carra	Breaghwy	Castlebar	IV.	127
51	Kilkenny	343 1 1	Roscommon	Athlone	Taghmaconnell	Athlone	IV.	185
23	Kilkenny Abbey	279 3 10	Westmeath	Kilkenny West	Kilkenny West	Athlone	I.	273
54, 62	Kilkennybeg	898 2 1	Tipperary, S.R.	Middlethird	St. Johnstown	Cashel	II.	330
22, 23	Kilkenny Lanesborough	122 3 11	Westmeath	Kilkenny West	Kilkenny West	Athlone	I.	273
19	KILKENNY CITY	—	—	—	—	Kilkenny	I.	117
22, 23	Kilkenny West	485 3 15b	Westmeath	Kilkenny West	Kilkenny West	Athlone	I.	273
143, 144	Kilkeran	560 1 13c	Cork, W.R.	Ibane and Barryroe	Rathbarry	Clonakilty	II.	150
41	Kilkere	154 1 12d	Sligo	Tirerrill	Kilmactranny	Boyle	IV.	240
68	Kilkerin	734 1 7	Clare	Clonderalaw	Killofin	Killadysert	II.	17
124	Kilkerran North	260 3 34	Cork, W.R.	Courceys	Ringrone	Kinsale	II.	147
124	Kilkerran South	230 0 9	Cork, W.R.	Courceys	Ringrone	Kinsale	II.	147
31	Kilkerrin	234 2 27	Galway	Tiaquin	Kilkerrin	Glennamaddy	IV.	77
39	Kilkerry	101 3 7	Kerry	Trughanacmy	Ballymacelligott	Tralee	II.	207
13	Kilkey	181 3 20	Carlow	Forth	Fennagh	Carlow	I.	4
42	Kilkieran	41 3 39	Clare	Bunratty Lower	Kilnasoolagh	Ennis	II.	6
64, 77	Kilkieran	2,255 0 33e	Galway	Ballynahinch	Moyrus	Clifden	IV.	13
29	Kilkieran	313 0 35	Kilkenny	Gowran	Inistioge	Thomastown	I.	96
14, 15	Kilkieran	749 0 1	Kilkenny	Gowran	Kilkieran	Kilkenny	I.	97
35, 41	Kilkillahara	578 2 16	Tipperary, N.R.	Eliogarty	Loughmoe West	Thurles	II.	271
140, 149	Kilkilleen	239 1 14	Cork, W.R.	West Carbery (E.D.)	Aghadown	Skibbereen	II.	137
2, 3	Kilkilloge	486 3 8	Sligo	Carbury	Ahamlish	Sligo	IV.	219
42	Kilkilvery	189 1 11	Galway	Clare	Kilkilvery	Tuam	IV.	20
28, 35	Kilkinamurry	1,174 1 13	Down	Upper Iveagh, Lr. pt.	Garvaghy	Banbridge	III.	173
42, 51	Kilkinlea Lower	807 0 17f	Limerick	Glenquin	Abbeyfeale	Newcastle	II.	244
42, 51	Kilkinlea Upper	818 1 23g	Limerick	Glenquin	Abbeyfeale	Newcastle	II.	244
127	Kilkinnikin East	331 2 36	Cork, W.R.	Bear	Kilnamanagh	Castletown	II.	126
127	KILKINNIKIN T.	—	Cork, W.R.	Bear	Kilnamanagh	Castletown	II.	126
127	Kilkinnikin West	401 0 24	Cork, W.R.	Bear	Kilnamanagh	Castletown	II.	126
23	Kilkip East	52 3 24	Tipperary, N.R.	Ikerrin	Killea	Roscrea	II.	275
23, 29	Kilkip West	124 1 4	Tipperary, N.R.	Ikerrin	Killea	Roscrea	II.	275
43	Kilkishen	129 0 5	Clare	Bunratty Lower	Kilmurry	Tulla	II.	6
43	Kilkishen Demesne	325 1 17h	Clare	Bunratty Lower	Kilmurry	Tulla	II.	6
43	Kilkishen Demesne	58 3 7	Clare	Tulla Lower	Clonlea	Tulla	II.	34
43	KILKISHEN T.	—	Clare	Tulla Lower	Clonlea	Tulla	II.	35
24	Kilkit	292 1 6	Monaghan	Cremorne	Aghamullen	Castleblayney	III.	258
135	Kilkittaun	224 0 23i	Galway	Leitrim	Clonrush	Scarriff	IV.	53
58	Kilkneedan	111 1 17	Kerry	Magunihy	Kilcredane	Killarney	II.	200
43	Kilknock	459 3 19	Antrim	Upper Toome	Drummaul	Ballymena	III.	34
13, 17	Kilknock	74 3 0	Carlow	Forth	Ballyellin	Carlow	I.	4
13, 17	Kilknock	883 1 33	Carlow	Forth	Kellistown	Carlow	I.	5
79	Kilknock	246 2 6j	Mayo	Carra	Breaghwy	Castlebar	IV.	127
102	Kilknock	315 2 23	Mayo	Costello	Bekan	Claremorris	IV.	139
57	Kilknock	296 1 38k	Tyrone	Omagh East	Kilskeery	Enniskillen	III.	313
33	Kilknockan	198 1 39	Cork, E.R.	Fermoy	Mallow	Mallow	II.	81
21	Kilknockan	199 3 21	Limerick	Kenry	Adare	Croom	II.	248
62, 70	Kilknockan	753 0 14	Tipperary, S.R.	Middlethird	Rathcool	Cashel	II.	329
38	Kilknockan	201 2 6	Waterford	Decies within Drum	Ardmore	Youghal	II.	350
15	Kilknockane	675 1 33	Cork, E.R.	Duhallow	Clonfert	Kanturk	II.	68
01, 07	Kill	486 3 15l	Cavan	Clanmahon	Crosserlough	Cavan	III.	76
84,85,96,97	Kill	224 1 34	Cork, E.R.	East Muskerry	Knockavilly	Bandon	II.	104

(a) Including 2A. 1R. 19P. water.
(b) Including 26A. 1R. 24P. water.
(c) Including 13A. 0R. 29P. water.
(d) Including 11A. 3R. 21P. water.
(e) Including 18A. 2R. 25P. water.
(f) Including 28A. 2R. 16P. water.
(g) Including 6A. 0R. 32P. water.
(h) Including 34A. 0R. 32P. water.
(i) Including 17A. 0R. 6P. water.
(j) Including 25A. 3R. 2P. water.
(k) Including 0A. 1R. 17P. water.
(l) Including 15A. 3R. 24P. water.

No. of Sheet of the Ordnance Survey Maps.	Townlands and Towns.	Area in Statute Acres. A. R. P.	County.	Barony.	Parish.	Poor Law Union in 1857.	Townland Census of 1851, Part I. Vol.	Page
71	Kill	224 3 32	Cork, W.R.	West Muskerry	Macroom	Macroom	II.	160
97	Kill	207 2 36	Donegal	Banagh	Kilcar	Glenties	III.	108
15,16,25,26	Kill	541 1 31	Donegal	Kilmacrenan	Clondahorky	Dunfanaghy	III.	123
26	Kill	549 3 17a	Donegal	Kilmacrenan	Mevagh	Milford	III.	130
35	Kill	289 3 15b	Galway	Ballynahinch	Ballindoon	Clifden	IV.	10
22, 35	Kill	274 0 15	Galway	Ballynahinch	Omey	Clifden	IV.	15
88, 100	Kill	120 3 19	Galway	Clonmacnowen	Clontuskert	Ballinasloe	IV.	24
99, 107	Kill	416 3 18	Galway	Longford	Kiltormer	Ballinasloe	IV.	60
118	Kill	325 2 29	Galway	Longford	Tiranascragh	Portumna	IV.	62
14, 20	Kill	30 0 19	Kerry	Clanmaurice	Ardfert	Tralee	II.	167
65	Kill	699 2 20	Kerry	Dunkerron North	Knockane	Killarney	II.	182
26	Kill	262 3 30	Kildare	Offaly West	Monasterevin	Athy	I.	73
2	Kill	331 3 18	Kilkenny	Fassadinin	Rathaspick	Castlecomer	I.	91
121, 122	Kill	193 2 27c	Mayo	Kilmaine	Moorgagagh	Ballinrobe	IV.	157
85	Kill	430 0 39	Mayo	Murrisk	Kilgeever	Westport	IV.	161
64	Kill	652 2 31d	Tyrone	Clogher	Aghalurcher	Clogher	III.	291
36	Kill	175 2 25	Westmeath	Clonlonan	Kilcleagh	Athlone	I.	261
11, 18	Kill	222 2 12	Westmeath	Moygoish	Kilbixy	Mullingar	I.	279
21, 27	Kill	215 0 21	Wicklow	Upper Talbotstown	Rathbran	Baltinglass	I.	365
86	Killaan	345 2 35	Galway	Kilconnell	Killaan	Ballinasloe	IV.	41
26	Killabban	673 1 9	Queen's Co.	Ballyadams	Killabban	Athy	I.	231
20	Killabeg	800 2 26e	Wexford	Scarawalsh	Clone	Enniscorthy	I.	322
37, 42	Killabeg	414 0 3	Wicklow	Shillelagh	Aghowle	Shillelagh	I.	356
7	Killabraher North	674 0 13	Cork, E.R.	Orrery and Kilmore	Shandrum	Kanturk	II.	110
7	Killabraher South	320 0 28	Cork, E.R.	Orrery and Kilmore	Shandrum	Kanturk	II.	110
31	Killabrick	167 1 2	Monaghan	Farney	Donaghmoyne	Carrickmacross	III.	270
102	Killabunane	563 1 26	Kerry	Glanarought	Kilcaskan	Kenmare	II.	187
87,88,96,97	Killabuonia	696 0 5	Kerry	Iveragh	Killemlagh	Cahersiveen	II.	196
30	Killachonna (Castlemaine)	77 1 21	Westmeath	Clonlonan	Ballyloughloe	Athlone	I.	260
30	Killachonna (Clibborn)	142 3 38	Westmeath	Clonlonan	Ballyloughloe	Athlone	I.	260
30	Killachonna (Potts)	10 1 25	Westmeath	Clonlonan	Ballyloughloe	Athlone	I.	260
107, 108	Killachunna	525 3 36	Galway	Longford	Kilquain	Portumna	IV.	60
73, 74	Killaclare	252 3 10	Mayo	Costello	Kilmovee	Swineford	IV.	142
58,59,71,72	Killaclogher	695 0 17	Galway	Tiaquin	Monivea	Tuam	IV.	79
47	Killaclohane	509 1 34	Kerry	Trughanacmy	Kilcolman	Killarney	II.	210
34, 39	Killacloran	1,386 2 13	Wicklow	Ballinacor South	Kilpipe	Rathdrum	I.	349
64, 75	Killacloyne	328 2 36	Cork, E.R.	Barrymore	Caherlag	Middleton	II.	52
75	Killacloyne	184 0 32	Cork, E.R.	Barrymore	Carrigtohill	Middleton	II.	52
70	Killaclug	215 3 34	Cork, W.R.	West Muskerry	Clondrohid	Macroom	II.	155
10	Killaclug East	189 3 5	Cork, E.R.	Condons&Clangibbon	Marshalstown	Mitchelstown	II.	63
10, 19	Killaclug West	202 0 9	Cork, E.R.	Condons&Clangibbon	Marshalstown	Mitchelstown	II.	63
46	Killacolla	369 0 3	Limerick	Connello Upper	Corcomohide	Kilmallock	II.	232
9, 18	Killacolla	666 1 37	Limerick	Shanid	Kilfergus	Glin	II.	256
17	Killacolla (Barker)	91 2 24	Limerick	Shanid	Kilfergus	Glin	II.	256
10, 16	Killaconin or Jonesborough	252 3 0	Meath	Upper Kells	Loughan or Castlekeeran	Kells	I.	207
6	Killaconner	107 3 24	Louth	Upper Dundalk	Inishkeen	Dundalk	I.	179
35	Killaconnigan	649 1 37	Meath	Lune	Killaconnigan	Trim	I.	208
142, 143	Killacoosane	66 3 20	Cork, W.R.	East Carbery (W.D.)	Kilfaughnabeg	Skibbereen	II.	133
37, 38	Killacorraun	1,282 3 18	Mayo	Tirawley	Crossmolina	Ballina	IV.	166
10, 16	Killacrim	211 3 32f	Kerry	Iraghticonnor	Dysert	Listowel	II.	190
22	Killacroy	209 1 5	Meath	Fore	Killallon	Oldcastle	I.	200
43	Killaculleen	1,296 2 27	Limerick	Glenquin	Killeedy	Newcastle	II.	246
74	Killadangan	220 1 34	Mayo	Costello	Castlemore	Castlereagh	IV.	140
87	Killadangan	218 3 14g	Mayo	Murrisk	Oughaval	Westport	IV.	162
14	Killadangan	781 2 31	Tipperary, N.R.	Lower Ormond	Killodiernan	Nenagh	II.	285
30, 31	Killadangan	400 3 12	Waterford	Decies without Drum	Kilgobnet	Dungarvan	II.	357
6	Killadden	226 2 5	Meath	Lower Slane	Loughbrackan	Ardee	I.	223
89	Killadeer	720 3 9h	Mayo	Carra	Ballintober	Castlebar	IV.	125
78, 89	Killadeer	870 1 14i	Mayo	Carra	Ballyhean	Castlebar	IV.	125
141,142,150,151	Killaderry	196 1 15j	Cork, W.R.	West Carbery (E.D.)	Castlehaven	Skibbereen	II.	138
61	Killaderry	590 1 26	Galway	Killian	Taghboy	Mountbellew	IV.	45
10, 18	Killaderry	322 2 38	King's Co.	Lower Philipstown	Killaderry	Tullamore	I.	143
44	Killaderry (Massy)	166 1 12	Clare	Tulla Lower	Kilseily	Limerick	II.	37
43, 44	Killaderry (O'Brien)	203 3 13	Clare	Tulla Lower	Kilseily	Limerick	II.	37
18	Killadiskert	155 1 25	Leitrim	Drumahaire	Inishmagrath	Manorhamilton	IV.	96
27, 28	Killadooley	357 1 10	Queen's Co.	Clandonagh	Donaghmore	Donaghmore	I.	233
27, 28	Killadooley	222 1 8k	Queen's Co.	Clandonagh	Skirk	Donaghmore	I.	235
11, 15	Killadoon	449 0 3l	Kildare	North Salt	Killadoon	Celbridge	I.	75
95, 105	Killadoon	438 0 1m	Mayo	Murrisk	Kilgeever	Westport	IV.	160
34	Killadoon	140 2 27	Sligo	Tirerrill	Killadoon	Boyle	IV.	239
25	Killadough	125 1 22	Leitrim	Carrigallen	Oughteragh	Bawnboy	IV.	92

(a) Including 6A. 1R. 13P. water.
(b) Including 14A. 3R. 32P. water.
(c) Including 10A. 2R. 5P. water.
(d) Including 3A. 2R. 34P. water.
(e) Including 7A. 1R. 0P. water.
(f) Including 12A. 0R. 0P. water.
(g) Including 7A. 2R. 26P. water.
(h) Including 3A. 0R. 35P. water.
(i) Including 41A. 3R. 16P. water.
(j) Including 0A. 1R. 8P. water.
(k) Including 24A. 2R. 17P. detached portion.
(l) Including 12A. 2R. 16P. water.
(m) Including 53A. 3R. 22P. water.

No. of Sheet of the Ordnance Survey Maps	Townlands and Towns.	Area in Statute Acres.	County.	Barony.	Parish.	Poor Law Union in 1857.	Townland Census of 1851, Part I. Vol.	Page
		A. R. P.						
8, 13	Killadoughran	420 2 2a	Westmeath	Delvin	Castletowndelvin	Castletowndelvin	I.	264
13, 19	Killadreenan	579 1 29	Wicklow	Newcastle	Newcastle Lower	Rathdrum	I.	353
31	Killadrown	157 0 1	King's Co.	Eglish	Drumcullen	Parsonstown	I.	134
43, 51	Killadroy	665 2 0	Tyrone	Omagh East	Clogherny	Omagh	III.	310
34	Killaduff	582 0 28	Wicklow	Ballinacor South	Kilpipe	Shillelagh	I.	349
107	Killadullisk	382 2 1	Galway	Longford	Kilquain	Portumna	IV.	60
59, 60	Killadysert	298 0 32b	Clare	Clonderalaw	Killadysert	Killadysert	II.	16
59, 60	KILLADYSERT T.	—	Clare	Clonderalaw	Killadysert	Killadysert	II.	16
129	Killafeen	157 1 32	Galway	Kiltartan	Kilbeacanty	Gort	IV.	47
33	Killafinta	52 1 20	Fermanagh	Clanawley	Kinawley	Enniskillen	III.	194
46, 51, 52	Killag	327 0 28	Wexford	Bargy	Killag	Wexford	I.	306
14	Killagally Glebe	195 1 14	King's Co.	Garrycastle	Wheery or Killagally	Parsonstown	I.	139
13, 20, 21	Killagh	851 3 16	Westmeath	Delvin	Killagh	Castletowndelvin	I.	265
7	Killaghaduff	99 1 27	Cavan	Tullyhaw	Kinawley	Bawnboy	III.	93
60	Killaghaun	209 0 37	Galway	Tiaquin	Ballymacward	Mountbellew	IV.	75
86	Killagh Beg	429 2 36	Galway	Kilconnell	Killallaghtan	Ballinasloe	IV.	41
7	Killaghintober	475 1 28	King's Co.	Garrycastle	Lemanaghan	Parsonstown	I.	136
86	Killagh More	1,016 2 28	Galway	Kilconnell	Killallaghtan	Ballinasloe	IV.	41
88	Killaghoor	264 2 24c	Mayo	Murrisk	Oughaval	Westport	IV.	162
98	Killaghtee	135 2 36	Donegal	Banagh	Killaghtee	Donegal	III.	109
36	Killaghteen	626 1 15	Limerick	Glenquin	Ardagh	Newcastle	II.	244
69	Killaghwaun	85 0 27d	Mayo	Carra	Islandeady	Castlebar	IV.	129
6	Killaghy	139 3 23	Armagh	Oneilland East	Shankill	Lurgan	III.	51
6	Killaghy	984 3 10e	Down	Ards Lower	Donaghadee	Newtownards	III.	158
40	Killaghy	60 0 36	Fermanagh	Coole	Galloon	Clones	III.	200
63	Killaghy	351 0 17	Tipperary, S.R.	Slievardagh	Kilvemnon	Callan	II.	335
25	Killaglasheen	57 1 36	Leitrim	Carrigallen	Oughteragh	Bawnboy	IV.	92
9	Killaglish	280 0 0	Queen's Co.	Portnahinch	Lea	Mountmellick	I.	244
20, 26	Killagoley	304 2 34	Wexford	Ballaghkeen	Templeshannon	Enniscorthy	I.	299
81	Killagoola	883 2 4	Galway	Moycullen	Moycullen	Galway	IV.	71
21, 27	Killagowan	274 1 4	Wexford	Ballaghkeen	Meelnagh	Gorey	I.	298
1, 2	Killagriff or Corgreagh	412 3 17	Meath	Lower Kells	Moybolgue	Kells	II.	203
24, 32, 33	Killagrohan	374 0 7	Cork, E.R.	Fermoy	Mallow	Mallow	II.	81
54, 67	Killaguile	1,062 0 11f	Galway	Moycullen	Killannin	Oughterard	IV.	69
89, 98	Killagurteen	338 0 32	Kerry	Iveragh	Dromod	Cahersiveen	II.	195
67, 75	Killaha	279 1 5	Kerry	Magunihy	Killaha	Killarney	II.	202
93, 102	Killaha East	459 1 23	Kerry	Glanarought	Tuosist	Kenmare	II.	189
35	Killahagan	471 0 24	Tipperary, N.R.	Eliogarty	Drom	Thurles	II.	269
29	Killahaly East	148 3 18	Waterford	Coshmore & Coshbride	Lismore and Mocollop	Lismore	II.	346
29	Killahaly West	243 3 7	Waterford	Coshmore & Coshbride	Lismore and Mocollop	Lismore	II.	346
15	Killahan	352 0 27	Kerry	Clanmaurice	Killahan	Tralee	II.	170
119, 120, 132, 133	Killahane	50 3 36	Cork, W.R.	West Carbery (E.D.)	Dromdaleague	Skibbereen	II.	140
48	Killahane	147 3 32	Kerry	Magunihy	Molahiffe	Killarney	II.	205
35, 41	Killahara	821 0 1	Tipperary, N.R.	Eliogarty	Loughmoe West	Thurles	II.	271
27	Killahard	80 0 24	Wexford	Ballaghkeen	Castle-ellis	Enniscorthy	I.	293
92,93,101,102	Killaha West	581 1 31	Kerry	Glanarought	Tuosist	Kenmare	II.	189
64, 75	Killahora	424 2 1	Cork, E.R.	Barrymore	Caherlag	Middleton	II.	52
18	Killahugh	279 2 2	Westmeath	Rathconrath	Rathconrath	Mullingar	I.	284
30	Killahurk	558 0 1g	Leitrim	Carrigallen	Carrigallen	Mohill	IV.	89
40, 45	Killahurler Lower	239 3 6	Wicklow	Arklow	Killahurler	Rathdrum	I.	345
39, 40, 45	Killahurler Upper	185 1 29	Wicklow	Arklow	Killahurler	Rathdrum	I.	345
12, 13	Killahy	464 3 2	Kilkenny	Crannagh	Killahy	Urlingford	I.	86
35	Killahy	234 3 6	Kilkenny	Knocktopher	Killahy	Waterford	I.	112
88	Killaidamee	156 0 37	Tipperary, S.R.	Iffa and Offa West	Ballybacon	Clogheen	II.	317
20	Killakane	821 1 39	Cork, E.R.	Condons & Clangibbon	Brigown	Mitchelstown	II.	59
3	Killakeady	87 2 25	Monaghan	Trough	Errigal Trough	Monaghan	III.	284
25	Killakee	661 0 27	Dublin	Uppercross	Cruagh	Dublin South	I.	39
15, 22	Killala	392 3 0h	Mayo	Tirawley	Killala	Killala	IV.	169
27	Killala	130 3 23	Sligo	Tirerrill	Ballysumaghan	Sligo	IV.	238
39	Killalahard	275 2 3i	Fermanagh	Coole	Galloon	Clones	III.	200
5	Killalane	233 0 32	Dublin	Balrothery East	Balrothery	Balrothery	I.	19
25	Killalane	318 1 21	Tipperary, N.R.	Owney and Arra	Killoscully	Nenagh	II.	295
22	KILLALA T.	—	Mayo	Tirawley	Killala	Killala	IV.	170
32	Killalea	20 2 32	Westmeath	Moycashel	Castletownkindalen	Mullingar	I.	277
66	Killalee	116 0 4	Kerry	Magunihy	Aghadoe	Killarney	II.	199
5	Killalee	40 1 22j	Limerick	Clanwilliam and Municipal Borough	St. John's	Limerick	II.	225
15	Killaleen	199 2 14	Leitrim	Drumahaire	Drumlease	Manorhamilton	IV.	94
27, 32	Killalish Lower	306 0 16	Wicklow	Upper Talbotstown	Kilranelagh	Baltinglass	I.	364
32	Killalish Upper	145 3 13	Wicklow	Upper Talbotstown	Kilranelagh	Baltinglass	I.	364
20	Killalies	212 2 24	Cavan	Clankee	Knockbride	Cootehill	III.	77
99	Killallaghtan	95 0 14	Galway	Clonmacnowen	Killallaghtan	Ballinasloe	IV.	26

(a) Including 10A. 2R. 14P. water.
(b) Including 1A. 2R. 16P. water.
(c) Including 0A. 3R. 23P. water.
(d) Including 7A. 2R. 38P. water.

(e) Including 6A. 2R. 0P. Mill Pond.
(f) Including 6A. 0R. 33P. water.
(g) Including 9A. 2R. 28P. water.
(h) Including 4A. 1R. 10P. water.

(i) Including 51A. 0R. 6P. water.
(j) { Within the Municipal Boundary, 30A. 2R. 10P. / Without the Municipal Boundary, 9A. 3R. 12P. }

No. of Sheet of the Ordnance Survey Maps.	Townlands and Towns.	Area in Statute Acres.	County.	Barony.	Parish.	Poor Law Union in 1857.	Townland Census of 1851, Part I.	
		A. R. P.					Vol.	Page
19, 20	Killalligan North .	146 2 32	Wexford . .	Scarawalsh . .	Monart . . .	Enniscorthy .	I.	324
19, 20	Killalligan South .	90 0 10	Wexford . .	Scarawalsh . .	Monart . . .	Enniscorthy .	I.	324
39	Killally . . .	148 1 18	Kerry . .	Trughanacmy .	Castleisland .	Tralee . .	II.	209
18, 19	Killally . .	307 2 16	Louth . .	Ferrard . . .	Clonmore . .	Drogheda .	I.	180
7, 12	Killally . . .	116 1 22	Louth . .	Upper Dundalk .	Ballybarrack .	Dundalk . .	I.	177
27, 28	Killally East .	283 2 2	Cork, E.R. .	Condons&Clangibbon	Kilworth . .	Fermoy . .	II.	62
27, 28	Killally West .	185 1 10	Cork, E.R. .	Condons&Clangibbon	Kilworth . .	Fermoy . .	II.	62
83	Killaloan Lower .	186 1 13a	Tipperary, S.R.	Iffa and Offa East .	Killaloan . .	Clonmel . .	II.	314
83	Killaloan Upper .	96 1 5	Tipperary, S.R.	Iffa and Offa East .	Killaloan . .	Clonmel . .	II.	314
22	Killaloe . .	299 1 33	Kilkenny . .	Shillelogher . .	Killaloe . .	Callan . .	I.	115
45	Killaloe T. . .	—	Clare . .	Tulla Lower . .	Killaloe . . .	Scarriff . .	II.	35
9	Killalongford . .	461 1 28	Carlow . .	Rathvilly . .	Clonmore . .	Shillelagh .	I.	10
22	Killaloo . .	270 2 10	Londonderry .	Tirkeeran . .	Cumber Lower .	Londonderry .	III.	249
18, 19	Killalooghan . .	198 1 6	Queen's Co. .	Stradbally . .	Dysartenos . .	Athy . .	I.	247
29, 43	Killaloonty . .	428 1 39	Galway . .	Clare . . .	Tuam . . .	Tuam . .	IV.	23
64	Killalough . .	149 3 7	Cork, E.R. .	Barrymore . .	Templeusque .	Cork . .	II.	59
109	Killaltanagh . .	374 0 21	Galway . .	Longford . .	Clonfert . .	Ballinasloe .	IV.	57
42	Killamanagh . .	128 1 11	Galway . .	Clare . . .	Donaghpatrick .	Tuam . .	IV.	19
3	Killamaster . .	194 3 6	Carlow . .	Carlow . . .	Killerrig . .	Carlow . .	I.	2
32, 35	Killamaun . .	406 2 39	Leitrim . .	Mohill . . .	Mohill . . .	Mohill . .	IV.	108
29	Killameen . .	263 1 16b	Leitrim . .	Carrigallen . .	Drumreilly . .	Bawnboy . .	IV.	91
30	Killamery . .	608 0 5	Kilkenny . .	Kells . . .	Killamery . .	Callan . .	I.	109
97	Killaminoge . .	551 0 22	Cork, E.R. .	Kinalea . . .	Templemichael .	Kinsale . .	II.	96
28, 33	Killamoat Lower .	281 1 30	Wicklow . .	Upper Talbotstown .	Kiltegan . .	Baltinglass .	I.	365
28, 33	Killamoat Upper .	224 2 5	Wicklow . .	Upper Talbotstown .	Kiltegan . .	Baltinglass .	I.	365
13, 14	Killamonan . .	32 3 20	Dublin . .	Castleknock . .	Mulhuddart . .	Dublin North .	I.	25
13, 14	Killamonan . .	76 1 26	Dublin . .	Castleknock . .	Ward . . .	Dublin North .	I.	25
34	Killamoyne . .	260 2 21	Tipperary, N.R.	Kilnamanagh Upper	Glenkeen . .	Thurles . .	II.	278
29	Killamuck . .	195 2 21	Queen's Co. .	Cullenagh . .	Abbeyleix . .	Abbeyleix .	I.	238
66, 77	Killamucky . .	334 0 16	Cork, E.R. .	Imokilly . . .	Mogeely . .	Middleton .	II.	90
59, 60, 73	Killamude East .	273 3 12	Galway . .	Tiaquin . . .	Ballymacward .	Mountbellew .	IV.	75
59	Killamude West .	62 3 34	Galway . .	Tiaquin . . .	Ballymacward .	Mountbellew .	IV.	75
53, 54	Killamurren . .	333 0 39	Cork, E.R. .	Barrymore . .	Gortroe . .	Fermoy . .	II.	55
28	Killan . .	226 3 1	Cavan . .	Clankee . . .	Bailieborough .	Bailieborough .	III.	71
21,22,27,28	Killanafinch . .	718 1 33	Tipperary, N.R.	Upper Ormond .	Kilkeary . .	Nenagh . .	II.	290
27, 28	Killanafinch . .	224 0 12	Tipperary, N.R.	Upper Ormond .	Latteragh . .	Nenagh . .	II.	292
21, 22	Killanahan . .	196 2 8	Limerick . .	Pubblebrien . .	Killeenoghty .	Croom . .	II.	253
110	Killanamaul . .	220 1 34	Cork, W.R. .	East Carbery (E.D.)	Kilbrittain . .	Bandon . .	II.	128
14, 15	Killananima . .	88 0 29	Leitrim . .	Drumahaire . .	Killanummery .	Manorhamilton	IV.	98
24, 32	Killananny . .	624 0 36	King's Co. .	Ballyboy . .	Killoughy . .	Tullamore .	I.	124
40	Killandrew . .	235 2 20	Kilkenny . .	Knocktopher . .	Rossinan . .	Waterford .	I.	113
38	Killandy . . .	125 3 30	Sligo . .	Corran . . .	Cloonoghil . .	Tobercurry .	IV.	225
32, 37	Killane . .	412 3 34	Antrim . .	Lower Toome . .	Ahoghill . .	Ballymena .	III.	32
17	Killane . .	6 3 21	Carlow . .	Forth . . .	Ballyellin . .	Carlow . .	I.	4
13, 17	Killane . .	133 3 30	Carlow . .	Forth . . .	Kellistown . .	Carlow . .	I.	5
9	Killane . .	156 1 18c	Londonderry .	Keenaght . .	Drumachose . .	NewTⁿLimavady	III.	235
24, 25	Killaneen . .	269 1 8d	Leitrim . .	Carrigallen . .	Oughteragh . .	Bawnboy . .	IV.	92
95	Killaneer . .	405 1 2	Cork, W.R. .	Kinalmeaky . .	Murragh . .	Bandon . .	II.	152
111, 124	Killaneetig . .	342 3 52	Cork, W.R. .	East Carbery (E.D.)	Ballinadee . .	Bandon . .	II.	126
43	Killanena . .	232 1 1e	Clare . .	Tulla Lower . .	Clonlea . .	Tulla . .	II.	34
12, 19	Killanena . .	1,656 2 10	Clare . .	Tulla Upper . .	Feakle . . .	Tulla . .	II.	39
15, 22	Killaney . . .	298 3 29f	Down . .	Castlereagh Upper .	Killaney . .	Lisburn . .	III.	165
27, 28	Killaney . . .	524 3 10	Down . .	Upper Iveagh, Lr. pt.	Garvaghy . .	Banbridge .	III.	172
58	Killaney Lower .	101 1 19	Tyrone . .	Clogher . . .	Clogher . .	Clogher . .	III.	293
58	Killaney Upper .	49 0 30	Tyrone . .	Clogher . . .	Clogher . .	Clogher . .	III.	293
142	Killangal . .	371 2 4	Cork, W.R. .	West Carbery (E.D.)	Castlehaven .	Skibbereen .	II.	138
29, 35	Killanigan . .	317 1 18	Tipperary, N.R.	Eliogarty . .	Loughmoe East .	Thurles . .	II.	271
22	Killanly . . .	316 1 30	Sligo . .	Tireragh . .	Castleconor .	Dromore West .	IV.	232
18, 19	Killann . . .	563 2 6	Wexford . .	Bantry . . .	Killann . .	Enniscorthy .	I.	300
22	Killannaduff . .	121 3 8	Wexford . .	Ballaghkeen . .	Donaghmore .	Gorey . .	I.	293
68	Killannin . .	410 1 17	Galway . .	Moycullen . .	Killannin . .	Oughterard .	IV.	69
10	Killanny . .	88 1 27	Louth . .	Ardee . . .	Killanny . .	Dundalk . .	I.	173
2, 3	Killanny . .	148 0 38	Monaghan .	Trough . . .	Errigal Trough .	Clogher . .	III.	284
35	Killanoordrane .	143 3 29	Kerry . .	Corkaguiny . .	Ballyduff . .	Dingle . .	II.	174
29	Killanthony . .	109 1 0	Waterford . .	Coshmore&Coshbride	Kilwatermoy .	Lismore . .	II.	343
86	Killanully . .	456 2 9	Cork, E.R. .	Kerrycurrihy . .	Killanully . .	Cork . .	II.	92
14, 15	Killanummery . .	243 0 26	Leitrim . .	Drumahaire . .	Killanummery .	Manorhamilton	IV.	98
9	Killanure . .	251 1 15	Wexford . .	Scarawalsh . .	St.Mary's NewTⁿBarry	Enniscorthy .	I.	325
111	Killany . .	230 1 33	Cork, E.R. .	Kinsale . . .	Dunderrow . .	Kinsale . .	II.	99
13	Killaphort . .	292 1 21	King's Co. .	Garrycastle . .	Clonmacnoise .	Parsonstown .	I.	135
25	Killaphort . .	207 3 11	Leitrim . .	Carrigallen . .	Drumreilly . .	Bawnboy . .	IV.	91
10	Killappoge . .	212 3 25	Roscommon .	Boyle . . .	Killummod . .	Boyle . .	IV.	196
17	Killaquill . .	53 3 28	Cavan . .	Tullygarvey . .	Drumgoon . .	Cootehill . .	III.	88
47	Killaraght . .	683 1 26	Sligo . .	Coolavin . .	Killaraght . .	Boyle . .	IV.	224

(a) Including 12A. 0R. 20P. water.　　(c) Including 3A. 0R. 23P. water.　　(e) Including 42A. 2R. 18P. water.
(b) Including 11A. 3R. 22P. water.　　(d) Including 9A. 3R. 3P. water.　　(f) Including 52A. 3R. 5P. water.

No. of Sheet of the Ordnance Survey Maps.	Townlands and Towns.	Area in Statute Acres.			County.	Barony.	Parish.	Poor Law Union in 1857.	Townland Census of 1851, Part I.	
		A.	R.	P.					Vol.	Page
13, 14	Killarah . . .	683	0	8a	Cavan . .	Tullyhunco . .	Kildallan . .	Bawnboy . .	III.	97
68, 81	Killarainy . .	213	2	5b	Galway . .	Moycullen . .	Moycullen . .	Galway . .	IV.	71
15, 16	Killaranny . .	650	2	9	King's Co. .	Ballycowan . .	Rahan . .	Tullamore .	I.	128
24	Killarbran . .	129	1	19	Fermanagh .	Magherastephana .	Aghalurcher .	Lisnaskea .	III.	216
27	Killarcan . .	339	2	15	Leitrim . .	Leitrim . . .	Kiltoghert . .	Cark. on Shannon	IV.	102
46	Killard . . .	627	2	26	Clare . .	Ibrickan . .	Killard . .	Kilrush . .	II.	23
62, 73, 74	Killard . . .	530	2	11	Cork, E.R. .	Cork . . .	Currykippane .	Cork . .	II.	64
39	Killard . . .	213	3	37c	Fermanagh .	Coole . . .	Galloon . .	Lisnaskea .	III.	200
28	Killard . . .	202	2	3	Limerick . .	Shanid . .	Ardagh . .	Newcastle .	II.	255
70	Killard . . .	84	3	25	Mayo . .	Carra . .	Turlough . .	Castlebar .	IV.	131
14	Killard . . .	265	0	13	Tipperary, N.R.	Lower Ormond .	Knigh . .	Nenagh . .	II.	285
32	Killard . . .	263	1	4	Westmeath .	Moycashel . .	Ardnurcher or Horse-leap . .	Mullingar .	I.	276
39	Killard Lower .	229	0	31	Down . .	Lecale Lower .	Ballyculter .	Downpatrick .	III.	178
38, 39	Killard Upper .	122	0	4	Down . .	Lecale Lower .	Ballyculter .	Downpatrick .	III.	178
36	Killaready . .	316	0	18	Limerick . .	Glenquin . .	Mahoonagh . .	Newcastle .	II.	246
24	Killarecastle .	508	3	20	Westmeath .	Rathconrath .	Killare . .	Mullingar .	I.	283
24	Killarechurch .	258	3	36	Westmeath .	Rathconrath .	Killare . .	Mullingar .	I.	283
2	Killaree . .	349	0	36	Cork, E.R. .	Orrery and Kilmore	Shandrum . .	Kilmallock .	II.	110
14	Killaree . .	656	2	28	Kilkenny .	Crannagh . .	Odagh . .	Kilkenny .	I.	86
86, 87	Killareeny . .	168	3	26	Galway . .	Kilconnell . .	Aughrim . .	Ballinasloe .	IV.	39
15	Killarga . .	59	3	25	Leitrim . .	Drumahaire . .	Killarga . .	Manorhamilton	IV.	98
10	Killarida . .	511	3	33	Kerry . .	Iraghticonnor .	Rattoo . .	Listowel . .	II.	193
21	Killark . .	119	3	24	Monaghan .	Dartree . .	Currin . .	Clones . .	III.	266
34	Killark . .	172	0	5	Monaghan .	Farney . .	Magheracloone .	Carrickmacross	III.	272
18, 26	Killarles . .	171	2	1	King's Co. .	Geashill . .	Geashill . .	Tullamore .	I.	140
5	Killarn . .	412	0	36	Down . .	Castlereagh Lower .	Newtownards .	Newtownards .	III.	163
66	Killarney . .	41	0	0	Kerry . .	Magunihy . .	Killarney . .	Killarney . .	II.	203
28	Killarney . .	155	0	34	Kilkenny .	Gowran . .	Killarney . .	Thomastown .	I.	97
40	Killarney . .	346	1	16	Roscommon .	Ballintober South .	Roscommon .	Roscommon .	IV.	190
4, 8	Killarney . .	183	2	9	Wicklow . .	Rathdown . .	Bray . .	Rathdown .	I.	354
66	KILLARNEY T. .	—			Kerry . .	Magunihy . .	Killarney . .	Killarney . .	II.	204
24, 31	Killaroo . .	195	2	4	Westmeath .	Rathconrath .	Killare . .	Mullingar .	I.	283
97	Killarriv . .	411	3	5	Galway . .	Athenry . .	Kiltullagh .	Loughrea .	IV.	5
19, 22	Killartery . .	213	1	1	Louth . .	Ferrard . .	Mayne . .	Drogheda .	I.	181
28	Killartry . .	44	2	34	Fermanagh .	Magherastephana .	Aghavea . .	Lisnaskea .	III.	219
28	Killarue . .	155	1	13	Monaghan .	Farney . .	Donaghmoyne .	Carrickmacross	III.	270
23, 31	Killarush . .	145	1	18	Cork, E.R. .	Duhallow . .	Clonmeen . .	Kanturk . .	II.	70
12	Killary . .	918	2	13	Meath . .	Lower Slane .	Killary . .	Ardee . .	I.	223
19	Killary . .	209	3	19	Tipperary, N.R.	Owney and Arra .	Templeachally .	Nenagh . .	II.	297
47	Killary Glebe .	119	0	6	Tyrone . .	Dungannon Middle .	Clonoe . .	Dungannon .	III.	300
19, 25	Killary (Hayes)	230	0	20	Tipperary, N.R.	Owney and Arra .	Templeachally .	Nenagh . .	II.	297
19	Killary (Smith)	88	1	15	Tipperary, N.R.	Owney and Arra .	Templeachally .	Nenagh . .	II.	297
27, 31	Killasanowl .	158	1	35	Leitrim . .	Leitrim . .	Kiltoghert .	Cark. on Shannon	IV.	102
84, 96	Killascaul . .	293	1	34	Galway . .	Athenry . .	Kiltullagh .	Loughrea .	IV.	5
28	Killashanbally .	143	2	23	Fermanagh .	Magherastephana .	Aghalurcher .	Lisnaskea .	III.	216
19	KILLASHANDRA T. .	—			Cavan . .	Tullyhunco . .	Killashandra .	Cavan . .	III.	99
24	Killashee . .	14	0	7	Kildare . .	Naas North .	Killashee . .	Naas . .	I.	62
24	Killashee . .	400	3	22	Kildare . .	Naas South .	Killashee . .	Naas . .	I.	65
13, 18	Killashee and Agha-keeran . .	371	1	9	Longford . .	Moydow . .	Killashee . .	Longford . .	I.	161
18	KILLASHEE T.	—			Longford . .	Moydow . .	Killashee . .	Longford . .	I.	162
46	Killaskillen .	1,484	3	27	Meath . .	Upper Moyfenrath .	Ballyboggan .	Edenderry .	I.	212
21,22,27,28	Killasmeestia .	199	1	37	Queen's Co. .	Clandonagh . .	Skirk . .	Donaghmore .	I.	235
31, 32	Killasmuggaun .	281	0	25	Galway . .	Tiaquin . .	Kilkerrin .	Glennamaddy .	IV.	77
10,11,15,16	Killasona . .	543	1	1	Longford . .	Granard . .	Granard . .	Granard . .	I.	156
39, 40	Killaspeenan .	147	2	5	Fermanagh .	Coole . .	Galloon . .	Clones . .	III.	200
15, 21	Killaspicktarvin	386	2	9	Kerry . .	Clanmaurice .	Kiltomy . .	Listowel . .	II.	172
13, 14	Killaspugbrone .	457	1	22	Sligo . .	Carbury . .	Killaspugbrone .	Sligo . .	IV.	222
15	Killaspuglonane	421	3	22	Clare . .	Corcomroe . .	Killaspuglonane .	Ennistimon .	II.	19
105	Killaspugmoylan	188	2	37	Galway . .	Dunkellin . .	Kilconickny .	Loughrea .	IV.	29
43	Killaspy . .	478	2	39	Kilkenny .	Ida . .	Dunkitt . .	Waterford .	I.	101
22	Killasseragh .	165	2	7	Cork, E.R. .	Duhallow . .	Kilmeen . .	Kanturk . .	II.	73
45, 54	Killasseragh .	340	2	2	Cork, E.R. .	Kinnatalloon .	Ballynoe . .	Fermoy . .	II.	97
24	Killastalliff .	134	2	35	Roscommon .	Ballintober North .	Kilglass . .	Strokestown .	IV.	186
82	Killasteever .	68	2	25	Donegal . .	Banagh . .	Inishkeel . .	Glenties . .	III.	106
21	Killaster . .	312	1	35	Roscommon .	Castlereagh . .	Kilcorkey .	Castlereagh .	IV.	199
22, 23	Killatee . .	319	0	21d	Cavan . .	Clankee . .	Drumgoon .	Cootehill . .	III.	72
13	Killateeaun .	211	1	3e	Galway . .	Ross . .	Ballinrobe .	Ballinrobe .	II.	72
27, 35	Killathy . .	614	3	1f	Cork, E.R. .	Fermoy . .	Killathy . .	Fermoy . .	II.	80
30, 34, 35	Killatoor . .	206	1	22	Waterford .	Decies within Drum	Aglish . .	Dungarvan .	II.	349
0	Killatten . .	70	0	22	Monaghan .	Monaghan . .	Tedavnet .	Monaghan .	III.	270
36	Killattimoriarty	307	3	37	Roscommon .	Ballintober South .	Kilgefin . .	Roscommon .	IV.	189

No. of Sheet of the Ordnance Survey Maps.	Townlands and Towns.	Area in Statute Acres.	County.	Barony.	Parish.	Poor Law Union in 1857.	Townland, Census of 1851, Part I.	
		A. R. P.					Vol.	Page
62, 72	Killaturly	856 2 37	Mayo	Costello	Kilbeagh	Swineford	IV.	140
35	Killaun	838 0 22	King's Co.	Eglish	Drumcullen	Parsonstown	I.	134
14	Killaun	339 3 10	Tipperary, N.R.	Lower Ormond	Dromineer	Nenagh	II.	283
29, 36	Killavackan	310 3 9	Roscommon	Roscommon	Cloonfinlough	Strokestown	IV.	209
10	Killavalla	19 3 36	Tipperary, N.R.	Lower Ormond	Borrisokane	Borrisokane	II.	282
27	Killavalla	89 3 26	Tipperary, N.R.	Upper Ormond	Aghnameadle	Nenagh	II.	289
27	Killavalla	91 3 21	Tipperary, N.R.	Upper Ormond	Kilnaneave	Nenagh	II.	291
23	Killavallig	339 0 32	Cork, E.R.	Duhallow	Castlemagner	Kanturk	II.	67
18, 19	Killavally	172 0 9	Queen's Co.	Stradbally	Dysartenos	Athy	I.	247
77, 78	Killavally	593 3 11	Tipperary, S.R.	Middlethird	Kiltinan	Clonmel	II.	328
38, 39	Killavally	817 2 32	Westmeath	Moycashel	Newtown	Mullingar	I.	279
89, 99	Killavally East	453 3 13a	Mayo	Carra	Ballintober	Castlebar	IV.	125
39	KILLAVALLY T.	—	Westmeath	Moycashel	Newtown	Mullingar	I.	279
89, 99	Killavally West	552 1 15b	Mayo	Carra	Ballintober	Castlebar	IV.	125
45	Killavarilly	372 0 22	Cork, E.R.	Kinnatalloon	Knockmourne	Fermoy	II.	98
63	Killavarrig	317 1 26	Cork, E.R.	Cork	Whitechurch	Cork	II.	66
123	Killavarrig	708 0 24	Cork, W.R.	East Carbery (E.D.)	Timoleague	Clonakilty	II.	130
18	Killavee	43 0 36	Donegal	Kilmacrenan	Clondavaddog	Millford	III.	125
120	Killaveenoge East	337 2 30	Cork, W.R.	West Carbery (E.D.)	Drinagh	Skibbereen	II.	139
120	Killaveenoge West	473 3 1	Cork, W.R.	West Carbery (E.D.)	Drinagh	Skibbereen	II.	139
38	Killavees	98 3 24	Down	Lecale Upper	Down	Downpatrick	III.	180
59	Killaveney	218 3 17c	Tyrone	Clogher	Errigal Trough	Clogher	III.	296
86	Killavenoge	43 0 29	Tipperary, S.R.	Iffa and Offa West	Shanrahan	Clogheen	II.	320
38,39,43,44	Killaveny	1,020 2 36	Wicklow	Ballinacor South	Kilpipe	Shillelagh	I.	349
39	Killavil	137 0 18	Sligo	Corran	Kilshalvy	Boyle	IV.	227
43	Killavilla	533 0 33	King's Co.	Ballybritt	Roscrea	Roscrea	I.	126
24, 30	Killavinoge	161 1 17	Tipperary, N.R.	Ikerrin	Killavinoge	Roscrea	II.	275
15, 17	Killavoggy	690 2 3	Leitrim	Drumahaire	Killanummery	Manorhamilton	IV.	98
17,18,30,31	Killavoher	954 2 17	Galway	Ballymoe	Dunmore	Glennamaddy	IV.	7
35, 36	Killavoy	158 2 14d	Clare	Tulla Lower	Killuran	Tulla	II.	36
31, 40	Killavoy	595 0 27	Cork, E.R.	Duhallow	Clonmeen	Kanturk	II.	70
29	Killawardy	469 2 3	Tipperary, N.R.	Ikerrin	Killea	Roscrea	II.	275
29	Killawardy	101 1 4	Tipperary, N.R.	Ikerrin	Templemore	Roscrea	II.	276
45	Killawillin	540 1 5	Cork, E.R.	Barrymore	Castlelyons	Fermoy	II.	53
34	KILLAWILLIN T.	—	Cork, E.R.	Fermoy	Monanimy	Mallow	II.	82
34	Killawinna	175 1 1	Clare	Bunratty Upper	Doora	Ennis	II.	8
27	Killawlan	63 2 34	Waterford	Gaultiere	Killea	Waterford	II.	363
89	Killawullaun East	331 2 15	Mayo	Carra	Ballintober	Castlebar	IV.	125
89, 99	Killawullaun Mountain	331 0 22e	Mayo	Carra	Ballintober	Castlebar	IV.	125
89	Killawullaun West	329 1 7	Mayo	Carra	Ballintober	Castlebar	IV.	125
42	Kill Beg	85 2 14	Meath	Lower Moyfenrath	Rathmolyon	Trim	I.	211
3, 7	Killcranny	195 3 35	Londonderry	Coleraine	Killowen	Coleraine	III.	232
31, 37	Kill Demesne	158 0 22f	Cavan	Clanmahon	Crosserlough	Cavan	III.	76
8	Killea	681 2 23	Leitrim	Rosclogher	Cloonclare	Manorhamilton	IV.	109
20, 29	Killea	159 2 36	Limerick	Connello Lower	Croagh	Rathkeale	II.	228
20	Killea	381 1 33	Londonderry	North West Liberties of Londonderry	Templemore	Londonderry	III.	246
42	Killea	58 0 30	Roscommon	Athlone	Kilmeane	Roscommon	IV.	182
29	Killea	79 2 11	Tipperary, N.R.	Ikerrin	Killea	Roscrea	II.	275
15	Killea	4 3 35	Tipperary, N.R.	Lower Ormond	Ardcrony	Nenagh	II.	282
6, 9	Killea	521 0 36g	Tipperary, N.R.	Lower Ormond	Finnoe	Borrisokane	II.	284
15	Killea	56 1 24	Tipperary, N.R.	Lower Ormond	Kilruane	Nenagh	II.	285
66	Killea	177 1 19	Tipperary, S.R.	Clanwilliam	Bruis	Tipperary	II.	305
37	Killea	264 0 38	Waterford	Coshmore and Coshbride	Templemichael	Youghal	II.	349
27	Killea	2 2 21	Waterford	Gaultiere	Killea	Waterford	II.	363
20	Killeacle	383 0 17	Kerry	Clanmaurice	Kilmoyly	Tralee	II.	171
43	Killeagh	631 0 16	Cork, E.R.	Barrymore	Ardnageehy	Fermoy	II.	50
65	Killeagh	147 1 0	Cork, E.R.	Barrymore	Ballycurrany	Middleton	II.	51
27	Killeagh	331 2 18	Cork, E.R.	Fermoy	Glanworth	Fermoy	II.	79
65, 76	Killeagh	427 1 18	Cork, E.R.	Imokilly	Middleton	Middleton	II.	89
112	Killeagh	74 0 17	Cork, E.R.	Kinalea	Kinure	Kinsale	II.	95
48	Killeagh	658 2 33	Kerry	Magunihy	Molahiffe	Killarney	II.	205
47	Killeagh	155 0 24	Kerry	Trughanacmy	Kiltallagh	Tralee	II.	212
17, 18	Killeagh	294 2 29	Kildare	Connell	Kilmeage	Naas	I.	55
23	Killeagh	195 3 25	Limerick	Clanwilliam	Ballybrood	Limerick	I.	221
22	Killeagh	157 3 30	Waterford	Decies without Drum	Modelligo	Dungarvan	II.	359
24, 31	Killeagh	120 1 35	Westmeath	Moycashel	Ardnurcher or Horseleap	Mullingar	I.	276
27	Killeagh	187 1 36	Wexford	Ballaghkeen	Ballyvaldon	Enniscorthy	I.	292
40	Killeagh	206 1 17	Wicklow	Arklow	Kilbride	Rathdrum	I.	344
35	Killeagh	313 3 7	Wicklow	Ballinacor South	Ballykine	Rathdrum	I.	348
22	Killeagh Common	1 2 36	Kildare	Offaly East	Grangeclare	Naas	I.	70

(a) Including 45A. 1R. 35P. water.
(b) Including 4A. 1R. 13P. water.
(c) Including 8A. 2R. 22P. water.
(d) Including 2A. 3R. 3P. water.
(e) Including 22A. 2R. 10P. water.
(f) Including 32A. 3R. 13P. water.
(g) Including 6A. 3R. 0P. water.

No. of Sheet of the Ordnance Survey Maps.	Townlands and Towns.	Area in Statute Acres.	County.	Barony.	Parish.	Poor Law Union in 1857.	Townland Census of 1851, Part I.	
		A. R. P.					Vol.	Page
22	Killeagh Common .	4 0 12	Kildare . .	Offaly East . .	Kildare . . .	Naas . .	I.	70
22	Killeagh Common .	3 0 3	Kildare . .	Offaly East . .	Rathangan . .	Naas . .	I.	71
66	Killeagh Gardens .	37 2 1	Cork, E.R. .	Imokilly . . .	Killeagh . .	Youghal . .	II.	88
66	KILLEAGH T. . .	—	Cork, E.R. .	Imokilly . . .	Killeagh . .	Youghal . .	II.	88
11	Killeague . .	223 0 33	Londonderry .	Coleraine . .	Aghadowey . .	Coleraine .	III.	229
44	Killeagy (Goonan) .	467 1 11	Clare . .	Tulla Lower . .	Killokennedy . .	Limerick . .	II.	35
36, 44	Killeagy (Ryan) .	487 3 25	Clare . .	Tulla Lower . .	Killokennedy . .	Limerick . .	II.	35
44	Killeagy (Stritch) .	112 3 19	Clare . .	Tulla Lower . .	Killokennedy . .	Limerick . .	II.	35
55	Killealy . . .	758 1 4	Antrim . .	Lower Massereene .	Killead . .	Antrim . .	III.	28
147, 152	Killeane . .	102 3 13	Cork, W.R. .	West Carbery (W.D.)	Kilmoe . .	Skull . .	II.	145
3	Killeanly . .	112 2 36	Monaghan .	Trough . . .	Errigal Trough .	Monaghan .	III.	284
5, 8, 9	Killeany . . .	102 2 19	Clare . .	Burren . . .	Killeany . .	Ballyvaghan .	II.	13
110,111,119	Killeany . . .	2,188 1 25	Galway . .	Aran . . .	Inishmore . .	Galway . .	IV.	3
50, 53	Killeany . . .	357 1 8	Meath . .	Upper Deece . .	Moyglare . .	Celbridge .	I.	194
23	Killeany . . .	1,232 0 31	Queen's Co. .	Maryborough West .	Clonenagh and Clonagheen . .	Abbeyleix .	I.	243
18	Killeany Beg .	164 3 1	Limerick . .	Shanid . . .	Kilfergus . .	Glin . . .	II.	256
18	Killeany More .	925 1 11	Limerick . .	Shanid . . .	Kilfergus . .	Glin . . .	II.	256
119	KILLEANY T. . .	—	Galway . .	Aran . . .	Inishmore . .	Galway . .	IV.	3
14, 19, 20	Kill East . .	181 1 26a	Kildare . .	South Salt . .	Kill . . .	Naas . .	I.	77
86,87,89,90	Killeatin . .	1,198 0 15	Tipperary, S.R. .	Iffa and Offa West .	Shanrahan . .	Clogheen .	II.	320
64	Killeaton . .	238 0 26	Antrim . .	Upper Belfast . .	Derryaghy . .	Lisburn . .	III.	10
71, 80	Killedan . . .	455 2 35	Mayo . .	Gallen . . .	Killedan . .	Swineford .	IV.	150
116	Killederdaowen .	67 1 23	Galway . .	Leitrim . . .	Duniry . .	Portumna .	IV.	53
20, 22, 23	Killedmond . .	511 0 16	Carlow . .	Idrone East . .	Kiltennell . .	Carlow . .	I.	7
23	KILLEDMOND T. .	—	Carlow . .	Idrone East . .	Kiltennell . .	Carlow . .	I.	8
10, 19	Killee . . .	631 1 33	Cork, E.R. .	Condons and Clangibbon . .	Marshalstown . .	Mitchelstown .	II.	63
22, 23	Killee . .	415 0 36b	Fermanagh .	Tirkennedy . .	Enniskillen . .	Enniskillen .	III.	222
16, 17	Killee . .	616 2 21c	Fermanagh .	Tirkennedy . .	Magheracross . .	Enniskillen .	III.	223
44	Killeedy North .	625 2 32	Limerick . .	Glenquin . .	Killeedy . .	Newcastle .	II.	246
44	Killeedy South .	465 1 29	Limerick . .	Glenquin . .	Killeedy . .	Newcastle .	II.	246
10	Killeef . . .	82 1 35	Monaghan .	Monaghan . .	Tehallan . .	Monaghan .	III.	280
11	Killeek . .	555 2 33	Dublin . .	Nethercross . .	Killeek . .	Balrothery .	I.	31
43	Killeelaun . .	437 1 32	Galway . .	Clare . . .	Tuam . .	Tuam . .	IV.	23
103	Killeely Beg .	288 3 9	Galway . .	Dunkellin . .	Killeely . .	Gort . .	IV.	29
103	Killeely More .	278 0 37	Galway . .	Dunkellin . .	Killeely . .	Gort . .	IV.	29
12, 16	Killeen . .	283 3 8	Armagh . .	Fews Lower . .	Lisnadill . .	Armagh . .	III.	47
29	Killeen . . .	1,009 0 5	Armagh . .	Orior Upper . .	Killevy . .	Newry . .	III.	58
17	Killeen . .	157 2 16	Clare . .	Inchiquin . .	Killinaboy . .	Corrofin .	II.	26
17, 25	Killeen . .	414 1 25d	Clare . .	Inchiquin . .	Rath . .	Corrofin .	II.	27
17, 25	Killeen . .	221 0 19e	Clare . .	Inchiquin . .	Ruan . .	Corrofin .	II.	28
43	Killeen . .	181 2 32	Clare . .	Tulla Lower . .	Clonlea . .	Tulla . .	II.	35
62	Killeen . .	264 3 36	Cork, E.R. .	East Muskerry . .	Matehy . .	Cork . .	II.	105
99	Killeen . .	37 1 8	Cork, E.R. .	Kerrycurrihy . .	Kilpatrick . .	Kinsale . .	II.	92
85, 97	Killeen . .	280 3 11	Cork, E.R. .	Kinalea . .	Inishannon . .	Bandon . .	II.	95
109, 122	Killeen . .	309 3 7	Cork, W.R. .	East Carbery (E.D.)	Desertserges .	Clonakilty .	II.	128
58	Killeen . .	156 3 13	Cork, W.R. .	West Muskerry .	Ballyvourney . .	Macroom .	II.	154
39, 40	Killeen . .	148 2 29	Cork, W.R. .	West Muskerry .	Kilcorney . .	Millstreet .	II.	158
107	Killeen . .	217 2 15	Donegal . .	Tirhugh . .	Kilbarron . .	Ballyshannon .	III.	148
5	Killeen . .	32 2 32	Down . .	Castlereagh Lower .	Dundonald . .	Belfast . .	III.	162
5	Killeen . .	137 2 17	Down . .	Castlereagh Lower .	Holywood . .	Belfast . .	III.	162
7	Killeen . .	229 0 3	Dublin . .	Balrothery West .	Clonmethan .	Balrothery .	I.	22
36, 37	Killeen . .	429 1 34f	Galway . .	Ballynahinch . .	Moyrus . .	Clifden . .	IV.	13
87	Killeen . .	118 2 13	Galway . .	Clonmacnowen .	Kilcloony . .	Ballinasloe .	IV.	25
16,17,29,30	Killeen . .	111 1 28	Galway . .	Dunmore . .	Tuam . .	Tuam . .	IV.	36
82	Killeen . .	125 0 31	Galway . .	Galway . .	Oranmore . .	Galway . .	IV.	37
81, 82	Killeen . .	86 3 33g	Galway . .	Galway . . .	Rahoon . .	Galway . .	IV.	38
60, 61	Killeen . .	203 2 25	Galway . .	Kilconnell . .	Ahascragh . .	Mountbellew .	IV.	39
129, 133	Killeen . .	462 3 4	Galway . .	Kiltartan . .	Beagh . .	Gort . .	IV.	46
106, 116	Killeen . .	269 0 9	Galway . .	Leitrim . .	Leitrim . .	Loughrea .	IV.	55
107	Killeen . .	120 1 8	Kerry . .	Dunkerron South .	Kilcrohane . .	Kenmare .	II.	184
58	Killeen . .	367 3 16	Kerry . .	Magunihy . .	Aghadoe . .	Killarney .	II.	199
76	Killeen . .	697 3 2	Kerry . .	Magunihy . .	Killaha . .	Killarney .	II.	202
29	Killeen . .	141 1 18	Kerry . .	Trughanacmy . .	Tralee . .	Tralee . .	II.	213
32	Killeen . .	542 0 29	Kildare . .	Narragh & RebanEast	Narraghmore . .	Athy . .	I.	66
18, 22	Killeen . .	860 2 23	Kilkenny . .	Crannagh . .	Kilmanagh . .	Callan . .	I.	86
32	Killeen . .	244 2 15	Kilkenny . .	Gowran . . .	Inistioge . .	Thomastown .	I.	96
35, 36	Killeen . .	208 3 23	Kilkenny . .	Knocktopher . .	Killahy . .	Waterford .	I.	112
38, 39, 43	Killeen . .	216 0 23	King's Co. .	Ballybritt . .	Aghancon . .	Roscrea .	I.	124
10,11,18,19	Killeen . .	357 1 21	King's Co. .	Coolestown . .	Monasteroris . .	Edenderry .	I.	133
10	Killeen . .	206 3 36	King's Co. .	Lower Philipstown .	Kilclonfert . .	Tullamore .	I.	142
33	Killeen . . .	186 1 34	King's Co. .	Upper Philipstown .	Clonyhurk . .	Mountmellick .	I.	143

(a) Including 14A. 3R. 22P. detached portion.   (d) Including 21A. 2R. 38P. water.   (f) Including 131A. 0R. 36P. water.
(b) Including 4A. 0R. 16P. water.   (e) Including 44A. 2R. 28P. water.   (g) Including 10A. 0R. 0P. water.
(c) Including 2A. 3R. 20P. water.

No. of Sheet of the Ordnance Survey Maps.	Townlands and Towns.	Area in Statute Acres.			County.	Barony.	Parish.	Poor Law Union in 1857.	Townland Census of 1851, Part I.	
		A.	R.	P.					Vol.	Page
15	Killeen	330	0	1	Leitrim	Drumahaire	Killanummery	Manorhamilton	IV.	98
49	Killeen	506	1	9	Limerick	Coshlea	Ballylanders	Mitchelstown	II.	237
48	Killeen	513	2	3	Limerick	Coshlea	Kilfinnane	Kilmallock	II.	240
21	Killeen	202	2	20	Limerick	Coshma	Adare	Croom	II.	241
45, 54	Killeen	298	0	23	Limerick	Glenquin	Killeedy	Newcastle	II.	246
11	Killeen	91	2	23	Limerick	Kenry	Kilcornan	Rathkeale	II.	249
20, 24	Killeen	733	0	36	Longford	Ardagh	Rathreagh	Ballymahon	I.	153
10	Killeen	678	2	18a	Longford	Granard	Granard	Granard	I.	156
8	Killeen	439	2	18	Longford	Longford	Clongesh	Longford	I.	158
11	Killeen	99	0	13	Louth	Louth	Louth	Dundalk	I.	184
90, 100	Killeen	124	1	12	Mayo	Carra	Drum	Castlebar	IV.	128
111, 112	Killeen	356	3	39	Mayo	Clanmorris	Crossboyne	Claremorris	IV.	133
92	Killeen	55	3	9	Mayo	Clanmorris	Knock	Claremorris	IV.	135
81	Killeen	155	0	17	Mayo	Costello	Aghamore	Swineford	IV.	137
62	Killeen	340	1	16	Mayo	Costello	Kilbeagh	Swineford	IV.	140
70	Killeen	315	0	10	Mayo	Gallen	Kildacommoge	Castlebar	IV.	148
50	Killeen	51	3	4	Mayo	Gallen	Killasser	Swineford	IV.	149
61, 71	Killeen	216	0	17	Mayo	Gallen	Meelick	Swineford	IV.	150
38	Killeen	364	1	14b	Mayo	Tirawley	Crossmolina	Ballina	IV.	166
7	Killeen	196	2	29	Mayo	Tirawley	Kilbride	Killala	IV.	168
37, 38	Killeen	1,264	1	0	Meath	Skreen	Killeen	Dunshaughlin	I.	221
26, 32	Killeen	442	1	5	Queen's Co.	Ballyadams	Killabban	Athy	I.	231
14	Killeen	232	2	36	Queen's Co.	Stradbally	Moyanna	Mountmellick	I.	247
11	Killeen	231	0	13	Queen's Co.	Upperwoods	Offerlane	Mountmellick	I.	252
7, 10	Killeen	197	2	13	Tipperary, N.R.	Lower Ormond	Borrisokane	Borrisokane	II.	282
5	Killeen	1,050	1	16	Tipperary, N.R.	Lower Ormond	Loughkeen	Parsonstown	II.	286
7	Killeen	128	2	19	Tipperary, N.R.	Lower Ormond	Terryglass	Borrisokane	II.	288
31, 37	Killeen	288	1	9	Tipperary, N.R.	Owney and Arra	Kilcomenty	Nenagh	II.	295
26, 32	Killeen	226	2	18	Tipperary, N.R.	Owney and Arra	Killoscully	Nenagh	II.	295
32, 38	Killeen	504	2	16	Tipperary, N.R.	Owney and Arra	Kilnarath	Nenagh	II.	296
27, 33	Killeen	501	1	21	Tipperary, N.R.	Upper Ormond	Kilnaneave	Nenagh	II.	291
48, 54	Killeen	1,565	2	30	Tipperary, S.R.	Slievardagh	Killenaule	Cashel	II.	334
47	Killeen	164	3	8	Tyrone	Dungannon Middle	Clonoe	Dungannon	III.	300
16	Killeen	466	2	21c	Tyrone	Strabane Lower	Ardstraw	Strabane	III.	319
25, 32	Killeen	170	2	2	Westmeath	Moycashel	Castletown Kindalen	Mullingar	I.	277
37	Killeen	134	3	21	Wexford	Shelmaliere East	Kilpatrick	Wexford	I.	331
64	Killeena	523	2	0	Cork, E.R.	Barrymore	Kilquane	Cork	II.	55
7, 14	Killeena	315	2	35	Mayo	Tirawley	Doonfeeny	Killala	IV.	167
41, 44	Killeenadeema	172	2	9	Roscommon	Athlone	Rahara	Roscommon	IV.	183
105, 115	Killeenadeema East	310	3	19	Galway	Loughrea	Killeenadeema	Loughrea	IV.	64
105, 115	Killeenadeema West	770	2	12	Galway	Loughrea	Killeenadeema	Loughrea	IV.	64
38, 47	Killeenafinnane	317	0	34	Kerry	Trughanacmy	Kiltallagh	Tralee	II.	212
6	Killeengarriff	278	2	30	Limerick	Clanwilliam	Killeenagarriff	Limerick	II.	224
65	Killeenagh	367	0	5	Clare	Moyarta	Moyarta	Kilrush	II.	34
45, 46	Killeenagh	465	3	5	Kerry	Corkaguiny	Ballinvoher	Dingle	II.	174
24	Killeenagh	92	1	33	Westmeath	Rathconrath	Killare	Mullingar	I.	283
34	Killeenaghmountain	301	1	29	Waterford	Coshmore&Coshbride	Kilcockan	Lismore	II.	343
34	Killeenagh North	323	0	29	Waterford	Coshmore&Coshbride	Kilcockan	Lismore	II.	343
34	Killeenagh South	268	0	7	Waterford	Coshmore&Coshbride	Kilcockan	Lismore	II.	343
24	Killeenagroagh	43	2	0	Westmeath	Rathconrath	Killare	Mullingar	I.	283
25	Killeenan	154	2	23	Clare	Inchiquin	Dysert	Ennis	II.	24
28	Killeenan	1,513	1	21	Tyrone	Dungannon Upper	Kildress	Cookstown	III.	309
16	Killeenan Beg	81	0	18	Galway	Dunmore	Tuam	Tuam	IV.	36
16, 17	Killeenan More	282	1	18	Galway	Dunmore	Tuam	Tuam	IV.	36
103	Killeenaran	211	0	33	Galway	Dunkellin	Drumacoo	Gort	IV.	28
68	Killeenasteena	363	0	29	Tipperary, S.R.	Middlethird	Killeenasteena	Cashel	II.	327
23, 30	Killeenatoor	193	1	39	Westmeath	Clonlonan	Ballyloughloe	Athlone	I.	260
9	Killeenatruan	119	1	28	Longford	Longford	Killoe	Longford	I.	159
103, 113	Killeenavarra	116	0	2	Galway	Dunkellin	Killeenavarra	Gort	IV.	30
24	Killeenavera	86	2	16	Limerick	Clanwilliam	Dromkeen	Limerick	II.	223
24	Killeenavera	129	0	22	Limerick	Clanwilliam	Grean	Limerick	II.	224
24, 31	Killeenbane or Tullagh Upper	55	0	13	Westmeath	Rathconrath	Killare	Mullingar	I.	283
14	Killeenbeg	82	1	38	Kildare	South Salt	Kill	Naas	I.	77
22	Killeenboy	84	3	21	King's Co.	Garrycastle	Gallen	Parsonstown	I.	136
23	Killeenboy	206	2	14	Longford	Shrule	Abbeyshrule	Ballymahon	I.	165
40	Killeenboy	589	2	24	Roscommon	Ballintober South	Kiltevan	Roscommon	IV.	190
17, 24	Killeenboy	271	3	27	Westmeath	Rathconrath	Killare	Ballymahon	I.	283
30, 36	Killeenboylegan	180	0	1	Westmeath	Clonlonan	Kilmanaghan	Athlone	I.	262
24	Killeenbrack	746	2	29	Westmeath	Rathconrath	Killare	Mullingar	I.	283
38	Killeenbreaghan	227	0	25	King's Co.	Ballybritt	Kilcolman	Parsonstown	I.	125
81, 82	Killeenbutler	249	1	39d	Tipperary, S.R.	Iffa and Offa West	Caher	Clogheen	II.	318
87, 88	Killeencoff	223	1	38	Mayo	Murrisk	Oughaval	Westport	IV.	162

(a) Including 23A. 0R. 15P. water.
(b) Including 1A. 2R. 14P. water.

(c) Including 3A. 2R. 39P. water.
(d) Including 3A. 2R. 5P. water.

4 D

No. of Sheet of the Ordnance Survey Maps	Townlands and Towns	Area in Statute Acres.			County.	Barony.	Parish.	Poor Law Union in 1857.	Townland Census of 1851, Part I.	
		A.	R.	P.					Vol.	Page
14	Killeencreevagh	15	0	25	Mayo	Tirawley	Rathreagh	Killala	IV.	171
63	Killeendaniel	320	1	3	Cork, E.R.	Cork	Kilcully	Cork	II.	64
65	Killeendooling	195	1	32	Cork, E.R.	Barrymore	Ballyspillane	Middleton	II.	51
23	Killeendowd	201	0	4	Longford	Moydow	Taghsheenod	Ballymahon	I.	162
11	Killeenduff	976	3	24	Sligo	Tireragh	Easky	Dromore West	IV.	233
21	Killeenduff	62	1	34	Sligo	Tirerrill	Kilross	Sligo	IV.	241
117	Killeen East	98	3	18	Galway	Longford	Killimorbologue	Portumna	IV.	59
26, 27	Killeen East	145	1	35	Kildare	Offaly West	Ballybrackan	Athy	I.	71
25, 29	Killeen East	116	3	17	Kilkenny	Gowran	Ullard	Thomastown	I.	100
22	Killeen East	197	2	31a	Roscommon	Roscommon	Shankill	Strokestown	IV.	213
96	Killeeneen Beg	217	0	24	Galway	Dunkellin	Killeeneen	Gort	IV.	30
95, 96, 104	Killeeneen More	735	2	24	Galway	Dunkellin	Killeeneen	Gort	IV.	30
19, 27	Killeenemer	414	2	5	Cork, E.R.	Fermoy	Killeenemer	Mitchelstown	II.	80
17, 24	Killeenerk	255	0	25	Westmeath	Rathconrath	Ballymorin	Mullingar	I.	282
113	Killeenhugh	275	3	22	Galway	Dunkellin	Killeenavarra	Gort	IV.	30
8	Killeen or Killeenly-nagh	149	3	39	Queen's Co.	Maryborough East	Straboe	Mountmellick	I.	242
8	Killeen or Killeenly-nagh	480	1	26	Queen's Co.	Portnahinch	Ardea	Mountmellick	I.	243
10, 11	Killeenlea	107	3	26	Kildare	North Salt	Killadoon	Celbridge	I.	75
23, 31	Killeenleagh	418	3	30	Cork, E.R.	Duhallow	Kilmeen	Kanturk	II.	73
143	Killeenleagh	101	1	1	Cork, W.R.	East Carbery (W.D.)	Ross	Clonakilty	II.	135
132	Killeenleagh	270	1	1	Cork, W.R.	West Carbery (W.D.)	Caheragh	Skibbereen	II.	142
80, 89, 90	Killeenleagh	596	2	29	Kerry	Iveragh	Dromod	Cahersiveen	II.	195
61	Killeenleigh	592	3	34	Cork, E.R.	East Muskerry	Donaghmore	Macroom	II.	103
35	Killeenleigh	162	1	22	Tipperary, N.R.	Eliogarty	Loughmoe East	Thurles	II.	271
31	Killeen and Lugnaboley	326	0	13	King's Co.	Ballyboy	Ballyboy	Parsonstown	I.	123
8	Killeenlynagh or Kil-leen	149	3	39	Queen's Co.	Maryborough East	Straboe	Mountmellick	I.	242
8	Killeenlynagh or Kil-leen	480	1	26	Queen's Co.	Portnahinch	Ardea	Mountmellick	I.	243
6, 7	Killeenmacoog North	32	3	26	Clare	Inchiquin	Kilkeedy	Corrofin	II.	26
6, 10	Killeenmacoog South	503	2	35	Clare	Inchiquin	Kilkeedy	Corrofin	II.	26
14	Killeenmore	363	0	17	Kildare	Naas North	Whitechurch	Naas	I.	63
17, 25	Killeenmore	1,489	2	5	King's Co.	Geashill	Geashill	Tullamore	I.	140
15, 22	Killeenmore	419	0	12b	Westmeath	Kilkenny West	Bunown	Athlone	I.	272
103	Killeenmunterlane North	173	2	35	Galway	Dunkellin	Kilcolgan	Gort	IV.	28
103	Killeenmunterlane South	150	1	23	Galway	Dunkellin	Kilcolgan	Gort	IV.	28
57	Killeennagallive	575	3	34	Tipperary, S.R.	Clanwilliam	Templebredon	Tipperary	II.	311
66	Killeennamanagh	303	3	22	Cork, E.R.	Imokilly	Mogeely	Middleton	II.	90
23	Killeennanam	177	2	13	Westmeath	Kilkenny West	Drumraney	Ballymahon	I.	273
21	Killeennashask	103	3	14	Mayo	Tirawley	Moygawnagh	Killala	IV.	171
129	Killeen North	380	3	7	Cork, W.R.	West Carbery (W.D.)	Kilcrohane	Bantry	II.	143
117, 126	Killeen North	252	0	3	Galway	Leitrim	Tynagh	Portumna	IV.	55
22	Killeenoghty	200	0	34c	Limerick	Pubblebrien	Killeenoghty	Croom	II.	253
104	Killeenpatrick	71	3	16	Galway	Loughrea	Isertkelly	Loughrea	IV.	63
74	Killeenreendowney	188	0	8	Cork, E.R.	Cork	St. Finbars	Cork	II.	66
111, 119	Killeenrevagh	505	3	20	Mayo	Clanmorris	Crossboyne	Claremorris	IV.	133
111, 119	Killeenrevagh	278	1	26	Mayo	Kilmaine	Kilcommon	Claremorris	IV.	154
42	Killeenrevagh	288	3	30	Roscommon	Athlone	Killinvoy	Roscommon	IV.	182
62,63,73,74	Killeens	943	1	7	Cork, E.R.	Cork	St. Marys Shandon	Cork	II.	66
124	Killeens	132	2	30	Cork, W.R.	East Carbery (E.D.)	Templetrine	Kinsale	II.	130
39	Killeens	253	1	14	Kerry	Trughanacmy	Currans	Killarney	II.	209
33	Killeens	78	2	17	Kilkenny	Ida	The Rower	Thomastown	I.	104
37, 42	Killeens	147	1	15	Wexford	Forth	St. Peters	Wexford	I.	314
109	Killeen's Island	0	3	20	Galway	Longford	Meelick	Portumna	IV.	62
129, 138	Killeen South	361	1	12	Cork, W.R.	West Carbery (W.D.)	Kilcrohane	Bantry	II.	143
117, 126	Killeen South	178	0	17	Galway	Leitrim	Tynagh	Portumna	IV.	55
48, 49	Killeentierna	565	3	9	Kerry	Trughanacmy	Killeentierna	Killarney	II.	211
117	Killeen West	52	0	31	Galway	Longford	Killimorbologue	Portumna	IV.	59
26	Killeen West	205	0	32	Kildare	Offaly West	Ballybrackan	Athy	I.	71
25, 29	Killeen West	292	0	15	Kilkenny	Gowran	Ullard	Thomastown	I.	100
22	Killeen West	221	3	0d	Roscommon	Roscommon	Shankill	Strokestown	IV.	213
13, 18	Killeeny	276	1	35	Longford	Moydow	Killashee	Longford	I.	161
46, 47	Killeenyarda	231	1	17	Tipperary, N.R.	Eliogarty	Holycross	Thurles	II.	270
31	Killeenycallaghan	109	3	18	Westmeath	Moycashel	Ardnurcher or Horse-leap	Mullingar	I.	276
7	Killeeshal	254	3	22e	Carlow	Idrone West	Cloydagh	Carlow	I.	9
30	Killeeshal	108	3	22	Waterford	Decies without Drum	Whitechurch	Dungarvan	II.	361
53	Killeeshil	521	2	10	Tyrone	Dungannon Lower	Killeeshil	Dungannon	III.	298
12, 17	Killeevan Glebe	108	0	6	Monaghan	Dartree	Killeevan	Clones	III.	268
24	Killegan	209	2	20f	Roscommon	Ballintober North	Kilglass	Strokestown	IV.	186

(a) Including 14A. 2R. 9P. water.
(b) Including 23A. 2R. 16P. water.
(c) Including 3A. 3R. 8P. water.
(d) Including 7A. 3R. 37P. water.
(e) Including 10A. 0R. 32P. River Barrow.
(f) Including 7A. 3R. 36P. water.

No. of Sheet of the Ordnance Survey Maps.	Townlands and Towns.	Area in Statute Acres. A. R. P.	County.	Barony.	Parish.	Poor Law Union in 1857.	Townland Census of 1851, Part I. Vol.	Page
40	Killegane	129 2 5	Kerry	Trughanacmy	Castleisland	Tralee	II.	208
3	Killegar	656 0 4	Wicklow	Rathdown	Powerscourt	Rathdown	I.	356
50	Killeglan	502 0 11	Roscommon	Athlone	Taghmaconnell	Ballinasloe	IV.	185
39, 45	Killegland	716 1 11	Meath	Ratoath	Killegland	Dunshaughlin	I.	218
24, 30	Killegney	1,014 3 23	Wexford	Bantry	Killegney	Enniscorthy	I.	301
12	Killegran	102 2 32	Wexford	Ballaghkeen	Ardamine	Gorey	I.	291
66, 67, 74, 75	Killegy Lower	146 1 34	Kerry	Magunihy	Killarney	Killarney	II.	203
74	Killegy Upper	303 3 9	Kerry	Magunihy	Killarney	Killarney	II.	203
112	Killehagh	356 1 13	Cork, E.R.	Kinalea	Kilmonoge	Kinsale	II.	95
28, 29	Killeheen	347 0 19	Limerick	Connello Lower	Kilscannell	Rathkeale	II.	228
54, 55	Killeheen	271 1 6	Tipperary, S.R.	Slievardagh	Ballingarry	Callan	II.	332
4	Killehenny	286 3 34	Kerry	Iraghticonnor	Killehenny	Listowel	II.	191
134	Killeigh	235 1 8	Cork, W.R.	East Carbery (W.D.)	Castleventry	Clonakilty	II.	131
25	Killeigh	1,186 2 39	King's Co.	Geashill	Geashill	Tullamore	I.	140
75	Killeigh	150 2 29	Tipperary, S.R.	Iffa and Offa West	Caher	Clogheen	II.	318
44	Killeighter	166 3 24	Galway	Clare	Killererin	Tuam	IV.	21
4	Killeighter	398 1 11	Kildare	Ikeathy&Oughterany	Cloncurry	Celbridge	I.	57
25	KILLEIGH T.	—	King's Co.	Geashill	Geashill	Tullamore	I.	140
15, 23	Killeinagh	44 3 3	Clare	Corcomroe	Clooney	Ennistimon	II.	18
21	Killeisk	119 0 39	Tipperary, N.R.	Upper Ormond	Ballymackey	Nenagh	II.	289
38	Killelan	48 2 13	Kildare	Kilkea and Moone	Killelan	Baltinglass	I.	60
32, 33	Killelan	274 0 35	Wexford	Ballaghkeen	St. Nicholas	Enniscorthy	I.	298
43	Killelane	105 3 38	Kerry	Corkaguiny	Dingle	Dingle	II.	175
79	Killelan East	353 2 34	Kerry	Iveragh	Caher	Cahersiveen	II.	194
79	Killelan West	324 1 34	Kerry	Iveragh	Caher	Cahersiveen	II.	194
36	Killeline	170 1 31	Limerick	Glenquin	Monagay	Newcastle	II.	247
26	Killellery	727 0 13	King's Co.	Geashill	Geashill	Tullamore	I.	140
37	Killelton	1,007 1 10	Kerry	Corkaguiny	Kilgobban	Tralee	II.	177
2	Killelton	192 3 22	Kerry	Iraghticonnor	Aghavallen	Listowel	II.	189
24, 32	Killelton	313 1 31	Waterford	Decies without Drum	Stradbally	Kilmacthomas	II.	361
75, 76	Killemly	208 3 2a	Tipperary, S.R.	Iffa and Offa West	Caher	Clogheen	II.	318
33	Killen	356 0 14b	Tyrone	Omagh West	Longfield West	Castlederg	III.	316
17	Killenagh	38 1 35	Wexford	Ballaghkeen	Killenagh	Gorey	I.	295
17	KILLENAGH T.	—	Wexford	Ballaghkeen	Killenagh	Gorey	I.	295
5	Killenaule	125 2 23	Tipperary, N.R.	Lower Ormond	Dorrha	Parsonstown	II.	283
5	Killenaule	126 3 31	Tipperary, N.R.	Lower Ormond	Loughkeen	Parsonstown	II.	286
54	Killenaule	324 3 24	Tipperary, S.R.	Slievardagh	Killenaule	Cashel	II.	334
54	KILLENAULE T.	—	Tipperary, S.R.	Slievardagh	Killenaule	Cashel	II.	334
23	Killen Far	327 2 15	Tyrone	Omagh West	Termonamongan	Castlederg	III.	317
11	Killenna Glebe	272 1 1	Leitrim	Drumahaire	Drumlease	Manorhamilton	IV.	94
22	Killennan	360 2 37	Londonderry	Tirkeeran	Cumber Lower	Londonderry	III.	249
23, 24	Killen Near	279 3 15	Tyrone	Omagh West	Termonamongan	Castlederg	III.	317
32	Killenny	112 0 12	Queen's Co.	Slievemargy	Killabban	Carlow	I.	245
13, 14	Killenny	288 1 22	Queen's Co.	Stradbally	Killenny	Mountmellick	I.	247
6	Killenny	225 2 11c	Tyrone	Strabane Lower	Donaghedy	Strabane	III.	321
35	Killenny Beg or Knocknagrally	130 3 33	Queen's Co.	Clarmallagh	Aghmacart	Abbeyleix	I.	236
35	Killenny More or Toberboe	621 1 18	Queen's Co.	Clarmallagh	Aghmacart	Abbeyleix	I.	236
8	Killenora	139 2 21	Carlow	Carlow	Kellistown	Carlow	I.	2
104, 117	Killenough	83 2 0	Cork, W.R.	Bear	Kilcaskan	Castletown	II.	123
52, 60	Killenure	354 0 18	Tipperary, S.R.	Kilnamanagh Lower	Oughterleague	Cashel	II.	324
109	Killeragh	188 0 16	Galway	Longford	Clonfert	Ballinasloe	IV.	57
9	Killerdoo	48 0 17	Roscommon	Boyle	Boyle	Boyle	IV.	194
7	Killerduff	304 0 12	Mayo	Tirawley	Doonfeeny	Killala	IV.	167
7	Killerguile	515 3 16	Waterford	Upperthird	Mothel	Carrick on Suir	II.	371
9	Killerk	16 1 32	Wicklow	Lower Talbotstown	Hollywood	Baltinglass	I.	360
41	Killerk East	219 0 38	Clare	Islands	Killone	Ennis	II.	30
70	Killerk North	468 0 13	Tipperary, S.R.	Middlethird	Donaghmore	Cashel	II.	326
70	Killerk South	4 3 34	Tipperary, S.R.	Middlethird	Donaghmore	Cashel	II.	326
41	Killerk West	230 2 22	Clare	Islands	Killone	Ennis	II.	30
29	Killermogh	266 2 24	Queen's Co.	Clarmallagh	Killermogh	Abbeyleix	I.	238
26	Killernam	72 0 35	Fermanagh	Clanawley	Killesher	Enniskillen	III.	192
31, 39	Killernan	668 2 0	Clare	Ibrickan	Kilmurry	Ennistimon	II.	23
118, 119, 121, 122	Killernan	531 3 39	Mayo	Kilmaine	Kilmainemore	Ballinrobe	IV.	156
4, 16	Killerneen	138 0 9	Galway	Dunmore	Addergoole	Tuam	IV.	33
33, 47	Killeroran	839 0 15	Galway	Killian	Killeroran	Mountbellew	IV.	44
34	Killerr	270 2 35	Roscommon	Ballymoe	Drumatemple	Castlereagh	IV.	191
3, 8	Killerrig	821 1 7	Carlow	Carlow	Killerrig	Carlow	I.	2
26	Killerrin	152 2 15	Leitrim	Carrigallen	Carrigallen	Bawnboy	IV.	89
15, 21	Killerry	1,974 2 14	Sligo	Tirerrill	Killerry	Sligo	IV.	239
97	Killescragh	309 0 30	Galway	Athenry	Killimordaly	Loughrea	IV.	4

(a) Including 2A. 0R. 24P. water.   (b) Including 2A. 3R. 38P. water.   (c) Including 2A. 2R. 7P. water.

4 D 2

No. of Sheet of the Ordnance Survey Maps.	Townlands and Towns.	Area in Statute Acres. A. R. P.	County.	Barony.	Parish.	Poor Law Union in 1857.	Townland Census of 1851, Part I. Vol.	Page
26, 32	Killesher	130 2 18	Fermanagh	Clanawley	Killesher	Enniskillen	III.	192
10	Killeshil	200 2 26	King's Co.	Lower Philipstown	Killaderry	Tullamore	I.	143
32, 37	Killeshin	715 3 4	Queen's Co.	Slievemargy	Killeshin	Carlow	I.	246
39	Killesk	467 2 22	Wexford	Shelburne	Killesk	New Ross	I.	327
44	Killester	147 2 24	Meath	Ratoath	Rathbeggan	Dunshaughlin	I.	219
19	Killester Demesne	56 1 24	Dublin	Coolock	Clontarf	Dublin North	I.	26
14,15,18,19	Killester North	150 3 37	Dublin	Coolock	Killester	Dublin North	I.	28
18, 19	Killester South	128 1 19	Dublin	Coolock	Killester	Dublin North	I.	28
45	Killestry	247 2 27	Clare	Tulla Lower	Killaloe	Scarriff	II.	35
40	Killeter	571 2 29	Cavan	Castlerahan	Mullagh	Kells	III.	70
9	Killeter	339 0 17	Longford	Longford	Killoe	Longford	I.	159
23	Killeter	427 3 29	Tyrone	Omagh West	Termonamongan	Castlederg	III.	317
32, 33	Killetra	344 1 13a	Cork, E.R.	Fermoy	Mallow	Mallow	II.	81
30	Killetragh	468 3 2b	Cork, E.R.	Duhallow	Dromtarriff	Millstreet	II.	71
100	Killevny	455 0 3	Galway	Longford	Clonfert	Ballinasloe	IV.	57
37, 45	Killey	352 3 31	Tyrone	Dungannon Middle	Pomeroy	Cookstown	III.	304
19, 20	Killhill	223 1 38	Kildare	South Salt	Kill	Naas	I.	77
8, 9, 18	Killhill and Rosskirk	561 2 18	Donegal	Kilmacrenan	Clondavaddog	Milford	III.	125
45	Killiaghan and Gort	764 1 14	Roscommon	Athlone	St. Johns	Athlone	IV.	183
25, 26	Killian	240 3 36c	Clare	Bunratty Upper	Templemaley	Ennis	II.	11
46	Killian	333 3 38	Galway	Killian	Killian	Mountbellew	IV.	44
107	Killiane	196 2 8	Galway	Longford	Killimorbologue	Portumna	IV.	59
42, 43	Killiane	259 2 4	Wexford	Forth	Killiane	Wexford	I.	310
42, 43	Killiane Little	259 2 0	Wexford	Forth	Killiane	Wexford	I.	310
24	Killibleught	447 2 30	Londonderry	Keenaght	Bovevagh	NewTⁿLimavady	III.	235
14	Killicar	192 0 34	Cavan	Lower Loughtee	Drumlane	Cavan	III.	80
13	Killickabawn	85 2 39	Wicklow	Newcastle	Kilcoole	Rathdrum	I.	352
153	Killickaforavane	39 2 26	Cork, W.R.	West Carbery (E.D.)	Clear-island	Skibbereen	II.	138
4, 5	Killickaweeny	495 3 37	Kildare	Ikeathy&Oughterany	Cloncurry	Celbridge	I.	57
29	Killierisk	48 2 0	Kerry	Trughanacmy	Ratass	Tralee	II.	213
8	Killilagh	95 3 36	Clare	Corcomroe	Killilagh	Ennistimon	II.	20
48	Killillane	92 3 32	Wexford	Forth	St. Helens	Wexford	I.	314
85	Killimor	697 3 0	Galway	Kilconnell	Killimordaly	Loughrea	IV.	42
120	Killimor	747 2 34d	Mayo	Kilmaine	Ballinchalla	Ballinrobe	IV.	152
107, 117	Killimor and Boleybeg	105 3 32	Galway	Longford	Killimorbologue	Portumna	IV.	59
107, 117	KILLIMOR T.	—	Galway	Longford	Killimorbologue	Portumna	IV.	59
8	Killimy	380 2 3	Queen's Co.	Portnahinch	Coolbanagher	Mountmellick	I.	244
92, 93	Killin	466 2 7	Donegal	Banagh	Inver	Donegal	III.	107
4	Killin	287 3 37	Donegal	Inishowen East	Clonca	Inishowen	III.	117
8	Killin	354 2 6	Louth	Lower Dundalk	Ballymascanlan	Dundalk	I.	176
4, 6, 7	Killin	196 2 21	Louth	Upper Dundalk	Kane	Dundalk'	I.	179
16	Killina	547 1 15	King's Co.	Ballycowan	Rahan	Tullamore	I.	128
12, 13	Killina	194 1 28	Monaghan	Dartree	Clones	Monaghan	III.	264
17	Killinaboy	159 1 24	Clare	Inchiquin	Killinaboy	Corrofin	II.	26
11, 17	Killinaddan	93 3 0	Roscommon	Roscommon	Aughrim	Carⁿ. on Shannon	IV.	207
89	Killinagh	40 3 12	Cork, E.R.	Imokilly	Cloyne	Middleton	II.	85
2, 3	Killinagh	494 1 5	Kildare	Carbury	Nurney	Edenderry	I.	53
5	Killinagh	728 3 28e	Westmeath	Moygoish	Rathaspick	Mullingar	I.	280
12	Killinagh Lower	651 1 1	Kildare	Carbury	Kilpatrick	Edenderry	I.	52
12	Killinagh Upper	507 2 1	Kildare	Carbury	Kilpatrick	Edenderry	I.	52
35, 37	Killinaker	77 2 19	Leitrim	Mohill	Mohill	Mohill	IV.	108
17	Killinakin	214 1 26	Down	Dufferin	Killinchy	Downpatrick	III.	166
16	Killinane	599 1 23f	Carlow	Idrone West	Killinane	Carlow	I.	9
30	Killinane	479 3 33	Cork, E.R.	Duhallow	Dromtarriff	Kanturk	II.	71
15	Killinane	243 3 4	Cork, E.R.	Duhallow	Knocktemple	Kanturk	II.	75
28, 32, 33	Killinane	474 2 37	Kildare	Kilcullen	Kilcullen	Naas	I.	58
49	Killinane	187 3 21	Limerick	Coshlea	Galbally	Mitchelstown	II.	239
41	Killinane	254 2 26	Tipperary, N.R.	Eliogarty	Thurles	Thurles	II.	273
103	Killinangel Beg	318 1 21	Donegal	Tirhugh	Drumhome	Ballyshannon	III.	146
103	Killinangel More	126 3 7	Donegal	Tirhugh	Drumhome	Ballyshannon	III.	146
2, 6	Killinaparson	819 2 23	Queen's Co.	Tinnahinch	Kilmanman	Mountmellick	I.	249
21, 24	Killinardan	515 1 11	Dublin	Uppercross	Tallaght	Dublin South	I.	41
71	Killinardrish	310 2 14g	Cork, E.R.	East Muskerry	Cannaway	Macroom	II.	102
39, 42	Killinaspick	265 1 35	Kilkenny	Iverk	Clonmore	Carrick on Suir	I.	105
15	Killinawas	174 3 29	Longford	Granard	Granard	Granard	I.	156
23	Killinbore	171 3 4	Longford	Shrule	Taghshinny	Ballymahon	I.	167
8, 13	Killincarrig	560 0 18	Wicklow	Rathdown	Delgany	Rathdown	I.	355
13	KILLINCARRIG T.	—	Wicklow	Rathdown	Delgany	Rathdown	I.	355
72	Killinch	117 3 6	Tipperary, S.R.	Slievardagh	Templemichael	Carrick on Suir	II.	336
17	Killinchy	555 0 30	Down	Dufferin	Killinchy	Downpatrick	III.	166
23, 30	Killinchy in the Woods	988 1 36	Down	Castlereagh Upper	Killyleagh	Downpatrick	III.	165
11	Killincoole	619 2 17	Louth	Louth	Killincoole	Dundalk	I.	184

(a) Including 18A. 1R. 8P. water.
(b) Including 5A. 0R. 0P. water.
(c) Including 37A. 2R. 3P. water.
(d) Including 15A. 3R. 0P. water.
(e) Including 36A. 0R. 39P. water.
(f) Including 17A. 3R. 8P. River Barrow.
(g) Including 6A. 1R. 32P. water.

No. of Sheet of the Ordnance Survey Maps.	Townlands and Towns.	Area in Statute Acres.			County.	Barony.	Parish.	Poor Law Union in 1857.	Townland Census of 1851, Part I.	
		A.	R.	P.					Vol.	Page
22, 28	Killincooly Beg	275	3	39	Wexford	Ballaghkeen	Killincooly	Enniscorthy	I.	295
28	Killincooly More	315	3	25	Wexford	Ballaghkeen	Killincooly	Enniscorthy	I.	295
41	Killindarragh	149	1	36	Donegal	Boylagh	Templecrone	Glenties	III.	115
31	Killindra	25	1	32	Kilkenny	Kells	Dunnamaggan	Callan	I.	108
39	Killined	38	2	19	Sligo	Corran	Kilshalvy	Boyle	IV.	227
23, 31	Killineen East	179	1	9	Waterford	Decies without Drum	Clonea	Dungarvan	II.	354
23, 31	Killineen West	338	2	36	Waterford	D.cies without Drum	Clonea	Dungarvan	II.	354
21, 24	Killineer	1,004	3	38	Louth	Drogheda	St. Peter's	Drogheda	I.	175
23, 26	Killiney	256	2	0	Dublin	Rathdown	Killiney	Rathdown	I.	36
35, 36	Killiney	817	1	39	Kerry	Corkaguiny	Killiney	Dingle	II.	178
23	KILLINEY T.	—			Dublin	Rathdown	Kill	Rathdown	I.	36
36	KILLINEY T.	—			Kerry	Corkaguiny	Killiney	Dingle	II.	178
133	Killinga	722	0	31a	Cork, W.R.	East Carbery (W.D.)	Kilmacabea	Skibbereen	II.	133
47	Killinick	24	0	39	Wexford	Forth	Killinick	Wexford	I.	310
47	KILLINICK T.	—			Wexford	Forth	Killinick	Wexford	I.	310
3, 7	Killinierin	249	1	27	Wexford	Gorey	Kilcavan	Gorey	I.	317
23	Killininneen	275	1	25	Westmeath	Kilkenny West	Drumraney	Ballymahon	I.	273
22	Killininny	194	2	11	Dublin	Uppercross	Tallaght	Dublin South	I.	41
40, 41	Killiniskyduff	187	1	37	Wicklow	Arklow	Kilbride	Rathdrum	I.	344
32	Killinlahan	375	2	23	Westmeath	Moycashel	Castletowndelaken	Mullingar	I.	277
14, 19	Killinlastra	94	0	19	Longford	Ardagh	Ardagh	Longford	I.	151
40	Killinleigh	57	1	32	Tipperary, N.R.	Kilnamanagh Upper	Moyaliff	Thurles	II.	279
65	Killinny	357	1	6	Clare	Moyarta	Moyarta	Kilrush	II.	34
27	Killinny	380	1	17	Kilkenny	Kells	Kells	Callan	I.	108
122	Killinny East	266	1	6	Galway	Kiltartan	Killinny	Gort	IV.	47
122	Killinny West	533	0	39	Galway	Kiltartan	Killinny	Gort	IV.	47
36	Killinoorin	84	0	24	Waterford	Decies within Drum	Ringagonagh	Dungarvan	II.	353
23, 29, 30	Killinordan	212	0	7	Roscommon	Roscommon	Bumlin	Strokestown	IV.	208
29	Killinordanbeg	245	1	17	Roscommon	Roscommon	Bumlin	Strokestown	IV.	208
12, 13	Killinpark	74	3	36	Wicklow	Newcastle	Kilcoole	Rathdrum	I.	352
34	Killinraghty Big	257	3	38	Roscommon	Ballymoe	Oran	Roscommon	IV.	192
34	Killinraghty Little	86	0	20	Roscommon	Ballymoe	Oran	Roscommon	IV.	192
30	Killinroan	142	3	20	Westmeath	Clonlonan	Ballyloughloe	Athlone	I.	260
26, 27	Killins	926	1	34b	Tyrone	Strabane Upper	Cappagh	Omagh	III.	325
22	Killins North	117	3	22	Antrim	Kilconway	Finvoy	Ballymoney	III.	26
22	Killins South	120	2	16	Antrim	Kilconway	Finvoy	Ballymoney	III.	26
12, 16, 17	Killinthomas	1,040	2	2	Kildare	Offaly East	Rathangan	Edenderry	I.	71
7, 12	Killintown	232	0	11c	Westmeath	Corkaree	Stonehall	Mullingar	I.	263
9, 15	Killinure	770	0	15	Down	Castlereagh Upper	Saintfield	Lisburn	III.	166
36	Killinure	232	3	37	King's Co.	Ballybritt	Seirkieran	Parsonstown	I.	127
14	Killinure	343	1	16	Limerick	Clanwilliam	Caherconlish	Limerick	II.	222
17	Killinure	194	2	4	Longford	Rathcline	Rathcline	Longford	I.	164
5, 9	Killinure	318	2	33	Queen's Co.	Portnahinch	Lea	Mountmellick	I.	244
11	Killinure	539	2	7	Queen's Co.	Upperwoods	Offerlane	Mountmellick	I.	252
81	Killinure	95	1	38	Tipperary, S.R.	Iffa and Offa West	Tubbrid	Clogheen	II.	321
25	Killinure	437	0	27d	Tyrone	Strabane Upper	Cappagh	Omagh	III.	325
37, 42	Killinure	1,767	1	0	Wicklow	Shillelagh	Aghowle	Shillelagh	I.	356
22	Killinure North	753	1	21	Westmeath	Kilkenny West	Bunown	Athlone	I.	272
22	Killinure South	115	2	26	Westmeath	Kilkenny West	Bunown	Athlone	I.	272
42	Killinvoy	350	1	22	Roscommon	Athlone	Killinvoy	Roscommon	IV.	182
26, 27	Killisk	787	0	30	Wexford	Ballaghkeen	Killisk	Enniscorthy	I.	296
16	Killiskea	223	3	19	King's Co.	Ballycowan	Kilbride	Tullamore	I.	127
19	Killiskey	104	2	31	Wicklow	Newcastle	Killiskey	Rathdrum	I.	352
26	Killissane	232	3	1	Cork, E.R.	Fermoy	Monanimy	Mallow	II.	81
61	Killstafford	157	0	22	Tipperary, S.R.	Middlethird	Brickendown	Cashel	II.	325
38	Killistristane	333	0	27	King's Co.	Clonlisk	Ettagh	Roscrea	I.	130
7	Killmaconnell	240	1	12	Londonderry	Coleraine	Macosquin	Coleraine	III.	233
42	Kill More	114	1	37	Meath	Lower Moyfenrath	Rathmolyon	Trim	I.	211
59	Killmountain	189	0	2	Cork, W.R.	West Muskerry	Clondrohid	Macroom	II.	155
109, 122	Kill North	136	2	24	Cork, W.R.	East Carbery (E.D.)	Desertserges	Clonakilty	II.	128
24, 33	Killoan	941	3	15e	Tyrone	Omagh West	Longfield West	Castlederg	III.	316
76	Killock	30	0	5	Tipperary, S.R.	Iffa and Offa East	Ballyclerahan	Clonmel	II.	312
79, 80	Killoe	612	2	17	Kerry	Iveragh	Caher	Cahersiveen	II.	194
9, 14	Killoe Glebe	129	1	0	Longford	Longford	Killoe	Longford	I.	159
68	Killotin	316	3	32	Clare	Clonderalaw	Killofin	Killadysert	I.	17
23	Kill of the Grange	263	1	39	Dublin	Rathdown	Kill	Rathdown	I.	36
14, 15	Killogeary	192	3	27	Mayo	Tirawley	Lackan	Killala	IV.	170
29, 30, 35, 36	Killogeenaghan	566	3	2	Westmeath	Clonlonan	Kilcleagh	Athlone	I.	261
2, 3	Killoghil	444	0	38	Clare	Burren	Drumcreehy	Ballyvaghan	II.	12
104	Killogilleen	93	1	1	Galway	Dunkellin	Killogilleen	Loughrea	IV.	31
70, 80	Killognaveen North	178	2	15	Kerry	Iveragh	Killinane	Cahersiveen	II.	197
80	Killognaveen South	396	2	9	Kerry	Iveragh	Killinane	Cahersiveen	II.	197

(a) Including 2A. 0R. 8P. water.
(b) Including 6A. 3R. 6P. water.
(c) Including 5A. 1R. 20P. water.
(d) Including 2A. 2R. 27P. w.ter.
(e) Including 4A. 3R. 19P. water.

No. of Sheet of the Ordnance Survey Maps.	Townlands and Towns.	Area in Statute Acres.			County.	Barony.	Parish.	Poor Law Union in 1857.	Townland Census of 1851, Part I.	
		A.	R.	P.					Vol.	Page
80, 89	Killogrone	340	0	29	Kerry	Iveragh	Caher	Cahersiveen	II.	194
21	Killogunra	98	3	17	Mayo	Tirawley	Killala	Killala	IV.	169
36, 44	Killokennedy	1,373	2	39	Clare	Tulla Lower	Killokennedy	Limerick	II.	35
54, 67	Killola	193	1	21	Galway	Moycullen	Killannin	Oughterard	IV.	69
88	Killoluaig	704	0	3	Kerry	Iveragh	Killemlagh	Cahersiveen	II.	196
5	Killomeerhoe	143	1	21	Kerry	Iraghticonnor	Lisselton	Listowel	II.	192
35	Killomenaghan	62	2	11	Westmeath	Clonlonan	Kilcleagh	Athlone	I.	261
122	Killomoran	266	3	7a	Galway	Kiltartan	Kilmacduagh	Gort	IV.	48
21, 22	Killonahan	320	3	22	Limerick	Pubblebrien	Killonahan	Croom	II.	253
6, 14	Killonan	218	3	34	Limerick	Clanwilliam	Derrygalvin	Limerick	II.	223
6, 14	Killonan	702	3	39	Limerick	Clanwilliam	Kilmurry	Limerick	II.	224
9, 13, 14	Killone	630	2	38	Queen's Co.	Stradbally	Killenny	Mountmellick	I.	247
16, 25	Killone	295	0	29	Waterford	Middlethird	Dunhill	Waterford	II.	367
96, 97	Killonecaha	227	0	11	Kerry	Iveragh	Killemlagh	Cahersiveen	II.	196
18	Killoneen	424	1	29	King's Co.	Lower Philipstown	Kilclonfert	Tullamore	I.	142
38	Killonerry	458	2	19	Kilkenny	Iverk	Whitechurch	Carrick on Suir	I.	107
35, 36	Killongford	209	2	25	Waterford	Decies without Drum	Dungarvan	Dungarvan	II.	355
59, 72	Killooaun	106	1	0	Galway	Tiaquin	Ballymacward	Mountbellew	IV.	75
72	Killooaun	302	0	32	Galway	Tiaquin	Clonkeen	Mountbellew	IV.	76
72	Killooaun (Browne)	128	2	21	Galway	Tiaquin	Ballymacward	Mountbellew	IV.	75
59, 72	Killooaun (Eyre)	403	0	17b	Galway	Tiaquin	Ballymacward	Mountbellew	IV.	75
23, 24	Killooly	1,347	2	23	King's Co.	Ballyboy	Killoughy	Tullamore	I.	124
16	Killooman	723	2	37	Leitrim	Drumahaire	Killarga	Manorhamilton	IV.	98
39	Killoon	131	0	8	Tyrone	Dungannon Upper	Ballyclog	Cookstown	III.	306
96, 104	Killora	172	2	23	Galway	Dunkellin	Killora	Loughrea	IV.	31
101, 109	Killoran	125	0	29	Galway	Longford	Clonfert	Ballinasloe	IV.	57
99	Killoran	642	0	2	Galway	Longford	Killoran	Ballinasloe	IV.	59
36	Killoran	1,594	2	35	Tipperary, N.R.	Eliogarty	Moyne	Thurles	II.	271
19	Killoran	148	3	4	Tipperary, N.R.	Owney and Arra	Castletownarra	Nenagh	II.	294
20	Killorane	69	1	19	Kerry	Clanmaurice	Ardfert	Tralee	II.	167
25	Killoran North	305	1	28	Sligo	Leyny	Killoran	Tobercurry	IV.	230
25, 32	Killoran South	241	0	23	Sligo	Leyny	Killoran	Tobercurry	IV.	230
31	Killorath	289	1	2	Limerick	Smallcounty	Glenogra	Croom	II.	260
56	KILLORGLIN T.	—			Kerry	Trughanacmy	Killorglin	Killarney	II.	211
59	Killoscobe	109	1	8	Galway	Tiaquin	Killoscobe	Mountbellew	IV.	78
26, 32	Killoscully	106	3	1	Tipperary, N.R.	Owney and Arra	Killoscully	Nenagh	II.	295
118	Killosheheen	249	0	21	Mayo	Kilmaine	Ballinrobe	Ballinrobe	IV.	153
8, 9, 13	Killoshulan	1,182	1	21	Kilkenny	Crannagh	Fertagh	Urlingford	I.	85
28, 34	Killoskehan	2,541	3	14	Tipperary, N.R.	Ikerrin	Killoskehan	Roscrea	II.	276
46, 60	Killosolan	1,799	0	19	Galway	Tiaquin	Killosolan	Mountbellew	IV.	78
30,31,35,36	Killosseragh	119	0	20	Waterford	Decies without Drum	Dungarvan	Dungarvan	II.	355
11	Killossery	252	2	20	Dublin	Nethercross	Killossery	Balrothery	I.	31
9, 17	Killoteran	282	2	12	Waterford	Middlethird	Killoteran	Waterford	II.	367
62, 66, 67	Killough	334	2	5	Antrim	Upper Massereene	Aghalee	Lurgan	III.	29
45	Killough	422	3	26c	Down	Lecale Upper	Rathmullan	Downpatrick	III.	181
92, 93	Killough	786	1	7	Galway	Moycullen	Moycullen	Galway	IV.	71
23	Killough	849	1	29	Tipperary, N.R.	Ikerrin	Templemore	Roscrea	II.	276
47	Killough	499	1	35	Tipperary, S.R.	Middlethird	Gaile	Cashel	II.	327
20	Killoughag	84	1	28	Antrim	Lower Glenarm	Layd	Ballycastle	III.	22
65	Killoughane	246	0	3	Kerry	Dunkerron North	Knockane	Killarney	II.	182
26, 35	Killoughcarran	598	2	12d	Donegal	Kilmacrenan	Kilmacrenan	Dunfanaghy	III.	129
127	Killough East	387	1	36	Cork, W.R.	Bear	Kilnamanagh	Castletown	II.	126
4	Killougher	320	3	23	Dublin	Balrothery East	Balscaddan	Balrothery	I.	20
7	Killough Lower	128	0	26e	Wicklow	Rathdown	Kilmacanoge	Rathdown	I.	355
19	Killoughrum	926	1	22	Wexford	Scarawalsh	Monart	Enniscorthy	I.	324
16	Killoughter	140	1	16	Cavan	Tullygarvey	Annagh	Cootehill	III.	87
19, 25	Killoughter	389	2	10	Wicklow	Newcastle	Rathnew	Rathdrum	I.	354
19, 20	Killoughternane	516	2	3	Carlow	Idrone East	Sliguff	Carlow	I.	8
127	KILLOUGH T.	—			Cork, W.R.	Bear	Kilnamanagh	Castletown	II.	126
45	KILLOUGH T.	—			Down	Lecale Upper	Rathmullan	Downpatrick	III.	181
30, 38	Killoughty	202	1	39	Limerick	Connello Upper	Ballingarry	Croom	II.	230
7	Killough Upper	230	3	24	Wicklow	Rathdown	Kilmacanoge	Rathdown	I.	355
127	Killough West	364	3	13	Cork, W.R.	Bear	Kilnamanagh	Castletown	II.	126
32	Killoughy	260	1	38	King's Co.	Ballyboy	Killoughy	Tullamore	I.	124
110	Killountain	483	3	16	Cork, W.R.	Kinalmeaky	Ballymodan	Bandon	II.	151
97	Killountane	245	2	15	Cork, E.R.	Kinalea	Inishannon	Bandon	II.	95
117	Killour	239	1	19	Mayo	Kilmaine	Ballinchalla	Ballinrobe	IV.	152
11	Killourney	329	0	39f	Clare	Inchiquin	Kilkeedy	Corrofin	II.	26
117	Killoveenoge	398	0	28	Cork, W.R.	West Carbery(W.D.)	Durrus	Bantry	II.	142
92	Killoveeny	391	1	35g	Mayo	Costello	Knock	Claremorris	IV.	143
34, 42	Killow	296	1	35	Clare	Islands	Clareabbey	Ennis	II.	23
14	Killowen	349	1	16	Cork, E.R.	Duhallow	Clonfert	Kanturk	II.	68
62	Killowen	601	3	17	Cork, E.R.	East Muskerry	Garrycloyne	Cork	II.	103

(a) Including 18A. 1R. 13P. water.
(b) Including 34A. 3R. 13P. water.
(c) Including 9A. 2R. 10P. water.

(d) Including 16A. 3R. 19P. water.
(e) Including 35A. 3R. 26P. detached portion.

(f) Including 2A. 3R. 14P. water.
(g) Including 4A. 2R. 15P. water.

No. of Sheet of the Ordnance Survey Maps.	Townlands and Towns.	Area in Statute Acres.			County.	Barony.	Parish.	Poor Law Union in 1857.	Townland Census of 1851, Part I.	
		A.	R.	P.					Vol.	Page
113	Killowen	418	2	23	Cork, E.R.	Kinalea	Ballyfoyle	Kinsale	II.	94
95, 109	Killowen	507	0	26	Cork, W.R.	Kinalmeaky	Killowen	Bandon	II.	152
39	Killowen	221	1	10	Cork, W.R.	West Muskerry	Drishane	Millstreet	II.	156
93	Killowen	301	0	36	Kerry	Glanarought	Kenmare	Kenmare	II.	186
4	Killowen	1,021	2	27	King's Co.	Warrenstown	Castlejordan	Edenderry	I.	145
17, 18, 26, 27	Killowen	353	3	10	Waterford	Middlethird	Drumcannon	Waterford	II.	366
4	Killowen	245	2	21	Waterford	Upperthird	Clonagam	Carrick on Suir	II.	369
6, 11	Killowen	349	3	38	Wexford	Gorey	Kilnahue	Gorey	I.	319
34	Killowen	233	3	25	Wexford	Shelburne	Whitechurch	New Ross	I.	329
37	Killowen	348	2	8	Wexford	Shelmaliere East	Tikillin	Wexford	I.	331
3	Killowen Lower	273	3	33	Wexford	Gorey	Kilgorman	Gorey	I.	318
54, 55	Killowen Mountains	666	2	33	Down	Upper Iveagh, Up.pt.	Kilbroney	Kilkeel	III.	175
3	Killowen Upper	197	2	31	Wexford	Gorey	Kilgorman	Gorey	I.	318
28, 29, 42, 43	Killower	315	2	14a	Galway	Clare	Killower	Tuam	IV.	21
22	Killowney Beg	103	3	27	King's Co.	Garrycastle	Gallen	Parsonstown	I.	136
15, 21	Killowney Big	141	3	34	Tipperary, N.R.	Upper Ormond	Ballymackey	Nenagh	II.	289
15, 21	Killowney Little	569	0	34	Tipperary, N.R.	Upper Ormond	Ballymackey	Nenagh	II.	289
22	Killowney More	371	0	38	King's Co.	Garrycastle	Gallen	Parsonstown	I.	136
124, 125, 147	Killowny	230	2	14	Cork, W.R.	Courceys	Kilroan	Kinsale	II.	147
42, 45	Killoy	123	3	37	Roscommon	Athlone	Killinvoy	Athlone	IV.	182
35, 36, 44, 45	Kill-saint-anne North	348	1	30	Cork, E.R.	Barrymore	Castlelyons	Fermoy	II.	53
44, 45	Kill-saint-anne South	496	1	9	Cork, E.R.	Barrymore	Castlelyons	Fermoy	II.	53
17	Kill St. Lawrence	36	1	19	Waterford	Gaultiere	Kill St. Lawrence	Waterford	II.	363
18	Kill St. Nicholas	189	3	16	Waterford	Gaultiere	Kill St. Nicholas	Waterford	II.	364
122	Kill South	139	2	30	Cork, W.R.	East Carbery (E.D.)	Desertserges	Clonakilty	II.	128
19	KILL T.	—			Kildare	South Salt	Kill	Naas	I.	77
25	KILL T.	—			Waterford	Decies without Drum	Kilbarrymeaden	Kilmacthomas	II.	356
9	Killua	935	2	16b	Westmeath	Delvin	Killua	Castletowndelvin	I.	265
28	Killucan	1,503	2	35	Tyrone	Dungannon Upper	Kildress	Cookstown	III.	309
20	Killucan	356	2	19	Westmeath	Farbill	Killucan	Mullingar	I.	267
20	KILLUCAN T.	—			Westmeath	Farbill	Killucan	Mullingar	I.	267
42	Killugger	47	2	8	Wexford	Forth	Kilmacree	Wexford	I.	311
11	Killukin	149	2	34	Roscommon	Boyle	Killukin	Carᵏ. on Shannon	IV.	195
28, 29	Killukin	193	0	36c	Roscommon	Roscommon	Killukin	Strokestown	IV.	211
13	Killulagh	131	2	4	Westmeath	Delvin	Killulagh	Castletowndelvin	I.	266
51	Killulla	380	1	32	Clare	Bunratty Lower	Clonloghan	Ennis	II.	3
24	Killult	451	0	36	Donegal	Kilmacrenan	Tullaghobegly	Dunfanaghy	III.	132
36	Killultagh	87	0	31	Roscommon	Roscommon	Cloonfinlough	Roscommon	IV.	209
97	Killultan	192	3	20	Donegal	Banagh	Killaghtee	Donegal	III.	109
11	Killummod	348	0	11	Roscommon	Boyle	Killummod	Carᵏ. on Shannon	IV.	196
85	Killumney	279	3	4	Cork, E.R.	East Muskerry	St. Finbars	Bandon	II.	106
93	Killunagher	555	1	15d	Mayo	Costello	Annagh	Claremorris	IV.	138
24, 30	Killunaght	609	3	20	Londonderry	Keenaght	Banagher	NewTᴺLimavady	III.	234
12	Killuney	209	0	28	Armagh	Oneilland West	Armagh	Armagh	III.	51
4	Killuney	635	0	4	Galway	Ballymoe	Dunmore	Glennamaddy	IV.	7
43, 44, 52, 53	Killuntin North	381	3	0	Cork, E.R.	Barrymore	Ardnageehy	Fermoy	II.	50
52, 53	Killuntin South	333	0	6	Cork, E.R.	Barrymore	Ardnageehy	Fermoy	II.	50
61, 74	Killuppaun (Clonbrock)	259	1	5	Galway	Clonmacnowen	Ahascragh	Ballinasloe	IV.	24
61, 74	Killuppaun (Mahon)	50	2	24	Galway	Clonmacnowen	Ahascragh	Ballinasloe	IV.	24
25, 26, 33	Killuragh	360	3	0	Cork, E.R.	Fermoy	Clenor	Mallow	II.	78
15, 24	Killuragh	736	1	5	Limerick	Owneybeg	Tuogh	Limerick	II.	251
36	Killuran	234	2	34	Clare	Tulla Lower	Killuran	Tulla	II.	36
36	Killuran Beg	231	3	2	Clare	Tulla Lower	Killuran	Tulla	II.	36
10	Killurane	642	1	29	Tipperary, N.R.	Lower Ormond	Modreeny	Borrisokane	II.	286
36	Killuran More	387	2	22	Clare	Tulla Lower	Killuran	Tulla	II.	36
7, 11	Killure	200	0	33	Londonderry	Coleraine	Macosquin	Coleraine	III.	233
36, 37	Killure	111	1	31	Sligo	Leyny	Kilmacteige	Tobercurry	IV.	231
17, 18	Killure	627	1	18	Waterford	Gaultiere	Killure	Waterford	II.	364
74	Killure Beg	441	2	33	Galway	Clonmacnowen	Kilgerrill	Ballinasloe	IV.	25
21	Killure or Bohernastrekaun	253	0	36	Kilkenny	Gowran	Wells	Kilkenny	I.	100
74	Killure Castle	636	0	17	Galway	Clonmacnowen	Kilgerrill	Ballinasloe	IV.	26
74, 87	Killure More	1,249	2	37	Galway	Clonmacnowen	Kilgerrill	Ballinasloe	IV.	26
24, 25	Killurin	2,463	2	8	King's Co.	Geashill	Geashill	Tullamore	I.	140
31, 32, 36, 37	Killurin	366	2	17	Wexford	Shelmaliere West	Killurin	Wexford	I.	334
88, 97	Killurly	733	0	7	Kerry	Iveragh	Prior	Cahersiveen	II.	198
69, 70	Killurly Commons	2,276	1	12e	Kerry	Iveragh	Killinane	Cahersiveen	II.	197
69, 70	Killurly East	340	0	10	Kerry	Iveragh	Killinane	Cahersiveen	II.	197
69	Killurly West	383	3	27	Kerry	Iveragh	Killinane	Cahersiveen	II.	197
71, 77, 78	Killurney	1,262	3	31	Tipperary, S.R.	Iffa and Offa East	Temple-etney	Clonmel	II.	316
77	Killurriga	171	2	3	Cork, E.R.	Imokilly	Ballyoughtera	Middleton	II.	84
70, 71, 78	Killusty North	739	0	21	Tipperary, S.R.	Middlethird	Kiltinan	Clonmel	II.	328
70, 71, 77, 78	Killusty South	616	3	37	Tipperary, S.R.	Middlethird	Kiltinan	Clonmel	II.	328

(a) Including 27ᴀ. 1ʀ. 18ᴘ. water.
(b) Including 14ᴀ. 3ʀ. 17ᴘ. water.
(c) Including 51ᴀ. 0ʀ. 34ᴘ. water.
(d) Including 5ᴀ. 0ʀ. 36ᴘ. water.
(e) Including 10ᴀ. 1ʀ. 12ᴘ. water.

No. of Sheet of the Ordnance Survey Maps.	Townlands and Towns.	Area in Statute Acres. A. R. P.	County.	Barony.	Parish.	Poor Law Union in 1857.	Townland Census of 1851, Part I. Vol.	Page
14 ,19	Kill West	378 3 21	Kildare	South Salt	Kill	Naas	I.	77
11, 15	Killybandrick	533 3 21a	Cavan	Tullygarvey	Annagh	Cavan	III.	87
24	Killybane	73 3 16	Fermanagh	Magherastephana	Aghalurcher	Lisnaskea	III.	216
46, 48	Killybasky	424 3 15	Londonderry	Loughinsholin	Lissan	Magherafelt	III.	242
48	Killybearn	417 0 35	Londonderry	Loughinsholin	Derryloran	Magherafelt	III.	240
8, 13	Killy Beg	439 1 36	Fermanagh	Magheraboy	Inishmacsaint	Ballyshannon	III.	213
27	Killybeg	388 3 22	Wicklow	Upper Talbotstown	Donaghmore	Baltinglass	I.	363
97	Killybegs	325 0 15	Donegal	Banagh	Killybegs Upper	Glenties	III.	110
13	Killybegs	219 3 34	Kildare	Clane	Killybegs	Naas	I.	54
3	Killybegs	215 2 0	Wexford	Gorey	Inch	Gorey	I.	316
3	Killybegs	213 0 9	Wexford	Gorey	Kilgorman	Gorey	I.	318
13	Killybegs Demesne	274 1 11	Kildare	Clane	Killybegs	Naas	I.	54
97	KILLYBEGS T.	—	Donegal	Banagh	Killybegs Upper	Glenties	III.	111
2, 3	Killybern	138 2 25	Monaghan	Trough	Errigal Trough	Clogher	III.	284
37, 42	Killyberry	299 1 30	Londonderry	Loughinsholin	Ballyscullion	Magherafelt	III.	239
50, 57	Killyberry	205 2 20	Tyrone	Clogher	Donacavey	Omagh	III.	294
37, 42	Killyberry Boyd	150 0 0	Londonderry	Loughinsholin	Ballyscullion	Magherafelt	III.	239
42	Killyberry Downing	134 3 2	Londonderry	Loughinsholin	Ballyscullion	Magherafelt	III.	239
32	Killyblane	134 3 27	Fermanagh	Clanawley	Killesher	Enniskillen	III.	193
57	Killyblunick Glebe	418 2 36	Tyrone	Omagh East	Kilskeery	Enniskillen	III.	313
18, 22	Killybodagh	370 2 13	Armagh	Orior Lower	Killevy	Newry	III.	56
41, 46	Killyboggin	303 1 9	Londonderry	Loughinsholin	Desertmartin	Magherafelt	III.	240
29	Killyboley	70 0 0	Monaghan	Farney	Inishkeen	Dundalk	III.	271
7	Killyboley	66 2 33	Monaghan	Trough	Donagh	Monaghan	III.	282
6	Killybough	89 1 19	Monaghan	Monaghan	Tedavnet	Monaghan	III.	279
35	Killybrack	541 0 30b	Tyrone	Strabane Upper	Cappagh	Omagh	III.	325
32	Killybracken	156 0 2	Fermanagh	Clanawley	Killesher	Enniskillen	III.	193
54	Killybracken	334 0 37	Tyrone	Dungannon Middle	Clonfeacle	Dungannon	III.	299
46, 54	Killybrackey	193 1 8c	Tyrone	Dungannon Middle	Drumglass	Dungannon	III.	303
10	Killybready	202 2 6	Londonderry	Keenaght	Aghanloo	NewTⁿLimavady	III.	234
28	Killybreagy	46 3 9	Fermanagh	Magherastephana	Aghavea	Lisnaskea	III.	219
22	Killybreed	47 2 15	Fermanagh	Magheraboy	Rossorry	Enniskillen	III.	214
3	Killybreen	212 1 21	Monaghan	Trough	Errigal Trough	Monaghan	III.	284
3	Killybressal	99 0 10	Monaghan	Trough	Errigal Trough	Monaghan	III.	284
15	Killybrone	101 2 1	Mayo	Tirawley	Killala	Killala	IV.	169
3	Killybrone	134 0 35	Monaghan	Trough	Errigal Trough	Clogher	III.	284
40	Killycanavan Lower	84 3 1	Tyrone	Dungannon Upper	Arboe	Cookstown	III.	305
40	Killycanavan Upper	145 3 34	Tyrone	Dungannon Upper	Arboe	Cookstown	III.	305
25	Killycannan	166 2 10	Cavan	Clanmahon	Denn	Cavan	III.	76
16	Killycapple	344 1 36	Armagh	Fews Lower	Lisnadill	Armagh	III.	47
6	Killycappy	51 3 23	Fermanagh	Lurg	Magheraculmoney	Lowtherstown	III.	208
20, 25	Killycard	180 3 28	Monaghan	Cremorne	Muckno	Castleblayney	III.	262
28, 29	Killycarn	875 1 33	Antrim	Lower Antrim	Skerry	Ballymena	III.	5
40, 43	Killycarnan	169 1 2	Fermanagh	Coole	Galloon	Clones	III.	200
10	Killycarnan	86 1 13	Monaghan	Monaghan	Tehallan	Monaghan	III.	280
5, 8	Killycarnan North	99 2 10	Monaghan	Monaghan	Tedavnet	Monaghan	III.	279
8	Killycarnan South	101 1 8	Monaghan	Monaghan	Tedavnet	Monaghan	III.	279
1, 2	Killycarney	221 0 16	Cavan	Tullyhaw	Killinagh	Enniskillen	III.	92
17	Killycarn Lower	187 2 0	Armagh	Orior Lower	Loughgilly	Newry	III.	56
17	Killycarn Upper	335 3 39d	Armagh	Orior Lower	Loughgilly	Newry	III.	56
3, 6	Killycarran	241 2 4	Monaghan	Trough	Errigal Trough	Monaghan	III.	284
21	Killycat	106 2 9	Fermanagh	Magheraboy	Rossorry	Enniskillen	III.	214
30, 31	Killycatron	156 1 20e	Cavan	Clanmahon	Drumlumman	Granard	III.	77
23	Killycleare	162 3 24	Cavan	Clankee	Drumgoon	Cootehill	III.	72
6	Killyclessy	75 1 12	Louth	Upper Dundalk	Creggan	Dundalk	I.	177
22, 27	Killycloghan	348 0 28f	Cavan	Clankee	Knockbride	Cootehill	III.	74
42	Killycloghan	99 2 22g	Fermanagh	Knockninny	Kinawley	Lisnaskea	III.	202
13	Killycloghan	57 3 7	Leitrim	Drumahaire	Cloonclare	Manorhamilton	IV.	93
35	Killyclogher	300 3 8	Tyrone	Strabane Upper	Cappagh	Omagh	III.	325
28	Killycloghy	157 0 35	Fermanagh	Magherastephana	Aghalurcher	Lisnaskea	III.	216
2	Killyclooney	768 1 32h	Tyrone	Strabane Lower	Donaghedy	Strabane	III.	321
39	Killyclowny	157 3 34i	Fermanagh	Coole	Galloon	Lisnaskea	III.	200
53	Killyclug	465 0 39	Donegal	Kilmacrenan	Conwal	Letterkenny	III.	126
13	Killycluggin	76 0 10	Cavan	Tullyhaw	Templeport	Bawnboy	III.	95
12	Killycoghill	141 3 30	Monaghan	Dartree	Clones	Monaghan	III.	264
28	Killycolman	135 1 4	Donegal	Kilmacrenan	Killygarvan	Millford	III.	128
38	Killycolp	113 2 29	Tyrone	Dungannon Upper	Desertcreat	Cookstown	III.	308
39, 40	Killycolpy	746 3 12	Tyrone	Dungannon Upper	Arboe	Cookstown	III.	305
10	Killycomain	195 0 24	Armagh	Oneilland East	Seagoe	Lurgan	III.	50
9	Killyconigan	87 0 24	Monaghan	Monaghan	Monaghan	Monaghan	III.	277
7	Killyconigan	203 1 17j	Monaghan	Trough	Donagh	Monaghan	III.	202
26	Killyconnan	216 0 28	Cavan	Upper Loughtee	Lavey	Cavan	III.	86
44	Killyconny	305 3 14	Cavan	Castlerahan	Loughan or Castlekeeran	Oldcastle	III.	69

(a) Including 55A. 0R. 34P. water.
(b) Including 1A. 0R. 32P. water.
(c) Including 1A. 1R. 3P. water.
(d) Including 11A. 2R. 24P. water.

(e) Including 5A. 2R. 16P. water.
(f) Including 4A. 0R. 8P. water.
(g) Including 2A. 2R. 26P. water.

(h) Including 4A. 2R. 32P. water.
(i) Including 39A. 2R. 10P. water.
(j) Including 44A. 3R. 24P. water.

No. of Sheet of the Ordnance Survey Maps.	Townlands and Towns.	Area in Statute Acres.			County.	Barony.	Parish.	Poor Law Union in 1857.	Townland Census of 1851, Part I.	
		A.	R.	P.					Vol.	Page
26, 31	Killycoogan	451	1	30	Antrim	Lower Toome	Ahoghill	Ballymena	III.	32
3, 6	Killycooly	271	0	28	Monaghan	Trough	Donagh	Monaghan	III.	282
12	Killycoonagh	231	3	19	Monaghan	Dartree	Killeevan	Clones	III.	268
23	Killycor	579	0	10	Londonderry	Tirkeeran	Cumber Upper	NewTLimavady	III.	249
3	Killycorran	40	2	34	Monaghan	Trough	Errigal Trough	Monaghan	III.	284
64	Killycorran	105	2	15a	Tyrone	Clogher	Clogher	Clogher	III.	293
27	Killycowan	664	3	35	Antrim	Kilconway	Rasharkin	Ballymena	III.	28
20	Killycracken	330	1	11	Monaghan	Cremorne	Muckno	Castleblayney	III.	262
17	Killycramph	65	0	25	Cavan	Tullygarvey	Drumgoon	Cootehill	III.	88
42	Killycramph	128	3	17b	Fermanagh	Knockninny	Kinawley	Lisnaskea	III.	202
28	Killycramph	86	3	6	Fermanagh	Magherastephana	Aghavea	Lisnaskea	III.	219
23, 27	Killycreen	791	2	26	Antrim	Kilconway	Rasharkin	Ballymena	III.	28
9	Killycreen	83	2	23	Monaghan	Monaghan	Tedavnet	Monaghan	III.	279
20, 25	Killycreen East	363	3	8	Fermanagh	Clanawley	Cleenish	Enniskillen	III.	191
20, 25	Killycreen West	692	3	31c	Fermanagh	Clanawley	Cleenish	Enniskillen	III.	191
17	Killycreeny	204	1	28	Cavan	Tullygarvey	Kildrumsherdan	Cootehill	III.	90
9	Killycrin	166	1	29d	Cavan	Tullyhaw	Templeport	Bawnboy	III.	95
19	Killycrom	156	0	27	Monaghan	Cremorne	Clontibret	Castleblayney	III.	260
12	Killycronaghan	108	3	4	Monaghan	Dartree	Killeevan	Clones	III.	268
21, 26	Killycroue	151	0	4	Cavan	Tullygarvey	Larah	Cavan	III.	91
6	Killycroney	155	3	10	Louth	Louth	Louth	Dundalk	I.	184
34	Killycrutteen	76	1	6	Fermanagh	Magherastephana	Aghalurcher	Lisnaskea	III.	216
17	Killyculla	557	3	32	Fermanagh	Tirkennedy	Enniskillen	Enniskillen	III.	222
21, 29	Killycurragh	773	1	11	Tyrone	Dungannon Upper	Derryloran	Cookstown	III.	307
35	Killycurragh	449	2	22	Tyrone	Strabane Upper	Cappagh	Omagh	III.	325
2	Killycurry	150	3	19e	Tyrone	Strabane Lower	Donaghedy	Strabane	III.	321
9, 13	Killycushil	72	2	5	Monaghan	Monaghan	Monaghan	Monaghan	III.	277
17, 25	Killydart	469	3	37	Tyrone	Strabane Lower	Ardstraw	Strabane	III.	319
45, 53	Killydesert	304	2	9	Donegal	Kilmacrenan	Kilmacrenan	Letterkenny	III.	129
3	Killydonagh	78	1	35	Monaghan	Trough	Errigal Trough	Monaghan	III.	284
46	Killydonnell	536	3	26	Donegal	Kilmacrenan	Aughnish	Millford	III.	122
26, 27	Killydonnelly	535	2	11	Antrim	Kilconway	Rasharkin	Ballymena	III.	28
8, 9	Killydonnelly	148	2	36	Monaghan	Monaghan	Tedavnet	Monaghan	III.	279
63, 64	Killydonoghoe	457	2	38	Cork, E.R.	Barrymore	Templeusque	Cork	II.	59
31, 37	Killydoon	163	1	34	Cavan	Clanmahon	Drumlumman	Granard	III.	77
31, 37	Killydream	271	1	30f	Cavan	Clanmahon	Drumlumman	Granard	III.	77
3	Killydreen	117	2	32	Monaghan	Trough	Errigal Trough	Clogher	III.	284
32	Killydressy	135	0	14	Down	Ards Upper	Witter	Downpatrick	III.	161
20	Killydrum	137	1	20	Fermanagh	Magheraboy	Boho	Enniskillen	III.	209
26	Killydrum	208	0	5g	Leitrim	Carrigallen	Carrigallen	Bawnboy	IV.	90
9, 13	Killydrutan	78	0	36	Monaghan	Monaghan	Monaghan	Monaghan	III.	277
33	Killyduff	201	2	21	Cavan	Castlerahan	Killinkere	Bailieborough	III.	69
48, 49	Killyfad	159	2	19	Antrim	Upper Toome	Drummaul	Antrim	III.	34
35	Killyfad	135	2	10	Leitrim	Mohill	Annaduff	Mohill	IV.	105
9, 14	Killyfad	200	3	5	Longford	Longford	Killoe	Longford	I.	159
16	Killyfaddy	375	0	15	Armagh	Fews Lower	Lisnadill	Armagh	III.	47
42, 46, 47	Killyfaddy	671	3	23	Londonderry	Loughinsholin	Magherafelt	Magherafelt	III.	243
58	Killyfaddy	154	3	32h	Tyrone	Clogher	Clogher	Clogher	III.	293
11, 15	Killyfana	324	0	10i	Cavan	Tullygarvey	Annagh	Cavan	III.	87
3	Killyfaragh	130	0	27	Monaghan	Trough	Errigal Trough	Monaghan	III.	284
16	Killyfargy	136	1	38j	Monaghan	Dartree	Currin	Clones	III.	266
38	Killyfassy	255	2	23	Cavan	Clanmahon	Ballymachugh	Cavan	III.	76
42, 43	Killyfast	290	3	11	Antrim	Upper Toome	Duneane	Ballymena	III.	35
29	Killyfea	548	0	26k	Leitrim	Carrigallen	Cloone	Mohill	IV.	90
14	Killyfern	119	0	8	Cavan	Lower Loughtee	Drumlane	Cavan	III.	80
38, 39	Killyfinla	232	2	13	Cavan	Castlerahan	Castlerahan	Oldcastle	III.	67
32	Killyflugh	213	3	19	Antrim	Lower Toome	Kirkinriola	Ballymena	III.	32
35	Killyfole	118	3	5l	Fermanagh	Clankelly	Clones	Clones	III.	196
12	Killyfuddy	207	3	2	Monaghan	Dartree	Killeevan	Clones	III.	268
50, 57	Killyfuddy	195	2	32	Tyrone	Omagh East	Kilskeery	Lowtherstown	III.	313
34	Killygally	183	2	34m	Monaghan	Farney	Magheracloone	Carrickmacross	III.	272
20, 26	Killyganard	297	3	23	Queen's Co.	Ballyadams	Ballyadams	Athy	I.	231
26, 30	Killygar	260	1	39n	Leitrim	Carrigallen	Carrigallen	Bawnboy	IV.	90
36	Killygarn	549	2	12	Antrim	Lower Toome	Ahoghill	Ballymena	III.	32
20,21,25,26	Killygarry	264	1	12	Cavan	Upper Loughtee	Annagelliff	Cavan	III.	82
16, 21	Killygarry	62	1	23	Cavan	Upper Loughtee	Castleterra	Cavan	III.	82
5, 6	Killygarry	145	2	33	Fermanagh	Lurg	Drumkeeran	Lowtherstown	III.	206
38	Killygarvan	139	3	35	Tyrone	Dungannon Upper	Desertcreat	Cookstown	III.	308
28	Killygarvan Lower	121	3	24	Donegal	Kilmacrenan	Killygarvan	Millford	III.	128
28	Killygarvan Upper	147	2	9	Donegal	Kilmacrenan	Killygarvan	Millford	III.	128
46	Killygavanagh	68	1	37	Tyrone	Dungannon Middle	Donaghmore	Dungannon	III.	302
6	Killygavna	285	2	3	Monaghan	Monaghan	Tedavnet	Monaghan	III.	279
35, 40	Killyglen	1,255	1	6	Antrim	Upper Glenarm	Grange of Killyglen	Larne	III.	24

(a) Including 1A. 1R. 20P. water.
(b) Including 11A. 2R. 26P. water.
(c) Including 15A. 2R. 30P. water.
(d) Including 1A. 1R. 12P. detached portion.
(e) Including 1A. 0R. 18P. water.

(f) Including 10A. 3R. 29P. water.
(g) Including 24A. 3R. 28P. water.
(h) Including 8A. 2R. 32P. water.
(i) Including 43A. 1R. 10P. water.
(j) Including 5A. 0R. 17P. water.

(k) Including 4A. 2R. 24P. water.
(l) Including 18A. 2R. 13P. water.
(m) Including 4A. 3R. 32P. water.
(n) Including 37A. 3R. 2P. water.

No. of Sheet of the Ordnance Survey Maps.	Townlands and Towns.	Area in Statute Acres.			County.	Barony.	Parish.	Poor Law Union in 1857.	Townland Census of 1851. Part I.	
		A.	R.	P.					Vol.	Page
20	Killygola	271	1	32a	Monaghan	Cremorne	Muckno	Castleblayney	III.	262
17	Killygone	100	3	12	Monaghan	Dartree	Killeevan	Clones	III.	268
39, 40	Killygonlan	513	3	29	Tyrone	Dungannon Upper	Arboe	Cookstown	III.	305
78	Killygordon	409	1	2b	Donegal	Raphoe	Donaghmore	Stranorlar	III.	138
57	Killygordon	581	2	33	Tyrone	Clogher	Clogher	Clogher	III.	293
78	KILLYGORDON T.	—			Donegal	Raphoe	Donaghmore	Stranorlar	III.	138
27, 28	Killygore	497	2	6	Antrim	Lower Antrim	Skerry	Ballymena	III.	5
14, 19	Killygorman	299	3	39	Cavan	Tullyhunco	Kildallan	Bawnboy	III.	97
12	Killygorman	75	1	30	Monaghan	Dartree	Killeevan	Clones	III.	268
35	Killygorman and Aghadrumsee	263	3	8c	Fermanagh	Clankelly	Clones	Clones	III.	194
19	Killygowan	112	0	17d	Cavan	Tullyhunco	Kildallan	Cavan	III.	97
20	Killygowan	288	2	2e	Cavan	Upper Loughtee	Kilmore	Cavan	III.	84
9	Killygowan	98	2	13	Monaghan	Monaghan	Monaghan	Monaghan	III.	277
33	Killygowan Island	71	2	37	Fermanagh	Tirkennedy	Cleenish	Lisnaskea	III.	220
18	Killygragy	137	1	21	Monaghan	Dartree	Aghabog	Cootehill	III.	263
9	Killygrallan	189	0	18	Monaghan	Monaghan	Tedavnet	Monaghan	III.	279
27	Killygrania	61	3	12	Fermanagh	Tirkennedy	Derrybrusk	Enniskillen	III.	220
14	Killygreagh	166	1	1	Cavan	Tullyhunco	Kildallan	Bawnboy	III.	97
38	Killygreagh	153	0	32	Fermanagh	Knockninny	Kinawley	Lisnaskea	III.	202
3, 4	Killygreen Lower	126	3	39	Londonderry	North East Liberties of Coleraine	Ballywillin	Coleraine	III.	245
4	Killygreen Upper	145	3	37	Londonderry	North East Liberties of Coleraine	Ballywillin	Coleraine	III.	245
26, 32	Killygrogan	341	3	10	Cavan	Upper Loughtee	Lavey	Cavan	III.	86
12, 17	Killyguire	624	3	7	Kildare	Offaly East	Rathangan	Edenderry	I.	71
34	Killygullan	67	2	38	Fermanagh	Magherastephana	Aghalurcher	Lisnaskea	III.	216
27, 33	Killygullib Glebe	966	2	39	Londonderry	Loughinsholin	Tamlaght O'Crilly	Ballymoney	III.	243
46, 54	Killyharry Glebe	255	1	10	Tyrone	Dungannon Middle	Donaghmore	Dungannon	III.	302
22, 27	Killyhevlin	152	2	36f	Fermanagh	Tirkennedy	Enniskillen	Enniskillen	III.	222
1	Killyhoman	151	3	18	Monaghan	Trough	Errigal Trough	Clogher	III.	284
21	Killyhommon	145	0	35g	Fermanagh	Magheraboy	Boho	Enniskillen	III.	209
31	Killykeeghan	1,336	3	17	Fermanagh	Clanawley	Killesher	Enniskillen	III.	192
37	Killykeen	59	2	22	Cavan	Clanmahon	Ballymachugh	Cavan	III.	76
37	Killykeen	54	3	18	Cavan	Clanmahon	Drumlumman	Granard	III.	77
19, 20	Killykeen	178	0	33	Cavan	Upper Loughtee	Kilmore	Cavan	III.	84
12, 13	Killykeeragh	111	3	24	Monaghan	Dartree	Clones	Monaghan	III.	264
28	Killykeeran	189	0	38	Fermanagh	Magherastephana	Aghavea	Lisnaskea	III.	219
18	Killykergan	308	3	18	Londonderry	Coleraine	Aghadowey	Coleraine	III.	230
12	Killykeskeame	127	2	10	Monaghan	Dartree	Killeevan	Monaghan	III.	268
46, 54	Killylack Glebe	55	0	10	Tyrone	Dungannon Middle	Drumglass	Dungannon	III.	303
35	Killylacky	96	0	19h	Fermanagh	Clankelly	Clones	Clones	III.	196
36, 42	Killylaes	86	1	20	Antrim	Upper Toome	Ballyscullion Grange	Ballymena	III.	33
39	Killylane	636	2	31	Antrim	Upper Antrim	Ballycor	Larne	III.	6
15	Killylane	509	3	37	Londonderry	Tirkeeran	Faughanvale	NewTᵉLimavady	III.	250
3	Killylaragh	107	1	36	Monaghan	Trough	Errigal Trough	Monaghan	III.	284
53	Killylastin	499	0	7	Donegal	Kilmacrenan	Conwal	Letterkenny	III.	126
15, 21	Killylaughnane	80	3	5	Tipperary, N.R.	Upper Ormond	Kilruane	Nenagh	II.	292
11	Killylea	449	2	27	Armagh	Armagh	Tynan	Armagh	III.	46
11	Killylea	250	2	30i	Cavan	Lower Loughtee	Annagh	Cavan	III.	79
5	Killylea	49	2	16	Fermanagh	Lurg	Magheraculmoney	Lowtherstown	III.	208
92	Killylea	102	1	31j	Mayo	Costello	Bekan	Claremorris	IV.	139
24	KILLYLEAGH T.	—			Down	Dufferin	Killyleagh	Downpatrick	III.	167
11	KILLYLEA T.	—			Armagh	Armagh	Tynan	Armagh	III.	46
3	Killyleck (Anketell)	86	2	24	Monaghan	Trough	Errigal Trough	Monaghan	III.	284
3	Killyleck (Lucas)	80	2	38	Monaghan	Trough	Errigal Trough	Monaghan	III.	284
9	Killyleen	139	1	20	Monaghan	Monaghan	Kilmore	Monaghan	III.	276
17	Killyleg	166	0	18	Monaghan	Dartree	Aghabog	Cootehill	III.	263
31	Killyless	547	0	37	Antrim	Lower Toome	Ahoghill	Ballymena	III.	32
53	Killylevin	255	1	0	Tyrone	Dungannon Middle	Donaghmore	Dungannon	III.	302
35	Killylifferbane Glebe	118	0	3	Fermanagh	Clankelly	Clones	Clones	III.	196
35	Killylifferdoo	73	2	8	Fermanagh	Clankelly	Clones	Clones	III.	196
23	Killyliss	57	0	7	Fermanagh	Tirkennedy	Enniskillen	Lisnaskea	III.	222
23	Killyliss	109	1	12	Monaghan	Cremorne	Aghnamullen	Cootehill	III.	258
50	Killyliss	231	1	25	Tyrone	Clogher	Donacavey	Omagh	III.	294
54	Killyliss	408	0	2k	Tyrone	Dungannon Middle	Donaghmore	Dungannon	III.	302
6	Killylough	296	0	18l	Monaghan	Monaghan	Tedavnet	Monaghan	III.	279
3	Killyloughavoy	97	1	23	Monaghan	Trough	Errigal Trough	Clogher	III.	284
8, 12	Killylyn	226	2	29	Armagh	Armagh	Grange	Armagh	III.	45
42	Killymackan	339	3	3m	Fermanagh	Knockninny	Kinawley	Lisnaskea	III.	202
21, 22	Killymaddy	274	1	4	Antrim	Kilconway	Finvoy	Ballymoney	III.	26
7	Killymaddy	221	3	11	Armagh	Tiranny	Eglish	Armagh	III.	60
53	Killymaddy (Evans)	186	3	23	Tyrone	Dungannon Middle	Donaghmore	Dungannon	III.	302

(a) Including 8A. 1R. 25P. water.
(b) Including 14A. 2R. 32P. water.
(c) Including 11A. 0R. 16P. water.
(d) Including 2A. 2R. 13P. water.
(e) Including 5A. 0R. 5P. water.

(f) Including 36A. 2R. 8P. water.
(g) Including 19A. 3R. 5P. water.
(h) Including 16A. 2R. 38P. water.
(i) Including 19A. 2R. 13P. water.

(j) Including 9A. 0R. 24P. water.
(k) Including 9A. 2R. 4P. water.
(l) Including 9A. 0R. 16P. water.
(m) Including 52A. 2R. 23P. water.

No. of Sheet of the Ordnance Survey Maps.	Townlands and Towns.	Area in Statute Acres.	County.	Barony.	Parish.	Poor Law Union in 1857.	Townland Census of 1851, Part I.
		A. R. P.					Vol. Page
54	Killymaddy (*Knox*)	333 3 19*a*	Tyrone . .	Dungannon Middle .	Donaghmore . .	Dungannon .	III. 302
21	Killymallaght .	571 2 23	Londonderry .	Tirkeeran .	Clondermot . .	Londonderry .	III. 248
29	Killymam .	156 2 31	Tyrone . .	Dungannon Upper .	Derryloran . .	Cookstown .	III. 307
9, 10	Killymarly .	180 2 34	Monaghan .	Monaghan . .	Monaghan . .	Monaghan .	III. 277
9	Killymarran .	75 2 26	Monaghan .	Monaghan . .	Tedavnet . .	Monaghan .	III. 279
52, 60	Killymasny .	1,445 0 5	Donegal . .	Raphoe . .	Conwal . . .	Letterkenny .	III. 137
54	Killymeal .	72 1 3	Tyrone . .	Dungannon Middle .	Drumglass . .	Dungannon .	III. 303
26	Killymeehan .	195 2 38	Cavan . .	Upper Loughtee .	Larah . . .	Cavan . .	III. 85
7	Killymeehin .	40 2 19	Leitrim . .	Rosclogher . .	Killasnet . .	Manorhamilton .	IV. 110
39	Killymenagh .	256 3 38	Tyrone . .	Dungannon Upper .	Arboe . . .	Cookstown .	III. 305
56	Killymendon .	247 2 5	Tyrone . .	Omagh East .	Kilskeery . .	Lowtherstown .	III. 313
16	Killymittan .	366 3 25	Fermanagh .	Tirkennedy .	Magheracross . .	Enniskillen .	III. 223
10	Killymonaghan .	143 2 19	Monaghan .	Cremorne . .	Clontibret . .	Monaghan .	III. 260
35, 36	Killymongaun .	491 0 14*b*	Galway . .	Ballynahinch .	Moyrus . .	Clifden . .	IV. 13
42, 50	Killymoonan .	207 3 29	Tyrone . .	Omagh East .	Donacavey .	Omagh . .	III. 310
29,30,38,39	Killymoon Demesne	589 3 2	Tyrone . .	Dungannon Upper .	Derryloran . .	Cookstown .	III. 307
13	Killy More .	395 1 14	Fermanagh .	Magheraboy . .	Inishmacsaint .	Ballyshannon .	III. 213
17, 18	Killymore .	448 3 7	Tyrone . .	Strabane Lower .	Ardstraw . .	Gortin . .	III. 319
52, 53	Killymorgan .	185 2 31	Tyrone . .	Clogher . .	Errigal Keerogue .	Clogher . .	III. 295
13	Killymoriarty .	160 3 37*c*	Cavan . .	Tullyhaw . .	Templeport . .	Bawnboy .	III. 95
53, 54	Killymoyle .	273 1 25	Tyrone . .	Dungannon Middle .	Donaghmore . .	Dungannon .	III. 302
49	Killymuck .	445 1 24	Londonderry .	Loughinsholin .	Ballinderry . .	Magherafelt .	III. 239
33	Killymuck Glebe .	572 2 0	Londonderry .	Loughinsholin .	Tamlaght O'Crilly .	Ballymoney .	III. 243
16	Killymullin .	259 2 2*d*	Cavan . .	Tullygarvey . .	Drung . . .	Cootehill .	III. 89
39	Killymurphy .	152 2 14	Tyrone . .	Dungannon Middle .	Donaghenry . .	Cookstown .	III. 301
3	Killymurry .	133 2 33	Monaghan .	Trough . . .	Errigal Trough .	Monaghan .	III. 284
39	Killynacran .	111 3 9*e*	Fermanagh .	Coole . . .	Galloon . .	Clones . .	III. 200
9, 10, 14	Killynaff .	133 1 38	Cavan . .	Tullyhaw . .	Templeport . .	Bawnboy . .	III. 95
22	Killynagh Beg .	124 1 3*f*	Roscommon .	Roscommon . .	Elphin . .	Strokestown .	IV. 209
22	Killynagh More .	173 1 19*g*	Roscommon .	Roscommon . .	Elphin . .	Strokestown .	IV. 209
5	Killynaght .	489 2 32	Tyrone . .	Strabane Lower .	Leckpatrick . .	Strabane . .	III. 322
14	Killynaher .	73 1 35*h*	Cavan . .	Lower Loughtee .	Drumlane . .	Cavan . .	III. 80
34	Killynamph .	176 0 14*i*	Fermanagh .	Magherastephana .	Aghalurcher . .	Lisnaskea .	III. 216
13, 19, 20	Killynan (*Cooke*)	1,090 3 17	Westmeath .	Moyashel and Magheradernon .	Rathconnell . .	Mullingar .	I. 276
6, 7	Killynann .	137 2 27	Wexford . .	Gorey . . .	Kilmakilloge . .	Gorey . .	I. 318
13, 20	Killynan (*Pratt*)	1,181 2 25	Westmeath .	Moyashel and Magheradernon .	Rathconnell . .	Mullingar .	I. 276
26, 32	Killynanum .	193 0 38	Cavan . .	Upper Loughtee .	Denn . . .	Cavan . .	III. 83
67	Killynaul .	334 0 27	Tyrone . .	Dungannon Lower .	Aghaloo . .	Dungannon .	III. 297
9	Killyneary .	151 3 37*j*	Cavan . .	Tullyhaw . .	Templeport . .	Bawnboy .	III. 95
20, 25	Killynebber .	217 0 32*k*	Cavan . .	Upper Loughtee .	Annagelliff . .	Cavan . .	III. 82
38	Killyneedan .	166 3 30	Tyrone . .	Dungannon Upper .	Desertcreat . .	Cookstown .	III. 308
60	Killyneery .	198 1 3	Tyrone . .	Dungannon Lower .	Carnteel . .	Clogher . .	III. 297
42	Killyncese .	285 0 29	Londonderry .	Loughinsholin .	Magherafelt . .	Magherafelt .	III. 243
10	Killyneill .	231 3 35	Monaghan .	Monaghan . .	Tehallan . .	Monaghan .	III. 280
54	Killyneill .	201 0 24	Tyrone . .	Dungannon Middle .	Drumglass . .	Dungannon .	III. 303
22	Killynenagh .	348 2 36*l*	Monaghan .	Dartree . .	Currin . . .	Cootehill .	III. 266
5, 10	Killynether .	151 0 5	Down . .	Castlereagh Lower .	Comber . .	Newtownards .	III. 162
42	Killynick .	241 1 36*m*	Fermanagh .	Knockninny . .	Kinawley . .	Lisnaskea .	III. 202
4, 5	Killynoogan .	75 2 30	Fermanagh .	Lurg . . .	Drumkeeran . .	Lowtherstown .	III. 206
39	Killynubber .	134 1 12*n*	Fermanagh .	Coole . . .	Galloon . .	Clones . .	III. 200
41	Killynumber .	180 0 33	Londonderry .	Loughinsholin .	Kilcronaghan . .	Magherafelt .	III. 241
12. 16	Killynure .	165 3 14	Armagh . .	Armagh . .	Lisnadill . .	Armagh . .	III. 45
32	Killynure .	369 1 26	Cavan . .	Castlerahan .	Crosserlough . .	Cavan . .	III. 68
12	Killynure .	187 1 37	Cavan . .	Tullygarvey . .	Annagh . .	Cavan . .	III. 87
22	Killynure .	134 2 34	Fermanagh .	Tirkennedy .	Enniskillen . .	Enniskillen .	III. 222
69	Killynure or Wilsons Fort . . .	356 3 33	Donegal . .	Raphoe . .	Convoy . .	Stranorlar .	III. 136
4	Killyon . .	270 3 29	Kildare . .	Carbury . . .	Dunfierth . .	Edenderry .	I. 52
36	Killyon . .	60 0 27	King's Co. .	Eglish . . .	Drumcullen . .	Parsonstown .	I. 134
41	Killyon . .	444 1 25	Meath . .	Upper Moyfenrath .	Killyon . .	Trim . .	I. 213
34	Killypaddy .	191 3 14*o*	Fermanagh .	Magherastephana .	Aghalurcher . .	Lisnaskea .	III. 217
25	Killyphort .	76 1 35	Fermanagh .	Clanawley .	Cleenish . .	Enniskillen .	III. 191
7	Killyquin .	110 2 36	Armagh . .	Tiranny . .	Eglish . .	Armagh . .	III. 59
54	Killyquinn .	70 1 38	Tyrone . .	Dungannon Middle .	Donaghmore . .	Dungannon .	III. 302
17	Killyramer .	213 0 22	Antrim . .	Upper Dunluce .	Ballymoney . .	Ballymoney .	III. 19
13	Killyrann .	329 3 36*p*	Cavan . .	Tullyhaw . .	Templeport . .	Bawnboy .	III. 95
39	Killyraw .	115 2 18*q*	Fermanagh .	Coole . . .	Galloon . .	Clones . .	III. 200
22, 27	Killyreagh .	56 3 28	Fermanagh .	Tirkennedy .	Derrybrusk . .	Enniskillen .	III. 220
7	Killyrean Lower .	103 3 10	Monaghan .	Trough . . .	Donagh . .	Monaghan .	III. 282
4, 7	Killyrean Upper .	173 0 25	Monaghan .	Trough . . .	Donagh . .	Monaghan .	III. 282
3	Killyreask .	68 2 35	Monaghan .	Trough . . .	Errigal Trough .	Clogher . .	III. 284

(*a*) Including 10A. 1R. 17P. water.
(*b*) Including 22A. 0R. 10P. water.
(*c*) Including 12A. 1R. 38P. water.
(*d*) Including 11A. 1R. 9P. water.
(*e*) Including 6A. 2R. 4P. water.
(*f*) Including 1A. 3R. 22P. water.

(*g*) Including 2A. 0R. 6P. water.
(*h*) Including 6A. 3R. 35P. water.
(*i*) Including 48A. 2R. 5P. water.
(*j*) Including 19A. 2R. 23P. Brackley Lough.
(*k*) Including 2A. 2R. 8P. water.
(*l*) Including 8A. 3R. 12P. water.

(*m*) Including 19A. 3R. 36P. water.
(*n*) Including 33A. 0R. 15P. water.
(*o*) Including 14A. 2R. 7P. water.
(*p*) Including 14A. 2R. 22P. water.
(*q*) Including 5A. 1R. 16P. water.

No. of Sheet of the Ordnance Survey Maps.	Townlands and Towns.	Area in Statute Acres.	County.	Barony.	Parish.	Poor Law Union in 1857.	Townland Census of 1851, Part I.	
		A. R. P.					Vol.	Page
16, 20	Killyreavy	357 3 9	Armagh	Armagh	Derrynoose	Armagh	III.	44
27	Killyree	346 1 8	Antrim	Kilconway	Dunaghy	Ballymena	III.	26
40	Killyroo	96 3 30	Fermanagh	Coole	Galloon	Clones	III.	200
28	Killyrover	164 3 29	Fermanagh	Magherastephana	Aghalurcher	Lisnaskea	III.	217
13	Killyruddan	230 1 37	Armagh	Fews Lower	Mullaghbrack	Armagh	III.	47
17,18,22,23	Killyrue	230 1 9a	Cavan	Clankee	Drumgoon	Cootehill	III.	72
16	Killyrue	133 1 12	Cavan	Tullygarvey	Drung	Cootehill	III.	89
33, 40	Killysavan	581 1 33	Down	Upper Iveagh, Up. pt.	Donaghmore	Newry	III.	175
2	Killyshane	115 0 32	Carlow	Carlow	Urglin	Carlow	I.	3
3	Killyslavan	95 1 38	Monaghan	Trough	Errigal Trough	Clogher	III.	284
20, 27	Killysorrell	231 3 16	Down	Lower Iveagh, Lr. pt.	Dromore	Banbridge	III.	168
21	Killytaggart	80 3 18b	Fermanagh	Magheraboy	Boho	Enniskillen	III.	209
19	Killytawny	137 0 8c	Cavan	Tullyhunco	Killashandra	Cavan	III.	98
26, 32	Killyteane	218 3 0	Cavan	Upper Loughtee	Denn	Cavan	III.	83
32	Killytogher	337 0 23	Cavan	Castlerahan	Crosserlough	Cavan	III.	68
36, 41	Killytoney	207 2 29	Londonderry	Loughinsholin	Kilcronaghan	Magherafelt	III.	241
8	Killytur	98 0 14	Monaghan	Monaghan	Tedavnet	Monaghan	III.	279
17, 18	Killyvaghan	338 3 38d	Cavan	Tullygarvey	Drumgoon	Cootehill	III.	88
22	Killyvahan	111 1 27	Cavan	Tullygarvey	Kildrumsherdan	Cootehill	III.	90
32	Killyvally	157 3 12	Cavan	Castlerahan	Denn	Oldcastle	III.	68
20, 25	Killyvally	107 0 12	Cavan	Upper Loughtee	Kilmore	Cavan	III.	84
18, 26	Killyvally	488 0 18	Londonderry	Coleraine	Desertoghill	Coleraine	III.	230
9, 10	Killyvane	96 2 15	Monaghan	Monaghan	Monaghan	Monaghan	III.	277
27	Killyvannan	117 2 16e	Fermanagh	Tirkennedy	Derryvullan	Enniskillen	III.	221
15, 20	Killyvanny	221 0 16	Cavan	Upper Loughtee	Castleterra	Cavan	III.	82
15	Killyveagh Glebe	327 3 7	Fermanagh	Magheraboy	Devenish	Enniskillen	III.	211
6	Killyveety	128 3 38	Londonderry	Coleraine	Dunboe	Coleraine	III.	231
33, 36	Killyvehy	671 1 2f	Leitrim	Mohill	Cloone	Mohill	IV.	106
46, 54	Killyverry	276 2 14	Donegal	Raphoe	Raymoghy	Londonderry	III.	142
36	Killyvilly	127 1 20	Fermanagh	Clankelly	Clones	Clones	III.	196
22	Killyvilly	242 1 7	Fermanagh	Tirkennedy	Enniskillen	Enniskillen	III.	222
12	Killyvolgan	322 2 16	Down	Ards Lower	Greyabbey	Newtownards	III.	158
9	Killywaum	101 3 37	Cavan	Tullyhaw	Templeport	Bawnboy	III.	95
13	Killywillin	201 3 37g	Cavan	Tullyhaw	Templeport	Bawnboy	III.	95
27	Killywillin	99 3 37h	Fermanagh	Clanawley	Cleenish	Enniskillen	III.	191
10	Killywilly	383 0 9i	Cavan	Lower Loughtee	Drumlane	Cavan	III.	80
15	Killywool	1,471 2 30	Londonderry	Tirkeeran	Faughanvale	NewTnLimavady	III.	250
39, 40	Killywoolaghan	659 3 9	Tyrone	Dungannon Upper	Arboe	Cookstown	III.	305
133, 142	Kilmacabea	354 2 27	Cork, W.R.	East Carbery (W.D.)	Kilmacabea	Skibbereen	II.	133
89	Kilmacahill	561 3 21	Cork, E.R.	Imokilly	Cloyne	Middleton	II.	85
20, 21	Kilmacahill	269 1 23	Kilkenny	Gowran	Kilmacahill	Kilkenny	I.	97
5, 6	Kilmacahill or Caraun	408 1 8	Westmeath	Moygoish	Rathaspick	Mullingar	I.	280
29	Kilmacananneny	422 3 30	Roscommon	Roscommon	Lissonuffy	Strokestown	IV.	212
30	Kilmacanearla North	460 1 25	Limerick	Connello Upper	Ballingarry	Croom	II.	230
30, 38	Kilmacanearla South	116 3 14	Limerick	Connello Upper	Ballingarry	Croom	II.	230
101, 111	Kilmacanelly	88 0 24	Mayo	Clanmorris	Crossboyne	Claremorris	IV.	133
8	Kilmacannon	280 0 19	Longford	Longford	Clongesh	Longford	I.	158
7	Kilmacannon	165 2 11j	Sligo	Carbury	Drumcliff	Sligo	IV.	221
7, 8	Kilmacanoge North	152 2 36h	Wicklow	Rathdown	Kilmacanoge	Rathdown	I.	355
7, 8	Kilmacanoge South	217 2 16	Wicklow	Rathdown	Kilmacanoge	Rathdown	I.	356
9	Kilmacanty	125 2 23	Armagh	Oneilland West	Kilmore	Armagh	III.	53
10	Kilmacar	813 0 32	Kilkenny	Fassadinin	Kilmacar	Castlecomer	I.	90
23	Kilmacaran	557 3 25l	Cavan	Clankee	Knockbride	Cootehill	III.	74
7	Kilmacarril	73 0 24	Roscommon	Boyle	Tumna	Carn. on Shannon	IV.	198
4, 5	Kilmacart	281 2 30	Carlow	Rathvilly	Hackettstown	Shillelagh	I.	11
4, 12	Kilmacat	218 2 7m	Limerick	Kenry	Ardcanny	Rathkeale	II.	248
35, 39, 40	Kilmacbrack	174 1 31n	Fermanagh	Coole	Galloon	Clones	III.	200
9, 14	Kilmacdermot	255 0 23	Wexford	Scarawalsh	St. Mary's Newtown-barry	Enniscorthy	I.	325
122, 128	Kilmacduagh	237 0 26o	Galway	Kiltartan	Kilmacduagh	Gort	IV.	48
121	Kilmacduagh	172 1 23	Mayo	Kilmaine	Kilmainebeg	Ballinrobe	IV.	155
47, 48, 58	Kilmacduane East	560 3 0	Clare	Moyarta	Kilmacduane	Kilrush	II.	33
47,48,57,58	Kilmacduane West	765 3 6	Clare	Moyarta	Kilmacduane	Kilrush	II.	33
17, 21	Kilmachugh	196 3 38	Armagh	Fews Lower	Kilclooney	Armagh	III.	46
12	Kilmachugh	265 3 9p	Armagh	Oneilland West	Grange	Armagh	III.	52
108, 109	Kilmachugh	336 0 18	Galway	Longford	Meelick	Portumna	IV.	61
89	Kilmackerrin East	633 2 28	Kerry	Iveragh	Dromod	Cahersiveen	II.	195
89	Kilmackerrin West	611 3 21	Kerry	Iveragh	Dromod	Cahersiveen	II.	195
26, 35	Kilmackilloo	444 1 32	Donegal	Kilmacrenan	Clondahorky	Dunfanaghy	III.	123
38	Kilmackilvenny,Barr of, or Monreagh	930 2 37	Donegal	Inishowen West	Fahan Upper	Londonderry	III.	121
102, 115	Kilmackowen	1,161 0 11	Cork, W.R.	Bear	Kilcatherine	Castletown	II.	124
27	Kilmacleague East	359 3 23	Waterford	Gaultiere	Kilmacleague	Waterford	II.	364

(a) Including 22A. 0R. 24P. water.
(b) Including 7A. 1R. 17P. water.
(c) Including 33A. 0R. 23P. water.
(d) Including 52A. 1R. 24P. water.
(e) Including 2A. 3R. 13P. water.
(f) Including 13A. 2R. 0P. water.

(g) Including 16A. 0R 24P. water.
(h) Including 26A. 1R. 34P. water.
(i) Including 96A. 3R. 12P. water.
(j) Including 16A. 2R. 22P. water.
(k) Including 6A. 0R. 0P. detached portion.

(l) Including 138A. 3R. 22P. water.
(m) Including 49A. 0R. 1P. water.
(n) Including 13A. 1R. 2P. water.
(o) Including 2A. 3R. 12P. water.
(p) Including 25A. 0R 1P. water.

No. of Sheet of the Ordnance Survey Maps.	Townlands and Towns.	Area in Statute Acres.			County.	Barony.	Parish.	Poor Law Union in 1857.	Townland Census of 1851, Part I.	
		A.	R.	P.					Vol.	Page
26, 27	Kilmacleague West .	360	2	26	Waterford .	Gaultiere . .	Kilmacleague . .	Waterford .	II.	364
24	Kilmaclenine . .	609	1	33	Cork, E.R. .	Orrery and Kilmore	Kilmaclenine . .	Mallow . .	II.	109
10,11,17,18	Kilmacnevan . .	240	0	4	Westmeath .	Moygoish . .	Kilmacnevan . .	Mullingar .	I.	280
16	Kilmacnoran . .	273	2	27	Cavan . .	Tullygarvey . .	Drung . . .	Cootehill . .	III.	89
33	Kilmacoe . .	625	3	33	Wexford . .	Shelmaliere East .	St. Margarets .	Wexford .	I.	331
24, 33	Kilmacogue . .	227	1	6	Limerick . .	Coonagh . .	Doon . . .	Tipperary .	II.	234
31	Kilmacogue . .	160	1	26	Tipperary, N.R.	Owney and Arra .	Kilnarath . .	Nenagh . .	II.	296
34	Kilmacoliver . .	347	2	8	Kilkenny . .	Kells . . .	Tullahought .	Carrick on Suir .	II.	110
18, 27	Kilmacomb . .	448	1	11	Waterford .	Gaultiere . .	Kilmacomb . .	Waterford .	II.	364
1	Kilmacomma . .	1,383	3	3a	Waterford .	Glenahiry . .	Inishlounaght .	Clonmel . .	II.	365
35	Kilmacoo . .	372	0	9	Wicklow . .	Arklow . . .	Castlemacadam .	Rathdrum .	I.	342
35	Kilmacoo . .	154	2	11	Wicklow . .	Arklow . . .	Redcross . .	Rathdrum .	I.	346
25	Kilmacoom . .	242	3	6	Cork, E.R. .	Fermoy . . .	Caherduggan .	Mallow . .	II.	77
35	Kilmacoo Upper .	279	2	8	Wicklow . .	Arklow . . .	Castlemacadam .	Rathdrum .	I.	342
22	Kilmacormick . .	152	0	2b	Fermanagh .	Tirkennedy . .	Trory . . .	Enniskillen .	III.	223
27	Kilmacot . .	68	0	7	Wexford . .	Ballaghkeen . .	Ballyvaldon . .	Enniscorthy .	I.	292
37, 46	Kilmacow . .	316	3	14	Cork, E.R. .	Kinnatalloon . .	Mogeely . .	Fermoy . .	II.	98
43	Kilmacow . .	246	1	24	Kilkenny . .	Iverk . . .	Kilmacow . .	Waterford .	I.	106
30	Kilmacow . .	1,078	1	35	Limerick . .	Connello Upper .	Ballingarry . .	Croom . .	II.	230
20	Kilmacowen . .	381	1	10	Sligo . . .	Carbury . . .	Kilmacowen . .	Sligo . .	IV.	222
43	Kilmacow T. .	—			Kilkenny . .	Iverk . . .	Kilmacow . .	Waterford .	I.	106
79	Kilmacrade . .	213	3	1c	Mayo . . .	Carra . . .	Breaghwy . .	Castlebar . .	IV.	127
106	Kilmacrah . .	329	1	11	Galway . .	Leitrim . . .	Leitrim . . .	Loughrea . .	IV.	55
30, 35	Kilmacrea Lower .	249	2	38	Wicklow . .	Arklow . . .	Redcross . .	Rathdrum .	I.	346
30	Kilmacrea Upper .	182	3	26	Wicklow . .	Arklow . . .	Redcross . .	Rathdrum .	I.	346
92, 98	Kilmacreddan . .	278	1	14	Donegal . .	Banagh . . .	Inver . . .	Donegal . .	III.	107
6, 11	Kilmacredock Lower	209	0	28	Kildare . .	North Salt . .	Kilmacredock .	Celbridge . .	I.	75
11	Kilmacredock Upper	269	3	38	Kildare . .	North Salt . .	Kilmacredock .	Celbridge . .	I.	75
11, 14	Kilmacree . .	65	2	3	Dublin . .	Nethercross . .	Kilsallaghan .	Balrothery .	I.	31
42	Kilmacree . .	108	0	15	Wexford . .	Forth . . .	Kilmacree . .	Wexford .	I.	311
45	Kilmacrenan . .	233	2	19	Donegal . .	Kilmacrenan . .	Kilmacrenan . .	Millford . .	III.	129
45	Kilmacrenan T. .	—			Donegal . .	Kilmacrenan . .	Kilmacrenan . .	Millford . .	III.	130
27	Kilmacrew . .	586	3	4	Down . . .	Lower Iveagh, Lr. pt.	Magherally . .	Banbridge .	III.	168
7	Kilmacrickard . .	376	3	28	Galway . .	Ballymoe . .	Ballynakill . .	Glennamaddy .	IV.	5
1, 3	Kilmacroy . .	402	1	19d	Roscommon .	Boyle . . .	Boyle . . .	Boyle . .	IV.	194
32	Kilmacshane . .	705	0	34e	Kilkenny . .	Gowran . . .	Inistioge . .	Thomastown .	I.	96
101, 109	Kilmacshane (Macklin)	272	1	15	Galway . .	Longford . .	Clonfert . . .	Ballinasloe .	IV.	57
101, 109	Kilmacshane (Turbett)	2,167	2	23	Galway . .	Longford . .	Clonfert . . .	Ballinasloe .	IV.	57
24	Kilmacsherwell .	174	3	35f	Leitrim . .	Mohill . . .	Fenagh . . .	Mohill . .	IV.	106
111	Kilmacsimon . .	219	0	35	Cork, W.R. .	East Carbery (E.D.)	Ballinadee . .	Bandon . .	II.	126
21	Kilmactalway . .	400	1	17	Dublin . .	Newcastle . .	Kilmactalway .	Celbridge .	I.	33
30, 36	Kilmacteige . .	2,158	3	34g	Sligo . . .	Leyny . . .	Kilmacteige . .	Tobercurry .	IV.	231
15	Kilmacthomas .	467	0	13	Waterford .	Decies without Drum	Rossmire . .	Kilmacthomas .	II.	360
15	Kilmacthomas T. .	—			Waterford .	Decies without Drum {	Ballylaneen } Rossmire }	Kilmacthomas .	II.	{354 {360
31	Kilmactrasna . .	139	2	17	Monaghan .	Farney . . .	Magheross . .	Carrickmacross .	III.	273
36	Kilmacuagh . .	80	3	8	Roscommon .	Ballintober South .	Kilgefin . . .	Roscommon .	IV.	189
29	Kilmacuagh (Castle-maine) . .	39	3	26h	Westmeath . .	Brawny . . .	St. Mary's . .	Athlone . .	I.	259
29	Kilmacuagh (Cooke)	50	0	11	Westmeath .	Brawny . . .	St. Mary's . .	Athlone . .	I.	259
29	Kilmacuagh (Mechum)	56	3	1	Westmeath .	Brawny . . .	St. Mary's . .	Athlone . .	I.	259
31, 36	Kilmacuddy . .	333	1	33	King's Co. .	Ballybritt . .	Letterluna . .	Parsonstown .	I.	126
23	Kilmacuddy . .	14	0	25	Tipperary, N.R.	Ikerrin . . .	Bourney . .	Roscrea . .	II.	274
23	Kilmacuddy . .	228	3	24	Tipperary, N.R.	Ikerrin . . .	Killea . . .	Roscrea . .	II.	275
22, 23	Kilmacud East . .	128	2	23	Dublin . .	Rathdown . .	Kilmacud . .	Rathdown .	I.	36
22, 23	Kilmacud West .	157	2	32	Dublin . .	Rathdown . .	Kilmacud . .	Rathdown .	I.	36
18	Kilmaculla . .	66	3	16	Cork, E.R. .	Fermoy . .	Kildorrery . .	Mitchelstown .	II.	80
13	Kilmacullagh . .	175	3	11	Wicklow . .	Newcastle . .	Newcastle Upper .	Rathdrum .	I.	353
16	Kilmacumsy . .	365	2	31	Roscommon .	Frenchpark . .	Kilmacumsy .	Boyle . .	IV.	203
11	Kilmacurkan . .	72	0	14	Sligo . . .	Tireragh . .	Easky . . .	Dromore West .	IV.	233
11	Kilmacurkan . .	345	2	5	Sligo . . .	Tireragh . .	Kilmacshalgan .	Dromore West .	IV.	235
30, 31	Kilmacurra East .	137	0	11	Wicklow . .	Arklow . . .	Dunganstown .	Rathdrum .	I.	343
40	Kilmacurrane . .	733	2	21	Cork, E.R. .	Duhallow . .	Clonmeen . .	Kanturk . .	II.	70
30	Kilmacurra West .	111	1	24	Wicklow . .	Arklow . . .	Dunganstown .	Rathdrum .	I.	343
27, 31	Kilmaddaroe . .	207	1	25i	Leitrim . .	Leitrim . . .	Kiltoghert . .	Cark. on Shannon	IV.	102
14	Kilmademoge . .	195	2	4	Kilkenny . .	Fassadinin . .	Kilmademoge .	Kilkenny . .	I.	90
10, 14	Kilmadum . .	358	3	5	Kilkenny . .	Fassadinin . .	Kilmadum . .	Kilkenny . .	I.	90
5	Kilmagamish . .	177	0	23	Armagh . .	Oneilland West .	Drumcree . .	Lurgan . .	III.	52
31	Kilmaganny . .	273	0	30	Kilkenny . .	Kells . . .	Kilmaganny . .	Callan . .	I.	109
31	Kilmaganny T. .	—			Kilkenny . .	Kells . . .	Kilmaganny . .	Callan . .	I.	109
15, 20	Kilmagar . .	615	0	31	Kilkenny . .	Gowran . . .	Clara . . .	Kilkenny . .	I.	94
15, 20	Kilmagar . .	342	0	25	Kilkenny . .	Gowran . . .	Kilderry . .	Kilkenny . .	I.	96
3, 8	Kilmagarvoge .	620	3	2	Carlow . .	Rathvilly . .	Tullowphelim .	Carlow . .	I.	12

(a) Including 2A. 1R. 1P. water.
(b) Including 33A. 2R. 1P. water.
(c) Including 13A. 2R. 36P. water.

(d) Including 76A. 2R. 7P. water.
(e) Including 17A. 0R. 4P. River Nore.
(f) Including 5A. 1R. 16P. water.

(g) Including 21A. 1R. 11P. water.
(h) Including 5A. 0R. 7P. detached portion.
(i) Including 13A. 1R. 29P. water.

No. of Sheet of the Ordnance Survey Maps.	Townlands and Towns.	Area in Statute Acres.	County.	Barony.	Parish.	Poor Law Union in 1857.	Townland Census of 1851, Part I.	
		A. R. P.					Vol.	Page
27	Kilmaghera . .	144 2 15	Leitrim . .	Leitrim . . .	Kiltoghert . .	Car^k. on Shannon	IV.	102
29	Kilmagibboge .	190 2 2	Waterford .	Decies within Drum	Kimolash . .	Dungarvan . .	II.	351
35, 40	Kilmagig Lower .	284 1 11	Wicklow . .	Arklow . .	Castlemacadam .	Rathdrum . .	I.	342
35, 40	Kilmagig Upper .	297 2 37	Wicklow . .	Arklow . .	Castlemacadam .	Rathdrum . .	I.	342
25	Kilmaglasderry .	192 2 6	Tipperary, N.R.	Owney and Arra .	Templeachally .	Nenagh . .	II.	297
12,13,16,17	Kilmaglin . .	298 2 31	Carlow . .	Idrone East . .	Fennagh . .	Carlow . .	I.	7
12	Kilmaglish . .	517 3 36	Westmeath .	Corkaree . .	Tyfarnham . .	Mullingar . .	I.	264
17	Kilmaglush . .	335 3 30	Carlow . .	Forth . .	Myshall . .	Carlow . .	I.	5
36	Kilmagner . .	765 3 5	Cork, E.R. .	Condons&Clangibbon	Castlelyons . .	Fermoy . .	II.	60
67	Kilmagner . .	164 3 16	Cork, E.R. .	Imokilly . .	Youghal . .	Youghal . .	II.	91
4, 5, 9, 10	Kilmagorroge . .	216 0 3	Kildare . .	Ikeathy&Oughterany	Cloncurry . .	Celbridge . .	I.	57
2	Kilmagoura . .	329 1 9	Cork, E.R. .	Orrery and Kilmore	Shandrum . .	Kanturk . .	II.	110
8	Kilmahamogue .	320 2 32	Antrim . .	Cary . .	Ballintoy . .	Ballycastle . .	III.	12
5	Kilmahon . .	355 3 15	Longford . .	Longford . .	Killoe . .	Longford . .	I.	159
17	Kilmahuddrick .	181 1 1	Dublin . .	Newcastle . .	Kilmahuddrick .	Dublin South .	I.	33
35, 36	Kilmaine . .	645 3 19	King's Co. .	Ballybritt . .	Seirkieran . .	Parsonstown .	I.	127
118, 121	Kilmaine . .	35 1 2	Mayo . .	Kilmaine . .	Kilmainemore .	Ballinrobe .	IV.	156
121	Kilmainepark . .	80 0 17	Mayo . .	Kilmaine . .	Kilmainemore .	Ballinrobe .	IV.	156
121	Kilmaine T. .	—	Mayo . .	Kilmaine . .	Kilmainemore .	Ballinrobe .	IV.	156
25, 31	Kilmainham . .	297 0 3	Cavan . .	Clanmahon . .	Crosserlough .	Cavan . .	III.	76
5	Kilmainham . .	33 3 22	Dublin . .	Balrothery East .	Balrothery . .	Balrothery . .	I.	19
18	Kilmainham . .	38 1 19	Dublin . .	Uppercross . .	St. James . .	Dublin South .	I.	41
17	Kilmainham . .	37 3 22	Meath . .	Upper Kells . .	Kells . . .	Kells . . .	I.	206
17	Kilmainham . .	1,294 3 17	Meath . .	Upper Kells . .	Teltown . .	Kells . . .	I.	207
8	Kilmainham . .	468 0 17	Queen's Co. .	Portnahinch . .	Ardea . .	Mountmellick .	I.	243
17	Kilmainham (Head-fort) . .	200 0 32	Meath . .	Upper Kells . .	Kells . . .	Kells . . .	I.	206
17	Kilmainham (Head-fort) . .	51 2 23	Meath . .	Upper Kells . .	Teltown . .	Kells . . .	I.	207
18	Kilmainham T. .	—	Dublin . .	Uppercross . .	St. James . .	Dublin South .	I.	41
5	Kilmainham T. .	—	Meath . .	Lower Kells . .	Kilmainham . .	Kells . . .	I.	203
2, 5	Kilmainhamwood .	280 1 2	Meath . .	Lower Kells . .	Kilmainham . .	Kells . . .	I.	203
45, 46	Kilmakardle . .	236 2 35	Tyrone . .	Dungannon Middle .	Pomeroy . .	Dungannon . .	III.	304
69	Kilmakaroge . .	228 1 17	Cork, W.R. .	West Muskerry .	Kilnamartry .	Macroom . .	II.	160
64	Kilmakee . .	377 0 3	Antrim . .	Upper Belfast . .	Derryaghy . .	Lisburn . .	III.	10
50, 51, 55	Kilmakee . .	690 1 35	Antrim . .	Upper Belfast . .	Templepatrick .	Antrim . .	III.	11
33, 34, 36	Kilmakenny . .	379 2 9a	Leitrim . .	Carrigallen . .	Cloone . . .	Mohill . .	IV.	90
12	Kilmakerrill . .	205 1 29	Leitrim . .	Drumahaire . .	Cloonclare . .	Manorhamilton .	IV.	93
41	Kilmakevoge . .	210 1 38	Kilkenny . .	Ida	Kilmakevoge .	Waterford . .	I.	103
42	Kilmakill . .	1,219 0 30	Tipperary, N.R.	Eliogarty . .	Moyne . . .	Thurles . .	II.	271
108	Kilmakilloge . .	342 1 33	Kerry . .	Glanarought . .	Tuosist . .	Kenmare . .	II.	189
18	Kilmakinlan . .	163 2 37	Longford . .	Moydow . .	Kilcommock . .	Ballymahon .	I.	161
2	Kilmalady Big .	515 0 2	King's Co. .	Kilcoursey . .	Ardnurcher or Horse-leap . . .	Tullamore .	I.	140
2	Kilmalady Little .	118 0 39	King's Co. .	Kilcoursey . .	Ardnurcher or Horse-leap . . .	Tullamore .	I.	140
27	Kilmalanophy .	116 0 21b	Fermanagh .	Tirkennedy . .	Cleenish . .	Enniskillen .	III.	220
27	Kilmalanophy .	14 2 4	Fermanagh .	Tirkennedy . .	Enniskillen . .	Enniskillen .	III.	222
74, 87	Kilmalaw . .	559 3 34	Galway . .	Clonmacnowen .	Kilgerrill . .	Ballinasloe .	IV.	26
51	Kilmaleery . .	111 2 17	Clare . .	Bunratty Lower .	Kilmaleery . .	Ennis . .	II.	6
32,33,40,41	Kilmaley . .	290 0 0	Clare . .	Islands . .	Kilmaley . .	Ennis . .	II.	31
3, 7	Kilmalin . .	375 1 25	Wicklow . .	Rathdown . .	Powerscourt .	Rathdown . .	I.	356
118	Kilmalinoge . .	215 2 30	Galway . .	Longford . .	Kilmalinoge .	Portumna . .	IV.	59
42, 43	Kilmalkedar . .	393 2 5	Kerry . .	Corkaguiny . .	Kilmalkedar .	Dingle . .	II.	178
47	Kilmallock . .	31 1 35	Limerick . .	Kilmallock . .	St.Peter's & St.Paul's	Kilmallock .	II.	250
32	Kilmallock . .	434 0 12	Wexford . .	Ballaghkeen . .	Kilmallock . .	Enniscorthy .	I.	296
47	Kilmallock Hill .	38 2 6	Limerick . .	Kilmallock . .	St.Peter's & St.Paul's	Kilmallock .	II.	250
47	Kilmallock T. .	—	Limerick . .	Kilmallock . .	St.Peter's & St.Paul's	Kilmallock .	II.	250
122, 123	Kilmaloda . .	634 3 28	Cork, W.R. .	East Carbery (E.D.)	Kilmaloda . .	Clonakilty .	II.	129
82	Kilmaloge . .	16 3 35	Tipperary, S.R.	Iffa and Offa West .	Ardfinnan . .	Clogheen . .	II.	317
82	Kilmaloge . .	559 3 21	Tipperary, S.R.	Iffa and Offa West .	Derrygrath . .	Clogheen . .	II.	318
82	Kilmaloge . .	127 1 26	Tipperary, S.R.	Iffa and Offa West .	Rochestown . .	Clogheen . .	II.	319
34	Kilmalogue . .	1,025 1 38	King's Co. .	Upper Philipstown .	Clonyhurk . .	Mountmellick .	I.	143
37, 38	Kilmaloo or Clash-ganny . .	191 1 27	Waterford .	Decies within Drum	Kinsalebeg . .	Youghal . .	II.	352
94	Kilmalooda . .	156 2 23	Cork, W.R. .	East Carbery (W.D.)	Fanlobbus . .	Dunmanway .	II.	132
37, 38	Kilmaloo East .	99 3 24	Waterford .	Decies within Drum	Kinsalebeg . .	Youghal . .	II.	352
37	Kilmaloo West .	266 2 34	Waterford .	Decies within Drum	Kinsalebeg . .	Youghal . .	II.	352
25	Kilmalum . .	458 0 3	Kildare . .	Naas South . .	Tipperkevin .	Naas . .	I.	65
18, 22	Kilmanagh . .	368 0 30	Kilkenny . .	Crannagh . .	Kilmanagh . .	Callan . .	I.	86
1, 2, 8	Kilmanaghan . .	465 0 21	King's Co. .	Kilcoursey . .	Kilmanaghan . .	Tullamore .	I.	141
18	Kilmanagh T. .	—	Kilkenny . .	Crannagh . .	Kilmanagh . .	Callan . .	I.	86
1	Kilmanahan . .	626 3 24c	Waterford .	Glenahiry . .	Kilronan . .	Clogheen . .	II.	365
24	Kilmanaheen . .	743 1 10	Kilkenny . .	Gowran . .	Dungarvan . .	Thomastown .	I.	94

(a) Including 22A. 3R. 7P. water.　　　　(b) Including 27 . 3R. 8P. water.　　　　(c) Including 14A. 0R. 0P. water.

No. of Sheet of the Ordnance Survey Maps.	Townlands and Towns.	Area in Statute Acres.	County.	Barony.	Parish.	Poor Law Union in 1857.	Townland Census of 1851, Part I. Vol.	Page
		A. R. P.						
35, 39	Kilmanahin	237 3 32	Kilkenny	Iverk	Fiddown	Carrick on Suir	I.	105
23	Kilmandil	133 2 32	Antrim	Kilconway	Killagan	Ballymoney	III.	27
88	Kilmancen	194 2 21a	Tipperary, S.R.	Iffa and Offa West	Ballybacon	Clogheen	II.	317
34	Kilmanicholas	161 1 12	Waterford	Coshmore&Coshbride	Kilcockan	Lismore	II.	343
23, 24	Kilmaniheen East	828 2 16b	Kerry	Trughanacmy	Brosna	Tralee	II.	208
23, 24	Kilmaniheen West	899 2 11c	Kerry	Trughanacmy	Brosna	Tralee	II.	208
2	Kilmanman	177 0 35	Queen's Co.	Tinnahinch	Kilmanman	Mountmellick	I.	249
42	Kilmannan	99 2 23	Wexford	Bargy	Kilmannan	Wexford	I.	306
42	Kilmannan Little	13 1 37	Wexford	Bargy	Kilmannan	Wexford	I.	306
93	Kilmannin	127 1 35d	Mayo	Costello	Bekan	Claremorris	IV.	139
39	Kilmannock	239 1 2	Wexford	Shelburne	Kilmokea	New Ross	I.	327
30	Kilmanoge	130 1 3	Wicklow	Arklow	Dunganstown	Rathdrum	I.	343
27	Kilmaquague	381 2 10	Waterford	Gaultiere	Rathmoylan	Waterford	II.	364
10, 13	Kilmartin	615 0 6	Dublin	Castleknock	Mulhuddart	Dublin North	I.	25
21	Kilmartin	666 1 9	Queen's Co.	Clandonagh	Kyle	Donaghmore	I.	233
19	Kilmartin	313 0 8	Wicklow	Newcastle	Killiskey	Rathdrum	I.	352
50, 61	Kilmartin Lower	367 3 29	Cork, E.R.	East Muskerry	Donaghmore	Macroom	II.	103
50	Kilmartin Upper	538 3 33	Cork, E.R.	East Muskerry	Donaghmore	Macroom	II.	103
40	Kilmascally	254 3 16	Tyrone	Dungannon Upper	Arboe	Cookstown	III.	305
22, 25	Kilmashogue	1,409 2 9	Dublin	Rathdown	Whitechurch	Dublin South	I.	38
45	Kilmass	85 0 6	Roscommon	Athlone	Rahara	Roscommon	IV.	183
25	Kilmastulla	377 2 1	Tipperary, N.R.	Owney and Arra	Kilmastulla	Nenagh	II.	295
7, 11	Kilmatroy	95 1 10	Armagh	Tiranny	Eglish	Armagh	III.	59
31, 35	Kilmead	487 3 30	Kildare	Narragh & RebanEast	Narraghmore	Athy	I.	66
8, 16	Kilmeadan	170 2 5	Waterford	Middlethird	Kilmeadan	Waterford	II.	368
18	Kilmeage	571 1 9	Kildare	Connell	Kilmeage	Naas	I.	55
13, 18	Kilmeage Little	6 1 26	Kildare	Connell	Kilmeage	Naas	I.	55
18	KILMEAGE T.	—	Kildare	Connell	Kilmeage	Naas	I.	55
7	Kilmeany	344 0 30	Carlow	Carlow	Ballinacarrig	Carlow	I.	1
11, 17	Kilmeany	869 1 4e	Kerry	Iraghticonnor	Knockanure	Listowel	II.	192
37, 45	Kilmeedy	191 3 22	Limerick	Connello Upper	Kilmeedy	Newcastle	II.	233
39, 48	Kilmeedy East	316 0 13	Cork, W.R.	West Muskerry	Drishane	Millstreet	II.	156
38	Kilmeedy East	200 3 35	Waterford	Decies within Drum	Kinsalebeg	Youghal	II.	352
37, 45	KILMEEDY T.	—	Limerick	Connello Upper	Kilmeedy	Newcastle	II.	233
39, 47, 48	Kilmeedy West	461 1 12	Cork, W.R.	West Muskerry	Drishane	Millstreet	II.	156
38	Kilmeedy West	118 1 1	Waterford	Decies within Drum	Kinsalebeg	Youghal	II.	352
21, 29	Kilmeelchon	391 1 36	King's Co.	Garrycastle	Lusmagh	Parsonstown	I.	137
25	Kilmeelickin	475 1 13	Galway	Ross	Ross	Oughterard	IV.	74
121	Kilmeen	261 0 30	Cork, W.R.	East Carbery (W.D)	Kilmeen	Clonakilty	II.	134
106	Kilmeen	699 1 36	Galway	Leitrim	Kilmeen	Loughrea	IV.	54
77	Kilmeena	141 2 18f	Mayo	Burrishoole	Kilmeena	Westport	IV.	122
47	Kilmelan	44 2 2	Tipperary, N.R.	Eliogarty	Moycarky	Thurles	II.	271
37	Kilmessan	754 1 9	Meath	Lower Deece	Kilmessan	Dunshaughlin	I.	192
37	KILMESSAN T.	—	Meath	Lower Deece	Kilmessan	Dunshaughlin	I.	192
32	Kilmichael	125 3 19	Cork, E.R.	Duhallow	Ballyclogh	Mallow	II.	67
126	Kilmichael	480 3 5	Cork, W.R.	Bear	Kilnamanagh	Castletown	II.	126
17	Kilmichael	182 2 28	Wexford	Ballaghkeen	Donaghmore	Gorey	I.	293
3, 7	Kilmichael	342 2 11g	Wexford	Gorey	Kilgorman	Gorey	I.	318
99	Kilmichael East	78 3 1	Cork, E.R.	Kerrycurrihy	Templebreedy	Kinsale	II.	93
6	Kilmichaelhill	213 1 18	Wexford	Gorey	Kilnahue	Gorey	I.	319
6	Kilmichael Lower	247 1 28	Wexford	Gorey	Kilnahue	Gorey	I.	319
126	KILMICHAEL T.	—	Cork, W.R.	Bear	Kilnamanagh	Castletown	II.	126
6	Kilmichael Upper	189 3 29	Wexford	Gorey	Kilnahue	Gorey	I.	319
99	Kilmichael West	175 3 29	Cork, E.R.	Kerrycurrihy	Templebreedy	Kinsale	II.	93
48	Kilmihil	830 0 7	Clare	Clonderalaw	Kilmihil	Kilrush	II.	17
37, 38	Kilmihil	435 2 31	Limerick	Connello Upper	Ballingarry	Croom	II.	231
47, 48, 55	Kilmihil	571 2 27	Limerick	Coshlea	Ballingaddy	Kilmallock	II.	237
48	KILMIHIL T.	—	Clare	Clonderalaw	Kilmihil	Kilrush	II.	17
27	Kilmilan	73 3 34	Queen's Co.	Clandonagh	Rathdowney	Donaghmore	I.	234
13	Kilminchy	382 3 22	Queen's Co.	Maryborough East	Straboe	Mountmellick	I.	242
28, 29	Kilminfoyle	407 0 16	Queen's Co.	Clarmallagh	Aghaboe	Abbeyleix	I.	236
13	Kilminioge	202 1 39	Down	Lower Iveagh, Up. pt.	Moira	Lurgan	III.	170
26	Kilminnick East	18 2 16	Kilkenny	Callan	Callan	Callan	I.	83
26	Kilminnick West	66 1 35	Kilkenny	Callan	Callan	Callan	I.	83
24	Kilminnin Lower	152 2 9	Waterford	Decies without Drum	Stradbally	Kilmacthomas	II.	361
31	Kilminnin North	55 2 33	Waterford	Decies without Drum	Dungarvan	Dungarvan	II.	355
31	Kilminnin South	100 3 30	Waterford	Decies without Drum	Dungarvan	Dungarvan	II.	355
24	Kilminnin Upper	163 0 12	Waterford	Decies without Drum	Stradbally	Kilmacthomas	II.	361
22, 23	Kilmissan	236 1 4	Carlow	St. Mullins Lower	St. Mullins	New Ross	I.	13
38	Kilmisten	92 0 34	Wexford	Shelmaliere East	Ardcolm	Wexford	I.	330
29	Kilmochonna	205 3 8	King's Co.	Garrycastle	Lusmagh	Parsonstown	I.	137
51, 52	Kilmocolmock	437 1 20	Roscommon	Athlone	Drum	Athlone	IV.	180
53	Kilmoculla	213 2 1	Clare	Tulla Lower	Kilseily	Limerick	II.	37

(a) Including 5A. 2R. 10P. River Suir.
(b) Including 10A. 2R. 23P. water.
(c) Including 19A. 1R. 11P. water.

(d) Including 12A. 0R. 22P. water.
(e) Including 25A. 3R. 6P. water.

(f) Including 30A. 0R. 17P. water.
(g) Including 3A. 0R. 32P. water.

No. of Sheet of the Ordnance Survey Maps.	Townlands and Towns.	Area in Statute Acres.	County.	Barony.	Parish.	Poor Law Union in 1857.	Townland Census of 1851, Part I.	
		A. R. P.					Vol.	Page
23	Kilmog or Racecourse	377 0 39	Kilkenny . .	Shillelogher . .	Grange . .	Kilkenny . .	I.	114
35	Kilmogue . .	654 2 22	Kilkenny . .	Knocktopher . .	Fiddown . .	Carrick on Suir	I.	111
29, 30	Kilmolash . .	61 1 36	Waterford . .	Decies without Drum	Kilmolash .	Dungarvan .	II.	357
76, 82	Kilmolash Lower .	293 1 21	Tipperary, S.R.	Iffa and Offa East .	Inishlounaght .	Clonmel . .	II.	313
76	Kilmolash Upper .	58 3 16	Tipperary, S.R.	Iffa and Offa East .	Inishlounaght .	Clonmel . .	II.	313
51, 62	Kilmona . . .	771 2 24	Cork, E.R. .	Barretts . . .	Grenagh . .	Cork . . .	II.	49
22	Kilmonaghan . .	182 1 23	Armagh . .	Orior Lower . .	Killevy . .	Newry . . .	III.	56
70	Kilmonaster Lower	212 3 24	Donegal . .	Raphoe . . .	Clonleigh . .	Strabane . .	III.	135
70, 79	Kilmonaster Middle	257 3 26	Donegal . .	Raphoe . . .	Clonleigh . .	Strabane . .	III.	135
86,87,98,99	Kilmoney . . .	1,430 2 37	Cork, E.R. .	Kerrycurrihy . .	Kilmoney . .	Kinsale . .	II.	92
17	Kilmoney North .	612 3 24	Kildare . .	Offaly East . .	Rathangan . .	Edenderry . .	I.	71
17, 22	Kilmoney South .	453 0 24	Kildare . .	Offaly East . .	Rathangan . .	Naas . . .	I.	71
16, 17	Kilmood and Bally-bunden . . .	921 0 9	Down . . .	Castlereagh Lower .	Kilmood . .	Newtownards .	III.	163
149, 153	Kilmoon . . .	223 0 38	Cork, W.R. .	West Carbery (E.D.)	Tullagh . .	Skibbereen .	II.	141
32, 33, 38	Kilmoon . . .	241 0 1	Meath . . .	Skreen . . .	Kilmoon . .	Dunshaughlin .	I.	221
4, 8	Kilmoon East . .	319 2 13	Clare . . .	Burren . . .	Kilmoon . .	Ennistimon .	II.	13
4, 8	Kilmoon West .	372 1 5	Clare . . .	Burren . . .	Kilmoon . .	Ennistimon .	II.	13
41	Kilmoraun . .	325 1 33	Clare . . .	Islands . . .	Killone . .	Ennis . . .	II.	30
20	Kilmore . . .	685 0 5	Antrim . .	Lower Glenarm .	Layd . . .	Ballycastle .	III.	22
8	Kilmore . . .	388 0 10	Armagh . .	Armagh . . .	Clonfeacle . .	Armagh . .	III.	43
9	Kilmore . . .	86 2 20	Armagh . .	Oneilland West .	Kilmore . .	Armagh . .	III.	53
32, 38	Kilmore . . .	285 3 0	Cavan . .	Castlerahan . .	Castlerahan . .	Oldcastle . .	III.	67
33, 39	Kilmore . . .	333 0 16a	Cavan . .	Castlerahan . .	Killinkere . .	Bailieborough .	III.	69
68	Kilmore . . .	349 2 7	Clare . . .	Clonderalaw . .	Kilmurry . .	Kilrush . .	II.	17
41	Kilmore . . .	129 2 27	Clare . . .	Islands . . .	Killone . .	Ennis . . .	II.	30
44, 53	Kilmore . . .	874 1 6	Clare . . .	Tulla Lower . .	Killokennedy .	Limerick . .	II.	36
27	Kilmore . . .	495 1 33	Clare . .	Tulla Upper . .	Tulla . . .	Tulla . . .	II.	41
1, 2	Kilmore . . .	334 1 6	Cork, E.R. .	Orrery and Kilmore	Kilbolane . .	Kanturk . .	II.	108
118	Kilmore . . .	233 2 24b	Cork, W.R. .	Bantry . . .	Kilmocomoge .	Bantry . .	II.	121
124	Kilmore . . .	418 3 34	Cork, W.R. .	Courceys . .	Templetrine .	Kinsale . .	II.	147
96	Kilmore . . .	692 3 18	Cork, E.R. .	Kinalmeaky . .	Brinny . .	Bandon . .	II.	151
119, 132	Kilmore . . .	338 0 33	Cork, W.R. .	West Carbery (E.D.)	Dromdaleague .	Skibbereen .	II.	140
81	Kilmore . . .	417 3 11c	Cork, W.R. .	West Muskerry .	Inchigeelagh .	Macroom . .	II.	158
44	Kilmore . . .	239 0 1d	Donegal . .	Kilmacrenan . .	Gartan . .	Letterkenny .	III.	127
30	Kilmore . . .	149 2 26	Down . . .	Castlereagh Upper .	Kilmore . .	Downpatrick .	III.	165
13	Kilmore . . .	1,514 0 37	Down . . .	Lower Iveagh(Up.pt.)	Shankill . .	Lurgan . .	III.	171
40	Kilmore . . .	167 0 38	Fermanagh .	Clankelly . .	Galloon . .	Clones . .	III.	198
1, 5	Kilmore . . .	94 0 12	Fermanagh .	Lurg . . .	Drumkeeran .	Lowtherstown .	III.	206
21	Kilmore . . .	217 3 35	Fermanagh .	Magheraboy . .	Devenish . .	Enniskillen .	III.	211
6	Kilmore . . .	442 3 38e	Galway . .	Ballymoe . .	Templetogher .	Glennamaddy .	IV.	9
29, 43	Kilmore . . .	440 0 3	Galway . .	Clare . . .	Tuam . . .	Tuam . . .	IV.	23
44	Kilmore . . .	474 3 9	Galway . .	Dunmore . .	Killererin . .	Tuam . . .	IV.	35
32, 33	Kilmore . . .	1,324 3 16	Galway . .	Killian . .	Killeroran . .	Mountbellew .	IV.	44
117	Kilmore . . .	349 1 26	Galway . .	Longford . .	Killimorbologue .	Portumna . .	IV.	59
13, 26	Kilmore . . .	194 3 17	Galway . .	Ross . . .	Ross . . .	Ballinrobe .	IV.	74
9	Kilmore . . .	590 0 27	Kerry . .	Clanmaurice . .	Killury . .	Listowel . .	II.	171
34,35,43,44	Kilmore . . .	1,598 0 18f	Kerry . .	Corkaguiny . .	Ballyduff . .	Dingle . .	II.	174
30	Kilmore . . .	330 2 2	Kerry . .	Trughanacmy .	O'Brennan . .	Tralee . .	II.	212
3	Kilmore . . .	711 1 31	Kildare . .	Carbury . .	Cadamstown .	Edenderry .	I.	51
7, 8	Kilmore . . .	127 3 33	Kildare . .	Carbury . .	Kilmore . .	Edenderry .	I.	52
24	Kilmore . . .	182 2 8	King's Co. .	Ballyboy . .	Killoughy . .	Tullamore .	I.	124
10	Kilmore . . .	140 0 17	Leitrim . .	Drumahaire . .	Drumlease . .	Manorhamilton	IV.	94
16, 18	Kilmore . . .	204 1 3	Leitrim . .	Drumahaire . .	Drumreilly . .	Carᵏ. on Shannon	IV.	95
18	Kilmore . . .	122 2 14	Leitrim . .	Drumahaire . .	Inishmagrath .	Manorhamilton	IV.	96
38	Kilmore . . .	965 3 6	Limerick . .	Connello Upper .	Ballingarry . .	Croom . .	II.	231
6	Kilmore . . .	581 1 20	Longford . .	Granard . .	Columbkille .	Granard . .	I.	156
72,73,81,82	Kilmore . . .	866 2 28	Mayo . . .	Costello . .	Kilmovee . .	Swineford .	IV.	142
60, 61	Kilmore . . .	550 2 34	Mayo . . .	Gallen . .	Toomore . .	Swineford .	IV.	151
43, 49	Kilmore . . .	760 0 7	Meath . . .	Upper Deece .	Kilmore . .	Dunshaughlin .	I.	193
41, 44	Kilmore . . .	503 2 20	Roscommon .	Athlone . . .	Athleague . .	Roscommon .	IV.	179
42	Kilmore . . .	127 3 2	Roscommon .	Athlone . .	Killinvoy . .	Athlone . .	IV.	182
12, 18	Kilmore . . .	69 3 0	Roscommon .	Ballintober North .	Kilmore . .	Carᵏ. on Shannon	IV.	187
19,20,25,26	Kilmore . . .	206 2 35	Roscommon .	Castlereagh . .	Kilkeevin . .	Castlereagh .	IV.	200
23	Kilmore . . .	216 1 23	Roscommon .	Roscommon . .	Bumlin . .	Strokestown .	IV.	208
45, 51	Kilmore . . .	638 1 29	Tipperary, N.R.	Kilnamanagh Upper	Toem . . .	Tipperary .	II.	280
26	Kilmore . . .	161 2 4	Tipperary, N.R.	Upper Ormond .	Kilmore . .	Nenagh . .	II.	291
77	Kilmore . . .	683 3 19	Tipperary, S.R.	Iffa and Offa East .	Lisronagh . .	Clonmel . .	II.	315
52	Kilmore . . .	125 3 18	Tipperary, S.R.	Kilnamanagh Lower	Clonoulty . .	Cashel . .	II.	323
61, 67	Kilmore . . .	398 0 16	Tyrone . .	Dungannon Lower .	Aghaloo . .	Dungannon .	III.	297
45, 46	Kilmore . . .	222 2 1	Tyrone . .	Dungannon Middle .	Pomeroy . .	Dungannon .	III.	304
34	Kilmore . . .	266 2 23g	Tyrone . .	Omagh East . .	Drumragh . .	Omagh . .	III.	312
34	Kilmore . . .	98 1 19	Waterford . .	Decies within Drum	Clashmore . .	Youghal . .	II.	351

(a) Including 8A. 2R. 32P. water.
(b) Including 20A. 3R. 4P. water.
(c) Including 21A. 3R. 33P. water.
(d) Including 5A. 0R. 26P. water.
(e) Including 1A. 3R. 35P. water.
(f) Including 9A. 0R. 30P. water.
(g) Including 1A. 0R. 6P. water.

No. of Sheet of the Ordnance Survey Maps.	Townlands and Towns.	Area in Statute Acres.	County.	Barony.	Parish.	Poor Law Union in 1857.	Townland Census of 1851, Part I.	
		A. R. P.					Vol.	Page
2	Kilmore . . .	630 0 18	Westmeath .	Moygoish . .	Street . . .	Granard . .	I.	281
14	Kilmore Big . .	359 2 11	Dublin . .	Coolock . .	Coolock . . .	Dublin North .	I.	27
3	Kilmorebrannagh .	342 1 5	Kildare . .	Carbury . . .	Cadamstown . .	Edenderry . .	I.	51
38	Kilmore Demesne .	112 0 10	Limerick . .	Conello Upper .	Ballingarry . .	Croom . .	II.	231
17, 18	Kilmore East . .	260 3 28a	Monaghan .	Dartree . . .	Ematris . . .	Cootehill . .	III.	267
9	Kilmore East . .	171 0 29	Monaghan .	Monaghan . .	Tedavnet . .	Monaghan . .	III.	279
28	Kilmore East . .	173 3 3	Waterford .	Coshmore & Coshbride	Tallow . . .	Lismore . .	II.	348
12	Kilmoreen . .	381 3 6	Limerick . .	Kenry . . .	Kildimo . . .	Rathkeale . .	II.	250
24	Kilmore (Irvine) .	373 1 1b	Tyrone . .	Omagh West . .	Longfield West .	Castlederg . .	III.	316
14	Kilmore Little . .	41 1 17	Dublin . .	Coolock . .	Coolock . . .	Dublin North .	I.	27
20, 25	Kilmore Lower .	143 0 12	Cavan . .	Upper Loughtee .	Kilmore . . .	Cavan . .	III.	84
13	Kilmore Lower .	379 1 5	Longford . .	Longford . .	Clongesh . .	Longford . .	I.	158
60	Kilmore Lower .	71 1 32	Tipperary, S.R.	Kilnamanagh Lower	Kilmore . .	Cashel . .	II.	323
30	Kilmoremoy . .	139 1 22	Mayo . .	Tirawley . . .	Kilmoremoy . .	Ballina . .	IV.	170
16	Kilmore North . .	499 1 18c	Clare . .	Corcomroe . .	Kiltoraght . .	Corrofin . .	II.	22
28	Kilmore North . .	238 2 19	Fermanagh .	Magherastephana .	Aghalurcher . .	Lisnaskea . .	III.	217
24	Kilmore (Robinson)	628 3 6d	Tyrone . .	Omagh West . .	Longfield West .	Castlederg . .	III.	316
16	Kilmore South . .	198 2 9	Clare . .	Corcomroe . .	Kiltoraght . .	Corrofin . .	II.	22
34	Kilmore South . .	212 1 28e	Fermanagh .	Magherastephana .	Aghalurcher . .	Lisnaskea . .	III.	217
30	KILMORE T. . .	—	Down . .	Castlereagh Upper .	Kilmore . . .	Downpatrick . .	III.	165
52	KILMORE T. . .	—	Wexford . .	Bargy . . .	Kilmore . . .	Wexford . .	I.	307
20, 25	Kilmore Upper .	226 2 36	Cavan . .	Upper Loughtee .	Kilmore . . .	Cavan . .	III.	84
13	Kilmore Upper .	389 3 26	Longford . .	Longford . .	Clongesh . .	Longford . .	I.	158
52, 60	Kilmore Upper .	757 2 34	Tipperary, S.R.	Kilnamanagh Lower	Kilmore . .	Cashel . .	II.	323
17	Kilmore West . .	252 1 14f	Monaghan .	Dartree . . .	Ematris . . .	Cootehill . .	III.	267
5, 8	Kilmore West . .	294 1 25g	Monaghan .	Monaghan . .	Tedavnet . .	Monaghan . .	III.	279
28	Kilmore West . .	185 2 29	Waterford .	Coshmore & Coshbride	Tallow . . .	Lismore . .	II.	348
34	Kilmorgan . .	220 2 10	Sligo . .	Corran . . .	Kilmorgan . .	Sligo . .	IV.	227
9	Kilmoriarty . .	326 1 30	Armagh . .	Oneilland West .	Drumcree . .	Lurgan . .	III.	52
26	Kilmorony . .	296 1 22h	Queen's Co. .	Ballyadams . .	Tankardstown .	Athy . .	I.	232
66, 77	Kilmountain . .	282 0 30	Cork, E.R. .	Imokilly . . .	Ballyoughtera .	Middleton . .	II.	84
73	Kilmovee . .	240 3 30	Mayo . .	Costello . .	Kilmovee . .	Swineford . .	IV.	142
8	Kilmovee . .	692 2 15	Waterford .	Upperthird . .	Guilcagh . .	Carrick on Suir	II.	370
18	Kilmoyangey . .	240 0 20	Antrim . .	Upper Dunluce .	Kilraghts . .	Ballymoney . .	III.	20
8, 16	Kilmoyemoge East .	324 0 28	Waterford .	Middlethird . .	Kilmeadan . .	Waterford . .	II.	368
8, 16	Kilmoyemoge West .	571 3 19	Waterford .	Middlethird . .	Kilmeadan . .	Waterford . .	II.	368
19	Kilmoylan . .	82 2 32	Limerick . .	Shanid . . .	Kilmoylan . .	Glin . .	II.	256
15, 16	Kilmoylan Lower .	366 1 24	Limerick . .	Coonagh . .	Doon . . .	Tipperary . .	II.	234
15, 16	Kilmoylan Upper .	246 3 37	Limerick . .	Coonagh . .	Doon . . .	Tipperary . .	II.	234
8	Kilmoyle . .	292 2 13	Antrim . .	Cary . . .	Grange of Drumtullagh	Ballycastle . .	III.	14
6, 7, 11, 12	Kilmoyle . .	222 2 2	Antrim . .	Lower Dunluce .	Ballyrashane . .	Coleraine . .	III.	15
12	Kilmoyle . .	330 1 24	Antrim . .	Lower Dunluce .	Dunluce . .	Ballymoney . .	III.	17
14	Kilmoyle . .	297 0 2	Longford . .	Longford . .	Killoe . . .	Longford . .	I.	159
12, 17	Kilmoyle Lower .	148 3 19	Antrim . .	Upper Dunluce .	Ballymoney . .	Ballymoney . .	III.	19
75	Kilmoyler . .	185 2 24	Tipperary, S.R.	Clanwilliam . .	Killardry . .	Tipperary . .	II.	308
122	Kilmoylerane North	306 3 26	Cork, W.R. .	East Carbery (E.D.)	Desertserges . .	Clonakilty . .	II.	128
122	Kilmoylerane South	324 3 30	Cork, W.R. .	East Carbery (E.D.)	Desertserges . .	Clonakilty . .	II.	128
12	Kilmoyle Upper or Kirkmoyle . .	149 2 10	Antrim . .	Upper Dunluce .	Ballymoney . .	Ballymoney . .	III.	19
15, 16, 24	Kilmoylin . .	551 3 18	Waterford .	Decies without Drum	Rossmire . .	Kilmacthomas .	II.	360
14	Kilmoyly North .	161 1 20	Kerry . .	Clanmaurice . .	Kilmoyly . .	Tralee . .	II.	171
14, 15, 20, 21	Kilmoyly South .	350 3 2	Kerry . .	Clanmaurice . .	Kilmoyly . .	Tralee . .	II.	171
8	Kilmucklin . .	592 3 1	King's Co. .	Kilcoursey . .	Kilbride . . .	Tullamore . .	I.	141
22	Kilmuckridge . .	291 3 38	Wexford . .	Ballaghkeen . .	Kilmuckridge . .	Enniscorthy . .	I.	296
4	Kilmulhane . .	152 2 34	Kerry . .	Iraghticonnor .	Kilehenny . .	Listowel . .	II.	191
5	Kilmullen . .	307 2 9	Queen's Co. .	Portnahinch . .	Lea . . .	Mountmellick .	I.	244
24	Kilmullin . .	359 3 37	Wicklow . .	Newcastle . .	Derrylossary . .	Rathdrum . .	I.	351
13	Kilmullin . .	348 2 24	Wicklow . .	Newcastle . .	Newcastle Lower .	Rathdrum . .	I.	353
41	Kilmur . .	317 2 4	Meath . .	Lune . . .	Killaconnigan . .	Trim . .	I.	208
2	Kilmurragh . .	132 2 31	King's Co. .	Kilcoursey . .	Kilcumreragh . .	Tullamore . .	I.	141
86	Kilmurriheen . .	218 1 6	Cork, E.R. .	Cork . . .	Inishkenny . .	Cork . .	II.	64
3	Kilmurrily . .	206 3 0	Kerry . .	Iraghticonnor .	Kilnaughtin . .	Glin . .	II.	191
25	Kilmurrin . .	264 2 23	Waterford .	Decies without Drum	Kilbarrymeaden .	Kilmacthomas .	II.	356
13, 17	Kilmurry . .	96 0 29	Carlow . .	Forth . . .	Ballon . . .	Carlow . .	I.	3
43	Kilmurry . .	200 3 27i	Clare . .	Bunratty Lower .	Kilmurry . .	Tulla . .	II.	6
61	Kilmurry . .	25 1 9	Cork, E.R. .	East Muskerry .	Inishcarra . .	Cork . .	II.	104
17, 30	Kilmurry . .	313 3 24	Galway . .	Ballymoe . .	Clonbern . .	Tuam . .	IV.	6
41	Kilmurry . .	63 1 15	Galway . .	Clare . . .	Cargin . . .	Tuam . .	IV.	18
105	Kilmurry . .	9 1 23	Galway . .	Dunkellin . .	Kilconickny . .	Loughrea . .	IV.	29
117	Kilmurry . .	113 0 14	Galway . .	Longford . .	Tynagh . . .	Portumna . .	IV.	62
35	Kilmurry . .	200 1 32	Kerry . .	Corkaguiny . .	Ballyduff . .	Dingle . .	II.	174
54	Kilmurry . .	50 2 33	Kerry . .	Corkaguiny . .	Minard . . .	Dingle . .	II.	180
93	Kilmurry . .	298 1 22	Kerry . .	Glanarought . .	Kenmare . .	Kenmare . .	II.	186

(a) Including 20A. 0R. 35P. water.
(b) Including 3A. 0R. 5P. water.
(c) Including 15A. 0R. 16P. water.
(d) Including 1A. 1R. 14P. water.
(e) Including 5UA. 2R. 4P. water.
(f) Including 57A. 2R. 26P. water.
(g) Including 8A. 1R. 20P. water.
(h) Including 5A. 3R. 12P. River Barrow.
(i) Including 9A. 1R. 7P. water.

4 F

No. of Sheet of the Ordnance Survey Maps.	Townlands and Towns.	Area in Statute Acres.			County.	Barony.	Parish.	Poor Law Union in 1857.	Townland Census of 1851, Part I.	
		A.	R.	P.					Vol.	Page
40	Kilmurry	398	2	12	Kerry	Trughanacmy	Ballincuslane	Tralee	II.	206
3, 4, 9	Kilmurry	1,010	2	28	Kildare	Carbury	Dunfierth	Edenderry	I.	52
9, 10, 13	Kilmurry	426	3	36	Kildare	Clane	Clane	Naas	I.	54
9, 10	Kilmurry	223	2	26	Kildare	Ikeathy & Oughterany	Donadea	Celbridge	I.	57
28	Kilmurry	371	2	24	Kilkenny	Gowran	Columbkille	Thomastown	I.	94
28	Kilmurry	28	2	36	Kilkenny	Gowran	Kilfane	Thomastown	I.	97
43, 46, 47	Kilmurry	1,239	3	36	Kilkenny	Ida	Rathpatrick	Waterford	I.	103
9, 10	Kilmurry	750	2	28	King's Co.	Lower Philipstown	Ballycommon	Tullamore	I.	142
48	Kilmurry	358	3	26	Limerick	Coshlea	Emlygrennan	Kilmallock	II.	258
48	Kilmurry	380	2	36	Meath	Lower Moyfenrath	Rathcore	Trim	I.	211
36	Kilmurry	727	0	11	Meath	Lower Moyfenrath	Trim	Trim	I.	212
28	Kilmurry	365	1	4a	Monaghan	Farney	Donaghmoyne	Carrickmacross	III.	270
14	Kilmurry	467	3	7	Queen's Co.	Stradbally	Kilteale	Mountmellick	I.	247
21, 27	Kilmurry	452	3	8	Roscommon	Castlereagh	Baslick	Castlereagh	IV.	199
76, 82	Kilmurry	93	0	25	Tipperary, S.R.	Iffa and Offa West	Derrygrath	Clonmel	II.	318
30	Kilmurry	250	0	20	Waterford	Decies without Drum	Dungarvan	Dungarvan	II.	355
7	Kilmurry	437	0	25	Wexford	Gorey	Kilmakilloge	Gorey	I.	318
12, 13, 18	Kilmurry	339	2	13	Wicklow	Newcastle	Newcastle Upper	Rathdrum	I.	353
27	Kilmurry	96	0	38	Wicklow	Upper Talbotstown	Baltinglass	Baltinglass	I.	362
45	Kilmurry (Archer)	351	1	37	Limerick	Connello Upper	Kilmeedy	Newcastle	II.	233
38	Kilmurry Beg	102	2	25	Mayo	Tirawley	Crossmolina	Ballina	IV.	166
45	Kilmurrybog	102	3	11	Limerick	Connello Upper	Kilmeedy	Newcastle	II.	233
58	Kilmurry East	137	3	11	Clare	Clonderalaw	Kilmurry	Killadysert	II.	17
42	Kilmurryely	306	0	19	King's Co.	Clonlisk	Kilmurryely	Roscrea	I.	131
45, 46	Kilmurry (Lane)	665	2	18	Limerick	Connello Upper	Kilmeedy	Newcastle	II.	233
45	Kilmurry Lower	172	3	18	Wicklow	Arklow	Arklow	Rathdrum	I.	341
27	Kilmurry Lower	326	1	26	Wicklow	Upper Talbotstown	Baltinglass	Baltinglass	I.	362
45	Kilmurry Middle	137	3	3	Wicklow	Arklow	Arklow	Rathdrum	I.	341
38	Kilmurry More	129	0	25	Mayo	Tirawley	Crossmolina	Ballina	IV.	166
28, 36	Kilmurry North	567	2	8	Cork, E.R.	Condons & Clangibbon	Leitrim	Fermoy	II.	62
31, 36	Kilmurry North	300	2	0	Wicklow	Arklow	Redcross	Rathdrum	I.	346
8	Kilmurry North	319	0	1	Wicklow	Rathdown	Kilmacanoge	Rathdown	I.	356
28, 36	Kilmurry South	521	0	4b	Cork, E.R.	Condons & Clangibbon	Leitrim	Fermoy	II.	62
36	Kilmurry South	214	2	39	Wicklow	Arklow	Redcross	Rathdrum	I.	346
7, 8	Kilmurry South	368	2	13	Wicklow	Rathdown	Kilmacanoge	Rathdown	I.	356
43	KILMURRY T.	—			Clare	Bunratty Lower	Kilmurry	Tulla	II.	6
45	Kilmurry Upper	124	2	32	Wicklow	Arklow	Arklow	Rathdrum	I.	341
27, 32	Kilmurry Upper	125	1	2	Wicklow	Upper Talbotstown	Baltinglass	Baltinglass	I.	362
58, 68	Kilmurry West	148	2	29	Clare	Clonderalaw	Kilmurry	Killadysert	II.	17
110	Kilmurry	1,769	1	24	Galway	Aran	Inishmore	Galway	IV.	3
8	Kilnabinnia	137	3	23	King's Co.	Kilcoursey	Kilbride	Tullamore	I.	141
16	Kilnabooley	130	0	23	Kildare	Offaly East	Rathangan	Edenderry	I.	71
109	Kilnaborris	382	3	22	Galway	Longford	Clonfert	Ballinasloe	IV.	57
39	Kilnabrack	76	2	8	Fermanagh	Knockninny	Kinawley	Lisnaskea	III.	202
63	Kilnabrack Lower	459	1	38	Kerry	Iveragh	Glanbehy	Cahersiveen	II.	196
63	Kilnabrack Upper	629	1	27	Kerry	Iveragh	Glanbehy	Cahersiveen	II.	196
33	Kilnacally	125	2	22	Clare	Islands	Drumcliff	Ennis	II.	30
133, 134	Kilnacally	384	3	9	Cork, W.R.	East Carbery (W.D.)	Kilmacabea	Skibbereen	II.	133
37	Kilnacappagh	183	1	11	Tipperary, N.R.	Owney and Arra	Kilvellane	Nenagh	II.	296
8	Kilnacarra	182	3	4	King's Co.	Kilcoursey	Kilbride	Tullamore	I.	141
88, 91	Kilnacarriga	1,204	2	3	Tipperary, S.R.	Iffa and Offa West	Newcastle	Clogheen	II.	319
29	Kilnacarriga	265	3	35	Waterford	Coshmore & Coshbride	Lismore and Mocollop	Lismore	II.	346
9	Kilnacarrow	244	2	10	Longford	Longford	Killoe	Longford	I.	159
12	Kilnacarrow	194	0	14c	Longford	Rathcline	Rathcline	Longford	I.	165
23	Kilnacarrow	164	1	33d	Longford	Shrule	Taghshinny	Ballymahon	I.	167
54, 61	Kilnacart	182	1	3	Tyrone	Dungannon Middle	Clonfeacle	Dungannon	III.	299
8	Kilnacash	154	1	0	Queen's Co.	Portnahinch	Ardea	Mountmellick	I.	243
68	Kilnacask Lower	86	2	32	Tipperary, S.R.	Clanwilliam	Relickmurry & Athassel	Tipperary	II.	310
68	Kilnacask Upper	137	2	17	Tipperary, S.R.	Clanwilliam	Relickmurry & Athassel	Tipperary	II.	310
133,141,142	Kilnaclasha	560	0	37	Cork, W.R.	West Carbery (E.D.)	Abbeystrowry	Skibbereen	II.	136
13	Kilnaclay	258	1	2	Monaghan	Monaghan	Drumsnat	Monaghan	III.	275
36, 40	Kilnacloghy	105	0	22	Roscommon	Ballintober South	Cloontuskert	Roscommon	IV.	188
111, 124	Kilnacloona	241	1	14	Cork, W.R.	Courceys	Ringrone	Kinsale	II.	147
9	Kilnacloy	136	2	1	Monaghan	Monaghan	Monaghan	Monaghan	III.	277
29, 33, 34	Kilnacolpagh	1,353	2	27	Antrim	Lower Antrim	Racavan	Ballymena	III.	4
26, 32	Kilnacor	273	1	35	Cavan	Upper Loughtee	Denn	Cavan	III.	83
40	Kilnacran	156	1	3	Fermanagh	Clankelly	Galloon	Clones	III.	198
14	Kilnacran	213	2	38	Monaghan	Monaghan	Tullycorbet	Monaghan	III.	281
14	Kilnacranagh	136	1	18e	Cavan	Lower Loughtee	Drumlane	Cavan	III.	80
95, 109	Kilnacranagh East	486	0	7	Cork, W.R.	East Carbery (W.D.)	Kinneigh	Bandon	II.	134
95, 100	Kilnacranagh West	420	2	55	Cork, W.R.	East Carbery (W.D.)	Kinneigh	Bandon	II.	134
42, 43	Kilnacrandy	160	0	17f	Clare	Bunratty Lower	Tomfinlough	Ennis	II.	7
42, 43	Kilnacrandy	131	3	17g	Clare	Bunratty Upper	Quin	Tulla	II.	10

(a) Including 5A. 3R. 7P. water.
(b) Including 10A. 3R. 17P. water.
(c) Including Islands.

(d) Including 7A. 0R. 2P. Inny River.
(e) Including 4A. 1R. 39P. water.

(f) Including 41A. 0R. 4P. water.
(g) Including 6A. 1R. 12P. water.

No. of Sheet of the Ordnance Survey Maps.	Townlands and Towns.	Area in Statute Acres.			County.	Barony.	Parish.	Poor Law Union in 1857.	Townland Census of 1851, Part I.	
		A.	R.	P.					Vol.	Page
28	Kilnacranfy	95	2	0	Monaghan	Farney	Donaghmoyne	Carrickmacross	III.	270
25, 26	Kilnacranna	172	2	36	Tipperary, N.R.	Owney and Arra	Kilmastulla	Nenagh	II.	295
52	Kilnacreagh	255	3	4	Clare	Bunratty Lower	Kilfinaghta	Limerick	II.	4
15, 20	Kilnacreeve	156	2	15a	Cavan	Upper Loughtee	Castleterra	Cavan	III.	83
31	Kilnacreevy	265	3	0b	Cavan	Clanmahon	Denn	Cavan	III.	76
26	Kilnacreevy	277	1	14	Cavan	Upper Loughtee	Larah	Cavan	III.	85
25, 26	Kilnacreevy	219	3	39c	Leitrim	Carrigallen	Drumreilly	Bawnboy	IV.	91
22	Kilnacrew	382	0	23	Cavan	Clankee	Knockbride	Cootehill	III.	74
28	Kilnacross	145	2	31d	Cavan	Clankee	Knockbride	Bailieborough	III.	74
16	Kilnacross	166	1	35	Cavan	Tullygarvey	Annagh	Cootehill	III.	87
21	Kilnacross	168	2	37	Cavan	Tullygarvey	Drung	Cootehill	III.	89
14	Kilnacross	112	0	6	Cavan	Tullyhunco	Kildallan	Bawnboy	III.	97
38	Kilnacrott	465	2	35	Cavan	Castlerahan	Crosserlough	Cavan	III.	68
20	Kilnadore	31	1	18	Antrim	Lower Glenarm	Layd	Ballycastle	III.	282
9	Kilnadreen	167	1	38	Monaghan	Trough	Donagh	Monaghan	III.	282
19	Kilnadrow	183	1	22	Cork, E.R.	Condons&Clangibbon	Kilgullane	Mitchelstown	II.	61
93, 94	Kilnadur	401	2	2	Cork, W.R.	East Carbery (W.D.)	Kilmichael	Dunmanway	II.	134
29	Kilnafaddoge	26	0	8	Westmeath	Brawny	St. Mary's	Athlone	I.	259
30, 35	Kilnafarna Lower	308	1	15	Waterford	Decies without Drum	Whitechurch	Dungarvan	II.	361
35	Kilnafarna Upper	143	1	8	Waterford	Decies without Drum	Whitechurch	Dungarvan	II.	362
23, 31	Kilnafrehan East	270	2	25	Waterford	Decies without Drum	Kilgobnet	Dungarvan	II.	357
23, 31	Kilnafrehan Middle	165	3	9	Waterford	Decies without Drum	Kilgobnet	Dungarvan	II.	357
23	Kilnafrehanmountain	324	2	25	Waterford	Decies without Drum	Kilgobnet	Dungarvan	II.	357
23, 31	Kilnafrehan West	393	0	1	Waterford	Decies without Drum	Kilgobnet	Dungarvan	II.	357
46	Kilnafurrery	256	1	19	Cork, E.R.	Kinnatalloon	Mogeely	Youghal	II.	98
23, 31	Kilnagall	428	1	6	King's Co.	Ballyboy	Ballyboy	Parsonstown	I.	123
56, 66	Kilnagalliagh	168	2	12	Clare	Moyarta	Kilfearagh	Kilrush	II.	32
41	Kilnagalliagh	270	2	3	Meath	Upper Moyfenrath	Clonard	Edenderry	I.	213
31	Kilnagalliagh	40	0	12	Westmeath	Moycashel	Ardnurcher or Horseleap	Mullingar	I.	276
115	Kilnagappagh	445	1	12	Galway	Loughrea	Killinan	Loughrea	IV.	64
21	Kilnagarbet	128	0	28	Cavan	Tullygarvey	Larah	Cootehill	III.	91
7	Kilnagarnagh	558	0	34	King's Co.	Garrycastle	Lemanaghan	Parsonstown	I.	136
18	Kilnagarns Lower	115	3	23	Leitrim	Drumahaire	Inishmagrath	Manorhamilton	IV.	96
18	Kilnagarns Upper	157	0	8	Leitrim	Drumahaire	Inishmagrath	Manorhamilton	IV.	96
79, 90	Kilnageer	163	1	1e	Mayo	Carra	Drum	Castlebar	IV.	128
3	Kilnageer	73	0	37	Monaghan	Trough	Errigal Trough	Monaghan	III.	284
14	Kilnaglare	237	2	26	Cavan	Lower Loughtee	Drumlane	Cavan	III.	80
15	Kilnaglare Lower	158	1	24	Cavan	Upper Loughtee	Castleterra	Cavan	III.	83
15	Kilnaglare Upper	57	2	11f	Cavan	Upper Loughtee	Castleterra	Cavan	III.	83
53	Kilnaglearagh	80	1	6	Kerry	Corkaguiny	Garfinny	Dingle	II.	177
87, 99	Kilnaglery	577	2	11	Cork, E.R.	Kerrycurrihy	Carrigaline	Kinsale	II.	92
29, 50	Kilnaglinny	332	1	16	King's Co.	Garrycastle	Lusmagh	Parsonstown	I.	137
73, 85	Kilnaglory	437	3	19	Cork, E.R.	East Muskerry	Kilnaglory	Cork	II.	104
96	Kilnagnady	712	1	17	Cork, W.R.	Kinalmeaky	Brinny	Bandon	II.	152
7	Kilnagoolny	739	3	39	King's Co.	Garrycastle	Lemanaghan	Parsonstown	I.	136
22	Kilnagornan	254	3	27	Kildare	Offaly East	Kildare	Naas	I.	70
132, 141	Kilnagospagh	346	2	9	Cork, W.R.	West Carbery(W.D.)	Caheragh	Skibbereen	II.	142
91	Kilnagower	179	3	38	Mayo	Clanmorris	Kilcolman	Claremorris	IV.	134
41, 44	Kilnagralta	201	2	37	Roscommon	Athlone	Tisrara	Roscommon	IV.	185
63, 71	Kilnagranagh	973	3	39	Tipperary, S.R.	Slievardagh	Cloneen	Callan	II.	332
15	Kilnagrange	1,336	1	8	Waterford	Decies without Drum	Fews	Kilmacthomas	II.	356
61	Kilnagrew	107	1	27g	Tyrone	Dungannon Middle	Clonfeacle	Dungannon	III.	299
28	Kilnagross	206	3	11	Leitrim	Leitrim	Kiltoghert	Cark. on Shannon	IV.	102
36	Kilnagross	118	0	29h	Meath	Upper Navan	Trim	Trim	I.	217
3	Kilnagullan	83	2	31	Monaghan	Trough	Errigal Trough	Monaghan	III.	284
39, 40, 44	Kilnagun	114	3	17	Cavan	Castlerahan	Lurgan	Oldcastle	III.	70
70, 71	Kilnagurteen	447	1	38	Cork, W.R.	West Muskerry	Macroom	Macroom	II.	160
9	Kilnahaltar	143	2	24	Monaghan	Monaghan	Kilmore	Monaghan	III.	276
37	Kilnahard	138	2	21	Cavan	Clanmahon	Ballymachugh	Cavan	III.	76
39	Kilnaharry	100	0	3	Sligo	Corran	Kilshalvy	Boyle	IV.	227
17	Kilnaharvey	122	3	30i	Monaghan	Dartree	Ematris	Cootehill	III.	267
51, 52	Kilnaheery	657	1	29	Tyrone	Clogher	Clogher	Clogher	III.	293
120	Kilnahera East	257	1	3j	Cork, W.R.	West Carbery (E.D.)	Dromdaleague	Skibbereen	II.	140
120	Kilnahera West	115	2	6	Cork, W.R.	West Carbery (E.D.)	Dromdaleague	Skibbereen	II.	140
30	Kilnahinch	300	2	11	Westmeath	Clonlonan	Kilmanaghan	Athlone	I.	262
86	Kilnahone	229	0	10	Cork, E.R.	Kerrycurrihy	Killanully	Cork	II.	92
54	Kilnahone	418	3	34	Tipperary, S.R.	Slievardagh	Crohane	Callan	II.	332
87, 99	Kilnahown	136	3	16	Galway	Clonmacnowen	Clontuskert	Ballinasloe	IV.	24
6, 11	Kilnahue	302	3	27	Wexford	Gorey	Kilnahue	Gorey	I.	319
22	Kilnahulla Beg	168	2	13	Cork, E.R.	Duhallow	Kilmeen	Kanturk	II.	73
22	Kilnahulla More	408	1	34	Cork, E.R.	Duhallow	Kilmeen	Kanturk	II.	73

(a) Including 7A. 1R. 0P. water.
(b) Including 8A. 1R. 16P. water.
(c) Including 8A. 1R. 4P. water.
(d) Including 13A. 0R. 10P. water.

(e) Including 22A. 3R. 9P. water.
(f) Including 3A. 2R. 8P. water.
(g) Including 4A. 3R. 0P. water.

(h) Including 6A. 1R. 32P. water.
(i) Including 8A. 2R. 25P. water.
(j) Including 1A. 0R. 16P. water.

4 F 2

No. of Sheet of the Ordnance Survey Maps.	Townlands and Towns.	Area in Statute Acres.			County.	Barony.	Parish.	Poor Law Union in 1857.	Townland Census of 1851, Part I.	
		A.	R.	P.					Vol.	Page
58	Kilnahusogue . .	595	1	1	Tyrone . .	Clogher . . .	Clogher . . .	Clogher . .	III.	293
38	Kilnakelly . .	272	0	2	Fermanagh .	Knockninny .	Kinawley . .	Lisnaskea . .	III.	202
40	Kilnakirk . .	172	3	9	Fermanagh .	Clankelly . .	Galloon . . .	Clones . .	III.	198
92	Kilnaknappoge . .	238	2	36	Cork, W.R. .	Bantry . .	Kilmocomoge .	Bantry . .	II.	121
38	Kilnalacka . .	111	2	3	King's Co. .	Clonlisk . .	Kilcolman .	Parsonstown .	I.	130
6	Kilnalag . . .	214	1	30	Galway . .	Ballymoe . .	Templetogher .	Glennamaddy .	IV.	9
5	Kilnalappa . .	351	3	36	Galway . .	Ballymoe . .	Dunmore . .	Glennamaddy .	IV.	7
37, 38	Kilnaleck . .	297	2	16a	Cavan . .	Castlerahan .	Crosserlough .	Cavan . .	III.	68
15	Kilnaleck . .	181	2	2b	Cavan . .	Lower Loughtee	Annagh . .	Cavan . .	III.	79
38	KILNALECK T. .	—			Cavan . .	Castlerahan .	Crosserlough .	Cavan . .	III.	68
21	Kilnaloo . . .	122	0	32	Fermanagh .	Magheraboy .	Rossorry . .	Enniskillen .	III.	214
36	Kilnalosset . .	116	3	21	Roscommon .	Ballintober South .	Kilgefin . .	Roscommon .	IV.	189
31	Kilnalug . . .	107	2	22	Westmeath .	Moycashel . .	Ardnurcher or Horse-leap . .	Mullingar .	I.	276
2	Kilnalun . . .	176	2	3	Meath . .	Morgallion . .	Enniskeen . .	Kells . .	I.	209
1	Kilnamack East .	710	3	24c	Waterford .	Glenahiry . .	Inishlounaght .	Clonmel . .	II.	365
1	Kilnamack West .	378	1	2d	Waterford .	Glenahiry . .	Inishlounaght .	Clogheen .	II.	365
21	Kilnamaddoo . .	179	0	22	Fermanagh .	Clanawley . .	Boho . . .	Enniskillen .	III.	189
22	Kilnamaddy . .	114	1	30	Fermanagh .	Tirkennedy . .	Derrybrusk . .	Enniskillen .	III.	220
12	Kilnamaddy . .	114	1	21	Monaghan .	Dartree . .	Killeevan . .	Clones . .	III.	268
13	Kilnamaddy . .	108	0	34	Monaghan .	Monaghan . .	Monaghan . .	Monaghan .	III.	277
14	Kilnamaddy . .	218	1	36	Monaghan .	Monaghan . .	Tullycorbet . .	Monaghan .	III.	281
22	Kilnamaddyroe .	118	1	14	Leitrim . .	Carrigallen .	Oughteragh . .	Bawnboy . .	IV.	92
21, 22	Kilnamanagh . .	621	2	21	Dublin . .	Uppercross . .	Tallaght . .	Dublin South .	I.	42
52	Kilnamanagh . .	356	0	25	Roscommon .	Athlone . .	St. Peters . .	Athlone . .	IV.	184
9, 15	Kilnamanagh . .	456	3	6	Roscommon .	Frenchpark . .	Kilnamanagh . .	Boyle . .	IV.	204
26	Kilnamanagh . .	388	2	25e	Sligo . .	Leyny . .	Ballysadare .	Sligo . .	IV.	230
30, 31	Kilnamanagh Beg .	337	2	11	Wicklow . .	Arklow . .	Glenealy . .	Rathdrum .	I.	344
21	Kilnamanagh Lower	200	1	26	Wexford . .	Ballaghkeen .	Kilnamanagh . .	Gorey . .	I.	297
30	Kilnamanagh More .	466	2	38	Wicklow . .	Arklow . .	Glenealy . .	Rathdrum .	I.	344
21	Kilnamanagh Upper	313	3	15	Wexford . .	Ballaghkeen .	Kilnamanagh . .	Gorey . .	I.	297
30	Kilnamarve . .	226	1	35f	Leitrim . .	Carrigallen .	Carrigallen . .	Bawnboy . .	IV.	90
23	Kilnambrahar . .	153	3	19	Fermanagh .	Tirkennedy . .	Enniskillen . .	Enniskillen .	III.	222
31	Kilnameel . .	194	1	26	Fermanagh .	Clanawley . .	Killesher . .	Enniskillen .	III.	192
109	Kilnameela . .	397	2	12	Cork, W.R. .	East Carbery (E.D.)	Desertserges .	Bandon . .	II.	128
33	Kilnamona . .	25	0	13	Clare . .	Inchiquin . .	Kilnamona . .	Ennis . .	II.	27
29, 37	Kilnamona . .	261	0	16	Limerick . .	Connello Upper .	Cloncagh . .	Newcastle .	II.	231
86	Kilnamona . .	146	0	32	Tipperary, S.R.	Iffa and Offa West .	Templetenny .	Clogheen . .	II.	320
9, 10	Kilnamoragh North	158	3	4	Kildare . .	Ikeathy&Oughterany	Donadea . .	Celbridge . .	I.	57
9, 10	Kilnamoragh South	426	1	23	Kildare . .	Ikeathy&Oughterany	Donadea . .	Celbridge . .	I.	57
16	Kilnamryall . .	398	3	38	Roscommon .	Roscommon . .	Shankill . .	Boyle . .	IV.	213
62, 73	Kilnamucky . .	257	3	34	Cork. E.R. .	East Muskerry .	Matehy . .	Cork . .	II.	105
107	Kilnamullaun . .	31	0	3	Galway . .	Longford . .	Abbeygormacan .	Ballinasloe .	IV.	56
107	Kilnamullaun . .	168	2	22	Galway . .	Longford . .	Killimorbologue .	Portumna .	IV.	59
47	Kilnanare . .	387	0	0	Kerry . .	Magunihy . .	Kilnanare . .	Killarney . .	II.	204
27	Kilnaneave . .	686	2	25	Tipperary, N.R.	Upper Ormond .	Kilnaneave . .	Nenagh . .	II.	291
22	Kilnanooan . .	171	2	30	Roscommon .	Roscommon . .	Elphin . .	Strokestown .	IV.	209
28	Kilnantoge Lower .	374	1	7	King's Co. .	Coolestown .	Clonsast . .	Edenderry .	I.	133
28	Kilnantoge Upper .	417	2	34	King's Co. .	Coolestown .	Clonsast . .	Edenderry .	I.	133
63, 74	Kilnap . . .	193	0	3	Cork, E.R. .	Cork . .	St. Annes Shandon .	Cork . .	II.	65
14	Kilnappy . .	198	3	6	Londonderry .	Tirkeeran . .	Faughanvale .	Londonderry .	III.	250
38	Kilnarainy . .	75	2	17g	Fermanagh .	Knockninny .	Kinawley . .	Lisnaskea . .	III.	202
82, 83	Kilnarovanagh . .	396	0	23	Cork, W.R. .	West Muskerry .	Macloneigh .	Macroom . .	II.	160
57	Kilnarovanagh . .	326	3	1	Kerry . .	Magunihy . .	Kilbonane . .	Killarney . .	II.	205
118	Kilnaruane . .	20	3	13	Cork, W.R. .	Bantry . .	Kilmocomoge .	Bantry . .	II.	121
14	Kilnasavoge . .	66	2	3	Longford . .	Ardagh . .	Templemichael .	Longford . .	I.	154
28, 34	Kilnaseer . .	645	1	23	Queen's Co. .	Clarmallagh .	Aghaboe . .	Abbeyleix . .	I.	236
28, 34	Kilnaseer . .	178	0	19	Queen's Co. .	Clarmallagh .	Aghmacart . .	Abbeyleix . .	I.	236
35	Kilnaseer . .	196	0	8	Tipperary, N.R.	Eliogarty . .	Loughmoe East .	Thurles . .	II.	271
27	Kilnashanally . .	106	3	3	Tipperary, N.R.	Upper Ormond .	Dolla . .	Nenagh . .	II.	290
30	Kilnashane . .	191	3	24	Queen's Co. .	Cullenagh . .	Dysartgallen .	Abbeyleix . .	I.	239
8	Kilnashee . .	273	1	19	Longford . .	Longford . .	Killoe . .	Longford . .	I.	159
36	Kilnasillagh . .	107	2	8	Roscommon .	Ballintober South .	Kilgefin . .	Roscommon .	IV.	189
46	Kilnaslee . .	301	3	38	Tyrone . .	Dungannon Middle .	Donaghmore .	Dungannon .	III.	302
16, 17	Kilnaslieve . .	329	0	16	Galway . .	Dunmore . .	Dunmore . .	Tuam . .	IV.	34
22, 28	Kilnasmuttaun . .	160	1	31	Wexford . .	Ballaghkeen .	Killincooly . .	Enniscorthy .	I.	295
42, 51	Kilnasoolagh . .	86	0	0	Clare . .	Bunratty Lower .	Kilnasoolagh .	Ennis . .	II.	6
66	Kilnasudry . .	23	3	0	Cork, E.R. .	Imokilly . .	Killeagh . .	Youghal . .	II.	88
11	Kilnatierney . .	122	0	17	Down . .	Ards Lower .	Greyabbey . .	Newtownards .	III.	158
67	Kilnatoora . .	128	2	31	Cork, E.R. .	Imokilly . .	Youghal . .	Youghal . .	II.	91
26	Kilnavar . .	184	3	28h	Cavan . .	Upper Loughtee .	Lavey . .	Cavan . .	III.	60
20, 23	Kilnavara . .	309	3	29i	Cavan . .	Upper Loughtee .	Urney . .	Cavan . .	III.	86
13	Kilnavert . .	188	1	38j	Cavan . .	Tullyhaw . .	Templeport .	Bawnboy . .	III.	95

(a) Including 4A. 2R. 37P. water.
(b) Including 27A. 2R. 9P. water.
(c) Including 8A. 3R. 18P. water.
(d) Including 14A. 1R. 12P. water.

(e) Including 3A. 3R. 16P. water.
(f) Including 10A. 1R. 32P. water.
(g) Including 1A. 3R. 17P. water.

(h) Including 5A. 0R. 28P. water.
(i) Including 19A. 1R. 5P. water.
(j) Including 5A. 1R. 6P. water

No. of Sheet of the Ordnance Survey Maps.	Townlands and Towns.	Area in Statute Acres.	County.	Barony.	Parish.	Poor Law Union in 1857.	Townland Census of 1851, Part I.	
		A. R. P.					Vol.	Page
33	Kilnew	199 3 29	Meath	Upper Duleek	Duleek Abbey	Drogheda	I.	198
27	Kilnew	191 3 18	Wexford	Ballaghkeen	Ballyvaldon	Enniscorthy	I.	292
27	Kilnew	194 2 0	Wexford	Ballaghkeen	Meenagh	Enniscorthy	I.	298
28, 36	Kilnoe	417 3 10a	Clare	Tulla Upper	Kilnoe	Scarriff	II.	40
47	Kilnoe	160 2 3	Tipperary, N.R.	Eliogarty	Moycarky	Thurles	II.	271
71	Kilnpark	64 3 6	Donegal	Raphoe	Clonleigh	Strabane	III.	135
85, 94	Kilpadder	73 0 36	Kerry	Glanarought	Kilgarvan	Kenmare	II.	187
32, 41	Kilpadder North	262 0 22	Cork, E.R.	Duhallow	Kilshannig	Mallow	II.	74
32, 41	Kilpadder South	344 2 7	Cork, E.R.	Duhallow	Kilshannig	Mallow	II.	74
3	Kilpaddoge	415 0 31	Kerry	Iraghticonnor	Kilnaughtin	Glin	II.	191
19, 20	Kilparteen	223 1 36	Tipperary, N.R.	Owney and Arra	Castletownarra	Nenagh	II.	294
1	Kilpatrick	169 1 25	Antrim	Cary	Rathlin Island	Ballycastle	III.	15
24, 32	Kilpatrick	122 3 16	Cork, E.R.	Duhallow	Castlemagner	Kanturk	II.	67
99	Kilpatrick	201 1 22	Cork, E.R.	Kinalea	Kilpatrick	Kinsale	II.	95
24, 32	Kilpatrick	290 0 32	Cork, E.R.	Orrery and Kilmore	Ballyclogh	Mallow	II.	106
96, 97	Kilpatrick	1,103 0 9	Cork, W.R.	Kinalmeaky	Brinny	Bandon	II.	152
148	Kilpatrick	123 2 12	Cork, W.R.	West Carbery (W.D.)	Skull	Skull	II.	146
59, 60	Kilpatrick	206 0 35	Cork, W.R.	West Muskerry	Clondrohid	Macroom	II.	155
93	Kilpatrick	148 3 11	Kerry	Glanarought	Kenmare	Kenmare	II.	186
8, 12	Kilpatrick	394 0 18	Kildare	Carbury	Kilpatrick	Edenderry	I.	52
26	Kilpatrick	130 0 11	Kildare	Offaly West	Ballybrackan	Athy	I.	71
7, 8, 15, 16	Kilpatrick	487 0 10	King's Co.	Ballycowan	Rahan	Tullamore	I.	129
17	Kilpatrick	360 3 35	Louth	Ardee	Kildemock	Ardee	I.	173
66	Kilpatrick	83 0 19	Tipperary, S.R.	Clanwilliam	Lattin	Tipperary	II.	309
51, 59	Kilpatrick	475 1 12	Tipperary, S.R.	Kilnamanagh Lower	Kilpatrick	Cashel	II.	324
11	Kilpatrick	472 3 3	Westmeath	Corkaree	Leny	Mullingar	I.	262
8, 13	Kilpatrick	843 1 30	Westmeath	Fore	Kilpatrick	Castletowndelvin	I.	270
18,19,25,26	Kilpatrick	772 2 18	Westmeath	Moyashel and Magheradernon	Mullingar	Mullingar	I.	275
31	Kilpatrick	132 0 7	Westmeath	Moycashel	Ardnurcher or Horseleap	Mullingar	I.	276
18	Kilpatrick	297 3 24	Westmeath	Rathconrath	Rathconrath	Mullingar	I.	284
21	Kilpatrick	238 2 0	Wexford	Ballaghkeen	Kilnamanagh	Gorey	I.	297
3, 7	Kilpatrick	248 1 26	Wexford	Gorey	Kilgorman	Gorey	I.	318
35, 36, 40	Kilpatrick	523 0 8	Wicklow	Arklow	Ennereilly	Rathdrum	I.	344
22	Kilpeacon	450 3 29	Limerick	Smallcounty	Kilpeacon	Croom	II.	260
13	Kilpedder East	125 1 19	Wicklow	Newcastle	Kilcoole	Rathdrum	I.	352
13	Kilpedder West	33 1 23	Wicklow	Newcastle	Kilcoole	Rathdrum	I.	352
52	Kilpheak	493 0 34	Donegal	Kilmacrenan	Conwal	Letterkenny	III.	126
61	Kilpheak	131 0 14	Tipperary, S.R.	Middlethird	St. Patricksrock	Cashel	II.	331
19	Kilphelan	122 2 11	Cork, E.R.	Condons and Clangibbon	Kilphelan	Mitchelstown	II.	62
10, 17	Kilphierish	269 2 36	Westmeath	Rathconrath	Piercetown	Ballymahon	I.	283
45, 46, 54	Kilphillibeen	535 2 5	Cork, E.R.	Kinnatalloon	Ballynoe	Fermoy	II.	97
16	Kilphrasoga	307 3 10	Galway	Dunmore	Liskeevy	Tuam	IV.	35
20, 26	Kilpierce	267 2 27	Wexford	Ballaghkeen	Templeshannon	Enniscorthy	I.	299
27	Kilpike	468 1 5	Down	Lower Iveagh, Lr. pt.	Seapatrick	Banbridge	III.	169
39	Kilpipe	694 3 0	Wicklow	Ballinacor South	Kilpipe	Shillelagh	I.	349
31	Kilpoole Hill	210 3 12	Wicklow	Arklow	Kilpoole	Rathdrum	I.	345
31	Kilpoole Lower	226 0 28	Wicklow	Arklow	Kilpoole	Rathdrum	I.	345
31	Kilpoole Upper	175 0 22	Wicklow	Arklow	Kilpoole	Rathdrum	I.	345
22, 28	Kilpurcel	336 2 11	Queen's Co.	Clandonagh	Donaghmore	Donaghmore	I.	233
13	Kilquade	350 3 0	Wicklow	Newcastle	Kilcoole	Rathdrum	I.	352
13	Kilquade	46 1 20	Wicklow	Newcastle	Newcastle Lower	Rathdrum	I.	353
104	Kilquain	220 1 39	Galway	Dunkellin	Kiltora	Loughrea	IV.	31
107, 108	Kilquain	373 0 14	Galway	Longford	Kilquain	Portumna	IV.	60
63	Kilquane	48 0 2	Clare	Bunratty Lower	St. Patricks	Limerick	II.	7
33	Kilquane	90 1 18	Clare	Islands	Drumcliff	Ennis	II.	30
42	Kilquane	523 0 32	Cork, E.R.	Barretts	Mourneabbey	Mallow	II.	50
64	Kilquane	269 0 1	Cork, E.R.	Barrymore	Kilquane	Cork	II.	55
26, 34	Kilquane	321 3 8	Cork, E.R.	Fermoy	Bridgetown	Fermoy	II.	77
34	Kilquane	288 1 15	Kerry	Corkaguiny	Kilquane	Dingle	II.	179
68	Kilquane	546 0 6	Kerry	Magunihy	Kilcummin	Killarney	II.	201
40, 41	Kilquane	1,048 0 33	Kerry	Trughanacmy	Ballincuslane	Tralee	II.	206
29, 30	Kilquane	133 2 10	Kerry	Trughanacmy	Ballymacelligott	Tralee	II.	207
19	Kilquane	96 1 6	Limerick	Connello Lower	Clonagh	Rathkeale	II.	227
35, 40	Kilqueeny	147 3 16	Wicklow	Arklow	Castlemacadam	Rathdrum	I.	342
37,38,42,43	Kilquiggin	364 0 38	Wicklow	Shillelagh	Mullinacuff	Shillelagh	I.	358
38	Kilquilly	243 0 33	Cavan	Castlerahan	Castlerahan	Oldcastle	III.	67
118	Kilquire Lower	331 1 28	Mayo	Kilmaine	Kilmanemore	Ballinrobe	IV.	156
118, 119	Kilquire Upper	195 1 2	Mayo	Kilmaine	Kilmainemore	Ballinrobe	IV.	156
17, 18	Kilraghts	424 3 8	Antrim	Upper Dunluce	Kilraghts	Ballymoney	III.	20
2, 3	Kilrainy	523 0 32	Kildare	Carbury	Kilrainy	Edenderry	I.	52

(a) Including 47A. 1R. 1P. water.   (b) Including 2A. 2R. 16P. water.

No. of Sheet of the Ordnance Survey Maps.	Townlands and Towns.	Area in Statute Acres.			County.	Barony.	Parish.	Poor Law Union in 1857.	Townland Census of 1851, Part I.	
		A.	R.	P.					Vol.	Page
27	Kilranelagh . .	221	1	26	Wicklow . .	Upper Talbotstown	Kilranelagh . .	Baltinglass .	I.	364
134	Kilrateera Lower .	146	3	7	Galway . .	Leitrim . . .	Inishcaltra . .	Scarriff .	IV.	55
134	Kilrateera Upper .	335	2	18	Galway . .	Leitrim . . .	Inishcaltra . .	Scarriff .	IV.	53
1, 2, 3	Kilrathmurry . .	756	1	5	Kildare . .	Carbury . . .	Kilrainy . .	Edenderry .	I.	52
22	Kilrea . . .	282	3	35	Armagh . .	Orior Lower .	Killevy . .	Newry .	III.	56
27	Kilrea . .	743	1	16	Londonderry .	Loughinsholin .	Kilrea . . .	Ballymoney .	III.	241
40	Kilready . .	116	1	4	Fermanagh .	Coole . . .	Galloon . .	Clones .	III.	200
24	Kilreal Lower .	116	2	29	Tyrone .	Omagh West .	Ardstraw . .	Castlederg .	III.	315
24	Kilreal Upper .	242	1	34	Tyrone .	Omagh West .	Ardstraw . .	Castlederg .	III.	315
67, 68	Kilrean . .	431	2	4	Donegal .	Raphoe . . .	Kilteevoge . .	Stranorlar .	III.	139
74	Kilrean Lower .	322	2	34	Donegal . .	Boylagh . . .	Killybegs Lower .	Glenties .	III.	114
74, 83	Kilrean Upper .	1,503	2	23	Donegal . .	Boylagh . . .	Killybegs Lower .	Glenties .	III.	114
28	Kilreash . .	127	1	0	Limerick .	Shanid . . .	Ardagh . . .	Newcastle .	II.	255
27	KILREA T. .	—			Londonderry .	Loughinsholin .	Kilrea . .	Ballymoney .	III.	241
16	Kilree . .	295	3	19a	Carlow . .	Idrone East .	Sliguff . .	Carlow .	I.	8
27	Kilree . .	420	0	0	Kilkenny .	Kells . . .	Kilree . .	Callan .	I.	109
23, 24	Kilree . .	785	3	22b	Kilkenny . .	Shillelogher .	Grangekilree .	Kilkenny .	I.	114
21, 22	Kilree . .	161	0	20	Roscommon .	Roscommon . .	Ogulla . .	Strokestown .	IV.	212
11, 14	Kilreesk . .	262	3	⅜	Dublin . .	Nethercross .	Finglas . .	Balrothery .	I.	30
4	Kilregane . .	610	1	31	Tipperary, N.R.	Lower Ormond .	Lorrha . . .	Borrisokane .	II.	285
35, 40	Kilridd . .	166	2	21	Fermanagh .	Clankelly . .	Clones . .	Clones .	III.	196
26, 27	Kilriffet . .	326	1	14	Tipperary, N.R.	Upper Ormond .	Dolla . . .	Nenagh .	II.	290
6	Kilriffin . .	173	0	30	Meath . .	Lower Slane .	Drumcondra . .	Ardee .	I.	222
8, 9	Kilrobert . .	347	3	3	Antrim . .	Cary . . .	Ramoan . .	Ballycastle .	III.	14
28	Kilrodane . .	141	2	27	Limerick . .	Shanid . . .	Ardagh . .	Newcastle .	II.	255
28	Kilrodane . .	161	0	8	Limerick . .	Shanid . . .	Newcastle . .	Newcastle .	II.	257
20	Kilroddan . .	204	2	33	Roscommon .	Frenchpark . .	Tibohine . .	Castlereagh .	IV.	205
32	Kilroe . .	248	1	4	Cork, E.R. .	Duhallow . .	Ballyclogh . .	Mallow .	II.	67
56	Kilroe . .	83	2	14	Galway . .	Clare . . .	Kilcoona . .	Tuam .	IV.	20
22	Kilroe . .	104	3	28	Mayo . .	Tirawley . .	Killala . .	Killala .	IV.	169
81, 87	Kilroe . .	428	3	34	Tipperary, S.R.	Iffa and Offa West .	Tubbrid . .	Clogheen .	II.	321
92	Kilroe East .	822	2	4c	Galway . .	Moycullen . .	Killannin . .	Galway .	IV.	70
92	Kilroe West .	910	2	7d	Galway . .	Moycullen . .	Killannin . .	Galway .	IV.	70
81, 87	Kilroewood . .	105	3	10	Tipperary, S.R.	Iffa and Offa West .	Tubbrid . .	Clogheen .	II.	321
82	Kilroghter . .	345	1	16	Galway . .	Galway . . .	Oranmore . .	Galway .	IV.	37
34	Kilronan . .	141	3	30	Fermanagh .	Magherastephana .	Aghalurcher . .	Lisnaskea .	III.	217
17	Kilronan . .	546	1	17	Waterford .	Middlethird .	Kilronan . .	Waterford .	II.	368
108, 121	Kilronane East .	476	1	12	Cork, W.R. .	East Carbery (W.D.)	Fanlobbus . .	Dunmanway .	II.	132
107, 108) 120, 121 }	Kilronane West .	562	3	22	Cork, W.R. .	East Carbery (W.D.)	Fanlobbus . .	Dunmanway .	II.	132
2, 4	Kilronan Mountain .	654	0	29	Roscommon .	Boyle . . .	Kilronan . .	Boyle .	IV.	197
111	KILRONAN T. .	—			Galway . .	Aran . . .	Inishmore . .	Galway .	IV.	3
13, 14	Kilrooan . .	144	0	33	Roscommon .	Frenchpark . .	Tibohine . .	Castlereagh .	IV.	205
7	Kilroosk . .	599	0	38e	Leitrim . .	Rosclogher .	Killasnet . .	Manorhamilton .	IV.	110
25	Kilrooskagh . .	179	0	8	Fermanagh .	Clanawley . .	Cleenish . .	Enniskillen .	III.	191
25	Kilrooskagh Island .	20	2	15	Fermanagh .	Clanawley . .	Cleenish . .	Enniskillen .	III.	192
40	Kilroosky . .	150	3	0f	Fermanagh .	Clankelly . .	Clones . .	Clones .	III.	196
36	Kilroosky . .	92	2	27	Roscommon .	Ballintober South .	Kilgefin . .	Roscommon .	IV.	189
53	Kilroot . .	625	3	7	Antrim . .	Lower Belfast .	Kilroot . .	Larne .	III.	9
40	Kilroot . .	106	0	15	Fermanagh .	Clankelly . .	Galloon . .	Clones .	III.	198
14	Kilrory . .	516	3	3	Queen's Co. .	Stradbally . .	Moyanna . .	Athy .	I.	247
69	Kilross . .	154	0	29	Donegal . .	Raphoe . . .	Stranorlar . .	Stranorlar .	III.	142
21	Kilross . .	208	0	16	Sligo . .	Tirerrill . .	Kilross . .	Sligo .	IV.	241
66, 73	Kilross . .	541	0	2	Tipperary, S.R.	Clanwilliam .	Clonbeg . .	Tipperary .	II.	305
66	Kilross . .	73	3	9	Tipperary, S.R.	Clanwilliam .	Lattin . .	Tipperary .	II.	309
23	Kilrossanty . .	358	3	27	Waterford .	Decies without Drum	Kilrossanty . .	Kilmacthomas .	II.	358
44, 45	Kilroughil . .	280	1	23	Clare . .	Tulla Lower . .	O'Briensbridge .	Limerick .	II.	38
134	Kilruane . .	272	1	7	Cork, W.R. .	Ibane and Barryroe	Ross . . .	Clonakilty .	II.	150
15	Kilruane . .	222	2	39	Tipperary, N.R.	Lower Ormond .	Kilruane . .	Nenagh .	II.	285
59, 65	Kilruddan . .	142	3	24	Tyrone . .	Clogher . .	Clogher . .	Clogher .	III.	293
8	Kilruddery Deerpark	271	1	10	Wicklow . .	Rathdown . .	Bray . .	Rathdown .	I.	354
8 8	Kilruddery Deerpark Kilruddery Demesne East . .	167 71	0 0	8 12	Wicklow . . Wicklow . .	Rathdown . . Rathdown . .	Delgany . . Bray . .	Rathdown . Rathdown .	I. I.	355 354
8	Kilruddery Demesne West . .	348	3	35	Wicklow . .	Rathdown . .	Bray . .	Rathdown .	I.	354
45	Kilrue . . .	612	1	19	Meath . .	Ratoath . .	Ratoath . .	Dunshaughlin .	I.	219
67	Kilrush . .	269	2	2	Clare . .	Moyarta . .	Kilrush . .	Kilrush .	II.	33
66	Kilrush . .	359	1	20	Cork, E.R. .	Imokilly . .	Mogeely . .	Middleton .	II.	90
109	Kilrush . .	189	3	19	Cork, W.R. .	East Carbery (E.D.)	Desertserges . .	Bandon .	II.	128
32	Kilrush . .	212	3	15	Kildare . .	Offaly West .	Kilrush . .	Athy .	I.	73
9, 13	Kilrush . .	423	1	25	Kilkenny . .	Crannagh . .	Clomantagh . .	Urlingford .	I.	85
25	Kilrush . .	146	3	3g	Leitrim . .	Carrigallen .	Oughteragh . .	Bawnboy .	IV.	92

(a) Including 9A. 0R. 22P. River Barrow.
(b) Including 4A. 3R. 30P. River Nore.
(c) Including 33A. 3R. 13P. water.

(d) Including 4A. 3R. 17P. water.
(e) Including 0A. 2R. 16P. water.

(f) Including 15A. 1R. 21P. water.
(g) Including 7A. 3R. 35P. water.

No. of Sheet of the Ordnance Survey Maps.	Townlands and Towns.	Area in Statute Acres. A. R. P.	County.	Barony.	Parish.	Poor Law Union in 1857.	Townland Census of 1851, Part I. Vol.	Page
5	Kilrush . . .	140 3 36a	Limerick . .	Pubblebrien and Municipal Borough .	St. Munchins . .	Limerick . .	II.	254
110, 111	Kilrush . . .	165 0 16b	Mayo . . .	Kilmaine . .	Kilcommon . .	Ballinrobe . .	IV.	155
41	Kilrush . . .	633 2 31	Tipperary, N.R.	Eliogarty . .	Thurles . .	Thurles . .	II.	273
12	Kilrusheighter . .	204 0 36	Sligo . . .	Tireragh . .	Templeboy . .	Dromore West .	IV.	236
30	Kilrush or Ironmills	1,548 3 13	Queen's Co. .	Cullenagh . .	Abbeyleix . .	Abbeyleix . .	I.	238
9	Kilrush Lower . .	478 1 27c	Westmeath .	Delvin . . .	Killua . .	Castletowndelvin	I.	265
31	Kilrush (Marquis) .	44 1 31	Waterford .	Decies without Drum	Kilrush . .	Dungarvan . .	II.	358
31	Kilrush (Power) .	38 1 2	Waterford .	Decies without Drum	Kilrush . .	Dungarvan . .	II.	358
67	KILRUSH T. .	—	Clare . .	Moyarta . .	Kilrush . .	Kilrush . .	II.	33
9	Kilrush Upper . .	444 0 5d	Westmeath .	Delvin . . .	Killua . .	Castletowndelvin	I.	265
64	Kilrussane . .	241 0 10	Cork, E.R. .	Barrymore . .	Killaspugmullane .	Cork . .	II.	55
25	Kilsallagh . .	75 1 11	Cavan . .	Clanmahon .	Kilmore . .	Cavan . .	III.	78
9	Kilsallagh . .	169 0 23	Cavan . .	Tullyhaw . .	Templeport . .	Bawnboy . .	III.	95
27	Kilsallagh . .	41 0 16	Fermanagh .	Tirkennedy . .	Derrybrusk . .	Enniskillen . .	III.	220
6, 7	Kilsallagh . .	951 1 21	Galway . .	Ballymoe . .	Kilcroan . .	Glennamaddy .	IV.	9
39	Kilsallagh . .	92 1 10	Kerry . .	Trughanacmy . .	Nohaval . .	Tralee . .	II.	212
20	Kilsallagh . .	538 0 6	Longford . .	Ardagh . . .	Mostrim . .	Granard . .	I.	152
27, 36	Kilsallagh . .	1,307 3 35e	Mayo . . .	Erris . . .	Kilcommon . .	Belmullet . .	IV.	144
39	Kilsallagh . .	118 0 3	Sligo . . .	Corran . .	Drumrat . .	Boyle . .	IV.	226
61	Kilsallagh . .	415 1 31	Tipperary, S.R.	Middlethird . .	Kilcommon . .	Cashel . .	II.	327
11	Kilsallaghan . .	353 3 35	Dublin . .	Nethercross . .	Kilsallaghan .	Balrothery . .	I.	31
86, 87	Kilsallagh Lower .	702 2 5	Mayo . . .	Murrisk . .	Oughaval . .	Westport . .	IV.	162
86, 96	Kilsallagh Upper .	347 1 6	Mayo . . .	Murrisk . .	Oughaval . .	Westport . .	IV.	162
39	Kilsalley . . .	373 2 17	Tyrone . .	Dungannon Upper .	Ballyclog . .	Cookstown . .	III.	306
67	Kilsampson . .	65 3 0	Tyrone . .	Dungannon Lower .	Aghaloo . .	Armagh . .	III.	297
61, 67	Kilsannagh . .	412 0 2	Tyrone . .	Dungannon Lower .	Aghaloo . . .	Dungannon . .	III.	297
30,31,36,37	Kilsaran . . .	436 0 8f	Cavan . .	Clanmahon . .	Drumlumman .	Granard . .	III.	77
15	Kilsaran . . .	491 2 33	Louth . .	Ardee . . .	Kilsaran . .	Ardee . .	I.	173
15	KILSARAN T. . .	—	Louth . .	Ardee . . .	Kilsaran . .	Ardee . .	I.	173
49, 59	Kilsarkan East .	665 3 1	Kerry . .	Trughanacmy . .	Dysert . .	Tralee . .	II.	210
49, 59	Kilsarkan West .	582 1 10	Kerry . .	Trughanacmy . .	Dysert . .	Tralee . .	II.	210
140, 141	Kilsarlaght . .	282 3 6g	Cork, W.R. .	West Carbery (E.D.)	Aghadown . .	Skibbereen . .	II.	137
50	Kilscanlan . .	349 0 14	Limerick . .	Coshlea . .	Galbally . .	Mitchelstown .	III.	239
35	Kilscanlan . .	527 2 18	Wexford . .	Bantry . . .	Kilscanlan . .	New Ross . .	I.	301
28	Kilscannell . .	617 3 24	Limerick . .	Connello Lower .	Kilscannell . .	Rathkeale . .	II.	228
61	Kilscobin . .	117 1 16	Tipperary, S.R.	Middlethird . .	St. Patricksrock .	Cashel . .	II.	331
111	Kilscohagh . .	318 3 25	Mayo . . .	Clanmorris . .	Crossboyne .	Claremorris . .	IV.	133
120, 133	Kilscohanagh . .	352 0 30	Cork, W.R. .	West Carbery (E.D.)	Dromdaleague .	Skibbereen . .	II.	140
48	Kilscoran . .	115 3 0	Wexford . .	Forth . . .	Kilscoran . .	Wexford . .	I.	311
44	Kilseily . . .	226 1 28	Clare . .	Tulla Lower . .	Kilseily . .	Limerick . .	II.	37
9	Kilsellagh . .	576 0 35	Sligo . . .	Carbury . . .	Drumcliff . .	Sligo . .	IV.	221
2	Kilshallow . .	122 0 10	Westmeath .	Moygoish . .	Street . .	Granard . .	I.	281
39, 44	Kilshalvy . .	510 1 11	Sligo . . .	Corran . . .	Kilshalvy . .	Boyle . .	IV.	227
3	Kilshanchoe . .	252 3 16	Kildare . .	Carbury . . .	Dunfierth . .	Edenderry . .	I.	52
14	Kilshane . . .	472 2 37	Dublin . .	Castleknock . .	Finglas . .	Dublin North .	I.	25
29, 37	Kilshane . . .	28 2 25	Limerick . .	Connello Upper .	Ballingarry . .	Croom . .	II.	231
67	Kilshane . . .	204 3 37	Tipperary, S.R.	Clanwilliam . .	Kilshane . .	Tipperary . .	II.	309
19, 27	Kilshannig . .	575 3 16	Kerry . .	Corkaguiny . .	Killiney . .	Dingle . .	II.	178
44	Kilshannig Lower .	123 0 35	Cork, E.R. .	Barrymore . .	Rathcormack .	Fermoy . .	II.	57
44	Kilshannig Upper .	238 1 9	Cork, E.R. .	Barrymore . .	Rathcormack .	Fermoy . .	II.	57
10,11,19,20	Kilshanny . .	377 2 3	Cork, E.R. .	Condons & Clangibbon	Brigown . .	Mitchelstown .	II.	59
15, 28	Kilshanvy . .	1,266 2 20	Galway . .	Dunmore . .	Kilconla . .	Tuam . .	IV.	35
27	Kilsharvan . .	199 3 9	Meath . .	Lower Duleek . .	Kilsharvan . .	Drogheda . .	I.	196
84	Kilsheelan . .	92 3 37h	Tipperary, S.R.	Iffa and Offa East .	Kilsheelan . .	Clonmel . .	II.	314
84	KILSHEELAN T. .	—	Tipperary, S.R.	Iffa and Offa East .	Kilsheelan . .	Clonmel . .	II.	315
16	Kilshenane . .	181 3 23	Kerry . .	Clanmaurice . .	Kilshenane . .	Listowel . .	II.	172
52, 60	Kilshenane . .	606 3 24	Tipperary, S.R.	Clanwilliam . .	Oughterleague .	Tipperary . .	II.	309
123	Kilshinahan . .	528 2 8	Cork, W.R. .	East Carbery (E.D.)	Kilbrittain . .	Bandon . .	II.	128
9, 10	Kilshruley . .	256 3 11	Longford . .	Granard . .	Clonbroney . .	Granard . .	I.	155
136	Kilsillagh . .	244 2 7	Cork, W.R. .	Ibane and Barryroe .	Kilsillagh . .	Clonakilty . .	II.	149
71	Kilskeagh . .	576 2 29	Galway . .	Clare . . .	Athenry . .	Galway . .	IV.	17
100	Kilskeagh . .	115 2 0	Mayo . . .	Carra . . .	Touaghty . .	Ballinrobe . .	IV.	130
16, 23	Kilskeer . .	1,590 3 30	Meath . .	Upper Kells . .	Kilskeer . .	Kells . .	I.	206
56	Kilskeery Glebe .	165 2 26	Tyrone . .	Omagh East . .	Kilskeery . .	Enniskillen . .	III.	313
6	Kilsmullan . .	263 1 12	Fermanagh .	Lurg . . .	Magheraculmoney .	Lowtherstown .	III.	208
9	Kilsob . . .	348 0 6i	Cavan . .	Tullyhaw . .	Templeport . .	Bawnboy . .	III.	95
5	Kilsough . .	65 0 12	Dublin . .	Balrothery East .	Balrothery . .	Balrothery . .	I.	19
25	Kilsteague . .	302 0 2	Waterford .	Middlethird . .	Dunhill . .	Kilmacthomas .	II.	366
44	Kilstraghlan or Ragwood . .	294 1 16	Sligo . . .	Coolavin . .	Kilfree . .	Boyle . .	IV.	224
16, 17	Kilstrule . .	924 2 4j	Tyrone . .	Strabane Lower .	Ardstraw . .	Strabane . .	III.	319
9	Kiltaan . . .	375 1 19	Clare . .	Burren . . .	Noughaval . .	Ballyvaghan . .	II.	13

(a) { Within the Municipal Boundary, 79A. 1R. 30P.
Without the Municipal Boundary, 61A. 2R. 6P.
(b) Including 5A. 1R. 26P. water.
(c) Including 17A. 3R. 10P. water.

(d) Including 7A. 2R. 30P. water.
(e) Including 12A. 3R. 13P. water.
(f) Including 12A. 2R. 27P. water.
(g) Including 2A. 2R. 14P. water.

(h) Including 6A. 1R. 3P. water.
(i) Including 2A. 3R. 33P. water.
(j) Including 8A. 0R. 38P. water.

No. of Sheet of the Ordnance Survey Maps.	Townlands and Towns.	Area in Statute Acres.			County.	Barony.	Parish.	Poor Law Union in 1857.	Townland Census of 1851, Part I.	
		A.	R.	P.					Vol.	Page
11	Kiltacky Beg . . .	338	1	38	Clare . .	Inchiquin . .	Kilkeedy . .	Corrofin . .	II.	26
6, 7, 10, 11	Kiltacky More . .	310	1	27	Clare . .	Inchiquin . .	Kilkeedy . .	Corrofin . .	II.	26
16, 17, 21	Kiltaghan North . .	306	3	8	Kildare . .	Offaly East . .	Rathangan . .	Edenderry . .	I.	71
16,17,21,22	Kiltaghan South . .	249	0	35	Kildare . .	Offaly East . .	Rathangan . .	Edenderry . .	I.	71
2	Kiltaglassan . .	173	2	29	Cavan . .	Tullyhaw . .	Killinagh . .	Enniskillen . .	III.	92
37	Kiltale . . .	857	1	29	Meath . .	Lower Deece . .	Kiltale . .	Dunshaughlin .	I.	192
30	Kiltallaghan . .	178	3	14	Kilkenny . .	Kells . .	Killamery . .	Callan . .	I.	109
21, 22	Kiltallaght . .	221	0	6	Louth . .	Ferrard . .	Drumshallon . .	Drogheda . .	I.	180
21, 24	Kiltalown . .	277	0	39	Dublin . .	Uppercross . .	Tallaght . .	Dublin South .	I.	42
80	Kiltamagh . .	267	2	0	Mayo . .	Gallen . .	Killedan . .	Swineford . .	IV.	150
80	KILTAMAGH T. . .	—			Mayo . .	Gallen . .	Killedan . .	Swineford .	IV.	150
42, 43	Kiltamnagh . .	327	3	4	Tyrone . .	Omagh East . .	Drumragh . .	Omagh . .	III.	312
86	Kiltankin . .	1,188	0	18	Tipperary, S.R.	Iffa and Offa West .	Templetenny . .	Clogheen . .	II.	320
37	Kiltanna . . .	370	0	37	Limerick . .	Glenquin . .	Clonelty . .	Newcastle .	II.	245
27, 35	Kiltanon . .	464	0	21	Clare . .	Tulla Upper . .	Tulla . .	Tulla . .	II.	41
2	Kiltareher . .	172	1	38	Westmeath .	Moygoish . .	Street . .	Granard . .	I.	281
67, 68	Kiltarnaght . .	136	0	13d	Mayo . .	Burrishoole . .	Burrishoole . .	Newport . .	IV.	119
41	Kiltarriff . .	206	0	17	Down . .	UpperIveagh(Up.pt.)	Drumgath . .	Newry . .	III.	175
99	Kiltarsaghaun . .	840	0	8b	Mayo . .	Carra . .	Ballintober . .	Castlebar . .	IV.	125
122, 123	Kiltartan . .	104	3	3	Galway . .	Kiltartan . .	Kiltartan . .	Gort . .	IV.	48
2, 7	Kiltass . . .	90	1	29	Cork, E.R. .	Orrery and Kilmore	Cooliney . .	Kilmallock .	II.	108
100	Kiltaugharaun . .	168	2	11	Mayo . .	Kilmaine . .	Robeen . .	Ballinrobe . .	IV.	157
13, 14	Kilteale . .	121	1	23	Queen's Co. .	Maryborough East .	Kilteale . .	Mountmellick .	II.	241
13, 14, 18	Kiltealy . .	1,080	1	0	Wexford . .	Scarawalsh . .	Templeshanbo .	Enniscorthy .	I.	326
13	KILTEALY T. . .				Wexford . .	Scarawalsh . .	Templeshanbo .	Enniscorthy .	I.	326
26	Kilteany . .	266	0	39c	Mayo . .	Erris . .	Kilcommon . .	Belmullet . .	IV.	144
3, 6	Kilteasheen . .	205	2	28	Roscommon .	Boyle . .	Kilbryan . .	Boyle . .	IV.	195
9, 10	Kiltean . .	681	0	25	Kerry . .	Iraghticonnor . .	Galey . .	Listowel . .	II.	190
20	Kilteel Lower . .	259	3	12	Kildare . .	South Salt . .	Kilteel . .	Naas . .	I.	77
20	KILTEEL T. . .	—			Kildare . .	South Salt . .	Kilteel . .	Naas . .	I.	77
20	Kilteel Upper . .	210	1	2	Kildare . .	South Salt . .	Kilteel . .	Naas . .	I.	77
33	Kilteely . .	199	1	38	Limerick . .	Coonagh . .	Kilteely . .	Kilmallock .	II.	235
33	KILTEELY T. . .				Limerick . .	Coonagh . .	Kilteely . .	Kilmallock .	II.	235
36,37,45,46	Kiltcenbane . .	1,186	3	37	Kerry . .	Corkaguiny . .	Kilgobban . .	Tralee . .	II.	177
33	Kilteen Glebe . .	84	2	28	Fermanagh .	Clanawley . .	Killesher . .	Enniskillen .	III.	193
9, 18	Kiltecry . .	579	3	12	Limerick . .	Shanid . .	Loghill . .	Glin . .	II.	257
40	Kilteevan . .	523	1	8	Roscommon .	Ballintober South .	Kilteevan . .	Roscommon .	IV.	190
77, 83	Kiltegan . .	116	2	29	Tipperary, S.R.	Iffa and Offa East .	Kiltegan . .	Clonmel . .	II.	315
27, 32	Kiltegan . .	284	3	27	Wicklow . .	Upper Talbotstown .	Kiltegan . .	Baltinglass .	I.	365
32	KILTEGAN T. . .	—			Wicklow . .	Upper Talbotstown .	Kiltegan . .	Baltinglass .	I.	365
12	Kiltemplan . .	162	0	5	Limerick . .	Pubblebrien . .	Kilkeedy . .	Limerick . .	II.	252
27, 28	Kiltenamullagh . .	145	0	20	Fermanagh .	Magherastephana .	Aghalurcher . .	Lisnaskea . .	III.	217
20,21,29,30	Kiltenan North . .	219	2	18	Limerick . .	Connello Lower .	Croagh . .	Rathkeale . .	II.	228
21, 30	Kiltenan South . .	248	2	33	Limerick . .	Connello Lower .	Croagh . .	Rathkeale . .	II.	228
9	Kiltennan North . .	42	2	8	Clare . .	Burren . .	Noughaval . .	Ballyvaghan .	II.	13
9	Kiltennan South . .	49	2	35	Clare . .	Burren . .	Noughaval . .	Ballyvaghan .	II.	13
12	Kiltennell . .	170	1	26	Wexford . .	Ballaghkeen . .	Kiltennell . .	Gorey . .	I.	297
22	Kiltennell &Ballinvally	298	0	10	Carlow . .	Idrone East . .	Kiltennell . .	New Ross . .	I.	7
64	Kiltermon . .	118	2	23	Tyrone . .	Clogher . .	Aghalurcher . .	Clogher . .	III.	291
10, 11	Kiltest . . .	607	1	4	Londonderry .	Coleraine . .	Aghadowey . .	Coleraine . .	III.	230
10, 15	Kilthomas . .	449	2	37	Wexford . .	Scarawalsh . .	Ferns . .	Enniscorthy .	I.	323
25, 26	Kiltiernan . .	354	2	0d	Dublin . .	Rathdown . .	Kiltiernan . .	Rathdown . .	I.	36
26	Kiltiernan Domain .	150	1	20	Dublin . .	Rathdown . .	Kiltiernan . .	Rathdown . .	I.	36
103	Kiltiernan East . .	488	3	10	Galway . .	Dunkellin . .	Kilcolgan . .	Gort . .	IV.	28
103	Kiltiernan West . .	198	2	30e	Galway . .	Dunkellin . .	Kilcolgan . .	Gort . .	IV.	28
6, 11	Kiltierney . .	323	2	13f	Fermanagh .	Lurg . .	Magheraculmoney .	Lowtherstown .	III.	208
5	Kiltillahan . .	570	0	9	Wexford . .	Scarawalsh . .	Carnew . .	Gorey . .	I.	322
29	Kiltillane . .	506	1	0	Tipperary, N.R.	Eliogarty . .	Templemore . .	Thurles . .	II.	272
29	Kiltilliha . .	195	2	8	Tipperary, N.R.	Eliogarty . .	Templemore . .	Thurles . .	II.	272
5, 10	Kiltilly . .	816	3	6	Wexford . .	Scarawalsh . .	Kilrush . .	Enniscorthy .	I.	324
19	Kiltimon . .	297	3	31	Wicklow . .	Newcastle . .	Killiskey . .	Rathdrum . .	I.	352
19	Kiltimon . .	5	2	24	Wicklow . .	Newcastle . .	Newcastle Upper .	Rathdrum . .	I.	353
70, 77	Kiltinan . .	801	0	37g	Tipperary, S.R.	Middlethird . .	Kiltinan . .	Clonmel . .	II.	328
3	Kiltinny Beg . .	83	2	9	Londonderry .	North East Liberties of Coleraine .	Ballyaghran . .	Coleraine . .	III.	244
7, 11	Kiltinny Lower . .	540	1	15	Londonderry .	Coleraine . .	Macosquin . .	Coleraine . .	III.	233
3	Kiltinny More . .	137	2	28	Londonderry .	North East Liberties of Coleraine .	Ballyaghran . .	Coleraine . .	III.	244
10, 11	Kiltinny Upper . .	666	0	37	Londonderry .	Coleraine . .	Macosquin . .	Coleraine . .	III.	233
21, 24	Kiltipper . .	193	0	19	Dublin . .	Uppercross . .	Tallaght . .	Dublin South .	I.	42
5	Kiltivna . .	191	2	21	Galway . .	Ballymoe . .	Dunmore . .	Glennamaddy .	IV.	7
43	Kiltober . .	99	0	19	Fermanagh .	Coole . .	Drummully . .	Clones . .	III.	199
23	Kiltober . .	58	2	23	Westmeath .	Kilkenny West . .	Drumraney . .	Ballymahon .	I.	273

(a) Including 2A. 0R. 1P. water.　　(d) Including 1A. 0R. 24P. detached portion.　　(f) Including 7A. 2R. 22P. water.
(b) Including 30A. 3R. 17P. water.　　(e) Including 6A. 1R. 16P. water.　　(g) Including 88A. 3R. 13P. detached portion.
(c) Including 14A. 3R. 7P. water.

No. of Sheet of the Ordnance Survey Maps.	Townlands and Towns.	Area in Statute Acres. A. R. P.	County.	Barony.	Parish.	Poor Law Union in 1857.	Townland Census of 1851, Part I. Vol.	Page
38	Kiltober . . .	380 2 20	Westmeath .	Moycashel .	Rahugh . .	Tullamore .	I.	279
38	Kiltober and Grange	296 3 29	Westmeath .	Moycashel .	Kilbeggan .	Tullamore .	I.	278
27	Kiltoghert . .	813 3 23a	Leitrim . .	Leitrim . .	Kiltoghert .	Carᵏ. on Shannon	IV.	102
27	KILTOGHERT T. .	—	Leitrim . .	Leitrim . .	Kiltoghert .	Carᵏ. on Shannon	IV.	103
121	Kiltogorra . .	305 0 33	Mayo . .	Kilmaine . .	Cong . .	Ballinrobe .	IV.	154
69, 70	Kiltole . . .	307 1 11	Donegal . .	Raphoe . .	Raphoe . .	Strabane . .	III.	141
1	Kiltomulty . .	167 3 16	Cavan . .	Tullyhaw . .	Killinagh .	Enniskillen .	III	92
15	Kiltomy . . .	177 1 11	Kerry . .	Clanmaurice .	Kiltomy . .	Listowel . .	II.	172
2	Kiltoohig . .	357 1 12	Cork, E.R. .	Orrery and Kilmore	Ballyhay . .	Kilmallock .	II.	106
45, 48	Kiltoom . .	115 0 34	Roscommon .	Athlone . .	Kiltoom . .	Athlone . .	IV.	183
7	Kiltoom . . .	536 3 28	Westmeath .	Fore . . .	Faughalstown .	Granard . .	I.	270
30, 36	Kiltoome . .	179 1 10	Meath . .	Upper Navan .	Kilcooly . .	Trim . .	I.	216
64, 73	Kiltooris . .	192 1 33b	Donegal . .	Boylagh . .	Inishkeel .	Glenties . .	III.	113
31, 32	Kiltorcan . .	976 3 32	Kilkenny . .	Knocktopher .	Derrynahinch .	Thomastown .	I.	111
99	Kiltormer East .	406 3 12	Galway . .	Longford . .	Kiltormer . .	Ballinasloe .	IV.	60
99	KILTORMER T. .	—	Galway . .	Longford . .	Kiltormer . .	Ballinasloe .	IV.	60
99	Kiltormer West .	196 2 31	Galway . .	Longford . .	Kiltormer . .	Ballinasloe .	IV.	60
33, 39	Kiltotan and Collinstown . . .	328 1 36	Westmeath .	Fartullagh .	Castlelost .	Mullingar .	I.	268
78	Kiltown . . .	206 1 2c	Donegal . .	Raphoe . .	Donaghmore .	Stranorlar .	III.	138
5	Kiltown . . .	730 0 14	Kilkenny . .	Fassadinin .	Castlecomer .	Castlecomer .	I.	88
33, 37	Kiltown . . .	350 2 25	Kilkenny . .	Ida . . .	The Rower .	New Ross .	I.	104
15	Kiltown . . .	200 3 12	Wexford . .	Scarawalsh .	Ferns . .	Enniscorthy .	I.	323
53	Kiltoy . . .	136 1 6	Donegal . .	Kilmacrenan .	Aghanunshin .	Letterkenny .	III.	122
45	Kiltra . . .	305 1 2	Wexford . .	Bargy . .	Bannow . .	Wexford . .	I.	304
24, 30	Kiltrasna . .	119 0 37	Cavan . .	Tullyhunco .	Killashandra .	Cavan . .	III.	98
55, 56	Kiltrasna . .	291 0 26	Galway . .	Clare . .	Killeany . .	Tuam . .	IV.	20
30, 34	Kiltrassy . .	395 1 27	Kilkenny . .	Kells . .	Kilamery . .	Callan . .	I.	109
19	Kiltrea . . .	443 1 12	Wexford . .	Scarawalsh .	Monart . .	Enniscorthy .	I.	324
71	Kiltrellig . .	570 1 13	Clare . .	Moyarta . .	Kilballyowen .	Kilrush . .	II.	31
71	KILTRELLIG T. .	—	Clare . .	Moyarta . .	Kilballyowen .	Kilrush . .	II.	32
19	Kiltrislane . .	267 3 19	Cork, E.R. .	Condons&Clangibbon	Brigown . .	Mitchelstown .	II.	59
70	Kiltroge . .	98 0 0	Galway . .	Clare . .	Claregalway .	Galway . .	IV.	18
70, 83	Kiltroge . .	446 0 20	Galway . .	Clare . .	Lackagh . .	Galway . .	IV.	23
110	Kiltrone . .	545 0 37d	Mayo . .	Kilmaine . .	Robeen . .	Ballinrobe .	IV.	157
20, 27	Kiltrough . .	135 3 13	Meath . .	Lower Duleek .	Colp . .	Drogheda .	I.	195
23	Kiltrustan . .	316 0 11	Roscommon .	Roscommon .	Kiltrustan .	Strokestown .	IV.	211
15	Kiltubbrid . .	307 1 21	Armagh . .	Tiranny . .	Tynan . .	Armagh . .	III.	60
24	Kiltubbrid . .	103 0 18	Leitrim . .	Leitrim . .	Kiltubbrid .	Carᵏ. on Shannon	IV.	104
13	Kiltubbrid . .	246 1 29	Monaghan .	Monaghan .	Kilmore . .	Monaghan .	III.	276
3, 6	Kiltubbrid . .	68 2 28	Monaghan .	Trough . .	Errigal Trough .	Monaghan .	III.	284
36	Kiltubbrid Island .	236 3 13	King's Co. .	Eglish . .	Drumcullen .	Parsonstown .	I.	134
82, 83	Kiltullagh . .	952 3 7	Galway . .	Dunkellin .	Oranmore .	Galway . .	IV.	32
18	Kiltullagh . .	696 3 9e	Galway . .	Tiaquin . .	Kilkerrin .	Glennamaddy .	IV.	77
25, 32	Kiltullagh . .	218 1 18	Roscommon .	Castlereagh .	Kiltullagh .	Castlereagh .	IV.	202
85, 97	Kiltullagh North .	590 3 29	Galway . .	Athenry . .	Kiltullagh .	Loughrea .	IV.	5
97	Kiltullagh South .	107 3 2	Galway . .	Athenry . .	Kiltullagh .	Loughrea .	IV.	5
35	Kiltultoge . .	694 1 35	Roscommon .	Ballymoe . .	Cloonygormican .	Roscommon .	IV.	191
48	Kiltumper . .	808 2 24	Clare . .	Clonderalaw .	Kilmihil . .	Kilrush . .	II.	17
34, 35	Kilturk North .	600 0 29f	Fermanagh .	Clankelly .	Galloon . .	Lisnaskea .	III.	198
40	Kilturk South .	188 0 22g	Fermanagh .	Clankelly .	Galloon . .	Clones . .	III.	198
39	Kilturk West .	237 0 36h	Fermanagh .	Coole . .	Galloon . .	Lisnaskea .	III.	200
38, 39	Kilturra . .	424 1 15	Sligo . .	Corran . .	Kilturra . .	Tobercurry .	IV.	227
27	Kiltybane or Lisleitrim . . .	447 3 37i	Armagh . .	Fews Upper .	Newtownhamilton .	Castleblayney .	III.	49
1	Kiltybannan . .	184 1 14	Galway . .	Ballymoe . .	Templetogher .	Glennamaddy .	IV.	9
24	Kiltybardan . .	390 1 8j	Leitrim . .	Carrigallen .	Oughteragh .	Bawnboy .	IV.	92
9	Kiltybegs . .	245 1 8	Longford . .	Ardagh . .	Templemichael .	Longford . .	I.	154
31, 32	Kiltybegs . .	301 3 24	Monaghan .	Farney . .	Donaghmoyne .	Carrickmacross	III.	270
7	Kiltybegs . .	124 1 34	Monaghan .	Trough . .	Donagh . .	Monaghan .	III.	282
93, 103	Kiltybo . . .	226 3 37	Mayo . .	Costello . .	Annagh . .	Claremorris .	IV.	138
13, 14	Kiltybranks . .	813 3 3	Roscommon .	Frenchpark .	Tibohine .	Castlereagh .	IV.	205
5	Kiltybrannock .	204 3 27	Roscommon .	Boyle . .	Boyle . .	Boyle . .	IV.	194
15	Kiltycahill . .	677 0 15k	Sligo . .	Carbury . .	Calry . .	Sligo . .	IV.	220
31	Kiltycarney . .	206 0 1	Leitrim . .	Leitrim . .	Kiltoghert .	Carᵏ. on Shannon	IV.	102
38	Kiltyclay . .	276 1 35	Tyrone . .	Dungannon Upper .	Desertcreat .	Cookstown .	III.	308
9	Kiltyclogh . .	264 0 32	Longford . .	Granard . .	Clonbroney .	Granard . .	I.	155
21, 27	Kiltycloghan . .	125 3 26	Sligo . .	Tirerrill . .	Ballysumaghan .	Sligo . .	IV.	238
8	Kiltyclogher . .	1,743 1 10	Leitrim . .	Rosclogher .	Cloonclare .	Manorhamilton .	IV.	109
38	Kiltyclogher . .	163 3 18	Tyrone . .	Dungannon Upper .	Desertcreat .	Cookstown .	III.	308
8	KILTYCLOGHER T. .	—	Leitrim . .	Rosclogher .	Cloonclare .	Manorhamilton .	IV.	109
2	Kiltycon . .	402 3 27l	Longford . .	Longford . .	Killoe . .	Longford . .	I.	159
8, 9, 14, 15	Kiltycooly . .	196 1 5	Sligo . .	Carbury . .	Drumcliff .	Sligo . .	IV.	221

4 G

No. of Sheet of the Ordnance Survey Maps.	Townlands and Towns.	Area in Statute Acres.	County.	Barony.	Parish.	Poor Law Union in 1857.	Townland Census of 1851, Part I.	
		A. R. P.					Vol.	Page
5	Kiltycreaghtan .	298 1 32	Roscommon .	Boyle . . .	Boyle . .	Boyle .	IV.	194
39	Kiltycreen .	108 2 35	Sligo . .	Corran . . .	Kilshalvy .	Boyle .	IV.	227
22	Kiltycreevagh .	110 2 39a	Leitrim . .	Carrigallen .	Oughteragh .	Bawnboy .	IV.	92
2, 5	Kiltycreevagh .	944 1 9b	Longford . .	Longford . .	Killoe .	Longford .	I.	159
41	Kiltycrose .	204 0 34c	Fermanagh .	Knockninny .	Kinawley .	Lisnaskea .	III.	202
81	Kiltyfanned .	383 0 19d	Donegal . .	Banagh . .	Glencolumbkille .	Glenties . .	III.	105
18	Kiltyfeenaghty Glebe	146 0 14e	Leitrim . .	Drumahaire .	Inishmagrath .	Manorhamilton .	IV.	96
25, 26	Kiltyfelan .	88 1 2	Fermanagh .	Clanawley .	Cleenish . .	Enniskillen .	III.	191
68, 77	Kiltyfergal .	449 1 39f	Donegal . .	Raphoe . .	Kilteevoge .	Stranorlar .	III.	139
24	Kiltyfinnan .	118 2 26	Leitrim . .	Mohill . .	Fenagh . .	Mohill .	IV.	106
25	Kiltygerry .	190 1 7g	Leitrim . .	Carrigallen .	Oughteragh .	Bawnboy .	IV.	92
22	Kiltyhugh .	231 2 21	Leitrim . .	Carrigallen .	Oughteragh .	Bawnboy .	IV.	92
15	Kiltykeary .	68 2 34	Longford . .	Granard . .	Clonbroney .	Granard .	I.	155
5	Kiltykere .	176 0 2	Sligo . .	Carbury . .	Ahamlish .	Sligo .	IV.	219
34	Kiltylough .	96 1 26h	Sligo . .	Tirerrill . .	Kilmacallan .	Boyle .	IV.	240
13	Kiltymaine .	330 1 31	Roscommon .	Frenchpark .	Tibohine . .	Castlereagh .	IV.	205
25	Kiltymoodan .	183 3 31	Leitrim . .	Carrigallen .	Oughteragh .	Bawnboy .	IV.	92
24	Kiltynashinnagh .	182 1 9	Leitrim . .	Carrigallen .	Oughteragh .	Bawnboy .	IV.	92
28	Kiltynashinnagh .	53 0 31	Leitrim . .	Leitrim . .	Kiltubbrid .	Carᵏ. on Shannon	IV.	104
13, 14	Kiltynaskellan .	547 3 4i	Cavan . .	Tullyhunco .	Kildallan .	Bawnboy .	III.	97
9, 14	Kiltyreher .	188 2 25	Longford . .	Longford . .	Killoe .	Longford .	I.	159
9, 14	Kiltyreher .	223 1 5	Longford . .	Longford . .	Templemichael .	Longford .	I.	160
77	Kiltyroe . .	199 2 39	Mayo . .	Burrishoole .	Kilmeena .	Newport .	IV.	122
26	Kiltyrome .	169 3 24	Tipperary, N.R.	Upper Ormond .	Kilmore . .	Nenagh .	II.	291
39	Kiltyteige .	48 2 23	Sligo . .	Corran . .	Drumrat . .	Boyle .	IV.	226
76	Kilva . .	261 3 0	Cork, E.R. .	Imokilly . .	Cloyne . .	Middleton .	II.	85
18	Kilvahan .	44 2 39	Queen's Co. .	Cullenagh .	Ballyroan .	Abbeyleix .	II.	239
18	Kilvahan .	80 2 13	Queen's Co. .	Cullenagh .	Kilcolmanbane .	Abbeyleix .	I.	240
74	Kilvanloon .	199 3 1	Mayo . .	Costello . .	Castlemore .	Castlereagh .	IV.	140
25, 32	Kilvarnet North .	254 0 24	Sligo . .	Leyny . .	Kilvarnet .	Tobercurry .	IV.	232
32	Kilvarnet South .	12 1 22	Sligo . .	Leyny . .	Kilvarnet .	Tobercurry .	IV.	232
32	Kilvealaton East .	118 2 35j	Cork, E.R. .	Duhallow .	Kilshannig .	Mallow .	II.	74
32	Kilvealaton West .	385 0 33k	Cork, E.R. .	Duhallow .	Kilshannig .	Mallow .	II.	74
63, 71	Kilvemnon .	653 2 35	Tipperary, S.R.	Slievardagh .	Kilvemnon .	Callan .	II.	335
6	Kilvergan .	218 0 26	Armagh . .	Oneilland East .	Seagoe . .	Lurgan .	III.	50
7	Kilvey . .	206 1 39l	Monaghan .	Trough . .	Donagh . .	Monaghan .	III.	282
52	Kilvickadownig .	421 3 21	Kerry . .	Corkaguiny .	Ventry . .	Dingle .	II.	180
17	Kilvickanease .	98 0 1	Cork, E.R. .	Fermoy . .	Doneraile .	Mallow .	II.	78
34, 35	Kilvilcorris .	401 3 0	Tipperary, N.R.	Eliogarty . .	Drom . .	Thurles .	II.	269
36, 42	Kilvillis . .	117 2 26	Antrim . .	Upper Toome .	Ballyscullion Grange	Ballymena .	III.	33
108	Kilvinane .	199 0 13	Cork, W.R. .	East Carbery (E.D.)	Ballymoney .	Dunmanway .	II.	127
110	Kilvindoney .	339 1 4m	Mayo . .	Kilmaine .	Robeen . .	Ballinrobe .	IV.	157
112, 113	Kilvine T. .	990 1 29	Mayo . .	Clanmorris .	Kilvine . .	Claremorris .	IV.	134
112	Kilvine T. .	—	Mayo . .	Clanmorris .	Kilvine . .	Claremorris .	IV.	134
32, 36	Kilvinoge .	508 1 21	Kilkenny . .	Knocktopher .	Jerpointchurch .	Thomastown .	I.	111
15,16,21,22	Kilvoy . .	483 0 5	Roscommon .	Roscommon .	Shankill . .	Castlereagh .	IV.	213
17	Kilvoydan .	164 3 34n	Clare . .	Inchiquin .	Killinaboy .	Corrofin .	II.	26
26	Kilvoydan North .	232 0 20	Clare . .	Bunratty Upper .	Inchicronan .	Ennis .	II.	9
26, 34	Kilvoydan South .	252 0 29	Clare . .	Bunratty Upper .	Inchicronan .	Ennis .	II.	9
108, 121	Kilvurra .	356 3 35	Cork, W.R. .	East Carbery (E.D.)	Ballymoney .	Dunmanway .	II.	127
8	Kilwalter .	84 2 12	Westmeath .	Delvin . .	Kilcumny .	Castletowndelvin	I.	265
20	Kilwarden .	364 0 39	Kildare . .	South Salt .	Kilteel . .	Naas .	I.	77
40,41,46,47	Kilwarden .	900 2 6	Meath . .	Upper Moyfenrath .	Clonard . .	Edenderry .	I.	213
36	Kilwarry .	88 1 1p	Donegal . .	Kilmacrenan .	Tullyfern .	Millford .	III.	133
33	Kilwatermoy .	202 3 20	Waterford .	Coshmore&Coshbride	Kilwatermoy .	Lismore .	II.	343
33	Kilwatermoymountain	206 3 24	Waterford .	Coshmore&Coshbride	Kilwatermoy .	Lismore .	II.	343
2, 3, 5, 6	Kilweelran .	652 2 14	Clare . .	Burren . .	Oughtmama .	Ballyvaghan .	II.	14
28	Kilwinny .	148 1 34	Waterford .	Coshmore&Coshbride	Tallow . .	Lismore .	II.	348
11	Kilwoghan .	110 3 37	Kildare . .	North Salt .	Kildrought .	Celbridge .	I.	74
27, 28	Kilworth .	175 2 17	Cork, E.R. .	Condons&Clangibbon	Kilworth .	Fermoy .	II.	62
27, 28	KILWORTH T. . .	—	Cork, E.R. .	Condons&Clangibbon	Kilworth .	Fermoy .	II.	62
42	Kilwullaun .	196 3 32	Galway . .	Clare . .	Donaghpatrick .	Tuam .	IV.	19
69, 79	Kimego East .	1,019 2 15	Kerry . .	Iveragh . .	Caher . .	Cahersiveen .	II.	194
69, 79	Kimego West .	695 3 14	Kerry . .	Iveragh . .	Caher . .	Cahersiveen .	II.	194
19	Kimeheer .	88 2 20	Limerick . .	Shanid . .	Robertstown .	Glin .	II.	258
22	Kimmage .	293 2 19	Dublin . .	Rathdown .	Rathfarnham .	Dublin South .	I.	37
22	Kimmage .	106 2 1	Dublin . .	Uppercross .	Crumlin . .	Dublin South .	I.	39
93	Kimmeenmore .	43 3 0	Galway . .	Galway . .	Rahoon . .	Galway .	IV.	38
29	Kimmeens .	17 3 22	Kildare . .	Naas South .	Ballymore Eustace .	Naas .	I.	64
105	Kimmid . .	255 2 10q	Donegal . .	Tirhugh . .	Templecarn .	Donegal .	III.	149
49, 50	Kimmins .	217 0 1	Meath . .	Upper Deece .	Moyglare .	Celbridge .	I.	194
29, 35	Kinoran .	380 1 24r	Fermanagh .	Clankelly .	Clones . .	Clones .	III.	196
71, 72	Kinaff . .	594 2 29	Mayo . .	Gallen . .	Kilconduff .	Swineford .	IV.	148

(a) Including 9A. 1R. 21P. water.
(b) Including 42A. 2R. 0P. water.
(c) Including 5A. 2R. 8P. water.
(d) Including 19A. 1R. 20P. water.
(e) Including 12A. 1R. 27P. water.
(f) Including 6A. 3R. 30P. water.

(g) Including 36A. 1R. 3P. water.
(h) Including 18A. 1R. 39P. water.
(i) Including 7A. 2R. 0P. water.
(j) Including 2A. 1R. 22P. water.
(k) Including 3A. 1R. 8P. water.
(l) Including 7A. 1R. 8P. water.

(m) Including 2A. 2R. 5P. water.
(n) Including 33A. 2R. 0P. water.
(o) Including 14A. 2R. 12P. water.
(p) Including 7A. 2R. 16P. water.
(q) Including 6A. 0R. 15P. water.
(r) Including 13A. 0R. 17P. water.

No. of Sheet of the Ordnance Survey Maps.	Townlands and Towns.	Area in Statute Acres.			County.	Barony.	Parish.	Poor Law Union in 1857.	Townland Census of 1851, Part I.	
		A.	R.	P.					Vol.	Page
11	Kinagha Beg	61	1	9	Cavan	Tullygarvey	Annagh	Cavan	III.	87
11, 15	Kinagha More	98	0	35	Cavan	Tullygarvey	Annagh	Cavan	III.	87
28	Kinallen	660	3	8	Down	Lower Iveagh, Lr. pt.	Dromore	Banbridge	III.	168
31	Kinallybane	162	2	32	Monaghan	Farney	Killanny	Carrickmacross	III.	271
31	Kinallyduff	138	3	9	Monaghan	Farney	Killanny	Carrickmacross	III.	271
17	Kinard	431	2	9	Limerick	Shanid	Kilfergus	Glin	II.	256
24	Kinard	434	3	19a	Longford	Ardagh	Rathreagh	Ballymahon	I.	153
38	Kinard	218	3	13	Mayo	Tirawley	Crossmolina	Ballina	IV.	166
10	Kinard	69	3	18	Monaghan	Cremorne	Tehallan	Monaghan	III.	262
16, 17	Kinard	234	3	1	Roscommon	Roscommon	Clooncraff	Strokestown	IV.	208
16	Kinard	142	2	25	Sligo	Tireragh	Kilglass	Dromore West	IV.	234
53, 54	Kinard East	358	2	28	Kerry	Corkaguiny	Kinard	Dingle	II.	179
97	Kinard East	400	3	27	Kerry	Iveragh	Prior	Cahersiveen	II.	198
53	Kinard West	175	2	24	Kerry	Corkaguiny	Kinard	Dingle	II.	179
97	Kinard West	525	3	33	Kerry	Iveragh	Prior	Cahersiveen	II.	198
21, 22	Kinarla	121	3	37b	Fermanagh	Magheraboy	Rossorry	Enniskillen	III.	214
84	Kinatevdilla	6	2	27	Mayo	Murrisk	Kilgeever	Westport	IV.	161
118	Kinathfineen	10	1	16	Cork, W.R.	Bantry	Kilmocomoge	Bantry	II.	121
33	Kinawley	187	2	34	Fermanagh	Clanawley	Kinawley	Enniskillen	III.	194
33	Kinbally	549	0	27	Antrim	Lower Antrim	Skerry	Ballymena	III.	5
41	Kincaslough	106	0	29c	Donegal	Boylagh	Templecrone	Glenties	III.	115
60	Kinclare	471	1	12	Galway	Tiaquin	Killosolan	Mountbellew	IV.	78
16	Kinclare	166	0	26	Roscommon	Roscommon	Shankill	Boyle	IV.	213
15, 16	Kinclare and Edenan	624	1	10	Roscommon	Roscommon	Shankill	Boyle	IV.	213
8, 9	Kincon	112	3	25	Armagh	Oneilland West	Kilmore	Armagh	III.	53
80, 81	Kincon	614	0	13	Mayo	Costello	Knock	Claremorris	IV.	143
14, 21	Kincon	498	0	9	Mayo	Tirawley	Kilfian	Killala	IV.	169
21	KINCON T.	—			Mayo	Tirawley	Kilfian	Killala	IV.	169
14, 15	Kincora	216	1	27	King's Co.	Garrycastle	Wheery or Killagally	Parsonstown	I.	139
8, 12	Kincorragh	83	2	30	Monaghan	Monaghan	Clones	Monaghan	III.	274
61, 62	Kincraigy	264	2	13	Donegal	Raphoe	Raymoghy	Letterkenny	III.	142
65	Kincrum	404	0	36	Donegal	Boylagh	Inishkeel	Glenties	III.	113
30, 36	Kincuillew	831	3	37d	Sligo	Leyny	Kilmacteige	Tobercurry	IV.	231
23	Kinculbrack	554	2	35	Londonderry	Tirkeeran	Cumber Upper	New Tⁿ Limavady	III.	249
97, 105	Kincullia	442	2	11	Galway	Loughrea	Loughrea	Loughrea	IV.	66
8, 13	Kindlestown Lower	177	0	10	Wicklow	Rathdown	Delgany	Rathdown	I.	355
8, 13	Kindlestown Upper	261	2	30	Wicklow	Rathdown	Delgany	Rathdown	I.	355
12	Kindroghed	414	1	7	Donegal	Inishowen East	Culdaff	Inishowen	III.	118
8	Kindrum	219	1	24e	Donegal	Kilmacrenan	Clondavaddog	Millford	III.	125
18	Kinduff	213	3	23	Monaghan	Dartree	Ematris	Cootehill	I.	267
23, 28	Kineagh	442	2	5f	Kildare	Kilcullen	Kilcullen	Naas	I.	58
55	Kinego	125	0	16	Tyrone	Dungannon Middle	Killyman	Dungannon	III.	303
88, 89	Kineigh	796	0	6	Kerry	Iveragh	Dromod	Cahersiveen	II.	195
14	Kineilty	403	1	2	Clare	Corcomroe	Kilmacrehy	Ennistimon	II.	20
27	Kinflea	133	1	22	Antrim	Kilconway	Dunaghy	Ballymena	III.	26
13	Kingarriff	306	1	15	Antrim	Upper Dunluce	Loughguile	Ballymoney	III.	20
59	Kingarrow	1,752	0	27g	Donegal	Boylagh	Inishkeel	Glenties	III.	113
26	Kingarrow	246	3	15	Tyrone	Strabane Upper	Cappagh	Omagh	III.	325
33, 38	Kingarrow North	143	2	34	Fermanagh	Knockninny	Kinawley	Lisnaskea	III.	202
39	Kingarrow South	80	2	6h	Fermanagh	Knockninny	Kinawley	Lisnaskea	III.	202
9	Kingarve	180	0	17	Armagh	Oneilland West	Drumcree	Lurgan	III.	52
46, 54	Kingarve	169	2	37i	Tyrone	Dungannon Middle	Drumglass	Dungannon	III.	303
42, 48	Kinghill	340	1	32	Down	Upper Iveagh, Lr. pt.	Clonduff	Newry	III.	171
33	Kinglass	278	2	29	Fermanagh	Clanawley	Kinawley	Enniskillen	III.	194
10	Kingorry	92	1	16	Monaghan	Monaghan	Tehallan	Monaghan	III.	280
51	Kingsbog	237	3	3	Antrim	Lower Belfast	Ballylinny	Antrim	III.	7
27	Kingsbog or Common	663	1	28	Kildare	Offaly East	Kildare	Naas	I.	70
34	Kingsborough	76	2	30	Sligo	Tirerrill	Killadoon	Boyle	IV.	239
34	Kingsbrook	236	1	5	Sligo	Tirerrill	Tawnagh	Sligo	IV.	241
35	KINGSCOURT T.	—			Cavan	Clankee	Enniskeen	Bailieborough	III.	73
39	Kingsfort	215	3	33j	Sligo	Corran	Toomour	Boyle	IV.	228
21	Kingsfort	103	0	0	Sligo	Tirerrill	Killerry	Sligo	IV.	239
19	Kingsfurze	424	1	10	Kildare	Naas North	Tipper	Naas	I.	63
5	King's Island	132	2	13h	Limerick	Limerick, Municipal Borough of	St. Munchins	Limerick	II.	262
25	King's Island	17	0	21	Longford	Rathcline	Cashel	Ballymahon	I.	163
32	King's Island	26	3	29	Wexford	Shelmaliere West	Clonmore	Enniscorthy	I.	333
86	Kingsland	117	1	23	Cork, E.R.	Kerrycurrihy	Ballinaboy	Cork	III.	91
12, 18	Kingsland	329	0	21	Kerry	Iraghticonnor	Duagh	Listowel	II.	190
32	Kingsland	108	3	13	Kildare	Narragh & Reban East	Usk	Naas	I.	67
20	Kingsland	88	2	10	Kilkenny	Gowran	Clara	Kilkenny	I.	94
19	Kingsland	104	2	23	Kilkenny	Gowran	St. John's	Kilkenny	I.	98
38	Kingsland	216	0	12	Limerick	Connello Upper	Ballingarry	Croom	II.	231

(a) Including 8A. 1R. 15P. water.
(b) Including 4A. 2R. 15P. water.
(c) Including 8A. 3R. 33P. water.
(d) Including 4A. 3R. 21P. water.

(e) Including 45A. 3R. 38P. water.
(f) Including 4A. 3A. 19P. water.
(g) Including 18A. 2R. 10P. water.
(h) Including 17A. 0R. 16P. water.

(i) Including 1A. 0R. 23P. water.
(j) Including 0A. 2R. 12P. water.
(k) Included in the Parish of St. Munchin.

4 G 2

No. of Sheet of the Ordnance Survey Maps.	Townlands and Towns.	Area in Statute Acres.	County.	Barony.	Parish.	Poor Law Union in 1857.	Townland Census of 1851, Part I.	
		A. R. P.					Vol.	Page
9	Kingsland	666 2 19	Roscommon	Frenchpark	Kilnamanagh	Boyle	IV.	204
13, 14, 18, 19	King-land East	161 3 5	Kilkenny	Crannagh	St. Canice	Kilkenny	I.	87
84	Kingsland North	90 3 0	Galway	Athenry	Athenry	Loughrea	IV.	4
84	Kingsland South	236 0 10	Galway	Athenry	Athenry	Loughrea	IV.	4
18	Kingsland West	75 2 23	Kilkenny	Crannagh	St. Canice	Kilkenny	I.	87
9, 17	Kingsmeadow	59 3 28	Waterford	Middlethird	Trinity Without	Waterford	II.	369
22	Kingsmountain	170 3 26	Meath	Fore	Killallon	Oldcastle	I.	200
9, 10	Kingsmountain	122 0 22	Meath	Upper Kells	Kilskeer	Kells	I	206
18	Kingsmountain	933 3 4	Sligo	Tireragh	Templeboy	Dromore West	IV.	236
35	Kingsmountain or Mylerstown	390 3 7	Kilkenny	Knocktopher	Aghaviller	Thomastown	I.	110
5, 6, 8, 9	Kingsmountain or Slievemore	704 1 19	Sligo	Carbury	Drumcliff	Sligo	IV.	221
26	Kingston	59 2 6	Dublin	Rathdown	Kiltiernan	Rathdown	I.	36
26	Kingston	92 2 26	Dublin	Rathdown	Tully	Rathdown	I.	38
35	Kingston	111 2 16	Wicklow	Arklow	Castlemacadam	Rathdown	I.	342
27, 35	Kingston's-fields	43 3 15	Cork, E.R.	Fermoy	Litter	Fermoy	II.	81
8	Kingstown	50 1 23	Dublin	Balrothery East	Lusk	Balrothery	I.	21
11	Kingstown	194 1 19	Dublin	Coolock	St. Margarets	Dublin North	I.	29
22	Kingstown	194 2 1	Dublin	Rathdown	Taney	Rathdown	I.	38
34	Kingstown	83 2 34	Fermanagh	Magherastephana	Aghalurcher	Lisnaskea	III.	217
25, 26	Kingstown and Carnuff Great	561 3 10	Meath	Skreen	Ardmulchan	Navan	I.	220
22, 35	Kingstown Glebe or Ballymaconry	78 1 37	Galway	Ballynahinch	Omey	Clifden	IV.	15
23	KINGSTOWN T.	—	Dublin	Rathdown	Monkstown	Rathdown	I.	37
21	Kingswood	35 0 32	Dublin	Uppercross	Cloudalkin	Dublin South	I.	39
21	Kingswood or Garranstown	122 3 1	Dublin	Uppercross	Tallaght	Dublin South	I.	41
21	Kingwilliamstown	254 0 38	Cork, E.R.	Duhallow	Nohavaldaly	Kanturk	II.	75
122, 123	Kinincha	103 1 5	Galway	Kiltartan	Kiltartan	Gort	IV.	48
49	Kinine	316 1 19	Tyrone	Omagh East	Kilskeery	Lowtherstown	III.	313
70, 83	Kiniska	505 0 22	Galway	Clare	Claregalway	Galway	IV.	18
35	Kinitty	865 1 4	Roscommon	Ballintober South	Kilbride	Roscommon	IV.	189
1	Kinkeel	131 0 20	Antrim	Cary	Rathlin Island	Ballycastle	III.	15
19	Kinkeel	143 0 22a	Cavan	Tullyhunco	Killashandra	Cavan	III.	98
89	Kinkeel Island	10 0 28	Donegal	Tirhugh	Kilbarron	Glenties	III.	148
4, 7, 8	Kinkillew	447 1 36b	Leitrim	Rosclogher	Rossinver	Manorhamilton	IV.	111
11	Kinkillew	64 3 8	Longford	Granard	Granard	Granard	I.	156
27	Kinkillew	262 0 26c	Sligo	Tirerrill	Ballynakill	Sligo	IV.	237
16	Kinkit	319 3 20	Tyrone	Strabane Lower	Urney	Strabane	III.	322
86, 96	Kinknock	279 1 0	Mayo	Murrisk	Kilgeever	Westport	IV.	160
58	Kinlea	240 0 34	Clare	Clonderalaw	Kilmurry	Kildysert	II.	17
78, 87	Kinletter	828 1 27d	Donegal	Raphoe	Donaghmore	Stranorlar	III.	138
28, 37	Kinletteragh	527 0 23	Donegal	Kilmacrenan	Killygarvan	Milford	III.	128
2	Kinlough	293 3 20	Leitrim	Rosclogher	Rossinver	Bally-hannon	IV.	111
122, 123	Kinlough	515 0 6	Mayo	Kilmaine	Shrule	Ballinrobe	IV.	108
2	KINLOUGH T.	—	Leitrim	Rosclogher	Rossinver	Ballyshannon	IV.	112
38	Kinmeen North	102 1 3	Fermanagh	Knockninny	Kinawley	Lisnaskea	III.	202
39	Kinmeen South	62 0 21e	Fermanagh	Knockninny	Kinawley	Lisnaskea	III.	202
114	Kinmona North	147 2 15	Galway	Dunkellin	Ardrahan	Gort	IV.	26
114	Kinmona South	108 0 9	Galway	Dunkellin	Ardrahan	Gort	IV.	26
34	Kinmore	438 1 9f	Fermanagh	Magherastephana	Aghalurcher	Lisnaskea	III.	217
2	Kinnabo	156 2 29	Cavan	Tullyhaw	Killinagh	Enniskillen	III.	92
54, 55, 62, 63	Kinnacally	323 1 39	Donegal	Raphoe	Taughboyne	Strabane	III.	143
68, 77	Kinnaderry	390 1 8g	Donegal	Raphoe	Kilteevoge	Stranorlar	III.	139
105	Kinnadoohy	525 2 19	Mayo	Murrisk	Kilgeever	Westport	IV.	160
2, 7	Kinnafad	626 3 8	Kildare	Carbury	Carrick	Edenderry	I.	52
4, 11, 12	Kinnafad	306 1 15	King's Co.	Warrenstown	Ballymacwilliam	Edenderry	I.	144
40, 45	Kinnagh	415 2 38	Wexford	Shelburne	Tintern	New Ross	I.	329
28	Kinnagillian	502 2 20	Tyrone	Dungannon Upper	Kildress	Cookstown	III.	309
25	Kinnagin	222 3 30	Monaghan	Cremorne	Clontibret	Castleblayney	III.	260
19, 29	Kinnagoe	497 1 3	Donegal	Inishowen West	Fahan Lower	Inishowen	III.	120
20, 26	Kinnagrelly	585 1 9	Sligo	Leyny	Ballysadare	Sligo	IV.	230
81	Kinnakillew	647 3 25	Donegal	Banagh	Glencolumbkille	Glenties	III.	105
105, 106	Kinnakillew	2,020 1 25h	Mayo	Murrisk	Kilgeever	Westport	IV.	160
4	Kinnakinelly	693 0 2	Galway	Dunmore	Addergoole	Tuam	IV.	33
16	Kinnalargy	115 3 6	Donegal	Kilmacrenan	Mevagh	Milford	III.	130
8, 17	Kinnalough	331 0 15i	Donegal	Kilmacrenan	Clondavaddog	Milford	III.	125
7, 11	Kinnara Glebe	181 3 12	Leitrim	Drumahaire	Drumlease	Manorhamilton	IV.	94
5	Kinnausy Island	1 2 22	Fermanagh	Lurg	Magheraculmoney	Lowtherstown	III.	208
21	Kinnavally	167 3 10	Mayo	Tirawley	Kilfian	Killala	IV.	169
87	Kinnaveelish	33 3 22	Galway	Kilconnell	Aughrim	Ballinasloe	IV.	39

(a) Including 10A. 0R. 10P. water.   (d) Including 27A. 2R. 5P. water.   (g) Including 2A. 0R. 4P. water.
(b) Including 4A. 3R. 20P. water.   (e) Including 5A. 2R. 38P. water.   (h) Including 10A. 2R. 18P. water.
(c) Including 8A. 0R. 3P. water.   (f) Including 15A. 3R. 15P. water.   (i) Including 61A. 0R. 2P. water.

No. of Sheet of the Ordnance Survey Maps.	Townlands and Towns.	Area in Statute Acres.			County.	Barony.	Parish.	Poor Law Union in 1857.	Townland Census of 1851, Part I.	
		A.	R.	P.					Vol.	Page
23	Kinnea . . .	236	1	38a	Cavan . .	Clankee . . .	Knockbride . .	Bailieborough .	III.	74
3, 10	Kinnea . . .	564	0	25	Donegal . .	Inishowen East .	Clonmany . .	Inishowen . .	III.	117
27, 28, 34	Kinnegad . .	1,358	3	28	Westmeath .	Farbill . .	Killucan . .	Mullingar . .	I.	267
27, 28	KINNEGAD T. .				Westmeath	Farbill . .	Killucan . .	Mullingar . .	I.	267
38, 39	Kinnegalliagh .	269	2	20	Antrim . .	Lower Antrim .	Glenwhirry . .	Ballymena . .	III.	4
28, 37	Kinnegar . .	32	2	3	Donegal . .	Kilmacrenan . .	Killygarvan . .	Milford . .	III.	128
8	Kinnegoe . .	293	3	19	Armagh . .	Armagh . .	Loughgall . .	Armagh . .	III.	45
3, 6	Kinnegoe . .	378	3	15	Armagh . .	Oneilland East .	Seagoe . .	Lurgan . .	III.	50
94	Kinneigh . .	428	0	15	Cork, W.R. .	East Carbery (W.D.)	Kinneigh . .	Dunmanway .	II.	134
77	*Kinnelly Islands* {	3	0	30	} Galway . .	Ballynahinch . .	Moyrus . . .	Clifden . .	IV.	14
		1	3	30						
		0	3	38						
98, 99	Kinnewry . .	1,035	3	14b	Mayo . .	Carra . .	Ballintober . .	Castlebar . .	IV.	125
36	KINNITTY T. . .	—			King's Co. .	Ballybritt . .	Kinnitty . .	Parsonstown .	I.	126
73, 82	Kinnoughty . .	205	1	29	Donegal . .	Banagh . .	Inishkeel . .	Glenties . .	III.	106
11	Kinnyglass . .	353	1	22	Londonderry .	Coleraine . .	Macosquin . .	Coleraine . .	III.	233
20	Kinnypottle . .	78	1	18c	Cavan . .	Upper Loughtee .	Urney . .	Cavan . .	III.	86
51	Kinoristown . .	63	2	19	Meath . .	Dunboyne . .	Dunboyne . .	Dunshaughlin .	I.	199
4, 7	Kinoud . . .	130	0	29	Dublin . .	Balrothery West .	Hollywood . .	Balrothery . .	I.	23
38,39,41,42	Kinoughtragh . .	301	1	26	Fermanagh .	Knockninny . .	Kinawley . .	Lisnaskea . .	III.	202
1	Kinramer North .	167	1	15	Antrim . .	Cary . .	Rathlin Island .	Ballycastle .	III.	15
1	Kinramer South .	173	2	21	Antrim . .	Cary . .	Rathlin Island .	Ballycastle .	III.	15
72	Kinreask . .	259	1	6	Galway . .	Tiaquin . .	Ballymacward .	Ballinasloe . .	IV.	75
42	Kinrush . . .	91	2	33d	Fermanagh .	Knockninny . .	Kinawley . .	Lisnaskea . .	III.	202
31, 40	Kinrush . . .	609	3	25	Tyrone . .	Dungannon Upper .	Arboe . .	Cookstown . .	III.	305
112, 125	KINSALE T. . .				Cork, E.R. .	Kinsale . .	{ Kinsale . . } { Ringcurran . }	Kinsale . .	II.	100
12, 15	Kinsaley . . .	713	3	33	Dublin . .	Coolock . .	Kinsaley . .	Balrothery . .	I.	28
15	Kinsellastown . .	264	2	10	Wicklow . .	Lower Talbotstown .	Crehelp . .	Baltinglass .	I.	359
28	Kintale . . .	76	1	33	Donegal . .	Kilmacrenan . .	Killygarvan . .	Milford . .	III.	128
1	Kinteera . . .	52	2	38	Cork, E.R. .	Orrery and Kilmore	Kilbolane . .	Kanturk . .	IV.	221
8	Kintogher . .	386	2	1	Sligo . .	Carbury . .	Drumcliff . .	Sligo . .	IV.	221
32, 39, 40	Kinturk . . .	959	3	15	Clare . .	Islands . .	Kilmaley . .	Ennis . .	II.	31
17	Kinturk . . .	118	2	3	Monaghan .	Dartree . .	Killeevan . .	Clones . .	III.	268
31	Kinturk . . .	188	2	32e	Tyrone . .	Dungannon Upper .	Arboe . .	Cookstown . .	III.	305
7	Kinturk Demesne .	818	3	35	Westmeath .	Fore . .	Rathgarve . .	Castletowndelvin	I.	271
89	Kinturk Lower .	119	3	35	Mayo . .	Carra . .	Ballyhean . .	Castlebar . .	IV.	125
89	Kinturk Upper .	28	1	14	Mayo . .	Carra . .	Ballyhean . .	Castlebar . .	IV.	125
14	Kinune . . .	381	0	5	Antrim . .	Lower Glenarm .	Grange of Layd .	Ballycastle .	III.	22
112, 125	Kinure . . .	448	1	14	Cork, E.R. .	Kinalea . .	Kinure . .	Kinsale . .	II.	95
112, 113	Kinvarra . .	338	1	0	Galway . .	Kiltartan . .	Kinvarradoorus .	Gort . .	IV.	49
65,66,78,79	Kinvarra . .	1,086	1	24f	Galway . .	Moycullen . .	Kilcummin . .	Oughterard .	IV.	67
113	KINVARRA T. . .	—			Galway . .	Kiltartan . .	Kinvarradoorus .	Gort . .	IV.	50
31	Kippagh . . .	198	2	13g	Cork, E.R. .	Duhallow . .	Dromtarriff . .	Kanturk . .	II.	71
22	Kippagh . . .	153	1	18	Cork, E.R. .	Duhallow . .	Kilmeen . .	Kanturk . .	II.	73
121	Kippagh . . .	856	1	6	Cork, W.R. .	East Carbery (W.D.)	Drinagh . .	Dunmanway .	II.	131
38, 47	Kippagh . . .	689	2	4	Cork, W.R. .	West Muskerry .	Drishane . .	Millstreet . .	II.	156
91	Kippaghingergill .	176	3	2	Cork, W.R. .	Bantry . .	Kilnocomoge . .	Bantry . .	II.	121
31, 32	Kippagh Middle .	95	0	15	Cork, E.R. .	Duhallow . .	Castlemagner .	Kanturk . .	II.	67
23, 31	Kippagh North .	137	2	27	Cork, E.R. .	Duhallow . .	Castlemagner .	Kanturk . .	II.	67
31, 32	Kippagh South .	60	1	8	Cork, E.R. .	Duhallow . .	Castlemagner .	Kanturk . .	II.	67
2	Kippane . . .	110	2	7	Cork, E.R. .	Orrery and Kilmore	Shandrum . .	Kilmallock .	II.	110
18, 31	Kippaunagh . .	273	3	27	Galway . .	Ballymoe . .	Dunmore . .	Glennamaddy .	IV.	7
8	Kippeenduff . .	56	3	24	King's Co. .	Kilcoursey . .	Kilmanaghan . .	Tullamore . .	I.	141
16	Kippin . . .	103	3	5	Westmeath .	Kilkenny West .	Noughaval . .	Ballymahon .	I.	274
32	Kippinduff . .	273	3	9	Westmeath .	Moycashel . .	Castletownkindalen	Mullingar . .	I.	277
22, 29	Kippinstown . .	60	0	2	Westmeath .	Brawny . .	St. Mary's . .	Athlone . .	I.	259
6	Kippure . . .	1,490	1	30	Wicklow . .	Lower Talbotstown .	Kilbride . .	Naas . .	I.	361
20	Kircassock . .	198	1	4	Down . .	Lower Iveagh, Upper part .	Magheralin . .	Lurgan . .	III.	170
21	Kircock . . .	76	1	16h	Louth . .	Ferrard . .	Drumshallon . .	Drogheda . .	I.	180
18	Kircubbin . .	528	0	4	Down . .	Ards Upper . .	Inishargy . .	Newtownards .	III.	160
18	KIRCUBBIN T. .				Down . .	Ards Upper . .	Inishargy . .	Newtownards .	III.	160
29	Kirikee . . .	716	0	34	Wicklow . .	Ballinacor North .	Knockrath . .	Rathdrum . .	I.	347
12	Kirkhill . . .	466	0	30	Antrim . .	Upper Dunluce .	Ballymoney . .	Ballymoney .	III.	19
32, 33	Kirkinriola . .	236	2	29	Antrim . .	Lower Toome .	Kirkinriola . .	Ballymena .	III.	32
18, 25	Kirkistown . .	1,036	0	35	Down . .	Ards Upper . .	Ardkeen . .	Downpatrick .	III.	159
8	Kirkistown . .	125	3	18	Londonderry .	North East Liberties of Coleraine .	Ballyrashane . .	Coleraine . .	III.	245
24	Kirkland and Toy .	264	2	21	Down . .	Dufferin . .	Kilyleagh . .	Downpatrick .	III.	167
12	Kirkmoyle or Kilmoyle Upper .	149	2	10	Antrim . .	Upper Dunluce .	Ballymoney . .	Ballymoney .	III.	19
60, 61	Kirkneedy . .	895	3	16	Donegal . .	Raphoe . .	Conwal . .	Letterkenny .	III.	137
53	Kirkstown . .	478	1	33	Donegal . .	Kilmacrenan . .	Conwal . .	Letterkenny .	III.	126

(a) Including 8A. 0R. 31P. water.
(b) Including 18A. 2R. 29P. water.
(c) Including 3A. 3R. 39P. detached portion.

(d) Including 5A. 3R. 12P. water.
(e) Including 0A. 3R. 22P. Island.
(f) Including 15A. 3R. 14P. water.

(g) Including 4A. 3R. 18P. water.
(h) Including 9A. 2R. 32P. water.

No. of Sheet of the Ordnance Survey Maps.	Townlands and Towns.	Area in Statute Acres.			County.	Barony.	Parish.	Poor Law Union in 1857.	Townland Census of 1851, Part I.	
		A.	R.	P.					Vol.	Page
29, 38	Kirktown (alias) Derryloran .	174	0	1	Tyrone .	Dungannon Upper .	Derryloran .	Cookstown .	III.	307
35, 36	Kirley . . .	520	0	27	Londonderry .	Loughinsholin .	Maghera . .	Magherafelt .	III.	242
24, 33	Kirlish . . .	497	2	36	Tyrone . .	Omagh West .	Longfield West .	Castlederg .	III.	316
14	Kirwan's Inch .	148	1	32	Kilkenny .	Fassadinin .	Dunmore . .	Kilkenny .	I.	89
45	Kish . .	78	2	8	Wicklow .	Arklow . .	Arklow . .	Rathdrum .	I.	341
48	Kisha . .	74	3	12	Wexford .	Forth . .	St. Iberius .	Wexford .	I.	314
4, 8	Kishaboy . .	11	1	33	Armagh .	Armagh . .	Loughgall .	Armagh .	III.	45
7, 8	Kishawanny Lower	263	2	6	Kildare .	Carbury . .	Kilmore . .	Edenderry .	I.	52
7, 8	Kishawanny Upper	333	1	25	Kildare .	Carbury . .	Kilmore . .	Edenderry .	I.	52
21	Kishkeam Lower .	306	3	19	Cork, E.R. .	Duhallow .	Kilmeen . .	Kanturk .	II.	73
21	Kishkeam Upper .	490	2	9	Cork, E.R. .	Duhallow .	Kilmeen . .	Kanturk .	II.	73
17	Kishoge . .	273	2	13	Dublin .	Newcastle .	Esker . .	Celbridge .	I.	33
14	Kishyquirk . .	288	1	31	Limerick .	Clanwilliam .	Abington .	Limerick .	II.	221
4	Kitchenstown .	196	0	3	Dublin .	Balrothery West .	Hollywood .	Balrothery .	I.	23
37	Kitestown . .	113	2	25	Wexford .	Shelmaliere East .	Kilpatrick .	Wexford .	I.	331
20	Kittybane . .	210	2	14	Londonderry .	Tirkeeran .	Clondermot .	Londonderry .	III.	248
35, 43	Kivlin . .	88	1	13a	Tyrone .	Omagh East .	Drumragh .	Omagh .	III.	312
12, 16	Kivvy . .	155	1	4	Cavan .	Tullygarvey .	Annagh . .	Cavan .	III.	87
30	Kivvy . .	189	2	7b	Leitrim .	Carrigallen .	Carrigallen .	Mohill .	IV.	90
107	Knader . .	788	3	37c	Donegal .	Tirhugh . .	Kilbarron .	Ballyshannon .	III.	148
11	Knappagh . .	237	3	9	Armagh .	Tiranny . .	Eglish . .	Armagh .	III.	59
18, 23	Knappagh . .	243	2	35	Cavan .	Clankee . .	Drumgoon .	Cootehill .	III.	72
35	Knappagh . .	88	0	15	Fermanagh .	Clankelly .	Clones . .	Clones .	III.	196
19	Knappagh . .	214	0	6d	Monaghan .	Cremorne .	Ballybay .	Castleblayney .	III.	259
88, 98	Knappagh Beg .	699	3	19e	Mayo . .	Murrisk . .	Aghagower .	Westport .	IV.	159
14	Knappagh Beg .	116	0	18	Sligo . .	Carbury .	St. John's .	Sligo .	IV.	223
88, 98	Knappaghmanagh .	494	3	13	Mayo . .	Murrisk . .	Aghagower .	Westport .	IV.	159
87,88,97,98	Knappagh More .	434	0	13	Mayo . .	Murrisk . .	Aghagower .	Westport .	IV.	159
14	Knappagh More .	141	1	5	Sligo . .	Carbury .	St. John's .	Sligo .	IV.	223
50	Knappoge . .	44	0	33	Clare . .	Clonderalaw .	Kilchreest .	Killadyseet .	II.	15
12, 13	Knappoge . .	621	1	5	Longford .	Longford .	Killashee .	Longford .	I.	158
23	Knappoge . .	177	1	39	Longford .	Shrule . .	Kilcommock .	Ballymahon .	I.	166
23, 29	Knapton . .	178	1	37	Queen's Co. .	Cullenagh .	Abbeyleix .	Abbeyleix .	I.	238
118	Knavagh . .	32	1	22	Galway .	Longford .	Tiranascragh .	Portumna .	IV.	62
22	Knavinstown .	618	3	25	Kildare .	Offaly West .	Knavinstown .	Athy .	I.	73
39	Knavinstown .	228	2	35	Meath . .	Ratoath . .	Crickstown .	Dunshaughlin .	I.	217
6, 7	Knawhill . .	345	2	9	Cork, E.R. .	Duhallow . .	Knocktemple .	Kanturk .	II.	75
3	Kneestown . .	201	2	18	Carlow .	Carlow . .	Killerrig .	Carlow .	I.	2
34	Knickeen . .	142	1	35	Kilkenny .	Kells . .	Tullahought .	Carrick on Suir .	I.	110
22	Knickeen . .	118	0	0	Wicklow .	Upper Talbotstown .	Donaghmore .	Baltinglass .	I.	363
14	Knigh . .	874	2	18	Tipperary, N.R. .	Lower Ormond .	Knigh . .	Nenagh .	II.	285
36	Knightsbrook .	473	3	14	Meath .	Lower Moyfenrath .	Laracor . .	Trim .	I.	210
4, 7	Knightstown .	184	2	15	Dublin .	Balrothery East .	Lusk . .	Balrothery .	I.	21
12, 18	Knightstown .	615	3	11	Meath .	Morgallion .	Kilshine . .	Navan .	I.	210
8	Knightstown or Ballinriddery .	279	2	11	Queen's Co. .	Portnahinch .	Ardea . .	Mountmellick .	I.	243
79	KNIGHT's TOWN T.	—			Kerry .	Iveragh . .	Valencia .	Cahersiveen .	II.	198
29, 37	Knightstreet .	104	1	0	Limerick .	Connello Upper .	Ballingarry .	Croom .	II.	231
12	Knightswood .	465	0	39f	Westmeath .	Corkaree .	Leny . .	Mullingar .	I.	263
10	Knock . .	105	2	22	Armagh .	Oneilland East .	Seagoe . .	Lurgan .	III.	50
68	Knock . .	319	0	36	Clare . .	Clonderalaw .	Kilmurry .	Kilrush .	II.	17
33, 41	Knock . .	367	3	18	Clare .	Islands . .	Drumcliff .	Ennis .	II.	30
40, 49	Knock . .	222	0	25	Cork, E.R. .	Duhallow . .	Clonmeen .	Kanturk .	II.	70
148	Knock . .	135	1	4	Cork, W.R. .	West Carbery(W.D.)	Skull . .	Skull .	II.	146
5	Knock . .	164	1	1	Donegal .	Inishowen East .	Culdaff .	Inishowen .	III.	118
78	Knock . .	280	3	4	Donegal .	Raphoe . .	Donaghmore .	Stranorlar .	III.	138
4, 5	Knock . .	288	0	16	Down .	Castlereagh Lower .	Knockbreda .	Belfast .	III.	163
5	Knock . .	183	1	20	Dublin .	Balrothery East .	Balrothery .	Balrothery .	I.	19
34, 35	Knock . .	46	1	19	Galway .	Ballynahinch .	Ballindoon .	Clifden .	IV.	10
44	Knock . .	203	0	38	Galway .	Clare . .	Killererin .	Tuam .	IV.	21
89	Knock . .	302	2	12	Galway .	Moycullen .	Killannin .	Oughterard .	IV.	70
80,81,92,93	Knock . .	956	2	29g	Galway .	Moycullen .	Moycullen .	Galway .	IV.	71
38, 39	Knock . .	501	1	17	King's Co. .	Ballybritt .	Ettagh . .	Roscrea .	I.	125
5	Knock . .	80	1	26	Limerick .	Pubblebrien .	St. Munchins .	Limerick .	II.	254
17	Knock . .	107	1	24	Longford .	Rathcline .	Rathcline .	Longford .	I.	164
114	Knock . .	366	1	9h	Mayo .	Murrisk . .	Inishbofin .	Clifden .	IV.	159
12	Knock . .	975	3	20	Meath . .	Morgallion .	Knock . .	Navan .	I.	210
50, 51, 54	Knock . .	679	3	34	Roscommon .	Athlone . .	Taghmaconnell .	Ballinasloe .	IV.	185
42	Knock . .	23	2	17	Wexford .	Forth . .	Rathaspick .	Wexford .	I.	312
86	Knockaarum .	125	3	20	Tipperary, S.R. .	Iffa and Offa West .	Shanrahan .	Clogheen .	II.	320
3	Knockabeany .	157	2	27	Monaghan .	Trough . .	Drumgal Trough .	Clogher .	III.	284
72	Knockaboy . .	77	1	4	Galway .	Tiaquin . .	Clonkeen .	Loughrea .	IV.	76

(a) Including 0A. 0R. 28P. water.
(b) Including 4A. 0R. 32P. water.
(c) Including 44A. 2R. 33P. water.

(d) Including 4A. 0R. 36P. water.
(e) Including 44A. 3R. 39P. water.
(f) Including 8A. 1R. 4P. water.

(g) Including 4A. 1R. 5P. water.
(h) Including 2A. 1R. 19P. water.

No. of Sheet of the Ordnance Survey Maps.	Townlands and Towns.	Area in Statute Acres. A. R. P.	County.	Barony.	Parish.	Poor Law Union in 1857.	Townland Census of 1851, Part I. Vol.	Page
13	Knockaboys . .	72 1 14	Louth . .	Ardee . . .	Clonkeen . .	Ardee . .	I.	172
54	Knockabritta . .	99 1 31	Tipperary, S.R.	Slievardagh . .	Crohane . .	Callan . .	II.	332
22	Knockacaharna .	310 0 39	Waterford .	Decies without Drum	Modelligo . .	Dungarvan .	II.	359
27	Knockacappul .	100 1 12	Cork, E.R. .	Condons&Clangibbon	Litter . . .	Fermoy . .	II.	62
26	Knockacappul .	183 3 25	Cork, E.R. .	Fermoy . . .	Wallstown . .	Mallow . .	II.	83
60, 68	Knockacappul .	355 2 8	Kerry . .	Magunihy . .	Kilcummin . .	Killarney . .	II.	201
18, 24	Knockacappul .	312 2 32	Sligo . .	Tireragh . .	Skreen . . .	Dromore West .	IV.	236
34, 35	Knockacappul .	113 2 9	Sligo . .	Tirerrill . .	Killadoon . .	Boyle . .	IV.	239
32, 38	Knockacappul .	405 1 4	Tipperary, N.R.	Owney and Arra	Kilnarath . .	Nenagh . .	II.	296
83	Knockacareigh .	186 3 1	Cork, W.R. .	West Muskerry .	Kilmurry . .	Macroom . .	II.	159
40, 46	Knockacarhanduff-Commons .	685 2 13	Tipperary, N.R.	Kilnamanagh Upper	Moyaliff . .	Thurles . .	II.	279
23	Knockacarn . .	439 1 1	Clare . .	Corcomroe . .	Clooney . .	Ennistimon .	II.	18
8	Knockacarn . .	93 2 34	Clare . .	Corcomroe . .	Killilagh . .	Ennistimon .	II.	20
30	Knockacarracoosh .	221 3 10	Cork, E.R. .	Duhallow . .	Cullen . .	Millstreet . .	II.	70
43	Knockacarrigeen .	288 0 30	Galway . .	Clare . . .	Belclare . .	Tuam . .	IV.	17
24,25,32,33	Knockacaurhin .	217 0 21	Clare . .	Inchiquin . .	Kilnamona . .	Ennis . .	II.	27
31	Knockachur . .	721 2 37	Kerry . .	Trughanacmy .	Ballincuslane .	Tralee . .	II.	206
26	Knockaclara . .	134 1 8	Clare . .	Bunratty Upper	Templemaley .	Ennis . .	II.	11
16, 22, 23	Knockaclare . .	797 1 0	Kerry . .	Clanmaurice .	Kilfeighny . .	Listowel . .	II.	170
4, 13	Knockaclarig . .	1,096 2 37	Cork, E.R. .	Duhallow . .	Kilmeen . .	Kanturk . .	II.	73
29	Knockaclogher .	67 3 5	Kerry . .	Trughanacmy .	Ardfert . .	Tralee . .	II.	205
29	Knockaclogher .	51 1 15	Kerry . .	Trughanacmy .	Clogherbrien .	Tralee . .	II.	209
27	Knockaclugga .	296 0 15	Limerick . .	Shanid . .	Kilmoylan . .	Glin . .	II.	256
13, 14	Knockacluggin .	739 2 21	Cork, E.R. .	Duhallow . .	Clonfert . .	Kanturk . .	II.	68
16	Knockacollier .	349 3 20	Queen's Co. .	Upperwoods .	Offerlane . .	Abbeyleix .	I.	252
11, 12	Knockacomortish .	651 3 15	Waterford .	Coshmore&Coshbride	Lismore and Mocollop	Lismore . .	II.	346
8	Knockaconey . .	145 1 2	Armagh . .	Armagh . .	Grange . .	Armagh . .	III.	45
9	Knockaconny .	100 1 39	Monaghan .	Monaghan . .	Monaghan . .	Monaghan .	III.	277
55	Knockacool . .	404 3 36	Cork, E.R. .	Kinnatalloon .	Mogeely . .	Youghal . .	II.	98
5, 13	Knockacoola . .	196 1 33	Waterford .	Glenahiry . .	Kilronan . .	Clonmel . .	II.	365
62	Knockacorbally .	216 0 2	Cork, E.R. .	East Muskerry .	Garrycloyne .	Cork . .	II.	103
10, 11	Knockacorha .	124 3 4	Roscommon .	Boyle . .	Killukin . .	Car.k on Shannon	IV.	195
18	Knockacosan .	74 0 27	Leitrim . .	Drumahaire .	Inishmagrath .	Manorhamilton .	IV.	96
27	Knockacraheen .	53 3 1	Tipperary, N.R.	Upper Ormond .	Kilnaneave .	Nenagh . .	II.	291
54	Knockacraig . .	453 3 28	Limerick . .	Connello Upper	Dromcolliher .	Newcastle . .	II.	233
24, 25	Knockacrin . .	339 0 26	Queen's Co. .	Cullenagh . .	Fossy or Timahoe .	Abbeyleix . .	I.	240
60, 71	Knockacroghera .	455 3 38	Cork, W.R. .	East Muskerry .	Aghinagh . .	Macroom . .	II.	154
78	Knockacroghery .	151 2 19	Mayo . .	Carra . .	Aglish . .	Castlebar . .	IV.	123
21, 22	Knockacronaun .	51 2 18	Waterford .	Decies without Drum	Affane . .	Lismore . .	II.	353
76,77,88,89	Knockacrump .	203 3 33	Cork, E.R. .	Imokilly . .	Cloyne . .	Middleton . .	II.	85
34, 42, 43	Knockacullata .	796 2 28	Cork, E.R. .	Fermoy . .	Monanimy . .	Mallow . .	II.	81
23, 24	Knockacullea North	199 1 18	Clare . .	Corcomroe . .	Clooney . .	Ennistimon .	II.	18
24	Knockacullea South	296 3 34	Clare . .	Corcomroe . .	Clooney . .	Ennistimon .	II.	18
21, 29	Knockaculleen .	172 0 15	Mayo . .	Tirawley . .	Moygawnagh .	Killala . .	IV.	171
11, 12	Knockaculleen .	227 2 21	Sligo . .	Tireragh . .	Kilmacshalgan .	Dromore West .	IV.	235
6, 10	Knockaculleen or Hollymount .	540 0 18	Roscommon .	Boyle . .	Ardcarn . .	Boyle . .	IV.	193
112	Knockacullen . .	210 0 31	Cork, E.R. .	Kinalea . .	Kinure . .	Kinsale . .	II.	95
108, 109, 121, 122	Knockacullen . .	381 3 38	Cork, W.R. .	East Carbery (E.D.)	Desertserges .	Clonakilty . .	II.	128
30	Knockacullen . .	113 2 16a	Waterford .	Decies without Drum	Whitechurch .	Dungarvan .	II.	362
58, 59	Knockacullig North	809 0 36	Kerry . .	Magunihy . .	Kilcummin . .	Killarney . .	II.	201
58, 59	Knockacullig South	333 2 13	Kerry . .	Magunihy . .	Kilcummin . .	Killarney . .	II.	201
115	Knockacullin . .	80 2 17	Cork, W.R. .	Bear . .	Killaconenagh .	Castletown .	II.	125
38	Knockacullin . .	462 3 10	Tipperary, N.R.	Owney and Arra	Kilnarath . .	Nenagh . .	II.	296
21	Knockacullion .	1,740 3 25	Leitrim . .	Carrigallen .	Oughteragh .	Bawnboy . .	IV.	92
15, 16	Knockacullion .	96 3 30	Leitrim . .	Drumahaire .	Killarga . .	Manorhamilton .	IV.	99
5	Knockacullion .	61 3 16	Monaghan .	Monaghan . .	Tedavnet . .	Monaghan . .	III.	279
15	Knockacully . .	48 0 14	Antrim . .	Lower Glenarm .	Layd . .	Ballycastle .	III.	23
14	Knockacummer .	405 1 30	Cork, E.R. .	Duhallow . .	Clonfert . .	Kanturk . .	II.	68
10	Knockacunnier .	70 1 10	Monaghan .	Monaghan . .	Tehallan . .	Monaghan . .	III.	280
38	Knockacunny . .	160 0 27	Tyrone . .	Dungannon Upper .	Derryloran .	Cookstown . .	III.	307
25	Knockacur . .	138 2 23	Cork, E.R. .	Fermoy . .	Doneraile . .	Mallow . .	II.	78
67	Knockacurra . .	93 2 25	Tipperary, S.R.	Clanwilliam .	Kilshane . .	Tipperary . .	II.	309
31, 32	Knockacurra . .	140 2 23	Westmeath .	Moycashel . .	Castletown Kindalen	Mullingar . .	I.	277
35	Knockacurrane .	126 0 4	Kerry . .	Corkaguiny .	Stradbally . .	Dingle . .	II.	180
100	Knockacurreen .	47 2 6	Mayo . .	Carra . .	Burriscarra .	Ballinrobe .	IV.	127
27	Knockacurrin . .	38 2 1	Waterford .	Gaultiere . .	Killea . .	Waterford . .	II.	363
6	Knockadaff . .	382 2 23	Roscommon .	Boyle . .	Ardcarn . .	Boyle . .	IV.	193
11	Knockadalteen .	148 0 23	Roscommon .	Boyle . .	Killucan . .	Car.k on Shannon	IV.	195
33	Knockadalteen .	245 3 30	Sligo . .	Corran . .	Emlaghfad . .	Sligo . .	IV.	226
32, 33	Knockadangan .	201 2 19b	Clare . .	Islands . .	Kilmaley . .	Ennis . .	II.	31

(a) Including 7A. 3R. 13P. detached portion.   (b) Including 3A. 0R. 16P. water.

No. of Sheet of the Ordnance Survey Maps.	Townlands and Towns.	Area in Statute Acres.			County.	Barony.	Parish.	Poor Law Union in 1857.	Townland Census of 1851, Part I.	
		A.	R.	P.					Vol.	Page
29	Knockadangan .	121	2	11	Mayo . .	Tirawley . .	Crossmolina . .	Ballina . .	IV.	166
41	Knockadangan .	823	2	23	Roscommon .	Athlone . .	Athleague . .	Roscommon .	IV.	179
105	Knockadaumore .	249	0	37	Galway . .	Dunkellin . .	Kilconickny .	Loughrea . .	IV.	29
52,53,65,66	Knockadav . .	4,595	0	22a	Galway . .	Moycullen . .	Kilcummin . .	Oughterard .	IV.	67
11	Knockadav .	394	0	1	Waterford .	Coshmore&Coshbride	Lismore and Mocollop	Lismore . .	II.	346
17, 22	Knockadawk . .	268	2	9	Wexford . .	Gorey . .	Kiltrisk . .	Gorey . .	I.	320
57	Knockadea . .	380	0	1	Limerick . .	Coshlea . .	Ballylanders .	Mitchelstown .	II.	237
58	Knockaderreen .	554	0	11	Clare . .	Clonderalaw .	Kilmurry . .	Kilrush . .	II.	17
45	Knockaderreen .	312	0	18	Clare . .	Tulla Lower .	O'Briensbridge .	Limerick . .	II.	38
17	Knockaderreen .	479	3	6	Kerry . .	Clanmaurice .	Duagh . .	Listowel . .	II.	168
33, 34	Knockaderry .	159	0	18	Clare . .	Bunratty Upper .	Templemaley .	Ennis . .	II.	11
48	Knockaderry .	379	1	26	Kerry . .	Magunihy . .	Molahiffe . .	Killarney . .	II.	205
28,29,36,37	Knockaderry .	706	1	27	Limerick . .	Glenquin . .	Clonelty . .	Newcastle .	II.	245
46	Knockaderry .	84	1	12	Tipperary, S.R.	Kilnamanagh Lower	Clogher . .	Cashel . .	II.	322
21, 27	Knockaderry .	405	2	4	Wicklow . .	Upper Talbotstown	Donaghmore .	Baltinglass .	I.	363
16	Knockaderry Lower	419	3	4	Waterford .	Middlethird .	Newcastle . .	Waterford .	II.	368
37	Knockaderry T. .	—			Limerick . .	Glenquin . .	Clonelty . .	Newcastle .	II.	245
16	Knockaderry Upper	87	1	24	Waterford .	Middlethird .	Newcastle . .	Waterford .	II.	368
27	Knockadigeen .	272	2	37	Tipperary, N.R.	Upper Ormond .	Kilnaneave .	Nenagh . .	II.	291
105, 106	Knockadileen .	286	0	14	Galway . .	Loughrea . .	Loughrea . .	Loughrea .	IV.	66
21	Knockadilly .	80	1	19	Wexford . .	Ballaghkeen .	Killincooly .	Gorey . .	I.	295
79	Knockadlough .	643	0	23b	Galway . .	Moycullen . .	Killannin . .	Galway . .	IV.	70
46	Knockadoo . .	690	1	24	Londonderry .	Loughinsholin .	Lissan . .	Magherafelt .	III.	242
5	Knockadoo . .	107	2	25	Roscommon .	Boyle . .	Boyle . .	Boyle . .	IV.	194
25	Knockadoo . .	808	3	19	Sligo . .	Leyny . .	Killoran . .	Tobercurry .	IV.	230
34	Knockadoo . .	43	2	33	Sligo . .	Tirerril . .	Tawnagh . .	Sligo . .	IV.	241
6, 10	Knockadoobrusna .	177	0	7	Roscommon .	Boyle . .	Boyle . .	Boyle . .	IV.	194
41	Knockadoois .	155	1	22	Fermanagh .	Knockninny .	Tomregan . .	Lisnaskea .	III.	203
83,84,95,96	Knockadooma .	264	2	15	Cork, W.R. .	Kinalmeaky .	Templemartin .	Bandon . .	II.	153
35	Knockadoon . .	134	3	27	Clare . .	Tulla Upper .	Tulla . .	Tulla . .	II.	42
78	Knockadoon . .	243	0	16	Cork, E.R. .	Imokilly . .	Kilmacdonogh .	Youghal . .	II.	88
112	Knockadoon . .	522	0	2	Mayo . .	Clanmorris .	Kilvine . .	Claremorris .	IV.	134
110	Knockadoon . .	126	0	25	Mayo . .	Kilmaine . .	Ballinrobe .	Ballinrobe .	IV.	153
11	Knockadoonlea .	322	1	35	Waterford .	Coshmore&Coshbride	Lismore and Mocollop	Lismore . .	II.	346
78	Knockadoon(Warren)	247	0	30	Cork, E.R. .	Imokilly . .	Kilmacdonogh .	Middleton .	II.	88
90, 100	Knockadorraghy .	432	3	0	Mayo . .	Clanmorris .	Mayo . .	Ballinrobe .	IV.	135
30	Knockalosan . .	249	3	10	Wicklow . .	Ballinacor North	Rathdrum . .	Rathdrum .	I.	347
60	Knockadreen .	105	0	38	Tyrone . .	Dungannon Lower .	Carnteel . .	Clogher . .	III.	297
18	Knockadreet .	296	2	16	Wicklow . .	Newcastle . .	Killiskey . .	Rathdrum .	I.	352
18	Knockadreet .	276	0	25	Wicklow . .	Newcastle . .	Newcastle Upper .	Rathdrum .	I.	353
3	Knockadrehid .	182	3	18	Roscommon .	Boyle . .	Ardcarn . .	Boyle . .	IV.	193
27, 31	Knockadrina . .	267	0	22	Kilkenny . .	Shillelogher .	Stonecarthy .	Thomastown .	I.	115
37	Knockadrinan .	106	0	23	Leitrim . .	Mohill . .	Mohill . .	Mohill . .	IV.	108
44	Knockadroleen .	43	2	1	Cork, E.R. .	Barrymore .	Rathcormack .	Fermoy . .	II.	57
25	Knockadromin .	324	0	4	Tipperary, N.R.	Owney and Arra .	Templeachally .	Nenagh . .	II.	297
125	Knockadrum . .	140	1	29	Galway . .	Leitrim . .	Ballynakill .	Loughrea .	IV.	51
88	Knockadrum . .	125	2	7	Mayo . .	Burrishoole .	Aghagower .	Westport .	IV.	118
24, 32	Knockadrumalea .	194	0	37	Waterford .	Decies without Drum	Stradbally .	Kilmacthomas .	II.	361
2	Knockadryan .	75	0	3	Roscommon .	Boyle . .	Kilronan . .	Boyle . .	IV.	197
11, 12	Knockaduff . .	308	3	11	Londonderry .	Coleraine . .	Aghadowey .	Coleraine .	III.	230
11, 20	Knockadullaun East	456	3	1	Waterford .	Coshmore&Coshbride	Lismore and Mocollop	Lismore . .	II.	346
11, 20	Knockadullaun West	166	2	34	Waterford .	Coshmore&Coshbride	Lismore and Mocollop	Lismore . .	II.	346
60, 70	Knockafall . .	130	3	24c	Mayo . .	Gallen . .	Templemore .	Castlebar .	IV.	151
22	Knockafarson or Broadlands .	230	0	7	Mayo . .	Tirawley . .	Ballysakeery .	Ballina . .	IV.	164
23,24,31,32	Knockafreaghaun .	741	2	3	Kerry . .	Trughanacmy .	Brosna . .	Tralee . .	II.	208
147	Knockagallane .	118	0	7	Cork, W.R. .	West Carbery(W.D.)	Kilmoe . .	Skull . .	II.	145
38	Knockagallane .	616	3	20	Cork, W.R. .	West Muskerry .	Drishane . .	Millstreet .	II.	156
93	Knockagar . .	263	2	6	Donegal . .	Banagh . .	Inver . .	Donegal . .	III.	107
69	Knockagarran .	331	0	27	Donegal . .	Raphoe . .	Convoy . .	Stranorlar .	III.	136
47, 57	Knockagarrane .	241	2	36	Kerry . .	Trughanacmy .	Kilcolman .	Killarney . .	II.	210
30	Knockagarrane East	118	0	31	Cork, E.R. .	Duhallow . .	Cullen . .	Millstreet .	II.	70
30	Knockagarrane West	105	1	38	Cork, E.R. .	Duhallow . .	Cullen . .	Millstreet .	II.	70
60, 70	Knockagarraun .	237	1	31	Mayo . .	Gallen . .	Templemore .	Castlebar .	IV.	151
29	Knockagarravaun .	228	2	32	Mayo . .	Tirawley . .	Crossmolina .	Ballina . .	IV.	166
11	Knockagarry . .	88	1	33	Carlow . .	Idrone West .	Oldleighlin .	Carlow . .	I.	9
10	Knockagarry . .	611	3	5	Cork, E.R. .	Condons&Clangibbon	Marshalstown .	Mitchelstown .	II.	63
26, 32	Knockageehan .	141	3	37	Fermanagh .	Clanawley .	Killesher . .	Enniskillen .	III.	193
23	Knockagh . .	262	1	18	Longford . .	Shrule . .	Taghshinny .	Ballymahon .	I.	167
3, 6	Knockagh . .	146	0	19	Louth . .	Upper Dundalk .	Kane . .	Dundalk .	I.	179
29, 35	Knockagh . .	1,096	0	37	Tipperary, N.R.	Eliogarty . .	Drom . .	Thurles . .	II.	269
76	Knockagh . .	311	3	7	Tipperary, S.R.	Iffa and Offa West .	Caher . .	Clogheen .	II.	318
94, 108	Knockaghaduff .	332	2	36	Cork, W.R. .	East Carbery (W.D.)	Fanlobbus . .	Dunmanway .	II.	132

(a) Including 201A. 1R. 38P. water.   (b) Including 18A. 2R. 24P. water.   (c) Including 1A. 0R. 33P. water.

No. of Sheet of the Ordnance Survey Maps.	Townlands and Towns.	Area in Statute Acres.			County.	Barony.	Parish.	Poor Law Union in 1857.	Townland Census of 1851, Part I.	
		A.	R.	P.					Vol.	Page
30	Knockaghy	368	3	34a	Cavan	Tullyhunco	Scrabby	Cavan	III.	99
66	Knockaginny	437	0	31	Tyrone	Dungannon Lower	Aghaloo	Armagh	III.	297
60	Knockaglana	1,035	3	12b	Mayo	Carra	Turlough	Castlebar	IV.	131
15	Knockagolig	504	1	23	Cork, E.R.	Duhallow	Kilbrin	Kanturk	II.	72
16	Knockagower	92	1	29	Sligo	Tireragh	Castleconor	Dromore West	IV.	232
57	Knockagowna	210	0	10	Kerry	Magunihy	Kilbonane	Killarney	II.	200
18	Knockagowny	70	3	30	Longford	Moydow	Ballymacormick	Longford	I.	161
11	Knockagraffy	24	3	6	Armagh	Armagh	Eglish	Armagh	III.	44
101	Knockagraffy	50	0	1	Mayo	Clanmorris	Tagheen	Claremorris	IV.	136
89	Knockagreenaun	90	1	8c	Mayo	Carra	Ballyhean	Castlebar	IV.	125
8	Knockaguilla	288	3	7	Clare	Corcomroe	Killilagh	Ennistimon	II.	20
31	Knockahavaun	107	2	21	Waterford	Decies without Drum	Dungarvan	Dungarvan	II.	355
13, 14	Knockahaw	207	3	1	Longford	Ardagh	Templemichael	Longford	I.	154
27, 33	Knockahaw	705	3	2	Queen's Co.	Clandonagh	Rathdowney	Donaghmore	I.	234
18	Knockaholet	530	3	15d	Antrim	Upper Dunluce	Loughguile	Ballymoney	III.	20
25	Knockahonagh	208	0	37	Queen's Co.	Stradbally	Tullomoy	Athy	I.	248
37	Knockahone	27	1	11	Wexford	Shelmaliere West	Carrick	Wexford	I.	332
37	Knockahoney	290	1	12	Sligo	Leyny	Kilmacteige	Tobercurry	IV.	231
4	Knockahorrea East	855	3	35	Cork, E.R.	Duhallow	Clonfert	Kanturk	II.	68
4	Knockahorrea West	832	3	28	Cork, E.R.	Duhallow	Clonfert	Kanturk	II.	68
21	Knockahunna	129	0	33	Tipperary, N.R.	Upper Ormond	Ballymackey	Nenagh	II.	289
39	Knockahurka	76	1	32	Sligo	Corran	Kilshalvy	Boyle	IV.	227
32	Knockainy East	71	3	22	Limerick	Smallcounty	Knockainy	Kilmallock	II.	261
32	KNOCKAINY T.	—			Limerick	Smallcounty	Knockainy	Kilmallock	II.	261
32, 40	Knockainy West	1,160	1	11	Limerick	Smallcounty	Knockainy	Kilmallock	II.	261
64, 65	Knockakeen	388	1	31	Cork, E.R.	Barrymore	Ballycurrany	Middleton	II.	51
88	Knockakeery	71	1	25	Mayo	Burrishoole	Aghagower	Westport	IV.	118
33, 34	Knockakelly	376	2	0	Tipperary, N.R.	Kilnamanagh Upper	Glenkeen	Thurles	II.	278
55	Knockakeo	296	0	25	Cork, E.R.	Kinnatalloon	Ballynoe	Fermoy	II.	97
102, 112	Knockakilleen	153	1	13	Galway	Kiltartan	Kinvarradoorus	Gort	IV.	49
41, 47	Knockakilly	141	3	21	Tipperary, N.R.	Eliogarty	Galbooly	Thurles	II.	270
3	Knockakirwan	98	3	3	Monaghan	Trough	Errigal Trough	Monaghan	III.	284
25	Knockakishta	123	1	3	Cavan	Upper Loughtee	Kilmore	Cavan	III.	84
2, 3	Knockalafalla	378	0	6	Waterford	Upperthird	Rathgormuck	Carrick on Suir	II.	371
27	Knockalaghta (Sandford)	233	1	21	Roscommon	Castlereagh	Ballintober	Castlereagh	IV.	198
27	Knockalaghta (Wills)	335	3	12	Roscommon	Castlereagh	Ballintober	Castlereagh	IV.	198
29, 30	Knockalahara	507	3	0	Waterford	Decies without Drum	Kilmolash	Lismore	II.	357
39	Knockalass	39	1	8	Sligo	Corran	Kilshalvy	Boyle	IV.	227
38	Knockalass	133	1	25	Sligo	Corran	Kilturra	Tobercurry	IV.	228
31	Knockalassa	935	1	36e	Clare	Inchiquin	Inagh	Ennistimon	II.	25
120	Knockalassa	89	0	2	Mayo	Kilmaine	Cong	Ballinrobe	IV.	154
19	Knockalassa	721	0	6	Waterford	Coshmore&Coshbride	Lismore and Mocollop	Lismore	II.	346
109	Knockaleanore	108	0	17	Mayo	Carra	Ballyovey	Ballinrobe	IV.	126
28,29,37,38	Knockaleery	432	2	11	Tyrone	Dungannon Upper	Kildress	Cookstown	III.	309
67	Knockalegan	112	2	24	Mayo	Burrishoole	Burrishoole	Newport	IV.	119
111	Knockalegan	360	2	9	Mayo	Kilmaine	Kilcommon	Ballinrobe	IV.	155
29, 38	Knockalegan	152	3	27	Mayo	Tirawley	Crossmolina	Ballina	IV.	166
57	Knockalegan	183	0	15	Tipperary, S.R.	Clanwilliam	Templebredon	Tipperary	II.	311
27	Knockalegan East	102	2	21	Roscommon	Castlereagh	Baslick	Castlereagh	IV.	199
27	Knockalegan West	126	3	8	Roscommon	Castlereagh	Baslick	Castlereagh	IV.	199
50	Knockalehid	90	3	1	Clare	Islands	Clondagad	Killadysert	II.	29
17, 20	Knockaleva	218	1	31	Louth	Ardee	Mosstown	Ardee	I.	174
58, 59	Knockalibade	548	2	20	Kerry	Magunihy	Kilcummin	Killarney	II.	201
100	Knockalinsky	141	0	37	Mayo	Kilmaine	Robeen	Ballinrobe	IV.	157
53, 63	Knockalisheen	445	3	12	Clare	Bunratty Lower	St. Munchins	Limerick	II.	6
28	Knockalisheen	84	2	1	Clare	Tulla Upper	Feakle	Scarriff	II.	39
86	Knockalisheen	225	2	24	Cork, E.R.	Cork	Inishkenny	Cork	II.	64
5, 6	Knockalisheen	564	3	13	Waterford	Glenahiry	Kilronan	Clonmel	II.	365
1, 5	Knockalisheen	1,251	0	5	Waterford	Upperthird	St. Marys, Clonmel	Clonmel	II.	372
26	Knockaloaghan	319	2	62	Clare	Bunratty Upper	Inchicronan	Tulla	II.	9
15,16,23,24	Knockalohert	339	0	7	Cork, E.R.	Duhallow	Kilbrin	Kanturk	II.	72
49, 55	Knockalonga	195	0	30	Tipperary, S.R.	Slievardagh	Ballingarry	Callan	II.	332
32	Knockalongford	25	1	1	Leitrim	Mohill	Mohill	Mohill	IV.	108
48	Knockalough	877	3	27	Clare	Clonderalaw	Kilmihil	Kilrush	II.	17
22	Knockalough	81	2	16	Fermanagh	Tirkennedy	Enniskillen	Enniskillen	III.	222
80, 81	Knockalough	1,121	1	4g	Galway	Moycullen	Moycullen	Galway	IV.	71
22	Knockalough	51	1	34	Mayo	Tirawley	Ballysakeery	Ballina	IV.	165
32, 33, 38	Knockalough	110	3	10h	Sligo	Corran	Cloonoghil	Tobercurry	IV.	225
17, 23	Knockalougha	1,244	1	15	Kerry	Clanmaurice	Duagh	Listowel	II.	168
40	Knockalough Commons	473	0	10	Tipperary, N.R.	Kilnamanagh Upper	Templebeg	Thurles	II.	279
30	Knockaloura East	216	0	22	Galway	Dunmore	Tuam	Tuam	IV.	36
30	Knockaloura West	215	2	15	Galway	Dunmore	Tuam	Tuam	IV.	36
16	Knockalt Lower	226	3	19	Wicklow	Lower Talbotstown	Boystown	Baltinglass	I.	359

(a) Including 5A. 3R. 20P. water. (d) Including 1A. 3R. 11P. water. (g) Including 85A. 1R. 32P. water.
(b) Including 33A. 1R. 18P. water. (e) Including 7A. 1R. 11P. water. (h) Including 31A. 0R. 0P. water.
(c) Including 6A. 2R. 17P. water. (f) Including 19A. 2R. 21P. water.

4 H

No. of Sheet of the Ordnance Survey Maps.	Townlands and Towns.	Area in Statute Acres.	County.	Barony.	Parish.	Poor Law Union in 1857.	Townland Census of 1851, Part I.	
		A.　R.　P.					Vol.	Page
21	Knockalton Lower .	114　3　10	Tipperary, N.R.	Upper Ormond .	Lisbunny .	Nenagh .	II.	292
21	Knockalton Upper .	478　1　13	Tipperary, N.R.	Upper Ormond .	Lisbunny .	Nenagh .	II.	292
16	Knockalt Upper .	162　3　2	Wicklow .	Lower Talbotstown	Boystown .	Baltinglass .	I.	359
26, 34	Knockaluskraun .	144　3　8	Clare .	Bunratty Upper .	Kilraghtis .	Ennis .	II.	9
3, 4	Knockamany .	306　3　7	Donegal .	Inishowen East .	Clonca .	Inishowen .	III.	117
11, 17	Knockamoohane .	207　1　38	Kerry .	Clanmaurice .	Finuge .	Listowel .	II.	169
22, 23	Knockamullin .	288　2　37	Queen's Co. .	Clarmallagh .	Aghaboe .	Abbeyleix .	I.	236
30	Knockan .	874　2　36	Londonderry .	Keenaght .	Banagher .	New[T]nLimavady	III.	234
15	Knockanabohilly .	70　3　18	Tipperary, N.R.	Upper Ormond .	Kilruane .	Nenagh .	II.	292
9, 14	Knockanacartan .	169　0　18a	Tipperary, N.R.	Lower Ormond .	Cloghprior .	Borrisokane .	II.	283
153	Knockanacohig .	62　0　33	Cork, W.R.	West Carbery (E.D.)	Clear-island .	Skibbereen .	II.	138
74	Knockanaconny .	284　2　37	Mayo .	Costello .	Castlemore .	Castlereagh .	IV.	140
10, 11	Knockanacree .	499　0　20	Tipperary, N.R.	Lower Ormond .	Modreeny .	Borrisokane .	II.	286
29	Knockanacuig .	49　2　19	Kerry .	Trughanacmy .	Tralee .	Tralee .	II.	213
14	Knockanacullin .	511　2　38	Waterford .	Decies without Drum	Kilrossanty .	Kilmacthomas .	II.	358
41	Knockanacunna .	31　0　14	Tipperary, N.R.	Eliogarty .	Rahelty .	Thurles .	II.	272
6, 10, 11	Knockanaddoge .	1,163　2　16	Kilkenny .	Fassadinin .	Dysart .	Castlecomer .	I.	89
6	Knockanaffrin .	1,254　2　31	Waterford .	Upperthird .	Rathgormuck .	Carrick on Suir	III.	371
16, 17	Knockanagh .	57　1　24	Waterford゛	Middlethird .	Kilmeadan .	Waterford .	II.	368
16, 17	Knockanagh .	103　3　28	Waterford .	Middlethird .	Lisnakill .	Waterford .	II.	368
39	Knockanaher .	192　1　13	Sligo .	Corran .	Drumrat .	Boyle .	IV.	226
30,31,38,39	Knockanalban .	939　1　27	Clare .	Ibrickan .	Kilmurry .	Ennistimon .	II.	23
4	Knockanally .	511　2　15	Kildare .	Ikeathy&Oughterany	Scullogestown .	Celbridge .	I.	58
101, 111	Knockananeel .	201　0　34	Mayo .	Clanmorris .	Crossboyne .	Claremorris .	IV.	133
35	Knockananig .	971　0　27	Cork, E.R.	Fermoy .	Litter .	Fermoy .	II.	81
11	Knockananima .	100　2　22	Roscommon .	Boyle .	Killukin ゛.	Car[k]. on Shannon	IV.	195
40	Knockananlig .	115　3　34	Kerry .	Trughanacmy .	Castleisland .	Tralee .	II.	209
20	Knockananna .	137　3　3	Waterford .	Coshmore&Coshbride	Lismore and Mocollop	Lismore .	II.	346
33	Knockananna .	267　1　2	Wicklow .	Ballinacor South .	Hacketstown .	Shillelagh .	I.	348
33, 42	Knockanannig .	593　2　29	Cork, E.R.	Fermoy .	Rahan .	Mallow .	II.	82
21, 29	Knockananny .	710　2　25b	Mayo .	Tirawley .	Moygawnagh .	Killala .	IV.	171
9	Knockananore .	200　2　13	Kerry .	Clanmaurice .	Rattoo .	Listowel .	II.	173
13	Knockananty .	240　1　2	Limerick .	Clanwilliam .	Derrygalvin .	Limerick .	II.	223
61	Knockanare .	340　1　0	Cork, E.R.	East Muskerry .	Donaghmore .	Macroom .	II.	103
17	Knockanare .	389　3　15	Cork, E.R.	Orrery and Kilmore	Buttevant .	Mallow .	II.	107
1	Knockanarra .	308　2　34	Galway .	Ballymoe .	Templetogher .	Glennamaddy .	IV.	9
103	Knockanarra .	145　3　5	Mayo .	Costello .	Annagh .	Claremorris .	IV.	138
46, 55	Knockanarrig .	215　2　5	Cork, E.R.	Kinnatalloon .	Mogeely .	Youghal .	II.	98
21, 22	Knockanarrigan .	253　2　30	Wicklow .	Upper Talbotstown	Donaghmore .	Baltinglass .	I.	363
67	Knockanarroor .	541　3　25	Kerry .	Magunihy .	Aghadoe .	Killarney .	II.	199
26, 27	Knockanarrow .	199　1　38	Sligo .	Tirerrill .	Kilmacallan .	Sligo .	IV.	240
11	Knockanasig .	194　2　9	Kerry .	Clanmaurice .	Finuge .	Listowel .	II.	169
54, 55	Knockanattin .	118　3　21	Tipperary, S.R.	Slievardagh .	Crohane .	Callan .	II.	332
44, 50	Knockanavar .	287　0　20	Tipperary, N.R.	Kilnamanagh Upper	Toem .	Tipperary .	II.	280
12, 17, 18	Knockanavery .	268　0　32	Antrim .	Upper Dunluce .	Kilraghts .	Ballymoney .	III.	20
93	Knockanavoddy .	191　3　10	Galway .	Moycullen .	Rahoon .	Galway .	IV.	72
6	Knookanbaun .	295　2　20	Limerick .	Clanwilliam .	Killeenagarriff .	Limerick .	II.	224
17	Knockanbaun .	191　3　17	Sligo .	Tireragh .	Kilmacshalgan .	Dromore West .	IV.	235
14, 15	Knockanbaun or Whitehill .	563　1　32	Longford .	Granard .	Clonbroney .	Granard .	I.	155
12	Knockanboy .	346　1　37	Antrim .	Lower Dunluce .	Derrykeighan .	Ballymoney .	III.	17
13	Knockanboy .	75　1　35	Longford .	Ardagh .	Ballymacormick .	Longford .	I.	152
5	Knockanbrack .	202　3　14	Tyrone .	Strabane Lower .	Leckpatrick .	Strabane .	III.	322
77, 78	Knockanclash .	354　0　4	Tipperary, S.R.	Iffa and Offa East .	Temple-etney .	Clonmel .	II.	316
37	Knockancullenagh .	363　1　2	Tipperary, N.R.	Owney and Arra .	Kilvellane .	Nenagh .	II.	296
21	Knockandarragh .	378　1　17	Wicklow .	Upper Talbotstown	Donaghmore .	Baltinglass .	I.	363
14, 15	Knockandort .	151　0　36	Wicklow .	Lower Talbotstown	Dunlavin .	Baltinglass .	I.	360
26	Knockanduff .	266　1　39	Waterford .	Middlethird .	Drumcannon .	Waterford .	II.	366
49, 50	Knockanduff .	100　1　27	Wexford .	Shelburne .	Templetown .	New Ross .	I.	328
40	Knockanduff .	102　1　17	Wicklow .	Arklow .	Castlemacadam .	Rathdrum .	I.	342
61, 62	Knockane .	214　3　24	Cork, E.R.	Barretts .	Donaghmore .	Cork .	II.	49
29, 30	Knockane .	151　1　9	Cork, E.R.	Duhallow .	Cullen .	Millstreet .	II.	70
61	Knockane .	280　2　32	Cork, E.R.	East Muskerry .	Inishcarra .	Cork .	II.	104
77	Knockane .	93　2　33	Cork, E.R.	Imokilly .	Ightermurragh .	Middleton .	II.	87
77	Knockane .	161　1　18	Cork, E.R.	Imokilly .	Killeagh .	Middleton .	II.	88
97	Knockane .	162　3　12	Cork, E.R.	Kinalea .	Ballymartle .	Kinsale .	II.	94
116	Knockane .	103　0　37	Cork, W.R.	Bear .	Killaconenagh .	Castletown .	II.	125
121	Knockane .	346　0　17	Cork, W.R.	East Carbery (W.D.)	Kilmeen .	Dunmanway .	II.	134
119	Knockane .	364　2　12	Cork, W.R.	West Carbery (E.D.)	Dromdaleague .	Skibbereen .	II.	140
82, 83	Knockane .	573　1　2	Cork, W.R.	West Muskerry .	Kilmichael .	Dunmanway .	II.	159
14	Knockane .	290　3　14	Kerry .	Clanmaurice .	Ballyheige .	Tralee .	II.	160
6, 10, 11	Knockane .	616　1　34	Kerry .	Iraghticonnor .	Listowel .	Listowel .	II.	193
36	Knockane .	166　0　15	Limerick .	Glenquin .	Monagay .	Newcastle .	II.	247

(a) Including 5A. 0R. 28P. water.　　　　　　(b) Including 4A. 0R. 24P. water.

No. of Sheet of the Ordnance Survey Maps.	Townlands and Towns.	Area in Statute Acres. A. R. P.	County.	Barony.	Parish.	Poor Law Union in 1857.	Townland Census of 1851, Part I. Vol.	Page
40	Knockane	201 3 17	Tipperary, N.R.	Kilnamanagh Upper	Templebeg	Thurles	II.	279
50, 51	Knockane	190 1 18	Tipperary, N.R.	Kilnamanagh Upper	Toem	Tipperary	II.	280
21, 22	Knockane	591 1 31	Tipperary, N.R.	Upper Ormond	Templedowney	Nenagh	II.	293
25	Knockane	266 2 2	Waterford	Decies without Drum	Kilbarrymeaden	Kilmacthomas	II.	356
25	Knockane	182 2 10	Waterford	Middlethird	Dunhill	Kilmacthomas	II.	367
8	Knockane	342 0 39	Waterford	Upperthird	Clonagam	Carrick on Suir	II.	369
14	Knockanea	343 0 21	Limerick	Clanwilliam	Caherconlish	Limerick	II.	222
29, 35	Knockanea	210 1 8	Westmeath	Clonlonan	Kilcleagh	Athlone	I.	261
38, 39, 48	Knockaneacoolteen	723 2 17	Kerry	Magunihy	Currans	Killarney	II.	200
108, 109	Knockaneady	393 2 19	Cork, W.R.	East Carbery (E.D.)	Ballymoney	Dunmanway	II.	127
52, 63	Knockaneag	311 2 18	Cork, E.R.	Cork	Whitechurch	Cork	II.	66
11	Knockaneagh	260 0 20	Armagh	Tiranny	Tynan	Armagh	III	60
133, 142	Knockaneagh	132 2 24	Cork, W.R.	West Carbery (E.D.)	Kilmacabea	Skibbereen	II.	140
84, 85	Knockaneamealgulla	237 0 29	Cork, E.R.	East Muskerry	Desertmore	Bandon	II.	102
34	Knockanean	336 3 9	Clare	Bunratty Upper	Doora	Ennis	II.	8
34, 35	Knockanearis	667 1 2	Waterford	Decies within Drum	Clashmore	Youghal	II.	351
5	Knockanearla	462 1 20	Monaghan	Monaghan	Tedavnet	Monaghan	III.	279
53	Knockaneasy	6 2 12	Wexford	Forth	Carn	Wexford	I.	309
81	Knockanebeg	50 2 28	Tipperary, S.R.	Iffa and Offa West	Tubbrid	Clogheen	II.	321
50	Knockanebrack	477 0 23	Limerick	Coshlea	Galbally	Mitchelstown	II.	239
91, 92	Knockanecosduff	266 0 18	Cork, W.R.	Bantry	Kilmocomoge	Bantry	II.	121
6, 15	Knockaneda	162 3 22	Cork, E.R.	Duhallow	Knocktemple	Kanturk	II.	75
16	Knockaneden	137 3 3	Clare	Corcomroe	Kiltoraght	Corrofin	II.	22
80	Knockaneden	399 1 25	Kerry	Iveragh	Killinane	Cahersiveen	II.	197
89	Knockaneden	238 2 8a	Mayo	Burrishoole	Islandeady	Westport	IV.	121
58	Knockaneduff	97 1 28	Tipperary, S.R.	Clanwilliam	Solloghodmore	Tipperary	II.	311
6	Knockaneek	120 2 4	Dublin	Balrothery West	Ballymadun	Dunshaughlin	I.	22
6	Knockaneglass East	213 0 14	Cork, E.R.	Duhallow	Tullylease	Kanturk	II.	76
6	Knockaneglass West	131 0 2	Cork, E.R.	Duhallow	Tullylease	Kanturk	II.	76
81	Knockane (Gurm)	69 3 18	Tipperary, S.R.	Iffa and Offa West	Tubbrid	Clogheen	II.	321
84	Knockaneleigh	284 0 13	Cork, E.R.	East Muskerry	Kilbonane	Bandon	II.	104
30	Knockanelo	146 3 17	Mayo	Tirawley	Ardagh	Ballina	IV.	163
136	Knockanemeeleen	97 3 6	Cork, W.R.	Ibane and Barryroe	Lislee	Clonakilty	II.	150
65	Knockanemore	80 0 11	Cork, E.R.	Barrymore	Dungourney	Middleton	II.	54
72,73,84,85	Knockanemore	962 3 22	Cork, E.R.	East Muskerry	Athnowen	Cork	II.	101
115	Knockane More	26 0 24	Cork, W.R.	Bear	Killaconenagh	Castletown	II.	125
88	Knockanemorney	227 2 11b	Cork, E.R.	Imokilly	Aghada	Middleton	II.	83
19	Knockanena	206 3 25	Clare	Tulla Upper	Feakle	Tulla	II.	39
19, 27	Knockanenabohilly	168 3 6	Cork, E.R.	Condons&Clangibbon	Kilcrumper	Fermoy	II.	61
133	Knockanenacrohy	158 0 0	Cork, W.R.	East Carbery (W.D.)	Kilmacabea	Skibbereen	II.	133
53	Knockanenafinoga	72 0 34	Cork, E.R.	Barrymore	Kilquane	Cork	II.	55
61	Knockanenagark	165 3 22	Cork, E.R.	East Muskerry	Magourney	Macroom	II.	105
55, 66	Knockanenakirka	448 2 38	Cork, E.R.	Imokilly	Dangandonovan	Middleton	II.	86
81	Knockane (Nash)	281 2 11	Tipperary, S.R.	Iffa and Offa West	Tubbrid	Clogheen	II.	321
72	Knockaneowen	72 0 34	Cork, E.R.	East Muskerry	Magourney	Macroom	II.	105
81	Knockane (Puttoge)	180 1 5	Tipperary, S.R.	Iffa and Offa West	Tubbrid	Clogheen	II.	321
82, 94	Knockanereagh	149 2 21	Cork, W.R.	West Muskerry	Kilmichael	Dunmanway	II.	159
22,23,30,31	Knockaneroe	317 1 22	Cork, E.R.	Duhallow	Kilmeen	Kanturk	II.	73
84	Knockaneroe	439 0 12	Cork, E.R.	East Muskerry	Moviddy	Bandon	II.	105
115	Knockaneroe	134 0 15	Cork, W.R.	Bear	Killaconenagh	Castletown	II.	125
124	Knockaneroe	127 3 11c	Cork, W.R.	East Carbery (E.D.)	Templetrine	Kinsale	II.	130
17, 23	Knockaneroe	159 3 22d	Kerry	Clanmaurice	Duagh	Listowel	II.	168
40	Knockaneroe	33 1 14	Tipperary, N.R.	Kilnamanagh Upper	Templebeg	Thurles	II.	279
89	Knockanerrew	68 1 39	Mayo	Carra	Ballyhean	Castlebar	IV.	125
7, 14, 15	Knockanerry	299 2 24	Limerick	Owneybeg	Abington	Limerick	II.	251
67	Knockanes	606 0 23	Kerry	Magunihy	Killaha	Killarney	II.	202
21	Knockanes	472 1 25	Limerick	Coshma	Adare	Croom	II.	241
65	Knockaneshane	66 3 31	Cork, E.R.	Barrymore	Templenacarriga	Middleton	II.	58
10, 19	Knockanevin	536 2 5	Cork, E.R.	Condons&Clangibbon	Templemolaga	Mitchelstown	II.	63
34	Knockanevin	215 0 35	Tipperary, N.R.	Kilnamanagh Upper	Glenkeen	Thurles	II.	278
27	Knockanevin	48 2 20	Wexford	Ballaghkeen	Castle-ellis	Enniscorthy	I.	293
70	Knockaneyouloo	968 1 34	Kerry	Iveragh	Killinane	Cahersiveen	II.	197
20	Knockanfoil More	38 0 10	Tipperary, N.R.	Owney and Arra	Youghalarra	Nenagh	II.	297
42	Knockangall	55 3 30	Wexford	Forth	Rathmacknee	Wexford	I.	313
21	Knockanglass	495 3 20	Tipperary, N.R.	Upper Ormond	Ballymackey	Nenagh	II.	289
49	Knockanglass	147 1 26	Tipperary, S.R.	Slievardagh	Buolick	Urlingford	II.	332
62	Knockanglass	651 0 2	Tipperary, S.R.	Slievardagh	Killenaule	Cashel	II.	334
30	Knockanillaun	169 0 20	Mayo	Tirawley	Ardagh	Ballina	IV.	164
105	Knockanima	117 2 26	Galway	Loughrea	Loughrea	Loughrea	IV.	66
42	Knockanimana	199 0 13	Clare	Islands	Clareabbey	Ennis	II.	29
39	Knockanimma	143 2 17	Sligo	Corran	Kilshalvy	Boyle	IV.	227
67	Knockanimrish	307 1 17	Kerry	Magunihy	Killaha	Killarney	II.	202
16, 17	Knockanina	437 3 33	Queen's Co.	Maryborough West	Clonenagh&Clonagheen	Mountmellick	I.	243

(a) Including 1A. 0R. 4P. water.
(b) Including 8A. 3R. 23P. water.
(c) Including 19A. 1R. 10P. detached portions.
(d) Including 3A. 3R. 8P. water.

4 H 2

No. of Sheet of the Ordnance Survey Maps.	Townlands and Towns.	Area in Statute Acres.			County.	Barony.	Parish.	Poor Law Union in 1857.	Townland Census of 1851, Part I.	
		A.	R.	P.					Vol.	Page
59	Knockaninane East	937	0	18	Kerry	Magunihy	Killarney	Killarney	II.	203
59, 67	Knockaninane West	777	3	0a	Kerry	Magunihy	Killarney	Killarney	II.	203
33, 41	Knockaninaun	271	3	35	Clare	Islands	Drumcliff	Ennis	II.	30
41	Knockanira	313	1	26	Clare	Islands	Killone	Ennis	II.	30
20	Knockaniska	135	2	8	Waterford	Coshmore & Coshbride	Lismore and Mocollop	Lismore	II.	346
35	Knockaniska	73	0	2	Waterford	Decies within Drum	Clashmore	Youghal	II.	351
11, 20	Knockaniska East	425	2	30	Waterford	Coshmore & Coshbride	Lismore and Mocollop	Lismore	II.	346
19	Knockaniska West	368	1	16	Waterford	Coshmore & Coshbride	Lismore and Mocollop	Lismore	II.	346
34	Knockannabinna	89	3	2	Tipperary, N.R.	Kilnamanagh Upper	Glenkeen	Thurles	II.	278
38	Knockannacreeva	170	2	1	Limerick	Coshma	Bruree	Kilmallock	II.	242
11	Knockannagad	194	0	34	Queen's Co.	Upperwoods	Offerlane	Mountmellick	I.	252
39, 40	Knockannagore	172	2	4	Kerry	Trughanacmy	Castleisland	Tralee	II.	209
153	Knockannamaurnagh	38	1	15	Cork, W.R.	West Carbery (E.D.)	Clear-island	Skibbereen	II.	138
20	Knockannamohilly	150	3	24	Tipperary, N.R.	Owney and Arra	Youghalarra	Nenagh	II.	297
12	Knockannanagh	500	1	23	Waterford	Coshmore & Coshbride	Lismore and Mocollop	Lismore	II.	346
81	Knockannapisha	44	1	19	Tipperary, S.R.	Iffa and Offa West	Tubbrid	Clogheen	II.	321
69	Knockannaveigh	289	2	23	Tipperary, S.R.	Middlethird	Knockgraffon	Cashel	II.	328
26	Knockanoark	288	0	18b	Cavan	Upper Loughtee	Lavey	Cavan	III.	86
35	Knockanode	247	0	39	Wicklow	Arklow	Castlemacadam	Rathdrum	I.	342
28	Knockanohill	113	3	3	Cork, E.R.	Condons & Clangibbon	Kilworth	Fermoy	II.	62
33	Knockanooker Lower	235	1	24	Wicklow	Ballinacor South	Hacketstown	Shillelagh	I.	348
33	Knockanooker Upper	338	2	0	Wicklow	Ballinacor South	Hacketstown	Shillelagh	I.	348
28	Knockanora	203	3	36	Tipperary, N.R.	Kilnamanagh Upper	Glenkeen	Thurles	II.	278
134	Knockanoran	80	1	19	Cork, W.R.	Ibane and Barryroe	Kilkerranmore	Clonakilty	II.	149
29	Knockanoran	470	2	2	Queen's Co.	Clarmallagh	Durrow	Abbeyleix	I.	237
31	Knockanore	141	0	9	Cavan	Clanmahon	Ballintemple	Cavan	III.	75
28	Knockanore	195	0	8c	Kilkenny	Gowran	Woolengrange	Thomastown	I.	100
34	Knockanore	157	1	7	Waterford	Coshmore & Coshbride	Kilcockan	Lismore	II.	343
11, 20	Knockanore	182	3	32	Waterford	Coshmore & Coshbride	Lismore and Mocollop	Lismore	II.	346
110, 118	Knockanotish	293	1	16d	Mayo	Kilmaine	Ballinrobe	Ballinrobe	IV.	153
58	Knockanoulort	191	2	20	Kerry	Magunihy	Kilcredane	Killarney	II.	200
150	Knockanoulty	64	3	25	Cork, W.R.	West Carbery (E.D.)	Tullagh	Skibbereen	II.	141
70	Knockanour	136	2	37	Mayo	Carra	Turlogh	Castlebar	IV.	131
26, 34	Knockanoura	582	1	4e	Clare	Bunratty Upper	Clooney	Tulla	II.	8
33	Knockanoura	55	1	12	Clare	Bunratty Upper	Templemaley	Ennis	II.	11
3	Knockanowl	123	3	16	Queen's Co.	Tinnahinch	Rearymore	Mountmellick	I.	250
27	Knockanpaddin	134	1	8	Waterford	Gaultiere	Rathmoylan	Waterford	II.	364
20	Knockanpierce	76	1	9	Tipperary, N.R.	Upper Ormond	Nenagh	Nenagh	II.	292
36	Knockanpower Lower	71	1	33	Waterford	Decies within Drum	Ringagonagh	Dungarvan	II.	353
22	Knockanpower Lower	471	3	11	Waterford	Decies without Drum	Colligan	Dungarvan	II.	354
36	Knockanpower Upper	172	1	35	Waterford	Decies within Drum	Ringagonagh	Dungarvan	II.	353
22	Knockanpower Upper	358	2	26	Waterford	Decies without Drum	Colligan	Dungarvan	II.	354
40, 45	Knockanrahan Lower	112	0	37	Wicklow	Arklow	Arklow	Rathdrum	I.	341
45	Knockanrahan Upper	184	2	29	Wicklow	Arklow	Arklow	Rathdrum	I.	341
67	Knockanrawley	212	3	15	Tipperary, S.R.	Clanwilliam	Cordangan	Tipperary	II.	306
110	Knockanreagh	139	3	12	Cork, W.R.	East Carbery (E.D.)	Ballymodan	Bandon	II.	127
26	Knockanreagh	221	1	38	Wicklow	Upper Talbotstown	Ballynure	Baltinglass	I.	362
45	Knockanree	71	3	5	Wicklow	Arklow	Arklow	Rathdrum	I.	341
35	Knockanree Lower	351	0	32	Wicklow	Arklow	Castlemacadam	Rathdrum	I.	342
35	Knockanree Upper	456	2	8	Wicklow	Arklow	Castlemacadam	Rathdrum	I.	342
52	Knockanroe	102	2	19	Cork, E.R.	Barretts	Whitechurch	Cork	II.	50
39, 40	Knockanroe	191	2	25	Cork, W.R.	West Muskerry	Kilcorney	Millstreet	II.	158
28	Knockanroe	59	0	4	Kilkenny	Gowran	Columbkille	Thomastown	I.	94
25	Knockanroe	97	1	14	Leitrim	Carrigallen	Oughteragh	Bawnboy	IV.	92
2	Knockanroe	48	2	31	Leitrim	Rosclogher	Rossinver	Ballyshannon	IV.	111
101, 111	Knockanroe	61	3	38	Mayo	Clanmorris	Tagheen	Claremorris	IV.	136
23, 29	Knockanroe	760	2	19	Tipperary, N.R.	Eliogarty	Templemore	Thurles	II.	272
26	Knockanroe	333	3	35	Tipperary, N.R.	Upper Ormond	Kilmore	Nenagh	II.	291
39	Knockanroe	147	0	13	Tyrone	Dungannon Upper	Ardtrea	Cookstown	III.	306
39	Knockanroe	20	1	18	Waterford	Decies within Drum	Ardmore	Dungarvan	II.	350
28	Knockanroe North	119	1	25	Kilkenny	Gowran	Kilfane	Thomastown	I.	97
28	Knockanroe South	24	2	30	Kilkenny	Gowran	Kilfane	Thomastown	I.	97
22	Knockanroger	394	3	8	Tipperary, N.R.	Ikerrin	Borrisnafarney	Roscrea	II.	274
94, 95	Knockanruddig	1,077	2	9	Kerry	Glanarought	Kilgarvan	Kenmare	II.	187
8, 13	Knockans	284	0	19	Antrim	Cary	Armoy	Ballycastle	III.	11
1	Knockans	257	0	3	Antrim	Cary	Rathlin Island	Ballycastle	III.	15
22	Knockans	819	0	24	Antrim	Kilconway	Finvoy	Ballymoney	III.	26
10	Knockans Lower	423	1	5	Clare	Burren	Carran	Ballyvaghan	II.	11
20	Knockans North	118	3	21	Antrim	Lower Glenarm	Layd	Ballycastle	III.	23
20	Knockans South	107	0	11	Antrim	Lower Glenarm	Layd	Ballycastle	III.	23
10	Knockans Upper	361	0	23	Clare	Burren	Carran	Ballyvaghan	II.	11
32	Knockansweeny	170	3	39	Cork, E.R.	Duhallow	Kilshannig	Mallow	II.	74
69	Knockantemple	154	0	31	Tipperary, S.R.	Middlethird	St. Patricksrock	Cashel	II.	331

(a) Including 7A. 2R. 32P. water.
(b) Including 0A. 2R. 30P. water.
(c) Including 5A. 0R. 28P. River Nore.
(d) Including 9A. 2R. 25P. water.
(e) Including 17A. 0R. 15P. water.

No. of Sheet of the Ordnance Survey Maps.	Townlands and Towns.	Area in Statute Acres.	County.	Barony.	Parish.	Poor Law Union in 1857.	Townland Census of 1851, Part I.	
		A. R. P.					Vol.	Page
7	Knockantern .	329 0 19	Londonderry .	North East Liberties of Coleraine . .	Coleraine .	Coleraine . .	III.	246
51	Knockantibrien .	87 1 37	Tipperary, S.R.	Kilnamanagh Lower	Aghacrew .	Tipperary . .	II.	322
51	Knockantota North	340 1 7	Cork, E.R.	Barretts . . .	Grenagh . .	Cork . .	II.	49
51	Knockantota South	407 1 10	Cork, E.R.	Barretts . . .	Grenagh . .	Cork . .	II.	49
94	Knockanuha .	626 2 18	Kerry .	Glanarought .	Kilgarvan .	Kenmare . .	II.	187
28	Knockanully .	480 0 29	Antrim .	Lower Antrim .	Skerry . .	Ballymena .	III.	5
16	Knockanulty .	176 3 25	Clare .	Corcomroe .	Clooney .	Ennistimon .	II.	18
29	Knockanumera .	167 2 17	Mayo .	Tirawley . .	Crossmolina .	Ballina . .	IV.	166
58, 59, 69, 70	Knockanure .	616 3 37	Cork, W.R.	West Muskerry .	Ballyvourney .	Macroom . .	II.	154
9, 10	Knockanure .	1,055 0 35	Wexford .	Scarawalsh .	Kilrush .	Enniscorthy .	I.	324
28, 29	Knockanush East .	446 0 20	Kerry .	Trughanacmy .	Clogherbrien .	Tralee . .	II.	209
28, 29	Knockanush West .	489 1 24	Kerry .	Trughanacmy .	Clogherbrien .	Tralee . .	II.	209
42, 45	Knockanyeonor .	311 3 21	Roscommon .	Athlone . .	St. Johns .	Athlone . .	IV.	183
77	KNOCKANYEVEEN T.	—	Mayo .	Burrishoole .	Kilmeena .	Westport, .	IV.	123
134, 135	Knockaphonery .	156 3 0	Cork, W.R.	Ibane and Barryroe	Rathbarry .	Clonakilty .	II.	150
136	Knockaphort .	119 3 18	Galway .	Leitrim . .	Inishcaltra .	Scarriff .	IV.	53
84, 96	Knockaphreaghane .	374 1 22	Cork, E.R.	East Muskerry .	Knockavilly .	Bandon . .	II.	105
150	Knockaphreaghane .	96 2 5	Cork, W.R.	West Carbery (E.D.)	Tullagh . .	Skibbereen .	II.	141
34	Knockaphreaghaun .	337 3 5	Clare .	Bunratty Upper .	Clooney .	Tulla . .	II.	8
52, 53	Knockaphreaghaun .	996 2 19a	Galway .	Moycullen .	Kilcummin .	Oughterard .	IV.	67
24	Knockaphrumpa .	320 1 11	Wicklow .	Newcastle .	Derrylossary .	Rathdrum .	I.	351
6, 7	Knockaphubble .	88 1 35	Monaghan .	Trough . .	Donagh . .	Monaghan .	III.	282
38	Knockaphuca .	82 2 0	Kildare .	Kilkea and Moone .	Castledermot .	Athy . .	I.	59
78	Knockaphunta .	380 1 12b	Mayo .	Carra . .	Aglish . .	Castlebar .	IV.	123
31	Knockaquirk .	42 3 39	Wicklow .	Arklow . .	Drumkay .	Rathdrum .	I.	343
89	Knockaraha .	163 2 28	Mayo .	Carra . .	Ballintober .	Castlebar .	IV.	125
13	Knockaraha .	99 0 25	Waterford .	Glenahiry .	Kilronan .	Clonmel . .	II.	365
87	Knockaraha East .	40 1 14	Mayo .	Murrisk . .	Oughaval .	Westport .	IV.	162
87	Knockaraha West .	52 2 0	Mayo .	Murrisk . .	Oughaval .	Westport .	IV.	162
43	Knockaraheen .	316 2 37	Cavan .	Castlerahan .	Munterconnaught .	Oldcastle .	III.	71
11	Knockaranny .	40 1 7	Meath .	Upper Kells .	Dulane . .	Kells . .	I.	205
81, 93	Knockarasser .	814 3 32c	Galway .	Moycullen .	Moycullen .	Galway . .	IV.	71
41, 42	Knockaraven .	394 0 22	Tyrone .	Omagh East .	Dromore .	Omagh . .	III.	311
28, 32	Knockard .	192 3 5	Kilkenny .	Gowran . .	Jerpointabbey .	Thomastown .	I.	96
2	Knockarda .	32 1 35	Carlow .	Carlow . .	Urglin . .	Carlow . .	I.	3
27	Knockardagannon Nth.	627 3 17	Queen's Co. .	Clandonagh .	Rathdowney .	Donaghmore .	I.	234
27, 33	Knockardagannon South .	291 0 35	Queen's Co. .	Clandonagh .	Rathdowney .	Donaghmore .	I.	234
24, 30	Knockardagur .	567 3 15	Queen's Co. .	Cullenagh .	Dysartgallen .	Abbeyleix .	I.	239
2, 3, 7, 8	Knockardamrum .	310 2 33	Cork, E.R.	Orrery and Kilmore	Ballyhay . .	Kilmallock .	II.	106
16	Knockardbane .	429 3 34	Cork, E.R.	Orrery and Kilmore	Liscarroll .	Mallow . .	II.	109
15	Knockardfree .	365 2 6	Cork, E.R.	Duhallow .	Kilbrin . .	Kanturk .	II.	72
10, 19	Knockardnacorlan .	240 3 24	Limerick .	Shanid . .	Robertstown .	Rathkeale .	II.	258
30, 31	Knockardrahan .	479 0 6	Cork, E.R.	Duhallow .	Dromtarriff .	Kanturk .	II.	71
24	Knockardsharriv .	268 3 1	Cork, E.R.	Duhallow .	Castlemagner .	Kanturk .	II.	67
31, 40	Knockardtry .	547 0 7	Kerry .	Trughanacmy .	Castleisland .	Tralee . .	II.	209
10	Knockaree .	245 2 5	Wexford .	Scarawalsh .	Kilrush .	Enniscorthy .	I.	324
39, 42	Knockarevan .	177 3 3	Fermanagh .	Knockninny .	Kinawley .	Lisnaskea .	III.	202
13	Knockarevan .	628 1 39	Fermanagh .	Magheraboy .	Inishmacsaint .	Ballyshannon .	III.	213
93, 94	Knockariblihane .	334 2 37	Cork, W.R.	East Carbery (W.D.)	Kilmichael .	Dunmanway .	II.	134
30	Knockariddane .	88 0 22	Kerry .	Trughanacmy .	O'Brennan .	Tralee . .	II.	212
30, 31	Knockariddera .	1,757 1 11	Kerry .	Trughanacmy .	Castleisland .	Tralee . .	II.	209
20	Knockarigg .	324 0 25	Wicklow .	Upper Talbotstown	Ballynure .	Baltinglass .	I.	362
20	Knockarigg Demesne	146 2 20	Wicklow .	Upper Talbotstown	Ballynure .	Baltinglass .	I.	362
20	Knockarigg Hill .	156 2 36	Wicklow .	Upper Talbotstown	Ballynure .	Baltinglass .	I.	362
39	Knockarley .	643 3 8	King's Co. .	Ballybritt .	Roscomroe .	Roscrea .	I.	126
22	Knockaroe .	220 2 38	Queen's Co. .	Clandonagh .	Aghaboe . .	Donaghmore .	I.	232
61, 67	Knockarogan Glebe	154 3 30	Tyrone .	Dungannon Middle .	Clonfeacle .	Dungannon .	III.	299
33	Knockaroura .	339 0 34	Cork, E.R.	Fermoy . .	Mallow . .	Mallow . .	II.	81
143	Knockarudane .	81 3 24	Cork, W.R.	East Carbery (W.D.)	Kilfaughnabeg .	Skibbereen .	II.	133
6, 10	Knockarush .	555 1 7	Roscommon .	Boyle . .	Boyle . .	Boyle . .	IV.	194
58, 66	Knockasarnet .	298 3 23	Kerry .	Magunihy .	Aghadoe . .	Killarney .	II.	199
115	Knockash .	164 1 30	Galway .	Loughrea .	Kilteskill .	Loughrea .	IV.	65
29, 30	Knockaskeehaun .	344 3 6	Mayo .	Tirawley . .	Kilfian .	Ballina .	IV.	169
28	Knockaskehane .	226 2 18	Cork, E.R.	Condons & Clangibbon	Leitrim .	Fermoy . .	II.	62
8	Knockaskeheen .	457 2 28	Clare .	Burren . .	Kilmoon .	Ennistimon .	II.	13
34	Knockaskibbole .	67 3 37	Clare .	Bunratty Upper .	Doora . .	Ennis . .	II.	8
69	Knockaskibbole .	479 2 25d	Mayo .	Carra . .	Aglish . .	Castlebar .	IV.	123
76	Knockasproha .	131 3 11	Mayo .	Burrishoole .	Kilmeena .	Westport .	IV.	122
44	Knockaspur .	155 1 10	King's Co. .	Clonlisk .	Templeharry .	Roscrea .	I.	132
36, 37	Knockastickane .	164 2 35	Cork, E.R.	Kinnatalloon .	Knockmourne .	Fermoy . .	II.	98
32, 41	Knockastoller .	560 0 37e	Donegal .	Kilmacrenan .	Tullaghobegly .	Dunfanaghy .	III.	132

(a) Including 129A. 2R. 9P. water.
(b) Including 8A. 3R. 16P. water.
(c) Including 7A. 0R. 12P. water.
(d) Including 8A. 1R. 8P. water.
(e) Including 21A. 3R. 13P. water.

No. of Sheet of the Ordnance Survey Maps	Townlands and Towns.	Area in Statute Acres.			County.	Barony.	Parish.	Poor Law Union in 1857.	Townland Census of 1851, Part I.	
		A.	R.	P.					Vol.	Page
30	Knockastuckane	315	2	4	Cork, E.R.	Duhallow	Cullen	Millstreet	II.	70
76, 77	Knockasturkeen	118	0	35	Cork, E.R.	Imokilly	Cloyne	Middleton	II.	85
76	Knockasturkeen	93	0	7	Cork, E.R.	Imokilly	Middleton	Middleton	II.	89
27	Knockataggart	858	2	22a	Cavan	Tullygarvey	Larah	Cootehill	III.	91
141, 150	Knockataggart	133	3	31	Cork, W.R.	West Carbery (E.D.)	Creagh	Skibbereen	II.	139
101	Knockataggart	87	0	38	Mayo	Clanmorris	Tagheen	Claremorris	IV.	136
58, 59	Knockataggle Beg	247	1	9	Kerry	Magunihy	Kilcummin	Killarney	II.	201
59	Knockataggle More	1,052	1	38	Kerry	Magunihy	Kilcummin	Killarney	II.	201
5	Knockatallan	405	1	36	Monaghan	Monaghan	Tedavnet	Monaghan	III.	279
14	Knockatancashlane	267	0	19	Limerick	Clanwilliam	Caherconlish	Limerick	II.	222
30	Knockatarriv	293	1	14	Kerry	Trughanacmy	Ballymacelligott	Tralee	II.	207
18	Knockatarry Brickeens	70	3	25	Longford	Moydow	Ballymacormick	Longford	I.	161
18	Knockatarry Poynton	167	2	19	Longford	Moydow	Ballymacormick	Longford	I.	161
147	Knockatassonig	94	0	22	Cork, W.R.	West Carbery (W.D.)	Kilmoe	Skull	II.	145
6, 11	Knockatavy	109	1	2	Louth	Upper Dundalk	Louth	Dundalk	I.	179
37	Knockataylor	47	1	8	Wexford	Shelmaliere West	Ardcandrisk	Wexford	I.	332
17	Knockateane	125	2	34	Cavan	Tullygarvey	Drumgoon	Cootehill	III.	88
15, 20, 21	Knockatee	52	2	14	Cavan	Upper Loughtee	Castleterra	Cavan	III.	83
32, 40, 41	Knockatee	668	3	12	Kerry	Trughanacmy	Ballincuslane	Tralee	II.	206
12	Knockatee	289	0	3	Westmeath	Corkaree	Taghmon	Mullingar	I.	264
12	Knockatee	7	0	39	Westmeath	Corkaree	Tyfarnham	Mullingar	I.	264
20	Knockateean	276	1	8	Leitrim	Drumahaire	Inishmagrath	Manorhamilton	IV.	96
5, 17	Knockatee East	194	0	20	Galway	Dunmore	Dunmore	Tuam	IV.	34
31	Knockateemore	155	0	12	Waterford	Decies without Drum	Dungarvan	Dungarvan	II.	355
15	Knockateery	207	1	12	Cavan	Tullygarvey	Annagh	Cavan	III.	87
5, 17	Knockatee West	286	2	17	Galway	Dunmore	Dunmore	Tuam	IV.	34
41	Knockateggal	270	3	21	Fermanagh	Knockninny	Tomregan	Lisnaskea	III.	203
39	Knockatelly	129	2	34	Sligo	Corran	Drumrat	Boyle	IV.	226
39, 43	Knockatemple	497	3	9	Cavan	Castlerahan	Munterconnaught	Oldcastle	III.	71
33	Knockatemple	138	1	14	Clare	Inchiquin	Kilnamona	Ennis	II.	27
70, 71	Knockatemple	299	1	3	Mayo	Gallen	Kildacommoge	Castlebar	IV.	148
18	Knockatemple	449	0	30	Wicklow	Newcastle	Calary	Rathdrum	I.	350
90	Knockatemple or Drum	208	0	9b	Mayo	Carra	Drum	Castlebar	IV.	128
18	Knockatermon	104	2	25	Clare	Inchiquin	Kilkeedy	Corrofin	II.	26
1, 2, 5, 6	Knockatillane	579	3	36	Wicklow	Lower Talbotstown	Kilbride	Naas	I.	361
30	Knockatinnole	150	2	7	Mayo	Tirawley	Ballysakeery	Ballina	IV.	165
43	Knockatinty	208	0	2c	Clare	Tulla Lower	Clonlea	Tulla	II.	35
29	Knockatippaun	140	1	12d	Kildare	Naas South	Brannockstown	Naas	I.	64
35, 43	Knockatloe	134	3	37e	Clare	Tulla Lower	Clonlea	Tulla	II.	35
121	Knockatlowig	312	0	26	Cork, W.R.	Ibane and Barryroe	Castleventry	Clonakilty	II.	148
18	Knockatober	220	1	7	Louth	Ardee	Cappoge	Ardee	I.	171
102	Knockatober	199	0	24	Mayo	Clanmorris	Kilcolman	Claremorris	IV.	134
21	Knockatober	102	0	31	Sligo	Tirerrill	Kilross	Sligo	IV.	241
18	Knockatober	441	3	8	Wexford	Bantry	Killann	Enniscorthy	I.	300
71	Knockatober or Pollboy	268	0	38	Galway	Tiaquin	Monivea	Tuam	IV.	79
85, 97	Knockatogher	679	2	21	Galway	Athenry	Kiltullagh	Loughrea	IV.	5
38, 43	Knockatomcoyle	1,132	2	34	Wicklow	Shillelagh	Mullinacuff	Shillelagh	I.	358
133	Knockatoo	251	1	19f	Galway	Kiltartan	Beagh	Gort	IV.	46
4	Knockatooan	641	3	8	Cork, E.R.	Duhallow	Clonfert	Kanturk	II.	68
133	Knockatoo Mountain	95	0	16	Galway	Kiltartan	Beagh	Gort	IV.	46
99	Knockatoor	312	0	30	Cork, E.R.	Kinalea	Kilpatrick	Kinsale	II.	95
96	Knockatoor	126	3	33	Galway	Dunkellin	Killeeneen	Loughrea	IV.	30
60	Knockatoor	66	3	32	Tipperary, S.R.	Clanwilliam	Relickmurry & Athassel	Tipperary	II.	310
35	Knockatoor	155	1	27	Waterford	Decies within Drum	Ardmore	Youghal	II.	350
33, 39	Knockatoora Commons	122	1	32	Tipperary, N.R.	Kilnamanagh Upper	Upperchurch	Thurles	II.	280
35, 43	Knockatooreen	405	0	35g	Clare	Tulla Lower	Clonlea	Tulla	II.	35
49	Knockatooreen	427	1	38	Tipperary, S.R.	Slievardagh	Kilcooly	Urlingford	II.	334
33, 37	Knockatore	279	2	2	Kilkenny	Ida	The Rower	New Ross	I.	104
100	Knockatotaun	173	2	5	Mayo	Carra	Rosslee	Ballinrobe	IV.	130
118, 121	Knockatotaun	38	2	39	Mayo	Kilmaine	Kilmainemore	Ballinrobe	IV.	156
25, 32	Knockatotaun	273	3	27	Sligo	Leyny	Killoran	Tobercurry	IV.	230
20	Knockatouk	181	1	36	Waterford	Coshmore&Coshbride	Lismore & Mocollop	Lismore	II.	346
6	Knockatoumpane	356	3	5	Cork, E.R.	Duhallow	Tullylease	Kanturk	II.	76
28	Knockatrasnane	518	1	3	Cork, E.R.	Condons&Clangibbon	Leitrim	Fermoy	II.	62
84, 85	Knockatreenane	237	2	30	Cork, E.R.	East Muskerry	Desertmore	Bandon	II.	102
5	Knockatrellane	174	1	15	Waterford	Glenahiry	Kilronan	Clonmel	II.	366
67	Knockattigan	87	3	21	Cork, E.R.	Imokilly	Youghal	Youghal	II.	91
11, 12	Knockattin	190	2	31	Louth	Upper Dundalk	Louth	Dundalk	I.	179
21	Knockatudor	224	3	3	Cavan	Tullygarvey	Larah	Cootehill	III.	91
23	Knockatullaghaun	381	2	35	Clare	Corcomroe	Clooney	Ennistimon	II.	18

(a) Including 4A. 2R. 32P. water.　　　　(d) Including 7A. 1R. 3P. water.　　　　(f) Including 22A. 2R. 2P. water.
(b) Including 0A. 1R. 32P. water.　　　　(e) Including 4A. 1R. 24P. water.　　　　(g) Including 54A. 0R. 7P. water.
(c) Including 41A. 2R. 28P. water.

No. of Sheet of the Ordnance Survey Maps.	Townlands and Towns.	Area in Statute Acres.			County.	Barony.	Parish.	Poor Law Union in 1857.	Townland Census of 1851, Part I.	
		A.	R.	P.					Vol.	Page
40	Knockatunna . .	852	2	17	Clare . .	Islands . . .	Kilmaley . .	Ennis . .	II.	31
12	Knockatunna . .	218	0	34a	Clare . .	Tulla Upper . .	Feakle . . .	Tulla . .	II.	39
13	Knockaturly . .	362	3	0b	Monaghan .	Monaghan . .	Monaghan . .	Monaghan .	III.	277
7, 15	Knockaturnory .	843	1	22	Waterford .	Upperthird . .	Mothel . . .	Carrick on Suir	II.	371
44	Knockauduff . .	215	1	9	Cork, E.R. .	Barrymore . .	Rathcormack . .	Fermoy . .	II.	57
28	Knockaulin . .	300	0	1	Kildare . .	Kilcullen . .	Kilcullen . .	Naas . .	I.	58
51	Knockaun . .	121	2	8	Clare . .	Bunratty Lower .	Clonloghan . .	Ennis . .	II.	3
51	Knockaun . .	142	1	18	Clare . .	Bunratty Lower .	Drumline . .	Ennis . .	II.	3
116	Knockaun . .	132	2	6	Galway . .	Leitrim . . .	Ballynakill . .	Loughrea . .	IV.	51
99, 107	Knockaun . .	246	2	7	Galway . .	Longford . .	Abbeygormacan .	Ballinasloe .	IV.	56
7	Knockaun . .	280	1	33	Mayo . .	Tirawley . .	Kilbride . . .	Killala . .	IV.	168
27, 34	Knockaun . .	182	0	3	Sligo . .	Tirerrill . .	Drumcolumb . .	Sligo . .	IV.	238
20	Knockaun . .	132	3	12c	Waterford .	Coshmore&Coshbride	Lismore and Mocollop	Lismore . .	II.	346
30	Knockaun . .	243	2	31	Waterford .	Decies without Drum	Whitechurch . .	Dungarvan .	II.	362
90	Knockaunabroona .	16	2	29	Mayo . .	Clanmorris . .	Mayo . . .	Claremorris .	IV.	135
11	Knockaunabulloga .	359	1	19	Waterford .	Coshmore&Coshbride	Lismore and Mocollop	Lismore . .	II.	346
92	Knockaunacat .	109	2	19d	Mayo . .	Costello . .	Bekan . . .	Claremorris .	IV.	139
44	Knockaunacorrin .	120	2	9	Cork, E.R. .	Barrymore . .	Rathcormack . .	Fermoy . .	II.	57
21	Knockaunacuit .	218	0	27	Waterford .	Coshmore&Coshbride	Lismore and Mocollop	Lismore . .	II.	346
16	Knockaunacurraheen	69	1	15	Kerry .	Clanmaurice . .	Dysert . . .	Listowel . .	II.	169
23	Knockaunagloon .	333	0	2	Waterford .	Decies without Drum	Kilgobnet . .	Dungarvan .	II.	357
91, 101	Knockaunakill .	448	0	37	Mayo . .	Clanmorris . .	Mayo . . .	Claremorris .	IV.	135
43	Knockaunalour .	545	1	31	Cork, E.R. .	Barrymore . .	Ardnageehy . .	Cork . .	II.	50
25	Knockaunanerrigal .	27	1	8	Clare . .	Inchiquin . .	Dysert . . .	Ennis . .	II.	24
33	Knockaunarainy .	158	1	0	Galway . .	Killian . . .	Athleague . .	Mountbellew .	IV.	43
11, 20	Knockaunarast .	267	3	18	Waterford .	Coshmore&Coshbride	Lismore and Mocollop	Lismore . .	II.	346
31, 40	Knockaunatee .	234	0	31	Kerry .	Trughanacmy . .	Castleisland . .	Tralee . .	II.	209
122	Knockaunatouk .	238	2	30	Galway . .	Kiltartan . .	Kilmacduagh . .	Gort . .	IV.	48
20, 29	Knockaunavad .	156	2	3	Limerick .	Connello Lower .	Rathkeale . .	Rathkeale .	II.	229
24	Knockaunavaddreen	432	2	15	Cork, E.R. .	Orrery and Kilmore	Kilmaclenine . .	Mallow . .	II.	109
49	Knockaunavlyman .	56	3	38	Limerick .	Coshlea . . .	Ballingarry . .	Kilmallock .	II.	237
39, 47	Knockaunavoddig .	226	3	1	Limerick .	Connello Upper .	Bruree . .	Kilmallock .	II.	231
23	Knockaunavogga .	70	2	6	Tipperary, N.R.	Ikerrin . . .	Bourney . .	Roscrea . .	II.	274
123	Knockaunawadda .	53	3	18	Galway . .	Kiltartan . .	Kilbeacanty . .	Gort . .	IV.	47
116, 125	Knockaunbaun .	87	1	19	Galway . .	Leitrim . . .	Ballynakill . .	Loughrea . .	IV.	51
116	Knockaunbaun .	100	1	15	Galway . .	Leitrim . . .	Kilteskill . .	Loughrea . .	IV.	55
25	Knockaunbaun .	1,234	2	16	Galway . .	Ross . . .	Ross . . .	Oughterard .	IV.	74
46	Knockaunbaun .	203	0	3	Mayo . .	Tirawley . .	Crossmolina . .	Ballina . .	IV.	166
5	Knockaunbrack .	345	2	10	Galway . .	Ballymoe . .	Dunmore . .	Glennamaddy .	IV.	7
17, 23	Knockaunbrack .	493	2	23	Kerry .	Clanmaurice . .	Duagh . . .	Listowel . .	II.	168
5, 6	Knockaunbrandaun	694	1	36	Waterford .	Decies without Drum	Seskinan . .	Dungarvan .	II.	360
125, 131	Knockauncarragh .	732	1	1	Galway . .	Leitrim . . .	Ballynakill . .	Loughrea . .	IV.	51
58, 71	Knockauncarragh .	370	2	24	Galway . .	Tiaquin . . .	Monivea . .	Tuam . .	IV.	79
59	Knockauncore .	268	0	5	Kerry .	Magunihy . .	Kilcummin . .	Killarney .	II.	201
122, 128	Knockauncoura .	123	0	23e	Galway . .	Kiltartan . .	Kilmacduagh . .	Gort . .	IV.	48
105	Knockauncoura .	132	3	30	Galway . .	Loughrea . .	Kilconickny . .	Loughrea . .	IV.	63
105	Knockauncoura .	28	0	19	Galway . .	Loughrea . .	Loughrea . .	Loughrea . .	IV.	66
83	Knockauncourt .	26	0	20	Tipperary, S.R.	Iffa and Offa East	St. Marys, Clonmel	Clonmel . .	II.	316
32, 41	Knockauncurragh .	1,705	3	5	Kerry .	Trughanacmy . .	Ballincuslane . .	Tralee . .	II.	206
116, 125	Knockaundarragh .	326	2	18	Galway . .	Leitrim . . .	Ballynakill . .	Loughrea . .	IV.	51
21	Knockaunderry .	100	1	0f	Mayo . .	Tirawley . .	Ballysakeery . .	Ballina . .	IV.	165
33	Knockaundoolis .	162	0	17	Limerick .	Coonagh . .	Templebredon .	Tipperary .	II.	236
21	Knockaun East .	121	0	25	Waterford .	Coshmore&Coshbride	Lismore and Mocollop	Lismore . .	II.	346
117	Knockauneevin and Ballywatteen .	367	0	13	Galway . .	Longford . .	Tynagh . .	Portumna .	IV.	62
20	Knockaunfargarve .	135	0	21	Waterford .	Coshmore&Coshbride	Lismore and Mocollop	Lismore . .	II.	346
12	Knockaungarriff .	341	2	31	Waterford .	Coshmore&Coshbride	Lismore and Mocollop	Lismore . .	II.	346
84	Knockaunglass .	29	0	1	Galway . .	Athenry . . .	Athenry . . .	Loughrea . .	IV.	4
63, 64	Knockaunglass .	128	3	1	Kerry .	Iveragh . . .	Killorglin . .	Killarney . .	II.	198
4, 16	Knockaunkeel .	33	2	27	Galway . .	Dunmore . .	Addergoole . .	Tuam . .	IV.	33
21	Knockaunmore .	100	0	18	Kerry .	Clanmaurice . .	O'Dorney . .	Tralee . .	II.	172
93	Knockaunnacarragh	113	0	6	Galway . .	Galway . . .	Rahoon . . .	Galway . .	IV.	38
75	Knockaunnacuddoge	171	1	21	Kerry .	Magunihy . .	Killaha . . .	Killarney . .	II.	202
49	Knockaunnacurraha	235	3	37	Limerick .	Coshlea . . .	Galbally . .	Mitchelstown .	II.	239
17	Knockaunnagat .	232	1	20	Galway . .	Dunmore . .	Dunmore . .	Tuam . .	IV.	34
6	Knockaunnageeha .	131	3	3	Galway . .	Ballymoe . .	Templetogher . .	Glennamaddy .	IV.	9
22	Knockaunnaglokee .	205	0	17	Waterford .	Decies without Drum	Modelligo . .	Dungarvan .	II.	359
38	Knockaunnagoun .	138	3	32	Waterford .	Decies within Drum	Lisgenan or Grange	Youghal . .	II.	352
27	Knockaunnagun .	161	3	19	Limerick .	Shanid . . .	Rathronan . .	Newcastle .	II.	257
125	Knockaunnakirkeen	34	1	3	Galway . .	Leitrim . . .	Ballynakill . .	Loughrea . .	IV.	51
23	Knockaunnanoon .	518	2	37	Kerry .	Clanmaurice . .	Duagh . . .	Listowel . .	II.	168
33	Knockaun North .	258	2	24	Waterford .	Coshmore&Coshbride	Kilwatermoy . .	Lismore . .	II.	343
67, 68	Knockaunranny .	1,356	3	37g	Galway . .	Moycullen . .	Moycullen . .	Galway . .	IV.	71

(a) Including 6A. 1R. 20P. water.
(b) Including 10A. 3R. 30P. water.
(c) Including 2A. 0R. 32P. water.

(d) Including 1A. 1R. 24P. water.
(e) Including 6A. 2R. 23P. water.

(f) Including 2A. 3R. 14P. water.
(g) Including 69A. 1R. 21P. water.

No. of Sheet of the Ordnance Survey Maps.	Townlands and Towns.	Area in Statute Acres. A. R. P.	County.	Barony.	Parish.	Poor Law Union in 1857.	Townland Census of 1851, Part I. Vol.	Page
25	Knockaunroe . .	169 2 8	Clare . .	Inchiquin . .	Dysert . .	Ennis . .	II.	24
10, 17	Knockaunroe . .	472 3 36	Clare . .	Inchiquin . .	Killinaboy . .	Corrofin . .	II.	26
61	Knockaunroe . .	107 3 30	Galway . .	Killian . .	Ahascragh . .	Ballinasloe . .	IV.	43
55, 63	Knockaunroe . .	83 3 14	Kerry . .	Iveragh . .	Killorglin . .	Killarney . .	II.	198
24, 33	Knockaunroe . .	110 0 30	Limerick . .	Coonagh . .	Grean . .	Tipperary . .	II.	235
19	Knockaunroe . .	189 0 11	Waterford .	Coshmore&Coshbride	Leitrim . .	Lismore . .	II.	344
79	Knockaunrory .	78 1 3	Kerry . .	Iveragh . .	Caher . .	Cahersiveen .	II.	194
41	Knockauns . .	133 3 10	Tipperary, N.R.	Eliogarty . .	Thurles . .	Thurles . .	II.	273
6	Knockauns East	219 2 39	Galway . .	Ballymoe . .	Boyounagh .	Glennamaddy .	IV.	6
4	Knockaunsmountain	689 0 33	Clare . .	Burren . .	Killonaghan .	Ballyvaghan .	II.	13
33	Knockaun South	410 2 23	Waterford .	Coshmore&Coshbride	Kilwatermoy .	Lismore . .	II.	343
6	Knockauns West	357 1 36	Galway . .	Ballymoe . .	Boyounagh .	Glennamaddy .	IV.	6
8	Knockaunvickteera .	108 3 29	Clare . .	Burren . .	Kilmoon . .	Ballyvaghan .	II.	13
54	Knockavadagh .	320 0 26	Tipperary, S.R.	Slievardagh .	Killenaule . .	Cashel . .	II.	334
41, 50	Knockavaddra .	1,084 3 5	Cork, E.R.	Duhallow . .	Kilshannig .	Mallow . .	II.	74
38	Knockavaddy .	236 1 2	Tyrone . .	Dungannon Upper .	Desertcreat .	Cookstown .	III.	308
9	Knockavaghig .	176 1 35	Kerry . .	Clanmaurice .	Rattoo . .	Listowel . .	II.	173
12	Knockavallan .	203 2 35	Antrim . .	Lower Dunluce .	Derrykeighan	Ballymoney .	III.	17
17	Knockavallig . .	194 2 20	Kerry . .	Clanmaurice .	Duagh . .	Listowel . .	II.	168
22, 35	Knockavally . .	202 0 38	Galway . .	Ballynahinch .	Omey . .	Clifden . .	IV.	15
22	Knockavally . .	82 3 17	Kilkenny . .	Shillelogher .	Tullaghanbrogue .	Callan . .	I.	116
76, 77	Knockavanloman .	97 1 26a	Mayo . .	Burrishoole .	Kilmeena . .	Westport .	IV.	122
5, 6	Knockavannia .	390 2 31	Waterford .	Decies without Drum	Seskinan . .	Dungarvan .	II.	360
5, 6, 13, 14	Knockavanniamountain .	519 0 18	Waterford .	Decies without Drum	Seskinan . .	Dungarvan .	II.	360
21, 25	Knockavannon .	771 0 37	Armagh . .	Fews Upper .	Ballymyre . .	Newry . .	III.	48
30	Knockavanny . .	173 0 9	Galway . .	Dunmore . .	Tuam . .	Tuam . .	IV.	36
36	Knockavea . .	50 2 15	Fermanagh .	Clankelly . .	Clones . .	Clones . .	III.	196
110	Knockaveale . .	563 1 22	Cork, W.R.	Kinalmeaky .	Ballymodan .	Bandon . .	II.	151
11	Knockaveelish .	1,071 3 28	Waterford .	Coshmore&Coshbride	Lismore and Mocollop	Lismore . .	II.	346
68	Knockaveely Glebe .	15 1 6	Mayo . .	Burrishoole .	Burrishoole .	Newport . .	IV.	119
18	Knockavegan . .	244 2 28	Longford .	Moydow . .	Kilcommock .	Ballymahon .	I.	161
18, 27	Knockavelish .	364 0 36	Waterford .	Gaultiere . .	Killea . .	Waterford .	II.	363
67	Knockaverry . .	112 2 5	Cork, E.R.	Imokilly . .	Youghal . .	Youghal . .	II.	91
59, 72	Knockavilla . .	256 0 28	Galway . .	Tiaquin . .	Killoscobe .	Mountbellew .	IV.	78
61	Knockavilla . .	141 3 37	Mayo . .	Gallen . .	Meelick . .	Swineford .	IV.	150
52, 60	Knockavilla . .	132 0 12	Tipperary, S.R.	Kilnamanagh Lower	Oughterleague .	Cashel . .	II.	324
29	Knockavilla . .	106 0 11	Wexford . .	Bantry . .	St. Mary's .	New Ross .	I.	302
26, 27	Knockaville . .	809 1 22b	Westmeath .	Farbill . .	Killucan . .	Mullingar .	I.	267
21, 22	Knockavilra or Fountainhill .	143 0 11	Galway . .	Ballynahinch .	Omey . .	Clifden, . .	IV.	15
29, 30	Knockavinnane .	136 2 6	Kerry . .	Trughanacmy .	Ballymacelligott	Tralee . .	II.	207
9	Knockavoarheen .	252 0 7	Clare . .	Burren . .	Noughaval .	Ballyvaghan .	II.	13
15	Knockavocka . .	213 0 25	Wexford . .	Gorey . .	Kilcormick .	Enniscorthy .	I.	317
133	Knockavoher . .	282 2 11	Cork, W.R.	East Carbery (W.D.)	Kilmacabea .	Skibbereen .	II.	133
25	Knockavolis . .	392 0 24c	Monaghan .	Cremorne . .	Clontibret .	Castleblayney .	III.	260
21	Knockavoreen .	408 0 25	Cork, E.R.	Duhallow . .	Kilmeen . .	Kanturk . .	II.	73
47, 57	Knockavota . .	355 3 39	Kerry . .	Trughanacmy .	Kilcolman .	Killarney . .	II.	210
7	Knockavota . .	170 1 12	Wexford . .	Gorey . .	Kilcavan . .	Gorey . .	I.	317
11	Knockavreaneen .	68 3 5	Roscommon .	Ballintober North	Kilmore . .	Carrick on Shannon	IV.	187
13, 18	Knockavrinnin .	288 0 0	Antrim . .	Upper Dunluce .	Loughguile .	Ballymoney .	III.	20
5	Knockavroe . .	232 3 36	Roscommon .	Boyle . .	Boyle . .	Boyle . .	IV.	194
43	Knockavrogeen East	290 1 38	Kerry . .	Corkaguiny .	Kildrum . .	Dingle . .	II.	177
43	Knockavrogeen West	291 2 1	Kerry . .	Corkaguiny .	Kildrum . .	Dingle . .	II.	177
70	Knockavrony . .	170 2 3	Mayo . .	Gallen . .	Kildacommoge .	Castlebar .	IV.	148
55	Knockavuddig .	190 0 19	Cork, E.R.	Barrymore .	Clonmult . .	Middleton .	II.	53
71, 72	Knockavullig .	465 0 4	Cork, E.R.	East Muskerry .	Cannaway, .	Macroom .	II.	102
20, 28	Knockavurra Glebe	115 1 8	Kerry . .	Clanmaurice .	Ardfert . .	Tralee . .	II.	167
36	Knockavurrea .	29 1 9	Roscommon .	Ballintober South	Kilgefin . .	Roscommon .	IV.	189
22	Knockavurrea .	122 3 11	Roscommon .	Roscommon .	Elphin . .	Strokestown .	IV.	209
27, 32	Knockavurrig .	187 0 6	Wicklow . .	Upper Talbotstown	Kiltegan . .	Baltinglass .	I.	365
84	Knockawaddra .	228 3 10	Cork, E.R.	East Muskerry .	Kilbonane .	Bandon . .	II.	104
121	Knockawaddra .	455 1 36d	Cork, W.R.	East Carbery (W.D.)	Kilmeen . .	Dunmanway .	II.	134
29	Knockawaddra East	111 1 21	Kerry . .	Trughanacmy .	Ratass . .	Tralee . .	II.	213
29	Knockawaddra Middle	88 2 36	Kerry . .	Trughanacmy .	Ratass . .	Tralee . .	II.	213
29	Knockawaddra West	174 2 4	Kerry . .	Trughanacmy .	Ratass . .	Tralee . .	II.	213
35, 40	Knockawaddy .	107 1 32	Fermanagh .	Clankelly . .	Clones . .	Clones . .	III.	196
8, 9	Knockawalky . .	70 2 5	Longford .	Longford . .	Templemichael .	Longford .	I.	160
15	Knockawillin . .	604 2 26	Cork, E.R. .	Duhallow . .	Clonfert . .	Kanturk . .	II.	68
5, 6	Knockawillin . .	479 1 8	Cork, E.R. .	Duhallow . .	Tullylease .	Kanturk . .	II.	76
32	Knockawinna . .	905 1 21	Kerry . .	Trughanacmy .	Brosna , .	Tralee . .	II.	202
95, 103	Knockawuddy .	67 0 0	Galway . .	Dunkellin . .	Ballynacourty .	Galway . .	IV.	27
76	Knockballagh .	104 2 24e	Mayo . .	Burrishoole .	Kilmeena . .	Westport .	IV.	122

(a) Including 7A. 1R. 12P. water.
(b) Including 17A. 2R. 10P. water.
(c) Including 9A. 0R. 3P. water.
(d) Including 4A. 3R. 24P. water.
(e) Including 0A. 2R. 3P. water.

No. of Sheet of the Ordnance Survey Maps.	Townlands and Towns.	Area in Statute Acres.	County.	Barony.	Parish.	Poor Law Union in 1857.	Townland Census of 1851, Part I.	
		A. R. P.					Vol.	Page
88, 91	Knockballiniry	741 0 4	Tipperary, S.R.	Iffa and Offa West	Ballybacon	Clogheen	II.	317
18	Knockballyboy	1,476 0 17	King's Co.	Geashill	Geashill	Tullamore	I.	140
113	Knockballyclery	83 3 36	Galway	Dunkellin	Killeenavarra	Gort	IV.	30
24	Knockballyfookeen	433 0 30	Limerick	Coonagh	Oola	Tipperary	II.	236
66, 73	Knockballymaloogh	280 1 25	Tipperary, S.R.	Clanwilliam	Clonbeg	Tipperary	II.	305
15,16,23,24	Knockballymartin	327 0 19	Cork, E.R.	Duhallow	Kilbrin	Kanturk	II.	72
63	Knockballynameath	107 2 8	Clare	Bunratty Lower	St. Patricks	Limerick	II.	7
67	Knockballynoe East	229 3 16	Tipperary, S.R.	Clanwilliam	Kilteakle	Tipperary	II.	308
67	Knockballynoe West	80 1 4	Tipperary, S.R.	Clanwilliam	Kilfeakle	Tipperary	II.	308
5, 6	Knockballyroney	796 3 14	Monaghan	Monaghan	Tedavnet	Monaghan	III.	279
9	Knockballystine	405 3 26	Carlow	Rathvilly	Clonmore	Shillelagh	I.	10
16	Knockballyvishteal	741 1 28	Galway	Dunmore	Dunmore	Tuam	IV.	34
15, 19	Knockbane	222 3 11	Armagh	Tiranny	Tynan	Armagh	III.	60
100, 104	Knockbane	125 3 10	Donegal	Tirhugh	Drumhome	Donegal	III.	146
68	Knockbane	241 3 5a	Galway	Moycullen	Moycullen	Galway	IV.	71
40	Knockbane	113 2 31	Kildare	Kilkea and Moone	Castledermot	Carlow	I.	59
46	Knockbane	84 1 14	King's Co.	Clonlisk	Borrisnafarney	Roscrea	I.	129
1	Knockbane	103 0 32	Wicklow	Lower Talbotstown	Kilbride	Naas	I.	361
106	Knockbaron	278 1 18	Galway	Leitrim	Kilmeen	Loughrea	IV.	54
17	Knockbarragh	328 1 0	Carlow	Forth	Barragh	Carlow	I.	4
51	Knockbarragh	921 1 0	Down	Upper Iveagh,Up. pt.	Kilbroney	Kilkeel	III.	175
31, 36	Knockbarron	1,328 1 33b	King's Co.	Eglish	Drumcullen	Parsonstown	I.	134
25	Knockbarron North	54 2 28c	Kilkenny	Gowran	Ullard	Thomastown	I.	100
25, 29	Knockbarron South	156 1 0d	Kilkenny	Gowran	Ullard	Thomastown	I.	100
16, 17	Knockbarry	330 0 23	Cork, E.R.	Orrery and Kilmore	Buttevant	Mallow	II.	107
16	Knockbarry	635 1 10	Cork, E.R.	Orrery and Kilmore	Liscarroll	Mallow	II.	109
71, 84	Knockbaun	214 0 31	Galway	Athenry	Athenry	Galway	IV.	4
22	Knockbaun	99 1 37	Galway	Ballynahinch	Omey	Clifden	IV.	15
115	Knockbaun	51 2 11	Galway	Loughrea	Killeenadeema	Loughrea	IV.	64
55	Knockbaun	77 1 38	Galway	Moycullen	Kilcummin	Oughterard	IV.	67
90	Knockbaun	151 2 39	Mayo	Carra	Drum	Castlebar	IV.	128
68, 69	Knockbaun	306 0 7	Mayo	Carra	Islandeady	Castlebar	IV.	129
92	Knockbaun	161 2 21	Mayo	Clanmorris	Knock	Claremorris	IV.	135
29	Knockbaun	156 2 13	Mayo	Tirawley	Crossmolina	Ballina	IV.	166
24,25,30,31	Knockbaun	1,042 0 36	Queen's Co.	Cullenagh	Dysartgallen	Abbeyleix	I.	239
19	Knockbaun	250 1 32	Waterford	Coshmore&Coshbride	Lismore and Mocollop	Lismore	II.	346
27	Knockbaun	68 3 38	Wexford	Ballaghkeen	Castle-ellis	Enniscorthy	I.	293
3	Knockbaun	106 2 31	Wexford	Gorey	Inch	Gorey	I.	316
11	Knockbaun & Knocknabranagh	711 3 35	Carlow	Idrone West	Oldleighlin	Carlow	I.	9
7	Knockbawn	78 2 3	Wicklow	Rathdown	Powerscourt	Rathdown	I.	356
21	Knockbawn	155 1 38	Wicklow	Upper Talbotstown	Freynestown	Baltinglass	I.	364
14, 20	Knock Beg	614 0 20	Fermanagh	Magheraboy	Devenish	Enniskillen	III.	211
120	Knockbeg	56 3 36	Mayo	Kilmaine	Cong	Ballinrobe	IV.	154
32	Knockbeg	228 2 38e	Queen's Co.	Slievemargy	Sleaty	Carlow	I.	246
26	Knockbeg East	249 2 36	Sligo	Tirerrill	Ballysadare	Sligo	IV.	237
26	Knockbeg West	449 1 37f	Sligo	Tirerrill	Ballysadare	Sligo	IV.	237
20	Knockbeha	886 2 6	Clare	Tulla Upper	Feakle	Scarriff	II.	39
13, 20	Knockbeha Mountain	466 3 38	Clare	Tulla Upper	Feakle	Scarriff	II.	39
41, 46	Knockbine	205 0 0	Wexford	Bargy	Ambrosetown	Wexford	I.	304
29	Knockbodaly	161 0 24g	Kilkenny	Gowran	Graiguenamanagh	Thomastown	I.	95
32, 37	Knockbodarra	117 1 16	Fermanagh	Clanawley	Kinawley	Enniskillen	III.	194
7, 12	Knockbody	336 3 21	Westmeath	Corkaree	Stonehall	Mullingar	I.	263
88	Knockboghil	69 3 8	Cork, E.R.	Imokilly	Titeskin	Middleton	II.	90
7	Knockboha	252 1 35	Mayo	Tirawley	Lackan	Killala	IV.	171
70	Knockboordan	163 2 19	Tipperary, S.R.	Middlethird	Fethard	Cashel	II.	327
28	Knockbounce	158 1 24	Kildare	Kilcullen	Kilcullen	Naas	I.	58
12	Knockbower	209 0 18	Carlow	Carlow	Tullowmagimma	Carlow	I.	2
28, 33	Knockboy	589 3 25	Antrim	Lower Antrim	Skerry	Ballymena	III.	5
4	Knockboy	431 0 27	Carlow	Rathvilly	Rathvilly	Baltinglass	I.	12
52	Knockboy	533 3 24	Cork, E.R.	Barrymore	Dunbulloge	Cork	II.	54
83	Knockboy	200 2 36	Cork, W.R.	West Muskerry	Kilmurry	Macroom	II.	159
34, 35	Knockboy	110 1 1	Fermanagh	Clankelly	Galloon	Lisnaskea	III.	198
63, 64, 77	Knockboy	914 2 0	Galway	Ballynahinch	Moyrus	Clifden	IV.	13
67	Knockboy	37 0 36	Mayo	Burrishoole	Burrishoole	Newport	IV.	119
77	Knockboy	109 1 22	Mayo	Burrishoole	Kilmeena	Westport	IV.	122
90, 100	Knockboy	146 0 35	Mayo	Carra	Drum	Castlebar	IV.	128
10	Knockboy	34 0 21	Monaghan	Monaghan	Tehallan	Monaghan	III.	280
49	Knockboy	151 0 18	Tipperary, S.R.	Slievardagh	Buolick	Urlingford	II.	332
12	Knockboy	492 1 23	Waterford	Coshmore&Coshbride	Lismore and Mocollop	Lismore	II.	346
31	Knockboy	27 2 10	Waterford	Decies without Drum	Dungarvan	Dungarvan	II.	355
13	Knockboy	752 0 20	Waterford	Decies without Drum	Seskinan	Dungarvan	II.	360
18	Knockboy	228 0 0	Waterford	Gaultiere	Ballygunner	Waterford	II.	362

(a) Including 59A. 1R. 8P. water.
(b) Including 34A. 2R. 35P. water.
(c) Including 3A. 2R. 30P. River Barrow.
(d) Including 4A. 0R. 26P. River Barrow.
(e) Including 9A. 2R. 4P. River Barrow.
(f) Including 13A. 3R. 12P. water.
(g) Including 5A. 3R. 6P. River Barrow.
(h) Including 61A. 3R. 3P. water.

No. of Sheet of the Ordnance Survey Maps.	Townlands and Towns.	Area in Statute Acres.			County.	Barony.	Parish.	Poor Law Union in 1857.	Townland Census of 1851, Part I.	
		A.	R.	P.					Vol.	Page
5, 9	Knockbrack	320	0	32a	Antrim	Cary	Culfeightrin	Ballycastle	III.	13
17	Knockbrack	377	2	38	Carlow	Forth	Myshall	Carlow	I.	5
15	Knockbrack	83	2	22	Clare	Corcomroe	Kilmanaheen	Ennistimon	II.	21
31	Knockbrack	246	2	15	Clare	Ibrickan	Kilfarboy	Ennistimon	II.	22
31, 40	Knockbrack	606	3	5	Cork, E.R.	Duhallow	Dromtarriff	Kanturk	II.	71
17	Knockbrack	103	1	32	Cork, E.R.	Fermoy	Doneraile	Mallow	II.	78
33,34,42,43	Knockbrack	1,286	1	13	Cork, E.R.	Fermoy	Rahan	Mallow	II.	82
17, 18	Knockbrack	226	2	33	Donegal	Kilmacrenan	Clondavaddog	Millford	III.	125
61	Knockbrack	447	2	7	Donegal	Raphoe	Leck	Letterkenny	III.	140
4	Knockbrack	303	0	20b	Dublin	Balrothery West	Hollywood	Balrothery	I.	23
22	Knockbrack	195	1	33	Galway	Ballynahinch	Omey	Clifden	IV.	15
86	Knockbrack	34	1	15	Galway	Kilconnell	Killaan	Ballinasloe	IV.	41
117, 126	Knockbrack	83	1	29	Galway	Leitrim	Tynagh	Portumna	IV.	55
71	Knockbrack	665	0	26	Galway	Tiaquin	Monivea	Loughrea	IV.	79
15, 21	Knockbrack	127	2	2	Kerry	Clanmaurice	Kilmoyly	Tralee	II.	171
38, 47	Knockbrack	704	3	15	Kerry	Magunihy	Molahiffe	Killarney	II.	205
23, 24, 31	Knockbrack	1,328	3	14	Kerry	Trughanacmy	Brosna	Tralee	II.	208
28	Knockbrack	42	3	39	Kilkenny	Gowran	Woolengrange	Thomastown	I.	100
40	Knockbrack	556	1	21	Kilkenny	Ida	Kilcolumb	Waterford	I.	102
44	Knockbrack	144	3	20	King's Co.	Clonlisk	Templeharry	Roscrea	I.	132
1	Knockbrack	23	0	35	Leitrim	Rosclogher	Rossinver	Ballyshannon	IV.	111
42, 43	Knockbrack	992	1	24c	Limerick	Glenquin	Abbeyfeale	Newcastle	II.	244
22	Knockbrack	488	2	7	Londonderry	Tirkeeran	Clondermot	Londonderry	III.	248
77, 88	Knockbrack	242	0	14d	Mayo	Burrishoole	Aghagower	Westport	IV.	118
101	Knockbrack	23	2	25	Mayo	Clanmorris	Tagheen	Claremorris	IV.	136
93, 103	Knockbrack	311	2	33	Mayo	Costello	Annagh	Claremorris	IV.	138
72	Knockbrack	126	3	23	Mayo	Costello	Kilmovee	Swineford	IV.	142
71	Knockbrack	121	1	12	Mayo	Gallen	Kilconduff	Swineford	IV.	148
37, 38	Knockbrack	410	3	2	Mayo	Tirawley	Crossmolina	Ballina	IV.	166
9, 15	Knockbrack	223	0	11	Meath	Fore	Loughcrew	Oldcastle	I.	201
16, 22	Knockbrack	326	2	6	Queen's Co.	Upperwoods	Offerlane	Abbeyleix	I.	252
39	Knockbrack	274	2	24	Sligo	Corran	Drumrat	Boyle	IV.	226
36	Knockbrack	643	1	15	Sligo	Leyney	Kilmacteige	Tobercurry	IV.	231
22	Knockbrack	293	1	29	Sligo	Tireragh	Castleconor	Dromore West	IV.	232
34	Knockbrack	109	3	13	Tipperary, N.R.	Kilnamanagh Upper	Glenkeen	Thurles	II.	278
21	Knockbrack	169	2	25	Tipperary, N.R.	Upper Ormond	Kilkeary	Nenagh	II.	290
70	Knockbrack	69	2	19	Tipperary, S.R.	Middlethird	Fethard	Cashel	II.	327
52	Knockbrack	87	0	15	Tyrone	Clogher	Errigal Keerogue	Clogher	III.	295
16	Knockbrack	102	1	27e	Tyrone	Omagh West	Ardstraw	Castlederg	III.	315
37, 38	Knockbrack	214	0	4	Waterford	Decies within Drum	Kinsalebeg	Youghal	II.	352
31	Knockbrack	34	3	27	Waterford	Decies without Drum	Dungarvan	Dungarvan	II.	355
42	Knockbrack	54	3	33	Wexford	Bargy	Kilmannan	Wexford	I.	306
2	Knockbrack	172	1	25	Wexford	Gorey	Kilnahue	Gorey	I.	319
21	Knockbrack East	75	1	30	Kerry	Clanmaurice	Kilflyn	Tralee	II.	170
6	Knockbrack East	173	1	3	Limerick	Clanwilliam	Killeenagarriff	Limerick	II.	224
6	Knockbrack East	16	0	30	Limerick	Clanwilliam	Stradbally	Limerick	II.	226
53	Knockbrack Lower	167	1	27	Clare	Tulla Lower	Kiltenanlea	Limerick	II.	37
62	Knockbrack or Trouthill	200	1	6	Mayo	Costello	Kilbeagh	Swineford	IV.	141
53	Knockbrack Upper	157	1	10	Clare	Tulla Lower	Kiltenanlea	Limerick	II.	37
21, 22	Knockbrack West	261	2	27	Kerry	Clanmaurice	Kilflyn	Tralee	II.	170
6	Knockbrack West	31	0	12	Limerick	Clanwilliam	Killeenagarriff	Limerick	II.	224
6	Knockbrack West	23	3	24	Limerick	Clanwilliam	Stradbally	Limerick	II.	226
6	Knockbrandon Lower	351	2	12	Wexford	Gorey	Rossminoge	Gorey	I.	321
6	Knockbrandon Upper	357	0	1	Wexford	Gorey	Rossminoge	Gorey	I.	321
67	Knockbreaga	146	3	37	Mayo	Burrishoole	Burrishoole	Newport	IV.	119
9	Knockbreckan	589	1	6	Down	Castlereagh Upper	Drumbo	Lisburn	III.	164
9	Knockbreckan	184	2	12	Down	Castlereagh Upper	Knockbreda	Lisburn	III.	165
27, 34	Knockbreenagher	288	0	32	Sligo	Tirerrill	Drumcolumb	Sligo	IV.	238
23, 28	Knockbride	386	0	30f	Cavan	Clankee	Knockbride	Bailieborough	III.	74
13, 14	Knockbrien	74	1	7	Limerick	Clanwilliam	Cahernarry	Limerick	II.	223
61, 62	Knockbrit	298	1	13	Tipperary, S.R.	Middlethird	Magorban	Cashel	II.	328
41	Knockbroad	78	0	34	Wexford	Shelmaliere West	Coolstuff	Wexford	I.	333
110	Knockbrogan	232	2	11	Cork, W.R.	Kinalmeaky	Kilbrogan	Bandon	II.	152
110, 123	Knockbrown	312	0	3	Cork, W.R.	East Carbery (E.D.)	Kilbrittain	Bandon	II.	128
110, 123	Knockbrown	510	0	11	Cork, W.R.	East Carbery (E.D.)	Kilmaloda	Bandon	II.	129
60	Knockbulloge	62	3	25	Tipperary, S.R.	Middlethird	St. Patricksrock	Cashel	II.	331
85	Knockburden	231	0	19	Cork, E.R.	East Muskerry	Kilnaglory	Cork	II.	104
16	Knockburrane	365	1	1	Kerry	Clanmaurice	Kilfeighny	Listowel	II.	170
30	Knockbutton	58	3	25	Kilkenny	Kells	Coolaghmore	Callan	I.	108
19, 28	Knockbweeheen	301	1	11	Limerick	Shanid	Kilcolman	Glin	II.	255
99, 99	Knockcahill	231	3	33g	Cork, E.R.	Duhallow	Dromtarriff	Millstreet	II.	71
59	Knockcairn	863	2	35	Antrim	Upper Massereene	Tullyrusk	Lisburn	III.	31

(a) Including 5A. 3R. 16P. water.
(b) Including 0A. 2R. 28P. detached portion.
(c) Including 11A. 3R. 4P. water.
(d) Including 7A. 3R. 8P. water.
(e) Including 3A. 0R. 24P. water.
(f) Including 25A. 3R. 20P. water.
(g) Including 2A. 3R. 32P. water.

No. of Sheet of the Ordnance Survey Maps.	Townlands and Towns.	Area in Statute Acres.			County.	Barony.	Parish.	Poor Law Union in 1857.	Townland Census of 1851, Part I.	
		A.	R.	P.					Vol.	Page
19	Knockclonagad	776	2	11	Carlow	Idrone East	Sliguff	Carlow	I.	8
15	Knockcloona	114	0	14	Cork, E.R.	Duhallow	Knocktemple	Kanturk	II.	75
58, 60	Knockcommane	293	0	28	Limerick	Coshlea	Kilbeheny	Mitchelstown	II.	239
26	Knockcommon	326	1	3	Meath	Lower Duleek	Knockcommon	Navan	I.	196
3	Knockconan	18	3	4	Monaghan	Trough	Errigal Trough	Monaghan	III.	284
52	Knockcoolkeare	675	3	15	Limerick	Glenquin	Killeedy	Kanturk	II.	246
3, 8	Knockcor	547	0	13	Kildare	Carbury	Mylerstown	Edenderry	I.	52
6	Knockcor	65	3	6	Louth	Upper Dundalk	Dunbin	Dundalk	I.	178
17	Knockcor	221	0	22a	Monaghan	Dartree	Aghabog	Cootehill	III.	263
6	Knockcor	130	0	16	Monaghan	Monaghan	Tedavnet	Monaghan	III.	279
23	Knockcorragh	131	0	4	Limerick	Clanwilliam	Caherelly	Limerick	II.	222
11, 20	Knockcorragh	375	0	35	Waterford	Coshmore&Coshbride	Lismore and Mocollop	Lismore	II.	346
71, 72	Knockcorrandoo	215	1	14	Galway	Tiaquin	Moylough	Tuam	IV.	80
42	Knockcroghery	217	2	28	Roscommon	Athlone	Killinvoy	Roscommon	IV.	182
42	KNOCKCROGHERY T.	—			Roscommon	Athlone	Killinvoy	Roscommon	IV.	182
37	Knockcumshin	24	2	38	Wexford	Shelmaliere West	Carrick	Wexford	I.	332
14	Knockcurlan	56	1	11	Louth	Ardee	Ardee	Ardee	I.	171
41	Knockcurra	60	1	38	Tipperary, N.R.	Eliogarty	Thurles	Thurles	II.	273
39	Knockcurraghbola Commons	821	1	19	Tipperary, N.R.	Kilnamanagh Upper	Upperchurch	Thurles	II.	280
39	Knockcurraghbola Crownlands	153	1	37	Tipperary, N.R.	Kilnamanagh Upper	Upperchurch	Thurles	II.	281
8, 12	Knockdav	169	1	27	Kilkenny	Galmoy	Fertagh	Urlingford	I.	92
24, 33	Knockderk	412	0	3	Limerick	Coonagh	Grean	Tipperary	II.	235
18	Knockdinnin	224	2	1	Louth	Ardee	Dromin	Ardee	I.	172
70	Knockdoebeg East	261	0	6	Galway	Clare	Lackagh	Galway	IV.	23
70	Knockdoebeg West	554	0	38	Galway	Clare	Lackagh	Galway	IV.	23
70	Knockdoemore	269	1	30	Galway	Clare	Claregalway	Galway	IV.	18
70	Knockdoemore	330	2	1	Galway	Clare	Lackagh	Galway	IV.	23
30	Knockdomny	687	1	19	Westmeath	Clonlonan	Ballyloughloe	Athlone	I.	260
53	Knockdonagh	265	1	18	Clare	Tulla Lower	O'Briensbridge	Limerick	II.	38
20	Knockdoo	287	0	39	Wicklow	Upper Talbotstown	Ballynure	Baltinglass	I.	362
35	Knockdoocunna	182	0	13	Clare	Tulla Upper	Tulla	Tulla	II.	42
59,60,67,68	Knockdoorah	755	2	37	Kerry	Magunihy	Kilcummin	Killarney	II.	201
17	Knockdoorish	290	2	2	Carlow	Forth	Barragh	Carlow	I.	4
34, 43	Knockdoorty	358	2	2	Cork, E.R.	Barrymore	Ardnageehy	Fermoy	II.	50
40,41,49,50	Knockdown	658	0	1	Kerry	Trughanacmy	Ballincuslane	Tralee	II.	206
27	Knockdown	1,076	3	19	Limerick	Shanid	Kilmoylan	Glin	II.	256
17, 20	Knockdramagh	424	0	30	Carlow	Forth	Myshall	Carlow	I.	5
3, 4	Knockdrin	1,221	3	36	King's Co.	Warrenstown	Castlejordan	Edenderry	I.	145
12	Knockdrin	71	2	25	Westmeath	Corkaree	Taghmon	Mullingar	I.	264
12	Knockdrin	58	0	22	Westmeath	Corkaree	Tyfarnham	Mullingar	I.	264
12, 19	Knockdrin	920	1	34b	Westmeath	Moyashel and Magheradernon	Rathconnell	Mullingar	I.	276
12, 19	Knockdrin Demesne	68	2	33c	Westmeath	Moyashel and Magheradernon	Mullingar	Mullingar	I.	275
41	Knockdrislagh	383	0	19	Cork, E.R.	Duhallow	Kilshannig	Mallow	II.	74
36	Knockdromaclogh	360	3	31	Cork, E.R.	Condons&Clangibbon	Castlelyons	Fermoy	II.	60
36	Knockdromaclogh	282	3	34	Cork, E.R.	Condons&Clangibbon	Clondulane	Fermoy	II.	60
20	Knockdromin	101	3	35	Limerick	Connello Lower	Cappagh	Rathkeale	II.	227
20	Knockdromin	148	2	17	Limerick	Connello Lower	Clonshire	Rathkeale	II.	227
142	Knockdrum	29	1	20	Cork, W.R.	West Carbery (E.D.)	Castlehaven	Skibbereen	II.	138
42	Knockdrumdonnell	82	3	30	Roscommon	Athlone	Kilmeane	Roscommon	IV.	182
35	Knockdrumleague	87	2	17	Clare	Tulla Upper	Tulla	Tulla	II.	42
23	Knockdrummagh North	99	2	3	Clare	Corcomroe	Clooney	Ennistimon	II.	18
23	Knockdrummagh South	101	0	22	Clare	Corcomroe	Clooney	Ennistimon	II.	18
125	Knockdrummore	54	2	27	Galway	Leitrim	Ballynakill	Loughrea	IV.	51
22	Knockduff	197	1	37	Armagh	Orior Lower	Killevy	Newry	III.	56
112, 125	Knockduff	271	3	36	Cork, E.R.	Kinsale	Ringcurran	Kinsale	II.	100
108	Knockduff	212	3	2	Cork, W.R.	East Carbery (W.D.)	Fanlobbus	Dunmanway	II.	132
16	Knockduff	54	2	2	Donegal	Kilmacrenan	Clondahorky	Dunfanaghy	III.	123
102	Knockduff	551	1	25	Kerry	Glanarought	Kilcaskan	Kenmare	II.	187
22, 30	Knockduff	164	3	13	Mayo	Tirawley	Ardagh	Ballina	IV.	164
39	Knockduff	206	0	37	Tipperary, N.R.	Kilnamanagh Upper	Toem	Tipperary	II.	280
12	Knockduff	66	1	5	Wexford	Ballaghkeen	Kilmakilloge	Gorey	I.	296
20	Knockduff	321	2	27	Wexford	Scarawalsh	Clone	Enniscorthy	I.	322
14	Knockduff	471	0	37	Wexford	Scarawalsh	Templeshanbo	Enniscorthy	I.	326
32	Knockduff	94	2	31	Wexford	Shelmaliere East	Artramon	Wexford	I.	330
32	Knockduff	21	3	0	Wexford	Shelmaliere East	Ballynaslaney	Enniscorthy	I.	330
25,26,31,32	Knockduff	331	1	35	Wexford	Shelmaliere West	Clonmore	Enniscorthy	I.	333
14	Knockduff Lower	812	3	33	Cork, E.R.	Duhallow	Clonfert	Kanturk	II.	68
29	Knockduff Lower	124	0	4	Cork, E.R.	Duhallow	Cullen	Millstreet	II.	70

(a) Including 51A. 0R. 17P. water.
(b) Including 119A. 3R. 7P. water.
(c) { Including 37A. 1R. 20P. water.
{ Including 0A. 3R. 25P. detached portion.

No. of Sheet of the Ordnance Survey Maps.	Townlands and Towns.	Area in Statute Acres.	County.	Barony.	Parish.	Poor Law Union in 1857.	Townland Census of 1851, Part I.	
		A. R. P.					Vol.	Page
24	Knockduff or Marley	881 3 23	Carlow .	St. Mullins Lower .	St. Mullins . .	New Ross . .	I.	13
5, 14	Knockduff Upper .	1,204 1 25	Cork, E.R. .	Duhallow . .	Clonfert . . .	Kanturk . .	II.	68
29	Knockduff Upper .	360 1 26	Cork, E.R. .	Duhallow . .	Cullen . . .	Millstreet . .	II.	70
34, 40	Knockdunnee . .	199 2 23	Tipperary, N.R.	Kilnamanagh Upper	Glenkeen . .	Thurles . .	II.	278
122	Knockea . .	545 3 14	Cork, W.R. .	East Carbery (W.D.)	Kilmeen . .	Clonakilty . .	II.	134
13	Knockea . .	62 0 13	Limerick . .	Clanwilliam . .	Cahernarry . .	Limerick . .	II.	223
39	Knockea . .	407 3 8	Wexford . .	Shelburne . .	Killesk . .	New Ross . .	I.	327
20, 28	Knockeanagh . .	434 3 39	Kerry . .	Trughanacmy .	Ardfert . .	Tralee . .	II.	205
5, 6	Knockearagh . .	828 1 20	Cork, E.R. .	Duhallow . .	Tullylease . .	Kanturk . .	II.	76
59, 67	Knockearagh . .	469 2 35	Kerry . .	Magunihy . .	Killarney . .	Killarney . .	II.	203
44	Knockearl . .	153 1 37	King's Co. .	Clonlisk . .	Templeharry . .	Roscrea . .	I.	132
24	Knockeen . .	374 2 14a	Carlow . .	St. Mullins Lower .	St. Mullins . .	New Ross . .	I.	13
6	Knockeen . .	141 1 18	Cork, E.R. .	Orrery and Kilmore	Kilbolane . .	Kanturk . .	II.	108
141	Knockeen . .	160 1 38	Cork, W.R. .	West Carbery (E.D.)	Aghadown . .	Skibbereen . .	II.	137
43, 53	Knockeen . .	67 3 31	Kerry . .	Corkaguiny . .	Dingle . .	Dingle . .	II.	175
39	Knockeen . .	337 3 32	Kerry . .	Trughanacmy . .	Castleisland . .	Tralee . .	II.	209
14	Knockeen . .	107 1 21	Limerick . .	Clanwilliam . .	Caherconlish . .	Limerick . .	II.	222
96	Knockeen . .	249 0 24	Mayo . .	Murrisk . .	Kilgeever . .	Westport . .	IV.	160
41	Knockeen . .	67 1 17	Tipperary, N.R.	Eliogarty . .	Thurles . .	Thurles . .	II.	273
88	Knockeen . .	152 1 20	Tipperary, S.R.	Iffa and Offa West .	Tullaghmelan . .	Clogheen . .	II.	321
17	Knockeen . .	876 0 17	Waterford .	Middlethird . .	Kilburne . .	Waterford . .	II.	367
37	Knockeen . .	83 0 11	Wexford . .	Shelmaliere West .	Kilbrideglynn . .	Wexford . .	I.	334
37	Knockeen . .	700 3 17	Wicklow . .	Shillelagh . .	Liscolman . .	Shillelagh . .	I.	357
21	KnockeenacurrigEast	186 3 31	Cork, E.R. .	Duhallow . .	Kilmeen . .	Kanturk . .	II.	73
21	Knockeenacurrig West	286 0 13	Cork, E.R. .	Duhallow . .	Kilmeen . .	Kanturk . .	II.	73
71	Knockeenacuttin .	157 3 23	Cork, W.R. .	East Muskerry . .	Aghinagh . .	Macroom . .	II.	154
29	Knockeenadallane .	275 3 10	Cork, E.R. .	Duhallow . .	Cullen . .	Millstreet . .	II.	70
21, 29	Knockeenadallane .	437 0 34	Cork, E.R. .	Duhallow . .	Kilmeen . .	Kanturk . .	II.	73
40	Knockeenatuder .	161 3 10	Cork, E.R. .	Duhallow . .	Clonmeen . .	Kanturk . .	II.	70
88	Knockeenawaddra .	158 0 21	Kerry . .	Iveragh . . .	Killemlagh . .	Cahersiveen . .	II.	196
18, 22	Knockeenbaun . .	538 2 30	Kilkenny . .	Crannagh . .	Kilmanagh . .	Callan . .	I.	86
120	Knockeenboy . .	263 0 5	Cork, W.R. .	East Carbery (W.D.)	Fanlobbus . .	Dunmanway . .	II.	132
120	KnockeenbweeLower	213 3 16b	Cork, W.R. .	West Carbery (E.D.)	Dromdaleague . .	Skibbereen . .	II.	140
107, 120	KnockeenbweeUpper	229 2 23	Cork, W.R. .	West Carbery (E.D.)	Dromdaleague . .	Skibbereen . .	II.	140
150	Knockeencon . .	108 0 19	Cork, W.R. .	West Carbery (E.D.)	Tullagh . .	Skibbereen . .	II.	141
31, 32	Knockeencreen . .	540 3 3	Kerry . .	Trughanacmy . .	Brosna . .	Tralee . .	II.	208
58	Knockeenduff . .	367 2 30	Kerry . .	Magunihy . .	Aghadoe . .	Killarney . .	II.	199
11, 20	Knockeengancan .	234 1 32	Waterford .	Coshmore&Coshbride	Lismore and Mocollop	Lismore . .	II.	346
18	Knockeenglass . .	282 3 11	Kilkenny . .	Crannagh . .	Kilmanagh . .	Callan . .	I.	86
29, 38	Knockeennagearagh	256 1 16	Cork, E.R. .	Duhallow . .	Cullen . .	Millstreet . .	II.	70
147	Knockeennagearagh	125 2 16	Cork, W.R. .	WestCarbery (W.D.)	Kilmoe . .	Skull . .	II.	145
67	Knockeennagowan .	345 0 34	Kerry . .	Magunihy . .	Aghadoe . .	Killarney . .	II.	199
53	Knockeennagroagh .	739 3 29	Cork, E.R. .	Barrymore . .	Gortroe . .	Fermoy . .	II.	55
49, 50	Knockeennahone .	829 2 13	Kerry . .	Trughanacmy . .	Ballinculsane . .	Tralee . .	II.	206
58	Knockeennalicka .	133 0 16	Kerry . .	Magunihy . .	Kilcummin . .	Killarney . .	II.	201
129, 130	Knockeens . .	313 3 13	Cork, W.R. .	WestCarbery (W.D.)	Kilcrohane . .	Bantry . .	II.	143
139	Knockeens . .	225 2 0	Cork, W.R. .	WestCarbery (W.D.)	Skull . .	Skull . .	II.	146
84, 85, 93	Knockeens . .	1,038 3 11	Kerry . .	Glanarought . .	Kilgarvan . .	Kenmare . .	II.	187
67	Knockeeragh . .	113 3 35	Mayo . .	Burrishoole . .	Burrishoole . .	Newport . .	IV.	119
76, 77	Knockeevan . .	661 0 23	Tipperary, S.R.	Iffa and Offa East .	Newchapel . .	Clonmel . .	II.	315
30	Knockegan andCloonagh Beg . .	178 0 21	Mayo . .	Tirawley . .	Ardagh . .	Ballina . .	IV.	164
5	Knockenagh North .	236 0 21	Kerry . .	Iraghticonnor .	Galey . .	Listowel . .	II.	190
5, 10	Knockenagh South .	332 2 34	Kerry . .	Iraghticonnor .	Galey . .	Listowel . .	II.	190
19, 20	Knockendrane . .	742 0 33	Carlow . .	Idrone East . .	Fennagh . .	Carlow . .	I.	7
17	Knockennis . .	309 3 20	Fermanagh .	Tirkennedy . .	Enniskillen . .	Enniskillen . .	III.	222
20	Knockeny . .	60 1 31	Antrim . .	Lower Glenarm . .	Layd . .	Ballycastle . .	III.	23
33	Knockeravella . .	11 3 13	Limerick . .	Coonagh . .	Templebredon .	Tipperary . .	II.	236
9, 15	Knockercreeveen .	163 2 14	Kerry . .	Clanmaurice . .	Rattoo . .	Listowel . .	II.	173
56	Knockereen . .	160 3 9	Galway . .	Clare . .	Kilcoona . .	Tuam . .	IV.	20
12	Knockergrana . .	161 0 11	Donegal . .	Inishowen East . .	Clonca . .	Inishowen . .	III.	117
19	Knockerk . .	465 0 6	Meath . .	Upper Slane . .	Slane . .	Navan . .	I.	225
57, 58	Knockerry East .	232 1 7c	Clare . .	Moyarta . .	Kilrush . .	Kilrush . .	II.	33
57, 58	Knockerry West .	463 3 27d	Clare . .	Moyarta . .	Kilrush . .	Kilrush . .	II.	33
46	Knockersally or Colehill . . .	1,761 2 0	Meath . .	Upper Moyfenrath .	Ballyboggan . .	Edenderry . .	I.	212
6	Knockertotan . .	133 3 14	Antrim . .	Lower Dunluce . .	Ballywillin . .	Coleraine . .	III.	15
4	Knockevagh . .	680 3 5	Carlow . .	Rathvilly . .	Rathvilly . .	Baltinglass . .	I.	12
15, 20	Knockfad . .	198 3 31e	Cavan . .	Upper Loughtee . .	Castleterra . .	Cavan . .	III.	83
15	Knockfadda . .	72 0 19	Cork, E.R. .	Duhallow . .	Clonfert . .	Kanturk . .	II.	68
49	Knockfadda . .	493 1 2	Mayo . .	Gallen . .	Killasser . .	Swineford . .	IV.	149
18	Knockfadda . .	1,069 0 17	Wicklow . .	Newcastle . .	Newcastle Upper .	Rathdrum . .	I.	353
69, 78	Knockfair . .	154 1 4f	Donegal . .	Raphoe . .	Stranorlar . .	Stranorlar . .	III.	142

(a) Including 2A. 2R.   3P. River Barrow.
(b) Including 12A. 3R. 19P. water.
(c) Including 9A. 1R. 18P. water.
(d) Including 1A. 1R. 10P. water.
(e) Including 0A. 1R.   2P. water.
(f) Including 3A. 2R. 13P. water.

No. of Sheet of the Ordnance Survey Maps.	Townlands and Towns.	Area in Statute Acres. A. R. P.	County.	Barony.	Parish.	Poor Law Union in 1857.	Townland Census of 1851, Part I. Vol.	Page
47	Knockfarnaght	447 0 19	Mayo	Tirawley	Addergoole	Castlebar	IV.	163
134	Knockfeen	188 0 9	Cork, W.R.	East Carbery (W.D.)	Castleventry	Clonakilty	II.	131
88	Knockfelim	66 2 7	Mayo	Burrishoole	Aghagower	Westport	IV.	118
23, 32	Knockfennell	238 2 27a	Limerick	Smallcounty	Monasteranenagh	Croom	II.	261
39	Knockfenora	336 0 39	Limerick	Connello Upper	Bruree	Kilmallock	II.	231
118	Knockfereen	84 3 12	Mayo	Kilmaine	Ballinrobe	Ballinrobe	IV.	153
40	Knockfield	404 1 38	Kildare	Kilkea and Moone	Graney	Baltinglass	I.	60
8	Knockfin	226 3 0	Cavan	Tullyhaw	Drumreilly	Bawnboy	III.	91
87, 88	Knockfin	96 1 30	Mayo	Murrisk	Oughaval	Westport	IV.	162
28, 34	Knockfin	367 0 10	Queen's Co.	Clarmallagh	Aghaboe	Abbeyleix	I.	236
27	Knockfinnisk	1,017 1 21	Limerick	Shanid	Dunmoylan	Newcastle	II.	255
67	Knockfobole	138 0 3	Tipperary, S.R.	Clanwilliam	Kilshane	Tipperary	II.	309
23, 24	Knockfola	1,167 2 16	Donegal	Kilmacrenan	Tullaghobegly	Dunfanaghy	III.	132
54, 62	Knockforlagh	236 2 33	Tipperary, S.R.	Slievardagh	St. John Baptist	Cashel	II.	336
74	Knockfree	27 3 8b	Cork, E.R.	Cork and Municipal Borough	St. Marys Shandon	Cork	II.	66
29, 30, 38, 39	Knockfree	327 2 28	Mayo	Tirawley	Kilbelfad	Ballina	IV.	168
32, 38	Knockfune	768 2 13	Tipperary, N.R.	Owney and Arra	Kilnarath	Nenagh	II.	296
27	Knockfune	80 2 21	Tipperary, N.R.	Upper Ormond	Aghnameadle	Nenagh	II.	289
112	KNOCKGARRA T.	—	Galway	Kiltartan	Kinvarradoorus	Gort	IV.	50
22, 30	Knockgarrauh (Hely)	109 3 39	Waterford	Decies without Drum	Modelligo	Lismore	II.	359
22	Knockgarraun (Sergeant)	59 1 18	Waterford	Decies without Drum	Modelligo	Lismore	II.	359
28	Knockgarve	159 1 15	Tipperary, N.R.	Upper Ormond	Aghnameadle	Nenagh	II.	289
77	Knockglass	554 3 33	Cork, E.R.	Imokilly	Ightermurragh	Middleton	II.	87
60	Knockglass	290 1 37	Cork, W.R.	East Muskerry	Aghabulloge	Macroom	II.	153
4	Knockglass	158 1 2	Donegal	Inishowen East	Clonca	Inishowen	III.	117
87	Knockglass	58 3 31	Galway	Clonmacnowen	Kilcloony	Ballinasloe	IV.	25
34	Knockglass	29 0 9	Kilkenny	Kells	Tullahought	Carrick on Suir	I.	110
53, 54	Knockglass	658 3 26	Limerick	Glenquin	Killagholehane	Newcastle	II.	245
67	Knockglass	72 0 7	Mayo	Burrishoole	Burrishoole	Newport	IV.	119
68, 77	Knockglass	200 3 30c	Mayo	Burrishoole	Kilnaclasser	Westport	IV.	121
110	Knockglass	311 1 30	Mayo	Kilmaine	Ballinrobe	Ballinrobe	IV.	153
29	Knockglass	325 0 15	Mayo	Tirawley	Crossmolina	Ballina	IV.	166
11	Knockglass	293 0 28	Meath	Upper Kells	Dulane	Kells	I.	205
9, 10, 15	Knockglass	995 3 18	Roscommon	Frenckpark	Kilcolagh	Boyle	IV.	203
37	Knockglass Beg	166 2 4	Kerry	Corkaguiny	Kilgobban	Tralee	II.	177
36, 37	Knockglass More	289 0 29	Kerry	Corkaguiny	Kilgobban	Tralee	II.	177
6, 8	Knockgorm	351 1 31d	Cavan	Tullyhaw	Templeport	Enniskillen	III.	95
76	Knockgorm	68 1 0	Cork, E.R.	Imokilly	Cloyne	Middleton	II.	85
55, 66	Knockgorm	145 3 35	Cork, E.R.	Imokilly	Killeagh	Youghal	II.	88
76	Knockgorm	94 3 12e	Cork, E.R.	Imokilly	Middleton	Middleton	II.	89
124	Knockgorm	107 3 21	Cork, W.R.	Courceys	Kilroan	Kinsale	II.	147
119	Knockgorm	421 3 10	Cork, W.R.	West Carbery (W.D.)	Caheragh	Skibbereen	II.	142
39	Knockgorm	94 2 35	Cork, W.R.	West Muskerry	Kilcorney	Millstreet	II.	158
27, 28, 34, 35	Knockgorm	493 0 37f	Down	Upper Iveagh, Lr. pt.	Garvaghy	Banbridge	III.	173
51, 59	Knockgorman	221 3 31	Tipperary, S.R.	Kilnamanagh Lower	Donohill	Tipperary	II.	323
14	Knockgrace	69 3 33	Kilkenny	Crannagh	Odagh	Kilkenny	I.	86
68, 75, 76	Knockgraffon	2,420 3 0	Tipperary, S.R.	Middlethird	Knockgraffon	Cashel	II.	328
39	Knockgrania	133 2 0	Sligo	Corran	Drumrat	Boyle	IV.	226
39	Knockgrania	222 3 27	Sligo	Corran	Kilturra	Tobercurry	IV.	228
24	Knockgrean	88 0 10	Limerick	Coonagh	Grean	Tipperary	II.	235
3	Knockgreany	182 1 15	Wexford	Gorey	Inch	Gorey	I.	316
76	Knockgriffin (Barrymore)	86 1 37	Cork, E.R.	Barrymore	Mogeesha	Middleton	II.	57
65, 76	Knockgriffin (Imokilly)	386 0 34	Cork, E.R.	Imokilly	Mogeesha	Middleton	II.	99
18, 24	Knockhall	1,653 3 10g	Roscommon	Ballintober North	Kilglass	Strokestown	IV.	186
26	Knockharley	291 0 15	Meath	Lower Duleek	Kentstown	Navan	I.	196
28	Knockheel	229 0 13	Queen's Co.	Clandonagh	Rathdowney	Donaghmore	I.	234
31	Knockhill & Drinagh	436 1 10	King's Co.	Ballyboy	Ballyboy	Parsonstown	I.	123
34	Knockhogan	209 3 11	Clare	Bunratty Upper	Doora	Ennis	II.	8
16	Knockhouse	310 1 17h	Waterford	Gaultiere	Kilmacomb	Waterford	II.	364
8, 16	Knockhouse	143 2 12	Waterford	Upperthird	Rossmire	Kilmacthomas	II.	371
9	Knockhouse Lower	293 2 25	Waterford	Middlethird	Killoteran	Waterford	II.	367
9	Knockhouse Upper	350 3 19	Waterford	Middlethird	Killoteran	Waterford	II.	367
47	Knockhowlin	24 1 33	Wexford	Forth	Ballymore	Wexford	I.	308
47, 48	Knockhowlin	95 2 9	Wexford	Forth	Ishartmon	Wexford	I.	309
5	Knockieran Lower	290 0 36	Wicklow	Lower Talbotstown	Blessington	Naas	I.	358
5	Knockieran Upper	192 1 26	Wicklow	Lower Talbotstown	Blessington	Naas	I.	358
15	Knockilly	681 3 10	Cork, E.R.	Duhallow	Clonfert	Kanturk	II.	68
54	Knockilterra	118 3 13	Tipperary, S.R.	Slievardagh	Crohane	Callan	II.	332
7	Knockina	240 3 7	Wexford	Gorey	Kilcavan	Gorey	I.	317
5	Knockinarvoer	185 3 15	Tyrone	Strabane Lower	Leckpatrick	Strabane	III.	322
32	Knockinelder	163 0 2	Down	Ards Upper	Ballyphilip	Downpatrick	III.	160

(a) Including 37A. 2R. 35P. Lough Gur.
(b) { Within the Municipal Boundary, 1A. 0R. 20P.
    { Without the Municipal Boundary, 26A. 2R. 28P.
(c) Including 6A. 1R. 17P. water.
(d) Including 6A. 1R. 38P. water.
(e) Including 1A. 1R. 12P. detached portion.
(f) Including 11A. 1R. 0P. water.
(g) Including 53A. 1R. 35P. water.
(h) Including 19A. 2R. 0P. water.

No. of Sheet of the Ordnance Survey Maps.	Townlands and Towns.	Area in Statute Acres.	County.	Barony.	Parish.	Poor Law Union in 1857.	Townland Census of 1851, Part I.	
		A. R. P.					Vol.	Page
10	Knockiniller	448 1 10	Tyrone	Strabane Lower	Ardstraw	Strabane	III.	319
82	Knockinrichard	27 3 14	Tipperary, S.R.	Iffa and Offa West	Derrygrath	Clogheen	II.	318
8	Knockinure	23 3 2	Monaghan	Monaghan	Clones	Monaghan	III.	275
34	Knockinure	242 3 10	Tipperary, N.R.	Kilnamanagh Upper	Glenkeen	Thurles	II.	278
27	Knock Island	154 2 17a	Fermanagh	Tirkennedy	Derryvullan	Enniskillen	III.	221
27	Knockisland	183 3 16	Meath	Lower Duleek	Duleek	Drogheda	I.	195
27	Knockisland	5 2 3	Meath	Upper Duleek	Duleek	Drogheda	I.	197
62, 70	Knockkelly	1,347 0 33	Tipperary, S.R.	Middlethird	Peppardstown	Cashel	II.	329
54	Knockkillaree	90 2 19	Galway	Moycullen	Kilcummin	Oughterard	IV.	67
9	Knock Killua	306 3 14	Westmeath	Delvin	Killua	Castletowndelvin	I.	265
22, 23, 28, 29	Knockkyle or Springfield	396 2 20	Queen's Co.	Clarmallagh	Aghaboe	Abbeyleix	I.	236
22	Knocklagh	285 2 25	Cork, E.R.	Duhallow	Kilmeen	Kanturk	II.	73
110, 118	Knocklahard	221 3 1	Mayo	Kilmaine	Ballinrobe	Ballinrobe	IV.	153
2, 3	Knocklahaun	106 2 3	Wexford	Gorey	Kilcavan	Gorey	I.	317
49	Knocklary	317 1 39	Limerick	Coshlea	Ballingarry	Kilmallock	II.	237
133	Knocklawrence	245 3 31	Galway	Kiltartan	Beagh	Gort	IV.	46
24, 25	Knocklead	786 3 30	Queen's Co.	Cullenagh	Fossy or Timahoe	Abbeyleix	I.	240
23	Knocklegan	60 3 6	Kilkenny	Shillelogher	Castleinch or Inchyolaghan	Kilkenny	I.	114
30	Knocklehaugh	270 2 19	Mayo	Tirawley	Kilmoremoy	Ballina	IV.	170
112	Knockleigh	379 3 1	Cork, E.R.	Kinalea	Kilmonoge	Kinsale	II.	95
4	Knocklishen Beg	319 1 7	Carlow	Rathvilly	Rathvilly	Baltinglass	I.	12
4	Knocklishen More	470 1 1	Carlow	Rathvilly	Rathvilly	Baltinglass	I.	12
37, 42	Knockloe	254 0 30	Wicklow	Shillelagh	Ardoyne	Shillelagh	I.	357
37	Knockloe	434 2 36	Wicklow	Shillelagh	Liscolman	Shillelagh	I.	357
82	Knocklofty Demesne	399 2 34b	Tipperary, S.R.	Iffa and Offa West	Tullaghmelan	Clogheen	II.	321
40	Knocklong	117 3 4	Limerick	Smallcounty	Kilfrush	Kilmallock	II.	260
40, 41	Knocklong East	559 2 21	Limerick	Coshlea	Knocklong	Kilmallock	II.	240
40, 41	Knocklong West	702 2 13	Limerick	Coshlea	Knocklong	Kilmallock	II.	240
14	Knocklore	197 1 24	Louth	Ardee	Charlestown	Ardee	I.	171
30, 31	Knockloskeraun	780 2 18	Clare	Ibrickan	Kilmurry	Ennistimon	II.	23
15	Knocklough	919 0 32c	Meath	Fore	Loughcrew	Oldcastle	I.	201
39	Knocklough	97 1 14d	Sligo	Corran	Toomour	Boyle	IV.	228
43	Knockloughlin	189 2 22	King's Co.	Ballybritt	Roscrea	Roscrea	I.	126
9	Knockloughlin	269 0 35	Longford	Longford	Templemichael	Longford	I.	160
67	Knockloughra	66 1 35	Mayo	Burrishoole	Burrishoole	Newport	IV.	119
1	Knocklucas	103 1 1	Waterford	Upperthird	St. Mary's Clonmel	Clonmel	II.	372
97, 98	Knocklucy	405 1 1	Cork, E.R.	Kinalea	Ballinaboy	Kinsale	II.	93
22	Knocklyon	429 2 33	Dublin	Uppercross	Tallaght	Dublin South	I.	42
35	Knockmacaroony Glebe	90 2 0e	Fermanagh	Clankelly	Clones	Clones	III.	196
40	Knockmackegan	87 3 23	Fermanagh	Clankelly	Galloon	Clones	III.	198
28, 29	Knockmacmanus	455 3 6	Fermanagh	Magherastephana	Aghavea	Lisnaskea	III.	219
10, 15	Knockmacolusky	73 1 7	Antrim	Cary	Culfeightrin	Ballycastle	III.	13
109	Knockmacool	241 3 35	Cork, W.R.	East Carbery (E.D.)	Desertserges	Bandon	II.	128
9	Knockmacoony	198 1 30	Meath	Fore	Oldcastle	Oldcastle	I.	202
37	Knockmacrory	60 1 13	Leitrim	Mohill	Mohill	Mohill	IV.	108
39	Knockmaddaroe	67 2 9f	Fermanagh	Coole	Galloon	Lisnaskea	III.	200
18	Knockmael East	390 0 39g	Clare	Bunratty Upper	Inchicronan	Gort	II.	9
18	Knockmael West	208 2 6h	Clare	Bunratty Upper	Inchicronan	Ennis	II.	9
25	Knockmahon	154 1 21	Waterford	Decies without Drum	Kilbarrymeaden	Kilmacthomas	II.	356
25	KNOCKMAHON T.	—	Waterford	Decies without Drum	Monksland	Kilmacthomas	II.	359
11	Knockmajor	804 2 25	Kilkenny	Fassadinin	Muckalee	Castlecomer	I.	91
22	Knockmanagh	318 3 30	Cork, E.R.	Duhallow	Kilmeen	Kanturk	II.	73
59	Knockmanagh	471 1 15	Kerry	Magunihy	Kilcummin	Killarney	II.	201
59, 67	Knockmanagh	261 0 8	Kerry	Magunihy	Killarney	Killarney	II.	203
50	Knockmanagh	164 3 3i	Mayo	Gallen	Killasser	Swineford	IV.	149
16	Knockmanoul	356 2 14	Fermanagh	Tirkennedy	Magheracross	Enniskillen	III.	223
20, 27	Knockmant	602 0 32	Westmeath	Farbill	Killucan	Mullingar	I.	267
19	Knockmanus	128 1 21	Carlow	Idrone East	Ballyellin	Carlow	I.	6
67	Knockmanus	155 1 33	Mayo	Burrishoole	Burrishoole	Newport	IV.	119
59	Knockmany	350 2 39	Tyrone	Clogher	Clogher	Clogher	III.	293
30	Knockmaon	146 0 30	Waterford	Decies without Drum	Whitechurch	Dungarvan	II.	362
47	Knockmaria or Addergoole	227 0 22	Mayo	Tirawley	Addergoole	Castlebar	IV.	163
38, 43, 44	Knockmark	670 1 33j	Meath	Lower Deece	Knockmark	Dunshaughlin	I.	192
39	Knockmaroe	908 2 16	Tipperary, N.R.	Kilnamanagh Upper	Upperchurch	Thurles	II.	281
25	Knockmarshal	255 2 35	Wexford	Bantry	St. John's	Enniscorthy	I.	302
8	Knockmartin	132 1 39	Longford	Longford	Clongesh	Longford	I.	158
19	Knockmascahill	564 3 9	Galway	Ballymoe	Ballynakill	Glennamaddy	IV.	5
13	Knockmay	88 3 14	Queen's Co.	Maryborough East	Borris	Mountmellick	I.	240
13	Knockmay	270 0 01	Queen's Co.	Maryborough East	Clonenagh and Clonagheen	Mountmellick	I.	241
17	Knockmeal	446 0 0	Kerry	Clanmaurice	Duagh	Listowel	II.	168

(a) Including 44A. 1R. 15P. water.
(b) Including 9A. 3R. 20P. water.
(c) Including 15A. 2R. 8P. water.
(d) Including 15A. 1R. 7P. water.

(e) Including 2A. 2R. 22P. water.
(f) Including 1A. 2R. 30P. water.
(g) Including 17A. 1R. 5P. water.

(h) Including 5A. 2R. 20P. water.
(i) Including 1A. 3R. 22P. water.
(j) Including 7A. 3R. 19P. detached portion.

No. of Sheet of the Ordnance Survey Maps.	Townlands and Towns.	Area in Statute Acres.			County.	Barony.	Parish.	Poor Law Union in 1857.	Townland Census of 1851, Part I.	
		A.	R.	P.					Vol.	Page
13	Knockmeal . .	611	3	29	Waterford .	Glenahiry .	Kilronan .	Clonmel . .	II.	366
12	Knockmealdown .	1,196	0	24	Waterford .	Coshmore&Coshbride	Lismore and Mocollop	Lismore . .	II.	346
25,26,31,32	Knockmeale . .	232	0	22	Tipperary, N.R.	Owney and Arra	Killoscully . .	Nenagh . .	II.	295
27	Knockmeale . .	143	1	11	Tipperary, N.R.	Upper Ormond .	Dolla . .	Nenagh . .	II.	290
41	Knockmeane . .	233	2	0	Roscommon .	Athlone . .	Kilmeane .	Roscommon .	IV.	182
38	Knockmeelmore .	278	3	4	Waterford .	Decies within Drum	Lisgenan or Grange	Youghal . .	II.	352
40	Knockmehill . .	213	1	13	Tipperary, N.R.	Kilnamanagh Upper	Templebeg . .	Thurles . .	II.	279
40	Knockmehill East .	17	3	5	Tipperary, N.R.	Kilnamanagh Upper	Templebeg . .	Thurles . .	II.	279
6, 10	Knockmenagh .	107	2	0	Armagh . .	Oneilland East .	Seagoe . .	Lurgan . .	III.	50
40	Knockmiller . .	172	2	31	Wicklow . .	Arklow . .	Killahurler .	Rathdrum .	I.	345
17, 21	Knockmitten . .	176	0	34	Dublin . .	Uppercross .	Clondalkin .	Dublin South .	I.	39
67	Knockmonalea East	285	0	10	Cork, E.R.	Imokilly . .	Clonpriest .	Youghal . .	II.	85
67	Knockmonalea West	265	3	6	Cork, E.R.	Imokilly . .	Clonpriest .	Youghal . .	II.	85
10	Knockmoody . .	85	3	15	Longford .	Granard . .	Clonbroney .	Granard . .	I.	155
19	Knockmooney .	147	1	20	Meath . .	Upper Slane .	Slane . .	Navan . .	I.	225
64, 68	Knockmore . .	521	0	16a	Antrim . .	Upper Massereene .	Blaris . .	Lisburn . .	III.	30
22, 23	Knockmore . .	380	2	2	Carlow . .	Idrone East .	Ballyellin .	New Ross . .	I.	6
9	Knockmore . .	273	1	9	Cavan . .	Tullyhaw .	Templeport .	Bawnboy . .	III.	95
48	Knockmore . .	880	1	20b	Clare . .	Clonderalaw .	Kilmihil . .	Kilrush . .	II.	17
24, 25	Knockmore . .	145	3	2	Clare . .	Inchiquin .	Dysert . .	Ennis . .	II.	24
32, 40	Knockmore . .	132	3	29c	Clare . .	Islands . .	Kilmaley . .	Ennis . .	II.	31
86	Knockmore . .	189	0	16	Cork, E.R.	Kerrycurrihy .	Carrigaline .	Cork . .	II.	92
120, 133	Knockmore . .	553	1	28	Cork, W.R.	East Carbery (W.D.)	Kilmacabea .	Skibbereen .	III.	133
14	Knock More . .	165	0	12	Fermanagh .	Magheraboy .	Devenish . .	Enniskillen .	III.	211
86	Knockmore . .	125	3	14	Galway . .	Kilconnell .	Killaan . .	Ballinasloe .	IV.	41
35,36,39,40	Knockmore . .	208	3	9	Kilkenny . .	Knocktopher .	Killahy . .	Waterford .	I.	112
39	Knockmore . .	225	0	10	Limerick .	Connello Upper .	Bruree . .	Kilmallock .	II.	231
11	Knockmore . .	25	1	26	Louth . .	Louth . .	Louth . .	Dundalk . .	I.	184
48	Knockmore . .	631	3	25	Mayo . .	Tirawley . .	Ballynahaglish .	Ballina . .	IV.	164
41	Knockmore . .	220	1	8	Sligo . .	Tirerrill . .	Kilmactranny .	Boyle . .	IV.	240
20	Knockmore . .	105	0	4	Tipperary, N.R.	Owney and Arra	Youghalarra .	Nenagh . .	II.	297
32, 38	Knockmore . .	403	1	20	Westmeath .	Moycashel .	Newtown . .	Mullingar .	I.	279
19, 25	Knockmore . .	573	1	34	Wexford . .	Bantry . .	Rossdroit .	Enniscorthy .	I.	302
38	Knockmore . .	74	0	39	Wexford . .	Shelmaliere East .	Ardcolm . .	Wexford . .	I.	330
79	Knockmore Eighter	114	2	33d	Mayo . .	Carra . .	Manulla . .	Castlebar .	IV.	129
79, 90	Knockmore Oughter	445	3	15e	Mayo . .	Carra . .	Manulla . .	Castlebar .	IV.	129
76	Knockmorris . .	147	1	36	Tipperary, S.R.	Iffa and Offa West .	Caher . .	Clogheen .	II.	318
11	Knockmorris . .	38	2	10	Westmeath .	Corkaree .	Lackan . .	Mullingar .	I.	262
32, 33	Knockmoy . .	44	2	34	Clare . .	Islands . .	Kilmaley . .	Ennis . .	II.	31
35, 36	Knockmoylan . .	1,382	0	1	Kilkenny . .	Knocktopher .	Kilkeasy . .	Thomastown .	I.	112
35	Knockmoylan . .	128	3	31	Kilkenny . .	Knocktopher .	Lismateige .	Thomastown .	I.	113
68	Knockmoyle . .	506	3	25	Mayo . .	Burrishoole .	Burrishoole .	Newport . .	IV.	119
77	Knockmoyle . .	94	1	16	Mayo . .	Burrishoole .	Kilmeena .	Newport . .	IV.	122
19, 20	Knockmoyle . .	3,799	1	4	Mayo . .	Tirawley . .	Kilfian . .	Killala . .	IV.	169
25, 26	Knockmoyle . .	86	0	15	Tyrone . .	Strabane Upper .	Cappagh . .	Omagh . .	III.	325
124, 125	Knockmoyle East .	626	1	0	Galway . .	Leitrim . .	Ballynakill .	Loughrea . .	IV.	51
77	Knockmoyleen .	79	3	27	Mayo . .	Burrishoole .	Kilmaclasser .	Westport . .	IV.	121
89	Knockmoyleen .	152	2	18	Mayo . .	Carra . .	Ballintober .	Castlebar .	IV.	125
34, 35, 44	Knockmoyleen .	1,458	3	19	Mayo . .	Erris . .	Kilcommon .	Newport . .	IV.	144
124	Knockmoyle West .	371	3	13	Galway . .	Leitrim . .	Ballynakill .	Loughrea . .	IV.	51
33, 34	Knockmoynagh .	412	1	23	Sligo . .	Corran . .	Kilmorgan .	Sligo . .	IV.	227
77	Knockmuinard .	162	3	14	Mayo . .	Burrishoole .	Kilmaclasser .	Westport . .	IV.	121
20	Knockmuldoney .	53	0	32f	Sligo . .	Leyny . .	Ballysadare .	Sligo . .	IV.	230
97	Knockmullane .	183	2	27	Cork, E.R.	Kinalea . .	Inishannon .	Bandon . .	II.	95
7, 12	Knockmullen . .	96	0	1	Wexford . .	Gorey . .	Kilmakilloge .	Gorey . .	I.	318
25, 29	Knockmullin . .	167	3	6	Leitrim . .	Leitrim . .	Fenagh . .	Mohill . .	IV.	100
49, 50	Knockmullin . .	64	1	28	Mayo . .	Gallen . .	Killasser .	Swineford .	IV.	149
26	Knockmullin . .	408	2	27g	Sligo . .	Tirerrill . .	Ballysadare .	Sligo . .	IV.	238
29, 34	Knockmullin . .	260	2	31	Wexford . .	Bantry . .	St. Mary's .	New Ross .	I.	302
6, 7	Knockmult . .	354	1	0	Londonderry .	Coleraine .	Dunboe . .	Coleraine . .	III.	231
50	Knockmurragha .	20	1	1	Clare . .	Bunratty Lower .	Kilnasoolagh .	Ennis . .	II.	8
27	Knockmurry . .	212	1	4	Roscommon .	Castlereagh .	Kilkeevin .	Castlereagh .	IV.	200
39	Knocknabansha .	500	3	4	Tipperary, N.R.	Kilnamanagh Upper	Upperchurch .	Thurles . .	II.	281
29	Knocknabarnaboy or Ashbrook . .	246	2	6	Roscommon .	Roscommon .	Lissonuffy .	Strokestown .	IV.	211
10	Knocknabeast .	61	1	5	Roscommon .	Boyle . .	Ardcarn . .	Boyle . .	IV.	193
51, 62	Knocknabehy . .	516	3	12	Cork, E.R.	Barretts . .	Grenagh . .	Cork . .	II.	49
124	Knocknabinny .	226	0	16	Cork, W.R.	Courceys .	Ringrone .	Kinsale . .	II.	147
27, 28	Knocknaboha . .	141	2	21	Limerick . .	Shanid . .	Ardagh . .	Newcastle .	II.	255
76	Knocknaboha . .	258	3	28	Tipperary, S.R.	Iffa and Offa West .	Mortlestown .	Clogheen . .	II.	319
74	Knocknabohilly .	100	1	17h	Cork and Municipal Borough	Cork, E.R.	St. Marys Shandon	Cork . .	II.	66
112	Knocknabohilly .	17	0	39	Cork, E.R.	Kinsale . .	Ringcurran .	Kinsale . .	II.	100

(a) Including 4A. 0R. 23P. water.
(b) Including 13A. 1R. 11P. water.
(c) Including 3A. 1R. 34P. water.

(d) Including 4A. 1R. 11P. water.
(e) Including 73A. 2R. 15P. water.
(f) Including 3A. 1R. 15P. water.

(g) Including 17A. 3R. 9P. water.
(h) { Within the Municipal Boundary, 54A. 1R. 21P.
     { Without the Municipal Boundary, 45A. 3R. 36P.

CENSUS OF IRELAND FOR THE YEAR 1851.

No. of Sheet of the Ordnance Survey Maps.	Townlands and Towns.	Area in Statute Acres.			County.	Barony.	Parish.	Poor Law Union in 1857.	Townland Census of 1851, Part I.	
		A.	R.	P.					Vol.	Page
86	Knocknaboley	63	3	5	Galway	Kilconnell	Grange	Loughrea	IV.	40
76, 77	Knocknaboley	315	1	21	Mayo	Burrishoole	Kilmeena	Newport	IV.	122
33, 38	Knocknaboley	715	2	20	Wicklow	Ballinacor South	Kilcommon	Shillelagh	I.	349
16	Knocknaboley	572	1	28	Wicklow	Lower Talbotstown	Hollywood	Baltinglass	I.	360
35, 44	Knocknabollan	180	2	30	Donegal	Kilmacrenan	Kilmacrenan	Milford	III.	129
56, 64	Knocknaboola	785	1	33a	Kerry	Dunkerron North	Killorglin	Killarney	II.	181
44	Knocknabooly	142	3	36	Cork, E.R.	Barrymore	Gortroe	Fermoy	II.	55
27	Knocknabooly	133	0	38	Kilkenny	Knocktopher	Ennisnag	Thomastown	I.	111
9, 18	Knocknabooly East	573	1	22	Limerick	Shanid	Loghill	Glin	II.	257
9, 18	Knocknabooly Middle	225	2	10	Limerick	Shanid	Loghill	Glin	II.	257
9, 18	Knocknabooly West	517	1	8	Limerick	Shanid	Loghill	Glin	II.	257
41, 50	Knocknaboul	1,274	2	32	Kerry	Trughanacmy	Ballincuslane	Tralee	II.	206
11, 20	Knocknaboul	455	2	18	Waterford	Coshmore&Coshbride	Lismore and Mocollop	Lismore	II.	346
11	Knocknabranagh and Knockbaun	711	3	35	Carlow	Idrone West	Oldleighlin	Carlow	I.	9
39	Knocknabrass	167	2	30b	Fermanagh	Coole	Galloon	Lisnaskea	III.	200
32	Knocknabrattoge or Greentown	209	1	24	Fermanagh	Clanawley	Killesher	Enniskillen	III.	193
68, 76	Knocknabro	1,465	0	5	Kerry	Magunihy	Killaha	Killarney	II.	202
28	Knocknabrogue	310	1	17	Tipperary, N.R.	Upper Ormond	Latteragh	Nenagh	II.	292
20	Knocknabrone	207	1	36	Waterford	Coshmore&Coshbride	Lismore and Mocollop	Lismore	II.	346
43	Knocknacaheragh	386	3	5	Cork, E.R.	Barrymore	Dunbulloge	Cork	II.	54
11,12,17,18	Knocknacaheragh	502	0	5	Kerry	Iraghticonnor	Duagh	Listowel	II.	190
67	Knocknacally	143	0	13	Cork, E.R.	Imokilly	Youghal	Youghal	II.	91
3	Knocknacarney	27	2	19	Monaghan	Trough	Errigal Trough	Monaghan	III.	284
58	Knocknacarney	169	3	14	Tyrone	Clogher	Clogher	Clogher	III.	293
93, 94	Knocknacarragh	134	2	21	Galway	Galway	Rahoon	Galway	IV.	38
15	Knocknacarriga	252	2	11	Limerick	Coonagh	Doon	Tipperary	II.	234
6, 7	Knocknacarrow	128	3	5	Roscommon	Boyle	Ardcarn	Boyle	IV.	193
15	Knocknacarry	155	0	22	Antrim	Lower Glenarm	Layd	Ballycastle	III.	23
15	KNOCKNACARRY T.	—			Antrim	Lower Glenarm	Layd	Ballycastle	III.	23
21	Knocknacaska	747	0	18	Kerry	Clanmaurice	O'Dorney	Tralee	II.	172
6	Knocknaclassagh	282	2	31	Leitrim	Rosclogher	Killasnet	Manorhamilton	IV.	110
45	Knocknaclogha	275	0	33	Tyrone	Dungannon Middle	Pomeroy	Dungannon	III.	304
5, 9	Knocknacloy	90	3	16	Roscommon	Boyle	Boyle	Boyle	IV.	194
61	Knocknacloy	220	1	15c	Tyrone	Dungannon Middle	Clonfeacle	Dungannon	III.	299
23	Knocknacolan	371	2	37	Cork, E.R.	Duhallow	Kilroe	Kanturk	II.	73
85	Knocknaconnery	163	2	8	Tipperary, S.R.	Iffa and Offa East	Carrick	Carrick on Suir	II.	312
17	Knocknacoska	126	2	4	Leitrim	Drumahaire	Inishmagrath	Manorhamilton	IV.	96
30, 31, 34	Knocknacran East	154	0	20	Monaghan	Farney	Magheracloone	Carrickmacross	III.	272
30, 31, 34	Knocknacran West	179	3	12	Monaghan	Farney	Magheracloone	Carrickmacross	III.	272
9	Knocknacree	154	1	39	Kerry	Clanmaurice	Rattoo	Listowel	II.	173
40	Knocknacree	47	0	8	Kildare	Kilkea and Moone	Castledermot	Athy	I.	59
40	Knocknacree	271	3	10	Kildare	Kilkea and Moone	Graney	Athy	I.	60
83, 84	Knocknacreeva	228	0	32	Galway	Clare	Athenry	Galway	IV.	17
2, 3, 7	Knocknacrcha	177	2	18	Waterford	Upperthird	Rathgormuck	Carrick on Suir	II.	371
118	Knocknacroagha	307	0	18	Mayo	Kilmaine	Ballinrobe	Ballinrobe	IV.	153
17	Knocknacrohy	302	0	27	Kerry	Clanmaurice	Duagh	Listowel	II.	168
24	Knocknacrohy	196	2	13	Limerick	Coonagh	Grean	Tipperary	II.	235
8	Knocknacrohy	254	2	22	Waterford	Upperthird	Guilcagh	Carrick on Suir	II.	370
30	KnocknacroohaLower	283	0	19	Waterford	Decies without Drum	Whitechurch	Dungarvan	II.	362
22, 30	KnocknacroohaUpper	387	0	11	Waterford	Decies without Drum	Whitechurch	Dungarvan	II.	362
34	Knocknacross	235	0	23	Sligo	Tirerrill	Kilmacallan	Sligo	IV.	240
14, 15	Knocknacrow	422	0	7	Antrim	Lower Glenarm	Grange of Layd	Ballycastle	III.	22
39	Knocknacroy	42	2	1	Sligo	Corran	Toomour	Sligo	IV.	228
74	Knocknacullen East	152	0	30	Cork, E.R.	Cork	St. Marys, Shandon	Cork	II.	66
74	Knocknacullen West	215	0	1	Cork, E.R.	Cork	St. Marys, Shandon	Cork	II.	66
112, 125	Knocknacurra	11	3	3	Cork, E.R.	Kinsale	Kinsale	Kinsale	II.	100
110, 111	Knocknacurra	422	1	15	Cork, W.R.	East Carbery (E.D.)	Ballinadee	Bandon	II.	126
22	Knocknacurra	232	1	21	Kerry	Trughanacmy	O'Brennan	Tralee	II.	212
21, 22	Knocknacurragh	381	3	15	Cork, E.R.	Duhallow	Kilmeen	Kanturk	II.	73
31, 32	Knocknadarriv	1,517	2	28	Kerry	Trughanacmy	Ballincuslane	Tralee	II.	206
97	Knocknadaula	117	2	24	Galway	Athenry	Killimordaly	Loughrea	IV.	4
97	Knocknadaula	252	3	8	Galway	Athenry	Kiltullagh	Loughrea	IV.	5
88	Knocknadempsey	75	0	13d	Tipperary, S.R.	Iffa and Offa West	Neddans	Clogheen	II.	319
43, 52	Knocknadiha	1,095	0	10	Limerick	Glenquin	Killeedy	Newcastle	II.	246
63, 64	Knocknadona	299	2	3	Antrim	Upper Massereene	Magheragall	Lisburn	III.	31
110	Knocknadrimna	83	1	12e	Mayo	Kilmaine	Ballinrobe	Ballinrobe	IV.	153
110	Knocknadrimna	209	2	3	Mayo	Kilmaine	Robeen	Ballinrobe	IV.	157
16, 22	Knocknadroose	3,084	1	2f	Wicklow	Lower Talbotstown	Hollywood	Baltinglass	I.	360
12	Knocknafallia	799	1	19	Waterford	Coshmore&Coshbride	Lismore and Mocollop	Lismore	II.	346
16, 95, 96	Knocknafaugher	000	0	13g	Donegal	Kilmacrenan	Clondahorky	Dunfanaghy	III.	123
36	Knocknafreeny	80	0	2	Waterford	Decies within Drum	Ardmore	Dungarvan	II.	350

(a) Including 12A. 0R. 21P. water.
(b) Including 20A. 2R. 2P. water.
(c) Including 2A. 2R. 37P. water.

(d) Including 5A. 2R. 24P. water.
(e) Including 8A. 2R. 33P. water.

(f) Including 8A. 0R. 22P. water.
(g) Including 18A. 0R. 29P. water.

No. of Sheet of the Ordnance Survey Maps.	Townlands and Towns.	Area in Statute Acres.			County.	Barony.	Parish.	Poor Law Union in 1857.	Townland Census of 1851, Part I.	
		A.	R.	P.					Vol.	Page
12, 21	Knocknafrehane	700	0	23	Waterford	Coshmore & Coshbride	Lismore and Mocollop	Lismore	II.	346
10	Knocknafushoga	321	2	14	Roscommon	Boyle	Estersnow	Boyle	IV.	195
110, 123	Knocknagallagh	886	3	36	Cork, W.R.	Kinalmeaky	Desertserges	Bandon	II.	152
22	Knocknagalliagh	285	2	34	Kildare	Offaly East	Kildare	Edenderry	I.	70
50, 58	Knocknagalty	1,754	3	13	Limerick	Coshlea	Kilbeheny	Mitchelstown	II.	239
119	Knocknaganny	133	2	9	Mayo	Kilmaine	Kilcommon	Ballinrobe	IV.	155
14	Knocknaganny	98	2	23	Sligo	Carbury	St. John's	Sligo	IV.	223
56	Knocknagappagh	479	3	19	Cork, E.R.	Imokilly	Ardagh	Youghal	II.	83
86	Knocknagappagh	88	2	38	Galway	Kilconnell	Killallaghtan	Ballinasloe	IV.	41
45	Knocknagapple	293	2	36	Cork, E.R.	Kinnatalloon	Aghern	Fermoy	II.	97
86	Knocknagapple	186	1	10	Tipperary, S.R.	Iffa and Offa West	Templetenny	Clogheen	II.	320
54	Knocknagapple	88	2	4	Tipperary, S.R.	Slievardagh	Crohane	Callan	II.	332
2	Knocknagapple	173	3	28	Wexford	Gorey	Kilnahue	Gorey	I.	319
111	Knocknagappul	507	1	36	Cork, W.R.	East Carbery (E.D.)	Ballinadee	Bandon	II.	126
143	Knocknagappul	102	2	8	Cork, W.R.	Ibane and Barryroe	Rathbarry	Clonakilty	II.	150
48, 49, 60	Knocknagappul	1,807	1	8	Cork, W.R.	West Muskerry	Clondrohid	Macroom	II.	155
20	Knocknagappul	217	2	17	Waterford	Coshmore & Coshbride	Lismore and Mocollop	Lismore	II.	346
38, 39	Knocknagappul	191	1	33	Waterford	Decies within Drum	Ardmore	Dungarvan	II.	350
18	Knocknagappul	115	3	30	Waterford	Gaultiere	Kill St. Nicholas	Waterford	II.	364
45, 54	Knocknagare	48	2	15	Cork, E.R.	Barrymore	Britway	Middleton	II.	52
65	Knocknagarhoon	405	1	37	Clare	Moyarta	Moyarta	Kilrush	II.	34
29	Knocknagarnaman	196	2	36	Monaghan	Farney	Inishkeen	Dundalk	III.	271
110	Knocknagarrane	461	3	15	Cork, W.R.	Kinalmeaky	Ballymodan	Bandon	II.	151
66	Knocknagarrivhan	839	0	10a	Galway	Moycullen	Kilcummin	Oughterard	IV.	67
39, 43	Knocknagartan	251	3	10	Cavan	Castlerahan	Munterconnaught	Oldcastle	III.	71
4, 8	Knocknagarvan	384	2	12	Antrim	Cary	Ballintoy	Ballycastle	III.	12
33	Knocknagarve	159	0	36	Tipperary, N.R.	Upper Ormond	Templederry	Nenagh	II.	293
23	Knocknagashel East	436	2	21	Kerry	Trughanacmy	Castleisland	Tralee	II.	209
23	Knocknagashel West	2,102	2	17	Kerry	Trughanacmy	Castleisland	Tralee	II.	209
17	Knocknagawna	344	2	21	Roscommon	Ballintober North	Kilmore	Carᵏ. on Shannon	IV.	187
39, 40	Knocknagee	479	3	3	Kildare	Kilkea and Moone	Ballaghmoon	Athy	I.	59
12, 13, 19	Knocknageeha	695	2	15	Clare	Tulla Upper	Feakle	Tulla	II.	39
50, 60	Knocknageeha	430	2	6	Kerry	Magunihy	Kilcummin	Killarney	II.	201
67, 68	Knocknageeha	126	1	13b	Mayo	Burrishoole	Burrishoole	Newport	IV.	119
121	Knocknageeha	357	2	7	Mayo	Kilmaine	Kilmainebeg	Ballinrobe	IV.	155
5	Knocknageeha	354	0	30	Monaghan	Monaghan	Tedavnet	Monaghan	III.	279
39	Knocknageeha	124	0	34	Sligo	Corran	Kilturra	Tobercurry	IV.	228
21, 27	Knocknageeha	177	3	22	Sligo	Tirerrill	Ballysumaghan	Sligo	IV.	238
30	Knocknageeha East	228	0	26	Cork, E.R.	Duhallow	Cullen	Millstreet	II.	70
30	Knocknageeha North	238	0	10	Cork, E.R.	Duhallow	Cullen	Millstreet	II.	70
30	Knocknageeha South	174	3	10	Cork, E.R.	Duhallow	Cullen	Millstreet	II.	70
29, 30	Knocknageeha West	168	3	37	Cork, E.R.	Duhallow	Cullen	Millstreet	II.	70
134, 143	Knocknageehy	247	0	12	Cork, W.R.	Ibane and Barryroe	Ross	Clonakilty	II.	150
79	Knocknageehy	54	0	39	Mayo	Carra	Breaghwy	Castlebar	IV.	127
38	Knocknageeragh or Summerhill	282	3	11	Waterford	Decies within Drum	Lisgenan or Grange	Youghal	II.	352
22	Knocknageragh	54	0	22	Waterford	Decies without Drum	Modelligo	Lismore	II.	359
33	Knocknagilky Lower	160	1	8	Wicklow	Ballinacor South	Hacketstown	Baltinglass	I.	318
33	Knocknagilky Upper	325	3	26	Wicklow	Ballinacor South	Hacketstown	Baltinglass	I.	349
26, 32	Knocknagillagh	71	2	30	Cavan	Upper Loughtee	Lavey	Cavan	III.	86
1, 2	Knocknagin	251	2	25	Dublin	Balrothery East	Balrothery	Balrothery	I.	19
41	Knocknagin	124	3	13	Londonderry	Loughinsholin	Desertmartin	Magherafelt	III.	240
23	Knocknaglogh	963	3	0	Kerry	Clanmaurice	Kilshenane	Listowel	II.	172
11	Knocknaglogh	185	2	33	Waterford	Coshmore & Coshbride	Lismore and Mocollop	Lismore	II.	346
35	Knocknaglogh Lower	454	0	23	Waterford	Decies within Drum	Ardmore	Dungarvan	II.	350
35	Knocknaglogh Upper	481	2	23	Waterford	Decies within Drum	Ardmore	Dungarvan	II.	350
54	Knocknaglohall	81	2	29	Cork, E.R.	Barrymore	Britway	Middleton	II.	52
21	Knocknagon	81	1	18	Mayo	Tirawley	Kilfian	Killala	IV.	169
1, 4, 5	Knocknagoney	845	0	33	Down	Castlereagh Lower	Holywood	Belfast	II.	162
27, 28	Knocknagoogh	176	1	31	Tipperary, N.R.	Upper Ormond	Latteragh	Nenagh	II.	292
109	Knocknagool	150	1	17	Mayo	Carra	Ballyovey	Ballinrobe	IV.	126
49	Knocknagoran	152	3	20	Tyrone	Omagh East	Kilskeery	Lowtherstown	III.	315
5	Knocknagoran	259	1	9	Louth	Lower Dundalk	Carlingford	Dundalk	I.	176
99	Knocknagore	327	3	8	Cork, E.R.	Kerrycurrihy	Templebreedy	Kinsale	II.	93
26	Knocknagore	713	3	30	Down	Lower Iveagh, Up.pt.	Tullylish	Banbridge	III.	171
39	Knocknagore	91	3	10	Sligo	Corran	Drumrat	Boyle	IV.	226
26, 27	Knocknagornagh	1,699	0	11	Limerick	Shanid	Kilmoylan	Glin	II.	256
6	Knocknagorteeny	439	1	39	Limerick	Owneybeg	Abington	Limerick	II.	251
73	Knocknagorty	180	1	27c	Cork, E.R.	Cork	Currykippane	Cork	II.	64
34	Knocknagoug	132	0	38	Clare	Bunratty Upper	Quin	Tulla	II.	10
72, 84	Knocknagoul	492	2	8	Cork, E.R.	East Muskerry	Aglish	Macroom	II.	101
22	Knocknagoum	573	1	5	Kerry	Trughanacmy	O'Brennan	Tralee	II.	212
49, 60	Knocknagoun	1,385	3	2	Cork, W.R.	East Muskerry	Aghabulloge	Macroom	II.	153

(a) Including 49A. 1R. 2P. water.   (b) Including 2A. 0R. 24P. water.   (c) Including 14A. 1R. 13P. water.

4 K

No. of Sheet of the Ordnance Survey Maps.	Townlands and Towns.	Area in Statute Acres.	County.	Barony.	Parish.	Poor Law Union in 1857.	Townland Census of 1851. Part I.	
		A. R. P.					Vol.	Page
68, 76, 77	Knocknagowan	1,367 2 3	Kerry	Magunihy	Killaha	Killarney	II.	202
35	Knocknagower	67 1 12	Kerry	Corkaguiny	Ballyduff	Dingle	II.	174
24	Knocknagraigue East	100 0 34	Clare	Corcomroe	Clooney	Corrofin	II.	18
15,16,23,24	Knocknagraigue West	305 1 34	Clare	Corcomroe	Clooney	Ennistimon	II.	18
35	Knocknagrally or Killenny Beg	130 3 33	Queen's Co.	Clarmallagh	Aghmacart	Abbeyleix	I.	236
31	Knocknagranagh	224 2 39	Waterford	Decies without Drum	Dungarvan	Dungarvan	II.	355
22, 31	Knocknagranshy	290 2 26	Limerick	Pubblebrien	Monasteranenagh	Croom	II.	253
8	Knocknagrat	78 0 16	Monaghan	Monaghan	Clones	Monaghan	III.	275
6	Knocknagrave	225 1 16	Monaghan	Trough	Donagh	Monaghan	III.	282
87	Knocknagreana	17 0 26	Galway	Clonmacnowen	Kilcloony	Ballinasloe	IV.	25
93	Knocknagreana	240 1 3	Galway	Moycullen	Rahoon	Galway	IV.	72
29	Knocknagree	448 1 29	Cork, E.R.	Duhallow	Nohavaldaly	Millstreet	II.	75
82	Knocknagree	46 3 25	Tipperary, S.R.	Iffa and Offa West	Tullaghmelan	Clogheen	II.	321
28	Knocknagree	119 1 5	Wicklow	Ballinacor South	Kiltegan	Baltinglass	I.	350
1	Knocknagriffin	49 3 8	Waterford	Upperthird	St. Marys Clonmel	Clonmel	II.	372
2, 5	Knocknagroagh	441 1 10	Clare	Burren	Drumcreehy	Ballyvaghan	II.	12
8, 13	Knocknagroagh	419 0 22	Queen's Co.	Maryborough East	Borris	Mountmellick	I.	240
26	Knocknagroagh	125 2 27a	Sligo	Corran	Kilmorgan	Sligo	IV.	227
25, 31	Knocknagross	122 0 19	Wexford	Bantry	Clonmore	Enniscorthy	I.	300
14, 15	Knocknagull	201 0 34	Wicklow	Lower Talbotstown	Dunlavin	Baltinglass	I.	360
47, 53 109,110, 117,118	Knocknagulliagh	406 0 39	Antrim	Lower Belfast	Templecorran	Larne	III.	9
	Knocknagulshy	240 0 30	Mayo	Kilmaine	Ballinrobe	Ballinrobe	IV.	153
21	Knocknagun	135 1 16	Kerry	Clanmaurice	O'Dorney	Tralee	II.	172
22	Knocknagundarragh or Scortreen	272 2 36	Carlow	Idrone East	Clonygoose	Carlow	I.	6
11, 15	Knocknaguppoge	285 0 33	Kilkenny	Gowran	Rathcoole	Kilkenny	I.	98
21, 29	Knocknahaha	169 0 30	Kerry	Trughanacmy	Clogherbrien	Tralee	II.	209
12, 13	Knocknahannee	205 1 36	Clare	Tulla Upper	Feakle	Tulla	II.	39
34	Knocknaharney	321 2 18	Tipperary, N.R.	Kilnamanagh Upper	Glenkeen	Thurles	II.	278
29	Knocknahattin	36 2 17	Meath	Lune	Athboy	Trim	I.	207
22	Knocknahaw	72 0 22	Galway	Ballynahinch	Ballynakill	Clifden	IV.	11
74	Knocknaheeny	181 1 6b	Cork, E.R.	Cork and Municipal Borough	St. Marys Shandon	Cork	II.	66
21, 22	Knocknahila	86 2 32	Kerry	Clanmaurice	Kilflyn	Tralee	II.	170
38, 39	Knocknahila Beg	319 3 36	Clare	Ibrickan	Kilmurry	Kilrush	II.	23
38, 39	Knocknahila More North	334 1 37	Clare	Ibrickan	Kilmurry	Kilrush	II.	23
39	Knocknahila More South	440 3 29	Clare	Ibrickan	Kilmurry	Kilrush	II.	23
84	Knocknahilan	338 3 23	Cork, E.R.	East Muskerry	Kilbonane	Bandon	II.	104
112	Knocknahilan	136 0 18	Cork, E.R.	Kinsale	Clontead	Kinsale	II.	99
13	Knocknahinch	316 1 38	Antrim	Upper Dunluce	Armoy	Ballymoney	III.	18
59, 67	Knocknahoe	468 0 2	Kerry	Magunihy	Killarney	Killarney	II.	203
44	Knocknahoo	178 3 34	Sligo	Coolavin	Kilfree	Boyle	IV.	224
58	Knocknahooan	179 3 25	Clare	Clonderalaw	Killimer	Kilrush	II.	16
58	Knocknahooan	212 3 20	Clare	Moyarta	Kilrush	Kilrush	II.	33
35	Knocknahoola	275 0 13	Waterford	Decies within Drum	Ardmore	Dungarvan	II.	350
63	Knocknahorgan	502 3 1	Cork, E.R.	Cork	Rathcooney	Cork	II.	65
63	KNOCKNAHORGAN T.	—	Cork, E.R.	Cork	Rathcooney	Cork	II.	65
41	Knocknahorn	533 0 29	Tyrone	Omagh East	Dromore	Omagh	III.	311
92, 98	Knocknahorna	123 1 9	Donegal	Banagh	Inver	Donegal	III.	107
30	Knocknahorna	133 2 3	King's Co.	Garrycastle	Reynagh	Parsonstown	I.	138
37	Knocknahorna	522 3 14	Mayo	Tirawley	Crossmolina	Ballina	IV.	166
5	Knocknahorna	245 1 3	Tyrone	Strabane Lower	Leckpatrick	Strabane	III.	322
43, 53	Knocknahow	147 2 1	Kerry	Corkaguiny	Kildrum	Dingle	II.	177
112	Knocknahowla Beg	182 2 26	Cork, E.R.	Kinalea	Kilmonoge	Kinsale	II.	95
112	Knocknahowla More	396 2 4	Cork, E.R.	Kinalea	Kilmonoge	Kinsale	II.	95
20	Knocknahunshin	278 0 33	Fermanagh	Magheraboy	Boho	Enniskillen	III.	209
14, 20	Knocknahur North	137 1 32	Sligo	Carbury	Kilmacowen	Sligo	IV.	222
20	Knocknahur South	152 3 0	Sligo	Carbury	Kilmacowen	Sligo	IV.	222
12	Knocknakearn	369 0 3	Queen's Co.	Maryborough West	Clonenagh and Clonagheen	Mountmellick	I.	243
8	Knocknakeeragh	196 0 6	Londonderry	North East Liberties of Coleraine	Ballyrashane	Coleraine	III.	245
36	Knocknakielt	616 2 28	Londonderry	Loughinsholin	Termoneeny	Magherafelt	III.	244
39	Knocknakill	276 0 16	Tipperary, N.R.	Kilnamanagh Upper	Templebeg	Thurles	II.	279
48	Knocknakilla	1,140 1 15	Cork, W.R.	West Muskerry	Drishane	Millstreet	II.	156
88	Knocknakillardy	119 0 2	Tipperary, S.R.	Iffa and Offa West	Neddans	Clogheen	II.	319
60, 70	Knocknakillew	95 0 27c	Mayo	Gallen	Templemore	Castlebar	IV.	151
109, 117	Knocknakillew	381 0 12	Mayo	Kilmaine	Ballinrobe	Ballinrobe	IV.	153
33, 39	Knocknakillew or Woodhill	311 3 29	Sligo	Corran	Cloonoghil	Tobercurry	IV.	225

(a) Including 4A. 2R. 22P. water.   (b) { Within the Municipal Boundary, 12A. 3R. 24P. / Without the Municipal Boundary, 168A. 1R. 22P.   (c) Including 8A. 2R. 31P. water.

No. of Sheet of the Ordnance Survey Maps.	Townlands and Towns.	Area in Statute Acres. A. R. P.	County.	Barony.	Parish.	Poor Law Union in 1857.	Townland Census of 1851, Part I. Vol.	Page
16	Knocknakilly . .	180 1 10	Kerry . .	Clanmaurice . .	Kilfeighny . .	Listowel . .	II.	170
42,43,51,52	Knocknalappa .	345 1 1a	Clare . .	Bunratty Lower .	Kilmurry . .	Tulla . .	II.	6
30	Knocknalear . .	87 2 35	Fermanagh .	Clankelly . .	Clones . .	Clones . .	III.	196
10	Knocknalina . .	317 2 33	Mayo . .	Erris . .	Kilmore . .	Belmullet . .	IV.	146
38	Knocknaloman .	651 1 34	Cork, W.R. .	West Muskerry .	Drishane . .	Millstreet . .	II.	156
19	Knocknalooricaun .	356 3 33	Waterford .	Coshmore&Coshbride	Lismore and Mocollop	Lismore . .	II.	346
23	Knocknalosset .	484 1 27	Cavan . .	Clankee . .	Knockbride . .	Cootehill . .	III.	74
35	Knocknalosset .	236 3 30	Fermanagh .	Clankelly . .	Clones . .	Clones . .	III.	196
11	Knocknalougha .	448 2 39	Waterford .	Coshmore&Coshbride	Lismore and Mocollop	Lismore . .	II.	346
5	Knocknalour . .	453 1 15	Wexford . .	Scarawalsh . .	Kilrush . .	Enniscorthy .	I.	324
11	Knocknalower .	760 3 36	Mayo . .	Erris . .	Kilcommon . .	Belmullet . .	IV.	144
5	Knocknalun . .	275 2 10	Monaghan .	Monaghan . .	Tedavnet . .	Monaghan . .	III.	279
98, 99	Knocknalurgan .	124 3 27	Cork, E.R. .	Kinalea . .	Carrigaline . .	Kinsale . .	II.	94
62	Knocknalyre . .	441 2 26	Cork, E.R. .	Barretts . .	Garrycloyne . .	Cork . .	II.	49
85	Knocknalyre . .	82 3 22	Cork, E.R. .	Cork . .	Ballinaboy . .	Cork . .	II.	63
29	Knocknalyre or Downhill .	60 0 37	Sligo . .	Tireragh . .	Kilmoremoy .	Ballina . .	IV.	235
35	Knocknamadderee .	261 3 31	Cork, E.R. .	Fermoy . .	Killathy . .	Fermoy . .	II.	80
76, 88	Knocknamadderee .	346 3 20	Cork, E.R. .	Imokilly . .	Cloyne . .	Middleton . .	II.	85
19	Knocknamaddy .	320 3 10b	Monaghan .	Cremorne . .	Ballybay . .	Castleblayney .	III.	259
86	Knocknamallavoge .	181 1 32	Cork, E.R. .	Cork . .	Inishkenny . .	Cork . .	II.	64
57	Knocknaman . .	289 1 4	Kerry . .	Magunihy . .	Kilbonane . .	Killarney . .	II.	200
99, 113	Knocknamanagh .	595 2 31	Cork, E.R. .	Kinalea . .	Tracton . .	Kinsale . .	II.	97
104	Knocknamanagh .	41 0 9	Galway . .	Dunkellin . .	Killogilleen . .	Loughrea . .	IV.	31
62, 73	Knocknamarriff .	191 3 23	Cork, E.R. .	East Muskerry .	Inishcarra . .	Cork . .	II.	104
41	Knocknamarshal .	23 1 27	Wexford . .	Shelmaliere West .	Taghmon . .	Wexford . .	I.	335
42, 43	Knocknamase or Goldengrove .	580 0 29	King's Co. .	Clonlisk . .	Ettagh . .	Roscrea . .	I.	130
22	Knocknamaulee .	212 0 19	Waterford .	Decies without Drum	Colligan . .	Dungarvan . .	III.	354
14	Knocknambraher .	165 3 25	Queen's Co. .	Stradbally . .	Stradbally . .	Athy . .	I.	247
33,34,39,40	Knocknamena Commons .	562 3 24	Tipperary, N.R. .	Kilnamanagh Upper	Upperchurch . .	Thurles . .	II.	281
23, 24, 29	Knocknamoe . .	396 3 38	Queen's Co. .	Cullenagh . .	Abbeyleix . .	Abbeyleix . .	I.	238
91	Knocknamoghalaun .	196 2 27	Mayo . .	Clanmorris . .	Mayo . .	Castlebar . .	IV.	135
141	Knocknamohalagh .	91 2 15	Cork, W.R. .	West Carbery (E.D.)	Aghadown . .	Skibbereen . .	III.	137
32	Knocknamoheragh .	372 0 36	Tipperary, N.R. .	Owney and Arra .	Kilnarath . .	Nenagh . .	II.	296
35, 40	Knocknamohill .	300 0 10	Wicklow . .	Arklow . .	Castlemacadam .	Rathdrum . .	I.	342
32, 41	Knocknamona .	411 1 16	Cork, E.R. .	Duhallow . .	Kilshannig . .	Mallow . .	II.	74
53	Knocknamona .	106 0 24	Donegal . .	Kilmacrenan . .	Conwal . .	Letterkenny . .	III.	126
30, 35	Knocknamona .	354 1 10	Waterford .	Decies within Drum	Ardmore . .	Dungarvan . .	II.	350
5	Knocknamota .	261 2 6	Wexford . .	Scarawalsh . .	Carnew . .	Gorey . .	I.	322
65	Knocknamouragh .	168 3 9	Cork, E.R. .	Barrymore . .	Templenacarriga .	Middleton . .	II.	58
11, 20	Knocknamuck .	259 2 27	Cork, E.R. .	Condons&Clangibbon	Brigown . .	Mitchelstown .	II.	60
6	Knocknamuck .	229 2 16	Cork, E.R. .	Duhallow . .	Knocktemple . .	Kanturk . .	II.	75
118	Knocknamuck .	103 3 36	Cork, W.R. .	Bantry . .	Kilmocomoge . .	Bantry . .	II.	121
13	Knocknamuck .	250 3 1	Kilkenny . .	Crannagh . .	Tullaroan . .	Kilkenny . .	I.	88
21	Knocknamucklagh .	225 2 37	Cork, E.R. .	Duhallow . .	Kilmeen . .	Kanturk . .	II.	73
47, 48	Knocknamucklagh .	323 3 21	Kerry . .	Magunihy . .	Kilnanare . .	Killarney . .	II.	204
117, 120	Knocknamucklagh .	355 3 16	Mayo . .	Kilmaine . .	Ballinchalla . .	Ballinrobe . .	IV.	152
20	Knocknamuck Lower	184 1 22	Wicklow . .	Upper Talbotstown .	Ballynure . .	Baltinglass . .	I.	362
10	Knocknamuckly .	254 1 29	Armagh . .	Oneilland East .	Seagoe . .	Lurgan . .	III.	50
28	Knocknamuck North	256 2 23	Waterford .	Coshmore&Coshbride	Lismore and Mocollop	Lismore . .	II.	346
28	Knocknamuck South	113 0 36	Waterford .	Coshmore&Coshbride	Lismore and Mocollop	Lismore . .	II.	346
20	Knocknamuck Upper	146 1 12	Wicklow . .	Upper Talbotstown .	Ballynure . .	Baltinglass . .	I.	362
26	Knocknamucky .	217 2 12	Clare . .	Bunratty Upper .	Inchicronan . .	Tulla . .	II.	9
87	Knocknamullagh .	335 1 7	Cork, E.R. .	Cork . .	Carrigaline . .	Cork . .	II.	64
25, 28	Knocknamullagh or Derryilan .	212 1 18	Monaghan .	Farney . .	Donaghmoyne .	Carrickmacross	III.	269
22	Knocknamunnion .	314 1 19	Wicklow . .	Upper Talbotstown .	Donaghmore . .	Baltinglass . .	I.	363
21	Knocknanagh Commons .	365 0 13	Cork, E.R. .	Duhallow . .	Kilmeen . .	Kanturk . .	II.	73
21	Knocknanagh East .	434 2 31	Cork, E.R. .	Duhallow . .	Kilmeen . .	Kanturk . .	II.	73
21	Knocknanagh West	416 2 12	Cork, E.R. .	Duhallow . .	Kilmeen . .	Kanturk . .	II.	73
28	Knocknanarney .	156 1 13	Kerry . .	Trughanacmy .	Ballynahaglish .	Tralee . .	II.	207
40, 46	Knocknanarny .	458 0 9	Down . .	Upper Iveagh, Up.pt.	Donaghmore . .	Newry . .	III.	175
12	Knocknanask . .	551 0 34	Waterford .	Coshmore&Coshbride	Lismore and Mocollop	Lismore . .	II.	346
112	Knocknanav . .	99 2 1	Cork, E.R. .	Kinalea . .	Kinure . .	Kinsale . .	II.	95
15	Knocknaneen . .	400 2 5	Monaghan .	Cremorne . .	Muckno . .	Castleblayney .	III.	262
83, 95	Knocknaneirk .	556 2 13	Cork, W.R. .	West Muskerry .	Kilmurry . .	Macroom . .	II.	159
48	Knocknanool . .	370 1 35	Roscommon .	Athlone . .	Kiltoom . .	Athlone . .	IV.	183
23	Knocknanuss . .	262 3 8	Cork, E.R. .	Duhallow . .	Subulter . .	Kanturk . .	II.	75
122	Knocknanuss . .	394 3 14	Cork, W.R. .	East Carbery (E.D.)	Desertserges . .	Clonakilty . .	II.	128
47, 53	Knocknanuss . .	365 0 18	Tipperary, N.R. .	Eliogarty . .	Moycarky . .	Thurles . .	II.	271
121	Knocknapisha . .	76 3 19	Mayo . .	Kilmaine . .	Kilmainebeg . .	Ballinrobe . .	IV.	155

(a) Including 94A. 0R. 28P. water.   (b) Including 33A. 0A. 12P. water.

4 K 2

No. of Sheet of the Ordnance Survey Maps.	Townlands and Towns.	Area in Statute Acres.	County.	Barony.	Parish.	Poor Law Union in 1857.	Townland Census of 1851, Part I.	
		A. R. P.					Vol.	Page
112, 125	Knocknapogaree	139 1 36	Cork, E.R.	Kinsale	Ringcurran	Kinsale	II.	100
76	Knocknaquill	165 1 37	Tipperary, S.R.	Middlethird	Knockgraffon	Cashel	II.	328
15	Knocknaraha	167 1 7	Clare	Corcomroe	Killaspuglonane	Ennistimon	II.	19
141	Knocknaraha	155 0 35	Cork, W.R.	West Carbery (E.D.)	Aghadown	Skibbereen	II.	137
28,29,33,34	Knocknaraha	185 3 7	Waterford	Coshmore&Coshbride	Kilwatermoy	Lismore	II.	343
8	Knocknaranhy	203 3 26	Clare	Corcomroe	Killilagh	Ennistimon	II.	20
63,64,67,68	Knocknarea	273 1 35	Antrim	Upper Massereene	Magheragall	Lisburn	III.	31
14	Knocknarea North	200 1 6	Sligo	Carbury	Killaspugbrone	Sligo	IV.	222
14	Knocknarea South	253 3 18	Sligo	Carbury	Killaspugbrone	Sligo	IV.	222
2, 6	Knocknaree	1,258 2 34	Waterford	Upperthird	Kilsheelan	Clonmel	II.	370
16. 24	Knocknareeha	111 3 27	Clare	Inchiquin	Rath	Corrofin	II.	27
60	Knocknarney	217 3 35	Tyrone	Dungannon Lower	Carnteel	Dungannon	III.	297
60, 61	Knocknaroy	526 2 36a	Tyrone	Dungannon Lower	Aghaloo	Dungannon	III.	297
31	Knocknasalla	16 1 18	Waterford	Decies without Drum	Dungarvan	Dungarvan	II.	355
3, 4, 7	Knocknasave	110 1 7	Monaghan	Trough	Donagh	Monaghan	III.	282
23, 27	Knocknasawna	135 3 17	Leitrim	Leitrim	Kiltoghert	Car[k]. on Shannon	IV.	102
58	Knocknascrow	1,571 2 22	Limerick	Coshlea	Kilbeheny	Mitchelstown	II.	239
60	Knocknaseed	353 0 5	Kerry	Magunihy	Nohavaldaly	Killarney	II.	205
22, 27	Knocknashammer	393 1 30	Cavan	Clankee	Drumgoon	Cootehill	III.	72
44	Knocknashammer	228 0 10	Sligo	Coolavin	Kilfree	Boyle	IV.	224
14, 20	Knocknashammer or Cloverhill	285 2 30b	Sligo	Carbury	Kilmacowen	Sligo	IV.	222
33	Knocknashamroge	276 3 11	Wicklow	Ballinacor South	Hacketstown	Shillelagh	I.	349
6	Knocknashane	208 0 34	Armagh	Oneilland East	Shankill	Lurgan	III.	51
107, 110	Knocknashangan	227 0 16	Donegal	Tirhugh	Kilbarron	Ballyshannon	III.	148
13, 19	Knocknashangan	403 0 39c	Fermanagh	Magheraboy	Devenish	Ballyshannon	III.	211
29	Knocknashannagh	302 1 0	Cork, E.R.	Duhallow	Cullen	Millstreet	II.	70
6	Knocknashee	117 0 14	Roscommon	Boyle	Boyle	Boyle	IV.	194
32	Knocknashee Common	48 2 36	Sligo	Leyny	Achonry	Tobercurry	IV.	229
12, 13	Knocknasheega	279 2 38	Waterford	Decies without Drum	Affane	Lismore	II.	353
27, 28	Knocknasilloge	491 0 14	Wexford	Ballaghkeen	Ballyvaldon	Enniscorthy	I.	292
54	Knocknaskagh	83 3 25	Cork, E.R.	Barrymore	Britway	Middleton	II.	52
66, 77	Knocknaskagh	180 0 20	Cork, E.R.	Imokilly	Killeagh	Youghal	II.	88
29, 30	Knocknaskagh Lower	257 0 3	Waterford	Decies without Drum	Kilmolash	Dungarvan	II.	357
30	Knocknaskagh Upper	198 1 35	Waterford	Decies without Drum	Kilmolash	Dungarvan	II.	357
19	Knocknaskea	75 2 2	Longford	Moydow	Kilglass	Ballymahon	I.	161
52,53,62,63	Knocknaskeagh	222 0 1	Clare	Bunratty Lower	Killeely	Limerick	II.	5
8, 15	Knocknaskeagh	354 1 21	Clare	Corcomroe	Kilshanny	Ennistimon	II.	21
50	Knocknaskeagh	338 1 6d	Mayo	Gallen	Killasser	Swineford	IV.	149
80	Knocknaskeagh	638 2 7	Mayo	Gallen	Killedan	Swineford	IV.	150
39, 44	Knocknaskeagh	309 2 39	Sligo	Coolavin	Kilfree	Boyle	IV.	224
15,16,20,21	Knocknaskeagh	304 1 32	Wexford	Gorey	Kilcormick	Enniscorthy	I.	317
33	Knocknaskeagh	267 2 14	Wicklow	Ballinacor South	Hacketstown	Shillelagh	I.	349
59, 67	Knocknaskeha	418 3 33	Kerry	Magunihy	Killarney	Killarney	II.	203
82	Knocknaskeharoe	33 2 19	Tipperary, S.R.	Iffa and Offa West	Ardfinnan	Clogheen	II.	317
30	Knocknasliggaun	370 0 35e	Sligo	Leyny	Kilmacteige	Tobercurry	IV.	231
34, 42	Knocknasnaa	1,825 3 34f	Limerick	Glenquin	Abbeyfeale	Newcastle	II.	244
17, 18, 24	Knocknastackan	291 1 27g	Fermanagh	Tirkennedy	Enniskillen	Lisnaskea	III.	222
109	Knocknastooka	118 1 13	Cork, W.R.	East Carbery (E.D.)	Desertserges	Bandon	II.	128
38	Knocknastooka	125 1 7	Waterford	Decies within Drum	Lisgenan or Grange	Youghal	II.	352
9	Knocknastreile	49 2 6	Wicklow	Lower Talbotstown	Hollywood	Baltinglass	I.	361
62	Knocknasuff	414 0 8	Cork, E.R.	East Muskerry	Garrycloyne	Cork	II.	103
68	Knocknatinnyweel	144 1 31h	Mayo	Burrishoole	Burrishoole	Newport	IV.	119
13	Knocknatubbrid	303 0 10	Carlow	Forth	Ardoyne	Carlow	I.	3
43	Knocknaveagh	422 3 31	Cavan	Castlerahan	Munterconnaught	Oldcastle	III.	71
90	Knocknaveagh	48 1 33	Mayo	Carra	Drum	Castlebar	IV.	128
27	Knocknavey	246 0 33	Wexford	Ballaghkeen	Killisk	Enniscorthy	I.	296
1, 6	Knocknavorahee	97 3 22	Cork, E.R.	Orrery and Kilmore	Kilbolane	Kanturk	II.	108
33, 39	Knocknawhishoge	98 2 6	Sligo	Corran	Toomour	Boyle	IV.	228
48	Knockpell	14 2 5	Wexford	Forth	Killinick	Wexford	I.	310
24	Knockneppy	172 1 33i	Clare	Corcomroe	Clooney	Ennistimon	II.	18
14	Knocknew	504 0 28	Kilkenny	Fassadinin	Kilmademoge	Kilkenny	I.	90
33	Knockninny	277 1 5	Fermanagh	Knockninny	Kinawley	Lisnaskea	III.	202
6	Knocknogher	261 3 9	Londonderry	Coleraine	Dunboe	Coleraine	III.	231
47, 52	Knocknoran	105 3 3	Wexford	Bargy	Kilmore	Wexford	I.	306
55	Knock North	84 0 9	Galway	Moycullen	Killannin	Oughterard	IV.	70
121	Knock North	274 3 29	Mayo	Kilmaine	Cong	Ballinrobe	IV.	154
39, 40	Knockoconor	145 0 33	Sligo	Corran	Toomour	Boyle	IV.	228
42	Knock of the Rocks	27 0 30	Wexford	Bargy	Kilmannan	Wexford	I.	306
24, 32	Knockognoe	252 1 7	Kerry	Trughanacmy	Brosna	Tralee	II.	108
51, 52	Knockogonnell	407 2 8	Clare	Inchiquin	Inagh	Ennistimon	II.	25
2, 7	Knockogonnell	451 0 12	Galway	Ballymoe	Kilcroan	Glennamaddy	IV.	9

(a) Including 10A. 2R. 20P. water.
(b) Including 6A. 0R. 21P. water.
(c) Including 1A. 2R. 29P. water.
(d) Including 0A. 1R. 11P. water.
(e) Including 10A. 0R. 30P. water.
(f) Including 3A. 3R. 8P. water.
(g) Including 4A. 1R. 30P. water.
(h) Including 5A. 3R. 16P. water.
(i) Including 4A. 2R. 20P. water.

No. of Sheet of the Ordnance Survey Maps.	Townlands and Towns.	Area in Statute Acres.	County.	Barony.	Parish.	Poor Law Union in 1857.	Townland Census of 1851, Part I.	
		A. R. P.					Vol.	Page
26, 31, 32	Knockoneill	1,713 0 7	Londonderry	Loughinsholin	Maghera	Magherafelt	III.	242
52	Knockonny	368 0 35	Tyrone	Clogher	Errigal Keerogue	Clogher	III.	295
66	Knockordan	234 2 37	Tipperary, S.R.	Clanwilliam	Lattin	Tipperary	II.	309
6	Knockough	242 1 24	Cork, E.R.	Orrery and Kilmore	Kilbolane	Kanturk	II.	108
114	Knockoura	821 3 36	Cork, W.R.	Bear	Killaconenagh	Castletown	II.	125
123, 124	Knockoura	845 2 0	Galway	Loughrea	Kilthomas	Gort	IV.	65
123	Knockouran	262 3 25	Galway	Kiltartan	Kilbeacanty	Gort	IV.	47
109	Knockowen	449 1 35	Kerry	Glanarought	Tuosist	Kenmare	II.	189
13	Knockown	96 1 11	Kilkenny	Crannagh	Freshford	Kilkenny	I.	85
18	Knockparson	83 3 23	Waterford	Gaultiere	Crooke	Waterford	II.	362
23	Knockpatrick	218 1 22	Clare	Corcomroe	Kilmanaheen	Ennistimon	II.	21
38, 40	Knockpatrick	422 1 28	Kildare	Kilkea and Moone	Graney	Baltinglass	I.	60
10	Knockpatrick	242 2 14	Limerick	Shanid	Robertstown	Glin	II.	258
50, 58	Knockphelagh	580 1 13	Tipperary, S.R.	Clanwilliam	Solloghodmore	Tipperary	II.	311
14	Knockphilip	91 0 19	Queen's Co.	Stradbally	Curraclone	Athy	I.	246
68	Knockphutteen	300 3 39	Clare	Clonderalaw	Killofin	Killadysert	II.	17
74	Knockpoge	9 3 8	Cork, E.R.	Cork	St. Annes Shandon	Cork	II.	65
85	Knockpoge	146 0 39	Cork, E.R.	East Muskerry	Kilnaglory	Cork	II.	104
64	Knockraha East	265 0 10	Cork, E.R.	Barrymore	Kilquane	Cork	II.	55
64	KNOCKRAHA T.	—	Cork, E.R.	Barrymore	Kilquane	Cork	II.	56
64	Knockraha West	188 1 4	Cork, E.R.	Barrymore	Kilquane	Cork	II.	55
48, 59	Knockraheen	999 1 10	Cork, W.R.	West Muskerry	Clondrohid	Macroom	II.	155
12, 18	Knockraheen	1,370 2 25	Wicklow	Newcastle	Calary	Rathdrum	I.	350
6	Knockramer	157 3 13	Armagh	Oneilland East	Seagoe	Lurgan	III.	50
7	Knockranny	131 1 23	Cavan	Tullyhaw	Kinawley	Bawnboy	III.	93
67,68,80,81	Knockranny	1,748 1 14a	Galway	Moycullen	Moycullen	Galway	IV.	71
72	Knockranny	223 1 2	Mayo	Gallen	Kilconduff	Swineford	IV.	148
88	Knockranny	183 1 3	Mayo	Murrisk	Oughaval	Westport	IV.	162
3, 4	Knockranny	376 0 5b	Roscommon	Boyle	Kilronan	Boyle	IV.	197
23, 24, 29	Knockrath Big	976 0 28	Wicklow	Ballinacor North	Knockrath	Rathdrum	I.	347
78	Knockrathkelly	90 3 27	Tipperary, S.R.	Iffa and Offa East	Kilcash	Clonmel	II.	313
26	Knockrathkyle	77 2 30	Wexford	Ballaghkeen	Ballyhuskard	Enniscorthy	I.	292
23,24,29,30	Knockrath Little	339 0 13	Wicklow	Ballinacor North	Knockrath	Rathdrum	I.	347
79	Knockrawer	46 3 34	Donegal	Raphoe	Donaghmore	Strabane	III.	138
78	Knockrawer	111 1 33	Mayo	Carra	Breaghwy	Castlebar	IV.	127
39	Knockrawer	81 0 20	Sligo	Corran	Kilshalvy	Boyle	IV.	227
38, 39	Knockrawer	119 3 14	Sligo	Corran	Kilturra	Tobercurry	IV.	228
26, 27	Knockrawer	231 3 18	Sligo	Tirerrill	Drumcolumb	Sligo	IV.	238
74	Knockrea	272 3 2c	Cork, E.R.	Cork and Municipal Borough	St. Nicholas	Cork	II.	66
24	Knockreagh	407 0 29	Clare	Inchiquin	Dysert	Ennis	II.	24
16	Knockreagh	115 3 8	Kerry	Clanmaurice	Kilfeighny	Listowel	II.	170
16	Knockreagh	231 1 31	Kerry	Clanmaurice	Kilshenane	Listowel	II.	172
21	Knockreagh	173 2 24	Kerry	Clanmaurice	O'Dorney	Tralee	II.	172
57	Knockreagh	400 3 23	Kerry	Magunihy	Kilcolman	Killarney	II.	200
49	Knockreagh	448 1 31	Kerry	Trughanacmy	Ballincuslane	Tralee	II.	206
22, 26	Knockreagh	363 3 32	Kilkenny	Shillelogher	Tullamaine	Callan	I.	116
29	Knockreagh	54 3 6	Monaghan	Farney	Inishkeen	Dundalk	III.	271
9, 10, 14, 15	Knockreagh	150 0 27	Wexford	Scarawalsh	Ballycarney	Enniscorthy	I.	322
25	Knockreagh Lower	142 1 9	Monaghan	Farney	Donaghmoyne	Castleblayney	III.	270
25, 28	Knockreagh Upper	183 3 8	Monaghan	Farney	Donaghmoyne	Carrickmacross	III.	270
26	Knockreddan	344 2 34d	Clare	Bunratty Upper	Inchicronan	Tulla	II.	9
25	Knockredmond	127 0 16	Wexford	Bantry	Rossdroit	Enniscorthy	I.	302
66	Knockreer	436 1 37	Kerry	Magunihy	Aghadoe	Killarney	II.	199
15,16,19,20	Knockrevan	342 0 6	Armagh	Armagh	Derrynoose	Armagh	III.	44
101	Knockrickard	88 0 13	Mayo	Clanmorris	Mayo	Claremorris	IV.	135
101	Knockrickard	47 3 5	Mayo	Clanmorris	Tagheen	Claremorris	IV.	136
20	Knockrinahan	128 0 2	Tipperary, N.R.	Owney and Arra	Youghalarra	Nenagh	II.	297
112	Knockrobin	192 2 15	Cork, E.R.	Kinsale	Clontead	Kinsale	II.	99
25	Knockrobin	110 1 17	Wicklow	Newcastle	Rathnew	Rathdrum	I.	354
16	Knockrobin Lower	205 2 9	Wexford	Scarawalsh	Toome	Gorey	I.	326
25	Knockrobin Murragh	17 2 4	Wicklow	Newcastle	Rathnew	Rathdrum	I.	354
16	Knockrobin Upper	250 2 27	Wexford	Scarawalsh	Toome	Gorey	I.	326
23	Knockroe	1,249 1 37	Carlow	Idrone East	Kiltennell	New Ross	I.	7
4	Knockroe	112 3 12	Carlow	Rathvilly	Rathvilly	Baltinglass	I.	12
11,12,15,16	Knockroe	40 3 38	Cavan	Tullygarvey	Annagh	Cavan	III.	87
7	Knockroe	228 2 16	Cavan	Tullyhaw	Kinawley	Bawnboy	III.	93
52	Knockroe	83 2 12	Clare	Bunratty Lower	Kilfintinan	Limerick	II.	5
62	Knockroe	107 2 9	Clare	Bunratty Lower	Killeely	Limerick	II.	5
24	Knockroe	75 2 39	Clare	Corcomroe	Clooney	Ennistimon	II.	18
16	Knockroe	612 3 17	Clare	Corcomroe	Kiltoraght	Corrofin	II.	22
6, 7, 10, 11	Knockroe	201 3 26	Clare	Inchiquin	Kilkeedy	Corrofin	II.	26
56	Knockroe	88 1 8	Clare	Moyarta	Kilfearagh	Kilrush	II.	32

(a) Including 5A. 3R. 22P. water.
(b) Including 89A. 1R. 30P. water.
(c) { Within the Municipal Boundary, 41A. 2R. 18P.
{ Without the Municipal Boundary, 231A. 0R. 24P.
(d) Including 7A. 0R. 24P. water.

No. of Sheet of the Ordnance Survey Maps.	Townlands and Towns.	Area in Statute Acres.	County.	Barony.	Parish.	Poor Law Union in 1857.	Townland Census of 1851, Part I.	
		A. R. P.					Vol.	Page
111	Knockroe	601 2 16	Cork, W.R.	East Carbery (E.D.)	Inishannon	Bandon	II.	128
140	Knockroe	433 3 16	Cork, W.R.	West Carbery(W.D.)	Kilcoe	Skull	II.	143
129, 138	Knockroe	218 1 18	Cork, W.R.	West Carbery(W.D.)	Kilcrohane	Bantry	II.	143
70	Knockroe	441 3 0	Cork, W.R.	West Muskerry	Kilnamartry	Macroom	II.	160
6	Knockroe	103 1 7	Fermanagh	Lurg	Drumkeeran	Lowtherstown	III.	206
17, 30	Knockroe	288 2 7a	Galway	Ballymoe	Clonbern	Tuam	IV.	6
87	Knockroe	197 1 14	Galway	Clonmacnowen	Kilcloony	Ballinasloe	IV.	25
104, 105	Knockroe	277 2 3	Galway	Dunkellin	Kilconickny	Loughrea	IV.	29
85	Knockroe	502 3 33	Galway	Kilconnell	Killimordaly	Loughrea	IV.	42
123	Knockroe	290 0 26b	Galway	Kiltartan	Kilbeacanty	Gort	IV.	47
125	Knockroe	48 2 25	Galway	Leitrim	Ballynakill	Loughrea	IV.	51
115	Knockroe	184 0 3	Galway	Loughrea	Killeenadeema	Loughrea	IV.	64
14	Knockroe	108 1 16	Kerry	Clanmaurice	Ardfert	Tralee	II.	167
80, 81	Knockroe	574 1 26	Kerry	Iveragh	Dromod	Cahersiveen	II.	195
39	Knockroe	299 0 2	Kildare	Kilkea and Moone	Dunmanoge	Athy	I.	59
38, 40	Knockroe	325 0 39	Kildare	Kilkea and Moone	Graney	Baltinglass	I.	60
18	Knockroe	83 3 22	Kilkenny	Crannagh	Ballinamara	Kilkenny	I.	84
9, 10	Knockroe	354 1 28	Kilkenny	Fassadinin	Rathbeagh	Castlecomer	I.	91
30	Knockroe	165 0 21	Kilkenny	Kells	Kilmaganny	Callan	I.	109
34	Knockroe	189 3 12	Kilkenny	Kells	Tullahought	Callan	I.	110
23	Knockroe	47 1 16	Limerick	Clanwilliam	Caherconlish	Limerick	II.	222
24, 33	Knockroe	555 1 38	Limerick	Coonagh	Kilteely	Tipperary	II.	235
12	Knockroe	174 2 36	Limerick	Kenry	Kildimo	Rathkeale	II.	250
92	Knockroe	116 3 29	Mayo	Clanmorris	Knock	Claremorris	IV.	135
101	Knockroe	582 3 17c	Mayo	Clanmorris	Mayo	Claremorris	IV.	135
92, 93	Knockroe	146 2 27	Mayo	Costello	Annagh	Claremorris	IV.	138
121	Knockroe	137 1 22	Mayo	Kilmaine	Kilmainebeg	Ballinrobe	IV.	155
119, 122	Knockroe	368 1 2	Mayo	Kilmaine	Kilmainemore	Ballinrobe	IV.	156
118	Knockroe	196 2 5	Mayo	Kilmaine	Kilmolara	Ballinrobe	IV.	157
14	Knockroe	70 2 4	Mayo	Tirawley	Templemurry	Killala	IV.	172
6	Knockroe	32 0 29	Roscommon	Boyle	Ardcarn	Boyle	IV.	193
10	Knockroe	304 3 25	Roscommon	Boyle	Estersnow	Boyle	IV.	195
10, 16	Knockroe	534 1 29d	Roscommon	Boyle	Killummod	Cark on Shannon	IV.	196
15, 21	Knockroe	274 3 28	Roscommon	Castlereagh	Kilcorkey	Castlereagh	IV.	199
26	Knockroe	71 0 36	Roscommon	Castlereagh	Kilkeevin	Castlereagh	IV.	200
40	Knockroe	209 3 11	Sligo	Tirerrill	Aghanagh	Boyle	IV.	237
26, 27	Knockroe	182 3 19	Sligo	Tirerrill	Kilmacallan	Sligo	IV.	240
35	Knockroe	508 3 18	Sligo	Tirerrill	Kilmactranny	Boyle	IV.	240
47	Knockroe	362 1 35	Tipperary, N.R.	Eliogarty	Moycarky	Thurles	II.	271
41	Knockroe	185 1 26	Tipperary, N.R.	Eliogarty	Rahelty	Thurles	II.	272
60	Knockroe	188 3 24	Tipperary, S.R.	Clanwilliam	Relickmurry & Athassel	Tipperary	II.	310
88	Knockroe	32 2 8	Tipperary, S.R.	Iffa and Offa West	Neddans	Clogheen	II.	319
51	Knockroe	84 0 12	Tipperary, S.R.	Kilnamanagh Lower	Kilpatrick	Cashel	II.	324
63	Knockroe	494 2 0	Tipperary, S.R.	Middlethird	Drangan	Cashel	II.	326
60	Knockroe	158 3 20	Tipperary, S.R.	Middlethird	Relickmurry & Athassel	Cashel	II.	330
10, 17	Knockroe	595 2 23e	Tyrone	Strabane Lower	Ardstraw	Strabane	III.	319
28	Knockroe	117 0 5	Waterford	Coshmore&Coshbride	Lismore and Mocollop	Lismore	II.	346
22	Knockroe	298 0 23	Waterford	Decies without Drum	Colligan	Dungarvan	II.	354
18	Knockroe	273 2 27	Waterford	Gaultiere	Kill St. Nicholas	Waterford	II.	364
3	Knockroe	36 3 6	Westmeath	Fore	Rathgarve	Granard	I.	271
12	Knockroe	89 1 20	Wexford	Ballaghkeen	Ardamine	Gorey	I.	291
30	Knockroe	471 2 35	Wexford	Bantry	Oldross	New Ross	I.	301
9	Knockroe	96 2 25	Wicklow	Lower Talbotstown	Hollywood	Baltinglass	I.	361
13	Knockroe	154 2 37	Wicklow	Newcastle	Kilcoole	Rathdrum	I.	352
11	Knockroe (Archdall)	106 2 21	Fermanagh	Lurg	Derryvullan	Lowtherstown	III.	204
104	Knockroebeg	19 1 8	Galway	Dunkellin	Kilconickny	Loughrea	IV.	29
114, 127	Knockroe East	357 1 34	Cork, W.R.	Bear	Kilnamanagh	Castletown	II.	126
11	Knockroe (Irvine)	48 0 21	Fermanagh	Lurg	Derryvullan	Lowtherstown	III.	204
23	Knockroe (Mason)	446 2 16	Limerick	Clanwilliam	Inch St. Lawrence	Limerick	II.	224
114, 127	Knockroe Middle	339 0 6	Cork, W.R.	Bear	Kilnamanagh	Castletown	II.	126
114, 127	Knockroe West	242 2 24f	Cork, W.R.	Bear	Kilnamanagh	Castletown	II.	126
23	Knockroe (Wilson)	269 1 6	Limerick	Clanwilliam	Inch St. Lawrence	Limerick	II.	224
6	Knockronaghan	195 3 7	Monaghan	Trough	Donagh	Monaghan	III.	282
28	Knockroosk	113 0 26g	Leitrim	Mohill	Fenagh	Mohill	IV.	106
88	Knockroosky	300 3 3h	Mayo	Burrishoole	Aghagower	Westport	IV.	118
16	Knockroundaly	173 2 30	Cork, E.R.	Orrery and Kilmore	Kilbroney	Mallow	II.	109
60, 61	Knockrour	937 1 13	Cork, W.R.	East Muskerry	Aghabulloge	Macroom	II.	153
58, 60	Knockrour	249 0 17	Limerick	Coshlea	Kilbeheny	Mitchelstown	II.	239
33	Knockrour	163 1 9	Waterford	Coshmore&Coshbride	Tallow	Lismore	II.	348
49, 50	Knockrower East	1,086 0 11	Kerry	Trughanacmy	Ballincuslane	Tralee	II.	206
49	Knockrower West	799 2 19	Kerry	Trughanacmy	Ballincuslane	Tralee	II.	206
42	Knockruth	72 1 6	Wexford	Forth	Rathmacknee	Wexford	I.	313
122	Knocks	540 3 5	Cork, W.R.	East Carbery (E.D.)	Desertserges	Clonakilty	II.	128

(a) Including 26A. 3R. 13P. water.
(b) Including 4A. 0R. 5P. water.
(c) Including 2A. 2R. 0P. water.

(d) Including 22A. 1R. 13P. water.
(e) Including 22A. 2R. 13P. water.
(f) Including 57A. 1R. 30P. detached portion.

(g) Including 19A. 3R. 14P. water.
(h) Including 5A. 2R. 29P. water.

No. of Sheet of the Ordnance Survey Maps.	Townlands and Towns.	Area in Statute Acres.			County.	Barony.	Parish.	Poor Law Union in 1857.	Townland Census of 1851, Part I.	
		A.	R.	P.					Vol.	Page
121	Knocks . .	309	3	1	Cork, W.R. .	East Carbery (W.D.)	Kilkerranmore	Clonakilty .	II.	133
121	Knocks . .	186	2	23	Cork, W.R. .	Ibane and Barryroe	Kilmean . .	Clonakilty .	II.	149
40	Knocks . .	133	2	18	Fermanagh .	Clankelly . .	Clones . .	Clones . .	III.	196
28,39,34,35	Knocks . .	193	1	16a	Fermanagh .	Magherastephana .	Aghalurcher .	Lisnaskea .	III.	217
22	Knocks . .	121	3	30	Leitrim . .	Carrigallen . .	Drumreilly .	Bawnboy . .	IV.	91
50	Knocks . .	223	1	25b	Mayo . .	Gallen . . .	Killasser . .	Swineford .	IV.	149
44	Knocks . .	82	2	11	Meath . .	Ratoath . .	Dunshaughlin .	Dunshaughlin .	I.	218
12	Knocks . .	160	0	1	Queen's Co. .	Maryborough West	Clonenagh and Clonagheen . .	Mountmellick .	I.	243
47	Knocks . .	108	2	0	Wexford . .	Bargy . .	Tomhaggard .	Wexford . .	I.	308
51	Knocksaggart .	149	0	38	Clare . .	Bunratty Lower .	Kilnasoolagh .	Ennis . .	II.	6
50	Knocksaggart .	331	0	39	Clare . .	Clonderalaw .	Kilchreest .	Killadysert .	II.	15
69, 70	Knocksaharn .	448	2	12	Cork, W.R. .	West Muskerry .	Kilnamartry .	Macroom .	II.	160
61	Knocksaintlour .	80	1	29	Tipperary, S.R. .	Middlethird .	St. John Baptist	Cashel . .	II.	330
70,79	Knocksaxon .	551	2	1	Mayo . .	Gallen . .	Templemore .	Castlebar .	IV.	151
30	Knocksbarrett .	147	1	11	Mayo . .	Tirawley . .	Kilmoremoy .	Ballina .	IV.	170
19, 20, 22	Knockscur or Knocksquire . .	713	0	27	Carlow . .	Idrone East .	Kiltennell .	Carlow . .	I.	7
21	Knocks East . .	78	0	35	Monaghan .	Dartree . .	Currin . .	Cootehill .	III.	266
11	Knocksedan .	98	3	25	Dublin . .	Nethercross .	Swords . .	Balrothery .	I.	32
22	Knockseera .	106	2	32	Queen's Co. .	Clandonagh .	Aghaboe . .	Donaghmore .	I.	232
6	Knocksentry .	221	2	30	Limerick . .	Clanwilliam .	Killeenagarriff	Limerick . .	II.	224
72, 84	Knockshanawee .	611	1	7	Cork, E.R. .	East Muskerry .	Aglish . .	Bandon . .	II.	101
68	Knockshanbally .	298	1	36c	Galway . .	Moycullen .	Moycullen .	Galway . .	IV.	71
11, 15	Knockshanbally .	453	0	6	Kilkenny . .	Gowran . .	Kilmadum .	Kilkenny .	I.	97
60, 70	Knockshanbally .	291	3	1	Mayo . .	Gallen . .	Templemore .	Castlebar .	IV.	151
10	Knockshanbo .	372	1	34	Mayo . .	Erris . .	Kilmore . .	Belmullet .	IV.	146
38, 39	Knockshanbrittas .	825	3	18	Tipperary, N.R. .	Kilnamanagh Upper	Doon . .	Tipperary .	II.	277
23, 29	Knockshangan .	122	1	0	Meath . .	Lune . . .	Athboy . .	Trim . .	I.	207
106	Knockshangarry .	59	1	28	Galway . .	Leitrim . .	Kilmeen . .	Loughrea .	IV.	54
106	Knockshangarry .	59	0	28	Galway . .	Loughrea . .	Loughrea . .	Loughrea .	IV.	66
40	Knockshannagh .	388	3	30	Kildare . .	Kilkea and Moone .	Graney . .	Baltinglass .	I.	60
44	Knockshanvo .	487	2	2	Clare . .	Tulla Lower .	Kilseily . .	Limerick . .	II.	37
5, 6	Knockshaunfin .	91	1	37	Wexford . .	Scarawalsh .	Carnew . .	Gorey . .	II.	322
28, 34	Knockshearoon .	252	3	11	Tipperary, N.R. .	Kilnamanagh Upper	Glenkeen .	Thurles . .	II.	278
8	Knockshigowna .	218	2	20	Tipperary, N.R. .	Lower Ormond .	Ballingarry .	Borrisokane .	II.	282
22	Knockshough Glebe	125	1	7	Kildare . .	Offaly East .	Kildare . .	Naas . .	I.	70
27	Knocksimon .	132	0	34	Westmeath .	Farbill . . .	Killucan . .	Mullingar .	I.	267
7	Knocks ink . .	40	1	15	Wicklow . .	Rathdown . .	Powerscourt .	Rathdown .	I.	356
122	Knockskagh .	489	0	8	Cork, W.R. .	East Carbery (E.D.)	Kilgarriff .	Clonakilty .	II.	129
133	Knockskagh .	826	2	15	Cork, W.R. .	East Carbery (W.D.)	Kilmacabea .	Skibbereen .	II.	133
76	Knockskagh .	150	3	14	Tipperary, S.R. .	Iffa and Offa West .	Mortlestown .	Clogheen .	II.	319
5, 6	Knockskavane .	910	0	18	Cork, E.R. .	Duhallow .	Clonfert . .	Kanturk .	II.	68
45, 46	Knockskehan .	235	2	35	Roscommon .	Athlone . .	St. John's .	Athlone . .	IV.	184
5, 6, 14, 15	Knockskeby .	797	2	8	Cork, E.R. .	Duhallow .	Clonfert . .	Kanturk .	II.	68
21	Knockskemolin .	151	0	19	Wexford . .	Ballaghkeen .	Kilnamanagh .	Gorey . .	I.	297
111	Knocksmall .	78	2	30	Cork, E.R. .	Kinalea . .	Dunderrow .	Kinsale . .	II.	94
4	Knocksoghey .	249	3	35d	Antrim . .	Cary . . .	Ballintoy .	Ballycastle .	III.	12
47	Knocksouna .	446	1	15	Limerick . .	Coshma . .	Tankardstown .	Kilmallock .	II.	244
92	Knock South .	605	1	9	Galway . .	Moycullen .	Killannin .	Galway . .	IV.	70
121	Knock South .	74	2	17	Mayo . .	Kilmaine . .	Cong . .	Ballinrobe .	IV.	154
19, 20, 22	Knocksquire or Knockscur . .	713	0	27	Carlow . .	Idrone East .	Kiltennell .	Carlow . .	I.	7
36,37,43,44	Knocksticken . .	453	2	24	Down . .	Kinelarty .	Loughinisland .	Downpatrick .	III.	177
37	Knockstown .	68	2	29	Meath . .	Lower Deece .	Kilmessan .	Dunshaughlin .	I.	192
37	Knockstown .	299	0	35	Meath . .	Lower Deece .	Trubley .	Trim . .	I.	192
43	Knockstown .	322	3	25	Meath . .	Upper Deece .	Kilmore . .	Dunshaughlin .	I.	193
24, 30	Knockstown .	558	0	10	Wexford . .	Bantry . .	Killegney .	Enniscorthy .	I.	301
47	Knockstowry .	34	1	27	Tipperary, N.R. .	Eliogarty .	Moycarky .	Thurles . .	II.	271
21	Knocks West .	162	2	35	Monaghan .	Dartree . .	Currin . .	Clones . .	III.	266
41	Knocktarton .	196	1	33	Wexford . .	Shelmaliere West .	Ballymitty .	Wexford . .	I.	332
78	Knockthomas .	201	1	33	Mayo . .	Carra . .	Aglish . .	Castlebar .	IV.	123
133	Knocktoby . .	191	1	12	Galway . .	Kiltartan .	Beagh . .	Gort . .	IV.	46
53, 54	Knocktoosh .	1,100	1	29	Limerick . .	Glenquin .	Killagholehane .	Newcastle .	II.	245
31	Knocktopherabbey .	228	0	36	Kilkenny .	Knocktopher .	Knocktopher .	Thomastown .	I.	112
31	Knocktopher Commons . .	187	3	11	Kilkenny .	Knocktopher .	Knocktopher .	Thomastown .	I.	112
31	Knocktophermanor	257	1	37e	Kilkenny .	Knocktopher .	Knocktopher .	Thomastown .	I.	112
31	KNOCKTOPHER T. .	—			Kilkenny .	Knocktopher .	Knocktopher .	Thomastown .	I.	112
40, 48	Knocktoran .	405	0	16	Limerick . .	Coshlea .	Knocklong .	Kilmallock .	II.	240
68	KNOCK T. . .	—			Clare . .	Clonderalaw .	Kilmurry .	Kilrush .	II.	18
46	Knocktown .	226	1	37	Wexford . .	Bargy . .	Duncormick .	Wexford . .	I.	305
53	Knockudder .	76	2	33	Meath . .	Dunboyne .	Dunboyne .	Dunshaughlin .	I.	199
19	Knockullard .	293	0	27	Carlow . .	Idrone East .	Sliguff . .	Carlow . .	I.	8

(a) Including 11A. 1R. 38P. water.
(b) Including 0A. 3R. 16P. water.
(c) Including 21A. 0R. 13P. water.
(d) Including 1A. 3R. 16P. Carrick-a-rede Island.
(e) Including 105A. 0R. 17P. detached portions.

No. of Sheet of the Ordnance Survey Maps.	Townlands and Towns.	Area in Statute Acres.			County.	Barony.	Parish.	Poor Law Union in 1857.	Townland Census of 1851, Part I.	
		A.	R.	P.					Vol.	Page
55, 56	Knockulty	317	0	24	Tipperary, S.R.	Slievardagh	Lismalin	Callan	II.	335
25	Knockumber	70	2	29	Meath	Lower Navan	Liscartan	Navan	I.	215
25	Knockumber	529	1	31	Meath	Lower Navan	Navan	Navan	I.	215
17	Knockundervaul	500	2	10	Kerry	Clanmaurice	Duagh	Listowel	II.	168
63	Knockuragh	330	0	38	Tipperary, S.R.	Middlethird	Drangan	Cashel	II.	326
39	Knockuregare	357	3	30	Limerick	Coshma	Uregare	Kilmallock	II.	244
6	Knockvicar	153	0	18	Roscommon	Boyle	Ardcarn	Boyle	IV.	193
34	Knockwatear	324	3	32	Cork, E.R.	Fermoy	Monanimy	Mallow	II.	81
31, 32	Knockwilliam	248	0	32	Kilkenny	Knocktopher	Derrynahinch	Thomastown	I.	111
34	Knockwilliam	94	0	10	Tipperary, N.R.	Kilnamanagh Upper	Glenkeen	Thurles	II.	278
53	Knockybrin	277	0	39	Donegal	Kilmacrenan	Aghanunshin	Letterkenny	III.	122
76	Knockycahillaun	34	3	25	Mayo	Burrishoole	Kilmeena	Westport	IV.	123
3, 6	Knockycallanan	519	2	30	Clare	Burren	Oughtmama	Ballyvaghan	II.	14
76, 77	Knockychottaun	208	3	34	Mayo	Burrishoole	Kilmeena	Westport	IV.	122
45	Knockyclovaun	250	2	38	Clare	Tulla Lower	Killaloe	Scarriff	II.	35
32	Knockycosker	440	2	19	Westmeath	Moycashel	Newtown	Mullingar	I.	279
41, 50	Knockyeala	848	2	19	Kerry	Trughanacmy	Ballincuslane	Tralee	II.	206
23	Knockyelan	452	1	30	Waterford	Decies without Drum	Kilrossanty	Kilmacthomas	II.	358
29	Knockyhena	595	0	22	Cork, E.R.	Duhallow	Nohavaldaly	Millstreet	II.	75
56	Knockyline	89	2	38	Kerry	Trughanacmy	Killorglin	Killarney	II.	211
24, 25	Knockymullgurry	933	0	7	Carlow	St. Mullins Lower	St. Mullins	New Ross	I.	13
21, 22	Knockyoolahan	157	1	16	Waterford	Decies without Drum	Affane	Lismore	II.	353
31, 32	Knockyoolahan East	164	0	36	Waterford	Decies without Drum	Clonea	Dungarvan	II.	354
31, 32	Knockyoolahan West	205	0	7	Waterford	Decies without Drum	Clonea	Dungarvan	II.	354
21	Knockyrourke	529	2	32	Cork, E.R.	Duhallow	Kilmeen	Kanturk	II.	73
50	Knockyrourke	316	1	1	Cork, E.R.	East Muskerry	Donaghmore	Macroom	II.	103
59, 67	Knockysheehan	493	3	13	Kerry	Magunihy	Aghadoe	Killarney	II.	199
76, 77	Knockysprickaun	128	2	36	Mayo	Burrishoole	Kilmeena	Westport	IV.	122
42, 43	Knopoge	495	1	32	Clare	Bunratty Upper	Quin	Tulla	II.	10
34, 43	Knoppoge	328	2	27	Cork, E.R.	Barrymore	Ardnageehy	Fermoy	II.	50
45	Knoppoge	11	3	39	Cork, E.R.	Barrymore	Gortroe	Fermoy	II.	55
15	Knoppoge	11	0	25	Cork, E.R.	Duhallow	Clonfert	Kanturk	II.	68
15	Knoppoge	197	1	37	Cork, E.R.	Duhallow	Kilcorcoran	Kanturk	II.	72
33	Knoppoge	399	0	37	Cork, E.R.	Fermoy	Mallow	Mallow	II.	81
111,123,124	Knoppoge	567	1	14	Cork, W.R.	East Carbery (E.D.)	Kilbrittain	Bandon	II.	128
9	Knoppoge	391	1	20	Kerry	Clanmaurice	Killury	Listowel	II.	171
80,81,89,90	Knoppoge	573	0	4	Kerry	Iveragh	Dromod	Cahersiveen	II.	195
58, 66	Knoppoge	329	3	35	Kerry	Magunihy	Aghadoe	Killarney	II.	199
32	Knoppoge	281	3	0	Kerry	Trughanacmy	Brosna	Tralee	II.	208
9	Knoppoge North	181	2	33	Kerry	Clanmaurice	Rattoo	Listowel	II.	173
9	Knoppoge South	161	3	21	Kerry	Clanmaurice	Rattoo	Listowel	II.	173
37	Knottown	228	0	33	Wexford	Shelmaliere East	Ardcavan	Wexford	I.	329
19	Knowth	313	0	16a	Meath	Upper Slane	Monknewtown	Drogheda	I.	224
20	Knoxspark	155	1	34b	Sligo	Leyny	Ballysadare	Sligo	IV.	230
14, 20	Knoxtershill	138	2	10	Wicklow	Upper Talbotstown	Ballynure	Baltinglass	I.	362
42, 43	Knuttery	807	2	26	Cork, E.R.	Fermoy	Rahan	Mallow	II.	82
18, 26	Kurin	453	3	4	Londonderry	Coleraine	Desertoghill	Coleraine	III.	230
17	Kye	350	0	6	Roscommon	Roscommon	Clooncraff	Strokestown	IV.	208
64, 72	Kylaglass	125	1	6	Tipperary, S.R.	Slievardagh	Kilvemnon	Callan	II.	335
125, 126	Kylagowan	328	1	24	Galway	Leitrim	Ballynakill	Loughrea	IV.	51
78	Kylanoreashy	382	3	22	Tipperary, S.R.	Iffa and Offa East	Kilcash	Clonmel	II.	313
2	Kylatallin	143	3	9	Kerry	Iraghticonnor	Aghavallen	Listowel	II.	189
71	Kylatlea	310	0	12	Tipperary, S.R.	Slievardagh	Kilvemnon	Callan	II.	335
71	Kylawilling	129	2	21	Tipperary, S.R.	Slievardagh	Kilvemnon	Callan	II.	335
22	Kyle	256	0	6	Carlow	St. Mullins Lower	Ballyellin	New Ross	I.	13
44	Kyle	307	3	36	Clare	Tulla Lower	Kilseily	Limerick	II.	37
67	Kyle	310	0	39	Cork, E.R.	Imokilly	Clonpriest	Youghal	II.	85
6	Kyle	181	3	21	Cork, E.R.	Orrery and Kilmore	Kilbolane	Kanturk	II.	108
31	Kyle	177	0	14	Kilkenny	Kells	Kilmaganny	Callan	I.	109
36	Kyle	604	2	8	King's Co.	Ballybritt	Kinnitty	Parsonstown	I.	125
40	Kyle	66	0	18	Limerick	Smallcounty	Knockainy	Kilmallock	II.	261
33, 34	Kyle	717	3	6	Queen's Co.	Clandonagh	Erke	Donaghmore	I.	233
15, 21	Kyle	379	3	17	Queen's Co.	Clandonagh	Kyle	Roscrea	I.	223
29	Kyle	435	3	36	Queen's Co.	Clarmallagh	Abbeyleix	Abbeyleix	I.	235
19	Kyle	275	3	34	Queen's Co.	Cullenagh	Fossy or Timahoe	Abbeyleix	I.	240
3	Kyle	7	2	35	Queen's Co.	Tinnahinch	Rearymore	Mountmellick	I.	250
41	Kyle	76	2	23	Tipperary, N.R.	Eliogarty	Rahelty	Thurles	II.	272
15	Kyle	314	2	8	Tipperary, N.R.	Lower Ormond	Ardcrony	Borrisokane	II.	282
15, 21	Kyle	56	1	26	Tipperary, N.R.	Upper Ormond	Kilruane	Nenagh	II.	292
58, 59	Kyle	422	2	0	Tipperary, N.R.	Clanwilliam	Solloghod-beg	Tipperary	II.	310
55, 63	Kyle	655	2	2	Tipperary, S.R.	Middlethird	Drangan	Cashel	II.	326
91	Kyle	298	3	33	Wexford	Ballaghkeen	Meelnagh	Enniscorthy	I.	298
9, 14	Kyle	365	2	2	Wexford	Scarawalsh	Templeshanbo	Enniscorthy	I.	326

(a) Including 3A. 3R. 0P. water.   (b) Including 6A. 2R. 39P. water.

No. of Sheet of the Ordnance Survey Maps.	Townlands and Towns.	Area in Statute Acres. A. R. P.	County.	Barony.	Parish.	Poor Law Union in 1857.	Townland Census of 1851. Part I. Vol.	Page
33, 38	Kyle	401 2 23	Wicklow	Ballinacor South	Kilcommon	Shillelagh	I.	349
32	Kylea	536 2 31a	Clare	Inchiquin	Inagh	Ennistimon	II.	25
26	Kyleadohir	249 2 35	Kilkenny	Kells	Coolaghmore	Callan	I.	108
63, 64	Kyleaduhir	224 2 20	Tipperary, S.R.	Slievardagh	Modeshil	Callan	II.	335
58, 59	Kyleagarry	111 2 24	Tipperary, S.R.	Clanwilliam	Solloghod-beg	Tipperary	II.	310
63, 64	Kyleaglanna	283 3 34	Tipperary, S.R.	Slievardagh	Modeshil	Callan	II.	335
116	Kyleaglannawood	164 1 34	Galway	Leitrim	Ballynakill	Loughrea	IV.	51
27	Kyleanullaun	146 2 36	Queen's Co.	Clandonagh	Rathsaran	Donaghmore	I.	235
23	Kyleandangan	95 3 36	Kilkenny	Shillelogher	Tullaghanbrogue	Callan	I.	116
23	Kyleannagh	191 0 21	Tipperary, N.R.	Ikerrin	Bourney	Roscrea	II.	274
11	Kyleashinnaun	251 1 9	Tipperary, N.R.	Lower Ormond	Modreeny	Borrisokane	II.	287
26	Kyleateera	197 2 21	Kilkenny	Kells	Mallardstown	Callan	I.	110
40, 41	Kyleatunna	639 0 34	Clare	Islands	Kilmaley	Ennis	II.	31
20	Kyleavarraga Middle	52 3 3	Limerick	Kenry	Adare	Rathkeale	II.	248
11	Kyleavarraga North	44 1 35	Limerick	Kenry	Adare	Rathkeale	II.	248
20	Kyleavarraga South	150 1 24	Limerick	Kenry	Adare	Rathkeale	II.	248
49	Kyleballygalvan	408 0 35	Tipperary, S.R.	Slievardagh	Ballingarry	Callan	II.	332
13	Kyleballynamoe	595 1 1	Kilkenny	Crannagh	Tubbridbritain	Urlingford	I.	87
18	Kyleballyoughter	295 3 6	Kilkenny	Crannagh	Tullaroan	Kilkenny	I.	88
28	Kylebeg	144 1 23	Cork, E.R.	Condons&Clangibbon	Leitrim	Fermoy	II.	62
106	Kylebeg	199 3 3	Galway	Leitrim	Tynagh	Loughrea	IV.	55
29	Kylebeg	132 3 37	Kerry	Trughanacmy	Ballymacelligott	Tralee	II.	207
20	Kylebeg	157 3 19	Kilkenny	Gowran	Gowran	Kilkenny	I.	95
19	Kylebeg	211 0 2	Kilkenny	Shillelogher	St. Patrick's	Kilkenny	I.	116
29	Kylebeg	314 0 9	Queen's Co.	Clarmallagh	Durrow	Abbeyleix	I.	237
14, 19	Kylebeg	106 1 32	Queen's Co.	Stradbally	Curraclone	Athy	I.	246
19	Kylebeg	56 1 1	Queen's Co.	Stradbally	Stradbally	Athy	I.	247
29	Kylebeg	17 2 3	Tipperary, N.R.	Eliogarty	Templemore	Thurles	II.	272
7	Kylebeg	190 2 21	Tipperary, N.R.	Lower Ormond	Aglishcloghane	Borrisokane	II.	281
10	Kylebeg	131 1 17	Tipperary, N.R.	Lower Ormond	Modreeny	Borrisokane	II.	287
20	Kylebeg	55 1 4	Tipperary, N.R.	Owney and Arra	Youghalarra	Nenagh	II.	297
27	Kylebeg	179 2 7	Tipperary, N.R.	Upper Ormond	Ballymaclogh	Nenagh	II.	290
21, 29	Kylebeg or Banagher	307 0 11	King's Co.	Garrycastle	Reynagh	Parsonstown	I.	138
31	Kyleboher	139 2 14	King's Co.	Ballyboy	Ballyboy	Parsonstown	I.	123
116	Kylebrack	6 0 39	Galway	Leitrim	Duniry	Loughrea	IV.	53
116	Kylebrack East	370 3 9	Galway	Leitrim	Leitrim	Loughrea	IV.	55
116	Kylebrack West	372 3 8	Galway	Leitrim	Leitrim	Loughrea	IV.	55
81	Kylebroghlan	307 3 20	Galway	Moycullen	Moycullen	Galway	IV.	71
11	Kylebwee	484 2 12	Kerry	Iraghticonnor	Listowel	Listowel	I.	193
13	Kyleclonhobert	283 0 18	Queen's Co.	Maryborough East	Borris	Mountmellick	I.	240
11	Kylecreen	653 2 36	Clare	Inchiquin	Kilkeedy	Corrofin	II.	26
26, 30	Kyle East	186 2 19	Kilkenny	Kells	Coolaghmore	Callan	I.	108
116	Kylegan	132 3 8	Galway	Leitrim	Duniry	Portumna	IV.	53
70	Kylefinchin	203 3 33	Cork, W.R.	West Muskerry	Kilnamartry	Macroom	II.	160
64	Kylefreaghane	195 2 33	Tipperary, S.R.	Slievardagh	Kilvennon	Callan	II.	335
115	Kylegarriff	97 3 19	Galway	Loughrea	Killeenadeema	Loughrea	IV.	64
15, 16	Kylegarve	320 3 36	Limerick	Coonagh	Doon	Tipperary	II.	234
44	Kyleglass	88 3 16	Clare	Tulla Lower	Killokennedy	Limerick	II.	36
13	Kylekiproe	125 3 17	Queen's Co.	Maryborough East	Borris	Mountmellick	I.	240
21, 27	Kyle Little	122 0 6	Wexford	Ballaghkeen	Meelnagh	Enniscorthy	I.	298
32	Kyle Lower	149 3 19	Wexford	Shelmaliere East	Kilpatrick	Wexford	I.	331
32	Kyle Middle	268 2 19	Wexford	Shelmaliere East	Kilpatrick	Wexford	I.	331
10,11,23,24	Kylemore	5,034 1 32c	Galway	Ballynahinch	Ballynakill	Clifden	IV.	11
117, 126	Kylemore	513 1 21	Galway	Leitrim	Ballynakill	Portumna	IV.	51
88, 100	Kylemore	1,411 1 20d	Galway	Longford	Clonfert	Ballinasloe	IV.	57
55, 68	Kylemore	454 1 30	Galway	Moycullen	Killannin	Oughterard	IV.	70
37	Kylemore	311 0 9	Kilkenny	Ida	The Rower	New Ross	I.	104
29	Kylemore	155 0 28	Tipperary, N.R.	Ikerrin	Templeree	Thurles	II.	277
25, 31	Kylenabehy	319 3 37	Queen's Co.	Ballyadams	Rathaspick	Athy	I.	232
125	Kylenagappa	157 3 28	Galway	Leitrim	Ballynakill	Loughrea	IV.	51
25, 33	Kylenagoneeny	273 0 22	Limerick	Coonagh	Oola	Tipperary	II.	236
15, 16	Kylenaheskeragh	542 0 37	Tipperary, N.R.	Upper Ormond	Ballygibbon	Nenagh	II.	289
34	Kylenahoory	95 3 30e	Cork, E.R.	Fermoy	Kilcummer	Fermoy	II.	80
132	Kylenamelly	403 3 38	Galway	Leitrim	Ballynakill	Portumna	IV.	51
5, 8	Kylenamuck	269 2 18	Tipperary, N.R.	Lower Ormond	Loughkeen	Parsonstown	II.	286
19	Kylenasaggart	61 0 2	Kilkenny	Crannagh	Ballycallan	Kilkenny	I.	84
22	Kylenaskeagh	374 0 29	Kilkenny	Shillelogher	Killaloe	Callan	I.	115
10	Kyleomadaun East	192 0 15	Tipperary, N.R.	Lower Ormond	Finnoe	Borrisokane	II.	284
10	Kyleomadaun West	226 3 21	Tipperary, N.R.	Lower Ormond	Finnoe	Borrisokane	II.	284
7, 10	Kyleonermody	106 1 24	Tipperary, N.R.	Lower Ormond	Borrisokane	Borrisokane	II.	282
14, 19	Kyleroe	170 2 22	Kilkenny	Gowran	St. John's	Kilkenny	I.	98
64, 77	Kylesalia	1,484 1 1	Galway	Ballynahinch	Moyrus	Clifden	IV.	13
14	Kylespiddoge	88 1 0	Queen's Co.	Stradbally	Moyanna	Athy	I.	247

(a) Including 34A. 0R. 32P. water.
(b) Including 89A. 2R. 30P. water.
(c) Including 18A. 1R. 7P. water.
(d) Including 9A. 1R. 24P. water.
(e) Including 1A. 0R. 32P. water.

4 L

No. of Sheet of the Ordnance Survey Maps	Townlands and Towns	Area in Statute Acres.			County.	Barony.	Parish.	Poor Law Union in 1857.	Townland Census of 1851, Part I.	
		A.	R.	P.					Vol.	Page
8, 13	Kyletalesha	711	3	26	Queen's Co.	Maryborough East	Borris	Mountmellick	I.	240
20, 29	Kyletaun	468	1	16a	Limerick	Connello Lower	Rathkeale	Rathkeale	II.	229
29	Kyletilloge	363	2	5	Queen's Co.	Clarmallagh	Aghaboe	Abbeyleix	I.	236
6, 7, 9, 10	Kyletombrickane	743	0	1	Tipperary, N.R.	Lower Ormond	Borrisokane	Borrisokane	II.	282
32, 37	Kyle Upper	229	0	38	Wexford	Shelmaliere East	Kilpatrick	Wexford	I.	331
31, 35	Kyleva	225	0	13	Kilkenny	Knocktopher	Aghaviller	Thomastown	I.	110
22	Kylevehagh Commons	83	1	8	Kilkenny	Callan	Callan	Callan	I.	83
26, 30	Kyle West	223	3	12	Kilkenny	Kells	Coolaghmore	Callan	I.	108
16	Labanasigh	139	3	29	Carlow	Idrone East	Dunleckny	Carlow	I.	7
19	Labanstown	372	0	26	Louth	Ferrard	Drumshallon	Drogheda	I.	180
68, 69	LABASHEEDA T.	—			Clare	Clonderalaw	Killofin	Killadysert	II.	17
64, 75	Labaun	13	0	39	Cork, E.R.	Barrymore	Carrigtohill	Middleton	II.	52
30	Labaun	288	2	0	Westmeath	Clonlonan	Ballyloughloe	Athlone	I.	260
27	Labbacallee	392	2	12	Cork, E.R.	Condons&Clangibbon	Litter	Fermoy	II.	62
58, 59	Labbadermody	541	0	24	Cork, W.R.	West Muskerry	Clondrohid	Macroom	II.	155
54, 62	Labbadish	314	0	21	Donegal	Raphoe	Raymoghy	Letterkenny	III.	142
69, 78	Labbadoo	216	2	11	Donegal	Raphoe	Convoy	Stranorlar	III.	136
10	Labbamolaga East	409	0	28	Cork, E.R.	Condons&Clangibbon	Templemolaga	Mitchelstown	II.	63
10	Labbamolaga Middle	443	2	9	Cork, E.R.	Condons&Clangibbon	Templemolaga	Mitchelstown	II.	63
10	Labbamolaga West	343	2	39	Cork, E.R.	Condons&Clangibbon	Templemolaga	Mitchelstown	II.	63
19	Labbanacallee	273	1	37	Waterford	Coshmore&Coshbride	Lismore and Mocollop	Lismore	II.	346
22	Labbinlee	175	0	20	Cavan	Tullygarvey	Kildrumsherdan	Cootehill	III.	90
40	Labby	597	1	32	Londonderry	Loughinsholin	Ballynascreen	Magherafelt	III.	239
28	Labbyeslin	61	3	5b	Leitrim	Mohill	Mohill	Mohill	IV.	108
42	Laboge	62	0	34	Roscommon	Athlone	Kilmeane	Roscommon	IV.	182
49, 59	Lack	464	1	26	Clare	Clonderalaw	Kilchreest	Killadysert	II.	15
6	Lack	224	0	16	Fermanagh	Lurg	Magheraculmoney	Lowtherstown	III.	208
16	Lack	177	1	24	Galway	Dunmore	Addergoole	Tuam	IV.	33
45, 46	Lack	1,765	1	14	Kerry	Corkaguiny	Ballinvoher	Dingle	II.	174
30	Lack	427	0	18	Roscommon	Ballintober North	Termonbarry	Strokestown	IV.	188
92	Lacka	766	1	11	Kerry	Dunkerron South	Templenoe	Kenmare	II.	185
1	Lacka	248	1	34	Limerick	Clanwilliam	Stradbally	Limerick	II.	226
22, 31	Lacka	162	0	28	Limerick	Pubblebrien	Monasteranenagh	Croom	II.	253
11	Lacka	238	3	16	Queen's Co.	Upperwoods	Offerlane	Mountmellick	I.	252
8	Lacka	51	3	25	Tipperary, N.R.	Lower Ormond	Ballingarry	Parsonstown	II.	282
8	Lacka	1,228	0	14	Tipperary, N.R.	Lower Ormond	Loughkeen	Parsonstown	II.	286
50, 61	Lackabane	576	1	7	Cork, E.R.	East Muskerry	Donaghmore	Macroom	II.	103
39	Lackabane	284	1	8	Cork, W.R.	West Muskerry	Drishane	Millstreet	II.	156
66	Lackabane	338	0	21	Kerry	Magunihy	Aghadoe	Killarney	II.	199
32	Lackabane	591	1	34	Kerry	Trughanacmy	Ballincuslane	Tralee	II.	206
93	Lackabaun	372	0	36	Cork, W.R.	East Carbery (W.D.)	Inchigeelagh	Dunmanway	II.	132
68	Lackabaun	396	1	16	Cork, W.R.	West Muskerry	Inchigeelagh	Macroom	II.	158
104, 105, 114, 115	Lackabaun	167	0	21	Galway	Dunkellin	Kilchreest	Loughrea	IV.	28
114, 115	Lackabaun	99	3	35	Galway	Dunkellin	Killinan	Loughrea	IV.	30
116	Lackabaun	182	0	32	Galway	Leitrim	Duniry	Portumna	IV.	53
30, 31, 39	Lackabaun	578	0	27	Kerry	Trughanacmy	Castleisland	Tralee	II.	209
18	Lackabeg	155	0	16	Carlow	St. Mullins Upper	Barragh	Shillelagh	I.	14
21	Lacka Beg	390	0	10	Kerry	Clanmaurice	O'Dorney	Tralee	II.	172
16	Lacka Beg	254	1	20	Limerick	Coonagh	Doon	Tipperary	II.	234
44	Lackabeha East	126	2	39	Cork, E.R.	Barrymore	Gortroe	Fermoy	II.	55
44	Lackabeha West	97	2	20	Cork, E.R.	Barrymore	Gortroe	Fermoy	II.	55
5	Lackaboy	160	3	38	Kerry	Iraghticonnor	Lisselton	Listowel	II.	192
26	Lackabrack	36	2	32	Cork, E.R.	Fermoy	Wallstown	Mallow	II.	83
7	Lackabrack	102	0	24	Tipperary, N.R.	Lower Ormond	Aglishcloghane	Borrisokane	II.	281
26, 32	Lackabrack	1,386	2	3	Tipperary, N.R.	Owney and Arra	Killoscully	Nenagh	II.	295
37	Lackabranner	479	1	13	Clare	Tulla Lower	Killaloe	Scarriff	II.	35
70, 71	Lackaduff	200	3	17	Cork, W.R.	West Muskerry	Macroom	Macroom	II.	160
59	Lackaduv	328	0	34	Cork, W.R.	West Muskerry	Clondrohid	Macroom	II.	155
9	Lacka East	38	0	21	Kerry	Clanmaurice	Rattoo	Listowel	II.	173
11, 17	Lacka East	514	0	38c	Kerry	Iraghticonnor	Duagh	Listowel	II.	190
5	Lacka East	180	3	38	Kerry	Iraghticonnor	Lisselton	Listowel	II.	192
25	Lackafin	207	2	32	Monaghan	Farney	Donaghmoyne	Castleblayney	III.	270
120, 121	Lackafinna	403	0	24	Mayo	Kilmaine	Cong	Ballinrobe	IV.	154
97	Lackafinna North	77	1	37	Galway	Loughrea	Kilconickny	Loughrea	IV.	63
97	Lackafinna South	321	2	17	Galway	Loughrea	Kilconickny	Loughrea	IV.	63
64	Lackagh	1,094	1	5d	Donegal	Boylagh	Inishkeel	Glenties	III.	113
98	Lackagh	83	1	14	Galway	Kilconnell	Killallaghtan	Ballinasloe	IV.	41
12, 15, 16	Lackagh	1,140	1	19e	Leitrim	Drumahaire	Killarga	Manorhamilton	IV.	99
24, 25	Lackagh	204	0	22	Londonderry	Keenaght	Dungiven	NewTⁿLimavady	III.	236

(a) Including 12A. 2R. 0P. water.
(b) Including 1A. 3R. 29P. water.
(c) Including 17A. 1R. 16P. water.
(d) Including 32A. 2R. 31P. water.
(e) Including 29A. 1R. 24P. water.

No. of Sheet of the Ordnance Survey Maps	Townlands and Towns.	Area in Statute Acres. A. R. P.	County.	Barony.	Parish.	Poor Law Union in 1857.	Townland Census of 1851. Part I. Vol.	Page
22	Lackagh . .	622 3 4	Londonderry .	Tirkeeran . .	Cumber Lower .	Londonderry .	III.	249
19	Lackagh . .	222 2 38	Monaghan .	Cremorne . .	Clontibret .	Castleblayney .	III.	261
11, 12	Lackagh . .	128 0 5	Roscommon .	Ballintober North .	Kilmore . .	Car¹. on Shannon	IV.	187
26, 27	Lackagh . .	240 0 31	Sligo . .	Corran . .	Kilmorgan .	Sligo . .	IV.	227
26, 32	Lackagh . .	272 2 34	Tipperary, N.R.	Owney and Arra .	Killoscully .	Nenagh . .	II.	295
51, 58	Lackagh . .	295 3 25	Tyrone . .	Clogher . .	Donacavey .	Omagh . .	III.	294
33	Lackagh . .	769 0 3a	Tyrone . .	Omagh West .	Longfield West .	Castlederg .	III.	316
150	Lackaghane .	185 1 32	Cork, W.R. .	West Carbery (E.D.)	Creagh . .	Skibbereen .	II.	139
74	Lackaghatermon .	613 3 19	Donegal . .	Boylagh . .	Inishkeel .	Glenties . .	III.	113
70	Lackagh Beg .	769 2 27	Galway . .	Clare . .	Lackagh . .	Galway . .	IV.	23
22	Lackagh Beg .	503 3 36	Kildare . .	Offaly West .	Lackagh . .	Athy . .	I.	73
6	Lackagh Beg .	441 2 39	King's Co. .	Garrycastle .	Lemanaghan .	Parsonstown .	I.	136
22	Lackaghbog .	21 3 34	Kildare . .	Offaly West .	Lackagh . .	Athy . .	I.	73
22	Lackaghboy .	121 2 27	Fermanagh .	Tirkennedy .	Derryvullan .	Enniskillen .	III.	221
70	Lackagh More .	550 1 10	Galway . .	Clare . .	Lackagh . .	Galway . .	IV.	23
22	Lackagh More .	486 2 1	Kildare . .	Offaly West .	Lackagh . .	Athy . .	I.	73
6, 7	Lackagh More .	579 1 12	King's Co. .	Garrycastle .	Lemanaghan .	Parsonstown .	I.	136
105	Lackakeely .	98 2 22	Mayo . .	Murrisk . .	Kilgeever .	Westport .	IV.	160
27, 28	Lackakera .	497 0 34	Tipperary, N.R.	Upper Ormond .	Latteragh .	Nenagh . .	II.	292
97, 105	Lackalea . .	725 3 18	Galway . .	Loughrea . .	Kilconickny .	Loughrea .	IV.	63
23	Lackaleigh .	96 0 12	Cork, E.R. .	Duhallow .	Subulter . .	Kanturk .	II.	75
54	Lacka Lower .	165 2 32	Limerick . .	Glenquin .	Killagholehane .	Newcastle .	II.	245
37	Lackalustraun .	807 2 23	Mayo . .	Tirawley .	Crossmolina .	Ballina .	IV.	166
23	Lackamore .	474 2 11b	Clare . .	Ibrickan . .	Kilfarboy .	Ennistimon .	II.	22
21	Lacka More .	527 1 34	Kerry . .	Clanmaurice .	O'Dorney .	Tralee . .	II.	172
8, 16	Lacka More .	310 1 9	Limerick . .	Coonagh . .	Doon . .	Tipperary .	II.	234
1, 3	Lackamore .	200 0 27	Queen's Co. .	Tinnahinch .	Castlebrack .	Mountmellick .	I.	248
19, 20	Lackamore .	181 1 8	Tipperary, N.R.	Owney and Arra .	Castletownarra .	Nenagh . .	II.	294
38	Lackamore .	340 2 2	Tipperary, N.R.	Owney and Arra .	Kilvellane .	Nenagh . .	II.	296
35	Lackamore .	89 3 37	Waterford .	Decies within Drum	Ardmore .	Youghal .	II.	350
35	Lackamore .	65 0 22	Waterford .	Decies within Drum	Clashmore .	Youghal .	II.	351
15	Lackan . .	405 3 11	Carlow . .	Idrone West .	Oldleighlin .	Carlow . .	I.	9
24, 30	Lackan . .	136 1 11	Cavan . .	Tullyhunco .	Killashandra .	Cavan . .	III.	98
42	Lackan . .	722 3 22c	Down . .	Upper Iveagh, Lr. pt.	Drumbally roney .	Banbridge .	III.	172
114	Lackan . .	173 1 6	Galway . .	Dunkellin .	Ardrahan .	Gort . .	IV.	26
125, 126	Lackan . .	378 1 11	Galway . .	Leitrim . .	Ballynakill .	Portumna .	IV.	51
9, 10	Lackan . .	264 1 25	King's Co. .	Lower Philipstown .	Kilclonfert .	Tullamore .	I.	142
14	Lackan . .	441 3 6	Longford . .	Ardagh . .	Mostrim . .	Granard .	I.	152
26, 27	Lackan . .	340 0 15d	Monaghan .	Cremorne .	Aghnamullen .	Castleblayney .	III.	258
3, 7	Lackan . .	193 2 27	Queen's Co. .	Tinnahinch .	Rosenallis .	Mountmellick .	I.	250
42	Lackan . .	216 0 11	Roscommon .	Athlone . .	Kilmeane .	Roscommon .	IV.	182
41,42,44,45	Lackan . .	494 0 15	Roscommon .	Athlone . .	Rahara . .	Roscommon .	IV.	183
10	Lackan . .	180 2 12	Roscommon .	Frenchpark .	Kilcolagh .	Boyle . .	IV.	203
11, 17	Lackan . .	337 1 28	Roscommon .	Roscommon .	Aughrim . .	Car¹. on Shannon	IV.	207
29, 36	Lackan . .	370 3 9	Roscommon .	Roscommon .	Cloonfinlough .	Roscommon .	IV.	209
10, 16	Lackan . .	421 3 6	Sligo . .	Tireragh . .	Kilglass . .	Dromore West .	IV.	234
6	Lackan . .	768 1 29c	Westmeath .	Corkaree . .	Lackan . .	Mullingar .	I.	262
15, 22	Lackan . .	163 3 7	Westmeath .	Kilkenny West .	Kilkenny West .	Athlone .	I.	273
6	Lackan . .	112 0 38	Wexford . .	Gorey . .	Kilmakilloge .	Gorey . .	I.	318
5, 10	Lackan . .	1,543 0 4	Wicklow . .	Lower Talbotstown .	Boystown .	Naas . .	I.	359
88	Lackanabrickane .	32 1 5	Tipperary, S.R.	Iffa and Offa West .	Ballybacon .	Clogheen .	II.	317
16	Lackanagoneeny .	286 1 22	Limerick . .	Coonagh . .	Doon . .	Tipperary .	II.	234
39	Lackanagrour .	117 1 16	Limerick . .	Coshma . .	Bruree . .	Kilmallock .	II.	242
33	Lackanalooha .	79 0 31	Cork, E.R. .	Fermoy . .	Mallow . .	Mallow . .	II.	81
122, 135	Lackanalooha .	209 2 11	Cork, W.R. .	East Carbery (E.D.)	Kilnagross .	Clonakilty .	II.	129
33	Lackanamona .	305 3 22f	Cork, E.R. .	Fermoy . .	Carrigleamleary .	Mallow . .	II.	77
24	Lackanascarry .	89 1 37	Limerick . .	Coonagh . .	Ballynaclogh .	Tipperary .	II.	234
36	Lackanash .	26 2 37	Meath . .	Upper Navan .	Trim . .	Trim . .	I.	217
94, 95	Lackanashinnagh .	224 1 23	Cork, W.R. .	East Carbery (W.D.)	Kinneigh .	Dunmanway .	II.	135
21, 29	Lackanastooka .	431 2 2	Cork, E.R. .	Duhallow .	Nohavaldaly .	Millstreet .	II.	75
16, 17	Lackanatlieve .	531 0 4	Sligo . .	Tireragh . .	Kilglass . .	Dromore West .	IV.	234
16	Lackancahill .	109 2 0	Sligo . .	Tireragh . .	Kilglass . .	Dromore West .	IV.	234
32	Lackanclare .	128 0 7	Cavan . .	Castlerahan .	Denn . .	Cavan . .	III.	68
40	Lackandarra .	14 1 33	Tipperary, N.R.	Kilnamanagh Upper	Moyaliff .	Thurles .	II.	279
13, 22	Lackandarra .	222 0 24	Waterford .	Decies without Drum	Seskinan .	Dungarvan .	II.	360
7	Lackandarragh Lower	228 3 7	Wicklow . .	Rathdown .	Powerscourt .	Rathdown .	I.	356
7	Lackandarragh Upper	204 0 24	Wicklow . .	Rathdown .	Powerscourt .	Rathdown .	I.	356
13, 22	Lackandarra Lower	574 2 37	Waterford .	Decies without Drum	Seskinan .	Dungarvan .	II.	360
13, 22	Lackandarra Upper	394 2 3	Waterford .	Decies without Drum	Seskinan .	Dungarvan .	II.	360
32	Lackanduff .	165 0 25	Cavan . .	Castlerahan .	Denn . .	Oldcastle .	III.	68
40, 41	Lackaneen .	284 1 23	Cork, E.R. .	Duhallow .	Kilshannig .	Mallow . .	II.	74
59, 70	Lackaneen .	308 3 38	Cork, W.R. .	West Muskerry .	Clondrohid .	Macroom .	II.	155
7	Lackanhill .	125 1 12	Mayo . .	Tirawley .	Lackan . .	Killala .	IV.	171

(a) Including 2A. 2R. 32P. water.
(b) Including 6A. 1R. 18P. water.
(c) Including 18A. 0R. 30P. water.
(d) Including 10A. 0R. 18P. water.
(e) Including 3A. 1R. 33P. water.
(f) Including 3A. 2R. 0P. water.

4 L 2

No. of Sheet of the Ordnance Survey Maps.	Townlands and Towns.	Area in Statute Acres. A. R. P.	County.	Barony.	Parish.	Poor Law Union in 1857.	Townland Census of 1851, Part I. Vol.	Page
2b, 31	Lackan Lower	339 1 4	Cavan	Clanmahon	Ballintemple	Cavan	III.	75
32	Lackanmore	399 2 18a	Cavan	Castlerahan	Denn	Oldcastle	III.	68
59, 60	Lackannashinnagh	445 3 16b	Clare	Clonderalaw	Killadysert	Killadysert	II.	16
31	Lackanoneen	466 0 17	Kerry	Trughanacmy	Ballincuslane	Tralee	II.	206
57	Lackanroe	99 3 17	Galway	Clare	Kilmoylan	Tuam	IV.	22
66	Lackantedane	123 3 30	Tipperary, S.R.	Clanwilliam	Clonpet	Tipperary	II.	306
31	Lackan Upper	185 0 15	Cavan	Clanmahon	Ballintemple	Cavan	III.	75
6	Lackanwood	306 3 32c	Westmeath	Corkaree	Lackan	Mullingar	I.	262
10	Lackareagh	224 2 0	Clare	Inchiquin	Killinaboy	Corrofin	II.	26
92	Lackareagh	268 0 30	Cork, W.R.	Bantry	Kilmocomoge	Bantry	II.	121
139	Lackareagh	326 0 29	Cork, W.R.	West Carbery (W.D.)	Skull	Skull	II.	146
83	Lackareagh	547 1 31	Cork, W.R.	West Muskerry	Kilmichael	Macroom	II.	159
20, 26	Lackareagh	338 1 34	Wicklow	Upper Talbotstown	Ballynure	Baltinglass	I.	362
44, 45	Lackareagh Beg	488 3 34	Clare	Tulla Lower	O'Briensbridge	Limerick	II.	38
44, 45	Lackareagh More	397 0 18	Clare	Tulla Lower	O'Briensbridge	Limerick	II.	38
87	Lackaroe	64 0 36	Cork, E.R.	Kerrycurrihy	Monkstown	Cork	II.	93
17	Lackaroe	155 3 10	Cork, E.R.	Orrery and Kilmore	Buttevant	Mallow	II.	107
16	Lackaroe	563 2 36	Cork, E.R.	Orrery and Kilmore	Liscarroll	Mallow	II.	109
93, 94	Lackaroe	608 1 8	Kerry	Glanarought	Kenmare	Kenmare	II.	186
36, 37	Lackaroe	151 3 31	King's Co.	Ballybritt	Letterluna	Parsonstown	I.	126
13	Lackaroe	121 3 34	Tipperary, N.R.	Owney and Arra	Castletownarra	Nenagh	II.	294
37	Lackaroe	25 0 6	Waterford	Coshmore&Coshbride	Templemichael	Youghal	II.	349
136	Lackarour	127 0 35	Cork, W.R.	Ibane and Barryroe	Lislee	Clonakilty	II.	150
88, 98	Lackaun	338 0 27	Mayo	Burrishoole	Aghagower	Westport	IV.	118
118,120,121	Lackaun	188 3 37	Mayo	Kilmaine	Ballinchalla	Ballinrobe	IV.	152
54	Lacka Upper	193 3 38	Limerick	Glenquin	Killagholehane	Newcastle	II.	245
80, 92	Lackavane	627 0 20	Cork, W.R.	Bantry	Kilmocomoge	Bantry	II.	121
104, 117	Lackavane	620 3 3	Cork, W.R.	Bear	Kilcaskan	Castletown	II.	123
138, 147	Lackavaun	222 2 9	Cork, W.R.	West Carbery (W.D.)	Kilmoe	Skull	II.	145
38, 39	Lackavrea	1,656 2 17d	Galway	Moycullen	Kilcummin	Oughterard	IV.	67
71	Lackavunaknick	200 0 34	Cork, W.R.	East Muskerry	Aghinagh	Macroom	II.	154
73	Lackaweer	158 2 31e	Donegal	Boylagh	Inishkeel	Glenties	III.	113
17	Lacka West	508 0 25	Kerry	Clanmaurice	Duagh	Listowel	II.	168
9	Lacka West	165 0 37	Kerry	Clanmaurice	Rattoo	Listowel	II.	173
5	Lacka West	172 2 14	Kerry	Iraghticonnor	Lisselton	Listowel	II.	192
69	Lack Beg	307 3 27	Cork, W.R.	West Muskerry	Kilnamartry	Macroom	II.	160
46	Lackbrack	84 3 35	Cork, E.R.	Kinnatalloon	Mogeely	Fermoy	II.	98
31, 32	Lackbrooder	1,118 2 9	Kerry	Trughanacmy	Ballincuslane	Tralee	II.	206
84, 93, 94	Lackcrom	828 2 39	Donegal	Banagh	Killymard	Donegal	III.	111
98, 108	Lackderg	181 0 7	Mayo	Murrisk	Aghagower	Westport	IV.	159
48	Lackdotia	411 3 3	Cork, W.R.	West Muskerry	Drishane	Millstreet	II.	156
48, 58	Lack East	756 1 21f	Clare	Clonderalaw	Kilmihil	Kilrush	II.	17
70	Lack East	273 3 4	Mayo	Carra	Turlough	Castlebar	IV.	131
16	Lackeel	159 1 27	Cork, E.R.	Duhallow	Kilbrin	Kanturk	II.	72
7, 16	Lackeen	279 3 19	Cork, E.R.	Orrery and Kilmore	Lackeen	Mallow	II.	109
92, 101	Lackeen	326 2 5	Kerry	Dunkerron South	Templenoe	Kenmare	II.	185
41	Lackelly East	153 0 32	Limerick	Coshlea	Galbally	Mitchelstown	II.	239
41	Lackelly West	305 0 38	Limerick	Coshlea	Galbally	Mitchelstown	II.	239
22	Lacken	193 1 0	Carlow	Idrone East	Kiltennell	Carlow	I.	7
22, 24	Lacken	89 0 12	Carlow	St. Mullins Lower	St. Mullins	New Ross	I.	13
48	Lacken	697 0 19g	Clare	Clonderalaw	Kilmihil	Kilrush	II.	17
46, 55	Lacken	262 0 20	Cork, E.R.	Kinnatalloon	Mogeely	Youghal	II.	98
18, 19	Lacken	267 0 29	Kilkenny	Crannagh	St. Canice	Kilkenny	I.	87
25	Lacken	102 0 32	Kilkenny	Gowran	Ullard	Thomastown	I.	100
19	Lacken	24 2 9h	Kilkenny	Gowran and Municipal Borough	St. John's	Kilkenny	I.	98
7	Lacken	354 2 20	Tipperary, N.R.	Lower Ormond	Terryglass	Borrisokane	II.	288
67	Lacken	309 2 20	Tipperary, S.R.	Clanwilliam	Cordangan	Tipperary	II.	306
59	Lacken	132 1 9	Tipperary, S.R.	Clanwilliam	Rathlynin	Tipperary	II.	309
88	Lacken	109 2 5i	Tipperary, S.R.	Iffa and Offa West	Neddans	Clogheen	II.	319
21	Lacken	168 0 11	Waterford	Decies without Drum	Affane	Lismore	II.	353
31	Lacken	202 1 22	Waterford	Decies without Drum	Dungarvan	Dungarvan	II.	355
17	Lacken	147 2 31	Waterford	Gaultiere	Kilbarry	Waterford	II.	363
32	Lacken	309 3 7	Wexford	Ballaghkeen	Kilmallock	Enniscorthy	I.	296
29, 30	Lacken	1,112 3 8	Wexford	Bantry	Oldross	New Ross	I.	301
46	Lacken	189 2 36	Wexford	Bargy	Duncormick	Wexford	I.	305
45, 51	Lackenacoombe	339 3 38	Tipperary, S.R.	Kilnamanagh Lower	Donohill	Tipperary	II.	323
45	Lackenacreena	301 0 19	Tipperary, S.R.	Kilnamanagh Lower	Donohill	Tipperary	II.	323
112	Lackenacummeen	286 3 28	Cork, E.R.	Kinsale	Clontead	Kinsale	II.	99
132	Lackenafasoge	282 3 19	Cork, W.R.	West Carbery (W.D.)	Caheragh	Skibbereen	II.	142
111, 112	Lackenagea	52 3 27	Cork, E.R.	Kinsale	Clontead	Kinsale	II.	99
135	Lackenagobidane	48 0 14	Cork, W.R.	East Carbery (E.D.)	Island	Clonakilty	II.	128
35	Lackenagreany	279 0 28	Waterford	Decies within Drum	Ardmore	Dungarvan	II.	350

(a) Including 52A. 1R. 19P. water.
(b) Including 7A. 0R. 32P. water.
(c) Including 31A. 2R. 28P. water.
(d) Including 190A. 3R. 9P. water.

(e) Including 15A. 0R. 28P. water.
(f) Including 30A. 3R. 30P. water.
(g) Including 27A. 1R. 22P. water.
(h) { Including 3A. 0R. 32P. River Nore. / Within the Municipal Boundary, 5A. 3R. 5P. / Without the Municipal Boundary, 18A. 3R. 4P
(i) Including 1A. 2R. 24P. water.

No. of Sheet of the Ordnance Survey Maps.	Townlands and Towns.	Area in Statute Acres. A. R. P.	County.	Barony.	Parish.	Poor Law Union in 1857.	Townland Census of 1851, Part I. Vol.	Page
147, 152	Lackenakea	112 3 0	Cork, W.R.	West Carbery(W.D.)	Kilmoe	Skull	II.	145
72, 73	Lackenareague	189 1 31	Cork, E.R.	East Muskerry	Athnowen	Cork	II.	101
25, 31	Lackenavea (Dunalley)	234 0 20	Tipperary, N.R.	Owney and Arra	Kilmastulla	Nenagh	II.	295
25, 31	Lackenavea (Egremont)	274 2 26	Tipperary, N.R.	Owney and Arra	Kilmastulla	Nenagh	II.	295
27	Lackenavorna	484 2 34	Tipperary, N.R.	Upper Ormond	Aghnameadle	Nenagh	II.	289
45	Lackenbaun	155 3 4	Clare	Tulla Lower	Killaloe	Scarriff	II.	35
65	Lackenbehy	306 2 9	Cork, E.R.	Barrymore	Carrigtohill	Middleton	II.	52
46	Lackenbehy	101 3 18	Cork, E.R.	Kinnatalloon	Mogeely	Fermoy	II.	98
37, 38	Lackendarra	78 2 37	Waterford	Decies within Drum	Kinsalebeg	Youghal	II.	352
32, 41	Lackendarragh	911 1 28	Cork, E.R.	Duhallow	Kilshannig	Mallow	II.	74
57, 58	Lackendarragh	1,165 0 17	Limerick	Coshlea	Kilbeheny	Mitchelstown	II.	239
10	Lackendarragh	179 0 24	Wexford	Scarawalsh	Kilrush	Enniscorthy	I.	324
43	Lackendarragh Middle	213 3 5	Cork, E.R.	Barrymore	Ardnageehy	Fermoy	II.	50
34,35,43,44	Lackendarragh North	1,445 2 24	Cork, E.R.	Barrymore	Ardnageehy	Fermoy	II.	50
43, 52	Lackendarragh South	364 1 16	Cork, E.R.	Barrymore	Ardnageehy	Fermoy	II.	50
31	Lackendragaun	285 3 30	Kilkenny	Kells	Dunnamaggan	Callan	I.	108
135	Lackenduff	251 0 0	Cork, W.R.	Ibane and Barryroe	Templeomalus	Clonakilty	II.	151
31	Lackenfune	94 3 3	Waterford	Decies without Drum	Kilrush	Dungarvan	II.	358
41	Lackennaskagh	165 0 12	Clare	Islands	Killone	Ennis	II.	30
21	Lackenrea	185 2 22	Waterford	Decies without Drum	Affane	Lismore	II.	353
64, 75	Lackenroe	451 1 0	Cork, E.R.	Barrymore	Caherlag	Cork	II.	52
73	Lackenshoneen	410 2 12a	Cork, E.R.	East Muskerry	Carrigrohanebeg	Cork	II.	102
34	Lackensillagh	221 2 8	Waterford	Decies within Drum	Aglish	Dungarvan	II.	349
15	Lackey	391 3 12	Queen's Co.	Clandonagh	Kyle	Roscrea	I.	233
17	Lackfrancis	113 3 35	Cork, E.R.	Orrery and Kilmore	Buttevant	Mallow	II.	107
75	Lacklea	611 2 0b	Donegal	Boylagh	Inishkeel	Glenties	III.	113
93	Lacklea	48 1 11	Galway	Galway	Rahoon	Galway	IV.	38
99, 103	Lacklom	256 1 13c	Donegal	Tirhugh	Drumhome	Ballyshannon	III.	146
29, 32	Lacklom	187 3 33	Monaghan	Farney	Inishkeen	Dundalk	III.	271
16, 17	Lackmelch	60 2 36	Meath	Upper Kells	Kells	Kells	I.	206
69	Lackmore	224 0 8	Cork, W.R.	West Muskerry	Kilnamartry	Macroom	II.	160
44	Lacknacoo	486 1 37d	Donegal	Kilmacrenan	Gartan	Letterkenny	III.	127
6	Lacknagreagh	83 2 38	Louth	Upper Dundalk	Barronstown	Dundalk	I.	177
60	Lacknahaghny	369 1 39	Cork, W.R.	East Muskerry	Aghabulloge	Macroom	II.	153
59	Lacktify	167 0 37	Cork, W.R.	West Muskerry	Clondrohid	Macroom	II.	155
6	Lack T.	—	Fermanagh	Lurg	Magheraculmoney	Lowtherstown	III.	209
48, 58	Lack West	1,375 0 6	Clare	Clonderalaw	Kilmihil	Kilrush	II	17
70	Lack West	232 1 38	Mayo	Carra	Turlough	Castlebar	IV.	131
40	Lacky	53 2 3	Fermanagh	Clankelly	Clones	Clones	III.	196
73, 82	Laconnell	592 1 25	Donegal	Banagh	Inishkeel	Glenties	III.	106
8, 12	Lacoon	863 0 23	Leitrim	Drumahaire	Cloonclare	Manorhamilton	IV.	93
75, 76	Lacroagh	583 2 35	Donegal	Boylagh	Inishkeel	Glenties	III.	113
27, 33	Lacystown	140 2 19	Meath	Upper Duleek	Stamullin	Drogheda	I.	198
8, 17	Laddan	137 0 11c	Donegal	Kilmacrenan	Clondavaddog	Milford	III.	125
25, 26	Ladestown	401 0 23	Westmeath	Moyashel and Magheradernon	Mullingar	Mullingar	I.	275
14	Ladycastle Lower	402 2 17f	Kildare	Naas North	Whitechurch	Naas	I.	63
14	Ladycastle Upper	315 3 28g	Kildare	Naas North	Whitechurch	Naas	I.	63
44, 50	Ladyhill	785 3 33	Antrim	Upper Antrim	Antrim	Antrim	III	5
14	Ladyhill	155 1 37	Kildare	Naas North	Bodenstown	Naas	I.	62
36	Lady Island	2 3 5	Meath	Lune	Kildalkey	Trim	I.	208
12, 18	Ladyrath	994 2 17	Meath	Upper Slane	Rathkenny	Navan	I.	225
88	Ladysabbey	16 0 7	Tipperary, S.R.	Iffa and Offa West	Ballybacon	Clogheen	II.	317
77	Lady's Bridge	4 3 12	Cork, E.R.	Imokilly	Ightermurragh	Middleton	II.	87
77	LADY'SBRIDGE T.	—	Cork, E.R.	Imokilly	Ightermurragh	Middleton	II.	87
99	Lady's Island	0 0 7	Mayo	Carra	Ballintober	Castlebar	IV.	125
53	Lady's Island	30 1 24	Wexford	Forth	Ladyisland	Wexford	I.	311
4	Ladystown	234 0 5	Carlow	Rathvilly	Baltinglass	Baltinglass	I.	10
61	Ladyswell	7 3 18	Tipperary, S.R.	Middlethird	St. John Baptist	Cashel	II.	330
18,19,23,24	Ladytown	1,147 0 11	Kildare	Connell	Ladytown	Naas	I.	55
59	Laffina	82 3 29	Tipperary, S.R.	Clanwilliam	Rathlynin	Tipperary	II.	309
46, 52	Laffina (Jones)	268 2 25	Tipperary, S.R.	Kilnamanagh Lower	Clogher	Cashel	II.	322
46, 52	Laffina (Lane)	285 0 1	Tipperary, S.R.	Kilnamanagh Lower	Clogher	Cashel	II.	322
20	Lafone	117 2 32	Waterford	Coshmore&Coshbride	Lismore andMocollop	Lismore	II.	346
17, 25	Lag	382 1 25	Cork, E.R.	Fermoy	Caherduggan	Mallow	II.	77
4	Lag	349 3 2	Donegal	Inishowen East	Clonca	Inishowen	III.	117
3, 4	Lagacurry	432 3 36	Donegal	Inishowen East	Clonmany	Inishowen	III.	117
90	Lagakilleen	56 0 37	Mayo	Carra	Drum	Castlebar	IV.	128
19, 20	Lagan	544 0 19	Armagh	Armagh	Keady	Armagh	III.	45
10	Lagan	174 1 33h	Cavan	Lower Loughtee	Drumlane	Cavan	III.	80
13	Lagan	157 3 35	Louth	Ardee	Clonkeen	Ardee	I.	172

(a) Including 20A. 0R. 2P. water.
(b) Including 17A. 1R. 24P. water.
(c) Including 4A. 1R. 2P. water.

(d) Including 15A. 3R. 2P. water.
(e) Including 2A. 2R. 38P. water.
(f) Including 8A. 2R. 30P. water.

(g) Including 2A. 1R. 7P. water.
(h) Including 2A. 2R. 23P. water.

No. of Sheet of the Ordnance Survey Maps.	Townlands and Towns.	Area in Statute Acres.	County.	Barony.	Parish.	Poor Law Union in 1857.	Townland Census of 1851, Part I.	
		A. R. P.					Vol.	Page
24, 25	Lagan	210 1 30a	Monaghan	Cremorne	Aghnamullen	Castleblayney	III.	258
83	Laganore	68 1 15	Tipperary, S.R.	Iffa and Offa East	Kilgrant	Clonmel	II.	314
90	Lagaturrin	138 1 1	Mayo	Clanmorris	Balla	Castlebar	IV.	132
5, 6	Lagavadder	361 2 18b	Tyrone	Strabane Lower	Leckpatrick	Strabane	III.	322
4	Lagavara	384 2 34	Antrim	Cary	Ballintoy	Ballycastle	III.	12
5	Lagavittal	213 1 16	Tyrone	Strabane Lower	Leckpatrick	Strabane	III.	322
24 {Louth Co.}	Lagavooren	648 2 24c	Meath	Drogheda and Municipal Borough	St. Mary's	Drogheda	I.	194
61, 62	Lagcurragh	681 0 24	Mayo	Gallen	Kilconduff	Swineford	IV.	148
35	Lagduff Beg	419 0 21	Mayo	Erris	Kilcommon	Newport	IV.	144
35	Lagduff More	1,028 2 12d	Mayo	Erris	Kilcommon	Newport	IV.	144
15	Lagflugh	70 1 39	Antrim	Lower Glenarm	Layd	Ballycastle	III.	23
68	Lagganstown Lower	603 1 24	Tipperary, S.R.	Clanwilliam	Relickmurry &Athassel	Tipperary	II.	310
68	Lagganstown Upper	367 3 17	Tipperary, S.R.	Clanwilliam	Relickmurry &Athassel	Tipperary	II.	310
124, 125	Laggoo	912 2 12	Galway	Leitrim	Ballynakill	Loughrea	IV.	51
15	Laghcloon	273 0 28	Clare	Corcomroe	Kilmacrehy	Ennistimon	II.	20
55	Laghey	113 3 3	Tyrone	Dungannon Middle	Killyman	Dungannon	III.	303
81	Laghil	147 2 28	Donegal	Banagh	Glencolumbkille	Glenties	III.	105
62	Laghile	89 0 4	Clare	Bunratty Lower	Kilfintinan	Limerick	II.	5
29, 35	Laghile	152 1 19	Tipperary, N.R.	Eliogarty	Loughmoe West	Thurles	II.	271
38, 39	Laghile	1,512 0 21	Tipperary, N.R.	Owney and Arra	Abington	Nenagh	II.	293
22	Laghile	458 3 21	Tipperary, N.R.	Upper Ormond	Aghnameadle	Nenagh	II.	289
87, 97	Laghloon	484 3 30e	Mayo	Murrisk	Aghagower	Westport	IV.	159
18, 22	Laghlooney	137 2 8	Longford	Moydow	Kilcommock	Ballymahon	I.	161
39	Laght	423 3 15	Cork, E.R.	Duhallow	Dromtarriff	Millstreet	II.	71
27	Laght	131 3 23	Cork, E.R.	Fermoy	Glanworth	Fermoy	II.	79
34	Laght	462 2 18	Tyrone	Omagh West	Longfield East	Omagh	III.	315
1, 2	Laghta	602 3 33	Leitrim	Rosclogher	Rossinver	Ballyshannon	IV.	111
46	Laghtacallow	184 3 8	Kerry	Trughanacmy	Kilgarrylander	Tralee	II.	211
30	Laghtadawannagh	185 3 0	Mayo	Tirawley	Kilmoremoy	Ballina	IV.	170
96	Laghta Eighter	1,675 0 39	Mayo	Murrisk	Kilgeever	Westport	IV.	160
41	Laghtagalla	93 0 14	Tipperary, N.R.	Eliogarty	Thurles	Thurles	II.	273
17	Laghtagoona	271 0 25	Clare	Inchiquin	Killinaboy	Corrofin	II.	26
22	Laghtanabba	207 0 11	Galway	Ballynahinch	Omey	Clifden	IV.	15
6	Laghtane East	250 1 31	Limerick	Clanwilliam	Killeenagarriff	Limerick	II.	224
6	Laghtane West	3 2 29	Limerick	Clanwilliam	Killeenagarriff	Limerick	II.	224
19,20,27,28	Laghtanvack	2,177 3 17	Mayo	Tirawley	Moygawnagh	Killala	IV.	171
96,97,106,107	Laghta Oughter	3,660 2 15	Mayo	Murrisk	Kilgeever	Westport	IV.	160
70	Laghtavarry	404 2 9	Mayo	Gallen	Kildacommoge	Castlebar	IV.	148
27	Laghtbrack	73 2 17	Kilkenny	Kells	Kells	Callan	I.	108
22	Laghtausk	420 2 29f	Roscommon	Roscommon	Elphin	Strokestown	IV.	209
19	Laghtea	214 3 19	Tipperary, N.R.	Owney and Arra	Castletownarra	Nenagh	II.	294
15	Laghtfoggy	637 0 31g	Tyrone	Omagh West	Termonamongan	Castlederg	III.	317
54	Laghtgannon	186 1 16	Galway	Moycullen	Killannin	Oughterard	IV.	70
70	Laghtgeorge	31 3 38	Galway	Clare	Claregalway	Galway	IV.	18
61, 71	Laghtmacdurkan	511 1 16h	Mayo	Gallen	Meelick	Swineford	IV.	150
15	Laghtmorris	640 1 18i	Tyrone	Omagh West	Termonamongan	Castlederg	III.	317
5	Laghtmurragha	1,269 3 9	Mayo	Erris	Kilcommon	Belmullet	IV.	144
8	Laghtmurreda	310 1 20j	Clare	Corcomroe	Killilagh	Ennistimon	II.	20
83, 95	Laghtneill	167 2 3	Cork, W.R.	West Muskerry	Kilmurry	Macroom	II.	159
72	Laghtonora	129 0 7	Galway	Tiaquin	Monivea	Loughrea	IV.	79
96	Laghtphilip	193 3 20	Galway	Dunkellin	Killeeneen	Gort	IV.	30
29	Laghtsigh	442 3 29	Cork, E.R.	Duhallow	Nohavaldaly	Millstreet	II.	75
12, 13	Laghty	231 1 5	Leitrim	Drumahaire	Cloonclare	Manorhamilton	IV.	93
8, 9	Laghty Barr	506 2 13	Leitrim	Drumahaire	Cloonclare	Manorhamilton	IV.	93
128, 129	Laghtyshaughnessy	312 0 10	Galway	Kiltartan	Beagh	Gort	IV.	46
15	Laghvally	115 1 31	Clare	Corcomroe	Kilmacrehy	Ennistimon	II.	20
100	Laghy	175 2 22	Donegal	Tirhugh	Drumhome	Donegal	III.	146
100	Laghy Barr or Ardbane	357 2 38	Donegal	Tirhugh	Drumhome	Donegal	III.	146
100	LAGHY T.	—	Donegal	Tirhugh	Drumhome	Donegal	III.	147
66	Lagile	136 0 13	Cork, E.R.	Imokilly	Killeagh	Youghal	II.	88
64	Lagmore	639 0 16	Antrim	Upper Belfast	Derryaghy	Lisburn	III.	10
5	Lagnagalloglagh	156 0 0	Tyrone	Strabane Lower	Leckpatrick	Strabane	III.	322
75	Lagnagillew	645 0 3k	Donegal	Boylagh	Inishkeel	Glenties	III.	113
31, 32, 38	Lagnaguppoge	221 3 11	Down	Lecale Lower	Ballyculter	Downpatrick	III.	178
36	Lagnagoushee	732 0 9	Waterford	Decies within Drum	Ardmore	Dungarvan	II.	350
90	Lagnamuck	173 0 38	Mayo	Clanmorris	Balla	Castlebar	IV.	132
78	Lagnavaddoge	35 0 34	Mayo	Carra	Aglish	Castlebar	IV.	124
81	Lagneeve	102 2 19l	Cork, W.R.	West Muskerry	Inchigeelagh	Dunmanway	II.	158
38, 44	Lagore Big	409 1 24	Meath	Ratoath	Ratoath	Dunshaughlin	I.	219
38, 44	Lagore Little	514 3 20	Meath	Ratoath	Ratoath	Dunshaughlin	I.	219
81, 82	Lagunna	837 2 25m	Donegal	Banagh	Inishkeel	Glenties	III.	106

(a) Including 4A. 0R. 34P. water.
(b) Including 6A. 3R. 16P. Moor Lough.
(c) { Within the Municipal Boundary, 119A. 0R. 0P.
     Without the Municipal Boundary, 529A. 2R. 24P.
(d) Including 10A. 1R. 16P. water.
(e) Including 2A. 3R. 6P. water.
(f) Including 23A. 0R. 33P. water.
(g) Including 8A. 0R. 29P. water.
(h) Including 18A. 3R. 27P. water.
(i) Including 3A. 1R. 31P. water.
(j) Including 9A. 1R. 29P. water.
(k) Including 24A. 0R. 26P. water.
(l) Including 22A. 0R. 0P. water.
(m) Including 35A. 1R. 36P. water.

No. of Sheet of the Ordnance Survey Maps	Townlands and Towns.	Area in Statute Acres. A. R. P.	County.	Barony.	Parish.	Poor Law Union in 1857.	Townland Census of 1851, Part I. Vol.	Page
46	Lahacrogher	125 0 0	Galway	Killian	Killian	Mountbellew	IV.	44
105, 118	Lahadane	68 3 35	Cork, W.R.	Bantry	Kilmocomoge	Bantry	II.	121
11, 17	Lahagboy	67 3 16	Roscommon	Roscommon	Aughrim	Carᵏ. on Shannon	IV.	207
29, 30	Lahagh	555 1 17	Tipperary, N.R.	Ikerrin	Templeree	Thurles	II.	277
19	Lahaghglass North	53 0 28	Galway	Ballymoe	Kilbegnet	Glennamaddy	IV.	8
19	Lahaghglass South	118 1 20	Galway	Ballymoe	Kilbegnet	Glennamaddy	IV.	8
41,42,50,51	Lahakinneen	379 1 5	Cork, E.R.	Barretts	Mourneabbey	Mallow	II.	50
13, 19	*Lahanacappul Island*	1 0 7	Sligo	Tireragh	Dromard	Dromore West	IV.	233
21	Lahanagh	196 1 7	Sligo	Carbury	St. John's	Sligo	IV.	223
120	Lahanaght	971 2 14	Cork, W.R.	West Carbery (E.D.)	Drinagh	Skibbereen	II.	139
40	*Lahan Island*	33 1 19	Donegal	Boylagh	Templecrone	Glenties	III.	116
6	*Lahan Island*	2 1 16	Roscommon	Boyle	Ardcarn	Boyle	IV.	193
52	Laharan	182 3 6	Cork, E.R.	Barrymore	Dunbulloge	Cork	II.	54
41	Laharan	759 1 22	Cork, E.R.	Duhallow	Kilshannig	Mallow	II.	74
27	Laharan	96 1 6	Cork, E.R.	Fermoy	Dunmahon	Fermoy	II.	79
130, 139	Laharan	225 1 26	Cork, W.R.	West Carbery (W.D.)	Skull	Skull	II.	146
39	Laharan	187 2 35	Cork, W.R.	West Muskerry	Kilcorney	Millstreet	II.	158
79, 88	Laharan	121 3 26	Kerry	Iveragh	Valencia	Cahersiveen	II.	198
57, 58	Laharan	176 1 32	Kerry	Magunihy	Aglish	Killarney	II.	200
57	Laharan	287 0 14	Kerry	Magunihy	Kilbonane	Killarney	II.	200
48	Laharan	218 0 4	Kerry	Trughanacmy	Killeentierna	Killarney	II.	211
56	Laharan	863 2 21	Kerry	Trughanacmy	Killorglin	Killarney	II.	211
38, 47	Laharan	250 2 8	Kerry	Trughanacmy	Kiltallagh	Tralee	II.	212
29	Laharan	142 1 2	Kerry	Trughanacmy	Ratass	Tralee	II.	213
138	Laharandota	67 0 29	Cork, W.R.	West Carbery (W.D.)	Kilcrohane	Bantry	II.	143
138	Laharandota Mountain	33 0 6	Cork, W.R.	West Carbery (W.D.)	Kilcrohane	Bantry	II.	144
22, 30	Laharan East	272 1 2	Cork, E.R.	Duhallow	Kilmeen	Kanturk	II.	73
105	Laharan East	51 3 2	Cork, W.R.	Bantry	Kilmocomoge	Bantry	II.	121
60	Laharankeal	182 3 8	Cork, W.R.	East Muskerry	Aghabulloge	Macroom	II.	153
69, 79	Laharan North	318 3 8	Kerry	Iveragh	Caher	Cahersiveen	II.	194
106	Laharanshermeen	175 0 20	Cork, W.R.	Bantry	Kilmocomoge	Bantry	II.	121
79,80,88,89	Laharan South	1,387 3 11	Kerry	Iveragh	Caher	Cahersiveen	II.	194
22	Laharan West	192 0 24	Cork, E.R.	Duhallow	Kilmeen	Kanturk	II.	73
105	Laharan West	91 2 36	Cork, W.R.	Bantry	Kilmocomoge	Bantry	II.	121
19, 24	Lahard	296 1 37	Cavan	Tullyhunco	Killashandra	Cavan	III.	98
100	Lahard	321 2 29	Cork, E.R.	Imokilly	Inch	Middleton	II.	87
57, 65	Lahard	721 2 37a	Kerry	Magunihy	Kilbonane	Killarney	II.	200
25	Lahard	151 1 23	Leitrim	Carrigallen	Oughteragh	Bawnboy	IV.	92
18	Lahardan	282 0 5	Clare	Bunratty Upper	Inchicronan	Ennis	II.	9
34	Lahardan	233 0 26	Sligo	Tirerrill	Killadoon	Boyle	IV.	239
8	Lahardan	593 0 23	Waterford	Upperthird	Kilmeadan	Carrick on Suir	II.	370
63, 74	Lahardane	208 1 4	Cork, E.R.	Cork	Rathcooney	Cork	II.	65
4	Lahardane	413 0 30	Kerry	Iraghticonnor	Killehenny	Listowel	II.	191
150, 151	Lahardane Beg	71 3 11	Cork, W.R.	West Carbery (E.D.)	Castlehaven	Skibbereen	II.	138
150, 151	Lahardane More	232 0 24	Cork, W.R.	West Carbery (E.D.)	Castlehaven	Skibbereen	II.	138
41, 42	Lahardan Lower	256 3 22	Tipperary, N.R.	Eliogarty	Twomileborris	Thurles	II.	273
41,42,47,48	Lahardan Upper	277 0 5	Tipperary, N.R.	Eliogarty	Twomileborris	Thurles	II.	274
35	Lahardaun	553 1 12b	Clare	Tulla Upper	Tulla	Tulla	II.	42
102, 103	Lahardaun	61 0 27	Galway	Dunkellin	Ballynacourty	Galway	IV.	27
114	Lahardaun	47 1 35	Galway	Dunkellin	Killinan	Loughrea	IV.	30
129	Lahardaun	541 3 17c	Galway	Kiltartan	Kilbeacanty	Gort	IV.	47
47	Lahardaun	461 2 3	Mayo	Tirawley	Addergoole	Castlebar	IV.	163
99, 113	Laharran	266 0 6	Cork, E.R.	Kinalea	Tracton	Kinsale	II.	97
19	Laheen	242 0 3	Cavan	Tullyhunco	Killashandra	Cavan	III.	98
103, 107	Laheen	356 3 5d	Donegal	Tirhugh	Kilbarron	Ballyshannon	III.	148
26, 30	Laheen	245 3 26e	Leitrim	Carrigallen	Carrigallen	Bawnboy	IV.	90
28	Laheen	119 3 5f	Leitrim	Leitrim	Kiltubbrid	Carᵏ. on Shannon	IV.	104
32	Laheennamona	19 1 30	Leitrim	Mohill	Mohill	Mohill	IV.	108
32	Laheen North	129 3 8	Leitrim	Leitrim	Mohill	Mohill	IV.	104
28	Laheen (*Peyton*)	80 0 34	Leitrim	Leitrim	Kiltubbrid	Carᵏ. on Shannon	IV.	104
32	Laheen South	94 0 10	Leitrim	Mohill	Mohill	Mohill	IV.	108
140, 141	Laheratanvally	123 1 12	Cork, W.R.	West Carbery (E.D.)	Aghadown	Skibbereen	II.	137
97	Laherfineen	139 0 32	Cork, E.R.	Kinalea	Inishannon	Bandon	II.	95
42, 52	Laherfree	102 3 29	Kerry	Corkaguiny	Ventry	Dingle	II.	180
111	Lahern	77 3 0	Cork, E.R.	Kinalea	Leighmoney	Kinsale	II.	96
150	Lahernathee	119 3 29	Cork, W.R.	West Carbery (E.D.)	Creagh	Skibbereen	II.	139
141	Lahertidaly	138 3 6	Cork, W.R.	West Carbery (E.D.)	Abbeystrowry	Skibbereen	II.	136
4, 5	Lahesheragh North	359 2 5	Kerry	Iraghticonnor	Lisselton	Listowel	II.	192
4, 5	Lahesheragh South	196 1 18	Kerry	Iraghticonnor	Lisselton	Listowel	II.	192
23	Lahesseragh	40 0 13	Tipperary, N.R.	Ikerrin	Killea	Roscrea	II.	275
9	Lahesseragh	83 0 22	Tipperary, N.R.	Lower Ormond	Kilbarron	Borrisokane	II.	234
20	Lahesseragh	392 0 39	Tipperary, N.R.	Upper Ormond	Nenagh	Nenagh	II.	292
26, 32	Lahid	737 3 2	Tipperary, N.R.	Upper Ormond	Kilmore	Nenagh	II.	291

(a) Including 14A. 2R. 36P. water.
(b) Including 14A. 0R. 38P. water.
(c) Including 10A. 3R. 30P. water.
(d) Including 8A. 0R. 22P. water.
(e) Including 10A. 3R. 22P. water.
(f) Including 7A. 0R. 14P. water.

No. of Sheet of the Ordnance Survey Maps.	Townlands and Towns.	Area in Statute Acres.	County.	Barony.	Parish.	Poor Law Union in 1857.	Townland Census of 1851, Part I.	
		A. R. P.					Vol.	Page
67	Lairakean . .	113 0 30	Tyrone . .	Dungannon Lower .	Aghaloo . . .	Armagh . .	III.	297
47	Lake . .	143 0 18	Wexford . .	Bargy . . .	Mulrankin . .	Wexford . .	I.	307
43	Lake Big . .	116 2 16	Wexford . .	Forth . . .	Rosslare . .	Wexford . .	I.	313
9	Lakefield . .	87 0 32a	Cavan . .	Tullyhaw . .	Templeport . .	Bawnboy . .	III.	95
88, 100	Lakefield . .	191 1 30	Galway . .	Clonmacnowen .	Clontuskert . .	Ballinasloe .	IV.	24
15	Lakefield . .	220 0 9	Meath . .	Fore . . .	Killallon . .	Oldcastle . .	I.	200
79	Lakeland Lower .	197 3 37b	Mayo . .	Carra . . .	Manulla . .	Castlebar . .	IV.	129
79	Lakeland Upper .	197 1 12c	Mayo . .	Carra . . .	Manulla . .	Castlebar . .	IV.	129
43	Lake Little . .	41 3 21	Wexford . .	Forth . . .	Rosslare . .	Wexford . .	I.	313
70, 83	Lakeview . .	353 1 3	Galway . .	Dunkellin . .	Claregalway . .	Galway . .	IV.	27
79, 80	Lakill . .	416 3 0	Mayo . .	Gallen . . .	Templemore . .	Castlebar . .	IV.	151
3, 4, 7, 8	Lakill and Moor-town . .	837 3 28d	Westmeath .	Fore . . .	St. Feighins . .	Castletowndelvin	I.	272
10	Lakingstown . .	268 0 6	Westmeath .	Moygoish . .	Kilmacnevan . .	Mullingar . .	I.	280
52	Lakyle . .	23 0 9	Clare . .	Bunratty Lower .	Killeely . .	Limerick . .	II.	5
53	Lakyle . .	108 2 25	Clare . .	Bunratty Lower .	St. Patricks . .	Limerick . .	II.	7
43	Lakyle . .	185 2 22e	Clare . .	Tulla Lower .	Clonlea . .	Tulla . .	II.	35
104	Lakyle . .	87 2 23	Galway . .	Dunkellin . .	Killogilleen . .	Loughrea . .	IV.	31
135	Lakyle . .	186 3 6f	Galway . .	Leitrim . .	Clonrush . .	Scarriff . .	IV.	53
22	Lakyle . .	58 0 29	Kilkenny . .	Shillelogher . .	Killaloe . .	Callan . .	I.	115
68	Lakyle North .	297 0 23	Clare . .	Clonderalaw .	Killofin . .	Killadysert .	II.	17
68	Lakyle South . .	212 1 16	Clare . .	Clonderalaw .	Killofin . .	Killadysert .	II.	17
24, 25	Lalistown . .	349 0 23	Westmeath .	Rathconrath .	Conry . . .	Mullingar . .	I.	282
61, 69	Lalor's-lot . .	817 0 22	Tipperary, S.R.	Middlethird .	St. John Baptist .	Cashel . .	II.	330
8	Lamagh . .	310 3 10	Longford . .	Longford . .	Clongesh . .	Longford . .	I.	158
9	Lambay Island .	595 3 0	Dublin . .	Nethercross . .	Portraine . .	Balrothery .	I.	31
64	Lambeg North .	188 3 16	Antrim . .	Upper Belfast .	Lambeg . . .	Lisburn . .	III.	10
64, 68	Lambeg South .	187 3 26	Antrim . .	Upper Massereene .	Lambeg . . .	Lisburn . .	III.	31
64	LAMBEG T. .	—	Antrim . .	Upper Belfast .	Lambeg . . .	Lisburn . .	III.	10
40, 45	Lamberton . .	126 0 35	Wicklow . .	Arklow . .	Arklow . .	Rathdrum . .	I.	341
18	Lamberton Demesne	366 1 7	Queen's Co. .	Maryborough East .	Dysartenos . .	Mountmellick .	I.	241
37	Lambertstown .	84 1 5	Meath . .	Lower Deece .	Kilmessan . .	Dunshaughlin .	I.	192
47	Lambertstown .	83 2 0	Wexford . .	Forth . . .	Mayglass . .	Wexford . .	I.	312
29	Lambhill . .	25 0 33	Galway . .	Dunmore . .	Tuam . . .	Tuam . .	IV.	36
23	Lamb Island .	0 1 35	Dublin . .	Rathdown . .	Dalkey . .	Rathdown . .	I.	35
79	Lamb Island .	2 3 16	Kerry . .	Iveragh . .	Caher . . .	Cahersiveen .	II.	194
66	Lamb Island .	1 2 19	Kerry . .	Magunihy . .	Aghadoe . .	Killarney . .	II.	199
56	Lamb Island .	3 3 38	Roscommon .	Moycarn . .	Moore . . .	Ballinasloe .	IV.	207
112	Lambs Island .	0 2 1	Galway . .	Kiltartan . .	Kinvarradoorus .	Gort . .	IV.	50
106	Lamb's Island .	10 0 6	Kerry . .	Dunkerron South .	Kilcrohane . .	Cahersiveen .	II.	184
32	Lambstown .	29 1 10	Queen's Co. .	Slievemargy . .	Killeshin . .	Carlow . .	I.	246
50	Lambstown .	245 0 2	Wexford . .	Shelburne . .	Templetown . .	New Ross . .	I.	328
31, 36, 37	Lambstown Great .	439 3 32	Wexford . .	Bantry . .	Whitechurchglynn .	Wexford . .	I.	303
36	Lambstown Little .	139 1 18	Wexford . .	Bantry . .	Whitechurchglynn .	Wexford . .	I.	303
14	Lambtown . .	73 3 21	Louth . .	Ardee . .	Mapastown . .	Ardee . .	I.	173
35, 40	Lammy . .	123 2 13	Fermanagh .	Clankelly . .	Clones . . .	Clones . .	III.	196
38, 46	Lammy . .	244 3 4	Tyrone . .	Dungannon Upper .	Desertcreat . .	Cookstown .	III.	308
34, 35	Lammy . .	153 3 6	Tyrone . .	Omagh East .	Drumragh . .	Omagh . .	III.	312
30, 34	Lamoge . .	468 3 25	Kilkenny . .	Kells . . .	Tullahought . .	Callan . .	I.	110
26	Lanaghran . .	90 1 39	Fermanagh .	Clanawley . .	Cleenish . .	Enniskillen .	III.	191
30, 31	Langlug . .	348 1 23	Tyrone . .	Dungannon Upper .	Ballinderry . .	Cookstown .	III.	306
12, 19	Landagivey . .	429 2 22	Londonderry .	Coleraine . .	Agivey . .	Coleraine . .	III.	230
11	Landahussy Lower .	306 0 20g	Tyrone . .	Strabane Upper .	Bodoney Upper .	Gortin . .	III.	324
11	Landahussy Upper .	281 2 22h	Tyrone . .	Strabane Upper .	Bodoney Upper .	Gortin . .	III.	324
40, 43	Landbrock . .	184 0 15i	Fermanagh .	Coole . .	Galloon . .	Clones . .	III.	200
13,14,18,19	Landenstown . .	568 0 25	Kildare . .	Clane . .	Brideschurch . .	Naas . .	I.	53
17	Landhead . .	306 0 21	Antrim . .	Upper Dunluce .	Ballymoney . .	Ballymoney .	III.	19
19	Landmore . .	102 1 0	Londonderry .	Coleraine . .	Aghadowey . .	Coleraine . .	III.	230
2	Landscape . .	141 0 26j	Waterford .	Upperthird . .	Kilsheelan . .	Carrick on Suir	II.	370
34	Landscape . .	160 2 19	Wexford . .	Bantry . .	Whitechurch . .	New Ross .	I.	303
19	Landsdown . .	139 3 17	Tipperary, N.R.	Owney and Arra .	Castletownarra .	Nenagh . .	II.	294
5	Lane . .	115 2 36	Dublin . .	Balrothery East .	Holmpatrick . .	Balrothery .	I.	20
5	Lane . .	28 2 25	Dublin . .	Balrothery East .	Lusk . .	Balrothery .	I.	21
53	Lanehead . .	9 0 33	Donegal . .	Kilmacrenan .	Aghanunshin . .	Letterkenny .	III.	122
17	Lanesborough .	32 0 28	Longford . .	Rathcline . .	Rathcline . .	Longford . .	I.	165
17	LANESBOROUGH T. .	—	Longford . .	Rathcline . .	Rathcline . .	Longford . .	I.	165
37	LANESBOROUGH T. .	—	Roscommon .	Ballintober South .	Cloontuskert . .	Roscommon .	IV.	188
48, 54	Lanespark . .	991 1 11	Tipperary, S.R.	Slievardagh .	Killenaule . .	Cashel . .	II.	334
12	Lanestown . .	480 2 20	Dublin . .	Nethercross . .	Donabate . .	Balrothery .	I.	30
14, 15	Laney . .	182 2 19	Antrim . .	Lower Glenarm .	Layd . .	Ballycastle .	III.	23
22	Langanoran . .	161 2 13	Waterford .	Decies without Drum	Modelligo . .	Dungarvan .	II.	359
59	Langarve . .	292 3 7	Antrim . .	Upper Massereene .	Camlin . . .	Antrim . .	III.	30
42	Langough . .	163 1 28	Clare . .	Bunratty Lower .	Tomfinlough . .	Ennis . .	II.	7

(a) Including 14A. 2R. 2P. water.
(b) Including 45A. 1R. 9P. water.
(c) Including 61A. 1R. 38P. water.
(d) Including 43A. 2R. 39P. water.

(e) Including 3A. 0R. 9P. Lough Avoher.
(f) Including 1A. 2R. 0P. water.
(g) Including 3A. 2R. 28P. water.

(h) Including 2A. 3R. 26P. water.
(i) Including 14A. 1R. 30P. water.
(j) Including 6A. 1R. 6P. water.

No. of Sheet of the Ordnance Survey Maps	Townlands and Towns.	Area in Statute Acres.			County.	Barony.	Parish.	Poor Law Union in 1857.	Townland Census of 1851, Part I.	
		A.	R.	P.					Vol.	Page
27	Lankill	235	0	8a	Fermanagh	Clanawley	Rossorry	Enniskillen	III.	194
88, 98	Lankill	253	2	33b	Mayo	Murrisk	Aghagower	Westport	IV.	159
2, 4	Lanliss	245	0	27	Cavan	Tullyhaw	Killinagh	Enniskillen	III.	92
32	Lanmore	69	0	27	Fermanagh	Clanawley	Killesher	Enniskillen	III.	193
88, 98	Lanmore	1,131	1	15c	Mayo	Murrisk	Aghagower	Westport	IV.	159
49, 50	Lanna	455	0	20	Clare	Islands	Clondagad	Killadysert	II.	29
47, 52	Lannagh	218	3	36	Wexford	Bargy	Kilmore	Wexford	I.	306
12	Lannaght	650	0	5	Clare	Tulla Upper	Feakle	Tulla	II.	39
36	Lannaght	100	3	20	Fermanagh	Clankelly	Clones	Clones	III.	196
8	Lannanerriagh	709	0	6	Cavan	Tullyhaw	Templeport	Bawnboy	III.	95
10	Lannat	512	0	1	Louth	Ardee	Killanny	Dundalk	I.	173
29	Lannat	184	2	17	Monaghan	Farney	Inishkeen	Dundalk	III.	271
23	Lansville	46	2	8	Dublin	Rathdown	Monkstown	Rathdown	I.	36
18, 19	Lantaur	193	3	21	Monaghan	Monaghan	Tullycorbet	Monaghan	III.	281
68, 77	Lappallagh	1,569	3	4d	Mayo	Carra	Islandeady	Westport	IV.	129
10	Lappan	102	1	37	Monaghan	Cremorne	Tehallan	Monaghan	III.	262
22	Lappanbane	297	1	7	Cavan	Tullygarvey	Drung	Cootehill	III.	89
22	Lappanduff	192	1	1	Cavan	Tullygarvey	Drung	Cootehill	III.	89
21, 28	Lappoges	330	2	25	Down	Lower Iveagh, Lr. pt.	Dromore	Lisburn	III.	168
36, 42	Laracor	392	2	7	Meath	Lower Moyfenrath	Laracor	Trim	I.	210
35	Laragh	224	3	22	Cavan	Clankee	Enniskeen	Bailieborough	III.	73
1, 2	Laragh	542	0	26	Cork, E.R.	Orrery and Kilmore	Kilbolane	Kanturk	II.	108
96, 110	Laragh	609	1	19	Cork, W.R.	Kinalmeaky	Kilbrogan	Bandon	II.	152
33	Laragh	130	3	15	Fermanagh	Clanawley	Kinawley	Enniskillen	III.	194
27	Laragh	283	1	6e	Fermanagh	Clanawley	Rossorry	Enniskillen	III.	194
16	Laragh	132	0	16	Fermanagh	Tirkennedy	Trory	Enniskillen	III.	223
85	Laragh	644	1	20	Galway	Kilconnell	Killimordaly	Loughrea	IV.	42
5, 10	Laragh	188	1	5	Kildare	Ikeathy & Oughterany	Kilcock	Celbridge	I.	57
28	Laragh	175	0	3f	Leitrim	Leitrim	Fenagh	Mohill	IV.	100
26, 32	Laragh	511	0	23	Londonderry	Coleraine	Desertoghill	Ballymoney	III.	230
22, 26	Laragh	155	1	5	Longford	Rathcline	Shrule	Ballymahon	I.	165
27, 28	Laragh	365	3	0	Monaghan	Cremorne	Aghnamullen	Castleblayney	III.	258
19, 24	Laragh	387	0	18	Monaghan	Cremorne	Ballybay	Castleblayney	III.	259
28	Laragh	159	1	27	Monaghan	Farney	Donaghmoyne	Carrickmacross	III.	270
12, 13	Laragh	122	3	17	Sligo	Tireragh	Skreen	Dromore West	IV.	236
43, 44	Laragh	485	3	24	Tyrone	Omagh East	Clogherny	Omagh	III.	310
17	Laragh	72	0	23	Tyrone	Strabane Lower	Ardstraw	Strabane	III.	319
31	Laragh	627	0	28	Westmeath	Moycashel	Kilcumreragh	Athlone	I.	278
11, 18	Laragh	147	0	13	Westmeath	Moygoish	Kilmacnevan	Mullingar	I.	280
38, 42, 43	Laragh	473	3	25	Wicklow	Shillelagh	Mullinacuff	Shillelagh	I.	358
8	Laraghakea	133	1	17	Clare	Corcomroe	Kilfenora	Ennistimon	II.	19
14	Laraghaleas	119	3	3	Londonderry	Tirkeeran	Faughanvale	Londonderry	III.	250
71	Laragh Beg	413	1	8	Galway	Clare	Abbeyknockmoy	Galway	IV.	16
5	Laraghbryan East	273	1	1	Kildare	North Salt	Laraghbryan	Celbridge	I.	75
5	Laraghbryan West	119	0	4	Kildare	North Salt	Laraghbryan	Celbridge	I.	75
17	Laraghcon	295	1	9g	Dublin	Newcastle	Leixlip	Celbridge	I.	33
5, 10	Laragh Demesne	639	3	31	Kildare	Ikeathy & Oughterany	Kilcock	Celbridge	I.	57
17, 18, 23, 24	Laragh East	2,202	2	4	Wicklow	Ballinacor North	Derrylossary	Rathdrum	I.	346
12	Laraghirril	364	3	28	Donegal	Inishowen East	Clonca	Inishowen	III.	117
58, 71	Laragh More	700	3	18	Galway	Clare	Abbeyknockmoy	Galway	IV.	16
34	Laragh and Ross	736	3	36	Roscommon	Ballymoe	Drumatemple	Castlereagh	IV.	191
7	Laraghshankill	104	3	22	Armagh	Tiranny	Eglish	Armagh	III.	59
11, 17	Laragh West	3,291	3	16h	Wicklow	Ballinacor North	Derrylossary	Rathdrum	I.	346
13, 17	Larah	307	0	16	Carlow	Forth	Ballon	Carlow	I.	3
21	Larah	136	0	25	Cavan	Upper Loughtee	Larah	Cavan	III.	85
2, 6	Laraheen	253	3	16	Wexford	Gorey	Kilcavan	Gorey	I.	317
2, 6	Laraheenhill	144	0	31	Wexford	Gorey	Kilcavan	Gorey	I.	317
82	Laralae	145	2	17	Mayo	Costello	Aghamore	Swineford	IV.	137
14	Larass or Strandhill	388	0	13	Sligo	Carbury	Killaspugbrone	Sligo	IV.	222
95	Laravoolta	390	3	15	Cork, W.R.	East Carbery (W.D.)	Kinneigh	Bandon	II.	135
23	Laraweehan	145	0	14i	Cavan	Clankee	Drumgoon	Cootehill	III.	72
35	Larchfield Glebe	49	0	27	Cavan	Clankee	Enniskeen	Bailieborough	III.	73
26	Larch Hill	119	1	1	Kildare	Offaly West	Ballybrackan	Athy	I.	71
16	Larch Hill	62	2	22	Queen's Co.	Upperwoods	Offerlane	Mountmellick	I.	252
2	Lareen	340	0	33	Leitrim	Rosclogher	Rossinver	Ballyshannon	IV.	111
20	Larga	86	3	22	Leitrim	Drumahaire	Inishmagrath	Manorhamilton	IV.	96
14	Largalinny	417	1	2j	Fermanagh	Magheraboy	Inishmacsaint	Ballyshannon	III.	213
31, 32	Largan	203	2	28	Cavan	Upper Loughtee	Denn	Cavan	III.	83
28, 42	Largan	602	3	25	Galway	Clare	Donaghpatrick	Tuam	IV.	19
23	Largan	169	3	23	Leitrim	Leitrim	Kiltoghert	Cark. on Shannon	IV.	102
59, 60	Largan	426	1	19	Mayo	Carra	Turlough	Castlebar	IV.	131
102, 103	Largan	103	2	20	Mayo	Costello	Annagh	Claremorris	IV.	138
64	Largan	829	3	34	Mayo	Costello	Kilcolman	Castlereagh	IV.	141

(a) Including 3A. 3R. 1P. water.
(b) Including 8A. 3R. 16P. water.
(c) Including 1A. 2R. 31P. water.
(d) Including 4A. 2R. 19P. water.

(e) Including 30A. 1R. 13P. water.
(f) Including 40A. 3R. 3½P. water.
(g) Including 5A. 3R. 8P. water.

(h) Including 23A. 0R. 25P. Lough Ouler.
(i) Including 17A. 3R. 3P. water.
(j) Including 24A. 2R. 12P. water.

No. of Sheet of the Ordnance Survey Maps	Townlands and Towns.	Area in Statute Acres.	County.	Barony.	Parish.	Poor Law Union in 1857.	Townland Census of 1851, Part I.	
		A. R. P.					Vol.	Page
80	Largan	200 2 4	Mayo	Gallen	Killedan	Swineford	IV.	150
3	Largan	108 1 31	Roscommon	Boyle	Kilbryan	Boyle	IV.	195
23	Largan	211 0 16	Roscommon	Roscommon	Kiltrustan	Strokestown	IV.	211
20, 26	Largan	468 3 5	Sligo	Leyny	Ballysadare	Sligo	IV.	230
30	Largan	798 3 11a	Sligo	Leyny	Kilmacteige	Tobercurry	IV.	231
32	Larganacarran	39 2 35	Fermanagh	Clanawley	Killesher	Enniskillen	III.	193
32	Larganacarran	66 1 15	Fermanagh	Clanawley	Kinawley	Enniskillen	III.	194
3	Larganavaddoge	441 0 18	Leitrim	Rosclogher	Rossinver	Ballyshannon	IV.	111
27	Largan Beg	421 0 11b	Mayo	Erris	Kilcommon	Belmullet	IV.	144
92, 93	Larganboy East	465 3 24	Mayo	Costello	Bekan	Claremorris	IV.	139
92	Larganboy West	385 3 27	Mayo	Costello	Bekan	Claremorris	IV.	139
18	Largandill	133 1 15	Leitrim	Drumahaire	Drumreilly	Carᵏ. on Shannon	IV.	95
3, 6	Largandoon	597 3 0c	Leitrim	Rosclogher	Killasnet	Manorhamilton	IV.	110
17	Largandoy	107 1 36	Fermanagh	Tirkennedy	Enniskillen	Enniskillen	III.	222
4, 5	Larganhugh	245 0 22	Leitrim	Rosclogher	Rossinver	Ballyshannon	IV.	111
19, 27	Largan More	1,675 2 36d	Mayo	Erris	Kilcommon	Belmullet	IV.	144
49	Larganmore	898 0 27e	Mayo	Gallen	Killasser	Swineford	IV.	149
20, 21, 23	Largan Mountain	164 3 36	Leitrim	Leitrim	Kiltoghert	Carᵏ. on Shannon	IV.	102
16	Larganreagh	115 0 37	Donegal	Kilmacrenan	Mevagh	Milford	III.	130
27	Larganreagh Barr or Meenacross	63 2 35	Donegal	Kilmacrenan	Mevagh	Milford	III.	130
6, 10	Largantea	698 2 8	Londonderry	Keenaght	Aghanloo	NewTⁿLimavady	III.	234
7	Largantemple	31 1 19	Leitrim	Rosclogher	Killasnet	Manorhamilton	IV.	110
36	Largantogher	189 1 34	Londonderry	Loughinsholin	Maghera	Magherafelt	III.	242
15	Largatreany	658 2 23	Donegal	Kilmacrenan	Clondahorky	Dunfanaghy	III.	123
14, 21	Large Park	984 2 36f	Down	Lower Iveagh, Up. pt.	Hillsborough	Lisburn	III.	169
59, 67	Largnalarkan	612 3 34	Donegal	Boylagh	Inishkeel	Glenties	III.	113
68	Largnalore	449 2 25	Donegal	Raphoe	Kilteevoge	Stranorlar	III.	139
58	Largy	409 0 21	Antrim	Lower Massereene	Killead	Antrim	III.	28
6	Largy	646 1 27	Fermanagh	Lurg	Magheraculmoney	Lowtherstown	III.	208
28	Largy	11 0 5	Fermanagh	Magherastephana	Aghavea	Lisnaskea	III.	219
22, 23	Largy	581 3 35g	Fermanagh	Tirkennedy	Derrybrusk	Enniskillen	III.	220
3, 4, 6, 7	Largy	1,705 1 10h	Leitrim	Rosclogher	Killasnet	Manorhamilton	IV.	110
16	Largy	672 3 36i	Londonderry	Keenaght	Tamlaght Finlagan	NewTⁿLimavady	III.	237
3	Largy	184 2 7	Meath	Lower Slane	Drumcondra	Ardee	I.	223
11	Largy	125 2 34	Monaghan	Dartree	Clones	Clones	III.	264
17	Largybeg	527 0 29	Tyrone	Strabane Lower	Ardstraw	Strabane	III.	319
81	Largybrack	1,043 2 27	Donegal	Banagh	Inishkeel	Glenties	III.	106
3, 4	Largydonnell	714 3 19	Leitrim	Rosclogher	Rossinver	Ballyshannon	IV.	111
16, 17	Largy or Forthenry	346 3 29	Cavan	Tullygarvey	Kildrumsherdan	Cootehill	III.	90
97	Largymore	252 3 7	Donegal	Banagh	Kilcar	Glenties	III.	108
14	Largymore	792 3 22j	Down	Castlereagh Upper	Blaris	Lisburn	III.	164
91, 97	Largynagreana	101 0 36	Donegal	Banagh	Killybegs Upper	Glenties	III.	110
10	Largyreagh	182 0 27	Londonderry	Keenaght	Drumachose	NewTⁿLimavady	III.	235
91, 97	Largysillagh	1,219 1 16	Donegal	Banagh	Killybegs Upper	Glenties	III.	110
20	Larha	33 3 1	Kerry	Clanmaurice	Ardfert	Tralee	II.	167
2, 5	Larha	873 2 37	Kerry	Iraghticonnor	Aghavallen	Listowel	II.	189
35	Larha North	8 0 37	Tipperary, N.R.	Eliogarty	Drom	Thurles	II.	269
35	Larha South	24 0 19	Tipperary, N.R.	Eliogarty	Drom	Thurles	II.	269
18, 22	Larkfield	13 0 30	Dublin	Uppercross	Crumlin	Dublin South	I.	39
11,12,15,16	Larkfield	2,064 3 15	Leitrim	Drumahaire	Cloonlogher	Manorhamilton	IV.	94
6	Larkfield	674 1 20k	Longford	Granard	Columbkille	Granard	I.	156
3, 4	Larkhill	202 2 30	Fermanagh	Lurg	Belleek	Ballyshannon	III.	203
19	Larkhill	402 0 27	Sligo	Leyny	Ballysadare	Sligo	IV.	230
12	Larkinstown	220 2 9	Westmeath	Corkaree	Stonehall	Mullingar	I.	263
42	Larkinstown	87 2 20	Wexford	Forth	St. Peters	Wexford	I.	314
5	Larmore	76 3 10	Fermanagh	Lurg	Drumkeeran	Lowtherstown	III.	206
40	LARNE T.	—	Antrim	{ Lower Belfast	Inver	} Larne	III.	{ 8
				{ Upper Glenarm	Larne	}		{ 25
116, 125	Larraga	206 0 18	Galway	Leitrim	Ballynakill	Loughrea	IV.	51
55, 68	Larragan	273 2 7	Galway	Moycullen	Killannin	Oughterard	IV.	70
2	Larragan	216 2 22	Queen's Co.	Tinnahinch	Kilmanman	Mountmellick	I.	249
46	Larrycormick	394 1 13	Londonderry	Loughinsholin	Desertlyn	Magherafelt	III.	240
21	Laskiltagh	43 3 37	Limerick	Coshma	Croom	Croom	II.	242
17	Lasmaconly	159 1 39	Carlow	Forth	Myshall	Carlow	I.	5
37, 46, 47	Lassaboy	608 1 1	Kerry	Trughanacmy	Kilgarrylander	Tralee	II.	211
34	Lassana	167 0 15	Clare	Bunratty Upper	Clooney	Tulla	II.	8
132, 141	Lassanaroe	374 0 35	Cork, W.R.	West Carbery(W.D.)	Caheragh	Skibbereen	II.	142
92	Lassanny	87 2 20l	Mayo	Costello	Bekan	Claremorris	IV.	139
58	Latbeg	235 1 0	Tyrone	Clogher	Clogher	Clogher	III.	293
25, 28	Latbirget	735 3 10	Armagh	Orior Upper	Forkill	Newry	III.	57
22	Latooster	100 0 0	Cavan	Castlerahan	Killenkere	Bailieborough	III.	69
87	Lateeve	790 3 32	Kerry	Iveragh	Killemlagh	Cahersiveen	II.	196

(a) Including 26ᴀ. 3ʀ. 32ᴘ. water.
(b) Including 6ᴀ. 2ʀ. 0ᴘ. water.
(c) Including 44ᴀ. 0ʀ. 32ᴘ. water.
(d) Including 15ᴀ. 1ʀ. 3ᴘ. water.

(e) Including 6ᴀ. 1ʀ. 36ᴘ. water.
(f) Including 41ᴀ. 2ʀ. 16ᴘ. water.
(g) Including 7ᴀ. 3ʀ. 16ᴘ. water.
(h) Including 88ᴀ. 2ʀ. 0ᴘ. water.

(i) Including 8ᴀ. 1ʀ. 25ᴘ. water.
(j) Including 9ᴀ. 2ʀ. 34ᴘ. water.
(k) Including 3ᴀ. 0ʀ. 3ᴘ. water.
(l) Including 5ᴀ. 0ʀ. 16ᴘ. water.

No. of Sheet of the Ordnance Survey Maps.	Townlands and Towns.	Area in Statute Acres.	County.	Barony.	Parish.	Poor Law Union in 1857.	Townland Census of 1851, Part I. Vol.	Page
		A. R. P.					Vol.	Page
42	Lateeve Beg . .	274 3 26	Kerry . .	Corkaguiny .	Kilmalkedar . .	Dingle . .	II.	178
42	Lateevemanagh .	298 2 34	Kerry . .	Corkaguiny .	Kilmalkedar . .	Dingle . .	II.	178
42	Lateeve More .	340 1 39	Kerry . .	Corkaguiny .	Kilmalkedar . .	Dingle . .	II.	178
21, 26	Lateever . .	231 1 4	Cavan . .	Upper Loughtee	Lavey . .	Cavan . .	III.	86
18	Lates . .	124 3 32	Kilkenny .	Crannagh .	Tullaroan . .	Kilkenny .	I.	88
12	Latgallan . .	48 0 21	Monaghan .	Dartree . .	Clones . .	Clones . .	III.	264
3	Latgee . .	9 1 26	Monaghan .	Trough . .	Errigal Trough .	Monaghan .	III.	284
27	Lathaleere .	209 0 7	Wicklow .	Upper Talbotstown .	Baltinglass .	Baltinglass .	I.	362
42	Latimerstown .	129 0 20	Wexford .	Forth . .	Rathaspick .	Wexford .	I.	312
30, 31	Latinalbany .	184 1 12a	Monaghan .	Farney . .	Maghcross .	Carrickmacross	III.	274
9	Latlorcan . .	151 3 18	Monaghan .	Monaghan .	Monaghan . .	Monaghan .	III.	277
16	Latmacollum .	289 2 5	Armagh .	Fews Lower .	Lisnadill . .	Armagh . .	III.	47
32	Latnadronagh .	330 3 2	Cavan . .	Castlerahan .	Crosserlough .	Cavan . .	III.	68
14, 15	Latnakelly .	140 3 19	Monaghan .	Cremorne .	Clontibret .	Castleblayney .	III.	261
13, 18	Latnamard .	322 3 17	Monaghan .	Dartree . .	Aghabog . .	Monaghan .	III.	263
42	Latoon North .	158 3 39	Clare . .	Bunratty Lower .	Kilnasoolagh .	Ennis . .	II.	6
42	Latoon South .	301 0 24	Clare . .	Bunratty Lower .	Kilnasoolagh .	Ennis . .	II.	6
12, 17	Latroe . .	110 3 35	Monaghan .	Dartree . .	Killeevan .	Clones . .	III.	268
22, 27	Latsey . .	437 2 14	Cavan . .	Clankee . .	Knockbride .	Cootehill .	III.	74
22, 26	Latt . .	306 0 4	Armagh .	Orior Upper .	Killevy . ○ .	Newry . .	III.	58
20	Latt . .	231 2 15b	Cavan . .	Upper Loughtee	Annagelliff .	Cavan . .	III.	82
16	Lattacapple .	134 2 2	Cavan . .	Tullygarvey .	Drung . .	Cootehill .	III.	89
24	Lattacrom .	396 0 38c	Monaghan .	Cremorne .	Aghnamullen .	Castleblayney .	III.	258
21	Lattacrossan .	169 2 0	Monaghan .	Dartree . .	Currin . .	Clones . .	III.	266
26, 32	Lattagloghan .	604 2 16	Cavan . .	Upper Loughtee	Lavey . .	Cavan . .	III.	86
18	Lattensbog .	194 1 9	Kildare .	Connell . .	Oldconnell .	Naas . .	I.	56
28	Latteragh .	476 0 13	Tipperary, N.R.	Upper Ormond .	Latteragh .	Nenagh . .	II.	292
23, 28	Latterriff .	122 0 21	Cavan . .	Clankee . .	Shercock .	Bailieborough .	III.	74
17	Lattery . .	289 0 9d	Armagh .	Fews Lower .	Mullaghbrack .	Armagh . .	III.	47
10	Lattigar . .	28 2 38	Monaghan .	Monaghan .	Monaghan . .	Monaghan .	III.	277
66	Lattin East .	206 2 18	Tipperary, S.R.	Clanwilliam .	Lattin . .	Tipperary .	II.	309
66	Lattin North .	264 1 14	Tipperary, S.R.	Clanwilliam .	Lattin . .	Tipperary .	II.	309
66	Lattin West .	180 2 2	Tipperary, S.R.	Clanwilliam .	Lattin . .	Tipperary .	II.	309
23	Latton . .	333 3 30e	Monaghan .	Cremorne .	Aghnamullen .	Cootehill .	III.	258
20	Lattonagh .	96 3 30	Fermanagh .	Magheraboy .	Boho . .	Enniskillen .	III.	209
3, 4	Lattone . .	98 2 15	Cavan . .	Tullyhaw .	Templeport .	Enniskillen .	III.	95
19, 20	Lattone . .	572 0 24f	Fermanagh .	Clanawley .	Cleenish . .	Ballyshannon .	III.	191
5, 8	Lattone . .	539 1 8	Leitrim .	Rosclogher .	Rossinver .	Manorhamilton .	IV.	111
24	Lattonfasky .	337 2 33g	Monaghan .	Cremorne .	Aghnamullen .	Castleblayney .	III.	258
32, 33	Lattoon . .	288 3 39h	Cavan . .	Castlerahan .	Lurgan . .	Oldcastle .	III.	70
60, 61	Lattoon . .	843 2 27	Galway .	Kilconnell .	Ahascragh .	Mountbellew .	IV.	39
28	Lattylanigan .	122 1 29i	Monaghan .	Farney . .	Donaghmoyne .	Carrickmacross	III.	270
17	Lattyloo . .	126 3 2	Cavan . .	Tullygarvey .	Drumgoon .	Cootehill .	III.	88
22	Latully . .	298 0 2	Cavan . .	Clankee . .	Drumgoon .	Cootehill .	III.	72
26	Laughanstown .	382 2 33	Dublin . .	Rathdown .	Tully . .	Rathdown .	I.	38
30, 31	Laughil . .	205 3 38	Galway .	Ballymoe .	Clonbern .	Glennamaddy .	IV.	6
96	Laughil . .	97 1 6	Galway .	Dunkellin .	Lickerrig .	Loughrea .	IV.	31
123, 129, 133	Laughil . .	347 2 0	Galway .	Kiltartan .	Beagh . .	Gort . .	IV.	46
125	Laughil . .	105 0 23	Galway .	Leitrim . .	Ballynakill .	Loughrea .	IV.	51
107	Laughil . .	82 2 32	Galway .	Longford .	Killimorbologue .	Portumna .	IV.	59
81	Laughil . .	1,155 3 23j	Galway .	Moycullen .	Moycullen .	Galway . .	IV.	71
45	Laughil . .	138 3 17	Galway .	Tiaquin .	Moylough .	Mountbellew .	IV.	80
43	Laughil . .	141 0 27	King's Co .	Ballybritt .	Roscrea . .	Roscrea . .	I.	126
31, 36	Laughil . .	186 1 18	King's Co. .	Eglish . .	Drumcullen .	Parsonstown .	I.	134
6	Laughil . .	367 3 28	King's Co. .	Garrycastle .	Lemanaghan .	Parsonstown .	I.	137
19	Laughil . .	112 1 33	Longford .	Ardagh . .	Ardagh . .	Longford .	I.	151
22	Laughil . .	245 2 15	Longford .	Rathcline .	Kilcommock .	Ballymahon .	I.	164
48, 60	Laughil . .	226 0 39	Mayo . .	Carra . .	Turlough .	Castlebar .	IV.	131
37	Laughil . .	320 1 2	Mayo . .	Tirawley .	Crossmolina .	Ballina . .	IV.	166
7	Laughil . .	93 2 33	Roscommon .	Boyle . .	Tumna . .	Car. on Shannon	IV.	198
25	Laughil . .	81 2 32	Roscommon .	Castlereagh .	Kiltullagh .	Castlereagh .	IV.	202
53	Laughil . .	162 0 39	Roscommon .	Moycarn .	Creagh . .	Ballinasloe .	IV.	206
24, 25, 31, 32	Laughil . .	2,184 1 2	Sligo . .	Leyny . .	Achonry . .	Tobercurry .	IV.	229
10, 15	Laughil (Adair) .	101 1 0	Longford .	Granard .	Clonbroney .	Granard .	I.	155
10, 15	Laughil (Edgeworth) .	171 0 29	Longford .	Granard .	Clonbroney .	Granard .	I.	155
7	Laughill . .	402 0 23	Fermanagh .	Magheraboy .	Inishmacsaint .	Ballyshannon .	III.	213
3	Laught or Commons .	236 0 39	Queen's Co. .	Tinnahinch .	Castlebrack .	Mountmellick .	I.	248
63, 64	Lauhir . .	266 1 33	Kerry . .	Iveragh . .	Glanbehy .	Killarney .	II.	196
31	*Launches Little Island* . .	6 3 26	Down . .	Lecale Lower .	Saul . .	Downpatrick .	III.	179
31	*Launches Long Island* . .	9 0 37	Down . .	Lecale Lower .	Saul . .	Downpatrick .	III.	179
3, 6	Launtaggart .	706 1 30	Leitrim .	Rosclogher .	Killasnet .	Manorhamilton .	IV.	110

(a) Including 6A. 2R. 25P. water.
(b) Including 4A. 0R. 32P. Drumgola Lough.
(c) Including 16A. 1R. 31P. water.
(d) Including 12A. 0R. 26P. water.

(e) Including 35A. 3R. 25P. water.
(f) Including 23A. 2R. 36P. water.
(g) Including 75A. 2R. 34P. water.

(h) Including 42A. 0R. 2P. water.
(i) Including 6A. 0R. 7P. water.
(j) Including 9A. 2R. 14F. water.

No. of Sheet of the Ordnance Survey Maps.	Townlands and Towns.	Area in Statute Acres. A. R. P.	County.	Barony.	Parish.	Poor Law Union in 1857.	Townland Census of 1851, Part I. Vol.	Page
8	Lauragh	88 2 32	Queen's Co.	Portnahinch	Ardea	Mountmellick	I.	243
30	Lauragh	308 2 22	Waterford	Decies without Drum	Whitechurch	Dungarvan	II.	362
108	Lauragh Lower	155 2 12	Kerry	Glanarought	Tuosist	Kenmare	II.	189
108	Lauragh Upper	383 1 35	Kerry	Glanarought	Tuosist	Kenmare	II.	189
56, 57	Laurclavagh	412 3 15	Galway	Clare	Cummer	Tuam	IV.	19
16	Laurelhill	77 3 22	Queen's Co.	Upperwoods	Offerlane	Mountmellick	I.	252
100	Laurencetown	267 3 10	Galway	Longford	Clonfert	Ballinasloe	IV.	57
4	Laurencetown	120 1 36	King's Co.	Warrenstown	Ballyburly	Edenderry	I.	144
48	Laurencetown North	340 2 10	Limerick	Coshlea	Particles	Kilmallock	II.	240
48, 56	Laurencetown South	423 3 38	Limerick	Coshlea	Particles	Kilmallock	II.	240
26	LAURENCETOWN T.	—	Down	Lower Iveagh, Up. pt.	Tullylish	Banbridge	III.	171
100	LAURENCETOWN T.	—	Galway	Longford	Clonfert	Ballinasloe	IV.	57
11	Laurestown	207 0 6	Dublin	Nethercross	Finglas	Balrothery	I.	30
42	Laurstown	169 3 9	Wexford	Forth	St. Peters	Wexford	I.	314
29	Laurlyer	261 1 33	Mayo	Tirawley	Ballysakeery	Ballina	IV.	165
37, 38	Lavagh	364 1 31	Cavan	Clanmahon	Ballymachugh	Cavan	III.	76
86, 87	Lavagh	182 3 20	Galway	Kilconnell	Killallaghtan	Ballinasloe	IV.	41
29	Lavagh	194 0 5	King's Co.	Garrycastle	Lusmagh	Parsonstown	I.	137
17	Lavagh	92 2 24	Leitrim	Drumahaire	Inishmagrath	Manorhamilton	IV.	97
31, 32	Lavagh	134 0 4a	Leitrim	Leitrim	Annaduff	Car*. on Shannon	IV.	99
18	Lavagh	536 0 35	Roscommon	Ballintober North	Kilglass	Strokestown	IV.	186
32	Lavagh	245 1 20	Sligo	Leyny	Achonry	Tobercurry	IV.	229
19	Lavagh	199 2 38	Sligo	Tireragh	Dromard	Dromore West	IV.	233
29	Lavagh Beg	51 2 18	King's Co.	Garrycastle	Lusmagh	Parsonstown	I.	137
30	Lavagilduff	252 0 6	Monaghan	Farney	Magheracloone	Carrickmacross	III.	272
50	Lavally	127 3 16	Clare	Clonderalaw	Kilchreest	Killadysert	II.	15
95	Lavally	410 0 37	Galway	Dunkellin	Killeely	Gort	IV.	29
122, 123	Lavally	133 0 21	Galway	Kiltartan	Beagh	Gort	IV.	46
123	Lavally	208 1 11	Galway	Kiltartan	Kiltartan	Gort	IV.	48
23	Lavally	160 3 12	Roscommon	Roscommon	Kiltrustan	Strokestown	IV.	211
33	Lavally	340 1 31b	Sligo	Carran	Toomour	Sligo	IV.	228
21, 27, 28	Lavally	1,360 3 25	Sligo	Tirerrill	Ballysumaghan	Sligo	IV.	238
21, 27	Lavally	629 0 24	Sligo	Tirerrill	Killerry	Sligo	IV.	239
104	Lavallyconor	125 3 17	Galway	Dunkellin	Killeely	Gort	IV.	29
33	Lavally Lower	119 2 15	Cork, E.R.	Fermoy	Rahan	Mallow	II.	82
76	Lavally Lower	224 0 32	Tipperary, S.R.	Iffa and Offa East	Newchapel	Clonmel	II.	315
49, 50	Lavally North	372 1 14	Clare	Islands	Clondagad	Killadysert	II.	29
49, 50	Lavally South	192 3 3	Clare	Islands	Clondagad	Killadysert	II.	29
33	Lavally Upper	808 3 23	Cork, E.R.	Fermoy	Rahan	Mallow	II.	82
76	Lavally Upper	180 1 29	Tipperary, S.R.	Iffa and Offa East	Newchapel	Clonmel	II.	315
5	Lavaran	66 3 5	Fermanagh	Lurg	Magheraculmoney	Lowtherstown	III.	208
29	Lavareen	226 2 28c	Leitrim	Carrigallen	Cloone	Mohill	IV.	90
23	Lavarreen	534 3 26	Clare	Corcomroe	Clooney	Ennistimon	II.	18
20, 23	Lavaur	226 3 33	Leitrim	Leitrim	Kiltoghert	Car*. on Shannon	IV.	102
26	Lavey	458 3 24d	Cavan	Upper Loughtee	Lavey	Cavan	III.	86
18	Lavin Lower	399 1 21	Antrim	Upper Dunluce	Loughguile	Ballymoney	III.	20
20, 21, 26	Lavinscartron	75 3 12	Sligo	Tirerrill	Kilross	Sligo	IV.	241
18	Lavin Upper	242 2 15	Antrim	Upper Dunluce	Loughguile	Ballymoney	III.	20
19, 20	Lavistown	255 1 27e	Kilkenny	Gowran	St. Martins	Kilkenny	I.	98
63	Lavy Beg	302 3 4	Mayo	Costello	Kilbeagh	Swineford	IV.	140
63	Lavy More	630 0 26	Mayo	Costello	Kilbeagh	Swineford	IV.	140
100	Lawarreen	20 1 4	Mayo	Carra	Burriscarra	Ballinrobe	IV.	127
112	Lawaus	426 2 12	Mayo	Clanmorris	Crossboyne	Claremorris	IV.	133
118	Lawaus	149 1 4	Mayo	Kilmaine	Ballinchalla	Ballinrobe	IV.	152
27	Lawcus	261 3 4	Kilkenny	Shillelogher	Ennisnag	Thomastown	I.	114
18	Lawlesstown	47 2 23	Louth	Ardee	Cappoge	Ardee	I.	171
77	Lawlesstown	226 3 37	Tipperary, S.R.	Iffa and Offa East	Kiltegan	Clonmel	II.	315
77, 83	Lawlesstown	179 0 29	Tipperary, S.R.	Iffa and Offa East	Rathronan	Clonmel	II.	316
10, 11	Lawrencetown or Oakleypark	741 3 2f	Meath	Upper Kells	Dulane	Kells	I.	205
15	Layd	219 3 8	Antrim	Lower Glenarm	Layd	Ballycastle	III.	23
8	Laytown	136 0 26	Dublin	Balrothery East	Baldongan	Balrothery	I.	19
32, 37	Lea	23 1 16	Fermanagh	Clanawley	Kinawley	Enniskillen	III.	194
5	Lea	1,097 3 12	Queen's Co.	Portnahinch	Lea	Mountmellick	I.	244
21	Leab	112 3 10g	Longford	Rathcline	Cashel	Ballymahon	I.	163
97	Leabaleaha	314 0 7	Kerry	Iveragh	Prior	Cahersiveen	II.	198
7, 15	Leabeg	751 3 24	King's Co.	Garrycastle	Lemanaghan	Parsonstown	I.	137
15, 23	Lea Beg	3,768 3 11h	King's Co.	Garrycastle	Wheery or Killagally	Parsonstown	I.	139
34	Leabeg	494 1 3	Roscommon	Ballymoe	Drumatemple	Castlereagh	IV.	191
13	Leabeg Lower	182 2 39	Wicklow	Newcastle	Newcastle Lower	Rathdrum	I.	353
13	Leabeg Middle	238 0 39	Wicklow	Newcastle	Newcastle Lower	Rathdrum	I.	353
13	Leabeg Upper	193 0 22	Wicklow	Newcastle	Newcastle Lower	Rathdrum	I.	353
40, 48	Leabgarrow	345 2 16	Donegal	Boylagh	Templecrone	Glenties	III.	115

(a) Including 4A. 2R. 38P. water.
(b) Including 16A. 0R. 31P. water.
(c) Including 29A. 2R. 20P. water.
(d) Including 26A. 0R. 4P. water.
(e) Including 3A. 1R. 4P. River Nore.
(f) Including 6A. 2R. 0P. water.
(g) Including 2A. 2R. 16P. water.
(h) Including 8A. 1R. 8P. water.

No. of Sheet of the Ordnance Survey Maps.	Townlands and Towns.	Area in Statute Acres. A. R. P.	County.	Barony.	Parish.	Poor Law Union in 1857.	Townland Census of 1851, Part I. Vol.	Page
48	Leabrannagh	63 2 17	Donegal	Boylagh	Templecrone	Glenties	III.	115
40	Leabrannagh Mountain North & Plughoge	113 1 9	Donegal	Boylagh	Templecrone	Glenties	III.	115
40, 48	Leabrannagh Mountain South & Plughoge	195 1 0	Donegal	Boylagh	Templecrone	Glenties	III.	115
47	Leachestown	122 0 27	Wexford	Forth	Mayglass	Wexford	I.	312
60	Leadawillin	455 2 7	Cork, W.R.	East Muskerry	Aghabulloge	Macroom	II.	153
54, 65	Leadinton	454 0 1	Cork, E.R.	Barrymore	Templenacarriga	Middleton	II.	58
57, 67	Leadmore East	341 3 27	Clare	Moyarta	Kilrush	Kilrush	II.	33
67	Leadmore West	296 2 0	Clare	Moyarta	Kilrush	Kilrush	II.	33
15	Leadymore	61 2 11	Mayo	Tirawley	Killala	Killala	IV.	169
10,11,16,17	Leaffony	1,484 0 0	Sligo	Tireragh	Kilglass	Dromore West	IV.	234
5	Leafin	93 0 24	Meath	Morgallion	Nobber	Kells	I.	210
47, 55	Leagane	152 1 34	Limerick	Coshma	Effin	Kilmallock	II.	243
19, 25	Leagane	354 0 0	Tipperary, N.R.	Owney and Arra	Templeachally	Nenagh	II.	297
92	Leagans	194 2 27	Donegal	Banagh	Inver	Donegal	III.	107
30, 31	Leagard North	224 0 17	Clare	Ibrickan	Kilfarboy	Ennistimon	II.	22
30	Leagard South	489 0 3	Clare	Ibrickan	Kilfarboy	Ennistimon	II.	22
22	Leagaun	122 2 30	Galway	Ballynahinch	Omey	Clifden	IV.	15
68	Leagaun	403 2 9	Galway	Moycullen	Moycullen	Galway	IV.	71
9	Leagh	191 3 23	Kerry	Clanmaurice	Rattoo	Listowel	II.	173
23	Leagh	100 2 22	Monaghan	Cremorne	Aghnamullen	Cootehill	III.	258
13	Leagh	168 2 10	Monaghan	Monaghan	Monaghan	Monaghan	III.	277
32	Leagh	442 2 30	Queen's Co.	Slievemargy	Killeshin	Carlow	I.	246
36	Leagh	218 3 9	Waterford	Decies within Drum	Ringagonagh	Dungarvan	III.	353
5, 6	Leaghan	101 0 8	Fermanagh	Lurg	Magheraculmoney	Lowtherstown	III.	208
27	Leaghan	917 2 36a	Tyrone	Strabane Upper	Bodoney Lower	Gortin	III.	323
12	Leagh or Ballybeg	148 1 23	Carlow	Forth	Tullowmagimma	Carlow	I.	5
48	Leaghcarrick	211 2 3b	Galway	Ballynahinch	Ballindoon	Clifden	IV.	10
22	Leaghin	203 2 26	Cavan	Tullygarvey	Kildrumsherdan	Cootehill	III.	90
9	Leagh Marshes	87 3 15	Kerry	Clanmaurice	Rattoo	Listowel	II.	173
112	Leagh North	233 2 33	Galway	Kiltartan	Kinvarradoorus	Gort	IV.	49
20	Leaghort	181 3 8	Clare	Tulla Upper	Feakle	Scarriff	II.	39
19, 20	Leaghort Beg	103 2 31	Clare	Tulla Upper	Feakle	Tulla	II.	39
19, 20	Leaghort More	209 0 6	Clare	Tulla Upper	Feakle	Tulla	II.	39
13	Leaghs	660 1 13	Tyrone	Strabane Upper	Bodoney Upper	Gortin	III.	324
112	Leagh South	408 3 1	Galway	Kiltartan	Kinvarradoorus	Gort	IV.	49
69,70,78,79	Leaght	588 3 6	Donegal	Raphoe	Donaghmore	Stranorlar	III.	138
142	League, The	3 2 22	Cork, W.R.	West Carbery (E.D.)	Myross	Skibbereen	II.	141
19	Leaha	662 0 30	Galway	Ballymoe	Kilbegnet	Glennamaddy	IV.	8
49, 50	Leaha	324 3 1	Kerry	Trughanacmy	Ballincuslane	Tralee	II.	206
56	Leaheen	167 1 35	Clare	Moyarta	Kilfearagh	Kilrush	II.	32
104, 117	Leahill	376 1 24	Cork, W.R.	Bear	Kilcaskan	Castletown	II.	123
9, 10	Leahys	470 2 37	Limerick	Shanid	Robertstown	Glin	II.	258
81	Lealetter	551 1 7c	Galway	Moycullen	Moycullen	Galway	IV.	71
40	Lealies	224 3 5	Antrim	Upper Glenarm	Kilwaughter	Larne	III.	25
25, 31	Leam	36 1 2	Cavan	Clanmahon	Ballintemple	Cavan	III.	75
17, 23	Leam	196 1 20	Fermanagh	Tirkennedy	Enniskillen	Enniskillen	III.	222
16	Leam	262 3 15d	Mayo	Erris	Kilmore	Belmullet	IV.	146
10	Leam	629 0 27	Roscommon	Boyle	Boyle	Boyle	IV.	194
30	Leamacrossan	820 2 8	Donegal	Inishowen East	Moville Upper	Inishowen	III.	119
46, 58	Leamadartaun	890 3 22	Mayo	Tirawley	Crossmolina	Ballina	IV.	166
82	Leamagowra	1,233 0 35	Donegal	Banagh	Inishkeel	Glenties	III.	106
9, 16	Leamaneh North	377 1 31	Clare	Inchiquin	Killinaboy	Corrofin	II.	26
16	Leamaneh South	187 2 12	Clare	Inchiquin	Killinaboy	Corrofin	II.	26
51	Leamaneigh Beg	95 2 3	Clare	Bunratty Lower	Clonloghan	Ennis	II.	3
51	Leamaneigh More	215 1 9	Clare	Bunratty Lower	Clonloghan	Ennis	II.	3
24, 28	Leamanish	276 0 15e	Leitrim	Mohill	Fenagh	Mohill	IV.	106
33	*Leamareha Island*	3 3 13	Mayo	Erris	Kilmore	Belmullet	IV.	146
15	Leamaskally	179 2 33f	Leitrim	Drumahaire	Killarga	Manorhamilton	IV.	99
21, 26	Leam Beg	110 1 11g	Fermanagh	Clanawley	Cleenish	Enniskillen	III.	191
27	Leambreslen	155 1 14	Fermanagh	Tirkennedy	Derryvullan	Enniskillen	III.	221
148	Leamcon	136 1 18	Cork, W.R.	West Carbery (W.D.)	Skull	Skull	II.	146
105, 106,} 115, 116 }	Leamcon	184 3 33	Galway	Leitrim	Kilteskill	Loughrea	IV.	55
53	Leam East	1,910 3 37h	Galway	Moycullen	Kilcummin	Oughterard	IV.	67
17	Leamgeltan	118 0 20	Cavan	Tullygarvey	Kildrumsherdan	Cootehill	III.	90
43	Leamirlea	265 3 10	Kerry	Corkaguiny	Kilmalkedar	Dingle	II.	178
64	Leamlara	278 3 22	Cork, E.R.	Barrymore	Ballycurrany	Middleton	II.	51
64	Leamlara	38 0 29	Cork, E.R.	Barrymore	Lisgoold	Middleton	II.	56
21, 26	Leam More	86 1 17	Fermanagh	Clanawley	Cleenish	Enniskillen	III.	191
48,.58	Leamnaguila	707 3 9	Kerry	Magunihy	Kilcredane	Killarney	II.	200

(a) Including 4A. 2R. 1P. water.
(b) Including 2A. 1R. 1P. water.
(c) Including 8A. 2R. 6P. water.
(d) Including 21A. 0R. 24P. water.
(e) Including 6A. 3R. 10P. water.
(f) Including 1A. 0R. 0P. water.
(g) Including 18A. 2R. 35P. water.
(h) Including 21A. 2R. 34P. water.

No. of Sheet of the Ordnance Survey Maps.	Townlands and Towns.	Area in Statute Acres.	County.	Barony.	Parish.	Poor Law Union in 1857.	Townland Census of 1851, Part I.	
		A. R. P.					Vol.	Page
110	Leamnahye Island	3 0 13	Mayo	Carra	Ballyovey	Ballinrobe	IV.	125
49	Leamnaleaha	586 3 7	Clare	Clonderalaw	Kilchreest	Killadysert	II.	15
26	Leamnamoyle	33 1 31	Fermanagh	Clanawley	Killesher	Enniskillen	III.	193
15, 23	Lea More	2,746 3 16	King's Co.	Garrycastle	Wheery or Killagally	Parsonstown	I.	139
34	Leamore	461 2 7a	Roscommon	Ballymoe	Ballynakill	Castlereagh	IV.	191
15, 20	Leamore or Glenville	83 3 9	Antrim	Lower Glenarm	Layd	Ballycastle	III.	22
13, 19	Leamore Lower	195 3 18	Wicklow	Newcastle	Newcastle Lower	Rathdrum	I.	353
19	Leamore Upper	349 3 2	Wicklow	Newcastle	Newcastle Lower	Rathdrum	I.	353
16, 22	Leampreaghane	399 1 6	Kerry	Clanmaurice	Kilfeighny	Listowel	II.	170
53	Leam West	2,348 2 11b	Galway	Moycullen	Kilcummin	Oughterard	IV.	67
31, 40	Leamydoody	317 2 8	Kerry	Trughanacmy	Ballincuslane	Tralee	II.	206
50, 60	Leanyglissane	189 1 5	Kerry	Magunihy	Aghadoe	Killarney	II.	199
49,50,59,60	Leamyglissane	624 3 5	Kerry	Magunihy	Kilcummin	Killarney	II.	201
10, 17	Leana	674 3 13	Clare	Inchiquin	Killinaboy	Corrofin	II.	26
3, 6	Leanamore	1,435 3 26	Kerry	Iraghticonnor	Aghavallen	Listowel	II.	189
1, 4	Leansaghane	208 0 7	Kerry	Iraghticonnor	Kilconly	Listowel	II.	191
14	Leany	862 1 10	Carlow	St. Mullins Upper	Moyacomb	Carlow	I.	14
53, 60	Leany	182 3 15	Tyrone	Dungannon Lower	Carnteel	Dungannon	III.	297
7, 16	Leap	133 3 2	Cork, E.R.	Orrery and Kilmore	Churchtown	Mallow	II.	107
39	Leap	158 2 19	King's Co.	Ballybritt	Aghancon	Roscrea	I.	124
28	Leap	73 1 33	Queen's Co.	Clarmallagh	Aghaboe	Abbeyleix	I.	236
14	Leapstown	187 0 26	Kilkenny	Fassadinin	Kilmademoge	Kilkenny	I.	90
142	LEAP T.	—	Cork, W.R.	East Carbery (W.D.) West Carbery (E.D.)	Kilmacabea	Skibbereen	II.	133 140
28	Lear	477 2 17c	Cavan	Clankee	Bailieborough	Bailieborough	III.	71
27	Lear	127 0 13	Cavan	Clankee	Knockbride	Cootehill	III.	74
36	Lear	249 1 1	Leitrim	Mohill	Cloone	Mohill	IV.	106
29	Lear	2,010 0 38	Londonderry	Tirkeeran	Cumber Upper	Londonderry	III.	249
7	Learden	106 3 10	Londonderry	Coleraine	Macosquin	Coleraine	III.	233
11, 18	Learden Lower	428 3 23d	Tyrone	Strabane Upper	Bodoney Upper	Gortin	III.	324
11, 18	Learden Upper	538 3 36e	Tyrone	Strabane Upper	Bodoney Upper	Gortin	III.	324
16, 24	Learmore	406 2 22f	Tyrone	Omagh West	Urney	Castlederg	III.	318
11	Leas	140 2 3	Dublin	Nethercross	Killossery	Balrothery	I.	31
33	Leaselands	87 2 33	Cork, E.R.	Fermoy	Mallow	Mallow	II.	81
7	Leastown	274 1 7	Dublin	Balrothery West	Westpalstown	Balrothery	I.	23
2, 3, 5	Leat	181 0 12	Tyrone	Strabane Lower	Donaghedy	Strabane	III.	321
17	Leat Beg	641 3 14	Donegal	Kilmacrenan	Clondavaddog	Millford	III.	125
21,22,29,30	Leath East	728 2 24	Kerry	Trughanacmy	Ratass	Tralee	II.	213
21, 29	Leath West	281 0 19	Kerry	Trughanacmy	Ratass	Tralee	II.	213
17	Leat More	188 0 31	Donegal	Kilmacrenan	Clondavaddog	Millford	III.	125
28	Lebally	224 0 31	Fermanagh	Magherastephana	Aghalurcher	Lisnaskea	III.	217
16	Lecade	95 1 24	Westmeath	Kilkenny West	Noughaval	Ballymahon	I.	274
47, 57	Lecarhoo	337 1 6	Kerry	Magunihy	Kilnanare	Killarney	II.	204
96	Lecarrow	78 2 5	Galway	Dunkellin	Killeeneen	Loughrea	IV.	30
104	Lecarrow	92 0 26	Galway	Dunkellin	Killora	Loughrea	IV.	31
96, 97	Lecarrow	150 2 39	Galway	Dunkellin	Lickerrig	Loughrea	IV.	31
46	Lecarrow	119 2 1	Galway	Kilconnell	Killosolan	Mountbellew	IV.	42
106	Lecarrow	3 2 13	Galway	Leitrim	Kilmeen	Loughrea	IV.	54
117	Lecarrow	162 0 19	Galway	Longford	Lickmolassy	Portumna	IV.	61
117	Lecarrow	173 0 39	Galway	Longford	Tynagh	Portumna	IV.	62
25, 26	Lecarrow	602 1 9	Galway	Ross	Ross	Oughterard	IV.	74
44, 45	Lecarrow	416 1 1g	Galway	Tiaquin	Moylough	Tuam	IV.	80
13	Lecarrow	227 1 31	King's Co.	Garrycastle	Clonmacnoise	Parsonstown	I.	135
68, 77	Lecarrow	401 1 19h	Mayo	Burrishoole	Burrishoole	Newport	IV.	119
90	Lecarrow	50 1 2	Mayo	Carra	Drum	Castlebar	IV.	128
70, 79	Lecarrow	74 2 24	Mayo	Carra	Kildacommoge	Castlebar	IV.	129
93, 105	Lecarrow	515 3 6	Mayo	Costello	Annagh	Claremorris	IV.	138
63	Lecarrow	434 2 35	Mayo	Costello	Kilbeagh	Swineford	IV.	140
92	Lecarrow	352 3 18	Mayo	Costello	Knock	Claremorris	IV.	143
71	Lecarrow	157 1 15	Mayo	Gallen	Meelick	Swineford	IV.	150
119	Lecarrow	255 2 22i	Mayo	Kilmaine	Kilcommon	Ballinrobe	IV.	155
118	Lecarrow	69 0 14	Mayo	Kilmaine	Kilmainemore	Ballinrobe	IV.	156
75, 84, 85	Lecarrow	594 0 19	Mayo	Murrisk	Kilgeever	Westport	IV.	161
38, 47	Lecarrow	83 0 18	Mayo	Tirawley	Addergoole	Castlebar	IV.	163
22	Lecarrow	107 2 14	Mayo	Tirawley	Ballysakeery	Ballina	IV.	165
29, 38	Lecarrow	276 2 9	Mayo	Tirawley	Crossmolina	Ballina	IV.	166
23, 24	Lecarrow	199 0 19j	Roscommon	Ballintober North	Kilglass	Strokestown	IV.	186
34	Lecarrow	36 3 21k	Roscommon	Ballymoe	Drumatemple	Castlereagh	IV.	191
5	Lecarrow	133 0 21	Roscommon	Boyle	Boyle	Boyle	IV.	194
34	Lecarrow	92 0 33	Roscommon	Castlereagh	Ballintober	Castlereagh	IV.	198
10, 11, 16	Lecarrow	236 2 25l	Roscommon	Frenchpark	Creeve	Car. on Shannon	IV.	203
19	Lecarrow	344 2 20	Roscommon	Frenchpark	Tibohine	Castlereagh	IV.	205
17, 18	Lecarrow	261 0 29m	Roscommon	Roscommon	Clooncraff	Strokestown	IV.	208
14	Lecarrow	182 1 27	Sligo	Carbury	Killaspugbrone	Sligo	IV.	222

(a) Including 13A. 0R. 34P. water.
(b) Including 138A. 2R. 1P. water.
(c) Including 14A. 1R. 7P. water.
(d) Including 4A. 3R. 1P. water.
(e) Including 5A. 1R. 0P. water.

(f) Including 1A. 1R. 8P. water.
(g) Including 11A. 3R. 1P. water.
(h) Including 17A. 0R. 15P. water.
(i) Including 19A. 0R. 24P. water.

(j) Including 2A. 1R. 33P. water.
(k) Including 10A. 0R. 14P. detached portion.
(l) Including 18A. 1R. 9P. water.
(m) Including 20A. 2R. 10P. water.

No. of Sheet of the Ordnance Survey Maps.	Townlands and Towns.	Area in Statute Acres.	County.	Barony.	Parish.	Poor Law Union in 1857.	Townland Census of 1851, Part I.	
		A. R. P.					Vol.	Page
38, 39	Lecarrow	214 1 15	Sligo	Corran	Cloonoghil	Tobercurry	IV.	225
33	Lecarrow	56 2 34	Sligo	Corran	Emlaghfad	Tobercurry	IV.	226
11,12,17,18	Lecarrow	377 2 21	Sligo	Tireragh	Kilmacshalgan	Dromore West	IV.	235
19	Lecarrow	220 1 4	Sligo	Tireragh	Skreen	Dromore West	IV.	236
40, 45	Lecarrow	382 0 28	Sligo	Tirerrill	Aghanagh	Boyle	IV.	237
34	Lecarrow	141 3 20a	Sligo	Tirerrill	Drumcolumb	Sligo	IV.	238
21	Lecarrowanteean	173 1 23	Mayo	Tirawley	Rathreagh	Killala	IV.	171
33, 41	Lecarrow Beg	116 1 8	Clare	Islands	Kilmaley	Ennis	II.	31
38	Lecarrowcloghagh	104 2 28	Mayo	Tirawley	Crossmolina	Ballina	IV.	166
29	Lecarrow Glebe or Britannia	157 3 7	King's Co.	Garrycastle	Reynagh	Parsonstown	I.	138
121	Lecarrowkilleen	246 0 3	Mayo	Kilmaine	Cong	Ballinrobe	IV.	154
28	Lecarrow Lower	555 2 29	Clare	Tulla Upper	Feakle	Scarriff	II.	39
73	Lecarrowmactully	165 3 6b	Galway	Kilconnell	Kilconnell	Ballinasloe	IV.	40
41	Lecarrow More	117 3 0	Clare	Islands	Kilmaley	Ennis	II.	31
70	Lecarrowmore	47 1 20	Galway	Clare	Claregalway	Galway	IV.	18
98	Lecarrownagappoge	139 2 24	Galway	Leitrim	Kilreekill	Loughrea	IV.	55
22	Lecarrownaveagh	131 3 0	Sligo	Tireragh	Castleconor	Dromore West	IV.	232
27	Lecarrow North	237 1 27c	Clare	Tulla Upper	Tulla	Tulla	II.	42
125	Lecarrow North	119 0 39	Galway	Leitrim	Ballynakill	Loughrea	IV.	51
7, 14	Lecarrowntemple	237 3 29	Mayo	Tirawley	Lackan	Killala	IV.	171
86	Lecarrowntruhaun	105 1 33	Galway	Kilconnell	Grange	Loughrea	IV.	40
29	Lecarrownwaddy	127 3 35	Mayo	Tirawley	Moygawnagh	Killala	IV.	171
35	Lecarrow South	106 0 33d	Clare	Tulla Upper	Tulla	Tulla	II.	42
125	Lecarrow South	131 1 6	Galway	Leitrim	Ballynakill	Loughrea	IV.	51
18	Lecarrow or Strandhill	54 2 39	Leitrim	Drumahaire	Inishmagrath	Manorhamilton	IV.	97
28	Lecarrow Upper	244 2 32	Clare	Tulla Upper	Feakle	Scarriff	II.	39
10, 14	Lecharrownahone	313 2 14e	Cavan	Tullyhaw	Templeport	Bawnboy	III.	95
32	Lecharry	355 3 22	Cavan	Castlerahan	Crosserlough	Cavan	III.	68
15	Lechurragh	208 3 39	Longford	Ardagh	Street	Granard	I.	153
17, 22	Leck	450 0 23	Antrim	Upper Dunluce	Ballymoney	Ballymoney	III.	19
1	Leck	86 2 30	Cavan	Tullyhaw	Killinagh	Enniskillen	III.	92
11	Leck	298 0 12	Londonderry	Coleraine	Macosquin	Coleraine	III.	233
10	Leck	504 2 0	Londonderry	Keenaght	Drumachose	New Tⁿ Limavady	III.	235
13	Leck	195 1 19	Monaghan	Monaghan	Kilmore	Monaghan	III.	276
39	Leck	72 1 21	Tyrone	Dungannon Upper	Ballyclog	Cookstown	III.	306
42, 47	Leckagh	108 0 31	Londonderry	Loughinsholin	Magherafelt	Magherafelt	III.	243
22	Leckan	292 3 21	Leitrim	Carrigallen	Drumreilly	Bawnboy	IV.	91
4, 7	Leckanarainey	852 2 10f	Leitrim	Rosclogher	Killasnet	Manorhamilton	IV.	110
60, 61	Leckaneen	147 0 20	Cork, W.R.	East Muskerry	Aghabulloge	Macroom	II.	153
86, 87	Leckanvy	786 0 0	Mayo	Murrisk	Oughaval	Westport	IV.	162
32, 33	Leckaun	658 1 19g	Clare	Inchiquin	Kilnamona	Ennis	II.	27
10, 11	Leckaun	220 2 19	Leitrim	Drumahaire	Drumlease	Manorhamilton	IV.	94
17	Leckaun	175 1 30	Leitrim	Drumahaire	Inishmagrath	Manorhamilton	IV.	97
27	Leckaun	232 3 16	Waterford	Gaultiere	Killea	Waterford	II.	363
48	Leckbeg	63 2 1	Donegal	Boylagh	Templecrone	Glenties	III.	115
60, 61	Leckee	402 0 23h	Mayo	Gallen	Toomore	Swineford	IV.	151
12	Leckemy or Carrowblagh	935 3 35	Donegal	Inishowen East	Moville Lower	Inishowen	III.	118
48, 49	Leckenagh	511 0 31i	Donegal	Boylagh	Templecrone	Glenties	III.	115
19	Leckin	330 1 32	Tyrone	Strabane Upper	Bodoney Lower	Gortin	III.	323
3, 6	Lecklasser	475 1 7	Sligo	Carbury	Rossinver	Sligo	IV.	223
12, 13	Lecklevera	284 3 7	Monaghan	Dartree	Killeevan	Monaghan	III.	268
4	Lecklintown	214 2 22	Dublin	Balrothery West	Naul	Balrothery	I.	23
114	Lecknabegga	105 2 10	Galway	Loughrea	Kilthomas	Loughrea	IV.	65
33	Lecknagh	95 0 23j	Leitrim	Mohill	Cloone	Mohill	IV.	106
10, 11, 24	Lecknavarna	1,275 3 6k	Galway	Ballynahinch	Ballynakill	Clifden	IV.	11
70	Leckneen	132 1 3	Mayo	Carra	Turlough	Castlebar	IV.	131
2, 5	Leckpatrick	551 0 20l	Tyrone	Strabane Lower	Leckpatrick	Strabane	III.	322
23, 28, 29	Lecks	505 0 37m	Cavan	Clankee	Shercock	Bailieborough	III	74
104	Lecky Rocks	11 0 25	Mayo	Murrisk	Inishbofin	Clifden	IV.	159
41, 46	Lecumpher	324 1 0	Londonderry	Loughinsholin	Desertmartin	Magherafelt	III.	240
9, 18	Lederg	1,180 1 26	Donegal	Inishowen West	Desertegny	Inishowen	III.	120
55	Lederg	40 1 5	Tyrone	Dungannon Middle	Killyman	Dungannon	III.	303
27	Ledonigan	197 1 22	Cavan	Clankee	Knockbride	Bailieborough	III.	74
22	Ledwithstown	579 1 13n	Longford	Rathcline	Kilcommock	Ballymahon	I.	164
22, 26	Ledwithstown	96 3 28	Longford	Rathcline	Shrule	Ballymahon	I.	165
25	Lee	769 2 0	Galway	Ross	Ross	Oughterard	IV.	74
6, 7, 10, 11	Leean	538 0 13	Leitrim	Drumahaire	Drumlease	Manorhamilton	IV.	94
101, 111	Leedaun	97 1 13	Mayo	Clanmorris	Crossboyne	Claremorris	IV.	133
31	Leeds	371 0 4	Clare	Ibrickan	Kilfarboy	Ennistimon	II.	22
32	Leeffa	135 2 23	Fermanagh	Clanawley	Killesher	Enniskillen	III.	193
34	Leeg	303 0 24	Monaghan	Farney	Killanny	Carrickmacross	III.	271

(a) Including 0A. 3R. 2P. water.
(b) Including 5A. 0R. 8P. water.
(c) Including 26A. 0R. 0P. water.
(d) Including 4A. 0R. 13P. water.
(e) Including 13A. 0R. 27P. water.

(f) Including 4A. 1R. 30P. water.
(g) Including 3A. 0R. 29P. water.
(h) Including 1A. 0R. 4P. water.
(i) Including 37A. 1R. 32P. water.
(j) Including 1A. 2R. 36P. water.

(k) Including 14A. 1R. 35P. water.
(l) Including 4A. 0R. 23P. water.
(m) Including 8A. 3R. 24P. water.
(n) Including 33A. 3R. 8P. water.

No. of Sheet of the Ordnance Survey Maps.	Townlands and Towns.	Area in Statute Acres.			County.	Barony.	Parish.	Poor Law Union in 1857.	Townland Census of 1851, Part I.	
		A.	R.	P.					Vol.	Page
40	Leegane . . .	102	3	3	Wexford . .	Shelmaliere West .	Clongeen . .	New Ross .	I.	333
4, 7	Leek . . .	204	0	9	Monaghan . .	Trough . . .	Donagh . .	Monaghan .	III.	282
6	Leeke . . .	182	1	38	Antrim . .	Lower Dunluce .	Dunluce . .	Coleraine .	III.	17
16	Leeke . . .	552	1	23	Londonderry .	Keenaght . .	Bovevagh . .	NewᵀⁿLimavady	III.	235
13, 19	Leekfield . .	367	0	18	Sligo . .	Tireragh . .	Skreen . .	Dromore West .	IV.	236
72	Leemount . .	103	1	38a	Cork, E.R. .	East Muskerry .	Magourney .	Macroom .	II.	105
147, 152	Leenane . . .	95	1	3	Cork, W.R. .	West Carbery(W.D.)	Kilmoe . .	Skull . .	II.	145
51	Leenane East .	37	0	7	Tipperary, S.R.	Clanwilliam .	Donohill . .	Tipperary .	II.	307
51	Leenane West .	56	0	19	Tipperary, S.R.	Kilnamanagh Lower	Donohill . .	Tipperary .	II.	323
11, 12, 24, 25	Leenaun . .	1,845	0	22	Galway . .	Ross . . .	Ross . .	Oughterard .	IV.	74
97, 107	Leenavesta .	905	2	38	Mayo . .	Murrisk . .	Oughaval .	Westport .	IV.	162
55	Lee's Island .	47	2	31	Galway . .	Moycullen . .	Killannin .	Oughterard .	IV.	70
21, 29	Lefanta . . .	52	2	16	Waterford . .	Decies without Drum	Affane . .	Lismore . .	II.	353
29	Lefanta Island .	8	0	0	Waterford . .	Decies without Drum	Affane . .	Lismore . .	II.	353
49	Lefinn . . .	185	0	33b	Donegal . .	Boylagh . .	Templecrone .	Glenties .	III.	115
9, 13	Legacorry or Rich Hill	347	2	24	Armagh . .	Oneilland West .	Kilmore . .	Armagh . .	III.	53
18	Legacurry .	226	1	29	Antrim . .	Upper Dunluce .	Kilraghts .	Ballymoney .	III.	20
99	Legacurry .	100	0	38	Donegal . .	Tirhugh . .	Drumhome .	Donegal .	III.	146
14, 15	Legacurry .	100	0	4	Down . .	Castlereagh Upper .	Drumbo . .	Lisburn .	III.	164
36	Legacurry .	35	0	3	Fermanagh .	Clankelly . .	Clones . .	Clones .	III.	196
19	Legacurry . .	164	3	15	Monaghan .	Monaghan . .	Tullycorbet .	Monaghan .	III.	281
6, 9	Legacurry .	183	1	9	Monaghan .	Trough . . .	Donagh . .	Monaghan .	III.	282
38	Legacurry .	137	0	7	Tyrone . .	Dungannon Upper .	Desertcreat .	Cookstown .	III.	308
43, 51	Legacurry .	500	1	11	Tyrone . .	Omagh East .	Clogherny .	Omagh . .	III.	310
17, 25	Legacurry .	334	1	14	Tyrone . .	Strabane Upper .	Cappagh . .	Omagh . .	III.	325
32, 37	Legaduff . .	47	3	0	Fermanagh .	Clanawley . .	Kinawley .	Enniskillen .	III.	194
6	Legaghory .	301	0	24	Armagh . .	Oneilland East .	Shankill . .	Lurgan . .	III.	51
22	Legaghory .	579	3	18	Londonderry .	Tirkeeran . .	Cumber Lower .	Londonderry .	III.	249
12	Legagilly or Tyross.	47	0	6	Armagh . .	Armagh . . .	Armagh . .	Armagh . .	III.	43
25, 31	Legaginny .	185	3	18	Cavan . .	Clanmahon .	Ballintemple .	Cavan . .	III.	75
19, 24	Legagrane .	954	0	37	Antrim . .	Kilconway . .	Dunaghy .	Ballymena .	III.	26
44, 45	Legagunnia .	127	1	13	Meath . .	Ratoath . .	Ratoath . .	Dunshaughlin .	I.	219
25	Legaland . .	225	0	25c	Cavan . .	Clanmahon .	Kilmore . .	Cavan . .	III.	78
107	Legaloscran .	62	3	17	Donegal . .	Tirhugh . .	Kilbarron .	Ballyshannon .	III.	148
4	Legalough .	108	1	18	Cavan . .	Tullyhaw . .	Killinagh .	Enniskillen .	III.	92
45, 46	Legaloy . .	205	2	19	Antrim . .	Lower Belfast .	Ballynure .	Larne . .	III.	7
107	Legaltan . .	254	0	14d	Donegal . .	Tirhugh . .	Kilbarron .	Ballyshannon .	III.	148
37, 44, 45	Legamaddy .	211	2	28	Down . .	Lecale Upper .	Bright . .	Downpatrick .	III.	180
58	Legamaghery .	290	2	11	Tyrone . .	Clogher . .	Donacavey .	Omagh . .	III.	294
28	Legan . .	241	3	28	Kilkenny . .	Gowran . .	Ballylinch .	Thomastown .	I.	93
23, 24	Legan . .	277	3	11	Longford . .	Shrule . .	Kilglass . .	Ballymahon .	I.	166
86	Legan . .	113	1	4	Mayo . .	Murrisk . .	Kilgeever .	Westport .	IV.	160
23, 24	Legan . .	452	2	15e	Roscommon .	Ballintober North .	Kilglass . .	Strokestown .	IV.	186
30	Legan . .	87	1	0	Westmeath .	Clonlonan .	Ballyloughloe .	Athlone .	I.	260
30	Legan . .	121	1	1f	Westmeath .	Clonlonan .	Kilmanaghan .	Athlone .	I.	262
22, 25	Leganamer .	81	3	22	Leitrim . .	Carrigallen .	Drumreilly .	Bawnboy .	IV.	91
35, 36	Legananny .	1,894	1	39g	Down . .	Upper Iveagh, Lr. pt.	Drumgooland .	Banbridge .	III.	172
33	Legananny .	527	2	27	Down . .	Upper Iveagh, Up.pt.	Aghaderg .	Banbridge .	III.	174
60, 61	Legane . .	371	0	0h	Tyrone . .	Dungannon Lower .	Aghaloo . .	Dungannon .	III.	297
9	Leganny . .	58	0	5	Armagh . .	Oneilland West .	Drumcree .	Lurgan . .	III.	52
33, 34	Leganvy . .	440	1	20i	Tyrone . .	Omagh West .	Longfield East .	Omagh . .	III.	315
12	Legarhill . .	141	0	23	Armagh . .	Armagh . .	Armagh . .	Armagh . .	III.	43
11, 12	Legarhill .	158	3	8	Monaghan .	Dartree . .	Clones . .	Clones . .	III.	264
53	Legaroe . .	443	2	19	Tyrone . .	Dungannon Lower .	Carnteel . .	Dungannon .	III.	297
50	Legatiggle .	302	3	19	Tyrone . .	Clogher . . .	Donacavey .	Omagh . .	III.	294
29	Legatillida .	304	2	2	Fermanagh .	Magherastephana .	Aghalurcher .	Lisnaskea .	III.	217
63	Legatirriff .	389	1	15	Antrim . .	Upper Massereene .	Ballinderry .	Lisburn .	III.	29
15, 23	Legatonegan .	493	3	26j	Tyrone . .	Omagh West .	Termonamongan .	Castlederg .	III.	317
6, 8	Legatraghta .	197	0	30	Cavan . .	Tullyhaw . .	Templeport .	Enniskillen .	III.	95
79, 90	Legaun . .	175	2	25	Mayo . .	Clanmorris .	Balla . .	Castlebar .	IV.	132
29	Legaun . .	76	1	37	Queen's Co. .	Clarmallagh .	Aghaboe . .	Abbeyleix .	I.	236
15, 23	Legavanuon .	383	2	10	Londonderry .	Tirkeeran . .	Faughanvale .	NewᵀⁿLimavady	III.	250
12, 13	Legavilly .	72	2	23	Armagh . .	Oneilland West .	Loughgall .	Armagh . .	III.	54
7, 9	Legavreagra .	467	2	39	Cavan . .	Tullyhaw . .	Kinawley .	Bawnboy .	III.	93
25, 31	Legaweel .	118	1	15	Cavan . .	Clanmahon .	Ballintemple .	Cavan . .	III.	75
17	Legboy . .	86	3	23	Donegal . .	Kilmacrenan .	Clondavaddog .	Milford .	III.	125
7, 12	Legcloghfin .	994	3	13k	Tyrone . .	Strabane Upper .	Bodoney Upper .	Gortin . .	III.	324
4	Legeelan . .	233	1	14	Cavan . .	Tullyhaw . .	Killinagh .	Enniskillen .	III.	92
20	Legg . . .	34	2	9	Antrim . .	Lower Glenarm .	Layd . .	Ballycastle .	III.	23
32, 37	Legg . .	637	3	18	Fermanagh .	Clanawley . .	Killesher .	Enniskillen .	III.	193
9	Legg . .	404	1	20l	Fermanagh .	Magheraboy .	Inishmacsaint .	Ballyshannon .	III.	213
2, 3	Leggagh . .	836	2	17m	Longford . .	Longford . .	Killoe . .	Longford .	I.	159
12	Leggagh . .	1,046	1	21	Meath . .	Morgallion .	Drakestown .	Navan . .	I.	209

(a) Including 3A. 2R. 11P. water.
(b) Including 5A. 0R. 38P. water.
(c) Including 4A. 1R. 0P. water.
(d) Including 9A. 2R. 20P. water.
(e) Including 29A. 2R. 32P. water.

(f) Including 0A. 3R. 37P. detached portion.
(g) Including 2A. 0R. 8P. water.
(h) Including 14A. 3R. 24P. water.
(i) Including 0A. 0R. 35P. water.

(j) Including 6A. 0R. 22P. water.
(k) Including 4A. 2R. 20P. water.
(l) Including 7A. 2R. 8P. water.
(m) Including 7A. 1R. 28P. water.

No. of Sheet of the Ordnance Survey Maps.	Townlands and Towns.	Area in Statute Acres.			County.	Barony.	Parish.	Poor Law Union in 1857.	Townland Census of 1851, Part I.	
		A.	R.	P.					Vol.	Page
25, 26, 32	Leggandenn or Dennmore	445	1	5	Cavan	Upper Loughtee	Denn	Cavan	III.	83
70	Leggandorragh	43	1	19	Donegal	Raphoe	Clonleigh	Strabane	III.	135
27	Legganhall	228	1	35	Meath	Upper Duleek	Moorechurch	Drogheda	I.	198
15	Leggatinty	773	0	17	Roscommon	Frenchpark	Tibohine	Castlereagh	IV.	205
19	Leggetsrath East	215	3	10	Kilkenny	Gowran	St. John's	Kilkenny	I.	98
19	Leggetsrath West	245	1	7a	Kilkenny	Gowran and Municipal Borough	St. John's	Kilkenny	I.	98
28, 31	Legghimore	178	0	8	Monaghan	Farney	Magheross	Carrickmacross	III.	274
4, 6	Legglass	216	1	13	Cavan	Tullyhaw	Templeport	Enniskillen	III	95
8	Leggs	92	2	27	Fermanagh	Lurg	Belleck	Ballyshannon	III.	203
16, 23	Leggygowan	1,165	1	34b	Down	Castlereagh Upper	Saintfield	Downpatrick	III.	166
11	Leggykelly	248	1	12c	Cavan	Tullygarvey	Annagh	Cavan	III.	87
94	Leghawny	643	0	12	Donegal	Tirhugh	Donegal	Donegal	III.	145
54	Legilly	263	0	14	Tyrone	Dungannon Middle	Clonfeacle	Dungannon	III	299
38	Leginn	169	2	14	Fermanagh	Knockninny	Kinawley	Lisnaskea	III.	202
27	Legland	461	0	13d	Cavan	Clankee	Knockbride	Cootehill	III.	74
28, 37	Legland	506	0	25	Donegal	Kilmacrenan	Killygarvan	Millford	III.	128
61, 69	Legland	313	1	14	Donegal	Raphoe	Convoy	Stranorlar	III.	136
14, 20	Legland	728	0	37	Fermanagh	Magheraboy	Devenish	Enniskillen	III.	211
25	Legland	659	3	29	Tyrone	Strabane Lower	Ardstraw	Strabane	III.	319
13	Leglehid	343	0	2	Fermanagh	Magheraboy	Inishmacsaint	Ballyshannon	III.	213
40	Legmacaffry	105	3	12	Fermanagh	Coole	Galloon	Clones	III.	200
13	Legmore	170	0	22	Down	Lower Iveagh, Up. pt.	Moira	Lurgan	III.	170
28, 31	Legmoylin	342	2	36	Armagh	Fews Upper	Creggan	Dundalk	III.	48
36	Legmuckduff	137	3	36	Donegal	Kilmacrenan	Tullyfern	Millford	III.	133
39	Legmurn	225	3	29	Tyrone	Dungannon Upper	Ballyclog	Cookstown	III.	306
17, 18	Legnabraid	548	0	28	Tyrone	Strabane Lower	Ardstraw	Gortin	III.	319
70, 79	Legnabraid or Cunninghamstown	100	0	20	Donegal	Raphoe	Clonleigh	Strabane	III.	135
31, 32, 37	Legnabrocky	940	2	35	Fermanagh	Clanawley	Killesher	Enniskillen	III.	193
29	Legnacash	89	0	37	Tyrone	Dungannon Upper	Kildress	Cookstown	III.	309
14	Legnacreeve	286	3	11	Monaghan	Monaghan	Monaghan	Monaghan	III.	277
6	Legnalerk	359	3	23	Cavan	Tullyhaw	Templeport	Enniskillen	III.	95
55	Legnaduff	54	2	15	Donegal	Raphoe	Killea	Londonderry	III.	139
6, 7, 11, 12	Legnagappoge	1,223	0	11	Tyrone	Strabane Lower	Donaghedy	Gortin	III.	321
20, 21	Legnagay Beg	1,127	0	36e	Fermanagh	Clanawley	Boho	Enniskillen	III.	189
21	Legnagay More	90	0	9	Fermanagh	Clanawley	Boho	Enniskillen	III.	189
16	Legnaglogh	205	1	7	Wexford	Ballaghkeen	Monamolin	Gorey	I.	298
28	Legnagooly	212	3	7	Antrim	Lower Antrim	Skerry	Ballymena	III.	5
4, 6	Legnagrow	830	1	21	Cavan	Tullyhaw	Templeport	Enniskillen	III.	95
44, 45, 53	Legnahoory	727	0	35	Donegal	Kilmacrenan	Kilmacrenan	Letterkenny	III.	129
32	Legnahorna	91	1	8	Fermanagh	Clanawley	Killesher	Enniskillen	III.	193
12	Legnakelly	238	3	29	Monaghan	Dartree	Clones	Clones	III.	264
70	Legnaneale	80	1	11	Donegal	Raphoe	Clonleigh	Strabane	III.	135
104	Legnanornoge	225	2	26f	Donegal	Tirhugh	Drumhome	Donegal	III.	146
62, 63	Legnatraw	466	0	8	Donegal	Raphoe	Taughboyne	Strabane	III.	143
32	Legnavea	133	3	18	Fermanagh	Clanawley	Killesher	Enniskillen	III	193
92	Legnawley Glebe	117	3	22	Donegal	Banagh	Inver	Donegal	III.	107
56, 60	Legoneil	916	1	5	Antrim	Upper Belfast	Shankill	Belfast	III.	10
56, 60	LEGONEIL T.	—			Antrim	Upper Belfast	Shankill	Belfast	III.	10
33, 34, 41, 42	Legphressy	615	0	33	Tyrone	Omagh West	Longfield East	Omagh	III.	315
11	Legvoy or Gardenstown	176	1	10	Roscommon	Boyle	Killukin	Car.k on Shannon	IV.	195
31	Legwee	281	0	15	Cavan	Clanmahon	Drumlumman	Granard	II.	77
32	Lehaknock	188	0	6g	Clare	Islands	Kilmaley	Ennis	II.	31
60	Lehanagh	414	3	21	Galway	Tiaquin	Killosolan	Mountbellew	IV.	78
90	Lehanagh	169	1	28	Mayo	Clanmorris	Mayo	Ballinrobe	IV.	135
37, 38	Lehanagh North	662	1	7h	Galway	Ballynahinch	Moyrus	Clifden	IV.	13
51	Lehanagh South	922	1	24i	Galway	Ballynahinch	Moyrus	Clifden	IV.	13
28	Lehardan	169	3	14	Donegal	Kilmacrenan	Killygarvan	Millford	III.	128
71	Lehenagh	404	1	17j	Cork, E.R.	East Muskerry	Carnaway	Macroom	II.	102
136, 145	Lehenagh	479	3	39	Cork, W.R.	Ibane and Barryroe	Abbeymahon	Clonakilty	II.	148
74, 86	Lehenagh Beg	122	2	1	Cork, E.R.	Cork	St. Finbars	Cork	II.	66
74, 86	Lehenagh More	1,021	3	35	Cork, E.R.	Cork	St. Finbars	Cork	II.	66
17, 21	Lehery	891	1	26k	Longford	Ratheline	Ratheline	Longford	I.	165
48, 49	Lehid	190	2	39l	Galway	Ballynahinch	Ballindoon	Clifden	IV.	10
16	Lehid	350	0	33	Galway	Dunmore	Kilbennan	Tuam	IV.	34
109, 1 103, 129	Lehid	683	2	1m	Kerry	Glanarought	Tuosist	Kenmare	II.	189
87	Lehid	218	1	11	Kerry	Iveragh	Killemlagh	Cahersiveen	II.	196
27	Le gill	58	1	25n	Fermanagh	Tirkennedy	Enniskillen	Enniskillen	III.	222
15, 25	Lehinch	275	1	27	Clare	Corcomroe	Kilmanaheen	Ennistimon	II.	21
39	Lehinch	125	3	8o	Fermanagh	Coole	Galloon	Clones	III.	200
101	Lehinch	59	2	0	Galway	Longford	Clonfert	Ballinasloe	IV.	57

(a) { Within the Municipal Boundary, 12A. 0R. 28P.
Without the Municipal Boundary, 233A. 0R. 19P.
(b) Including 4A. 0R. 21P. water.
(c) Including 10A. 0R. 18P. water.
(d) Including 7A. 1R. 36P. water.
(e) Including 2A. 3R. 10P. water.

(f) Including 12A. 2R. 30P. water.
(g) Including 1A. 3R. 31P. water.
(h) Including 57A. 0R. 32P. water.
(i) Including 19A. 3R. 21P. water.
(j) Including 2A. 3R. 36P. water.

(k) Including 24A. 0R. 0P. water.
(l) Including 25A. 0R. 3P. water.
(m) Including 7A. 0R. 17P. water.
(n) Including 15A. 3R. 0P. water.
(o) Including 7A. 3R. 21P. water.

No. of Sheet of the Ordnance Survey Maps.	Townlands and Towns.	Area in Statute Acres.	County.	Barony.	Parish.	Poor Law Union in 1857.	Townland Census of 1851, Part I.	
							Vol.	Page
		A. R. P.						
31	Lehinch . . .	202 3 27	Galway . .	Tiaquin . . .	Kilkerrin . .	Glennamaddy .	IV.	77
8	Lehinch . . .	239 2 31	King's Co. .	Kilcoursey . .	Kilbride . .	Tullamore .	I.	141
1	Lehinch . . .	3 3 26	Tipperary, N.R.	Lower Ormond .	Dorrha . .	Parsonstown .	II.	283
3, 4	Lehinch . . .	761 1 32	Tipperary, N.R.	Lower Ormond .	Lorrha . .	Borrisokane .	II.	285
110, 111	Lehinch Demesne .	595 2 28	Mayo . . .	Kilmaine . .	Kilcommon . .	Ballinrobe .	IV.	155
23	LEHINCH T. . .	—	Clare . .	Corcomroe . {	Kilmacrehy . Kilmanaheen . }	Ennistimon .	II.	{20 {21
18	Lehurick . . .	155 3 20a	Galway . .	Tiaquin . . .	Kilkerrin . .	Glennamaddy .	IV.	77
42, 48	Leigh . . .	2,140 2 3	Tipperary, N.R.	Eliogarty . .	Twomileborris .	Thurles . .	II.	274
15	Leighan . . .	336 3 35	Fermanagh .	Magheraboy . .	Devenish . .	Enniskillen .	III.	211
140, 141	Leighcloon . .	207 0 0	Cork, W.R. .	West Carbery (E.D.)	Aghadown . .	Skibbereen .	II.	137
12, 16	Leighlinbridge . .	302 3 13b	Carlow . .	Idrone East . .	Agha . . .	Carlow . .	I.	6
12	LEIGHLINBRIDGE T.	—	Carlow . . {	Idrone East . Idrone West . }	Agha . . . Wells . . .	Carlow . .	I.	{6 {10
111	Leighmoney Beg .	143 1 22	Cork, E.R. .	Kinalea . . .	Leighmoney .	Kinsale . .	II.	96
111	Leighmoney More .	321 3 13	Cork, E.R. .	Kinalea . . .	Dunderrow .	Kinsale . .	II.	94
111	Leighmoney More .	30 0 30	Cork, E.R. .	Kinalea . . .	Leighmoney .	Kinsale . .	II.	96
78	Leighon Island . .	10 0 24	Galway . .	Moycullen . .	Killannin . .	Oughterard .	IV.	70
35, 37	Leinsterlodge . .	290 0 3	Kildare . .	Kilkea and Moone .	Tankardstown .	Athy . .	I.	61
28, 34	Leiter . . .	186 3 12	Cavan . .	Clankee . . .	Bailieborough .	Bailieborough .	III.	71
28,29,34,35	Leiter . . .	630 0 19	Cavan . .	Clankee . . .	Enniskeen .	Bailieborough .	III.	73
26	Leiter . . .	164 0 14	Cavan . .	Upper Loughtee .	Lavey . . .	Cavan . .	III.	86
4	Leiterra . . .	160 0 21	Roscommon .	Boyle . . .	Ardcarn . .	Boyle . .	IV.	193
8, 9	Leitra . . .	82 3 1	Cavan . .	Tullyhaw . .	Templeport .	Bawnboy . .	III.	95
10	Leitra . . .	507 2 2c	Clare . .	Inchiquin . .	Kilkeedy . .	Corrofin . .	II.	26
13	Leitra . . .	1,227 0 2	King's Co. .	Garrycastle . .	Clonmacnoise .	Parsonstown .	I.	135
23	Leitra . . .	156 0 14	Leitrim . .	Leitrim . . .	Kiltubbrid .	Cark. on Shannon	IV.	104
12, 17	Leitrim . . .	277 0 36	Antrim . .	Upper Dunluce .	Ballymoney .	Ballymoney .	III.	19
49	Leitrim . . .	165 3 29	Antrim . .	Upper Toome . .	Drummaul . .	Antrim . .	III.	34
44	Leitrim . . .	637 1 30	Cavan . .	Castlerahan . .	Loughan or Castle-keeran .	Kells . .	III.	69
34	Leitrim . . .	229 2 38	Cavan . .	Clankee . . .	Moybolgue .	Bailieborough .	III.	74
47, 48	Leitrim . . .	982 2 29	Clare . .	Clonderalaw . .	Kilmihil . .	Kilrush . .	II.	17
44, 53	Leitrim . . .	403 0 30	Clare . .	Tulla Lower . .	Killokennedy .	Limerick . .	II.	36
28, 36	Leitrim . . .	376 3 0	Cork, E.R. .	Condons&Clangibbon	Leitrim . . .	Fermoy . .	II.	62
12	Leitrim . . .	806 1 4	Donegal . .	Inishowen East .	Culdaff . .	Inishowen .	III.	118
47, 55	Leitrim . . .	293 1 1d	Donegal . .	Raphoe . . .	Allsaints . .	Londonderry .	III.	134
52, 55	Leitrim . . .	773 1 17	Down . .	Mourne . . .	Kilkeel . .	Kilkeel . .	III.	183
48. 52	Leitrim . . .	2,978 0 1	Down . .	Upper Iveagh, Lr. pt.	Clonduff . .	Newry . .	III.	171
35, 36, 43	Leitrim . . .	1,199 3 30	Down . .	Upper Iveagh, Lr. pt.	Drumgooland .	Banbridge .	III.	172
40, 43	Leitrim . . .	199 0 22	Fermanagh .	Coole . . .	Galloon . .	Clones . .	III.	200
20, 21	Leitrim . . .	175 0 30	Fermanagh .	Magheraboy . .	Boho . . .	Enni-killen .	III.	210
11	Leitrim . . .	1,313 2 25	King's Co. .	Coolestown . .	Monasteroris .	Edenderry .	I.	133
27	Leitrim . . .	139 2 14	Leitrim . .	Leitrim . . .	Kiltoghert .	Cark. on Shannon	IV.	102
24	Leitrim . . .	101 1 22	Leitrim . .	Leitrim . . .	Kiltubbrid .	Cark. on Shannon	IV.	104
42	Leitrim . . .	923 3 6	Londonderry .	Loughinsholin .	Ballyscullion .	Magherafelt .	III.	239
9	Leitrim . . .	123 2 0	Longford . .	Granard . . .	Clonbroney .	Granard . .	I.	155
10, 15	Leitrim . . .	498 2 31	Longford . .	Granard . . .	Granard . .	Granard . .	I.	156
8	Leitrim . . .	447 3 23	Longford . .	Longford . . .	Clongesh . .	Longford . .	I.	158
34	Leitrim . . .	153 0 11e	Monaghan .	Farney . . .	Magheracloone .	Carrickmacross	III.	272
10	Leitrim . . .	287 2 28	Monaghan .	Monaghan . .	Tehallan . .	Monaghan .	III.	280
28,29,35,36	Leitrim . . .	124 0 28	Roscommon .	Ballintober South .	Kilbride . .	Roscommon .	IV.	189
14, 15, 21	Leitrim . . .	1,491 3 2	Roscommon .	Frenchpark . .	Tibohine . .	Castlereagh .	IV.	205
23	Leitrim . . .	252 0 30	Tyrone . .	Omagh West . .	Termonamongan .	Castlederg .	III.	317
3	Leitrim . . .	266 1 29f	Tyrone . .	Strabane Lower .	Donaghedy .	Strabane .	III.	321
22	Leitrim . . .	355 3 30	Wicklow . .	Upper Talbotstown .	Donaghmore .	Baltinglass .	I.	363
103, 104	Leitrim Beg . .	173 2 37	Cork, W.R. .	Bear . . .	Kilcaskan .	Castletown .	II.	123
116	Leitrim Beg . .	258 2 0	Galway . .	Leitrim . . .	Leitrim . .	Loughrea . .	IV.	55
6, 7	Leitrim or Corbaun	466 1 15	Longford . .	Granard . . .	Columbkille .	Granard . .	I.	155
6	Leitrim East . .	609 2 13	Kerry . .	Iraghticonnor . .	Murher . .	Glin . .	II.	193
28, 32	Leitrim Lower . .	182 1 25	Leitrim . .	Mohill . . .	Mohill . .	Mohill . .	IV.	108
1, 4	Leitrim Lower . .	268 1 32	Meath . .	Lower Kells . .	Moynalty .	Kells . .	I.	204
6	Leitrim Middle . .	644 1 2	Kerry . .	Iraghticonnor . .	Murher . .	Glin . .	II.	193
103, 116	Leitrim More . .	93 0 15	Cork, W.R. .	Bear . . .	Kilcaskan .	Castletown .	II.	123
116	Leitrim More . .	286 1 36	Galway . .	Leitrim . . .	Leitrim . .	Loughrea . .	IV.	55
31, 32	Leitrim North . .	443 3 6	Sligo . .	Leyny . . .	Achonry . .	Tobercurry .	IV.	229
38	Leitrim South . .	735 0 22	Sligo . .	Leyny . . .	Achonry . .	Tobercurry .	IV.	229
27	LEITRIM T. . .	—	Leitrim . .	Leitrim . . .	Kiltoghert .	Cark. on Shannon	IV	103
52	Leitrim Upper . .	422 0 1	Down . .	Mourne . . .	Kilkeel . .	Kilkeel . .	III.	183
28, 32	Leitrim Upper . .	177 3 25	Leitrim . .	Mohill . . .	Mohill . .	Mohill . .	IV.	108
4	Leitrim Upper . .	199 0 12	Meath . .	Lower Kells . .	Moynalty .	Kells . .	I.	204
6	Leitrim West . .	535 2 18	Kerry . .	Iraghticonnor . .	Murher . .	Glin . .	II.	193
106, 107, 119, 120	Leitry Lower . .	357 0 4	Cork, W.R. .	West Carbery (E.D.)	Dromdaleague .	Skibbereen .	II.	140

(a) Including 45A. 1R. 30P. water.
(b) Including 11A. 3R. 32P. River Barrow.
(c) Including 9A. 1R. 9P. water.
(d) Including 17A. 2R. 20P. water.
(e) Including 10A. 1R. 24P. water.
(f) Including 2A. 1R. 38P. water.

No. of Sheet of the Ordnance Survey Maps.	Townlands and Towns.	Area in Statute Acres.	County.	Barony.	Parish.	Poor Law Union in 1857.	Townland Census of 1851, Part I.	
		A. R. P.					Vol.	Page
106,107,119	Leitry Upper	383 1 7	Cork, W.R.	West Carbery (E.D.)	Dromdaleague	Skibbereen	II.	140
6, 11	Leixlip	604 3 5a	Kildare	North Salt	Leixlip	Celbridge	I.	75
11	Leixlip Demesne	238 2 39b	Kildare	North Salt	Leixlip	Celbridge	I.	75
11	LEIXLIP T.	—	Kildare	North Salt	Leixlip	Celbridge	I.	75
5	Lelagh	366 0 22	Tipperary, N.R.	Lower Ormond	Dorrha	Parsonstown	II.	283
7, 15	Lemanaghan	2,265 3 13	King's Co.	Garrycastle	Lemanaghan	Parsonstown	I.	137
14, 15	Lemgare	427 3 15	Monaghan	Cremorne	Clontibret	Castleblayney	III.	261
3, 4	Lemnagh Beg	224 3 15	Antrim	Cary	Ballintoy	Ballycastle	III.	12
3, 4	Lemnagh More	403 2 25	Antrim	Cary	Ballintoy	Ballycastle	III.	12
11	Lemnagore	255 3 9	Armagh	Tiranny	Tynan	Armagh	III.	60
10, 11, 23	Lemnaheltia	736 0 3	Galway	Ballynahinch	Ballynakill	Clifden	IV.	11
25	Lemnalary	191 3 35	Antrim	Lower Glenarm	Ardclinis	Larne	III.	21
25	Lemnalary Mountain	885 0 25c	Antrim	Lower Glenarm	Ardclinis	Larne	III.	21
37, 42	Lemnaroy	238 1 28	Londonderry	Loughinsholin	Termoneeny	Magherafelt	III.	244
54	Lemonfield	388 2 30	Galway	Moycullen	Kilcummin	Oughterard	IV.	67
13	Lemonfield	434 2 21	Limerick	Pubblebrien	Knocknagaul	Limerick	II.	253
26	Lemongrove or Rathcam	263 2 14	Westmeath	Fartullagh	Enniscoffey	Mullingar	I.	268
30, 31	Lemonstown	382 3 31	Kilkenny	Kells	Kilmaganny	Callan	I.	109
9, 15	Lemonstown	686 3 37	Wicklow	Lower Talbotstown	Crehelp	Baltinglass	I.	359
23, 24	Lemybrien	537 2 30	Waterford	Decies without Drum	Kilrossanty	Kilmacthomas	II.	358
24	Lemybrien	13 3 7	Waterford	Decies without Drum	Stradbally	Kilmacthomas	II.	361
93	Lenabower	38 1 31	Galway	Galway	Rahoon	Galway	IV.	38
31	Lenaboy	101 2 17	Galway	Ballymoe	Clonbern	Glennamaddy	IV.	6
94	Lenaboy	52 1 4	Galway	Galway	Rahoon	Galway	IV.	38
19	Lenaboy	138 1 32	Longford	Ardagh	Ardagh	Longford	I.	151
87	Lenacraigaboy	230 0 20	Mayo	Murrisk	Oughaval	Westport	IV.	162
27	Lenaderg	335 0 1	Down	Lower Iveagh, Up.pt.	Tullylish	Banbridge	III.	171
10	Lenadoon	51 1 15	Sligo	Tireragh	Easky	Dromore West	IV.	233
47	Lenadremnagh	110 0 4	Tyrone	Dungannon Middle	Clonoe	Dungannon	III.	300
74, 87	Lenafin	338 3 24	Galway	Clonmacnowen	Kilgerrill	Ballinasloe	IV.	26
43, 44	Lenagh	569 2 5	Antrim	Upper Toome	Drummaul	Antrim	III.	34
3	Lenagh	106 0 7	Monaghan	Trough	Errigal Trough	Monaghan	III.	284
19, 26, 27	Lenagh	1,182 0 16	Tyrone	Strabane Upper	Bodoney Lower	Gortin	III.	323
9	Lenaghan	298 1 24d	Fermanagh	Magheraboy	Inishmacsaint	Ballyshannon	III.	213
21	Lenaghan	168 0 30e	Fermanagh	Magheraboy	Rossorry	Enniskillen	III.	214
27	Lenagorra	184 2 33	Kildare	Offaly West	Harristown	Athy	I.	72
12,13,16,17	Lenalea	285 1 25	Armagh	Fews Lower	Mullaghbrack	Armagh	III.	47
60	Lenalea	385 2 26	Donegal	Raphoe	Conwal	Letterkenny	III.	137
73, 74	Lenaloughra	124 1 35	Galway	Kilconnell	Fohanagh	Mountbellew	IV.	40
4, 11	Lenamarran	255 0 31	King's Co.	Warrenstown	Ballymacwilliam	Edenderry	I.	144
16	Lenamore	130 1 16	Galway	Dunmore	Tuam	Tuam	IV.	36
85	Lenamore	238 1 33	Galway	Kilconnell	Killimordaly	Loughrea	IV.	42
101	Lenamore	65 3 28	Galway	Longford	Clonfert	Ballinasloe	IV.	57
71, 72	Lenamore	950 2 32	Galway	Tiaquin	Monivea	Loughrea	IV.	79
25	Lenamore	1,010 3 9	Londonderry	Keenaght	Dungiven	NewT. Limavady	III.	236
1, 5	Lenamore	188 3 31	Londonderry	Keenaght	Magilligan	NewT. Limavady	III.	237
102	Lenamore	167 3 3	Mayo	Costello	Bekan	Claremorris	IV.	139
18, 26	Lenamore	1,276 0 12f	Tyrone	Strabane Upper	Bodoney Lower	Gortin	III.	323
24	Lenamore	49 1 19	Westmeath	Rathconrath	Ballymorin	Mullingar	I.	282
9,10,18,19	Lenan	1,583 1 10	Donegal	Inishowen East	Clonmany	Inishowen	III.	117
111	Lenanaboll	86 1 4	Mayo	Clanmorris	Tagheen	Claremorris	IV.	136
18,19,26,27	Lenanadurtaun	607 0 0	Mayo	Erris	Kilcommon	Belmullet	IV.	144
97	Lenanadurtaun	1,066 2 1y	Mayo	Murrisk	Oughaval	Westport	IV.	162
44	Lenanamalla	125 0 31	Roscommon	Athlone	Tisrara	Roscommon	IV.	185
69	Lenanasillagh	292 2 14	Mayo	Carra	Islandeady	Castlebar	IV.	129
59, 69	Lenanavea	875 2 26	Mayo	Carra	Aglish	Castlebar	IV.	124
40	Lenanavragh	223 3 13h	Cavan	Castlerahan	Mullagh	Kells	III.	70
19	Lenanmarla	285 2 3i	Galway	Ballymoe	Kilbegnet	Glennamaddy	IV.	8
72, 85	Lenareagh	364 1 3	Galway	Tiaquin	Clonkeen	Loughrea	IV.	76
72, 85	Lenareagh	126 2 29	Galway	Tiaquin	Killimordaly	Loughrea	IV.	77
19	Lenarevagh	102 3 26	Galway	Ballymoe	Kilbegnet	Glennamaddy	IV.	8
93	Lenarevagh	101 0 8	Galway	Galway	Rahoon	Galway	IV.	38
12, 19	Lenarevagh	2,344 2 11j	Mayo	Erris	Kilcommon	Belmullet	IV.	144
42, 48	Lenish	343 0 24	Down	Upper Iveagh, Lr.pt.	Clonduff	Newry	III.	171
33	Lennaght	103 0 22	Kilkenny	Ida	The Rower	New Ross	I.	104
5, 8	Lennaght	257 1 5	Monaghan	Monaghan	Tedavnet	Monaghan	III.	279
19	Lennan	156 1 22	Monaghan	Monaghan	Tullycorbet	Monaghan	III.	281
6, 11	Leny	294 2 18	Westmeath	Corkaree	Lackan	Mullingar	I.	262
6, 11	Leny	163 2 17	Westmeath	Corkaree	Leny	Mullingar	I.	263
29	Lenynarnan and Aghilly	377 3 8	Donegal	Inishowen West	Fahan Lower	Inishowen	III.	120
103	Leo	387 1 36	Mayo	Costello	Annagh	Claremorris	IV.	138

(a) Including 4A. 2R. 6P. River Liffey.
(b) Including 9A. 0R. 16P. River Liffey.
(c) Including 39A. 1R. 20P. water.
(d) Including 24A. 1R. 32P. water.
(e) Including 2A. 2R. 8P. water.
(f) Including 9A. 2R. 10P. water.
(g) Including 67A. 0R. 19P. water.
(h) Including 21A. 0R. 0P. water.
(i) Including 29A. 0R. 10P. water.
(j) Including 27A. 1R. 35P. water.

4 N 2

No. of Sheet of the Ordnance Survey Maps.	Townlands and Towns.	Area in Statute Acres. A. R. P.	County.	Barony.	Parish.	Poor Law Union in 1857.	Townland Census of 1851, Part I. Vol.	Page
47	Leode . . .	382 3 0	Down .	Upper Iveagh, Lr. pt.	Clonduff . .	Newry . .	III.	171
22	Leoh . . .	1,010 1 2	Wicklow .	Upper Talbotstown .	Donaghmore .	Baltinglass .	I.	363
15	Leonagh . . .	241 1 21a	Leitrim .	Drumahaire .	Killarga .	Manorhamilton	IV.	99
12	Leonards Island .	100 1 18	Monaghan	Dartree . .	Clones . .	Clones . .	III.	264
43, 49	Leonardstown .	184 2 3	Meath .	Upper Deece .	Kilmore . .	Dunshaughlin .	I.	193
31, 34	Leons Beg . .	80 2 3	Monaghan	Farney . .	Magheracloone .	Carrickmacross	III.	272
31, 34	Leons Garve or Leons (M'Kenna) .	270 1 15	Monaghan	Farney . .	Magheracloone .	Carrickmacross	III.	272
31, 34	Leons (M'Kenna) or Leons Garve .	270 1 15	Monaghan	Farney . .	Magheracloone .	Carrickmacross	III.	272
23, 26	Leopardstown and Carnanhall .	277 2 35	Dublin .	Rathdown .	Tully . .	Rathdown .	I.	38
27	Leperstown . .	825 3 33	Waterford .	Gaultiere . .	Killea . .	Waterford .	II.	363
34	Leraw . . .	81 2 28	Fermanagh .	Magherastephana .	Aghalurcher .	Lisnaskea .	III.	217
96	Lergadaghtan . .	112 0 21	Donegal .	Banagh . .	Glencolumbkille .	Glenties .	III.	105
96	Lergadaghtan . .	94 3 16	Donegal .	Banagh . .	Kilcar . .	Glenties .	III.	108
90, 96	Lergadaghtan Mountain .	209 1 6	Donegal .	Banagh . .	Glencolumbkille .	Glenties .	III.	105
8	Lergan . . .	338 3 11	Fermanagh .	Magheraboy .	Inishmacsaint .	Ballyshannon .	III.	213
82	Lerginacarha . .	342 2 31b	Donegal .	Banagh . .	Inishkeel .	Glenties .	III.	106
81, 82	Lergynasearhagh .	621 3 9	Donegal .	Banagh . .	Inishkeel .	Glenties .	III.	106
18, 31	Lerhin . . .	279 3 35	Galway .	Ballymoe .	Clonbern .	Glennamaddy .	IV.	6
20, 21	Lerrig North .	495 3 23	Kerry .	Clanmaurice .	Kilmoyly .	Tralee .	II.	171
20, 21	Lerrig South .	468 3 24	Kerry .	Clanmaurice .	Kilmoyly .	Tralee .	II.	171
21	LERRIG T. . .	—	Kerry .	Clanmaurice .	Kilmoyly .	Tralee .	II.	171
22	Lesh . . .	198 0 19	Armagh .	Orior Lower .	Killevy .	Newry .	III.	56
21, 22	Lesh . . .	201 2 34	Armagh .	Orior Lower .	Loughgilly .	Newry .	III.	56
38, 44	Leshemstown .	482 0 20	Meath .	Ratoath . .	Dunshaughlin .	Dunshaughlin .	I.	218
21, 26	Lesky . . .	196 2 3	Fermanagh .	Clanawley .	Boha . .	Enniskillen .	III.	189
21, 29	Lessanny . .	191 3 20	Mayo .	Tirawley .	Moygawnagh .	Killala .	IV.	171
15, 16	Lessans . .	492 3 15	Down .	Castlereagh Upper .	Saintfield .	Lisburn .	III.	166
2	Letachmentgallon .	84 3 8	Meath .	Lower Kells .	Moybolgue .	Kells .	I.	203
42	Letalian . . .	502 3 6	Down .	Upper Iveagh, Lr. pt.	Kilcoo .	Kilkeel .	III.	173
51	Letfern . . .	425 0 16	Tyrone .	Omagh East .	Clogherny .	Omagh .	III.	310
6	Letfordspark . .	53 3 19	Roscommon .	Boyle . .	Boyle . .	Boyle .	IV.	194
6	Letgonnelly . .	61 1 12	Monaghan	Trough . .	Donagh . .	Monaghan .	III.	282
7	Letloonigan . .	12 2 24	Monaghan	Trough . .	Donagh . .	Monaghan .	III.	282
23	Lettan . . .	201 0 24	Fermanagh .	Tirkennedy .	Enniskillen .	Enniskillen .	III.	222
122	Letter . . .	367 1 39	Cork, W.R. .	East Carbery (W.D.)	Kilmeen . .	Clonakilty .	II.	134
147	Letter . . .	219 2 22	Cork, W.R. .	West Carbery (W.D.)	Kilmoe . .	Skull .	II.	145
139, 140	Letter . . .	703 1 39	Cork, W.R. .	West Carbery (W.D.)	Skull . .	Skull .	II.	145
96	Letter . . .	191 0 6	Donegal .	Banagh . .	Kilcar . .	Glenties .	III.	108
91	Letter . . .	63 0 7	Donegal .	Banagh . .	Killybegs Upper .	Glenties .	III.	110
9, 10	Letter . . .	851 1 21	Donegal .	Inishowen East .	Clonmany .	Inishowen .	III.	117
38	Letter . . .	625 3 28	Donegal .	Inishowen West .	Fahan Upper .	Londonderry .	III.	121
45	Letter . . .	453 1 14	Donegal .	Kilmacrenan .	Kilmacrenan .	Milford .	III.	129
4	Letter . . .	192 0 3	Fermanagh .	Lurg . .	Templecarn .	Lowtherstown .	III.	209
9	Letter . . .	246 2 15	Fermanagh .	Magheraboy .	Inishmacsaint .	Ballyshannon .	III.	213
67, 80	Letter . . .	1,692 1 20c	Galway .	Moycullen .	Killannin .	Galway .	IV.	70
83, 92	Letter . . .	1,301 2 33d	Kerry .	Dunkerron South .	Templenoe .	Kenmare .	II.	185
2	Letter . . .	111 2 19	Kerry .	Iraghticonnor .	Aghavallen .	Listowel .	II.	189
79	Letter . . .	683 3 19	Kerry .	Iveragh . .	Caher . .	Cahersiveen .	II.	194
36, 37	Letter . . .	225 2 1	King's Co. .	Ballybritt .	Letterluna .	Parsonstown .	I.	126
17	Letter . . .	310 2 31	Leitrim .	Drumahaire .	Inishmagrath .	Manorhamilton	IV.	97
77	Letter . . .	875 0 17	Mayo .	Burrishoole .	Islandeady .	Westport .	IV.	121
18	Lettera . . .	434 0 25	Galway .	Ballymoe .	Clonbern .	Glennamaddy .	IV.	6
1	Lettera . . .	261 2 14	Galway .	Ballymoe .	Templetogher .	Glennamaddy .	IV.	9
44	Lettera . . .	2,981 2 9	Mayo .	Erris . .	Kilcommon .	Newport .	IV.	144
41	Lettera or Crossaun	86 0 24	Galway .	Clare . .	Killursa .	Tuam .	IV.	21
40	Letteragh .	2,072 2 23	Clare .	Islands . .	Kilmaley .	Ennis .	II.	31
82, 94	Letteragh .	117 2 25	Galway .	Galway . .	Rahoon . .	Galway .	IV.	38
14	Letteragh .	120 3 19	Monaghan	Cremorne .	Clontibret .	Monaghan .	III.	261
40,41,45,46	Letteran .	715 0 15	Londonderry .	Loughinsholin .	Lissan . .	Magherafelt .	III.	242
63	Letterard .	840 3 9e	Galway .	Ballynahinch .	Moyrus . .	Clifden .	IV.	13
115, 116	Letterass .	2,059 0 32	Mayo .	Murrisk . .	Aghagower .	Westport .	IV.	159
116	Letterass Island .	0 1 9	Mayo .	Murrisk . .	Aghagower .	Westport .	IV.	159
17	Letterbailey .	556 3 25	Fermanagh .	Tirkennedy .	Enniskillen .	Enniskillen .	III.	222
14, 19	Letterbane .	276 1 22	Monaghan	Cremorne .	Clontibret .	Monaghan .	III.	261
93	Letterbarra .	212 3 13	Donegal .	Banagh . .	Inver . .	Donegal .	III.	107
9	Letter Beg .	231 2 34	Galway .	Ballynahinch .	Ballynakill .	Clifden .	IV.	11
24	Letterbeg .	179 2 25	Mayo .	Erris . .	Kilmore .	Belmullet .	IV.	140
16,17,24,25	Letterbin .	707 2 8	Tyrone .	Strabane Lower .	Ardstraw .	Strabane .	III.	319
5, 6	Letterboy .	178 3 4	Fermanagh .	Lurg . .	Magheraculmoney .	Lowtherstown .	III.	208
11	Letterbrat .	708 1 16f	Tyrone .	Strabane Upper .	Bodoney Upper .	Gortin .	III.	324

(a) Including 58A. 1R. 32P. water.
(b) Including 35A. 2R. 21P. water.
(c) Including 18A. 1R. 25P. water.
(d) Including 14A. 0R. 24P. water.
(e) Including 11A. 2R. 2P. water.
(f) Including 4A. 3R. 28P. water.

No. of Sheet of the Ordnance Survey Maps.	Townlands and Towns.	Area in Statute Acres.			County.	Barony.	Parish.	Poor Law Union in 1857.	Townland Census of 1851, Part I.	
		A.	R.	P.					Vol.	Page
24	Letterbreckaun	1,610	3	13	Galway	Ballynahinch	Ballynakill	Cliflen	IV.	11
26	Letterbreen	141	0	5	Fermanagh	Clanawley	Cleenish	Enniskillen	III.	191
67	Letterbrick	1,070	2	3	Donegal	Raphoe	Kilteevoge	Stranorlar	III.	139
46	Letterbrick	1,149	0	35	Mayo	Tirawley	Crossmolina	Ballina	IV.	166
12	Letterbrickaun	451	0	38	Galway	Ross	Ross	Oughterard	IV.	74
97	Letterbrock	1,081	3	24	Mayo	Murrisk	Aghagower	Westport	IV.	159
36	Letterbrone	1,289	2	28a	Sligo	Leyny	Kilmacteige	Tobercurry	IV.	231
77, 78, 90	Lettercallow	1,245	1	4	Galway	Moycullen	Killannin	Oughterard	IV.	70
85, 86	Lettercannon	998	1	33	Kerry	Glanarought	Kilgarvan	Kenmare	II.	187
24, 33	Lettercarn	512	2	20b	Tyrone	Omagh West	Ardstraw	Castlederg	III.	315
49	Lettercau	343	0	7c	Donegal	Boylagh	Templecrone	Glenties	III.	115
50, 51	Lettercaunus	351	0	13	Galway	Ballynahinch	Moyrus	Clifden	IV.	13
39, 47	Letterclery	141	1	31	Tyrone	Dungannon Middle	Donaghenry	Cookstown	III.	301
123, 136	Lettercollum	209	3	4	Cork, W.R.	Ibane and Barryroe	Timoleague	Clonakilty	II.	151
53, 54	Lettercraff	1,374	1	6d	Galway	Moycullen	Kilcummin	Oughterard	IV.	67
66, 67	Lettercraffroe	1,154	0	1e	Galway	Moycullen	Kilcummin	Oughterard	IV.	67
102	Lettercran	526	0	27f	Donegal	Tirhugh	Templecarn	Donegal	III.	149
35	Letterdeen	278	0	38g	Galway	Ballynahinch	Omey	Clifden	IV.	15
76, 77	Letterdeskert	282	2	8	Galway	Ballynahinch	Moyrus	Clifden	IV.	13
50	Letterdife	1,590	2	20h	Galway	Ballynahinch	Moyrus	Clifden	IV.	13
102	Letterdunane	350	1	36	Kerry	Glanarought	Kilcaskan	Kenmare	II.	187
138	Letter East	259	0	16	Cork, W.R.	West Carbery (W.D.)	Kilcrohane	Bantry	II.	144
63, 71	Letter East	215	0	34	Kerry	Iveragh	Glanbehy	Cahersiveen	II.	196
3, 13	Lettereeneen	1,235	2	20i	Galway	Ross	Ballinrobe	Ballinrobe	IV.	72
115	Lettereeragh	1,405	3	25	Mayo	Murrisk	Kilgeever	Westport	IV.	160
10, 11	Letterettrin	399	2	26j	Galway	Ballynahinch	Ballynakill	Clifden	IV.	11
84, 93	Letterfad	1,520	0	3k	Donegal	Banagh	Inver	Donegal	III.	107
35, 44, 45	Letterfad	277	0	33	Donegal	Kilmacrenan	Kilmacrenan	Milford	III.	129
24, 28	Letterfine	135	3	2l	Leitrim	Leitrim	Kiltubbrid	Car^k. on Shannon	IV.	104
91	Letterfinish	382	1	10	Kerry	Dunkerron South	Kilcrohane	Kenmare	II.	184
80, 92	Letterfir	2,296	1	3m	Galway	Moycullen	Killannin	Galway	IV.	70
39, 40, 53	Letterfore	2,274	3	26n	Galway	Moycullen	Kilcummin	Oughterard	IV.	67
23	Letterfrack	1,239	1	6o	Galway	Ballynahinch	Ballynakill	Clifden	IV.	11
81, 82	Lettergarriv	951	3	39p	Kerry	Dunkerron North	Knockane	Cahersiveen	II.	182
41, 49	Lettergash	613	1	35	Tyrone	Omagh East	Dromore	Lowtherstown	III.	311
5	Lettergeeragh	186	0	27	Longford	Longford	Killoe	Longford	I.	159
10, 11	Lettergesh East	2,180	2	28q	Galway	Ballynahinch	Ballynakill	Clifden	IV.	11
10	Lettergesh West	1,186	0	0r	Galway	Ballynahinch	Ballynakill	Clifden	IV.	11
5	Lettergonnell	651	0	35	Longford	Longford	Killoe	Longford	I.	159
121	Lettergorman	737	0	37s	Cork, W.R.	East Carbery (W.D.)	Drinagh	Dunmanway	II.	131
39, 40	Lettergreen	180	2	13	Fermanagh	Coole	Galloon	Clones	III.	200
62	Lettergull	557	1	18	Donegal	Raphoe	Taughboyne	Strabane	III.	143
5	Lettergullion	494	1	20	Longford	Longford	Killoe	Longford	I.	159
81, 93	Lettergunnet	852	0	16t	Galway	Moycullen	Rahoon	Galway	IV.	72
65, 74	Letterilly	1,904	3	0u	Donegal	Boylagh	Inishkeel	Glenties	III.	113
39, 53	Letterkeeghaun	433	0	12	Galway	Moycullen	Kilcummin	Oughterard	IV.	67
58, 59	Letterkeeghaun	1,254	1	33	Mayo	Tirawley	Addergoole	Castlebar	IV.	163
5	Letterkeen	308	2	36	Fermanagh	Lurg	Drumkeeran	Lowtherstown	III.	206
45, 46, 57	Letterkeen	3,032	3	21	Mayo	Burrishoole	Burrishoole	Newport	IV.	119
31	Letterkelly	856	3	24	Clare	Inchiquin	Inagh	Ennistimon	II.	25
53	Letterkenny	410	0	21	Donegal	Kilmacrenan	Conwal	Letterkenny	III.	126
53	LETTERKENNY T.	—			Donegal	Kilmacrenan	Conwal	Letterkenny	III.	127
61	Letterleague	599	2	7	Donegal	Raphoe	Conwal	Letterkenny	III.	137
118, 131	Letterlicky East	320	1	23	Cork, W.R.	West Carbery (W.D.)	Kilmocomoge	Bantry	II.	144
118, 131	Letterlicky Middle	647	0	12	Cork, W.R.	West Carbery (W.D.)	Kilmocomoge	Bantry	II.	144
131	Letterlicky West	525	3	17	Cork, W.R.	West Carbery (W.D.)	Kilmocomoge	Bantry	II.	144
11	Letterloan	548	0	26	Londonderry	Coleraine	Macosquin	Coleraine	III.	233
23	Letterlogher	291	3	11	Londonderry	Tirkeeran	Cumber Upper	New Tⁿ Limavady	III.	249
68	Letterlough	326	1	25	Mayo	Burrishoole	Burrishoole	Newport	IV.	119
138	Letter Lower	49	1	2	Cork, W.R.	West Carbery (W.D.)	Kilcrohane	Bantry	II.	144
93, 94	Letter Lower	367	1	27	Kerry	Glanarought	Kenmare	Kenmare	II.	186
57, 67	Lettermaghera North	1,160	0	35	Mayo	Burrishoole	Burrishoole	Newport	IV.	119
57, 67	Lettermaghera South	914	2	7v	Mayo	Burrishoole	Burrishoole	Newport	IV.	119
107, 108	Lettermaginskin	1,059	1	25	Mayo	Murrisk	Aghagower	Westport	IV.	159
69, 78	Lettermakenny	427	0	35	Donegal	Raphoe	Stranorlar	Stranorlar	III.	142
80	Lettermas	846	2	36w	Galway	Moycullen	Moycullen	Galway	IV.	71
22, 23	Lettermire	399	2	39	Londonderry	Tirkeeran	Cumber Lower	Londonderry	III.	249
91	Lettermoreel	311	1	13	Kerry	Dunkerron South	Kilcrohane	Kenmare	II.	184
11, 16	Lettermoney	209	1	13	Fermanagh	Tirkennedy	Magheracross	Lowtherstown	III.	223
16	Lettermore	229	1	26	Cavan	Tullygarvey	Kildrumsherdan	Cootehill	III.	90
84, 93	Lettermore	578	3	9	Donegal	Banagh	Inver	Donegal	III.	107
69	Lettermore	604	1	7	Donegal	Raphoe	Convoy	Stranorlar	III.	136
9	Letter More	236	3	8	Galway	Ballynahinch	Ballynakill	Clifden	IV.	11

(a) Including 6A. 3R. 33P. water.
(b) Including 16A. 1R. 5P. water.
(c) Including 58A. 3R. 3P. water.
(d) Including 3A. 0R. 4P. water.
(e) Including 436A. 3R. 21P. water.
(f) Including 20A. 3R. 23P. water.
(g) Including 6A. 3R. 13P. water.
(h) Including 58A. 2R. 23P. water.
(i) Including 18A. 3R. 21P. water.
(j) Including 3A. 0R. 6P. water.
(k) Including 10A. 3R. 15P. water.
(l) Including 3A. 2R. 10P. water.
(m) Including 193A. 1R. 4P. water.
(n) Including 85A. 2R. 19P. water.
(o) Including 18A. 0R. 15P. water.
(p) Including 107A. 0R. 9P. water.
(q) Including 35A. 0R. 2P. water.
(r) Including 21A. 3R. 38P. water.
(s) Including 8A. 1R. 15P. water.
(t) Including 6A. 1R. 19P. water.
(u) Including 39A. 3R. 30P. water.
(v) Including 7A. 3R. 37P. water.
(w) Including 16A. 2R. 19P. water.

No. of Sheet of the Ordnance Survey Maps.	Townlands and Towns.	Area in Statute Acres. A. R. P.	County.	Barony.	Parish.	Poor Law Union in 1857.	Townland Census of 1851, Part I. Vol.	Page
53, 66	Lettermore	1,259 2 37a	Galway	Moycullen	Kilcummin	Oughterard	IV.	67
78	Lettermore	1,008 2 5	Galway	Moycullen	Killannin	Oughterard	IV.	70
129, 138	Letter-mountain	233 3 0	Cork, W.R.	West Carbery (W.D.)	Kilcrohane	Bantry	II.	144
22, 23, 28	Lettermuck	587 3 14	Londonderry	Tirkeeran	Cumber Upper	Londonderry	III.	249
63, 78, 79	Lettermuckoo	2,496 0 4b	Galway	Moycullen	Kilcummin	Oughterard	IV.	67
89	Lettermullan	787 2 5	Galway	Moycullen	Kilcummin	Oughterard	IV.	69
93	Letternacahy	159 1 23	Donegal	Banagh	Inver	Donegal	III.	107
91, 100	Letternadarriv	706 1 16	Kerry	Dunkerron South	Kilcrohane	Kenmare	II.	184
37, 46	Letterneevoge	516 2 9c	Mayo	Tirawley	Crossmolina	Ballina	IV.	166
22, 35	Letternoosh	397 1 16d	Galway	Ballynahinch	Omey	Clifden	IV.	15
80	Letterpeak	595 3 10e	Galway	Moycullen	Moycullen	Galway	IV.	71
64, 77	Letterpibrum	607 3 7f	Galway	Ballynahinch	Moyrus	Clifden	IV.	13
141	Letterscanlan	97 1 30	Cork, W.R.	West Carbery (E.D.)	Aghadown	Skibbereen	II.	137
11, 24	Lettershanbally	1,382 0 10g	Galway	Ballynahinch	Ballynakill	Clifden	IV.	11
60,61,68,69	Lettershanbo	575 0 34	Donegal	Raphoe	Convoy	Stranorlar	III.	136
68	Lettershanbo	1,300 0 12	Donegal	Raphoe	Kilteevoge	Stranorlar	III.	139
35	Lettershanna	189 2 27	Galway	Ballynahinch	Omey	Clifden	IV.	15
36	Lettershea	629 0 14	Galway	Ballynahinch	Moyrus	Clifden	IV.	13
14, 22	Lettershendony	299 1 16	Londonderry	Tirkeeran	Cumber Lower	Londonderry	III.	249
51, 52	Lettershinna	4,396 1 34h	Galway	Ballynahinch	Moyrus	Clifden	IV.	13
142	Lettertinlish	397 2 1i	Cork, W.R.	West Carbery (E.D.)	Castlehaven	Skibbereen	II.	138
45, 46	Lettertrask	1,350 0 29j	Mayo	Tirawley	Crossmolina	Ballina	IV.	166
84, 93	Lettertreane	569 2 12k	Donegal	Banagh	Inver	Donegal	III.	107
17,18,23,24	Letterunshin	1,756 0 21	Sligo	Tireragh	Kilmacshalgan	Dromore West	IV.	235
93, 94	Letter Upper	407 2 10	Kerry	Glanarought	Kenmare	Kenmare	II.	186
138	Letter West	117 2 37	Cork, W.R.	West Carbery (W.D.)	Kilcrohane	Bantry	II.	144
63, 70, 71	Letter West	1,770 0 6l	Kerry	Iveragh	Glanbehy	Cahersiveen	II.	196
36, 37	Lettery	951 1 32m	Galway	Ballynahinch	Moyrus	Clifden	IV.	13
52, 59	Lettery	182 1 32	Tyrone	Clogher	Errigal Keerogue	Clogher	III.	295
41	Lettery	579 0 24	Tyrone	Omagh East	Dromore	Omagh	III.	311
23	Lettreen	155 1 28	Roscommon	Roscommon	Kiltrustan	Strokestown	IV.	211
36	Lettybrook or Clooneen	331 0 7	King's Co.	Ballybritt	Letterluna	Parsonstown	I.	126
13, 14	Leugh	418 2 22	Kilkenny	Crannagh	Odagh	Kilkenny	I.	86
44, 45	Leugh	434 1 0	Tipperary, N.R.	Kilnamanagh Upper	Doon	Tipperary	II.	277
9, 10	Levaghery	286 2 39n	Armagh	Oncilland East	Seagoe	Lurgan	III.	50
22	Levaghy	85 2 39	Fermanagh	Tirkennedy	Derryvullan	Enniskillen	III.	221
8	Levalleglish	222 1 33o	Armagh	Oneiland West	Loughgall	Armagh	III.	54
60, 70	Levallinree	355 3 25p	Mayo	Carra	Turlough	Castlebar	IV.	131
43	Levnlly	110 0 38	Galway	Clare	Belclare	Tuam	IV.	17
110, 118	Levally	331 2 19q	Mayo	Kilmaine	Ballinrobe	Ballinrobe	IV.	153
47	Levally	241 1 31	Mayo	Tirawley	Addergoole	Castlebar	IV.	163
34	Levally	345 1 15	Queen's Co.	Clarmallagh	Erke	Donaghmore	I.	237
51, 54	Levallyclanone	145 2 36	Down	Upper Iveagh, Up. pt.	Kilbroney	Kilkeel	III.	176
30	Levally East	392 3 17	Galway	Ballymoe	Tuam	Tuam	IV.	10
15, 21	Levally Lower	160 3 2	Fermanagh	Magheraboy	Devenish	Enniskillen	III.	211
28	Levallymore	262 0 27	Armagh	Orior Upper	Forkill	Newry	III.	57
87	Levallynearl or Foats	224 1 38	Galway	Kilconnell	Aughrim	Ballinasloe	IV.	39
28	Levallyreagh	507 1 14	Down	Lower Iveagh, Lr. pt.	Dromara	Banbridge	III.	167
51	Levallyreagh	151 1 9	Down	Upper Iveagh, Up. pt	Kilbroney	Kilkeel	III.	176
112	Levallyroe	266 2 30	Mayo	Clanmorris	Kilvine	Claremorris	IV.	134
103, 113	Levallyroe	887 2 10r	Mayo	Costello	Annagh	Claremorris	IV.	138
15, 21	Levally Upper	155 0 13	Fermanagh	Magheraboy	Devenish	Enniskillen	III.	211
30	Levally West	230 3 31	Galway	Ballymoe	Tuam	Tuam	IV.	10
74	Levcelick	193 1 28	Mayo	Costello	Kilmovee	Swineford	IV.	142
20, 26	Levcelick	251 2 14	Roscommon	Castlereagh	Kilkeevin	Castlereagh	IV.	200
25	Leveran Island	0 1 30	Longford	Ratheline	Cashel	Ballymahon	I.	163
15,16,21,22	Levern	215 0 35	Wicklow	Upper Talbotstown	Donaghmore	Baltinglass	I.	363
9, 15	Leveroge	340 0 18	Down	Castlereagh Upper	Drumbo	Lisburn	III.	164
37	Levitstown	653 1 18s	Kildare	Kilkea and Moone	Dunmanoge	Athy	I.	59
37	Levitstown	384 0 28t	Kildare	Kilkea and Moone	Tankardstown	Athy	I.	61
41, 46	Levitstown	139 0 9	Wexford	Bargy	Duncormick	Wexford	I.	305
42	Levitstown	91 2 13	Wexford	Forth	Drinagh	Wexford	I.	309
41	Lewagh Beg	198 1 18	Tipperary, N.R.	Eliogarty	Thurles	Thurles	II.	273
41	Lewagh More	296 3 36	Tipperary, N.R.	Eliogarty	Thurles	Thurles	II.	273
46, 52	Lewellensland	158 3 37	Meath	Upper Moyfenrath	Castlejordan	Edenderry	I.	212
23	Lewistown	523 3 27	Kildare	Connell	Ladytown	Naas	I.	55
49	Lewistown	209 2 29	Wexford	Shelburne	Templetown	New Ross	I.	329
32	Leymore	365 3 31	Antrim	Lower Toome	Ahoghill	Ballymena	III.	32
18, 19	Liafin	489 3 15	Donegal	Inishowen West	Desertegny	Inishowen	III.	91
29, 30	Libbert East	194 2 9	Antrim	Lower Glenarm	Tickmacrevan	Larne	III	24
29	Libbert West	42 2 24	Antrim	Lower Glenarm	Tickmacrevan	Larne	III.	24
5, 8, 9	Liberties of Carlingford	2,321 3 2	Louth	Lower Dundalk	Carlingford	Dundalk	I.	176

(a) Including 7A. 3R. 23P. water.
(b) Including 283A. 0R. 38P. water.
(c) Including 12A. 3R. 38P. water.
(d) Including 4A. 1R. 37P. water.
(e) Including 60A. 2R. 0P. water.
(f) Including 62A. 1R. 24P. water.
(g) Including 1A. 0R. 2P. water.

(h) Including 462A. 2R. 17P. water.
(i) Including 8A. 0R. 8P. water.
(j) Including 54A. 2R. 18P. water.
(k) Including 6A. 3R. 10P. water.
(l) Including 132A. 0R. 36P. water.
(m) Including 59A. 3R. 24P. water.
(n) Including 6A. 3R. 21P. water.

(o) Including 0A. 2R. 2P. water.
(p) Including 101A. 3R. 27P. water.
(q) Including 6A. 2R. 16P. water.
(r) Including 10A. 1R. 8P. water.
(s) Including 6A. 3R. 8P. water.
(t) Including 9A. 2R. 0P. River Barrow.

No. of Sheet of the Ordnance Survey Maps.	Townlands and Towns.	Area in Statute Acres.			County.	Barony.	Parish.	Poor Law Union in 1857.	Townland Census of 1851, Part I.	
		A.	R.	P.					Vol.	Page
54	Liberty	258	1	3	Roscommon	Moycarn	Moore	Ballinasloe	IV.	207
52	Libgate	118	2	36	Wexford	Bargy	Kilmore	Wexford	I.	306
13	Lickadoon	671	3	2	Limerick	Clanwilliam	Caheravally	Limerick	II.	221
89	Lickane	65	3	12	Cork, E.R.	Imokilly	Cloyne	Middleton	II.	85
127	Lickbarrahane	241	1	37	Cork, W.R.	Bear	Kilnamanagh	Castletown	II.	146
3	Lickbla	397	1	6	Westmeath	Fore	Lickbla	Granard	I.	270
71, 72	Lickeen	570	2	27	Kerry	Iveragh	Glanbehy	Cahersiveen	II.	196
24	Lickeen	163	1	22	Wicklow	Ballinacor North	Knockrath	Rathdrum	II.	347
16	Lickeen East	651	2	32a	Clare	Corcomroe	Kilfenora	Ennistimon	II.	19
90	Lickeen East	222	1	10	Cork, W.R.	Bear	Kilcaskan	Bantry	II.	123
15, 16	Lickeen West	205	1	16	Clare	Corcomroe	Kilfenora	Ennistimon	II.	19
90	Lickeen West	149	2	0	Cork, W.R.	Bear	Kilcaskan	Bantry	II.	123
96, 97	Lickerrig	265	1	25	Galway	Dunkellin	Lickerrig	Loughrea	IV.	31
45, 46	Licketstown	342	2	22	Kilkenny	Iverk	Portnascully	Waterford	I.	106
45	Licketstown T.	—			Kilkenny	Iverk	Portnascully	Waterford	I.	106
54	Lickfinn	340	1	13	Tipperary, S.R.	Slievardagh	Crohane	Urlingford	II.	332
48, 54	Lickfinn	575	2	11	Tipperary, S.R.	Slievardagh	Lickfinn	Urlingford	II.	335
27, 35, 36	Licklash	191	1	10b	Cork, E.R.	Condons&Clangibbon	Clondulane	Fermoy	II.	60
117	Lickmolassy	109	0	33	Galway	Longford	Lickmolassy	Portumna	IV.	61
25	Licknaun	321	2	12	Clare	Bunratty Upper	Templemaley	Ennis	II.	11
141, 150	Licknavar	284	1	4	Cork, W.R.	West Carbery (E.D.)	Creagh	Skibbereen	II.	139
3	Lickny	52	2	31	Westmeath	Fore	Mayne	Granard	I.	271
13, 22	Lickoran	215	0	31	Waterford	Decies without Drum	Lickoran	Lismore	II.	358
13, 22	Lickoranmountain	96	2	24	Waterford	Decies without Drum	Lickoran	Lismore	II.	358
151	Lickowen	139	0	13	Cork, W.R.	West Carbery (E.D.)	Castlehaven	Skibbereen	II.	138
19	Liffane	392	0	10	Limerick	Connello Lower	Lismakeery	Rathkeale	II.	228
18	Liffeybank	4	1	14c	Dublin	Dublin, Municipal Borough of	St. James	Dublin North	I.	44
2	Lillock	108	0	24	Londonderry	Coleraine	Dunboe	Coleraine	III.	231
33	Lifford	451	1	0	Clare	Islands	Drumcliff	Ennis	II.	30
71	Lifford	148	1	3	Donegal	Raphoe	Clonleigh	Strabane	III.	135
57	Lifford	515	2	34	Tyrone	Omagh East	Kilskeery	Enniskillen	III.	313
71	Lifford Bog	54	2	16	Donegal	Raphoe	Clonleigh	Strabane	III.	135
70, 71	Lifford Common	360	3	26	Donegal	Raphoe	Clonleigh	Strabane	III.	135
71	Lifford T.	—			Donegal	Raphoe	Clonleigh	Strabane	III.	135
10	Ligadaughtan	149	0	31	Antrim	Cary	Culfeightrin	Ballycastle	III.	13
12, 19, 20	Ligatraght	697	3	14	Tyrone	Strabane Upper	Bodoney Lower	Gortin	III.	323
5, 10, 11	Ligfordrum or Douglas	3,883	1	17	Tyrone	Strabane Lower	Ardstraw	Strabane	III.	319
14	Ligg	140	3	3	Londonderry	Tirkeeran	Faughanvale	Londonderry	III.	250
9, 10	Liggartown	261	0	26d	Tyrone	Strabane Lower	Urney	Strabane	III.	322
12, 19	Liggins	433	0	22	Tyrone	Strabane Upper	Bodoney Lower	Gortin	III.	323
21	Lightfield	64	1	12	Longford	Rathcline	Cashel	Ballymahon	I.	163
78	Lightford	77	1	25	Mayo	Carra	Breaghwy	Castlebar	IV.	127
3	Light House Island	40	1	32	Down	Ards Lower	Bangor	Newtownards	III.	157
40	Lighthouse Lot	82	0	27	Donegal	Boylagh	Templecrone	Glenties	III.	115
10	Lignameeltoge	129	0	36	Fermanagh	Lurg	Derryvullan	Lowtherstown	III.	204
25, 32	Lilliput or Nure	244	1	22	Westmeath	Moycashel	Dysart	Mullingar	I.	278
40	Lillybrook	66	1	31	Sligo	Tirerrill	Aghanagh	Boyle	IV.	237
27, 28	Limavallaghan	238	3	11	Antrim	Kilconway	Dunaghy	Ballymena	III.	26
106, 116	Limehill	653	3	10	Galway	Leitrim	Duniry	Loughrea	IV.	53
37	Limehill	1,436	2	30	Tyrone	Dungannon Upper	Desertcreat	Cookstown	III.	308
37, 46	Limekilnclose	41	3	26	Cork, E.R.	Kinnatalloon	Mogeely	Lismore	II.	98
28	Limekilnclose	111	0	36	Waterford	Coshmore&Coshbride	Tallow	Lismore	II.	348
22	Limekilnfarm	102	0	4	Dublin	Uppercross	Crumlin	Dublin South	I.	40
25	Limekilnhill	154	1	12e	Meath	Lower Navan	Navan	Navan	I.	215
114	Limepark North	258	2	6	Galway	Kiltartan	Kilthomas	Loughrea	IV.	49
114	Limepark South	86	0	12	Galway	Loughrea	Kilthomas	Loughrea	IV.	65
2, 3	Limerick	172	1	13	Wexford	Gorey	Kilcavan	Gorey	I.	317
5	LIMERICK CITY	—			—	—	—	Limerick	II.	262
37, 38	Liminary	743	2	3	Antrim	Lower Antrim	Ballyclug	Ballymena	III.	3
45	Limnagh	365	1	10	Sligo	Tirerrill	Aghanagh	Boyle	IV.	237
31, 36, 37	Limnaharry	386	2	6	Antrim	Lower Toome	Ahoghill	Ballymena	III.	32
58	Lindsay's Farm	107	3	28	Galway	Tiaquin	Abbeyknockmoy	Tuam	IV.	75
24	Linfield	334	1	0	Limerick	Coonagh	Grean	Tipperary	II.	235
34, 35	Linford	659	2	17	Antrim	Upper Glenarm	Carncastle	Larne	III.	24
29	Ling	507	3	0	Londonderry	Tirkeeran	Cumber Upper	Londonderry	III.	249
48	Ling, Ford of	18	1	28	Wexford	Forth	Ballybrennan	Wexford	I.	308
48	Ling, Ford of	45	3	34	Wexford	Forth	Kilscoran	Wexford	I.	311
47, 52	Lingstown Lower	58	0	13	Wexford	Forth	Ishartmon	Wexford	I.	309
47	Lingstown Upper	72	3	16	Wexford	Forth	Ishartmon	Wexford	I.	309
12	Linkardstown	498	3	14	Carlow	Carlow	Tullowmagimma	Carlow	I.	2
2, 3, 6, 7	Linnanagh	154	2	20	Wexford	Gorey	Kilcavan	Gorey	I.	317
15	Linns	188	3	11f	Louth	Ardee	Gernonstown	Ardee	I.	172

(a) Including 113A. 0R. 1P. water.
(b) Including 4A. 0R. 0P. water.
(c) Included in the Parish of St. James.
(d) Including 12A. 1R. 31P. water.
(e) Including 5A. 2R. 26P. water.
(f) Including 17A. 0R. 18P. water.

No. of Sheet of the Ordnance Survey Maps.	Townlands and Towns.	Area in Statute Acres.			County.	Barony.	Parish.	Poor Law Union in 1857.	Townland Census of 1851, Part I.	
		A.	R.	P.					Vol.	Page
39	Linnyglass	102	1	21	Tyrone	Dungannon Upper	Ballyclog	Cookstown	III.	306
18,19,28,29	Linsfort	331	3	5	Donegal	Inishowen West	Desertegny	Inishowen	III.	120
22	Lintaun	86	1	33	Kilkenny	Callan	Callan	Callan	I.	83
47	Linziestown	69	2	28	Wexford	Forth	Ballymore	Wexford	I.	308
47	Linziestown	102	3	38	Wexford	Forth	Ishartmon	Wexford	I.	310
41	Lionsden	345	1	4a	Meath	Upper Moyfenrath	Castlerickard	Trim	I.	213
92, 93	Lippa	388	0	15	Galway	Moycullen	Moycullen	Galway	IV.	71
32	Lipstown	198	3	13	Kildare	Narragh & Reban East	Narraghmore	Athy	I.	66
32	Lipstown Lower	409	0	16	Kildare	Narragh & Reban East	Davidstown	Athy	I.	66
32	Lipstown Upper	216	2	5	Kildare	Narragh & Reban East	Davidstown	Athy	I.	66
16, 17	Lisabuck	129	0	38b	Monaghan	Dartree	Killeevan	Clones	III.	268
26	Lisachrin	461	3	12	Londonderry	Coleraine	Desertoghill	Ballymoney	III.	250
35	Lisachunny	53	1	5	Cavan	Clankee	Enniskeen	Bailieborough	III.	73
47	Lisaclare	185	1	37	Tyrone	Dungannon Middle	Clonoe	Dungannon	III.	300
16	Lisacoghil	208	3	8	Leitrim	Drumahaire	Inishmagrath	Manorhamilton	IV.	97
35, 43	Lisacoppin	140	2	2c	Tyrone	Omagh East	Cappagh	Omagh	III.	310
27	Lisacullion	259	3	24d	Monaghan	Farney	Magheross	Carrickmacross	III.	274
60	Lisadavil	100	1	14	Tyrone	Dungannon Lower	Carnteel	Clogher	III.	298
28	Lisadearny	126	2	11	Fermanagh	Magherastephana	Aghalurcher	Lisna-kea	III.	217
32	Lisaderg	198	1	21	Cavan	Upper Loughtee	Lavey	Cavan	III.	86
18	Lisaderg or Corweelis	207	2	28	Cavan	Tullygarvey	Drumgoon	Cootehill	III.	88
12	Lisadian	197	1	33	Armagh	Armagh	Eglish	Armagh	III.	44
21	Lisadian	693	2	27	Armagh	Orior Upper	Loughgilly	Newry	III.	58
14	Lisadian	392	1	2	Down	Lower Iveagh, Up. pt.	Hillsborough	Lisburn	III.	169
17	Lisadlooey	37	2	31	Leitrim	Drumahaire	Inishmagrath	Manorhamilton	IV.	97
20	Lisaghmore	295	2	7	Londonderry	Tirkeeran	Clondermot	Londonderry	III.	248
14	Lisaginny	103	0	32	Monaghan	Cremorne	Clontibret	Monaghan	III.	261
29	Lisagoan	696	3	8	Cavan	Clankee	Enniskeen	Bailieborough	III.	73
25	Li-agore	100	2	26	Monaghan	Farney	Donaghmoyne	Castleblayney	III.	270
41, 46	Lisalbanagh	223	2	35	Londonderry	Loughinsholin	Desertlyn	Magherafelt	III.	240
17	Lisalea	111	1	30	Monaghan	Dartree	Killeevan	Clones	III.	268
30	Lisamry	135	3	19c	Armagh	Fews Upper	Creggan	Castleblayney	III.	48
34	Lisanalsk	247	3	39	Cavan	Clankee	Bailieborough	Bailieborough	III.	71
35	Lisanelly	288	2	8f	Tyrone	Strabane Upper	Cappagh	Omagh	III.	325
31	Lisanisk	206	0	28g	Monaghan	Farney	Magheross	Carrickmacross	III.	274
35	Lisanisky	112	3	3	Cavan	Clankee	Enniskeen	Bailieborough	III.	73
30	Lisanny	210	0	33h	Cavan	Clanmahon	Drumlumman	Granard	III.	77
23	Li-aquil	169	2	19	Longford	Shrule	Kilglass	Ballymahon	I.	166
25	Lisaquiil	70	2	30	Monaghan	Farney	Donaghmoyne	Castleblayney	III.	270
24	Li-ard	76	1	6	Waterford	Decies without Drum	Ballylaneen	Kilmacthomas	II.	354
17	Lisarearke	149	1	26	Monaghan	Dartree	Currin	Clones	III.	266
16	Lisarney	242	0	12	Cavan	Tullygarvey	Drung	Cootehill	III.	89
12	Lisarrilly	118	3	37	Monaghan	Dartree	Killeevan	Monaghan	III.	268
35	Li-asturrin	83	1	30	Cavan	Clankee	Enniskeen	Bailieborough	III.	73
23, 29	Lisataggart	94	2	29	Cavan	Clankee	Shercock	Bailieborough	III.	74
21	Lisatawan	126	1	35	Cavan	Upper Loughtee	Larah	Cavan	III.	85
30, 31	Lisatlister	163	2	20	Monaghan	Farney	Magheracloone	Carrickmacross	III.	272
21	Lisatoo	150	3	19	Cavan	Upper Loughtee	Larah	Cavan	III.	85
92	Lisavaddy	164	3	12	Donegal	Banagh	Killaghtee	Donegal	III.	109
51	Lisavaddy	38	0	7	Tyrone	Clogher	Donacavey	Omagh	III.	294
9, 13	Lisavague	336	2	13	Armagh	Orior Lower	Kilmore	Banbridge	III.	56
3	Lisavargy	70	2	24	Monaghan	Trough	Errigal Trough	Monaghan	III.	284
17	Lisawaum	69	1	11i	Cavan	Tullygarvey	Drumgoon	Cootehill	III.	88
59, 67	Li-babe	554	2	35	Kerry	Magunihy	Aghadoe	Killarney	II.	199
44	Lisbalecly	267	3	29	Sligo	Coolavin	Kilfree	Boyle	IV.	224
28	Lisball	799	1	11	Cavan	Clankee	Bailieborough	Bailieborough	III.	71
4, 5	Lisballyard	610	2	12	Tipperary, N.R.	Lower Ormond	Dorrha	Parsonstown	II.	283
13, 18	Lisballyfroot	544	0	18	Kilkenny	Crannagh	Tullaroan	Kilkenny	I.	88
7, 8, 16, 17	Lisballynny	514	3	17	Cork. E.R.	Fermoy	Imphrick	Mallow	II.	80
78	Lisbalting	144	0	39	Tipperary, S.R.	Iffa and Offa East	Kilcash	Clonmel	II.	313
27	Lisbanagher	141	2	0	Sligo	Tirerrill	Kilmacallan	Sligo	IV.	240
61	Lisbancarney	79	0	13	Tyrone	Dungannon Middle	Clonfeacle	Dungannon	III.	299
14	Lisbane	242	3	9	Armagh	Orior Lower	Ballymore	Banbridge	III.	55
11, 12	Lisbane	111	0	16	Armagh	Tiranny	Eglish	Armagh	III.	59
2	Lisbane	214	1	30	Down	Ards Lower	Bangor	Newtownards	III.	157
25	Lisbane	258	1	26j	Down	Ards Upper	Ardkeen	Downpatrick	III.	159
10,11,16,17	Lisbane	661	3	18	Down	Castlereagh Lower	Tullynakill	Newtownards	III.	163
15, 22	Lisbane	788	3	20k	Down	Castlereagh Upper	Killaney	Lisburn	III.	165
31	Lisbane	156	1	27	Down	Lecale Lower	Saul	Downpatrick	III.	179
70	Lisbane	434	1	19	Kerry	Iveragh	Killinane	Cahersiveen	II.	197
19	Lisbane	370	2	8	Limerick	Shanid	Dunmoylan	Rathkeale	II.	255
9	Lisbane	36	3	17	Monaghan	Monaghan	Kilmore	Monaghan	III.	276
59, 65	Lisbane	120	3	33	Tyrone	Clogher	Clogher	Clogher	III.	293

(a) Including 4A. 0R. 32P. water.
(b) Including 7A. 1R. 32P. water.
(c) Including 2A. 0R. 11P. water.
(d) Including 5A. 1R. 2P. water.

(e) Including 40A. 2R. 37P. water.
(f) Including 7A. 1R. 10P. water.
(g) Including 7A. 0R. 36P. water.
(h) Including 19A. 0R. 38P. water.

(i) Including 1A. 0R. 24P. water.
(j) Including 7A. 0R. 5P. water.
(k) Including 15A. 2R. 7P. water.

No. of Sheet of the Ordnance Survey Maps.	Townlands and Towns.	Area in Statute Acres.			County.	Barony.	Parish.	Poor Law Union in 1857.	Townland Census of 1851, Part I.	
		A.	R.	P.					Vol.	Page
61	Lisbanlemneigh	88	2	6	Tyrone	Dungannon Middle	Clonfeacle	Dungannon	III.	299
12, 16	Lisbanoe	177	2	17	Armagh	Armagh	Lisnadill	Armagh	III.	45
10, 16	Lisbarnet	632	2	17	Down	Castlereagh Lower	Kilmood	Newtownards	III.	163
28, 36	Lisbarreen	466	2	8a	Clare	Tulla Upper	Kilnoe	Scarriff	II.	40
101	Lisbaun	64	1	10	Mayo	Clanmorris	Kilcolman	Claremorris	IV.	134
61, 71	Lisbaun	102	1	22	Mayo	Gallen	Meelick	Swineford	IV.	150
48	Lisbaun	298	2	3	Roscommon	Athlone	Kiltoom	Athlone	IV.	183
93	Lisbaun East	93	0	31	Mayo	Costello	Bekan	Claremorris	IV.	139
92	Lisbaun West	30	3	33b	Mayo	Costello	Bekan	Claremorris	IV.	139
108, 121	Lisbealad East	536	0	8	Cork, W.R.	East Carbery (W.D.)	Drinagh	Dunmanway	II.	131
120, 121	Lisbealad West	347	0	22	Cork, W.R.	East Carbery (W.D.)	Drinagh	Dunmanway	II.	131
100, 101	Lisbeg	353	0	30	Galway	Longford	Clonfert	Ballinasloe	IV.	57
59, 60	Lisbeg	233	2	13	Tyrone	Dungannon Lower	Carnteel	Clogher	III.	298
109, 122	Lisbehegh	255	2	4	Cork, W.R.	East Carbery (E.D.)	Desertserges	Clonakilty	II.	128
3	Lisbellanagroagh Beg	209	3	0	Antrim	Cary	Ballintoy	Ballycastle	III.	12
3	Lisbellanagroagh More	188	1	19	Antrim	Cary	Ballintoy	Ballycastle	III.	12
27	LISBELLAW T.	—			Fermanagh	Tirkennedy	Cleenish	Enniskillen	III.	220
32, 40	Lisbiggeen	102	1	3	Clare	Islands	Kilmaley	Ennis	II.	31
29, 50	Lisbigney	531	0	12	Queen's Co.	Cullenagh	Abbeyleix	Abbeyleix	I.	238
26, 32	Lisblake	317	0	2	Fermanagh	Clanawley	Killesher	Enniskillen	III.	193
90	Lisblowick	168	3	0	Mayo	Carra	Drum	Castlebar	IV.	128
16	Lisboduff	186	3	3	Cavan	Tullygarvey	Drung	Cootehill	III.	89
26	Lisbofin	77	3	9	Fermanagh	Clanawley	Cleenish	Enniskillen	III.	191
8	Lisbofin or Blackwatertown	259	0	31	Armagh	Armagh	Clonfeacle	Armagh	III.	43
52	Lisbook	80	1	18	Tipperary, N.R.	Eliogarty	Holycross	Cashel	II.	270
17	Lisboy	202	3	2	Antrim	Upper Dunluce	Kilraghts	Ballymoney	III.	20
31	Lisboy	117	3	9	Down	Lecale Lower	Saul	Downpatrick	III.	179
23	Lisboy	138	3	30	Fermanagh	Magherastephana	Aghavea	Lisnaskea	III.	219
18	Lisboy	117	1	19	Londonderry	Coleraine	Aghadowey	Coleraine	III.	230
6, 12	Lisboy	83	0	11	Meath	Lower Slane	Siddan	Ardee	I.	224
6	Lisboy	82	2	31	Monaghan	Trough	Donagh	Monaghan	III.	282
27	Lisboy	207	2	17	Roscommon	Castlereagh	Kilkeevin	Castlereagh	IV.	200
16, 22	Lisboy	235	0	2	Roscommon	Roscommon	Shankill	Strokestown	IV.	213
58	Lisboy	247	3	23	Tyrone	Clogher	Clogher	Clogher	III.	293
46	Lisboy	70	1	35	Tyrone	Dungannon Middle	Donaghmore	Dungannon	III.	302
39	Lisboy	152	2	14	Tyrone	Dungannon Upper	Artrea	Cookstown	III.	306
35, 43	Lisboy	272	2	10c	Tyrone	Omagh East	Cappagh	Omagh	III.	310
69, 70	Lisboy Beg	434	2	4	Cork, W.R.	West Muskerry	Kilnamartry	Macroom	II.	160
69	Lisboy More	533	2	15	Cork, W.R.	West Muskerry	Kilnamartry	Macroom	II.	160
8	Lisbrack	45	3	38	Longford	Longford	Clongesh	Longford	I.	158
13	Lisbrack	42	1	27	Longford	Longford	Templemichael	Longford	I.	160
22	Lisbrannan	159	1	23d	Monaghan	Dartree	Ematris	Cootehill	III.	267
16	Lisbree	238	1	12	Cavan	Tullygarvey	Drung	Cootehill	III.	89
28	Lisbreen	118	1	19	Antrim	Lower Antrim	Skerry	Ballymena	III.	5
28	Lisbreen Half Quarter	123	2	21	Antrim	Lower Antrim	Skerry	Ballymena	III.	5
40	Lisbride	254	3	3	Roscommon	Ballintober South	Roscommon	Roscommon	IV.	190
20, 26	Lisbrien	123	1	2	Tipperary, N.R.	Upper Ormond	Kilmore	Nenagh	IV.	291
7	Lisbrin	104	0	37	Mayo	Tirawley	Doonfeeny	Killala	IV.	167
123	Lisbrine	735	3	35	Galway	Kiltartan	Kilbeacanty	Gort	IV.	47
23	Lisbrockan	69	3	1	Leitrim	Leitrim	Kiltoghert	Cars. on Shannon	IV.	102
61	Lisbrogan	119	0	0	Mayo	Gallen	Meelick	Swineford	IV.	150
7	Lisbryan	13	3	10	Tipperary, N.R.	Lower Ormond	Aglishcloghane	Borrisokane	II.	281
7, 8	Lisbryan	460	2	20	Tipperary, N.R.	Lower Ormond	Ballingarry	Borrisokane	II.	282
28, 29	Lisbunny	849	3	14	Londonderry	Tirkeeran	Cumber Upper	Londonderry	III.	249
20, 21	Lisbunny	535	3	29	Tipperary, N.R.	Upper Ormond	Lisbunny	Nenagh	II.	292
68	LISBURN T.	—			Antrim	Upper Massereene	Blaris	Lisburn	III.	30
14	LISBURN T.	—			Down	Castlereagh Upper	Blaris	Lisburn	III.	164
39	Lisbush	123	2	34	Kildare	Kilkea and Moone	Ballaghmoon	Athy	I.	59
18	Liscabble	517	3	31	Tyrone	Strabane Upper	Bodoney Lower	Gortin	III.	323
39, 48	Liscahane	767	0	33	Cork, W.R.	West Muskerry	Drishane	Millstreet	II.	156
20, 21, 28, 29	Liscahane	915	0	34	Kerry	Trughanacmy	Ardfert	Tralee	II.	206
112	Liscahane Beg	87	1	30	Cork, E.R.	Kinsale	Clontead	Kinsale	II.	99
111, 112	Liscahane More	61	0	20	Cork, E.R.	Kinsale	Clontead	Kinsale	II.	99
20	Liscahill	241	0	28	Longford	Ardagh	Mostrim	Granard	I.	152
41	Liscahill	90	0	21	Tipperary, N.R.	Eliogarty	Thurles	Thurles	II.	273
31	Liscalgat	220	0	27	Armagh	Fews Upper	Creggan	Castleblayney	III.	48
18	Liscall	441	2	0	Londonderry	Coleraine	Errigal	Coleraine	III.	232
31	Liscallyroan	151	1	13	Leitrim	Leitrim	Kiltoghert	Cars. on Shannon	III.	102
45, 48	Liscam	69	0	6	Roscommon	Athlone	Cam	Athlone	IV.	180
69, 70	Liscananaun	951	1	32	Galway	Clare	Lackagh	Galway	IV.	23
14, 15, 22, 23	Liscannor	171	0	14	Clare	Corcomroe	Kilmacrehy	Ennistimon	II.	20
14, 15	LISCANNOR T.	—			Clare	Corcomroe	Kilmacrehy	Ennistimon	II.	20

(a) Including 11A. 3R. 10P. water.
(b) Including 1A. 1R. 21P. water.
(c) Including 5A. 3R. 12P. water.
(d) Including 19A. 3R. 28P. water.

No. of Sheet of the Ordnance Survey Maps	Townlands and Towns.	Area in Statute Acres.	County.	Barony.	Parish.	Poor Law Union in 1857.	Townland Census of 1851, Part I.	
		A. R. P.					Vol.	Page
87	Liscappul	121 1 22	Galway	Clonmacnowen	Kilcloony	Ballinasloe	IV.	25
24	Liscarban	203 3 7	Leitrim	Leitrim	Kiltubbrid	Car*. on Shannon	IV.	104
34	Liscarnan	128 1 8	Monaghan	Farney	Magheracloone	Carrickmacross	III.	272
35	Liscarney	182 1 12	Kerry	Corkaguiny	Ballyduff	Dingle	II.	174
97, 98	Liscarney	393 1 12a	Mayo	Murrisk	Aghagower	Westport	IV.	159
9	Liscarney	60 2 14	Monaghan	Monaghan	Tehallan	Monaghan	III.	280
58, 59	Liscarrigane	553 2 1	Cork, W.R.	West Muskerry	Clondrohid	Macroom	II.	155
16	Liscarroll	116 2 22	Cork, E.R.	Orrery and Kilmore	Liscarroll	Mallow	II.	109
16	LISCARROLL T.	—	Cork, E.R.	Orrery and Kilmore	Liscarroll	Mallow	II.	109
24, 25	Liscartan	771 1 15	Meath	Lower Navan	Liscartan	Navan	I.	215
40, 49	Liscasey	2,064 3 1b	Clare	Islands	Clondagad	Killadysert	II.	29
92	Liscat	419 1 0	Mayo	Costello	Aghamore	Claremorris	IV.	137
12, 13	Liscat	58 1 7	Monaghan	Monaghan	Drumsnat	Monaghan	III.	275
39	Liscausy	107 2 30	Tyrone	Dungannon Upper	Artrea	Cookstown	III.	306
62	Lisclamerty	417 1 17	Donegal	Raphoe	Raymoghy	Letterkenny	III.	142
23	Lisclogher	230 0 29	Cavan	Clankee	Drumgoon	Cootehill	III.	72
14	Lisclogher Great	1,565 1 2	Westmeath	Delvin	Castletowndelvin	Castletowndelvin	I.	264
14	Lisclogher Little or Earlsmeadow	199 0 18	Westmeath	Delvin	Castletowndelvin	Castletowndelvin	I.	264
21	Lisclone	179 2 9	Cavan	Tullygarvey	Larah	Cootehill	III.	91
35	Liscloonadea	224 1 35c	Leitrim	Mohill	Mohill	Mohill	IV.	108
13,14,21,22	Lisclooney	785 2 33	King's Co.	Garrycastle	Tisaran	Parsonstown	I.	138
3	Liscloon Lower	269 2 13	Tyrone	Strabane Lower	Donaghedy	Strabane	III.	321
46	Liscloonmeeltoge	165 0 14	Galway	Killian	Moylough	Mountbellew	IV.	45
3	Liscloon Upper	346 0 35	Tyrone	Strabane Lower	Donaghedy	Strabane	III.	321
77	Lisclovaun	98 0 26	Mayo	Burrishoole	Kilmeenagh	Westport	IV.	122
102	Liscluman	152 3 39	Mayo	Costello	Bekan	Claremorris	IV.	139
41, 44	Liscoffy (Kelly)	222 2 33	Roscommon	Athlone	Athleague	Roscommon	IV.	179
44	Liscoffy (Madden)	152 2 22	Roscommon	Athlone	Athleague	Roscommon	IV.	179
7	Liscolman	340 1 34	Antrim	Lower Dunluce	Billy	Ballymoney	III.	16
37	Liscolman	947 3 16	Wicklow	Shillelagh	Liscolman	Shillelagh	I.	357
11	Liscolvan	86 1 25	Roscommon	Ballintober North	Kilmore	Car*. on Shannon	IV.	187
10	Lisconduff	113 2 38	Monaghan	Cremorne	Tehallan	Monaghan	III.	262
60	Lisconduff	205 3 3	Tyrone	Dungannon Lower	Carnteel	Dungannon	III.	298
22, 23	Liscongill	247 1 26	Cork, E.R.	Duhallow	Clonfert	Kanturk	II.	68
16	Lisconly	61 0 7	Galway	Dunmore	Tuam	Tuam	IV.	36
12	Lisconnan	492 2 19	Antrim	Lower Dunluce	Derrykeighan	Ballymoney	III.	17
26	Lisconny	242 3 17	Sligo	Tirerrill	Drumcolumb	Sligo	IV.	238
51	Lisconor	102 3 17	Clare	Bunratty Lower	Clonloghan	Ennis	II.	3
27	Lisconor	96 3 17	Leitrim	Leitrim	Kiltoghert	Car*. on Shannon	IV.	102
50, 57	Lisconrea	146 3 36	Tyrone	Clogher	Donacavey	Omagh	III.	294
39	Lisconry	85 3 18	Sligo	Corran	Drumrat	Boyle	IV.	226
78, 79	Liscooly	127 1 5d	Donegal	Raphoe	Donaghmore	Stranorlar	III.	138
4	Liscoonera	153 1 12	Clare	Burren	Killonaghan	Ballyvaghan	II.	13
59	Liscormick	275 3 4e	Clare	Clonderalaw	Killadysert	Killadysert	II.	16
23	Liscormick	188 0 34	Longford	Shrule	Agharra	Ballymahon	I.	166
6	Liscorran	183 0 34	Armagh	Oneilland East	Shankill	Lurgan	III.	51
31	Liscorran	28 1 19	Monaghan	Farney	Magheracloone	Carrickmacross	III.	273
21	Liscorry	61 2 37	Louth	Drogheda	St. Peter's	Drogheda	I.	175
28	Liscosker	27 2 26	Fermanagh	Magherastephana	Aghavea	Lisnaskea	III.	219
72, 81	Liscosker	160 2 38	Mayo	Costello	Aghamore	Swineford	IV.	137
71	Liscottle	119 3 17	Mayo	Gallen	Kilconduff	Swineford	IV.	148
106, 107	Liscoyle	517 1 7	Galway	Longford	Abbeygormacan	Ballinasloe	IV.	56
39	Liscreagh	405 1 28	Cork, W.R.	West Muskerry	Drishane	Millstreet	II.	156
7	Liscreagh	146 2 22	Limerick	Owneybeg	Abington	Limerick	II.	251
34, 35, 41	Liscreagh	257 1 19	Tipperary, N.R.	Eliogarty	Inch	Thurles	II.	270
10	Liscreevaghan or Cla- dy-sproul	121 2 20f	Tyrone	Strabane Lower	Ardstraw	Strabane	III.	319
10, 11	Liscreevin	198 2 10	Fermanagh	Lurg	Derryvullan	Lowtherstown	III.	204
69,70,78,79	Liscromwell	259 1 20	Mayo	Carra	Aglish	Castlebar	IV.	124
121, 122	Liscubba	462 2 11	Cork, W.R.	East Carbery W.D.	Kilmeen	Clonakilty	II.	134
22, 25	Liscuilfea	97 3 2g	Leitrim	Carrigallen	Oughteragh	Bawnboy	IV.	92
32, 46	Liscuill	640 3 37	Galway	Killian	Killian	Mountbellew	IV.	44
18	Liscuillew Lower	168 2 31	Leitrim	Drumahaire	Inishmagrath	Manorhamilton	IV.	97
17, 18, 20	Liscuillew Upper	265 3 28	Leitrim	Drumahaire	Inishmagrath	Manorhamilton	IV.	97
2	Liscullane	257 3 3	Cork, E.R.	Orrery and Kilmore	Shandrum	Kilmallock	II.	110
15	Liscullane	371 0 20	Kerry	Clanmaurice	Kilcaragh	Listowel	II.	169
15	Liscullane	219 0 1	Kerry	Clanmaurice	Kiltomy	Listowel	II.	172
17, 25	Liscullaun	133 1 26	Clare	Inchiquin	Rath	Corrofin	II.	27
35	Liscullaun	510 2 13h	Clare	Tulla, Upper	Tulla	Tulla	II.	42
13, 18	Liscumasky	321 3 5	Monaghan	Dartree	Aghabog	Monaghan	III.	263
73	Liscune Lower	369 2 22	Galway	Kilconnell	Ballymacward	Ballinasloe	IV.	39
73	Liscune Upper	291 2 30	Galway	Kilconnell	Ballymacward	Ballinasloe	IV.	39

(a) Including 10A. 1R. 3P. water.
(b) Including 7A. 2R. 28P. water.
(c) Including 10A. 3R. 4P. water.
(d) Including 6A. 1R. 8P. water.
(e) Including 9A. 0R. 6P. water.
(f) Including 3A. 1R. 21P. water.
(g) Including 4A. 1R. 28P. water.
(h) Including 2A. 0R. 3P. water.

No. of Sheet of the Ordnance Survey Maps	Townlands and Towns.	Area in Statute Acres.	County.	Barony.	Parish.	Poor Law Union in 1857.	Townland Census of 1851, Part I. Vol.	Page
		A. R. P.						
89	Liscunnell	149 1 22	Mayo	Carra	Ballyhean	Castlebar	IV.	125
5	Liscurry	79 3 15	Tyrone	Strabane Lower	Leckpatrick	Strabane	III.	322
23	Lisdachon	282 3 6	Westmeath	Kilkenny West	Kilkenny West	Athlone	I.	273
32, 33, 35	Lisdadanan	136 0 21a	Leitrim	Mohill	Mohill	Mohill	IV.	108
15, 16	Lisdalgan	481 3 27	Down	Castlereagh Upper	Saintfield	Lisburn	III.	166
30	Lisdalleen & Drummin	596 2 36	Tipperary, N.R.	Ikerrin	Templetouhy	Thurles	II.	277
14	Lisdaly	196 1 19	King's Co.	Garrycastle	Tisaran	Parsonstown	I.	138
10	Lisdaly	361 2 16b	Roscommon	Boyle	Killummod	Boyle	IV.	196
22	Lisdangan	345 2 36	Cork, E.R.	Duhallow	Clonfert	Kanturk	II.	68
20	Lisdaran	125 0 38	Cavan	Upper Loughtee	Urney	Cavan	III.	86
43, 44	Lisdargan	902 1 24	Kerry	Corkaguiny	Cloghane	Dingle	II.	175
17	Lisdarragh	146 1 37	Monaghan	Dartree	Killeevan	Clones	III.	268
5, 8	Lisdarush	608 3 19	Leitrim	Rosclogher	Rossinver	Manorhamilton	IV.	111
31	Lisdauky	103 0 17	Leitrim	Leitrim	Kiltoghert	Cark. on Shannon	IV.	102
42	Lisdaulan	709 3 26	Roscommon	Athlone	Killinvoy	Roscommon	IV.	182
46, 47	Lisdavuck	70 2 31	King's Co.	Clonlish	Castletownely	Roscrea	I.	129
14	Lisdead	95 2 8	Fermanagh	Magheraboy	Devenish	Enniskillen	III.	211
21	Lisdeegin	84 2 5	Cavan	Upper Loughtee	Castleterra	Cavan	III.	83
56	Lisdeen	774 2 35	Clare	Moyarta	Kilfearagh	Kilrush	II.	32
107	Lisdeligny	656 3 30	Galway	Longford	Killimorbologue	Portumna	IV.	59
51	Lisdergan	23 0 9	Tyrone	Clogher	Donacavey	Omagh	III.	294
14, 22	Lisderg or Bellmount	420 2 18	King's Co.	Garrycastle	Tisaran	Parsonstown	I.	138
14, 15	Lisdermot	368 1 33	King's Co.	Garrycastle	Wheery or Killagally	Parsonstown	I.	139
54	Lisdermot	95 2 11	Tyrone	Dungannon Middle	Clonfeacle	Dungannon	III.	299
26, 32	Lisderry	195 0 10	Fermanagh	Clanawley	Killesher	Enniskillen	III.	193
21, 22	Lisdillon	1,590 3 26	Londonderry	Tirkeeran	Clondermot	Londonderry	III.	248
51, 52	Lisdillure	263 3 33	Roscommon	Athlone	Drum	Athlone	IV.	180
2	Lisdivin Lower	149 1 28c	Tyrone	Strabane Lower	Donaghedy	Strabane	III.	321
2	Lisdivin Upper	102 2 19	Tyrone	Strabane Lower	Donaghedy	Strabane	III.	321
32	Lisdivrick	160 0 4	Fermanagh	Clanawley	Killesher	Enniskillen	III.	193
23	Lisdoagh	101 3 11d	Cavan	Clankee	Drumgoon	Cootehill	III.	72
59	Lisdoart	190 0 21	Tyrone	Dungannon Lower	Carnteel	Clogher	III.	298
42	Lisdonagh	258 0 31e	Galway	Clare	Donaghpatrick	Tuam	IV.	19
23, 28	Lisdonan	220 2 12f	Cavan	Clankee	Knockbride	Bailieborough	III.	74
73	Lisdonnellroe	130 0 6g	Galway	Kilconnell	Kilconnell	Ballinasloe	IV.	40
32	Lisdonnish	134 3 11	Cavan	Castlerahan	Crosserlough	Cavan	III.	68
20	Lisdonny	282 3 14h	Monaghan	Cremorne	Muckno	Castleblayney	III.	262
36	Lisdonowley	462 0 8	Tipperary, N.R.	Eliogarty	Moyne	Thurles	II.	271
12	Lisdonwilly	145 3 24	Armagh	Armagh	Grange	Armagh	III.	45
7	Lisdoo	120 2 1	Louth	Upper Dundalk	Dundalk	Dundalk	I.	178
49	Lisdoo	153 2 39	Tyrone	Omagh East	Kilskeery	Lowtherstown	III.	313
5	Lisdoo	166 2 1	Tyrone	Strabane Lower	Leckpatrick	Strabane	III.	322
9	Lisdoo	340 3 22	Tyrone	Strabane Lower	Urney	Strabane	III.	322
108	Lisdooaun	318 2 1	Galway	Longford	Donanaghta	Portumna	IV.	58
14, 15, 20, 21	Lisdoodan	188 1 22	Fermanagh	Magheraboy	Devenish	Enniskillen	III.	211
33, 34, 40	Lisdoogan	226 0 21	Sligo	Corran	Kilmorgan	Sligo	IV.	227
15, 16	Lisdoonan	518 1 20	Down	Castlereagh Upper	Saintfield	Lisburn	III.	166
28	Lisdoonan	169 0 11	Monaghan	Farney	Donaghmoyne	Carrickmacross	III.	270
8	Lisdoonvarna	635 2 3	Clare	Burren	Kilmoon	Ballyvaghan	II.	13
8, 9	Lisdoony East	59 0 4	Clare	Corcomroe	Kilfenora	Ennistimon	II.	19
8, 15	Lisdoony West	257 2 23	Clare	Corcomroe	Kilfenora	Ennistimon	II.	19
84	Lisdoran	72 1 10	Galway	Tiaquin	Monivea	Loughrea	IV.	79
27, 28	Lisdornan	835 0 36	Meath	Upper Duleek	Moorechurch	Drogheda	I.	198
16, 23	Lisdossan	455 1 12	Westmeath	Kilkenny West	Noughaval	Ballymahon	I.	274
11, 12	Lisdown	131 3 20	Armagh	Tiranny	Eglish	Armagh	III.	59
4, 9	Lisdowney	1,755 1 18	Kilkenny	Galmoy	Aharney	Urlingford	I.	91
9	LISDOWNEY T.	—	Kilkenny	Galmoy	Aharney	Urlingford	I.	91
19	Lisdreenagh	192 0 27	Longford	Ardagh	Kilglass	Longford	I.	152
24	Lisdromacrone	108 1 13	Leitrim	Leitrim	Kiltubbrid	Cark. on Shannon	IV.	104
28, 32	Lisdromafarna	184 0 13	Leitrim	Leitrim	Kiltoghert	Cark. on Shannon	IV.	102
28, 32	Lisdromarea North	265 0 5i	Leitrim	Leitrim	Kiltoghert	Cark. on Shannon	IV.	102
28, 32	Lisdromarea South	57 1 20	Leitrim	Leitrim	Kiltoghert	Cark. on Shannon	IV.	102
28	Lisdrum	107 3 34	Fermanagh	Magherastephana	Aghavea	Lisnaskea	III.	219
11, 12	Lisdrumard	272 1 25	Armagh	Armagh	Lisnadill	Armagh	III.	45
15, 16	Lisdrumbrughas	511 0 26	Armagh	Armagh	Derrynoose	Armagh	III.	44
21	Lisdrumchor Lower	147 0 7	Armagh	Fews Lower	Loughgilly	Armagh	II.	47
21	Lisdrumchor Upper	501 3 15j	Armagh	Fews Lower	Loughgilly	Armagh	II.	47
23	Lisdrumcleve	331 1 34k	Monaghan	Cremorne	Aghnamullen	Castleblayney	III.	258
10	Lisdrumdoagh	103 1 36	Monaghan	Monaghan	Monaghan	Monaghan	III.	277
23	Lisdrumfad	160 1 10	Cavan	Clankee	Shercock	Bailieborough	III.	74
32	Lisdrumgivel Lower	77 3 22	Leitrim	Leitrim	Mohill	Mohill	IV.	104
28, 32	Lisdrumgivel Upper	94 1 6	Leitrim	Leitrim	Mohill	Mohill	IV.	104
14, 15	Lisdrumgormly	255 3 20	Monaghan	Cremorne	Clontibret	Castleblayney	III.	261

(a) Including 16A. 3R. 39P. water.　　(e) Including 32A. 1R. 27P. water.　　(i) Including 16A. 1R. 16P. water.
(b) Including 10A. 3R. 34P. water.　　(f) Including 16A. 3R. 10P. water.　　(j) Including 16A. 3R. 24P. water.
(c) Including 4A. 0R. 27P. water.　　(g) Including 14A. 3R. 36P. water.　　(k) Including 23A. 3R. 7P. water.
(d) Including 11A. 3R. 10P. water.　　(h) Including 6A. 0R. 15P. water.

No. of Sheet of the Ordnance Survey Maps.	Townlands and Towns.	Area in Statute Acres.			County.	Barony.	Parish.	Poor Law Union in 1857.	Townland Census of 1851, Part I.	
		A.	R.	P.					Vol.	Page
17, 18	Lisdrumgran .	90	1	19	Leitrim . .	Drumahaire . .	Inishmagrath . .	Manorhamilton .	IV.	97
26	Lisdrumgullion	500	2	21a	Armagh . .	Orior Upper . .	Newry . . .	Newry . .	III.	59
26	Lisdrumliska .	306	0	30	Armagh . .	Orior Upper . .	Newry . . .	Newry . .	III.	59
14	Lisdrumneill .	329	2	10	Roscommon .	Frenchpark . .	Tibohine . .	Castlereagh .	IV.	205
23	Lisdrumskea .	248	2	37b	Cavan . .	Clankee . .	Shercock . .	Bailieborough .	III.	74
30	Lisdrumturk . .	337	0	35	Monaghan . .	Farney . .	Magheross . .	Carrickmacross	III.	274
38	Lisduane . .	677	2	36	Limerick . .	Connello Upper .	Ballingarry . .	Croom . .	II.	231
43, 44	Lisduff . . .	267	0	4	Cavan . .	Castlerahan . .	Lurgan . .	Oldcastle . .	III.	70
37, 38	Lisduff . . .	471	2	20	Cavan . .	Clanmahon . .	Ballymachugh .	Cavan . .	III.	76
25	Lisduff . . .	125	1	19	Cavan . .	Upper Loughtee .	Kilmore . .	Cavan . .	III.	84
51	Lisduff . . .	264	2	6	Clare . .	Bunratty Lower .	Kilnasoolagh . .	Ennis . .	II.	6
11	Lisduff . . .	257	0	4c	Clare . .	Inchiquin . .	Killinaboy . .	Corrofin . .	II.	27
17	Lisduff . . .	103	1	22	Clare . .	Inchiquin . .	Ruan . .	Corrofin . .	II.	28
53, 54	Lisduff . . .	180	2	17	Clare . .	Tulla Lower . .	Kiltenanlea . .	Limerick . .	II.	37
35	Lisduff . . .	314	3	11	Clare . .	Tulla Upper . .	Tulla . .	Tulla . .	II.	42
144	Lisduff . . .	161	0	27	Cork, W.R. .	Ibane and Barryroe	Rathbarry . .	Clonakilty .	II.	150
46	Lisduff . . .	278	1	24	Down . .	Lordship of Newry .	Newry . .	Newry . .	III.	182
28	Lisduff . . .	87	0	27	Fermanagh .	Magherastephana .	Aghalurcher .	Lisnaskea .	III.	217
20	Lisduff . . .	104	0	15	Galway . .	Ballymoe . .	Kilbegnet . .	Roscommon .	IV.	8
5	Lisduff . . .	304	1	12	Galway . .	Dunmore . .	Dunmore . .	Tuam . .	IV.	34
85	Lisduff . . .	204	1	13	Galway . .	Kilconnell . .	Killimordaly . .	Loughrea .	IV.	42
107, 117	Lisduff . . .	264	0	2	Galway . .	Longford . .	Tynagh . .	Portumna .	IV.	62
97, 105	Lisduff . . .	211	1	18	Galway . .	Loughrea . .	Loughrea . .	Loughrea . .	IV.	66
14	Lisduff . . .	284	2	17	Kerry . .	Clanmaurice . .	Killury . .	Listowel . .	II.	171
9	Lisduff . . .	69	1	9	Kilkenny . .	Fassadinin . .	Grangemaccomb .	Urlingford .	I.	89
38	Lisduff . . .	398	2	2	King's Co. .	Clonlisk . .	Kilcolman . .	Parsonstown .	I.	130
31	Lisduff . . .	295	0	8	King's Co. .	Eglish . .	Drumcullen . .	Parsonstown .	I.	134
14	Lisduff . . .	155	1	8	King's Co. .	Garrycastle . .	Tisaran . .	Parsonstown .	I.	138
32	Lisduff . . .	97	0	21	Leitrim . .	Leitrim . .	Annaduff . .	Cark. on Shannon	IV.	99
31	Lisduff . . .	77	3	38	Leitrim . .	Leitrim . .	Kiltoghert . .	Cark. on Shannon	IV.	102
30	Lisduff . . .	106	0	7	Limerick . .	Connello Upper .	Ballingarry . .	Croom . .	II.	231
14, 19	Lisduff . . .	67	3	8	Longford . .	Ardagh . .	Ardagh . .	Longford . .	I.	151
13, 14	Lisduff . . .	343	0	36	Longford . .	Ardagh . .	Ballymacormick .	Longford . .	I.	152
10, 15	Lisduff . . .	195	0	35	Longford . .	Granard . .	Clonbroney . .	Granard . .	I.	155
17	Lisduff . . .	47	0	24	Longford . .	Rathcline . .	Rathcline . .	Longford . .	I.	165
67	Lisduff . . .	26	2	29	Mayo . .	Burrishoole . .	Burrishoole . .	Newport . .	IV.	120
112	Lisduff . . .	360	2	28	Mayo . .	Clanmorris . .	Crossboyne . .	Claremorris .	IV.	133
101	Lisduff . . .	228	0	3	Mayo . .	Clanmorris . .	Kilcolman . .	Claremorris .	IV.	134
103	Lisduff . . .	159	0	1	Mayo . .	Costello . .	Annagh . .	Claremorris .	IV.	138
71, 72, 80	Lisduff . . .	287	3	17	Mayo . .	Gallen . .	Killedan . .	Swineford .	IV.	150
61	Lisduff . . .	216	1	32d	Mayo . .	Gallen . .	Meelick . .	Swineford .	IV.	150
118	Lisduff . . .	66	3	10	Mayo . .	Kilmaine . .	Kilmainemore .	Ballinrobe .	IV.	156
24	Lisduff . . .	270	1	6	Monaghan . .	Cremorne . .	Aghnamullen .	Castleblayney .	III.	258
27, 33	Lisduff . . .	832	2	29	Queen's Co. .	Clandonagh . .	Rathdowney .	Donaghmore .	I.	234
41, 44	Lisduff . . .	221	2	0	Roscommon .	Athlone . .	Tisrara . .	Roscommon .	IV.	185
14, 15	Lisduff . . .	297	3	27	Roscommon .	Frenchpark . .	Tibohine . .	Castlereagh .	IV.	205
23	Lisduff . . .	207	2	4	Roscommon .	Roscommon . .	Kiltrustan . .	Strokestown .	IV.	211
9, 15	Lisduff . . .	275	2	21	Sligo . .	Carbury . .	Calry . .	Sligo . .	IV.	220
20	Lisduff . . .	152	2	4	Sligo . .	Leyny . .	Ballysadare .	Sligo . .	IV.	230
41, 42	Lisduff . . .	230	1	6	Tipperary, N.R.	Eliogarty . .	Rahelty . .	Thurles . .	II.	272
16,17,22,23	Lisduff . . .	263	2	27	Tipperary, N.R.	Ikerrin . .	Rathnaveoge . .	Roscrea . .	II.	276
4, 7	Lisduff . . .	508	0	11	Tipperary, N.R.	Lower Ormond .	Aglishcloghane .	Borrisokane .	II.	281
26	Lisduff . . .	40	2	37	Tipperary, N.R.	Upper Ormond .	Kilmore . .	Nenagh . .	II.	291
66	Lisduff . . .	236	1	3	Tipperary, S.R.	Clanwilliam . .	Lattin . .	Tipperary . .	II.	309
43	Lisduff . . .	638	1	1	Tipperary, S.R.	Slievardagh . .	Kilcooly . .	Urlingford .	II.	334
61	Lisduff . . .	76	1	2	Tyrone . .	Dungannon Middle .	Clonfeacle . .	Dungannon .	III.	299
2	Lisduff . . .	142	2	26	Westmeath .	Moygoish . .	Street . .	Granard . .	I.	281
19	Lisduff (Montgomery)	355	0	2	Longford . .	Moydow . .	Ardagh . .	Longford . .	I.	160
117	Lisduff South . .	80	2	14	Galway . .	Leitrim . .	Tynagh . .	Portumna .	IV.	55
17	Lisduggan . .	58	0	11	Waterford . .	Middlethird . .	Kilburne . .	Waterford .	II.	367
9	Lisduggan Big .	198	1	24	Waterford . .	Middlethird . .	Trinity Without .	Waterford .	II.	369
9	Lisduggan Little .	9	0	10	Waterford . .	Middlethird . .	Trinity Without .	Waterford .	II.	369
23, 24	Lisduggan North .	221	3	11	Cork, E.R. .	Duhallow . .	Castlemagner .	Kanturk . .	II.	67
23	Lisduggan South .	304	3	25	Cork, E.R. .	Duhallow . .	Castlemagner .	Kanturk . .	II.	67
118	Lisduneen . .	23	0	9	Galway . .	Longford . .	Tiranascragh . .	Portumna .	IV.	62
21	Lisdunvis Glebe .	67	2	18	Cavan . .	Upper Loughtee .	Castleterra . .	Cavan . .	III.	83
116	Lisdurra . .	91	0	18	Galway . .	Leitrim . .	Ballynakill . .	Loughrea . .	IV.	52
61	Lisdurraun . .	151	3	35	Mayo . .	Gallen . .	Meelick . .	Swineford .	IV.	150
39, 48	Lisduvoge . .	295	2	8e	Mayo . .	Tirawley . .	Kilbelfad . .	Ballina . .	IV.	168
20	Liscenan . .	362	2	24	Monaghan . .	Cremorne . .	Muckno . .	Castleblayney .	III.	262
11	Lisoggorton . .	151	1	55f	Monaghan . .	Dartree . .	Clones . .	Clones . .	III.	264
21	Lisegny . .	135	2	25	Cavan . .	Tullygarvey . .	Larah . .	Cootehill . .	III.	91
47	Lisfannan . .	487	3	37	Donegal . .	Inishowen West .	Burt . .	Londonderry .	III.	120

(a) Including 19A. 0R. 8P. water.   (c) Including 18A. 0R. 22P. water.   (e) Including 17A. 1R. 32P. water.

(b) Including 13A. 0R. 23P. water.   (d) Including 15A. 2R. 5P. water.   (f) Including 8A. 2R. 34P. water.

No. of Sheet of the Ordnance Survey Maps.	Townlands and Towns.	Area in Statute Acres. A. R. P.	County.	Barony.	Parish.	Poor Law Union in 1857.	Townland Census of 1851, Part I. Vol.	Page
29, 38	Lisfannan	553 2 14	Donegal	Inishowen West	Fahan Upper	Londonderry	III.	121
14	Lisfarrell	319 1 13	Longford	Ardagh	Templemichael	Longford	I.	154
7	Lisfarrellboy	42 1 26	Roscommon	Boyle	Tumna	Boyle	IV.	198
53	Lisfearty	175 3 1	Tyrone	Dungannon Lower	Killeeshil	Dungannon	III.	298
98	Lisfehill	302 2 21	Cork, E.R.	Kinalea	Ballinaboy	Kinsale	II.	93
45	Lisfelim	806 1 14a	Roscommon	Athlone	St. John's	Athlone	IV.	184
31	Lisfennel	8 1 11	Waterford	Decies without Drum	Dungarvan	Dungarvan	II.	355
31	Lisfennel	110 2 13	Waterford	Decies without Drum	Kilrush	Dungarvan	II.	358
108	Lisfinny	192 3 38	Galway	Longford	Donanaghta	Portumna	IV.	58
28	Lisfinny	115 1 13	Waterford	Coshmore & Coshbride	Lismore and Mocollop	Lismore	II.	346
17, 18, 20	Lisfuiltaghan	360 2 25	Leitrim	Drumahaire	Inishmagrath	Manorhamilton	IV.	97
86	Lisfunshion	722 0 11	Tipperary, S.R.	Iffa and Offa West	Templetenny	Clogheen	II.	320
12	Lisgall	67 2 16	Monaghan	Dartree	Clones	Clones	III.	264
28	Lisgall	155 1 23	Monaghan	Farney	Donaghmoyne	Carrickmacross	III.	270
53, 54, 60	Lisgallon	258 0 13	Tyrone	Dungannon Middle	Donaghmore	Dungannon	III.	302
32	Lisgally	61 0 19	Fermanagh	Clanawley	Killesher	Enniskillen	III.	193
21	Lisgannon	294 0 17	Cavan	Tullygarvey	Drung	Cootehill	III.	89
28	Lisgar	299 1 39	Cavan	Clankee	Bailieborough	Bailieborough	III.	71
100	Lisgar	98 0 16	Galway	Longford	Clonfert	Ballinasloe	IV.	57
31	Lisgarney	95 1 20	Leitrim	Leitrim	Kiltoghert	Cark. on Shannon	IV.	102
15, 21	Lisgarode	318 2 15	Tipperary, N.R.	Upper Ormond	Kilruane	Nenagh	II.	292
10, 15	Lisgarriff	81 3 38	Tipperary, N.R.	Lower Ormond	Ardcrony	Borrisokane	II.	282
27, 33	Lisgarriff	91 0 27	Tipperary, N.R.	Upper Ormond	Dolla	Nenagh	II.	290
27, 33	Lisgarriff East	154 3 25	Tipperary, N.R.	Upper Ormond	Dolla	Nenagh	II.	290
27, 33	Lisgarriff West	380 2 22	Tipperary, N.R.	Upper Ormond	Dolla	Nenagh	II.	290
17	Lisgarvan	217 3 1	Carlow	Forth	Gilbertstown	Carlow	I.	4
16	Lisgarve	218 1 7	Roscommon	Frenchpark	Kilmacumsy	Boyle	IV.	203
16	Lisgaugh	139 1 22	Limerick	Coonagh	Doon	Tipperary	II.	234
17	Lisgavneen	386 0 11	Leitrim	Drumahaire	Killarga	Manorhamilton	IV.	99
68	Lisgibbon	327 0 23	Tipperary, S.R.	Clanwilliam	Relickmurry & Athassel	Tipperary	II.	310
44	Lisgillalea	180 1 9	Roscommon	Athlone	Tisrara	Roscommon	IV.	185
18	Lisgillan	295 0 16b	Monaghan	Cremorne	Aghnamullen	Cootehill	III.	258
29	Lisgillock Glebe	1,063 0 25c	Leitrim	Mohill	Cloone	Mohill	IV.	106
59, 60	Lisginny	113 2 22	Tyrone	Dungannon Lower	Carnteel	Clogher	III.	298
66	Lisglasheen	49 1 31	Cork, E.R.	Imokilly	Killeagh	Youghal	II.	88
20, 21	Lisglass	554 1 18	Londonderry	Tirkeeran	Clondermot	Londonderry	III.	248
34	Lisglass	64 2 11	Waterford	Coshmore & Coshbride	Kilcockan	Lismore	II.	343
14	Lisglassan	138 3 13	Monaghan	Cremorne	Clontibret	Monaghan	III.	261
23	Lisglassock	113 0 38	Longford	Shrule	Kilcommock	Ballymahon	I.	166
17	Lisglenbeha	151 3 6	Tipperary, N.R.	Ikerrin	Corbally	Roscrea	II.	275
22	Lisglennon	361 3 39d	Mayo	Tirawley	Ballysakeery	Ballina	IV.	165
15	Lisglynn	248 3 11	Armagh	Armagh	Derrynoose	Armagh	III.	44
7	Lisgoagh	102 0 33	Monaghan	Trough	Donagh	Monaghan	III.	282
36, 40	Lisgobban	256 1 37	Roscommon	Ballintober South	Kilbride	Roscommon	IV.	189
61	Lisgobban	135 0 6	Tyrone	Dungannon Middle	Clonfeacle	Dungannon	III.	299
52, 53	Lisgonnell	121 3 4	Tyrone	Clogher	Errigal Keerogue	Clogher	III.	295
5	Lisgoogan	223 1 33	Clare	Burren	Rathborney	Ballyvaghan	II.	14
1	Lisgool	28 1 18	Leitrim	Rosclogher	Rossinver	Ballyshannon	IV.	112
65	Lisgoold East	367 1 29	Cork, E.R.	Barrymore	Lisgoold	Middleton	II.	56
65	Lisgoold North	325 3 9	Cork, E.R.	Barrymore	Lisgoold	Middleton	II.	56
65	Lisgoold West	213 3 26	Cork, E.R.	Barrymore	Lisgoold	Middleton	II.	56
22, 27	Lisgoole	135 0 10e	Fermanagh	Clanawley	Rossorry	Enniskillen	III.	194
28	Lisgordan	216 2 29	Limerick	Shanid	Rathronan	Glin	II.	257
15	Lisgorey	85 2 4	Sligo	Carbury	Calry	Sligo	IV.	220
32, 33	Lisgorgan Glebe	179 1 16	Londonderry	Loughinsholin	Tamlaght O'Crilly	Ballymoney	III.	243
11, 15	Lisgorman	849 2 35	Leitrim	Drumahaire	Cloonlogher	Manorhamilton	IV.	94
71	Lisgormin	184 3 10	Mayo	Gallen	Bohola	Swineford	IV.	147
18	Lisgorran	196 2 30	Monaghan	Cremorne	Aghnamullen	Cootehill	III.	258
65	Lisgorran	219 0 12	Tyrone	Clogher	Clogher	Clogher	III.	293
79	Lisgowel	167 3 33	Mayo	Carra	Breaghwy	Castlebar	IV.	127
33, 39	Lisgrea	391 1 9f	Cavan	Castlerahan	Lurgan	Oldcastle	III.	70
6	Lisgreaghan	60 0 37	Roscommon	Boyle	Ardcarn	Boyle	IV.	193
3	Lisgrew	51 2 6	Monaghan	Trough	Errigal Trough	Monaghan	III.	284
16	Lisgriffin	308 1 16	Cork, E.R.	Orrery and Kilmore	Buttevant	Mallow	II.	107
35	Lisgriffin	161 2 9	Waterford	Decies within Drum	Aglish	Dungarvan	II.	349
22, 25	Lisgruddy	216 3 12	Leitrim	Carrigallen	Drumreilly	Bawnboy	IV.	91
60, 73	Lisgub East	473 1 8	Galway	Kilconnell	Ballymacward	Mountbellew	IV.	39
60, 73	Lisgub (Ward)	46 0 12	Galway	Tiaquin	Ballymacward	Mountbellew	IV.	75
60, 73	Lisgub West	112 1 36	Galway	Tiaquin	Ballymacward	Mountbellew	IV.	75
47	Lisgullaun	292 1 24	Sligo	Coolavin	Killaraght	Boyle	IV.	224
56	Lisgurreen	439 1 29	Clare	Ibrickan	Killard	Kilrush	II.	23
18	Lisgurry	98 1 9	Longford	Moydow	Moydow	Longford	I.	162
22, 26	Lisheegan	610 2 11	Antrim	Kilconway	Finvoy	Ballymoney	III.	26

(a) Including 33A. 2R. 11P. water.
(b) Including 37A. 0R. 17F. water.
(c) Including 31A. 1R. 2P. water.
(d) Including 11A. 2R. 25P. water.
(e) Including 19A. 0R. 5P. water.
(f) Including 3A. 3R. 3P. water.

No. of Sheet of the Ordnance Survey Maps.	Townlands and Towns.	Area in Statute Acres.	County.	Barony.	Parish.	Poor Law Union in 1857.	Townland Census of 1851, Part I.	
		A. R. P.					Vol.	Page
41, 50	Lisheen	959 0 13	Clare	Islands	Clondagad	Killadysert	II.	29
34, 35	Lisheen	211 0 20	Cork, E.R.	Fermoy	Killathy	Fermoy	II.	80
105, 106	Lisheen	590 2 8	Cork, W.R.	Bantry	Kilmocomoge	Bantry	II.	121
124	Lisheen	44 1 25	Cork, W.R.	East Carbery (E.D.)	Templetrine	Kinsale	II.	130
128	Lisheen	414 2 21	Galway	Kiltartan	Kilmacduagh	Gort	IV.	48
60	Lisheen	128 0 4	Galway	Tiaquin	Ballymacward	Mountbellew	IV.	76
60	Lisheen	788 1 7	Kerry	Magunihy	Nohavaldaly	Killarney	II.	205
35	Lisheen	415 0 35	King's Co.	Eglish	Eglish	Parsonstown	I.	135
24	Lisheen	84 0 4	Limerick	Coonagh	Ballynaclogh	Tipperary	II.	234
27	Lisheen	199 2 12	Roscommon	Castlereagh	Baslick	Castlereagh	IV.	199
23	Lisheen	198 2 12a	Roscommon	Roscommon	Kiltrustan	Strokestown	IV.	211
35, 36	Lisheen	990 2 13	Tipperary, N.R.	Eliogarty	Moyne	Thurles	II.	272
46	Lisheen	245 2 5	Tipperary, N.R.	Kilnamanagh Upper	Moyaliff	Cashel	II.	279
7	Lisheen	181 1 0	Tipperary, N.R.	Lower Ormond	Aglishcloghane	Borrisokane	II.	281
4, 5	Lisheen	180 0 25	Tipperary, N.R.	Lower Ormond	Dorrha	Parsonstown	II.	283
7	Lisheen	378 1 22	Tipperary, N.R.	Lower Ormond	Uskane	Borrisokane	II.	288
60	Lisheen	151 3 6	Tipperary, S.R.	Clanwilliam	Ballygriffin	Tipperary	II.	305
68, 75	Lisheen	69 3 0	Tipperary, S.R.	Clanwilliam	Clonbullogue	Tipperary	II.	306
59	Lisheen	103 0 35	Tipperary, S.R.	Clanwilliam	Templenoe	Tipperary	II.	312
2	Lisheen	54 2 39	Waterford	Upperthird	Killaloan	Clonmel	II.	370
61	Lisheenabrone	493 1 14	Mayo	Gallen	Meelick	Swineford	IV.	150
115	Lisheenaclara	82 3 20	Galway	Loughrea	Kilteskill	Loughrea	IV.	65
20, 26	Lisheenacloonta	173 1 22	Tipperary, N.R.	Upper Ormond	Kilmore	Nenagh	II.	291
20	Lisheenacooravan	53 3 27	Sligo	Carbury	Kilmacowen	Sligo	IV.	222
122	Lisheenacrannagh	182 2 20b	Galway	Kiltartan	Kilmacduagh	Gort	IV.	48
140	Lisheenacrehig	196 0 17	Cork, W.R.	West Carbery (W.D.)	Kilcoe	Skull	II.	143
30	Lisheenafeela	317 2 27	Cork, E.R.	Duhallow	Cullen	Millstreet	II.	70
15	Lisheenagower	214 3 24	Tipperary, N.R.	Upper Ormond	Ballymackey	Nenagh	II.	289
99, 107	Lisheenaguile	319 0 4	Galway	Longford	Kiltormer	Ballinasloe	IV.	60
98	Lisheenahevnia	111 1 39	Galway	Leitrim	Abbeygormacan	Loughrea	IV.	50
81	Lisheenakeeran	47 2 20	Galway	Galway	Rahoon	Galway	IV.	38
123	Lisheenaleen	267 0 17	Cork, W.R.	East Carbery (E.D.)	Rathclarin	Bandon	II.	130
116	Lisheenaleen	365 3 5	Galway	Leitrim	Kilteskill	Loughrea	IV.	55
59	Lisheenaleen	49 2 28	Tipperary, S.R.	Clanwilliam	Donohill	Tipperary	II.	307
28, 29	Lisheenanierin	90 2 15	Roscommon	Roscommon	Cloonfinlough	Strokestown	IV.	209
69	Lisheenanoran	686 0 7c	Galway	Clare	Annaghdown	Galway	IV.	16
88	Lisheenanoul	185 2 10d	Tipperary, S.R.	Iffa and Offa West	Ballybacon	Clogheen	II.	317
35	Lisheenataggart	463 2 16	Tipperary, N.R.	Eliogarty	Loughmoe West	Thurles	II.	271
83	Lisheenavalla	546 1 3	Galway	Clare	Lackagh	Galway	IV.	23
78, 89	Lisheenaveelish	25 2 28	Mayo	Carra	Ballyhean	Castlebar	IV.	126
39, 48	Lisheenbaun	424 3 26	Kerry	Trughanacmy	Dysert	Tralee	II.	210
60	Lisheen Beg	162 3 1	Tipperary, S.R.	Clanwilliam	Ballygriffin	Tipperary	II.	305
7	Lisheenboy	54 3 32	Tipperary, N.R.	Lower Ormond	Aglishcloghane	Borrisokane	II.	281
19	Lisheenbrien	149 1 24	Tipperary, N.R.	Owney and Arra	Castletownarra	Nenagh	II.	294
65, 66	Lisheencrony	1,242 3 20	Clare	Moyarta	Moyarta	Kilrush	II.	34
59	Lisheendarby	69 1 17	Tipperary, S.R.	Clanwilliam	Donohill	Tipperary	II.	307
4, 5	Lisheeneagh	55 3 21	Clare	Burren	Kilmoon	Ballyvaghan	II.	13
113	Lisheeneenaun East	156 3 33	Galway	Dunkellin	Killeenavarra	Gort	IV.	30
113	Lisheeneenaun West	243 0 39	Galway	Dunkellin	Killeenavarra	Gort	IV.	30
114	Lisheeneynaun	115 3 23	Galway	Loughrea	Ardrahan	Loughrea	IV.	62
59	Lisheenfrankagh	179 2 9	Tipperary, S.R.	Clanwilliam	Donohill	Tipperary	II.	307
65, 66	Lisheenfurroor	855 2 4	Clare	Moyarta	Moyarta	Kilrush	II.	34
122	Lisheenielagaun	122 3 39	Mayo	Kilmaine	Moorgagagh	Ballinrobe	IV.	157
59	Lisheenkyle	70 0 14	Tipperary, S.R.	Clanwilliam	Solloghod-beg	Tipperary	II.	310
83	Lisheenkyle East	174 2 38	Galway	Clare	Athenry	Galway	IV.	17
83	Lisheenkyle West	514 2 15	Galway	Clare	Athenry	Galway	IV.	17
94	Lisheenleigh	462 1 17	Cork, W.R.	East Carbery (W.D.)	Fanlobbus	Dunmanway	II.	132
35	Lisheenloughtin	16 2 20	Roscommon	Ballintober South	Kilbride	Roscommon	IV.	189
140, 149	Lisheen Lower	61 3 4	Cork, W.R.	West Carbery (E.D.)	Aghadown	Skibbereen	II.	137
118	Lisheenmanus	80 1 26	Mayo	Kilmaine	Kilcommon	Ballinrobe	IV.	155
48, 58	Lisheennacannina	366 1 31	Kerry	Magunihy	Molahiffe	Killarney	II.	205
131	Lisheennacreagh	656 3 38	Cork, W.R.	West Carbery (W.D.)	Skull	Skull	II.	146
116	Lisheennagat	69 2 17	Galway	Leitrim	Duniry	Portumna	IV.	53
55, 56	Lisheennageeha	324 2 32	Galway	Clare	Killeany	Tuam	IV.	20
6, 18	Lisheennaheltia	1,090 0 37	Galway	Ballymoe	Boyounagh	Glennamaddy	IV.	6
58	Lisheennamalausa	128 2 17	Tipperary, S.R.	Clanwilliam	Solloghod-more	Tipperary	II.	311
141	Lisheennapingina	92 0 36	Cork, W.R.	West Carbery (E.D.)	Abbeystrowry	Skibbereen	II.	136
47, 57	Lisheennashingane	324 0 3	Kerry	Magunihy	Kilbonane	Killarney	II.	200
99	Lisheennavannoge (Blake)	44 1 12	Galway	Clonmacnowen	Clontuskert	Ballinasloe	IV.	24
99	Lisheennavannoge (Clancarty)	78 2 33	Galway	Clonmacnowen	Clontuskert	Ballinasloe	IV.	25
116	Lisheen North	75 1 18	Galway	Leitrim	Duniry	Loughrea	IV.	53

(a) Including 7A. 2R. 13P. water.
(b) Including 10A. 2R. 11P. water.
(c) Including 2A. 0R. 22P. Lough Afoor.
(d) Including 2A. 1R. 39P. water.

No. of Sheet of the Ordnance Survey Maps.	Townlands and Towns.	Area in Statute Acres.	County.	Barony.	Parish.	Poor Law Union in 1857.	Townland Census of 1851, Part I.	
		A. R. P.					Vol.	Page
31	Lisheenoona . .	51 0 13	Waterford .	Decies without Drum	Dungarvan .	Dungarvan .	II.	355
51	Lisheenowen . .	120 0 7	Cork, E.R. .	Barretts . . .	Whitechurch .	Cork . .	II.	50
15, 23	Lisheenowen . .	238 2 5	Cork, E.R. .	Duhallow . .	Kilcorcoran .	Kanturk .	II.	72
88	Lisheenpower . .	142 0 37	Tipperary, S.R.	Iffa and Offa West .	Ballybacon .	Clogheen .	II.	317
64	Lisheenroe . .	115 0 15	Cork, E.R. .	Barrymore . .	Kilquane .	Cork . .	II.	55
141, 142, 150, 151	Lisheenroe . .	167 3 1a	Cork, W.R. .	West Carbery (E.D.)	Castlehaven .	Skibbereen .	II.	138
73	Lisheens . . .	118 2 0	Cork, E.R. .	East Muskerry .	Athnowen .	Cork . .	II.	101
73	Lisheens . . .	11 3 3	Cork, E.R. .	East Muskerry .	Kilnaglory .	Cork . .	II.	104
1	Lisheens . . .	373 0 36	Wicklow . .	Lower Talbotstown .	Kilbride . .	Naas . .	I.	361
45	Lisheensheela . .	250 3 3	Limerick . .	Connello Upper .	Kilmeedy .	Newcastle .	II.	233
116	Lisheen South . .	71 1 5	Galway . .	Leitrim . .	Duniry . .	Loughrea .	IV.	53
33	Lisheenteige . .	230 0 34b	Galway . .	Killian . .	Killeroran .	Mountbellew .	IV.	44
65, 66	LISHEEN T. . .	—	Clare . .	Moyarta . .	Moyarta . .	Kilrush . .	II.	34
19	Lisheentyrone . .	49 0 27	Tipperary, N.R.	Owney and Arra .	Castletownnarra .	Nenagh .	II.	294
19	Lisheentyrone South	10 0 32	Tipperary, N.R.	Owney and Arra .	Castletownnarra .	Nenagh .	II.	294
140, 141, 149, 150	Lisheen Upper . .	187 0 35	Cork, W.R. .	West Carbery (E.D.)	Aghadown .	Skibbereen .	II.	137
17	Lisheenvicknaheeha	75 2 23	Clare . .	Inchiquin .	Ruan . .	Corrofin .	II.	28
116	Lisheeny . . .	81 2 28	Galway . .	Leitrim . .	Ballynakill .	Loughrea .	IV.	52
58	Lisheenydeen . .	222 1 4	Clare . .	Clonderalaw .	Kilmurry .	Kilrush . .	II.	17
32	Lishenry . .	150 0 25c	Cavan . .	Castlerahan .	Denn . .	Oldcastle .	III.	68
16, 17	Lishugh . . .	124 3 15	Roscommon .	Roscommon .	Aughrim .	Cark. on Shannon	IV.	207
10	Lisillaun . . .	1 0 16	Limerick . .	Connello Lower .	Morgans . .	Rathkeale .	II.	228
8	Lisinan . .	97 3 36	Monaghan .	Monaghan .	Clones . .	Monaghan .	III.	275
23, 24	Lisinaw . . .	525 3 0d	Down . .	Dufferin . .	Killyleagh .	Downpatrick .	III.	167
5	Lisingle . . .	71 3 32	Fermanagh .	Lurg . .	Magheraculmoney .	Lowtherstown .	III.	208
16	Lisinigan . .	50 0 0	Cavan . .	Tullygarvey .	Drung . .	Cootehill .	III.	89
26, 27	Lisinisky . .	302 2 39e	Monaghan .	Cremorne .	Aghnamullen .	Carrickmacross	III	258
27	Lisirril . . .	282 0 1f	Monaghan .	Farney . .	Magheross .	Carrickmacross	III.	274
6	Liskea . . .	211 1 15	Galway . .	Ballymoe .	Templetogher .	Glennamaddy .	IV.	9
8	Liskeabrick . .	56 2 25	Monaghan .	Monaghan .	Clones . .	Monaghan .	III.	275
45	Liskeagh . .	124 3 25	Sligo . .	Corran . .	Kilshalvy .	Boyle . .	IV.	227
38	Liskeelty . .	85 1 21	Waterford .	Decies within Drum	Ardmore . .	Youghal .	II.	350
38	Liskeelty . .	117 2 35	Waterford .	Decies within Drum	Ballymacart .	Youghal .	II.	351
73	Liskeeraghan . .	324 1 30	Donegal . .	Banagh . .	Inishkeel .	Glenties .	III.	106
16	Liskeevy . .	619 2 22	Galway . .	Dunmore .	Liskeevy .	Tuam . .	IV.	35
16	Liskelly . .	111 0 34	Cork, E.R. .	Orrery and Kilmore	Kilbroney .	Mallow . .	II.	109
87, 99	Liskelly . .	205 1 24	Galway . .	Clonmacnowen .	Clontuskert .	Ballinasloe .	IV.	25
3	Liskenna . .	76 0 31	Monaghan .	Trough . .	Errigal Trough .	Monaghan .	III.	285
30, 38	Liskennett East .	235 1 20	Limerick . .	Connello Upper .	Ballingarry .	Croom . .	II.	231
30, 38	Liskennett West .	301 1 13	Limerick . .	Connello Upper .	Ballingarry .	Croom . .	II.	231
68, 69	Liskeran . .	722 0 38	Donegal . .	Raphoe . .	Stranorlar .	Stranorlar .	III.	142
9, 16	Lisket . . .	262 3 14	Clare . .	Corcomroe .	Kilfenora .	Ennistimon .	II.	19
47, 48, 54	Liskeveen . .	1,453 1 32	Tipperary, N.R.	Eliogarty . .	Ballymurreen .	Thurles .	II.	269
104	Liskevin . .	126 2 38	Galway . .	Dunkellin .	Kilcolgan .	Gort . .	IV.	28
70	Liskey . . .	139 2 38	Donegal . .	Raphoe . .	Clonleigh .	Strabane .	III.	135
85	Liskillea . .	444 0 23	Cork, E.R. .	Kerrycurrihy .	Ballinaboy .	Cork . .	II.	91
110	Liskilleen . .	543 0 25	Mayo . .	Kilmaine .	Ballinrobe .	Ballinrobe .	IV.	153
28	Liskilleen (Dickson)	72 1 1	Limerick . .	Shanid . .	Ardagh . .	Newcastle .	II.	255
28	Liskilleen (O'Brien)	151 1 31	Limerick . .	Shanid . .	Ardagh . .	Rathkeale .	II.	255
36	Liskilly . .	92 0 39	Fermanagh .	Clankelly .	Clones . .	Clones . .	III.	196
21	Liskilly . .	179 2 4	Limerick . .	Coshma . .	Adare . .	Croom . .	II.	241
5	Liskinbwee . .	140 3 14	Tyrone . .	Strabane Lower .	Camus . .	Strabane .	III.	320
44	Liskincon . .	96 3 19g	Tyrone . .	Omagh East .	Termonmaguirk .	Omagh . .	III.	314
10	Liskinlahan . .	332 3 22	Tipperary, N.R.	Lower Ormond .	Borrisokane .	Borrisokane .	II.	282
47	Liskittle . .	89 0 13	Tyrone . .	Dungannon Middle .	Donaghenry .	Cookstown .	III.	301
50, 51	Lisky . .	88 3 13	Tyrone . .	Clogher . .	Donacavey .	Omagh . .	III.	294
10	Lisky . .	375 2 21h	Tyrone . .	Strabane Lower .	Camus . .	Strabane .	III.	320
9, 13	Liskyborough . .	277 2 7	Armagh . .	Oneilland West .	Kilmore . .	Armagh . .	III.	53
33	Lisky Glebe . .	108 1 3i	Tyrone . .	Omagh West .	Longfield West .	Castlederg .	III.	316
23	Lislaban . .	409 0 9	Antrim . .	Kilconway .	Loughguile .	Ballymoney .	III.	27
61, 71	Lislackagh . .	160 3 16	Mayo . .	Gallen . .	Meelick . .	Swineford .	IV.	150
61	Lisladeen . .	422 1 2	Cork, E.R. .	East Muskerry .	Inishcarra .	Cork . .	II.	104
4, 5, 9, 10	Lisladraun . .	53 0 31	Kerry . .	Iraghticonnor .	Lisselton .	Listowel .	II.	192
17	Lislaferty . .	216 0 14	Tyrone . .	Strabane Lower .	Ardstraw .	Strabane .	III.	319
17	Lislagan Lower .	101 1 6	Antrim . .	Upper Dunluce .	Ballymoney .	Ballymoney .	III.	19
17	Lislagan Upper .	100 3 35	Antrim . .	Upper Dunluce .	Ballymoney .	Ballymoney .	III.	19
8, 9	Lislahelly . .	546 0 25	Sligo . .	Carbury . .	Drumcliff .	Sligo . .	IV.	221
22, 25	Lislahy . .	99 2 26	Leitrim . .	Carrigallen .	Drumreilly .	Bawnboy .	IV.	91
15, 23	Lislaird . .	451 2 23j	Tyrone . .	Omagh West .	Termonamongan .	Castlederg .	III.	317
17	Lislane . .	153 3 22	Londonderry .	Keenaght .	Balteagh .	NewTⁿLimavady	III.	234
58	Lislane . .	898 2 20k	Tyrone . .	Clogher . .	Clogher . .	Clogher . .	III.	293

(a) Including 19A. 3R. 14P. water.
(b) Including 1A. 0R. 20P. water.
(c) Including 1A. 2R. 39P. water.
(d) Including 8A. 2R. 2P. Clay Lake North.

(e) Including 41A. 2R. 15P. water.
(f) Including 58A. 2R. 29P. water.
(g) Including 1A. 1R. 27P. water.
(h) Including 11A. 1R. 12P. water.

(i) Including 2A. 2R. 26P. water.
(j) Including 12A. 1R. 9P. water.
(k) Including 2A. 0R. 32P. water.

No. of Sheet of the Ordnance Survey Maps.	Townlands and Towns.	Area in Statute Acres.			County.	Barony.	Parish.	Poor Law Union in 1857.	Townland Census of 1851, Part I.	
		A.	R.	P.					Vol.	Page
19, 20	Lislanly . . .	193	1	6a	Monaghan .	Cremorne . .	Clontibret . .	Castleblayney .	III.	261
12	Lislannan . .	66	0	35	Monaghan .	Dartree . . .	Clones . . .	Clones . .	III.	264
18, 26	Lislap East . .	866	0	12	Tyrone . .	Strabane Upper .	Cappagh . .	Omagh . .	III.	325
17	Lislap West . .	212	1	7b	Tyrone . .	Strabane Upper .	Cappagh . .	Omagh . .	III.	325
5	Lislarheenbeg . .	214	0	3	Clare . .	Burren . . .	Kilieany . .	Ballyvaghan .	II.	13
5	Lislarheenmore .	504	3	31	Clare . .	Burren . . .	Rathborney .	Ballyvaghan .	II.	14
40	Lislarris . . .	57	1	39	Fermanagh .	Coole . . .	Galloon . .	Clones . .	III.	200
4	Lislary . . .	347	3	26	Sligo . .	Carbury . .	Ahamlish . .	Sligo . .	IV.	219
8	Lislasly . . .	211	1	20	Armagh . .	Armagh . .	Loughgall . .	Armagh . .	III.	46
120	Lislaughera . .	243	0	8	Mayo . .	Kilmaine . .	Cong . . .	Ballinrobe .	IV.	154
62	Lislaughna . .	291	2	1	Mayo . .	Gallen . . .	Killasser . .	Swineford .	IV.	149
2, 3, 6	Lislaughtin . .	867	1	15	Kerry . .	Iraghticonnor .	Aghavallen . .	Listowel . .	II.	189
16	Lislea . . .	257	1	23	Armagh . .	Armagh . .	Lisnadill . .	Armagh . .	III.	45
16	Lislea . . .	249	1	0	Armagh . .	Fews Upper .	Lisnadill . .	Armagh . .	III.	49
25, 28	Lislea . . .	497	0	33	Armagh . .	Orior Upper .	Killevy . .	Newry . .	III.	58
19	Lislea . . .	202	0	21	Armagh . .	Tiranny . .	Derrynoose . .	Armagh . .	III.	59
39, 40	Lislea . . .	486	2	14	Cavan . .	Castlerahan . .	Lurgan . .	Oldcastle .	III.	70
17	Lislea . . .	186	2	7	Cavan . .	Tullygarvey .	Kildrumsherdan .	Cootehill .	III.	90
21	Lislea . . .	221	2	13	Cavan . .	Tullygarvey .	Larah . . .	Cootehill .	III.	91
32	Lislea . . .	211	0	0	Cavan . .	Upper Loughtee .	Denn . . .	Cavan . .	III.	83
51	Lislea . . .	133	3	39	Clare . .	Bunratty Lower .	Clonloghan . .	Ennis . .	II.	3
40	Lislea . . .	117	2	24c	Fermanagh .	Clankelly . .	Galloon . .	Clones . .	III.	198
28	Lislea . . .	231	2	3	Fermanagh .	Magherastephana .	Aghalurcher .	Lisnaskea .	III.	217
60	Lislea . . .	302	3	3	Galway . .	Kilconnell . .	Killosolan . .	Mountbellew .	IV.	42
32	Lislea . . .	57	1	4	Leitrim . .	Leitrim . .	Annaduff . .	Car^k. on Shannon	IV.	99
27, 33	Lislea . . .	917	3	38	Londonderry .	Loughinsholin .	Kilrea . .	Ballymoney .	III.	241
5, 9, 10	Lislea . . .	425	2	14	Longford . .	Granard . .	Clonbroney . .	Granard . .	I.	155
23	Lislea . . .	495	2	30	Longford . .	Moydow . .	Kilcommock . .	Ballymahon .	I.	161
1, 2, 4, 5	Lislea . . .	562	3	13	Louth . .	Lower Dundalk .	Carlingford . .	Dundalk . .	I.	176
2	Lislea . . .	102	2	26	Meath . .	Lower Kells .	Enniskeen . .	Kells . .	I.	202
17	Lislea . . .	105	2	15	Monaghan .	Dartree . .	Aghabog . .	Cootehill .	III.	263
16, 21	Lislea . . .	75	0	2	Monaghan .	Dartree . .	Currin . .	Clones . .	III.	266
2	Lislea . . .	99	2	17	Roscommon .	Boyle . .	Kilronan . .	Boyle . .	IV.	197
32	Lislea . . .	367	1	30d	Sligo . .	Corran . .	Clocnoghil . .	Tobercurry .	IV.	225
36, 37	Lislea . . .	354	3	36	Sligo . .	Leyny . .	Kilmacteige . .	Tobercurry .	IV.	231
51	Lislea . . .	171	1	35	Tyrone . .	Clogher . .	Clogher . .	Clogher . .	III.	293
43	Lislea . . .	76	1	8e	Tyrone . .	Omagh East . .	Cappagh . .	Omagh . .	III.	310
19, 27	Lisleagh . . .	184	2	32	Cork, E.R. .	Fermoy . .	Kilgullane . .	Fermoy . .	II.	80
24	Lisleagh . . .	403	2	15	Cork, E.R. .	Orrery and Kilmore	Ballyclogh . .	Mallow . .	II.	106
13, 22	Lisleagh . . .	263	3	0	Waterford .	Decies without Drum	Lickoran . .	Lismore . .	II.	358
13	Lisleaghmountain .	156	2	0	Waterford .	Decies without Drum	Lickoran . .	Lismore . .	II.	358
11, 18	Lislea North and South . .	426	0	4f	Tyrone . .	Strabane Upper .	Bodoney Upper .	Gortin . .	III.	324
39	Lislee . . .	124	3	15	Tyrone . .	Dungannon Middle .	Donaghenry . .	Cookstown .	III.	301
136, 137	Lisleecourt . .	420	2	15	Cork, W.R. .	Ibane and Barryroe	Lislee . .	Clonakilty .	II.	150
10	Lisleen . . .	455	3	33	Down . .	Castlereagh Lower .	Comber . .	Newtownards .	III.	162
24	Lisleen . . .	213	1	19	Tyrone . .	Omagh West . .	Ardstraw . .	Castlederg .	III.	315
136	Lisleetemple . .	193	3	6	Cork, W.R. .	Ibane and Barryroe	Lislee . .	Clonakilty .	II.	150
29, 30	Lislehane . .	175	2	23	Cork, E.R. .	Duhallow . .	Cullen . .	Millstreet .	II.	70
65, 73	Lisleibane . .	616	1	19	Kerry . .	Dunkerron North .	Knockane . .	Killarney .	II.	182
10	Lisleighbeg . .	220	1	18	Tipperary, N.R.	Lower Ormond .	Borrisokane . .	Borrisokane .	II.	282
14	Lisleitrim . .	145	1	16	Monaghan .	Monaghan . .	Monaghan . .	Monaghan .	III.	277
27	Lisleitrim or Kilty-bane . . .	447	3	37g	Armagh . .	Fews Upper . .	Newtownhamilton .	Castleblayney .	III.	49
136	Lislevane . .	600	1	28	Cork, W.R. .	Ibane and Barryroe	Abbeymahon .	Clonakilty .	II.	148
136	LISLEVANE T. .	—			Cork, W.R. .	Ibane and Barryroe	Abbeymahon .	Clonakilty .	II.	148
27	Lisliddy . . .	155	0	32	Roscommon .	Castlereagh .	Kilkeevin . .	Castlereagh .	IV.	200
25, 34	Lislimnaghan .	108	2	8h	Tyrone . .	Strabane Upper .	Cappagh . .	Omagh . .	III.	325
40	Lislin . . .	305	0	24	Cavan . .	Castlerahan . .	Mullagh . .	Kells . .	III.	70
16	Lislin . . .	101	1	12	Cavan . .	Tullygarvey .	Drung . .	Cootehill .	III.	89
22, 23	Lislom . . .	220	1	13	Longford . .	Shrule . .	Kilcommock . .	Ballymahon .	I.	166
89	Lislonane . .	145	3	5	Kerry . .	Iveragh . .	Dromod . .	Cahersiveen .	II.	195
17	Lislongfield . .	169	2	23	Monaghan .	Dartree . .	Aghabog . .	Cootehill .	III.	263
11, 15	Lisloony . . .	154	1	29	Armagh . .	Tiranny . .	Tynan . .	Armagh . .	III.	60
29	Lisloose . . .	180	1	30	Kerry . .	Trughanacmy .	Tralee . .	Tralee . .	II.	213
52, 60	Lisloran . . .	392	2	18	Tipperary, S.R. .	Clanwilliam .	Ballygriffin . .	Cashel . .	II.	305
14	Lislorkan North .	310	2	30	Clare . .	Corcomroe .	Kilmacrehy . .	Ennistimon .	II.	20
14	Lislorkan South .	194	3	18	Clare . .	Corcomroe .	Kilmacrehy . .	Ennistimon .	II.	20
59, 60, 73	Lisloughlin . .	581	0	3	Galway . .	Tiaquin . .	Ballymacward .	Mountbellew .	IV.	76
56	Lisluinaghan . .	847	3	5	Clare . .	Moyarta . .	Kilfearagh . .	Kilrush . .	II.	32
44	Lislunnan . .	708	3	16	Antrim . .	Lower Antrim .	Connor . .	Antrim . .	III.	3
18	Lislynchahan . .	145	2	29	Monaghan .	Dartree . .	Ematris . .	Cootehill .	III.	267
2	Lismacaffry . .	110	3	10	Westmeath .	Moygoish . .	Street . . .	Granard . .	I.	281

(a) Including 14A. 3R. 17P. water.　　　　(d) Including 30A. 0R. 13P. water.　　　　(g) Including 29A. 2R. 28P. water.
(b) Including 3A. 0R. 10P. water.　　　　(e) Including 1A. 2R. 25P. water.　　　　(h) Including 1A. 3R. 15P. water.
(c) Including 14A. 3R. 10P. water.　　　　(f) Including 7A. 1R. 28P. water.

No. of Sheet of the Ordnance Survey Maps.	Townlands and Towns.	Area in Statute Acres.			County.	Barony.	Parish.	Poor Law Union in 1857.	Townland Census of 1851, Part I.	
		A.	R.	P.					Vol.	Page
38, 42	Lismacanigan Lower	386	1	11	Cavan	Castlerahan	Castlerahan	Oldcastle	III.	67
38	Lismacanigan Upper	236	2	13	Cavan	Castlerahan	Castlerahan	Oldcastle	III.	67
22	Lismacarol	516	3	18	Londonderry	Tirkeeran	Clondermot	Londonderry	III.	248
19	Lismacbryan	318	1	20	Sligo	Tireragh	Dromard	Dromore West	IV.	233
57	Lismacfinnin	187	2	6	Kerry	Magunihy	Killorglin	Killarney	II.	204
51, 61	Lismacleane	109	3	31	Clare	Bunratty Lower	Clonloghan	Ennis	II.	3
42, 48	Lismacloskey	330	0	30	Antrim	Upper Toome	Duneane	Ballymena	III.	35
21	Lismacmanus	140	3	24	Longford	Ratheline	Ratheline	Longford	I.	165
22, 23	Lismacmurrogh	123	3	5	Longford	Shrule	Kilcommock	Ballymahon	I.	166
16	Lismacool	378	2	31	Roscommon	Frenchpark	Kilmacumsy	Boyle	IV.	203
13, 14	Lismacrerk	137	0	14	Monaghan	Monaghan	Monaghan	Monaghan	III.	277
7, 8	Lismacrory	619	2	9	Tipperary, N.R.	Lower Ormond	Ballingarry	Borrisokane	II.	282
2, 5	Lismacsheedy	385	3	7	Clare	Burren	Rathborney	Ballyvaghan	II.	14
36	Lismacsheela	90	1	5	Fermanagh	Clankelly	Clones	Clones	III.	196
2, 5	Lismacteige	402	2	33	Clare	Burren	Rathborney	Ballyvaghan	II.	14
106, 107	Lismacteige	162	3	37	Galway	Longford	Abbeygormacan	Ballinasloe	IV.	56
67, 68	Lismacue	241	1	24	Tipperary, S.R.	Clanwilliam	Templeneiry	Tipperary	II.	311
108	Lismafadda	101	3	13	Galway	Longford	Meelick	Portumna	IV.	61
81	Lismaganshion	128	3	24	Mayo	Costello	Aghamore	Swineford	IV.	137
25	Lismagawley	42	2	25	Longford	Ratheline	Cashel	Ballymahon	I.	163
25	Lismagawley Bog	25	1	32	Longford	Ratheline	Cashel	Ballymahon	I.	163
25	Lismagawley Meadow	32	2	34	Longford	Ratheline	Cashel	Ballymahon	I.	163
16	Lismageevoge	108	2	27	Roscommon	Frenchpark	Creeve	Car*. on Shannon	IV.	203
33	Lismagiril	377	2	31	Cavan	Castlerahan	Killinkere	Bailieborough	III.	69
15	Lismagoneen	121	3	16	Longford	Granard	Clonbroney	Granard	I.	155
18	Lismagonway	136	2	3	Monaghan	Dartree	Aghabog	Cootehill	III.	263
20, 21	Lismagratty	182	2	6	Cavan	Upper Loughtee	Castleterra	Cavan	III.	83
42	Lismagroon	49	1	8	Roscommon	Athlone	Killinvoy	Roscommon	IV.	182
19	Lismagunshin	151	1	37a	Monaghan	Cremorne	Clontibret	Monaghan	III.	261
41, 44	Lismaha	239	0	13b	Roscommon	Athlone	Tisrara	Roscommon	IV.	186
61, 72	Lismahane	161	3	13	Cork, E.R.	East Muskerry	Inishcarra	Cork	II.	104
44, 50	Lismahon	229	0	20	Meath	Ratoath	Rathregan	Dunshaughlin	I.	219
20	Lismaine	294	3	31	Down	Lower Iveagh, Up. pt.	Magheralin	Lurgan	III.	170
9, 10	Lismaine	316	3	27	Kilkenny	Fassadinin	Cooleraheen	Kilkenny	I.	89
27	Lismakeegan	119	2	33	Leitrim	Leitrim	Kiltoghert	Car*. on Shannon	IV.	102
19, 20	Lismakeery	522	1	16	Limerick	Connello Lower	Lismakeery	Rathkeale	II.	228
34	Lismakeeve	122	0	33	Tipperary, N.R.	Kilnamanagh Upper	Glenkeen	Thurles	II.	278
17	Lismakin	316	0	36	Tipperary, N.R.	Ikerrin	Corbally	Roscrea	II.	275
7	Lismalady	174	0	4	Westmeath	Corkaree	Multyfarnham	Mullingar	I.	263
77	Lismalaghlin	185	0	12	Cork, E.R.	Imokilly	Mogeely	Middleton	II.	90
55, 63	Lismalin	554	2	20	Tipperary, S.R.	Slievardagh	Lismalin	Callan	II.	335
7, 8	Lismaline	210	1	33	Tipperary, N.R.	Lower Ormond	Uskane	Borrisokane	II.	288
28	Lismalore	364	2	37	Fermanagh	Magherastephana	Aghavea	Lisnaskea	III.	219
27, 31	Lismannagh	103	1	17	Leitrim	Leitrim	Annaduff	Car*. on Shannon	IV.	99
88, 100	Lismanny	1,938	1	8c	Galway	Longford	Clontuskert	Ballinasloe	IV.	58
18	Lismanus	136	3	6	Louth	Ardee	Mosstown	Ardee	I.	174
35	Lismateige	1,180	3	24	Kilkenny	Knocktopher	Lismateige	Thomastown	I.	113
12	Lismeagh	55	1	2	Monaghan	Dartree	Clones	Clones	III.	264
81	Lismeegaun	250	0	20	Mayo	Costello	Aghamore	Swineford	IV.	137
27, 35	Lismeehan or Maryfort	297	1	5d	Clare	Tulla Upper	Tulla	Tulla	II.	42
29	Lismeehy	123	3	4	Roscommon	Roscommon	Lissonuffy	Strokestown	IV.	212
22, 23	Lismeelcunnin	760	2	19	Cork, E.R.	Duhallow	Clonfert	Kanturk	II.	68
32,33,38,39	Lismeen	331	0	26e	Cavan	Castlerahan	Lurgan	Oldcastle	III.	70
32	Lismeen	60	0	3	Cavan	Upper Loughtee	Denn	Cavan	III.	83
10	Lismenan	24	1	22	Monaghan	Monaghan	Monaghan	Monaghan	III.	277
45, 46	Lismenary	330	2	7	Antrim	Lower Belfast	Ballynure	Larne	III.	7
47	Lismerraun	198	3	11	Sligo	Coolavin	Killaraght	Boyle	IV.	224
117	Lismihil	208	2	20	Galway	Longford	Killimorbologue	Portumna	IV.	59
103, 104	Lismintan or Bally-ruddelly	377	3	1	Donegal	Tirhugh	Drumhome	Donegal	III.	146
71	Lismiraun	326	0	21	Mayo	Gallen	Bohola	Swineford	IV.	147
15	Lismire	752	2	29	Cork, E.R.	Duhallow	Clonfert	Kanturk	II.	68
59	Lismoes	190	1	33	Galway	Tiaquin	Killoscobe	Mountbellew	IV.	78
54, 62	Lismoghry	352	1	1	Donegal	Raphoe	Raymoghy	Strabane	III.	142
9	Lismoher	153	1	9	Clare	Burren	Noughaval	Ballyvaghan	II.	13
88, 89	Lismolin	100	0	37	Mayo	Burrishoole	Islandeady	Westport	IV.	121
55, 61	Lismonaghan	155	2	9	Donegal	Raphoe	Leck	Letterkenny	III.	140
33	Lismonaghan	93	1	22	Fermanagh	Clanawley	Kinawley	Enniskillen	III.	194
56	Lismoney	680	1	8	King's Co.	Ballybritt	Kinnitty	Parsonstown	I.	125
48	Lismoney	338	3	22	Londonderry	Loughinsholin	Lissan	Magherafelt	III.	212
66	Lismongane	159	3	15	Kerry	Magunihy	Aghadoe	Killarney	II.	199
70	Lismontigley	178	0	26	Donegal	Raphoe	Raphoe	Strabane	III.	141

(a) Including 12A. 0R. 2P. water.
(b) Including 12A. 2R. 8P. water.
(c) Including 29A. 3R. 3P. water.
(d) Including 2A. 2R. 1P. water.
(e) Including 8A. 3R. 2P. water.

4 P

No. of Sheet of the Ordnance Survey Maps.	Townlands and Towns.	Area in Statute Acres.			County.	Barony.	Parish.	Poor Law Union in 1857.	Townland Census of 1851, Part I.	
		A.	R.	P.					Vol.	Page
32	Lismoonly	139	0	34	Fermanagh	Clanawley	Killesher	Enniskillen	III.	193
4, 5	Lismorahaun	223	1	20	Clare	Burren	Kilmoon	Ballyvaghan	II.	13
61	Lismoran	439	0	24a	Mayo	Gallen	Killasser	Swineford	IV.	149
38	Lismore	366	1	7	Down	Lecale Lower	Dunsfort	Downpatrick	III.	179
29	Lismore	267	2	25	Kerry	Trughanacmy	Ratass	Tralee	II.	213
8, 13	Lismore	155	0	16	Longford	Longford	Clongesh	Longford	I.	158
22	Lismore	180	3	7	Queen's Co.	Clandonagh	Aghaboe	Donaghmore	I.	232
21	Lismore	225	3	31	Tipperary, N.R.	Upper Ormond	Ballymackey	Nenagh	II.	289
64	Lismore	135	1	23	Tyrone	Clogher	Clogher	Clogher	III.	293
59	Lismore	311	0	35	Tyrone	Clogher	Errigal Keerogue	Clogher	III.	295
21	Lismore	139	0	10b	Waterford	Coshmore&Coshbride	Lismore & Mocollop	Lismore	II.	346
9, 17	Lismore	155	3	34	Waterford	Middlethird	Killoteran	Waterford	II.	367
25	Lismore Demesne	332	1	10c	Cavan	Clanmahon	Kilmore	Cavan	III.	78
108, 109	Lismore Demesne	465	2	12	Galway	Longford	Clonfert	Ballinasloe	IV.	57
21	LISMORE T.	—			Waterford	Coshmore&Coshbride	Lismore & Mocollop	Lismore	II.	348
40,41,49,50	Lismorris	339	0	10	Clare	Islands	Clondagad	Killadysert	II.	29
8, 13	Lismorrity	167	2	32	Antrim	Cary	Grange of Drumtullagh	Ballycastle	III.	14
62	Lismortagh	447	3	15	Tipperary, S.R.	Middlethird	Cooleagh	Cashel	II.	326
8	Lismoy	459	3	19	Longford	Longford	Clongesh	Longford	I.	158
104	Lismoylan	138	1	17	Galway	Dunkellin	Killinan	Loughrea	IV.	30
123	Lismoyle	42	1	14	Galway	Kiltartan	Kilbeacanty	Gort	IV.	47
45, 59	Lismoyle	210	1	11	Galway	Tiaquin	Killoscobe	Mountbellew	IV.	78
31	Lismoyle	185	0	13	Leitrim	Leitrim	Annaduff	Cark. on Shannon	IV.	99
26, 27	Lismoyle	925	2	1	Londonderry	Loughinsholin	Tamlaght O'Crilly	Ballymoney	III.	243
45	Lismoyle	61	1	21	Roscommon	Athlone	Cam	Athlone	IV.	180
62	Lismoynan	463	1	29	Tipperary, S.R.	Middlethird	St. Johnstown	Cashel	II.	330
37	Lismoyny	214	2	28	Westmeath	Moycashel	Ardnurcher or Horseleap	Tullamore	I.	277
17, 25	Lismuinga East	54	3	24	Clare	Inchiquin	Ruan	Corrofin	II.	28
17, 25	Lismuinga West	109	1	19	Clare	Inchiquin	Ruan	Corrofin	II.	28
41	Lismulbreeda	415	3	29	Clare	Islands	Killone	Ennis	II.	30
6	Lismulkeare	131	2	16	Roscommon	Boyle	Ardcarn	Boyle	IV.	193
66, 67	Lismulladown	385	2	25	Tyrone	Dungannon Lower	Aghaloo	Dungannon	III.	297
14	Lismullane	267	0	31	Limerick	Clanwilliam	Abington	Limerick	II.	221
21, 26	Lismullig	90	2	39	Cavan	Upper Loughtee	Annagelliff	Cavan	III.	82
31, 32	Lismullin	938	3	11	Meath	Skreen	Lismullin	Navan	I.	221
78, 87	Lismullyduff	778	0	28	Donegal	Raphoe	Donaghmore	Stranorlar	III.	138
54	Lismulrevy	175	0	4	Tyrone	Dungannon Middle	Clonfeacle	Dungannon	III.	299
37	Lismurnaghan	275	2	1	Antrim	Lower Toome	Ahoghill	Ballymena	III.	32
7	Lismurphy	124	3	6	Londonderry	Coleraine	Macosquin	Coleraine	III.	233
59	Lismurphy	20	0	13	Tipperary, S.R.	Clanwilliam	Donohill	Tipperary	II.	307
33	Lismurragha	160	2	26	Queen's Co.	Clandonagh	Rathdowney	Donaghmore	I.	234
102, 112	Lismurrew	209	2	5	Mayo	Clanmorris	Kilcolman	Claremorris	IV.	134
28	Lismurtagh	217	0	17	Roscommon	Castlereagh	Baslick	Castlereagh	IV.	199
28	Lismurtagh	164	1	1	Roscommon	Roscommon	Ogulla	Strokestown	IV.	212
56	Lismuse	398	3	5	Clare	Ibrickan	Killard	Kilrush	II.	23
23	Lisnabane	235	0	30	Fermanagh	Magherastephana	Aghavea	Lisnaskea	III.	219
95, 96	Lisnabanree	227	2	20	Cork, W.R.	Kinalmeaky	Kilbrogan	Bandon	II.	152
39	Lisnabantry	233	2	37	Cavan	Castlerahan	Killinkere	Bailieborough	III.	69
39	Lisnabantry	135	3	11	Cavan	Castlerahan	Mullagh	Bailieborough	III.	70
70	Lisnabert	130	0	7	Donegal	Raphoe	Donaghmore	Strabane	III.	138
67	Lisnabilla	87	2	34	Antrim	Upper Massereene	Magheramesk	Lisburn	III.	31
20	Lisnabin	276	3	1	Westmeath	Farbill	Killucan	Mullingar	I.	267
8, 13	Lisnabo	123	2	6	Longford	Longford	Clongesh	Longford	I.	158
2	Lisnabo	184	1	5	Meath	Lower Kells	Enniskeen	Kells	I.	202
101	Lisnaboley	49	1	25	Mayo	Clanmorris	Kilcolman	Claremorris	IV.	134
16	Lisnaboll	97	3	34	Roscommon	Frenchpark	Kilmacumsy	Boyle	IV.	203
1, 2	Lisnaboy	50	1	3	Meath	Lower Kells	Moybolgue	Kells	I.	203
29	Lisnaboy Lower	247	0	34	Cork, E.R.	Duhallow	Cullen	Millstreet	II.	70
29, 38	Lisnaboy Upper	267	3	33	Cork, E.R.	Duhallow	Cullen	Millstreet	II.	70
31	Lisnabrack	42	3	15	Leitrim	Leitrim	Kiltoghert	Cark. on Shannon	IV.	102
7	Lisnabrack	582	1	31	Leitrim	Rosclogher	Killasnet	Manorhamilton	IV.	110
33	Lisnabrague	563	0	12d	Down	Upper Iveagh, Up.pt.	Aghaderg	Banbridge	III.	174
7, 12	Lisnabraugh	188	1	19	Antrim	Lower Dunluce	Derrykeighan	Ballymoney	III.	17
9	Lisnabreeny	956	1	39	Down	Castlereagh Upper	Knockbreda	Lisburn	III.	165
46	Lisnabrinlodge	28	3	7	Cork, E.R.	Kinnatalloon	Mogeely	Fermoy	II.	98
37, 46	Lisnabrin Lower	114	0	16	Cork, E.R.	Kinnatalloon	Mogeely	Fermoy	II.	98
38, 42	Lisnabrinnia	140	2	12	Cavan	Clanmahon	Kilbride	Oldcastle	III.	78
46	Lisnabrin North	217	0	0	Cork, E.R.	Kinnatalloon	Mogeely	Fermoy	II.	98
121	Lisnabrinny	346	3	12	Cork, W.R.	East Carbery (W.D.)	Kilmeen	Dunmanway	III.	134
46	Lisnabrin South	180	3	25	Cork, E.R.	Kinnatalloon	Mogeely	Fermoy	II.	98
50, 51	Lisnabuherey	59	2	26	Tyrone	Clogher	Donacavey	Omagh	III.	294
59	Lisnabunny	56	3	18	Tyrone	Clogher	Errigal Keerogue	Clogher	III.	295

(a) Including 12A. 1R. 20P. water.
(b) Including 1A. 0R. 8P. water.
(c) Including 3A. 2R. 35P. water.
(d) Including 46A. 2R. 0P. Lough Shark.

No. of Sheet of the Ordnance Survey Maps.	Townlands and Towns.	Area in Statute Acres.			County.	Barony.	Parish.	Poor Law Union in 1857.	Townland Census of 1851, Part I.	
		A.	R.	P.					Vol.	Page
21	Lisnacark	65	1	24	Cavan	Upper Loughtee	Castleterra	Cavan	III.	83
17	Lisnacask	167	3	37	Westmeath	Rathconrath	Rathconrath	Mullingar	I.	284
46, 47	Lisnaclassagh	162	0	37	Galway	Kilconnell	Killosolan	Mountbellew	IV.	42
18, 23	Lisnaclea	324	2	16	Cavan	Clankee	Drumgoon	Cootehill	III.	72
29, 35	Lisnaclea	180	0	7	Cavan	Clankee	Enniskeen	Bailieborough	III.	73
30	Lisnaclea	171	2	10	Monaghan	Farney	Magheracloone	Carrickmacross	III.	273
54	Lisnaclin	88	0	39	Tyrone	Dungannon Middle	Drumglass	Dungannon	III.	303
15	Lisnacloon	445	0	28*d*	Tyrone	Omagh West	Termonamongan	Castlederg	III.	317
30, 31	Lisnacon	425	2	35	Cork, E.R.	Duhallow	Dromtarriff	Kanturk	II.	71
25, 34	Lisnacreaght	866	3	25	Tyrone	Strabane Lower	Ardstraw	Omagh	III.	319
11, 18	Lisnacreaght	764	2	9*b*	Tyrone	Strabane Upper	Bodoney Upper	Gortin	III.	324
55	Lisnacree	257	2	18	Down	Mourne	Kilkeel	Kilkeel	III.	183
51	Lisnacreeve	507	1	26	Tyrone	Clogher	Donacavey	Omagh	III.	294
34, 41	Lisnacreevy	577	3	5	Down	Upper Iveagh, Lr. pt.	Drumballyroney	Banbridge	III.	172
23	Lisnacreevy	268	3	14	Longford	Moydow	Taghsheenod	Ballymahon	I.	162
112	Lisnacrilla	169	0	32	Cork, E.R.	Kinsale	Clontead	Kinsale	II.	99
27	Lisnacrogher	400	3	21	Antrim	Lower Antrim	Skerry	Ballymena	III.	5
39	Lisnacroghy or Gallowstown	229	0	10	Roscommon	Ballintober South	Roscommon	Roscommon	IV.	190
41, 42	Lisnacroppan	306	0	29	Down	Upper Iveagh, Lr. pt.	Drumballyroney	Banbridge	III.	172
61	Lisnacroy	102	3	39	Tyrone	Dungannon Middle	Clonfeacle	Dungannon	III.	299
82	Lisnacuddy	227	0	26	Cork, W.R.	West Muskerry	Kilmichael	Dunmanway	II.	159
19, 28	Lisnacullia	131	2	34	Limerick	Connello Lower	Clonagh	Rathkeale	II.	227
25	Lisnacullia	48	0	36	Limerick	Coonagh	Doon	Tipperary	II.	234
25	Lisnacullia	88	3	37	Limerick	Coonagh	Oola	Tipperary	II.	236
109, 122	Lisnacunna	529	2	20	Cork, W.R.	East Carbery (E.D.)	Desertserges	Bandon	II.	128
89	Lisnacurley	136	0	8*c*	Mayo	Carra	Ballyhean	Castlebar	IV.	126
17, 21	Lisnacush	269	3	38	Longford	Ratheline	Ratheline	Longford	I.	165
23	Lisnadarragh	117	3	27*d*	Cavan	Clankee	Shercock	Bailieborough	III.	74
41	Lisnadarragh	183	3	15	Cavan	Clanmahon	Drumlumman	Granard	III.	77
27	Lisnadarragh	274	0	30	Monaghan	Cremorne	Aghnamullen	Carrickmacross	III.	258
16	Lisnadill	324	3	19	Armagh	Fews Upper	Lisnadill	Armagh	III.	49
97	Lisnadrisha	256	2	16	Galway	Dunkellin	Kileonierin	Loughrea	IV.	29
43	Lisnadurk Glebe North	142	0	26	Fermanagh	Clankelly	Currin	Clones	III.	197
43	Lisnadurk Glebe South	6	2	38	Fermanagh	Clankelly	Currin	Clones	III.	197
43	Lisnadurk Middle	1	1	28	Fermanagh	Clankelly	Currin	Clones	III.	197
49, 59	Lisnafaha	220	2	27	Clare	Clonderalaw	Killadysert	Killadysert	II.	16
33, 39	Lisnafana	243	0	8	Cavan	Castlerahan	Lurgan	Oldcastle	III.	70
27, 30	Lisnafeddaly	201	1	33	Monaghan	Farney	Magheross	Carrickmacross	III.	274
7, 11	Lisnafeedy	159	1	5	Armagh	Tiranny	Eglish	Armagh	III.	59
26, 27	Lisnafiffy	430	2	31	Down	Lower Iveagh, Lr. pt.	Seapatrick	Banbridge	III.	169
26, 27	Lisnafiffy	213	3	37	Down	Lower Iveagh, Up. pt.	Tullylish	Banbridge	III.	171
32, 37	Lisnafillon	342	3	16	Antrim	Lower Toome	Ahoghill	Ballymena	III.	32
10, 17	Lisnafin	766	1	33	Tyrone	Strabane Lower	Ardstraw	Gortin	III.	319
28	Lisnafinelly	72	3	10	Monaghan	Farney	Donaghmoyne	Carrickmacross	III.	270
44, 53	Lisnafulla	240	0	32	Limerick	Glenquin	Killeedy	Newcastle	II.	246
10	Lisnafunshin	425	0	9	Kilkenny	Fassadinin	Mothell	Castlecomer	I.	90
33	Lisnagade	430	1	19	Down	Upper Iveagh, Up. pt.	Aghaderg	Banbridge	III.	174
23	Lisnagalliagh	239	1	2	Monaghan	Cremorne	Aghnamullen	Cootehill	III.	258
8	Lisnagalt	283	0	20	Londonderry	North East Liberties of Coleraine	Ballyrashane	Coleraine	III.	245
2	Lisnagappagh	71	2	33	Westmeath	Moygoish	Street	Granard	I.	281
22	Lisnagard	180	0	35	Roscommon	Roscommon	Elphin	Strokestown	IV.	209
44	Lisnagar Demesne	459	2	39*e*	Cork, E.R.	Barrymore	Rathcormack	Fermoy	II.	57
51	Lisnagardy	107	1	19	Tyrone	Clogher	Donacavey	Omagh	III.	294
31	Lisnagarran	355	1	8	Antrim	Lower Toome	Ahoghill	Ballymena	III.	32
64, 68	Lisnagarvy	434	3	12*f*	Antrim	Upper Massereene	Blaris	Lisburn	III.	30
7, 8	Lisnagat	183	1	8	Antrim	Cary	Grange of Drumtullagh	Ballycastle	III.	14
17, 21	Lisnagat	434	3	38	Armagh	Fews Lower	Kilclooney	Armagh	III.	46
95, 96	Lisnagat	395	2	0	Cork, W.R.	Kinalmeaky	Templemartin	Bandon	II.	153
31	Lisnagat	43	0	32	Leitrim	Leitrim	Kiltoghert	Car*k*. on Shannon	IV.	102
67, 74	Lisnagaul	590	0	1	Tipperary, S.R.	Clanwilliam	Cordangan	Tipperary	II.	306
26	Lisnagaver	419	3	14	Antrim	Kilconway	Rasharkin	Ballymoney	III.	28
44	Lisnagavragh	393	2	19*g*	Roscommon	Athlone	Tisrara	Roscommon	IV.	186
28, 32	Lisnagea	189	3	16	Leitrim	Leitrim	Kiltoghert	Car*k*. on Shannon	IV.	102
78	Lisnageeha or Antigua	157	0	17*h*	Mayo	Carra	Aglish	Castlebar	IV.	124
26, 32	Lisnageenly	765	0	30	Tipperary, N.R.	Upper Ormond	Kilmore	Nenagh	II.	291
17	Lisnageer	162	0	9*i*	Cavan	Tullygarvey	Drumgoon	Cootehill	III.	88
16, 17	Lisnageer	198	2	15	Cavan	Tullygarvey	Kildrumsherdan	Cootehill	III.	90
7, 18, 19	Lisnageeragh	594	2	8	Galway	Ballymoe	Ballynakill	Glennamaddy	IV.	5
2	Lisnageeragh	188	2	37	Galway	Ballymoe	Kilcroan	Glennamaddy	IV.	9

(*a*) Including 6A. 1R. 2P. water.
(*b*) Including 9A. 0R. 37P. water.
(*c*) Including 2A. 1R. 0P. water.

(*d*) Including 7A. 0R. 25P. water.
(*e*) Including 13A. 3R. 4P. water.
(*f*) Including 4A. 2R. 23P. water.

(*g*) Including 20A. 2R. 32P. Lough Croan.
(*h*) Including 7A. 3R. 35P. water.
(*i*) Including 1A. 1R. 15P. water.

No. of Sheet of the Ordnance Survey Maps.	Townlands and Towns.	Area in Statute Acres.	County.	Barony.	Parish.	Poor Law Union in 1857.	Townland Census of 1851, Part I.	
		A. R. P.					Vol.	Page
42	Lisnageeragh . .	507 3 14	King's Co. .	Clonlisk . .	Roscrea . .	Roscrea . .	I.	131
15	Lisnageeragh . .	429 3 26	Longford . .	Ardagh . .	Mostrim . .	Granard . .	I.	152
20	Lisnagelvin . .	36 3 27	Londonderry .	Tirkeeran . .	Clondermot .	Londonderry .	III.	248
24	Lisnageragh . .	427 2 35	Waterford .	Decies without Drum	Ballylaneen .	Kilmacthomas .	II.	354
25, 34	Lisnagirr . .	515 0 34a	Tyrone . .	Strabane Upper .	Cappagh . .	Omagh . .	III.	325
41	Lisnagirra . .	263 0 16	Roscommon .	Athlone . .	Athleague .	Roscommon .	IV.	179
26	Lisnaglea . .	219 1 15	Cavan . .	Upper Loughtee .	Larah . .	Cavan . .	III.	85
46	Lisnagleer . .	237 1 21	Tyrone . .	Dungannon Middle .	Pomeroy . .	Dungannon .	III.	304
104	Lisnagloos . .	74 2 39	Galway . .	Dunkellin . .	Killora . .	Loughrea . .	IV.	31
28, 34	Lisnagole . .	199 1 4	Fermanagh .	Magherastephana .	Aghalurcher .	Lisnaskea .	III.	217
24	Lisnagomman . .	179 0 25	Queen's Co. .	Cullenagh . .	Dysartgallen .	Abbeyleix .	I.	239
24	Lisnagomman or Coole	63 0 1	Queen's Co. .	Cullenagh . .	Dysartgallen .	Abbeyleix .	I.	239
9, 10	Lisnagon . .	278 1 1	Meath . .	Upper Kells .	Kilskeer . .	Kells . .	I.	206
9, 15	Lisnagoneeny . .	207 3 6	Kerry . .	Clanmaurice .	Rattoo . .	Listowel . .	II.	173
33, 34, 41	Lisnagonnell . .	349 2 33	Down . .	Upper Iveagh, Up. pt.	Aghaderg .	Banbridge .	III.	174
41, 47	Lisnagonoge . .	261 1 14	Tipperary, N.R.	Eliogarty . .	Holycross .	Thurles . .	II.	270
18, 23	Lisnagoon . .	158 3 9	Cavan . .	Tullygarvey .	Drumgoon .	Cootehill . .	III.	88
26	Lisnagoorneen . .	183 3 14	Cork, E.R. .	Fermoy . .	Carrigdownane .	Fermoy . .	II.	77
26	Lisnagoorneen . .	482 2 31	Cork, E.R. .	Fermoy . .	Castletownroche .	Fermoy . .	II.	77
17	Lisnagore . .	275 2 10	Monaghan .	Dartree . .	Killeevan .	Clones . .	III.	268
32, 38	Lisnagowan . .	130 2 17	Sligo . .	Corran . .	Cloonoghil .	Tobercurry .	IV.	225
16	Lisnagowan . .	151 1 36	Cavan . .	Upper Loughtee .	Castleterra .	Cavan . .	III.	83
15	Lisnagowan . .	157 3 12b	Leitrim . .	Drumahaire .	Killarga . .	Manorhamilton .	IV.	99
46	Lisnagowan . .	132 0 31	Tyrone . .	Dungannon Middle .	Donaghmore .	Dungannon .	III.	302
8	Lisnagower . .	280 3 31	Tipperary, N.R.	Lower Ormond .	Ballingarry .	Borrisokane .	II.	282
104	Lisnagranshy . .	182 1 23	Galway . .	Dunkellin . .	Kilcolgan .	Gort . .	IV.	28
68	Lisnagrave . .	276 2 13	Kerry . .	Magunihy . .	Kilcummin .	Killarney . .	II.	201
18, 22	Lisnagree . .	241 2 36	Armagh . .	Orior Lower .	Ballymore .	Newry . .	III	55
60	Lisnagree . .	217 0 7	Galway . .	Tiaquin . .	Killosolan .	Mountbellew .	IV.	78
36	Lisnagree . .	103 3 33	Kerry . .	Corkaguiny .	Killiney . .	Dingle . .	II.	178
19	Lisnagree . .	123 3 37	Waterford .	Coshmore&Coshbride	Lismore and Mocollop	Lismore . .	II.	346
31	Lisnagree . .	403 0 37	Westmeath .	Moycashel .	Kilcunrreragh .	Athlone . .	I.	278
55	Lisnagree Upper .	37 0 17	Down . .	Mourne . .	Kilkeel . .	Kilkeel . .	III.	183
15, 20	Lisnagreeve . .	197 2 22	Monaghan .	Cremorne . .	Clontibret .	Castleblayney .	III.	261
43	Lisnagreggan . .	240 0 3	Antrim . .	Upper Toome . .	Drummaul .	Antrim . .	III.	34
6, 10	Lisnagrib . .	314 3 23	Londonderry .	Keenaght . .	Aghanloo .	NewTⁿLimavady	III.	234
15, 20	Lisnagrish . .	442 1 18	Longford . .	Ardagh . .	Mostrim . .	Granard . .	I.	152
39, 41	Lisnagroagh . .	66 1 20	Roscommon .	Athlone . .	Fuerty . .	Roscommon .	IV.	181
27, 33	Lisnagroat . .	906 3 15	Londonderry .	Loughinsholin .	Tamlaght O'Crilly .	Ballymoney .	III.	243
25, 32	Lisnagroob . .	198 3 32	Roscommon .	Castlereagh .	Kiltullagh .	Castlereagh .	IV.	202
81	Lisnagross . .	192 1 0	Mayo . .	Costello . .	Aghamore .	Swineford .	IV.	137
25	Lisnagrough . .	133 1 37	Cork, E.R. .	Fermoy . .	Caherduggan .	Mallow . .	II.	77
40, 46, 47	Lisnagrough . .	231 2 14	Tipperary, N.R.	Eliogarty . .	Holycross .	Thurles . .	II.	270
2	Lisnagrow . .	144 2 2	Meath . .	Lower Kells .	Enniskeen .	Kells . .	I.	202
106, 116	Lisnagry . .	341 2 34	Galway . .	Leitrim . .	Leitrim . .	Loughrea . .	IV.	55
6	Lisnagry . .	429 2 9	Limerick . .	Clanwilliam .	Stradbally .	Limerick . .	II.	226
28, 31	Lisnaguiveragh . .	179 2 32	Monaghan .	Farney . .	Magheross .	Carrickmacross	III.	274
28	Lisnagunnion . .	134 3 14	Monaghan .	Farney . .	Donaghmoyne .	Carrickmacross	III.	270
3, 7	Lisnagunogue Lower	379 3 37	Antrim . .	Cary . .	Billy . .	Ballycastle .	III.	12
3, 7	Lisnagunogue Upper	365 3 13	Antrim . .	Cary . .	Billy . .	Ballycastle .	III.	12
122	Lisnagyreeny . .	141 1 30	Galway . .	Kiltartan . .	Kilmacduagh .	Gort . .	IV.	48
30, 39	Lisnahall . .	98 2 1	Tyrone . .	Dungannon Upper .	Artrea . .	Cookstown .	III.	306
49, 56	Lisnahanna . .	297 2 32	Tyrone . .	Omagh East .	Kilskeery .	Lowtherstown .	III.	313
18, 26	Lisnaharney . .	409 2 17	Tyrone . .	Strabane Upper .	Cappagh . .	Omagh . .	III.	325
30	Lisnahay North .	345 2 19	Antrim . .	Upper Glenarm .	Carncastle .	Larne . .	III.	24
30	Lisnahay South .	355 0 21	Antrim . .	Upper Glenarm .	Carncastle .	Larne . .	III.	24
33, 34, 39, 40	Lisnahederna . .	281 2 3	Cavan . .	Castlerahan .	Mullagh . .	Bailieborough .	III.	70
35	Lisnahederna . .	119 2 17	Cavan . .	Clankee . .	Enniskeen .	Bailieborough .	III.	73
33, 38	Lisnahilt . .	136 1 22	Antrim . .	Lower Antrim .	Racavan . .	Ballymena .	III.	4
29	Lisnahirka . .	101 1 21c	Roscommon .	Roscommon .	Cloonfinlough .	Strokestown .	IV.	209
42	Lisnahoon . .	70 0 3	Roscommon .	Athlone . .	Killinvoy .	Roscommon .	IV.	182
63	Lisnahorna . .	191 1 14	Cork, E.R. .	Cork . .	Rathcooney .	Cork . .	II.	65
55	Lisnahoy . .	48 1 28	Tyrone . .	Dungannon Middle .	Killyman .	Dungannon .	III.	303
54	Lisnahull . .	118 1 36	Tyrone . .	Dungannon Middle .	Donaghmore .	Dungannon .	III.	302
26, 31	Lisnahunshin . .	744 1 8	Antrim . .	Lower Toome .	Aghoghill .	Ballymena .	III.	32
14	Lisnakea . .	96 0 19	Armagh . .	Orior Lower .	Ballymore .	Banbridge .	III.	55
25, 26	Lisnakealwee . .	922 1 24	Kerry . .	Corkaguiny .	Cloghane .	Dingle . .	II.	175
30, 33	Lisnakeeny . .	189 2 35	Monaghan .	Farney . .	Magheracloone .	Carrickmacross	III.	273
31	Lisnakelly . .	158 0 31	Monaghan .	Farney . .	Killanny . .	Carrickmacross	III.	271
17	Lisnakill . .	200 0 23	Waterford .	Middlethird .	Lisnakill . .	Waterford .	II.	368
9	Lisnakilly . .	100 0 17d	Londonderry .	Keenaght . .	Tamlaght Finlagan .	NewTⁿLimavady	III.	237
78	Lisnakirka or Mile-bush . . .	214 3 6e	Mayo . .	Carra . .	Aglish . .	Castlebar .	IV.	124

(a) Including 5A. 1R. 22P. water.   (c) Including 17A. 0R. 15P. water.   (e) Including 1A. 3R. 33P. water.
(b) Including 8A. 0R. 32P. water.   (d) Including 0A. 2R. 7P. water.

No. of Sheet of the Ordnance Survey Maps.	Townlands and Towns.	Area in Statute Acres.			County.	Barony.	Parish.	Poor Law Union in 1857.	Townland Census of 1851, Part I.	
		A.	R.	P.					Vol.	Page
39, 40	Lisnaknock	123	3	22	Fermanagh	Coole	Galloon	Clones	III.	200
57	Lisnalanniv	365	2	32	Limerick	Coshlea	Kilbeheny	Mitchelstown	II.	239
41	Lisnalannow	64	3	25	Roscommon	Athlone	Athleague	Roscommon	IV.	179
34	Lisnalea	143	3	0a	Cavan	Clankee	Bailieborough	Bailieborough	III.	71
13, 18	Lisnalea	286	1	6	Kilkenny	Crannagh	Tullaroan	Kilkenny	I.	88
21, 22	Lisnalee	152	1	5	Armagh	Orior Lower	Forkill	Newry	III.	56
21, 22	Lisnalee	312	3	4	Armagh	Orior Lower	Loughgilly	Newry	III.	56
16	Lisnalee	225	2	18	Monaghan	Dartree	Currin	Clones	III.	266
13	Lisnalee	145	0	20	Monaghan	Monaghan	Kilmore	Monaghan	III.	276
35	Lisnalegan	150	3	6	Roscommon	Ballymoe	Cloonygormican	Roscommon	IV.	191
51	Lisnalinchy	1,018	1	15	Antrim	Lower Belfast	Ballylinny	Antrim	III.	7
23	Lisnalong	150	2	8b	Monaghan	Cremorne	Aghnamullen	Cootehill	III.	258
14	Lisnalurg	180	1	36	Sligo	Carbury	Drumcliff	Sligo	IV.	221
25, 28	Lisnamacka	99	0	22	Monaghan	Farney	Donaghmoyne	Carrickmacross	III.	270
59	Lisnamaghery	184	1	30c	Tyrone	Clogher	Clogher	Clogher	III.	293
14	Lisnamaine or Sycamore Fields	55	0	1	Cavan	Lower Loughtee	Drumlane	Cavan	III.	80
35	Lisnamallard	137	0	24	Fermanagh	Clankelly	Clones	Clones	III.	196
35	Lisnamallard	175	0	16d	Tyrone	Strabane Upper	Cappagh	Omagh	III.	325
25	Lisnamandra	89	1	7	Cavan	Upper Loughtee	Kilmore	Cavan	III.	85
80	Lisnamaneeagh	115	2	14	Mayo	Gallen	Killedan	Swineford	IV.	150
24, 28	Lisnamanny	692	1	23	Antrim	Kilconway	Dunaghy	Ballymena	III.	26
37	Lisnamaul	278	3	1	Down	Lecale Upper	Down	Downpatrick	III.	180
30, 44	Lisnaminaun	263	0	24	Galway	Clare	Killererin	Tuam	IV.	21
10	Lisnamintry	173	3	18	Armagh	Oneilland East	Seagoe	Lurgan	III.	50
21	Lisnamoe	219	2	24	Tipperary, N.R.	Upper Ormond	Ballymackey	Nenagh	II.	289
86	Lisnamoltaun	351	0	33	Galway	Kilconnell	Killaan	Ballinasloe	IV.	41
54	Lisnamonaghan	132	2	38	Tyrone	Dungannon Middle	Donaghmore	Dungannon	III.	302
30	Lisnamore	246	0	30	Down	Castlereagh Upper	Kilmore	Downpatrick	III.	165
47	Lisnamorrow	384	3	7	Londonderry	Loughinsholin	Artrea	Magherafelt	III.	238
35	Lisnamovaun	241	3	32	Kerry	Corkaguiny	Cloghane	Dingle	II.	175
111, 119	Lisnamoyle	167	2	18	Mayo	Kilmaine	Kilcommon	Ballinrobe	IV.	155
28	Lisnamoyle Etra	150	3	15	Monaghan	Farney	Donaghmoyne	Carrickmacross	III.	270
28	Lisnamoyle Otra	149	0	9	Monaghan	Farney	Donaghmoyne	Carrickmacross	III.	270
49, 55	Lisnamrock	317	2	16	Tipperary, S.R.	Slievardagh	Ballingarry	Callan	II.	332
20	Lisnamuck	363	3	11	Limerick	Connello Lower	Croagh	Rathkeale	II.	228
11	Lisnamuck	302	3	22	Londonderry	Coleraine	Aghadowey	Coleraine	III.	230
36	Lisnamuck	284	0	26	Londonderry	Loughinsholin	Maghera	Magherafelt	III.	242
13, 14	Lisnamuck	265	2	19	Longford	Ardagh	Templemichael	Longford	I.	154
82	Lisnamuck	367	2	15	Tipperary, S.R.	Iffa and Offa West	Derrygrath	Clogheen	II.	318
47	Lisnamucklagh	28	1	16	Roscommon	Athlone	Dysart	Athlone	IV.	181
47	Lisnamucklagh	244	0	15	Roscommon	Athlone	Taghboy	Athlone	IV.	184
79	Lisnamulligan	260	2	36	Donegal	Raphoe	Donaghmore	Strabane	III.	138
47, 48	Lisnamulligan	692	2	7	Down	Upper Iveagh, Lr.pt.	Clonduff	Newry	III.	171
39	Lisnamult	261	2	11	Roscommon	Ballintober South	Roscommon	Roscommon	IV.	190
33	Lisnamurrikin	601	1	25	Antrim	Lower Antrim	Racavan	Ballymena	III.	4
14	Lisnanagh	630	2	22	Longford	Granard	Killoe	Granard	I.	157
31	Lisnananagh	209	1	34	Cavan	Clanmahon	Ballintemple	Cavan	III.	75
21, 26	Lisnananagh	167	0	34	Cavan	Upper Loughtee	Larah	Cavan	III.	85
38	Lisnanane	319	0	26	Tyrone	Dungannon Upper	Desertcreat	Cookstown	III.	308
2	Lisnanard	127	1	18	Clare	Burren	Drumcreehy	Ballyvaghan	II.	12
40	Lisnanarriagh	335	3	3	Roscommon	Ballintober South	Cloontuskert	Roscommon	IV.	188
15, 16, 18	Lisnanaw	83	2	20	Leitrim	Drumahaire	Inishmagrath	Manorhamilton	IV.	97
15, 16	Lisnaneane	87	1	8	Longford	Granard	Granard	Granard	I.	156
22, 28	Lisnaneane	255	1	0e	Roscommon	Roscommon	Kilcooley	Strokestown	IV.	210
53	Lisnanees Lower	129	2	9	Donegal	Kilmacrenan	Aghanunshin	Letterkenny	III.	122
53	Lisnanees Upper	192	2	11	Donegal	Kilmacrenan	Aghanunshin	Letterkenny	III.	122
9	Lisnanore	46	3	20	Monaghan	Monaghan	Tehallan	Monaghan	III.	280
16, 18	Lisnanorrus	88	3	32	Leitrim	Drumahaire	Inishmagrath	Manorhamilton	IV.	97
38, 47	Lisnanoul	145	1	9	Kerry	Trughanacmy	Kiltallagh	Tralee	II.	212
9	Lisnanroum	103	3	29	Clare	Burren	Kilcorney	Ballyvaghan	II.	12
11, 17	Lisnanuran	200	3	7	Roscommon	Roscommon	Aughrim	Cark. on Shannon	IV.	207
99,100,104	Lisnapaste	569	0	28f	Donegal	Tirhugh	Drumhome	Donegal	III.	146
78, 89	Lisnaponra North	155	3	16	Mayo	Carra	Ballyhean	Castlebar	IV.	126
89	Lisnaponra South	91	1	38	Mayo	Carra	Ballyhean	Castlebar	IV.	126
51	Lisnarable	341	1	2	Tyrone	Clogher	Clogher	Clogher	III.	293
6	Lisnaragh Irish	616	2	33g	Tyrone	Strabane Lower	Donaghedy	Gortin	III.	321
6	Lisnaragh Scotch	172	1	21	Tyrone	Strabane Lower	Donaghedy	Gortin	III.	321
79	Lisnaran	111	0	29	Mayo	Carra	Breaghwy	Castlebar	IV.	127
19	Lisnarawer	195	3	12	Sligo	Tireragh	Dromard	Dromore West	IV.	233
69	Lisnaree	26	2	23	Donegal	Raphoe	Convoy	Stranorlar	III.	136
69	Lisnaree	68	2	15	Donegal	Raphoe	Stranorlar	Stranorlar	III.	143
41	Lisnaree	314	0	9	Down	Lordship of Newry	Newry	Newry	III.	182

(a) Including 4A. 3R. 3P. water.
(b) Including 4A. 1R. 13P. water.
(c) Including 0A. 2R. 32P. water.
(d) Including 7A. 2R. 13P. water.
(e) Including 8A. 2R. 25P. water.
(f) Including 15A. 2R. 14P. water.
(g) Including 6A. 2 t. 4P. water.

No. of Sheet of the Ordnance Survey Maps.	Townlands and Towns.	Area in Statute Acres.			County.	Barony.	Parish.	Poor Law Union in 1857.	Townland Census of 1851, Part I.	
		A.	R.	P.					Vol.	Page
27, 34	Lisnaree . . .	437	3	14	Down . .	Upper Iveagh, Up. pt.	Seapatrick . .	Banbridge . .	III.	176
29	Lisnareelin . .	60	0	11	Tipperary, N.R.	Ikerrin . .	Killea . . .	Roscrea . .	II.	275
6, 11	Lisnarick . .	101	2	11	Antrim . .	Lower Dunluce .	Ballyrashane .	Coleraine . .	III.	15
2	Lisnarode . .	157	3	17	Queen's Co. .	Tinnahinch . .	Kilmanman . .	Mountmellick .	I.	249
11	Lisnaroe Far . .	83	3	12	Monaghan .	Dartree . . .	Clones . . .	Clones . .	III.	264
11	Lisnaroe Near .	131	0	32a	Monaghan .	Dartree . . .	Clones . . .	Clones . .	III.	265
10	LISNARRICK T. .	—			Fermanagh .	Lurg . . .	Derryvullan . .	Lowtherstown .	III.	205
27, 35	Lisnasallagh . .	129	1	32	Cork, E.R. .	Condons&Clangibbon	Clondulane . .	Fermoy . .	II.	60
27, 35	Lisnasallagh . .	33	1	15	Cork, E.R. .	Fermoy . . .	Kilcrumper . .	Fermoy . .	II.	80
15, 16	Lisnasallagh . .	81	2	1b	Down . .	Castlereagh Upper .	Saintfield . .	Lisburn . .	III.	166
17	Lisnasaran . .	84	2	32c	Cavan . .	Tullygarvey . .	Drumgoon . .	Cootehill . .	III.	88
35	Lisnassonagh .	105	1	12	Cavan . .	Clankee . .	Enniskeen . .	Bailieborough .	III.	73
22, 23	Lisnascreen . .	143	1	0	Westmeath .	Kilkenny West .	Kilkenny West .	Athlone . .	I.	273
61	Lisnascreena . .	275	0	2	Galway . .	Kilconnell . .	Fohanagh . .	Mountbellew .	IV.	40
25, 26	Lisnascreghog .	752	1	26	Londonderry .	Coleraine . .	Errigal . .	Coleraine . .	III.	232
40	Lisnasella . .	106	1	6	Tipperary, N.R.	Kilnamanagh Upper	Ballycahill . .	Thurles . .	II.	277
61	Lisnashandrum East	129	2	35	Cork, E.R. .	East Muskerry .	Inishcarra . .	Cork . .	II.	104
61	Lisnashandrum West	102	1	21	Cork, E.R. .	East Muskerry .	Inishcarra . .	Cork . .	II.	104
20	Lisnashanker . .	301	2	31	Down . .	Lower Iveagh, Up. pt.	Magheralin . .	Lurgan . .	III.	170
16, 21	Lisnashanna . .	176	2	5d	Cavan . .	Upper Loughtee .	Castleterra . .	Cavan . .	III.	83
31	Lisnashannagh .	106	1	0	Monaghan .	Farney . . .	Killanny . .	Carrickmacross	III.	271
13	Lisnashannagh .	194	1	28	Monaghan .	Monaghan . .	Kilmore . .	Monaghan . .	III.	276
4	Lisnasharragh .	182	3	27	Down . .	Castlereagh Upper .	Knockbreda . .	Belfast . .	III.	165
30, 39	Lisnashearshane .	296	0	23e	Cork, E.R. .	Duhallow . .	Cullen . .	Millstreet . .	II.	70
40	Lisnashillida . .	126	1	32	Fermanagh .	Clankelly . .	Galloon . .	Clones . .	III.	198
41	Lisnasillagh . .	245	1	4	Roscommon .	Athlone . .	Athleague . .	Roscommon .	IV.	179
34	LISNASKEA T. .	—			Fermanagh .	Magherastephana .	Aghalurcher .	Lisnaskea . .	III.	218
34	Lisnasliggan . .	568	1	7	Down . .	Upper Iveagh, Up. pt.	Annaclone . .	Banbridge . .	III.	174
23	Lisnasoo . .	222	0	28	Antrim . .	Kilconway . .	Grange of Dundermot	Ballymena . .	III.	27
10	Lisnascoolmoy .	248	3	19	Tipperary, N.R.	Lower Ormond .	Ardcrony . .	Borrisokane .	II.	282
47	Lisnastrane . .	248	1	33	Tyrone . .	Dungannon Middle .	Clonoe . .	Dungannon .	III.	300
14, 15	Lisnastrean . .	413	3	2	Down . .	Castlereagh Upper .	Drumbo . .	Lisburn . .	III.	164
20	Lisnasure . .	246	2	13	Down . .	Lower Iveagh, Up. pt.	Magheralin . .	Lurgan . .	III.	170
55	Lisnataylor . .	856	1	14	Antrim . .	Lower Massereene .	Killead . .	Antrim . .	III.	28
41	Lisnatea . .	146	0	11f	Roscommon .	Athlone . .	Fuerty . .	Roscommon .	IV.	181
40, 41	Lisnatierny . .	415	1	24	Down . .	Upper Iveagh, Up. pt.	Aghaderg . .	Banbridge . .	III.	174
37	Lisnatinny . .	148	2	11	Cavan . .	Clannahon . .	Drumlumman .	Granard . .	III.	77
8, 14	Lisnatrunk . .	27	3	33g	Down . .	Castlereagh Upper .	Blaris . .	Lisburn . .	III.	164
8, 9, 14, 15	Lisnatrunk . .	300	3	0	Down . .	Castlereagh Upper .	Lambeg . .	Lisburn . .	III.	166
77, 78	Lisnatubbrid . .	540	0	11	Tipperary, S.R.	Iffa and Offa East .	Temple-etney .	Clonmel . .	II.	316
25	Lisnatullagh . .	330	2	3h	Leitrim . .	Carrigallen . .	Oughteragh . .	Bawnboy . .	IV.	92
17	Lisnatunny Glebe .	485	1	8i	Tyrone . .	Strabane Lower .	Ardstraw . .	Gortin . .	III.	319
35, 41, 42	Lisnavaghrog . .	432	2	38	Down . .	Upper Iveagh, Lr. pt.	Drumballyroney .	Banbridge . .	III.	172
18	Lisnaveane . .	206	0	30	Monaghan .	Cremorne . .	Tullycorbet . .	Monaghan . .	III.	263
18	Lisnaveane . .	283	0	0	Monaghan .	Dartree . . .	Ematris . .	Cootehill . .	III.	267
29	Lisnaviddoge North	89	1	22	Tipperary, N.R.	Eliogarty . .	Templemore . .	Thurles . .	II.	272
29	Lisnaviddoge South	59	3	22	Tipperary, N.R.	Eliogarty . .	Templemore . .	Thurles . .	II.	272
36	Lisnavoe . .	67	0	30j	Fermanagh .	Clankelly . .	Clones . .	Clones . .	III.	196
27	Lisnaward . .	413	3	10	Down . .	Lower Iveagh, Lr. pt.	Dromore . .	Banbridge . .	III.	168
59	Lisnawery . .	96	3	30	Tyrone . .	Clogher . . .	Errigal Keerogue .	Clogher . .	III.	295
36	Lisnawesnagh .	41	3	1	Fermanagh .	Clankelly . .	Clones . .	Clones . .	III.	196
38	Lisnawhiggel . .	364	0	26	Antrim . .	Lower Antrim .	Connor . .	Ballymena . .	III.	3
7	Lisnawully . .	283	1	24	Louth . .	Upper Dundalk .	Dundalk . .	Dundalk . .	I.	178
14, 20	Lisneal . .	153	0	32	Londonderry .	Tirkeeran . .	Clondermot . .	Londonderry .	III.	248
8, 9	Lisneany . .	216	2	28	Armagh . .	Oneilland West .	Loughgall . .	Armagh . .	III.	54
39	Lisneight . .	49	1	38	Tyrone . .	Dungannon Middle .	Donaghenry . .	Cookstown . .	III.	301
53	Lisnenan . .	232	1	29	Donegal . .	Kilmacrenan .	Conwal . .	Letterkenny .	III.	126
3, 4, 9	Lisnevagh . .	1,110	1	3	Carlow . .	Rathvilly . .	Rathvilly . .	Baltinglass .	I.	12
43, 44	Lisnevanagh . .	741	3	9	Antrim . .	Upper Toome . .	Shilvodan Grange .	Antrim . .	III.	35
11	Lisnisk . .	307	2	27	Antrim . .	Lower Dunluce .	Ballyrashane . .	Ballymoney .	III.	15
18	Lisnisk . .	335	0	16	Antrim . .	Upper Dunluce .	Loughguile . .	Ballymoney .	III.	20
17	Lisnisk . .	185	0	22	Armagh . .	Orior Lower . .	Loughgilly . .	Newry . .	III.	56
42	Lisnisk . .	475	3	21k	Down . .	Upper Iveagh, Lr. pt.	Drumballyroney .	Banbridge . .	III.	172
6, 10	Lisnisky . .	184	2	9	Armagh . .	Oneilland East .	Seagoe . .	Lurgan . .	III.	50
70	Lisnoble . .	22	0	31	Donegal . .	Raphoe . .	Raphoe . .	Strabane . .	III.	141
15	Lisnode . .	253	0	31	Down . .	Castlereagh Upper .	Drumbo . .	Lisburn . .	III.	164
14	Lisnoe . .	153	3	26	Down . .	Castlereagh Upper .	Blaris . .	Lisburn . .	III.	164
79, 90	Lisnolan . .	338	3	3l	Mayo . .	Carra . .	Manulla . .	Castlebar . .	IV.	129
1	Lisnugent . .	62	0	39	Westmeath .	Fore . .	Foyran . .	Granard . .	I.	270
12	Lisoarty . .	112	1	26	Monaghan .	Dartree . .	Clones . .	Clones . .	III.	283
45	Lisoid . .	280	3	24	Down . .	Lecale Upper .	Bright . .	Downpatrick .	III.	100
28	Lisoivan . .	72	0	3	Fermanagh .	Magherastephana .	Aghavea . .	Lisnaskea . .	III.	219
28,29,32,33	Lisomadaun . .	159	3	30	Leitrim . .	Mohill . .	Mohill . .	Mohill . .	IV.	108

(a) Including 15A. 3R. 0P. water.
(b) Including 5A. 3R. 10P. water.
(c) Including 4A. 2R. 3P. water.
(d) Including 6A. 0R. 22P. water.

(e) Including 1A. 2R. 16P. water.
(f) Including 10A. 0R. 12P. water.
(g) Including 0A. 2R. 12P. water.
(h) Including 17A. 0R. 30P. water.

(i) Including 9A. 3R. 21P. water.
(j) Including 3A. 1R. 31P. water.
(k) Including 12A. 2R. 24P. water.
(l) Including 2A. 2R. 19P. water.

No. of Sheet of the Ordnance Survey Maps.	Townlands and Towns.	Area in Statute Acres. A. R. P.	County.	Barony.	Parish.	Poor Law Union in 1857.	Townland Census of 1851, Part I. Vol.	Page
34	Lisoneill . . .	145 2 0	Fermanagh	Magherastephana	Aghalurcher . .	Lisnaskea	III.	217
23	Lisowen . . .	911 3 38	Down . .	Castlereagh Upper .	Saintfield	Downpatrick .	III.	166
92	Lispatrick . .	37 3 6a	Mayo . .	Costello . .	Knock . .	Claremorris .	IV.	143
124, 137	Lispatrick Lower .	304 2 4	Cork, W.R.	Courceys . .	Ringrone . .	Kinsale . .	II.	147
137	Lispatrick Upper .	271 2 26	Cork, W.R.	Courceys . .	Ringrone . .	Kinsale . .	II.	147
100	Lispheasty . .	118 2 22	Galway . .	Longford . .	Clonfert . . .	Ballinasloe	IV.	57
16	Lisphilip . .	146 3 0	Roscommon .	Frenchpark .	Kilmacumsy .	Boyle . .	IV.	203
7, 11	Lispopple . .	611 1 33	Dublin . .	Nethercross .	Killossery . .	Balrothery .	I.	31
3, 6, 7	Lispopple . .	238 1 10	Westmeath .	Fore . .	Mayne . .	Granard .	I.	271
40	Lispuckaun . .	319 0 11	Clare . .	Islands . .	Kilmaley . .	Ennis . .	II.	31
14, 19	Lisquigny . .	133 0 17	Monaghan .	Monaghan . .	Tullycorbet . .	Monaghan .	III.	281
9	Lisquillibeen .	384 1 10	Tipperary, N.R.	Lower Ormond .	Kilbarron . .	Borrisokane .	III.	284
77, 78	Lisquinlan . .	756 3 8	Cork, E.R.	Imokilly . .	Ightermurragh .	Middleton .	II.	87
123	Lisrabirra . .	43 0 32	Galway . .	Kiltartan . .	Kiltartan . .	Gort . .	IV.	48
35, 40	Lisrace . . .	146 0 0	Fermanagh .	Clankelly . .	Clones . .	Clones . .	III.	196
10, 15	Lisraghtigan .	140 3 16	Longford . .	Granard . .	Clonbroney . .	Granard .	I.	155
3	Lisraherty . .	144 1 25	Longford . .	Granard . .	Killoe . .	Granard .	I.	157
18	Lisraw . . .	366 0 13	Armagh . .	Orior Lower .	Ballymore .	Newry . .	III.	55
18	Lisready (Clare) .	322 3 27	Limerick . .	Shanid . .	Loghill . .	Glin . .	II.	257
18	Lisready (Cripps) .	475 0 12	Limerick . .	Shanid . .	Loghill . .	Glin . .	II.	257
25, 26	Lisreagh . .	155 2 29	Cavan . .	Upper Loughtee .	Annagelliff . .	Cavan . .	III.	82
22, 27	Lisreagh . .	233 1 26	Fermanagh .	Tirkennedy . .	Derryvullan .	Enniskillen .	III.	221
14	Lisrenny . .	3 1 13	Louth . .	Ardee . .	Charlestown .	Ardee . .	I.	171
14	Lisrenny . .	848 3 0	Louth . .	Ardee . .	Tallanstown .	Ardee . .	I.	175
17	Lisrevagh . .	290 0 6	Longford . .	Rathcline . .	Rathcline . .	Longford .	I.	165
6	Lisrivis . . .	446 1 23	Galway . .	Ballymoe . .	Templetogher .	Glennamaddy .	IV.	9
55, 62	Lisroan . .	133 3 34	Tyrone . .	Dungannon Middle .	Clonfeacle . .	Dungannon .	III.	299
90, 100	Lisrobert . .	214 0 2b	Mayo . .	Carra . .	Drum . .	Castlebar .	IV.	128
101	Lisrobert . .	64 3 22	Mayo . .	Clanmorris .	Tagheen . .	Claremorris .	IV.	136
22	Lisrobin East .	297 1 32	Cork, E.R.	Duhallow . .	Kilmeen . .	Kanturk . .	II.	73
22	Lisrobin West .	527 3 3	Cork, E.R.	Duhallow . .	Kilmeen . .	Kanturk . .	II.	73
31	Lisrodden . .	265 2 37	Antrim . .	Lower Toome .	Ahoghill . .	Ballymena .	III.	32
26	Lisroddy . .	39 1 20	Fermanagh .	Clanawley . .	Rossorry . .	Enniskillen .	III.	194
15, 16	Lisroe . .	205 2 13	Clare . .	Corcomroe .	Clooney . .	Ennistimon .	II.	18
40	Lisroe . .	538 1 19	Clare . .	Islands . .	Kilmaley . .	Ennis . .	II.	31
122	Lisroe . .	91 3 33	Cork, W.R.	East Carbery (E.D.)	Kilgarriff . .	Clonakilty .	II.	129
17	Lisroe . .	521 0 10	Kerry . .	Clanmaurice .	Duagh . .	Listowel . .	II.	168
58	Lisroe . .	151 0 22	Kerry . .	Magunihy . .	Kilcummin .	Killarney .	II.	201
22	Lisroe . .	238 2 39	Waterford .	Decies without Drum	Modelligo .	Dungarvan .	II.	359
77	Lisronagh . .	573 2 19	Tipperary, S.R.	Iffa and Offa East .	Lisronagh .	Clonmel . .	II.	315
36	Lisroon . .	72 1 1	Fermanagh .	Clankelly . .	Clones . .	Clones . .	III.	196
3	Lisroosky . .	105 1 1	Monaghan .	Trough . .	Errigal Trough .	Monaghan .	III.	285
22, 25	Lisroughty . .	149 1 38	Leitrim . .	Carrigallen .	Drumreilly .	Bawnboy .	IV.	91
23, 29	Lisroyne . .	448 2 37c	Roscommon .	Roscommon .	Bumlin . .	Strokestown .	IV.	208
26	Lisruntagh . .	133 3 6	Sligo . .	Tirerrill . .	Ballysadare .	Sligo . .	IV.	238
15, 16	Lisryan . .	411 0 4	Longford . .	Ardagh . .	Street . .	Granard .	I.	153
19	Liss . . .	402 2 23	Clare . .	Tulla Upper .	Feakle . .	Tulla . .	II.	39
42, 56	Liss . . .	416 2 3	Galway . .	Clare . .	Killeany . .	Tuam . .	IV.	20
116, 125	Liss . . .	309 2 6	Galway . .	Leitrim . .	Ballynakill .	Loughrea .	IV.	52
58	Liss . . .	486 0 18	Galway . .	Tiaquin . .	Abbeyknockmoy .	Tuam . .	IV.	75
99, 107	Liss . . .	633 0 19	Kerry . .	Dunkerron South .	Kilcrohane .	Kenmare .	II.	184
34	Liss . . .	321 1 30	Tipperary, N.R.	Kilnamanagh Upper	Glenkeen . .	Thurles . .	II.	278
19	Liss . . .	316 0 36	Waterford .	Coshmore&Coshbride	Lismore and Mocollop	Lismore . .	II.	347
139	Lissacaha . .	779 0 16	Cork, W.R.	West Carbery (W.D.)	Skull . .	Skull . .	II.	146
139	Lissacaha (North) .	349 3 30	Cork, W.R.	West Carbery (W.D.)	Skull . .	Skull . .	II.	146
39	Lissacapia . .	55 1 21	Cork. W.R.	West Muskerry .	Kilcorney .	Millstreet .	II.	158
33	Lissacapple . .	186 1 4	Cavan . .	Castlerahan .	Killinkere .	Bailieborough .	III.	69
18, 31	Lissacarha . .	263 2 38	Galway . .	Tiaquin . .	Kilkerrin . .	Glennamaddy .	IV.	77
22, 25	Lissacarn . .	254 0 13d	Leitrim . .	Carrigallen .	Oughteragh .	Bawnboy .	IV.	92
39	Lissacarrow . .	178 3 12	Roscommon .	Athlone . .	Fuerty . .	Roscommon .	IV.	181
107, 110	Lissacholly . .	612 2 25	Donegal . .	Tirhugh . .	Kilbarron .	Ballyshannon .	III.	148
132, 141	Lissaclarig East .	360 0 38	Cork, W.R.	West Carbery(W.D.)	Kilcoe . .	Skull . .	II.	143
131, 132, ⎱ 140, 141 ⎰	Lissaclarig West .	392 1 6	Cork, W.R.	West Carbery(W.D.)	Kilcoe . . .	Skull . .	II.	143
70	Lissacresig . .	251 3 13	Cork, W.R.	West Muskerry .	Clondrohid .	Macroom .	II.	155
108	Lissacroneen .	213 0 15	Cork, W.R.	East Carbery (W.D.)	Kinneigh . .	Dunmanway .	II.	135
66, 77	Lissacrue . .	138 2 15	Cork, E.R.	Imokilly . .	Killeagh . .	Youghal . .	II.	88
98	Lissacullaun . .	109 0 19	Galway . .	Kilconnell .	Killallaghtan .	Ballinasloe	IV.	41
98	Lissacullaun . .	45 0 3	Galway . .	Longford . .	Killoran . .	Ballinasloe	IV.	59
14	Lissacurkia . .	382 2 21	Roscommon .	Frenchpark .	Tibohine . .	Castlereagh .	IV.	205
28	Lissacurkia . .	133 3 23	Roscommon .	Roscommon .	Kilcooley . .	Strokestown .	IV.	210
5, 8	Lissadill . .	634 2 7	Sligo . .	Carbury . .	Drumcliff .	Sligo . .	IV.	221
78, 79	Lissadober . .	375 2 39	Tipperary, S.R.	Iffa and Offa East .	Kilmurry . .	Carrick on Suir	II.	314

(a) Including 6A. 3R. 20P. water.
(b) Including 7A. 0R. 8P. water.
(c) Including 16A. 2R. 23P. water.
(d) Including 13A. 0R. 12P. water.

No. of Sheet of the Ordnance Survey Maps.	Townlands and Towns.	Area in Statute Acres.			County.	Barony.	Parish.	Poor Law Union in 1857.	Townland Census of 1851, Part I.	
		A.	R.	P.					Vol.	Page
114	Lissadoill	211	0	13	Galway	Loughrea	Kilthomas	Gort	IV.	65
11	Lissadonna	403	2	5a	Tipperary, N.R.	Lower Ormond	Ballingarry	Borrisokane	II.	282
16, 17	Lissadorn	572	2	10	Roscommon	Roscommon	Aughrim	Carᵏ. on Shannon	IV.	207
7, 14	Lissadrone East	240	1	17	Mayo	Tirawley	Lackan	Killala	IV.	171
7, 14	Lissadrone West	322	3	13	Mayo	Tirawley	Lackan	Killala	IV.	171
114	Lissadulta	131	3	6	Galway	Kiltartan	Kilthomas	Gort	IV.	49
4	Lissagadda	167	2	10	Tipperary, N.R.	Lower Ormond	Lorrha	Borrisokane	II.	285
35, 39	Lissagallan	1,000	1	29	Roscommon	Athlone	Fuerty	Roscommon	IV.	181
11, 15	Lissagally	418	1	30	Armagh	Armagh	Derrynoose	Armagh	III.	44
25, 29	Lissagarvan	1,090	1	18	Leitrim	Mohill	Cloone	Mohill	IV.	106
8	Lissagernal	224	3	35	Longford	Longford	Clongesh	Longford	I.	158
14, 19	Lissaghanedan	199	2	8	Longford	Ardagh	Ardagh	Longford	I.	151
12	Lissaghmore	207	3	28	Londonderry	Coleraine	Agivey	Coleraine	III.	230
34	Lissagorry Glebe	80	2	29	Fermanagh	Clankelly	Galloon	Lisnaskea	III.	198
147	Lissagriffin	344	3	4	Cork, W.R.	West Carbery(W.D.)	Kilmoe	Skull	II.	145
97	Lissagroom	300	0	27	Cork, E.R.	Kinalea	Knockavilly	Bandon	II.	96
81	Lissagurraun	157	0	14	Galway	Moycullen	Moycullen	Galway	IV.	71
16	Lissahane	525	2	15	Kerry	Clanmaurice	Kilfeighny	Listowel	II.	170
16	Lissahane	305	1	24	Waterford	Decies without Drum	Newcastle	Kilmacthomas	II.	359
14	Lissahawley	142	1	9	Londonderry	Tirkeeran	Clondermot	Londonderry	III.	248
22	Lissakillen North	131	3	22	Westmeath	Kilkenny West	Bunown	Athlone	I.	272
22	Lissakillen South	180	0	15	Westmeath	Kilkenny West	Bunown	Athlone	I.	272
32	Lissakilly	191	1	38	Westmeath	Moycashel	Castletownkindalen	Mullingar	I.	277
23	Lissakit	145	0	18	Longford	Moydow	Taghsheenod	Ballymahon	I.	162
81	Lissakyle	70	3	19b	Tipperary, S.R.	Iffa and Offa West	Caher	Clogheen	II.	318
90	Lissalacaun	132	0	22c	Mayo	Carra	Drum	Castlebar	IV.	128
16	Lissaleen	227	0	32	Galway	Dunmore	Kilbennan	Tuam	IV.	34
12, 21	Lissaleen	199	2	39	Limerick	Pubblebrien	Croom	Limerick	II.	252
22	Lissalican	548	1	35	Carlow	St. Mullins Lower	Ballyellin	New Ross	I.	13
132, 133,} 141, 142 }	Lissalohorig	419	2	25	Cork, W.R.	West Carbery (E.D.)	Abbeystrowry	Skibbereen	II.	136
96, 97	Lissalondoon	115	2	8	Galway	Dunkellin	Kilconierin	Loughrea	IV.	29
25	Lissalough	152	1	14	Sligo	Leyny	Killoran	Tobercurry	IV.	230
71	Lissalougha	77	3	36	Clare	Moyarta	Kilballyowen	Kilrush	II.	32
98	Lissalumma	170	6	22	Galway	Leitrim	Abbeygormacan	Loughrea	IV.	50
21, 27	Lissalway	1,525	1	12	Roscommon	Castlereagh	Baslick	Castlereagh	IV.	199
9, 14	Lissameen	303	3	11	Longford	Granard	Clonbroney	Granard	I.	155
153	Lissamona	176	0	25	Cork, W.R.	West Carbery (E.D.)	Clear-island	Skibbereen	II.	138
29, 30	Lissamota	607	2	9	Limerick	Connello Upper	Ballingarry	Croom	II.	231
22	Lissan	559	2	9	Fermanagh	Tirkennedy	Derryvullan	Enniskillen	III.	221
54	Lissan	147	2	11	Tyrone	Dungannon Middle	Clonfeacle	Dungannon	III.	299
29	Lissan	220	3	12	Tyrone	Dungannon Upper	Lissan	Cookstown	III.	309
35, 43	Lissan	217	2	22d	Tyrone	Omagh East	Drumragh	Omagh	III.	312
10ˢ	Lissanacody	507	0	15	Galway	Longford	Donanaghta	Portumna	IV.	58
48, 58	Lissanair	435	3	28	Clare	Clonderalaw	Kilmihil	Kilrush	II.	17
13	Lissanalta	238	0	3	Limerick	Pubblebrien	Knocknagaul	Limerick	II.	253
15, 16	Lissananny	618	1	22e	Galway	Dunmore	Kilbennan	Tuam	IV.	34
20	Lissananny	545	2	5	Roscommon	Frenchpark	Tibohine	Castlereagh	IV.	205
39	Lissananny Beg	403	1	5	Sligo	Corran	Emlaghfad	Boyle	IV.	226
33, 39	Lissananny More	195	3	9	Sligo	Corran	Emlaghfad	Sligo	IV.	226
117	Lissanard East	228	3	7	Galway	Leitrim	Tynagh	Portumna	IV.	55
117	Lissanard West	67	3	23	Galway	Leitrim	Tynagh	Portumna	IV.	55
50	Lissanarroor	161	0	16	Limerick	Coshlea	Galbally	Mitchelstown	II.	239
45, 46, 48	Lissan Demesne	171	1	20	Londonderry	Loughinsholin	Lissan	Magherafelt	III.	242
3	Lissanduff or Bushfoot	225	2	3	Antrim	Lower Dunluce	Dunluce	Coleraine	III.	17
32	Lissaneagh	141	1	15	Sligo	Leyny	Achonry	Tobercurry	IV.	229
21, 29	Lissanearla East	235	1	16	Kerry	Trughanacmy	Tralee	Tralee	II.	213
21, 29	Lissanearla West	229	0	16	Kerry	Trughanacmy	Tralee	Tralee	II.	213
41, 42	Lissan East	214	0	33	Clare	Islands	Clareabbey	Ennis	II.	29
39	Lissaneaville	500	2	15	Roscommon	Athlone	Fuerty	Roscommon	IV.	181
50	Lissaneden	315	2	16	Tyrone	Omagh East	Dromore	Omagh	III.	311
26	Lissaneena	362	3	8f	Sligo	Tirerrill	Ballysadare	Sligo	IV.	238
27	Lissaneeny	160	1	20	Sligo	Tirerrill	Ballynakill	Sligo	IV.	237
132, 133	Lissane Lower	246	0	12	Cork, W.R.	West Carbery (E.D.)	Caheragh	Skibbereen	II.	137
119,132,133	Lissane Upper	281	1	4	Cork, W.R.	West Carbery (E.D.)	Caheragh	Skibbereen	II.	137
132	Lissangle	443	3	33	Cork, W.R.	West Carbery(W.D.)	Caheragh	Skibbereen	II.	142
39, 43	Lissanierin	572	2	27	King's Co.	Ballybritt	Aghancon	Roscrea	I.	124
29,30,38,39	Lissaniska	149	2	11g	Cork, E.R.	Duhallow	Cullen	Millstreet	II.	70
125	Lissaniska	148	2	39	Galway	Leitrim	Ballynakill	Loughrea	IV.	52
58	Lissaniska	211	2	3	Galway	Tiaquin	Abbeyknockmoy	Tuam	IV.	75
93	Lissaniska	231	2	21	Kerry	Glanarought	Kenmare	Kenmare	II.	186
11	Lissaniska	767	2	22	Kerry	Iraghticonnor	Knockanure	Listowel	II.	192
13, 14	Lissaniska	142	3	0	King's Co.	Garrycastle	Tisaran	Parsonstown	I.	138

(a) Including 10A. 1R. 6P. water.　　(d) Including 10A. 2R. 9P. water.　　(f) Including 0A. 1R. 21P. water.
(b) Including 1A. 2R. 24P. water.　　(e) Including 20A. 1R. 24P. water.　　(g) Including 2A. 0R. 12P. water.
(c) Including 6A. 2R. 35P. water.

No. of Sheet of the Ordnance Survey Maps.	Townlands and Towns.	Area in Statute Acres. A. R. P.	County.	Barony.	Parish.	Poor Law Union in 1857.	Townland Census of 1851, Part I. Vol.	Page
90	Lissaniska	168 2 8	Mayo	Carra	Drum	Castlebar	IV.	128
79	Lissaniska	357 0 23	Mayo	Carra	Kildacommoge	Castlebar	IV.	129
92, 102	Lissaniska	826 2 14a	Mayo	Costello	Bekan	Claremorris	IV.	139
71	Lissaniska	72 0 30	Mayo	Gallen	Bohola	Swineford	IV.	147
100	Lissaniska	257 0 36	Mayo	Kilmaine	Robeen	Ballinrobe	IV.	157
38	Lissaniska	94 0 25	Waterford	Decies within Drum	Lisgnan or Grange	Youghal	II.	352
36, 37	Lissaniska East	328 3 36	Limerick	Glenquin	Clonelty	Newcastle	II.	245
48	Lissaniska East	353 3 2	Mayo	Tirawley	Ballynahaglish	Ballina	IV.	164
107	Lissaniska North	408 2 14	Galway	Longford	Killimorbologue	Portumna	IV.	59
107, 117	Lissaniska South	630 2 15	Galway	Longford	Killimorbologue	Portumna	IV.	59
36	Lissaniska West	292 1 27	Limerick	Glenquin	Clonelty	Newcastle	II.	245
48	Lissaniska West	363 0 27	Mayo	Tirawley	Ballynahaglish	Ballina	IV.	164
75, 87	Lissanisky	94 2 39	Cork, E.R.	Barrymore	Clonmel	Cork	II.	53
25, 33	Lissanisky	301 1 15	Cork, E.R.	Fermoy	Carrigleamleary	Mallow	II.	77
96, 97	Lissanisky	485 3 4	Cork, E.R.	Kinalea	Knockavilly	Bandon	II.	96
2, 8	Lissanisky	626 2 32	King's Co.	Kilcoursey	Kilbride	Tullamore	I.	141
14, 19	Lissanisky	92 3 39	Longford	Ardagh	Ardagh	Longford	I.	151
22, 26	Lissanisky	55 0 9	Longford	Ratcline	Shrule	Ballymahon	I.	165
118	Lissanisky	311 0 16	Mayo	Kilmaine	Ballinrobe	Ballinrobe	IV.	153
42	Lissanisky	105 0 31	Roscommon	Athlone	Kilmeane	Roscommon	IV.	182
34, 38	Lissanisky	103 2 4	Roscommon	Ballymoe	Oran	Roscommon	IV.	192
21	Lissanisky	272 0 28	Tipperary, N.R.	Upper Ormond	Ballymackey	Nenagh	II.	289
88	Lissanly	169 1 32	Cork, E.R.	Imokilly	Inch	Middleton	II.	87
23	Lissanode	592 2 38	Westmeath	Kilkenny West	Drumraney	Athlone	I.	273
141	Lissanoohig	314 0 15	Cork, W.R.	West Carbery (E.D.)	Abbeystrowry	Skibbereen	II.	136
15	Lissanore	234 0 15	Longford	Ardagh	Mostrim	Granard	I.	152
9, 13	Lissanover	299 1 35	Cavan	Tullyhaw	Templeport	Bawnboy	III.	95
71	Lissanumera	97 0 3	Mayo	Gallen	Kilconduff	Swineford	IV.	148
20	Lissanure	556 3 2	Longford	Ardagh	Mostrim	Granard	I.	153
30	Lissanure	186 1 36	Tipperary, N.R.	Ikerrin	Killavinoge	Thurles	II.	275
30	Lissanure	504 2 0	Tipperary, N.R.	Ikerrin	Templetouhy	Thurles	II.	277
13	Lissanurlan	180 0 7	Longford	Longford	Templemichael	Longford	I.	160
41	Lissan West	385 0 23	Clare	Islands	Clareabbey	Ennis	II.	29
33	Lissanymore	760 1 16	Cavan	Upper Loughtee	Killinkere	Bailieborough	III.	84
99, 100	Lissapharson	83 3 0	Galway	Longford	Kiltormer	Ballinasloe	IV.	60
29	Lissaphobble	64 2 27	Roscommon	Roscommon	Lissonuffy	Strokestown	IV.	212
110	Lissaphooca	513 0 16	Cork, W.R.	East Carbery (E.D.)	Ballymodan	Bandon	II	127
106	Lissaphuca	194 3 5	Galway	Leitrim	Kilmeen	Loughrea	IV.	54
47	Lissaphuca	148 0 3	Roscommon	Athlone	Taghboy	Athlone	IV.	184
28	Lissaphuca	111 0 15	Roscommon	Roscommon	Kilcooley	Strokestown	IV.	210
16	Lissaquill	114 2 36	Westmeath	Kilkenny West	Noughaval	Ballymahon	I.	274
23, 30	Lissara	145 2 3	Down	Castlereagh Upper	Kilmore	Downpatrick	III.	165
142	Lissarankin	144 0 15	Cork, W.R.	West Carbery (E.D.)	Castlehaven	Skibbereen	II.	138
30	Lissaraw	260 0 25	Armagh	Fews Upper	Creggan	Castleblayney	III.	48
25	Lissaraw	348 2 22	Armagh	Orior Upper	Killevy	Newry	III.	58
13	Lissaraw	193 1 29	Monaghan	Monaghan	Monaghan	Monaghan	III.	277
42, 51	Lissard	1,121 1 37	Cork, E.R.	Barretts	Grenagh	Cork	II.	49
111	Lissard	204 2 7	Cork, E.R.	Kinalea	Leighmoney	Kinsale	II.	96
134	Lissard	87 2 1	Cork, W.R.	East Carbery (W.D.)	Ross	Clonakilty	II.	135
73, 86	Lissard	245 1 24	Galway	Kilconnell	Kilconnell	Ballinasloe	IV.	40
41, 49	Lissard	684 3 23	Limerick	Coshlea	Galbally	Mitchelstown	II.	239
15	Lissard	258 1 30	Longford	Granard	Clonbroney	Granard	I.	155
83	Lissardagh	456 0 17	Cork, W.R.	West Muskerry	Kilmurry	Macroom	II.	159
38	Lissardboola	376 3 6	Kerry	Trughanacmy	Ballyseedy	Tralee	II.	208
40	Lissard More	117 0 37b	Mayo	Gallen	Kilgarvan	Ballina	IV.	148
14	Lissardowlan	153 2 37	Longford	Ardagh	Templemichael	Longford	I.	154
99, 100	Lissareaghaun or Belview	969 2 25	Galway	Longford	Kiltormer	Ballinasloe	IV.	60
149	Lissaree	137 0 24	Cork, W.R.	West Carbery (E.D.)	Aghadown	Skibbereen	II.	137
118	Lissareemig	78 0 3	Cork, W.R.	Bantry	Durrus	Bantry	II.	119
40, 41	Lissaroon	296 1 28	Tipperary, N.R.	Eliogarty	Inch	Thurles	II.	270
95	Lissarourke	512 2 25	Cork, W.R.	East Carbery (W.D.)	Kinneigh	Bandon	II.	135
38	Lissarow	127 1 30c	Waterford	Decies within Drum	Ardmore	Youghal	II.	350
38	Lissarow	175 3 1	Waterford	Decies within Drum	Ballymacart	Youghal	II.	351
83	Lissarulla	365 3 29	Galway	Dunkellin	Claregalway	Galway	IV.	27
3, 7	Lissasmuttaun	375 3 19	Waterford	Upperthird	Clonagam	Carrick on Suir	II.	369
39	Lissataggle	376 3 22	Kerry	Trughanacmy	Currans	Killarney	II.	209
29	Lissatanvally	153 0 24	Kerry	Trughanacmy	Ratass	Tralee	II.	213
111	Lissatava	692 0 23	Mayo	Kilmaine	Kilcommon	Ballinrobe	IV.	155
81, 90	Lissatinnig	480 1 38	Kerry	Iveragh	Dromod	Cahersiveen	II.	195
19	Lissatotan	33 0 9	Limerick	Connello Lower	Clonagh	Rathkeale	II.	227
19	Lissatotan	286 3 1	Limerick	Shanid	Kilbradran	Rathkeale	II.	255
15	Lissatunna	221 1 39	Clare	Corcomroe	Kilmanaheen	Ennistimon	II.	21

(a) Including 64A. 0R. 26P. water.   (b) Including 19A. 0R. 19P. water.   (c) Including 22A. 1R. 17P. detached portion.

4 Q

No. of Sheet of the Ordnance Survey Maps.	Townlands and Towns.	Area in Statute Acres.	County.	Barony.	Parish.	Poor Law Union in 1857.	Townland Census of 1851, Part I.	
		A. R. P.					Vol.	Page
114	Lissatunny . .	151 3 2	Galway . .	Kiltartan . .	Kiltartan . .	Gort . .	IV.	48
21	Lissatunny . .	252 3 11	Tipperary, N.R.	Upper Ormond .	Ballynaclogh .	Nenagh . .	II.	290
22	Lissatunny . .	142 2 0	Westmeath .	Kilkenny West .	Kilkenny West .	Athlone . .	I.	273
75, 81	Lissava . .	808 3 5	Tipperary, S.R.	Iffa and Offa West .	Caher . .	Clogheen . .	II.	318
14	Lissavaddy . .	110 3 11	Longford . .	Longford . .	Killoe . .	Longford . .	I.	159
87, 99	Lissavahaun .	171 3 28	Galway . .	Clonmacnowen .	Aughrim . .	Ballinasloe .	IV.	24
44	Lissavally . .	189 2 4	Galway . .	Clare . .	Killererin . .	Tuam . .	IV.	21
44	Lissavally Glebe .	85 3 12	Galway . .	Clare . .	Killererin . .	Tuam . .	IV.	21
29	Lissavally (Jackson)	258 0 13	Galway . .	Dunmore . .	Tuam . .	Tuam . .	IV.	36
29	Lissavally (Vesey) .	195 3 30	Galway . .	Dunmore . .	Tuam . .	Tuam . .	IV.	36
57	Lissavane East .	352 3 21	Kerry . .	Magunihy . .	Kilbonane . .	Killarney . .	II.	200
57	Lissavane West .	410 1 21	Kerry . .	Magunihy . .	Kilbonane . .	Killarney . .	II.	200
29, 30	Lissavarra . .	152 2 39	Limerick . .	Connello Upper .	Ballingarry . .	Croom . .	II.	231
17	Lissavilla . .	116 2 31	Roscommon .	Roscommon . .	Aughrim . .	Cark. on Shannon	IV.	207
25	Lissaviron . .	191 3 33	Waterford .	Middlethird . .	Dunhill . .	Kilmacthomas .	II.	367
25	Lissavironbog .	66 3 29	Waterford .	Middlethird . .	Dunhill . .	Kilmacthomas .	II.	367
51	Lissavoura . .	488 1 10	Cork, E.R. .	Barretts . .	Grenagh . .	Cork . .	II.	49
31	Lissavra Big .	177 3 38	Westmeath .	Moycashel .	Ardnurcher or Horse-leap . .	Mullingar . .	II.	
31	Lissavra Little .	52 2 4	Westmeath .	Moycashel .	Ardnurcher or Horse-leap . .	Mullingar . .	I.	276
32	Lissavruggy . .	516 0 0	Galway . .	Killian . .	Killian . .	Mountbellew .	I.	277
							IV.	44
21,22,27,28	Lissawaddy . .	214 2 30	Roscommon .	Castlereagh .	Baslick . .	Castlereagh .	IV.	199
24	Lissawarriff . .	336 2 34a	Longford . .	Shrule . .	Agharra . .	Ballymahon .	I.	166
17, 21	Lissawly or St. Albans	91 3 23	Longford . .	Rathcline . .	Rathcline . .	Longford . .	I.	165
99	Lissawullaun . .	186 1 8	Galway . .	Clonmacnowen .	Killallaghtan .	Ballinasloe .	IV.	26
14	Lissawully . .	59 3 11	Sligo . .	Carbury . .	Killaspugbrone .	Sligo . .	IV.	222
3	Lisseagh . .	56 2 36	Monaghan .	Trough . .	Errigal Trough .	Monaghan . .	III.	285
31	Lisseeghan . .	140 1 16	Leitrim . .	Leitrim . .	Kiltoghert . .	Cark. on Shannon	IV.	102
47	Lisseenamanragh .	126 3 35	Roscommon .	Athlone . .	Taghboy . .	Athlone . .	IV.	184
1	Lisseevin . .	110 0 3	Roscommon .	Boyle . .	Kilronan . .	Boyle . .	IV.	197
26, 27	Lisselan . .	578 2 39	Waterford .	Middlethird . .	Drumcannon .	Waterford . .	II.	366
122	Lisselane . .	429 2 36	Cork, W.R. .	East Carbery (E.D.)	Kilnagross . .	Clonakilty . .	II.	129
26, 27	Lisselty . .	247 2 7	Waterford .	Gaultiere . .	Rathmoylan .	Waterford . .	II.	364
20, 26	Lissenhall . .	242 3 37	Tipperary, N.R.	Upper Ormond .	Kilmore . .	Nenagh . .	II.	291
11, 12	Lissenhall Great .	260 1 11	Dublin . .	Nethercross . .	Swords . .	Balrothery .	I.	32
11, 12	Lissenhall Little .	326 1 33	Dublin . .	Nethercross . .	Swords . .	Balrothery .	I.	32
40, 41	Lisserboy . .	204 3 32	Down . .	Lordship of Newry .	Newry . .	Newry . .	III.	182
5, 9	Lisserdrea . .	611 0 31	Roscommon .	Boyle . .	Boyle . .	Boyle . .	IV.	194
21, 27	Lissergloon . .	164 3 36b	Sligo . .	Tirerrill . .	Ballysumaghan .	Sligo . .	IV.	258
14	Lissergool . .	678 2 28	Roscommon .	Frenchpark .	Tibohine . .	Castlereagh .	IV.	205
47	Lisserlough . .	148 2 30	Sligo . .	Coolavin . .	Killaraght . .	Boyle . .	IV.	224
3	Lisserluss . .	258 0 23	Antrim . .	Cary . .	Billy . .	Ballycastle .	III.	12
4, 5	Lissernane . .	609 1 3	Tipperary, N.R.	Lower Ormond .	Lorrha . .	Borrisokane .	II.	285
110	Lisseveleen&Skeheen	92 1 10	Mayo . .	Kilmaine . .	Robeen . .	Ballinrobe .	IV.	157
15	Lissheagh or Mount Irwin . .	160 3 3	Armagh . .	Tiranny . .	Tynan . .	Armagh . .	III.	60
111	Lissheeda . .	227 0 26	Cork, E.R. .	Kinalea . .	Leighmoney .	Kinsale . .	II.	96
8, 9	Lissheffield . .	44 0 35	Armagh . .	Oneilland West .	Kilmore . .	Armagh . .	III.	53
8, 9	Lissheffield . .	143 2 35	Armagh . .	Oneilland West .	Loughgall . .	Armagh . .	III.	54
{ 74 } {Mayo Co.}	Lissian . .	387 3 26	Roscommon .	Frenchpark .	Castlemore .	Castlereagh .	IV.	202
94	Lissicorrane . .	337 3 25	Cork, W.R. .	East Carbery (W.D.)	Kinneigh . .	Dunmanway .	II.	155
8, 12	Lissinagroagh . .	791 0 17	Leitrim . .	Rosclogher .	Cloonclare .	Manorhamilton .	IV.	109
104	Lissindragan . .	90 0 37	Galway . .	Dunkellin . .	Killora . .	Loughrea . .	IV.	31
69	Lissinisk . .	53 2 17	Donegal . .	Raphoe . .	Convoy . .	Stranorlar .	III.	136
4	Lissiniska . .	384 2 36	Leitrim . .	Rosclogher .	Rossinver . .	Manorhamilton .	IV.	112
61, 69	Lissinore . .	78 0 34	Donegal . .	Raphoe . .	Convoy . .	Stranorlar .	III.	136
21	Lissireen . .	187 0 37	Kerry . .	Clanmaurice .	Kiltomy . .	Tralee . .	II.	172
41	Lissize . .	283 3 14c	Down . .	Upper Iveagh, Lr. pt.	Drumballyroney .	Newry . .	III.	172
41	Lissize . .	197 2 25	Down . .	Upper Iveagh, Up. pt.	Drumgath . .	Newry . .	III.	175
15	Lisslanly . .	113 3 29	Armagh . .	Tiranny . .	Tynan . .	Armagh . .	III.	60
70, 80	Liss Lower . .	353 0 22	Kerry . .	Iveragh . .	Killinane . .	Cahersiveen .	II.	197
66	Lissobihane . .	568 2 21	Tipperary, S.R.	Clanwilliam .	Emly . .	Tipperary .	II.	308
28	Lissodeige . .	411 1 9	Kerry . .	Trughanacmy .	Ballynahaglish .	Tralee . .	II.	207
35	Lissofin . .	294 0 28	Clare . .	Tulla Upper .	Tulla . .	Tulla . .	II.	42
29	Lissonuffy . .	168 2 26	Roscommon .	Roscommon . .	Lissonuffy . .	Strokestown .	IV.	212
30	Lissooleen . .	28 3 11	Kerry . .	Trughanacmy .	Ballymacelligott .	Tralee . .	II.	207
37	Lissoughter . .	1,386 0 13d	Galway . .	Ballynahinch .	Moyrus . .	Clifden . .	IV.	13
16	Lissowen . .	189 3 22	Limerick . .	Coonagh . .	Doon . .	Tipperary .	II.	234
15,16,22,23	Lissoy . .	254 2 36e	Westmeath .	Kilkenny West .	Kilkenny West .	Athlone . .	I.	273
18, 10	Lissoy . .	45 3 19	Westmeath .	Kilkenny West .	Noughaval . .	Athlone . .	I.	274
67, 68	Lissue or Teraghafeeva	428 0 16f	Antrim . .	Upper Massereene .	Blaris . .	Lisburn . .	III.	30
22	Lissummon . .	567 3 5	Armagh . .	Orior Lower .	Killevy . .	Newry . .	III.	56

(a) Including 11A. 2R. 26P. water.
(b) Including 6A. 0R. 8P. water.
(c) Including 2A. 1R. 2P. water.
(d) Including 88A. 1R. 39P. water.
(e) Including 4A. 1R. 14P. water.
(f) Including 2A. 1R. 0P. water.

No. of Sheet of the Ordnance Survey Maps.	Townlands and Towns.	Area in Statute Acres.	County.	Barony.	Parish.	Poor Law Union in 1857.	Townland Census of 1851, Part I.	
		A. R. P.					Vol.	Page
70, 80	Liss Upper	81 3 15	Kerry	Iveragh	Killinane	Cahersiveen	II.	197
45	Lissurla	173 3 5	Cork, E.R.	Barrymore	Gortroe	Fermoy	II.	55
43, 44	Lissurland	174 3 16	Limerick	Glenquin	Monagay	Newcastle	II.	247
17	Lissybroder	379 3 16	Galway	Dunmore	Dunmore	Tuam	IV.	34
93	Lissyclearig Lower	196 2 12	Kerry	Glanarought	Kenmare	Kenmare	II.	186
84, 93	Lissyclearig Upper	258 2 2	Kerry	Glanarought	Kenmare	Kenmare	II.	186
60	Lissyconnor	353 1 33	Kerry	Magunihy	Nohavaldaly	Killarney	II.	205
5, 6, 18	Lissyconor	337 3 39	Galway	Ballymoe	Dunmore	Glennamaddy	IV.	7
34	Lissycoyne	137 3 20	Sligo	Tirerrill	Kilmacallan	Sligo	IV.	240
136	Lissycrimeen	532 0 2	Cork, W.R.	Ibane and Barryroe	Lislee	Clonakilty	II.	150
14, 15	Lissycurrig	285 3 12	Kerry	Clanmaurice	Killury	Listowel	II.	171
13	Lissydaly	153 3 1	Roscommon	Frenchpark	Tibohine	Castlereagh	IV.	205
131, 140	Lissydonnell	223 2 21	Cork, W.R.	West Carbery (W.D.)	Skull	Skull	II.	146
61	Lissyegan (Hodson)	453 3 5	Galway	Killian	Ahascragh	Ballinasloe	IV.	43
61	Lissyegan (Mahon)	169 3 15	Galway	Killian	Ahascragh	Ballinasloe	IV.	43
48	Lissygreaghan	103 1 28	Roscommon	Athlone	Kiltoom	Athlone	IV.	183
26	Lissyleamy	43 1 13	Tipperary, N.R.	Upper Ormond	Kilmore	Nenagh	II.	291
25	Lissyline	43 3 35	Clare	Inchiquin	Ruan	Corrofin	II.	28
9	Lissylisheen	457 0 31	Clare	Burren	Rathborney	Ballyvaghan	II.	14
63	Lissymulgee	228 2 11	Mayo	Costello	Kilbeagh	Swineford	IV.	140
38	Lissyneillan	193 0 6	Clare	Ibrickan	Kilmurry	Kilrush	II.	23
67	Lissyviggeen	552 0 22	Kerry	Magunihy	Killarney	Killarney	II.	203
59	Lissyvurriheen	426 2 23	Clare	Clonderalaw	Killadysert	Killadysert	II.	16
29	Lissywollen	196 0 31	Westmeath	Brawny	St. Marys	Athlone	I.	260
61	Listack	497 2 2	Donegal	Raphoe	Conwal	Letterkenny	III.	137
55	Listamlet	166 2 21	Tyrone	Dungannon Middle	Clonfeacle	Dungannon	III.	299
62	Listannagh	99 2 2	Donegal	Raphoe	Taughboyne	Strabane	III.	143
19	Listarkelt	477 1 27	Armagh	Tiranny	Derrynoose	Armagh	III.	59
142	Listarkin	163 2 13	Cork, W.R.	West Carbery (E.D.)	Myross	Skibbereen	II.	141
38, 40	Listeige	151 3 33	Waterford	Decies within Drum	Lisgenan or Grange	Youghal	II.	352
12	Listellan	146 2 21	Monaghan	Dartree	Killeevan	Clones	III.	268
53, 61	Listellian	651 0 3	Donegal	Raphoe	Leck	Letterkenny	III.	140
21, 29	Listellick North	425 3 37	Kerry	Trughanacmy	Tralee	Tralee	II.	213
29	Listellick South	179 0 26	Kerry	Trughanacmy	Tralee	Tralee	II.	213
36, 37	Listerlin	1,407 2 36	Kilkenny	Ida	Listerlin	New Ross	I.	103
61, 62	Listernan	134 3 33	Mayo	Gallen	Killasser	Swineford	IV.	149
27	Listhomasroe	164 0 14	Roscommon	Castlereagh	Kilkeevin	Castlereagh	IV.	200
55	Listicall Lower	187 1 30	Donegal	Raphoe	Taughboyne	Londonderry	III.	143
54, 55	Listicall Upper	302 0 30	Donegal	Raphoe	Taughboyne	Londonderry	III.	143
14	Listiernan	290 0 25	Cavan	Tullyhunco	Kildallan	Bawnboy	III.	97
10, 14	Listinny	105 3 23	Monaghan	Cremorne	Clontibret	Monaghan	III.	261
23	Listobit	267 2 7	Longford	Shrule	Taghshinny	Ballymahon	I.	167
21, 24	Listoke	124 1 23	Louth	Drogheda	St. Peters	Drogheda	I.	175
23, 30	Listooder	510 3 37	Down	Castlereagh Upper	Kilmore	Downpatrick	III.	165
10, 11	Listowel	311 3 7a	Kerry	Iraghticonnor	Listowel	Listowel	II.	193
10	LISTOWEL T.	—	Kerry	Iraghticonnor	Listowel	Listowel	II.	193
9, 10	Listraghee	166 3 6	Longford	Granard	Clonbroney	Granard	I.	155
10, 14	Listraheagny	89 0 39	Monaghan	Monaghan	Monaghan	Monaghan	III.	277
22, 23	Listress	314 3 30	Londonderry	Tirkeeran	Comber Lower	Londonderry	III.	249
28	Listrim	695 0 36	Kerry	Trughanacmy	Ardfert	Tralee	II.	206
28	Listrim	232 3 27	Kerry	Trughanacmy	Ballynahaglish	Tralee	II.	207
71	Listrisnan	198 2 6	Mayo	Gallen	Bohola	Swineford	IV.	147
14	Listroar	134 2 4	Monaghan	Cremorne	Clontibret	Monaghan	III.	261
39	Listrolin	489 2 31	Kilkenny	Iverk	Muckalee	Carrick on Suir	I.	106
39	Listrolin	699 1 36	Kilkenny	Iverk	Rathkieran	Carrick on Suir	I.	107
39	Listrush	91 2 36	Sligo	Corran	Drumrat	Boyle	IV.	226
57	Listry	717 1 31	Kerry	Magunihy	Kilbonane	Killarney	II.	200
18	Listulk	78 3 20	Louth	Ardee	Mosstown	Ardee	I.	174
20, 21	Listullycurran	621 3 14	Down	Lower Iveagh, Lr.pt.	Dromore	Lisburn	III.	168
16	Listymore	809 2 17	Tyrone	Strabane Lower	Ardstraw	Castlederg	III.	319
66	Listymurragh	63 3 17	Kerry	Magunihy	Killarney	Killarney	II.	203
73	Lisvarrinane	661 3 10	Tipperary, S.R.	Clanwilliam	Clonbeg	Tipperary	II.	305
8	Liswatty Lower	408 1 6	Londonderry	North East Liberties of Coleraine	Ballyrashane	Coleraine	III.	245
8	Liswatty Upper	148 2 25	Londonderry	North East Liberties of Coleraine	Ballyrashane	Coleraine	III.	245
44, 47	Liswilliam	259 0 5	Roscommon	Athlone	Taghboy	Athlone	IV.	184
22	Litter Beg	124 0 8	Wexford	Ballaghkeen	Kilmuckridge	Gorey	I.	297
22	Litter More	122 3 24	Wexford	Ballaghkeen	Kilmuckridge	Gorey	I.	297
45, 51, 52	Little Ballymena	837 1 6	Antrim	Lower Belfast	Ballynure	Larne	III.	7
26	Little Bray	33 2 1	Dublin	Rathdown	Oldconnaught	Rathdown	I.	37
26	LITTLE BRAY T.	—	Dublin	Rathdown	Oldconnaught	Rathdown	I.	37
47	Littlebridge	87 0 16	Wexford	Forth	Ballymore	Wexford	I.	308

(a) Including 14A. 0R. 3P. water.

No. of Sheet of the Ordnance Survey Maps	Townlands and Towns.	Area in Statute Acres.			County.	Barony.	Parish.	Poor Law Union in 1857.	Townland Census of 1851, Part I.	
		A.	R.	P.					Vol.	Page
47	Littlebridge . .	21	2	7	Wexford . .	Forth . .	Ishartmon . .	Wexford . .	I.	310
21	Littlebridge Inches .	53	0	38	Waterford .	Decies without Drum	Affane . .	Lismore . .	II.	353
23	Littleconnell . .	376	2	11	Kildare . .	Connell . .	Oldconnell . .	Naas . .	I.	56
17	Little Derry . .	502	2	36	Londonderry .	Keenaght . .	Balteagh . .	NewTⁿLimavady	III.	234
10, 14	Littlefield . .	74	3	10	Kilkenny . .	Fassadinin .	Mayne . .	Kilkenny . .	I.	90
49	Littlefield . .	179	1	37	Tipperary, S.R.	Slievardagh .	Buolick . .	Urlingford .	II.	332
6	Little Glebe . .	97	2	3	Londonderry .	Coleraine . .	Dunboe . .	Coleraine . .	III.	231
37	Littlegrace . .	50	0	38	Cork, E.R. .	Kinnatalloon .	Knockmourne .	Lismore . .	II.	98
28	Littlegrace . .	20	3	20	Waterford .	Coshmore&Coshbride	Lismore and Mocollop	Lismore . .	II.	347
23, 24	Littlegrange . .	352	0	38	Louth . .	Ferrard . .	Tullyallen . .	Drogheda . .	I.	183
28	Littlehill . .	29	2	0	Fermanagh .	Magherastephana .	Aghalurcher .	Lisnaskea . .	III.	217
126	Little Island . .	1	2	26	Cork, W.R. .	Bear . .	Kilnamanagh .	Castletown .	II.	126
144	Little-island . .	48	3	21	Cork, W.R. .	Ibane and Barryroe	Ardfield . .	Clonakilty .	II.	148
143	Little-island . .	111	2	20	Cork, W.R. .	Ibane and Barryroe	Rathbarry . .	Clonakilty .	II.	150
16	Little Island . .	0	3	23	Donegal . .	Kilmacrenan .	Clondahorky .	Dunfanaghy .	III.	124
21	Little Island . .	1	2	31	Longford . .	Rathcline . .	Rathcline . .	Longford . .	I.	165
10, 18	Little Island . .	289	1	10	Waterford .	Gaultiere . .	Ballynakill . .	Waterford . .	II.	362
47	Little Island . .	10	2	39	Wexford . .	Bargy . .	Kilcowan . .	Wexford . .	I.	305
7	Littlemill . .	103	2	8	Louth . .	Upper Dundalk .	Ballybarrack .	Dundalk . .	I.	177
17	Little Minnis's Island	3	2	24	Down . .	Ards Upper .	Ardkeen . .	Downpatrick .	III.	159
28	Littlemount . .	248	1	32	Fermanagh .	Magherastephana .	Aghavea . .	Lisnaskea . .	III.	219
13	Littlepace . .	97	0	8	Dublin . .	Castleknock .	Mulhuddart .	Dublin North .	I.	25
62	Little Quay Island .	0	3	17	Clare . .	Bunratty Lower	Bunratty . .	Ennis . .	II.	3
14	Littlerath . .	170	1	15	Kildare . .	Naas North .	Bodenstown .	Naas . .	I.	62
36, 37	Littlerath . .	266	1	2	Meath . .	Upper Navan .	Kilcooly . .	Trim . .	I.	216
96	Littlesilver . .	177	2	31	Cork, W.R. .	Kinalmeaky .	Kilbrogan . .	Bandon . .	II.	152
48	LITTLETON T. .	—			Tipperary, N.R.	Eliogarty . .	Twomileborris .	Thurles . .	II.	274
13	Littletown . .	175	2	28	Kildare . .	Connell . .	Kilmeage . .	Naas . .	I.	55
15	Littletown . .	256	2	37	Westmeath .	Kilkenny West .	Kilkenny West .	Ballymahon .	I.	273
47	Littletown . .	90	3	3	Wexford . .	Bargy . .	Tomhaggard .	Wexford . .	I.	308
51	Little Venture .	1	2	6	Clare . .	Bunratty Lower	Kilmaleery .	Ennis . .	II.	5
1, 3	Littlewood . .	203	2	30	Westmeath .	Fore . .	Lickbla . .	Granard . .	I.	270
12, 13	Livery Lower .	234	3	32	Antrim . .	Lower Dunluce .	Derrykeighan .	Ballymoney .	III.	17
12, 13	Livery Upper .	270	3	0	Antrim . .	Lower Dunluce .	Derrykeighan .	Ballymoney .	III.	17
15, 16	Lixnaw . .	148	1	0	Kerry . .	Clanmaurice .	Kilcaragh . .	Listowel . .	II.	169
16	LIXNAW T. . .	—			Kerry . .	Clanmaurice .	{ Kilcaragh . . Kiltomy . . }	Listowel . .	II. {	169 172
16, 17	Lloyd Commons of .	509	1	3	Meath . .	Upper Kells .	Kells . .	Kells . .	I.	206
29	Lloydsborough .	247	3	36	Tipperary, N.R.	Ikerrin . .	Killea . .	Roscrea . .	II.	276
29	Lloydsborough .	322	0	18	Tipperary, N.R.	Ikerrin . .	Templemore .	Roscrea . .	II.	276
31, 32	Loan . .	506	2	33	Antrim . .	Lower Toome .	Ahoghill . .	Ballymena .	III.	32
1, 2, 5, 6	Loan . .	872	1	14	Kilkenny . .	Fassadinin .	Castlecomer .	Castlecomer .	I.	88
22	Lobawn . .	411	2	38	Wicklow . .	Upper Talbotstown .	Donaghmore .	Baltinglass .	I.	363
78	Lobinish . .	0	2	0	Galway . .	Moycullen .	Killannin .	Oughterard .	IV.	70
12	Lobinstown . .	466	3	7	Meath . .	Lower Slane .	Killary . .	Ardee . .	I.	223
21	Lockard Big . .	62	3	11	Fermanagh .	Magheraboy .	Rossorry . .	Enniskillen .	III.	214
21	Lockard Little .	74	0	14	Fermanagh .	Magheraboy .	Rossorry . .	Enniskillen .	III.	214
24	Lockardstown .	204	2	19	Westmeath .	Rathconrath .	Conry . .	Mullingar .	I.	282
25	Lockclose or Grange	166	0	31	King's Co. .	Geashill . .	Geashill . .	Tullamore .	I.	140
21	Lock House Island .	0	2	4	King's Co. .	Garrycastle .	Gallen . .	Parsoustown .	I.	136
46, 47	Lockstown . .	521	3	26	Antrim . .	Lower Belfast .	Templecorran .	Larne . .	III.	9
10, 16	Lockstown Lower .	324	2	2	Wicklow . .	Lower Talbotstown .	Hollywood .	Baltinglass .	I.	361
16	Lockstown Upper .	736	3	37	Wicklow . .	Lower Talbotstown .	Hollywood .	Baltinglass .	I.	361
32, 33	Lodge . .	287	3	18	Cork, E.R. .	Fermoy . .	Mallow . .	Mallow . .	II.	81
42	Lodge . .	107	2	0	Galway . .	Clare . .	Kilkilvery .	Tuam . .	IV.	20
9	Lodge . .	311	2	1	Kilkenny . .	Galmoy . .	Balleen . .	Urlingford .	I.	91
32, 33	Lodge . .	543	2	14	Limerick . .	Smallcounty .	Hospital . .	Kilmallock .	II.	260
7	Lodge . .	140	0	6	Londonderry .	North East Liberties of Coleraine .	Coleraine . .	Coleraine . .	III.	246
11	Lodge . .	203	3	31	Roscommon .	Boyle . .	Killukin . .	Car^k. on Shannon	IV.	196
14	Lodge . .	263	3	4a	Tipperary, N.R.	Lower Ormond .	Killodiernan .	Nenagh . .	II.	285
88	Lodge . .	155	1	8	Tipperary, S.R.	Iffa and Offa West .	Ballybacon .	Clogheen .	II.	317
9	Lodge Demesne East	146	1	12	Kilkenny . .	Crannagh .	Sheffin . .	Urlingford .	I.	86
9	Lodge Demesne West	169	3	11	Kilkenny . .	Galmoy . .	Sheffin . .	Urlingford .	I.	93
37	Lodgefarm . .	720	0	38	Kildare . .	Kilkea and Moone .	Kilkea . .	Athy . .	I.	60
10, 14	Lodgepark . .	233	0	4b	Kildare . .	North Salt .	Straffan . .	Celbridge .	I.	76
15	Lodgewood . .	246	0	24	Wexford . .	Scarawalsh .	Ferns . .	Enniscorthy .	I.	323
45	Loftusacre . .	2	0	20	Wexford . .	Bargy . .	Bannow . .	Wexford . .	I.	304
49, 54	Loftushall . .	305	2	6	Wexford . .	Shelburne .	Hook . .	New Ross .	I.	327
36, 37	Loganstown . .	283	0	27c	Meath . .	Upper Navan .	Kilcooly . .	Trim . .	I.	216
13, 22	Logavinshire . .	135	1	1	Limerick . .	Pubblebrien .	Crecora . .	Croom . .	II.	252
27, 33	Logg . .	83	2	38	Tipperary, N.R.	Upper Ormond .	Kilmore . .	Nenagh . .	II.	291
2	Loggan Lower .	401	0	2	Wexford . .	Gorey . .	Crosspatrick .	Gorey . .	I.	316

(a) Including 10A. 2R. 20P. water.　　　(b) Including 6A. 3R. 3P. water.　　　(c) Including 13A. 1R. 24P. water.

No. of Sheet 'of the Ordnance Survey Maps.	Townlands and Towns.	Area in Statute Acres. A. R. P.	County.	Barony.	Parish.	Poor Law Union in 1857.	Townland Census of 1851. Part I. Vol.	Page
2	Loggan Upper	748 0 29	Wexford . .	Gorey . . .	Crosspatrick . .	Gorey . . .	I.	316
28, 29	Loghill . .	508 3 2	Limerick . .	Connello Lower .	Rathkeale . .	Rathkeale . .	II.	229
9, 18	Loghill . .	645. 3 18	Limerick . .	Shanid . . .	Loghill . . .	Glin . . .	II.	257
9	LOGHILL T. . .	—	Limerick . .	Shanid . . .	Loghill . . .	Glin . . .	II.	257
53	Loginsherd .	38 0 17a	Wexford . .	Forth . . .	Carn . . .	Wexford . .	I.	309
20	Logleagh . .	268 1 8	Waterford .	Coshmore&Coshbride	Lismore and Mocollop	Lismore . .	II.	347
9'	Logloss . .	27 1 27	Waterford .	Middlethird . .	Trinity Without .	Waterford . .	II.	369
41	Lognafulla .	60 0 33	Tipperary, N.R.	Eliogarty . .	Thurles . . .	Thurles . .	II.	273
131, 132	Lognagappul .	383 1 2	Cork, W.R. .	West Carbery (W.D.)	Caheragh . .	Skibbereen . .	II.	142
28, 29	Logstown .	170 0 18b	Kildare . .	Naas South . .	Carnalway . .	Naas . . .	I.	64
3	Loguestown .	86 2 8	Londonderry .	North East Liberties of Coleraine . .	Ballywillin . .	Coleraine . .	III.	245
3, 7	Loguestown .	73 2 36	Londonderry .	North East Liberties of Coleraine . .	Coleraine . .	Coleraine . .	III.	246
101	Lohart . .	482 0 18	Kerry . .	Glanarought .	Tuosist . .	Kenmare . .	II.	189
98, 106	Loher . .	623 1 12	Kerry . .	Dunkerron South .	Kilcrohane . .	Cahersiveen . .	II.	184
29	Lohercannan .	471 0 21	Kerry . .	Trughanacmy .	Annagh . .	Tralee . .	II.	205
24, 32	Lohort East .	250 3 11c	Cork, E.R. .	Duhallow . .	Castlemagner .	Kanturk . .	II.	67
24, 32	Lohort West .	228 0 31	Cork, E.R. .	Duhallow . .	Castlemagner .	Kanturk . .	II.	67
94	Lomanagh . .	588 3 14	Kerry . .	Glanarought .	Kilgarvan . .	Kenmare . .	II.	187
87	Lomanagh .	363 1 25	Kerry . .	Iveragh . .	Killemlagh . .	Cahersiveen . .	II.	196
90, 99	Lomanagh North	489 2 38	Kerry . .	Dunkerron South .	Kilcrohane . .	Kenmare . .	II.	184
90, 99	Lomanagh South	456 0 7	Kerry . .	Dunkerron South .	Kilcrohane . .	Kenmare . .	II.	184
30	Lomaunaghbaun .	342 3 17	Galway . .	Ballymoe . .	Clonbern . .	Tuam . .	IV.	6
30	Lomaunaghroe .	375 0 39	Galway . .	Ballymoe . .	Clonbern . .	Tuam . .	IV.	6
32	Lombardstown .	358 2 0d	Cork, E.R. .	Duhallow . .	Kilshannig . .	Mallow . .	II.	74
14, 23	Lombardstown .	199 1 26	Limerick . .	Clanwilliam .	Caherconlish .	Limerick . .	II.	222
46	Lomcloon . .	348 1 34e	Sligo . .	Coolavin . .	Killaraght . .	Boyle . .	IV.	224
9	Lomond . .	191 3 28f	Londonderry .	Keenaght . .	Tamlaght Finlagan .	NewT⁰Limavady	III.	237
135	Lonagh . .	33 3 34	Cork, W.R. .	Ibane and Barryroe	Island . . .	Clonakilty . .	II.	149
56	Lonart . .	482 3 32g	Kerry . .	Trughanacmy .	Killorglin . .	Killarney . .	II.	211
20	Londonderry .	199 3 30	Londonderry .	North West Liberties of Londonderry .	Templemore . .	Londonderry .	III.	246
20	LONDONDERRY T. .	—	Londonderry .	{ North West Liberties of Londonderry . } { Tirkeeran . . }	} Templemore . { Clondermot . . }	} Londonderry . {	III.	{ 247 { 248 { 248
17	Long . .	167 2 20	Cavan . .	Tullygarvey .	Kildrumsherdan .	Cootehill . .	III.	90
22	Longacre .	214 3 26h	Cork, E.R. .	Duhallow . .	Clonfert . .	Kanturk . .	II.	68
9	Longcourse .	52 0 15i	Waterford .	Middlethird and Municipal Borough .	Trinity Without .	Waterford . .	II.	369
29	Longfield . .	85 2 31	Antrim . .	Lower Glenarm .	Tickmacrevan .	Larne . .	III.	24
28, 31	Longfield .	394 1 32	Armagh . .	Orior Upper .	Forkill . . .	Newry . .	III.	57
16	Longfield .	93 1 35	Cavan . .	Tullygarvey .	Drung . . .	Cootehill . .	III.	89
21	Longfield .	141 3 16	Cavan . .	Tullygarvey .	Larah . . .	Cootehill . .	III.	91
73	Longfield .	112 3 17	Donegal . .	Banagh . .	Inishkeel . .	Glenties . .	III.	106
65	Longfield .	60 1 5	Donegal . .	Boylagh . .	Lettermacward .	Glenties . .	III.	114
24	Longfield .' .	199 1 7	Fermanagh . .	Magherastephana .	Aghalurcher .	Lisnaskea . .	III.	217
47, 48	Longfield .	193 3 31	Kerry . .	Magunihy . .	Kilnanare . .	Killarney . .	II.	204
26, 30	Longfield .	148 3 33	Leitrim . .	Carrigallen .	Carrigallen . .	Bawnboy . .	IV.	90
41	Longfield .	441 1 9	Londonderry .	Loughinsholin .	Desertmartin .	Magherafelt .	III.	240
15, 20	Longfield .	373 1 30	Longford . .	Ardagh . .	Mostrim . .	Granard . .	I.	153
60, 70	Longfield .	156 3 37j	Mayo . .	Gallen . .	Templemore . .	Castlebar . .	IV.	151
25	Longfield .	374 2 29	Monaghan .	Cremorne . .	Muckno . .	Castleblayney .	III.	262
12	Longfield .	164 0 19	Monaghan .	Dartree . .	Clones . . .	Clones . .	III.	265
45	Longfield .	127 0 21	Roscommon .	Athlone . .	Rahara . .	Roscommon .	IV.	183
52	Longfield .	240 0 22	Tipperary, S.R.	Middlethird .	Ardmayle . .	Cashel . .	II.	324
15	Longfield Beg .	115 3 22	Londonderry .	Tirkeeran .	Faughanvale .	Londonderry .	III.	•250
28, 31	Longfield Etra .	139 1 22	Monaghan .	Farney . .	Donaghmoyne .	Carrickmacross .	III.	270
15	Longfield Level(Intake)	365 2 3	Londonderry .	Tirkeeran .	Faughanvale .	Londonderry .	III	250
15	Longfield More .	203 0 4	Londonderry .	Tirkeeran .	Faughanvale .	Londonderry .	III.	250
31	Longfield Otra .	146 2 2l	Monaghan .	Farney . .	Donaghmoyne .	Carrickmacross .	III.	270
46	Longford .	334 3 12	Galway . .	Killian . .	Ballynakill . .	Mountbellew .	IV.	43
108, 118	Longford .	930 1 0	Galway . .	Longford . .	Tiranascragh .	Portumna . .	IV.	62
39	Longford . .	146 1 2l	King's Co. .	Ballybritt . .	Roscomroe . .	Parsonstown .	I.	126
25	Longford .	4 0 5	Limerick . .	Coonagh . .	Doon . . .	Tipperary . .	II.	234
29, 38	Longford .	155 1 30	Mayo . .	Tirawley . .	Crossmolina .	Ballina . .	IV.	166
27	Longford .	69 2 3	Meath . .	Lower Duleek .	Duleek . .	Drogheda . .	I.	195
11, 16	Longford .	275 0 20	Queen's Co. .	Upperwoods .	Offerlane . .	Mountmellick .	I.	252
26, 27	Longford .	394 1 12	Roscommon .	Castlereagh .	Kilkeevin . .	Castlereagh .	IV.	200
23	Longford .	369 2 28	Tipperary, N.R.	Ikerrin . .	Bourney . .	Roscrea . .	II.	274
23	Longford .	53 1 14	Tipperary, N.R.	Ikerrin . .	Rathnaveoge .	Roscrea . .	II.	276
73	Longford .	752 1 33	Tipperary, S.R.	Clanwilliam .	Clonbeg . .	Tipperary . .	II.	305
67	Longford .	75 2 15	Tipperary, S.R.	Clanwilliam .	Cordangan . .	Tipperary . .	II.	306
39	Longford Big .	377 2 18	King's Co. .	Ballybritt . .	Seirkieran . .	Parsonstown .	I.	127
19	Longford Demesne .	201 0 38	Sligo . .	Tireragh . .	Dromard . .	Dromore West .	IV.	233

(a) Including 11A. 3R. 39P. detached portion.
(b) Including 3A. 1R. 18P. water.
(c) Including 64A. 3R. 27P. detached portion.
(d) Including 9A. 2R. 4P. water.

(e) Including 7A. 1R. 27P. water.
(f) Including 1A. 3R. 27P. water.
(g) Including 6A. 2R. 38P. water.
(h) Including 3A. 3R. 0P. detached portion.

(i) { Within the Municipal Boundary, 10A. 2R. 20P. { Without the Municipal Boundary, 41A. 1R. 35P.
(j) Including 6A. 1R. 19P. water.

No. of Sheet of the Ordnance Survey Maps.	Townlands and Towns.	Area in Statute Acres.	County.	Barony.	Parish.	Poor Law Union in 1857.	Townland Census of 1851, Part I.	
		A. R. P.					Vol.	Page
25	Longford East	100 1 16	Limerick	Coonagh	Oola	Tipperary	II.	236
39	Longford Little	80 3 24	King's Co.	Ballybritt	Seirkieran	Parsonstown	I.	127
42	Longfordpass East	101 3 13	Tipperary, N.R.	Eliogarty	Kilcooly	Thurles	II.	270
36, 42	Longfordpass North	1,345 2 25	Tipperary, N.R.	Eliogarty	Kilcooly	Thurles	II.	270
42	Longfordpass South	1,068 1 28	Tipperary, N.R.	Eliogarty	Kilcooly	Thurles	II.	270
13	LONGFORD T.	—	Longford	Ardagh } Longford }	Templemichael	Longford	I.	{154 {160
25	Longford West	95 1 7	Limerick	Coonagh	Oola	Tipperary	II.	236
23	Longford Wood	243 0 24	Tipperary, N.R.	Ikerrin	Bourney	Roscrea	II.	274
40	Longgraigue	537 3 34	Wexford	Shelmaliere West	Clongeen	New Ross	I.	333
37	Longhill	70 1 1	Donegal	Kilmacrenan	Tullyfern	Millford	III.	133
41	Longhill	141 3 16	Tyrone	Omagh East	Dromore	Omagh	III.	311
7	Longhill Commons	7 1 1	Wicklow	Rathdown	Kilmacanoge	Rathdown	I.	356
126	Long Island	6 3 14	Cork, W.R.	Bear	Kilnamanagh	Castletown	II.	126
148	Long Island	341 2 5	Cork, W.R.	West Carbery (W.D.)	Skull	Skull	II.	146
24	Long Island	5 0 38	Down	Ards Upper	Ardkeen	Downpatrick	III.	159
17	Long Island	11 1 5	Down	Castlereagh Lower	Tullynakill	Newtownards	III.	163
15	Long Island	8 0 23	Fermanagh	Tirkennedy	Trory	Enniskillen	III.	224
109	Long Island	1 1 4	Galway	Longford	Meelick	Portumna	IV.	62
87	Long Island	9 0 4	Kerry	Iveragh	Killemlagh	Cahersiveen	II.	196
25	Long Island	2 3 38	Longford	Rathcline	Cashel	Ballymahon	I.	163
109	Long Island	13 1 25	Mayo	Carra	Ballyovey	Ballinrobe	IV.	126
52, 55	Long Island	144 2 9	Roscommon	Athlone	St. Peter's	Athlone	IV.	184
56	Long Island	29 1 15	Roscommon	Moycarn	Moore	Ballinasloe	IV.	207
1	Long Island	38 3 19	Tipperary, N.R.	Lower Ormond	Lorrha	Borrisokane	II.	285
52	Long Island Little	1 0 36	Roscommon	Athlone	St. Peter's	Athlone	IV.	184
55	Long Island North	1 0 0	Galway	Clare	Cargin	Tuam	IV.	18
33	Longjohnshill	582 2 15	Tipperary, N.R.	Upper Ormond	Kilnaneave	Nenagh	II.	291
10, 11	Longlands	94 1 39	Down	Castlereagh Lower	Comber	Newtownards	III.	162
18	Longmeadows	45 0 25a	Dublin	Castleknock	St. James	Dublin North	I.	25
28, 29	Longmore	2,187 2 18	Antrim	Lower Antrim	Skerry	Ballymena	III.	5
42	Longnamuck	231 3 38	Roscommon	Athlone	Killinvoy	Roscommon	IV.	182
30, 36	Longorchard	836 1 35	Tipperary, N.R.	Ikerrin	Templetouhy	Thurles	II.	277
59	Longridge	75 1 17	Tyrone	Clogher	Clogher	Clogher	I.I.	293
47	Longridge	68 2 12	Wexford	Bargy	Kilcowan	Wexford	I.	305
15	Longrob	118 0 6	Fermanagh	Magheraboy	Devenish	Enniskillen	III.	211
2, 6	Long's Glebe	91 1 38	Londonderry	Coleraine	Dunboe	Coleraine	III.	231
12	Longstone	20 3 15	Armagh	Armagh	Armagh	Armagh	III.	43
51, 52	Longstone	356 3 28	Cork, E.R.	Barretts	Whitechurch	Cork	II.	50
29	Longstone	170 2 11	Kildare	Naas South	Ballymore-eustace	Naas	I.	64
23, 24	Longstone	91 0 15	Limerick	Clanwilliam	Grean	Limerick	II.	224
26, 32	Longstone	149 2 8	Tipperary, N.R.	Owney and Arra	Killoscully	Nenagh	II.	295
58	Longstone	183 0 14	Tipperary, S.R.	Clanwilliam	Cullen	Tipperary	II.	307
58	Longstone	505 1 30	Tipperary, S.R.	Clanwilliam	Kilcornan	Tipperary	II.	308
25	Longstones	110 3 3	Leitrim	Carrigallen	Oughteragh	Bawnboy	IV.	92
21	Longstones	0 3 6	Louth	Ferrard	Mullary	Drogheda	I.	182
64, 75	Longstown	128 0 20	Cork, E.R.	Barrymore	Carrigtohill	Middleton	II.	52
25	Longtown	40 1 5	Antrim	Lower Glenarm	Ardclinis	Larne	III.	21
10, 14	Longtown	64 0 3	Kildare	North Salt	Straffan	Celbridge	I.	76
49	Longtown	125 1 33	Meath	Upper Deece	Kilclone	Dunshaughlin	I.	193
13, 14	Longtown Demesne	326 3 3b	Kildare	Clane	Killybegs	Naas	I.	54
13, 14	Longtown North	124 0 2	Kildare	Clane	Killybegs	Naas	I.	54
13, 14	Longtown South	305 3 27	Kildare	Clane	Killybegs	Naas	I.	54
32	Longueville	317 0 7c	Cork, E.R.	Duhallow	Ballyclogh	Mallow	II.	67
46	Longueville North	355 3 20	Cork, E.R.	Kinnatalloon	Ballynoe	Fermoy	II.	97
46	Longueville South	271 2 23	Cork, E.R.	Kinnatalloon	Ballynoe	Fermoy	II.	97
41, 47	Longwood	296 2 31d	Meath	Upper Moyfenrath	Castlerickard	Trim	I.	213
41, 47	Longwood	540 3 15	Meath	Upper Moyfenrath	Clonard	Trim	I.	213
47	LONGWOOD T.	—	Meath	Upper Moyfenrath	Castlerickard } Clonard }	Trim	I.	213
26, 32	Longnogs	300 2 3	Cavan	Upper Loughtee	Denn	Cavan	III.	83
7, 10	Looart	148 1 26	Monaghan	Trough	Donagh	Monaghan	III.	282
62	Loobnamuck	139 1 2e	Mayo	Gallen	Killasser	Swineford	IV.	149
84, 96	Loobroe	49 3 14	Galway	Athenry	Athenry	Loughrea	IV.	4
90	Loona Beg	214 1 0f	Mayo	Carra	Drum	Castlebar	IV.	128
61	Loonaghtan (Kelly)	94 3 31	Galway	Killian	Ahascragh	Mountbellew	IV.	43
61	Loonaghtan (Mahon)	194 1 29	Galway	Killian	Ahascragh	Mountbellew	IV.	43
90	Loona More	290 2 17g	Mayo	Carra	Drum	Castlebar	IV.	128
44, 45	Loonburn	286 2 17	Antrim	Upper Antrim	Kilbride	Antrim	III.	6
17	Loortan	54 0 21	Cavan	Tullygarvey	Kildrumsherdan	Cootehill	III.	90
132	Looscaun	363 0 23	Galway	Leitrim	Ballynakill	Portumna	IV.	52
73, 74, 83, 84	Looscaunagh	523 0 3h	Kerry	Dunkerron South	Knockane	Killarney	II.	184
48, 60	Loosky Island	2 3 5	Mayo	Carra	Turlough	Castlebar	IV.	131

(a) Including 9A. 0R. 32P. water.
(b) Including 6A. 2R. 26P. detached portion.
(c) Including 4A. 2R. 8P. River Blackwater.
(d) Including 2A. 0R. 2P. detached portion.
(e) Including 5A. 3R. 32P. water.
(f) Including 5A. 3R. 4P. water.
(g) Including 20A. 1R. 21P. water.
(h) Including 30A. 0R. 18P. water.

No. of Sheet of the Ordnance Survey Maps.	Townlands and Towns.	Area in Statute Acres.			County.	Barony.	Parish.	Poor Law Union in 1857.	Townland Census of 1851, Part I.	
		A.	R.	P.					Vol.	Page
23	Loran	485	2	24	Tipperary, N.R.	Ikerrin	Bourney	Roscrea	II.	274
95	*Lord Fitzgerald's Island*	0	0	26	Galway	Dunkellin	Oranmore	Galway	IV.	32
15	Lordstown	167	2	9	Meath	Fore	Diamor	Oldcastle	I.	200
4	Lorrha	1,636	1	15a	Tipperary, N.R.	Lower Ormond	Lorrha	Borrisokane	II.	285
4	LORRHA T.	—			Tipperary, N.R.	Lower Ormond	Lorrha	Borrisokane	II.	285
15	Lorrug	157	3	32	Wicklow	Lower Talbotstown	Dunlavin	Baltinglass	I.	360
19	Lorum	349	0	11	Carlow	Idrone East	Lorum	Carlow	I.	8
36, 39	Loskeran	369	2	18b	Waterford	Decies within Drum	Ardmore	Dungarvan	II.	350
9	Losset	177	3	35	Antrim	Cary	Culfeightrin	Ballycastle	III.	13
24, 30	Losset	123	2	7	Cavan	Tullyhunco	Killashandra	Cavan	III.	98
35, 44	Losset	1,291	0	3	Donegal	Kilmacrenan	Gartan	Letterkenny	III.	127
4, 5	Losset	253	3	24c	Meath	Lower Kells	Moybolgue	Kells	I.	203
18	Losset	172	3	16	Monaghan	Dartree	Ematris	Cootehill	III.	267
31	Losset	181	3	5d	Monaghan	Farney	Magheracloone	Carrickmacross	III.	273
13, 18	Losset	124	0	17	Monaghan	Monaghan	Kilmore	Monaghan	III.	276
45	Losset	152	3	12	Tipperary, N.R.	Kilnamanagh Upper	Doon	Tipperary	II.	277
45	Losset	171	2	21	Tipperary, N.R.	Kilnamanagh Upper	Toem	Tipperary	II.	280
58, 64	Losset	184	1	37	Tyrone	Clogher	Clogher	Clogher	III.	293
37	Lossetkillew	86	3	19	Cavan	Clanmahon	Ballymachugh	Cavan	III.	76
30, 31	Lossets	99	0	18	Monaghan	Farney	Magheross	Carrickmacross	III.	274
74	Lota Beg	201	1	19	Cork, E.R.	Cork	Rathcooney	Cork	II.	65
74	Lota More	539	0	7	Cork, E.R.	Cork	Rathcooney	Cork	II.	65
39	Lotteragh Lower	106	2	0	Limerick	Connello Upper	Bruree	Kilmallock	II.	231
39	Lotteragh Upper	311	2	23	Limerick	Connello Upper	Bruree	Kilmallock	II.	231
53	Lough	123	0	12	Kerry	Corkaguiny	Garfinny	Dingle	II.	177
8	Lough	293	3	3	Kilkenny	Galmoy	Erke	Urlingford	I.	92
8, 9	Lough	473	3	26	Queen's Co.	Portnahinch	Lea	Mountmellick	I.	244
46	Lough	213	0	8	Wexford	Bargy	Bannow	Wexford	I.	304
46	Lough	163	3	22	Wexford	Bargy	Duncormick	Wexford	I.	305
48	Lough	64	0	4	Wexford	Forth	Kilscoran	Wexford	I.	311
31	Loughabor	276	3	38	Kildare	Offaly West	Fontstown	Athy	I.	72
9	Loughachork	296	1	1e	Fermanagh	Magheraboy	Inishmacsaint	Ballyshannon	III.	213
73	Loughaclerybeg	155	0	15	Galway	Kilconnell	Kilconnell	Ballinasloe	IV.	40
64, 65	Loughaconeera	1,434	2	26f	Galway	Ballynahinch	Moyrus	Clifden	IV.	13
25	Loughaconnick	161	2	12	Cavan	Upper Loughtee	Kilmore	Cavan	III.	85
81	Loughacutteen	147	2	25	Tipperary, S.R.	Iffa and Offa West	Whitechurch	Clogheen	II.	321
77	Loughaderry	189	2	25g	Cork, E.R.	Imokilly	Ballyoughtera	Middleton	II.	84
33	Loughatian	553	3	9	Down	Upper Iveagh, Up. pt.	Aghaderg	Banbridge	III.	174
35, 44	Loughadoon	203	1	26h	Kerry	Corkaguiny	Ballyduff	Dingle	II.	174
45, 53	Loughagannon	358	2	1	Donegal	Kilmacrenan	Aghanunshin	Letterkenny	III.	122
19	Loughagar Beg	108	2	9	Westmeath	Moyashel and Magheradernon	Rathconnell	Mullingar	I.	276
12, 13, 19, 20	Loughagar More	906	0	29	Westmeath	Moyashel and Magheradernon	Rathconnell	Mullingar	I.	276
49, 50	Loughagher	1,510	2	37i	Donegal	Boylagh	Templecrone	Glenties	III.	115
13, 18	Loughakeo	173	0	37	Queen's Co.	Maryborough East	Dysartenos	Mountmellick	I.	241
10	Loughan	111	0	7	Antrim	Cary	Culfeightrin	Ballycastle	III.	14
25	Loughan	25	3	4	Antrim	Lower Glenarm	Ardclinis	Larne	III.	21
1, 2	Loughan	113	3	36	Cavan	Tullyhaw	Killinagh	Enniskillen	III.	92
45, 47	Loughan	702	0	8	King's Co.	Clonlisk	Finglas	Roscrea	I.	130
23	Loughan	168	0	4	Longford	Moydow	Taghsheenod	Ballymahon	I.	162
10	Loughan	587	2	19j	Meath	Upper Kells	Loughan or Castlekeeran	Kells	I.	207
17, 18	Loughan	347	0	26k	Westmeath	Rathconrath	Rathconrath	Mullingar	I.	284
118, 121	Loughanaganky	133	3	28	Mayo	Kilmaine	Ballinchalla	Ballinrobe	IV.	152
32, 38	Loughanagore	313	1	5	Westmeath	Moycashel	Kilbeggan	Tullamore	I.	278
3	Loughanalla	129	1	24	Westmeath	Fore	Rathgarve	Castletowndelvin	I.	271
58, 60	Loughananna	457	2	21	Limerick	Coshlea	Kilbeheny	Mitchelstown	II.	239
29	Loughanaskin	31	2	9	Westmeath	Brawny	St. Mary's	Athlone	I.	260
3, 7	Loughanavagh or Newpark	172	3	14	Westmeath	Fore	St. Feighins	Castletowndelvin	I.	272
12	Loughanavatta	214	1	15	Tipperary, N.R.	Ikerrin	Bourney	Roscrea	II.	276
92	Loughanboy	188	1	20	Mayo	Costello	Bekan	Claremorris	IV.	139
118	Loughanboy	177	1	0	Mayo	Kilmaine	Kilmainemore	Ballinrobe	IV.	156
22	Loughanbrean	223	3	38	Meath	Fore	Killallon	Oldcastle	I.	200
22, 23	Loughanderg	282	0	3	Meath	Fore	Killallon	Oldcastle	I.	201
29	Loughandonning	183	2	7	Westmeath	Brawny	St. Mary's	Athlone	I.	260
22	Loughandys	105	3	8	Kildare	Offaly East	Kildare	Naas	I.	70
77, 89	Loughane	287	3	29	Cork, E.R.	Imokilly	Bohillane	Middleton	II.	84
127	Loughane Beg	276	3	21	Cork, W.R.	Bear	Kilnamanagh	Castletown	II.	126
62	Loughane East	501	1	9	Cork, E.R.	East Muskerry	Matehy	Cork	II.	105
27, 33	Loughane Lower	123	3	16	Tipperary, N.R.	Upper Ormond	Kilnaneave	Nenagh	IV.	291
15	Loughanelteen	335	3	32l	Sligo	Carbury	Calry	Sligo	IV.	220
126, 127	Loughane More	387	3	37	Cork, W.R.	Bear	Kilnamanagh	Castletown	II.	126

No. of Sheet of the Ordnance Survey Maps.	Townlands and Towns.	Area in Statute Acres.	County.	Barony.	Parish.	Poor Law Union in 1857.	Townland Census of 1851, Part I.	
		A. R. P.					Vol.	Page
5, 10	Loughanes	385 1 10	Kerry	Iraghticonnor	Lisselton	Listowel	II.	192
27, 33	Loughane Upper	223 3 0	Tipperary, N.R.	Upper Ormond	Kilnancave	Nenagh	II.	291
62	Loughane West	541 2 33	Cork, E.R.	East Muskerry	Matehy	Cork	II.	105
3, 7	Loughan Hill	29 0 3	Londonderry	North East Liberties of Coleraine	Coleraine	Coleraine	III.	246
31	Loughaniska	80 3 34	Waterford	Decies without Drum	Dungarvan	Dungarvan	II.	355
12	Loughanleagh	78 0 9	Limerick	Pubblebrien	Mungret	Limerick	II.	254
32, 38	Loughanlewnaght	144 2 26	Westmeath	Moycashel	Newtown	Mullingar	I.	279
14, 15	Loughanmore	147 3 8	Louth	Louth	Mansfieldstown	Ardee	I.	185
8	Loughanmore	186 1 29	Louth	Lower Dundalk	Ballymascanlan	Dundalk	I.	176
19	Loughannacrannoge	44 3 11	Sligo	Tireragh	Dromard	Dromore West	IV.	233
7, 8	Loughanreagh North	124 0 6	Londonderry	North East Liberties of Coleraine	Kildollagh	Coleraine	III.	246
7, 8	Loughanreagh South	149 0 26	Londonderry	North East Liberties of Coleraine	Kildollagh	Coleraine	III.	246
26	Loughans	1,338 3 28	Down	Lower Iveagh. Up. pt.	Tullylish	Banbridge	III	171
60	Loughans	397 2 29	Tyrone	Dungannon Lower	Carnteel	Clogher	III.	298
43	Loughanspark	17 1 6	Galway	Clare	Belclare	Tuam	IV.	17
22	Loughanstown	108 2 14	Limerick	Clanwilliam	Caheravally	Limerick	II.	221
22	Loughanstown	11 1 28	Limerick	Clanwilliam	Fedamore	Limerick	II.	223
32	Loughanstown	397 2 19	Meath	Skreen	Rathfeigh	Dunshaughlin	I.	221
12	Loughanstown	357 1 21	Westmeath	Corkaree	Portnashangan	Mullingar	I.	263
9, 14	Loughanstown	275 2 18a	Westmeath	Delvin	Castletowndelvin	Castletowndelvin	I.	264
3	Loughanstown	134 3 36	Westmeath	Fore	Rathgarve	Granard	I.	271
6	Loughanstown	155 0 24	Westmeath	Moygoish	Russagh	Granard	I.	280
5, 6	Loughanstown Lower or Slievelahan	145 1 12	Westmeath	Moygoish	Russagh	Granard	I.	280
11	Loughantarve	119 0 35	Louth	Upper Dundalk	Louth	Dundalk	I.	179
31	Loughanunna	51 3 16	Waterford	Decies without Drum	Dungarvan	Dungarvan	II.	355
41, 49	Loughanure	941 1 20b	Donegal	Boylagh	Templecrone	Glenties	III.	115
14	Loughanure Commons	108 2 13	Kildare	Clane	Clane	Naas	I.	54
8, 12	Loughaphonta	73 2 30	Leitrim	Rosclogher	Cloonclare	Manorhamilton	IV.	109
8	Loughaphonta Barr	394 0 38	Leitrim	Rosclogher	Cloonclare	Manorhamilton	IV.	109
44	Loughaphreaghaun	80 3 38	Cork, E.R.	Barrymore	Rathcormack	Fermoy	II.	57
43, 48	Loughard	75 2 10	Wexford	Forth	Ballybrennan	Wexford	I.	308
26	Lougharuane	304 0 29	Cork, E.R.	Fermoy	Castletownroche	Fermoy	II.	77
3, 6	Loughash	1,173 0 9c	Tyrone	Strabane Lower	Donaghedy	Gortin	III.	321
44	Loughaskerry	261 3 11	Donegal	Kilmacrenan	Kilmacrenan	Millford	III.	129
76	Loughatalia	218 0 21	Cork, E.R.	Imokilly	Middleton	Middleton	II.	89
124, 125, 130, 131	Loughatorick North	3,193 0 9d	Galway	Leitrim	Ballynakill	Loughrea	IV.	52
130,131,134	Loughatorick South	2,949 1 11e	Galway	Leitrim	Ballynakill	Loughrea	IV.	52
115	Loughaun	42 0 16	Galway	Loughrea	Kilteskill	Loughrea	IV.	65
8	Loughaun	552 2 14	King's Co.	Ballycowan	Durrow	Tullamore	I.	127
20	Loughaun	95 0 19	Limerick	Connello Lower	Nantinan	Rathkeale	II.	229
7	Loughaun	40 2 31	Tipperary, N.R.	Lower Ormond	Aglishcloghane	Borrisokane	II.	281
10, 11	Loughaun	596 3 12	Tipperary, N.R.	Lower Ormond	Modreeny	Borrisokane	II.	287
20	Loughaun	115 2 3	Tipperary, N.R.	Owney and Arra	Youghalarra	Nenagh	II.	298
76	Loughaun	42 1 34	Tipperary, S.R.	Iffa and Offa West	Caher	Clogheen	II.	318
23, 35, 36	Loughauna	1,050 2 20f	Galway	Ballynahinch	Omey	Clifden	IV.	15
108	Loughaunacreen	160 3 32	Kerry	Glanarought	Tuosist	Kenmare	II.	189
114	Loughaunawadda	145 1 5g	Galway	Kiltartan	Kilthomas	Gort	IV.	49
91, 92	Loughaun Beg	1,762 1 1h	Galway	Moycullen	Killannin	Galway	IV.	70
46, 60	Loughaunboy	139 0 22	Galway	Kilconnell	Killosolan	Mountbellew	IV.	42
99	Loughaunbrean	68 0 4	Galway	Clonmacnowen	Clontuskert	Ballinasloe	IV.	25
73	Loughaunbrean	191 2 27	Galway	Kilconnell	Kilconnell	Ballinasloe	IV.	40
71, 84	Loughaunenaghan	156 2 11	Galway	Athenry	Athenry	Galway	IV.	4
103	Loughaun Island	2 1 34	Galway	Dunkellin	Kilcolgan	Gort	IV.	28
102	Loughaunnaman	223 0 38	Mayo	Clanmorris	Kilcolman	Claremorris	IV.	134
86	Loughaunnavaag	147 0 2	Galway	Kilconnell	Killallaghtan	Ballinasloe	IV.	41
17, 25	Loughaunnaweelaun	295 3 34	Clare	Inchiquin	Ruan	Corrofin	II.	28
19, 27	Loughaun North	501 0 3	Clare	Tulla Upper	Tulla	Tulla	II.	42
117, 126	Loughaunroe East	246 2 35	Galway	Leitrim	Tynagh	Portumna	IV.	55
117, 126	Loughaunroe West	79 2 20	Galway	Leitrim	Tynagh	Portumna	IV.	55
35	Loughaun South	37 1 17	Clare	Tulla Upper	Tulla	Tulla	II.	42
104	Loughavaul	518 0 20i	Cork, W.R.	Bear	Kilcaskan	Bantry	II.	123
64	Loughawee	1,100 3 36j	Galway	Ballynahinch	Moyrus	Clifden	IV.	13
15	Loughbally	452 2 29k	Roscommon	Frenchpark	Kilcolagh	Boyle	IV.	203
5	Loughbarn	128 0 32	Dublin	Balrothery East	Balrothery	Balrothery	I.	19
50,51,58,59	Loughbarra or Croagheen	2,020 1 24l	Donegal	Kilmacrenan	Gartan	Letterkenny	III.	127
87	Loughbeg	145 0 12	Cork, E.R.	Kerrycurrihy	Barnahely	Cork	II.	91
27	Loughbeg	86 3 0	Kerry	Corkaguiny	Killiney	Dingle	II.	178
27, 31	Loughbeg	30 1 39	Kilkenny	Kells	Dunnamaggan	Callan	I.	108

(a) Including 4A. 1R. 32P. water.
(b) Including 142A. 1R. 32P. water.
(c) Including 15A. 0R. 37P. water.
(d) Including 37A. 0R. 25P. water.

(e) Including 7A. 0R. 16P. water.
(f) Including 61A. 0R. 37P. water.
(g) Including 7A. 1R. 12P. water.
(h) Including 81A. 2R. 11P. water.

(i) Including 18A. 3R. 11P. water.
(j) Including 55A. 3R. 7P. water.
(k) Including 92A. 0R. 39P. water.
(l) Including 56A. 0R. 18P. water.

No. of Sheet of the Ordnance Survey Maps.	Townlands and Towns.	Area in Statute Acres. A. R. P.	County.	Barony.	Parish.	Poor Law Union in 1857.	Townland Census of 1851, Part I. Vol.	Page
41, 42	Loughbeg T	72 1 28	Tipperary, N.R.	Eliogarty	Rahelty	Thurles	II.	272
87	LOUGHBEG T.	—	Cork, E.R.	Kerrycurrihy	Barnahely	Cork	II.	91
14	Loughbollard Commons	32 0 5	Kildare	Clane	Clane	Naas	I.	54
24	Loughboreen	212 1 14	Kilkenny	Gowran	Tullaherin	Thomastown	I.	100
35, 36	Loughborough	320 1 27a	Clare	Tulla Lower	Killuran	Tulla	II.	36
87	Loughbown	299 2 14	Galway	Clonmacnowen	Kilcloony	Ballinasloe	IV.	25
19	Loughboy	109 1 11	Kilkenny	Shillelogher	St. Patrick's	Kilkenny	I.	116
39	Loughbrack	367 2 35	Tipperary, N.R.	Kilnamanagh Upper	Templebeg	Thurles	II.	279
6	Loughbrackan	530 0 21b	Meath	Lower Slane	Loughbrackan	Ardee	I.	223
15	Loughbrattoge	343 3 18	Monaghan	Cremorne	Muckno	Castleblayney	III.	262
33, 34	LOUGHBRICKLAND T.	—	Down	Upper Iveagh, Up.pt.	Aghaderg	Banbridge	III.	174
23	Loughbrown	186 1 17	Kildare	Offaly East	Pollardstown	Naas	I.	70
32	Loughburke	238 2 21c	Clare	Islands	Kilmaley	Ennis	II.	31
104	Loughburke	19 0 39	Galway	Loughrea	Killinan	Loughrea	IV.	64
70, 77	Loughcapple	259 3 7	Tipperary, S.R.	Middlethird	Kiltinan	Clonmel	II.	328
8	Lough Common	10 2 29	Dublin	Balrothery East	Lusk	Balrothery	I.	21
28, 33	Loughconnelly	1,163 2 1	Antrim	Lower Antrim	Skerry	Ballymena	III.	5
23,24,27,28	Loughconway	91 0 5d	Leitrim	Leitrim	Kiltubbrid	Car. on Shannon	IV.	104
128, 129	Loughcooter Demesne	884 3 3	Galway	Kiltartan	Beagh	Gort	IV.	46
15	Loughcrew	1,013 1 2	Meath	Fore	Loughcrew	Oldcastle	I.	201
65, 74	Loughcrillan	508 3 14	Donegal	Boylagh	Inishkeel	Glenties	III.	113
120	Loughcrot	213 2 7	Cork, W.R.	West Carbery (E.D.)	Dromdaleague	Skibbereen	II.	140
94, 95	Loughcuill	408 3 28e	Donegal	Tirhugh	Donegal	Donegal	III.	145
113	Loughcurra North	287 3 1	Galway	Kiltartan	Kinvarradoorus	Gort	IV.	49
113	Loughcurra South	336 1 11	Galway	Kiltartan	Kinvarradoorus	Gort	IV.	49
30, 31	Loughdawan	454 0 8f	Cavan	Clanmahon	Drumlumman	Granard	III.	77
105	Loughdeeveen	74 0 32	Cork, W.R.	Bantry	Kilmocomoge	Bantry	II.	121
16, 17	Loughdeheen	734 0 23	Waterford	Middlethird	Lisnakill	Waterford	II.	368
30	Loughderry and Derrymullin	369 1 5g	King's Co.	Eglish	Eglish	Parsonstown	I.	134
65, 74	Loughderryduff	600 0 30h	Donegal	Boylagh	Inishkeel	Glenties	III.	113
36	Loughdoo	83 3 2	Donegal	Kilmacrenan	Tullyfern	Milford	III.	133
25	Loughdoo	171 1 0i	Down	Ards Upper	Castleboy	Downpatrick	III.	160
11	Loughdooly	125 1 9	Cavan	Lower Loughtee	Drumlane	Cavan	III.	80
34, 35	Loughduff	596 0 29	Antrim	Upper Glenarm	Carncastle	Larne	III.	24
17	Lougheagle	167 0 22	Cork, E.R.	Fermoy	Doneraile	Mallow	II.	78
94	Lougheask Demesne	258 1 11	Donegal	Banagh	Killymard	Donegal	III.	111
45	Lougher	991 2 2	Kerry	Corkaguiny	Ballinvoher	Dingle	II.	174
26	Lougher	639 2 28j	Meath	Lower Duleek	Duleek	Drogheda	I.	195
81	Lougheraherk	355 3 39k	Donegal	Banagh	Glencolumbkille	Glenties	III.	105
2,4	Lougherbraghy	595 3 35	Donegal	Inishowen East	Clonca	Inishowen	III.	117
50	Loughermore	142 0 38	Antrim	Upper Antrim	Nilteen Grange	Antrim	III.	6
15,16,23,24	Loughermore	1,116 3 31	Londonderry	Tirkeeran	Faughanvale	New Tn Limavady	III.	250
64	Loughermore Glebe	68 1 5	Tyrone	Clogher	Aghalurcher	Clogher	III.	291
66	Loagherrig	804 2 39l	Donegal	Boylagh	Inishkeel	Glenties	III.	113
64,65,73,74	Loughfad	905 1 3m	Donegal	Boylagh	Inishkeel	Glenties	III.	113
101, 105	Loughfad	673 1 21n	Donegal	Tirhugh	Templecarn	Donegal	III.	149
21	Loughfarm	122 2 5	Longford	Ratheline	Cashel	Ballymahon	I.	163
60, 61	Loughfeedora	139 0 21	Tipperary, S.R.	Middlethird	St. Patricksrock	Cashel	II.	331
8	Loughgall	131 3 11o	Armagh	Oneilland West	Loughgall	Armagh	III.	54
8	LOUGHGALL T.	—	Armagh	Oneilland West	Loughgall	Armagh	III.	54
35	Loughgare	216 3 9p	Fermanagh	Clankelly	Clones	Clones	III.	196
26	Loughgerald	107 2 29	Wexford	Bantry	Clonmore	Enniscorthy	I.	300
20	Loughglinn	137 0 39	Roscommon	Frenchpark	Tibohine	Castlereagh	IV.	205
14, 20	Loughglinn Demesne	1,105 0 0q	Roscommon	Frenchpark	Tibohine	Castlereagh	IV.	205
20	LOUGHGLINN T.	—	Roscommon	Frenchpark	Tibohine	Castlereagh	IV.	205
47	Loughgunnen Great	137 3 39	Wexford	Forth	Mayglass	Wexford	I.	312
47	Loughgunnen Little	79 3 33	Wexford	Forth	Mayglass	Wexford	I.	312
32	Loughgur	1,285 0 16r	Limerick	Smallcounty	Knockainy	Kilmallock	II.	261
23	Loughhill	168 1 18	Antrim	Kilconway	Killagan	Ballymoney	III.	27
78	Lough Hill	57 0 32s	Donegal	Raphoe	Stranorlar	Stranorlar	III.	143
34	Lough Hill	35 1 26t	Fermanagh	Magherastephana	Aghalurcher	Lisnaskea	III.	217
73	Lough Hill or Drumalough	166 3 33u	Donegal	Banagh	Inishkeel	Glenties	III.	106
1,5	Loughill	431 2 10	Kilkenny	Fassadinin	Abbeyleix	Castlecomer	I.	88
1,5	Loughill	599 0 33	Kilkenny	Fassadinin	Attanagh	Castlecomer	I.	88
1	Loughill	48 1 26	Kilkenny	Fassadinin	Rosconnell	Castlecomer	I.	91
93	Loughinch	77 2 6	Galway	Galway	Rahoon	Galway	IV.	38
31, 38	Loughkeelan	378 0 19	Down	Lecale Lower	Ballyculter	Downpatrick	III.	178
8	Loughkeen	226 0 13	Tipperary, N.R.	Lower Ormond	Loughkeen	Parsonstown	II.	286
69	Loughkent East	250 2 19	Tipperary, S.R.	Middlethird	Knockgraffon	Cashel	II.	328
69, 76	Loughkent Lower	328 3 35	Tipperary, S.R.	Middlethird	Knockgraffon	Cashel	II.	328
68, 69	Loughkent West	265 1 26	Tipperary, S.R.	Middlethird	Knockgraffon	Cashel	II.	328

(a) Including 49A. 2R. 10P. water.
(b) Including 25A. 1R. 8P. water.
(c) Including 13A. 3R. 14P. water.
(d) Including 7A. 0R. 19P. water.
(e) Including 10A. 1R. 34P. water.
(f) Including 17A. 3R. 11P. water.
(g) Including 42A. 0R. 14P. water.
(h) Including 36A. 0R. 1P. water.

(i) Including 10A. 2R. 35P. Lough Doo.
(j) Including 2A. 2R. 0P. water.
(k) Including 22A. 1R. 11P. water.
(l) Including 24A. 2R. 39P. water.
(m) Including 36A. 3R. 13P. water.
(n) Including 26A. 0R. 28P. water.
(o) Including 7A. 3R. 13P. water.

(p) Including 36A. 2R. 7P. water.
(q) Including 161A. 3R. 30P. water.
(r) Including 110A. 3R. 23P. Loughgar.
(s) Including 7A. 3R. 8P. water.
(t) Including 5A. 2R. 20P. water.
(u) Including 9A. 0R. 25P. water.
(v) Including 15A. 1R. 10P. water.

No. of Sheet of the Ordnance Survey Maps.	Townlands and Towns.	Area in Statute Acres. A. R. P.	County.	Barony.	Parish.	Poor Law Union in 1857.	Townland Census of 1851, Part I. Vol.	Page
40	Loughkillygreen	180 2 33a	Fermanagh	Clankelly	Galloon	Clones	III.	198
94, 100	Loughkip	112 0 11	Donegal	Tirhugh	Donegal	Donegal	III.	145
54	Loughlackagh	156 1 18	Roscommon	Moycarn	Moore	Ballinasloe	IV.	207
41	Loughlahan	38 1 11	Tipperary, N.R.	Eliogarty	Thurles	Thurles	II.	273
5	Loughland	41 0 8	Dublin	Balrothery East	Lusk	Balrothery	I.	21
19, 25	Loughlass	138 1 3	Queen's Co.	Ballyadams	Ballyadams	Athy	I.	231
17	Loughlea	432 1 0	Cork, E.R.	Fermoy	Imphrick	Mallow	II.	80
71, 72	Loughleigh	512 2 3b	Cork, E.R.	East Muskerry	Cannaway	Macroom	II.	102
32	Loughlin Island	1 0 0	Donegal	Kilmacrenan	Tullaghobegly	Dunfanaghy	III.	132
22	Loughlinnan	78 2 0	Cavan	Tullygarvey	Drung	Cootehill	III.	89
26	Loughlinstown	422 3 21	Dublin	Rathdown	Killiney	Rathdown	I.	36
11	Loughlinstown	248 2 34	Kildare	South Salt	Donaghcumper	Celbridge	I.	76
38	Loughlinstown	267 3 24	Meath	Ratoath	Kilbrew	Dunshaughlin	I.	218
45	Loughlinstown	301 2 12	Meath	Ratoath	Ratoath	Dunshaughlin	I.	219
26	Loughlinstown Commons	8 2 32c	Dublin	Rathdown	Killiney	Rathdown	I.	36
26	Loughlinstown Commons	19 3 12d	Dublin	Rathdown	Rathmichael	Rathdown	I.	37
22	Loughlion	78 0 27	Kildare	Offaly East	Kildare	Naas	I.	70
76, 82	Loughlohery	904 2 11	Tipperary, S.R.	Iffa and Offa West	Caher	Clogheen	II.	318
28, 33	Loughloughan	526 3 4	Antrim	Lower Antrim	Skerry	Ballymena	III.	5
7	Loughlynch	347 2 24e	Antrim	Lower Dunluce	Billy	Ballymoney	III.	16
19	Loughmacask	56 0 28	Kilkenny	Crannagh	St. Canice	Kilkenny	I.	87
27, 36	Loughmacrory	1,651 2 11f	Tyrone	Omagh East	Termonmaguirk	Omagh	III.	314
32	Loughmagarry	362 2 12	Antrim	Lower Toome	Ahoghill	Ballymena	III.	32
4	Loughmain	119 2 21	Dublin	Balrothery West	Naul	Balrothery	I.	23
5	Loughmansland Glebe	132 0 12	Queen's Co.	Portnahinch	Lea	Mountmellick	I.	244
141	Loughmarsh	112 0 3g	Cork, W.R.	West Carbery (E.D.)	Aghadown	Skibbereen	II.	137
14, 19	Loughmerans	369 1 6h	Kilkenny	Gowran	St. John's	Kilkenny	I.	98
22	Loughminane	101 1 5	Kildare	Offaly East	Kildare	Naas	I.	70
35	LOUGHMOE T.	—	Tipperary, N.R.	Eliogarty	Loughmoe West	Thurles	II.	271
15, 21	Loughmogue Lower	190 1 27	Wicklow	Lower Talbotstown	Dunlavin	Baltinglass	I.	360
15	Loughmogue Upper	302 1 12	Wicklow	Lower Talbotstown	Dunlavin	Baltinglass	I.	360
31, 38	Loughmoney	304 0 3	Down	Lecale Lower	Ballee	Downpatrick	III.	178
31	Loughmore	23 3 16	Waterford	Decies without Drum	Kilrush	Dungarvan	II.	358
13	Loughmore Common	38 0 0	Limerick	Pubblebrien	Mungret	Limerick	II.	254
66	Loughmuck	295 2 2i	Donegal	Boylagh	Inishkeel	Glenties	III.	113
34,35,42,43	Loughmuck (Alcorn)	336 1 1j	Tyrone	Omagh East	Drumragh	Omagh	III.	312
42, 43	Loughmuck (Wallace)	165 1 8k	Tyrone	Omagh East	Drumragh	Omagh	III.	312
92	Loughmuilt	467 3 24	Donegal	Banagh	Killaghtee	Donegal	III.	109
3, 4	Loughnuirran	438 2 32	Leitrim	Rosclogher	Rossinver	Ballyshannon	IV.	112
30, 39	Loughnacappagh	36 2 11	Kerry	Trughanacmy	Ballymaccelligott	Tralee	II.	207
8	Loughnacush	189 3 21	Kildare	Carbury	Ardkill	Edenderry	I.	51
61	Loughnafina	18 0 19	Tipperary, S.R.	Middlethird	St. John Baptist	Cashel	II.	330
19, 24	Loughnafin or Rockfield	378 0 8l	Cavan	Tullyhunco	Killashandra	Cavan	III.	98
40	Loughnageer	902 0 9	Wexford	Shelmaliere West	Clongeen	New Ross	I.	333
53	Loughnagin	278 0 6	Donegal	Kilmacrenan	Aghanunshin	Letterkenny	III.	122
39	Loughnagore	146 0 34	Kerry	Trughanacmy	Killeentierna	Killarney	II.	211
24	Loughnagowan	302 1 11	Clare	Inchiquin	Rath	Ennistimon	II.	27
17, 25	Loughnahelly	478 3 37m	Mayo	Erris	Kilcommon	Belmullet	IV.	144
27	Loughnahilly	175 1 5	Cork, E.R.	Fermoy	Kilcrumper	Fermoy	II.	80
36	Loughnakey	108 2 31n	Donegal	Kilmacrenan	Tullyfern	Millford	III.	133
82	Loughnalughraman	243 2 34o	Donegal	Banagh	Inishkeel	Glenties	III.	106
58, 66	Loughnambraddan	362 1 3p	Donegal	Boylagh	Inishkeel	Glenties	III.	113
29	Loughnamuck	4 3 17	Queen's Co.	Clarmallagh	Durrow	Abbeyleix	I.	237
96	Loughnamucka	691 1 30q	Mayo	Murrisk	Kilgeever	Westport	IV.	160
39	Loughnaneane	184 2 35	Roscommon	Ballintober South	Roscommon	Roscommon	IV.	190
28	Loughnasollis Lower	115 3 22	Waterford	Coshmore&Coshbride	Tallow	Lismore	II.	348
28	Loughnasollis Upper	116 3 36	Waterford	Coshmore&Coshbride	Tallow	Lismore	II.	348
28, 33	Loughnatouse	128 0 38	Waterford	Coshmore&Coshbride	Tallow	Lismore	II.	348
2	Loughneas	264 0 19r	Tyrone	Strabane Lower	Leckpatrick	Strabane	III.	322
26	Loughooly	23 3 19	Kilkenny	Callan	Callan	Callan	I.	83
12	Loughoony	66 1 10s	Monaghan	Dartree	Clones	Clones	III.	265
41	Loughorne	465 2 18t	Down	Lordship of Newry	Newry	Newry	III.	182
14, 15	Loughourna	1,062 3 14u	Tipperary, N.R.	Lower Ormond	Knigh	Nenagh	II.	285
6	Loughpark	292 2 21	Galway	Ballymoe	Boyounagh	Glennamaddy	IV.	6
29, 30	Loughpark	86 2 7	Galway	Dunmore	Tuam	Tuam	IV.	36
125	Loughpark	115 3 28v	Galway	Leitrim	Ballynakill	Loughrea	IV.	52
90	Loughpark	82 2 21w	Mayo	Carra	Rosslee	Castlebar	IV.	130
12	Loughpark	48 3 29	Tipperary, N.R.	Ikerrin	Roscrea	Roscrea	II.	270
7	Loughpark	171 3 4	Westmeath	Fore	St. Feighins	Castletowndelvin	I.	272
26	Loughquin	179 0 16	Cork, E.R.	Fermoy	Wallstown	Mallow	II.	83

(a) Including 14A. 0R. 39P. water.
(b) Including 12A. 0R. 5P. water.
(c) Including 3A. 1R. 28P. detached portion.
(d) Including 1A. 0R. 28P. detached portion.
(e) Including 7A. 0R. 29P. water.
(f) Including 45A. 2R. 10P. water.
(g) Including 5A. 1R. 38P. water.
(h) Including 8A. 1R. 32P. River Nore.

(i) Including 26A. 1R. 20P. water.
(j) Including 5A. 3R. 20P. water.
(k) Including 28A. 2R. 33P. water.
(l) Including 61A. 2R. 20P. water.
(m) Including 12A. 2R. 32P. water.
(n) Including 6A. 2R. 8P. water.
(o) Including 66A. 2R. 38P. water.
(p) Including 28A. 0R. 0P. water.

(q) Including 7A. 0R. 36P. water.
(r) Including 4A. 0R. 0P. water.
(s) Including 4A. 0R. 0P. water.
(t) Including 39A. 3R. 13P. water.
(u) Including 18A. 1R. 12P. water.
(v) Including 15A. 0R. 8P. water.
(w) Including 13A. 3R. 22P. water.

No. of Sheet of the Ordnance Survey Maps.	Townlands and Towns.	Area in Statute Acres. A. R. P.	County.	Barony.	Parish.	Poor Law Union in 1857.	Townland Census of 1851, Part I. Vol.	Page
2	Loughrask	282 3 11	Clare	Burren	Drumcreehy	Ballyvaghan	II.	12
105	Loughrea	163 0 11	Galway	Loughrea	Loughrea	Loughrea	IV.	66
105	LOUGHREA T.	—	Galway	Loughrea	Loughrea	Loughrea	IV.	66
63	Loughrelisk	616 2 39	Antrim	Upper Massereene	Ballinderry	Lisburn	III.	29
6	Loughriscouse	1,115 0 38	Down	Ards Lower	Newtownards	Newtownards	III.	159
16	Loughroe	234 1 26	King's Co.	Ballycowan	Rahan	Tullamore	I.	129
8, 9, 12, 13	Loughros	681 2 4	Leitrim	Drumahaire	Cloonclare	Manorhamilton	IV.	93
36	Loughros Glebe	200 0 16	Donegal	Kilmacrenan	Tullyfern	Millford	III.	133
30	Loughross	251 0 5a	Armagh	Fews Upper	Creggan	Castleblayney	III.	48
69	Loughrusheen	426 2 2b	Mayo	Carra	Aglish	Castlebar	IV.	124
38	Loughry	46 1 0	Tyrone	Dungannon Upper	Derryloran	Cookstown	III.	307
38	Loughry	87 2 6	Tyrone	Dungannon Upper	Desertcreat	Cookstown	III.	308
38	Loughry Demesne	128 3 19	Tyrone	Dungannon Upper	Derryloran	Cookstown	III.	307
77, 86	Loughsallagh	910 0 7c	Donegal	Raphoe	Kilteevoge	Stranorlar	III.	139
50, 51	Loughsallagh	165 3 4	Meath	Dunboyne	Dunboyne	Dunshaughlin	I.	199
57	Loughsalt	141 2 32d	Donegal	Boylagh	Templecrone	Glenties	III.	115
24, 28	Loughscur	97 3 31e	Leitrim	Leitrim	Kiltubbrid	Car". on Shannon	IV.	104
23	Loughsheedan	103 2 17	Longford	Moydow	Taghsheenod	Ballymahon	I.	162
5, 8	Loughshinny	98 1 13	Dublin	Balrothery East	Lusk	Balrothery	I.	21
8	LOUGHSHINNY T.	—	Dublin	Balrothery East	Lusk	Balrothery	I.	21
27, 31	Loughsollish	239 3 14	Kilkenny	Kells	Dunamaggan	Callan	I.	108
8	Loughstown	89 0 7	Westmeath	Delvin	Kilcumny	Castletowndelvin	I.	265
82	Loughtally	536 2 13f	Tipperary, S.R.	Iffa and Offa East	Inishlounaght	Clonmel	II.	313
11	Loughtate	59 2 4	Louth	Ardee	Louth	Dundalk	I.	173
18, 19	Loughteeog	428 3 21	Queen's Co.	Stradbally	Dysartenos	Athy	I.	247
56	Loughterush	302 3 29	Tyrone	Omagh East	Kilskeery	Lowtherstown	III.	313
29, 30	Loughtilube	481 2 2	Londonderry	Tirkeeran	Banagher	Londonderry	III.	247
10	Loughtown	235 0 24	Kildare	Ikeathy&Oughterany	Clonshanbo	Celbridge	I.	57
17, 20, 21	Loughtown Lower	166 3 29	Dublin	Newcastle	Kilmactalway	Celbridge	I.	33
17, 21	Loughtown Upper	94 3 5	Dublin	Newcastle	Kilmactalway	Celbridge	I.	33
99	Loughturk East	33 1 19	Galway	Clonmacnowen	Clontuskert	Ballinasloe	IV.	25
99	Loughturk West	130 3 25	Galway	Clonmacnowen	Clontuskert	Ballinasloe	IV.	25
105	Loughultan	795 0 11g	Donegal	Tirhugh	Templecarn	Donegal	III.	149
116	*Loughure Island*	2 0 24	Cork, W.R.	Bear	Kilcaskan	Castletown	II.	123
33	Loughvella	209 3 14	Clare	Islands	Drumcliff	Ennis	II.	30
38,39,42,43	Loughwheelion or Moneyadda	246 3 21	King's Co	Clonlisk	Aghancon	Roscrea	I.	129
86	LOUISBURGH T.	—	Mayo	Murrisk	Kilgeever	Westport	IV.	161
29, 30	Loumanagh North	211 1 15	Cork, E.R.	Duhallow	Kilmeen	Millstreet	II.	73
29, 30	Loumanagh South	528 0 30	Cork, E.R.	Duhallow	Kilmeen	Millstreet	II.	73
93, 94	Lounaghan	1,040 0 12	Kerry	Glanarought	Kilgarvan	Kenmare	II.	187
19	Lousybush	107 1 30	Kilkenny	Crannagh	St. Canice	Kilkenny	I.	87
118	*Lousy Castle Island*	0 0 27	Cork, W.R.	Bantry	Kilmocomoge	Bantry	II.	121
11, 14	Louth Hall	1,027 0 5h	Louth	Ardee	Tallanstown	Ardee	I.	175
23	Louth Hill or Mellifont Park	129 1 1	Louth	Ferrard	Tullyallen	Drogheda	I.	183
11	LOUTH T.	—	Louth	Louth	Louth	Dundalk	I.	185
18	Lovescharity	24 2 1i	Dublin	Dublin Municipal Borough of	St. George	Dublin North	I.	44
18, 19	Love's Corkey	794 0 36	Antrim	Upper Dunluce	Loughguile	Ballymoney	III.	20
32	Lowberry	106 3 30	Roscommon	Castlereagh	Kiltullagh	Castlereagh	IV.	202
38	Low Cross	175 3 4	Tyrone	Dungannon Upper	Desertcreat	Cookstown	III.	308
100	Lower Barr and Carrick Upper	1,142 3 16j	Donegal	Tirhugh	Drumhome	Donegal	III.	146
14	Lower Broghindrumminor Tavnaghranny	186 1 31	Antrim	Lower Glenarm	Grange of Layd	Ballycastle	III.	22
30	Lower Heath	174 2 31	King's Co.	Eglish	Eglish	Parsonstown	I.	135
24	Lowerton Beg	360 0 15	King's Co.	Ballyboy	Killoughy	Tullamore	I.	124
24	Lowerton More	457 3 26	King's Co.	Ballyboy	Killoughy	Tullamore	I.	124
139, 148	Lowertown	431 3 2	Cork, W.R.	West Carbery (W.D.)	Skull	Skull	II.	146
12	Lowertown	64 1 17	Monaghan	Dartree	Clones	Clones	III.	265
54, 55	Lowertown	185 1 11	Tyrone	Dungannon Middle	Killyman	Dungannon	III.	303
38, 40	Lowertown	300 2 5	Westmeath	Moycashel	Rahugh	Tullamore	I.	279
23, 27, 28	Lower Tullykittagh	425 3 3	Antrim	Kilconway	Dunaghy	Ballymena	III.	26
36	Lowerwood	233 3 32	Westmeath	Clonlonan	Kilcleagh	Athlone	I.	261
4, 5	Lowery	223 0 21	Fermanagh	Lurg	Drumkeeran	Lowtherstown	III.	206
8	Lowerybane	248 2 19k	Fermanagh	Lurg	Belleek	Ballyshannon	III.	203
69	Lowesgreen	230 2 15	Tipperary, S.R.	Middlethird	Kilbragh	Cashel	II.	327
12	Lowfield	93 3 36l	Roscommon	Ballintober North	Kilmore	Car". on Shannon	IV.	187
7	Lowforge or Drumconra	189 2 36	Cavan	Tullyhaw	Kinawley	Bawnboy	III.	93
151	*Low Island*	1 3 21	Cork, W.R.	West Carbery (E.D.)	Myross	Skibbereen	II.	141
68	*Low Island*	0 0 39	Mayo	Carra	Islandeady	Castlebar	IV.	129
21, 27	Lowlough	53 1 35	Wexford	Ballaghkeen	Meelnagh	Enniscorthy	I.	298

(a) Including 16A. 3R. 22P. water.
(b) Including 7A. 2R. 14P. water.
(c) Including 8A. 3R. 2P. water.
(d) Including 8A. 0R. 2P. water.

(e) Including 23A. 1R. 16P. water.
(f) Including 7A. 2R. 22P. water.
(g) Including 28A. 1R. 32P. water.
(h) Including 15A. 3R. 27P. water.

(i) Included in the Parish of St. George.
(j) Including 61A. 3R. 25P. water.
(k) Including 7A. 3R. 26P. water.
(l) Including 21A. 2R. 0P. water.

No. of Sheet of the Ordnance Survey Maps.	Townlands and Towns.	Area in Statute Acres.	County.	Barony.	Parish.	Poor Law Union in 1857.	Townland Census of 1851. Part I.	
		A. R. P.					Vol.	Page
98, 99	Lowpark	372 3 6	Galway	Longford	Killoran	Ballinasloe	IV.	59
63	Lowpark	285 3 39	Mayo	Costello	Kilbeagh	Swineford	IV.	140
15, 22	Lowpark or Ballyboy	262 0 27	Westmeath	Kilkenny West	Kilkenny West	Athlone	I.	273
5, 6	Lowparks	68 3 17	Roscommon	Boyle	Boyle	Boyle	IV.	194
22	Lowran	553 2 38	Queen's Co.	Upperwoods	Offerlane	Abbeyleix	I.	252
11	Lowrath North	326 3 26	Louth	Louth	Louth	Dundalk	I.	184
11	Lowrath South	35 2 4	Louth	Louth	Louth	Dundalk	I.	184
11	LOWTHERSTOWN T.	—	Fermanagh	Lurg	Derryvullan	Lowtherstown	III.	205
40	Lowtown	177 1 23	Antrim	Upper Glenarm	Kilwaughter	Larne	III.	25
13	Lowtown	504 1 14	Kildare	Connell	Kilmeage	Naas	I.	55
30	Lowtown	743 1 28d	Kildare	Narragh&RebanWest	Kilberry	Athy	I.	68
20	Lowtown	241 0 31	Wicklow	Upper Talbotstown	Ballynure	Baltinglass	I.	362
27	Lowtown or Balleighter	395 0 1	Westmeath	Farbill	Killucan	Mullingar	I.	267
51, 54	Lowtown Kilcashel	939 3 32	Roscommon	Moycarn	Moore	Ballinasloe	IV.	207
61, 73, 74	Lowville	1,555 2 1	Galway	Kilconnell	Fohanagh	Ballinasloe	IV.	40
56, 57, 61	Low Wood	388 1 6	Antrim	Upper Belfast	Shankill	Belfast	III.	10
29	Loy	135 3 38	Tyrone	Dungannon Upper	Derryloran	Cookstown	III.	307
47	Loyer	162 1 13	King's Co.	Clonlisk	Castletownely	Roscrea	I.	129
18	Loyst	224 1 18	Monaghan	Monaghan	Kilmore	Monaghan	III.	276
83, 84	Luaghnabrogue	1,020 0 4	Donegal	Banagh	Inver	Donegal	III.	107
14,15,19,20	Lubitavish	195 1 13	Antrim	Lower Glenarm	Layd	Ballycastle	III.	23
17	Lucan Demesne	152 1 2b	Dublin	Newcastle	Lucan	Celbridge	I.	33
17	Lucan & Pettycanon	259 3 27c	Dublin	Newcastle	Lucan	Celbridge	I.	33
17	LUCAN T.	—	Dublin	Newcastle	Lucan	Celbridge	I.	33
26	Lucas's Park	68 0 5	Wexford	Bantry	St. John's	Enniscorthy	I.	302
29, 38	Luddan	519 1 31	Donegal	Inishowen West	Fahan Lower	Inishowen	III.	120
14, 23	Ludden Beg	243 2 37	Limerick	Clanwilliam	Ludden	Limerick	II.	225
14, 23	Ludden More	437 0 26	Limerick	Clanwilliam	Ludden	Limerick	II.	225
43, 44	Luffany	237 3 15	Kilkenny	Ida	Rathpatrick	Waterford	I.	103
42, 45	Luffany	444 3 20	Kilkenny	Iverk	Portnascully	Waterford	I.	106
14, 20	Luffertan	136 3 28	Sligo	Carbury	Killaspugbrone	Sligo	IV.	222
89, 99	Luffertaun	136 3 28	Mayo	Carra	Ballintober	Castlebar	IV.	125
9	Lug	99 3 32	King's Co.	Ballycowan	Durrow	Tullamore	I.	127
33, 34	Lugacaha	77 0 22	Sligo	Corran	Kilmorgan	Sligo	IV.	227
23, 24	Lugacaha	175 1 18d	Westmeath	Rathconrath	Ballymore	Ballymahon	I.	282
4	Lugadoo	91 0 20	Kildare	Ikeathy&Oughterany	Cloncurry	Celbridge	I.	57
24	Lugadowden	78 1 33	Kildare	Naas South	Tipperkevin	Naas	I.	65
21	Lugakeeran	368 3 34	Roscommon	Castlereagh	Kilcorkey	Castlereagh	IV.	199
112	Lugalisheen North	190 2 13	Mayo	Clanmorris	Crossboyne	Claremorris	IV.	133
112	Lugalisheen South	131 0 10	Mayo	Clanmorris	Crossboyne	Claremorris	IV.	133
11	Lugalustran	72 3 26	Leitrim	Drumahaire	Drumlease	Manorhamilton	IV.	94
24	Lugamarla	320 1 26	King's Co.	Ballyboy	Killoughy	Tullamore	I.	124
31	Luganiska	331 0 21	King's Co.	Ballyboy	Ballyboy	Parsonstown	I.	123
78,79,89,90	Lugaphuill	250 3 37e	Mayo	Carra	Ballyhean	Castlebar	IV.	126
89, 90	Lugaphuill	215 0 2f	Mayo	Carra	Drum	Castlebar	IV.	128
8	Lugasnaghta	565 2 23	Leitrim	Rosclogher	Cloonclare	Manorhamilton	IV.	109
119	Lugatallin	140 0 34	Mayo	Kilmaine	Kilcommon	Ballinrobe	IV.	155
17	Lugateane	185 3 9	Roscommon	Roscommon	Aughrim	Carᵏ. on Shannon	IV.	207
101	Lugatemple	206 3 15	Mayo	Clanmorris	Kilcolman	Claremorris	IV.	134
9	Lugatober	223 3 7	Sligo	Carbury	Drumcliff	Sligo	IV.	221
14, 15	Lugatryna	252 1 4	Wicklow	Lower Talbotstown	Dunlavin	Baltinglass	I.	360
20	Lugawarry	311 3 36	Sligo	Leyny	Ballysadare	Sligo	IV.	230
19	Lugbaun	381 0 38g	Sligo	Tireragh	Dromard	Dromore West	IV.	233
47, 50, 51	Lugboy	445 3 36	Roscommon	Athlone	Taghmaconnell	Athlone	IV.	185
22, 23	Lugboy	257 0 20h	Roscommon	Roscommon	Elphin	Strokestown	IV.	209
103	Lugboy Demesne	244 2 17	Mayo	Costello	Annagh	Claremorris	IV.	138
81	Lugbrack	52 3 10	Mayo	Costello	Aghamore	Swineford	IV.	137
8	Lugbriscan	42 0 28	Louth	Lower Dundalk	Carlingford	Dundalk	I.	176
12, 18	Lugdoon	665 1 28	Sligo	Tireragh	Templeboy	Dromore West	IV.	236
16, 22, 23	Lugduff	2,354 0 30i	Wicklow	Ballinacor North	Derrylossery	Rathdrum	I.	346
38, 43	Lugduff	384 0 0	Wicklow	Ballinacor South	Kilcommon	Shillelagh	I.	349
88, 100	Lugfree	92 2 16	Cork, E.R.	Imokilly	Inch	Middleton	II.	87
21, 24	Lugg	315 1 8	Dublin	Newcastle	Saggart	Celbridge	I.	34
19, 25	Luggacurren	1,838 1 15	Queen's Co.	Stradbally	Tullomoy	Athy	I.	248
67	Luggakeeraun	564 0 22	Galway	Moycullen	Killannin	Oughterard	IV.	70
66	Lugganaffrin	652 1 6j	Galway	Moycullen	Kilcummin	Oughterard	IV.	67
33	Lugganammer	454 3 8	Leitrim	Carrigallen	Cloone	Mohill	IV.	90
70, 79	Lugganashlere	181 0 6	Mayo	Carra	Turlough	Castlebar	IV.	131
66	Lugganimma	1,139 3 27k	Galway	Moycullen	Kilcummin	Oughterard	IV.	67
24	Luggatarriff	526 1 7	Galway	Ballynahinch	Ballynakill	Clifden	IV.	11
55	Luggawannia	969 0 1	Galway	Clare	Cargin	Tuam	IV.	18
24	Lugglass	145 1 25	King's Co.	Ballyboy	Killoughy	Tullamore	I.	124
16	Lugglass Lower	241 2 1	Wicklow	Lower Talbotstown	Hollywood	Baltinglass	I.	361

(a) Including 17A. 3R. 16P. water.
(b) Including 13A. 2R. 16P. water.
(c) Including 1A. 3R. 32P. water.
(d) Including 33A. 3R. 8P. water.

(e) Including 2A. 3R. 24P. water.
(f) Including 1A. 0R. 18P. water.
(g) Including 4A. 1R. 16P. water.
(h) Including 2A. 3R. 8P. water.

(i) { Including 50A. 0R. 35P. Upper Lake.
   Including 3A. 3R. 24P. Lower Lake.
(j) Including 29A. 2R. 19P. water.
(k) Including 40A. 3R. 30P. water.

No. of Sheet of the Ordnance Survey Maps	Townlands and Towns	Area in Statute Acres. A. R. P.	County.	Barony.	Parish.	Poor Law Union in 1857.	Townland Census of 1851. Part I. Vol.	Page
16	Lugglass Upper	240 2 13	Wicklow	Lower Talbotstown	Hollywood	Baltinglass	I.	361
23	Luggs	64 3 22	Roscommon	Roscommon	Kiltrustan	Strokestown	IV.	211
17	Luggygalla	82 0 17	Westmeath	Rathconrath	Rathconrath	Mullingar	I.	284
60	Lughanagh	100 1 35	Galway	Kilconnell	Killosolan	Mountbellew	IV.	42
12	Lughawagh	45 1 26	Leitrim	Drumahaire	Cloonclare	Manorhamilton	IV.	93
28	Lugher	65 2 8	Donegal	Kilmacrenan	Killygarvan	Millford	III.	128
26	Lughil	275 2 37	Kildare	Offaly West	Ballybrackan	Athy	I.	71
12, 13	Lughinny	382 1 38	Kilkenny	Crannagh	Killahy	Urlingford	I.	86
66, 67	Lughveen	826 3 27	Donegal	Boylagh	Inishkeel	Glenties	III.	113
15, 17	Lugmeeltan	235 0 27	Leitrim	Drumahaire	Inishmagrath	Manorhamilton	IV.	97
17, 18	Lugmeen	50 3 17	Leitrim	Drumahaire	Inishmagrath	Manorhamilton	IV.	97
21, 24	Lugmore	122 1 32	Dublin	Uppercross	Tallaght	Dublin South	I.	42
1	Lugmore	107 1 10	Fermanagh	Lurg	Drumkeeran	Lowtherstown	III.	206
18, 26	Lugmore	67 2 12	King's Co.	Geashill	Geashill	Tullamore	I.	140
18, 20	Lugmore	72 0 28	Leitrim	Drumahaire	Inishmagrath	Manorhamilton	IV.	97
31	Lugnaboley & Killeen	326 0 13	King's Co.	Ballyboy	Ballyboy	Parsonstown	I.	123
19, 20	Lugnadeffa	359 1 4	Sligo	Leyny	Ballysadare	Sligo	IV.	230
77	Lugnafahy	110 2 32	Mayo	Burrishoole	Kilmaclasser	Westport	IV.	121
6	Lugnafaughery	422 0 31	Leitrim	Rosclogher	Killasnet	Manorhamilton	IV.	110
9	Lugnagall	241 2 15	Sligo	Carbury	Drumcliff	Sligo	IV.	221
44, 54	Lugnagappul	148 1 14	Kerry	Corkaguiny	Minard	Dingle	II.	180
26	Lugnagon	368 2 12	Leitrim	Carrigallen	Carrigallen	Bawnboy	IV.	90
9, 10	Lugnagroagh	227 0 20	Wicklow	Lower Talbotstown	Boystown	Naas	I.	359
18	Lugnagullagh	70 0 1	Westmeath	Corkaree	Tyfarnham	Mullingar	I.	264
5	Lugnagun Great	518 1 30	Wicklow	Lower Talbotstown	Blessington	Naas	I.	358
5	Lugnagun Little	120 0 24	Wicklow	Lower Talbotstown	Blessington	Naas	I.	358
13	Lugnalettin	1,704 1 11	Mayo	Tirawley	Doonfeeny	Killala	IV.	*167
20, 26	Lugnamackan	325 1 14	Sligo	Leyny	Ballysadare	Sligo	IV.	230
22	Lugnamannow	22 3 21	Sligo	Tireragh	Castleconor	Ballina	IV.	232
6	Lugnamuddagh or Cashelfinoge	211 2 36	Roscommon	Boyle	Boyle	Boyle	IV.	194
22, 28	Lugnaquillia	874 0 24	Wicklow	Upper Talbotstown	Donaghmore	Baltinglass	I.	363
10	Lugnashammer	151 2 31	Roscommon	Boyle	Killukin	Boyle	IV.	196
15	Lugnaskeehan	269 0 12	Leitrim	Drumahaire	Killarga	Manorhamilton	IV.	99
70, 79	Lugnavaddoge	173 0 3	Mayo	Carra	Turlough	Castlebar	IV.	131
88	Lugrevagh	64 3 5	Mayo	Burrishoole	Aghagower	Westport	IV.	118
56	Luimnagh East	121 2 38	Galway	Clare	Kilcoona	Tuam	IV.	20
56	Luimnagh West	234 1 18	Galway	Clare	Kilcoona	Tuam	IV.	20
12, 17	Lullybeg	2,203 0 8	Kildare	Offaly East	Cloncurry	Edenderry	I.	69
12, 17	Lullymore East	1,090 0 34	Kildare	Offaly East	Lullymore	Edenderry	I.	70
12	Lullymore West	1,566 0 28	Kildare	Offaly East	Lullymore	Edenderry	I.	70
16, 17	Lumcloon	237 0 5	Carlow	Idrone East	Fennagh	Carlow	I.	7
22, 23	Lumcloon	2,248 1 17a	King's Co.	Garrycastle	Gallen	Parsonstown	I.	136
37, 42	Lumcloon	221 3 0	Wicklow	Shillelagh	Aghowle	Shillelagh	I.	356
68, 69	Lumnagh Beg	76 1 30	Cork, W.R.	West Muskerry	Ballyvourney	Macroom	II.	154
58, 68, 69	Lumnagh More	183 2 12	Cork, W.R.	West Muskerry	Ballyvourney	Macroom	II.	154
11	Lumville	346 0 7	King's Co.	Coolestown	Monasteroris	Edenderry	I.	133
27, 33	Lunderstown	287 3 7	Meath	Upper Duleek	Duleek	Drogheda	I.	197
20	Lunestown	177 3 3	Westmeath	Farbill	Killucan	Castletowndelvin	I.	267
41	Luney	383 0 18	Londonderry	Loughinsholin	Desertmartin	Magherafelt	III.	240
74	Lung	855 1 27	Mayo	Costello	Castlemore	Castlereagh	IV.	140
58, 64	Lungs	218 1 26b	Tyrone	Clogher	Clogher	Clogher	III.	293
32	Lunniagh	507 2 9c	Donegal	Kilmacrenan	Tullaghobegly	Dunfanaghy	III.	132
8, 14, 15	Luogh North	611 2 35d	Clare	Corcomroe	Killilagh	Ennistimon	II.	20
14	Luogh South	457 0 5e	Clare	Corcomroe	Killilagh	Ennistimon	II.	20
3	Luppan	125 3 22	Monaghan	Trough	Errigal Trough	Clogher	III.	285
128	Lurga	166 1 34	Galway	Kiltartan	Beagh	Gort	IV.	46
33	Lurga	156 1 23	Leitrim	Mohill	Cloone	Mohill	IV.	106
4, 7	Lurga	195 2 35	Roscommon	Boyle	Tumna	Carbon Shannon	IV.	198
123	Lurgabaun	122 1 23	Galway	Kiltartan	Kilbeacanty	Gort	IV.	47
17	Lurgaboy	224 2 14	Armagh	Fews Lower	Mullaghbrack	Armagh	III.	47
2, 4	Lurgaboy	111 2 8	Roscommon	Boyle	Kilronan	Boyle	IV.	197
46, 54	Lurgaboy	139 3 15	Tyrone	Dungannon Middle	Drumglass	Dungannon	III.	303
15	Lurgabrack	709 1 24	Donegal	Kilmacrenan	Clondahorky	Dunfanaghy	III.	123
24	Lurgachamlough	218 0 20f	Monaghan	Cremorne	Aghnamullen	Castleblayney	III.	258
17	Lurgacloghan	246 2 24	Donegal	Kilmacrenan	Clondavaddog	Millford	III.	125
16	Lurgacloy	274 1 2g	Mayo	Erris	Kilmore	Belmullet	IV.	146
53	Lurgacullion	289 1 4	Tyrone	Dungannon Lower	Killeeshil	Dungannon	III.	298
63, 73	Lurga Lower	452 2 31	Mayo	Costello	Kilbeagh	Swineford	IV.	141
6	Lurgan	88 1 14	Armagh	Oneilland East	Shankill	Lurgan	III.	51
39	Lurgan	127 2 24	Cavan	Castlerahan	Lurgan	Oldcastle	III.	70
103	Lurgan	484 2 12h	Donegal	Tirhugh	Drumhome	Ballyshannon	III.	146
25	Lurgan	54 0 23	Fermanagh	Clanawley	Cleenish	Enniskillen	III.	191

(a) Including 3A. 1R. 20P. water.
(b) Including 0A. 0R. 32P. water.
(c) Including 6A. 0R. 6P. water.

(d) Including 5A. 2R. 24P. water.
(e) Including 2A. 1R. 18P. water.
(f) Including 17A. 2R. 29P. water.

(g) Including 7A. 1R. 31P. water.
(h) Including 11A. 0R. 16P. water.

No. of Sheet of the Ordnance Survey Maps.	Townlands and Towns.	Area in Statute Acres.			County.	Barony.	Parish.	Poor Law Union in 1857.	Townland Census of 1851, Part I.	
		A.	R.	P.					Vol.	Page
28	Lurgan	61	3	33	Fermanagh	Magherastephana	Aghavea	Lisnaskea	III.	219
105	Lurgan	131	3	26	Galway	Dunkellin	Kilconickny	Loughrea	IV.	29
16	Lurgan	245	0	23	Galway	Dunmore	Addergoole	Tuam	IV.	33
16, 17	Lurgan	315	3	2	Galway	Dunmore	Dunmore	Tuam	IV.	34
60	Lurgan	639	1	9	Galway	Kilconnell	Killosolan	Mountbellew	IV.	42
123	Lurgan	226	1	25a	Galway	Kiltartan	Kilbeacanty	Gort	IV.	47
1	Lurgan	444	3	3	King's Co.	Kilcoursey	Kilmanaghan	Tullamore	I.	141
12	Lurgan	674	0	28b	Leitrim	Drumahaire	Cloonclare	Manorhamilton	IV.	93
24	Lurgan	73	2	32	Longford	Ardagh	Rathreagh	Ballymahon	I.	153
81	Lurgan	318	3	28	Mayo	Costello	Aghamore	Swineford	IV.	137
93	Lurgan	305	1	18	Mayo	Costello	Annagh	Claremorris	IV.	138
102	Lurgan	339	1	1	Mayo	Costello	Bekan	Claremorris	IV.	139
2	Lurgan	81	1	39	Roscommon	Boyle	Kilronan	Boyle	IV.	197
15	Lurgan	294	0	14	Roscommon	Frenchpark	Kilcolagh	Boyle	IV.	203
22	Lurgan	215	0	6c	Roscommon	Roscommon	Shankill	Strokestown	IV.	213
39	Lurgan	111	1	19d	Sligo	Corran	Toomour	Boyle	IV.	228
27	Lurgan	119	3	12	Sligo	Tirerrill	Ballysumaghan	Sligo	IV.	238
15, 22	Lurgan	57	2	9	Westmeath	Kilkenny West	Kilkenny West	Athlone	I.	273
24	Lurgan	108	1	6	Westmeath	Rathconrath	Killare	Mullingar	I.	283
21, 25	Lurgana	314	0	7	Armagh	Fews Upper	Ballymyre	Newry	III.	48
51	Lurganaglare	319	2	22	Tyrone	Clogher	Clogher	Clogher	III.	293
36, 37, 42	Lurganagoose	214	2	15	Londonderry	Loughinsholin	Termoneeny	Magherafelt	III.	244
33	Lurgananure	326	0	38	Cavan	Castlerahan	Killinkere	Bailieborough	III.	69
40, 46	Lurganare	341	0	30	Down	Upper Iveagh, Up. pt.	Donaghmore	Newry	III.	175
34	Lurganaveele	221	1	20	Cavan	Castlerahan	Killinkere	Bailieborough	III.	69
34	Lurganbane	119	2	22	Cavan	Clankee	Bailieborough	Bailieborough	III.	71
21	Lurganbane	553	3	30	Down	Lower Iveagh, Lr. pt.	Dromore	Banbridge	III.	168
23	Lurganbane	218	0	38	Fermanagh	Magherastephana	Aghalurcher	Lisnaskea	III.	217
107	Lurgan Beg	113	2	18	Galway	Longford	Abbeygormacan	Ballinasloe	IV.	56
43	Lurganboy	272	2	8	Cavan	Castlerahan	Munterconnaught	Oldcastle	III.	71
23	Lurganboy	176	0	38	Cavan	Clankee	Drumgoon	Cootehill	III.	72
20, 25	Lurganboy	46	2	33	Cavan	Upper Loughtee	Urney	Cavan	III.	86
74, 83	Lurganboy	71	0	25	Donegal	Banagh	Killybegs Lower	Glenties	III.	110
9, 18	Lurganboy	82	2	6	Donegal	Kilmacrenan	Clondavaddog	Millford	III.	125
28	Lurganboy	576	0	0	Donegal	Kilmacrenan	Killygarvan	Millford	III.	128
99	Lurganboy	86	3	29	Donegal	Tirhugh	Donegal	Donegal	III.	145
40	Lurganboy	183	2	25	Fermanagh	Coole	Galloon	Clones	III.	200
1	Lurganboy	64	3	3	Fermanagh	Lurg	Drumkeeran	Lowtherstown	III.	206
6	Lurganboy	128	1	8	Fermanagh	Lurg	Magheraculmoney	Lowtherstown	III.	208
19	Lurganboy	164	2	14	Louth	Ferrard	Port	Drogheda	I.	182
15, 22	Lurganboy	127	1	6	Meath	Fore	Moylagh	Oldcastle	I.	201
15	Lurganboy	188	1	1	Monaghan	Cremorne	Muckno	Castleblayney	III.	262
17	Lurganboy	217	2	4	Monaghan	Dartree	Currin	Cootehill	III.	266
50, 57	Lurganboy	141	3	35	Tyrone	Clogher	Donacavey	Omagh	III.	294
44, 45, 52	Lurganboy	663	3	4	Tyrone	Clogher	Errigal Keerogue	Clogher	III.	295
39	Lurganboy	89	3	33	Tyrone	Dungannon Upper	Artrea	Cookstown	III.	306
16	Lurganboy	304	0	24	Tyrone	Strabane Lower	Ardstraw	Castlederg	III.	319
17, 25	Lurganboy	150	3	29e	Tyrone	Strabane Upper	Cappagh	Omagh	III.	325
28	Lurganboys	232	2	13f	Monaghan	Farney	Donaghmoyne	Carrickmacross	III.	270
7	LURGANBOY T.	—			Leitrim	Rosclogher	Killasnet	Manorhamilton	IV.	110
18, 28	Lurganbrack	295	0	32	Donegal	Kilmacrenan	Clondavaddog	Millford	III.	125
41, 47	Lurganeahone	558	0	9	Down	Upper Iveagh, Up. pt.	Drumgath	Newry	III.	175
51	Lurgancanty	179	3	25	Down	Upper Iveagh, Up. pt.	Clonallan	Newry	III.	174
18	Lurganclabby	195	3	33	Fermanagh	Tirkennedy	Enniskillen	Enniskillen	III.	222
57	Lurganconary	109	0	25g	Down	Mourne	Kilkeel	Kilkeel	III.	183
9	Lurgancot	218	1	36	Armagh	Oneilland West	Kilmore	Armagh	III.	53
28, 31	Lurgancullenboy	652	2	35	Armagh	Fews Upper	Creggan	Dundalk	III.	48
44, 45	Lurgandarragh	1,176	0	32	Mayo	Erris	Kilcommon	Newport	IV.	144
21	Lurgandarragh Big	150	0	4	Fermanagh	Magheraboy	Cleenish	Enniskillen	III.	210
21	Lurgandarragh Little	40	3	32	Fermanagh	Magheraboy	Rossorry	Enniskillen	III.	214
15, 20	Lurganearly	325	3	12	Monaghan	Cremorne	Muckno	Castleblayney	III.	262
37, 45	Lurganeden	298	3	4	Tyrone	Dungannon Middle	Pomeroy	Cookstown	III.	304
39	Lurgan Glebe	44	2	30	Cavan	Castlerahan	Lurgan	Oldcastle	III.	70
99	Lurgan Great	302	3	12	Galway	Clonmacnowen	Killallaghtan	Ballinasloe	IV.	26
24, 25	Lurgangreen	328	3	28	Monaghan	Cremorne	Aghnamullen	Castleblayney	III.	258
12	LURGANGREEN T.	—			Louth	Louth	Dromiskin	Dundalk	I.	183
3, 4	Lurgankeel	611	0	5	Louth	Upper Dundalk	Faughart	Dundalk	I.	178
99	Lurgan Little	217	0	35	Galway	Clonmacnowen	Killallaghtan	Ballinasloe	IV.	26
107	Lurgan More	640	0	11	Galway	Longford	Abbeygormacan	Ballinasloe	IV.	56
20	Lurganmore	181	2	12	Monaghan	Cremorne	Muckno	Castleblayney	III.	262
57	Lurganreagh	218	0	16	Down	Mourne	Kilkeel	Kilkeel	III.	183
31	Lurgans	273	3	34	Monaghan	Farney	Magheross	Carrickmacross	III.	274
66, 67	Lurgansemanus	120	3	3	Antrim	Upper Massereene	Aghalee	Lurgan	III.	29

(a) Including 0A. 2R. 4P. water.
(b) Including 4A. 2R. 25P. water.
(c) Including 9A. 3R. 33P. water.

(d) Including 8A. 2R. 7P. water.
(e) Including 1A. 2R. 21P. water.

(f) Including 9A. 2R. 11P. water.
(g) Including 3A. 0R. 21P. detached portion.

No. of Sheet of the Ordnance Survey Maps.	Townlands and Towns.	Area in Statute Acres.	County.	Barony.	Parish.	Poor Law Union in 1857.	Townland Census of 1851, Part I.	
							Vol.	Page
		A. R. P.						
70	Lurganshannagh	137 1 23	Donegal	Raphoe	Clonleigh	Strabane	III.	135
107	Lurganshanny	90 3 28	Galway	Longford	Abbeygormacan	Ballinasloe	IV.	56
38,39,52,53	Lurgan or Shindilla	1,121 0 22	Galway	Moycullen	Kilcummin	Oughterard	IV.	67
20	Lurgantamry	202 2 19	Down	Lower Iveagh, Up. pt.	Donaghcloney	Lurgan	III.	169
6	Lurgantarry	175 3 36	Armagh	Oneilland East	Shankill	Lurgan	III.	51
59, 63	Lurganteneil	637 2 27	Antrim	Upper Massereene	Ballinderry	Lisburn	III.	29
6	LURGAN T.	—	Armagh	Oneilland East	Shankill	Lurgan	III.	51
67	Lurganure	346 1 31	Antrim	Upper Massereene	Blaris	Lisburn	III.	30
13, 20	Lurganville	585 2 3	Down	Lower Iveagh, Up. pt.	Moira	Lurgan	III.	170
43, 49	Lurgan West	221 3 3	Antrim	Upper Toome	Drummaul	Antrim	III.	34
73	Lurga Upper	632 3 5	Mayo	Costello	Kilbeagh	Swineford	IV.	141
62, 63	Lurgill	470 1 33	Antrim	Upper Massereene	Ballinderry	Lisburn	III.	29
48, 53, 54	Lurgoe	1,375 3 22	Tipperary, S.R.	Slievardagh	Graystown	Cashel	II.	333
61	Lurgy	278 0 27	Donegal	Raphoe	Leck	Letterkenny	III.	140
38,39,46,47	Lurgy	292 2 10	Tyrone	Dungannon Middle	Donaghenry	Cookstown	III.	301
53, 61	Lurgybrack	81 1 21	Donegal	Raphoe	Leck	Letterkenny	III.	140
45	Lurgylea	412 2 2	Tyrone	Dungannon Middle	Pomeroy	Dungannon	III.	304
40	Lurgyroe	197 0 2	Tyrone	Dungannon Upper	Arboe	Cookstown	III.	305
21	Lurgyross	216 0 5	Armagh	Fews Lower	Loughgilly	Armagh	III.	47
12	Lurgyvallen	184 1 0	Armagh	Armagh	Armagh	Armagh	III.	43
8	Lurraga	115 2 8	Clare	Corcomroe	Killilagh	Ennistimon	II.	20
20	Lurraga	97 0 11	Limerick	Connello Lower	Nantinan	Rathkeale	II.	229
12	Lurraga	155 3 0	Limerick	Pubblebrien	Croom	Limerick	II.	252
13	Lurraga	25 3 2	Limerick	Pubblebrien	Mungret	Limerick	II.	254
1	Lurraga	103 3 10	Roscommon	Boyle	Kilronan	Boyle	IV.	197
88	Lurrig	97 3 15	Cork, E.R.	Imokilly	Rostellan	Middleton	II.	90
31, 32	Lurrig	108 1 19	Westmeath	Moycashel	Castletownkindalen	Mullingar	I.	277
141, 142	Lurriga	165 0 9	Cork, W.R.	West Carbery (E.D.)	Abbeystrowry	Skibbereen	II.	136
13, 14	Lushkinnagh	160 1 33	Kilkenny	Crannagh	Odagh	Kilkenny	I.	86
8	Lusk	701 1 8a	Dublin	Balrothery East	Lusk	Balrothery	I.	21
31	Luskanargid	52 0 14	Waterford	Decies without Drum	Kilrush	Dungarvan	II.	358
8	LUSK T.	—	Dublin	Balrothery East	Lusk	Balrothery	I.	21
23	Lustia	153 2 35b	Leitrim	Leitrim	Kiltoghert	Cark. on Shannon	IV.	102
7	Lustia	290 1 19	Roscommon	Boyle	Tumna	Cark. on Shannon	IV.	198
50	Lustown	109 3 0	Meath	Dunboyne	Dunboyne	Dunshaughlin	I.	199
33	Lusty Beg	25 3 34	Fermanagh	Tirkennedy	Cleenish	Enniskillen	III.	220
4	Lusty Beg Island	48 1 39	Fermanagh	Lurg	Drumkeeran	Lowtherstown	III.	207
33	Lusty More	50 1 20	Fermanagh	Tirkennedy	Cleenish	Enniskillen	III.	220
4, 9	Lusty More Island	71 1 5	Fermanagh	Lurg	Templecarn	Lowtherstown	III.	209
48	Lyalbeg	5 0 11	Galway	Ballynahinch	Ballindoon	Clifden	IV.	11
48	Lyalmore	14 1 29	Galway	Ballynahinch	Ballindoon	Clifden	IV.	11
11, 18	Lyan	613 1 36	Clare	Inchiquin	Kilkeedy	Corrofin	II.	26
19	Lyanmore	168 1 9	Longford	Ardagh	Ardagh	Longford	I.	151
28	Lybagh	381 1 18	Wicklow	Ballinacor South	Kiltegan	Baltinglass	I.	350
112	Lybe	327 2 14	Cork, E.R.	Kinalea	Kilmonoge	Kinsale	II.	95
17	Lybes	122 3 32	Kerry	Clanmaurice	Duagh	Listowel	II.	168
83	Lydacan	852 2 26	Galway	Dunkellin	Claregalway	Galway	IV.	27
113	Lydacan	213 0 7	Galway	Kiltartan	Ardrahan	Gort	IV.	45
5, 6	Lyle	651 3 0	Sligo	Carbury	Ahamlish	Sligo	IV.	219
10	Lylo	117 0 13	Armagh	Oneilland East	Seagoe	Lurgan	III.	50
50	Lynaghstown	160 2 0	Meath	Ratoath	Ballymaglassan	Dunshaughlin	I.	217
16	Lynally Glebe	528 3 31	King's Co.	Ballycowan	Lynally	Tullamore	I.	128
31, 32, 36	Lynamsgarden	125 3 29	Kildare	Narragh and Reban East	Narraghmore	Athy	I.	66
110	Lynchsacres	61 2 39	Mayo	Kilmaine	Robeen	Ballinrobe	IV.	157
18	Lyneen	424 2 12	Longford	Moydow	Killashee	Ballymahon	I.	162
19, 26	Lynn	1,204 3 36	Westmeath	Fartullagh	Lynn	Mullingar	I.	269
20	Lyons	120 1 11	Dublin	Newcastle	Newcastle	Celbridge	I.	34
15	Lyons	540 1 15c	Kildare	South Salt	Lyons	Celbridge	I.	77
19	Lyons	40 0 12d	Kilkenny	Kilkenny, Municipal Borough of	St. Canice	Kilkenny	I.	117
3	Lyonstown	191 2 34	Roscommon	Boyle	Ardcarn	Boyle	IV.	193
61, 69	Lyonstown	492 2 4	Tipperary, S.R.	Middlethird	St. Patricksrock	Cashel	II.	331
22	Lyracrumpane	980 3 32	Kerry	Clanmaurice	Kilfeighny	Listowel	II.	170
51	Lyradane	1,481 1 20	Cork, E.R.	Barretts	Grenagh	Cork	II.	49
1	Lyragh	171 1 32	Cork, E.R.	Orrery and Kilmore	Kilbolane	Kanturk	II.	108
6	Lyrane	298 3 36	Wexford	Gorey	Kilnahue	Gorey	I.	319
4	Lyraneag	771 1 37	Cork, E.R.	Duhallow	Clonfert	Kanturk	II.	68
1, 2	Lyranearla	449 2 7	Waterford	Upperthird	St. Mary's Clonmel	Clonmel	II.	372
72	Lyranes Lower	270 1 38	Kerry	Dunkerron North	Knockane	Cahersiveen	II.	182
72	Lyranes Upper	427 1 7	Kerry	Dunkerron North	Knockane	Cahersiveen	II.	182
19, 20	Lyrath	128 0 31	Kilkenny	Gowran	Blackrath	Kilkenny	I.	93
19, 20	Lyrath	74 0 18	Kilkenny	Gowran	St. John's	Kilkenny	I.	98

(a) Including 70A. 0R. 3P. detached portions.
(b) Including 8A. 0R. 13P. water.
(c) Including 22A. 2R. 12P. water.
(d) Included in the Parish of St. Canice.

No. of Sheet of the Ordnance Survey Maps.	Townlands and Towns.	Area in Statute Acres.	County.	Barony.	Parish.	Poor Law Union in 1857.	Townland Census of 1851, Part I.	
		A. R. P.					Vol.	Page
20	Lyrath	63 2 23	Kilkenny	Gowran	St. Martins	Kilkenny	I.	98
13, 22	Lyrattin	594 2 27	Waterford	Decies without Drum	Lickoran	Lismore	II.	358
43	Lyravarrig	495 3 14	Cork, E.R.	Barrymore	Ardnageehy	Cork	II.	50
30, 39	Lyravuckane	227 1 23	Cork, E.R.	Duhallow	Cullen	Millstreet	II.	70
52	Lyre	929 3 39	Cork, E.R.	Barrymore	Dunbulloge	Cork	II.	54
20, 28	Lyre	576 1 13	Cork, E.R.	Condons&Clangibbon	Macroney	Fermoy	II.	63
40	Lyre	503 2 17	Cork, E.R.	Duhallow	Clonmeen	Kanturk	II.	70
6, 15	Lyre	77 0 14	Cork, E.R.	Duhallow	Knocktemple	Kanturk	II.	75
46	Lyre	160 3 4	Cork, E.R.	Kinnatalloon	Mogeely	Youghal	II.	98
90	Lyre	201 1 37	Cork, W.R.	Bear	Kilcaskan	Bantry	II.	123
116	Lyre	82 0 39	Cork, W.R.	Bear	Killaconenagh	Castletown	II.	125
141	Lyre	212 2 9	Cork, W.R.	West Carbery (E.D.)	Aghadown	Skibbereen	II.	137
5	Lyre	183 3 18	Kerry	Iraghticonnor	Lisselton	Listowel	II.	192
47, 57	Lyre	187 2 11	Kerry	Magunihy	Kilcolman	Killarney	II.	200
31, 32, 40	Lyre	561 2 39	Kerry	Trughanacmy	Ballincuslane	Tralee	II.	206
48	Lyre	188 2 0	Kerry	Trughanacmy	Killeentierna	Killarney	II.	211
49	Lyre	69 2 11	Limerick	Coshlea	Galbally	Mitchelstown	II.	239
73	Lyre	557 1 16	Tipperary, S.R.	Clanwilliam	Clonbeg	Tipperary	II.	305
35	Lyre	237 2 7	Waterford	Decies within Drum	Ardmore	Dungarvan	II.	350
15	Lyre	205 1 39	Waterford	Decies without Drum	Kilrossanty	Kilmacthomas	II.	358
19, 20	Lyre	90 3 13	Wexford	Scarawalsh	Monart	Enniscorthy	I.	324
20, 28	Lyre (Barry)	648 2 28	Cork, E.R.	Condons&Clangibbon	Macroney	Fermoy	II.	63
72, 73	Lyreboy	967 3 8	Kerry	Dunkerron North	Killorglin	Cahersiveen	II.	181
38	Lyredaowen	489 2 11	Cork, E.R.	Duhallow	Nohavaldaly	Millstreet	II.	75
21	Lyre East	613 1 0	Waterford	Coshmore&Coshbride	Lismore and Mocollop	Lismore	II.	347
6	Lyre East	296 3 30	Waterford	Decies without Drum	Seskinan	Dungarvan	II.	360
20, 28	Lyreen	304 3 26	Cork, E.R.	Condons&Clangibbon	Macroney	Fermoy	II.	63
86, 89	Lyrefune	1,272 1 20	Tipperary, S.R.	Iffa and Offa West	Templetenny	Clogheen	II.	320
46, 55	Lyre Mountain	360 2 20	Cork, E.R.	Kinnatalloon	Mogeely	Youghal	II.	98
6, 14	Lyre Mountain	1,419 1 27	Waterford	Decies without Drum	Seskinan	Dungarvan	II.	360
21	Lyrenacallee East	141 0 17	Waterford	Coshmore&Coshbride	Lismore and Mocollop	Lismore	II.	347
21	Lyrenacallee West	150 0 20	Waterford	Coshmore&Coshbride	Lismore and Mocollop	Lismore	II.	347
33, 34	Lyrenacarriga	275 2 6	Waterford	Coshmore&Coshbride	Kilwatermoy	Lismore	II.	344
68, 80	Lyrenageeha	484 2 39	Cork, W.R.	West Muskerry	Inchigeelagh	Macroom	II.	158
19	Lyrenaglogh	292 2 19	Waterford	Coshmore&Coshbride	Lismore and Mocollop	Lismore	II.	347
52	Lyrenamon	189 3 19	Cork, E.R.	Barrymore	Dunbulloge	Cork	II.	54
20	Lyre West	110 0 35	Waterford	Coshmore&Coshbride	Lismore and Mocollop	Lismore	II.	347
6	Lyre West	351 3 28	Waterford	Decies without Drum	Seskinan	Dungarvan	II.	360
60	Lyroe	490 3 28	Cork, W.R.	East Muskerry	Aghabulloge	Macroom	II.	153
27, 28, 33	Lyroge	280 3 4	Queen's Co.	Clandonagh	Rathsaran	Donaghmore	I.	235
65	Lysaghtstown	270 2 37	Cork, E.R.	Barrymore	Carrigtohill	Middleton	II.	52
45	Lysterfield	453 2 7a	Roscommon	Athlone	Cam	Athlone	IV.	180
17	Lythe Rock	0 1 36	Down	Ards Upper	Ardkeen	Newtownards	III.	159
65, 74	Maas	643 0 26b	Donegal	Boylagh	Inishkeel	Glenties	III.	113
35	Mabbotstown	93 0 14	Kilkenny	Knocktopher	Aghaviller	Thomastown	I.	110
12	Mabestown	44 2 38	Dublin	Coolock	Kinsaley	Balrothery	I.	28
45, 51	Mabestown	207 2 34	Meath	Dunboyne	Kilbride	Dunshaughlin	I.	200
8	Mabestown	316 1 36	Westmeath	Delvin	Castletowndelvin	Castletowndelvin	I.	264
32	Mabrista	125 3 1	Westmeath	Moycashel	Castletownkindalen	Mullingar	I.	277
13	Macantrim	167 3 26	Armagh	Fews Lower	Mullaghbrack	Armagh	III.	47
2, 5	Mac Crackens	40 2 21	Tyrone	Strabane Lower	Leckpatrick	Strabane	III.	322
76	Mace	251 2 20c	Galway	Ballynahinch	Moyrus	Clifden	IV.	13
56, 69	Mace	430 0 36d	Galway	Clare	Annaghdown	Galway	IV.	16
5, 6	Mace	201 0 17e	Westmeath	Moygoish	Rathaspick	Mullingar	I.	280
9	Macecrump	144 3 33	Mayo	Erris	Kilmore	Belmullet	IV.	146
9	Macecrump Common	25 2 33	Mayo	Erris	Kilmore	Belmullet	IV.	146
91	Mace Lower	511 1 16	Mayo	Clanmorris	Kilcolman	Claremorris	IV.	134
91	Mace Middle	377 1 12	Mayo	Clanmorris	Kilcolman	Claremorris	IV.	134
88	Mace North	181 2 13	Mayo	Burrishoole	Aghagower	Westport	IV.	118
88	Mace South	352 3 32	Mayo	Burrishoole	Aghagower	Westport	IV.	118
31	Macetown	316 2 22	Meath	Lower Navan	Ardsallagh	Navan	I.	214
32, 38	Macetown	1,248 1 19	Meath	Skreen	Macetown	Dunshaughlin	I.	221
19	Macetown	985 0 33	Westmeath	Moyashel and Magheradernon	Rathconnell	Mullingar	I.	276
13	Macetown Middle	93 0 27	Dublin	Castleknock	Mulhuddart	Dublin North	I.	25
13	Macetown North	48 0 31	Dublin	Castleknock	Mulhuddart	Dublin North	I.	25
13	Macetown South	41 1 17	Dublin	Castleknock	Mulhuddart	Dublin North	I.	25
91, 92	Mace Upper	356 1 1	Mayo	Clanmorris	Kilcolman	Claremorris	IV.	134
16	Macfinn Lower	104 2 6	Antrim	Upper Dunluce	Ballymoney	Ballymoney	III.	15
8, 12	Macfinn Lower	30 3 20	Londonderry	North East Liberties of Coleraine	Ballymoney	Ballymoney	III.	245

(a) Including 18A. 3R. 24P. water.
(b) Including 13A. 2R. 34P. water.
(c) Including 15A. 3R. 8P. water.
(d) Including 12A. 3R. 25P. water.
(e) Including 5A. 1R. 16P. water.

No. of Sheet of the Ordnance Survey Maps.	Townlands and Towns.	Area in Statute Acres. A. R. P.	County.	Barony.	Parish.	Poor Law Union in 1857.	Townland Census of 1851, Part I. Vol.	Page
16	Macfinn Upper	82 2 6	Antrim	Upper Dunluce	Ballymoney	Ballymoney	III.	19
14, 19	Mackan	176 0 6	Cavan	Tullyhunco	Kildallan	Bawnboy	III.	97
27	Mackan	82 1 1	Leitrim	Leitrim	Kiltoghert	Cark. on Shannon	IV.	102
73, 74	Mackanagh Lower	231 3 30	Tipperary, S.R.	Clanwilliam	Clonbeg	Tipperary	II.	305
73, 74	Mackanagh Upper	595 1 8	Tipperary, S.R.	Clanwilliam	Clonbeg	Tipperary	II.	305
33	Mackan Glebe	266 0 27a	Fermanagh	Clanawley	Killesher	Enniskillen	III.	193
6	Mackanhill	30 2 1	Meath	Lower Slane	Inishmot	Ardee	I.	223
30	Mackanrany	131 2 18	Westmeath	Clonlonan	Ballyloughloe	Athlone	I.	260
29	Mackenny	175 3 27	Tyrone	Dungannon Upper	Kildress	Cookstown	III.	309
47	Mackenstown	13 3 96	Wexford	Forth	Mayglass	Wexford	I.	312
55	Mackinawood	203 0 26	Tipperary, S.R.	Slievardagh	Lismalin	Callan	II.	335
31, 32	Mackmine	863 2 9	Wexford	Shelmaliere West	Clonmore	Enniscorthy	I.	333
34	Macknagh	92 1 31	Fermanagh	Magherastephana	Aghalurcher	Lisnaskea	III.	217
32	Macknagh	492 0 21	Londonderry	Loughinsholin	Maghera	Magherafelt	III.	242
14	Macknan	77 2 29	Cavan	Lower Loughtee	Drumlane	Cavan	III.	80
87	Mackney	198 3 33	Galway	Clonmacnowen	Kilcloony	Ballinasloe	IV.	25
31, 37	Mackney (Bourke)	43 0 10	Tipperary, N.R.	Owney and Arra	Kilnarath	Nenagh	II.	296
87	Mackney (Clancarty)	282 2 21	Galway	Clonmacnowen	Clontuskert	Ballinasloe	IV.	25
87	Mackney (Kelly)	102 2 37	Galway	Clonmacnowen	Clontuskert	Ballinasloe	IV.	25
31	Mackney (O'Brien)	31 1 1	Tipperary, N.R.	Owney and Arra	Kilnarath	Nenagh	II.	296
14	M'Lean and Partners Division	100 3 12	Londonderry	Tirkeeran	Faughanvale	Londonderry	III.	250
7, 11	Macleary	349 3 33	Londonderry	Coleraine	Macosquin	Coleraine	III.	233
69	Macmeenstown	149 3 38	Donegal	Raphoe	Convoy	Stranorlar	III.	136
29	Macmurroughs	162 2 37	Wexford	Bantry	St. Mary's	New Ross	I.	302
29	Macmurroughsisland	135 0 38	Wexford	Bantry	St. Mary's	New Ross	I.	302
10	Macnadille	114 3 4	Roscommon	Boyle	Killukin	Cark. on Shannon	IV.	196
29	Macnahanny or Ashgrove	389 2 37	King's Co.	Garrycastle	Lusmagh	Parsonstown	I.	137
29	Macnahanny or Fulough	438 3 12	King's Co.	Garrycastle	Lusmagh	Parsonstown	I.	137
21	Macoghlans Island	25 3 10	King's Co.	Garrycastle	Reynagh	Parsonstown	I.	138
7	Macosquin	19 1 21	Londonderry	Coleraine	Macosquin	Coleraine	III.	233
3	Macoyle Lower	116 3 14	Wexford	Gorey	Kilgorman	Gorey	I.	318
3, 7	Macoyle Upper	159 1 8	Wexford	Gorey	Kilgorman	Gorey	I.	318
79	Macreary	809 3 30	Tipperary, S.R.	Iffa and Offa East	Kilmurry	Carrick on Suir	II.	314
34	Macreddin East	441 3 27	Wicklow	Ballinacor South	Ballykine	Rathdrum	I.	348
34	Macreddin West	186 1 3	Wicklow	Ballinacor South	Ballykine	Rathdrum	I.	348
28	Macroney Lower	578 0 1	Cork, E.R.	Condons&Clangibbon	Macroney	Fermoy	II.	63
28	Macroney Upper	738 3 10	Cork, E.R.	Condons&Clangibbon	Macroney	Fermoy	II.	63
70, 71	MACROOM T.	—	Cork, W.R.	West Muskerry	Macroom	Macroom	II.	160
44, 45	M'Vickersland	348 3 36	Antrim	Upper Antrim	Kilbride	Antrim	III.	6
122	Madame	273 0 5	Cork, W.R.	East Carbery (E.D.)	Kilmaloda	Clonakilty	II.	129
122	Madame	41 3 11	Cork, W.R.	East Carbery (E.D.)	Kilnagross	Clonakilty	II.	129
70	Madamsland	39 3 26	Tipperary, S.R.	Middlethird	Redcity	Cashel	II.	329
34, 42	Madara	59 3 30	Clare	Bunratty Upper	Quin	Tulla	II.	10
65	Madavagh	296 2 8c	Donegal	Boylagh	Lettermacward	Glenties	III.	114
24	Maddadoo	160 1 5	Westmeath	Rathconrath	Killare	Ballymahon	I.	283
15	Maddan	460 3 26	Armagh	Armagh	Derrynoose	Armagh	III.	44
27	Maddenstown Demesne	200 3 22	Kildare	Offaly East	Ballysax	Naas	I.	69
27	Maddenstown Middle	392 3 18	Kildare	Offaly East	Ballysax	Naas	I.	69
27, 28	Maddenstown North	368 3 38	Kildare	Offaly East	Ballysax	Naas	I.	69
27	Maddenstown South	662 1 8	Kildare	Offaly East	Ballysax	Naas	I.	69
20	Maddockstown	593 0 32d	Kilkenny	Gowran	Blackrath	Kilkenny	I.	93
8	Maddoxgarden	1 3 6	Louth	Lower Dundalk	Carlingford	Dundalk	I.	176
8	Maddoxland	108 2 2	Louth	Lower Dundalk	Carlingford	Dundalk	I.	176
3	Maddybenny Beg	77 3 30	Londonderry	North East Liberties of Coleraine	Ballyaghran	Coleraine	III.	244
3	Maddybenny More	108 2 32	Londonderry	North East Liberties of Coleraine	Ballyaghran	Coleraine	III.	244
14	Maddyboy	84 0 17	Limerick	Clanwilliam	Abington	Limerick	II.	221
6, 14	Maddyboy	609 3 30	Limerick	Clanwilliam	Clonkeen	Limerick	II.	223
21	Maddydoo Lower or New Buildings	90 2 30	Antrim	Kilconway	Finvoy	Ballymoney	III.	26
21, 22	Maddydoo Upper	249 3 30	Antrim	Kilconway	Finvoy	Ballymoney	III.	26
40	Maddydrumbrist	182 0 26	Down	Upper Iveagh, Up. pt.	Donaghmore	Newry	III.	175
21	Maddykeel Lower	107 3 34	Antrim	Kilconway	Finvoy	Ballymoney	III.	26
21, 22	Maddykeel Upper	257 2 25	Antrim	Kilconway	Finvoy	Ballymoney	III.	26
132	Madore	208 0 8	Cork, W.R.	West Carbery(W.D.)	Caheragh	Skibbereen	II.	142
133	Madranna	128 1 34	Cork, W.R.	East Carbery (W.D.)	Kilmacabea	Skibbereen	II.	133
24	Maelra	130 2 15	Limerick	Coonagh	Oola	Tipperary	II.	236
22	Magaha	312 3 5	Waterford	Decies without Drum	Whitechurch	Lismore	II.	362
37, 39	Maganey Lower	246 0 33e	Kildare	Kilkea and Moone	Dunmanoge	Athy	I.	59
37, 39	Maganey Upper	174 2 31	Kildare	Kilkea and Moone	Dunmanoge	Athy	I.	59

(a) Including 3A. 3R. 15P. water.
(b) Including 4A. 1R. 11P. detached portion.
(c) Including 32A. 1R. 32P. water.
(d) Including 6A. 3R. 2P. River Nore.
(e) Including 10A. 2R. 0P. water.

4 S

No. of Sheet of the Ordnance Survey Maps.	Townlands and Towns.	Area in Statute Acres.			County.	Barony.	Parish.	Poor Law Union in 1857.	Townland Census of 1851, Part I.	
		A.	R.	P.					Vol.	Page
5	Magaraty	132	2	35	Armagh	Oneilland West	Tartaraghan	Armagh	III.	55
67	Maghaberry	353	3	25	Antrim	Upper Massereene	Magheramesk	Lisburn	III.	31
46, 47	Maghadone	439	3	35	Londonderry	Loughinsholin	Artrea	Magherafelt	III.	238
35, 44	Maghanaboe	1,088	0	24	Kerry	Corkaguiny	Ballyduff	Dingle	II.	174
64, 72	Maghancoosaun	199	1	12a	Kerry	Dunkerron North	Killorglin	Cahersiveen	II.	181
22, 30	Maghanknockane	982	0	35	Kerry	Trughanacmy	O'Brennan	Tralee	II.	212
72, 82	Maghanlawaun	447	3	14	Kerry	Dunkerron North	Knockane	Killarney	II.	182
25, 34	Maghanveel	1,299	3	8	Kerry	Corkaguiny	Cloghane	Dingle	II.	175
26	Maghareagh	143	0	29	Queen's Co.	Ballyadams	Tankardstown	Athy	I.	232
34	Magharenny	933	2	13	Tyrone	Omagh West	Longfield East	Omagh	III.	315
36	Maghasheela	191	0	14	Kerry	Corkaguiny	Killiney	Dingle	II.	178
39	Magh East	142	2	13	Kerry	Trughanacmy	Ballymacelligott	Tralee	II.	207
62	Magheestown	233	3	37	Donegal	Raphoe	Raphoe	Strabane	III.	141
26, 27, 34	Maghera	1,460	3	1	Clare	Bunratty Upper	Clooney	Tulla	II.	8
23	Maghera	326	2	28	Clare	Corcomroe	Kilmanaheen	Ennistimon	II.	21
24, 32	Maghera	668	3	26	Clare	Inchiquin	Inagh	Ennistimon	II.	25
16, 24	Maghera	146	3	1	Clare	Inchiquin	Rath	Corrofin	II.	27
19	Maghera	1,713	1	4b	Clare	Tulla Upper	Feakle	Tulla	II.	40
72,73,81,82	Maghera	1,806	3	3c	Donegal	Banagh	Inishkeel	Glenties	III.	106
21	Maghera	85	1	6	Limerick	Pubblebrien	Croom	Croom	II.	252
33	Maghera	56	2	7	Sligo	Corran	Emlaghfad	Sligo	IV.	226
15, 16	Maghera	403	0	3	Westmeath	Kilkenny West	Noughaval	Ballymahon	I.	274
37	Magherabane	333	3	5	King's Co.	Ballybritt	Letterluna	Parsonstown	I.	126
22	Magherabane	244	2	6	King's Co.	Garrycastle	Gallen	Parsonstown	I.	136
31, 32	Magherabaun	642	2	37	Clare	Inchiquin	Inagh	Ennistimon	II.	25
19, 27	Magherabaun	958	2	33	Clare	Tulla Upper	Feakle	Scarriff	II.	40
43	Magherabeg	564	3	11	Antrim	Upper Toome	Drummaul	Antrim	III.	34
38	Magherabeg	295	2	9	Donegal	Inishowen West	Fahan Upper	Londonderry	III.	121
16	Magherabeg	328	3	32	Donegal	Kilmacrenan	Mevagh	Millford	III.	130
54	Maghera Beg	269	1	22	Donegal	Raphoe	Raymoghy	Letterkenny	III.	142
20, 21	Magherabeg	863	0	27	Down	Lower Iveagh, Lr. pt.	Dromore	Banbridge	III.	168
54	Maghera Beg	218	2	0	Galway	Moycullen	Kilcummin	Oughterard	IV.	67
26, 27	Magherabeg	804	3	27	Kerry	Corkaguiny	Killiney	Dingle	II.	178
31	Maghera Beg	173	1	38	Wicklow	Arklow	Dunganstown	Rathdrum	I.	344
26	Magherablad	201	0	12	Donegal	Kilmacrenan	Clondahorky	Dunfanaghy	III.	123
4	Magheraboy	180	0	9	Antrim	Cary	Ballintoy	Ballycastle	III.	12
23, 24	Magheraboy	477	2	10	Antrim	Kilconway	Dunaghy	Ballymena	III.	26
22, 26	Magheraboy	615	1	19	Antrim	Kilconway	Rasharkin	Ballymoney	III.	28
78, 79	Magheraboy	321	0	14	Donegal	Raphoe	Donaghmore	Stranorlar	III.	138
55	Magheraboy	21	1	20	Donegal	Raphoe	Killea	Londonderry	III.	139
53, 54, 61	Magheraboy	319	0	28	Donegal	Raphoe	Leck	Letterkenny	III.	140
62, 70	Magheraboy	38	0	8	Donegal	Raphoe	Raphoe	Strabane	III.	141
25, 31	Magheraboy	328	2	2	Londonderry	Keenaght	Dungiven	New Tn Limavady	III.	236
3	Magheraboy	97	1	12	Londonderry	North East Liberties of Coleraine	Ballywillin	Coleraine	III.	245
92	Magheraboy	110	0	16	Mayo	Clanmorris	Kilcolman	Claremorris	IV.	134
74	Magheraboy	176	3	22	Mayo	Costello	Kilcolman	Castlereagh	IV.	141
73, 74, 83	Magheraboy	516	2	33	Mayo	Costello	Kilmovee	Swineford	IV.	142
49	Magheraboy	105	2	38	Mayo	Gallon	Killasser	Swineford	IV.	149
31	Magheraboy	170	3	15	Monaghan	Farney	Magheross	Carrickmacross	III.	274
14	Magheraboy	327	0	39	Sligo	Carbury	St. John's	Sligo	IV.	223
3, 7	Magheraboy or Bushmills	23	3	36	Antrim	Cary	Billy	Coleraine	III.	12
55	Magheraboy Glebe	34	0	21	Donegal	Raphoe	Killea	Londonderry	III.	139
12,13,17,18	Magheraboy Lower	226	1	1	Antrim	Upper Dunluce	Kilraghts	Ballymoney	III.	20
37, 41	Magheraboy Lower	236	3	17	Cavan	Clanmahon	Drumlumman	Granard	III.	77
14	MAGHERABOY T.	—			Sligo	Carbury	St. John's	Sligo	IV.	223
17	Magheraboy Upper	415	2	35	Antrim	Upper Dunluce	Kilraghts	Ballymoney	III.	20
41	Magheraboy Upper	263	1	17	Cavan	Clanmahon	Drumlumman	Granard	III.	77
22	Magherabrack	126	1	18	Mayo	Tirawley	Ballysakeery	Ballina	IV.	165
16, 17	Magherabrack	358	3	37	Sligo	Tireragh	Kilglass	Dromore West	IV.	234
20, 21	Magheracanon	115	2	22	Londonderry	Tirkeeran	Clondermot	Londonderry	III.	248
106, 109	Magheracar	918	0	4	Donegal	Tirhugh	Inishmacsaint	Ballyshannon	III.	147
4, 8	Magheracashel	413	2	34	Antrim	Cary	Ballintoy	Ballycastle	III.	12
3	Magheraclay	25	3	37	Londonderry	North East Liberties of Coleraine	Ballyaghran	Coleraine	III.	244
32	Magheraclogher	563	1	2	Donegal	Kilmacrenan	Tullaghobegly	Dunfanaghy	III.	132
76, 77	Magheracloigh	319	2	38	Donegal	Raphoe	Kilteevoge	Stranorlar	III.	139
62	Magheracloy	103	2	32	Donegal	Raphoe	Taughboyne	Strabane	III.	144
17	Magheracoltan	762	0	13	Tyrone	Strabane Lower	Ardstraw	Strabane	III.	319
21, 22	Magheraconluce	571	3	4	Down	Lower Iveagh, Lr. pt.	Annahilt	Lisburn	III.	167
69	Magheracorran	547	3	23	Donegal	Raphoe	Convoy	Stranorlar	III.	150
30	Magheracranmoney	861	1	38	Down	Lecale Lower	Inch	Downpatrick	III.	179

(a) Including 1A. 2R. 9P. water.   (b) Including 28A. 2R. 7P. water.   (c) Including 20A. 3R. 29P. water.

No. of Sheet of the Ordnance Survey Maps.	Townlands and Towns.	Area in Statute Acres.	County.	Barony.	Parish.	Poor Law Union in 1857.	Townland Census of 1851, Part I.	
		A. R. P.					Vol.	Page
16, 24	Magheracreggan	355 0 23	Tyrone	Strabane Lower	Ardstraw	Castlederg	III.	319
2	Magheracross	47 1 19	Antrim	Lower Dunluce	Dunluce	Coleraine	III.	17
16	Magheracross	306 3 22	Fermanagh	Tirkennedy	Magheracross	Lowtherstown	III.	223
16, 23	Magheracuirknagh	5 3 27	Westmeath	Kilkenny West	Kilkenny West	Athlone	I.	273
14	Magheradartin	420 0 2	Down	Lower Iveagh, Up.pt.	Hillsborough	Lisburn	III.	169
29	Magheradrool	503 0 4	Down	Kinelarty	Magheradrool	Downpatrick	III.	177
11, 20, 21	Magheradrumman	1,916 0 24	Donegal	Inishowen East	Donagh	Inishowen	III.	113
8, 17	Magheradrumman	324 0 39a	Donegal	Kilmacrenan	Clondavaddog	Millford	III.	125
36	Magheradrumman	270 2 31b	Donegal	Kilmacrenan	Tullyfern	Millford	III.	133
21	Magheradunbar	240 0 19	Fermanagh	Magheraboy	Devenish	Enniskillen	III.	211
89	Magherafadda	174 1 8	Mayo	Carra	Ballyhean	Castlebar	IV.	126
42	MAGHERAFELT T.	—	Londonderry	Loughinsholin	Magherafelt	Magherafelt	III.	243
41, 42, 47	Magherafelt, Town-parks of	1,219 1 12	Londonderry	Loughinsholin	Magherafelt	Magherafelt	III.	243
63, 67	Magheragall	265 2 4	Antrim	Upper Massereene	Magheragall	Lisburn	III.	31
32	Magheragallan	412 3 33	Donegal	Kilmacrenan	Tullaghobegly	Dunfanaghy	III.	132
21	Magheragannon	109 1 19	Fermanagh	Magheraboy	Devenish	Enniskillen	III.	211
9	Magheragar	353 1 32	Tyrone	Strabane Lower	Urney	Strabane	III.	322
50	Magheragart	122 0 0	Tyrone	Omagh East	Dromore	Omagh	III.	311
50	Magheragart (Donnell)	281 1 1c	Tyrone	Omagh East	Dromore	Omagh	III.	311
50	Magheragart or Sessiaghs	190 3 9	Tyrone	Omagh East	Dromore	Omagh	III.	311
14	Magherageery	423 2 36d	Down	Lower Iveagh,Up.pt.	Blaris	Lisburn	III.	169
15	Magheraghanrush or Deer Park	270 2 37	Sligo	Carbury	Calry	Sligo	IV.	220
8	Magheragillerneeve or Springfield	306 1 34	Sligo	Carbury	Drumcliff	Sligo	IV.	221
29, 37, 38	Magheraglass	286 1 33	Tyrone	Dungannon Upper	Kildress	Cookstown	III.	309
70	Magherahaan	282 2 1	Donegal	Raphoe	Raphoe	Strabane	III.	141
15	Magherahar	151 1 0	Fermanagh	Magheraboy	Inishmacsaint	Enniskillen	III.	213
70	Magherahee	384 1 8	Donegal	Raphoe	Raphoe	Strabane	III.	141
13	Magherahinch	132 1 35	Down	Lower Iveagh,Up. pt.	Moira	Lurgan	III.	170
13, 14	Magherahoney	826 1 0	Antrim	Upper Dunluce	Loughguile	Ballymoney	III.	20
23	Magherakeel	443 2 1e	Tyrone	Omagh West	Termonamongan	Castlederg	III.	317
22	Magheraknock	799 2 39	Down	Kinelarty	Magheradrool	Lisburn	III.	177
35	Magheralackagh	217 0 31	Sligo	Tirerrill	Kilmactranny	Boyle	IV.	240
37	Magheralagan	377 0 25f	Down	Lecale Upper	Down	Downpatrick	III.	180
30	Magheralahan	140 2 31	Donegal	Inishowen East	Moville Upper	Inishowen	III.	119
47	Magheralamfield	277 0 16	Tyrone	Dungannon Middle	Clonoe	Dungannon	III.	300
43	Magheralane	1,122 2 36g	Antrim	Upper Toome	Drummaul	Antrim	III.	34
64	Magheralave	743 1 7	Antrim	Upper Belfast	Derryaghy	Lisburn	III.	10
64	Magheralave	157 3 37h	Antrim	Upper Massereene	Derryaghy	Lisburn	III.	30
13	MAGHERALIN T.	—	Down	Lower Iveagh,Up. pt.	Magheralin	Lurgan	III.	170
63, 67	Magheraliskmisk	794 3 24	Antrim	Upper Massereene	Magheragall	Lisburn	III.	31
27	Magherally	491 1 3	Down	Lower Iveagh, Lr. pt.	Magherally	Banbridge	III.	168
30	Magheralone	871 1 9i	Down	Kinelarty	Kilmore	Downpatrick	III.	177
56	Magheralough	196 2 24j	Tyrone	Omagh East	Kilskeery	Lowtherstown	III.	314
24	Magheralough	248 0 27	Tyrone	Strabane Lower	Ardstraw	Castlederg	III.	319
16, 26	Magheramagorgan	380 0 12	Donegal	Kilmacrenan	Mevagh	Millford	III.	130
1	Magheramason	230 0 10	Tyrone	Strabane Lower	Donaghedy	Strabane	III.	321
42, 43	Magheramayo	752 2 34k	Down	Upper Iveagh, Lr. pt.	Drumgooland	Banbridge	III.	172
25	Magheramenagh	278 2 15l	Donegal	Kilmacrenan	Clondahorky	Dunfanaghy	III.	123
8	Magheramenagh	209 0 7m	Fermanagh	Lurg	Belleek	Ballyshannon	III.	203
3	Magheramenagh	91 0 7	Londonderry	North East Liberties of Coleraine	Ballywillin	Coleraine	III.	245
67	Magheramesk	498 1 10	Antrim	Upper Massereene	Magheramesk	Lisburn	III.	31
8	Magheramore	538 3 27	Antrim	Cary	Ramoan	Ballycastle	III.	14
73	Magheramore	580 0 28n	Donegal	Boylagh	Inishkeel	Glenties	III.	113
54	Maghera More	70 0 35	Donegal	Raphoe	Raymoghy	Letterkenny	III.	142
40	Magheramore	105 3 13	Fermanagh	Clankelly	Galloon	Clones	III.	198
107	Magheramore	374 0 17	Galway	Longford	Killimorbologue	Portumna	IV.	59
54, 67	Maghera More	929 0 27o	Galway	Moycullen	Kilcummin	Oughterard	IV.	67
42	Magheramore	93 2 22	King's Co.	Clonlisk	Kilmurryely	Roscrea	I.	131
3, 4	Magheramore	246 3 21	Leitrim	Rosclogher	Rossinver	Ballyshannon	IV.	112
18, 26	Magheramore	494 1 10	Londonderry	Coleraine	Desertoghill	Coleraine	III.	230
30, 31	Magheramore	909 1 27	Londonderry	Keenaght	Banagher	NewTⁿLimavady	III.	234
16	Magheramore	464 3 17	Londonderry	Keenaght	Tamlaghtfinlagan	NewTⁿLimavady	III.	237
15	Magheramore	159 0 35	Londonderry	Tirkeeran	Faughanvale	NewTⁿLimavady	III.	250
92, 102	Magheramore	522 3 35	Mayo	Costello	Knock	Claremorris	IV.	143
30	Magheramore	269 0 28	Westmeath	Clonlonan	Ballyloughloe	Athlone	I.	260
31	Maghera More	506 2 21	Wicklow	Arklow	Dunganstown	Rathdrum	I.	344
47	Magheramulkenny	197 2 4	Tyrone	Dungannon Middle	Clonoe	Dungannon	III.	300
28, 33	Magheramully	356 0 6	Antrim	Lower Antrim	Skerry	Ballymena	III.	5
55, 56	Magheramurphy	378 0 5	Down	Mourne	Kilkeel	Kilkeel	III.	183

(a) Including 17A. 0R. 26P. water.
(b) Including 18A. 3R. 29P. water.
(c) Including 1A. 0R. 5P. water.
(d) Including 4A. 2R. 6P. water.
(e) Including 0A. 3R. 8P. water.

(f) Including 20A. 3R. 34P. water.
(g) Including 19A. 1R. 25P. water.
(h) Including 0A. 1R. 27P. detached portion.
(i) Including 18A. 3R. 0P. water.
(j) Including 4A. 0R. 26P. water.

(k) Including 5A. 1R. 30P. water.
(l) Including 14A. 1R. 5P. water.
(m) Including 17A. 3R. 2P. water.
(n) Including 20A. 0R. 30P. water.
(o) Including 21A. 3R. 1P. water.

No. of Sheet of the Ordnance Survey Maps.	Townlands and Towns.	Area in Statute Acres.	County.	Barony.	Parish.	Poor Law Union in 1857.	Townland Census of 1851, Part I.	
		A. R. P.					Vol.	Page
30, 36	Magheramurry	135 1 19	Westmeath	Clonlonan	Kilmanaghan	Athlone	I.	262
52, 53	Magheran	532 0 35	Donegal	Kilmacrenan	Conwal	Letterkenny	III.	126
19, 20	Magherana	739 1 34	Down	Lower Iveagh, Up. pt.	Donaghcloney	Lurgan	III.	169
78, 89	Magheranagay	110 1 27	Mayo	Carra	Ballyhean	Castlebar	IV.	126
21	Magheranageeragh	103 0 25	Fermanagh	Magheraboy	Devenish	Enniskillen	III.	211
23	Magheranageeragh	399 3 24a	Tyrone	Omagh West	Termonamongan	Castlederg	III.	317
28	Magheranakilly	84 3 14	Donegal	Kilmacrenan	Killygarvan	Milford	III.	128
53	Magheranan	77 3 17	Donegal	Kilmacrenan	Aghanunshin	Letterkenny	III.	122
69	Magheranappan	425 0 29	Donegal	Raphoe	Convoy	Stranorlar	III.	136
33	Magheranaskeagh	276 0 13	King's Co.	Upper Philipstown	Clonyhurk	Mountmellick	I.	143
4	Magheranaul	233 0 31	Donegal	Inishowen East	Clonmany	Inishowen	III.	117
108	Magheranearla	289 0 5	Galway	Longford	Tiranascragh	Portumna	IV.	62
15	Magheranenagh	250 3 37	Tipperary, N.R.	Lower Ormond	Ardcrony	Nenagh	II.	282
29	Magheranerla	12 1 39	Westmeath	Brawny	St. Mary's	Athlone	I.	260
38	Magheranore	301 1 19	Sligo	Leyny	Achonry	Tobercurry	IV.	229
10, 11, 17	Magheranraheen or Rockforest	511 1 2b	Clare	Inchiquin	Kilkeedy	Corrofin	II.	26
17	Magheranure	204 3 30	Cavan	Tullygarvey	Drumgoon	Cootehill	III.	88
12	Magheranure	113 0 25c	Monaghan	Dartree	Clones	Clones	III.	265
78	Magherapaste	50 3 18	Donegal	Raphoe	Stranorlar	Stranorlar	III.	143
44, 45	Magherareagh	342 3 21	Clare	Tulla Lower	O'Briensbridge	Limerick	II.	38
79	Magherareagh	217 1 12d	Donegal	Raphoe	Donaghmore	Strabane	III.	138
40	Magherareagh	85 2 33	Fermanagh	Clankelly	Galloon	Clones	III.	198
134	Magherareagh	358 1 36	Galway	Leitrim	Inishcaltra	Scarriff	IV.	54
42	Magherareagh	160 0 26	King's Co.	Clonlisk	Kilmurryely	Roscrea	I.	131
40	Magherareagh	36 3 18	Limerick	Smallcounty	Athneasy	Kilmallock	II.	258
40	Magherareagh	21 0 22	Limerick	Smallcounty	Kilbreedy Major	Kilmallock	II.	260
34	Magherareagh	273 3 10	Tipperary, N.R.	Eliogarty	Inch	Thurles	II.	270
88	Magherareagh	54 2 30e	Tipperary, S.R.	Iffa and Offa West	Ardfinnan	Clogheen	II.	317
81,82,87,88	Magherareagh	332 1 10f	Tipperary, S.R.	Iffa and Offa West	Tubbrid	Clogheen	II.	321
2	Magherareagh	361 3 11g	Tyrone	Strabane Lower	Donaghedy	Strabane	III.	321
12	Magherarny	248 0 1h	Monaghan	Dartree	Clones	Clones	III.	265
26	Magheraroarty	221 3 27i	Donegal	Kilmacrenan	Clondahorky	Dunfanaghy	III.	123
24	Magheraroarty	908 0 38j	Donegal	Kilmacrenan	Tullaghobegly	Dunfanaghy	III.	132
24, 33	Magheraroarty Mountain	1,389 3 22k	Donegal	Kilmacrenan	Tullaghobegly	Dunfanaghy	III.	132
16	Magherarville	169 1 22	Armagh	Armagh	Lisnadill	Armagh	III.	45
43	Magherasaul	573 1 4l	Down	Lecale Upper	Kilmegan	Downpatrick	III.	181
10, 16	Magherascouse	1,284 2 9m	Down	Castlereagh Lower	Comber	Newtownards	III.	162
46	Magherascullion	327 3 1	Londonderry	Loughinsholin	Desertlyn	Magherafelt	III.	240
22	Magherashaghry	177 0 16	Monaghan	Dartree	Currin	Cootehill	III.	266
70, 79	Magherashanvally	271 1 36	Donegal	Raphoe	Donaghmore	Strabane	III.	138
9, 10	Magheraskeagh	91 2 20	Londonderry	Keenaght	Aghanloo	NewT'Limavady	III.	234
62, 70	Magherasollus	364 0 10	Donegal	Raphoe	Raphoe	Strabane	III.	141
72, 82	Magherasrahan	157 0 36	Kerry	Dunkerron North	Knockane	Killarney	II.	182
29	Magheratimpany	523 3 7	Down	Kinelarty	Magheradrool	Downpatrick	III.	177
43	MAGHERA T.	—	Down	Upper Iveagh, Lr. pt.	Maghera	Kilkeel	III.	173
36	MAGHERA T.	—	Londonderry	Loughinsholin	Maghera	Magherafelt	III.	243
68, 69	Magheravall or Midcut	268 2 33	Donegal	Raphoe	Convoy	Stranorlar	III.	136
17, 18	Magheraveen	302 1 12	Longford	Ratheline	Ratheline	Longford	I.	165
18	Magherawardan	675 2 22	Donegal	Kilmacrenan	Clondavaddog	Milford	III.	125
9	Magheraweeleen	105 0 35	Clare	Burren	Kilcorney	Ballyvaghan	II.	12
49	Maghereagh	73 3 16	Antrim	Upper Toome	Antrim	Antrim	III.	33
43, 49	Maghereagh	557 1 2	Antrim	Upper Toome	Drummaul	Antrim	III.	34
56	Maghereagh	642 2 22	Down	Mourne	Kilkeel	Kilkeel	III.	183
6	Maghereagh	259 1 37	Louth	Upper Dundalk	Barronstown	Dundalk	I.	177
71	Maghereen	32 0 28	Cork, W.R.	West Muskerry	Macroom	Macroom	II.	160
15	Maghereeroy	80 0 34	Antrim	Lower Glenarm	Layd	Ballycastle	III.	23
9	Magherindonnel	71 0 7	Antrim	Cary	Culfeightrin	Ballycastle	III.	14
16	Magherintemple	93 2 39	Cavan	Tullygarvey	Drung	Cootehill	III.	89
7	Magherintendry	359 1 6	Antrim	Lower Dunluce	Billy	Coleraine	III.	16
17	Maghernacaldry	65 3 3	Cavan	Tullygarvey	Drumgoon	Cootehill	III.	88
34	Maghernacloy	152 2 8	Monaghan	Farney	Magheracloone	Carrickmacross	III.	273
44	Maghernagran	136 3 25	Donegal	Kilmacrenan	Conwal	Letterkenny	III.	126
4, 8	Maghernahar	299 1 31	Antrim	Cary	Ballintoy	Ballycastle	III.	12
18	Maghernaharny	404 3 24	Monaghan	Dartree	Ematris	Cootehill	III.	267
26	Maghernahely	266 3 4	Armagh	Orior Upper	Killevy	Newry	III.	58
22	Maghernakelly	125 0 29	Monaghan	Dartree	Ematris	Cootehill	III.	267
25	Maghernakill	148 2 38	Monaghan	Farney	Donaghmoyne	Castleblayney	III.	270
8, 17	Maghernaloght	90 2 00	Donegal	Kilmacrenan	Clondavaddog	Milford	III.	125
43, 44	Maghernashangan	814 3 26n	Donegal	Kilmacrenan	Gartan	Letterkenny	III.	127
22	Maghernaskeagh or Bushfield	258 0 33	Queen's Co.	Clandonagh	Aghaboe	Donaghmore	I.	232

(a) Including 7A. 3R. 15P. water.
(b) Including 12A. 3R. 9P. water.
(c) Including 4A. 2R. 30P. water.
(d) Including 3A. 0R. 5P. water.
(e) Including 5A. 1R. 16P. water.

(f) Including 5A. 3R. 0P. water.
(g) Including 1A. 1R. 6P. water.
(h) Including 11A. 1R. 22P. water.
(i) Including 10A. 2R. 20P. water.
(j) Including 397A. 2R. 8P. of Peninsula.

(k) Including 46A. 0R. 21P. water.
(l) Including 15A. 2R. 8P. water.
(m) Including 14A. 0R. 38P. water.
(n) Including 14A. 0R. 3P. water.

No. of Sheet of the Ordnance Survey Maps.	Townlands and Towns.	Area in Statute Acres.			County.	Barony.	Parish.	Poor Law Union in 1857.	Townland Census of 1851, Part I.	
		A.	R.	P.					Vol.	Page
31	Magheross	136	0	20	Monaghan	Farney	Magheross	Carrickmacross	III.	274
1, 2	Maghery	324	0	39*a*	Armagh	Oneilland West	Tartaraghan	Lurgan	III.	55
55	Maghery	283	3	28	Down	Mourne	Kilkeel	Kilkeel	III.	183
8	Maghery	114	0	33*b*	Monaghan	Monaghan	Clones	Monaghan	III.	275
2, 4	Magheryard	413	3	25	Donegal	Inishowen East	Clonca	Inishowen	III.	117
79	Magherycallaghan	144	0	15*c*	Donegal	Raphoe	Urney	Strabane	III.	144
13, 17	Magherydogherty	443	3	16*d*	Armagh	Fews Lower	Mullaghbrack	Armagh	III.	47
48, 56	Maghery Glebe	511	0	6*e*	Donegal	Boylagh	Templecrone	Glenties	III.	115
11,12,15,16	Maghery Kilcrany	335	2	38	Armagh	Armagh	Derrynoose	Armagh	III.	44
2	MAGHERY T.	—			Armagh	Oneilland West	Tartaraghan	Lurgan	III.	55
17	Maghnavery	378	1	0	Armagh	Orior Lower	Kilclooney	Armagh	III.	56
9	Magho	414	0	38	Fermanagh	Magheraboy	Inishmacsaint	Ballyshannon	III.	213
9	Maghon	291	0	17	Armagh	Oneilland West	Drumcree	Lurgan	III.	52
23, 26	Maghon	497	0	33*f*	Monaghan	Cremorne	Aghnamullen	Cootehill	III.	258
39	Magh West	196	1	38	Kerry	Trughanacmy	Ballymacelligott	Tralee	II.	207
90, 99	Maghygreenane	2,156	3	37*g*	Kerry	Iveragh	Dromod	Cahersiveen	II.	195
7, 11	Magillstown	325	2	30	Dublin	Nethercross	Swords	Balrothery	I.	32
69, 76	Maginstown	475	2	27	Tipperary, S.R.	Middlethird	Mora	Cashel	II.	329
4, 5	Magirr	211	2	14*h*	Tyrone	Strabane Lower	Urney	Strabane	III.	322
39	Maglass	93	1	34	Kerry	Trughanacmy	Nohaval	Tralee	II.	212
30, 39	Maglass East	235	2	15	Kerry	Trughanacmy	Ballymacelligott	Tralee	II.	207
30, 39	Maglass West	291	1	31	Kerry	Trughanacmy	Ballymacelligott	Tralee	II.	207
73, 85	Maglin	331	1	15	Cork, E.R.	East Muskerry	St. Nicholas	Cork	II.	106
21	Magmore	31	3	17	Wexford	Ballaghkeen	Kilnamanagh	Gorey	I.	297
67	Magnershill	62	0	17	Cork, E.R.	Imokilly	Youghal	Youghal	II.	91
29	Magoney	200	1	38	Monaghan	Farney	Inishkeen	Dundalk	III.	271
23	Magonragh	225	0	22*i*	Fermanagh	Tirkennedy	Enniskillen	Enniskillen	III.	222
72	Magooly	432	3	2*j*	Cork, E.R.	East Muskerry	Inishcarra	Cork	II.	104
61, 62	Magorban	225	1	25	Tipperary, S.R.	Middlethird	Magorban	Cashel	II.	328
25	Magowna	89	1	6	Clare	Inchiquin	Kilnamona	Ennis	II.	27
33, 41	Magowna	357	3	37	Clare	Islands	Kilmaley	Ennis	II.	31
25	Magowna East	15	3	28	Clare	Inchiquin	Dysert	Ennis	II.	24
25	Magowna West	84	2	5	Clare	Inchiquin	Dysert	Ennis	II.	24
62, 63	Magowry	663	0	16	Tipperary, S.R.	Middlethird	Magowry	Cashel	II.	328
13	Maguin's Island	13	0	38	Sligo	Carbury	Killaspugbrone	Sligo	IV.	222
23	MAGUIRES BRIDGE T.	—			Fermanagh	Magherastephana	Aghalurcher	Lisnaskea	III.	218
10, 11	Magurk	222	0	22	Leitrim	Drumahaire	Drumlease	Manorhamilton	IV.	94
71, 72	Mahallagh	276	3	31	Cork, E.R.	East Muskerry	Cannaway	Macroom	II.	102
15, 16	Mahanagh	135	3	11	Cork, E.R.	Duhallow	Kilbrin	Kanturk	II.	72
30, 31	Mahanagh	222	0	34	Galway	Ballymoe	Cloabern	Tuam	IV.	6
43, 57	Mahanagh	210	0	29*k*	Galway	Clare	Cummer	Tuam	IV.	19
18	Mahanagh	196	2	31*l*	Leitrim	Drumahaire	Inishmagrath	Manorhamilton	IV.	97
23	Mahanagh	263	0	39	Leitrim	Leitrim	Kiltoghert	Car*k*. on Shannon	IV.	102
88, 89	Mahanagh	126	1	17	Mayo	Burrishoole	Aghagower	Westport	I.	118
44, 45	Mahanagh	869	2	22*m*	Sligo	Coolavin	Kilfree	Boyle	IV.	224
27	Mahanagh	35	2	28	Wexford	Ballaghkeen	Castle-ellis	Enniscorthy	I.	293
17	Mahee Island	176	3	38	Down	Castlereagh Lower	Tullynakill	Newtownards	III.	163
74, 75	Mahon	266	3	5*n*	Cork, E.R.	Cork	St. Finbars	Cork	II.	66
33, 41	Mahonburgh	242	3	21	Clare	Islands	Drumcliff	Ennis	II.	30
11	Mahonstown	254	3	19	Meath	Upper Kells	Dulane	Kells	I.	205
26, 33	Mahonstown	507	3	39	Westmeath	Fartullagh	Enniscoffey	Mullingar	I.	268
36	Mahoonagh Beg	91	1	36	Limerick	Glenquin	Mahoonagh	Newcastle	II.	246
36	Mahoonagh More	311	3	35	Limerick	Glenquin	Mahoonagh	Newcastle	II.	246
36	MAHOONAGH T.	—			Limerick	Glenquin	Mahoonagh	Newcastle	II.	246
24	Maidenhall	160	3	32*o*	Kilkenny	Shillelogher	Danesfort	Thomastown	I.	114
25,26,31,32	Maidenhead	326	2	31	Queen's Co.	Slievemargy	Killabban	Carlow	I.	245
19	Maidenhill	45	1	35*p*	Kilkenny	Shillelogher and Municipal Borough	St. Canice	Kilkenny	I.	115
23	*Maiden Rock*	0	1	13	Dublin	Rathdown	Dalkey	Rathdown	I.	35
39	Maidstown	380	0	9	Limerick	Coshma	Dromin	Kilmallock	II.	243
15	Maine	671	0	36*q*	Louth	Ardee	Kilsaran	Ardee	I.	173
26, 35	Maine	475	1	11	Tyrone	Strabane Upper	Cappagh	Omagh	III.	325
1, 2	Maine North	815	2	7	Cork, E.R.	Orrery and Kilmore	Kilbolane	Kanturk	II.	108
17	Maine North	413	2	37	Londonderry	Keenaght	Balteagh	Newt*n*Limavady	III.	234
1, 2	Maine South	493	0	10	Cork, E.R.	Orrery and Kilmore	Kilbolane	Kanturk	II.	108
17	Maine South	230	1	5	Londonderry	Keenaght	Balteagh	Newt*n*Limavady	III.	234
10, 14	Mainham	172	2	36	Kildare	Ikeathy &Oughterany	Mainham	Celbridge	I.	58
7	Mainscourt	377	2	30	Dublin	Balrothery West	Ballyboghill	Balrothery	I.	22
79, 85	Mainstown	279	3	13	Tipperary, S.R.	Iffa and Offa East	Newtownlennan	Carrick on Suir	II.	315
56	Makenny	810	1	17*r*	Tyrone	Omagh East	Kilskeery	Lowtherstown	III.	314
19	Makief	99	0	12	Cavan	Tullyhunco	Kildallan	Bawnboy	III.	97
12	Malahide	503	0	4	Dublin	Coolock	Malahide	Balrothery	I.	28
12	Malahide Demesne	215	2	31	Dublin	Coolock	Malahide	Balrothery	I.	28

(*a*) Including 8A. 0R. 2P. water.
(*b*) Including 7A. 3R. 8P. water.
(*c*) Including 4A. 3R. 9P. water.
(*d*) Including 16A. 3R. 18P. water.
(*e*) Including 41A. 0R. 0P. water.
(*f*) Including 50A. 3R. 1P. water.
(*g*) Including 239A. 3R. 26P. water.

(*h*) Including 10A. 3R. 39P. water.
(*i*) Including 19A. 2R. 23P. water.
(*j*) Including 2A. 0R. 19P. River Lee.
(*k*) Including 42A. 1R. 4P. water.
(*l*) Including 7A. 0R. 8P. water.
(*m*) Including 7A. 0R. 26P. water.

(*n*) Including 21A. 2R. 0P. detached portion.
(*o*) Including 2A. 1R. 19P. River Nore.
(*p*) { Within the Municipal Boundary, 5A. 1R. 22P. Without the Municipal Boundary, 40A. 0R. 13P.
(*q*) Including 14A. 3R. 34P. water.
(*r*) Including 4A. 2R. 33P. water.

No. of Sheet of the Ordnance Survey Maps.	Townlands and Towns.	Area in Statute Acres. A. R. P.	County.	Barony.	Parish.	Poor Law Union in 1857.	Townland Census of 1851, Part I. Vol.	Page
12	MALAHIDE T.	—	Dublin	Coolock	Malahide	Balrothery	I.	28
88	Malapardas	7 2 1	Cork, E.R.	Imokilly	Cloyne	Middleton	II.	85
5	Malheney	102 3 12	Dublin	Balrothery East	Balrothery	Balrothery	I.	19
89, 90, 96	Malin Beg	3,112 2 37	Donegal	Banagh	Glencolumbkille	Glenties	III.	105
80, 89	Malin More	3,020 2 25a	Donegal	Banagh	Glencolumbkille	Glenties	III.	105
4	MALIN T.	—	Donegal	Inishowen East	Clonca	Inishowen	III.	117
58	Mallabeny	328 1 36	Tyrone	Clogher	Clogher	Clogher	III.	293
93, 107	Mallabracka	333 0 36	Cork, W.R.	East Carbery (W.D.)	Fanlobbus	Dunmanway	II.	132
4, 7	Mallahow	601 1 36	Dublin	Balrothery West	Hollywood	Balrothery	I.	23
66	Mallaranny	1,085 2 15	Mayo	Burrishoole	Burrishoole	Newport	IV.	119
26, 27	Mallardstown	258 0 25	Kilkenny	Kells	Mallardstown	Callan	I.	110
26, 27	Mallardstown East	77 1 0b	Kilkenny	Kells	Mallardstown	Callan	I.	110
26, 27	Mallardstown Great	316 3 8c	Kilkenny	Kells	Mallardstown	Callan	I.	110
26, 27	Mallardstown Lower	245 0 23	Kilkenny	Kells	Mallardstown	Callan	I.	110
26	Mallardstown Upper	207 3 15	Kilkenny	Kells	Mallardstown	Callan	I.	110
26	Mallardstown West	86 2 29	Kilkenny	Kells	Mallardstown	Callan	I.	110
119	Mallaroe	101 0 23	Mayo	Kilmaine	Kilcommon	Ballinrobe	IV.	155
152	Mallavoge	254 0 18	Cork, W.R.	West Carbery (W.D.)	Kilmoe	Skull	II.	145
141	Mallavonea	26 1 14	Cork, W.R.	West Carbery (E.D.)	Abbeystrowry	Skibbereen	II.	136
141	Mallavonea	140 1 23	Cork, W.R.	West Carbery (E.D.)	Aghadown	Skibbereen	II.	137
7	Mallendober	81 3 37	Antrim	Lower Dunluce	Billy	Coleraine	III.	16
33	Mallow	172 2 0	Cork, E.R.	Fermoy	Mallow	Mallow	II.	81
94	Mallow	233 0 5	Cork, W.R.	East Carbery (W.D.)	Kinneigh	Dunmanway	II.	135
95, 96	Mallowgaton	327 2 30	Cork, W.R.	Kinalmeaky	Kilbrogan	Bandon	II.	152
33	MALLOW T.	—	Cork, E.R.	Fermoy	Mallow	Mallow	II.	81
3, 4	Mallybreen	688 0 4d	Fermanagh	Lurg	Belleek	Ballyshannon	III.	203
19, 32	Mallyree	110 3 35	Galway	Killian	Athleague	Mountbellew	IV.	43
60, 61, 64, 65	Malone Lower	1,880 2 6	Antrim	Upper Belfast	Shankill	Belfast	III.	35
64, 65	Malone Upper	1,384 1 38e	Antrim	Upper Belfast	Shankill	Lisburn	III.	10
29	Maloon	164 2 2	Tyrone	Dungannon Upper	Derryloran	Cookstown	III.	307
21	*Malthooa*	5 3 23	Galway	Ballynahinch	Omey	Clifden	IV.	15
17	Malthousepark	8 1 37	Westmeath	Rathconrath	Piercetown	Ballymahon	I.	283
101	Maltpool	249 0 12	Mayo	Clanmorris	Tagheen	Claremorris	IV.	136
82, 94	Mamucky	221 3 34	Cork, W.R.	West Muskerry	Kilmichael	Dunmanway	II.	159
14	Managhbeg	121 3 13	Londonderry	Tirkeeran	Clondermot	Londonderry	III.	248
11	Managher	132 3 21	Londonderry	Coleraine	Aghadowey	Coleraine	III.	230
14	Managhmore	105 3 31	Londonderry	Tirkeeran	Clondermot	Londonderry	III.	248
108	Manch East	321 0 22	Cork, W.R.	East Carbery (W.D.)	Fanlobbus	Dunmanway	II.	132
108	Manch Middle	265 0 24	Cork, W.R.	East Carbery (W.D.)	Fanlobbus	Dunmanway	II.	132
108	Manch West	531 0 23	Cork, W.R.	East Carbery (W.D.)	Fanlobbus	Dunmanway	II.	132
6, 7	Mandistown	831 1 33	Meath	Lower Slane	Inishmot	Ardee	I.	223
9	Mandoran	488 3 10	Wexford	Scarawalsh	St. Marys Newtownbarry	Enniscorthy	I.	325
72	Mangan	257 2 34	Tipperary, S.R.	Slievardagh	Templemichael	Carrick on Suir	II.	336
6	Mangan	253 1 9	Wexford	Gorey	Kilnahue	Gorey	I.	319
22	Mangan	51 0 4	Wexford	Gorey	Kiltrisk	Gorey	I.	320
19	Mangan	786 3 37	Wexford	Scarawalsh	Templeshanbo	Enniscorthy	I.	326
17	Mangan Lower	261 3 38	Wexford	Ballaghkeen	Donaghmore	Gorey	I.	293
38	Mangans	386 1 35	Wicklow	Ballinacor South	Kilcommon	Shillelagh	I.	349
17	Mangan Upper	128 1 19	Wexford	Ballaghkeen	Donaghmore	Gorey	I.	293
7	Manger	298 1 3	Fermanagh	Magheraboy	Inishmacsaint	Ballyshannon	III.	213
25	Manger	43 2 2	Queen's Co.	Stradbally	Tullomoy	Athy	I.	248
21	Manger	221 1 30	Wicklow	Upper Talbotstown	Rathbran	Baltinglass	I.	365
74, 75, 84, 85	Mangerton	2,598 2 5	Kerry	Glanarought	Kilgarvan	Kenmare	II.	187
8, 13	Manister	208 0 22	Antrim	Cary	Grange of Drumtullagh	Ballycastle	III.	14
14	Manistown	86 2 8	Louth	Ardee	Ardee	Ardee	I.	171
29	Manna North	131 2 27	Tipperary, N.R.	Eliogarty	Templemore	Thurles	II.	272
33	Mannanstown	217 1 34	Meath	Upper Duleek	Ardcath	Drogheda	I.	197
29	Manna South	225 2 3	Tipperary, N.R.	Eliogarty	Templemore	Thurles	II.	272
104	Mannin	251 3 18	Galway	Dunkellin	Ardrahan	Loughrea	IV.	26
81, 92	Mannin	274 2 9	Mayo	Costello	Aghamore	Swineford	IV.	137
16, 22	Mannin	508 2 9	Queen's Co.	Upperwoods	Offerlane	Abbeyleix	I.	252
104	Manninard	215 2 4	Galway	Dunkellin	Ardrahan	Loughrea	IV.	26
35, 49	Mannin Beg	326 0 11f	Galway	Ballynahinch	Ballindoon	Clifden	IV.	10
27	Manning	393 3 6	Cork, E.R.	Condons & Clangibbon	Glanworth	Fermoy	I.	61
140	*Mannin Island*	13 2 10	Cork, W.R.	West Carbery (W.D.)	Kilcoe	Skull	II.	143
35, 49	Mannin More	578 1 32g	Galway	Ballynahinch	Ballindoon	Clifden	IV.	10
130	*Mannions Island Large*	3 0 31	Cork, W.R.	West Carbery (W.D.)	Durrus	Bantry	II.	142
130	*Mannions Island Small*	0 0 17	Cork, W.R.	West Carbery (W.D.)	Durrus	Bantry	II.	143
15	Manofwar	99 1 2	Wicklow	Lower Talbotstown	Tober	Baltinglass	I.	361
22	Manola Wood	103 1 20	Antrim	Kilconway	Finvoy	Ballymoney	III.	26
5	Manoo	80 1 23	Fermanagh	Lurg	Magheraculmoney	Lowtherstown	III.	208
11	Manooney	257 1 11	Armagh	Armagh	Tynan	Armagh	III.	46

(a) Including 39A. 3R. 4P. water.
(b) Including 6A. 2R. 24P. detached portion.
(c) Including 19A. 0R. 27P. detached portion.
(d) Including 63A. 1R. 35P. water.
(e) Including 22A. 2R. 21P. water.
(f) Including 2A. 3R. 23P. water.
(g) Including 54A. 3R. 20P. water.

No. of Sheet of the Ordnance Survey Maps.	Townlands and Towns.	Area in Statute Acres.	County.	Barony.	Parish.	Poor Law Union in 1857.	Townland Census of 1851, Part I.	
							Vol.	Page
		A. R. P.						
28	Manor	470 1 8	Roscommon	Roscommon	Killukin	Strokestown	IV.	211
9	Manor	64 3 19a	Waterford	Gaultiere and Municipal Borough	St. Johns Without	Waterford	II.	365
54	Manorcunningham	202 0 28	Donegal	Raphoe	Raymoghy	Letterkenny	III.	142
54	Manorcunningham Churchland	87 0 38	Donegal	Raphoe	Raymoghy	Letterkenny	III.	142
54	Manorcunningham Churchland Isle	43 3 34	Donegal	Raphoe	Raymoghy	Letterkenny	III.	142
54	MANORCUNNINGHAM T.	—	Donegal	Raphoe	Raymoghy	Letterkenny	III.	142
29	Manor East	161 2 22	Kerry	Trughanacmy	Ratass	Tralee	II.	213
7, 11	Manorhamilton	175 2 1	Leitrim	Drumahaire	Cloonclare	Manorhamilton	IV.	93
7, 11	MANORHAMILTON T.	—	Leitrim	{ Drumahaire { Rosclogher	Cloonclare Killasnet	} Manorhamilton	IV. {	94 110
36	Manorland 1st Division	87 0 35b	Meath	Lower Moyfenrath	Trim	Trim	I.	212
36	Manorland 2nd Division	216 1 1	Meath	Lower Moyfenrath	Trim	Trim	I.	212
34	Manor Water House	45 2 28	Fermanagh	Coole	Galloon	Lisnaskea	III.	200
29	Manor West	154 2 34	Kerry	Trughanacmy	Ratass	Tralee	II.	213
4	Manragh Lower	80 1 18	Cavan	Tullyhaw	Killinagh	Enniskillen	III.	92
16	Manraghrory	157 2 28	Mayo	Erris	Kilmore	Belmullet	IV.	146
4	Manragh Upper	115 1 6	Cavan	Tullyhaw	Killinagh	Enniskillen	III	92
36	Manselscourt	229 0 28	Kilkenny	Knocktopher	Kilbeacon	Waterford	I.	112
42	Manselstown	360 0 27	Tipperary, N.R.	Eliogarty	Moyne	Thurles	II.	272
54	Manserghshill	326 3 15	Tipperary, S.R.	Slievardagh	St. John Baptist	Cashel	II.	336
112	Mansfield's-land	9 0 18	Cork, E.R.	Kinsale	Kinsale	Kinsale	I.	100
112	Mansfield's-land	71 3 16	Cork, E.R.	Kinsale	Ringcurran	Kinsale	I.	100
14, 15	Mansfieldstown	551 0 16	Louth	Louth	Mansfieldstown	Ardee	I.	185
15	MANSFIELDSTOWN T.	—	Louth	Louth	Mansfieldstown	Ardee	I.	185
30	Mantingstown	81 1 9	Kilkenny	Kells	Coolaghmore	Callan	I.	108
60	Mantlehill Great	678 1 7	Tipperary, S.R.	Clanwilliam	Relickmurry & Athassel	Tipperary	II.	310
60	Mantlehill Little	167 0 31	Tipperary, S.R.	Clanwilliam	Relickmurry & Athassel	Tipperary	II.	310
5	Mantlin	162 3 12	Fermanagh	Lurg	Magheraculmoney	Lowtherstown	III.	208
12	Mantua	22 2 7	Dublin	Nethercross	Swords	Balrothery	I.	32
15	Mantuar	327 2 0c	Roscommon	Frenchpark	Kilcolagh	Boyle	IV.	203
79	Manulla	194 2 18d	Mayo	Carra	Manulla	Castlebar	IV.	129
79	MANULLA T.	—	Mayo	Carra	Manulla	Castlebar	IV.	129
42, 56	Manuslown	537 1 11	Galway	Clare	Kilcoona	Tuam	IV.	20
42	Manusmore	922 0 20	Clare	Islands	Clareabbey	Ennis	II.	29
14	Mapastown	224 1 36	Louth	Ardee	Mapastown	Ardee	I.	173
10	Maperath	173 1 15	Meath	Upper Kells	Dulane	Kells	I.	205
10	Maperath	511 1 2	Meath	Upper Kells	Loughan or Castlekeeran	Kells	I.	207
30, 31	Mapestown	191 0 23	Waterford	Decies without Drum	Kilrush	Dungarvan	II.	358
28	Maphoner	458 0 22	Armagh	Orior Upper	Forkill	Newry	III.	57
1, 3	Maplestown	485 2 0	Carlow	Rathvilly	Rahill	Baltinglass	I.	12
35	Marahill	91 2 26	Cavan	Clankee	Enniskeen	Bailieborough	III.	73
31	Marahill	88 1 6	Cavan	Clanmahon	Ballintemple	Cavan	III.	75
24, 25	Marahill	362 0 2e	Cavan	Upper Loughtee	Kilmore	Cavan	III.	85
16	Marblehill	105 0 19	Donegal	Kilmacrenan	Clondahorky	Dunfanaghy	III.	123
125	Marblehill	503 2 18	Galway	Leitrim	Ballynakill	Loughrea	IV.	52
29, 35	Mardyke	173 0 4	Tipperary, N.R.	Eliogarty	Loughmoe East	Thurles	II.	271
54	Mardyke	115 1 28	Tipperary, S.R.	Slievardagh	Graystown	Callan	II.	333
54	MARDYKE T.	—	Tipperary, S.R.	Slievardagh	Graystown	Callan	II.	333
15	Marfagh	109 2 31	Donegal	Kilmacrenan	Clondahorky	Dunfanaghy	III.	123
31	Marganure	250 1 34	Galway	Tiaquin	Killerrin	Glennamaddy	IV.	77
19	Margaret's-fields	34 0 1	Kilkenny	Shillelogher	St. Patrick's	Kilkenny	I.	116
5	Margaretstown	73 0 33	Dublin	Balrothery East	Balrothery	Balrothery	I.	19
1, 5	Margymonaghan	209 1 5	Londonderry	Keenaght	Magilligan	NewT.Limavady	III.	237
42	Marhin	748 0 7	Kerry	Corkaguiny	Marhin	Dingle	II.	179
5, 6	Mariavilla	297 2 4	Kildare	North Salt	Laraghbryan	Celbridge	I.	75
75	Marino	329 0 21	Cork, E.R.	Barrymore	Clonmel	Cork	II.	53
14, 18	Marino	218 2 20	Dublin	Coolock	Clonturk	Dublin North	I.	27
18	MARINO T.	—	Dublin	Coolock	Clontarf	Dublin North	I.	26
17	MARKETHILL T.	—	Armagh	Fews Lower	{ Kilclooney { Mullaghbrack	} Armagh	III. {	46 47
26	Markree Demesne	507 0 24	Sligo	Tirerrill	Ballysadare	Sligo	IV.	238
13	Marlacoo Beg	306 1 21f	Armagh	Oneilland West	Mullaghbrack	Banbridge	III.	54
13	Marlacoo More	403 0 0g	Armagh	Oneilland West	Mullaghbrack	Banbridge	III.	54
45	Marlay	465 2 34	Galway	Tiaquin	Moylough	Mountbellew	IV.	80
18	Marlay	205 2 19	Louth	Ferrard	Marlestown	Drogheda	I.	181
25, 31	Marlbank	587 2 25	Fermanagh	Clanawley	Killesher	Enniskillen	III.	193
22	Marlbrook	37 1 22	Limerick	Pubblebrien	Crecora	Croom	II.	252
29	Marley	97 2 33	Galway	Dunmore	Tuam	Tuam	IV.	36

(a) { Within the Municipal Boundary, 31A. 2R. 6P. { Without the Municipal Boundary, 33A. 1R. 13P.
(b) Including 1A. 1R. 0P. water.
(c) Including 41A. 0R. 16P. water.
(d) Including 7A. 3R. 27P. water.
(e) Including 10A. 1R. 18P. water.
(f) Including 13A. 2R. 5P. water.
(g) Including 10A. 2R. 26P. water.

No. of Sheet of the Ordnance Survey Maps.	Townlands and Towns.	Area in Statute Acres.			County.	Barony.	Parish.	Poor Law Union in 1857.	Townland Census of 1851, Part I.	
		A.	R.	P.					Vol.	Page
19	Marley . . .	132	1	39	Wexford . .	Scarawalsh . .	Monart . .	Enniscorthy .	I.	324
24	Marley or Knockduff	881	3	23	Carlow . .	St. Mullins Lower .	St. Mullins . .	New Ross .	I.	13
24	Marlfield . .	214	3	20	Down . .	Ards Upper . .	Ardquin . .	Downpatrick .	III.	159
82, 83	Marlfield . .	436	2	10a	Tipperary, S.R.	Iffa and Offa East .	Inishlounaght .	Clonmel . .	II.	313
82	Marlhill . . .	304	2	17	Tipperary, S.R.	Iffa and Offa West .	Ardfinnan . .	Clogheen . .	II.	317
68, 69	Marlhill . . .	673	3	26	Tipperary, S.R.	Middlethird . .	Knockgraffon .	Cashel . .	II.	328
19, 26	Marlinstown . .	673	0	13	Westmeath . .	Moyashel and Magheradernon .	Mullingar . .	Mullingar . .	I.	275
19	Marlinstown Bog .	117	0	31	Westmeath .	Moyashel and Magheradernon .	Mullingar . .	Mullingar . .	I.	275
46	Marlow . . .	390	1	28	Tipperary, S.R.	Kilnamanagh Lower	Clogher . .	Cashel . .	II.	322
2	Marnellsgrove .	328	0	14	Galway . .	Ballymoe . .	Kilcroan . .	Glennamaddy .	IV.	9
19	Marnellsmeadows .	19	0	35b	Kilkenny . .	Shillelogher and Municipal Borough .	St. Canice .	Kilkenny . .	I.	115
11	Marrassit or College Hall . . .	271	0	30	Armagh . .	Armagh . .	Tynan . .	Armagh . .	III.	46
33, 41	Marrock Glebe .	149	0	36c	Tyrone . .	Omagh West . .	Longfield West .	Castlederg .	III.	316
141	Marsh . . .	154	3	13	Cork, W.R.	West Carbery (E.D.)	Abbeystrowry .	Skibbereen .	II.	136
40	Marsh . . .	199	3	37	Wicklow . .	Arklow . .	Kilbride . .	Rathdrum .	I.	345
18	Marshallrath . .	171	1	35	Louth . .	Ardee . .	Mosstown . .	Ardee . .	I.	174
94, 95	Marshallspark .	26	2	36	Galway . .	Dunkellin . .	Ballynacourty .	Galway . .	IV.	27
37	Marshallstown .	247	0	21d	Down . .	Lecale Upper . .	Down . .	Downpatrick .	III.	181
11,12,14,15	Marshallstown .	120	1	28	Dublin . .	Nethercross . .	Swords . .	Balrothery .	I.	32
37	Marshallstown or Crumpstown .	354	2	24	Meath . .	Lower Deece . .	Scurlockstown .	Trim . .	I.	192
19	Marshalstown .	480	0	24	Cork, E.R.	Condons&Clangibbon	Marshalstown .	Mitchelstown .	II.	63
38	Marshalstown .	353	0	20	Kildare . .	Kilkea and Moone .	Killelan . .	Baltinglass .	I.	60
53	Marshalstown .	70	3	32	Tipperary, S.R.	Middlethird . .	Ballysheehan .	Cashel . .	II.	325
19, 20	Marshalstown .	695	1	25	Wexford . .	Scarawalsh . .	Monart . .	Enniscorthy .	I.	324
40, 41	Marshalstown .	166	1	8	Wexford . .	Shelmaliere West .	Ballymitty . .	Wexford . .	I.	332
7	Marshes Lower .	590	0	13	Louth . .	Upper Dundalk .	Dundalk . .	Dundalk . .	I.	178
7	Marshes Upper .	795	1	4	Louth . .	Upper Dundalk .	Dundalk . .	Dundalk . .	I.	178
29, 34	Marshmeadows .	160	1	9	Wexford . .	Bantry . .	St. Mary's . .	New Ross .	I.	302
7	Marsh North .	337	3	36	Louth . .	Upper Dundalk .	Dundalk . .	Dundalk . .	I.	178
7	Marsh South .	790	1	39	Louth . .	Upper Dundalk .	Dundalk . .	Dundalk . .	I.	178
37	Marshtown . .	331	0	36	Cork, E.R.	Condons&Clangibbon	Lismore and Mocollop	Fermoy . .	II.	62
2	Martara . .	105	0	9	Kerry . .	Iraghticonnor .	Aghavallen . .	Listowel . .	II.	189
39	Martara . .	87	3	21	Kerry . .	Trughanacmy . .	Ballymacelligott .	Tralee . .	II.	207
32	Martingale . .	120	0	39	Wexford . .	Ballaghkeen . .	Ballynaslaney .	Enniscorthy .	I.	292
28	Martinstown .	188	1	33	Antrim . .	Lower Antrim .	Skerry . .	Ballymena .	III.	5
3, 4	Martinstown .	315	0	26	Kildare . .	Carbury . .	Cadamstown .	Edenderry .	I.	51
28	Martinstown .	53	0	31	Kildare . .	Offaly East . .	Ballysax . .	Athy . .	I.	69
28	Martinstown .	374	3	19	Kildare . .	Offaly East . .	Ballyshannon .	Athy . .	I.	69
28	Martinstown .	274	1	13	Kildare . .	Offaly East . .	Carn . .	Athy . .	I.	69
28	Martinstown .	150	3	39	Kildare . .	Offaly East . .	Tully . .	Athy . .	I.	71
48	Martinstown .	527	3	19	Limerick . .	Coshlea . .	Athneasy . .	Kilmallock .	II.	237
15,16,18,19	Martinstown .	265	2	22	Louth . .	Ferrard . .	Port . .	Drogheda .	I.	182
15, 16	Martinstown .	262	1	4	Meath . .	Fore . .	Diamor . .	Oldcastle .	I.	200
37, 43	Martinstown .	237	0	10	Meath . .	Lower Deece .	Galtrim . .	Trim . .	I.	191
23, 29	Martinstown .	789	1	20	Meath . .	Lune . .	Athboy . .	Trim . .	I.	207
49	Martinstown .	18	1	37	Meath . .	Upper Deece .	Kilmore . .	Dunshaughlin .	I.	193
12	Martinstown .	532	1	22	Westmeath . .	Corkaree . .	Stonehall . .	Mullingar .	I.	263
13, 14	Martinstown .	376	2	2	Westmeath . .	Delvin . .	Castletowndelvin .	Castletowndelvin	I.	265
3	Martinstown .	33	0	29	Westmeath .	Fore . .	Lickbla . .	Castletowndelvin	I.	270
4, 8	Martinstown .	592	0	30e	Westmeath .	Fore . .	St. Mary's . .	Castletowndelvin	I.	272
48	Martinstown .	48	2	32	Wexford .	Forth . .	Ballybrennan .	Wexford . .	I.	308
27, 36	Martramane . .	140	0	0	Kerry . .	Corkaguiny . .	Killiney . .	Dingle . .	II.	178
53	Martray . .	250	0	35f	Tyrone . .	Dungannon Lower .	Carnteel . .	Clogher . .	III.	298
24	Martry . .	414	1	12	Clare . .	Inchiquin . .	Rath . .	Ennistimon .	II.	27
17, 24	Martry . .	754	1	39	Meath . .	Lower Navan . .	Martry . .	Kells . .	I.	215
16	Martry . .	194	2	17	Roscommon .	Frenchpark . .	Creeve . .	Cark. on Shannon	IV.	203
11	Marvelstown .	267	3	23	Meath . .	Lower Kells . .	Kilbeg . .	Kells . .	I.	202
74, 86	Maryborough .	264	2	10	Cork, E.R.	Cork . .	Carrigaline .	Cork . .	II.	64
13	Maryborough .	391	1	37	Queen's Co.	Maryborough East .	Borris . .	Mountmellick .	I.	240
13	MARYBOROUGH T. .	—			Queen's Co.	Maryborough East .	Borris . .	Mountmellick .	I.	241
23	Marybrook . .	171	0	7	Cork, E.R.	Duhallow . .	Kilbrin . .	Kanturk . .	II.	72
27, 35	Maryfort or Lismeehan . .	297	1	5g	Clare . .	Tulla Upper . .	Tulla . .	Tulla . .	II.	42
32	Maryglen . .	98	0	19	Tipperary, N.R.	Owney and Arra .	Killoscully .	Neuagh . .	II.	295
33	Maryland . .	49	0	6	Meath . .	Upper Duleek .	Ardcath . .	Drogheda .	I.	197
39	Marymount .	161	1	35	King's Co.	Ballybritt . .	Aghancon . .	Roscrea . .	I.	124
16	Marymount . .	357	1	28	Queen's Co.	Upperwoods .	Offerlane . .	Mountmellick .	I.	252
20	Marystown . .	189	1	15	Roscommon .	Castlereagh . .	Kiltullagh .	Castlereagh .	IV.	202
9, 16	Maryville . .	143	2	17	Clare . .	Corcomroe . .	Kilfenora . .	Ennistimon .	II.	19

(a) Including 24A. 3R. 30P. water.
(b) { Within the Municipal Boundary, 18A. 3R. 39P.
{ Without the Municipal Boundary, 0A. 0R. 36P.
(c) Including 2A. 3R. 2P. water.
(d) Including 20A. 3R. 33P. detached portion.
(e) Including 26A. 1R. 16P. water.
(f) Including 15A. 1R. 13P. water.
(g) Including 2A. 2R. 1P. water.

No. of Sheet of the Ordnance Survey Maps.	Townlands and Towns.	Area in Statute Acres.	County.	Barony.	Parish.	Poor Law Union in 1857.	Townland Census of 1851. Part I.	
		A. R. P.					Vol.	Page
27	Maryville	89 2 29	Cork, E.R.	Condons&Clangibbon	Kilworth	Fermoy	II.	62
19	Maryville	118 3 2	Dublin	Coolock	Raheny	Dublin North	I.	28
22	Maryville	143 1 30	Limerick	Pubblebrien	Ballycahane	Croom	II.	251
71	Mashanaglass	935 1 0a	Cork, W.R.	East Muskerry	Aghinagh	Macroom	II.	154
26	Masiness	314 3 21	Donegal	Kilmacrenan	Clondahorky	Dunfanaghy	III.	123
29	Masmore	106 0 14	Galway	Dunmore	Tuam	Tuam	IV.	36
105, 106	Masonbrook	298 0 25	Galway	Loughrea	Kilteskill	Loughrea	IV.	65
76	Mason Island	92 0 26	Galway	Ballynahinch	Moyrus	Clifden	IV.	14
34	Mason Lodge	43 0 11b	Monaghan	Farney	Magheracloone	Carrickmacross	III.	273
13, 19	Masreagh	279 3 39	Sligo	Tireragh	Skreen	Dromore West	IV.	236
70	Mass Beg	126 3 17	Donegal	Raphoe	Clonleigh	Strabane	III.	135
47, 59	Massbrook Lower	765 2 33c	Mayo	Tirawley	Addergoole	Castlebar	IV.	163
47, 59	Massbrook South	723 3 30	Mayo	Tirawley	Addergoole	Castlebar	IV.	163
47, 59	Massbrook Upper	677 3 35d	Mayo	Tirawley	Addergoole	Castlebar	IV.	163
50	MASSEREENE T.	—	Antrim	Lower Massereene	Muckamore (Grange of)	Antrim	III.	29
71	Masshill	91 2 10	Donegal	Raphoe	Clonleigh	Strabane	III.	135
70	Mass More	123 1 24	Donegal	Raphoe	Clonleigh	Strabane	III.	135
45	Masspool	141 2 3	Meath	Ratoath	Greenoge	Dunshaughlin	I.	218
45	Massreagh	249 3 5	Donegal	Kilmacrenan	Kilmacrenan	Millford	III.	129
3, 7	Masteragwee	178 3 4	Londonderry	Coleraine	Dunboe	Coleraine	III.	231
59	Mastergeeha	1,109 3 31	Kerry	Magunihy	Kilcummin	Killarney	II.	201
89	Mastergeehy	220 3 2	Kerry	Iveragh	Dromod	Cahersiveen	II.	195
68, 75	Masterstown	530 1 14	Tipperary, S.R.	Clanwilliam	Relickmurry and Athassel	Tipperary	II.	310
4	Matt	153 3 6	Dublin	Balrothery East	Balscaddan	Balrothery	I.	20
25, 26	Matthewstown	178 0 14	Waterford	Middlethird	Reisk	Waterford	II.	369
38	*Mattle Island*	1 2 26	Clare	Ibrickan	Kilmurry	Kilrush	II.	23
21, 27	Mattymount	130 1 22	Wicklow	Upper Talbotstown	Rathbran	Baltinglass	I.	365
51	Maudemount	195 0 24	Tipperary, S.R.	Kilnamanagh Lower	Kilpatrick	Cashel	II.	324
10	Maudlin	319 1 2	Kilkenny	Fassadinin	Kilmacar	Castlecomer	I.	90
10	Maudlin	88 0 23	Kilkenny	Fassadinin	Mothell	Castlecomer	I.	90
36	Maudlin	105 2 11e	Meath	Lower Moyfenrath	Trim	Trim	I.	212
17	Maudlin	59 3 30	Meath	Upper Kells	Kells	Kells	I.	206
19	Maudlings	361 1 12	Kildare	Naas North	Naas	Naas	I.	62
29	Maudlins	83 2 35	Wexford	Bantry	St. Mary's	New Ross	I.	302
19	Maudlinsland	53 0 15f	Kilkenny	Gowran	St. John's	Kilkenny	I.	98
29	MAUDLINS T.	—	Wexford	Bantry	St. Mary's	New Ross	I.	302
40, 45	Maudlintown	258 1 28	Wexford	Bargy	Kilcavan	New Ross	I.	305
37,38,42,43	Maudlintown	125 1 27	Wexford	Forth	Maudlintown	Wexford	I.	312
78, 84	Mauganstown	292 1 11	Tipperary, S.R.	Iffa and Offa East	Kilsheelin	Clonmel	II.	314
107	Maugh	85 1 39	Cork, W.R.	East Carbery (W.D.)	Fanlobbus	Dunmanway	II.	132
92	Maugha	411 1 20	Cork, W.R.	Bantry	Kilmocomoge	Bantry	II.	121
92, 106	Maughanaclea	1,592 1 5	Cork, W.R.	Bantry	Kilmocomoge	Bantry	II.	121
91, 92	Maughanasilly	313 0 10	Cork, W.R.	Bantry	Kilmocomoge	Bantry	II.	121
60	Maughantoorig	346 2 13	Kerry	Magunihy	Kilcummin	Killarney	II.	201
143	Maul	114 2 4	Cork, W.R.	East Carbery (W.D.)	Ross	Clonakilty	II.	135
139	Mauladinna	319 1 4	Cork, W.R.	West Carbery (W.D.)	Skull	Skull	II.	146
132	Maulagallane	155 3 23	Cork, W.R.	West Carbery (W.D.)	Caheragh	Skibbereen	II.	142
90,91,99,100	Maulagallane	601 3 11	Kerry	Dunkerron South	Kilcrohane	Kenmare	II.	184
66	Maulagh	164 3 7	Kerry	Magunihy	Aghadoe	Killarney	II.	199
89	Maulagirkane	195 3 27	Kerry	Iveragh	Dromod	Cahersiveen	II.	195
142	Maulagow	205 1 13g	Cork, W.R.	East Carbery (W.D.)	Kilfaughnabeg	Skibbereen	II.	133
120	Maulagow	269 2 18	Cork, W.R.	West Carbery (E.D.)	Drinagh	Skibbereen	II.	139
101, 109	Maulagowna	1,061 3 39h	Kerry	Glanarought	Tuosist	Kenmare	II.	189
44	Maulane East	191 0 14	Cork, E.R.	Barrymore	Rathcormack	Fermoy	II.	57
44	Maulane West	220 0 33	Cork, E.R.	Barrymore	Rathcormack	Fermoy	II.	57
120	Maulanimirish	621 0 34	Cork, W.R.	East Carbery (W.D.)	Fanlobbus	Dunmanway	II.	132
106	Maularaha	205 3 38	Cork, W.R.	Bantry	Kilmocomoge	Bantry	II.	121
107, 108	Maulashangarry	107 1 28	Cork, W.R.	East Carbery (W.D.)	Fanlobbus	Dunmanway	II.	132
121, 134	Maulatanvally	622 3 21	Cork, W.R.	East Carbery (W.D.)	Ross	Clonakilty	II.	135
143	Maulatrahane	79 2 0	Cork, W.R.	Ibane and Barryroe	Rathbarry	Clonakilty	II.	150
133	Maulatrahane	345 0 8	Cork, W.R.	West Carbery (E.D.)	Kilmacabea	Skibbereen	II.	140
92	Maulavanig	444 2 20	Cork, W.R.	Bantry	Kilmocomoge	Bantry	II.	121
75, 87	Maulbaun	143 1 8	Cork, E.R.	Kerrycurrihy	Monkstown	Cork	II.	93
141	Maulbrack	450 2 39	Cork, W.R.	West Carbery (E.D.)	Abbeystrowry	Skibbereen	II.	136
109	Maulbrack East	100 3 11	Cork, W.R.	East Carbery (E.D.)	Desertserges	Bandon	II.	128
109	Maulbrack West	242 0 20	Cork, W.R.	East Carbery (E.D.)	Desertserges	Bandon	II.	128
91, 92	Maulcallee	1,230 1 0	Kerry	Dunkerron South	Kilcrohane	Kenmare	II.	184
121	Maulcorragh	35 0 34	Cork, W.R.	East Carbery (W.D.)	Kilmeen	Dunmanway	II.	134
142	Maulicarrane	114 3 30	Cork, W.R.	West Carbery (E.D.)	Myross	Skibbereen	II.	141
106	Maulikeeve	194 2 7	Cork, W.R.	Bantry	Kilmocomoge	Bantry	II.	121
8, 14	Maulin	432 0 9	Kerry	Clanmaurice	Ballyheige	Tralee	II.	168
80, 89	Maulin	463 0 35	Kerry	Iveragh	Dromod	Cahersiveen	II.	195

(a) Including 15A. 2R. 20P. River Lee.
(b) Including 2A. 2R. 37P. water.
(c) Including 86A. 1R. 36P. water.

(d) Including 102A. 1R. 29P. water.
(e) Including 1A. 3R. 32P. detached portion.
(f) Including 3A. 1R. 16P. River Nore.

(g) Including 6A. 2R. 34P. water.
(h) Including 6A. 3R. 23P. water.

No. of Sheet of the Ordnance Survey Maps.	Townlands and Towns.	Area in Statute Acres.			County.	Barony.	Parish.	Poor Law Union in 1857.	Townland Census of 1851, Part I.	
		A.	R.	P.					Vol.	Page
118, 131	Maulinward	219	2	29	Cork, W.R.	West Carbery (W.D.)	Kilmocomoge	Bantry	II.	144
135, 136	Maulmacredmond	389	2	28	Cork, W.R.	Ibane and Barryroe	Templequinlan	Clonakilty	II.	151
110, 123	Maulmane	219	3	36	Cork, W.R.	East Carbery (E.D.)	Kilbrittain	Bandon	II.	128
143	Maulmareen	73	0	21	Cork, W.R.	East Carbery (W.D.)	Kilfaughnabeg	Skibbereen	II.	133
135, 136	Maulmore	105	2	13	Cork, W.R.	Ibane and Barryroe	Templequinlan	Clonakilty	II.	151
80	Maulmore	207	2	11	Cork, W.R.	West Muskerry	Inchigeelagh	Macroom	II.	158
81	Maulnabrack	646	2	31	Kerry	Iveragh	Dromod	Cahersiveen	II.	195
122	Maulnagearagh	135	2	12	Cork, W.R.	East Carbery (E.D.)	Kilnagross	Clonakilty	II.	129
133	Maulnagirra	211	3	28	Cork, W.R.	West Carbery (E.D.)	Kilmacabea	Skibbereen	II.	140
92	Maulnagower	253	0	30	Kerry	Dunkerron South	Templenoe	Kenmare	II.	185
48, 59	Maulnagrough	381	0	12	Cork, W.R.	West Muskerry	Clondrohid	Macroom	II.	155
89	Maulnahone	362	0	3	Kerry	Iveragh	Dromod	Cahersiveen	II.	195
48, 49, 59	Maulnahorna	1,633	0	16	Cork, W.R.	West Muskerry	Clondrohid	Macroom	II.	155
92	Maulnahorna	412	2	21	Kerry	Dunkerron South	Templenoe	Kenmare	II.	185
109	Maulnarouga North	81	3	38	Cork, W.R.	East Carbery (E.D.)	Desertserges	Bandon	II.	128
109, 122	Maulnarouga South	374	3	11	Cork, W.R.	East Carbery (E.D.)	Desertserges	Bandon	II.	128
132	Maulnaskeha	275	1	15	Cork, W.R.	West Carbery (E.D.)	Dromdaleague	Skibbereen	II.	140
135	Maulnaskehy	14	1	5	Cork, W.R.	East Carbery (E.D.)	Kilgarriff	Clonakilty	II.	129
130	Maulnaskehy	535	2	32	Cork, W.R.	West Carbery (W.D.)	Kilcrohane	Bantry	II.	144
51	Maulrane	214	2	15	Cork, E.R.	Barretts	Grenagh	Cork	II.	49
122	Maulrour	244	2	17	Cork, W.R.	East Carbery (E.D.)	Desertserges	Clonakilty	II.	128
122, 123	Maulrour	340	0	5	Cork, W.R.	East Carbery (E.D.)	Kilmaloda	Clonakilty	II.	129
110, 123	Maulskinlahane	245	2	23	Cork, W.R.	East Carbery (E.D.)	Kilbrittain	Bandon	II.	128
134	Maulvirane	302	2	10	Cork, W.R.	East Carbery (W.D.)	Castleventry	Clonakilty	II.	131
59	Maulyarkane	658	2	4	Kerry	Magunihy	Kilcummin	Killarney	II.	201
30	Maulyclickeen	353	0	13	Cork, E.R.	Duhallow	Kilmeen	Millstreet	II.	73
135	Maulycorcoran	136	0	25	Cork. W.R.	Ibane and Barryroe	Kilkerranmore	Clonakilty	II.	149
59	Maulykeavane	522	3	28	Kerry	Magunihy	Kilcummin	Killarney	II.	201
83, 92	Maulyneill	924	0	21	Kerry	Dunkerron South	Templenoe	Kenmare	II.	185
121, 134	Maulyregan	681	0	22	Cork, W.R.	East Carbery (W.D.)	Ross	Clonakilty	II.	135
35	Maum	304	0	20*a*	Galway	Ballynahinch	Ballindoon	Clifden	IV.	10
75, 85	Maum	104	2	38	Mayo	Murrisk	Kilgeever	Westport	IV.	161
44	Maumagarrane	304	0	22	Kerry	Corkaguiny	Minard	Dingle	II.	180
42	Maumanorig	130	2	13	Kerry	Corkaguiny	Marhin	Dingle	II.	179
45	Maumaratta	2,796	1	35	Mayo	Erris	Kilcommon	Newport	IV.	144
25, 26	Maum East	481	2	37	Galway	Ross	Ross	Oughterard	IV.	74
78, 89, 90	Maumeen	3,510	2	4*b*	Galway	Moycullen	Killannin	Oughterard	IV.	70
99	Maumeen	273	0	21	Mayo	Carra	Ballintober	Castlebar	IV.	125
22	Maumfin	107	1	25	Galway	Ballynahinch	Ballynakill	Clifden	IV.	11
25	Maumgawnagh	725	3	36	Galway	Ross	Ross	Oughterard	IV.	74
36, 45	Maumnahaltora	122	3	19	Kerry	Corkaguiny	Kilgobban	Tralee	II	177
54, 55	Maumnaman	569	2	22*c*	Mayo	Burrishoole	Achill	Newport	IV.	117
12, 13	Maumtra-na	1,648	2	23	Galway	Ross	Ross	Ballinrobe	IV.	74
25	Maum West	355	1	11	Galway	Ross	Ross	Oughterard	IV.	74
132	Maune	142	0	5	Cork, W.R.	West Carbery (W.D.)	Caheragh	Skibbereen	II.	142
119	Maunvough	230	9	18	Cork. W.R.	West Carbery (W.D.)	Caheragh	Skibbereen	II.	142
44, 53	Mauricetown	893	2	21	Limerick	Glenquin	Kil eedy	Newcastle	II.	246
43, 48	Mauritiustown	68	3	6	Wexford	Forth	Rosslare	Wexford	I.	313
42	Mausnarylaan	280	3	23*d*	Clare	Bunratty Lower	Tomfinlough	Ennis	II.	7
56	Mausrevagh	378	1	30	Galway	Clare	Kilcoona	Tuam	IV.	20
60	Mausrower	613	3	26	Kerry	Magunihy	Kilcummin	Killarney	II.	201
38	Mauteoge	103	1	19	Mayo	Tirawley	Crossmolina	Ballina	IV.	166
4	Mautiagh	411	1	31	Leitrim	Rosclogher	Rossinver	Manorhamilton	IV.	112
17	Mavemacullen	398	2	38	Armagh	Orior Lower	Ballymore	Banbridge	III.	55
17	Mavemacullen	239	1	30	Armagh	Orior Lower	Loughgilly	Banbridge	III.	56
22	Maw	424	3	37	Galway	Ballynahinch	Omey	Clifden	IV.	15
109	Mawbeg East	222	1	3	Cork, W.R.	Kinalmeaky	Kill wen	Bandon	II.	152
109	Mawbeg West	110	1	8	Cork, W.R.	Kinalmeaky	Killowen	Bandon	II.	152
88	Mawbrin	76	1	9	Cork. E.R.	Imokilly	Titeskin	Middleton	II.	90
46, 48, 49	Mawillian	499	3	15	Londonderry	Loughinsholin	Artrea	Magherafelt	III.	238
109	Mawmore East	208	2	19	Cork, W.R.	Kinalmeaky	Killowen	Bandon	II.	152
109	Mawmore West	215	1	36	Cork, W.R.	Kinalmeaky	Killowen	Bandon	II.	152
5	Maws	527	0	14	Kildare	North Salt	Laraghbryan	Celbridge	I	75
46	Maxboley	187	3	17	Wexford	Bargy	Ambrosetown	Wexford	I.	304
26	Maxtown	119	2	4	Kilkenny	Callan	Callan	Callan	I.	83
38, 44	Maxwellswalls	1,419	1	9	Antrim	Lower Antrim	Connor	Antrim	III	3
11, 18	Mayboy	134	3	19	Londonderry	Coleraine	Aghadowey	Coleraine	III.	230
18	Mayboy	312	2	34	Londonderry	Coleraine	Errigal	Coleraine	III.	232
7, 8	Maydown	158	0	17	Armagh	Tiranny	Eglish	Armagh	III.	59
14	Maydown	167	0	7*e*	Londonderry	Tirkeeran	Clondermot	Londonderry	III.	248
101	Mayfield	309	1	6*f*	Mayo	Clanmorris	Crossboyne	Claremorris	IV.	133
22, 26, 27	Mayfield or Ballyna- galliagh	303	1	22	Kildare	Offaly West	Duneany	Athy	I.	72

(*a*) Including 1A. 2R. 29P. water.
(*b*) Including 241A. 0R. 38P. water.
(*c*) Including 1A. 2R. 14P. water.
(*d*) Including 12A. 0R. 23P. water.
(*e*) Including 7A. 2R. 37P. Lough Enagh East.
(*f*) Including 18A. 0R. 19P. water.

No. of Sheet of the Ordnance Survey Maps.	Townlands and Towns.	Area in Statute Acres.	County.	Barony.	Parish.	Poor Law Union in 1857.	Townland Census of 1851, Part I.	
		A. R. P.					Vol.	Page
4, 8	Mayfield or Rockets-castle	495 2 8	Waterford	Upperthird	Clonagam	Carrick on Suir	II.	369
78	Mayladstown	576 1 37	Tipperary, S.R.	Iffa and Offa East	Kilcash	Clonmel	II.	313
54	Maylin	63 3 36	Donegal	Raphoe	Raymoghy	Londonderry	III.	142
45	Mayne	107 1 35	Limerick	Glenquin	Mahoonagh	Newcastle	II.	246
19, 22	Mayne	217 0 14	Louth	Ferrard	Mayne	Drogheda	I.	181
51	Mayne	419 3 34	Meath	Dunboyne	Dunboyne	Dunshaughlin	I.	199
2, 3	Mayne	540 0 14a	Westmeath	Fore	Mayne	Granard	I.	271
34	Maynebog	172 3 20	Queen's Co.	Clarmallagh	Aghmacart	Abbeyleix	I.	236
15	Maynetown	235 2 3	Dublin	Coolock	Baldoyle	Dublin North	I.	26
13	Maynooth	234 1 22	Armagh	Oneilland West	Kilmore	Armagh	III.	53
5, 6	Maynooth	483 3 23	Kildare	North Salt	Laraghbryan	Celbridge	I.	75
5	Maynooth South	36 2 5	Kildare	North Salt	Laraghbryan	Celbridge	I.	75
5	MAYNOOTH T.	—	Kildare	North Salt	Laraghbryan	Celbridge	I.	75
17, 18	Mayo	174 0 36	Cavan	Tullygarvey	Drumgoon	Cootehill	III.	88
47, 51	Mayo	674 1 28	Down	Upper Iveagh, Up. pt.	Clonallan	Newry	III.	174
24, 25	Mayo	439 0 12h	Leitrim	Carrigallen	Oughteragh	Bawnboy	IV.	92
31, 36	Mayo	677 1 39	Queen's Co.	Slievemargy	Killabban	Carlow	I.	245
18	Mayogher	442 1 10	Londonderry	Coleraine	Aghadowey	Coleraine	III.	230
90, 91	Mayo Parks	80 3 18	Mayo	Clanmorris	Mayo	Claremorris	IV.	135
21	Maytone	370 0 24	Armagh	Orior Lower	Loughgilly	Newry	III.	57
22, 26	Maytown	278 2 4	Armagh	Orior Upper	Killevy	Newry	III.	58
89	Maytown	372 0 22	Cork, E.R.	Imokilly	Ballintemple	Middleton	II.	84
48	Maytown	133 3 20	Wexford	Forth	Rosslare	Wexford	I.	313
14	Maze	1,563 0 18c	Down	Lower Iveagh, Up. pt.	Blaris	Lisburn	III.	169
8, 13	Mazes	590 1 37	Antrim	Cary	Grange of Drumtullagh	Ballycastle	III.	14
40	Meadagh	142 1 14	Limerick	Coshma	Uregare	Kilmallock	II.	244
38	Meadowpark	63 1 25	Westmeath	Moycashel	Kilbeggan	Tullamore	I.	278
6	Meadow Parks	26 3 3	Antrim	Lower Dunluce	Ballywillin	Coleraine	III.	15
3	Meadow Parks	46 2 16	Antrim	Lower Dunluce	Dunluce	Coleraine	III.	17
18	Meadstown	492 0 26	Cork, E.R.	Fermoy	Farahy	Mitchelstown	II.	79
86, 98	Meadstown	982 2 26	Cork, E.R.	Kerrycurrihy	Liscleary	Kinsale	II.	92
30	Meadstown	1,254 0 18	Meath	Upper Navan	Clonmacduff	Trim	I.	216
22	Meaghsland	42 3 34d	Louth	Ferrard	Termonfeckin	Drogheda	I.	182
16, 24	Meaghy	908 1 31e	Tyrone	Strabane Lower	Ardstraw	Strabane	III.	319
14	Meakstown	174 0 9	Dublin	Coolock	Santry	Dublin North	I.	29
51	Mealclye	105 2 35	Tipperary, S.R.	Kilnamanagh Lower	Donohill	Cashel	II.	323
133	Mealisheen	58 3 2	Cork, W.R.	West Carbery (E.D.)	Kilmacabea	Skibbereen	II.	140
34	Meallaghmore	209 1 8	Kilkenny	Kells	Tullahought	Callan	I.	110
30, 34	Meallaghmore Lower	175 2 21	Kilkenny	Kells	Killamery	Callan	I.	109
30	Meallaghmore Upper	149 2 9	Kilkenny	Kells	Killamery	Callan	I.	109
65, 73	Meallis	1,277 2 20f	Kerry	Dunkerron North	Knockane	Killarney	II.	182
9, 15	Mealough	827 2 10g	Down	Castlereagh Upper	Drumbo	Lisburn	III.	165
53	Meanagh	249 1 8	Clare	Tulla Lower	Kilseily	Limerick	II.	37
98	Meanus	147 0 3	Galway	Leitrim	Kilreekill	Loughrea	IV.	55
57, 65	Meanus	238 2 35	Kerry	Dunkerron North	Killorglin	Killarney	II.	181
57, 65	Meanus	324 0 24h	Kerry	Dunkerron North	Knockane	Killarney	II.	182
39	Meanus	156 3 9	Kerry	Trughanacmy	Castleisland	Tralee	II.	209
39, 48	Meanus	309 3 19i	Kerry	Trughanacmy	Currans	Killarney	II.	209
47	Meanus	105 2 38	Kerry	Trughanacmy	Kiltallagh	Tralee	II.	212
31	Meanus	298 1 27	Limerick	Smallcounty	Glenogra	Croom	II.	260
3	Meath Hill	958 3 36j	Meath	Lower Slane	Ardagh	Kells	I.	222
53	Meath Moor of	90 3 12	Meath	Dunboyne	Dunboyne	Dunshaughlin	I.	199
11, 18	Meavemanougher	176 3 19	Londonderry	Coleraine	Aghadowey	Coleraine	III.	230
16	Medophall	256 3 16	Wexford	Scarawalsh	Toome	Gorey	I.	326
11, 16	Medophall Demesne	163 3 33	Wexford	Scarawalsh	Toome	Gorey	I.	326
2	Meedanmore	341 3 16	Donegal	Inishowen East	Clonca	Inishowen	III.	117
33	Meedian	460 3 25	Westmeath	Fartullagh	Clonfad	Mullingar	I.	268
22, 29	Meehan	267 3 18	Westmeath	Brawny	St. Mary's	Athlone	I.	260
42	Meehaun	74 2 35	Roscommon	Athlone	Killinvoy	Roscommon	IV.	182
17	Meclaghans	1,386 1 27	King's Co.	Geashill	Geashill	Tullamore	IV.	140
97	Meelagulleen	234 2 6	Kerry	Iveragh	Prior	Cahersiveen	II.	198
23	Meelaherragh	403 1 1	Cork, E.R.	Duhallow	Clonfert	Kanturk	II.	68
3	Meelcon	164 0 4	Kerry	Iraghticonnor	Kilnaughtin	Glin	II.	191
37, 38	Meeldrum	131 2 19	Westmeath	Moycashel	Kilbeggan	Tullamore	I.	278
64	Meeleen	361 3 18	Cork, E.R.	Barrymore	Kilquane	Cork	II.	55
24	Meelgarrow	254 3 33	Wexford	Bantry	Templeludigan	New Ross	I.	303
62	Meelick	789 1 19	Clare	Bunratty Lower	Killeely	Limerick	II.	5
24	Meelick	52 0 38	Clare	Inchiquin	Inagh	Ennistimon	II.	25
135, 137	Meelick	443 1 11	Galway	Leitrim	Clonrush	Scarriff	IV.	53
108	Meelick	416 2 15	Galway	Longford	Meelick	Portumna	IV.	61
6	Meelick	591 0 19	Galway	Tiaquin	Boyounagh	Glennamaddy	IV.	76
46, 60	Meelick	240 1 11	Galway	Tiaquin	Killosolan	Mountbellew	IV.	78

(a) Including 5A. 2R. 10P. water.
(b) Including 38A. 3R. 20P. water.
(c) Including 6A. 1R. 16P. water.
(d) Including 2A. 3R. 17P. detached portion.

(e) Including 7A. 3R. 39P. water.
(f) Including 16A. 3R. 15P. water.
(g) Including 0A. 2R. 20P. water.

(h) Including 5A. 3R. 15P. water.
(i) Including 0A. 3R. 24P. detached portion.
(j) Including 38A. 1R. 34P. water.

No. of Sheet of the Ordnance Survey Maps.	Townlands and Towns.	Area in Statute Acres.			County.	Barony.	Parish.	Poor Law Union in 1857.	Townland Census of 1851, Part I.	
		A.	R.	P.					Vol.	Page
85	Meelick	520	3	28	Kerry	Glanarought	Kilgarvan	Kenmare	II.	187
28	Meelick	131	3	14	Leitrim	Leitrim	Mohill	Mohill	IV.	104
18	Meelick	63	1	1	Longford	Moydow	Ballymacormick	Longford	I.	161
69, 70	Meelick	208	3	0a	Mayo	Carra	Turlough	Castlebar	IV.	131
112	Meelick	448	2	24b	Mayo	Clanmorris	Crossboyne	Claremorris	IV.	133
71	Meelick	122	2	9	Mayo	Gallen	Meelick	Swineford	IV.	150
22	Meelick	207	2	31c	Mayo	Tirawley	Killala	Killala	IV.	169
13	Meelick	99	3	12	Queen's Co.	Maryborough East	Borris	Mountmellick	I.	240
13, 18	Meelick	292	3	22	Queen's Co.	Maryborough East	Kilcolmanbane	Mountmellick	I.	241
3	Meelick	1,442	2	21	Queen's Co.	Tinnahinch	Rosenallis	Mountmellick	I.	250
17, 18	Meelick	122	3	38d	Roscommon	Ballintober North	Kilmore	Carᵏ. on Shannon	IV.	187
24	Meelick	316	0	16	Roscommon	Ballintober North	Termonbarry	Strokestown	IV.	188
25	Meelick	33	2	21	Roscommon	Castlereagh	Kiltullagh	Castlereagh	IV.	202
19, 20	Meelick	203	1	39	Roscommon	Frenchpark	Tibohine	Castlereagh	IV.	205
9	Meelick	90	1	4e	Tipperary, N.R.	Lower Ormond	Kilbarron	Borrisokane	II.	284
26	Meelickaduff	99	3	0	Roscommon	Castlereagh	Kilkeevin	Castlereagh	IV.	200
30, 31	Meelickbeg	154	3	35	Galway	Ballymoe	Clonbern	Tuam	IV.	6
102, 112	Meelick Beg	80	3	7	Mayo	Clanmorris	Kilcolman	Claremorris	IV.	134
30	Meelick East	127	3	33	Galway	Dunmore	Tuam	Tuam	IV.	36
30, 31	Meelickmore	264	1	36	Galway	Ballymoe	Dunmore	Tuam	IV.	7
101,102,112	Meelick More	305	3	25	Mayo	Clanmorris	Kilcolman	Claremorris	IV.	134
38	Meelick Park	58	2	1	Sligo	Corran	Cloonoghil	Tobercurry	IV.	225
32, 33	Meelickroe	248	2	28	Roscommon	Castlereagh	Kiltullagh	Castlereagh	IV.	202
16, 29	Meelick West	137	1	30	Galway	Dunmore	Tuam	Tuam	IV.	36
136	Meelmane	226	0	3	Cork, W.R.	Ibane and Barryroe	Lisl:e	Clonakilty	II.	150
27	Meelnagh	11	1	16	Wexford	Ballaghkeen	Meelnagh	Enniscorthy	I.	298
110	Meelon	428	1	18	Cork, W.R.	Kinalmeaky	Ballymodan	Bandon	II.	151
37	Meelragh (Nagur)	262	0	14	Leitrim	Mohill	Mohill	Mohill	IV.	108
35, 37	Meelragh (Saggart)	166	2	36	Leitrim	Mohill	Mohill	Mohill	IV.	108
77	Meelshane	257	0	24	Cork, E.R.	Imokilly	Ballyoughtera	Middleton	II.	84
19	Meeltanagh	124	2	16	Longford	Ardagh	Ardagh	Longford	I.	151
18	Meeltanagh	99	1	14	Longford	Moydow	Moydow	Longford	I.	162
14	Meeltoge	45	0	29f	Cavan	Lower Loughtee	Drumlane	Cavan	III.	80
49	Meeltogues	144	3	11	Tyrone	Omagh East	Kilskeery	Lowtherstown	III.	314
81	Meeltran	325	2	16	Mayo	Costello	Aghamore	Claremorris	IV.	137
32	Meeltraun (Daniel Kelly)	138	0	4	Roscommon	Castlereagh	Kiltullagh	Castlereagh	IV.	202
32	Meeltraun (Denis Kelly)	125	1	37	Roscommon	Castlereagh	Kiltullagh	Castlereagh	IV.	202
32	Meeltraun (O'Flyn)	111	2	24	Roscommon	Castlereagh	Kiltullagh	Castlereagh	IV.	202
32	Meeltraun (Wills)	212	2	18	Roscommon	Castlereagh	Kiltullagh	Castlereagh	IV.	202
6, 11	Meen	552	1	19	Kerry	Iraghticonnor	Listowel	Listowel	II.	193
20, 30	Meenabaltin	463	3	37	Donegal	Inishowen East	Moville Upper	Inishowen	III.	119
14, 15	Meenablagh or Fourth Corgary	766	1	27g	Tyrone	Omagh West	Termonamongan	Castlederg	III.	317
82	Meenaboll	197	2	5	Donegal	Banagh	Inishkeel	Glenties	III.	106
59	Meenaboll	492	0	1	Donegal	Kilmacrenan	Conwal	Letterkenny	III.	126
49, 57	Meenabollagan	914	1	5h	Donegal	Boylagh	Templecrone	Glenties	III.	115
92	Meenabrock	447	1	11	Donegal	Banagh	Killaghtee	Donegal	III.	109
75, 76	Meenabrock	736	0	4i	Donegal	Boylagh	Inishkeel	Glenties	III.	113
95	Meenabrock	918	3	7j	Donegal	Tirhugh	Donegal	Donegal	III.	145
83	Meenacahan	486	0	23	Donegal	Banagh	Inver	Donegal	III.	107
93	Meenacally	175	2	26	Donegal	Banagh	Killymard	Donegal	III.	111
100	Meenacargagh or Raneany Barr	991	3	10k	Donegal	Tirhugh	Drumhome	Donegal	III.	146
57, 65	Meenacarn	389	3	25l	Donegal	Boylagh	Lettermacward	Glenties	III.	114
74	Meenachallow	701	1	0	Donegal	Boylagh	Killybegs Lower	Glenties	III.	114
92	Meenacharbet	82	1	10	Donegal	Banagh	Inver	Donegal	III.	107
81, 90	Meenacharvey	1,289	0	7	Donegal	Banagh	Glencolumbkille	Glenties	III.	105
66, 67, 75	Meenachuit	370	2	10	Donegal	Boylagh	Inishkeel	Glenties	III.	113
91	Meenachullalan	252	2	28	Donegal	Banagh	Killybegs Upper	Glenties	III.	110
50, 58, 59	Meenachullion	2,348	3	18m	Donegal	Boylagh	Inishkeel	Glenties	III.	113
23, 24	Meenaclady	1,955	2	22	Donegal	Kilmacrenan	Tullaghobegly	Dunfanaghy	III.	132
56, 57	Meenacloghcor	152	3	28n	Donegal	Boylagh	Templecrone	Glenties	III.	115
75, 84	Meenacloghspar	286	1	6	Donegal	Banagh	Inver	Donegal	III.	107
83, 92	Meenacloy	300	3	27	Donegal	Banagh	Killaghtee	Donegal	III.	109
32	Meenacloy	416	2	9o	Tyrone	Omagh West	Longfield West	Castlederg	III.	316
13, 14	Meenacloyabane	1,337	1	16p	Fermanagh	Magheraboy	Inishmacsaint	Ballyshannon	III.	213
12	Meenacrane	716	3	3q	Tyrone	Strabane Upper	Bodoney Upper	Gortin	III.	324
81	Meenacross	330	1	36	Donegal	Banagh	Glencolumbkille	Glenties	III.	105
57	Meenacross	254	3	29r	Donegal	Boylagh	Templecrone	Glenties	III.	115
27	Meenacross or Larganreagh Barr	63	2	35	Donegal	Kilmacrenan	Mevagh	Millford	III.	130
51, 59	Meenacung	593	3	16	Donegal	Kilmacrenan	Conwal	Letterkenny	III.	126

(a) Including 0A. 0R. 39P. water.	(g) Including 4A. 0R. 20P. water.	(m) Including 44A. 3R. 30P. water.
(b) Including 5A. 1R. 9P. water.	(h) Including 111A. 0R. 36P. water.	(n) Including 13A. 3R. 0P. water.
(c) Including 7A. 0R. 12P. water.	(i) Including 37A. 3R. 5P. water.	(o) Including 2A. 1R. 7P. water.
(d) Including 2A. 3R. 30P. water.	(j) Including 15A. 1R. 27P. water.	(p) Including 5A. 0R. 38P. water.
(e) Including 9A. 0R. 16P. water.	(k) Including 30A. 2R. 3P. water.	(q) Including 4A. 0R. 10P. water.
(f) Including 1A. 3R. 22P. water.	(l) Including 8A. 0R. 2P. water.	(r) Including 4A. 3R. 15P. water.

No. of Sheet of the Ordnance Survey Maps.	Townlands and Towns.	Area in Statute Acres.	County.	Barony.	Parish.	Poor Law Union in 1857.	Townland Census of 1851, Part I. Vol.	Page
		A. R. P.					Vol.	Page
33, 42	Meenacung	1,170 2 18a	Donegal	Kilmacrenan	Tullaghobegly	Dunfanaghy	III.	132
72,73,81,82	Meenacurrin	1,795 2 37b	Donegal	Banagh	Inishkeel	Glenties	III.	106
83, 92	Meenacurrin	226 1 13c	Donegal	Banagh	Inver	Donegal	III.	107
60	Meenadaura or Drumnahough Mountain	491 1 27	Donegal	Raphoe	Conwal	Stranorlar	III.	137
81	Meenadiff	386 1 8d	Donegal	Banagh	Glencolumbkille	Glenties	III.	105
10, 19	Meenadiff	420 1 30	Donegal	Inishowen West	Mintiaghs or Barr of Inch	Inishowen	III.	121
58, 59	Meenadoan	998 2 34	Donegal	Boylagh	Inishkeel	Glenties	III.	113
32, 33	Meenadoan	731 3 30e	Tyrone	Omagh West	Longfield West	Castlederg	III.	316
11, 18	Meenadoo	1,047 0 4f	Tyrone	Strabane Upper	Bodoney Lower	Gortin	III.	323
81	Meenadreen	197 1 11	Donegal	Banagh	Glencolumbkille	Glenties	III.	105
83	Meenadreen	309 3 16	Donegal	Banagh	Killaghtee	Donegal	III.	109
94	Meenadreen	805 1 13	Donegal	Tirhugh	Donegal	Donegal	III.	145
115	Meenaduff	32 0 23	Cork, W.R.	Bear	Killaconenagh	Castletown	II.	125
32, 41	Meenaduff	298 0 33	Donegal	Kilmacrenan	Tullaghobegly	Dunfanaghy	III.	132
22	Meenafergus	697 2 31	Tyrone	Omagh West	Termonamongan	Castlederg	III.	317
51, 59	Meenagannive	484 0 6	Donegal	Kilmacrenan	Gartan	Letterkenny	III.	127
50	Meenagar	434 0 35	Tyrone	Omagh East	Dromore	Omagh	III.	311
11	Meenagarragh	207 1 35	Tyrone	Strabane Upper	Bodoney Upper	Gortin	III.	324
8, 9	Meenagh	425 2 0	Leitrim	Drumahaire	Cloonclare	Manorhamilton	IV.	93
47	Meenagh	292 1 16	Tyrone	Dungannon Middle	Clonoe	Dungannon	III.	300
1	Meenagh Hill	251 1 8	Tyrone	Strabane Lower	Donaghedy	Strabane	III.	321
13, 14	Meenagleragh	700 2 29g	Fermanagh	Magheraboy	Devenish	Ballyshannon	III.	211
23, 24, 31	Meenagleragh	890 0 12	Sligo	Leyny	Kilmacteige	Tobercurry	IV.	231
30, 31	Meenaglogh	994 0 28	Sligo	Leyny	Kilmacteige	Tobercurry	IV.	231
29	Meenagloghrane	365 0 8	Cork, E.R.	Duhallow	Cullen	Millstreet	II.	70
82	Meenagolan	809 1 32	Donegal	Banagh	Inishkeel	Glenties	III.	106
92	Meenagolan	183 1 2h	Donegal	Banagh	Killaghtee	Donegal	III.	109
67	Meenagolan	625 3 23	Donegal	Boylagh	Inishkeel	Glenties	III.	113
87	Meenagolan	1,147 1 34	Donegal	Raphoe	Donaghmore	Stranorlar	III.	138
34, 43	Meenagoppoge	569 1 14	Donegal	Kilmacrenan	Tullaghobegly	Dunfanaghy	III.	132
11	Meenagorp	296 1 35	Tyrone	Strabane Upper	Bodoney Upper	Gortin	III.	324
19, 29	Meenagory	736 2 13	Donegal	Inishowen West	Fahan Lower	Inishowen	III.	120
65	Meenagowan	195 2 29i	Donegal	Boylagh	Lettermacward	Glenties	III.	114
49	Meenagowan	209 2 34	Tyrone	Omagh East	Dromore	Omagh	III.	311
40	Meenagowna	69 1 30j	Donegal	Boylagh	Templecrone	Glenties	III.	115
83,84,92,93	Meenagrau	944 2 28	Donegal	Banagh	Inver	Donegal	III.	107
83, 92	Meenagranoge	737 3 7k	Donegal	Banagh	Inver	Donegal	III.	107
4	Meenagraun	439 1 37	Leitrim	Rosclogher	Rossinver	Manorhamilton	IV.	112
77	Meenagrauv	614 1 0l	Donegal	Raphoe	Kilteevoge	Stranorlar	III.	139
68, 69	Meenagrauv	346 3 1	Donegal	Raphoe	Stranorlar	Stranorlar	III.	143
73, 74	Meenagrillagh	742 2 14m	Donegal	Boylagh	Inishkeel	Glenties	III.	113
22, 23	Meenagrogan	333 2 6n	Tyrone	Omagh West	Termonamongan	Castlederg	III.	317
66, 75	Meenagrubby	348 0 20	Donegal	Boylagh	Inishkeel	Glenties	III.	113
84	Meenaguse Beg	302 3 18	Donegal	Banagh	Inver	Donegal	III.	107
75, 84	Meenaguse More	737 3 14	Donegal	Banagh	Killymard	Donegal	III.	111
41	Meenaheery Glebe	137 0 12o	Tyrone	Omagh West	Longfield West	Castlederg	III.	316
87	Meenahinnis	247 3 35	Donegal	Raphoe	Donaghmore	Stranorlar	III.	138
70, 79	Meenahoney	183 3 39	Donegal	Raphoe	Donaghmore	Stranorlar	III.	138
50	Meenahony	996 1 34	Cork, E.R.	East Muskerry	Donaghmore	Macroom	II.	103
68	Meenahorna	963 2 30	Donegal	Raphoe	Kilteevoge	Stranorlar	III.	139
14, 22	Meenakeeran	2,305 2 27p	Tyrone	Omagh West	Termonamongan	Castlederg	III.	317
82	Meenakillew	548 2 20	Donegal	Banagh	Inishkeel	Glenties	III.	106
74, 75, 83	Meenakilwirra	442 3 27	Donegal	Boylagh	Killybegs Lower	Glenties	III.	114
68	Meenalaban	563 0 9	Donegal	Raphoe	Convoy	Stranorlar	III.	136
65, 74	Meenalargan	434 1 8	Donegal	Boylagh	Inishkeel	Glenties	III.	113
20, 21	Meenaleavin	588 3 4q	Donegal	Inishowen East	Moville Upper	Inishowen	III.	119
41	Meenalecky	498 1 0	Donegal	Boylagh	Templecrone	Glenties	III.	115
66, 75, 76	Meenaleenaghan	495 0 34	Donegal	Boylagh	Inishkeel	Glenties	III.	113
67	Meenalig	466 0 3	Donegal	Raphoe	Kilteevoge	Stranorlar	III.	139
18	Meenalooban	130 2 11	Donegal	Inishowen West	Desertegny	Inishowen	III.	120
24	Meenamaddoo	461 1 21	Sligo	Leyny	Kilmacteige	Tobercurry	IV.	231
66, 75	Meenamalragh	593 3 13	Donegal	Boylagh	Inishkeel	Glenties	III.	113
66, 75	Meenamanragh	622 0 37	Donegal	Boylagh	Inishkeel	Glenties	III.	113
29	Meenamullaghan	323 0 31	Donegal	Inishowen West	Fahan Lower	Inishowen	III.	120
23, 32	Meenamullan	629 2 31r	Tyrone	Omagh West	Termonamongan	Castlederg	III.	317
33,34,40,41	Meenan	391 0 28	Down	Upper Iveagh, Up. pt	Aghaderg	Banbridge	III.	174
74, 75	Meenanall	307 1 19s	Donegal	Boylagh	Inishkeel	Glenties	III.	113
68	Meenanamph	510 3 25	Donegal	Raphoe	Kilteevoge	Stranorlar	III.	139
17	Meenanare	596 3 29	Kerry	Clanmaurice	Duagh	Listowel	II.	168
66, 67	Meenanarwa	550 1 20	Donegal	Boylagh	Inishkeel	Glenties	III.	113
53	Meenane	559 0 0	Cork, E.R.	Barrymore	Ardnageehy	Fermoy	II.	50

No. of Sheet of the Ordnance Survey Maps.	Townlands and Towns.	Area in Statute Acres.			County.	Barony.	Parish.	Poor Law Union in 1857.	Townland Census of 1851, Part I.	
		A.	R.	P.					Vol.	Page
28	Meenanea	344	0	31	Tyrone	Dungannon Upper	Kildress	Cookstown	III.	309
81, 90	Meenaneary	823	2	38	Donegal	Banagh	Glencolumbkille	Glenties	III.	105
100, 101	Meenannellison	2,188	1	9a	Donegal	Tirhugh	Templecarn	Donegal	III.	149
32, 33	Meenanillar	564	0	19	Donegal	Kilmacrenan	Tullaghobegly	Dunfanaghy	III.	132
68	Meenanilta	257	1	30	Donegal	Raphoe	Stranorlar	Stranorlar	III.	143
82, 91	Meenapeaky	302	1	36	Donegal	Banagh	Inishkeel	Glenties	III.	106
6	Meenaphuill	375	1	6b	Leitrim	Rosclogher	Killasnet	Manorhamilton	IV.	110
20	Meenarainy	313	2	6	Fermanagh	Clanawley	Cleenish	Ballyshannon	III.	191
12, 13	Meenarodda	2,157	1	28	Tyrone	Strabane Upper	Bodoney Lower	Gortin	III.	324
91	Meenaroshin	444	1	25c	Donegal	Banagh	Killybegs Upper	Glenties	III.	111
28	Meenascallagh	302	1	15	Tyrone	Dungannon Upper	Kildress	Cookstown	III.	309
72, 81	Meenasillagh	653	2	5	Donegal	Banagh	Glencolumbkille	Glenties	III.	105
3, 5	Meenaslieve	211	1	33	Cavan	Tullyhaw	Killinagh	Enniskillen	III.	92
67	Meenasrone North	498	0	30d	Donegal	Boylagh	Inishkeel	Glenties	III.	113
76	Meenasrone South	308	3	10	Donegal	Boylagh	Inishkeel	Glenties	III.	113
84	Meenataggart	172	0	14	Donegal	Banagh	Killymard	Donegal	III.	111
14, 22	Meenatarriff	127	0	35	Cork, E.R.	Duhallow	Clonfert	Kanturk	II.	68
66, 67	Meenatawy	458	1	19	Donegal	Boylagh	Inishkeel	Glenties	III.	113
82	Meenateia	367	0	13	Donegal	Banagh	Inishkeel	Glenties	III.	106
59	Meenatinny	1,503	3	2	Donegal	Kilmacrenan	Conwal	Letterkenny	III.	126
45	Meenatole	199	2	37	Donegal	Kilmacrenan	Conwal	Millford	III.	126
3	Meenatully	550	0	22e	Fermanagh	Lurg	Belleek	Ballyshannon	III.	203
90	Meenavaghran	757	3	29f	Donegal	Banagh	Glencolumbkille	Glenties	III.	105
75	Meenavale	420	0	32	Donegal	Boylagh	Inishkeel	Glenties	III.	113
82, 83	Meenavally	684	1	7	Donegal	Banagh	Inishkeel	Glenties	III.	106
69	Meenavally	149	3	31	Donegal	Raphoe	Convoy	Stranorlar	III.	136
30	Meenavanaghan	352	2	21	Donegal	Inishowen East	Moville Upper	Inishowen	III.	119
100	Meenavanaghan or Greaghs Barr	232	1	5	Donegal	Tirhugh	Drumhome	Donegal	III.	146
89, 90	Meenavean	440	2	3	Donegal	Banagh	Glencolumbkille	Glenties	III.	105
69	Meenavoy	837	3	30	Donegal	Raphoe	Stranorlar	Stranorlar	III.	143
74, 83	Meenawannia	270	3	16	Donegal	Boylagh	Killybegs Lower	Glenties	III.	114
20, 25	Meenawargy	215	3	22	Fermanagh	Clanawley	Cleenish	Enniskillen	III.	191
84	Meenawilderg	159	3	19	Donegal	Banagh	Killymard	Donegal	III.	111
52	Meenawilligan	221	1	14	Donegal	Kilmacrenan	Gartan	Letterkenny	III.	127
91	Meenawley	137	0	6	Donegal	Banagh	Killybegs Upper	Glenties	III.	111
92	Meenawullaghan	368	2	23	Donegal	Banagh	Inver	Donegal	III.	108
68	Meenbane	804	3	20	Donegal	Raphoe	Stranorlar	Stranorlar	III.	143
41, 49	Meenbannad	1,607	2	28g	Donegal	Boylagh	Templecrone	Glenties	III.	115
23, 31	Meenbannivane	1,473	1	8	Kerry	Trughanacmy	Castleisland	Tralee	II.	209
77, 86, 95	Meenbog	4,444	1	6	Donegal	Raphoe	Donaghmore	Stranorlar	III.	138
68	Meenbog	442	2	10	Donegal	Raphoe	Kilteevoge	Stranorlar	III.	139
32	Meenbog	881	2	32h	Tyrone	Omagh West	Longfield West	Castlederg	III.	316
91, 97	Meenboy	199	0	31	Donegal	Banagh	Kilcar	Glenties	III.	108
35	Meenbunone	571	3	39	Donegal	Kilmacrenan	Kilmacrenan	Millford	III.	129
59, 60	Meencargagh	358	0	35	Donegal	Kilmacrenan	Conwal	Stranorlar	III.	126
77	Meencargagh	764	0	15	Donegal	Raphoe	Stranorlar	Stranorlar	III.	143
24	Meencargagh	502	3	14	Tyrone	Omagh West	Longfield West	Castlederg	III.	316
23, 32	Meencarriga	334	3	29	Tyrone	Omagh West	Termonamongan	Castlederg	III.	317
32	Meenclogher	401	1	3d	Tyrone	Omagh West	Termonamongan	Castlederg	III.	317
34	Meencoolasheskin	186	1	1	Donegal	Kilmacrenan	Raymunterdoney	Dunfanaghy	III.	131
41,42,49,50	Meencorwick	1,013	2	21j	Donegal	Kilmacrenan	Tullaghobegly	Dunfanaghy	III.	132
10	Meencraig	368	0	17	Londonderry	Coleraine	Aghadowey	Coleraine	III.	230
10, 17	Meencraig	569	2	31	Londonderry	Coleraine	Errigal	Coleraine	III.	232
77, 86	Meencrumlin	620	3	6	Donegal	Raphoe	Stranorlar	Stranorlar	III.	143
19,20,29,30	Meendacalliagh	1,435	0	17	Donegal	Inishowen West	Fahan Lower	Inishowen	III.	120
6, 11	Meendamph	1,640	2	24	Tyrone	Strabane Lower	Donaghedy	Gortin	III.	321
33, 42	Meenderrygamph	1,300	3	10	Donegal	Kilmacrenan	Tullaghobegly	Dunfanaghy	III.	132
49,50,57,58	Meenderryherk Glebe	900	1	20k	Donegal	Boylagh	Templecrone	Glenties	III.	115
41	Meenderrynasloe	1,005	3	9	Donegal	Boylagh	Templecrone	Glenties	III.	115
41	Meenderryowan	507	2	14l	Donegal	Boylagh	Templecrone	Glenties	III.	115
10, 19	Meendoran	1,050	3	21m	Donegal	Inishowen East	Clonmany	Inishowen	III.	117
57	Meendrain	482	3	24n	Donegal	Boylagh	Templecrone	Glenties	III.	115
21	Meendurragha	276	0	28	Cork, E.R.	Duhallow	Kilmeen	Kanturk	II.	73
108, 118	Meeneen	358	2	21	Galway	Longford	Fahy	Portumna	IV.	58
14	Meeneeshal	686	2	24	Cork, E.R.	Duhallow	Clonfert	Kanturk	II.	68
27, 35, 36	Meenformal	766	0	38o	Donegal	Kilmacrenan	Mevagh	Millford	III.	130
82, 83, 92	Meengilcarry	337	0	12	Donegal	Banagh	Inishkeel	Glenties	III.	106
59, 67	Meengilcarry	450	0	34	Donegal	Boylagh	Inishkeel	Glenties	III.	113
14	Meengorman	495	2	6	Cork, E.R.	Duhallow	Kilteevoge	Stranorlar	III.	139
59	Meenirroy	543	0	34	Donegal	Kilmacrenan	Conwal	Letterkenny	III.	126
38	Meeniska	58	3	2	Westmeath	Moycashel	Kilbeggan	Tullamore	I.	278
5, 14	Meenkearagh	635	3	6	Cork, E.R.	Duhallow	Clonfert	Kanturk	II.	69

(a) Including 236A. 1R. 17P. water.
(b) Including 70A. 0R. 16P. water.
(c) Including 14A. 0R. 37P. water.
(d) Including 20A. 0R. 28P. water.
(e) Including 68A. 2R. 18P. water.
(f) Including 37A. 3R. 28P. water.
(g) Including 86A. 0R. 31P. water.
(h) Including 22A. 2R. 37P. water.
(i) Including 5A. 1R. 30P. water.
(j) Including 21A. 0R. 6P. water.
(k) Including 15A. 1R. 15P. water.
(l) Including 32A. 3R. 35P. water.
(m) Including 112A. 3R. 8P. water.
(n) Including 28A. 2R. 19P. water.
(o) Including 13A. 2R. 10P. water.

No. of Sheet of the Ordnance Survey Maps.	Townlands and Towns.	Area in Statute Acres.			County.	Barony.	Parish.	Poor Law Union in 1857.	Townland Census of 1851, Part I.	
		A.	R.	P.					Vol.	Page
29	Meenkeeragh . .	812	1	38	Donegal . .	Inishowen West .	Fahan Lower . .	Inishowen .	III.	120
12, 13	Meenkeeragh . .	619	0	32a	Leitrim . .	Drumahaire . .	Clooncläre . .	Manorhamilton .	IV.	93
10, 16	Meenlagh . .	285	3	19	Meath . .	Upper Kells . .	Loughan or Castle-keeran . .	Kells . .	I.	207
35, 36	Meenlaragh . .	412	1	31	Donegal . .	Kilmacrenan . .	Mevagh . . .	Millford . .	III.	130
24	Meenlaragh . .	381	3	31	Donegal . .	Kilmacrenan . .	Tullaghobegly . .	Dunfanaghy .	III.	132
5, 17	Meenleana . .	252	3	27	Galway . .	Dunmore . .	Dunmore . .	Tuam . .	IV.	34
57	Meenlecknalore . .	840	0	18b	Donegal . .	Boylagh . .	Templecrone . .	Glenties . .	III.	115
31	Meenleitrim North .	684	2	37	Kerry . .	Trughanacmy .	Castleisland . .	Tralee . .	II.	209
31	Meenleitrim South .	786	3	32	Kerry . .	Trughanacmy . .	Castleisland . .	Tralee . .	II.	209
12, 13	Meenletterbale .	1,259	0	9	Donegal . .	Inishowen East .	Moville Lower . .	Inishowen . .	III.	119
78, 79	Meenlougher . .	328	0	18c	Donegal . .	Raphoe . . .	Donaghmore . .	Strabane . .	III.	138
48, 49	Meenmore . .	1,548	2	34d	Donegal . .	Boylagh . .	Templecrone . .	Glenties . .	III.	115
6	Meenmore . .	226	2	36	Fermanagh .	Lurg . . .	Magheraculmoney .	Lowtherstown .	III.	208
45	Meenmore . .	21ı	3	22	Sligo . .	Corran . .	Toomour . .	Boyle . .	IV.	228
58,59,66,67	Meenmore East .	1,125	1	31	Donegal . .	Boylagh . .	Inishkeel . .	Glenties . .	III.	113
58, 66	Meenmore West .	1,260	1	10	Donegal . .	Boylagh . .	Inishkeel . .	Glenties . .	III.	113
33, 41	Meenmossogue Glebe	347	0	0e	Tyrone . .	Omagh West .	Longfield West .	Castlederg .	III.	316
57, 67	Meennacloghfinny .	1,337	1	15f	Mayo . .	Burrishoole .	Burrishoole . .	Newport . .	IV.	119
60	Meennagishagh .	154	1	4	Kerry . .	Magunihy . .	Kilcummin . .	Killarney . .	II.	201
17, 23	Meennahorna .	352	3	6	Kerry . .	Clanmaurice .	Duagh . .	Listowel . .	II.	168
4	Meennaraheeny .	813	2	30	Cork, E.R. .	Duhallow . .	Clonfert . .	Kanturk . .	II.	68
36	Meennascarty . .	147	3	34	Kerry . .	Corkaguiny .	Killiney . .	Dingle . .	II.	178
8, 9	Meenogahane . .	625	2	17	Kerry . .	Clanmaurice .	Killury . .	Listowel . .	II.	171
55	Meenoughter . .	278	2	33	Cork, E.R. .	Imokilly . .	Ardagh . .	Youghal . .	II.	83
91	Meenreagh . .	876	3	0g	Donegal . .	Banagh . .	Killybegs Upper .	Glenties . .	III.	111
28, 37	Meenreagh . .	176	0	31	Donegal . .	Kilmacrenan .	Killygarvan . .	Millford . .	III.	128
35, 36	Meenreagh . .	439	2	7h	Donegal . .	Kilmacrenan . .	Kilmacrenan . .	Millford . .	III.	129
87	Meenreagh . .	1,738	0	39	Donegal . .	Raphoe . .	Donaghmore . .	Stranorlar .	III.	138
5, 14	Meenroe . .	244	3	10	Cork, E.R. .	Duhallow . .	Clonfert . .	Kanturk . .	II.	69
21, 29	Meenross . .	538	0	35	Clare . .	Tulla Upper .	Moynoe . .	Scarriff .	II.	40
14	Meens . . .	787	0	4	Cork, E.R. .	Duhallow . .	Clonfert . .	Kanturk . .	II.	69
21, 22	Meens . . .	323	1	25	Cork, E.R. .	Duhallow . .	Kilmeen . .	Kanturk . .	II.	73
17, 23	Meenscovane . .	277	1	6i	Kerry . .	Clanmaurice .	Duagh . .	Listowel . .	II.	168
100, 101, 104, 105	Meensheefin .	2,992	1	15j	Donegal . .	Tirhugh . .	Templecarn . .	Donegal . .	III.	149
30	Meenskeha East .	222	3	17	Cork, E.R. .	Duhallow . .	Cullen . .	Millstreet .	II.	70
30	Meenskeha West .	250	0	22	Cork, E.R. .	Duhallow . .	Cullen . .	Millstreet .	II.	70
84	Meentacor . .	299	2	17	Donegal . .	Banagh . .	Inver . .	Donegal . .	III.	108
84	Meentacreeghan .	408	0	11	Donegal . .	Banagh . .	Inver . .	Donegal . .	III.	108
82, 91	Meentadun . .	202	0	21	Donegal . .	Banagh . .	Killybegs Upper .	Glenties . .	III.	111
28	Meentagh . .	274	1	9	Donegal . .	Kilmacrenan .	Clondavaddog .	Millford .	III.	125
28	Meentaghconlan .	252	2	31	Donegal . .	Kilmacrenan .	Clondavaddog .	Millford .	III.	125
28	Meentaghmore .	269	0	7	Donegal . .	Kilmacrenan .	Clondavaddog .	Millford .	III.	125
96, 97	Meentakeeraghan .	92	3	31	Donegal . .	Banagh . .	Kilcar . .	Glenties . .	III.	108
83	Meentanadea . .	217	0	37	Donegal . .	Banagh . .	Killybegs Lower .	Glenties . .	III.	110
83	Meentanakill . .	296	2	27k	Donegal . .	Banagh . .	Inver . .	Donegal . .	III.	108
82	Meentashesk . .	338	1	6l	Donegal . .	Banagh . .	Inishkeel . .	Glenties . .	III.	106
5, 14	Meentinny East .	560	2	17	Cork, E.R. .	Duhallow . .	Clonfert . .	Kanturk . .	II.	69
4, 5, 13, 14	Meentinny West .	1,403	3	6	Cork, E.R. .	Duhallow . .	Clonfert . .	Kanturk . .	II.	69
60	Meentoges . .	394	2	16	Kerry . .	Magunihy . .	Kilcummin . .	Killarney . .	II.	201
7	Meentolla . .	494	1	35	Limerick . .	Owneybeg . .	Abington . .	Limerick . .	II.	251
1	Meentullyclogh .	90	2	19	Fermanagh .	Lurg . .	Drumkeeran .	Lowtherstown .	III.	206
82,83,91,92	Meentullynagarn .	366	3	31	Donegal . .	Banagh . .	Killaghtee . .	Glenties . .	III.	109
60, 68	Meentycat . .	1,577	1	30	Donegal . .	Raphoe . .	Convoy . .	Stranorlar .	III.	136
21, 29	Meentyflugh . .	347	1	26	Cork, E. R. .	Duhallow . .	Kilmeen . .	Kanturk . .	II.	73
59	Meentygrannagh .	839	3	31	Donegal . .	Kilmacrenan .	Couwal . .	Stranorlar .	III.	126
66, 67	Meentymorgal .	469	0	28m	Donegal . .	Boylagh . .	Inishkeel . .	Glenties . .	III.	113
139	Meenvane . .	154	1	0	Cork, W.R. .	We-t Carbery(W.D.)	Skull . .	Skull . .	II.	146
30	Meenwaun . .	68	1	2	King's Co. .	Garrycastle . .	Reynagh . .	Parsonstown .	I.	138
30	Meenyanly . .	642	2	26	Donegal . .	Inishowen West .	Muff . .	Londonderry .	III.	121
83, 92	Meenybraddan .	668	2	21m	Donegal . .	Banagh . .	Inver . .	Donegal . .	III.	108
90, 91	Meenychanon . .	471	1	24	Donegal . .	Banazh . .	Kilcar . .	Glenties . .	III.	109
91, 97	Meenyhooghan .	180	2	28	Donegal . .	Banagh . .	Killybegs Upper .	Glenties . .	III.	111
35, 43	Meenyline North .	957	1	24	Limerick . .	Glenquin . .	Monagay . .	Newcastle .	II.	247
43	Meenyline South .	531	2	5	Limerick . .	Glenquin . .	Monagay . .	Newcastle .	II.	247
11, 12, 16	Meenymore . .	1,044	0	37o	Leitrim . .	Drumahaire . .	Clooncläre . .	Manorhamilton .	IV.	93
23, 24	Meenyvoughaun .	567	0	35	Kerry . .	Trughanacmy .	Brosna . .	Tralee . .	II.	208
11	Meera . .	174	1	39	Roscommon .	Boyle . .	Tumna . .	Car'.on Shannon	IV.	198
87	Meermihil . .	51	2	26	Mayo . .	Murrisk . .	Oughaval . .	Westport . .	IV.	162
38	Meersparkfarm or Demesne . .	238	2	0	Westmeath .	Moycashel . .	Kilbeggan . .	Tullamore .	I.	278
61	Meeshal . .	215	3	0	Cork, E.D. .	East Muskerry .	Magourney . .	Macroom . .	II.	105

(a) Including 12A. 3R. 22P. water.
(b) Including 18A. 1R. 34P. water.
(c) Including 1A. 3R. 31P. water.
(d) Including 137A. 2P. water.
(e) Including 26A. 2R. 15F. water.

(f) Including 6ı. 1ı. 38P. water.
(g) Including 4A. 1R. 35P. water.
(h) Including 1A. 2R. 28P. water.
(i) Including 4A. 2R. 0P. water.
(j) Including 55A. 2R. 22P. water.

(k) Including 3A. 2R. 10P. water.
(l) Including 4A. 0R. 4P. water.
(m) Including 58A. 3R. 18P. water.
(n) Including 4A. 1R. 36P. water.
(o) Including 7A. 0R. 29P. water.

No. of Sheet of the Ordnance Survey Maps.	Townlands and Towns.	Area in Statute Acres.	County.	Barony.	Parish.	Poor Law Union in 1857.	Townland Census of 1851, Part I.	
		A.　R.　P.					Vol.	Page
35	Meetinghouse-hill .	83　3　14	Tyrone . .	Omagh East . .	Drumragh . .	Omagh . .	III.	312
35	Meetings . .	343　0　37	Wicklow . .	Ballinacor North .	Rathdrum . .	Rathdrum . .	I.	347
41, 46	Megargy . .	441　3　38	Londonderry .	Loughinsholin .	Magherafelt . .	Magherafelt .	III.	243
10	Meggagh East .	31　3　3	Clare . .	Burren . . .	Carran . .	Ballyvaghan .	II.	11
9, 10	Meggagh West .	119　1　19	Clare . .	Burren . . .	Carran . .	Ballyvaghan .	II.	11
114	Meheranspark .	178　2　17	Galway . .	Loughrea . .	Isertkelly . .	Loughrea . .	IV.	63
29	Meigh . .	434　1　8	Armagh . .	Orior Upper . .	Killevy . .	Newry . .	III.	58
61	Meldrum . .	589　2　15	Tipperary, S.R.	Middlethird . .	Brickendown . .	Cashel . .	II.	325
5	Melkagh . .	183　3　13	Longford . .	Longford . .	Killoe . .	Longford . .	I.	159
16	Melkernagh . .	81　1　22	Longford . .	Granard . .	Granard . .	Granard . .	I.	156
24	Mell . .	1,141　0　2a	Louth . .	Ferrard & Municipal Borough of Drogheda	Tullyallen . .	Drogheda . .	I.	183
40	Mellamore . .	18　2　23	Donegal . .	Boylagh . . .	Templecrone . .	Glenties . .	III.	115
44, 45	Mellefontstown .	566　1　7	Cork, E.R. .	Barrymore . .	Gortroe . .	Fermoy . .	II.	55
20,21,23,24	Mellifont . .	367　0　5	Louth . .	Ferrard . .	Tullyallen . .	Drogheda . .	I.	183
13, 19	Mellifont . .	264　3　19	Meath . .	Upper Slane . .	Monknewtown .	Drogheda . .	I.	224
13, 19	Mellifont . .	460　1　6	Meath . .	Upper Slane . .	Tullyallen . .	Drogheda . .	I.	225
23	Mellifont Park or Louth Hill .	129　1　1	Louth . .	Ferrard . .	Tullyallen . .	Drogheda . .	I.	183
111	Mellifontstown .	323　1　36	Cork, E.R. .	Kinsale . .	Dunderrow . .	Kinsale . .	II.	99
111, 112	Mellifontstown .	282　1　24	Cork, E.R. .	Kinsale . .	Ringcurran . .	Kinsale . .	II.	100
48, 49	Mellisson . .	635　1　30	Tipperary, S.R.	Slievardagh . .	Buolick . .	Urlingford . .	II.	332
4	Mellon . .	580　2　28	Limerick . .	Kenry . .	Ardcanny . .	Rathkeale . .	II.	248
7, 8	Melmore . .	374　1　6b	Donegal . .	Kilmacrenan . .	Mevagh . .	Millford . .	III.	130
40, 43	Melville . . .	270　3　11	Kilkenny . .	Ida . . .	Dunkitt . .	Waterford . .	I.	101
31	Memory . .	43　3　37	Kilkenny . .	Kells . .	Kilmaganny . .	Callan . .	I.	109
18	Menagh . . .	10　0　0	Londonderry .	Coleraine . .	Aghadowey . .	Coleraine . .	III.	230
98	Menamny . .	127　1　7	Donegal . .	Banagh . .	Killaghtee . .	Donegal . .	III.	109
88	Meneen . . .	154　1　22	Mayo . .	Burrishoole . .	Aghagower . .	Westport . .	IV.	118
82	Menlough . .	921　1　27c	Galway . .	Galway . .	Oranmore . .	Galway . .	IV.	37
59	Menlough Commons	223　2　9	Galway . .	Tiaquin . .	Killoscobe . .	Mountbellew .	IV.	78
59	Menlough Eighter .	476　2　31	Galway . .	Tiaquin . .	Killoscobe . .	Mountbellew .	IV.	78
59	Menlough Oughter .	303　1　37	Galway . .	Tiaquin . .	Killoscobe . .	Mountbellew .	IV.	78
82	MENLOUGH T. .	—	Galway . .	Galway . .	Oranmore . .	Galway . .	IV.	37
6, 7	Mentrim . .	280　3　37	Meath . .	Lower Slane . .	Inishmot . .	Ardee . .	I.	223
17	Menus . . .	152　1　33	Galway . .	Dunmore . .	Dunmore . .	Tuam . .	IV.	34
17	Menus Park . .	99　1　30	Galway . .	Dunmore . .	Dunmore . .	Tuam . .	IV.	34
12	Meoul . . .	252　1　31	Waterford . .	Coshmore &Coshbride	Lismore and Mocollop	Lismore . .	II.	347
56	Merchantstown Glebe	344　0　3	Tyrone . .	Omagh East . .	Termonmaguirk .	Omagh . .	III.	314
12, 13	Merepark . .	81　0　2	Wicklow . .	Newcastle . .	Newcastle Upper .	Rathdrum . .	I.	353
15	Merginstown . .	163　2　16	Wicklow . .	Lower Talbotstown .	Dunlavin . .	Baltinglass . .	I.	360
15	Merginstown Demesne	198　1　12	Wicklow . .	Lower Talbotstown .	Dunlavin . .	Baltinglass . .	I.	360
15, 21	Merginstown Glen .	303　3　20	Wicklow . .	Lower Talbotstown .	Dunlavin . .	Baltinglass . .	I.	360
82, 94	Merlinpark . .	323　0　39	Galway . .	Galway . .	Oranmore . .	Galway . .	IV.	37
18,19,22,23	Merrion . .	197　1　39	Dublin . .	Dublin . .	Donnybrook . .	Dublin South .	I.	30
23	Merrion . . .	102　0　28	Dublin . .	Rathdown . .	Booterstown . .	Rathdown . .	I.	35
18,19,22,23	MERRION T. . .	—	Dublin . .	Dublin . .	Donnybrook . .	Dublin South .	I.	30
14	Merryfalls . .	133　0　25	Dublin . .	Coolock . .	St. Margarets . .	Dublin North .	I.	29
25	Merrymeeting .	175　2　10	Wicklow . .	Newcastle . .	Rathnew . .	Rathdrum . .	I.	354
44	Merrywell . .	16　3　16	Meath . .	Lower Deece . .	Knockmark . .	Dunshaughlin .	I.	192
44	Merrywell . .	122　3　33	Meath . .	Ratoath . .	Dunshaughlin . .	Dunshaughlin .	I.	218
44	Mersheen . .	243　3　27	Wexford . .	Shelburne . .	St.James&Dunbrody	New Ross . .	I.	328
10	Mertonhall . .	369　1　2	Tipperary, N.R.	Lower Ormond .	Modreeny . .	Borrisokane .	II.	287
32	Merville or Brewel East . . .	418　0　35	Kildare . .	Narragh & Reban East	Usk . . .	Naas . .	I.	67
18	Metticaa Glebe .	370　1　7	Londonderry .	Coleraine . .	Errigal . .	Coleraine . .	III.	232
16	Mevagh . . .	155　2　2	Donegal . .	Kilmacrenan . .	Mevagh . .	Millford . .	III.	130
3	*Mew Island* . .	31　2　4	Down . .	Ards Lower . .	Bangor . .	Newtownards .	III.	157
27	Mewlaghmore .	124　3　15	Roscommon .	Castlereagh . .	Kilkeevin . .	Castlereagh .	IV.	201
18, 19	Michaelschurch .	278　2　17	Kilkenny . .	Crannagh . .	Ballycallan . .	Kilkenny . .	I.	84
33	Micknanstown .	164　2　28	Meath . .	Upper Duleek . .	Ardcath . .	Drogheda . .	I.	197
33	Micknanstown .	362　3　17	Meath . .	Upper Duleek . .	Clonalvy . .	Drogheda . .	I.	197
68, 69	Midcut or Maghera-vall . . .	268　2　33	Donegal . .	Raphoe . . .	Convoy . .	Stranorlar . .	III.	136
47	Middleborough .	133　0　34	Meath . .	Upper Moyfenrath .	Clonard . .	Trim . .	I.	213
46, 52	Middle Division .	3,868　0　13d	Antrim . .	Carrickfergus . .	Carrickfergus . .	Larne . .	III.	11
19	Middle Gortnagross	33　2　25	Antrim . .	Lower Glenarm .	Layd . . .	Ballycastle .	III.	23
68	*Middle Island* . .	4　1　39	Galway . .	Moycullen . .	Killannin . .	Oughterard .	IV.	70
19	Middleknock . .	55　1　24	Kilkenny . .	Gowran . .	St. John's . .	Kilkenny . .	I.	98
134, 136	Middleline North .	467　3　2	Galway . .	Leitrim . .	Inishcaltra . .	Scarriff . .	IV.	54
136	Middleline South .	214　0　7	Galway . .	Leitrim . .	Inishcaltra . .	Scarriff . .	IV.	54
90	Middlemount . .	190　0　9	Queen's Co. .	Clarmallagh . .	Aghaboe . .	Donaghmore .	I.	236
28	Middlemount or Bal-lyvoghlaun . .	434　0　22	Queen's Co. .	Clarmallagh . .	Coolkerry . .	Donaghmore .	I.	237

(a) { Within the Municipal Boundary,　26A. 0R. 37P. / Without the Municipal Boundary, 1,114A. 3R. 5P.　(b) Including 7A. 3R. 18P. water. / (c) Including 71A. 1R. 17P. water.　(d) Including { 1,386A. 2R. 12P. / 170A. 3R. 1P. } detached portions.

No. of Sheet of the Ordnance Survey Maps.	Townlands and Towns.	Area in Statute Acres.	County.	Barony.	Parish.	Poor Law Union in 1857.	Townland Census of 1851, Part I.	
		A. R. P.					Vol.	Page
20	Middle Park . .	34 0 19	Antrim . .	Lower Glenarm .	Layd . . .	Ballycastle .	III.	23
27	Middleplough . .	136 1 0	Tipperary, N.R.	Upper Ormond .	Templederry . .	Nenagh . .	II.	293
114	Middlequarter .	612 2 0a	Mayo . .	Murrisk . . .	Inishbofin . .	Clifden . .	IV.	159
26, 32	Middlequarter .	486 1 4	Tipperary, N.R.	Owney and Arra .	Killoscully . .	Nenagh . .	II.	295
88, 91	Middlequarter .	2,270 3 27b	Tipperary, S.R.	Iffa and Offa West .	Newcastle . .	Clogheen . .	II.	319
31, 36	Middlequarter .	97 3 24	Waterford .	Decies without Drum	Dungarvan . .	Dungarvan . .	II.	355
13	Middleton .	382 2 24	Longford . .	Moydow . . .	Kilashee . .	Longford . .	I.	162
76	MIDDLETON T. .	—	Cork, E.R. .	Imokilly . .	{ Middleton } { Mogeesha }	Middleton .	II.	{ 89 } { 90 }
15	Middletown . .	118 2 18	Armagh . .	Tiranny . . .	Tynan . . .	Armagh . .	III.	60
30, 31	Middletown . .	225 0 17c	Cavan . .	Clanmahon . .	Drumlumman .	Granard . .	III.	77
64	Middletown . .	166 0 26	Donegal . .	Boylagh . . .	Inishkeel . .	Glenties . .	III.	113
14, 15	Middletown . .	148 3 11	Dublin . .	Coolock . . .	Cloghran . .	Balrothery .	I.	26
5	Middletown . .	57 0 29	Fermanagh .	Lurg . . .	Drumkeeran . .	Lowtherstown .	III.	206
79	Middletown . .	134 1 23	Mayo . .	Carra . . .	Kildacommoge .	Castlebar . .	IV.	129
10	Middletown . .	219 3 16	Tipperary, N.R.	Lower Ormond .	Uskane . . .	Borrisokane .	II.	288
12	Middletown . .	177 1 19	Wexford . .	Ballaghkeen . .	Ardamine . .	Gorey . .	I.	291
26	Middletown . .	260 1 19	Wexford . .	Ballaghkeen . .	Ballyhuskard .	Enniscorthy .	I.	292
47	Middletown . .	79 0 31	Wexford . .	Forth . . .	Mayglass . .	Wexford . .	I.	312
15	MIDDLETOWN T. .	—	Armagh . .	Tiranny . . .	Tynan . . .	Armagh . .	III.	61
15	Middlewalk . .	695 0 38	Tipperary, N.R.	Upper Ormond .	Ballygibbon .	Nenagh . .	II.	289
29	Midgefield or Glenna-meeltoge . .	90 2 5	Roscommon .	Roscommon .	Cloonfinlough .	Strokestown .	IV.	209
87, 97	Midgefield or Tawny-nameeltoge . .	209 3 20d	Mayo . .	Murrisk . . .	Aghagower '	Westport . .	IV.	159
34	Midhill . . .	94 1 0	Fermanagh .	Clankelly . .	Galloon . . .	Lisnaskea . .	III.	198
11	Mid Island . .	15 1 28	Down . .	Ards Lower . .	Greyabbey . .	Newtownards .	III.	158
23	Mien . . .	479 0 33	Tipperary, N.R.	Ikerrin . . .	Killea . . .	Roscrea . .	II.	276
17, 23	Mihanagh . .	167 0 28e	Roscommon .	Roscommon .	Kiltrustan . .	Strokestown .	IV.	211
51, 52	Mihanboy . .	278 3 33	Roscommon .	Athlone . .	Drum . . .	Athlone . .	IV.	180
107, 120	Milane . . .	1,034 3 20	Cork, W.R. .	East Carbery (W.D.)	Fanlobbus . .	Dunmanway .	II.	132
67	Milcum . . .	79 3 9	Mayo . .	Burrishoole . .	Burrishoole . .	Newport . .	IV.	119
78	Milebush or Lisna-kirka . . .	214 3 6f	Mayo . .	Carra . . .	Aglish . . .	Castlebar .	IV.	124
5	Milecross . .	407 0 24	Down . .	Castlereagh Lower .	Newtownards .	Newtownards .	III.	163
19	Milehouse . .	246 2 25	Wexford . .	Scarawalsh . .	Monart . . .	Enniscorthy .	I.	324
28, 29	Milemill . . .	7 3 19	Kildare . .	Naas South . .	Gilltown . .	Naas . .	I.	65
135	Miles . . .	268 0 11	Cork, W.R. .	East Carbery (E.D.)	Kilgarriff . .	Clonakilty .	II.	129
94	Milestone . .	1 2 19	Galway . .	Galway . . .	St. Nicholas .	Galway . .	IV.	38
1	Milestown . .	96 2 29	Dublin . .	Balrothery East .	Balscaddan . .	Balrothery .	I.	20
15	Milestown . .	352 2 35	Louth . .	Ardee . . .	Kilsaran . .	Ardee . .	I.	173
50, 53	Milestown . .	277 1 25	Meath . .	Dunboyne . .	Dunboyne . .	Dunshaughlin .	I.	199
18	Milestown . .	170 2 31	Meath . .	Upper Kells . .	Donaghpatrick .	Navan . .	I.	205
70, 71	Milestown . .	345 1 19	Tipperary, S.R.	Middlethird . .	Cloneen . .	Cashel . .	II.	325
42, 41	Milestown . .	38 3 22	Wexford . .	Forth . . .	Rathmacknee .	Wexford . .	I.	313
26	Milford . . .	65 0 13g	Queen's Co. .	Ballyadams . .	Tankardstown .	Athy . .	I.	232
7	Milford . . .	81 0 37	Tipperary, N.R.	Lower Ormond .	Aglishcloghane .	Borrisokane .	II.	281
119, 122	Milford Demesne .	460 1 37	Mayo . .	Kilmaine . .	Kilmainemore .	Ballinrobe .	IV.	156
1	MILFORD T. . .	—	Cork, E.R. .	Orrery and Kilmore .	Kilbolane . .	Kanturk . .	II.	108
2	Milkernagh . .	376 2 27	Westmeath .	Moygoish . .	Street . . .	Granard . .	I.	281
53	Milk Isle . .	25 2 31	Donegal . .	Kilmacrenan . .	Conwal . . .	Letterkenny .	III.	126
37	Millbanks . .	198 0 2	Kilkenny . .	Ida . . .	Rosbercon . .	New Ross .	I.	103
67	Millberry . .	255 0 38	Tyrone . .	Dungannon Lower .	Aghaloo . .	Armagh . .	III.	297
91, 105	Mill Big . . .	200 3 39	Cork, W.R. .	Bantry . . .	Kilmocomoge .	Bantry . .	II.	121
37	Millbrook . .	41 3 25	Donegal . .	Kilmacrenan . .	Killygarvan .	Milford . .	III.	128
25	Millbrook . .	112 2 25	King's Co. .	Geashill . .	Ballykeane . .	Tullamore .	I.	139
101	Millbrook . .	43 3 24	Mayo . .	Clanmorris . .	Crossboyne . .	Claremorris .	IV.	133
27	Millbrook . .	452 3 17	Tipperary, N.R.	Upper Ormond .	Kilnaneave . .	Nenagh . .	II.	291
7	Millburn . . .	122 0 10	Londonderry .	North East Liberties of Coleraine .	Coleraine . .	Coleraine . .	III.	246
3	Millcastle . .	228 3 8	Westmeath .	Fore . . .	Rathgarve . .	Castletowndelvin	I.	271
38	Mill and Churchquar-ter . . .	72 2 25	Waterford .	Decies within Drum	Lisgenan or Grange	Youghal . .	II.	352
70, 82	Milleen . . .	342 2 25	Cork, W.R. .	West Muskerry .	Inchigeelagh .	Macroom . .	II.	158
133, 134	Milleenahilan . .	85 0 30	Cork, W.R. .	East Carbery (W.D.)	Kilmacabea . .	Skibbereen .	II.	133
107, 108	Milleenannig . .	448 2 25	Cork, W.R. .	East Carbery (W.D.)	Fanlobbus . .	Dunmanway .	II.	132
142	Milleenanimrish .	14 3 36	Cork, W.R. .	West Carbery (E.D.)	Kilmacabea . .	Skibbereen .	II.	140
132, 133	Milleenawillin . .	219 2 28	Cork, W.R. .	West Carbery (E.D.)	Abbeystrowry .	Skibbereen .	II.	136
4	Milleenboy . .	822 1 5	Cork, E.R. .	Duhallow . .	Clonfert . .	Kanturk . .	II.	69
138, 147	Milleen and Carriga-cat . . .	838 2 27	Cork, W.R. .	West Carbery (W.D.)	Kilmoe . . .	Skull . .	II.	144
118	Milleencoola . .	18 1 34	Cork, W.R. .	Bantry . . .	Kilmocomoge .	Bantry . .	II.	121
4, 5	Milleenduff . .	1,346 2 5	Cork, E.R. .	Duhallow . .	Clonfert . .	Kanturk . .	II.	69
121	Milleennagun . .	489 1 14h	Cork, W.R. .	East Carbery (W.D.)	Kilmeen . . .	Dunmanway .	II.	134

(a) Including 8A. 0R. 32P. water.   (d) Including 3A. 3R. 37P. water.   (g) Including 3A. 0R. 24P. River Barrow.
(b) Including 9A. 0R. 32P. water.   (e) Including 11A. 3R. 5P. water.   (h) Including 4A. 0R. 32P. water.
(c) Including 12A. 3R. 26P. water.   (f) Including 1A. 3R. 33P. water.

4 U

No. of Sheet of the Ordnance Survey Maps.	Townlands and Towns.	Area in Statute Acres.			County.	Barony.	Parish.	Poor Law Union in 1857.	Townland Census of 1851, Part I.	
		A.	R.	P.					Vol.	Page
133	Milleennahorna	195	3	23	Cork, W.R.	West Carbery (E.D.)	Abbeystrowry	Skibbereen	II.	136
132	Milleennahorna	119	3	28	Cork, W.R.	West Carbery (W.D.)	Caheragh	Skibbereen	II.	142
102	Milleens	305	1	26	Kerry	Glanarought	Kilcaskan	Kenmare	II.	187
57, 58, 69	Milleeny	1,504	2	30	Cork, W.R.	West Muskerry	Ballyvourney	Macroom	II.	154
30	Milleenylegane	122	3	35	Cork, E.R.	Duhallow	Cullen	Millstreet	II.	70
7	Miller Hill	46	2	0	Down	Ards Lower	Donaghadee	Newtownards	III.	158
89	Millerhill	116	1	9	Mayo	Carra	Ballintober	Castlebar	IV.	125
24	Millerstown	203	1	22	Waterford	Decies without Drum	Stradbally	Kilmacthomas	II.	361
20	Millerstown	72	0	4	Westmeath	Farbill	Killucan	Mullingar	I.	267
79	Millfarm	28	0	23	Donegal	Raphoe	Urney	Strabane	III.	144
32	Millfarm	193	2	1	Kildare	Offaly West	Kilrush	Athy	I.	73
21	Millfarm	23	0	25	Kildare	Offaly West	Lackagh	Athy	I.	73
32, 40	Millfarm	212	1	3	Limerick	Smallcounty	Hospital	Kilmallock	II.	260
13	Mill Five Acres	11	3	28	Antrim	Cary	Armoy	Ballycastle	III.	11
36	Millford	203	1	5	Donegal	Kilmacrenan	Tullyfern	Millford	III.	133
19, 20	Millford	250	0	25	Galway	Ballymoe	Kilbegnet	Glennamaddy	IV.	8
36	MILLFORD T.	—			Donegal	Kilmacrenan	Tullyfern	Millford	III.	133
8, 9	Millgrange	339	2	5	Louth	Lower Dundalk	Carlingford	Dundalk	I.	176
27	Mill Grove	99	0	37	King's Co.	Coolestown	Clonsast	Edenderry	I.	133
11, 14	Millhead	64	3	32	Dublin	Coolock	St. Margarets	Dublin North	I.	29
14	Millicent Demesne	247	3	6a	Kildare	Clane	Clane	Naas	I.	54
14	Millicent North	97	2	27	Kildare	Clane	Clane	Naas	I.	54
14	Millicent South	325	0	29b	Kildare	Clane	Clane	Naas	I.	54
5, 8	Milligan	96	1	29	Monaghan	Monaghan	Tedavnet	Monaghan	III.	279
36	Milligans	110	3	37	Fermanagh	Clankelly	Clones	Clones	III.	196
26	Mill Island	24	3	26	Kilkenny	Kells	Mallardstown	Callan	I.	110
7	MILL ISLE T.				Down	Ards Lower	Donaghadee	Newtownards	III.	158
52, 53	Millix	1,230	2	37	Tyrone	Clogher	Errigal Keerogue	Dungannon	III.	295
48, 53	Millknock	46	3	25	Wexford	Forth	Tacumshin	Wexford	I.	315
98	Mill-land	57	2	21	Cork, E.R.	Kinalea	Ballymartle	Kinsale	II.	94
44	Mill Land	116	2	6	Meath	Ratoath	Rathbeggan	Dunshaughlin	I.	219
14	Mill-land	54	1	36	Queen's Co.	Stradbally	Curraclone	Athy	I.	246
20, 27	Mill Land	37	1	1	Westmeath	Farbill	Killucan	Mullingar	I.	267
43, 44	Mill Land	117	1	8	Wicklow	Ballinacor South	Crosspatrick	Shillelagh	I.	348
23, 24, 29	Mill Land and Cur-leyland	173	0	1	Meath	Lune	Athboy	Trim	I.	207
32	Mill Lands	156	2	29	Wexford	Ballaghkeen	Ballynaslaney	Enniscorthy	I.	292
7, 12	Mill Lands	137	2	26	Wexford	Ballaghkeen	Kilmakilloge	Gorey	I.	296
105	Mill Little	120	3	17	Cork, W.R.	Bantry	Kilmocomoge	Bantry	II.	121
7, 8	Mill Loughan	164	3	31	Londonderry	North East Liberties of Coleraine	Kildollagh	Coleraine	III.	246
47, 48	Millmount	241	3	39	Limerick	Coshlea	Ballingaddy	Kilmallock	II.	237
17	Millockstown	600	1	5c	Louth	Ardee	Kildemock	Ardee	I.	173
96	Millpark	63	1	4	Galway	Athenry	Athenry	Loughrea	IV.	4
19	Millpark	14	2	5	Galway	Ballymoe	Kilbegnet	Glennamaddy	IV.	8
108	Millpark	37	3	31	Galway	Longford	Meelick	Portumna	IV.	61
27	Millpark	9	1	35	Galway	Ross	Ross	Oughterard	IV.	74
32	Millpark	41	2	10	Leitrim	Leitrim	Annaduff	Mohill	IV.	99
11	Millpark	117	2	24	Louth	Upper Dundalk	Louth	Dundalk	I.	179
12	Millpark	83	3	5	Tipperary, N.R.	Ikerrin	Roscrea	Roscrea	II.	276
95	Millplot	4	1	37	Galway	Dunkellin	Oranmore	Galway	IV.	32
17	Millquarter	163	0	17	Antrim	Upper Dunluce	Ballymoney	Ballymoney	III.	19
36, 42	Mill Quarter	560	2	18	Antrim	Upper Toome	Ballyscullion Grange	Ballymena	III.	33
30, 35	Millquarter	647	0	21	Wexford	Bantry	Oldross	New Ross	I.	301
6	Millquarter	145	0	26	Wexford	Gorey	Kilnahue	Gorey	I.	319
70	Millsessiagh	54	3	29	Donegal	Raphoe	Clonleigh	Strabane	III.	135
39	MILLSTREET T.	—			Cork, W.R.	West Muskerry	Drishane	Millstreet	II.	156
34	Milltate	55	3	11	Fermanagh	Coole	Galloon	Lisnaskea	III.	200
11	Milltate	101	0	19	Fermanagh	Lurg	Derryvullan	Lowtherstown	III.	204
22	Milltate	80	2	0	Fermanagh	Tirkennedy	Derryvullan	Enniskillen	III.	221
25	Mill Tenement	1	1	1	Antrim	Lower Glenarm	Ardclinis	Larne	III.	21
17	Milltown	402	3	5	Carlow	Forth	Barragh	Carlow	I.	4
17, 19, 20	Milltown	336	0	21	Carlow	Idrone East	Fennagh	Carlow	I.	7
14	Milltown	129	3	16	Cavan	Lower Loughtee	Drumlane	Cavan	III.	80
27, 35	Milltown	465	2	31	Clare	Tulla Upper	Tulla	Tulla	II.	42
7	Milltown	80	0	14	Cork, E.R.	Orrery and Kilmore	Aglishdrinagh	Kilmallock	II.	106
2, 7	Milltown	291	0	26	Cork, E.R.	Orrery and Kilmore	Cooliney	Kilmallock	II.	108
134, 143, 144	Milltown	106	2	39	Cork, W.R.	Ibane and Barryroe	Rathbarry	Clonakilty	II.	150
93, 94	Milltown	46	3	2	Donegal	Banagh	Killymard	Donegal	III.	111
44, 52	Milltown	54	1	12	Donegal	Kilmacrenan	Gartan	Letterkenny	III.	127
69	Milltown	50	3	1	Donegal	Raphoe	Convoy	Stranorlar	III.	158
60, 61	Milltown	311	2	0	Donegal	Raphoe	Conwal	Letterkenny	III.	137
70	Milltown	38	0	38	Donegal	Raphoe	Raphoe	Strabane	III.	141

(a) Including 6A. 1R. 24P. water.   (b) Including 0A. 2R. 16P. water.   (c) Including 0A. 3R. 35P. detached portion.

No. of Sheet of the Ordnance Survey Maps.	Townlands and Towns.	Area in Statute Acres.			County.	Barony.	Parish.	Poor Law Union in 1857.	Townland Census of 1851, Part I.	
		A.	R.	P.					Vol.	Page
54	Milltown	93	3	25	Donegal	Raphoe	Raymoghy	Londonderry	III.	142
94	Milltown	98	3	3	Donegal	Tirhugh	Donegal	Donegal	III.	145
51	Milltown	472	2	20a	Down	Upper Iveagh, Up. pt.	Clonallan	Newry	III.	174
17, 21	Milltown	496	0	35b	Dublin	Newcastle	Kilmactalway	Celbridge	I.	33
18, 22	Milltown	185	2	13	Dublin	Uppercross	St. Peters	Dublin South	I.	41
38	Milltown	100	0	17	Fermanagh	Knockninny	Kinawley	Lisnaskea	III.	202
16	Milltown	102	3	20	Galway	Dunmore	Addergoole	Tuam	IV.	33
31, 32	Milltown	439	0	18	Galway	Tiaquin	Kilkerrin	Glennamaddy	IV.	77
21	Milltown	207	1	25	Kerry	Clanmaurice	O'Dorney	Tralee	II.	172
43, 53	Milltown	391	1	7	Kerry	Corkaguiny	Dingle	Dingle	II.	175
47	Milltown	54	0	20	Kerry	Trughanacmy	Kilcolman	Killarney	II.	210
18, 23	Milltown	378	0	15	Kildare	Connell	Feighcullen	Naas	I.	55
34, 35	Milltown	460	3	36c	Kildare	Narragh&Reban West	Churchtown	Athy	I.	67
25	Milltown	577	2	18d	Kilkenny	Gowran	Ullard	Thomastown	I.	100
41	Milltown	195	0	28	Kilkenny	Ida	Ballygurrim	New Ross	I.	101
43	Milltown	507	3	9	Kilkenny	Ida	Dunkitt	Waterford	I.	101
35, 39	Milltown	939	3	19	Kilkenny	Knocktopher	Muckalee	Carrick on Suir	I.	113
42	Milltown	252	1	25	King's Co.	Clonlisk	Shinrone	Roscrea	I.	131
30	Milltown	191	3	37	King's Co.	Garrycastle	Reynagh	Parsonstown	I.	138
7, 11	Milltown	116	3	8	Leitrim	Rosclogher	Killasnet	Manorhamilton	IV.	110
5, 6, 13, 14	Milltown	141	3	14	Limerick	Clanwilliam	Derrygalvin	Limerick	II.	223
5, 6	Milltown	30	1	6	Limerick	Clanwilliam	Kilmurry	Limerick	II.	224
29, 30	Milltown	239	0	8	Limerick	Connello Lower	Croagh	Rathkeale	II.	228
23, 24, 33	Milltown	149	3	18	Limerick	Coonagh	Aglishcormick	Tipperary	II.	233
24	Milltown	51	2	2	Limerick	Coonagh	Doon	Tipperary	II.	234
48	Milltown	57	3	5	Limerick	Coshlea	Ballingaddy	Kilmallock	II.	237
40	Milltown	118	2	33	Limerick	Coshma	Uregare	Kilmallock	II.	244
3, 11	Milltown	360	0	30	Limerick	Kenry	Iverus	Rathkeale	II.	249
32, 40	Milltown	117	2	33	Limerick	Smallcounty	Knockainy	Kilmallock	II.	261
5	Milltown	157	2	27	Londonderry	Keenaght	Magilligan	New Tn Limavady	III.	237
18, 19	Milltown	127	2	33	Louth	Ferrard	Dysart	Drogheda	I.	181
21, 22	Milltown	287	3	18	Louth	Ferrard	Termonfeckin	Drogheda	I.	182
12	Milltown	369	2	39	Louth	Louth	Dromiskin	Dundalk	I.	183
6	Milltown	59	3	25	Louth	Upper Dundalk	Barronstown	Dundalk	I.	177
15	Milltown	630	3	30	Meath	Fore	Moylagh	Oldcastle	I.	201
37	Milltown	126	0	28	Meath	Lower Deece	Galtrim	Trim	I.	191
24	Milltown	424	3	36	Meath	Lune	Rathmore	Trim	I.	208
39, 45	Milltown	530	2	2e	Meath	Ratoath	Donaghmore	Dunshaughlin	I.	218
49	Milltown	180	1	4	Meath	Upper Deece	Kilclone	Dunshaughlin	I.	193
27, 33	Milltown	189	1	25	Meath	Upper Duleek	Duleek Abbey	Drogheda	I.	198
17, 24	Milltown	208	3	23	Meath	Upper Kells	Balrathboyne	Kells	I.	204
18	Milltown	191	0	19	Monaghan	Dartree	Ematris	Cootehill	III.	267
25	Milltown	345	2	18	Queen's Co.	Ballyadams	Rathaspick	Athy	I.	232
47, 50	Milltown	1,048	2	32	Roscommon	Athlone	Dysart	Athlone	IV.	181
18	Milltown	118	1	37f	Roscommon	Ballintober North	Kilmore	Carn. on Shannon	IV.	187
27, 28	Milltown	640	3	11	Roscommon	Castlereagh	Baslick	Castlereagh	IV.	199
32	Milltown	144	0	7	Roscommon	Castlereagh	Kiltullagh	Castlereagh	IV.	202
58	Milltown	236	2	2	Tipperary, S.R.	Clanwilliam	Cullen	Tipperary	II.	307
58	Milltown	93	1	34	Tipperary, S.R.	Clanwilliam	Solloghodmore	Tipperary	II.	311
46, 52	Milltown	295	1	30	Tipperary, S.R.	Kilnamanagh Lower	Clogher	Cashel	II.	322
17	Milltown	610	1	6g	Tyrone	Strabane Lower	Ardstraw	Strabane	III.	319
5	Milltown	15	0	37h	Tyrone	Strabane Lower	Camus	Strabane	III.	320
2	Milltown	147	3	4i	Tyrone	Strabane Lower	Donaghedy	Strabane	III.	321
5	Milltown	181	3	6	Tyrone	Strabane Lower	Leckpatrick	Strabane	III.	322
33, 34	Milltown	1,115	2	3	Westmeath	Fartullagh	Pass of Kilbride	Mullingar	I.	269
7	Milltown	775	0	27	Westmeath	Fore	Faughalstown	Castletowndelvin	I.	270
23	Milltown	195	2	16	Westmeath	Rathconrath	Ballymore	Ballymahon	I.	282
25	Milltown	701	1	5	Westmeath	Rathconrath	Churchtown	Mullingar	I.	282
17, 18	Milltown	310	3	0	Westmeath	Rathconrath	Rathconrath	Mullingar	I.	284
18	Milltown	118	0	36	Wexford	Bantry	Killann	Enniscorthy	I.	300
42	Milltown	87	2	16	Wexford	Forth	Kildavin	Wexford	I.	310
48	Milltown	121	0	19	Wexford	Forth	Kilscoran	Wexford	I.	311
15	Milltown	199	0	38	Wexford	Scarawalsh	Kilbride	Enniscorthy	I.	323
39	Milltown	70	2	19	Wexford	Shelburne	Ballybrazil	New Ross	I.	327
45	Milltown	161	0	15	Wexford	Shelburne	Tintern	New Ross	I.	329
14, 15	Milltown	257	1	15	Wicklow	Lower Talbotstown	Dunlavin	Baltinglass	I.	360
69	Milltown Beg	184	2	30	Tipperary, S.R.	Middlethird	Mora	Cashel	II.	329
15	Milltown Blaney	116	2	24	Fermanagh	Magheraboy	Inishmacsaint	Enniskillen	III.	213
6	Milltown Bog	13	0	31	Louth	Upper Dundalk	Barronstown	Dundalk	I.	177
77	Milltown Britton	736	2	39	Tipperary, S.R.	Middlethird	Baptistgrange	Clonmel	II.	325
43	Milltown, Commons of	58	2	37	Kerry	Corkaguiny	Dingle	Dingle	II.	175
12	Milltown Grange	247	1	1	Louth	Louth	Dromiskin	Dundalk	I.	183
30	MILLTOWN MALBAY T.	—			Clare	Ibrickan	Kilfarboy	Ennistimon	II.	22

(a) Including 7A. 3R. 8P. water.
(b) Including 23A. 2R. 14P. detached portion.
(c) Including 11A. 3R. 8P. River Barrow.
(d) Including 11A. 3R. 0P. River Barrow.
(e) Including 6A. 3R. 22P. detached portion.
(f) Including 4A. 2R. 0P. water.
(g) Including 13A. 1R. 36P. water.
(h) Including 0A. 2R. 35P. water.
(i) Including 2A. 0R. 10P. water.

4 U 2

No. of Sheet of the Ordnance Survey Maps.	Townlands and Towns.	Area in Statute Acres.	County.	Barony.	Parish.	Poor Law Union in 1857.	Townland Census of 1851, Part I.	
		A. R. P.					Vol.	Page
69	Milltown More	241 0 20	Tipperary, S.R.	Middlethird	Mora	Cashel	II.	329
19, 20	Milltown North	192 3 37	Limerick	Connello Lower	Lismakeery	Rathkeale	II.	228
25	Milltown North	308 2 37	Wicklow	Newcastle	Rathnew	Rathdrum	I.	354
12	Milltown Old	49 3 38	Louth	Louth	Dromiskin	Dundalk	I.	183
62	Milltown St. John	403 3 9	Tipperary, S.R.	Middlethird	Cooleagh	Cashel	II.	326
19, 20	Milltown South	140 3 22	Limerick	Connello Lower	Lismakeery	Rathkeale	II.	228
25	Milltown South	68 3 22	Wicklow	Newcastle	Rathnew	Rathdrum	I.	354
2	Milltown T.	—	Armagh	Oneilland West	Tartaraghan	Lurgan	III.	55
22	Milltown T.	—	Dublin	Uppercross	St. Peters	Dublin South	I.	41
47	Milltown T.	—	Kerry	Trughanacmy	Kilcolman	Killarney	II.	210
33, 34	Milltown T.	—	Westmeath	Fartullagh	Pass of Kilbride	Mullingar	I.	269
28	Millwood	185 2 35	Fermanagh	Magherastephana	Aghalurcher	Lisnaskea	III.	217
69, 81	Milmorane	431 2 17	Cork, W.R.	West Muskerry	Inchigeelagh	Macroom	II.	158
16	Milshoge	217 2 26	Wexford	Scarawalsh	Toome	Gorey	I.	326
11	Miltonsfields	82 1 36	Dublin	Nethercross	Swords	Balrothery	I.	32
29, 30	Miltron Glebe	337 0 27	Leitrim	Carrigallen	Cloone	Mohill	IV.	90
5	Milverton	92 0 27	Dublin	Balrothery East	Baldongan	Balrothery	I.	19
5	Milverton	277 1 5	Dublin	Balrothery East	Holmpatrick	Balrothery	I.	20
5	Milverton Demesne	136 0 36	Dublin	Balrothery East	Holmpatrick	Balrothery	I.	20
99	Minane	106 1 36	Cork, E.R.	Kinalea	Tracton	Kinsale	II.	97
115	Minane Island	2 3 19	Cork, W.R.	Bear	Killaconenagh	Castletown	II.	125
115	Minanekeal	0 1 27	Cork, W.R.	Bear	Killaconenagh	Castletown	II.	125
120, 133	Minanes	569 3 36	Cork, W.R.	West Carbery (E.D.)	Drinagh	Skibbereen	II.	139
99	Minane T.	—	Cork, E.R.	Kinalea	Tracton	Kinsale	II.	97
8, 13	Minard	159 1 0	Longford	Longford	Clongesh	Longford	I.	158
54	Minard East	147 1 27	Kerry	Corkaguiny	Minard	Dingle	II.	180
54	Minard West	510 2 38	Kerry	Corkaguiny	Minard	Dingle	II.	180
81,82,93,94	Mincloon	170 1 36a	Galway	Galway	Rahoon	Galway	IV.	38
5	Minearny	190 2 18	Londonderry	Keenaght	Magilligan	NewTⁿLimavady	III.	237
15	Minegallagher Glebe	275 1 20	Londonderry	Tirkeeran	Faughanvale	NewTⁿLimavady	III.	250
30, 39	Minehill	165 1 26	Cork, E.R.	Duhallow	Dromtarriff	Millstreet	II.	71
46	Mineveigh	152 2 38	Tyrone	Dungannon Middle	Tullyniskin	Dungannon	III.	305
67	Minish	522 1 26	Kerry	Magunihy	Killarney	Killarney	II.	203
28	Minister's-land	175 3 0	Limerick	Shanid	Ardagh	Newcastle	II.	255
21, 28	Ministown	280 0 2	Meath	Lower Duleek	Julianstown	Drogheda	I.	196
31	Minkill	97 1 27	Leitrim	Leitrim	Kiltoghert	Carᵏ. on Shannon	IV.	102
42, 43	Minmore	19 2 32	Wicklow	Shillelagh	Aghowle	Shillelagh	I.	356
43	Minmore	30 1 30	Wicklow	Shillelagh	Carnew	Shillelagh	I.	357
42,43,46,47	Minmore	229 1 22	Wicklow	Shillelagh	Moyacomb	Shillelagh	I.	358
91	Minna	903 2 13b	Galway	Moycullen	Kilcummin	Galway	IV.	67
26	Minnauns	197 1 38	Kilkenny	Callan	Callan	Callan	I.	83
30	Minnis North	59 2 29	Antrim	Lower Glenarm	Tickmacrevan	Larne	III.	24
30	Minnis North	102 2 2	Antrim	Upper Glenarm	Carncastle	Larne	III.	24
17	Minnis's Island Great	3 3 28	Down	Ards Upper	Ardkeen	Downpatrick	III.	159
17	Minnis's Island Little	3 2 24	Down	Ards Upper	Ardkeen	Downpatrick	III.	159
30	Minnis South	55 0 4	Antrim	Upper Glenarm	Carncastle	Larne	III.	24
78	Minorstown	235 1 13	Tipperary, S.R.	Iffa and Offa East	Kilsheelan	Clonmel	II.	314
9, 14	Minran	178 0 4	Fermanagh	Magheraboy	Inishmacsaint	Ballyshannon	III.	213
21, 22	Minus Island	69 1 5	King's Co.	Garrycastle	Gallen	Parsonstown	I.	136
9, 10	Minvaud Lower	305 2 10	Carlow	Rathvilly	Clonmore	Shillelagh	I.	10
9, 10	Minvaud Upper	292 2 4	Carlow	Rathvilly	Clonmore	Shillelagh	I.	10
70, 71	Mira	512 0 7	Galway	Clare	Athenry	Galway	IV.	17
42	Mirehill	307 0 2	Galway	Clare	Donaghpatrick	Tuam	IV.	19
96	Mishells	604 2 38	Cork, W.R.	Kinalmeaky	Kilbrogan	Bandon	II.	152
21	Miskaun Glebe	327 0 6	Leitrim	Carrigallen	Oughteragh	Bawnboy	IV.	92
29	Miskish Beg	95 1 34	Monaghan	Farney	Inishkeen	Dundalk	III.	271
29	Miskish More	75 1 36	Monaghan	Farney	Inishkeen	Dundalk	III.	271
30, 35	Misterin	548 2 2	Wexford	Bantry	Adamstown	New Ross	I.	299
39	Mistyburn	423 1 35	Antrim	Lower Antrim	Glenwhirry	Ballymena	III.	4
53	Mitchellsfort	903 1 37	Cork, E.R.	Barrymore	Kilquane	Cork	II.	56
10, 19	Mitchelstown	840 0 5	Cork, E.R.	Condons and Clangibbon	Brigown	Mitchelstown	II.	60
10, 19	Mitchelstown	393 1 29	Cork, E.R.	Condons and Clangibbon	Marshalstown	Mitchelstown	II.	63
14	Mitchelstown	154 2 30	Dublin	Castleknock	Castleknock	Dublin North	I.	24
11	Mitchelstown	127 0 27	Limerick	Kenry	Iveruss	Rathkeale	II.	249
19	Mitchelstown	150 1 5	Louth	Ferrard	Dunany	Ardee	I.	180
37	Mitchelstown	158 3 17	Meath	Lower Deece	Galtrim	Trim	I.	191
12	Mitchelstown	355 2 24	Meath	Lower Slane	Mitchelstown	Ardee	I.	223
29, 30	Mitchelstown	776 1 1	Meath	Lune	Athboy	Trim	I.	207
9, 14	Mitchelstown	298 2 39	Westmeath	Delvin	Castletowndelvin	Castletowndelvin	I.	265
49	Mitchelstowndown	100 0 12	Limerick	Coshlea	Ballingarry	Kilmallock	II.	237
49	Mitchel-towndown East	144 3 4	Limerick	Coshlea	Knocklong	Kilmallock	II.	240

(a) Including 1A. 2R. 38P. water.　　　　　　(b) Including 21A. 2R. 18P. water.

No. of Sheet of the Ordnance Survey Maps.	Townlands and Towns.	Area in Statute Acres. A. R. P.	County.	Barony.	Parish.	Poor Law Union in 1857.	Vol.	Page
40,41,48,49	Mitchelstowndown North .	277 1 29	Limerick .	Coshlea . . .	Knocklong .	Kilmallock .	II.	240
41, 48, 49	Mitchelstowndown West .	277 0 3	Limerick .	Coshlea . . .	Knocklong .	Kilmallock .	II.	240
112	Mitchelstown East .	250 2 1	Cork, E.R.	Kinsale . . .	Clontead .	Kinsale . .	II.	99
19	MITCHELSTOWN T..	—	Cork, E.R.	Condons&Clangibbon	Brigown . .	Mitchelstown .	II.	60
112	Mitchelstown West.	172 3 39	Cork, E.R.	Kinsale . .	Clontead .	Kinsale . .	II.	99
2	Moanabricka .	306 2 16	Cork, E.R.	Orrery and Kilmore	Kilbolane .	Kanturk . .	II.	108
7	Moanacurragh .	43 0 32	Carlow .	Carlow . . .	Ballinacarrig .	Carlow . .	I.	1
25	Moanahila .	177 2 1	Limerick .	Coonagh . .	Oola . .	Tipperary .	II.	236
8	Moanalow .	161 3 1	Carlow .	Carlow . . .	Grangeford .	Carlow . .	I.	2
8	Moanamanagh .	162 1 31	Carlow .	Carlow . . .	Grangeford .	Carlow . .	I.	2
26	Moanamought Commons	53 0 29	Kilkenny .	Callan . . .	Callan . .	Callan . .	I.	83
23, 24	Moananagh .	299 0 22	Clare .	Corcomroe .	Clooney . .	Ennistimon .	II.	18
1	Moanarnane .	179 1 9	Cork, E.R.	Orrery and Kilmore	Kilbolane .	Kanturk . .	II.	108
110	Moanarone .	235 1 32	Cork, W.R.	East Carbery (E.D.)	Ballymodan .	Bandon . .	II.	127
1	Moanaspick .	282 3 12	Wicklow .	Lower Talbotstown	Kilbride . .	Naas . .	I.	361
25	Moanaviddoge .	98 1 35	Limerick .	Coonagh . .	Oola . .	Tipperary .	II.	236
4	Moanavoth .	220 1 37	Carlow .	Rathvilly . .	Rathvilly .	Baltinglass .	I.	12
1	Moanavraca .	209 1 6	Cork, E.R.	Orrery and Kilmore	Kilbolane .	Kanturk . .	II.	108
38	Moanballyshivane .	44 2 30	Waterford .	Decies within Drum	Lisgenan or Grange	Youghal . .	II.	352
70	Moanbarron .	73 3 32	Tipperary, S.R.	Middlethird .	Kiltinan . .	Clonmel . .	II.	328
53, 64	Moanbaun .	400 3 18	Cork, E.R.	Barrymore .	Ballycurrany .	Middleton .	II.	51
84	Moanbaun .	603 1 17	Galway .	Athenry . .	Athenry . .	Loughrea . .	IV.	4
20	Moanbeg .	26 2 25	Tipperary, N.R.	Upper Ormond .	Nenagh . .	Nenagh . .	II.	292
70	Moan Beg .	62 3 26	Tipperary, S.R.	Middlethird .	Fethard . .	Cashel . .	II.	327
36	Moanbrack .	140 3 1	Waterford .	Decies within Drum	Ardmore . .	Dungarvan .	II.	350
88	Moancrea .	328 1 30	Tipperary, S.R.	Iffa and Offa West .	Neddans . .	Clogheen .	II.	319
59	Moandoherdagh .	212 2 4	Tipperary, S.R.	Clanwilliam .	Donohill . .	Tipperary .	II.	307
11, 15, 16	Moanduff .	90 3 24	Carlow .	Idrone West .	Killinane .	Carlow . .	I.	9
11, 15	Moanduff .	288 0 11	Carlow .	Idrone West .	Oldleighlin .	Carlow . .	I.	9
25	Moanduff .	135 1 0	Limerick .	Coonagh .	Castletown .	Tipperary .	II.	234
22	Moanfad . .	70 3 34	Queen's Co. .	Clandonagh .	Aghaboe . .	Donaghmore .	I.	232
21	Moanfin . .	309 0 38	Tipperary, N.R.	Upper Ormond .	Kilruane . .	Nenagh . .	II.	292
59	Moanflugh .	415 3 2	Cork, W.R.	West Muskerry .	Clondrohid .	Macroom . .	II.	155
39	Moanfoun .	134 2 28	Waterford .	Decies within Drum	Ardmore . .	Dungarvan .	II.	350
28	Moanfune .	105 0 22	Waterford .	Coshmore&Coshbride	Tallow . .	Lismore . .	II.	348
83	Moangarriff .	125 0 17	Tipperary, S.R.	Iffa and Offa East .	Kilgrant . .	Clonmel . .	II.	314
26	Moangarve .	200 3 25	Kilkenny .	Kells . .	Mallardstown .	Callan . .	I.	110
26	Moankeal Commons	44 3 20	Kilkenny .	Callan . .	Callan . .	Callan . .	I.	83
34	Moankeenane .	243 0 11	Tipperary, N.R.	Kilnamanagh Upper	Glenkeen .	Thurles . .	II.	278
43, 44	Moanlahan .	522 3 35	Cork, E.R.	Barrymore .	Rathcormack .	Fermoy . .	II.	57
66	Moanlahan .	48 3 32	Cork, E.R.	Imokilly . .	Killeagh . .	Youghal . .	II.	88
36, 44	Moanleana .	451 2 26	Limerick .	Glenquin .	Mahoonagh .	Newcastle .	II.	246
83	Moanmehill .	72 3 27a	Tipperary, S.R.	Iffa and Offa East .	Kilgrant . .	Clonmel . .	II.	314
13, 17	Moanmore .	194 0 27	Carlow .	Forth . .	Fennagh . .	Carlow . .	I.	4
15	Moanmore .	618 3 9	Carlow .	Idrone West .	Oldleighlin .	Carlow . .	I.	9
15	Moanmore .	74 1 13	Carlow .	Idrone West .	Wells . .	Carlow . .	I.	10
105, 106	Moanmore .	184 1 36	Galway .	Loughrea .	Kilteskill .	Loughrea . .	IV.	65
39, 40	Moanmore .	195 3 16	Kerry .	Trughanacmy .	Castleisland .	Tralee . .	II.	209
31	Moanmore .	386 2 32	Kilkenny .	Kells . .	Dunnamaggan .	Callan . .	I.	108
59	Moanmore .	212 2 24	Limerick .	Coshlea . .	Particles . .	Kilmallock .	II.	240
22	Moanmore .	100 2 7	Limerick .	Smallcounty .	Fedamore . .	Croom . .	II.	259
65, 66	Moanmore .	1,413 2 7	Tipperary, S.R.	Clanwilliam .	Emly . . .	Tipperary .	II.	308
58	Moanmore .	507 0 24	Tipperary, S.R.	Clanwilliam .	Solloghodmore .	Tipperary .	II.	311
82	Moanmore .	323 0 7	Tipperary, S.R.	Iffa and Offa West .	Tullaghmelan .	Clogheen .	II.	321
70	Moanmore .	16 0 17	Tipperary, S.R.	Middlethird .	Fethard . .	Cashel . .	II.	327
26	Moanmore Commons	281 2 20	Kilkenny .	Callan . .	Callan . .	Callan . .	I.	83
105, 106	Moanmore East .	198 1 30	Galway .	Loughrea .	Loughrea .	Loughrea . .	IV.	66
57	Moanmore Lower .	441 2 38	Clare .	Moyarta .	Kilrush . .	Kilrush . .	II.	33
57	Moanmore North .	405 2 32b	Clare .	Moyarta .	Kilrush . .	Kilrush . .	II.	33
57	Moanmore South .	1,175 3 32	Clare .	Moyarta .	Kilrush . .	Kilrush . .	II.	33
57	Moanmore Upper .	368 1 4	Clare .	Moyarta .	Kilrush . .	Kilrush . .	II.	33
105	Moanmore West .	152 3 38	Galway .	Loughrea .	Loughrea .	Loughrea . .	IV.	66
126	Moanakeeba East .	457 1 20	Galway .	Leitrim .	Tynagh . .	Portumna .	IV.	55
126	Moanakeeba West	477 3 38	Galway .	Leitrim .	Tynagh . .	Portumna .	IV.	55
36	Moanogeenagh .	337 2 20	Clare .	Tulla Lower .	Killuran . .	Tulla . .	II.	36
25	Moanoola .	133 2 18	Limerick .	Coonagh . .	Oola . .	Tipperary .	II.	236
66, 73	Moanour .	632 3 32	Tipperary, S.R.	Clanwilliam .	Clonbeg . .	Tipperary .	II.	305
67	Moanreagh .	60 0 9	Tipperary, S.R.	Clanwilliam .	Clonpet . .	Tipperary .	II.	306
67	Moanreagh .	54 1 26	Tipperary, S.R.	Clanwilliam .	Cordangan .	Tipperary .	II	306
24	Moanreel North .	355 3 12	Clare .	Inchiquin .	Rath . .	Ennistimon .	II	28
24	Moanreel South .	508 0 18	Clare .	Inchiquin .	Rath . .	Ennistimon .	II.	28

(a) Including 4A. 2R. 8P. water.　　　　(b) Including 30A. 3R. 3P. water.

No. of Sheet of the Ordnance Survey Maps.	Townlands and Towns.	Area in Statute Acres.	County.	Barony.	Parish.	Poor Law Union in 1857.	Townland Census of 1851, Part I.	
		A. R. P.					Vol.	Page
24, 32	Moanroe	202 1 38	Cork, E.R.	Duhallow	Ballyclogh	Mallow	II.	67
77	Moanroe	111 1 23	Cork, E.R.	Imokilly	Garryvoe	Middleton	II.	87
99	Moanroe	240 0 35	Cork, E.R.	Kerrycurrihy	Kilpatrick	Kinsale	II.	92
16	Moanroe	75 0 28	Cork, E.R.	Orrery and Kilmore	Churchtown	Mallow	II.	107
1	Moanroe	116 1 20	Cork, E.R.	Orrery and Kilmore	Kilbolane	Kanturk	II.	108
43	Moanroe	53 1 6a	Kilkenny	Ida	Kilcolumb	Waterford	I.	102
23	Moanroe	56 1 27	Limerick	Clanwilliam	Dromkeen	Limerick	II.	223
25	Moanroe	309 2 15	Limerick	Coonagh	Oola	Tipperary	II.	236
77	Moanroe	191 3 0	Tipperary, S.R.	Iffa and Offa East	Lisronagh	Clonmel	II.	315
44	Moanroe Beg	182 0 14	Limerick	Glenquin	Killeedy	Newcastle	II.	246
31, 32	Moanroe Commons	68 1 30	Kilkenny	Knocktopher	Knocktopher	Thomastown	I.	112
44	Moanroe More	379 0 15	Limerick	Glenquin	Killeedy	Newcastle	II.	246
60	Moanteen	242 1 3	Tipperary, S.R.	Clanwilliam	Relickmurry & Athassel	Tipperary	II.	310
25, 29	Moanteenmore	454 2 17	Kilkenny	Gowran	Dungarvan	Thomastown	I.	94
26, 27, 34	Moanvane	1,068 1 15	King's Co.	Upper Philipstown	Ballykean	Mountmellick	I.	143
32	Moanvane	135 2 33	Roscommon	Castlereagh	Kiltullagh	Castlereagh	IV.	202
45	Moanvaun	540 1 11	Tipperary, N.R.	Kilnamanagh Upper	Doon	Tipperary	II.	277
51	Moanvaun	247 3 27	Tipperary, N.R.	Kilnamanagh Upper	Toem	Tipperary	II.	280
15, 21	Moanvawn	237 3 20	Wicklow	Upper Talbotstown	Freynestown	Baltinglass	I.	364
55, 63	Moanvurrin	461 1 35	Tipperary, S.R.	Middlethird	Drangan	Cashel	II.	326
29	Moanwing	98 2 32	Limerick	Connello Lower	Rathkeale	Rathkeale	II.	229
33	Moarhaun	58 0 10	Clare	Inchiquin	Kilnamona	Ennis	II.	27
37, 41	Moat	161 1 14	Cavan	Clanmahon	Ballymachugh	Cavan	III.	76
19	Moat	454 0 9b	Galway	Ballymoe	Kilbegnet	Glennamaddy	IV.	8
87	Moat	238 3 20	Galway	Kilconnell	Aughrim	Ballinasloe	IV.	39
117	Moat	208 0 27	Galway	Longford	Killimorbologue	Portumna	IV.	59
45	Moat	649 2 37	Galway	Tiaquin	Moylough	Glennamaddy	IV.	80
13	Moat	140 2 14	Kilkenny	Crannagh	Freshford	Kilkenny	I.	85
89	Moat	339 3 23	Mayo	Carra	Ballintober	Castlebar	IV.	125
90	Moat	210 0 36	Mayo	Clanmorris	Balla	Castlebar	IV.	132
102, 103	Moat	251 2 33	Mayo	Costello	Annagh	Claremorris	IV.	138
8	Moat	792 0 37	Meath	Fore	Killeagh	Oldcastle	I.	201
5, 11	Moat	340 3 24	Meath	Lower Kells	Kilbeg	Kells	I.	202
42	Moat	275 2 21	Meath	Lower Moyfenrath	Rathmolyon	Trim	I.	211
10	Moat	302 2 14	Meath	Upper Kells	Dulane	Kells	I.	205
30	Moat	570 2 11	Queen's Co.	Cullenagh	Dysartgallen	Abbeyleix	I.	239
36	Moat	24 0 5	Waterford	Decies within Drum	Ringagonagh	Dungarvan	II.	353
59	Moatabulcane	50 1 15	Tipperary, S.R.	Clanwilliam	Templenoe	Tipperary	II.	312
8	Moatalusha or Inchisland	233 0 35	Carlow	Carlow	Grangeford	Carlow	I.	2
15	Moatavally	231 1 24	Longford	Ardagh	Street	Granard	I.	153
38	Moatavanny	217 3 34	Kildare	Kilkea and Moone	Castledermot	Baltinglass	I.	59
14	Moat Commons	22 3 26	Kildare	Clane	Clane	Naas	I.	54
30, 36	Moategranoge	374 2 7	Westmeath	Clonlonan	Kilcleagh	Athlone	I.	261
30	MOATE T.	—	Westmeath	Clonlonan	{ Kilcleagh	Athlone	I.	262
					Kilmanaghan }			
14, 15	Moatfarrell	769 2 23	Longford	Granard	Clonbroney	Granard	I.	155
10	Moatfield	18 1 27	Longford	Granard	Granard	Granard	I.	156
25	Moathill	41 1 15	Meath	Lower Navan	Navan	Navan	I.	215
4, 5	Moatpark	217 0 35	Kilkenny	Fassadinin	Donaghmore	Castlecomer	I.	89
16, 22	Moatquarter	215 0 16	Tipperary, N.R.	Ikerrin	Rathnaveoge	Roscrea	II.	276
51, 59	Moatquarter	93 0 5	Tipperary, S.R.	Clanwilliam	Donohill	Tipperary	II.	307
59, 60, 67	Moatquarter	388 3 33	Tipperary, S.R.	Clanwilliam	Kilfeakle	Tipperary	II.	308
34, 35	Moatstown	113 0 9d	Kildare	Narragh & Reban West	Churchtown	Athy	I.	67
36	Moat Town	512 2 34	Meath	Lune	Kildalkey	Trim	I.	208
100, 108	Moaty	191 0 9	Galway	Longford	Clonfert	Ballinasloe	IV.	57
99	Moaty	218 2 1	Galway	Longford	Kiltormer	Ballinasloe	IV.	60
61, 62	Mobarnan	536 2 24	Tipperary, S.R.	Middlethird	Magorban	Cashel	II.	328
26, 31	Moboy	577 1 0	Antrim	Lower Toome	Ahoghill	Ballymena	III.	33
37	Moboy	961 0 25e	Tyrone	Dungannon Upper	Kildress	Cookstown	III.	309
45, 46	Mobuy	1,409 3 18	Londonderry	Loughinsholin	Lissan	Magherafelt	III.	242
40	Mockbeggar	27 0 1	Fermanagh	Coole	Galloon	Clones	III.	200
61	Mocklershill	417 2 32	Tipperary, S.R.	Middlethird	Magorban	Cashel	II.	328
69, 76	Mocklerstown	711 2 37	Tipperary, S.R.	Middlethird	Colman	Cashel	II.	325
5, 6	Mocmoyne	202 2 12	Roscommon	Boyle	Boyle	Boyle	IV.	194
121, 123	Mocollagan	185 0 6f	Mayo	Kilmaine	Shrule	Ballinrobe	IV.	158
19, 20	Mocollop	375 0 7g	Waterford	Coshmore & Coshbride	Lismore and Mocollop	Lismore	II.	347
121, 123	Mocorha	603 0 11	Mayo	Kilmaine	Shrule	Ballinrobe	IV.	158
14	Mocurry East	243 2 17	Wexford	Scarawalsh	Templeshanbo	Enniscorthy	I.	326
13, 14, 18, 19	Mocurry West	449 0 25	Wexford	Scarawalsh	Templeshanbo	Enniscorthy	I.	326
36	Moddybeg	45 0 24	Wexford	Shelmaliere West	Taghmon	Wexford	I.	335
23	Modeonagh	179 0 11	Fermanagh	Tirkennedy	Enniskillen	Enniskillen	III.	222
19, 20	Modeese	218 3 29	Monaghan	Cremorne	Clontibret	Castleblayney	III.	261

(a) Including 4A. 3R. 0P. water.
(b) Including 9A. 0R. 30P. water.
(c) Including 20A. 2R. 18P. water.

(d) Including 5A. 0R. 36P. River Barrow.
(e) Including 14A. 1R. 19P. Lough Bracken.

(f) Including 26A. 0R. 20P. water.
(g) Including 13A. 3R. 36P. water.

No. of Sheet of the Ordnance Survey Maps.	Townlands and Towns.	Area in Statute Acres.			County.	Barony.	Parish.	Poor Law Union in 1857.	Townland Census of 1851, Part I.	
		A.	R.	P.					Vol.	Page
55,56,63,64	Modeshil (*Ayre*)	1,032	2	23	Tipperary, S.R.	Slievardagh	Modeshil	Callan	II.	335
55, 63	Modeshil (*Sankey*)	377	2	25	Tipperary, S.R.	Slievardagh	Modeshil	Callan	II.	335
18	Modorragh	151	1	38	Leitrim	Drumahaire	Inishmagrath	Manorhamilton	IV.	97
17	Modranstown	122	1	28	Westmeath	Rathconrath	Rathconrath	Mullingar	I.	284
10, 15	Modreeny	255	1	22	Tipperary, N.R.	Lower Ormond	Modreeny	Borrisokane	II.	287
20	Moe	42	2	30	Clare	Tulla Upper	Feakle	Scarriff	II.	40
66	Mogeely	259	1	22	Cork, E.R.	Imokilly	Mogeely	Middleton	II.	90
37, 46	Mogeely Lower	304	1	5	Cork, E.R.	Kinnatalloon	Mogeely	Fermoy	II.	98
46	Mogeely Upper	247	0	38	Cork, E.R.	Kinnatalloon	Mogeely	Fermoy	II.	98
59, 60	Mogh	292	2	7	Tipperary, S.R.	Clanwilliam	Rathlynin	Tipperary	II.	309
45, 53	Moghan	178	3	8	Tyrone	Dungannon Middle	Donaghmore	Dungannon	III.	302
34, 40	Mogland	180	3	5	Tipperary, N.R.	Kilnamanagh Upper	Upperchurch	Thurles	II.	281
62	Moglass	49	2	20	Tipperary, S.R.	Middlethird	Cooleagh	Cashel	II.	326
62	Moglass	372	3	12	Tipperary, S.R.	Slievardagh	Killenaule	Cashel	II.	334
10	Mogouhy	86	2	5	Clare	Burren	Carran	Ballyvaghan	II.	11
51	Mogullaan	82	3	14	Clare	Bunratty Lower	Drumline	Ennis	II.	3
82, 83	Mogumna	201	2	8	Donegal	Banagh	Killybegs Lower	Glenties	III.	110
83	Mogumna Mountain	108	1	37	Donegal	Banagh	Killybegs Lower	Glenties	III.	110
141	Mohanagh	675	2	0	Cork, W.R.	West Carbery (E.D.)	Aghadown	Skibbereen	II.	137
10,11,16,17	Moheedian	344	2	10*a*	Roscommon	Frenchpark	Creeve	Car*k*. on Shannon	IV.	203
14	Moher	99	0	36	Cavan	Lower Loughtee	Drumlane	Cavan	III.	80
8	Moher	939	3	13	Cavan	Tullyhaw	Drumreilly	Bawnboy	III.	91
9, 10	Moher	218	0	30	Cavan	Tullyhaw	Tomregan	Bawnboy	III.	96
26	Moher	202	2	6	Cavan	Upper Loughtee	Denn	Cavan	III.	83
26, 32, 33	Moher	590	3	30	Cavan	Upper Loughtee	Lavey	Cavan	III.	86
30	Moher	427	1	13	Cork, E.R.	Duhallow	Cullen	Millstreet	II.	70
32	Moher	113	1	13	Fermanagh	Clanawley	Killesher	Enniskillen	III.	193
32, 33	Moher	219	0	3	Fermanagh	Clanawley	Kinawley	Enniskillen	III.	194
87	Moher	154	3	13	Galway	Clonmacnowen	Kilcloony	Ballinasloe	IV.	25
44	Moher	211	1	32	Galway	Tiaquin	Abbeyknockmoy	Tuam	IV.	75
6	Moher	225	0	26	Kerry	Iraghticonnor	Murher	Glin	II.	193
24, 25	Moher	146	1	25	Leitrim	Carrigallen	Oughteragh	Bawnboy	IV.	92
35	Moher	130	2	22	Leitrim	Mohill	Annaduff	Mohill	IV.	105
37	Moher	70	2	27	Leitrim	Mohill	Mohill	Mohill	IV.	108
2, 4	Moher	191	0	3	Leitrim	Rosclogher	Rossinver	Ballyshannon	IV.	112
7, 15	Moher	481	2	1	Limerick	Owneybeg	Abington	Limerick	II.	251
24	Moher	240	1	13	Roscommon	Ballintober North	Kilglass	Strokestown	IV.	186
36, 37	Moher	521	3	17	Roscommon	Ballintober South	Cloontuskert	Roscommon	IV.	188
29	Moher	347	1	37*b*	Roscommon	Roscommon	Cloonfinlough	Strokestown	IV.	209
40	Moher	592	0	6	Tipperary, N.R.	Kilnamanagh Upper	Upperchurch	Thurles	II.	281
86	Moher	98	3	39	Tipperary, S.R.	Iffa and Offa West	Templetenny	Clogheen	II.	320
36, 45	Mohera	904	3	5	Cork, E.R.	Barrymore	Castlelyons	Fermoy	II.	53
23, 27	Moheracreevy Glebe	94	3	8	Leitrim	Leitrim	Kiltoghert	Car*k*. on Shannon	IV.	102
45, 51	Moheragh	1,340	0	30	Tipperary, S.R.	Kilnamanagh Lower	Donohill	Tipperary	II.	323
9, 10	Moheramoylan	189	1	8	Clare	Burren	Carran	Ballyvaghan	II.	11
37	Moheranea	76	2	33	Fermanagh	Clanawley	Kinawley	Enniskillen	III.	194
9, 10	Moheraroon	138	0	20	Clare	Burren	Carran	Ballyvaghan	II.	12
16	Moherbullog	30	3	28	Clare	Inchiquin	Rath	Corrofin	II.	28
34	Mohercrom	215	2	31	Cavan	Clankee	Enniskeen	Bailieborough	III.	73
11	Moher East	335	0	35	Queen's Co.	Upperwoods	Offerlane	Mountmellick	I.	252
44,45,50,51	Moher East	326	3	0*c*	Tipperary, N.R.	Kilnamanagh Upper	Toem	Tipperary	II.	280
32	Mohereen	486	3	12*d*	Cork, E.R.	Duhallow	Kilshannig	Mallow	II.	74
21, 24	Moher (*Gregg*)	465	3	26	Leitrim	Leitrim	Kiltubbrid	Car*k*. on Shannon	IV.	104
9	Moherloob	111	1	9	Cavan	Tullyhaw	Templeport	Bawnboy	III.	95
18	Mohernagh	822	3	8	Limerick	Shanid	Kilmoylan	Glin	II.	256
32	Mohernameela	72	1	12	Leitrim	Leitrim	Mohill	Mohill	IV.	104
7, 9	Moherreagh	195	2	20	Cavan	Tullyhaw	Templeport	Bawnboy	III.	95
35	Moherrevan	221	0	10*e*	Leitrim	Mohill	Annaduff	Mohill	IV.	105
23, 24	Moherrevogagh	157	2	23	Leitrim	Leitrim	Kiltubbrid	Car*k*. on Shannon	IV.	104
11	Moher West	316	0	37	Queen's Co.	Upperwoods	Offerlane	Mountmellick	I.	252
50	Moher West	36	2	12	Tipperary, N.R.	Kilnamanagh Upper	Toem	Tipperary	II.	280
10, 14	Mohil	294	1	9	Kilkenny	Fassadinin	Kilmademoge	Kilkenny	I.	90
32	Mohill	116	2	20	Leitrim	Mohill	Mohill	Mohill	IV.	108
32	Mohill T.	—			Leitrim	Mohill	Mohill	Mohill	IV.	109
55	Mohober	959	2	27	Tipperary, S.R.	Slievardagh	Lismalin	Callan	II.	335
107,108,120	Mohona	424	2	29	Cork, W.R.	East Carbery (W.D.)	Fanlobbus	Dunmanway	II.	132
22	Mohullen	173	0	27	Carlow	St. Mullins Lower	Ballyellin	New Ross	I.	13
19	Moig	305	2	29	Limerick	Shanid	Kilmoylan	Glin	II.	256
11	Moig East	116	3	23	Limerick	Kenry	Kilcornan	Rathkeale	II.	249
11	Moig East Glebe	77	1	9	Limerick	Kenry	Kilcornan	Rathkeale	II.	249
14, 15, 23	Moigh	209	0	9	Limerick	Clanwilliam	Caherconlish	Limerick	II.	222
7	Moigh	171	2	39	Roscommon	Boyle	Tumna	Car*k*. on Shannon	IV.	198
32	Moigh Lower	170	2	37	Roscommon	Castlereagh	Kiltullagh	Castlereagh	IV.	202

(*a*) Including 10A. 2R. 23P. water.　　　(*c*) Including 1A. 0R. 28P. detached portion.　　　(*e*) Including 13A. 1R. 31P. water.
(*b*) Including 3A. 1R. 32P. water.　　　(*d*) Including 11A. 3R. 4P. water.

No. of Sheet of the Ordnance Survey Maps.	Townlands and Towns.	Area in Statute Acres.	County.	Barony.	Parish.	Poor Law Union in 1857.	Townland Census of 1851, Part I.	
		A. R. P.					Vol.	Page
32	Moigh Upper . .	167 0 21a	Roscommon .	Castlereagh . .	Kiltullagh . .	Castlereagh .	IV.	202
11	Moig North . .	244 2 35	Limerick . .	Connello Lower .	Askeaton . .	Rathkeale .	II.	226
10, 11	Moig South . .	811 1 35	Limerick . .	Connello Lower .	Askeaton . .	Rathkeale .	II.	227
11	Moig West . .	218 1 2	Limerick . .	Kenry . . .	Kilcornan . .	Rathkeale .	II.	249
13	MOIRA T. . .	—	Down . . .	Lower Iveagh, Up. pt.	Moira . . .	Lurgan . .	III.	170
31, 34	Mokecran . .	158 0 6	Monaghan . .	Farney . . .	Magheracloone .	Carrickmacross	III.	273
26	Molassy . . .	169 0 7	Kilkenny . .	Callan . . .	Callan . . .	Callan . .	I.	83
43	Moleena . . .	58 1 25	Fermanagh .	Clankelly . .	Drummully . .	Clones . .	III.	197
41	Molerick . . .	626 3 30	Meath . . .	Upper Moyfenrath .	Clonard . .	Edenderry .	I.	213
25	Mollaneen . .	260 2 12	Clare . . .	Inchiquin . .	Dysert . . .	Ennis . .	II.	24
38	Molly . . .	298 3 31	Fermanagh .	Knockninny . .	Kinawley . .	Lisnaskea .	III.	202
5, 6, 10	Molly . . .	513 0 24	Longford . .	Granard . . .	Columbkille . .	Granard . .	I.	156
2, 3, 6	Mollyglass . .	127 0 2	Longford . .	Granard . . .	Columbkille . .	Granard . .	I.	156
4	Mollynadinta . .	195 1 7	Leitrim . .	Rosclogher . .	Rossinver . .	Ballyshannon .	IV.	112
19	Mollyroe . .	66 0 19	Longford . .	Moydow . . .	Moydow . . .	Longford . .	I.	162
38	Molosky . . .	583 0 9	Clare . . .	Ibrickan . .	Kilmurry . .	Kilrush . .	II.	23
67	Molougha . .	508 2 33b	Clare . . .	Moyarta . . .	Kilrush . . .	Kilrush . .	II.	33
88	Moloughabbey . .	292 3 18	Tipperary, S.R. .	Iffa and Offa West .	Molough . . .	Clogheen . .	II.	318
88	Moloughnewtown .	272 0 18c	Tipperary, S.R. .	Iffa and Offa West .	Molough . . .	Clogheen . .	II.	318
39,40,42,43	Molum . . .	702 0 28	Kilkenny . .	Iverk . . .	Ullid . . .	Waterford .	I.	107
56	Molusk, Grange of .	928 3 33d	Antrim . . .	Lower Belfast . .	Templepatrick .	Belfast . .	III.	9
62	Momeen . . .	509 1 10	Donegal . .	Raphoe . . .	Taughboyne . .	Strabane . .	III.	144
28, 31	Momony . . .	89 2 14	Monaghan . .	Farney . . .	Donoghmoyne .	Carrickmacross	III.	270
17	Monablanchameen .	151 2 38	Kilkenny . .	Crannagh . .	Tubbridbritain .	Urlingford .	I.	87
30	Monaboul . .	187 3 29	Kilkenny . .	Kells . . .	Kilmaganny . .	Callan . .	I.	109
66	Monabraher . .	79 0 1	Cork, E.R. . .	Imokilly . .	Ardagh . . .	Youghal . .	II.	83
66	Monabraher . .	99 2 37	Cork, E.R. . .	Imokilly . . .	Killeagh . .	Youghal . .	II.	88
5	Monabraher . .	142 1 8e	Limerick . .	Pubblebrien and Municipal Borough .	Killeely . . .	Limerick . .	II.	253
21	Monabreeka . .	141 2 32	Waterford . .	Coshmore&Coshbride	Lismore and Mocollop	Lismore . .	II.	347
9, 13	Monabrika . .	150 3 7	Kilkenny . .	Crannagh . .	Freshford . .	Kilkenny . .	I.	85
13	Monabrogue . .	236 1 2	Kilkenny . .	Crannagh . .	Ballylarkin . .	Kilkenny . .	I.	85
39, 44	Monacahee . .	303 1 32	Wexford . .	Shelburne . .	Rathroe . . .	New Ross . .	I.	328
1	Monacallee . .	20 3 27	Waterford . .	Upperthird . .	St. Marys Clonmel .	Clonmel . .	II.	372
43	Monacappa . .	43 1 36	Kerry . . .	Corkaguiny . .	Dingle . . .	Dingle . .	II.	175
31	Monachunna . .	107 0 34	Kilkenny . .	Kells . . .	Dunnamaggan .	Callan . .	I.	108
111, 112	Monaclarig . .	41 2 10	Cork, E.R. . .	Kinsale . . .	Clontead . .	Kinsale . .	II.	99
39	Monaclaudy . .	187 1 13	Kildare . .	Kilkea and Moone .	Ballaghmoon .	Athy . .	I.	59
5	Monaclinoe . .	94 0 0	Limerick . .	Clanwilliam . .	St. Lawrence's .	Limerick . .	II.	225
62	Monacnapa . .	268 1 16	Cork, E.R. . .	East Muskerry .	Garrycloyne . .	Cork . .	II.	103
41	Monacocka . .	69 1 38	Tipperary, N.R. .	Eliogarty . .	Thurles . . .	Thurles . .	II.	273
30	Monacow . .	228 3 38	Galway . .	Dunmore . .	Tuam . . .	Tuam . .	IV.	36
77	Monacreagh . .	193 0 10	Cork, E.R. . .	Imokilly . . .	Ightermurragh .	Middleton .	II.	87
35	Monacullee . .	364 1 17	Waterford . .	Decies within Drum	Ardmore . .	Dungarvan .	II.	350
15, 20	Monadarragh . .	454 2 29	Longford . .	Ardagh . . .	Mostrim . .	Granard . .	I.	153
75, 81	Monaderreen . .	652 0 34	Tipperary, S.R. .	Iffa and Offa West .	Caher . . .	Clogheen . .	II.	318
2, 3	Monadiha . .	388 2 36	Waterford . .	Upperthird . .	Rathgormuck . .	Carrick on Suir	II.	371
61	Monadreela . .	120 0 38	Tipperary, S.R. .	Middlethird . .	St. Patricksrock .	Cashel . .	III.	331
27, 28	Monadrishane . .	214 3 34	Cork, E.R. . .	Condons&Clangibbon	Kilworth . .	Fermoy . .	II.	62
27	Monadubbaun . .	155 1 26	Kilkenny . .	Kells . . .	Dunnamaggan .	Callan . .	I.	108
5	Monaduff . .	263 3 21	Longford . .	Longford . .	Killoe . . .	Longford . .	I.	159
31	Monaduff . .	170 3 14	Westmeath . .	Moycashel . .	Ardnurcher or Horseleap . .	Mullingar .	I.	277
21	Monafehadee . .	158 0 33	Waterford . .	Coshmore&Coshbride	Lismore and Mocollop	Lismore . .	II.	347
14	Monaferrick . .	165 2 17	Queen's Co. .	Stradbally . .	Curraclone . .	Athy . .	I.	246
14	Monafrica . .	41 2 19	Kilkenny . .	Crannagh . .	Odagh . . .	Kilkenny . .	I.	86
41, 47	Monagalliagh . .	20 2 4f	Meath . . .	Upper Moyfenrath .	Clonard . .	Edenderry .	I.	213
35	Monagally East .	156 1 1	Waterford . .	Decies within Drum	Aglish . . .	Dungarvan .	II.	349
34, 35	Monagally West .	287 0 10	Waterford . .	Decies within Drum	Aglish . . .	Dungarvan .	II.	349
69	Monagarraun . .	492 1 38g	Mayo . . .	Carra . . .	Islandeady . .	Castlebar .	IV.	129
3	Monagarrow Little .	71 1 8	Wexford . .	Gorey . . .	Kilgorman . .	Gorey . .	I.	318
3, 7	Monagarrow Lower	195 2 0	Wexford . .	Gorey . . .	Kilgorman . .	Gorey . .	I.	318
3	Monagarrow Upper	182 3 34	Wexford . .	Gorey . . .	Kilgorman . .	Gorey . .	I.	318
23	Monage . . .	82 0 25	Monaghan . .	Dartree . . .	Ematris . . .	Cootehill .	III.	267
6	Monagead . .	164 1 18h	Westmeath . .	Moygoish . .	Street . . .	Granard . .	I.	281
20	Monagear . .	196 0 24	Wexford . .	Scarawalsh . .	Clone . . .	Enniscorthy .	I.	322
60	Monagee . . .	157 2 1	Tipperary, S.R. .	Middlethird . .	St. Patricksrock .	Cashel . .	II.	331
35	Monageela . .	437 1 39	Waterford . .	Decies within Drum	Ardmore . .	Dungarvan .	II.	350
27, 32	Monaghan . .	160 2 37	Antrim . . .	Lower Toome . .	Kirkinriola . .	Ballymena .	III.	32
21	Monaghan . .	182 0 39	Fermanagh .	Magheraboy . .	Devenish . .	Enniskillen .	II.	211
27,28,33,34	Monaghanoose . .	648 2 27i	Cavan . . .	Clankee . . .	Bailieborough .	Bailieborough .	III.	71
25, 32	Monaghanstown .	707 0 21	Westmeath . .	Moycashel . .	Dysart . . .	Mullingar .	I.	278
9	MONAGHAN T. .	—	Monaghan . .	Monaghan . .	Monaghan . .	Monaghan .	III.	277

(a) Including 6A. 0R. 0P. water.
(b) Including 23A. 2R. 39P. water.
(c) Including 10A. 1R. 16P. water.
(d) Including 9A. 1R. 18P. water.

(e) { Within the Municipal Boundary, 10A. 0R. 36P.
  { Without the Municipal Boundary, 132A. 0R. 12P.
(f) Including 6A. 0R. 30P. detached portion.

(g) Including 3A. 3R. 32P. water.
(h) Including 11A. 0R. 3P. water.
(i) Including 5A. 0R. 0P. water.

No. of Sheet of the Ordnance Survey Maps.	Townlands and Towns.	Area in Statute Acres.	County.	Barony.	Parish.	Poor Law Union in 1857.	Townland Census of 1851, Part I.	
		A. R. P.					Vol.	Page
35	Monagilleeny . .	163 2 17	Waterford .	Decies within Drum	Ardmore . .	Youghal . .	II.	350
40	Monaglogh _ . .	297 2 37	Wicklow . .	Arklow . . .	Killahurler . .	Rathdrum . .	I.	345
19,20,24,25	Monagor . .	186 3 10	Monaghan .	Cremorne . .	Clontibret . .	Castleblayney .	III.	261
18	Monagormly . .	367 2 39a	Galway . .	Tiaquin . .	Kilkerrin . .	Glennamaddy .	IV.	77
78	Monagoul . .	184 1 8	Cork, E.R. .	Imokilly . .	Kilmacdonogh .	Youghal . .	II.	88
39	Monagoush . .	270 0 36	Waterford .	Decies within Drum	Ardmore . .	Dungarvan . .	II.	350
45, 46	Monagown . .	491 0 36	Cork, E.R. .	Kinnatalloon .	Knockmourne .	Fermoy . .	II.	93
16	Monagreany Lower	306 3 15	Wexford . .	Gorey . . .	Monamolin . .	Gorey . .	I.	321
16	Monagreany Upper	352 0 22	Wexford . .	Gorey . . .	Monamolin . .	Gorey . .	I.	321
30	Monaguillagh .	130 0 1	Armagh . .	Fews Upper .	Creggan . .	Castleblayney .	III.	43
89	Monagurra . .	287 2 38	Cork, E.R. .	Imokilly . .	Kilnahon . .	Middleton . .	II.	89
12, 17, 18	Monaincha . .	1,778 1 35b	Tipperary, N.R.	Ikerrin . .	Corbally . .	Roscrea . .	II.	275
18, 31	Monairmore . .	126 3 7	Galway . .	Tiaquin . .	Kilkerrin . .	Glennamaddy .	IV.	77
41	Monakeeba . .	165 0 0	Tipperary, N.R.	Eliogarty . .	Thurles . .	Thurles . .	II.	273
24	Monakirka . .	155 1 12	Waterford .	Decies without Drum	Stradbally . .	Kilmacthomas .	II.	361
51, 62	Monalahy . .	202 3 29	Cork, E.R. .	Barretts . .	Grenagh . .	Cork . .	I.	49
2	Monalee . .	256 2 13	Wexford . .	Gorey . . .	Kilnenor . .	Gorey . .	I.	319
14, 19	Monalee . .	390 3 37	Wexford . .	Scarawalsh .	Templeshanbo .	Enniscorthy .	I.	326
1, 2	Monaleehill . .	434 2 27	Wexford . .	Gorey . . .	Kilnenor . .	Gorey . .	I.	319
28	Monalia . .	164 1 4	Monaghan .	Farney . . .	Donaghmoyne .	Carrickmacross	III.	270
13	Monalin . .	152 2 20	Wicklow . .	Newcastle .	Newcastle Upper .	Rathdrum . .	I.	353
16	Monalla . .	35 0 36	Fermanagh .	Tirkennedy .	Derryvullan .	Enniskillen .	III.	221
71	Monallig . .	252 0 0c	Cork, E.R. .	East Muskerry .	Cannaway . .	Macroom . .	II.	102
55	Monaloo . .	438 1 8	Cork, E.R. .	Kinnatalloon .	Mogeely . .	Youghal . .	II.	99
80, 86	Monaloughra .	156 1 19	Tipperary, S.R.	Iffa and Offa West .	Shanrahan . .	Clogheen . .	II.	320
21	Monalour Lower	180 3 38	Waterford .	Coshmore & Coshbride	Lismore and Mocollop	Lismore . .	II.	347
12, 21	Monalour Upper	234 1 27	Waterford .	Coshmore & Coshbride	Lismore and Mocollop	Lismore . .	II.	347
31	Monaltybane .	130 0 38d	Monaghan .	Farney . . .	Killanny . .	Carrickmacross	III.	271
31	Monaltyduff . .	130 0 5e	Monaghan .	Farney . . .	Killanny . .	Carrickmacross	III.	271
3	Monalug . .	75 1 10	Wexford . .	Gorey . . .	Kilgorman . .	Gorey . .	I.	318
35	Monalummery .	257 0 36	Waterford .	Decies within Drum	Ardmore . .	Dungarvan . .	II.	350
52	Monalumpera .	110 0 11	Tipperary, S.R.	Middlethird .	Ardmayle . .	Cashel . .	II.	324
21	Monaman Lower	141 2 33	Waterford .	Coshmore & Coshbride	Lismore and Mocollop	Lismore . .	II.	347
25	Monamanry . .	89 2 24	Queen's Co. .	Stradbally . .	Tullomoy . .	Athy . .	I.	248
21	Monaman Upper	168 0 22	Waterford .	Coshmore & Coshbride	Lismore and Mocollop	Lismore . .	II.	347
73, 86	Monambraher .	90 0 18	Galway . .	Kilconnell .	Kilconnell . .	Ballinasloe .	IV.	40
61	Monameagh . .	258 1 15	Tipperary, S.R.	Middlethird .	St. Patricksrock .	Cashel . .	II.	331
35, 38	Monameean . .	476 0 25	Waterford .	Decies within Drum	Ardmore . .	Dungarvan . .	II.	350
25	Monameelagh .	219 2 11	Waterford .	Middlethird .	Islandikane .	Waterford . .	II.	367
17, 18	Monamintra . .	356 2 1	Waterford .	Gaultiere . .	Monamintra .	Waterford . .	II.	364
46, 47	Monamoe . .	314 1 22	Tipperary, N.R.	Eliogarty . .	Holycross . .	Thurles . .	II.	270
18, 24	Monamolin . .	714 0 21	Wexford . .	Bantry . . .	Templeludigan .	New Ross . .	I.	303
16	MONAMOLIN T. .	—	Wexford . .	Ballaghkeen .	Monamolin . .	Gorey . .	I.	298
27	Monamonra . .	429 1 1	Queen's Co. .	Clandonagh .	Rathdowney .	Donaghmore .	I.	234
88	Monamore . .	101 3 16	Mayo . .	Murrisk . .	Aghagower . .	Westport . .	IV.	159
36	Monamraher . .	183 1 30	Waterford .	Decies within Drum	Ardmore . .	Dungarvan . .	·II.	350
5	Monamuck . .	31 0 4f	Limerick . .	Clanwilliam and Municipal Borough .	St. John's . .	Limerick . .	II.	225
10	Monamuck . .	446 0 35	Wicklow . .	Lower Talbotstown .	Boystown . .	Baltinglass .	I.	359
34, 35	Monanacloy . .	104 3 4	Fermanagh .	Clankelly . .	Galloon . .	Lisnaskea . .	III.	198
28	Monanagirr . .	174 0 28g	Monaghan .	Farney . . .	Donaghmoyne .	Carrickmacross	III.	270
10, 17	Monanaleen . .	287 0 38	Clare . .	Inchiquin . .	Killinaboy . .	Corrofin . .	II.	27
19	Monanameal . .	543 0 28	Tyrone . .	Strabane Upper .	Bodoney Lower .	Gortin . .	III.	324
53	Monananig . .	713 1 30	Cork, E.R. .	Barrymore .	Gortroe . .	Fermoy . .	II.	55
53	Monananig . .	67 1 0	Cork, E.R. .	Barrymore .	Templebodan .	Fermoy . .	II.	58
27	Monanarrig . .	289 3 32	Wexford . .	Ballaghkeen .	Ballyvaldon .	Enniscorthy .	I.	292
8	Monanclogh . .	536 0 26	Antrim . .	Cary . . .	Armoy . .	Ballycastle .	III.	11
64	Monaneague . .	163 1 26	Cork, E.R. .	Barrymore .	Kilquane . .	Cork . .	II.	55
41	Monanearla . .	65 0 27	Tipperary, N.R.	Eliogarty . .	Thurles . .	Thurles . .	II.	273
35, 38	Monaneea . .	171 0 7	Waterford .	Decies within Drum	Ardmore . .	Dungarvan . .	II.	350
34	Monang . .	83 1 30	Waterford .	Coshmore & Coshbride	Kilcockan . .	Lismore . .	II.	343
31	Monang . .	52 0 17	Waterford .	Decies without Drum	Dungarvan . .	Dungarvan . .	II.	355
34	Monanimy Lower	439 2 25h	Cork, E.R. .	Fermoy . .	Monanimy . .	Mallow . .	II.	81
26, 34	Monanimy Upper	388 0 23	Cork, E.R. .	Fermoy . .	Monanimy . .	Mallow . .	II.	81
31	Monanny . .	159 1 16	Monaghan .	Farney . . .	Donaghmoyne .	Carrickmacross	III.	270
34	Monanoe . .	232 0 13	Clare . .	Bunratty Upper .	Doora . .	Ennis . .	II.	8
12	Monanooag . .	104 3 13	Limerick . .	Kenry . . .	Kildimo . .	Rathkeale . .	II.	250
22, 28	Monanore . .	426 3 25	Tipperary, N.R.	Upper Ormond .	Aghnameadle .	Nenagh . .	II.	289
18, 19	Monantin . .	142 0 27	Monaghan .	Cremorne . .	Ballybay . .	Castleblayney .	III.	259
40, 41	Monanveel . .	463 0 13	Cork, E.R. .	Duhallow . .	Kilshannig . .	Mallow . .	II.	74
42	Monaparson . .	354 3 38	Cork, E.R. .	Barretts . .	Mourneabbey .	Mallow . .	II.	50
27, 31	Monapheeby or Boherbaun Upper .	374 1 24	Kildare . .	Offaly West .	Harristown . .	Athy . .	I.	72

(a) Including 30A. 3R. 26P. water.
(b) Including 49A. 1R. 31P. water.
(c) Including 15A. 0R. 0P. water.
(d) Including 12A. 3R. 11P. water.

(e) Including 19A. 3R. 18P. water.
(f) { Within the Municipal Boundary, 30A. 3R. 10P.
   { Without the Municipal Boundary, 0A. 0R. 34P.

(g) Including 7A. 0R. 34P. water.
(h) Including 18A. 0R. 14P. water.

4 X

No. of Sheet of the Ordnance Survey Maps.	Townlands and Towns.	Area in Statute Acres.			County.	Barony.	Parish.	Poor Law Union in 1857.	Townland Census of 1851, Part I.	
		A.	R.	P.					Vol.	Page
27	Monaquill	416	2	22	Tipperary, N.R.	Upper Ormond	Kilnaneave	Nenagh	II.	291
75,76,81,82	Monaraha	187	1	38	Tipperary, S.R.	Iffa and Offa West	Caher	Clogheen	II.	318
42	Monaraheen	181	0	8	Tipperary, N.R.	Eliogarty	Twomileborris	Thurles	II.	274
26	Monarche Commons	389	3	5	Kilkenny	Callan	Callan	Callan	I.	83
63	Monard	868	1	18	Cork, E.R.	Cork	Whitechurch	Cork	II.	66
70	Monard	116	3	15	Galway	Clare	Lackagh	Galway	IV.	23
91	Monard	82	1	30	Mayo	Clanmorris	Mayo	Castlebar	IV.	135
58	Monard	313	0	33	Tipperary, S.R.	Clanwilliam	Solloghodmore	Tipperary	II.	311
11	Monard	369	1	15	Waterford	Coshmore&Coshbride	Lismore and Mocollop	Lismore	II.	347
72	Monareagh	159	2	4	Cork, E.R.	East Muskerry	Magourney	Macroom	II.	105
3	Monareagh	95	3	21	Wexford	Gorey	Inch	Gorey	I.	316
43, 52, 53	Monaree	183	3	7	Kerry	Corkaguiny	Kildrum	Dingle	II.	177
83	Monargan Glebe	361	3	4	Donegal	Banagh	Killybegs Lower	Glenties	III.	110
20, 26	Monaroan	325	1	29	Tipperary, N.R.	Upper Ormond	Kilmore	Nenagh	II.	291
19	Monart East	836	1	2	Wexford	Scarawalsh	Monart	Enniscorthy	I.	324
19	Monart West	252	2	9	Wexford	Scarawalsh	Monart	Enniscorthy	I.	324
23, 31	Monarud	239	3	32	Waterford	Decies without Drum	Kilgobnet	Dungarvan	II.	357
23	Monarudmountain	331	2	6	Waterford	Decies without Drum	Kilgobnet	Dungarvan	II.	357
18	Monascallaghan	286	0	27	Longford	Moydow	Moydow	Longford	I.	162
19	Monascreeban	293	0	18	Queen's Co.	Ballyadams	Ballyadams	Athy	I.	231
4	Monascreebe	434	2	16	Louth	Lower Dundalk	Ballymascanlan	Dundalk	I.	176
2, 6	Monaseed	143	0	19	Wexford	Gorey	Kilnahue	Gorey	I.	319
6	Monaseed Demesne	267	2	8	Wexford	Gorey	Kilnahue	Gorey	I.	319
28	Monashinnagh	51	2	24	Limerick	Shanid	Ardagh	Newcastle	II.	255
53	Monaskeha	218	0	33	Clare	Tulla Lower	Kiltenanlea	Limerick	II.	37
10	Monasootagh	793	1	16	Wexford	Scarawalsh	Kilcomb	Gorey	I.	323
11	Monasop	239	3	3	Queen's Co.	Upperwoods	Offerlane	Mountmellick	I.	252
30, 31	Monassa	281	2	15	Kilkenny	Kells	Ballytobin	Callan	I.	107
38, 39, 40	Monasset	912	3	27	Westmeath	Moycashel	Rahugh	Tullamore	I.	279
21	Monasterboice	276	2	3	Louth	Ferrard	Monasterboice	Drogheda	I.	181
21, 26	Monasterevin	208	1	32	Kildare	Offaly West	Monasterevin	Athy	I.	73
26, 27	Monasterevin Bog	153	0	24	Kildare	Offaly West	Monasterevin	Athy	I.	73
21, 26	MONASTEREVIN T.	—			Kildare	Offaly West	Monasterevin	Athy	I.	73
33	Monasternalea or Abbeygrey	503	1	14	Galway	Killian	Athleague	Mountbellew	IV.	43
33	Monasternalea or Abbeygrey	157	3	37	Galway	Killian	Killeroran	Mountbellew	IV.	44
31	Monaster North	262	0	10	Limerick	Pubblebrien	Monsteranenagh	Croom	II.	253
11, 12	Monasteroris	1,017	1	26	King's Co.	Coolestown	Monasteroris	Edenderry	I.	133
6	Monasterowen	185	1	18	Galway	Ballymoe	Templetogher	Glennamaddy	IV.	9
44, 46	Monasterredan	675	3	2	Sligo	Coolavin	Kilcolman	Boyle	IV.	223
46	Monasterredan or Annaghbeg	119	2	25a	Sligo	Coolavin	Kilcolman	Boyle	IV.	223
31	Monaster South	381	1	25	Limerick	Coshma	Monasteranenagh	Croom	II.	243
3, 7	Monastery	527	0	29	Wicklow	Rathdown	Powerscourt	Rathdown	I.	356
5	Monastill	92	0	6	Carlow	Rathvilly	Hacketstown	Shillelagh	I.	11
61	Monataggart	372	3	16	Cork, E.R.	East Muskerry	Donaghmore	Macroom	II.	103
20	Monataggart	153	1	14	Waterford	Coshmore&Coshbride	Lismore and Mocollop	Lismore	II.	347
20, 21	Monatarriv East	230	0	26	Waterford	Coshmore&Coshbride	Lismore and Mocollop	Lismore	II.	347
20	Monatarriv West	268	1	23	Waterford	Coshmore&Coshbride	Lismore and Mocollop	Lismore	II.	347
41	Monatierna	83	2	21	Tipperary, N.R.	Eliogarty	Twomileborris	Thurles	II.	274
58	Monatogher	74	1	8	Tipperary, S.R.	Clanwilliam	Solloghodmore	Tipperary	II.	311
53, 64	Monatooreen	182	3	35	Cork, E.R.	Barrymore	Kilquane	Cork	II.	55
31	Monatore	88	0	16	Kildare	Narragh and Reban East	Narraghmore	Athy	I.	66
26	Monatore	209	3	33	Wicklow	Upper Talbotstown	Ballynure	Baltinglass	I.	362
13	Monatouk or Bonatouk	135	3	30	Waterford	Decies without Drum	Seskinan	Lismore	II.	360
40	Monatray East	205	0	5	Waterford	Decies within Drum	Kinsalebeg	Youghal	II.	352
40	Monatray Middle	293	0	37	Waterford	Decies within Drum	Kinsalebeg	Youghal	II.	352
40	Monatray West	163	0	28	Waterford	Decies within Drum	Kinsalebeg	Youghal	II.	352
28, 29	Monatrim Lower	159	1	19	Waterford	Coshmore&Coshbride	Lismore and Mocollop	Lismore	II.	347
29	Monatrim Upper	200	2	10	Waterford	Coshmore&Coshbride	Lismore and Mocollop	Lismore	II.	347
3	Monature	232	3	37	Wexford	Gorey	Inch	Gorey	I.	316
14, 18	Monaughrim	982	1	8	Carlow	St. Mullins Upper	Moyacomb	Shillelagh	I.	14
13	Monavadaroe	169	0	25	Kilkenny	Crannagh	Tullaroan	Kilkenny	I.	88
81, 93	Monavaddra	476	3	1	Cork, W.R.	West Muskerry	Inchigeelagh	Dunmanway	II.	158
22, 23	Monavaddra	158	3	12	Kilkenny	Shillelogher	Tullaghanbrogue	Callan	I.	116
19	Monavaha	96	2	36	Limerick	Shanid	Robertstown	Glin	II.	258
19	Monavaha	77	0	29	Limerick	Shanid	Shanagolden	Glin	II.	258
11	Monavallet	193	1	39	Louth	Louth	Louth	Dundalk	I.	184
29	Monavally	40	0	17	Kerry	Trughanacmy	Tralee	Tralee	II.	213
61	Monavanshere	170	0	15	Cork, E.R.	East Muskerry	Donaghmore	Macroom	II.	103
55	Monavarnoge	333	0	8	Cork, E.R.	Imokilly	Ardagh	Youghal	II.	83
24, 32	Monavaud	56	2	25	Waterford	Decies without Drum	Stradbally	Kilmacthomas	II.	361

(a) Including 5A. 1R. 33P. water.

No. of Sheet of the Ordnance Survey Maps.	Townlands and Towns.	Area in Statute Acres.	County.	Barony.	Parish.	Poor Law Union in 1857.	Townland Census of 1851, Part I.	
		A. R. P.					Vol.	Page
31, 36	Monavea	1,004 0 13	Queen's Co.	Slievemargy	Killabban	Carlow	I.	245
39	Monavinnaun	156 1 29	Kilkenny	Iverk	Muckalee	Carrick on Suir	I.	106
32	Monavoddagh	49 2 23	Wexford	Ballaghkeen	Ballynaslaney	Enniscorthy	I.	292
6	Monavreece	144 0 23	Fermanagh	Lurg	Drumkeeran	Lowtherstown	III.	206
21	Monavugga	140 0 34	Waterford	Coshmore&Coshbride	Lismore and Mocollop	Lismore	II.	347
14	Monawilkin	208 3 28a	Fermanagh	Magheraboy	Inishmacsaint	Ballyshannon	III.	213
21, 27	Monawilling Lower	254 3 24	Wexford	Ballaghkeen	Kilcormick	Enniscorthy	I.	294
21	Monawilling Upper	223 2 15	Wexford	Ballaghkeen	Kilcormick	Enniscorthy	I.	294
26	Monawinnia	32 3 28	Kilkenny	Kells	Mallardstown	Callan	I.	110
6	Monbay Lower	283 3 4	Wexford	Gorey	Rossminoge	Gorey	I.	321
6	Monbay Upper	281 0 11	Wexford	Gorey	Rossminoge	Gorey	I.	321
14, 19	Monbeg	595 1 35	Wexford	Scarawalsh	Templeshanbo	Enniscorthy	I.	326
12, 21	Monboy	158 3 15	Waterford	Coshmore&Coshbride	Lismore and Mocollop	Lismore	II.	347
6, 10	Monbrief	291 1 31	Armagh	Oneilland East	Shankill	Lurgan	III.	51
14, 18	Monclone	245 1 24	Armagh	Orior Lower	Ballymore	Banbridge	III.	55
54	Monclink	237 1 25	Donegal	Raphoe	Raymoghy	Letterkenny	III.	142
44	Mondaniel	602 3 36	Cork, E.R.	Barrymore	Rathcormack	Fermoy	II.	57
26, 27	Mondaniel	197 3 11	Wexford	Ballaghkeen	Ballyhuskard	Enniscorthy	I.	292
12, 21	Mondellihy	342 3 34	Limerick	Coshma	Adare	Croom	II.	241
62	Mondooey Lower	154 2 25	Donegal	Raphoe	Raymoghy	Letterkenny	III.	142
62	Mondooey Middle	333 1 25	Donegal	Raphoe	Raymoghy	Letterkenny	III.	142
62	Mondooey Upper	482 1 14	Donegal	Raphoe	Raymoghy	Letterkenny	III.	142
15, 16, 22	Mondrehid	393 2 21	Queen's Co.	Upperwoods	Offerlane	Abbeyleix	I.	252
24, 25	Monduff	169 3 19	Wicklow	Newcastle	Rathnew	Rathdrum	I.	354
15, 21	Monea	141 0 28	Fermanagh	Magheraboy	Devenish	Enniskillen	III.	211
38, 40	Monea	432 0 22b	Waterford	Decies within Drum	Ardmore	Youghal	II.	350
88, 89	Monearaniska	31 1 18	Cork, E.R.	Imokilly	Cloyne	Middleton	II.	85
21	Monearla	172 0 14	Limerick	Coshma	Adare	Croom	II.	241
67	Monearmore	85 1 37	Cork, E.R.	Imokilly	Clonpriest	Youghal	II.	85
105	Monearmore	9 3 25	Galway	Loughrea	Kilconickny	Loughrea	IV.	63
105	Monearmore	53 1 5	Galway	Loughrea	Loughrea	Loughrea	IV.	66
66	Monearmore	21 1 0	Kerry	Magunihy	Killarney	Killarney	II.	203
58	Monearmore	42 0 21	Tipperary, S.R.	Clanwilliam	Cullen	Tipperary	II.	307
26	Monebrock	179 0 35	Queen's Co.	Ballyadams	Tankardstown	Athy	I.	232
33, 42	Monee East	404 2 33	Cork, E.R.	Fermoy	Rahan	Mallow	II.	82
3, 5	Moneen	652 2 12c	Cavan	Tullyhaw	Killinagh	Enniskillen	III.	92
3	Moneen	446 3 13d	Clare	Burren	Abbey	Ballyvaghan	II.	11
71	Moneen	145 1 15	Clare	Moyarta	Kilballyowen	Kilrush	II.	32
27	Moneen	277 0 30	Cork, E.R.	Fermoy	Glanworth	Fermoy	II.	79
96	Moneen	101 3 5	Cork, W.R.	Kinalmeaky	Brinny	Bandon	II.	152
84, 96	Moneen	589 2 9	Cork, W.R.	Kinalmeaky	Templemartin	Bandon	II.	153
70	Moneen	138 3 21	Donegal	Raphoe	Clonleigh	Strabane	III.	135
26, 52	Moneen	99 3 30	Fermanagh	Clanawley	Killesher	Enniskillen	III.	193
7	Moneen	81 0 23	Galway	Ballymoe	Ballynakill	Glennamaddy	IV.	5
1	Moneen	292 3 23	Galway	Ballymoe	Templetogher	Glennamaddy	IV.	9
43, 57	Moneen	125 0 33	Galway	Clare	Cummer	Tuam	IV.	19
59, 60	Moneen	85 1 34	Galway	Tiaquin	Ballymacward	Mountbellew	IV.	76
59	Moneen	522 0 2	Galway	Tiaquin	Killoscobe	Mountbellew	IV.	78
25, 29	Moneen	364 3 15	Kilkenny	Gowran	Graiguenamanagh	Thomastown	I.	95
1, 2	Moneen	273 1 22	Leitrim	Rosclogher	Rossinver	Ballyshannon	IV.	112
56	Moneen	119 0 17	Limerick	Coshlea	Particles	Kilmallock	II.	240
86	Moneen	154 0 17	Mayo	Murrisk	Kilgeever	Westport	IV.	160
14	Moneen	101 1 14	Mayo	Tirawley	Rathreagh	Killala	IV.	171
36	Moneen	48 3 9	Roscommon	Ballintober South	Cloontuskert	Roscommon	IV.	188
36	Moneen	191 1 19	Westmeath	Clonlonan	Kilcleagh	Athlone	I.	261
5, 6	Moneenabrone	138 3 37	Cavan	Tullyhaw	Templeport	Enniskillen	III.	95
24, 30	Moneenacully	80 3 28	Roscommon	Roscommon	Bumlin	Strokestown	IV.	208
8, 12	Moneenageer	177 1 11	Leitrim	Drumahaire	Cloonclare	Manorhamilton	IV.	93
14	Moneenagunnell	121 3 39	King's Co.	Garrycastle	Tisaran	Parsonstown	I.	139
100	Moneenaheeltia	92 0 32	Galway	Longford	Clonfert	Ballinasloe	IV.	57
21	Moneenalion Commons Lower	55 2 3	Dublin	Newcastle	Saggart	Celbridge	I.	34
21	Moneenalion Commons Upper	73 2 4	Dublin	Newcastle	Saggart	Celbridge	I.	35
1	Moneenally	285 0 37	Galway	Ballymoe	Templetogher	Glennamaddy	IV.	9
17, 18, 20	Moneenatieve	510 2 19	Galway	Drumahaire	Inishmagrath	Manorhamilton	IV.	97
9	Moneenaun	148 1 39	Kilkenny	Galmoy	Rathbeagh	Urlingford	I.	93
107	Moneenaveena	94 1 25	Galway	Longford	Killimorbologue	Portumna	IV.	59
32, 37	Moneenbane	95 1 9	Fermanagh	Clanawley	Kinawley	Enniskillen	III.	194
24	Moneenbog	113 2 0	Roscommon	Ballintober North	Termonbarry	Strokestown	IV.	188
78	Moneenbradagh	136 2 16	Mayo	Carra	Aglish	Castlebar	IV.	124
31	Moneenderg	74 2 4	King's Co.	Eglish	Drumcullen	Parsonstown	I.	134
8	Moneendogue	466 0 27	Fermanagh	Magheraboy	Inishmacsaint	Ballyshannon	III.	213

(a) Including 23A. 0R. 39P. water.
(b) Including 2A. 3R. 32P. detached portion.
(c) Including 7A. 0R. 8P. water.
(d) Including 19A. 3R. 11P. water.

No. of Sheet of the Ordinance Survey Maps.	Townlands and Towns.	Area in Statute Acres.	County.	Barony.	Parish.	Poor Law Union in 1857.	Townland Census of 1851, Part I.	
		A. R. P.					Vol.	Page
104, 114	Moneen East .	325 3 25	Galway .	Loughrea .	Ardrahan .	Loughrea .	IV.	62
3	Moneengaugagh .	136 0 33	Leitrim .	Rosclogher .	Rossinver .	Ballyshannon .	IV.	112
12	Moneenlom .	384 0 19	Leitrim .	Drumahaire .	Cloonclare .	Manorhamilton .	IV.	93
25,26,38,39	Moneenmore .	660 2 32	Galway .	Ross .	Cong .	Oughterard .	IV.	73
52	Moneennagliggin North or Boston .	129 1 28	Clare .	Bunratty Lower .	Killeely .	Limerick .	II.	5
52, 62	Moneennagliggin South .	89 1 9	Clare .	Bunratty Lower .	Killeely .	Limerick .	II.	5
135	Moneennamucky .	101 3 4	Cork, W.R.	Ibane and Barryroe	Ardfield .	Clonakilty .	II.	148
17	Moneenpollagh .	38 3 23	Galway .	Dunmore .	Dunmore .	Tuam .	IV.	34
18, 20	Moneenreave .	208 2 31	Leitrim .	Drumahaire .	Inishmagrath .	Manorhamilton .	IV.	97
19, 20	Moneenroe .	161 2 3	Galway .	Ballymoe .	Kilbegnet .	Glennamaddy .	IV.	8
6	Moneenroe .	1,303 1 11	Kilkenny .	Fassadinin .	Castlecomer .	Castlecomer .	I.	88
110	Moneens .	259 3 7	Cork, W.R.	Kinalmeaky .	Desertserges .	Bandon .	II.	152
6, 8	Moneensauran .	1,739 3 33	Cavan .	Tullyhaw .	Templeport .	Enniskillen .	III.	95
7, 8, 12	Moneenshinnagh .	484 1 19	Leitrim .	Drumahaire .	Cloonclare .	Manorhamilton .	IV.	93
5	Moneenterriff .	332 0 5	Cavan .	Tullyhaw .	Killinagh .	Enniskillen .	III.	92
114	Moneen West .	113 0 28	Galway .	Loughrea .	Ardrahan .	Loughrea .	IV.	63
42	Monee West .	430 3 26	Cork, E.R.	Fermoy .	Rahan .	Mallow .	II.	82
15, 23	Monehanegan .	430 1 30	Londonderry .	Tirkeeran .	Faughanvale .	Londonderry .	III.	250
78, 87	Monellan .	381 1 2	Donegal .	Raphoe .	Donaghmore .	Stranorlar .	III.	138
11	Monelly .	142 2 9	Queen's Co.	Upperwoods .	Offerlane .	Mountmellick .	I.	252
21, 26	Monelty .	161 1 13	Cavan .	Tullygarvey .	Larah .	Cootehill .	III.	91
22	Monennican .	116 1 12	Meath .	Fore .	Killallon .	Oldcastle .	I.	201
37, 43	Monenstown .	179 3 36	Meath .	Lower Deece .	Galtrim .	Trim .	I.	191
11	Monereagh .	287 3 34	Sligo .	Tireragh .	Easky .	Dromore West .	IV.	233
1, 3	Monesk .	1,077 1 7	Cavan .	Tullyhaw .	Killinagh .	Enniskillen .	III.	92
47	Moness .	369 0 10	Donegal .	Inishowen West .	Burt .	Londonderry .	III.	120
63	Moness .	125 1 20	Donegal .	Raphoe .	Taughboyne .	Strabane .	III.	144
13	Moneteen .	71 3 32	Limerick .	Pubblebrien .	Mungret .	Limerick .	II.	254
9	Money .	173 1 32	Armagh .	Oneilland West .	Kilmore .	Armagh .	III.	53
14, 15	Money .	103 3 21a	Cavan .	Lower Loughtee .	Drumlane .	Cavan .	III.	80
31	Money .	1,046 1 17	King's Co.	Ballyboy .	Ballyboy .	Parsonstown .	I.	123
76	Money .	215 0 30	Mayo .	Burrishoole .	Kilmeena .	Westport .	IV.	122
23	Money .	235 0 18b	Monaghan .	Cremorne .	Aghnamullen .	Cootehill .	III.	258
1	Money .	268 3 17	Westmeath .	Fore .	Foyran .	Granard .	I.	270
5	Money .	698 1 32	Wexford .	Scarawalsh .	Carnew .	Gorey .	I.	322
38,39,42,43	Moneyadda or Loughwheelion .	246 3 21	King's Co.	Clonlisk .	Aghancon .	Roscrea .	I.	129
21	Moneyatta Commons	19 1 28	Dublin .	Newcastle .	Saggart .	Celbridge .	I.	35
13	Moneyballytyrrell .	41 1 8	Queen's Co.	Maryborough East .	Borris .	Mountmellick .	I.	240
16	Moneybeg .	363 1 16c	Carlow .	Idrone East .	Dunleckny .	Carlow .	I.	7
42	Money Beg .	466 0 39d	Donegal .	Kilmacrenan .	Tullaghobegly .	Dunfanaghy .	III.	132
1	Moneybeg .	261 1 9	Westmeath .	Fore .	Foyran .	Granard .	I.	270
76	*Moneybeg Island*	9 1 36	Mayo .	Burrishoole .	Kilmeena .	Westport .	IV.	123
45	Money Big .	208 1 2	Wicklow .	Arklow .	Arklow .	Rathdrum .	I.	341
21, 27	Moneyboe .	210 1 2	Wexford .	Ballaghkeen .	Meelnagh .	Gorey .	I.	298
22, 28	Moneyboy .	167 3 2e	Roscommon .	Roscommon .	Kilcooley .	Strokestown .	IV.	210
11	Moneybrannon .	183 1 13	Londonderry .	Coleraine .	Aghadowey .	Coleraine .	III.	230
63, 64	Moneybroom .	431 2 39	Antrim .	Upper Massereene .	Magheragall .	Lisburn .	III.	31
17, 22	Moneycanon .	754 2 7	Antrim .	Kilconway .	Finvoy .	Ballymoney .	III.	26
3	Moneycanon .	406 2 20	Tyrone .	Strabane Lower .	Donaghedy .	Strabane .	III.	321
36, 43	Moneycarragh .	700 0 7	Down .	Lecale Upper .	Kilmegan .	Downpatrick .	III.	181
18	Moneycarrie Lower .	148 2 4	Londonderry .	Coleraine .	Aghadowey .	Coleraine .	III.	230
18	Moneycarrie Upper .	155 2 19	Londonderry .	Coleraine .	Aghadowey .	Coleraine .	III.	230
13	Moneycarroll .	79 2 25	Wicklow .	Newcastle .	Newcastle Upper .	Rathdrum .	I.	353
21, 22, 27	Moneycass Glebe .	314 3 10	Cavan .	Tullygarvey .	Larah .	Cootehill .	III.	91
30	Moneycleare .	38 3 39	Queen's Co.	Cullenagh .	Dysartgallen .	Abbeyleix .	I.	239
30	Moneycleare .	214 0 20	Queen's Co.	Cullenagh .	Rosconnell .	Abbeyleix .	I.	240
39, 40	Moneyconey .	1,123 1 21	Londonderry .	Loughinsholin .	Ballynascreen .	Magherafelt .	III.	239
10, 11	Moneycooly .	408 0 14	Kildare .	North Salt .	Laraghbryan .	Celbridge .	I.	75
8	Moneycree .	98 1 26	Armagh .	Armagh .	Grange .	Armagh .	III.	45
5	Moneycrockroe .	378 0 10	Louth .	Lower Dundalk .	Ballymascanlan .	Dundalk .	I.	176
11	Moneycross Lower .	184 2 17	Wexford .	Gorey .	Liskinfere .	Gorey .	I.	320
11	Moneycross Upper .	196 3 1	Wexford .	Gorey .	Liskinfere .	Gorey .	I.	320
63	Moneycrumog .	412 3 19	Antrim .	Upper Massereene .	Ballinderry .	Lisburn .	III.	29
82	Moneycusker .	417 2 34	Cork, W.R.	West Muskerry .	Kilmichael .	Dunmanway .	II.	159
12, 21	Moneydarragh .	2,596 3 0f	Donegal .	Inishowen East .	Culdaff .	Inishowen .	III.	118
40	Moneydass .	130 3 13	Tipperary, N.R.	Eliogarty .	Ballycahill .	Thurles .	II.	269
18,19,26,27	Moneydig .	415 3 19	Londonderry .	Coleraine .	Desertoghill .	Coleraine .	III.	200
52	Moneydullog .	133 2 15	Antrim .	Lower Toome .	Ahoghill .	Ballymena .	III.	32
53, 56	Moneydorragh Beg .	599 1 25	Down .	Mourne .	Kilkeel .	Kilkeel .	III.	183
53, 56	Moneydorragh More .	1,375 1 4	Down .	Mourne .	Kilkeel .	Kilkeel .	III.	183

(a) Including 12A. 3R. 2P. water.
(b) Including 15A. 1R. 30P. water.

(c) Including 10A. 3R. 12P. River Barrow.
(d) Including 116A. 1R. 38P. water.

(e) Including 3A. 0R. 34P. water.
(f) Including 12A. 2R. 29P. water.

No. of Sheet of the Ordnance Survey Maps.	Townlands and Towns.	Area in Statute Acres.	County.	Barony.	Parish.	Poor Law Union in 1857.	Townland Census of 1851, Part I.	
		A. R. P.					Vol.	Page
53	Moneydorragh More Upper	1,044 1 9	Down	Mourne	Kilkeel	Kilkeel	III.	183
23	Moneyduff	274 0 17	Antrim	Kilconway	Dunaghy	Ballymena	III.	26
95	Moneyduff	74 1 10	Galway	Dunkellin	Oranmore	Galway	IV.	32
79	Moneyduff	54 0 7	Kerry	Iveragh	Caher	Cahersiveen	II.	194
13	Moneyduff	167 2 31	Leitrim	Drumahaire	Cloonclare	Manorhamilton	IV.	93
10, 11	Moneyduff	279 2 22	Leitrim	Drumahaire	Drumlease	Manorhamilton	IV.	95
11	Moneyduff	84 0 16	Roscommon	Ballintober North	Kilmore	Carᵏon Shannon	IV.	187
10, 15	Moneydurtlow	306 0 36	Wexford	Scarawalsh	Kilrush	Enniscorthy	I.	324
22, 26	Moneyfad	61 2 17	Longford	Rathcline	Shrule	Ballymahon	I.	165
73	Moneyflugh	224 1 7	Cork, E.R.	East Muskerry	Inishcarra	Cork	II.	104
90, 93	Moneyflugh	1,249 3 10	Kerry	Dunkerron South	Kilcrohane	Kenmare	II.	184
94, 95	Moneygaff East	666 1 38	Cork, W.R.	East Carbery (W.D.)	Kinneigh	Dunmanway	II.	135
94	Moneygaff West	602 1 33	Cork, W.R.	East Carbery (W.D.)	Kinneigh	Dunmanway	II.	135
46, 47	Moneygall	663 0 0	King's Co.	Clonlisk	Cullenwaine	Roscrea	I.	129
46, 47	MONEYGALL, T.	—	King's Co.	Clonlisk	Cullenwaine	Roscrea	I.	129
56, 57	Moneygar	504 3 3	Tyrone	Omagh East	Kilskeery	Lowtherstown	III.	314
37, 38	Moneygaragh	166 3 5	Tyrone	Dungannon Upper	Desertcreat	Cookstown	III.	308
4	Moneygashel	328 3 34	Cavan	Tullyhaw	Killinagh	Enniskillen	III.	92
42	Moneyglass	688 2 18	Antrim	Upper Toome	Duneane	Ballymena	III.	35
17	Moneygobbin	130 2 24	Antrim	Upper Dunluce	Ballymoney	Ballymoney	III.	19
5	Moneygold	471 2 2	Sligo	Carbury	Ahamlish	Sligo	IV.	219
42	Moneygore	361 0 9	Down	Upper Iveagh, Lr.pt.	Drumballyroney	Newry	III.	172
43	Moneygorm	653 0 33	Cork, E.R.	Barrymore	Ardnagechy	Fermoy	II.	50
21, 22	Moneygorm	202 0 35	Waterford	Decies without Drum	Affane	Lismore	II.	353
22	Moneygorm East	253 0 33	Waterford	Decies without Drum	Affane	Lismore	II.	353
12	Moneygorm North	166 2 26	Waterford	Coshmore & Coshbride	Lismore and Mocollop	Lismore	II.	347
12, 21	Moneygorm South	219 0 10	Waterford	Coshmore & Coshbride	Lismore and Mocollop	Lismore	II.	347
21, 22	Moneygorm West	141 1 17	Waterford	Decies without Drum	Affane	Lismore	II.	353
27	Moneygran	748 0 20	Londonderry	Loughinsholin	Kilrea	Ballymoney	III.	241
46	Moneygreggan	237 0 32	Donegal	Raphoe	Allsaints	Londonderry	III.	134
17	Moneygrogh	91 0 23	Carlow	Forth	Barragh	Enniscorthy	I.	4
17	Moneyguiggy	735 3 10	Londonderry	Keenaght	Balteagh	NewTᵐLimavady	III.	234
36	Moneyguiggy	461 1 0	Londonderry	Loughinsholin	Ballynascreen	Magherafelt	III.	239
86, 87	Moneygurney	911 2 7	Cork. E.R.	Cork	Carrigaline	Cork	II.	64
36	Moneyguyneen	183 3 21	King's Co.	Ballybritt	Letterluna	Parsonstown	I.	126
54	Moneyhaughly	256 3 13	Donegal	Raphoe	Raymoghy	Letterkenny	III.	142
48	Moneyhaw	285 1 22	Londonderry	Loughinsholin	Arboe	Magherafelt	III.	238
48	Moneyhaw	246 1 29	Londonderry	Loughinsholin	Lissan	Magherafelt	III.	242
25	Moneyheer	291 0 31	Wexford	Bantry	St. John's	Enniscorthy	I.	302
40	Moneyhenry	121 0 38	Kilkenny	Knocktopher	Killahy	Waterford	I.	112
30	Moneyhoghan	382 0 16	Londonderry	Tirkeeran	Banagher	Londonderry	III.	247
15, 16	Moneyhoolaghan	122 3 9	Longford	Ardagh	Street	Granard	I.	153
19, 25	Moneyhore	323 2 6	Wexford	Bantry	Rossdroit	Enniscorthy	I.	302
11	Moneykee	179 3 21	Fermanagh	Lurg	Derryvullan	Lowtherstown	III.	205
8, 13	Moneylagan	236 3 29	Longford	Longford	Clongesh	Longford	I.	158
5, 6	Moneylahan	501 1 39	Sligo	Carbury	Rossinver	Sligo	IV.	223
43, 44	Moneylane	610 3 29	Down	Lecale Upper	Kilmegan	Downpatrick	III.	181
45	Moneylane	98 2 22	Wicklow	Arklow	Arklow	Rathdrum	I.	341
11	Moneylawn Lower	161 2 25	Wexford	Gorey	Liskinfere	Gorey	I.	320
11	Moneylawn Upper	173 1 23	Wexford	Gorey	Liskinfere	Gorey	I.	320
93	Moneylea	249 3 38	Cork, W.R.	East Carbery (W.D.)	Inchigeelagh	Dunmanway	II.	132
21, 22	Moneylea	235 3 25	Roscommon	Roscommon	Elphin	Castlereagh	IV.	209
12	Moneylea	5 3 7	Westmeath	Moyashel and Magheraderuon	Rathconnell	Mullingar	I.	276
26	Moneyleck	289 0 12	Antrim	Kilconway	Rasharkin	Ballymoney	III.	28
45	Money Little	97 0 29	Wicklow	Arklow	Arklow	Rathdrum	I.	341
18	Money Lower	240 1 6	Queen's Co.	Stradbally	Fossy or Timahoe	Athy	I.	247
42	Money Lower	485 0 12	Wicklow	Shillelagh	Aghowle	Shillelagh	I.	356
34	Moneymakinn	57 1 30	Fermanagh	Magherastephana	Aghalurcher	Lisnaskea	III.	217
29, 34	Moneymeen	517 2 26	Wicklow	Ballinacor South	Ballinacor	Rathdrum	I.	348
18	Moneymohill	624 3 20	Limerick	Shanid	Dunmoylan	Glin	II.	255
42	Money More	492 0 16	Donegal	Kilmacrenan	Tullaghobegly	Dunfanaghy	III.	132
54	Moneymore	395 3 25	Donegal	Raphoe	Raymoghy	Londonderry	III.	142
103	Moneymore	127 0 38	Donegal	Tirhugh	Drumhome	Ballyshannon	III.	146
40	Moneymore	178 2 11	Down	Upper Iveagh, Upper part	Donaghmore	Newry	III.	175
46, 48	Moneymore	283 0 5	Londonderry	Loughinsholin	Artrea	Magherafelt	III.	238
46	Moneymore	244 1 33	Londonderry	Loughinsholin	Desertlyn	Magherafelt	III.	240
36	Moneymore	271 3 7	Londonderry	Loughinsholin	Maghera	Magherafelt	III.	242
24	Moneymore	710 2 24c	Louth	Drogheda and Municipal Borough	St. Peter's	Drogheda	I.	175
93	Moneymore	202 2 16	Mayo	Costello	Annagh	Claremorris	IV.	138
36, 42	Moneymore	200 2 28	Meath	Lower Moyfenrath	Rathmolyon	Trim	I.	211

(a) Including 6A. 1R. 9P. water.
(b) Including 79A. 2R. 36P. water.

(c) { Within the Municipal Boundary 191A. 3R. 11P.
{ Without the Municipal Boundary 518A. 3R. 13P.

No. of Sheet of the Ordnance Survey Maps.	Townlands and Towns.	Area in Statute Acres.	County.	Barony.	Parish.	Poor Law Union in 1857.	Townland Census of 1851, Part I.	
		A. R. P.					Vol.	Page
41, 47	Moneymore	227 2 29a	Meath	Upper Moyfenrath	Clonard	Trim	I.	213
21	Moneymore	316 2 8	Queen's Co.	Clandonagh	Kyle	Donaghmore	I.	233
42	Moneymore	408 2 25	Roscommon	Athlone	Kilmeane	Roscommon	IV.	182
20	Moneymore	404 0 28	Wicklow	Upper Talbotstown	Ballynure	Baltinglass	I.	362
95	Moneymore East	622 0 35	Galway	Dunkellin	Oranmore	Galway	IV.	32
46	MONEYMORE T.	—	Londonderry	Loughinsholin	{ Artrea } { Desertlynn }	Magherafelt	III.	{ 238 } { 240 }
95	Moneymore West	324 0 36	Galway	Dunkellin	Oranmore	Galway	IV.	32
28, 29	Moneynabane	1,236 1 32b	Down	Upper Iveagh, Lr. pt.	Dromara	Banbridge	III.	172
73	Moneynaboola	896 3 28c	Tipperary, S.R.	Clanwilliam	Clonbeg	Tipperary	II.	305
95	Moneynacroha	382 2 17	Cork, W.R.	East Carbery (W.D.)	Kinneigh	Dunmanway	II.	135
23	Moneynamanagh or Umma Beg	207 3 20	Westmeath	Rathconrath	Ballymore	Athlone	I.	282
24	Moneynamough	391 0 19	Wexford	Bantry	Templeludigan	New Ross	I.	303
3, 8	Moneynamuck or Cooloultha	465 1 23	Kilkenny	Galmoy	Erke	Urlingford	I.	92
3, 8	Moneynamuck (Stopford)	491 1 21	Kilkenny	Galmoy	Erke	Urlingford	I.	92
18, 23	Moneyneagh	581 1 13	Antrim	Kilconway	Loughguile	Ballymoney	III.	27
35	Moneyneany	2,204 1 22	Londonderry	Loughinsholin	Ballynascreen	Magherafelt	III.	239
23, 24	Moneyneddy	31 3 36	Fermanagh	Magherastephana	Aghalurcher	Lisnaskea	III.	217
48, 49	Moneynick	297 0 38	Antrim	Upper Toome	Duneane	Antrim	III.	35
27, 28, 36	Moneynicrin	1,431 3 13d	Mayo	Tirawley	Crossmolina	Ballina	IV.	166
22	Moneynoe Glebe or Chanterhill	126 1 3	Fermanagh	Tirkennedy	Enniskillen	Enniskillen	III.	222
9	Moneynure	90 3 16e	Cavan	Tullyhaw	Templeport	Bawnboy	III.	95
23	Moneynure	32 1 3	Leitrim	Leitrim	Kiltoghert	Carᵏ. on Shannon	IV.	102
26	Moneyouragan	132 2 33	Fermanagh	Clanawley	Cleenish	Enniskillen	III.	191
70	Moneypark	40 0 5	Tipperary, S.R.	Middlethird	Fethard	Cashel	II.	327
16	Moneypatrick	60 2 26	Armagh	Armagh	Lisnadill	Armagh	III.	45
1, 3	Moneyquid	768 2 35	Queen's Co.	Tinnahinch	Castlebrack	Mountmellick	I.	248
16	Moneyquin	209 2 14	Armagh	Armagh	Lisnadill	Armagh	III.	45
9	Moneyrannel	187 2 38	Londonderry	Keenaght	Tamlaghtfinlagan	NewTᵈLimavady	III.	237
10	Moneyreagh	672 0 19	Down	Castlereagh Lower	Comber	Newtownards	III.	162
93	Moneyreague	720 0 24	Cork, W.R.	East Carbery (W.D.)	Fanlobbus	Dunmanway	II.	132
3	Moneyribbin	198 2 8	Wexford	Gorey	Inch	Gorey	I.	316
43	Moneyrod	225 2 29f	Antrim	Upper Toome	Duneane	Antrim	III.	35
28	Moneyroe	54 2 25	Leitrim	Mohill	Mohill	Mohill	IV.	108
27, 33	Moneysallin	702 0 22	Londonderry	Loughinsholin	Tamlaght O'Crilly	Ballymoney	III.	244
43, 49	Moneyscalp	901 2 39	Down	Upper Iveagh, Lr. pt.	Kilcoo	Kilkeel	III.	173
112	Moneyscreebagh or Mountscribe	465 3 15	Galway	Kiltartan	Kinvarradoorus	Gort	IV.	49
36	Moneyshanere	569 0 27	Londonderry	Loughinsholin	Kilcronaghan	Magherafelt	III.	241
52	Moneysharvan	376 1 7	Londonderry	Loughinsholin	Killelagh	Magherafelt	III.	241
38, 42	Moneyshingaun	54 0 38	King's Co.	Clonlisk	Kilmurryely	Roscrea	I.	131
35, 42	Moneyslane	1,060 0 32g	Down	Upper Iveagh, Lr. pt.	Drumgooland	Banbridge	III.	172
33, 37	Moneystaghan Ellis	496 2 18	Londonderry	Loughinsholin	Tamlaght O'Crilly	Magherafelt	III.	244
33, 37	Moneystaghan Mac-peake	410 0 27	Londonderry	Loughinsholin	Tamlaght O'Crilly	Magherafelt	III.	244
41	Moneysterling and Annagh	408 1 15	Londonderry	Loughinsholin	Desertmartin	Magherafelt	III.	240
24	Moneystown Hill	364 3 16	Wicklow	Newcastle	Derrylossary	Rathdrum	I.	351
24	Moneystown North	375 0 32	Wicklow	Newcastle	Derrylossary	Rathdrum	I.	351
24	Moneystown South	176 3 2	Wicklow	Newcastle	Derrylossary	Rathdrum	I.	351
96	Moneyteige	471 2 0	Galway	Dunkellin	Killeeneen	Loughrea	IV.	30
39	Moneyteige Middle	297 1 15	Wicklow	Arklow	Ballintemple	Rathdrum	I.	342
39	Moneyteige North	260 0 34	Wicklow	Arklow	Ballintemple	Rathdrum	I.	342
39	Moneyteige South	328 0 19	Wicklow	Arklow	Ballintemple	Rathdrum	I.	342
25	Moneytucker	711 2 15	Wexford	Bantry	Rossdroit	Enniscorthy	I.	302
18	Money Upper	159 2 34	Queen's Co.	Stradbally	Fossy or Timahoe	Athy	I.	247
42	Money Upper	953 0 19	Wicklow	Shillelagh	Aghowle	Shillelagh	I.	356
15, 20	Moneyvart	84 2 4	Antrim	Lower Glenarm	Layd	Ballycastle	III.	23
73	Moneyveen	746 3 25	Galway	Kilconnell	Kilconnell	Ballinasloe	IV.	40
6, 10	Moneyvennon or Freehall	209 1 15	Londonderry	Keenaght	Aghanloo	NewTᵈLimavady	III.	234
19	Moneyvolan	181 2 6h	Monaghan	Cremorne	Clontibret	Castleblayney	III.	261
142	Moneyvollahane	342 0 23	Cork, W.R.	West Carbery (E.D.)	Castlehaven	Skibbereen	II.	138
46, 54	Monfad	238 2 3	Donegal	Raphoe	Allsaints	Londonderry	III.	134
74,75,86,87	Monfieldstown	431 2 39	Cork, E.R.	Cork	Carrigaline	Cork	II.	64
25, 26	Monfin	206 2 24	Wexford	Bantry	St. John's	Enniscorthy	I.	302
27	Mong	274 0 34	Leitrim	Leitrim	Kiltoghert	Carᵏ. on Shannon	IV.	102
30	Mongagh	341 0 10i	Roscommon	Roscommon	Lissonuffy	Strokestown	IV.	212
40	Mongan	256 1 1	Wicklow	Arklow	Arklow	Rathdrum	I.	341
27, 34	Monganstown	483 0 38	Westmeath	Farbill	Killucan	Mullingar	I.	267

(a) Including 5A. 2R. 32P. River Boyne.   (d) Including 50A. 0R. 22P. Lough Dahybaun.   (g) Including 5A. 0R. 37P. water.
(b) Including 4A. 3R. 14P. water.   (e) Including 15A. 2R. 35P. Brackley Lough.   (h) Including 16A. 2R. 38P. water.
(c) Including 5A. 1R. 19P. water.   (f) Including 3A. 3R. 13P. water.   (i) Including 3A. 2R. 8P. water.

No. of Sheet of the Ordnance Survey Maps.	Townlands and Towns.	Area in Statute Acres.			County.	Barony.	Parish.	Poor Law Union in 1857.	Townland Census of 1851, Part I.	
		A.	R.	P.					Vol.	Page
41	Mongaun	109	1	24	Wexford	Shelmaliere West	Taghmon	Wexford	I.	335
63	Mongavlin	125	1	13	Donegal	Raphoe	Taughboyne	Strabane	III.	144
7, 15	Mongfune	590	2	0	Limerick	Owneybeg	Abington	Limerick	II.	251
23	Mongibbaghan	200	2	25	Fermanagh	Magherastephana	Aghalurcher	Lisnaskea	III.	217
55	Monglass	345	2	26	Donegal	Raphoe	Allsaints	Londonderry	III.	134
19	Monglass	382	2	5	Wexford	Scarawalsh	Monart	Enniscorthy	I.	324
34, 35	Mongnacool Lower	317	1	30	Wicklow	Ballinacor South	Ballykine	Rathdrum	I.	348
34, 35	Mongnacool Upper	223	1	24	Wicklow	Ballinacor South	Ballykine	Rathdrum	I.	348
62	Mongorry	530	2	28	Donegal	Raphoe	Raphoe	Letterkenny	III.	141
6, 11	Monicknew	660	1	33	Queen's Co.	Upperwoods	Offerlane	Mountmellick	I.	252
18	Monintin	240	0	19	Monaghan	Cremorne	Aghnamullen	Cootehill	III.	258
7, 12	Monintown	425	3	26	Westmeath	Corkaree	Multyfarnham	Mullingar	I.	263
7, 12	Monintown	116	1	0	Westmeath	Corkaree	Stonehall	Mullingar	I.	263
71, 72	Monivea Demesne	924	3	17a	Galway	Tiaquin	Monivea	Tuam	IV.	79
71	Monivea T.	—			Galway	Tiaquin	Monivea	Tuam	IV.	79
31	Monkeal	12	0	37	Waterford	Decies without Drum	Dungarvan	Dungarvan	II.	355
19	Monknewtown	1,086	0	3	Meath	Upper Slane	Monknewtown	Drogheda	I.	224
104	Monksfield	319	0	22	Galway	Dunkellin	Killogilleen	Loughrea	IV.	31
82	Monksgrange	415	0	7	Tipperary. S.R.	Iffa and Offa East	Inishlounaght	Clogheen	II.	313
15	Monks Island	1	0	31	Sligo	Carbury	Calry	Sligo	IV.	220
8, 9	Monksland	302	0	24	Louth	Lower Dundalk	Carlingford	Dundalk	I.	176
49, 52	Monksland	1,333	0	6	Roscommon	Athlone	St. Peter's	Athlone	IV.	184
52, 57	Monkstown	811	0	34	Antrim	Lower Belfast	Carnmoney	Belfast	III.	8
87	Monkstown	206	2	20	Cork, E.R.	Kerrycurrihy	Monkstown	Cork	II.	93
23	Monkstown	212	3	10b	Dublin	Rathdown	Monkstown	Rathdown	I.	36
76,77,82,83	Monkstown	94	1	19	Tipperary, S.R.	Iffa and Offa East	Inishlounaght	Clonmel	II.	313
83	Monkstown	13	0	17	Tipperary, S.R.	Iffa and Offa East	Kiltegan	Clonmel	II.	315
12	Monkstown	589	3	3	Westmeath	Corkaree	Taghmon	Mullingar	I.	264
87	Monkstown (Castle Farm)	257	1	20	Cork, E.R.	Kerrycurrihy	Monkstown	Cork	II.	93
23	Monkstown Castlefarm	33	0	35	Dublin	Rathdown	Monkstown	Rathdown	I.	36
23	Monkstown Housefarm	22	3	36	Dublin	Rathdown	Monkstown	Rathdown	I.	36
87	MONKSTOWN T.	—			Cork, E.R.	Kerrycurrihy	Monkstown	Cork	II.	93
36	Monktown	244	3	31c	Meath	Lower Moyfenrath	Trim	Trim	I.	212
26, 32	Monktown	1,036	2	30	Meath	Skreen	Monktown	Navan	I.	221
2, 3	Monktown	379	3	14d	Westmeath	Fore	Mayne	Granard	I.	271
9, 10, 15, 16	Monlough	732	3	26e	Down	Castlereagh Lower	Comber	Newtownards	III.	162
26	Monloum	47	0	4	Waterford	Middlethird	Drumcannon	Waterford	II.	366
7	Monninane	663	2	35	Waterford	Upperthird	Mothel	Carrick on Suir	II.	371
17	Monmore	181	0	17	Wexford	Ballaghkeen	Donaghmore	Gorey	I.	293
32	Monmore	319	0	7	Wexford	Shelmaliere East	Artramon	Wexford	I.	330
32	Monmore	41	3	15	Wexford	Shelmaliere East	Kilpatrick	Wexford	I.	331
23, 28	Monmurry	115	1	16	Fermanagh	Magherastephana	Aghavea	Lisnaskea	III.	219
4, 7	Monmurry	246	0	24	Monaghan	Trough	Donagh	Monaghan	III.	282
15	Monnaboy	395	0	6	Londonderry	Tirkeeran	Faughanvale	Londonderry	III.	250
16	Monnagh	243	2	6	Queen's Co.	Upperwoods	Offerlane	Mountmellick	I.	252
18	Monneill	117	1	14	Monaghan	Dartree	Ematris	Cootehill	III.	267
25	Monnery Lower	258	2	24f	Cavan	Upper Loughtee	Kilmore	Cavan	III.	85
25	Monnery Upper	212	2	36g	Cavan	Upper Loughtee	Kilmore	Cavan	III.	85
30	Monog	228	0	36	Armagh	Fews Upper	Creggan	Castleblaney	III.	48
9	Monphole	68	3	12	Kilkenny	Galmoy	Sheffin	Urlingford	I.	93
19	Monread North	299	0	5	Kildare	Naas North	Naas	Naas	I.	62
19	Monread South	296	1	31	Kildare	Naas North	Naas	Naas	I.	62
18	Monreagh	398	3	29	Clare	Inchiquin	Kilkeedy	Corrofin	II.	26
55	Monreagh	272	0	19	Donegal	Raphoe	Taughboyne	Londonderry	III.	144
38	Monreagh or Barr of Kilmackilvenny	930	2	37	Donegal	Inishowen West	Fahan Upper	Londonderry	III.	121
20	Monree	163	0	14	Down	Lower Iveagh, Up. pt.	Donaghcloney	Lurgan	III.	169
70	Monroe	315	1	23	Galway	Clare	Lackagh	Galway	IV.	23
34, 40	Monroe	63	2	13	Tipperary, N.R.	Eliogarty	Inch	Thurles	II.	270
14, 20	Monroe	411	0	11	Tipperary, N.R.	Owney and Arra	Youghalarra	Nenagh	II.	298
81	Monroe	85	1	12	Tipperary, S.R.	Iffa and Offa West	Tubbrid	Clogheen	II.	321
46, 52	Monroe	114	2	3	Tipperary, S.R.	Kilnamanagh Lower	Clonoulty	Cashel	II.	323
70	Monroe	138	0	17	Tipperary, S.R.	Middlethird	Barrettsgrange	Cashel	II.	325
11	Monroe	167	2	7	Westmeath	Corkaree	Portloman	Mullingar	I.	263
26	Monroe	266	1	10	Wexford	Ballaghkeen	Edermine	Enniscorthy	I.	294
27, 33	Monroe	155	0	6	Wexford	Ballaghkeen	Killisk	Enniscorthy	I.	296
16, 17	Monroe	160	1	26	Wexford	Gorey	Ballycanew	Gorey	I.	316
32	Monroe	10	0	0	Wexford	Shelmaliere East	Ardcavan	Wexford	I.	329
21	Monroe	92	3	39	Wicklow	Upper Talbotstown	Donaghmore	Baltinglass	I.	363
88	Monroe East	328	3	15	Tipperary, S.R.	Iffa and Offa West	Ballybacon	Clogheen	II.	317
31	Monroe Glebe	9	3	21	Waterford	Decies without Drum	Dungarvan	Dungarvan	II.	355

(a) Including 6A. 1R. 30P. water.
(b) Including 67A. 2R. 24P. detached portions.
(c) Including 7A. 1R. 24P. water.
(d) Including 1A. 1R. 14P. water.
(e) Including 29A. 0R. 5P. water.
(f) Including 5A. 2R. 0P. water.
(g) Including 0A. 2R. 0P. water.

No. of Sheet of the Ordnance Survey Maps.	Townlands and Towns.	Area in Statute Acres.			County.	Barony.	Parish.	Poor Law Union in 1857.	Townland Census of 1851, Part I.	
		A.	R.	P.					Vol.	Page
11, 18	Monroe or Johnstown (Nugent)	113	3	34	Westmeath	Moygoish	Templeoran	Mullingar	I.	281
87, 88	Monroe West	76	2	19	Tipperary, S.R.	Iffa and Offa West	Ballybacon	Clogheen	II.	317
29	Monrush	160	0	35	Tyrone	Dungannon Upper	Derryloran	Cookstown	III.	307
14, 20	Monsea	642	2	37	Tipperary, N.R.	Lower Ormond	Monsea	Nenagh	II.	287
54	Mouslatt	192	1	17	Tipperary, S.R.	Slievardagh	Killenaule	Cashel	II.	334
21	Montanagay	146	2	16	Kerry	Clanmaurice	O'Dorney	Tralee	II.	173
67, 74	Montanavoe	91	0	17	Tipperary, S.R.	Clanwilliam	Templeneiry	Tipperary	II.	311
122, 123	Monteen	589	2	36	Cork, W.R.	East Carbery (E.D.)	Kilmaloda	Clonakilty	II.	129
90, 104	Monteensudder	130	1	31	Cork, W.R.	Bear	Kilcaskan	Bantry	II.	123
61, 69	Montgomery's Fort or Calhame	146	2	35	Donegal	Raphoe	Convoy	Stranorlar	III.	136
42	Montiagh	1,446	1	9	Sligo	Leyny	Achonry	Tobercurry	IV.	229
69	Montiagh North	454	2	17	Galway	Clare	Claregalway	Galway	IV.	18
1	Montiaghroe	272	1	35	Fermanagh	Lurg	Drumkeeran	Lowtherstown	III.	206
62, 66	Montiaghs	1,543	3	9	Antrim	Upper Massereene	Aghagallon	Lurgan	III.	29
69	Montiagh South	331	2	23	Galway	Dunkellin	Claregalway	Galway	IV.	28
17, 23	Montore	264	1	27	Tipperary, N.R.	Ikerrin	Rathnaveoge	Roscrea	II.	276
23	Montpelier	23	0	10	Dublin	Rathdown	Monkstown	Rathdown	I.	36
71, 84	Montpelier	305	2	6	Galway	Athenry	Athenry	Galway	IV.	4
1	Montpelier	263	3	16	Limerick	Clanwilliam	Stradbally	Limerick	II.	226
1	MONTPELIER T.	—			Limerick	Clanwilliam	Stradbally	Limerick	II.	226
38, 39	Montrath	983	2	25	Westmeath	Moycashel	Rahugh	Tullamore	I.	279
67	Montymeane	622	3	39	Donegal	Boylagh	Inishkeel	Glenties	III.	113
16	Monument	104	1	10	Kerry	Clanmaurice	Kilcaragh	Listowel	II.	169
30, 44	Monumentpark	125	3	13	Galway	Dunmore	Tuam	Tuam	IV.	36
70	Monumentpark	66	0	29	Mayo	Carra	Turlough	Castlebar	IV.	131
37	Monure	106	3	6	Queen's Co.	Slievemargy	Killeshin	Carlow	I.	246
29	Monvore	83	2	9	Waterford	Coshmore & Coshbride	Lismore and Mocollop	Lismore	II.	347
26	Monvoy	242	2	20	Waterford	Middlethird	Drumcannon	Waterford	II.	366
6, 7	Monydoo or Tonycrom	444	3	35	Cavan	Tullyhaw	Kinawley	Bawnboy	III.	93
25, 28	Monyglen	221	2	39	Monaghan	Farney	Donaghmoyne	Carrickmacross	III.	270
25	Monygorbet	48	3	24	Monaghan	Farney	Donaghmoyne	Castleblayney	III.	270
31	Monyheige Commons	30	1	30	Kilkenny	Knocktopher	Knocktopher	Thomastown	I.	112
29	Monyvroe	361	2	12	Waterford	Decies without Drum	Affane	Dungarvan	II.	353
13, 14	Moodoge	181	2	20	Armagh	Orior Lower	Ballymore	Banbridge	III.	55
38	Moodoge	99	2	9	Cavan	Castlerahan	Castlerahan	Oldcastle	III.	67
6	Moodoge	798	3	7	Sligo	Carbury	Rossinver	Sligo	IV.	223
13	Moods	383	3	29	Kildare	Clane	Downings	Naas	I.	54
42	Mooghaun North	233	0	22a	Clare	Bunratty Lower	Tomfinlough	Ennis	II.	7
42	Mooghaun South	426	2	34b	Clare	Bunratty Lower	Tomfinlough	Ennis	II.	7
23	Mooghna	698	3	6c	Clare	Corcomroe	Clooney	Ennistimon	II.	18
4	Moohane	127	1	34	Kerry	Iraghticonnor	Killehenny	Listowel	II.	191
32	Moohane	170	2	18	Limerick	Smallcounty	Cahercorney	Kilmallock	II.	259
42	Mooncoin	43	0	10	Kilkenny	Iverk	Pollrone	Waterford	I.	106
42	MOONCOIN T.	—			Kilkenny	Iverk	Pollrone	Waterford	I.	106
36, 38	Moone	2,877	1	31	Kildare	Kilkea and Moone	Moone	Athy	I.	61
68	Mooneennahasragh	378	3	15	Donegal	Raphoe	Kilteevoge	Stranorlar	III.	139
36	MOONE T.	—			Kildare	Kilkea and Moone	Moone	Athy	I.	61
4, 11	Mooneysland or Grovesend	92	2	25	King's Co.	Warrenstown	Ballyburly	Edenderry	I.	144
3, 6	Mooneystown	465	3	1	Meath	Lower Slane	Drumcondra	Ardee	I.	223
24	Mooneystown	369	3	30	Meath	Lune	Rathmore	Trim	I.	208
20	Moonhall	157	0	37	Kilkenny	Gowran	Tiscoffin	Kilkenny	I.	99
45	Moonveen	326	0	30	Kilkenny	Iverk	Portnascully	Waterford	I.	106
83	Moor	658	1	32	Galway	Clare	Athenry	Galway	IV.	17
116	Moor	107	0	11	Galway	Leitrim	Duniry	Portumna	IV.	53
19	Moor	138	3	19	Longford	Ardagh	Ardagh	Longford	I.	151
20, 21	Moor	227	3	11	Roscommon	Castlereagh	Kilkeevin	Castlereagh	IV.	201
61	Moor	4	2	29	Tipperary, S.R.	Middlethird	St. Patricksrock	Cashel	II.	331
12	Moor	136	0	14	Wexford	Ballaghkeen	Ardamine	Gorey	I.	291
47	Moor	156	1	5	Wexford	Bargy	Mulrankin	Wexford	I.	307
73	Moorabbey	225	1	6	Tipperary, S.R.	Clanwilliam	Clonbeg	Tipperary	II.	305
48, 49	Moorbrook	281	2	20d	Mayo	Gallen	Toomore	Swineford	IV.	151
37	Moord	62	3	37	Waterford	Decies within Drum	Kinsalebeg	Youghal	II.	352
40	Moordyke	244	1	22	Antrim	Upper Glenarm	Kilwaughter	Larne	III.	25
26	Mooreabbey Demesne	1,267	0	5	Kildare	Offaly West	Monasterevin	Athy	I.	73
28	Moorechurch	203	0	27	Meath	Upper Duleek	Moorechurch	Drogheda	I.	198
21	Mooreenaruggan	21	2	32	Dublin	Uppercross	Clondalkin	Dublin South	I.	39
100	Moorehall or Muckloon	130	2	34	Mayo	Carra	Burriscarra	Ballinrobe	IV.	127
28, 29	Moorehill	255	0	6	Waterford	Coshmore & Coshbride	Kilwatermoy	Lismore	II.	344
22	Moore Lodge	58	0	6	Antrim	Kilconway	Finvoy	Ballymoney	III.	96
19	Mooremount	167	2	20	Louth	Ardee	Cappoge	Ardee	I.	171
18	Mooremount	177	1	33	Louth	Ardee	Dromin	Ardee	I.	172

(a) Including 5A. 3R. 8P. water.
(b) Including 5A. 1R. 0P. water.

(c) Including 6A. 0R. 24P. water.

(d) Including 11A. 3R. 19P. water.

No. of Sheet of the Ordnance Survey Maps.	Townlands and Towns.	Area in Statute Acres.			County	Barony.	Parish.	Poor Law Union in 1857.	Townland Census of 1851, Part I.	
		A.	R.	P.					Vol.	Page
54	Moore North	303	1	26	Roscommon	Moycarn	Moore	Ballinasloe	IV.	207
28	Moorepark	223	3	3	Cork, E.R.	Condons&Clangibbon	Kilcrumper	Fermoy	II.	61
27, 28	Moorepark	233	1	38	Cork, E.R.	Condons&Clangibbon	Kilworth	Fermoy	II.	62
33	Moorepark	763	1	26	Meath	Upper Duleek	Piercetown	Dunshaughlin	I.	198
27	Moorepark West	84	2	30	Cork, E.R.	Fermoy	Kilcrumper	Fermoy	II.	80
33	Moorerow or Tonlegee	297	1	31	Westmeath	Fartullagh	Kilbride	Mullingar	I.	268
66	Mooresfort	805	1	12	Tipperary, S.R.	Clanwilliam	Lattin	Tipperary	II.	309
39, 40	Mooreshill	335	2	39	Wicklow	Arklow	Killahurler	Rathdrum	I.	345
33, 39	Mooresides	265	0	36	Meath	Upper Duleek	Clonalvy	Drogheda	I.	197
54	Moore South	571	2	13	Roscommon	Moycarn	Moore	Ballinasloe	IV.	207
3	Moorestown	145	1	13	Carlow	Carlow	Killerrig	Carlow	I.	2
33, 34	Moorestown	265	3	35	Kerry	Corkaguiny	Kilquane	Dingle	II.	179
48, 49	Moorestown	817	3	20	Limerick	Coshlea	Kilfinnane	Kilmallock	II.	240
13, 14	Mooretown	71	2	0a	Dublin	Castleknock	Mulhuddart	Dublin North	I.	25
11	Mooretown	309	3	32	Dublin	Nethercross	Swords	Balrothery	I.	32
22, 27	Mooretown	524	2	12	Kildare	Offaly East	Kildare	Naas	I.	70
12	Mooretown	965	2	37	Louth	Louth	Dromiskin	Dundalk	I.	183
37,38,43,44	Mooretown	260	3	14	Meath	Lower Deece	Knockmark	Dunshaughlin	I.	192
7, 13	Mooretown	306	2	33	Meath	Lower Slane	Siddan	Ardee	I.	224
44	Mooretown	303	2	1	Meath	Ratoath	Ratoath	Dunshaughlin	I.	219
25	Mooretown	279	3	37	Meath	Skreen	Athlumney	Navan	I.	220
33	Mooretown	194	3	36	Meath	Upper Duleek	Ardcath	Drogheda	I.	197
19	Mooretown	204	0	11	Meath	Upper Slane	Slane	Navan	I.	225
13	Mooretown	400	1	27b	Westmeath	Delvin	Castletowndelvin	Castletowndelvin	I.	265
1	Moorfield	567	1	34	Galway	Ballymoe	Templetogher	Glennamaddy	IV.	9
108	Moorfield	211	1	35	Galway	Longford	Fahy	Portumna	IV.	58
23	Moorfield	437	1	7	Kildare	Connell	Morristownbiller	Naas	I.	56
49	Moorfield	499	1	23	Tyrone	Omagh East	Kilskeery	Lowtherstown	III.	314
108	Moorfield or Gortnamona	109	2	20	Galway	Longford	Fahy	Portumna	IV.	58
108	Moorfield or Gortnamona	460	2	10	Galway	Longford	Kilquain	Portumna	IV.	60
35	Moorfields	388	1	30	Wexford	Bantry	Oldross	New Ross	I.	301
42	Moorfields	99	0	30	Wexford	Forth	Rathaspick	Wexford	I.	312
121, 122	Moorgagagh	101	0	15c	Mayo	Kilmaine	Moorgagagh	Ballinrobe	IV.	157
29	Moorhill	225	1	1	Kildare	Naas South	Gilltown	Naas	I.	65
29	Moorhill	206	0	3	Kildare	Naas South	Jago	Naas	I.	65
55	*Moor Island*	2	0	20	Galway	Moycullen	Kilcummin	Oughterard	IV.	69
55	*Moor Island*	1	3	13	Galway	Moycullen	Kilcummin	Oughterard	IV.	69
2	Moorlagh	75	1	37	Meath	Lower Kells	Kilmainham	Kells	I.	203
7	Moorland	161	1	22d	Louth	Upper Dundalk	Dundalk	Dundalk	I.	178
34, 39	Moorlough	203	3	38e	Fermanagh	Clankelly	Galloon	Lisnaskea	III.	198
22	Moorneen	276	3	25f	Galway	Ballynahinch	Omey	Clifden	IV.	15
7	Moorock	973	0	25	King's Co.	Garrycastle	Lemanaghan	Parsonstown	I.	137
53	Moor of Meath	90	3	12	Meath	Dunboyne	Dunboyne	Dunshaughlin	I.	199
21, 22	Moorspark	85	0	17	Wicklow	Upper Talbotstown	Donaghmore	Baltinglass	I.	363
76, 82	Moorstown	133	2	35	Tipperary, S.R.	Iffa and Offa East	Caher	Clonmel	II.	312
76	Moorstown	507	3	38	Tipperary, S.R.	Iffa and Offa East	Inishlounaght	Clonmel	II.	313
69, 70	Moorstown	632	2	32	Tipperary, S.R.	Middlethird	Mora	Cashel	II.	329
19	Moorstown	119	0	39	Wicklow	Newcastle	Killiskey	Rathdrum	I.	352
27	Moorstown	147	2	28	Wicklow	Upper Talbotstown	Donaghmore	Baltinglass	I.	363
7	Moortown	291	1	10	Dublin	Balrothery West	Clonmethan	Balrothery	I.	22
18	Moortown	205	1	38g	Kildare	Connell	Ladytown	Naas	I.	55
10	Moortown	382	3	22	Kildare	Ikeathy&Oughterany	Mainham	Celbridge	I.	58
28	Moortown	378	0	1	Kildare	Kilcullen	Tully	Naas	I.	58
11	Moortown	206	2	10	Kildare	North Salt	Kildrought	Celbridge	I.	74
18	Moortown	193	0	12	Meath	Morgallion	Kilberry	Navan	I.	209
77	Moortown	108	0	7	Tipperary, S.R.	Iffa and Offa East	Kilgrant	Clonmel	II.	314
53	Moortown	15	2	14	Wexford	Forth	Carn	Wexford	I.	309
47	Moortown	67	1	19	Wexford	Forth	Mayglass	Wexford	I.	312
28	Moortowncastle	372	2	8	Kildare	Kilcullen	Tully	Athy	I.	58
41, 46	Moortown Great	292	2	14	Wexford	Bargy	Ambrosetown	Wexford	I.	304
47	Moortown Great	232	1	37	Wexford	Bargy	Tomhaggard	Wexford	I.	308
3, 4, 7, 8	Moortown and Lakill	837	3	28h	Westmeath	Fore	St. Feighins	Castletowndelvin	I.	272
41	Moortown Little	258	0	24	Wexford	Bargy	Ambrosetown	Wexford	I.	304
47	Moortown Little	119	1	26	Wexford	Bargy	Tomhaggard	Wexford	I.	308
20	Moraghy	121	2	14	Monaghan	Cremorne	Muckno	Castleblayney	III.	262
24	Moranspark	8	1	30	Westmeath	Rathconrath	Killare	Mullingar	I.	283
10, 11	Moranstown	47	0	31	Westmeath	Moygoish	Kilbixy	Mullingar	I.	279
108, 121	Moreagh	261	0	20	Cork, W.R.	East Carbery (W.D.)	Fanlobbus	Dunmanway	II.	132
38, 46	Moree	263	3	14	Tyrone	Dungannon Upper	Desertcreat	Cookstown	III.	308
30, 38	Morenane	859	3	19	Limerick	Connello Upper	Ballingarry	Croom	II.	231

(a) Including 2A. 3R. 25P. detached portion.
(b) Including 15A. 0R. 2P. water.
(c) Including 20A. 0R. 36P. water.

(d) Including 11A. 2R. 3P. water.
(e) Including 34A. 3R. 19P. water.
(f) Including 1A. 2R. 26P. water.

(g) Including 3A. 1R. 3P. water.
(h) Including 43A. 2R. 39P. water.

4 Y

No. of Sheet of the Ordnance Survey Maps.	Townlands and Towns.	Area in Statute Acres.	County.	Barony.	Parish.	Poor Law Union in 1857.	Townland Census of 1851, Part I.	
		A. R. P.					Vol.	Page
11	Morerah . . .	592 0 39	Leitrim . .	Drumahaire . .	Drumlease . .	Manorhamilton	IV.	95
37, 38	Moress . . .	316 3 1a	Donegal . .	Inishowen West .	Inch . .	Londonderry .	III.	121
8, 9, 13 14	Morett . . .	1,938 2 7	Queen's Co. .	Portnahinch . .	Coolbanagher .	Mountmellick .	I.	244
13	Morgan's Island .	0 3 32	Galway . .	Kiltartan . .	Kinvarradoorus .	Gort . .	IV.	50
10	Morgans North .	807 0 23	Limerick . .	Connello Lower .	Morgans . .	Rathkeale .	II.	228
10	Morgans South .	405 0 36	Limerick . .	Connello Lower .	Morgans . .	Rathkeale .	II.	228
24	Morganstown . .	96 0 30	Kildare . .	Naas South . .	Kill . .	Naas . .	I.	65
18	Morganstown . .	82 1 28	Louth . .	Ferrard . .	Dysart . .	Drogheda .	I	181
41	Mormeal . .	515 1 3	Londonderry .	Loughinsholin .	Kilcronaghan .	Magherafelt .	III.	241
11	Mornane . .	751 3 25	Limerick . .	Kenry . .	Kilcornan . .	Rathkeale .	II.	249
19, 23	Mornin . . .	847 2 14	Longford . .	Moydow . .	Taghsheenod .	Ballymahon .	I.	162
21	Mornington . .	1,155 0 24	Meath . .	Lower Duleek .	Colp . .	Drogheda .	I.	195
21	MORNINGTON T. .	—	Meath . .	Lower Duleek .	Colp . .	Drogheda .	I.	195
6, 7	Moroe . . .	135 0 0	Limerick . .	Owneybeg . .	Abington . .	Limerick .	II.	251
7	MOROE T. . .	—	Limerick . .	Owneybeg . .	Abington . .	Limerick .	II.	251
6, 7	Moroewood . .	241 0 4	Limerick . .	Owneybeg . .	Abington . .	Limerick .	II.	251
17	Moross . . .	309 1 0	Donegal . .	Kilmacrenan . .	Clondavaddog .	Millford .	III.	125
25, 31	Morrell . . .	204 1 6	Meath . .	Skreen . .	Kilcarn . .	Navan .	I.	220
22	Morriscastle . .	246 0 28	Wexford . .	Ballaghkeen . .	Kilmuckridge .	Gorey .	I.	297
29	Morrissysland .	26 2 16	Wexford . .	Bantry . .	St. Mary's .	New Ross .	I.	302
19	Morristown . .	101 3 1	Kildare . .	South Salt . .	Forenaghts . .	Naas .	I.	77
23	Morristownbiller	435 1 14	Kildare . .	Connell . .	Morristownbiller .	Naas .	I.	56
18	Morristown Little	59 0 32b	Kildare . .	Connell . .	Oldconnell . .	Naas .	I.	56
18	Morristown Lower .	200 2 9c	Kildare . .	Connell . .	Oldconnell . .	Naas .	I.	56
18, 23	Morristown Upper .	332 0 26	Kildare . .	Connell . .	Oldconnell . .	Naas .	I.	56
7	Mortarstown Lower	206 0 10d	Carlow . .	Carlow . .	Carlow . .	Carlow .	I.	1
7	Mortarstown Upper	400 3 1 e	Carlow . .	Carlow . .	Carlow . .	Carlow .	I.	1
22, 31	Mortgage . .	358 1 28	Limerick . .	Smallcounty . .	Fedamore . .	Croom .	II.	259
37, 38, 40	Mortgage . .	148 2 39	Waterford . .	Decies within Drum	Kinsalebeg . .	Youghal .	II.	352
19	Mortgage Fields .	48 3 28	Kilkenny . .	Shillelogher . .	St. Patrick's .	Kilkenny .	I.	116
48, 56	Mortlestown . .	819 3 22	Limerick . .	Coshlea . .	Particles . .	Kilmallock .	II.	240
76	Mortlestown . .	325 2 12	Tipperary, S.R.	Iffa and Offa West .	Mortlestown . .	Clogheen .	II.	319
54, 62	Mortle-town . .	754 3 2	Tipperary, S.R.	Middlethird . .	Cooleagh . .	Cashel .	II.	326
76	Mortlestown Little .	54 3 35	Tipperary, S.R.	Iffa and Offa West .	Mortlestown . .	Clogheen .	II.	319
3	Mortyclogh . .	285 0 26	Clare . .	Burren . .	Abbey . .	Ballyvaghan .	II.	11
88	Mosestown . .	158 1 13	Cork, E.R. .	Imokilly . .	Aghada . .	Middleton .	II.	83
84, 96	Moskeagh . .	652 0 24	Cork, W.R. .	Kinalmeaky . .	Templemartin .	Bandon .	II.	153
28	Mosney . . .	200 3 15	Meath . .	Upper Duleek .	Moorechurch .	Drogheda .	I.	198
91, 101	Mossbrook . .	371 1 19	Mayo . .	Clanmorris . .	Mayo . .	Claremorris .	IV.	135
52	Mossfield . .	47 2 10	Donegal . .	Kilmacrenan . .	Gartan . .	Letterkenny .	III.	127
38, 39	Mossfield . .	395 3 39	King's Co. .	Ballybritt . .	Seirkieran . .	Parsonstown .	I.	127
16	Mossfield or Urbal .	238 3 19	Fermanagh .	Tirkennedy . .	Trory . .	Enniskillen .	III.	224
95, 96	Mos-grove . .	789 3 34	Cork, W.R. .	Kinalmeaky . .	Templemartin .	Bandon .	II.	153
61	Mossmore . .	190 1 31	Tyrone . .	Dungannon Middle	Clonfeacle . .	Dungannon .	III.	299
7, 8, 12, 13	Moss-side . .	284 2 24	Antrim . .	Cary . .	Grange of Drumtullagh	Ballycastle .	III.	14
45	Moss-side . .	125 3 11	Antrim . .	Upper Antrim .	Kilbride . .	Antrim .	III.	6
7	MOSS-SIDE T. .	—	Antrim . .	Cary . .	Grange of Drumtullagh	Ballycastle .	III.	14
18, 22	Mosstown . .	183 2 22	Longford . .	Moydow . .	Kilcommock .	Ballymahon .	I.	161
22	Mosstown . .	491 2 4f	Longford . .	Rathcline . .	Kilcommock .	Ballymahon .	I.	164
24	Mosstown or Ballinkeeny	212 1 18	Westmeath .	Rathconrath . .	Killare . .	Mullingar .	I.	283
24	Mosstown Demesne .	140 0 3	Westmeath .	Rathconrath . .	Killare . .	Mullingar .	I.	283
18	Mosstown North .	234 3 14g	Louth . .	Ardee . .	Mosstown . .	Ardee .	I.	174
18	Mosstown South .	52 3 9	Louth . .	Ardee . .	Mosstown . .	Ardee .	I.	174
13	Mossy Glen . .	793 1 25	Donegal . .	Inishowen East .	Moville Lower .	Inishowen .	III.	119
12, 13	Mostragee . .	300 0 39	Antrim . .	Lower Dunluce .	Derrykeighan .	Ballymoney .	III.	17
6, 9	Mota . . .	201 0 20	Tipperary, N.R.	Lower Ormond .	Kilbarron . .	Borrisokane .	II.	284
26	Motabeg or Salville	140 0 25	Wexford . .	Ballaghkeen . .	Templeshannon .	Enniscorthy .	I.	299
5, 6	Motalower . .	325 3 12	Wexford . .	Gorey . .	Carnew . .	Shillelagh .	I.	316
41	M talee . .	344 1 33	Londonderry .	Loughinsholin .	Desertmartin .	Magherafelt .	III.	240
40, 41, 42	Mote Demesne .	1,263 3 3	Roscommon .	Athlone . .	Kilmeane . .	Roscommon .	IV.	182
3, 7	Mothel . . .	259 1 21	Waterford . .	Upperthird . .	Mothel . .	Carrick on Suir .	II.	371
25	Mough . . .	175 2 38	Leitrim . .	Leitrim . .	Fenagh . .	Mohill .	IV.	100
16, 24	Mough or Greatwood	132 3 20	King's Co. .	Ballyboy . .	Killoughy . .	Tullamore .	I.	124
34	Moughley . .	42 0 23	Fermanagh .	Magherastephana .	Aghalurcher .	Lisnaskea .	III.	217
99, 100	Moularustig . .	195 2 30	Kerry . .	Dunkerron South .	Kilcrohane . .	Kenmare .	II.	184
37, 40, 41	Mouler-town or Ballyvoulera	323 1 26	Kilkenny . .	Ida . .	Kilcoan . .	Waterford .	I.	102
50	Mount . . .	138 2 3	Clare . .	Clonderalaw . .	Kilchreest . .	Kiladysert .	II.	15
61	Mountain . .	60 0 27	Galway . .	Clonmacnowen .	Ahascragh . .	Ballinasloe .	IV.	24
98	Mountain . .	81 3 30	Galway . .	Kilconnell . .	Killallaghtan .	Ballinasloe .	IV.	41
93	Mountain . .	221 1 23h	Mayo . .	Costello . .	Bekan . .	Claremorris .	IV.	139

(a) Including 8A. 1R. 24P. reclaimed land.
(b) Including 2A. 2R. 11P. water.
(c) Including 5A. 1R. 20P. water.
(d) Including 9A. 0R. 16P. River Barrow.
(e) Including 14A. 3R. 5P. River Barrow.
(f) Including 14A. 2R. 16P. water.
(g) Including 13A. 3R. 8P. water.
(h) Including 38A. 1R. 8P. water.

No. of Sheet of the Ordnance Survey Maps.	Townlands and Towns.	Area in Statute Acres.	County.	Barony.	Parish.	Poor Law Union in 1857.	Townland Census of 1851, Part I.
		A. R. P.					Vol. / Page
22	Mountaincastle North	165 3 0	Waterford	Decies without Drum	Modelligo	Dungarvan	II. 359
22	Mountaincastle South	184 3 20	Waterford	Decies without Drum	Modelligo	Dungarvan	II. 359
135, 144	Mountain Common	324 0 29	Cork, W.R.	Ibane and Barryroe	Ardfield	Clonakilty	II. 148
81,82,92,93	Mountaincommon	942 2 28	Mayo	Costello	Aghamore	Swineford	IV. 137
94	Mountain Common	290 1 22	Mayo	Murrisk	Kilgeever	Westport	IV. 161
11	Mountainfarm	625 0 14	Queen's Co.	Upperwoods	Offerlane	Mountmellick	I. 252
12, 21	Mountainfarm	232 0 8	Waterford	Coshmore&Coshbride	Lismore and Mocollop	Lismore	II. 347
42	Mountaingate	64 3 13	Wexford	Bargy	Kilmannan	Wexford	I. 306
23	Mountain Lodge Demesne	484 3 18	Monaghan	Cremorne	Aghnamullen	Cootehill	III. 258
25, 26	Mountain Lower	424 2 21	Roscommon	Castlereagh	Kiltullagh	Castlereagh	IV. 202
31, 36	Mountainmuck	252 3 9	Wexford	Bantry	Whitechurchglynn	Wexford	I. 303
84	Mountain North	220 0 7	Galway	Athenry	Athenry	Galway	IV. 4
78	Mountainpark	106 1 36	Donegal	Raphoe	Donaghmore	Stranorlar	III. 138
62	Mountainpark	178 2 16	Donegal	Raphoe	Raphoe	Strabane	III. 141
125	Mountainpark	171 2 39	Galway	Leitrim	Ballynakill	Loughrea	IV. 52
10, 16	Mountainpole	340 2 2	Meath	Upper Kells	Dulane	Kells	I. 205
10,11,16,17	Mountainpole or Rochfortsland	84 1 35	Meath	Upper Kells	Kells	Kells	I. 206
20	Mountain Rea	112 2 12	Waterford	Coshmore&Coshbride	Lismore and Mocollop	Lismore	II. 347
96	Mountain South	177 1 26	Galway	Athenry	Athenry	Loughrea	IV. 4
11, 12	Mountainstown	495 3 3	Meath	Morgallion	Kilshine	Navan	I. 210
7, 11	Mountainthird	159 2 14	Leitrim	Rosclogher	Killasnet	Manorhamilton	IV. 110
18	Mountaintown	206 2 10	Louth	Ferrard	Dunleer	Ardee	I. 181
25, 26	Mountain Upper	392 2 0	Roscommon	Castlereagh	Kiltullagh	Castlereagh	IV. 202
83, 95	Mountain West	198 0 33	Galway	Dunkellin	Athenry	Galway	IV. 27
10	Mount Alexander	408 2 25a	Down	Castlereagh Lower	Comber	Newtownards	III. 162
12	Mountalexander	299 1 12	Wexford	Ballaghkeen	Kiltennell	Gorey	I. 297
2	Mountallen	137 3 5	Roscommon	Boyle	Kilronan	Boyle	IV. 197
35, 43	Mountallon	180 0 1	Clare	Tulla Lower	Clonlea	Tulla	II. 35
40	Mountalt	32 0 36	Tipperary, N.R.	Kilnamanagh Upper	Ballycahill	Thurles	II. 277
11	Mountambrose Great	49 3 1	Dublin	Nethercross	Killeek	Balrothery	I. 31
11	Mountambrose Little	31 1 9	Dublin	Nethercross	Killeek	Balrothery	I. 31
87, 90	Mountanglesby	971 2 17	Tipperary, S.R.	Iffa and Offa West	Shanrahan	Clogheen	II. 320
3	Mount Anketell	60 0 33	Monaghan	Trough	Errigal Trough	Monaghan	III. 285
37	Mountanna	86 0 8	Wexford	Shelmaliere East	Kilpatrick	Wexford	I. 331
22	Mountanville	92 1 24	Dublin	Rathdown	Taney	Rathdown	I. 38
9, 10	Mountarmstrong	368 3 23	Kildare	Ikeathy&Oughterany	Mainham	Celbridge	I. 58
16	Mountarmstrong	54 3 19	King's Co.	Ballycowan	Rahan	Tullamore	I. 129
23	Mountashton	72 0 15	Dublin	Rathdown	Monkstown	Rathdown	I. 36
54	Mountaylor	109 0 16	Tipperary, S.R.	Slievardagh	Killenaule	Cashel	II. 334
8	Mountbagnall	347 2 4	Louth	Lower Dundalk	Carlingford	Dundalk	I. 176
66, 77	Mountbell	244 2 31	Cork, E.R.	Imokilly	Killeagh	Youghal	II. 88
45, 46	Mountbellew Demesne	73 3 36b	Galway	Killian	Ballynakill	Mountbellew	IV. 43
45, 46	Mountbellew Demesne	480 2 18c	Galway	Killian	Moylough	Mountbellew	IV. 45
46	MOUNTBELLEW T.	—	Galway	Killian	Moylough	Mountbellew	IV. 45
72	Mountbernard	109 1 30	Galway	Tiaquin	Ballymacward	Mountbellew	IV. 76
16	Mount Bernard	50 2 24d	Tyrone	Omagh West	Urney	Castlederg	III. 318
47	Mountblakeney	562 2 27	Limerick	Coshma	Kilbreedy Minor	Kilmallock	II. 243
4	Mountbolton	658 2 14	Waterford	Upperthird	Clonagam	Carrick on Suir	II. 369
24	MOUNTBOLUS T.	—	King's Co.	Ballyboy	Killoughy	Tullamore	I. 124
16	Mountbridget	240 1 28	Cork, E.R.	Orrery and Kilmore	Churchtown	Mallow	II. 107
88	Mountbrown	304 2 27	Mayo	Burrishoole	Aghagower	Westport	IV. 118
71	Mountbrowne	294 2 0	Galway	Clare	Abbeyknockmoy	Galway	IV. 16
31	Mountcampbell	157 0 4	Leitrim	Leitrim	Annaduff	Cark on Shannon	IV. 99
23	Mount Carmel	183 3 18	Monaghan	Cremorne	Aghnamullen	Cootehill	III. 258
29	Mountcarteret or Feeghroe	52 3 9	King's Co.	Garrycastle	Reynagh	Parsonstown	I. 138
43	Mountcashel	92 2 11	Clare	Bunratty Lower	Kilfinaghta	Tulla	II. 4
2	Mountcastle	188 1 34	Tyrone	Strabane Lower	Donaghedy	Strabane	III. 321
53, 63	Mountcatherine	232 0 6	Clare	Tulla Lower	Kiltenanlea	Limerick	II. 37
44, 53	Mountcatherine	319 0 25	Cork, E.R.	Barrymore	Kilshanahan	Fermoy	II. 56
24	Mountcatherine	26 2 19	Limerick	Coonagh	Ballynaclogh	Tipperary	II. 234
24	Mountcatherine	17 3 13	Limerick	Coonagh	Grean	Tipperary	II. 235
40	Mountcatherine	50 0 3	Tipperary, N.R.	Eliogarty	Inch	Thurles	II. 270
93, 99	Mountcharles	650 0 32e	Donegal	Banagh	Inver	Donegal	III. 108
93, 99	MOUNTCHARLES T.	—	Donegal	Banagh	Inver	Donegal	III. 108
16	Mountcoal	595 0 24	Kerry	Clanmaurice	Kilshenane	Listowel	II. 172
52	Mountcollins	1,025 3 23	Limerick	Glenquin	Killeedy	Newcastle	II. 246
8, 9, 16, 17	Mountcongreve	118 2 32	Waterford	Middlethird	Kilmeadan	Waterford	II. 368
17	Mountcongreve	65 0 15	Waterford	Middlethird	Lisnakill	Waterford	II. 368
48	Mountcoote	310 2 4	Limerick	Coshlea	Ardpatrick	Kilmallock	II. 236
16	Mountcorbitt	175 0 19	Cork, E.R.	Orrery and Kilmore	Churchtown	Mallow	II. 107

(a) Including 0A. 1R. 0P. water.
(b) Including 2A. 2R. 27P. water.
(c) Including 60A. 3R. 12P. water.
(d) Including 1A. 3R. 10P. water.
(e) Including 20A. 0R. 11P. water.

4 Y 2

No. of Sheet of the Ordnance Survey Maps.	Townlands and Towns.	Area in Statute Acres.			County.	Barony.	Parish.	Poor Law Union in 1857.	Townland Census of 1851, Part I.	
		A.	R.	P.					Vol.	Page
78	Mountcotton . .	203	3	11	Cork, E.R. .	Imokilly . . .	Kilmacdonogh .	Youghal . .	II.	88
47	Mountcross . .	41	1	14	Wexford . .	Bargy . . .	Mulrankin . .	Wexford . .	I.	307
35	Mount Darby . .	132	3	19a	Fermanagh .	Clankelly . .	Clones . . .	Clones . .	III.	196
9, 10, 18, 19	Mountdavid . .	327	0	17	Limerick . .	Shanid . . .	Shanagolden . .	Glin . . .	II.	258
12, 17	Mountdavis . .	528	2	17	Longford . .	Rathcline . .	Rathcline . .	Longford . .	I.	165
31	Mountdelvin . .	457	1	34	Roscommon .	Castlereagh .	Kiltullagh . .	Castlereagh .	IV.	202
73, 74	Mount Desert . .	413	1	32b	Cork, E.R. .	Cork . . .	Currykippane .	Cork . . .	II.	64
29,30,36,37	Mountdillon . .	1,369	2	26	Roscommon .	Roscommon . .	Lissonuffy . .	Strokestown .	IV.	212
15, 18	Mountdoyle . .	124	2	2	Louth . .	Ardee . . .	Drumcar . .	Ardee . .	I.	172
21	Mountdruid . .	212	2	3	Roscommon .	Castlereagh .	Kilcorkey . .	Castlereagh .	IV.	199
22, 23	Mountdrum . .	174	1	22	Fermanagh .	Tirkennedy . .	Derryvullan .	Enniskillen .	III.	221
39, 47	Mounteagle . .	167	0	1	Limerick . .	Connello Upper .	Bruree . . .	Kilmallock .	II.	231
23, 24	Mounteagle . .	124	2	15	Queen's Co. .	Cullenagh . .	Ballyroan . .	Abbeyleix .	I.	239
23, 24	Mounteagle . .	348	0	9	Queen's Co. .	Cullenagh . .	Clonenagh&Clonagheen	Abbeyleix .	I.	239
7	Mounteagle or Drumanilra . .	312	1	33c	Roscommon .	Boyle . . .	Tumna . .	Car\. on Shannon	IV.	198
5	Mountedward or Drangan . .	307	0	26	Sligo . .	Carbury . .	Ahamlish . .	Sligo . .	IV.	219
20	Mount Edwards . .	58	0	15	Antrim . .	Lower Glenarm .	Layd . . .	Ballycastle .	III.	23
29	Mountelliott . .	469	3	24	Wexford . .	Bantry . .	St. Marys . .	New Ross .	I.	302
10	Mountfalcon . .	432	2	4	Tipperary, N.R.	Lower Ormond .	Ardcrony . .	Borrisokane .	II.	282
17, 23	Mountfead . .	253	1	35	Queen's Co. .	Maryborough West .	Clonenagh&Clonagheen	Abbeyleix .	I.	243
14, 15	Mountfin Lower or Ballinturner . .	437	0	27d	Wexford . .	Scarawalsh .	Ballycarney . .	Enniscorthy .	I.	322
8, 12	Mountfinn . .	328	0	18	Kilkenny . .	Galmoy . .	Urlingford . .	Urlingford .	I.	93
14	Mountfin Upper .	345	1	29	Wexford . .	Scarawalsh .	Ballycarney . .	Enniscorthy .	I.	322
11	Mountforest . .	164	1	1	Wexford . .	Gorey . . .	Liskinfere . .	Gorey . .	I.	320
13	Mountfortescue . .	245	3	26	Meath . .	Upper Slane . .	Grangegeeth . .	Ardee . .	I.	224
39, 47	Mountfox . .	291	0	11	Limerick . .	Kilmallock . .	St. Peters & St. Pauls	Kilmallock .	II.	250
23	Mountfrisco . .	174	0	11	Tipperary, N.R.	Ikerrin . . .	Bourney . .	Roscrea . .	II.	274
139, 140	Mountgabriel . .	758	3	5	Cork, W.R. .	West Carbery (W.D.)	Skull . . .	Skull . .	II.	146
40	Mountgaffeny . .	71	3	4	Sligo . .	Tirerrill . .	Aghanagh . .	Boyle . .	IV.	237
18	Mountgale . .	456	0	8	Kilkenny . .	Crannagh . .	Ballycallan . .	Kilkenny . .	I.	85
71	Mountgarret . .	173	1	20	Galway . .	Tiaquin . .	Monivea . .	Loughrea .	IV.	79
29	Mountgarrett . .	86	3	19	Wexford . .	Bantry . .	St. Marys . .	New Ross .	I.	302
34	Mountgeorge . .	25	2	9	Tipperary, N.R.	Kilnamanagh Upper	Glenkeen . .	Thurles . .	II.	278
16	Mountgeorge . .	158	2	38	Wexford . .	Gorey . . .	Kilcormick . .	Enniscorthy .	I.	317
53, 62, 63	Mountgordon . .	141	2	22	Clare . .	Bunratty Lower .	St. Munchins .	Limerick . .	II.	6
12	Mountgorry . .	119	3	10	Dublin . .	Nethercross . .	Swords . . .	Balrothery .	I.	32
69, 78	Mountgregory . .	109	1	17e	Mayo . .	Carra . . .	Aglish . . .	Castlebar .	IV.	124
78, 87	Mounthall . .	591	1	39	Donegal . .	Raphoe . .	Donaghmore . .	Stranorlar .	III.	138
11	Mounthall . .	189	2	18	Queen's Co. .	Upperwoods . .	Offerlane . .	Mountmellick .	I.	252
23	Mount Hamilton .	685	1	23	Antrim . .	Kilconway . .	Killagan . .	Ballymoney .	III.	27
7	Mounthamilton . .	217	3	27	Louth . .	Upper Dundalk .	Dundalk . .	Dundalk . .	I.	178
29	Mounthanover . .	136	2	0	Wexford . .	Bantry . .	Ballyanne . .	New Ross .	I.	299
29	Mounthawk . .	132	3	29	Kerry . .	Trughanacmy .	Tralee . . .	Tralee . .	II.	214
59,60,72,73	Mounthazel . .	422	2	0	Galway . .	Tiaquin . .	Ballymacward .	Mountbellew .	IV.	76
42, 45	Mountheaton . .	449	1	37	King's Co. .	Clonlisk . .	Corbally . .	Roscrea . .	I.	129
42, 45	Mountheaton . .	237	0	39	King's Co. .	Clonlisk . .	Dunkerrin . .	Roscrea . .	I.	130
47	Mounthenry . .	135	1	30	Kerry . .	Magunihy . .	Kilnanare . .	Killarney .	II.	204
30	Mounthenry . .	55	2	18	King's Co. .	Eglish . . .	Eglish . . .	Parsonstown .	I.	135
123	Mounthenry . .	235	0	16	Mayo . .	Kilmaine . .	Shrule . . .	Ballinrobe .	IV.	158
31	Mounthill . .	526	1	3	Armagh . .	Fews Upper . .	Creggan . .	Dundalk . .	III.	48
31,32,40,41	Mounthillary . .	115	1	29	Cork, E.R. .	Duhallow . .	Kilshannig . .	Mallow . .	II.	74
74, 86	Mounthovel . .	178	2	21	Cork, E.R. .	Cork . . .	Carrigaline . .	Cork . .	II.	64
16	Mounthoward Lower	435	2	1	Wexford . .	Gorey . . .	Monamolin . .	Gorey . .	I.	321
16	Mounthoward Upper	200	3	39	Wexford . .	Gorey . . .	Monamolin . .	Gorey . .	I.	321
52	Mountievers . .	348	2	37	Clare . .	Bunratty Lower .	Kilfinaghta . .	Limerick . .	II.	4
52	Mountievers . .	27	2	32	Clare . .	Bunratty Lower .	Kilfintinan . .	Limerick . .	II.	5
29	Mountinfant . .	311	2	12	Cork, E.R. .	Duhallow . .	Nohavaldaly . .	Millstreet .	II.	75
39, 44	Mount Irvine . .	338	1	10	Sligo . .	Coolavin . .	Kilfree . .	Boyle . .	IV.	224
15	Mount Irwin or Lissheagh . .	160	3	3	Armagh . .	Tiranny . .	Tynan . . .	Armagh . .	III.	60
27	Mountisland . .	193	0	23	Tipperary, N.R.	Upper Ormond .	Kilmore . .	Nenagh . .	II.	291
18	Mountjerome . .	28	1	11	Dublin . .	Uppercross . .	St. Catherines .	Dublin South .	I.	40
18	Mountjessop . .	260	3	28	Longford . .	Moydow . .	Moydow . . .	Longford . .	I.	162
19	Mountjohn . .	82	2	31	Wicklow . .	Newcastle . .	Newcastle Upper .	Rathdrum .	I.	353
26, 35	Mountjoy Forest East Division . .	1,751	3	2f	Tyrone . .	Strabane Upper .	Cappagh . .	Omagh . .	III.	325
25,26,34,35	Mountjoy Forest West Division . .	1,018	2	8g	Tyrone . .	Strabane Upper .	Cappagh . .	Omagh . .	III.	325
33, 34	*Mountjoy Island* .	3	1	0	Fermanagh .	Magherastephana .	Aghalurcher .	Lisnaskea .	III.	218
60	Mountjudkin . .	49	3	13	Tipperary, S.R.	Middlethird .	St. Patricksrock .	Cashel . .	II.	331

(a) Including 11A. 3R. 36P. water.　　(d) Including 6A. 3R. 9P. water.　　(f) Including 18A. 3R. 24P. water.
(b) Including 15A. 3R. 12P. water.　　(e) Including 10A. 0R. 21P. water.　　(g) Including 22A. 2R. 25P. water.
(c) Including 12A. 1R. 39P. water.

No. of Sheet of the Ordnance Survey Maps.	Townlands and Towns.	Area in Statute Acres.			County.	Barony.	Parish.	Poor Law Union in 1857.	Townland Census of 1851, Part I.	
		A.	R.	P.					Vol.	Page
27, 28	Mountjuliet or Walton's Grove . .	536	0	6a	Kilkenny .	Knocktopher .	Jerpointchurch	Thomastown	I.	111
14	Mountkeeffe . .	707	0	8	Cork, E.R.	Duhallow .	Clonfert . .	Kanturk .	II.	69
1, 4	Mountkelly . .	446	1	17	Carlow .	Rathvilly .	Rathvilly . .	Baltinglass .	I.	12
18	Mountkelly . .	457	2	16b	Galway .	Ballymoe .	Boyounagh .	Glennamaddy .	IV.	6
13	Mount Kennedy Demesne . .	39	2	16	Wicklow .	Newcastle .	Kilcoole . . .	Rathdrum .	I.	352
13	Mount Kennedy Demesne . .	412	2	3	Wicklow .	Newcastle .	Newcastle Upper .	Rathdrum .	I.	353
5	Mountkennet . .	21	0	1c	Limerick .	Limerick, Municipal Borough of .	St. Michaels .	Limerick .	II.	262
37	Mountland or Butterhouse . .	107	2	32	Meath .	Lower Deece .	Scurlockstown .	Trim .	I.	192
39, 48	Mountleader . .	254	0	7	Cork, W.R.	West Muskerry .	Drishane . .	Millstreet .	II.	156
25	Mountloftus . .	48	0	23	Kilkenny .	Gowran . .	Powerstown .	Thomastown .	I.	98
112	Mountlong . .	80	1	17	Cork, E.R.	Kinalea . .	Kilmonoge .	Kinsale .	II.	95
11, 18, 19	Mountlucas or Drumcaw . .	1,250	1	4	King's Co.	Coolestown .	Ballynakill .	Edenderry .	I.	132
79	Mountluke . .	117	0	39	Kerry .	Iveragh .	Caher . .	Cahersiveen .	II.	194
30	Mountlusk . .	105	1	9	Wicklow .	Arklow .	Kilcommon .	Rathdrum .	I.	345
23, 26	Mount Mapas or Scalpwilliam .	146	3	10	Dublin .	Rathdown .	Kill . .	Rathdown .	I.	36
12, 16	Mountmelican . .	61	2	38	Carlow .	Idrone East .	Fennagh . .	Carlow .	I.	7
12, 21	Mountmelleray . .	555	1	34	Waterford .	Coshmore&Coshbride	Lismore and Mocollop	Lismore .	II.	347
8	MOUNTMELLICK T. .	—			Queen's Co.	Portnahinch . Tinnahinch .	Ardea . . Rosenallis . }	Mountmellick .	I.	244 250
22, 23	Mountmerrion or Callary . .	376	1	5	Dublin . .	Rathdown .	Taney . .	Rathdown .	I.	38
22, 23	Mountmerrion South	4	1	8	Dublin .	Rathdown .	Taney . .	Rathdown .	I.	38
23	Mountminnett . .	286	0	5	Limerick .	Clanwilliam .	Ballybrood .	Limerick .	II.	221
9	Mountmisery . .	52	2	27d	Waterford .	Gaultiere and Municipal Borough	Kilculliheen .	Waterford .	II.	363
11	Mountmurray . .	357	1	23	Westmeath .	Corkaree .	Portnashangan .	Mullingar .	I.	263
82, 83	Mountmusic . .	502	2	22	Cork, W.R.	West Muskerry .	Kilmichael .	Dunmanway .	II.	159
25, 33	Mountnagle . .	307	1	16	Cork, E.R.	Fermoy . .	Carrigleamleary .	Mallow .	II.	77
6	Mountnebo . .	304	0	10	Wexford .	Gorey . .	Kilnahue .	Gorey .	I.	319
1, 4	Mountneill . .	207	1	39	Carlow .	Rathvilly .	Rathvilly .	Baltinglass .	I.	12
45, 46	Mountneill . .	315	1	38	Kilkenny .	Iverk .	Aglish . .	Waterford .	I.	105
39	Mountnicholas .	108	1	5	Kerry .	Trughanacmy .	Ballymacelligott	Tralee .	II.	207
17, 21	Mountnorris . .	556	2	19	Armagh .	Orior Lower .	Loughgilly .	Newry .	III.	57
21	MOUNT NORRIS T. .	—			Armagh .	Orior Lower .	Loughgilly .	Newry .	III.	57
24	Mount North . .	535	2	23	Cork, E.R.	Orrery and Kilmore	Ballyclogh .	Mallow .	II.	106
38	Mount Nugent .	137	1	13	Cavan .	Clanmahon .	Kilbride . .	Oldcastle .	III.	78
15	Mountnugent Lower	214	1	26	Kilkenny .	Gowran . .	Rathcoole .	Kilkenny .	I.	98
38	MOUNT NUGENT T. .	—			Cavan .	Clanmahon .	Kilbride .	Oldcastle .	III.	78
15	Mountnugent Upper	246	1	25	Kilkenny .	Gowran . .	Rathcoole .	Kilkenny .	I.	98
30	Mountodell . .	192	1	36	Waterford .	Decies without Drum	Whitechurch .	Dungarvan .	II.	362
15	Mountolive . .	40	3	38	Dublin .	Coolock .	Raheny . .	Dublin North .	I.	28
28	Mountoliver . .	8	2	24	Queen's Co.	Clandonagh .	Rathdowney .	Donaghmore .	I.	234
28	Mountoliver . .	59	1	12	Queen's Co.	Clandonagh .	Rathsaran .	Donaghmore .	I.	235
36	Mountoven . .	392	1	26	Kerry .	Corkaguiny .	Kilgobban .	Tralee .	II.	177
42	Mountpallas . .	248	1	21	Cavan .	Clanmahon .	Kilbride . .	Oldcastle .	III.	78
22, 25	Mountpelier . .	919	3	13	Dublin .	Uppercross .	Tallaght . .	Dublin South .	I.	42
31	Mountphilips . .	259	2	12	Tipperary, N.R.	Owney and Arra	Kilvellane .	Nenagh .	II.	296
52	Mountpill . .	173	1	4	Wexford .	Bargy .	Tomhaggard .	Wexford .	I.	308
52	Mountpill Burrow .	29	0	39	Wexford .	Bargy .	Tomhaggard .	Wexford .	I.	308
16, 17	Mountpleasant . .	139	3	11	Carlow .	Idrone East .	Fennagh . .	Carlow .	I.	7
105	Mountpleasant . .	154	0	0	Galway .	Loughrea .	Loughrea . .	Loughrea .	IV.	66
24	Mountpleasant . .	677	3	0e	King's Co.	Ballyboy .	Killoughy .	Tullamore .	I.	124
4, 12	Mountpleasant .	172	0	9	Limerick .	Kenry .	Ardcanny .	Rathkeale .	II.	248
100	Mountpleasant . .	117	1	21f	Mayo .	Carra .	Touaghty .	Ballinrobe .	IV.	130
29	Mountpleasant . .	245	2	37g	Roscommon	Roscommon .	Kilbride . .	Strokestown .	IV.	210
43	Mountpleasant . .	202	1	23	Wicklow .	Shillelagh .	Crosspatrick .	Shillelagh .	I.	357
47	Mountpleasant or Tagunnan . .	190	1	27	Wexford .	Forth . .	Mayglass .	Wexford .	I.	312
52	Mountpleasure . .	82	0	18	Donegal .	Kilmacrenan .	Gartan . .	Letterkenny .	III.	127
53	Mountplummer .	1,171	3	11	Limerick .	Glenquin .	Monagay .	Newcastle .	II.	247
42	Mountplunkett . .	451	0	3	Roscommon	Athlone .	Killinvoy .	Athlone .	IV.	182
29	Mountpotter . .	93	3	18	Galway .	Dunmore .	Tuam . .	Tuam .	IV.	36
38	Mountprospect . .	353	2	31	Cavan .	Castlerahan .	Castlerahan .	Oldcastle .	III.	67
46	Mountprospect . .	102	3	25	Cork, E.R.	Kinnatalloon .	Mogeely . .	Fermoy .	II.	99
17	Mountprospect . .	249	1	3	Kildare .	Offaly East .	Rathangan .	Edenderry .	I.	71
3	Mountprospect . .	99	2	34	Roscommon	Boyle . .	Ardcarn . .	Boyle .	IV.	193
38, 39	Mount Prospect or Tullyoran . .	135	2	9	Fermanagh .	Knockninny .	Kinawley .	Lisnaskea .	III.	202

(a) Including 13A. 3R. 8P. River Nore.
(b) Including 5A. 3R. 7P. water.
(c) Included in the Parish of St. Michael.
(d) { Within the Municipal Boundary, 21A. 3R. 29P. / Without the Municipal Boundary, 30A. 2R. 38P.
(e) Including 36A. 1R. 21P. water.
(f) Including 8A. 3R. 14P. water.
(g) Including 4A. 0R. 13P. water.

No. of Sheet of the Ordnance Survey Maps.	Townlands and Towns.	Area in Statute Acres.	County.	Barony.	Parish.	Poor Law Union in 1857.	Townland Census of 1851, Part I.	
		A. R. P.					Vol.	Page
17	Mountrath	1,186 1 5	Queen's Co.	Maryborough West	Clonenagh&Clonagheen	Mountmellick	I.	243
16, 17	Mountrath	240 0 13	Queen's Co.	Upperwoods	Offerlane	Mountmellick	I.	252
17	MOUNTRATH T.	—	Queen's Co.	Maryborough West	Clonenagh&Clonagheen	Mountmellick	I.	243
44, 53	Mountrice	317 1 11	Clare	Tulla Lower	Kilseily	Limerick	II.	37
21, 22	Mountrice	632 3 27	Kildare	Offaly West	Lackagh	Athy	I.	73
22	Mountrice Bog	43 3 19	Kildare	Offaly West	Lackagh	Athy	I.	73
47	Mountrivers	943 2 27	Clare	Ibrickan	Killard	Kilrush	II.	23
27,28,35,36	Mount Rivers	155 1 4a	Cork, E.R.	Condons&Clangibbon	Clondulane	Fermoy	II	60
60, 61	Mountrivers	473 0 24	Cork, W.R.	East Muskerry	Aghabulloge	Macroom	II.	153
37	Mountrivers	23 1 32	Tipperary, N.R.	Owney and Arra	Kilvellane	Nenagh	II.	296
29	Mountrivers	48 1 2	Waterford	Decies without Drum	Affane	Lismore	II.	353
21, 29	*Mountrivers Islands*	12 3 13b	Waterford	Decies without Drum	Affane	Lismore	II.	353
19	Mountrobert	143 3 2	Westmeath	Moyashel and Magh-eradernon	Rathconnell	Mullingar	I.	276
55	Mountross	416 2 36	Galway	Clare	Killeany	Tuam	IV.	20
13, 14	Mountrush	181 0 34	Louth	Ardee	Clonkeen	Ardee	I.	172
25	Mountrussell	43 1 11	Cork. E.R.	Fermoy	Carrigleamleary	Mallow	II.	77
55, 56	Mountrussell	1,134 2 24	Limerick	Coshlea	Ballingaddy	Kilmallock	II.	237
20, 26	Mountsack	98 3 3	Tipperary, N.R.	Owney and Arra	Burgesbeg	Nenagh	II.	294
7	Mount Sandel	230 1 39	Londonderry	North East Liberties of Coleraine	Coleraine	Coleraine	III.	246
112	Mountscribe or Moneyscreebagh	465 3 15	Galway	Kiltartan	Kinvarradoorus	Gort	IV.	49
16	Mountseaton	83 0 30	Wexford	Scarawalsh	Kilbride	Enniscorthy	I.	323
24	Mountseskin	715 2 36	Dublin	Uppercross	Tallaght	Dublin South	I.	42
49	Mount Shalgus	112 3 11	Antrim	Upper Toome	Drummaul	Antrim	III	34
134, 136	Mountshannon	255 2 20	Galway	Leitrim	Inishcaltra	Scarriff	IV.	54
6	Mountshannon	2 1 10	Limerick	Clanwilliam	Killeenagarriff	Limerick	II.	224
6	Mountshannon	318 1 3c	Limerick	Clanwilliam	Stradbally	Limerick	II.	226
68	Mountshannon East	513 1 6	Clare	Clonderalaw	Killofin	Killadysert	II.	17
134, 136	MOUNTSHANNON T.	—	Galway	Leitrim	Inishcaltra	Scarriff	IV.	54
68	Mountshannon West	417 1 21	Clare	Clonderalaw	Killofin	Killadysert	II.	17
45	Mountsilk	106 2 27	Galway	Tiaquin	Moylough	Mountbellew	IV.	80
24	Mountsion	7 2 39	Limerick	Clanwilliam	Dromkeen	Limerick	II.	223
24	Mountsion	176 3 10	Limerick	Clanwilliam	Grean	Limerick	II.	224
40	Mountsion	25 0 39	Tipperary, N.R.	Kilnamanagh Upper	Ballycahill	Thurles	II.	277
9	Mountsion	69 0 19d	Waterford	Gaultiere and Municipal Borough	Kilculliheen	Waterford	II.	363
11	Mount Stewart	780 1 24	Down	Ards Lower	Greyabbey	Newtownards	III.	158
51, 58	Mount Stewart	634 2 31	Tyrone	Clogher	Clogher	Clogher	III.	293
11	Mountstuart	68 0 28	Dublin	Nethercross	Killossery	Balrothery	I.	31
35	Mountstuart	196 2 29	Waterford	Decies within Drum	Ardmore	Dungarvan	II.	350
44	Mount Talbot	657 0 25e	Roscommon	Athlone	Tisrara	Roscommon	IV.	186
2, 5	Mount Temple	410 1 27	Sligo	Carbury	Ahamlish	Sligo	IV.	219
30	Mount Temple	580 2 14	Westmeath	Clonlonan	Ballyloughloe	Athlone	I.	260
34, 35	Mount Town	384 1 35	Sligo	Tirerrill	Killadoon	Boyle	IV.	239
9	Mounttrenchard	525 1 38	Limerick	Shanid	Loghill	Glin	II.	257
55, 66	Mountuniacke	35 1 4	Cork, E.R.	Imokilly	Ardagh	Youghal	II.	83
55, 66	Mountuniacke	192 0 1	Cork, E.R.	Imokilly	Killeagh	Youghal	II.	88
25	Mountusher	109 0 6	Wicklow	Newcastle	Rathnew	Rathdrum	I.	354
73	Mountventure	76 1 38	Galway	Tiaquin	Ballymacward	Ballinasloe	IV.	76
21	Mountwilliam	59 3 15	Limerick	Coshma	Adare	Croom	II	241
59	Mountwilliam	92 1 3	Tipperary, S.R.	Clanwilliam	Kilfeacle	Tipperary	II.	308
4, 11	Mountwilson	416 0 34	King's Co.	Warrenstown	Ballymacwilliam	Edenderry	I.	144
8, 13	Mountwolseley or Crosslow	809 1 13	Carlow	Rathvilly	Tullowphelim	Carlow	I.	12
15	Mournbeg	48 3 19f	Tyrone	Omagh West	Termonamongan	Castlederg	III.	317
42	Mourneabbey	81 1 31	Cork, E.R.	Barretts	Mourneabbey	Mallow	II.	50
48,49,52,53	Mourne Mountains East	6,713 1 22g	Down	Mourne	Kilkeel	Kilkeel	III.	183
52	Mourne Mountains Middle	3,198 0 38	Down	Mourne	Kilkeel	Kilkeel	III.	183
52, 55	Mourne Mountains West	4,093 1 13	Down	Mourne	Kilkeel	Kilkeel	III.	183
55	Mourne Park or Ballyrogan	1,141 3 3	Down	Mourne	Kilkeel	Kilkeel	III.	182
47	Mousetown	143 2 13	Tyrone	Dungannon Middle	Clonoe	Dungannon	III.	300
19, 27	Movanagher	608 3 8	Londonderry	Coleraine	Kilrea	Ballymoney	III.	232
1	Movarran	129 2 9	Fermanagh	Lurg	Drumkeeran	Lowtherstown	III.	206
38	Moveagh	323 2 3	Tyrone	Dungannon Upper	Derryloran	Cookstown	III.	307
36	Moveedy	121 2 35	Limerick	Glenquin	Grange	Newcastle	II.	245
55,56,65,66	Moveen East	1,066 0 8	Clare	Moyarta	Moyarta	Kilrush	II	34
55, 65	Moveen West	1,113 0 1	Clare	Moyarta	Moyarta	Kilrush	II.	34
18	Movenis	375 2 13	Londonderry	Coleraine	Desertoghill	Coleraine	III.	230

(a) Including 7A. 1R. 10P. water.
(b) Four Islands in Blackwater River.
(c) Including 17A. 0R. 29P. detached portion.
(d) { Within the Municipal Boundary, 21A. 1R. 6P.
      { Without the Municipal Boundary, 47A. 3R. 13P.
(e) Including 27A. 0R. 0P. water.
(f) Including 4A. 1R. 19P. water.
(g) Including 36A. 3R. 0P. Lough Shannagh.

No. of Sheet of the Ordnance Survey Maps	Townlands and Towns.	Area in Statute Acres.			County.	Barony.	Parish.	Poor Law Union in 1857.	Townland Census of 1851. Part I.	
		A.	R.	P.					Vol.	Page
6	Movilla	171	0	7	Down	Ards Lower	Newtownards	Newtownards	III.	159
21, 22	MOVILLE T.	—			Donegal	Inishowen East	Moville Lower	Inishowen	III.	119
15, 16	Mowillin	402	2	17	Armagh	Armagh	Derrynoose	Armagh	III.	44
58. 59	Moy	713	2	14	Clare	Clonderalaw	Kilfiddane	Killadysert	II.	15
83	Moy	84	0	18	Donegal	Banagh	Killybegs Lower	Glenties	III.	110
112, 113	Moy	270	2	2	Galway	Kiltartan	Kinvarradoorus	Gort	IV.	49
42, 43	Moy	159	3	16	Meath	Lower Moyfenrath	Laracor	Trim	I.	210
20	Moy	225	3	12	Monaghan	Cremorne	Muckno	Castleblayney	III	262
1, 3	Moy	165	1	9	Monaghan	Trough	Errigal Trough	Clogher	III.	285
62	Moy	237	3	23	Tyrone	Dungannon Middle	Clonfeacle	Dungannon	III.	299
52, 55	Moyad	458	1	1	Down	Mourne	Kilkeel	Kilkeel	III.	183
42, 48, 49	Moyad	1,556	0	17	Down	Upper Iveagh. Lr. pt	Kilcoo	Kilkeel	III.	173
50, 51	Moyadam	685	3	33	Antrim	Upper Antrim	Nilteen Grange	Antrim	III.	7
25, 31	Moyadd	724	2	7	Queen's Co.	Cullenagh	Dysartgallen	Abbeyleix	I.	239
57, 67	Moyadda Beg	242	3	18	Clare	Moyarta	Kilrush	Kilrush	II.	33
57	Moyadda More	413	1	14	Clare	Moyarta	Kilrush	Kilrush	II.	33
52	Moyad Upper	326	3	39	Down	Mourne	Kilkeel	Kilkeel	III.	183
37	Moyagall	792	0	8	Londonderry	Loughinsholin	Maghera	Magherafelt	III.	242
36, 45	Moyagh	304	2	5a	Donegal	Kilmacrenan	Tullyfern	Milford	III.	133
2	Moyagh	155	1	34d	Tyrone	Strabane Lower	Donaghedy	Strabane	III.	321
24	Moyagher	385	1	14	Meath	Lune	Rathmore	Trim	I.	208
24	Moyagher Lower	386	3	30	Meath	Lune	Rathmore	Trim	I.	208
33	Moyagoney	740	1	20	Londonderry	Loughinsholin	Kilrea	Ballymoney	III.	241
40, 46	Moyaliff	1,207	1	9	Tipperary, N.R.	Kilnamanagh Upper	Moyaliff	Thurles	II.	279
19, 26	Moyallan	415	0	7	Down	Lower Iveagh, Up. pt.	Tullylish	Banbridge	III.	171
1, 2	Moyally	343	3	3	King's Co.	Kilcoursey	Kilmanaghan	Tullamore	I.	141
14	Movanna	258	0	19	Queen's Co.	Stradbally	Moyanna	Athy	I.	247
22, 23	Moyard	1,172	1	4	Galway	Ballynahinch	Ballynakill	Clifden	IV.	11
39,40,44,45	Moyard	1,580	2	15	Londonderry	Loughinsholin	Ballynascreen	Magherafelt	III.	239
61	Moyard	228	1	25	Tyrone	Dungannon Middle	Clonfeacle	Dungannon	III.	299
8	Moyarget Lower	752	0	21	Antrim	Cary	Ramoan	Ballycastle	III.	14
8	Moyarget Upper	823	2	12	Antrim	Cary	Ramoan	Ballycastle	III.	14
65	Moyarta East	241	0	13	Clare	Moyarta	Moyarta	Kilrush	II.	34
65	Moyarta West	540	3	20	Clare	Moyarta	Moyarta	Kilrush	II.	34
72,73,85,86	Moyarwood	728	3	2	Galway	Kilconnell	Ballymacward	Ballinasloe	IV.	39
11, 16, 17	Moyassa	315	3	39	Kerry	Clanmaurice	Finuge	Listowel	II.	169
32	Moyasset	235	0	21	Antrim	Lower Toome	Ahoghill	Ballymena	III.	32
56, 57	Moyasta	904	3	29	Clare	Moyarta	Kilfearagh	Kilrush	II.	32
13	Moyaver Lower	395	3	25	Antrim	Upper Dunluce	Armoy	Ballymoney	III.	18
13	Moyaver Upper	430	3	8	Antrim	Upper Dunluce	Armoy	Ballymoney	III.	18
30	Moybane	342	3	20	Armagh	Fews Upper	Creggan	Castleblayney	III.	48
21	Moybane	207	1	33	Fermanagh	Clanawley	Cleenish	Enniskillen	III.	191
23	Moy Beg	304	0	9	Clare	Ibrickan	Kilfarboy	Ennistimon	II.	22
36	Moybeg Kirley	162	2	22	Londonderry	Loughinsholin	Kilcronaghan	Magherafelt	III.	241
5, 10	Moybella North	458	0	2	Kerry	Iraghticonnor	Lisselton	Listowel	II.	192
5, 10	Moybella South	314	2	4	Kerry	Iraghticonnor	Lisselton	Listowel	II.	192
28	Moybrick Lower	480	0	30	Down	Lower Iveagh, Lr. pt.	Dromara	Banbridge	III.	167
28	Moybrick Upper	522	0	21	Down	Upper Iveagh, Lr. pt.	Dromara	Banbridge	III.	172
21	Moybroue	273	2	18	Fermanagh	Clanawley	Cleenish	Enniskillen	III.	191
14	Moybuy	421	2	5c	Londonderry	Tirkeeran	Faughanvale	Londonderry	III.	250
47	Moycarky	518	3	29	Tipperary, N.R.	Eliogarty	Moycarky	Thurles	II.	271
37, 38	Moycashel	680	0	10	Westmeath	Moycashel	Ardnurcher or Horseleap	Tullamore	I.	277
14	Moyclare	717	2	13	King's Co.	Garrycastle	Wheery or Killagally	Parsonstown	I.	139
104, 105	Moycola	160	1	4	Galway	Dunkellin	Killogilleen	Loughrea	IV.	31
7	Moycraig Hamilton	232	3	29	Antrim	Cary	Billy	Ballycastle	III.	12
12	Moycraig Lower	363	0	35	Antrim	Cary	Billy	Ballycastle	III.	12
7, 12	Moycraig Macallister	277	1	20	Antrim	Cary	Billy	Ballycastle	III.	12
7, 8	Moycraig Upper	441	1	28	Antrim	Cary	Billy	Ballycastle	I.I.	13
68, 81	Moycullen	426	1	21d	Galway	Moycullen	Moycullen	Galway	IV.	71
21, 28	Moydalgan	531	3	8	Down	Lower Iveagh, Lr. pt.	Dromara	Lisburn	III.	168
35	Moydamlaght	980	2	15	Londonderry	Loughinsholin	Ballynascreen	Magherafelt	III.	239
36, 37	Moydilliga	1,200	3	37	Cork, E.R.	Condons&Clangibbon	Knockmourne	Fermoy	II.	62
11	Moydorragh	184	2	34	Meath	Lower Kells	Cruicetown	Kells	I.	202
44	Moydough	181	2	9	Sligo	Colavin	Kilfree	Boyle	IV.	224
41, 42	Moydow	151	3	0	Roscommon	Athlone	Kilmeane	Roscommon	IV.	182
19	Moydow Glebe	94	2	10	Longford	Moydow	Moydow	Longford	I.	162
37, 41	Moydristan	219	0	36	Cavan	Clanmahon	Ballymachugh	Cavan	III.	76
29	Moydrum	474	1	37	Westmeath	Brawny	St. Mary's	Athlone	I.	260
29	Moydrum	598	3	24	Westmeath	Clonlonan	Ballyloughloe	Athlone	I.	260
46	Moydrum or Bogstown	369	0	11	Meath	Upper Moyfenrath	Clonard	Edenderry	I.	213
23	Moyduff	213	0	35e	Cavan	Clankee	Drumgoon	Cootehill	III.	72

No. of Sheet of the Ordnance Survey Maps.	Townlands and Towns.	Area in Statute Acres.			County.	Barony.	Parish.	Poor Law Union in 1857.	Townland Census of 1851. Part I.	
		A.	R.	P.					Vol.	Page
9, 14	Moyeady	90	2	4*a*	Wexford	Scarawalsh	St. Mary's NewTⁿBarry	Enniscorthy	I.	325
66	Moyeightragh	70	3	10	Kerry	Magunihy	Killarney	Killarney	II.	203
34, 35	Moyer	350	0	29	Cavan	Clankee	Enniskeen	Bailieborough	III.	73
36, 41	Moyesset	159	3	29	Londonderry	Loughinsholin	Kilcronaghan	Magherafelt	III.	241
10, 14	Moy Etra	160	2	11	Monaghan	Cremorne	Clontibret	Monaghan	III.	261
69	Moyfadda	425	0	25	Clare	Clonderalaw	Kilfiddane	Killadysert	II.	15
35, 36	Moyfeagher	371	0	19*b*	Meath	Lune	Killaconnigan	Trim	I.	208
41	Moyfin	389	1	9*c*	Meath	Upper Moyfenrath	Clonard	Trim	I.	213
50, 53	Moygaddy	581	1	35	Meath	Upper Deece	Moyglare	Celbridge	I.	194
43, 52	Moygalla	261	1	13	Clare	Bunratty Lower	Kiltinaghta	Tulla	II.	4
20	Moygannon	461	3	7	Down	Lower Iveagh, Up.pt.	Donaghcloney	Lurgan	III.	169
51, 54	Moygannon	187	1	9	Down	Upper Iveagh, Up. pt.	Kilbroney	Kilkeel	III.	176
44	Moygara	1,174	2	7	Sligo	Coolavin	Kilfree	Boyle	IV.	224
63	Moygarriff	334	1	24	Antrim	Upper Massereene	Ballinderry	Lisburn	III.	29
54	Moygashel	315	1	1*d*	Tyrone	Dungannon Middle	Clonfeacle	Dungannon	III.	299
7	Moyge	840	2	13	Cork, E.R.	Orrery and Kilmore	Liscarroll	Mallow	II.	109
18	Moygh	125	0	19	Longford	Moydow	Killashee	Longford	I.	162
26, 27	Moygh	350	0	14*e*	Longford	Rathcline	Shrule	Ballymahon	I.	165
49, 50, 53	Moyglare	914	3	17	Meath	Upper Deece	Moyglare	Celbridge	I.	194
21	Moyglass	71	3	18	Fermanagh	Magheraboy	Devenish	Enniskillen	III.	211
21	Moyglass	68	2	18	Fermanagh	Magheraboy	Rossorry	Enniskillen	III.	214
125	Moyglass	878	1	4	Galway	Leitrim	Ballynakill	Loughrea	IV.	52
23	Moyglass	402	2	32	Roscommon	Ballintober North	Kilglass	Strokestown	IV.	186
12	Moyglass	230	2	6*f*	Roscommon	Ballintober North	Kilmore	Carⁿ. on Shannon	IV.	187
38, 39	Moyglass Beg	200	0	15	Clare	Ibrickan	Kilmurry	Kilrush	II.	23
39	Moyglass More	263	0	25	Clare	Ibrickan	Kilmurry	Kilrush	II.	24
9, 10	Moygowna	233	3	39	Clare	Burren	Carran	Ballyvaghan	II.	12
9	Moygrehan Lower	259	3	11	Westmeath	Delvin	Killua	Castletowndelvin	I.	265
9	Moygrehan Upper	237	3	19	Westmeath	Delvin	Killua	Castletowndelvin	I.	266
88	Moyhastin	398	1	35*g*	Mayo	Burrishoole	Aghagower	Westport	IV.	118
35,36,40,41	Moyheeland	525	0	6	Londonderry	Loughinsholin	Ballynascreen	Magherafelt	III.	239
70, 79	Moyhenna	162	1	31	Mayo	Carra	Kildacommoge	Castlebar	IV.	129
62	Moyhill	430	2	31	Clare	Bunratty Lower	Kilfintinan	Limerick	II.	5
24, 25	Moyhill	601	0	9	Clare	Inchiquin	Rath	Corrofin	II.	28
1, 2	Moyhill	202	0	1	Meath	Lower Kells	Moybolgue	Kells	I.	203
1, 5, 6	Moyhora	1,172	1	5	Kilkenny	Fassadinin	Castlecomer	Castlecomer	I.	89
24, 25	Moyhullin	166	3	19	Clare	Inchiquin	Dysert	Ennis	II.	24
21, 26	Moykeel	185	3	36	Fermanagh	Clanawley	Cleenish	Enniskillen	III.	191
40	Moykeeran	192	1	10	Londonderry	Loughinsholin	Ballynascreen	Magherafelt	III.	239
27, 33	Moyknock	611	2	20	Londonderry	Loughinsholin	Kilrea	Ballymoney	III.	241
14, 15	Moylagh	384	0	7	Meath	Fore	Moylagh	Oldcastle	I.	201
43, 51	Moylagh	536	2	19	Tyrone	Omagh East	Clogherny	Omagh	III.	310
114	Moylanboy	1	1	15	Mayo	Murrisk	Inishbofin	Clifden	IV.	159
27, 32	Moylarg	332	0	9	Antrim	Lower Toome	Ahoghill	Ballymena	III.	32
106	Moylaun Island	12	1	8	Kerry	Dunkerron South	Kilcrohane	Cahersiveen	II.	184
36	Moyle	333	2	15*h*	Donegal	Kilmacrenan	Tullyfern	Milford	III.	133
46, 54	Moyle	214	1	5	Donegal	Raphoe	Allsaints	Londonderry	III.	134
36	Moyleabbey	197	3	37	Kildare	Narragh&Reban East	Narraghmore	Baltinglass	I.	66
23	Moyle Beg	145	0	30	Monaghan	Cremorne	Aghnamullen	Cootehill	III.	258
7, 8	Moyle Big	521	1	11	Carlow	Carlow	Kellistown	Carlow	I.	2
105, 106	Moyleen	360	0	10	Galway	Loughrea	Loughrea	Loughrea	IV.	66
44, 50	Moyleggan	154	2	30	Meath	Ratoath	Rathregan	Dunshaughlin	I.	219
72, 82	Moyleglass	520	3	11*i*	Kerry	Dunkerron North	Knockane	Killarney	II.	182
17	Moyle Glebe	410	0	31*j*	Tyrone	Strabane Lower	Ardstraw	Gortin	III.	319
21, 26	Moylehid	613	3	11	Fermanagh	Clanawley	Cleenish	Enniskillen	III.	191
36	Moylehill	156	3	31*k*	Donegal	Kilmacrenan	Tullyfern	Milford	III.	133
7, 8	Moyle Little	150	0	16	Carlow	Carlow	Kellistown	Carlow	I.	2
23	Moyle More	157	2	26	Monaghan	Cremorne	Aghnamullen	Cootehill	III.	258
46	Moylemoss	115	2	30	Donegal	Raphoe	Allsaints	Londonderry	III.	134
23	Moylemuck	147	2	18*l*	Monaghan	Cremorne	Aghnamullen	Cootehill	III.	258
8, 9, 14	Moyleroe Big	298	0	20	Westmeath	Delvin	Castletowndelvin	Castletowndelvin	I.	265
9	Moyleroe Little	60	2	16	Westmeath	Delvin	Castletowndelvin	Castletowndelvin	I.	265
29	Moyles	121	3	10	Monaghan	Farney	Donaghmoyne	Carrickmacross	III.	270
9, 10, 14	Moyles	241	1	15	Monaghan	Monaghan	Monaghan	Monaghan	III.	277
26	Moyletra Kill	518	0	32	Londonderry	Coleraine	Desertoghill	Coleraine	III.	230
26	Moyletra Toy	557	3	13	Londonderry	Coleraine	Desertoghill	Ballymoney	III.	231
27, 33	Moylett	561	1	25*m*	Cavan	Upper Loughtee	Killinkere	Cavan	III.	84
50	Moylinny	129	3	3	Antrim	Upper Antrim	Antrim	Antrim	III.	5
5	Moylish	73	3	21	Limerick	Pubblebrien	St. Munchins	Limerick	II.	254
42, 46	Moylisha	628	3	13	Wicklow	Shillelagh	Moyacomb	Shillelagh	I.	358
60, 41	Moylisa	323	2	35	Roscommon	Athlone	Fuerty	Roscommon	IV.	181
45	Moylough	68	3	14	Galway	Tiaquin	Moylough	Mountbellew	IV.	80
34	Moylough	103	1	29	Monaghan	Farney	Magheracloone	Carrickmacross	III.	273

(*a*) Including 1A. 0R. 32P. water.
(*b*) Including 12A. 2R. 38P. water.
(*c*) Including 8A. 1R. 24P. water.
(*d*) Including 2A. 1R. 23P. water.
(*e*) Including 1A. 0R. 1P. water.

(*f*) Including 12A. 3R. 2P. water.
(*g*) Including 7A. 3R. 2P. water.
(*h*) Including 52A. 2R. 6P. water.
(*i*) Including 3A. 2R. 18P. water.

(*j*) Including 14A. 1R. 35P. water.
(*k*) Including 51A. 3R. 24P. water.
(*l*) Including 12A. 0R. 32P. water.
(*m*) Including 28A. 0R. 26P. water.

No. of Sheet of the Ordnance Survey Maps.	Townlands and Towns.	Area in Statute Acres.			County.	Barony.	Parish.	Poor Law Union in 1857.	Townland Census of 1851, Part I.	
		A.	R.	P.					Vol.	Page
38, 43	Moylough	1,497	0	27	Sligo	Leyny	Achonry	Tobercurry	IV.	229
45	Moylough Beg	351	1	18	Galway	Tiaquin	Moylough	Mountbellew	IV.	80
45	Moylough More	524	3	36	Galway	Tiaquin	Moylough	Mountbellew	IV.	80
30	Moymet	906	0	34	Meath	Upper Navan	Moymet	Trim	I.	216
26	Moymlough	409	1	30	Sligo	Leyny	Killoran	Sligo	IV.	230
23	Moy More	208	3	27	Clare	Ibrickan	Kilfarboy	Ennistimon	II.	22
25	Moymore	275	2	20	Clare	Inchiquin	Ruan	Corrofin	II.	28
35	Moymore	306	3	21	Clare	Tulla Upper	Tulla	Tulla	II.	42
63	Moymore	115	1	28	Donegal	Raphoe	Taughboyne	Strabane	III.	144
24	Moymore	285	0	30	Down	Dufferin	Killyleagh	Downpatrick	III.	167
24	Moymore	133	1	39	Limerick	Coonagh	Grean	Tipperary	II.	235
37	Moymore	592	2	27a	Tyrone	Dungannon Upper	Desertcreat	Cookstown	III.	308
15	Moymore North	510	2	34	Clare	Corcomroe	Killaspuglonane	Ennistimon	II.	19
15	Moymore South	24	3	34	Clare	Corcomroe	Killaspuglonane	Ennistimon	II.	19
46	Moymucklemurry	302	2	6	Londonderry	Loughinsholin	Desertlyn	Magherafelt	III.	240
76	Moyna	193	2	3	Mayo	Burrishoole	Kilmeena	Westport	IV.	122
5	Moynagh	135	0	39	Meath	Morgallion	Castletown	Kells	I.	209
38	Moynagh	111	0	31	Tyrone	Dungannon Upper	Desertcreat	Cookstown	III.	308
10, 11	Moynaghan North	221	1	31b	Fermanagh	Lurg	Derryvullan	Lowtherstown	III.	205
10, 15	Moynaghan South	128	1	28	Fermanagh	Lurg	Derryvullan	Lowtherstown	III.	205
37	Moynagh Lower	302	3	13	Cavan	Clanmahon	Drumlumman	Granard	III.	77
37, 41	Moynagh Upper	366	2	10	Cavan	Clanmahon	Drumlumman	Granard	III.	77
10, 11	Moynalty	483	1	7	Meath	Lower Kells	Moynalty	Kells	I.	204
11	MOYNALTY T.	—			Meath	Lower Kells	Moynalty	Kells	I.	204
43	Moynalvy	740	2	11	Meath	Upper Deece	Kilmore	Dunshaughlin	I.	193
36	Moynasboy	149	2	17	Meath	Lower Moyfenrath	Trim	Trim	I.	212
67	Moyne	302	3	5	Clare	Moyarta	Kilrush	Kilrush	II.	33
100	Moyne	276	0	2	Donegal	Tirhugh	Drumhome	Donegal	III.	146
44, 58	Moyne	536	2	33c	Galway	Tiaquin	Abbeyknockmoy	Tuam	IV.	75
10	Moyne	141	3	20	Kilkenny	Fassadinin	Kilmacar	Castlecomer	I.	90
2, 3	Moyne	502	0	18d	Longford	Granard	Killoe	Longford	I.	157
123	Moyne	880	3	25e	Mayo	Kilmaine	Shrule	Ballinrobe	IV.	158
22	Moyne	394	1	36	Mayo	Tirawley	Killala	Killala	IV.	169
29	Moyne	287	1	27	Queen's Co.	Clarmallagh	Durrow	Abbeyleix	I.	237
14	Moyne	731	3	21	Roscommon	Frenchpark	Tibohine	Castlereagh	IV.	205
54,55,62,63	Moyne	269	1	30	Tipperary, S.R.	Middlethird	Magowry	Cashel	II.	328
33	Moyne	351	3	36	Wicklow	Ballinacor South	Moyne	Shillelagh	I.	350
36, 42	Moyneard	711	0	26	Tipperary, N.R.	Eliogarty	Moyne	Thurles	II.	272
25	Moynehall	195	3	34	Cavan	Upper Loughtee	Annagelliff	Cavan	III.	82
20	Moyne Lower	261	0	24	Wexford	Scarawalsh	St.MarysEnniscorthy	Enniscorthy	I.	325
20	Moyne Middle	238	1	15	Wexford	Scarawalsh	St.MarysEnniscorthy	Enniscorthy	I.	325
36	Moynetemple	416	2	35	Tipperary, N.R.	Eliogarty	Moyne	Thurles	II.	272
36	MOYNE T.	—			Tipperary, N.R.	Eliogarty	Moyne	Thurles	II.	272
20	Moyne Upper	200	2	5	Wexford	Scarawalsh	St.MarysEnniscorthy	Enniscorthy	I.	325
35	Moyng	388	0	22	Waterford	Decies within Drum	Ardmore	Youghal	II.	350
35	Moyng Little	125	1	2	Waterford	Decies within Drum	Ardmore	Dungarvan	II.	350
66	Moynish More	61	2	18	Mayo	Burrishoole	Burrishoole	Newport	IV.	120
21, 29	Moynoe	417	1	2	Clare	Tulla Upper	Moynoe	Scarriff	II.	40
18	Moynsha	96	2	3f	Kerry	Clanmaurice	Duagh	Listowel	II.	168
24	Moyntiagh	284	2	1	Wicklow	Newcastle	Derrylossary	Rathdrum	I.	351
42	Moynure	112	2	23	King's Co.	Clonlisk	Kilmurryely	Roscrea	I.	131
42	Moynure	156	0	5	King's Co.	Clonlisk	Roscrea	Roscrea	I.	131
52	Moynure	156	0	16	Roscommon	Athlone	Drum	Athlone	IV.	180
7	Moyny	217	1	11	Mayo	Tirawley	Kilbride	Killala	IV.	168
119	Moyny East	318	2	0	Cork, W.R.	West Carbery (E.D.)	Dromdaleague	Skibbereen	II.	140
119	Moyny Lower	216	3	29	Cork, W.R.	West Carbery (E.D.)	Dromdaleague	Skibbereen	II.	140
119	Moyny Middle	107	1	38	Cork, W.R.	West Carbery (E.D.)	Dromdaleague	Skibbereen	II.	140
119	Moyny Upper	225	3	17	Cork, W.R.	West Carbery (E.D.)	Dromdaleague	Skibbereen	II.	140
96	Moyode	824	0	17	Galway	Athenry	Kilconierin	Loughrea	IV.	4
96	Moyode Demesne	599	1	13	Galway	Athenry	Kilconierin	Loughrea	IV.	4
4	Moyoran	210	0	12	Roscommon	Boyle	Tumna	Cark. on Shannon	IV.	198
14	Moy Otra	112	3	34	Monaghan	Cremorne	Clontibret	Monaghan	III.	261
76	Moyour	225	3	22	Mayo	Burrishoole	Kilmeena	Westport	IV.	122
108	Moyower	314	0	14	Galway	Longford	Meelick	Portumna	IV.	61
19	Moyra and Fortmill	168	0	2	Longford	Ardagh	Ardagh	Longford	I.	151
25, 34	Moyra Glebe	1,709	3	23	Donegal	Kilmacrenan	Raymunterdoney	Dunfanaghy	III.	131
10	Moyrahan	990	3	33	Mayo	Erris	Kilmore	Belmullet	IV.	146
29, 35, 36	Moyrath	966	1	18	Meath	Lune	Kildalkey	Trim	I.	208
6, 10	Moyraverty	374	3	22	Armagh	Oneilland East	Seagoe	Lurgan	III.	50
18	Moyree Commons	522	2	24g	Clare	Inchiquin	Ruan	Corrofin	II.	28
18, 27	Moyreen	509	1	32	Limerick	Shanid	Dunmoylan	Glin	II.	255
34	Moyriesk	77	2	13	Clare	Bunratty Upper	Clooney	Ennis	II.	8
34	Moyriesk	575	3	11	Clare	Bunratty Upper	Doora	Ennis	II.	8

(a) Including 8A. 0R. 11P. Lough Bracken.
(b) Including 26A. 1R. 32P. water.
(c) Including 4A. 2R. 32P. water.

(d) Including 6A. 3R. 0P. water.
(e) Including 10A. 3R. 28P. water.

(f) Including 6A. 0R. 3P. water.
(g) Including 19A. 3R. 19P. water.

No. of Sheet of the Ordnance Survey Maps.	Townlands and Towns.	Area in Statute Acres.			County.	Barony.	Parish.	Poor Law Union in 1857.	Townland Census of 1851. Part I.	
		A.	R.	P.					Vol.	Page
87, 96	Moyrisk . . .	303	0	36	Kerry . . .	Iveragh . .	Killemlagh . .	Cahersiveen .	II.	196
20	Moyroe . . .	51	2	6	Tipperary, N.R.	Lower Ormond .	Nenagh . . .	Nenagh . .	II.	287
55	Moyroe . . .	136	0	12	Tyrone . . .	Dungannon Middle .	Killyman . .	Dungannon .	III.	303
13, 17	Moyrourkan . .	395	0	21	Armagh . .	Oneilland West .	Mullaghbrack .	Banbridge .	III.	54
63, 76	Moyrus . . .	1,313	0	37a	Galway . .	Ballynahinch .	Moyrus . .	Clifden . .	IV.	13
32	Moyrush . . .	304	2	26	Sligo . . .	Corran . .	Cloonoghil . .	Tobercurry .	IV.	225
67	Moyrusk . . .	311	3	10	Antrim . .	Upper Massereene .	Magheragall .	Lisburn . .	III.	31
45	Moys . . .	261	0	19	Clare . . .	Tulla Lower .	Killaloe . .	Scarriff . .	II.	35
16	Moys . . .	821	2	22	Londonderry .	Keenaght . .	Tamlaght Finlagan	NewTⁿLimavady	III.	237
17, 18	Moysnaght . .	905	0	16	Fermanagh .	Tirkennedy .	Enniskillen .	Enniskillen .	III.	222
14	Moysnaght . .	121	2	14	Monaghan .	Cremorne .	Clontibret . .	Monaghan .	III.	261
16	Moys T. . .	—			Londonderry .	Keenaght . .	Tamlaght Finlagan	NewTⁿLimavady	III.	238
21, 22	Moystown Demesne	578	3	3	King's Co. .	Garrycastle .	Tisaran . .	Parsonstown .	I.	139
35	Moytirra East .	195	2	18	Sligo . . .	Tirerrill . .	Kilmactranny .	Boyle . .	IV.	240
34, 35	Moytirra West .	334	2	31	Sligo . . .	Tirerrill . .	Kilmactranny .	Boyle . .	IV.	240
62	Moy T. . .	—			Tyrone . . .	Dungannon Middle .	Clonfeacle . .	Dungannon .	III.	300
60	Moyure . . .	43	3	31	Galway . .	Tiaquin . .	Ballymacward .	Mountbellew .	IV.	76
22, 23	Moyvally . .	171	2	36	Carlow . .	Idrone East .	Kiltennell . .	Carlow . .	I.	7
1, 3	Moyvally . .	1,363	0	4	Kildare . .	Carbury . .	Ballynadrumny .	Edenderry .	I.	51
6, 11	Moyvane North .	447	2	21	Kerry . . .	Iraghticonnor .	Murher . .	Listowel .	II.	193
6, 11	Moyvane South .	422	2	7	Kerry . . .	Iraghticonnor .	Murher . .	Listowel .	II.	193
45, 48, 49	Moyvannan . .	600	1	36	Roscommon .	Athlone . .	Kiltoom . .	Athlone .	IV.	183
83, 95, 96	Moyveela . .	893	2	22	Galway . .	Dunkellin .	Athenry . .	Galway . .	IV.	27
95	Moyveela . .	500	0	37	Galway . .	Dunkellin .	Stradbally .	Galway . .	IV.	32
54	Moyvoon East .	81	1	31	Galway . .	Moycullen .	Kilcummin .	Oughterard .	IV.	67
54	Moyvoon West .	60	1	3	Galway . .	Moycullen .	Kilcummin .	Oughterard .	IV.	67
17	Moyvore . .	1,483	3	10	Westmeath .	Rathconrath .	Templepatrick .	Ballymahon .	I.	284
17	Moyvore T. .	—			Westmeath .	Rathconrath .	Templepatrick .	Ballymahon .	I.	284
23, 30, 31	Moyvoughly . .	1,911	0	12	Westmeath .	Rathconrath .	Ballymore .	Athlone .	I.	282
104	Muccurragh . .	309	2	5	Cork, W.R. .	Bear . . .	Kilcaskan .	Bantry . .	II.	123
9	Muchgrange . .	316	2	6	Louth . .	Lower Dundalk .	Carlingford .	Dundalk .	I.	176
43, 48	Muchknock . .	21	1	29	Wexford . .	Forth . .	Killinick . .	Wexford .	I.	310
48	Muchrath . .	79	2	9	Wexford . .	Forth . .	Killinick . .	Wexford .	I.	310
46	Muchtown . .	68	2	16	Wexford . .	Bargy . .	Kilcowan . .	Wexford .	I.	305
35, 41	Muchwood . .	433	1	2b	Meath . .	Lune . . .	Killaconnigan .	Trim . .	I.	208
37	Muchwood . .	145	1	20	Wexford . .	Shelmaliere West .	Ardcandrisk .	Wexford .	I.	332
22	Muck . . .	157	1	36	Kilkenny . .	Crannagh .	Tullaghanbrogue .	Callan . .	I.	87
10, 11	Muckalee . .	1,123	1	23	Kilkenny . .	Fassadinin .	Muckalee . .	Castlecomer .	I.	91
50	Muckamore . .	390	2	27	Antrim . .	Lower Massereene .	Muckamore(Grange of)	Antrim . .	III.	28
108, 118	Muckanagh . .	373	1	6	Galway . .	Longford .	Fahy . . .	Portumna .	IV.	58
33, 36	Muckanagh . .	196	1	6	Leitrim . .	Mohill . .	Cloone . .	Mohill . .	IV.	106
68	Muckanagh . .	1,053	1	24	Mayo . .	Carra . .	Islandeady .	Castlebar .	IV.	129
60	Muckanagh . .	698	1	1	Mayo . .	Carra . .	Turlough .	Castlebar .	IV.	131
17, 18, 23	Muckanagh . .	405	0	38	Roscommon .	Ballintober North .	Kilglass . .	Strokestown .	IV.	186
15	Muckanagh . .	634	3	39c	Westmeath .	Kilkenny West .	Noughaval .	Athlone .	I.	274
42, 51	Muckanagh (Butler)	111	0	29d	Clare . . .	Bunratty Lower .	Tomfinlough .	Ennis . .	II.	7
65, 78	Muckanaghederdauhaulia .	470	1	15	Galway . .	Moycullen .	Kilcummin .	Oughterard .	IV.	67
66, 79	Muckanaghkillew .	1,238	3	7e	Galway . .	Moycullen .	Kilcummin .	Oughterard .	IV.	67
33, 47	Muckanagh North .	624	2	2f	Galway . .	Killian . .	Killeroran .	Mountbellew .	IV.	44
47	Muckanagh South .	346	0	32	Galway . .	Killian . .	Killeroran .	Mountbellew .	IV.	44
42, 51	Muckanagh (Studdert) .	140	0	33g	Clare . . .	Bunratty Lower .	Tomfinlough .	Ennis . .	II.	7
42	Muckanagh (Vandeleur) .	325	1	25h	Clare . . .	Bunratty Lower .	Tomfinlough .	Ennis . .	II.	7
56	Muckcoort . .	648	3	9	Galway . .	Clare . .	Killeany .	Tuam . .	IV.	20
16	Muckduff . .	168	3	36	Sligo . . .	Tireragh . .	Castleconor .	Dromore West .	IV.	232
27, 28	Muckduff Lower .	368	3	15	Wicklow . .	Upper Talbotstown .	Kiltegan . .	Baltinglass .	I.	365
27, 28	Muckduff Upper .	483	2	15	Wicklow . .	Upper Talbotstown .	Kiltegan . .	Baltinglass .	I.	365
32	Muckelty . .	278	0	21	Sligo . . .	Leyny . .	Achonry . .	Tobercurry .	IV.	229
6	Muckenagh . .	463	1	1	Cork. E.R. .	Duhallow .	Tullylease .	Kanturk .	II.	76
21	Muckenagh . .	216	1	23i	Fermanagh .	Magheraboy .	Boho . .	Enniskillen .	III.	210
8, 12, 13	Muckenagh . .	311	0	0	Fermanagh .	Magheraboy .	Inishmacsaint .	Ballyshannon .	III.	213
16	Muckenagh . .	318	0	12	Kerry . . .	Clanmaurice .	Kilfeighny .	Listowel .	II.	170
9, 15	Muckenagh . .	611	2	7	Kerry . . .	Clanmaurice .	Kiltomy . .	Listowel .	II.	172
29, 32	Mucker . . .	101	1	15	Monaghan .	Farney . .	Donaghmoyne .	Carrickmacross .	III.	270
101	Muckera . .	329	1	22	Kerry . . .	Glanarought .	Tuosist . .	Kenmare .	II.	189
10	Muckerstaff . .	351	3	8	Longford .	Granard . .	Granard . .	Granard .	I.	156
45	Muckerstown . .	359	3	31	Meath . .	Ratoath . .	Donaghmore .	Dunshaughlin .	I.	218
5	Muckery . .	349	2	6j	Armagh . .	Oneilland West .	Drumcree .	Lurgan . .	III.	52
34	Muckinish . .	422	1	3k	Clare . . .	Bunratty Upper .	Clooney . .	Ennis . .	II.	8
94	Muckinish . .	204	1	0l	Clare . . .	Inchiquin .	Inagh . .	Ennistimon .	II.	25
8	*Muckinish* . .	12	2	1	Fermanagh .	Magheraboy .	Inishmacsaint .	Ballyshannon .	III.	213

(a) Including 75A. 0R. 22P. water.
(b) Including 5A. 1R. 34P. water.
(c) Including 20A. 2R. 10P. water.
(d) Including 54A. 2R. 0P. water.

(e) Including 193A. 3R. 34P. water.
(f) Including 38A. 2R. 6P. water.
(g) Including 16A. 0R. 32P. water.
(h) Including 142A. 0R. 25P. water.

(i) Including 4A. 1R. 5P. water.
(j) Including 22A. 0R. 9P. water.
(k) Including 15A. 2R. 26P. water.
(l) Including 41A. 1R. 36P. water.

No. of Sheet of the Ordnance Survey Maps.	Townlands and Towns.	Area in Statute Acres. A. R. P.	County.	Barony.	Parish.	Poor Law Union in 1857.	Townland Census of 1851, Part I. Vol.	Page
21	*Muckinish*	48 1 21	King's Co.	Garrycastle	Lusmagh	Parsonstown	I.	137
21	*Muckinish*	27 1 24	Longford	Rathcline	Cashel	Ballymahon	I.	163
67	*Muckinish*	25 3 38	Mayo	Burrishoole	Burrishoole	Newport	IV.	120
3	Muckinish East	365 0 30	Clare	Burren	Drumcreehy	Ballyvaghan	II.	12
2, 3	Muckinish West	747 2 20	Clare	Burren	Drumcreehy	Ballyvaghan	II.	12
40	*Muck Island*	21 2 11	Sligo	Tirerrill	Kilmactranny	Boyle	IV.	241
10	Mucklagh	324 1 35	Cavan	Tullyhaw	Tomregan	Bawnboy	III.	96
16, 24	Mucklagh	370 3 39	King's Co.	Ballycowan	Lynally	Tullamore	I.	128
9	Mucklagh	99 0 15	Louth	Lower Dundalk	Carlingford	Dundalk	I.	176
76	Mucklagh	101 1 1	Mayo	Burrishoole	Kilmeena	Westport	IV.	122
22	Mucklagh	57 2 31	Monaghan	Dartree	Currin	Cootehill	III.	266
29, 34	Mucklagh	784 0 38	Wicklow	Ballinacor South	Ballinacor	Rathdrum	I.	348
39	Mucklagh	500 1 33	Wicklow	Ballinacor South	Kilpipe	Shillelagh	I.	349
32	Mucklaghan Glebe	129 1 0*a*	Leitrim	Leitrim	Annaduff	Carᵏ. on Shannon	IV.	100
11, 15	Mucklagh or Fairview	235 3 13*b*	Armagh	Tiranny	Tynan	Armagh	III.	60
43	Muckleramer	300 0 19	Antrim	Upper Toome	Drummaul	Ballymena	III.	34
14	Muckletown	10 2 30	Westmeath	Delvin	Castletowndelvin	Castletowndelvin	I.	265
26,27,32,33	Mucklin	487 3 6	Tipperary, N.R.	Upper Ormond	Kilmore	Nenagh	II.	291
20	Mucklin	131 3 39	Westmeath	Delvin	Killucan	Castletowndelvin	I.	266
4, 9	Mucklon	739 1 6	Kildare	Carbury	Dunfierth	Edenderry	I.	52
3	Mucklone	328 2 31	Queen's Co.	Tinnahinch	Castlebrack	Mountmellick	I.	248
41, 44	Mucklone East	106 3 17	King's Co.	Clonlisk	Kilcomin	Roscrea	I.	131
41, 44	Mucklone West	268 0 31	King's Co.	Clonlisk	Kilcomin	Roscrea	I.	131
47	Muckloon	905 0 17*c*	Galway	Killian	Taghboy	Mountbellew	IV.	45
4	Muckloon	246 2 5	Tipperary, N.R.	Lower Ormond	Terryglass	Borrisokane	II.	288
6, 7	Muckloonmodderee	721 2 29	Tipperary, N.R.	Lower Ormond	Terryglass	Borrisokane	II.	288
100	Muckloon or Moorehall	130 2 34	Mayo	Carra	Burriscarra	Ballinrobe	IV.	127
32	Mucklougher	84 1 2*d*	Leitrim	Mohill	Mohill	Mohill	IV.	108
12	Mucklow	151 2 23	Wexford	Ballaghkeen	Kiltennell	Gorey	I.	297
22	Muckmeadows	27 1 2	Kilkenny	Shillelogher	Tullaghanbrogue	Callan	I.	116
9	Mucknagh	265 1 9	Longford	Longford	Killoe	Longford	I.	159
48	Muckranstown	44 3 37	Meath	Forth	Kilscoran	Wexford	I.	311
67	Muckridge	220 1 4	Cork, E.R.	Imokilly	Youghal	Youghal	II.	91
67	Muckridge Demesne	128 1 29	Cork, E.R.	Imokilly	Youghal	Youghal	II.	91
42	Muckrim	160 2 24	Antrim	Upper Toome	Duneane	Ballymena	III.	35
96	Muckros	213 1 18	Donegal	Banagh	Kilcar	Glenties	III.	109
99	Muckros	62 1 0	Donegal	Tirhugh	Donegal	Donegal	III.	145
5	Muckros	252 0 6	Fermanagh	Lurg	Drumkeeran	Lowtherstown	III.	206
24	Muckros	262 0 11*e*	Leitrim	Leitrim	Fenagh	Mohill	IV.	100
66, 74	Muckross	759 2 25*f*	Kerry	Magunihy	Killarney	Killarney	II.	203
1, 3	Muckrum	217 1 4	Leitrim	Rosclogher	Rossinver	Ballyshannon	IV.	112
69	Muckrush	303 0 2	Galway	Clare	Annaghdown	Galway	IV.	16
135	Muckruss	99 3 9	Cork, W.R.	Ibane and Barryroe	Ardfield	Clonakilty	II.	148
120, 121	Muckrussaun	249 3 14	Mayo	Kilmaine	Ballinchalla	Ballinrobe	IV.	152
93, 102	Mucksna	705 2 4	Kerry	Glanarought	Kenmare	Kenmare	II.	186
48	Muckstown	46 0 3	Wexford	Forth	Tacumshin	Wexford	I.	315
35	Muff	128 3 14*g*	Cavan	Clankee	Enniskeen	Bailieborough	III.	73
22	Muff	279 1 26	Cavan	Tullygarvey	Kildrumsherdan	Cootehill	III.	90
4, 5	Muff	470 0 4	Donegal	Inishowen East	Culdaff	Inishowen	III.	118
39	Muff	588 0 12	Donegal	Inishowen West	Muff	Londonderry	III.	121
48	Muff	222 3 19	Londonderry	Loughinsholin	Lissan	Magherafelt	III.	242
14, 15	Muff	318 0 32	Londonderry	Tirkeeran	Faughanvale	Londonderry	III.	250
11	Muff	185 2 7	Louth	Ardee	Louth	Dundalk	I.	173
5	Muff	604 1 24*h*	Meath	Morgallion	Nobber	Kells	I.	210
29	Muff	75 1 13	Monaghan	Farney	Donaghmoyne	Carrickmacross	III.	270
39, 41	Muff	306 3 29*i*	Roscommon	Athlone	Fuerty	Roscommon	IV.	181
39	Muff T.	—	Donegal	Inishowen West	Muff	Londonderry	III.	121
14, 15	Muff T.	—	Londonderry	Tirkeeran	Faughanvale	Londonderry	III.	250
13	Muggalnagrow	831 3 32	Fermanagh	Magheraboy	Inishmacsaint	Ballyshannon	III.	213
103	Muggaunagh	145 1 16	Galway	Dunkellin	Kilcolgan	Gort	IV.	28
23	*Muglins*	0 2 31	Dublin	Rathdown	Dalkey	Rathdown	I.	35
9	Muinaghan	232 3 19	Cavan	Tullyhaw	Templeport	Bawnboy	III.	95
18	Muineagh	244 2 21	Donegal	Inishowen West	Desertegny	Inishowen	III.	120
17	Muineagh	253 3 27	Donegal	Kilmacrenan	Clondavaddog	Milford	III.	125
9	Muineal	105 3 5	Cavan	Tullyhaw	Templeport	Bawnboy	III.	95
100, 101	Muing	146 1 18	Galway	Longford	Clonfert	Ballinasloe	IV.	57
13	Muingacarreen	309 2 13	Clare	Tulla Upper	Feakle	Scarriff	II.	40
7, 8	Muingacurry	805 1 14	Limerick	Owneybeg	Doon	Limerick	II.	251
72	Muingagarha	118 0 3	Kerry	Dunkerron North	Knockane	Killarney	II.	182
27, 36	Muingaghel	2,140 1 37	Mayo	Erris	Kilcommon	Belmullet	IV.	144
13	Muinganierin	1,027 0 6	Mayo	Tirawley	Doonfeeny	Killala	IV.	167
12, 13, 21	Muinganine	1,063 3 8	Cork, E.R.	Duhallow	Nohavaldaly	Kanturk	II.	75
56, 64	Muingaphuca	662 3 15	Kerry	Iveragh	Killorglin	Killarney	II.	198

(a) Including 6A. 3R. 22P. water.　　(d) Including 9A. 3R. 17P. water.　　(g) Including 2A. 2R. 33P. water.
(b) Including 2A. 0R. 37P. water.　　(e) Including 96A. 0R. 13P. water.　　(h) Including 2A. 3R. 27P. water.
(c) Including 2A. 0R. 10P. water.　　(f) Including 17A. 0R. 16P. water.　　(i) Including 8A. 3R. 39P. water.

No. of Sheet of the Ordnance Survey Maps.	Townlands and Towns.	Area in Statute Acres.	County.	Barony.	Parish.	Poor Law Union in 1857.	Townland Census of 1851, Part I.	
		A. R. P.					Vol.	Page
22	Muingatlaunlush	325 3 9	Kerry	Trughanacmy	O'Brennan	Tralee	II.	212
97, 107	Muingatogher	1,129 1 27a	Mayo	Murrisk	Oughaval	Westport	IV.	162
30	Muingavrannig	94 3 12	Kerry	Trughanacmy	O'Brennan	Tralee	II.	212
117, 118	Muingbaun	661 3 19	Galway	Longford	Kilquain	Portumna	IV.	60
44	Muingboy	430 0 27	Clare	Tulla Lower	Killokennedy	Limerick	II.	36
29	Muing East	52 0 24	Kerry	Trughanacmy	Ratass	Tralee	II.	213
6	Muingelly	311 1 23	Mayo	Tirawley	Doonfeeny	Killala	IV.	167
11	Muingerroon North	153 2 12	Mayo	Erris	Kilcommon	Belmullet	IV.	144
11, 18	Muingerroon South	1,453 3 20	Mayo	Erris	Kilcommon	Belmullet	IV.	144
11,12,18,19	Muingingaun	2,190 0 19b	Mayo	Erris	Kilcommon	Belmullet	IV.	144
17, 25	Muingmore	2,227 0 33	Mayo	Erris	Kilcommon	Belmullet	IV.	144
4, 5, 11, 12	Muingnabo	2,991 1 17	Mayo	Erris	Kilcommon	Belmullet	IV.	144
26, 35	Muingnahalloona	1,599 0 28	Mayo	Erris	Kilcommon	Belmullet	IV.	144
30	Muingnaminnane	1,019 0 38	Kerry	Trughanacmy	Ballymacelligott	Tralee	II.	207
26, 35	Muingnanarnad	1,058 0 15c	Mayo	Erris	Kilcommon	Belmullet	IV.	144
30	Muingnatee	230 3 27	Kerry	Trughanacmy	Ballymacelligott	Tralee	II.	207
7	Muingrevagh	198 0 31	Mayo	Tirawley	Kilbride	Killala	IV.	168
10, 17	Muings	914 1 9	Mayo	Erris	Kilcommon	Belmullet	IV.	144
31	Muingvautia	710 3 28	Kerry	Trughanacmy	Castleisland	Tralee	II.	209
23	Muingwee	287 0 14	Kerry	Clanmaurice	Duagh	Listowel	II.	168
29	Muing West	78 0 39	Kerry	Trughanacmy	Ratass	Tralee	II.	213
22, 23	Muingwore	1,086 0 28	Sligo	Tireragh	Castleconor	Dromore West	IV.	232
88	Muingydowda	156 1 6	Kerry	Iveragh	Prior	Cahersiveen	II.	198
40	Muingyroogeen	218 3 8	Cork, E.R.	Duhallow	Clonmeen	Kanturk	II.	70
17	Muiniagh	217 0 12	King's Co.	Ballycowan	Kilbride	Tullamore	I.	127
54	Mulboy	173 0 36	Tyrone	Dungannon Middle	Clonfeacle	Dungannon	III.	299
23	Mulchanstown	47 1 17	Dublin	Rathdown	Kill	Rathdown	I.	36
13	Mulchanstown	110 0 18	Westmeath	Delvin	Killulagh	Castletowndelvin	I.	266
23	Mulderg	434 3 28	Londonderry	Tirkeeran	Cumber Upper	NewTⁿLimavady	III.	249
10, 19	Mulderricksfield	178 2 35	Limerick	Shanid	Kilmoylan	Rathkeale	II.	256
10	Mulderricksfield	118 0 13	Limerick	Shanid	Robertstown	Rathkeale	II.	258
23, 24	Muldonagh	2,127 3 7	Londonderry	Keenaght	Bovevagh	NewTⁿLimavady	III.	235
19, 20	Muldrumman	194 0 21	Monaghan	Cremorne	Clontibret	Castleblayney	III.	261
37, 42	Mulgannon	210 0 39	Wexford	Forth	Mauldintown	Wexford	I.	312
4, 9	Mulgeeth	835 1 11	Kildare	Carbury	Dunfierth	Edenderry	I.	52
49	Mulhussey	881 3 36	Meath	Upper Deece	Kilclone	Dunshaughlin	I.	193
6, 7	Mulkaun	383 1 13	Leitrim	Rosclogher	Killasnet	Manorhamilton	IV.	110
9	Mulkeeragh	335 3 24	Londonderry	Keenaght	Tamlaght Finlagan	NewTⁿLimavady	III.	237
13	Mullabane	171 0 28	Louth	Ardee	Clonkeen	Ardee	I.	172
9	Mullabane	174 3 2	Louth	Lower Dundalk	Carlingford	Dundalk	I.	176
6	Mullabohy	151 2 25	Louth	Louth	Louth	Dundalk	I.	184
22, 23	Mullaboy	640 0 19	Londonderry	Tirkeeran	Cumber Lower	Londonderry	III.	249
26	Mullabrack	435 3 7	Down	Lower Iveagh,Up. pt.	Tullylish	Banbridge	III.	171
12	Mullabrack	95 1 3	Monaghan	Monaghan	Clones	Monaghan	III.	275
6, 9	Mullabrack (Scott)	88 0 36	Monaghan	Trough	Donagh	Monaghan	III.	282
6	Mullabrack (Shaw)	100 1 18	Monaghan	Trough	Donagh	Monaghan	III.	282
3	Mullabryan	220 2 10	Monaghan	Trough	Errigal Trough	Monaghan	III.	285
17, 20	Mullacapple	154 0 10	Louth	Ardee	Mosstown	Ardee	I.	174
24	Mullacash Middle	265 1 9	Kildare	Naas South	Killashee	Naas	I.	65
24	Mullacash North	159 2 20	Kildare	Naas South	Killashee	Naas	I.	65
24	Mullacash South	276 2 23	Kildare	Naas South	Killashee	Naas	I.	65
32, 38	Mullacastle	345 2 12d	Cavan	Castlerahan	Crosserlough	Cavan	III.	68
14	Mullacloe	217 3 7	Louth	Ardee	Shanlis	Ardee	I.	174
11	Mullacrew	106 2 33	Louth	Louth	Louth	Dundalk	I.	184
11	MULLACREW T.	—	Louth	Louth	Louth	Dundalk	I.	185
16	Mullacroghery	231 2 15e	Cavan	Tullygarvey	Annagh	Cootehill	III.	87
17	Mullacurry	115 1 27	Louth	Ardee	Dromin	Ardee	I.	172
3	Mulladermot	119 0 35	Monaghan	Trough	Errigal Trough	Monaghan	III.	285
17	Mulladrillen	55 1 28	Louth	Ardee	Ardee	Ardee	I.	171
9, 13	Mulladry	748 0 35	Armagh	Oneilland West	Kilmore	Armagh	III.	53
12	Mulladuff	101 2 28	Monaghan	Monaghan	Clones	Monaghan	III.	275
22	Mullafarry	322 2 37	Mayo	Tirawley	Ballysakeery	Ballina	IV.	165
27	Mullafernaghan	500 0 31	Down	Lower Iveagh, Lr. pt.	Magherally	Banbridge	III.	168
61, 62	Mullafin	175 2 9	Donegal	Raphoe	Raphoe	Letterkenny	III.	141
14	Mullagarry	162 1 3	Monaghan	Cremorne	Clontibret	Monaghan	III.	261
40, 44	Mullagh	668 0 34f	Cavan	Castlerahan	Mullagh	Kells	III.	70
98	Mullagh	213 3 16	Cork, E.R.	Kinalea	Ballymartle	Kinsale	II.	94
118	Mullagh	173 3 35	Cork, W.R.	Bantry	Durrus	Bantry	II.	119
31	Mullagh	432 3 27	Down	Dufferin	Killyleagh	Downpatrick	III.	167
29	Mullagh	536 3 8	Galway	Dunmore	Kilbennan	Tuam	IV.	34
10,11,14,15	Mullagh	860 1 0g	Leitrim	Dromahaire	Drumlease	Manorhamilton	IV.	95
35	Mullagh	210 2 4	Leitrim	Mohill	Annaduff	Mohill	IV.	105
19	Mullagh	312 0 2	Limerick	Shanid	Kilmoylan	Rathkeale	II.	256

(a) Including 63A. 2R. 20P. water.
(b) Including 6A. 0R. 16P. water.
(c) Including 21A. 0R. 16P. water.
(d) Including 7A. 1R. 11P. water.
(e) Including 8A. 1R. 31P. water.
(f) Including 29A. 0R. 37P. water.
(g) Including 11A. 2R. 19P. water.

No. of Sheet of the Ordnance Survey Maps.	Townlands and Towns.	Area in Statute Acres.			County.	Barony.	Parish.	Poor Law Union in 1857.	Townland Census of 1851, Part I.	
		A.	R.	P.					Vol.	Page
9, 16	Mullagh . . .	155	0	26a	Londonderry .	Keenaght . .	Tamlaght Finlagan .	NewTⁿLimavady	III.	237
36	Mullagh . . .	681	0	17	Londonderry .	Loughinsholin .	Termoneeny . .	Magherafelt .	III.	244
13	Mullagh . . .	196	1	0	Longford . .	Longford . .	Templemichael .	Longford . .	I.	160
96	Mullagh . . .	339	3	38	Mayo . .	Murrisk . .	Oughaval . .	Westport . .	IV.	162
15	Mullagh . . .	87	2	17	Meath . .	Fore . .	Loughcrew . .	Oldcastle . .	I.	201
43, 49	Mullagh . . .	496	3	27	Meath . .	Upper Deece .	Kilmore . . .	Dunshaughlin .	I.	193
48	Mullagh . . .	42	2	29	Roscommon .	Athlone . .	Kiltoom . .	Athlone . .	IV.	183
84, 85	Mullagh . . .	451	0	39	Tipperary, S.R.	Iffa and Offa East	Kilmurry . .	Carrick on Suir	II.	314
24	Mullagh . . .	119	3	27	Tyrone . .	Strabane Lower .	Ardstraw . .	Strabane . .	III.	319
3	Mullagh . . .	278	3	26	Westmeath .	Fore . .	Lickbla . .	Granard . .	I.	270
18	Mullagha . .	586	0	18	Meath . .	Upper Slane .	Rathkenny . .	Navan . .	I.	225
3	Mullaghacall North	263	0	19	Londonderry .	North East Liberties of Coleraine .	Ballyaghran .	Coleraine .	III.	244
3	Mullaghacall South	68	1	10	Londonderry .	North East Liberties of Coleraine .	Ballyaghran .	Coleraine .	III.	244
54	Mullaghadrolly .	90	1	16b	Tyrone . .	Dungannon Middle .	Donaghmore .	Dungannon .	III.	302
69	Mullaghadrum .	35	3	11	Galway . .	Clare . .	Annaghdown .	Galway . .	IV.	16
9	Mullaghadun .	115	2	14	Monaghan .	Monaghan . .	Monaghan . .	Monaghan .	III.	277
54	Mullaghadun .	139	0	9	Tyrone . .	Dungannon Middle .	Drumglass . .	Dungannon .	III.	303
69, 78	Mullaghagarry .	256	2	5	Donegal . .	Raphoe . .	Stranorlar . .	Stranorlar .	III.	143
1, 2	Mullaghahy . .	103	2	29	Cavan . .	Tullyhaw . .	Killinagh . .	Enniskillen .	III.	92
21, 22	Mullaghakaraun .	261	1	17	King's Co. .	Garrycastle . .	Reynagh . .	Parsonstown .	I.	138
30	Mullaghakaraun Bog	74	0	21	King's Co. .	Garrycastle . .	Reynagh . .	Parsonstown .	I.	138
54	Mullaghanagh .	160	3	0c	Tyrone . .	Dungannon Middle .	Donaghmore .	Dungannon .	III.	302
3, 7	Mullaghanard or Derreen . .	188	0	12	Queen's Co. .	Tinnahinch . .	Rosenallis . .	Mountmellick .	I.	250
32	Mullaghanarry .	317	3	10	Sligo . .	Leyny . .	Achonry . .	Tobercurry .	IV.	229
78, 87	Mullaghaneary .	293	1	32	Donegal . .	Raphoe . .	Donaghmore .	Stranorlar .	III.	138
25	Mullaghanee . .	222	3	26	Monaghan .	Cremorne . .	Clontibret . .	Castleblaney .	III.	261
28	Mullaghaneigh .	58	3	34	Leitrim . .	Leitrim . .	Kiltubbrid . .	Car^k. on Shannon	IV.	104
70	Mullaghanny . .	247	0	31	Donegal . .	Raphoe . .	Clonleigh . .	Strabane . .	III.	135
23	Mullaghard . .	288	3	24d	Cavan . .	Clankee . .	Drumgoon . .	Cootehill . .	III.	72
25	Mullaghard . .	67	3	27	Meath . .	Upper Kells .	Donaghpatrick .	Navan . .	I.	205
44, 47	Mullaghardagh .	223	3	39	Roscommon .	Athlone . .	Taghboy . .	Athlone . .	IV.	184
7, 12	Mullagharlin . .	242	2	33	Louth . .	Upper Dundalk .	Dundalk . .	Dundalk . .	I.	178
34	Mullagharn . .	251	0	36	Tyrone . .	Omagh East .	Drumragh . .	Omagh . .	III.	312
34	Mullagharn (Young)	81	1	5	Tyrone . .	Omagh East .	Drumragh . .	Omagh . .	III.	312
13	Mullagharoy . .	283	3	19	Meath . .	Upper Slane .	Grangegeeth .	Ardee . .	I.	224
10	Mullagharush . .	202	0	21	King's Co. .	Lower Philipstown .	Kilclonfert . .	Tullamore .	I.	142
11	Mullaghatinny or Elm Park . .	197	2	29	Armagh . .	Tiranny . .	Eglish . . .	Armagh . .	III.	59
5, 8	Mullaghattin . .	282	1	7	Louth . .	Lower Dundalk .	Ballymascanlan .	Dundalk . .	I.	176
8	Mullaghattin . .	175	3	22	Louth . .	Lower Dundalk .	Carlingford . .	Dundalk . .	I.	176
2, 5	Mullaghavally . .	267	1	10	Meath . .	Lower Kells .	Moybolgue . .	Kells . .	I.	203
13	Mullaghavorneen .	264	0	4	Longford . .	Ardagh . .	Ballymacormick .	Longford . .	I.	152
39, 40	Mullaghawny . .	555	1	33	Mayo . .	Gallen . .	Attymass . .	Ballina . .	IV.	147
13	Mullaghbane . .	103	1	34	Armagh . .	Fews Lower .	Mullaghbrack .	Armagh . .	III.	47
12	Mullaghbane . .	369	2	10e	Armagh . .	Oneilland West .	Loughgall . .	Armagh . .	III.	54
28, 31	Mullaghbane . .	674	3	9	Armagh . .	Orior Upper .	Forkill . .	Newry . .	III.	57
25	Mullaghbane . .	211	0	2	Fermanagh .	Clanawley . .	Killesher . .	Enniskillen .	III.	193
6, 7	Mullaghbane . .	168	3	9	Monaghan .	Trough . .	Donagh . .	Monaghan .	III.	282
53	Mullaghbane . .	245	0	19	Tyrone . .	Dungannon Lower .	Carnteel . .	Clogher . .	III.	298
53, 54	Mullaghbane . .	280	2	0	Tyrone . .	Dungannon Middle .	Donaghmore .	Dungannon .	III.	302
42	Mullaghbane . .	690	1	26	Tyrone . .	Omagh East .	Dromore . .	Omagh . .	III.	311
18	Mullaghbaun . .	98	1	35	Leitrim . .	Drumahaire .	Inishmagrath .	Manorhamilton	IV.	97
98, 106	Mullagh Beg . .	183	3	30	Galway . .	Longford . .	Abbeygormacan .	Ballinasloe .	IV.	56
40	Mullaghblaney .	64	0	23	Fermanagh .	Coole . .	Galloon . .	Clones . .	III.	200
13	Mullagh Bog . .	107	2	3	Longford . .	Longford . .	Templemichael .	Longford . .	I.	160
41	Mullaghboy . .	251	2	28	Antrim . .	Lower Belfast .	Islandmagee .	Larne . .	III.	8
31	Mullaghboy . .	225	2	31	Cavan . .	Clanmahon .	Ballintemple .	Cavan . .	III.	75
37	Mullaghboy . .	301	3	30	Cavan . .	Clanmahon .	Ballymachugh .	Cavan . .	III.	76
14	Mullaghboy . .	65	0	25	Cavan . .	Lower Loughtee .	Drumlane . .	Cavan . .	III.	80
16, 17	Mullaghboy . .	234	3	23	Cavan . .	Tullygarvey .	Kildrumsherdan .	Cootehill . .	III.	90
4	Mullaghboy . .	303	1	33f	Cavan . .	Tullyhaw . .	Killinagh . .	Enniskillen .	III.	92
24, 30	Mullaghboy . .	126	0	10	Cavan . .	Tullyhunco .	Killashandra .	Cavan . .	III.	98
39	Mullaghboy . .	99	2	8g	Fermanagh .	Coole . .	Galloon . .	Lisnaskea .	III.	200
29	Mullaghboy . .	147	0	29h	Kildare . .	Naas South .	Carnalway . .	Naas . .	I.	64
25, 29	Mullaghboy . .	474	3	24i	Leitrim . .	Carrigallen .	Drumreilly . .	Bawnboy . .	IV.	91
28	Mullaghboy . .	123	2	27	Leitrim . .	Leitrim . .	Kiltubbrid . .	Car^k. on Shannon	IV.	104
37	Mullaghboy . .	568	0	30	Londonderry .	Loughinsholin .	Ballyscullion .	Magherafelt .	III.	239
41, 42	Mullaghboy . .	58	0	1	Londonderry .	Loughinsholin .	Magherafelt .	Magherafelt .	III.	243
25	Mullaghboy . .	74	2	6	Meath . .	Lower Navan .	Navan . .	Navan . .	I.	215
2, 5	Mullaghboy . .	104	0	16j	Meath . .	Morgallion .	Enniskeen . .	Kells . .	I.	209
17	Mullaghboy . .	108	1	37	Monaghan .	Dartree . .	Killeevan . .	Clones . .	III.	268

(a) Including 3A. 2R. 22P. water.
(b) Including 2A. 2R. 23P. water.
(c) Including 3A. 3R. 20P. water.
(d) Including 41A. 3R. 0P. water.

(e) Including 10A. 3R. 29P. water.
(f) Including 7A. 1R. 19P. water.
(g) Including 4A. 0R. 23P. water.

(h) Including 11A. 0R. 35P. water.
(i) Including 6A. 2R. 25P. water.
(j) Including 1A. 1R. 11P. water.

No. of Sheet of the Ordnance Survey Maps.	Townlands and Towns.	Area in Statute Acres.			County.	Barony.	Parish.	Poor Law Union in 1857.	Townland Census of 1851, Part I.	
		A.	R.	P.					Vol.	Page
7	Mullaghboy	121	3	39	Monaghan	Trough	Donagh	Monaghan	III.	282
61, 62	Mullaghboy	174	1	4	Tyrone	Dungannon Middle	Clonfeacle	Dungannon	III.	299
13, 17	Mullaghbrack	257	0	26	Armagh	Fews Lower	Mullaghbrack	Armagh	III.	47
33	Mullaghbrack	326	2	31	Leitrim	Mohill	Cloone	Mohill	IV.	106
36	Mullaghbrady	87	1	7a	Fermanagh	Clankelly	Clones	Clones	III.	196
40	Mullaghbreedin	34	3	31	Fermanagh	Clankelly	Galloon	Clones	III.	198
34	Mullaghcapple	31	0	23	Fermanagh	Clankelly	Galloon	Lisna-kea	III.	198
34	Mullaghcapple Glebe	10	1	19	Fermanagh	Clankelly	Galloon	Lisnaskea	III.	198
63, 67	Mullaghcarton	632	2	2	Antrim	Upper Massereene	Magheragall	Lisburn	III.	31
18	Mullaghcashel	58	2	0	Leitrim	Drumahaire	Inishmagrath	Manorhamilton	IV.	97
17, 24	Mullaghcloc	633	1	29b	Westmeath	Rathconrath	Killare	Ballymahon	I.	283
29, 30	Mullaghconnelly	196	1	38	Antrim	Lower Glenarm	Tickmacrevan	Larne	III.	24
36	Mullaghconnelly	96	1	20	Fermanagh	Clankelly	Clones	Clones	III.	196
54	Mullaghconor Glebe	190	1	4	Tyrone	Dungannon Middle	Donaghmore	Dungannon	III.	302
3	Mullaghcor	121	3	15	Monaghan	Trough	Errigal Trough	Monaghan	III.	285
33, 39	Mullaghcor	132	1	20	Sligo	Corran	Toomour	Boyle	IV.	228
54	Mullaghcreevy	231	2	1	Tyrone	Dungannon Middle	Donaghmore	Dungannon	III.	302
30	Mullaghcroghery	321	2	34	Monaghan	Farney	Magheross	Carrickmacross	III.	274
9	Mullaghcroghery	53	2	28	Monaghan	Monaghan	Monaghan	Monaghan	III.	277
24	Mullaghcrohy	249	3	19	King's Co.	Ballyboy	Killoughy	Tullamore	I.	124
8, 13	Mullaghcroy	526	0	4	Westmeath	Delvin	Castletowndelvin	Castletowndelvin	I.	255
54	Mullaghdaly	200	1	17	Tyrone	Dungannon Middle	Clonfeacle	Dungannon	III.	299
32	Mullaghdarrig	63	1	3	Wexford	Ballaghkeen	Kilmallock	Enniscorthy	I.	296
41	Mullaghderg	539	3	13c	Donegal	Boylagh	Templecrone	Glenties	III.	115
41	Mullaghderg Mountain Pasture	847	3	8d	Donegal	Boylagh	Templecrone	Glenties	III.	115
19	Mullaghdillon	264	0	12	Meath	Upper Slane	Slane	Navan	I.	225
47	Mullaghdoo	283	1	0	Antrim	Lower Belfast	Islandmagee	Larne	III.	9
19	Mullaghdoo	272	2	0	Cavan	Tullyhunco	Kildallan	Bawnboy	III.	97
14	Mullaghdoo	173	2	21	Leitrim	Drumahaire	Killanummery	Manorhamilton	IV.	98
41	Mullaghdoo Irish	91	3	3	Donegal	Boylagh	Templecrone	Glenties	III.	115
41	Mullaghdoo Scotch	304	2	19e	Donegal	Boylagh	Templecrone	Glenties	III.	115
21,22,28,29	Mullaghdrin	549	3	12	Down	Lower Iveagh, Lr. pt.	Dromara	Lisburn	III.	168
13	Mullaghduff	146	2	14	Antrim	Lower Dunluce	Derrykeighan	Ballymoney	III.	17
27	Mullaghduff	332	1	19	Armagh	Fews Upper	Newtownhamilton	Castleblayney	III.	49
10	Mullaghduff	252	3	18	Cavan	Tullyhaw	Tomregan	Bawnboy	III.	96
19, 20	Mullaghduff	159	3	3f	Monaghan	Cremorne	Clontibret	Castleblayney	III.	261
6, 7	Mullaghduff	117	2	24	Monaghan	Trough	Donagh	Monaghan	III.	282
13	Mullaghduff (Big)	197	2	5	Antrim	Cary	Armoy	Ballycastle	III.	11
13	Mullaghduff (Little)	89	3	15	Antrim	Cary	Armoy	Ballycastle	III.	11
26	Mullaghdun	61	0	15	Fermanagh	Clanawley	Cleenish	Enniskillen	III.	191
45	Mullagheep	142	1	0	Donegal	Kilmacrenan	Tullyfern	Milford	III.	133
11, 17	Mullaghey	115	1	23	Meath	Upper Kells	Kells	Kells	I.	206
29, 30	Mullaghfad	1,642	3	26g	Fermanagh	Magherastephana	Aghalurcher	Lisnaskea	III.	217
20	Mullaghfadda	67	1	33	Leitrim	Drumahaire	Inishmagrath	Manorhamilton	IV.	97
40	Mullaghfarna	159	2	6	Sligo	Tirerrill	Aghanagh	Boyle	IV.	237
6	Mullaghfarne	70	0	2	Fermanagh	Lurg	Magheraculmoney	Lowtherstown	III.	208
61	Mullaghfin	218	3	7	Donegal	Raphoe	Convoy	Stranorlar	III.	136
26	Mullaghfin	252	2	10	Meath	Lower Duleek	Duleek	Drogheda	I.	195
21	Mullaghfin	56	1	38	Sligo	Tirerrill	Killerry	Sligo	IV.	239
46	Mullaghfurtherland	161	0	8	Tyrone	Dungannon Middle	Donaghmore	Dungannon	III.	302
15	Mullaghgar	62	1	7	Sligo	Carbury	Calry	Sligo	IV.	220
40, 43	Mullaghgare	76	3	18h	Fermanagh	Coole	Galloon	Clones	III.	200
33	Mullaghgarrow	177	1	34	Fermanagh	Clanawley	Kinawley	Enniskillen	III.	194
21, 24	Mullaghgarve	836	3	21	Leitrim	Leitrim	Kiltubbrid	Cark. on Shannon	IV.	104
34	Mullaghgarve	119	2	11	Monaghan	Farney	Magheracloone	Carrickmacross	III.	273
48, 49	Mullaghgaun	176	3	0	Antrim	Upper Toome	Duneane	Antrim	III.	35
64	Mullaghglass	920	0	32	Antrim	Upper Belfast	Derryaghy	Lisburn	III.	10
14, 18	Mullaghglass	700	1	23	Armagh	Orior Lower	Ballymore	Banbridge	III.	55
22, 26	Mullaghglass	682	3	27	Armagh	Orior Upper	Killevy	Newry	III.	58
36	Mullaghglass	116	0	19	Fermanagh	Clankelly	Clones	Clones	III.	197
10	Mullaghglass	874	1	37	Galway	Ballynahinch	Ballynakill	Clifden	IV.	12
39	Mullaghglass	245	2	11	Tyrone	Dungannon Upper	Arboe	Cookstown	III.	305
17, 18	Mullaghgreenan	176	3	19i	Monaghan	Dartree	Aghabog	Cootehill	III.	263
18, 19	Mullaghinch	504	1	22	Londonderry	Coleraine	Aghadowey	Coleraine	III.	230
6	Mullaghinshigo	206	0	12j	Monaghan	Monaghan	Tedavnet	Monaghan	III.	279
38, 39	Mullaghinshogagh	162	1	16	Fermanagh	Knockninny	Kinawley	Lisnaskea	III.	202
31	Mullaghkeel	48	1	38	Cavan	Clanmahon	Crosserlough	Cavan	III.	76
34	Mullaghkeel or Ballymackilroy	119	2	27	Fermanagh	Magherastephana	Aghalurcher	Lisnaskea	III.	217
27	Mullaghkippin	121	1	33k	Fermanagh	Magherastephana	Aghalurcher	Lisnaskea	III.	217
9	Mullaghlea	399	0	10l	Cavan	Tullyhaw	Templeport	Bawnboy	III.	95
5, 6	Mullaghlea Glen	238	0	5	Cavan	Tullyhaw	Templeport	Enniskillen	III.	95

No. of Sheet of the Ordnance Survey Maps.	Townlands and Towns.	Area in Statute Acres.			County.	Barony.	Parish.	Poor Law Union in 1857.	Townland Census of 1851, Part I.	
		A.	R.	P.					Vol.	Page
40	Mullaghlehan . .	78	2	4	Fermanagh .	Coole . .	Galloon . . .	Clones . .	III.	200
21	Mullaghlevin .	91	3	35	Fermanagh .	Magheraboy . .	Rossorry .	Enniskillen .	III.	214
61	Mullaghlongfield .	111	1	39	Tyrone .	Dungannon Middle .	Clonfeacle .	Dungannon .	III.	299
4	Mullaghlusky . .	55	3	14	Roscommon .	Boyle . . .	Kilronan . .	Boyle . .	IV.	197
31	Mullaghmacateer .	155	0	4	Monaghan .	Farney . . .	Killanny .	Carrickmacross .	III.	272
18, 24	Mullaghmacormick.	596	1	15	Roscommon .	Ballintober North .	Kilglass . . .	Strokestown .	IV.	186
26	Mullaghmaddy . .	56	2	3	Fermanagh .	Clanawley . .	Cleenish . .	Enniskillen .	III.	191
28	Mullaghmakevy .	78	3	14a	Fermanagh .	Magherastephana .	Aghalurcher .	Lisnaskea .	III.	217
46	Mullaghmarget .	70	0	3	Tyrone .	Dungannon Middle .	Tullyniskan .	Dungannon .	III.	305
17	Mullaghmarkagh .	66	0	9	Galway .	Dunmore . .	Dunmore . .	Tuam . .	IV.	34
30,31,39,40	Mullaghmarky . .	406	1	30	Kerry .	Trughanacmy .	Castleisland .	Tralee . .	II.	209
9	Mullaghmatt . .	68	3	35	Monaghan .	Monaghan . .	Monaghan . .	Monaghan .	III.	277
14, 15	Mullaghmeen . .	114	3	31	Cavan .	Lower Loughtee .	Drumlane . .	Cavan . .	III.	80
16, 22	Mullaghmeen . .	399	0	0	Fermanagh .	Tirkennedy .	Magheracross .	Enniskillen .	III.	223
31	Mullaghmeen . .	119	1	12	Monaghan .	Farney . .	Killanny . .	Carrickmacross	III.	272
1	Mullaghmeen . .	436	1	36	Westmeath .	Fore . . .	Foyran . . .	Granard . .	I.	270
34	Mullaghmenagh Lower	127	2	4	Tyrone .	Omagh East .	Drumragh .	Omagh . .	III.	312
34	Mullaghmenagh Upper	228	0	24	Tyrone .	Omagh East .	Drumragh .	Omagh . .	III.	312
106	Mullaghnesha .	423	1	4	Cork, W.R. .	West Carbery (E.D.)	Dromdaleague .	Skibbereen .	II.	140
9	Mullaghmonaghan .	92	2	20	Monaghan .	Monaghan . .	Monaghan . .	Monaghan .	III.	277
8	Mullaghmore . .	168	0	11	Armagh .	Armagh . .	Loughgall . .	Armagh . .	III.	46
17, 21	Mullaghmore . .	337	0	26b	Armagh .	Orior Lower .	Loughgilly .	Newry . .	III.	57
38, 39	Mullaghmore . .	248	2	12	Cavan .	Castlerahan .	Castlerahan .	Oldcastle .	III.	67
39	Mullaghmore . .	62	3	29	Cavan .	Castlerahan .	Lurgan . .	Oldcastle .	III.	70
9	Mullaghmore . .	205	1	13c	Cavan .	Tullyhaw .	Templeport .	Bawnboy .	III.	95
14	Mullaghmore . .	459	3	1	Cavan .	Tullyhunco .	Kildallan .	Bawnboy .	III.	97
119, 132	Mullaghmore . .	271	1	15	Cork, W.R. .	West Carbery (W.D.)	Caheragh . .	Skibbereen .	II.	142
47, 51	Mullaghmore . .	681	2	29	Down .	Upper Iveagh. Lr. pt.	Clonduff . .	Newry . .	III.	171
21	Mullaghmore . .	147	0	1	Fermanagh .	Clanawley . .	Cleenish . .	Enniskillen .	III.	191
5	Mullaghmore . .	157	3	10	Fermanagh .	Lurg . .	Drumkeeran .	Lowtherstown .	III.	206
28	Mullaghmore . .	46	2	39	Fermanagh .	Magherastephana .	Aghalurcher .	Lisnaskea .	III.	217
98,99,106,107	Mullagh More . .	394	0	14	Galway .	Longford .	Abbeygormacan .	Ballinasloe .	IV.	56
29, 30	Mullaghmore . .	211	3	36d	Leitrim .	Carrigallen .	Drumreilly .	Bawnboy .	IV.	91
15	Mullaghmore . .	422	0	36	Leitrim .	Drumahaire .	Killarga . .	Manorhamilton	IV.	99
12	Mullaghmore . .	234	0	14	Londonderry .	Coleraine . .	Agivey . .	Coleraine .	III.	230
3	Mullaghmore . .	269	1	21	Meath .	Lower Slane .	Drumcondra .	Ardee . .	I.	223
17	Mullaghmore . .	176	0	38e	Monaghan .	Dartree . .	Aghabog . .	Cootehill .	III.	263
10	Mullaghmore . .	122	2	30	Monaghan .	Monaghan . .	Tehallan . .	Monaghan .	III.	280
1, 3	Mullaghmore . .	85	2	20	Monaghan .	Trough . .	Errigal Trough .	Clogher . .	III.	285
25	Mullaghmore . .	273	1	4	Queen's Co. .	Ballyadams .	Rathaspick .	Athy . .	I.	232
11	Mullaghmore . .	180	2	2	Roscommon .	Boyle . .	Killukin . .	Cark. on Shannon	IV.	196
2, 3	Mullaghmore . .	886	1	17	Sligo .	Carbury . .	Ahamlish .	Sligo . .	IV.	219
27	Mullaghmore . .	247	1	34	Sligo .	Tirerrill .	Ballynakill .	Sligo . .	IV.	237
64	Mullaghmore . .	266	3	14	Tyrone .	Clogher . .	Aghalurcher .	Clogher . .	III.	291
59	Mullaghmore . .	269	0	12	Tyrone .	Clogher . .	Clogher . .	Clogher . .	III.	293
46, 54	Mullaghmore . .	397	0	20	Tyrone .	Dungannon Middle .	Donaghmore .	Dungannon .	III.	302
43, 51	Mullaghmore . .	646	3	7	Tyrone .	Omagh East .	Clogherny .	Omagh . .	III.	310
42	Mullaghmore . .	215	2	27f	Tyrone .	Omagh East .	Drumragh .	Omagh . .	III.	312
35	Mullaghmore . .	453	3	16g	Tyrone .	Strabane Upper .	Cappagh . .	Omagh . .	III.	325
24,25,30,31	Mullaghmore or Allerstown .	189	2	27	Meath .	Lower Navan .	Ardbraccan .	Navan . .	I.	214
45	Mullaghmore East .	824	1	3	Galway .	Tiaquin . .	Moylough .	Mountbellew .	IV.	80
9	Mullaghmore East .	115	1	23h	Monaghan .	Monaghan . .	Tedavnet .	Monaghan .	III.	279
67	Mullaghmore East .	347	1	2	Tyrone .	Dungannon Lower .	Aghaloo . .	Armagh .	III.	297
12	Mullaghmore Glebe	120	3	3	Londonderry .	Coleraine . .	Agivey . .	Coleraine .	III.	230
46, 54	Mullaghmore Glebe	204	3	5i	Tyrone .	Dungannon Middle .	Donaghmore .	Dungannon .	III.	302
45	Mullaghmore North	238	0	23	Galway .	Tiaquin . .	Moylough .	Mountbellew .	IV.	80
6, 9	Mullaghmore North	285	3	3j	Monaghan .	Monaghan . .	Tedavnet .	Monaghan .	III.	279
45, 59	Mullaghmore South	443	3	16	Galway .	Tiaquin . .	Moylough .	Mountbellew .	IV.	80
45	Mullaghmore West .	496	0	4	Galway .	Tiaquin . .	Moylough .	Mountbellew .	IV.	80
9	Mullaghmore West .	146	1	5	Monaghan .	Monaghan . .	Tedavnet .	Monaghan .	III.	279
2	Mullaghmore West .	133	3	1	Sligo .	Carbury . .	Ahamlish .	Sligo . .	IV.	219
60	Mullaghmore West .	127	2	22	Tyrone .	Dungannon Lower .	Aghaloo . .	Clogher . .	III.	297
66, 67	Mullaghmossagh .	193	2	27	Tyrone .	Dungannon Lower .	Aghaloo . .	Armagh .	III.	297
47	Mullaghmossan .	247	2	35	Antrim .	Lower Belfast .	Glynn . .	Larne . .	III.	8
61, 62	Mullaghmossog Glebe	62	1	7	Tyrone .	Dungannon Middle .	Clonfeacle .	Dungannon .	III.	300
47	Mullaghmoyle .	319	3	11	Tyrone .	Dungannon Middle .	Donaghenry .	Dungannon .	III.	301
28, 32	Mullaghmoyne East	187	0	9	Kildare .	Offaly West .	Ballyshannon .	Athy . .	I.	72
27,28,31,32	Mullaghmoyne West	201	3	22	Kildare .	Offaly West .	Ballyshannon .	Athy . .	I.	72
19	Mullaghmullen .	106	1	10	Cavan .	Tullyhunco .	Kildallan .	Cavan . .	III.	97
26	Mullaghnabreena .	140	3	3k	Sligo .	Tirerrill . .	Ballysadare .	Sligo . .	IV.	238
3	Mullaghnahegny .	105	3	22	Monaghan .	Trough . .	Errigal Trough .	Monaghan .	III.	285
25	Mullaghnameely .	108	3	36	Leitrim .	Leitrim . .	Fenagh . .	Mohill . .	IV.	100

(a) Including 3A. 1R. 1P. Lough Corban.
(b) Including 23A. 0R. 24P. water.
(c) { Including 27A. 2R. 20P. Lakefield Lough.
    { Including 35A. 2R. 8P. Bellaboy Lough.
(d) Including 4A. 2R. 1P. water.
(e) Including 12A. 0R. 0P. water.
(f) Including 2A. 3R. 13P. water.
(g) Including 6A. 0R. 14P. water.
(h) Including 3A. 2R. 20P. water.
(i) Including 10A. 1R. 24P. water.
(j) Including 24A. 3R. 24P. water.
(k) Including 12A. 3R. 27P. water.

No. of Sheet of the Ordnance Survey Maps.	Townlands and Towns.	Area in Statute Acres.			County.	Barony.	Parish.	Poor Law Union in 1857.	Townland Census of 1851, Part I.	
		A.	R.	P.					Vol.	Page
33, 37	Mullaghnamoyagh .	89	3	0	Londonderry .	Loughinsholin .	Tamlaght O'Crilly .	Magherafelt .	III.	244
5	Mullaghnaneane .	912	0	34	Sligo . .	Carbury . .	Drumcliff . .	Sligo . .	IV.	221
14, 20	Mullaghnashee .	423	1	10	Roscommon .	Frenchpark . .	Tibohine . .	Castlereagh .	IV.	205
53, 60	Mullaghnese .	180	3	15a	Tyrone . .	Dungannon Lower .	Carnteel . .	Dungannon .	III.	298
76	Mullaghnoney .	119	0	35	Tipperary, S.R.	Iffa and Offa East .	Newchapel .	Clonmel . .	II.	315
37	Mullaghoran .	722	3	21	Cavan . .	Clanmahon .	Drumlumman .	Granard . .	III.	77
3	Mullagh Otra .	130	3	39	Monaghan .	Trough . .	Errigal Trough .	Clogher . .	III.	285
6	Mullaghpeak .	129	1	12	Monaghan .	Trough . .	Donagh . .	Monaghan .	III.	282
34	Mullaghrafferty .	121	3	24	Monaghan .	Farney . .	Magheracloone .	Carrickmacross	III.	273
5	Mullaghreagh .	94	0	6	Meath . .	Lower Kells .	Kilbeg . .	Kells . .	I.	202
21, 22	Mullaghree .	113	0	21	Fermanagh .	Magheraboy .	Rossorry .	Enniskillen .	III.	214
37, 38	Mullaghreelan .	500	2	23	Kildare . .	Kilkea and Moone .	Kilkea . .	Athy . .	I.	60
32, 33	Mullaghrigny .	63	1	1	Leitrim .	Mohill . .	Mohill . .	Mohill . .	IV.	108
46	Mullaghroddan .	227	1	37	Tyrone . .	Dungannon Middle .	Donaghmore .	Dungannon .	III.	302
72	Mullaghroe .	204	3	2	Cork, E.R. .	East Muskerry .	Athnowen .	Cork . .	II.	101
24	Mullaghroe .	336	1	9	Mayo . .	Erris . .	Kilmore . .	Belmullet .	IV.	146
18	Mullaghroe .	117	0	13	Meath . .	Upper Slane .	Gernonstown .	Navan . .	I.	224
44, 45	Mullaghroe .	432	3	32	Sligo . .	Coolavin .	Kilfree . .	Boyle . .	IV.	224
21	Mullaghroe Lower .	106	0	19	Kildare .	Offaly West .	Lackagh . .	Athy . .	I.	73
29	Mullaghroe North .	166	0	30	Cork. E.R. .	Duhallow .	Cullen . .	Millstreet .	II.	71
29	Mullaghroe South .	186	1	9	Cork, E.R. .	Duhallow .	Cullen . .	Millstreet .	II.	71
21	Mullaghroe Upper .	105	0	34	Kildare . .	Offaly West .	Lackagh . .	Athy . .	I.	73
70	Mullaghruttery .	180	0	16	Galway . .	Clare . .	Claregalway .	Galway . .	IV.	18
27	Mullaghsallagh .	90	2	21	Leitrim .	Leitrim . .	Kiltoghert .	Cark. on Shannon	IV.	102
34, 35	Mullaghsandall .	798	3	0	Antrim . .	Upper Glenarm .	Kilwaughter .	Larne . .	III.	25
3	Mullaghselsana .	46	2	11	Monaghan .	Trough . .	Errigal Trough .	Clogher . .	III.	285
38	Mullaghshantullagh .	42	3	37	Tyrone . .	Dungannon Upper .	Desertcreat .	Cookstown .	III.	308
18	Mullaghsillogagh .	338	0	32	Fermanagh .	Tirkennedy .	Enniskillen .	Enniskillen .	III.	222
36	Mullaghslin Glebe .	2,368	1	30	Tyrone . .	Omagh East .	Clogherny .	Omagh . .	III.	310
23,24,29,30	Mullaghstones .	195	1	19	Meath . .	Lune . .	Athboy . .	Trim . .	I.	207
27,28,33,34	Mullaghteelin .	536	3	4	Meath . .	Upper Duleek .	Moorechurch .	Drogheda .	I.	198
46, 54	Mullaghteige .	175	2	35b	Tyrone . .	Dungannon Middle .	Killyman .	Dungannon .	III.	303
59, 65	Mullaghtinny .	187	0	14	Tyrone . .	Clogher . .	Clogher . .	Clogher . .	III.	293
30, 39	Mullaghtironey .	254	0	37	Tyrone . .	Dungannon Upper .	Tamlaght .	Cookstown .	III.	309
41, 44	MULLAGH T. . .	—			Cavan . .	Castlerahan .	Mullagh . .	Kells . .	III.	70
38	MULLAGH T. . .	—			Clare . .	Ibrickan . .	Kilmurry .	Kilrush . .	II.	24
28, 29	Mullaghunshinagh .	365	3	33	Monaghan .	Farney . .	Donaghmoyne .	Carrickmacross	III.	270
34, 43	Mullaghveal .	1,362	1	21c	Kerry . .	Corkaguiny .	Cloghane .	Dingle . .	II.	175
7, 13	Mullaghwillin .	105	3	28	Meath . .	Lower Slane .	Siddan . .	Ardee . .	I.	224
30,31,39,40	Mullaghwotragh .	247	3	7	Tyrone . .	Dungannon Upper .	Arboe . .	Cookstown .	III.	305
26, 27	Mullaghy .	113	3	30	Fermanagh .	Clanawley .	Rossorry .	Enniskillen .	III.	194
24	Mullaghycullen .	215	3	18d	Leitrim . .	Leitrim . .	Kiltubbrid .	Cark. on Shannon	IV.	104
8	Mullaglassan .	108	0	8	Monaghan .	Monaghan .	Clones . .	Monaghan .	III.	275
10, 14	Mullahead .	864	0	17	Armagh . .	Orior Lower .	Kilmore . .	Banbridge .	III.	56
13	Mullalelish .	620	3	36	Armagh . .	Oneilland West .	Kilmore . .	Armagh . .	III.	53
9	Mullaletragh .	221	0	7	Armagh . .	Oneilland West .	Kilmore . .	Armagh . .	III.	53
7	Mullaliss .	123	2	5	Monaghan .	Trough . .	Donagh . .	Monaghan .	III.	282
6, 9	Mullaloughan . .	182	2	2	Monaghan .	Trough . .	Donagh . .	Monaghan .	III.	282
10, 18	Mullalough or Cavemount	778	1	6	King's Co. .	Lower Philipstown .	Kilclonfert .	Tullamore .	I.	142
16	Mullalougher .	296	2	28	Cavan . .	Tullygarvey .	Annagh . .	Cootehill .	III.	87
36	Mullamast .	1,451	1	20	Kildare . .	Kilkea and Moone .	Narraghmore .	Athy . .	I.	61
17	Mullameelan .	88	1	25	Louth . .	Ardee . .	Ardee . .	Ardee . .	I.	171
14	Mullamore .	103	0	27	Louth . .	Ardee . .	Tallanstown .	Ardee . .	I.	175
9	Mullamurphy .	110	2	26	Monaghan .	Trough . .	Donagh . .	Monaghan .	III.	282
15	Mullan . . .	355	2	3	Armagh . .	Tiranny . .	Tynan . .	Armagh . .	III.	60
23	Mullan . . .	109	2	33	Cavan . .	Clankee . .	Drumgoon .	Cootehill .	III.	72
12	Mullan . . .	4	2	24	Dublin . .	Nethercross .	Donabate .	Balrothery .	I.	30
25	Mullan . . .	128	1	39	Fermanagh .	Clanawley .	Cleenish .	Enniskillen .	III.	191
32, 37	Mullan . . .	141	3	22	Fermanagh .	Clanawley .	Kinawley .	Enniskillen .	III.	194
41, 42	Mullan . . .	97	2	5	Fermanagh .	Knockninny .	Kinawley .	Lisnaskea .	III.	202
11	Mullan . . .	230	1	4	Londonderry .	Coleraine .	Aghadowey .	Coleraine .	III.	230
19, 27	Mullan . . .	425	0	6	Londonderry .	Coleraine .	Kilrea . .	Ballymoney .	III.	232
19	Mullan . . .	242	1	37	Monaghan .	Monaghan .	Tullycorbet .	Monaghan .	III.	281
3, 4	Mullan . . .	71	3	5	Monaghan .	Trough . .	Errigal Trough .	Monaghan .	III.	285
14	Mullanabattog .	129	3	21	Monaghan .	Monaghan .	Monaghan .	Monaghan .	III.	277
15, 23	Mullanabreen .	291	2	35e	Tyrone . .	Omagh West .	Termonamongan .	Castlederg .	III.	317
38	Mullanabreena .	426	2	19	Sligo . .	Leyny . .	Achonry .	Tobercurry .	IV.	229
82	Mullanacarry .	53	0	36	Donegal . .	Banagh . .	Inishkeel .	Glenties .	III.	106
3	Mullanacask .	140	2	9	Monaghan .	Trough . .	Errigal Trough .	Clogher .	III.	285
22	Mullanacaw .	74	0	5f	Fermanagh .	Magheraboy .	Rossorry .	Enniskillen .	III.	214
ʃʃ	Mullanachose .	133	0	36	Donegal . .	Raphoe . .	Stranorlar .	Stranorlar .	III.	143
82, 83	Mullanacloy .	120	1	7	Donegal . .	Banagh . .	Killybegs Lower .	Glenties .	III.	110
12	Mullanacloy . .	145	2	17	Monaghan .	Dartree . .	Clones . .	Clones . .	III.	265

(a) Including 10A. 2R. 26P. water.　　　　(c) Including 44A. 0R. 26P. water.　　　　(e) Including 1A. 3R. 24P. water.
(b) Including 1A. 1R. 9P. water.　　　　(d) Including 18A. 0R. 16P. water.　　　　(f) Including 5A. 0R. 32P. water.

No. of Sheet of the Ordnance Survey Maps.	Townlands and Towns.	Area in Statute Acres. A. R. P.	County.	Barony.	Parish.	Poor Law Union in 1857.	Townland Census of 1851, Part I. Vol.	Page
28	Mullanacranna	239 3 22	Wicklow	Upper Talbotstown	Kiltegan	Baltinglass	I.	365
9, 10	Mullanacre Lower	314 2 5	Cavan	Tullyhaw	Tomregan	Bawnboy	III.	96
9, 10	Mullanacre Upper	552 1 39	Cavan	Tullyhaw	Tomregan	Bawnboy	III.	96
35	Mullanacross	198 0 3a	Cavan	Clankee	Enniskeen	Bailieborough	III.	73
99, 163	Mullanacross	259 3 8	Donegal	Tirhugh	Drumhome	Ballyshannon	III.	146
9, 12, 13	Mullanacross	136 3 37	Monaghan	Monaghan	Drumsnat	Monaghan	III.	275
3	Mullanacross	137 0 36	Monaghan	Trough	Errigal Trough	Clogher	III.	285
30, 34	Mullanadarragh	443 3 136	Leitrim	Carrigallen	Carrigallen	Mohill	IV.	90
30,31,35,36	Mullanafawnia	173 0 2	King's Co.	Eglish	Drumcullen	Parsonstown	I.	134
10, 14	Mullanaffrin	127 2 19c	Cavan	Lower Loughtee	Drumlane	Cavan	III.	80
1, 3	Mullanafinnog	58 2 29	Monaghan	Trough	Errigal Trough	Clogher	III.	285
18	Mullanagore	225 2 32	Monaghan	Cremorne	Aghnamullen	Cootehill	III.	258
32	Mullanagower	186 0 31	Wexford	Shelmaliere East	Ardcavan	Wexford	I.	329
36	Mullanahinch	205 1 9d	Fermanagh	Clankelly	Clones	Clones	III.	197
40	Mullanahoe	321 1 8	Tyrone	Dungannon Upper	Arboe	Cookstown	III.	305
3	Mullanakill	125 2 31	Westmeath	Fore	Rathgarve	Castletowndelvin	I.	271
94	Mullanalamphry	186 1 36	Donegal	Tirhugh	Donegal	Donegal	III.	145
2	Mullanaleck	122 1 38	Leitrim	Rosclogher	Rossinver	Ballyshannon	IV.	112
11	Mullanamoy	80 2 26	Monaghan	Dartree	Clones	Clones	III.	265
3	Mullananailog	101 2 14	Monaghan	Trough	Errigal Trough	Monaghan	III.	285
24	Mullananalt	216 2 28	Monaghan	Cremorne	Aghnamullen	Castleblayney	III.	258
69	Mullanard	212 0 32	Donegal	Raphoe	Convoy	Stranorlar	III.	136
6	Mullanarockan	113 3 5e	Monaghan	Monaghan	Tedavnet	Monaghan	III.	279
31	Mullanarry	125 2 22	Monaghan	Farney	Magheross	Carrickmacross	III.	274
8	Mullanary	288 1 22	Armagh	Armagh	Clonfeacle	Armagh	III.	43
17	Mullanary	233 0 22	Armagh	Orior Lower	Ballymore	Banbridge	III.	55
15	Mullanary	158 3 0	Armagh	Tiranny	Tynan	Armagh	III.	60
24	Mullanarycortannel	270 1 39	Monaghan	Cremorne	Aghnamullen	Castleblayney	III.	258
23	Mullanary Glebe	182 1 8f	Monaghan	Cremorne	Aghnamullen	Cootehill	III.	258
5	Mullanasaggart	81 3 2	Fermanagh	Lurg	Magheraculmoney	Lowtherstown	III.	208
19, 20	Mullanashee	262 2 39	Sligo	Leyny	Ballysadare	Sligo	IV.	230
12, 13	Mullanasilla	363 0 7	Armagh	Oneilland West	Loughgall	Armagh	III.	54
22	Mullanaskea	249 0 15	Fermanagh	Tirkennedy	Enniskillen	Enniskillen	III.	222
14	Mullanaskeagh	121 3 29	Leitrim	Drumahaire	Killanummery	Manorhamilton	IV.	98
99	Mullanasole	181 0 24	Donegal	Tirhugh	Drumhome	Donegal	III.	146
100	Mullanasole Barr	299 2 31g	Donegal	Tirhugh	Drumhome	Donegal	III.	146
25, 34	Mullanatoomog	645 1 21h	Tyrone	Omagh East	Drumragh	Omagh	III.	312
28	Mullanavannog	78 1 25i	Monaghan	Farney	Donaghmoyne	Carrickmacross	III.	270
13	Mullanavannog	113 2 5	Monaghan	Monaghan	Drumsnat	Monaghan	III.	275
15, 16	Mullanavarnoge	94 1 12	Cavan	Tullygarvey	Annagh	Cavan	III.	87
26	Mullanavehy	233 3 35	Fermanagh	Clanawley	Killesher	Enniskillen	III.	193
2, 4	Mullanavockaun	165 1 24	Leitrim	Rosclogher	Rossinver	Ballyshannon	IV.	112
20, 25	Mullanawinna	232 2 3	Fermanagh	Clanawley	Cleenish	Enniskillen	III.	191
36	Mullanbeg	342 3 19	Tyrone	Omagh East	Termonmaguirk	Omagh	III.	314
79	Mullanboy	57 3 5j	Donegal	Raphoe	Donaghmore	Strabane	III.	138
79	Mullanboy	60 2 9k	Donegal	Raphoe	Urney	Strabane	III.	144
42,43,50,51	Mullanboy	478 1 25	Tyrone	Clogher	Donacavey	Omagh	III.	294
42	Mullanboy	231 1 29	Tyrone	Omagh East	Dromore	Omagh	III.	311
92, 93, 98	Mullanboys	248 0 36	Donegal	Banagh	Inver	Donegal	III.	108
32	Mullan or Bumper Lodge	57 1 16	Fermanagh	Clanawley	Killesher	Enniskillen	III.	193
8	Mullandavagh	139 1 38l	Monaghan	Monaghan	Clones	Monaghan	III.	275
3	Mullanderg	141 2 17	Monaghan	Trough	Errigal Trough	Monaghan	III.	285
78	Mullandrait	194 3 12m	Donegal	Raphoe	Stranorlar	Stranorlar	III.	143
1	Mullandreenagh or Thornhill	168 3 35	Cavan	Tullyhaw	Killinagh	Enniskillen	III.	92
10	Mullane	148 1 8	Londonderry	Keenaght	Drumachose	NewTⁿLimavady	III.	235
6	Mullanfad	315 3 9	Sligo	Carbury	Rossinver	Sligo	IV.	223
43	Mullangore	207 2 37n	Donegal	Kilmacrenan	Gartan	Letterkenny	III.	127
3, 7	Mullanhead	56 1 22	Londonderry	Coleraine	Dunboe	Coleraine	III.	231
7	Mullanlary	95 2 3	Monaghan	Trough	Donagh	Monaghan	III.	282
31	Mullan Lower	288 2 25	Tyrone	Dungannon Upper	Ballinderry	Cookstown	III.	306
1	Mullanmeen Middle	74 1 13	Fermanagh	Lurg	Drumkeeran	Lowtherstown	III.	207
1	Mullanmeen Under	191 0 23	Fermanagh	Lurg	Drumkeeran	Lowtherstown	III.	207
1	Mullanmeen Upper	122 3 29	Fermanagh	Lurg	Drumkeeran	Lowtherstown	III.	207
75	Mullanmore	247 3 22	Donegal	Boylagh	Inishkeel	Glenties	III.	113
36	Mullanmore	888 1 36	Tyrone	Omagh East	Termonmaguirk	Omagh	III.	314
22,23,24,25	Mullannagaun	284 1 34	Carlow	St. Mullins Lower	St. Mullins	New Ross	I.	13
24	Mullannaskeagh	180 0 31	Carlow	St. Mullins Lower	St. Mullins	New Ross	I.	13
38	Mullannaskeagh	263 0 30	Wicklow	Ballinacor South	Kilcommon	Shillelagh	I.	349
24	Mullannavode	114 2 31	Carlow	St. Mullins Lower	St. Mullins	New Ross	I.	13
42	Mullanour	135 2 18	Wexford	Forth	Rathaspick	Wexford	I.	312

(a) Including 17A. 2R. 35P. water.
(b) Including 11A. 1R. 8P. water.
(c) Including 19A. 3R. 35P. water.
(d) Including 4A. 1R. 0P. water.
(e) Including 6A. 3R. 23P. detached portions.
(f) Including 43A. 1R. 31P. water.
(g) Including 4A. 1R. 29P. water.
(h) Including 10A. 0R. 3P. water.
(i) Including 5A. 1R. 25P. water.
(j) Including 1A. 0R. 22P. water.
(k) Including 0A. 3R. 26P. water.
(l) Including 12A. 2R. 36P. water.
(m) Including 3A. 2R. 30P. water.
(n) Including 74A. 0R. 0P. water.

5 A

No. of Sheet of the Ordnance Survey Maps.	Townlands and Towns.	Area in Statute Acres.	County.	Barony.	Parish.	Poor Law Union in 1857.	Townland Census of 1851. Part I.	
		A. R. P.					Vol.	Page
6	Mullanrody	217 0 6	Fermanagh	Lurg	Magheraculmoney	Lowtherstown	III.	208
22	Mullans	731 2 38	Antrim	Kilconway	Finvoy	Ballymoney	III.	26
93	Mullans	134 2 28	Donegal	Banagh	Killymard	Donegal	III.	111
100	Mullans	41 2 12	Donegal	Tirhugh	Drumhome	Donegal	III.	146
107	Mullans	302 2 14a	Donegal	Tirhugh	Kilbarron	Ballyshannon	III.	148
35, 36	Mullans	104 0 23	Fermanagh	Clankelly	Clones	Clones	III.	197
4	Mullans	367 0 13	Fermanagh	Lurg	Templecarn	Lowtherstown	III.	209
32	Mullans	82 3 12	Limerick	Smallcounty	Knockainy	Kilmallock	II.	261
10, 14	Mullans	66 1 28	Monaghan	Cremorne	Clontibret	Monaghan	III.	261
59	Mullans	142 2 36	Tyrone	Clogher	Clogher	Clogher	III.	293
50	Mullans	82 0 36	Tyrone	Clogher	Donacavey	Omagh	III.	294
15	Mullans	7 2 10	Wicklow	Upper Talbotstown	Rathsallagh	Baltinglass	I.	365
20	Mullanshellistragh	141 0 23	Fermanagh	Clanawley	Cleenish	Enniskillen	III.	191
58	Mullans (Killyfaddy)	163 1 33	Tyrone	Clogher	Clogher	Clogher	III.	293
38	Mullans North	548 0 11	Wicklow	Ballinacor South	Kilcommon	Shillelagh	I.	349
38	Mullans South	536 0 5	Wicklow	Ballinacor South	Kilcommon	Shillelagh	I.	349
14	Mullanstown	368 1 37	Louth	Ardee	Ardee	Ardee	I.	171
47	Mullantain	99 3 12	Tyrone	Dungannon Middle	Donaghenry	Cookstown	III.	301
74	Mullantiboyle	98 0 10	Donegal	Boylagh	Killybegs Lower	Glenties	III.	114
6, 9	Mullantimore	122 3 36	Monaghan	Monaghan	Tedavnet	Monaghan	III.	279
9	Mullantine	276 3 22	Armagh	Oneilland West	Drumcree	Lurgan	III.	52
17	Mullantine	137 0 11	Kildare	Offaly East	Rathangan	Edenderry	I.	71
33	Mullantlavan	159 2 18	Monaghan	Farney	Magheracloone	Carrickmacross	III.	273
30, 33	Mullantornan	157 3 30	Monaghan	Farney	Magheracloone	Carrickmacross	III.	273
29, 35	Mullantra	61 1 8	Cavan	Clankee	Enniskeen	Bailieborough	III.	73
14	Mullantur	104 1 27	Armagh	Orior Lower	Ballymore	Banbridge	III.	55
7, 11	Mullantur	158 3 11	Armagh	Tiranny	Eglish	Armagh	III.	59
31	Mullan Up er	276 2 5	Tyrone	Dungannon Upper	Ballinderry	Cookstown	III.	306
29	Mullanvaum	562 0 23b	Fermanagh	Clankelly	Clones	Clones	III.	197
10	Mullanwary	62 1 25c	Cavan	Lower Loughtee	Drumlane	Cavan	III.	80
7	Mullanyduff	157 2 16	Leitrim	Rosclogher	Killasnet	Manorhamilton	IV.	110
1	Mullanyduff	158 2 6	Leitrim	Rosclogher	Rossinver	Ballyshannon	IV.	112
67	Mullarie	250 2 5	Cork, E.R.	Imokilly	Clonpriest	Youghal	II.	85
40	Mullarney	99 0 9	Kildare	Kilkea and Moone	Castledermot	Athy	I.	59
19	Mullaroe	117 2 22	Sligo	Tireragh	Skreen	Dromore West	IV.	236
53, 56	Mullartown	1,292 1 23	Down	Mourne	Kilkeel	Kilkeel	III.	183
53	Mullartown Upper	679 3 38	Down	Mourne	Kilkeel	Kilkeel	III.	183
9	Mullarts	71 0 20	Antrim	Cary	Ramoan	Ballycastle	III.	14
15	Mullarts	80 0 19	Antrim	Lower Glenarm	Layd	Ballycastle	III.	23
50	Mullasiloga	144 0 13	Tyrone	Clogher	Donacavey	Omagh	III.	294
8, 9	Mullatee	160 0 32	Louth	Lower Dundalk	Carlingford	Dundalk	I.	176
8	Mullatigorry	160 2 26d	Monaghan	Monaghan	Tedavnet	Monaghan	III.	279
8, 9	Mullatishaughlin	178 1 18e	Monaghan	Monaghan	Tedavnet	Monaghan	III.	279
8, 12	Mullaun	220 2 34	Leitrim	Drumahaire	Cloonclare	Manorhamilton	IV.	93
31	Mullaun	37 1 5	Leitrim	Leitrim	Annaduff	Cark. on Shannon	IV.	100
28	Mullaun	63 1 23	Leitrim	Mohill	Mohill	Mohill	IV.	108
68	Mullaun	50 0 16	Mayo	Burrishoole	Burrishoole	Newport	IV.	119
2, 4	Mullaun	166 1 24	Roscommon	Boyle	Kilronan	Boyle	IV.	197
24, 31	Mullaun	1,740 1 38f	Sligo	Leyny	Achonry	Tobercurry	IV.	229
26	Mullaun	75 2 34	Wexford	Ballaghkeen	Edermine	Enniscorthy	I.	294
3	Mullaun	230 3 37	Wexford	Gorey	Kilnenor	Gorey	I.	319
12	Mullaunattina	257 0 1	Kilkenny	Galmoy	Urlingford	Urlingford	I.	93
41	Mullaunbrack	240 0 30	Tipperary, N.R.	Eliogarty	Thurles	Thurles	II.	273
6	Mullaunfin	100 0 17	Wexford	Gorey	Kilnahue	Gorey	I.	319
26	Mullaunglass	4 1 16	Kilkenny	Callan	Callan	Callan	I.	83
24	Mullaun Glebe	185 0 28	Leitrim	Leitrim	Kiltubbrid	Cark. on Shannon	IV.	104
9, 14	Mullaunnasmear	327 2 15	Wexford	Scarawalsh	St. Marys Newtown-barry	Enniscorthy	I.	325
16	Mullaunreagh	335 0 0	Wexford	Gorey	Monamolin	Gorey	I.	321
17	Mullauns	20 3 24	Dublin	Newcastle	Kilmactalway	Celbridge	I.	33
30	Mullauns	63 0 19g	Mayo	Tirawley	Kilmoremoy	Ballina	IV.	170
29	Mullauns	154 3 16	Sligo	Tireragh	Kilmoremoy	Ballina	IV.	235
41	Mullauns	212 3 27	Tipperary, N.R.	Eliogarty	Thurles	Thurles	II.	273
11	Mullavally	285 3 7	Louth	Louth	Louth	Dundalk	I.	184
35	Mullavea Glebe	60 0 28	Fermanagh	Clankelly	Clones	Clones	III.	197
13	Mullavilly	159 1 34	Armagh	Orior Lower	Kilmore	Banbridge	III.	56
42	Mullawinny	411 2 1	Tyrone	Omagh East	Donacavey	Omagh	III.	310
22, 26	Mullawornia	245 2 5	Longford	Rathcline	Shrule	Ballymahon	I.	165
40, 49	Mullen	833 2 33	Kerry	Trughanacmy	Ballinuuslane	Tralee	II.	206
15	Mullen	1,426 3 7	Roscommon	Frenchpark	Tibohine	Castlereagh	IV.	205
43	Mullenaboree	883 1 22	Cork, E.R.	Barrymore	Ardnageehy	Cork	II.	90
43	Mullenaglemig	134 2 9	Kerry	Corkaguiny	Dingle	Dingle	II.	175
1, 4	Mullenakill North	229 1 5	Armagh	Oneilland West	Killyman	Armagh	III.	53

(a) Including 24A. 1R. 13P. water.   (d) Including 9A. 2R. 0P. water.   (f) Including 18A. 0R. 26P. water.
(b) Including 2A. 0R. 34P. water.   (e) Including 26A. 0R. 8P. water.   (g) Including 11A. 1R. 13P. water.
(c) Including 2A. 1R. 9P. water.

No. of Sheet of the Ordnance Survey Maps.	Townlands and Towns.	Area in Statute Acres.	County.	Barony.	Parish.	Poor Law Union in 1857.	Townland Census of 1851, Part I.	
		A. R. P.					Vol.	Page
4	Mullenakill South	280 0 22	Armagh	Oneilland West	Killyman	Armagh	III.	53
1, 4	Mullenakill West	123 1 24	Armagh	Oneilland West	Killyman	Armagh	III.	53
77	Mullenaranky	423 0 29	Tipperary, S.R.	Iffa and Offa East	Lisronagh	Clonmel	II.	315
35, 44	Mullenataura	955 2 33	Cork, E.R.	Barrymore	Rathcormack	Fermoy	II.	57
35, 39	Mullenbeg	743 0 37	Kilkenny	Iverk	Fiddown	Carrick on Suir	I.	105
15	Mullenduff	251 1 38	Roscommon	Frenchpark	Kilcolagh	Boyle	IV.	203
112	Mullendunny	74 1 26	Cork, E.R.	Kinsale	Clontead	Kinsale	II.	99
10, 15	Mullenkeagh	75 0 19	Tipperary, N.R.	Lower Ormond	Modreeny	Borrisokane	II.	287
62	Mullenmadoge	332 3 2	Mayo	Costello	Kilbeagh	Swineford	IV.	141
23, 24	Mullenmeehan	523 0 39	Westmeath	Rathconrath	Ballymore	Ballymahon	I.	282
38	Mullenmore North	251 1 3	Mayo	Tirawley	Crossmolina	Ballina	IV.	166
38	Mullenmore South	245 0 5	Mayo	Tirawley	Crossmolina	Ballina	IV.	166
40, 41	Mullenahone	295 0 20	Kilkenny	Ida	Kilmakevoge	Waterford	I.	103
36	Mullenakill	849 2 2	Kilkenny	Knocktopher	Jerpoint West	New Ross	I.	111
20, 21	Mullenan	829 3 18	Londonderry	North West Liberties of Londonderry	Templemore	Londonderry	III.	246
59	Mullenroe	689 1 14	Cork, W.R.	West Muskerry	Clondrohid	Macroom	II.	155
46, 47	Mulleny	434 2 18	Donegal	Inishowen West	Burt	Londonderry	III.	120
38	Mullies	69 0 15	Fermanagh	Knockninny	Kinawley	Lisnaskea	III.	202
10	Mullies	134 2 13	Fermanagh	Lurg	Derryvullan	Lowtherstown	III.	205
7	Mullies	191 0 7	Leitrim	Rosclogher	Killasnet	Manorhamilton	IV.	110
8, 9	Mulliganstown	552 2 34	Westmeath	Delvin	Clonarney	Castletowndelvin	I.	265
43	Mullinabro	207 0 40	Kilkenny	Ida	Dunkitt	Waterford	I.	101
18	Mullinabrone	352 0 4	Londonderry	Coleraine	Aghadowey	Coleraine	III.	230
63	Mullinahone	199 1 7	Tipperary, S.R.	Slievardagh	Kilvemnon	Callan	II.	335
63	MULLINAHONE T.	—	Tipperary, S.R.	Slievardagh	Kilvemnon	Callan	II.	335
44, 45	Mullinan	392 2 13	Meath	Ratoath	Ratoath	Dunshaughlin	I.	219
19	Mullinaskeagh	104 1 24	Antrim	Lower Glenarm	Layd	Ballycastle	III.	23
40	Mullinavat	32 0 38	Kilkenny	Knocktopher	Kilbeacon	Waterford	I.	112
40	MULLINAVAT T.	—	Kilkenny	Knocktopher	Kilbeacon	Waterford	I.	112
12, 18	Mullinaveige	735 3 14	Wicklow	Ballinacor North	Calary	Rathdrum	I.	346
15, 18	Mullincross	509 3 38	Louth	Ardee	Kilsaran	Ardee	I.	173
40	Mullinderry	90 3 3	Wexford	Shelmaliere West	Inch	New Ross	I.	333
1	Mullindress	46 2 30	Antrim	Cary	Rathlin Island	Ballycastle	III.	15
78	Mullingar	91 2 5	Donegal	Raphoe	Donaghmore	Stranorlar	III.	138
19	Mullingar	857 1 0	Westmeath	Moyashel and Magheradernon	Mullingar	Mullingar	I.	275
19	MULLINGAR T.	—	Westmeath	Moyashel and Magheradernon	Mullingar	Mullingar	I.	275
10	Mullingee	55 2 25	Longford	Granard	Granard	Granard	I.	156
32	Mullinnagore or Oilgate	101 2 28	Wexford	Ballaghkeen	Edermine	Enniscorthy	I.	294
63	Mullinoly	203 2 52	Tipperary, S.R.	Slievardagh	Kilvemnon	Callan	II.	335
37	Mullinree	26 0 15	Wexford	Shelmaliere West	Kilbrideglynn	Wexford	I.	334
6	Mullinroe	425 3 14d	Longford	Granard	Columbkille	Granard	I.	156
31	Mullinsallagh	644 0 37	Antrim	Lower Toome	Ahoghill	Ballymena	III.	32
67	Mullintor	208 3 38	Tyrone	Dungannon Lower	Aghaloo	Dungannon	III.	297
13	Mullolagher	208 2 17	Longford	Longford	Templemichael	Longford	I.	160
13, 17	Mullurg	192 0 25	Armagh	Fews Lower	Mullaghbrack	Armagh	III.	47
75	Mully	458 1 20	Donegal	Boylagh	Inishkeel	Glenties	III.	113
24,25,30,31	Mullyamly	135 3 10	Cavan	Clanmahon	Ballintemple	Cavan	III.	75
6	Mullyandrew	100 2 28	Meath	Lower Slane	Drumconrath	Ardee	I.	223
19, 23	Mullyard	795 3 24	Armagh	Tiranny	Derrynoose	Armagh	III.	59
25	Mullyard	317 0 16b	Fermanagh	Clanawley	Cleenish	Enniskillen	III.	191
26	Mullyardlougher	73 3 7	Fermanagh	Clanawley	Cleenish	Enniskillen	III.	191
15, 20	Mullyash	337 0 23	Monaghan	Cremorne	Muckno	Castleblayney	III.	262
26	Mullyaster	163 2 4	Leitrim	Carrigallen	Carrigallen	Bawnboy	IV.	90
23	Mullybrack	280 0 28c	Cavan	Clankee	Knockbride	Cootchill	III.	74
10	Mullybrack	43 3 34	Fermanagh	Lurg	Derryvullan	Lowtherstown	III.	205
54	Mullybrannon	277 3 39	Tyrone	Dungannon Middle	Clonfeacle	Dungannon	III.	300
11	Mullybreslen	47 1 33	Fermanagh	Lurg	Derryvullan	Lowtherstown	III.	205
27	Mullybritt	64 0 15	Fermanagh	Tirkennedy	Cleenish	Enniskillen	III.	220
15	Mullyeagh Lower	341 3 33	Wicklow	Lower Talbotstown	Hollywood	Baltinglass	I.	361
15	Mullyeagh Upper	394 0 38	Wicklow	Lower Talbotstown	Hollywood	Baltinglass	I.	361
54, 61	Mullycar	304 2 24d	Tyrone	Dungannon Middle	Clonfeacle	Dungannon	III.	300
60,61,66,67	Mullycarnan	372 1 20e	Tyrone	Dungannon Lower	Aghaloo	Dungannon	III.	297
54	Mullycarnan	123 0 4	Tyrone	Dungannon Middle	Clonfeacle	Dungannon	III.	300
36	Mullycavan	143 0 0	Fermanagh	Clankelly	Clones	Clones	III.	197
26	Mullycovet	56 2 17	Fermanagh	Clanawley	Cleenish	Enniskillen	III.	191
14, 18, 19	Mullycrock	165 2 11	Monaghan	Monaghan	Tullycorbet	Monaghan	III.	281
46	Mullycrunnet	100 2 34	Tyrone	Dungannon Middle	Donaghmore	Dungannon	III.	302
40	Mullydiunity	25 2 9	Fermanagh	Coole	Galloon	Clones	III.	200
40	Mullyduff	121 1 39	Fermanagh	Coole	Galloon	Clones	III.	200
8, 9	Mullyera	57 3 17	Monaghan	Monaghan	Tedavnet	Monaghan	III.	279

(a) Including 8A. 0R. 11P. water.   (c) Including 60A. 1R. 16P. water.   (e) Including 29A. 1R. 3P. water.
(b) Including 1A. 0R. 7P. water.   (d) Including 9A. 2R. 19P. water.

5 A 2

No. of Sheet of the Ordnance Survey Maps.	Townlands and Towns.	Area in Statute Acres. A. R. P.	County.	Barony.	Parish.	Poor Law Union in 1857.	Townland Census of 1851, Part I. Vol.	Page
6	Mullyera	65 3 18	Monaghan	Monaghan	Tedavnet	Monaghan	III.	279
22	Mullyfabeg	564 2 38a	Tyrone	Omagh West	Termonamongan	Castlederg	III.	317
22	Mullyfamore	798 0 4b	Tyrone	Omagh West	Termonamongan	Castlederg	III.	317
21	Mullygarry	168 2 39	Fermanagh	Clanawley	Cleenish	Enniskillen	III.	191
27, 28	Mullygollan	162 2 4	Roscommon	Castlereagh	Baslick	Castlereagh	IV.	199
46	Mullygruen	118 2 7c	Tyrone	Dungannon Middle	Donaghmore	Dungannon	III.	302
7	Mullyjordan	193 1 11	Monaghan	Trough	Donagh	Monaghan	III.	282
15	Mullykivet	46 2 35	Fermanagh	Magheraboy	Devenish	Enniskillen	III.	211
13	Mullyknock	162 2 18	Monaghan	Monaghan	Monaghan	Monaghan	III.	277
22, 23	Mullyknock or Topped Mountain	730 1 10d	Fermanagh	Tirkennedy	Enniskillen	Enniskillen	III.	222
8	Mullyleggan	180 1 20	Armagh	Armagh	Clonfeacle	Armagh	III.	43
22, 27	Mullylogan	80 1 23	Fermanagh	Magheraboy	Rossory	Enniskillen	III.	214
7, 8, 11	Mullyloughan	90 2 20	Armagh	Tiranny	Eglish	Armagh	III.	59
12	Mullyloughran	305 0 17	Armagh	Oneilland West	Armagh	Armagh	III.	51
6	Mully Lower	123 0 17	Cavan	Tullyhaw	Templeport	Enniskillen	III.	95
38, 39	Mullylun	190 3 16	Fermanagh	Knockninny	Kinawley	Lisnaskea	III.	202
20, 25	Mullylusty	401 0 22	Fermanagh	Clanawley	Cleenish	Enniskillen	III.	191
34	Mullylusty	171 2 3	Monaghan	Farney	Magheracloone	Carrickmacross	III.	273
17	Mullymagaraghan	95 3 19e	Monaghan	Dartree	Aghabog	Cootehill	III.	263
26	Mullymagowan	544 3 38	Cavan	Upper Loughtee	Lavey	Cavan	III.	86
26, 27	Mullymesker	261 2 28	Fermanagh	Clanawley	Cleenish	Enniskillen	III.	191
35, 39	Mullymucks	1,541 0 11	Roscommon	Ballintober South	Kilbride	Roscommon	IV.	189
34, 35	Mullynaburtlan	248 2 12	Fermanagh	Magherastephana	Aghalurcher	Lisnaskea	III.	217
39, 42	Mullynacoagh	265 0 13f	Fermanagh	Knockninny	Kinawley	Lisnaskea	III.	202
33	Mullynadrumman	75 2 20	Leitrim	Mohill	Cloone	Mohill	IV.	106
14	Mullynagolman	109 3 36g	Cavan	Lower Loughtee	Tomregan	Bawnboy	III.	81
40	Mullynagowan	132 3 33	Fermanagh	Clankelly	Galloon	Clones	III.	198
38	Mullynaherb	200 1 38	Fermanagh	Knockninny	Kinawley	Lisnaskea	III.	202
9	Mullynahinch	139 2 26	Monaghan	Monaghan	Kilmore	Monaghan	III.	276
32	Mullynahunshin	129 0 18	Fermanagh	Clanawley	Killesher	Enniskillen	III.	193
35	Mullynalughoge	78 1 23h	Fermanagh	Clankelly	Clones	Clones	III.	197
28, 34	Mullynascarty	127 2 12	Fermanagh	Magherastephana	Aghalurcher	Lisnaskea	III.	217
14	Mullynaskeagh	57 3 28	Fermanagh	Magheraboy	Devenish	Ballyshannon	III.	211
5	Mullynaval	33 1 34	Fermanagh	Lurg	Drumkeeran	Lowtherstown	III.	207
24, 29, 30	Mullynavale	1,972 1 20	Fermanagh	Magherastephana	Aghalurcher	Lisnaskea	III.	217
40	Mullynavannoge	99 2 3i	Fermanagh	Clankelly	Galloon	Clones	III.	198
20	Mullynavarnoge	88 1 34	Fermanagh	Clanawley	Cleenish	Enniskillen	III.	191
67	Mullynaveagh	128 0 21	Tyrone	Dungannon Lower	Aghaloo	Armagh	III.	297
39	Mullyned	44 3 30	Fermanagh	Coole	Galloon	Lisnaskea	III.	200
38	Mullyneeny	328 0 10	Fermanagh	Knockninny	Kinawley	Lisnaskea	III.	202
61, 67	Mullyneill	339 0 11j	Tyrone	Dungannon Lower	Aghaloo	Dungannon	III.	297
12	Mullynure	295 3 20	Armagh	Armagh	Grange	Armagh	III.	45
3	Mullynure	81 2 16	Monaghan	Trough	Errigal Trough	Clogher	III.	285
37, 38	Mullynure	164 0 4	Tyrone	Dungannon Upper	Desertcreat	Cookstown	III.	308
34	Mullyore	141 1 14	Monaghan	Farney	Magheracloone	Carrickmacross	III.	273
53, 60	Mullyroddan	308 2 13	Tyrone	Dungannon Lower	Killeeshil	Dungannon	III.	298
53	Mullysilly	139 1 25	Tyrone	Dungannon Lower	Killeeshil	Dungannon	III.	298
5	Mullystaghan	150 0 6	Meath	Lower Kells	Moybolgue	Kells	I.	203
6	Mully Upper	151 3 19	Cavan	Tullyhaw	Templeport	Enniskillen	III.	95
64, 73	Mullyvea	495 0 12k	Donegal	Boylagh	Inishkeel	Glenties	III.	113
36	Mulmontry	247 1 21	Wexford	Shelmaliere West	Taghmon	Wexford	I.	335
83	Mulmosog or Altnagapple	766 2 21	Donegal	Banagh	Inishkeel	Glenties	III.	106
28, 29	Mulnadoran	195 0 2	Fermanagh	Magherastephana	Aghavea	Lisnasken	III.	219
27	Mulnafye	327 2 19	Tyrone	Omagh East	Termonmaguirk	Omagh	III.	314
105	Mulnagoad	91 0 2l	Donegal	Tirhugh	Templecarn	Donegal	III.	149
50	Mulnagoagh	246 2 36m	Tyrone	Omagh East	Dromore	Omagh	III.	311
46	Mulnagore	291 1 23	Tyrone	Dungannon Middle	Pomeroy	Dungannon	III.	304
56	Mulnagork	122 2 0	Tyrone	Omagh East	Kilskeery	Enniskillen	III.	314
70	Mulnagung	277 0 24	Donegal	Raphoe	Clonleigh	Strabane	III.	135
40	Mulnahorn	95 3 19	Fermanagh	Coole	Galloon	Clones	III.	200
60, 66	Mulnahorn	455 2 11	Tyrone	Dungannon Lower	Aghaloo	Clogher	III.	297
53	Mulnahunch	245 2 1	Tyrone	Dungannon Lower	Killeeshil	Dungannon	III.	298
65	Mulnamin Beg	379 3 18	Donegal	Boylagh	Inishkeel	Glenties	III.	113
65	Mulnamin More	237 1 7	Donegal	Boylagh	Inishkeel	Glenties	III.	113
12, 16	Mulnanarragh	136 2 13	Cavan	Tullygarvey	Annagh	Cavan	III.	87
21	Mulnasillagh	110 0 4	Leitrim	Carrigallen	Oughteragh	Bawnboy	IV.	92
22	Mulnavannoge	175 0 9	Leitrim	Carrigallen	Oughteragh	Bawnboy	IV.	92
70	Mulnaveagh	313 2 36	Donegal	Raphoe	Clonleigh	Strabane	III.	135
35, 40	Mulnavoo	296 0 2	Londonderry	Loughinsholin	Ballynascreen	Magherafelt	III	939
47	Mulphedder	704 2 18	Meath	Upper Moyfenrath	Clonard	Edenderry	I.	213
84, 96	Mulpit	181 3 5	Galway	Athenry	Athenry	Loughrea	IV.	4

(a) Including 2A. 2R. 11P. water.
(b) Including 5A. 0R. 16P. water.
(c) Including 6A. 0R. 7P. water.
(d) Including 4A. 1R. 27P. water.
(e) Including 5A. 3R. 37F. water.

(f) Including 24A. 2R. 3P. water.
(g) Including 9A. 2R. 3P. water.
(h) Including 6A. 0R. 28P. water.
(i) Including 2A. 3R. 6P. water.

(j) Including 5A. 2R. 37P. water.
(k) Including 41A. 1R. 7P. water.
(l) Including 3A. 2R. 16P. water.
(m) Including 4A. 3R. 12P. water.

No. of Sheet of the Ordnance Survey Maps.	Townlands and Towns.	Area in Statute Acres.			County.	Barony.	Parish.	Poor Law Union in 1857.	Townland Census of 1851, Part I.	
		A.	R.	P.					Vol.	Page
47	Mulrankin	291	1	23	Wexford	Bargy	Mulrankin	Wexford	I.	307
30, 26	Mulrick	341	0	29	Cavan	Tullyhunco	Scrabby	Granard	III.	99
27	Mulrod	135	0	32a	Fermanagh	Tirkennedy	Derryvullan	Enniskillen	III.	221
113	*Mulroney's Island*	6	0	38	Galway	Kiltartan	Kinvarradoorus	Gort	IV.	50
103	Mulroog East	378	2	28	Galway	Dunkellin	Kilcolgan	Gort	IV.	28
103	Mulroog West	400	3	20	Galway	Dunkellin	Kilcolgan	Gort	IV.	28
92	Multins	468	0	29	Donegal	Banagh	Killaghtee	Donegal	III.	109
6, 7	Multyfarnham	185	0	39	Westmeath	Corkaree	Multyfarnham	Mullingar	I.	263
7, 12	Multyfarnham or Fearbranagh	142	2	34	Westmeath	Corkaree	Stonehall	Mullingar	I.	263
7, 12	Multyfarnham or Fearbranagh	116	3	23	Westmeath	Corkaree	Tyfarnham	Mullingar	I.	264
6, 7	MULTYFARNHAM T.	—			Westmeath	Corkaree	Multyfarnham	Mullingar	I.	263
4	Multyhogy	169	3	5	Down	Castlereagh Upper	Knockbreda	Belfast	III.	165
10, 17	Mulvin	232	3	12b	Tyrone	Strabane Lower	Ardstraw	Strabane	III.	319
12	Munakill	447	0	10c	Leitrim	Drumahaire	Cloonclare	Manorhamilton	IV.	93
45, 54	Mundellihy	890	2	28	Limerick	Connello Upper	Dromcolliher	Newcastle	II.	233
37, 38, 43, 46	Munderrydoe	255	3	12	Tyrone	Dungannon Middle	Pomeroy	Cookstown	III.	304
36	Munga	902	3	12d	Galway	Ballynahinch	Ballindoon	Clifden	IV.	10
42, 43	Mungacullin	450	1	25	Wicklow	Shillelagh	Aghowle	Shillelagh	I.	356
33	Mungau	302	0	7	Kilkenny	Ida	The Rower	New Ross	I.	104
37	Mungaun	949	3	29	Mayo	Tirawley	Crossmolina	Ballina	IV.	166
28	Mungmacody	552	3	0	Kilkenny	Gowran	Columbkille	Thomastown	I.	94
24	Munie	158	1	29	Tyrone	Omagh West	Urney	Castlederg	III.	318
29	Munie North	192	2	36	Antrim	Lower Glenarm	Tickmacrevan	Larne	III.	24
29	Munie South	481	3	7	Antrim	Lower Glenarm	Tickmacrevan	Larne	III.	24
9	Munlough North	105	1	4	Cavan	Tullyhaw	Templeport	Bawnboy	III.	95
9	Munlough South	68	2	13	Cavan	Tullyhaw	Templeport	Bawnboy	III.	95
7	Munlusk	326	0	36	Tipperary, N.R.	Lower Ormond	Aglishcloghane	Borrisokane	II.	281
17	Munmahoge	191	2	31	Waterford	Middlethird	Kilbride	Waterford	II.	367
17	Munmahoge	288	3	23	Waterford	Middlethird	Kilburne	Waterford	II.	367
121	Munnadesha	105	0	34	Mayo	Kilmaine	Kilmolara	Ballinrobe	IV.	157
12	Munnagashel	183	3	32	Leitrim	Drumahaire	Cloonclare	Manorhamilton	IV.	93
141	Munnane	210	2	26	Cork, W.R.	West Carbery (E.D.)	Aghadown	Skibbereen	II.	137
3	Munnia	388	0	6	Clare	Burren	Abbey	Ballyvaghan	II.	11
7, 8	Munnia	154	3	20	Tipperary, N.R.	Lower Ormond	Ballingarry	Borrisokane	II.	282
31	Munnia	381	0	4	Tipperary, N.R.	Owney and Arra	Killoscully	Nenagh	II.	295
141, 150	Munnig North	354	1	38	Cork, W.R.	West Carbery (E.D.)	Creagh	Skibbereen	II.	139
150	Munnig South	77	0	35	Cork, W.R.	West Carbery (E.D.)	Creagh	Skibbereen	II.	139
17	Munnilly	98	3	13	Cavan	Tullygarvey	Drumgoon	Cootehill	III.	88
16	Munnilly	149	1	32	Monaghan	Dartree	Clones	Clones	III.	265
7	Munsburrow	870	0	6	Waterford	Upperthird	Mothel	Carrick on Suir	II.	371
15, 16	Muntermellan	1,122	3	30	Donegal	Kilmacrenan	Clondahorky	Dunfanaghy	III.	123
98, 99	Munterneese	315	1	8	Donegal	Banagh	Inver	Donegal	III.	108
12, 25	Munterowen East	744	1	13	Galway	Ross	Ross	Oughterard	IV.	74
12, 25	Munterowen Middle	531	0	32	Galway	Ross	Ross	Oughterard	IV.	74
12, 25	Munterowen West	265	1	17	Galway	Ross	Ross	Oughterard	IV.	74
62, 70	Muntertinny	382	2	39	Donegal	Raphoe	Raphoe	Strabane	III.	141
29	Muntober	613	3	36	Tyrone	Dungannon Upper	Kildress	Cookstown	III.	309
34	Munville	71	1	2	Fermanagh	Magherastephana	Aghalurcher	Lisnaskea	III.	217
67	Murgasty	151	0	39	Tipperary, S.R.	Clanwilliam	Tipperary	Tipperary	II.	312
23	Murhaun	226	1	28	Leitrim	Leitrim	Kiltoghert	Carrick on Shannon	IV.	102
6, 11	Murher	583	1	20	Kerry	Iraghticonnor	Murher	Listowel	II.	193
39, 40	Murhy	298	2	19	Sligo	Corran	Toomour	Boyle	IV.	228
27, 34	Murillyroe	215	3	36	Sligo	Tirerrill	Tawnagh	Sligo	IV.	241
26	Murrirrigane	730	3	27	Kerry	Corkaguiny	Cloghane	Dingle	II.	175
46	Murlough	70	0	38	Donegal	Raphoe	Allsaints	Londonderry	III.	134
70	Murlough	185	3	1	Donegal	Raphoe	Clonleigh	Strabane	III.	135
43, 44	Murlough Lower	859	2	16	Down	Lecale Upper	Kilmegan	Downpatrick	III.	181
43, 49	Murlough Upper	569	3	10	Down	Upper Iveagh, Lr. pt.	Maghera	Kilkeel	III.	173
39	Murmod	746	2	17	Cavan	Castlerahan	Lurgan	Oldcastle	III.	70
58, 69	Murnaghbeg	281	1	24	Cork, W.R.	West Muskerry	Ballyvourney	Macroom	II.	154
91	Murneen North	737	2	38	Mayo	Clanmorris	Kilcolman	Claremorris	IV.	134
91	Murneen South	393	3	9	Mayo	Clanmorris	Kilcolman	Claremorris	IV.	134
28, 37	Murnells	770	3	2	Tyrone	Dungannon Upper	Kildress	Cookstown	III.	309
36	Murntown	133	1	7	Wexford	Shelmaliere West	Kilbrideglynn	Wexford	I.	334
42	Murntown Lower	125	1	14	Wexford	Forth	Kildavin	Wexford	I.	310
42	Murntown Upper	82	1	2	Wexford	Forth	Kildavin	Wexford	I.	310
22, 23, 25, 26	Murphystown	406	1	34	Dublin	Rathdown	Tully	Rathdown	I.	38
109	Murragh	408	2	10	Cork, W.R.	East Carbery (W.D.)	Murragh	Bandon	II.	135
7	Murragh	327	0	2	Dublin	Balrothery West	Westpalstown	Balrothery	I.	23
108	*Murragh*	9	1	39	Galway	Longford	Meelick	Portumna	IV.	62
16	Murragh	400	2	15	King's Co.	Ballycowan	Rahan	Tullamore	I.	129

(a) Including 2A. 3R. 2P. water.
(b) Including 18A. 0R. 15P. water.
(c) Including 51A. 2R. 4P. water.
(d) Including 52A. 0R. 9P. water.

No. of Sheet of the Ordnance Survey Maps.	Townlands and Towns.	Area in Statute Acres. A. R. P.	County.	Barony.	Parish.	Poor Law Union in 1857.	Townland Census of 1851, Part I. Vol.	Page
131, 140	Murrahin	138 0 7	Cork, W.R.	West Carbery (W.D.)	Skull	Skull	II.	146
140	Murrahin North	214 0 2	Cork, W.R.	West Carbery (W.D.)	Kilcoe	Skull	II.	143
140	Murrahin South	162 1 25	Cork, W.R.	West Carbery (W.D.)	Kilcoe	Skull	II.	143
130, 131	Murreagh	180 0 13	Cork, W.R.	West Carbery (W.D.)	Durrus	Bantry	II.	142
33, 42	Murreagh	379 2 14	Kerry	Corkaguiny	Kilmalkedar	Dingle	II.	178
88,89,97,98	Murreagh	773 3 32	Kerry	Iveragh	Dromod	Cahersiveen	II.	195
8, 9, 17	Murren	388 0 19	Donegal	Kilmacrenan	Clondavaddog	Millford	III.	125
14	Murrens	206 2 13	Meath	Fore	Moylough	Oldcastle	I.	201
56, 66	Murrevagh	1,014 3 21	Mayo	Burrishoole	Burrishoole	Newport	IV.	119
87	Murrisk Demesne	33 1 4	Mayo	Murrisk	Oughaval	Westport	IV.	162
87	Murrisknaboll	87 2 30	Mayo	Murrisk	Oughaval	Westport	IV.	162
15, 25	Murroe	1,300 0 29a	Donegal	Kilmacrenan	Clondahorky	Dunfanaghy	III.	123
94	Murroogh	245 1 25	Galway	Galway	Oranmore	Galway	IV.	37
1, 2	Murrooghkilly	1,049 1 32	Clare	Burren	Gleninagh	Ballyvaghan	II.	12
1, 2	Murrooghtoohy North	619 1 4	Clare	Burren	Gleninagh	Ballyvaghan	II.	12
1	Murrooghtoohy South	517 3 11	Clare	Burren	Gleninagh	Ballyvaghan	II.	12
19, 20	Murroo or Gortnagross Lower	67 1 27	Antrim	Lower Glenarm	Layd	Ballycastle	II.	22
44	Murtaghstown	153 3 10	Kilkenny	Ida	Rathpatrick	Waterford	I.	103
30, 37	Murvaclogher or Broaghclogh	648 1 15	Down	Kinelarty	Kilmore	Downpatrick	III.	177
78	*Murvagh Island*	4 0 3	Galway	Moycullen	Kilannin	Oughterard	IV.	70
99	Murvagh Lower	549 3 32	Donegal	Tirhugh	Drumhome	Donegal	III.	147
99	Murvagh Upper Glebe	291 2 16	Donegal	Tirhugh	Drumhome	Donegal	III.	147
49,50,62,63	Murvey	1,087 0 32b	Galway	Ballynahinch	Moyrus	Clifden	IV.	13
48	Mushera	649 2 10	Cork, W.R.	West Muskerry	Drishane	Millstreet	II.	156
48, 49	Mushera	452 0 11	Cork, W.R.	West Muskerry	Kilcorney	Millstreet	II.	158
119,121,122	Musicfield	76 1 2	Mayo	Kilmaine	Kilmainemore	Ballinrobe	IV.	156
38, 43	Muskeagh	557 3 32	Wicklow	Ballinacor South	Kilcommon	Shillelagh	I.	349
33	Mutton Island	158 2 26	Clare	Ibrickan	Kilmurry	Kilrush	II	23
63	*Mutton Island*	1 2 16	Galway	Ballynahinch	Moyrus	Clifden	IV.	14
94	*Mutton Island*	4 0 19	Galway	Galway	Rahoon	Galway	IV.	38
33	Mweelagarraun	35 0 10	Clare	Inchiquin	Kilnamona	Ennis	II.	27
36	Mweelahorna	127 2 25	Waterford	Decies within Drum	Ardmore	Dungarvan	II.	350
36	Mweelahorna	248 1 8	Waterford	Decies within Drum	Ringagonagh	Dungarvan	II.	353
84, 85	*Mweelaun Island*	4 0 26	Mayo	Murrisk	Kilgeever	Westport	IV.	161
2, 6	Mweelbane	99 0 29	Fermanagh	Lurg	Drumkeeran	Lowtherstown	III.	207
57	Mweelcaha	131 1 5c	Kerry	Dunkerron North	Knockane	Killarney	II.	182
23	Mweelin	652 3 29	Galway	Ballynahinch	Ballynakill	Clifden	IV.	12
88	Mweelin	79 0 31	Kerry	Iveragh	Prior	Cahersiveen	II.	198
54, 55	Mweelin	1,444 3 28d	Mayo	Burrishoole	Achill	Newport	IV.	117
105,106,115	Mweelin	765 0 27	Mayo	Murrisk	Kilgeever	Westport	IV.	160
38	Mweeling	117 1 20	Waterford	Decies within Drum	Ardmore	Dungarvan	II.	350
30	Mweelinroe	38 0 14	Kerry	Trughanacmy	Ballymacelligott	Tralee	II.	207
118	Mweelis	127 3 2	Mayo	Kilmaine	Kilmainemore	Ballinrobe	IV.	156
94, 102	Mweeloon	221 1 28	Galway	Dunkellin	Ballynacourty	Galway	IV.	27
24	Mweelra	91 2 30	Westmeath	Rathconrath	Conry	Mullingar	I.	282
44, 45	Mweelroe	234 1 1	Sligo	Coolavin	Kilfree	Boyle	IV.	224
103	*Mweenisharan*	13 2 7	Galway	Dunkellin	Drumacoo	Gort	IV.	28
76	Mweenish Island	572 0 29e	Galway	Ballynahinch	Moyrus	Clifden	IV.	14
102	Mweenish Island	53 2 25	Galway	Dunkellin	Ballynacourty	Galway	IV.	27
30, 39	Mweennalaa	253 3 2	Kerry	Trughanacmy	Nohaval	Tralee	II.	212
9	Mweevoo	114 1 25	Kerry	Iraghticonnor	Ballyconry	Listowel	II.	190
9, 10	Mweevuck	200 1 4	Kerry	Iraghticonnor	Ballyconry	Listowel	II.	190
65	Mweewillin	1,284 0 29	Mayo	Burrishoole	Achill	Newport	IV.	117
15, 20	Myaugh	249 0 38	Wexford	Gorey	Kilcormick	Enniscorthy	I.	317
20	Myaugh	79 1 14	Wexford	Scarawalsh	Clone	Enniscorthy	I.	322
85	Mylane	598 1 26	Cork, E.R.	East Muskerry	St. Finbars	Bandon	II.	106
34, 35	Mylerspark	881 2 9	Wexford	Bantry	Oldross	New Ross	I.	301
3, 8	Mylerstown	499 0 12	Kildare	Carbury	Mylerstown	Edenderry	I.	52
13, 18	Mylerstown	792 0 24	Kildare	Connell	Rathernan	Naas	I.	56
24	Mylerstown	338 0 22	Kildare	Naas South	Killashee	Naas	I.	65
27, 31	Mylerstown	244 2 37	Kildare	Offally West	Harristown	Athy	I.	72
77, 83	Mylerstown	185 1 31	Tipperary, S.R.	Iffa and Offa East	Kilgrant	Clonmel	II.	314
76	Mylerstown	102 2 27	Tipperary, S.R.	Iffa and Offa East	Newchapel	Clonmel	II.	315
35	Mylerstown or Kingsmountain	390 3 7	Kilkenny	Knocktopher	Aghaviller	Thomastown	I.	110
121, 122	Mylesestate	44 0 23	Mayo	Kilmaine	Kilmainemore	Ballinrobe	IV.	156
57	Mylespark	115 1 3	Galway	Clare	Cummer	Tuam	IV.	19
20	Mylestown	144 2 32	Westmeath	Farbill	Killucan	Mullingar	I.	267
88	Mynagh	101 0 9	Kildare	Offally West	Lackagh	Athy	I.	73
22	Mynagh	50 1 19	Kildare	Offally West	Rathangan	Athy	I.	74
5, 9	Myroe Level (*Intake*)	661 2 39	Londonderry	Keenaght	Tamlaght Finlagan	New T^n Limavady	III.	237

(a) Including 17A. 2R. 34P. water.
(b) Including 36A. 0R. 5P. water.
(c) Including 6A. 3R. 29P. water.
(d) Including 7A. 3R. 32P. water.
(e) Including 11A. 0R. 0P. water.

No. of Sheet of the Ordinance Survey Maps.	Townlands and Towns.	Area in Statute Acres.	County.	Barony.	Parish.	Poor Law Union in 1857.	Townland Census of 1851, Part I.	
		A. R. P.					Vol.	Page
142, 151	Myross . .	226 1 2	Cork, W.R.	West Carbery (E.D.)	Myross . .	Skibbereen .	II.	141
99	Myrtleville .	79 2 12	Cork, E.R.	Kerrycurrihy .	Templebreedy .	Kinsale .	II.	93
17, 20	Myshall . .	970 0 5	Carlow .	Forth . .	Myshall . .	Carlow .	I.	5
17	MYSHALL T. .	—	Carlow .	Forth . .	Myshall . .	Carlow .	I.	5
33	*Naan East and South*	0 3 10	Fermanagh .	Magherastephana .	Aghalurcher .	Lisnaskea .	III.	218
33	Naan West .	97 3 14	Fermanagh .	Magherastephana .	Aghalurcher .	Lisnaskea .	III.	218
19, 24	Naas East .	524 1 28	Kildare .	Naas North .	Naas . .	Naas .	I.	62
19	NAAS T. .	—	Kildare .	Naas North .	Naas . .	Naas .	I.	62
19	Naas West .	538 0 36	Kildare .	Naas North .	Naas . .	Naas .	I.	62
40, 49	Nadanuller Beg	498 2 10	Cork, E.R.	Duhallow .	Clonmeen .	Kanturk .	II.	70
40	Nadanuller More	682 0 29	Cork, E.R.	Duhallow .	Clonmeen .	Kanturk .	II.	70
22,23,28,29	Nadnaveagh .	261 1 12*d*	Roscommon .	Roscommon .	Killukin .	Strokestown .	IV.	211
38	Nadneagh .	109 0 8	King's Co.	Clonlisk .	Kilcolman .	Parsonstown .	I.	130
72	Nadrid . .	545 3 21*b*	Cork, E.R.	East Muskerry .	Magourney .	Macroom .	II.	105
31	Nafarty . .	263 1 1	Monaghan .	Farney .	Magheross .	Carrickmacross	III.	274
37	Naghan . .	336 1 24	Down .	Kinelarty .	Loughinisland .	Downpatrick .	III.	177
12, 13	Naghill . .	155 3 29	Monaghan .	Monaghan .	Drumsnat .	Monaghan .	III.	275
26	Naglesborough	224 0 37	Cork, E.R.	Fermoy .	Castletownroche	Fermoy .	II.	77
14	Naglesland .	63 3 21	Kilkenny .	Crannagh .	Odagh . .	Kilkenny .	I.	86
27	Nahana . .	610 2 5	King's Co.	Coolestown .	Clonsast . .	Edenderry .	I.	133
15, 20	Naheelis . .	88 3 6*c*	Cavan .	Lower Loughtee	Drumlane .	Cavan .	III.	80
30	Nahod Little .	156 2 31	Westmeath .	Clonlonan .	Ballyloughloe .	Athlone .	I.	260
30	Nahod More .	183 0 9	Westmeath .	Clonlonan .	Ballyloughloe .	Athlone .	I.	260
107	Nail or Inga .	200 2 21	Galway .	Longford .	Killimorbologue	Portumna .	IV.	59
24, 33	Nakil or Surgeview	221 2 24	Mayo .	Erris .	Kilmore .	Belmullet .	IV.	146
17, 21	Nangor . .	171 1 28	Dublin .	Uppercross .	Clondalkin .	Dublin South .	I.	39
57	Nantinan .	568 1 22	Kerry .	Magunihy .	Killorglin .	Killarney .	II.	204
20	Nantinan .	71 0 2	Limerick .	Connello Lower	Nantinan .	Rathkeale .	II.	229
14, 19	Nappagh .	255 2 8	Longford .	Moydow . .	Ardagh . .	Longford .	I.	160
20, 25	Nappan Mountain	738 2 22	Antrim .	Lower Glenarm	Ardclinis .	Larne .	III.	21
20	Nappan North	44 2 12	Antrim .	Lower Glenarm	Ardclinis .	Larne .	III.	21
20, 25	Nappan South	38 2 31	Antrim .	Lower Glenarm	Ardclinis .	Larne .	III.	21
64	Naran . .	495 3 13*d*	Donegal .	Boylagh .	Iniskeel .	Glenties .	III.	113
3	Nare . .	46 2 16	Londonderry	North East Liberties of Coleraine .	Ballyaghran .	Coleraine .	III.	244
43	Narrabaun North	126 1 7	Kilkenny .	Iverk .	Kilmacow .	Waterford .	I.	106
43	Narrabaun South	247 0 13	Kilkenny .	Iverk .	Kilmacow .	Waterford .	I.	106
38	Narraghbeg .	202 2 28	Kildare .	Kilkea and Moone .	Killelan .	Baltinglass .	I.	60
32, 36	Narraghmore .	589 3 21	Kildare .	Narragh & Reban East	Narraghmore .	Athy .	I.	66
32	Narraghmore Demesne	307 1 34	Kildare .	Narragh & Reban East	Narraghmore .	Athy .	I.	66
51, 54	Narrow Water	348 1 35	Down .	Upper Iveagh, Up. pt.	Warrenspoint .	Newry .	III.	176
8	Nart . .	105 0 5	Monaghan .	Monaghan .	Clones .	Monaghan .	III.	275
18	Nart . .	177 1 17	Monaghan .	Monaghan .	Kilmore .	Monaghan .	III.	276
34, 35, 40	Nash . .	1,152 3 2	Wexford .	Shelburne .	Owenduff .	New Ross .	I.	328
4	Nashesquarter	211 3 10	Carlow .	Rathvilly .	Haroldstown .	Shillelagh .	I.	11
11	Naul . .	433 1 28	Armagh .	Armagh .	Tynan .	Armagh .	III.	46
4	Naul . .	376 0 4	Dublin .	Balrothery West	Naul .	Balrothery .	I.	23
33, 34	Naul . .	707 2 8	Meath .	Upper Duleek	Clonalvy .	Drogheda .	I.	197
50	Naulswood .	63 3 29	Meath .	Dunboyne .	Dunboyne .	Dunshaughlin .	I.	199
4	NAUL T. .	—	Dublin .	Balrothery West	Naul .	Balrothery .	I.	23
12	Navan . .	155 2 29	Armagh .	Armagh .	Eglish .	Armagh .	III.	44
4, 7	Navan . .	140 3 15	Louth .	Lower Dundalk	Ballymascanlan	Dundalk .	I.	176
25	NAVAN T. .	—	Meath .	{ Lower Navan . Skreen .	{ Donaghmore . Navan . Athlumney . }	Navan .	I. {	214 215 220
78	Navenny .	340 3 10*e*	Donegal .	Raphoe .	Donaghmore .	Stranorlar .	III.	138
118, 121	Nealepark .	444 2 15	Mayo .	Kilmaine .	Kilmolara .	Ballinrobe .	IV.	157
15	Nealstown or Ballaghlyragh .	148 2 2	Queen's Co.	Upperwoods .	Offerlane .	Mountmellick .	I.	250
93, 94	Neaskin . .	398 2 4	Cork, W.R.	East Carbery (W.D.)	Fanlobbus .	Dunmanway .	II.	132
13, 19	Ned . .	323 1 25	Cavan .	Tullyhunco .	Killashandra .	Bawnboy .	III.	98
33, 38	Ned . .	117 3 7	Fermanagh .	Knockninny .	Kinawley .	Lisnaskea .	III.	202
9, 16	Ned . .	356 0 36	Londonderry	Keenaght .	Tamlaght Finlagan	New T° Limavady	III.	237
107	Nedanone .	173 0 7	Kerry .	Dunkerron South	Kilcrohane .	Kenmare .	II.	184
16	Neddaingh .	204 3 31	Cavan .	Tullygarvey .	Annagh .	Cootehill .	III.	87
88	Neddans (*Farran*)	239 0 2*f*	Tipperary, S.R.	Iffa and Offa West	Neddans .	Clogheen .	II.	319
82, 88	Neddans (*Nagle*)	396 0 26	Tipperary, S.R.	Iffa and Offa West	Neddans .	Clogheen .	II.	319
108	Nedinagh East	427 3 4	Cork, W.R.	East Carbery (W.D.)	Fanlobbus .	Dunmanway .	II.	132
108	Nedinagh West	433 2 2	Cork, W.R.	East Carbery (W.D.)	Fanlobbus .	Dunmanway .	II.	132
6	Nedsherry .	151 1 31	Fermanagh .	Lurg . .	Magheraculmoney	Lowtherstown .	III.	208

(*a*) Including 7A. 0R. 10P. water.
(*b*) Including 15A. 1R. 6P. water.
(*c*) Including 22A. 0R. 20P. water.
(*d*) Including 20A. 3R. 25P. water.
(*e*) Including 3A. 1R. 20P. water.
(*f*) Including 8A. 3R. 7P. water.

No. of Sheet of the Ordnance Survey Maps.	Townlands and Towns.	Area in Statute Acres.	County.	Barony.	Parish.	Poor Law Union in 1857.	Townland Census of 1851, Part I.	
		A. R. P.					Vol.	Page
54, 55	*Needle Island or Snahadaun* . .	1 2 24	Galway . .	Moycullen .	Kilcummin . .	Oughterard . .	IV.	69
71	Neesha . . .	1,319 0 27	Kerry . .	Iveragh . .	Glanbehy . .	Cahersiveen . .	II.	196
24, 25	Neigham . .	470 0 0	Kilkenny . .	Gowran . .	Dungarvan . .	Thomastown .	I.	94
17	Neillstown .	146 0 8	Dublin . .	Uppercross .	Clondalkin . .	Dublin South .	I.	39
24	Neillstown . .	484 0 34	Meath . .	Lower Navan .	Ardbraccan . .	Navan . .	I.	214
30, 36	Neillstown . .	186 0 4	Meath . .	Lune . .	Kildalkey . .	Trim . .	I.	208
25	Neillstown Park .	20 1 12	Meath . .	Lower Navan .	Ardbraccan . .	Navan . .	I.	214
52	Nemestown . .	246 0 16	Wexford . .	Bargy . .	Kilmore . .	Wexford . .	I.	306
20, 21	Nenagh North .	776 0 30	Tipperary, N.R.	Lower Ormond .	Nenagh . .	Nenagh . .	II.	287
20	Nenagh South .	64 2 37*d*	Tipperary, N.R.	Upper Ormond .	Nenagh . .	Nenagh . .	II.	293
20, 21	NENAGH T. . .	—	Tipperary, N.R.	{ Lower Ormond { Upper Ormond }	Nenagh . .	Nenagh . .	II.	{ 287 { 293
63	Nethertown . .	113 1 35	Donegal . .	Raphoe . .	Taughboyne .	Strabane . .	III.	144
53	Nethertown .	99 0 15	Wexford . .	Forth . .	Carn . .	Wexford . .	I.	309
71, 72	Nettleville Demesne	508 1 25*b*	Cork, E.R. .	East Muskerry .	Cannaway . .	Macroom . .	II.	102
16, 17	Nevillescourt .	121 3 36*c*	Wexford . .	Gorey . .	Ballycanew . .	Gorey . .	I.	316
25	Nevinstown . .	239 3 30	Meath . .	Lower Navan .	Donaghmore .	Navan . .	I.	214
11, 14	Nevinstown East .	138 1 0	Dublin . .	Nethercross .	Swords . .	Balrothery . .	I.	32
11	Nevinstown West .	33 3 31	Dublin . .	Nethercross .	Swords . .	Balrothery . .	I.	32
4, 7	Nevitt . . .	351 2 31	Dublin . .	Balrothery East .	Lusk . .	Balrothery . .	I.	21
28, 29	Newabbey . .	203 2 0*c*	Kildare . .	Naas South .	Brannockstown .	Naas . .	I.	64
2	Newacre . . .	76 0 32*d*	Carlow . .	Carlow . .	Painestown . .	Carlow . .	I.	2
69, 78	Newantrim . .	206 3 30*e*	Mayo . .	Carra . .	Aglish . .	Castlebar . .	IV.	124
11	Newbarn . .	374 3 26	Dublin . .	Nethercross .	Kilsallaghan .	Balrothery . .	I.	31
35	Newbawn . .	1,124 0 27	Wexford . .	Shelmaliere West	Newbawn . .	New Ross . .	I.	334
30	Newbawn . .	419 1 9	Wicklow . .	Arklow . .	Dunganstown .	Rathdrum . .	I.	344
37, 42	Newbay . . .	138 3 3	Wexford . .	Forth . .	St. Peters . .	Wexford . .	I.	314
32	Newberry . .	294 2 3*f*	Cork, E.R. .	Duhallow . .	Kilshannig . .	Mallow . .	II.	74
48	NEW BIRMINGHAM T.	—	Tipperary, S.R.	Slievardagh .	Kilcooly . .	Urlingford . .	II.	334
17	Newbliss . .	317 1 35	Monaghan . .	Dartree . .	Killeevan . .	Clones . .	III.	268
17	NEWBLISS T. . .	—	Monaghan . .	Dartree . .	Killeevan . .	Clones . .	III.	268
112	Newborough . .	137 2 23	Cork, E.R. .	Kinalea . .	Kilmonoge . .	Kinsale . .	II.	95
32, 46	Newbridge . .	200 3 9	Galway . .	Killian . .	Killian . .	Mountbellew .	IV.	45
11	Newbridge . .	183 2 19	Wexford . .	Gorey . .	Toome . .	Gorey . .	I.	321
12	Newbridge Demesne	349 2 11	Dublin . .	Nethercross .	Donabate . .	Balrothery . .	I.	30
23	NEWBRIDGE T. .	—	Kildare . .	Connell . .	Great Connell . Morristown Biller }	Naas . .	I.	{ 155 { 156
17	Newbristy North .	126 2 6	Westmeath .	Rathconrath .	Ballymorin . .	Mullingar . .	I.	282
17, 24	Newbristy South .	55 2 37	Westmeath .	Rathconrath .	Ballymorin . .	Mullingar . .	I.	282
15	Newbrook . .	53 2 2	Dublin . .	Coolock . .	Coolock . .	Dublin North .	I.	27
27	Newbrook . .	114 3 25	Leitrim . .	Leitrim . .	Kiltoghert . .	Carr. on Shannon	IV.	102
47	Newbrook . .	82 0 17	Tipperary, N.R.	Eliogarty . .	Galbooly . .	Thurles . .	II.	270
29, 30	New Buildings .	123 0 25	Tyrone . .	Dungannon Upper	Derryloran . .	Cookstown . .	III.	307
21	New Buildings or Maddydoo Lower	90 2 30	Antrim . .	Kilconway .	Finvoy . .	Ballymoney . .	III.	26
11, 12	New Buildings North	319 1 31	Antrim . .	Upper Dunluce .	Ballymoney .	Ballymoney . .	III.	19
17	New Buildings South	466 0 4	Antrim . .	Upper Dunluce .	Ballymoney .	Ballymoney . .	III.	19
20	NEW BUILDINGS T.	—	Londonderry .	Tirkeeran . .	Clondermot .	Londonderry .	III.	248
62	Newcastle . .	477 0 8	Cork, E.R. .	Barretts . .	Grenagh . .	Cork . .	II.	49
25, 32	Newcastle . .	226 2 22	Down . .	Ards Upper .	Slanes . .	Downpatrick .	III.	161
82, 94	Newcastle . .	512 2 35*g*	Galway . .	Galway . .	Rahoon . .	Galway . .	IV.	38
86, 87	Newcastle . .	611 2 25	Galway . .	Kilconnell .	Aughrim . .	Ballinasloe .	IV.	39
86	Newcastle . .	136 0 11	Galway . .	Kilconnell .	Killallaghtan .	Ballinasloe .	IV.	41
31, 32	Newcastle . .	232 3 0	Galway . .	Tiaquin . .	Kilkerrin . .	Glennamaddy .	IV.	77
71, 72	Newcastle . .	218 2 10	Galway . .	Tiaquin . .	Monivea . .	Loughrea . .	IV.	79
5, 6	Newcastle . .	697 0 21	Limerick . .	Clanwilliam .	Kilmurry . .	Limerick . .	II.	225
27	Newcastle . .	530 1 21*h*	Longford . .	Shrule . .	Forgney . .	Ballymahon .	I.	166
71	Newcastle . .	438 1 15	Mayo . .	Gallen . .	Meelick . .	Swineford . .	IV.	150
9	Newcastle . .	808 2 26*i*	Meath . .	Fore . .	Oldcastle . .	Oldcastle . .	I.	202
4	Newcastle . .	474 3 15	Meath . .	Lower Kells .	Moynalty . .	Kells . .	I.	204
48	Newcastle . .	1,359 3 30	Meath . .	Lower Moyfenrath .	Rathcore . .	Trim . .	I.	211
2, 5	Newcastle . .	176 1 36*j*	Meath . .	Morgallion .	Enniskeen . .	Kells . .	I.	209
86	Newcastle . .	162 1 5	Tipperary, S.R.	Iffa and Offa West .	Templetenny .	Clogheen . .	II.	320
36	Newcastle . .	67 0 26	Westmeath .	Clonlonan .	Kilcleagh . .	Athlone . .	I.	261
33	Newcastle . .	508 2 6	Westmeath .	Fartullagh .	Clonfad . .	Mullingar . .	I.	268
3	Newcastle . .	358 0 26	Westmeath .	Fore . .	Lickbla . .	Granard . .	I.	270
42, 47	Newcastle . .	237 0 17	Wexford . .	Bargy . .	Kilmannan . .	Wexford . .	I.	306
37	Newcastle . .	102 1 35	Wexford . .	Shelmaliere East	Kilpatrick . .	Wexford . .	I.	331
35, 40	Newcastle . .	845 2 3	Wexford . .	Shelmaliere West	Clongeen . .	New Ross . .	I.	333
20	Newcastle Demesne	136 2 6	Dublin . .	Newcastle .	Newcastle . .	Celbridge . .	I.	04
90	Newcastle Farm .	208 1 36	Dublin . .	Newcastle .	Newcastle . .	Celbridge . .	I.	34
37	Newcastle Lower .	72 1 16	Wexford . .	Shelmaliere East	Tikillin . .	Wexford . .	I.	231
13, 19	Newcastle Lower .	189 0 4	Wicklow . .	Newcastle .	Newcastle Lower .	Rathdrum . .	I.	353

(*a*) Including 1A. 0R. 37P. detached portion.
(*b*) Including 15A. 1R. 1P. water.
(*c*) Including 6A. 2R. 19P. water.
(*d*) Including 3A. 1R. 0P. River Barrow.

(*e*) Including 8A. 3R. 5P. water.
(*f*) Including 3A. 0R. 30P. water.
(*g*) Including 42A. 3R. 15P. water.

(*h*) Including 4A. 2R. 36P. water.
(*i*) Including 3A. 3R. 10P. detached portion.
(*j*) Including 16A. 3R. 38P. water.

No. of Sheet of the Ordnance Survey Maps.	Townlands and Towns.	Area in Statute Acres. A. R. P.	County.	Barony.	Parish.	Poor Law Union in 1857.	Townland Census of 1851, Part I. Vol.	Page
13, 19	Newcastle Middle	295 0 0	Wicklow	Newcastle	Newcastle Lower	Rathdrum	I.	353
20, 21	Newcastle North	151 1 39	Dublin	Newcastle	Newcastle	Celbridge	I.	34
20, 21	Newcastle South	183 0 15	Dublin	Newcastle	Newcastle	Celbridge	I.	34
49	NEWCASTLE T.	—	Down	Upper Iveagh, Lr. pt.	Kilcoe	Kilkeel	III.	173
20, 21	NEWCASTLE T.	—	Dublin	Newcastle	Newcastle	Celbridge	I.	34
36	NEWCASTLE T.	—	Limerick	Glenquin	Monagay / Newcastle	Newcastle	II.	{247 / 248
88	NEWCASTLE T.	—	Tipperary, S.R.	Iffa and Offa West	Newcastle	Clogheen	II.	319
19	NEWCASTLE T.	—	Wicklow	Newcastle	Newcastle Lower	Rathdrum	I.	353
37	Newcastle Upper	208 3 6	Wexford	Shelmaliere East	Tikillin	Wexford	I.	331
19	Newcastle Upper	351 2 39	Wicklow	Newcastle	Newcastle Lower	Rathdrum	I.	353
95	Newcestown	666 0 38	Cork, W.R.	Kinalmeaky	Murragh	Bandon	II.	152
76, 77	Newchapel	233 1 36	Tipperary, S.R.	Iffa and Offa East	Newchapel	Clonmel	II.	315
31, 35	Newchurch	394 0 0	Kilkenny	Kells	Kilmaganny	Carrick on Suir	I.	109
96	Newchurch Glebe	2 0 23	Donegal	Banagh	Kilcar	Glenties	III.	109
4, 8	Newcourt	369 3 7	Wicklow	Rathdown	Bray	Rathdown	I.	354
20, 26, 27	Newdown	1,406 0 14	Westmeath	Farbill	Killucan	Mullingar	I.	267
13, 18	Newengland	308 3 1	Kilkenny	Crannagh	Tullaroan	Kilkenny	I.	88
37	Newfarm	54 1 21	Kilkenny	Ida	The Rower	New Ross	I.	104
67	Newfield	151 2 36	Mayo	Burrishoole	Burrishoole	Newport	IV.	119
84	Newford	219 2 15	Galway	Athenry	Athenry	Loughrea	IV.	4
32	Newforest	995 2 19	Galway	Tiaquin	Kilkerrin	Glennamaddy	IV.	77
33	Newfort	195 3 12	Wexford	Ballaghkeen	Castle-ellis	Enniscorthy	I.	293
2	Newgarden	209 1 37a	Carlow	Carlow	Painestown	Carlow	I.	2
1, 6	Newgarden North	203 2 39	Limerick	Clanwilliam	Stradbally	Limerick	II.	226
43	Newgarden or Pollaturk	425 0 23	Galway	Clare	Belclare	Tuam	IV.	17
6	Newgarden South	6 3 38	Limerick	Clanwilliam	Stradbally	Limerick	II.	226
75	NEW GLANMIRE T.	—	Cork, E.R.	Barrymore	Caherlag	Cork	II.	52
36	New Glebe	17 0 35	Roscommon	Ballintober South	Kilgefin	Roscommon	IV.	189
19, 26	Newgrange	782 3 39b	Meath	Upper Slane	Monknewtown	Drogheda	I.	224
19, 27	Newgrove	320 0 32	Cork, E.R.	Condons&Clangibbon	Glanworth	Mitchelstown	II.	61
32, 46	Newgrove	154 3 36	Galway	Killian	Killian	Mountbellew	IV.	45
98	Newgrove	619 0 26	Galway	Leitrim	Kilreekill	Loughrea	IV.	55
33, 37	Newgrove	409 1 27	Kilkenny	Ida	Dysartmoon	New Ross	I.	101
9	Newgrove	144 3 28	Monaghan	Monaghan	Tedavnet	Monaghan	III.	279
23	Newgrove	34 1 32	Westmeath	Kilkenny West	Drumraney	Ballymahon	I.	273
26,27,34,35	Newgrove or Ballyslattery	754 0 12c	Clare	Tulla Upper	Tulla	Tulla	II.	41
8	Newhaggard	363 2 7d	Dublin	Balrothery East	Lusk	Balrothery	I.	21
3	Newhaggard	119 2 36	Dublin	Balrothery West	Garristown	Dunshaughlin	I.	22
36	Newhaggard	622 0 7e	Meath	Lower Moyfenrath	Trim	Trim	I.	212
27	Newhaggard	188 3 39	Meath	Upper Duleek	Kilsharvan	Drogheda	I.	198
41	Newhall	561 1 39f	Clare	Islands	Killone	Ennis	II.	30
114, 123	Newhall	168 1 15	Galway	Kiltartan	Kiltartan	Gort	IV.	48
18, 19	Newhall	570 0 0g	Kildare	Connell	Ladytown	Naas	I.	55
18	Newhall	7 0 29	Kildare	Connell	Oldconnell	Naas	I.	56
18	Newhall	94 3 7	Louth	Ferrard	Dunleer	Ardee	I.	181
43, 49	Newhall	105 0 10	Tipperary, S.R.	Slievardagh	Kilcooly	Urlingford	II.	334
38	Newhall or Gorteenafoly	125 0 39	King's Co.	Clonlisk	Ettagh	Roscrea	I.	130
17	Newhill	99 1 34	Antrim	Upper Dunluce	Ballymoney	Ballymoney	III.	19
42, 48	Newhill	636 0 2	Tipperary, N.R.	Eliogarty	Twomileborris	Thurles	II.	274
20, 21	Newhouse	176 1 26	Kilkenny	Gowran	Gowran	Kilkenny	I.	95
24, 28	Newhouse	598 3 34	Kilkenny	Gowran	Tullaherin	Thomastown	I.	100
21, 22	Newhouse	225 1 5	Louth	Ferrard	Termonfeckin	Drogheda	I.	182
46, 47	Newhouse	202 0 20	Wexford	Bargy	Kilcowan	Wexford	I.	305
47	Newhouse	48 2 39	Wexford	Forth	Ballymore	Wexford	I.	308
48	Newhouses	55 2 18	Wexford	Forth	Kilrane	Wexford	I.	311
48	Newhouses	46 3 29	Wexford	Forth	St. Helens	Wexford	I.	314
69	NEWINN T.	—	Tipperary, S.R.	Middlethird	Knockgraffon	Cashel	II.	328
24	Newland North	757 2 6	Kildare	Naas South	Killashee	Naas	I.	65
40,41,46,47	Newlands	446 3 30	Antrim	Lower Belfast	Glynn	Larne	III.	8
21	Newlands	56 2 11	Dublin	Uppercross	Clondalkin	Dublin South	I.	39
23	Newlands	148 0 11	Kilkenny	Shillelogher	Burnchurch	Callan	I.	113
21	Newlands Demesne	55 2 27	Dublin	Uppercross	Clondalkin	Dublin South	I.	39
21	Newlands Demesne	70 1 11	Dublin	Uppercross	Tallaght	Dublin South	I.	42
24	Newland South	144 0 15	Kildare	Naas South	Killashee	Naas	I.	65
24	Newland West	205 0 39	Kildare	Naas South	Killashee	Naas	I.	65
6	Newlawn	300 2 35	Tipperary, N.R.	Lower Ormond	Terryglass	Borrisokane	II.	288
42, 51	Newmarket	181 0 33	Clare	Bunratty Lower	Tomfinlough	Ennis	II.	7
14, 22	Newmarket	144 3 14	Cork, E.R.	Duhallow	Clonfert	Kanturk	II.	69
31	Newmarket	185 1 37	Kilkenny	Knocktopher	Aghaviller	Thomastown	I.	111
51	NEWMARKET ON FERGUS T.	—	Clare	Bunratty Lower	Tomfinlough	Ennis	II.	7

(a) Including 5A. 0R. 16P. River Barrow.
(b) Including 31A. 3R. 32P. water.
(c) Including 13A. 3R. 33P. water.
(d) Including 26A. 0R. 7P. detached portion.
(e) Including 20A. 0R. 8P. water.
(f) Including 26A. 0R. 21P. water.
(g) Including 3A. 0R. 22P. water.

5 B

No. of Sheet of the Ordnance Survey Maps.	Townlands and Towns.	Area in Statute Acres.	County.	Barony.	Parish.	Poor Law Union in 1857.	Townland Census of 1851, Part I.	
		A. R. P.					Vol.	Page
14, 22	NEWMARKET T.	—	Cork, E.R.	Duhallow	Clonfert	Kanturk	II.	69
46	Newmill	289 2 13	Donegal	Kilmacrenan	Aughnish	Milford	III.	122
14, 19	Neworchard	208 3 3	Kilkenny	Gowran	St. John's	Kilkenny	I.	98
5	Newpaddocks	77 3 32	Wicklow	Lower Talbotstown	Blessington	Naas	I.	358
50	New Park	80 2 1	Antrim	Upper Antrim	Antrim	Antrim	III.	5
52	Newpark	201 2 16	Clare	Bunratty Lower	Feenagh	Ennis	II.	4
33, 34	Newpark	106 0 13	Clare	Bunratty Upper	Templemaley	Ennis	II.	11
11	Newpark	351 3 31	Dublin	Castleknock	Ward	Dublin North	I.	25
23	Newpark	121 0 8	Dublin	Rathdown	Kill	Rathdown	I.	36
1, 5	Newpark	47 0 10	Fermanagh	Lurg	Drumkeeran	Lowtherstown	III.	207
17, 18	Newpark	220 3 24	Kildare	Connell	Kilmeage	Naas	I.	55
30	Newpark	67 0 20	Kilkenny	Kells	Kilmaganny	Callan	I.	109
20, 29	Newpark	111 0 38	Limerick	Connello Lower	Croagh	Rathkeale	II.	228
47, 55	Newpark	139 1 25	Limerick	Coshlea	Effin	Kilmallock	II.	238
21	Newpark	470 0 0	Longford	Rathcline	Cashel	Ballymahon	I.	163
61, 62	Newpark	468 1 15	Mayo	Gallen	Kilconduff	Swineford	IV.	148
33	Newpark	276 2 39	Sligo	Corran	Kilmorgan	Sligo	IV.	227
53, 61	Newpark	667 2 21	Tipperary, S.R.	Middlethird	Ballysheehan	Cashel	II.	325
49	Newpark	307 0 34	Tipperary, S.R.	Slievardagh	Kilcooly	Urlingford	II.	334
49	New Park	339 0 7a	Tyrone	Omagh East	Dromore	Omagh	III.	311
21, 22	Newpark	211 3 28	Wicklow	Upper Talbotstown	Donaghmore	Baltinglass	I.	363
3, 7	Newpark or Loughanavagh	172 3 14	Westmeath	Fore	St. Feighins	Castletowndelvin	I.	272
19	Newpark Lower	151 3 32b	Kilkenny	Gowran and Municipal Borough	St. Maul's	Kilkenny	I.	99
19	Newpark Upper	160 1 35	Kilkenny	Gowran	St. Maul's	Kilkenny	I.	99
5	Newpass Demesne	131 1 30	Westmeath	Moygoish	Rathaspick	Granard	I.	280
24	Newport	387 3 24c	Longford	Ardagh	Rathreagh	Ballymahon	I.	153
67, 68	Newport	69 0 12	Mayo	Burrishoole	Burrishoole	Newport	IV.	119
31, 37	Newport	303 3 10	Tipperary, N.R.	Owney and Arra	Kilvellane	Newport	II.	296
34, 37	Newport East	329 3 25	Waterford	Coshmore & Coshbride	Kilcockan	Lismore	II.	343
68	NEWPORT T.	—	Mayo	Burrishoole	Burrishoole	Newport	IV.	120
37	NEWPORT T.	—	Tipperary, N.R.	Owney and Arra	Kilvellane	Nenagh	II.	296
34, 37	Newport West	137 1 38	Waterford	Coshmore & Coshbride	Kilcockan	Lismore	II.	343
2, 3	Newquay	291 0 13	Clare	Burren	Oughtmama	Ballyvaghan	II.	14
11	Newragh	13 2 12	Louth	Louth	Louth	Dundalk	I.	184
12, 15	Newrath	494 3 35	Louth	Louth	Dromiskin	Dundalk	I.	183
11	Newrath	77 3 24	Louth	Louth	Louth	Dundalk	I.	184
11	Newrath	267 0 32	Meath	Lower Kells	Kilbeg	Kells	I.	203
19	Newrath	195 0 25	Meath	Upper Slane	Slane	Navan	I.	225
9	Newrath	553 0 5	Waterford	Gaultiere	Kilculliheen	Waterford	II.	363
25	Newrath	267 2 16	Wicklow	Newcastle	Rathnew	Rathdrum	I.	354
7	Newrath Big	103 2 19	Meath	Lower Slane	Siddan	Ardee	I.	224
16	Newrath Big	153 0 4	Meath	Upper Kells	Kells	Kells	I.	206
16, 17	Newrath Little	117 3 39	Meath	Upper Kells	Kells	Kells	I.	206
31	Newross	299 3 0	Tipperary, N.R.	Owney and Arra	Kilnarath	Nenagh	II.	296
29	Newross	102 1 23	Wexford	Bantry	St. Mary's	New Ross	I.	302
29	New Ross T.		Wexford	Bantry	St. Mary's	New Ross	I.	302
63, 71	Newrow	122 3 38	Donegal	Raphoe	Clonleigh	Strabane	III.	135
70	Newrow	47 2 39	Donegal	Raphoe	Raphoe	Strabane	III.	141
20	Newrow	70 1 5	Kildare	South Salt	Kilteel	Naas	I.	77
58, 64	Newry	161 3 34	Tyrone	Clogher	Clogher	Clogher	III.	293
42, 46	Newry	1,274 1 27	Wicklow	Shillelagh	Moyacomb	Shillelagh	I.	358
26	NEWRY T.	—	Armagh	Orior Upper	Newry	Newry	III.	59
46, 50	NEWRY T.	—	Down	Lordship of Newry	Newry	Newry	III.	182
3, 6	Newstone	721 3 10	Meath	Lower Slane	Drumcondra	Ardee	I.	223
14	Newstown	646 1 28	Carlow	Forth	Ardoyne	Carlow	I.	223
26, 32	Newtate or Drummon	210 2 23	Fermanagh	Clanawley	Killesher	Enniskillen	III.	192
25	Newtown	34 3 17	Antrim	Lower Glenarm	Ardclinis	Larne	III.	21
29	Newtown	425 2 2	Armagh	Orior Upper	Killevy	Newry	III.	58
12, 16	Newtown	887 0 22	Carlow	Idrone East	Agha	Carlow	I.	6
24	Newtown	823 3 28	Carlow	St. Mullins Lower	St. Mullins	New Ross	I.	13
25	Newtown	107 3 25	Cavan	Clanmahon	Kilmore	Cavan	III.	78
7	Newtown	56 0 19	Cavan	Tullyhaw	Kinawley	Bawnboy	III.	93
9	Newtown	93 2 20d	Cavan	Tullyhaw	Templeport	Bawnboy	III.	95
26, 32	Newtown	120 0 23	Cavan	Upper Loughtee	Denn	Cavan	III.	84
2, 5	Newtown	805 3 32	Clare	Burren	Drumcreehy	Ballyvaghan	II.	12
36	Newtown	138 2 13	Clare	Tulla Lower	Killuran	Tulla	II.	36
53	Newtown	264 2 30	Clare	Tulla Lower	Kiltenanlea	Limerick	II.	37
32	Newtown	78 3 32	Cork, E.R.	Duhallow	Mallow	Mallow	II.	75
8	Newtown	520 3 39	Cork, E.R.	Fermoy	Ballyhay	Mitchelstown	II.	76
17	Newtown	203 0 11	Cork, E.R.	Fermoy	Doneraile	Mallow	II.	73
118	Newtown	330 0 3	Cork, W.R.	Bantry	Kilmocomoge	Bantry	II.	121

(a) Including 7A. 1R. 3P. water.
(b) { Within the Municipal Boundary, 68A. 2R. 15P.
  { Without the Municipal Boundary, 83A. 1R. 17P.
(c) Including 17A. 0R. 39P. water.
(d) Including 17A. 3R. 23P. water.

No. of Sheet of the Ordnance Survey Maps.	Townlands and Towns.	Area in Statute Acres.			County.	Barony.	Parish.	Poor Law Union in 1857.	Townland Census of 1851, Part I.	
		A.	R.	P.					Vol.	Page
51, 52, 54	Newtown	432	3	2	Down	Upper Iveagh, Up. pt.	Kilbroney	Kilkeel	III.	176
1, 4	Newtown	247	0	16	Dublin	Balrothery East	Balscaddan	Balrothery	I.	20
3, 6	Newtown	741	3	34	Dublin	Balrothery West	Garristown	Dunshaughlin	I.	22
7	Newtown	309	0	17	Dublin	Balrothery West	Westpalstown	Balrothery	I.	23
15	Newtown	199	0	30	Dublin	Coolock	Coolock	Dublin North	I.	27
14	Newtown	340	3	37	Dublin	Coolock	St. Margarets	Dublin North	I.	29
11, 12	Newtown	232	3	30a	Dublin	Nethercross	Swords	Balrothery	I.	32
25, 26	Newtown	230	2	19	Dublin	Rathdown	Kiltiernan	Rathdown	I.	36
22, 25	Newtown	450	0	30	Dublin	Uppercross	Cruagh	Dublin South	I.	39
15	Newtown	172	0	27	Fermanagh	Magheraboy	Devenish	Enniskillen	III.	211
7	Newtown	497	1	18	Galway	Ballymoe	Ballynakill	Glennamaddy	IV.	5
46, 47	Newtown	88	3	2	Galway	Killian	Killeroran	Mountbellew	IV.	44
122	Newtown	226	2	6	Galway	Kiltartan	Kilmacduagh	Gort	IV.	48
114, 123	Newtown	192	1	2	Galway	Kiltartan	Kiltartan	Gort	IV.	48
118	Newtown	70	2	28	Galway	Longford	Kilmalinoge	Portumna	IV.	59
68	Newtown	391	1	5	Galway	Moycullen	Moycullen	Galway	IV.	71
58	Newtown	385	3	33	Galway	Tiaquin	Abbeyknockmoy	Tuam	IV.	75
4	Newtown	427	0	25	Kildare	Ikeathy&Oughterany	Cloncurry	Celbridge	I.	57
40	Newtown	47	0	39	Kildare	Kilkea and Moone	Castledermot	Athy	I.	59
38	Newtown	207	1	29	Kildare	Kilkea and Moone	Killelan	Baltinglass	I.	60
40	Newtown	452	2	28	Kildare	Kilkea and Moone	Kineagh	Baltinglass	I.	61
19, 20	Newtown	74	0	22	Kildare	Naas North	Rathmore	Naas	I.	62
19, 20	Newtown	534	1	1	Kildare	Naas North	Tipper	Naas	I.	63
19, 24	Newtown	206	1	11	Kildare	Naas South	Killashee	Naas	I.	65
5, 10	Newtown	347	2	8	Kildare	North Salt	Laraghbryan	Celbridge	I.	75
6, 11	Newtown	216	0	4	Kildare	North Salt	Leixlip	Celbridge	I.	75
22, 27	Newtown	267	1	17	Kildare	Offaly East	Kildare	Naas	I.	70
17	Newtown	525	3	39	Kildare	Offaly East	Rathangan	Edenderry	I.	71
17, 22	Newtown	380	1	20	Kildare	Offaly East	Tully	Naas	I.	71
27, 28	Newtown	373	3	11	Kildare	Offaly West	Ballyshannon	Athy	I.	72
11, 15	Newtown	289	1	28b	Kildare	South Salt	Donaghcumper	Celbridge	I.	76
19	Newtown	95	1	6	Kildare	South Salt	Kill	Naas	I.	77
9, 13	Newtown	133	3	21	Kilkenny	Crannagh	Clomantagh	Urlingford	I.	85
12, 17	Newtown	328	1	23	Kilkenny	Crannagh	Kilcooly	Kilkenny	I.	86
19	Newtown	902	2	19	Kilkenny	Crannagh	St. Canice	Kilkenny	I.	87
10	Newtown	291	2	35	Kilkenny	Fassadinin	Mothell	Castlecomer	I.	90
29	Newtown	197	1	27	Kilkenny	Gowran	Graiguenamanagh	Thomastown	I.	95
19	Newtown	134	0	19	Kilkenny	Gowran	St. John's	Kilkenny	I.	98
28	Newtown	500	0	13	Kilkenny	Gowran	Thomastown	Thomastown	I.	99
43	Newtown	82	2	20	Kilkenny	Ida	Dunkitt	Waterford	I.	101
43	Newtown	76	2	22	Kilkenny	Iverk	Kilmacow	Waterford	I.	106
31	Newtown	189	0	22	Kilkenny	Kells	Dunnamaggan	Callan	I.	108
39	Newtown	1,199	1	29	King's Co.	Ballybritt	Roscomroe	Parsonstown	I.	126
16	Newtown	413	2	4	King's Co.	Ballycowan	Rahan	Tullamore	I.	129
45	Newtown	125	3	32	King's Co.	Clonlisk	Kilcomin	Roscrea	I.	131
11, 19	Newtown	822	0	1	King's Co.	Coolestown	Castlejordan	Edenderry	I.	132
29	Newtown	319	3	9	King's Co.	Garrycastle	Lusmagh	Parsonstown	I.	137
17, 25	Newtown	812	3	34	King's Co.	Geashill	Geashill	Tullamore	I.	140
2	Newtown	510	0	2	King's Co.	Kilcoursey	Kilcumreragh	Tullamore	I.	141
1	Newtown	249	3	22	King's Co.	Kilcoursey	Kilmanaghan	Tullamore	I.	141
23	Newtown	22	1	17	Limerick	Clanwilliam	Caherconlish	Limerick	II.	222
23	Newtown	56	1	14	Limerick	Clanwilliam	Inch St. Lawrence	Limerick	II.	224
5, 6	Newtown	457	3	28	Limerick	Clanwilliam	Kilmurry	Limerick	II.	225
24, 33	Newtown	410	3	30	Limerick	Coonagh	Tuogheluggin	Tipperary	II.	236
49	Newtown	289	0	1	Limerick	Coshlea	Galbally	Mitchelstown	II.	239
31, 32	Newtown	143	2	9	Limerick	Coshma	Bruff	Kilmallock	II.	242
11	Newtown	365	2	31	Limerick	Kenry	Kilcornan	Rathkeale	II.	249
4	Newtown	1,664	2	18	Limerick	Pubblebrien	Kilkeedy	Limerick	II.	252
40	Newtown	289	1	22	Limerick	Smallcounty	Hospital	Kilmallock	II.	260
22	Newtown	243	3	28	Limerick	Smallcounty	Kilpeacon	Croom	II.	260
24	Newtown	102	0	22	Longford	Ardagh	Rathreagh	Ballymahon	I.	153
18	Newtown	181	3	36	Longford	Moydow	Ballymacormick	Longford	I.	161
13	Newtown	101	0	30	Longford	Moydow	Killashee	Longford	I.	162
11	Newtown	65	2	0	Louth	Ardee	Louth	Dundalk	I.	173
22, 25	Newtown	451	2	27	Louth	Ferrard	Termonfeckin	Drogheda	I.	182
6, 11	Newtown	330	3	23	Louth	Louth	Louth	Dundalk	I.	184
99, 109	Newtown	517	0	1c	Mayo	Carra	Ballyovey	Ballinrobe	IV.	126
89, 90, 99	Newtown	475	1	30	Mayo	Carra	Burriscarra	Castlebar	IV.	127
24	Newtown	494	3	7	Mayo	Erris	Kilmore	Belmullet	IV.	146
39	Newtown	290	1	28d	Mayo	Tirawley	Kilbelfad	Ballina	IV.	168
15, 22	Newtown	279	0	23	Meath	Fore	Killallon	Oldcastle	I.	201
15	Newtown	261	3	6	Meath	Fore	Loughcrew	Oldcastle	I.	201
20	Newtown	129	2	13	Meath	Lower Duleek	Culp	Drogheda	I.	195

(a) Including 63A. 0R. 6P. detached portions.
(b) Including 7A. 2R. 32P. water.

(c) Including 103A. 2R. 5P. water.
(d) Including 10A. 1R. 7P. water.

No. of Sheet of the Ordnance Survey Maps.	Townlands and Towns.	Area in Statute Acres.			County.	Barony.	Parish.	Poor Law Union in 1857.	Townland Census of 1851, Part I.	
		A.	R.	P.					Vol.	Page
27	Newtown	344	3	14	Meath	Lower Duleek	Duleek	Drogheda	I.	195
26	Newtown	709	3	0	Meath	Lower Duleek	Knockcommon	Navan	I.	196
5, 11	Newtown	234	0	17	Meath	Lower Kells	Cruicetown	Kells	I.	202
5	Newtown	335	0	21	Meath	Lower Kells	Kilmainham	Kells	I.	203
11	Newtown	566	2	34	Meath	Lower Kells	Newtown	Kells	I.	204
44	Newtown	71	3	36	Meath	Ratoath	Ratoath	Dunshaughlin	I.	219
27, 33	Newtown	214	2	12	Meath	Upper Duleek	Ardcath	Drogheda	I.	197
36	Newtown	119	3	2a	Meath	Upper Navan	Newtownclonbun	Trim	I.	216
29, 35	Newtown	842	2	15	Queen's Co.	Clarmallagh	Aghmacart	Abbeyleix	I.	236
14	Newtown	158	0	13	Queen's Co.	Stradbally	Stradbally	Athy	I.	247
16, 22	Newtown	309	3	24	Queen's Co.	Upperwoods	Offerlane	Abbeyleix	I.	252
51	Newtown	140	0	21	Roscommon	Athlone	Drum	Athlone	IV.	180
24, 30	Newtown	566	1	7b	Roscommon	Ballintober North	Termonbarry	Strokestown	IV.	188
40, 42	Newtown	355	1	22	Roscommon	Ballintober South	Kilteevan	Roscommon	IV.	190
34	Newtown	593	1	14	Roscommon	Ballymoe	Oran	Roscommon	IV.	192
53	Newtown	278	3	34	Roscommon	Moycarn	Creagh	Ballinasloe	IV.	206
29	Newtown	381	2	35	Roscommon	Roscommon	Bumlin	Strokestown	IV.	208
5	Newtown	154	3	8	Sligo	Carbury	Ahamlish	Sligo	IV.	219
22	Newtown	410	3	34	Sligo	Tireragh	Castleconor	Dromore West	IV.	232
47, 48	Newtown	160	3	25	Tipperary, N.R.	Eliogarty	Ballymurreen	Thurles	II.	269
46, 47	Newtown	303	0	5	Tipperary, N.R.	Eliogarty	Holycross	Thurles	II.	270
18, 24	Newtown	105	3	4	Tipperary, N.R.	Ikerrin	Bourney	Roscrea	II.	274
18	Newtown	158	0	4	Tipperary, N.R.	Ikerrin	Corbally	Roscrea	II.	275
40	Newtown	99	1	9	Tipperary, N.R.	Kilnamanagh Upper	Ballycahill	Thurles	II.	277
40	Newtown	63	1	16	Tipperary, N.R.	Kilnamanagh Upper	Templebeg	Thurles	II.	279
1, 4	Newtown	189	2	19	Tipperary, N.R.	Lower Ormond	Dorrha	Parsonstown	II.	283
19	Newtown	259	1	39	Tipperary, N.R.	Owney and Arra	Templeachally	Nenagh	II.	297
14, 20	Newtown	352	2	8	Tipperary, N.R.	Owney and Arra	Youghalarra	Nenagh	II.	298
21	Newtown	150	1	2	Tipperary, N.R.	Upper Ormond	Ballymackey	Nenagh	II.	289
66,67,73,74	Newtown	405	2	25	Tipperary, S.R.	Clanwilliam	Clonbeg	Tipperary	II.	305
59	Newtown	212	3	14	Tipperary, S.R.	Clanwilliam	Solloghod-beg	Tipperary	II.	310
77, 83	Newtown	156	0	19	Tipperary, S.R.	Iffa and Offa East	Killaloan	Clonmel	II.	314
51	Newtown	56	1	32	Tipperary, S.R.	Kilnamanagh Lower	Aghacrew	Tipperary	II.	322
70	Newtown	107	3	28	Tipperary, S.R.	Middlethird	Baptistgrange	Cashel	II.	325
53	Newtown	313	1	23	Tipperary, S.R.	Middlethird	Erry	Cashel	II.	326
69, 76	Newtown	159	2	39	Tipperary, S.R.	Middlethird	Knockgraffon	Cashel	II.	328
37	Newtown	154	2	18	Waterford	Coshmore&Coshbride	Templemichael	Youghal	II.	349
38	Newtown	233	3	9	Waterford	Decies within Drum	Ardmore	Youghal	II.	350
37	Newtown	211	1	25	Waterford	Decies within Drum	Kinsalebeg	Youghal	II.	352
36	Newtown	96	1	2	Waterford	Decies without Drum	Dungarvan	Dungarvan	II.	355
22	Newtown	172	2	39	Waterford	Decies without Drum	Modelligo	Lismore	II.	359
15, 16	Newtown	227	2	36	Waterford	Decies without Drum	Rossmire	Kilmacthomas	II.	360
24	Newtown	157	0	7	Waterford	Decies without Drum	Stradbally	Kilmacthomas	II.	361
18	Newtown	272	1	2	Waterford	Gaultiere	Crooke	Waterford	II.	362
9, 10	Newtown	112	3	8	Waterford	Gaultiere	Kilcullihen	Waterford	II.	363
9	Newtown	148	2	1c	Waterford	Gaultiere and Municipal Borough	St. Johns Without	Waterford	II.	365
26	Newtown	344	2	36	Waterford	Middlethird	Drumcannon	Waterford	II.	366
25	Newtown	208	1	23	Waterford	Middlethird	Islandikane	Kilmacthomas	II.	367
8, 16	Newtown	142	3	11	Waterford	Middlethird	Kilmeadan	Waterford	II.	368
9	Newtown	395	2	37d	Westmeath	Delvin	Castletowndelvin	Castletowndelvin	I.	265
3	Newtown	131	0	19	Westmeath	Fore	Mayne	Granard	I.	271
19, 26	Newtown	181	0	27	Westmeath	Moyashel and Magheradernon	Mullingar	Mullingar	I.	275
16,17,23,24	Newtown	525	1	30	Westmeath	Rathconrath	Ballymore	Ballymahon	I.	282
17, 22	Newtown	201	2	9	Wexford	Ballaghkeen	Donaghmore	Gorey	I.	293
21	Newtown	205	2	31	Wexford	Ballaghkeen	Kilmuckridge	Gorey	I.	297
31	Newtown	345	0	25	Wexford	Bantry	Adamstown	New Ross	I.	299
18	Newtown	545	1	23	Wexford	Bantry	Killann	Enniscorthy	I.	300
45	Newtown	453	2	17	Wexford	Bargy	Bannow	Wexford	I.	304
46	Newtown	59	3	14	Wexford	Bargy	Killag	Wexford	I.	306
52	Newtown	114	1	37	Wexford	Bargy	Kilmore	Wexford	I.	306
52	Newtown	122	1	17	Wexford	Bargy	Kilturk	Wexford	I.	307
41	Newtown	245	3	31	Wexford	Bargy	Taghmon	Wexford	I.	307
48	Newtown	94	0	20	Wexford	Forth	Kilscoran	Wexford	I.	311
42	Newtown	82	0	26	Wexford	Forth	Rathmacknee	Wexford	I.	313
37	Newtown	34	3	30	Wexford	Forth	St. Peters	Wexford	I.	314
15	Newtown	247	2	21	Wexford	Scarawalsh	Ferns	Enniscorthy	I.	323
19	Newtown	422	3	6	Wexford	Scarawalsh	Monart	Enniscorthy	I.	324
37	Newtown	342	1	23	Wexford	Shelmaliere West	Carrick	Wexford	I.	332
31	Newtown	106	3	33	Wicklow	Arklow	Drumkay	Rathdrum	I.	343
9	Newtown	393	3	16	Wicklow	Lower Talbotstown	Hollywood	Baltinglass	I.	361
7	Newtown	150	2	5	Wicklow	Rathdown	Kilmacanoge	Rathdown	I.	356

(a) Including 4A. 2R. 25P. water.
(b) Including 3A. 2R. 22P. water.
(c) { Within the Municipal Boundary, 145A. 1R. 11P.
{ Without the Municipal Boundary, 3A. 0R. 30P.
(d) Including 5A. 2r. 38P. water.

No. of Sheet of the Ordnance Survey Maps.	Townlands and Towns.	Area in Statute Acres.			County.	Barony.	Parish.	Poor Law Union in 1857.	Townland Census of 1851. Part I.	
		A.	R.	P.					Vol.	Page
38, 43	Newtown	393	2	35	Wicklow	Shillelagh	Mullinacuff	Shillelagh	I.	358
21	Newtown	130	2	8	Wicklow	Upper Talbotstown	Donaghmore	Baltinglass	I.	363
27	Newtown	127	2	27	Wicklow	Upper Talbotstown	Kilranelagh	Baltinglass	I.	364
82	Newtownadam	327	3	14	Tipperary, S.R.	Iffa and Offa West	Caher	Clogheen	II.	318
39	Newtownallen	602	3	35	Kildare	Kilkea and Moone	Ballaghmoon	Athy	I.	59
14	NEWTOWN ANDERSON T.	—			Sligo	Carbury	Calry	Sligo	IV.	220
77, 83	Newtown nanner Demesne	227	0	19	Tipperary, S.R.	Iffa and Offa East	Kilsheelan	Clonmel	II.	314
5, 6	NEWTOWN ARDS T.	—			Down	Ards Lower / Castlereagh Lower	Newtownards	Newtownards	III.	{159 163}
7, 12	Newtownbabe	187	2	29	Louth	Upper Dundalk	Ballybarrack	Dundalk	I.	177
23, 27	Newtown (Baker)	647	2	16	Kilkenny	Shillelogher	Earlstown	Callan	I.	114
29, 30	Newtown or Ballyfallon	650	1	11	Meath	Lune	Athboy	Trim	I.	207
13	Newtown or Ballynoe	573	2	22	Carlow	Forth	Ardoyne	Carlow	I.	3
6, 7	Newtownbalregan	733	1	26a	Louth	Upper Dundalk	Castletown	Dundalk	I.	177
24	Newtown Baltracey	102	0	31	Kildare	Naas North	Tipper	Naas	I.	63
9	Newtownbarry	329	2	8b	Wexford	Scarawalsh	St. Marys Newtownbarry	Enniscorthy	I.	325
9	NEWTOWNBARRY T.	—			Wexford	Scarawalsh	St. Marys Newtownbarry	Enniscorthy	I.	325
45	NEWTOWN BELLEW T.	—			Galway	Tiaquin	Moylough	Mountbellew	IV.	80
31, 35	Newtownbert	813	3	6	Kildare	Narragh&Reban West	Kilberry	Athy	I.	68
46, 47	Newtown Big	170	2	34	Wexford	Bargy	Kilcowan	Wexford	I.	305
23	Newtown Blackrock	3	1	1	Dublin	Dublin	Monkstown	Rathdown	J.	30
23	Newtown Blackrock	127	2	34	Dublin	Rathdown	Monkstown	Rathdown	I.	36
114, 123	Newtownblake	202	1	23	Galway	Loughrea	Kilthomas	Gort	IV.	65
14	Newtownbond	385	1	16	Longford	Granard	Killoe	Granard	I.	157
19, 25	Newtownboswell	166	2	17	Wicklow	Newcastle	Killiskey	Rathdrum	I.	352
116	Newtownbracklagh	139	0	33	Galway	Leitrim	Duniry	Portumna	IV.	53
9	NEWTOWNBREDA T.	—			Down	Castlereagh Upper	Knockbreda	Lisburn	III.	165
73	Newtownburke	128	3	12	Donegal	Banagh	Inishkeel	Glenties	III.	106
40	NEWTOWN BUTLER T.	—			Fermanagh	Coole	Galloon	Clones	III.	200
—	NEWTOWN BUTLER T.	—			Galway	Dunkellin	Oranmore	Galway	IV.	32
28	Newtown Carradoan	101	3	17	Donegal	Kilmacrenan	Killygarvan	Milford	III.	128
38, 39	Newtowncarrigans	231	0	15	Roscommon	Ballymoe	Dunamon	Roscommon	IV.	191
23	Newtown Castlebyrn	84	3	1	Dublin	Rathdown	Monkstown	Rathdown	I.	37
2	Newtowncliffony	105	0	30	Sligo	Carbury	Ahamlish	Sligo	IV.	219
30, 36	Newtownclonbun	267	3	23	Meath	Upper Navan	Newtownclonbun	Trim	I.	216
41	Newtown or Cloncen	351	2	28	Meath	Upper Moyfenrath	Killyon	Trim	I.	213
45	Newtown Commons	300	3	32	Meath	Ratoath	Greenoge	Dunshaughlin	I.	218
29	Newtown or Commons	698	3	38	Wexford	Bantry	St. Mary's	New Ross	I.	302
8	Newtowncorduff	263	0	4	Dublin	Balrothery East	Lusk	Balrothery	I.	21
24	NEWTOWN CROMMELIN T.	—			Antrim	Kilconway	Newtown Crommelin	Ballymena	III.	27
46, 54	Newtowncunningham	247	1	8	Donegal	Raphoe	Allsaints	Londonderry	III.	134
46	NEWTOWN CUNNINGHAM T.	—			Donegal	Raphoe	Allsaints	Londonderry	III.	134
30	Newtown (Darcy)	277	1	2	Galway	Dunmore	Dunmore	Tuam	IV.	34
30	Newtown (Darcy)	41	3	29	Galway	Dunmore	Tuam	Tuam	IV.	36
11,12,14,15	Newtowndarver	703	1	36	Louth	Louth	Darver	Dundalk	I.	183
63	NEWTOWN DILLON T.	—			Mayo	Costello	Kilbeagh	Swineford	IV.	141
13, 18	Newtowndonore	873	1	32	Kildare	Clane	Downings	Naas	I.	54
63	Newtowndrangan	784	2	25	Tipperary, S.R.	Middlethird	Drangan	Cashel	II.	326
93	Newtowndrumgornan	339	2	15	Donegal	Banagh	Killymard	Donegal	III.	111
66	Newtown East	183	2	35	Clare	Moyarta	Moyarta	Kilrush	II.	34
99	Newtowneyre	181	2	6	Galway	Longford	Kiltormer	Ballinasloe	IV.	60
12	Newtownfane	131	1	17	Louth	Upper Dundalk	Louth	Dundalk	I.	179
28, 35	Newtown Farragher	759	3	23	Roscommon	Ballymoe	Cloonygormican	Castlereagh	IV.	191
22	Newtownflanigan	134	0	4	Longford	Ratheline	Cashel	Ballymahon	I.	163
8	NEWTOWN FORBES T.	—			Longford	Longford	Clongesh	Longford	I.	158
45	Newtowntore	117	1	26	Donegal	Kilmacrenan	Aughnish	Letterkenny	III.	122
23, 24	Newtown Girley	675	3	28	Meath	Upper Kells	Girley	Kells	I.	205
122, 128	Newtown (Glynn)	102	3	10c	Galway	Kiltartan	Kilmacduagh	Gort	IV.	48
26	Newtowngore	171	2	2.d	Leitrim	Carrigallen	Carrigallen	Bawnboy	IV.	90
26	NEWTOWN GORE T.	—			Leitrim	Carrigallen	Carrigallen	Bawnboy	IV.	90
24, 25	Newtown Great	469	1	25	Kildare	Naas North	Rathmore	Naas	I.	62
45	Newtowngrove or Grovehall	196	3	6	Donegal	Kilmacrenan	Kilmacrenan	Millford	III.	129
11	Newtown (Guest)	212	0	31	Tipperary, N.R.	Lower Ormond	Modreeny	Borrisokane	II.	287
55	Newtownhamilton	52	1	14	Donegal	Raphoe	Killea	Londonderry	III.	139
24, 25	NEWTOWN HAMILTON T.	—			Armagh	Fews Upper	Newtownhamilton	Castleblayney	III.	49
11	Newtown (Hodgins)	198	3	1	Tipperary, N.R.	Lower Ormond	Modreeny	Borrisokane	II.	287
9	Newtownhortland	255	3	26	Kildare	Ikeathy&Oughterany	Scullogestown	Celbridge	I.	58
99	Newtownkelly	51	0	29	Galway	Clonmacnowen	Clontuskert	Ballinasloe	IV.	25
54	Newtown Kilcashel	282	1	29	Roscommon	Moycarn	Moore	Ballinasloe	IV.	207

(a) Including 47A. 0R. 20P. water.
(b) Including 5A. 3R. 1P. water.
(c) Including 5A. 1R. 28P. water.
(d) Including 2A. 3R. 8P. water.

No. of Sheet of the Ordnance Survey Maps.	Townlands and Towns.	Area in Statute Acres.	County.	Barony.	Parish.	Poor Law Union in 1857.	Townland Census of 1851, Part I.	
		A. R. P.					Vol.	Page
103	Newtown Kilcolgan	132 3 25	Galway	Dunkellin	Kilcolgan	Gort	IV.	28
17, 20	Newtown Knockaleva	328 3 16	Louth	Ardee	Mosstown	Ardee	I.	174
10	Newtownlaragh	86 0 1	Kildare	Ikeathy&Oughterany	Kilcock	Celbridge	I.	57
9	Newtown Limavady (alias) Rathbrady Beg	293 0 35a	Londonderry	Keenaght	Drumachose	NewT⁰Limavady	III.	235
9	NEWTOWN LIMA-VADY T.	—	Londonderry	Keenaght	Drumachose	NewT⁰Limavady	III.	235
25	Newtown Little	107 1 39	Dublin	Rathdown	Kilgobbin	Rathdown	I.	35
22	Newtown Little	178 1 16	Dublin	Rathdown	Rathfarnham	Dublin South	I.	37
25	Newtown Little	23 0 0	Kildare	Naas North	Rathmore	Naas	I.	62
46, 47	Newtown Little	63 0 0	Wexford	Bargy	Kilcowan	Wexford	I.	305
38	Newtownlow	190 0 35	Westmeath	Moycashel	Newtown	Mullingar	I.	279
20, 21, 24	Newtown Lower	132 1 39	Dublin	Newcastle	Saggart	Celbridge	I.	35
79	Newtown Lower	380 2 39	Tipperary, S.R.	Iffa and Offa East	Newtownlennan	Carrick on Suir	II.	315
3	Newtown Lower	251 3 5	Wexford	Gorey	Inch	Gorey	I.	316
37	Newtown Lower	130 0 30	Wexford	Shelmaliere East	Tikillin	Wexford	I.	331
102, 112	Newtownlynch	85 2 3	Galway	Kiltartan	Kinvarradoorus	Gort	IV.	49
30	Newtown (Lynott)	181 0 20	Galway	Dunmore	Dunmore	Tuam	IV.	34
10	Newtownmacabe	324 0 10	Kildare	North Salt	Taghadoe	Celbridge	I.	76
21	Newtown Monaster-boice	868 1 0	Louth	Ferrard	Monasterboice	Drogheda	I.	181
9	Newtownmoneenlug-gagh	128 2 25	Kildare	Ikeathy&Oughterany	Scullogestown	Celbridge	I.	58
13	Newtownmountken-nedy	103 0 25	Wicklow	Newcastle	Newcastle Upper	Rathdrum	I.	353
13	NEWTOWN MOUNT-KENNEDY T.	—	Wicklow	Newcastle	Newcastle Upper	Rathdrum	I.	353
49	Newtownmoyaghy	312 0 28	Meath	Upper Deece	Moyglare	Celbridge	I.	194
49	Newtownmoyaghy	293 0 7	Meath	Upper Deece	Rodanstown	Celbridge	I.	194
36, 42	Newtownmoynagh	533 1 5b	Meath	Lower Moyfenrath	Trim	Trim	I.	212
2	Newtown North	228 2 7	Cork, E.R.	Orrery and Kilmore	Shandrum	Kanturk	II.	110
125	Newtown North	134 1 12	Galway	Leitrim	Ballynakill	Loughrea	IV.	52
24, 33	Newtown North	276 3 13	Limerick	Coonagh	Oola	Tipperary	II.	236
111, 112	Newtown North	84 0 38	Mayo	Clanmorris	Crossboyne	Claremorris	IV.	133
51	Newtown North	281 2 27	Tipperary, S.R.	Kilnamanagh Lower	Donohill	Tipperary	II.	323
23	Newtownpark	20 3 31	Dublin	Rathdown	Kill	Rathdown	I.	36
25	Newtownpark	270 1 32	Kildare	Naas North	Rathmore	Naas	I.	62
23	NEWTOWN PARK T.	—	Dublin	Rathdown	Stillorgan	Rathdown	I.	38
39	Newtownpilsworth	287 3 32c	Kildare	Kilkea and Moone	Dunmanoge	Athy	I.	59
49	Newtownrathganley	491 0 34	Meath	Upper Deece	Kilmore	Dunshaughlin	I.	193
122, 128	Newtown (Regan)	140 1 39	Galway	Kiltartan	Kilmacduagh	Gort	IV.	48
6	NEWTOWN SANDES T.	—	Kerry	Iraghticonnor	Murher	Listowel	II.	193
27	Newtownsaunders	356 2 27	Wicklow	Upper Talbotstown	Baltinglass	Baltinglass	I.	362
27	Newtown (Shea)	577 2 10	Kilkenny	Shillelogher	Earlstown	Callan	I.	114
21	Newtown or Skirk	599 1 26	Queen's Co.	Clandonagh	Skirk	Donaghmore	I.	235
2	Newtown South	229 1 4	Cork, E.R.	Orrery and Kilmore	Shandrum	Kanturk	II.	110
125	Newtown South	70 1 12	Galway	Leitrim	Ballynakill	Loughrea	IV.	52
33	Newtown South	18 2 9	Limerick	Coonagh	Oola	Tipperary	II.	236
111, 112	Newtown South	191 2 17	Mayo	Clanmorris	Crossboyne	Claremorris	IV.	133
51	Newtown South	47 3 31	Tipperary, S.R.	Kilnamanagh Lower	Donohill	Tipperary	II.	323
17	Newtown Springfield	122 2 21	Donegal	Kilmacrenan	Clondavaddog	Milford	III.	125
24, 25	Newtownstalaban	112 3 31	Louth	Ferrard	Beaulieu	Drogheda	I.	180
21, 24, 25	Newtownstalaban	953 0 11	Louth	Ferrard	Tullyallen	Drogheda	I.	183
17	Newtown Stewart	540 3 7d	Tyrone	Strabane Lower	Ardstraw	Strabane	III.	319
17	NEWTOWN STEWART T.	—	Tyrone	Strabane Lower	Ardstraw	Strabane	III.	319
2	NEWTOWN T.	—	Cork, E.R.	Orrery and Kilmore	Shandrum	Kanturk	II.	110
27	NEWTOWN T.	—	Down	Lower Iveagh, Lr. pt.	Seapatrick	Banbridge	III.	169
29	NEWTOWN T.	—	King's Co.	Garrycastle	Lusmagh	Parsonstown	I.	137
51, 52	Newtown Upper	213 0 39	Down	Upper Iveagh, Up. pt.	Kilbroney	Kilkeel	III.	176
21, 24	Newtown Upper	319 2 19e	Dublin	Newcastle	Saggart	Celbridge	I.	35
79	Newtown Upper	277 1 0	Tipperary, S.R.	Iffa and Offa East	Newtownlennan	Carrick on Suir	II.	315
3	Newtown Upper	157 3 39	Wexford	Gorey	Inch	Gorey	I.	316
37	Newtown Upper	74 0 1	Wexford	Shelmaliere East	Tikillin	Wexford	I.	331
8	NEWTOWN VEVAY T.	—	Wicklow	Rathdown	Bray	Rathdown	I.	355
66	Newtown West	151 1 35	Clare	Moyarta	Moyarta	Kilrush	II.	34
22	Newtownwhite	328 3 24	Mayo	Tirawley	Ballysakeery	Ballina	IV.	165
93	Newvillage	60 3 2	Galway	Galway	Rahoon	Galway	IV.	38
32	Newvillage	136 3 6	Galway	Killian	Killian	Mountbellew	IV.	45
40, 54	Newvillage	1,010 2 1½f	Galway	Moycullen	Kilcummin	Oughterard	IV.	67
44, 50	Niblock	321 1 24	Antrim	Upper Antrim	Antrim	Antrim	III.	5
46	Nicharee	183 3 17	Wexford	Bargy	Duncormick	Wexford	I.	305
4, 5	Nicholastown	538 2 17	Kildare	Ikeathy&Oughterany	Cloncurry	Celbridge	I.	57
28	Nicholastown	425 0 1g	Kildare	Kilcullen	Kilcullen	Naas	I.	58

(a) Including 10A. 2R. 15P. water.
(b) Including 3A. 2R. 20P. water.
(c) Including 6A. 1R. 8P. water.
(d) Including 16A. 2R. 21P. water.
(e) Including 10A. 0R. 9P. detached portion.
(f) Including 4A. 1R. 36P. water.
(g) Including 2A. 1R. 28P. water.

No. of Sheet of the Ordnance Survey Maps.	Townlands and Towns.	Area in Statute Acres.	County.	Barony.	Parish.	Poor Law Union in 1857.	Townland Census of 1851, Part I.	
		A. R. P.					Vol.	Page
35, 37	Nicholastown . .	962 2 17	Kildare . .	Kilkea and Moone .	Tankardstown .	Athy . .	I.	61
5	Nicholastown . .	113 2 28	Kilkenny . .	Fassadinin . .	Kilmenan . .	Castlecomer .	I.	90
43	Nicholastown . .	623 1 4	Kilkenny . .	Ida . . .	Kilcolumb . .	Waterford .	I.	102
39, 42	Nicholastown . .	184 0 31	Kilkenny . .	Iverk . . .	Pollrone . .	Carrick on Suir	I.	106
10, 11	Nicholastown . .	501 3 29	Louth . . .	Ardee . .	Philipstown .	Ardee . .	I.	174
19	Nicholastown . .	225 3 16	Louth . . .	Ferrard . . .	Port . .	Drogheda .	I.	182
82	Nicholastown . .	426 2 35	Tipperary, S.R.	Iffa and Offa West .	Derrygrath .	Clogheen .	II.	318
22	Nicholastown . .	46 0 18	Waterford . .	Decies without Drum	Whitechurch .	Lismore .	II.	362
16	Nicholastown . .	33 1 3	Westmeath . .	Kilkenny West .	Noughaval .	Ballymahon .	I.	274
18, 25	Nicholastown . .	163 1 30	Westmeath . .	Rathconrath . .	Churchtown .	Mullingar .	I.	282
24	Nicker . . .	194 3 13	Limerick . .	Coonagh . .	Grean . . .	Tipperary .	II.	235
66	Nickeres . . .	80 0 16	Tipperary, S.R.	Clanwilliam . .	Emly . . .	Tipperary .	II.	308
24	NICKER T. . .	—	Limerick . .	Coonagh . .	Grean . . .	Tipperary .	II.	235
21, 28	Ninch . . .	686 1 17a	Meath . . .	Lower Duleek .	Julianstown .	Drogheda .	I.	196
70	Nineacres . .	16 1 38	Galway . . .	Clare . . .	Annaghdown .	Galway .	IV.	16
53	Nineacres . .	20 1 28	Wexford . .	Forth . . .	Carn . . .	Wexford .	I.	309
72	Ninemilehouse .	57 1 17	Tipperary, S.R.	Slievardagh . .	Templemichael .	Callan .	II.	336
72	NINEMILEHOUSE T.	—	Tipperary, S.R.	Slievardagh . .	Grangemockler / Templemichael .	Carrick on Suir / Callan .	II. }	333 / 336
53	Nineteenacres . .	31 2 26	Wexford . .	Forth . . .	Carn . . .	Wexford .	I.	309
53, 54	Noan . . .	931 1 7	Tipperary, S.R.	Slievardagh . .	Graystown .	Cashel .	II.	333
42, 48	Noard . . .	1,017 3 31b	Tipperary, N.R.	Eliogarty . .	Twomileborris .	Thurles .	II.	274
5, 6	Nobber . . .	501 0 24	Meath . . .	Morgallion . .	Nobber . .	Kells . .	I.	210
5, 6	NOBBER T. . .	—	Meath . . .	Morgallion . .	Nobber . .	Kells . .	I.	210
52, 53	Nodstown . .	995 0 7	Tipperary, S.R.	Middlethird . .	Ardmayle .	Cashel .	II.	324
52, 53	Nodstown North .	22 0 27	Tipperary, S.R.	Middlethird . .	Ardmayle .	Cashel .	II.	324
53	Nodstown South .	168 1 20	Tipperary, S.R.	Middlethird . .	Ardmayle .	Cashel .	II.	324
14, 22	Noggusboy . .	687 1 15	King's Co. .	Garrycastle . .	Gallen . .	Parsonstown .	I.	136
14, 22	Noggusduff . .	313 3 19	King's Co. .	Garrycastle . .	Gallen . .	Parsonstown .	I.	136
11	Noghan . . .	189 3 11c	Cavan . . .	Lower Loughtee .	Drumlane .	Cavan .	III.	80
112, 113	Nohaval . . .	344 3 17	Cork, E.R. .	Kinalea . .	Nohaval . .	Kinsale .	II.	96
29, 38	Nohavaldaly . .	964 3 8d	Cork, E.R. .	Duhallow . .	Nohavaldaly .	Millstreet .	II.	75
29, 38	Nohaval Lower .	414 3 28	Cork, E.R. .	Duhallow . .	Nohavaldaly .	Millstreet .	II.	75
30	Nohaval North .	108 1 34	Kerry . . .	Trughanacmy .	Nohaval . .	Tralee .	II.	212
30, 39	Nohaval South .	375 1 38	Kerry . . .	Trughanacmy .	Nohaval . .	Tralee .	II.	212
112, 113	NOHAVAL T. . .	—	Cork, E.R. .	Kinalea . .	Nohaval . .	Kinsale .	II.	96
29, 38	Nohaval Upper .	477 0 4	Cork, E.R. .	Duhallow . .	Nohavaldaly .	Millstreet .	II.	75
28	Nolagh . . .	751 2 35	Cavan . . .	Clankee . .	Shercock .	Bailieborough .	III.	74
3, 7	Nonsuch . .	220 2 32	Westmeath . .	Fore . . .	Mayne . .	Granard .	I.	271
33	Nooan East . .	130 0 34	Clare . . .	Islands . .	Drumcliff .	Ennis .	II.	30
33	Nooan West . .	187 3 25	Clare . . .	Islands . .	Drumcliff .	Ennis .	II.	30
16, 17	Nooan . . .	452 1 6e	Clare . . .	Inchiquin . .	Killinaboy .	Corrofin .	II.	27
25	Nooan . . .	400 2 18f	Clare . . .	Inchiquin . .	Ruan . .	Corrofin .	II.	28
12	Nook . . .	85 1 24	Monaghan . .	Dartree . .	Clones . .	Clones .	III.	285
39, 44	Nook . . .	517 3 39	Wexford . .	Shelburne . .	St. James & Dunbrody	New Ross .	I.	328
11	Norbrinstown or Normanstown . .	287 2 21	Meath . . .	Upper Kells .	Kells . .	Kells . .	I.	206
121, 122	Normangrove . .	568 1 31	Galway . . .	Kiltartan . .	Killinny . .	Gort . .	IV.	47
50, 51	Normansgrove .	74 1 15g	Meath . . .	Dunboyne . .	Dunboyne .	Dunshaughlin .	I.	199
11	Normanstown or Norbrinstown .	287 2 21	Meath . . .	Upper Kells .	Kells . .	Kells . .	I.	206
4	Norrira . . .	489 3 31h	Donegal . .	Inishowen East .	Clonca . .	Inishowen .	III.	117
21, 29	Norrisland . .	113 1 39	Waterford . .	Coshmore & Coshbride	Lismore and Mocollop	Lismore .	II.	347
11, 16	Norrismount . .	279 1 1	Wexford . .	Scarawalsh . .	Toome . .	Gorey .	I.	326
41,42,46,47	Norristown . .	197 0 20	Wexford . .	Bargy . .	Kilmannan .	Wexford .	I.	306
113	Northampton . .	112 2 16	Galway . . .	Kiltartan . .	Kinvarradoorus .	Gort . .	IV.	49
87	Northbrook . .	415 0 16	Galway . . .	Kilconnell . .	Aughrim .	Ballinasloe .	IV.	39
19	*North Bull Islands* .	6 0 34i	Dublin . .	Coolock . .	Raheny . .	Dublin North .	I.	29
19	North Bull or The Island . .	120 3 21	Dublin . .	Coolock . .	Clontarf . .	Dublin North .	I.	26
46,47,52,53	North East Division	3,296 3 8j	Antrim . .	Carrickfergus .	Carrickfergus .	Larne .	III.	11
11	Northgrove . .	188 0 29	Queen's Co. .	Upperwoods .	Offerlane .	Mountmellick .	I.	252
77, 78	North Island . .	11 1 13	Galway . . .	Ballynahinch .	Moyrus . .	Clifden .	IV.	14
11, 18	North & South Lislea	426 0 4k	Tyrone . .	Strabane Upper .	Bodoney Upper .	Gortin .	III.	324
29, 30	Northyard . .	441 1 22	Roscommon . .	Roscommon .	Bumlin . .	Strokestown .	IV.	208
34	Noughaval . .	200 0 36	Clare . . .	Bunratty Upper .	Doora . .	Ennis .	II.	8
9	Noughaval . .	500 1 6	Clare . . .	Burren . .	Noughaval .	Ballyvaghan .	II.	13
16	Noughaval . .	557 2 26	Westmeath . .	Kilkenny West .	Noughaval .	Ballymahon .	I.	274
4, 8	Novally . . .	399 0 34	Antrim . .	Cary . . .	Ramoan . .	Ballycastle .	III.	14
17	Nugentstown . .	236 3 0	Meath . . .	Upper Kells .	Balrathboyne .	Kells . .	I.	204
101	Nunsacre . .	5 2 16	Galway . . .	Longford . .	Clonfert . .	Ballinasloe .	IV.	57
15	*Nuns Island* . .	4 1 17	Westmeath . .	Kilkenny West .	Bunown . .	Athlone .	I.	272
24	Nunsland . .	87 3 4	Kildare . .	Naas North .	Rathmore .	Naas .	I.	62
18	Nun's Quarter .	178 1 2	Down . . .	Ards Upper .	Inishargy .	Newtownards .	III.	160

(a) Including 15A. 1R. 16P. detached portion.
(b) Including 129A. 1R. 16P. detached portions.
(c) Including 17A. 1R. 7P. water.
(d) Including 9A. 3R. 15P. water.

(e) Including 64A. 3R. 18P. water.
(f) Including 5A. 0R. 9P. water.
(g) Including 6A. 0R. 16P. detached portion.
(h) Including 37A. 3R. 29P. detached portion.

(i) Three small Islands, North Bull.
(j) Including 89A. 3R. 22P. Lough Morne.
(k) Including 7A. 1R. 28P. water.

No. of Sheet of the Ordnance Survey Maps.	Townlands and Towns.	Area in Statute Acres.	County.	Barony.	Parish.	Poor Law Union in 1857.	Townland Census of 1851. Part I.	
		A. R. P.					Vol.	Page
66	Nunstown . .	170 2 34	Kerry . .	Magunihy . .	Aghadoe . .	Killarney . .	II.	199
64	Nurchossy Irish .	250 2 25	Tyrone . .	Clogher . .	Clogher . .	Clogher . .	III.	293
64	Nurchossy Scotch .	141 0 32a	Tyrone . .	Clogher . .	Clogher . .	Clogher . .	III.	293
7	Nure . . .	299 1 25	Leitrim . .	Rosclogher . .	Killasnet . .	Manorhamilton	IV.	110
30	Nure . . .	70 0 9	Mayo . .	Tirawley . .	Ardagh . .	Ballina . .	IV.	164
31	Nure Beg . .	47 2 0	Monaghan .	Farney . .	Killanny . .	Carrickmacross	III.	272
31	Nure Beg . .	85 1 14	Monaghan .	Farney . .	Magheracloone	Carrickmacross	III.	273
25, 32	Nure or Lilliput .	244 1 22	Westmeath .	Moycashel . .	Dysart . .	Mullingar .	I.	278
31	Nure More . .	128 3 24b	Monaghan .	Farney . .	Killanny . .	Carrickmacross	III.	272
31	Nure More . .	118 2 32c	Monaghan .	Farney . .	Magheracloone	Carrickmacross	III.	273
12	Nurney . . .	209 0 10	Carlow . .	Idrone East .	Agha . .	Carlow . .	I.	6
12	Nurney . . .	289 3 31	Carlow . .	Idrone East .	Nurney . .	Carlow . .	I.	8
3	Nurney . . .	364 2 17	Kildare . .	Carbury . .	Nurney . .	Edenderry .	I.	53
27, 31	Nurney . . .	258 2 6	Kildare . .	Offaly West .	Nurney . .	Athy . .	I.	74
27	Nurney Bog .	147 2 15	Kildare . .	Offaly West .	Nurney . .	Athy . .	I.	74
27	Nurney Demesne .	334 1 2	Kildare . .	Offaly West .	Nurney . .	Athy . .	I.	74
12	NURNEY T. . .	—	Carlow . .	Idrone East .	Nurney . .	Carlow . .	I.	8
27	NURNEY T. . .	—	Kildare . .	Offaly West .	Nurney . .	Athy . .	I.	74
71	Nurserypark or Corrabaun . .	48 2 27	Galway . .	Tiaquin . .	Monivea . .	Tuam . .	IV.	79
41, 42	Nursetown Beg .	254 3 23	Cork, E.R. .	Duhallow . .	Kilshannig .	Mallow . .	II.	74
41	Nursetown More .	356 1 9	Cork, E.R. .	Duhallow . .	Kilshannig .	Mallow . .	II.	74
21, 22	Nutfield . . .	109 1 14d	Cavan . .	Tullygarvey .	Drung . .	Cootehill .	III.	89
25	Nutfield . . .	219 2 28e	Clare . .	Bunratty Upper .	Templemaley .	Corrofin . .	II.	11
28	Nutfield . . .	130 0 4	Fermanagh .	Magherastephana .	Aghavea . .	Lisnaskea .	III.	219
19	Nutgrove . .	229 2 21	Cork, E.R. .	Condons & Clangibbon	Kilgullane .	Mitchelstown .	II.	61
3	Nutgrove . .	177 1 25	Queen's Co. .	Tinnahinch .	Rosenallis .	Mountmellick .	I.	259
117	Nutgrove or Feebrack . .	264 3 36	Galway . .	Longford . .	Tynagh . .	Portumna .	IV.	62
126	Nut Island . .	0 3 16	Galway . .	Longford . .	Lickmolassy .	Portumna .	IV.	61
25	Nut Island . .	15 3 18	Longford . .	Rathcline . .	Cashel . .	Ballymahon .	I.	163
3, 6, 7	Nutstown . .	759 2 11	Dublin . .	Balrothery West .	Ballymadun .	Dunshaughlin .	I.	22
51	Nuttstown . .	301 0 31	Meath . .	Dunboyne . .	Kilbride . .	Dunshaughlin .	I.	200
27	Nymphhall . .	56 0 26	Waterford .	Gaultiere . .	Killea . .	Waterford .	II.	363
120	Nymphsfield . .	192 0 39f	Mayo . .	Kilmaine . .	Cong . .	Ballinrobe .	IV.	154
3	Nyra . . .	268 3 15	Queen's Co. .	Tinnahinch .	Rosenallis .	Mountmellick .	I.	250
19	Oaghmonicroy .	756 3 24g	Tyrone . .	Strabane Upper .	Bodoney Lower .	Gortin . .	III.	324
53	Oakfield . . .	260 2 8	Clare . .	Tulla Lower .	Kiltenanlea .	Limerick . .	II.	37
26	Oakfield . . .	199 1 31	Fermanagh .	Clanawley . .	Cleenish . .	Enniskillen .	III.	191
28, 29	Oakfield . . .	283 1 6h	Roscommon .	Roscommon .	Cloonfinlough .	Strokestown .	IV.	209
62, 70	Oakfield Demesne .	231 0 31	Donegal . .	Raphoe . .	Raphoe . .	Strabane .	III.	141
14	Oakfield or Derrydarragh . .	344 3 0	Sligo . .	Carbury . .	St. John's .	Sligo . .	IV.	223
55	Oakfield or Gortnandarragh . .	259 0 19	Galway . .	Moycullen . .	Killannin . .	Oughterard .	IV.	70
31	Oakhampton .	386 0 10	Tipperary, N.R.	Owney and Arra .	Kilnarath . .	Nenagh . .	II.	296
29	Oaklands . .	185 3 28	Tyrone . .	Dungannon Upper .	Kildress . .	Cookstown .	III.	309
29, 34	Oaklands . .	171 3 33	Wexford . .	Bantry . .	St. Mary's .	New Ross .	I.	302
11	Oakleypark . .	103 3 33	Kildare . .	North Salt .	Kildrought .	Celbridge .	I.	74
35,36,38,39	Oakleypark . .	753 1 22	King's Co. .	Ballybritt . .	Seirkieran .	Parsonstown .	I.	127
10, 11	Oakleypark or Lawrencetown . .	741 3 2i	Meath . .	Upper Kells .	Dulane . .	Kells . .	I.	205
2	Oakpark or Painestown . .	1,296 0 12j	Carlow . .	Carlow . .	Painestown .	Carlow . .	I.	2
6	Oakport Demesne .	587 1 28k	Roscommon .	Boyle . .	Ardcarn . .	Boyle . .	IV.	193
30, 36	Oakstown . .	183 2 23	Meath . .	Upper Navan .	Trim . .	Trim . .	I.	217
11	Oaktate . .	126 2 31	Louth . .	Ardee . .	Louth . .	Dundalk .	I.	173
16, 17	Oakwood . .	1,721 2 9	Wicklow . .	Lower Talbotstown .	Hollywood .	Baltinglass .	I.	361
15, 20	Oakwood or Drummully . .	182 3 2	Cavan . .	Upper Loughtee .	Castleterra .	Cavan . .	III.	83
58	Oakwood North .	369 3 35	Galway . .	Tiaquin . .	Abbeyknockmoy	Tuam . .	IV.	75
58	Oakwood South .	89 1 1	Galway . .	Tiaquin . .	Abbeyknockmoy	Tuam . .	IV.	75
76	Oatencake . .	94 3 1	Cork, E.R. .	Imokilly . .	Mogeesha . .	Middleton .	II.	90
43, 52, 53	Oatfield . .	871 1 31l	Clare . .	Tulla Lower .	Clonlea . .	Limerick . .	II.	35
86,87,98,99	Oatfield . .	894 3 34	Galway . .	Kilconnell . .	Aughrim . .	Ballinasloe .	IV.	39
13	Oatlands . .	115 0 5	Limerick . .	Clanwilliam .	Cahervally .	Limerick . .	II.	221
5, 8	Oberstown . .	281 3 4	Dublin . .	Balrothery East .	Lusk . .	Balrothery .	I.	21
17	Oberstown . .	220 1 10	Louth . .	Ardee . .	Shanlis . .	Ardee . .	I.	174
32	Obertstown . .	538 3 2	Meath . .	Skreen . .	Skreen . .	Dunshaughlin .	I.	221
45, 54	O'Briensbridge .	740 1 30	Clare . .	Tulla Lower .	O'Briensbridge .	Limerick . .	II.	38
54	O'BRIENSBRIDGE T.	—	Clare . .	Tulla Lower .	O'Briensbridge .	Limerick . .	II.	38
26	Obrienscastle .	213 2 27m	Clare . .	Bunratty Upper .	Inchicronan .	Tulla . .	II.	9

No. of Sheet of the Ordnance Survey Maps.	Townlands and Towns.	Area in Statute Acres.	County.	Barony.	Parish.	Poor Law Union in 1857.	Townland Census of 1851, Part I.	
		A. R. P.					Vol.	Page
35	O'CALLAGHANSMILLST.	—	Clare . .	Tulla Lower . .	Killuran . . .	Tulla . . .	II.	36
12	Ockanaroe . .	108 3 23	Queen's Co. .	Maryborough West .	Clonenagh&Clonagheen	Mountmellick .	I.	243
14	Odagh . .	1 2 22	Kilkenny . .	Crannagh . .	Odagh . . .	Kilkenny . .	I.	86
81, 93	Oddacres . .	84 3 2	Galway . .	Galway . . .	Rahoon . .	Galway . .	IV.	38
31, 37	Odder . .	595 2 37	Meath . .	Skreen . . .	Tara . . .	Navan . .	I.	222
94	O'Donnell's Island .	0 2 32	Donegal . .	Tirhugh . .	Donegal . . .	Donegal . .	III.	145
60	O'Donnell's Island or Illaunbeg . .	8 0 36	Clare . .	Clonderalaw . .	Killadysert . .	Killadysert .	II.	16
1, 3	Oggal . .	265 3 25	Cavan . .	Tullyhaw . .	Killinagh . .	Enniskillen .	III.	92
38, 39	Ogham . .	475 2 34	Sligo . .	Corran . . .	Kilturra . .	Tobercurry .	IV.	228
34	Ogham . .	244 2 27	Sligo . .	Tirerrill . .	Tawnagh . .	Sligo . .	IV.	241
38	Oghambaun . .	412 1 35	Sligo . .	Leyny . . .	Achonry . .	Tobercurry .	IV.	229
93, 94	Ogherbeg . .	690 1 4	Donegal . .	Banagh . .	Killymard . .	Donegal . .	III.	111
79	Oghermong . .	496 0 31	Kerry . .	Iveragh . .	Caher . . .	Cahersiveen .	II.	194
68	Oghery . .	439 1 11a	Galway . .	Moycullen . .	Moycullen . .	Galway . .	IV.	71
22, 27	Oghil . .	1,186 0 33	Kildare . .	Offaly West . .	Monasterevin . .	Athy . .	I.	73
9	Oghil . .	761 1 27	Longford . .	Longford . .	Killoe . . .	Longford . .	I.	159
17	Oghil . .	204 2 0	Sligo . .	Tireragh . .	Kilglass . .	Dromore West .	IV.	234
100	Oghil Beg . .	437 1 33	Galway . .	Longford . .	Clonfert . .	Ballinasloe .	IV.	57
31	Oghill . .	335 3 18b	Cavan . .	Clanmahon . .	Ballintemple . .	Cavan . .	III.	75
36	Oghill . .	263 2 18c	Donegal . .	Kilmacrenan . .	Tullyfern . .	Milford . .	III.	133
6	Oghill . .	196 0 24	Fermanagh .	Lurg . . .	Drumkeeran . .	Lowtherstown .	III.	207
15, 16	Oghill . .	82 1 30	Fermanagh .	Lurg . . .	Trory . . .	Lowtherstown .	III.	209
34	Oghill . .	33 3 4	Fermanagh .	Magherastephana .	Aghalurcher . .	Lisnaskea .	III.	217
110, 111	Oghill . .	1,799 2 18d	Galway . .	Aran . . .	Inishmore . .	Galway . .	IV.	3
28, 32	Oghill . .	119 3 26	Leitrim . .	Mohill . .	Mohill . . .	Mohill . .	IV.	108
9, 16	Oghill . .	69 1 26	Londonderry .	Keenaght . .	Tamlaght Finlagan	NewTeLimavady	III.	237
14, 22	Oghill . .	271 3 20	Londonderry .	Tirkeeran . .	Cumber Lower . .	Londonderry .	III.	249
19, 24	Oghill . .	289 0 36	Monaghan .	Cremorne . .	Clontibret . .	Castleblayney .	III.	261
28, 29, 32	Oghill . .	91 3 17	Monaghan .	Farney . .	Donaghmoyne . .	Carrickmacross	III.	270
39	Oghill . .	164 0 11	Tyrone . .	Dungannon Upper .	Ballyclog . .	Cookstown .	III.	306
57, 67	Oghillees . .	842 1 18	Mayo . .	Burrishoole . .	Burrishoole . .	Newport . .	IV.	119
2	Oghillicartan . .	121 1 35	Fermanagh .	Lurg . . .	Drumkeeran . .	Lowtherstown .	III.	207
35, 36	Oghil Lower . .	387 3 6	Wicklow . .	Arklow . .	Redcross . .	Rathdrum .	I.	346
132	Oghilly . .	326 3 27	Galway . .	Leitrim . .	Ballynakill . .	Portumna .	IV.	52
100	Oghil More . .	368 3 25	Galway . .	Longford . .	Clonfert . .	Ballinasloe .	IV.	57
35	Oghil Upper . .	219 3 11	Wicklow . .	Arklow . .	Redcross . .	Rathdrum .	I.	346
63	Oghly Island . .	12 2 16	Galway . .	Ballynahinch .	Moyrus . .	Clifden . .	IV.	14
60	O'Grady's Island or Inishoul . .	1 1 35	Clare . .	Clonderalaw . .	Killadysert . .	Killadysert .	II.	16
22, 28	Ogulla . .	235 1 15	Roscommon .	Roscommon . .	Ogulla . . .	Strokestown .	IV.	212
32	Oilgate or Mullinna-gore . .	101 2 28	Wexford . .	Ballaghkeen . .	Edermine . .	Enniscorthy .	I.	294
32	OILGATE T. . .	—	Wexford . .	Ballaghkeen . .	Edermine . .	Enniscorthy .	I.	294
29	Okyle . .	175 2 16	Waterford .	Coshmore &Coshbride	Lismore and Mocollop	Lismore . .	II.	347
85	Oldabbey . .	347 3 16	Cork, E.R. .	East Muskerry . .	Inishkenny . .	Cork . .	II.	104
19	Oldabbey . .	547 0 37	Limerick . .	Shanid . .	Robertstown . .	Glin . .	II.	258
14, 20	Old Barr . .	604 3 38	Fermanagh .	Magheraboy . .	Devenish . .	Enniskillen .	III.	211
21, 22	Oldbawn . .	615 1 9	Dublin . .	Uppercross . .	Tallaght . .	Dublin South .	I.	42
36	Oldboley . .	326 3 23	Wexford . .	Shelmaliere West .	Taghmon . .	Wexford . .	I.	335
2, 3, 6, 7	Oldboleys . .	1,165 1 4	Wicklow . .	Rathdown . .	Powerscourt . .	Rathdown .	I.	356
16	Oldborris . .	112 2 9	Queen's Co. .	Upperwoods . .	Offerlane . .	Abbeyleix .	I.	252
20	Oldbridge . .	732 0 16e	Meath . .	Lower Duleek . .	Donore . .	Drogheda .	I.	195
1	Oldbridge . .	51 2 23f	Waterford .	Upperthird and Municipal Borough .	St. Marys Clonmel .	Clonmel . .	II.	372
15	Oldcamp . .	98 1 10	Queen's Co. .	Clandonagh . .	Kyle . . .	Roscrea . .	I.	233
6	Oldcarton . .	288 0 14	Kildare . .	North Salt . .	Laraghbryan . .	Celbridge .	I.	75
61	Oldcastle . .	417 2 38	Cork, E.R. .	East Muskerry . .	Magourney . .	Macroom . .	II.	105
96, 97	Oldcastle . .	103 2 7	Galway . .	Dunkellin . .	Kilconierin . .	Loughrea .	IV.	29
61	Oldcastle . .	270 0 33g	Mayo . .	Gallen . .	Meelick . .	Swineford .	IV.	150
9	Oldcastle . .	1,257 1 5	Meath . .	Fore . . .	Oldcastle . .	Oldcastle .	I.	202
17, 23	Oldcastle . .	503 3 2	Tipperary, N.R. .	Ikerrin . .	Bourney . .	Roscrea .	II.	274
45, 51	Oldcastle . .	339 0 26	Tipperary, N.R.	Kilnamanagh Upper	Toem . . .	Tipperary .	II.	280
72, 79	Oldcastle . .	77 1 8	Tipperary, S.R. .	Slievardagh . .	Newtownlennan .	Carrick on Suir	II.	335
30, 34	Oldcastle Lower .	172 2 37	Kilkenny . .	Kells . .	Killamery . .	Callan . .	I.	109
18	Oldcastletown . .	864 1 14	Cork, E.R. .	Condons&Clangibbon	Kildorrery . .	Mitchelstown .	II.	61
9	OLDCASTLE T. .	—	Meath . .	Fore . . .	Oldcastle . .	Oldcastle . .	I.	202
30	Oldcastle Upper .	195 1 36	Kilkenny . .	Kells . .	Killamery . .	Callan . .	I.	109
29	Old Church . .	104 0 27	Antrim . .	Lower Glenarm . .	Tickmacrevan . .	Larne . .	III.	24
96	Old Church Glebe .	1 2 10	Donegal . .	Banagh . .	Kilcar . . .	Glenties . .	III.	109
36	Old Church Yard .	0 2 10	Tyrone . .	Omagh East . .	Termonmaguirk .	Omagh . .	III.	314
26, 28	Oldconnaught . .	726 0 14	Dublin . .	Rathdown . .	Oldconnaught . .	Rathdown .	I.	37
18, 23	Oldconnell . .	677 2 37h	Kildare . .	Connell . .	Oldconnell . .	Naas . .	I.	56
75	Oldcourt . .	17 2 9	Cork, E.R. .	Barrymore . .	Clonmel . .	Cork . .	II.	53

(a) Including 0A. 1R. 34P. water.
(b) Including 20A. 0R. 8P. water.
(c) Including 6A. 1R. 32P. water.
(d) Including 10A. 2R. 1P. water.
(e) Including 21A. 0R. 18P. water.

(f) { Within the Municipal Boundary, 16A. 2R. 0P.
Including 5A. 1R. 31P. water.
Without the Municipal Boundary, 35A. 0R. 23P.
Including 3A. 0R. 10P. water. }

(g) Including 3A. 3R. 32P. water.
(h) Including 25A. 3R. 3P. water.

5 C

No. of Sheet of the Ordnance Survey Maps.	Townlands and Towns.	Area in Statute Acres.			County.	Barony.	Parish.	Poor Law Union in 1857.	Townland Census of 1851, Part I.	
		A.	R.	P.					Vol.	Page
54	Oldcourt	470	1	0	Cork, E.R.	Barrymore	Templebodan	Middleton	II.	58
75, 87	Oldcourt	344	1	17	Cork, E.R.	Cork	Carrigaline	Cork	II.	64
17	Oldcourt	240	1	2	Cork, E.R.	Fermoy	Doneraile	Mallow	II.	79
124	Oldcourt	334	0	7	Cork, W.R.	Courceys	Ringrone	Kinsale	II.	147
141, 150	Oldcourt	218	3	19	Cork, W.R.	West Carbery (E.D.)	Creagh	Skibbereen	II.	139
22, 25	Oldcourt	435	3	23	Dublin	Uppercross	Tallaght	Dublin South	I.	42
7, 8	Oldcourt	361	2	21	Kildare	Carbury	Kilmore	Edenderry	I.	52
31, 35	Oldcourt	646	2	20	Kildare	Narragh&RebanWest	Kilberry	Athy	I.	68
33	Oldcourt	345	3	32	Kilkenny	Ida	Clonamery	Thomastown	I.	101
35, 39	Oldcourt	517	0	31	Kilkenny	Iverk	Fiddown	Carrick on Suir	I.	105
29, 29	Oldcourt	147	3	26	Limerick	Connello Lower	Croagh	Rathkeale	II.	228
26	Oldcourt	155	3	32	Queen's Co.	Ballyadams	Killabban	Athy	I.	231
9, 10	Oldcourt	455	3	8a	Tipperary, N.R.	Lower Ormond	Finnoe	Borrisokane	II.	284
30, 31	Oldcourt	719	3	35	Wexford	Bantry	Adamstown	New Ross	I.	299
34	Oldcourt	491	2	8	Wexford	Shelburne	Whitechurch	New Ross	I.	329
5	Oldcourt	873	0	18	Wicklow	Lower Talbotstown	Blessington	Naas	I.	358
4, 8	Oldcourt	316	0	26	Wicklow	Rathdown	Bray	Rathdown	I.	355
14, 15	Oldcourt	244	1	7	Wicklow	Upper Talbotstown	Rathsallagh	Baltinglass	I.	365
65	Oldcourt East	173	1	34	Cork, E.R.	Barrymore	Templenacarriga	Middleton	II.	58
65	Oldcourt West	120	1	26	Cork, E.R.	Barrymore	Templenacarriga	Middleton	II.	58
10	Oldcroghan	649	1	23	King's Co.	Lower Philipstown	Croghan	Edenderry	I.	142
32, 37	Oldderrig	343	3	21	Queen's Co.	Slievemargy	Killeshin	Carlow	I.	246
64	Oldforge	356	0	6b	Antrim	Upper Belfast	Drumbeg	Lisburn	III.	10
67	Oldforge	146	2	9	Kerry	Magunihy	Killarney	Killarney	II.	203
112, 125	Old-fort	33	3	26	Cork, E.R.	Kinsale	Ringrone	Kinsale	II.	101
34, 35, 39, 40	Old Freehold	2,143	1	12	Antrim	Upper Glenarm	Kilwaughter	Larne	III.	25
28, 29	Oldglass	754	2	28	Queen's Co.	Clarmallagh	Aghaboe	Donaghmore	I.	236
28	Oldglass	172	1	35	Queen's Co.	Clarmallagh	Bordwell	Donaghmore	I.	237
36	Old Glebe or Cartron	54	3	28	Roscommon	Ballintober South	Kilgefin	Roscommon	IV.	189
50	Oldgraigue	158	1	5	Meath	Upper Deece	Moyglare	Celbridge	I.	194
32	Oldgrange	15	0	11	Kildare	Narragh & RebanEast	Fontstown	Athy	I.	66
31, 32	Oldgrange	363	1	2	Kildare	Narragh & RebanEast	Narraghmore	Athy	I.	66
21	Oldgrange	402	2	12	Kildare	Offaly West	Monasterevin	Athy	I.	73
25, 29	Oldgrange	717	1	4	Kilkenny	Gowran	Graiguenamanagh	Thomastown	I.	95
11	Oldgrange	262	2	25	Sligo	Tireragh	Easky	Dromore West	IV.	234
82	Oldgrange	190	3	14	Tipperary, S.R.	Iffa and Offa West	Tullaghmelan	Clogheen	II.	321
7	Oldgrange	572	2	13	Waterford	Upperthird	Mothel	Carrick on Suir	II.	371
47	Oldhall	89	0	30	Wexford	Bargy	Mulrankin	Wexford	I.	307
86	Oldhead	244	3	31	Mayo	Murrisk	Kilgeever	Westport	IV.	160
137	Oldhead or Downmacpatrick	202	1	10	Cork, W.R.	Courceys	Ringrone	Kinsale	II.	147
28	Oldkilcullen	792	1	29	Kildare	Kilcullen	Kilcullen	Naas	I.	58
32	Oldleagh	222	3	23	Queen's Co.	Slievemargy	Killabban	Carlow	I.	245
11, 15	Oldleighlin	302	3	23	Carlow	Idrone West	Oldleighlin	Carlow	I.	9
11	OLDLEIGHLIN T.	—			Carlow	Idrone West	Oldleighlin	Carlow	I.	9
19	Oldmill	330	2	12	Queen's Co.	Stradbally	Dysartenos	Athy	I.	247
48	Oldmill	18	2	23	Wexford	Forth	Kilrane	Wexford	I.	311
35	OLD MILLS T.	—			Antrim	Upper Glenarm	Carncastle	Larne	III.	24
20	Oldmilltown	165	0	11	Kildare	South Salt	Kilteel	Naas	I.	77
22	Oldorchard	123	2	26	Dublin	Rathdown	Rathfarnham	Dublin South	I.	37
5	Oldpaddocks	41	3	7	Wicklow	Lower Talbotstown	Blessington	Naas	I.	358
56, 60, 61	Old Park	787	3	22	Antrim	Upper Belfast	Shankill	Belfast	III.	10
19	Oldpark	17	2	31	Kilkenny	Crannagh	St. Canice	Kilkenny	I.	87
33, 39	Oldrock or Shancarrigeen	205	1	26	Sligo	Corran	Cloonoghill	Tobercurry	IV.	225
50, 55	Oldstone	411	2	31	Antrim	Lower Massereene	Muckamore(Grange of)	Antrim	III.	28
117, 118	Oldstreet	207	2	37	Galway	Longford	Kilquain	Portumna	IV.	60
6, 7	Oldtown	122	2	12	Antrim	Lower Dunluce	Ballyrashane	Coleraine	III.	15
19, 22	Oldtown	72	2	14	Carlow	Idrone East	Ballyellin	Carlow	I.	6
12	Oldtown	674	3	18	Carlow	Idrone East	Nurney	Carlow	I.	8
9	Oldtown	193	3	26	Carlow	Rathvilly	Clonmore	Shillelagh	I.	10
3	Oldtown	195	2	20	Carlow	Rathvilly	Kineagh	Baltinglass	I.	11
53	Oldtown	100	0	2	Donegal	Raphoe	Leck	Letterkenny	III.	140
7	Oldtown	358	0	25c	Dublin	Balrothery West	Clonmethan	Balrothery	I.	22
15	Oldtown	74	2	29	Dublin	Coolock	Artaine	Dublin North	I.	26
15	Oldtown	43	2	15	Dublin	Coolock	Coolock	Dublin North	I.	27
11	Oldtown	165	2	13	Dublin	Nethercross	Swords	Balrothery	I.	32
23	Oldtown	179	2	10	Kildare	Connell	Greatconnell	Naas	I.	55
19	Oldtown	134	0	0	Kildare	Naas North	Naas	Naas	I.	62
24	Oldtown	169	3	17	Kildare	Naas South	Killashee	Naas	I.	65
11	Oldtown	251	1	21	Kildare	North Salt	Kildrought	Celbridge	I.	74
20	Oldtown	31	2	8	Kildare	South Salt	Kilteel	Naas	I.	77
18	Oldtown	282	3	33	Kilkenny	Crannagh	Tullaroan	Kilkenny	I.	88

(a) Including 0A. 3R. 15P. water.   (b) Including 4A. 1R. 16P. water.   (c) Including 47A. 0R. 28P. detached portions.

No. of Sheet of the Ordnance Survey Maps.	Townlands and Towns.	Area in Statute Acres.			County.	Barony.	Parish.	Poor Law Union in 1857.	Townland Census of 1851, Part I.	
		A.	R.	P.					Vol.	Page
9, 10	Oldtown	556	2	24	Kilkenny	Fassadinin	Grangemaccomb	Castlecomer	I.	89
27, 28	Oldtown	296	2	15	Kilkenny	Knocktopher	Jerpointchurch	Thomastown	I.	111
23	Oldtown	390	1	24	Kilkenny	Shillelogher	Burnchurch	Callan	I.	113
16, 24	Oldtown	130	0	12	King's Co.	Ballycowan	Rahan	Tullamore	I.	129
18	Oldtown	443	2	11	King's Co.	Lower Philipstown	Killaderry	Tullamore	I.	143
14, 19	Oldtown	325	0	27	Longford	Ardagh	Ardagh	Longford	I.	151
24	Oldtown	170	1	3	Meath	Lower Navan	Martry	Kells	I.	215
25, 31	Oldtown	509	1	18	Meath	Skreen	Kilcarn	Navan	I.	220
49	Oldtown	55	1	34	Meath	Upper Deece	Gallow	Trim	I.	193
48, 49	Oldtown	267	0	3	Meath	Upper Deece	Rathcore	Trim	I.	194
27	Oldtown	98	2	28	Queen's Co.	Clandonagh	Rathsaran	Donaghmore	I.	235
34, 35	Oldtown	764	3	27	Queen's Co.	Clarmallagh	Aghmacart	Abbeyleix	I.	236
17	Oldtown	420	1	19	Queen's Co.	Maryborough West	Clonenagh and Clonagheen	Abbeyleix	I.	243
10, 16	Oldtown	239	2	20	Roscommon	Frenchpark	Kilmacumsy	Boyle	IV.	204
29	Oldtown	354	1	21	Tipperary, N.R.	Eliogarty	Templemore	Thurles	II.	272
33	Oldtown	364	2	21	Westmeath	Fartullagh	Castlelost	Mullingar	I.	268
22	Oldtown	148	0	21	Wexford	Ballaghkeen	Donaghmore	Gorey	I.	293
52	Oldtown	34	2	24	Wexford	Bargy	Tomhaggard	Wexford	I.	308
38	Oldtown	94	0	3	Wexford	Shelmaliere East	Ardcolm	Wexford	I.	330
20, 26	Oldtown	214	1	14	Wicklow	Upper Talbotstown	Ballynure	Baltinglass	I.	362
32,33,40,41	Oldtown (Bennett)	541	0	7	Limerick	Smallcounty	Hospital	Kilmallock	II.	260
25	Oldtown or Cornagleragh	126	1	7	Cavan	Upper Loughtee	Annagelliff	Cavan	III.	81
10	Oldtown Curralane	145	1	35	Wexford	Scarawalsh	Kilrush	Enniscorthy	I.	324
37, 42	Old Town Deer Park	202	0	34	Londonderry	Loughinsholin	Ballyscullion	Magherafelt	III.	239
19	Oldtown Demesne	161	1	27	Kildare	Naas North	Naas	Naas	I.	62
13, 18	Oldtowndonore	1,015	1	18	Kildare	Clane	Downings	Naas	I.	54
37, 42	Old Town Downing	222	3	18	Londonderry	Loughinsholin	Ballyscullion	Magherafelt	III.	239
18	Oldtownhill	403	3	5	Kilkenny	Crannagh	Tullaroan	Kilkenny	I.	88
54	Oldtown Kilcashel	403	3	26	Roscommon	Moycarn	Moore	Ballinasloe	IV.	207
23	Oldtown or Puddingstreet	111	2	19	Westmeath	Kilkenny West	Drumraney	Ballymahon	I.	273
32, 33	Oldtown (Ryan)	212	3	26	Limerick	Smallcounty	Hospital	Kilmallock	II.	260
7	OLDTOWN T.	—			Dublin	Balrothery West	Clonmethan	Balrothery	I.	22
9	Oldtully	216	1	33	Meath	Fore	Oldcastle	Oldcastle	I.	202
68	Old Warren	446	1	20a	Cavan	Upper Massereene	Blaris	Lisburn	III.	30
22	Ollatrim	47	0	39	Tipperary, N.R.	Upper Ormond	Aghnameadle	Nenagh	II.	289
42	Oltore	192	2	37b	Galway	Clare	Donaghpatrick	Tuam	IV.	19
35	Omagh	31	3	15c	Tyrone	Omagh East	Drumragh	Omagh	III.	312
35	OMAGH T.	—			Tyrone	Omagh East	Drumragh	Omagh	III.	313
37, 38	Omard	965	2	14d	Cavan	Clanmahon	Ballymachugh	Cavan	III.	76
44	Omaun Beg	303	2	39	Galway	Clare	Killecrin	Tuam	IV.	21
44	Omaun More	350	1	35	Galway	Clare	Killererin	Tuam	IV.	21
9	O'Meara's Acres	75	2	34	Tipperary, N.R.	Lower Ormond	Kilbarron	Borrisokane	II.	284
21	Omey Island, Cartoorbeg	73	3	26	Galway	Ballynahinch	Omey	Clifden	IV.	15
21	Omey Island, Cloon	94	2	5e	Galway	Ballynahinch	Omey	Clifden	IV.	15
21	Omey Island, Gooreen	145	2	17f	Galway	Ballynahinch	Omey	Clifden	IV.	15
21	Omey Island, Gooreenatinny	117	0	28g	Galway	Ballynahinch	Omey	Clifden	IV.	15
21	Omey Island, Sturrakeen	91	0	24h	Galway	Ballynahinch	Omey	Clifden	IV.	15
7	Omoresforest	1,074	0	12	Queen's Co.	Maryborough West	Clonenagh and Clonagheen	Mountmellick	I.	243
51	Onagh	834	3	37	Roscommon	Athlone	Taghmaconnell	Athlone	IV.	185
7	Onagh	188	0	33	Wicklow	Rathdown	Powerscourt	Rathdown	I.	356
110	Onaght	1,767	3	33	Galway	Aran	Inishmore	Galway	IV.	3
24, 30	Ongenstown	1,267	0	34	Meath	Lower Navan	Ardbraccan	Navan	I.	214
27	Ongenstown	203	1	9	Meath	Upper Duleek	Duleek	Drogheda	I.	197
20, 25	Onomy	125	3	8	Monaghan	Cremorne	Muckno	Castleblayney	III.	262
17, 25	Ooankeagh	115	2	37	Clare	Inchiquin	Ruan	Corrofin	II.	28
64	Oolagh East	1,072	0	26i	Kerry	Dunkerron North	Knockane	Cahersiveen	II.	182
64	Oolagh West	703	0	7j	Kerry	Dunkerron North	Knockane	Cahersiveen	II.	182
25	Oolahills East	530	0	23	Limerick	Coonagh	Oola	Tipperary	II.	236
25	Oolahills West	73	1	24	Limerick	Coonagh	Oola	Tipperary	II.	236
25	OOLA T.	—			Limerick	Coonagh	Oola	Tipperary	II.	236
38, 52	Oorid	1,514	0	2l	Galway	Moycullen	Kilcummin	Oughterard	IV.	67
10	Oorla	97	2	24	Limerick	Shanid	Robertstown	Rathkeale	II.	258
11, 12	Oort	754	3	13	Donegal	Inishowen East	Culdaff	Inishowen	III.	118
100, 101	Oory	455	1	37	Mayo	Clanmorris	Taghccn	Claremorris	IV.	136
20, 25	Ora Beg	119	2	10	Fermanagh	Clanawley	Cleenish	Enniskillen	III.	191
20	Oram	255	1	6	Monaghan	Cremorne	Muckno	Castleblayney	III.	262

(a) Including 10A. 2R. 36P. water.
(b) Including 25A. 0R. 11P. water.
(c) Including 3A. 1R. 0P. water.
(d) Including 18A. 0R. 18P. water.

(e) Including 16A. 0R. 28P. water.
(f) Including 13A. 3R. 11P. water.
(g) Including 10A. 2R. 31P. water.
(h) Including 20A. 3R. 24P. water.

(i) Including 50A. 3R. 11P. water.
(j) Including 43A. 2R. 14P. water.
(k) Including 188A. 2R. 27P. water.

No. of Sheet of the Ordnance Survey Maps.	Townlands and Towns.	Area in Statute Acres.	County.	Barony.	Parish.	Poor Law Union in 1857.	Townland Census of 1851, Part I.	
		A. R. P.					Vol.	Page
34	Oran . . .	275 2 11	Roscommon .	Ballymoe . .	Oran . . .	Roscommon .	IV.	192
83, 95	Oran Beg . .	519 1 1	Galway . .	Dunkellin . .	Oranmore . .	Galway . .	IV.	32
95	Oranhill . .	346 0 0	Galway . .	Dunkellin . .	Oranmore . .	Galway . .	IV.	32
81	Oranhill . .	33 2 19	Galway . .	Galway . .	Rahoon . .	Galway . .	IV.	38
95	Oran More .	315 3 4	Galway . .	Dunkellin . .	Oranmore . .	Galway . .	IV.	32
95	ORANMORE T.	—	Galway . .	Dunkellin . .	Oranmore . .	Galway . .	IV.	32
50, 53	Oranstown . .	156 3 13	Meath . .	Dunboyne . .	Dunboyne . .	Dunshaughlin .	I.	199
12	Orchard . .	316 3 23a	Carlow . .	Idrone East .	Nurney . .	Carlow . .	I.	8
14, 18	Orchard . .	416 1 21	Carlow . .	St. Mullins Upper .	Moyacomb .	Carlow . .	I.	14
6	Orchard Island .	7 3 2	Roscommon .	Boyle . .	Ardcarn . .	Boyle . .	IV.	193
19, 25	Orchard Lower .	390 2 26	Queen's Co. .	Cullenagh . .	Fossy or Timahoe .	Abbeyleix .	I.	240
18, 27	Orchardstown .	251 3 33	Waterford .	Gaultiere . .	Kilmacleague .	Waterford .	II.	364
17	Orchardstown .	206 3 36	Waterford .	Middlethird .	Kilburne .	Waterford .	II.	367
77	Orchardstown East .	135 2 18	Tipperary, S.R.	Iffa and Offa East	Newchapel .	Clonmel .	II.	315
77	Orchardstown West	220 2 28	Tipperary, S.R.	Iffa and Offa East	Newchapel .	Clonmel .	II.	315
25	Orchard Upper .	91 2 16	Queen's Co. .	Cullenagh . .	Fossy or Timahoe .	Abbeyleix .	I.	240
54	Ordnance Ground .	6 2 15	Galway . .	Moycullen . .	Kilcummin .	Oughterard .	IV.	68
2	O'Reilly's Island .	12 2 11	Roscommon .	Boyle . .	Kilronan .	Boyle . .	IV.	197
29, 35	Ories . . .	378 2 17	Westmeath .	Clonlonan . .	Kilcleagh .	Athlone .	I.	262
64	Orinish Island .	4 1 24	Donegal . .	Boylagh . .	Inishkeel .	Glenties .	III.	114
17	Oristown . .	133 1 27	Meath . .	Morgallion .	Clongill . .	Navan . .	I.	209
11, 17	Oristown . .	1,835 2 3	Meath . .	Upper Kells .	Teltown . .	Kells . .	I.	207
17	ORISTOWN T. .	—	Meath . .	Upper Kells .	Teltown . .	Kells . .	I.	207
29	Oritor . .	289 2 38	Tyrone . .	Dungannon Upper .	Kildress . .	Cookstown .	III.	309
23	Orkneys . .	91 3 4	Tipperary, N.R.	Ikerrin . .	Bourney . .	Roscrea .	II.	274
22, 25	Orlagh . .	43 2 5	Dublin . .	Uppercross .	Cruagh . .	Dublin South .	I.	39
2	Orlock . .	183 0 17	Down . .	Ards Lower .	Bangor . .	Newtownards .	III.	157
101	Ormond's Island .	19 2 36	Kerry . .	Glanarought .	Tuosist . .	Kenmare .	II.	189
20, 25	Oro More or Tully-brack . .	443 0 39b	Fermanagh .	Clanawley . .	Cleenish . .	Enniskillen .	III.	191
42, 47	Orristown . .	235 0 14	Wexford . .	Forth . .	Kilmacree .	Wexford .	I.	311
116	Orthon's Island .	0 2 13	Cork, W.R. .	Bear . .	Kilcaskan .	Castletown .	II.	123
19	Osberstown . .	1,316 1 28c	Kildare . .	Naas North .	Naas . .	Naas . .	I.	62
44	O'Shea's Acres .	137 2 19	Clare . .	Tulla Lower .	Kilseily . .	Limerick .	II.	37
36	Osierbrook . .	108 0 12	King's Co. .	Ballybritt .	Seirkieran .	Parsonstown .	I.	127
15	Ossoryhill . .	518 1 12	Kilkenny . .	Gowran . .	Kilderry .	Kilkenny .	I.	96
35	Otter Island .	0 0 6	Leitrim . .	Mohill . .	Annaduff .	Mohill . .	IV.	105
126	Otters Island .	0 3 9	Galway . .	Longford . .	Lickmolassy .	Portumna .	IV.	61
29	Otterstown . .	183 1 25	Meath . .	Lune . .	Athboy . .	Trim . .	I.	207
19	Oughaval . .	327 1 20	Queen's Co. .	Stradbally .	Stradbally .	Athy . .	I.	247
36	Oughaval . .	187 0 20	Sligo . .	Leyny . .	Kilmacteige .	Tobercurry .	IV.	231
7	Oughtagh . .	627 0 18	Galway . .	Ballymoe . .	Ballynakill .	Glennamaddy .	IV.	5
19, 20	Oughtagh . .	77 3 19	Galway . .	Ballymoe . .	Kilbegnet .	Roscommon .	IV.	8
22, 23	Oughtagh . .	668 2 25	Londonderry .	Tirkeeran .	Cumber Lower .	Londonderry .	III.	249
71	Oughtagh . .	291 1 32	Mayo . .	Gallen . .	Templemore .	Castlebar .	IV.	151
6	Oughtagorey .	596 2 25	Sligo . .	Carbury . .	Rossinver .	Sligo . .	IV.	223
7, 12	Oughtboy . .	964 0 30d	Tyrone . .	Strabane Upper .	Bodoney Upper .	Gortin . .	III.	324
100, 101	Oughtcarn . .	1,051 3 8e	Donegal . .	Tirhugh . .	Templecarn .	Donegal .	III.	149
4	Oughtdarra . .	289 1 24	Clare . .	Corcomroe .	Killilagh .	Ennistimon .	II.	20
7, 12	Oughtdoorish .	1,848 3 30f	Tyrone . .	Strabane Upper .	Bodoney Upper .	Gortin . .	III.	324
15, 23	Oughter . .	494 3 9	King's Co. .	Garrycastle .	Lemanaghan .	Parsonstown .	I.	137
25	Oughteragh . .	263 3 30g	Leitrim . .	Carrigallen .	Oughteragh .	Bawnboy .	IV.	92
65, 72	Oughterard . .	537 0 12	Clare . .	Moyarta . .	Kilballyowen .	Kilrush .	II.	32
15	Oughterard . .	388 2 13	Kildare . .	South Salt .	Oughterard .	Naas . .	I.	78
38	Oughterard . .	152 3 1	Tyrone . .	Dungannon Upper .	Desertcreat .	Cookstown .	III.	308
41	Oughterard . .	326 3 17	Tyrone . .	Omagh East .	Dromore .	Omagh .	III.	311
60	Oughterard or Caurans Upper .	119 3 38h	Mayo . .	Carra . .	Turlough .	Castlebar .	IV.	130
54	OUGHTERARD T. .	—	Galway . .	Moycullen . .	Kilcummin .	Oughterard .	IV.	69
8	Oughterdrum .	125 1 21	Fermanagh .	Lurg . .	Belleek .	Ballyshannon .	III.	203
28, 37	Oughterlin .	777 1 25	Donegal . .	Kilmacrenan .	Killygarvan .	Milford .	III.	128
49, 60	Oughtihery .	1,031 0 19	Cork, W.R. .	East Muskerry .	Aghabulloge .	Macroom .	II.	153
89, 98, 99	Oughtiv . .	1,048 1 0	Kerry . .	Iveragh . .	Dromod .	Cahersiveen .	II.	195
3	Oughtmama .	821 3 0	Clare . .	Burren . .	Oughtmama .	Ballyvaghan .	II.	14
7, 12	Oughtmame .	823 3 26	Tyrone . .	Strabane Upper .	Bodoney Upper .	Gortin . .	III.	324
49, 57	Oughtmeen .	1,139 1 2i	Donegal . .	Boylagh . .	Templecrone .	Glenties .	III.	115
146, 147	Oughtminnee .	167 1 19	Cork, W.R. .	West Carbery(W.D.)	Kilmoe . .	Skull .	II.	145
99, 100	Oughtnadrin .	145 1 1	Donegal . .	Tirhugh . .	Drumhome .	Donegal .	III.	147
100, 101	Oughtnadrin Barr, Tullygallen, and Tullywee .	1,434 2 38j	Donegal . .	Tirhugh . .	Drumhome .	Donegal .	III.	147
7, 8, 12, 13	Oughtnamwella .	1,368 3 36	Tyrone . .	Strabane Upper .	Bodoney Upper .	Gortin . .	III.	324
131	Oughtohig .	182 0 9	Cork, W.R. .	West Carbery(W.D.)	Kilcoe . .	Skull .	II.	143

(a) Including 10A. 2R. 16P. River Barrow.
(b) Including 15A. 3R. 2P. water.
(c) Including 15A. 3R. 2P. River Liffey.
(d) Including 0A. 1R. 30P. water.

(e) Including 59A. 3R. 36P. water.
(f) Including 5A. 2R. 35P. water.
(g) Including 22A. 1R. 26P. water.

(h) Including 13A. 0R. 4P. water.
(i) Including 56A. 0R. 27P. water.
(j) Including 15A. 2R. 7P. water.

No. of Sheet of the Ordnance Survey Maps.	Townlands and Towns.	Area in Statute Acres. A. R. P.	County.	Barony.	Parish.	Poor Law Union in 1857.	Townland Census of 1851, Part I. Vol.	Page
97, 107	Oughty	1,277 0 38	Mayo	Murrisk	Oughaval	Westport	IV.	162
1, 2	Oughtymore	246 0 14	Londonderry	Keenaght	Magilligan	New Tn Limavady	III.	237
5	Oughtymoyle	248 3 14	Londonderry	Keenaght	Magilligan	New Tn Limavady	III.	237
21, 27	Oulart	404 0 37	Wexford	Ballaghkeen	Meelnagh	Enniscorthy	I.	298
3	Oulart	278 1 0	Wexford	Gorey	Kilnenor	Gorey	I.	320
20	Oulartard	327 1 27	Wexford	Scarawalsh	Clone	Enniscorthy	I.	322
26	Oulartleigh	296 1 18	Wexford	Ballaghkeen	Ballyhuskard	Enniscorthy	I.	292
21	OULART T.	—	Wexford	Ballaghkeen	Meelnagh	Enniscorthy	I.	298
20, 21	Oulartwick Beg	112 3 32	Wexford	Ballaghkeen	Kilcormick	Enniscorthy	I.	294
20, 21	Oulartwick More	210 2 32	Wexford	Ballaghkeen	Kilcormick	Enniscorthy	I.	294
21	Ouley	82 1 27	Cavan	Upper Loughtee	Castleterra	Cavan	III.	83
15	Ouley	746 2 20	Down	Castlereagh Upper	Saintfield	Lisburn	III.	166
41	Ouley	444 1 0	Down	Lordship of Newry	Newry	Newry	III.	182
119, 122	Oultauns	203 0 13	Mayo	Kilmaine	Kilcommon	Ballinrobe	IV.	155
126	Oultort	471 0 16	Galway	Longford	Lickmolassy	Portumna	IV.	61
14, 19, 24	Ouna or Eagle Hill	2,888 2 31	Antrim	Lower Glenarm	Layd	Ballycastle	III.	23
30, 31	Ounagh	831 2 2	Sligo	Leyny	Kilmacteige	Tobercurry	IV.	231
8, 13	Ouragh	412 1 15	Carlow	Rathvilly	Tullowphelim	Carlow	I.	12
45	Ouris	144 3 21	King's Co.	Clonlisk	Dunkerron	Roscrea	I.	130
27	Outal	158 0 0	Antrim	Kilconway	Grange of Dundermot	Ballymena	III.	27
75, 76	Outeragh	1,033 1 7	Tipperary, S.R.	Middlethird	Outeragh	Cashel	II.	329
6	Outhill	224 3 22	Antrim	Lower Dunluce	Ballyrashane	Coleraine	III.	15
16	Outlack	449 2 0	Armagh	Fews Lower	Lisnadill	Armagh	III.	47
11	Outlands	79 2 0	Dublin	Nethercross	Swords	Balrothery	I.	32
39	Outlands of Grevally	63 2 39	Tyrone	Dungannon Middle	Donaghenry	Cookstown	III.	301
25	Outleckan	759 0 20	Armagh	Fews Upper	Ballymyre	Newry	III.	48
19, 23	Outrath	528 2 13	Kilkenny	Shillelogher	Outrath	Kilkenny	I.	115
27	Ouvry	190 3 30	Monaghan	Farney	Magheross	Carrickmacross	III.	274
16, 22	Ovaun	104 0 19a	Roscommon	Roscommon	Shankill	Strokestown	IV.	213
23, 27	Ovenstown	610 0 12	Kilkenny	Shillelogher	Earlstown	Callan	I.	114
4	Ovidstown	334 3 2	Kildare	Ikeathy & Oughterany	Cloncurry	Celbridge	I.	57
10, 14	Ovidstown	54 1 34	Kildare	North Salt	Straffan	Celbridge	I.	76
10, 14	Ovidstown	211 2 6	Kildare	North Salt	Taghadoe	Celbridge	I.	76
24, 30	Ovil	941 1 22	Londonderry	Keenaght	Dungiven	New Tn Limavady	III.	236
5, 12	Owenanirragh	1,413 0 3b	Mayo	Erris	Kilcommon	Belmullet	IV.	144
86	Owenavaddy or Riverstick	71 1 11	Galway	Kilconnell	Killaan	Loughrea	IV.	41
24	Owenbeg	601 2 28	Londonderry	Keenaght	Dungiven	New Tn Limavady	III.	236
11, 17	Owenbeg	1,466 3 13	Sligo	Tireragh	Easky	Dromore West	IV.	234
84	Owenbeg	288 2 31	Donegal	Banagh	Killymard	Donegal	III.	111
19, 20	Owenboy	2,021 0 33	Donegal	Inishowen West	Fahan Lower	Inishowen	III.	120
28, 37	Owenboy	1,239 0 34	Mayo	Tirawley	Crossmolina	Ballina	IV.	166
28	Owenbreedin	78 2 0	Fermanagh	Magherastephana	Aghavea	Lisnaskea	III.	219
113	Owenbristy	69 1 23	Galway	Dunkellin	Ardrahan	Gort	IV.	27
8	Owencam	314 1 19	Cavan	Tullyhaw	Templeport	Bawnboy	III.	95
34, 39	Owencloghy	1,658 0 24	Antrim	Lower Glenarm	Tickmacrevan	Larne	III.	24
55, 56, 66	Owenduff	2,023 2 11c	Mayo	Burrishoole	Achill	Newport	IV.	117
36, 44, 45	Owenduff	2,138 1 31d	Mayo	Erris	Kilcommon	Newport	IV.	144
9, 13	Owengallees	469 2 24e	Cavan	Tullyhaw	Templeport	Bawnboy	III.	95
35	Owenglass	1,306 3 13	Mayo	Erris	Kilcommon	Newport	IV.	144
29, 38	Owenkillew and Barnahone	584 2 37	Donegal	Inishowen West	Fahan Lower	Inishowen	III.	120
78, 87	Owennagadragh	460 2 17	Donegal	Raphoe	Donaghmore	Stranorlar	III.	138
40	Owenreagh	759 3 25	Londonderry	Loughinsholin	Ballynascreen	Magherafelt	III.	239
5, 10	Owenreagh	767 0 0	Tyrone	Strabane Lower	Leckpatrick	Strabane	III.	322
61	Owen's & Bigg's-Lot	143 0 27	Tipperary, S.R.	Middlethird	St. John Baptist	Cashel	II.	330
130	Owen's Island	1 1 6	Cork, W.R.	West Carbery(W.D.)	Kilcrohane	Bantry	II.	144
24	Owenskerry	165 1 0	Fermanagh	Magherastephana	Aghalurcher	Lisnaskea	III.	217
45	Owensland	282 3 22	Antrim	Upper Antrim	Kilbride	Antrim	III.	6
50, 53	Owenstown	108 1 21	Meath	Upper Deece	Moyglare	Celbridge	I.	194
42, 47	Owenstown	98 1 22	Wexford	Forth	Rathmacknee	Wexford	I.	313
22, 23	Owenstown or Trimleston	75 2 8	Dublin	Rathdown	Taney	Rathdown	I.	38
81, 82	Owenteskiny	1,353 3 29	Donegal	Banagh	Inishkeel	Glenties	III.	106
97	Owenwee	1,561 0 0	Mayo	Murrisk	Oughaval	Westport	IV.	162
17, 23	Owenykeevan or Tawnamaddoo	844 0 17	Sligo	Tireragh	Easky	Dromore West	IV.	234
41	Ower	668 3 18	Galway	Clare	Killursa	Tuam	IV.	22
55, 68	Ower	1,149 1 34f	Galway	Moycullen	Killannin	Oughterard	IV.	70
40	Owey Island	301 1 29	Donegal	Boylagh	Templecrone	Glenties	III.	116
22	Owlbeg	71 1 15	Carlow	Idrone East	Clonygoose	Carlow	I.	6
10, 15	Owl Island	22 1 38	Fermanagh	Magheraboy	Inishmacsaint	Enniskillen	III.	213
56, 57, 64	Ownagarry	1,100 2 21g	Kerry	Dunkerron North	Killorglin	Killarney	II.	181
34,35,38,39	Owning	799 2 33	Kilkenny	Iverk	Owning	Carrick on Suir	I.	106

(a) Including 2A. 0R. 27P. water.
(b) Including 33A. 2R. 29P. water.
(c) Including 21A. 2R. 21P. water.
(d) Including 25A. 1R. 26P. water.
(e) { Including 60A. 0R. 24P. Bunerky Lough.
{ Including 40A. 0R. 17P. Lakefield Lough.
(f) Including 31A. 0R. 37P. water.
(g) Including 1A. 1R. 35P. water.

No. of Sheet of the Ordnance Survey Maps.	Townlands and Towns.	Area in Statute Acres. A.	R.	P.	County.	Barony.	Parish.	Poor Law Union in 1857.	Townland Census of 1851, Part I. Vol.	Page
80	Oxford	319	3	5	Mayo	Gallen	Killedan	Swineford	IV.	150
107	Oxgrove	89	2	17	Galway	Longford	Killimorbologue	Portumna	IV.	59
114	Ox Island	1	2	1	Mayo	Murrisk	Inishbofin	Clifden	IV.	159
10,11,15,16	Oxpark	217	1	36	Tipperary, N.R.	Lower Ormond	Modreeny	Borrisokane	II.	287
27, 36	Oxtown	350	2	24	Tyrone	Omagh East	Termonmaguirk	Omagh	III.	314
112	Oysterhaven	48	3	4	Cork, E.R.	Kinalea	Kilmonoge	Kinsale	II.	95
8	Oyster Island	32	3	32	Sligo	Carbury	Killaspugbrone	Sligo	IV.	222
23	Paal East	247	1	14	Cork, E.R.	Duhallow	Kilmeen	Kanturk	II.	73
23, 31	Paal West	393	1	33	Cork, E.R.	Duhallow	Kilmeen	Kanturk	II.	73
50, 51	Pace	225	0	3	Meath	Dunboyne	Dunboyne	Dunshaughlin	I.	199
50, 51	Paddingstown	33	0	21	Meath	Dunboyne	Dunboyne	Dunshaughlin	I.	199
10, 17	Paddinstown Lower	410	3	28	Westmeath	Rathconrath	Rathconrath	Ballymahon	I.	284
10, 17	Paddinstown Upper	172	2	28	Westmeath	Rathconrath	Rathconrath	Ballymahon	I.	284
20	Paddock	321	3	9	Cavan	Upper Loughtee	Urney	Cavan	III.	86
120	Paddock	179	2	28	Cork, W.R.	East Carbery (W.D.)	Drinagh	Skibbereen	II.	131
94	Paddock	269	0	17	Cork, W.R.	East Carbery (W.D.)	Kinneigh	Dunmanway	II.	135
140, 141	Paddock	194	1	15	Cork, W.R.	West Carbery (E.D.)	Aghadown	Skibbereen	II.	137
17	Paddock	79	1	19	Galway	Dunmore	Dunmore	Tuam	IV.	34
53	Paddock	59	0	15	Kerry	Corkaguiny	Kildrum	Dingle	II.	177
23	Paddock	60	1	25	Kilkenny	Shillelogher	Burnchurch	Callan	I.	113
21	Paddock	93	2	30	Louth	Ferrard	Monasterboice	Drogheda	I.	181
45	Paddock	160	3	36	Meath	Ratoath	Ratoath	Dunshaughlin	I.	219
11	Paddock	568	2	27	Queen's Co.	Upperwoods	Offerlane	Mountmellick	I.	252
6	Paddock	9	1	10	Roscommon	Boyle	Ardcarn	Boyle	IV.	193
31, 40	Paddock	37	3	31	Tipperary, N.R.	Kilnamanagh Upper	Glenkeen	Thurles	II.	278
28	Paddock	100	0	9	Waterford	Coshmore&Coshbride	Kilwatermoy	Lismore	II.	344
8	Paddock	31	2	35	Wicklow	Rathdown	Delgany	Rathdown	I.	355
19, 20	Paddocks	161	2	13	Waterford	Coshmore&Coshbride	Lismore and Mocollop	Lismore	II.	347
49	Padinstown	291	2	1	Meath	Upper Deece	Balfeaghan	Celbridge	I.	193
49, 50	Pagestown	439	2	2	Meath	Upper Deece	Kilclone	Dunshaughlin	I.	193
10	Painestown	554	2	20	Kildare	Ikeathy&Oughterany	Balraheen	Celbridge	I.	56
14, 19	Painestown	423	2	35	Kildare	South Salt	Kill	Naas	I.	77
17, 18	Painestown	284	3	31	Louth	Ardee	Dromin	Ardee	I.	172
19	Painestown	208	0	6	Louth	Ferrard	Clonmore	Drogheda	I.	180
20, 21	Painestown	160	1	4	Meath	Lower Duleek	Colp	Drogheda	I.	195
19, 26	Painestown	1,487	2	4a	Meath	Lower Duleek	Painestown	Navan	I.	196
12	Painestown	550	3	27	Meath	Morgallion	Castletown	Navan	I.	209
32, 38	Painestown	616	3	9	Meath	Skreen	Macetown	Dunshaughlin	I.	221
2	Painestown or Oakpark	1,296	0	12b	Carlow	Carlow	Painestown	Carlow	I.	2
3, 7	Pakenhamhall or Tullynally	471	3	27	Westmeath	Fore	Mayne	Granard	I.	271
109	Palaceanne	211	0	38	Cork, W.R.	East Carbery (W.D.)	Kinneigh	Bandon	II.	135
30	Palace East	195	1	34	Wexford	Bantry	Oldross	New Ross	I.	301
30	Palace West	353	1	37	Wexford	Bantry	Oldross	New Ross	I.	301
32	Pallas	620	2	18c	Cork, E.R.	Duhallow	Roskeen	Kanturk	II.	75
135	Pallas	105	3	25	Cork, W.R.	Ibane and Barryroe	Ardfield	Clonakilty	II.	148
135	Pallas	25	1	33	Cork, W.R.	Ibane and Barryroe	Island	Clonakilty	II.	149
60, 73	Pallas	631	1	38	Galway	Kilconnell	Fohanagh	Mountbellew	IV.	40
117	Pallas	636	1	2	Galway	Leitrim	Tynagh	Portumna	IV.	55
126	Pallas	197	3	35	Galway	Longford	Lickmolassy	Portumna	IV.	61
16, 22	Pallas	1,078	2	29	Kerry	Clanmaurice	Kilfeighny	Listowel	II.	170
24	Pallas	120	1	37	King's Co.	Ballyboy	Killoughy	Tullamore	I.	124
37, 45	Pallas	270	0	2	Limerick	Connello Upper	Kilmeedy	Newcastle	II.	233
24	Pallas	171	3	16	Limerick	Coonagh	Grean	Tipperary	II.	235
3, 11	Pallas	366	1	19	Limerick	Kenry	Chapelrussell	Rathkeale	II.	248
3, 11	Pallas	66	3	37	Limerick	Kenry	Kilcornan	Rathkeale	II.	249
5, 8	Pallas	141	2	4	Tipperary, N.R.	Lower Ormond	Loughkeen	Parsonstown	II.	286
59	Pallas	370	3	6	Tipperary, S.R.	Clanwilliam	Donohill	Tipperary	II.	307
38	Pallas	303	0	15	Westmeath	Moycashel	Durrow	Tullamore	I.	277
15, 24	Pallasbeg	492	3	26	Limerick	Owneybeg	Tuogh	Limerick	II.	251
23, 27	Pallas Beg	222	0	7d	Longford	Shrule	Forgney	Ballymahon	I.	166
20	Pallas Beg	239	0	4	Tipperary, N.R.	Owney and Arra	Youghalarra	Nenagh	II.	298
12, 13	Pallas Big	556	2	10	Queen's Co.	Maryborough East	Clonenagh and Clonagheen	Mountmellick	I.	241
38, 39	Pallasboy	481	0	12	Westmeath	Moycashel	Rahugh	Tullamore	I.	279
21, 22	Pallas East	151	1	4	Tipperary, N.R.	Upper Ormond	Templedowney	Nenagh	II.	293
24	PALLAS GREAN T.	—			Limerick	Coonagh	Grean	Tipperary	II.	235
24	Pallashill	128	0	2	Limerick	Coonagh	Grean	Tipperary	II.	235
40	Pallashill	417	2	1	Tipperary, N.R.	Illoguarty	Ileih	Thurles	II.	270
3, 11	PALLASKENRY T.	—			Limerick	Kenry	Chapelrussell	Rathkeale	II.	248

(a) Including 5A. 3R. 16P. water.
(b) Including 20A. 0R. 0P. water.
(c) Including 25A. 1R. 0P. water.
(d) Including 6A. 2R. 29P. water.

No. of Sheet of the Ordnance Survey Maps.	Townlands and Towns.	Area in Statute Acres. A. R. P.	County.	Barony.	Parish.	Poor Law Union in 1857.	Townland Census of 1851, Part I. Vol.	Page
12	Pallas Little . .	339 1 21	Queen's Co. .	Maryborough East .	Clonenagh and Clonagheen . .	Mountmellick .	I.	241
34	Pallas Lower .	314 2 3	Tipperary, N.R.	Kilnamanagh Upper	Glenkeen . .	Thurles . .	II.	278
23, 27	Pallas More . .	306 1 25a	Longford . .	Shrule . .	Forgney . .	Ballymahon .	I.	166
20	Pallas More .	578 0 38	Tipperary, N.R.	Owney and Arra .	Youghalarra . .	Nenagh . .	II.	298
24	Pallaspark .	279 3 37b	King's Co. .	Ballyboy . .	Killoughy . .	Tullamore .	I.	124
—	PALLAS T. . .	—	Cork, E.R. .	Kinalea . .	Kinure . .	Kinsale . .	II.	96
34	Pallas Upper . .	367 3 38	Tipperary, N.R.	Kilnamanagh Upper	Glenkeen . .	Thurles . .	II.	278
21, 22	Pallas West . .	184 2 37	Tipperary, N.R.	Upper Ormond .	Templedowney .	Nenagh . .	II.	293
65, 66	Pallis . .	171 2 22c	Kerry . .	Magunihy . .	Aghadoe . .	Killarney .	II.	199
29	Pallis . .	62 3 37	Waterford .	Coshmore&Coshbride	Lismore and Mocollop	Lismore . .	II.	347
2	Pallishill . .	211 0 0	Wexford . .	Gorey . .	Kilnenor . .	Gorey . .	I.	320
2	Pallis Lower . .	340 3 55	Wexford . .	Gorey . .	Kilnenor . .	Gorey . .	I.	320
2	Pallis Upper .	279 1 39	Wexford . .	Gorey . .	Kilnenor . .	Gorey . .	I.	320
22	Palmershill . .	201 2 9	Queen's Co. .	Clarmallagh .	Aghaboe . .	Donaghmore .	I.	236
61	Palmer's-hill .	56 1 20	Tipperary, S.R.	Middlethird .	St. Patricksrock .	Cashel . .	II.	331
6	Palmersland . .	93 0 19	Louth . .	Louth . .	Louth . .	Dundalk . .	I.	184
17, 18	Palmerston Lower .	268 1 26d	Dublin . .	Uppercross .	Palmerston .	Dublin South .	I.	40
17	PALMERSTON T. .	—	Dublin . .	Uppercross .	Palmerston .	Dublin South .	I.	40
17	Palmerston Upper .	204 0 37	Dublin . .	Uppercross .	Palmerston .	Dublin South .	I.	40
5, 8	Palmerstown . .	249 2 16	Dublin . .	Balrothery East .	Balrothery . .	Balrothery .	I.	19
6, 7	Palmerstown . .	558 2 16	Dublin . .	Balrothery West .	Palmerstown . .	Balrothery .	I.	23
83, 95	Palmerstown . .	449 0 36	Galway . .	Dunkellin . .	Athenry . .	Galway . .	IV.	27
19	Palmerstown . .	119 0 38	Kildare . .	Naas North . .	Johnstown . .	Naas . .	I.	62
19	Palmerstown . .	162 3 22	Kilkenny . .	Crannagh . .	St. Canice . .	Kilkenny . .	I.	87
19	Palmerstown . .	57 3 21	Kilkenny . .	Shillelogher .	St. Patrick's .	Kilkenny . .	I.	116
19	Palmerstown Demesne . .	691 1 18	Kildare . .	Naas North . .	Johnstown . .	Naas . .	I.	62
40	Palmira or Cornaglare . .	389 3 2	Cavan . .	Castlerahan .	Mullagh . .	Kells . .	III.	70
47	Paradise . .	56 2 19	Wexford . .	Forth . .	Ishartmon . .	Wexford . .	I.	310
47	Paradise Little .	4 3 24	Wexford . .	Forth . .	Ishartmon . .	Wexford . .	I.	310
18	Parcellstown . .	727 1 15	Westmeath .	Moygoish .	Templecran . .	Mullingar .	I.	281
17	Parcellstown . .	123 3 27	Westmeath .	Rathconrath .	Rathconrath . .	Mullingar .	I.	284
15	Parisee . .	467 3 17e	Cavan . .	Lower Loughtee .	Annagh . .	Cavan . .	III.	79
25, 29	Parishagh . .	118 1 6	Antrim . .	Lower Glenarm .	Tickmacrevan .	Larne . .	III.	24
15	Paris Island Big .	13 1 6	Fermanagh .	Lurg . .	Trory . .	Lowtherstown .	III.	209
15	Paris Island Little .	3 3 1	Fermanagh .	Lurg . .	Trory . .	Lowtherstown .	III.	209
9	Paristown . .	120 2 29	Westmeath .	Delvin . .	Killua . .	Castletowndelvin	I.	266
13	Park . .	182 0 35	Antrim . .	Cary . .	Armoy . .	Ballycastle .	III.	11
7	Park . .	437 1 30	Carlow . .	Carlow . .	Ballinacarrig .	Carlow . .	I.	1
22	Park . .	457 2 23	Cork, E.R. .	Duhallow .	Clonfert . .	Kanturk . .	II.	69
29	Park . .	233 0 37	Cork, E.R. .	Duhallow .	Nohavaldaly .	Millstreet .	II.	75
87	Park . .	43 1 1	Cork, E.R. .	Kerrycurrihy .	Monkstown . .	Cork . .	II.	93
45	Park . .	119 1 29	Cork, E.R. .	Kinnatalloon .	Aghern . .	Fermoy . .	II.	97
115, 116	Park . .	198 1 27	Cork, W.R. .	Bear . .	Killaconenagh .	Castletown .	II.	125
84	Park . .	554 1 33	Galway . .	Athenry . .	Athenry . .	Loughrea .	IV.	4
19, 20	Park . .	167 2 22	Galway . .	Ballymoe . .	Kilbegnet . .	Glennamaddy .	IV.	8
69	Park . .	165 3 7	Galway . .	Clare . .	Annaghdown .	Galway . .	IV.	16
99	Park . .	207 2 0	Galway . .	Clonmacnowen .	Killallaghtan .	Ballinasloe .	IV.	26
16	Park . .	40 3 19	Galway . .	Dunmore . .	Kilbennan . .	Tuam . .	IV.	34
55	Park . .	486 1 22	Galway . .	Moycullen .	Killannin . .	Oughterard .	IV.	70
92, 93	Park . .	456 0 32	Galway . .	Moycullen .	Moycullen . .	Galway . .	IV.	71
66, 67	Park . .	353 2 34	Kerry . .	Magunihy .	Killarney . .	Killarney .	II.	203
31	Park . .	149 2 37	King's Co. .	Ballyboy . .	Ballyboy . .	Parsonstown .	I.	123
21, 22	Park . .	587 3 28	King's Co. .	Garrycastle .	Gallen . .	Parsonstown .	I.	136
1, 3	Park . .	276 1 17	Leitrim . .	Rosclogher .	Rossinver . .	Ballyshannon .	IV.	112
6	Park . .	72 2 27	Limerick . .	Clanwilliam .	Stradbally . .	Limerick . .	II.	226
5	Park . .	240 2 32f	Limerick . .	Clanwilliam and Municipal Borough .	St. Patrick's .	Limerick . .	II.	225
49, 50	Park . .	454 1 34	Limerick . .	Coshlea . .	Galbally . .	Mitchelstown .	II.	239
18, 27	Park . .	634 1 25	Limerick . .	Shanid . .	Dunmoylan .	Glin . .	II.	255
70	Park . .	183 2 28	Mayo . .	Carra . .	Turlough . .	Castlebar .	IV.	131
63	Park . .	102 0 25	Mayo . .	Costello . .	Kilbeagh . .	Swineford .	IV.	141
46	Park . .	718 3 1	Meath . .	Upper Moyfenrath .	Ballyboggan .	Edenderry .	I.	212
46	Park . .	71 1 10g	Meath . .	Upper Moyfenrath .	Clonard . .	Edenderry .	I.	213
27	Park . .	118 0 3	Queen's Co. .	Clandonagh .	Rathsaran . .	Donaghmore .	I.	235
29	Park . .	121 2 0	Queen's Co. .	Clarmallagh .	Aghaboe . .	Abbeyleix .	I.	236
29	Park . .	15 2 0	Queen's Co. .	Clarmallagh .	Killermogh .	Abbeyleix .	I.	238
14, 19	Park . .	241 1 36	Queen's Co. .	Stradbally .	Curraclone .	Athy . .	I.	246
23, 29	Park . .	436 2 26	Tipperary, N.R.	Ikerrin . .	Killea . .	Roscrea . .	II.	276
22	Park . .	312 3 9	Tipperary, N.R.	Upper Ormond .	Aghnameadle .	Nenagh . .	II.	289
22	Park . .	173 2 15	Tipperary, N.R.	Upper Ormond .	Ballymackey .	Nenagh . .	II.	259
82	Park . .	315 1 32	Tipperary, S.R.	Iffa and Offa West .	Tullaghmelan .	Clogheen .	II.	321

(a) Including 6A. 3R. 13P. water.
(b) Including 24A. 0R. 24P. water.
(c) Including 1A. 1R. 8P. water.

(d) Including 12A. 2R. 0P. water.
(e) Including 148A. 1R. 14P. water.

(f) { Within the Municipal Boundary, 215A. 2R. 17P.
     { Without the Municipal Boundary, 25A. 0R. 15P.
(g) Including 11A. 3R. 32P. detached portion.

No. of Sheet of the Ordnance Survey Maps.	Townlands and Towns.	Area in Statute Acres. A. R. P.	County.	Barony.	Parish.	Poor Law Union in 1857.	Townland Census of 1851, Part I. Vol.	Page
24, 32	Park	177 1 2	Waterford	Decies without Drum	Stradbally	Kilmacthomas	II.	361
2	Park	546 0 7	Waterford	Upperthird	Rathgormuck	Carrick on Suir	II.	371
25, 26	Park	323 2 15	Wexford	Bantry	Clonmore	Enniscorthy	I.	300
46, 51	Park	45 1 11	Wexford	Bargy	Killag	Wexford	I.	306
5	Park	246 1 11	Wexford	Scarawalsh	Carnew	Gorey	I.	322
37	Park	249 2 8	Wexford	Shelmaliere West	Carrick	Wexford	I.	332
45	Park	229 2 30	Wicklow	Arklow	Arklow	Rathdrum	I.	341
42, 46, 47	Park	469 2 21	Wicklow	Shillelagh	Moyacomb	Shillelagh	I.	358
26	Parkacunna	84 1 39	Cork, E.R.	Fermoy	Castletownroche	Fermoy	II.	77
58, 59	Parkacurry	323 0 25	Galway	Tiaquin	Monivea	Tuam	IV.	79
33	Parkadallane	70 3 19	Cork, E.R.	Fermoy	Mallow	Mallow	II.	81
81	Parkaderreen	40 1 32	Tipperary, S.R.	Iffa and Offa West	Shanrahan	Clogheen	II.	320
81	Parkaderreen	61 0 9	Tipperary, S.R.	Iffa and Offa West	Tubbrid	Clogheen	II.	321
116	Parkagarraun	68 0 2	Galway	Leitrim	Ballynakill	Loughrea	IV.	52
19, 25	Parkahoughill	187 1 6	Queen's Co.	Ballyadams	Ballyadams	Athy	I.	231
65	Parkalassa	57 3 11	Kerry	Dunkerron North	Killorglin	Killarney	II.	181
26	Parkalough	88 0 7a	Clare	Bunratty Upper	Inchicronan	Tulla	II.	9
104	Parkaloughan	72 1 29	Galway	Dunkellin	Kilcolgan	Gort	IV.	28
118, 131	Parkana	218 1 23	Cork, W.R.	West Carbery (W.D.)	Kilmocomoge	Bantry	II.	144
56	Parkanallacan	95 0 37	Galway	Clare	Kilcoona	Tuam	IV.	20
70	Parkanillane	154 3 30	Cork, W.R.	West Muskerry	Kilnamartyra	Macroom	II.	160
17	Parkannesley Lower	271 3 1	Wexford	Ballaghkeen	Donaghmore	Gorey	I.	293
17	Parkannesley Upper	182 0 25	Wexford	Ballaghkeen	Donaghmore	Gorey	I.	293
22	Parkaree	51 0 8	Limerick	Pubblebrien	Monasteranenagh	Croom	II.	253
7	Parkaree or Boherfadda	285 1 11	King's Co.	Garrycastle	Lemanaghan	Parsonstown	I.	137
103, 113	Parkatleva	217 0 11	Galway	Dunkellin	Kilcolgan	Gort	IV.	28
101	Parkatleva	72 1 23	Mayo	Clanmorris	Kilcolman	Claremorris	IV.	134
31	Parkatluggera	17 0 2	Waterford	Decies without Drum	Dungarvan	Dungarvan	II.	355
20	Parkatobeen	128 3 2	Waterford	Coshmore & Coshbride	Lismore and Mocollop	Lismore	II.	347
22	Parkatotaun	49 3 22	Limerick	Clanwilliam	Cahervally	Limerick	II.	221
22	Parkatotaun	74 0 10	Limerick	Clanwilliam	Fedamore	Limerick	II.	223
17, 23	Parkavilla	170 0 25	Queen's Co.	Maryborough West	Clonenagh & Clonagheen	Abbeyleix	I.	243
58, 66	Parkavonear	124 1 9	Kerry	Magunihy	Aghadoe	Killarney	II.	199
18	Parkbaun	351 2 30	Galway	Ballymoe	Clonbern	Glennamaddy	IV.	6
6	Parkbaun	51 0 0	Galway	Ballymoe	Templetogher	Glennamaddy	IV.	9
104	Parkbaun	121 1 7	Galway	Dunkellin	Kilcolgan	Gort	IV.	28
3, 7	Parkbaun	129 0 1	Wexford	Gorey	Kilcavan	Gorey	I.	317
29	Parkbawn	60 0 11	Queen's Co.	Clarmallagh	Abbeyleix	Abbeyleix	I.	235
1	Parkbeg	242 0 4	Queen's Co.	Tinnahinch	Castlebrack	Mountmellick	I.	248
20	Parkbeg	17 2 30	Tipperary, N.R.	Owney and Arra	Youghalarra	Nenagh	II.	298
2	Parkbeg	172 2 13	Waterford	Upperthird	Rathgormuck	Carrick on Suir	II.	371
29	Parkboy	81 2 32	Kerry	Trughanacmy	Clogherbrien	Tralee	II.	209
89	Parkboy	35 1 18	Mayo	Carra	Ballyhean	Castlebar	IV.	126
25	Parkboy	15 1 22	Meath	Lower Navan	Navan	Navan	I.	215
9	Parkboy	169 0 13	Tipperary, N.R.	Lower Ormond	Cloghprior	Borrisokane	II.	283
28	Parkdotia	297 1 33	Waterford	Coshmore & Coshbride	Tallow	Lismore	II.	348
13	Park or Dunamase	338 2 0	Queen's Co.	Maryborough East	Dysartenos	Mountmellick	I.	241
10, 16	Parke	124 0 6	Sligo	Tireragh	Kilglass	Dromore West	IV.	234
30	Parkearagh	56 2 38	Kerry	Trughanacmy	O'Brennan	Tralee	II.	212
6	Park East	181 0 25	Antrim	Lower Dunluce	Dunluce	Coleraine	III.	17
18, 31	Park East	357 3 25	Galway	Ballymoe	Clonbern	Glennamaddy	IV.	7
14, 20	Parkeel	271 1 3	Roscommon	Frenchpark	Tibohine	Castlereagh	IV.	205
31	Parkeenaflugh	13 3 26	Waterford	Decies without Drum	Dungarvan	Dungarvan	II.	355
30	Parkeenagarra	74 3 1	Waterford	Decies without Drum	Whitechurch	Dungarvan	II.	362
31	Parkeenalougha	10 3 22	Waterford	Decies without Drum	Kilrush	Dungarvan	II.	358
15	Parkeennaglogh	251 0 34	Waterford	Decies without Drum	Rossmire	Kilmacthomas	II.	360
103	Parkeighter	26 2 19	Galway	Dunkellin	Kilcolgan	Gort	IV.	28
39, 47	Parker's Farm	16 0 5	Tyrone	Dungannon Middle	Donaghenry	Cookstown	III.	301
87	Parkgarriff	255 1 1	Cork, E.R.	Kerrycurrihy	Monkstown	Cork	II.	93
28, 33	Parkgarriff	51 3 31	Waterford	Coshmore & Coshbride	Tallow	Lismore	II.	348
58	Parkgarve	148 3 18	Galway	Clare	Kilmoylan	Tuam	IV.	22
70, 71	Parkgarve	57 0 17	Galway	Clare	Lackagh	Galway	IV.	23
41	Parkgarve or Coarse-park	118 3 3	Galway	Clare	Killursa	Tuam	IV.	21
50	Park Hall	128 1 35	Antrim	Upper Antrim	Antrim	Antrim	III.	5
107	Parkhill	204 1 32	Donegal	Tirhugh	Kilbarron	Ballyshannon	III.	148
6	Parkhill	177 2 15b	Fermanagh	Lurg	Magheraculmoney	Lowtherstown	III.	208
31	Parklane	8 2 9	Waterford	Decies without Drum	Dungarvan	Dungarvan	II.	355
44, 58	Parklaur	103 3 15	Galway	Tiaquin	Abbeyknockmoy	Tuam	IV.	75
112	Parklaurence	20 1 5	Cork, E.R.	Kinsale	Clontead	Kinsale	II.	99
29	Parklewis	47 3 37	Limerick	Connello Lower	Rathkeale	Rathkeale	II	229
14	Park Lower	199 2 15	Queen's Co.	Stradbally	Dysartenos	Athy	I.	247
27, 28	Parkmeen	151 1 35	King's Co.	Coolestown	Clonsast	Edenderry	I.	133

(a) Including 22A. 1R. 35P. water.   (b) Including 7A. 1R. 10P. water.

No. of Sheet of the Ordnance Survey Maps.	Townlands and Towns.	Area in Statute Acres. A. R. P.	County.	Barony.	Parish.	Poor Law Union in 1857.	Townland Census of 1851, Part I. Vol.	Page
20	Parkmore	57 3 20	Clare	Tulla Upper	Feakle	Scarriff	II.	40
84	Parkmore	172 2 21	Cork, E.R.	East Muskerry	Kilbonane	Bandon	II.	104
16	Parkmore	132 3 19	Donegal	Kilmacrenan	Clondahorky	Dunfanaghy	III.	123
29, 43	Parkmore	130 1 11	Galway	Clare	Tuam	Tuam	IV.	23
82	Parkmore	194 0 5	Galway	Galway	St. Nicholas	Galway	IV.	38
21	Parkmore	59 1 15	Kerry	Clanmaurice	Killahan	Tralee	II.	170
21	Parkmore	43 3 20	Kerry	Clanmaurice	Kiltomy	Tralee	II.	172
19, 23	Parkmore	160 0 0	Kilkenny	Shillelogher	Castleinch or Inchyolaghan	Kilkenny	I.	114
30, 31	Parkmore	230 3 3	King's Co.	Eglish	Eglish	Parsonstown	I.	135
19	Parkmore	66 0 2	Limerick	Shanid	Robertstown	Glin	II.	258
19	Parkmore	59 0 20	Limerick	Shanid	Shangolden	Glin	II.	258
53	Parkmore	293 0 32	Roscommon	Moycarn	Creagh	Ballinasloe	IV.	206
40	Parkmore	103 2 12	Sligo	Tirerrill	Aghanagh	Boyle	IV.	237
12, 17	Parkmore	338 2 29	Tipperary, N.R.	Ikerrin	Roscrea	Roscrea	II.	276
22	Parkmore	63 1 23	Waterford	Decies without Drum	Modelligo	Lismore	II.	359
24	Parkmore	662 1 30	Wicklow	Newcastle	Derrylossary	Rathdrum	I.	351
47	Parkmore	150 1 27	Wicklow	Shillelagh	Carnew	Shillelagh	I.	357
19, 24	Parkmore or Aganlane	1,835 3 14	Antrim	Lower Glenarm	Layd	Ballycastle	III.	23
12	Parkmore or Demesne	222 1 10	Armagh	Armagh	Armagh	Armagh	III.	43
43, 47	Parkmore (Page)	143 2 22	Wicklow	Shillelagh	Carnew	Shillelagh	I.	357
55	Parkmountain	71 2 13	Cork, E.R.	Imokilly	Ardagh	Youghal	II.	88
67	Parkmountain	84 2 35	Cork, E.R.	Imokilly	Youghal	Youghal	II.	91
16, 17	Parknabinnia	356 3 26	Clare	Inchiquin	Killinaboy	Corrofin	II.	27
12	Parknacross	146 1 35	Wexford	Ballaghkeen	Ardamine	Gorey	I.	291
31	Parknagappul	14 2 0	Waterford	Decies without Drum	Dungarvan	Dungarvan	II.	356
15, 21	Parknageragh	243 0 24	Kerry	Clanmaurice	Killahan	Tralee	II.	170
74	Parknaglantane	8 3 37a	Cork, E.R.	Cork	St. Marys Shandon	Cork	II.	66
117	Parknahown	90 2 29	Galway	Leitrim	Tynagh	Portumna	IV.	55
34, 35	Parknahown	415 0 32	Queen's Co.	Clarmallagh	Aghmacart	Abbeyleix	I.	236
77	Parknahyla	116 2 5	Cork, E.R.	Imokilly	Ightermurragh	Middleton	II.	87
11, 20	Parknakilla	151 3 35	Cork, E.R.	Condons and Clangibbon	Brigown	Mitchelstown	II.	60
110, 111	Parknakillew	227 0 16b	Mayo	Clanmorris	Tagheen	Claremorris	IV.	136
11	Parknakyle	471 3 24	Carlow	Idrone West	Oldleighlin	Carlow	I.	9
57, 67	Parknamoney	180 3 19	Clare	Moyarta	Kilrush	Kilrush	II.	33
39,40,48,49	Parknamulloge	293 1 11	Kerry	Trughanacmy	Dysert	Tralee	II.	210
77, 83	Parknascaddane	16 3 33	Tipperary, S.R.	Iffa and Offa East	Kiltegan	Clonmel	II.	315
40	Parknashaw	164 0 10	Wicklow	Arklow	Castlemacadam	Rathdrum	I.	342
90	Parknashingaun	31 3 15	Mayo	Carra	Rosslee	Castlebar	IV.	130
17	Parknashoge	199 2 19	Wexford	Ballaghkeen	Killenagh	Gorey	I.	295
3, 7	Parknasilloge	122 1 8	Wicklow	Rathdown	Powerscourt	Rathdown	I.	356
48	Parknasmuttaun	159 3 26	Kerry	Trughanacmy	Dysert	Killarney	II.	210
74	Parknock	4 2 1c	Cork, E.R.	Cork, Municipal Borough of	St. Marys Shandon	Cork	II.	111
21	Parknoe	105 1 19	Waterford	Coshmore & Coshbride	Lismore and Mocollop	Lismore	II.	347
17, 18	Park North	309 3 1	Cork, E.R.	Fermoy	Doneraile	Mallow	II.	79
76	Park North	138 3 8	Cork, E.R.	Imokilly	Middleton	Middleton	II.	89
23	Parkplace	164 3 14	Longford	Moydow	Taghsheenod	Ballymahon	I.	162
53	Parkroe	67 2 37	Clare	Bunratty Lower	St. Patricks	Limerick	II.	7
103, 104	Parkroe	63 0 6	Galway	Dunkellin	Killeely	Gort	IV.	30
113	Parkroe	92 2 26	Galway	Dunkellin	Killeenavarra	Gort	IV.	30
96	Parkroe	95 3 24	Galway	Dunkellin	Killeeneen	Gort	IV.	30
96	Parkroe	94 1 11	Galway	Dunkellin	Killora	Loughrea	IV.	31
95	Parkroe	106 1 14	Galway	Dunkellin	Oranmore	Galway	IV.	32
13	Parkroe	215 2 0	Limerick	Clanwilliam	Cahervally	Limerick	II.	221
39	Parkroe	33 1 27	Limerick	Coshma	Dromin	Kilmallock	II.	243
51	Parkroe	199 3 7	Tipperary, N.R.	Kilnamanagh Upper	Toem	Tipperary	II.	280
24	Parkroe	532 1 21	Wicklow	Newcastle	Derrylossary	Rathdrum	I.	351
12	Parks	86 0 7	Kilkenny	Crannagh	Tubbridbritain	Urlingford	I.	87
100	Parks	439 0 17d	Mayo	Carra	Toughty	Ballinrobe	IV.	130
4, 9, 10	Parksgrove	603 1 25	Kilkenny	Galmoy	Aharney	Urlingford	I.	91
17, 18	Park South	191 0 37	Cork, E.R.	Fermoy	Doneraile	Mallow	II.	79
76	Park South	112 1 25	Cork, E.R.	Imokilly	Middleton	Middleton	II.	89
35	Parkstown	346 3 32	Meath	Lune	Killaconnigan	Trim	I.	208
47, 48	Parkstown	624 0 5	Tipperary, N.R.	Eliogarty	Ballymurreen	Thurles	II.	269
40, 41	Parkstown Lower	187 0 5	Kilkenny	Ida	Kilmakevoge	Waterford	I.	103
40	Parkstown Upper	169 0 29	Kilkenny	Ida	Kilmakevoge	Waterford	I.	103
10, 18	Parkswood Lower	128 3 6	Waterford	Gaultiere	Kill St. Nicholas	Waterford	II.	364
10, 18	Parkswood Upper	163 3 7	Waterford	Gaultiere	Kill St. Nicholas	Waterford	II.	364
13, 14	Park Upper	426 1 20	Queen's Co.	Stradbally	Dysartenos	Athy	I.	247
77	Parkville	70 1 4	Tipperary, S.R.	Iffa and Offa East	Rathronan	Clonmel	II.	316
18	Park West	177 1 29	Galway	Ballymoe	Clonbern	Glenamaddy	IV.	7

(a) { Within the Municipal Borough, 3A. 3R. 6P.
{ Without the Municipal Borough, 5A. 0R. 31P.
(b) Including 4A. 0R. 32P. water.
(c) Included in the Parish of St. Marys Shandon.
(d) Including 65A. 2R. 6P. water.

No. of Sheet of the Ordnance Survey Maps.	Townlands and Towns.	Area in Statute Acres.			County.	Barony.	Parish.	Poor Law Union in 1857.	Townland Census of 1851, Part I.	
		A.	R.	P.					Vol.	Page
1, 2	Parkwood	234	3	13	King's Co.	Kilcoursey	Kilcumreragh	Tullamore	I.	141
6	Parkwood	20	3	36	Limerick	Clanwilliam	Stradbally	Limerick	II.	226
4, 7	Parnelstown	167	0	14	Dublin	Balrothery East	Lusk	Balrothery	I.	21
13	Parslickstown	202	2	24	Dublin	Castleknock	Mulhuddart	Dublin North	I.	25
32	Parson Hall	37	1	4	Down	Ards Upper	Ballytrustan	Downpatrick	III.	160
40, 43	Parson's Green Glebe	92	0	24	Fermanagh	Coole	Galloon	Clones	III.	200
129	Parsons Island	3	2	8	Galway	Kiltartan	Beagh	Gort	IV.	46
8	Parsonstown	510	0	28	Kildare	Carbury	Ardkill	Edenderry	I.	51
11	Parsonstown	126	3	10a	Kildare	North Salt	Donaghcumper	Celbridge	I.	74
19	Parsonstown	259	2	21	Louth	Ferrard	Parsonstown	Drogheda	I.	182
44	Parsonstown	438	1	2	Meath	Ratoath	Rathregan	Dunshaughlin	I.	219
12	Parsonstown	413	1	1	Westmeath	Corkaree	Tyfarnham	Mullingar	I.	264
35	PARSONSTOWN OR BIRR T.	—			King's Co.	Ballybritt	Birr	Parsonstown	I.	125
12	ParsonstownDemesne	643	0	3	Meath	Lower Slane	Killary	Ardee	I.	223
63	Parteen	132	1	25	Clare	Bunratty Lower	St. Patricks	Limerick	II.	7
17	Parton Island	2	3	6	Down	Ards Upper	Ardkeen	Downpatrick	III.	159
26	Paslicktown	272	0	23	Westmeath	Fartullagh	Moylisker	Mullingar	I.	269
62, 63	Pass	69	1	11	Clare	Bunratty Lower	Killeely	Limerick	II.	5
36	Pass	198	3	0	King's Co.	Eglish	Drumcullen	Parsonstown	I.	134
18	Pass	228	3	12	Queen's Co.	Cullenagh	Ballyroan	Abbeyleix	I.	239
18	Pass	126	0	29	Queen's Co.	Cullenagh	Kilcolmanbane	Abbeyleix	I.	240
18	Passage East	5	2	14	Waterford	Gaultiere	Kill St. Nicholas	Waterford	II.	364
18	PASSAGE T.	—			Waterford	Gaultiere	Kill St. Nicholas	Waterford	II.	364
18	Passage West	3	2	24	Waterford	Gaultiere	Kill St. Nicholas	Waterford	II.	364
75, 87	PASSAGE WEST T.				Cork, E.R.	Kerrycurrihy	{ Marmullane { Monkstown	Cork	II.	{ 92 { 93
13	Passifyoucan	88	2	18	Dublin	Newcastle	Leixlip	Celbridge	I.	33
21	Passlands	104	3	10	Kildare	Offaly West	Monasterevin	Athy	I.	73
27, 34	Pass of Kilbride	1,999	0	37	Westmeath	Fartullagh	Pass of Kilbride	Mullingar	I.	269
9, 17	Pastimeknock	49	1	21	Waterford	Middlethird	Trinity Without	Waterford	II.	369
18	Patch	418	1	22	Galway	Ballymoe	Clonbern	Glennamaddy	IV.	7
31	Patch	101	3	14	Galway	Tiaquin	Kilkerrin	Glennamaddy	IV.	77
45	Patch	272	3	3b	Galway	Tiaquin	Moylough	Mountbellew	IV.	80
17	Patch	143	0	19	Kerry	Clanmaurice	Duagh	Listowel	II.	168
11, 17	Patch	186	1	10	Sligo	Tireragh	Kilmacshalgan	Dromore West	IV.	235
21	Patches	153	3	15	Galway	Ballynahinch	Omey	Clifden	IV.	15
9	Patricks Island	0	0	14	Leitrim	Drumahaire	Cloonclare	Manorhamilton	IV.	94
9, 15	Patrickstown	1,055	1	4	Meath	Fore	Diamor	Oldcastle	I.	200
4	Patrickswell	205	2	19	Carlow	Rathvilly	Rathvilly	Baltinglass	I.	12
32	Patrickswell	473	3	1	Limerick	Smallcounty	Knockainy	Kilmallock	II.	261
20	Patrickswell	121	1	13	Tipperary, N.R.	Owney and Arra	Burgesbeg	Nenagh	II.	294
82, 83	Patrickswell	330	1	26c	Tipperary, S.R.	Iffa and Offa East	Inishlounaght	Clonmel	II.	313
103	Pattenspark	137	3	35	Mayo	Costello	Annagh	Claremorris	IV.	138
35	Paudeenourstown	52	0	14d	Kildare	Narragh and Reban West	Kilberry	Athy	I.	68
17	Paughanstown	19	1	14	Louth	Ardee	Dromin	Ardee	I.	172
17	Paughanstown	517	0	37	Louth	Ardee	Kildemock	Ardee	I.	173
43	Paulbeg	372	1	20	Wicklow	Shillelagh	Carnew	Shillelagh	I.	357
23	Paulsacres	40	2	11	Waterford	Decies without Drum	Kilrossanty	Kilmacthomas	II.	358
16, 21	Paulstown	1,074	2	28	Kilkenny	Gowran	Kilmacahill	Kilkenny	I.	97
16	PAULSTOWN T.	—			Kilkenny	Gowran	{ Kilmacahill { Shankill	Kilkenny	I.	{ 97 { 99
24	Pavle Island	49	2	11	Down	Dufferin	Killyleagh	Downpatrick	III.	167
26	Pawlerth	53	1	25	Kilkenny	Callan	Callan	Callan	I.	83
9	Peacockbank	154	1	15	Tyrone	Strabane Lower	Urney	Strabane	III.	323
45	Peacockstown	247	1	10	Meath	Ratoath	Ratoath	Dunshaughlin	I.	219
54	Peafield	22	2	0	Cork, E.R.	Barrymore	Gortroe	Fermoy	II.	55
54	Peafield	1,153	0	25	Cork, E.R.	Barrymore	Templebodan	Middleton	II.	58
88	Peafield	17	1	19	Cork, E.R.	Imokilly	Aghada	Middleton	II.	83
16, 22	Peafield	209	1	16	Queen's Co.	Upperwoods	Offerlane	Abbeyleix	I.	252
5	Peafield	41	1	2	Limerick	Clanwilliam	Kilmurry	Limerick	II.	225
81	Peahill	73	3	35	Tipperary, S.R.	Iffa and Offa West	Whitechurch	Clogheen	II.	322
70	Peak	220	2	0	Galway	Clare	Claregalway	Galway	IV.	18
44	Peak	133	2	35	Galway	Clare	Killererin	Tuam	IV.	21
71	Peak	223	0	33	Galway	Tiaquin	Monivea	Tuam	IV.	79
34	Peak	48	1	31	Roscommon	Ballymoe	Cloonygormican	Roscommon	IV.	191
15, 21	Peak	387	1	39	Roscommon	Castlereagh	Kilcorkey	Castlereagh	IV.	200
61, 72	Peake	361	3	23	Cork, W.R.	East Muskerry	Aghabulloge	Macroom	II.	153
53	Peake	257	2	12	Tipperary, S.R.	Middlethird	Ballysheehan	Cashel	II.	325
83, 84	Peakroe	145	0	3	Galway	Clare	Athenry	Galway	IV.	17
21	Peamount	88	1	29	Dublin	Newcastle	Newcastle	Celbridge	I.	34
22	Pearsonsbrook	208	0	15	Westmeath	Kilkenny West	Kilkenny West	Athlone	I.	273
27, 28	Peast	211	1	21	Monaghan	Farney	Maghercloss	Carrickmacross	III.	274

(a) Including 2A. 1R. 3P. water.
(b) Including 7A. 3R. 38P. water.

(c) Including 1A. 1R. 36P. water.
(d) Including 7A. 3R. 21P. water.

No. of Sheet of the Ordnance Survey Maps.	Townlands and Towns.	Area in Statute Acres.			County.	Barony.	Parish.	Poor Law Union in 1857.	Townland Census of 1851, Part I.	
		A.	R.	P.					Vol.	Page
90	Peenoge . . .	103	3	6a	Mayo . .	Carra . . .	Rosslee . . .	Castlebar . .	IV.	130
59	Pegsborough . .	37	1	12	Tipperary, S.R.	Clanwilliam . .	Tipperary . .	Tipperary . .	II.	312
14, 18	Pelletstown . .	259	3	6	Dublin . .	Castleknock . .	Castleknock . .	Dublin North .	I.	24
44	Pelletstown . .	455	2	0	Meath . .	Ratoath . .	Dunshaughlin .	Dunshaughlin .	I.	218
45	Pellick . .	324	1	6	Cork, E.R. .	Barrymore . .	Castlelyons . .	Fermoy . .	II.	53
75, 87	Pembroke . .	243	2	7	Cork, E.R. .	Kerrycurrihy . .	Marmullane . .	Cork . .	II.	92
17	Pembrokestown .	191	2	39	Waterford . .	Middlethird . .	Lisnakill . .	Waterford . .	II.	368
46	Pembrokestown .	133	1	21	Wexford . .	Bargy . . .	Killag . .	Wexford . .	I.	306
42	Pembrokestown .	96	2	31	Wexford . .	Forth . .	Maudlintown .	Wexford . .	I.	312
29, 35	Penane . . .	172	0	4	Tipperary, N.R.	Eliogarty . .	Loughmoe East .	Thurles . .	II.	271
19	Pennefatherslot .	87	2	34b	Kilkenny . .	Gowran and Municipal Borough	St. John's . .	Kilkenny . .	I.	98
40	Pennefatherswood .	195	1	6	Tipperary, N.R.	Kilnamanagh Upper	Moyaliff . .	Thurles . .	II.	279
13, 20	Pennyburn . .	123	0	19	Londonderry .	North West Liberties of Londonderry .	Templemore . .	Londonderry .	III.	246
17, 22	Peppardscastle .	392	3	3	Wexford . .	Ballaghkeen . .	Donaghmore .	Gorey . .	I.	293
62	Peppardstown .	201	1	11	Tipperary, S.R.	Middlethird . .	Peppardstown .	Cashel . .	II.	329
16	Pepperhill . .	136	2	19	Cork, E.R. .	Orrery and Kilmore	Buttevant . .	Mallow . .	II.	107
14	Pepperstown .	544	1	23	Louth . .	Ardee . .	Charlestown . .	Ardee . .	I.	171
16, 17	Pepperstown .	104	0	23	Meath . .	Upper Kells . .	Burry . .	Kells . .	I.	205
3	Perrymount . .	98	3	37	Wexford . .	Gorey . .	Inch . .	Gorey . .	I.	316
22	Perrystown . .	93	3	7	Dublin . .	Uppercross . .	Crumlin . .	Dublin South .	I.	40
74, 87	Perssepark . .	303	1	31	Galway . .	Clonmacnowen .	Kilcloony . .	Ballinasloe .	IV.	25
60	Persse's-lot . .	136	1	37	Tipperary, S.R.	Clanwilliam . .	Relickmurry & Athassel	Tipperary . .	II.	310
11	Peru . . .	93	1	30	Meath . .	Lower Kells . .	Newtown . .	Kells . .	I.	204
26, 27	Petersburg or Cappaghnagapple .	655	0	36	Galway . .	Ross . . .	Ross . . .	Oughterard .	IV.	73
30, 36	Peterstown . .	178	1	22	Meath . .	Upper Navan .	Newtownclonbun .	Trim . .	I.	216
36	Peterstown . .	28	1	11	Meath . .	Upper Navan .	Trim . .	Trim . .	I.	217
8	Petestown . .	60	0	37	Louth . .	Lower Dundalk .	Carlingford . .	Dundalk . .	I.	176
47	Petitstown . .	72	1	7	Wexford . .	Forth . .	Mayglass . .	Wexford . .	I.	312
19	Petitswood . .	552	1	25	Westmeath . .	Moyashel and Magheradernon .	Mullingar . .	Mullingar . .	I.	275
105	Pettigoe . . .	72	0	19	Donegal . .	Tirhugh . .	Templecarn . .	Donegal . .	III.	149
105 ⎱ 4 ⎰	PETTIGOE T. . .	—			⎰ Donegal . . ⎱ Fermanagh .	Tirhugh . . Lurg . .	Templecarn . . Drumkeeran . .	Donegal . . Lowherstown .	III. III.	149 207
17	Pettycanon and Lucan	259	3	27c	Dublin . .	Newcastle . .	Lucan . .	Celbridge . .	I.	33
39	Phaleesh . .	191	0	39	Sligo . .	Corran . .	Kilshalvy . .	Boyle . .	IV.	227
108	Phale Lower . .	287	0	24	Cork, W.R. .	East Carbery (E.D.)	Ballymoney . .	Dunmanway .	II.	127
108	Phale Upper . .	234	0	23	Cork, W.R. .	East Carbery (E.D.)	Ballymoney . .	Dunmanway .	II.	127
18	Pharis . . .	388	0	7	Antrim . .	Upper Dunluce .	Loughguile . .	Ballymoney .	III.	20
78	Pheasanthill . .	149	3	2	Mayo . .	Carra . .	Aglish . .	Castlebar . .	IV.	124
49	Phepotstown .	702	0	16d	Meath . .	Upper Deece .	Kilmore . .	Dunshaughlin .	I.	193
25	Pherson's Island .	13	3	16	Down . .	Ards Upper . .	Ardkeen . .	Downpatrick .	III.	159
13	Phibblestown or Hansfield . .	223	1	36	Dublin . .	Castleknock . .	Clonsilla . .	Celbridge . .	I.	24
14	Philibenstown .	214	2	0	Louth . .	Ardee . .	Mapastown . .	Ardee . .	I.	173
41	Philippintown .	143	0	26	Wexford . .	Bargy . . .	Ballyconnick .	Wexford . .	I.	304
51	Philipston . .	431	0	7	Tipperary, S.R.	Kilnamanagh Lower	Donohill . .	Tipperary . .	II.	323
25	Philipstown . .	175	3	31	Kildare . .	Naas North . .	Rathmore . .	Naas . .	I.	62
17, 18	Philipstown . .	308	0	29	Louth . .	Ardee . .	Mosstown . .	Ardee . .	I.	174
11	Philipstown . .	194	2	28	Louth . .	Ardee . .	Philipstown . .	Ardee . .	I.	174
21, 24	Philipstown . .	268	1	29	Louth . .	Ferrard . .	Philipstown . .	Drogheda . .	I.	182
3, 6	Philipstown . .	406	1	11	Louth . .	Upper Dundalk .	Philipstown . .	Dundalk . .	I.	179
15	Philipstown . .	292	3	7	Meath . .	Fore . .	Diamor . .	Oldcastle . .	I.	200
18	PHILIPSTOWN T. .	—			King's Co. .	Lower Philipstown .	Killaderry . .	Tullamore . .	I.	143
30, 36	Phillinstown .	256	2	12	Meath . .	Upper Navan .	Trim . .	Trim . .	I.	217
3	Phillipstown . .	253	3	14	Carlow . .	Rathvilly . .	Kineagh . .	Baltinglass .	I.	11
36	Phillistown . .	92	1	17	Meath . .	Upper Navan .	Trim . .	Trim . .	I.	217
31	Philpotstown .	115	0	18	Meath . .	Lower Navan .	Ardsallagh . .	Navan . .	I.	214
30	Philpotstown .	224	1	30	Meath . .	Lower Navan .	Rataine . .	Navan . .	I.	215
31	Philpotstown .	323	1	34	Meath . .	Skreen . .	Dowdstown . .	Navan . .	I.	220
17, 24	Phœnixtown .	440	3	5	Meath . .	Lower Navan .	Martry . .	Kells . .	I.	215
26	Phrompstown . .	199	1	15	Dublin . .	Rathdown . .	Oldconnaught .	Rathdown . .	I.	37
26	Physicianstown .	286	0	4	Kilkenny . .	Kells . .	Coolaghmore . .	Callan . .	I.	108
11, 14	Pickardstown . .	184	1	5	Dublin . .	Coolock . .	St. Margaret's .	Dublin North .	I.	29
17, 26	Pickardstown . .	247	3	38	Waterford . .	Middlethird . .	Drumcannon . .	Waterford . .	II.	366
13	Picketstown . .	115	0	11	Kilkenny . .	Crannagh . .	Tullaroan . .	Kilkenny . .	I.	88
8	Piedmont . .	428	1	20	Louth . .	Lower Dundalk .	Ballymascanlan .	Dundalk . .	I.	176
11	Piercefield . .	255	2	35	Westmeath . .	Corkaree . .	Portnashangan .	Mullingar . .	I.	263
11	Piercefield or Temploran . .	740	3	28	Westmeath . .	Moygoish . .	Templeoran . .	Mullingar . .	I.	281
62	Piercetown . .	308	2	32	Cork, E.R. .	Cork . .	St. Annes Shandon .	Cork . .	II.	65
98	Piercetown . .	307	3	7	Cork, E.R. .	Kinalea . .	Cullen . .	Kinsale . .	II.	94

(a) Including 6A. 1R. 27P. water.
(b) { Within the Municipal Boundary, 57A. 3R. 8P.
{ Without the Municipal Boundary, 29A. 3R. 26P.

(c) Including 1A. 3R. 32P. water.
(d) Including 14A. 3R. 19P. water.

No. of Sheet of the Ordnance Survey Maps.	Townlands and Towns.	Area in Statute Acres.			County.	Barony.	Parish.	Poor Law Union in 1857.	Townland Census of 1851, Part I.	
		A.	R.	P.					Vol.	Page
5	Piercetown	41	1	34	Dublin	Balrothery East	Holmpatrick	Balrothery	I.	20
5	Piercetown	36	1	1	Dublin	Balrothery East	Lusk	Balrothery	I.	21
23	Piercetown	165	0	28	Kildare	Connell	Morristownbiller	Naas	I.	56
44, 50	Piercetown	668	2	36	Meath	Dunboyne	Dunboyne	Dunshaughlin	I.	199
6	Piercetown	294	2	15	Meath	Lower Slane	Inishmot	Ardee	I.	223
49	Piercetown	323	0	23	Meath	Upper Deece	Balfeaghan	Celbridge	I.	193
33	Piercetown	159	0	31	Meath	Upper Duleek	Piercetown	Dunshaughlin	I.	198
16,17,23,24	Piercetown	548	0	23	Meath	Upper Kells	Balrathboyne	Kells	I.	204
42	Piercetown	320	3	3	Tipperary, N.R.	Eliogarty	Rahelty	Thurles	II.	272
52	Piercetown	273	1	10	Tipperary, S.R.	Kilnamanagh Lower	Clonoulty	Cashel	II.	323
33	Piercetown	313	1	4	Westmeath	Fartullagh	Castlelost	Mullingar	I.	268
10, 17	Piercetown	233	0	18	Westmeath	Rathconrath	Piercetown	Ballymahon	I.	283
42	Piercetown	92	3	35	Wexford	Forth	Rathmacknee	Wexford	I.	313
64	Pigeonhill	52	2	36	Cork, E.R.	Barrymore	Kilquane	Cork	II.	56
25	Pigeonhouse	68	2	13	King's Co.	Geashill	Geashill	Tullamore	I.	140
18	*Pigeon Island*	10	0	5	Roscommon	Ballintober North	Termonbarry	Strokestown	IV.	188
23	Pigeonpark	260	2	38	Kilkenny	Shillelogher	Danesfort	Thomastown	I.	114
61	Pigeonpark	30	2	27	Tipperary, S.R.	Middlethird	St. Patricksrock	Cashel	II.	331
18, 19	Pigeonpark or Scrub	535	1	33	King's Co.	Upper Philipstown	Geashill	Edenderry	I.	144
36, 37	Pigeonstown	626	3	32	King's Co.	Ballybritt	Letterluna	Parsonstown	I.	126
18, 19	Pighill	125	1	17	Meath	Upper Slane	Stackallan	Navan	I.	225
109	*Pig Island*	5	2	23	Mayo	Carra	Ballyovey	Ballinrobe	IV.	126
1, 4	*Pig Island*	6	2	24	Mayo	Erris	Kilcommon	Belmullet	IV.	145
15, 22	Pigotstown	236	2	34	Meath	Fore	Killallon	Oldcastle	I.	201
3	*Pigott's Island*	3	1	16	Limerick	Kenry	Kilcornan	Rathkeale	II.	249
29	Pigotts or Tanyard	80	0	14	Wexford	Bantry	St. Mary's	New Ross	I.	302
124	Pikesland	67	3	38	Cork, W.R.	Courceys	Ringrone	Kinsale	II.	147
11	Pilgrimhill	343	1	4	Kerry	Iraghticonnor	Duagh	Listowel	II.	190
16	Pilgrimhill	40	2	14	Queen's Co.	Upperwoods	Offerlane	Abbeyleix	II.	252
78	Pillmore	398	0	25	Cork, E.R.	Imokilly	Clonpriest	Youghal	II.	85
37	Pillpark	16	2	39	Waterford	Decies within Drum	Clashmore	Youghal	II.	351
21	Pilltown	288	2	2	Meath	Lower Duleek	Colp	Drogheda	I.	195
37, 38	Pilltown	337	2	2	Waterford	Decies within Drum	Kinsalebeg	Youghal	II.	352
39	PILLTOWN T.	—			Kilkenny	Iverk	Fiddown	Carrick on Suir	I.	105
27	Pinnacle	95	0	7	Wicklow	Upper Talbotstown	Baltinglass	Baltinglass	I.	362
12, 17	Pintown	173	3	21	Tipperary, N.R.	Ikerrin	Roscrea	Roscrea	II	276
29	Pinure	84	0	24	Kerry	Trughanacmy	Clogherbrien	Tralee	II	209
45	Piperhill	382	2	3	Tipperary, N.R.	Kilnamanagh Upper	Toem	Tipperary	II.	280
67	Pipersbog	38	1	39	Cork, E.R.	Imokilly	Youghal	Youghal	II.	91
20, 25	Pipershall	176	2	15	Kildare	Naas North	Rathmore	Naas	I.	62
40	Pipers Hill	28	2	6	Fermanagh	Coole	Galloon	Clones	III.	200
25	Piperstown	381	0	8	Dublin	Uppercross	Tallaght	Dublin South	I.	42
21	Piperstown	355	1	19	Louth	Ferrard	Drumshallon	Drogheda	I.	180
23	Pishanagh	128	0	29	Westmeath	Kilkenny West	Drumraney	Ballymahon	I.	273
17	Pishanagh	73	0	29	Westmeath	Rathconrath	Rathconrath	Mullingar	I.	284
5	Pitchfordstown	408	2	12	Kildare	Ikeathy and Oughterany	Cloncurry	Celbridge	I.	57
60	Plaister	226	2	34	Tyrone	Dungannon Lower	Carnteel	Clogher	III.	298
54	Plaster	155	3	33	Donegal	Raphoe	Allsaints	Londonderry	III.	134
4	Plaster	312	1	20	Louth	Lower Dundalk	Ballymascanlan	Dundalk	I.	176
6	Plaster	225	1	3	Louth	Upper Dundalk	Barronstown	Dundalk	I.	177
20, 27	Platin	1,405	1	18	Meath	Lower Duleek	Duleek	Drogheda	I.	195
3	Plattinstown	113	2	2	Wexford	Gorey	Inch	Gorey	I.	316
24	Plaukarauka	133	3	25	Limerick	Coonagh	Grean	Tipperary	II.	235
54	Plea Isle	59	2	17	Donegal	Raphoe	Raymoghy	Letterkenny	III.	142
32	Pleberstown	659	0	13	Kilkenny	Gowran	Pleberstown	Thomastown	I.	97
15	Plezica	211	2	25	Wicklow	Lower Talbotstown	Dunlavin	Baltinglass	I.	360
26	Plodstown	52	0	25	Westmeath	Fartullagh	Mullingar	Mullingar	I.	269
19, 26	Plodstown	167	3	6	Westmeath	Moyashel and Magheradernon	Mullingar	Mullingar	I.	275
19	Ploopluck	153	3	12	Kildare	Naas North	Naas	Naas	I.	62
15	Ploresk	14	1	6	Kerry	Clanmaurice	Kilmoyly	Tralee	II.	171
42	Plot	67	2	13	Wexford	Bargy	Kilmannan	Wexford	I.	306
4	Ploverhill	66	3	16	Tipperary, N.R.	Lower Ormond	Lorrha	Borrisokane	II.	285
53,54,61,62	Pluck	129	2	36	Donegal	Raphoe	Leck	Letterkenny	III.	140
50, 51	Pluckanes East	366	0	4	Cork, E.R.	Barretts	Donaghmore	Cork	II.	49
50, 51	Pluckanes North	1,042	1	36	Cork, E.R.	Barretts	Donaghmore	Cork	II.	49
50	Pluckanes South	175	0	7	Cork, E.R.	Barretts	Donaghmore	Cork	II.	49
50	Pluckanes West	357	3	27	Cork, E.R.	Barretts	Donaghmore	Cork	II.	49
29	Pluckeen	25	2	10	Kerry	Trughanacmy	Tralee	Tralee	II.	214
17, 18	Pluckerstown	565	0	9	Kildare	Connell	Kilmeage	Naas	I.	55
17	Pluckerstown	346	0	32	Kildare	Offaly East	Kilmeage	Naas	I.	70
3	Pluckhimin	131	1	2	Dublin	Balrothery West	Garristown	Dunshaughlin	I.	22

No. of Sheet of the Ordnance Survey Maps.	Townlands and Towns.	Area in Statute Acres.			County.	Barony.	Parish.	Poor Law Union in 1857.	Townland Census of 1851, Part I.	
		A.	R.	P.					Vol.	Page
33	Pluckhimin or Ballymuck	156	2	2	Meath	Upper Duleek	Piercetown	Dunshaughlin	I.	198
15	Pluckstown	195	2	36	Kildare	South Salt	Lyons	Celbridge	I.	77
29	Pinckstown	380	1	38	Meath	Lune	Athboy	Trim	I.	207
52	Pludboher	23	3	32	Wexford	Bargy	Tomhaggard	Wexford	I.	308
48	Plughoge	52	2	23	Donegal	Boylagh	Templecrone	Glenties	III.	115
40	Plughoge and Leabrannagh Mountain North	113	1	9	Donegal	Boylagh	Templecrone	Glenties	III.	115
40, 48	Plughoge and Leabrannagh Mountain South	195	1	0	Donegal	Boylagh	Templecrone	Glenties	III.	115
18	Plunketsland	72	2	33	Louth	Ardee	Drumcar	Ardee	I.	172
11	Plunketsland	29	3	24	Louth	Louth	Louth	Dundalk	I.	184
38, 40	Plunketstown Lower	295	1	26	Kildare	Kilkea and Moone	Graney	Baltinglass	I.	60
38, 40	Plunketstown Upper	342	1	3	Kildare	Kilkea and Moone	Graney	Baltinglass	I.	60
15	Plush	230	0	37	Cavan	Upper Loughtee	Castleterra	Cavan	III.	83
98	Point	231	0	34	Donegal	Banagh	Inver	Donegal	III.	108
97	Point	290	3	18	Donegal	Banagh	Killaghtee	Donegal	III.	109
26	Point	66	1	21	Fermanagh	Clanawley	Cleenish	Enniskillen	III.	191
7	Point	153	2	14	Louth	Upper Dundalk	Dundalk	Dundalk	I.	178
9	Point	115	3	32	Monaghan	Monaghan	Kilmore	Monaghan	III.	276
130, 139	Pointabulloge	1	0	31	Cork, W.R.	West Carbery (W.D.)	Kilcrohane	Bantry	II.	144
18 } 33 }	Pointz Pass T.	—			{ Armagh	Orior Lower	Ballymore	Newry	III.	56
					{ Down	Upper Iveagh, Up. pt.	Aghaderg	Banbridge	III.	174
6, 12	Polecastle	173	2	38	Meath	Lower Slane	Siddan	Ardee	I.	224
64	Poleglass	188	1	37	Antrim	Upper Belfast	Derryaghy	Lisburn	III.	10
37	Polehore	335	1	17	Wexford	Shelmaliere West	Ardcandrisk	Wexford	I.	332
42	Polepatrick	101	2	4	Londonderry	Loughinsholin	Magherafelt	Magherafelt	III.	243
21, 26	Poles	292	3	4	Cavan	Upper Loughtee	Annagelliff	Cavan	III.	82
50	Polfore	333	3	6	Tyrone	Omagh East	Dromore	Omagh	III.	311
17, 22	Polintanny	280	0	23	Antrim	Upper Dunluce	Ballymoney	Ballymoney	III.	19
25	Pollabane	352	3	34	Cavan	Upper Loughtee	Kilmore	Cavan	III.	85
84	Pollacappul	171	2	19	Galway	Athenry	Athenry	Loughrea	IV.	4
10, 23	Pollacappul	1,077	0	36a	Galway	Ballynahinch	Ballynakill	Clifden	IV.	12
44	Pollacappul	219	0	37	Galway	Clare	Killererin	Tuam	IV.	21
103	Pollacappul	110	3	36	Mayo	Costello	Annagh	Claremorris	IV.	138
3, 10	Pollacappul	415	2	25	Mayo	Erris	Kilmore	Belmullet	IV.	146
29	Pollacorragune	1,003	2	14b	Galway	Dunmore	Kilbennan	Tuam	IV.	34
57	Pollacossaun Eighter	50	2	23	Galway	Clare	Cummer	Tuam	IV.	19
57	Pollacossaun Oughter	60	3	34	Galway	Clare	Cummer	Tuam	IV.	19
59, 72	Pollacrossaun	321	1	33	Galway	Tiaquin	Moylough	Mountbellew	IV.	80
42	Pollacullaire	121	2	23	Galway	Clare	Kilkilvery	Tuam	IV.	20
114	Pollacurra	67	3	2	Galway	Loughrea	Ardrahan	Loughrea	IV.	63
44	Polladooey	156	0	22c	Galway	Tiaquin	Killererin	Tuam	IV.	77
3, 6	Polladooey	240	3	0	Longford	Granard	Columbkille	Granard	I.	156
28, 29, 38	Polladoohy	461	0	3d	Mayo	Tirawley	Crossmolina	Ballina	IV.	166
32	Pollafree	243	1	18	Cavan	Upper Loughtee	Denn	Cavan	III.	84
10,11,17,18	Pollagarraun	523	2	10	Mayo	Erris	Kilcommon	Belmullet	IV.	144
43	Pollagh	115	0	16e	Clare	Bunratty Lower	Killinaghta	Limerick	II.	4
84	Pollagh	133	3	34	Galway	Athenry	Athenry	Galway	IV.	4
103	Pollagh	335	2	13f	Galway	Dunkellin	Killeenavarra	Gort	IV.	30
81	Pollagh	163	1	26	Galway	Galway	Rahoon	Galway	IV.	38
129	Pollagh	227	0	10	Galway	Kiltartan	Beagh	Gort	IV.	46
116	Pollagh	58	0	9	Galway	Leitrim	Ballynakill	Loughrea	IV.	52
55, 68	Pollagh	662	3	39	Galway	Moycullen	Killannin	Oughterard	IV.	70
81	Pollagh	51	1	4	Galway	Moycullen	Moycullen	Galway	IV.	71
6	Pollagh	207	2	37	Kerry	Iraghticonnor	Galey	Listowel	II.	190
18, 22	Pollagh	597	2	0	Kilkenny	Crannagh	Kilmanagh	Callan	I.	86
25	Pollagh	639	1	26g	Kilkenny	Gowran	Powerstown	Thomastown	I.	98
30	Pollagh	35	2	1	Kilkenny	Kells	Killamery	Callan	I.	109
26	Pollagh	30	1	39	Kilkenny	Kells	Mallardstown	Callan	I.	110
15	Pollagh	907	3	18	King's Co.	Garrycastle	Lemanaghan	Parsonstown	I.	137
25	Pollagh	274	1	17	Longford	Rathcline	Cashel	Ballymahon	I.	163
60	Pollagh	320	0	0h	Mayo	Gallen	Templemore	Castlebar	IV.	151
34	Pollagh	274	0	0	Tipperary, N.R.	Eliogarty	Inch	Thurles	II.	270
25, 31	Pollagh	133	2	31	Tipperary, N.R.	Owney and Arra	Kilcomenty	Nenagh	II.	295
37	Pollagh	81	1	0	Tipperary, N.R.	Owney and Arra	Kilvellane	Nenagh	II.	296
74	Pollagh	133	1	17	Tipperary, S.R.	Clanwilliam	Templeneiry	Tipperary	II.	311
22	Pollaghadoo	475	0	21	Wicklow	Upper Talbotstown	Donaghmore	Baltinglass	I.	363
27	Pollaghaglass	52	3	19	King's Co.	Coolestown	Clonsast	Edenderry	I.	133
12, 13	Pollaghanumera	224	3	26	Clare	Tulla Upper	Feakle	Tulla	II.	40
63,64,71,72	Pollagh (Blunden)	79	0	21	Tipperary. S.R.	Slievardagh	Kilvemnon	Callan	II.	335
27, 28, 34	Pollaghnagraigue	182	2	16	King's Co.	Coolestown	Clonsast	Edenderry	I.	133

(a) Including 20A. 0R. 25P. water.
(b) Including 13A. 0R. 9P. Aclaureen Lough.
(c) Including 6A. 0R. 0P. water.

(d) Including 3A. 0R. 1P. Brackloon Lough.
(e) Including 3A. 3R. 25P. water.
(f) Including 13A. 3R. 34P. water.

(g) Including 7A. 0R. 32P. River Barrow.
(h) Including 13A. 2R. 32P. water.

No. of Sheet of the Ordnance Survey Maps.	Townlands and Towns.	Area in Statute Acres.			County.	Barony.	Parish.	Poor Law Union in 1857.	Townland Census of 1851, Part I.	
		A.	R.	P.					Vol.	Page
30	Pollaghoole	148	3	18	King's Co.	Garrycastle	Reynagh	Parsonstown	I.	128
64, 72	Pollagh (Pennefather)	30	0	19	Tipperary, S.R.	Slievardagh	Kilvemnon	Callan	II.	335
69, 82	Pollaghrevagh	417	3	28	Galway	Dunkellin	Claregalway	Galway	IV.	28
5	Pollaginnive	25	2	20	Fermanagh	Lurg	Drumkeeran	Lowtherstown	III.	207
83	Pollagooil	97	3	39	Galway	Clare	Athenry	Galway	IV.	17
13, 20, 21	Pollagoona Mountain	2,825	0	23a	Clare	Tulla Upper	Moynoe	Scarriff	II.	40
21	Pollagorteen	276	1	39	Kildare	Offaly West	Lackagh	Athy	I.	73
15	Pollaguill	324	2	25	Donegal	Kilmacrenan	Clondahorky	Dunfanaghy	III.	123
40	Pollahoney	366	1	13	Wicklow	Arklow	Arklow	Rathdrum	I.	341
42	Pollakeel	193	2	3	Cavan	Clanmahon	Kilbride	Oldcastle	III.	78
26	Pollakeel	500	3	22	Cavan	Upper Loughtee	Denn	Cavan	III.	84
48	Pollalaher	657	2	25b	Roscommon	Athlone	Cam	Athlone	IV.	180
90, 100	Pollalena	74	0	4	Mayo	Carra	Drum	Castlebar	IV.	128
33, 39	Pollamalady	264	0	29	Cavan	Castlerahan	Lurgan	Oldcastle	III.	70
20, 21, 25, 26	Pollamore Far	256	1	2	Cavan	Upper Loughtee	Annagelliff	Cavan	III.	82
20, 25	Pollamore Near	247	0	27	Cavan	Upper Loughtee	Annagelliff	Cavan	III.	82
31	Pollanalty East	366	3	37	Roscommon	Castlereagh	Kiltullagh	Castlereagh	IV.	202
31	Pollanalty West	342	1	38	Roscommon	Castlereagh	Kiltullagh	Castlereagh	IV.	202
32	Pollanaroo	184	3	24	Roscommon	Castlereagh	Kiltullagh	Castlereagh	IV.	202
79	Poilanaskan	186	1	13	Mayo	Carra	Breaghwy	Castlebar	IV.	127
59	Pollandoo	573	2	9c	Donegal	Kilmacrenan	Gartan	Letterkenny	III.	127
25	Pollanea Lower	152	3	3	Roscommon	Castlereagh	Kiltullagh	Castlereagh	IV.	202
25, 32	Pollanea Upper	123	2	23	Roscommon	Castlereagh	Kiltullagh	Castlereagh	IV.	202
6	Pollaneyster	298	3	32	Galway	Ballymoe	Templetogher	Glennamaddy	IV.	9
101	Pollaniska	78	0	27	Mayo	Clanmorris	Crossboyne	Claremorris	IV.	133
27	Pollanorman	433	2	20	Tipperary, N.R.	Upper Ormond	Ballynaclogh	Nenagh	II.	290
26, 27	Pollanorman	283	1	1	Tipperary, N.R.	Upper Ormond	Dolla	Nenagh	II.	290
97	Pollanoughty	916	1	15	Mayo	Murrisk	Oughaval	Westport	IV.	162
52	Pollans	161	3	26	Donegal	Kilmacrenan	Conwal	Letterkenny	III.	126
17	Pollaphuca	66	0	3	Galway	Dunmore	Dunmore	Tuam	IV.	34
30	Pollaphuca	200	2	13	Galway	Dunmore	Tuam	Tuam	IV.	36
31	Pollaphuca	196	0	1	Roscommon	Castlereagh	Kiltullagh	Castlereagh	IV.	202
35, 40	Pollaphuca	117	1	19	Wicklow	Arklow	Castlemacadam	Rathdrum	I.	342
6	Pollarassa	154	3	9	Galway	Ballymoe	Templetogher	Glennamaddy	IV.	9
20	Pollardstown	488	0	19	Cork, E.R.	Condons&Clangibbon	Brigown	Mitchelstown	II.	60
23	Pollardstown	1,063	1	29	Kildare	Offaly East	Pollardstown	Naas	I.	70
31, 32	Pollareagh	244	2	12	Cavan	Castlerahan	Crosserlough	Cavan	III.	68
38	Pollareagh	137	0	25	Cavan	Clanmahon	Kilbride	Oldcastle	III.	78
113	Pollataggle	63	3	12	Galway	Kiltartan	Ardrahan	Gort	IV.	45
98	Pollatlugga	188	1	9	Galway	Clonmacnowen	Killallaghtan	Ballinasloe	IV.	26
11	Pollatomich or Kilcommon	672	2	30	Mayo	Erris	Kilcommon	Belmullet	IV.	144
20	Pollatrumpa	179	2	12	Clare	Tulla Upper	Feakle	Scarriff	II.	40
16	Pollaturick	261	1	19	Galway	Dunmore	Addergoole	Tuam	IV.	33
43	Pollaturk or Newgarden	425	0	23	Galway	Clare	Belclare	Tuam	IV.	17
79, 80, 90, 91	Pollavaddy	388	0	8d	Mayo	Clanmorris	Balla	Castlebar	IV.	132
71	Pollavullaun	84	1	11	Galway	Tiaquin	Monivea	Tuam	IV.	79
89	Pollawaddy	160	1	4	Mayo	Carra	Ballintober	Castlebar	IV.	125
100, 101	Pollawaddy	47	0	32	Mayo	Clanmorris	Mayo	Claremorris	IV.	135
58	Pollawarla	261	1	3	Galway	Tiaquin	Abbeyknockmoy	Tuam	IV.	75
47, 59	Pollawarla	482	1	7e	Mayo	Tirawley	Addergoole	Castlebar	IV.	163
111	Pollaweela	207	0	12	Mayo	Kilmaine	Kilcommon	Ballinrobe	IV.	155
44	Pollbaun	132	3	18	Galway	Clare	Killererin	Tuam	IV.	21
111, 119	Pollbaun	320	0	13	Mayo	Kilmaine	Kilcommon	Ballinrobe	IV.	155
87, 88	Pollboy	856	2	38f	Galway	Clonmacnowen	Kilcloony	Ballinasloe	IV.	25
7, 11	Pollboy	222	3	10	Leitrim	Drumahaire	Cloonlogher	Manorhamilton	IV.	94
74	Pollboy	170	1	28	Mayo	Costello	Castlemore	Castlereagh	IV.	140
12	Pollboy	192	0	21	Mayo	Erris	Kilcommon	Belmullet	IV.	144
71	Pollboy or Knockatober	268	0	38	Galway	Tiaquin	Monivea	Tuam	IV.	79
42	Pollbrean	73	2	30	Wexford	Forth	Drinagh	Wexford	I.	309
15	Pollbrock	106	3	12	Louth	Ardee	Stabannan	Ardee	I.	174
43	Polldarragh	223	2	21	Galway	Clare	Belclare	Tuam	IV.	17
32	Polldarrig	163	1	6	Wexford	Shelmaliere East	Ballynaslaney	Enniscorthy	I.	330
113	Polldonoghoe	76	1	14	Galway	Kiltartan	Ardrahan	Gort	IV.	45
40	Polldoon	165	3	2	Wexford	Shelmaliere West	Ballylannan	New Ross	I.	332
30	Polldorragha	326	1	5	Galway	Dunmore	Tuam	Tuam	IV.	36
101	Polldrian	164	3	36	Mayo	Clanmorris	Tagheen	Claremorris	IV.	136
39	Pollduff	888	0	33	King's Co.	Ballybritt	Roscomroe	Parsonstown	I.	125
6	Polleagh North	112	0	39	Galway	Ballymoe	Templetogher	Glennamaddy	IV.	9
6	Polleagh South	134	2	39g	Galway	Ballymoe	Templetogher	Glennamaddy	IV.	9
50	Polleban	107	3	17	Meath	Ratoath	Ballymaglassan	Dunshaughlin	I.	217
28, 33	Pollee	413	3	22	Antrim	Lower Antrim	Skerry	Ballymena	III.	5
16	Polleens	67	0	36	Galway	Dunmore	Tuam	Tuam	IV.	36

(a) Including 132A. 2R. 3P. water.
(b) Including 2A. 2R. 32P. water.
(c) Including 24A. 3R. 0R. water.

(d) Including 3A. 1R. 4P. water.
(e) Including 29A. 1R. 35P. water.

(f) Including 21A. 1R. 6P. water.
(g) Including 14A. 3R. 23P. water.

No. of Sheet of the Ordnance Survey Maps.	Townlands and Towns.	Area in Statute Acres.	County.	Barony.	Parish.	Poor Law Union in 1857.	Townland Census of 1851, Part I.	
		A. R. P.					Vol.	Page
93	Polleeny . . .	941 3 24a	Galway . .	Moycullen . .	Rahoon . . .	Galway . .	IV.	72
68, 81	Polleha . . .	341 2 15b	Galway . .	Moycullen . .	Moycullen . .	Galway . .	IV.	71
18	Polleighter . .	298 0 9	Galway . .	Ballymoe . .	Clonbern . .	Glennamaddy .	IV.	7
2, 7	Pollerton Big .	381 1 23	Carlow . .	Carlow . . .	Carlow . .	Carlow . .	I.	1
2, 7	Pollerton Little	299 0 7	Carlow . .	Carlow . . .	Carlow . .	Carlow . .	I.	1
9	Pollet . . .	164 0 25c	Donegal . .	Kilmacrenan .	Clondavaddog .	Millford . .	III.	125
117	Pollfeeneen . .	38 0 19	Galway . .	Longford . .	Tynagh . .	Portumna .	IV.	62
43	Pollintemple .	98 3 25	Cavan . .	Castlerahan .	Lurgan . .	Oldcastle .	III.	70
82	Pollkeen . . .	606 3 14	Galway . .	Galway . .	Oranmore . .	Galway . .	IV.	37
47	Pollmanagh Great .	135 2 32	Wexford . .	Bargy . . .	Kilmannan .	Wexford . .	I.	306
47	Pollmanagh Little .	73 2 11	Wexford . .	Bargy . . .	Kilmannan . .	Wexford . .	I.	306
96	Pollnabanny .	278 0 9	Galway . .	Dunkellin . .	Killora . . .	Loughrea . .	IV.	31
59	Pollnabrone .	486 2 11	Galway . .	Tiaquin . .	Killoscobe . .	Mountbellew .	IV.	78
121	Pollnabunny .	155 3 23	Mayo . .	Kilmaine . .	Kilmainebeg .	Ballinrobe .	IV.	155
111	Pollnacartan .	23 3 15	Mayo . .	Kilmaine . .	Kilcommon .	Ballinrobe .	IV.	155
81	Pollnaclogha .	1,391 3 12d	Galway . .	Moycullen .	Moycullen .	Galway . .	IV.	71
93	Pollnacroaghy .	79 2 35	Mayo . .	Costello . .	Bekan . . .	Claremorris .	IV.	139
31	Pollnagappul . .	24 2 23	Leitrim . .	Leitrim . .	Kiltoghert .	Car^k. on Shannon	IV.	102
104	Pollnagarragh East .	175 0 6	Galway . .	Dunkellin .	Killeely . .	Gort . . .	IV.	30
104	Pollnagarragh West	149 0 8	Galway . .	Dunkellin .	Killeely . .	Gort . . .	IV.	30
61	Pollnagawna . .	204 0 26e	Mayo . .	Gallen . .	Meelick . . .	Swineford .	IV.	150
11	Pollnagh . .	342 3 5	Armagh . .	Tiranny . .	Tynan . .	Armagh . .	III.	60
84	Pollnagrongh .	355 1 9	Galway . .	Athenry . .	Athenry . .	Loughrea . .	IV.	4
42	Pollnahallia .	733 1 30	Galway . .	Clare . . .	Donaghpatrick .	Tuam . .	IV.	19
117	Pollnahincha .	80 3 5	Galway . .	Longford . .	Killimorbologue .	Portumna .	IV.	59
29	Pollnamal . .	175 1 4	Galway . .	Clare . . .	Belclare . .	Tuam . .	IV.	17
29, 43	Pollnamal . .	487 1 16	Galway . .	Clare . . .	Killower . .	Tuam . .	IV.	21
17	Pollnamoghil .	66 2 18	Roscommon .	Roscommon .	Aughrim . .	Car^k. on Shannon	IV.	207
47	Pollnamuckaor Charlestown . .	88 0 10	Galway . .	Killian . .	Killeroran . .	Mountbellew .	IV.	43
104	Pollnaranny .	1,348 3 12f	Donegal . .	Tirhugh . .	Drumhome . .	Donegal . .	III.	147
94	Pollnarooma East .	81 0 17	Galway . .	Galway . .	Rahoon . . .	Galway . .	IV.	38
94	Pollnarooma West .	166 1 16	Galway . .	Galway . .	Rahoon . .	Galway . .	IV.	38
104	Pollnashinnagh .	116 0 19	Galway . .	Dunkellin .	Killinan . .	Loughrea . .	IV.	30
111, 112	Pollnasillagh .	115 0 31	Mayo . .	Clanmorris .	Crossboyne .	Claremorris .	IV.	133
113	Pollnavengh .	178 1 3	Galway . .	Kiltartan . .	Kinvarradoorus .	Gort . .	IV.	49
2	Pollockstown .	96 2 36	Tyrone . .	Strabane Lower .	Leckpatrick .	Strabane . .	III.	322
6	Pollower . .	29 0 23	Roscommon .	Boyle . . .	Ardcarn . .	Boyle . .	IV.	193
6	Pollower . .	101 0 29	Roscommon .	Boyle . .	Kilbryan . .	Boyle . .	IV.	195
24	Pollpeasty . .	361 2 29	Wexford . .	Bantry . .	Killegney . .	Enniscorthy .	I.	361
111	Pollraddy .	147 3 18	Mayo . .	Kilmaine .	Kilcommon .	Ballinrobe .	IV.	155
47, 52	Pollrane . .	142 3 0	Wexford . .	Bargy . .	Kilturk . .	Wexford . .	I.	307
48	Pollrankin .	126 1 23	Wexford . .	Forth . .	St. Michael's .	Wexford . .	I.	314
27	Pollranny .	138 2 35	Roscommon .	Castlereagh .	Baslick . .	Castlereagh .	IV.	199
55	Pollranny (Lynchaghan) . .	897 0 31	Mayo . .	Burrishoole .	Achill . .	Newport . .	IV.	117
55, 65	Pollranny (Sweeny)	1,104 2 23g	Mayo . .	Burrishoole .	Achill . .	Newport . .	IV.	117
32, 33	Pollregan .	155 2 18	Wexford . .	Shelmaliere East .	Ardcolm . .	Wexford . .	I.	330
1, 6	Pollremon .	345 2 14h	Galway . .	Ballymoe . .	Templetogher .	Glennamaddy .	IV.	9
48	Pollrevagh .	158 1 39i	Galway . .	Ballynahinch .	Ballindoon .	Clifden . .	IV.	10
105	Pollroebuck .	39 1 4	Galway . .	Loughrea .	Loughrea . .	Loughrea . .	IV.	66
71, 80	Pollronahan Beg .	79 3 17	Mayo . .	Gallen . .	Killedan . .	Swineford .	IV.	150
71, 80	Pollronahan More .	236 0 21	Mayo . .	Gallen . .	Killedan . .	Swineford .	IV.	150
42	Pollrone . . .	699 2 35	Kilkenny . .	Iverk . .	Pollrone . .	Waterford .	I.	106
34	Pollrone . . .	253 3 21	Kilkenny .	Kells . .	Tullahought .	Carrick on Suir	I.	110
42	POLLRONE T. .	—	Kilkenny . .	Iverk . .	Pollrone . .	Waterford .	I.	106
42	Pollsallagh .	182 2 27	Wexford .	Forth . .	Rathmacknee .	Wexford . .	I.	313
61	Pollsharvoge .	365 0 21j	Mayo . .	Gallen . .	Meelick . .	Swineford .	IV.	150
6	Pollshask .	121 1 7	Galway . .	Ballymoe . .	Templetogher .	Glennamaddy .	IV.	9
58	Pollsillagh .	303 3 24	Galway . .	Clare . .	Kilmoylan .	Tuam . .	IV.	22
58	POLLSILLAGH T. .	—	Galway . .	Clare . .	Kilmoylan .	Tuam . .	IV.	22
117	Polltalloon East	58 3 14	Galway . .	Leitrim . .	Tynagh . .	Portumna .	IV.	55
117	Polltalloon West .	93 1 27	Galway . .	Leitrim . .	Tynagh . .	Portumna .	IV.	56
47	Pollwitch .	29 2 13	Wexford .	Forth . .	Mayglass . .	Wexford . .	I.	312
1	Pollynoon .	114 0 35	Galway . .	Ballymoe . .	Templetogher .	Glennamaddy .	IV.	10
23, 29	Pollymount .	220 1 22	Roscommon .	Roscommon .	Bumlin . .	Strokestown .	IV.	208
37	Pomeroy . .	57 2 23	Tyrone . .	Dungannon Middle .	Pomeroy . .	Cookstown .	III.	304
37	Pomeroy . .	273 3 0	Tyrone . .	Dungannon Upper .	Desertcreat .	Cookstown .	III.	308
37	POMEROY T. .	—	Tyrone . .	Dungannon Middle .	Pomeroy . .	Cookstown .	III.	304
29	Pondfields .	12 3 10	Wexford .	Bantry . .	St. Mary's .	New Ross .	I.	302
22	PONDS T. .	—	Dublin . .	Rathdown . .	Rathfarnham .	Dublin South .	I.	37
66, 67	Poobles . .	482 2 38k	Antrim . .	Upper Massereene .	Aghalee . .	Lurgan . .	III.	29
107, 120	Pookeen . .	448 1 3	Cork, W.R. .	East Carbery (W.D.)	Fanlobbus . .	Dunmanway .	II.	132

(a) Including 19A. 2R. 33P. water.
(b) Including 9A. 0R. 33P. water.
(c) Including 2A. 3R. 32P. water.
(d) Including 19A. 0R. 10P. water.

(e) Including 10A. 2R. 16P. water.
(f) Including 98A. 2R. 34P. water.
(g) Including 1A. 0R. 20P. water.
(h) Including 2A. 3R. 19P. water.

(i) Including 5A. 0R. 33P. water.
(j) Including 11A. 1R. 34P. water.
(k) Including 34A. 0R. 15P. Broad Water.

No. of Sheet of the Ordnance Survey Maps.	Townlands and Towns.	Area in Statute Acres.			County.	Barony.	Parish.	Poor Law Union in 1857.	Townland Census of 1851, Part I.	
		A.	R.	P.					Vol.	Page
150	Pookeen . . .	159	3	38	Cork, W.R. .	West Carbery (E.D.)	Tullagh . . .	Skibbereen	II.	141
23	Poormansbridge .	277	2	27	Queen's Co. .	Cullenagh . .	Abbeyleix . .	Abbeyleix .	I.	238
5, 8	Popeshall . .	70	0	6	Dublin . .	Balrothery East .	Lusk . . .	Balrothery .	I.	21
32	Poplar . . .	12	2	30	Wexford . .	Shelmaliere East .	Artramon . .	Wexford . .	I.	330
14	Poppintree . .	16	1	18a	Dublin . .	Castleknock . .	Finglas . .	Dublin North .	I.	25
14	Poppintree . .	118	3	17	Dublin . .	Coolock . .	Santry . .	Dublin North .	I.	29
98	Poppyhill . .	13	2	18	Galway . .	Kilconnell . .	Killallaghtan .	Ballinasloe .	IV.	41
98, 99	Poppyhill . .	381	1	35	Galway . .	Longford . .	Killoran . .	Ballinasloe .	IV.	59
4	Porchavodda . .	91	1	19	Carlow . .	Rathvilly . .	Hacketstown .	Shillelagh .	I.	11
54, 55	Porridgetown East .	240	2	0	Galway . .	Moycullen . .	Killannin . .	Oughterard .	IV.	70
54, 55	Porridgetown West	135	2	24	Galway . .	Moycullen . .	Killannin . .	Oughterard .	IV.	70
15	Porsoon . . .	65	2	32	Clare . .	Corcomroe . .	Kilshanny . .	Ennistimon .	II.	21
1	Port . . .	168	3	0	Cavan . .	Tullyhaw . .	Killinagh . .	Enniskillen .	III.	92
9, 13	Port . . .	335	0	36b	Cavan . .	Tullyhaw . .	Templeport . .	Bawnboy . .	III.	95
72, 81	Port . . .	300	2	14	Donegal . .	Banagh . .	Glencolumbkille .	Glenties . .	III.	105
98	Port . . .	107	0	32	Donegal . .	Banagh . .	Inver . .	Donegal . .	III.	108
15, 25, 26	Port . . .	527	3	33c	Donegal . .	Kilmacrenan .	Clondahorky .	Dunfanaghy .	III.	123
27	Port . . .	70	0	6	Leitrim . .	Leitrim . .	Kiltoghert . .	Carᵏ. on Shannon	IV.	102
34, 42	Port . . .	1,205	1	22d	Limerick . .	Glenquin . .	Abbeyfeale . .	Newcastle .	II.	244
21	Port . . .	64	2	5	Limerick . .	Kenry . .	Adare . .	Croom . .	II.	248
19	Port . . .	703	1	7	Louth . .	Ferrard . .	Port . .	Drogheda .	I.	182
54	Portacarron . .	233	2	37	Galway . .	Moycullen . .	Kilcummin . .	Oughterard .	IV.	68
54	Portacarron Beg .	48	3	33	Galway . .	Moycullen . .	Kilcummin . .	Oughterard .	IV.	68
15	Portacloghan . .	132	2	37e	Cavan . .	Lower Loughtee .	Drumlane . .	Cavan . .	III.	80
1, 4	Portacloy . .	922	2	0	Mayo . .	Erris . .	Kilcommon . .	Belmullet .	IV.	144
9	PORTADOWN T. .	—			Armagh . .	{ Oneilland East . } { Oneilland West . }	{ Seagoe . . } { Drumcree . . }	Lurgan . .	III.	{ 50 } { 52 }
32	PORTAFERRY T. .	—			Down . .	Ards Upper . .	Ballyphilip . .	Downpatrick .	III.	160
90, 91	Portagh . .	326	2	20	Mayo . .	Clanmorris . .	Mayo . .	Claremorris .	IV.	135
14, 15	Portaghard . .	518	3	31	Roscommon .	Frenchpark . .	Tibohine . .	Castlereagh .	IV.	205
11	Portaghbradagh .	177	0	21	Sligo . .	Tireragh . .	Kilmacshalgan .	Dromore West .	IV.	235
19	Portaliff Glebe .	10	1	33f	Cavan . .	Tullyhunco . .	Killashandra .	Cavan . .	III.	98
19	Portaliff or Town-parks . .	326	3	35g	Cavan . .	Tullyhunco . .	Killashandra .	Cavan . .	III.	98
27	Portally . .	116	2	31	Waterford . .	Gaultiere . .	Killea . .	Waterford .	II.	363
32	Portan . .	128	1	7h	Cavan . .	Castlerahan . .	Crosserlough .	Cavan . .	III.	68
51	Portan . .	102	3	8	Meath . .	Dunboyne . .	Dunboyne . .	Dunshaughlin .	I.	199
35, 41	Portan . .	391	1	2i	Meath . .	Lune . .	Killaconnigan .	Trim . .	I.	208
44	Portan . .	345	0	31	Meath . .	Ratoath . .	Rathregan . .	Dunshaughlin .	I.	219
35	Portanab . .	563	3	34	Meath . .	Lune . .	Kildalkey . .	Trim . .	I.	208
25	Portanclogh . .	85	0	30	Meath . .	Lower Navan . .	Navan . .	Navan . .	I.	215
25	Portane . .	24	1	28	Limerick . .	Coonagh . .	Doon . .	Tipperary .	II.	234
25	Portane . .	112	2	22	Limerick . .	Coonagh . .	Oola . .	Tipperary .	II.	236
22	Portaneena . .	219	1	11	Westmeath . .	Kilkenny West .	Kilkenny West .	Athlone . .	I.	273
27, 31	Portancoght . .	78	1	19	Leitrim . .	Leitrim . .	Kiltoghert . .	Carᵏ. on Shannon	IV.	102
30, 36	Portanure . .	371	3	13j	Cavan . .	Tullyhunco . .	Scrabby . .	Granard . .	III.	99
25, 26	Portanure . .	356	1	33	Longford . .	Rathcline . .	Cashel . .	Ballymahon .	I.	164
25	Portanure Bog .	54	0	11	Longford . .	Rathcline . .	Cashel . .	Ballymahon .	I.	164
34	PORTARLINGTON T. .	—			{ King's Co . } { Queen's Co. . }	{ Upper Philipstown . } { Portnahinch . . }	{ Cloneyhurk . } { Lea . . }	Mountmellick .	I.	{ 143 } { 244 }
4, 5										
47	Portauns . .	357	1	23	Limerick . .	Kilmallock . .	St.Peter's & St.Paul's	Kilmallock .	II.	250
54	Portavarrig . .	12	3	5	Cork, E.R. .	Barrymore . .	Britway . .	Middleton .	II.	52
54	Partavarrig . .	145	1	36	Cork, E.R. .	Barrymore . .	Templebodan .	Middleton .	II.	58
13	Portavaud . .	140	1	25	Sligo . .	Tireragh . .	Skreen . .	Dromore West .	IV.	236
2	Portavoe . .	544	2	36	Down . .	Ards Lower . .	Bangor . .	Newtownards .	III.	157
18, 25	Portavogie . .	615	0	13	Down . .	Ards Upper . .	St. Andrews alias Ballyhalbert	Newtownards .	III.	161
21, 29	Portavrolla and Curraghavarna .	235	1	11	King's Co. .	Garrycastle . .	Reynagh . .	Parsonstown .	I.	138
33	Portbeg . .	63	2	3	Fermanagh .	Clanawley . .	Kinawley . .	Enniskillen .	III.	194
32	Portboy . .	136	1	29	Limerick . .	Smallcounty . .	Ballynamona .	Kilmallock .	II.	259
101, 105	Portcreevy . .	333	0	27h	Donegal . .	Tirhugh . .	Templecarn . .	Donegal . .	III.	149
1	Portcrusha . .	286	0	10	Limerick . .	Clanwilliam . .	Stradbally . .	Limerick . .	II.	226
68	Portdarragh . .	440	0	24	Galway . .	Moycullen . .	Moycullen . .	Galway . .	IV.	71
62	Portdrine . .	570	2	11	Clare . .	Bunratty Lower .	Kilfintinan .	Limerick . .	II.	5
44	Portduff . .	162	2	10	Cork, E.R. .	Barrymore . .	Rathcormack .	Fermoy . .	II.	57
39	Portduff . .	122	2	28	Kerry . .	Trughanacmy .	Castleisland .	Tralee . .	II.	209
47, 50	Porteen and Ballyrevagh . .	305	1	4	Roscommon .	Athlone . .	Dysart . .	Athlone . .	IV.	181
50	Porteen and Ballyrevagh West	363	0	38l	Roscommon .	Athlone . .	Dysart . .	Athlone . .	IV.	181
49, 54	Portersgate . .	174	0	17	Wexford . .	Shelburne . .	Hook . .	New Ross .	I.	327
36	Portersize . .	514	2	20	Kildare . .	Narragh & RebanEast	Timolin . .	Baltinglass .	I.	67
29	Portersland . .	81	1	0	Wexford . .	Bantry . .	St. Marys . .	New Ross .	I.	302

(a) Including 7ᴀ. 0ʀ. 37ᴘ. detached portion.
(b) Including 49ᴀ. 3ʀ. 13ᴘ. water.
(c) Including 27ᴀ. 2ʀ. 26ᴘ. water.
(d) Including 2ᴀ. 1ʀ. 0ᴘ. water.

(e) Including 11ᴀ. 1ʀ. 18ᴘ. water.
(f) Including 0ᴀ. 2ʀ. 16ᴘ. detached portion.
(g) Including 59ᴀ. 2ʀ. 16ᴘ. water.
(h) Including 13ᴀ. 2ʀ. 1ᴘ. water.

(i) Including 0ᴀ. 2ʀ. 38ᴘ. water.
(j) Including 14ᴀ. 1ʀ. 27ᴘ. water.
(k) Including 19ᴀ. 3ʀ. 13ᴘ. water.
(l) Including 28ᴀ. 1ʀ. 29ᴘ. water.

No. of Sheet of the Ordnance Survey Maps.	Townlands and Towns.	Area in Statute Acres.			County.	Barony.	Parish.	Poor Law Union in 1857.	Townland Census of 1851, Part I.	
		A.	R.	P.					Vol.	Page
13, 17	Porterstown	219	1	37	Dublin	Castleknock	Castleknock	Dublin North	I.	24
20	Porterstown	98	3	32	Kildare	South Salt	Kilteel	Naas	I.	77
44	Porterstown	202	3	12	Meath	Ratoath	Rathbeggan	Dunshaughlin	I.	219
50	Porterstown	49	2	22	Meath	Upper Deece	Moyglare	Celbridge	I.	194
33	Porterstown	88	3	13	Meath	Upper Duleek	Ardcath	Drogheda	I.	197
20, 27	Porterstown (Cooke)	367	2	13	Westmeath	Farbill	Killucan	Mullingar	I.	267
27	Porterstown (Napper)	157	1	31	Westmeath	Farbill	Killucan	Mullingar	I.	267
14, 19	Port or Glasstown	118	2	30	Cavan	Tullyhunco	Kildallan	Cavan	III.	97
31 } 33 }	PORTGLENONE T.	—			{ Antrim { Londonderry	Lower Toome Loughinsholin	Ahoghill Tamlaght O'Crilly	Ballymena Magherafelt	III. III.	32 244
5	Portgloriam	479	1	27	Kildare	Ikeathy&Oughterany	Kilcock	Celbridge	I.	57
63, 71	Porthall	470	1	7	Donegal	Raphoe	Clonleigh	Strabane	III.	135
6, 7	Portinaghy	123	1	32a	Monaghan	Trough	Donagh	Monaghan	III.	282
33	Portinch	184	3	28b	Sligo	Corran	Emlaghfad	Tobercurry	IV.	226
5	Portinode	298	1	18	Fermanagh	Lurg	Drumkeeran	Lowtherstown	III.	207
70, 79	Portinure	85	1	9	Donegal	Raphoe	Clonleigh	Strabane	III.	135
1	Port Island	0	2	0	Cavan	Tullyhaw	Killinagh	Enniskillen	III.	92
114	Port Island	20	3	2	Mayo	Murrisk	Inishbofin	Clifden	IV.	159
7	Portjack	123	0	5	Westmeath	Fore	Mayne	Granard	I.	271
4	Portland	1,048	3	10	Tipperary, N.R.	Lower Ormond	Lorrha	Borrisokane	II.	285
1, 4	Portland Island	64	0	12	Tipperary, N.R.	Lower Ormond	Lorrha	Borrisokane	II.	285
1, 4	Portland Little	482	3	39	Tipperary, N.R.	Lower Ormond	Lorrha	Borrisokane	II.	285
15	Portlawney	139	3	28c	Cavan	Lower Loughtee	Drumlane	Cavan	III.	80
8	PORTLAW T.	—			Waterford	Upperthird	Clonagam	Carrick on Suir	II.	369
25	Portlecka	228	1	7d	Clare	Inchiquin	Ruan	Corrofin	II.	28
48, 49	Portlee	235	3	35	Antrim	Upper Toome	Drummaul	Antrim	III.	34
48	Portlee (part of)	166	2	33	Antrim	Upper Toome	Drummaul	Antrim	III.	34
36, 45	Portleen	667	2	11e	Donegal	Kilmacrenan	Kilmacrenan	Millford	III.	129
35	Portlester	609	2	39f	Meath	Lune	Killaconnigan	Trim	I.	208
22	Portlick	373	2	14	Westmeath	Kilkenny West	Bunown	Athlone	I.	272
11, 18	Portloman	267	3	0	Westmeath	Corkaree	Portloman	Mullingar	I.	263
19, 24	Portlongfield	762	3	9g	Cavan	Tullyhunco	Killashandra	Cavan	III.	98
47, 55	Portlough	282	2	0h	Donegal	Raphoe	Allsaints	Londonderry	III.	134
31	Portloughan	221	2	26	Down	Lecale Lower	Saul	Downpatrick	III.	179
87	Portmagee	140	1	3	Kerry	Iveragh	Killemlagh	Cahersiveen	II.	196
87	PORTMAGEE T.	—			Kerry	Iveragh	Killemlagh	Cahersiveen	II.	196
51	Portmanna	119	2	19i	Meath	Dunboyne	Dunboyne	Dunshaughlin	I.	199
15	Portmarnock	386	1	33	Dublin	Coolock	Portmarnock	Balrothery	I.	28
14	Portmellick	108	0	4	Dublin	Coolock	St. Margarets	Dublin North	I.	29
62, 63	Portmore	562	3	0j	Antrim	Upper Massereene	Ballinderry	Lurgan	III.	29
41	Portmuck	235	1	25k	Antrim	Lower Belfast	Islandmagee	Larne	III.	9
21	Portmush	112	1	28	Fermanagh	Magheraboy	Rossorry	Enniskillen	III.	214
4	Portnablahy	280	3	8	Fermanagh	Lurg	Templecarn	Lowtherstown	III.	209
4	Portnaboe	284	1	1	Waterford	Upperthird	Fenoagh	Carrick on Suir	II.	370
9	Portnacloyaduff	394	1	32	Fermanagh	Magheraboy	Inishmacsaint	Ballyshannon	III.	213
9	Portnacrinnaght	144	3	39l	Roscommon	Frenchpark	Kilnamanagh	Boyle	IV.	204
4	Portnahinch	175	1	9	Queen's Co.	Portnahinch	Ardea	Mountmellick	I.	243
40	Portnahinch	152	1	35	Roscommon	Ballintober South	Cloontuskert	Roscommon	IV.	188
43, 46	Portnahully	288	3	17	Kilkenny	Iverk	Aglish	Waterford	I.	105
19	Portnaquin	53	3	18	Cavan	Tullyhunco	Killashandra	Cavan	III.	98
7, 15	Portnard	2,123	1	22	Limerick	Owneybeg	Tuogh	Limerick	II.	251
42, 45	Portnascully	131	3	10	Kilkenny	Iverk	Pollrone	Waterford	I.	106
42, 45	Portnascully	265	0	8	Kilkenny	Iverk	Portnascully	Waterford	I.	106
12	Portnashangan	498	2	27m	Westmeath	Corkaree	Portnashangan	Mullingar	I.	263
27	Portnasnow Glebe	31	0	32n	Fermanagh	Tirkennedy	Enniskillen	Enniskillen	III.	222
107	Portnason	57	3	22	Donegal	Tirhugh	Inishmacsaint	Ballyshannon	III.	147
15	Portnelligan	160	2	17o	Armagh	Tiranny	Tynan	Armagh	III.	60
53	Portnick	122	0	21p	Roscommon	Moycarn	Creagh	Ballinasloe	IV.	206
18	Portobello	107	0	5q	Dublin	Uppercross and Municipal Borough	St. Peters	Dublin South	I.	41
10, 16	Portobello	474	2	15	Roscommon	Frenchpark	Creeve	Cark. on Shannon	IV.	203
22	Portora	116	0	35r	Fermanagh	Magheraboy	Rossorry	Enniskillen	III.	214
8	Portraine	110	1	14	Dublin	Nethercross	Portraine	Balrothery	I.	31
12	Portraine Demesne	229	0	23	Dublin	Nethercross	Donabate	Balrothery	I.	30
8, 12	Portraine Demesne	241	3	22	Dublin	Nethercross	Portraine	Balrothery	I.	31
33	Portreagh	57	0	14s	Fermanagh	Clanawley	Kinawley	Enniskillen	III.	194
14	Portree	119	1	8t	Queen's Co.	Stradbally	Curraclone	Athy	I.	246
19	PORTROE T.	—			Tipperary, N.R.	Owney and Arra	Castletownarra	Nenagh	II.	294
99	Portroyal	443	0	16u	Mayo	Carra	Ballyovey	Ballinrobe	IV.	126
11	Portruan	111	0	37v	Cavan	Lower Loughtee	Annagh	Cavan	III.	79
42	Portrunny	10	1	34	Roscommon	Athlone	Kilmeane	Roscommon	IV.	182
2, 6	Port Rush	214	3	17	Antrim	Lower Dunluce	Ballywillin	Coleraine	III.	15
4	Portrushen Lower	339	2	36	Carlow	Rathvilly	Kiltegan	Baltinglass	I.	11

(a) Including 6A. 3R. 16P. water.
(b) Including 7A. 3R. 9P. water.
(c) Including 18A. 0R. 24P. water.
(d) Including 24A. 2R. 29P. water.
(e) Including 146A. 2R. 4P. water.
(f) Including 0A. 2R. 38P. water.
(g) Including 107A. 3R. 9P. water.
(h) Including 32A. 1R. 7P. water.

(i) Including 44A. 1R. 5P. detached portions.
(j) Including 118A. 0R. 19P. Portmore Lough.
(k) Including 11A. 0R. 39P. Isle of Muck.
(l) Including 9A. 0R. 25P. water.
(m) Including 9A. 0R. 24P. water.
(n) Including 2A. 2R. 21P. water.
(o) Including 24A. 1R. 14P. water.
(p) Including 7A. 0R. 24P. water.

(q) { Within the Municipal Boundary, 51A. 3R. 31P. { Without the Municipal Boundary, 55A. 0R. 14P.
(r) Including 31A. 3R. 16P. water.
(s) Including 3A. 3R. 37P. water.
(t) Including 3A. 1R. 12P. River Barrow.
(u) Including 48A. 2R. 12P. water.
(v) Including 18A. 2R. 24P. water.

5 E

No. of Sheet of the Ordnance Survey Maps.	Townlands and Towns.	Area in Statute Acres. A.	R.	P.	County.	Barony.	Parish.	Poor Law Union in 1857.	Townland Census of 1851, Part I. Vol.	Page
4	Portrushen Upper	220	3	13	Carlow	Rathvilly	Kiltegan	Baltinglass	I.	11
2	Port Rush T.	—			Antrim	Lower Dunluce	Ballywillin	Coleraine	III.	16
39	Ports	221	1	13a	Fermanagh	Coole	Galloon	Lisnaskea	III.	200
3	Port Stewart T.	—			Londonderry	North East Liberties of Coleraine	Ballyaghran	Coleraine	III.	245
98	Port T.	—			Donegal	Banagh	Inver	Donegal	III.	108
19	Port T.	—			Louth	Ferrard	Port	Drogheda	I.	182
117,126,127	Portumna	783	2	17	Galway	Longford	Lickmolassy	Portumna	IV.	61
126,127	Portumna Demesne	1,400	0	19	Galway	Longford	Lickmolassy	Portumna	IV.	61
127	Portumna T.	—			Galway	Longford	Lickmolassy	Portumna	IV.	61
13	Porturlan	67	2	14	Cavan	Tullyhaw	Templeport	Bawnboy	III.	95
1, 4, 5	Porturlin	2,120	2	15	Mayo	Erris	Kilcommon	Belmullet	IV.	144
25	Posey	48	2	8	Kilkenny	Gowran	Ullard	Thomastown	I.	100
10, 11	Posseckstown	252	1	31	Kildare	North Salt	Killadoon	Celbridge	I.	75
48	Posseckstown	1,046	3	24	Meath	Lower Moyfenrath	Rathcore	Trim	I.	211
6	Posseckstown	1,261	3	14	Meath	Morgallion	Nobber	Kells	I.	210
30	Potaley	17	2	39	Kerry	Trughanacmy	Ballymacelligott	Tralee	II.	207
55	Potatoe Island	1	2	36	Galway	Moycullen	Kilcummin	Oughterard	IV.	69
3,7	Pottagh	148	0	17	Londonderry	Coleraine	Dunboe	Coleraine	III.	231
31	Pottahee	145	3	1	Cavan	Clanmahon	Ballintemple	Cavan	III.	75
44, 50	Potterswalls	173	2	28	Antrim	Upper Antrim	Antrim	Antrim	III.	5
36	Pottiagh	101	3	36	Fermanagh	Clankelly	Clones	Clones	III.	197
17	Pottiaghan Commons	153	1	13	Westmeath	Rathconrath	Killare	Ballymahon	I.	283
32	Pottle	130	3	24	Cavan	Castlerahan	Denn	Oldcastle	III.	68
22,23,27,28	Pottle	81	3	34	Cavan	Clankee	Knockbride	Cootehill	III.	74
30	Pottle	136	0	32	Cavan	Tullyhunco	Killashandra	Cavan	III.	98
21	Pottle	87	3	17	Cavan	Upper Loughtee	Annagelliff	Cavan	III.	82
20	Pottle	56	0	11	Cavan	Upper Loughtee	Kilmore	Cavan	III.	85
37, 41	Pottlebane	271	1	39	Cavan	Clanmahon	Drumlumman	Granard	III.	77
10, 16	Pottlebane	511	1	16	Meath	Upper Kells	Kilskeer	Kells	I.	206
37	Pottleboy	91	3	8	Cavan	Clanmahon	Ballymachugh	Cavan	III.	76
17	Pottleboy	74	0	6	Cavan	Tullygarvey	Kildrumsherdan	Cootehill	III.	90
21	Pottleboy	40	1	15	Cavan	Upper Loughtee	Castleterra	Cavan	III.	83
27	Pottlebrack	185	2	39	Cavan	Clankee	Knockbride	Bailieborough	III.	74
33, 34	Pottleduff	51	2	22	Cavan	Castlerahan	Killinkere	Bailieborough	III.	69
16	Pottle East	89	0	4	Cavan	Tullygarvey	Drung	Cootehill	III.	89
28, 34	Pottle Lower	244	2	20	Cavan	Clankee	Bailieborough	Bailieborough	III.	71
18, 22	Pottlerath	1,016	1	38	Kilkenny	Crannagh	Kilmanagh	Callan	I.	86
17, 18	Pottlereagh	98	3	31	Cavan	Tullygarvey	Drumgoon	Cootehill	III.	88
10	Pottlereagh	311	2	36	Meath	Upper Kells	Kilskeer	Kells	I.	206
32	Pottle Soden	43	1	34	Cavan	Upper Loughtee	Denn	Cavan	III.	84
28, 34	Pottle Upper	252	0	23	Cavan	Clankee	Bailieborough	Bailieborough	III.	71
16	Pottle West	150	0	34	Cavan	Tullygarvey	Drung	Cootehill	III.	89
21	Pottore	299	1	18	Leitrim	Carrigallen	Oughteragh	Bawnboy	IV.	92
5	Poulacapple	327	3	27	Clare	Burren	Rathborney	Ballyvaghan	II.	14
64	Poulacapple East	747	2	7	Tipperary, S.R.	Slievardagh	Kilvemnon	Callan	II.	335
63, 64	Poulacapple West	769	2	8	Tipperary, S.R.	Slievardagh	Kilvemnon	Callan	II.	335
9	Poulacarran	319	1	17	Clare	Burren	Carran	Ballyvaghan	II.	12
75, 81	Poulaculleare	395	3	15	Tipperary, S.R.	Iffa and Offa West	Whitechurch	Clogheen	II.	322
63, 64, 74	Poulacurry North	175	1	27	Cork, E.R.	Cork	Rathcooney	Cork	II.	65
63,64,74,75	Poulacurry South	238	0	20	Cork, E.R.	Cork	Rathcooney	Cork	II.	65
52, 53	Pouladown	171	0	24	Cork, E.R.	Barrymore	Templeusque	Cork	II.	59
27, 35	Poulaforia	112	2	26	Clare	Tulla Upper	Tulla	Tulla	II.	42
28	Poulagower	481	1	4	Clare	Tulla Upper	Tomgraney	Scarriff	II.	41
74, 84	Poulagower	1,314	2	20	Kerry	Magunihy	Killarney	Killarney	II.	203
22, 27, 28	Poulakerry	273	2	25	Tipperary, N.R.	Upper Ormond	Kilkeary	Nenagh	II.	230
84	Poulakerry	291	0	4c	Tipperary, S.R.	Iffa and Offa East	Kilsheelan	Clonmel	II.	314
40	Poulanassy	0	3	13	Kilkenny	Iverk	Kilmacow	Waterford	I.	106
5, 9	Poulanine	208	0	25	Clare	Burren	Kilcorney	Ballyvaghan	II.	12
76	Poulaniska	53	0	6	Cork, E.R.	Barrymore	Carrigtohill	Middleton	II.	52
10	Poulaphuca	179	0	17	Clare	Burren	Carran	Ballyvaghan	II.	12
6	Poulaphuca	148	1	19	Clare	Burren	Oughtmama	Ballyvaghan	II.	14
50	Poulaphuca	64	3	32	Clare	Clonderalaw	Kilchreest	Killadysert	II.	15
83, 95	Poularick	726	1	31	Cork, W.R.	West Muskerry	Kilmurry	Macroom	II.	159
7	Poulataggle	470	1	6d	Clare	Inchiquin	Kilkeedy	Corrofin	II.	26
88	Poulatar	162	2	38	Tipperary, S.R.	Iffa and Offa West	Ballybacon	Clogheen	II.	317
80, 81	Poulavala	289	2	35	Tipperary, S.R.	Iffa and Offa West	Tubbrid	Clogheen	II.	321
6	Poulavare	164	2	36	Cork, E.R.	Duhallow	Tullylease	Kanturk	II.	76
2	Poulavone	237	1	31	Waterford	Upperthird	Rathgormuck	Clonmel	II.	371
9	Poulawack	226	1	2	Clare	Burren	Carran	Ballyvaghan	II.	12
38	Poulawaddra	821	3	1	Kerry	Trughanacmy	Ballyseedy	Tralee	II.	208
30, 31	Poulawillan	444	0	6	Clare	Ibrickan	Kilfarboy	Ennistimon	II.	22
5, 6	Poulbaun	392	1	31	Clare	Burren	Kilcorney	Ballyvaghan	II.	12

(a) Including 15A. 2R. 15P. water.
(b) Including 6A. 0R. 15P. water.
(c) Including 7A. 2R. 8P. water.
(d) Including 4A. 0R. 21P. water.

No. of Sheet of the Ordnance Survey Maps.	Townlands and Towns.	Area in Statute Acres.			County.	Barony.	Parish.	Poor Law Union in 1857.	Townland Census of 1851, Part I.	
		A.	R.	P.					Vol.	Page
25	Poulbaun	124	2	2	Clare	Inchiquin	Rath	Corrofin	II.	28
22	Poulbautia	277	0	38	Waterford	Decies without Drum	Affane	Lismore	II.	353
31	Poulboy	80	3	5	Kilkenny	Kells	Kilmaganny	Callan	I.	109
1, 2	Poulboy	123	1	0a	Waterford	Upperthird	St. Marys Clonmel	Clonmel	II.	372
9	Poulcaragharush	181	2	5	Clare	Burren	Carran	Ballyvaghan	II.	12
47	Pouldine	120	2	33	Tipperary, N.R.	Eliogarty	Moycarky	Thurles	II.	271
6, 7	Pouleenacoona	191	1	7	Clare	Inchiquin	Kilkeedy	Corrofin	II.	26
12, 21	Poulfadda	229	1	30	Waterford	Coshmore & Coshbride	Lismore and Mocollop	Lismore	II.	347
5	Poulgorm	343	0	13	Clare	Burren	Kilcorney	Ballyvaghan	II.	12
19	Poulgour	131	3	3	Kilkenny	Shillelogher	St. Patrick's	Kilkenny	I.	116
4, 8	Pouliskaboy	61	3	16	Clare	Corcomroe	Killilagh	Ennistimon	II.	20
18	Poulleagh	49	0	4	Cork, E.R.	Fermoy	Farahy	Mallow	II.	79
18	Poulleagh	96	1	34	Cork, E.R.	Fermoy	Templeroan	Mallow	II.	82
11	Poulmacrih	47	1	3	Clare	Inchiquin	Kilkeedy	Corrofin	II.	26
79	Poulmaleen	380	0	36	Tipperary, S.R.	Iffa and Offa East	Newtownlennan	Carrick on Suir	II.	315
39	Poulmaloe	243	0	27	Wexford	Shelburne	Whitechurch	New Ross	I.	329
36, 41	Poulmarl	293	2	37	Wexford	Shelmaliere West	Taghmon	Wexford	I.	335
5, 9	Poulnabrone	166	1	4	Clare	Burren	Kilcorney	Ballyvaghan	II.	12
5	Poulnabrucky	272	3	24	Clare	Burren	Rathborney	Ballyvaghan	II.	14
149	Poulnacallee	153	1	30	Cork, W.R.	West Carbery (E.D.)	Aghadown	Skibbereen	II.	137
67, 68	Poulnadarree	315	3	38	Clare	Clonderalaw	Killimer	Kilrush	II.	16
8	Poulnagun	477	1	34	Clare	Corcomroe	Killilagh	Ennistimon	II.	20
1, 2	Poulnagunoge	670	2	12	Waterford	Upperthird	St. Marys Clonmel	Clonmel	II.	372
10, 16	Poulnahaha	110	3	19	Kerry	Iraghticonnor	Dysert	Listowel	II.	190
10	Poulnalour	618	1	22	Clare	Inchiquin	Killinaboy	Corrofin	II.	27
66	Poulnamuck	81	2	39	Kerry	Magunihy	Killarney	Killarney	II.	203
24	Poulnareagha	139	3	20	Cork, E.R.	Orrery and Kilmore	Buttevant	Mallow	II.	107
9	Poulnaskagh	120	2	39	Clare	Burren	Kilcorney	Ballyvaghan	II.	12
36	Poulpeasty	308	1	25	Wexford	Bantry	Whitechurchglynn	Wexford	I.	303
11	Poulroe	467	2	3b	Clare	Inchiquin	Kilkeedy	Corrofin	II.	26
22	Poultalloon	188	1	10	Limerick	Smallcounty	Fedamore	Croom	II.	259
87, 88	Pound	609	1	32	Kerry	Iveragh	Killemlagh	Cahersiveen	II.	196
25	Poundcartron	809	0	1	Galway	Ross	Ross	Oughterard	IV.	74
46	Poundfields	15	2	16	Cork, E.R.	Kinnatalloon	Mogeely	Fermoy	II.	99
7	Poundhill	74	2	31	Leitrim	Rosclogher	Killasnet	Manorhamilton	IV.	110
141, 150	Poundlick	362	3	34	Cork, W.R.	West Carbery (E.D.)	Creagh	Skibbereen	II.	139
65	Poundquarter	88	3	16	Cork, E.R.	Barrymore	Lisgoold	Middleton	II.	56
44	Powderlough	400	3	39	Meath	Ratoath	Rathbeggan	Dunshaughlin	I.	219
38	Powellsborough	1,041	3	22	Sligo	Leyny	Achonry	Tobercurry	IV.	229
7	Powellshill	59	2	6	Roscommon	Boyle	Tumna	Carᵏ. on Shannon	IV.	198
18	Powelstown	107	2	13	Queen's Co.	Stradbally	Dysartenos	Athy	I.	247
18	Powelstown	43	0	32	Queen's Co.	Stradbally	Fossy or Timahoe	Athy	I.	247
22	Powerfield	22	1	30	Limerick	Smallcounty	Monasteranenagh	Croom	II.	261
7	Powerscourt Demesne	811	0	27	Wicklow	Rathdown	Powerscourt	Rathdown	I.	356
2, 6, 7, 12	Powerscourt Mountain	7,590	0	10c	Wicklow	Rathdown	Powerscourt	Rathdown	I.	356
7, 12	Powerscourt Paddock	1,017	0	33	Wicklow	Rathdown	Calary	Rathdown	I.	355
16, 17	Powersknock	295	2	3	Waterford	Middlethird	Kilmeadan	Waterford	II.	368
12	Powerstown	551	2	21d	Carlow	Carlow	Clonmelsh	Carlow	I.	1
25, 26	Powerstown	385	2	24	Cork, E.R.	Fermoy	Clenor	Mallow	II.	78
13	Powerstown	358	2	20	Dublin	Castleknock	Mulhuddart	Dublin North	I.	25
77, 83	Powerstown	133	0	32	Tipperary, S.R.	Iffa and Offa East	Kilgrant	Clonmel	II.	314
77, 83	Powerstown Demesne	110	0	39	Tipperary, S.R.	Iffa and Offa East	Kilgrant	Clonmel	II.	314
83	Powerstown Demesne	141	3	27	Tipperary, S.R.	Iffa and Offa East	St. Marys Clonmel	Clonmel	II.	316
25	Powerstown East	399	1	27	Kilkenny	Gowran	Powerstown	Thomastown	I.	98
25	Powerstown West	15	3	11	Kilkenny	Gowran	Powerstown	Thomastown	I.	98
32	Powerswood	665	3	30	Kilkenny	Gowran	Inistioge	Thomastown	I.	96
48	Poyntstown	170	3	0	Tipperary, S.R.	Slievardagh	Buolick	Urlingford	II.	332
48	Poyntstown	571	3	19	Tipperary, S.R.	Slievardagh	Fennor	Urlingford	II.	333
22	Prabagh	169	1	11	Leitrim	Carrigallen	Oughteragh	Bawnboy	IV.	92
46	Prablin	34	2	19	Donegal	Kilmacrenan	Aughnish	Millford	III.	122
44	Prap	180	0	8	Cork, E.R.	Barrymore	Rathcormack	Fermoy	II.	57
38	Prap	162	0	22	Waterford	Decies within Drum	Ardmore	Youghal	II.	350
34, 39	Preban	277	2	38	Wicklow	Ballinacor South	Preban	Shillelagh	I.	350
49	Prebaun	258	3	11	Mayo	Gallen	Killasser	Swineford	IV.	149
26	Prebaun	40	2	9	Westmeath	Fartullagh	Moylisker	Mullingar	I.	269
125	Preghane	546	2	23	Cork, E.R.	Kinsale	Ringcurran	Kinsale	II.	100
20	Prehen	222	0	35	Londonderry	Tirkeeran	Clondermot	Londonderry	III.	248
68	Pribbaun	211	0	28	Galway	Moycullen	Killannin	Oughterard	IV.	70
61, 69	Price's-lot	454	0	17	Tipperary, S.R.	Middlethird	St. John Baptist	Cashel	II.	330
39	Priesthaggard	249	0	35	Wexford	Shelburne	Kilmokea	New Ross	I.	327
22, 23	Priesthouse	277	3	36	Dublin	Rathdown	Donnybrook	Dublin South	I.	35
6, 7	Priestland East	175	0	8	Antrim	Lower Dunluce	Dunluce	Coleraine	III.	17
6, 7	Priestland West	229	0	2	Antrim	Lower Dunluce	Dunluce	Coleraine	III.	17

(a) Including 3A. 2R. 31P. water.
(b) Including 36A. 0R. 21P. water.
(c) { Including 64A. 3R. 0P. Lough Bray, Lower. / Including 28A. 2R. 24P. Lough Bray, Upper.
(d) Including 7A. 0R. 20P. River Barrow.

No. of Sheet of the Ordnance Survey Maps.	Townlands and Towns.	Area in Statute Acres.			County.	Barony.	Parish.	Poor Law Union in 1857.	Townland Census of 1851. Part I.	
		A.	R.	P.					Vol.	Page
9, 16	Priestsessagh . .	456	0	37	Tyrone . .	Strabane Lower .	Ardstraw . .	Castlederg . .	III.	319
132	Priests Island . .	1	0	17	Galway . .	Leitrim . . .	Ballynakill . .	Portumna . .	IV.	52
21	Priests Island . .	4	2	5	Longford . .	Ratheline . .	Cashel . . .	Ballymahon . .	I.	164
13	Priestsnewtown . .	347	3	12	Wicklow . .	Newcastle . .	Kilcoole . . .	Rathdrum . .	I.	352
60	Priest's Rock . .	0	2	0	Clare . .	Bunratty Lower .	Kilconry . . .	Ennis . . .	II.	4
69	Prieststown . .	88	0	26	Donegal . .	Raphoe . . .	Convoy . . .	Stranorlar . .	III.	136
29	Priestsvalley . .	82	0	13	Kilkenny . .	Gowran . . .	Graiguenamanagh .	Thomastown . .	I.	95
24	Priest Town . .	214	3	10	Down . .	Ards Upper . .	Ardquin . . .	Downpatrick . .	III.	159
21	Priest Town . .	64	1	10	Dublin . .	Uppercross . .	Clondalkin . .	Dublin South . .	I.	39
21	Priest Town . .	382	1	25	Louth . .	Ferrard . . .	Mullary . . .	Drogheda . .	I.	182
45, 51	Priest Town . .	456	0	38	Meath . .	Dunboyne . .	Kilbride . . .	Dunshaughlin . .	I.	200
88, 91	Priesttown . .	457	1	0	Tipperary, S.R. .	Iffa and Offa West .	Newcastle . .	Clogheen . .	II.	319
63	Priesttown . .	124	1	13	Tipperary, S.R. .	Middlethird . .	Drangan . . .	Cashel . .	II.	326
20	Priesttown . .	224	1	35	Westmeath . .	Farbill . . .	Killucan . . .	Mullingar . .	I.	267
63	Priesttown Demesne	335	0	38	Tipperary, S.R. .	Middlethird . .	Drangan . . .	Cashel . .	II.	326
22	Primatepark . .	43	3	16	Louth . .	Ferrard . . .	Termonfeckin . .	Drogheda . .	I.	183
33, 38, 39	Primatestown . .	646	0	5	Meath . .	Skreen . . .	Kilmoon . . .	Dunshaughlin . .	I.	221
48	Primestown . .	4	3	38	Wexford . .	Forth . . .	Tacumshin . .	Wexford . .	I.	315
20	Primity . . .	189	2	15	Londonderry . .	Tirkeeran . .	Clondermot . .	Londonderry . .	III.	248
14, 20	Primrosegrange . .	101	3	33	Sligo . .	Carbury . . .	Killaspugbrone . .	Sligo . . .	IV.	222
33	Princetown . .	224	0	2	Meath . .	Upper Duleek .	Ardcath . . .	Drogheda . .	I.	197
13	Printinstown . .	323	1	34a	Westmeath . .	Delvin . . .	Castletowndelvin .	Castletowndelvin .	I.	265
4	Priorland . .	45	3	34	Dublin . .	Balrothery East .	Balscaddan . .	Balrothery . .	I.	20
7	Priorland . .	171	2	24	Louth . .	Upper Dundalk .	Dundalk . . .	Dundalk . .	I.	178
9, 14	Priorpark . .	207	3	31b	Tipperary, N.R. .	Lower Ormond .	Cloghprior . .	Borrisokane . .	II.	283
9	Priorsknock . .	51	1	26	Waterford . .	Gaultiere . .	St. Johns Without .	Waterford . .	II.	365
5	Prior's-land . .	61	2	17c	Limerick . .	Limerick, Municipal Borough of .	Killeely . . .	Limerick . .	II.	262
5	Prior's-land . .	226	1	9d	Limerick . .	Limerick, Municipal Borough of .	St. Michaels . .	Limerick . .	II.	262
11	Priorstate . .	118	0	37	Louth . .	Louth . . .	Louth . . .	Dundalk . .	I.	184
21, 22	Priorstown . .	259	3	37	Louth . .	Ferrard . . .	Drumshallon . .	Drogheda . .	I.	180
21, 22	Priorstown . .	91	2	28e	Louth . .	Ferrard . . .	Termonfeckin . .	Drogheda . .	I.	183
78, 84	Priorstown . .	217	3	35f	Tipperary, S.R. .	Iffa and Offa East .	Killaloan . .	Clonmel . .	II.	314
14, 15	Priorswood . .	68	1	14	Dublin . .	Coolock . . .	Coolock . . .	Dublin North . .	I.	27
29	Priory Demesne .	288	1	38	Tipperary, N.R. .	Eliogarty . .	Templemore . .	Thurles . .	II.	272
27	Prioryland . .	428	3	34	Meath . .	Lower Duleek .	Duleek . . .	Drogheda . .	I.	195
79	Prison East . .	181	1	25	Mayo . .	Carra . . .	Manulla . . .	Castlebar . .	IV.	129
79	Prison North . .	340	3	26	Mayo . .	Carra . . .	Manulla . . .	Castlebar . .	IV.	129
79	Prison South . .	254	0	69	Mayo . .	Carra . . .	Manulla . . .	Castlebar . .	IV.	129
37, 43	Procklis . . .	318	0	26	Antrim . .	Upper Toome .	Drummaul . .	Ballymena . .	III.	34
52	Procklis . . .	429	1	19	Donegal . .	Kilmacrenan . .	Conwal . . .	Letterkenny . .	III.	126
45	Procklis . . .	179	3	33	Donegal . .	Kilmacrenan . .	Kilmacrenan . .	Milford . .	III.	129
33,34,42,43	Procklis . . .	1,733	1	22h	Donegal . .	Kilmacrenan . .	Tullaghobegly . .	Dunfanaghy . .	III.	132
1	Procklis . . .	194	3	34	Fermanagh . .	Lurg . . .	Drumkeeran . .	Lowtherstown . .	III.	207
141	Prohoness . .	288	1	19	Cork, W.R. .	West Carbery (E.D.) .	Aghadown . .	Skibbereen . .	II.	137
30, 39	Prohus . . .	312	1	33i	Cork, E.R. .	Duhallow . .	Dromtarriff . .	Millstreet . .	II.	71
70	Prohus . . .	278	0	17	Cork, W.R. .	West Muskerry .	Clondrohid . .	Macroom . .	II.	155
6	Prohust . . .	609	3	24	Cork, E.R. .	Orrery and Kilmore .	Kilbolane . .	Kanturk . .	II.	108
4, 7	Proleek . . .	439	2	16	Louth . .	Lower Dundalk .	Ballymascanlan .	Dundalk . .	I.	176
4	Proleek Acres . .	59	3	9	Louth . .	Lower Dundalk .	Ballymascanlan .	Dundalk . .	I.	176
26	Prologue . .	39	0	22	Kilkenny . .	Callan . . .	Callan . . .	Callan . .	I.	83
3, 4, 7, 8	Prolusk . . .	433	1	20	Antrim . .	Cary . . .	Ballintoy . .	Ballycastle . .	III.	12
58	Prolusk . . .	239	1	15	Tyrone . .	Clogher . .	Clogher . . .	Clogher . .	III.	293
47	Proonts . . .	27	1	19	Limerick . .	Kilmallock . .	St. Peter's & St. Paul's .	Kilmallock . .	II.	250
28	Propoge . . .	802	0	5	Cork, E.R. .	Condons&Clangibbon	Leitrim . . .	Fermoy . .	II.	62
67	Propoge . . .	76	2	39	Cork, E.R. .	Imokilly . .	Youghal . . .	Youghal . .	II.	91
34	Propoge . . .	284	0	25	Waterford . .	Coshmore&Coshbride	Templemichael . .	Youghal . .	II.	349
17	Prospect . .	158	3	30	Antrim . .	Upper Dunluce .	Ballymoney . .	Ballymoney . .	III.	19
9	Prospect . .	229	1	10j	Cavan . .	Tullyhaw . .	Templeport . .	Bawnboy . .	III.	95
58, 68	Prospect . .	133	2	33	Clare . .	Clonderalaw . .	Kilmurry . .	Killadysert . .	II.	18
18	Prospect . .	42	1	15	Dublin . .	Coolock . . .	Glasnevin . .	Dublin North . .	I.	27
18	Prospect . .	9	2	20	Dublin . .	Coolock . . .	St. Georges . .	Dublin North . .	I.	29
84	Prospect . .	53	1	28	Galway . .	Athenry . . .	Athenry . . .	Loughrea . .	IV.	4
5, 17	Prospect . .	105	3	26	Galway . .	Dunmore . .	Dunmore . .	Tuam . .	IV.	34
128, 129	Prospect . .	243	1	0	Galway . .	Kiltartan . .	Beagh . . .	Gort . .	IV.	46
14	Prospect . .	223	1	0	Kildare . .	Naas North . .	Sherlockstown . .	Naas . .	I.	63
1, 6	Prospect . .	289	2	32	Limerick . .	Clanwilliam . .	Stradbally . .	Limerick . .	II.	226
33	Prospect . .	99	3	18	Limerick . .	Coonagh . . .	Oola . . .	Tipperary . .	II.	236
38	Prospect . .	144	1	3k	Mayo . .	Tirawley . .	Crossmolina . .	Ballina . .	IV.	166
63	Prospect . .	196	1	29	Tipperary, S.R. .	Middlethird . .	Drangan . . .	Cashel . .	II.	326
63, 70	Prospect . .	174	1	17	Tipperary, S.R. .	Middlethird . .	Rathcool . .	Cashel . .	II.	329
9	Prospect . .	130	2	29	Tyrone . .	Strabane Lower .	Urney . . .	Strabane . .	III.	323

(a) Including 13A. 1R. 5P. water.
(b) Including 1A. 3R. 24P. water.
(c) Included in the Parish of Killeely.
(d) Included in the Parish of St. Michael.
(e) Including 2A. 2R. 3P. detached portion.
(f) Including 5A. 3R. 38P. water.
(g) Including 37A. 1R. 11P. water.
(h) Including 168A. 2R. 14P. water.
(i) Including 8A. 0R. 18P. water.
(j) Including 129A. 3R. 18P. Brackley Lough.
(k) Including 3A. 1R. 9P. water.

No. of Sheet of the Ordnance Survey Maps.	Townlands and Towns.	Area in Statute Acres.			County.	Barony.	Parish.	Poor Law Union in 1857.	Townland Census of 1851, Part I.	
		A.	R.	P.					Vol.	Page
7, 12	Prospect .	342	2	0	Wexford .	Ballaghkeen .	Kiltennell	Gorey .	I.	297
4, 5	Prospect or Coolmela	1,059	3	20	Wexford .	Scarawalsh .	Moyacomb	Shillelagh .	I.	325
108	Prospect Demesne .	55	2	15	Galway .	Longford	Meelick .	Portumna	IV.	61
14	Prospect East .	189	2	12	Tipperary, N.R.	Lower Ormond .	Cloghprior	Nenagh .	II.	283
37, 40	Prospecthall .	358	1	24	Waterford .	Decies within Drum	Kinsalebeg	Youghal .	II.	352
94, 95	Prospecthill .	282	1	13	Galway .	Dunkellin .	Ballynacourty	Galway .	IV.	27
19	Prospect Lower	122	2	26	Wicklow .	Newcastle .	Newcastle Upper	Rathdrum	I.	353
19	Prospect Upper	52	2	11	Wicklow .	Newcastle .	Newcastle Upper	Rathdrum	I.	353
14	Prospect West .	207	2	3a	Tipperary, N.R.	Lower Ormond .	Cloghprior	Nenagh .	II.	283
13	PROSPEROUS T. .	—			Kildare .	Clane . .	Clane . .	Naas .	I.	54
20	Proudfootstown	208	2	24b	Meath .	Upper Slane .	Dowth .	Drogheda .	I.	224
18, 25	Proudstown .	710	2	12	Meath .	Lower Navan .	Donaghmore .	Navan .	I.	214
32	Proudstown .	670	1	8	Meath .	Skreen .	Skreen .	Dunshaughlin .	I.	221
8	Prucklish .	266	0	2	Longford .	Longford .	Clongesh	Longford .	I.	158
10	Prucklishtown	178	0	15	Longford .	Granard . .	Clonbroney .	Granard .	I.	155
28	Prughlish .	239	3	3	Leitrim .	Leitrim . .	Kiltubbrid	Car^k. on Shannon	IV.	104
47, 59	Prughlish .	433	2	21	Mayo .	Tirawley .	Addergoole .	Castlebar .	IV.	163
33	Prughlish .	478	2	5	Tyrone .	Omagh West .	Longfield West	Castlederg	III.	316
40	Prumpelstown Lower	286	3	23	Kildare .	Kilkea and Moone .	Castledermot .	Athy .	I.	59
39, 40	Prumpelstown Upper	218	1	24	Kildare .	Kilkea and Moone .	Castledermot .	Athy .	I.	59
3, 8	Pruntus . . .	481	0	25	Cork, E.R.	Fermoy . .	Ballyhay	Mitchelstown .	II.	76
35	Prusselstown .	69	3	21	Kildare .	Narragh&Reban West	Kilberry .	Athy .	I.	68
35	Prusselstown .	173	0	21	Kildare .	Narragh&Reban West	St. Michaels .	Athy .	I.	68
23	Pubble . . .	270	1	20	Fermanagh .	Tirkennedy .	Enniskillen	Enniskillen .	III.	222
17	Pubble . . .	425	0	10c	Tyrone .	Strabane Lower .	Ardstraw	Gortin .	III.	319
60	Pubblehill .	128	2	14	Tipperary, S.R.	Clanwilliam .	Oughterleague	Tipperary .	II.	309
35, 36	Pubblestown .	220	3	16	Meath .	Lune . .	Kildalkey .	Trim .	I.	208
126	Puckady Island .	0	3	12	Galway .	Longford .	Lickmolassy .	Portumna .	IV.	61
111	Puckane . .	119	2	11	Cork, E.R.	Kinalea . .	Ringcurran .	Kinsale .	II.	96
7	Puckane . .	224	2	4	Limerick .	Owneybeg .	Abington .	Limerick .	II.	251
14	PUCKAUN T. . .	—			Tipperary, N.R.	Lower Ormond .	Killodiernan .	Nenagh .	II.	285
89	Puck Island .	6	2	24	Galway .	Moycullen .	Killannin .	Oughterard .	IV.	70
44	Puckisland .	601	0	31d	Kerry .	Corkaguiny .	Minard .	Dingle .	II.	180
14, 18	Puckstown .	123	0	4	Dublin .	Coolock .	Artaine .	Dublin North .	I.	26
18	Puckstown .	139	1	13	Louth .	Ardee . .	Mosstown	Ardee .	I.	174
67	Puddingfield .	172	2	4	Tipperary, S.R.	Clanwilliam .	Kilshane .	Tipperary .	II.	309
23	Puddingstreet or Oldtown	111	2	19	Westmeath .	Kilkenny West .	Drumraney .	Ballymahon .	I.	273
96	Puffin Island .	125	1	20	Kerry .	Iveragh . .	Killemlagh .	Cahersiveen .	II.	196
35, 36	Pulla . . .	270	0	0	Waterford .	Decies within Drum	Ardmore .	Dungarvan .	II.	350
6	Pullagh . .	653	1	14	Clare .	Burren . .	Carran .	Ballyvaghan .	II.	12
27, 31	Pullagh . . .	208	1	35	Kildare .	Offaly West .	Harristown	Athy .	I.	72
15, 24	Pullagh . .	283	3	30	Limerick .	Coonagh . .	Doon .	Tipperary .	II.	234
30	Pullagh . .	218	3	14	Limerick .	Coshma . .	Croom .	Croom .	II.	242
32	Pullagh . .	216	0	6	Sligo .	Leyny . .	Achonry	Tobercurry .	IV.	229
14	Pullans . .	192	2	17	Monaghan .	Cremorne .	Clontibret .	Monaghan .	III.	261
8	Pullans North .	161	2	10	Londonderry .	North East Liberties of Coleraine .	Kildollagh .	Coleraine .	III.	246
8	Pullans South .	102	0	27	Londonderry .	North East Liberties of Coleraine .	Kildollagh .	Coleraine .	III.	246
5, 6	Pullateebee .	270	3	3e	Tyrone .	Strabane Lower .	Leckpatrick .	Strabane .	III.	322
23	Pulleen . .	343	3	23	Cork, E.R.	Duhallow .	Castlemagner .	Kanturk .	II.	67
3	Pulleen . .	317	3	3	Kerry .	Iraghticonnor .	Kilnaughtin .	Glin .	II.	191
47	Pullingtown .	99	3	20	Wexford .	Bargy . .	Kilmore .	Wexford .	I.	306
53	Pullingtown .	22	0	32f	Wexford .	Forth . .	Carn .	Wexford .	I.	309
19	Pullinstown Big .	171	2	15	Wexford .	Scarawalsh .	Monart .	Enniscorthy .	I.	324
19	Pullinstown Little .	161	0	9	Wexford .	Scarawalsh .	Monart .	Enniscorthy .	I.	324
6	Pullis . . .	222	1	28	Monaghan .	Trough . .	Donagh .	Monaghan .	III.	282
15, 16	Pullyernan .	1,359	2	33	Tyrone .	Omagh West .	Urney .	Castlederg .	III.	318
62	Punchbowl .	134	2	9	Clare .	Bunratty Lower .	Killeely .	Limerick .	II.	5
17	Punchersgrange .	710	2	6	Kildare .	Connell . .	Feighcullen .	Naas .	I.	55
24	Punchestown . .	52	1	21	Kildare .	Naas South .	Tipperkevin .	Naas .	I.	65
24	Punchestown Great	323	0	3	Kildare .	Naas North .	Rathmore .	Naas / .	I.	63
24	Punchestown Little	121	3	21	Kildare .	Naas North .	Rathmore .	Naas .	I.	63
20	Punchestown Lower	467	1	32	Kildare .	Naas North .	Rathmore .	Naas .	I.	63
20	Punchestown Upper	264	1	3	Kildare .	Naas North .	Rathmore .	Naas .	I.	63
63	Puntabeg . .	153	1	12	Mayo .	Costello . .	Kilbeagh .	Swineford .	IV.	141
13, 14	Purcellsgarden .	194	0	19g	Kilkenny .	Crannagh .	Odagh .	Kilkenny .	I.	86
19	Purcellsinch .	177	2	3h	Kilkenny .	Gowran . .	St. John's .	Kilkenny .	I.	98
17	Purcellstown .	158	3	9	Louth .	Ardee . .	Smarmore .	Ardee .	I.	174
9	PURDYSBURN T. .	—			Down . .	Castlereagh Upper .	Drumbo .	Lisburn .	III.	165
111	Purrauns . .	547	1	21	Mayo .	Kilmaine .	Kilcommon .	Ballinrobe .	IV.	155
15	Pushen Island .	5	2	34	Fermanagh .	Magheraboy .	Inishmacsaint .	Ballyshannon .	III.	213

(a) Including 5A. 0R. 18P. water.
(b) Including 4A. 0R. 34P. water.
(c) Including 9A. 3R. 27P. water.
(d) Including 5A. 3R. 6P. water.
(e) Including 5A. 1R. 32P. Moor Lough.
(f) Including 6A. 1R. 8P. detached portion.
(g) Including 1A. 1R. 36P. detached portion.
(h) Including 5A. 2R. 8P. River Nore.

No. of Sheet of the Ordnance Survey Maps.	Townlands and Towns.	Area in Statute Acres.	County.	Barony.	Parish.	Poor Law Union in 1857.	Townland Census of 1851, Part I.	
		A. R. P.					Vol.	Page
14	Pust North . .	180 2 33	Limerick . .	Clanwilliam . .	Caherconlish .	Limerick . .	II.	222
14	Pust North . .	46 3 15	Limerick . .	Clanwilliam . .	Inch St. Lawrence .	Limerick . .	II.	224
14, 23	Pust South . .	21 1 21	Limerick . .	Clanwilliam . .	Caherconlish .	Limerick . .	II.	222
14, 23	Pust South . .	49 2 11	Limerick . .	Clanwilliam . .	Inch St. Lawrence .	Limerick . .	II.	224
15	Putiaghan Lower .	88 3 11*a*	Cavan . .	Lower Loughtee .	Urney . .	Cavan . .	III.	81
15	Putiaghan Upper .	121 2 11*b*	Cavan . .	Lower Loughtee .	Urney . .	Cavan . .	III.	81
17	Puttaghan . .	486 2 11	King's Co. .	Ballycowan .	Kilbride . .	Tullamore .	I.	128
10	Puttaghan . .	114 1 3	King's Co. .	Lower Philipstown .	Kilclonfert .	Tullamore .	I.	142
17	PUTTAGHAN T.	—	King's Co. .	Ballycowan .	Kilbride . .	Tullamore .	I.	128
7, 11	Quakerstown . .	324 0 5	Clare . .	Inchiquin .	Kilkeedy .	Corrofin . .	II.	26
8, 11	Quakerstown . .	370 1 10	Tipperary, N.R.	Lower Ormond .	Ballingarry .	Borrisokane .	II.	282
42	Quanstown . .	96 1 17	Wexford . .	Forth . .	Rathaspick .	Wexford . .	I.	313
149	*Quarantine Island* .	1 1 37	Cork, W.R. .	West Carbery (E.D.)	Tullagh . .	Skibbereen .	II.	141
15	Quarry . .	33 1 37	Dublin . .	Coolock . .	Howth . .	Dublin North .	I.	28
34, 35	Quarry . .	224 1 31	Kildare . .	Narragh&RebanWest	Churchtown .	Athy . .	I.	67
12, 19	Quarry . .	201 2 35*c*	Westmeath .	Moyashel and Magh-eradernon .				
16	Quarry . .	130 3 4	Wexford . .	Scarawalsh .	Mullingar .	Mullingar .	I.	275
11	Quarryfarm or Drim-hill .	71 2 35	Queen's Co. .	Upperwoods .	Kilbride . .	Enniscorthy .	I.	323
38	Quarryfield . .	629 0 33	Sligo . .	Corran . .	Offerlane .	Mountmellick .	I.	251
117	Quarryhill . .	85 0 37	Galway . .	Leitrim . .	Cloonoghil .	Tobercurry .	IV.	225
19	Quarryland . .	19 0 3*d*	Kilkenny .	Gowran . .	Tynagh . .	Portumna .	IV.	56
44, 50	Quarryland . .	402 2 2	Meath . .	Dunboyne .	St. John's .	Kilkenny . .	I.	98
16	Quarrymount . .	149 2 33	Galway . .	Dunmore .	Dunboyne .	Dunshaughlin .	I.	199
1, 3	Quarrymount . .	117 1 39	Queen's Co. .	Tinnahinch .	Dunmore .	Tuam . .	IV.	34
					Castlebrack .	Mountmellick .	I.	248
17	Quarryvale . .	53 2 26*e*	Dublin . .	Uppercross .	Palmerston .	Dublin South .	I.	40
17	Quarter . .	136 0 1	Galway . .	Dunmore .	Dunmore .	Tuam . .	IV.	34
29	Quarter . .	79 1 37	Waterford .	Decies without Drum	Affane . .	Lismore . .	II.	353
37	Quarter Cormick .	179 2 30	Down . .	Lecale Upper .	Down . .	Downpatrick .	III.	181
70	Quartercross . .	225 2 7	Tipperary, S.R.	Middlethird .	Coolmundry .	Cashel . .	II.	326
17, 24	Quarterland . .	148 0 38	Down . .	Dufferin .	Killinchy .	Downpatrick .	III.	166
43, 44	Quarter Lenagh .	99 2 22	Antrim . .	Upper Toome .	Antrim . .	Antrim . .	III.	33
32, 33	Quartertown Lower	494 2 25*f*	Cork, E.R. .	Fermoy . .	Mourneabbey .	Mallow . .	II.	82
33, 42	Quartertown Upper	493 0 22	Cork, E.R. .	Fermoy . .	Mourneabbey .	Mallow . .	II.	82
8, 12	Quay . . .	62 1 27	Dublin . .	Nethercross .	Portraine .	Balrothery .	I.	31
29	Quaybaun . .	110 3 26	Galway . .	Dunmore .	Dunmore .	Tuam . .	IV.	34
64	Quaybaun . .	120 3 19	Kerry . .	Iveragh . .	Killorglin .	Killarney .	II.	198
62	*Quay Island* . .	22 0 18	Clare . .	Bunratty Lower .	Bunratty .	Ennis . .	II.	3
117	Queensacres . .	26 0 30	Galway . .	Longford .	Lickmolassy .	Portumna .	IV.	61
17, 29, 30	Queensfort . .	269 2 3	Galway . .	Dunmore .	Tuam . .	Tuam . .	IV.	36
15, 16	Queensland . .	93 3 17	Longford .	Ardagh . .	Street . .	Granard . .	I.	153
87	QUEENSTOWN T.	—	Cork, E.R. .	Barrymore .	{ Clonmel . .	Cork . .	II.	{ 153 / 159 }
					Templerobin . }			
66	Querrin . .	1,532 2 11	Clare . .	Moyarta . .	Moyarta . .	Kilrush . .	II.	34
10, 16	Quigabar . .	168 2 26	Sligo . .	Tireragh .	Kilglass . .	Dromore West .	IV.	234
10	Quigaboy . .	249 1 6	Sligo . .	Tireragh .	Kilglass . .	Dromore West .	IV.	234
4, 5	Quigelagh . .	324 1 7	Meath . .	Lower Kells .	Moynalty .	Kells . .	I.	204
42	Quigginroe . .	193 1 32	Wicklow . .	Shillelagh .	Aghowle . .	Shillelagh .	I.	357
12	Quiggy . .	613 3 30*g*	Tyrone . .	Strabane Upper .	Bodoney Upper .	Gortin . .	III.	324
9	Quiglough . .	103 0 38*h*	Monaghan .	Monaghan .	Tedavnet .	Monaghan .	III.	279
22, 29	Quignalecka . .	231 0 14	Sligo . .	Tireragh .	Kilmoremoy .	Ballina . .	IV.	235
22	Quignalegan . .	413 2 14	Sligo . .	Tireragh .	Kilmoremoy .	Ballina . .	IV.	235
22, 29	Quignamanger .	180 0 31	Sligo . .	Tireragh .	Kilmoremoy .	Ballina . .	IV.	235
22, 29	Quignashee . .	555 3 30	Sligo . .	Tireragh .	Kilmoremoy .	Ballina . .	IV.	235
7	Quilley Lower .	190 2 27	Londonderry	Coleraine .	Dunboe . .	Coleraine .	III.	231
7	Quilley Upper .	177 3 28	Londonderry	Coleraine .	Dunboe . .	Coleraine .	III.	232
17, 26	Quillia . .	289 0 31	Waterford .	Middlethird .	Drumcannon .	Waterford .	II.	366
20, 27	Quilly . .	811 1 24	Down . .	Lower Iveagh, Lr. pt.	Dromore .	Banbridge .	III.	168
46	Quilly . .	282 2 29	Londonderry	Loughinsholin .	Desertlyn .	Magherafelt .	III.	240
39, 41	Quiltinan . .	67 2 19	Roscommon	Athlone . .	Fuerty . .	Roscommon .	IV.	181
65, 72	Quilty . .	291 0 26	Clare . .	Moyarta . .	Kilballyowen .	Kilrush . .	II.	32
30, 38	Quilty East . .	363 1 2	Clare . .	Ibrickan . .	Kilmurry .	Kilrush . .	II.	24
30, 38	Quilty West . .	303 2 19	Clare . .	Ibrickan . .	Kilmurry .	Kilrush . .	II.	24
42	Quin . . .	40 1 1	Clare . .	Bunratty Upper .	Quin . .	Tulla . .	II.	10
7	Quinagh . .	643 2 10	Carlow . .	Carlow . .	Ballinacarrig .	Carlow . .	I.	1
4, 5	Quinaltagh . .	721 1 36	Galway . .	Dunmore .	Addergoole .	Tuam . .	IV.	33
42	Quingardens . .	170 0 15	Clare . .	Bunratty Upper .	Quin . .	Tulla . .	II.	10
15, 20	Quinsborough . .	147 1 18	Kildare . .	South Salt .	Oughterard .	Naas . .	I.	78
21	Quinsborough or Cool-sicken .	617 2 16	Kildare . .	Offaly West .	Lackagh .	Athy . .	I.	73
76	*Quinsheen Island* .	2 0 33	Mayo . .	Burrishoole .	Kilmeena .	Westport .	IV.	123

No. of Sheet of the Ordnance Survey Maps.	Townlands and Towns.	Area in Statute Acres.			County.	Barony.	Parish.	Poor Law Union in 1857.	Townland Census of 1851, Part I.	
		A.	R.	P.					Vol.	Page
53, 63	Quinspool North	165	2	34	Clare	Bunratty Lower	St. Patricks	Limerick	II.	7
63	Quinspool South	125	1	29	Clare	Bunratty Lower	St. Patricks	Limerick	II.	7
46	Quintinmanus	61	0	18	Tyrone	Dungannon Middle	Tullyniskan	Dungannon	III.	305
42	Quin T.	—			Clare	Bunratty Upper	Quin	Tulla	II.	10
34	Quinville North	48	0	10	Clare	Bunratty Upper	Quin	Tulla	II.	10
34, 42	Quinville South	23	2	12	Clare	Bunratty Upper	Quin	Tulla	II.	10
46	Quitchery Great	155	2	1	Wexford	Bargy	Kilcavan	Wexford	I.	305
41, 46	Quitchery Little	106	3	12	Wexford	Bargy	Kilcavan	Wexford	I.	305
9, 18	Quitrent Mountain	1,195	2	28	Cork, E.R.	Condons and Clangibbon	Farahy	Mitchelstown	II.	60
11	Quivvy	484	2	25a	Cavan	Lower Loughtee	Drumlane	Cavan	III.	80
24	Quivvy	65	0	11	Cavan	Tullyhunco	Killashandra	Cavan	III.	98
31, 38	Quoile	469	3	26	Down	Lecale Lower	Saul	Downpatrick	III.	179
24,25,28,29	Quolie	2,545	3	9	Antrim	Lower Antrim	Skerry	Ballymena	III.	5
28	Rabane	81	2	35	Cavan	Clankee	Knockbride	Bailieborough	III.	74
28	Rabane	175	0	37b	Cavan	Clankee	Shercock	Bailieborough	III.	75
72	Rabaun	229	0	28	Mayo	Gallen	Meelick	Swineford	IV.	150
66	Rabbit or Brown Island	12	0	35	Kerry	Magunihy	Aghadoe	Killarney	II.	199
16	Rabbitburrow	310	3	5	King's Co.	Ballycowan	Rahan	Tullamore	I.	129
25	Rabbitburrow	114	2	28	Roscommon	Castlereagh	Kiltullagh	Castlereagh	IV.	202
29	Rabbit Island	4	1	1	Clare	Tulla Upper	Moynoe	Scarriff	II.	40
118	Rabbit Island	2	1	18	Cork, W.R.	Bantry	Kilmocomoge	Bantry	II.	121
142	Rabbit Island	17	2	6	Cork, W.R.	West Carbery (E.D.)	Myross	Skibbereen	II.	141
40, 43	Rabbit Island	67	0	1	Fermanagh	Clankelly	Drummully	Clones	III.	197
5	Rabbit Island	10	3	36	Fermanagh	Lurg	Magheraculmoney	Lowtherstown	III.	208
10	Rabbit Island	17	2	20	Fermanagh	Magheraboy	Inishmacsaint	Enniskillen	III.	213
34	Rabbit Island	4	3	37	Fermanagh	Magherastephana	Aghalurcher	Lisnaskea	III.	218
69	Rabbit Island	14	3	6	Galway	Clare	Annaghdown	Galway	IV.	17
132	Rabbit Island	3	2	13	Galway	Leitrim	Ballynakill	Portumna	IV.	52
55	Rabbit Island	18	1	32	Galway	Moycullen	Kilcummin	Oughterard	IV.	69
55	Rabbit Island	1	2	38	Galway	Moycullen	Killannin	Oughterard	IV.	70
67	Rabbit Island	14	2	1	Mayo	Burrishoole	Burrishoole	Newport	IV.	120
76	Rabbit Island	20	2	35	Mayo	Burrishoole	Kilmeena	Westport	IV.	123
24	Rabbit Island	1	2	2	Roscommon	Ballintober North	Termonbarry	Strokestown	IV.	188
35	Rabbit Island or Inchmurrin	27	1	2	Leitrim	Mohill	Annaduff	Mohill	IV.	105
123	Rabbit Islands	1	3	18b	Mayo	Kilmaine	Cong	Ballinrobe	IV.	154
		0	0	36b						
19, 20	Rabbitpark	55	0	10	Galway	Ballymoe	Kilbegnet	Glennamaddy	IV.	8
14, 19	Rabbit Park	223	2	4	Longford	Ardagh	Ardagh	Longford	I.	151
17	Rabows	70	0	6	Monaghan	Dartree	Killeevan	Clones	III.	268
25	Rabrackan	36	2	39	Cavan	Clanmahon	Ballintemple	Cavan	III.	75
34	Rabradagh	166	0	18	Roscommon	Ballymoe	Oran	Roscommon	IV.	192
21	Rabron	112	0	19	Fermanagh	Magheraboy	Devenish	Enniskillen	III.	211
9	Rabstown	206	1	2	Tyrone	Strabane Lower	Urney	Strabane	III.	323
29	Racarbry	634	2	26	Armagh	Armagh	Keady	Armagh	III.	45
17	Racaulfield	99	0	14	Monaghan	Dartree	Killeevan	Clones	III.	268
33, 34, 38	Racavan	1,368	2	13	Antrim	Lower Antrim	Racavan	Ballymena	III.	4
24	Race	48	3	18	Limerick	Coonagh	Grean	Tipperary	II.	235
24	Racebeg	19	2	28	Limerick	Coonagh	Ballynaclogh	Tipperary	II.	234
117	Racecourse	117	1	23	Galway	Leitrim	Tynagh	Portumna	IV.	56
41	Racecourse	186	1	11	Tipperary, N.R.	Eliogarty	Thurles	Thurles	II.	273
68, 69	Racecourse	171	3	0	Tipperary, S.R.	Middlethird	St. John Baptist	Cashel	II.	330
28, 33	Racecourse	143	3	8	Waterford	Coshmore & Coshbride	Tallow	Lismore	II.	348
48	Racecourse	53	2	27	Wexford	Forth	St. Iberius	Wexford	I.	314
2	Racecourse	133	0	29	Wexford	Gorey	Kilnahue	Gorey	I.	319
8	Racecourse Common	121	0	11	Dublin	Balrothery East	Lusk	Balrothery	I.	21
60,61,68,69	Racecourse Demesne	150	0	11	Tipperary, S.R.	Middlethird	St. John Baptist	Cashel	II.	330
23	Racecourse or Kilmog	377	0	39	Kilkenny	Shillelogher	Grange	Kilkenny	I.	114
45	Race End	99	2	0	Donegal	Kilmacrenan	Conwal	Letterkenny	III.	126
28, 32	Racefield	192	3	26	Kildare	Offaly West	Ballyshannon	Athy	I.	72
42	Racepark	40	3	31	Galway	Clare	Kilkilvery	Tuam	IV.	20
45, 48	Rackans	178	1	5	Roscommon	Athlone	Cam	Athlone	IV.	180
24	Rackavra	501	0	0	Westmeath	Rathconrath	Killare	Mullingar	I.	283
38	Rackenstown	229	3	1	Meath	Ratoath	Ratoath	Dunshaughlin	I.	219
12	Rackethall	229	3	30c	Tipperary, N.R.	Ikerrin	Corbally	Roscrea	II.	275
14	Rackwallace	308	1	3	Monaghan	Monaghan	Monaghan	Monaghan	III.	277
42	Raclaghy	165	1	25	Cavan	Clanmahon	Kilbride	Oldcastle	III.	78
35	Racolpa	457	2	5	Tyrone	Strabane Upper	Cappagh	Omagh	III.	325
58	Racomane East	246	3	22	Kerry	Magunihy	Aglish	Killarney	II.	200
58	Racomane West	262	3	0	Kerry	Magunihy	Aglish	Killarney	II.	200

(a) Including 33A. 2R. 34P. water.   (b) Including 5A. 0R. 20P. water.   (c) Including 3A. 3R. 8P. water.

No. of Sheet of the Ordnance Survey Maps.	Townlands and Towns.	Area in Statute Acres.			County.	Barony.	Parish.	Poor Law Union in 1857.	Townland Census of 1851, Part I.	
		A.	R.	P.					Vol.	Page
9	Raconnell	225	3	23	Monaghan	Monaghan	Tedavnet	Monaghan	III.	279
57, 70	Racoona	117	3	34	Galway	Clare	Annaghdown	Galway	IV.	16
26	Racorcraun	41	2	12	Clare	Bunratty Upper	Kilraghtis	Ennis	II.	9
50	Racrane	73	1	33	Tyrone	Clogher	Donacavey	Omagh	III.	294
38	Racraveen	105	2	4	Cavan	Clanmahon	Kilbride	Oldcastle	III.	78
22	Racreeghan or Fastry	284	0	10a	Monaghan	Dartree	Ematris	Cootehill	III.	267
33	Racullen	299	0	0	Leitrim	Mohill	Cloone	Mohill	IV.	106
17	Radeerpark	255	0	25	Monaghan	Dartree	Killeevan	Clones	III.	268
12	Radeery	139	2	21b	Monaghan	Dartree	Aghabog	Monaghan	III.	264
23, 30	Rademan	788	2	20	Down	Kinelarty	Kilmore	Downpatrick	III.	177
44, 52	Radergan	919	3	10	Tyrone	Omagh East	Clogherny	Omagh	III.	310
14	Radestown North	584	0	4	Kilkenny	Gowran	St. John's	Kilkenny	I.	98
14	Radestown South	168	2	23	Kilkenny	Gowran	St. John's	Kilkenny	I.	98
67	Radrinagh	106	1	14	Kerry	Magunihy	Killarney	Killarney	II.	203
13	Radrum	164	1	3	Monaghan	Monaghan	Kilmore	Monaghan	III.	276
31	Radrumskean	112	3	32	Monaghan	Farney	Killanny	Carrickmacross	III.	272
86	Radullaan	110	2	33	Galway	Kilconnell	Killaan	Ballinasloe	IV.	41
106	Rafarn	443	1	12	Galway	Leitrim	Kilneen	Loughrea	IV.	54
106	Rafarn	13	1	14	Galway	Leitrim	Leitrim	Loughrea	IV.	55
16	Rafeehan	53	0	9	Meath	Upper Kells	Burry	Kells	I.	205
9	Rafeenan	272	0	6	Monaghan	Monaghan	Tedavnet	Monaghan	III.	279
30	Raferagh	551	1	30c	Monaghan	Farney	Magheross	Carrickmacross	III.	274
129	Raferigeen	197	2	10	Cork, W.R.	West Carbery (W.D.)	Kilcrohane	Bantry	II.	144
87	Raffeen	550	0	23	Cork, E.R.	Kerrycurrihy	Liscleary	Cork	II.	92
11, 12	Raffin	272	3	25	Meath	Morgallion	Drakestown	Navan	I.	209
39	Raffony	279	1	10	Cavan	Castlerahan	Mullagh	Bailieborough	III.	70
16, 23	Raffrey	1,396	1	17	Down	Castlereagh Upper	Killinchy	Downpatrick	III.	165
10, 14	Rafian	159	0	31	Cavan	Lower Loughtee	Drumlane	Cavan	III.	80
23, 24	Rafintan	207	2	2	Fermanagh	Magherastephana	Aghalurcher	Lisnaskea	III.	217
1, 3	Raflacony	72	1	9	Monaghan	Trough	Errigal Trough	Clogher	III.	285
24	Rafline	274	1	32	Clare	Inchiquin	Rath	Corrofin	II.	28
92, 98	Rafoarty	157	0	6	Donegal	Banagh	Inver	Donegal	III.	108
99, 100	Rafoarty	94	0	6	Donegal	Tirhugh	Drumhome	Donegal	III.	147
85, 97	Raford	431	3	1	Galway	Athenry	Kiltullagh	Loughrea	IV.	5
93,94,99,100	Raforker	93	0	36	Donegal	Tirhugh	Donegal	Donegal	III.	145
42, 56	Rafwee	412	2	33	Galway	Clare	Killeany	Tuam	IV.	20
32	Ragamus	164	1	28	Limerick	Smallcounty	Knockainy	Kilmallock	II.	261
20	Ragaskin	156	1	9	Cavan	Upper Loughtee	Castleterra	Cavan	III.	83
19	Raggetsland	97	3	20	Kilkenny	Shillelogher	St. Patrick's	Kilkenny	I.	116
30	Raggettstown	293	2	14	Queen's Co.	Cullenagh	Dysartgallen	Abbeyleix	I.	239
7	Raghly	169	2	5	Sligo	Carbury	Drumcliff	Sligo	IV.	221
13	Raghra	399	2	7	King's Co.	Garrycastle	Clonmacnoise	Parsonstown	I.	135
56	Raghrabeg	1,172	3	6d	Roscommon	Moycarn	Moore	Ballinasloe	IV.	207
44	Ragwood or Kilstraghlan	294	1	16	Sligo	Coolavin	Kilfree	Boyle	IV.	224
54, 67	Raha	226	3	36e	Galway	Moycullen	Kilcummin	Oughterard	IV.	68
8	Rahaberna	252	0	2	Sligo	Carbury	Drumcliff	Sligo	IV.	221
64	Rahack Glebe	195	1	7f	Tyrone	Clogher	Aghalurcher	Clogher	III.	291
17	Rahadorrish	153	3	9	Westmeath	Rathconrath	Templepatrick	Ballymahon	I.	284
14	Rahaghan	53	1	39g	Cavan	Lower Loughtee	Drumlane	Cavan	III.	80
15	Rahaghy	102	3	25	Meath	Fore	Loughcrew	Oldcastle	I.	201
32	Rahale	137	3	33	Wexford	Ballaghkeen	Ballynaslaney	Enniscorthy	I.	292
48,49,59,60	Rahalisk	1,075	3	27	Cork, W.R.	West Muskerry	Macroom	Macroom	II.	160
11	Rahall	370	0	26	Fermanagh	Lurg	Derryvullan	Lowtherstown	III.	205
26	Rahalian	280	3	25	Fermanagh	Clanawley	Cleenish	Enniskillen	III.	191
86, 98	Rahally	191	0	35	Galway	Kilconnell	Grange	Loughrea	IV.	40
15	Rahalton	84	3	16h	Fermanagh	Magheraboy	Inishmacsaint	Enniskillen	III.	213
114	Rahaly	407	1	20	Galway	Kiltartan	Kilthomas	Gort	IV.	49
33, 34	Rahan	1,263	1	11	Cork, E.R.	Fermoy	Rahan	Mallow	II.	82
36, 44	Rahanagh	166	1	6	Limerick	Glenquin	Killeedy	Newcastle	II.	246
59	Rahanane	508	3	34	Kerry	Magunihy	Kilcummin	Killarney	II.	201
24	Rahanavannagh	596	3	17i	Queen's Co.	Cullenagh	Ballyroan	Abbeyleix	I.	239
16	Rahan Demesne	391	1	36	King's Co.	Ballycowan	Rahan	Tullamore	I.	129
28	Rahandrick Lower	96	0	8	Queen's Co.	Clarmallagh	Bordwell	Donaghmore	I.	237
28	Rahandrick Upper	299	2	9	Queen's Co.	Clarmallagh	Bordwell	Donaghmore	I.	237
103	Rahaneena	75	3	30	Galway	Dunkellin	Stradbally	Gort	IV.	32
98	Rahan Far	157	1	17	Donegal	Banagh	Killaghtee	Donegal	III.	109
33	Rahanine	568	2	23	Westmeath	Fartullagh	Castlelost	Mullingar	I.	268
55, 66	Rahaniska	245	0	24	Clare	Moyarta	Moyarta	Kilrush	II.	34
76	Rahaniskey	89	2	35	Tipperary, S.R.	Iffa and Offa East	Newchapel	Clonmel	II.	315
63	Rahanisky	376	3	18	Cork, E.R.	Cork	Kilcully	Cork	II.	64
92	Rahanlacky	146	2	32	Donegal	Banagh	Killaghtee	Donegal	III.	109
14	Rahanna	144	3	22	Louth	Ardee	Charlestown	Ardee	I.	171

No. of Sheet of the Ordnance Survey Maps.	Townlands and Towns.	Area in Statute Acres. A. R. P.	County.	Barony.	Parish.	Poor Law Union in 1857.	Townland Census of 1851, Part I. Vol.	Page
98	Rahan Near	213 2 3	Donegal	Banagh	Killaghtee	Donegal	III.	109
30, 39	Rahans	237 0 27a	Mayo	Tirawley	Ballynahaglish	Ballina	IV.	164
28, 31	Rahans	249 0 23b	Monaghan	Farney	Donaghmoyne	Carrickmacross	III.	270
34	Rahans	164 2 28c	Monaghan	Farney	Magheracloone	Carrickmacross	III.	273
45	Rahara	617 3 10	Roscommon	Athlone	Rahara	Roscommon	IV.	183
84, 96	Rahard	398 0 38	Galway	Athenry	Athenry	Loughrea	IV.	4
40, 43	Rahard	401 2 2	Kilkenny	Ida	Dunkitt	Waterford	I.	101
33	Rahard	81 0 7	Limerick	Coonagh	Tuogheluggin	Tipperary	II.	236
117, 118	Rahard	254 1 31	Mayo	Kilmaine	Ballinrobe	Ballinrobe	IV.	153
111,118,119	Rahard	151 0 33d	Mayo	Kilmaine	Kilcommon	Ballinrobe	IV.	155
110	Rahard	305 0 28e	Mayo	Kilmaine	Robeen	Ballinrobe	IV.	157
9	Rahard	560 2 30	Meath	Fore	Oldcastle	Oldcastle	I.	202
36	Rahard	149 2 13	Wexford	Bantry	Whitechurch Glynn	Wexford	I.	303
27	Rahardagh	332 3 10	Roscommon	Castlereagh	Baslick	Castlereagh	IV.	199
40	Rahard East	26 0 35	Kilkenny	Ida	Rossinan	Waterford	I.	104
39	Rahardrum	324 3 11	Cavan	Castlerahan	Lurgan	Oldcastle	III.	70
40	Rahard West	254 1 1	Kilkenny	Ida	Rossinan	Waterford	I.	104
20, 21	Raharney	243 1 22	Westmeath	Farbill	Killucan	Mullingar	I.	267
20, 21	Raharney Little	56 2 10	Westmeath	Farbill	Killucan	Castletowndelvin	I.	267
20, 21	RAHARNEY T.		Westmeath	Farbill	Killucan	Mullingar	I.	267
31	Raharverty	76 2 22	Cavan	Clanmahon	Crosserlough	Cavan	III.	76
96, 104	Rahasane	522 1 27	Galway	Dunkellin	Killeely	Gort	IV.	30
36	Rahaval	137 1 9	Wicklow	Arklow	Redcross	Rathdrum	I.	346
4, 5	Rahavanig	259 3 10	Kerry	Iraghticonnor	Kilconly	Listowel	II.	191
9	Rahealy	215 0 36	Kerry	Clanmaurice	Rattoo	Listowel	II.	173
21, 26	Raheelagh	305 0 33f	Cavan	Upper Loughtee	Larah	Cavan	III.	85
11	Raheelan	133 3 25g	Cavan	Lower Loughtee	Drumlane	Cavan	III.	80
5, 8	Raheelin	639 2 13	Leitrim	Rosclogher	Rossinver	Manorhamilton	IV.	112
14, 15	Raheely	350 2 12	Roscommon	Frenchpark	Tibohine	Castlereagh	IV.	205
17, 18	Raheen	215 0 0	Carlow	Forth	Barragh	Enniscorthy	I.	4
11	Raheen	329 1 35	Carlow	Idrone West	Oldleighlin	Carlow	I.	9
9	Raheen	183 2 35	Carlow	Rathvilly	Clonmore	Shillelagh	I.	10
4, 9	Raheen	408 0 11	Carlow	Rathvilly	Haroldstown	Shillelagh	I.	11
29	Raheen	406 1 16	Clare	Tulla Upper	Tomgraney	Scarriff	II.	41
51	Raheen	86 3 24	Cork, E.R.	Barretts	Whitechurch	Cork	II.	50
44	Raheen	107 2 5	Cork, E.R.	Barrymore	Rathcormack	Fermoy	II.	57
6	Raheen	372 3 16	Cork, E.R.	Duhallow	Tullylease	Kanturk	II.	76
84, 85	Raheen	372 2 16	Cork, E.R.	East Muskerry	Knockavilly	Bandon	II.	105
97	Raheen	73 0 19	Cork, E.R.	Kinalea	Ballinaboy	Kinsale	II.	93
118, 119	Raheen	301 2 11	Cork, W.R.	Bantry	Kilmocomoge	Bantry	II.	121
142	Raheen	256 3 24	Cork, W.R.	West Carbery (E.D.)	Castlehaven	Skibbereen	II.	138
142	Raheen	159 1 2¾	Cork, W.R.	West Carbery (E.D.)	Myross	Skibbereen	II.	141
107	Raheen	99 0 13	Donegal	Tirhugh	Kilbarron	Ballyshannon	III.	148
24	Raheen	328 1 5	Dublin	Newcastle	Saggart	Celbridge	I.	35
17	Raheen	94 2 12	Dublin	Uppercross	Clondalkin	Dublin South	I.	39
84	Raheen	151 1 2	Galway	Athenry	Athenry	Loughrea	IV.	4
42	Raheen	252 1 33	Galway	Clare	Donaghpatrick	Tuam	IV.	19
107, 108	Raheen	542 0 5	Galway	Longford	Kilquain	Portumna	IV.	60
107, 117	Raheen	42 3 12	Galway	Longford	Tynagh	Portumna	IV.	62
52	Raheen	92 3 36	Kerry	Corkaguiny	Ventry	Dingle	II.	180
98	Raheen	334 3 20	Kerry	Dunkerron South	Kilcrohane	Cahersiveen	II.	184
59	Raheen	234 1 22	Kerry	Magunihy	Aghadoe	Killarney	II.	199
68	Raheen	501 1 33	Kerry	Magunihy	Kilcummin	Killarney	II.	201
10	Raheen	157 2 32	Kildare	Ikeathy &Oughterany	Balraheen	Celbridge	I.	56
18	Raheen	382 0 14	Kilkenny	Crannagh	Tullaroan	Kilkenny	I.	88
37, 41	Raheen	269 0 24	Kilkenny	Ida	Rosbercon	New Ross	I.	103
39	Raheen	584 0 19	Kilkenny	Iverk	Fiddown	Carrick on Suir	I.	105
27, 31	Raheen	175 1 9	Kilkenny	Kells	Dunnamaggan	Callan	I.	108
2, 8	Raheen	649 0 12	King's Co.	Kilcoursey	Kilbride	Tullamore	I.	141
26	Raheen	296 2 38	King's Co.	Upper Philipstown	Ballykean	Mountmellick	I.	143
13	Raheen	394 2 2	Limerick	Clanwilliam	Caheravally	Limerick	II.	221
6	Raheen	115 2 21	Limerick	Clanwilliam	Killeenagarriff	Limerick	II.	224
29	Raheen	357 3 39	Limerick	Connello Lower	Croagh	Rathkeale	II.	228
41, 49	Raheen	268 3 39	Limerick	Coshlea	Ballyscaddan	Kilmallock	II.	238
31, 32	Raheen	324 2 21	Limerick	Coshma	Tullabracky	Croom	II.	244
28	Raheen	26 0 7	Queen's Co.	Clandonagh	Rathdowney	Donaghmore	I.	234
13, 14	Raheen	155 1 17	Queen's Co.	Maryborough East	Kilteale	Mountmellick	I.	241
17, 23	Raheen	201 3 28	Queen's Co.	Maryborough West	Clonenagh&Clonagheen	Abbeyleix	I.	243
16, 22	Raheen	204 3 22	Roscommon	Roscommon	Elphin	Strokestown	IV.	209
40,41,46,47	Raheen	247 0 8	Tipperary, N.R.	Eliogarty	Holycross	Thurles	II.	270
68	Raheen	200 3 19	Tipperary, S.R.	Clanwilliam	Clonbulloge	Tipperary	II.	306
88	Raheen	150 2 6	Tipperary, S.R.	Iffa and Offa West	Ballybacon	Clogheen	II.	317
75, 81	Raheen	563 0 12	Tipperary, S.R.	Iffa and Offa West	Caher	Clogheen	II.	318

(a) Including 5A. 1R. 10P. water.
(b) Including 9A. 2R. 36P. water.
(c) Including 33A. 3R. 28P. water.

(d) Including 5A. 3R. 14P. water.
(e) Including 1A. 2R. 24P. water.
(f) Including 28A. 1R. 1P. water.

(g) Including 8A. 3R. 33P. water.
(h) Including 13A. 3R. 19P. water.

5 F

No. of Sheet of the Ordnance Survey Maps.	Townlands and Towns.	Area in Statute Acres.			County.	Barony.	Parish.	Poor Law Union in 1857.	Townland Census of 1851. Part I.	
		A.	R.	P.					Vol.	Page
53	Raheen	93	1	35	Tipperary, S.R.	Middlethird	Ballysheehan	Cashel	II.	325
78, 79	Raheen	94	0	8	Tipperary, S.R.	Slievardagh	Garrangibbon	Carrick on Suir	II.	333
63, 64	Raheen	63	1	0	Tipperary, S.R.	Slievardagh	Kilvemnon	Callan	II.	335
37	Raheen	13	0	0	Waterford	Decies within Drum	Clashmore	Youghal	II.	351
18	Raheen	200	1	25	Waterford	Gaulticre	Crooke	Waterford	II.	362
1	Raheen	97	3	32a	Waterford	Upperthird	St. Marys Clonmel	Clonmel	II.	372
23, 24, 30, 31	Raheen	682	0	8	Westmeath	Rathconrath	Ballymore	Athlone	I.	282
11, 12	Raheen	284	3	15	Wexford	Ballaghkeen	Killenagh	Gorey	I.	295
25, 31	Raheen	494	0	37	Wexford	Bantry	Chapel	Enniscorthy	I.	299
5, 6, 10, 11	Raheen	515	0	0	Wexford	Scarawalsh	Kilcomb	Gorey	I.	323
9, 10	Raheen	458	0	26	Wexford	Scarawalsh	Kilrush	Enniscorthy	I.	324
41	Raheen	205	1	0	Wexford	Shelmaliere West	Taghmon	Wexford	I.	335
40	Raheen	57	1	15	Wicklow	Arklow	Kilbride	Rathdrum	I.	345
18	Raheen	334	1	16	Wicklow	Ballinacor North	Derrylossary	Rathdrum	I.	346
21	Raheen	172	2	7	Wicklow	Upper Talbotstown	Donaghmore	Baltinglass	I.	363
26, 27	Raheen	350	0	18	Wicklow	Upper Talbotstown	Rathbran	Baltinglass	I.	365
100	Raheenabbeyland	84	0	35	Mayo	Kilmaine	Robeen	Ballinrobe	IV.	157
23, 24	Raheenabrogue	290	0	26	Queen's Co.	Cullenagh	Ballyroan	Abbeyleix	I.	239
30, 35	Raheenaclonagh	692	0	20	Wexford	Bantry	Newbawn	New Ross	I.	301
30	Raheenacrehy	234	2	26	Meath	Upper Navan	Trim	Trim	I.	217
3	Raheenadaw	284	1	36	Carlow	Rathvilly	Kineagh	Baltinglass	I.	12
34	Raheenadeeragh	367	0	34	Kildare	Narragh & Reban West	Churchtown	Athy	I.	67
44	Raheenagh	895	3	8	Limerick	Glenquin	Killeedy	Newcastle	II.	246
7, 12	Raheenagurren East	187	2	18	Wexford	Ballaghkeen	Kilmakilloge	Gorey	I.	296
7, 12	Raheenagurren West	248	1	7	Wexford	Ballaghkeen	Kilmakilloge	Gorey	I.	296
30	Raheenahennedy	306	3	23	Wexford	Bantry	Newbawn	New Ross	I.	301
13	Raheenahoran	270	0	30	Queen's Co.	Maryborough East	Kilteale	Mountmellick	I.	241
27	Raheenakeeran	1,340	0	16	King's Co.	Upper Philipstown	Geashill	Tullamore	I.	144
42, 43	Raheenakit	205	3	31	Wicklow	Shillelagh	Aghowle	Shillelagh	I.	357
14	Raheenaniska	461	3	21	Queen's Co.	Stradbally	Moyanna	Athy	I.	247
18, 19	Raheenanisky	351	0	3	Queen's Co.	Stradbally	Dysartenos	Athy	I.	247
19, 23	Raheenapisha	212	1	33	Kilkenny	Shillelogher	Castleinch or Inchyolaghan	Kilkenny	I.	114
30	Raheenarostia or Rochestown	149	1	16	Wexford	Bantry	Newbawn	New Ross	I.	301
35	Raheenarran	409	2	13	Kilkenny	Kells	Kilmaganny	Carrick on Suir	I.	109
35	Raheenavine	135	2	33	Wicklow	Arklow	Castlemacadam	Rathdrum	I.	342
82	Raheenballindoney	154	3	21	Tipperary, S.R.	Iffa and Offa West	Ardfinnan	Clogheen	II.	317
19, 25	Raheenbarnagh	31	2	30	Queen's Co.	Stradbally	Tullomoy	Athy	I.	248
69	Raheen Barr	594	0	13	Mayo	Carra	Islandeady	Castlebar	IV.	129
118	Raheen Beg	74	3	27	Cork, W.R.	Bantry	Kilmocomoge	Bantry	II.	121
18, 26	Raheenbeg	352	0	20	King's Co.	Upper Philipstown	Geashill	Tullamore	I.	144
3	Raheen Beg	115	0	33	Westmeath	Fore	Rathgarve	Granard	I.	271
17	Raheen Beg	133	2	0	Wexford	Ballaghkeen	Killenagh	Gorey	I.	295
15, 21	Raheen or Charleville	219	1	5	Queen's Co.	Clandonagh	Kyle	Donaghmore	I.	233
74	Raheen and Cooleen	10	3	39	Cork, E.R.	Cork	St. Nicholas	Cork	II.	66
20, 23	Raheendarragh	968	2	35	Carlow	Idrone East	Kiltennell	Carlow	I.	7
21	Raheendarrig	367	2	8	Wexford	Ballaghkeen	Monamolin	Gorey	I.	298
113, 122	Raheen Demesne	313	1	32	Galway	Kiltartan	Ardrahan	Gort	IV.	45
29, 33	Raheendonore	2,256	2	19	Kilkenny	Gowran	Graiguenamanagh	Thomastown	I.	95
7, 12	Raheendoran	137	1	22	Carlow	Idrone West	Cloydagh	Carlow	I.	9
33, 37	Raheenduff	223	2	18	Kilkenny	Ida	The Rower	New Ross	I.	104
23	Raheenduff	219	1	18	Kilkenny	Shillelogher	Grange	Kilkenny	I.	114
25, 26	Raheenduff	396	0	33	King's Co.	Geashill	Geashill	Tullamore	I.	140
6	Raheenduff	64	1	30	Leitrim	Rosclogher	Killasnet	Manorhamilton	IV.	110
100	Raheenduff	88	2	36b	Mayo	Carra	Burriscarra	Ballinrobe	IV.	127
29, 30, 35	Raheenduff	207	0	15	Queen's Co.	Clarmallagh	Rosconnell	Abbeyleix	I.	238
14, 19	Raheenduff	348	2	19	Queen's Co.	Stradbally	Dysartenos	Athy	I.	247
21	Raheenduff	336	2	23	Wexford	Ballaghkeen	Kilcormick	Gorey	I.	294
31	Raheenduff	644	0	12	Wexford	Bantry	Adamstown	New Ross	I.	299
35, 40	Raheenduff	368	3	15	Wexford	Shelmaliere West	Horetown	New Ross	I.	333
18, 24	Raheenduff Big	319	1	23	Queen's Co.	Cullenagh	Fossy or Timahoe	Abbeyleix	I.	240
18, 24	Raheenduff Little	171	1	20	Queen's Co.	Cullenagh	Fossy or Timahoe	Abbeyleix	I.	240
105	Raheen Eighter	206	2	9	Galway	Dunkellin	Kilconickny	Loughrea	IV.	29
87	Raheenering	127	2	38	Cork, E.R.	Kerrycurrihy	Carrigaline	Cork	II.	92
30, 31	Raheenglass	404	1	36	King's Co.	Eglish	Drumcullen	Parsonstown	I.	134
43	Raheenglass	178	3	39	Wicklow	Shillelagh	Crosspatrick	Shillelagh	I.	357
46	Raheengraney	655	3	9	Wicklow	Shillelagh	Moyacomb	Shillelagh	I.	358
113, 114	Raheen Kilkelly	232	1	2	Galway	Kiltartan	Ardrahan	Gort	IV.	45
17	Raheenkillane	213	3	3	Carlow	Forth	Ballyellin	Carlow	I.	4
20, 23	Raheenkyle	987	1	35	Carlow	Idrone East	Kiltennell	Carlow	I.	7
35	Raheenleagh	387	1	29	Queen's Co.	Clarmallagh	Aghmacart	Abbeyleix	I.	236
39, 44	Raheenleagh	426	1	24	Wicklow	Arklow	Killahurler	Rathdrum	I.	345

(a) Including 6A. 3R. 17P. water. (b) Including 15A. 3R. 31P. water.

No. of Sheet of the Ordnance Survey Maps.	Townlands and Towns.	Area in Statute Acres.	County.	Barony.	Parish.	Poor Law Union in 1857.	Townland Census of 1851, Part I.	
		A. R. P.					Vol.	Page
20	Raheenliegh	918 3 8	Carlow	Forth	Myshall	Carlow	I.	5
28	Raheen Lower	219 2 13	Queen's Co.	Clandonagh	Donaghmore	Donaghmore	I.	233
59	Raheen Lower	123 0 25	Tipperary, S.R.	Clanwilliam	Solloghod-beg	Tipperary	II.	310
22	Raheenlusk	231 3 21	Wexford	Ballaghkeen	Donaghmore	Ballyboy	I.	294
31	Raheenmeel	156 0 34	King's Co.	Ballyboy	Ballyboy	Parsonstown	I.	123
12	Raheen Moor	244 2 30	Wexford	Ballaghkeen	Killenagh	Gorey	I.	295
53	Raheenmoor	67 3 1	Wexford	Forth	Carn	Wexford	I.	309
118	Raheen More	218 1 11	Cork, W.R.	Bantry	Kilmocomioge	Bantry	II.	121
10	Raheenmore	136 1 30	King's Co.	Lower Philipstown	Kilclonfert	Tullamore	I.	142
3	Raheen More	132 3 27	Westmeath	Fore	Rathgarve	Castletowndelvin	I.	271
17	Raheen More	169 2 9	Wexford	Ballaghkeen	Killenagh	Gorey	I.	295
31	Raheenmore	27 0 5	Wicklow	Arklow	Drumkay	Rathdrum	I.	343
10	Raheennagee	91 1 2	Wexford	Scarawalsh	Ferns	Enniscorthy	I.	323
19	Raheennagun	46 1 17	Kilkenny	Crannagh	St. Canice	Kilkenny	I.	87
31	Raheennahoon	300 3 33	Wexford	Bantry	Kilcowanmore	Enniscorthy	I.	300
19, 25	Raheennahown	342 1 24	Queen's Co.	Stradbally	Tullomoy	Athy	I.	248
9, 14	RaheennahownNorth	157 0 28	Queen's Co.	Stradbally	Moyanna	Athy	I.	247
14	RaheennahownSouth	38 0 16	Queen's Co.	Stradbally	Moyanna	Athy	I.	247
41, 49	Raheennamadra	397 1 37	Limerick	Coshlea	Knocklong	Kilmallock	II.	240
21	Raheennaskeagh Lower	259 0 23	Wexford	Ballaghkeen	Kilnamanagh	Gorey	I.	297
21	Raheennaskeagh Upper	166 3 8	Wexford	Ballaghkeen	Kilnamanagh	Gorey	I.	297
10	Raheen Old	67 3 33	Kildare	Ikeathy & Oughterany	Balraheen	Celbridge	I.	56
105	Raheen Oughter	142 3 32	Galway	Loughrea	Kilconickny	Loughrea	IV.	63
17	Raheenpark	135 2 13	Wexford	Ballaghkeen	Killenagh	Gorey	I.	295
28	Raheenphelan Glebe	142 3 16	Queen's Co.	Clandonagh	Donaghmore	Donaghmore	I.	233
24,25,28,29	Raheenroche	740 3 1	Kilkenny	Gowran	Dungarvan	Thomastown	I.	94
139, 140	Raheenroe	242 2 24	Cork, W.R.	West Carbery (W.D.)	Skull	Skull	II.	146
56	Raheenroe	40 2 38	Limerick	Coshlea	Kilflyn	Kilmallock	II.	240
56	Raheenroe	84 2 16	Limerick	Coshlea	Particles	Kilmallock	II.	240
21	Raheenroe	43 0 17	Mayo	Tirawley	Kilfian	Killala	IV.	169
80, 86	Raheenroe	185 2 29	Tipperary, S.R.	Iffa and Offa West	Shanrahan	Clogheen	II.	320
70	Raheenroe	25 3 27	Tipperary. S.R.	Middlethird	Coolnundry	Cashel	II.	326
87	Raheens	175 1 43	Cork, E.R.	Kerrycurrihy	Carrigaline	Cork	II.	92
80	Raheens	312 3 7	Kerry	Iveragh	Killinane	Cahersiveen	II.	197
18	Raheens	540 0 21a	Kildare	Clane	Carragh	Naas	I.	53
78	Raheens	290 2 30	Mayo	Carra	Islandeady	Castlebar	IV.	129
21, 22	Raheens	146 1 7	Mayo	Tirawley	Ballysakeery	Ballina	IV.	165
12	Raheens	30 2 21	Tipperary, N.R.	Ikerrin	Roscrea	Roscrea	II.	276
16	Raheens	569 0 12	Waterford	Middlethird	Kilmeadan	Waterford	II.	368
87	Raheens East	34 0 18	Cork, E.R.	Kerrycurrihy	Carrigaline	Cork	II.	92
27	Raheensheara	60 1 36	Queen's Co.	Clandonagh	Donaghmore	Donaghmore	I.	233
27	Raheensheara	51 2 32	Queen's Co.	Clandonagh	Rathdowney	Donaghmore	I.	234
38	Raheenteige	277 0 17	Wicklow	Ballinacor South	Kilcommon	Shillelagh	I.	349
28	Raheen Upper	238 2 3	Queen's Co.	Clandonagh	Donaghmore	Donaghmore	I.	233
59	Raheen Upper	123 1 3	Tipperary, S.R.	Clanwilliam	Solloghod-beg	Tipperary	II.	310
16, 17	Raheenwood	228 1 14	Carlow	Idrone East	Myshall	Carlow	I.	8
11, 15	Raheenwood	302 3 17	Carlow	Idrone West	Oldleighlin	Carlow	I.	9
53	Raheenyhooig	121 0 12	Kerry	Corkaguiny	Dingle	Dingle	II.	175
35	Raheevarren	503 2 22	Wexford	Shelmaliere West	Newbawn	New Ross	I.	334
42	Raheever	348 3 23	Cavan	Clanmahon	Kilbride	Oldcastle	III.	78
16, 21	Raheg	224 2 29b	Cavan	Upper Loughtee	Castleterra	Cavan	III.	83
15	Rahellistin	126 0 25	Cavan	Tullygarvey	Annagh	Cavan	III.	87
5, 8	Rahelly	204 1 39	Sligo	Carbury	Drumcliff	Sligo	IV.	221
13, 18	Rahelty	298 0 10	Kilkenny	Crannagh	Ballinamara	Kilkenny	I.	84
35,36,41,42	Rahelty	819 2 24	Tipperary, N.R.	Eliogarty	Rahelty	Thurles	II.	272
29, 37	Rahena Beg	292 0 13	Clare	Tulla Lower	Ogonnelloe	Scariff	II.	38
37	Rahena More	222 1 6	Clare	Tulla Lower	Ogonnelloe	Scariff	II.	38
10	Rahendrick	499 1 4	Meath	Upper Kells	Loughan or Castle-keeran	Kells	I.	207
8	Raheny	166 1 15	Dublin	Balrothery East	Lusk	Balrothery	I.	21
15	Raheny North	130 3 15	Dublin	Coolock	Raheny	Dublin North	I.	28
15, 19	Raheny South	95 1 35	Dublin	Coolock	Raheny	Dublin North	I.	29
15	RAHENY T.	—	Dublin	Coolock	Raheny	Dublin North	I.	29
36	Raherd	29 3 17	Wicklow	Arklow	Dunganstown	Rathdrum	I.	344
36	Raherd	95 0 24	Wicklow	Arklow	Ennereilly	Rathdrum	I.	344
97	Raherneen	124 3 14	Galway	Dunkellin	Kilconierin	Loughrea	IV.	29
74	Raherolus	239 1 33	Mayo	Costello	Kilmovee	Swineford	IV.	142
1, 3, 4	Rahill	651 1 27	Carlow	Rathvilly	Rahill	Baltinglass	I.	12
26	Rahill	74 0 13	Meath	Lower Duleek	Duleek	Drogheda	I.	195
22	Rahilla Commons	8 3 19	Kildare	Offaly East	Dunmurry	Naas	I.	69
22	Rahilla Commons	11 3 13	Kildare	Offaly East	Kildare	Naas	I.	70
22	Rahilla Glebe	506 1 25	Kildare	Offaly East	Kildare	Naas	I.	70
40	Rahillakeen	269 3 15	Kilkenny	Ida	Dunkitt	Waterford	I.	101

(a) Including 33A. 0R. 10P. detached portion. (b) Including 1A. 1R. 27P. water.

5 F 2

No. of Sheet of the Ordnance Survey Maps.	Townlands and Towns.	Area in Statute Acres.	County.	Barony.	Parish.	Poor Law Union in 1857.	Townland Census of 1851. Part I.	
		A. R. P.					Vol.	Page
40	Rahillakeen	122 3 0	Kilkenny	Ida	Rossinan	Waterford	I.	104
8	Rahillion	100 0 10	Dublin	Nethercross	Portraine	Balrothery	I.	31
2	Rahin	656 1 0	Kildare	Carbury	Carrick	Edenderry	I.	52
25, 26	Rahin	627 0 30	Queen's Co.	Ballyadams	Killabban	Athy	I.	231
12	Rahina	58 2 9	Limerick	Pubblebrien	Kilkeedy	Limerick	II.	252
69	Rahinaghmore	84 0 30	Tipperary, S.R.	Middlethird	Knockgraffon	Cashel	II.	328
7, 8	Rahinane	280 3 12	Tipperary, N.R.	Lower Ormond	Ballingarry	Borrisokane	II.	282
7	Rahinane	24 0 32	Tipperary, N.R.	Lower Ormond	Uskane	Borrisokane	II.	288
38	Rahinashane and Spittaltown	141 3 19	Westmeath	Moycashel	Newtown	Mullingar	I.	279
38	Rahinashurock	96 1 5	Westmeath	Moycashel	Newtown	Mullingar	I.	279
47, 48	Rahinch	183 3 16	Tipperary, N.R.	Eliogarty	Ballymurreen	Thurles	II.	269
33, 39	Rahincuill	486 1 11	Westmeath	Fartullagh	Newtown	Mullingar	I.	269
141	Rahine	158 2 34	Cork, W.R.	West Carbery (E.D.)	Aghadown	Skibbereen	II.	137
38	Rahinmore	169 2 2	Westmeath	Moycashel	Newtown	Mullingar	I.	279
42, 52	Rahinnane	235 0 33	Kerry	Corkaguiny	Ventry	Dingle	II.	180
42, 52	Rahinnane West	305 0 32	Kerry	Corkaguiny	Ventry	Dingle	II.	180
59, 60	Rahins	158 1 30	Galway	Tiaquin	Killsscobe	Mountbellew	IV.	78
42, 48	Rahinstown	569 2 35	Meath	Lower Moyfenrath	Rathcore	Trim	I.	211
30	Rahogarty North	161 1 21	Galway	Dunmore	Tuam	Tuam	IV.	36
30	Rahogarty South	166 3 22	Galway	Dunmore	Tuam	Tuam	IV.	36
27	Raholland	215 2 5	Meath	Upper Duleek	Moorechurch	Drogheda	I.	198
31	Raholp	535 1 18	Down	Lecale Lower	Ballyculter	Downpatrick	III.	178
65, 72	Rahona East	416 3 7	Clare	Moyarta	Moyarta	Kilrush	II.	34
65, 72	Rahona West	391 1 17	Clare	Moyarta	Moyarta	Kilrush	II.	34
14	Rahone	57 0 26	Tipperary, N.R.	Lower Ormond	Cloghprior	Borrisokane	II.	283
20, 28	Rahoneen	298 0 26	Kerry	Clanmaurice	Ardfert	Tralee	II.	167
50	Rahony	734 0 0	Tyrone	Omagh East	Dromore	Omagh	III.	311
5, 11, 12	Rahood	599 2 36	Meath	Morgallion	Castletown	Kells	I.	209
81, 82, 94	Rahoon	754 3 6	Galway	Galway	Rahoon	Galway	IV.	38
4, 9	Rahoonagh	209 3 8	Kerry	Iraghticonnor	Killehenny	Listowel	II.	191
69	Rahoonagh East	331 3 11	Cork, W.R.	West Muskerry	Ballyvourney	Macroom	II.	154
58, 69	Rahoonagh West	367 1 19	Cork, W.R.	West Muskerry	Ballyvourney	Macroom	II.	154
29	Rahoonane	96 0 36	Kerry	Trughanacmy	Tralee	Tralee	II.	214
32, 36	Rahoonbeak	325 3 29	Kildare	Narragh & RebanEast	Narraghmore	Athy	I.	66
37	Rahora	236 2 38	Kilkenny	Ida	Listerlin	New Ross	I.	103
16	Rahoran	52 2 22	Cavan	Tullygarvey	Drung	Cootehill	III.	89
57,58,63,64	Rahoran	307 1 7	Tyrone	Clogher	Clogher	Clogher	III.	293
38, 40	Rahugh	271 1 36	Westmeath	Moycashel	Rahugh	Tullamore	I.	279
12, 15	Rahulk	135 1 7	Dublin	Coolock	Kinsaley	Balrothery	I.	28
20	Rahultan	153 2 21a	Cavan	Upper Loughtee	Urney	Cavan	III.	86
107	Rahyconor	136 1 1	Galway	Longford	Tynagh	Portumna	IV.	62
82, 94	Rahylin Glebe	28 3 17	Galway	Galway	St. Nicholas	Galway	IV.	38
51	Rahyvira	88 1 39	Tipperary, S.R.	Kilnamanagh Lower	Donohill	Tipperary	II.	323
25	Raigh	358 1 4	Galway	Ross	Ross	Oughterard	IV.	74
67	Raigh	84 1 13	Mayo	Burrishoole	Burrishoole	Newport	IV.	119
98	Raigh	435 2 8	Mayo	Murrisk	Aghagower	Westport	IV.	159
5, 6, 10, 11	Railpark	366 3 34	Kildare	North Salt	Laraghbryan	Celbridge	I.	75
69	Railstown	96 2 36	Tipperary, S.R.	Middlethird	Kilbragh	Cashel	II.	327
61	Railstown	125 0 19	Tipperary, S.R.	Middlethird	Kilconnell	Cashel	II.	327
61, 69	Railstown	408 2 23	Tipperary, S.R.	Middlethird	Railstown	Cashel	II.	329
3	Rainestown	620 3 14	Carlow	Carlow	Killerrig	Carlow	I.	2
17	*Rainey Island*	39 3 19	Down	Ards Upper	Ardkeen	Newtownards	III.	159
30	Raish	86 2 23	Mayo	Tirawley	Kilmoremoy	Ballina	IV.	170
17, 22	Rakane	310 2 15b	Cavan	Tullygarvey	Kildrumsherdan	Cootehill	III.	90
18	Rakean	138 0 15	Monaghan	Dartree	Aghabog	Cootehill	III.	264
10	Rakeelan	125 2 20c	Cavan	Tullyhaw	Tomregan	Bawnboy	III.	96
22	Rakeelan Glebe	107 0 15d	Fermanagh	Tirkennedy	Enniskillen	Enniskillen	III.	222
18	Rakeeragh	107 0 34	Monaghan	Dartree	Ematris	Cootehill	III.	267
30, 31	Rakeeragh	163 0 3	Monaghan	Farney	Magheross	Carrickmacross	III.	274
13	Rakeeragh	137 2 32	Monaghan	Monaghan	Monaghan	Monaghan	III.	277
42	Rakeeragh	142 3 30e	Tyrone	Omagh East	Drumragh	Omagh	III.	312
50	Rakeeranbeg	180 2 2	Tyrone	Omagh East	Dromore	Omagh	III.	311
34	Rakeevan	727 1 11	Cavan	Clankee	Bailieborough	Bailieborough	III.	71
17	Rakeevan	70 1 25f	Monaghan	Dartree	Aghabog	Cootehill	III.	264
3	Rakelly	51 3 13	Monaghan	Trough	Errigal Trough	Clogher	III.	285
17	Rakelly	316 3 35	Tyrone	Strabane Lower	Ardstraw	Strabane	III.	319
16,17,21,22	Rakenny	339 0 9g	Cavan	Tullygarvey	Drung	Cootehill	III.	89
123	Rakerin	338 2 32	Galway	Kiltartan	Kilbeacanty	Gort	IV.	47
22, 25	Ralaghan	243 3 34	Cavan	Clankee	Drumgoon	Cootehill	III.	72
28	Ralaghan	632 3 32	Cavan	Clankee	Shercock	Bailieborough	III.	75
3	Ralaghan	163 1 26	Monaghan	Trough	Errigal Trough	Monaghan	III.	285
3	Ralappane	211 1 18	Kerry	Iraghticonnor	Kilnaughtin	Glin	II.	191

(a) Including 26A. 2R. 29P. water.
(b) Including 8A. 1R. 18P. water.
(c) Including 3A. 0R. 3P. water.

(d) Including 6A. 1R. 0P. water.
(e) Including 1A. 3R. 29P. water.

(f) Including 5A. 2R. 16P. water.
(g) Including 8A. 3R. 3P. water.

No. of Sheet of the Ordnance Survey Maps.	Townlands and Towns.	Area in Statute Acres. A. R. P.	County.	Barony.	Parish.	Poor Law Union in 1857.	Townland Census of 1851, Part I. Vol.	Page
13, 19	Raleagh . . .	285 1 27	Cavan .	Tullyhunco . .	Kildallan . .	Bawnboy . .	III.	97
22,23,29,30	Raleagh . . .	665 0 5	Down . .	Kinelarty . .	Kilmore . .	Downpatrick .	III.	177
70	Raleigh North .	267 2 21	Cork, W.R. .	West Muskerry .	Kilnamartry .	Macroom . .	II.	160
70	Raleigh South .	340 1 17	Cork, W.R. .	West Muskerry .	Kilnamartry .	Macroom . .	II.	160
24, 30	Ralish . . .	430 0 23	Queen's Co. .	Cullenagh . .	Dysartgallen .	Abbeyleix . .	I.	239
30	Rallagh . . .	423 3 39	Londonderry .	Keenaght . .	Banagher . .	NewTⁿLimavady	III.	234
5, 8	Rallekaystown .	173 1 32a	Dublin . .	Balrothery East .	Lusk . . .	Balrothery .	I.	21
2	Raloaghan . .	632 1 2	Meath . .	Morgallion . .	Enniskeen . .	Kells . . .	I.	209
20, 28	Ralph . . .	79 2 18	Waterford .	Coshmore&Coshbride	Lismore and Mocollop	Lismore . .	II.	347
50	Ralph . . .	283 3 4	Wexford .	Shelburne . .	Fethard . .	New Ross . .	I.	327
8	Ralphsdale . .	163 1 28	Westmeath .	Delvin . . .	Kilcumny . .	Castletowndelvin	I.	265
46, 47	Ralphtown . .	162 0 33	Wexford . .	Bargy . . .	Kilcowan . .	Wexford . .	I.	305
17	Raludan . .	68 0 23	Cavan . .	Tullygarvey . .	Kildrumsherdan .	Cootehill . .	III.	90
28, 42	Ralusk . . .	73 2 37	Galway . .	Clare . . .	Donaghpatrick .	Tuam . .	IV.	19
36, 44	Ramackan . .	1,208 3 35b	Tyrone . .	Omagh East . .	Termonmaguirk .	Omagh . .	III.	314
66, 67	Ramaket . .	143 0 36	Tyrone . .	Dungannon Lower .	Aghaloo . .	Armagh . .	III.	297
17, 18	Ramaley . .	753 0 36	Fermanagh .	Tirkennedy . .	Enniskillen . .	Enniskillen .	III.	222
13	Ramanny . .	114 3 28	Monaghan .	Monaghan . .	Monaghan . .	Monaghan . .	III.	277
38	Ramoan or Barr	206 3 28	Fermanagh .	Knockninny . .	Kinawley . .	Lisnaskea . .	III.	201
121, 122	Ramolin . .	620 1 25c	Mayo . .	Kilmaine . .	Shrule . .	Ballinrobe .	IV.	158
38	Ramonan . .	194 0 0	Cavan . .	Castlerahan . .	Castlerahan . .	Oldcastle . .	III.	67
11	Ramooney . .	159 1 0	Leitrim . .	Drumahaire . .	Cloonclare . .	Manorhamilton .	IV.	93
12	Ramoy . . .	46 3 2	Monaghan .	Dartree . . .	Clones . .	Clones . .	III.	265
8	Rampark . .	412 1 7	Louth . .	Lower Dundalk .	Ballymascanlan .	Dundalk . .	I.	176
26, 27	Rampark . .	52 0 5	Roscommon .	Castlereagh . .	Kilkeevin . .	Castlereagh .	IV.	201
20,21,26,27	Rampere . .	345 3 18	Wicklow . .	Upper Talbotstown .	Rathbran . .	Baltinglass .	I.	365
6, 7	Ramsfortpark or Ballowen . . .	324 3 31	Wexford . .	Gorey . . .	Kilmakilloge .	Gorey . . .	I.	318
44	Ramsgrange . .	1,230 1 16	Wexford . .	Shelburne . .	St. James and Dunbrody . .	New Ross . .	I.	325
44	RAMSGRANGE T. .	—	Wexford . .	Shelburne . .	St. James and Dunbrody . .	New Ross . .	I.	328
58	*Rams Island* . .	6 3 23d	Antrim . .	Upper Massereene .	Glenavy . .	Antrim . .	III.	30
14	*Rams Island* . .	7 0 12	Galway . .	Ross . . .	Ross . . .	Oughterard .	IV.	74
50	Ramstown . .	521 2 23	Wexford . .	Shelburne . .	Fethard . .	New Ross . .	I.	327
6, 7, 11 12	Ramstown Lower .	200 2 1	Wexford . .	Gorey . . .	Kilmakilloge .	Gorey . . .	I.	318
11, 12	Ramstown Upper .	220 1 18	Wexford . .	Gorey . . .	Kilmakilloge .	Gorey . . .	I.	318
11, 12, 15	Ramulligan . .	129 0 11	Cavan . .	Tullygarvey . .	Annagh . .	Cavan . .	III.	87
24	Ramult . . .	239 2 3	Fermanagh .	Magherastephana .	Aghalurcher .	Lisnaskea . .	III.	217
59	Ranacrohy . .	16 3 14	Tipperary, S.R.	Clanwilliam . .	Kilmucklin . .	Tipperary . .	II.	309
59	Ranacrohy . .	149 3 15	Tipperary, S.R.	Clanwilliam . .	Templenoe . .	Tipperary . .	II.	312
42, 48, 49	Ranaghan . .	111 3 6	Antrim . .	Upper Toome . .	Duneane . .	Antrim . .	III.	35
17, 18	Ranaghan . .	419 3 8e	Clare . .	Inchiquin . .	Ruan . .	Corrofin . .	II.	28
11	Ranaghan . .	277 2 3	Longford . .	Granard . . .	Abbeylara . .	Granard . .	I.	154
46, 54	Ranaghan . .	137 1 38	Tyrone . .	Dungannon Middle .	Drumglass . .	Dungannon . .	III.	303
7, 8	Ranaghan . .	641 3 13	Westmeath .	Fore . . .	St. Feighins .	Castletowndelvin	I.	272
11	Ranaghanbaun .	40 3 1	Longford . .	Granard . . .	Abbeylara . .	Granard . .	I.	154
26	Ranaghan Beg .	75 2 18	Sligo . .	Leyny . . .	Kilvarnet . .	Tobercurry .	IV.	232
26	Ranaghan More .	174 0 28f	Sligo . .	Leyny . . .	Kilvarnet . .	Tobercurry .	IV.	232
68, 77	Ranaghy . .	274 0 35	Mayo . .	Burrishoole . .	Islandeady . .	Westport . .	IV.	121
73, 74	Ranagissaun .	287 3 12	Mayo . .	Costello . .	Kilmovee . .	Swineford . .	IV.	142
19	Ranahan . .	322 2 30	Limerick . .	Connello Lower .	Rathkeale . .	Rathkeale . .	II.	229
7, 15	Ranahinch . .	261 2 39	Westmeath .	Fore . . .	Faughalstown .	Castletowndelvin	I.	270
49	Ranaleen . .	375 3 10	Kerry . .	Trughanacmy .	Killeentierna .	Killarney . .	II.	211
48	Ranalough . .	393 1 39	Kerry . .	Trughanacmy .	Killeentierna .	Killarney . .	II.	211
116	Ranamackan . .	231 2 5	Galway . .	Leitrim . .	Duniry . .	Loughrea . .	IV.	53
15	Rananagh . .	72 2 38	Antrim . .	Lower Glenarm .	Layd . .	Ballycastle .	III.	23
62,63,72,73	Rananranny . .	167 2 21	Mayo . .	Costello . .	Kilbeagh . .	Swineford . .	IV.	141
32	Randallsmill . .	90 0 23	Wexford . .	Shelmaliere East .	Tikillin . .	Wexford . .	I.	331
15	Randalshough .	138 1 13	Fermanagh .	Magheraboy . .	Devenish . .	Enniskillen .	III.	211
43, 49	Randal-town . .	130 1 4h	Antrim . .	Upper Toome . .	Drummaul . .	Antrim . .	III.	34
18, 25	Randalstown . .	939 0 0	Meath . .	Upper Kells . .	Donaghpatrick .	Navan . .	I.	205
47	Randalstown . .	206 0 39	Wexford . .	Forth . . .	Mayglass . .	Wexford . .	I.	312
21	Randalstown . .	233 0 1	Wicklow . .	Upper Talbotstown .	Donaghmore . .	Baltinglass .	I.	363
43	RANDALSTOWN T. .	—	Antrim . .	Upper Toome . .	Drummaul . .	Antrim . .	III.	34
55	Randox . .	396 3 35	Antrim . .	Lower Massereene .	Killead . .	Antrim . .	III.	28
100	Raneany Barr or Meenacargagh . .	991 3 10i	Donegal . .	Tirhugh . .	Drumhome . .	Donegal . .	III.	146
100	Raneany East . .	139 1 22	Donegal . .	Tirhugh . .	Drumhome . .	Donegal . .	III.	147
100	Raneany West .	181 2 38	Donegal . .	Tirhugh . .	Drumhome . .	Donegal . .	III.	147
98	Raneely . . .	218 3 33	Donegal . .	Banagh . .	Inver . .	Donegal . .	III.	108
51	Raneese . .	419 1 20	Tyrone . .	Clogher . . .	Donacavey . .	Omagh . .	III.	294
16	Raneevoge . .	217 1 30	Meath . .	Upper Kells . .	Kil-keer . .	Oldcastle . .	I.	206
52	Ranelagh . .	71 1 29	Roscommon .	Athlone . .	St. Peter's . .	Athlone . .	IV.	184

(a) Including 10A. 1R. 20P. detached portions.   (d) Including 0A. 1R. 3P. Duck Island.   (g) Including 7A. 0R. 15P. water.
(b) Including 8A. 1R. 5P. water.   (e) Including 51A. 1R. 14P. water.   (h) Including 2A. 0R. 10P. water.
(c) Including 45A. 2R. 34P. water.   (f) Including 2A. 0R. 2P. water.   (i) Including 30A. 2R. 3P. water.

No. of Sheet of the Ordnance Survey Maps.	Townlands and Towns.	Area in Statute Acres.	County.	Barony.	Parish.	Poor Law Union in 1857.	Townland Census 1851, Part I.	
		A. R. P.					Vol.	Page
39	Ranelagh . .	71 1 18	Roscommon .	Ballintober South .	Roscommon .	Roscommon .	IV.	190
18	Ranelagh North .	121 1 38a	Dublin .	Uppercross and Municipal Borough .	St. Peters .	Dublin South .	I.	41
18	Ranelagh South .	53 2 20	Dublin .	Uppercross .	St. Peters .	Dublin South .	I.	41
18	RANELAGH T. .	—	Dublin .	Uppercross .	St. Peters .	Dublin South .	I.	41
43	Ranelly . .	315 0 20b	Tyrone .	Omagh East .	Clogherny .	Omagh .	III.	310
64	Ranenly . .	116 1 1	Tyrone .	Clogher .	Clogher .	Clogher .	III.	293
91	Rangaroe . .	197 2 24	Cork, W.R. .	Bantry .	Kilmocomoge .	Bantry .	II.	121
56, 64	Rangue . .	576 3 2	Kerry .	Trughanacmy .	Killorglin .	Killarney .	II.	211
61	Rann . .	517 2 39	Donegal .	Raphoe .	Leck .	Letterkenny .	III.	140
15	Rannagh . .	253 2 26	Clare .	Corcomroe .	Killaspuglonane .	Ennistimon .	II.	19
15	Rannagh . .	176 2 16	Clare .	Corcomroe .	Kilmacrehy .	Ennistimon .	II.	20
35	Rannagh . .	228 2 7	Clare .	Tulla Upper .	Tulla .	Tulla .	II.	42
6, 10	Rannagh East .	416 1 26	Clare .	Burren .	Carran .	Ballyvaghan .	II.	12
48	Rannagh and Toories	338 3 20	Donegal .	Boylagh .	Templecrone .	Glenties .	III.	116
6, 10	Rannagh West .	896 3 30	Clare .	Burren .	Carran .	Ballyvaghan .	II.	12
35	Rannatruffaun East	199 2 25	Sligo .	Tirerrill .	Killadoon .	Boyle .	IV.	239
34, 35	Rannatruffaun West	205 1 4	Sligo .	Tirerrill .	Killadoon .	Boyle .	IV.	239
89	Ranns . .	128 2 8	Mayo .	Carra .	Ballintober .	Castlebar .	IV.	125
57, 65	Ranny . .	588 1 13	Donegal .	Boylagh .	Lettermacward .	Glenties .	III.	114
27	Ranny . .	286 2 30	Donegal .	Kilmacrenan .	Tullyfern .	Millford .	III.	133
32	Ranrenagh . .	189 1 35	Cavan .	Upper Loughtee .	Denn .	Cavan .	III.	84
18	Ransborough .	139 0 27	Cork, E.R. .	Fermoy .	St. Nathlash .	Mitchelstown .	II.	82
40, 44	Rantavan . .	672 0 24d	Cavan .	Castlerahan .	Mullagh .	Kells .	III.	70
24	Rantoge Glebe .	293 2 34	Leitrim .	Leitrim .	Kiltubbrid .	Cark. on Shannon	IV.	104
67	Rapepark . .	51 1 13	Clare .	Moyarta .	Kilrush .	Kilrush .	II.	33
70	Raphoe Demesne .	126 1 21	Donegal .	Raphoe .	Raphoe .	Strabane .	III.	141
70	RAPHOE T. .	—	Donegal .	Raphoe .	Raphoe .	Strabane .	III.	141
62, 70	Raphoe Townparks .	306 1 1	Donegal .	Raphoe .	Raphoe .	Strabane .	III.	141
34	Rapla . .	367 2 10	Queen's Co. .	Clarmallagh .	Aghmacart .	Abbeyleix .	I.	236
15	Rapla . .	93 1 39	Tipperary, N.R. .	Upper Ormond .	Kilruane .	Nenagh .	II.	292
15	Rapla North .	163 3 36	Tipperary, N.R. .	Upper Ormond .	Kilruane .	Nenagh .	II.	292
15, 21	Rapla South .	417 2 29	Tipperary, N.R. .	Upper Ormond .	Kilruane .	Nenagh .	II.	292
32	Rappa . .	146 1 37	Queen's Co. .	Slievemargy .	Shrule .	Carlow .	I.	246
29, 30	Rappacastle .	288 3 24	Mayo .	Tirawley .	Ardagh .	Ballina .	IV.	164
17, 18	Rapparehill .	671 0 23	Longford .	Moydow .	Killashee .	Longford .	I.	162
29	Raragh . .	114 1 19	Cavan .	Clankee .	Enniskeen .	Bailieborough .	III.	73
60, 61	Rareagh . .	1,038 1 7	Donegal .	Raphoe .	Conwal .	Letterkenny .	III.	137
20, 21	Rareagh . .	54 1 19	Kerry .	Clanmaurice .	Kilmoyly .	Tralee .	II.	171
52	Rarogan . .	305 3 8	Tyrone .	Clogher .	Errigal Keerogue .	Clogher .	III.	295
43	Rarone . .	153 2 13	Tyrone .	Omagh East .	Clogherny .	Omagh .	III.	310
99, 100	Raroocy . .	105 2 38	Donegal .	Tirhugh .	Donegal .	Donegal .	III.	145
97, 105	Raruddy East .	328 3 9	Galway .	Loughrea .	Kilconickny .	Loughrea .	IV.	63
97, 105	Raruddy West .	354 1 27	Galway .	Loughrea .	Kilconickny .	Loughrea .	IV.	63
6	Rarutagh . .	117 3 8	Monaghan .	Trough .	Donagh .	Monaghan .	III.	282
9	Rascahan . .	85 3 38	Londonderry .	Keenaght .	Tamlaght Finlagan .	NewTnLimavady	III.	237
21	Rascalstreet .	234 2 13	Cork, E.R. .	Duhallow .	Kilmeen .	Kanturk .	II.	73
26	RASHARKIN T. .	—	Antrim .	Kilconway .	Rasharkin .	Ballymoney .	III.	28
52, 60	Rashedoge .	46 3 20	Donegal .	Raphoe .	Conwal .	Letterkenny .	III.	137
45	Rashee . .	739 0 5	Antrim .	Upper Antrim .	Rashee .	Antrim .	III.	7
3, 4, 10, 11	Rashenny .	791 3 1	Donegal .	Inishowen East .	Clonmany .	Inishowen .	III.	117
6, 7, 15	Rashinagh .	462 2 23	King's Co. .	Garrycastle .	Lemanaghan .	Parzonstown .	I.	137
8, 14	Rasillagh .	240 3 9e	Meath .	Fore .	Killeagh .	Oldcastle .	I.	201
4	Raskeagh . .	247 2 0	Louth .	Upper Dundalk .	Faughart .	Dundalk .	I.	178
21	Raskill . .	216 3 9	Cavan .	Upper Loughtee .	Larah .	Cavan .	III.	85
22, 28	Raspberry Hill .	167 0 11	Londonderry .	Tirkeeran .	Cumber Upper .	Londonderry .	III.	249
19	Raspberryhill .	169 2 20f	Waterford .	Coshmore&Coshbride .	Lismore .	Lismore .	II.	344
76	Rassakeeran .	78 1 13	Mayo .	Burrishoole .	Kilmeena .	Westport .	IV.	122
32, 38	Rassan . .	392 1 11	Cavan .	Castlerahan .	Crosserlough .	Cavan .	III.	68
3, 6	Rassan . .	640 1 11	Louth .	Upper Dundalk .	Creggan .	Dundalk .	I.	178
38	Rassan or Corglass .	96 0 35	Cavan .	Castlerahan .	Crosserlough .	Oldcastle .	III.	68
101	Rassaraun .	42 1 0	Mayo .	Clanmorris .	Taghcen .	Claremorris .	IV.	136
33, 36	Rassaun . .	440 2 38	Leitrim .	Carrigallen .	Cloone .	Mohill .	IV.	90
4, 7	Rassaun East .	377 1 34	Leitrim .	Rosclogher .	Killasnet .	Manorhamilton .	IV.	110
4, 7	Rassaun West .	505 1 6g	Leitrim .	Rosclogher .	Killasnet .	Manorhamilton .	IV.	110
38, 39	Rasuddan .	227 3 29	Cavan .	Castlerahan .	Castlerahan .	Oldcastle .	III.	67
30, 31	Rataine . .	718 0 38	Meath .	Lower Navan .	Rataine .	Navan .	I.	215
18, 25	Ratallagh .	352 2 2	Down .	Ards Upper .	Ardkeen .	Downpatrick .	III.	159
10	Ratallen . .	718 1 28	Roscommon .	Frenchpark .	Kilcolagh .	Boyle .	IV.	203
13, 17	Ratarnet . .	204 1 18	Armagh .	Fews Lower .	Mullaghbrack .	Armagh .	III.	47
29	Ratass . .	128 3 0	Kerry .	Trughanacmy .	Ratass .	Tralee .	II.	213
48	Ratawragh .	148 3 31	Roscommon .	Athlone .	Kiltoom .	Athlone .	IV.	183
35	Rateen . .	89 3 5h	Fermanagh .	Clankelly .	Clones .	Clones .	III.	197

No. of Sheet of the Ordnance Survey Maps.	Townlands and Towns.	Area in Statute Acres.	County.	Barony.	Parish.	Poor Law Union in 1857.	Townland Census of 1851, Part I.	
		A. R. P.					Vol.	Page
17	Rateerbane	136 2 29	Monaghan	Dartree	Killeevan	Clones	III.	268
15, 28	RATESH T.	—	Galway	Dunmore	Kilconla	Tuam	IV.	35
25	Rath	221 0 13	Clare	Inchiquin	Rath	Corrofin	II.	28
55,56,66,67	Rath	386 3 33	Cork, E.R.	Imokilly	Ardagh	Youghal	II.	83
7, 16	Rath	287 0 2	Cork, E.R.	Orrery and Kilmore	Churchtown	Mallow	II.	107
100, 104	Rath	125 3 18	Donegal	Tirhugh	Drumhome	Donegal	III.	147
1	Rath	166 3 23a	Dublin	Balrothery East	Balscaddan	Balrothery	I.	20
11	Rath	187 0 36	Dublin	Nethercross	Killossery	Balrothery	I.	31
105	Rath	571 3 25	Kerry	Dunkerron South	Kilcrohane	Cahersiveen	II.	184
102	Rath	465 3 8	Kerry	Glanarought	Kilcaskan	Kenmare	II.	187
46	Rath	161 0 12	King's Co.	Clonlisk	Cullenwaine	Roscrea	I.	129
14, 15	Rath	377 0 16	Limerick	Owneybeg	Abington	Limerick	II.	251
27	Rath	566 0 22	Longford	Shrule	Forgney	Ballymahon	I.	166
8	Rath	89 2 15	Louth	Lower Dundalk	Carlingford	Dundalk	I.	176
7	Rath	75 1 22	Louth	Upper Dundalk	Ballybarrack	Dundalk	I.	177
81, 82	Rath	659 1 14b	Mayo	Costello	Aghamore	Swineford	IV.	137
39	Rath	174 3 36	Meath	Ratoath	Cookstown	Dunshaughlin	I.	217
45	Rath	246 3 15	Meath	Ratoath	Greenoge	Dunshaughlin	I.	218
33	Rath	213 0 20	Meath	Upper Duleek	Ardcath	Drogheda	I.	197
29	Rath	215 3 34	Queen's Co.	Clarmallagh	Durrow	Abbeyleix	I.	237
5	Rath	169 0 13	Tipperary, N.R.	Lower Ormond	Dorrha	Parsonstown	II.	283
37, 38, 40	Rath	419 0 16	Waterford	Decies within Drum	Kinsalebeg	Youghal	II.	352
3	Rath	292 2 22	Waterford	Upperthird	Fenoagh	Carrick on Suir	III.	370
23	Rath	352 0 23	Westmeath	Kilkenny West	Kilkenny West	Athlone	I.	275
11	Rath	112 1 0	Westmeath	Moygoish	Kilbixy	Mullingar	I.	279
2, 6	Rath	652 0 12	Westmeath	Moygoish	Street	Granard	I.	281
46	Rath	140 2 19	Wexford	Bargy	Duncormick	Wexford	I.	305
37, 42	Rath	283 3 11	Wicklow	Shillelagh	Ardoyne	Shillelagh	I.	357
40	Rathaglish	44 1 36	Kilkenny	Ida	Kilcolumb	Waterford	I.	102
25	Rathaldron	243 3 16	Meath	Lower Navan	Donaghmore	Navan	I.	214
23	Rathaleek	169 3 5	Kilkenny	Shillelogher	Castleinch or Inchyolaghan	Kilkenny	I.	114
53, 54	Rathaneague	360 1 33	Cork, E.R.	Barrymore	Gortroe	Fermoy	II.	55
16, 17	Rathangan	1,004 3 5c	Kildare	Offaly East	Rathangan	Edenderry	I.	71
46	Rathangan	461 2 33	Wexford	Bargy	Duncormick	Wexford	I.	305
17	Rathangan Demesne	561 3 7	Kildare	Offaly East	Rathangan	Edenderry	I.	71
17	RATHANGAN T.	—	Kildare	Offaly East	Rathangan	Edenderry	I.	71
11	Rathaniska	6 2 9	Westmeath	Corkaree	Lackan	Mullingar	I.	262
11	Rathaniska	114 1 33	Westmeath	Corkaree	Leyny	Mullingar	I.	263
87	Rathanker	320 2 7	Cork, E.R.	Kerrycurrihy	Monkstown	Cork	II.	93
114	Rathanlon	69 1 10	Galway	Dunkellin	Ardrahan	Gort	IV.	27
23	Rathanna	1,149 3 37	Carlow	Idrone East	Kiltennell	Carlow	I.	8
30	Rathanny	257 2 21	Kerry	Trughanacmy	Ballymacelligott	Tralee	II.	207
40	Rathanny	713 2 21	Limerick	Smallcounty	Knockainy	Kilmallock	II.	261
67	Rathanny	154 1 6	Tipperary, S.R.	Clanwilliam	Cordangan	Tipperary	II.	306
16, 25	Rathanny	418 1 7	Waterford	Decies without Drum	Kilbarrymeaden	Kilmacthomas	II.	356
33	Rathanure	114 1 23	Tipperary, N.R.	Upper Ormond	Templederry	Nenagh	II.	293
84	Rathard	773 3 29	Cork, E.R.	East Muskerry	Kilbonane	Bandon	II.	104
76	Rathard	115 3 29	Tipperary, S.R.	Iffa and Offa West	Mortlestown	Clogheen	II.	319
16	Rathardeagher	90 0 3	Roscommon	Frenchpark	Creeve	Cark on Shannon	IV.	203
23	Ratharney	321 0 9d	Longford	Shrule	Abbeyshrule	Ballymahon	I.	165
110, 111	Ratharoon East	810 1 28	Cork, W.R.	East Carbery (E.D.)	Ballinadee	Bandon	II.	126
110	Ratharoon West	383 2 22	Cork, W.R.	East Carbery (E.D.)	Ballinadee	Bandon	II.	126
8	Rathartan	105 0 25	Dublin	Balrothery East	Lusk	Balrothery	I.	21
19, 24	Rathasker	132 1 27	Kildare	Naas North	Killashee	Naas	I.	62
24	Rathasker	167 0 14	Kildare	Naas North	Naas	Naas	I.	62
25	Rathaspick	95 3 10	Queen's Co.	Ballyadams	Rathaspick	Athy	I.	232
5, 6	Rathaspick	126 3 17	Westmeath	Moygoish	Rathaspick	Mullingar	I.	280
42	Rathaspick	216 2 13	Wexford	Forth	Rathaspick	Wexford	I.	313
9, 15	Rathattin	431 3 3	Wicklow	Lower Talbotstown	Hollywood	Baltinglass	I.	361
62, 70	Rathavin	170 2 22	Tipperary, S.R.	Middlethird	Rathcool	Cashel	II.	329
5, 6, 12, 13	Rathavisteen	1,735 2 2e	Mayo	Tirawley	Doonfeeny	Killala	IV.	167
30	Rathbal	833 2 9f	Mayo	Tirawley	Ballysakeery	Ballina	IV.	165
10	Rathballylong	187 1 20	Wicklow	Lower Talbotstown	Boystown	Naas	I.	359
20	Rathbane	447 0 0	Kildare	South Salt	Kilteel	Naas	I.	77
3	Rathbane	472 1 11	Kilkenny	Galmoy	Erke	Urlingford	I.	92
4, 5, 10, 11	Rathbane	360 2 0	Meath	Lower Kells	Moynalty	Kells	I.	204
33	Rathbane	336 3 12	Wicklow	Ballinacor South	Hacketstown	Shillelagh	I.	349
5, 13	Rathbane North	359 2 34g	Limerick	Clanwilliam and Municipal Borough	St. Nicholas	Limerick	II.	225
13	Rathbane South	159 2 31	Limerick	Clanwilliam	St. Nicholas	Limerick	II.	225
27	Rathbarna	183 1 12	Roscommon	Castlereagh	Kilkeevin	Castlereagh	IV.	201
25	Rathbarran	402 3 35	Sligo	Leyny	Killoran	Tobercurry	IV.	231

(a) Including 41A. 2R. 20P. detached portion.
(b) Including 12A. 2R. 22P. water.
(c) Including 47A. 3R. 3P. detached portion.
(d) Including 3A. 3R. 4P. River Inny.
(e) Including 9A. 0R. 10P. water.
(f) Including 11A. 3R. 7P. water.
(g) { Within the Municipal Boundary, 64A. 1R. 29P. { Without the Municipal Boundary, 295A. 1R. 5P.

No. of Sheet of the Ordnance Survey Maps.	Townlands and Towns.	Area in Statute Acres.	County.	Barony.	Parish.	Poor Law Union in 1857.	Townland Census of 1851, Part I.	
		A. R. P.					Vol.	Page
36	Rathbarry	47 1 32	Cork, E.R.	Barrymore	Castlelyons	Fermoy	II.	53
8	Rathbaun	594 3 17	Carlow	Carlow	Grangeford	Carlow	I.	2
8	Rathbaun	110 3 23	Clare	Burren	Kilmoon	Ballyvaghan	II.	13
114	Rathbaun	394 0 19	Galway	Dunkellin	Ardrahan	Gort	IV.	27
60	Rathbaun	267 0 0	Galway	Tiaquin	Killosolan	Mountbellew	IV.	78
14	Rathbaun	289 2 8	Leitrim	Drumahaire	Killanummery	Manorhamilton	IV.	98
69, 78	Rathbaun	131 2 9a	Mayo	Carra	Aglish	Castlebar	IV.	124
39, 48	Rathbaun	391 3 37b	Mayo	Tirawley	Ballynahaglish	Ballina	IV.	164
39	Rathbaun	239 3 16c	Mayo	Tirawley	Kilbelfad	Ballina	IV.	168
14	Rathbaun	20 3 2	Mayo	Tirawley	Rathreagh	Killala	IV.	171
14	Rathbaun	211 3 19	Mayo	Tirawley	Templemurry	Killala	IV.	172
26, 33	Rathbaun	716 0 3d	Sligo	Leyny	Kilvarnet	Tobercurry	IV.	232
39	Rathbaun North	108 2 29	Sligo	Corran	Kilturra	Tobercurry	IV.	228
38, 39	Rathbaun South	85 0 15	Sligo	Corran	Kilturra	Tobercurry	IV.	228
14, 15	Rathbawn	111 0 28	Wicklow	Lower Talbotstown	Dunlavin	Baltinglass	I.	360
9, 10	Rathbeagh	648 0 0	Kilkenny	Galmoy	Rathbeagh	Urlingford	I.	93
11	Rathbeal	554 2 7	Dublin	Nethercross	Swords	Balrothery	I.	32
50	Rathbeg	178 2 6	Antrim	Upper Antrim	Donegore	Antrim	III.	6
50	Rathbeg	3 2 17	Antrim	Upper Antrim	Nilteen Grange	Antrim	III.	7
51, 52	Rath Beg	148 0 18	Clare	Bunratty Lower	Feenagh	Tulla	II.	4
112	Rath Beg	39 3 14	Cork, E.R.	Kinsale	Ringcurran	Kinsale	II.	100
68	Rath Beg	1,072 0 10	Kerry	Magunihy	Kilcummin	Killarney	II.	201
47	Rath Beg	216 1 2	Kerry	Magunihy	Kilnanare	Killarney	II.	204
38	Rath Beg	1,155 2 37	King's Co.	Clonlisk	Kilcolman	Parsonstown	I.	130
42, 43	Rathbeg	648 0 19	Tipperary, S.R.	Slievardagh	Fennor	Urlingford	II.	333
44	Rathbeggan	683 2 21	Meath	Ratoath	Rathbeggan	Dunshaughlin	I.	219
11	Rathbennett	333 3 16	Westmeath	Corkaree	Leny	Mullingar	I.	263
11, 14	Rathbody	284 1 4	Louth	Ardee	Tallanstown	Ardee	I.	175
20	Rathbourn or Rathcenmore	201 1 1	Kilkenny	Gowran	St. Martins	Kilkenny	I.	99
22	Rathbrack	419 3 25	Meath	Fore	Killallon	Oldcastle	I.	201
15, 22	Rathbrack	103 0 26	Meath	Fore	Moylagh	Oldcastle	I.	201
10, 16	Rathbrack	187 1 5	Meath	Upper Kells	Dulane	Kells	I.	205
20	Rathbrack	38 2 20	Westmeath	Farbill	Kilucan	Mullingar	I.	267
6, 10	Rathbrackan	305 1 10	Longford	Granard	Abbeylara	Granard	I.	154
9	Rathbrady Beg (alias) Newtown Limavady	293 0 35e	Londonderry	Keenaght	Drumachose	NewTⁿLimavady	III.	235
9	Rathbrady More	326 1 21	Londonderry	Keenaght	Drumachose	NewTⁿLimavady	III.	235
14	Rathbraghan	262 1 13	Sligo	Carbury	Calry	Sligo	IV.	220
20, 21	Rathbran	378 2 21	Wicklow	Upper Talbotstown	Rathbran	Baltinglass	I.	365
21	Rathbranagh	443 3 7	Limerick	Coshma	Croom	Croom	II.	242
13	Rathbran Beg	608 2 11	Meath	Lower Slane	Killary	Ardee	I.	223
12, 13	Rathbranchurch	831 2 29	Meath	Lower Slane	Killary	Ardee	I.	223
13	Rathbran More	694 1 0	Meath	Lower Slane	Killary	Ardee	I.	223
13	Rathbrennan	141 3 7	Queen's Co.	Maryborough East	Straboe	Mountmellick	I.	242
39	Rathbrennan	315 3 13	Roscommon	Ballintober South	Roscommon	Roscommon	IV.	190
17,18,22,23	Rathbride	1,052 0 19	Kildare	Offaly East	Tully	Naas	I.	71
11, 14	Rathbrist	569 1 31	Louth	Louth	Louth	Ardee	I.	184
61	Rathbrit	315 0 3	Tipperary, S.R.	Middlethird	Kilconnell	Cashel	II.	327
25	Rathcabaun	205 3 11	Clare	Inchiquin	Ruan	Corrofin	II.	28
38, 42	Rathcahill	186 0 38	King's Co.	Clonlisk	Kilmurryely	Roscrea	I.	131
36, 42, 44	Rathcahill East	746 0 25	Limerick	Glenquin	Monagay	Newcastle	II.	247
43	Rathcahill West	1,041 3 17	Limerick	Glenquin	Monagay	Newcastle	II.	247
10	Rathcaled	383 2 38	Westmeath	Rathconrath	Rathconrath	Mullingar	I.	284
77	Rathcallan	244 0 12	Cork, E.R.	Imokilly	Ightermurragh	Middleton	II.	87
26	Rathcam or Lemongrove	263 2 14	Westmeath	Fartullagh	Enniscoffey	Mullingar	I.	268
55, 66	Rathcanning	507 2 16	Cork, E.R.	Imokilly	Dungourney	Middleton	II.	86
31, 39	Rathcannon	2,130 3 17	Limerick	Coshma	Athlacca	Kilmallock	II.	241
21, 22	Rathcarbry	326 0 29	Armagh	Orior Lower	Loughgilly	Newry	III.	57
34	Rathcardan	164 3 16	Tipperary, N.R.	Kilnamanagh Upper	Glenkeen	Thurles	II.	278
24	Rathcarra	34 3 15	Westmeath	Rathconrath	Ballymorin	Mullingar	I.	282
30	Rathcarran	778 2 24	Meath	Lune	Athboy	Trim	I.	207
34	Rathcarran	121 1 33	Roscommon	Ballymoe	Drumatemple	Castlereagh	IV.	191
110, 118	Rathcarreen	116 0 14	Mayo	Kilmaine	Ballinrobe	Ballinrobe	IV.	153
14	Rathcarrick	134 0 25	Sligo	Carbury	Killaspugbrone	Sligo	IV.	222
33	Rathcarstown	121 0 10	Meath	Upper Duleek	Clonalvy	Drogheda	I.	197
20	Rathcash	36 0 39	Kilkenny	Gowran	Blanchvilleskill	Kilkenny	I.	93
14, 21, 22	Rathcash	324 3 20	Mayo	Tirawley	Killala	Killala	IV.	169
20	Rathcash East	198 2 36	Kilkenny	Gowran	Tiscoffin	Kilkenny	I.	99
20	Rathcash Little	11 1 23	Kilkenny	Gowran	Tiscoffin	Kilkenny	I.	99
20	Rathcash West	149 0 4	Kilkenny	Gowran	Tiscoffin	Kilkenny	I.	99
11	Rathcassan	187 2 8	Louth	Louth	Louth	Dundalk	I.	184

(a) Including 4A. 2R. 18P. water.
(b) Including 3A. 3R. 39P. water.
(c) Including 4A. 0R. 31P. water.
(d) Including 3½A. 3R. 26P. water.
(e) Including 10A. 2R. 15P. water.

No. of Sheet of the Ordnance Survey Maps.	Townlands and Towns.	Area in Statute Acres.			County.	Barony.	Parish.	Poor Law Union in 1857.	Townland Census of 1851, Part I.	
		A.	R.	P.					Vol.	Page
17	Rathcastle	145	2	10	Westmeath	Rathconrath	Rathconrath	Mullingar	I.	284
16, 17	Rathclare	443	0	39	Cork, E.R.	Orrery and Kilmore	Buttevant	Mallow	II.	107
79	Rathclarish	314	3	1	Tipperary, S.R.	Iffa and Offa East	Kilmurry	Carrick on Suir	II.	314
12	Rathclevin	137	3	29	Kilkenny	Crannagh	Tubbridbritain	Urlingford	I.	87
17	Rathcline	1,168	1	22	Longford	Rathcline	Rathcline	Longford	I.	165
5, 6, 10, 11	Rathclittagh	227	0	38a	Westmeath	Moygoish	Rathaspick	Mullingar	I.	280
23	Rathclogh	582	2	20	Kilkenny	Shillelogher	Danesfort	Thomastown	I.	114
53, 61	Rathclogh North	162	1	35	Tipperary, S.R.	Middlethird	Ballysheehan	Cashel	II.	325
61	Rathclogh South	172	0	39	Tipperary, S.R.	Middlethird	Ballysheehan	Cashel	II.	325
60, 68	Rathcloheen	365	2	21	Tipperary, S.R.	Clanwilliam	Relickmurry & Athassel	Tipperary	II.	310
11, 19	Rathclonbrackan or Rathvilla	720	3	18	King's Co.	Coolestown	Monasteroris	Edenderry	I.	133
26	Rathclooney	737	0	3b	Clare	Bunratty Upper	Clooney	Tulla	II.	8
53, 54	Rathcobane	21	2	20	Cork, E.R.	Barrymore	Gortroe	Middleton	II.	55
53, 54	Rathcobane	558	3	31	Cork, E.R.	Barrymore	Templebodan	Middleton	II.	58
11	Rathcobican	675	2	3	King's Co.	Warrenstown	Ballymacwilliam	Edenderry	I.	144
2, 3	Rathcoffey	189	0	5	Queen's Co.	Tinnahinch	Rearymore	Mountmellick	I.	250
10	Rathcoffey Demesne	222	0	3	Kildare	Ikeathy & Oughterany	Balraheen	Celbridge	I.	56
10	Rathcoffey North	216	1	8	Kildare	Ikeathy & Oughterany	Balraheen	Celbridge	I.	56
10	Rathcoffey South	255	2	1	Kildare	Ikeathy & Oughterany	Balraheen	Celbridge	I.	56
17	Rathcogue	188	3	36	Westmeath	Rathconrath	Piercetown	Ballymahon	I.	283
18, 19	Rathcolman	307	0	1	Westmeath	Moyashel and Magheradernon	Mullingar	Mullingar	I.	275
31	Rathconnell	374	2	7	Kildare	Offaly West	Fontstown	Athy	I.	72
19	Rathconnell	575	0	22c	Westmeath	Moyashel and Magheradernon	Rathconnell	Mullingar	I.	276
31	Rathconnell Wood	517	3	13	Kildare	Offaly West	Fontstown	Athy	I.	72
24, 30	Rathconny	335	2	35	Meath	Lune	Rathmore	Trim	I.	208
35	Rathconor	1,045	3	27	Roscommon	Ballintober South	Kilbride	Roscommon	IV.	189
17, 18	Rathconrath	152	2	12	Westmeath	Rathconrath	Rathconrath	Mullingar	I.	284
18	RATHCONRATH T.	—			Westmeath	Rathconrath	Rathconrath	Mullingar	I.	284
17, 18	Rathconvil	322	1	13	Armagh	Orior Lower	Loughgilly	Newry	III.	57
30, 39	Rathcool	979	2	15d	Cork, E.R.	Duhallow	Dromtarriff	Millstreet	II.	71
139, 140	Rathcool	401	0	29	Cork, W.R.	West Carbery (W.D.)	Skull	Skull	II.	146
45	Rathcool	129	2	16	Meath	Ratoath	Ratoath	Dunshaughlin	I.	219
62, 70	Rathcool	364	3	16	Tipperary, S.R.	Middlethird	Rathcool	Cashel	II.	329
50	Rathcoola East	554	3	2	Cork, E.R.	East Muskerry	Donaghmore	Macroom	II.	103
50	Rathcoola West	493	1	6	Cork, E.R.	East Muskerry	Donaghmore	Macroom	II.	103
21	Rathcoole	417	1	19	Dublin	Newcastle	Rathcoole	Celbridge	I.	34
17, 18	Rathcoole	218	1	31	Louth	Ardee	Dromin	Ardee	I.	172
21	RATHCOOLE T.	—			Dublin	Newcastle	Rathcoole	Celbridge	I.	34
18	Rathcoon	613	3	28	Meath	Morgallion	Kilberry	Navan	I.	209
63	Rathcooney	229	0	38	Cork, E.R.	Cork	Rathcooney	Cork	II.	65
41	Rathcooney	27	3	29	Tipperary, N.R.	Eliogarty	Thurles	Thurles	II.	273
10	Rathcor	164	1	1	Longford	Granard	Granard	Granard	I.	157
8	Rathcor	654	1	4	Louth	Lower Dundalk	Carlingford	Dundalk	I.	176
12, 13	Rathcorbally	175	1	2	Westmeath	Corkaree	Taghmon	Mullingar	I.	264
42, 48	Rathcore	828	3	12	Meath	Lower Moyfenrath	Rathcore	Trim	I.	211
25	Rathcore	163	3	27	Westmeath	Rathconrath	Churchtown	Mullingar	I.	282
25	Rathcorick	207	1	36	Cavan	Upper Loughtee	Annagelliff	Cavan	III.	82
44	Rathcormack	202	1	17	Cork, E.R.	Barrymore	Rathcormack	Fermoy	II.	57
35, 44	Rathcormack-mountain	481	2	4	Cork, E.R.	Barrymore	Rathcormack	Fermoy	II.	57
44	RATHCORMACK T.	—			Cork, E.R.	Barrymore	Rathcormack	Fermoy	II.	57
29, 35	Rathcormick	622	0	32	Meath	Lune	Kildalkey	Trim	I.	208
24	Rathcorrig or Rathcusack	170	2	8e	Kilkenny	Gowran	Woolengrange	Thomastown	I.	100
8	RATHCOR T.	—			Louth	Lower Dundalk	Carlingford	Dundalk	I.	177
104	Rathcosgry	369	1	28	Galway	Dunkellin	Ardrahan	Loughrea	IV.	27
33	Rathcot	138	0	21	Wicklow	Ballinacor South	Hacketstown	Shillelagh	I.	349
60	Rathcoun	318	2	33	Tipperary, S.R.	Middlethird	St. Patricksrock	Cashel	II.	331
76	Rathcoursey East	252	0	1	Cork, E.R.	Imokilly	Garranekinnefeake	Middleton	II.	86
76	RATHCOURSEY T.	—			Cork, E.R.	Imokilly	Garranekinnefeake	Middleton	II.	86
76	Rathcoursey West	214	2	7	Cork, E.R.	Imokilly	Garranekinnefeake	Middleton	II.	86
28, 33	Rathcoyle Lower	359	3	2	Wicklow	Ballinacor South	Kiltegan	Baltinglass	I.	350
28, 33	Rathcoyle Upper	272	2	3	Wicklow	Ballinacor South	Kiltegan	Baltinglass	I.	350
33	Rathcraggaun	188	1	3	Clare	Islands	Drumcliff	Ennis	II.	30
9, 14	Rathcrea	404	1	6	Queen's Co.	Stradbally	Moyanna	Athy	I.	247
21	Rathcreedan	274	3	30	Dublin	Newcastle	Rathcoole	Celbridge	I.	34
3	Rathcreevagh	437	0	4	Westmeath	Fore	Lickbla	Castletowndelvin	I.	270
35, 41	Rathcriddoge	220	0	4	Tipperary, N.R.	Eliogarty	Rahelty	Thurles	II.	272
20	Rathcrihane	18	0	27	Kerry	Clanmaurice	Ardfert	Tralee	II.	167
7	Rathcrogue	422	0	8	Carlow	Carlow	Tullowmagimma	Carlow	I.	2
10, 11	Rathcronan	201	2	29	Longford	Granard	Granard	Granard	I.	157
40	Rathcrony	357	2	24	Clare	Islands	Kilmaley	Ennis	II.	31

(a) Including 4A. 1R. 32P. water.
(b) Including 27A. 3R. 16P. water.
(c) Including 5A. 0R. 18P. water.
(d) Including 5A. 1R. 14P. water.
(e) Including 4A. 2R. 3P. River Nore.

5 G

No. of Sheet of the Ordnance Survey Maps.	Townlands and Towns.	Area in Statute Acres.	County.	Barony.	Parish.	Poor Law Union in 1857.	Townland Census of 1851, Part I.	
		A. R. P.					Vol.	Page
27	Rathculbin . .	646 2 35	Kilkenny . .	Kells . . .	Mallardstown . .	Callan . .	I.	110
84	Rathculleen . .	225 0 23	Cork, E.R. .	East Muskerry .	Kilbonane . .	Bandon . .	II.	104
9, 10	Rathculliheen . .	305 2 18	Waterford . .	Gaultiere . .	Kilculliheen . .	Waterford . .	II.	363
19	Rathcumber . .	213 1 5	Armagh . .	Tiranny . .	Tynan . . .	Armagh . .	III.	60
42, 48	Rathcunikeen . .	160 1 10	Tipperary, N.R. .	Eliogarty . .	Ballymurreen . .	Thurles . .	II.	269
24	Rathcunningham .	221 1 24	Down . .	Dufferin . .	Killyleagh . .	Downpatrick .	III.	167
88	Rathcuppoge . .	102 1 3	Cork, E.R. .	Imokilly . .	Cloyne . . .	Middleton . .	II.	85
88	Rathcuppoge . .	32 2 12	Cork, E.R. .	Imokilly . .	Titeskin . .	Middleton . .	II.	90
42	Rathcurby North .	124 3 24	Kilkenny . .	Iverk . . .	Rathkieran . .	Waterford . .	I.	107
42, 43	Rathcurby South .	277 2 9	Kilkenny . .	Iverk . . .	Rathkieran . .	Waterford . .	I.	107
24	Rathcusack or Rath-corrig . .	170 2 8a	Kilkenny . .	Gowran . .	Woolengrange . .	Thomastown .	I.	100
27	Rathdaggan . .	69 0 21	Cork, E.R. .	Fermoy . .	Glanworth . .	Fermoy . .	II.	79
28	Rathdangan . .	298 0 16	Wicklow . .	Upper Talbotstown .	Kiltegan . .	Baltinglass .	I.	365
3	Rathdaniel . .	588 3 13	Carlow . .	Rathvilly . .	Kineagh . .	Baltinglass .	I.	12
20, 21	Rathdaniel . .	726 3 15	Louth . .	Ferrard . .	Mullary . .	Drogheda . .	I.	182
67	Rathdermot . .	119 0 39	Tipperary, S.R. .	Clanwilliam . .	Templeneiry . .	Tipperary . .	II.	311
6	Rathdiveen . .	102 0 9	Roscommon . .	Boyle . . .	Ardcarn . .	Boyle . .	IV.	193
6	Rathdiveen . .	91 2 39	Roscommon . .	Boyle . . .	Kilbryan . .	Boyle . .	IV.	195
44,45,52,53	Rathdonnell . .	684 2 33	Donegal . .	Kilmacrenan . .	Kilmacrenan . .	Letterkenny .	III.	129
22	Rathdonnell . .	145 2 25	Sligo . .	Tireragh . .	Castleconor . .	Ballina . .	IV.	232
33	Rathdoony Beg .	316 1 19	Sligo . .	Corran . .	Emlaghfad . .	Sligo . .	IV.	226
33	Rathdoony More .	496 1 23	Sligo . .	Corran . .	Emlaghfad . .	Sligo . .	IV.	226
28	Rathdowney . .	553 1 6	Queen's Co. .	Clandonagh . .	Rathdowney . .	Donaghmore .	I.	234
48	Rathdowney . .	43 2 18	Wexford . .	Forth . . .	Ballybrennan . .	Wexford . .	I.	308
48	Rathdowney . .	62 0 16	Wexford . .	Forth . . .	Ladysisland . .	Wexford . .	I.	311
48	Rathdowney . .	77 2 20	Wexford . .	Forth . . .	St. Michael's . .	Wexford . .	I.	314
28	RATHDOWNEY T. .	—	Queen's Co. .	Clandonagh . .	Rathdowney . .	Donaghmore .	I.	234
8	Rathdown Lower .	378 0 16	Wicklow . .	Rathdown . .	Delgany . .	Rathdown . .	I.	355
8	Rathdown Upper .	497 1 0	Wicklow . .	Rathdown . .	Delgany . .	Rathdown . .	I.	355
26	Rathdrinagh . .	757 3 28	Meath . .	Lower Duleek . .	Knockcommon . .	Navan . .	I.	196
25	Rathdrishoge . .	382 2 16	Westmeath . .	Moycashel . .	Castletownkindalen	Mullingar .	I.	277
111	Rathdrought . .	1,242 0 30	Cork, W.R. .	East Carbery (E.D.) .	Ballinadee . .	Bandon . .	II.	126
45, 54	Rathdrum . .	336 2 37	Cork, E.R. .	Kinnatalloon . .	Ballynoe . .	Fermoy . .	II.	97
45, 54	Rathdrum . .	339 1 11	Cork, E.R. .	Kinnatalloon . .	Britway . .	Fermoy . .	II.	98
9, 10, 17, 18	Rathdrum . .	735 2 34	King's Co. .	Lower Philipstown .	Ballycommon . .	Tullamore .	I.	142
70	Rathdrum . .	236 3 16	Tipperary, S.R. .	Middlethird . .	Colman . .	Cashel . .	II.	325
30	Rathdrum . .	291 0 28	Wicklow . .	Ballinacor North .	Rathdrum . .	Rathdrum . .	I.	347
12, 13	Rathdrumgran . .	185 0 3	Armagh . .	Oneilland West .	Loughgall . .	Armagh . .	III.	54
18	Rathdrumin . .	146 1 3	Louth . .	Ferrard . .	Rathdrumin . .	Drogheda . .	I.	182
30	RATHDRUM T. .	—	Wicklow . .	Ballinacor North .	Rathdrum . .	Rathdrum . .	I.	347
38	Rathduane . .	788 3 23b	Cork, W.R. .	West Muskerry .	Drishane . .	Millstreet . .	II.	156
16	Rathduff . .	383 0 7 .	Carlow . .	Idrone East . .	Dunleckny . .	Carlow . .	I.	7
51	Rathduff . .	799 3 13	Cork, E.R. .	Barretts . .	Grenagh . .	Cork . .	II.	49
45	Rathduff . .	136 1 22	Kerry . .	Corkaguiny . .	Ballinvoher . .	Dingle . .	II.	174
5	Rathduff . .	148 1 9	Kilkenny . .	Fassadinin . .	Donaghmore . .	Castlecomer .	I.	89
28	Rathduff . .	373 2 1	Kilkenny . .	Gowran . .	Woolengrange . .	Thomastown .	I.	100
27	Rathduff . .	55 0 36	Kilkenny . .	Kells . . .	Stonecarthy . .	Thomastown .	I.	110
3, 4	Rathduff . .	180 3 24	Louth . .	Upper Dundalk .	Roche . . .	Dundalk . .	I.	179
90, 91	Rathduff . .	431 2 39	Mayo . .	Clanmorris . .	Balla . . .	Castlebar . .	IV.	132
91	Rathduff . .	193 1 22	Mayo . .	Clanmorris . .	Mayo . . .	Castlebar . .	IV.	135
39	Rathduff . .	262 1 30c	Mayo . .	Tirawley . .	Kilbelfad . .	Ballina . .	IV.	168
32	Rathduff . .	40 3 17	Queen's Co. .	Slievemargy . .	Killeshin . .	Carlow . .	I.	246
32	Rathduff . .	114 3 5	Queen's Co. .	Slievemargy . .	Shrule . .	Carlow . .	I.	246
58	Rathduff . .	74 1 11	Tipperary, S.R. .	Clanwilliam . .	Cullen . .	Tipperary . .	II.	307
68	Rathduff . .	71 0 16	Tipperary, S.R. .	Clanwilliam . .	Kilfeakle . .	Tipperary . .	II.	308
68	Rathduff . .	105 0 29	Tipperary, S.R. .	Clanwilliam . .	Relickmurry & Athassel	Tipperary . .	II.	310
30	Rathduff . .	148 0 6	Westmeath . .	Clonlonan . .	Ballyloughloe . .	Athlone . .	I.	261
17, 18	Rathduff . .	295 1 7	Westmeath . .	Rathconrath . .	Rathconrath . .	Mullingar .	I.	284
18	Rathduff . .	517 3 6	Wexford . .	Bantry . .	Killann . .	Enniscorthy .	I.	300
26	Rathduff or Anneville	335 0 8	Westmeath . .	Fartullagh . .	Moylisker . .	Mullingar .	I.	269
27	Rathduff (Bayley) .	75 3 19	Kilkenny . .	Kells . . .	Kells . . .	Callan . .	I.	108
33	Rathduffbeg . .	314 2 32	Wicklow . .	Upper Talbotstown .	Kiltegan . .	Baltinglass .	I.	365
27	Rathduff Lower .	92 0 0	Kilkenny . .	Kells . . .	Kells . . .	Callan . .	I.	108
77	Rathduff Lower .	22 0 28	Tipperary, S.R. .	Iffa and Offa East .	Rathronan . .	Clonmel . .	II.	316
27	Rathduff (Madden) .	99 0 23	Kilkenny . .	Kells . . .	Kells . . .	Callan . .	I.	108
33	Rathduffmore . .	291 3 8	Wicklow . .	Ballinacor South .	Hacketstown . .	Shillelagh .	I.	349
27	Rathduff Upper .	304 3 27	Kilkenny . .	Kells . . .	Kells . . .	Callan . .	I.	108
77	Rathduff Upper .	50 3 7	Tipperary, S.R. .	Iffa and Offa East .	Rathronan . .	Clonmel . .	II.	316
5	Rathe . .	401 2 23	Meath . .	Morgallion . .	Nobber . .	Kells . .	I.	210
16, 17	Rathea . . .	1,665 0 34	Kerry . .	Clanmaurice . .	Kilshenane . .	Listowel . .	II.	172
13	Rathealy . .	596 2 36	Kilkenny . .	Crannagh . .	Tullaroan . .	Kilkenny . .	I.	88
69	Rath East . .	344 1 19	Cork, W.R. .	West Muskerry .	Ballyvourney . .	Macroom . .	II.	154

(a) Including 4A. 2R. 3P. River Nore.   (b) Including 7A. 0R. 20P. water.   (c) Including 21A. 3R. 3P. water.

No. of Sheet of the Ordnance Survey Maps.	Townlands and Towns.	Area in Statute Acres. A. R. P.	County.	Barony.	Parish.	Poor Law Union in 1857.	Townland Census of 1851, Part I. Vol.	Page
37, 42	Rath East	399 2 14	Wicklow	Shillelagh	Liscolman	Shillelagh	I.	357
12, 16	Rathedan	639 3 1	Carlow	Idrone East	Agha	Carlow	I.	6
14	Rathedmond	191 0 7	Sligo	Carbury	St. John's	Sligo	IV.	223
20	Ratheenmore or Rathbourn	201 1 1	Kilkenny	Gowran	St. Martins	Kilkenny	I.	99
13	Ratheeragh	207 3 13	Carlow	Forth	Ardoyne	Carlow	I.	3
12, 16	Rathellin	739 3 34a	Carlow	Idrone East	Agha	Carlow	I.	6
44, 46	Rathenny	258 1 32	King's Co.	Clonlisk	Cullenwaine	Roscrea	I.	129
50	Rathenraw	91 1 20	Antrim	Upper Antrim	Antrim	Antrim	III.	5
17	Rathercan	141 0 16	Carlow	Idrone East	Fennagh	Carlow	I.	7
18	Rathernan	511 0 13	Kildare	Connell	Rathernan	Naas	I.	56
20	Ratherrig	246 1 2	Queen's Co.	Ballyadams	Ballyadams	Athy	I.	231
17, 18	Rathescar Middle	319 0 6	Louth	Ardee	Mosstown	Ardee	I.	174
18	Rathescar North	130 0 31	Louth	Ardee	Mosstown	Ardee	I.	174
18, 21	Rathescar South	26 0 3	Louth	Ardee	Mosstown	Ardee	I.	174
14, 21	Ratheskin	612 1 13	Mayo	Tirawley	Kilfian	Killala	IV.	169
13	Ratheven	158 1 36	Queen's Co.	Maryborough East	Borris	Mountmellick	I.	240
13	Ratheven	25 3 6	Queen's Co.	Maryborough East	Straboe	Mountmellick	I.	242
11, 17	Rathevin	62 2 38	Roscommon	Ballintober North	Kilmore	Carᵏ. on Shannon	IV.	187
5, 6	Rathfad	166 1 16	Londonderry	Keenaght	Aghanloo	NewᵀⁿLimavady	III.	234
9	Rathfaddan	53 3 32	Waterford	Middlethird	Trinity Without	Waterford	II.	369
21	Rathfalla	285 2 24	Tipperary, N.R.	Upper Ormond	Lisbunny	Nenagh	II.	292
22	Rathfarnham	603 3 13	Dublin	Rathdown	Rathfarnham	Dublin South	I.	37
22	RATHFARNHAM T.	—	Dublin	Rathdown	Rathfarnham	Dublin South	I.	37
19	Rathfarra	75 1 39	Limerick	Shanid	Shanagolden	Glin	II	258
70, 71	Rathfee	449 0 37	Galway	Clare	Lackagh	Galway	IV.	23
32	Rathfeigh	1,330 2 27	Meath	Skreen	Rathfeigh	Dunshaughlin	I.	221
84	Rathfelane	237 3 30	Cork, E.R.	East Muskerry	Kilbonane	Bandon	II.	104
18	Rathfeston	966 2 32	King's Co.	Upper Philipstown	Geashill	Tullamore	I.	144
106	Rathfield	141 3 33	Kerry	Dunkerron South	Kilcrohane	Cahersiveen	II.	184
53, 64	Rathfilode	301 0 32	Cork, E.R.	Barrymore	Kilquane	Cork	II.	56
42	Rathflesk	300 0 24	Meath	Lower Moyfenrath	Rathmolyon	Trim	I.	211
42, 51	Rathfolan	323 1 15	Clare	Bunratty Lower	Kilnasoolagh	Ennis	II.	6
65, 66	Rathfootera	179 1 8	Cork, E.R.	Barrymore	Dungourney	Middleton	II.	54
103	Rathfragan	67 3 15	Donegal	Tirhugh	Drumhome	Ballyshannon	III.	147
43, 51	Rathfraggan	393 1 17	Tyrone	Clogher	Donacavey	Omagh	III.	294
15	Rathfran	295 3 29	Mayo	Tirawley	Templemurry	Killala	IV.	172
15	Rathfranpark	127 2 27	Mayo	Tirawley	Templemurry	Killala	IV.	172
5	Rathfrask	201 2 30	Sligo	Carbury	Ahamlish	Sligo	IV.	219
36, 37	Rathfreedy	268 0 8	Limerick	Glenquin	Clonelty	Newcastle	II.	245
41	RATHFRYLAND T.	—	Down	{ Upper Iveagh, Lr.pt. Upper Iveagh, Up. pt.	Drumballyroney } Drumgath	Newry	III.	{ 172 175
21	Rathfuadagh	337 2 1	Roscommon	Castlereagh	Baslick	Castlereagh	IV.	199
38, 39	Rathfure	74 2 7	Fermanagh	Knockninny	Kinawley	Lisnaskea	III.	202
19, 25	Rathfylane	349 3 34	Wexford	Bantry	Rossdroit	Enniscorthy	I.	302
68	Rathgallen	351 1 5	Tipperary, S.R.	Clanwilliam	Relickmurry & Athassel	Tipperary	II.	310
6, 7, 11	Rathganny	498 0 18	Westmeath	Corkaree	Multyfarnham	Mullingar	I.	263
22	Rathgar	304 2 39	Dublin	Rathdown	Rathfarnham	Dublin South	I.	37
30	Rathgaroge	494 1 10	Wexford	Bantry	Ballyanne	New Ross	I.	299
33, 39	Rathgarrett	2,582 1 17	Westmeath	Fartullagh	Newtown	Mullingar	I.	269
1, 5	Rathgarry	249 0 20	Kilkenny	Fassadinin	Abbeyleix	Castlecomer	I.	88
20	Rathgarvan or Clifden	484 2 32	Kilkenny	Gowran	Clara	Kilkenny	I.	94
3	Rathgarve	97 3 14	Westmeath	Fore	Rathgarve	Castletowndelvin	I.	271
69, 81	Rathgaskig	607 3 1	Cork, W.R.	West Muskerry	Inchigeelagh	Macroom	II.	158
21	Rathgeean	267 3 11	Sligo	Tirerrill	Killerry	Sligo	IV.	239
13	Rathgeenan	147 0 13	Louth	Ardee	Clonkeen	Ardee	I.	172
22, 23, 25	Rathgeran	1,151 3 14	Carlow	St. Mullins Lower	St. Mullins	New Ross	I.	13
36	Rathgibbon North	226 1 10	King's Co.	Eglish	Drumcullen	Parsonstown	I.	134
36	Rathgibbon South	332 1 22	King's Co.	Eglish	Drumcullen	Parsonstown	I.	134
19,20,25,26	Rathgilbert	512 2 20	Queen's Co.	Ballyadams	Ballyadams	Athy	I.	231
2	Rathgill	312 2 25	Down	Ards Lower	Bangor	Newtownards	III.	157
5, 6	Rathgillon	578 3 22	Meath	Morgallion	Nobber	Kells	I.	210
65	Rathgire	143 3 22	Cork, E.R.	Barrymore	Templenacarriga	Middleton	II.	58
13	Rathglass	348 0 33	Carlow	Rathvilly	Tullowphelim	Carlow	I.	12
107, 110	Rathglass	175 2 18	Donegal	Tirhugh	Inishmacsaint	Ballyshannon	III.	147
86, 98	Rathglass	502 3 32	Galway	Kilconnell	Killaan	Loughrea	IV.	41
29	Rathglass	111 3 25	Mayo	Tirawley	Kilfian	Ballina	IV.	69
22	Rathglass	336 1 17	Sligo	Tireragh	Castleconor	Dromore West	IV.	232
12	Rathglass	227 0 14	Sligo	Tireragh	Templeboy	Dromore West	IV.	236
3	Rathglassane	296 2 2	Cork, E.R.	Fermoy	Ard-keagh	Mallow	II.	76
22	Rathglass East	158 0 23	Mayo	Tirawley	Ballysakeery	Ballina	IV.	165
22, 30	Rathglass West	158 2 2	Mayo	Tirawley	Ballysakeery	Ballina	IV.	165
2, 3	Rathgoggan Middle	529 1 18	Cork, E.R.	Orrery and Kilmore	Rathgoggan	Kilmallock	II.	109

(a) Including 6A. 2R. 7P. River Barrow.

5 G 2

No. of Sheet of the Ordnance Survey Maps.	Townlands and Towns.	Area in Statute Acres.			County.	Barony.	Parish.	Poor Law Union in 1857.	Townland Census of 1851, Part I.	
		A.	R.	P.					Vol.	Page
2, 3	Rathgoggan North .	685	1	26	Cork, E.R. .	Orrery and Kilmore	Rathgoggan .	Kilmallock .	II.	109
2, 3	Rathgoggan South .	335	1	28	Cork, E.R. .	Orrery and Kilmore	Rathgoggan .	Kilmallock .	II.	109
28	Rathgoonan .	66	3	1	Limerick .	Connello Lower	Clonagh .	Rathkeale .	II.	227
17,18,23,24	Rathgoonaun .	1,529	0	21	Sligo .	Tireragh .	Kilmacshalgan	Dromore West	IV.	235
96	Rathgorgin .	604	3	15	Galway .	Athenry .	Kilconierin .	Loughrea .	IV.	4
24	Rathgorman .	56	0	0	Down .	Dufferin .	Killinchy .	Downpatrick .	III.	166
3	Rathgormuck .	112	0	34	Waterford .	Upperthird .	Rathgormuck .	Carrick on Suir	II.	371
3	RATHGORMUCK T. .	—			Waterford .	Upperthird .	Mothel . Rathgormuck .	Carrick on Suir	II.	371
20	Rathgorragh .	159	3	14	Kildare .	South Salt .	Kill .	Naas .	I.	77
28	Rathgorragh Lower	428	0	15	Wicklow .	Upper Talbotstown .	Kiltegan .	Baltinglass .	I.	365
28	Rathgorragh Upper	241	3	28	Wicklow .	Upper Talbotstown .	Kiltegan .	Baltinglass .	I.	365
17	Rathgory .	92	3	10	Donegal .	Kilmacrenan .	Clondavaddog	Milford .	III.	125
17	Rathgory .	39	0	20	Louth .	Ardee .	Ardee .	Ardee .	I.	171
18, 21	Rathgory .	269	0	12	Louth .	Ferrard .	Mullary .	Drogheda .	I.	182
19	Rathgowan or Farranshock .	85	3	38	Westmeath .	Moyashel and Magheradernon	Mullingar .	Mullingar .	I.	275
25, 26	Rathgran .	309	0	34	Sligo .	Leyny .	Kilvarnet .	Tobercurry .	IV.	232
119	Rathgranagher(Lindsay) .	277	3	13	Mayo .	Kilmaine .	Kilmainemore	Ballinrobe .	IV.	156
119, 122	Rathgranagher (Miller .	672	3	17	Mayo .	Kilmaine .	Kilmainemore	Ballinrobe .	IV.	156
119	RATHGRANAGHER T.	—			Mayo .	Kilmaine .	Kilmainemore	Ballinrobe .	IV.	156
4	Rath Great .	193	1	27	Dublin .	Balrothery West	Naul .	Balrothery .	I.	23
11, 12	Rathgreedan .	151	0	3	King's Co. .	Coolestown .	Monasteroris .	Edenderry .	I.	133
31, 35	Rathgrumly .	210	3	13	Kildare .	Narragh&RebanWest	Narraghmore .	Athy .	I.	68
77	Rathhaha .	185	1	9	Cork, E.R. .	Imokilly .	Garryvoe .	Middleton .	II.	87
35	Rath-healy .	222	1	11a	Cork, E.R. .	Condons&Clangibbon	Clondulane .	Fermoy .	II.	60
44	Rath Hill .	258	1	8	Meath .	Ratoath .	Dunshaughlin .	Dunshaughlin .	I.	218
21, 24	Rath, Hill of .	230	2	9	Louth .	Ferrard .	Tullyallen .	Drogheda .	I.	183
5	Rathhugh .	247	2	33	Sligo .	Carbury .	Ahamlish .	Sligo .	IV.	219
6, 11, 12	Rathiddy .	182	3	35	Louth .	Upper Dundalk	Louth .	Dundalk .	I.	179
11	Rathingle .	113	0	5	Dublin .	Nethercross .	Swords .	Balrothery .	I.	32
10	Rathinree Lower .	332	2	39	Meath .	Lower Kells .	Moynalty .	Kells .	I.	204
10, 11	Rathinree Upper .	363	3	24	Meath .	Lower Kells .	Moynalty .	Kells .	I.	204
41, 44	Rathinure .	574	3	19	Kilkenny .	Ida .	Kilcolumb .	Waterford .	I.	102
42	Rathjarney .	126	2	11	Wexford .	Forth .	Rathmacknee .	Wexford .	I.	313
23, 32	Rathjordan .	813	1	15	Limerick .	Clanwilliam .	Rathjordan .	Limerick .	II.	225
66	Rathkea .	282	3	19	Tipperary, S.R.	Clanwilliam .	Bruis .	Tipperary .	II.	305
20, 29	Rathkeale .	302	2	0	Limerick .	Connello Lower	Rathkeale .	Rathkeale .	II.	229
20, 29	Rathkeale Commons .	46	3	34	Limerick .	Connello Lower	Rathkeale .	Rathkeale .	II.	229
29	RATHKEALE T. .	—			Limerick .	Connello Lower	Rathkeale .	Rathkeale .	II.	230
33	Rathkeel .	519	0	9	Antrim .	Lower Antrim .	Racavan .	Ballymena .	III.	4
30	Rathkeelan .	338	2	27	Armagh .	Fews Upper .	Creggan .	Castleblayney .	III.	48
23, 28	Rathkeelan .	390	0	7	Fermanagh .	Magherastephana	Aghavea .	Lisnaskea .	III.	219
24	Rathkeeragan .	106	2	8	King's Co. .	Ballyboy .	Killoughy .	Tullamore .	I.	124
14	Rathkeery .	332	1	21	Roscommon .	Frenchpark .	Tibohine .	Castlereagh .	IV.	205
36	Rathkeevan .	77	3	10	Fermanagh .	Clankelly .	Clones .	Clones .	III.	197
76, 82	Rathkeevin .	481	2	18	Tipperary, S.R.	Iffa and Offa East	Rathronan .	Clonmel .	II.	316
118	Rathkelly .	181	1	4b	Mayo .	Kilmaine .	Ballinrobe .	Ballinrobe .	IV.	153
35	Rathkenna .	344	1	10	Meath .	Lune .	Kildalkey .	Trim .	I.	208
46	Rathkennan .	699	3	8	Tipperary, S.R.	Kilnamanagh Lower	Rathkenny .	Cashel .	II.	324
46	Rathkennanwood .	86	3	18	Tipperary, S.R.	Kilnamanagh Lower	Rathkenny .	Cashel .	II.	324
27, 28	Rathkenny .	521	2	0	Antrim .	Lower Antrim .	Skerry .	Ballymena .	III.	5
21	Rathkenny .	508	3	18	Kerry .	Clanmaurice .	O'Dorney .	Tralee .	II.	173
12, 18	Rathkenny .	1,598	3	3	Meath .	Upper Slane .	Rathkenny .	Navan .	I.	225
62, 63	Rathkenny .	1,075	3	0	Tipperary, S.R.	Middlethird .	Peppardstown .	Cashel .	II.	329
70, 77	Rathkenty .	201	2	1	Tipperary, S.R.	Middlethird .	Kiltinan .	Cashel .	II.	328
41	Rathkerry .	205	3	35	Clare .	Islands .	Drumcliff .	Ennis .	II.	30
22, 28	Rathkeva .	202	0	20	Roscommon .	Roscommon .	Ogulla .	Strokestown .	IV.	212
87, 96	Rathkieran .	295	1	0	Kerry .	Iveragh .	Killemlagh .	Cahersiveen .	II.	196
42	Rathkieran .	319	0	5	Kilkenny .	Iverk .	Rathkieran .	Waterford .	I.	107
43, 49	Rathkilmore .	277	1	5	Meath .	Upper Deece .	Kilmore .	Dunshaughlin .	I.	193
21	Rathkineely .	276	1	22	Roscommon .	Castlereagh .	Kilcorkey .	Castlereagh .	IV.	200
29	Rathkip .	290	2	9	Sligo .	Tireragh .	Kilmoremoy .	Ballina .	IV.	235
5, 10	Rathkyle .	769	1	38	Kilkenny .	Fassadinin .	Kilmacar .	Castlecomer .	I.	90
31, 36	Rathkyle .	474	3	27	Wexford .	Shelmaliere West	Kilgarvan .	New Ross .	I.	334
7, 8	Rathlackan .	642	1	38	Mayo .	Tirawley .	Kilcummin .	Killala .	IV.	168
7, 8	RATHLACKAN T. .	—			Mayo .	Tirawley .	Kilcummin .	Killala .	IV.	168
3	Rathlagan .	101	2	0	Meath .	Lower Slane .	Ardagh .	Kells .	I.	222
3	Rathlagan .	57	3	6	Meath .	Lower Slane .	Drumconrath .	Kells .	I.	223
49, 51	Rathlaheen North .	42	2	24a	Clare .	Bunratty Lower	Tomfinlough .	Ennis .	II.	7
42, 51	Rathlaheen South .	1,425	0	3d	Clare .	Bunratty Lower	Tomfinlough .	Ennis .	II.	7
18	Rathland East .	40	2	5	Dublin .	Uppercross .	St. Catherines .	Dublin South .	I.	40

(a) Including 10A. 1R. 38P. water.
(b) Including 5A. 2R. 18P. water.
(c) Including 26A. 2R. 32P. water.
(d) Including 57A. 0R. 0P. water.

No. of Sheet of the Ordnance Survey Maps.	Townlands and Towns.	Area in Statute Acres.	County.	Barony.	Parish.	Poor Law Union in 1857.	Townland Census of 1851, Part I.	
		A. R. P.					Vol.	Page
18	Rathland West	37 2 0	Dublin	Uppercross	St. Catherines	Dublin South	I.	40
42	Rathlannon	263 0 10	Wexford	Forth	Kildavin	Wexford	I.	310
38	Rathlead	278 1 14	Waterford	Decies within Drum	Ardmore	Dungarvan	II.	350
13, 18	Rathleague	527 3 13	Queen's Co.	Maryborough East	Kilcolmanbane	Mountmellick	I.	241
13	Rathleague	93 0 20	Queen's Co.	Maryborough East	Straboe	Mountmellick	I.	242
5, 9	Rathleash	322 2 7	Queen's Co.	Portnahinch	Lea	Mountmellick	I.	244
34, 35	Rathleasty	382 2 2	Tipperary, N.R.	Eliogarty	Drom	Thurles	II.	269
10, 11	Rathlee	928 0 7	Sligo	Tireragh	Easky	Dromore West	IV.	234
50, 53	Rathleek	279 2 18	Meath	Dunboyne	Dunboyne	Dunshaughlin	I.	199
29, 33	Rathleen	272 1 21	Kilkenny	Gowran	Inistioge	Thomastown	I.	96
26, 27	Rathleg	182 0 23	Roscommon	Castlereagh	Kilkeevin	Castlereagh	IV.	201
32	Rathlena	342 0 30	Roscommon	Castlereagh	Kiltullagh	Castlereagh	IV.	202
12	Rathlevanagh	256 0 5	Westmeath	Corkaree	Portnashangan	Mullingar	I.	263
24	Rathlihen	409 2 29	King's Co.	Ballyboy	Killoughy	Tullamore	I.	124
89	RathlinO'BirneIsland	50 0 38	Donegal	Tirhugh	Kilbarron	Glenties	III.	148
4	Rath Little	140 1 34	Dublin	Balrothery West	Naul	Balrothery	I.	23
8	Rathlogan	146 1 36	Kilkenny	Galmoy	Glashare	Urlingford	I.	92
8	Rathlogan	484 3 7	Kilkenny	Galmoy	Rathlogan	Urlingford	I.	93
83	Rathloose	80 3 19	Tipperary, S.R.	Iffa and Offa East	Kilgrant	Clonmel	II.	314
8	Rath Lower	156 0 4	Louth	Lower Dundalk	Carlingford	Dundalk	I.	176
21	Rath Lower	114 1 8	Waterford	Coshmore&Coshbride	Lismore and Mocollop	Lismore	II.	347
16	Rath Lower	121 0 11	Westmeath	Kilkenny West	Noughaval	Ballymahon	I.	274
43	Rathluby	123 0 32a	Clare	Bunratty Upper	Quin	Tulla	II.	10
11, 19	Rathlumber	389 1 28	King's Co.	Coolestown	Monasteroris	Edenderry	I.	133
17	Rathlust	258 1 8	Louth	Ardee	Kildemock	Ardee	I.	173
8, 9	Rathlyon	413 3 35	Carlow	Rathvilly	Tullowphelim	Carlow	I.	12
17, 18	Rathmacan	656 3 13	Kilkenny	Crannagh	Tullaroan	Kilkenny	I.	88
69	Rathmacarty East	86 1 33	Tipperary, S.R.	Middlethird	Kilbragh	Cashel	II.	327
69	Rathmacarty West	177 2 1	Tipperary, S.R.	Middlethird	Kilbragh	Cashel	II.	327
42, 47	Rathmacknee Great	167 3 29	Wexford	Forth	Rathmacknee	Wexford	I.	313
42, 47	Rathmacknee Little	108 2 28	Wexford	Forth	Rathmacknee	Wexford	I.	313
38	Rathmacostello	110 3 26	Mayo	Tirawley	Crossmolina	Ballina	IV.	166
25	Rathmactiernan	143 1 37	Sligo	Leyny	Killoran	Tobercurry	IV.	231
86	Rathmacullig East	214 3 6	Cork, E.R.	Cork	Killanully	Cork	II.	64
86	Rathmacullig West	241 1 23	Cork, E.R.	Cork	Killanully	Cork	II.	64
44	Rathmadder	162 3 24	Sligo	Coolavin	Kilfree	Boyle	IV.	224
37, 42	Rathmagurry	553 2 31	Sligo	Leyny	Achonry	Tobercurry	IV.	229
23	Rathmaher	98 3 27	Cork, E.R.	Duhallow	Castlemagner	Kanturk	II.	67
19	Rathmaiden	257 0 26	Meath	Upper Slane	Slane	Navan	I.	225
15	Rathmaiden	647 2 1	Waterford	Decies without Drum	Fews	Kilmacthomas	II.	356
29	Rathmakelly Glebe	197 2 6	Queen's Co.	Clarmallagh	Killermogh	Abbeyleix	I.	238
12, 13	Rathnale	183 2 14	Limerick	Pubblebrien	Mungret	Limerick	II.	254
118, 119	Rathmalikeen	129 2 5	Mayo	Kilmaine	Kilcommon	Ballinrobe	IV.	155
45	Rathmalode	47 3 19	Kerry	Corkaguiny	Ballinvoher	Dingle	II.	174
10	Rath (Malone)	37 2 6	Westmeath	Rathconrath	Piercetown	Mullingar	I.	283
41, 42	Rathmanna	45 3 0	Tipperary, N.R.	Eliogarty	Rahelty	Thurles	II.	272
41, 42	Rathmanna	240 3 18	Tipperary, N.R.	Eliogarty	Twomileborris	Thurles	II.	274
5, 11	Rathmanoo	388 1 19	Meath	Lower Kells	Moynalty	Kells	I.	204
8, 14	Rathmea	246 0 17b	Meath	Fore	Killeagh	Oldcastle	I.	201
33	Rathmeague	163 1 9	Wicklow	Ballinacor South	Hacketstown	Shillelagh	I.	349
41	Rathmeehan	55 2 14	Clare	Islands	Killone	Ennis	II.	30
11	Rathmeel	82 0 20	Sligo	Tireragh	Easky	Dromore West	IV.	234
22	Rathmeel	123 2 33	Sligo	Tireragh	Kilmoremoy	Ballina	IV.	235
45, 46	Rathmelton	534 0 2	Donegal	Kilmacrenan	Aughnish	Milford	III.	122
45, 46	RATHMELTON T.	—	Donegal	Kilmacrenan	Aughnish	Milford	III.	122
34	Rathmew	170 3 36	Roscommon	Ballymoe	Oran	Roscommon	IV.	192
26	Rathmichael	409 1 26	Dublin	Rathdown	Rathmichael	Rathdown	I.	37
5, 9	Rathmiles	179 3 26	Queen's Co.	Portnahinch	Lea	Mountmellick	I.	244
18, 22	Rathmines East	117 1 10	Dublin	Uppercross	St. Peters	Dublin South	I.	41
22	Rathmines Great	88 2 15	Dublin	Rathdown	Taney	Rathdown	I.	38
22	Rathmines Little	68 3 25	Dublin	Rathdown	Taney	Rathdown	I.	38
22	Rathmines South	194 3 22	Dublin	Uppercross	St. Peters	Dublin South	I.	41
18, 22	RATHMINES T.	—	Dublin	Uppercross	St. Peters	Dublin South	I.	41
18, 22	Rathmines West	102 2 2	Dublin	Uppercross	St. Peters	Dublin South	I.	41
42	Rathmolyon	198 3 11	Meath	Lower Moyfenrath	Rathmolyon	Trim	I.	211
42	RATHMOLYON T.	—	Meath	Lower Moyfenrath	Rathmolyon	Trim	I.	211
21	Rathmoney	150 0 17	Sligo	Tirerrill	Killerry	Sligo	IV.	239
54, 62	Rathmooley	288 3 35	Tipperary, S.R.	Slievardagh	Killenaule	Cashel	II.	334
26	Rathmoon	281 1 31	Wicklow	Upper Talbotstown	Baltinglass	Baltinglass	I.	362
5, 8	Rathmooney	413 2 36	Dublin	Balrothery East	Lusk	Balrothery	I.	21
35	Rathmoran	84 3 11c	Fermanagh	Clankelly	Clones	Clones	III.	197
50	Rathmore	67 1 36	Antrim	Upper Antrim	Donegore	Antrim	III.	6
50	Rathmore	298 3 32	Antrim	Upper Antrim	Nilteen Grange	Antrim	III.	7

(a) Including 23A. 2R. 7P. water.   (b) Including 11A. 2R. 5P. water.   (c) Including 3A. 3R. 5P. water.

No. of Sheet of the Ordnance Survey Maps.	Townlands and Towns.	Area in Statute Acres.			County.	Barony.	Parish.	Poor Law Union in 1857.	Townland Census of 1851, Part I.	
		A.	R.	P.					Vol.	Page
3	Rathmore	815	0	39	Carlow	Rathvilly	Rathmore	Baltinglass	I.	12
51, 52	Rath More	352	0	9a	Clare	Bunratty Lower	Feenagh	Tulla	II.	4
74	Rathmore	103	2	34b	Cork, E.R.	Cork, Municipal Borough of	St. Annes Shandon	Cork	II.	111
112	Rathmore	47	3	29	Cork, E.R.	Kinsale	Kinsale	Kinsale	II.	100
112, 125	Rathmore	336	0	14	Cork, E.R.	Kinsale	Ringcurran	Kinsale	II.	100
150	Rathmore	709	1	39	Cork, W.R.	West Carbery (E.D.)	Tullagh	Skibbereen	II.	141
107	Rathmore	481	2	7	Donegal	Tirhugh	Inishmacsaint	Ballyshannon	III.	147
8	Rathmore	77	1	13c	Fermanagh	Lurg	Belleek	Ballyshannon	III.	203
43, 57	Rathmore	231	0	35	Galway	Clare	Cummer	Tuam	IV.	19
60, 68	Rath More	785	0	36	Kerry	Magunihy	Kilcummin	Killarney	II.	201
47	Rath More	235	0	7	Kerry	Magunihy	Kilnanare	Killarney	II.	204
22, 30	Rathmore	964	0	2	Kerry	Trughanacmy	O'Brennan	Tralee	II.	212
8	Rathmore	521	2	19	Kildare	Carbury	Ardkill	Edenderry	I.	51
14	Rathmore	417	3	17d	Kildare	Naas North	Bodenstown	Naas	I.	62
38	Rath More	792	3	30	King's Co.	Clonlisk	Kilcolman	Parsonstown	I.	130
11, 12	Rathmore	216	2	35	King's Co.	Coolestown	Monasteroris	Edenderry	I.	133
33	Rathmore	248	2	27	King's Co.	Upper Philipstown	Clonyhurk	Mountmellick	I.	143
5, 6	Rathmore	649	0	6e	Longford	Granard	Columbkille	Longford	I.	156
26, 27	Rathmore	849	0	20f	Longford	Shrule	Noughaval	Ballymahon	I.	166
6	Rathmore	319	3	35	Louth	Upper Dundalk	Philipstown	Dundalk	I.	179
29	Rathmore	626	0	35	Mayo	Tirawley	Crossmolina	Ballina	IV.	166
24, 30	Rathmore	915	3	6	Meath	Lune	Rathmore	Trim	I.	208
28	Rathmore	160	1	31	Monaghan	Farney	Donaghmoyne	Carrickmacross	III.	270
19	Rathmore	175	2	4	Queen's Co.	Ballyadams	Ballyadams	Athy	I.	231
22, 28	Rathmore	409	0	28	Queen's Co.	Clandonagh	Donaghmore	Donaghmore	I.	233
14	Rathmore	407	0	16	Queen's Co.	Stradbally	Stradbally	Athy	I.	247
35	Rathmore	292	3	13	Roscommon	Ballintober South	Kilbride	Roscommon	IV.	189
28	Rathmore	342	3	4	Roscommon	Roscommon	Killukin	Strokestown	IV.	211
17, 23	Rathmore	262	0	36g	Roscommon	Roscommon	Kiltrustan	Strokestown	IV.	211
26	Rathmore	368	3	32	Sligo	Leyny	Killoran	Tobercurry	IV.	231
7, 10	Rathmore	372	3	29	Tipperary, N.R.	Lower Ormond	Borrisokane	Borrisokane	II.	282
76	Rathmore	120	1	19	Tipperary, S.R.	Iffa and Offa West	Caher	Clogheen	II.	318
11, 17, 18	Rathmore	204	2	0	Westmeath	Moygoish	Kilmacnevan	Mullingar	I.	280
48	Rathmore	121	3	11	Wexford	Forth	St. Iberius	Wexford	I.	314
19	Rathmore	194	0	28	Wicklow	Newcastle	Killiskey	Rathdrum	I.	352
107	Rathmoreahanduff	88	2	19	Galway	Longford	Killimorbologue	Portumna	IV.	59
107	Rathmore Demesne	302	2	15	Galway	Longford	Killimorbologue	Portumna	IV.	59
20	Rathmore East	377	1	1	Kildare	Naas North	Rathmore	Naas	I.	63
22, 31	Rathmore North	718	0	11	Limerick	Smallcounty	Monasteranenagh	Croom	II.	261
31	Rathmore South	594	1	22	Limerick	Smallcounty	Monasteranenagh	Croom	II.	261
19, 20, 25	Rathmore West	927	2	16	Kildare	Naas North	Rathmore	Naas	I.	63
3, 8	Rathmorgan	541	0	16	Cork, E.R.	Orrery and Kilmore	Ballyhay	Kilmallock	II.	106
18	Rathmorgan	965	0	16	Mayo	Erris	Kilcommon	Belmullet	IV.	144
14, 15	Rathmorrel	236	2	33	Kerry	Clanmaurice	Killury	Listowel	II.	171
84	Rathmorrissy	617	1	7	Galway	Athenry	Athenry	Loughrea	IV.	4
30, 31	Rathmount	38	2	10	King's Co.	Eglish	Drumcullen	Parsonstown	I.	134
100, 104	Rath Mountain	710	3	8h	Donegal	Tirhugh	Drumhome	Donegal	III.	147
34	Rathmoy	456	0	37	Tipperary, N.R.	Kilnamanagh Upper	Glenkeen	Thurles	II.	279
27	Rathmoylan	280	1	23	Waterford	Gaultiere	Rathmoylan	Waterford	II.	364
104	Rathmoyle	67	3	30	Galway	Dunkellin	Killeely	Gort	IV.	30
13, 18	Rathmoyle	374	0	3	Kilkenny	Crannagh	Ballinamara	Kilkenny	I.	84
46	Rathmoyle	102	0	15	King's Co.	Clonlisk	Borrisnafarney	Roscrea	I.	129
11	Rathmoyle	343	1	29	King's Co.	Warrenstown	Ballyburly	Edenderry	I.	144
29	Rathmoyle	123	1	9	Mayo	Tirawley	Crossmolina	Ballina	IV.	166
23, 24	Rathmoyle	774	1	39	Queen's Co.	Cullenagh	Abbeyleix	Abbeyleix	I.	238
21	Rathmoyle	545	1	22	Roscommon	Castlereagh	Baslick	Castlereagh	IV.	199
27	Rathmuck	297	0	7	Kildare	Offaly West	Duneany	Athy	I.	72
37	Rathmullan	484	0	36	Donegal	Kilmacrenan	Killygarvan	Milford	III.	128
20	Rathmullan	776	0	28	Meath	Lower Duleek	Donore	Drogheda	I.	195
44	Rathmullan Lower	743	1	34	Down	Lecale Upper	Rathmullan	Downpatrick	III.	181
37	RATHMULLAN T.	—			Donegal	Kilmacrenan	Killygarvan	Milford	III.	128
44	Rathmullan Upper	207	0	30	Down	Lecale Upper	Rathmullan	Downpatrick	III.	181
27, 34	Rathmulpatrick	224	0	30	Sligo	Tirerrill	Kilmacallan	Sligo	IV.	240
22	Rathmurphy	104	2	8	Sligo	Tireragh	Castleconor	Dromore West	IV.	232
24, 32	Rathmurragh	184	3	15	King's Co.	Ballyboy	Killoughy	Tullamore	I.	124
5	Rathnabo	121	1	10	Wicklow	Lower Talbotstown	Blessington	Naas	I.	358
7	Rathnacally	319	2	17	Cork, E.R.	Orrery and Kilmore	Cooliney	Kilmallock	II.	108
26	Rathnacarton	293	0	4	Cork, E.R.	Fermoy	Castletownroche	Mallow	II.	78
39	Rathnaconeen	193	0	32i	Mayo	Tirawley	Ballynahaglish	Ballina	IV.	164
90, 100	Rathnacreeva	694	2	38	Mayo	Carra	Rosslee	Ballinrobe	IV.	130
21	Rathnadoffy	183	0	23	Mayo	Tirawley	Rathreagh	Killala	IV.	171
5	Rathnafushoge	256	2	5	Carlow	Rathvilly	Hacketstown	Shillelagh	I.	11

(a) Including 0A. 2R. 20P. water.
(b) Included in the Parish of St. Anne Shandon.
(c) { Including 4A. 2R. 35P. White Island.
       Including 16A. 1R. 17P. water.
(d) Including 11A. 0R. 18P. water.
(e) Including 3A. 0R. 13P. water.
(f) Including 9A. 2R. 27P. water.
(g) Including 19A. 2R. 15P. water.
(h) Including 40A. 2R. 12P. water.
(i) Including 3A. 3R. 34P. water.

No. of Sheet of the Ordnance Survey Maps.	Townlands and Towns.	Area in Statute Acres.			County.	Barony.	Parish.	Poor Law Union in 1857.	Townland Census of 1851, Part I.	
		A.	R.	P.					Vol.	Page
15	Rathnagard	239	0	35	Cork, E.R.	Duhallow	Kilbrin	Kanturk	II.	72
20	Rathnageeragh	684	0	23	Carlow	Idrone East	Fennagh	Carlow	I.	7
35	Rathnageeragh	468	2	35	Wexford	Shelburne	Owenduff	New Ross	I.	328
22	Rathnaglye	234	3	37	Roscommon	Roscommon	Ogulla	Strokestown	IV.	212
19, 28	Rathnagore	78	1	12	Limerick	Shanid	Kilbradran	Rathkeale	II.	255
5	Rathnagrew Lower	226	1	35	Carlow	Rathvilly	Hacketstown	Shillelagh	I.	11
5	Rathnagrew Upper	380	1	35	Carlow	Rathvilly	Hacketstown	Shillelagh	I.	11
118	Rathnaguppaun	282	0	10	Mayo	Kilmaine	Ballinrobe	Ballinrobe	IV.	153
33	Rathnakelliga	48	1	18	Sligo	Corran	Emlaghfad	Sligo	IV.	226
20, 21	Rathnaleen North	392	2	39	Tipperary, N.R.	Upper Ormond	Lisbunny	Nenagh	II.	292
21	Rathnaleen South	327	2	35	Tipperary, N.R.	Upper Ormond	Lisbunny	Nenagh	II.	292
27	Rathnaleugh	269	2	6	Queen's Co.	Clandonagh	Rathdowney	Donaghmore	I.	234
21	Rathnallog	412	0	28	Roscommon	Castlereagh	Kilcorkey	Castlereagh	IV.	200
31, 37	Rathnally	394	3	33a	Meath	Upper Navan	Kilcooly	Trim	I.	216
76	Rathnalour	79	0	8	Tipperary, S.R.	Iffa and Offa East	Newchapel	Clonmel	II.	315
27, 34	Rathnalulleagh	334	3	13	Roscommon	Castlereagh	Ballintober	Castlereagh	IV.	198
29	Rathnamagh	752	1	12	Mayo	Tirawley	Kilfian	Ballina	IV.	169
13	Rathnamanagh	391	3	33	Queen's Co.	Maryborough East	Borris	Mountmellick	I.	240
36	Rathnameneenagh	364	2	4	Waterford	Decies within Drum	Ardmore	Dungarvan	II.	350
36	Rathnameneenagh	254	1	12	Waterford	Decies within Drum	Ringagonagh	Dungarvan	II.	353
25	Rathnamuddagh	1,538	2	4	Westmeath	Moyashel and Magheradernon	Dysart	Mullingar	I.	274
36	Rathnaneane	116	0	36	Limerick	Glenquin	Monagay	Newcastle	II.	247
2, 7	Rathnapish	368	2	10	Carlow	Carlow	Carlow	Carlow	I.	1
17	Rathnarovanagh	182	0	26b	Roscommon	Ballintober North	Kilmore	Cark. on Shannon	IV.	187
20	Rathnarrow	107	3	39	Westmeath	Farbill	Killucan	Mullingar	I.	267
26	Rathnarrow (Brett)	218	3	27	Sligo	Leyny	Kilvarnet	Tobercurry	IV.	232
26	Rathnarrow (O'Hara)	283	2	18	Sligo	Leyny	Kilvarnet	Tobercurry	IV.	232
97	Rathnaruogy	421	1	31	Cork, E.R.	Kinalea	Inishannon	Bandon	II.	95
29	Rathnaseer	483	0	37	Limerick	Connello Lower	Nantinan	Rathkeale	II.	229
8	Rathnashannagh	165	0	25	Carlow	Carlow	Grangeford	Carlow	I.	2
24	Rathnaskilloge	223	0	14	Waterford	Decies without Drum	Stradbally	Kilmacthomas	II.	361
77	Rathnasliggeen	120	2	19	Tipperary, S.R.	Iffa and Offa East	Kiltegan	Clonmel	II.	315
40, 43	Rathnasmolagh	337	0	8	Kilkenny	Ida	Dunkitt	Waterford	I.	101
17	Rathnaveoge Lower	520	1	18	Tipperary, N.R.	Ikerrin	Rathnaveoge	Roscrea	II.	276
17	Rathnaveoge Upper	428	1	23	Tipperary, N.R.	Ikerrin	Rathnaveoge	Roscrea	II.	276
14	Rathnawooraun	120	0	9	Mayo	Tirawley	Templemurry	Killala	IV.	172
59	Rathneaveen (Ormond)	148	3	16	Tipperary, S.R.	Clanwilliam	Tipperary	Tipperary	II.	312
59	Rathneaveen (Ryan)	195	0	19	Tipperary, S.R.	Clanwilliam	Tipperary	Tipperary	II.	312
52	Rathnedan	71	3	39	Wexford	Forth	Ballymore	Wexford	I.	308
24	Rathnee	178	1	37	Cork, E.R.	Orrery and Kilmore	Ballyclogh	Mallow	II.	106
11, 14	Rathneestin	634	2	35	Louth	Ardee	Philipstown	Ardee	I.	174
11	Rathneety	181	2	22	Louth	Louth	Killincoole	Dundalk	I.	184
11	Rathneety	27	0	25	Louth	Louth	Louth	Dundalk	I.	184
24	Rathnew	92	2	34	Westmeath	Rathconrath	Conry	Mullingar	I.	282
25	RATHNEW T.	—			Wicklow	Newcastle	Rathnew	Rathdrum	I.	354
32	Rathnugent	107	3	33	Westmeath	Moycashel	Castletownkindalen	Mullingar	I.	277
32, 33	Rathnure	197	3	26	Westmeath	Fartullagh	Clonfad	Mullingar	I.	268
25	Rathnure	265	2	30	Wexford	Bantry	Rossdroit	Enniscorthy	I.	302
18, 24	Rathnure Lower	477	0	17	Wexford	Bantry	Killann	Enniscorthy	I.	300
18, 24	Rathnure Upper	382	0	26	Wexford	Bantry	Killann	Enniscorthy	I.	300
88	Rathokelly	207	2	34c	Tipperary, S.R.	Iffa and Offa West	Molough	Clogheen	II.	318
88	Rathokelly	35	1	17d	Tipperary, S.R.	Iffa and Offa West	Neddans	Clogheen	II.	319
48	Ratholm	97	3	11	Wexford	Forth	Ballybrennan	Wexford	I.	308
21	Rathoma	626	2	30e	Mayo	Tirawley	Ballysakeery	Ballina	IV.	165
71, 72	Rathonoane	408	2	13	Cork, E.R.	East Muskerry	Cannaway	Macroom	II.	102
14	Rathonoragh	106	2	3	Sligo	Carbury	Killaspugbrone	Sligo	IV.	222
7, 14	Rathoonagh	551	3	20	Mayo	Tirawley	Kilbride	Killala	IV.	168
12, 17, 18	Rathoran	354	1	39f	Kerry	Iraghticonnor	Duagh	Listowel	II.	190
61	Rathordan	842	3	4	Tipperary, S.R.	Middlethird	St. Patricksrock	Cashel	II.	331
54, 65	Rathorgan	323	3	0	Cork, E.R.	Barrymore	Dungourney	Middleton	II.	54
12	Rathornan	319	2	13g	Carlow	Idrone West	Tullowcreen	Carlow	I.	9
13, 14	Rathory	227	1	13	Louth	Ardee	Tallanstown	Ardee	I.	175
8	Rathoscar	90	2	18	Kilkenny	Galmoy	Fertagh	Urlingford	I.	92
19, 25, 26	Rathosey	1,012	0	3	Sligo	Leyny	Killoran	Tobercurry	IV.	231
8	Rathosheen	132	2	10	Kilkenny	Galmoy	Erke	Urlingford	I.	92
6	Rathowen	307	3	1	Westmeath	Moygoish	Rathaspick	Granard	I.	280
6	Rathowen	59	3	5	Westmeath	Moygoish	Russagh	Granard	I.	280
22	Rathowen East	246	3	29	Mayo	Tirawley	Killala	Killala	IV.	170
6	Rathowen (Edward)	93	3	19	Westmeath	Moygoish	Rathaspick	Granard	I.	280
6	RATHOWEN T.	—			Westmeath	Moygoish	Rathaspick	Granard	I.	280
21, 22	Rathowen West	221	1	19	Mayo	Tirawley	Killala	Killala	IV.	170
45	Rathpalatine	347	2	24	Limerick	Glenquin	Mahoonagh	Newcastle	II.	246

(a) Including 13A. 2R. 13P. water. (d) Including 3A. 3R. 0P. water. (f) Including 3A. 0R. 16P. water.
(b) Including 7A. 3R. 8P. water. (e) Including 0A. 1R. 33P. water. (g) Including 6A. 0R. 32P. River Barrow.
(c) Including 0A. 2R. 32P. water.

No. of Sheet of the Ordnance Survey Maps.	Townlands and Towns.	Area in Statute Acres.	County.	Barony.	Parish.	Poor Law Union in 1857.	Townland Census of 1851, Part I.	
		A. R. P.					Vol.	Page
3, 7, 8	Rathpatrick	988 3 36	Kilkenny	Galmoy	Erke	Urlingford	I.	92
43, 44	Rathpatrick	365 3 25	Kilkenny	Ida	Rathpatrick	Waterford	I.	103
63, 74	Rathpeacon	719 2 12	Cork, E.R.	Cork	Whitechurch	Cork	II.	66
54	Rathpeak	761 0 7	Roscommon	Moycarn	Moore	Ballinasloe	IV.	207
24	Rathphaudin	545 1 18	Wexford	Bantry	Templeludigan	New Ross	I.	303
22	Rathphelan	222 1 2	Queen's Co.	Upperwoods	Offerlane	Abbeyleix	I.	252
2, 3	Rathpierce Hill	315 3 10	Wexford	Gorey	Kilnenor	Gorey	I.	320
3	Rathpierce Lower	169 3 19	Wexford	Gorey	Kilnenor	Gorey	I.	320
3	Rathpierce Upper	235 3 12	Wexford	Gorey	Kilnenor	Gorey	I.	320
28	Rathpiper North	6 0 35	Queen's Co.	Clarmallagh	Rathdowney	Donaghmore	I.	238
28, 34	Rathpiper South	92 1 26	Queen's Co.	Clandonagh	Rathdowney	Donaghmore	I.	234
47	Rathpoge East	212 1 26	Kerry	Trughanacmy	Kilcolman	Killarney	II.	210
47	Rathpoge West	191 2 16	Kerry	Trughanacmy	Kilcolman	Killarney	II.	210
8	Rathpoleen	269 1 0	Kilkenny	Galmoy	Erke	Urlingford	I.	92
25	Rathquage	269 2 30	Waterford	Decies without Drum	Kilbarrymeaden	Kilmacthomas	II.	356
14	Rathquarter	212 3 29	Sligo	Carbury	Calry	Sligo	IV.	220
23	Rathranna	434 1 28	Cork, E.R.	Duhallow	Clonfert	Kanturk	II.	69
3, 8	Rathreagh	621 2 38	Kilkenny	Galmoy	Erke	Urlingford	I.	92
14, 21	Rathreagh	199 1 30	Mayo	Tirawley	Rathreagh	Killala	IV.	171
28	Rathreagh Beg	171 3 20	Limerick	Connello Lower	Clonagh	Rathkeale	II.	227
28	Rathreagh More	300 1 38	Limerick	Connello Lower	Clonagh	Rathkeale	II.	227
79	Rathredmond	144 2 36	Mayo	Carra	Manulla	Castlebar	IV.	129
110, 118	Rathredmond	331 2 7	Mayo	Kilmaine	Ballinrobe	Ballinrobe	IV.	153
31	Rathreedaun	659 3 19	Mayo	Gallen	Kilgarvan	Ballina	IV.	148
44	Rathregan	655 2 18	Meath	Ratoath	Rathregan	Dunshaughlin	I.	219
6	Rathreynolds	107 3 24	Meath	Lower Slane	Siddan	Ardee	I.	224
20, 26	Rathrippin	124 2 20	Sligo	Tirerrill	Ballysadare	Sligo	IV.	238
11, 12	Rathroal	118 3 31	Louth	Upper Dundalk	Haynestown	Dundalk	I.	178
24, 32	Rathrobin	991 2 21	King's Co.	Ballyboy	Killoughy	Tullamore	I.	124
30, 39	Rathroe	223 1 1	Cork, E.R.	Duhallow	Cullen	Millstreet	II.	71
97	Rathroe	151 0 27	Cork, E.R.	Kinalea	Ballinaboy	Kinsale	II.	93
4, 5	Rathroe	159 2 2	Kerry	Iraghticonnor	Lisselton	Listowel	II.	192
21	Rathroe	184 0 2	Mayo	Tirawley	Kilfian	Killala	IV.	169
16	Rathroe	142 2 9	Roscommon	Roscommon	Shankill	Strokestown	IV.	213
54	Rathroe	137 3 12	Tipperary, S.R.	Slievardagh	Killenaule	Cashel	II.	334
22, 30	Rathroeen	709 0 36a	Mayo	Tirawley	Ballysakeery	Ballina	IV.	165
48	Rathrolan	13 2 16	Wexford	Forth	Ballymore	Wexford	I.	308
48	Rathrolan	67 1 13	Wexford	Forth	Tacumshin	Wexford	I.	315
77	Rathronan	395 2 1	Tipperary, S.R.	Iffa and Offa East	Rathronan	Clonmel	II.	316
47	Rathronan	207 3 28	Wexford	Bargy	Mulrankin	Wexford	I.	307
77	Rathronan Demesne	256 0 12	Tipperary, S.R.	Iffa and Offa East	Rathronan	Clonmel	II.	316
9	Rathronshin	827 3 28	Queen's Co.	Portnahinch	Lea	Mountmellick	I.	244
71	Rathrowan	293 3 0	Mayo	Gallen	Bohola	Swineford	IV.	147
131, 140	Rathruane Beg	302 0 18	Cork, W.R.	West Carbery (W.D.)	Skull	Skull	II.	146
140	Rathruane More	267 3 26	Cork, W.R.	West Carbery (W.D.)	Skull	Skull	II.	146
13	Rathrush	970 0 33	Carlow	Forth	Gilbertstown	Carlow	I.	4
60, 61	Rathrushel	129 3 7b	Mayo	Gallen	Templemore	Castlebar	IV.	151
23	Rathsallagh	186 1 22	Longford	Shrule	Abbeyshrule	Ballymahon	I.	165
69	Rathsallagh	368 3 38	Tipperary, S.R.	Middlethird	Tullamain	Cashel	II.	331
14, 15	Rathsallagh	246 1 34	Wicklow	Upper Talbotstown	Rathsallagh	Baltinglass	I.	365
14, 20	Rathsallagh Demesne	248 3 29	Wicklow	Upper Talbotstown	Rathsallagh	Baltinglass	I.	365
27, 28	Rathsaran Glebe	183 1 17	Queen's Co.	Clandonagh	Rathsaran	Donaghmore	I.	235
67	Rathsasseragh	59 0 26	Tipperary, S.R.	Clanwilliam	Corroge	Tipperary	II.	306
62	Rathscanlan	252 2 30	Mayo	Gallen	Kilconduff	Swineford	IV.	148
37, 38	Rathscanlan	604 2 6	Sligo	Leyny	Achonry	Tobercurry	IV.	229
15, 21	Rathscannel	258 0 33	Kerry	Clanmaurice	Killahan	Tralee	II.	170
1	Rathshane	175 3 36	Westmeath	Fore	Foyran	Granard	I.	270
33, 38	Rathshanmore East	295 2 28	Wicklow	Ballinacor South	Hacketstown	Shillelagh	I.	349
33, 38	Rathshanmore South	225 2 30	Wicklow	Ballinacor South	Hacketstown	Shillelagh	I.	349
33, 38	Rathshanmore West	184 0 12	Wicklow	Ballinacor South	Hacketstown	Shillelagh	I.	349
28	Rathsherry	514 3 13	Antrim	Lower Antrim	Skerry	Ballymena	III.	5
53	Rathshillane	101 0 2	Wexford	Forth	Tacumshin	Wexford	I.	315
35, 36	Rathsillagh	466 2 1	Wexford	Shelmaliere West	Kilgarvan	New Ross	I.	334
31, 32	Rathsillagh Lower	173 1 4	Kildare	Narragh & Reban East	Fontstown	Athy	I.	66
31, 32	Rathsillagh Upper	342 2 25	Kildare	Narragh & Reban East	Fontstown	Athy	I.	66
24	Rathskeagh Lower	181 2 26	Westmeath	Rathconrath	Killare	Mullingar	I.	283
24	Rathskeagh Upper	438 1 11	Westmeath	Rathconrath	Killare	Mullingar	I.	283
71, 80	Rathslevin	312 1 6	Mayo	Gallen	Bohola	Swineford	IV.	147
33, 37	Rathsnagadan	246 2 8	Kilkenny	Ida	The Rower	New Ross	I.	104
4, 5, 11	Rathstephen	234 1 9	Meath	Lower Kells	Moynalty	Kells	I.	204
35	Rathstewart	52 3 38	Kildare	Narragh&Reban West	St. Michaels	Athy	I.	68
47	Rathtermon	271 0 3	Sligo	Coolavin	Killaraght	Boyle	IV.	224
32	Rathtillig	304 0 23	Queen's Co.	Slievmargy	Killabban	Carlow	I.	245

(a) Including 20A. 2R. 8P. water.   (b) Including 6A. 3R. 18P. water.

No. of Sheet of the Ordnance Survey Maps.	Townlands and Towns.	Area in Statute Acres.			County.	Barony.	Parish.	Poor Law Union in 1857.	Townland Census of 1851, Part I.	
		A.	R.	P.					Vol.	Page
47	Rathtinaun . .	75	1	33	Sligo . .	Coolavin . .	Killaraght . .	Boyle . .	IV.	224
99	Rathtinny Glebe .	90	2	5	Donegal . .	Tirhugh . . .	Drumhome . .	Donegal . .	III.	147
8, 13	Rathtoe . . .	877	0	11	Carlow . .	Forth . . .	Gilbertstown . .	Carlow . .	I.	4
20	Rathtoole . .	425	1	34	Wicklow . .	Upper Talbotstown .	Rathtoole . .	Baltinglass .	I.	365
27, 31	Rathtooterny or Floodhall . .	394	1	11	Kilkenny . .	Knocktopher . .	Jerpointchurch .	Thomastown .	I.	111
3, 6	Rathtrasna . .	243	0	2a	Meath . .	Lower Slane . .	Drumcondra . .	Ardee . .	I.	223
15	Rathtrillick . .	125	1	7	Armagh . .	Tiranny . . .	Tynan . . .	Armagh . .	III.	60
18	Rathtrim . .	129	0	18	Westmeath . .	Rathconrath . .	Rathconrath . .	Mullingar . .	I.	284
48	Rathtroane . .	709	3	30	Meath . .	Lower Moyfenrath .	Rathcore . .	Trim . .	I.	211
30	Rathturtin . .	1,007	0	38	Wexford . .	Bantry . . .	Killegney . .	Enniscorthy .	I.	301
39, 40	Rathumney . .	1,152	0	21	Wexford . .	Shelburne . .	Owenduff . .	New Ross .	I.	328
21	Rath Upper . .	118	2	33	Waterford . .	Coshmore and Coshbride .	Lismore and Mocollop	Lismore . .	II.	347
16, 23	Rath Upper . .	174	1	9	Westmeath . .	Kilkenny West .	Noughaval . .	Ballymahon .	I.	274
13	Rathurd . . .	139	2	32	Limerick . .	Clanwilliam . .	Donaghmore . .	Limerick . .	II.	223
13	Rathurd . . .	189	3	25	Limerick . .	Clanwilliam . .	St. Nicholas . .	Limerick . .	II.	225
35, 36	Rathure North .	273	2	25	King's Co. .	Eglish . . .	Drumcullen . .	Parsonstown .	I.	134
35, 36	Rathure South .	209	2	1	King's Co. .	Eglish . . .	Drumcullen . .	Parsonstown .	I.	134
21	Rathurles . .	291	0	4	Tipperary, N.R.	Upper Ormond .	Kilruane . .	Nenagh . .	II.	292
15, 21	Rathurles Commonage	19	1	38	Tipperary, N.R.	Upper Ormond .	Kilruane . .	Nenagh . .	II.	292
12, 18	Rathurlisk . .	103	3	37	Sligo . .	Tireragh . .	Templeboy . .	Dromore West .	IV.	236
14, 19	Rathvaldron . .	142	2	26	Longford . .	Ardagh . .	Ardagh . .	Longford . .	I.	151
112	Rathvallikeen .	18	3	10	Cork, E.R. .	Kinsale . . .	Ringcurran . .	Kinsale . .	II.	100
13, 14	Rathvarrin . .	434	0	13	Carlow . .	Forth . . .	Ardoyne . .	Carlow . .	I.	3
18	Rathvergin . .	203	3	15	Clare . .	Inchiquin . .	Ruan . .	Corrofin . .	II.	28
11, 19	Rathvilla or Rathclonbrackan . .	720	3	18	King's Co. .	Coolestown . .	Monasteroris .	Edenderry .	I.	133
3, 4	Rathvilly . .	120	3	28	Carlow . .	Rathvilly . .	Rathvilly . .	Baltinglass .	I.	12
4	RATHVILLY T. .				Carlow . .	Rathvilly . .	Rathvilly . .	Baltinglass .	I.	12
12	Rathvinden . .	11	1	11	Carlow . .	Idrone West .	Tullowcreen .	Carlow . .	I.	9
12	Rathvinden . .	173	0	31b	Carlow . .	Idrone West .	Wells . .	Carlow . .	I.	10
12	Rathwade . .	345	0	12	Carlow . .	Idrone East .	Agha . .	Carlow . .	I.	6
22	Rathwalkin . .	245	2	28	Kildare . .	Offaly East .	Kildare . .	Edenderry .	I.	70
82	Rathwalter . .	28	3	14	Tipperary, S.R.	Iffa and Offa West .	Tullaghmelan .	Clogheen . .	II.	321
50	Rathwarren . .	228	3	5	Tyrone . .	Clogher . .	Donacavey . .	Omagh . .	III.	294
69	Rath West . .	259	1	19	Cork, W.R. .	West Muskerry .	Ballyvourney .	Macroom . .	II.	154
128, 133	Rathwilladoon .	368	3	23	Galway . .	Kiltartan . .	Beagh . .	Gort . .	IV.	46
20, 27	Rathwire Lower .	369	2	2	Westmeath .	Farbill . . .	Killucan . .	Mullingar . .	I.	267
20	RATHWIRE T. .	—			Westmeath .	Farbill . . .	Killucan . .	Mullingar . .	I.	267
20, 27	Rathwire Upper .	437	1	18	Westmeath .	Farbill . . .	Killucan . .	Mullingar . .	I.	267
15	Rathwood . .	280	1	14	Limerick . .	Owneybeg . .	Abington . .	Limerick . .	II.	251
47	Rathyark . .	160	3	20	Wexford . .	Bargy . .	Mulrankin . .	Wexford . .	I.	307
18	Rat Island . .	0	0	2	Roscommon .	Ballintober North .	Kilmore . .	Car². on Shannon	IV.	187
40	Ratoal . .	76	1	27	Fermanagh .	Clankelly . .	Galloon . .	Clones . .	III.	198
38,39,44,45	Ratoath . .	978	1	11	Meath . .	Ratoath . .	Ratoath . .	Dunshaughlin .	I.	219
45	Ratoath Manor .	16	2	12c	Meath . .	Ratoath . .	Ratoath . .	Dunshaughlin .	I.	219
44	RATOATH T. .	—			Meath . .	Ratoath . .	Ratoath . .	Dunshaughlin .	I.	219
21	Ratona . .	198	0	20d	Fermanagh .	Magheraboy . .	Rossorry . .	Enniskillen .	III.	214
139	Ratooragh . .	1,183	2	1	Cork, W.R. .	West Carbery (W.D.)	Skull . .	Skull . .	II.	146
17, 23	Ratoran . .	587	3	9	Fermanagh .	Tirkennedy . .	Enniskillen .	Enniskillen .	III.	222
58	Ratory . .	156	1	1	Tyrone . .	Clogher . .	Clogher . .	Clogher . .	III.	293
8, 14	Ratra . .	325	2	0	Roscommon .	Frenchpark . .	Tibohine . .	Castlereagh .	IV.	205
21	Ratrass . .	218	0	38	Westmeath .	Farbill . . .	Killucan . .	Castletowndelvin .	I.	267
22	Ratrussan . .	605	2	26	Cavan . .	Tullygarvey . .	Kildrumsherdan .	Cootehill . .	III.	90
63	Ratteen . .	103	1	21	Donegal . .	Raphoe . .	Taughboyne . .	Strabane . .	III.	144
27, 34	Rattin . .	1,528	0	18	Westmeath .	Farbill . . .	Killucan . .	Mullingar . .	I.	267
23	Rattinagh . .	185	0	34	Roscommon .	Ballintober North .	Kilglass . .	Strokestown .	IV.	186
9	Rattoo . .	379	0	37	Kerry . .	Clanmaurice .	Rattoo . .	Listowel . .	II.	173
9	Rattoo Island .	0	3	0	Kerry . .	Clanmaurice .	Rattoo . .	Listowel . .	II.	173
16, 24	Ratyn . .	198	3	2	Tyrone . .	Strabane Lower .	Ardstraw . .	Castlederg .	III.	319
118	Rausakeera North .	83	1	10	Mayo . .	Kilmaine . .	Kilmainemore .	Ballinrobe .	IV.	156
118, 121	Rausakeera South .	79	0	16	Mayo . .	Kilmaine . .	Kilmainemore .	Ballinrobe .	IV.	156
19	Rausker . .	175	3	34	Monaghan .	Cremorne . .	Clontibret . .	Castleblayney .	III.	261
85	Ravakeel . .	77	0	36	Cork, E.R. .	East Muskerry .	Kilnaglory . .	Cork . .	II.	104
11	Ravanny . .	84	0	19	Louth . .	Ardee . .	Louth . .	Dundalk . .	I.	173
16	Ravara . .	1,246	0	13	Down . .	Castlereagh Lower .	Killinchy . .	Newtownards .	III.	163
51	Raveagh . .	240	2	10	Tyrone . .	Clogher . .	Donacavey . .	Clogher . .	III.	294
27	Raveege . .	213	3	16	Roscommon .	Castlereagh . .	Ballintober . .	Castlereagh .	IV.	198
18	Ravel . .	305	3	30	Louth . .	Ferrard . .	Dunleer . .	Ardee . .	I.	181
60	Ravellea . .	470	1	10	Tyrone . .	Dungannon Lower .	Carnteel . .	Clogher . .	III.	298
31, 32	Ravenfield or Aghadoon . .	69	0	7	Cavan . .	Upper Loughtee .	Denn . .	Cavan . .	III.	83
6	Ravensdale . .	186	2	8	Kildare . .	North Salt . .	Laraghbryan . .	Celbridge . .	I.	75

(a) Including 5A. 1R. 19P. water.   (c) Including 3A. 0R. 11P. detached portion.
(b) Including 5A. 1R. 16P. River Barrow.   (d) Including 1A. 1R. 23P. water.

5 H

No. of Sheet of the Ordnance Survey Maps.	Townlands and Towns.	Area in Statute Acres.	County.	Barony.	Parish.	Poor Law Union in 1857.	Townland Census of 1851, Part I.	
		A. R. P.					Vol.	Page
1, 4, 5	Ravensdale Park or Anaverna	2,343 0 18a	Louth	Lower Dundalk	Ballymascanlan	Dundalk	I.	176
26	Ravenswell	47 2 12	Dublin	Rathdown	Oldconnaught	Rathdown	I.	37
14	Ravernet	401 1 10	Down	Lower Iveagh, Up. pt.	Blaris	Lisburn	III.	169
6, 11	Raw	123 0 13b	Fermanagh	Lurg	Magheraculmoney	Lowtherstown	III.	208
24, 29	Raw	147 3 10	Fermanagh	Magherastephana	Aghalurcher	Lisnaskea	III.	217
23	Raw	151 2 4c	Monaghan	Cremorne	Aghnamullen	Cootehill	III.	258
43	Raw	367 0 12	Tyrone	Omagh East	Clogherny	Omagh	III.	310
19	Rawes	332 0 12	Armagh	Tiranny	Tynan	Armagh	III.	60
23, 32	Rawleystown	261 2 5	Limerick	Smallcounty	Cahercorney	Kilmallock	II.	259
17	Rawros	216 1 22	Donegal	Kilmacrenan	Mevagh	Millford	III.	130
79, 88	Raws Lower	236 2 4	Donegal	Raphoe	Donaghmore	Strabane	III.	138
79, 88	Raws Upper	455 0 34	Donegal	Raphoe	Donaghmore	Strabane	III.	138
13	Ray	143 2 39d	Cavan	Tullyhaw	Templeport	Bawnboy	III.	95
37	Ray	574 2 30	Donegal	Kilmacrenan	Aughnish	Millford	III.	122
45	Ray	167 2 17	Donegal	Kilmacrenan	Kilmacrenan	Millford	III.	129
25, 34	Ray	1,847 1 10	Donegal	Kilmacrenan	Raymunterdoney	Dunfanaghy	III.	131
86, 87	Rayhill	144 3 18	Galway	Kilconnell	Killallaghtan	Ballinasloe	IV.	41
54	Raymoghy	372 0 21	Donegal	Raphoe	Raymoghy	Letterkenny	III.	142
39	Raymondstown	186 3 13	Limerick	Coshma	Dromin	Kilmallock	II.	243
44	Raynestown	362 2 18	Meath	Ratoath	Rathbeggan	Dunshaughlin	I.	219
45	Raystown	301 2 24	Meath	Ratoath	Ratoath	Dunshaughlin	I.	219
142, 151	Rea	266 0 16	Cork, W.R.	West Carbery (E.D.)	Abbeystrowry	Skibbereen	II.	136
21, 22	Rea	248 3 22	Kerry	Clanmaurice	Kilflyn	Tralee	II.	170
11, 17	Rea	259 0 32	Kerry	Iraghticonnor	Duagh	Listowel	II.	190
21, 22	Rea-allen	293 0 2	Cork, E.R.	Duhallow	Kilmeen	Kanturk	II.	73
50	Reaboy	366 1 3	Kerry	Magunihy	Kilcummin	Killarney	II.	201
92	Reacashlagh	232 0 11	Kerry	Dunkerron South	Templenoe	Kenmare	II.	185
70	Reacaslagh	432 0 33	Kerry	Iveragh	Killinane	Cahersiveen	II.	197
32	Reacaslagh	1,224 1 38	Kerry	Trughanacmy	Ballincuslane	Tralee	II.	206
20	Reacaumaglanna	200 1 3	Waterford	Coshmore & Coshbride	Lismore and Mocollop	Lismore	II.	347
30, 31	Readesbarn	247 0 34	Kilkenny	Kells	Kilmaganny	Callan	I.	109
36	Readoty	86 3 13	Waterford	Decies within Drum	Ringagonagh	Dungarvan	II.	353
67, 68	Readrinagh	376 0 23	Kerry	Magunihy	Kilcummin	Killarney	II.	201
38, 44	Readsland	123 1 21	Meath	Ratoath	Dunshaughlin	Dunshaughlin	I.	218
36,37,42,43	Readstown	433 2 11	Meath	Lower Moyfenrath	Laracor	Trim	I.	210
39, 45	Reafadda	837 0 39	Tipperary, N.R.	Kilnamanagh Upper	Toem	Tipperary	II.	280
138	Reagh	221 1 37	Cork, W.R.	West Carbery (W.D.)	Kilcrohane	Bantry	II.	144
29, 36	Reagh	163 0 29	Roscommon	Roscommon	Cloonfinlough	Roscommon	IV.	209
116, 117	Reaghan	493 1 31	Galway	Leitrim	Tynagh	Portumna	IV.	56
18, 25, 26	Reaghan	567 0 38	Tyrone	Strabane Upper	Cappagh	Omagh	III.	325
41	Reaghfa	74 1 36	Clare	Islands	Killone	Ennis	II.	30
11, 17	Reagh Island	127 3 10	Down	Castlereagh Lower	Tullynakill	Newtownards	III.	164
10,11,13,14	Reaghstown	735 1 11	Louth	Ardee	Philipstown	Ardee	I.	174
45	Reagoulane	179 0 28	Tipperary, N.R.	Kilnamanagh Upper	Toem	Tipperary	II.	280
61	Reagrellagh	358 0 9	Cork, E.R.	East Muskerry	Inishcarra	Cork	II.	104
113	Reagrove	421 3 6	Cork, E.R.	Kinalea	Ballyfoyle	Kinsale	II.	94
46, 51	Reahouse	149 3 29	Wexford	Bargy	Killag	Wexford	I.	306
26	Realtoge	249 1 34	Meath	Skreen	Brownstown	Navan	I.	220
56	Realtons	292 3 13e	Tyrone	Omagh East	Kilskeery	Enniskillen	III.	314
36	Reamanagh	169 2 17	Waterford	Decies within Drum	Ballymacart	Dungarvan	II.	351
35	Reamanagh East	258 0 26	Waterford	Decies within Drum	Ardmore	Dungarvan	II.	350
35	Reamanagh West	422 0 33	Waterford	Decies within Drum	Ardmore	Dungarvan	II.	350
12	Reanabarna	344 1 0	Waterford	Coshmore&Coshbride	Lismore and Mocollop	Lismore	II.	347
68	Reanabobul	662 3 23	Cork, W.R.	West Muskerry	Ballyvourney	Macroom	II.	154
35	Reanaboola	255 3 11	Waterford	Decies within Drum	Ardmore	Youghal	II.	350
53	Reanabrone	116 2 11	Clare	Bunratty Lower	St. Patricks	Limerick	II.	7
82, 94	Reanacaheragh	438 2 36	Cork, W.R.	West Muskerry	Kilmichael	Dunmanway	II.	159
38, 39	Reanaclogheen	224 1 19	Waterford	Decies within Drum	Ardmore	Dungarvan	II.	350
20	Reanacoolagh East	261 3 22	Waterford	Coshmore&Coshbride	Lismore and Mocollop	Lismore	II.	347
11, 20	Reanacoolagh West	400 2 30	Waterford	Coshmore&Coshbride	Lismore and Mocollop	Lismore	II.	347
5, 13	Reanadampaun Commons	1,003 3 0	Waterford	Decies without Drum	Seskinan	Dungarvan	II.	360
5, 13	Reanadampaun Commons	873 3 6	Waterford	Glenahiry	Kilronan	Clonmel	II.	366
21, 22	Reanagashel	341 1 3	Cork, E.R.	Duhallow	Kilmeen	Kanturk	II.	73
52	Reanagillee Commons	320 2 32	Limerick	Glenquin	Killeedy	Newcastle	II.	246
32, 40	Reanagishagh	650 1 6	Clare	Islands	Kilmaley	Ennis	II.	31
22, 30	Reanagowan	1,093 1 11	Kerry	Trughanacmy	Ballymacelligott	Tralee	II.	207
35	Reanagullee	305 0 38	Waterford	Decies within Drum	Ardmore	Dungarvan	II.	350
5	Reanahoun	880 2 30	Cork, E.R.	Duhallow	Clonfert	Kanturk	II.	69
13	Reanahumana	170 0 16	Clare	Tulla Upper	Feakle	Tulla	II.	40
69	Reananerree	469 0 1	Cork, W.R.	West Muskerry	Kilnamartry	Macroom	II.	160

(a) Including 7A. 1R. 3P. water.
(b) Including 6A. 2R. 6P. water.
(c) Including 2A. 1R. 29P. water.
(d) Including 23A. 3R. 10P. water.
(e) Including 0A. 2R. 4P. water.

No. of Sheet of the Ordnance Survey Maps.	Townlands and Towns.	Area in Statute Acres.	County.	Barony.	Parish.	Poor Law Union in 1857.	Townland Census of 1851, Part I.	
		A. R. P.					Vol.	Page
134	Reanascreena North	365 1 22	Cork, W.R.	East Carbery (W.D.)	Ross	Clonakilty	II.	135
134	Reanascreena South	421 3 25	Cork, W.R.	East Carbery (W.D.)	Ross	Clonakilty	II.	135
35, 38	Reanaskeha	203 3 11	Waterford	Decies within Drum	Ardmore	Dungarvan	II.	350
50, 60	Reanasup	870 3 10	Kerry	Magunihy	Nohavaldaly	Killarney	II.	205
35	Reanaviddoge	196 0 20	Waterford	Decies within Drum	Ardmore	Dungarvan	II.	350
21	Reandallane	242 3 27	Cork, E.R.	Duhallow	Kilmeen	Kanturk	II.	73
55	Reanduff	318 1 34	Cork, E.R.	Kinnatalloon	Mogeely	Youghal	II.	99
113	Reaniesglen	195 2 27	Cork, E.R.	Kinalea	Nohaval	Kinsale	II.	96
113	Reanieshouse	186 2 3	Cork, E.R.	Kinalea	Ballyfoyle	Kinsale	II.	94
133	Rearahinagh	357 1 20	Cork, W.R.	West Carbery (E.D.)	Caheragh	Skibbereen	II.	137
133	Rearahinagh	290 3 13	Cork, W.R.	West Carbery (E.D.)	Dromdaleague	Skibbereen	II.	140
38	Reardnogy Beg	434 0 9	Tipperary, N.R.	Owney and Arra	Abington	Nenagh	II.	293
38	Reardnogy More	682 2 23	Tipperary, N.R.	Owney and Arra	Abington	Nenagh	II.	293
86, 87, 89, 90	Rearoe	698 1 34	Tipperary, S.R.	Iffa and Offa West	Shanrahan	Clogheen	II.	320
84, 96	Rearour	601 2 8	Cork, E.R.	East Muskerry	Kilbonane	Bandon	II.	104
85, 86, 97, 98	Rearour and Barrettshill	608 1 11	Cork, E.R.	Kerrycurrihy	Ballinaboy	Cork	II.	91
46, 55	Rearour North	208 3 28	Cork, E.R.	Kinnatalloon	Mogeely	Youghal	II.	99
55	Rearour South	223 3 33	Cork, E.R.	Kinnatalloon	Mogeely	Youghal	II.	99
3	Reary Beg	947 2 22a	Queen's Co.	Tinnahinch	Rearymore	Mountmellick	I.	250
2, 3	Reary More	585 2 32	Queen's Co.	Tinnahinch	Rearymore	Mountmellick	I.	250
1, 3	Rearyvalley or Clonygark	582 1 32	Queen's Co.	Tinnahinch	Rearymore	Mountmellick	I.	250
25, 26	Reask	104 2 19	Cavan	Upper Loughtee	Annagelliff	Cavan	III.	82
117	Reask	117 0 13	Galway	Leitrim	Tynagh	Portumna	IV.	56
101, 109	Reask	626 2 7	Galway	Longford	Clonfert	Ballinasloe	IV.	57
42	Reask	259 1 11	Kerry	Corkaguiny	Marhin	Dingle	II.	179
24	Reask	386 3 30	Limerick	Coonagh	Tuoghcluggin	Tipperary	II.	236
92	Reask	478 0 26b	Mayo	Costello	Bekan	Claremorris	IV.	139
26, 27, 32, 33	Reask	191 3 19	Meath	Lower Duleek	Duleek	Drogheda	I.	195
11	Reask	91 2 28	Meath	Lower Kells	Emlagh	Kells	I.	202
38	Reask	805 3 6	Meath	Ratoath	Kilbrew	Dunshaughlin	I.	218
47	Reask	297 0 38	Sligo	Coolavin	Killaraght	Boyle	IV.	224
25, 33	Reaskaun	101 0 29	Clare	Bunratty Upper	Templemaley	Ennis	II.	11
51	Reaskavalla	92 3 22	Tipperary, S.R.	Clanwilliam	Solloghodmore	Tipperary	II.	311
52	Reaskcamoge	490 3 18	Clare	Bunratty Lower	Kilfinaghta	Limerick	II.	4
54	Reaskcor	168 0 5	Tyrone	Dungannon Middle	Donaghmore	Dungannon	III.	302
114	Reaskgarriff	45 0 16	Galway	Dunkellin	Ardrahan	Gort	IV.	27
104	Reaskmore	85 1 11	Galway	Dunkellin	Killora	Loughrea	IV.	31
108	Reaskmore	306 3 20	Galway	Longford	Meelick	Portumna	IV.	61
54	Reaskmore	327 2 34	Tyrone	Dungannon Middle	Donaghmore	Dungannon	III.	302
105	Reaskrevagh	45 1 23	Galway	Dunkellin	Kilchreest	Loughrea	IV.	28
3, 4	Reatagh	149 3 31	Waterford	Upperthird	Fenoagh	Carrick on Suir	II.	370
48	Reavaun	423 3 26	Kerry	Magunihy	Killeentierna	Killarney	II.	204
134	Reavilleen	204 1 7	Cork, W.R.	East Carbery (W.D.)	Ross	Clonakilty	II.	135
120, 133	Reavouler	800 1 34	Cork, W.R.	East Carbery (W.D.)	Kilmacabea	Skibbereen	II.	133
27	Rebane	272 1 26	Monaghan	Cremorne	Aghnamullen	Castleblayney	III.	258
5	Reboge	226 1 36c	Limerick	Clanwilliam and Municipal Borough	St. Patrick's	Limerick	II.	225
5	Reboge Island	78 2 18d	Limerick	Limerick, Municipal Borough of	St. Patrick's	Limerick	II.	262
5	Reboge Meadows	29 1 14	Limerick	Clanwilliam	St. Patrick's	Limerick	II.	225
35	Recarson	405 3 19e	Tyrone	Omagh East	Cappagh	Omagh	III.	310
45, 53	Reclain	298 0 25	Tyrone	Dungannon Middle	Donaghmore	Dungannon	III.	302
35, 39, 40	Redacres North	239 0 38	Kilkenny	Knocktopher	Killahy	Waterford	I.	112
39	Redacres South	116 2 5	Kilkenny	Knocktopher	Killahy	Waterford	I.	112
67, 78	Redbarn	281 2 23	Cork, E.R.	Imokilly	Clonpriest	Youghal	II.	85
20	Red Bay	100 0 7	Antrim	Lower Glenarm	Layd	Ballycastle	III.	23
10	Redbog	284 0 17	Carlow	Rathvilly	Clonmore	Shillelagh	I.	10
20, 25	Redbog	459 0 38	Kildare	Naas North	Rathmore	Naas	I.	63
21	Redbog	136 2 3	Kilkenny	Gowran	Gowran	Kilkenny	I.	95
21	Redbog	95 0 10	Kilkenny	Gowran	Kilmacahill	Kilkenny	I.	97
10	Redbog	220 2 2	Louth	Ardee	Louth	Dundalk	I.	173
38	Redbog	209 2 33	Meath	Ratoath	Dunshaughlin	Dunshaughlin	I.	218
1	Redbrae	78 1 21	Leitrim	Rosclogher	Rossinver	Ballyshannon	IV.	112
12, 17	Redcastle	510 2 15	Queen's Co.	Maryborough West	Clonenagh and Clonagheen	Mountmellick	I.	243
70	Redcity	453 1 22	Tipperary, S.R.	Middlethird	Redcity	Cashel	II.	329
17, 21	Redcow	141 1 31	Dublin	Uppercross	Clondalkin	Dublin South	I.	39
4, 7	Redcow	164 1 17	Louth	Upper Dundalk	Dundalk	Dundalk	I.	178
17	Redcowfarm	183 1 13	Dublin	Uppercross	Palmerston	Dublin South	I.	40
35	Redcross	344 2 29	Wicklow	Arklow	Redcross	Rathdrum	I.	346
35	REDCROSS T.	—	Wicklow	Arklow	Redcross	Rathdrum	I.	346
59	Reddanswalk	229 0 8	Tipperary, S.R.	Clanwilliam	Templenoe	Tipperary	II.	312

(a) Including 7A. 1R. 6P. water.
(b) Including 20A. 3R. 4P. water.
(c) { Within the Municipal Boundary, 19A. 3R. 32P. / Without the Municipal Boundary, 206A. 2R. 4P.
(d) Included in the Parish of St. Patrick.
(e) Including 4A. 1R. 9P. water.

No. of Sheet of the Ordnance Survey Maps.	Townlands and Towns.	Area in Statute Acres.	County.	Barony.	Parish.	Poor Law Union in 1857.	Townland Census of 1851, Part I.
		A. R. P.					Vol. / Page
32	Reddina . . .	206 3 24	Wexford . .	Shelmaliere West .	Killurin . . .	Enniscorthy .	I. / 334
29	Reddysland . .	18 3 31	Wexford . .	Bantry . . .	St. Mary's . .	New Ross .	I. / 302
18	Redeen . . .	69 3 14	Kilkenny . .	Crannagh . .	Ballycallan . .	Kilkenny .	I. / 85
5, 12	Redford Glebe .	474 1 21	Donegal . .	Inishowen East .	Clonca . .	Inishowen .	III. / 117
21, 24	Redgap . . .	175 1 30	Dublin . .	Newcastle . .	Rathcoole . .	Celbridge .	I. / 34
44	Redgap . . .	33 0 2	Kilkenny . .	Ida . . .	Kilcolumb . .	Waterford .	I. / 103
47	Redhall . . .	571 3 17	Antrim . .	Lower Belfast .	Templecorran .	Larne .	III. / 9
102	Redhill . . .	215 0 0	Mayo . .	Costello . .	Annagh . .	Claremorris .	IV. / 138
70	Redhill . . .	173 3 26	Mayo . .	Gallen . .	Templemore .	Castlebar .	IV. / 151
12, 16	Redhill Demesne .	185 2 18a	Cavan . .	Tullygarvey .	Annagh . .	Cavan .	III. / 87
22	Redhills . . .	332 0 3	Kildare . .	Offaly East .	Kildare . .	Edenderry .	I. / 70
24	Redhills . . .	40 1 6	Queen's Co. .	Cullenagh . .	Abbeyleix . .	Abbeyleix .	I. / 238
12, 16	REDHILL T. .	—	Cavan . .	Tullygarvey .	Annagh . .	Cavan .	III. / 87
22	Redhouse . .	232 1 7	Kilkenny . .	Shillelogher .	Killaloe . .	Callan .	I. / 115
29	Redhouse . .	93 0 1	Wexford . .	Bantry . .	St. Mary's . .	New Ross .	I. / 302
29	Red Island . .	11 2 22	Clare . .	Tulla Upper .	Inishcaltra .	Scarriff .	II. / 40
26	Red Island . .	6 2 7	Donegal . .	Kilmacrenan .	Clondahorky .	Dunfanaghy .	III. / 124
50	Red Island . .	1 2 13	Galway . .	Ballynahinch .	Moyrus . .	Clifden .	IV. / 14
24	Red Island . .	3 0 32	Galway . .	Ballynahinch .	Moyrus . .	Clifden .	IV. / 14
27	Red Island . .	16 0 21	Galway . .	Ross . .	Ross . .	Oughterard .	IV. / 74
25	Red Island . .	1 3 1	Longford . .	Rathcline .	Cashel . .	Ballymahon .	I. / 164
123	Red Island . .	6 2 39	Mayo . .	Kilmaine .	Shrule . .	Ballinrobe .	IV. / 158
77, 83	Redmondstown .	403 1 20	Tipperary, S.R.	Iffa and Offa East .	Kilgrant . .	Clonmel .	II. / 314
24, 25	Redmondstown .	659 3 20	Westmeath .	Rathconrath .	Churchtown .	Mullingar .	I. / 282
42	Redmondstown .	131 3 22	Wexford . .	Forth . .	Rathaspick .	Wexford .	I. / 313
32	Redmondstown .	201 3 19	Wexford . .	Shelmaliere East .	Ballynaslaney .	Enniscorthy .	I. / 330
46	Redmoor . .	219 0 29	Wexford . .	Bargy . .	Killag . .	Wexford .	I. / 306
27	Redmountain .	100 0 6	Meath . .	Lower Duleek .	Duleek . .	Drogheda .	I. / 195
117	Redpark . . .	142 1 12	Galway . .	Leitrim . .	Tynagh . .	Portumna .	IV. / 56
85	Redtrench North .	772 1 19	Kerry . .	Glanarought .	Kilgarvan .	Kenmare .	II. / 188
94	Redtrench South .	333 0 16	Kerry . .	Glanarought .	Kilgarvan .	Kenmare .	II. / 188
24, 27	Reduff . . .	214 1 10	Monaghan .	Cremorne .	Aghnamullen .	Castleblayney .	III. / 258
1, 4	Redwood . .	3,003 0 36	Tipperary, N.R.	Lower Ormond .	Dorrha . .	Parsonstown .	II. / 283
1, 4	Redwood . .	1,537 2 25	Tipperary, N.R.	Lower Ormond .	Lorrha . .	Parsonstown .	II. / 285
12	Ree . . .	302 3 9	Londonderry .	Coleraine .	Agivey . .	Coleraine .	III. / 230
81, 82	Reechestown .	198 3 26b	Tipperary, S.R.	Iffa and Offa West .	Rochestown .	Clogheen .	II. / 319
53	Reedstown . .	160 0 33c	Wexford . .	Forth . .	Tacumshin .	Wexford .	I. / 315
15	Reen . . .	168 2 10	Armagh . .	Tiranny . .	Tynan . .	Armagh .	III. / 60
116	Reen . . .	40 2 22	Cork, W.R. .	Bear . .	Kilcaskan .	Castletown .	II. / 123
142, 151	Reen . . .	252 2 29	Cork, W.R. .	West Carbery (E.D.)	Myross . .	Skibbereen .	II. / 141
83, 92	Reen . . .	865 1 12	Kerry . .	Dunkerron South .	Templenoe .	Kenmare .	II. / 185
66	Reen . . .	283 3 32	Kerry . .	Magunihy .	Killarney .	Killarney .	II. / 203
56	Reen . . .	554 1 34	Kerry . .	Trughanacmy .	Killorglin .	Killarney .	II. / 211
116	Reenabulliga .	334 0 36	Cork, W.R. .	Bear . .	Kilcaskan .	Castletown .	II. / 123
130	Reenacappul .	185 3 33	Cork, W.R. .	West Carbery (W.D.)	Kilcrohane .	Bantry .	II. / 144
105	Reenadisert .	130 0 20	Cork, W.R. .	Bantry . .	Kilmocomoge .	Bantry .	II. / 121
117, 118	Reenaknock .	120 0 1	Cork, W.R. .	Bantry . .	Kilmocomoge .	Bantry .	II. / 121
79	Reenard . . .	647 2 25	Kerry . .	Iveragh . .	Caher . .	Cahersiveen .	II. / 194
16	Reenavanna East .	378 2 38	Limerick . .	Coonagh . .	Doon . .	Tipperary .	II. / 234
8, 16	Reenavanna West .	279 0 14	Limerick . .	Coonagh . .	Doon . .	Tipperary .	II. / 234
105, 118	Reenavanny .	149 1 10	Cork, W.R. .	Bantry . .	Kilmocomoge .	Bantry .	II. / 121
53	Reenbeg . . .	112 0 20	Kerry . .	Corkaguiny .	Dingle . .	Dingle .	II. / 175
43	Reenboy . . .	192 3 18	Kerry . .	Corkaguiny .	Cloghane .	Dingle .	II. / 175
87	Reencaheragh .	270 3 24	Kerry . .	Iveragh . .	Killemlagh .	Cahersiveen .	II. / 196
43	Reenconnell .	359 1 3	Kerry . .	Corkaguiny .	Kilmalkedar .	Dingle .	II. / 178
141	Reencorreen .	347 0 13	Cork, W.R. .	West Carbery (E.D.)	Abbeystrowry .	Skibbereen .	II. / 136
150	Reendacussane .	94 3 14	Cork, W.R. .	West Carbery (E.D.)	Castlehaven .	Skibbereen .	II. / 138
105	Reenearagh .	218 3 3	Kerry . .	Dunkerron South .	Kilcrohane .	Cahersiveen .	II. / 184
122, 123	Reengarrigeen .	560 3 13	Cork, W.R. .	East Carbery (E.D.)	Kilmaloda .	Clonakilty .	II. / 129
108	Reenkilla . .	491 3 4	Kerry . .	Glanarought .	Tuosist . .	Kenmare .	II. / 189
90, 91, 104, 105	Reenmeen East .	133 1 33	Cork, W.R. .	Bear . .	Kilcaskan .	Bantry .	II. / 123
90, 104	Reenmeen West .	104 2 18	Cork, W.R. .	Bear . .	Kilcaskan .	Bantry .	II. / 123
150	Reenmore Island .	41 2 12	Cork, W.R. .	West Carbery (E.D.)	Creagh . .	Skibbereen .	II. / 139
141	Reenmurragha .	500 1 38	Cork, W.R. .	West Carbery (E.D.)	Aghadown .	Skibbereen .	II. / 137
88	Reennacoola .	116 0 8	Kerry . .	Iveragh . .	Prior . .	Cahersiveen .	II. / 198
19	Reennafardarrig .	6 1 39	Kerry . .	Corkaguiny .	Killiney . .	Dingle .	II. / 178
63	Reennanallagane .	299 2 15	Kerry . .	Iveragh . .	Glanbehy .	Cahersiveen .	II. / 196
143	Reenogrena .	253 1 37	Cork, W.R. .	East Carbery (W.D.)	Kilfaughnabeg .	Skibbereen .	III. / 133
122	Reenroe . . .	123 3 23	Cork, W.R. .	East Carbery (E.D.)	Kilgarriff .	Clonakilty .	II. / 129
132	Reenroe . . .	238 3 29	Cork, W.R. .	West Carbery (E.D.)	Dromdaleague .	Skibbereen .	II. / 140
88, 97	Reenroe . . .	128 1 12	Kerry . .	Iveragh . .	Prior . .	Cahersiveen .	II. / 198
118	Reenrour East .	21 1 9	Cork, W.R. .	Bantry . .	Kilmocomoge .	Bantry .	II. / 121

(a) Including 7A. 2R. 32P. water.   (b) Including 4A. 2R. 30P. water.   (c) Including 5A. 3R. 32P. water.

No. of Sheet of the Ordnance Survey Maps.	Townlands and Towns.	Area in Statute Acres.			County.	Barony.	Parish.	Poor Law Union in 1857.	Townland Census of 1851, Part I.	
		A.	R.	P.					Vol.	Page
118	Reenrour West	77	2	10	Cork, W.R.	Bantry	Kilmocomoge	Bantry	II.	121
28	Reens East	167	3	17	Limerick	Connello Lower	Kilscannell	Rathkeale	II.	228
28	Reens West	169	2	22	Limerick	Connello Lower	Kilscannell	Rathkeale	II.	228
114	Reentrusk	1,424	2	20	Cork, W.R.	Bear	Kilnamanagh	Castletown	II.	126
2, 3	Reenturk	135	3	34	Kerry	Iraghticonnor	Kilnaughtin	Glin	II.	191
105	Reenydonagan	198	0	36a	Cork, W.R.	Bantry	Kilmocomoge	Bantry	II.	121
28	Reerasta North	72	3	30	Limerick	Shanid	Ardagh	Newcastle	II.	255
28	Reerasta South	83	1	7	Limerick	Shanid	Ardagh	Newcastle	II.	255
11, 15	Reevanagh	1,029	2	9	Kilkenny	Gowran	Tiscoffin	Kilkenny	I.	99
14, 15	Reeves	221	1	16b	Kilkenny	South Salt	Donaghcumper	Celbridge	I.	76
53	Regaile	174	3	35	Tipperary, S.R.	Middlethird	Guile	Cashel	II.	327
42, 47	Regan	116	1	2	Wexford	Bargy	Kilmannan	Wexford	I.	306
8	Regeens	109	3	32	Dublin	Balrothery East	Lusk	Balrothery	I.	21
8	Regles	229	3	30c	Dublin	Balrothery East	Lusk	Balrothery	I.	21
60	Rehaghy	579	2	25d	Tyrone	Dungannon Lower	Aghaloo	Dungannon	III.	297
80	Rehill	428	0	10	Kerry	Iveragh	Caher	Cahersiveen	II.	194
80,81,86,87	Rehill	789	0	1	Tipperary, S.R.	Iffa and Offa West	Shanrahan	Clogheen	II.	320
81	Rehill	13	2	20	Tipperary, S.R.	Iffa and Offa West	Tubbrid	Clogheen	II.	321
65, 72	Rehy East	669	3	9	Clare	Moyarta	Kilballyowen	Kilrush	II.	32
72	Rehy West	653	1	38	Clare	Moyarta	Kilballyowen	Kilrush	II.	32
39	Reilly	108	1	24e	Fermanagh	Knockninny	Kinawley	Lisnaskea	III.	202
14	Reillys Trench	106	0	23	Down	Lower Iveagh, Up.pt.	Hillsborough	Lisburn	III.	169
33, 39	Reisk	832	0	31	Tipperary, N.R.	Kilnamanagh Upper	Upperchurch	Thurles	II.	281
17, 26	Reisk	273	0	36	Waterford	Middlethird	Reisk	Waterford	II.	369
22	Relagh	121	1	39	Fermanagh	Tirkennedy	Enniskillen	Enniskillen	III.	222
16, 22	Relagh	170	2	4	Fermanagh	Tirkennedy	Magheracross	Enniskillen	III.	223
56	Relagh	279	0	20	Tyrone	Omagh East	Kilskeery	Enniskillen	III.	314
34, 40	Relagh Beg	173	3	25	Cavan	Clankee	Moybolgue	Bailieborough	III.	74
43	Relaghdooey	226	1	37f	Tyrone	Omagh East	Drumragh	Omagh	III.	313
56	Relagh Guinness	458	3	22g	Tyrone	Omagh East	Kilskeery	Lowtherstown	III.	314
34	Relagh More	114	0	10	Cavan	Clankee	Moybolgue	Bailieborough	III.	74
102, 110	Releagh	816	3	6	Kerry	Glanarought	Kilcaskan	Kenmare	II.	187
64	Relessy	354	2	25h	Tyrone	Clogher	Aghalurcher	Clogher	III.	291
10, 17	Relick (Longworth)	215	0	39	Westmeath	Rathconrath	Piercetown	Ballymahon	I.	284
10, 17	Relick (Malone)	36	3	1	Westmeath	Rathconrath	Piercetown	Ballymahon	I.	284
36	Rellan	103	0	16	Fermanagh	Clankelly	Clones	Clones	III.	197
46	Reloagh	160	0	3	Tyrone	Dungannon Middle	Donaghmore	Dungannon	III.	302
18	Remeen	51	0	16	Kilkenny	Crannagh	Ballinamara	Kilkenny	I.	84
18	Remeen	222	1	25	Kilkenny	Crannagh	Tullaroan	Kilkenny	I.	88
43, 49	Renaghmore	364	3	14	Tipperary, S.R.	Slievardagh	Kilcooly	Urlingford	II.	334
24	Renalicka	118	2	1i	Clare	Corcomroe	Clooney	Ennistimon	II.	18
34	Renny Lower	175	1	24j	Cork, E.R.	Fermoy	Kilcummer	Fermoy	II.	80
26, 34	Renny Upper	366	0	29	Cork, E.R.	Fermoy	Kilcummer	Fermoy	II.	80
43	Renogher Glebe	74	2	11	Fermanagh	Clankelly	Currin	Clones	III.	197
115, 116, 128, 129	Rerrin	291	1	33	Cork, W.R.	Bear	Killaconenagh	Castletown	II.	125
60, 61	Reskatirriff	306	3	22k	Tyrone	Dungannon Lower	Carnteel	Dungannon	III.	298
29	Retreat	89	3	14	Westmeath	Brawny	St. Mary's	Athlone	I.	260
19	Retreat or Cloghglass	406	3	23	Antrim	Lower Glenarm	Layd	Ballycastle	III.	23
6, 7	Revallagh North	205	3	7	Antrim	Lower Dunluce	Ballyrashane	Coleraine	III.	15
6, 7	Revallagh South	214	1	24	Antrim	Lower Dunluce	Ballyrashane	Coleraine	III.	15
19	Reviewfields	138	2	14	Kilkenny	Shillelogher	St. Patrick's	Kilkenny	I.	116
93	Revlin	100	3	4	Donegal	Banagh	Killymard	Donegal	III.	111
6	Reycroftspark	85	1	2	Roscommon	Boyle	Ardcarn	Boyle	IV.	193
20, 21	Reyfad	825	1	22	Fermanagh	Magheraboy	Boho	Enniskillen	III.	210
124	Reynabrone	406	2	29	Galway	Leitrim	Ballynakill	Loughrea	IV.	52
131, 134	Reynclamper	397	0	18	Galway	Leitrim	Ballynakill	Portumna	IV.	52
13, 20	Reynella	611	3	29l	Westmeath	Moyashel and Magheradernon	Rathconnell	Mullingar	I.	276
4	Reynoldstown	128	2	4	Dublin	Balrothery West	Naul	Balrothery	I.	23
19	Reynoldstown	318	2	1	Louth	Ferrard	Mayne	Drogheda	I.	181
123, 124	Reyrawer	579	3	3	Galway	Kiltartan	Kilthomas	Gort	IV.	49
9	Rhine	781	3	21	Longford	Longford	Killoe	Longford	I.	159
44	Ribstown	201	3	4	Meath	Ratoath	Rathregan	Dunshaughlin	I.	219
25	Ricehill or Coolnagor	128	1	18	Cavan	Upper Loughtee	Kilmore	Cavan	III.	84
31	Ricesland	65	3	3m	Kilkenny	Knocktopher	Knocktopher	Thomastown	I.	112
12	Ricetown	69	2	33	Meath	Lower Slane	Killary	Ardee	I.	223
12	Ricetown	283	0	18	Meath	Lower Slane	Mitchelstown	Ardee	I.	223
17, 25	Richardstown	371	1	27	Cork, E.R.	Fermoy	Caherduggan	Mallow	II.	77
7, 8	Richardstown	474	0	2	Dublin	Balrothery East	Lusk	Balrothery	I.	21
10, 14	Richardstown	587	1	12	Kildare	Ikeathy&Oughterany	Mainham	Celbridge	I.	58
17	Richardstown	80	1	17	Louth	Ardee	Dromin	Ardee	I.	172
14,15,17,18	Richardstown	1,089	2	38	Louth	Ardee	Richardstown	Ardee	I.	174

(a) Including 31A. 1R. 6P. water.
(b) Including 1A. 3R. 8P. water.
(c) Including 21A. 3R. 5P. detached portion.
(d) Including 22A. 0R. 16P. water.
(e) Including 6A. 2R. 38P. water.

(f) Including 7A. 2R. 0P. water.
(g) Including 3A. 3R. 23P. water.
(h) Including 0A. 0R. 22P. water.
(i) Including 1A. 3R. 21P. water.

(j) Including 10A. 0R. 22P. water.
(k) Including 8A. 3R. 21P. water.
(l) Including 15A. 2R. 22P. water.
(m) Including 49A. 2R. 27P. detached portions.

No. of Sheet of the Ordnance Survey Maps.	Townlands and Towns.	Area in Statute Acres.	County.	Barony.	Parish.	Poor Law Union in 1857.	Townland Census of 1851, Part I. Vol.	Page
		A. R. P.						
28	Richardstown	101 0 15	Meath	Upper Duleek	Moorechurch	Drogheda	I.	198
11	Richard Taaffes Holding	318 3 21	Louth	Louth	Louth	Dundalk	I.	184
46, 51	Richfield	247 1 10	Wexford	Bargy	Killag	Wexford	I.	306
46,47,51,52	Richfield (*Reclaimed*)	146 3 28	Wexford	Bargy	Killag	Wexford	I.	306
19	Richfort or Cooleeshil	289 2 38	Longford	Ardagh	Ardagh	Longford	I.	151
6	Richhill	64 3 8	Limerick	Clanwilliam	Stradbally	Limerick	II.	226
9, 13	Rich Hill or Legacorry	347 2 24	Armagh	Oneilland West	Kilmore	Armagh	III.	53
13	RICH HILL T.	—	Armagh	Oneilland West	Kilmore	Armagh	III.	53
18	Richmond	110 0 22	Dublin	Coolock	Clonturk	Dublin North	I.	27
31	Richmond	422 2 38	Galway	Tiaquin	Kilkerrin	Glennamaddy	IV.	77
38	Richmond	201 1 14	Mayo	Tirawley	Crossmolina	Ballina	IV.	166
20	Richmond	339 0 12	Tipperary, N.R.	Lower Ormond	Monsea	Nenagh	II.	287
52, 59	Richmond	266 3 4	Tyrone	Clogher	Errigal Keerogue	Clogher	III.	295
18	RICHMOND T.	—	Dublin	Coolock	Clonturk	Dublin North	I.	27
12,13,21,22	Richmondvilla	135 1 27	Limerick	Pubblebrien	Crecora	Croom	II.	252
5, 9	Richmount or Aghavellan	123 1 13	Armagh	Oneilland West	Drumcree	Lurgan	III.	52
50,51,55,56	Rickamore	1,245 0 33	Antrim	Upper Belfast	Templepatrick	Antrim	III.	11
40, 41	Rickardsland North	45 1 25	Kilkenny	Ida	Kilcoan	Waterford	I.	102
41	Rickardsland South	42 2 15	Kilkenny	Ida	Kilcoan	Waterford	I.	102
23	Rickardstown	145 1 39	Kildare	Connell	Morristownbiller	Naas	I.	56
8, 13	Rickardstown	839 3 9	Westmeath	Delvin	Killulagh	Castletowndelvin	I.	266
52	Rickardstown	154 2 39	Wexford	Bargy	Kilmore	Wexford	I.	307
27, 31	Rickardstown Lower	490 2 8	Kildare	Offaly West	Harristown	Athy	I.	72
27	Rickardstown Upper	232 3 11*a*	Kildare	Offaly West	Harristown	Athy	I.	72
1, 3	Ricketstown	220 3 20	Carlow	Rathvilly	Rahill	Baltinglass	I.	12
3	Ricketstown or Bettyfield	198 2 12	Carlow	Rathvilly	Kineagh	Baltinglass	I.	12
3	Ricketstown North	282 2 10	Carlow	Rathvilly	Kineagh	Baltinglass	I.	12
3	Ricketstown South	270 2 18	Carlow	Rathvilly	Kineagh	Baltinglass	I.	12
129	*Ricks Island*	0 3 24	Galway	Kiltartan	Beagh	Gort	IV.	46
19,20,28,29	Riddlestown	819 3 14	Limerick	Connello Lower	Doondonnell	Rathkeale	II.	228
11, 15	Ridge	1,542 2 1	Carlow	Idrone West	Oldleighlin	Carlow	I.	9
12	Ridge	184 1 9	Kilkenny	Galmoy	Borrismore	Urlingford	I.	92
23, 31	Ridgemount or Ballybrackan	513 1 35	King's Co.	Ballyboy	Ballyboy	Parsonstown	I.	123
54	Riesk	383 1 28	Cork, E.R.	Barrymore	Templebodan	Middleton	II.	58
18	Riesk	190 1 39	Kilkenny	Crannagh	Ballycallan	Kilkenny	I.	85
22	Riesk	86 0 32	Kilkenny	Shillelogher	Killaloe	Callan	I.	115
22	Riesk	37 2 13	Kilkenny	Shillelogher	Tullaghanbrogue	Callan	I.	116
27	Riesk	3 2 35	Wexford	Ballaghkeen	Castle-ellis	Enniscorthy	I.	293
27	Riesk	120 2 4	Wexford	Ballaghkeen	Killila	Enniscorthy	I.	295
46	Riesk	28 3 35	Wexford	Bargy	Killag	Wexford	I.	306
21	Rigg	232 3 28	Fermanagh	Magheraboy	Rossorry	Enniskillen	III.	214
38	Riggins	121 1 10	Meath	Ratoath	Kilbrew	Dunshaughlin	I.	218
38	Riggins	126 0 27	Meath	Skreen	Macetown	Dunshaughlin	I.	221
97	Rigsdale	686 3 36	Cork, E.R.	Kinalea	Dunderrow	Kinsale	II.	94
23	Rin	661 2 18*b*	King's Co.	Garrycastle	Gallen	Parsonstown	I.	136
48	Rinagall	9 0 29	Mayo	Tirawley	Kilbelfad	Ballina	IV.	168
2, 3, 7, 8	Rinaghan	51 0 35	Kildare	Carbury	Carrick	Edenderry	I.	52
48	Rinagry	431 2 35	Mayo	Tirawley	Kilbelfad	Ballina	IV.	168
48	Rinakilleen	26 1 10	Mayo	Tirawley	Kilbelfad	Ballina	IV.	168
16	Rinanagh	218 1 35*c*	Mayo	Erris	Kilmore	Belmullet	IV.	146
100	Rinaneel	180 3 18	Mayo	Carra	Burriscarra	Ballinrobe	IV.	127
42	*Rinanny Island*	37 1 21	Roscommon	Ballintober South	Kilteevan	Roscommon	IV.	190
11	Rinawade Lower	47 1 17	Kildare	North Salt	Donaghcumper	Celbridge	I.	74
11	Rinawade Upper	87 2 37	Kildare	North Salt	Donaghcumper	Celbridge	I.	74
32, 33	Rinbaun	876 3 14	Sligo	Leyny	Achonry	Tobercurry	IV.	229
8	Rinboy	183 1 21*d*	Donegal	Kilmacrenan	Clondavaddog	Millford	III.	125
61	Rinbrack	515 2 3*e*	Mayo	Gallen	Meelick	Swineford	IV.	150
15	Rinclevan	260 1 32	Donegal	Kilmacrenan	Clondahorky	Dunfanaghy	III.	123
11, 16	Rincoolagh	662 3 15	Longford	Granard	Granard	Granard	I.	157
37	Rincrew	265 0 30	Waterford	Coshmore&Coshbride	Templemichael	Youghal	II.	349
10, 19	Rincullia	151 3 12	Limerick	Shanid	Robertstown	Rathkeale	II.	258
122, 123, 128, 129	Rindifin	236 1 35	Galway	Kiltartan	Beagh	Gort	IV.	46
42	Rine	88 3 36	Clare	Bunratty Upper	Quin	Tulla	II.	10
2, 3	Rine	325 2 1*f*	Clare	Burren	Oughtmama	Ballyvaghan	II.	14
35	Rine	69 1 34	Clare	Tulla Upper	Tulla	Tulla	II.	42
51, 60, 61	Rineanna North	595 3 35	Clare	Bunratty Lower	Kilconry	Ennis	II.	4
61	Rineanna South	460 2 39	Clare	Bunratty Lower	Kilconry	Ennis	II.	4

(*a*) Including 1A. 3R. 32P. detached portion.
(*b*) Including 6A. 1R. 24P. water.
(*c*) Including 39A. 2R. 21P. water.
(*d*) Including 7A. 3R. 3P. water.
(*e*) Including 14A. 3R. 10P. water.
(*f*) Including 34A. 3R. 27P. water.

No. of Sheet of the Ordnance Survey Maps.	Townlands and Towns.	Area in Statute Acres.	County.	Barony.	Parish.	Poor Law Union in 1857.	Townland Census of 1851, Part I.	
							Vol.	Page
		A. R. P.						
11, 17, 18	Rinecaha	515 2 26a	Clare	Inchiquin	Kilkeedy	Corrofin	II.	26
135	Rineen	28 1 23	Cork, W.R.	Ibane and Barryroe	Island	Clonakilty	II.	149
61	*Rineenacolla*	1 0 13	Clare	Bunratty Lower	Kilconry	Ennis	II.	4
18	Rinelea	279 3 5b	Clare	Inchiquin	Ruan	Corrofin	II.	28
65	Rinemackaderrig	260 2 7	Clare	Moyarta	Moyarta	Kilrush	II.	34
38	Rineroe	78 3 5	Clare	Ibrickan	Kilmurry	Kilrush	II.	24
53	Rineroe	62 2 5	Clare	Tulla Lower	Kiltenanlea	Limerick	II.	37
21	Rineroe	431 3 21	Limerick	Coshma	Adare	Croom	II.	241
25, 33	Rinerrinagh	97 0 22c	Clare	Inchiquin	Dysert	Ennis	II.	24
78	Ring	314 0 23	Cork, E.R.	Imokilly	Kilmacdonogh	Youghal	II.	88
4, 5	Ring	244 1 34	Dublin	Balrothery East	Balscaddan	Balrothery	I.	20
27	Ring	108 3 7d	Fermanagh	Tirkennedy	Derrybrusk	Enniskillen	III.	220
27	Ring	266 2 38e	Fermanagh	Tirkennedy	Enniskillen	Enniskillen	III.	222
22	Ring	91 1 1f	Fermanagh	Tirkennedy	Trory	Enniskillen	III.	223
53	Ring	137 2 20	Wexford	Forth	Carn	Wexford	I.	309
47	Ring	36 1 12	Wexford	Forth	Ishartmon	Wexford	I.	310
47, 48	Ring	67 1 23	Wexford	Forth	Tacumshin	Wexford	I.	315
99	Ringabella	478 0 30	Cork, E.R.	Kinalea	Tracton	Kinsale	II.	97
87	Ringacoltig	135 3 38	Cork, E.R.	Barrymore	Clonmel	Cork	II.	53
47	Ringaheen	79 0 12	Wexford	Forth	Rathmacknee	Wexford	I.	513
31	Ringaphuca	9 3 32	Waterford	Decies without Drum	Dungarvan	Dungarvan	II.	356
89	Ringarraun	179 0 27g	Mayo	Carra	Ballyhean	Castlebar	IV.	126
87	Ringaskiddy	246 3 26	Cork, E.R.	Kerrycurrihy	Barnahely	Cork	II.	91
38	Ringawaddy	236 0 28	Down	Lecale Lower	Dunsfort	Downpatrick	III.	179
31	Ringbane	134 3 7	Down	Lecale Lower	Saul	Downpatrick	III.	179
41	Ringbane	221 2 14h	Down	Upper Iveagh, Up. pt.	Donaghmore	Newry	III.	175
52	Ringbaun	121 1 4	Wexford	Bargy	Kilturk	Wexford	I.	307
52	Ringbaun Burrow	29 3 26	Wexford	Bargy	Kilturk	Wexford	I.	307
40, 41	Ringclare	280 2 15	Down	Upper Iveagh, Up. pt.	Donaghmore	Newry	III.	175
4, 5	Ring Commons	180 3 22	Dublin	Balrothery East	Balscaddan	Balrothery	I.	20
4	Ring Commons (1st Division)	24 2 10	Dublin	Balrothery West	Hollywood	Balrothery	I.	23
4	Ring Commons (2nd Division)	8 2 14	Dublin	Balrothery West	Hollywood	Balrothery	I.	23
10, 11	Ringcreevy	347 1 26	Down	Castlereagh Lower	Comber	Newtownards	III.	162
31	Ringcrehy	64 0 11	Waterford	Decies without Drum	Dungarvan	Dungarvan	II.	356
24	Ringdufferin	241 1 24	Down	Dufferin	Killyleagh	Downpatrick	III.	167
112	Ring East	103 1 0	Cork, E.R.	Kinalea	Kinure	Kinsale	II.	96
103	Ringeelaun	211 1 1	Galway	Dunkellin	Drumacoo	Gort	IV.	28
45	Ringfad	181 1 5	Down	Lecale Lower	Ardglass	Downpatrick	III.	178
124	Ringfinnan	120 2 2	Cork, E.R.	Kinsale	Ringrone	Kinsale	II.	101
53	Ring Green	44 2 20	Wexford	Forth	Carn	Wexford	I.	309
17, 24	Ringhaddy	96 1 13	Down	Dufferin	Killinchy	Downpatrick	III.	166
48	Ringknock	35 0 31	Wexford	Forth	Tacumshin	Wexford	I.	315
31, 31	Ringlestown	812 0 24	Meath	Lower Deece	Kilmessan	Dunshaughlin	I.	192
53	Ring Little	20 1 8	Wexford	Forth	Carn	Wexford	I.	309
51, 54	Ringmackilroy	301 0 26	Down	Upper Iveagh, Up.pt.	Warrenspoint	Newry	III.	176
87	Ringmeen	251 0 4	Cork, E.R.	Barrymore	Clonmel	Cork	II.	53
3	Ringmoylan	99 1 9	Limerick	Kenry	Ardcanny	Rathkeale	II.	248
3	Ringmoylan	113 3 12	Limerick	Kenry	Kilcornan	Rathkeale	II.	249
112	Ringnanean	361 1 32	Cork, E.R.	Kinalea	Kilmonoge	Kinsale	II.	95
31	Ringnasilloge	34 0 33	Waterford	Decies without Drum	Dungarvan	Dungarvan	II.	356
11, 17	Ringneill	455 1 19i	Down	Castlereagh Lower	Tullynakill	Newtownards	III.	163
41	Ringolish	276 2 20	Down	Upper Iveagh, Up. pt.	Donaghmore	Newry	III.	175
15	Ringowny	727 2 8	Longford	Ardagh	Mostrim	Granard	I.	153
7	Ringrash Beg	152 1 22	Londonderry	Coleraine	Macosquin	Coleraine	III.	233
7	Ringrash More	240 2 37	Londonderry	Coleraine	Macosquin	Coleraine	III.	233
37	Ringreagh	153 0 1	Down	Lecale Upper	Kilclief	Downpatrick	III.	181
113	Ringroe	180 1 18	Cork, E.R.	Kinalea	Ballyfoyle	Kinsale	II.	94
10	Ringroe	250 0 13	Tipperary, N.R.	Lower Ormond	Ardcrony	Borrisokane	II.	282
124, 125	Ringrone	160 2 14	Cork, E.R.	Kinsale	Ringrone	Kinsale	II.	101
18	Ringsend	53 0 14	Dublin	Dublin	Donnybrook	Dublin South	I.	30
53	Ringsherane	31 2 19	Wexford	Forth	Carn	Wexford	I.	309
12, 17	Ringstown	1,062 3 9	Queen's Co.	Maryborough West	Clonenagh and Clonagheen	Mountmellick	I.	243
7	Ringstown	235 2 30	Westmeath	Fore	Faughalstown	Castletowndelvin	I.	270
40	Ringvilla	119 3 15	Fermanagh	Clankelly	Galloon	Clones	III.	198
112, 125	Ringville	186 1 24	Cork, E.R.	Kinalea	Kilmonoge	Kinsale	II.	95
44	Ringville	213 0 19	Kilkenny	Ida	Kilcolumb	Waterford	I.	103
36	RINGVILLE OR BALLY-NAGAULBEG T.	—	Waterford	Decies within Drum	Ringagonagh	Dungarvan	II.	353
112	Ring West	86 1 36	Cork, E.R.	Kinalea	Kinure	Kinsale	II.	96
20	Ringwood	95 1 35	Dublin	Newcastle	Newcastle	Celbridge	I.	34
37	Ringwood	206 3 37	Kilkenny	Ida	The Rower	New Ross	I.	104

(a) Including 71A. 3R. 39P. water.
(b) Including 77A. 2R. 12P. water.
(c) Including 15A. 0R. 13P. water.
(d) Including 34A. 1R. 15P. water.
(e) Including 79A. 1R. 26P. water.
(f) Including 7A. 1R. 19P. water.
(g) Including 12A. 2R. 31P. water.
(h) Including 14A. 1R. 24P. water.
(i) Including 1A. 1R. 13P. water.

No. of Sheet of the Ordnance Survey Maps	Townlands and Towns	Area in Statute Acres	County	Barony	Parish	Poor Law Union in 1857	Townland Census of 1851. Part I.	
		A. R. P.					Vol.	Page
18,19,21,22	Rinkinstown	95 0 31	Louth	Ferrard	Rathdrumin	Drogheda	I.	182
43	Rinkippeen	181 0 30	Galway	Dunmore	Tuam	Tuam	IV.	36
8	Rinmore	315 3 8a	Donegal	Kilmacrenan	Clondavaddog	Milford	III.	125
94	Rinmore	465 1 5b	Galway	Galway	St. Nicholas	Galway	IV.	38
48	Rinmore	181 1 6	Mayo	Tirawley	Kilbelfad	Ballina	IV.	168
19, 20	Rinn	183 0 2c	Cavan	Lower Loughtee	Drumlane	Cavan	III.	81
103, 104	Rinn	433 3 16	Galway	Dunkellin	Killeely	Gort	IV.	30
95	Rinn	347 2 25	Galway	Dunkellin	Oranmore	Galway	IV.	32
32,33,35,36	Rinn	415 1 1d	Leitrim	Mohill	Cloone	Mohill	IV.	106
72, 81	Rinn	185 0 6e	Mayo	Costello	Aghamore	Swineford	IV.	137
3	Rinn	284 1 21	Queen's Co.	Tinnahinch	Rosenallis	Mountmellick	I.	250
6, 10	Rinn	560 2 31	Roscommon	Boyle	Ardcarn	Boyle	IV.	193
14	Rinn	27 2 24	Sligo	Carbury	Killaspugbrone	Sligo	IV.	222
39	Rinn	126 1 35	Sligo	Corran	Kilshalvy	Boyle	IV.	227
20	Rinn	55 1 13f	Sligo	Leyny	Ballysadare	Sligo	IV.	230
31	Rinnacurreen	183 3 10	Leitrim	Leitrim	Kiltoghert	Car^. on Shannon	IV.	102
41	Rinnafarset	557 1 17g	Donegal	Boylagh	Templecrone	Glenties	III.	116
42, 43, 46	Rinnagan	765 2 17	Roscommon	Athlone	St. Johns	Athlone	IV.	184
35	Rinnagowna	194 0 1	Leitrim	Mohill	Mohill	Mohill	IV.	108
69	Rinnaharney	160 3 2	Galway	Clare	Annaghdown	Galway	IV.	16
79	Rinnahulty	160 2 31h	Mayo	Carra	Manulla	Castlebar	IV.	129
96	Rinnakill	183 1 10	Donegal	Banagh	Glencolumbkille	Glenties	III.	105
55	Rinnaknock	82 2 23	Galway	Clare	Killursa	Tuam	IV.	22
10, 17	Rinnamona	429 0 24	Clare	Inchiquin	Killinaboy	Corrofin	II.	27
48, 49	Rinnananny	444 2 16i	Mayo	Gallen	Toomore	Swineford	IV.	151
16	Rinnaraw	78 1 26j	Donegal	Kilmacrenan	Clondahorky	Dunfanaghy	III.	123
39	Rinnarogue	180 3 17	Sligo	Corran	Cloonoghil	Tobercurry	IV.	225
77. 78	Rinnaseer	180 1 6k	Mayo	Burrishoole	Islandeady	Westport	IV.	121
10, 11, 17	Rinnashinnagh	551 0 1	Mayo	Erris	Kilcommon	Belmullet	IV.	144
26	Rinnasligo	225 2 23l	Donegal	Kilmacrenan	Clondahorky	Dunfanaghy	III.	123
13	Rinn and Clogher	261 0 23	Longford	Longford	Killashee	Longford	I.	158
34	Rinneen	49 1 38	Clare	Bunratty Upper	Quin	Tulla	II.	10
22, 23	Rinneen	392 0 2	Clare	Corcomroe	Kilmanaheen	Ennistimon	II.	21
17	Rinneen	462 1 15m	Clare	Inchiquin	Ruan	Corrofin	II.	28
123	Rinneen	192 1 21	Galway	Kiltartan	Kiltartan	Gort	IV.	48
112	Rinneen	140 3 22	Galway	Kiltartan	Kinvarradoorus	Gort	IV.	49
68	Rinneen	250 2 17n	Galway	Moycullen	Moycullen	Galway	IV.	71
105, 106	Rinneen	450 1 4	Kerry	Dunkerron South	Kilcrohane	Cahersiveen	II.	184
15	Rinnenny	138 3 14	Longford	Ardagh	Mostrim	Granard	I.	153
40	Rinnerroon	72 3 23	Galway	Moycullen	Kilcummin	Oughterard	IV.	68
40	Rinrainy Island	19 2 3	Donegal	Boylagh	Templecrone	Glenties	III.	116
17	Rinroe	193 1 26o	Clare	Inchiquin	Kilkeedy	Corrofin	II.	26
11, 16	Rinroe	263 2 26	Longford	Granard	Granard	Granard	I.	157
22	Rinroe	196 0 15	Sligo	Tireragh	Castleconor	Dromore West	IV.	232
123	Rinrush	134 2 18	Galway	Kiltartan	Kiltartan	Gort	IV.	48
78	Rinshinna	161 1 11	Mayo	Carra	Breaghwy	Castlebar	IV.	127
135	Rinskea	133 0 22	Galway	Leitrim	Clonrush	Scarriff	IV.	53
11, 20	Rintulla	128 2 34	Limerick	Kenry	Kilcornan	Rathkeale	II.	249
15	Rinvanny	258 1 17	Longford	Ardagh	Clonbroney	Granard	I.	152
95	Rinville East	248 3 17	Galway	Dunkellin	Oranmore	Galway	IV.	32
94	RINVILLE T.	—	Galway	Dunkellin	Oranmore	Galway	IV.	32
94, 95	Rinville West	820 3 2	Galway	Dunkellin	Oranmore	Galway	IV.	32
48	Riscrann	23 0 30	Wexford	Forth	St. Helens	Wexford	I.	314
6, 7	Risk	157 3 18	Antrim	Lower Dunluce	Ballyrashane	Coleraine	III.	15
13	Risk	320 1 5p	Down	Lower Iveagh, Up. pt.	Moira	Lurgan	III.	170
19	Risk	68 2 22	Londonderry	Coleraine	Aghadowey	Coleraine	III.	230
12	RIVERCHAPEL T.		Wexford	Ballaghkeen	Ardamine	Gorey	I.	291
21, 28	Riverdale	1,695 2 25	Westmeath	Farbill	Killucan	Castletowndelvin	I.	267
109	River Island	6 2 5	Mayo	Carra	Ballyovey	Ballinrobe	IV.	126
15, 21	Riverlawn	71 3 14	Tipperary, N.R.	Upper Ormond	Ballymackey	Nenagh	II.	289
18, 19	Riverlyons or Clonarrow	1,897 3 14	King's Co.	Lower Philipstown	Kilclonfert	Tullamore	I.	142
6	Rivers	21 0 11	Limerick	Clanwilliam	Killeenagarriff	Limerick	II.	224
6	Rivers	317 3 3	Limerick	Clanwilliam	Kilmurry	Limerick	II.	225
6	Rivers	118 3 19	Limerick	Clanwilliam	Stradbally	Limerick	II.	226
46, 47	Riversdale	116 2 2	Galway	Killian	Killeroran	Mountbellew	IV.	44
26	Riversfield	69 0 6	Kilkenny	Callan	Callan	Callan	I.	84
48	Riversfield	159 1 19	Limerick	Coshlea	Ardpatrick	Kilmallock	II.	236
86	Riverstick or Owenavaddy	71 1 11	Galway	Kilconnell	Killaan	Loughrea	IV.	41
64	Riverstown	56 0 26	Cork, E.R.	Barrymore	Ballydeloher	Cork	II.	51
63, 64, 75	Riverstown	449 1 39	Cork, E.R.	Barrymore	Templeusque	Cork	II.	59
26	Riverstown	240 3 35q	Kildare	Offaly West	Ballybrackan	Athy	I.	71

(a) Including 29A. 0R. 18P. water.
(b) Including 11A. 0R. 32P. water.
(c) Including 46A. 2R. 10P. water.
(d) Including 167A. 2R. 20P. water.
(e) Including 2A. 1R. 17P. water.
(f) Including 5A. 0R. 26P. water.

(g) Including 34A. 2R. 17P. water.
(h) Including 37A. 0R. 3P. water.
(i) Including 13A. 0R. 7P. water.
(j) Including 9A. 1R. 22P. water.
(k) Including 9A. 2R. 26P. water.
(l) Including 5A. 3R. 11P. water.

(m) Including 60A. 2R. 5P. water.
(n) Including 70A. 1R. 4P. water.
(o) Including 19A. 2R. 30P. water.
(p) Including 19A. 2R. 25P. water.
(q) Including 12A. 3R. 12P. water.

No. of Sheet of the Ordnance Survey Maps.	Townlands and Towns.	Area in Statute Acres.	County.	Barony.	Parish.	Poor Law Union in 1857.	Townland Census of 1851, Part I.	
		A. R. P.					Vol.	Page
14	Riverstown	383 1 20	Louth	Ardee	Ardee	Ardee	I.	171
31	Riverstown	907 3 39	Meath	Skreen	Tara	Navan	I.	222
33	Riverstown	412 3 37	Meath	Upper Duleek	Duleek	Drogheda	I.	198
33	Riverstown	79 0 36	Meath	Upper Duleek	Piercetown	Dunshaughlin	I.	198
39, 44	Riverstown	333 2 2	Sligo	Corran	Kilshalvy	Boyle	IV.	227
42	Riverstown	57 1 8a	Tyrone	Omagh East	Drumragh	Omagh	III.	313
20, 27	Riverstown	457 0 35	Westmeath	Farbill	Killucan	Mullingar	I.	267
46	Riverstown	94 2 22	Wexford	Bargy	Killag	Wexford	I.	306
64, 75	Riverstown T.	—	Cork, E.R.	Barrymore	Templeusque	Cork	II.	59
27	Riverstown T.	—	Sligo	Tirerrill	{ Drumcolumb	} Sligo	IV.	{238
					Kilmacallan			240}
5	Riverstown T.	—	Tipperary, N.R.	Lower Ormond	Loughkeen	Parsonstown	II.	286
26	Riverview	100 0 33	Wexford	Ballaghkeen	Edermine	Enniscorthy	I.	294
15	Rivory	312 0 19b	Cavan	Upper Loughtee	Urney	Cavan	III.	86
19	Roachpond	31 3 39c	Kilkenny	Gowran and Municipal Borough	St. John's	Kilkenny	I.	98
11	Road	175 0 33	King's Co.	Warrenstown	Ballyburly	Edenderry	I.	144
8	Roadford T.	—	Clare	Corcomroe	Killilagh	Ennistimon	II.	20
33	Roadmain	222 0 13	Meath	Skreen	Cushinstown	Dunshaughlin	I.	220
26	Roadquarter	70 0 26	Roscommon	Castlereagh	Kiltullagh	Castlereagh	IV.	202
62, 70	Roads	637 2 36d	Kerry	Iveragh	Killinane	Cahersiveen	II.	197
38	Roadstown or Ballinvally	213 1 34	Sligo	Corran	Cloonoghil	Tobercurry	IV.	225
40	Roan	119 3 7	Tipperary, N.R.	Kilnamanagh Upper	Upperchurch	Thurles	II.	281
54	Roan	272 1 39	Tipperary, S.R.	Slievardagh	Killenaule	Cashel	II.	334
61	Roan	127 1 39	Tyrone	Dungannon Middle	Clonfeacle	Dungannon	III.	300
64, 73	Roancarrick Island	5 1 34	Donegal	Boylagh	Inishkeel	Glenties	III.	114
116	Roancarrig-beg (rock)	—	Cork, W.R.	Bear	Kilcaskan	Bantry	II.	123
116	Roancarrig-more (rock)	—	Cork, W.R.	Bear	Kilcaskan	Bantry	II.	123
64	Roanish Island	21 0 4	Donegal	Boylagh	Inishkeel	Glenties	III.	114
50	Roanstown	276 3 33	Meath	Ratoath	Ballymaglassan	Dunshaughlin	I.	217
110	Robeen	142 1 28e	Mayo	Kilmaine	Robeen	Ballinrobe	IV.	157
110, 111	Robeenard	443 3 30	Mayo	Kilmaine	Kilcommon	Ballinrobe	IV.	155
19	Robertshill	67 1 25f	Kilkenny	Shillelogher and Municipal Borough	St. Canice	Kilkenny	I.	115
98	Robertstown	430 0 3	Cork, E.R.	Kinalea	Ballyfeard	Kinsale	II.	93
10, 19	Robertstown	285 3 39	Limerick	Shanid	Robertstown	Rathkeale	II.	258
5, 11	Robertstown	1,678 3 11g	Meath	Lower Kells	Kilbeg	Kells	I.	203
45	Robertstown	293 0 10	Meath	Ratoath	Donaghmore	Dunshaughlin	I.	218
23, 24	Robertstown	191 1 22	Waterford	Decies without Drum	Killrossanty	Kilmacthomas	II.	358
7, 8, 15, 16	Robertstown	535 3 20	Waterford	Decies without Drum	Rossmire	Kilmacthomas	II.	360
13	Robertstown East	336 1 9	Kildare	Connell	Kilmeage	Naas	I.	55
13	Robertstown T.	—	Kildare	Connell	Kilmeage	Naas	I.	55
13	Robertstown West	269 3 12	Kildare	Connell	Kilmeage	Naas	I.	55
18, 22	Robinhood	77 2 7	Dublin	Uppercross	Drimnagh	Dublin South	I.	40
26	Robinhood or Cloonlish	257 0 5	Roscommon	Castlereagh	Kiltullagh	Castlereagh	IV.	201
25	Robinrath	120 2 30	Meath	Lower Navan	Navan	Navan	I.	215
41	Robinstown	323 1 3	Kilkenny	Ida	Kilmakevoge	Waterford	I.	103
11	Robinstown	159 1 27	Longford	Granard	Granard	Granard	I.	157
35	Robinstown	515 3 33	Meath	Lune	Killaconnigan	Trim	I.	208
16, 23	Robinstown	759 0 18	Meath	Upper Kells	Kilskeer	Kells	I.	206
8	Robinstown	393 1 23	Westmeath	Delvin	Kilcumny	Castletowndelvin	I.	265
25,26,32,33	Robinstown	318 2 3	Westmeath	Fartullagh	Carrick	Mullingar	I.	267
32, 33	Robinstown	20 2 24	Westmeath	Fartullagh	Clonfad	Mullingar	I.	268
3	Robinstown	152 0 25	Westmeath	Fore	Lickbla	Castletowndelvin	I.	270
46	Robinstown	325 3 19	Wexford	Bargy	Duncormick	Wexford	I.	305
9, 14	Robinstown Great	98 0 20	Westmeath	Delvin	Castletowndelvin	Castletowndelvin	I.	265
30	Robinstown Great	661 0 33	Wexford	Bantry	Oldross	New Ross	I.	301
19	Robinstown (Levinge)	306 1 6	Westmeath	Moyashel and Magheradernon	Mullingar	Mullingar	I.	275
9	Robinstown Little	23 1 16	Westmeath	Delvin	Castletowndelvin	Castletowndelvin	I.	265
30	Robinstown Little	341 0 38	Wexford	Bantry	Oldross	New Ross	I.	301
3	Robinstown Lower	98 2 9	Westmeath	Fore	Rathgarve	Castletowndelvin	I.	271
19	Robinstown (Tyrrell)	250 2 3	Westmeath	Moyashel and Magheradernon	Mullingar	Mullingar	I.	275
3	Robinstown Upper	125 0 18	Westmeath	Fore	Rathgarve	Castletowndelvin	I.	271
12	Robswalls	191 1 12	Dublin	Coolock	Portmarnock	Balrothery	I.	28
3	Roche	35 1 36	Louth	Upper Dundalk	Kane	Dundalk	I.	179
3	Roche	230 0 39	Louth	Upper Dundalk	Roche	Dundalk	I.	179
23, 26	Rocheshill	122 3 15	Dublin	Rathdown	Kill	Rathdown	I.	36
75, 87	Rochestown	505 0 27	Cork, E.R.	Cork	Carrigaline	Cork	II.	64
124, 137	Rochestown	104 0 29	Cork, W.R.	East Carbery (E.D.)	Templetrine	Kinsale	II.	130
23	Rochestown	95 0 24h	Dublin	Rathdown	Kill	Rathdown	I.	36
29	Rochestown	113 3 25i	Kildare	Naas South	Gilltown	Naas	I.	65

(a) Including 2A. 1R. 0P. water.
(b) Including 33A. 0R. 25P. water.
(c) { Within the Municipal Boundary, 28A. 0R. 20P. { Without the Municipal Boundary, 3A. 3R. 19P.
(d) Including 1A. 0R. 8P. water.
(e) Including 4A. 1R. 18P. water.
(f) { Within the Municipal Boundary, 67A. 1R. 4P. { Without the Municipal Boundary, 0A. 0R. 21P.
(g) Including 5A. 1R. 8P. water.
(h) Including 63A. 2R. 30P. detached portion.
(i) Including 5A. 3R. 25P. water.

No. of Sheet of the Ordnance Survey Maps.	Townlands and Towns.	Area in Statute Acres.			County.	Barony.	Parish.	Poor Law Union in 1857.	Townland Census of 1851, Part I.	
		A.	R.	P.					Vol.	Page
44	Rochestown	862	0	33	Kilkenny	Ida	Kilcolumb	Waterford	I.	103
39	Rochestown	486	3	1	Kilkenny	Iverk	Rathkieran	Waterford	I.	107
22, 23	Rochestown	465	2	4	Limerick	Clanwilliam	Rochestown	Limerick	II.	225
18	Rochestown	405	1	6	Meath	Upper Slane	Gernonstown	Navan	I.	224
81, 82	Rochestown	633	3	3a	Tipperary, S.R.	Iffa and Offa West	Rochestown	Clogheen	II.	319
3	Rochestown	154	2	13	Westmeath	Fore	Lickbla	Granard	I.	270
34, 35	Rochestown	685	3	21	Wexford	Bantry	Oldross	New Ross	I.	301
46	Rochestown	140	0	34	Wexford	Bargy	Duncormick	Wexford	I.	305
41	Rochestown	504	2	3	Wexford	Bargy	Taghmon	Wexford	I.	307
42	Rochestown	89	3	13	Wexford	Forth	Drinagh	Wexford	I.	309
40	Rochestown	228	3	13	Wexford	Shelmaliere West	Ballylannan	New Ross	I.	332
23	Rochestown Domain	113	2	22	Dublin	Rathdown	Kill	Rathdown	I.	36
30	Rochestown or Raheenarostia	149	1	16	Wexford	Bantry	Newbawn	New Ross	I.	301
85, 86	Rochfordstown	538	0	27	Cork, E.R.	Cork	Inishkenny	Cork	II.	64
33	ROCHFORTBRIDGE T.	—			Westmeath	Fartullagh	Castlelost	Mullingar	I.	268
26	Rochfort Demesne	450	0	3	Westmeath	Fartullagh	Moylisker	Mullingar	I.	269
10,11,16,17	Rochfortsland or Mountainpole	84	1	35	Meath	Upper Kells	Kells	Kells	I.	206
98, 99	Rock	194	3	35	Donegal	Banagh	Inver	Donegal	III.	108
14	Rock	12	1	4	Dublin	Coolock	Santry	Dublin North	I.	29
32	Rock	188	1	31	Kildare	Offaly West	Kilrush	Athy	I.	73
14	Rock	67	0	22	Louth	Ardee	Ardee	Ardee	I.	171
11	Rock	25	1	34	Roscommon	Boyle	Killukin	Cark. on Shannon	IV.	196
31, 32	Rockbarton	245	2	31	Limerick	Coshma	Tullabracky	Croom	II.	244
31	Rockbarton	241	3	34	Limerick	Smallcounty	Glenogra	Croom	II.	260
45	Rock Big	251	2	21	Wicklow	Arklow	Arklow	Rathdrum	I.	341
45	Rockbog	88	2	20	Wicklow	Arklow	Arklow	Rathdrum	I.	341
70	Rockborough	115	2	34	Cork, W.R.	West Muskerry	Macroom	Macroom	II.	160
27	Rockbrook	231	1	25	Sligo	Tirerrill	Ballynakill	Sligo	IV.	237
18	ROCKCORRY T.	—			Monaghan	Dartree	Ematris	Cootehill	III.	267
38	Rockdale	123	1	13	Tyrone	Dungannon Upper	Desertcreat	Cookstown	III.	308
29, 35	Rocker	125	1	7	Tipperary, N.R.	Eliogarty	Loughmoe West	Thurles	II.	271
4, 8	Rocketscastle or Mayfield	495	2	8	Waterford	Upperthird	Clonagam	Carrick on Suir	II.	369
23	Rockfarm	60	1	36	Limerick	Clanwilliam	Ballybrood	Limerick	II.	221
32	Rockfield	159	2	16	Cavan	Castlerahan	Crosserlough	Cavan	III.	68
55, 63	Rockfield	105	3	18	Donegal	Raphoe	Taughboyne	Strabane	III.	144
23	Rockfield	79	0	9	Dublin	Rathdown	Monkstown	Rathdown	I.	37
34, 35	Rockfield	124	1	2	Fermanagh	Clankelly	Galloon	Lisnaskea	III.	198
15, 16	Rockfield	188	2	22	Fermanagh	Lurg	Trory	Lowtherstown	III.	209
96	Rockfield	253	3	5	Galway	Dunkellin	Killeeneen	Loughrea	IV.	30
30, 39	Rockfield	305	0	14	Kerry	Trughanacmy	Ballymacelligott	Tralee	II.	207
22	Rockfield	129	1	8	Limerick	Smallcounty	Ballycahane	Croom	II.	259
88	Rockfield	237	0	23	Mayo	Burrishoole	Aghagower	Westport	IV.	118
70	Rockfield	365	2	26	Mayo	Carra	Turlough	Castlebar	IV.	131
91, 92, 102	Rockfield	874	2	21b	Mayo	Clanmorris	Kilcolman	Claremorris	IV.	134
16, 17	Rockfield	180	0	9	Meath	Upper Kells	Kells	Kells	I.	206
30	Rockfield	131	2	4	Waterford	Decies without Drum	Modelligo	Lismore	II.	359
5	Rockfield or Crumlin	297	1	9c	Westmeath	Moygoish	Rathaspick	Mullingar	I.	280
31	Rockfield East	319	1	1	Galway	Tiaquin	Kilkerrin	Glennamaddy	IV.	77
57, 58	Rockfield East	435	0	22	Kerry	Magunihy	Kilbonane	Killarney	II.	200
19, 24	Rockfield or Loughnafin	378	0	8d	Cavan	Tullyhunco	Killashandra	Cavan	III.	98
57	Rockfield Middle	315	0	13	Kerry	Magunihy	Kilbonane	Killarney	II.	200
31	Rockfield West	161	2	31	Galway	Tiaquin	Kilkerrin	Glennamaddy	IV.	77
57	Rockfield West	118	1	5	Kerry	Magunihy	Kilbonane	Killarney	II.	200
25, 26	Rockfinlough	260	1	23	Sligo	Leyny	Kilvarnet	Tobercurry	IV.	232
67	Rockfleet	92	0	13e	Mayo	Burrishoole	Burrishoole	Newport	IV.	119
18	Rockforest	830	0	15	Tipperary, N.R.	Ikerrin	Corbally	Roscrea	II.	275
33	Rockforest East	255	1	17f	Cork, E.R.	Fermoy	Rahan	Mallow	II.	82
10, 11, 17	Rockforest or Magheranraheen	511	1	2g	Clare	Inchiquin	Kilkeedy	Corrofin	II.	26
33	Rockforest West	170	3	39h	Cork, E.R.	Fermoy	Rahan	Mallow	II.	82
96, 97	Rockfort	308	0	14	Cork, W.R.	East Carbery (E.D.)	Brinny	Bandon	II.	127
71, 72	Rockgrove	189	0	31	Cork, E.R.	East Muskerry	Magourney	Macroom	II.	105
38	Rockhead	82	2	29	Tyrone	Dungannon Upper	Derryloran	Cookstown	III.	307
16	Rockhill	121	3	37i	Donegal	Kilmacrenan	Clondahorky	Dunfanaghy	III.	123
53, 61	Rockhill	249	3	13	Donegal	Raphoe	Leck	Letterkenny	III.	140
103, 104	Rockhill	763	2	17j	Donegal	Tirhugh	Drumhome	Ballyshannon	III.	147
95	Rockhill	50	3	28	Galway	Dunkellin	Oranmore	Galway	IV	32
2, 4	Rockhill	98	3	9	Roscommon	Boyle	Kilronan	Boyle	IV.	197
4, 5	Rockhill East	779	2	32	Cork, E.R.	Duhallow	Clonfert	Kanturk	II.	69
38	ROCKHILL T.	—			Limerick	Connello Upper	Bruree	Kilmallock	II.	231

(a) Including 6A. 0R. 0P. water. (e) Including 9A. 3R. 31P. water. (h) Including 5A. 3R. 8P. water.
(b) Including 32A. 2R. 39P. water. (f) Including 7A. 3R. 16P. water. (i) Including 15A. 2R. 33P. water.
(c) Including 52A. 1R. 39P. water. (g) Including 12A. 3R. 9P. water. (j) Including 31A. 1R. 31P. water.
(d) Including 61A. 2R. 20P. water.

No. of Sheet of the Ordnance Survey Maps.	Townlands and Towns.	Area in Statute Acres. A. R. P.	County.	Barony.	Parish.	Poor Law Union in 1857.	Townland Census of 1851, Part I. Vol.	Page
4, 5	Rockhill West	1,329 3 3	Cork, E.R.	Duhallow	Clonfert	Kanturk	II.	69
111	Rockhouse	82 2 19a	Cork, W.R.	East Carbery (E.D.)	Ballinadee	Bandon	II.	126
147	Rock Island	61 0 34	Cork, W.R.	West Carbery (W.D.)	Kilmoe	Skull	II.	145
110	*Rock Island*	34 3 34	Galway	Aran	Inishmore	Galway	IV.	3
50, 51	Rockland	332 1 13	Roscommon	Athlone	Taghmaconnell	Athlone	IV.	185
95	Rocklands	75 3 28	Galway	Dunkellin	Oranmore	Galway	IV.	32
—	ROCKLEY T.	—	Sligo	Carbury	Drumcliff	Sligo	IV.	222
45	Rock Little	138 3 35	Wicklow	Arklow	Arklow	Rathdrum	I.	341
70	Rocklow	81 1 12	Tipperary, S.R.	Middlethird	Rathcool	Cashel	II.	329
13	Rockmacreeny	280 3 13	Armagh	Oneilland West	Kilmore	Armagh	III.	53
8	Rockmarshall	568 2 30	Louth	Lower Dundalk	Ballymascanlan	Dundalk	I.	176
18	ROCKMILLS T.	—	Cork, E.R.	Fermoy	St. Nathlash	Mitchelstown	II.	82
40, 41	Rock of Ballingly	111 3 12	Wexford	Bargy	Kilcavan	Wexford	I.	305
122	Rockpark	85 0 10	Galway	Kiltartan	Kilmacduagh	Gort	IV.	48
19, 20, 23, 24	Rockpeyton	64 3 27	Longford	Ardagh	Kilglass	Ballymahon	I.	152
13	Rocks	41 2 34	Armagh	Fews Lower	Mullaghbrack	Armagh	III.	47
25	Rocks	81 2 13	Cavan	Clanmahon	Kilmore	Cavan	III.	78
22	Rocksavage	88 1 32	Carlow	St. Mullins Lower	St. Mullins	New Ross	I.	13
135, 136	Rocksavage	166 1 10	Cork, W.R.	Ibane and Barryroe	Templequinlan	Clonakilty	II.	151
37, 42, 43	Rocksborough	178 0 31	Wexford	Forth	Maudlintown	Wexford	I.	312
110	Rocksborough North	109 2 0	Mayo	Kilmaine	Ballinrobe	Ballinrobe	IV.	153
110	Rocksborough South	177 1 11	Mayo	Kilmaine	Ballinrobe	Ballinrobe	IV.	153
9	Rockshire	137 3 19b	Waterford	Gaultiere and Municipal Borough	Kilculliheen	Waterford	II.	363
15, 16	Rockspring	350 3 6	Cork, E.R.	Orrery and Kilmore	Liscarroll	Mallow	II.	109
16	Rockspring	178 2 2	Wexford	Scarawalsh	Kilbride	Enniscorthy	I.	323
22, 23	Rockstown	233 2 6	Limerick	Clanwilliam	Fedamore	Limerick	II.	223
23	Rockstown	52 0 9	Limerick	Clanwilliam	Rochestown	Limerick	II.	225
30, 35	Rockstown Lower	114 2 16	Wicklow	Arklow	Castlemacadam	Rathdrum	I.	342
30, 35	Rockstown Upper	258 0 29	Wicklow	Arklow	Castlemacadam	Rathdrum	I.	342
37	Rocktown	757 1 32	Londonderry	Loughinsholin	Maghera	Magherafelt	III.	242
11	Rockvale	457 1 28c	Clare	Inchiquin	Kilkeedy	Corrofin	II.	26
31, 37	Rockvale	66 3 33	Tipperary, N.R.	Owney and Arra	Kilnarath	Nenagh	II.	296
5	Rockview	241 3 7	Tipperary, N.R.	Lower Ormond	Dorrha	Parsonstown	II.	283
14	Rockview	119 2 15	Tipperary, N.R.	Lower Ormond	Knigh	Nenagh	II.	285
72	Rockview	121 1 2	Tipperary, S.R.	Slievardagh	Templemichael	Callan	II.	336
17	Rockville	196 3 12d	Roscommon	Roscommon	Aughrim	Cark. on Shannon	IV.	207
68, 69	Rockwell	338 0 21e	Tipperary, S.R.	Middlethird	Knockgraffon	Cashel	II.	328
82	Rockwood	41 0 34	Galway	Dunkellin	Claregalway	Galway	IV.	28
87	*Rocky Island*	2 2 5	Cork, E.R.	Barrymore	Templerobin	Cork	II.	58
49	Rodanstown	214 1 23	Meath	Upper Deece	Rodanstown	Celbridge	I.	194
12, 18	Roddans	395 2 27	Down	Ards Upper	St. Andrews *alias* Ballyhalbert	Newtownards	III.	161
34, 39	Roddenagh	846 3 11	Wicklow	Ballinacor South	Kilpipe	Shillelagh	I.	349
115	Rodeen	564 1 17	Cork, W.R.	Bear	Killaconenagh	Castletown	II.	125
17	Rodeen	118 3 5f	Roscommon	Roscommon	Aughrim	Cark. on Shannon	IV.	207
38	Rodeen	40 2 10	Waterford	Decies within Drum	Ardmore	Youghal	II.	350
9, 10	Rodeen Lower	263 0 2	Tipperary, N.R.	Lower Ormond	Finnoe	Borrisokane	II.	284
10	Rodeen Upper	207 1 24	Tipperary, N.R.	Lower Ormond	Finnoe	Borrisokane	II.	284
4	Roden	351 3 22	Tipperary, N.R.	Lower Ormond	Dorrha	Parsonstown	II.	283
24	Rodstown	263 0 27	Meath	Lower Navan	Martry	Kells	I.	215
16	Rodstown	76 1 17	Meath	Upper Kells	Burry	Kells	I.	205
65	Rodus	85 0 6	Tipperary, S.R.	Clanwilliam	Emly	Tipperary	II.	308
42	Roebuck	440 3 30	Cavan	Clanmahon	Kilbride	Oldcastle	III.	78
22	Roebuck	6 0 17	Dublin	Dublin	Taney	Rathdown	I.	30
22	Roebuck	814 0 23	Dublin	Rathdown	Taney	Rathdown	I.	38
22	Roebuck	35 1 7	Dublin	Uppercross	Crumlin	Dublin South	I.	40
70	Roebuck's-land	123 0 16	Tipperary, S.R.	Middlethird	Coolmundry	Cashel	II.	326
82, 91	Roechrow	352 3 25	Donegal	Banagh	Inishkeel	Glenties	III.	106
82	Roechrow	300 3 25	Donegal	Banagh	Killybegs Upper	Glenties	III.	111
7	Roegarraun	187 2 11	Tipperary, N.R.	Lower Ormond	Terryglass	Borrisokane	II.	288
55	*Roeillan*	2 2 39	Mayo	Burrishoole	Achill	Newport	IV.	117
87	*Roeillan*	3 2 18	Mayo	Murrisk	Oughaval	Westport	IV.	162
9, 10, 22, 23	*Roeillaun*	36 2 7	Galway	Ballynahinch	Ballynakill	Clifden	IV.	12
10	*Roeillaun*	3 1 20	Galway	Ballynahinch	Ballynakill	Clifden	IV.	12
21	*Roeillaun*	3 1 12	Galway	Ballynahinch	Omey	Clifden	IV.	15
54	*Roeillaun*	18 0 17	Galway	Moycullen	Kilcummin	Oughterard	IV.	69
65	*Roeillaun*	3 0 32	Galway	Moycullen	Kilcummin	Oughterard	IV.	69
66	*Roeillaun*	15 3 36	Mayo	Burrishoole	Burrishoole	Newport	IV.	120
40	*Roeillaunbaun*	1 2 34	Galway	Ross	Cong	Oughterard	IV.	73
40	*Roeillaundoo*	5 1 39	Galway	Ross	Cong	Oughterard	IV.	73
40	*Roeillaun East*	2 0 0	Galway	Ross	Cong	Oughterard	IV.	73
17	*Roe Island*	20 2 9	Down	Ards Upper	Ardkeen	Downpatrick	III.	159

(a) Including 10A. 0R. 14P. detached portion.
(b) { Within the Municipal Boundary, 10A. 2R. 37P.
      { Without the Municipal Boundary, 127A. 0R. 22P.

(c) Including 35A. 0R. 5P. water.
(d) Including 8A. 0R. 7P. water.

(e) Including 20A. 2R. 8P. water.
(f) Including 7A. 3R. 0P. water.

No. of Sheet of the Ordnance Survey Maps.	Townlands and Towns.	Area in Statute Acres.	County.	Barony.	Parish.	Poor Law Union in 1857.	Townland Census of 1851, Part I.	
		A.　R.　P.					Vol.	Page
38	*Roe Island* . .	5　3　4	Mayo . .	Tirawley . .	Crossmolina . .	Ballina . .	IV.	167
77	Roekilmeena .	220　2　0	Mayo . .	Burrishoole . .	Kilmeena . .	Westport . .	IV.	122
96	Roelough . .	130　0　29	Donegal . .	Banagh . . .	Kilcar . .	Glenties . .	III.	109
77	Roemore . .	132　2　4	Mayo . .	Burrishoole . .	Kilmeena . .	Newport . .	IV.	122
79	Roemore . .	88　1　19	Mayo . .	Carra . . .	Breaghwy . .	Castlebar . .	IV.	127
93	Roes . . .	289　3　37	Donegal . .	Banagh . . .	Inver . .	Donegal . .	III.	108
66	Roesborough .	337　1　4	Tipperary, S.R.	Clanwilliam .	Tipperary . .	Tipperary . .	II.	312
5	Roestown . .	228　2　16	Kildare . .	Ikeathy&Oughterany	Kilcock . .	Celbridge . .	I.	57
17	Roestown . .	421　1　26	Louth . .	Ardee . . .	Kildemock . .	Ardee . .	I.	173
38, 44	Roestown . .	398　3　13	Meath . .	Ratoath . .	Dunshaughlin .	Dunshaughlin .	I.	218
18	Roestown . .	166　3　14	Meath . .	Upper Slane .	Gernonstown .	Navan . .	I.	224
95, 103	Roevehagh . .	679　1　13	Galway . .	Dunkellin . .	Killeely . .	Gort . .	IV.	30
79	Roganspark . .	9　0　26	Donegal . .	Raphoe . .	Urney . .	Strabane . .	III.	144
11	Roganstown . .	178　2　7	Dublin . .	Nethercross .	Swords . .	Balrothery .	I.	32
15	Rogary . .	35　0　19*a*	Cavan . .	Lower Loughtee .	Drumlane . .	Cavan . .	III.	81
42, 56	Rogersfield or Gortrory	52　3　32	Galway . .	Clare . . .	Killeany . .	Tuam . .	IV.	20
8	Rogerstown . .	345　2　8	Dublin . .	Balrothery East .	Lusk . . .	Balrothery .	I.	21
31	Rogerstown . .	296　0　21	Kilkenny . .	Kells . . .	Kilmaganny .	Callan . .	I.	109
11	Rogerstown . .	355　1　18	King's Co. .	Coolestown . .	Monasteroris .	Edenderry .	I.	133
13	Rogerstown . .	242　2　16	Louth . .	Ardee . . .	Clonkeen . .	Ardee . .	I.	172
20, 27, 28	Rogerstown . .	518　3　13	Meath . .	Lower Duleek .	Julianstown .	Drogheda .	I.	196
25	Rogerstown . .	133　0　15	Westmeath .	Rathconrath .	Churchtown .	Mullingar .	I.	282
38, 39	Rogerstown & Belline	648　2　38	Kilkenny . .	Iverk . . .	Fiddown . .	Carrick on Suir	I.	105
18, 21	Rokeby . . .	245　3　14	Louth . .	Ferrard . .	Marlestown .	Drogheda .	I.	181
2	Rolagh . .	174　1　3	Meath . .	Morgallion . .	Enniskeen . .	Kells . .	I.	209
17	*Rolly Island* . .	21　0　16	Down . .	Castlereagh Lower .	Tullynakill .	Newtownards .	III.	164
87	*Roman Island* . .	8　2　22	Mayo . .	Murrisk . .	Oughaval . .	Westport . .	IV.	162
17	Ronanstown . .	91　0　28	Dublin . .	Uppercross . .	Clondalkin .	Dublin South .	I.	39
16	Ronard . .	76　2　39	Cavan . .	Tullygarvey .	Drung . .	Cootehill .	III.	89
1, 3	Roo . . .	419　0　23	Cavan . .	Tullyhaw . .	Killinagh . .	Enniskillen .	III.	92
96, 104	Roo . . .	742　3　36	Galway . .	Dunkellin . .	Killora . .	Loughrea .	IV.	31
122	Roo . . .	847　3　21	Galway . .	Kiltartan . .	Kilmacdungh .	Gort . .	IV.	48
24	Roo . . .	171　0　22	Monaghan .	Cremorne . .	Aghnamullen .	Castleblayney .	III.	258
17, 18	Roo . . .	145　3　16*b*	Roscommon .	Ballintober North .	Kilmore . .	Car*k*.on Shannon	IV.	187
22	Rooan . .	86　2　32	Westmeath .	Kilkenny West .	Bunown . .	Athlone .	I.	272
98	Rooaun . .	175　2　27	Galway . .	Kilconnell . .	Killallaghtan .	Ballinasloe .	IV.	41
108, 109	Rooaun . .	636　3　31	Galway . .	Longford . .	Clonfert . .	Ballinasloe .	IV.	57
43	Rooaun . .	74　3　14	King's Co. .	Ballybritt . .	Roscrea . .	Roscrea . .	I.	126
23, 24	Rooaun . .	237　1　37	Roscommon .	Ballintober North .	Kilglass . .	Strokestown .	IV.	186
53	Rooaun . .	142　0　34	Roscommon .	Moycarn . .	Creagh . .	Ballinasloe .	IV.	206
123	Rooaunalaghta .	68　0　8	Mayo . .	Kilmaine . .	Shrule . .	Ballinrobe .	IV.	158
53	Rooaun Bog and Meadow . .	90　0　29*c*	Roscommon .	Moycarn . .	Creagh . .	Ballinasloe .	IV.	206
70	Rooaunmore . .	250　2　1	Galway . .	Clare . . .	Claregalway .	Galway . .	IV.	18
113	Rooaunmore . .	251　1　4	Galway . .	Dunkellin . .	Ardrahan . .	Gort . .	IV.	27
112	Roo Demesne . .	309　3　25	Galway . .	Kiltartan . .	Kinvarradoorus .	Gort . .	IV.	49
14	Roodstown . .	685　1　27	Louth . .	Ardee . . .	Stabannon .	Ardee . .	I.	174
53	Roo East . .	246　2　10	Clare . .	Tulla Lower .	O'Briensbridge .	Limerick .	II.	38
33	Rooghan . .	655　2　14	Antrim . .	Lower Antrim .	Racavan . .	Ballymena .	III.	4
100	Rooghan . .	170　3　24	Galway . .	Longford . .	Clonfert . .	Ballinasloe .	IV.	57
14, 21	Rooghan . .	149　1　6	Mayo . .	Tirawley . .	Rathreagh . .	Killala . .	IV.	171
27	Rooghan . .	763　3　8	Sligo . .	Tirerrill . .	Ballynakill .	Sligo . .	IV.	237
104, 114	Rooghaun . .	215　3　27	Galway . .	Dunkellin . .	Ardrahan . .	Gort . .	IV.	27
100	Rooghaun . .	127　1　19	Mayo . .	Carra . .	Burriscarra .	Ballinrobe .	IV.	127
98	Rooghaun . .	334　3　28	Mayo . .	Murrisk . .	Aghagower .	Westport .	IV.	159
20, 33	Rookwood or Bellagad	316　3　20*d*	Galway . .	Killian . .	Athleague .	Mountbellew .	IV.	43
25	Roolagh . .	158　3　20	Tipperary, N.R.	Owney and Arra .	Templeachally .	Nenagh . .	II.	297
95, 96	Roonah . .	847　1　14*e*	Mayo . .	Murrisk . .	Kilgeever . .	Westport . .	IV.	160
99	*Rooney's Island* .	33　2　25	Donegal . .	Tirhugh . .	Drumhome . .	Donegal . .	III.	147
1	Roonivoolin . .	130　3　37*f*	Antrim . .	Cary . .	Rathlin Island .	Ballycastle .	III.	15
105	Roonkeel . .	74　1　4	Mayo . .	Murrisk . .	Kilgeever . .	Westport . .	IV.	160
10, 15	Roos . .	250　3　15	Longford . .	Granard . .	Clonbroney .	Granard . .	I.	155
119	Roos . .	639　0　27	Mayo . .	Kilmaine . .	Kilcommon .	Ballinrobe .	IV.	155
81	Roosca (*Burke*) .	323　3　27	Tipperary, S.R.	Iffa and Offa West .	Tubbrid . .	Clogheen .	II.	321
81	Roosca (*Hickey*) .	194　1　32	Tipperary, S.R.	Iffa and Offa West .	Tubbrid . .	Clogheen .	II.	321
81	Roosca (*Miles*) .	106　0　28	Tipperary, S.R.	Iffa and Offa West .	Tubbrid . .	Clogheen .	II.	321
116, 117	Roosk . .	437　0　39	Cork, W.R. .	Bear . . .	Kilcaskan . .	Castletown .	II.	123
10	Roosk . .	177　2　10	Kildare . .	North Salt . .	Taghadoe . .	Celbridge . .	I.	76
4, 11	Roosk . .	244　1　30	King's Co. .	Warrenstown .	Ballymacwilliam .	Edenderry .	I.	144
8	Rooska . .	200　3　8	Clare . .	Burren . .	Kilmoon . .	Ballyvaghan .	II.	13
117, 118	Rooska East . .	293　1　12	Cork, W.R. .	Bantry . .	Durrus . .	Bantry . .	II.	119
77, 89	Rooskagh . .	237　0　34	Cork, E.R. .	Imokilly . .	Bohillane . .	Middleton .	II.	84
48, 51	Rooskagh . .	1,252　1　29	Roscommon .	Athlone . .	St. Peter's .	Athlone .	IV.	184

(*a*) Including 6A. 0R. 29P. water.　　　(*c*) Including 4A. 0R. 24P. water.　　　(*e*) Including 102A. 2R. 13P. water.
(*b*) Including 11A. 1R. 12P. water.　　(*d*) Including 22A. 1R. 0P. water.　　　(*f*) Including 6A. 0R. 30P. water.

No. of Sheet of the Ordnance Survey Maps.	Townlands and Towns.	Area in Statute Acres.	County.	Barony.	Parish.	Poor Law Union in 1857.	Townland Census of 1851, Part I.	
		A. R. P.					Vol.	Page
35, 36	Rooskagh East	1,022 0 20	Limerick	Shanid	Ardagh	Newcastle	II.	255
33	Rooskagh North	146 1 32	Fermanagh	Clanawley	Kinawley	Enniskillen	III.	194
32, 37	Rooskagh South	59 3 24	Fermanagh	Clanawley	Kinawley	Enniskillen	III.	194
35	Rooskagh West	921 3 7	Limerick	Shanid	Ardagh	Newcastle	II.	255
117	Rooska West	295 1 7	Cork, W.R.	Bantry	Durrus	Bantry	II.	119
22, 23, 28	Roosky	202 3 23a	Cavan	Clankee	Knockbride	Cootehill	III.	74
10, 19	Roosky	1,239 1 19	Donegal	Inishowen East	Clonmany	Inishowen	III.	117
30, 31	Roosky	212 3 9	Donegal	Inishowen East	Moville Upper	Inishowen	III.	119
29, 38	Roosky	525 1 37	Donegal	Inishowen West	Fahan Upper	Londonderry	III.	121
26, 35	Roosky	388 3 11b	Donegal	Kilmacrenan	Clondahorky	Dunfanaghy	III.	123
47, 55	Roosky	458 1 20c	Donegal	Raphoe	Allsaints	Londonderry	III.	134
62	Roosky	601 3 12	Donegal	Raphoe	Raymoghy	Letterkenny	III.	142
15	Roosky	121 2 16	Fermanagh	Magheraboy	Devenish	Enniskillen	III.	211
15	Roosky	86 2 27	Fermanagh	Magheraboy	Inishmacsaint	Enniskillen	III.	213
32, 33	Roosky	119 0 0d	Leitrim	Mohill	Mohill	Mohill	IV.	108
2, 4	Roosky	190 1 26	Leitrim	Rosclogher	Rossinver	Ballyshannon	IV.	112
101	Roosky	222 0 10	Mayo	Clanmorris	Crossboyne	Claremorris	IV.	133
51, 52, 63	Roosky	1,688 0 14	Mayo	Costello	Kilbeagh	Swineford	IV.	141
81, 92	Roosky	644 0 30	Mayo	Costello	Knock	Claremorris	IV.	143
49	Roosky	867 1 11e	Mayo	Gallen	Attymass	Ballina	IV.	147
21	Roosky	240 0 27	Mayo	Tirawley	Moygawnagh	Killala	IV.	171
3	Roosky	252 2 33	Meath	Lower Slane	Drumcondra	Ardee	I.	223
12	Roosky	226 1 1f	Monaghan	Dartree	Killeevan	Clones	III.	268
13	Roosky	119 1 1	Monaghan	Monaghan	Drumsnat	Monaghan	III.	275
9	Roosky	154 1 38	Monaghan	Monaghan	Monaghan	Monaghan	III.	277
18, 24	Roosky	209 2 6	Roscommon	Ballintober North	Termonbarry	Strokestown	IV.	188
{ 74, 83 } (MayoCo.)	Roosky	490 3 9	Roscommon	Frenchpark	Castlemore	Castlereagh	IV.	202
101	Rooskybeg	69 2 10g	Mayo	Clanmorris	Crossboyne	Claremorris	IV.	133
39	Roosky Beg	58 0 14	Sligo	Corran	Drumrat	Boyle	IV.	226
69, 70	Roosky Lower	135 3 19	Donegal	Raphoe	Raphoe	Strabane	III.	141
39	Roosky More	109 3 32	Sligo	Corran	Drumrat	Boyle	IV.	226
35	Rooskynamona	407 0 4h	Leitrim	Mohill	Mohill	Mohill	IV.	108
24	Roosky New	190 0 29	Roscommon	Ballintober North	Termonbarry	Strokestown	IV.	188
37 } 24 }	Roosky T.	—	{ Leitrim	Mohill	Mohill	Mohill	IV.	109
			{ Roscommon	Ballintober North	Termonbarry	Strokestown	IV.	188
69, 70	Roosky Upper	738 0 1	Donegal	Raphoe	Raphoe	Strabane	III.	141
31	Rootagh	163 0 18	Tipperary, N.R.	Owney and Arra	Kilnarath	Nenagh	II.	296
10, 11	Rootate	165 2 4	Louth	Ardee	Louth	Dundalk	I.	173
13	Rootiagh	179 3 14	Limerick	Pubblebrien	Crecora	Limerick	II.	252
23, 32	Rootiagh	274 1 26	Limerick	Smallcounty	Ballinard	Kilmallock	II.	259
54	Rooty	158 0 39	Roscommon	Moycarn	Moore	Ballinasloe	IV.	207
72	Rooves Beg	396 3 25	Cork, E.R.	East Muskerry	Aglish	Macroom	II.	101
72	Rooves More	612 1 15i	Cork, E.R.	East Muskerry	Aglish	Macroom	II.	101
53	Roo West	214 3 32	Clare	Tulla Lower	O'Briensbridge	Limerick	II.	38
25, 32, 33	Ropefield or Falnasoogaun	384 0 38	Sligo	Leyny	Kilvarnet	Tobercurry	IV.	232
26	Roperstown	100 3 5	Wexford	Ballaghkeen	Edermine	Enniscorthy	I.	294
7	Roran	499 1 10	Tipperary, N.R.	Lower Ormond	Terryglass	Borrisokane	II.	288
25	Roran	287 1 2	Tipperary, N.R.	Owney and Arra	Templeachally	Nenagh	II.	297
16	Roranna	137 3 17	Monaghan	Dartree	Drummully	Clones	III.	266
35	Rorardstown Lower	291 3 4	Tipperary, N.R.	Eliogarty	Drom	Thurles	II.	269
35	Rorardstown Upper	245 2 37	Tipperary, N.R.	Eliogarty	Drom	Thurles	II.	269
36	Roristown	259 2 0j	Meath	Lower Moyfenrath	Trim	Trim	I.	212
40	Rory's Glen	389 0 32	Antrim	Upper Glenarm	Kilwaughter	Larne	III.	25
29, 34	Rosahane	488 2 6	Wicklow	Ballinacor South	Ballinacor	Rathdrum	I.	348
38	Rosbane	496 0 28	Wicklow	Ballinacor South	Kilcommon	Shillelagh	I.	349
67, 76	Rosbarnagh Island	52 3 3	Mayo	Burrishoole	Burrishoole	Newport	IV.	120
76	Rosbeg	26 3 0	Mayo	Burrishoole	Kilmeena	Newport	IV.	122
37	Rosbercon	110 0 34	Kilkenny	Ida	Rosbercon	New Ross	I.	103
37	Rosbercon T.		Kilkenny	Ida	Rosbercon	New Ross	I.	103
18, 23	Rosberry	1,054 2 26k	Kildare	Connell	Morristownbiller	Naas	I.	56
34, 35, 37	Rosbran	91 3 36	Kildare	Narragh&RebanWest	St. John's	Athy	I.	68
20	Rosbran	101 3 36	Queen's Co.	Ballyadams	St. John's	Athy	I.	232
76	Roscahill	240 0 1	Mayo	Burrishoole	Kilmeena	Westport	IV.	122
7	Roscall	238 0 23	Dublin	Balrothery West	Ballyboghil	Balrothery	I.	22
94	Roscam	408 0 26	Galway	Galway	Oranmore	Galway	IV.	37
24	Roscarban	279 1 5l	Leitrim	Leitrim	Kiltubbrid	Cark. on Shannon	IV.	104
8, 15	Roscat	712 2 30	Carlow	Rathvilly	Ardristan	Carlow	I.	10
31	Roscath	226 3 26	Wicklow	Arklow	Dunganstown	Rathdrum	I.	344
43,44,51,52	Roscavey	1,126 0 26	Tyrone	Omagh East	Clogherny	Omagh	III.	310
67, 76	Rosclave	108 0 27m	Mayo	Burrishoole	Burrishoole	Newport	IV.	119
2	Rosclogher	119 0 23	Leitrim	Rosclogher	Rossinver	Ballyshannon	IV.	112

(a) Including 12A. 2R. 4P. water.
(b) Including 11A. 1R. 3P. water.
(c) Including 48A. 0R. 25P. water.
(d) Including 18A. 0R. 31P. water.
(e) Including 13A. 1R. 8P. water.

(f) Including 11A. 3R. 22P. water.
(g) Including 8A. 3R. 15P. water.
(h) Including 13A. 2R. 24P. water.
(i) Including 9A. 0R. 19P. water.
(j) Including 6A. 0R. 32P. water.

(k) { Including 195A. 3R. 35P. detached portions.
Including 6A. 0R. 11P. water.
(l) Including 83A. 0R. 0P. water.
(m) Including 7A. 0R. 1P. detached portion.

No. of Sheet of the Ordnance Survey Maps.	Townlands and Towns.	Area in Statute Acres. A. R. P.	County.	Barony.	Parish.	Poor Law Union in 1857.	Townland Census of 1851, Part I. Vol.	Page
38	Roscolvin	191 3 13	Kildare	Kilkea and Moone	Castledermot	Baltinglass	I.	59
39	ROSCOMMON T.	—	Roscommon	Ballintober South	Roscommon	Roscommon	IV.	190
39	Roscomroe	414 3 17	King's Co.	Ballybritt	Roscomroe	Parsonstown	I.	126
30	Roscon	283 3 19	Kilkenny	Kells	Killamery	Callan	I.	109
29, 30	Rosconnell Glebe	155 0 11	Queen's Co.	Clarmallagh	Rosconnell	Abbeyleix	I.	238
56	Roscor	251 3 22	Tyrone	Omagh East	Magheracross	Lowtherstown	III.	314
16	Roscore Demesne	356 2 32	King's Co.	Ballycowan	Rahan	Tullamore	I.	129
22, 23	Roscrea	122 3 25	Galway	Ballynahinch	Ballynakill	Clifden	IV.	12
12	ROSCREA T.	—	Tipperary, N.R.	Ikerrin	Roscrea	Roscrea	II.	276
33	Roscrib East	187 3 30	Sligo	Corran	Toomour	Sligo	IV.	228
33	Roscrib West	141 1 1a	Sligo	Corran	Toomour	Sligo	IV.	228
46	Roscullen Island	56 2 2	Kerry	Trughanacmy	Kilgarrylander	Tralee	II.	211
23	Roscunnish	136 0 36b	Leitrim	Leitrim	Kiltoghert	Carⁿ. on Shannon	IV.	102
24	Roscunnish	137 3 23	Leitrim	Leitrim	Kiltubbrid	Carⁿ. on Shannon	IV.	104
7, 19	Rosdaul	125 2 29	Galway	Ballymoe	Ballynakill	Glennamaddy	IV.	5
22, 23	Rosdellig	369 2 6	Carlow	Idrone East	Kiltennell	Carlow	I.	8
4, 11	Rosdoagh	1,446 0 37	Mayo	Erris	Kilcommon	Belmullet	IV.	144
76, 77	Rosdooaun	230 2 13	Mayo	Burrishoole	Kilmeena	Newport	IV.	122
32	Rosdoowaun	179 3 34	Leitrim	Mohill	Mohill	Mohill	IV.	108
46	Rosdrehid	116 3 12	King's Co.	Clonlisk	Cullenwaine	Roscrea	I.	129
3	Rosduff	743 0 13	Longford	Granard	Columbkille	Granard	I.	156
12	Rosebrook or Annaghboy	42 0 0	Armagh	Armagh	Armagh	Armagh	III.	43
23	Rosedermot	692 0 12	Antrim	Kilconway	Dunaghy	Ballymena	III.	26
9	Rosefield	178 2 14	Monaghan	Monaghan	Kilmore	Monaghan	III.	276
40, 45	Rosegarland	752 0 39	Wexford	Shelmaliere West	Ballylannan	New Ross	I.	332
69	Rosegreen	350 3 38	Tipperary, S.R.	Middlethird	Tullamain	Cashel	II.	331
40, 44	Rosehill	795 1 10	Cavan	Castlerahan	Mullagh	Kells	III.	70
13	Rosehill	56 1 8c	Cavan	Tullyhaw	Templeport	Bawnboy	III.	95
48	Rosehill	33 2 22	Wexford	Forth	Rosslare	Wexford	I.	313
47	Roseland	15 2 10	Wexford	Forth	Kildavin	Wexford	I.	310
3	Roselick Beg	48 1 31	Londonderry	North East Liberties of Coleraine	Ballyaghran	Coleraine	III.	244
3	Roselick More	178 3 5	Londonderry	North East Liberties of Coleraine	Ballyaghran	Coleraine	III.	244
15	Rosemaryhill	80 3 30	Wexford	Scarawalsh	Ferns	Enniscorthy	I.	323
63, 64	Rosemeilan	199 1 15	Tyrone	Clogher	Clogher	Clogher	III.	293
11, 12	Rosemount	284 0 17	Down	Ards Lower	Greyabbey	Newtownards	III.	158
3, 7	Rosenallis	66 0 0	Queen's Co.	Tinnahinch	Rosenallis	Mountmellick	I.	250
3	ROSENALLIS T.	—	Queen's Co.	Tinnahinch	Rosenallis	Mountmellick	I.	250
5	Rosepark	8 0 32	Dublin	Balrothery East	Balrothery	Balrothery	I.	19
16, 17	Rosepenna	543 0 10	Donegal	Kilmacrenan	Mevagh	Millford	III.	130
23	Rosetown	416 0 33d	Kildare	Connell	Greatconnell	Naas	I.	55
37	Rosetown	429 0 38	Kildare	Kilkea and Moone	Tankardstown	Athy	I.	61
43, 48	Rosetown	71 1 37	Wexford	Forth	Rosslare	Wexford	I.	313
39, 44	Rosetown	517 0 32	Wexford	Shelburne	St. James & Dunbrody	New Ross	I.	328
12	Roseyards	179 0 0	Antrim	Upper Dunluce	Ballymoney	Ballymoney	III.	19
15	Rosfaraghan	422 2 29	King's Co.	Garrycastle	Wheery or Killagally	Parsonstown	I.	139
2	Rosfriar	263 2 33	Leitrim	Rosclogher	Rossinver	Ballyshannon	IV.	112
66, 67	Rosgalliv	275 1 29	Mayo	Burrishoole	Burrishoole	Newport	IV.	120
41	Rosgarran	251 3 31	Londonderry	Loughinsholin	Desertmartin	Magherafelt	III.	241
67	Rosgibbileen	102 0 19	Mayo	Burrishoole	Burrishoole	Newport	IV.	120
28	Rosgoordagh	127 0 25	Tipperary, N.R.	Upper Ormond	Aghnameadle	Nenagh	II.	289
32, 33	Rosharry	224 0 12	Leitrim	Mohill	Mohill	Mohill	IV.	108
97	Roshin	344 1 14	Donegal	Banagh	Killybegs Upper	Glenties	III.	111
25	Roshin	644 3 4e	Donegal	Kilmacrenan	Clondahorky	Dunfanaghy	III.	123
52	Roshin	128 2 25	Donegal	Kilmacrenan	Conwal	Letterkenny	III.	126
44, 52	Roshin	307 2 28f	Donegal	Kilmacrenan	Gartan	Letterkenny	III.	127
48, 49	Roshin Acres	235 1 30g	Donegal	Boylagh	Templecrone	Glenties	III.	116
40, 48	Roshin Lodge	67 3 21	Donegal	Boylagh	Templecrone	Glenties	III.	116
40, 48	Roshin North	58 3 32	Donegal	Boylagh	Templecrone	Glenties	III.	116
48, 56	Roshin South	198 3 29h	Donegal	Boylagh	Templecrone	Glenties	III.	116
41	Roshure	217 0 33	Londonderry	Loughinsholin	Desertmartin	Magherafelt	III.	241
65, 78	Roskeeda	199 3 31	Galway	Moycullen	Kilcummin	Oughterard	IV.	68
32	Roskeen	334 0 12i	Cork, E.R.	Duhallow	Roskeen	Kanturk	II.	75
1	Roskeen	938 1 31	Queen's Co.	Tinnahinch	Castlebrack	Mountmellick	I.	248
40	Roskeen	375 2 31	Tipperary, N.R.	Kilnamanagh Upper	Moyaliff	Thurles	II.	279
40	Roskeen Little	9 1 4	Tipperary, N.R.	Kilnamanagh Upper	Moyaliff	Thurles	II.	279
67	Roskeen North	202 1 5	Mayo	Burrishoole	Burrishoole	Newport	IV.	120
40	Roskeen North	13 0 0	Tipperary, N.R.	Kilnamanagh Upper	Moyaliff	Thurles	II.	279
67	Roskeen South	127 1 39	Mayo	Burrishoole	Burrishoole	Newport	IV.	120
40	Roskeen South	4 2 32	Tipperary, N.R.	Kilnamanagh Upper	Moyaliff	Thurles	II.	279
79, 90	Roslahan Lower	165 3 29j	Mayo	Carra	Drum	Castlebar	IV.	128

(a) Including 2A. 3R. 16P. water.
(b) Including 8A. 25P. water.
(c) Including 4A. 0R. 1P. water.
(d) Including 18A. 0R. 16P. water.

(e) Including 25A. 2R. 3P. water.
(f) Including 71A. 3R. 10P. water.
(g) Including 9A. 3R. 26P. water.

(h) Including 16A. 0R. 2P. water.
(i) Including 9A. 0R. 32P. water.
(j) Including 29A. 0R. 12P. water.

No. of Sheet of the Ordnance Survey Maps.	Townlands and Towns.	Area in Statute Acres.			County.	Barony.	Parish.	Poor Law Union in 1857.	Townland Census of 1851, Part I.	
		A.	R.	P.					Vol.	Page
79, 90	Roslahan Upper	159	2	36	Mayo	Carra	Drum	Castlebar	IV.	128
76	Roslaher	51	0	26	Mayo	Burrishoole	Kilmeena	Newport	IV.	122
22, 23	Rosleague	218	3	2	Galway	Ballynahinch	Ballynakill	Clifden	IV.	12
67	Roslynagh	15	1	27	Mayo	Burrishoole	Burrishoole	Newport	IV.	120
53, 63	Rosmadda East	180	2	27	Clare	Bunratty Lower	St. Patricks	Limerick	II.	7
53, 63	Rosmadda West	139	1	9	Clare	Bunratty Lower	St. Patricks	Limerick	II.	7
9, 14	Rosmead and Cavestown	1,346	0	17	Westmeath	Delvin	Castletowndelvin	Castletowndelvin	I.	264
16	Rosmearan	169	3	12	Galway	Dunmore	Addergoole	Tuam	IV.	33
27	Rosmeen	354	0	17	Roscommon	Castlereagh	Ballintober	Castlereagh	IV.	198
76	Rosmindle	83	0	2	Mayo	Burrishoole	Kilmeena	Westport	IV.	122
76	Rosmoney	120	3	22	Mayo	Burrishoole	Kilmeena	Westport	IV.	122
126, 132	Rosmore	1,011	0	19	Galway	Leitrim	Ballynakill	Portumna	IV.	52
67	Rosmore	77	2	34	Mayo	Burrishoole	Burrishoole	Newport	IV.	120
27	Rosmore	332	3	15	Sligo	Tirerrill	Kilmacallan	Sligo	IV.	240
7, 8	Rosmoylan	54	0	17	Galway	Ballymoe	Dunamon	Roscommon	IV.	7
7, 19	Rosmoylan	464	2	15a	Galway	Ballymoe	Kilbegnet	Roscommon	IV.	8
65, 78	Rosmuck	523	2	34	Galway	Moycullen	Kilcummin	Oughterard	IV.	68
40	Rosmult	360	0	24	Tipperary, N.R.	Kilnamanagh Upper	Moyaliff	Thurles	II.	279
66	Rosmurrevagh	28	1	27	Mayo	Burrishoole	Burrishoole	Newport	IV.	120
46	Rosnacananee	107	2	5	Tipperary, N.R.	Kilnamanagh Upper	Moyaliff	Thurles	II.	279
57, 58, 65, 66	Rosnacartan Beg	170	1	14	Kerry	Magunihy	Kilbonane	Killarney	II.	200
57	Rosnacartan More	159	2	28	Kerry	Magunihy	Kilbonane	Killarney	II.	200
26	Rosnagleragh	355	0	35b	Mayo	Erris	Kilcommon	Belmullet	IV.	144
9, 17	Rosnagowloge or Tirinchinan	218	1	8	King's Co.	Ballycowan	Kilbride	Tullamore	I.	128
32	Rosnagussane	124	3	14	Cork, E.R.	Duhallow	Ballyclogh	Mallow	II.	67
17	Rosnakill	320	2	39c	Donegal	Kilmacrenan	Clondavaddog	Milford	III.	125
76	Rosnakilly	51	3	28	Mayo	Burrishoole	Kilmeena	Westport	IV.	122
26	Rosnamuck	219	3	19	Tyrone	Strabane Upper	Cappagh	Omagh	III.	325
9, 14	Rosnamullane	556	3	0	Queen's Co.	Stradbally	Moyanna	Athy	I.	247
34	Rosnamulteeny	244	1	18	Tipperary, N.R.	Kilnamanagh Upper	Glenkeen	Thurles	II.	279
71	Rosnascalp	215	1	17d	Cork, W.R.	East Muskerry	Aghinagh	Macroom	II.	154
22	Rosnashane	475	0	19	Antrim	Kilconway	Finvoy	Ballymoney	III.	26
43, 44	Rosnastraw	710	3	1	Wicklow	Ballinacor South	Kilpipe	Shillelagh	I.	349
36	Rosneillan	65	1	3	Clare	Tulla Lower	Killuran	Tulla	II.	36
43, 52	Rosroe	275	2	2	Clare	Bunratty Lower	Kilmurry	Tulla	II.	6
10, 11	Rosroe	296	2	18	Galway	Ballynahinch	Ballynakill	Clifden	IV.	12
50, 63	Rosroe	1,049	3	9e	Galway	Ballynahinch	Moyrus	Clifden	IV.	13
38	Ross	538	1	28	Antrim	Lower Antrim	Connor	Antrim	III.	3
25	Ross	137	3	39f	Clare	Inchiquin	Dysert	Corrofin	II.	24
64, 71	Ross	489	2	11	Clare	Moyarta	Kilballyowen	Kilrush	II.	32
45	Ross	402	1	24	Clare	Tulla Lower	O'Briensbridge	Limerick	II.	38
28	Ross	100	1	0	Clare	Tulla Upper	Feakle	Scarriff	II.	40
45	Ross	365	1	6	Down	Lecale Lower	Kilclief	Downpatrick	III.	179
19	Ross	156	0	35g	Fermanagh	Clanawley	Boho	Ballyshannon	III.	189
27	Ross	160	0	17	Fermanagh	Clanawley	Cleenish	Enniskillen	III.	191
21	Ross	282	1	36h	Fermanagh	Magheraboy	Devenish	Enniskillen	III.	211
9, 22	Ross	138	1	26	Galway	Ballynahinch	Ballynakill	Clifden	IV.	12
41	Ross	29	0	29	Galway	Clare	Killursa	Tuam	IV.	22
116	Ross	83	3	9	Galway	Leitrim	Ballynakill	Loughrea	IV.	52
46, 47	Ross	131	2	37	Kerry	Trughanacmy	Kilgarrylander	Tralee	II.	211
24	Ross	777	1	22	King's Co.	Ballycowan	Lynally	Tullamore	I.	128
30, 35	Ross	147	3	16	King's Co.	Eglish	Eglish	Parsonstown	I.	135
11	Ross	287	3	36	Leitrim	Drumahaire	Cloonclare	Manorhamilton	IV.	94
16	Ross	64	2	28	Leitrim	Drumahaire	Inishmagrath	Manorhamilton	IV.	97
15	Ross	293	2	29	Mayo	Tirawley	Killala	Killala	IV.	170
8	Ross	958	1	32	Meath	Fore	Killeagh	Oldcastle	I.	201
31, 37, 38	Ross	472	2	31	Meath	Skreen	Skreen	Dunshaughlin	I.	221
32, 38	Ross	119	1	0	Meath	Skreen	Tara	Navan	I.	222
12	Ross	656	2	3	Queen's Co.	Maryborough East	Clonenagh and Clonagheen	Mountmellick	I.	241
2, 6	Ross	498	2	11	Queen's Co.	Tinnahinch	Rearymore	Mountmellick	I.	250
47	Ross	273	0	20	Sligo	Coolavin	Killaraght	Boyle	IV.	224
19	Ross	232	0	5	Sligo	Tireragh	Skreen	Dromore West	IV.	236
5	Ross	241	1	28	Tipperary, N.R.	Lower Ormond	Dorrha	Parsonstown	II.	283
67, 68	Ross	132	3	36	Tipperary, S.R.	Clanwilliam	Kilfeakle	Tipperary	II.	308
39, 46, 47	Ross	180	1	37	Tyrone	Dungannon Middle	Donaghenry	Cookstown	III.	301
20	Ross	78	0	37	Waterford	Coshmore & Coshbride	Lismore and Mocollop	Lismore	II.	347
30	Ross	79	1	29	Waterford	Decies without Drum	Whitechurch	Dungarvan	II.	362
16	Ross	433	3	37	Waterford	Middlethird	Newcastle	Waterford	II.	368
6, 7	Ross	1,024	2	18i	Waterford	Upperthird	Mothel	Carrick on Suir	II.	371
15	Ross	93	0	2	Westmeath	Kilkenny West	Noughaval	Athlone	I.	274

(a) Including 1A. 2R. 27P. water.
(b) Including 12A. 2R. 24P. water.
(c) Including 8A. 0R. 35P. water.

(d) Including 3A. 0R. 28P. water.
(e) Including 7A. 3R. 16P. water.
(f) Including 48A. 3R. 37P. water.

(g) Including 2A. 3R. 8P. water.
(h) Including 60A. 3R. 34P. water.
(i) Including 11A. 2R. 2P. water.

No. of Sheet of the Ordnance Survey Maps.	Townlands and Towns.	Area in Statute Acres.	County.	Barony.	Parish.	Poor Law Union in 1857.	Townland Census of 1851, Part I.	
		A. R. P.					Vol.	Page
25	Rossaa	163 1 17	Fermanagh	Clanawley	Killesher	Enniskillen	III.	193
10	Rossachrin	130 0 25	Fermanagh	Lurg	Derryvullan	Lowtherstown	III.	205
22, 23	Rossacon	691 2 15	Cork, E.R.	Duhallow	Clonfert	Kanturk	II.	69
92	Rossacoosane	1,173 1 17	Kerry	Dunkerron South	Templenoe	Kenmare	II.	185
67, 68, 76	Rossacroo	229 2 22	Kerry	Magunihy	Aghadoe	Killarney	II.	199
67, 68	Rossacroobeg	145 3 12	Kerry	Magunihy	Killaha	Killarney	II.	202
85	Rossacroonaloo	441 0 3	Kerry	Magunihy	Killaha	Killarney	II.	202
51	Rossacrow	193 0 6	Tipperary, S.R.	Kilnamanagh Lower	Aghacrew	Tipperary	II.	322
51	Rossacrow	91 2 2	Tipperary, S.R.	Kilnamanagh Lower	Donohill	Tipperary	II.	323
17, 20	Rossacurra	431 3 26	Carlow	Forth	Myshall	Carlow	I.	5
21, 22	Rossadillisk	185 2 34	Galway	Ballynahinch	Omey	Clifden	IV.	15
11	Rossadown	314 0 12	Queen's Co.	Upperwoods	Offerlane	Mountmellick	I.	252
74, 80	Rossadrehid	2,690 0 34a	Tipperary, S.R.	Clanwilliam	Templeneiry	Tipperary	II.	311
17	Rossagh East	260 1 22	Cork, E.R.	Fermoy	Doneraile	Mallow	II.	79
17	Rossaghroe	265 3 33	Cork, E.R.	Fermoy	Doneraile	Mallow	II.	79
17	Rossagh West	307 1 15	Cork, E.R.	Fermoy	Doneraile	Mallow	II.	79
31	Rossaguile	89 3 10	Tipperary, N.R.	Owney and Arra	Killoscully	Nenagh	II.	295
31	Rossaguile	305 2 23	Tipperary, N.R.	Owney and Arra	Kilnarath	Nenagh	II.	296
16, 22	Rossahilly	227 3 12	Fermanagh	Tirkennedy	Trory	Enniskillen	III.	223
11	Rossalee	223 3 36	Queen's Co.	Upperwoods	Offerlane	Mountmellick	I.	252
3	Rossalia	468 0 24	Clare	Burren	Abbey	Ballyvaghan	II.	11
75	Rossalia	234 1 39b	Kerry	Magunihy	Killaha	Killarney	II.	202
80	Rossalougha	923 2 34c	Cork, W.R.	West Muskerry	Inchigeelagh	Macroom	II.	158
41	Rossamine	193 3 9	King's Co.	Clonlisk	Shinrone	Roscrea	I.	131
16	Rossan	291 3 14	Longford	Granard	Abbeylara	Granard	I.	154
46	Rossan	638 3 9	Meath	Upper Moyfenrath	Clonard	Edenderry	I.	213
25	Rossana Lower	130 2 39	Wicklow	Newcastle	Rathnew	Rathdrum	I.	354
25	Rossana Upper	80 3 35	Wicklow	Newcastle	Rathnew	Rathdrum	I.	354
71	Rossane	165 2 12	Tipperary, S.R.	Slievardagh	Kilvemnon	Callan	II.	335
48	Rossanean	300 1 39	Kerry	Magunihy	Killeentierna	Killarney	II.	204
48	Rossanean	273 1 8	Kerry	Magunihy	Molahiffe	Killarney	II.	205
30	Rossaneny (Morris)	187 1 7	Kilkenny	Kells	Killamery	Callan	I.	109
30	Rossaneny (Reade)	510 3 12	Kilkenny	Kells	Killamery	Callan	I.	109
76, 77	Rossanrubble	174 0 26	Mayo	Burrishoole	Burrishoole	Newport	IV.	120
28	Rossanure	147 2 14	Clare	Tulla Upper	Feakle	Scarriff	II.	40
140	Rossard	63 2 6	Cork, W.R.	West Carbery(W.D.)	Kilcoe	Skull	II.	143
101, 109	Rossard	947 2 0d	Kerry	Glanarought	Tuosist	Kenmare	II.	189
14	Rossard	22 2 31	Limerick	Clanwilliam	Ludden	Limerick	II.	225
9, 14	Rossard	900 0 16	Wexford	Scarawalsh	Templeshanbo	Enniscorthy	I.	326
6, 7	Rossarrell	133 3 0	Monaghan	Trough	Donagh	Monaghan	III.	282
37	Rossary Beg	79 2 19	Tipperary, N.R.	Owney and Arra	Kilvellane	Nenagh	II.	296
37	Rossary More	129 0 35	Tipperary, N.R.	Owney and Arra	Kilvellane	Nenagh	II.	296
27	Rossavally	234 1 36	Fermanagh	Clanawley	Cleenish	Enniskillen	III.	191
90, 91	Rossaveel	809 3 14e	Galway	Moycullen	Kilcummin	Galway	IV.	68
46	Rossbane	140 3 15	Limerick	Connello Upper	Corcomohide	Croom	II.	232
35	Ross or Barrack-quarter	160 1 24	Queen's Co.	Clarmallagh	Aghmacart	Abbeyleix	I.	236
15	Rossbaun	381 3 36	Queen's Co.	Clandonagh	Kyle	Roscrea	I.	233
64, 73	Rossbeg	325 0 20f	Donegal	Boylagh	Inishkeel	Glenties	III.	113
8, 9	Rossbeg	173 3 23	Fermanagh	Lurg	Belleek	Ballyshannon	III.	203
34	Rossbeg	149 2 23g	Fermanagh	Magherastephana	Aghalurcher	Lisnaskea	III.	217
36, 38	Ross Beg	435 2 6	Leitrim	Mohill	Cloone	Mohill	IV.	106
87, 88	Rossbeg	136 2 33	Mayo	Murrisk	Oughaval	Westport	IV.	162
22	Ross Beg	297 2 21	Roscommon	Roscommon	Elphin	Strokestown	IV.	209
51	Rossbeg	88 1 18	Tipperary, S.R.	Kilnamanagh Lower	Kilpatrick	Cashel	II.	324
46	Ross Beg	207 2 3	Tyrone	Dungannon Middle	Drumglass	Dungannon	III.	303
39	Rossbeg	95 1 27	Westmeath	Moycashel	Rahugh	Tullamore	I.	279
18	Ross Beg Glebe	60 2 22	Leitrim	Drumahaire	Inishmagrath	Manorhamilton	IV.	97
55, 63	Rossbehy	980 0 27h	Kerry	Iveragh	Glanbehy	Cahersiveen	II.	196
74	Rossbog	938 2 39	Tipperary, S.R.	Clanwilliam	Clonbeg	Tipperary	II.	305
15	Ross (Bourke)	133 1 11	Mayo	Tirawley	Killala	Killala	IV.	170
84, 93	Rossboy	173 2 22	Kerry	Glanarought	Kenmare	Kenmare	II.	186
53, 54	Rossbrackan	247 3 30i	Donegal	Raphoe	Leck	Letterkenny	III.	140
13, 14	Rossbressal or Bella-heady	222 0 5j	Cavan	Tullyhunco	Kildallan	Bawnboy	III.	96
35, 40	Rossbrick Glebe	216 1 27	Fermanagh	Clankelly	Clones	Clones	III.	197
13	Rossbrien	323 1 18	Limerick	Pubblebrien	St. Michaels	Limerick	II.	254
140, 149	Rossbrin	276 1 20	Cork, W.R.	West Carbery (W.D.)	Skull	Skull	II.	146
26	Rosscad	125 2 14k	Donegal	Kilmacrenan	Clondahorky	Dunfanaghy	III.	123
5	Rosscah	60 1 24	Fermanagh	Lurg	Magheraculmoney	Lowtherstown	III.	208
67, 68	Rosscahill East	330 0 3	Galway	Moycullen	Killannin	Oughterard	IV.	70
55, 67, 68	Rosscahill West	324 2 30l	Galway	Moycullen	Killannin	Oughterard	IV.	70
103	Rosscanlan	27 1 5	Donegal	Tirhugh	Drumhome	Ballyshannon	III.	147

(a) Including 25A. 2R. 32P. Muskry Lough.
(b) Including 2A. 0R. 21P. water.
(c) Including 28A. 0R. 18P. water.
(d) Including 50A. 0R. 16P. water.
(e) Including 34A. 1R. 35P. water.
(f) Including 12A. 3R. 20P. water.
(g) Including 11A. 3R. 10P. water.
(h) Including 31A. 1R. 8P. water.
(i) Including 6A. 3R. 18P. Haugheys Isle.
(j) Including 10A. 0R. 0P. water.
(k) Including 7A. 1R. 25P. water.
(l) Including 5A. 0R. 25P. water.

No. of Sheet of the Ordnance Survey Maps.	Townlands and Towns.	Area in Statute Acres.	County.	Barony.	Parish.	Poor Law Union in 1857.	Townland Census of 1851, Part I.	
		A. R. P.					Vol.	Page
143	Ross CARDERY T.	—	Cork, W.R.	East Carbery (W.D.)	Ross	Clonakilty	II.	136
27	Rosscarn	246 2 24a	Fermanagh	Clanawley	Rossorry	Enniskillen	III.	194
103	Rosscat	204 1 16	Donegal	Tirhugh	Kilbarron	Ballyshannon	III.	148
15	Rossclare	110 3 31	Fermanagh	Lurg	Derryvullan	Lowtherstown	III.	205
50	Rosscliff	188 1 4	Clare	Clonderalaw	Kilchreest	Killadysert	II.	15
5	Rosscolban	336 2 27	Fermanagh	Lurg	Magheraculmoney	Lowtherstown	III.	208
25	Rosscolgan	111 0 34	Cavan	Upper Loughtee	Urney	Cavan	III.	86
21	Rosscoltan	239 3 31	Fermanagh	Magheraboy	Devenish	Enniskillen	III.	211
30	Rossconor	215 0 7	Down	Kinelarty	Kilmore	Downpatrick	III.	177
41, 42	Rossconor	218 3 17	Down	Upper Iveagh, Lr. pt.	Drumballyroney	Newry	III.	172
8	Rosscor	362 3 55b	Fermanagh	Magheraboy	Inishmacsaint	Ballyshannon	III.	213
8	Rosscor Island	10 2 16	Fermanagh	Magheraboy	Inishmacsaint	Ballyshannon	III.	213
25	Rosscorkey Island	27 1 25	Fermanagh	Clanawley	Cleenish	Enniskillen	III.	192
4	Rosscrennagh	93 0 20	Fermanagh	Lurg	Templecarn	Lowtherstown	III.	269
10, 15	Rossdagamph or St. Catherines	219 3 19c	Fermanagh	Magheraboy	Inishmacsaint	Enniskillen	III.	213
18,19,22,23	Rossdama	246 3 25	Kilkenny	Shillelogher	Grange	Kilkenny	I.	114
32, 33	Rossdanean	126 0 2	Fermanagh	Clanawley	Kinawley	Enniskillen	III.	194
34	Rossdarragh	908 0 30	Queen's Co.	Clandonagh	Erke	Donaghmore	I.	233
68	Ross Demesne	477 1 39d	Galway	Moycullen	Killannin	Oughterard	IV.	70
100	Rossdohan	453 0 34	Kerry	Dunkerron South	Kilcrohane	Kenmare	II.	184
100	Rossdohan Island	134 1 5	Kerry	Dunkerron South	Kilcrohane	Kenmare	II.	184
27, 33	Rossdoney	245 3 27e	Fermanagh	Clanawley	Cleenish	Enniskillen	III.	191
94	Rossdoo Island	2 3 18	Donegal	Banagh	Killymard	Donegal	III.	112
15	Rossdorragha	407 2 18	Queen's Co.	Clandonagh	Kyle	Roscrea	I.	233
31	Rossdreenagh	279 2 8f	Monaghan	Farney	Donaghmoyne	Carrickmacross	III.	271
18	Rossduff	196 3 16	Waterford	Gaultiere	Rossduff	Waterford	II.	364
60, 70	Ross East	273 1 6	Mayo	Carra	Turlough	Castlebar	IV.	131
125	Rosseeshal	49 2 21g	Galway	Leitrim	Ballynakill	Loughrea	IV.	52
85	Rosseightragh	539 3 17	Kerry	Glanarought	Kilgarvan	Kenmare	II.	188
32	Rossena	299 1 26	Queen's Co.	Slievemargy	Killabban	Carlow	I.	245
31	Rossenarra	146 1 35	Kilkenny	Kells	Kilmaganny	Callan	I.	109
31	Rossenarra Demesne	953 3 34	Kilkenny	Kells	Kilmaganny	Callan	I.	109
22, 30	Rosserk	1,074 0 19h	Mayo	Tirawley	Ballysakeery	Ballina	IV.	165
8	Rosses Lower	492 1 8i	Sligo	Carbury	Drumcliff	Sligo	IV.	221
35, 41	Rossestown	587 3 32	Tipperary, N.R.	Eliogarty	Shyane	Thurles	II.	272
8	Rosses Upper	373 3 14j	Sligo	Carbury	Drumcliff	Sligo	IV.	221
8	ROSSES UPPER T.	—	Sligo	Carbury	Drumcliff	Sligo	IV.	222
16	Rossfad	290 2 12	Fermanagh	Lurg	Derryvullan	Lowtherstown	III.	205
15	Ross (Fallon)	169 3 27	Mayo	Tirawley	Killala	Killala	IV.	170
25, 31	Rossfinch	413 3 39	Tipperary, N.R.	Owney and Arra	Kilnarath	Nenagh	II.	296
34	Rossgad	176 0 20k	Fermanagh	Magherastephana	Aghalurcher	Lisnaskea	III.	217
15	Ross (Gardiner)	124 3 39	Mayo	Tirawley	Killala	Killala	IV.	170
36	Rossgarrow	276 3 28	Donegal	Kilmacrenan	Tullyfern	Milford	III.	133
70, 71	Rossgeir	281 1 14	Donegal	Raphoe	Clonleigh	Strabane	III.	135
30, 31	Rossglass	184 1 39l	Cork, E.R.	Duhallow	Drontarriff	Kanturk	II.	71
45	Rossglass	349 1 37	Down	Lecale Upper	Kilclief	Downpatrick	III.	181
4, 5	Rossgole	97 0 9	Fermanagh	Lurg	Drumkeeran	Lowtherstown	III.	207
15	Ross (Goodwin)	243 0 22	Mayo	Tirawley	Killala	Killala	IV.	170
29	Rossgrilla	83 0 0	Waterford	Coshmore&Coshbride	Lismore and Mocollop	Lismore	II.	347
10	Rossgweer	281 0 38	Fermanagh	Lurg	Derryvullan	Lowtherstown	III.	205
4	Rossharbour	339 1 28	Fermanagh	Lurg	Belleek	Ballyshannon	III.	203
4	Rossharbour Old	116 0 15	Fermanagh	Lurg	Templecarn	Lowtherstown	III.	209
27	Rosshill	139 1 39	Galway	Ross	Ross	Oughterard	IV.	74
10	Rossigh	77 1 22	Fermanagh	Lurg	Derryvullan	Lowtherstown	III.	205
99	Rossilly	147 2 16	Donegal	Tirhugh	Drumhome	Donegal	III.	147
100	Rossilly Barr	301 3 20	Donegal	Tirhugh	Drumhome	Donegal	III.	147
40, 43	Rossinan	182 0 32	Kilkenny	Knocktopher	Rossinan	Waterford	I.	113
10, 15	Rossinnan	108 1 21	Fermanagh	Lurg	Derryvullan	Lowtherstown	III.	205
15	Ross Inner	162 2 33	Fermanagh	Magheraboy	Devenish	Enniskillen	III.	211
14	Rossinure Beg	891 0 1m	Fermanagh	Magheraboy	Devenish	Enniskillen	III.	211
14, 20	Rossinure More	1,123 1 26	Fermanagh	Magheraboy	Devenish	Enniskillen	III.	211
66	Ross Island	158 2 25	Kerry	Magunihy	Killarney	Killarney	II.	203
15	Rosskeeragh	183 1 8n	Cavan	Lower Loughtee	Annagh	Cavan	III.	79
17	Rosskelton	940 2 10	Queen's Co.	Maryborough West	Clonenagh and Clonagheen	Abbeyleix	I.	243
129, 130	Rosskerrig	577 1 15	Cork, W.R.	West Carbery (W.D.)	Kilcrohane	Bantry	II.	144
129, 130	Rosskerrig Mountain	283 3 12	Cork, W.R.	West Carbery (W.D.)	Kilcrohane	Bantry	II.	144
8, 9, 18	Rosskirk and Killhill	561 2 18	Donegal	Kilmacrenan	Clondavaddog	Milford	III.	125
12	Rosskit Island	33 3 12	Fermanagh	Magheraboy	Inishmacsaint	Ballyshannon	III.	213
75, 87	Rosslague	226 3 26	Cork, E.R.	Barrymore	Templerobin	Cork	II.	58
27	Rosslara	318 3 16o	Clare	Tulla Upper	Tulla	Tulla	II.	42
34	Ross and Laragh	736 3 36	Roscommon	Ballymoe	Drumatemple	Castlereagh	IV.	191

(a) Including 48A. 3R. 16P. water.
(b) Including 26A. 1R. 4P. water.
(c) Including 6A. 0R. 8P. water.
(d) Including 99A. 0R. 0P. water.
(e) Including 4A. 1R. 29P. River Erne.
(f) Including 11A. 1R. 5P. water.

(g) Including 7A. 2R. 24P. water.
(h) Including 16A. 2R. 10P. water.
(i) Including 13A. 0R. 24P. Lough Curraghmore.
(j) {Including 7A. 0R. 22P. detached portion. / Including 3A. 1R. 0P. Lough Curraghmore.}

(k) Including 8A. 0R. 1P. water.
(l) Including 6A. 0R. 36P. water.
(m) Including 7A. 1R. 20P. water.
(n) Including 14A. 3R. 36P. water.
(o) Including 25A. 2R. 33P. water.

5 K

No. of Sheet of the Ordnance Survey Maps.	Townlands and Towns.	Area in Statute Acres.	County.	Barony.	Parish.	Poor Law Union in 1857.	Townland Census of 1851, Part I.	
		A. R. P.					Vol.	Page
38	Rosslarefort	17 0 26	Wexford	Forth	Rosslare	Wexford	I.	313
36	Rosslea	92 2 11	Fermanagh	Clankelly	Clones	Clones	III.	197
13	Rossleaghan	309 1 38	Queen's Co.	Maryborough East	Borris	Mountmellick	II.	240
36	ROSSLEA T.	—	Fermanagh	Clankelly	Clones	Clones	III.	197
17	Rosslee	485 0 36	Carlow	Forth	Myshall	Carlow	I.	5
33, 34	Rosslevan	266 2 22	Clare	Bunratty Upper	Kilraghtis	Ennis	II.	9
23	Rossline	128 2 23	Cork, E.R.	Duhallow	Clonfert	Kanturk	II.	69
15, 23	Rossline	450 2 38	Cork, E.R.	Duhallow	Kilcorcoran	Kanturk	II.	72
6, 10, 11	Rosslough	355 3 33	Louth	Ardee	Louth	Dundalk	I.	173
34	Rossmacaffry	186 2 0a	Fermanagh	Magherastephana	Aghalurcher	Lisnaskea	III.	217
34	Rossmacall	58 2 8b	Fermanagh	Magherastephana	Aghalurcher	Lisnaskea	III.	217
26	Rossmacawinny	273 3 19	Fermanagh	Clanawley	Killesher	Enniskillen	III.	193
102,115,116	Rossmackowen Commons	2,453 3 0	Cork, W.R.	Bear	Killaconenagh	Castletown	II.	125
34	Rossmacole	95 1 28	Fermanagh	Magherastephana	Aghalurcher	Lisnaskea	III.	217
12	Rossmakay	397 1 33	Louth	Upper Dundalk	Louth	Dundalk	I.	179
52, 62	Rossmanagher	789 1 27	Clare	Bunratty Lower	Feenagh	Ennis	II.	4
11, 17	Rossmeen	887 2 20	Meath	Upper Kells	Kells	Kells	I.	206
6, 11	Rossminoge North	298 0 16	Wexford	Gorey	Rossminoge	Gorey	I.	321
11	Rossminoge South	238 2 23	Wexford	Gorey	Rossminoge	Gorey	I.	321
75, 76	Rossmore	384 0 23	Cork, E.R.	Barrymore	Mogeesha	Middleton	II.	57
121	Rossmore	456 0 12	Cork, W.R.	East Carbery (W.D.)	Kilmeen	Clonakilty	II.	134
130	Rossmore	307 3 11	Cork, W.R.	West Carbery (W.D.)	Durrus	Bantry	II.	142
81, 82	Rossmore	492 3 3	Cork, W.R.	West Muskerry	Inchigeelagh	Macroom	II.	158
99, 100	Rossmore	89 2 25	Donegal	Tirhugh	Drumhome	Donegal	III.	147
8, 9	Rossmore	358 0 22	Fermanagh	Lurg	Belleek	Ballyshannon	III.	203
10	Rossmore	130 1 7	Fermanagh	Lurg	Derryvullan	Lowtherstown	III.	205
48	Rossmore	280 3 31	Kerry	Maguniby	Molahiffe	Killarney	II.	205
22	Rossmore	421 2 17	Kilkenny	Shillelogher	Killaloe	Callan	I.	115
18	Ross More	124 3 15	Leitrim	Drumahaire	Inishmagrath	Manorhamilton	IV.	97
36, 38	Ross More	172 0 9	Leitrim	Mohill	Cloone	Mohill	IV.	106
37,38,45,46	Rossmore	231 0 35	Limerick	Connello Upper	Corcomohide	Croom	II.	232
48	Rossmore	224 3 19	Londonderry	Loughinsholin	Lissan	Magherafelt	III.	242
27	Rossmore	435 3 3	Queen's Co.	Clandonagh	Rathsaran	Donaghmore	I.	235
7, 12	Rossmore	162 2 13	Queen's Co.	Maryborough West	Clonenagh and Clonagheen	Mountmellick	I.	243
37	Rossmore	1,734 2 1	Queen's Co.	Slievemargy	Killeshin	Carlow	I.	246
9	Rossmore	291 0 28	Queen's Co.	Stradbally	Moyanna	Athy	I.	247
88, 91	Rossmore	383 2 28	Tipperary, S.R.	Iffa and Offa West	Newcastle	Clogheen	II.	319
46, 52	Rossmore	475 1 19	Tipperary, S.R.	Kilnamanagh Lower	Clonoulty	Cashel	II.	323
46	Ross More	111 0 11	Tyrone	Dungannon Middle	Drumglass	Dungannon	III.	303
22	Ross More East	329 2 35c	Roscommon	Roscommon	Elphin	Strokestown	IV.	210
100	Rossmore Island	318 2 38	Kerry	Dunkerron South	Kilcrohane	Kenmare	II.	184
22	Ross More West	250 3 24	Roscommon	Roscommon	Elphin	Strokestown	IV.	210
15	Rossnabarnagh	126 0 22	Queen's Co.	Clandonagh	Kyle	Roscrea	I.	233
36	Rossnabrone	60 0 17d	Cork, E.R.	Condons & Clangibbon	Castlelyons	Fermoy	II.	60
130	Rossnacaheragh	846 3 0	Cork, W.R.	West Carbery (W.D.)	Kilcrohane	Bantry	II.	144
16	Rossnaclonagh Inside	196 0 22	Queen's Co.	Upperwoods	Offerlane	Mountmellick	I.	252
16	Rossnaclonagh Out-side	330 0 29	Queen's Co.	Upperwoods	Offerlane	Mountmellick	I.	252
15, 16	Rossnacreena	208 3 32	Queen's Co.	Upperwoods	Offerlane	Mountmellick	I.	252
16	Rossnadough	234 0 20	Queen's Co.	Upperwoods	Offerlane	Mountmellick	I.	252
15	Rossnafarsan	112 1 13	Fermanagh	Magheraboy	Devenish	Enniskillen	III.	211
7, 12	Rossnagad	201 1 7	Queen's Co.	Maryborough West	Clonenagh and Clonagheen	Mountmellick	I.	243
20, 21	Rossnagalliagh	201 1 3	Londonderry	Tirkeeran	Clondermot	Londonderry	III.	248
18	Rossnaglogh East	125 1 33	Monaghan	Dartree	Aghabog	Cootehill	III.	264
17	Rossnaglogh West	110 0 19	Monaghan	Dartree	Aghabog	Cootehill	III.	264
141	Rossnagoose	86 3 34	Cork, W.R.	West Carbery (E.D.)	Aghadown	Skibbereen	II.	137
90	Rossnagrena	429 0 18	Cork, W.R.	Bear	Kilcaskan	Bantry	II.	123
74	Rossnahowgarry	130 3 11	Kerry	Maguniby	Killarney	Killarney	II.	203
82	Rossnakilla	246 1 23	Cork, W.R.	West Muskerry	Kilmichael	Dunmanway	II.	159
23	Rossnamanniff Lower	55 2 2	Tipperary, N.R.	Eliogarty	Templemore	Thurles	II.	272
23	Rossnamanniff Upper	44 2 10	Tipperary, N.R.	Eliogarty	Templemore	Thurles	II.	272
16	Rossnanarney	336 2 37	Cork, E.R.	Orrery and Kilmore	Liscarroll	Mallow	II.	109
33, 37	Rossnanowl	119 0 21	Kilkenny	Ida	The Rower	New Ross	I.	104
19, 26	Rossnaree	694 3 39c	Meath	Lower Duleek	Knockcommon	Navan	I.	196
57	Rossnareen	258 0 25	Tyrone	Omagh East	Kilskeery	Enniskillen	III.	314
90, 104	Rossnashunsoge	160 0 18	Cork, W.R.	Bear	Kilcaskan	Bantry	II.	123
103	Rossnowlagh Lower	401 2 31	Donegal	Tirhugh	Drumhome	Ballyshannon	III.	147
103	Rossnowlagh Upper or Crockahany	389 2 10	Donegal	Tirhugh	Drumhome	Ballyshannon	III.	147
22	Rossola	96 0 27f	Fermanagh	Magheraboy	Rossory	Enniskillen	III.	214
19, 24	Rossolus	192 1 6	Monaghan	Cremorne	Clontibret	Castleblayney	III.	261
22	Rossorry	164 3 27g	Fermanagh	Magheraboy	Rossory	Enniskillen	III.	214

(a) Including 12A. 1R. 6P. water.
(b) Including 12A. 1R. 28P. water.
(c) Including 4A. 3R. 19P. water.

(d) Including 4A. 3R. 0P. water.
(e) Including 25A. 0R. 20P. water.

(f) Including 16A. 0R. 1P. water.
(g) Including 16A. 3R. 9P. water.

No. of Sheet of the Ordnance Survey Maps.	Townlands and Towns.	Area in Statute Acres. A. R. P.	County.	Barony.	Parish.	Poor Law Union in 1857.	Townland Census of 1851, Part I. Vol.	Page
40	Rossoulty	312 1 12	Tipperary, N.R.	Kilnamanagh Upper	Templebeg	Thurles	II.	279
15,16,21,22	Ross Outer	185 2 34	Fermanagh	Magheraboy	Devenish	Enniskillen	III.	211
76, 77	Rossow	181 2 18	Mayo	Burrishoole	Kilmeena	Newport	IV.	122
40	Rosspile	445 1 39	Wexford	Shelmaliere West	Ballylannan	New Ross	I.	332
15	Rosspoint or Cosbystown East	117 1 1	Fermanagh	Magheraboy	Inishmacsaint	Enniskillen	III.	213
45, 46	Rossreagh	76 0 14	Donegal	Kilmacrenan	Tullyfern	Milford	III.	133
81	Rossrehill	7 1 30	Tipperary, S.R.	Iffa and Offa West	Shanrahan	Clogheen	II.	320
80, 81	Rossrehill	149 3 34	Tipperary, S.R.	Iffa and Offa West	Tubbrid	Clogheen	II.	321
28, 29	Rossroe	147 0 5	Kilkenny	Gowran	Inistioge	Thomastown	I.	96
78	Rossroe Island	57 3 30	Galway	Moycullen	Kilcummin	Oughterard	IV.	69
31, 39	Rosstemple	354 1 34	Limerick	Coshma	Athlacca	Kilmallock	II.	241
31	Rosstemple	65 2 7	Limerick	Coshma	Croom	Croom	II.	242
32	Rosstillegane	50 2 17	Queen's Co.	Slievemargy	Killabban	Carlow	I.	245
64	Ross T.	—	Clare	Moyarta	Kilballyowen	Kilrush	II.	32
51, 54	Rosstrevor	510 1 35	Down	Upper Iveagh, Up. pt.	Kilbroney	Kilkeel	III.	176
51,52,54,55	Rosstrevor Mountains	2,129 0 0	Down	Upper Iveagh, Up. pt.	Kilbroney	Kilkeel	III.	176
54	ROSSTREVOR T.	—	Down	Upper Iveagh, Up. pt.	Kilbroney	Kilkeel	III.	176
51, 54	Rosstrevor Upper	1,066 0 28	Down	Upper Iveagh, Up. pt.	Kilbroney	Kilkeel	III.	176
60, 69, 70	Ross West	438 1 35	Mayo	Carra	Turlough	Castlebar	IV.	131
24	Rossy	288 3 32a	Leitrim	Leitrim	Kiltubbrid	Cark. on Shannon	IV.	104
93, 99	Rossylongan	154 0 6	Donegal	Banagh	Killymard	Donegal	III.	111
87	Rossymailley	42 0 34	Mayo	Murrisk	Oughaval	Westport	IV.	162
67	Rossyvera	74 3 21	Mayo	Burrishoole	Burrishoole	Newport	IV.	120
99, 100	Rossyvolan	83 3 34	Donegal	Tirhugh	Drumhome	Donegal	III.	147
22	Rossyvullan	62 0 28	Fermanagh	Tirkennedy	Enniskillen	Enniskillen	III.	222
38	Rostalla	272 1 24	Westmeath	Moycashel	Durrow	Tullamore	I.	277
88	Rostellan	31 3 7	Cork, E.R.	Imokilly	Garranekinnefeake	Middleton	II.	86
88	Rostellan	799 3 7b	Cork, E.R.	Imokilly	Rostellan	Middleton	II.	90
132	Rostollus	194 3 26	Galway	Leitrim	Ballynakill	Portumna	IV.	52
53	Rostonstown	70 3 22	Wexford	Forth	Tacumshin	Wexford	I.	315
53	Rostonstown Burrow	65 3 5	Wexford	Forth	Tacumshin	Wexford	I.	315
76	Rostoohy	57 3 27	Mayo	Burrishoole	Kilmeena	Westport	IV.	122
66	Rosturk	795 0 27	Mayo	Burrishoole	Burrishoole	Newport	IV.	120
67	Rosturk	34 1 15	Mayo	Burrishoole	Burrishoole	Newport	IV.	120
126	Rosturra	511 2 39	Galway	Leitrim	Ballynakill	Loughrea	IV.	52
21,22,27,28	Rostyduff Lower	271 2 1	Wicklow	Upper Talbotstown	Donaghmore	Baltinglass	I.	363
27, 28	Rostyduff Upper	306 1 4	Wicklow	Upper Talbotstown	Donaghmore	Baltinglass	I.	363
40	Rostygah	265 0 22	Wicklow	Arklow	Arklow	Rathdrum	I.	341
37, 46	Rosybower	105 2 37	Cork, E.R.	Kinnatalloon	Mogeely	Fermoy	II.	99
15, 21	Rottenhill	243 3 33	Wicklow	Upper Talbotstown	Rathsallagh	Baltinglass	I.	365
97	Rotten Island	0 3 12	Donegal	Banagh	Killybegs Upper	Glenties	III.	111
1, 2	Rotten Mountain	354 2 10	Fermanagh	Lurg	Drumkeeran	Lowtherstown	III.	207
90, 104	Rougham	1,068 0 8	Cork, W.R.	Bear	Kilcaskan	Bantry	II.	123
16	Rougham	292 3 0	Armagh	Armagh	Derrynoose	Armagh	III.	44
5, 9	Rougham	228 1 19	Armagh	Oneilland West	Drumcree	Lurgan	III.	52
9	Rougham	128 3 8	Clare	Corcomroe	Kilfenora	Ennistimon	II.	19
45, 46	Rougham	68 1 26	Donegal	Kilmacrenan	Tullyfern	Milford	III.	133
46	Rougham	117 2 5	Donegal	Raphoe	Allsaints	Londonderry	III.	134
71	Rougham	66 1 6	Donegal	Raphoe	Clonleigh	Strabane	III.	135
60, 61	Rougham	138 3 29	Donegal	Raphoe	Conwal	Letterkenny	III.	137
1, 4	Rougham	138 1 28	Tipperary, N.R.	Lower Ormond	Dorrha	Parsonstown	II.	283
50	Rougham	105 3 19	Tyrone	Clogher	Donacavey	Omagh	III.	294
59	Rougham	257 3 19	Tyrone	Clogher	Errigal Keerogue	Clogher	III.	295
46, 47	Rougham	312 2 25c	Tyrone	Dungannon Middle	Donaghenry	Dungannon	III.	301
46	Rougham Glebe	103 0 5	Donegal	Raphoe	Allsaints	Londonderry	III.	134
16, 17	Roughaun	127 1 28	Clare	Inchiquin	Killinaboy	Corrofin	II.	27
20	Roughfield	80 2 12	Kilkenny	Gowran	Blanchvilleskill	Kilkenny	I.	93
19,20,26,27	Roughgrange	763 0 24d	Meath	Lower Duleek	Duleek	Drogheda	II.	195
96	Roughgrove East	400 1 13	Cork, W.R.	Kinalmeaky	Kilbrogan	Bandon	II.	152
96	Roughgrove West	375 2 12	Cork, W.R.	Kinalmeaky	Kilbrogan	Bandon	II.	152
8	Rough Hill	64 3 18	Monaghan	Monaghan	Clones	Monaghan	III.	275
59	Rough Hill	59 2 22	Tyrone	Clogher	Errigal Keerogue	Clogher	III.	295
27	Rough Island	6 0 27	Donegal	Kilmacrenan	Tullyfern	Milford	III.	133
11	Rough Island	6 2.35	Down	Castlereagh Lower	Comber	Newtownards	III.	162
9	Rough Island	4 1 25	Fermanagh	Lurg	Belleek	Ballyshannon	III.	204
66	Rough Island	1 2 3	Kerry	Magunihy	Killarney	Killarney	II.	204
42	Roughmead	8 2 13	Wexford	Forth	Drinagh	Wexford	I.	309
53	Roughpark	171 3 32	Donegal	Kilmacrenan	Aghanunshin	Letterkenny	III.	122
45, 46	Roughpark	73 0 16	Donegal	Kilmacrenan	Aughnish	Milford	III.	122
71	Roundfield	210 3 16	Galway	Tiaquin	Monivea	Tuam	IV.	79
110	Roundhill	126 1 32	Cork, W.R.	Kinalmeaky	Ballymodan	Bandon	II.	151
31	Roundhill	82 3 32	King's Co.	Eglish	Drumcullen	Parsonstown	I.	134

(a) Including 57A. 0R. 23P. water.
(b) Including 3A. 3R. 2P. water.
(c) Including 10A. 2R. 7P. Lough Roughan.
(d) Including 22A. 0R. 0P. water.

5 K 2

No. of Sheet of the Ordnance Survey Maps.	Townlands and Towns.	Area in Statute Acres.			County.	Barony.	Parish.	Poor Law Union in 1857.	Townland Census of 1851. Part I.	
		A.	R.	P.					Vol.	Page
5	Roundhill	131	1	18	Tyrone	Strabane Lower	Leckpatrick	Strabane	III.	322
35, 37	Roundhills	59	2	19	Kildare	Narragh and Reban West	St. Johns	Athy	I.	68
110	ROUNDHILL T.	—			Cork, W.R.	Kinalmeaky	Ballymodan	Bandon	II.	151
24	Round Island	2	0	24	Down	Ards Upper	Ardkeen	Downpatrick	III.	159
50, 63	Roundstone	210	3	6a	Galway	Ballynahinch	Moyrus	Clifden	IV.	13
50, 63	ROUNDSTONE T.	—			Galway	Ballynahinch	Moyrus	Clifden	IV.	14
22	ROUND TOWN T.	—			Dublin	Rathdown	Rathfarnham	Dublin South	I.	37
11	Roundwood	230	2	33	Queen's Co.	Upperwoods	Offerlane	Mountmellick	I.	252
18	Roundwood	1,208	1	13	Wicklow	Ballinacor North	Derrylossary	Rathdrum	I.	346
134, 143	Rouryglen	263	3	15	Cork, W.R.	East Carbery (W.D.)	Ross	Clonakilty	II.	135
60	Rousky	133	2	22	Tyrone	Dungannon Lower	Carnteel	Clogher	III.	298
38	Rousky	112	2	35	Tyrone	Dungannon Middle	Donaghenry	Cookstown	III.	301
6	Rousky	322	3	37b	Tyrone	Strabane Lower	Donaghedy	Strabane	III.	321
19	Rousky	295	1	29c	Tyrone	Strabane Upper	Bodoney Lower	Gortin	III.	324
39	Rouskyroe	67	3	35	Tyrone	Dungannon Middle	Donaghenry	Cookstown	III.	301
13	Routagh	345	0	27	Limerick	Clanwilliam	Donaghmore	Limerick	II.	223
35	Rover	569	3	0	Sligo	Tirerrill	Kilmactranny	Boyle	IV.	240
44, 45	Roverkilly	222	2	26	Roscommon	Athlone	Rahara	Roscommon	IV.	183
2	Rover Lower	306	1	1	Roscommon	Boyle	Kilronan	Boyle	IV.	197
2	Rover Upper	146	0	31	Roscommon	Boyle	Kilronan	Boyle	IV.	197
19	Rowan	484	0	9	Armagh	Tiranny	Derrynoose	Armagh	III.	59
51	Rowan	180	3	25	Meath	Dunboyne	Dunboyne	Dunshaughlin	I.	199
4, 5	Rowans Big	252	2	14	Dublin	Balrothery East	Lusk	Balrothery	I.	21
4, 5	Rowans Little	156	2	8	Dublin	Balrothery East	Lusk	Balrothery	I.	21
10	Rowanstown	130	2	29	Kildare	North Salt	Laraghbryan	Celbridge	I.	75
107, 110	Rowantreehill	193	1	3	Donegal	Tirhugh	Kilbarron	Ballyshannon	III.	148
21	Rower Beg	250	2	23	Limerick	Coshma	Adare	Croom	II.	241
21	Rower More	182	3	33	Limerick	Coshma	Adare	Croom	II.	241
42	Rowestown	124	1	7	Wexford	Forth	Drinagh	Wexford	I.	309
37	Rowestown	180	3	11	Wexford	Shelmaliere West	Kilbrideglynn	Wexford	I.	334
24	Rowe or Toordillon	60	2	29	Westmeath	Rathconrath	Killare	Mullingar	I.	283
75	Rowgarrane	240	0	18	Cork, E.R.	Barrymore	Caherlag	Cork	II.	52
17	Rowlagh	102	3	37	Dublin	Uppercross	Esker	Dublin South	I.	40
17	Rowlandstown	290	0	13	Westmeath	Rathconrath	Rathconrath	Mullingar	I.	284
33	Rowlestown	98	0	6	Meath	Upper Duleek	Ardcath	Drogheda	I.	197
7, 11	Rowlestown East	121	2	36	Dublin	Nethercross	Killossery	Balrothery	I.	31
7, 11	Rowlestown West	217	3	31	Dublin	Nethercross	Killossery	Balrothery	I.	31
5	Rowls Aldworth	166	1	3	Cork, E.R.	Duhallow	Clonfert	Kanturk	II.	69
5	Rowls Allen	412	2	6	Cork, E.R.	Duhallow	Clonfert	Kanturk	II.	69
5, 14	Rowls Daunt	254	1	8	Cork, E.R.	Duhallow	Clonfert	Kanturk	II.	69
5	Rowls Langford (North)	1,125	0	28	Cork, E.R.	Duhallow	Clonfert	Kanturk	II.	69
5	Rowls Langford (South)	1,314	1	27	Cork, E.R.	Duhallow	Clonfert	Kanturk	II.	69
5, 14	Rowls Noonan	641	3	36	Cork, E.R.	Duhallow	Clonfert	Kanturk	II.	69
5	Rowls Shaddock	250	2	4	Cork, E.R.	Duhallow	Clonfert	Kanturk	II.	69
18	Rowreagh	638	1	6	Down	Ards Upper	Inishargy	Newtownards	III.	160
65, 76	Roxborough	124	2	20	Cork, E.R.	Barrymore	Inchinabacky	Middleton	II.	55
104, 114	Roxborough	392	2	11	Galway	Loughrea	Killinan	Loughrea	IV.	64
48	Roxborough	249	1	22	Kerry	Magunihy	Molahiffe	Killarney	II.	205
13	Roxborough	526	2	5	Limerick	Clanwilliam	Cahervally	Limerick	II.	221
21	Roxborough	134	1	24	Louth	Ferrard	Mullary	Drogheda	I.	182
35,36,39,40	Roxborough	1,076	3	4	Roscommon	Ballintober South	Kilbride	Roscommon	IV.	189
82, 88	Roxborough	189	3	15d	Tipperary, S.R.	Iffa and Offa West	Tullaghmelan	Clogheen	II.	321
28	Roxborough or Dorsy (Cavan O'Hanlon)	147	0	31	Armagh	Fews Upper	Newtownhamilton	Castleblayney	III.	49
90, 96	Roxborough Glebe	500	0	34	Donegal	Banagh	Kilcar	Glenties	III.	109
17, 24, 25	Roxton	452	1	31	Clare	Inchiquin	Rath	Corrofin	II.	28
17	Roy	242	1	0	Galway	Dunmore	Dunmore	Tuam	IV.	34
25, 34	Roy	2,403	2	22e	Mayo	Erris	Kilcommon	Belmullet	IV.	144
59	Roy	65	1	19	Tyrone	Clogher	Clogher	Clogher	III.	293
1, 3	Royaloak	362	1	10	Kildare	Carbury	Ballynadrumny	Edenderry	I.	51
16	ROYAL OAK T.	—			Carlow	Idrone West	Killinane	Carlow	I.	9
103	Roymore	25	1	30	Galway	Dunkellin	Kilcolgan	Gort	IV.	28
1, 6	Ruan	67	0	24	Limerick	Clanwilliam	Stradbally	Limerick	II.	226
53	Ruanard	176	2	29	Clare	Tulla Lower	Kiltenanlea	Limerick	II.	37
25	Ruan Commons	15	3	35	Clare	Inchiquin	Ruan	Corrofin	II.	28
32	Ruanes	133	3	6	Cork, E.R.	Duhallow	Ballyclogh	Mallow	II.	67
21, 22	Ruaunmore	258	2	27	Wexford	Ballaghkeen	Killincooly	Gorey	I.	295
10, 11	Rubbal	168	3	5f	Leitrim	Drumahaire	Drumlease	Manorhamilton	IV.	95
61	Rubble	245	0	3g	Mayo	Gallen	Killasser	Swineford	IV.	149
27, 33	Rudder	294	2	34	Meath	Upper Duleek	Duleek Abbey	Drogheda	I.	198
31	Rue	51	0	2	Leitrim	Leitrim	Kiltoghert	Cark. on Shannon	IV.	102

(a) Including 1A. 0R. 32P. water.
(b) Including 2A. 2R. 27P. water.
(c) Including 0A. 2R. 25P. water.

(d) Including 4A. 2R. 12P. water.
(e) Including 15A. 2R. 33P. water.

(f) Including 2A. 3R. 10P. water.
(g) Including 22A. 3R. 33P. water.

No. of Sheet of the Ordnance Survey Maps.	Townlands and Towns.	Area in Statute Acres.			County.	Barony.	Parish.	Poor Law Union in 1857.	Townland Census of 1851, Part I.	
		A.	R.	P.					Vol.	Page
37	Rue . . .	721	3	16	Sligo .	Leyny . .	Kilmacteige .	Tobercurry .	IV.	231
34, 35	Runnabackan .	285	2	11	Roscommon .	Ballymoe .	Oran . .	Roscommon .	IV.	192
9, 15	Runnabehy .	328	1	23	Roscommon .	Frenchpark .	Kilnamanagh .	Castlereagh .	IV.	204
10, 16	Runnaboll .	322	3	4	Roscommon .	Frenchpark .	Kilcolagh .	Boyle . .	IV.	203
16	Runnacocka .	132	1	1	Roscommon .	Frenchpark .	Kilmacumsy .	Boyle . .	IV.	204
9	Runnameelta .	139	2	7	Roscommon .	Frenchpark .	Kilnamanagh .	Castlereagh .	IV.	204
34, 35	Runnamoat .	460	2	13	Roscommon .	Ballymoe .	Cloonygormican .	Roscommon .	IV.	191
9	Runnaroddan .	126	2	14	Roscommon .	Frenchpark .	Kilnamanagh .	Boyle . .	IV.	204
16	Runnaroddaun .	76	1	17	Roscommon .	Frenchpark .	Kilmacumsy .	Boyle . .	IV.	204
22	Runnaruag .	148	0	7	Roscommon .	Roscommon .	Elphin . .	Stroke-town .	IV.	210
16	Runnateggal or Rye-field . .	178	1	37	Roscommon .	Frenchpark .	Creeve . .	Cark. on Shannon	IV.	203
8, 9	Runnawillin or Callow . .	632	1	24a	Roscommon .	Frenchpark .	Kilnamanagh .	Castlereagh .	IV.	204
28	Ruppa . .	268	1	6	Kilkenny .	Gowran .	Columbkille .	Thomastown .	I.	94
53	Rupperagh .	252	1	19	Cork, E.R. .	Barrymore .	Kilquane .	Cork . .	II.	56
56, 57	Ruppulagh .	1,094	3	32	Limerick .	Coshlea .	Darragh .	Kilmallock .	II.	238
8	Rush . .	1,171	2	26	Dublin .	Balrothery East .	Lusk . .	Balrothery .	I.	21
142	Rushanes .	168	0	19	Cork, W.R. .	East Carbery (W.D.)	Kilfaughnabeg .	Skibbereen .	II.	133
32, 33	Rushaun .	260	0	38b	Clare .	Inchiquin .	Kilnamona .	Ennis . .	II.	27
77	Rushbrook .	104	3	28c	Mayo .	Burrishoole .	Kilmaclasser .	Westport .	IV.	121
101, 111	Rushbrook East .	151	0	6	Mayo .	Clanmorris .	Crossboyne .	Claremorris .	IV.	133
101, 111	Rushbrook West .	42	0	6	Mayo .	Clanmorris .	Crossboyne .	Claremorris .	IV.	133
8	Rush Demesne .	452	1	25	Dublin .	Balrothery East .	Lusk . .	Balrothery .	I.	21
9	Rusheen .	142	2	30	Clare .	Burren .	Noughaval .	Ballyvaghan .	II.	14
59	Rusheen .	210	2	19	Clare .	Clonderalaw .	Killadysert .	Killadysert .	II.	16
15, 23	Rusheen .	280	1	18	Cork, E.R. .	Duhallow .	Kilcorcoran .	Kanturk .	II.	72
2	Rusheen .	439	3	13	Cork, E.R. .	Orrery and Kilmore	Corcomohide .	Kanturk .	II.	108
60, 71	Rusheen .	287	0	2	Cork, W.R. .	East Muskerry .	Aghabulloge .	Macroom .	II.	153
21	Rusheen .	61	0	5d	Galway .	Ballynahinch .	Omey . .	Clifden .	IV.	15
93	Rusheen .	27	2	23	Galway .	Galway .	Rahoon .	Galway .	IV.	38
94, 103	Rusheen .	417	3	8	Kerry .	Glanarought .	Kilgarvan .	Kenmare .	II.	188
2, 3	Rusheen .	214	2	14	Kerry .	Iraghticonnor .	Aghavallen .	Listowel .	II.	189
47	Rusheen .	415	2	38	Kerry .	Magunihy .	Kilnanare .	Killarney .	II.	204
48, 58	Rusheen .	286	0	24	Kerry .	Magunihy .	Molahiffe .	Killarney .	II.	205
41, 44	Rusheen .	130	2	23	King's Co. .	Clonlisk .	Kilcomin .	Roscrea .	I.	131
76, 87	Rusheen .	232	1	16	Mayo .	Burrishoole .	Kilmeena .	Westport .	IV.	122
101	Rusheen .	39	3	6	Mayo .	Clanmorris .	Tagheen .	Claremorris .	IV.	136
6, 10	Rusheen .	379	2	3	Roscommon .	Boyle .	Ardcarn .	B . .	IV.	192
27	Rusheen .	231	2	24	Roscommon .	Castlereagh .	Baslick .	Castlereagh .	IV.	199
27	Rusheen .	301	2	15	Sligo .	Tirerrill .	Ballynakill .	Sligo .	IV.	237
27	Rusheen .	342	3	6	Sligo .	Tirerrill .	Drumcolumb .	Sligo .	IV.	238
130, 131	Rusheenaniska .	83	2	18	Cork, W.R. .	West Carbery (W.D.)	Durrus .	Bantry .	I	142
75	Rusheen Beg .	231	1	6	Kerry .	Magunihy .	Killaha .	Killarney .	II.	202
34	Rusheen Beg .	232	1	8	Tipperary, N.R.	Kilnamanagh Upper	Glenkeen .	Thurles .	II.	279
9, 10	Rusheenduff .	287	3	23e	Galway .	Ballynahinch .	Ballynakill .	Clifden .	IV.	12
27	Rusheen East .	202	2	27	Galway .	Ross .	Ross . .	Oughterard .	IV.	74
23	Rusheen Island .	4	0	35	Mayo .	Erris .	Kilmore .	Belmullet .	IV.	146
75	Rusheen More .	678	1	13	Kerry .	Magunihy .	Killaha .	Killarney .	II.	202
34	Rusheen More .	289	2	13	Tipperary, N.R.	Kilnamanagh Upper	Glenkeen .	Thurles .	II.	279
76, 77	Rusheennacholla .	78	2	36	Galway .	Ballynahinch .	Moyrus .	Clifden .	IV.	14
77	Rusheennamanagh .	926	1	20f	Galway .	Ballynahinch .	Moyrus .	Clifden .	IV.	13
2	Rusheenpark .	89	1	1	Kerry .	Iraghticonnor .	Aghavallen .	Listowel .	II.	189
93, 102	Rusheens .	315	2	37	Kerry .	Glanarought .	Kenmare .	Kenmare .	II.	186
67	Rusheens .	18	2	4	Mayo .	Burrishoole .	Burrishoole .	Newport .	IV.	120
22	Rusheens .	271	2	15	Mayo .	Tirawley .	Ballysakeery .	Ballina .	IV.	165
38	Rusheens .	114	1	20	Waterford .	Decies within Drum	Ardmore .	Dungarvan .	II.	350
73, 74	Rusheens East .	121	2	34	Mayo .	Costello .	Kilmovee .	Swineford .	IV.	142
43	Rusheens North .	315	1	29	Galway .	Clare .	Tuam .	Tuam .	IV.	23
43	Rusheens South .	195	0	20	Galway .	Clare .	Tuam .	Tuam .	IV.	23
73	Rusheens West .	161	1	3	Mayo .	Costello .	Kilmovee .	Swineford .	IV.	142
90, 100	Rusheen or Thomastown . .	212	0	1g	Mayo .	Carra .	Drum . .	Castlebar .	IV.	128
27	Rusheen West .	123	3	37	Galway .	Ross .	Ross . .	Oughterard .	IV.	74
107	Rusheeny .	121	2	5	Galway .	Longford .	Killimorbologue .	Portumna .	IV.	59
54, 67	Rusheeny .	1,673	2	36h	Galway .	Moycullen .	Kilcummin .	Oughterard .	IV.	68
77	Rusheenyvulligan .	103	3	34i	Galway .	Ballynahinch .	Moyrus .	Clifden .	IV.	13
104, 105	Rushen .	996	3	15j	Donegal .	Tirhugh .	Templecarn .	Donegal .	III.	149
31	Rushes . .	393	0	1	Queen's Co. .	Slievemargy .	Killabban .	Carlow .	I.	245
32	Rushestown .	882	3	16k	Galway .	Killian .	Killian .	Mountbellew .	IV.	45
21, 22	Rushey Hill .	78	2	24	Antrim .	Kilconway .	Finvoy .	Ballymoney .	III.	26
95	Rushfield .	216	2	12	Cork, W.R. .	East Carbery (W.D.)	Kinneigh .	Bandon .	II.	135
16, 22	Rush Hall .	747	0	33	Queen's Co. .	Upperwoods .	Offerlane .	Abbeyleix .	I.	252

(a) Including 7A. 1R. 21P. water.
(b) Including 6A. 3R. 27P. water.
(c) Including 24A. 3R. 19P. water.
(d) Including 20A. 3R. 36P. water.

(e) Including 17A. 2R. 5P. water.
(f) Including 105A. 1R. 39P. water.
(g) Including 8A. 2R. 11P. water.
(h) Including 19A. 1R. 2P. water.

(i) Including 3A. 0R. 16P. water.
(j) Including 68A. 3R. 37P. water.
(k) Including 6A. 1R. 0P. water.

No. of Sheet of the Ordnance Survey Maps.	Townlands and Towns.	Area in Statute Acres.			County.	Barony.	Parish.	Poor Law Union in 1857.	Townland Census of 1851, Part I.	
		A.	R.	P.					Vol.	Page
79	Rush Hill	127	2	15	Mayo	Carra	Manulla	Castlebar	IV.	129
4	Rush Hill	68	3	3	Roscommon	Boyle	Kilronan	Boyle	IV.	197
11,12,16,17	Rushin	746	2	18	Queen's Co.	Upperwoods	Offerlane	Mountmellick	I.	252
1	Rushinbane	168	1	26	Fermanagh	Lurg	Drumkeeran	Lowtherstown	III.	207
1	Rushindoo	158	2	37	Fermanagh	Lurg	Drumkeeran	Lowtherstown	III.	207
27	Rushin East	203	2	36a	Fermanagh	Clanawley	Cleenish	Enniskillen	III.	191
25	Rushin West	113	0	11	Fermanagh	Clanawley	Cleenish	Enniskillen	III.	191
28, 35	Rushpark Farragher	208	2	18	Roscommon	Ballymoe	Cloonygormican	Castlereagh	IV.	191
18	Rushport	176	0	36b	Roscommon	Ballintober North	Kilmore	Carᵏ. on Shannon	IV.	187
8	Rush T.	—			Dublin	Balrothery East	Lusk	Balrothery	I.	21
54	Rushveala	151	3	27	Galway	Moycullen	Kilcummin	Oughterard	IV.	68
18, 19	Rushwee	105	0	32	Meath	Upper Slane	Slane	Navan	I.	225
18, 19	Rushwee	212	3	15	Meath	Upper Slane	Stackallan	Navan	I.	225
78, 87	Rushyhill	208	2	24	Donegal	Raphoe	Donaghmore	Stranorlar	III.	138
50	Rusk	194	2	38	Meath	Dunboyne	Dunboyne	Dunshaughlin	I.	199
10	Ruskey	170	2	22	Londonderry	Keenaght	Drumachose	NewTⁿLimavady	III.	235
11, 12	Rusky	116	0	36	Londonderry	Coleraine	Aghadowey	Coleraine	III.	230
49	Rusky Lower	146	1	21	Londonderry	Loughinsholin	Tamlaght	Magherafelt	III.	243
49	Rusky Upper	169	1	11	Londonderry	Loughinsholin	Tamlaght	Magherafelt	III.	243
24	Russa	79	2	35	Clare	Corcomroe	Clooney	Ennistimon	II.	18
141,142,150	Russagh	431	0	22c	Cork, W.R.	West Carbery (E.D.)	Abbeystrowry	Skibbereen	II.	136
2	Russagh	363	0	24	King's Co.	Kilcoursey	Ardnurcher or Horseleap	Tullamore	I.	140
6	Russagh	240	2	18	Westmeath	Moygoish	Russagh	Granard	I.	280
123, 129	Russaun	236	0	25d	Galway	Kiltartan	Kilbeacanty	Gort	IV.	47
5, 9, 10	Russborough	431	1	36e	Wicklow	Lower Talbotstown	Burgage	Naas	I.	359
84, 96, 97	Russelhill	656	1	33	Cork, E.R.	East Muskerry	Knockavilly	Bandon	II.	105
31, 36	Russellspenn	113	2	13	King's Co.	Eglish	Drumcullen	Parsonstown	I.	134
38	Russells Quarter	98	3	4	Down	Lecale Upper	Down	Downpatrick	III.	181
31	Russells Quarter North	78	3	35	Down	Lecale Lower	Saul	Downpatrick	III.	179
31	Russells Quarter South	65	2	16	Down	Lecale Lower	Saul	Downpatrick	III.	179
3, 8	Russellstown	349	0	4	Carlow	Carlow	Killerrig	Carlow	I.	2
18	Russellstown	382	0	30	Kildare	Connell	Rathernan	Naas	I.	56
35	Russellstown	196	3	25	Kildare	Narragh & Reban West	Kilberry	Athy	I.	68
4, 5	Russellstown	331	0	18	Kilkenny	Fassadinin	Kilmenan	Castlecomer	I.	90
33, 37	Russellstown	198	3	24	Kilkenny	Ida	The Rower	New Ross	I.	104
1	Russellstown	1,722	3	30	Waterford	Glenahiry	Kilronan	Clonmel	II.	366
26	Russellstown	455	1	9	Westmeath	Fartullagh	Mullingar	Mullingar	I.	269
46	Russellstown	179	0	37	Wexford	Bargy	Kilcowan	Wexford	I.	305
5, 10	Russellstown	233	0	11f	Wicklow	Lower Talbotstown	Burgage	Naas	I.	359
26	Russellstown Little	37	1	11	Westmeath	Fartullagh	Mullingar	Mullingar	I.	269
1	Russellstown New	890	0	25	Waterford	Glenahiry	Kilronan	Clonmel	II.	366
2	Russellswood	151	1	10	Kildare	Carbury	Carrick	Edenderry	I.	52
16	Russelstown	652	3	3	Galway	Dunmore	Addergoole	Tuam	IV.	33
58	Russelstown	215	3	26	Tipperary, S.R.	Clanwilliam	Solloghod-more	Tipperary	II.	311
10, 14	Ruthstown	348	2	8	Kilkenny	Fassadinin	Kilmademoge	Kilkenny	I.	90
14	Ruthstown	157	1	5	Kilkenny	Fassadinin	Kilmadum	Kilkenny	I.	90
42, 45	Rutland	171	2	36	King's Co.	Clonlisk	Kilcomin	Roscrea	I.	131
48	Rutland Island or Inishmacadurn	312	3	9	Donegal	Boylagh	Templecrone	Glenties	III.	116
2, 3, 7, 8	Rutland or Urglin	726	2	11	Carlow	Carlow	Urglin	Carlow	I.	3
47	Ryan	391	1	7	Down	Lordship of Newry	Newry	Newry	III.	182
26, 32	Ryane	255	2	29	Wexford	Ballaghkeen	Edermine	Enniscorthy	I.	294
84	Ryecourt	283	1	14	Cork, E.R.	East Muskerry	Moviddy	Bandon	I.	105
43	Ryefield	923	0	1	Cavan	Castlerahan	Munterconnaught	Oldcastle	III.	71
52	Ryefield East	346	1	29	Cork, E.R.	Barrymore	Whitechurch	Cork	II.	59
16	Ryefield or Runnateggal	178	1	37	Roscommon	Frenchpark	Creeve	Carᵏ.on Shannon	IV.	203
52	Ryefield West	163	1	0	Cork, E.R.	Barrymore	Whitechurch	Cork	II.	59
26	RyefortorAghateggal	109	0	20	Cavan	Upper Loughtee	Denn	Cavan	III.	83
30	Ryehill	302	2	33	Galway	Dunmore	Tuam	Tuam	IV.	36
58	Ryehill Demesne	172	2	12	Galway	Tiaquin	Monivea	Tuam	IV.	79
54	Ryelands	453	0	32	Donegal	Raphoe	Raymoghy	Strabane	III.	142
23	Ryelanes	164	0	4	Kilkenny	Shillelogher	Tullaghanbrogue	Callan	I.	116
26	Rylagh	756	2	15	Tyrone	Strabane Upper	Cappagh	Omagh	III.	325
9	Ryland Lower	428	2	14g	Wexford	Scarawalsh	St. Marys Newtown-barry	Enniscorthy	I.	325
34,35,42,43	Rylands	242	2	32h	Tyrone	Omagh East	Drumragh	Omagh	III.	313
18	Rylands	632	0	10i	Tyrone	Strabane Upper	Bodoney Lower	Gortin	III.	324
9	Ryland Upper	487	1	11j	Wexford	Scarawalsh	St. Marys Newtown-barry	Enniscorthy	I.	325
26, 34	Rylane	849	2	29	Clare	Bunratty Upper	Clooney	Tulla	II.	8
49, 60, 61	Rylane	1,340	3	4	Cork, W.R.	East Muskerry	Aghabulloge	Macroom	II.	153
17	Rylane	554	0	13	Kerry	Clanmaurice	Duagh	Listowel	II.	168

(a) Including 26A. 1R. 8P. water.
(b) Including 1A. 0R. 22P. water.
(c) Including 28A. 3R. 10P. water.
(d) Including 5A. 2R. 20P. water.

(e) Including 3A. 2R. 21P. water.
(f) Including 4A. 1R. 11P. water.
(g) Including 12A. 2R. 28P. water.

(h) Including 0A. 3R. 0P. water.
(i) Including 6A. 1R. 4P. water.
(j) Including 8A. 1R. 12P. water.

No. of Sheet of the Ordnance Survey Maps.	Townlands and Towns.	Area in Statute Acres.	County.	Barony.	Parish.	Poor Law Union in 1857.	Townland Census of 1851, Part I.	
		A. R. P.					Vol.	Page
29	Rylanes . . .	207 1 1	Limerick . .	Connello Lower .	Rathkeale . .	Croom . .	II.	229
29	Rylanes . . .	88 1 23	Limerick . .	Connello Upper .	Ballingarry . .	Croom . .	II.	231
29	Ryleen . . .	521 3 37	Wexford . .	Bantry . . .	St. Mary's . .	New Ross .	I.	302
25	Ryninch Lower .	102 2 28	Tipperary, N.R.	Owney and Arra .	Templeachally .	Nenagh . .	II.	297
.9, 25	Ryninch Upper .	475 0 21	Tipperary, N.R.	Owney and Arra .	Templeachally .	Nenagh . .	II.	297
41, 49	Ryves Castle . .	390 1 1	Limerick . .	Coshlea . . .	Ballyscaddan . .	Kilmallock .	II.	238
20, 21	Sackville . .	382 0 12	Kerry . . .	Clanmaurice . .	Ardfert . . .	Tralee . .	II.	167
33, 34	Saddlestown . .	163 1 27	Meath . . .	Upper Duleek .	Stamullin . .	Drogheda .	I.	198
59, 67	Sadleirswells . .	383 0 5	Tipperary, S.R.	Clanwilliam .	Tipperary . .	Tipperary .	II.	312
21	Saggart . . .	576 1 8	Dublin . .	Newcastle . .	Saggart . .	Celbridge .	I.	35
21	SAGGART T. . .	—	Dublin . .	Newcastle . .	Saggart . .	Celbridge .	I.	35
17, 21	St. Albans or Lissawly	91 3 23	Longford . .	Rathcline . .	Rathcline . .	Longford .	I.	165
8	St. Annes Glebe .	86 3 21	Longford . .	Longford . .	Clongesh . .	Longford .	I.	158
53	St. Awaries . .	6 1 27	Wexford . .	Forth . . .	Ladysisland . .	Wexford .	I.	311
32	St. Brendan's or Creg-ganagrogy . .	530 0 17	Galway . .	Killian . .	Killian . .	Mountbellew .	IV.	45
6, 11	St. Catherines .	25 2 38	Kildare . .	North Salt . .	Confey . .	Celbridge .	I.	74
17	St. Catherine's Park	195 1 12a	Dublin . .	Newcastle . .	Leixlip . .	Celbridge .	I.	33
11	St. Catherine's Park	79 0 30b	Kildare . .	North Salt . .	Leixlip . .	Celbridge .	I.	75
10, 15	St. Catherines or Rossdagamph .	219 3 19c	Fermanagh . .	Magheraboy . .	Inishmacsaint .	Enniskillen .	III.	213
96,97,104,105	Saintclerans . .	626 3 9	Galway . .	Dunkellin .	Lickerrig . .	Loughrea .	IV.	31
35	Saint Cunning .	107 3 30	Antrim . .	Upper Glenarm .	Carncastle . .	Larne . .	III.	24
61	St. Dominicks Abbey	2 1 11	Tipperary, S.R.	Middlethird . .	St. Patricksrock .	Cashel . .	II.	331
15	Saintdoolaghs .	202 0 14	Dublin . .	Coolock . .	Balgriffin . .	Dublin North .	I.	26
15	ST. DOOLAGHS T. .	—	Dublin . .	Coolock . .	Balgriffin . .	Dublin North .	I.	26
32, 37	St. Edmond's .	88 3 27	Wexford . .	Shelmaliere East .	Artramon . .	Wexford .	I.	330
17	St. Edmondsbury .	129 1 17	Dublin . .	Newcastle . .	Esker . .	Celbridge .	I.	33
17	St. Edmondsbury .	71 0 14d	Dublin . .	Newcastle . .	Lucan . .	Celbridge .	I.	33
71, 84	Saintellen . .	90 2 8	Galway . .	Athenry . .	Athenry . .	Galway . .	IV.	4
16, 23	Saintfield Parks .	236 1 12e	Down . .	Castlereagh Upper .	Saintfield . .	Lisburn . .	III.	166
16	SAINTFIELD T. .	—	Down . .	Castlereagh Upper .	Saintfield . .	Lisburn . .	III.	166
5	St. Francisabbey .	10 3 38f	Limerick . .	Limerick, Municipal Borough of .	St. Mary's . .	Limerick . .	II.	262
61	St. Francisabbey .	12 1 3	Tipperary, S.R.	Middlethird . .	St. John Baptist .	Cashel . .	II.	330
12, 15	Sainthelens . .	192 0 19	Dublin . .	Coolock . .	Portmarnock . .	Balrothery .	I.	28
48	St. Helens . .	22 2 23	Wexford . .	Forth . .	St. Helens . .	Wexford .	I.	314
48	St. Iberius . .	32 0 0	Wexford . .	Forth . .	St. Iberius . .	Wexford .	I.	314
18	St. James' (Phœnix Park, part of) .	499 3 15	Dublin . .	Castleknock . .	St. James . .	Dublin North .	I.	25
38, 40	Saintjohn's . .	458 2 31	Kildare . .	Kilkea and Moone .	Castledermot . .	Baltinglass .	I.	59
36	Saintjohn's . .	58 1 4g	Meath . .	Lower Moyfenrath .	Laracor . .	Trim . .	I.	210
26	Saintjohn's . .	325 0 24	Wexford . .	Bantry . .	St. John's . .	Enniscorthy .	I.	302
6	Saintjohnsfort .	180 0 30	Meath . .	Lower Slane . .	Siddan . .	Ardee . .	I.	224
45	Saint Johns Point .	290 2 23	Down . .	Lecale Upper .	Rathmullan . .	Downpatrick .	III.	181
11	St. Johns Rath .	157 3 34	Meath . .	Lower Kells . .	Staholmog . .	Kells . .	I.	204
55, 63	Saintjohnstown .	279 1 23	Donegal . .	Raphoe . .	Taughboyne . .	Strabane . .	III.	144
62	St. Johnstown .	818 1 21	Tipperary, S.R.	Middlethird . .	St. Johnstown .	Cashel . .	II.	330
9	Saintjohnstown or Ballinalee . .	161 3 10	Longford . .	Granard . .	Clonbroney . .	Granard . .	I.	154
63	SAINT JOHNSTOWN T.	—	Donegal . .	Raphoe . .	Taughboyne . .	Strabane . .	III.	144
45	Saintkierans . .	469 3 2	Wexford . .	Shelburne . .	Tintern . .	New Ross .	I.	329
17, 18	Saintlaurence . .	200 2 9h	Dublin . .	Uppercross . .	Palmerston . .	Dublin South .	I.	40
105	St. Laurencesfields .	54 0 8	Galway . .	Loughrea . .	Loughrea . .	Loughrea .	IV.	66
40, 45	Saintleonards . .	438 2 11	Wexford . .	Shelburne . .	Tintern . .	New Ross .	I.	329
76	St. Macdara's Island	60 2 9	Galway . .	Ballynahinch . .	Moyrus . .	Clifden .	IV.	14
11, 14	St. Margarets .	150 1 21	Dublin . .	Coolock . .	St. Margarets .	Dublin North .	I.	29
48, 53	St. Margarets .	170 2 16	Wexford . .	Forth . .	St. Margarets .	Wexford .	I.	314
24, 26	St. Mullin's . .	151 0 20i	Carlow . .	St. Mullins Lower .	St. Mullin's .	New Ross .	I.	13
5	St. Patrick's Island .	15 1 1	Dublin . .	Balrothery East .	Holmpatrick .	Balrothery .	I.	20
60, 61	St. Patricksrock .	162 3 28	Tipperary, S.R.	Middlethird . .	St. Patricksrock .	Cashel . .	II.	331
12	ST. PATRICKSWELL T.	—	Limerick . .	Pubblebrien . .	{ Kilkeedy . . / Killonahan . . / Mungret . .	{ Limerick . . / Croom . . / Limerick . . }	II.	{ 252 / 253 / 254 }
61	Saints Island .	13 3 6	Clare . .	Bunratty Lower .	Bunratty . .	Ennis . .	II.	3
101	Saints Island .	10 1 16	Donegal . .	Tirhugh . .	Templecarn .	Donegal .	III.	149
26	Saints Island .	205 2 33	Longford . .	Rathcline . .	Cashel . .	Ballymahon .	I.	164
120	Saints Island .	11 1 30	Mayo . .	Kilmaine . .	Cong . . .	Ballinrobe .	IV.	154
46	St. Tenants . .	189 1 18	Wexford . .	Bargy . . .	Ballyconnick .	Wexford .	I.	304
63	Saint Thomas' Island	21 0 39	Clare . .	Bunratty Lower .	St. Patricks . .	Limerick . .	II.	7

(a) Including 2A. 2R. 24P. River Liffey.
(b) Including 0A. 0R. 12P. water.
(c) Including 6A. 0R. 8P. water.
(d) Including 3A. 0R. 8P. water.
(e) Including 2A. 2R. 5P. water.
(f) Included in the Parish of St. Mary.
(g) Including 3A. 0R. 24P. water.
(h) Including 5A. 2R. 24P. water.
(i) Including 1A. 0R. 32P. River Barrow.

No. of Sheet of the Ordnance Survey Maps.	Townlands and Towns.	Area in Statute Acres.			County	Barony.	Parish.	Poor Law Union in 1857.	Townland Census of 1851. Part I.	
		A.	R.	P.					Vol.	Page
53	St. Vogues'	25	3	0	Wexford	Forth	Carn	Wexford	I.	309
11	St. Wolstans	110	1	20a	Kildare	South Salt	Donaghcumper	Celbridge	I.	76
78	Saleen	83	0	32b	Mayo	Carra	Aglish	Castlebar	IV.	124
118	Saleen	33	1	19	Mayo	Kilmaine	Ballinrobe	Ballinrobe	IV.	153
50, 53	Salestown	302	3	28	Meath	Dunboyne	Dunboyne	Dunshaughlin	I.	199
55	Salia	1,898	2	13c	Mayo	Burrishoole	Achill	Newport	IV.	117
35	Salisbury	63	0	27	Kildare	Narragh&RebanWest	Kilberry	Athy	I.	68
35	Sallagh	723	0	8	Antrim	Upper Glenarm	Carncastle	Larne	III.	24
53	Sailaghagrane	208	1	18	Donegal	Kilmacrenan	Conwal	Letterkenny	III.	126
19, 24	Sallaghan	177	0	16	Cavan	Tullyhunco	Killashandra	Cavan	III.	98
30	Sallaghan	356	0	30d	Cavan	Tullyhunco	Scrabby	Granard	III.	99
31	Sallaghan	23	1	22	Leitrim	Leitrim	Kiltoghert	Carª. on Shannon	IV.	102
69, 70	Sallagher	146	1	8	Mayo	Carra	Turlough	Castlebar	IV.	131
32	Sallaghill	181	3	22e	Cavan	Castlerahan	Crosserlough	Cavan	III.	68
34, 39	Sallaghy	53	3	11	Fermanagh	Coole	Galloon	Lisnaskea	III.	200
89	Sallahig	184	3	1	Kerry	Iveragh	Dromod	Cahersiveen	II.	195
14, 19	Sallins	206	3	21	Kildare	Naas North	Bodenstown	Naas	I.	62
19	SALLINS T.	—			Kildare	Naas North	Bodenstown) Naas)	Naas	I.	62
16	Salloon	224	1	38	Fermanagh	Tirkennedy	Magheracross	Lowtherstown	III.	223
29	Sallowilly	412	3	17	Londonderry	Tirkeeran	Cumber Upper	Londonderry	III.	249
35	Sallow Island	0	1	8	Leitrim	Mohill	Annaduff	Mohill	IV.	105
8	Sallow Island	0	1	2	Longford	Longford	Clongesh	Longford	I.	158
84, 93	Sallows	2,469	2	7	Donegal	Banagh	Inver	Donegal	III.	108
47	Sallsquarter	116	3	9	Tipperary, S.R.	Middlethird	Gaile	Cashel	II.	327
44, 53	Sallybank (Merritt) or Drumsillagh	523	2	1	Clare	Tulla Lower	Kilseily	Limerick	II.	36
44, 53	Sallybank (Parker) or Drumsillagh	588	3	28	Clare	Tulla Lower	Kilseily	Limerick	II.	36
43	Sallybog	204	1	26	Tipperary, S.R.	Slievardagh	Kilcooly	Urlingford	II.	334
54	Sallybrook	66	1	10	Donegal	Raphoe	Raymoghy	Londonderry	III.	142
6	Sallybrook	133	1	39	Meath	Lower Slane	Drumcondra	Ardee	I.	223
63	SALLYBROOK T.	—			Cork, E.R.	Cork	Rathcooney	Cork	II.	65
81, 92	Sallyhernaun	248	1	23	Mayo	Costello	Knock	Claremorris	IV.	143
20	Sally Island	4	0	0	Cavan	Upper Loughtee	Kilmore	Cavan	III.	85
129	Sally Island	0	1	9	Galway	Kiltartan	Beagh	Gort	IV.	46
18	Sallymount	10	0	32	Dublin	Uppercross	Donnybrook	Dublin South	I.	40
6	Sallymount	68	1	21	Limerick	Clanwilliam	Stradbally	Limerick	II.	226
36, 41	Sallymount	384	1	10	Wicklow	Arklow	Ennereilly	Rathdrum	I.	344
29	Sallymount Demesne	223	2	8	Kildare	Naas South	Brannockstown	Naas	I.	64
23	SALLY NOGGINS T. or GLENAGAREY	—			Dublin	Rathdown	Monkstown	Rathdown	I.	37
16	Sally Park	249	0	0	Cork, E.R.	Orrery and Kilmore	Liscarroll	Mallow	II.	109
27, 28	Sallypark	199	1	0	Tipperary, N.R.	Upper Ormond	Latteragh	Nenagh	II.	292
23	SALLYS CROSS ROADS T.	—			Cork, E.R.	Duhallow	Castlemagner	Kanturk	II.	67
32	Sallysgrove	91	3	14	Fermanagh	Clanawley	Killesher	Enniskillen	III.	193
42, 47	Sallystown	152	1	3	Wexford	Forth	Kildavin	Wexford	I.	310
78, 87	Sallywood	391	0	34	Donegal	Raphoe	Donaghmore	Stranorlar	III.	138
5	Salmon	251	0	26	Dublin	Balrothery East	Balrothery	Balrothery	I.	19
10	Salrock	288	3	28f	Galway	Ballynahinch	Ballynakill	Clifden	IV.	12
16	Salry	213	2	38	Fermanagh	Tirkennedy	Magheracross	Enniskillen	III.	223
51	Saltee Island Great	215	3	9	Wexford	Bargy	Kilmore	Wexford	I.	307
51	Saltee Island Little	93	1	23	Wexford	Bargy	Kilmore	Wexford	I.	307
21	Salterbridge	402	2	0	Waterford	Coshmore&Coshbride	Lismore and Mocollop	Lismore	II.	347
8, 12	Salters Grange	308	1	23	Armagh	Oneilland West	Grange	Armagh	III.	52
15, 16, 19	Salterstown	1,047	3	17	Louth	Ferrard	Salterstown	Ardee	I.	182
99	Salthill Demesne	308	1	26	Donegal	Banagh	Inver	Donegal	III.	108
31	Salt Island	51	0	15	Down	Lecale Lower	Saul	Downpatrick	III.	180
39	Saltmills	320	0	14	Wexford	Shelburne	St.James&Dunbrody	New Ross	I.	328
45	Saltmills	272	3	38	Wexford	Shelburne	Tintern	New Ross	I.	329
45	SALTMILLS T.	—			Wexford	Shelburne	Tintern	New Ross	I.	329
48,49,56,57	Saltpans	167	0	26	Donegal	Boylagh	Templecrone	Glenties	III.	116
28	Saltpans	262	0	4g	Donegal	Kilmacrenan	Killygarvan	Milford	III.	128
14	Salt Works	40	2	5	Londonderry	Tirkeeran	Faughanvale	Londonderry	III.	250
26	Salville or Motabeg	140	0	25	Wexford	Ballaghkeen	Templeshannon	Enniscorthy	I.	299
28	Samphire Island	1	1	28	Kerry	Trughanacmy	Fenit	Tralee	II.	210
28	Samphire Island Little	0	3	32	Kerry	Trughanacmy	Fenit	Tralee	II.	210
21	Samsonagh	232	2	29	Fermanagh	Clanawley	Cleenish	Enniskillen	III.	191
61	Sanaghanroe	206	0	32	Tyrone	Dungannon Middle	Clonfeacle	Dungannon	III.	300
47	Sanctuary	13	0	24	Wexford	Forth	Killinick	Wexford	I.	310
13	Sandbrook or Ballygarret	258	3	25	Carlow	Forth	Ballon	Carlow	I.	3
73	Sandfield	605	1	14h	Donegal	Boylagh	Inishkeel	Glenties	III.	113

(a) Including 4A. 1R. 32P. water.
(b) Including 14A. 3R. 11P. water.
(c) Including 20A. 2R. 20P. water.

(d) Including 10A. 2R. 7P. water.
(e) Including 3A. 1R. 11P. water.
(f) Including 24A. 3R. 34P. water.

(g) Including 10A. 1R. 18P. water.
(h) Including 31A. 2R. 7P. water.

No. of Sheet of the Ordnance Survey Maps.	Townlands and Towns.	Area in Statute Acres.			County.	Barony.	Parish.	Poor Law Union in 1857.	Townland Census of 1851, Part I.	
		A.	R.	P.					Vol.	Page
10	Sandfield	80	2	26	Louth	Ardee	Louth	Dundalk	I.	173
14, 15	Sandfordscourt	596	3	25	Kilkenny	Gowran	Rathcoole	Kilkenny	I.	98
15, 16	Sandhill	77	3	23	Donegal	Kilmacrenan	Clondahorky	Dunfanaghy	III.	123
14	Sandhill	257	1	4	Fermanagh	Magheraboy	Inishmacsaint	Enniskillen	III.	213
67	Sandhill	73	1	6	Mayo	Burrishoole	Burrishoole	Newport	IV.	120
16	Sandhills	78	3	39	Monaghan	Fartree	Currin	Clones	III.	266
1, 2	Sandhills and Corcas	125	3	10	Kerry	Iraghticonnor	Kilconly	Listowel	II.	191
40	Sandholes	98	1	4a	Fermanagh	Coole	Galloon	Clones	III.	200
73	Sand Island	9	0	5	Donegal	Banagh	Inishkeel	Glenties	III.	106
25	Sand Island	5	3	6	Longford	Ratheline	Cashel	Ballymahon	I.	164
39	Sandpits	158	1	22	Kilkenny	Iverk	Fiddown	Carrick on Suir	I.	105
26, 27	Sandville	470	2	25	Cork, E.R.	Fermoy	Glanworth	Fermoy	II.	79
2	Sandville	113	2	4	Tyrone	Strabane Lower	Donaghedy	Strabane	III.	321
125	Sandy Cove Island	18	1	29	Cork, E.R.	Kinsale	Kilroan	Kinsale	II.	100
125	SANDY COVE T.	—			Cork, E.R.	Kinsale	Kilroan / Ringrone	Kinsale	II.	100 / 101
65	Sandyhill	325	2	21	Cork, E.R.	Barrymore	Dungourney	Middleton	II.	54
55	Sandyhill	263	1	13	Cork, E.R.	Kinnatalloon	Mogeely	Youghal	II.	99
14	Sandyhill	173	0	10	Dublin	Coolock	St. Margarets	Dublin North	I.	29
42	Sandyhill	308	0	14	Leyny		Achonry	Tobercurry	IV.	229
15	Sandyhills	229	1	5	Wicklow	Lower Talbotstown	Tober	Baltinglass	I.	361
149	Sandy Island	10	1	9	Cork, W.R.	West Carbery (E.D.)	Tullagh	Skibbereen	II.	141
14	Sandylane	267	3	11	Limerick	Clanwilliam	Abington	Limerick	II.	221
14	Sandylane	171	2	1	Limerick	Clanwilliam	Caherconlish	Limerick	II.	222
18, 19	Sandymount	242	3	37	Dublin	Dublin	Donnybrook	Dublin South	I.	30
67, 68	Sandymount	48	2	29	Mayo	Burrishoole	Burrishoole	Newport	IV.	120
29	Sandymount	50	3	34	Tipperary, N.R.	Eliogarty	Templemore	Thurles	II.	272
18, 19	SANDYMOUNT T.	—			Dublin	Dublin	Donnybrook	Dublin South	I.	30
14	Santry	26	1	32b	Dublin	Coolock	Coolock	Dublin North	I.	27
14	Santry	631	0	7	Dublin	Coolock	Santry	Dublin North	I.	29
14	Santry Demesne	273	0	11	Dublin	Coolock	Santry	Dublin North	I.	29
5	Santryhill	36	0	28	Wicklow	Lower Talbotstown	Blessington	Naas	I.	358
14	SANTRY T.	—			Dublin	Coolock	Santry	Dublin North	I.	29
28, 29	Sapperton North	210	0	18	Waterford	Coshmore&Coshbride	Kilwatermoy	Lismore	II.	344
29, 34	Sapperton South	202	0	20	Waterford	Coshmore&Coshbride	Kilwatermoy	Lismore	II.	344
69	Sarnaght	431	3	29c	Mayo	Carra	Aglish	Castlebar	IV.	124
50	Sarney	247	2	36	Meath	Dunboyne	Dunboyne	Dunshaughlin	I.	199
19	Sarsanstown	124	3	0	Westmeath	Moyashel and Magheradernon	Mullingar	Mullingar	I.	275
63, 64	Sarsfieldscourt	621	2	37	Cork. E.R.	Barrymore	Templeusque	Cork	II.	59
28	Sarsfieldstown	425	0	27	Meath	Upper Duleek	Moorechurch	Drogheda	I.	198
20, 27	Sarsfieldstown	76	0	1	Westmeath	Farbill	Killucan	Mullingar	I.	267
52	Sarshill	181	2	15	Wexford	Bargy	Kilmore	Wexford	I.	307
13	Sart	379	1	1	Kilkenny	Crannagh	Ballinamara	Kilkenny	I.	84
13	Sart	355	1	11	Kilkenny	Crannagh	Clashacrow	Kilkenny	I.	85
121, 134	Sarue	494	3	23	Cork. W.R.	East Carbery (W.D.)	Castleventry	Clonakilty	II.	131
11	Saucerstown	211	3	16	Dublin	Nethercross	Swords	Balrothery	I.	32
70	Saucestown	246	2	38	Tipperary, S.R.	Middlethird	Peppardstown	Cashel	II.	329
70	Saucestown	96	2	15	Tipperary, S.R.	Middlethird	Rathcool	Cashel	II.	329
31, 38	Saul	488	1	20d	Down	Lecale Lower	Saul	Downpatrick	III.	179
38	Saul Quarter	90	2	26	Down	Lecale Upper	Down	Downpatrick	III.	181
37	Saunderscourt	440	2	29	Wexford	Shelmaliere East	Kilpatrick	Wexford	I.	331
21	Saundersgrove	205	0	19	Wicklow	Upper Talbotstown	Rathbran	Baltinglass	I.	365
21, 27	Saundersgrove Hill	189	0	11	Wicklow	Upper Talbotstown	Rathbran	Baltinglass	I.	365
25	Savagetown	201	3	36	Waterford	Middlethird	Dunhill	Kilmacthomas	II.	367
14	Savagh	121	3	10	Antrim	Lower Glenarm	Layd	Ballycastle	III.	23
47	Saval Beg	365	0	14	Down	Lordship of Newry	Newry	Newry	III.	182
41, 47	Saval More	364	1	18	Down	Lordship of Newry	Newry	Newry	III.	182
13	Sawelabeg	456	0	37	Tyrone	Strabane Upper	Bodoney Upper	Gortin	III.	324
126	Sawnagh	367	0	20	Galway	Longford	Lickmolassy	Portumna	IV.	61
35	Sawyerswood	206	0	32	Kildare	Narragh&RebanWest	Kilberry	Athy	I.	68
82	Scaddaman	203	0	37	Donegal	Banagh	Inishkeel	Glenties	III.	106
22	Scaffog	43	2	17	Fermanagh	Magheraboy	Rossorry	Enniskillen	III.	214
67	Scalaheen	105	0	21	Tipperary, S.R.	Clanwilliam	Cordangan	Tipperary	II.	306
38	Scalestown	186	1	15	Meath	Skreen	Trevet	Dunshaughlin	I.	222
30	Scalkill	365	1	19	Monaghan	Farney	Magheracloone	Carrickmacross	III.	273
17, 18, 24, 25	Scallanstown	389	0	1	Meath	Lower Navan	Liscartan	Navan	I.	215
49, 56	Scallen	312	3	39	Tyrone	Omagh East	Kilskeery	Lowtherstown	III.	314
12, 13	Scalp	285	0	14	Clare	Tulla Upper	Feakle	Tulla	II.	40
96	Scalp	153	1	31	Galway	Dunkellin	Killeeneen	Gort	IV.	30
114	Scalp	211	1	36	Galway	Loughrea	Ardrahan	Gort	IV.	63
9, 15	Scalp	350	3	11	Wicklow	Lower Talbotstown	Hollywood	Baltinglass	I.	361
19	Scalpnagown	2,234	1	15	Clare	Bunratty Upper	Inchicronan	Tulla	II.	9

(a) Including 9A. 0R. 29P. water.
(b) Including 4A. 3R. 11P. detached portion.
(c) Including 6A. 2R. 3P. water.
(d) Including 3A. 2R. 0F. water.

No. of Sheet of the Ordnance Survey Maps.	Townlands and Towns.	Area in Statute Acres.		County.	Barony.	Parish.	Poor Law Union in 1857.	Townland Census of 1851, Part I.	
		A.	R. P.					Vol.	Page
23, 26	Scalpwilliam or Mount Mapas	146	3 10	Dublin	Rathdown	Kill	Rathdown	I.	36
11, 12	Scalty	99	2 5	Londonderry	Coleraine	Aghadowey	Coleraine	III.	230
15	Scandally	251	2 22	Fermanagh	Magheraboy	Devenish	Enniskillen	III.	211
2	Scanlan's Island	70	2 33	Clare	Burren	Oughtmama	Ballyvaghan	II.	14
10	Scanlansland	171	3 35	Kilkenny	Fassadinin	Muckalee	Castlecomer	I.	91
46	Scar	393	3 6	Wexford	Bargy	Duncormick	Wexford	I.	305
15, 20	Scarawalsh	496	3 24a	Wexford	Scarawalsh	Ballycarney	Enniscorthy	I.	322
14	Scardan Beg	150	2 32	Sligo	Carbury	Killaspugbrone	Sligo	IV.	222
14	Scardan More	200	2 6	Sligo	Carbury	Killaspugbrone	Sligo	IV.	222
3	Scardans Lower	470	2 34b	Fermanagh	Lurg	Belleek	Ballyshannon	III.	203
3, 4	Scardans Upper	294	1 25c	Fermanagh	Lurg	Belleek	Ballyshannon	III.	203
28	Scardaun	253	2 12d	Leitrim	Leitrim	Kiltubbrid	Carr on Shannon	IV.	104
82	Scardaun	230	3 6e	Mayo	Costello	Aghamore	Swineford	IV.	137
45	Scardaun	1,274	1 1f	Mayo	Erris	Kilcommon	Newport	IV.	144
41	Scardaun	200	2 6	Roscommon	Athlone	Athleague	Roscommon	IV.	179
111	Scardaun East	243	2 20	Mayo	Clanmorris	Crossboyne	Claremorris	IV.	133
111	Scardaun West	180	2 21	Mayo	Clanmorris	Crossboyne	Claremorris	IV.	133
105	Scariff	366	1 2	Kerry	Dunkerron South	Kilcrohane	Cahersiveen	II.	184
29	Scark	210	2 24	Wexford	Bantry	Ballyanne	New Ross	I.	299
23	Scarletstown	216	2 4g	Kildare	Connell	Morristownbiller	Naas	I.	56
6	Scarnageeragh or Emyvale	119	2 4	Monaghan	Trough	Donagh	Monaghan	III.	282
3	Scarnagh Lower	317	2 30	Wexford	Gorey	Inch	Gorey	I.	316
3	Scarnagh Upper	222	1 18	Wexford	Gorey	Inch	Gorey	I.	316
9	Scarragh	77	1 38	Tipperary, N.R.	Lower Ormond	Kilbarron	Borrisokane	II.	284
60	Scarreth	105	0 27	Galway	Kilconnell	Ballymacward	Mountbellew	IV.	39
76	Scarriff	192	3 5	Cork, E.R.	Imokilly	Cloyne	Middleton	II.	85
84, 96	Scarriff	327	2 13	Cork, W.R.	Kinalmeaky	Templemartin	Bandon	II.	153
128, 133	Scarriff	158	3 38	Galway	Kiltartan	Beagh	Gort	IV.	46
89, 98	Scarriff	321	1 4	Kerry	Iveragh	Dromod	Cahersiveen	II.	195
28, 29	SCARRIFF T.	—		Clare	Tulla Upper	Tomgraney	Scarriff	II.	41
2, 6	Scarroon	738	2 19	Queen's Co.	Tinnahinch	Kilmanman	Mountmellick	I.	249
51	Scarrough	332	2 1	Tipperary, S.R.	Kilnamanagh Lower	Donohill	Tipperary	II.	323
31	Scarry	62	1 5	King's Co.	Ballyboy	Ballyboy	Parsonstown	I.	123
18	Scart	511	2 8	Cork, E.R.	Condons & Clangibbon	Kildorrery	Mitchelstown	II.	61
97	Scart	219	2 2	Cork, E.R.	Kinalea	Ballynartle	Kinsale	II.	94
112	Scart	120	1 21	Cork, E.R.	Kinsale	Clontead	Kinsale	II.	99
24	Scart	595	3 36	Cork, E.R.	Orrery and Kilmore	Ballyclogh	Mallow	II.	106
1	Scart	221	2 4	Cork, E.R.	Orrery and Kilmore	Kilbolane	Kanturk	II.	108
116	Scart	19	2 12	Cork, W.R.	Bear	Killaconenagh	Castletown	II.	125
107	Scart	113	3 17	Kerry	Dunkerron South	Kilcrohane	Kenmare	II.	184
48, 58	Scart	330	1 1	Kerry	Magunihy	Kilcredane	Killarney	II.	200
39	Scart	376	1 3	Kerry	Trughanacmy	Nohaval	Tralee	II.	212
20	Scart	48	2 26	Kilkenny	Gowran	Blackrath	Kilkenny	I.	93
20	Scart	48	1 29	Kilkenny	Gowran	Clara	Kilkenny	I.	94
24	Scart	481	2 11	Kilkenny	Gowran	Dungarvan	Thomastown	I.	94
40	Scart	388	1 13	Kilkenny	Knocktopher	Rossinan	Waterford	I.	113
13, 14	Scart	183	0 20	Limerick	Clanwilliam	Cahernarry	Limerick	II.	223
6, 14	Scart	234	2 11	Limerick	Clanwilliam	Derrygalvin	Limerick	II.	223
20	Scart	141	0 33	Limerick	Connello Lower	Nantinan	Rathkeale	II.	229
24, 33	Scart	195	1 14	Limerick	Coonagh	Kilteely	Tipperary	II.	235
17	Scart	128	2 17	Tipperary, N.R.	Ikerrin	Corbally	Roscrea	II.	275
67	Scart	177	1 7	Tipperary, S.R.	Clanwilliam	Killardry	Tipperary	II.	308
81, 87	Scart	420	1 17	Tipperary, S.R.	Iffa and Offa West	Tubbrid	Clogheen	II.	321
34	Scart	185	1 10	Waterford	Coshmore & Coshbride	Kilcockan	Lismore	II.	343
29	Scart	42	2 29	Waterford	Coshmore & Coshbride	Lismore and Mocollop	Lismore	II.	347
31	Scart	32	2 6	Waterford	Decies without Drum	Dungarvan	Dungarvan	II.	356
30	Scart	166	1 13	Waterford	Decies without Drum	Whitechurch	Dungarvan	II.	362
24	Scartacrooka	99	1 39	Waterford	Decies without Drum	Stradbally	Kilmacthomas	II.	361
135	Scartagh	186	0 34	Cork, W.R.	East Carbery (E.D.)	Kilgarriff	Clonakilty	II.	129
49	Scartaglin	687	1 35	Kerry	Trughanacmy	Castleisland	Tralee	II.	209
49	SCARTAGLIN T.			Kerry	Trughanacmy	Castleisland	Tralee	II.	209
81	Scartana	337	1 39	Tipperary, S.R.	Iffa and Offa West	Whitechurch	Clogheen	II.	322
44, 53	Scartbarry	706	2 0	Cork, E.R.	Barrymore	Kilshanahan	Fermoy	II.	56
118	Scartbaun	240	1 37	Cork, W.R.	West Carbery (W.D.)	Kilmocomoge	Bantry	II.	144
81, 87	Scartbeg	20	2 34	Tipperary, S.R.	Iffa and Offa West	Tubbrid	Clogheen	II.	321
87	Scart East	174	3 18	Tipperary, S.R.	Iffa and Offa West	Shanrahan	Clogheen	II.	320
61	Scarteen	217	2 9	Cork, E.R.	East Muskerry	Donaghmore	Macroom	II.	103
32, 33	Scarteen	160	1 17	Cork, E.R.	Fermoy	Mallow	Mallow	II.	81
83, 92	Scarteen	1,211	0 7h	Kerry	Dunkerron South	Templenoe	Kenmare	II.	185
58	Scarteen	175	3 18	Kerry	Magunihy	Aghadoe	Killarney	II.	199
41	Scarteen	242	1 24	Limerick	Coshlea	Ballyscaddan	Kilmallock	II.	238

(a) Including 11A. 2R. 21P. water.   (d) Including 12A. 2R. 28P. water.   (g) Including 111A. 1R. 32P. detached portions.
(b) Including 2A. 1R. 30P. water.   (e) Including 47A. 0R. 1P. water.   (h) Including 7A. 2R. 21P. water.
(c) Including 2A. 0R. 16P. water.   (f) Including 9A. 3R. 13P. water.

No. of Sheet of the Ordnance Survey Maps.	Townlands and Towns.	Area in Statute Acres.			County.	Barony.	Parish.	Poor Law Union in 1857.	Townland Census of 1851, Part I.	
		A.	R.	P.					Vol.	Page
131, 132	Scarteenakillin	452	0	32	Cork, W.R.	West Carbery (W.D.)	Skull	Skull	II.	146
14, 22	Scarteen Lower	702	1	9	Cork, E.R.	Duhallow	Clonfert	Kanturk	II.	69
14	Scarteen Upper	730	0	28	Cork, E.R.	Duhallow	Clonfert	Kanturk	II.	69
22	Scart (Hely)	95	3	9	Waterford	Decies without Drum	Modelligo	Lismore	II.	359
66, 67	Scartlea	126	3	28	Kerry	Magunihy	Killarney	Killarney	II.	203
2	Scartlea	214	1	19	Waterford	Upperthird	Dysert	Clonmel	II.	369
88	Scartlea Lower	78	0	25	Cork, E.R.	Imokilly	Garranekinnefeake	Middleton	II.	86
88	SCARTLEA T.	—			Cork, E.R.	Imokilly	Garranekinnefeake	Middleton	II.	86
76, 88	Scartlea Upper	104	1	12	Cork, E.R.	Imokilly	Garranekinnefeake	Middleton	II.	86
10	Scartleigh	93	2	13a	Kerry	Iraghticonnor	Dysert	Listowel	II.	190
84	Scart Lower	109	3	5	Cork, E.R.	East Muskerry	Kilbonane	Bandon	II.	104
12, 13, 21, 22	Scartmountain	1,209	2	5	Waterford	Decies without Drum	Modelligo	Lismore	II.	359
20	Scartnacrooha	140	3	5b	Waterford	Coshmore&Coshbride	Lismore and Mocollop	Lismore	II.	347
13, 14	Scartnadriny	185	0	7	Waterford	Decies without Drum	Kilgobnet	Dungarvan	II.	357
14	Scartnadrinymountain	530	2	6	Waterford	Decies without Drum	Kilgobnet	Dungarvan	II.	357
74, 75, 81	Scartnaglorane	1,700	1	0	Tipperary, S.R.	Iffa and Offa West	Whitechurch	Clogheen	II.	322
64	Scartnamackagh	69	3	39	Kerry	Iveragh	Killorglin	Killarney	II.	198
44	Scartnamoe	76	0	28	Kilkenny	Ida	Kilcolumb	Waterford	I.	103
96	Scartnamuck	550	0	13	Cork, W.R.	Kinalmeaky	Templemartin	Bandon	II.	153
31	Scartore	67	2	12	Waterford	Decies without Drum	Dungarvan	Dungarvan	II.	356
22	Scart (Sergeant)	76	3	29	Waterford	Decies without Drum	Modelligo	Lismore	II.	359
84	Scart Upper	301	2	35	Cork, E.R.	East Muskerry	Kilbonane	Bandon	II.	104
86, 87	Scart West	192	1	25	Tipperary, S.R.	Iffa and Offa West	Shanrahan	Clogheen	II.	320
33	Scarva	680	3	25	Down	Upper Iveagh, Up. pt.	Aghaderg	Banbridge	III.	174
16	Scarvagherin	451	3	27c	Tyrone	Strabane Lower	Ardstraw	Castlederg	III.	319
33	SCARVA T.	—			Down	Upper Iveagh, Up. pt.	Aghaderg	Banbridge	III.	174
17	Scarvy	140	2	30	Monaghan	Dartree	Killeevan	Clones	III.	268
25	Scaryhill	218	1	29	Antrim	Lower Glenarm	Ardclinis	Larne	III.	21
7	Scatternagh	171	0	25	Dublin	Nethercross	Killossery	Balrothery	I.	31
33	Scatternagh	253	1	30	Meath	Upper Duleek	Duleek	Drogheda	I.	198
67	Scattery Island	179	0	19	Clare	Moyarta	Kilrush	Kilrush	II.	33
42	Scaughmolin	105	3	1	Wexford	Forth	Rathaspick	Wexford	I.	313
22	Scholarstown	200	2	39	Dublin	Uppercross	Rathfarnham	Dublin South	I.	40
77	Schoolgardens	29	3	23	Cork, E.R.	Imokilly	Ightermurragh	Middleton	II.	87
76	School-land	16	2	37	Cork, E.R.	Imokilly	Middleton	Middleton	II.	89
9	School Land	96	2	7	Longford	Granard	Clonbroney	Granard	I.	155
112	Scilly	6	0	10	Cork, E.R.	Kinsale	Ringcurran	Kinsale	II.	100
13	Scilly Island	4	0	29	Tipperary, N.R.	Owney and Arra	Castletownarra	Nenagh	II.	294
151	Scobaun	180	2	9	Cork, W.R.	West Carbery (E.D.)	Castlehaven	Skibbereen	II.	138
14	Scogganstown	69	0	7	Louth	Ardee	Ardee	Ardee	I.	171
44	Scolboa	268	2	19	Antrim	Lower Antrim	Connor	Antrim	III.	3
21	Scollagh	129	2	22	Wexford	Ballaghkeen	Kilcormick	Enniscorthy	I.	294
24	Sconce	72	0	28	King's Co.	Ballyboy	Killoughy	Tullamore	I.	124
6	Sconce	459	0	16	Londonderry	Coleraine	Dunboe	Coleraine	III.	232
12	Sconce Lower	225	3	17	Queen's Co.	Maryborough West	Clonenagh and Clonagheen	Mountmellick	I.	243
6, 7, 11, 12	Sconce Upper	679	0	29	Queen's Co.	Maryborough West	Clonenagh and Clonagheen	Mountmellick	I.	243
24, 25	Scool	290	3	19d	Clare	Inchiquin	Rath	Corrofin	II.	28
16	Scor Beg	233	0	23	Roscommon	Frenchpark	Kilmacumsy	Boyle	IV.	204
36	Scordaun	127	3	34	Waterford	Decies within Drum	Ardmore	Dungarvan	II.	351
42	Scorduff	231	0	29	King's Co.	Clonlisk	Kilmurryely	Roscrea	I.	131
16	Scor More	212	2	3	Roscommon	Frenchpark	Kilmacumsy	Boyle	IV.	204
22	Scortreen or Knocknagundarragh	272	2	36	Carlow	Idrone East	Clonygoose	Carlow	I.	6
39	Scotchfort	155	3	36	Mayo	Tirawley	Kilbelfad	Ballina	IV.	168
20	Scotch Island	1	3	1	Cavan	Upper Loughtee	Kilmore	Cavan	III.	85
23, 24	Scotchomerbane	701	0	34	Antrim	Kilconway	Newtowncrommelin	Ballymena	III.	27
23	Scotchrath	449	2	8	Queen's Co.	Maryborough West	Clonenagh and Clonagheen	Abbeyleix	I.	243
5	Scotchtown	283	0	22e	Londonderry	Keenaght	Magilligan	New Tn Limavady	III.	237
29	Scotchtown	20	1	5	Tyrone	Dungannon Upper	Derryloran	Cookstown	III.	307
10	Scotchtown or Gortaweel	137	1	28f	Cavan	Tullyhaw	Tomregan	Bawnboy	III.	96
5	Scotland	183	0	11	Carlow	Rathvilly	Hacketstown	Shillelagh	I.	11
79	Scotland	46	3	39	Donegal	Raphoe	Donaghmore	Stranorlar	III.	138
18	Scotland	193	0	30	Galway	Ballynoe	Boyounagh	Glennamaddy	IV.	6
25	Scotland	119	1	7	Queen's Co.	Stradbally	Tullomoy	Athy	I.	248
22, 26	Scotsborough	303	1	37	Kilkenny	Shillelogher	Killaloe	Callan	I.	115
46	Scotsland	74	0	20	Wexford	Bargy	Duncormick	Wexford	I.	305
9	Scotstown	84	3	1	Tyrone	Strabane Lower	Urney	Strabane	III.	323
9	SCOTSTOWN T.	—			Monaghan	Monaghan	Tedavnet	Monaghan	III.	280
18	Scottstown	389	2	25	Meath	Upper Slane	Rathkenny	Navan	I.	225
39	Scoul	35	1	38	Limerick	Coshma	Dromin	Kilmallock	II.	243
39	Scoul	37	0	39	Limerick	Coshma	Uregare	Kilmallock	II.	244

(a) Including 12A. 3R. 8P. water.
(b) Including 4A. 3R. 36P. water.
(c) Including 12A. 1R. 17P. water.
(d) Including 6A. 1R. 6P. water.
(e) Including 21A. 2R. 26P. water.
(f) Including 2A. 0R. 30P. water.

CENSUS OF IRELAND FOR THE YEAR 1851.

No. of Sheet of the Ordnance Survey Maps.	Townlands and Towns.	Area in Statute Acres.	County.	Barony.	Parish.	Poor Law Union in 1857.	Townland Census of 1851, Part I.	
		A. R. P.					Vol.	Page
28	Scrabbagh	51 1 19a	Leitrim	Leitrim	Kiltubbrid	Car^k. on Shannon	IV.	104
17	Scrabbagh	110 2 26	Roscommon	Ballintober North	Kilmore	Car^k. on Shannon	IV.	187
9	Scrabby	191 1 38b	Cavan	Tullyhaw	Templeport	Bawnboy	III.	95
30, 36	Scrabby	306 3 12c	Cavan	Tullyhunco	Scrabby	Granard	III.	99
30	SCRABBY T.	—	Cavan	Tullyhunco	Scrabby	Granard	III.	99
5, 6	Scrabo	316 0 15	Down	Castlereagh Lower	Newtownards	Newtownards	III.	163
19, 25, 26	Scragg	432 0 22	Tipperary, N.R.	Owney and Arra	Kilmastulla	Nenagh	II.	295
35	Scraggane	284 1 7	Kerry	Corkaguiny	Stradbally	Dingle	II.	180
61	Scraggaun	96 3 33	Tipperary, S.R.	Middlethird	St. John Baptist	Cashel	II.	330
37	Scraggeen	783 1 0	Tipperary, N.R.	Owney and Arra	Kilvellane	Nenagh	II.	296
32, 33	Scraghy	2,081 1 13d	Tyrone	Omagh West	Termonamongan	Castlederg	III.	317
51	Scrahallia	191 1 12	Galway	Ballynahinch	Moyrus	Clifden	IV.	13
29	Scrahan	304 2 1	Cork, E.R.	Duhallow	Nohavalddaly	Millstreet	II.	75
81, 82	Scrahan	130 3 15	Cork, W.R.	West Muskerry	Inchigeelagh	Dunmanway	II.	158
17	Scrahan	373 2 18	Kerry	Clanmaurice	Duagh	Listowel	II.	168
15	Scrahan	470 3 15	Waterford	Decies without Drum	Rossmire	Kilmacthomas	II.	360
90, 91	Scrahanagnave	392 0 35	Kerry	Dunkerron South	Kilcrohane	Kenmare	II.	184
57, 68, 69	Scrahanagown	416 0 22	Cork, W.R.	West Muskerry	Ballyvourney	Macroom	II.	154
60	Scrahanagullaun	228 2 29	Kerry	Magunihy	Kilcummin	Killarney	II.	201
59	Scrahanard	350 3 30	Cork, W.R.	West Muskerry	Clondrohid	Macroom	II.	155
60	Scrahanaveal	413 1 2	Kerry	Magunihy	Kilcummin	Killarney	II.	201
66	Scrahane	96 0 15e	Kerry	Magunihy	Killarney	Killarney	II.	203
59, 60	Scrahanfadda	1,044 2 18	Kerry	Magunihy	Kilcummin	Killarney	II.	202
80	Scrahanmore	187 0 23	Cork, W.R.	West Muskerry	Inchigeelagh	Macroom	II.	158
91, 100	Scrahannagaur	533 3 1	Kerry	Dunkerron South	Kilcrohane	Kenmare	II.	184
38	Scrahans	285 2 32	Waterford	Decies within Drum	Ardmore	Dungarvan	II.	351
21	Scrahans East	154 1 17	Waterford	Coshmore & Coshbride	Lismore and Mocollop	Lismore	II.	347
21	Scrahans West	160 0 0	Waterford	Coshmore & Coshbride	Lismore and Mocollop	Lismore	II.	347
131	Scrahanyleary	433 0 24	Cork, W.R.	West Carbery (W.D.)	Skull	Skull	II.	146
23	Scralea	272 3 18	Tyrone	Omagh West	Termonamongan	Castlederg	III.	317
36	Scrallaghbeg	153 1 11	Kerry	Corkaguiny	Kilgobban	Tralee	II.	177
29	Scramoge	290 1 10	Roscommon	Roscommon	Bumlin	Strokestown	IV.	208
26	Scrarour	66 0 38	Cork, E.R.	Fermoy	Castletownroche	Fermoy	II.	78
36	Scratenagh	153 2 12	Wicklow	Arklow	Ennereilly	Rathdrum	I.	344
93, 99	Scrawhill	61 0 1	Donegal	Banagh	Killymard	Donegal	III.	111
23	Screeboge	200 2 9	Longford	Shrule	Taghsheenod	Ballymahon	I.	166
5	Screeboge	245 2 9	Meath	Lower Kells	Moynalty	Kells	I.	204
47	Screeboge or Ashfield	270 0 37	Meath	Upper Moyfenrath	Clonard	Edenderry	I.	213
64	Screeby	242 1 8f	Tyrone	Clogher	Clogher	Clogher	III.	293
56	Screeby	306 3 33	Tyrone	Omagh East	Kilskeery	Enniskillen	III.	314
34	Screevagh	117 1 34g	Fermanagh	Coole	Galloon	Lisnaskea	III.	200
82	Scregg	231 0 20	Mayo	Costello	Aghamore	Swineford	IV.	137
93, 103	Scregg	400 2 34	Mayo	Costello	Annagh	Claremorris	IV.	138
42, 45	Scregg	662 2 28h	Roscommon	Athlone	Killinvoy	Roscommon	IV.	182
11	Scregg	174 3 13	Roscommon	Boyle	Killukin	Car^k. on Shannon	IV.	196
25	Scregg	53 1 35	Roscommon	Castlereagh	Kiltullagh	Castlereagh	IV.	202
50, 57, 58	Screggagh	509 2 11	Tyrone	Clogher	Donacavey	Omagh	III.	294
16, 24	Screggan	335 0 3	King's Co.	Ballycowan	Lynally	Tullamore	I.	128
31	Scregg East	327 3 10	Galway	Tiaquin	Kilkerrin	Glennamaddy	IV.	77
31	Scregg West	308 1 27	Galway	Tiaquin	Kilkerrin	Glennamaddy	IV.	77
30	Screhan	273 1 8	Kilkenny	Kells	Coolaghmore	Callan	I.	108
112	Screhaneroe	73 3 37	Cork, E.R.	Kinsale	Clontead	Kinsale	II.	99
36	Scrib	525 0 4	Down	Kinelarty	Loughinisland	Downpatrick	III.	177
13, 19	Scribbagh	820 2 29i	Fermanagh	Magheraboy	Devenish	Ballyshannon	III.	211
14	Scribblestown	272 0 35	Dublin	Castleknock	Castleknock	Dublin North	I.	24
36	Scribby	91 0 16	Fermanagh	Clankelly	Clones	Clones	III.	197
53, 61	Scribly	213 3 2	Donegal	Raphoe	Leck	Letterkenny	III.	140
9	Scriboge	59 2 34j	Tipperary, N.R.	Lower Ormond	Kilbarron	Borrisokane	II.	284
25	Scriggan	267 1 13	Londonderry	Keenaght	Dungiven	New T^o Limavady	III.	236
126	Scrivoge	210 2 6	Cork, W.R.	Bear	Kilnamanagh	Castletown	II.	126
29, 35	Scroghil	54 2 30	Westmeath	Clonlonan	Kilcleagh	Athlone	I.	262
59	Scronagare	212 1 16	Cork, W.R.	West Muskerry	Clondrohid	Macroom	II.	155
1	Scrothea East	163 1 9	Waterford	Upperthird	St. Marys Clonmel	Clonmel	II.	372
1	SCROTHEA T.	—	Waterford	Upperthird	St. Marys Clonmel	Clonmel	II.	372
1	Scrothea West	132 1 20	Waterford	Upperthird	St. Marys Clonmel	Clonmel	II.	372
58	Scrownore	377 3 15	Limerick	Coshlea	Kilbeheny	Mitchelstown	II.	239
34, 35	Scrub and Glenmacolla	394 3 36	Queen's Co.	Clarmallagh	Aghmacart	Abbeyleix	I.	236
18, 19	Scrub or Pigeonpark	335 1 33	King's Co.	Upper Philipstown	Geashill	Edenderry	I.	144
35	Scullaboge	789 0 26	Wexford	Shelmaliere West	Newbawn	New Ross	I.	334
76, 88	Sculleen	270 1 38	Cork, E.R.	Imokilly	Cloyne	Middleton	II.	85
26	Scurlocksbush	139 0 29	Wexford	Ballaghkeen	Edermine	Enniscorthy	I.	294
5, 6	Scurlocksleap	630 3 34	Wicklow	Lower Talbotstown	Kilbride	Naas	I.	361
36, 37	Scurlockstown	667 1 13k	Meath	Lower Deece	Scurlockstown	Trim	I.	192

(a) Including 0A. 2R. 30P. water.
(b) Including 26A. 3R. 6P. Brackley Lough.
(c) Including 52A. 3R. 16P. water.
(d) Including 22A. 2R. 31P. water.

(e) Including 2A. 0R. 0P. water.
(f) Including 6A. 1R. 24P. water.
(g) Including 12A. 0R. 35P. water.
(h) Including 2A. 0R. 28P. water.

(i) Including 1A. 3R. 33P. water.
(j) Including 32A. 3R. 3P. detached portions.
(k) Including 4A. 2R. 16P. water.

No. of Sheet of the Ordnance Survey Maps.	Townlands and Towns.	Area in Statute Acres.			County.	Barony.	Parish.	Poor Law Union in 1857.	Townland Census of 1851, Part I.	
		A.	R.	P.					Vol.	Page
16, 23	Scurlockstown	425	2	25	Meath	Upper Kells	Burry	Kells	I.	205
11, 18	Scurlockstown	151	2	24	Westmeath	Corkaree	Portloman	Mullingar	I.	263
8	Scurlockstown	575	3	1	Westmeath	Delvin	Clonarney	Castletowndelvin	I.	265
46	Scurlogebush	339	3	6	Wexford	Bargy	Duncormick	Wexford	I.	305
21	Scurlogue	153	3	18	Wicklow	Upper Talbotstown	Rathbran	Baltinglass	I.	365
16	Scurmore	330	0	7	Sligo	Tireragh	Castleconor	Dromore West	IV.	232
40, 41	Seabank	265	2	35	Wicklow	Arklow	Kilbride	Rathdrum	I.	345
17	Seaboughan	139	0	13	Armagh	Fews Lower	Kilclooney	Armagh	III.	46
54, 55	Seacash	1,168	1	13	Antrim	Lower Massereene	Killead	Antrim	III.	28
11,12,16,17	Seacon Beg	232	3	0	Antrim	Upper Dunluce	Ballymoney	Ballymoney	III.	19
11, 16	Seacon Lower	283	3	39	Antrim	Upper Dunluce	Ballymoney	Ballymoney	III.	19
8	Seacon Lower	23	0	36	Londonderry	North East Liberties of Coleraine	Ballymoney	Ballymoney	III.	245
11	Seacon More	208	0	26	Antrim	Upper Dunluce	Ballymoney	Ballymoney	III.	19
8	Seaconmore	5	3	5	Londonderry	North East Liberties of Coleraine	Ballymoney	Ballymoney	III.	245
52, 60	Seacor	386	2	25	Donegal	Kilmacrenan	Conwal	Letterkenny	III.	126
101, 105	Seadavog Mountain	745	0	8	Donegal	Tirhugh	Templecarn	Donegal	III.	149
38	Seafield	165	2	11a	Clare	Ibrickan	Kilmurry	Kilrush	II.	24
67	Seafield	80	3	15	Cork, E.R.	Imokilly	Youghal	Youghal	II.	91
118	Seafield	177	3	13	Cork, W.R.	Bantry	Kilmocomoge	Bantry	II.	121
95	Seafield	85	1	9	Galway	Dunkellin	Ballynacourty	Galway	IV.	27
14, 20	Seafield	218	1	2	Sligo	Carbury	Kilmacowen	Sligo	IV.	222
24	Seafield	341	2	21	Waterford	Decies without Drum	Ballylaneen	Kilmacthomas	III.	354
7, 12	Seafield	126	1	10	Wexford	Ballaghkeen	Kiltennell	Gorey	I.	297
46	Seafield	66	3	6	Wexford	Bargy	Duncormick	Wexford	I.	305
19	SEAFIELD AVENUE T.	—			Dublin	Coolock	Clontarf	Dublin North	I.	26
26, 29	Seafin	539	1	26	Armagh	Orior Upper	Killevy	Newry	III.	58
35, 42	Seafin	399	2	21	Down	Upper Iveagh, Lr. pt.	Drumballyroney	Banbridge	III.	172
36, 37	Seaforde Demesne	1,013	3	18b	Down	Kinelarty	Loughinisland	Downpatrick	III.	177
37	SEAFORDE T.	—			Down	Kinelarty	Loughinisland	Downpatrick	III.	177
16	Seagahan	886	1	39	Armagh	Fews Lower	Lisnadill	Armagh	III.	47
5, 6, 9, 10	Seagoe Lower	290	2	22c	Armagh	Oneilland East	Seagoe	Lurgan	III.	50
9, 10	Seagoe Upper	130	1	22d	Armagh	Oneilland East	Seagoe	Lurgan	III.	50
48	Sea, Hill of	89	0	12	Wexford	Forth	Rosslare	Wexford	I.	313
98	Seahill and Tuckmill Hill	118	0	3	Donegal	Banagh	Inver	Donegal	III.	108
112	Seal Island	3	2	18	Galway	Kiltartan	Kinvarradoorus	Gort	IV.	50
12	Seamount	127	0	10	Wexford	Ballaghkeen	Ardamine	Gorey	I.	291
12	Seapoint	33	3	10	Dublin	Nethercross	Swords	Balrothery	I.	32
93	Seapoint	17	3	32	Galway	Galway	Rahoon	Galway	IV.	38
23	Seapoint or Temple-hill	52	2	33	Dublin	Rathdown	Monkstown	Rathdown	I.	37
17	Searkin	118	1	12	Monaghan	Dartree	Killeevan	Clones	III.	268
13	Seasonspark	116	0	35	Wicklow	Newcastle	Newcastle Upper	Rathdrum	I.	353
24, 29	Seasons	114	3	34	Kildare	Naas South	Ballymore Eustace	Naas	I.	64
12	Seatown East	22	2	21	Dublin	Nethercross	Swords	Balrothery	I.	32
11, 12	Seatown West	92	1	26	Dublin	Nethercross	Swords	Balrothery	I.	32
30	Seavaghan	569	3	8	Down	Kinelarty	Loughinisland	Downpatrick	III.	177
7, 10	Seaveagh	143	2	0	Monaghan	Monaghan	Tehallan	Monaghan	III.	280
17	Seaview	178	2	5	Wexford	Ballaghkeen	Donaghmore	Gorey	I.	294
13	Seaview	55	3	9	Wicklow	Newcastle	Kilcoole	Rathdrum	I.	352
14	Second Croagh or Sixth Corgary	2,111	2	1e	Tyrone	Omagh West	Termonamongan	Castlederg	III.	317
35	Sedennan	182	3	27	Tyrone	Omagh East	Drumragh	Omagh	III.	313
17	Sedenrath	214	1	30	Meath	Upper Kells	Kells	Kells	I.	206
15	Sedgemoor	56	0	16g	Tipperary, N.R.	Lower Ormond	Knigh	Nenagh	II.	285
49	Sedgy Island	2	2	4	Roscommon	Athlone	Kiltoom	Athlone	IV.	183
12, 16	See	168	0	25	Cavan	Tullygarvey	Drung	Cootehill	III.	89
21	Seeaghanbaun	109	0	31	Mayo	Tirawley	Kilfian	Killala	IV.	169
21	Seeaghandeo	163	3	25	Mayo	Tirawley	Kilfian	Killala	IV.	169
66, 67	Seecon	1,828	3	34h	Galway	Moycullen	Killannin	Oughterard	IV.	70
52	Seeconglas	770	0	12	Limerick	Glenquin	Killeedy	Newcastle	II.	246
8	Seecrin	33	0	11	Louth	Lower Dundalk	Carlingford	Dundalk	I.	176
17	Seedagh	130	2	28	Donegal	Kilmacrenan	Clondavaddog	Milford	III.	125
6	Seeds	276	2	17	Cork, E.R.	Orrery and Kilmore	Kilbolane	Kanturk	II.	108
27	Seefin	593	1	12i	Cavan	Clankee	Knockbride	Bailieborough	III.	74
104	Seefin	309	3	8	Galway	Dunkellin	Killogilleen	Loughrea	IV.	31
35	Seefin	143	1	1	King's Co.	Ballybritt	Birr	Parsonstown	I.	125
111, 119	Seefin	508	1	8	Mayo	Clanmorris	Crossboyne	Claremorris	IV.	133
44, 45	Seefin	195	0	33	Sligo	Coolavin	Kilfree	Boyle	IV.	224
35	SEEFIN T.	—			King's Co.	Ballybritt	Birr	Parsonstown	I.	125
23	Seegronan	700	3	35	Tyrone	Omagh West	Termonamongan	Castlederg	III.	317
119	Seehanes	307	1	7	Cork, W.R.	West Carbery (E.D.)	Dromdaleague	Skibbereen	II.	140

No. of Sheet of the Ordnance Survey Maps.	Townlands and Towns.	Area in Statute Acres.			County.	Barony.	Parish.	Poor Law Union in 1857.	Townland Census of 1851, Part I.	
		A.	R.	P.					Vol.	Page
40	Seeharan	371	2	17	Cavan	Castlerahan	Mullagh	Bailieborough	III.	70
9, 10	Seein	461	1	25a	Tyrone	Strabane Lower	Urney	Strabane	III.	323
9	SEEIN T.	—			Tyrone	Strabane Lower	Urney	Strabane	III.	323
11	Seemochuda	248	1	31	Waterford	Coshmore & Coshbride	Lismore and Mocollop	Lismore	II.	347
30, 36	Seeoge	150	0	13	Westmeath	Clonlonan	Kilcleagh	Athlone	I.	262
29	Seeola	129	1	3	Monaghan	Farney	Inishkeen	Dundalk	III.	271
27	Seeoran	459	0	7b	Cavan	Clankee	Knockbride	Cootehill	III.	74
109	Seerillaun	3	1	3	Mayo	Carra	Ballyovey	Ballinrobe	IV.	126
51, 52	Seersha	60	3	5	Clare	Bunratty Lower	Feenagh	Ennis	II.	4
57, 58	Seersha	108	2	16	Kerry	Magunihy	Aglish	Killarney	II.	200
93	Seershin	286	3	34	Galway	Moycullen	Rahoon	Galway	IV.	72
19, 25	Seevness	711	1	6	Sligo	Leyny	Killoran	Tobercurry	IV.	231
20	Segravescastle	30	1	22	Kildare	Naas North	Rathmore	Naas	I.	63
33, 34, 42	Segully	513	3	0	Tyrone	Omagh West	Longfield East	Omagh	III.	316
19	Seixeslough	49	0	38c	Kilkenny	Gowran and Municipal Borough	St. John's	Kilkenny	I.	98
6	Seller	287	2	23	Meath	Morgallion	Nobber	Kells	I.	210
134	Sellernaun East	372	3	31	Galway	Leitrim	Inishcaltra	Scarriff	IV.	54
134	Sellernaun West	370	3	25	Galway	Leitrim	Inishcaltra	Scarriff	IV.	54
8	Selloo	65	1	18	Monaghan	Monaghan	Clones	Monaghan	III.	275
9	Selshion	172	1	22	Armagh	Oneilland West	Drumcree	Lurgan	III.	52
17	Seltan	499	3	13	Leitrim	Drumahaire	Inishmagrath	Manorhamilton	IV.	97
28, 29	Seltan	145	0	26d	Leitrim	Mohill	Mohill	Mohill	IV.	108
19, 21	Seltanahunshin	824	3	18	Leitrim	Carrigallen	Oughteragh	Bawnboy	IV.	92
28	Seltan (McDonald)	69	3	35e	Leitrim	Leitrim	Kiltubbrid	Cark. on Shannon	IV.	104
28	Seltan (Moran)	65	0	10f	Leitrim	Leitrim	Kiltubbrid	Cark. on Shannon	IV.	104
17, 18, 20	Seltannasaggart or Corry Mountain	131	3	36	Leitrim	Drumahaire	Inishmagrath	Manorhamilton	IV.	97
20	Seltannaskeagh	47	3	36	Leitrim	Drumahaire	Inishmagrath	Manorhamilton	IV.	97
2	Seltannaveeny	300	1	15	Roscommon	Boyle	Kilronan	Boyle	IV.	197
17	Semicock	46	2	19	Antrim	Upper Dunluce	Ballymoney	Ballymoney	III.	19
7	Seneirl	114	3	11	Antrim	Lower Dunluce	Dunluce	Coleraine	III.	17
26	Seneschalstown	425	0	7	Meath	Lower Duleek	Painstown	Navan	I.	196
22	Sentryhill	457	3	33	Queen's Co.	Clandonagh	Aghaboe	Donaghmore	I.	233
15, 16, 22, 23	Seraghstown	363	1	10	Meath	Fore	Killallon	Oldcastle	I.	201
60	Sergeant's Lot	110	3	21	Tipperary, S.R.	Clanwilliam	Relickmurry & Athassel	Tipperary	II.	310
127	Scrough Island	0	0	16	Cork, W.R.	Bear	Kilnamanagh	Castletown	II.	126
22	Serse	447	1	35	Armagh	Orior Lower	Killevy	Newry	III.	56
22, 24	Seskin	74	3	3	Carlow	St. Mullins Lower	St. Mullins	New Ross	I.	13
4	Seskin	480	1	39	Kilkenny	Galmoy	Aharney	Urlingford	I.	91
30	Seskin	296	3	7	Kilkenny	Kells	Killamery	Callan	I.	109
33, 34, 39	Seskin	228	3	22	Tipperary, N.R.	Kilnamanagh Upper	Upperchurch	Thurles	II.	281
50, 58, 59	Seskin	237	0	5	Tipperary, S.R.	Clanwilliam	Solloghod-more	Tipperary	II.	311
78, 84	Seskin	975	0	20	Tipperary, S.R.	Iffa and Offa East	Kilsheelan	Clonmel	II.	315
37, 38, 42, 43	Seskin	355	0	19	Wicklow	Shillelagh	Mullinacuff	Shillelagh	I.	358
22	Seskin	255	0	2	Wicklow	Upper Talbotstown	Donaghmore	Baltinglass	I.	363
4, 9	Seskin Little	36	2	12	Kilkenny	Galmoy	Aharney	Urlingford	I.	91
11, 12	Seskin Lower	352	1	7	Carlow	Idrone West	Oldleighlin	Carlow	I.	9
19, 20	Seskinnamadra	693	0	0	Carlow	Idrone East	Sliguff	Carlow	I.	8
4, 9	Seskin North	402	1	38	Kilkenny	Galmoy	Aharney	Urlingford	I.	91
43, 51	Seskinore	870	1	0	Tyrone	Omagh East	Clogherny	Omagh	III.	310
51	SESKINORE T.	—			Tyrone	Omagh East	Clogherny	Omagh	III.	310
11	Seskinrea	597	2	25	Carlow	Idrone West	Oldleighlin	Carlow	I.	9
16	Seskinryan	475	0	29	Carlow	Idrone East	Dunleckny	Carlow	I.	7
16, 19	Seskinryan	86	2	10	Carlow	Idrone East	Lorum	Carlow	I.	8
4, 9	Seskin South	342	1	32	Kilkenny	Galmoy	Aharney	Urlingford	I.	91
11	Seskin Upper	690	0	6	Carlow	Idrone West	Oldleighlin	Carlow	I.	9
70	Sesnacully	55	2	17	Donegal	Raphoe	Raphoe	Strabane	III.	141
9, 16	Sesnagh	130	1	35	Londonderry	Keenaght	Tamlaght Finlagan	NewTnLimavady	III.	237
63, 64	Sess	311	1	32	Tyrone	Clogher	Clogher	Clogher	III.	293
59	Sess	70	2	32	Tyrone	Clogher	Errigal Keerogue	Clogher	III.	295
10, 17	Sessagh of Gallan	205	2	13	Tyrone	Strabane Lower	Ardstraw	Gortin	III.	319
59	Sessia	92	3	23	Tyrone	Clogher	Clogher	Clogher	III.	293
38, 39	Sessia	73	3	24	Tyrone	Dungannon Middle	Donaghenry	Cookstown	III.	301
46	Sessia	52	3	6	Tyrone	Dungannon Middle	Tullyniskan	Dungannon	III.	305
40	Sessia	137	3	8	Tyrone	Dungannon Upper	Arboe	Cookstown	III.	305
30	Sessia	56	1	3	Tyrone	Dungannon Upper	Arboe	Cookstown	III.	305
45	Sessiadonaghy	420	1	8	Tyrone	Dungannon Middle	Pomeroy	Dungannon	III.	304
8	Sessiagh	101	2	16	Donegal	Kilmacrenan	Clondavaddog	Milford	III.	125
70, 79	Sessiagh	103	2	3	Donegal	Raphoe	Donaghmore	Strabane	III.	138
30, 34	Sessiagh	120	0	32g	Leitrim	Carrigallen	Carrigallen	Mohill	IV.	90
101	Sessiagh	140	0	3	Mayo	Clanmorris	Tagheen	Claremorris	IV.	136
43	Sessiagh	107	0	28	Tyrone	Clogher	Donacavey	Omagh	III.	294

(a) Including 9A. 1R. 32P. water.
(b) Including 20A. 3R. 1P. water.
(c) { Within the Municipal Boundary, 0A. 0R. 1P.
Without the Municipal Boundary, 49A. 0R. 37P.
(d) Including 15A. 2R. 13P. water.
(e) Including 5A. 2R. 16P. water.
(f) Including 5A. 0R. 37P. water.
(g) Including 5A. 3R. 24P. water

No. of Sheet of the Ordnance Survey Maps.	Townlands and Towns.	Area in Statute Acres.	County.	Barony.	Parish.	Poor Law Union in 1857.	Townland Census of 1851, Part I. Vol.	Page
		A. R. P.						
79	Sessiagh (Allison)	123 3 16	Donegal	Raphoe	Donaghmore	Strabane	III.	138
33	Sessiagh East	347 2 29a	Fermanagh	Tirkennedy	Cleenish	Enniskillen	III.	220
101, 105	Sessiaghkeelta	515 0 37	Donegal	Tirhugh	Templecarn	Donegal	III.	149
70, 79	Sessiagh (Long)	208 0 19	Donegal	Raphoe	Donaghmore	Strabane	III.	138
78	Sessiagh (O'Neill)	224 2 4	Donegal	Raphoe	Donaghmore	Stranorlar	III.	138
11	Sessiaghs	170 1 15	Fermanagh	Lurg	Magheracross	Lowtherstown	III.	207
50	Sessiaghs or Magheragart	190 3 9	Tyrone	Omagh East	Dromore	Omagh	III.	311
26, 27	Sessiagh West	332 1 12	Fermanagh	Clanawley	Cleenish	Enniskillen	III.	191
61	Sessiamagaroll	268 1 34b	Tyrone	Dungannon Middle	Clonfeacle	Dungannon	III.	300
39	Sessia (Murphy)	83 1 34	Tyrone	Dungannon Upper	Desertcreat	Cookstown	III.	308
38	Sessia (Scott)	178 1 23	Tyrone	Dungannon Upper	Desertcreat	Cookstown	III.	308
52	Sess Kilgreen	57 2 30	Tyrone	Clogher	Errigal Keerogue	Clogher	III.	295
31, 37	Sessuecommon	1,315 2 6c	Sligo	Leyny	Achonry	Tobercurry	IV.	229
24, 31, 37	Sessuegarry	2,531 3 6d	Sligo	Leyny	Achonry	Tobercurry	IV.	229
31, 37	Sessuegilroy	1,424 3 11	Sligo	Leyny	Achonry	Tobercurry	IV.	229
16,17,22,23	Sevenchurches or Camaderry	4,518 3 38e	Wicklow	Ballinacor North	Derrylossary	Rathdrum	I.	346
1	Sevenparks (1st Division)	4 0 18	Dublin	Balrothery East	Balscaddan	Balrothery	I.	20
1	Sevenparks (2nd Division)	4 2 7	Dublin	Balrothery East	Balscaddan	Balrothery	I.	20
1	Sevenparks (3rd Division)	0 2 24	Dublin	Balrothery East	Balscaddan	Balrothery	I.	20
8, 12	Sevensisters	224 2 0	Kilkenny	Galmoy	Fertagh	Urlingford	I.	92
21	Sevitsland	74 1 9	Meath	Lower Duleek	Julianstown	Drogheda	I.	196
18	Seygorry	204 0 30	Londonderry	Coleraine	Aghadowey	Coleraine	III.	230
55	Seyloran	93 3 11	Tyrone	Dungannon Middle	Clonfeacle	Dungannon	III.	300
16	Seymourstown Black	458 0 32	Meath	Upper Kells	Kilskeer	Kells	I.	206
16	Seymourstown White	246 1 1	Meath	Upper Kells	Kilskeer	Kells	I.	206
8, 13	Shaen	1,024 3 29	Queen's Co.	Maryborough East	Straboe	Mountmellick	I.	242
10	Shallany	167 0 11f	Fermanagh	Lurg	Derryvullan	Lowtherstown	III.	205
33	Shallee	260 1 27	Clare	Inchiquin	Kilnamona	Ennis	II.	27
26	Shallee (Coughlan)	687 3 19	Tipperary, N.R.	Owney and Arra	Killoscully	Nenagh	II.	295
26	Shallee Lower and Upper	487 3 35	Tipperary, N.R.	Owney and Arra	Killoscully	Nenagh	II.	295
26	Shallee (White)	424 0 4	Tipperary, N.R.	Owney and Arra	Killoscully	Nenagh	II.	295
66	Shallogan Beg	698 3 9	Donegal	Boylagh	Inishkeel	Glenties	III.	113
66	Shallogan More	2,194 2 34	Donegal	Boylagh	Inishkeel	Glenties	III.	113
11	Shallon	56 3 13	Dublin	Castleknock	Finglas	Dublin North	I.	25
11	Shallon	152 3 37	Dublin	Nethercross	Kilsallaghan	Balrothery	I.	31
27	Shallon	434 0 1	Meath	Lower Duleek	Kilsharvan	Drogheda	I.	196
29	Shallowspark	46 1 9	Wexford	Bantry	St. Mary's	New Ross	I.	302
18	Shalvanstown	252 1 26	Meath	Upper Slane	Gernonstown	Navan	I.	224
97	Shalwy	182 2 35	Donegal	Banagh	Kilcar	Glenties	III.	109
72	Shammerbaun	411 2 20g	Mayo	Costello	Kilmovee	Swineford	IV.	142
72	Shammerdoo	955 3 0h	Mayo	Costello	Kilmovee	Swineford	IV.	142
18	Shamrockhill	90 3 18	Louth	Ferrard	Dunleer	Ardee	I.	181
17	Shamrock Island	2 3 36	Down	Dufferin	Killinchy	Downpatrick	III.	166
35	Shamrocklodge	25 3 27	Kildare	Narragh&RebanWest	St. Johns	Athy	I.	68
55	Shanaboola	190 1 31	Cork, E.R.	Kinnatalloon	Ballynoe	Fermoy	II.	97
94	Shanacashel	751 3 34	Cork, W.R.	West Muskerry	Kilmichael	Dunmanway	II.	159
72	Shanacashel	641 2 15	Kerry	Dunkerron North	Knockane	Cahersiveen	II.	182
82, 94	Shanacashelkneeves	336 0 22	Cork, W.R.	West Muskerry	Kilmichael	Dunmanway	II.	159
44	Shanaclogh	88 3 8	Cork, E.R.	Barrymore	Rathcormack	Fermoy	II.	57
95	Shanaclogh	145 3 39	Cork, W.R.	East Carbery (W.D.)	Kinneigh	Dunmanway	II.	135
21, 30	Shanaclogh	147 3 4	Limerick	Connello Upper	Croom	Croom	II.	232
22	Shanaclogh	193 0 25	Limerick	Pubblebrien	Crecora	Croom	II.	232
25	Shanaclogh East	78 3 2	Limerick	Coonagh	Oola	Tipperary	II.	236
25	Shanaclogh West	106 2 4	Limerick	Coonagh	Oola	Tipperary	II.	236
16, 25	Shanaclone	361 1 26	Waterford	Middlethird	Dunhill	Kilmacthomas	II.	367
27,28,35,36	Shanacloon	304 2 39	Cork, E.R.	Condons&Clangibbon	Clondulane	Fermoy	II.	60
58, 69	Shanacloon	342 3 2	Cork, W.R.	West Muskerry	Ballyvourney	Macroom	II.	154
65	Shanacloon	315 2 23	Kerry	Dunkerron North	Knockane	Killarney	II.	182
22, 27	Shanacloon	189 1 25	Kildare	Offaly East	Bailyshannon	Naas	I.	69
30	Shanacloon	107 2 3	King's Co.	Eglish	Eglish	Parsonstown	I.	135
7, 15, 16	Shanacloon	355 3 27	Limerick	Coonagh	Doon	Tipperary	II.	234
47	Shanacloon	176 2 22	Tipperary, N.R.	Eliogarty	Galbooly	Thurles	II.	270
23	Shanacloon	336 3 6	Tipperary, N.R.	Ikerrin	Bourney	Roscrea	II.	274
44, 50	Shanacloon	296 0 15	Tipperary, N.R.	Kilnamanagh Upper	Toem	Tipperary	II.	280
36	Shanacloon	33 2 9	Waterford	Decies within Drum	Ringagonagh	Dungarvan	II.	353
44	Shanacloon	61 1 13	Wexford	Shelburne	St.James&Dunbrody	New Ross	I.	328
96	Shanacloyne	355 1 13	Cork, W.R.	Kinalmeaky	Templemartin	Bandon	II.	155
11	Shanacool	34 0 5i	Kerry	Iraghticonnor	Knockanure	Listowel	II.	192

(a) Including 15A. 2R. 31P. water.
(b) Including 5A. 0R. 0P. water.
(c) Including 9A. 2R. 33P. water.
(d) Including 15A. 0R. 35P. water.

(e) { Including 51A. 1R. 24P. Lough Nahanagan.
Including 48A. 1R. 16P. Upper Lake.
Including 7A. 2R. 24P. Lower Lake. }
(f) Including 11A. 0R. 16P. water.

(g) Including 20A. 2R. 35P. water.
(h) Including 12A. 0R. 16P. water.
(i) Including 8A. 0R. 10P. water.

No. of Sheet of the Ordnance Survey Maps.	Townlands and Towns.	Area in Statute Acres.			County.	Barony.	Parish.	Poor Law Union in 1857.	Townland Census of 1851, Part I.	
		A.	R.	P.					Vol.	Page
24, 32	Shanacool	173	0	25	Waterford	Decies without Drum	Stradbally	Kilmacthomas	II.	361
37	Shanacoole	455	0	23	Waterford	Decies within Drum	Clashmore	Youghal	II.	351
115	Shanacoumha	28	1	24	Cork, W.R.	Bear	Killaconenagh	Castletown	II.	125
93	Shanacrane East	866	0	35	Cork, W.R.	East Carbery (W.D.)	Inchigeelagh	Dunmanway	II.	132
93	Shanacrane West	528	1	25	Cork, W.R.	East Carbery (W.D.)	Inchigeelagh	Dunmanway	II.	132
26	Shanadullaun	372	3	35	Galway	Ross	Ross	Oughterard	IV.	74
12, 13	Shanafaraghaun	1,641	1	29	Galway	Ross	Ross	Oughterard	IV.	74
17, 23	Shanafona	186	0	24	Kerry	Clanmaurice	Duagh	Listowel	II.	168
89	Shanagarry	27	0	36	Cork, E.R.	Imokilly	Bohillane	Middleton	II.	84
89	Shanagarry North	439	1	26	Cork, E.R.	Imokilly	Kilmahon	Middleton	II.	89
89	Shanagarry South	179	1	39	Cork, E.R.	Imokilly	Kilmahon	Middleton	II.	89
89	SHANAGARRY T.	—			Cork, E.R.	Imokilly	Kilmahon	Middleton	II.	89
18	Shanagh	276	3	7	Cork, E.R.	Fermoy	Templeroan	Mallow	II.	82
94, 108	Shanagh	363	3	23	Cork, W.R.	East Carbery (W.D.)	Fanlobbus	Dunmanway	II.	132
88	Shanagh	15	0	10	Mayo	Burrishoole	Aghagower	Westport	IV.	118
73	Shanaghan	191	3	18a	Donegal	Banagh	Inishkeel	Glenties	III.	106
81, 92	Shanaghmoyle	161	1	37	Mayo	Costello	Knock	Claremorris	IV.	143
136, 145	Shanaghobarravane	173	0	14	Cork, W.R.	Ibane and Barryroe	Lislee	Clonakilty	II.	150
35	Shanaghy	52	0	17	Fermanagh	Clankelly	Clones	Clones	III.	197
34, 39	Shanaghy	134	0	10	Fermanagh	Magherastephana	Aghalurcher	Lisnaskea	III.	217
10	Shanaghy	837	0	31b	Mayo	Erris	Kilmore	Belmullet	IV.	146
71	Shanaghy	189	2	31	Mayo	Gallen	Bohola	Swineford	IV.	147
7	Shanaghy	128	0	30	Mayo	Tirawley	Kilbride	Killala	IV.	168
23	Shanaghy	324	0	17	Tyrone	Omagh West	Termonamongan	Castlederg	III.	317
29	Shanaghy or Ardnaree	522	2	4c	Sligo	Tireragh	Kilmoremoy	Ballina	IV.	235
21	Shanaghy Lower or Artiferty	62	3	28	Antrim	Kilconway	Finvoy	Ballymoney	III.	26
21, 22	Shanaghy Upper	293	1	3	Antrim	Kilconway	Finvoy	Ballymoney	III.	26
19	Shanagolden	57	3	1	Limerick	Shanid	Shanagolden	Glin	II.	258
19	Shanagolden Demesne	13	0	6	Limerick	Shanid	Robertstown	Glin	II.	258
10, 19	Shanagolden Demesne	259	1	34	Limerick	Shanid	Shanagolden	Glin	II.	258
19	SHANAGOLDEN T.	—			Limerick	Shanid	Shanagolden	Glin	II.	258
86, 98	Shanagraigue	465	3	5	Cork, E.R.	Kerrycurrihy	Liscleary	Kinsale	II.	92
88, 100	Shanance	168	3	3	Cork, E.R.	Imokilly	Inch	Middleton	II.	87
37, 46	Shanahill	929	1	13d	Kerry	Trughanacmy	Kilgarrylander	Tralee	II.	211
46	Shanahill East	110	3	36	Kerry	Trughanacmy	Kilgarrylander	Tralee	II.	211
23	Shanahoe	718	1	36	Queen's Co.	Maryborough West	Clonenagh&Clonagheen	Abbeyleix	I.	243
31, 32	Shanahona	210	0	0	Wexford	Shelmaliere West	Killurin	Wexford	I.	334
37, 46	Shanakeal	1,234	2	1	Kerry	Trughanacmy	Kilgarrylander	Tralee	II.	211
35	Shanakeever	259	3	35e	Galway	Ballynahinch	Omey	Clifden	IV.	15
74	Shanakiel	178	2	23f	Cork, E.R.	Cork and Municipal Borough	St. Marys Shandon	Cork	II.	66
78	Shanakill	304	2	9	Cork, E.R.	Imokilly	Kilmacdonogh	Youghal	II.	88
123	Shanakill	197	0	17	Cork, W.R.	East Carbery (E.D.)	Rathclarin	Bandon	II.	130
60, 71	Shanakill	461	2	29	Cork, W.R.	East Muskerry	Aghinagh	Macroom	II.	154
39, 40	Shanakill	255	3	9	Cork, W.R.	West Muskerry	Kilcorney	Millstreet	II.	158
29	Shanakill	49	3	7	Kerry	Trughanacmy	Tralee	Tralee	II.	214
23	Shanakill	872	0	30	Tipperary, N.R.	Ikerrin	Killavinoge	Roscrea	II.	275
34	Shanakill	303	2	2	Waterford	Decies within Drum	Aglish	Dungarvan	II.	349
36	Shanakill	114	2	34	Waterford	Decies within Drum	Ringagonagh	Dungarvan	II.	353
35	Shanakill	86	0	27	Waterford	Decies without Drum	Dungarvan	Dungarvan	II.	356
15,16,24,25	Shanakill	614	3	3	Waterford	Decies without Drum	Rossmire	Kilmacthomas	II.	360
6, 7	Shanakill	455	1	11	Waterford	Upperthird	Rathgormuck	Carrick on Suir	II.	371
37, 46	Shanakill Lower	244	0	25	Cork, E.R.	Kinnatalloon	Mogeely	Fermoy	II.	99
6	Shanakill Lower	155	2	28	Tipperary, N.R.	Lower Ormond	Terryglass	Borrisokane	II.	288
46	Shanakill Upper	244	1	35	Cork, E.R.	Kinnatalloon	Mogeely	Fermoy	II.	99
6	Shanakill Upper	157	0	20	Tipperary, N.R.	Lower Ormond	Terryglass	Borrisokane	II.	288
38, 39	Shanaknock	348	0	26	Cork, E.R.	Duhallow	Drishane	Millstreet	II.	71
105	Shanaknock	59	2	10	Cork, W.R.	Bantry	Kilmocomoge	Bantry	II.	121
98	Shanaknock	927	1	0	Kerry	Dunkerron South	Kilcrohane	Cahersiveen	II.	184
30	Shanaknock	149	2	8	Kerry	Trughanacmy	O'Brennan	Tralee	II.	212
51	Shanaknock	193	2	18	Tipperary, S.R.	Kilnamanagh Lower	Aghacrew	Tipperary	II.	322
51	Shanaknock	51	1	9	Tipperary, S.R.	Kilnamanagh Lower	Donohill	Tipperary	II.	323
34	Shanakyle	76	3	3	Kerry	Corkaguiny	Kilquane	Dingle	II.	179
62	Shanakyle	288	1	32	Tipperary, S.R.	Middlethird	Magowry	Cashel	II.	328
60	Shanalurg	103	3	2	Tyrone	Dungannon Lower	Carnteel	Dungannon	III.	298
33	Shanapollagh	62	2	30	Waterford	Coshmore&Coshbride	Kilwatermoy	Lismore	II.	344
140	Shanavagh	256	1	31	Cork, W.R.	West Carbery (W.D.)	Skull	Skull	II.	146
43, 44	Shanavagha	226	0	12	Cork, E.R.	Barrymore	Rathcormack	Fermoy	II.	57
60, 71	Shanavagha	107	2	7	Cork, W.R.	East Muskerry	Aghinagh	Macroom	II.	154
77	Shanavagroon	114	1	19	Cork, E.R.	Imokilly	Dohillane	Middleton	II.	84
132, 141	Shanavalla	128	3	10	Cork, W.R.	West Carbery (W.D.)	Caheragh	Skibbereen	II.	142
97, 98	Shanavally	308	2	3	Cork, E.R.	Kinalea	Ballymartle	Kinsale	II.	94

(a) Including 8A. 1R. 8P. water.
(b) Including 0A. 2R. 5P. Islands.
(c) Including 1A. 3R. 19P. River Moy.

(d) Including 4A. 1R. 30P. detached portion.
(e) Including 16A. 3R. 7P. water.

(f) Including 5A. 1R. 4P. water.
Within the Municipal Boundary, 2A. 1R. 3P.
Without the Municipal Boundary, 176A. 1R. 20P.

No. of Sheet of the Ordnance Survey Maps.	Townlands and Towns.	Area in Statute Acres.	County.	Barony.	Parish.	Poor Law Union in 1857.	Townland Census of 1851, Part I.	
		A. R. P.					Vol.	Page
97, 111	Shanavally	175 2 33	Cork, E.R.	Kinalea	Leighmoney	Kinsale	II.	96
147	Shanavally	85 0 26	Cork, W.R.	West Carbery (W.D.)	Kilmoe	Skull	II.	145
39	Shanavally	269 0 8	Kerry	Trughanacmy	Ballymacelligott	Tralee	II.	207
9	Shanavally	94 3 26	Tipperary, N.R.	Lower Ormond	Cloghprior	Borrisokane	II.	283
115	Shanavallyleigh	85 1 11	Cork, W.R.	Bear	Killaconenagh	Castletown	II.	125
11, 12	Shanavaur	212 2 15	Queen's Co.	Upperwoods	Offerlane	Mountmellick	I.	252
10	Shanaveag	287 1 39	Galway	Ballynahinch	Ballynakill	Clifden	IV.	12
31, 39	Shanavogh East	866 1 9	Clare	Ibrickan	Kilmurry	Ennistimon	II.	24
31, 39	Shanavogh West	432 0 30	Clare	Ibrickan	Kilmurry	Ennistimon	II.	24
21	Shanavoher	483 2 11	Cork, E.R.	Duhallow	Kilmeen	Kanturk	II.	73
41	Shanavoher	774 0 39	Cork, E.R.	Duhallow	Kilshannig	Mallow	II.	74
20	Shanavoola	170 3 4	Waterford	Coshmore&Coshbride	Lismore and Mocollop	Lismore	II.	347
54, 65	Shanavougha	174 2 20	Cork, E.R.	Barrymore	Templenacarriga	Middleton	II.	58
109	Shanaway East	386 1 18	Cork, W.R.	East Carbery (E.D.)	Ballymoney	Dunmanway	II.	127
3	Shanaway East	176 3 20	Kerry	Iraghticonnor	Kilnaughtin	Glin	II.	191
108, 109	Shanaway Middle	296 3 27	Cork, W.R.	East Carbery (E.D.)	Ballymoney	Dunmanway	II.	127
108, 109	Shanaway West	266 0 12	Cork, W.R.	East Carbery (E.D.)	Ballymoney	Dunmanway	II.	127
3	Shanaway West	244 0 30	Kerry	Iraghticonnor	Kilnaughtin	Glin	II.	192
49	Shanawillen	79 3 24	Kerry	Trughanacmy	Killeentierna	Killarney	II.	211
72	Shanballard	254 1 35	Galway	Tiaquin	Clonkeen	Loughrea	IV.	76
23	Shanbally	164 0 15	Clare	Corcomroe	Kilmanaheen	Ennistimon	II.	21
44	Shanbally	97 1 33	Cork, E.R.	Barrymore	Rathcormack	Fermoy	II.	57
29	Shanbally	428 1 37	Cork, E.R.	Duhallow	Nohavaldaly	Millstreet	II.	75
87	Shanbally	353 1 27	Cork, E.R.	Kerrycurrihy	Carrigaline	Cork	II.	92
90, 96	Shanbally	819 3 1	Donegal	Banagh	Glencolumbkille	Glenties	III.	106
56	Shanbally	165 3 17	Galway	Clare	Annaghdown	Galway	IV.	16
96	Shanbally	213 0 19	Galway	Dunkellin	Killeeneen	Gort	IV.	30
96	Shanbally	71 1 8	Galway	Dunkellin	Killora	Loughrea	IV.	31
116	Shanbally	213 0 2	Galway	Leitrim	Duniry	Portumna	IV.	53
118	Shanbally	122 0 11	Galway	Longford	Kilquain	Portumna	IV.	60
18	Shanbally	183 3 14a	Kerry	Clanmaurice	Duagh	Listowel	II.	168
11	Shanbally	265 2 31	Limerick	Kenry	Kilcornan	Rathkeale	II.	249
34	Shanbally	61 2 29	Queen's Co.	Clarmallagh	Aghmacart	Abbeyleix	I.	236
47	Shanbally	107 1 26	Tipperary, N.R.	Owney and Arra	Moycarky	Thurles	II.	271
25, 31	Shanbally	85 1 37b	Tipperary, N.R.	Owney and Arra	Kilcomenty	Nenagh	II.	295
21	Shanbally	141 1 38	Tipperary, N.R.	Upper Ormond	Ballymackey	Nenagh	II.	289
77	Shanbally	510 1 37	Tipperary, S.R.	Iffa and Offa East	Lisronagh	Clonmel	II.	315
78	Shanbally	618 2 25	Tipperary, S.R.	Iffa and Offa East	Temple-etney	Clonmel	II.	316
86	Shanbally	371 3 18	Tipperary, S.R.	Iffa and Offa West	Shanrahan	Clogheen	II.	320
21	Shanbally	178 0 24	Waterford	Coshmore&Coshbride	Lismore and Mocollop	Lismore	II.	347
38	Shanbally	84 1 23	Waterford	Decies within Drum	Lisgenan or Grange	Youghal	II.	352
36	Shanbally	179 2 6	Waterford	Decies within Drum	Ringagonagh	Dungarvan	II.	353
23, 31	Shanbally	313 1 21	Waterford	Decies without Drum	Kilrossanty	Kilmacthomas	II.	358
5, 6	Shanballyanne	359 2 24	Waterford	Decies without Drum	Seskinan	Dungarvan	II.	360
27	Shanballyard	157 3 32	Tipperary, N.R.	Upper Ormond	Aghnameadle	Nenagh	II.	289
76	Shanballyard	322 1 9	Tipperary, S.R.	Iffa and Offa East	Inishlounaght	Clonmel	II.	313
7	Shanballybaun	267 2 28c	Roscommon	Boyle	Tumna	Car'. on Shannon	IV.	198
47	Shanballybeg	35 2 36	Galway	Killian	Killian	Mountbellew	IV.	45
34	Shanballycleary	10 2 19	Tipperary, N.R.	Kilnamanagh Upper	Glenkeen	Thurles	II.	279
98	Shanballycolman	45 0 33	Galway	Kilconnell	Killallaghtan	Ballinasloe	IV.	41
93	Shanballyduff	46 0 10	Galway	Galway	Rahoon	Galway	IV.	38
36, 42	Shanballyduff	341 2 36	Tipperary, N.R.	Eliogarty	Rahelty	Thurles	II.	272
40	Shanballyduff	306 3 15	Tipperary, N.R.	Kilnamanagh Upper	Moyaliff	Thurles	II.	279
60, 68	Shanballyduff	663 3 26	Tipperary, S.R.	Middlethird	Dangandargan	Cashel	II.	326
7	Shanballyeden	39 2 28	Galway	Ballymoe	Dunamon	Roscommon	IV.	7
38	Shanballyedmond	866 3 36	Tipperary, N.R.	Owney and Arra	Abington	Nenagh	II.	293
72	Shanballyeeshal	261 1 9	Galway	Tiaquin	Clonkeen	Loughrea	IV.	76
41	Shanbally or Greenfield	199 0 28	Galway	Clare	Killursa	Tuam	IV.	21
47	Shanballylosky	95 1 14	Roscommon	Athlone	Taghboy	Athlone	IV.	184
5	Shanballymore	727 3 19	Galway	Dunmore	Addergoole	Tuam	IV.	33
47	Shanballymore	218 3 30	Galway	Killian	Killeroran	Mountbellew	IV.	44
40	Shanballymore	24 1 22	Galway	Moycullen	Kilcummin	Oughterard	IV.	68
72	Shanballymore	263 0 15	Galway	Tiaquin	Clonkeen	Loughrea	IV.	76
36, 40	Shanballymore	88 2 3	Roscommon	Ballintober South	Cloontuskert	Roscommon	IV.	188
59	Shanballymore	199 3 32	Tipperary, S.R.	Clanwilliam	Kilmucklin	Tipperary	II.	309
18, 26	ShanballymoreLower	250 3 31	Cork, E.R.	Fermoy	Templeroan	Mallow	II.	82
18	SHANBALLYMORE T.	—	Cork, E.R.	Fermoy	Templeroan	Mallow	II.	82
18	Shanballymore Upper	354 2 9	Cork. E.R.	Fermoy	Templeroan	Mallow	II.	82
17, 23	Shanballynahagh	170 1 6	Tipperary, N.R.	Ikerrin	Bourney	Roscrea	II.	274
1	Shanballynakill	48 2 6	King's Co.	Kilcoursey	Kilmanaghan	Tullamore	I.	141
53, 64	Shanballyreagh	422 0 16	Cork, E.R.	Barrymore	Kilquane	Cork	II.	56
18	Shanballysallagh	348 2 1	Clare	Inchiquin	Kilkeedy	Corrofin	II.	26

(a) Including 8A. 0R. 24P. water.　　(b) Including 3A. 2R. 34P. detached portion.　　(c) Including 21A. 1R. 35P. water.

5 M

No. of Sheet of the Ordnance Survey Maps.	Townlands and Towns.	Area in Statute Acres. A. R. P.	County.	Barony.	Parish.	Poor Law Union in 1857.	Townland Census of 1851, Part I. Vol.	Page
3	Shanbeg . . .	198 2 31	Queen's Co. .	Tinnahinch . .	Rosenallis . .	Mountmellick .	I.	250
31	Shanbo . . .	290 1 35	Meath . .	Lower Navan . .	Rataine . .	Navan . .	I.	215
21, 22	Shanboe . .	458 1 13	Queen's Co. .	Clandonagh . .	Aghaboe . .	Donaghmore .	I.	233
37, 41	Shanbogh Lower	328 3 31	Kilkenny . .	Ida . . .	Shanbogh . .	New Ross .	I.	104
37, 41	Shanbogh Upper	649 2 24	Kilkenny .	Ida . . .	Shanbogh . .	New Ross .	I.	104
74	Shanboley .	351 1 13a	Galway . .	Clonmacnowen .	Ahascragh . .	Ballinasloe .	IV.	24
9, 22	Shanboolard .	283 1 14b	Galway . .	Ballynahinch . .	Ballynakill . .	Clifden . .	IV.	12
4, 10, 11	Shancarnan .	749 3 7	Meath . .	Lower Kells . .	Moynalty . .	Kells . .	I.	204
15	Shancarrick .	85 0 9	Leitrim .	Drumahaire . .	Killarga . .	Manorhamilton	IV.	99
33, 39	Shancarrigeen or Oldrock . .	205 1 26	Sligo . .	Corran . .	Clconoghil . .	Tobercurry .	IV.	225
31	Shancashlaun .	25 3 23	Kilkenny .	Kells . .	Kilmaganny . .	Callan . .	I.	109
112	Shanclogh .	250 0 30	Galway . .	Kiltartan . .	Kinvarradoorus .	Gort . .	IV.	49
39, 48	Shanclogh .	203 0 10c	Mayo . .	Tirawley . .	Ballynahaglish .	Ballina . .	IV.	164
28	Shancloon .	464 1 4d	Galway . .	Clare . .	Donaghpatrick .	Tuam . .	IV.	19
23	Shanco . .	270 1 37e	Fermanagh .	Tirkennedy . .	Enniskillen . .	Enniskillen .	III.	222
15, 16, 22, 23	Shanco . . .	324 3 3	Meath . .	Fore . .	Killallon . .	Oldcastle .	I.	201
35	Shanco . .	333 1 1	Meath . .	Lune . .	Kildalkey . .	Trim . .	I.	208
12, 17	Shanco . .	70 0 28	Monaghan .	Dartree . .	Killeevan . .	Clones . .	III.	268
27, 30	Shanco . .	429 3 19	Monaghan .	Farney . .	Magheross . .	Carrickmacross	III.	274
3	Shanco . .	88 2 3	Monaghan .	Trough . .	Errigal Trough .	Monaghan .	III.	285
64, 65	Shanco . .	160 3 30	Tyrone . .	Clogher . .	Clogher . .	Clogher . .	III.	293
28, 29, 31, 32	Shancobane .	125 3 25	Monaghan .	Farney . .	Donaghmoyne .	Carrickmacross	III.	271
29, 32	Shancoduff .	135 3 35	Monaghan .	Farney . .	Donaghmoyne .	Carrickmacross	III.	271
31	Shancor . .	127 3 16	Cavan . .	Clannahon . .	Kilmore . .	Cavan . .	III.	78
24	Shancor . .	165 3 37	Cavan . .	Tullyhunco . .	Killashandra .	Cavan . .	III.	98
5	Shancor . .	248 0 30	Meath . .	Lower Kells . .	Kilmainham . .	Kells . .	I.	203
15	Shancorn .	97 0 14f	Cavan . .	Lower Loughtee .	Annagh . .	Cavan . .	III.	79
11	Shancorry .	69 2 32g	Cavan . .	Lower Loughtee .	Annagh . .	Cavan . .	III.	79
25	Shancough .	237 2 32	Sligo . .	Leyny . .	Killoran . .	Tobercurry .	IV.	231
35	Shancough .	146 3 15	Sligo . .	Tirerrill . .	Shancough . .	Boyle . .	IV.	241
19	Shancroaghan .	145 1 9h	Cavan . .	Tullyhunco . .	Killashandra .	Cavan . .	III.	99
6	Shancrock .	778 2 39	Sligo . .	Carbury . .	Rossinver . .	Sligo . .	IV.	223
7	Shancurragh .	45 0 12	Leitrim . .	Rosclogher . .	Killasnet . .	Manorhamilton	IV.	110
7	Shancurragh, Barr of	53 3 3	Leitrim . .	Rosclogher . .	Killasnet . .	Manorhamilton	IV.	110
23	Shancurry .	270 2 27	Leitrim . .	Leitrim . .	Kiltoghert . .	Cark. on Shannon	IV.	102
43	Shandangan .	43 0 16	Clare . .	Bunratty Upper .	Quin . .	Tulla . .	II.	10
17	Shandangan .	320 2 17	Clare . .	Inchiquin . .	Killinaboy . .	Corrofin . .	II.	27
24	Shandangan .	14 3 0	Limerick . .	Coonagh . .	Tuoghcluggin .	Tipperary .	II.	236
51	Shandangan .	119 2 1	Tipperary, S.R.	Clanwilliam . .	Donohill . .	Tipperary .	II.	307
43	Shandangan East .	203 3 33i	Clare . .	Bunratty Lower .	Kilmurry . .	Tulla . .	II.	6
71, 83	Shandangan East .	605 3 33	Cork, E.R. .	East Muskerry .	Cannaway . .	Macroom .	II.	102
43	Shandangan West .	208 3 39j	Clare . .	Bunratty Lower .	Kilmurry . .	Tulla . .	II.	6
71, 83	Shandangan West .	494 3 25	Cork, E.R. .	East Muskerry .	Cannaway . .	Macroom .	II.	102
33, 34	Shanderry .	1,020 0 9	King's Co. .	Upper Philipstown .	Clonyhurk . .	Mountmellick .	I.	143
16	Shanderry .	101 0 4	Queen's Co. .	Upperwoods . .	Offerlane . .	Mountmellick .	I.	252
31	Shandon .	160 2 37	Waterford .	Decies without Drum	Dungarvan . .	Dungarvan .	II.	356
31	Shandon Island	2 1 6	Waterford .	Decies without Drum	Dungarvan . .	Dungarvan .	II.	356
19	Shandrim .	1,323 3 25k	Donegal . .	Inishowen West .	Fahan Lower .	Inishowen .	III.	120
38	Shandrum .	437 0 5	Clare . .	Ibrickan . .	Kilmurry . .	Kilrush . .	II.	24
2	Shandrum .	625 3 6	Cork, E.R. .	Orrery and Kilmore .	Shandrum . .	Kilmallock .	II.	110
120	Shandrum .	243 3 2	Cork, W.R. .	East Carbery (W.D.)	Drinagh . .	Skibbereen .	II.	131
94	Shandrum .	393 0 24	Kerry . .	Glanarought . .	Kilgarvan . .	Kenmare . .	II.	188
77	Shandrum .	198 3 23	Mayo . .	Burrishoole . .	Kilmeena . .	Newport . .	IV.	122
105	Shandrum Beg .	130 2 0l	Cork, W.R. .	Bantry . .	Kilmocomoge .	Bantry . .	II.	121
105	Shandrum More .	212 1 33	Cork, W.R. .	Bantry . .	Kilmocomoge .	Bantry . .	II.	121
24	Shane . . .	180 3 26	Monaghan .	Cremorne . .	Ballybay . .	Castleblayney .	III.	259
17	Shanecrackan Beg .	258 3 29	Armagh . .	Oneilland West .	Mullaghbrack .	Banbridge .	III.	54
17	Shanecrackan More	307 0 26	Armagh . .	Oneilland West .	Mullaghbrack .	Banbridge .	III.	54
18	Shaneglish .	239 1 36	Armagh . .	Orior Lower . .	Ballymore . .	Banbridge .	III.	55
42	Shanemullagh .	263 3 32	Londonderry .	Loughinsholin .	Magherafelt . .	Magherafelt .	III.	243
14	Shanemullagh .	125 0 34	Monaghan .	Cremorne . .	Clontibret . .	Monaghan .	III.	261
50, 55	Shaneoguestown .	526 2 6	Antrim . .	Lower Massereene .	Muckamore (Grange of)	Antrim . .	III.	29
13, 14	Shanes . .	1,169 1 6	Antrim . .	Upper Dunluce .	Loughguile . .	Ballymoney .	III.	20
49	Shanes Castle .	131 1 37	Antrim . .	Upper Toome . .	Antrim . .	Antrim . .	III.	33
43, 49	Shane's Castle Park	1,913 0 23m	Antrim . .	Upper Toome . .	Drummaul . .	Antrim . .	III.	34
20, 21	Shanettra . .	1,420 1 9	Mayo . .	Tirawley . .	Kilfian . .	Killala . .	IV.	169
66	Shanganagh .	174 0 16	Clare . .	Moyarta . .	Moyarta . .	Kilrush . .	II.	34
26	Shanganagh .	702 2 36	Dublin . .	Rathdown . .	Rathmichael .	Rathdown .	I.	37
20, 26	Shanganagh Beg .	297 0 25m	Queen's Co. .	Ballyadams . .	Tankardstown .	Athy . .	I.	232
20, 26	Shanganagh More .	358 0 33	Queen's Co. .	Ballyadams . .	Tankardstown .	Athy . .	I.	232
14	Shanganhill . .	137 1 28	Dublin . .	Coolock . .	St. Margarets .	Dublin North .	I.	29
10	Shanganny . .	50 0 16	Kilkenny .	Fassadinin . .	Coolcraheen .	Kilkenny . .	I.	89

(a) Including 7A. 2R. 2P. water.
(b) Including 19A. 1R. 26P. water.
(c) Including 7A. 3R. 8P. water.
(d) Including 47A. 3R. 13P. water.
(e) Including 19A. 1R. 4P. water.

(f) Including 20A. 2R. 0P. water.
(g) Including 3A. 0R. 23P. water.
(h) Including 45A. 3R. 18P. water.
(i) Including 13A. 1R. 13P. water.
(j) Including 3A. 2R. 28P. water.

(k) Including 7A. 1R. 6P. water.
(l) Including 0A. 2R. 25P. water.
(m) Including 53A. 2R. 8P. water.
(n) Including 1A. 2R. 16P. River Barrow.

No. of Sheet of the Ordnance Survey Maps.	Townlands and Towns.	Area in Statute Acres.	County.	Barony.	Parish.	Poor Law Union in 1857.	Townland Census of 1851, Part I.	
		A. R. P.					Vol.	Page
10	Shanganny	264 2 33	Kilkenny	Fassadinin	Grangemaccomb	Kilkenny	I.	89
10	Shanganny	104 0 8	Kilkenny	Fassadinin	Mayne	Kilkenny	I.	90
17	Shangarry	678 0 37	Carlow	Forth	Myshall	Carlow	I.	5
106	Shangarry	409 3 2	Galway	Leitrim	Abbeygormacan	Loughrea	IV.	50
106	Shangarry	183 0 5	Galway	Leitrim	Tynagh	Loughrea	IV.	56
36	Shangarry	201 3 17	Limerick	Glenquin	Monagay	Newcastle	II.	247
55	Shangarry	1,156 0 4	Tipperary, S.R.	Slievardagh	Mowney	Callan	II.	335
117	Shangorman or Inishangan	16 3 38	Mayo	Kilmaine	Ballinrobe	Ballinrobe	IV.	153
93, 94	Shangort	48 3 31	Galway	Galway	Rahoon	Galway	IV.	38
99, 109	Shangort	265 1 27	Mayo	Carra	Ballyovey	Ballinrobe	IV.	126
16	Shangownagh	67 1 29	Queen's Co.	Upperwoods	Offerlane	Abbeyleix	I.	252
18, 19	Shanid Lower	552 0 37	Limerick	Shanid	Kilmoylan	Glin	II.	256
19	Shanid Upper	159 2 18	Limerick	Shanid	Kilmoylan	Glin	II.	256
14	Shaninish	134 0 35	Antrim	Lower Glenarm	Layd	Ballycastle	III.	23
38, 39	Shankey	95 3 27	Tyrone	Dungannon Middle	Donaghenry	Cookstown	III.	301
6	Shankill	173 3 28	Armagh	Oneilland East	Shankill	Lurgan	III.	51
37	Shankill	100 2 17	Cavan	Clanmahon	Ballymachugh	Cavan	III.	76
34, 41	Shankill	723 0 14	Down	Upper Iveagh, Up. pt.	Aghaderg	Banbridge	III.	174
26	Shankill	1,182 0 39	Dublin	Rathdown	Rathmichael	Rathdown	I.	37
15	Shankill	213 2 27	Fermanagh	Magheraboy	Devenish	Enniskillen	III.	211
22	Shankill	206 1 35	Fermanagh	Tirkennedy	Derryvullan	Enniskillen	III.	221
69	Shankill	198 1 28	Galway	Clare	Annaghdown	Galway	IV.	16
45,46,59,60	Shankill	535 3 30	Galway	Killian	Moylough	Mountbellew	IV.	45
16, 21	Shankill	1,880 0 7	Kilkenny	Gowran	Shankill	Kilkenny	I.	99
27	Shankill	259 1 19	Monaghan	Cremorne	Aghnamullen	Carrickmacross	III.	258
8, 12	Shankill	243 0 25d	Monaghan	Dartree	Clones	Clones	III.	265
16, 22	Shankill	365 0 6	Roscommon	Roscommon	Shankill	Strokestown	IV.	213
2, 6	Shankill	1,338 1 25	Wicklow	Lower Talbotstown	Kilbride	Naas	I.	361
31	Shankill East	308 2 0	Galway	Tiaquin	Kilkerrin	Glennamaddy	IV.	77
21	Shankill Lower	235 3 06	Cavan	Upper Loughtee	Annagelliff	Cavan	III.	82
21	Shankill Upper	276 1 10	Cavan	Upper Loughtee	Annagelliff	Cavan	III.	82
31	Shankill West	301 3 32c	Galway	Tiaquin	Kilkerrin	Glennamaddy	IV.	77
26,27,33,34	Shankough	373 1 12	Roscommon	Ballymoe	Drumatemple	Castlereagh	IV.	191
94	Shanlaragh	374 0 35	Cork, W.R.	East Carbery (W.D.)	Kilmichael	Dunmanway	II.	134
17	Shanlis	904 0 39	Louth	Ardee	Shanlis	Ardee	I.	174
47	Shanliss Lower	134 2 28	Tyrone	Dungannon Middle	Clonoe	Dungannon	III.	300
47	Shanliss Upper	141 0 0	Tyrone	Dungannon Middle	Clonoe	Dungannon	III.	300
11, 18	Shanlongford	295 2 34	Londonderry	Coleraine	Aghadowey	Coleraine	III.	230
11, 18	Shanlongford	360 1 24	Londonderry	Coleraine	Errigal	Coleraine	III.	232
36	Shanlothe	72 3 23	Meath	Lower Moyfenrath	Trim	Trim	I.	212
51	Shanlyre	195 3 15	Cork, E.R.	Barretts	Whitechurch	Cork	II.	50
45	Shanmaghry	426 3 10	Tyrone	Dungannon Middle	Pomeroy	Dungannon	III.	304
61	Shanmoy	118 2 25	Tyrone	Dungannon Middle	Clonfeacle	Dungannon	III.	300
26	Shanmullagh	94 0 29	Fermanagh	Clanawley	Cleenish	Enniskillen	III.	191
6	Shanmullagh	67 0 32	Fermanagh	Lurg	Magheraculmoney	Lowtherstown	III.	208
16	Shanmullagh	200 2 33	Fermanagh	Tirkennedy	Trory	Enniskillen	III.	223
2, 5	Shanmullagh	783 2 8	Longford	Longford	Killoe	Longford	I.	159
3, 6	Shanmullagh	229 3 22	Louth	Upper Dundalk	Creggan	Dundalk	I.	178
10, 14	Shanmullagh	143 3 3	Monaghan	Cremorne	Clontibret	Monaghan	III.	261
31	Shanmullagh	127 2 36d	Monaghan	Farney	Killanny	Carrickmacross	III.	272
14	Shanmullagh	213 0 39	Monaghan	Monaghan	Tullycorbet	Monaghan	III.	281
3	Shanmullagh	161 0 16	Monaghan	Trough	Errigal Trough	Clogher	III.	285
8	Shanmullagh or Ballycullen	239 0 27	Armagh	Armagh	Clonfeacle	Armagh	III.	43
49	Shanmullagh East	532 3 38	Tyrone	Omagh East	Kilskeery	Lowtherstown	III.	314
50	Shanmullagh Glebe	142 2 39	Tyrone	Omagh East	Dromore	Omagh	III.	311
8	Shanmullagh North	36 3 30	Monaghan	Monaghan	Clones	Monaghan	III.	275
12	Shanmullagh South	159 1 8	Monaghan	Dartree	Clones	Clones	III.	265
49	Shanmullagh West	508 2 27	Tyrone	Omagh East	Kilskeery	Lowtherstown	III.	314
5	Shannabooly	146 0 17	Limerick	Pubblebrien	St. Munchins	Limerick	II.	254
59	Shannacool	449 1 16	Clare	Clonderalaw	Killadysert	Killadysert	II.	16
41	Shannacool	95 2 36	Clare	Islands	Killone	Ennis	II.	30
64	Shannadonnell	530 3 7c	Galway	Ballynahinch	Moyrus	Clifden	IV.	13
53, 66	Shannadullaghaun	555 2 11f	Galway	Moycullen	Kilcummin	Oughterard	IV.	68
93	Shannafreaghoge	185 2 10	Galway	Moycullen	Rahoon	Galway	IV.	72
90	Shannagh	309 1 32	Donegal	Banagh	Kilcar	Glenties	III.	109
70	Shannagh	115 0 17	Donegal	Raphoe	Raphoe	Strabane	III.	141
100, 104	Shannagh	961 2 22	Donegal	Tirhugh	Drumhome	Donegal	III.	147
32	Shannagh	84 1 16	Leitrim	Mohill	Mohill	Mohill	IV.	108
35	Shannaghan	878 3 31	Down	Upper Iveagh, Lr.pt.	Newry	Banbridge	III.	173
18	Shannagh Beg	298 2 3	Galway	Tiaquin	Kilkerrin	Glennamaddy	IV.	77
8, 9	Shannaghdoo	364 0 30g	Donegal	Kilmacrenan	Clondavaddog	Millford	III.	125

(a) Including 23A. 0R. 22P. water.
(b) Including 5A. 0R. 7P. water.
(c) Including 1A. 3R. 1P. water.
(d) Including 5A. 2R. 30P. water.
(e) Including 11A. 3R. 5P. water.
(f) Including 33A. 2R. 19P. water.
(g) Including 36A. 2R. 11P. water.

No. of Sheet of the Ordnance Survey Maps.	Townlands and Towns.	Area in Statute Acres.			County.	Barony.	Parish.	Poor Law Union in 1857.	Townland Census of 1851, Part I.	
		A.	R.	P.					Vol.	Page
18	Shannagh More .	500	0	17	Galway . .	Tiaquin . . .	Kilkerrin . .	Glennamaddy .	IV.	77
80, 92	Shannagurraun .	1,225	2	16a	Galway .	Moycullen .	Moycullen . .	Galway . .	IV.	71
69	Shannakea Beg .	296	2	26	Clare . .	Clonderalaw .	Kilfiddane . .	Killadysert .	II.	15
69	Shannakea More .	822	3	10b	Clare . .	Clonderalaw .	Kilfiddane . .	Killadysert .	II.	15
38, 52	Shannakeela .	1,907	2	34c	Galway .	Ballynahinch . .	Moyrus . .	Clifden . .	IV.	13
36, 44	Shannaknock .	243	1	13	Clare . .	Tulla Lower .	Killokennedy . .	Limerick . .	II.	36
63	Shannakyle .	275	3	28	Clare . .	Bunratty Lower .	St. Patricks .	Limerick . .	II.	7
49	Shannanagower .	139	3	25d	Galway .	Ballynahinch . .	Ballindoon .	Clifden . .	IV.	10
66, 67, 79	Shannapheasteen .	3,104	2	39e	Galway .	Moycullen .	Kilcummin . .	Galway . .	IV.	68
42	Shannaragh .	936	1	32	Tyrone .	Omagh East .	Dromore . .	Omagh . .	III.	311
48	Shannasmore .	329	3	9	Mayo . .	Tirawley .	Ballynahaglish .	Ballina . .	IV.	164
38, 39	Shannaunnafeola .	2,888	2	1f	Galway .	Moycullen .	Kilcummin . .	Oughterard .	IV.	68
52	Shannavarra .	929	2	4g	Galway .	Moycullen .	Kilcummin . .	Oughterard .	IV.	68
39	Shannawagh .	100	2	1	Galway .	Moycullen .	Kilcummin . .	Oughterard .	IV.	68
64	Shannawirra .	796	1	31h	Galway .	Ballynahinch . .	Moyrus . .	Clifden . .	IV.	13
53, 66	Shannawona .	1,121	3	12i	Galway .	Moycullen .	Kilcummin . .	Oughterard .	IV.	68
92	Shannawoneen .	1,030	2	31j	Galway .	Moycullen .	Killannin . .	Galway . .	IV.	70
64, 65	Shannera Lower .	829	1	25	Kerry .	Dunkerron North .	Killorglin .	Cahersiveen .	II.	181
64,65,72,73	Shannera Upper .	709	3	34	Kerry .	Dunkerron North .	Killorglin .	Cahersiveen .	II.	181
35, 40	Shannock .	77	2	24	Fermanagh .	Clankelly . .	Clones . .	Clones . .	III.	197
40	Shannock Green .	62	0	34	Fermanagh .	Clankelly . .	Clones . .	Clones . .	III.	197
13	SHANNONBRIDGE T.	—			King's Co. .	Garrycastle . .	Clonmacnoise .	Parsonstown .	I.	135
14	Shannon Eighter .	174	0	13	Sligo . .	Carbury . .	Calry . .	Sligo . .	IV.	220
3	Shannongrove .	476	1	21	Limerick . .	Kenry . . .	Ardcanny . .	Rathkeale .	II.	248
14	Shannonhall .	105	1	15	Tipperary, N.R. .	Lower Ormond .	Dromineer .	Nenagh . .	II.	283
22	SHANNONHARBOUR T.				King's Co. .	Garrycastle . .	Gallen . .	Parsonstown .	I.	136
70	Shannon Lower .	185	2	24	Donegal . .	Raphoe . .	Clonleigh . .	Strabane . .	III.	135
70	Shannon Middle .	197	2	38	Donegal . .	Raphoe . .	Clonleigh . .	Strabane . .	III.	135
13	Shannon Navigation	0	2	27	King's Co. .	Garrycastle . .	Clonmacnoise .	Parsonstown .	I.	135
14, 15	Shannon Oughter .	184	2	12	Sligo . .	Carbury . .	Calry . .	Sligo . .	IV.	220
86, 87	Shannonpark . .	201	2	29	Cork, E.R. .	Kerrycurrihy . .	Carrigaline .	Cork . .	II.	92
11	Shannonspark East .	34	0	7	Sligo . .	Tireragh . .	Easky . .	Dromore West .	IV.	234
11	Shannonspark West .	10	2	38	Sligo . .	Tireragh . .	Easky . .	Dromore West .	IV.	234
14	Shannonvale . .	180	2	28	Tipperary, N.R. .	Lower Ormond .	Dromineer .	Nenagh . .	II.	283
10, 11	Shannonview . .	31	3	13	Limerick . .	Connello Lower .	Askeaton . .	Rathkeale .	II.	227
25	Shannow . .	178	2	26	Cavan . .	Clanmahon . .	Denn . .	Cavan . .	III.	76
31	Shannow Lower .	283	1	35	Cavan . .	Clanmahon . .	Ballintemple .	Cavan . .	III.	75
31	Shannow Upper .	167	2	17	Cavan . .	Clanmahon . .	Ballintemple .	Cavan . .	III.	75
15, 16	Shannow Wood .	218	0	34	Cavan . .	Tullygarvey . .	Annagh . .	Cavan . .	III.	87
23, 24	Shanog . .	68	3	32	Tyrone .	Omagh West . .	Ardstraw . .	Castlederg .	III.	315
18	Shanonagh . .	533	2	35	Westmeath .	Moygoish . .	Templeoran .	Mullingar .	I.	281
10, 17	Shanonny East .	338	1	39	Tyrone .	Strabane Lower .	Ardstraw . .	Gortin . .	III.	319
10, 17	Shanonny West .	273	1	18	Tyrone .	Strabane Lower .	Ardstraw . .	Strabane . .	III.	319
46	Shanoo . . .	111	3	25	Wexford .	Bargy . . .	Kilcowan . .	Wexford . .	I.	305
36	Shanowle . .	630	3	27	Wexford .	Shelmaliere West .	Horetown . .	New Ross .	I.	333
3, 4, 11 12	Shanpallas . .	221	1	1	Limerick . .	Kenry . . .	Chapelrussell .	Rathkeale .	II.	248
33	Shanraa . .	87	2	35	Fermanagh .	Clanawley . .	Kinawley . .	Enniskillen .	III.	194
25	Shanragh . .	250	2	11	Queen's Co. .	Ballyadams . .	Rathaspick .	Athy . .	I.	232
31	Shanrah . .	129	2	29	Monaghan .	Farney . .	Killanny . .	Carrickmacross .	III.	272
87, 90	Shanrahan . .	3,870	1	6	Tipperary, S.R. .	Iffa and Offa West .	Shanrahan . .	Clogheen . .	II.	320
35	Shanraheen . .	164	2	25	Kildare . .	Narragh&RebanWest	Kilberry . .	Athy . .	I.	68
35	Shanrath . .	6	3	15	Kildare . .	Narragh&RebanWest	St. Johns . .	Athy . .	I.	68
36, 44	Shanrath . .	343	0	23	Limerick . .	Glenquin . .	Mahoonagh .	Newcastle .	II.	246
35	Shanrath East .	123	3	1	Kildare . .	Narragh&RebanWest	St. Michaels .	Athy . .	I.	68
35	Shanrath West .	111	0	2	Kildare . .	Narragh&RebanWest	St. Michaels .	Athy . .	I.	68
28	Shanraw . .	109	3	30	Leitrim . .	Leitrim . . .	Kiltubbrid .	Car^k. on Shannon	IV.	104
90	Shanrawy . .	100	0	11	Mayo . .	Carra . . .	Rosslee . .	Castlebar .	IV.	130
9	Shanreagh . .	157	3	28k	Londonderry .	Keenaght . .	Tamlaght Finlagan .	New T^nLimavady	III.	237
28, 35	Shanrod . .	668	0	16	Down . .	Upper Iveagh, Lr. pt.	Garvaghy . .	Banbridge .	III.	173
28, 31	Shanroe . .	590	0	2	Armagh . .	Orior Upper . .	Forkhill . .	Newry . .	III.	57
8	Shanroe . .	83	3	2	Monaghan .	Monaghan . .	Clones . .	Monaghan .	III.	275
36	Shantalliv . .	115	0	13	Kerry . .	Corkaguiny . .	Killiney . .	Dingle . .	II.	178
18, 31	Shantallow . .	154	1	5	Galway .	Ballymoe . .	Clonbern . .	Glennamaddy .	IV.	7
43, 44	Shantallow . .	287	2	14	Galway .	Clare . . .	Killererin .	Tuam . .	IV.	21
104	Shantallow . .	114	2	7	Galway .	Dunkellin . .	Ardrahan . .	Gort . .	IV.	27
95	Shantallow . .	198	0	34	Galway .	Dunkellin . .	Athenry . .	Galway . .	IV.	27
94	Shantallow . .	123	2	22	Galway .	Galway . .	Rahoon . .	Galway . .	IV.	38
58	Shantallow . .	117	2	2	Galway .	Tiaquin . .	Abbeyknockmoy .	Tuam . .	IV.	75
13	Shantallow . .	1,178	0	27	Londonderry .	North West Liberties of Londonderry .	Templemore .	Londonderry .	III.	247
111	Shantallow . .	330	0	10	Mayo . .	Kilmaine . .	Kilcommon . .	Ballinrobe .	IV.	155
15	Shantally . .	166	3	11	Armagh . .	Tiranny . .	Tynan . .	Armagh . .	III.	60
60	Shantavny . .	160	1	2	Tyrone .	Dungannon Lower .	Carnteel . .	Clogher . .	III.	298

(a) Including 24A. 3R. 4P. water.　　(e) Including 21A. 3R. 0P. water.　　(i) Including 44A. 3R. 9P. water.
(b) Including 11A. 1R. 25P. water.　　(f) Including 55A. 0R. 36P. water.　　(j) Including 6A. 1R. 38P. water.
(c) Including 72A. 1R. 24P. water.　　(g) Including 37A. 1R. 35P. water.　　(k) Including 3A. 1R. 15P. water.
(d) Including 3A. 0R. 20P. water.　　(h) Including 39A. 3R. 39P. water.

No. of Sheet of the Ordnance Survey Maps.	Townlands and Towns.	Area in Statute Acres. A. R. P.	County.	Barony.	Parish.	Poor Law Union in 1857.	Townland Census of 1851, Part I. Vol.	Page
52	Shantavny Irish	790 0 16	Tyrone	Clogher	Errigal Keerogue	Clogher	III.	295
52	Shantavny Scotch	587 0 39	Tyrone	Clogher	Errigal Keerogue	Clogher	III.	295
21	Shantemon	396 0 15a	Cavan	Upper Loughtee	Castleterra	Cavan	III.	83
27	Shantonagh	220 1 0b	Monaghan	Cremorne	Aghnamullen	Castleblayney	III.	258
18	Shantonagh	150 1 14	Monaghan	Cremorne	Ballybay	Castleblayney	III.	259
58	Shantonagh	346 0 27	Tyrone	Clogher	Clogher	Clogher	III.	293
27	Shantony	151 0 23c	Monaghan	Cremorne	Aghnamullen	Carrickmacross	III.	258
45	Shantraud	202 1 32	Clare	Tulla Lower	Killaloe	Scarriff	II.	35
12, 21	Shantraud	40 1 21	Limerick	Kenry	Adare	Croom	II.	248
33	Shantulla	72 2 1	Clare	Islands	Drumcliff	Ennis	II.	30
130, 139	Shantullig North	271 3 20	Cork, W.R.	West Carbery (W.D.)	Skull	Skull	II.	146
139	Shantullig South	737 1 34	Cork, W.R.	West Carbery (W.D.)	Skull	Skull	II.	146
25	Shantully	56 0 36	Cavan	Clanmahon	Kilmore	Cavan	III.	78
20	Shantum	179 0 10	Longford	Ardagh	Mostrim	Granard	I.	153
81	Shanvaghera	449 0 32	Mayo	Costello	Knock	Claremorris	IV.	143
28	Shanvaghey	184 3 8	Queen's Co.	Clarmallagh	Bordwell	Donaghmore	I.	237
33	Shanvally	101 2 38	Fermanagh	Clanawley	Kinawley	Enniskillen	III.	194
30	Shanvally	85 1 3	Galway	Dunmore	Tuam	Tuam	IV.	36
114	Shanvally	59 2 32d	Galway	Kiltartan	Kilthomas	Gort	IV.	49
126	Shanvally	211 2 3	Galway	Longford	Lickmolassy	Portumna	IV.	61
66	Shanvally	1,006 2 8e	Galway	Moycullen	Kilcummin	Oughterard	IV.	68
24	Shanvally	107 3 34	King's Co.	Ballycowan	Lynally	Tullamore	I.	128
78	Shanvally	57 3 10	Mayo	Carra	Breaghwy	Castlebar	IV.	127
71, 80	Shanvally	275 2 37	Mayo	Gallen	Killedan	Swineford	IV.	150
32	Shanvally	66 0 24	Queen's Co.	Slievemargy	Killeshin	Carlow	I.	246
7	Shanvally	138 3 2	Tipperary, N.R.	Lower Ormond	Terryglass	Borrisokane	II.	288
109	Shanvallyard	589 0 1	Mayo	Carra	Ballyovey	Ballinrobe	IV.	126
118	Shanvallybeg	47 1 0	Cork, W.R.	Bantry	Kilmocomoge	Bantry	II.	121
10	*Shanvallybeg*	10 3 28	Galway	Ballynahinch	Ballynakill	Clifden	IV.	12
77	*Shanvallybeg*	77 1 4f	Mayo	Burrishoole	Kilmeena	Westport	IV.	122
97, 107	Shanvallybeg	1,170 1 26g	Mayo	Murrisk	Oughaval	Westport	IV.	162
112	Shanvallyboght	118 0 33	Mayo	Clanmorris	Kilvine	Claremorris	IV.	134
13	Shanvallycahill	497 2 21h	Galway	Ross	Ballinchalla	Ballinrobe	IV.	72
67	Shanvallyhugh	126 0 28	Mayo	Burrishoole	Burrishoole	Newport	IV.	120
70	Shanvallyshane	234 3 7	Cork, W.R.	West Muskerry	Kilnamartry	Macroom	II.	160
7	Shanvaus	220 2 25	Leitrim	Rosclogher	Killasnet	Manorhamilton	IV.	110
5, 6	Shanvey	203 3 24i	Londonderry	Keenaght	Aghanloo	NewTⁿLimavady	III.	234
20, 28	Shanvodinnaun	2,277 3 29	Mayo	Tirawley	Moygawnagh	Killala	IV.	171
33	Shanvogh	254 1 16	Clare	Islands	Drumcliff	Ennis	II.	30
106	Shanvoher	35 2 25	Galway	Leitrim	Duniry	Loughrea	IV.	53
28	Shanvolahan	1,196 0 9	Mayo	Tirawley	Crossmolina	Ballina	IV.	166
87	Shanvoley	42 1 13	Galway	Clonmacnowen	Clontuskert	Ballinasloe	IV.	25
59	Shanvoley	677 0 24	Mayo	Carra	Turlough	Castlebar	IV.	131
3	Shanvoley	25 3 21	Roscommon	Boyle	Kilbryan	Boyle	IV.	195
49, 61	Shanwar	328 1 18j	Mayo	Gallen	Toomore	Swineford	IV.	151
10, 18, 19	Sharagore	798 1 33	Donegal	Inishowen West	Desertegny	Inishowen	III.	120
38	Sharavogue	472 0 2	King's Co.	Clonlisk	Kilcolman	Parsonstown	I.	130
31	*Shark Island*	3 1 11	Down	Lecale Lower	Saul	Downpatrick	III.	180
54	Sharon Glebe	103 2 4	Donegal	Raphoe	Raymoghy	Londonderry	III.	142
4, 5	Sharragh	774 0 0	Tipperary, N.R.	Lower Ormond	Dorrha	Parsonstown	II.	283
13, 18	Sharvoge	242 1 32	Longford	Moydow	Killashee	Longford	I.	162
37, 43	Sharvogues	854 0 22k	Antrim	Upper Toome	Drummaul	Antrim	III.	34
4	Shasgar	248 3 14	Leitrim	Rosclogher	Rossinver	Ballyshannon	IV.	112
7, 8	Shasmore	356 3 22	Leitrim	Rosclogher	Rossinver	Manorhamilton	IV.	112
16	Shass	315 3 10	Leitrim	Drumahaire	Inishmagrath	Manorhamilton	IV.	97
33	*Shave Island*	3 2 10	Fermanagh	Tirkennedy	Cleenish	Enniskillen	III.	220
36	Shawstown	147 2 1	Wexford	Shelmaliere West	Horetown	New Ross	I.	333
20	Sheaffield North	138 3 11	Kilkenny	Gowran	Gowran	Kilkenny	I.	95
20	Sheaffield South	20 2 2	Kilkenny	Gowran	Gowran	Kilkenny	I.	95
28, 31	Shean	985 1 32	Armagh	Orior Upper	Forkill	Newry	III.	57
37	Shean	75 1 22	Cork, E.R.	Condons&Clangibbon	Lismore and Mocollop	Fermoy	II.	62
120	Shean	63 0 27	Cork, W.R.	East Carbery (W.D.)	Fanlobbus	Dunmanway	II.	132
9	Shean	587 0 6	Fermanagh	Magheraboy	Inishmacsaint	Ballyshannon	III.	213
12, 20	Shean	695 0 26	King's Co.	Coolestown	Monasteroris	Edenderry	I.	133
20, 28	Shean Beg	163 3 27	Waterford	Coshmore&Coshbride	Lismore and Mocollop	Lismore	II.	347
77	Sheanliss	252 3 12	Cork, E.R.	Imokilly	Cloyne	Middleton	II.	85
62, 73	Shean Lower	237 1 4	Cork, E.R.	East Muskerry	Garrycloyne	Cork	II.	103
20, 28	Shean More	480 0 34	Waterford	Coshmore&Coshbride	Lismore and Mocollop	Lismore	II.	347
58	Sheans East	252 1 11	Kerry	Magunihy	Aglish	Killarney	II.	200
58	Sheans West	116 1 38	Kerry	Magunihy	Aglish	Killarney	II.	200
62	Shean Upper	230 1 11	Cork, E.R.	East Muskerry	Garrycloyne	Cork	II.	103
19,20,23,24	Sheastown	599 2 22l	Kilkenny	Shillelogher	Kilferagh	Kilkenny	I.	115
40,41,45,46	Sheastown	180 3 17	Wexford	Bargy	Kilcavan	Wexford	I.	305

(a) Including 6A. 0R. 19P. water.
(b) Including 27A. 0R. 30P. water.
(c) Including 50A. 3R. 13P. water.
(d) Including 6A. 2R. 8P. water.

(e) Including 34A. 3R. 8P. water.
(f) Including 6A. 2R. 33P. water.
(g) Including 45A. 1R. 3P. water.
(h) Including 20A. 0R. 34P. water.

(i) Including 6A. 0R. 32P. water.
(j) Including 20A. 3R. 15P. water.
(k) Including 9A. 2R. 38P. water.
(l) Including 18A. 3R. 16P. River Nore.

No. of Sheet of the Ordnance Survey Maps.	Townlands and Towns.	Area in Statute Acres.			County.	Barony.	Parish.	Poor Law Union in 1857.	Townland Census of 1851, Part I.	
		A.	R.	P.					Vol.	Page
6	Shee	196	1	31	Monaghan	Monaghan	Tedavnet	Monaghan	III.	279
17, 20	Sheean	262	0	18	Carlow	Forth	Myshall	Carlow	I.	5
34	Sheean	163	3	36	Kildare	Narragh & Reban West	Churchtown	Athy	I.	67
31	Sheean	426	1	25	Kildare	Narragh & Reban West	Kilberry	Athy	I.	68
16, 17	Sheean	316	1	18	Kildare	Offaly East	Rathangan	Edenderry	I.	71
1	Sheean	38	3	9	Leitrim	Rosclogher	Rossinver	Ballyshannon	IV.	112
77, 88	Sheean	381	0	25	Mayo	Burrishoole	Islandeady	Westport	IV.	121
27, 36	Sheean	2,096	2	6a	Mayo	Erris	Kilcommon	Belmullet	IV.	144
51	Sheean	94	1	10	Roscommon	Athlone	Taghmaconnell	Athlone	IV.	185
35, 36	Sheean	56	2	16	Westmeath	Clonlonan	Kilcleagh	Athlone	I.	262
17	Sheean	75	1	39	Westmeath	Rathconrath	Rathconrath	Ballymahon	I.	284
34	Sheeanabeg (Robeck)	121	1	30	Wicklow	Ballinacor South	Ballykine	Rathdrum	I.	348
34	Sheeanabeg (Whaley)	127	1	12	Wicklow	Ballinacor South	Ballykine	Rathdrum	I.	348
34	Sheeana More	590	1	25	Wicklow	Ballinacor South	Ballykine	Rathdrum	I.	348
44	Sheeanmore	2,650	3	21	Mayo	Erris	Kilcommon	Newport	IV.	144
13	Sheeanmore	169	3	19	Sligo	Tireragh	Skreen	Dromore West	IV.	236
59	Sheeans	868	0	24	Mayo	Carra	Turlough	Castlebar	IV.	131
48	Sheeaun	1,302	3	4b	Clare	Clonderalaw	Kilmihil	Kilrush	II.	17
40	Sheeaun	708	2	18	Clare	Islands	Kilmaley	Ennis	II.	31
20,21,28,29	Sheeaun	631	0	31	Clare	Tulla Upper	Moynoe	Scarriff	II.	40
122, 128	Sheeaun	356	3	35	Galway	Kiltartan	Kilmacduagh	Gort	IV.	48
118	Sheeaun	51	3	9	Galway	Longford	Kilmalinoge	Portumna	IV.	59
72, 85	Sheeaun	178	1	39	Galway	Tiaquin	Clonkeen	Loughrea	IV.	76
71	Sheeaunpark	118	3	14	Galway	Clare	Lackagh	Galway	IV.	23
92	Sheeaunroe	192	1	34	Galway	Moycullen	Moycullen	Galway	IV.	71
117	Sheeaunrush	54	2	5	Galway	Longford	Lickmolassy	Portumna	IV.	61
22	Sheeauns	666	2	11c	Galway	Ballynahinch	Ballynakill	Clifden	IV.	12
34	Sheebeg	126	2	18	Fermanagh	Magherastephana	Aghalurcher	Lisnaskea	III.	217
24, 28	Sheebeg	109	2	12	Leitrim	Leitrim	Kiltubbrid	Car*. on Shannon	IV.	104
12	Sheefin	295	1	24	Westmeath	Corkaree	Taghmon	Mullingar	I.	264
28	Sheegeeragh	182	3	30	Roscommon	Roscommon	Killukin	Strokestown	IV.	211
3, 5, 6	Sheegorey	716	2	30	Roscommon	Boyle	Boyle	Boyle	IV.	194
107	Sheegys	224	1	2	Donegal	Tirhugh	Kilbarron	Ballyshannon	III.	148
12	Sheehane	73	2	29	Tipperary, N.R.	Ikerrin	Roscrea	Roscrea	II.	276
36	Sheehaun (Hughes)	17	0	34	Roscommon	Ballintober South	Kilgefin	Roscommon	IV.	189
36	Sheehaun (Morton)	172	0	11	Roscommon	Ballintober South	Kilgefin	Roscommon	IV.	189
33	Sheehinny	125	1	21	Fermanagh	Knockninny	Kinawley	Lisnaskea	III.	202
3	Sheelagh	290	0	23	Louth	Upper Dundalk	Creggan	Dundalk	I.	178
17	Sheelah's Island	0	1	38	Down	Ards Upper	Inishargy	Newtownards	III.	160
117	Sheelane Island	1	1	24	Cork, W.R.	Bear	Kilcaskan	Castletown	II.	123
6	Sheehruddera	103	2	0	Tipperary, N.R.	Lower Ormond	Terryglass	Borrisokane	II.	288
27	Sheemore	321	0	25	Leitrim	Leitrim	Kiltoghert	Car*. on Shannon	IV.	102
6	Sheemuldoon	400	3	23	Fermanagh	Lurg	Magheraculmoney	Lowtherstown	III.	208
17, 18	Sheena	121	2	23	Leitrim	Drumahaire	Inishmagrath	Manorhamilton	IV.	97
39, 40	Sheeny	80	3	0	Fermanagh	Coole	Galloon	Clones	III.	200
16	Sheeny	154	1	25	Meath	Upper Kells	Kells	Kells	I.	206
23, 24	Sheepgrange	496	1	37	Louth	Ferrard	Tullyallen	Drogheda	I.	183
13, 14	Sheephill	349	1	28	Dublin	Castleknock	Castleknock	Dublin North	I.	24
20	Sheephouse	373	3	19	Meath	Lower Duleek	Donore	Drogheda	I.	195
47	Sheephouse	92	0	31	Wexford	Bargy	Mulrankin	Wexford	I.	307
40, 45	Sheephouse	82	0	8	Wicklow	Arklow	Arklow	Rathdrum	I.	341
45	Sheepland Beg	170	2	3	Down	Lecale Lower	Dunsfort	Downpatrick	III.	179
38, 45	Sheepland More	615	3	29	Down	Lecale Lower	Dunsfort	Downpatrick	III.	179
13, 17	Sheepmoor	161	0	16	Dublin	Castleknock	Clonsilla	Celbridge	I.	24
40	Sheep Park	115	3	39d	Donegal	Boylagh	Templecrone	Glenties	III.	116
31	Sheepstown	572	1	38	Kilkenny	Knocktopher	Knocktopher	Thomastown	I.	112
8	Sheepstown	385	3	23	Westmeath	Delvin	Clonarney	Castletowndelvin	I.	265
46, 47	Sheeptown	598	2	8	Down	Lordship of Newry	Newry	Newry	III.	182
22	Sheeptown	95	0	22	Kilkenny	Crannagh	Kilmanagh	Callan	I.	86
22	Sheeptown	28	1	28	Kilkenny	Crannagh	Tullaghanbrogue	Callan	I.	87
65, 66	Sheepwalk	269	1	21	Cork, E.R.	Barrymore	Dungourney	Middleton	II.	54
43	Sheepwalk	51	0	39	Fermanagh	Clankelly	Drummully	Clones	III.	197
99	Sheepwalk	145	0	17	Galway	Clonmacnowen	Clontuskert	Ballinasloe	IV.	25
9	Sheepwalk	91	3	28	Kerry	Clanmaurice	Rattoo	Listowel	II.	173
11	Sheepwalk	42	2	32	Louth	Louth	Louth	Dundalk	I.	184
9, 15	Sheepwalk	715	0	21	Roscommon	Frenchpark	Tibohine	Castlereagh	IV.	205
42	Sheepwalk	147	1	26	Wexford	Forth	Killiane	Wexford	I.	310
40	Sheepwalk	165	2	28	Wicklow	Arklow	Kilbride	Rathdrum	I.	345
27, 35	Sheepwalk East	311	1	30	Cork, E.R.	Condons&Clangibbon	Litter	Fermoy	II.	62
27, 35	Sheepwalk West	75	1	7	Cork, E.R.	Fermoy	Litter	Fermoy	II.	81
70	Sheereloon	121	3	36	Donegal	Raphoe	Clonleigh	Strabane	III.	135
16	Sheerevagh	225	2	37	Roscommon	Frenchpark	Kilnacumsy	Boyle	IV.	204
34	Sheerevagh	140	1	39	Sligo	Tirerrill	Kilmacallan	Sligo	IV.	240

(a) Including 11A. 2R. 5P. water.
(b) Including 14A. 2R. 14P. water.
(c) Including 33A. 3R. 30P. water.
(d) Including 3A. 3R. 17P. water.

No. of Sheet of the Ordnance Survey Maps.	Townlands and Towns.	Area in Statute Acres.	County.	Barony.	Parish.	Poor Law Union in 1857.	Townland Census of 1851, Part I.	
		A. R. P.					Vol.	Page
15	Sheeroe	29 2 12	Longford	Granard	Clonbroney	Granard	I.	155
23	Sheeroe	41 2 10	Longford	Shrule	Agharra	Ballymahon	I.	166
88	Sheeroe	138 2 24	Mayo	Murrisk	Aghagower	Westport	IV.	159
27	Sheetrim	817 0 38a	Armagh	Fews Upper	Creggan	Castleblayney	III.	48
15, 19	Sheetrim	202 2 37	Armagh	Tiranny	Tynan	Armagh	III.	60
33, 38	Sheetrim	163 1 12	Fermanagh	Knockninny	Kinawley	Lisnaskea	III.	202
24, 25	Sheetrim	224 1 2	Monaghan	Cremorne	Clontibret	Castleblayney	III.	261
9, 13	Sheetrim	142 3 39	Monaghan	Monaghan	Monaghan	Monaghan	III.	277
6, 9	Sheetrim	287 0 7	Monaghan	Monaghan	Tedavnet	Monaghan	III.	279
15	Sheevannan	359 1 12	Roscommon	Frenchpark	Tibohine	Castlereagh	IV.	205
27	Sheffield	181 0 2	Leitrim	Leitrim	Kiltoghert	Cark. on Shannon	IV.	103
66, 67	Sheheree	221 1 2	Kerry	Magunihy	Killarney	Killarney	II.	203
92, 93	Shehy Beg	720 1 8	Cork, W.R.	East Carbery (W.D.)	Inchigeelagh	Dunmanway	II.	132
93	Shehy More	645 0 23b	Cork, W.R.	East Carbery (W.D.)	Inchigeelagh	Dunmanway	II.	132
30	Sheiland	91 1 39	Armagh	Fews Upper	Creggan	Castleblayney	III.	48
33	Sheilstown	639 1 15	Wicklow	Ballinacor South	Moyne	Shillelagh	I.	356
39,40,44,45	Shelbaggan	1,151 2 37	Wexford	Shelburne	Rathroe	New Ross	I.	328
29	Shelbourne	35 2 30	King's Co.	Garrycastle	Lusmagh	Parsonstown	I.	137
12	Shellfield	35 0 33	Antrim	Lower Dunluce	Dunluce	Ballymoney	III.	17
46	Shellfield	54 3 33	Donegal	Kilmacrenan	Aughnish	Milford	III.	122
19	Shellumsrath	128 3 1	Kilkenny	Shillelogher	St. Patrick's	Kilkenny	I.	116
37, 42	ShelmaliereCommons	393 3 39	Wexford	Shelmaliere West	Carrick	Wexford	I.	332
37, 42	ShelmaliereCommons	760 0 5	Wexford	Shelmaliere West	Kilbrideglynn	Wexford	I.	334
41, 42	ShelmaliereCommons	606 3 12	Wexford	Shelmaliere West	Taghmon	Wexford	I.	335
40	Shelton	202 3 2	Wicklow	Arklow	Kilbride	Rathdrum	I.	345
40	Shelton Abbey	728 1 17	Wicklow	Arklow	Kilbride	Rathdrum	I.	345
13,14,18,19	Shelton North	929 0 31	Antrim	Upper Dunluce	Loughguile	Ballymoney	III.	20
14, 18, 19	Shelton South	776 0 9	Antrim	Upper Dunluce	Loughguile	Ballymoney	III.	20
10	Shelvins	163 1 10	Monaghan	Monaghan	Tehallan	Monaghan	III.	280
5	Shenick's Island	15 1 23	Dublin	Balrothery East	Holmpatrick	Balrothery	I.	20
21	Shepherdshill	199 0 9	Wicklow	Upper Talbotstown	Freynestown	Baltinglass	I.	364
23	SHERCOCK T.	—	Cavan	Clankee	Shercock	Bailieborough	III.	75
56	Sheridan	91 3 29	Tyrone	Omagh East	Magheracross	Lowtherstown	III.	314
38	Sheriffhill	393 1 2	Kildare	Kilkea and Moone	Kilelan	Baltinglass	I.	60
40	Sheriff's Land	73 0 16	Antrim	Upper Glenarm	Kilwaughter	Larne	III.	25
107, 108	Sherky Island	82 1 19	Kerry	Dunkerron South	Kilcrohane	Kenmare	II.	184
14, 19	Sherlockstown	556 0 22	Kildare	Naas North	Sherlockstown	Naas	I.	63
14	Sherlockstown Common	138 0 30	Kildare	Naas North	Sherlockstown	Naas	I.	63
13, 20	Sherriff's Mountain	408 1 38	Londonderry	North West Liberties of Londonderry	Templemore	Londonderry	III.	247
38, 46	Sherrigrim	399 0 27	Tyrone	Dungannon Middle	Donaghenry	Cookstown	III.	301
47	Sherwood	47 0 24	Wexford	Forth	Mayglass	Wexford	I.	312
17, 18	Sherwood or Dukespark	334 1 7	Carlow	Forth	Barragh	Enniscorthy	I.	4
13, 17	Sherwoodpark	115 1 34c	Carlow	Forth	Aghade	Carlow	I.	3
17	Sherwoodpark	38 3 14	Carlow	Forth	Barragh	Carlow	I.	4
13, 19	Shesharoe	202 3 33	Tipperary, N.R.	Owney and Arra	Castletownarra	Nenagh	II.	294
20	Shesheraghkeale	201 2 27	Tipperary, N.R.	Lower Ormond	Nenagh	Nenagh	II.	287
10	Shesheraghmore	544 3 39	Tipperary, N.R.	Lower Ormond	Borrisokane	Borrisokane	II.	282
10	Shesheraghscanlan	115 1 25	Tipperary, N.R.	Lower Ormond	Finnoe	Borrisokane	II.	284
3, 6	Sheshia	320 3 27d	Clare	Burren	Abbey	Ballyvaghan	II.	11
45	Sheshiv	181 1 21	Limerick	Connello Upper	Clonerew	Newcastle	II.	232
10	Sheshodonnell East	41 1 37	Clare	Burren	Carran	Ballyvaghan	II.	12
9, 10	Sheshodonnell West	106 3 34	Clare	Burren	Carran	Ballyvaghan	II.	12
27, 28	Sheshoon	316 0 24	Kildare	Offaly East	Ballysax	Naas	I.	69
9, 16	Sheshymore	715 2 37	Clare	Burren	Noughaval	Corrofin	II.	14
1, 3	Sheskernagh	104 2 15	Westmeath	Fore	Rathgarve	Castletowndelvin	I.	271
6	Sheskin	203 2 32	Cork, E.R.	Orrery and Kilmore	Tullylease	Kanturk	II.	110
118	Sheskin	318 3 15	Cork, W.R.	Bantry	Kilmocomoge	Bantry	II.	121
32, 37	Sheskin	517 0 29	King's Co.	Ballybritt	Letterluna	Parsonstown	I.	126
15	Sheskin	94 3 31	Leitrim	Drumahaire	Killarga	Manorhamilton	IV.	99
12,13,19,20	Sheskin	7,012 3 17	Mayo	Erris	Kilcommon	Belmullet	IV.	144
5, 8	Sheskin	418 3 15	Monaghan	Monaghan	Tedavnet	Monaghan	III.	279
41	Sheskin	237 0 6	Tipperary, N.R.	Eliogarty	Thurles	Thurles	II.	273
21, 29	Sheskin	152 1 1	Waterford	Decies without Drum	Affane	Lismore	II.	353
32	Sheskin	200 1 35	Waterford	Decies without Drum	Stradbally	Kilmacthomas	II.	361
3	Sheskin	600 3 23	Waterford	Upperthird	Kilmoleran	Carrick on Suir	II.	370
20, 23	Sheskinacurry	145 3 11	Leitrim	Leitrim	Kiltoghert	Cark. on Shannon	IV.	103
62	Sheskinapoll	158 3 1	Donegal	Raphoe	Raymoghy	Strabane	III.	142
49	Sheskinarone	1,313 3 34e	Donegal	Boylagh	Templecrone	Glenties	III.	116
84	Sheskinatawy	195 0 14	Donegal	Banagh	Inver	Donegal	III.	108
32	Sheskinbeg	215 1 13	Donegal	Kilmacrenan	Tullaghobegly	Dunfanaghy	III.	132

(a) Including 46A. 2R. 5P. water.
(b) Including 6A. 2R. 37P. water.
(c) Including 7A. 0R. 30P. detached portion.
(d) Including 6A. 0R. 1P. water.
(e) Including 50A. 0R. 24P. water.

No. of Sheet of the Ordnance Survey Maps.	Townlands and Towns.	Area in Statute Acres. A. R. P.	County.	Barony.	Parish.	Poor Law Union in 1857.	Townland Census of 1851, Part I. Vol.	Page
22, 26	Sheskin Commons .	7 2 14	Kilkenny .	Callan . . .	Callan . .	Callan . .	I.	84
19, 27	Sheskinshule .	824 1 25	Tyrone .	Strabane Upper .	Bodoney Lower .	Gortin . .	III.	324
3	Shesknan .	481 2 36	Leitrim .	Rosclogher .	Rossinver . .	Ballyshannon .	IV.	112
113	Shessanagirba .	148 1 0	Galway .	Kiltartan .	Kinvarradoorus .	Gort . .	IV.	49
113	Shessareagh .	93 2 20	Galway .	Dunkellin .	Killeenavarra .	Gort . .	IV.	30
49, 59	Shessiv . .	258 1 32	Clare .	Clonderalaw .	Killadysert .	Killadysert .	II.	16
25	Shessiv . .	174 0 38a	Clare .	Inchiquin .	Rath . .	Corrofin .	II.	28
113	Shessy North .	145 3 0	Galway .	Kiltartan .	Ardrahan .	Gort . .	IV.	45
113	Shessy South .	108 1 16	Galway .	Kiltartan .	Ardrahan .	Gort . .	IV.	45
39, 40	Shevry . .	961 3 30	Tipperary, N.R.	Kilnamanagh Upper	Upperchurch .	Thurles .	II.	281
13	Shewis . .	214 2 34	Armagh .	Oneilland West .	Kilmore . .	Armagh .	III.	53
17	Shibbilis . .	116 1 7b	Cavan .	Tullygarvey .	Drumgoon .	Cootehill .	III.	88
122	Shigaunagh .	588 3 22c	Galway .	Kiltartan .	Killinny .	Gort . .	IV.	47
53	Shilbrack .	11 1 13	Wexford .	Forth . .	Carn . .	Wexford .	I.	309
34, 39	Shillanavogy .	1,475 2 29	Antrim .	Lower Antrim .	Racavan . .	Ballymena .	III.	4
23	Shillanmore .	152 0 12	Fermanagh .	Tirkennedy .	Enniskillen .	Enniskillen .	III.	222
43	SHILLELAGH T. .	—	Wicklow .	Shillelagh .	Carnew . .	Shillelagh .	I.	357
48	Shilmaine .	171 0 3	Wexford .	Forth . .	Kilscoran .	Wexford .	I.	311
53	Shilmore .	57 3 36d	Wexford .	Forth . .	Carn . .	Wexford .	I.	309
96, 110	Shinagh . .	471 2 4	Cork, W.R.	Kinalmeaky .	Kilbrogan .	Bandon .	II.	152
23	Shinan . .	255 1 0e	Cavan .	Clankee . .	Shercock .	Bailieborough .	III.	75
7, 8	Shinanagh .	312 1 6	Cork, E.R.	Fermoy . .	Imphrick .	Mallow .	II.	80
2, 7	Shinanagh .	231 3 27	Cork, E.R.	Orrery and Kilmore	Shandrum .	Kanturk .	II.	110
21, 22	Shindala .	158 2 12	Kildare .	Offaly West .	Lackagh . .	Athy . .	I.	73
38,39,52,53	Shindilla or Lurgan	1,121 0 22	Galway .	Moycullen .	Kilcummin .	Oughterard .	IV.	67
90, 91	Shinganagh .	269 3 12	Mayo .	Clanmorris .	Mayo . .	Claremorris .	IV.	135
74	Shinganagh .	72 1 14	Tipperary, S.R.	Clanwilliam .	Templeneiry .	Tipperary .	II.	311
17	Shinganagh .	155 0 19	Waterford .	Middlethird .	Lisnakill .	Waterford .	II.	368
19, 20	Shingaun .	72 1 5	Wexford .	Scarawalsh .	Monart . .	Enniscorthy .	I.	324
14	Shingaunagh North	105 1 26	Clare .	Corcomroe .	Kilmacrehy .	Ennistimon .	II.	20
14	Shingaunagh South	82 0 23	Clare .	Corcomroe .	Kilmacrehy .	Ennistimon .	II.	20
16, 17, 24	Shinglis . .	1,581 1 9f	Westmeath .	Rathconrath .	Ballymore .	Ballymahon .	I.	282
41, 47	Shinn . .	463 0 10	Down .	Lordship of Newry .	Newry . .	Newry .	III.	182
109	Shinnagh .	477 0 34	Kerry .	Glanarought .	Tuosist . .	Kenmare .	II.	189
60, 68	Shinnagh .	772 0 23	Kerry .	Magunihy .	Nohavaldaly .	Killarney .	II.	205
70	Shinnagh .	175 1 11g	Mayo .	Carra . .	Turlough .	Castlebar .	IV.	131
22	Shinnanagh .	639 0 20	Galway .	Ballynahinch .	Omey . .	Clifden .	IV.	15
42	Shinrone .	724 2 11	King's Co.	Clonlisk . .	Shinrone .	Roscrea .	I.	131
42	SHINRONE T. .	—	King's Co.	Clonlisk . .	Shinrone .	Roscrea .	I.	131
117	Shintilla .	1 1 13	Mayo .	Kilmaine .	Ballinchalla .	Ballinrobe .	IV.	152
107	Shiplough .	423 0 36	Cork, W.R.	East Carbery (W.D.)	Fanlobbus .	Dunmanway .	II.	132
111	Ship-pool .	235 2 13	Cork, E.R.	Kinalea . .	Leighmoney .	Kinsale .	II.	96
3	Shirsheen .	170 1 33	Wexford .	Gorey . .	Inch . .	Gorey . .	I.	316
15	Shivdelagh .	158 1 3	Leitrim .	Drumahaire .	Inishmagrath .	Manorhamilton .	IV.	97
28, 29	Shivdilla .	113 1 4	Leitrim .	Mohill . .	Mohill . .	Mohill .	IV.	108
38	Shivey . .	151 1 13	Tyrone .	Dungannon Upper .	Desertcreat .	Cookstown .	III.	308
32	Shoalmore .	121 3 20h	Leitrim .	Mohill . .	Mohill . .	Mohill .	IV.	108
71,72,84,85	Shoodaun .	542 2 18	Galway .	Tiaquin . .	Moniyea .	Loughrea .	IV.	79
60	Shore Island .	28 0 12	Clare .	Clonderalaw .	Killadysert .	Killadysert .	II.	16
105	Shore Island .	0 1 24	Galway .	Loughrea .	Killeenadeema .	Loughrea .	IV.	64
27, 31	Shortallstown .	304 0 3	Kilkenny .	Kells . .	Kilree . .	Callan .	I.	109
42, 47	Shortalstown .	113 0 27	Wexford .	Forth . .	Rathmacknee .	Wexford .	I.	313
82, 88	Shortcastle .	65 3 30i	Tipperary, S.R.	Iffa and Offa West .	Ardfinnan .	Clogheen .	II.	317
76	Shortcastle .	58 0 31	Tipperary, S.R.	Iffa and Offa West .	Mortlestown .	Clogheen .	II.	319
3	Shortstone East .	201 3 2	Louth .	Upper Dundalk .	Roche . .	Dundalk .	I.	179
3	Shortstone West .	349 2 36	Louth .	Upper Dundalk .	Roche . .	Dundalk .	I.	179
14	Shortwood .	104 3 28	Kildare .	Naas North .	Whitechurch .	Naas . .	I.	63
47	Shouks . .	27 2 7	Wexford .	Bargy . .	Mulrankin .	Wexford .	I.	307
31, 37	Shower . .	644 1 11	Tipperary, N.R.	Owney and Arra .	Kilvellane .	Nenagh .	II.	296
142	Shreelane .	403 2 34j	Cork, W.R.	West Carbery (E.D.)	Kilmacabea .	Skibbereen .	II.	140
75	Shronaboy .	1,165 0 7	Kerry .	Magunihy .	Killaha . .	Killarney .	II.	202
119, 120	Shronacarton .	216 3 24	Cork, W.R.	West Carbery (E.D.)	Dromdaleague .	Skibbereen .	II.	140
131	Shronagree .	495 0 12	Cork, W.R.	West Carbery (W.D.)	Skull . .	Skull . .	II.	147
92	Shronagreehy .	348 0 4	Cork, W.R.	Bantry . .	Kilmocomoge .	Bantry .	II.	121
82	Shronahiree Beg .	586 3 3	Kerry .	Dunkerron North .	Knockane .	Cahersiveen .	II.	182
72, 82	Shronahiree More .	871 0 18	Kerry .	Dunkerron North .	Knockane .	Cahersiveen .	II.	182
81	Shronaloughane .	785 0 35	Kerry .	Iveragh . .	Dromod .	Cahersiveen .	II.	195
104	Shrone . .	394 1 24	Cork, W.R.	Bear . .	Kilcaskan .	Bantry .	II.	123
6	Shrone . .	115 3 29	Kerry .	Iraghticonnor .	Aghavallen .	Listowel .	II.	189
47,48,57,58	Shrone . .	148 2 38	Kerry .	Magunihy .	Kilbonane .	Killarney .	II.	200
68	Shrone Beg .	1,110 2 31	Kerry .	Magunihy .	Killcummin .	Killarney .	II.	201
31	Shronebeha .	518 2 12	Cork, E.R.	Duhallow .	Clonmeen .	Kanturk .	II.	70
11, 17	Shronebeirne .	412 2 27k	Kerry .	Iraghticonnor .	Duagh . .	Listowel .	II.	190

(a) Including 9A. 1R. 18P. water.
(b) Including 3A. 2R. 28P. water.
(c) Including 3A. 2R. 8P. water.
(d) Including 2A. 2R. 4P. detached portion.
(e) Including 19A. 0R. 30P. water.
(f) Including 26A. 2R. 16P. water.
(g) Including 11A. 0R. 23P. water.
(h) Including 23A. 2R. 3P. water.
(i) Including 2A. 0R. 0P. water.
(j) Including 17A. 3R. 39P. water.
(k) Including 12A. 3R. 32P. water.

No. of Sheet of the Ordnance Survey Maps.	Townlands and Towns.	Area in Statute Acres. A. R. P.	County.	Barony.	Parish.	Poor Law Union in 1857.	Townland Census of 1851, Part I. Vol.	Page
108, 111	Shronebirrane	1,204 2 25	Kerry	Glanarought	Tuosist	Kenmare	II.	189
67, 68	Shronedarragh	482 2 12	Kerry	Magunihy	Aghadoe	Killarney	II.	199
10	Shrone East	203 0 15	Kerry	Iraghticonnor	Galey	Listowel	II.	190
66	Shronell	99 3 39	Tipperary, S.R.	Clanwilliam	Bruis	Tipperary	II.	305
66	Shronell	50 0 21	Tipperary, S.R.	Clanwilliam	Shronell	Tipperary	II.	310
66	Shronell Beg	558 3 24	Tipperary, S.R.	Clanwilliam	Shronell	Tipperary	II.	310
66	Shronell More	155 2 8	Tipperary, S.R.	Clanwilliam	Shronell	Tipperary	II.	310
10	Shrone Middle	132 0 22	Kerry	Iraghticonnor	Galey	Listowel	II.	190
68, 76	Shrone More	1,145 0 34a	Kerry	Magunihy	Kilcummin	Killarney	II.	202
1, 6	Shronepookeen	276 1 28	Cork, E.R.	Orrery and Kilmore	Kilbolane	Kanturk	II.	108
10	Shrone West	298 1 16	Kerry	Iraghticonnor	Galey	Listowel	II.	190
66, 73	Shrough	494 3 24	Tipperary, S.R.	Clanwilliam	Bruis	Tipperary	II.	305
2, 6	Shrubbywood	280 1 27b	Westmeath	Fore	Mayne	Granard	I.	271
55	Shrub Island	1 1 1	Galway	Clare	Killursa	Tuam	IV.	22
14	Shrubs	79 1 36	Dublin	Coolock	Coolock	Dublin North	I.	27
5	Shrule	91 3 34	Galway	Dunmore	Dunmore	Tuam	IV.	34
26	Shrule	55 2 32c	Longford	Ratheline	Shrule	Ballymahon	I.	165
122	Shrule	161 2 12	Mayo	Kilmaine	Shrule	Ballinrobe	IV.	158
32	Shrule	166 0 14d	Queen's Co.	Slievmargy	Shrule	Carlow	I.	246
17, 22	Shrule	109 0 8	Wexford	Ballaghkeen	Donaghmore	Gorey	I.	294
6	Shrule	261 3 37	Wexford	Gorey	Rossminoge	Gorey	I.	321
5, 6, 11	Shrule	119 2 33	Wexford	Scarawalsh	Kilcomb	Gorey	I.	323
28, 42	Shrulegrove	214 1 39	Galway	Clare	Donaghpatrick	Tuam	IV.	19
122	SHRULE T.	—	Mayo	Kilmaine	Shrule	Ballinrobe	IV.	158
38	Shureen and Bally-nasuddery	171 0 36	Westmeath	Moycashel	Kilbeggan	Tullamore	I.	278
30	Shurock	257 0 38	Westmeath	Clonlonan	Ballyloughloe	Athlone	I.	261
31, 32	Shurock	109 3 39	Westmeath	Moycashel	Castletownkindalen	Mullingar	I.	277
30, 31	Shuters Islands	3 1 37 / 7 3 15	Down	Lecale Lower	Inch	Downpatrick	III.	179
14	Siberia or Slieveroe	147 0 8	Sligo	Carbury	Killaspugbrone	Sligo	IV.	222
19	Sibylhill	77 1 38	Dublin	Coolock	Clontarf	Dublin North	I.	26
26	Sicily	445 2 0	Meath	Lower Duleek	Danestown	Navan	I.	195
16	Sidaire	326 0 4	Fermanagh	Tirkennedy	Magheracross	Lowtherstown	III.	223
6	Siddan	242 2 31	Meath	Lower Slane	Siddan	Ardee	I.	224
6	SIDDAN T.	—	Meath	Lower Slane	Siddan	Ardee	I.	224
47,48,52,53	Sigginstown	24 0 23	Wexford	Forth	Ishartmon	Wexford	I.	310
52, 53	Sigginstown	197 2 13	Wexford	Forth	Tacumshin	Wexford	I.	315
52, 53	Sigginstown Island Great	24 2 17	Wexford	Forth	Tacumshin	Wexford	I.	315
52	Sigginstown Island Little	1 3 21	Wexford	Forth	Tacumshin	Wexford	I.	315
41	Siginshaggard	260 3 2	Wexford	Shelmaliere West	Coolstuff	Wexford	I.	333
24	Sileshaun East	283 1 31	Clare	Inchiquin	Inagh	Ennistimon	II.	25
24	Sileshaun West	375 1 33	Clare	Inchiquin	Inagh	Ennistimon	II.	25
24	Sillagh	326 2 13	Kildare	Naas South	Kill	Naas	I.	65
1, 5	Sillaheens	394 3 21	Waterford	Glenahiry	Kilronan	Clonmel	II.	366
107	Sillahertane	464 2 27	Cork, W.R.	East Carbery (W.D.)	Fanlobbus	Dunmanway	II.	132
95	Sillahertane	1,718 3 18	Kerry	Glanarought	Kilgarvan	Kenmare	II.	188
23, 24	Silliothill	258 3 1	Kildare	Naas South	Carnalway	Naas	I.	64
22	Silliothill	166 3 11	Kildare	Offaly East	Moone	Naas	I.	70
7	Sillis	310 3 6	Monaghan	Trough	Donagh	Monaghan	III.	282
14	Silloge	215 1 5	Dublin	Coolock	Santry	Dublin North	I.	29
21	Silloge	102 2 20	Louth	Ferrard	Monasterboice	Drogheda	I.	181
18	Silloge	624 0 10	Meath	Morgallion	Kilberry	Navan	I.	209
61	Silverfort	231 3 35	Tipperary, S.R.	Middlethird	Magorban	Cashel	II.	328
35, 36	Silvergrove	533 3 9e	Clare	Tulla Lower	Killuran	Tulla	II.	36
69,70,81,82	Silvergrove	395 1 6	Cork, W.R.	West Muskerry	Inchigeelagh	Macroom	II.	158
31	Silverhill	411 2 35	Clare	Ibrickan	Kilfarboy	Ennistimon	II.	22
21, 22	Silverhill	295 1 21	Fermanagh	Magheraboy	Devenish	Enniskillen	III.	211
48	Silverhill	159 2 22f	Galway	Ballynahinch	Ballindoon	Clifden	IV.	10
46	Silverhill	124 3 13	King's Co.	Clonlisk	Cullenwaine	Roscrea	I.	129
5	Silverhill	149 3 35	Sligo	Carbury	Ahamlish	Sligo	IV.	219
5	Silverhill	151 0 28	Tyrone	Strabane Lower	Leckpatrick	Strabane	III.	322
29	Silverhill Lower	83 2 8g	Kildare	Naas South	Ballymore Eustace	Naas	I.	64
29	Silverhill Upper	146 0 4	Kildare	Naas South	Ballymore Eustace	Naas	I.	64
126	Silver Island	0 1 25	Galway	Longford	Lickmolassy	Portumna	IV.	61
26	SILVERMINES T.	—	Tipperary, N.R.	Upper Ormond	Kilmore	Nenagh	II.	291
47	Silverspring	166 2 11	Wexford	Forth	Mayglass	Wexford	I.	312
42	Silverspring or Afaddy	165 0 27	Kilkenny	Iverk	Ballytarsney	Waterford	I.	105
42	Silverspring or Afaddy	77 3 2	Kilkenny	Iverk	Pollrone	Waterford	I.	106
125	Silverstream	33 2 4	Galway	Leitrim	Ballynakill	Loughrea	IV.	52
6	Silverwood	198 3 25	Armagh	Oneilland East	Seagoe	Lurgan	III.	50
18, 22	Simmonscourt	81 0 9	Dublin	Rathdown	Donnybrook	Dublin South	I.	35

(a) Including 7A. 0R. 32P. water.
(b) Including 8A. 0R. 32P. water.
(c) Including 5A. 3R. 3P. water.

(d) Including 4A. 3R. 22P. River Barrow.
(e) Including 59A. 2R. 18P. water.

(f) Including 13A. 0R. 27P. water.
(g) Including 1A. 1R. 18P. water.

5 N

No. of Sheet of the Ordnance Survey Maps.	Townlands and Towns.	Area in Statute Acres.			County.	Barony.	Parish.	Poor Law Union in 1857.	Townland Census of 1851, Part I.	
		A.	R.	P.					Vol.	Page
11	Simmonstown	300	2	35	Kildare	South Salt	Donaghcumper	Celbridge	I.	76
24	*Simmy Island*	8	1	24	Down	Dufferin	Killyleagh	Downpatrick	III.	167
14	Simonsland	86	3	23	Kilkenny	Crannagh	Odagh	Kilkenny	I.	86
18	Simonstown	170	2	38	Louth	Ardee	Drumcar	Ardee	I.	172
18, 25	Simonstown	516	0	27	Meath	Lower Navan	Donaghmore	Navan	I.	214
20	Simonstown	47	0	7	Westmeath	Farbill	Killucan	Mullingar	I.	267
26	Simonstown	230	3	11	Westmeath	Fartullagh	Enniscoffey	Mullingar	I.	268
26, 33	Simonstown	126	0	31	Westmeath	Fartullagh	Kilbride	Mullingar	I.	268
3, 7	Simonstown	285	2	33	Westmeath	Fore	Mayne	Granard	I.	271
18	Simonstown	279	1	18	Westmeath	Rathconrath	Rathconrath	Mullingar	I.	284
38	Simonstown East	62	0	16	Kildare	Kilkea and Moone	Killelan	Baltinglass	I.	60
36, 38	Simonstown West	413	2	36	Kildare	Kilkea and Moone	Killelan	Baltinglass	I.	60
5	Singland	523	2	13a	Limerick	Clanwilliam and Municipal Borough	St. Patrick's	Limerick	II.	225
106	Single Street T.	—			Donegal	Tirhugh	Inishmacsaint	Ballyshannon	III.	147
33	Sinnottsmill	69	3	35	Wexford	Shelmaliere East	Ardcavan	Wexford	I.	330
42	Sinnottstown	159	3	28	Wexford	Forth	Drinagh	Wexford	I.	309
6	Sion	164	1	27	Kildare	North Salt	Laraghbryan	Celbridge	I.	75
28	Sion	80	0	3b	Waterford	Coshmore & Coshbride	Lismore and Mocollop	Lismore	II.	347
32	Sion	102	2	29	Wexford	Shelmaliere East	Kilpatrick	Wexford	I.	331
19	Sionhermitage	30	0	8c	Kilkenny	Gowran	St. John's	Kilkenny	I.	98
20	Sionhill	398	1	39	Westmeath	Farbill	Killucan	Mullingar	I.	267
9, 16	Sistrakeel	964	3	4	Londonderry	Keenaght	Tamlaght Finlagan	New Town Limavady	III.	237
48	Sixacre	13	0	16	Wexford	Forth	Rosslare	Wexford	I.	313
52	Sixmilebridge	294	0	39	Clare	Bunratty Lower	Kilfinaghta	Ennis	II.	4
52	Sixmilebridge T.	—			Clare	Bunratty Lower	Kilfinaghta	Ennis	II.	4
23	Sixmilebridge T.	—			Limerick	Smallcounty	Monasteranenagh	Croom	II.	261
44	Six Mile Cross	199	0	9	Tyrone	Omagh East	Termonmaguirk	Omagh	III.	315
44	Six Mile Cross T.	—			Tyrone	Omagh East	Termonmaguirk	Omagh	III.	315
105	Sixnoggins	682	3	19	Mayo	Murrisk	Kilgeever	Westport	IV.	160
14	Sixth Corgary or Second Croagh	2,111	2	1d	Tyrone	Omagh West	Termonamongan	Castlederg	III.	317
71	Sixty Acres	73	3	24	Donegal	Raphoe	Clonleigh	Strabane	III.	135
30	Skagh	296	2	8	Cork, E.R.	Duhallow	Cullen	Millstreet	II.	71
21, 30	Skagh	383	1	15	Limerick	Coshma	Croom	Croom	II.	242
17	Skaghardgannon	182	0	1	Cork, E.R.	Fermoy	Doneraile	Mallow	II.	79
24, 32	Skaghvickinerow	387	2	11e	Clare	Inchiquin	Inagh	Ennistimon	II.	25
74	Skahabeg North	55	1	5	Cork, E.R.	Cork	St. Nicholas	Cork	II.	66
74	Skahabeg South	29	0	21	Cork, E.R.	Cork	St. Nicholas	Cork	II.	66
105	Skahanagh	59	2	13	Cork, W.R.	Bantry	Kilmocomoge	Bantry	II.	122
142	Skahanagh	173	3	15	Cork, W.R.	West Carbery (E.D.)	Myross	Skibbereen	II.	141
38	Skahanagh	239	3	34	Kerry	Trughanacmy	Ratass	Tralee	II.	213
17	Skahanagh Beg	463	3	13	Cork, E.R.	Fermoy	Doneraile	Mallow	II.	79
105	Skahanagh Beg	39	2	12	Cork, W.R.	Bantry	Kilmocomoge	Bantry	II.	122
105	Skahanagh Lower	44	0	4	Cork, W.R.	Bantry	Kilmocomoge	Bantry	II.	122
17, 18	Skahanagh More	550	1	25	Cork, E.R.	Fermoy	Doneraile	Mallow	II.	79
105, 106	Skahanagh More	167	0	28	Cork, W.R.	Bantry	Kilmocomoge	Bantry	II.	122
53	Skahanagh North	561	0	14	Cork, E.R.	Barrymore	Kilshanahan	Fermoy	II.	56
53	Skahanagh South	791	3	15	Cork, E.R.	Barrymore	Kilshanahan	Fermoy	II.	56
19	Skahanrane	221	0	25	Carlow	Idrone East	Lorum	Carlow	I.	8
14	Skahard	149	3	16	Limerick	Clanwilliam	Caherconlish	Limerick	I.	222
48	Skahies	305	1	6	Kerry	Magunihy	Molahiffe	Killarney	II.	205
97, 111	Skanagore	261	1	4	Cork, E.R.	Kinalea	Leighmoney	Kinsale	II.	96
32, 41	Skarragh	538	2	10	Cork, E.R.	Duhallow	Kilshannig	Mallow	II.	74
26, 27	Skea	566	1	29	Fermanagh	Clanawley	Cleenish	Enniskillen	III.	191
1	Skea	160	3	25	Fermanagh	Lurg	Drumkeeran	Lowthertown	III.	207
46	Skea	200	0	13	Tyrone	Dungannon Middle	Pomeroy	Dungannon	III.	304
17	Skeachorn	121	3	24	Monaghan	Dartree	Killeevan	Clones	III.	268
110, 123	Skeaf	452	2	1	Cork, W.R.	East Carbery (E.D.)	Kilmaloda	Clonakilty	II.	129
123	Skeaf East	371	2	6	Cork, W.R.	East Carbery (E.D.)	Kilmaloda	Clonakilty	II.	129
123	Skeaf West	477	3	20	Cork, W.R.	East Carbery (E.D.)	Kilmaloda	Clonakilty	II.	129
9, 13	Skeagarvey	76	0	7	Monaghan	Monaghan	Monaghan	Monaghan	III.	277
34	Skeagh	794	1	15	Antrim	Upper Glenarm	Kilwaughter	Larne	III.	25
28	Skeagh	691	1	8f	Cavan	Clankee	Knockbride	Bailieborough	III.	74
4	Skeagh	170	0	35	Cavan	Tullyhaw	Killinagh	Enniskillen	III.	92
132, 141	Skeagh	552	2	2	Cork, W.R.	West Carbery (E.D.)	Abbeystrowry	Skibbereen	II.	136
139	Skeagh	483	1	0	Cork, W.R.	West Carbery (W.D.)	Skull	Skull	II.	147
35	Skeagh	331	1	13	Donegal	Kilmacrenan	Clondahorky	Dunfanaghy	III.	123
28	Skeagh	828	2	15	Down	Lower Iveagh, Lr. pt.	Dromore	Banbridge	III.	168
20	Skeagh	122	3	4	Dublin	Newcastle	Newcastle	Celbridge	I.	34
28	Skeagh	266	3	9	Fermanagh	Magherastephana	Aghavea	Lisnaskea	III.	219
15	Skeagh	65	1	1	Kildare	South Salt	Lyons	Celbridge	I.	77
8, 9, 12	Skeagh	134	2	34	Monaghan	Monaghan	Drumsnat	Monaghan	III.	275
22	Skeagh	326	0	31	Queen's Co.	Clarmallagh	Aghaboe	Donaghmore	I.	236

(a) { Within the Municipal Boundary, 0A. 2R. 10P.
Without the Municipal Boundary, 523A. 0R. 3P.
(b) Including 8A. 1R. 2P. detached portion.

(c) Including 2A. 3R. 3P. River Nore.
(d) Including 5A. 3R. 28P. water.

(e) Including 11A. 0R. 20P. water.
(f) Including 91A. 0R. 2P. water.

No. of Sheet of the Ordnance Survey Maps.	Townlands and Towns.	Area in Statute Acres.	County.	Barony.	Parish.	Poor Law Union in 1857.	Townland Census of 1851, Part I.	
		A. R. P.					Vol.	Page
12, 18	Skeagh	306 2 22	Roscommon	Ballintober North	Kilmore	Car^k. on Shannon	IV.	187
35	Skeagh	44 2 4	Tipperary, N.R.	Eliogarty	Loughmoe East	Thurles	II.	271
22, 26	Skeaghacloran	204 2 33	Kilkenny	Callan	Callan	Callan	I.	84
84	Skeaghaderreen	169 2 3	Galway	Athenry	Athenry	Galway	IV.	4
140	Skeaghanore East	332 3 18	Cork, W.R.	West Carbery (W.D.)	Kilcoe	Skull	II.	143
140	Skeaghanore West	378 0 30	Cork, W.R.	West Carbery (W.D.)	Kilcoe	Skull	II.	143
93	Skeaghard	116 0 2	Mayo	Costello	Bekan	Claremorris	IV.	139
97	Skeagharcgan	112 3 10	Galway	Dunkellin	Kilconierin	Loughrea	IV.	29
23, 24	Skeaghaturrish	187 3 22	Kilkenny	Shillelogher	Danesfort	Thomastown	I.	114
42, 56	Skeaghbeg	117 3 22	Galway	Clare	Kilkilvery	Tuam	IV.	20
17	Skeagh Beg	52 2 1	Westmeath	Rathconrath	Rathconrath	Mullingar	I.	284
12, 17	Skeaghcroum	70 0 23	Kilkenny	Crannagh	Tubbridbritain	Urlingford	I.	87
18	Skeaghmore	83 3 5	Louth	Ardee	Drumcar	Ardee	I.	172
17	Skeagh More	397 0 29	Westmeath	Rathconrath	Rathconrath	Mullingar	I.	284
38	Skeahanagh	237 3 15	Westmeath	Moycashel	Kilbeggan	Tullamore	I.	278
15	Skeahanagh or Farmley	330 0 3a	Wexford	Scarawalsh	Ballycarney	Enniscorthy	I.	322
118	Skealoghan	301 1 11	Mayo	Kilmaine	Kilcommon	Ballinrobe	IV.	155
32	Skeamartin	17 2 23	Leitrim	Leitrim	Mohill	Mohill	IV.	104
149	*Skeam East*	49 3 0	Cork, W.R.	West Carbery (E.D.)	Aghadown	Skibbereen	II.	137
149	*Skeam West*	30 3 19	Cork, W.R.	West Carbery (E.D.)	Aghadown	Skibbereen	II.	137
48, 51	Skeanamuck	224 1 27b	Roscommon	Athlone	Taghmaconnell	Athlone	IV.	185
16	Skeanavart	122 0 8	Roscommon	Frenchpark	Kilmacumsy	Boyle	IV.	204
22	Skeanaveane	32 3 32	Westmeath	Kilkenny West	Bunown	Athlone	I.	272
43	Skeard	295 3 8	Kilkenny	Ida	Dunkitt	Waterford	I.	101
4	Skearke	312 1 36	Meath	Lower Kells	Moynalty	Kells	I.	204
42	Skeaterpark	102 0 21	Wexford	Bargy	Kilmannan	Wexford	I.	306
5, 8	Skeatry	76 1 2	Monaghan	Monaghan	Clones	Monaghan	III.	275
47, 48, 51	Skeavaily	413 1 24	Roscommon	Athlone	Taghmaconnell	Athlone	IV.	185
36	Skeboy	262 0 18	Tyrone	Omagh East	Termonmaguirk	Omagh	III.	315
99,107,108	Skecoor	432 2 38	Galway	Longford	Kiltormer	Ballinasloe	IV.	60
18, 22	Skegatillida	222 0 16	Armagh	Orior Lower	Ballymore	Newry	III.	55
56,57,60,61	Skegoneill	620 0 9	Antrim	Upper Belfast	Shankill	Belfast	III.	10
13	Skehacreggaun	99 2 25	Limerick	Pubblebrien	Mungret	Limerick	II.	254
31	Skehacrine (*Humble*)	77 1 36	Waterford	Decies without Drum	Dungarvan	Dungarvan	II.	356
31	Skehacrine (*Marquis*)	8 0 39	Waterford	Decies without Drum	Dungarvan	Dungarvan	II.	356
19	Skehaghard	278 1 2c	Galway	Ballymoe	Kilbegnet	Glennamaddy	IV.	8
99	Skehahagh	128 1 17	Mayo	Carra	Ballintober	Castlebar	IV.	125
1, 5	Skehana	925 3 4	Kilkenny	Fassadinin	Castlecomer	Castlecomer	I.	89
33,34,41,42	Skehanagh	545 0 13	Clare	Islands	Clareabbey	Ennis	II.	29
97	Skehanagh	381 1 2	Cork, E.R.	Kinalea	Dunderrow	Kinsale	II.	95
114	Skehanagh	60 1 8	Galway	Kiltartan	Kiltartan	Gort	IV.	48
114	Skehanagh	324 1 7d	Galway	Kiltartan	Kilthomas	Gort	IV.	49
108	Skehanagh	41 1 34	Galway	Longford	Fahy	Portuma	IV.	58
108	Skehanagh	100 3 0	Galway	Longford	Kilquain	Portuma	IV.	60
117	Skehanagh	115 0 27	Galway	Longford	Tynagh	Portuma	IV.	62
59	Skehanagh	550 0 11	Galway	Tiaquin	Moylough	Mountbellew	IV.	80
107	Skehanagh	170 3 36	Kerry	Dunkerron South	Kilcrohane	Kenmare	II.	184
14	Skehanagh	123 1 33	King's Co.	Garrycastle	Wheery or Killagally	Parsonstown	I.	139
28	Skehanagh	406 1 27	Limerick	Connello Lower	Kilscannell	Rathkeale	II.	228
22	Skehanagh	136 0 10	Limerick	Pubblebrien	Ballycahane	Croom	II.	251
22	Skehanagh	110 1 20	Limerick	Pubblebrien	Kilpeacon	Croom	II.	253
25, 26	Skehanagh	574 3 29	Queen's Co.	Ballyadams	Killabban	Athy	I.	231
23	Skehanagh	325 0 26	Tipperary, N.R.	Ikerrin	Killavinoge	Roscrea	II.	275
9	Skehanagh	70 0 6	Tipperary, N.R.	Lower Ormond	Kilbarron	Borrisokane	II.	284
8	Skehanagh	250 2 14	Tipperary, N.R.	Lower Ormond	Loughkeen	Parsonstown	II.	286
78	Skehanagh	21 1 10	Tipperary, S.R.	Iffa and Offa East	Kilsheelan	Clonmel	II.	315
52	Skehanagh	191 1 15	Tipperary, S.R.	Kilnamanagh Lower	Clonoulty	Cashel	II.	323
89, 99	Skehanagh Lower	258 0 30	Mayo	Carra	Ballintober	Castlebar	IV.	125
86	Skehanagh North	209 1 18	Galway	Kilconnell	Killaan	Loughrea	IV.	41
23	Skehanagh North	182 3 31	Tipperary, N.R.	Ikerrin	Killea	Roscrea	II.	276
86	Skehanagh South	104 2 9	Galway	Kilconnell	Killaan	Loughrea	IV.	41
23	Skehanagh South	73 1 22	Tipperary, N.R.	Ikerrin	Killea	Roscrea	II.	276
114	SKEHANAGH. T.	---	Galway	Kiltartan	Kilthomas	Gort	IV.	49
89, 99	Skehanagh Upper	174 2 7e	Mayo	Carra	Ballintober	Castlebar	IV.	125
31	Skehanard (*Barron*)	29 2 12	Waterford	Decies without Drum	Dungarvan	Dungarvan	II.	356
31	Skehanard (*Humble*)	23 0 26	Waterford	Decies without Drum	Dungarvan	Dungarvan	II.	356
11	Skehanicrin (*Egan*)	221 1 38	Kerry	Iraghticonnor	Listowel	Listowel	II.	193
11	Skehanicrin Lower	73 1 21	Kerry	Iraghticonnor	Listowel	Listowel	II.	193
11	Skehanicrin (*Stokes*)	143 1 38	Kerry	Iraghticonnor	Listowel	Listowel	II.	193
111, 112	Skehavaud	211 0 22	Mayo	Clanmorris	Crossboyne	Claremorris	IV.	133
20	Skeheen	478 1 3	Cork, E.R.	Condons & Clangibbon	Brigown	Mitchelstown	II.	60
73, 74	Skeheen	180 0 19	Mayo	Costello	Kilmovee	Swineford	IV.	142

(a) Including 6A. 2R. 1P. water.
(b) Including 36A. 3R. 8P. water.
(c) Including 29A. 1R. 34P. water.
(d) Including 2A. 1R. 32P. water.
(e) Including 9A. 1R. 39P. water.

No. of Sheet of the Ordnance Survey Maps.	Townlands and Towns.	Area in Statute Acres.			County.	Barony.	Parish.	Poor Law Union in 1857.	Townland Census of 1851. Part I.	
		A.	R.	P.					Vol.	Page
80, 86	Skeheenaranky .	3,024	1	16	Tipperary, S.R.	Iffa and Offa West .	Templetenny .	Clogheen .	II.	320
31	Skeheen (*Evans*) .	132	0	12	Westmeath	Moycashel	Ardnurcher or Horse-leap . . .	Mullingar .	I.	277
110	Skeheen and Lisse-veleen . .	92	1	10	Mayo .	Kilmaine .	Robeen . .	Ballinrobe .	IV.	157
31	Skeheen (*Nagle*) .	229	0	6	Westmeath	Moycashel .	Ardnurcher or Horse-leap . . .	Mullingar .	I.	277
20	Skeheen Upper .	1,207	0	32	Cork, E.R.	Condons&Clangibbon	Brigown .	Mitchelstown .	II.	60
90	Skehil . . .	323	0	39	Cork, W.R.	Bear . . .	Kilcaskan .	Bantry .	II.	123
58	Skelgagh . .	225	0	34	Tyrone .	Clogher . .	Clogher . .	Clogher .	III.	293
50	Skelgagh . .	234	3	39	Tyrone .	Omagh East .	Donacavey .	Omagh .	III.	310
104	*Skelligg Rock Great* .	44	1	28	Kerry .	Iveragh . .	Killemlagh .	Cahersiveen .	II.	196
104	*Skelligg Rock Little* .	16	3	18	Kerry .	Iveragh . .	Killemlagh .	Cahersiveen .	II.	196
79, 88	Skelpy . . .	278	0	29	Donegal .	Raphoe . .	Urney . .	Strabane .	III.	144
99, 100	Skenageehy .	123	1	21	Galway .	Longford .	Kiltormer .	Ballinasloe .	IV.	60
38	Skenagun . .	222	3	4	Kildare .	Kilkea and Moone .	Castledermot .	Baltinglass .	I.	59
37, 38	Skenahergny .	258	0	18	Tyrone .	Dungannon Upper .	Desertcreat .	Cookstown .	III.	308
26	Skenakilla .	317	1	19	Cork, E.R.	Fermoy . .	Castletownroche .	Fermoy .	II.	78
38	Skenarget . .	93	2	37	Tyrone .	Dungannon Upper .	Desertcreat .	Cookstown .	III.	308
47	Skeoge . . .	188	2	8	Donegal .	Inishowen West .	Burt . .	Londonderry .	III.	120
28	Skeoge . . .	231	3	28	Fermanagh .	Magherastephana .	Aghavea .	Lisnaskea .	III.	219
50, 57	Skeogue . .	467	3	10	Tyrone .	Omagh East .	Dromore .	Lowtherstown .	III.	311
11	Skephubble .	135	3	20	Dublin .	Nethercross .	Finglas . .	Balrothery .	I.	31
58, 68	Skerdagh Lower .	515	1	37	Mayo .	Burrishoole .	Burrishoole .	Newport .	IV.	120
58, 68	Skerdagh Upper .	1,186	0	31	Mayo .	Burrishoole .	Burrishoole .	Newport .	IV.	120
17	Skerrick East .	74	0	39	Monaghan	Dartree . .	Currin . .	Clones .	III.	266
21	Skerrick West .	106	0	0	Monaghan	Dartree . .	Currin . .	Clones .	III.	266
2	*Skerries* . .	24	1	9	Antrim .	Lower Dunluce .	Ballywillin .	Coleraine .	III.	16
15, 19	Skerries . .	218	0	3	Armagh .	Tiranny . .	Tynan . .	Armagh .	III.	60
31	Skerries North .	506	1	19	Kildare .	Narragh&RebanWest	Narraghmore .	Athy .	I.	68
31	Skerries South .	301	0	12	Kildare .	Narragh&RebanWest	Narraghmore .	Athy .	I.	68
5	SKERRIES T. .	—			Dublin .	Balrothery East .	Holmpatrick .	Balrothery .	I.	20
24, 27	Skerriff (*Tichburn*) .	419	0	5	Armagh .	Fews Upper .	Newtownhamilton .	Castleblayney .	III.	49
24, 27	Skerriff (*Trueman*) .	341	2	17	Armagh .	Fews Upper .	Newtownhamilton .	Castleblayney .	III.	49
18	Skerrig . .	169	2	27	Cavan .	Tullygarvey .	Drumgoon .	Cootehill .	III.	88
36, 45	Skerry . . .	184	1	31*a*	Donegal .	Kilmacrenan .	Kilmacrenan .	Milford .	III.	129
7	Skerry . . .	1,150	3	3	Queen's Co.	Tinnahinch .	Rosenallis .	Mountmellick .	I.	250
24	Skerry East .	2,017	0	35	Antrim .	Kilconway .	Newtown Crommelin	Ballymena .	III.	27
9	Skerryglass .	87	0	17	Tyrone .	Strabane Lower .	Urney . .	Strabane .	III.	323
20	Skerrymore .	213	3	9	Monaghan	Cremorne .	Muckno . .	Castleblayney .	III.	262
24	Skerry West .	727	1	4	Antrim .	Kilconway .	Newtown Crommelin	Ballymena .	III.	27
39	Skerrywhirry .	2,236	0	24	Antrim .	Lower Antrim .	Glenwhirry .	Ballymena .	III.	4
12	Skervan . .	116	0	0	Monaghan	Monaghan .	Drumsnat .	Monaghan .	III.	275
17	*Sketrick Island* .	40	3	35	Down .	Ards Upper .	Ardkeen .	Newtownards .	III.	159
96, 97	Skevanish .	359	0	23	Cork, W.R.	East Carbery (E.D.) .	Inishannon .	Bandon .	II.	128
60	Skey . . .	262	3	31	Tyrone .	Dungannon Lower .	Carnteel .	Clogher .	III.	298
9	Skibbereen .	110	1	35	Waterford	Middlethird .	Kilrossanty .	Waterford .	II.	367
141	SKIBBEREEN T. .	—			Cork, W.R.	WestCarbery(E.D.) {	Abbeystrowry . Creagh . }	Skibbereen .	II. {	136 139
13	Skibbolecorragh .	44	3	34	Sligo .	Tireragh . .	Skreen .	Dromore West .	IV.	236
18	Skibbolmore .	82	0	8	Louth .	Ferrard . .	Dunleer .	Ardee .	I.	181
79	Skiddernagh .	290	3	2*b*	Mayo .	Carra . .	Manulla .	Castlebar .	IV.	129
151	*Shiddy Island* .	1	2	34	Cork, W.R.	West Carbery (E.D.) .	Myross .	Skibbereen .	II.	141
7, 11	Skidoo . .	658	3	3	Dublin .	Nethercross .	Swords .	Balrothery .	I.	32
45	Skilganaban .	577	0	15	Antrim .	Lower Belfast .	Ballynure .	Larne .	III.	7
27, 28	Skillyscolban .	450	3	27	Down .	Lower Iveagh, Lr. pt.	Dromore .	Banbridge .	III.	168
10	Skinboy . .	152	1	29	Tyrone .	Strabane Lower .	Ardstraw .	Strabane .	III.	319
10	Skinboy Mountain .	242	2	19	Tyrone .	Strabane Lower .	Ardstraw .	Strabane .	III.	319
10	Skinnagin .	85	0	34	Monaghan	Monaghan .	Tehallan .	Monaghan .	III.	280
6	Skinnagin .	94	0	23	Monaghan	Trough . .	Donagh . .	Monaghan .	III.	282
1, 5	Skinnahergna .	112	0	23	Monaghan	Trough . .	Errigal Trough .	Clogher .	III.	285
17	Skinnew . .	248	2	18	Wexford .	Gorey . .	Monamolin .	Gorey .	I.	321
9	Skinstown .	176	1	5	Kilkenny .	Galmoy .	Rathbeagh .	Urlingford .	I.	93
21	Skirk Glebe or Erris	105	0	8	Queen's Co.	Clandonagh .	Skirk . .	Donaghmore .	I.	235
21	Skirk or Newtown .	599	1	26	Queen's Co.	Clandonagh .	Skirk . .	Donaghmore .	I.	235
21, 26	Skirteen . .	89	0	39	Kildare .	Offaly West .	Monasterevin .	Athy .	I.	73
22, 23	Skool . . .	292	3	28	Limerick .	Smallcounty .	Fedamore .	Limerick .	II.	259
22, 23	Skoolhill . .	214	1	35	Limerick .	Smallcounty .	Fedamore .	Limerick .	II.	259
94, 100	Skreen . . .	360	3	37	Donegal .	Tirhugh . .	Drumhome .	Donegal .	III.	147
26	Skreen . . .	119	1	36	Fermanagh .	Clanawley .	Cleenish .	Enniskillen .	III.	191
32	Skreen . . .	99	0	10	Fermanagh .	Clanawley .	Killesher .	Enniskillen .	III.	193
32	Skreen . . .	1,266	2	19	Meath .	Skreen . .	Skreen . .	Dunshaughlin .	I.	221
42	Skreen . . .	201	3	24	Tyrone .	Omagh East .	Donacavey .	Omagh .	III.	310
13	Skreen Beg .	96	0	0	Sligo .	Tireragh . .	Skreen . .	Dromore West .	IV.	236

(*a*) Including 20A. 2R. 0P. water.   (*b*) Including 17A. 0R. 7P. water.

No. of Sheet of the Ordnance Survey Maps.	Townlands and Towns.	Area in Statute Acres.	County.	Barony.	Parish.	Poor Law Union in 1857.	Townland Census of 1851, Part I.	
		A. R. P.					Page	Vol.
36	Skreen Lower	442 2 36a	Donegal	Kilmacrenan	Kilmacrenan	Millford	III.	129
13, 19	Skreen More	106 0 22	Sligo	Tireragh	Skreen	Dromore West	IV.	236
32	SKREEN T.	—	Meath	Skreen	Skreen	Dunshaughlin	I.	221
36	Skreen Upper	223 0 29b	Donegal	Kilmacrenan	Kilmacrenan	Millford	III.	129
7, 11	Skreeny	151 2 7	Leitrim	Drumahaire	Cloonclare	Manorhamilton	IV.	94
7	Skreeny	58 1 36	Leitrim	Rosclogher	Killasnet	Manorhamilton	IV.	110
7	Skreeny Little	144 2 12	Leitrim	Drumahaire	Cloonclare	Manorhamilton	IV.	94
20	Skrillagh	75 1 1	Kerry	Clanmaurice	Ardfert	Tralee	II.	167
41, 42, 44	Skrine	874 3 28	Roscommon	Athlone	Kilmeane	Roscommon	IV.	182
5	Skrinny	105 3 11	Fermanagh	Lurg	Drumkeeran	Lowtherstown	III.	207
139, 148	Skull	674 3 36	Cork, W.R.	West Carbery (W.D.)	Skull	Skull	II.	147
139, 148	SKULL T.	—	Cork, W.R.	West Carbery (W.D.)	Skull	Skull	II.	147
48	Slad	123 0 3	Wexford	Forth	Kilscoran	Wexford	I.	311
70, 77	Sladagh	141 1 3	Tipperary, S.R.	Middlethird	Baptistgrange	Cashel	II.	325
21	Slade	142 2 8	Dublin	Newcastle	Saggart	Celbridge	I.	35
26	Slade	157 0 7	Kilkenny	Callan	Callan	Callan	I.	84
54	Slade	241 3 8	Wexford	Shelburne	Hook	New Ross	I.	327
24	Slademore	101 3 8	Dublin	Newcastle	Rathcoole	Celbridge	I.	34
54	SLADE T.	—	Wexford	Shelburne	Hook	New Ross	I.	327
10	Sladoo	243 3 15	Clare	Burren	Carran	Ballyvaghan	II.	12
19	Sladran	1,267 3 0	Donegal	Inishowen West	Fahan Lower	Inishowen	III.	120
40	Slaghbooly	482 3 29	Clare	Islands	Kilmaley	Ennis	II.	31
37	Slaght	672 3 22	Antrim	Lower Antrim	Connor	Ballymena	III.	3
84, 85, 94	Slaght	812 1 0	Kerry	Glanarought	Kilgarvan	Kenmare	II.	188
34	Slaght	213 1 14	Wexford	Bantry	Oldross	New Ross	I.	301
108, 118	Slaghta	135 2 35	Galway	Longford	Fahy	Portumna	IV.	58
26	Slaghtaverty	259 1 36	Londonderry	Coleraine	Errigal	Coleraine	III.	232
20, 21	Slaghtfreeden	2,302 1 32c	Tyrone	Dungannon Upper	Lissan	Cookstown	III.	309
23	Slaghtmanus	2,115 1 17	Londonderry	Tirkeeran	Cumber Lower	Londonderry	III.	249
32	Slaghtneill	954 2 27	Londonderry	Loughinsholin	Killelagh	Magherafelt	III.	241
36, 37	Slaghtybogy	462 2 11	Londonderry	Loughinsholin	Maghera	Magherafelt	III.	242
94	Slaheny	760 1 9	Kerry	Glanarought	Kilgarvan	Kenmare	II.	188
62	Slainstown North	154 3 6	Tipperary, S.R.	Middlethird	Rathcool	Cashel	II.	329
62	Slainstown South	14 0 7	Tipperary, S.R.	Middlethird	Rathcool	Cashel	II.	329
32	Slanduff	264 1 5	Meath	Skreen	Monktown	Navan	I.	221
29	Slane	823 2 24	Antrim	Lower Antrim	Skerry	Ballymena	III.	5
19	Slane	745 3 20d	Meath	Upper Slane	Slane	Navan	I.	225
18	Slane Beg	308 0 20	Westmeath	Moyashel and Magheradernon	Dysart	Mullingar	I.	274
19	Slanecastle Demesne	563 3 33e	Meath	Upper Slane	Slane	Navan	I.	225
18	Slane More	408 1 3	Westmeath	Moyashel and Magheradernon	Dysart	Mullingar	I.	274
25	Slanes	197 2 18	Down	Ards Upper	Slanes	Downpatrick	III.	161
32	Slanestown	141 3 25	Meath	Skreen	Rathfeigh	Dunshaughlin	I.	221
18	Slanestown	478 3 26	Westmeath	Moyashel and Magheradernon	Mullingar	Mullingar	I.	275
19	SLANE T.	—	Meath	Upper Slane	Slane	Navan	I.	225
27	Slaneypark	90 3 20	Wicklow	Upper Talbotstown	Baltinglass	Baltinglass	I.	362
8	Slaneyquarter	373 0 2	Carlow	Carlow	Grangeford	Carlow	I.	2
24, 25	Slanore	129 3 16f	Cavan	Upper Loughtee	Kilmore	Cavan	III.	85
20	Slapragh	705 0 26	Fermanagh	Clanawley	Cleenish	Ballyshannon	III.	191
9, 10	Slatady	177 3 19	Down	Castlereagh Upper	Knockbreda	Belfast	III.	165
64	Slatbeg	753 0 24g	Tyrone	Clogher	Clogher	Clogher	III.	293
13, 19	Slate	130 0 22	Wicklow	Newcastle	Newcastle Lower	Rathdrum	I.	353
125	Slatefield	185 2 34h	Galway	Leitrim	Ballynakill	Loughrea	IV.	52
52	Slatefield	85 3 38	Tipperary, S.R.	Middlethird	Ardmayle	Cashel	II.	324
46, 54	Slatehill	68 2 2	Donegal	Raphoe	Allsaints	Londonderry	III.	134
20, 25	Slate House	43 0 32	Antrim	Lower Glenarm	Ardclinis	Larne	III.	21
20	Slatequarries	143 3 17	Kildare	Naas North	Rathmore	Naas	I.	63
24	Slate Quarries	18 1 25	Kildare	Naas South	Tipperkevin	Naas	I.	65
64	Slatmore	405 1 9i	Tyrone	Clogher	Clogher	Clogher	III.	293
24	Slattagh Beg	175 3 27	Roscommon	Ballintober North	Kilglass	Strokestown	IV.	186
24	Slattagh More	865 2 22	Roscommon	Ballintober North	Kilglass	Strokestown	IV.	186
19	Slattinagh	305 0 8	Fermanagh	Magheraboy	Devenish	Ballyshannon	III.	211
13, 19	Slattinagh, Barr of	244 0 19	Fermanagh	Magheraboy	Devenish	Ballyshannon	III.	210
31	Slatt Lower	896 0 30	Queen's Co.	Slievemargy	Rathaspick	Carlow	I.	246
31	Slatt Upper	857 1 3	Queen's Co.	Slievemargy	Rathaspick	Carlow	I.	246
77, 88	Slaugar	213 0 15	Mayo	Burrishoole	Kilmeena	Westport	IV.	122
8	Slawin	154 0 2	Fermanagh	Magheraboy	Inishmacsaint	Ballyshannon	III.	213
8, 13	Slawin, Barr of	240 3 12j	Fermanagh	Magheraboy	Inishmacsaint	Ballyshannon	III.	212
22	Sleadycastle	77 0 33	Waterford	Decies without Drum	Modelligo	Dungarvan	II.	359
12, 18	Sleamaine or Ballinvalla	540 3 19	Wicklow	Ballinacor North	Calary	Rathdrum	I.	346
24	Sleanaglogh	440 0 30	Wicklow	Newcastle	Derrylossary	Rathdrum	I.	351

(a) Including 23A. 1R. 0P. water.
(b) Including 31A. 0R. 39P. water.
(c) Including 59A. 3R. 21P. Lough Fea.
(d) Including 8A. 1R. 1P. water.

(e) Including 19A. 2R. 10P. water.
(f) Including 4A. 0R. 0P. water.
(g) Including 0A. 2R. 0P. water.

(h) Including 9A. 2R. 16P. water.
(i) Including 0A. 1R. 8P. water.
(j) Including 5A. 3R. 39P. water.

No. of Sheet of the Ordnance Survey Maps.	Townlands and Towns.	Area in Statute Acres.			County.	Barony.	Parish.	Poor Law Union in 1857.	Townland Census of 1851, Part I.	
		A.	R.	P.					Vol.	Page
15	Sleans	109	2	21	Antrim	Lower Glenarm	Layd	Ballycastle	III.	23
32	Sleaty	442	1	13a	Queen's Co.	Slievemargy	Sleaty	Carlow	I.	246
32	SLEATYCRAIGUE T.	—			Queen's Co.	Slievemargy	Killeshin	Carlow	I.	246
27, 33	Slee	162	2	2b	Fermanagh	Tirkennedy	Derryvullan	Enniskillen	III.	221
27	Slee	152	1	22c	Fermanagh	Tirkennedy	Enniskillen	Enniskillen	III.	222
42, 47	Sleedagh	284	3	24	Wexford	Bargy	Kilmannan	Wexford	I.	306
32, 33	Sleeghan	214	1	6	Donegal	Kilmacrenan	Tullaghobegly	Dunfanaghy	III.	132
19, 20	Sleehaun	425	2	1	Longford	Ardagh	Rathreagh	Ballymahon	I.	153
19, 20, 24	Sleehaun (Sankey)	95	0	18	Longford	Ardagh	Rathreagh	Ballymahon	I.	153
26	Sleemana	198	3	14	Cork, E.R.	Fermoy	Castletownroche	Fermoy	II.	78
94	Sleenoge	118	3	21	Cork, W.R.	East Carbery (W.D.)	Kinneigh	Dunmanway	II.	135
77, 89	Sleveen	247	0	39	Cork, E.R.	Imokilly	Cloyne	Middleton	II.	86
112	Sleveen	18	1	27	Cork, E.R.	Kinsale	Ringcurran	Kinsale	II.	100
121, 122	Sleveen	360	2	12	Cork, W.R.	Ibane and Barryroe	Kilmeen	Clonakilty	II.	149
9, 15	Sleveen	386	3	18	Kerry	Clanmaurice	Rattoo	Listowel	II.	173
10	Sleveen	133	3	17	Kilkenny	Fassadinin	Kilmacar	Castlecomer	I.	90
15	Sleveen	77	0	33	Leitrim	Drumahaire	Killarga	Manorhamilton	IV.	99
34	Sleveen	82	2	6	Waterford	Coshmore&Coshbride	Kilcockan	Lismore	II.	343
25	Sleveen	225	3	3	Waterford	Decies without Drum	Kilbarrymeaden	Kilmacthomas	II.	356
71	Sleveen East	528	1	10	Cork, W.R.	West Muskerry	Macroom	Macroom	II.	160
70, 71	Sleveen West	226	3	15	Cork, W.R.	West Muskerry	Macroom	Macroom	II.	160
25	SLEVEEN T.	—			Waterford	Decies without Drum	Kilbarrymeaden	Kilmacthomas	II.	356
27, 28	Slevin	448	3	4	Roscommon	Castlereagh	Baslick	Castlereagh	IV.	199
39	Slevinagee	103	2	36	Roscommon	Ballintober South	Roscommon	Roscommon	IV.	190
3, 4, 6, 7	Slevoir	435	3	12	Tipperary, N.R.	Lower Ormond	Terryglass	Borrisokane	II.	288
41	Slevoy	626	0	8	Wexford	Shelmaliere West	Taghmon	Wexford	I.	335
35	Slievadrehid	203	0	35	Kerry	Corkaguiny	Cloghane	Dingle	II.	175
83, 92	Slievaduff	764	1	0	Kerry	Dunkerron South	Templenoe	Kenmare	II.	185
9	Slievawaddra	154	3	38	Kerry	Clanmaurice	Rattoo	Listowel	II.	173
17, 18	Slieve	573	2	8	Galway	Ballymoe	Dunmore	Glennamaddy	IV.	7
13	Slieve	332	2	1	Longford	Longford	Killashee	Longford	I.	158
3, 6	Slieve	140	1	4	Louth	Upper Dundalk	Kane	Dundalk	I.	179
46	Slieveadoctor	260	3	8	Cork, E.R.	Kinnatalloon	Mogeely	Fermoy	II.	99
32	Slievealoughaun	232	3	26	Clare	Islands	Kilmaley	Ennis	II.	31
80, 81	Slieveancena	2,993	3	4d	Galway	Moycullen	Moycullen	Galway	IV.	71
13	Slieveanore	3,168	0	10e	Clare	Tulla Upper	Feakle	Scarriff	II.	40
95	Slieveaun	185	3	17	Galway	Dunkellin	Stradbally	Galway	IV.	32
6, 11	Slievebane	330	2	35f	Fermanagh	Lurg	Magheraculmoney	Lowtherstown	III.	208
29, 30	Slievebane and Drumnagreagh	1,127	3	20	Antrin	Upper Glenarm	Carncastle	Larne	III.	24
18	Slievebaun	161	3	11	Wexford	Bantry	Killann	Enniscorthy	I.	300
6	Slievebaun	204	0	30	Wexford	Gorey	Kilnahue	Gorey	I.	319
18	Slieveboy	89	3	11	Louth	Ferrard	Dunleer	Ardee	I.	181
3, 7	Slieveboy	491	0	20	Westmeath	Fore	Rathgarve	Castletowndelvin	I.	271
28	Slieveboy Lower	321	1	0	Wicklow	Ballinacor South	Kiltegan	Baltinglass	I.	350
28	Slieveboy Upper	204	0	21	Wicklow	Ballinacor South	Kiltegan	Baltinglass	I.	350
14	Slievebrickan	132	2	17	Cavan	Lower Loughtee	Tomregan	Bawnboy	III.	81
62	Slievebuck	140	2	32	Donegal	Raphoe	Raphoe	Letterkenny	III.	141
35,36,49,50	Slieveburke	1,460	3	34g	Galway	Ballynahinch	Ballindoon	Clifden	IV.	10
34	Slieveburth	72	1	32	Waterford	Coshmore&Coshbride	Kilwatermoy	Lismore	II.	344
15	Slievebwee	181	1	24	Kerry	Clanmaurice	Killahan	Tralee	II.	170
37	Slievecarragh	262	1	26	Kilkenny	Ida	Dysartmoon	New Ross	I.	102
6	Slievecarran	657	1	33	Clare	Burren	Oughtmama	Ballyvaghan	II.	14
34	Slieve-iiltia Commons	183	2	34	Wexford	Shelburne	Whitechurch	New Ross	I.	329
34, 38	Slieve and Corbally	1,181	2	31h	Roscommon	Ballymoe	Ballynakill	Roscommon	IV.	191
9, 10, 15, 16	Slievecorragh	773	3	5	Wicklow	Lower Talbotstown	Hollywood	Baltinglass	I.	361
29	Slievedarragh	116	0	8	Galway	Dunmore	Dunmore	Tuam	IV.	34
14, 22	Slievedoo	4,559	3	14i	Tyrone	Omagh West	Termonamongan	Castlederg	III.	317
69	Slievedooley	522	1	38	Clare	Clonderalaw	Killofin	Kilrush	II.	17
51	Slievedotia	712	3	16	Cork, E.R.	Barretts	Whitechurch	Cork	II.	50
86, 98	Slievedotia	72	3	28	Galway	Kilconnell	Grange	Loughrea	IV.	40
40, 45	Slieveduff	263	1	10	Wicklow	Arklow	Inch	Rathdrum	I.	344
24	Slievedurda	92	1	15	Carlow	St. Mullins Lower	St. Mullins	New Ross	I.	13
36, 45	Slieve East	1,128	1	35	Kerry	Corkaguiny	Kilgobban	Tralee	II.	177
57, 69, 70	Slievefin	503	1	2	Galway	Clare	Annaghdown	Galway	IV.	16
39,40,44,45	Slievefoore	412	2	14	Wicklow	Arklow	Killahurler	Rathdrum	I.	345
97, 111	Slievegallane	461	0	34	Cork, E.R.	Kinalea	Leighmoney	Kinsale	II.	96
13	Slievegar	235	2	7	Wexford	Scarawalsh	Templeshanbo	Enniscorthy	I.	326
57	Slievegaura	234	1	34	Kerry	Magunihy	Kilbonane	Killarney	II.	200
25, 26, 34	Slieveglass	485	3	10	Kerry	Corkaguiny	Cloghane	Dingle	II.	175
44, 45	Slievegorm	125	1	0j	Galway	Tiaquin	Killererin	Tuam	IV.	77
28, 29	Slieve Gullion	987	1	30	Armagh	Orior Upper	Forkill	Newry	III.	57

(a) Including 3A. 1R. 10P. River Barrow.
(b) Including 39A. 0R. 27P. water.
(c) Including 23A. 3R. 35P. water.
(d) Including 91A. 0R. 25P. water.

(e) Including 45A. 0R. 1P. water.
(f) Including 10A. 3R. 27P. water.
(g) Including 316A. 3R. 3P. water.

(h) Including 14A. 1R. 2P. water.
(i) Including 37A. 1R. 16P. water.
(j) Including 1A. 3R. 24P. water.

No. of Sheet of the Ordnance Survey Maps.	Townlands and Towns.	Area in Statute Acres. A. R. P.	County.	Barony.	Parish.	Poor Law Union in 1857.	Townland Census of 1851, Part I. Vol.	Page
5, 6	Slievelahan or Loughanstown Lower	145 1 12	Westmeath	Moygoish	Russagh	Granard	I.	280
28	Slievemaan	571 2 32	Wicklow	Ballinacor South	Kiltegan	Baltinglass	I.	350
153	Slievemore	283 3 6	Cork, W.R.	West Carbery (E.D.)	Tullagh	Skibbereen	II.	141
41, 42, 54	Slievemore	3,722 3 21a	Mayo	Burrishoole	Achill	Newport	IV.	117
5, 6, 8, 9	Slievemore or Kingsmountain	704 1 19	Sligo	Carbury	Drumcliff	Sligo	IV.	221
19, 32, 33	Slievemurry	1,162 1 7	Galway	Killian	Killeroran	Mountbellew	IV.	44
33, 34	Slievemweel	376 2 37	Wicklow	Ballinacor South	Moyne	Shillelagh	I.	350
9	Slievenabillog	35 1 8	Clare	Burren	Killeany	Ballyvaghan	II.	13
35	Slievenaboley	1,193 1 38b	Down	Upper Iveagh, Lr. pt.	Drumgooland	Banbridge	III.	172
92	Slievenabrehan	153 3 36	Mayo	Clanmorris	Knock	Claremorris	IV.	135
60, 64	Slievenacloy	240 0 9	Antrim	Upper Belfast	Derryaghy	Lisburn	III.	10
60, 64	Slievenacloy	439 1 9	Antrim	Upper Massereene	Derryaghy	Lisburn	III.	30
30	Slievenagark	218 1 4	Mayo	Tirawley	Ardagh	Ballina	IV.	164
14	Slievenageeragh	250 0 37	Clare	Corcomroe	Kilmacrehy	Ennistimon	II.	20
31, 36	Slievenagh	407 1 31	Antrim	Lower Toome	Ahoghill	Ballymena	III.	32
22, 26	Slievenaghy	595 3 23	Antrim	Kilconway	Finvoy	Ballymoney	III.	26
10	Slievenaglasha	249 1 23	Clare	Inchiquin	Killinaboy	Corrofin	II.	27
27	Slievenagorea	239 3 32	Wexford	Ballaghkeen	Ballyhuskard	Enniscorthy	I.	292
27	Slievenagrane	341 3 35	Wexford	Ballaghkeen	Castle-ellis	Enniscorthy	I.	293
60	Slievenagravery	323 3 32	Antrim	Upper Belfast	Derryaghy	Lisburn	III.	10
38	Slievenagriddle	237 3 21	Down	Lecale Lower	Ballee	Downpatrick	III.	178
8	Slievenagry	197 3 10	Clare	Corcomroe	Kilfenora	Ennistimon	II.	19
19, 21	Slievenakilla	2,805 0 39c	Leitrim	Drumahaire	Drumreilly	Cark on Shannon	IV.	95
42, 43	Slievenalargy	477 3 8d	Down	Upper Iveagh, Lr. pt.	Kilcoo	Kilkeel	III.	173
23, 31	Slievenalicka	322 0 15e	Clare	Ibrickan	Kilfarboy	Ennistimon	II.	22
28, 33	Slievenamough	354 3 26	Wicklow	Ballinacor South	Kiltegan	Baltinglass	I.	350
28, 33	Slievenamough Plain	178 2 28	Wicklow	Ballinacor South	Kiltegan	Baltinglass	I.	350
90, 99	Slievenashaska	1,493 3 11f	Kerry	Dunkerron South	Kilcrohane	Kenmare	II.	184
28, 29	Slievenavadoge	185 1 15	Kerry	Trughanacmy	Clogherbrien	Tralee	II.	209
40	Slievenavode	82 2 7	Wicklow	Arklow	Castlemacadam	Rathdrum	I.	342
36	Slievenisky	1,198 2 31	Down	Upper Iveagh, Lr. pt.	Kilmegan	Downpatrick	III.	173
94	Slieveowen	335 0 32	Cork, W.R.	West Muskerry	Kilmichael	Dunmanway	II.	159
58	Slievereagh	1,646 1 38	Cork, W.R.	West Muskerry	Ballyvourney	Macroom	II.	154
28	Slievereagh Lower	266 2 21	Wicklow	Upper Talbotstown	Kiltegan	Baltinglass	I.	365
28	Slievereagh Upper	259 0 30	Wicklow	Upper Talbotstown	Kiltegan	Baltinglass	I.	365
98	Slieveroe	551 2 3	Cork, E.R.	Kinalea	Cullen	Kinsale	II.	94
41	Slieveroe	461 3 33	Galway	Clare	Killursa	Tuam	IV.	22
96	Slieveroe	275 2 34	Galway	Dunkellin	Killora	Loughrea	IV.	31
31	Slieveroe	191 1 3	Galway	Tiaquin	Kilkerrin	Glennamaddy	IV.	77
24, 25	Slieveroe	282 0 32	Kildare	Naas South	Tipperkevin	Naas	I.	65
13, 18	Slieveroe	264 0 3	Monaghan	Monaghan	Kilmore	Monaghan	III.	276
8, 9	Slieveroe	220 0 1	Roscommon	Frenchpark	Kilnamanagh	Castlereagh	IV.	204
17	Slieveroe	239 1 32	Waterford	Middlethird	Lisnakill	Waterford	II.	368
30	Slieveroe	194 2 34	Wicklow	Arklow	Kilcommon	Rathdrum	I.	345
33, 38	Slieveroe	513 0 1	Wicklow	Ballinacor South	Moyne	Shillelagh	I.	350
14	Slieveroe or Siberia	147 0 8	Sligo	Carbury	Killaspugbrone	Sligo	IV.	222
24	Slievethoul	403 1 25	Dublin	Newcastle	Rathcoole	Celbridge	I.	34
36, 45	Slieve West	607 1 9	Kerry	Corkaguiny	Kilgobban	Tralee	II.	177
14	Sliganagh	140 3 19	Leitrim	Drumahaire	Killanummery	Manorhamilton	IV.	98
31	Sligaunagh	31 0 20	Waterford	Decies without Drum	Dungarvan	Dungarvan	II.	356
14	SLIGO T.	—	Sligo	Carbury	Calry / St. Johns	Sligo	IV.	{220 223}
19	Sliguff	784 2 19d	Carlow	Idrone East	Lorum	Carlow	I.	8
16, 19	Sliguff	478 0 22h	Carlow	Idrone East	Sliguff	Carlow	I.	8
86, 98	Slihaun Beg	74 2 7	Galway	Kilconnell	Killallaghtan	Ballinasloe	IV.	41
86, 98	Slihaun More	207 2 12	Galway	Kilconnell	Killallaghtan	Ballinasloe	IV.	41
3, 4	Slimag	162 1 35	Londonderry	North East Liberties of Coleraine	Ballywillin	Coleraine	III.	245
77	Slinaun	179 3 32	Mayo	Burrishoole	Kilmaclasser	Westport	IV.	121
77	Slinaunroe	286 3 24	Mayo	Burrishoole	Kilmaclasser	Westport	IV.	121
118	Slip	24 3 21	Cork, W.R.	Bantry	Kilmocomoge	Bantry	II.	122
37	Slipperygreen	30 1 13	Wexford	Forth	St. Peters	Wexford	I.	314
13, 14	Slisgarrow	293 0 3i	Fermanagh	Magheraboy	Devenish	Ballyshannon	III.	211
13	Slisgarrow	428 3 18	Fermanagh	Magheraboy	Inishmacsaint	Ballyshannon	III.	213
100	Slishmeen	79 3 23	Mayo	Carra	Rosslee	Ballinrobe	IV.	130
15, 21	Slishwood	374 3 1	Sligo	Tirerrill	Killerry	Sligo	IV.	239
21	Slishwood Islands	{0 2 13 / 0 1 15}	Sligo	Tirerrill	Killerry	Sligo	IV.	239
2	Sliss	129 0 37	Kerry	Iraghticonnor	Aghavallen	Listowel	II.	189
6, 7, 11, 12	Sloanstown	261 0 17	Down	Ards Lower	Donaghadee	Newtownards	III.	158
132	Sloe Island	0 3 21	Galway	Leitrim	Ballynakill	Portumna	IV.	52
33	Sloughan	687 2 25	Tyrone	Omagh West	Longfield West	Castlederg	III.	316

(a) Including 26A. 1R. 16P. water.
(b) Including 9A. 2R. 33P. water.
(c) Including 8A. 2R. 11P. water.
(d) Including 36A. 3R. 12P. water.
(e) Including 8A. 1R. 29P. water.
(f) Including 20A. 0R. 17P. water.
(g) Including 7A. 0R. 24P. River Barrow.
(h) Including 11A. 3R. 35P. River Barrow.
(i) Including 7A. 0R. 8P. water.

No. of Sheet of the Ordnance Survey Maps.	Townlands and Towns.	Area in Statute Acres.	County.	Barony.	Parish.	Poor Law Union in 1857.	Townland Census of 1851, Part I.	
		A. R. P.					Vol.	Page
36, 37, 45	Sluggan .	1,176 0 20	Tyrone .	Omagh East . .	Termonmaguirk	Omagh .	III.	315
21, 29	Sluggara .	135 2 26	Waterford .	Decies without Drum	Affane .	Lismore .	II.	353
13	Sluggary .	347 3 12	Limerick .	Pubblebrien .	Mungret .	Limerick .	II.	254
17	Sluicequarter .	261 3 34a	Kerry .	Iraghticonnor .	Duagh .	Listowel .	II.	190
28, 34	Slush Hill .	337 2 39	Fermanagh .	Magherastephana .	Aghalurcher .	Lisnaskea .	III.	217
18	Slutsend or West Farm	125 0 12b	Dublin .	Coolock and Municipal Borough	Glasnevin .	Dublin North .	I.	27
35	Smaghraan .	178 1 27	Roscommon .	Ballintober South .	Kilbride .	Roscommon .	IV.	189
31, 35	Smallford .	351 1 38	Kildare .	Narragh&RebanWest	Kilberry .	Athy .	I.	68
39, 42	*Small Island* .	4 0 24	Fermanagh .	Knockninny .	Galloon .	Lisnaskea .	III.	201
42	Small Island .	3 2 22	Londonderry .	Loughinsholin .	Ballyscullion .	Magherafelt .	III.	240
14	Small Park .	68 0 20c	Down .	Lower Iveagh, Up. pt.	Hillsborough .	Lisburn .	III.	169
17, 18	Smallquarter .	376 0 33	Antrim .	Upper Dunluce .	Kilraghts .	Ballymoney .	III.	20
5	Smallquarter .	68 1 17	Waterford .	Glenahiry .	Kilronan .	Clonmel .	II.	366
17, 20	Smarmore .	1,119 1 15	Louth .	Ardee .	Smarmore .	Ardee .	I.	174
43	Smartscastle East .	76 3 37	Kilkenny .	Ida .	Dunkitt .	Waterford .	I.	101
43	Smartscastle West .	110 0 1	Kilkenny .	Ida .	Dunkitt .	Waterford .	I.	101
2, 3	Smear .	1,072 1 0	Longford .	Granard .	Columbkille .	Granard .	I.	156
33, 42	Smerwick .	457 0 36	Kerry .	Corkaguiny .	Dunurlin .	Dingle .	II.	176
107	Sminver .	99 3 1	Donegal .	Tirhugh .	Kilbarron .	Ballyshannon .	III.	148
12	SMITHBOROUGH T. .	—	Monaghan .	Monaghan .	Clones .	Monaghan .	III.	275
32	Smithfield .	198 3 2	Cork, E.R. .	Duhallow .	Kilshannig .	Mallow .	II.	74
23, 24	Smithfield .	104 3 0	Longford .	Ardagh .	Kilglass .	Ballymahon .	I.	152
47	Smithsfarm .	18 3 14	Tipperary, N.R. .	Eliogarty .	Moycarky .	Thurles .	II.	271
40	*Smith's Island* .	2 1 15	Galway .	Ross .	Cong .	Oughterard .	IV.	73
19	Smithsland North .	106 1 5	Kilkenny .	Shillelogher .	St. Patrick's .	Kilkenny .	I.	116
19	Smithsland South .	66 1 7	Kilkenny .	Shillelogher .	St. Patrick's .	Kilkenny .	I.	116
51	Smithstown .	309 2 31	Clare .	Bunratty Lower .	Drumline .	Ennis .	II.	3
8, 15	Smithstown .	285 0 25	Clare .	Corcomroe .	Kilshanny .	Ennistimon .	II.	22
10	Smithstown .	232 0 3	Kildare .	North Salt .	Taghadoe .	Celbridge .	I.	76
5, 6, 10, 11	Smithstown .	689 0 11	Kilkenny .	Fassadinin .	Dysart .	Castlecomer .	I.	89
20, 24	Smithstown .	375 1 25	Kilkenny .	Gowran .	Dunbell .	Kilkenny .	I.	94
24	Smithstown .	9 3 34	Kilkenny .	Gowran .	Tullaherin .	Thomastown .	I.	100
36, 40	Smithstown .	169 3 17	Kilkenny .	Knocktopher .	Kilbeacon .	Waterford .	I.	112
36, 40	Smithstown .	777 1 26	Kilkenny .	Knocktopher .	Listerlin .	New Ross .	I.	113
14, 22	Smithstown .	128 3 13	King's Co. .	Garrycastle .	Gallen .	Parsonstown .	I.	136
20,21,27,28	Smithstown .	518 1 38	Meath .	Lower Duleek .	Julianstown .	Drogheda .	I.	196
38	Smithstown .	294 1 25	Meath .	Skreen .	Killeen .	Dunshaughlin .	I.	221
16	Smithstown .	440 1 23	Meath .	Upper Kells .	Kilskeer .	Kells .	I.	206
28	Smithstown Lower .	98 0 31	Kilkenny .	Gowran .	Thomastown .	Thomastown .	I.	99
28	Smithstown Upper .	358 1 1	Kilkenny .	Gowran .	Thomastown .	Thomastown .	I.	99
16	Smoor Beg .	122 3 31	Waterford .	Middlethird .	Dunhill .	Kilmacthomas .	II.	367
16	Smoor More .	248 0 15	Waterford .	Middlethird .	Dunhill .	Kilmacthomas .	II.	367
142	Smorane .	223 0 12	Cork, W.R. .	West Carbery (E.D.)	Castlehaven .	Skibbereen .	II.	138
141, 142	Smorane .	214 3 35	Cork, W.R. .	West Carbery (E.D.)	Creagh .	Skibbereen .	II.	139
18, 22	Smotscourt .	277 1 16	Dublin .	Dublin .	Donnybrook .	Dublin South .	I.	30
17, 25	Smulgedon .	495 3 4	Londonderry .	Keenaght .	Balteagh .	NewTnLimavady	III.	234
79, 90	Smuttanagh .	244 3 11	Mayo .	Carra .	Manulla .	Castlebar .	IV.	129
3	Smutternagh .	363 0 6	Roscommon .	Boyle .	Kilbryan .	Boyle .	IV.	195
54, 55	Snahadaun or Needle Island .	1 2 24	Galway .	Moycullen .	Kilcummin .	Oughterard .	IV.	69
19	Snakeel .	255 2 15	Cavan .	Upper Loughtee .	Kilmore .	Cavan .	III.	85
43	Snaty (*Cooper*) .	344 1 17	Clare .	Tulla Lower .	Kilseily .	Limerick .	II.	37
43	Snaty (*Massy*) .	324 0 35	Clare .	Tulla Lower .	Kilseily .	Limerick .	II.	37
43	Snaty (*Wilson*) .	294 1 3	Clare .	Tulla Lower .	Kilseily .	Limerick .	II.	37
65	Snauvbo .	444 2 9	Galway .	Moycullen .	Kilcummin .	Oughterard .	IV.	68
105	Snave .	247 1 30	Cork, W.R. .	Bantry .	Kilmocomoge .	Bantry .	II.	122
100	SNEEM T. .	—	Kerry .	Dunkerron South .	Kilcrohane .	Kenmare .	II.	184
26, 32	Sneeoge .	236 0 21	Meath .	Lower Duleek .	Duleek .	Drogheda .	I.	195
39	Sniggeen .	54 0 38	Sligo .	Corran .	Drumrat .	Boyle .	IV.	226
23, 24	Snimnagorta .	265 3 35	Westmeath .	Rathconrath .	Ballymore .	Ballymahon .	I.	282
28	Snowhill .	193 2 35	Fermanagh .	Tirkennedy .	Cleenish .	Enniskillen .	III.	220
15	Snug .	60 2 37	Dublin .	Coolock .	Raheny .	Dublin North .	I.	29
10	Snugborough .	496 0 39	Cavan .	Tullyhaw .	Tomregan .	Bawnboy .	III.	96
42	Snugborough .	226 3 2d	Clare .	Bunratty Lower .	Tomfinlough .	Ennis .	II.	7
74, 83	Snugborough .	406 2 22	Donegal .	Banagh .	Killybegs Lower .	Glenties .	III.	110
13, 14	Snugborough .	53 0 19	Dublin .	Castleknock .	Castleknock .	Dublin North .	I.	24
15	Snugborough .	102 3 24	Dublin .	Coolock .	Balgriffin .	Dublin North .	I.	26
44, 46	Snugborough .	58 1 32	King's Co. .	Clonlisk .	Cullenwaine .	Roscrea .	I.	129
38, 42	Snugborough .	67 0 5	King's Co. .	Clonlisk .	Kilmurryely .	Roscrea .	I.	131
49	Snugborough .	169 1 29	Limerick .	Coshlea .	Galbally .	Mitchelstown .	II.	239
18, 22	Snugborough .	36 0 22	Longford .	Moydow .	Kilcommock .	Ballymahon .	I.	161
78	Snugborough .	370 3 15e	Mayo .	Carra .	Aglish .	Castlebar .	IV.	124
29	Snugborough .	114 0 20	Waterford .	Coshmore&Coshbride	Kilwatermoy .	Lismore .	II.	344

(a) Including 12A. 1R. 24P. water.
(b) { Within the Municipal Boundary, 0A. 2R. 15P.
    { Without the Municipal Boundary, 124A. 1R. 37P.

(c) Including 9A. 3R. 25P. water.
(d) Including 2A. 0R. 32P. water.
(e) Including 36A. 0R. 17P. water.

No. of Sheet of the Ordnance Survey Maps.	Townlands and Towns.	Area in Statute Acres.	County.	Barony.	Parish.	Poor Law Union in 1857.	Townland Census of 1851. Part I.	
		A. R. P.					Vol.	Page
35, 40	Snugborough . .	147 3 16	Wicklow . .	Arklow . .	Kilbride . . .	Rathdrum .	I.	345
21	Snugborough . .	271 3 24	Wicklow . .	Upper Talbotstown .	Donaghmore . .	Baltinglass .	I.	363
37	Snugburrow . .	225 2 23	Kildare . .	Kilkea and Moone .	Tankardstown .	Athy . .	I.	61
39	Soarn . . .	102 0 26	Tyrone . .	Dungannon Middle .	Donaghenry . .	Cookstown .	III.	301
52	Sockar . . .	1,047 3 20	Donegal . .	Kilmacrenan .	Kilmacrenan . .	Letterkenny .	III.	129
15	Socknalougher .	80 0 2	Leitrim . .	Drumahaire .	Killarga . . .	Manorhamilton .	IV.	99
15	Socks . . .	84 3 32	Leitrim . .	Drumahaire .	Killarga . . .	Manorhamilton .	IV.	99
61	Sod Island . .	0 1 26	Clare . .	Bunratty Lower .	Bunratty . .	Ennis . .	II.	3
3, 6	Sogher . . .	82 3 25	Monaghan .	Trough . . .	Errigal Trough .	Monaghan .	III.	285
25	Soheen . . .	213 2 39	Clare . .	Inchiquin .	Kilnamona . .	Ennis . .	II.	27
6	Soho . . .	118 3 25	Westmeath .	Corkaree . .	Multyfarnham .	Mullingar .	I.	263
30	Solar . . .	42 3 19	Antrim . .	Upper Glenarm .	Carncastle . .	Larne . .	III.	24
51, 59	Solloghodbeg .	858 2 22	Tipperary, S.R.	Clanwilliam .	Sollophed-beg .	Tipperary .	II.	310
2	Sollus . . .	136 3 33	Tyrone . .	Strabane Lower .	Donaghedy . .	Strabane .	III.	321
20	Solsborough . .	148 2 28	Tipperary, N.R.	Lower Ormond .	Nenagh . .	Nenagh .	II.	287
20	Solsborough . .	265 0 30a	Wexford . .	Scarawalsh .	Clone . .	Enniscorthy .	I.	322
99, 100	Somerset . .	543 3 3	Galway . .	Longford .	Clontuskert .	Ballinasloe .	IV.	58
7	Somerset . .	409 3 27	Londonderry .	Coleraine .	Macosquin . .	Coleraine .	III.	233
9	Somervillestown .	89 1 29	Tyrone . .	Strabane Lower .	Urney . .	Strabane .	III.	323
7	Sonnagh . .	139 0 13	Galway . .	Ballymoe .	Ballynakill .	Glennamaddy .	IV.	5
7, 19	Sonnagh . .	282 1 24	Galway . .	Ballymoe .	Kilbegnet . .	Glennamaddy .	IV.	8
74	Sonnagh . .	308 2 5	Galway . .	Clonmacnowen .	Fohanagh . .	Ballinasloe .	IV.	25
30	Sonnagh . .	121 3 39	Leitrim . .	Carrigallen .	Carrigallen .	Mohill .	IV.	90
6	Sonnagh . .	526 0 20	Longford .	Granard . .	Columbkille .	Granard .	I.	156
62, 63	Sonnagh . .	1,480 2 39	Mayo . .	Costello . .	Kilbeagh . .	Swineford .	IV.	141
38	Sonnagh . .	190 2 14	Westmeath .	Moycashel .	Rahugh . .	Tullamore .	I.	279
11, 18	Sonnagh Demesne .	478 2 2	Westmeath .	Moygoish .	Templeoran .	Mullingar .	I.	281
19	Sonnagh East .	231 2 21	Galway . .	Ballymoe .	Boyounagh .	Glennamaddy .	IV.	6
115	Sonnagh New .	503 0 13	Galway . .	Loughrea .	Kilceenadeema .	Loughrea .	IV.	64
115	Sonnagh Old .	1,640 2 10	Galway . .	Loughrea .	Killeenadeema .	Loughrea .	IV.	64
19	Sonnagh West .	139 0 38	Galway . .	Ballymoe .	Boyounagh .	Glennamaddy .	IV.	6
73	Sonvolaun . .	681 0 26	Mayo . .	Costello . .	Kilmovee .	Swineford .	IV.	142
13	Soodry . .	268 1 34	Sligo . .	Tireragh .	Skreen . .	Dromore West .	IV.	236
27	Sooey . . .	151 1 8	Sligo . .	Tirerrill . .	Ballynakill .	Sligo .	IV.	237
52	Sooreeny . .	187 0 10	Clare . .	Bunratty Lower .	Kilfinaghta .	Tulla .	II.	4
39	Soppog . .	606 3 27	Donegal . .	Inishowen West .	Muff . . .	Londonderry .	III.	121
7, 10, 11	Sopwell . .	1,113 1 6b	Tipperary, N.R.	Lower Ormond .	Uskane . .	Borrisokane .	II.	288
5, 9	Soran . . .	1,204 1 4	Longford .	Longford .	Killoe . .	Longford .	I.	159
29, 30	Sorne . . .	691 2 5	Donegal . .	Inishowen West .	Fahan Lower .	Inishowen .	III.	120
8	Sorrel . . .	436 0 5	Cork, E.R.	Fermoy . .	Ballyhay . .	Mitchelstown .	II.	76
40, 48, 49	Sorrel Island or Illaunatoo .	276 1 20	Clare . .	Clonderalaw .	Kilmihil . .	Ennis . .	II.	17
52	Soughane . .	162 3 18	Wexford . .	Bargy . .	Kilturk . .	Wexford .	I.	307
29	Sousheen Common .	7 3 8c	Kildare . .	Naas South .	Ballymore Eustace .	Naas . .	I.	64
19	Southfield . .	216 1 30	Queen's Co. .	Ballyadams .	Ballyadams .	Athy .	I.	231
22	Southgreen . .	20 3 15	Kildare . .	Offaly East .	Kildare . .	Naas .	I.	70
22	Southgreen . .	164 0 2	Kildare . .	Offaly East .	Tully . .	Naas .	I.	71
15, 21	Southhill . .	121 3 16	Tipperary, N.R.	Upper Ormond .	Kilruane . .	Nenagh .	II.	292
14	South Hill . .	174 3 32	Westmeath .	Delvin . .	Castletowndelvin .	Castletowndelvin .	I.	265
11	South Island . .	20 2 30	Down . .	Ards Lower .	Greyabbey . .	Newtownards .	III.	158
29, 34	Southknock . .	116 2 5	Wexford . .	Bantry . .	St. Mary's .	New Ross .	I.	302
18	South Lots . .	31 0 12	Dublin . .	Dublin . . .	St. Marks . .	Dublin South .	I.	30
20	Southpark . .	126 2 20d	Waterford .	Coshmore&Coshbride .	Lismore & Mocollop .	Lismore .	II.	347
27	Southpark Demesne .	763 3 32	Roscommon .	Castlereagh .	Kilkeevin .	Castlereagh .	IV.	201
135	South-ring . .	246 2 11	Cork, W.R.	Ibane and Barryroe .	Templeomalus .	Clonakilty .	II.	151
125	Sovereign Island .	0 2 10	Cork, E.R.	Kinalea . .	Kinure . .	Kinsale .	II.	96
125	Sovereign Islands .	{ 1 0 37 { 1 2 38	Cork, E.R.	Kinsale . .	Ringcurran .	Kinsale .	II.	100
5, 6	Spa . . .	257 1 39	Roscommon .	Boyle . .	Boyle . .	Boyle .	IV.	194
1	Spa . . .	66 2 0	Waterford .	Upperthird .	St. Marys Clonmel .	Clonmel .	II.	372
93	Spaddagh . .	203 1 12	Mayo . .	Costello . .	Annagh . .	Claremorris .	IV.	138
107	Spaddan . .	68 3 38	Donegal . .	Tirhugh .	Kilbarron .	Ballyshannon .	III.	148
61	Spafield . .	76 0 31	Tipperary, S.R.	Middlethird .	St. John Baptist .	Cashel .	II.	330
25, 33	Spaglen . .	438 2 32	Cork. E.R.	Fermoy . .	Mallow . .	Mallow .	II.	81
19, 22	Spahill . .	559 3 6	Carlow . .	Idrone East .	Kiltennell .	Carlow .	I.	8
8	Spahill . .	201 1 24	Kilkenny . .	Galmoy . .	Balleen . .	Urlingford .	I.	91
19, 20	Spaightspark . .	42 1 33	Clare . .	Tulla Upper .	Feakle . .	Tulla .	II.	40
16	Spamount . .	88 0 2e	Tyrone . .	Omagh West .	Ardstraw . .	Castlederg .	III.	315
34	SPANCELHILL T. .	—	Clare . .	Bunratty Upper .	Clooney . .	Ennis .	II.	8
147	Spanishcove . .	84 1 23	Cork, W.R.	West Carbery (W.D.) .	Kilmoe . .	Skull .	II.	145
149	Spanish Island .	119 3 38	Cork, W.R.	West Carbery (E.D.) .	Creagh . .	Skibbereen .	II.	139
35	Spaquarter . .	177 0 25	Queen's Co. .	Clarmallagh .	Aghmacart .	Abbeyleix .	I.	236
131	Sparrograda . .	262 0 35	Cork, W.R.	West Carbery (W.D.) .	Skull . . .	Skull .	II.	147

(a) Including 4A. 0R. 0P. water.
(b) Including 9A. 2R. 8P. water.
(c) Including 1A. 0R. 36P. water.
(d) Including 9A. 2R. 16P. water.
(e) Including 4A. 2R. 25P. water.

No. of Sheet of the Ordnance Survey Maps.	Townlands and Towns.	Area in Statute Acres.			County.	Barony.	Parish.	Poor Law Union in 1857.	Townland Census of 1851, Part I.	
		A.	R.	P.					Vol.	Page
31	Sparrowsland	84	1	16	Wexford	Bantry	Clonmore	Enniscorthy	I.	300
31	Sparrowsland	185	0	33	Wexford	Bantry	Kilcowanmore	Enniscorthy	I.	300
23	Spaug	154	3	5	Clare	Corcomroe	Clooney	Ennistimon	II.	18
63	Speck	128	3	19	Mayo	Costello	Kilbeagh	Swineford	IV.	141
47	Speenoge	522	1	31	Donegal	Inishowen West	Burt	Londonderry	III.	120
23	Speerholme	163	0	16a	Tyrone	Omagh West	Termonamongan	Castlederg	III.	317
5, 8	Spellickanee	299	3	19	Louth	Lower Dundalk	Ballymascanlan	Dundalk	I.	176
42	Spelsherstown	81	1	13	Wexford	Bargy	Kilmannan	Wexford	I.	306
5, 6, 11, 12	Spiddal	731	1	35	Meath	Morgallion	Nobber	Kells	I.	210
92	Spiddle East	377	1	29	Galway	Moycullen	Moycullen	Galway	IV.	71
92	Spiddle Middle	338	0	17	Galway	Moycullen	Moycullen	Galway	IV.	71
92	SPIDDLE T.	—			Galway	Moycullen	Moycullen	Galway	IV.	72
92	Spiddle West	727	1	13	Galway	Moycullen	Moycullen	Galway	IV.	71
94	Spierstown	103	1	39	Donegal	Tirhugh	Donegal	Donegal	III.	145
87	Spike Island	98	3	34	Cork, E.R.	Barrymore	Templerobin	Cork	II.	58
27	Spinans East	180	1	14	Wicklow	Upper Talbotstown	Donaghmore	Baltinglass	I.	363
21, 27	Spinans Hill	130	1	37	Wicklow	Upper Talbotstown	Donaghmore	Baltinglass	I.	363
27	Spinans Middle	194	1	32	Wicklow	Upper Talbotstown	Donaghmore	Baltinglass	I.	363
27	Spinans West	76	2	30	Wicklow	Upper Talbotstown	Donaghmore	Baltinglass	I.	363
127	Spindillaun	0	1	25	Galway	Longford	Lickmolassy	Portumna	IV.	61
37	Spink	191	1	9	King's Co.	Ballybritt	Letterluna	Parsonstown	I.	126
88	Spital	92	1	15	Cork, E.R.	Imokilly	Cloyne	Middleton	II.	86
17	Spital	505	2	15	Cork, E.R.	Orrery and Kilmore	Buttevant	Mallow	II.	107
136	Spital & Aghmanister	153	1	7	Cork, W.R.	Ibane and Barryroe	Abbeymahon	Clonakilty	II.	148
70	Spitalfield	21	0	38	Tipperary, S.R.	Middlethird	Fethard	Cashel	II.	327
112	Spital-land	47	2	23	Cork, E.R.	Kinsale	Ringcurran	Kinsale	II.	100
5	Spital-land	185	3	20b	Limerick	Clanwilliam and Municipal Borough	St. Laurence's	Limerick	II.	225
60	Spital-land	8	3	20	Tipperary, S.R.	Clanwilliam	Relickmurry & Athassel	Tipperary	II.	310
67	Spital-land	26	1	8c	Tipperary, S.R.	Clanwilliam	Tipperary	Tipperary	II.	312
82, 88	Spital-land	15	1	14	Tipperary, S.R.	Iffa and Offa West	Ardfinnan	Clogheen	II.	317
74	Spital-lands	112	2	20d	Cork, E.R.	Cork and Municipal Borough	St. Nicholas	Cork	II.	66
31	Spittaltown	254	0	8	Westmeath	Moycashel	Ardnurcher or Horseleap	Mullingar	I.	277
38	Spittaltown & Rahinashane	141	3	19	Westmeath	Moycashel	Newtown	Mullingar	I.	279
49	Spittle	607	3	23	Limerick	Coshlea	Ballylanders	Mitchelstown	II.	237
56, 57	Spittle	368	2	24	Limerick	Coshlea	Darragh	Kilmallock	II.	238
38	Spittle Ballee	222	3	6	Down	Lecale Lower	Ballee	Downpatrick	III.	178
19	Spittlefield or Springfield	274	3	15	Westmeath	Moyashel & Magheradernon	Mullingar	Mullingar	I.	275
3, 7	Spittle Hill	176	0	25	Londonderry	North East Liberties of Coleraine	Coleraine	Coleraine	III.	246
38	Spittle Quarter	97	0	33	Down	Lecale Lower	Ballee	Downpatrick	III.	178
17	Spollanstown	362	1	39	King's Co.	Ballycowan	Kilbride	Tullamore	I.	128
17	Sporthouse	339	2	39	Waterford	Middlethird	Kilbride	Waterford	II.	367
7	Sportsmanshall	124	3	31	Louth	Upper Dundalk	Dundalk	Dundalk	I.	178
26	Spotfield	318	3	29c	Sligo	Tirerrill	Ballysadare	Sligo	IV.	238
32, 36	Spratstown	319	2	34	Kildare	Narragh & Reban East	Narraghmore	Baltinglass	I.	66
10,11,13,14	Spricklestown	122	1	22	Dublin	Castleknock	Ward	Dublin North	I.	25
31	Spring (Duke)	29	0	1f	Waterford	Decies without Drum	Kilrush	Dungarvan	II.	358
50	Spring Farm	93	3	37	Antrim	Upper Antrim	Antrim	Antrim	III.	5
30, 35	Springfarm	239	1	19	Wicklow	Arklow	Redcross	Rathdrum	I.	346
52	Springfield	63	1	27	Clare	Bunratty Lower	Feenagh	Ennis	II.	4
53, 63	Springfield	306	2	20	Clare	Tulla Lower	Kiltenanlea	Limerick	II.	37
67	Springfield	56	3	28	Cork, E.R.	Imokilly	Youghal	Youghal	II.	91
112	Springfield	186	0	0	Cork, E.R.	Kinalea	Nohaval	Kinsale	II.	96
98	Springfield	35	2	12	Cork, E.R.	Kinalea	Tracton	Kinsale	II.	97
8, 17	Springfield	341	1	34	Donegal	Kilmacrenan	Clondavaddog	Milford	III.	125
6	Springfield	166	3	19	Galway	Ballymoe	Templetogher	Glennamaddy	IV.	10
99	Springfield	463	1	16	Galway	Longford	Killoran	Ballinasloe	IV.	59
30	Springfield	338	2	4	King's Co.	Eglish	Drumcullen	Parsonstown	I.	134
32	Springfield	77	0	9	Leitrim	Mohill	Mohill	Mohill	IV.	108
45, 54	Springfield	414	2	10	Limerick	Glenquin	Killagholehane	Newcastle	II.	245
78	Springfield	50	0	34	Mayo	Carra	Aglish	Castlebar	IV.	124
12	Springfield	214	0	14	Queen's Co.	Maryborough West	Clonenagh&Clonagheen	Mountmellick	I.	243
34	Springfield	55	2	1	Sligo	Tirerrill	Tawnagh	Sligo	IV.	241
28, 34	Springfield	101	2	3	Tipperary, N.R.	Kilnamanagh Upper	Glenkeen	Thurles	II.	279
10	Springfield	232	3	9	Tipperary, N.R.	Lower Ormond	Finnoe	Borrisokane	II.	284
59, 67	Springfield	117	3	5	Tipperary, S.R.	Clanwilliam	Tipperary	Tipperary	II.	312
69, 76	Springfield	355	3	17	Tipperary, S.R.	Middlethird	Knockgraffon	Cashel	II.	328
54, 55	Springfield	144	1	17	Tipperary, S.R.	Slievardagh	Ballingarry	Callan	II.	222
43, 49	Springfield	118	0	37	Tipperary, S.R.	Slievardagh	Kilcooly	Urlingford	II.	334
28	Springfield	85	3	31	Waterford	Coshmore&Coshbride	Tallow	Lismore	II.	348
29	Springfield	76	0	33	Waterford	Decies without Drum	Affane	Lismore	II.	353

(a) Including 6A. 1R. 26P. water.
(b) { Within the Municipal Boundary, 60A. 0R. 25P.
{ Without the Municipal Boundary, 125A. 2R. 35P.
(c) { Including 2A. 1R. 20P. water.
{ Including 11A. 2R. 34P. detached portion.
(d) { Within the Municipal Boundary, 72A. 3R. 38P.
{ Without the Municipal Boundary, 39A. 2R. 22P.
(e) Including 9A. 0R. 27P. water.
(f) Including 6A. 1R. 12P. detached portion.

No. of Sheet of the Ordnance Survey Maps.	Townlands and Towns.	Area in Statute Acres.			County.	Barony.	Parish.	Poor Law Union in 1857.	Townland Census of 1851, Part I.	
		A.	R.	P.					Vol.	Page
45	Springfield	143	3	9	Wicklow	Arklow	Arklow	Rathdrum	I.	341
7, 8	Springfield	20	2	20	Wicklow	Rathdown	Bray	Rathdown	I.	355
11, 19	Springfield or Ballyhugh	185	2	22	King's Co.	Coolestown	Ballynakill	Edenderry	I.	132
10	Springfield Glebe	46	3	10	Tipperary, N.R.	Lower Ormond	Finnoe	Borrisokane	II.	284
22,23,28,29	Springfield or Knockkyle	396	2	20	Queen's Co.	Clarmallagh	Aghaboe	Abbeyleix	I.	236
37, 38, 40	Springfield Lower	92	2	0	Waterford	Decies within Drum	Kinsalebeg	Youghal	II.	352
8	Springfield or Magheragilderneeve	306	1	34	Sligo	Carbury	Drumcliff	Sligo	IV.	221
19	Springfield or Spittlefield	274	3	15	Westmeath	Moyashel & Magheradernon	Mullingar	Mullingar	I.	275
60	SPRINGFIELD T.	—			Antrim	Upper Belfast	Shankill	Belfast	III.	10
40	Springfield Upper	15	3	34	Waterford	Decies within Drum	Kinsalebeg	Youghal	II.	352
116, 117	Spring Garden	275	0	35	Galway	Leitrim	Tynagh	Portumna	IV.	56
19	Spring Garden	361	3	25	Sligo	Tireragh	Dromard	Dromore West	IV.	233
32	Spring Gardens	197	0	28	Roscommon	Castlereagh	Kiltullagh	Castlereagh	IV.	202
23	Spring Grove	263	2	35	Cork, E.R.	Duhallow	Kilroe	Kanturk	II.	73
36	Spring Grove	293	0	27	Fermanagh	Clankelly	Clones	Clones	III.	197
107	Spring Grove or Timsallagh	740	3	26	Galway	Longford	Kilquain	Portumna	IV.	60
15	Springhall	154	3	25	Meath	Fore	Moylagh	Oldcastle	I.	201
64, 75	Springhill	165	2	11	Cork, E.R.	Barrymore	Carrigtohill	Middleton	II.	52
99	Springhill	97	3	3	Cork, E.R.	Kinalea	Tracton	Kinsale	II.	97
70	Springhill	100	0	25	Donegal	Raphoe	Clonleigh	Strabane	III.	135
15	Springhill	64	0	2	Dublin	Coolock	Cloghran	Balrothery	I.	26
14	Springhill	156	3	22	Kilkenny	Fassadinin	Odagh	Kilkenny	I.	91
19	Springhill	148	1	12	Kilkenny	Shillelogher	St. Patrick's	Kilkenny	I.	116
20	Spring Hill	55	1	25	Londonderry	North West Liberties of Londonderry	Templemore	Londonderry	III.	247
21	Springhill	133	0	15	Mayo	Tirawley	Rathreagh	Killala	IV.	171
32, 37	Springhill	782	0	21a	Queen's Co.	Slievemargy	Killeshin	Carlow	I.	246
15, 21, 22	Springhill	170	1	32	Queen's Co.	Upperwoods	Offerlane	Donaghmore	I.	252
54	Springhill	44	3	22	Tipperary, S.R.	Slievardagh	Graystown	Cashel	II.	333
54	Springhill	126	3	34	Tipperary, S.R.	Slievardagh	Killenaule	Cashel	II.	334
67	Springhouse	471	2	16	Tipperary, S.R.	Clanwilliam	Kilshane	Tipperary	II.	309
32, 45, 46	Springlawn	1,124	3	19	Galway	Killian	Ballynakill	Mountbellew	IV.	43
22	Springlodge	79	2	12	Limerick	Pubblebrien	Monasteranenagh	Croom	II.	253
31	Spring (Marquis)	32	3	28	Waterford	Decies without Drum	Kilrush	Dungarvan	II.	358
27	Spring Mount	162	2	38	Antrim	Kilconway	Grange of Dundermot	Ballymena	III.	27
44, 53	Springmount	347	2	32	Clare	Tulla Lower	Killokennedy	Limerick	II.	36
14, 18	Springmount	131	2	12	Dublin	Castleknock	Finglas	Dublin North	I.	25
39	Springmount	279	3	33	Kerry	Trughanacmy	Killeentierna	Killarney	II.	211
23	Springmount	165	1	20	Queen's Co.	Maryborough West	Clonenagh and Clonagheen	Abbeyleix	I.	243
9	Springmount	128	0	12	Tipperary, N.R.	Lower Ormond	Cloghprior	Borrisokane	II.	283
60	Springmount	97	2	23	Tipperary, S.R.	Clanwilliam	Relickmurry &Athassel	Tipperary	II.	310
31	Springmount	7	3	8	Waterford	Decies without Drum	Kilrush	Dungarvan	II.	358
18	Springmount	460	2	32	Wexford	Bantry	Killann	Enniscorthy	I.	300
7	Springpark	262	2	22	King's Co.	Garrycastle	Lemanaghan	Parsonstown	I.	137
8, 11	Springpark	112	2	32	Tipperary, N.R.	Lower Ormond	Ballingarry	Borrisokane	II.	282
30	Springpark	531	0	26	Wexford	Bantry	Oldross	New Ross	I.	301
37, 38	Springtown	327	2	12	Fermanagh	Knockninny	Kinawley	Enniskillen	III.	202
4, 5	Springtown	179	0	22	Fermanagh	Lurg	Drumkeeran	Lowtherstown	III.	207
13	Spring Town	227	2	34	Londonderry	North West Liberties of Londonderry	Templemore	Londonderry	III.	247
11	Springtown	665	3	32	Longford	Granard	Granard	Granard	I.	157
59, 65	Springtown	164	0	38b	Tyrone	Clogher	Clogher	Clogher	III.	293
9, 18	Springvale	237	2	34	Cork, E.R.	Fermoy	Kildorrery	Mitchelstown	II.	80
12	Springvale	356	3	17	Down	Ards Upper	Ballywalter	Newtownards	III.	160
118	Springvale	27	0	26c	Mayo	Kilmaine	Ballinrobe	Ballinrobe	IV.	153
14	Springvale or Glennameenagh	283	1	24	Wexford	Scarawalsh	Ballycarney	Enniscorthy	I.	322
43	Springvalley	308	0	15	Meath	Lower Moyfenrath	Laracor	Trim	I.	210
23	Springville	72	0	11	Cork, E.R.	Duhallow	Kilbrin	Kanturk	II.	72
16	Springville or Dandlestown	462	0	34	Meath	Upper Kells	Burry	Kells	I.	205
27	Spruceshay	56	2	16	Kilkenny	Kells	Mallardstown	Callan	I.	110
89, 98	Spunkane	795	3	15	Kerry	Iveragh	Dromod	Cahersiveen	II.	195
36, 45	Spurree	276	2	2	Cork, E.R.	Barrymore	Castlelyons	Fermoy	II.	53
39	Spurtown (Duke)	132	2	20	Sligo	Corran	Kilshalvy	Tobercurry	IV.	227
39	Spurtown Lower	260	2	14	Sligo	Corran	Kilshalvy	Boyle	IV.	227
24	Sra	225	1	25	Monaghan	Cremorne	Aghnamullen	Castleblayney	III.	258
2	Srabra	109	1	34	Roscommon	Boyle	Kilronan	Boyle	IV.	197
2	Srabragan	247	0	30	Roscommon	Boyle	Kilronan	Boyle	IV.	197

(a) Including 11A. 2R. 12P. detached portion.   (b) Including 1A. 2R. 3P. water.   (c) Including 1A. 1R. 21P. water.

No. of Sheet of the Ordnance Survey Maps.	Townlands and Towns.	Area in Statute Acres. A. R. P.	County.	Barony.	Parish.	Poor Law Union in 1857.	Townland Census of 1851, Part I. Vol.	Page
11	Srabrick	340 1 34	Leitrim	Drumahaire	Cloonlogher	Manorhamilton	IV.	94
4	Sracleighreen	537 3 18a	Leitrim	Rosclogher	Killasnet	Manorhamilton	IV.	110
9	Sracocka	127 1 3	Roscommon	Frenchpark	Kilnamanagh	Castlereagh	IV.	204
6	Sracreeghan	443 2 36b	Leitrim	Rosclogher	Killasnet	Manorhamilton	IV.	110
14, 15, 17	Sracummer	203 3 22	Leitrim	Drumahaire	Killanummery	Manorhamilton	IV.	98
2	Sracummer	159 1 23	Leitrim	Rosclogher	Rossinver	Ballyshannon	IV.	112
14	Sradoon	250 1 37	Leitrim	Drumahaire	Killanummery	Manorhamilton	IV.	98
20, 21	Sradrinagh	1,174 2 4	Leitrim	Drumahaire	Drumreilly	Cark. on Shannon	IV.	95
22	Sradrinan	145 1 21	Leitrim	Carrigallen	Drumreilly	Bawnboy	IV.	91
8, 12	Sradrine	262 2 18	Leitrim	Drumahaire	Cloonclare	Manorhamilton	IV.	94
51, 54	Sraduff	345 3 15	Roscommon	Athlone	Taghmaconnell	Athlone	IV.	185
5	Sraduff	342 3 6	Tipperary, N.R.	Lower Ormond	Dorrha	Parsonstown	II.	283
31	Sraduff	249 1 36	Westmeath	Moycashel	Castletownkindalen	Mullingar	I.	277
8	Sraduffy	257 1 33	Leitrim	Rosclogher	Cloondare	Manorhamilton	IV.	109
28	Sragarn	196 1 10	Leitrim	Mohill	Mohill	Mohill	IV.	108
8	Sragarrow	52 0 35	Longford	Longford	Clongesh	Longford	I.	158
2	Sragarve	29 3 37	Leitrim	Rosclogher	Rossinver	Ballyshannon	IV.	112
13, 17	Sragh	231 3 22	Carlow	Forth	Ballon	Carlow	I.	3
47, 57	Sragh	1,483 1 8	Clare	Ibrickan	Killard	Kilrush	II.	23
12, 17	Sragh	287 2 10	Kilkenny	Crannagh	Tubbridbritain	Urlingford	I.	87
44, 45	Sragh	264 3 18	Sligo	Coolavin	Kilfree	Boyle	IV.	224
9, 10	Sragh	134 3 32	Tipperary, N.R.	Lower Ormond	Finnoe	Borrisokane	II.	284
27	Sragh	190 1 27	Tipperary, N.R.	Upper Ormond	Ballynaclogh	Nenagh	II.	290
26	Sragh	74 3 6	Tipperary, N.R.	Upper Ormond	Kilmore	Nenagh	II.	291
22, 23	Sraghcumber	317 2 34c	Tyrone	Omagh West	Termonamongan	Castlederg	III.	317
20, 21	Sraghgaddy	313 0 6	Kilkenny	Gowran	Kilmacahill	Kilkenny	I.	97
12	Sraghmore	1,074 2 0	Wicklow	Ballinacor North	Calary	Rathdrum	I.	346
74	Srah	31 2 30	Galway	Clonmacnowen	Kilgerrill	Ballinasloe	IV.	26
104, 105	Srah	188 3 28	Galway	Dunkellin	Kilconickny	Loughrea	IV.	29
114	Srah	196 1 29	Galway	Kiltartan	Kiltartan	Gort	IV.	48
126, 132	Srah	444 0 2	Galway	Leitrim	Ballynakill	Portumna	IV.	52
17	Srah	453 3 12	King's Co.	Ballycowan	Kilbride	Tullamore	I.	128
4	Srah	262 0 30	King's Co.	Warrenstown	Ballyburly	Edenderry	I.	144
99, 109	Srah	912 3 38d	Mayo	Carra	Ballyovey	Ballinrobe	IV.	126
92, 102	Srah	67 2 15	Mayo	Costello	Knock	Claremorris	IV.	143
17, 25	Srah	1,378 2 0	Mayo	Erris	Kilcommon	Belmullet	IV.	144
48	Srah	178 1 29e	Mayo	Tirawley	Ballynahaglish	Ballina	IV.	164
34	Srah	532 1 8	Queen's Co.	Clarmallagh	Erke	Donaghmore	I.	237
42	Srah	88 1 0	Roscommon	Athlone	Killinvoy	Roscommon	IV.	182
25	Srah	70 2 38	Roscommon	Castlereagh	Kiltullagh	Castlereagh	IV.	202
56,57,66,67	Srahacorick	756 0 14	Mayo	Burrishoole	Burrishoole	Newport	IV.	120
34, 40	Srahan	204 0 28	Cavan	Clankee	Moybolgue	Bailieborough	III.	74
26	Srahanarry	197 1 14f	Mayo	Erris	Kilcommon	Belmullet	IV.	144
10, 11	Srahanboy	707 3 28	Queen's Co.	Upperwoods	Offerlane	Mountmellick	I.	252
38	Srahanbrogagh	343 0 20	King's Co.	Clonlisk	Ettagh	Roscrea	I.	130
14	Srahane	234 3 43	Limerick	Clanwilliam	Carrigparson	Limerick	II.	223
14	Srahane East	218 2 1	Limerick	Clanwilliam	Caherconlish	Limerick	II.	222
14	Srahane West	63 3 23	Limerick	Clanwilliam	Caherconlish	Limerick	II.	222
10	Sraharla	384 2 17	Cork, E.R.	Condons&Clangibbon	Templemolaga	Mitchelstown	II.	63
34, 35	Sraharory	59 2 34	Fermanagh	Magherastephana	Aghalurcher	Lisnaskea	III.	217
4, 5, 12	Srahataggle	4,167 2 18	Mayo	Erris	Kilcommon	Belmullet	IV.	144
18, 26	Srahataggle South	649 2 6	Mayo	Erris	Kilcommon	Belmullet	IV.	145
116	Srahatloe	1,432 2 1	Mayo	Murrisk	Aghagower	Westport	IV.	159
100, 101	Srahaun	175 1 3	Galway	Longford	Clonfert	Ballinasloe	IV.	57
115, 116	Srahaunananta	203 3 16	Galway	Leitrim	Kilteskill	Loughrea	IV.	55
33	Srahaunnagort or Thornfield	121 2 12g	Galway	Killian	Athleague	Mountbellew	IV.	43
45	Srahauns	127 2 23	Roscommon	Athlone	Kiltoom	Athlone	IV.	183
46, 52	Srahavarrella	373 0 2	Tipperary, S.R.	Kilnamanagh Lower	Clonoulty	Cashel	II.	323
34	Srahbaun	226 2 4	Queen's Co.	Clarmallagh	Erke	Donaghmore	I.	237
2, 6	Srahcullen	291 0 31	Queen's Co.	Tinnahinch	Rearymore	Mountmellick	I.	250
106	Srahdoo	67 3 10	Galway	Leitrim	Kilmeen	Loughrea	IV.	54
2	Srahduff Glebe	229 3 7	Queen's Co.	Tinnahinch	Kilmanman	Mountmellick	I.	249
44,45,56,57	Srahduggaun	3,435 3 35h	Mayo	Erris	Kilcommon	Newport	IV.	145
35	Srahederdaowen	341 2 20	Mayo	Erris	Kilcommon	Newport	IV.	145
34	Sraheen	230 1 27	Clare	Bunratty Upper	Clooney	Tulla	II.	8
98, 108	Sraheen	1,127 3 1i	Mayo	Burrishoole	Aghagower	Westport	IV.	118
48	Sraheen	675 2 20j	Mayo	Tirawley	Ballynahaglish	Ballina	IV.	164
97	Sraheendoo	69 0 33	Galway	Athenry	Kiltullagh	Loughrea	IV.	5
55, 65	Sraheens	2,207 1 19k	Mayo	Burrishoole	Achill	Newport	IV.	117
73	Sraheens	278 2 1	Mayo	Costello	Kilmovee	Swineford	IV.	142
80	Sraheens	251 1 5	Mayo	Gallen	Bohola	Swineford	IV.	147
11	Sraheens	73 2 5	Sligo	Tireragh	Easky	Dromore West	IV.	234

(a) Including 52A. 0R. 28P. water.
(b) Including 21A. 3R. 9P. water.
(c) Including 5A. 2R. 13P. water.
(d) Including 8A. 1R. 8P. water.
(e) Including 11A. 1R. 1P. water.
(f) Including 13A. 2R. 24P. water.
(g) Including 4A. 3R. 11P. water.
(h) Including 116A. 3R. 38P. water.
(i) Including 11A. 0R. 13P. water.
(j) Including 7A. 0R. 9P. water.
(k) Including 20A. 3R. 12P. water.

No. of Sheet of the Ordnance Survey Maps.	Townlands and Towns.	Area in Statute Acres. A. R. P.	County.	Barony.	Parish.	Poor Law Union in 1857.	Townland Census of 1851, Part I. Vol.	Page
16	Srahenny	226 2 35	Fermanagh	Tirkennedy	Trory	Enniskillen	III.	223
26	Srahenry	7 3 30	Westmeath	Moyashel and Magh-eradernon	Mullingar	Mullingar	I.	275
61	Srahgarve	158 3 31a	Galway	Killian	Taghboy	Mountbellew	IV.	45
26	Srahgraddy	1,262 3 5b	Mayo	Erris	Kilcommon	Belmullet	IV.	145
12, 13	Srahlaghy	1,229 0 27	Mayo	Tirawley	Doonfeeny	Killala	IV.	167
107, 108	Srahlea	321 3 3	Mayo	Murrisk	Aghagower	Westport	IV.	159
34	Srahleagh	197 0 28	Queen's Co.	Clarmallagh	Erke	Donaghmore	I.	237
3, 7	Srahleagh	231 3 21	Queen's Co.	Tinnahinch	Rosenallis	Mountmellick	I.	250
61	Srahlouglura	367 1 11c	Galway	Killian	Ahascragh	Ballinasloe	IV.	43
51, 63	Srah Lower	322 1 31	Mayo	Costello	Kilbeagh	Swineford	IV.	141
13, 20	Srahmeen	1,792 0 25	Mayo	Tirawley	Kilfian	Killala	IV.	169
65	Srahmore	353 2 26d	Mayo	Burrishoole	Achill	Newport	IV.	117
45, 57	Srahmore	3,352 3 18	Mayo	Burrishoole	Burrishoole	Newport	IV.	120
26	Srahmore	590 2 15e	Mayo	Erris	Kilcommon	Belmullet	IV.	145
96	Srahnacloy	1,101 1 10	Mayo	Murrisk	Kilgeever	Westport	IV.	160
19, 20, 27	Srahnakilly	3,395 1 3f	Mayo	Erris	Kilcommon	Belmullet	IV.	145
35	Srahnamanragh	1,050 2 28	Mayo	Erris	Kilcommon	Newport	IV.	145
96	Srahnanagh	106 0 21	Mayo	Murrisk	Kilgeever	Westport	IV.	160
12, 19	Srahnaplaia	1,985 1 4	Mayo	Erris	Kilcommon	Belmullet	IV.	145
86	Srahnashasky	83 3 9	Mayo	Murrisk	Kilgeever	Westport	IV.	160
45,46,57,58	Srahrevagh	1,288 0 4	Mayo	Burrishoole	Burrishoole	Newport	IV.	120
96	Srahrevagh	719 2 18	Mayo	Murrisk	Kilgeever	Westport	IV.	160
106	Srahroosky	1,032 2 29g	Mayo	Murrisk	Kilgeever	Westport	IV.	160
51, 63	Srah Upper	541 1 2	Mayo	Costello	Kilbeagh	Swineford	IV.	141
96	Srahwee	507 3 28h	Mayo	Murrisk	Kilgeever	Westport	IV.	160
37, 38, 47	Srahyconigaun	540 1 26	Mayo	Tirawley	Crossmolina	Ballina	IV.	166
6, 7, 13	Sralagagh East	36 2 3	Mayo	Tirawley	Doonfeeny	Killala	IV.	167
6, 13	Sralagagh West	1,662 3 35	Mayo	Tirawley	Doonfeeny	Killala	IV.	167
7	Sralahan	133 3 3	Cavan	Tullyhaw	Kinawley	Bawnboy	III.	93
9	Sralahan or The Common	207 1 3	Cavan	Tullyhaw	Tomregan	Bawnboy	III.	96
53, 54, 56	Sralea	204 3 33	Roscommon	Moycarn	Creagh	Ballinasloe	IV.	206
39, 40	Sralea	60 1 24	Sligo	Corran	Drumrat	Boyle	IV.	226
5	Sraleagh	115 2 36	Kilkenny	Fassadinin	Donaghmore	Castlecomer	I.	89
85	Sraleigh	164 3 12	Cork. E.R.	East Muskerry	Inishkenny	Cork	II.	104
22	Sraloughan	199 1 12	Leitrim	Carrigallen	Drumreilly	Bawnboy	IV.	91
35	Sramcen	43 2 30	Westmeath	Brawny	St. Mary's	Athlone	I.	260
6, 10	Sramore	681 3 11	Leitrim	Drumahaire	Drumlease	Manorhamilton	IV.	95
22	Sranabell	432 2 22	Meath	Fore	Killallon	Oldcastle	I.	201
37	Sranacally	654 1 6	Mayo	Tirawley	Crossmolina	Ballina	IV.	166
15	Sranacrannaghy	196 1 19	Leitrim	Drumahaire	Killarga	Manorhamilton	IV.	99
29	Sranadarragh	279 2 37	Leitrim	Carrigallen	Drumreilly	Bawnboy	IV.	91
18	Sransgalloon	451 0 5	Clare	Bunratty Upper	Inchicronan	Ennis	II.	9
19	Sranagarvanagh	647 0 13	Leitrim	Drumahaire	Drumreilly	Car'. on Shannon	IV.	95
12, 13	Sranagross	300 2 20	Leitrim	Drumahaire	Cloonclare	Manorhamilton	IV.	94
12	Sranahaw	822 1 17	Galway	Ross	Ross	Oughterard	IV.	74
38	Sranalaghta North	35 2 8	Mayo	Tirawley	Crossmolina	Ballina	IV.	166
38	Sranalaghta South	70 1 10	Mayo	Tirawley	Crossmolina	Ballina	IV.	166
69, 70	Sranalee	183 0 18i	Mayo	Carra	Turlough	Castlebar	IV.	131
27	Srananagh	301 1 19	Sligo	Tirerrill	Ballysumaghan	Sligo	IV.	238
7	Srananny	157 2 37	Monaghan	Trough	Donagh	Monaghan	III.	282
2	Srananroan	119 0 29	Roscommon	Boyle	Kilronan	Boyle	IV.	197
95, 109	Sranaviddoge	619 0 14	Cork. W.R.	East Carbery (W.D.)	Murragh	Bandon	II.	135
42	Sranayalloge	31 0 8	Cavan	Clanmahon	Kilbride	Oldcastle	III.	78
6	Sranea	77 3 16	Leitrim	Rosclogher	Killasnet	Manorhamilton	IV.	110
31, 32	Sraneeg	264 3 8	Westmeath	Moycashel	Castletownkindalen	Mullingar	I.	277
14	Sranill	199 1 30	Fermanagh	Magheraboy	Devenish	Enniskillen	III.	211
26	Sranure	388 1 4	King's Co.	Upper Philipstown	Ballykean	Mountmellick	I.	143
5	Srarevagh	74 1 21	Sligo	Carbury	Ahamlish	Sligo	IV.	219
28	Sratrissaun North	137 0 6	Leitrim	Mohill	Mohill	Mohill	IV.	108
28, 32	Sratrissaun South	96 1 22	Leitrim	Mohill	Mohill	Mohill	IV.	108
5	Sraud (Conolly)	106 1 14	Leitrim	Rosclogher	Rossinver	Ballyshannon	IV.	112
5	Sraud (Ferguson)	92 2 3	Leitrim	Rosclogher	Rossinver	Ballyshannon	IV.	112
12	Sravrannes	144 1 38	Leitrim	Drumahaire	Cloonclare	Manorhamilton	IV.	94
63	Srawickeen	361 1 15	Clare	Tulla Lower	Kiltenanlea	Limerick	II.	37
5	Sreelane	111 1 19	Limerick	Clanwilliam	Kilmurry	Limerick	II.	225
27	Sreenty	459 2 11j	Monaghan	Farney	Magheross	Carrickmacross	III.	274
10, 14	Sriff	222 2 7	Leitrim	Drumahaire	Drumlease	Manorhamilton	IV.	95
11	Sroankeeragh	73 1 10	Roscommon	Boyle	Tumna	Car'. on Shannon	IV.	198
8	Sronagh	55 3 18	Queen's Co.	Portnahinch	Ardea	Mountmellick	I.	243
19, 20	Sronscull	181 3 7	Queen's Co.	Ballyadams	Ballyadams	Athy	I.	231
15	Sroohil	49 2 4	Clare	Corcomroe	Kilmanaheen	Ennistimon	II.	21

(a) Including 16A. 0R. 0P. water.
(b) Including 8A. 2R. 31P. water.
(c) Including 16A. 2R. 0P. water.
(d) Including 16A. 2R. 27P. water.

(e) Including 19A. 0R. 35P. water.
(f) Including 49A. 3R. 26P. water.
(g) Including 8A. 3R. 4P. water.

(h) Including 28A. 0R. 13P. water.
(i) Including 3A. 3R. 24P. water.
(j) Including 15A. 3R. 21P. water.

No. of Sheet of the Ordnance Survey Maps.	Townlands and Towns.	Area in Statute Acres.			County.	Barony.	Parish.	Poor Law Union in 1857.	Townland Census of 1851, Part I.	
		A.	R.	P.					Vol.	Page
10, 19	Sroolane	216	3	34	Limerick .	Shanid . .	Shanagolden .	Rathkeale .	II.	258
10	Sroolane North	81	0	19	Limerick .	Shanid . .	Robertstown .	Rathkeale .	II.	258
10, 19	Sroolane South	20	3	33	Limerick .	Shanid . .	Robertstown .	Rathkeale .	II.	258
104	Sroove . .	76	2	13	Galway .	Dunkellin .	Kilcolgan .	Gort .	IV.	28
28	Sroove . .	249	2	29	Roscommon	Roscommon .	Killukin .	Strokestown	IV.	211
44, 46	Sroove . .	1,670	3	32	S'igo .	Coolavin .	Kilcolman .	Boyle .	IV.	224
5, 10	Sroughan .	497	3	29	Wicklow .	Lower Talbotstown .	Boystown .	Naas .	I.	359
14	Sroughmore .	186	1	37	Wexford .	Scarawalsh .	Monart .	Enniscorthy	I.	324
14	Sroughmore .	310	0	36	Wexford .	Scarawalsh .	Templeshanbo	Enniscorthy	I.	326
35	Sroughmore .	376	2	20	Wicklow .	Arklow .	Castlemacadam	Rathdrum .	I.	342
35	Srowland .	121	2	8a	Kildare .	Narragh&RebanWest	Kilberry .	Athy .	I.	68
55	Srue . .	339	3	35	Galway .	Moycullen .	Kilcummin .	Oughterard .	IV.	68
75,76,84,85	Sruell . .	2,772	2	29b	Donegal .	Banagh .	Killymard .	Donegal .	III.	112
25	Sruell or Corragarry	311	2	35c	Monaghan .	Farney .	Donaghmoyne .	Castleblayney	III.	269
30, 31	Srughawadda .	137	1	38	Kilkenny .	Kells .	Kilmaganny .	Callan .	I.	109
80	Srugreana .	366	0	24	Kerry .	Iveragh .	Killinane .	Cahersiveen .	II.	197
13	Sruhagh .	324	3	6d	Cavan .	Tullyhaw .	Templeport .	Bawnboy .	III.	95
5	Sruhanagh .	405	2	20	Cavan .	Tullyhaw .	Killinagh .	Enniskillen .	III.	92
52	Sruhane .	33	0	30	Tipperary, S.R.	Middlethird .	Ardmayle .	Cashel .	II.	324
51, 52	Sruhangarrow	248	3	2	Donegal .	Kilmacrenan .	Gartan .	Letterkenny .	III.	127
51	Sruhangarrow Mountain .	325	3	39	Donegal .	Kilmacrenan .	Gartan .	Letterkenny .	III.	128
24, 33	Sruhanreagh .	296	0	9	Donegal .	Kilmacrenan .	Tullaghobegly .	Dunfanaghy .	III.	132
9	Sruhanure .	316	0	39	Fermanagh .	Magheraboy .	Inishmacsaint .	Ballyshannon	III.	213
28, 29	Sruhaun . .	226	2	22e	Leitrim .	Leitrim .	Fenagh .	Mohill .	IV.	100
27	Sruhaun . .	190	1	3	Wicklow .	Upper Talbotstown .	Baltinglass .	Baltinglass .	I.	362
60	Sruhaunfusta .	127	2	11	Galway .	Kilconnell .	Killosolan .	Mountbellew .	IV.	42
21	Sruh East .	173	2	39	Waterford .	Coshmore&Coshbride	Lismore and Mocollop	Lismore .	II.	347
21	Sruh West .	123	3	16	Waterford .	Coshmore&Coshbride	Lismore and Mocollop	Lismore .	II.	347
3	Srunahella .	212	2	15f	Westmeath .	Fore .	Rathgarve .	Castletowndelvin	I.	271
8	Sruveel . .	131	1	38g	Monaghan .	Monaghan .	Tedavnet .	Monaghan .	III.	279
14,15,17,18	Stabannan .	498	3	29	Louth .	Ardee .	Stabannan .	Ardee .	I.	174
15	STABANNAN T.	—			Louth .	Ardee .	Stabannan .	Ardee .	I.	174
17, 22	Stable . .	185	3	35	Wexford .	Ballaghkeen .	Donaghmore .	Gorey .	I.	294
18,19,25,26	Stackallan .	944	3	34h	Meath .	Upper Slane .	Stackallan .	Navan .	I.	225
52	Stackarnagh .	503	2	37	Donegal .	Kilmacrenan .	Conwal .	Letterkenny .	III.	126
22	Stack's-mountain .	846	0	27	Kerry .	Clanmaurice .	Kilflyn .	Tralee .	II.	170
22, 25	Stackstown .	175	3	32	Dublin .	Rathdown .	Whitechurch .	Dublin South .	I.	38
11	Stacumny .	155	3	39	Kildare .	South Salt .	Stacumny .	Celbridge .	I.	78
11	Stacumny Cottage .	135	0	24	Kildare .	South Salt .	Stacumny .	Celbridge .	I.	78
28, 34	Stadalt . .	382	2	0	Meath .	Upper Duleek .	Stamullin .	Drogheda .	I.	198
37	Stael . .	60	0	29	Waterford .	Coshmore&Coshbride	Templemichael .	Youghal .	II.	349
33	Staff Island .	7	2	32	Fermanagh .	Tirkennedy .	Cleenish .	Lisnaskea .	III.	220
49	Staffordstown .	169	2	17	Antrim .	Upper Toome .	Duneane .	Antrim .	III.	35
8	Staffordstown .	105	2	37	Dublin .	Balrothery East	Lusk .	Balrothery .	I.	21
50	Staffordstown .	253	3	17	Meath .	Ratoath .	Ballymaglassan	Dunshaughlin .	I.	217
26, 32	Staffordstown .	616	3	7	Meath .	Skreen .	Staffordstown .	Navan .	I.	221
50	Staffordstown Little	144	3	7	Meath .	Ratoath .	Ballymaglassan	Dunshaughlin .	I.	217
8, 12	Staffordstown Turvey	134	3	8	Dublin .	Balrothery East	Lusk .	Balrothery .	I.	21
44, 52	Staghall . .	133	3	21i	Donegal .	Kilmacrenan .	Gartan .	Letterkenny .	III.	128
43, 51	Staghall Mountain .	423	1	6	Donegal .	Kilmacrenan .	Gartan .	Letterkenny .	III.	128
43, 44	Staghall Mountain East .	332	2	25	Donegal .	Kilmacrenan .	Gartan .	Letterkenny .	III.	128
43	Staghall Mountain West .	1,683	0	6j	Donegal .	Kilmacrenan .	Gartan .	Dunfanaghy .	III.	128
3	Stag Island .	8	1	38	Roscommon	Boyle .	Boyle .	Boyle .	IV.	194
60, 68	Stagmount .	708	2	16	Kerry .	Magunihy .	Kilcummin .	Killarney .	II.	202
19	Stag Park .	306	0	18	Cork, E.R.	Condons&Clangibbon	Brigown .	Mitchelstown .	II.	60
20	Stagreenan .	130	0	30	Meath .	Lower Duleek .	Colp .	Drogheda .	I.	195
114	Stags of Bofin .	7	1	9	Mayo .	Murrisk .	Inishbofin .	Clifden .	IV.	159
11	Staholmog .	576	2	15	Meath .	Lower Kells .	Staholmog .	Kells .	I.	204
22	Staigbraud .	53	2	2	Waterford .	Decies without Drum	Modelligo .	Lismore .	II.	359
99, 107	Staigue . .	1,107	2	19	Kerry .	Dunkerron South .	Kilcrohane .	Kenmare .	II.	184
25	Stakally . .	356	1	35	Kilkenny .	Gowran .	Powerstown .	Thomastown .	I.	98
53, 54	Stakernagh .	235	1	32k	Tyrone .	Dungannon Middle	Donaghmore .	Dungannon .	III.	302
20, 27	Stalleen . .	792	1	26l	Meath .	Lower Duleek .	Donore .	Drogheda .	I.	195
20, 21	Stameen . .	361	2	5	Meath .	Lower Duleek .	Colp .	Drogheda .	I.	195
28	Stampspark .	16	1	27m	Kilkenny .	Gowran .	Thomastown .	Thomastown .	I.	99
1	Stamullin .	109	2	15	Dublin .	Balrothery East	Balscaddan .	Balrothery .	I.	20
28, 34	Stamullin .	392	2	22	Meath .	Upper Duleek .	Stamullin .	Drogheda .	I.	199
34	STAMULLIN T.	—			Meath .	Upper Duleek .	Stamullin .	Drogheda .	I	199
5, 7	Standane .	92	2	8	Antrim .	Lower Dunluce .	Dunluce .	Coleraine .	III.	17
48, 52	Stang . .	1,783	3	12	Down .	Upper Iveagh, Lr. pt.	Clonduff .	Newry .	III.	171

(a) Including 3A. 3R. 36P. water.
(b) Including 41A. 1R. 11P. water.
(c) Including 33A. 3R. 17P. water.
(d) Including 102A. 3R. 18P. water.
(e) Including 3A. 0R. 14P. water.

(f) Including 36A. 1R. 6P. water.
(g) Including 2A. 2R. 28P. water.
(h) Including 13A. 2R. 19P. water.
(i) Including 67A. 2R. 37P. water.

(j) Including 33A. 0R. 6P. water.
(k) Including 3A. 3R. 8P. water.
(l) Including 13A. 2R. 17P. water.
(m) Including 0A. 2R. 16P. River Nore.

No. of Sheet of the Ordnance Survey Maps	Townlands and Towns	Area in Statute Acres.	County.	Barony.	Parish.	Poor Law Union in 1857.	Townland Census of 1851, Part I. Vol.	Page
		A. R. P.						
14	Stang	41 2 26	Dublin	Castleknock	Finglas	Dublin North	I.	25
17	Stangaun	139 2 12	Leitrim	Drumahaire	Inishmagrath	Manorhamilton	IV.	97
54	Stangmore (Knox)	214 1 34	Tyrone	Dungannon Middle	Clonfeacle	Dungannon	III.	300
62	Stangmore (Mayec)	90 3 32	Tyrone	Dungannon Middle	Clonfeacle	Dungannon	III.	300
20, 21	Stangs	119 0 31	Kilkenny	Gowran	Gowran	Kilkenny	I.	95
26	Stangs	68 1 30	Tipperary, N.R.	Upper Ormond	Kilmore	Nenagh	II.	291
18, 22	Stannaway	162 1 30	Dublin	Uppercross	Crumlin	Dublin South	I.	40
32	Stanney	110 2 26	Queen's Co.	Slievemargy	Killeshin	Carlow	I.	246
7	Staplestown	233 2 29	Carlow	Carlow	Ballinacarrig	Carlow	I.	1
9	Staplestown	625 1 1	Kildare	Clane	Ballynafagh	Naas	I.	53
47	Staplestown	20 0 15	Wexford	Forth	Ballymore	Wexford	I.	308
42	Staplestown (Greaves)	208 3 24	Wexford	Forth	Kildavin	Wexford	I.	310
42	Staplestown (Morgan)	90 1 8	Wexford	Forth	Kildavin	Wexford	I.	310
42	Staplestown (Ram)	61 3 14	Wexford	Forth	Kildavin	Wexford	I.	310
15	Stapolin	245 0 23	Dublin	Coolock	Baldoyle	Dublin North	I.	26
13	Starinagh	1,117 1 12	Meath	Upper Slane	Collon	Ardee	I.	224
40, 43	Starraghan	136 3 9a	Fermanagh	Coole	Galloon	Clones	III.	200
61, 69	Starritstown	71 1 22	Donegal	Raphoe	Convoy	Stranorlar	III.	136
42	Starvehall	117 0 10	Wexford	Forth	Rathaspick	Wexford	I.	313
101	*Station Island*	0 3 26	Donegal	Tirhugh	Templecarn	Donegal	III.	149
55	*Staunton's Island or Clydagh*	2 0 28	Galway	Clare	Cargin	Tuam	IV.	18
39, 47	Steales	143 3 25	Limerick	Kilmallock	St. Peter's & St. Paul's	Kilmallock	II.	250
56, 57	Stealroe	140 3 14	Kerry	Trughanacmy	Killorglin	Killarney	II.	211
15	Steelaun	168 1 17	Mayo	Tirawley	Templemurry	Killala	IV.	172
20	Steelstown	152 3 10	Dublin	Newcastle	Newcastle	Celbridge	I.	34
50	Steeple	182 1 21	Antrim	Upper Antrim	Antrim	Antrim	I I.	5
30, 36	Steeplestown	155 1 6	Meath	Upper Navan	Trim	Trim	I.	217
124	Steilaneigh	42 2 0	Cork. W.R.	East Carbery (E.D.)	Templetrine	Kinsale	II.	130
22	Steill	291 0 9	Roscommon	Roscommon	Ogulla	Strokestown	IV.	212
25	STEPASIDE T.	—	Dublin	Rathdown	Kilgobbin	Rathdown	I.	35
29	Stephensland	21 1 27	Wexford	Bantry	St. Mary's	New Ross	I.	302
5	Stephenstown	310 3 15	Dublin	Balrothery East	Balrothery	Balrothery	I.	19
40	Stephenstown	170 1 6	Limerick	Coshlea	Athneasy	Kilmallock	II.	237
11, 12	Stephenstown	201 0 37	Louth	Upper Dundalk	Louth	Dundalk	I.	179
6, 12	Stephenstown	372 0 35	Meath	Morgallion	Castletown	Navan	I.	209
61, 69	Stephenstown	164 2 34	Tipperary, S.R.	Middlethird	St. John Baptist	Cashel	II.	330
9	Stephenstown	125 2 126	Tyrone	Strabane Lower	Urney	Strabane	III.	323
42, 47	Stephenstown	71 0 20	Wexford	Forth	Kilmacree	Wexford	I.	311
61	Stephenstownbeg	114 2 22	Tipperary, S.R.	Middlethird	Railstown	Cashel	II.	329
24	Stephenstown North	252 3 4	Kildare	Naas South	Killashee	Naas	I.	65
24	Stephenstown South	236 3 9	Kildare	Naas South	Killashee	Naas	I.	65
20	Stereame	77 1 38	Tipperary, N.R.	Lower Ormond	Nenagh	Nenagh	II.	287
39	Stevenson's Dowery	106 1 5	Tyrone	Dungannon Middle	Donaghenry	Cookstown	III.	301
29	Stewartsgrove	115 0 32	Queen's Co.	Clarmallagh	Abbeyleix	Abbeyleix	I.	235
29	Stewartsgrove	19 1 25	Queen's Co.	Clarmallagh	Durrow	Abbeyleix	I.	237
39, 47	STEWARTSTOWN T.	—	Tyrone	Dungannon Middle	Donaghenry	Cookstown	III.	301
14, 17	Stickillin	730 2 29	Louth	Ardee	Stickillin	Ardee	I.	175
18	Stickins	279 2 7	Kildare	Clane	Carragh	Naas	I.	53
17	Stifyans	46 3 17	Louth	Ardee	Mosstown	Ardee	I.	174
13	Stilebawn	159 2 38	Wicklow	Newcastle	Kilcoole	Rathdrum	I.	352
7	Stilebawn	183 3 15	Wicklow	Rathdown	Kilmacanoge	Rathdown	I.	356
50	Stiles	89 0 1	Antrim	Upper Antrim	Antrim	Antrim	III.	5
69	Stillimity	37 0 20	Tipperary, S.R.	Middlethird	Mora	Cashel	II.	329
29	*Still Island*	2 1 39	King's Co.	Garrycastle	Lusmagh	Parsonstown	I.	137
23	Stillorgan Grove	148 2 9	Dublin	Rathdown	Stillorgan	Rathdown	I.	37
23	Stillorgan North	63 3 13	Dublin	Rathdown	Stillorgan	Rathdown	I.	37
23	Stillorgan Park	182 2 7	Dublin	Rathdown	Stillorgan	Rathdown	I.	37
23	Stillorgan South	73 3 4	Dublin	Rathdown	Stillorgan	Rathdown	I.	37
23	STILLORGAN T.	—	Dublin	Rathdown	Stillorgan	Rathdown	I.	38
61	Stiloga	439 0 12	Tyrone	Dungannon Middle	Clonfeacle	Dungannon	III.	300
15, 22	Stirrupstown	301 3 16	Meath	Fore	Killallon	Oldcastle	I.	201
18	Stirue	46 0 8c	Louth	Ardee	Mosstown	Ardee	I.	174
18, 21	Stirue	203 1 39	Louth	Ferrard	Mullary	Drogheda	I.	182
14	Stockens	49 1 36	Dublin	Castleknock	Finglas	Dublin North	I.	25
14, 15	Stockhole	225 3 4	Dublin	Coolock	Cloghran	Balrothery	I.	26
29	Stocks	236 0 18	Meath	Lune	Athboy	Trim	I.	207
59	Stokaun	147 2 7	Tipperary, S.R.	Clanwilliam	Templenoe	Tipperary	II.	312
10, 19	Stokesfield	182 3 19	Limerick	Shanid	Robertstown	Rathkeale	II.	258
12	Stokesquarter	62 1 8	Meath	Morgallion	Castletown	Navan	I.	209
50, 51	Stokestown	212 0 27d	Meath	Dunboyne	Dunboyne	Dunshaughlin	I.	199
36, 42	Stokestown	408 1 11	Meath	Lower Moyfenrath	Laracor	Trim	I.	210

(a) Including 16A. 2R. 39P. water.　　　　　(c) Including 5A. 1R. 6P. detached portion.
(b) Including 3A. 1R. 13P. water.　　　　　(d) Including 10A. 2R. 11P. detached portion.

No. of Sheet of the Ordnance Survey Maps.	Townlands and Towns.	Area in Statute Acres.			County.	Barony.	Parish.	Poor Law Union in 1857.	Townland Census of 1851, Part I.	
		A.	R.	P.					Vol.	Page
25	Stokestown	288	2	20	Westmeath	Moyashel and Magheradernon	Mullingar	Mullingar	I.	275
34	Stokestown	604	1	36	Wexford	Bantry	Whitechurch	New Ross	I.	303
6, 11	Stonebrack	571	0	25	Tyrone	Strabane Lower	Donaghedy	Gortin	III.	321
27	Stonecarthy East	317	2	7	Kilkenny	Shillelogher	Stonecarthy	Thomastown	I.	115
27	Stonecarthy West	405	0	3	Kilkenny	Shillelogher	Stonecarthy	Thomastown	I.	115
28	Stoneen	77	0	22	Kilkenny	Gowran	Kilfane	Thomastown	I.	97
9, 10, 15	Stonefield	892	2	34	Meath	Fore	Oldcastle	Oldcastle	I.	202
4	Stonefort	58	2	29	Fermanagh	Lurg	Templecarn	Lowtherstown	III.	209
51	Stonehall	330	0	34	Clare	Bunratty Lower	Kilconry	Ennis	II.	4
11	Stonehall	201	1	23a	Limerick	Kenry	Kilcornan	Rathkeale	II.	249
48	Stonehall	242	1	2	Mayo	Tirawley	Ballynahaglish	Ballina	IV.	164
36	Stonehall	28	3	34	Meath	Lower Moyfenrath	Trim	Trim	I.	212
7, 12	Stonehall	387	0	24b	Westmeath	Corkaree	Stonehall	Mullingar	I.	263
20	Stonehall or Carrownageeragh	208	2	6	Sligo	Leyny	Ballysadare	Sligo	IV.	230
11	STONEHALL T.	—			Limerick	Kenry	Kilcornan	Rathkeale	II.	249
4	Stonehouse	270	2	37	King's Co.	Warrenstown	Castlejordan	Edenderry	I.	145
18, 21	Stonehouse	487	2	18	Louth	Ferrard	Mullary	Drogheda	I.	182
8	Stonehouse	459	2	36	Waterford	Middlethird	Kilmeadan	Waterford	II.	368
45, 50	Stonehouse	172	1	38	Wexford	Shelburne	Fethard	New Ross	I.	327
38	Stonehousefarm	125	1	19	Westmeath	Moycashel	Kilbeggan	Tullamore	I.	278
16	Stonepark	68	0	28	Cavan	Tullygarvey	Annagh	Cavan	III.	87
62	Stonepark	98	3	25	Clare	Bunratty Lower	Killeely	Limerick	II.	5
27	Stonepark	94	3	21	Clare	Tulla Upper	Feakle	Scarriff	II.	40
38	Stonepark	80	2	21	Fermanagh	Knockninny	Kinawley	Lisnaskea	III.	202
6	Stonepark	117	3	24	Galway	Ballymoe	Boyounagh	Glennamaddy	IV.	6
58	Stonepark	81	2	24	Galway	Tiaquin	Monivea	Tuam	IV.	79
10, 14	Stonepark	396	2	5	Leitrim	Drumahaire	Drumlease	Manorhamilton	IV.	95
23	Stonepark	132	0	39	Limerick	Clanwilliam	Ludden	Limerick	II.	225
13	Stonepark	195	1	37	Longford	Ardagh	Ballymacormick	Longford	I.	152
18, 22	Stonepark	71	3	10	Longford	Moydow	Kilcommock	Ballymahon	I.	161
90	Stonepark	72	2	1	Mayo	Carra	Rosslee	Castlebar	IV.	130
100	Stonepark	92	1	25	Mayo	Carra	Touaghty	Ballinrobe	IV.	130
39, 41	Stonepark	724	3	7	Roscommon	Ballintober South	Roscommon	Roscommon	IV.	190
4	Stonepark	125	1	7	Roscommon	Boyle	Kilronan	Boyle	IV.	197
25, 26	Stonepark	144	0	29	Roscommon	Castlereagh	Kiltullagh	Castlereagh	IV.	202
16	Stonepark	41	3	12	Roscommon	Frenchpark	Kilmacumsy	Boyle	IV.	204
20	Stonepark	106	1	0	Roscommon	Frenchpark	Tibohine	Castlereagh	IV.	205
45	Stonepark	213	1	31	Sligo	Coolavin	Killaraght	Boyle	IV.	224
6	Stonepark	49	3	25	Tipperary, N.R.	Lower Ormond	Terryglass	Borrisokane	II.	288
74	Stonepark	849	2	4	Tipperary, S.R.	Clanwilliam	Clonbeg	Tipperary	II.	305
61	Stonepark	29	0	7	Tipperary, S.R.	Middlethird	St. John Baptist	Cashel	II.	330
25	Stonepark	91	3	36	Wexford	Bantry	Clonmore	Enniscorthy	I.	300
42	Stonepark or Bawnmore	101	1	5	Galway	Clare	Donaghpatrick	Tuam	IV.	19
32	Stonepark North	45	3	1	Roscommon	Castlereagh	Kiltullagh	Castlereagh	IV.	202
33	Stoneparks	85	1	18	Sligo	Corran	Emlaghfad	Sligo	IV.	226
32	Stonepark South	85	3	38	Roscommon	Castlereagh	Kiltullagh	Castlereagh	IV.	202
22, 23	Stonestown	2,485	3	33	King's Co.	Garrycastle	Gallen	Parsonstown	I.	136
30	Stonestown	407	0	34	Meath	Upper Navan	Moymet	Trim	I.	216
5	Stonestown	85	1	31	Tipperary, N.R.	Lower Ormond	Loughkeen	Parsonstown	II.	286
14	Stonestown	242	0	20c	Westmeath	Delvin	Castletowndelvin	Castletowndelvin	I.	265
8, 9	Stonestown	521	1	29	Westmeath	Delvin	Clonarney	Castletowndelvin	I.	265
13	Stonestown	61	3	13	Westmeath	Delvin	Killulagh	Castletowndelvin	I.	266
3	Stonestown	288	2	28	Westmeath	Fore	Rathgarve	Castletowndelvin	I.	271
6, 18	Stonetown	274	1	37d	Galway	Ballymoe	Boyounagh	Glennamaddy	IV.	6
5	Stonetown	30	0	36e	Limerick	Limerick, Municipal Borough of	St. Nicholas	Limerick	II.	262
10, 11	Stonetown Lower	181	0	11	Louth	Ardee	Louth	Dundalk	I.	173
11	Stonetown Upper	62	3	0	Louth	Ardee	Louth	Dundalk	I.	173
26	Stoneville	191	0	27	Limerick	Connello Lower	Nantinan	Rathkeale	II.	229
20	Stoneville	98	1	32	Limerick	Connello Lower	Rathkeale	Rathkeale	II.	229
9, 16	Stonewalls	130	3	13	Tyrone	Strabane Lower	Ardstraw	Strabane	III.	319
5	Stongaluggaun	29	0	30	Westmeath	Moygoish	Rathaspick	Mullingar	I.	280
16	Stonyacre	400	3	18	Tipperary, N.R.	Lower Ormond	Modreeny	Borrisokane	II.	287
37	Stonybatter	40	3	4	Wexford	Shelmaliere West	Carrick	Wexford	I.	332
9, 16	Stonyfalls	183	2	29	Tyrone	Strabane Lower	Ardstraw	Strabane	III.	319
3, 6	Stonyfalls	123	0	18f	Tyrone	Strabane Lower	Donaghedy	Strabane	III.	321
48	Stonyford	78	2	27	Wexford	Forth	Kilscoran	Wexford	I.	311
27	STONYFORD T.	—			Kilkenny	Knocktopher	Stonecarthy / Ennisnag	Thomastown	I.	113 / 114
25	Stony Hill	86	2	17	Antrim	Lower Glenarm	Tickmacrevan	Larne	III.	24
126	Stonyisland	557	1	29	Galway	Longford	Lickmolassy	Portumna	IV.	61

(a) Including 3A. 2R. 19P. water.　　　　(c) Including 2A. 3R. 19P. water.　　　　(e) Included in the Parish of St. Nicholas.
(b) Including 8A. 2R. 24P. water.　　　　(d) Including 2A. 2R. 32P. water.　　　　(f) Including 2A. 1R. 20P. water.

No. of Sheet of the Ordnance Survey Maps.	Townlands and Towns.	Area in Statute Acres.			County.	Barony.	Parish.	Poor Law Union in 1857.	Townland Census of 1851, Part I.	
		A.	R.	P.					Vol.	Page
17	Stonylane	180	1	25	Louth	Ardee	Ardee	Ardee	I.	171
2	Stonypath	90	0	27	Tyrone	Strabane Lower	Leckpatrick	Strabane	III.	322
15	Stooagh	387	2	3	Queen's Co.	Upperwoods	Offerlane	Mountmellick	I.	252
22, 28	Stook	290	2	12	Tipperary, N.R.	Upper Ormond	Aghnameadle	Nenagh	II.	289
97	Stookeen	81	3	21	Cork, E.R.	Kinalea	Ballinaboy	Kinsale	II.	93
48	Stookeens	147	3	22	Limerick	Coshlea	Kilbreedy Major	Kilmallock	II.	239
43, 47	Stoops	208	2	23	Wicklow	Shillelagh	Carnew	Shillelagh	I.	357
14	Stormanstown	248	2	35	Dublin	Coolock	Santry	Dublin North	I.	29
13, 14	Stormanstown	536	0	13	Louth	Ardee	Clonkeen	Ardee	I.	172
74, 83	Stormhill	100	3	39	Donegal	Banagh	Killybegs Lower	Glenties	III.	110
140	Stouke	247	3	38	Cork, W.R.	West Carbery(W.D.)	Skull	Skull	II.	147
44	Stowelodge	261	1	8	Galway	Clare	Killererin	Tuam	IV.	21
107, 108	Stowlin	539	3	18	Galway	Longford	Kilquain	Portumna	IV.	60
50	Strabane	136	1	23	Tyrone	Cloger	Donacavey	Omagh	III.	294
5	Strabane Bog	84	1	32a	Tyrone	Strabane Lower	Leckpatrick	Strabane	III.	322
5	STRABANE T.	—			Tyrone	Strabane Lower	{ Camus / Leckpatrick / Urney }	} Strabane	III.	{ 320 / 322 / 323 }
4, 5	Strabane, Townparks of	417	1	86b	Tyrone	Strabane Lower	Camus	Strabane	III.	320
3, 8	Straboe	1,104	0	24	Carlow	Rathvilly	Straboe	Baltinglass	I.	12
8, 13	Straboe	575	3	28	Queen's Co.	Maryborough East	Straboe	Mountmellick	I.	242
72, 81	Straboy	1,212	2	8c	Donegal	Banagh	Glencolumbkille	Glenties	III.	106
65,66,74,75	Straboy	1,391	0	31d	Donegal	Boylagh	Inishkeel	Glenties	III.	113
90, 96, 97	Strabrinna Lower	188	2	32	Donegal	Banagh	Kilcar	Glenties	III.	109
90,91,96,97	Strabrinna Upper	211	1	6	Donegal	Banagh	Kilcar	Glenties	III.	109
66, 75	Stracashel	391	2	9	Donegal	Boylagh	Inishkeel	Glenties	III.	113
5	Straclevan	106	3	27	Monaghan	Monaghan	Tedavnet	Monaghan	III.	279
5, 6, 8, 9	Stracruncion	93	3	22	Monaghan	Monaghan	Tedavnet	Monaghan	III.	279
41	Stradavoher	94	0	24	Tipperary, N.R.	Eliogarty	Thurles	Thurles	II.	273
14, 19	Stradbally	522	0	39	Queen's Co.	Stradbally	Stradbally	Athy	I.	248
32	Stradbally Beg	246	0	30	Waterford	Decies without Drum	Stradbally	Kilmacthomas	II.	361
95, 103	Stradbally East	164	2	22	Galway	Dunkellin	Stradbally	Galway	IV.	32
24, 32	Stradbally More	503	2	3	Waterford	Decies without Drum	Stradbally	Kilmacthomas	II.	361
35	Stradbally Mountain	593	0	15e	Kerry	Corkaguiny	Stradbally	Dingle	II.	180
95, 103	Stradbally North	395	2	20	Galway	Dunkellin	Stradbally	Galway	IV.	32
1, 6	Stradbally North	180	2	16	Limerick	Clanwilliam	Stradbally	Limerick	II.	226
103	Stradbally South	284	2	38	Galway	Dunkellin	Stradbally	Galway	IV.	32
1, 6	Stradbally South	3	2	13	Limerick	Clanwilliam	Stradbally	Limerick	II.	226
103	STRADBALLY T.	—			Galway	Dunkellin	Oranmore	Galway	IV.	32
35	STRADBALLY T.	—			Kerry	Corkaguiny	Stradbally	Dingle	II.	180
14, 19	STRADBALLY T.	—			Queen's Co.	Stradbally	Stradbally	Athy	I.	248
24, 32	STRADBALLY T.	—			Waterford	Decies without Drum	Stradbally	Kilmacthomas	II.	361
103	Stradbally West	144	2	38	Galway	Dunkellin	Stradbally	Gort	IV.	32
23	Stradbrook	33	3	2	Dublin	Rathdown	Monkstown	Rathdown	I.	37
70	Strade	500	1	6f	Mayo	Gallen	Templemore	Castlebar	IV.	151
31	Stradeen	117	2	8	Monaghan	Farney	Killanny	Carrickmacross	III.	272
25	Stradermot	125	3	29g	Leitrim	Carrigallen	Oughteragh	Bawnboy	IV.	92
26	STRADONE T.	—			Cavan	Upper Loughtee	Larah	Cavan	III.	85
26, 27	Stradowan	1,309	0	2	Tyrone	Strabane Upper	Bodoney Lower	Gortin	III.	324
6, 10	Stradreagh	765	1	1	Londonderry	Keenaght	Aghanloo	New T. Limavady	III.	234
14	Stradreagh Beg	57	2	30h	Londonderry	Tirkeeran	Clondermot	Londonderry	III.	248
14	Stradreagh More	130	2	4i	Londonderry	Tirkeeran	Clondermot	Londonderry	III.	248
17	Straduff	196	1	11	Carlow	Forth	Myshall	Carlow	I.	5
7, 15	Straduff	582	1	34	King's Co.	Garrycastle	Lemanaghan	Parsonstown	I.	137
35	Straduff	746	2	7	Sligo	Tirerrill	Kilmactranny	Boyle	IV.	240
41, 42	Straduff	324	1	10	Tyrone	Omagh East	Dromore	Omagh	III.	311
10, 14	Straffan	215	2	6	Kildare	North Salt	Straffan	Celbridge	I.	76
14	Straffan Demesne	214	3	20j	Kildare	North Salt	Straffan	Celbridge	I.	76
76	Stragally	270	0	12	Donegal	Raphoe	Kilteevoge	Stranorlar	III.	139
91, 92	Stragar	908	2	27	Donegal	Banagh	Killybegs Upper	Glenties	III.	111
20, 21	Stragelliff	236	1	34k	Cavan	Upper Loughtee	Annagelliff	Cavan	III.	82
9	Straghan or Cornasore	124	2	11	Monaghan	Trough	Donagh	Monaghan	III.	283
5	Stragolan	105	1	13	Fermanagh	Lurg	Drumkeeran	Lowtherstown	III.	207
17	Stragole	101	1	20	Fermanagh	Tirkennedy	Enniskillen	Enniskillen	III.	222
33	Stragowna	149	0	20	Fermanagh	Clanawley	Kinawley	Enniskillen	III.	194
35, 44	Stragraddy	1,847	3	38	Donegal	Kilmacrenan	Kilmacrenan	Milford	III.	129
67	Stragrane	172	1	34	Tyrone	Dungannon Lower	Aghaloo	Armagh	III.	297
5, 10	Stragullin	174	3	35l	Tyrone	Strabane Lower	Camus	Strabane	III.	320
4, 8	Strahard	625	1	22	Queen's Co.	Portnahinch	Ardea	Mountmellick	I.	243
9, 10, 14, 15	Strahart	171	0	34m	Wexford	Scarawalsh	Ballycarney	Enniscorthy	I.	322
11, 15	Straheglin	263	3	24n	Cavan	Lower Loughtee	Annagh	Cavan	III.	79
12, 13	Strahull	361	3	18	Tyrone	Strabane Upper	Bodoney Upper	Gortin	III.	324
17	Strahulter	319	0	7o	Tyrone	Strabane Lower	Ardstraw	Gortin	III.	319

(a) Including 3A. 1R. 18P. water.
(b) { Including 20A. 2R. 25P. Lyons Island. / Including 40A. 3R. 17P. River Mourne. / Including 5A. 3R. 24P. Tideway.
(c) Including 2A. 3R. 36P. water.
(d) Including 12A. 2R. 29P. water.
(e) Including 6A. 0R. 13P. water.
(f) Including 3A. 3R. 6P. water.
(g) Including 8A. 3R. 20P. water.
(h) Including 10A. 2R. 12P. Lough Enagh East.
(i) { Including 4A. 1R. 4P. Lough Enagh East. / Including 4A. 3R. 2P. Lough Enagh West.
(j) Including 8A. 2R. 16P. water.
(k) Including 10A. 1R. 25P. Beaghy Lough.
(l) Including 15A. 2R. 27P. water.
(m) Including 6A. 3R. 20P. water.
(n) Including 30A. 1R. 34P. water.
(o) Including 8A. 3R. 25P. water.

5 P

No. of Sheet of the Ordnance Survey Maps.	Townlands and Towns.	Area in Statute Acres. A. R. P.	County.	Barony.	Parish.	Poor Law Union in 1857.	Townland Census of 1851, Part I. Vol.	Page
15	Straid	69 1 31a	Antrim	Lower Glenarm	Layd	Ballycastle	III.	23
37	Straid	339 2 39	Antrim	Upper Toome	Ahoghill	Ballymena	III.	33
10, 19	Straid	3,171 0 29	Donegal	Inishowen East	Clonmany	Inishowen	III.	117
6	Straid	148 0 33	Galway	Ballymoe	Templetogher	Glennamaddy	IV.	10
23, 29, 30	Straid	682 1 18	Londonderry	Tirkeeran	Banagher	Londonderry	III.	247
50, 55	Straidballymorris	449 3 38	Antrim	Upper Belfast	Templepatrick	Antrim	III.	11
7	Straidbilly	213 2 19	Antrim	Lower Dunluce	Billy	Ballymoney	III	16
80	Straid or Glebe	83 0 32	Donegal	Banagh	Glencolumbkille	Glenties	III.	106
55	Straidhavern	482 1 8	Antrim	Lower Massereene	Killead	Antrim	III.	28
45,46,51,52	Straidland	1,983 1 2	Antrim	Lower Belfast	Ballynure	Larne	III.	7
51, 52	Straidnahanna	191 1 27	Antrim	Lower Belfast	Ballylinny	Antrim	III.	7
84	Strake	431 0 30	Mayo	Murrisk	Kilgeever	Westport	IV.	161
32, 33	Strakeenagh	556 0 0	Donegal	Kilmacrenan	Tullaghobegly	Dunfanaghy	III.	132
20, 21	Stralahan	555 0 14b	Fermanagh	Clanawley	Boho	Enniskillen	III.	189
11	Straleek	9 2 0	Kildare	South Salt	Donaghcumper	Celbridge	I.	76
90	Straleel	855 2 33	Donegal	Banagh	Kilcar	Glenties	III.	109
90	Straleel Glebe	3 1 35	Donegal	Banagh	Kilcar	Glenties	III.	109
90	Straleel North	879 2 30	Donegal	Banagh	Glencolumbkille	Glenties	III.	106
90	Straleel South	709 0 5c	Donegal	Banagh	Glencolumbkille	Glenties	III.	106
91	Straleeny	58 2 19	Donegal	Banagh	Killybegs Upper	Glenties	III.	111
17, 18	Straletterdallan	685 2 20d	Tyrone	Strabane Lower	Ardstraw	Gortin	III.	319
75	Stralinchy	159 2 35	Donegal	Boylagh	Inishkeel	Glenties	III.	113
61	Stralongford	756 3 35	Donegal	Raphoe	Convoy	Stranorlar	III.	136
21	Stralongford	365 0 33	Leitrim	Carrigallen	Oughteragh	Bawnboy	IV.	92
49	Stralongford	288 3 22	Tyrone	Omagh East	Kilskeery	Lowtherstown	III.	314
4	Stralusky	115 3 21	Carlow	Rathvilly	Haroldstown	Shillelagh	I.	11
40	Stralustrin	51 3 12	Fermanagh	Clankelly	Clones	Clones	III.	197
32	Stramackilmartin	217 3 9	Donegal	Kilmacrenan	Tullaghobegly	Dunfanaghy	III.	132
5	Stramackilroy	635 1 16	Monaghan	Monaghan	Tedavnet	Monaghan	III.	279
33, 39	Stramaquerty	180 1 22	Cavan	Castlerahan	Killinkere	Oldcastle	III.	69
43	Stramatt	127 1 8	Cavan	Castlerahan	Lurgan	Oldcastle	III.	70
38	Stramatt	95 0 10	Fermanagh	Knockninny	Kinawley	Lisnaskea	III.	202
26	Stramillian	106 3 14	Kildare	Offaly West	Monasterevin	Athy	I.	73
51	Stramore	198 3 38	Donegal	Kilmacrenan	Gartan	Letterkenny	III.	128
6	Stramore	176 3 27	Monaghan	Trough	Donagh	Monaghan	III.	283
51	Stramore Upper	911 0 8	Donegal	Kilmacrenan	Gartan	Letterkenny	III.	128
67, 68	Stranabrattoge	647 2 3	Donegal	Raphoe	Kilteevoge	Stranorlar	III.	139
32, 33	Stranabrooey	392 1 29	Donegal	Kilmacrenan	Tullaghobegly	Dunfanaghy	III.	132
2	Stranabrosny	132 0 21e	Tyrone	Strabane Lower	Donaghedy	Strabane	III.	321
14, 19, 20	Stranacally	511 1 22	Fermanagh	Magheraboy	Devenish	Ballyshannon	III.	211
7	Stranacarry	72 1 23	Louth	Upper Dundalk	Castletown	Dundalk	I.	177
29	Stranaclea	389 0 29	Donegal	Inishowen West	Fahan Lower	Inishowen	III.	120
32	Stranacorcragh	336 1 4	Donegal	Kilmacrenan	Tullaghobegly	Dunfanaghy	III.	132
9, 13	Stranadarragh	155 0 11	Cavan	Tullyhaw	Templeport	Bawnboy	III.	95
2, 6	Stranadarriff	452 1 3	Fermanagh	Lurg	Magheraculmoney	Lowtherstown	III.	208
28	Stranafeley	320 3 27	Fermanagh	Magherastephana	Aghavea	Lisnaskea	III.	219
6, 7	Stranagalwilly	3,129 1 37	Tyrone	Strabane Lower	Cumber Upper	Gortin	III.	320
3, 5	Stranagap	44 0 32	Cavan	Tullyhaw	Killinagh	Enni-killen	III.	92
41	Stranagard	170 0 25	Londonderry	Loughinsholin	Desertmartin	Magherafelt	III.	241
81	Stranagartan	119 0 39	Donegal	Banagh	Glencolumbkille	Glenties	III.	106
12	Stranagarvagh	58 2 33	Monaghan	Dartree	Clones	Clones	III.	265
65, 74, 75	Stranaglogh	730 2 11	Donegal	Boylagh	Inishkeel	Glenties	III.	113
67	Stranagoppoge	353 2 28	Donegal	Boylagh	Inishkeel	Glenties	III.	113
49, 56	Stranagummer	260 1 13	Tyrone	Omagh East	Kilskeery	Lowtherstown	III.	314
22	Stranahely	375 2 39	Wicklow	Upper Talbotstown	Donaghmore	Baltinglass	I.	365
2, 6	Stranahone	469 0 20	Fermanagh	Lurg	Magheraculmoney	Lowtherstown	III.	208
38, 43	Stranakelly	591 0 31	Wicklow	Shillelagh	Mullinacuff	Shillelagh	I.	358
90	Stranakirk	310 2 15	Donegal	Banagh	Kilcar	Glenties	III.	109
3	Stranamart	636 3 28	Cavan	Tullyhaw	Killinagh	Enniskillen	III.	92
79	Stranamuck	104 0 6f	Donegal	Raphoe	Donaghmore	Strabane	III.	138
35	Strananerriagh	558 1 26	Fermanagh	Clankelly	Clones	Clones	III.	197
58	Stranasaggart	269 2 7	Donegal	Boylagh	Lettermacward	Glenties	III.	114
30	Stranatona	150 1 27	Monaghan	Farney	Magheracloone	Carrickmacross	III.	272
34	Strancally	256 1 16	Waterford	Coshmore&Coshbride	Kilcockan	Lismore	II.	343
29, 34	Strancally Demesne	196 3 28	Waterford	Coshmore&Coshbride	Kilcockan	Lismore	II.	343
45	Strand	360 2 39g	Down	Lecale Upper	Bright	Downpatrick	III.	180
42	Strandfield	58 2 32	Wexford	Forth	Kerloge	Wexford	I.	310
120	Strandhill	176 0 14h	Mayo	Kilmaine	Cong	Ballinrobe	IV.	154
14	Strandhill or Larass	388 0 13	Sligo	Carbury	Killaspugbrone	Sligo	IV.	222
18	Strandhill or Lecarrow	54 2 39	Leitrim	Drumahaire	Inishmagrath	Manorhamilton	IV.	97
80	Strandsend	113 3 6	Kerry	Iveragh	Killinane	Cahersiveen	II.	197
4	Strandtown	335 3 22	Down	Castlereagh Lower	Holywood	Belfast	III.	162
18	St ANDVILLE AVENUE T.	—	Dublin	Coolock	Clontarf	Dublin North	I.	26

(a) Including 0A. 2R. 8P. detached portions.
(b) Including 8A. 1R. 21P. water.
(c) Including 4A. 2R. 18P. water.
(d) Including 16A. 1R. 0P. water.
(e) Including 4A. 1R. 20P. water.
(f) Including 3A. 2R. 2P. water.
(g) Including 17A. 0R. 14P. water.
(h) Including 12A. 1R. 7P. water.

No. of Sheet of the Ordnance Survey Maps.	Townlands and Towns.	Area in Statute Acres.	County.	Barony.	Parish.	Poor Law Union in 1857.	Townland Census of 1851, Part I.	
		A. R. P.					Vol.	Page
94	Straness	413 0 0	Donegal	Tirhugh	Drumhome	Donegal	III.	147
31, 32	Strangford Lower	261 3 25	Down	Lecale Lower	Ballyculter	Downpatrick	III.	178
31, 32	STRANGFORD T.	—	Down	Lecale Lower	Ballyculter	Downpatrick	III.	178
31	Strangford Upper	277 0 10	Down	Lecale Lower	Ballyculter	Downpatrick	III.	178
43	Strangsmill	109 0 12	Kilkenny	Ida	Dunkitt	Waterford	I.	101
50, 57	Stranisk	778 3 37	Tyrone	Clogher	Donacavey	Omagh	III.	294
5	Stranisk	159 2 1	Tyrone	Strabane Lower	Leckpatrick	Strabane	III.	322
12	Stranocum	434 2 28	Antrim	Upper Dunluce	Ballymoney	Ballymoney	III.	19
12	STRANOCUM T.	—	Antrim	Upper Dunluce	Ballymoney	Ballymoney	III.	19
13	Stranoodan	202 1 16	Monaghan	Monaghan	Kilmore	Monaghan	III.	276
70	Stranorlaghan	78 0 13	Donegal	Raphoe	Raphoe	Strabane	III.	141
78	Stranorlar	259 3 3a	Donegal	Raphoe	Stranorlar	Stranorlar	III.	143
78	STRANORLAR T.	—	Donegal	Raphoe	Stranorlar	Stranorlar	III.	143
42	Strany Beg	135 3 12	Meath	Lower Moyfenrath	Rathmolyon	Trim	I.	211
42	Strany More	178 2 37	Meath	Lower Moyfenrath	Rathmolyon	Trim	I.	211
75	Strasallagh	623 0 31b	Donegal	Boylagh	Inishkeel	Glenties	III.	113
21	Stratford	341 1 32	Wicklow	Upper Talbotstown	Rathbran	Baltinglass	I.	365
26, 27	Stratfordlodge	277 3 20	Wicklow	Upper Talbotstown	Baltinglass	Baltinglass	I.	362
21	STRATFORD T.	—	Wicklow	Upper Talbotstown	Rathbran	Baltinglass	I.	365
22	Strathall	205 2 37	Londonderry	Tirkeeran	Cumber Lower	Londonderry	III.	249
4, 10, 11	Straths	374 2 6	Donegal	Inishowen East	Clonmany	Inishowen	III.	117
50	Stratigore	111 3 29	Tyrone	Clogher	Donacavey	Omagh	III.	294
14	Stratonagher	544 2 24c	Fermanagh	Magheraboy	Devenish	Enniskillen	III.	211
14, 15	Stratore	339 3 12	Fermanagh	Magheraboy	Devenish	Enniskillen	III.	211
18, 25	Strattonstown	375 2 37	Westmeath	Moyashel and Magheradernon	Mullingar	Mullingar	I.	275
34, 35	Straughroy	186 0 16d	Tyrone	Strabane Upper	Capnagh	Omagh	III.	325
81, 82	Stravally	922 1 21	Donegal	Banagh	Inishkeel	Glenties	III.	106
26, 32, 33	Stravicnabo	537 2 18	Cavan	Upper Loughtee	Lavey	Cavan	III.	86
16, 24	Straw	242 0 20	Londonderry	Keenaght	Bovevagh	New T. Limavady	III.	235
40	Straw	432 2 28	Londonderry	Loughinsholin	Ballynascreen	Magherafelt	III.	239
22	Strawberryhill or Drishoge	182 1 12	King's Co.	Garrycastle	Gallen	Parsonstown	I.	136
2, 7	Strawhall	373 1 9e	Carlow	Carlow	Carlow	Carlow	I.	1
35, 36	Strawhall	573 0 10f	Cork, E.R.	Condons&Clangibbon	Clondulane	Fermoy	II.	60
22, 23	Strawhall	40 0 26	Kildare	Offaly East	Kildare	Naas	I.	70
68	Straw Island	2 2 4	Galway	Moycullen	Killannin	Oughterard	IV.	70
35, 40	Strawmore	530 1 9	Londonderry	Loughinsholin	Ballynascreen	Magherafelt	III.	239
40, 41	Straw Mountain	421 0 12	Londonderry	Loughinsholin	Ballynascreen	Magherafelt	III.	239
74, 83	Strawoaghter Glebe	720 3 3g	Donegal	Banagh	Killybegs Lower	Glenties	III.	110
45	Strawpark	57 1 14	Antrim	Upper Antrim	Kilbride	Antrim	III.	6
100	Stream	47 2 16	Galway	Clonmacnowen	Clontuskert	Ballinasloe	IV.	25
8, 17	Streamhill East	1,623 2 12	Cork, E.R.	Fermoy	Doneraile	Mallow	II.	79
8, 17	Streamhill West	896 1 3	Cork, E.R.	Fermoy	Doneraile	Mallow	II.	79
85, 86	Streamsford	237 1 25	Galway	Kilconnell	Grange	Loughrea	IV.	40
85, 86	Streamsford	278 1 4	Galway	Kilconnell	Killimordaly	Loughrea	IV.	42
12, 15	Streamstown	67 3 12	Dublin	Coolock	Kinsaley	Balrothery	I.	28
123	Streamstown	132 2 10	Galway	Kiltartan	Kilbeacanty	Gort	IV.	47
106, 116	Streamstown	396 3 21	Galway	Leitrim	Duniry	Loughrea	IV.	53
36	Streamstown	570 2 31	King's Co.	Eglish	Drumcullen	Parsonstown	I.	134
21, 22	Streamstown	59 2 19	King's Co.	Garrycastle	Reynagh	Parsonstown	I.	138
21, 22	Streamstown	92 1 24	Longford	Ratheline	Cashel	Ballymahon	I.	164
23	Streamstown	89 1 37	Longford	Shrule	Taghshinny	Ballymahon	I.	167
14	Streamstown	154 1 17	Louth	Ardee	Mapastown	Ardee	I.	173
101	Streamstown	295 3 8	Mayo	Clanmorris	Kilcolman	Claremorris	IV.	134
87	Streamstown	136 2 22	Mayo	Murrisk	Oughaval	Westport	IV.	162
32	Streamstown	200 3 30	Sligo	Leyny	Achonry	Tobercurry	IV.	229
20	Streamstown	369 2 4	Sligo	Leyny	Ballysadare	Sligo	IV.	230
7, 12	Streamstown	468 3 22	Westmeath	Fore	Faughalstown	Castletowndelvin	I.	270
23	Streamstown	110 1 8	Westmeath	Kilkenny West	Drumraney	Ballymahon	I.	273
16, 23	Streamstown	69 1 14	Westmeath	Kilkenny West	Noughaval	Ballymahon	I.	274
31	Streamstown	958 3 4	Westmeath	Moycashel	Ardnurcher or Horseleap	Mullingar	I.	277
48	Streamstown	70 0 2	Wexford	Forth	Rosslare	Wexford	I.	313
22	Streamstown or Barratrough	1,000 3 8h	Galway	Ballynahinch	Omey	Clifden	IV.	15
7	Streanduff	31 3 1	Monaghan	Trough	Donagh	Monaghan	III.	283
5	Streedagh	490 1 37	Sligo	Carbury	Ahamlish	Sligo	IV.	219
36	Streefe Glebe	376 2 39	Tyrone	Omagh East	Termonmaguirk	Omagh	III.	315
9, 10	Streeve	119 0 39	Londonderry	Keenaght	Drumachose	New T. Limavady	III.	235
38	Straws	391 1 32	Tyrone	Dungannon Upper	Kildress	Cookstown	III.	309
38	Strifehill	66 1 14	Tyrone	Dungannon Upper	Derryloran	Cookstown	III.	307
5	Strifeland	138 2 22	Dublin	Balrothery East	Holmpatrick	Balrothery	I.	20
70	Strike Lower	100 1 26	Tipperary, S.R.	Middlethird	Coolmundry	Cashel	II.	326

(a) Including 10A. 3R. 9P. water.
(b) Including 47A. 3R. 11P. water.
(c) Including 12A. 0R. 11P. water.
(d) Including 10A. 1R. 35P. water.
(e) Including 7A. 2R. 0P. River Barrow.
(f) Including 1A. 2R. 10P. water.
(g) Including 12A. 1R. 38P. water.
(h) Including 16A. 1R. 23P. water.

No. of Sheet of the Ordnance Survey Maps.	Townlands and Towns.	Area in Statute Acres.	County.	Barony.	Parish.	Poor Law Union in 1857.	Townland Census of 1851. Part I.	
		A. R. P.					Vol.	Page
70	Strike Upper	269 0 15	Tipperary, S.R.	Middlethird	Coolmundry	Cashel	II.	326
26, 27	String	240 0 20	Cork, E.R.	Fermoy	Glanworth	Fermoy	II.	79
29	Stripe	240 1 33	Fermanagh	Magherastephana	Aghalurcher	Lisnaskea	III.	217
57	Stripe	156 1 21	Galway	Clare	Cummer	Tuam	IV.	19
30	Stripe	77 2 29	Galway	Dunmore	Tuam	Tuam	IV.	36
93	Stripe	71 2 7	Galway	Moycullen	Rahoon	Galway	IV.	72
62, 72	Stripe	194 1 20	Mayo	Costello	Kilbeagh	Swineford	IV.	141
4	Stripe North	339 1 38a	Galway	Dunmore	Dunmore	Tuam	IV.	34
37	Stripes	55 3 15	Kilkenny	Ida	The Rower	New Ross	I.	104
30	Stripe South	38 2 18	Galway	Dunmore	Dunmore	Tuam	IV.	34
8, 13	Stroan	383 2 8	Antrim	Cary	Armoy	Ballycastle	III.	11
24, 28	Stroan	208 2 34	Kilkenny	Gowran	Kilfane	Thomastown	I.	97
42, 43	Stroancarbadagh	206 0 28	Tyrone	Omagh East	Drumragh	Omagh	III.	313
15	Stroane	158 2 2b	Cavan	Lower Loughtee	Annagh	Cavan	III.	79
76	Stroangarrow	1,155 0 12	Donegal	Raphoe	Kilteevoge	Stranorlar	III.	139
60,61,68,69	Stroangibbagh	447 1 0	Donegal	Raphoe	Convoy	Stranorlar	III.	136
76	Stroangibbagh	359 3 31	Donegal	Raphoe	Kilteevoge	Stranorlar	III.	140
12	Stroan Lower	153 0 25	Antrim	Lower Dunluce	Derrykeighan	Ballymoney	III.	17
12	Stroan Upper	253 0 24	Antrim	Lower Dunluce	Derrykeighan	Ballymoney	III.	17
29	Strogue	712 1 16	Tipperary, N.R.	Ikerrin	Templeree	Thurles	II.	277
22	Stroke	210 1 5	Leitrim	Carrigallen	Drumreilly	Bawnboy	IV.	91
23, 29	STROKESTOWN T.	—	Roscommon	Roscommon	{ Bumlin / Kiltrustan }	Strokestown	IV.	{ 208 / 211 }
13	Stroove	1,052 0 4	Donegal	Inishowen East	Moville Lower	Inishowen	III.	119
78	Struaun	59 0 17	Mayo	Carra	Aglish	Castlebar	IV.	124
38	Struell	365 0 21	Down	Lecale Upper	Down	Downpatrick	III.	181
39	Stuart Hall	143 2 2	Tyrone	Dungannon Upper	Arboe	Cookstown	III.	305
31	Stuccolane	3 1 23	Waterford	Decies without Drum	Dungarvan	Dungarvan	II.	356
32	Stuck	130 1 12	Leitrim	Mohill	Mohill	Mohill	IV.	108
100	Stuckeen	183 3 11	Mayo	Carra	Touaghty	Ballinrobe	IV.	130
15	Studfield North	132 2 34	Wicklow	Lower Talbotstown	Donard	Baltinglass	I.	360
15, 21	Studfield South	35 2 0	Wicklow	Lower Talbotstown	Donard	Baltinglass	I.	360
46	Stughan	141 3 9	Tyrone	Dungannon Middle	Tullyniskan	Dungannon	III.	305
3, 4, 6, 7	Stumpa	122 0 16	Louth	Upper Dundalk	Kane	Dundalk	I.	179
66, 76, 77	Stumphill	360 0 5	Cork, E.R.	Barrymore	Inchinabacky	Middleton	II.	55
30	Stump of the Castle	804 2 6	Wicklow	Newcastle	Kilcommon	Rathdrum	I.	351
37	Stumpys Hill	87 3 0	Fermanagh	Clanawley	Kinawley	Enniskillen	III.	194
25	Sturgan	396 2 28	Armagh	Orior Upper	Killevy	Newry	III.	58
21	Sturrakeen	91 0 24c	Galway	Ballynahinch	Omey	Clifden	IV.	15
23, 24	Subulter	382 2 27	Cork, E.R.	Duhallow	Subulter	Kanturk	II.	75
74	Suburbs of Cork	0 0 8	Cork, E.R.	Cork	St. Annes Shandon	Cork	II.	65
74	Suburbs of Cork	2 1 9	Cork, E.R.	Cork	St. Finbars	Cork	II.	66
74	Suburbs of Cork	1 0 25	Cork, E.R.	Cork	St. Marys Shandon	Cork	II.	66
74	Suburbs of Cork	1 0 3	Cork, E.R.	Cork	St. Nicholas	Cork	II.	66
53	Suckfield	127 3 39d	Roscommon	Moycarn	Creagh	Ballinasloe	IV.	206
35	Sugarhill	1,467 3 14	Limerick	Glenquin	Monagay	Newcastle	II.	247
22	Sugarloaf	163 1 30	Wicklow	Upper Talbotstown	Donaghmore	Baltinglass	I.	363
19	Sugarloaf Hill	6 1 14e	Kilkenny	Kilkenny Municipal Borough of	St. Canice	Kilkenny	I.	117
24, 28	Sugarstown	263 2 5	Kilkenny	Gowran	Kilfane	Thomastown	I.	97
68	Suirville	256 1 37	Tipperary, S.R.	Clanwilliam	Relickmurry & Athassel	Tipperary	II.	310
29	Sullenboy	55 1 39	Tyrone	Dungannon Upper	Derryloran	Cookstown	III.	307
27,28,36,37 9, 15	Sultan	2,252 3 35f	Tyrone	Omagh East	Termonmaguirk	Omagh	III.	315
	Summerbank or Drumsawry	809 1 38	Meath	Fore	Loughcrew	Oldcastle	I.	201
67	Summerfield	179 3 10	Cork, E.R.	Imokilly	Youghal	Youghal	II.	91
69,70,82,83	Summerfield or Cahergowan	841 0 25	Galway	Dunkellin	Claregalway	Galway	IV.	27
7	Summergrove or Garroon	239 1 4	Queen's Co.	Tinnahinch	Rosenallis	Mountmellick	I.	250
54	Summerhill	230 1 7	Clare	Tulla Lower	Kiltenanlea	Limerick	II.	37
99	Summerhill	261 1 22	Donegal	Banagh	Killymard	Donegal	III.	112
40	Summerhill	95 2 32	Fermanagh	Clankelly	Clones	Clones	III.	197
32, 46	Summerhill	225 1 28	Galway	Killian	Killian	Mountbellew	IV.	45
11	Summerhill	289 2 21	Louth	Louth	Louth	Dundalk	I.	184
43	Summerhill	176 1 14	Meath	Lower Moyfenrath	Laracor	Trim	I.	210
17, 23	Summerhill	382 3 35	Tipperary, N.R.	Ikerrin	Rathnaveoge	Roscrea	II.	276
34	Summerhill	151 3 18	Tipperary, N.R.	Kilnamanagh Upper	Glenkeen	Thurles	II.	279
83	Summerhill	64 1 2	Tipperary, S.R.	Iffa and Offa East	Kiltegan	Clonmel	II.	315
13	Summerhill or Aghnaharna	134 2 18	Queen's Co.	Maryborough East	Borris	Mountmellick	I.	240
42, 43, 49	Summerhill Demesne	755 1 36	Meath	Lower Moyfenrath	Laracor	Trim	I.	210
38	Summerhill or Knocknageeragh	282 3 11	Waterford	Decies within Drum	Lisgenan or Grange	Youghal	II.	352
6	Summerhill Lower	195 3 16	Meath	Lower Slane	Loughbracken	Ardee	I.	223

(a) Including 13A. 2R. 29P. water.
(b) Including 32A. 0R. 18P. water.
(c) Including 20A. 3R. 24P. water.
(d) Including 2A. 0R. 7P. water.
(e) Included in the Parish of St. Canice.
(f) Including 7A. 2R. 34P. water.

No. of Sheet of the Ordnance Survey Maps.	Townlands and Towns.	Area in Statute Acres.	County.	Barony.	Parish.	Poor Law Union in 1857.	Townland Census of 1851, Part I.	
		A. R. P.					Vol.	Page
100	Summerhill North .	258 1 8	Mayo . .	Kilmaine . .	Mayo . . .	Ballinrobe .	IV.	157
100	Summerhill South .	437 3 13	Mayo . .	Kilmaine . .	Mayo . . .	Ballinrobe .	IV.	157
43	SUMMERHILL T. .	—	Meath . .	Lower Moyfenrath .	Laracor . .	Trim . .	I.	210
6	Summerhill Upper .	493 1 3	Meath . .	Lower Slane . .	Loughbrackan .	Ardee . .	I.	223
30	Summerslane . .	115 1 11	Kilkenny .	Kells . .	Coolaghmore .	Callan . .	I.	108
36, 42	Summerstown . .	456 2 10	Meath . .	Lower Moyfenrath .	Laracor . .	Trim . .	I.	210
53	Summerstown .	29 3 36	Wexford . .	Forth . .	Carn . .	Wexford . .	I.	309
48	Summertown . .	61 1 4	Wexford . .	Forth . .	St. Margaret's .	Wexford . .	I.	314
45	Summerville . .	342 2 38a	Galway . .	Tiaquin . .	Moylough . .	Mountbellew .	IV.	80
3, 11	Summerville . .	258 3 2	Limerick . .	Kenry . .	Kilcornan . .	Rathkeale .	II.	249
27	Summerville . .	61 1 29	Waterford . .	Gaultiere . .	Ballynakill .	Waterford .	II.	362
64, 73	Summy . . .	447 2 8b	Donegal . .	Boylagh . .	Inishkeel . .	Glenties .	III.	113
28	Suncroft . . .	81 3 39	Kildare . .	Offaly East . .	Carn . .	Naas . .	I.	69
7, 16	Sunfort . . .	230 1 18	Cork, E.R. .	Duhallow . .	Knocktemple .	Kanturk . .	II.	75
24	Sunglen . . .	131 3 37	Limerick . .	Coonagh . .	Grean . .	Tipperary .	II.	235
44, 58	Sunhill . . .	162 1 37	Galway . .	Tiaquin . .	Abbeyknockmoy .	Tuam . .	IV.	75
23	Sunhill . . .	47 1 8	Kilkenny . .	Shillclogher .	Burnchurch .	Callan . .	I.	113
21	Sunlawn . . .	93 1 8	Waterford . .	Decies without Drum .	Affane . .	Lismore . .	II.	353
18, 26	Sunnagh . . .	218 1 37	Clare . .	Bunratty Upper .	Inchicronan .	Tulla . .	II.	9
29, 33	Sunnagh Beg . .	290 2 18	Leitrim . .	Mohill . .	Cloone . .	Mohill . .	IV.	106
29	Sunnaghconner .	179 1 35	Leitrim . .	Carrigallen . .	Cloone . .	Mohill . .	IV.	90
33	Sunnagh More .	1,434 3 9c	Leitrim . .	Mohill . .	Cloone . .	Mohill . .	IV.	106
28	Sunnyhill . . .	394 3 14	Kildare . .	Kilcullen . .	Kilcullen . .	Naas . .	I.	58
89	Sunville . . .	51 0 39	Cork, E.R. .	Imokilly . .	Cloyne . .	Middleton .	II.	86
24	Sunville . . .	37 3 21	Limerick . .	Coonagh . .	Grean . .	Tipperary .	II.	235
48, 56	Sunville Lower .	287 2 37	Limerick . .	Coshlea . .	Particles . .	Kilmallock .	II.	241
56	Sunville Upper .	554 0 6	Limerick . .	Coshlea . .	Particles . .	Kilmallock .	II.	241
11	Surgalstown North .	224 1 12	Dublin . .	Nethercross . .	Killossery .	Balrothery .	I.	31
11	Surgalstown South .	203 0 7	Dublin . .	Nethercross . .	Killossery .	Balrothery .	I.	31
24, 33	Surgeview or Nakil	221 2 24	Mayo . .	Erris . .	Kilmore . .	Belmullet .	IV.	146
88	Sussa . . .	717 0 23	Kerry . .	Iveragh . .	Prior . .	Cahersiveen .	II.	198
39	Sutherland . .	182 3 25	Meath . .	Ratoath . .	Crickstown .	Dunshaughlin .	I.	217
15, 19	Sutton North . .	116 1 20	Dublin . .	Coolock . .	Howth . .	Dublin North .	I.	28
76	Suttonrath . .	204 0 14	Tipperary, S.R. .	Iffa and Offa West .	Caher . .	Clogheen .	II.	318
15, 19	Sutton South . .	352 2 2	Dublin . .	Coolock . .	Howth . .	Dublin North .	I.	28
14	Suttonsrath . .	223 0 11	Kilkenny . .	Fassadinin . .	Odagh . .	Kilkenny .	I.	91
37	Swainstown . .	321 3 28	Meath . .	Lower Deece .	Kilmessan .	Dunshaughlin .	I.	192
6	Swallow Island .	4 1 18	Roscommon .	Boyle . .	Ardcarn . .	Boyle . .	IV.	193
29	Swan . . .	96 0 36	Queen's Co. .	Clarmallagh .	Durrow . .	Abbeyleix .	I.	237
129	Swan Island . .	0 0 21	Galway . .	Kiltartan . .	Beagh . .	Gort . .	IV.	46
6	Swan Island . .	0 0 8	Longford . .	Granard . .	Columbkille .	Granard .	I.	156
7	SWANLINBAR T. .	—	Cavan . .	Tullyhaw . .	Kinawley . .	Bawnboy .	III.	93
15	Swansnest . .	89 1 38	Dublin . .	Coolock . .	Kilbarrack .	Dublin North .	I.	28
26, 32	Swatragh . .	413 1 18	Londonderry .	Loughinsholin .	Maghera . .	Magherafelt .	III.	242
32	SWATRAGH T. .	—	Londonderry .	Loughinsholin .	Maghera . .	Magherafelt .	III.	243
26	Sweetfarm . .	161 3 20	Wexford . .	Bantry . .	St. John's .	Enniscorthy .	I.	302
67	Sweetfields . .	53 1 16	Cork. E.R. .	Imokilly . .	Youghal . .	Youghal .	II.	91
9	Sweethill . .	259 1 8	Kilkenny . .	Galmoy . .	Rathbeagh .	Urlingford .	I.	93
15	Sweetwood Little .	90 3 8	Leitrim . .	Drumahaire .	Killarga . .	Manorhamilton .	IV.	99
15	Sweetwood Lower .	129 3 8	Leitrim . .	Drumahaire .	Killarga . .	Manorhamilton .	IV.	99
15	Sweetwood Upper .	95 3 6	Leitrim . .	Drumahaire .	Killarga . .	Manorhamilton .	IV.	99
20, 25	Swellan Lower .	248 0 10d	Cavan . .	Upper Loughtee .	Urney . .	Cavan . .	III.	86
20	Swellan Upper .	107 1 33e	Cavan . .	Upper Loughtee .	Urney . .	Cavan . .	III.	86
18	Swiftsacre . .	14 0 14	Galway . .	Ballymoe . .	Boyounagh .	Glennamaddy .	IV.	6
10	Swiftsheath . .	593 2 38	Kilkenny . .	Fassadinin . .	Coolcrahcen .	Kilkenny .	I.	89
13	Swilly . . .	122 1 25	Donegal . .	Raphoe . .	Taughboyne .	Strabane .	III.	144
26	Swillybrin . .	152 0 11	Donegal . .	Kilmacrenan .	Clondahorky .	Dunfanaghy .	III.	123
32	Swinefield . .	230 2 26	Roscommon .	Castlereagh .	Kiltullagh .	Castlereagh .	IV.	202
62	Swineford . .	95 2 10	Mayo . .	Gallen . .	Kilconduff .	Swineford .	IV.	148
62	SWINEFORD T. .	—	Mayo . .	Gallen . .	Kilconduff .	Swineford .	IV.	148
21	Swinestown . .	86 0 26	Louth . .	Ferrard . .	Marlestown .	Drogheda .	I.	181
24	Swordlestown North .	549 0 19	Kildare . .	Naas South .	Kill . .	Naas . .	I.	65
24	Swordlestown South .	476 3 11	Kildare . .	Naas South .	Kill . .	Naas . .	I.	65
11, 12	Swords Demesne .	114 2 14	Dublin . .	Nethercross .	Swords . .	Balrothery .	I.	32
11	Swords Glebe . .	9 1 21f	Dublin . .	Nethercross .	Swords . .	Balrothery .	I.	32
11	SWORDS T. . .	—	Dublin . .	Nethercross .	Swords . .	Balrothery .	I.	32
17	Sycamore . .	132 1 8	Cork, E.R. .	Fermoy . .	Doneraile .	Mallow . .	II.	79
14	Sycamore Fields or Lisnamaine .	55 0 1	Cavan . .	Lower Loughtee .	Drumlane .	Cavan . .	III.	80
100	Sycamorehill . .	520 2 1	Galway . .	Longford . .	Clonfert . .	Ballinasloe .	IV.	57
54, 61	Syerla . . .	174 2 10	Tyrone . .	Dungannon Middle .	Clonfeacle .	Dungannon .	III.	300
29	Sylaun . . .	273 2 9	Galway . .	Clare . .	Belclare . .	Tuam . .	IV.	17
29	Sylaun . . .	36 3 37	Galway . .	Clare . .	Killower . .	Tuam . .	IV.	21

(a) Including 18A. 0R. 23P. water.
(b) Including 30A. 0R. 3P. water.
(c) Including 11A. 1R. 24P. water.
(d) Including 18A. 3R. 32P. water.
(e) Including 5A. 3R. 35P. water.
(f) Including 0A. 1R. 3P. detached portion.

No. of Sheet of the Ordnance Survey Maps.	Townlands and Towns.	Area in Statute Acres.			County.	Barony.	Parish.	Poor Law Union in 1857.	Townland Census of 1851, Part I.	
		A.	R.	P.					Vol.	Page
29	Sylaun . . .	68	1	9a	Galway .	Dunmore .	Kilbennan .	Tuam .	IV.	34
69, 82	Sylaun . . .	479	0	1	Galway .	Galway .	Oranmore .	Galway .	IV.	37
17	Sylaun East .	230	3	3	Galway .	Dunmore .	Dunmore .	Tuam .	IV.	34
17	Sylaunnagran .	186	2	18	Galway .	Dunmore .	Dunmore .	Tuam .	IV.	34
17	Sylaun West .	90	3	3	Galway .	Dunmore .	Dunmore .	Tuam .	IV.	34
53	Synone . . .	620	2	1	Tipperary, S.R.	Middlethird .	Ballysheehan .	Cashel .	II.	325
31	Syonan . .	100	3	5	Westmeath	Moycashel	Ardnurcher or Horse-leap .	Mullingar .	I.	277
50	Syonee . .	190	3	24	Tyrone .	Clogher .	Donacavey .	Omagh .	III.	294
50, 51	Syonfin . .	249	1	35	Tyrone .	Clogher .	Donacavey .	Omagh .	III.	294
58, 64	Syunshin .	286	3	11	Tyrone .	Clogher .	Clogher .	Clogher .	III.	293
32	Taash . .	187	0	16	Leitrim .	Leitrim .	Annaduff .	Mohill .	IV.	100
15	Tabagh . .	68	0	13	Fermanagh	Magheraboy .	Inishmacsaint .	Enniskillen .	III.	213
22	Table Mountain .	508	3	2	Wicklow .	Upper Talbotstown .	Donaghmore .	Baltinglass .	I.	363
3	Taboe Glebe .	681	3	32	Tyrone .	Strabane Lower .	Donaghedy .	Strabane .	III.	321
53	Tacumshin .	211	3	1	Wexford .	Forth .	Tacumshin .	Wexford .	I.	315
51	Taduff East .	115	3	0	Roscommon .	Athlone .	Drum .	Athlone .	IV.	180
51	Taduff West .	193	2	11	Roscommon .	Athlone .	Drum .	Athlone .	IV.	180
50, 51	Taggartsland and Cromy .	185	3	23	Antrim .	Upper Antrim .	Donegore .	Antrim .	III.	6
10	Taghadoe .	506	0	5	Kildare .	North Salt .	Taghadoe .	Celbridge .	I.	76
21	Tagharina .	120	3	9	Londonderry .	Tirkeeran .	Clondermot .	Londonderry .	III.	248
29	Taghart North or Closnabraddan .	431	2	27b	Cavan .	Clankee .	Enniskeen .	Bailieborough .	III.	73
28, 29	Taghart South .	872	0	25	Cavan .	Clankee .	Enniskeen .	Bailieborough .	III.	73
44	Taghboy .	849	0	32c	Roscommon .	Athlone .	Taghboy .	Athlone .	IV.	184
24, 25	Taghboyne .	172	3	31	Westmeath .	Rathconrath .	Churchtown .	Mullingar .	I.	282
111	Tagheen East .	94	1	36	Mayo .	Clanmorris .	Tagheen .	Claremorris .	IV.	136
111	Tagheen West .	83	2	0	Mayo .	Clanmorris .	Tagheen .	Claremorris .	IV.	136
16	Taghey . .	214	2	27	Antrim .	Upper Dunluce .	Ballymoney .	Ballymoney .	III.	19
51, 54	Taghmaconnell .	728	0	14	Roscommon .	Athlone .	Taghmaconnell .	Athlone .	IV.	185
12, 13	Taghmon .	1,120	3	28	Westmeath .	Corkaree .	Taghmon .	Mullingar .	I.	264
41	Taghmon .	252	1	7	Wexford .	Shelmalicre West .	Taghmon .	Wexford .	I.	335
36, 41	TAGHMON T. .	—			Wexford .	Shelmalicre West .	Taghmon .	Wexford .	I.	335
14	Taghnabrick .	352	3	39	Down .	Castlereagh Upper .	Blaris .	Lisburn .	III.	164
24	Taghnafearagh .	170	1	10	Westmeath .	Rathconrath .	Killare .	Mullingar .	I.	283
19, 25	Taghnarra .	647	0	31	Roscommon .	Castlereagh .	Kilkeevin .	Castlereagh .	IV.	201
6	Taghnevan .	276	2	7	Armagh .	Oneilland East .	Shankill .	Lurgan .	III.	51
19	Taghnoose .	442	2	30	Roscommon .	Castlereagh .	Kilkeevin .	Castlereagh .	IV.	201
23	Taghsheenod Glebe	47	3	10	Longford .	Moydow .	Taghsheenod .	Ballymahon .	I.	162
23	Taghshinny .	372	0	10	Longford .	Shrule .	Taghshinny .	Ballymahon .	I.	167
47	Tagunnan or Mount-pleasant .	190	1	27	Wexford .	Forth .	Mayglass .	Wexford .	I.	312
100	Tahilla . .	352	1	31	Kerry .	Dunkerron South .	Kilcrohane .	Kenmare .	II.	184
100	TAHILLA T. .	—			Kerry .	Dunkerron South .	Kilcrohane .	Kenmare .	II.	184
20	Talbotshill .	207	3	23	Kilkenny .	Gowran .	Gowran .	Kilkenny .	I.	95
14, 19	Talbotsinch .	303	3	30d	Kilkenny .	Crannagh and Municipal Borough .	St. Canice .	Kilkenny .	I.	87
47	Talbotstown .	97	2	0	Wexford .	Forth .	Kilmacree .	Wexford .	I.	311
27	Talbotstown Lower .	258	2	23	Wicklow .	Upper Talbotstown .	Kilranelagh .	Baltinglass .	I.	364
27	Talbotstown Upper .	318	3	14	Wicklow .	Upper Talbotstown .	Kilranelagh .	Baltinglass .	I.	364
31	Tallacoolbeg .	56	2	15	Waterford .	Decies without Drum	Dungarvan .	Dungarvan .	II.	356
31	Tallacoolmore .	151	0	33	Waterford .	Decies without Drum	Kilgobnet .	Dungarvan .	II.	357
43, 44	Tallagh . .	1,759	1	33	Mayo .	Erris .	Kilcommon .	Newport .	IV.	145
9, 10	Tallagh . .	1,429	2	30	Mayo .	Erris .	Kilmore .	Belmullet .	IV.	146
21, 22	Tallaght . .	1,952	1	36	Dublin .	Uppercross .	Tallaght .	Dublin South .	I.	42
21	TALLAGHT T. .	—			Dublin .	Uppercross .	Tallaght .	Dublin South .	I.	42
105	Tallavbaun .	524	3	29	Mayo .	Murrisk .	Kilgeever .	Westport .	IV.	160
105	Tallavbaun Island .	11	1	1	Mayo .	Murrisk .	Kilgeever .	Westport .	IV.	161
19, 32	Tallavnamraher .	231	0	38	Galway .	Ballymoe .	Kilbegnet .	Glennamaddy .	IV.	8
28	Tallow . .	74	1	30	Waterford .	Coshmore&Coshbride	Tallow .	Lismore .	II.	348
28	Tallowbridge Lands	104	2	18e	Waterford .	Coshmore&Coshbride	Lismore and Mocollop	Lismore .	II.	347
28	TALLOWBRIDGE T. .	—			Waterford .	Coshmore&Coshbride	Lismore and Mocollop	Lismore .	II.	348
96	Tallowroe .	368	1	17	Galway .	Dunkellin .	Killeeneen .	Gort .	IV.	30
28	TALLOW T. .				Waterford .	Coshmore&Coshbride	Tallow .	Lismore .	II.	348
26	Tallyho . .	69	1	7	Westmeath .	Fartullagh .	Moylisker .	Mullingar .	I.	269
47	Tamary . .	645	2	38	Down .	Upper Iveagh, Lr. pt.	Clonduff .	Newry .	III.	171
26	Tamlaght .	545	3	24	Antrim .	Kilconway .	Rasharkin .	Ballymoney .	III.	28
20	Tamlaght .	271	0	6	Antrim .	Lower Glenarm .	Ardclinis .	Larne .	III.	21
37, 43	Tamlaght .	326	2	23	Antrim .	Upper Toome .	Drummaul .	Ballymena .	III.	34
15	Tamlaght .	301	0	1	Armagh .	Armagh .	Derrynoose .	Armagh .	III.	44
11, 12	Tamlaght .	166	2	34	Armagh .	Armagh .	Eglish .	Armagh .	III.	44

(a) Including 17A. 1R. 18P. water.
(b) Including 5A. 2R. 32P. water.
(c) Including 9A. 0R. 18P. water.

(d) { Including 8A. 3R. 32P. River Nore.
Within the Municipal Boundary,　4A. 3R. 32P.
Without the Municipal Boundary, 298A. 3R. 38P.
(e) Including 1A. 3R. 2P. detached portions.

No. of Sheet of the Ordnance Survey Maps.	Townlands and Towns.	Area in Statute Acres.	County.	Barony.	Parish.	Poor Law Union in 1857.	Townland Census of 1851, Part I.	
		A. R. P.					Vol.	Page
27	Tamlaght	185 0 36a	Fermanagh	Tirkennedy	Derryvullan	Enniskillen	III.	221
19	Tamlaght	245 3 29	Londonderry	Coleraine	Aghadowey	Ballymoney	III.	230
5, 6	Tamlaght	288 3 37	Londonderry	Keenaght	Magilligan	Newtᵈ Limavady	III.	237
9, 16	Tamlaght	299 1 29	Londonderry	Keenaght	Tamlaght Finlagan	Newtᵈ Limavady	III.	237
48, 49	Tamlaght	248 1 21	Londonderry	Loughinsholin	Tamlaght	Magherafelt	III.	243
51, 52	Tamlaght	383 2 35	Tyrone	Clogher	Clogher	Clogher	III.	293
29	Tamlaght	142 1 20	Tyrone	Dungannon Upper	Kildress	Cookstown	III.	309
34	Tamlaght	462 3 27	Tyrone	Omagh East	Drumragh	Omagh	III.	313
32	Tamlaghtavally	160 0 17	Leitrim	Mohill	Mohill	Mohill	IV.	108
32	Tamlaght Beg	154 0 20	Leitrim	Mohill	Mohill	Mohill	IV.	108
37	Tamlaghtduff	679 2 21	Londonderry	Loughinsholin	Ballyscullion	Magherafelt	III.	239
20	Tamlaghtmore	68 1 34	Antrim	Lower Glenarm	Ardclinis	Larne	III.	21
32, 35	Tamlaght More	297 2 13	Leitrim	Mohill	Mohill	Mohill	IV.	108
48	Tamlaghtmore	225 3 6	Londonderry	Loughinsholin	Derryloran	Magherafelt	III.	240
55	Tamlaghtmore	526 2 5b	Tyrone	Dungannon Middle	Kildyman	Dungannon	III.	303
39	Tamlaghtmore	261 0 5	Tyrone	Dungannon Upper	Arboe	Cookstown	III.	305
33	Tamlaght T.	—	Londonderry	Loughinsholin	Tamlaght O'Crilly	Magherafelt	III.	244
23	Tamlat	199 0 28	Monaghan	Cremorne	Aghnamullen	Cootehill	III.	258
9, 13	Tamlat	107 2 29	Monaghan	Monaghan	Monaghan	Monaghan	III.	277
10	Tamlat	136 2 6	Monaghan	Monaghan	Tehallan	Monaghan	III.	280
6	Tamlat	121 2 6	Monaghan	Trough	Errigal Trough	Monaghan	III.	285
1, 2	Tamnabrady	322 1 18	Tyrone	Strabane Lower	Donaghedy	Strabane	III.	321
2	Tamnabryan	237 1 37	Tyrone	Strabane Lower	Donaghedy	Strabane	III.	321
1	Tamnaclare	315 3 37	Tyrone	Strabane Lower	Donaghedy	Strabane	III.	321
42	Tamnadeese	438 2 11	Londonderry	Loughinsholin	Magherafelt	Magherafelt	III.	243
48, 49	Tamnaderry	144 1 13	Antrim	Upper Toome	Duneane	Antrim	III.	35
46	Tamnadooey	317 3 38	Londonderry	Loughinsholin	Desertlyn	Magherafelt	III.	240
6	Tamnaficarbet	122 3 3	Armagh	Oneilland East	Seagoe	Lurgan	III.	50
6	Tamnafiglassan	178 3 18	Armagh	Oneilland East	Seagoe	Lurgan	III.	50
29, 30	Tamnagh	2,592 1 8	Londonderry	Tirkeeran	Banagher	Londonderry	III.	247
25	Tamnagh	186 3 13	Tyrone	Strabane Lower	Ardstraw	Strabane	III.	319
26, 29	Tamnaghbane	338 2 8c	Armagh	Orior Upper	Killevy	Newry	III.	58
42	Tamnaghmore	370 2 3	Antrim	Upper Toome	Duneane	Ballymena	III.	35
13	Tamnaghmore	534 3 30	Armagh	Orior Lower	Kilmore	Banbridge	III.	56
13	Tamnaghvelton	378 1 5	Armagh	Orior Lower	Kilmore	Banbridge	III.	56
47, 51	Tamnaharry	636 2 28	Down	Upper Iveagh, Up. pt.	Clonallan	Newry	III.	174
14, 15, 23	Tamnaherin	790 3 37	Londonderry	Tirkeeran	Cumber Lower	Londonderry	III.	249
1, 2	Tamnakeery	239 1 37	Tyrone	Strabane Lower	Donaghedy	Strabane	III.	321
7	Tamnamoney	111 2 2	Londonderry	Coleraine	Macosquin	Coleraine	III.	233
38	Tamnaskeeny	393 3 33	Tyrone	Dungannon Upper	Kildress	Cookstown	III.	309
39, 40	Tamnavally	249 0 5	Tyrone	Dungannon Upper	Arboe	Cookstown	III.	305
70	Tamnawood	64 2 10	Donegal	Raphoe	Clonleigh	Strabane	III.	135
42	Tamniaran	753 1 2	Londonderry	Loughinsholin	Ballyscullion	Magherafelt	III.	239
31	Tamniarin	657 3 13	Londonderry	Keenaght	Dungiven	Newtᵈ Limavady	III.	236
30	Tamnyagan	362 0 36	Londonderry	Tirkeeran	Banagher	Newtᵈ Limavady	III.	247
36, 41	Tamnyaskey	239 1 14	Londonderry	Loughinsholin	Kilcronaghan	Magherafelt	III.	241
29	Tamnyhagan	45 0 7	Tyrone	Dungannon Upper	Lissan	Cookstown	III.	309
39	Tamnyleunan	167 2 7	Tyrone	Dungannon Middle	Donaghenry	Cookstown	III.	301
36	Tamnymartin	124 0 37	Londonderry	Loughinsholin	Maghera	Magherafelt	III.	242
18	Tamnymore	402 3 8	Londonderry	Coleraine	Errigal	Coleraine	III.	232
20	Tamnymore	254 3 11	Londonderry	Tirkeeran	Clondermot	Londonderry	III.	248
22	Tamnymore	346 1 37	Londonderry	Tirkeeran	Cumber Lower	Londonderry	III.	249
32, 36	Tamnymullan	445 2 12	Londonderry	Loughinsholin	Maghera	Magherafelt	III.	242
26	Tamnyrankin	417 3 30	Londonderry	Coleraine	Desertoghill	Ballymoney	III.	231
14	Tamnyreagh	231 1 29	Londonderry	Tirkeeran	Cumber Lower	Londonderry	III.	249
66	Tamnyvane	146 3 7	Antrim	Upper Massereene	Aghagallon	Lurgan	III.	29
55	Tamnyveagh	154 2 22	Down	Upper Iveagh, Up. pt.	Kilbroney	Kilkeel	III.	176
83	Tamur	608 1 20d	Donegal	Banagh	Inver	Donegal	III.	108
104, 105	Tamur	1,365 1 13e	Donegal	Tirhugh	Templecarn	Donegal	III.	149
28,29,33,34	Tamybuck	1,480 2 28	Antrim	Lower Antrim	Racavan	Ballymena	III.	4
2, 6	Tanderagee	42 2 1	Antrim	Lower Dunluce	Dunluce	Coleraine	III.	17
16, 20	Tanderagee	302 1 25	Armagh	Fews Lower	Lisnadill	Armagh	III.	47
34	Tanderagee	251 1 8f	Cavan	Clankee	Bailieborough	Bailieborough	III.	71
3	Tanderagee	190 3 17	Kildare	Carbury	Mylerstown	Edenderry	I.	52
42	Tanderagee	273 2 27	Meath	Lower Moyfenrath	Rathmolyon	Trim	I.	211
12	Tanderagee	149 2 20	Monaghan	Dartree	Clones	Clones	III.	265
37	Tanderagee	279 0 34	Tyrone	Dungannon Middle	Pomeroy	Cookstown	III.	304
44	Tanderagee	565 1 20	Tyrone	Omagh East	Termonmaguirk	Omagh	III.	315
13	Tanderageebane	166 3 25	Monaghan	Monaghan	Monaghan	Monaghan	III.	277
13	Tanderageebrack	136 3 16	Monaghan	Monaghan	Monaghan	Monaghan	III.	277
14	Tanderagee T.	—	Armagh	Orior Lower	Ballymore	Banbridge	III.	56
75	Tangaveane	351 0 5g	Donegal	Boylagh	Inishkeel	Glenties	III.	113
50, 57, 58	Tangaveane	1,634 2 37h	Donegal	Boylagh	Templecrone	Glenties	III.	116

(a) Including 3A. 2R. 21P. water.
(b) Including 6A. 1R. 33P. water.
(c) Including 4A. 0R. 3P. water.

(d) Including 23A. 3R. 19P. water.
(e) Including 100A. 0R. 15P. water.
(f) Including 11A. 2R. 13P. water.

(g) Including 7A. 2R. 36P. water.
(h) Including 123A. 0R. 36P. water.

No. of Sheet of the Ordnance Survey Maps.	Townlands and Towns.	Area in Statute Acres.			County.	Barony.	Parish.	Poor Law Union in 1857.	Townland Census of 1851, Part I.	
		A.	R.	P.					Vol.	Page
96, 97	Tangincartoor	234	2	17	Mayo	Murrisk	Oughaval	Westport	IV.	162
18	Tankardrath	134	1	37	Meath	Morgallion	Kilberry	Navan	I.	209
18	Tankardsgarden	507	3	0a	Kildare	Connell	Oldconnell	Naas	I.	56
6, 7	Tankardsrock	332	3	8	Louth	Upper Dundalk	Castletown	Dundalk	I.	177
8, 9	Tankardstown	1,411	3	28	Carlow	Rathvilly	Tullowphelim	Carlow	I.	12
18	Tankardstown	600	2	2	Cork, E.R.	Fermoy	Farahy	Mitchelstown	II.	79
2, 5	Tankardstown	203	2	13	Dublin	Balrothery East	Balrothery	Balrothery	I.	19
38	Tankardstown	331	2	26	Kildare	Kilkea and Moone	Kineagh	Baltinglass	I.	61
40	Tankardstown	311	2	6	Limerick	Smallcounty	Uregare	Kilmallock	II.	261
17, 24	Tankardstown	568	1	10	Meath	Lower Navan	Donaghpatrick	Navan	I.	214
45	Tankardstown	123	2	10	Meath	Ratoath	Ratoath	Dunshaughlin	I.	219
33	Tankardstown	93	3	5	Meath	Upper Duleek	Clonalvy	Drogheda	I.	197
12, 18, 19	Tankardstown	691	0	2	Meath	Upper Slane	Gernonstown	Navan	I.	224
26	Tankardstown	949	2	66b	Queen's Co.	Ballyadams	Tankardstown	Athy	I.	232
25	Tankardstown	235	0	17	Waterford	Decies without Drum	Kilbarrymeaden	Kilmacthomas	II.	356
39, 47	Tankardstown North	430	1	28	Limerick	Coshma	Tankardstown	Kilmallock	II.	244
47	Tankardstown South	196	2	13	Limerick	Coshma	Tankardstown	Kilmallock	II.	244
75	Tankerstown	249	1	15	Tipperary, S.R.	Clanwilliam	Clonbulloge	Tipperary	II.	306
18, 23	Tanmacnally	170	0	23c	Monaghan	Dartree	Ematris	Cootehill	III.	267
60, 61	Tannagh	258	1	32	Tyrone	Dungannon Lower	Aghaloo	Dungannon	III.	297
67	Tannaghlane	365	0	14	Tyrone	Dungannon Lower	Aghaloo	Armagh	III.	297
43	Tannaghmore	330	3	1	Antrim	Upper Toome	Drummaul	Ballymena	III.	34
17	Tannaghmore	315	3	32d	Armagh	Oneilland West	Mullaghbrack	Banbridge	III.	54
29,30,36,37	Tannaghmore	282	1	32	Down	Kinelarty	Loughinisland	Downpatrick	III.	177
6	Tannaghmore North	230	1	26	Armagh	Oneilland East	Shankill	Lurgan	III.	51
6	Tannaghmore South	205	2	26	Armagh	Oneilland East	Shankill	Lurgan	III.	51
6	Tannaghmore West	209	2	14	Armagh	Oneilland East	Seagoe	Lurgan	III.	50
77	Tannersrath	89	1	23	Tipperary, S.R.	Iffa and Offa East	Kilgrant	Clonmel	II.	314
17, 18	Tannyoky	181	0	3	Armagh	Orior Lower	Ballymore	Newry	III.	55
19	Tanrego East or Carrowmore	167	2	5	Sligo	Tireragh	Dromard	Dromore West	IV.	233
19	Tanrego West	297	0	37	Sligo	Tireragh	Dromard	Dromore West	IV.	233
30	Tanseyclose	159	0	35	Wicklow	Ballinacor North	Rathdrum	Rathdrum	I.	347
17, 23	Tansyfield	132	3	4	Roscommon	Roscommon	Elphin	Strokestown	IV.	210
25, 26	Tantramurry	230	1	9e	Tyrone	Strabane Upper	Cappagh	Omagh	III.	325
40	Tantybulk	78	3	17	Fermanagh	Clankelly	Galloon	Clones	III.	198
29	Tanyard or Pigotts	80	0	14	Wexford	Bantry	St. Mary's	New Ross	I.	302
28, 35	Tap	605	2	9	Sligo	Tirerrill	Shancough	Boyle	IV.	241
25, 28	Taplagh	139	0	39	Monaghan	Farney	Donaghmoyne	Carrickmacross	III.	271
32	Tara	275	1	27	Down	Ards Upper	Witter	Downpatrick	III.	161
8	Tara	518	1	14	King's Co.	Ballycowan	Durrow	Tullamore	I.	127
7	Tarahill	296	2	17	Wexford	Ballaghkeen	Kilcavan	Gorey	I.	294
7	Tarahill	152	0	31	Wexford	Ballaghkeen	Kiltennell	Gorey	I.	297
31	TARA T.	—			Meath	Skreen	Tara	Navan	I.	222
3	Tarbert	367	2	30	Kerry	Iraghticonnor	Kilnaughtin	Glin	II.	192
17	Tarbert	190	2	17	Queen's Co.	Maryborough West	Clonenagh&Clonagheen	Abbeyleix	I.	243
3	Tarbert Island	63	0	35	Kerry	Iraghticonnor	Kilnaughtin	Glin	II.	192
3	TARBERT T.	—			Kerry	Iraghticonnor	Kilnaughtin	Glin	II.	192
44	Tardree	730	1	7	Antrim	Lower Antrim	Connor	Antrim	III.	3
34	Tarlum	252	1	24	Tyrone	Omagh East	Drumragh	Omagh	III.	313
58, 68	Tarmon	666	3	24f	Clare	Clonderalaw	Killimer	Kilrush	II.	16
3, 6	Tarmon East	937	2	0	Kerry	Iraghticonnor	Kilnaughtin	Glin	II.	192
3	Tarmon Hill	174	2	11	Kerry	Iraghticonnor	Kilnaughtin	Glin	II.	192
6	Tarmon West	314	0	14	Kerry	Iraghticonnor	Kilnaughtin	Glin	II.	192
95	Tarramud	451	1	33	Galway	Dunkellin	Stradbally	Galway	IV.	32
103, 113	Tarrea	312	0	3	Galway	Dunkellin	Killeenavarra	Gort	IV.	30
26, 35	Tarsaghaun Beg North	948	0	3	Mayo	Erris	Kilcommon	Newport	IV.	145
35	Tarsaghaun Beg South	822	1	25	Mayo	Erris	Kilcommon	Newport	IV.	145
26,27,35,36	Tarsaghaun More	5,439	0	30	Mayo	Erris	Kilcommon	Belmullet	IV.	145
5, 6	Tarsan	203	2	0g	Armagh	Oneilland East	Seagoe	Lurgan	III.	50
54, 55	Tarsna	236	3	14	Tipperary, S.R.	Slievardagh	Crohane	Callan	II.	332
15, 16	Tartan	513	2	13	Roscommon	Frenchpark	Kilmacumsy	Boyle	IV.	204
5	Tarthlogue	118	1	37	Armagh	Oneilland West	Tartaraghan	Lurgan	III.	55
55	Tartlaghan	144	3	30	Tyrone	Dungannon Middle	Killyman	Dungannon	III.	303
9, 16	Tartnakilly	1,024	1	29	Londonderry	Keenaght	Tamlaght Finlagan	New Tn Limavady	III.	237
16, 20	Tassagh	633	3	28	Armagh	Armagh	Keady	Armagh	III.	45
14	Tassan	500	2	33	Monaghan	Cremorne	Clontibret	Castleblayney	III.	261
3	Tatebane	232	1	21	Louth	Upper Dundalk	Roche	Dundalk	I.	179
7	Tateetra	106	2	11	Louth	Upper Dundalk	Castletown	Dundalk	I.	177
6, 7, 11, 12	Tates and Carrans Park	132	3	35	Louth	Upper Dundalk	Dunbin	Dundalk	I.	178
21, 22	Tate's Fort	60	0	34	Antrim	Kilconway	Finvoy	Ballymoney	III.	26
17, 18, 25	Tatestown	339	3	14	Meath	Upper Kells	Donaghpatrick	Navan	I.	205
3	Tatnadarra	52	0	14	Louth	Upper Dundalk	Roche	Dundalk	I.	179

(a) Including 6A. 1R. 21P. water.
(b) Including 8A. 3R. 2P. River Barrow.
(c) Including 8A. 1R. 34P. water.

(d) Including 26A. 0R. 28P. water.
(e) Including 8A. 2R. 19P. water.

(f) Including 14A. 2R. 0P. water.
(g) Including 2A. 2R. 1P. River Bann.

No. of Sheet of the Ordnance Survey Maps.	Townlands and Towns.	Area in Statute Acres.	County.	Barony.	Parish.	Poor Law Union in 1857.	Townland Census of 1851, Part I.	
		A. R. P.					Vol.	Page
51, 58	Tatnadaveny . .	743 1 28	Tyrone . .	Clogher . . .	Clogher . . .	Clogher . .	III.	293
29	Tatnagilta . .	127 2 18	Tyrone . .	Dungannon Upper .	Lissan . . .	Cookstown . .	III.	309
27	Tatnamallaght . .	52 1 11	Fermanagh .	Tirkennedy . .	Derryvullan . .	Enniskillen .	III.	221
57, 58, 64	Tattanafinnell . .	827 0 26	Tyrone . .	Clogher . . .	Clogher . . .	Clogher . .	III.	293
64	Tattanellan . .	111 2 14a	Tyrone . .	Clogher . . .	Aghalurcher . .	Clogher . .	III.	291
34	Tatteevagh . .	55 2 39	Fermanagh .	Magherastephana .	Aghalurcher . .	Lisnaskea .	III.	217
24, 29	Tattenabuddagh . .	589 3 25	Fermanagh .	Magherastephana .	Aghalurcher . .	Lisnaskea .	III.	217
24	Tattenaheglish . .	200 0 38	Fermanagh .	Magherastephana .	Aghalurcher . .	Lisnaskea .	III.	217
23, 24	Tattenalee . .	236 3 11	Fermanagh .	Magherastephana .	Aghalurcher . .	Lisnaskea .	III.	217
26, 32	Tattenamona . .	223 1 13	Fermanagh .	Clanawley . .	Killesher . .	Enniskillen .	III.	193
23, 28	Tattenamona . .	157 3 8	Fermanagh .	Magherastephana .	Aghavea . . .	Lisnaskea .	III.	219
28	Tattendillur . .	66 3 27	Fermanagh .	Magherastephana .	Aghavea . . .	Lisnaskea .	III.	219
36	Tattinbarr . .	70 0 17	Fermanagh .	Clankelly . .	Clones . . .	Clones . .	III.	197
28	Tattinbarr . .	181 2 19	Fermanagh .	Magherastephana .	Aghavea . . .	Lisnaskea .	III.	219
22	Tattincake . .	217 3 36	Monaghan .	Dartree . . .	Currin . . .	Cootehill .	III.	266
28	Tattinderry . .	62 1 12	Fermanagh .	Magherastephana .	Aghalurcher . .	Lisnaskea .	III.	217
9	Tattindonagh . .	208 0 32	Monaghan .	Monaghan . .	Tedavnet . .	Monaghan .	III.	279
23	Tattinfree . .	369 1 18	Fermanagh .	Magherastephana .	Aghavea . . .	Lisnaskea .	III.	219
15, 20	Tattintlieve . .	281 1 17	Monaghan .	Cremorne . .	Muckno . . .	Castleblayney .	III.	262
13	Tattintlieve . .	219 1 29	Monaghan .	Dartree . . .	Aghabog . .	Monaghan .	III.	264
35, 36	Tattintonegan . .	48 1 4	Fermanagh .	Clankelly . .	Clones . . .	Clones . .	III.	197
17, 23	Tattinweer . .	249 0 27	Fermanagh .	Tirkennedy . .	Enniskillen . .	Enniskillen .	III.	222
25	Tattraconnaghty . .	253 0 37b	Tyrone . .	Strabane Upper .	Cappagh . . .	Omagh . .	III.	325
28, 29	Tattyboy . .	479 1 13	Monaghan .	Farney . . .	Donaghmoyne . .	Carrickmacross	III.	271
14	Tattyboys . .	105 2 22	Louth . .	Ardee . . .	Clonkeen . .	Ardee . .	I.	172
23	Tattybrack . .	207 3 10c	Monaghan .	Cremorne . .	Aghnamullen . .	Cootehill .	III.	258
35	Tattycam . .	134 1 37d	Fermanagh .	Clankelly . .	Galloon . . .	Clones . .	III.	198
50	Tattycor . . .	355 0 34	Tyrone . .	Omagh East . .	Dromore . . .	Omagh . .	III.	311
34	Tattygare . .	106 3 23	Fermanagh .	Clankelly . .	Galloon . . .	Lisnaskea .	III.	198
27	Tattygare . .	156 1 1	Fermanagh .	Tirkennedy . .	Derryvullan . .	Enniskillen .	III.	221
24, 25	Tattygare . .	286 3 27	Monaghan .	Cremorne . .	Clontibret . .	Castleblayney .	III.	261
17, 22	Tattygare . .	104 3 3e	Monaghan .	Dartree . . .	Ematris . . .	Cootehill .	III.	267
9	Tattygare . .	107 3 0	Monaghan .	Monaghan . .	Tedavnet . .	Monaghan .	III.	279
21	Tattygare Glebe .	105 3 33	Monaghan .	Magheraboy . .	Rossorry . . .	Enniskillen .	III.	214
36	Tattygormican . .	98 1 13f	Fermanagh .	Clankelly . .	Clones . . .	Clones . .	III.	197
29, 38	Tattykeel . .	321 2 16	Tyrone . .	Dungannon Upper .	Kildress . . .	Cookstown .	III.	309
43	Tattykeel . .	302 0 32g	Tyrone . .	Omagh East . .	Drumragh . . .	Omagh . .	III.	313
34, 42	Tattykeel (Buchannan)	319 3 16	Tyrone . .	Omagh East . .	Drumragh . . .	Omagh . .	III.	313
5	Tattykeel Lower .	68 3 30	Fermanagh .	Lurg . . .	Magheraculmoney .	Lowtherstown .	III.	208
34, 42	Tattykeel (Rogers) .	688 2 0	Tyrone . .	Omagh East . .	Drumragh . . .	Omagh . .	III.	313
5	Tattykeel Upper .	36 3 25	Fermanagh .	Lurg . . .	Magheraculmoney .	Lowtherstown .	III.	208
23	Tattykeeran . .	459 3 9	Fermanagh .	Magherastephana .	Aghavea . . .	Lisnaskea .	III.	219
35, 43	Tattykeeran . .	603 3 9	Tyrone . .	Omagh East . .	Clogherny . .	Omagh . .	III.	310
22,23,27,28	Tattymacall . .	413 3 10	Fermanagh .	Tirkennedy . .	Derryvullan . .	Enniskillen .	III.	221
36	Tattymore . .	188 1 33	Fermanagh .	Clankelly . .	Clones . . .	Clones . .	III.	197
35, 40	Tattymorris . .	50 1 3	Fermanagh .	Clankelly . .	Clones . . .	Clones . .	III.	197
50, 57	Tattymoyle Lower .	502 1 1	Tyrone . .	Clogher . . .	Donacavey . .	Omagh . .	III.	294
50, 57	Tattymoyle Middle .	561 1 32	Tyrone . .	Clogher . . .	Donacavey . .	Omagh . .	III.	294
57	Tattymoyle Upper .	468 1 5	Tyrone . .	Clogher . . .	Donacavey . .	Omagh . .	III.	294
42	Tattymulmona . .	241 2 5	Tyrone . .	Omagh East . .	Donacavey . .	Omagh . .	III.	310
35	Tattynacunnian . .	52 0 6	Fermanagh .	Clankelly . .	Clones . . .	Clones . .	III.	197
12	Tattynagall . .	167 1 7	Monaghan .	Dartree . . .	Killeevan . .	Monaghan .	III.	268
35	Tattynageeragh . .	70 2 34	Fermanagh .	Clankelly . .	Clones . . .	Clones . .	III.	197
35	Tattynagolan . .	74 0 4	Fermanagh .	Clankelly . .	Clones . . .	Clones . .	III.	197
25, 26	Tattynagole . .	129 0 33h	Tyrone . .	Strabane Upper .	Cappagh . . .	Omagh . .	III.	325
6	Tattynaskeagh or Thornfield . .	179 2 1	Louth . .	Upper Dundalk .	Inishkeen . .	Dundalk . .	I.	179
24	Tattynuckle . .	279 1 1i	Fermanagh .	Magherastephana .	Aghalurcher . .	Lisnaskea .	III.	217
25, 26	Tattynure . .	373 1 9j	Tyrone . .	Strabane Upper .	Cappagh . . .	Omagh . .	III.	325
28	Tattyreagh . .	241 3 22	Cavan . .	Clankee . .	Knockbride . .	Bailieborough .	III.	74
24	Tattyreagh . .	256 0 34k	Fermanagh .	Magherastephana .	Aghalurcher . .	Lisnaskea .	III.	217
43	Tattyreagh Glebe .	906 0 8l	Tyrone . .	Omagh East . .	Drumragh . . .	Omagh . .	III.	313
15, 20	Tattyreagh North .	305 2 37	Monaghan .	Cremorne . .	Clontibret . .	Castleblayney .	III.	261
19	Tattyreagh South .	123 3 5	Monaghan .	Cremorne . .	Clontibret . .	Castleblayney .	III.	261
42	Tattysallagh . .	949 2 6m	Tyrone . .	Omagh East . .	Drumragh . . .	Omagh . .	III.	313
14, 21	Taughblane . .	512 2 22	Down . .	Lower Iveagh, Up. pt.	Hillsborough . .	Lisburn . .	III.	170
77, 86	Taughboy . .	484 1 27	Donegal . .	Raphoe . . .	Donaghmore . .	Stranorlar .	III.	138
20	Taughlumny . .	274 1 36	Down . .	Lower Iveagh, Up. pt.	Magheralin . .	Lurgan . .	III.	170
13	Taughrane . .	196 3 17	Down . .	Lower Iveagh, Up. pt.	Magheralin . .	Lurgan . .	III.	170
45	Taulaght . .	240 3 6	Wexford . .	Shelburne . .	Tintern . . .	New Ross .	I.	329
13	Taurbeg . .	410 1 2	Cork, E.R. .	Duhallow . .	Clonfert . . .	Kanturk .	II.	69
13, 14	Taurmore . .	1,135 2 24	Cork, E.R. .	Duhallow . .	Clonfert . . .	Kanturk .	II.	69
9	Tavanagh . .	149 1 31n	Armagh . .	Oneilland West .	Drumcree . .	Lurgan . .	III.	52

(a) Including 6A. 3R. 18P. water.
(b) Including 4A. 0R. 19P. water.
(c) Including 16A. 1R. 0P. water.
(d) Including 4A. 0R. 13P. water.
(e) Including 8A. 3R. 18P. water.
(f) Including 16A. 0R. 19P. water.
(g) Including 3A. 3R. 22P. water.
(h) Including 2A. 2R. 8P. water.
(i) Including 14A. 1R. 31P. water.
(j) Including 6A. 0R. 21P. water.
(k) Including 19A. 3R. 12P. water.
(l) Including 5A. 2R. 24P. water.
(m) Including 1A. 1R. 1P. water.
(n) Including 4A. 2R. 34P. water.

No. of Sheet of the Ordnance Survey Maps.	Townlands and Towns.	Area in Statute Acres.	County.	Barony.	Parish.	Poor Law Union in 1857.	Townland Census of 1851. Part I.	
		A. R. P.					Vol.	Page
1, 3	Tavanagh	104 3 37	Monaghan	Trough	Errigal Trough	Clogher	III.	285
15, 20	Tavanaskea	405 3 11	Monaghan	Cremorne	Muckno	Castleblayney	III.	262
20	Tavnaghan	64 2 23	Antrim	Lower Glenarm	Layd	Ballycastle	III.	28
19, 20	Tavnagharry	141 1 0	Antrim	Lower Glenarm	Layd	Ballycastle	III.	23
8, 9	Tavnaghboy	221 3 29	Antrim	Cary	Ramoan	Ballycastle	III.	15
14, 15	Tavnaghdrissagh	116 0 12	Antrim	Lower Glenarm	Layd	Ballycastle	III.	23
43, 44	Tavnaghmore	612 1 29	Antrim	Upper Toome	Shilvodan Grange	Antrim	III.	35
14	Tavnaghoney	174 2 9	Antrim	Lower Glenarm	Layd	Ballycastle	III.	23
15, 20	Tavnaghowen	69 3 4	Antrim	Lower Glenarm	Layd	Ballycastle	III.	23
14	Tavnaghranny or Lower Broghindrummin	186 1 31	Antrim	Lower Glenarm	Grange of Layd	Ballycastle	III.	22
73, 82	Tavraun	1,127 0 34	Mayo	Costello	Kilmovee	Swineford	IV.	142
102	Tawin East	179 1 5	Galway	Dunkellin	Ballynacourty	Galway	IV.	27
102	Tawin West	217 3 29	Galway	Dunkellin	Ballynacourty	Galway	IV.	27
19	Tawlagh or Cornaclea	63 0 18a	Cavan	Tullyhunco	Kildallan	Cavan	III.	96
37	Tawlaght	300 0 22	Cavan	Clanmahon	Ballymachugh	Cavan	III.	76
15	Tawlaght	89 3 29b	Cavan	Lower Loughtee	Drumlane	Cavan	III.	81
101, 105	Tawlaght	575 3 24	Donegal	Tirhugh	Templecarn	Donegal	III.	149
28	Tawlaght	94 0 23	Kerry	Trughanacmy	Ardfert	Tralee	II.	206
28	Tawlaght	373 2 21	Kerry	Trughanacmy	Ballynahaglish	Tralee	II.	207
11	Tawlaght	84 2 4	Roscommon	Boyle	Killukin	Cark. on Shannon	IV.	196
2	Tawlaght	154 1 34	Roscommon	Boyle	Kilronan	Boyle	IV.	197
1	Tawly	1,713 3 35c	Leitrim	Rosclogher	Rossinver	Ballyshannon	IV.	112
79	Tawnacrom	190 0 0d	Donegal	Raphoe	Donaghmore	Strabane	III.	138
18, 24	Tawnadremira	1,060 2 33e	Sligo	Tireragh	Kilmacshalgan	Dromore West	IV.	235
9	Tawnagh	146 2 21	Cavan	Tullyhaw	Templeport	Bawnboy	III.	95
94, 100	Tawnagh	120 1 38f	Donegal	Tirhugh	Donegal	Donegal	III.	145
2, 5	Tawnagh	482 3 5	Longford	Longford	Killoe	Longford	I.	159
88	Tawnagh	66 0 19	Mayo	Burrishoole	Aghagower	Westport	IV.	118
109	Tawnagh	557 1 9	Mayo	Carra	Ballyovey	Ballinrobe	IV.	126
91	Tawnagh	80 2 31	Mayo	Clanmorris	Kilcolman	Claremorris	IV.	134
101	Tawnagh	95 3 38	Mayo	Clanmorris	Tagheen	Claremorris	IV.	136
81	Tawnagh	60 2 0	Mayo	Costello	Aghamore	Swineford	IV.	137
102	Tawnagh	185 2 21	Mayo	Costello	Bekan	Claremorris	IV.	139
121	Tawnagh	58 0 26	Mayo	Kilmaine	Kilmainemore	Ballinrobe	IV.	156
47	Tawnagh	511 0 4	Mayo	Tirawley	Addergoole	Castlebar	IV.	163
48, 51	Tawnagh	554 2 39g	Roscommon	Athlone	Taghmaconnell	Athlone	IV.	185
39	Tawnagh	146 2 21	Sligo	Corran	Kilshalvy	Boyle	IV.	227
34	Tawnagh	441 0 17	Sligo	Tirerrill	Tawnagh	Sligo	IV.	241
71, 80	Tawnaghaknaff	155 2 11	Mayo	Gallen	Bohola	Swineford	IV.	147
50, 51	Tawnaghbaun	259 1 7	Galway	Ballynahinch	Moyrus	Clifden	IV.	13
44, 58	Tawnaghbaun	160 3 24	Galway	Tiaquin	Abbeyknockmoy	Tuam	IV.	75
119	Tawnaghbaun	170 2 16	Mayo	Kilmaine	Kilcommon	Ballinrobe	IV.	155
57	Tawnaghbeg	43 3 12	Galway	Clare	Cummer	Tuam	IV.	19
39, 53	Tawnaghbeg	194 2 12h	Galway	Moycullen	Kilcummin	Oughterard	IV.	68
52, 64	Tawnaghbeg	832 0 13i	Galway	Costello	Kilbeagh	Swineford	IV.	141
60	Tawnagh Beg	1,033 1 2j	Mayo	Gallen	Templemore	Castlebar	IV.	151
122, 128	Tawnagh East	158 3 29	Galway	Kiltartan	Kilmacduagh	Gort	IV.	48
112	Tawnagh East	111 3 37	Galway	Kiltartan	Kinvarradoorus	Gort	IV.	49
122	Tawnagh East	243 3 29	Mayo	Kilmaine	Kilmainemore	Ballinrobe	IV.	156
85, 94	Tawnaghgorm	173 0 13	Donegal	Tirhugh	Donegal	Donegal	III.	145
4, 9	Tawnaghlahan	162 1 4	Fermanagh	Lurg	Belleek	Ballyshannon	III.	203
94	Tawnaghlahan	126 1 23	Donegal	Tirhugh	Donegal	Donegal	III.	145
91	Tawnaghlahard	259 0 21	Mayo	Clanmorris	Kilcolman	Claremorris	IV.	134
37, 38	Tawnaghmore	600 2 33	Galway	Ballynahinch	Moyrus	Clifden	IV.	13
57	Tawnaghmore	410 0 20	Galway	Clare	Kilmoylan	Tuam	IV.	22
35	Tawnagh More	272 1 28k	Leitrim	Mohill	Cloone	Mohill	IV.	106
93	Tawnaghmore	463 2 18l	Mayo	Costello	Bekan	Claremorris	IV.	139
27	Tawnaghmore	1,813 1 33m	Mayo	Erris	Kilcommon	Belmullet	IV.	145
79	Tawnagh More	307 2 13	Mayo	Gallen	Templemore	Castlebar	IV.	151
48	Tawnaghmore	457 0 33	Mayo	Tirawley	Kilbelfad	Ballina	IV.	168
11	Tawnagh More	96 2 18n	Roscommon	Ballintober North	Kilmore	Cark. on Shannon	IV.	187
39, 44	Tawnaghmore	185 1 26	Sligo	Corran	Kilshalvy	Boyle	IV.	227
22	Tawnaghmore Lower	266 3 19	Mayo	Tirawley	Killala	Killala	IV.	170
22	Tawnaghmore Upper	120 3 0	Mayo	Tirawley	Killala	Killala	IV.	170
37	Tawnaghs	709 1 10	Mayo	Tirawley	Crossmolina	Ballina	IV.	166
122	Tawnagh West	66 1 7	Galway	Kiltartan	Kilmacduagh	Gort	IV.	48
102, 112	Tawnagh West	242 0 13o	Galway	Kiltartan	Kinvarradoorus	Gort	IV.	49
72	Tawnaglass	200 3 1	Mayo	Gallen	Kilconduff	Swineford	IV.	148
58, 68	Tawnagrania	596 1 5	Mayo	Burrishoole	Burrishoole	Newport	IV.	120
10, 16	Tawnahoney	104 1 26	Leitrim	Drumahaire	Killarga	Manorhamilton	IV.	99
46	Tawnakeel	388 1 17p	Mayo	Tirawley	Crossmolina	Ballina	IV.	166

No. of Sheet of the Ordnance Survey Maps.	Townlands and Towns.	Area in Statute Acres. A. R. P.	County.	Barony.	Parish.	Poor Law Union in 1857.	Townland Census of 1851, Part I. Vol.	Page
17, 23	Tawnalaghta . .	1,109 1 3	Sligo . .	Tireragh . . .	Kilglass . . .	Dromore West .	IV.	234
99, 100	Tawnalary . .	66 0 8	Donegal .	Tirhugh . .	Donegal . .	Donegal . .	III.	145
4, 5	Tawnaleck . .	165 3 8	Leitrim .	Rosclogher . .	Rossinver . .	Ballyshannon .	IV.	112
12	Tawnaleen . .	1,399 3 21	Galway .	Ross . . .	Ross . . .	Oughterard .	IV.	74
39,40,44,45	Tawnalion . .	134 0 35	Sligo . .	Corran . .	Drumrat . .	Boyle . .	IV.	226
6	Tawnamachugh .	575 0 4	Leitrim .	Rosclogher . .	Killasnet . .	Manorhamilton	IV.	110
17, 23	Tawnamaddoo or Owenykeevan .	844 0 17	Sligo . .	Tireragh . .	Easky . . .	Dromore West .	IV.	234
58, 68	Tawnamartola .	115 2 33	Mayo . .	Burrishoole .	Burrishoole .	Newport . .	IV.	120
3	Tawnamore . .	180 0 2	Louth . .	Upper Dundalk .	Creggan . .	Dundalk . .	I.	178
17, 23	Tawnamore . .	1,722 0 28a	Sligo . .	Tireragh . .	Kilmacshalgan .	Dromore West .	IV.	235
62	Tawnamullagh .	83 3 6	Mayo . .	Gallen . . .	Kilconduff .	Swineford .	IV.	148
68	Tawnameeltoge .	104 0 32	Mayo . .	Burrishoole .	Burrishoole .	Newport . .	IV.	120
35,36,44,45	Tawnasheffin .	795 3 22	Mayo . .	Erris . . .	Kilcommon .	Newport . .	IV.	145
26, 35	Tawnasool . .	1,567 0 11	Mayo . .	Erris . . .	Kilcommon .	Belmullet .	IV.	145
23,24,30,31	Tawnaneilleen .	646 3 36	Sligo . .	Leyny . . .	Kilmacteige .	Tobercurry .	IV.	231
97	Tawnasligo . .	97 3 4	Donegal .	Banagh . . .	Killybegs Upper	Glenties . .	III.	111
18,19,24,25	Tawnatrohaun .	1,417 1 9b	Sligo . .	Tireragh . .	Skreen . . .	Dromore West .	IV.	236
17	Tawnatruffaun .	971 3 28c	Sligo . .	Tireragh . .	Kilmacshalgan .	Dromore West .	IV.	235
32	Tawnavoultry .	128 2 10½	Sligo . .	Leyny . . .	Achonry . .	Tobercurry .	IV.	229
4	Tawnawanny . .	114 0 4	Fermanagh .	Lurg . . .	Templecarn .	Lowtherstown .	III.	209
68	Tawnawoggaun .	191 1 35	Mayo . .	Burrishoole .	Burrishoole .	Newport . .	IV.	120
85, 86, 94	Tawnawully Mountains	6,053 3 15d	Donegal .	Tirhugh . . .	Donegal . .	Donegal . .	III.	145
135	Tawnies Lower .	238 3 24	Cork, W.R.	East Carbery (E.D.)	Kilgarriff . .	Clonakilty .	II.	129
135	Tawnies Upper .	321 0 23	Cork, W.R.	East Carbery (E.D.)	Kilgarriff . .	Clonakilty .	II.	129
31, 32	Tawnrush . .	223 2 20	Kildare .	Offaly West .	Kilrush . .	Athy . .	I.	73
96	Tawny . . .	585 0 26	Donegal .	Banagh . . .	Kilcar . .	Glenties . .	III.	109
17	Tawny . . .	237 1 17e	Donegal .	Kilmacrenan .	Clondavaddog .	Millford . .	III.	125
107	Tawnyard . .	682 2 32f	Mayo . .	Murrisk . .	Oughaval . .	Westport .	IV.	162
38	Tawnybrack . .	825 2 23	Antrim .	Lower Antrim .	Connor . .	Ballymena .	III.	3
69,78	Tawnycoolawee .	152 3 7	Mayo . .	Carra . . .	Aglish . .	Castlebar .	IV.	124
20	Tawnycorragh .	105 2 11	Leitrim .	Drumahaire .	Inishmagrath .	Manorhamilton	IV.	97
107	Tawnycrower .	945 1 16	Mayo . .	Murrisk . .	Oughaval . .	Westport .	IV.	162
27	Tawnycurry . .	87 1 7	Leitrim .	Leitrim . .	Kiltoghert .	Cark. on Shannon	IV.	103
105, 106	Tawnydoogan .	751 1 32	Mayo . .	Murrisk . .	Kilgeever .	Westport .	IV.	160
1	Tawnydorragh .	132 2 2	Fermanagh .	Lurg . . .	Drumkeeran .	Lowtherstown .	III.	207
32	Tawnyeely . .	35 1 8	Leitrim .	Mohill . .	Mohill . .	Mohill . .	IV.	108
69, 78	Tawnyeeny . .	703 2 9g	Mayo . .	Carra . . .	Islandeady .	Castlebar .	IV.	129
77	Tawnyemon . .	145 2 15h	Mayo . .	Burrishoole .	Kilmaclasser .	Westport .	IV.	121
7, 8	Tawnyfeacle . .	509 1 21	Leitrim .	Rosclogher .	Cloonclare .	Manorhamilton	IV.	109
92	Tawnygorm . .	126 0 39	Donegal .	Banagh . .	Inver . .	Donegal . .	III.	108
11, 15	Tawnyhoosy . .	108 2 18	Leitrim .	Drumahaire .	Killarga . .	Manorhamilton	IV.	99
73	Tawnyinah Lower	282 0 18	Mayo . .	Costello . .	Kilbeagh .	Swineford .	IV.	141
73	Tawnyinah Middle .	397 0 34	Mayo . .	Costello . .	Kilbeagh .	Swineford .	IV.	141
73	Tawnyinah Upper .	627 3 14	Mayo . .	Costello . .	Kilbeagh .	Swineford .	IV.	141
106, 115	Tawnyinlough .	723 0 21i	Mayo . .	Murrisk . .	Kilgeever .	Westport .	IV.	160
59, 60	Tawnykinaff .	813 0 5	Mayo . .	Carra . . .	Turlough . .	Castlebar .	IV.	131
69, 70	Tawnylaheen .	411 2 16	Mayo . .	Carra . . .	Aglish . .	Castlebar .	IV.	124
69, 70	Tawnylaheen .	20 2 32	Mayo . .	Carra . . .	Turlough . .	Castlebar .	IV.	131
15, 16	Tawnylea . .	193 3 4	Leitrim .	Drumahaire .	Killarga . .	Manorhamilton	IV.	99
91	Tawnylough . .	496 3 22j	Mayo . .	Clanmorris .	Mayo . .	Claremorris .	IV.	135
45	Tawny Lower .	179 1 27	Donegal .	Kilmacrenan .	Kilmacrenan .	Millford . .	III.	129
8, 12	Tawnylust . .	123 1 33	Leitrim .	Rosclogher .	Cloonclare .	Manorhamilton	IV.	109
8	Tawnylust Barr	135 2 14	Leitrim .	Rosclogher .	Cloonclare .	Manorhamilton	IV.	109
8	Tawnylust Barr Upper . .	165 1 21	Leitrim .	Rosclogher .	Cloonclare .	Manorhamilton	IV.	109
96	Tawnymackan .	501 1 20k	Mayo . .	Murrisk . .	Kilgeever .	Westport .	IV.	160
4	Tawnymakelly .	138 0 28l	Cavan .	Tullyhaw . .	Killinagh .	Enniskillen .	III.	92
11	Tawnymanus . .	272 3 4	Leitrim .	Drumahaire .	Cloonclare .	Manorhamilton	IV.	94
45	Tawny Middle .	79 1 32	Donegal .	Kilmacrenan .	Kilmacrenan .	Millford . .	III.	129
59, 65	Tawnymore . .	350 0 35m	Tyrone .	Clogher . .	Clogher . .	Clogher . .	III.	293
7, 11	Tawnymoyle . .	613 2 39	Leitrim .	Rosclogher .	Killasnet . .	Manorhamilton	IV.	110
46	Tawnymucklagh .	626 3 8n	Sligo . .	Coolavin . .	Kilcolman .	Boyle . .	IV.	224
5	Tawnynaboll . .	451 3 15o	Mayo . .	Tirawley . .	Doonfeeny .	Killala . .	IV.	167
99	Tawnynagry . .	499 1 26p	Mayo . .	Carra . . .	Ballintober .	Castlebar .	IV.	125
36, 45	Tawnynahulty .	1,249 0 13q	Mayo . .	Tirawley . .	Crossmolina .	Ballina . .	IV.	166
87, 97	Tawnynameeltoge or Midgefield .	209 3 20r	Mayo . .	Murrisk . .	Aghagower .	Westport .	IV.	159
5	Tawnyneden . .	147 2 30	Roscommon .	Boyle . . .	Boyle . . .	Boyle . .	IV.	194
106, 115	Tawnynoran . .	1,117 2 29s	Mayo . .	Murrisk . .	Kilgeever .	Westport .	IV.	160
8	Tawnynoran Glebe .	276 2 17t	Fermanagh .	Lurg . . .	Belleek . .	Ballyshannon .	III.	203
27	Tawnyreagh . .	234 0 32u	Fermanagh .	Tirkennedy .	Derrybrusk .	Enniskillen .	III.	220
20	Tawnyrover . .	113 1 11	Roscommon .	Frenchpark .	Tibohine . .	Castlereagh .	IV.	205

(a) Including 2A. 2R. 16P. Lough Ice.
(b) Including 8A. 1R. 14P. water.
(c) Including 9A. 3R. 24P. Lough Ice.
(d) Including 81A. 0R. 22P. water.
(e) Including 18A. 0R. 12P. water.
(f) Including 68A. 0R. 26P. water.
(g) Including 1A. 2R. 14P. water.
(h) Including 17A. 2R. 24P. water.
(i) Including 24A. 1R. 17P. water.
(j) Including 27A. 3R. 23P. water.
(k) Including 4A. 0R. 24P. water.
(l) Including 8A. 0R. 21P. water.
(m) Including 3A. 2R. 16P. water.
(n) Including 3A. 2R. 18P. water.
(o) Including 12A. 2R. 27P. water.
(p) Including 50A. 0R. 33P. water.
(q) Including 25A. 2R. 29P. water.
(r) Including 3A. 3R. 37P. water.
(s) Including 17A. 3R. 34P. water.
(t) Including 26A. 2R. 39P. water.
(u) Including 53A. 2R. 18P. water.

No. of Sheet of the Ordnance Survey Maps.	Townlands and Towns.	Area in Statute Acres.			County.	Barony.	Parish.	Poor Law Union in 1857.	Townland Census of 1851, Part I.	
		A.	R.	P.					Vol.	Page
˙69	Tawnyshane . .	408	2	4a	Mayo . .	Carra . . .	Turlough . .	Castlebar .	IV.	131
96, 97	Tawnyslinnaun .	747	3	5	Mayo . .	Murrisk . .	Oughaval . .	Westport . .	IV.	162
1	Tawnytallan . .	118	1	33	Leitrim . .	Rosclogher .	Rossinver . .	Ballyshannon .	IV.	112
6	Tawnytaskin . .	232	2	14	Roscommon .	Boyle . .	Boyle . .	Boyle . .	IV.	194
8, 12	Tawnyunshinagh .	223	3	33	Leitrim . .	Rosclogher .	Cloonclare .	Manorhamilton .	IV.	109
36, 45	Tawny Upper .	169	2	28b	Donegal . .	Kilmacrenan .	Kilmacrenan .	Millford . .	III.	129
94	Tawnyvorgal . .	135	3	1	Donegal . .	Banagh . .	Killymard .	Donegal . .	III.	112
20, 21, 28	Tawnywaddyduff .	1,352	0	15	Mayo . .	Tirawley . .	Moygawnagh .	Killala . .	IV.	171
45	Tawran . .	684	1	1	Sligo . .	Coolavin . .	Killaraght .	Boyle . .	IV.	224
22, 25	Taylorsgrange .	451	3	39	Dublin . .	Rathdown . .	Whitechurch .	Dublin South .	I.	38
42, 43	Taylorstown .	1,237	0	38	Antrim . .	Upper Toome .	Ballyscullion Grange	Ballymena .	III.	33
99	Taylorstown .	101	1	30	Galway . .	Clonmacnowen .	Clontuskert .	Ballinasloe .	IV.	25
52	Taylorstown .	171	2	21	Roscommon .	Athlone . .	Drum . .	Athlone . .	IV.	180
40	Taylorstown .	441	2	25	Wexford . .	Shelburne . .	Tintern . .	New Ross . .	I.	329
76	Tead Beg .	25	0	7	Cork, E.R. .	Imokilly . .	Cloyne . .	Middleton .	II.	86
109	Teadies Lower .	204	2	5	Cork, W.R. .	East Carbery (W.D.)	Kinneigh . .	Bandon . .	II.	135
95, 109	Teadies Upper .	595	2	39	Cork, W.R. .	East Carbery (W.D.)	Kinneigh . .	Bandon . .	II.	135
76·	Tead More . .	144	0	19	Cork, E.R. .	Imokilly . .	Cloyne . .	Middleton .	II.	86
5	Teagy . .	212	2	13	Armagh . .	Oneilland West .	Tartaraghan .	Armagh . .	III.	55
69	Teangue . .	53	3	13	Donegal . .	Raphoe . .	Stranorlar .	Stranorlar .	III.	143
61	*Tearaght Island* .	47	0	7	Kerry . .	Corkaguiny .	Dunquin . .	Dingle . .	II.	176
30	Teconnaught .	745	1	24c	Down . .	Kinelarty . .	Kilmore . .	Downpatrick .	III.	177
118	Tedagh . .	187	0	10	Cork, W.R. .	Bantry . .	Durrus . .	Bantry . .	II.	119
6	Tedavnet . .	46	3	11	Monaghan .	Monaghan . .	Tedavnet .	Monaghan .	III.	279
6, 11	Tedd . .	572	1	18	Fermanagh .	Lurg . .	Derryvullan .	Lowtherstown .	III.	205
31	Tedeehan Lower .	45	3	0	Cavan . .	Clanmahon .	Crosserlough .	Cavan . .	III.	76
31	Tedeehan Middle .	70	2	33	Cavan . .	Clanmahon .	Crosserlough .	Cavan . .	III.	76
31	Tedeehan Upper .	149	3	18	Cavan . .	Clanmahon .	Crosserlough .	Cavan . .	III.	76
53	Tedwards . .	15	0	34	Wexford . .	Forth . .	Carn . .	Wexford . .	I.	309
30, 31, 35	Teeavan . .	2,709	0	39	Londonderry .	Keenaght . .	Banagher .	NewTⁿLimavady	III.	234
3	Teebane . .	1,363	1	1d	Cavan . .	Tullyhaw . .	Killinagh .	Enniskillen .	III.	92
19, 20	Teebane . .	143	2	3	Fermanagh .	Clanawley .	Cleenish .	Ballyshannon .	III.	191
28	Teebane . .	361	0	35	Tyrone . .	Dungannon Upper .	Kildress . .	Cookstown .	III.	309
19, 20	Teebane East .	779	0	24e	Tyrone . .	Strabane Upper .	Bodoney Lower .	Gortin . .	III.	324
19, 27	Teebane West .	1,077	3	27	Tyrone . .	Strabane Upper .	Bodoney Lower .	Gortin . .	III.	324
9	Teeboy . .	472	1	33f	Cavan . .	Tullyhaw . .	Templeport .	Bawnboy . .	III.	95
11, 16	Teehill . .	128	0	5	Monaghan .	Dartree . .	Clones . .	Clones . .	III.	265
3, 8	Teelough . .	128	2	28	Kildare . .	Carbury . .	Kilmore . .	Edenderry .	I.	52
13	Teemore . .	281	2	34	Armagh . .	Oneilland West .	Mullaghbrack .	Banbridge .	III.	54
11	Teemore . .	108	1	0g	Cavan . .	Lower Loughtee .	Drumlane .	Cavan . .	III.	81
1, 2	Teemore . .	71	2	35	Cavan . .	Tullyhaw . .	Killinagh .	Enniskillen .	III.	92
41, 42	Teemore . .	117	1	17	Fermanagh .	Knockninny .	Kinawley .	Lisnaskea .	III.	202
10	Teemore . .	64	1	16	Longford . .	Granard . .	Granard . .	Granard . .	I.	157
23, 29	Teenaght . .	333	2	33	Londonderry .	Tirkeeran .	Cumber Lower .	Londonderry .	III.	249
94, 108	Teenah . .	284	1	17	Cork, W.R. .	East Carbery (W.D.)	Kinneigh . .	Dunmanway .	II.	135
27	Teer . .	248	1	9h	Armagh . .	Fews Upper .	Creggan . .	Castleblayney .	III.	48
43	Teer . .	89	0	20	Fermanagh .	Clankelly .	Drummully .	Clones . .	III.	197
25, 26	Teer . .	1,106	2	7	Kerry . .	Corkaguiny .	Cloghane . .	Dingle . .	II.	175
17	Teer . .	64	3	36	Monaghan .	Dartree . .	Killeevan .	Clones . .	III.	268
1, 6	Teeracurra .	143	0	15	Cork, E.R. .	Orrery and Kilmore	Kilbolane .	Kanturk . .	II.	108
14	Teeraghbeg .	130	2	19	Clare . .	Corcomroe .	Kilmacrehy .	Ennistimon .	II.	20
70, 80	Teeraha . .	314	2	32	Kerry . .	Iveragh . .	Killinane .	Cahersiveen .	II.	197
82	Teeranassig .	294	1	36	Cork, W.R. .	West Muskerry .	Inchigeelagh .	Dunmanway .	II.	158
90	Teeranea . .	1,613	1	30i	Galway . .	Moycullen .	Killannin .	Oughterard .	IV.	70
26	Teeranea . .	540	1	34j	Galway . .	Ross . .	Ross . .	Oughterard .	IV.	74
42	Teeravane . .	378	2	14	Kerry . .	Corkaguiny .	Dunurlin .	Dingle . .	II.	176
12	Teeraw . .	195	0	34	Armagh . .	Armagh . .	Grange . .	Armagh . .	III.	45
70	Teerbeg . .	176	0	4	Cork, W.R. .	West Muskerry .	Clondrohid .	Macroom .	II.	155
35	Teerbrin . .	154	2	19	Kerry . .	Corkaguiny .	Stradbally .	Dingle . .	II.	180
83	Teereeven . .	394	2	17	Cork, W.R. .	West Muskerry .	Kilmurry .	Macroom .	II.	159
82	Teerelton . .	452	0	19	Cork, W.R. .	West Muskerry .	Kilmichael .	Dunmanway .	II.	159
70, 82	Teergay . .	235	3	31	Cork, W.R. .	West Muskerry .	Inchigeelagh .	Macroom .	II.	158
8	Teergonean .	348	1	11	Clare . .	Corcomroe .	Kilfilagh .	Ennistimon .	II.	20
27	Teer Island .	127	2	15k	Armagh . .	Fews Upper .	Creggan . .	Castleblayney .	III.	45
16, 24	Teerleheen .	196	0	28	Clare . .	Corcomroe .	Clooney . .	Ennistimon .	II.	18
41	Teermaclane .	602	2	10	Clare . .	Islands . .	Killone . .	Ennis . .	II.	30
36	Teermena . .	234	0	31	Limerick . .	Glenquin . .	Monagay . .	Newcastle .	II.	247
48	Teermore . .	371	2	16	Limerick . .	Coshlea . .	Kilbreedy Major .	Kilmallock .	II.	239
16	Teermore . .	99	0	27	Roscommon .	Frenchpark .	Kilmacumsy .	Boyle . .	IV.	204
31	Teermore . .	95	2	19	Westmeath .	Moycashel .	Ardnurcher or Horse-leap	Mullingar .	I.	277
17	Teermulmoney .	53	0	18	Clare . .	Inchiquin . .	Ruan . .	Corrofin .	II.	28
67	Teernaboul .	635	3	15	Kerry . .	Magunihy .	Killarney .	Killarney .	II.	203

(a) Including 4A. 3R. 18P. water.
(b) Including 16A. 2R. 20P. water.
(c) Including 8A. 3R. 8P. water.
(d) Including 7A. 2R. 38P. water.

(e) Including 4A. 1R. 32P. water.
(f) Including 48A. 0R. 0P. Bunerky Lough.
(g) Including 5A. 2R. 8P. water.
(h) Including 24A. 0R. 35P. water.

(i) Including 38A. 0R. 29P. water.
(j) Including 12A. 2R. 24P. water.
(k) Including 37A. 2R. 15P. water.

No. of Sheet of the Ordnance Survey Maps.	Townlands and Towns.	Area in Statute Acres. A. R. P.	County.	Barony.	Parish.	Poor Law Union in 1857.	Townland Census of 1851, Part I. Vol.	Page
32, 38	Teernacreeve . .	303 0 39	Westmeath .	Moycashel . .	Castletownkindalen	Mullingar .	I.	277
57, 58	Teernagloghane .	423 3 20	Clare . .	Moyarta . .	Kilmacduane . .	Kilrush .	II.	33
70, 80	Teernahila . .	513 2 13	Kerry . .	Iveragh . .	Killinane . .	Cahersiveen .	II.	197
37	Teernahilla . .	433 2 14	Limerick . .	Connello Upper .	Cloncagh . .	Newcastle .	II.	231
114	Teernahillane .	282 0 8	Cork, W.R. .	Bear . . .	Killaconenagh .	Castletown .	II.	125
25, 38	Teernakill North .	1,125 0 20	Galway . .	Ross . . .	Ross . .	Oughterard .	IV.	74
38, 39	Teernakill South .	4,766 1 31	Galway . .	Ross . . .	Ross . .	Oughterard .	IV.	74
17	Teernea . . .	166 1 6a	Clare . .	Inchiquin . .	Ruan . .	Corrofin .	II.	28
17	Teernea Commons .	108 3 31	Clare . .	Inchiquin . .	Ruan . .	Corrofin .	II.	28
70,71,80,81	Teeromoyle . .	2,246 1 16	Kerry . .	Iveragh . .	Killinane . .	Cahersiveen .	II.	197
25	Teeronaun . .	37 0 32	Clare . .	Inchiquin . .	Dysert . .	Ennis .	II.	24
35, 43	Teeronea . .	664 0 36b	Clare . .	Tulla Lower .	Clonlea . .	Tulla .	II.	35
28	Teeroneer . .	65 0 37c	Clare . .	Tulla Upper .	Tomgraney .	Scarriff .	II.	41
35, 36, 43	Teerovannan .	470 2 17	Clare . .	Tulla Lower .	Killuran . .	Tulla .	II.	36
68	Teervarna . .	88 1 39	Clare . .	Clonderalaw .	Killimer . .	Kilrush .	II.	16
37	Teervena . .	104 1 15	Limerick . .	Connello Upper .	Cloncagh . .	Newcastle .	II.	231
8, 14	Teesan . . .	159 2 16	Sligo . .	Carbury . .	Drumcliff . .	Sligo .	IV.	221
32	Teeshan . .	389 0 8	Antrim . .	Lower Toome .	Ahoghill . .	Ballymena .	III.	32
10	Teeskagh . .	376 0 0	Clare . .	Inchiquin . .	Killinaboy .	Corrofin .	II.	27
32	Teesnaghtan .	89 1 24	Fermanagh .	Clanawley . .	Kinawley .	Enniskillen .	III.	194
58	Teevaloughan .	903 3 29d	Mayo . .	Burrishoole .	Burrishoole .	Newport .	IV.	120
7	Teeveeny . .	829 2 31	Cork, E.R. .	Orrery and Kilmore	Shandrum . .	Kanturk .	II.	110
87, 97	Teevenacroaghy .	817 2 36	Mayo . .	Murrisk . .	Oughaval .	Westport .	IV.	162
69	Teevickmoy . .	520 3 21	Donegal . .	Raphoe . .	Stranorlar .	Stranorlar .	III.	143
88, 98	Teevinish East .	775 0 34	Mayo . .	Burrishoole .	Aghagower .	Westport .	IV.	118
98	Teevinish West .	784 2 24	Mayo . .	Burrishoole .	Aghagower .	Westport .	IV.	118
67, 68	Teevmore . .	155 2 30	Mayo . .	Burrishoole .	Burrishoole .	Newport .	IV.	120
106, 115	Teevnabinnia .	321 1 2e	Mayo . .	Murrisk . .	Kilgeever .	Westport .	IV.	160
8, 14	Teevnacreeva .	271 0 20	Roscommon .	Frenchpark .	Tibohine . .	Castlereagh .	IV.	205
7	Teevrevagh . .	96 3 36	Westmeath .	Fore . . .	Rathgarve .	Castletowndelvin	I.	271
1	Teevurcher . .	469 2 7	Meath . .	Lower Kells .	Moybolgue .	Kells .	I.	203
26	Tehorney . .	132 3 8	Antrim . .	Kilconway .	Rasharkin .	Ballymoney .	III.	28
9	Telaydan . .	121 0 7f	Monaghan .	Monaghan . .	Tedavnet . .	Monaghan .	III.	279
7	Telaydan . .	193 0 4	Monaghan .	Trough . .	Donagh . .	Monaghan .	III.	283
34, 35	Tellarought . .	1,176 1 12	Wexford . .	Shelburne .	Tellarought .	New Ross .	I.	328
29, 36	Telton . .	79 0 27	Roscommon .	Roscommon .	Cloonfinlough .	Strokestown .	IV.	209
17	Teltown . . .	626 0 0	Meath . .	Upper Kells .	Teltown . .	Kells .	I.	207
17	Temain . . .	503 0 17	Londonderry .	Keenaght . .	Balteagh . .	NewTnLimavady	III.	234
31	Temora . . .	163 1 32	King's Co. .	Ballyboy . .	Ballyboy .	Parsonstown .	I.	123
55	Tempanroe . . .	122 0 18	Tyrone . .	Dungannon Middle .	Killyman .	Dungannon .	III.	303
7	Templanstown .	179 1 18	Westmeath .	Fore . . .	Faughalstown .	Castletowndelvin	I.	270
3, 4	Templanstown .	205 3 37	Westmeath .	Fore . . .	St. Feighins .	Castletowndelvin	I.	272
3	Templastragh .	149 1 22	Antrim . .	Cary . . .	Ballintoy .	Ballycastle .	III.	12
72, 85	Temple . . .	203 2 16	Galway . .	Tiaquin . .	Clonkeen .	Loughrea .	IV.	76
63	Temple . . .	200 1 27	Mayo . .	Costello . .	Kilbeagh .	Swineford .	IV.	141
27, 35	Templeathea East .	1,656 0 34	Limerick . .	Shanid . .	Rathronan .	Newcastle .	II.	257
26,27,34,35	Templeathea West .	1,453 0 20	Limerick . .	Shanid . .	Rathronan .	Newcastle .	II.	257
11	Templebannagh .	280 2 33g	Clare . .	Inchiquin . .	Kilkeedy .	Corrofin .	II.	26
54	Templebodan .	253 3 5	Cork, E.R. .	Barrymore .	Templebodan .	Middleton .	II.	58
33	Templebredon .	66 3 22	Limerick . .	Coonagh . .	Templebredon .	Tipperary .	II.	236
122, 135	Templebryan North	436 1 36	Cork, W.R. .	East Carbery (E.D.)	Templebryan .	Clonakilty .	II.	130
122, 135	Templebryan South	363 1 18	Cork, W.R. .	East Carbery (E.D.)	Templebryan .	Clonakilty .	II.	130
8	Templecarrig Lower	256 1 22	Wicklow . .	Rathdown .	Delgany .	Rathdown .	I.	355
8	Templecarrig Upper	103 0 33	Wicklow . .	Rathdown .	Delgany .	Rathdown .	I.	355
16	Templeconnell .	226 2 30	Cork, E.R. .	Orrery and Kilmore	Kilbroney .	Mallow .	II.	109
63	Templecormac .	242 2 1	Antrim . .	Upper Massereene .	Ballinderry .	Lisburn .	III.	29
27	Templederry .	150 1 19	Tipperary, N.R.	Upper Ormond .	Templederry .	Nenagh .	II.	293
22	Templederry .	174 2 5	Wexford . .	Ballaghkeen .	Donaghmore .	Gorey .	I.	294
52	Templedouglas .	26 2 33	Donegal . .	Kilmacrenan .	Conwal .	Letterkenny .	III.	126
47	Temple-effin .	203 2 10	Antrim . .	Lower Belfast .	Islandmagee .	Larne .	III.	9
77	Temple-etney .	99 . 2 1	Tipperary, S.R. .	Iffa and Offa East .	Temple-etney .	Clonmel .	II.	316
43	Templeglentan East	789 3 25	Limerick . .	Glenquin .	Monagay .	Newcastle .	II.	247
43	Templeglentan West	1,380 0 4	Limerick . .	Glenquin .	Monagay .	Newcastle .	II.	247
23	Templehill or Sea-point . .	52 2 33	Dublin . .	Rathdown .	Monkstown .	Rathdown .	I.	37
32, 33	Templehouse Demesne	568 2 21	Sligo . .	Leyny . .	Kilvarnet .	Tobercurry .	IV.	232
24	Templeludigan .	1,108 3 27	Wexford . .	Bantry . .	Templeludigan .	New Ross .	I.	303
35, 40	Templelusk . .	351 1 18	Wicklow . .	Arklow . .	Castlemacadam .	Rathdrum .	I.	342
36	Templelyon Lower .	220 3 16	Wicklow . .	Arklow . .	Redcross .	Rathdrum .	I.	346
36	Templelyon Upper .	163 1 27	Wicklow . .	Arklow . .	Redcross .	Rathdrum .	I.	346
31	Templemacateer	136 3 33	Westmeath .	Moycashel .	Ardnurcher or Horse-leap . . .	Mullingar .	I.	277
96	Templemartin .	413 2 34	Galway . .	Dunkellin .	Killora . .	Loughrea .	IV.	31

(a) Including 20A. 0R. 7P. water.
(b) Including 16A. 2R. 33P. water.
(c) { Including 36A. 2R. 16P. water. / Including 11A. 1R. 23P. Island O'Grady.
(d) Including 5A. 0R. 39P. water.
(e) Including 16A. 1R. 29P. water.
(f) Including 5A. 2R. 20P. water.
(g) Including 14A. 1R. 37P. water.

No. of Sheet of the Ordnance Survey Maps.	Townlands and Towns.	Area in Statute Acres.			County.	Barony.	Parish.	Poor Law Union in 1857.	Townland Census of 1851, Part I.	
		A.	R.	P.					Vol.	Page
20	Templemartin .	82	1	2	Kilkenny . .	Gowran . . .	Blackrath . .	Kilkenny . .	I.	93
19, 20	Templemartin .	28	1	24	Kilkenny . .	Gowran . . .	St. John's .	Kilkenny . .	I.	98
20	Templemartin .	210	1	30	Kilkenny . .	Gowran . . .	St. Martins .	Kilkenny . .	I.	99
16	Templemary .	754	1	7	Cork, E.R. .	Orrery and Kilmore	Buttevant .	Mallow . .	II.	107
52, 63	Templemichael .	542	1	20	Cork, E.R. .	Barrymore .	St. Michaels .	Cork . .	II.	57
14	Templemichael .	280	2	13	Limerick . .	Clanwilliam .	Caherconlish .	Limerick . .	II.	222
72	Templemichael .	183	1	10	Tipperary, S.R.	Slievardagh .	Templemichael	Carrick on Suir	II.	336
37	Templemichael .	119	1	14	Waterford .	Coshmore&Coshbride	Templemichael	Youghal . .	II.	349
40	Templemichael .	174	0	34	Wicklow . .	Arklow . .	Kilbride . .	Rathdrum . .	I.	345
13, 14	Templemichael Glebe	163	2	17	Longford . .	Ardagh . .	Templemichael	Longford . .	I.	154
29	Templemore Demesne	386	1	12a	Tipperary, N.R.	Eliogarty . .	Templemore .	Thurles . .	II.	272
29	TEMPLEMORE T. .	—			Tipperary, N.R.	Eliogarty . .	Templemore .	Thurles . .	II.	272
4, 11	Templemoyle . .	1,013	0	7	Donegal . .	Inishowen East	Clonca . .	Inishowen .	III.	117
71, 84	Templemoyle .	151	1	17	Galway . .	Tiaquin . .	Monivea . .	Loughrea . .	IV.	79
45	Templemoyle .	82	1	12b	Galway . .	Tiaquin . .	Moylough . .	Mountbellew .	IV.	80
30,31,34,35	Templemoyle .	1,645	3	5	Londonderry .	Keenaght . .	Banagher . .	NewTⁿLimavady	III.	234
16	Templemoyle .	498	0	5	Londonderry .	Keenaght . .	Bovevagh .	NewTⁿLimavady	III.	235
14	Templemoyle .	144	0	23	Londonderry .	Tirkeeran .	Faughanvale .	Londonderry .	III.	250
26	Templenaboe .	154	1	11	Carlow . .	St. Mullins Lower .	St. Mullins .	New Ross . .	I.	13
20	Templenabree .	55	3	27	Sligo . .	Carbury . .	Kilmacowen .	Sligo . .	IV.	222
65	Templenacarriga North	175	2	12	Cork, E.R. .	Barrymore . .	Templenacarriga	Middleton .	II.	58
65	Templenacarriga South	205	2	13	Cork, E.R. .	Barrymore . .	Templenacarriga	Middleton .	II.	58
30	Templenacroha .	848	1	32	Wexford . .	Bantry . .	Adamstown .	New Ross .	I.	299
25	Templenaffrin .	150	0	8	Fermanagh .	Clanawley .	Cleenish . .	Enniskillen .	III.	191
67, 68	Templenahurney .	592	1	14	Tipperary, S.R.	Clanwilliam .	Clonbullogue .	Tipperary .	II.	306
107	Templenew .	100	0	7c	Donegal . .	Tirhugh . .	Kilbarron .	Ballyshannon .	III.	148
27, 35	Templenoe .	397	3	8d	Cork, E.R. .	Fermoy . .	Litter . .	Fermoy . .	II.	81
59	Templenoe .	206	0	6	Tipperary, S.R.	Clanwilliam .	Templenoe .	Tipperary .	II.	312
68	Templenoe .	366	1	34	Tipperary, S.R.	Middlethird .	Killeenasteena .	Cashel . .	II.	327
22	Templeogue .	671	0	21	Dublin . .	Uppercross .	Tallaght . .	Dublin South .	I.	42
33	Templeoran North .	280	0	36	Westmeath .	Fartullagh .	Clonfad . .	Mullingar .	I.	268
11	Templeoran or Piercefield	740	3	28	Westmeath .	Moygoish .	Templeoran .	Mullingar .	I.	281
33	Templeoran South .	40	3	16	Westmeath .	Fartullagh .	Clonfad . .	Mullingar .	I.	268
35, 39	Templeorum .	252	1	1	Kilkenny .	Iverk . .	Fiddown . .	Carrick on Suir	I.	105
8	Templeowen .	32	0	36e	Carlow . .	Rathvilly .	Fennagh . .	Carlow . .	I.	11
87	Templepark .	118	1	10	Galway . .	Clonmacnowen .	Clontuskert .	Ballinasloe .	IV.	25
50, 51	Templepatrick .	618	3	30	Antrim . .	Upper Belfast .	Templepatrick .	Antrim . .	III.	11
7	Templepatrick .	32	0	19	Down . .	Ards Lower .	Donaghadee .	Newtownards .	III.	158
17	Templepatrick .	272	3	11	Westmeath .	Rathconrath .	Templepatrick .	Ballymahon .	I.	284
50, 51	TEMPLEPATRICK T.	—			Antrim . .	Upper Belfast .	Templepatrick .	Antrim . .	III.	11
12, 13	Templepeter .	65	0	4	Carlow . .	Forth . .	Gilbertstown .	Carlow . .	I.	4
12, 13	Templepeter .	104	3	32	Carlow . .	Forth . .	Templepeter .	Carlow . .	I.	5
11	TEMPLE PLACE T. .				Kildare . .	South Salt .	Donaghcumper .	Celbridge . .	I.	76
33	Templequain .	376	2	18	Queen's Co. .	Clandonagh .	Rathdowney .	Donaghmore .	I.	234
40	Templerainy .	242	0	21	Wicklow . .	Arklow . .	Kilbride . .	Rathdrum . .	I.	345
39	Templereagh .	85	0	31	Tyrone . .	Dungannon Middle	Donaghenry .	Cookstown .	III.	301
19, 25	Templescoby .	855	2	23	Wexford . .	Bantry . .	Templescoby .	Enniscorthy .	I.	303
20, 26	Templeshannon .	332	3	2f	Wexford . .	Ballaghkeen .	Templeshannon	Enniscorthy .	I.	299
30	Templeshelin .	790	2	10	Wexford . .	Bantry . .	Adamstown .	New Ross . .	I.	299
22	*Temple's Island* .	2	3	1	Westmeath .	Kilkenny West .	Kilkenny West .	Athlone . .	I.	273
12	Templetate .	136	3	20	Monaghan .	Dartree . .	Clones . .	Clones . .	III.	265
10	Templetate .	50	2	39	Monaghan .	Monaghan .	Tehallan . .	Monaghan .	III.	280
13, 18	Templeton Glebe .	379	2	2	Longford . .	Moydow . .	Killashee . .	Longford . .	I.	162
30	TEMPLETOUHY T. .	—			Tipperary, N.R.	Ikerrin . .	Templetouhy .	Thurles . .	II.	277
14	Templetown .	184	2	25g	Londonderry .	Tirkeeran .	Clondermot .	Londonderry .	III.	248
8, 9	Templetown .	436	3	22	Louth . .	Lower Dundalk .	Carlingford .	Dundalk . .	I.	177
49, 50	Templetown .	689	0	17	Wexford . .	Shelburne .	Templetown .	New Ross . .	I.	329
63	Templeusque .	458	1	12	Cork, E.R. .	Barrymore .	Templeusque .	Cork . .	II.	59
46	Templevally .	330	1	18	Cork, E.R. .	Kinnatalloon .	Mogeely .	Fermoy . .	II.	99
40	Templevanny .	177	3	17h	Sligo . .	Corran . .	Toomour . .	Boyle . .	IV.	228
24, 25	Templeyvrick .	279	1	4	Waterford .	Decies without Drum	Ballylaneen .	Kilmacthomas .	II.	354
23	TEMPO T. .	—			Fermanagh .	Tirkennedy .	Enniskillen .	Enniskillen .	III.	223
47	Tenacre .	27	1	11	Wexford . .	Bargy . .	Tomhaggard .	Wexford . .	I.	308
48	Tenacre .	123	2	11	Wexford . .	Forth . .	Kilrane . .	Wexford . .	I.	311
14	Tenaghs .	623	1	26	Antrim . .	Cary . .	Culfeightrin .	Ballycastle .	III.	14
42	Tenchspit .	122	3	17	Wexford . .	Forth . .	Rathaspick .	Wexford . .	I.	313
23	Tennalick .	546	3	28i	Longford . .	Shrule . .	Taghshinny .	Ballymahon .	I.	167
23	Tennalough .	316	3	2	Longford . .	Shrule . .	Agharra . .	Ballymahon .	I.	166
11	Tennyphobble .	43	1	25	Longford . .	Granard . .	Granard . .	Granard . .	I.	157
9	Tentore .	238	3	21	Kilkenny . .	Galmoy . .	Sheffin . .	Urlingford .	I.	93
8	Tents . .	363	2	16	Cavan . .	Tullynaw . .	Killnagh . .	Enniskillen .	III.	92
26	Tents . .	191	3	12	Fermanagh .	Clanawley .	Cleenish . .	Enniskillen .	III.	191
20	Tents . .	178	0	14	Leitrim . .	Drumahaire .	Inishmagrath .	Manorhamilton	IV.	97

(a) Including 16A. 0R. 16P. water.
(b) Including 4A. 0R. 17P. water.
(c) Including 4A. 3R. 33P. water.
(d) Including 4A. 1R. 29P. water.

(e) Including 3A. 2R. 23P. detached portions.
(f) Including 3A. 1R. 0P. water.
(g) { Including 29A. 3R. 30P. Lough Enagh East.
    { Including 9A. 0R. 2P. Lough Enagh West.

(h) Including 4A. 0R. 19P. water.
(i) Including 9A. 0R. 20P. River Inny.

No. of Sheet of the Ordnance Survey Maps.	Townlands and Towns.	Area in Statute Acres.	County.	Barony.	Parish.	Poor Law Union in 1857.	Townland Census of 1851, Part I. Vol.	Page
		A. R. P.						
67, 68	Teraghafeeva or Lissue	428 0 16a	Antrim	Upper Massereene	Blaris	Lisburn	III.	30
9	Teraverty	154 3 10	Monaghan	Monaghan	Tedavnet	Monaghan	III.	279
18, 22	Terenure	569 0 9	Dublin	Rathdown	Rathfarnham	Dublin South	I.	37
2	Termon	238 3 31	Cavan	Tullyhaw	Killinagh	Enniskillen	III.	92
33	Termon	755 0 20b	Cavan	Upper Loughtee	Killinkere	Bailieborough	III.	84
6, 10	Termon	908 3 9	Clare	Burren	Carran	Ballyvaghan	II.	12
48	Termon	301 1 16	Donegal	Boylagh	Templecrone	Glenties	III.	116
128	Termon	645 1 27c	Galway	Kiltartan	Kilmacduagh	Gort	IV.	48
24, 33	Termon	1,033 1 25	Mayo	Erris	Kilmore	Belmullet	IV.	146
5, 6	Termon	207 1 7	Roscommon	Boyle	Boyle	Boyle	IV.	194
20	Termonbacca	464 0 3	Londonderry	North West Liberties of Londonderry	Templemore	Londonderry	III.	247
21, 27	Termon Beg	330 0 22	Roscommon	Castlereagh	Kilkeevin	Castlereagh	IV.	201
9	Termoncarragh	618 3 34	Mayo	Erris	Kilmore	Belmullet	IV.	146
9	TERMONCARRAGH T.	—	Mayo	Erris	Kilmore	Belmullet	IV.	146
56	Termon East	201 1 24	Clare	Moyarta	Kilfearagh	Kilrush	II.	32
22	Termonfeckin	1,096 3 20d	Louth	Ferrard	Termonfeckin	Drogheda	I.	183
22	TERMONFECKIN T.	—	Louth	Ferrard	Termonfeckin	Drogheda	I.	183
20,21,26,27	Termon More	643 1 1	Roscommon	Castlereagh	Kilkeevin	Castlereagh	IV.	201
36	TERMON ROCK T.	—	Tyrone	Omagh East	Termonmaguirk	Omagh	III.	315
89, 98	Termons	713 0 19	Kerry	Iveragh	Dromod	Cahersiveen	II.	195
56	Termon West	765 2 31	Clare	Moyarta	Kilfearagh	Kilrush	II.	32
17, 25	Ternamuck	201 3 25	Londonderry	Keenaght	Balteagh	NewTⁿLimavady	III.	234
44	Terrampunt	127 1 30	Cork, E.R.	Barrymore	Rathcormack	Fermoy	II.	57
12	Terraskane	309 1 22	Armagh	Armagh	Eglish	Armagh	III.	44
53, 54	Terrenew	248 2 24	Tyrone	Dungannon Middle	Donaghmore	Dungannon	III.	302
48	Terressan	186 1 0	Londonderry	Loughinsholin	Derryloran	Magherafelt	III.	240
58, 59	Terrew	63 1 11	Tyrone	Clogher	Clogher	Clogher	III.	293
48, 60	Terrybaun	303 2 31e	Mayo	Tirawley	Addergoole	Castlebar	IV.	163
10	Terrycaffe	166 2 27	Monaghan	Monaghan	Tehallan	Monaghan	III.	280
17	Terrydoo Clyde	455 3 26	Londonderry	Keenaght	Balteagh	NewTⁿLimavady	III.	234
10, 17	Terrydoo Walker	484 1 38	Londonderry	Keenaght	Balteagh	NewTⁿLimavady	III.	234
30	Terrydreen	826 2 17	Londonderry	Tirkeeran	Banagher	Londonderry	III.	247
16, 17	Terrydremont North	291 2 16f	Londonderry	Keenaght	Balteagh	NewTⁿLimavady	III.	234
16, 17	Terrydremont South	327 0 11g	Londonderry	Keenaght	Balteagh	NewTⁿLimavady	III.	234
16	Terrydrum	234 3 15	Londonderry	Keenaght	Tamlaght Finlagan	NewTⁿLimavady	III.	238
47,48,59,60	Terryduff	693 2 25	Mayo	Tirawley	Addergoole	Castlebar	IV.	163
14	Terrygeely	195 0 26	Monaghan	Monaghan	Tullycorbet	Monaghan	III.	281
6	Terryglass	577 0 38	Tipperary, N.R.	Lower Ormond	Terryglass	Borrisokane	II.	288
61	Terryglassog	263 3 19h	Tyrone	Dungannon Middle	Clonfeacle	Dungannon	III.	300
43	Terrygowan	141 0 18	Antrim	Upper Toome	Drummaul	Ballymena	III.	34
19	Terrygreeghan	248 1 29i	Monaghan	Cremorne	Ballybay	Castleblayney	III.	259
14	Terryhoogan	376 3 2	Armagh	Orior Lower	Ballymore	Banbridge	III.	55
82, 94	Terryland	218 3 25j	Galway	Galway	St. Nicholas	Galway	IV.	38
61	Terryscollop	240 0 34	Tyrone	Dungannon Middle	Clonfeacle	Dungannon	III.	300
75, 76	Terry's-land	269 0 14k	Cork, E.R.	Barrymore	Carrigtohill	Middleton	II.	52
31	Terrysstang	4 3 38	Waterford	Decies without Drum	Dungarvan	Dungarvan	II.	356
9	Terrytole	70 0 30l	Monaghan	Monaghan	Tedavnet	Monaghan	III.	279
29, 38	Terrywinny	120 1 23	Tyrone	Dungannon Upper	Kildress	Cookstown	III.	309
5	Tervillin	120 3 10	Antrim	Cary	Culfeightrin	Ballycastle	III.	14
4, 12	Tervoe	526 0 12	Limerick	Pubblebrien	Kilkeedy	Limerick	II.	252
13	Tetoppa	104 3 10	Monaghan	Monaghan	Kilmore	Monaghan	III.	276
13, 20	Tevrin	343 2 25	Westmeath	Moyashel and Magheradernon	Rathconnell	Mullingar	I.	276
37	The Bonn	58 0 24	Tyrone	Dungannon Middle	Pomeroy	Cookstown	III.	304
126	*The Bull Island*	1 0 8	Cork, W.R.	Bear	Kilnamanagh	Castletown	II.	126
126	*The Calf Island*	0 1 33	Cork, W.R.	Bear	Kilnamanagh	Castletown	II.	126
149	*The Catalogues*	4 3 13	Cork, W.R.	West Carbery (E.D.)	Tullagh	Skibbereen	II.	141
126	*The Cow Island*	1 3 2	Cork, W.R.	Bear	Kilnamanagh	Castletown	II.	126
42, 43, 47	The Creagh (*Etre and Otre*)	2,298 3 10	Londonderry	Loughinsholin	Artrea	Magherafelt	III.	238
42	The Creagh (*Etre and Otre*) (*Intake*)	215 2 27	Londonderry	Loughinsholin	Artrea	Magherafelt	III.	238
42, 43, 47	The Creagh (*Etre and Otre*) (*Intake*)	98 1 38	Londonderry	Loughinsholin	Artrea	Magherafelt	III.	238
15, 16	The Derries	234 1 20	Queen's Co.	Upperwoods	Offerlane	Abbeyleix	I.	252
9	The Derries or Ballyshaneduff	618 3 16	Queen's Co.	Portnahinch	Lea	Mountmellick	I.	244
26	The Division	124 3 30	Tipperary, N.R.	Upper Ormond	Kilmore	Nenagh	II.	291
31	The Gort *alias* Eglish	74 1 8	Tyrone	Dungannon Upper	Ballinderry	Cookstown	III.	306
17	*The Hassans*	0 1 4	Donegal	Kilmacrenan	Clondavaddog	Millford	III.	125
41	The Heath	103 1 27	Tipperary, N.R.	Eliogarty	Thurles	Thurles	II.	273
19	The Island or North Bull	120 3 21	Dublin	Coolock	Clontarf	Dublin North	I.	26

(a) Including 2A. 1R. 0P. water.
(b) Including 4A. 0R. 16P. water.
(c) Including 6A. 1R. 17P. water.
(d) Including 7A. 0R. 7P. detached portion.

(e) Including 8A. 0R. 24P. water.
(f) Including 3A. 0R. 38P. water.
(g) Including 0A. 3R. 5P. water.
(h) Including 0A. 2R. 39P. detached portion.

(i) Including 18A. 1R. 18P. water.
(j) Including 36A. 0R. 17P. water.
(k) Including 35A. 3R. 31P. detached portion.
(l) Including 6A. 1R. 10P. water.

No. of Sheet of the Ordnance Survey Maps.	Townlands and Towns.	Area in Statute Acres.	County.	Barony.	Parish.	Poor Law Union in 1857.	Townland Census of 1851, Part I.	
		A. R. P.					Vol.	Page
85	*The Islands* . .	28 1 7*a*	Tipperary, S.R. .	Iffa and Offa East .	Carrick . . .	Carrick on Suir .	II.	313
142	The League . .	3 2 22	Cork, W.R. .	West Carbery (E.D.) .	Myross . . .	Skibbereen . .	II.	141
25	THE LITTLE FURZE T.	—	Meath . .	Skreen . . .	Athlumney . .	Navan . .	I.	220
121	THE NEALE T. .	—	Mayo . .	Kilmaine . .	Kilmolara . .	Ballinrobe .	IV.	157
32	Theoil . . .	122 3 17	Wexford . .	Ballaghkeen . .	Ballynaslaney .	Enniscorthy .	I.	292
32	Theoil . . .	24 0 25	Wexford . .	Ballaghkeen . .	Edermine . .	Enniscorthy .	I.	294
120, 121	The Pike . .	363 0 30*b*	Cork, W.R. .	West Carbery (E.D.) .	Drinagh . .	Skibbereen . .	II.	139
54	The Point Park .	144 0 1	Down . .	Upper Iveagh, Up.pt.	Kilbroney . .	Kilkeel . .	III.	176
38	The Raven . .	550 2 37	Wexford . .	Shelmaliere East .	St. Margaret's .	Wexford . .	I.	331
38	*The Ridge* . .	4 1 5	Wexford . .	Shelmaliere East .	St. Margaret's .	Wexford . .	I.	331
33	THE ROWER T. .	—	Kilkenny . .	Ida . . .	The Rower . .	New Ross .	I.	104
17, 18	The Sheehys . .	898 2 24	Tipperary, N.R.	Ikerrin . .	Corbally . .	Roscrea . .	II.	275
36	The Walk . .	330 3 32	King's Co. .	Ballybritt . .	Kinnitty . .	Parsonstown .	I.	126
43	The-wood . .	72 3 8	Kerry . .	Corkaguiny . .	Dingle . .	Dingle . .	II.	176
101, 102	The Woods & Faunkill	370 0 5	Cork, W.R. .	Bear . . .	Kilcatherine .	Castletown .	II.	124
120	*Thick Island* . .	0 2 1	Mayo . .	Kilmaine . .	Ballinchalla .	Ballinrobe .	IV.	152
25	Thomascourt or Drumroosk . .	59 2 7	Cavan . .	Upper Loughtee .	Kilmore . .	Cavan . .	III.	85
57, 67	Thomastown . .	137 2 34	Clare . .	Moyarta . .	Kilrush . .	Kilrush . .	II.	23
24, 25	Thomastown . .	340 0 26*c*	Down . .	Ards Upper . .	Ardquin . .	Downpatrick .	III.	159
5, 8	Thomastown . .	159 3 16	Dublin . .	Balrothery East .	Lusk . .	Balrothery .	I.	21
23	Thomastown . .	213 0 29	Dublin . .	Rathdown . .	Monkstown .	Rathdown .	I.	37
22, 27	Thomastown . .	105 3 2	Fermanagh .	Tirkennedy , .	Derrybrusk .	Enniskillen .	III.	220
43	Thomastown . .	114 2 15	Galway . .	Clare . .	Belclare . .	Tuam . .	IV.	18
3, 4	Thomastown . .	566 0 0	Kildare . .	Carbury . .	Cadamstown .	Edenderry .	I.	51
18	Thomastown . .	148 3 11*d*	Kildare . .	Clane . .	Carragh . .	Naas . .	I.	53
28	Thomastown . .	396 3 25	Kildare . .	Kilcullen . .	Tully . .	Athy . .	I.	58
28	Thomastown . .	16 1 10*e*	Kilkenny . .	Gowran . .	Thomastown .	Thomastown .	I.	99
11	Thomastown . .	330 1 17	King's Co. .	Warrenstown .	Ballymacwilliam .	Edenderry .	I.	144
56	Thomastown . .	1,027 0 1	Limerick . .	Coshlea . .	Kilfinnane .	Kilmallock .	II.	240
47	Thomastown . .	952 3 39	Limerick . .	Coshma . .	Kilbreedy Minor .	Kilmallock .	II.	243
11	Thomastown . .	407 3 4	Louth . .	Ardee . .	Phillipstown .	Ardee . .	I.	174
11	Thomastown . .	65 1 5	Louth . .	Ardee . .	Tallanstown .	Ardee . .	I.	175
7	Thomastown . .	136 0 29	Louth . .	Upper Dundalk .	Dunbin . .	Dundalk .	I.	178
119	Thomastown . .	319 0 2	Mayo . .	Kilmaine . .	Kilcommon .	Ballinrobe .	IV.	155
118	Thomastown . .	168 2 34	Mayo . .	Kilmaine . .	Kilmainemore .	Ballinrobe .	IV.	156
15	Thomastown . .	593 3 24	Meath . .	Fore . .	Loughcrew .	Oldcastle .	I.	201
26	Thomastown . .	226 3 13	Meath . .	Lower Duleek .	Duleek . .	Drogheda .	I.	195
11	Thomastown . .	417 1 28	Meath . .	Lower Kells .	Kilbeg . .	Kells . .	I.	203
38	Thomastown . .	187 3 19	Meath . .	Ratoath . .	Dunshaughlin .	Dunshaughlin .	I.	218
82	Thomastown . .	174 2 36	Tipperary, S.R.	Iffa and Offa West .	Derrygrath .	Clogheen .	II.	318
27	Thomastown . .	68 3 25	Westmeath .	Farbill . .	Killucan . .	Mullingar .	I.	267
40, 45	Thomastown . .	299 1 19	Wicklow . .	Arklow . .	Arklow . .	Rathdrum .	I.	341
31, 36	Thomastown Demesne	720 3 29	King's Co. .	Eglish . .	Drumcullen .	Parsonstown .	I.	134
51, 54	Thomastown Demesne	658 0 13	Roscommon .	Athlone . .	Drum . .	Athlone .	IV.	180
60, 68	Thomastown Demesne	423 2 33	Tipperary, S.R.	Clanwilliam .	Relickmurry & Athassel	Tipperary .	II.	310
59, 60, 67, 68	Thomastown Demesne North . . .	419 2 5	Tipperary, S.R.	Clanwilliam .	Kilfeakle . .	Tipperary .	II.	308
67, 68	Thomastown Demesne South . . .	641 2 18	Tipperary, S.R.	Clanwilliam .	Kilfeakle . .	Tipperary .	II.	308
17, 22	Thomastown East .	583 0 15	Kildare . .	Offaly East .	Thomastown .	Edenderry .	I.	71
90, 100	Thomastown or Rusheen	212 0 11*f*	Mayo . .	Carra . .	Drum . .	Castlebar .	IV.	128
28	THOMASTOWN T. .	—	Kilkenny . .	Gowran . .	{ Columbkille . { Thomastown . }	Thomastown .	I.	{ 94 { 99
60	THOMASTOWN T. .	—	Tipperary, S.R.	Clanwilliam .	Relickmurry & Athassel	Tipperary .	II.	310
22	Thomastown West .	270 0 25	Kildare . .	Offaly East .	Thomastown .	Edenderry .	I.	71
7, 8	Thomondtown .	163 3 6	Dublin . .	Balrothery East .	Lusk . .	Balrothery .	I.	21
20	Thornberry . .	159 0 12	Kildare . .	South Salt .	Kill . .	Naas . .	I.	77
117	Thornfield . .	198 0 25	Galway . .	Longford . .	Lickmolassy .	Portumna .	IV.	61
6	Thornfield . .	101 2 38	Limerick . .	Clanwilliam .	Killeenagarriff .	Limerick . .	II.	224
33	Thornfield or Sra- haunnagort . .	121 2 12*g*	Galway . .	Killian . .	Athleague .	Mountbellew .	IV.	43
6	Thornfield or Tatty- naskeagh . .	179 2 1	Louth . .	Upper Dundalk .	Inishkeen .	Dundalk .	I.	179
115, 116	Thornhill . .	219 1 4	Cork, W.R. .	Bear . .	Killaconenagh .	Castletown .	II.	125
11	Thornhill . .	45 2 7	Kildare . .	North Salt .	Kildrought .	Celbridge .	I.	74
87	Thornhill . .	307 3 14	Mayo . .	Murrisk . .	Oughaval .	Westport .	IV.	162
8, 9, 12, 13	Thornhill . .	40 0 38	Monaghan .	Monaghan .	Drumsnat .	Monaghan .	III.	275
31	Thornhill . .	137 3 23	Tipperary, N.R.	Owney and Arra .	Kilcomenty .	Nenagh .	II.	295
16, 22	Thornhill Glebe .	110 1 9	Fermanagh .	Tirkennedy .	Trory . .	Enniskillen .	III.	223
46	Thornhill Glebe .	118 0 18	Tyrone . .	Dungannon Middle .	Pomeroy . .	Dungannon .	III.	304
1	Thornhill or Mullan- dreenagh . .	168 3 35	Cavan . .	Tullyhaw . .	Killinagh .	Enniskillen .	III.	92
11	Thorntown . .	268 0 27	Dublin . .	Nethercross .	Killsallaghan .	Balrothery .	I.	31
11	Thornwell . .	303 0 15	King's Co. .	Warrenstown .	Ballymacwilliam .	Edenderry .	I.	144

(*a*) Nine Islands in the River Suir.
(*b*) Including 33A. 0R. 2P. water.
(*c*) Including 15A. 0R. 5P. Lough Cowey.

(*d*) Including 2A. 2R. 8P. water.
(*e*) Including 1A. 1R. 37P. River Nore.

(*f*) Including 8A. 2R. 11P. water.
(*g*) Including 4A. 3R. 11P. water.

No. of Sheet of the Ordnance Survey Maps.	Townlands and Towns.	Area in Statute Acres. (A. R. P.)	County.	Barony.	Parish.	Poor Law Union in 1857.	Townland Census of 1851, Part I. Vol.	Page
53	Threeacres	12 0 20	Wexford	Forth	Carn	Wexford	I.	309
27	Three Carvaghs	224 1 26a	Cavan	Clankee	Knockbride	Cootehill	III.	74
13, 14	Threecastles	457 2 36	Kilkenny	Crannagh	Odagh	Kilkenny	I.	86
1, 5	Threecastles	669 3 38	Wicklow	Lower Talbotstown	Blessington	Naas	I.	358
14	Threecastles Demesne	198 2 24	Kilkenny	Crannagh	Odagh	Kilkenny	I.	86
133	Three-gneeves	178 3 14	Cork, W.R.	East Carbery (W.D.)	Kilmacabea	Skibbereen	II.	133
31	Threemilewater	171 1 34	Wicklow	Arklow	Dunganstown	Rathdrum	I.	344
30, 39	Three Trees	1,121 3 4	Donegal	Inishowen West	Muff	Londonderry	III.	121
34	Threewells	861 3 11	Wicklow	Ballinacor South	Ballykine	Rathdrum	I.	348
16	*Thulla Island*	0 3 22	Dublin	Coolock	Howth	Dublin North	I.	28
52, 53, 61	Thurlesbeg	1,014 0 7	Tipperary, S.R.	Middlethird	St. Patricksrock	Cashel	II.	331
41	THURLES T.	—	Tipperary, N.R.	Eliogarty	Thurles	Thurles	II.	273
41	Thurles Townparks	365 3 27	Tipperary, N.R.	Eliogarty	Thurles	Thurles	II.	273
19, 26	Thurstianstown	882 3 2b	Meath	Lower Duleek	Painstown	Navan	I.	196
72	Tiaquin Demesne	427 1 36c	Galway	Tiaquin	Monivea	Loughrea	IV.	79
10,11,17,18	Tibaran	1,287 0 1	Londonderry	Coleraine	Errigal	Coleraine	III.	232
44	Tibarney	202 0 9d	Roscommon	Athlone	Tisrara	Roscommon	IV.	186
38, 39	Tibberaghny	1,147 2 18	Kilkenny	Iverk	Tibberaghny	Carrick on Suir	I.	107
35, 36	Tibberedoge Glebe	98 2 8	Fermanagh	Clankelly	Clones	Clones	III.	197
64	Tibbotstown	228 1 15	Cork, E.R.	Barrymore	Carrigtohill	Middleton	II.	52
14	Tibohine	305 3 18	Roscommon	Frenchpark	Tibohine	Castlereagh	IV.	205
25	Tibradden	842 3 31	Dublin	Uppercross	Cruagh	Dublin South	I.	39
8, 12	Ticknevin	2,335 3 22	Kildare	Carbury	Kilpatrick	Edenderry	I.	52
30, 35	Ticlash	148 1 6	Wicklow	Arklow	Kilcommon	Rathdrum	I.	345
29	Ticloy	966 2 21	Antrim	Lower Antrim	Skerry	Ballymena	III.	5
46, 60	Ticooly (*Carr*)	221 0 24	Galway	Kilconnell	Killosolan	Mountbellew	IV.	42
46, 60	Ticooly (*O'Kelly*)	710 1 35	Galway	Tiaquin	Killosolan	Mountbellew	IV.	78
9	Ticor	91 2 23	Waterford	Middlethird	Trinity Without	Waterford	II.	369
24, 30	Ticosker	406 1 38e	Cavan	Tullyhunco	Killashandra	Cavan	III.	99
24	Ticosker Glebe	43 1 16f	Cavan	Tullyhunco	Killashandra	Cavan	III.	99
46, 47	Ticroghan	1,409 3 34	Meath	Upper Moyfenrath	Clonard	Edenderry	I.	213
13	Tiduff	1,060 0 0	Kerry	Clanmaurice	Ballyheige	Tralee	II.	168
3	Tieraclea Lower	298 3 37	Kerry	Iraghticonnor	Kilnaughtin	Glin	II.	192
3	Tieraclea Upper	163 0 26	Kerry	Iraghticonnor	Kilnaughtin	Glin	II.	192
43	Tiermore	102 0 6	Kilkenny	Iverk	Ullid	Waterford	I.	107
19	Tiermore	115 0 7	Limerick	Shanid	Shanagolden	Glin	II.	258
27	Tiermoyle	313 0 12	Tipperary, N.R.	Upper Ormond	Aghnameadle	Nenagh	II.	289
8, 14	Tiershanaghan	702 3 0	Kerry	Clanmaurice	Ballyheige	Tralee	II.	168
83, 84	Tievachorky	274 2 34	Donegal	Banagh	Inver	Donegal	III.	108
28	Tievadinna and Cloghoge	302 2 38g	Monaghan	Farney	Donaghmoyne	Carrickmacross	III.	269
24, 27	Tievaleny	234 0 25h	Monaghan	Cremorne	Aghnamullen	Castleblayney	III.	258
1	Tievaveeny	241 1 37	Fermanagh	Lurg	Drumkeeran	Lowtherstown	III.	207
8	Tievealough Glebe	79 0 12i	Fermanagh	Lurg	Belleek	Ballyshannon	III.	203
38	Tievebane	447 0 0	Donegal	Inishowen West	Fahan Upper	Londonderry	III.	121
23, 36	Tievebaun	1,136 2 20	Galway	Ballynahinch	Omey	Clifden	IV.	15
70	Tieveboy	133 1 7	Donegal	Raphoe	Clonleigh	Strabane	III.	135
33, 39	Tieveboy	159 3 24	Sligo	Corran	Emlaghfad	Boyle	IV.	226
79, 88	Tievebrack	307 2 35	Donegal	Raphoe	Donaghmore	Strabane	III.	138
104	Tievebrack	222 1 7	Donegal	Tirhugh	Drumhome	Ballyshannon	III.	147
13, 20	Tievebrack	1,220 3 18	Tyrone	Strabane Upper	Bodoney Lower	Gortin	III.	324
23,24,36,37	Tievebreen	1,561 2 31	Galway	Ballynahinch	Moyrus	Clifden	IV.	13
20	Tievebunnan	616 2 37	Fermanagh	Clanawley	Boho	Ballyshannon	III.	189
86, 87	Tievecloghoge	1,511 3 32	Donegal	Raphoe	Donaghmore	Stranorlar	III.	138
31, 32	Tievecrom	787 0 38	Armagh	Orior Upper	Forkill	Newry	III.	57
59	Tievedeevan	458 1 20	Donegal	Boylagh	Inishkeel	Glenties	III.	113
92	Tievedooly	224 1 3	Donegal	Banagh	Inver	Donegal	III.	108
9, 22	Tievegarriff	118 3 38	Galway	Ballynahinch	Ballynakill	Clifden	IV.	12
94	Tievegarriff	46 2 15	Galway	Galway	Rahoon	Galway	IV.	38
43	Tievegarrow	40 1 10	Fermanagh	Clankelly	Drummully	Clones	III.	197
56, 57	Tievegarvlagh	241 1 24j	Donegal	Boylagh	Templecrone	Glenties	III.	116
75	Tievelough	240 0 15k	Donegal	Boylagh	Inishkeel	Glenties	III.	113
101, 102	Tievemore	2,194 2 7	Donegal	Tirhugh	Templecarn	Donegal	III.	149
22	Tievemore	48 2 12	Galway	Ballynahinch	Ballynakill	Clifden	IV.	12
30, 37	Tievenadarragh	1,269 3 39l	Down	Kinelarty	Loughinisland	Downpatrick	III.	177
39	Tievenagh	76 3 31m	Tyrone	Dungannon Upper	Artrea	Cookstown	III.	306
39	Tievenagh (*part of*)	26 1 34	Tyrone	Dungannon Upper	Artrea	Cookstown	III.	306
33	Tievenaman	446 3 17	Cavan	Castlerahan	Killinkere	Bailieborough	III.	69
20, 23, 24	Tievenamara	421 3 8n	Armagh	Tiranny	Keady	Armagh	III.	60
12,13,19,20	Tievenameena	844 2 15	Tyrone	Strabane Upper	Bodoney Lower	Gortin	III.	324
23, 32	Tievenameenta	275 3 2o	Tyrone	Omagh West	Termonamongan	Castlederg	III.	317
22, 27	Tievenanass	543 0 15	Cavan	Tullygarvey	Kildrumsherdan	Cootehill	III.	90
1	Tievenavarnog	152 2 4	Fermanagh	Lurg	Drumkeeran	Lowtherstown	III.	207

(a) Including 9A. 3R. 6P. water.
(b) Including 4A. 3R. 24P. water.
(c) Including 11A. 3R. 24P. water.
(d) Including 6A. 0R. 12P. water.
(e) Including 54A. 3R. 28P. water.
(f) Including 11A. 0R. 8P. water.

(g) Including 11A. 0R. 16P. water.
(h) Including 5A. 2R. 34P. water.
(i) Including 19A. 0R. 0P. water.
(j) Including 6A. 3R. 21P. water.
(k) Including 35A. 1R. 34P. water.

(l) Including 27A. 0R. 16P. water.
(m) Exclusive of detached portion.
(n) Including 14A. 1R. 28P. water.
(o) { Including 0A. 1R. 3P. water.
{ Including 2A. 2R. 9P. detached portion.

No. of Sheet of the Ordnance Survey Maps.	Townlands and Towns.	Area in Statute Acres.	County.	Barony.	Parish.	Poor Law Union in 1857.	Townland Census of 1851, Part I.	
		A. R. P.					Vol.	Page
17	Tievenaveagh . .	60 1 14	Cavan . .	Tullygarvey . .	Drumgoon . .	Cootehill . .	III.	88
16	Tievenny . .	475 2 6a	Tyrone . .	Strabane Lower .	Ardstraw . .	Strabane . .	III.	319
66, 67	Tievereagh . .	206 0 3	Donegal . .	Boylagh . .	Inishkeel . .	Glenties . .	III.	113
32	Tieveshilly . .	289 2 1	Down . .	Ards Upper . .	Witter . .	Downpatrick . .	III.	161
82, 91	Tieveskeelta . .	496 0 37	Donegal . .	Banagh . .	Killybegs Upper .	Glenties . .	III.	111
95, 101	Tievetooey . .	1,257 0 39	Donegal . .	Tirhugh . .	Templecarn . .	Donegal . .	III.	149
9	Tifeaghna (Browne)	110 1 7	Kilkenny . .	Galmoy . .	Sheffin . .	Urlingford . .	I.	93
9	Tifeaghna (Mt. Garret)	212 2 17	Kilkenny . .	Galmoy . .	Sheffin . .	Urlingford . .	I.	93
19	Tiglin . . .	122 2 19	Wicklow . .	Newcastle . .	Killiskey . .	Rathdrum . .	I.	352
18, 24	Tiglin . . .	472 0 4	Wicklow . .	Newcastle . .	Killiskey . .	Rathdrum . .	I.	352
19	Tiglin . . .	151 0 9	Wicklow . .	Newcastle . .	Newcastle Lower .	Rathdrum . .	I.	353
44	Tigreenaun . .	391 0 16	Galway . .	Clare . .	Killererin . .	Tuam . .	IV.	21
8	Tigroe . .	291 2 27	Waterford . .	Middlethird . .	Kilmeadan . .	Waterford . .	II.	368
35	Tigroney East .	320 0 31	Wicklow . .	Arklow . .	Castlemacadam .	Rathdrum . .	I.	342
35	Tigroney West .	376 3 4	Wicklow . .	Arklow . .	Castlemacadam .	Rathdrum . .	I.	342
29	Tikerlevan . .	831 0 20	Kilkenny . .	Gowran . .	Graiguenamanagh .	Thomastown . .	I.	95
37	Tikillin . .	288 2 3	Wexford . .	Shelmaliere East .	Tikillin . .	Wexford . .	I.	331
2	Tikincor Lower .	115 2 26b	Waterford . .	Upperthird . .	Killaloan . .	Clonmel . .	II.	370
2	Tikincor Upper .	264 0 20	Waterford . .	Upperthird . .	Killaloan . .	Clonmel . .	II.	370
26	Tiknick . .	204 0 38	Dublin . .	Rathdown . .	Tully . .	Rathdown . .	I.	38
4	Tiknock . .	855 1 33	Carlow . .	Rathvilly . .	Rathvilly . .	Baltinglass . .	I.	12
87	Tiknock . .	23 2 1	Cork, E.R. .	Barrymore . .	Templerobin . .	Cork . .	II.	58
22, 25	Tiknock . .	627 0 20	Dublin . .	Rathdown . .	Taney . .	Rathdown . .	I.	38
37	Tiknock . .	453 3 23	Waterford . .	Decies within Drum	Clashmore . .	Youghal . .	II.	351
20, 21	Tiknock . .	277 2 4	Wexford . .	Ballaghkeen . .	Kilcormick . .	Enniscorthy . .	I.	294
40	Tiknock . .	168 2 32	Wicklow . .	Arklow . .	Kilbride . .	Rathdrum . .	I.	345
38,39,44,45	Tildarg . .	2,725 0 34c	Antrim . .	Upper Antrim .	Rashee . .	Antrim . .	III.	7
126	Tilickafinna . .	510 0 4	Cork, W.R. .	Bear . .	Kilnamanagh . .	Castletown . .	II.	126
52	Tilladavin . .	163 2 13	Wexford . .	Bargy . .	Tomhaggard . .	Wexford . .	I.	308
19	Timacat . .	486 0 24	Galway . .	Tiaquin . .	Kilkerrin . .	Glennamaddy . .	IV.	77
27, 32, 33	Timaconway . .	594 1 21	Londonderry .	Loughinsholin .	Tamlaght O'Crilly .	Ballymoney . .	III.	244
17, 18, 31	Timadoaoun . .	594 2 36	Galway . .	Ballymoe . .	Dunmore . .	Glennamaddy . .	IV.	8
18, 19, 24	Timahoe . .	510 2 8	Queen's Co. .	Cullenagh . .	Fossy or Timahoe .	Abbeyleix . .	I.	240
8, 9	Timahoe East .	2,193 3 25	Kildare . .	Clane . .	Timahoe . .	Naas . .	I.	54
8, 9	Timahoe West .	795 1 8	Kildare . .	Clane . .	Timahoe . .	Naas . .	I.	54
5, 9	Timakeel . .	199 0 23	Armagh . .	Oneilland West .	Drumcree . .	Lurgan . .	III.	52
27, 34	Timanagh . .	403 2 32	Roscommon .	Castlereagh . .	Ballintober . .	Castlereagh . .	IV.	198
18, 31	Timard . .	295 3 39d	Galway . .	Ballymoe . .	Clonbern . .	Glennamaddy . .	IV.	7
5	Timard . .	129 1 16	Kildare . .	North Salt . .	Laraghbryan . .	Celbridge . .	I.	75
12	Timeighter . .	323 0 21	Tipperary, N.R.	Ikerrin . .	Roscrea . .	Roscrea . .	II.	276
50	Timlins . .	36 2 21	Meath . .	Upper Deece . .	Moyglare . .	Dunshaughlin . .	I.	194
19	Timmore . .	299 2 34	Wicklow . .	Newcastle . .	Newcastle Upper .	Rathdrum . .	I.	353
19	Timogue . .	682 1 17	Queen's Co. .	Stradbally . .	Timogue . .	Athy . .	I.	248
123, 136	Timoleague . .	185 1 35	Cork, W.R. .	Ibane and Barryroe	Timoleague . .	Clonakilty . .	II.	151
123, 136	TIMOLEAGUE T. .	—	Cork, W.R. .	Ibane and Barryroe	Timoleague . .	Clonakilty . .	II.	151
36	Timolin . .	1,102 2 7	Kildare . .	Narragh & Reban East	Timolin . .	Baltinglass . .	I.	67
22, 30	Timolin . .	686 2 28	King's Co. .	Garrycastle . .	Reynagh . .	Parsonstown . .	I.	138
13, 21	Timolin or Derry-holmes and Derry-haran . .	533 2 18	King's Co. .	Garrycastle . .	Tisaran . .	Parsonstown . .	I.	138
36	TIMOLIN T. .	—	Kildare . .	Narragh & Reban East	Timolin . .	Baltinglass . .	I. .	67
18	Timoney . .	699 2 15	Tipperary, N.R.	Ikerrin . .	Corbally . .	Roscrea . .	II.	275
18	Timoney Hills .	206 2 32	Tipperary, N.R.	Ikerrin . .	Corbally . .	Roscrea . .	II.	275
32, 33	Timoole . .	535 3 36	Meath . .	Skreen . .	Timoole . .	Dunshaughlin . .	I.	222
14	Timpan . .	156 3 19	Antrim . .	Lower Glenarm .	Layd . .	Ballycastle . .	III.	23
64	Timpany . .	248 3 20	Tyrone . .	Clogher . .	Aghalurcher . .	Clogher . .	III.	291
2	Timpaun . .	136 3 0	Roscommon .	Boyle . .	Kilronan . .	Boyle . .	IV.	197
107	Timsallagh or Spring Grove . .	740 3 26,	Galway . .	Longford . .	Kilquain . .	Portumna . .	IV.	60
5	Timulkenny . .	64 0 23	Armagh . .	Oneilland West .	Drumcree . .	Lurgan . .	III.	52
21	Timullen . .	161 3 6	Louth . .	Ferrard . .	Monasterboice . ?	Drogheda . .	I.	181
30	Timullin . .	127 2 33	Wicklow . .	Arklow . .	Kilcommon . .	Rathdrum . .	I.	345
5	Tinacarra . .	135 1 10	Roscommon .	Boyle . .	Boyle . .	Boyle . .	IV.	194
34	Tinacrannagh . .	375 1 7	King's Co. .	Upper Philipstown .	Clonyhurk . .	Mountmellick . .	I.	143
105, 115	Tinageeragh . .	201 1 21	Galway . .	Loughrea . .	Killeenadeema . .	Loughrea . .	IV.	64
53	Tinageragh . .	468 2 16	Cork, E.R. .	Barrymore . .	Ardnageehy . .	Fermoy . .	II.	51
40, 45	Tinahask Lower .	117 2 39	Wicklow . .	Arklow . .	Arklow . .	Rathdrum . .	I.	341
45	Tinahask Upper .	138 3 24	Wicklow . .	Arklow . .	Arklow . .	Rathdrum . .	I.	341
38, 43	Tinahely . .	216 0 22	Wicklow . .	Ballinacor South .	Kilcommon . .	Shillelagh . .	I.	349
38	TINAHELY T. .	—	Wicklow . .	Ballinacor South .	Kilcommon . .	Shillelagh . .	I.	349
25	Tinakelly . .	233 1 23	Wicklow . .	Newcastle . .	Rathnew . .	Rathdrum . .	I.	051
25	Tinakelly Murragh	67 2 8	Wicklow . .	Newcastle . .	Rathnew . .	Rathdrum . .	I.	351
29, 30, 35	Tinakilly or Wood-house . .	464 2 7	Waterford . .	Decies within Drum	Kilmolash . .	Dungarvan . .	II.	351

No. of Sheet of the Ordnance Survey Maps.	Townlands and Towns.	Area in Statute Acres. A. R. P.	County.	Barony.	Parish.	Poor Law Union in 1857.	Townland Census of 1851, Part I. Vol.	Page
10	Tinalintan	253 0 18	Kilkenny	Fassadinin	Kilmacar	Castlecomer	I.	90
22	Tinalira	307 0 12	Waterford	Decies without Drum	Modelligo	Dungarvan	II.	359
1, 7	Tinamuck East	369 3 38	King's Co.	Kilcoursey	Kilmanaghan	Tullamore	I.	141
7	Tinamuck South	210 3 33	King's Co.	Kilcoursey	Kilmanaghan	Tullamore	I.	141
1, 7	Tinamuck West	489 3 1	King's Co.	Kilcoursey	Kilmanaghan	Tullamore	I.	141
12	Tinary	145 2 14	Monaghan	Dartree	Aghabog	Clones	III.	264
37	Tincarraun	178 2 36	Kilkenny	Ida	The Rower	New Ross	I.	104
12	Tincashel	329 1 23	Kilkenny	Galmoy	Urlingford	Urlingford	I.	93
37	Tincone	48 1 38	Wexford	Shelmaliere East	Ardcavan	Wexford	I.	330
32	Tincoon	218 0 39	Wexford	Ballaghkeen	Edermine	Enniscorthy	I.	294
25	Tincouse	132 0 18a	Kilkenny	Gowran	Powerstown	Thomastown	I.	98
41, 42	Tincurra	434 0 25	Wexford	Shelmaliere West	Taghmon	Wexford	I.	335
7	Tincurragh	67 0 35	Wexford	Gorey	Kilcavan	Gorey	I.	317
7	Tincurragh	30 2 21	Wexford	Gorey	Kilgorman	Gorey	I.	318
81	Tincurry	401 0 9	Tipperary, S.R.	Iffa and Offa West	Whitechurch	Clogheen	II.	322
15	Tincurry	1,015 0 22b	Wexford	Scarawalsh	Ballycarney	Enniscorthy	I.	322
18	Tinderry	427 3 34	Tipperary, N.R.	Ikerrin	Corbally	Roscrea	II.	275
42, 47	Ting	94 1 23	Wexford	Forth	Rathmacknee	Wexford	I.	313
17	Tingar	127 1 23	Wexford	Ballaghkeen	Donaghmore	Gorey	I.	294
22	Tingarran	187 2 36	Kilkenny	Shillelogher	Killaloe	Callan	I.	115
3, 4	Tinhalla	363 3 31	Waterford	Upperthird	Fenoagh	Carrick on Suir	II.	370
30	Tinkershill	195 0 7	Galway	Dunmore	Tuam	Tuam	IV.	36
54	Tinklersford	59 2 21	Donegal	Raphoe	Raymoghy	Londonderry	III.	142
5	Tinlough	404 0 36	Tipperary, N.R.	Lower Ormond	Loughkeen	Parsonstown	II.	286
71	Tinlough	265 2 22	Tipperary, S.R.	Slievardagh	Grangemockler	Carrick on Suir	II.	333
2	Tinnabaun	299 0 27	Wexford	Gorey	Kilnenor	Gorey	I.	320
28	Tinnaberna	163 0 15	Wexford	Ballaghkeen	Killincooly	Enniscorthy	I.	295
37	Tinnabinna	264 0 17	Waterford	Decies within Drum	Clashmore	Youghal	II.	351
35	Tinnacarrick	849 1 6	Wexford	Shelburne	Owenduff	New Ross	I.	328
22, 24	Tinnacarrig	676 2 9	Carlow	St. Mullins Lower	Ullard	New Ross	I.	13
13	Tinnaclash	37 1 23	Carlow	Forth	Templepeter	Carlow	I.	5
4	Tinnaclash	255 0 37	Carlow	Rathvilly	Kiltegan	Baltinglass	I.	11
28	Tinnaclohy	167 2 38	Queen's Co.	Clandonagh	Rathdowney	Donaghmore	I.	234
22	Tinnacree	233 3 21c	Wexford	Ballaghkeen	Kilmuckridge	Gorey	I.	297
30, 31	Tinnacross	67 3 4	King's Co.	Eglish	Drumcullen	Parsonstown	I.	134
20	Tinnacross	367 2 0	Wexford	Scarawalsh	Clone	Enniscorthy	I.	322
11, 20	Tinnacullia	247 1 38	Limerick	Kenry	Kilcornan	Rathkeale	II.	249
15	Tinnagarney	211 1 38	Carlow	Idrone West	Wells	Carlow	I.	10
21	Tinnagroun	88 3 12	Waterford	Coshmore&Coshbride	Lismore and Mocollop	Lismore	II.	347
56, 57	Tinnahally	386 0 32	Kerry	Trughanacmy	Killorglin	Killarney	II.	211
32	Tinnahask	135 3 36	Wexford	Ballaghkeen	Ballynaslaney	Enniscorthy	I.	292
24	Tinnahinch	349 1 31d	Carlow	St. Mullins Lower	St. Mullins	New Ross	I.	13
3, 6, 7	Tinnahinch	2,908 0 26	Queen's Co.	Tinnahinch	Rearymore	Mountmellick	I.	250
35	Tinnahinch	111 1 25	Wicklow	Arklow	Castlemacadam	Rathdrum	I.	342
24	TINNAHINCH T.	—	Carlow	St. Mullins Lower	St. Mullins	New Ross	I.	13
51	Tinnahinchy	118 2 19	Tipperary, S.R.	Kilnamanagh Lower	Donohill	Tipperary	II.	323
25	Tinnakeenly	188 0 15	Kilkenny	Gowran	Powerstown	Thomastown	I.	98
31	Tinnakill	229 1 22	Kildare	Narragh&RebanWest	Narraghmore	Athy	I.	68
17	Tinnakill	142 0 23	Queen's Co.	Maryborough West	Clonenagh&Clonagheen	Abbeyleix	I.	243
4, 8	Tinnakill	800 2 19	Queen's Co.	Portnahinch	Ardea	Mountmellick	I.	243
16	Tinnakill	682 0 2	Queen's Co.	Upperwoods	Offerlane	Mountmellick	I.	252
18	Tinnakilla	596 3 13	Limerick	Shanid	Kilmoylan	Glin	II.	256
32	Tinnakilla	325 1 35	Wexford	Shelmaliere West	Killurin	Enniscorthy	I.	334
39	Tinnakilly	262 2 23	Kilkenny	Iverk	Fiddown	Carrick on Suir	I.	105
22	Tinnakilly	228 0 20	Kilkenny	Shillelogher	Killaloe	Callan	I.	115
5, 8	Tinnakilly	404 0 31	Tipperary, N.R.	Lower Ormond	Loughkeen	Parsonstown	II.	286
71	Tinnakilly	297 0 1	Tipperary, S.R.	Middlethird	Cloneen	Cashel	II.	325
70	Tinnakilly	301 1 33	Tipperary, S.R.	Middlethird	Peppardstown	Cashel	II.	329
37	Tinnakilly Big	216 3 24	Kilkenny	Ida	Rosbercon	New Ross	I.	103
37	Tinnakilly Little	17 3 0	Kilkenny	Ida	Rosbercon	New Ross	I.	103
34, 39	Tinnakilly Lower	362 0 6	Wicklow	Ballinacor South	Ballykine	Rathdrum	I.	348
34, 39	Tinnakilly Upper	586 1 16	Wicklow	Ballinacor South	Ballykine	Rathdrum	I.	348
5	Tinnalintan	234 0 7	Kilkenny	Fassadinin	Donaghmore	Castlecomer	I.	89
38	Tinnalyra	282 3 32e	Waterford	Decies within Drum	Lisgenan or Grange	Youghal	II.	352
26	Tinnamoona	59 1 29	Kilkenny	Callan	Callan	Callan	I.	84
29	Tinnapark	179 2 11	Kilkenny	Gowran	Graiguenamanagh	Thomastown	I.	95
13	Tinnapark Demesne	309 0 22	Wicklow	Newcastle	Kilcoole	Rathdrum	I.	352
28	Tinnaragh	23 2 29	Queen's Co.	Clarmallagh	Aghaboe	Donaghmore	I.	236
28	Tinnaragh	16 3 12	Queen's Co.	Clarmallagh	Bordwell	Donaghmore	I.	237
29	Tinnaraheen	180 0 23	Queen's Co.	Clarmallagh	Aghaboe	Abbeyleix	I.	236
37	Tinnaranny	826 0 9	Kilkenny	Ida	Rosbercon	New Ross	I.	103
40	Tinnarath	256 3 18	Wexford	Shelmaliere West	Inch	New Ross	I.	333
16	Tinnascart	405 2 17	Cork, E.R.	Orrery and Kilmore	Buttevant	Mallow	II.	107

(a) Including 1A. 2R. 13P. River Barrow.　　(c) Including 21A. 0R. 0P. water.　　(e) Including 22A. 3R. 18P. detached portion.
(b) Including 7A. 0R. 27P. water.　　(d) Including 15A. 3R. 0P. River Barrow.

5 R 2

No. of Sheet of the Ordnance Survey Maps.	Townlands and Towns.	Area in Statute Acres.			County.	Barony.	Parish.	Poor Law Union in 1857.	Townland Census of 1851, Part I.	
		A.	R.	P.					Vol.	Page
34	Tinnascart	653	3	9	Waterford	Decies within Drum	Aglish	Dungarvan	II.	349
9	Tinnascarty	112	1	4	Kilkenny	Galmoy	Sheffin	Urlingford	I.	93
33, 37	Tinnascolly	300	0	30	Kilkenny	Ida	The Rower	New Ross	I.	104
6, 7	Tinnashinnagh	170	3	0	Wexford	Gorey	Kilmakilloge	Gorey	I.	318
10, 15	Tinnashrule	394	1	11	Wexford	Scarawalsh	Ferns	Enniscorthy	I.	323
4, 9	Tinnaslatty	771	3	25	Kilkenny	Galmoy	Aharney	Urlingford	I.	91
37	Tinnaslatty	257	2	33	Kilkenny	Ida	The Rower	New Ross	I.	104
32	Tinnasragh	129	3	17	Queen's Co.	Slievemargy	Killabban	Carlow	I.	245
15	Tinnatarriff	318	3	30	Limerick	Owneybeg	Tuogh	Limerick	II.	251
134	Tinneel	133	2	24	Cork, W.R.	East Carbery (W.D.)	Ross	Clonakilty	II.	135
3, 7	Tinneel	174	0	22	Queen's Co.	Tinnahinch	Rosenallis	Mountmellick	I.	250
7	Tinnehinch	25	2	33	Wicklow	Rathdown	Kilmacanoge	Rathdown	I.	356
7	Tinnehinch	49	0	9	Wicklow	Rathdown	Powerscourt	Rathdown	I.	356
21	Tinnehinch	66	0	9	Wicklow	Upper Talbotstown	Donaghmore	Baltinglass	I.	363
27	Tinnick	46	2	17	Wexford	Ballaghkeen	Ballyvaldon	Enniscorthy	I.	292
78, 87	Tinnies Lower East	211	1	38	Kerry	Iveragh	Valencia	Cahersiveen	II.	198
78, 87	Tinnies Lower West	173	2	32	Kerry	Iveragh	Valencia	Cahersiveen	II.	198
78, 87	Tinnies Upper	221	3	1	Kerry	Iveragh	Valencia	Cahersiveen	II.	198
39	Tinnock	528	3	9	Wexford	Shelburne	Killesk	New Ross	I.	327
7	Tinnock Lower	336	1	1	Wexford	Gorey	Kilcavan	Gorey	I.	317
7	Tinnock Upper	183	2	1	Wexford	Gorey	Kilcavan	Gorey	I.	317
17	Tinnybeg	71	0	3	Leitrim	Drumahaire	Inishmagrath	Manorhamilton	IV.	97
94	Tinnycahil	113	0	35	Donegal	Tirhugh	Donegal	Donegal	III.	145
29	Tinnycross	67	3	23	Kildare	Naas South	Ballymore Eustace	Naas	I.	64
9, 17	Tinnycross or Bally-nasrah	510	2	28	King's Co.	Ballycowan	Kilbride	Tullamore	I.	127
15, 20	Tinnynarr	416	0	38	Longford	Ardagh	Mostrim	Granard	I.	153
55	Tinock	382	2	33	Tipperary, S.R.	Slievardagh	Ballingarry	Callan	II.	332
2, 6	Tinode	723	0	5	Westmeath	Moygoish	Street	Granard	I.	281
1	Tinode	1,250	3	9	Wicklow	Lower Talbotstown	Kilbride	Naas	I.	361
20, 26	Tinoranhill North	246	0	38	Wicklow	Upper Talbotstown	Ballynure	Baltinglass	I.	362
26	Tinoranhill South	258	3	5	Wicklow	Upper Talbotstown	Ballynure	Baltinglass	I.	362
26, 27	Tinraheen	486	2	16	Wexford	Ballaghkeen	Killisk	Enniscorthy	I.	296
7, 12	Tinriland	545	1	27	Carlow	Carlow	Tullowmagimma	Carlow	I.	2
41, 46	Tintagh	1,070	1	18	Londonderry	Loughinsholin	Lissan	Magherafelt	III.	242
3	Tintagh	473	2	13	Roscommon	Boyle	Boyle	Boyle	IV.	194
45	Tintern	600	1	1	Wexford	Shelburne	Tintern	New Ross	I.	329
22	Tinteskin	128	2	28	Wexford	Ballaghkeen	Killincooly	Gorey	I.	295
37	Tintine	265	3	35	Kilkenny	Ida	The Rower	New Ross	I.	104
28, 29	Tintore	181	2	37	Queen's Co.	Clarmallagh	Aghaboe	Abbeyleix	I.	236
28, 29	Tintore	664	0	30	Queen's Co.	Clarmallagh	Killermogh	Abbeyleix	I.	238
135	Tintrim	206	2	27a	Galway	Leitrim	Clonrush	Scarriff	IV.	53
21	Tintur	125	2	3	Waterford	Coshmore&Coshbride	Lismore and Mocollop	Lismore	II.	347
21	Tinure	347	1	8	Louth	Ferrard	Mullary	Drogheda	I.	182
85	Tinvane	161	1	8	Tipperary, S.R.	Iffa and Offa East	Carrick	Carrick on Suir	II.	312
43	Tinvaucoosh	320	2	21	Kilkenny	Ida	Dunkitt	Waterford	I.	101
27, 31	Tinvaun	419	2	33	Kilkenny	Kells	Kilree	Callan	I.	109
35	Tinvoher	1,087	1	14	Tipperary, N.R.	Eliogarty	Loughmoe West	Thurles	II.	271
35	Tinwear	406	0	7	Queen's Co.	Clarmallagh	Durrow	Abbeyleix	I.	237
28, 32	Tippeenan Lower	185	3	29	Kildare	Offaly West	Fontstown	Athy	I.	72
32	Tippeenan Upper	185	2	30	Kildare	Offaly West	Fontstown	Athy	I.	72
25, 26	Tipper	120	2	39	Longford	Rathcline	Cashel	Ballymahon	I.	164
23	Tipper	80	3	16	Longford	Shrule	Kilcommock	Ballymahon	I.	166
59, 67	Tipperary Hills	37	1	3	Tipperary, S.R.	Clanwilliam	Tipperary	Tipperary	II.	312
67	TIPPERARY T.	—			Tipperary, S.R.	Clanwilliam	Cordangan / Corroge / Tipperary	Tipperary	II.	306 / 306 / 312
19	Tipper East	249	2	28	Kildare	Naas North	Tipper	Naas	I.	63
24	Tipperkevin	278	0	21	Kildare	Naas South	Tipperkevin	Naas	I.	65
19	Tipper North	176	0	17	Kildare	Naas North	Tipper	Naas	I.	63
19, 24	Tipper South	433	0	13	Kildare	Naas North	Tipper	Naas	I.	63
23	Tipperstown	119	3	33	Dublin	Rathdown	Kill	Rathdown	I.	36
14, 15	Tipperstown	99	0	13	Kildare	South Salt	Castledillon	Celbridge	I.	76
19	Tipper West	173	0	12	Kildare	Naas North	Tipper	Naas	I.	63
4, 5	Tirachorka	189	1	10	Meath	Lower Kells	Moybolgue	Kells	I.	203
39	Tiraffy	70	2	2b	Fermanagh	Coole	Galloon	Lisnaskea	III.	200
31	Tiragarvan	222	0	35	Monaghan	Farney	Magheross	Carrickmacross	III.	274
129	Tiraloughan	97	2	39c	Galway	Kiltartan	Beagh	Gort	IV.	46
23	Tiraltan	293	2	25	Fermanagh	Tirkennedy	Enniskillen	Enniskillen	III.	222
6	Tiramoan	113	2	30d	Monaghan	Trough	Donagh	Monaghan	III.	283
9	Tiranagher Beg	217	2	18e	Fermanagh	Magheraboy	Inishmacsaint	Ballyshannon	III.	213
9, 9	Tiranagher More	155	1	28f	Fermanagh	Magheraboy	Inishmacsaint	Ballyshannon	III.	213
118	Tiranascragh	1,006	1	37	Galway	Longford	Tiranascragh	Portumna	IV.	62

No. of Sheet of the Ordnance Survey Maps.	Townlands and Towns.	Area in Statute Acres. A. R. P.	County.	Barony.	Parish.	Poor Law Union in 1857.	Townland Census of 1851, Part I. Vol.	Page
49, 61	Tiraninny	302 1 22	Mayo	Gallen	Killasser	Swineford	IV.	149
13, 18	Tirardan	123 1 23	Monaghan	Monaghan	Kilmore	Monaghan	III.	276
34	Tiraree	89 3 9	Sligo	Corran	Kilmorgan	Sligo	IV.	227
44	Tirargus	1,126 3 16a	Donegal	Kilmacrenan	Kilmacrenan	Milford	III.	129
33, 38	Tiraroe	249 1 34	Fermanagh	Knockninny	Kinawley	Lisnaskea	III.	202
21	Tiratick	134 1 19	Sligo	Tirerrill	Killerry	Sligo	IV.	239
24	Tiraun	436 3 10	Mayo	Erris	Kilmore	Belmullet	IV.	146
33	Tiravally Glebe	366 0 19	Fermanagh	Clanawley	Kinawley	Enniskillen	III.	194
7, 10	Tiravera	191 0 22	Monaghan	Monaghan	Tehellan	Monaghan	III.	280
10	Tiravray	155 1 22	Monaghan	Monaghan	Monaghan	Monaghan	III.	277
32	Tiravree Glebe	114 3 28	Fermanagh	Clanawley	Kinawley	Enniskillen	III.	194
2	Tirawinnea	160 2 27b	Meath	Lower Kells	Moybolgue	Kells	I.	203
29, 43	Tirboy	154 3 24	Galway	Clare	Tuam	Tuam	IV.	23
14, 22	Tirbracken	300 0 17	Londonderry	Tirkeeran	Clondermot	Londonderry	III.	248
7	Tircahan	169 1 36	Cavan	Tullyhaw	Kinawley	Bawnboy	III.	93
69, 78	Tircallan	131 3 29	Donegal	Raphoe	Stranorlar	Stranorlar	III.	143
64	Tircar	179 3 7	Tyrone	Clogher	Aghalurcher	Clogher	III.	291
107	Tirconeen	28 2 19	Donegal	Tirhugh	Kilbarron	Ballyshannon	III.	148
21	Tirconnell	25 2 36	Fermanagh	Magheraboy	Devenish	Enniskillen	III.	211
47	Tirconnellbeg	79 0 35	Roscommon	Athlone	Dysart	Athlone	IV.	181
3	Tirconnelly	259 0 9	Tyrone	Strabane Lower	Donaghedy	Strabane	III.	321
12	Tircooney	88 3 17	Monaghan	Dartree	Clones	Clones	III.	265
5, 6, 9, 10	Tircorran	187 0 30	Londonderry	Keenaght	Aghanloo	NewTⁿLimavady	III.	234
6	Tircreven	828 1 35	Londonderry	Keenaght	Magilligan	NewTⁿLimavady	III.	237
25	Tircullen	125 3 29	Cavan	Upper Loughtee	Kilmore	Cavan	III.	85
28	Tircullen Lower	105 0 33	Waterford	Coshmore&Coshbride	Kilwatermoy	Lismore	II.	344
28	Tircullen Upper	80 3 32	Waterford	Coshmore&Coshbride	Kilwatermoy	Lismore	II.	344
26	Tircur	400 2 10	Tyrone	Strabane Upper	Cappagh	Omagh	III.	325
8	Tireagerty	68 1 28	Armagh	Armagh	Clonfeacle	Armagh	III.	44
12	Tirearly	213 2 23	Armagh	Armagh	Lisnadill	Armagh	III.	45
12	Tiredigan	104 2 12	Monaghan	Dartree	Killeevan	Monaghan	III.	268
24	Tireeghan	261 1 18	Fermanagh	Magherastephana	Aghalurcher	Lisnaskea	III.	217
50	Tireenan	251 0 8	Tyrone	Clogher	Donacavey	Omagh	III.	294
35	Tireevil	107 0 19c	Fermanagh	Clankelly	Clones	Clones	III.	197
29, 30	Tireighter	611 1 20	Londonderry	Tirkeeran	Cumber Upper	Londonderry	III.	249
60	Tirelugan	487 2 23	Tyrone	Dungannon Lower	Carnteel	Clogher	III.	298
23	Tirenny	208 2 7	Fermanagh	Magherastephana	Aghalurcher	Lisnaskea	III.	217
3	Tireran	150 2 11	Monaghan	Trough	Errigal Trough	Clogher	III.	285
26, 32	Tirernan	444 1 34	Queen's Co.	Slievemargy	Killabban	Carlow	I.	245
18, 28	Tirevlin	51 3 28	Donegal	Kilmacrenan	Clondavaddog	Milford	III.	125
42	Tirfergus	267 1 2	Down	Upper Iveagh, Lr. pt.	Drumballyroney	Banbridge	III.	172
10	Tirfinnog	93 0 20	Monaghan	Monaghan	Monaghan	Monaghan	III.	277
46	Tirgan	625 0 32	Londonderry	Loughinsholin	Desertmartin	Magherafelt	III.	241
12	Tirgarriff	27 2 19	Armagh	Armagh	Eglish	Armagh	III.	44
8	Tirgarve	196 2 22	Armagh	Armagh	Grange	Armagh	III.	45
32, 33	Tirgarvil	435 3 36	Londonderry	Loughinsholin	Maghera	Magherafelt	III.	242
23, 30	Tirglassan	459 0 17	Londonderry	Tirkeeran	Banagher	NewTⁿLimavady	III.	247
25	Tirgoland	374 1 19	Londonderry	Keenaght	Dungiven	NewTⁿLimavady	III.	236
10	Tirgormly	209 0 7	Cavan	Lower Loughtee	Drumlane	Cavan	III.	81
50	Tirgracey	459 2 0	Antrim	Lower Massereene	Muckamore(Grange of)	Antrim	III.	29
54	Tirharon	148 3 26	Donegal	Raphoe	Raymoghy	Letterkenny	III.	142
5	Tirhogar	566 3 34	Queen's Co.	Portnahinch	Lea	Mountmellick	I.	244
27, 36	Tirhomin	577 1 30	Donegal	Kilmacrenan	Tullyfern	Milford	III.	133
32	Tirhugh	765 1 19	Londonderry	Loughinsholin	Killelagh	Magherafelt	III.	241
8	Tirigannon Glebe	132 2 10d	Fermanagh	Lurg	Belleek	Ballyshannon	III.	203
9, 17	Tirinchinan or Rosnagowloge	218 1 8	King's Co.	Ballycowan	Kilbride	Tullamore	I.	128
79	Tirinisk	252 2 29e	Donegal	Raphoe	Donaghmore	Strabane	III.	138
32, 36	Tirkane	1,258 2 24	Londonderry	Loughinsholin	Killelagh	Magherafelt	III.	241
9	Tirkeenan	125 1 2	Monaghan	Monaghan	Monaghan	Monaghan	III.	277
70, 79	Tirkeeran	92 1 20	Donegal	Raphoe	Clonleigh	Strabane	III.	135
18, 26	Tirkeeran	275 1 36	Londonderry	Coleraine	Desertoghill	Coleraine	III.	231
21	Tirkeeveny	227 0 10	Londonderry	Tirkeeran	Clondermot	Londonderry	III.	248
42	Tirkelly	548 3 12	Down	Upper Iveagh, Lr.pt.	Drumballyroney	Banbridge	III.	172
5, 6	Tirkernaghan	906 1 26f	Tyrone	Strabane Lower	Donaghedy	Strabane	III.	321
44	Tirkillin	457 0 33	Donegal	Kilmacrenan	Kilmacrenan	Milford	III.	130
14	Tirkilly	100 0 37	Antrim	Lower Glenarm	Layd	Ballycastle	III.	23
26, 27	Tirlahode Lower	529 2 14	Cavan	Upper Loughtee	Larah	Cavan	III.	85
26, 27	Tirlahode Upper	487 0 22	Cavan	Upper Loughtee	Larah	Cavan	III.	85
18, 28	Tirlaydan	465 3 30	Donegal	Kilmacrenan	Clondavaddog	Milford	III.	125
22, 23	Tirlickeen	852 2 10	Longford	Rathcline	Shrule	Ballymahon	I.	165
20	Tirliffin	232 3 33	Cavan	Lower Loughtee	Drumlane	Cavan	III.	81
26, 35	Tirlin	75 1 6	Donegal	Kilmacrenan	Clondahorky	Dunfanaghy	III.	123

(a) Including 84A. 1R. 4P. water.
(b) Including 7A. 3R. 29P. water.
(c) Inc'uling 6A. 1R. 38P. water.
(d) Including 38A. 1R. 10P. water.
(e) Including 3A. 0R. 14P. water.
(f) Including 5A. 2R. 0P. water.

No. of Sheet of the Ordnance Survey Maps.	Townlands and Towns.	Area in Statute Acres.			County.	Barony.	Parish.	Poor Law Union in 1857.	Townland Census of 1851, Part I.	
		A.	R.	P.					Vol.	Page
17	Tirloughan	421	0	26	Donegal	Kilmacrenan	Mevagh	Millford	III.	130
10, 14	Tirmacmoe	110	2	11	Monaghan	Cremorne	Clontibret	Monaghan	III.	261
9, 16	Tirmacoy	254	1	4	Londonderry	Tirkeeran	Faughanvale	NewTⁿLimavady	III.	250
8	Tirmacrannon	163	1	22	Armagh	Armagh	Loughgall	Armagh	III.	46
5, 12	Tirmacroragh	664	2	38	Donegal	Inishowen East	Culdaff	Inishowen	III.	118
29	Tirmacshane	71	2	29	Tyrone	Dungannon Upper	Kildress	Cookstown	III.	309
2	Tirmacspird	450	0	6	Fermanagh	Lurg	Drumkeeran	Lowtherstown	III.	207
27	Tirmactiernan	32	1	1	Leitrim	Leitrim	Kiltoghert	Carᵏ. on Shannon	IV.	103
9, 13	Tirmadown	164	2	33	Monaghan	Monaghan	Kilmore	Monaghan	III.	276
10	Tirmaquin	184	0	36	Londonderry	Keenaght	Drumachose	NewTⁿLimavady	III.	235
17	Tirmegan	125	0	23a	Tyrone	Strabane Lower	Ardstraw	Strabane	III.	319
4, 9	Tirmoghan Common	46	1	37	Kildare	Ikeathy&Oughterany	Cloncurry	Celbridge	I.	57
37, 38	Tirmonen	173	2	10	Fermanagh	Knockninny	Kinawley	Enniskillen	III.	202
26	Tirmurty	459	2	25	Tyrone	Strabane Upper	Cappagh	Omagh	III.	325
30	Tirnadrola	92	1	2	Monaghan	Farney	Magheross	Carrickmacross	III.	274
32, 33	Tirnageeragh	410	3	18	Londonderry	Loughinsholin	Maghera	Magherafelt	III.	242
79	Tirnagushoge or Bick- etstown	140	0	4	Donegal	Raphoe	Donaghmore	Strabane	III.	138
11, 12	Tirnahinch Far	166	1	32b	Monaghan	Dartree	Clones	Clones	III.	265
11	Tirnahinch Near	166	2	35c	Monaghan	Dartree	Clones	Clones	III.	265
8, 9	Tirnamona	61	3	10	Monaghan	Monaghan	Tedavnet	Monaghan	III.	279
136	Tirnanean	165	1	33	Cork, W.R.	Ibane and Barryroe	Lislee	Clonakilty	II.	150
6, 9	Tirnaneill	232	2	23	Monaghan	Trough	Donagh	Monaghan	III.	283
12	Tirnascobe	536	3	36d	Armagh	Oneilland West	Armagh	Armagh	III.	51
52, 53	Tirnaskea	319	0	30	Tyrone	Clogher	Errigal Keerogue	Clogher	III.	295
37, 38	Tirnaskea	149	1	0	Tyrone	Dungannon Upper	Desertcreat	Cookstown	III.	308
38	Tirnaskea (*Bayly*)	279	2	14	Tyrone	Dungannon Upper	Desertcreat	Cookstown	III.	308
6	Tirnaskea North	120	2	26	Monaghan	Monaghan	Tedavnet	Monaghan	III.	279
8	Tirnaskea South	66	1	8	Monaghan	Monaghan	Tedavnet	Monaghan	III.	280
9	Tirnawannagh	337	3	7e	Cavan	Tullyhaw	Templeport	Bawnboy	III.	95
122	Tirneevin	118	0	20	Galway	Kiltartan	Kilmacduagh	Gort	IV.	48
32, 36	Tirnony	519	2	23	Londonderry	Loughinsholin	Killelagh	Magherafelt	III.	241
25	Tiroe	326	3	0	Kilkenny	Gowran	Ullard	Thomastown	I.	100
72	Tiroe	77	2	13	Tipperary, S.R.	Slievardagh	Newtownlennan	Carrick on Suir	II.	335
19	Tiromedan	195	0	3f	Monaghan	Monaghan	Tullycorbet	Monaghan	III.	281
63, 71	Tironeill	179	1	12	Donegal	Raphoe	Clonleigh	Strabane	III.	135
33	Tiroogan	67	1	10	Fermanagh	Clanawley	Kinawley	Enniskillen	III.	194
36, 44	Tiroony	323	3	14	Tyrone	Omagh East	Termonmaguirk	Omagh	III.	315
25	Tirourkan	111	2	12	Cavan	Upper Loughtee	Annagelliff	Cavan	III.	82
25	Tirquin	147	3	7g	Cavan	Upper Loughtee	Annagelliff	Cavan	III.	82
35	Tirquin	528	1	31	Tyrone	Strabane Upper	Cappagh	Omagh	III.	325
37	Tirroddy	158	3	25	Donegal	Kilmacrenan	Tullyfern	Millford	III.	133
55	Tirroddy	170	2	17	Donegal	Raphoe	Taughboyne	Londonderry	III.	144
100	Tirrooaun	311	3	36	Galway	Longford	Clontuskert	Ballinasloe	IV.	58
6	Tirsogue	74	0	24	Armagh	Oneilland East	Shankill	Lurgan	III.	51
46	Tirur	333	2	24	Galway	Killian	Killian	Mountbellew	IV.	45
2, 6	Tirwinny	181	0	0	Fermanagh	Lurg	Drumkeeran	Lowtherstown	III.	207
42	Tirygory	479	3	19h	Down	Upper Iveagh, Lr. pt.	Drumballyroney	Banbridge	III.	172
12, 21	Tiryrone	964	0	17	Donegal	Inishowen East	Moville Upper	Inishowen	III.	119
71, 84	Tisaxon	470	2	32	Galway	Tiaquin	Monivea	Loughrea	IV.	79
111	Tisaxon Beg	128	0	17	Cork, E.R.	Kinsale	Tisaxon	Kinsale	II.	101
111, 124	Tisaxon More	313	1	6	Cork, E.R.	Kinsale	Tisaxon	Kinsale	II.	101
66	Tiscallen	323	3	24	Antrim	Upper Massereene	Aghagallon	Lurgan	III.	29
88	Titeskin	237	1	25	Cork, E.R.	Imokilly	Titeskin	Middleton	II.	90
12	Tithewer	687	0	28	Wicklow	Newcastle	Calary	Rathdrum	I.	350
5	Tivannagh	239	1	6	Roscommon	Boyle	Boyle	Boyle	IV.	194
19	Tivnacree	345	1	31	Armagh	Tiranny	Derrynoose	Armagh	III.	59
14	Toanreagh	320	1	27	Kerry	Clanmaurice	Ballyheige	Tralee	II.	168
4	Tobeen	234	0	24	Dublin	Balrothery West	Garristown	Dunshaughlin	I.	22
38	Tober	109	0	38	Cork, W.R.	West Muskerry	Drishane	Millstreet	II.	156
54	Tober	275	2	31	Donegal	Raphoe	Taughboyne	Londonderry	III.	144
103, 104	Tober	1,529	0	21i	Donegal	Tirhugh	Kilbarron	Ballyshannon	III.	148
20	Tober	61	3	17	Fermanagh	Magheraboy	Boho	Enniskillen	III.	210
46	Tober	54	0	38	Kerry	Trughanacmy	Kilgarrylander	Tralee	II.	211
1, 2	Tober	289	1	15	King's Co.	Kilcoursey	Kilmanaghan	Tullamore	I.	141
10	Tober	256	1	29	Longford	Granard	Abbeylara	Granard	I.	154
81	Tober	149	2	23	Mayo	Costello	Aghamore	Swineford	IV.	137
71	Tober	1,006	1	17	Tipperary, S.R.	Middlethird	Cloneen	Cashel	II.	325
20, 28	Tober	151	3	27	Waterford	Coshmore&Coshbride	Lismore and Mocollop	Lismore	II.	347
7	Tober	192	2	5	Westmeath	Corkaree	Multyfarnham	Mullingar	I.	263
104	Toberacreggaun	78	2	15	Galway	Dunkellin	Ardrahan	Gort	IV.	27
47, 52, 53	Toberadora	577	3	17	Tipperary, S.R.	Middlethird	Gaile	Cashel	II.	327
6, 14	Toberagarriff	265	0	33	Limerick	Owneybeg	Abington	Limerick	II.	251

(a) Including 2A. 1R. 19P. water.
(b) Including 6A. 3R. 8P. water.
(c) Including 6A. 3R. 28P. water.
(d) Including 10A. 1R. 1P. water.

(e) { Including 49A. 3R. 19P. Brackly Lough. / Including 26A. 0R. 0P. Bunerky Lough.
(f) Including 5A. 2R. 16P. water.

(g) Including 4A. 1R. 36P. water.
(h) Including 13A. 2R. 11P. water.
(i) Including 261A. 2R. 29P. water.

No. of Sheet of the Ordnance Survey Maps.	Townlands and Towns.	Area in Statute Acres.	County.	Barony.	Parish.	Poor Law Union in 1857.	Townland Census of 1851, Part I.	
							Vol.	Page
		A. R. P.						
50, 51, 56	Toberagnee . .	560 0 20	Antrim . .	Upper Belfast .	Ballymartin . .	Antrim . .	III.	9
37	Toberagoole . .	15 2 29	Waterford . .	Decies within Drum	Kinsalebeg . .	Youghal . .	II.	352
83	Toberaheena . .	115 3 37	Tipperary, S.R.	Iffa and Offa East .	Inishlounaght . .	Clonmel . .	II.	313
77, 83	Toberaheena . .	83 3 4	Tipperary, S.R.	Iffa and Offa East .	Kiltegan . .	Clonmel . .	II.	315
83	TOBERAHEENA T. .	—	Tipperary, S.R.	Iffa and Offa East .	Inishlounaght . .	Clonmel . .	II.	313
21	Toberanania . .	295 0 26	Sligo . .	Tirerrill . . .	Killerry . . .	Sligo . .	IV.	239
44	Toberaneague .	286 3 23	Cork, E.R. .	Barrymore . .	Rathcormack . .	Fermoy . .	II.	57
49	Toberaniddaun .	383 3 36	Clare . . .	Islands . . .	Clondagad . .	Killadysert . .	II.	29
11	Toberanierin Lower	257 3 39	Wexford . .	Gorey . . .	Liskinfere . .	Gorey . .	I.	320
11	Toberanierin Upper	193 2 38	Wexford . .	Gorey . . .	Liskinfere . .	Gorey . .	I.	321
12	Toberaquill . .	363 1 33	Westmeath . .	Corkaree . .	Taghmon . .	Mullingar .	I.	264
6, 7	Toberataravan .	116 2 16	Roscommon . .	Boyle . . .	Tunna . . .	Boyle . .	IV.	198
6, 7	Toberatooreen .	851 0 10	Kerry . . .	Iraghticonnor .	Murher . . .	Listowel . .	II.	193
41	Toberavaddy . .	302 1 18a	Roscommon . .	Athlone . .	Fuerty . . .	Roscommon . .	IV.	181
31	Toberaviller . .	107 1 22	Wicklow . .	Arklow . .	Drumkay . .	Rathdrum . .	I.	343
13	Toberawnaun . .	173 2 22	Sligo . . .	Tireragh . . .	Skreen . . .	Dromore West .	IV.	236
27	Toberbeg . .	2 2 5	Wexford . .	Ballaghkeen .	Castle-ellis . .	Enniscorthy .	I.	293
27	Toberbeg . .	49 2 0	Wexford . .	Ballaghkeen .	Killisk . . .	Enniscorthy .	I.	296
15	Toberbeg . .	251 2 39	Wicklow . .	Lower Talbotstown.	Dunlavin . .	Baltinglass .	I.	360
8	Toberbilly . .	287 3 19	Antrim . .	Cary . . .	Ramoan . . .	Ballycastle . .	III.	15
17, 18	Toberbilly . .	205 0 6	Antrim . .	Upper Dunluce .	Kilraghts . .	Ballymoney . .	III.	20
27	Toberbiroge .	178 1 25	Galway . .	Ross . . .	Cong . . .	Oughterard . .	IV.	73
35	Toberboe or Killenny More . . .	621 1 18	Queen's Co. .	Clarmallagh . .	Aghmacart . .	Abbeyleix . .	I.	236
95	Toberbrackan .	181 3 6	Galway . .	Dunkellin . .	Killeely . . .	Gort . . .	IV.	30
18, 22	Toberbreedia . .	201 0 30	Kilkenny . .	Crannagh . .	Ballycallan . .	Kilkenny . .	I.	85.
16	Toberbride . .	233 3 2	Carlow . .	Idrone East . .	Dunleckny . .	Carlow . .	I.	7
26	Toberbride . .	138 2 8	Sligo . . .	Tirerrill . . .	Ballysadare . .	Sligo . . .	IV.	238
14	Toberbunny . .	156 3 21	Dublin . .	Coolock . . .	Cloghran . .	Balrothery .	I.	26
11	Toberburr . .	220 1 23	Dublin . .	Nethercross . .	Finglas . . .	Balrothery .	I.	31
22	Toberclare . .	463 3 11	Westmeath . .	Kilkenny West .	Kilkenny West .	Athlone . .	I.	273
22	Tobercocka . .	88 3 3	Kildare . .	Offaly West . .	Lackagh . . .	Athy . .	I.	73
84, 96	Toberconnelly .	21 1 8	Galway . .	Athenry . . .	Athenry . . .	Loughrea . .	IV.	4
44	Toberconor . .	167 0 7	Roscommon . .	Athlone . .	Rahara . . .	Roscommon . .	IV.	183
17, 24	Tobercormick . .	501 2 25	Westmeath . .	Rathconrath . .	Ballymorin . .	Mullingar .	I.	282
37, 44	Tobercorran .	381 1 17	Down . .	Lecale Upper . .	Down . . .	Downpatrick .	III.	181
41	Tobercrossaun .	119 0 27	Galway . .	Clare . . .	Killursa . .	Tuam . .	IV.	22
38	Tobercurry . .	736 2 34	Sligo . . .	Leyny . . .	Achonry . . .	Tobercurry . .	IV.	229
38	TOBERCURRY T. .	—	Sligo . . .	Leyny . . .	Achonry . . .	Tobercurry . .	IV.	230
10, 11	Toberdaly . .	1,552 1 0	King's Co. .	Warrenstown . .	Castlejordan . .	Edenderry .	I.	145
45	Toberdan . .	519 3 2	Roscommon . .	Athlone . .	St. Johns . .	Athlone . .	IV.	184
9, 15	Tober Demesne .	260 1 17	Wicklow . .	Lower Talbotstown.	Tober . . .	Baltinglass .	I.	361
7, 12	Toberdoney . .	257 2 20	Antrim . .	Lower Dunluce .	Billy . . .	Ballymoney . .	III.	16
17, 18	Toberdoney . .	222 1 18	Louth . .	Ardee . . .	Dromin . . .	Ardee . .	I.	172
6	Toberdornan . .	130 0 3	Antrim . .	Lower Dunluce .	Ballywillin . .	Coleraine . .	III.	16
45, 46	Toberdowney . .	184 3 9	Antrim . .	Lower Belfast .	Ballynure . .	Larne . .	III.	7
7	Toberduff . .	176 3 18	Wexford . .	Gorey . . .	Kilcavan . . .	Gorey . .	I.	317
27	Toberelva . .	125 2 38	Roscommon . .	Castlereagh . .	Baslick . . .	Castlereagh .	IV.	199
11	Toberfelim . .	166 0 31	Longford . .	Granard . . .	Granard . . .	Granard . .	I.	157
32	Toberfinnick . .	120 0 34	Wexford . .	Shelmaliere East .	Artramon . .	Wexford . .	I.	330
16, 21	Tobergal . .	375 3 38	Wexford . .	Gorey . . .	Kilcormick . .	Enniscorthy .	I.	317
44, 50	Tobergill . .	1,044 2 38	Antrim . .	Upper Antrim .	Donegore . .	Antrim . .	III.	6
3, 6	Tobergregan . .	626 0 23	Dublin . .	Balrothery West .	Garristown . .	Dunshaughlin .	I.	22
87	Tobergrellan .	83 2 19	Galway . .	Clonmacnowen .	Kilcloony . .	Ballinasloe . .	IV.	25
42	Toberhead . .	728 0 8	Londonderry .	Loughinsholin .	Maghera . .	Magherafelt .	III.	243
6	Toberhewny . .	205 2 27	Armagh . .	Oneilland East .	Shankill . .	Lurgan . .	III.	51
54	Toberiheen . .	163 2 35	Roscommon . .	Moycarn . .	Moore . . .	Ballinasloe . .	IV.	207
43	Toberjarlath . .	114 2 1	Galway . .	Clare . . .	Tuam . . .	Tuam . .	IV.	23
7, 8	Toberkeagh . .	247 1 25	Antrim . .	Cary . . .	Ballintoy . .	Ballycastle . .	III.	12
41	Toberkeagh . .	277 1 25	Roscommon . .	Athlone . .	Athleague . .	Roscommon . .	IV.	179
27	Toberkeagh . .	163 3 22	Roscommon . .	Castlereagh . .	Ballintober . .	Castlereagh .	IV.	198
49, 57	Toberkeen . .	461 3 4b	Donegal . .	Boylagh . .	Templecrone . .	Glenties . .	III.	116
29	Toberlane . .	192 1 0	Tyrone . .	Dungannon Upper .	Derryloran . .	Cookstown . .	III.	307
17, 18	Toberleheen . .	350 3 29	King's Co. .	Geashill . .	Geashill . .	Tullamore . .	I.	140
27	Toberlomina . .	270 3 36	Wexford . .	Ballaghkeen . .	Meelnagh . .	Enniscorthy .	I.	298
15	Tober Lower . .	133 1 27	Wicklow . .	Lower Talbotstown .	Tober . . .	Baltinglass .	I.	361
39, 44	Toberlownagh .	917 2 8	Wicklow . .	Ballinacor South .	Kilpipe . . .	Shillelagh . .	I.	349
13	Toberlyan . .	171 3 13c	Cavan . .	Tullyhaw . .	Templeport . .	Bawnboy . .	III.	95
13	Toberlyan Duffin .	160 0 11d	Cavan . .	Tullyhaw . .	Templeport . .	Bawnboy . .	III.	95
47,48,50,51	Tobermacloughlin .	459 2 37	Roscommon . .	Athlone . .	Taghmaconnell .	Athlone . .	IV.	185
17	Tobermaclugg . .	85 3 20	Dublin . .	Newcastle . .	Lucan . . .	Celbridge . .	I.	33
40	Tobermaing . .	259 3 18	Kerry . . .	Trughanacmy .	Castleisland . .	Tralee . .	II.	209
34	Tobermakee . .	228 3 8	Roscommon . .	Ballymoe . .	Drumatemple . .	Castlereagh .	IV.	191

(a) Including 14A. 1R. 30P. water.
(b) Including 31A. 2R. 25P. water.

(c) Including 17A. 3R. 32P. water.
(d) Including 2A. 3R. 7P. water.

No. of Sheet of the Ordnance Survey Maps.	Townlands and Towns.	Area in Statute Acres.	County.	Barony.	Parish.	Poor Law Union in 1857.	Townland Census of 1851, Part I.	
		A. R. P.					Vol.	Page
14	Tobermalug . .	279 0 35	Limerick . .	Clanwilliam . .	Caherconlish . .	Limerick . .	II.	222
61, 62	Tobermesson Glebe .	250 0 15	Tyrone . .	Dungannon Middle .	Clonfeacle . .	Dungannon .	III.	300
42, 43	Tobermina . .	190 0 23	Galway . .	Clare . .	Belclare . .	Tuam . .	IV.	18
38	Tobermoney . .	231 3 5a	Down . .	Lecale Upper .	Down . .	Downpatrick .	III.	181
36	Tobermore . .	295 0 29	Londonderry .	Loughinsholin .	Kilcronaghan .	Magherafelt .	III.	241
29, 38	Tobermore . .	313 1 6	Mayo . .	Tirawley . .	Crossmolina .	Ballina . .	IV.	166
36	TOBERMORE T. .	—	Londonderry .	Loughinsholin .	Kilcronaghan .	Magherafelt .	III.	241
11	Tobermurry . .	230 2 32	Limerick . .	Kenry . .	Kildimo . .	Rathkeale .	II.	250
39	Tobernabrone . .	602 0 8	Kilkenny . .	Iverk . .	Fiddown . .	Carrick on Suir	I.	105
5, 6, 17	Tobernaclug . .	392 3 0	Galway . .	Ballymoe . .	Dunmore . .	Glennamaddy .	IV.	8
122	Tobernadarry . .	182 1 23	Mayo . .	Kilmaine . .	Moorgagagh .	Ballinrobe .	IV.	157
39	Tobernafauna or Cashel . .	79 2 0	Kilkenny . .	Iverk . .	Fiddown . .	Carrick on Suir	I.	105
20, 28, 29	Tobernagat . .	857 3 15	Clare . .	Tulla Upper .	Moynoe . .	Scarriff . .	II.	40
23	Tobernagauhoge .	118 2 10	Westmeath .	Kilkenny West	Kilkenny West .	Athlone . .	I.	273
34	Tobernaglashy .	83 3 31	Sligo . .	Tirerrill . .	Kilmacallan .	Sligo . .	IV.	240
18	Tobernagola . .	419 3 36	Antrim . .	Upper Dunluce .	Loughguile .	Ballymoney .	III.	20
99, 103	Tobernahoory . .	147 2 30	Donegal . .	Tirhugh . .	Drumhome .	Donegal . .	III.	147
19	Tobernahulla . .	452 1 22	Waterford .	Coshmore&Coshbride	Lismore and Mocollop	Lismore . .	II.	347
43, 53, 54	Tobernamoodane .	343 0 7	Kerry . .	Corkaguiny .	Kinard . .	Dingle . .	II.	179
9, 13	Tobernapeastia .	219 3 31	Kilkenny . .	Crannagh . .	Freshford . .	Kilkenny . .	I.	85
118, 121	Tobernashee . .	104 3 32	Mayo . .	Kilmaine . .	Kilmolara .	Ballinrobe .	IV.	157
83, 84	Tobernavean . .	363 0 8	Galway . .	Clare . .	Athenry . .	Galway . .	IV.	17
44	Tobernaveen . .	362 3 0	Antrim . .	Upper Toome .	Shilvodan Grange .	Antrim . .	III.	35
47	Tobernaveen . .	768 1 10	Mayo . .	Tirawley . .	Addergoole .	Castlebar .	IV.	163
14	Tobernaveen . .	58 0 14	Sligo . .	Carbury . .	Kilmacowen .	Sligo . .	IV.	222
47	Tobernea . .	45 1 7	Limerick . .	Coshma . .	Kilbreedy Minor .	Kilmallock .	II.	243
47	Tobernea East .	465 0 9	Limerick . .	Coshma . .	Effin . .	Kilmallock .	II.	243
47	Tobernea Middle .	211 1 30	Limerick . .	Coshma . .	Effin . .	Kilmallock .	II.	243
47, 55	Tobernea West .	458 1 7	Limerick . .	Coshma . .	Effin . .	Kilmallock .	II.	243
28, 29	Toberogan . .	154 2 33	Kildare . .	Kilcullen .	Kilcullen . .	Naas . .	I.	58
25	Toberona . .	209 2 2	Wexford . .	Bantry . .	Templescoby .	Enniscorthy .	I.	303
70	Toberoneill . .	225 1 38	Donegal . .	Raphoe . .	Clonleigh .	Strabane . .	III.	135
23	Toberpatrick . .	515 3 25	Roscommon .	Roscommon .	Kiltrustan .	Strokestown .	IV.	211
13	Toberpatrick . .	183 2 17	Sligo . .	Tireragh . .	Skreen . .	Dromore West .	IV.	236
39, 44	Toberpatrick . .	744 1 18	Wicklow . .	Ballinacor South .	Kilpipe . .	Shillelagh .	I.	349
128	TOBERREENDONEY T.	—	Galway . .	Kiltartan . .	Beagh . .	Gort . .	IV.	46
42	Toberreeoge . .	71 2 35	Roscommon .	Athlone . .	Kilmeane .	Roscommon .	IV.	182
37	Toberroddy . .	233 2 9	Sligo . .	Leyny . .	Kilmacteige .	Tobercurry .	IV.	231
83, 84	Toberroe . .	482 1 5	Galway . .	Athenry . .	Athenry . .	Loughrea .	IV.	4
28	Toberroe . .	390 3 33	Galway . .	Dunmore . .	Kilconla . .	Tuam . .	IV.	35
7	Toberroe East .	114 0 29	Galway . .	Ballymoe . .	Ballynakill .	Glennamaddy .	IV.	5
7	Toberroe West .	167 0 8	Galway . .	Ballymoe . .	Ballynakill .	Glennamaddy .	IV.	5
10, 18	Toberronan . .	139 1 24	King's Co. .	Lower Philipstown .	Killaderry .	Tullamore .	I.	143
88, 98	Toberrooaun . .	543 2 24	Mayo . .	Burrishoole .	Aghagower .	Westport . .	IV.	118
22	Toberrory . .	574 0 4	Roscommon .	Roscommon .	Elphin . .	Strokestown .	IV.	210
26	TOBERSCANAVAN T.	—	Sligo . .	Tirerrill . .	Ballysadare .	Sligo . .	IV.	238
32, 38	Toberscardan . .	358 0 31	Sligo . .	Leyny . .	Achonry .	Tobercurry .	IV.	229
55	Toberslane . .	168 3 10	Donegal . .	Raphoe . .	Killea . .	Londonderry .	III.	139
1	Tobersool . .	223 0 20	Dublin . .	Balrothery East	Balscaddan .	Balrothery .	I.	20
1	Tobertaskin . .	67 0 23b	Dublin . .	Balrothery East	Balscaddan .	Balrothery .	I.	20
32, 38	Tobertelly . .	714 1 17	Sligo . .	Leyny . .	Achonry .	Tobercurry .	IV.	229
19	Toberton . .	131 2 19	Kildare . .	Naas North .	Johnstown .	Naas . .	I.	62
1, 4	Tobertown . .	365 1 2	Dublin . .	Balrothery East	Balscaddan .	Balrothery .	I.	20
7	TOBER T. . .	—	Galway . .	Ballymoe . .	Kilcroan .	Glennamaddy .	IV.	9
42	Tobertynan . .	747 1 24	Meath . .	Lower Moyfenrath .	Rathmolyon .	Trim . .	I.	211
16, 17	Toberultan . .	147 0 7	Meath . .	Upper Kells .	Burry . .	Kells . .	I.	205
15	Tober Upper . .	305 3 29	Wicklow . .	Lower Talbotstown .	Tober . .	Baltinglass .	I.	361
24, 25	Toberwine . .	49 1 27	Antrim . .	Lower Glenarm .	Layd . .	Ballycastle .	III.	23
13	Toberyquin . .	221 0 15	Limerick . .	Clanwilliam .	Caheravally .	Limerick . .	II.	221
27	Tobinsgarden . .	17 1 5	Tipperary, N.R.	Upper Ormond .	Latteragh .	Nenagh . .	II.	292
3, 4, 8, 9	Tobinstown . .	845 2 8	Carlow . .	Rathvilly . .	Rathvilly .	Baltinglass .	I.	12
2	Tobinstown . .	89 3 36	Galway . .	Ballymoe . .	Kilcroan .	Glennamaddy .	IV.	9
21	Tobradan . .	151 1 17	Fermanagh .	Clanawley .	Boho . .	Enniskillen .	III.	189
151	Toehead . .	219 3 37	Cork, W.R. .	West Carbery (E.D.)	Castlehaven .	Skibbereen .	II.	138
50	Toem . . .	98 2 16	Tipperary, N.R.	Kilnamanagh Upper	Toem . .	Tipperary .	II.	280
13	Togan . . .	167 2 39	Monaghan .	Monaghan . .	Drumsnat .	Monaghan .	III.	275
32	Togher . . .	454 1 36	Cavan . .	Castlerahan .	Crosserlough .	Cavan . .	III.	68
34	Togher . . .	299 1 31	Cavan . .	Castlerahan .	Killinkere .	Bailieborough .	III.	69
93	Togher . . .	661 2 36	Cork, W.R. .	East Carbery (W.D.)	Fanlobbus .	Dunmanway .	II.	132
69	Togher . . .	171 0 36	Cork, W.R. .	West Muskerry .	Ballyvourney .	Macroom . .	II.	154
6, 7	Togher . . .	140 2 8	King's Co. .	Garrycastle .	Lemanaghan .	Parsonstown .	I.	137
10, 11	Togher . . .	350 1 17	King's Co. .	Lower Philipstown .	Ballyburly .	Edenderry .	I.	142

(a) Including 3A. 0R. 32P. water.   (b) Including 4A. 1R. 39P. detached portion.

No. of Sheet of the Ordnance Survey Maps.	Townlands and Towns.	Area in Statute Acres.	County.	Barony.	Parish.	Poor Law Union in 1857.	Townland Census of 1851, Part I.	
		A. R. P.					Vol.	Page
19	Togher . . .	330 0 13	Louth . .	Ferrard . . .	Clonmore . .	Drogheda . .	I.	180
93	Togher . . .	162 3 34a	Mayo . .	Costello . .	Bekan . .	Claremorris .	IV.	139
100, 110	Togher . . .	556 2 4	Mayo . .	Kilmaine . .	Robeen . .	Ballinrobe .	IV.	158
13, 18	Togher . . .	831 3 19	Queen's Co. .	Maryborough East .	Borris . .	Mountmellick .	I.	240
50, 53	Togher . . .	509 3 18	Roscommon .	Athlone . .	Taghmaconnell .	Ballinasloe .	IV.	185
24, 30	Togher . . .	348 3 31	Tipperary, N.R.	Ikerrin . . .	Templetouhy .	Thurles . .	II.	277
1	Togher . . .	676 0 18	Westmeath .	Fore . . .	Foyran . .	Granard . .	I.	270
36	Togher . . .	65 1 4	Wicklow . .	Arklow . . .	Dunganstown .	Rathdrum .	I.	344
10, 16	Togher . . .	648 2 4	Wicklow . .	Lower Talbotstown .	Boystown . .	Baltinglass .	I.	359
14, 15	Togherbane . .	329 0 3	Kerry . .	Clanmaurice . .	Kilmoyly . .	Tralee . .	II.	171
44	Togher Beg . .	191 0 29	Galway . .	Clare . . .	Killererin . .	Tuam . .	IV.	21
18	Togher Beg . .	91 2 34	Wicklow . .	Ballinacor North .	Derrylossary .	Rathdrum .	I.	346
20, 25	Togher or Danesfort Demesne . .	202 1 18b	Cavan . .	Upper Loughtee .	Kilmore . .	Cavan . .	III.	85
21, 22	Toghereen . .	152 1 10	Kildare . .	Offaly West .	Lackagh . .	Athy . .	I.	73
46, 47	Toghergar . .	42 3 4	Galway . .	Killian . .	Killian . .	Mountbellew .	IV.	45
43, 44	Togher More . .	360 0 33	Galway . .	Clare . . .	Killererin . .	Tuam . .	IV.	21
18	Togher More . .	222 0 29	Wicklow . .	Ballinacor North .	Derrylossary .	Rathdrum .	I.	346
37, 41	Toghernaross . .	276 2 32	Cavan . .	Clanmahon . .	Drumlumman .	Granard .	III.	77
22	Togherorymore .	143 3 11	Kildare . .	Offaly West .	Lackagh . .	Athy . .	I.	73
24, 25	Togherstown . .	606 2 14	Westmeath .	Rathconrath .	Conry . .	Mullingar .	I.	282
14, 18	Tolka . . .	213 0 25	Dublin . .	Castleknock . .	Finglas . .	Dublin North .	I.	25
18	Tolka Park . .	37 0 12	Dublin . .	Coolock . .	Glasnevin . .	Dublin North .	I.	27
14, 18	TOLKA T. . .	—	Dublin . .	Castleknock . .	Finglas . .	Dublin North .	I.	25
38, 45	Tollumgrange Lower	173 1 23	Down . .	Lecale Lower . .	Dunsfort . .	Downpatrick .	III.	179
38, 45	Tollumgrange Upper	163 0 24	Down . .	Lecale Lower . .	Dunsfort . .	Downpatrick .	III.	179
43, 49	Tollymore . .	538 2 3	Down . .	Upper Iveagh, Lr. pt.	Maghera . .	Kilkeel . .	III.	173
43, 49	Tollymore Park .	1,128 1 25	Down . .	Upper Iveagh, Lr.pt.	Kilcoo . .	Kilkeel . .	III.	173
38	Tolvin . . .	175 3 28	Tyrone . .	Dungannon Upper .	Desertcreat .	Cookstown .	III.	308
43, 47	Tomacork . .	894 0 20	Wicklow . .	Shillelagh . .	Carnew . .	Shillelagh .	I.	357
15, 20	Tomacurry . .	397 3 12c	Wexford . .	Scarawalsh . .	Monart . .	Enniscorthy .	I.	324
14, 15, 19, 20	Tomadilly . .	554 0 20	Wexford . .	Scarawalsh . .	Monart . .	Enniscorthy .	I.	324
16, 17	Tomagaddy . .	379 3 29	Wexford . .	Gorey . .	Monamolin .	Gorey . .	I.	321
16	Tomagaddy Little .	12 2 28	Wexford . .	Gorey . .	Monamolin .	Gorey . .	I.	321
10	Tomakeany . .	191 0 18	Kilkenny . .	Fassadinin .	Kilmacar . .	Castlecomer .	I.	90
39	Tomanierin Lower .	138 0 8	Wicklow . .	Ballinacor South .	Kilpipe . .	Rathdrum .	I.	349
39	Tomanierin Upper .	149 1 36	Wicklow . .	Ballinacor South .	Kilpipe . .	Rathdrum .	I.	349
18, 24	Tomanine . .	299 2 36	Wexford . .	Bantry . .	Templeludigan .	New Ross .	I.	303
14	Tomanoole . .	389 0 20	Wexford . .	Scarawalsh . .	Monart . .	Enniscorthy .	I.	324
17	Tomany . . .	170 2 16d	Monaghan .	Dartree . .	Ematris . .	Cootehill .	III.	267
116, 125	Tomany Beg . .	200 2 4	Galway . .	Leitrim . .	Ballynakill .	Loughrea .	IV.	52
116	Tomany More . .	347 1 21	Galway . .	Leitrim . .	Ballynakill .	Loughrea .	IV.	52
116	Tomanynambraher .	101 0 6	Galway . .	Leitrim . .	Ballynakill .	Loughrea .	IV.	52
35	Tomard . . .	413 2 15	Kildare . .	Narragh and Reban West . . .	Kilberry . .	Athy . .	I.	68
6, 11	Tomard or Booly-rathornan . .	286 3 16	Carlow . .	Idrone West .	Tullowcreen .	Carlow . .	I.	9
6, 11, 12	Tomard Lower .	495 1 36e	Carlow . .	Idrone West .	Tullowcreen .	Carlow . .	I.	10
6, 11, 12	Tomard Upper .	596 1 6f	Carlow . .	Idrone West .	Tullowcreen .	Carlow . .	I.	10
10	Tomascotha . .	35 3 5	Kilkenny . .	Fassadinin .	Muckalee .	Castlecomer .	I.	91
10	Tomassan . .	135 2 25g	Cavan . .	Lower Loughtee .	Drumlane .	Cavan . .	III.	81
14	Tomatee . . .	208 3 22	Wexford . .	Scarawalsh . .	Templeshanbo .	Enniscorthy .	I.	326
2, 3	Tomathone Lower .	202 1 34	Wexford . .	Gorey . .	Kilnenor . .	Gorey . .	I.	320
2, 3	Tomathone Upper .	129 2 27	Wexford . .	Gorey . . .	Kilnenor . .	Gorey . .	I.	320
6	Tombay . . .	154 0 38	Wexford . .	Gorey . .	Kilnahue . .	Gorey . .	I.	319
4	Tombeagh . .	700 0 36	Carlow . .	Rathvilly . .	Hacketstown .	Shillelagh .	I.	11
62	Tomboholla . .	670 3 38h	Mayo . .	Costello . .	Kilbeagh . .	Swineford .	IV.	141
10, 15	Tombrack . .	478 0 5	Wexford . .	Scarawalsh . .	Ballycarney .	Enniscorthy .	I.	322
15	Tombrackwood .	200 2 29	Wexford . .	Scarawalsh . .	Ballycarney .	Enniscorthy .	I.	322
47	Tombreen . .	1,184 1 16	Wicklow . .	Shillelagh . .	Carnew . .	Shillelagh .	I.	357
9, 14, 15	Tombrick . .	877 1 18i	Wexford . .	Scarawalsh . .	Ballycarney .	Enniscorthy .	I.	322
7, 10	Tombrickane . .	1,284 2 15	Tipperary, N.R.	Lower Ormond .	Borrisokane .	Borrisokane .	II.	282
36	Tomcool . . .	49 2 36	Wexford . .	Shelmaliere West .	Coolstuff . .	Wexford .	I.	333
36	Tomcool Big . .	170 3 17	Wexford . .	Shelmaliere West .	Kilbrideglynn .	Wexford .	I.	334
36	Tomcool Little .	77 3 28	Wexford . .	Shelmaliere West .	Kilbrideglynn .	Wexford .	I.	334
2, 3	Tomcoyle . .	256 2 15	Wexford . .	Gorey . .	Kilnenor . .	Gorey . .	I.	320
11	Tomcoyle . .	156 2 7	Wexford . .	Gorey . .	Liskinfere .	Gorey . .	I.	321
39	Tomcoyle . .	464 0 5	Wicklow . .	Ballinacor South .	Preban . .	Shillelagh .	I.	350
2, 3	Tomcoylehill . .	137 1 32	Wexford . .	Gorey . . .	Kilnenor . .	Gorey . .	I.	320
18, 19	Tomcoyle Lower .	204 0 35	Wicklow . .	Newcastle . .	Killiskey . .	Rathdrum .	I.	352
18	Tomcoyle Upper .	128 0 39	Wicklow . .	Newcastle . .	Killiskey . .	Rathdrum .	I.	352
18	Tomdarragh . .	661 0 32	Wicklow . .	Ballinacor North .	Derrylossary .	Rathdrum .	I.	346
19, 22	Tomdarragh and Ballyellin . .	1,067 3 35j	Carlow . .	Idrone East .	Ballyellin . .	Carlow . .	I.	6

(a) Including 40A. 0R. 31P. water.
(b) Including 2A. 3R. 36P. water.
(c) Including 4A. 1R. 13P. water.
(d) Including 20A. 3R. 23P. water.

(e) Including 200A. 3R. 12P. detached portions.
(f) { Including 4A. 0R. 32P. River Barrow. / Including 9A. 3R. 38P. detached portion.
(g) Including 26A. 2R. 5P. water.

(h) Including 7A. 0R. 19P. water.
(i) Including 14A. 3R. 18P. water.
(j) Including 25A. 1R. 16P. River Barrow.

CENSUS OF IRELAND FOR THE YEAR 1851.

No. of Sheet of the Ordnance Survey Maps.	Townlands and Towns.	Area in Statute Acres.	County.	Barony.	Parish.	Poor Law Union in 1857.	Townland Census of 1851, Part I.	
		A. R. P.					Vol.	Page
10, 11	Tomdeely North	776 1 6	Limerick	Connello Lower	Tomdeely	Rathkeale	II.	230
10	Tomdeely South	306 2 1	Limerick	Connello Lower	Tomdeely	Rathkeale	II.	230
19,20,22,23	Tomduff	241 0 2	Carlow	Idrone East	Kiltennell	Carlow	I.	8
17	Tomduff	179 3 35	Wexford	Ballaghkeen	Killenagh	Gorey	I.	295
25, 26	Tomduff	134 1 31	Wexford	Bantry	St. John's	Enniscorthy	I.	302
27	Tome	176 0 24	Clare	Tulla Upper	Tulla	Tulla	II.	42
24,25,30,31	Tomfarney	724 1 22	Wexford	Bantry	Chapel	Enniscorthy	I.	299
31	Tomfarney Lower	182 2 23	Wexford	Bantry	Kilcowanmore	Enniscorthy	I.	300
31	Tomfarney Upper	282 0 24	Wexford	Bantry	Kilcowanmore	Enniscorthy	I.	300
11, 16	Tomgar	252 2 25	Wexford	Gorey	Ballycanew	Gorey	I.	316
21	Tomgarrow	247 1 2	Wexford	Ballaghkeen	Killincooly	Gorey	I.	295
21	Tomgarrow	45 0 26	Wexford	Ballaghkeen	Kilnamanagh	Gorey	I.	297
30,31,35,36	Tomgarrow	570 3 13	Wexford	Bantry	Adamstown	New Ross	I.	299
14, 15	Tomgarrow	490 3 14	Wexford	Scarawalsh	Ballycarney	Enniscorthy	I.	322
28	Tomgraney	421 1 29a	Clare	Tulla Upper	Tomgraney	Scarriff	II.	41
28	Tomgraney T.	—	Clare	Tulla Upper	Tomgraney	Scarriff	II.	41
47	Tomhaggard	230 2 16	Wexford	Bargy	Tomhaggard	Wexford	I.	308
66	Tomies East	136 1 12b	Kerry	Dunkerron North	Aghadoe	Killarney	II.	181
65, 66	Tomies West	252 2 24c	Kerry	Dunkerron North	Aghadoe	Killarney	II.	181
66	Tomies Wood	267 3 29	Kerry	Dunkerron North	Aghadoe	Killarney	II.	181
24, 25, 30	Tominearly	1,021 2 3	Wexford	Bantry	Killegney	Enniscorthy	I.	301
34	Tomiska	104 1 24	Monaghan	Farney	Magheracloone	Carrickmacross	III.	273
4	Tomisky	273 3 23	Longford	Longford	Mohill	Longford	I.	160
10, 14	Tomkinroad	146 1 15d	Cavan	Lower Loughtee	Drumlane	Cavan	III.	81
26, 32	Tomlane	189 3 37	Wexford	Ballaghkeen	Edermine	Enniscorthy	I.	294
24, 25	Tomloskan	203 2 21e	Leitrim	Carrigallen	Oughteragh	Bawnboy	IV.	93
61, 69	Tommyscroft or Craigs	143 0 4	Donegal	Raphoe	Convoy	Stranorlar	III.	136
16, 21	Tomnaboley Lower	301 0 10	Wexford	Gorey	Kilcormick	Enniscorthy	I.	317
16, 21	Tomnaboley Upper	107 0 15	Wexford	Gorey	Kilcormick	Enniscorthy	I.	317
43	Tomnafinnoge	537 2 35	Wicklow	Shillelagh	Carnew	Shillelagh	I.	357
20, 26	Tomnafunshoge	554 3 3	Wexford	Scarawalsh	Templeshannon	Enniscorthy	I.	326
25	Tomnahaha	231 0 27	Kilkenny	Gowran	Powerstown	Thomastown	I.	98
7	Tomnahealy	181 0 18	Wexford	Gorey	Kilcavan	Gorey	I.	317
7	Tomnahealy Little	94 2 15	Wexford	Gorey	Kilcavan	Gorey	I.	317
56, 57	Tomnahulla	617 2 1	Galway	Clare	Annaghdown	Tuam	IV.	16
20	Tomnakippeen	66 0 34	Wexford	Scarawalsh	Monart	Enniscorthy	I.	325
25, 26	Tomnalossett	219 3 31	Wexford	Bantry	St. John's	Enniscorthy	I.	302
17	Tomnamuck	176 0 7	Wexford	Ballaghkeen	Donaghmore	Gorey	I.	294
39	Tomnaskela	339 3 4	Wicklow	Ballinacor South	Kilpipe	Shillelagh	I.	349
12	Tomnaslough	69 2 29	Carlow	Idrone West	Wells	Carlow	I.	10
15	Tomnasock	329 3 36	Carlow	Idrone West	Oldleighlin	Carlow	I.	9
19	Tomoclavin	123 2 0	Queen's Co.	Stradbally	Tullomoy	Athy	I.	248
64	Tom of the Tae-End	22 1 3	Antrim	Upper Belfast	Shankill	Belfast	III.	10
15, 20	Tomogrow	257 2 32	Monaghan	Cremorne	Muckno	Castleblayney	III.	262
14	Tomona	111 3 18	Tipperary, N.R.	Lower Ormond	Monsea	Nenagh	II.	287
14, 19	Tomona	386 0 37	Wexford	Scarawalsh	Templeshanbo	Enniscorthy	I.	326
45	Tomree	595 1 10f	Galway	Tiaquin	Moylough	Mountbellew	IV.	80
18, 24	Tomriland	1,321 2 27	Wicklow	Ballinacor North	Derrylossary	Rathdrum	I.	346
7	Tomrud	209 2 36	Leitrim	Rosclogher	Killasnet	Manorhamilton	IV.	110
15, 20	Tomsallagh	1,049 1 23	Wexford	Scarawalsh	Clone	Enniscorthy	I.	322
12	Tomsilla Lower	213 3 14	Wexford	Ballaghkeen	Kiltennell	Gorey	I.	297
12	Tomsilla Upper	250 0 39	Wexford	Ballaghkeen	Kiltennell	Gorey	I.	297
10	Tom's Island	6 0 7	Fermanagh	Lurg	Magheraculmoney	Lowtherstown	III.	208
81, 82, 93	Tonabrocky	435 2 33g	Galway	Galway	Rahoon	Galway	IV.	38
112	Tonabuska	47 3 28	Cork, E.R.	Kinalea	Kinure	Kinsale	II.	96
100	Tonacartron	77 0 13	Mayo	Kilmaine	Mayo	Ballinrobe	IV.	157
28, 42	Tonacooleen	378 2 8	Galway	Clare	Donaghpatrick	Tuam	IV.	19
90	Tonacrick	101 1 25	Galway	Moycullen	Kilcummin	Galway	IV.	68
47	Tonacrock	319 3 15	Mayo	Tirawley	Addergoole	Castlebar	IV.	163
46	Tonacurra	305 3 35	Galway	Killian	Killian	Mountbellew	IV.	45
81, 82	Tonacurragh	316 0 37½	Galway	Galway	Oranmore	Galway	IV.	37
89	Tonaderrew	229 0 28	Mayo	Carra	Ballintober	Castlebar	IV.	125
9	Tonadooravaun	259 3 7	Galway	Ballynahinch	Ballynakill	Clifden	IV.	12
9, 14	Tonafarna	263 2 5	Queen's Co.	Stradbally	Moyanna	Athy	I.	247
107	Tonafora	169 3 15	Cork, W.R.	East Carbery (W.D.)	Fanlobbus	Dunmanway	II.	132
120, 133	Tonafora	83 0 19	Cork, W.R.	West Carbery (E.D.)	Dromdaleague	Skibbereen	II.	140
14, 20	Tonafortes	86 0 4	Sligo	Carbury	St. Johns	Sligo	IV.	223
69	Tonagarraun	546 2 16	Galway	Clare	Annaghdown	Galway	IV.	16
64, 68	Tonagh	240 0 27	Antrim	Upper Massereene	Blaris	Lisburn	III.	30
42	Tonagh	374 1 23	Cavan	Clanmahon	Kilbride	Oldcastle	III.	78
15	Tonagh	163 1 17i	Cavan	Upper Loughtec	Castleterra	Cavan	III.	83
55	Tonagh	554 1 12	Donegal	Raphoe	Taughboyne	Londonderry	III.	144

(a) Including 3A. 3R. 3P. water.
(b) Including 2A. 2R. 16P. water.
(c) Including 2A. 2R. 16P. water.

(d) Including 36A. 2R. 24P. water.
(e) Including 57A. 1R. 26P. water.
(f) Including 1A. 3R. 24P. water.

(g) Including 6A. 3R. 35P. water.
(h) Including 63A. 2R. 12P. water.
(i) Including 6A. 1R. 18P. water

No. of Sheet of the Ordnance Survey Maps.	Townlands and Towns.	Area in Statute Acres.	County.	Barony.	Parish.	Poor Law Union in 1857.	Townland Census of 1851, Part I.	
							Vol.	Page
		A. R. P.						
42	Tonagh . . .	33 3 39	King's Co. .	Clonlisk . . .	Kilmurryely .	Roscrea . . .	I.	131
14	Tonagh . . .	258 2 20	Monaghan .	Cremorne . .	Clontibret . .	Castleblayney .	III.	261
18	Tonagh . . .	251 1 23	Monaghan .	Dartree . .	Aghabog . .	Cootehill . .	III.	264
15, 22	Tonagh . . .	446 2 33*c*	Westmeath .	Kilkenny West .	Kilkenny West .	Athlone . .	I.	273
17	Tonaghbane . .	274 2 39*b*	Cavan . .	Tullygarvey .	Kildrumsherdan .	Cootehill . .	III.	90
32, 33	Tonagh Glebe . .	59 2 10	Fermanagh .	Clanawley . .	Kinawley . .	Enniskillen .	III.	194
15,16,22,23	Tonaghmore . .	1,043 3 9*c*	Down . .	Castlereagh Upper .	Saintfield . .	Lisburn . .	III.	166
27	Tonaghmore . .	594 1 10*d*	Down . .	Lower Iveagh, Lr. pt.	Magherally .	Banbridge . .	III.	168
1, 3, 4	Tonaghmore and Hammondstown .	546 0 36	Westmeath .	Fore . . .	St. Feighins .	Castletowndelvin	I.	272
40	Tonaght . . .	325 3 11	Londonderry .	Loughinsholin .	Ballynascreen .	Magherafelt .	III.	239
22	Tonagimsy . .	118 2 11*e*	Monaghan .	Dartree . .	Ematris . .	Cootehill . .	III.	267
3, 13	Tonaglanna . .	480 1 22	Galway . .	Ross . . .	Ballinrobe .	Ballinrobe .	IV.	72
36	Tonakilly . .	47 2 35	Kerry . .	Corkaguiny .	Kilgobban . .	Tralee . .	II.	177
15	Tonaknick . .	36 3 25	Roscommon .	Frenchpark .	Kilcolagh . .	Boyle . .	IV.	203
15, 21	Tonaknock . .	222 1 30	Kerry . .	Clanmaurice .	Killahan . .	Tralee . .	II.	170
120, 121	Tonaleeaun . .	69 1 2	Mayo . .	Kilmaine . .	Cong . . .	Ballinrobe .	IV.	154
53, 54	Tonalig . . .	464 3 28	Roscommon .	Moycarn . .	Creagh . .	Ballinasloe .	IV.	206
19	Tonaloy . . .	327 0 34	Cavan . .	Tullyhunco .	Kildallan .	Bawnboy . .	III.	97
56, 69	Tonamace . .	241 2 34	Galway . .	Clare . . .	Annaghdown .	Galway . .	IV.	16
57	Tonamace . .	108 3 39	Galway . .	Clare . . .	Kilmoylan .	Tuam . .	IV.	22
9	Tonamace . .	216 3 12	Mayo . .	Erris . . .	Kilmore . .	Belmullet .	IV.	146
9	Tonamace Common	18 1 14	Mayo . .	Erris . . .	Kilmore . .	Belmullet .	IV.	146
20	Tonamaddy . .	78 2 39	Galway . .	Ballymoe .	Kilbegnet .	Roscommon .	IV.	8
30	Tonaneeve . .	309 0 14	Monaghan .	Farney . .	Magheracloone .	Carrickmacross	III.	273
6	Tonanilt . . .	31 1 18	Cavan . .	Tullyhaw .	Kinawley . .	Enniskillen .	III.	93
14	Tonanoran . .	110 1 17	Fermanagh .	Magheraboy .	Devenish . .	Ballyshannon .	III.	211
38	Tonaphort . .	238 3 24	Westmeath .	Moycashel .	Kilbeggan .	Tullamore .	I.	278
14	Tonaphubble . .	111 0 13	Sligo . .	Carbury . .	St. Johns . .	Sligo . .	IV.	223
24	Tonaphuca or Flemingtown South .	448 0 1	Kildare . .	Naas South .	Killashee . .	Naas . .	I.	65
39, 40	Tonaponra . .	106 0 23	Sligo . .	Corran . .	Toomour . .	Boyle . .	IV.	228
76	Tonaraha East .	29 3 30	Mayo . .	Burrishoole .	Kilmeena .	Westport . .	IV.	122
76	Tonaraha West .	69 0 29	Mayo . .	Burrishoole .	Kilmeena .	Westport . .	IV.	122
26	Tonardrum . .	93 0 19	Fermanagh .	Clanawley .	Cleenish . .	Enniskillen .	III.	191
33	Tonaree . . .	64 3 5	Limerick . .	Coonagh . .	Templebredon .	Tipperary .	II.	236
105	Tonaroasty . .	58 3 30	Galway . .	Loughrea .	Loughrea .	Loughrea . .	IV.	66
2, 5	Tonarussa . .	259 0 31	Clare . .	Burren . .	Drumcreehy .	Ballyvaghan .	II.	12
1, 3, 4	Tonashammer .	539 1 3*f*	Westmeath .	Fore . . .	St. Feighins .	Castletowndelvin	I.	272
43, 55	Tonatanvally . .	2,068 1 14*g*	Mayo . .	Burrishoole .	Achill . .	Newport . .	IV.	117
115	Tonatleva . .	954 3 36	Mayo . .	Murrisk . .	Kilgeever . .	Westport . .	IV.	160
28	Tonavally . .	85 2 15	Fermanagh .	Magherastephana .	Aghavea . .	Lisnaskea .	III.	219
29, 38	Tonavane . .	1,270 1 26	Kerry . .	Trughanacmy .	Annagh . .	Tralee . .	II.	205
68	Tonavoher . .	531 0 15	Clare . .	Clonderalaw .	Killimer . .	Kilrush . .	II.	118
8	Tonbane Glebe .	143 2 12	Donegal .	Kilmacrenan .	Clondavaddog .	Milford . .	III.	125
105	Tonbaun . .	108 0 39	Galway . .	Dunkellin .	Kilconickny .	Loughrea .	IV.	29
21, 22	Tonbaun . .	115 1 38	Limerick . .	Pubblebrien .	Crecora . .	Croom . .	II.	252
89	Tonbaun . .	47 2 17	Mayo . .	Carra . . .	Ballintober .	Castlebar .	IV.	125
28	Tonbaun . .	294 2 27	Roscommon .	Ballymoe .	Cloonygormican .	Castlereagh .	IV.	191
40	Tonbwee . .	127 2 14	Kerry . .	Trughanacmy .	Castleisland .	Tralee* . .	II.	209
3	Tonduff . . .	207 1 1	Antrim . .	Cary . . .	Billy . .	Ballycastle .	III.	13
10, 18, 19	Tonduff . . .	699 3 2*h*	Donegal .	Inishowen West .	Desertegney .	Inishowen .	III.	120
76, 77	Tonduff . . .	290 0 2	Donegal .	Raphoe . .	Kilteevoge .	Stranorlar .	III.	140
23, 24	Tonduff . . .	704 1 9	Queen's Co. .	Cullenagh .	Abbeyleix .	Abbeyleix .	I.	238
3	Tonduff Mountain .	156 3 1	Antrim . .	Cary . . .	Billy . .	Ballycastle .	III.	13
67, 68, 77	Tonduff (*Thompson*)	207 3 28	Donegal .	Raphoe . .	Kilteevoge .	Stranorlar .	III.	140
120	Toneagh . . .	247 1 12	Cork, W.R. .	West Carbery (E.D.)	Dromdaleague .	Skibbereen .	II.	140
22	Toneduff . .	503 3 20	Londonderry .	Tirkeeran .	Cumber Lower .	Londonderry .	III.	249
20, 21	Toneel North .	184 0 19	Fermanagh .	Magheraboy .	Boho . .	Enniskillen .	III.	210
21	Toneel South .	36 2 0	Fermanagh .	Clanawley .	Boho . .	Enniskillen .	III.	189
11, 16	Toneen . . .	181 1 20	Longford .	Granard . .	Granard . .	Granard . .	I.	157
18, 19	Toneen . . .	215 3 30	Longford .	Moydow . .	Moydow . .	Longford .	I.	162
36, 44	Tonegan . .	396 3 13	Tyrone . .	Omagh East .	Termonmaguirk .	Omagh . .	III.	315
27	Tonereagh . .	82 3 30	Roscommon .	Castlereagh .	Baslick . .	Castlereagh .	IV.	199
34	Toney . . .	46 2 31	Fermanagh .	Magherastephana .	Aghalurcher .	Lisnaskea .	III.	217
18	Tonguefield . .	4 1 25	Dublin . .	Uppercross .	Crumlin . .	Dublin South .	I.	40
3	Tonintlieve . .	175 0 23	Monaghan .	Trough . .	Errigal Trough .	Clogher . .	III.	285
13, 14	Toniscoffy . .	441 3 8	Monaghan .	Monaghan .	Monaghan .	Monaghan .	III.	277
35, 36	Tonity Bog . .	51 1 27	Fermanagh .	Clankelly .	Clones . .	Clones . .	III.	197
35, 40	Tonitygorman .	146 2 36	Fermanagh .	Clankelly .	Clones . .	Clones . .	III.	197
9	Tonlegee . .	135 0 16	Cavan . .	Tullyhaw .	Templeport .	Bawnboy . .	III.	95
49, 59	Tonlegee . .	564 2 1	Clare . .	Clonderalaw .	Kilchreest .	Killadysert .	II.	15
24	Tonlegee . .	20 0 12	Clare . .	Inchiquin .	Rath . . .	Corrofin . .	II.	28

(*a*) Including 1A. 0R. 8P. water.
(*b*) Including 7A. 3R. 0P. water.
(*c*) Including 13A. 1R. 4P. water.

(*d*) Including 6A. 2R. 30P. water.
(*e*) Including 5A. 0R. 37P. water.
(*f*) Including 13A. 1R. 3P. water.

(*g*) Including 167A. 3R. 10P. water.
(*h*) Including 1A. 3R. 0P. detached portion.

No. of Sheet of the Ordnance Survey Maps.	Townlands and Towns.	Area in Statute Acres.	County.	Barony.	Parish.	Poor Law Union in 1857.	Townland Census of 1851, Part I.	
		A. R. P.					Vol.	Page
17	Tonlegee	51 1 2a	Clare	Inchiquin	Ruan	Corrofin	II.	28
15	Tonlegee	242 3 30	Dublin	Coolock	Coolock	Dublin North	I.	27
11	Tonlegee	80 1 0	Dublin	Nethercross	Swords	Balrothery	I.	32
29	Tonlegee	117 3 14	Galway	Dunmore	Kilbennan	Tuam	IV.	34
26	Tonlegee	343 0 33	Galway	Ross	Ross	Oughterard	IV.	74
35	Tonlegee	71 1 26	Kildare	Narragh&Reban West	St. Johns	Athy	I.	68
12, 16	Tonlegee	844 2 36b	Leitrim	Drumahaire	Inishmagrath	Manorhamilton	IV.	97
12	Tonlegee	98 1 2c	Limerick	Kenry	Kildimo	Rathkeale	II.	250
98, 99	Tonlegee	755 2 1d	Mayo	Burrishoole	Aghagower	Westport	IV.	118
35	Tonlegee	744 1 12	Roscommon	Ballintober South	Kilbride	Roscommon	IV.	189
40	Tonlegee	369 1 7	Roscommon	Ballintober South	Kilteevan	Roscommon	IV.	190
16	Tonlegee	76 0 38	Westmeath	Kilkenny West	Noughaval	Ballymahon	I.	274
36	Tonlegee	112 3 8	Wicklow	Arklow	Dunganstown	Rathdrum	I.	344
33	Tonlegee or Moorerow	297 1 31	Westmeath	Fartullagh	Kilbride	Mullingar	I.	268
22	Tonlemone	505 2 20	King's Co.	Garrycastle	Gallen	Parsonstown	I.	136
53, 54	Tonlemone	147 0 2	Roscommon	Moycarn	Creagh	Ballinasloe	IV.	206
17	Tonlemony	104 2 25	Westmeath	Rathconrath	Templepatrick	Ballymahon	I.	284
21	Tonlisderritt	203 3 4	Fermanagh	Clanawley	Cleenish	Enniskillen	III.	191
9, 10	Tonmore	297 3 4	Mayo	Erris	Kilmore	Belmullet	IV.	146
16	Tonmoyle	445 3 26	Galway	Dunmore	Tuam	Tuam	IV.	36
34	Tonnaboy	163 2 18	Fermanagh	Clankelly	Galloon	Lisnaskea	III.	198
33	Tonnacroob	51 0 2	Fermanagh	Knockninny	Kinawley	Lisnaskea	III.	202
11	Tonnagh	218 1 15	Armagh	Armagh	Eglish	Armagh	III.	44
14, 15	Tonnagh	376 1 33	Fermanagh	Magheraboy	Inishmacsaint	Ballyshannon	III.	213
27, 31	Tonnagh	86 1 16e	Leitrim	Leitrim	Kiltoghert	Cark. on Shannon	IV.	103
51, 63	Tonnagh	499 1 27	Mayo	Costello	Kilbeagh	Swineford	IV.	141
22	Tonnagh	59 0 4	Monaghan	Dartree	Ematris	Cootehill	III.	267
50	Tonnaghbane	38 3 39	Tyrone	Clogher	Donacavey	Omagh	III.	294
50	Tonnagh Beg	227 0 33	Tyrone	Clogher	Donacavey	Omagh	III.	294
30, 36	Tonnaghboy	144 2 37	Fermanagh	Clankelly	Clones	Clones	III.	197
50	Tonnagh More	317 1 17	Tyrone	Omagh East	Donacavey	Omagh	III.	310
133	Tonranny	102 3 18f	Galway	Kiltartan	Beagh	Gort	IV.	46
88	Tonranny	178 0 28	Mayo	Murrisk	Aghagower	Westport	IV.	159
133	Tonranny Mountain	58 2 31	Galway	Kiltartan	Beagh	Gort	IV.	46
47	Tonreagh	163 1 21	Kerry	Trughanacmy	Kiltallagh	Tralee	II.	212
29, 30	Tonreagh Lower	157 0 2	Kerry	Trughanacmy	Ballymacelligott	Tralee	II.	207
29, 30	Tonreagh Upper	137 0 6	Kerry	Trughanacmy	Ballymacelligott	Tralee	II.	207
21	Tonree	97 3 24	Mayo	Tirawley	Moygawnagh	Killala	IV.	171
92, 98	Tonregee	226 2 36	Donegal	Banagh	Inver	Donegal	III.	108
107	Tonregee	65 2 4	Donegal	Tirhugh	Kilbarron	Ballyshannon	III.	148
103	Tonregee	372 0 29	Mayo	Costello	Annagh	Claremorris	IV.	138
64	Tonregee	346 0 38	Mayo	Costello	Kilcolman	Castlereagh	IV.	141
55, 56	Tonregee East	762 1 20g	Mayo	Burrishoole	Achill	Newport	IV.	117
33	Tonregee Island	3 2 23	Fermanagh	Tirkennedy	Cleenish	Lisnaskea	III.	220
55	Tonregee West	566 0 13	Mayo	Burrishoole	Achill	Newport	IV.	117
30	Tonrevagh	291 2 29	Galway	Dunmore	Tuam	Tuam	IV.	36
20, 21	Tonrevagh	167 0 4	Roscommon	Castlereagh	Kilkeevin	Castlereagh	IV.	201
42	Tonroe	196 0 1	Galway	Clare	Kilkilvery	Tuam	IV.	20
103, 104, 113, 114	Tonroe	209 1 36	Galway	Dunkellin	Ardrahan	Gort	IV.	27
95	Tonroe	682 0 36	Galway	Dunkellin	Ballynacourty	Galway	IV.	27
116	Tonroe	291 0 29	Galway	Leitrim	Ballynakill	Loughrea	IV.	52
63	Tonroe	240 3 15	Mayo	Costello	Kilbeagh	Swineford	IV.	141
71	Tonroe	65 0 6	Mayo	Gallen	Kilconduff	Swineford	IV.	148
21, 22, 27	Tonroe	211 2 38	Roscommon	Castlereagh	Baslick	Castlereagh	IV.	199
9	Tonroe or Creen	306 2 22	Roscommon	Frenchpark	Kilnamanagh	Boyle	IV.	204
9	Tonroe or Feenagh	217 3 35	Roscommon	Frenchpark	Kilnamanagh	Boyle	IV.	204
14, 21	Tonroe Lower	125 3 29	Mayo	Tirawley	Rathreagh	Killala	IV.	171
14, 21	Tonroe Upper	108 0 27	Mayo	Tirawley	Rathreagh	Killala	IV.	171
23	Tonteere	228 2 8	Limerick	Clanwilliam	Ballybrood	Limerick	II.	221
38	Tonteheige	160 2 31	Waterford	Decies within Drum	Lisgenan or Grange	Youghal	II.	352
54	Tonvey	298 0 15	Roscommon	Moycarn	Moore	Ballinasloe	IV.	207
54	Tonwee	66 3 5	Galway	Moycullen	Kilcummin	Oughterard	IV.	68
54	Tonweeroe	49 0 34	Galway	Moycullen	Kilcummin	Oughterard	IV.	68
2	Tonwore	290 1 18	Fermanagh	Lurg	Drumkeeran	Lowtherstown	III.	207
14	Tonyarraher	136 1 39	Cavan	Lower Loughtee	Drumlane	Cavan	III.	81
39, 48	Tonybaun	293 3 11h	Mayo	Tirawley	Ballynahaglish	Ballina	IV.	164
5, 6	Tonyclea	588 2 11	Monaghan	Monaghan	Tedavnet	Monaghan	III.	280
21	Tonyconnelly	158 3 0	Cavan	Tullygarvey	Larah	Cootehill	III.	91
6	Tonycoogan	107 1 8	Monaghan	Trough	Donagh	Monaghan	III.	283
6, 7	Tonycrom or Monydoo	444 3 35	Cavan	Tullyhaw	Kinawley	Bawnboy	III.	93
29	Tonycurneen	66 1 33	Roscommon	Roscommon	Lissonuffy	Strokestown	IV.	212
35	Tonydrummallard	76 3 35	Fermanagh	Clankelly	Clones	Clones	III.	197

(a) Including 15A. 0R. 18P. water.
(b) Including 16A. 0R. 27P. water.
(c) Including 20A. 1R. 17P. water.
(d) Including 29A. 0R. 3P. water.
(e) Including 1A. 0R. 3P. water.
(f) Including 0A. 3R. 17P. water.
(g) Including 4A. 1R. 19P. water.
(h) Including 11A. 0R. 30P. water.

No. of Sheet of the Ordnance Survey Maps.	Townlands and Towns.	Area in Statute Acres.			County.	Barony.	Parish.	Poor Law Union in 1857.	Townland Census of 1851, Part I.	
		A.	R.	P.					Vol.	Page
27	Tonyduff	414	2	21	Cavan	Clankee	Knockbride	Cootehill	III.	74
28	Tonyellida	125	2	2	Monaghan	Farney	Donaghmoyne	Carrickmacross	III.	271
6	Tonyfinnigan	185	1	21	Monaghan	Trough	Donagh	Monaghan	III.	283
3	Tonyfohanan	84	3	13	Monaghan	Trough	Errigal Trough	Monaghan	III.	285
27, 33	Tonyfoyle	440	0	21	Cavan	Clankee	Knockbride	Bailieborough	III.	74
3, 7	Tonygarrow	685	2	20	Wicklow	Rathdown	Powerscourt	Rathdown	I.	356
6	Tonygarvey	114	3	10	Monaghan	Trough	Donagh	Monaghan	III.	283
17	Tonyglaskan	524	0	33	Fermanagh	Tirkennedy	Enniskillen	Enniskillen	III.	222
19	Tonyglassan	220	0	23a	Monaghan	Cremorne	Ballybay	Castleblayney	III.	259
19	Tonyglassan	128	0	3	Monaghan	Cremorne	Clontibret	Castleblayney	III.	261
47	Tonyhabboc	94	3	12	Donegal	Raphoe	Allsaints	Londonderry	III.	134
9, 13	Tonyhallagh	37	3	3	Cavan	Tullyhaw	Templeport	Bawnboy	III.	95
7	Tonyhamigan	74	1	19b	Monaghan	Trough	Donagh	Monaghan	III.	283
22	Tonyhull	226	1	36	Cavan	Clankee	Drumgoon	Cootehill	III.	72
17, 22	Tonyin	269	2	25c	Cavan	Tullygarvey	Kildrumsherdan	Cootehill	III.	90
31,32,37,38	Tonylion	127	3	38	Cavan	Castlerahan	Crosserlough	Cavan	III.	68
27	Tonyloman	253	0	25d	Fermanagh	Clanawley	Cleenish	Enniskillen	III.	191
17, 22	Tonymacgilduff	159	0	24	Cavan	Tullygarvey	Kildrumsherdan	Cootehill	III.	90
27	Tonymalloe	77	3	33e	Fermanagh	Tirkennedy	Cleenish	Enniskillen	III.	220
20, 25	Tonymore	405	0	25f	Cavan	Upper Loughtee	Kilmore	Cavan	III.	85
42	Tonymore	149	1	6g	Fermanagh	Knockninny	Kinawley	Lisnaskea	III.	202
38, 41	Tonymore	443	2	5	Fermanagh	Knockninny	Tomregan	Lisnaskea	III.	203
11	Tonymore North	211	3	12	Longford	Granard	Abbeylara	Granard	I.	154
11	Tonymore South	463	2	37	Longford	Granard	Abbeylara	Granard	I.	154
38	Tonynelt	114	0	11	Fermanagh	Knockninny	Kinawley	Lisnaskea	III.	202
6	Tonynumery	87	2	0	Monaghan	Trough	Errigal Trough	Monaghan	III.	285
1	Tonyowen Lower	157	0	28	Westmeath	Fore	Foyran	Granard	I.	270
1, 3	Tonyowen Upper	196	1	6	Westmeath	Fore	Foyran	Granard	I.	270
7	Tonyquin	29	3	31	Cavan	Tullyhaw	Kinawley	Bawnboy	III.	93
13	Tonyrevan	55	0	27	Cavan	Tullyhaw	Templeport	Bawnboy	III.	95
19	Tonyscallan	172	3	13h	Monaghan	Cremorne	Clontibret	Castleblayney	III.	261
4, 7	Tonyshandeny	106	3	4	Monaghan	Trough	Donagh	Monaghan	III.	283
6	Tonysillogagh	145	2	23	Monaghan	Trough	Donagh	Monaghan	III.	283
5	Tonystackan	252	1	30	Monaghan	Monaghan	Tedavnet	Monaghan	III.	280
22	Tonystick	146	3	4i	Fermanagh	Tirkennedy	Enniskillen	Enniskillen	III.	222
22	Tonytallagh	135	0	24j	Monaghan	Dartree	Currin	Cootehill	III.	266
27	Tonyteige	200	1	28	Fermanagh	Clanawley	Cleenish	Enniskillen	III.	191
38	Tonyvarnog	206	2	27	Fermanagh	Knockninny	Kinawley	Lisnaskea	III.	202
33, 38	Tonywall	154	3	14	Fermanagh	Knockninny	Kinawley	Lisnaskea	III.	202
10, 15	Tonywardan	559	3	21	Longford	Granard	Granard	Granard	I.	157
27	Tooa	284	2	4	Monaghan	Cremorne	Aghnamullen	Castleblayney	III.	258
64, 74	Toobrackan	744	2	34	Mayo	Costello	Kilcolman	Castlereagh	IV.	141
71, 80	Toocananagh	1,266	0	33	Mayo	Gallen	Bohola	Swineford	IV.	147
10	Toohana	276	0	29	Kerry	Iraghticonnor	Ballyconry	Listowel	II.	190
10, 11	Toolestown	186	0	25	Kildare	North Salt	Taghadoe	Celbridge	I.	76
15, 21	Toolestown	214	1	3	Wicklow	Upper Talbotstown	Freynestown	Baltinglass	I.	364
28	Toolinn	74	1	31	Fermanagh	Magherastephana	Aghavea	Lisnaskea	III.	219
97	Tooloobaunbeg	454	0	33	Galway	Loughrea	Lickerrig	Loughrea	IV.	65
97	Tooloobauntemple	244	1	25	Galway	Athenry	Kilconickny	Loughrea	IV.	4
69	Tooloone	127	2	33	Tipperary, S.R.	Middlethird	Knockgraffon	Cashel	II.	328
12	Tooloscan	149	0	38	Roscommon	Ballintober North	Kilmore	Car\k. on Shannon	IV.	187
108	Toom	474	3	35	Cork, W.R.	East Carbery (W.D.)	Fanlobbus	Dunmanway	II.	132
20	Toom	152	2	19	Wexford	Scarawalsh	Clone	Enniscorthy	I.	322
29, 33	Tooma	240	0	11	Leitrim	Mohill	Cloone	Mohill	IV.	106
16, 25	Toomaline Lower	495	1	6	Limerick	Coonagh	Doon	Tipperary	II.	234
16	Toomaline Upper	276	2	16	Limerick	Coonagh	Doon	Tipperary	II.	234
4	Tooman	231	0	23k	Dublin	Balrothery East	Lusk	Balrothery	I.	21
36, 38	Tooman	907	0	17	Leitrim	Mohill	Cloone	Mohill	IV.	106
13	Tooman	101	3	20	Wicklow	Newcastle	Kilcoole	Rathdrum	I.	352
74	Toomanagh	151	0	30	Mayo	Costello	Castlemore	Castlereagh	IV.	140
24, 28	Toomans	320	0	15l	Leitrim	Leitrim	Kiltubbrid	Car\k. on Shannon	IV.	104
32	Toomard	253	2	29m	Galway	Killian	Killian	Mountbellew	IV.	45
50	Toombeola	461	3	14n	Galway	Ballynahinch	Moyrus	Clifden	IV.	13
42, 48	Toome	180	0	27	Antrim	Upper Toome	Duneane	Ballymena	III.	35
65	Toome	541	3	38o	Donegal	Boylagh	Lettermacward	Glenties	III.	114
8	Toome	357	3	3p	Donegal	Kilmacrenan	Clondavaddog	Millford	III.	125
30	Toome	332	2	10	Leitrim	Carrigallen	Drumreilly	Bawnboy	IV.	91
6, 7	Toome	557	3	4	Longford	Granard	Columbkille	Granard	I.	156
23, 27	Toome	307	1	36	Longford	Shrule	Taghshinny	Ballymahon	I.	167
19, 24	Toome	216	1	26q	Monaghan	Cremorne	Clontibret	Castleblayney	III.	261
25	Toome	257	2	12r	Monaghan	Farney	Donaghmoyne	Castleblayney	III.	271
11	Toomes	344	0	21	Louth	Louth	Louth	Dundalk	I.	184
42	Toome T.	—			Antrim	Upper Toome	Duneane	Ballymena	III.	35

No. of Sheet of the Ordnance Survey Maps.	Townlands and Towns.	Area in Statute Acres.	County.	Barony.	Parish.	Poor Law Union in 1857.	Townland Census of 1851, Part I.	
		A. R. P.					Vol.	Page
45, 46, 53	Toomog . . .	217 0 27	Tyrone . .	Dungannon Middle .	Donaghmore . .	Dungannon .	III.	302
22, 28	Toomona . .	300 0 4	Roscommon .	Roscommon . .	Ogulla . . .	Strokestown .	IV.	212
61	Toomore . .	302 2 30a	Mayo . . .	Gallen . . .	Toomore . .	Swineford .	IV.	151
17	Toomore . .	456 0 0b	Roscommon .	Roscommon . .	Aughrim . .	Cark. on Shannon	IV.	207
40	Toomour . .	508 1 16	Sligo . .	Corran . . .	Toomour . .	Boyle . .	IV.	228
70, 71	Toomsbeg . .	128 2 8	Cork, W.R. .	West Muskerry .	Macloneigh .	Macroom .	II.	160
71, 83	Tooms East . .	609 0 12	Cork, W.R. .	West Muskerry .	Macloneigh .	Macroom .	II.	160
70,71,82,83	Tooms West .	592 3 11	Cork, W.R. .	West Muskerry .	Macloneigh .	Macroom .	II.	160
8	Toomullin . .	127 2 36	Clare . .	Corcomroe .	Killilagh .	Ennistimon .	II.	20
22	Toomyvara T. .	—	Tipperary, N.R.	Upper Ormond .	Aghnameadle .	Nenagh .	II.	289
70, 80	Toon . . .	253 3 1	Kerry . .	Iveragh . .	Killinane .	Cahersiveen .	II.	197
34, 35	Toonagh . .	710 0 36	Clare . .	Bunratty Upper .	Clooney . .	Tulla . .	II.	8
25	Toonagh . .	232 2 15	Clare . .	Inchiquin . .	Dysert . .	Ennis . .	II.	24
25	Toonagh Commons .	74 1 17	Clare . .	Inchiquin . .	Dysert . .	Ennis . .	II.	24
58, 69	Toonlane . .	254 1 17	Cork, W.R. .	West Muskerry .	Ballyvourney .	Macroom .	II.	154
23	Toor . . .	397 0 37	Clare . .	Ibrickan . .	Kilfarboy .	Ennistimon .	II.	22
20, 28	Toor . . .	716 3 31	Cork, E.R. .	Condons&Clangibbon	Kilworth .	Fermoy .	II.	62
146, 147	Toor . . .	213 1 25	Cork, W.R. .	West Carbery (W.D.)	Kilmoe . .	Skull . .	II.	145
17	Toor . . .	599 0 6	Kerry . .	Clanmaurice .	Duagh . .	Listowel .	II.	168
98, 106	Toor . . .	213 3 20	Kerry . .	Dunkerron South .	Kilcrohane .	Cahersiveen .	II.	184
56	Toor . . .	492 2 24	Limerick . .	Coshlea . .	Particles . .	Kilmallock .	II.	241
46	Toor . . .	468 1 12	Meath . .	Upper Moyfenrath .	Castlejordan .	Edenderry .	I.	212
41	Toor . . .	48 0 25	Tipperary, N.R.	Eliogarty . .	Thurles . .	Thurles .	II.	273
20	Toor . . .	52 2 17	Tipperary, N.R.	Owney and Arra .	Youghalarra .	Nenagh .	II.	298
66	Toor . . .	275 3 2	Tipperary, S.R.	Clanwilliam . .	Bruis . .	Tipperary .	II.	305
71, 78	Toor . . .	1,026 1 27	Tipperary, S.R.	Iffa and Offa East .	Kilcash . .	Clonmel .	II.	313
19	Toor . . .	209 1 19	Waterford .	Coshmore&Coshbride	Lismore and Mocollop	Lismore .	II.	347
35, 38	Toor . . .	211 3 14	Waterford .	Decies within Drum	Lisgenan or Grange	Youghal .	II.	352
22	Toor . . .	67 2 37	Waterford .	Decies without Drum	Modelligo .	Lismore .	II.	359
2	Toor . . .	367 3 5	Waterford .	Upperthird . .	Dysert . .	Clonmel .	II.	369
15, 16	Toor . . .	1,012 0 10	Wicklow .	Lower Talbotstown .	Hollywood .	Baltinglass .	I.	361
41	Toora . . .	930 2 36	King's Co. .	Clonlisk . .	Shinrone .	Roscrea .	II.	131
14	Tooracappul .	21 1 13	Mayo . . .	Tirawley . .	Templemurry .	Killala .	IV.	172
71, 81	Tooracladane .	1,481 0 27	Kerry . .	Iveragh . .	Dromod . .	Cahersiveen .	II.	195
5	Tooracurragh .	206 0 16	Waterford .	Glenahiry . .	Kilronan .	Clonmel .	II.	366
34, 35	Tooradoo . .	509 1 12	Limerick . .	Shanid . . .	Rathronan .	Newcastle .	II.	257
20	Tooradoo . .	124 3 6	Waterford .	Coshmore&Coshbride	Lismore and Mocollop	Lismore .	II.	347
5	Toorala . .	194 0 39	Waterford .	Glenahiry . .	Kilronan .	Clonmel .	II.	366
57	Tooraleagan .	250 2 32	Limerick . .	Coshlea . .	Ballylanders .	Mitchelstown .	II.	237
12	Tooranaraheen .	955 1 10	Waterford .	Coshmore&Coshbride	Lismore and Mocollop	Lismore .	II.	347
13	Tooraneena .	318 1 30	Waterford .	Decies without Drum	Seskinan .	Dungarvan .	II.	360
14, 15	Toorard . .	922 3 16	Cork, E.R. .	Duhallow . .	Clonfert . .	Kanturk .	II.	69
49	Toorard . .	114 0 12	Mayo . . .	Gallen . . .	Killasser .	Swineford .	IV.	149
123	Toorard . .	408 3 9	Mayo . . .	Kilmaine . .	Shrule . .	Ballinrobe .	IV.	158
19	Toorard . .	65 3 11	Sligo . .	Tireragh . .	Dromard .	Dromore West .	IV.	233
93	Tooraree . .	401 2 7c	Mayo . . .	Costello . .	Bekan . .	Claremorris .	IV.	139
18, 27	Tooraree Lower	907 3 1	Limerick . .	Shanid . . .	Kilfergus .	Glin . .	II.	256
18, 27	Tooraree Upper	621 0 20	Limerick . .	Shanid . . .	Kilfergus .	Glin . .	II.	256
23, 35, 36	Tooraskeheen .	715 0 16	Galway .	Ballynahinch .	Omey . .	Clifden .	IV.	15
32	Toorataggart .	144 1 0	Tipperary, N.R.	Owney and Arra .	Killoscully .	Nenagh .	II.	295
10	Toor Beg . .	287 2 14	Kilkenny .	Fassadinin .	Kilmacar .	Castlecomer .	I.	90
80, 86	Toor Beg . .	337 0 29	Tipperary, S.R.	Iffa and Offa West .	Shanrahan .	Clogheen .	II.	320
23, 30	Toorbeg . .	218 2 30	Westmeath .	Kilkenny West .	Drumraney .	Athlone .	I.	273
38, 47	Toorboney .	367 1 0	Cork, W.R. .	West Muskerry .	Drishane .	Millstreet .	II.	156
11	Toorboy . .	109 0 33	Sligo . .	Tireragh . .	Kilmacshalgan .	Dromore West .	IV.	235
28	Toorboy . .	467 2 4	Wicklow .	Ballinacor South .	Kiltegan .	Baltinglass .	I.	350
88, 89	Toorbuck . .	164 3 39	Mayo . . .	Burrishoole .	Aghagower .	Westport .	IV.	118
104	Toorclogher .	59 0 28	Galway .	Dunkellin .	Killogilleen .	Loughrea .	IV.	31
24	Toorcoffey .	13 2 8	Westmeath .	Rathconrath .	Killare . .	Mullingar .	I.	283
11	Toor Commons .	14 0 22	Westmeath .	Moygoish .	Kilbixy . .	Mullingar .	I.	279
24	Toordillon or Rowe .	60 2 29	Westmeath .	Rathconrath .	Killare . .	Mullingar .	I.	283
28	Tooreagh . .	24 3 26	Queen's Co. .	Clarmallagh .	Aghaboe . .	Donaghmore .	I.	236
33	Tooreagh . .	176 0 39	Tipperary, N.R.	Upper Ormond .	Templederry .	Nenagh .	II.	293
98	Tooree . .	163 3 11	Galway .	Kilconnell .	Killallaghtan .	Ballinasloe .	IV.	41
34	Tooreen . .	138 2 20	Clare . .	Bunratty Upper .	Kilraghtis .	Ennis . .	II.	9
8	Tooreen . .	244 0 29d	Clare . .	Corcomroe .	Kilshanny .	Ennistimon .	II.	22
23, 31	Tooreen . .	458 3 14e	Clare . .	Ibrickan . .	Kilfarboy .	Ennistimon .	II.	22
53	Tooreen . .	149 0 20	Clare . .	Tulla Lower .	Killokennedy .	Limerick .	II.	36
36	Tooreen . .	112 3 9	Clare . .	Tulla Lower .	Killuran .	Tulla . .	II.	36
31, 40	Tooreen . .	221 1 11	Cork, E.R. .	Duhallow . .	Clonmeen .	Kanturk .	II.	70
34, 43	Tooreen . .	350 1 36	Cork, E.R. .	Fermoy . .	Monanimy .	Mallow .	II.	82
97	Tooreen . .	146 0 8	Cork, E.R. .	Kinalea . .	Dunderrow .	Kinsale .	II.	95
91, 92	Tooreen . .	292 2 2	Cork, W.R. .	Bantry . .	Kilmocomoge .	Bantry .	II.	122

(a) Including 4A. 0R. 30P. water.   (c) Including 11A. 1R. 18P. water.   (e) Including 11A. 0R. 0P. water.
(b) Including 35A. 0R. 2P. water.   (d) Including 6A. 3R. 22P. water.

No. of Sheet of the Ordnance Survey Maps.	Townlands and Towns.	Area in Statute Acres.			County.	Barony.	Parish.	Poor Law Union in 1857.	Townland Census of 1851, Part I.	
		A.	R.	P.					Vol.	Page
90	Tooreen	556	0	14	Cork, W.R.	Bear	Kilcaskan	Bantry	II.	123
116	Tooreen	9	0	8	Cork, W.R.	Bear	Killaconenagh	Castletown	II.	125
93	Tooreen	152	0	10	Cork, W.R.	East Carbery (W.D.)	Inchigeelagh	Dunmanway	II.	132
132, 133	Tooreen	521	1	11	Cork, W.R.	West Carbery (E.D.)	Caheragh	Skibbereen	II.	137
138	Tooreen	319	2	38	Cork, W.R.	West Carbery (W.D.)	Kilcrohane	Bantry	II.	144
147	Tooreen	121	2	21	Cork, W.R.	West Carbery (W.D.)	Kilmoe	Skull	II.	145
22	Tooreen	757	1	38a	Galway	Ballynahinch	Ballynakill	Clifden	IV.	12
22, 35	Tooreen	148	0	31	Galway	Ballynahinch	Omey	Clifden	IV.	15
17	Tooreen	43	3	5	Galway	Dunmore	Dunmore	Tuam	IV.	34
86	Tooreen	236	2	31	Galway	Kilconnell	Killaan	Ballinasloe	IV.	41
129	Tooreen	163	0	25	Galway	Kiltartan	Beagh	Gort	IV.	46
117	Tooreen	33	2	10	Galway	Leitrim	Tynagh	Portumna	IV.	56
17	Tooreen	435	1	18	Kerry	Clanmaurice	Duagh	Listowel	II.	169
21, 22	Tooreen	525	3	21	Kerry	Clanmaurice	Kilflyn	Tralee	II.	170
96, 97	Tooreen	137	0	8	Kerry	Iveragh	Killemlagh	Cahersiveen	II.	196
30	Tooreen	170	3	29	Kerry	Trughanacmy	Ballymacelligott	Tralee	II.	207
26, 27	Tooreen	291	2	27	King's Co.	Upper Philipstown	Geashill	Tullamore	I.	144
4	Tooreen	179	1	25	King's Co.	Warrenstown	Ballyburly	Edenderry	I.	144
13, 14	Tooreen	436	2	27	Limerick	Clanwilliam	Carrigparson	Limerick	II.	223
30, 31	Tooreen	706	2	16	Limerick	Coshma	Croom	Croom	II.	242
109	Tooreen	353	1	37	Mayo	Carra	Ballyovey	Ballinrobe	IV.	126
82	Tooreen	203	1	38	Mayo	Costello	Aghamore	Swineford	IV.	137
86	Tooreen	53	2	7	Mayo	Murrisk	Kilgeever	Westport	IV.	160
29	Tooreen	502	1	4	Mayo	Tirawley	Crossmolina	Ballina	IV.	167
14, 15	Tooreen	153	0	24	Mayo	Tirawley	Templemurry	Killala	IV.	172
29	Tooreen	75	0	35	Roscommon	Roscommon	Lissonuffy	Strokestown	IV.	212
41	Tooreen	202	0	30	Tipperary, N.R.	Eliogarty	Thurles	Thurles	II.	273
45	Tooreen	148	1	8	Tipperary, N.R.	Kilnamanagh Upper	Toem	Tipperary	II.	280
26, 27	Tooreen	67	1	13	Tipperary, N.R.	Upper Ormond	Dolla	Nenagh	II.	290
73, 74	Tooreen	160	2	31	Tipperary, S.R.	Clanwilliam	Clonbeg	Tipperary	II.	305
51	Tooreen	131	1	31	Tipperary, S.R.	Kilnamanagh Lower	Donohill	Cashel	II.	323
51	Tooreen	10	3	0	Tipperary, S.R.	Kilnamanagh Lower	Kilpatrick	Cashel	II.	324
77	Tooreen	112	0	17	Tipperary, S.R.	Middlethird	Baptistgrange	Clonmel	II.	325
10	Tooreena	885	3	33	Galway	Ballynahinch	Ballynakill	Clifden	IV.	12
24	Tooreena	539	3	1	Galway	Ballynahinch	Ballynakill	Clifden	IV.	12
31, 32	Tooreenagowan	796	0	36	Kerry	Trughanacmy	Ballincuslane	Tralee	II.	206
81, 93	Tooreenalour	532	1	26	Cork, W.R.	West Muskerry	Inchigeelagh	Dunmanway	II.	158
98, 99	Tooreenard	116	0	32	Galway	Clonmacnowen	Killallaghtan	Ballinasloe	IV.	26
31	Tooreenard	540	0	27	Kerry	Trughanacmy	Castleisland	Tralee	II.	209
21, 22	Tooreenavuscaun	388	1	15	Cork, E.R.	Duhallow	Kilmeen	Kanturk	II.	73
39, 48	Tooreenbane	594	1	1	Cork, W.R.	West Muskerry	Drishane	Millstreet	II.	156
115	Tooreen Beg	155	0	17	Cork, W.R.	Bear	Killaconenagh	Castletown	II.	125
84	Tooreenbreanla	272	0	32b	Kerry	Glanarought	Kenmare	Kenmare	II.	186
38	Tooreenbrien Lower	253	0	37	Tipperary, N.R.	Owney and Arra	Kilvellane	Nenagh	II.	296
38	Tooreenbrien Upper	508	3	2	Tipperary, N.R.	Owney and Arra	Kilvellane	Nenagh	II.	296
50	Tooreencahill	622	0	21	Kerry	Magunihy	Nohavaldaly	Killarney	II.	205
29	Tooreenclassagh	587	3	38	Cork, E.R.	Duhallow	Nohavaldaly	Kanturk	II.	75
14	Tooreencormack	145	0	7	Cork, E.R.	Duhallow	Clonfert	Kanturk	II.	69
39, 40, 46	Tooreencullinagh	83	2	8	Tipperary, N.R.	Kilnamanagh Upper	Moyaliff	Thurles	II.	279
14	Tooreendermot	360	2	35	Cork, E.R.	Duhallow	Clonfert	Kanturk	II.	69
5, 14	Tooreen Donnell	140	0	7	Cork, E.R.	Duhallow	Clonfert	Kanturk	II.	69
27	Tooreendonnell	808	3	22	Limerick	Shanid	Kilmoylan	Glin	II.	256
21	Tooreenduff	516	3	31	Cork, E.R.	Duhallow	Kilmeen	Kanturk	II.	73
80	Tooreenduff	437	2	26	Cork, W.R.	West Muskerry	Inchigeelagh	Dunmanway	II.	158
71	Tooreenealagh	1,676	1	28c	Kerry	Iveragh	Glanbehy	Cahersiveen	II.	196
25, 33	Tooreen East	131	2	23	Clare	Inchiquin	Kilnamona	Ennis	II.	27
103, 113	Tooreen East	288	3	1d	Galway	Dunkellin	Killeenavarra	Gort	IV.	30
6, 14	Tooreen East	621	3	21	Waterford	Decies without Drum	Seskinan	Dungarvan	II.	360
13	Tooreenfineen	1,240	1	15	Cork, E.R.	Duhallow	Kilmeen	Kanturk	II.	73
50	Tooreengarriv	713	1	18	Kerry	Trughanacmy	Ballincuslane	Tralee	II.	206
21, 29	Tooreenglanahee	789	3	16	Cork, E.R.	Duhallow	Nohavaldaly	Kanturk	II.	75
80	Tooreenlahard	139	2	8	Cork, W.R.	West Muskerry	Inchigeelagh	Macroom	II.	158
4, 5	Tooreenmacauliffe	1,174	3	9	Cork, E.R.	Duhallow	Clonfert	Kanturk	II.	69
80	Tooreenmore	371	2	17	Kerry	Iveragh	Caher	Cahersiveen	II.	194
31	Tooreenmore	1,186	1	8	Kerry	Trughanacmy	Castleisland	Tralee	II.	209
115	Tooreen More East	188	2	7	Cork, W.R.	Bear	Killaconenagh	Castletown	II.	125
115	Tooreen More West	167	3	25	Cork, W.R.	Bear	Killaconenagh	Castletown	II.	125
6, 14	Tooreenmountain	704	1	16	Waterford	Decies without Drum	Seskinan	Dungarvan	II.	360
32	Tooreennablauha	450	1	22	Kerry	Trughanacmy	Brosna	Tralee	II.	208
82, 91	Tooreennafersha	445	2	24	Kerry	Dunkerron South	Templenoe	Kenmare	II.	185
53	Tooreennagreana	890	1	37	Limerick	Glenquin	Killeedy	Newcastle	II.	246
4, 13	Tooreennagrena	624	0	17	Cork, E.R.	Duhallow	Clonfert	Kanturk	II.	69
104	Tooreennagrena	504	3	26	Cork, W.R.	Bear	Kilcaskan	Castletown	II.	123

(a) Including 47A. 3R. 1P. water.
(b) Including 3A. 1R. 23P. water.
(c) Including 118A. 0R. 4P. water.
(d) Including 21A. 3R. 19P. water.

No. of Sheet of the Ordnance Survey Maps.	Townlands and Towns.	Area in Statute Acres. A. R. P.	County.	Barony.	Parish.	Poor Law Union in 1857.	Townland Census of 1851, Part I. Vol.	Page
14	Tooreennaguppoge	313 3 38	Cork, E.R.	Duhallow	Clonfert	Kanturk	II.	69
82, 91	Tooreennahone	365 3 27	Kerry	Dunkerron South	Templenoe	Kenmare	II.	185
14	Tooreennamire	230 0 24	Cork, E.R.	Duhallow	Clonfert	Kanturk	II.	69
50, 60	Tooreennamult	743 2 30	Kerry	Magunihy	Kilcummin	Killarney	II.	202
80	Tooreennanean	201 2 7	Cork, W.R.	West Muskerry	Inchigeelagh	Dunmanway	II.	158
32, 41	Tooreennascarty	755 1 21	Kerry	Trughanacmy	Ballincuslane	Tralee	II.	206
142	Tooreennasillane	166 3 34	Cork, W.R.	West Carbery (E.D.)	Abbeystrowry	Skibbereen	II.	136
56, 64	Tooreennasliggaun	468 2 14	Kerry	Iveragh	Killorglin	Killarney	II.	198
30	Tooreennastooka	136 1 38	Kerry	Trughanacmy	Ballymacelligott	Tralee	II.	207
42, 51	Tooreen North	1,133 0 34	Cork, E.R.	Barretts	Mourneabbey	Mallow	II.	50
116	Tooreen North	103 0 37	Galway	Leitrim	Ballynakill	Loughrea	IV.	52
22, 30	Tooreenphilip	111 1 21	Mayo	Tirawley	Ballysakeery	Ballina	IV.	165
29	Tooreenreaghy	143 1 20	Cork, E.R.	Duhallow	Nohavaldaly	Millstreet	II.	75
98, 99	Tooreens	1,801 2 8a	Kerry	Dunkerron South	Kilcrohane	Cahersiveen	II.	184
42, 43, 51	Tooreen South	980 0 23	Cork, E.R.	Barretts	Mourneabbey	Mallow	II.	50
106, 119	Tooreen South	131 1 34	Cork, W.R.	Bantry	Kilmocomoge	Bantry	II.	122
116	Tooreen South	192 2 1	Galway	Leitrim	Ballynakill	Loughrea	IV.	52
25, 33	Tooreen West	127 1 36	Clare	Inchiquin	Kilnamona	Ennis	II.	27
103, 113	Tooreen West	214 0 38b	Galway	Dunkellin	Killeenavarra	Gort	IV.	30
6	Tooreen West	318 0 29	Waterford	Decies without Drum	Seskinan	Dungarvan	II.	360
81	Tooreeny	422 1 27	Galway	Moycullen	Moycullen	Galway	IV.	71
98, 99	Tooreenyduneen	559 3 35	Kerry	Dunkerron South	Kilcrohane	Cahersiveen	II.	184
15	Tooreigh	165 2 30	Tipperary, N.R.	Upper Ormond	Ballymackey	Nenagh	II.	289
16	Toorevagh	148 0 29	Westmeath	Rathconrath	Ballymore	Ballymahon	I.	282
30	Toorfelim	279 0 23	Westmeath	Clonlonan	Kilmanaghan	Athlone	I.	262
33, 39	Toorfiba	123 1 19	Tipperary, N.R.	Kilnamanagh Upper	Upperchurch	Thurles	II.	281
14	Toorfin	112 3 29	Longford	Ardagh	Templemichael	Longford	I.	154
20	Toorfune	72 2 12	Tipperary, N.R.	Owney and Arra	Burgesbeg	Nenagh	II.	294
43	Toorgarriff	644 0 34	Cork, E.R.	Barrymore	Ardnageehy	Fermoy	II.	51
77	Toorgarve	114 1 39	Mayo	Burrishoole	Kilmaclasser	Westport	IV.	121
17	Toorglass	383 1 11	Mayo	Erris	Kilcommon	Belmullet	IV.	145
48	Toories and Rannagh	338 3 20	Donegal	Boylagh	Templecrone	Glenties	III.	116
84, 85	Toorkeel	111 2 0	Galway	Tiaquin	Monivea	Loughrea	IV.	79
125, 131	Toorleitra	3,358 0 28	Galway	Leitrim	Ballynakill	Loughrea	IV.	52
37	Toorlestraun	256 0 17	Sligo	Leyny	Kilmacteige	Tobercurry	IV.	231
32, 38	Toorlisnamore	583 2 32	Westmeath	Moycashel	Castletownkindalen	Mullingar	I.	277
26	Toorloggagh	735 3 12	Galway	Ross	Ross	Oughterard	IV.	74
7	Toorlougher	492 0 1	Limerick	Owneybeg	Abington	Limerick	II.	251
86	Toormacleane	103 3 29	Galway	Kilconnell	Grange	Loughrea	IV.	40
115, 124	Toormacnevin	1,175 0 27	Galway	Loughrea	Killeenadeema	Loughrea	IV.	64
109	Toormakeady East	200 1 37	Mayo	Carra	Ballyovey	Ballinrobe	IV.	126
108, 109	Toormakeady Mountain	1,051 1 12	Mayo	Carra	Ballyovey	Ballinrobe	IV.	126
109	Toormakeady West	104 3 18	Mayo	Carra	Ballyovey	Ballinrobe	IV.	126
16	Toormore	448 1 38	Clare	Corcomroe	Kiltoraght	Corrofin	II.	22
25	Toormore	38 0 14	Clare	Inchiquin	Ruan	Corrofin	II.	28
33, 34	Toormore	209 3 28	Cork, E.R.	Fermoy	Monanimy	Mallow	II.	82
141	Toormore	142 0 31	Cork, W.R.	West Carbery (E.D.)	Aghadown	Skibbereen	II.	137
138,139,147,148	Toormore	601 3 34	Cork, W.R.	West Carbery (W.D.)	Kilmoe	Skull	II.	145
86, 98	Toormore	135 3 18	Galway	Kilconnell	Killallaghtan	Ballinasloe	IV.	41
118	Toormore	65 3 20	Galway	Longford	Kilmalinoge	Portumna	IV.	59
59	Toormore	522 3 27	Kerry	Magunihy	Kilcummin	Killarney	II.	202
5, 10	Toor More	423 3 20	Kilkenny	Fassadinin	Kilmacar	Castlecomer	I.	90
10, 11	Toormore	116 0 4	Roscommon	Boyle	Killukin	Cark. on Shannon	IV.	196
80, 86	Toor More	286 0 8	Tipperary, S.R.	Iffa and Offa West	Shanrahan	Clogheen	II.	320
70	Toormore East	261 1 9	Mayo	Carra	Turlough	Castlebar	IV.	131
70	Toormore West	194 0 32	Mayo	Carra	Turlough	Castlebar	IV	131
46	Toornafolla	123 3 37	Meath	Upper Moyfenrath	Castlejordan	Edenderry	I.	212
43, 52	Toornafulla	1,544 0 35	Limerick	Glenquin	Killeedy	Newcastle	II.	246
20	Toornageeha	173 3 11	Waterford	Coshmore&Coshbride	Lismore and Mocollop	Lismore	II.	347
16	Toornageehy	572 1 11	Kerry	Clanmaurice	Kilshenane	Listowel	II.	172
21	Toornagoppoge	86 3 32	Waterford	Coshmore&Coshbride	Lismore and Mocollop	Lismore	II.	347
8	Toornahooan	160 3 11	Clare	Corcomroe	Killilagh	Ennistimon	II.	20
8	Toornamongan	79 1 37	Kilkenny	Galmoy	Erke	Urlingford	I.	92
49, 59, 60	Toornanaunagh	807 1 35	Kerry	Magunihy	Kilcummin	Killarney	II.	202
71, 72	Toornaneaskagh	418 1 22	Kerry	Iveragh	Glanbehy	Cahersiveen	II.	196
48	Toornanoulagh	202 3 7	Kerry	Trughanacmy	Killeentierna	Killarney	II.	211
35	Toor North	658 2 33	Waterford	Decies within Drum	Ardmore	Dungarvan	II.	351
71, 80	Tooromin	509 2 33	Mayo	Gallen	Bohola	Swineford	IV.	147
10	Toorreagh	251 2 30	Cork, E.R.	Condons&Clangibbon	Templemolaga	Mitchelstown	II.	63
5, 13	Toorreagh	251 2 16	Waterford	Glenahiry	Kilronan	Clonmel	II.	366
71, 81	Toorsaleen	943 2 35	Kerry	Iveragh	Dromod	Cahersiveen	II.	195
125	Toorsmuttaun	95 1 9	Galway	Leitrim	Ballynakill	Loughrea	IV.	52

(a) Including 15A. 2R. 32P. water.　　　　　(b) Including 11A. 1R. 31P. water.

No. of Sheet of the Ordnance Survey Maps.	Townlands and Towns.	Area in Statute Acres. A. R. P.	County.	Barony.	Parish.	Poor Law Union in 1857.	Townland Census of 1851, Part I. Vol.	Page
35	Toor South	356 1 9	Waterford	Decies within Drum	Ardmore	Youghal	II.	351
2	Toortane	308 0 12	Kilkenny	Fassadinin	Rathaspick	Castlecomer	I.	91
20, 28	Toortane	184 0 22	Waterford	Coshmore & Coshbride	Lismore and Mocollop	Lismore	II.	347
15, 16	Toortaun	99 1 35	Queen's Co.	Upperwoods	Offerlane	Abbeyleix	I.	252
36	Toorydonnellan	111 2 16	Westmeath	Clonlonan	Kilcleagh	Athlone	I.	262
11	Toorymartin	92 0 28	Roscommon	Boyle	Killukin	Cark. on Shannon	IV.	196
59, 60	Tooslenagh	312 0 21	Donegal	Raphoe	Conwal	Stranorlar	III.	137
102, 112	Tootagh	278 3 5	Mayo	Clanmorris	Kilcolman	Claremorris	IV.	134
21	Tootenhill	215 2 15	Dublin	Newcastle	Rathcoole	Celbridge	I.	34
20, 25	Toppan	399 1 19a	Fermanagh	Clanawley	Cleenish	Enniskillen	III.	191
22, 23	Topped Mountain or Mullyknock	730 1 10b	Fermanagh	Tirkennedy	Enniskillen	Enniskillen	III.	222
17	Topp Lower	113 1 25	Antrim	Upper Dunluce	Ballymoney	Ballymoney	III.	19
12, 17	Topp Upper	118 0 38	Antrim	Upper Dunluce	Ballymoney	Ballymoney	III.	19
6	Toprass	139 3 7	Louth	Upper Dundalk	Inishkeen	Dundalk	I.	179
70	Tops	262 2 9	Donegal	Raphoe	Raphoe	Strabane	III.	141
70	Tops Demesne	134 2 13	Donegal	Raphoe	Raphoe	Strabane	III.	141
42, 50	Tor	3,115 3 35c	Donegal	Kilmacrenan	Tullaghobegly	Dunfanaghy	III.	132
26,27,35,36	Toragh	213 3 26	Donegal	Kilmacrenan	Mevagh	Millford	III.	130
46	Toragh	365 1 4	Tipperary, S.R.	Kilnamanagh Lower	Clonoulty	Cashel	II.	323
80, 81	Toralaydan Island	2 1 37	Donegal	Banagh	Glencolumbkille	Glenties	III.	106
42	Toralt	68 3 22	Fermanagh	Knockninny	Kinawley	Lisnaskea	III.	202
19, 23	Torboy	350 3 8	Longford	Moydow	Taghsheenod	Ballymahon	I.	162
74	Torc	362 0 14	Kerry	Magunihy	Killarney	Killarney	II.	204
10	Torcorr	154 3 27	Antrim	Cary	Culfeightrin	Ballycastle	III.	14
17	Torduff	260 3 7	Wexford	Ballaghkeen	Donaghmore	Gorey	I.	294
5, 9	Torglass	174 3 6	Antrim	Cary	Culfeightrin	Ballycastle	III.	14
32	Torglass Island	2 2 39	Donegal	Kilmacrenan	Tullaghobegly	Dunfanaghy	III.	132
13	Torman and Ardbearn	121 2 3	Carlow	Forth	Kellistown	Carlow	I.	4
85	Tormaun	78 1 22	Galway	Kilconnell	Killimordaly	Loughrea	IV.	42
6, 9	Tormore	659 2 38d	Sligo	Carbury	Drumcliff	Sligo	IV.	222
72	Tormore Island	4 1 22	Donegal	Banagh	Glencolumbkille	Glenties	III.	106
5, 9	Tornabodagh	73 0 11	Antrim	Cary	Culfeightrin	Ballycastle	III.	14
32	Tornacolpagh Island	2 1 27	Donegal	Kilmacrenan	Tullaghobegly	Dunfanaghy	III.	132
60	Tornagrough	297 1 30	Antrim	Upper Massereene	Derryaghy	Lisburn	III.	30
10, 15	Tornamoney	170 3 24	Antrim	Cary	Culfeightrin	Ballycastle	III.	14
26	Tornanstown	130 1 12	Westmeath	Fartullagh	Lynn	Mullingar	I.	269
15	Tornant Lower	274 2 13	Wicklow	Lower Talbotstown	Dunlavin	Baltinglass	I.	360
15	Tornant Upper	366 0 21	Wicklow	Lower Talbotstown	Dunlavin	Baltinglass	I.	360
5, 9	Tornaroan	112 1 12	Antrim	Cary	Culfeightrin	Ballycastle	III.	14
60	Tornaroy	291 1 4	Antrim	Upper Belfast	Derryaghy	Lisburn	III.	10
44, 47	Torpan Beg	233 0 3	Roscommon	Athlone	Taghboy	Athlone	IV.	184
44, 47	Torpan More	241 0 31	Roscommon	Athlone	Taghboy	Athlone	IV.	184
38	Torque	157 3 15	Westmeath	Moycashel	Newtown	Mullingar	I.	279
9	Torrewa	22 2 12	Cavan	Tullyhaw	Templeport	Bawnboy	III.	95
21, 22	Toryhill	298 0 16	Limerick	Pubblebrien	Croom	Croom	II.	252
6	Tory Island	785 1 16e	Donegal	Kilmacrenan	Tullaghobegly	Dunfanaghy	III.	132
24	Tossy	233 3 3	Monaghan	Cremorne	Aghnamullen	Castleblayney	III.	258
36, 41	Tottenhamgreen	581 2 39	Wexford	Shelmaliere West	Horetown	New Ross	I.	333
120	Toughbaun	441 3 11	Cork, W.R.	East Carbery (W.D.)	Drinagh	Skibbereen	II.	131
120	Toughmacdermody	255 1 36	Cork, W.R.	West Carbery (E.D.)	Drinagh	Skibbereen	II.	139
119	Toughraheen	277 0 14	Cork, W.R.	West Carbery (E.D.)	Dromdaleague	Skibbereen	II.	140
31	Touknockane	55 2 6	Tipperary, N.R.	Owney and Arra	Kilcomenty	Nenagh	II.	295
47	Toulett	552 0 23	Donegal	Inishowen West	Burt	Londonderry	III.	120
82	Touloure	110 3 36	Tipperary, S.R.	Iffa and Offa West	Ardfinnan	Clogheen	II.	317
19	Tountinna	367 0 17	Tipperary, N.R.	Owney and Arra	Templeachally	Nenagh	II.	297
75	Toureen	978 3 34	Tipperary, S.R.	Clanwilliam	Killardry	Tipperary	II.	308
29	Tourin	89 2 3	Waterford	Coshmore & Coshbride	Lismore and Mocollop	Lismore	II.	348
29	Tourin Demesne	451 1 16	Waterford	Coshmore & Coshbride	Lismore and Mocollop	Lismore	II.	348
9	Tournagee	192 3 37f	Roscommon	Frenchpark	Kilnamanagh	Boyle	IV.	204
31	Tournore	62 1 31g	Waterford	Decies without Drum	Dungarvan	Dungarvan	II.	356
5	Towas	357 1 11	Meath	Lower Kells	Kilmainham	Kells	I.	203
13	Tower Beg	317 2 34	Fermanagh	Magheraboy	Devenish	Ballyshannon	III.	211
17	Towergare	409 0 24	Waterford	Middlethird	Kilburne	Waterford	II.	367
100	Towerhill Demesne	340 0 7i	Mayo	Carra	Touaghty	Ballinrobe	IV.	130
13, 19	Tower More	184 1 36j	Fermanagh	Magheraboy	Devenish	Ballyshannon	III.	211
36, 45	Towermore Lower	160 1 2	Cork, E.R.	Barrymore	Castlelyons	Fermoy	II.	53
36	Towermore Upper	246 1 25	Cork, E.R.	Barrymore	Castlelyons	Fermoy	II.	53
46, 47	Towlaght	723 1 38	Meath	Upper Moyfenrath	Clonard	Edenderry	I.	213
5	Towlerton	119 2 29	Limerick	Clanwilliam	Kilmurry	Limerick	II.	225
31, 32	Towlerton	1,054 2 2	Queen's Co.	Slievemargy	Killabban	Carlow	I.	245
58	Townagh	91 1 21	Tyrone	Clogher	Clogher	Clogher	III.	293
41, 42	Townagha	139 2 25	Tipperary, N.R.	Eliogarty	Rahelty	Thurles	II.	272

(a) Including 3A. 2R. 20P. water.
(b) Including 4A. 1R. 27P. water.
(c) Including 19A. 2R. 11P. water.
(d) Including 56A. 3R. 36P. water.

(e) Including 16A. 2R. 12P. water.
(f) Including 3A. 2R. 38P. water.
(g) Including 11A. 3R. 18P. detached portions.

(h) Including 12A. 1R. 25P. water.
(i) Including 12A. 3R. 0P. water.
(j) Including 4A. 2R. 13P. water.

No. of Sheet of the Ordnance Survey Maps.	Townlands and Towns.	Area in Statute Acres. A. R. P.	County.	Barony.	Parish.	Poor Law Union in 1857.	Townland Census of 1851, Part I. Vol.	Page
22,23,35,36	Townaloughra	261 3 22a	Galway	Ballynahinch	Omey	Clifden	IV.	15
25	Townamuiloge	417 3 11	Wexford	Bantry	Rossdroit	Enniscorthy	I.	302
7	Townend	156 3 9	Antrim	Lower Dunluce	Dunluce	Coleraine	III.	17
15, 16	Townfields	333 0 20	Tipperary, N.R.	Lower Ormond	Modreeny	Borrisokane	II.	287
11	Townhill	67 2 12	Fermanagh	Lurg	Derryvullane	Lowtherstown	III.	205
143	Town Lands	53 3 38	Cork, W.R.	East Carbery(W.D.)	Ross	Clonakilty	II.	136
23, 24	Townleyhall	924 3 27	Louth	Ferrard	Tullyallen	Drogheda	I.	183
67	Town Lot	9 1 34	Tipperary, S.R.	Clanwilliam	Tipperary	Tipperary	II.	312
118	Town Lots	90 0 20	Cork, W.R.	Bantry	Kilmocomoge	Bantry	II.	122
19	Townlough Lower	200 0 6	Tipperary, N.R.	Owney and Arra	Castletownarra	Nenagh	II.	294
19	Townlough Upper	327 3 28	Tipperary, N.R.	Owney and Arra	Castletownarra	Nenagh	II.	294
60, 61	Townparks	1,769 1 35b	Antrim	Belfast, Municipal Borough of	Shankill	Belfast	III.	35
4, 5, 8, 9	Town Parks	663 1 16	Antrim	Cary	Ramoan	Ballycastle	III.	15
29, 30	Town Parks	109 3 29	Antrim	Lower Glenarm	Tickmacrevan	Larne	III.	24
32, 37	Town Parks	452 3 12	Antrim	Lower Toome	Kirkinriola	Ballymena	III.	33
50	Town Parks	1,163 0 7	Antrim	Upper Antrim	Antrim	Antrim	III.	5
17	Townparks	882 3 30	Antrim	Upper Dunluce	Ballymoney	Ballymoney	III.	19
35, 40	Town Parks	322 1 5	Antrim	Upper Glenarm	Larne	Larne	III.	25
15,16,20,21	Townparks	196 2 1	Cavan	Upper Loughtee	Castleterra	Cavan	III.	83
20	Townparks	38 2 33	Cavan	Upper Loughtee	Urney	Cavan	III.	86
88	Townparks	107 2 34	Cork, E.R.	Imokilly	Cloyne	Middleton	II.	86
76	Townparks	316 0 35	Cork, E.R.	Imokilly	Middleton	Middleton	II.	89
70, 71	Town Parks	120 0 7c	Donegal	Raphoe	Clonleigh	Strabane	III.	135
107	Townparks	295 1 19d	Donegal	Tirhugh	Kilbarron	Ballyshannon	III.	148
10	Town Parks	491 1 2e	Down	Castlereagh Lower	Comber	Newtownards	III.	162
5	Townparks	545 1 29	Dublin	Balrothery East	Holmpatrick	Balrothery	I.	20
11	Townparks	104 0 24	Dublin	Nethercross	Swords	Balrothery	I.	32
87, 88	Townparks	119 3 38f	Galway	Clonmacnowen	Kilcloony	Ballinasloe	IV.	25
94	Townparks	379 3 4g	Galway	Galway	Rahoon	Galway	IV.	38
82, 94	Townparks	501 1 25h	Galway	Galway	St. Nicholas	Galway	IV.	38
108	Townparks	117 2 11	Galway	Longford	Donanaghta	Portumna	IV.	58
40	Townparks	95 3 7	Kildare	Kilkea and Moone	Castledermot	Athy	I.	59
35	Townparks	128 0 6i	Kildare	Narragh and Reban West	Churchtown	Athy	I.	67
35	Townparks	118 2 7	Kildare	Narragh and Reban West	St. Michaels	Athy	I.	68
35	Townparks	824 2 29	King's Co.	Ballybritt	Birr	Parsonstown	I.	125
10, 18	Townparks	1,198 2 5	King's Co.	Lower Philipstown	Killaderry	Tullamore	I.	143
31	Townparks	289 3 32j	Leitrim	Leitrim	Kiltoghert	Cark. on Shannon	IV.	103
13	Townparks	402 0 14	Longford	Ardagh	Templemichael	Longford	I.	154
8	Townparks	137 1 0	Longford	Longford	Clongesh	Longford	I.	158
14, 17	Townparks	1,123 3 13	Louth	Ardee	Ardee	Ardee	I.	171
7	Townparks	435 2 21k	Louth	Upper Dundalk	Dundalk	Dundalk	I.	178
25	Townparks	324 1 11l	Meath	Lower Navan	Navan	Navan	I.	215
29	Town Parks	267 0 26	Meath	Lune	Athboy	Trim	I.	207
16, 17	Town Parks	1,198 3 12	Meath	Upper Kells	Kells	Kells	I.	206
21, 22	Townparks	695 2 9	Queen's Co.	Clandonagh	Aghaboe	Donaghmore	I.	233
4, 7, 8	Townparks	773 1 1	Queen's Co.	Tinnahinch	Rosenallis	Mountmellick	I.	250
53	Townparks	183 3 35m	Roscommon	Moycarn	Creagh	Ballinasloe	IV.	206
12	Townparks	138 2 9	Tipperary, N.R.	Ikerrin	Roscrea	Roscrea	II.	276
85	Town Parks	222 3 1	Tipperary, S.R.	Iffa and Offa East	Carrick	Carrick on Suir	II.	313
75, 81	Townparks	358 2 12n	Tipperary, S.R.	Iffa and Offa West	Caher	Clogheen	II.	318
5	Town Parks	443 2 28o	Tyrone	Strabane Lower	Leckpatrick	Strabane	III.	322
21, 28, 29	Townparks	171 1 19	Waterford	Coshmore&Coshbride	Lismore and Mocollop	Lismore	II.	348
3, 7	Townparks	391 3 23	Westmeath	Fore	Rathgarve	Castletowndelvin	I.	271
37	Townparks	525 0 10	Wexford	Forth	St. John's	Wexford	I.	315
37	Townparks	87 2 11	Wexford	Forth	St. Michael's of Feagh	Wexford	I.	315
37	Townparks	23 3 4	Wexford	Forth	St. Peter's	Wexford	I.	314
21, 29	Townparks East	210 1 6	Waterford	Coshmore&Coshbride	Lismore and Mocollop	Lismore	II.	348
28	Townparks East	251 1 26	Waterford	Coshmore&Coshbride	Tallow	Lismore	II.	348
29	Townparks (5th Division)	191 0 2	Galway	Dunmore	Tuam	Tuam	IV.	36
29	Townparks (1st Division)	148 0 7	Galway	Dunmore	Tuam	Tuam	IV.	36
29	Townparks (4th Division)	14 1 13	Galway	Clare	Tuam	Tuam	IV.	23
36	Townparks North	64 1 25p	Meath	Upper Navan	Trim	Trim	I.	217
2, 3	Town Parks of Donaghadee	632 1 29	Down	Ards Lower	Donaghadee	Newtownards	III.	158
41, 42, 47	Townparks of Magherafelt	1,219 1 12	Londonderry	Loughinsholin	Magherafelt	Magherafelt	III.	243
4, 5	Townparks of Strabane	417 1 8q	Tyrone	Strabane Lower	Camus	Strabane	III.	320
19	Townparks or Portaliff	326 3 35r	Cavan	Tullyhunco	Killashandra	Cavan	III.	98

(a) Including 26A. 2R. 23P. water.
(b) Included in the Parish of Shankill.
(c) Including 4A. 1R. 8P. water.
(d) Including 16A. 2R. 25P. water.
(e) Including 10A. 0R. 11P. water.
(f) Including 7A. 1R. 24P. water.
(g) Including 6A. 1R. 23P. water.

(h) Including 40A. 1R. 21P. water.
(i) Including 5A. 0R. 8P. River Barrow.
(j) Including Islands.
(k) Including 14A. 1R. 8P. water.
(l) Including 2A. 0R. 39P. water.
(m) Including 29A. 3R. 20P. water.
(n) Including 10A. 3R. 14P. water.

(o) Including 6A. 0R. 9P. water.
(p) { Including 0A. 2R. 32P. detached portion.
{ Including 3A. 2R. 32P. water.
{ Including 20A. 2R. 25P. Lyons Island.
(q) { Including 40A. 3R. 17P. River Mourne.
{ Including 5A. 3R. 24P. Tideway.
(r) { Including 59A. 2R. 16P. water.

No. of Sheet of the Ordnance Survey Maps.	Townlands and Towns.	Area in Statute Acres.	County.	Barony.	Parish.	Poor Law Union in 1857.	Townland Census of 1851, Part I.	
		A. R. P.					Vol.	Page
29, 43	Townparks(2nd Division)	102 2 28	Galway	Clare	Tuam	Tuam	IV.	23
36	Townparks South	35 1 27a	Meath	Lower Moyfenrath	Trim	Trim	I.	212
29, 43	Townparks (3rd Division)	34 0 34	Galway	Clare	Tuam	Tuam	IV.	23
20, 21, 28	Townparks West	181 0 27	Waterford	Coshmore&Coshbride	Lismore and Mocollop	Lismore	II.	348
28	Townparks West	321 3 18	Waterford	Coshmore&Coshbride	Tallow	Lismore	II.	348
112	Townplots	54 3 33	Cork, E.R.	Kinsale	Kinsale	Kinsale	II.	100
22	Townplots East	25 2 17	Mayo	Tirawley	Killala	Killala	IV.	170
15, 22	Townplots West	581 0 25	Mayo	Tirawley	Killala	Killala	IV.	170
21, 24	Townrath	426 1 15	Louth	Drogheda	St. Peter's	Drogheda	I.	175
24	Toy and Kirkland	264 2 21	Down	Dufferin	Killyleagh	Downpatrick	III.	167
100	Trabolgan	662 0 35	Cork, E.R.	Imokilly	Trabolgan	Middleton	II.	90
104	Tracashel	166 2 15	Cork, W.R.	Bear	Kilcaskan	Bantry	II.	123
99	TRACTON T.	—	Cork, E.R.	Kinalea	Tracton	Kinsale	II.	97
41	Tracystown East	204 3 30	Wexford	Shelmaliere West	Taghmon	Wexford	I.	335
36, 41	Tracystown West	401 1 15	Wexford	Shelmaliere West	Taghmon	New Ross	I.	335
116, 117	Trafrask East	194 0 16	Cork, W.R.	Bear	Kilcaskan	Castletown	II.	123
116	Trafrask West	122 0 24	Cork, W.R.	Bear	Kilcaskan	Castletown	II.	123
108	Tragalee	104 3 15	Kerry	Glanarought	Tuosist	Kenmare	II.	189
29	Tralee	374 1 37	Kerry	Trughanacmy	Tralee	Tralee	II.	214
48, 49	Tralee	163 0 27	Londonderry	Loughinsholin	Artrea	Magherafelt	III.	238
29	TRALEE T.	—	Kerry	Trughanacmy	{ Ratass } { Tralee }	Tralee	II.	{ 213 { 214
47, 48	Tralia	260 3 16	Kerry	Magunihy	Kilnanare	Killarney	II.	204
143	Tralong	283 1 19	Cork, W.R.	East Carbery (W.D.)	Ross	Clonakilty	II.	136
26	Tramore Burrow	217 0 3	Waterford	Middlethird	Drumcannon	Waterford	II.	366
26	Tramore East	155 3 24	Waterford	Middlethird	Drumcannon	Waterford	II.	366
26	Tramore West	138 2 0	Waterford	Middlethird	Drumcannon	Waterford	II.	366
48	Trane	28 1 1	Wexford	Forth	St. Iberius	Wexford	I.	314
34, 39	Trannish	126 0 30	Fermanagh	Magherastephana	Aghalurcher	Lisnaskea	III.	218
53, 64	Trantstown	500 0 9	Cork, E.R.	Barrymore	Killaspugmullane	Cork	II.	55
34	Trascan	1,481 2 26	King's Co.	Upper Philipstown	Clonyhurk	Mountmellick	I.	143
24	Trasgarve	426 3 1	Sligo	Tireragh	Kilmacshalgan	Dromore West	IV.	235
106	Traskernagh	241 3 28	Galway	Leitrim	Kilmeen	Loughrea	IV.	54
23	Trasna	310 3 15	Fermanagh	Magherastephana	Aghavea	Lisnaskea	III.	219
17	Trasnagh Island	24 3 11	Down	Ards Upper	Ardkeen	Newtownards	III.	159
39	Trasna Island	103 3 15	Fermanagh	Knockninny	Kinawley	Lisnaskea	III.	203
22	Trasna Island	12 3 31	Fermanagh	Tirkennedy	Trory	Enniskillen	III.	224
45	Trasternagh North	153 2 35	Galway	Tiaquin	Moylough	Mountbellew	IV.	80
45	Trasternagh South	330 0 38	Galway	Tiaquin	Moylough	Glennamaddy	IV.	80
26, 27	Traverston	295 1 18	Tipperary, N.R.	Upper Ormond	Dolla	Nenagh	II.	290
118, 119	Trawlebane	499 2 24	Cork, W.R.	West Carbery (W.D.)	Caheragh	Skibbereen	II.	142
118	Trawnahaha	199 0 15b	Cork, W.R.	Bantry	Kilmocomoge	Bantry	II.	122
91, 105	Trawnamaddree	562 2 3	Cork, W.R.	Bantry	Kilmocomoge	Bantry	II.	122
9	Trawnish Island	2 1 30	Leitrim	Drumahaire	Clooclare	Manorhamilton	IV.	94
12	Tray	205 0 16	Armagh	Armagh	Eglish	Armagh	III.	44
28	Tray	130 0 11	Monaghan	Farney	Donaghmoyne	Carrickmacross	III.	271
5, 10	Treadstown	195 1 23	Kildare	North Salt	Laraghbryan	Celbridge	I.	75
6	Treagh	253 2 35	Louth	Upper Dundalk	Creggan	Dundalk	I.	178
22	Trean	105 1 10c	Galway	Ballynahinch	Omey	Clifden	IV.	15
13, 14	Trean	256 1 35	Galway	Ross	Ballinrobe	Ballinrobe	IV.	72
33	Trean	208 0 5	Leitrim	Mohill	Cloone	Mohill	IV.	106
18	Trean	158 1 1	Louth	Ferrard	Dunleer	Ardee	I.	181
42	Trean	76 3 19	Roscommon	Athlone	Kilmeane	Roscommon	IV.	182
62, 63	Treanacally or Hagfield	860 0 5	Mayo	Costello	Kilbeagh	Swineford	IV.	141
29	Treanacreeve	191 3 13	Roscommon	Roscommon	Lissonuffy	Strokestown	IV.	212
21, 29	Treanagh	329 0 32	Mayo	Tirawley	Kilfian	Killala	IV.	169
10	Treanagry	287 1 6d	Roscommon	Boyle	Estersnow	Boyle	IV.	195
3, 6	Treanakillew	630 0 24e	Leitrim	Rosclogher	Killasnet	Manorhamilton	IV.	110
10	Treanamarly	260 2 18f	Roscommon	Boyle	Estersnow	Boyle	IV.	195
78	Treanamullin	188 1 39g	Donegal	Raphoe	Stranorlar	Stranorlar	III.	143
117	Treananearla	391 1 37	Galway	Longford	Killimorbologue	Portumna	IV.	59
43, 44	Treanaree	252 1 19	Kilkenny	Ida	Kilcolumb	Waterford	I.	103
61	Treanavinny	165 3 38	Donegal	Raphoe	Leck	Letterkenny	III.	140
29	Treanbaun	140 2 32	Galway	Clare	Belclare	Tuam	IV.	18
29, 43	Treanbaun	285 1 30h	Galway	Clare	Killower	Tuam	IV.	21
86, 98	Treanbaun	172 0 21	Galway	Kilconnell	Killaan	Loughrea	IV.	41
44, 52	Treanbeg	229 1 2	Donegal	Kilmacrenan	Conwal	Letterkenny	III.	126
57, 58, 67	Treanbeg	725 2 18	Mayo	Burrishoole	Burrishoole	Newport	IV.	120
61	Treanboy	155 0 14	Donegal	Raphoe	Convoy	Stranorlar	III.	136
7	Treanboy	397 3 28i	Galway	Ballymoe	Kilcroan	Glennamaddy	IV.	9
36	Treanboy	123 1 13	Limerick	Glenquin	Monagay	Newcastle	II.	247

(a) Including 1A. 1R. 0P. water. (d) Including 39A. 3R. 8P. water. (g) Including 2A. 3R. 35P. water.
(b) Including 2A. 3R. 20P. water. (e) Including 42A. 0R. 0P. water. (h) Including 24A. 3R. 4P. water.
(c) Including 12A. 0R. 10P. water. (f) Including 13A. 0R. 34P. water. (i) Including 1A. 0R. 4P. water.

5 T 2

No. of Sheet of the Ordnance Survey Maps.	Townlands and Towns.	Area in Statute Acres.	County.	Barony.	Parish.	Poor Law Union in 1857.	Townland Census of 1851, Part I.	
		A. R. P.					Vol.	Page
13	Treanboy	76 2 9	Longford	Moydow	Killashee	Longford	I.	162
11, 19, 20	Treanfasy or Glasalt	1,448 3 10	Donegal	Inishowen East	Donagh	Inishowen	III.	118
71	Treanfohanaun	574 3 32	Mayo	Gallen	Bohola	Swineford	IV.	147
63, 64	Treangarriv	570 1 1	Kerry	Iveragh	Glanbehy	Killarney	II.	196
29	Treangarrow	146 1 28	Mayo	Tirawley	Kilfian	Ballina	IV.	169
111	Treangarve	199 2 15	Mayo	Clanmorris	Crossboyne	Claremorris	IV.	133
60	Treankeel	567 3 22	Donegal	Raphoe	Conwal	Stranorlar	III.	137
71, 80	Treankeel	262 1 24a	Mayo	Gallen	Killedan	Swineford	IV.	150
96	Treankyle	31 1 28	Galway	Dunkellin	Kilconierin	Loughrea	IV.	29
94, 95	Treanlaur	179 3 21	Galway	Dunkellin	Ballynacourty	Galway	IV.	27
57, 58	Treanlaur	923 3 6	Mayo	Burrishoole	Burrishoole	Newport	IV.	120
109	Treanlaur	383 2 6	Mayo	Carra	Ballyovey	Ballinrobe	IV.	126
40	Treanlaur	117 3 14	Mayo	Gallen	Attymass	Ballina	IV.	147
72	Treanlaur	400 3 33	Mayo	Gallen	Kilconduff	Swineford	IV.	148
47	Treanlewis	172 2 31	Limerick	Kilmallock	St.Peter's & St.Paul's	Kilmallock	II.	250
34, 40	Treanmacmurtagh	585 0 24	Sligo	Tirerrill	Drumcolumb	Boyle	IV.	238
39	Treanmanagh	476 3 24b	Clare	Ibrickan	Kilmurry	Kilrush	II.	24
10, 11, 17	Treanmanagh	150 3 21c	Clare	Inchiquin	Kilkeedy	Corrofin	II.	26
63, 64	Treanmanagh	600 1 38d	Kerry	Iveragh	Glanbehy	Killarney	II.	196
24, 33	Treanmanagh	225 1 17	Limerick	Coonagh	Grean	Tipperary	II.	235
33	Treanmanagh	73 2 1	Limerick	Coonagh	Tuoghcluggin	Tipperary	II.	236
32	Treanmore	170 3 39	Leitrim	Mohill	Mohill	Mohill	IV.	108
40	Treanmore	437 2 30e	Sligo	Corran	Toomour	Boyle	IV.	228
35, 41	Treanmore	129 3 6	Sligo	Tirerrill	Kilmactranny	Boyle	IV.	240
15, 17	Treannadullagh	177 0 25	Leitrim	Drumahaire	Killarga	Manorhamilton	IV.	99
80	Treannagleragh	1,115 0 21	Mayo	Gallen	Killedan	Swineford	IV.	150
51	Treannahow	275 1 30	Clare	Bunratty Lower	Kilnasoolagh	Ennis	II.	6
112	Treannaskehy	181 3 13	Mayo	Clanmorris	Kilvine	Claremorris	IV.	134
40, 49	Treanoughter	277 2 29	Mayo	Gallen	Attymass	Ballina	IV.	147
55, 63	Treanoughtragh	74 3 20	Kerry	Iveragh	Killorglin	Killarney	II.	198
7	Treanpark	105 2 7	Galway	Ballymoe	Ballynakill	Glennamaddy	IV.	5
46	Treanrevagh	82 3 14	Galway	Killian	Moylough	Mountbellew	IV.	45
102	Treanrevagh	50 1 29	Mayo	Costello	Bekan	Claremorris	IV.	139
49	Treanrevagh	338 0 37	Mayo	Gallen	Killasser	Swineford	IV.	149
62	Treansallagh	297 2 2	Donegal	Raphoe	Taughboyne	Strabane	III.	144
40	Treanscrabbagh	411 1 32	Sligo	Tirerrill	Aghanagh	Boyle	IV.	237
61, 69	Treantaboy	901 1 16	Donegal	Raphoe	Convoy	Stranorlar	III.	136
62	Treantagh	249 3 38	Donegal	Raphoe	Taughboyne	Strabane	III.	144
54, 62	Treantaghmucklagh	352 0 32	Donegal	Raphoe	Taughboyne	Strabane	III.	144
60, 70	Treanybrogaun	285 1 16	Mayo	Carra	Turlough	Castlebar	IV.	131
16	Treehoo	163 1 30	Cavan	Tullygarvey	Annagh	Cootehill	III.	87
68	Tree Island	1 0 26	Mayo	Carra	Islandeady	Castlebar	IV.	129
21, 26	Treel	325 3 37	Fermanagh	Clanawley	Boho	Enniskillen	III.	189
14, 19	Treel	192 3 24	Longford	Ardagh	Ardagh	Longford	I.	151
23	Treel	59 0 3	Longford	Ardagh	Kilglass	Ballymahon	I.	152
8	Treel	87 1 7	Longford	Longford	Clongesh	Longford	I.	158
57, 67	Treel	1,634 3 15	Mayo	Burrishoole	Burrishoole	Newport	IV.	120
23	Treenearla Commons	375 2 19	Waterford	Decies without Drum	Kilrossanty	Kilmacthomas	II.	358
112	Trellick	227 3 5	Galway	Kiltartan	Kinvarradoorus	Gort	IV.	49
36	Tremblestown	427 2 10	Meath	Upper Navan	Trim	Trim	I.	217
37	Tremoge	1,889 1 19f	Tyrone	Omagh East	Termonmaguirk	Omagh	III.	315
13, 18	Trenchardstown	429 1 21	Kilkenny	Crannagh	Tullaroan	Kilkenny	I.	88
26, 30	Treuchmore	422 3 2	Kilkenny	Kells	Coolaghmore	Callan	I.	108
109	Treveg Island	0 1 5	Galway	Longford	Meelick	Portumna	IV.	62
38	Trevet	731 0 38	Meath	Skreen	Trevet	Dunshaughlin	I.	222
38	Trevet Grange	537 0 19	Meath	Ratoath	Trevet	Dunshaughlin	I.	220
29	Trianglepark	5 1 26	Wexford	Bantry	St. Mary's	New Ross	I.	302
39, 40	Trickvallen	279 2 12	Tyrone	Dungannon Upper	Arboe	Cookstown	III.	305
32	Trien	734 2 34	Fermanagh	Clanawley	Killesher	Enniskillen	III.	193
11	Trien	276 2 29	Kerry	Iraghticonnor	Knockanure	Listowel	II.	192
26	Trien	483 1 5	Roscommon	Castlereagh	Kilkeevin	Castlereagh	IV.	201
26, 27	Trienaltenagh	288 3 10	Londonderry	Coleraine	Desertoghill	Coleraine	III.	231
15, 23	Trienamongan	290 0 26g	Tyrone	Omagh West	Termonamongan	Castlederg	III.	317
11, 17	Trienearagh	1,708 0 27h	Kerry	Clanmaurice	Duagh	Listowel	II.	169
135, 136	Trieneens	81 2 4	Cork, W.R.	Ibane and Barryroe	Templequinlan	Clonakilty	II.	151
6	Trienieragh	270 1 16	Cork, E.R.	Orrery and Kilmore	Kilbolane	Kanturk	II.	108
47	Trihill East	273 2 11	Galway	Killian	Killeroran	Mountbellew	IV.	44
47	Trihill West	506 3 22	Galway	Killian	Killeroran	Mountbellew	IV.	44
36	Trilacroghan	322 1 19	Roscommon	Ballintober South	Kilgefin	Roscommon	IV.	189
29	Trila (Dillon)	318 2 21	Roscommon	Roscommon	Lissonuffy	Strokestown	IV.	212
29	Trila (Martin)	296 1 39	Roscommon	Roscommon	Lissonuffy	Strokestown	IV.	212
29, 38	Trillick	444 0 4	Donegal	Inishowen West	Fahan Lower	Inishowen	III.	120
26	Trillick	117 0 24	Fermanagh	Clanawley	Cleenish	Enniskillen	III.	191

(a) Including 29A. 0R. 31P. detached portion.
(b) Including 3A. 2R. 10P. water.
(c) Including 14A. 0R. 34P. water.

(d) Including 7A. 0R. 13P. water.
(e) Including 5A. 3R. 21P. Lough Labe.
(f) Including 11A. 0R. 0P. water.

(g) Including 3A. 3R. 3P. water.
(h) Including 31A. 1R. 30P. water.

No. of Sheet of the Ordnance Survey Maps.	Townlands and Towns.	Area in Statute Acres.	County.	Barony.	Parish.	Poor Law Union in 1857.	Townland Census of 1851. Part I.	
		A. R. P.					Vol.	Page
13,14,18,19	Trillickacurry .	369 2 2	Longford . .	Moydow . .	Ballymacormick .	Longford . .	I.	161
13, 18	Trillickatemple .	236 3 9	Longford . .	Moydow . .	Ballymacormick .	Longford . .	I.	161
56	TRILLICK T. . .	—	Tyrone . .	Omagh East . .	Kilskeery . .	Lowherstown .	III.	314
22, 23	Trimleston or Owens-town . . .	75 2 8	Dublin . .	Rathdown . .	Taney . .	Rathdown . .	I.	38
48	Trimmer . .	150 1 15	Wexford . .	Forth . . .	Kilscoran . .	Wexford . .	I.	311
53	Trimragh . .	324 2 14	Donegal . .	Raphoe . .	Leck . .	Letterkenny .	III.	140
36	TRIM T. . . .	—	Meath . .	{ Lower Moyfenrath } Upper Navan .	Trim . . .	Trim . .	I. {	212 217
11, 18	Trinamadan . .	956 3 28a	Tyrone . .	Strabane Upper .	Bodoney Lower .	Gortin . .	III.	324
19, 20	Trinity Island .	122 2 11	Cavan . .	Upper Loughtee .	Kilmore . .	Cavan . .	III.	85
6	*Trinity Island* .	1 3 13	Roscommon .	Boyle . .	Kilbryan . .	Boyle . .	IV.	195
9	Trinity Without .	68 3 24b	Waterford .	Waterford,Municipal Borough of .	Trinity Without .	Waterford .	II.	373
58	Trippeenagh . .	148 1 34	Kerry . .	Magunihy . .	Aglish . .	Killarney .	II.	200
1, 4	Trippul East . .	266 3 37	Kerry . .	Iraghticonnor .	Kilconly . .	Listowel . .	II.	191
1, 4	Trippul West . .	213 2 19	Kerry . .	Iraghticonnor .	Kilconly . .	Listowel . .	II.	191
87, 99	Tristaun . .	751 2 38	Galway . .	Clonmacnowen .	Clontuskert . .	Ballinasloe .	IV.	25
11	Tristernagh . .	158 3 0	Westmeath .	Moygoish . .	Kilbixy . .	Mullingar .	I.	279
11	Tristernagh Demesne	380 1 0	Westmeath .	Moygoish . .	Kilbixy . .	Mullingar .	I.	280
17,18,25,26	Tristia . . .	3,495 3 18	Mayo . .	Erris . .	Kilcommon .	Belmullet .	IV.	145
37, 46, 47	Tristia . . .	1,355 3 38c	Mayo . .	Tirawley . .	Crossmolina .	Ballina . .	IV.	167
1, 2, 4, 5	Trohanny . .	493 1 21	Meath . .	Lower Kells . .	Moynalty . .	Kells . .	I.	204
30	Tromaty . .	586 0 38	Donegal . .	Inishowen East .	Moville Upper .	Inishowen .	III.	119
30	Tromaty . .	432 2 17d	Donegal . .	Inishowen West .	Muff . .	Inishowen .	III.	121
39, 41	Tromaun . .	716 3 38	Roscommon .	Athlone . .	Athleague .	Roscommon .	IV.	179
41	TROMAUN T. .	—	Roscommon .	Athlone . .	Athleague .	Roscommon .	IV.	179
42	Tromman . .	632 2 18	Meath . .	Lower Moyfenrath .	Rathmolyon .	Trim . .	I.	211
31, 32, 37	Tromogagh . .	782 2 16	Fermanagh .	Clanawley . .	Killesher .	Enniskillen .	III.	193
14, 15	Tromra . . .	203 1 3	Antrim . .	Lower Glenarm .	Layd . .	Ballycastle .	III.	23
10, 11	Tromra . . .	423 2 25	Longford . .	Granard . .	Granard . .	Granard . .	I.	157
3	Tromra . . .	607 3 34	Westmeath .	Fore . .	Rathgarve .	Granard . .	I.	271
38	Tromracastle .	170 1 18	Clare . .	Ibrickan . .	Kilmurry . .	Kilrush . .	II.	24
38	Tromra East . .	222 2 13	Clare . .	Ibrickan . . .	Kilmurry . .	Kilrush . .	II.	24
38	Tromra West . .	139 1 19	Clare . .	Ibrickan . . .	Kilmurry . .	Kilrush . .	II.	24
10	Trooperfield .	105 3 30	Down . .	Castlereagh Lower .	Comber . .	Newtownards .	III.	162
112	Troopers-close .	9 3 13	Cork, E.R. .	Kinsale . .	Ringcurran .	Kinsale . .	II.	100
24	Trooperstown .	1,531 3 17	Wicklow . .	Ballinacor North .	Knockrath .	Rathdrum .	I.	347
16, 22	Trory . . .	335 1 32	Fermanagh .	Tirkennedy . .	Trory . .	Enniskillen .	III.	224
31	Trostan . . .	114 2 15e	Monaghan .	Farney . .	Magheross .	Carrickmacross .	III.	274
16	Trotts . . .	47 0 23	Sligo . .	Tireragh . .	Kilglass . .	Dromore West .	IV.	234
53	Trough . . .	393 3 35	Clare . .	Tulla Lower . .	O'Briensbridge .	Limerick . .	II.	38
62	Trouthill or Knock-brack . . .	200 1 6	Mayo . .	Costello . . .	Kilbeagh . .	Swineford .	IV.	141
14, 19	Troyswood . .	507 2 30f	Kilkenny . .	Crannagh . .	St. Canice .	Kilkenny .	I.	87
31, 37	Trubley . . .	471 0 9g	Meath . .	Lower Deece . .	Trubley . .	Trim . .	I.	192
13, 19	Trudder . . .	240 1 30	Wicklow . .	Newcastle . .	Newcastle Upper .	Rathdrum .	I.	353
55	True . . .	174 0 0	Tyrone . .	Dungannon Middle .	Killyman . .	Dungannon .	III.	303
100	Trumman East .	832 0 30h	Donegal . .	Tirhugh . .	Drumhome .	Donegal . .	III.	147
99, 100	Trumman West .	270 1 18	Donegal . .	Tirhugh . .	Drumhome .	Donegal . .	III.	147
100	Trumman West Barr	344 0 9	Donegal . .	Tirhugh . .	Drumhome .	Donegal . .	III.	147
50, 60	*Trummer* . .	3 0 39	Clare . .	Clonderalaw .	Killadysert .	Killadysert .	II.	16
67	Trummery . .	592 2 23	Antrim . .	Upper Massereene .	Magheramesk .	Lisburn . .	III.	31
17	Trumra . . .	1,444 1 2	Queen's Co. .	Maryborough West .	Clonenagh and Clonagheen . .	Mountmellick .	I.	243
77,78,86,87	Trusk . . .	1,326 2 19i	Donegal . .	Raphoe . .	Donaghmore .	Stranorlar .	III.	138
34,35,48,49	Truska . . .	415 0 19j	Galway . .	Ballynahinch .	Ballindoon .	Clifden . .	IV.	10
92	Truskaunnagappul .	189 2 6	Galway . .	Moycullen . .	Moycullen . .	Galway . .	IV.	71
65	Trusklieve . .	521 1 24	Clare . .	Moyarta . .	Kilballyowen .	Kilrush . .	II.	32
65	Trusklieve . .	328 3 27	Clare . .	Moyarta . .	Moyarta . .	Kilrush . .	II.	34
93	Trusky East . .	305 0 9k	Galway . .	Galway . .	Rahoon . .	Galway . .	IV.	38
93	Trusky West . .	294 2 26	Galway . .	Galway . .	Rahoon . .	Galway . .	IV.	38
73	Trust . . .	238 0 5	Galway . .	Kilconnell . .	Kilconnell .	Ballinasloe .	IV.	40
29	Trustan . . .	99 2 0	Fermanagh .	Magherastephana .	Aghavea . .	Lisnaskea .	III.	219
33	Trustan Glebe .	164 3 28	Fermanagh .	Clanawley . .	Killesher .	Enniskillen .	III.	193
2	Tuam . . .	564 2 13	Cavan . .	Tullyhaw . .	Killinagh .	Enniskillen .	III.	92
36	Tuam . . .	467 2 22	Roscommon .	Ballintober South .	Kilgefin . .	Roscommon .	IV.	189
1, 2	*Tuam Island* .	10 0 10	Cavan . .	Tullyhaw . .	Killinagh .	Enniskillen .	III.	92
29, 43	TUAM T. . .	—	Galway . .	{ Clare . . } { Dunmore . . }	Tuam . .	Tuam . .	IV.	{ 23 { 36
98, 99	Tubbrid . . .	355 2 29	Cork, E.R. .	Kinalea . .	Tracton . .	Kinsale . .	II.	97
5	Tubbrid . . .	170 3 12	Fermanagh .	Lurg . .	Drumkeeran .	Lowherstown .	III.	207
57	Tubbrid . . .	105 1 3l	Kerry . .	Dunkerron North .	Knockane .	Killarney .	II.	182
93	Tubbrid . . .	151 2 4	Kerry . .	Dunkerron South .	Templenoe .	Kenmare .	II.	185

(a) Including 3A. 2R. 32P. water.
(b) Included in the Parish of Trinity Without.
(c) Including 29A. 3R. 5P. water.
(d) Including 206A. 1R. 31P. detached portion.

(e) Including 17A. 0R. 10P. water.
(f) Including 19A. 0R. 22P. River Nore.
(g) Including 10A. 0R. 8P. water.
(h) Including 11A. 2R. 20P. water.

(i) Including 29A. 1R. 39P. water.
(j) Including 11A. 0R. 16P. water.
(k) Including 10A. 1R. 34P. water.
(l) Including 5A. 3R. 23P. water.

No. of Sheet of the Ordnance Survey Maps.	Townlands and Towns.	Area in Statute Acres.			County.	Barony.	Parish.	Poor Law Union in 1857.	Townland Census of 1851, Part I.	
		A.	R.	P.					Vol.	Page
39, 42	Tubbrid . . .	344	1	8	Kilkenny . .	Iverk . . .	Tubbrid . . .	Carrick on Suir	I.	107
42	Tubbrid . . .	327	1	11	King's Co. . .	Clonlisk . . .	Kilmurryely . .	Roscrea . .	I.	131
19	Tubbrid . . .	172	3	37	Limerick . .	Shanid . . .	Kilmoylan . .	Rathkeale . .	II.	256
8, 14	Tubbrid . . .	662	1	27	Meath . .	Fore . . .	Killeagh . .	Oldcastle . .	I.	201
15	Tubbrid . . .	174	1	26	Queen's Co. .	Clandonagh . .	Kyle . . .	Roscrea . .	I.	233
81, 87	Tubbrid . . .	543	2	5	Tipperary, S.R.	Iffa and Offa West .	Tubbrid . . .	Clogheen . .	II.	321
29	Tubbrid . . .	80	2	6	Waterford . .	Coshmore & Coshbride	Lismore and Mocollop	Lismore . .	II.	348
36, 37	Tubbrid Beg . .	1,346	2	30a	Mayo . . .	Tirawley . . .	Crossmolina . .	Ballina . .	IV.	167
12, 13	Tubbrid Lower .	475	0	13	Kilkenny . .	Crannagh . . .	Tubbridbritain .	Urlingford . .	I.	87
36, 37	Tubbrid More .	1,110	2	20b	Mayo . .	Tirawley . . .	Crossmolina . .	Ballina . .	IV.	167
12, 13	Tubbrid Upper .	497	2	37	Kilkenny . .	Crannagh . . .	Tubbridbritain .	Urlingford . .	I.	87
29, 35	Tubbrit . . .	86	3	4	Westmeath . .	Clonlonan . .	Kilcleagh . .	Athlone . .	I.	262
21	Tubrid Beg . .	613	1	9	Kerry . .	Clanmaurice . .	Ardfert . . .	Tralee . .	II.	167
9	Tubride . . .	346	3	20	Meath . .	Fore . . .	Oldcastle . .	Oldcastle . .	I.	202
20, 21, 29	Tubrid More .	993	3	15	Kerry . .	Clanmaurice . .	Ardfert . . .	Tralee . .	II.	167
3, 8	Tuckamine . .	111	2	2	Carlow . .	Rathvilly . .	Rathvilly . .	Baltinglass . .	I.	12
27	Tuckmill Hill .	226	3	32	Wicklow . .	Upper Talbotstown	Rathbran . .	Baltinglass . .	I.	365
98	Tuckmill Hill and Seahill . . .	118	0	3	Donegal . .	Banagh . . .	Inver . . .	Donegal . .	III.	108
21, 27	Tuckmill Lower .	278	2	32	Wicklow . .	Upper Talbotstown	Rathbran . .	Baltinglass . .	I.	365
11	Tuckmillpark . .	26	1	25	Leitrim . .	Drumahaire . .	Cloonclare . .	Manorhamilton	IV.	94
10	Tuckmilltate . .	29	0	6	Monaghan . .	Monaghan . .	Tehallan . .	Monaghan . .	III.	280
15	Tuckmilltown . .	245	2	13	Kildare . .	South Salt . .	Oughterard . .	Naas . .	I.	78
27	Tuckmill Upper .	390	3	8	Wicklow . .	Upper Talbotstown	Rathbran . .	Baltinglass . .	I.	365
24	Tuftarney . .	508	1	2	Antrim . .	Kilconway . .	Dunaghy . .	Ballymena . .	III.	26
26	Tuiterath . .	202	1	24	Meath . .	Lower Duleek .	Kentstown . .	Navan . .	I.	196
31	Tuitestown . .	172	3	8	Kilkenny . .	Kells . . .	Dunnamaggan .	Thomastown .	I.	108
7, 8, 12, 13	Tuitestown . .	543	0	17	Westmeath . .	Fore . . .	Kilpatrick . .	Castletowndelvin	I.	270
18, 25	Tuitestown . .	729	3	17	Westmeath . .	Moyashel and Magheradernon . .	Mullingar . .	Mullingar . .	I.	275
31	Tuitestown Little .	61	2	33	Kilkenny . .	Kells . . .	Dunnamaggan .	Callan . .	I.	108
32	Tulcon . . .	198	3	6c	Leitrim . .	Leitrim . . .	Mohill . .	Mohill . .	IV.	104
35, 36	Tulcon . . .	570	3	32d	Leitrim . .	Mohill . . .	Cloone . . .	Mohill . .	IV.	106
9, 10	Tulfarris . .	449	0	38e	Wicklow . .	Lower Talbotstown	Boystown . .	Naas . .	I.	359
7	Tulla . . .	565	3	35	Clare . .	Inchiquin . .	Kilkeedy . .	Corrofin . .	II.	26
35	Tulla . . .	297	0	29	Clare . .	Tulla Upper . .	Tulla . . .	Tulla . .	II.	42
125	Tulla . . .	160	3	27	Galway . .	Leitrim . . .	Ballynakill . .	Loughrea . .	IV.	52
57	Tulla . . .	774	1	31	Limerick . .	Coshlea . . .	Darragh . .	Kilmallock . .	II.	238
26	Tulla . . .	167	3	36	Tipperary, N.R.	Upper Ormond .	Kilmore . .	Nenagh . .	II.	291
65, 66	Tulla . . .	210	1	25	Tipperary, S.R.	Clanwilliam . .	Emly . . .	Tipperary . .	II.	308
47	Tullabards Great .	262	3	27	Wexford . .	Bargy . . .	Kilturk . .	Wexford . .	I.	307
47	Tullabards Little .	138	3	31	Wexford . .	Bargy . . .	Kilturk . .	Wexford . .	I.	307
1, 4	Tulla Beg . .	205	2	18	Kerry . .	Iraghticonnor .	Kilconly . .	Listowel . .	II.	191
24	Tullabeg . .	68	3	29	Limerick . .	Coonagh . .	Ballynaclogh .	Tipperary . .	II.	234
11, 16	Tullabeg . .	213	0	11	Wexford . .	Gorey . . .	Toome . . .	Gorey . .	I.	321
57	Tullabrack . .	979	1	29	Clare . .	Moyarta . .	Kilrush . .	Kilrush . .	II.	33
57	Tullabrack East .	382	0	39f	Clare . .	Moyarta . .	Kilmacduane .	Kilrush . .	II.	33
57	Tullabrack West .	490	3	38	Clare . .	Moyarta . .	Kilmacduane .	Kilrush . .	II.	33
31, 32	Tullabracky . .	377	2	32	Limerick . .	Coshma . .	Tullabracky .	Kilmallock . .	II.	244
27	Tullacommon . .	101	0	24	Queen's Co. .	Clandonagh . .	Donaghmore .	Donaghmore .	I.	233
24	Tullacondra . .	220	2	36	Cork, E.R.	Orrery and Kilmore	Ballyclogh . .	Mallow . .	II.	106
21	Tullacrimeen . .	184	1	39	Kerry . .	Clanmaurice . .	Kiltomy . .	Listowel . .	II.	172
39, 40	Tulla and Crumlin .	822	2	24	King's Co. . .	Ballybritt . .	Kinnitty . .	Parsonstown .	I.	126
7	Tulladuff . .	359	3	35	Cork, E.R.	Duhallow . .	Knocktemple .	Kanturk . .	II.	75
6	Tullagee . .	184	1	21g	Louth . .	Louth . . .	Louth . . .	Dundalk . .	I.	184
33	Tullagh . . .	138	0	35	Clare . .	Islands . . .	Drumcliff . .	Ennis . .	II.	30
88, 89	Tullagh . . .	111	2	25	Cork, E.R.	Imokilly . . .	Ballintemple .	Middleton . .	II.	84
88, 89	Tullagh . . .	219	0	39	Cork, E.R.	Imokilly . . .	Cloyne . . .	Middleton . .	II.	86
88, 89	Tullagh . . .	27	3	27	Cork, E.R.	Imokilly . . .	Inch . . .	Middleton . .	II.	87
93	Tullagh . . .	406	1	15	Cork, W.R.	East Carbery (W.D.)	Inchigeelagh .	Dunmanway .	II.	132
3, 10	Tullagh . . .	711	2	34	Donegal . .	Inishowen East .	Clonmany . .	Inishowen . .	III.	117
27	Tullagh . . .	1,109	0	32h	Donegal . .	Kilmacrenan . .	Mevagh . .	Milford . .	III.	130
29	Tullagh . . .	158	1	0	Tyrone . .	Dungannon Upper .	Derryloran . .	Cookstown .	III.	307
39, 40	Tullaghaboy . .	646	2	0	Clare . .	Islands . . .	Kilmaley . .	Ennis . .	II.	31
39, 53	Tullaghaboy . .	254	1	1	Galway . .	Moycullen . .	Kilcummin . .	Oughterard .	IV.	68
91, 92	Tullaghacullion .	176	0	18	Donegal . .	Banagh . . .	Killybegs Upper .	Glenties . .	III.	111
30, 31	Tullaghaglass .	1,092	3	14i	Sligo . .	Leyny . . .	Kilmacteige . .	Tobercurry .	IV.	231
21	Tullaghaloyst .	110	2	28	Monaghan . .	Dartree . . .	Currin . . .	Cootehill . .	III.	266
1	Tullaghan . .	120	2	37	Leitrim . .	Rosclogher . .	Rossinver . .	Ballyshannon .	IV.	112
8, 9	Tullaghan . .	112	3	27	Monaghan . .	Monaghan . .	Tedavnet . .	Monaghan . .	III.	280
9	Tullaghan . .	116	0	5	Queen's Co. .	Portnahinch . .	Lea . . .	Mountmellick .	I.	244
21	Tullaghan . .	326	1	37	Roscommon .	Castlereagh . .	Kilcorkey . .	Castlereagh .	IV.	200
9, 10	Tullaghan . .	317	3	1	Roscommon .	Frenchpark . .	Kilnamanagh .	Boyle . .	IV.	204

(a) Including 26A. 2R. 0P. water.
(b) Including 32A. 2R. 15P. water.
(c) Including 3A. 0R. 38P. water.

(d) Including 145A. 2R. 22P. water.
(e) Including 9A. 2R. 13P. water.
(f) Including 8A. 3R. 6P. water.

(g) Including 2A. 3R. 34P. water.
(h) Including 12A. 1R. 0P. water.
(i) Including 9A. 1R. 9P. water.

No. of Sheet of the Ordnance Survey Maps.	Townlands and Towns.	Area in Statute Acres.	County.	Barony.	Parish.	Poor Law Union in 1857.	Townland Census of 1851, Part I.	
		A. R. P.					Vol.	Page
19,20.25,26	Tullaghan	380 3 13	Sligo	Leyny	Ballysadare	Sligo	IV.	230
22, 23	Tullaghan	142 3 12	Westmeath	Kilkenny West	Kilkenny West	Athlone	I.	273
18, 19	Tullaghan	633 0 17	Westmeath	Moyashel and Magheradernon	Mullingar	Mullingar	I.	275
34	Tullaghanbaun	597 1 2	Mayo	Erris	Kilcommon	Belmullet	IV.	145
25, 34	Tullaghanduff	1,283 0 24	Mayo	Erris	Kilcommon	Belmullet	IV.	145
32	Tullaghanmore	122 3 12	Westmeath	Moycashel	Castletownkindalen	Mullingar	I.	277
64, 74	Tullaghanmore or Edmondstown Demesne	440 2 12	Mayo	Costello	Kilcolman	Castlereagh	IV.	141
30	Tullaghanoge	1,183 3 22	Meath	Upper Navan	Tullaghanoge	Trim	I.	217
64, 74	Tullaghanrock	668 2 2	Mayo	Costello	Kilcolman	Castlereagh	IV.	141
22	Tullaghans	896 0 32	Antrim	Kilconway	Finvoy	Ballymoney	III.	26
16, 18	Tullaghans	151 2 7	Leitrim	Drumahaire	Inishmagrath	Manorhamilton	IV.	97
30	Tullaghanshanlin	162 1 6	Westmeath	Clonlonan	Ballyloughloe	Athlone	I.	261
32	Tullaghansleek	51 2 34	Westmeath	Moycashel	Castletownkindalen	Mullingar	I.	277
24, 30	Tullaghanstown	726 1 1	Meath	Upper Navan	Clonmacduff	Trim	I.	216
1	TULLAGHAN T.	—	Leitrim	Rosclogher	Rossinver	Ballyshannon	IV.	112
31	Tullaghaun	124 2 21	Galway	Tiaquin	Kilkerrin	Glennamaddy	IV.	77
103	Tullaghaun	207 3 7	Mayo	Costello	Annagh	Claremorris	IV.	138
26	Tullaghaunnashammer	848 2 35	Mayo	Erris	Kilcommon	Belmullet	IV.	145
23	Tullaghbane	239 0 14	Antrim	Kilconway	Dunaghy	Ballymena	III.	26
48	Tullaghbeg	101 0 20	Antrim	Upper Toome	Duneane	Antrim	III.	35
5, 6, 13	Tullaghbeg	980 0 35a	King's Co.	Garrycastle	Clonmacnoise	Parsonstown	I.	135
46, 47	Tullagh Beg	257 0 10b	Tyrone	Dungannon Middle	Donaghenry	Cookstown	III.	301
93, 99	Tullaghcullion	66 0 25	Donegal	Tirhugh	Donegal	Donegal	III.	145
36, 37	Tullagher	367 3 8	Kilkenny	Ida	Dysartmoon	New Ross	I.	102
10,11,17,18	Tullagherin	937 2 20	Tyrone	Strabane Upper	Bodoney Upper	Gortin	III.	324
37	TULLAGHER T.	—	Kilkenny	Ida	Dysartmoon	New Ross	I.	102
37	Tullaghgarley	315 1 18	Antrim	Lower Antrim	Ahoghill	Ballymena	III.	3
37	Tullaghgarley	279 2 32	Antrim	Lower Antrim	Connor	Ballymena	III.	3
27, 32	Tullaghgarley	652 0 24	Antrim	Lower Toome	Ahoghill	Ballymena	III.	32
11, 12	Tullaghgore	432 2 0	Antrim	Upper Dunluce	Tullaghgore	Ballymoney	III.	20
16	Tullagh Lower	142 3 26	Clare	Corcomroe	Kilfenora	Corrofin	II.	19
105	Tullagh Lower	67 1 17	Galway	Loughrea	Loughrea	Loughrea	IV.	66
50	Tullaghlumman Beg	394 1 31c	Galway	Ballynahinch	Moyrus	Clifden	IV.	13
50	Tullaghlumman More	787 1 31d	Galway	Ballynahinch	Moyrus	Clifden	IV.	13
37, 43	Tullaghmedan	477 2 32	Meath	Lower Deece	Derrypatrick	Dunshaughlin	I.	191
82, 88	Tullaghmelan	97 2 19	Tipperary, S.R.	Iffa and Offa West	Tullaghmelan	Clogheen	II.	321
39	Tullaghmore	441 3 22e	Galway	Moycullen	Kilcummin	Oughterard	IV.	68
46, 47	Tullagh More	235 3 7f	Tyrone	Dungannon Middle	Donaghenry	Cookstown	III.	301
3	Tullaghmurry East	84 0 35	Londonderry	North East Liberties of Coleraine	Ballyaghran	Coleraine	III.	245
3	Tullaghmurry West	91 3 36	Londonderry	North East Liberties of Coleraine	Ballyaghran	Coleraine	III.	245
9, 15	Tullaghna	434 1 8	Kerry	Clanmaurice	Rattoo	Listowel	II.	173
32	Tullaghnacrossan	77 3 20	Westmeath	Moycashel	Castletownkindalen	Mullingar	I.	277
30	Tullaghnageeragh	55 2 30	Westmeath	Clonlonan	Kilcleagh	Athlone	I.	262
24,25,33,34	Tullaghobegly Irish	2,448 1 38g	Donegal	Kilmacrenan	Tullaghobegly	Dunfanaghy	III.	132
25, 34	Tullaghobegly Scotch	1,425 3 15h	Donegal	Kilmacrenan	Tullaghobegly	Dunfanaghy	III.	132
4, 5	Tullaghomeath	719 0 2	Louth	Lower Dundalk	Carlingford	Dundalk	I.	177
8, 13	Tullaghore	345 2 28	Antrim	Cary	Armoy	Ballycastle	III.	11
16	Tullagh Upper	222 3 8	Clare	Corcomroe	Kilfenora	Corrofin	II.	19
105	Tullagh Upper	86 2 10	Galway	Loughrea	Loughrea	Loughrea	IV.	66
24, 31	Tullagh Upper or Killeenbane	55 0 13	Westmeath	Rathconrath	Killare	Mullingar	I.	283
5	Tullaghyrory	173 0 37	Cavan	Tullyhaw	Killinagh	Enniskillen	III.	92
57, 58	Tullagower	881 0 20	Clare	Moyarta	Kilrush	Kilrush	II.	33
75	Tullagnageeragh	113 3 3	Cork, E.R.	Barrymore	Carrigtohill	Middleton	II.	52
24	Tullagroe	78 3 30	Clare	Corcomroe	Clooney	Corrofin	II.	18
30, 31	Tullagubbeen	796 3 6	Kerry	Trughanacmy	Castleisland	Tralee	II.	209
102	Tullaha	188 1 29	Kerry	Glanarought	Kilcaskan	Kenmare	II.	187
67, 75	Tullaha	835 0 9i	Kerry	Magunihy	Killaha	Killarney	II.	202
44,45,53,54	Tullaha	379 0 1	Limerick	Glenquin	Killagholehane	Newcastle	II.	245
20	Tullahedy	569 0 4	Tipperary, N.R.	Upper Ormond	Kilmore	Nenagh	II.	291
88, 100	Tullaheen Beg	43 0 39	Cork, E.R.	Imokilly	Inch	Middleton	II.	87
88, 100	Tullaheen More	67 1 33	Cork, E.R.	Imokilly	Inch	Middleton	II.	87
2, 5	Tullahennel North	1,220 2 33	Kerry	Iraghticonnor	Aghavallen	Listowel	II.	189
5	Tullahennel South	971 3 35	Kerry	Iraghticonnor	Aghavallen	Listowel	II.	189
46, 56, 57	Tullaher	1,675 2 16j	Clare	Ibrickan	Killard	Kilrush	II.	23
24	Tullaherin	759 1 26	Kilkenny	Gowran	Tullaherin	Thomastown	I.	100
34	Tullahought	211 0 26	Kilkenny	Kells	Tullahought	Carrick on Suir	I.	110
91	Tullakeel	264 1 18	Kerry	Dunkerron South	Kilcrohane	Kenmare	II.	184
13	Tullakeel	716 3 17	Louth	Ardee	Clonkeen	Ardee	I.	172
24	Tullaloughan	90 1 1	Clare	Corcomroe	Clooney	Corrofin	II.	18

(a) Including 74A. 0R. 0P. water.
(b) Including 24A. 3R. 6P. water.
(c) Including 154A. 0R. 32P. water.
(d) Including 312A. 1R. 22P. water.

(e) Including 3A. 0R. 4P. water.
(f) Including 15A. 2R. 0P. Lough Roughan.
(g) Including 117A. 1R. 7P. water.

(h) Including 5A. 0R. 3P. water.
(i) Including 3A. 3R. 8P. Lough Doo.
(j) Including 45A. 0R. 5P. Tullaher Lough.

No. of Sheet of the Ordnance Survey Maps.	Townlands and Towns.	Area in Statute Acres.	County.	Barony.	Parish.	Poor Law Union in 1857.	Townland Census of 1851, Part I.	
		A. R. P.					Vol.	Page
69	Tullamain	95 1 32	Tipperary, S.R.	Middlethird	Kilbragh	Cashel	II.	327
69	Tullamain	998 1 9	Tipperary, S.R.	Middlethird	Tullamaine	Cashel	II.	331
22, 23, 26, 27	Tullamaine (*Ashbrook*)	670 0 1	Kilkenny	Shillelogher	Tullamaine	Callan	I.	116
26	Tullamaine (*Flood*)	138 0 6	Kilkenny	Shillelogher	Tullamaine	Callan	I.	116
15	Tullamore	102 0 4	Clare	Corcomroe	Killaspuglonane	Ennistimon	II.	19
5, 6, 10, 11	Tullamore	1,902 0 10	Kerry	Iraghticonnor	Galey	Listowel	II.	190
4, 5	Tulla More	663 0 28	Kerry	Iraghticonnor	Kilconly	Listowel	II.	191
17	Tullamore	411 3 36	King's Co.	Ballycowan	Kilbride	Tullamore	I.	128
20	Tullamore	354 3 24	Tipperary, N.R.	Owney and Arra	Monsea	Nenagh	II.	296
17	TULLAMORE T.	—	King's Co.	Ballycowan	Kilbride	Tullamore	I.	128
27	Tullamoylin	66 1 7	Tipperary, N.R.	Upper Ormond	Ballynaclogh	Nenagh	II.	290
26, 27	Tullamoylin	234 1 28	Tipperary, N.R.	Upper Ormond	Dolla	Nenagh	II.	290
71	Tullanacorra	411 1 35	Mayo	Gallen	Kilconduff	Swineford	IV.	148
20, 25	Tullanacrunat	132 2 1	Monaghan	Cremorne	Muckno	Castleblayney	III.	262
25	Tullanacrunat North	86 2 10	Monaghan	Farney	Donaghmoyne	Castleblayney	III.	271
25	Tullanacrunat South	82 0 20	Monaghan	Farney	Donaghmoyne	Castleblayney	III.	271
51, 52	Tullanafoile	515 0 10*a*	Tyrone	Clogher	Clogher	Clogher	III.	293
6	Tullanaginn	133 3 31	Fermanagh	Lurg	Magheraculmoney	Lowtherstown	III.	208
6, 11	Tullanaglare	60 3 34	Fermanagh	Lurg	Magheraculmoney	Lowtherstown	III.	208
5, 6	Tullanaglug	94 2 27	Fermanagh	Lurg	Magheraculmoney	Lowtherstown	III.	208
37	Tullanaglug	579 2 5	Sligo	Leyny	Kilmacteige	Tobercurry	IV.	231
5, 6, 10, 11	Tullanaguiggy	251 3 7	Fermanagh	Lurg	Magheraculmoney	Lowtherstown	III.	208
52	Tullanascreen	135 1 28	Donegal	Kilmacrenan	Conwal	Letterkenny	III.	126
58, 64	Tullanavert	246 2 0	Tyrone	Clogher	Clogher	Clogher	III.	293
9	Tullandreen	115 0 4	Cavan	Tullyhaw	Templeport	Bawnboy	III.	95
15	Tullance	307 2 26	Londonderry	Tirkeeran	Faughanvale	Londonderry	III.	250
5	Tullanierin	143 1 15	Cavan	Tullyhaw	Killinagh	Enniskillen	III.	92
19, 26	Tullanisky	759 2 34	Westmeath	Fartullagh	Lynn	Mullingar	I.	269
11	Tullanree	581 1 34	Donegal	Inishowen East	Donagh	Inishowen	III.	118
7, 8	Tullans	458 0 25	Londonderry	North East Liberties of Coleraine	Coleraine	Coleraine	III.	246
3, 5	Tullantanty	174 0 34	Cavan	Tullyhaw	Killinagh	Enniskillen	III.	92
3, 5	Tullanteen	130 1 39	Cavan	Tullyhaw	Killinagh	Enniskillen	III.	92
5	Tullantintin	128 2 14	Cavan	Tullyhaw	Killinagh	Enniskillen	III.	92
8	Tullanvoolty	435 1 5	Kilkenny	Galmoy	Erke	Urlingford	I.	92
36	Tullaree	151 1 16	Kerry	Corkaguiny	Killiney	Dingle	II.	178
18	Tullaroan	443 1 29	Kilkenny	Crannagh	Tullaroan	Kilkenny	I.	88
56, 66	Tullaroe	1,036 2 9	Clare	Moyarta	Moyarta	Kilrush	II.	34
39	Tullaroe	191 0 4	King's Co.	Ballybritt	Ettagh	Roscrea	I.	125
12, 17	Tullaskeagh	113 1 29	Tipperary, N.R.	Ikerrin	Roscrea	Roscrea	II.	276
33	Tullassa	481 0 22	Clare	Islands	Drumcliff	Ennis	II.	30
35	TULLA T.	—	Clare	Tulla Upper	Tulla	Tulla	II.	42
70	Tullatreada	349 1 29	Cork, W.R.	West Muskerry	Macroom	Macroom	II.	160
16	Tullavally	252 0 32	Cavan	Tullygarvey	Drung	Cootehill	III.	89
73	Tullawicky	182 3 12	Galway	Kilconnell	Ballymacward	Ballinasloe	IV.	39
50	Tulleague	212 2 1	Mayo	Gallen	Killasser	Swineford	IV.	149
12	Tulleevin	65 3 12	Monaghan	Dartree	Clones	Monaghan	III.	265
23	Tullen	147 2 18	Roscommon	Roscommon	Kiltrustan	Strokestown	IV.	211
54	Tullequane	104 0 33	Tipperary, S.R.	Slievardagh	Lickfinn	Urlingford	II.	335
31, 39	Tullerboy	583 1 29	Limerick	Coshma	Athlacca	Kilmallock	II.	241
39, 40	Tullerstown	205 2 16	Wexford	Shelburne	Tintern	New Ross	I.	329
65	Tullig	1,057 3 34	Clare	Moyarta	Kilballyowen	Kilrush	II.	32
65	Tullig	14 1 27	Clare	Moyarta	Moyarta	Kilrush	II.	34
51	Tullig	213 2 30	Cork, E.R.	Barretts	Whitechurch	Cork	II.	50
16	Tullig	177 3 10	Cork, E.R.	Orrery and Kilmore	Bregoge	Mallow	II.	106
122	Tullig	135 1 5	Cork, W.R.	East Carbery (E.D.)	Kilmaloda	Clonakilty	II.	129
134	Tullig	402 1 3	Cork, W.R.	East Carbery (W.D.)	Kilmacabea	Skibbereen	II.	133
130	Tullig	192 3 20	Cork, W.R.	West Carbery (W.D.)	Durrus	Bantry	II.	142
130	Tullig	23 2 12	Cork, W.R.	West Carbery (W.D.)	Kilcrohane	Bantry	II.	144
39, 48	Tullig	1,730 2 6	Cork, W.R.	West Muskerry	Drishane	Millstreet	II.	156
16, 22	Tullig	710 3 11	Kerry	Clanmaurice	Kilfeighny	Listowel	II.	170
45	Tullig	211 1 5	Kerry	Corkaguiny	Ballinvoher	Dingle	II.	174
36	Tullig	321 2 12	Kerry	Corkaguiny	Killiney	Dingle	II.	178
57, 65	Tullig	347 0 35*b*	Kerry	Dunkerron North	Knockane	Killarney	II.	182
84, 93	Tullig	391 1 7	Kerry	Glanarought	Kenmare	Kenmare	II.	186
102, 110	Tullig	787 3 15	Kerry	Glanarought	Kilcaskan	Kenmare	II.	187
88, 89	Tullig	971 0 0	Kerry	Iveragh	Dromod	Cahersiveen	II.	195
70	Tullig	295 0 31	Kerry	Iveragh	Killinane	Cahersiveen	II.	197
66, 67	Tullig	319 1 18	Kerry	Magunihy	Killarney	Killarney	II.	204
40	Tullig	659 2 20	Kerry	Trughanacmy	Castleisland	Tralee	II.	209
61	Tullig Beg	73 0 15	Cork, E.R.	East Muskerry	Magourney	Macroom	II.	105
86, 98	Tullig Beg	150 3 27	Cork, E.R.	Kerrycurrihy	Ballinaboy	Cork	II.	91
56, 64	Tullig Beg	1,314 1 25	Kerry	Trughanacmy	Killorglin	Killarney	II.	211

(*a*) Including 0A. 2R. 32P. water.   (*b*) Including 13A. 0R. 10P. water.

No. of Sheet of the Ordnance Survey Maps.	Townlands and Towns.	Area in Statute Acres.	County.	Barony.	Parish.	Poor Law Union in 1857.	Townland Census of 1851. Part I.	
		A. R. P.					Vol.	Page
81	Tulligealane . .	1,246 3 35	Kerry . .	Iveragh . .	Dromod . . .	Cahersiveen .	II.	195
134, 135	Tulligee . . .	131 3 0	Cork, W.R. .	East Carbery (W.D.)	Ross . . .	Clonakilty .	II.	136
45	Tulligmacthomas .	677 3 38	Limerick . .	Connello Upper .	Dromcolliher .	Newcastle .	II.	233
61	Tullig More . .	481 2 25	Cork, E.R. .	East Muskerry .	Magourney .	Macroom .	II.	105
86, 98	Tullig More . .	447 3 0	Cork, E.R. .	Kerrycurrihy .	Ballinaboy .	Cork . .	II.	91
56	Tullig More . .	535 2 16	Kerry . .	Trughanacmy .	Killorglin .	Killarney .	II.	211
35, 43	Tulligoline North .	1,054 1 12	Limerick . .	Glenquin . .	Monagay . .	Newcastle .	II.	247
43	Tulligoline South .	674 3 18d	Limerick . .	Glenquin . .	Monagay . .	Newcastle .	II.	247
22, 29	Tullin . . .	108 1 5	Westmeath .	Brawny . .	St. Mary's .	Athlone . .	I.	260
21, 28	Tullindoney . .	391 0 37	Down . .	Lower Iveagh, Lr. pt.	Dromore . .	Banbridge .	III.	168
15, 20	Tullinearly . .	152 3 15	Monaghan .	Cremorne . .	Muckno . .	Castleblayney .	III.	262
45	Tullinespick . .	49 3 38	Down . .	Lecale Upper .	Bright . .	Downpatrick .	III.	180
28	Tullinisky . .	697 3 32	Down . .	Lower Iveagh, Lr. pt.	Garvaghy .	Banbridge .	III.	168
98, 99	Tullinlagan . .	141 1 4	Donegal . .	Banagh . .	Inver . .	Donegal . .	III.	108
108, 118	Tullinlicky . .	363 1 6	Galway . .	Longford . .	Fahy . .	Portumna .	IV.	58
83, 84	Tullinlough . .	156 3 38b	Donegal . .	Banagh . .	Inver . .	Donegal . .	III.	108
15	Tullinloughan . .	238 2 18	Leitrim . .	Drumahaire .	Killarga .	Manorhamilton	IV.	99
8	Tullintaggart . .	106 3 6	Leitrim . .	Rosclogher .	Cloonclare .	Manorhamilton	IV.	109
34	Tullintanvally . .	810 2 0	Down . .	Upper Iveagh, Up. pt.	Annaclone .	Banbridge .	III.	174
83, 92	Tullinteane . .	1,011 2 10	Donegal . .	Banagh . .	Killaghtee .	Donegal . .	III.	109
20	Tullinteskin . .	72 0 2	Fermanagh .	Clanawley .	Cleenish . .	Ballyshannon .	III.	191
20	Tullintlisny . .	191 0 39	Monaghan .	Cremorne . .	Muckno . .	Castleblayney .	III.	262
8	Tullintloy . .	541 3 22c	Leitrim . .	Rosclogher .	Cloonclare .	Manorhamilton	IV.	109
16	Tullintowell . .	435 0 36	Leitrim . .	Drumahaire .	Inishmagrath .	Manorhamilton	IV.	97
23, 29	Tullintrain . .	571 3 13	Londonderry .	Tirkeeran .	Cumber Upper .	Londonderry .	III.	249
15, 20	Tullintrat . .	250 2 22	Monaghan .	Cremorne . .	Muckno . .	Castleblayney .	III.	262
22	Tullintuppeen . .	246 0 6	Roscommon .	Roscommon .	Elphin . .	Strokestown .	IV.	210
15, 16	Tullinwannia . .	265 0 12	Leitrim . .	Drumahaire .	Killarga .	Manorhamilton	IV.	99
15	Tullinwillin . .	159 1 30	Leitrim . .	Drumahaire .	Killarga .	Manorhamilton	IV.	99
20	Tullinwonny . .	75 0 37	Fermanagh .	Magheraboy .	Boho . .	Enniskillen .	III.	210
114	Tullira . . .	541 2 0	Galway . .	Dunkellin .	Ardrahan .	Gort . .	IV.	27
41	Tullispark . .	134 3 10	Wexford . .	Bargy . .	Kilmannan .	Wexford .	I.	306
34	Tullog . . .	508 1 38	Meath . .	Upper Duleek .	Stamullin .	Drogheda .	I.	199
71, 78	Tullohea . . .	578 0 5	Tipperary, S.R.	Iffa and Offa East .	Garrangibbon .	Clonmel .	II.	313
68	Tullokyne . .	171 1 24	Galway . .	Moycullen .	Moycullen .	Galway . .	IV.	71
19	Tullomoy . .	677 3 32	Queen's Co. .	Ballyadams .	Tullomoy .	Athy . .	I.	232
24	Tullore . . .	199 2 28	Queen's Co. .	Cullenagh .	Ballyroan .	Abbeyleix .	I.	239
59, 67	Tullorum . .	97 0 12	Kerry . .	Magunihy .	Killarney .	Killarney .	II.	204
30, 31	Tullovin . . .	100 3 1	Limerick . .	Coshma . .	Anhid . .	Croom . .	II.	241
30, 31	Tullovin . . .	601 2 37	Limerick . .	Coshma . .	Croom . .	Croom . .	II.	242
37	Tullow . . .	229 0 24	Tipperary, N.R.	Owney and Arra .	Kilvellane .	Nenagh .	II.	296
87, 88	Tullow . . .	328 2 22	Tipperary, S.R.	Iffa and Offa West .	Ballybacon .	Clogheen .	II.	317
70	Tullow . . .	192 2 10	Tipperary, S.R.	Middlethird .	Kiltinan .	Clonmel .	II.	328
8, 13	Tullowbeg . .	547 0 23	Carlow . .	Rathvilly .	Fennagh .	Carlow .	I.	11
15	Tullowbrin . .	984 2 14	Kilkenny . .	Gowran . .	Rathcoole .	Kilkenny .	I.	98
42	Tullowclay . .	290 2 23	Wicklow . .	Shillelagh .	Ardoyne .	Shillelagh .	I.	357
62, 63	Tullowcossaun .	453 1 0	Tipperary, S.R.	Middlethird .	Cloneen . .	Cashel .	II.	325
10, 14	Tullowglass . .	286 0 11	Kilkenny . .	Fassadinin .	Mayne . .	Kilkenny .	I.	90
30	Tullowmacjames .	2,077 2 0	Tipperary, N.R.	Ikerrin . .	Templetouhy .	Thurles .	II.	277
8	Tullowphelim . .	1,525 2 28	Carlow . .	Rathvilly .	Tullowphelim .	Carlow .	I.	12
8	TULLOW T. . .	—	Carlow . .	Rathvilly .	{ Fennagh . . { Tullowphelim . }	Carlow .	I.	{ 11 { 12
38	Tully . . .	744 0 20	Antrim . .	Lower Antrim .	Ballyclug .	Ballymena .	III.	3
20	Tully . . .	90 1 11	Antrim . .	Lower Glenarm .	Layd . .	Ballycastle .	III.	23
29	Tully . . .	307 1 3	Antrim . .	Lower Glenarm .	Tickmacrevan .	Larne .	III.	24
55	Tully . . .	952 3 25	Antrim . .	Lower Massereene .	Killead . .	Antrim .	III.	28
14,15,19,20	Tully . . .	105 3 18d	Cavan . .	Lower Loughtee .	Drumlane .	Cavan .	III.	81
19, 24	Tully . . .	264 2 11	Cavan . .	Tullyhunco .	Killashandra .	Cavan .	III.	99
20	Tully . . .	90 2 28	Cavan . .	Upper Loughtee .	Kilmore . .	Cavan .	III.	85
17	Tully . . .	166 3 23	Donegal . .	Kilmacrenan .	Clondavaddog .	Milford .	III.	125
61, 62	Tully . . .	129 1 17	Donegal . .	Raphoe . .	Raymoghy .	Letterkenny .	III.	142
94, 100	Tully . . .	195 2 33	Donegal . .	Tirhugh . .	Donegal . .	Donegal .	III.	145
107	Tully . . .	88 1 39	Donegal . .	Tirhugh . .	Kilbarron .	Ballyshannon .	III.	148
27	Tully . . .	172 1 6e	Fermanagh .	Clanawley .	Cleenish . .	Enniskillen .	III.	191
32	Tully . . .	64 2 29	Fermanagh .	Clanawley .	Killesher .	Enniskillen .	III.	193
35	Tully . . .	989 3 19f	Fermanagh .	Clankelly .	Clones . .	Clones .	III.	197
38	Tully . . .	269 1 16	Fermanagh .	Knockninny .	Kinawley .	Lisnaskea .	III.	202
15, 16	Tully . . .	70 0 25	Fermanagh .	Lurg . .	Trory . .	Lowtherstown .	III.	209
10	Tully . . .	345 0 18	Fermanagh .	Magheraboy .	Inishmacsaint .	Ballyshannon .	III.	213
27	Tully . . .	64 1 24g	Fermanagh .	Tirkennedy .	Derryvullan .	Enniskillen .	III.	221
33	Tully . . .	358 2 17h	Galway . .	Killian . .	Killeroran .	Mountbellew .	IV.	44
32, 46	Tully . . .	106 0 34	Galway . .	Killian . .	Killian . .	Mountbellew .	IV.	45
168	Tully . . .	122 0 32	Galway . .	Longford . .	Meelick . .	Portumna .	IV.	61

(a) Including 5A. 3R. 19P. detached portion.   (d) Including 36A. 0R. 9P. water.   (g) Including 7A. 0R. 21P. water.
(b) Including 11A. 2R. 6P. water.   (e) Including 54A. 2R. 16P. water.   (h) Including 5A. 0R. 0P. water.
(c) Including 7A. 2R. 36P. water.   (f) Including 6A. 2R. 7P. water.

5 U

No. of Sheet of the Ordnance Survey Maps.	Townlands and Towns.	Area in Statute Acres. A. R. P.	County.	Barony.	Parish.	Poor Law Union in 1857.	Townland Census of 1851, Part I. Vol.	Page
91	Tully	518 0 37a	Galway	Moycullen	Killannin	Galway	IV.	70
2	Tully	274 1 11	King's Co.	Kilcoursey	Ardnurcher or Horseleap	Tullamore	I.	140
2	Tully	24 1 2	King's Co.	Kilcoursey	Kilmanaghan	Tullamore	I.	141
25	Tully	107 1 0	Leitrim	Carrigallen	Oughteragh	Bawnboy	IV.	93
14, 15	Tully	232 1 1	Leitrim	Drumahaire	Killanummery	Manorhamilton	IV.	98
24, 25	Tully	212 0 27b	Leitrim	Leitrim	Fenagh	Mohill	IV.	100
31	Tully	179 1 23	Leitrim	Leitrim	Kiltoghert	Cark. on Shannon	IV.	103
7	Tully	386 3 15	Leitrim	Rosclogher	Killasnet	Manorhamilton	IV.	110
9	Tully	117 2 2	Londonderry	Keenaght	Tamlaght Finlagan	NewTnLimavady	III.	238
14	Tully	250 2 1	Londonderry	Tirkeeran	Faughanvale	Londonderry	III.	250
15	Tully	487 1 7	Longford	Granard	Granard	Granard	I.	157
13	Tully	376 1 38	Longford	Longford	Clongesh	Longford	I.	158
23	Tully	207 0 35	Longford	Shrule	Kilglass	Ballymahon	I.	166
13	Tully	115 3 22	Louth	Ardee	Clonkeen	Ardee	I.	172
10, 11	Tully	765 3 28	Louth	Louth	Louth	Dundalk	I.	184
78	Tully	202 3 6c	Mayo	Carra	Aglish	Castlebar	IV.	124
79, 90	Tully	119 1 3	Mayo	Carra	Drum	Castlebar	IV.	128
96	Tully	327 0 10	Mayo	Murrisk	Kilgeever	Westport	IV.	160
8	Tully	102 2 39	Meath	Fore	Killeagh	Oldcastle	I.	201
9	Tully	94 0 31	Monaghan	Monaghan	Monaghan	Monaghan	III.	277
6, 9	Tully	50 2 0	Monaghan	Monaghan	Tedavnet	Monaghan	III.	280
6	Tully	197 1 0d	Monaghan	Trough	Donagh	Monaghan	III.	283
23, 24	Tully	413 2 28	Roscommon	Ballintober North	Kilglass	Strokestown	IV.	186
17, 18	Tully	255 0 34e	Roscommon	Ballintober North	Kilmore	Cark. on Shannon	IV.	187
28, 29, 36	Tully	228 1 8f	Roscommon	Ballintober South	Kilbride	Roscommon	IV.	189
21	Tully	1,182 0 15	Roscommon	Castlereagh	Kilcorkey	Castlereagh	IV.	200
19	Tully	916 2 23g	Roscommon	Frenchpark	Tibohine	Castlereagh	IV.	205
54	Tully	204 1 10	Roscommon	Moycarn	Moore	Ballinasloe	IV.	207
15	Tully	271 2 20	Sligo	Carbury	Calry	Sligo	IV.	220
8	Tully	208 1 5	Sligo	Carbury	Drumcliff	Sligo	IV.	222
14	Tully	122 3 29	Sligo	Carbury	Killaspugbrone	Sligo	IV.	222
40	Tully	456 3 15	Sligo	Corran	Toomour	Boyle	IV.	228
34	Tully	98 0 19	Sligo	Tirerrill	Killadoon	Boyle	IV.	239
59	Tully	148 1 24	Tyrone	Clogher	Clogher	Clogher	III.	293
60, 66	Tully	236 3 36	Tyrone	Dungannon Lower	Carnteel	Clogher	III.	298
38	Tully	76 0 28	Tyrone	Dungannon Upper	Desertcreat	Cookstown	III.	308
33	Tully	747 1 36h	Tyrone	Omagh West	Longfield West	Castlederg	III.	316
25, 34	Tully	409 3 35	Tyrone	Strabane Upper	Cappagh	Omagh	III.	325
29, 30	Tully	535 0 4	Westmeath	Clonlonan	Ballyloughloe	Athlone	I.	261
38, 42	Tullyagan	132 1 34	Cavan	Clanmahon	Kilbride	Oldcastle	III.	78
25	Tullyah	480 3 35	Armagh	Orior Upper	Loughgilly	Newry	III.	58
17, 21	Tullyallen	251 2 39i	Armagh	Orior Lower	Loughgilly	Newry	III.	57
21, 24	Tullyallen	941 3 29	Louth	Ferrard	Tullyallen	Drogheda	I.	183
31, 34	Tullyallen	136 0 31j	Monaghan	Farney	Magheracloone	Carrickmacross	III.	273
53	Tullyallen	224 3 14	Tyrone	Dungannon Middle	Donaghmore	Dungannon	III.	302
24	TULLYALLEN T.	—	Louth	Ferrard	Tullyallen	Drogheda	I.	183
21, 31	Tullyally	1,062 3 20k	Donegal	Inishowen East	Moville Upper	Inishowen	III.	119
20	Tullyally Lower	238 2 27	Londonderry	Tirkeeran	Clondermot	Londonderry	III.	248
20	Tullyally Upper	126 3 8	Londonderry	Tirkeeran	Clondermot	Londonderry	III.	248
12, 16	Tullyalt	90 3 3	Cavan	Tullygarvey	Drung	Cootehill	III.	89
13	Tullyanaghan	184 0 4	Down	Lower Iveagh, Up. pt.	Magheralin	Lurgan	III.	170
54, 55	Tullyannan	218 1 9	Donegal	Raphoe	Allsaints	Londonderry	III.	134
54, 55	Tullyannan Glebe	148 0 3	Donegal	Raphoe	Allsaints	Londonderry	III.	134
15	Tullyanog	155 0 14l	Cavan	Lower Loughtee	Drumlane	Cavan	III.	81
46	Tullyaran	288 3 11	Tyrone	Dungannon Middle	Donaghmore	Dungannon	III.	302
12	Tullyard	247 1 10	Armagh	Armagh	Grange	Armagh	III.	45
27, 30	Tullyard	187 0 26	Armagh	Fews Upper	Creggan	Castleblayney	III.	48
17, 22	Tullyard	136 3 39	Cavan	Tullygarvey	Kildrumsherdan	Cootehill	III.	90
74	Tullyard	1,108 1 24	Donegal	Boylagh	Inishkeel	Glenties	III.	113
79, 88	Tullyard	130 2 5	Donegal	Raphoe	Urney	Strabane	III.	144
15	Tullyard	378 1 17	Down	Castlereagh Upper	Drumbo	Lisburn	III.	165
13, 20	Tullyard	369 1 14	Down	Lower Iveagh, Up. pt.	Moira	Lurgan	III.	170
21	Tullyard	262 3 23	Louth	Ferrard	Termonfeckin	Drogheda	I.	183
30	Tullyard	161 3 28	Meath	Upper Navan	Trim	Trim	I.	217
17	Tullyard	191 1 26	Monaghan	Dartree	Killeevan	Cootehill	III.	268
13	Tullyard	285 2 15	Monaghan	Monaghan	Monaghan	Monaghan	III.	277
6	Tullyard	103 3 15	Monaghan	Trough	Donagh	Monaghan	III.	283
38	Tullyard	154 1 16	Tyrone	Dungannon Upper	Desertcreat	Cookstown	III.	308
24, 33	Tullyard	411 2 20m	Tyrone	Omagh West	Longfield West	Castlederg	III.	316
2, 3	Tullyard	487 2 18n	Tyrone	Strabane Lower	Donaghedy	Strabane	III.	321
5	Tullyard	248 3 13	Tyrone	Strabane Lower	Leckpatrick	Strabane	III.	322
12	Tullyargle	31 2 12	Armagh	Armagh	Armagh	Armagh	III.	43

(a) Including 44A. 3R. 1P. water.
(b) Including 16A. 2R. 12P. water.
(c) Including 29A. 2R. 5P. water.
(d) Including 8A. 0R. 30P. water.
(e) Including 19A. 3R. 15P. water.

(f) Including 2A. 3R. 32P. water.
(g) Including 89A. 1R. 14P. water.
(h) Including 22A. 2R. 39P. water.
(i) Including 6A. 2R. 24P. water.
(j) Including 7A. 2R. 10P. water.

(k) Including 12A. 1R. 16P. water.
(l) Including 30A. 3R. 36P. water.
(m) Including 0A. 0R. 24P. water.
(n) Including 6A. 1R. 17P. water.

No. of Sheet of the Ordnance Survey Maps.	Townlands and Towns.	Area in Statute Acres.	County.	Barony.	Parish.	Poor Law Union in 1857.	Townland Census of 1851, Part I. Vol.	Page
		A. R. P.					Vol.	Page
9, 10	Tullyarmon	268 0 28	Londonderry	Keenaght	Aghanloo	New Ta Limavady	III.	234
4	Tullyarran	89 2 2	Meath	Lower Kells	Moynalty	Kells	I.	204
29	Tullyarvan	828 0 23	Donegal	Inishowen West	Fahan Lower	Inishowen	III.	120
4	Tullyattin	219 0 27	Meath	Lower Kells	Moynalty	Kells	I.	204
16	Tullyavy	172 3 21	Fermanagh	Tirkennedy	Trory	Enniskillen	III.	224
62, 63	Tullyballydonnell	369 0 31	Antrim	Upper Massereene	Ballinderry	Lurgan	III.	29
12, 13	Tullybane	183 1 11	Antrim	Lower Dunluce	Derrykeighan	Ballymoney	III.	17
30	Tullybane	299 0 21	Westmeath	Clonlonan	Ballyloughloe	Athlone	I.	261
10	Tullybaun	71 1 5	Longford	Granard	Clonbroney	Granard	I.	155
74	Tully Beg	1,024 3 26a	Donegal	Boylagh	Inishkeel	Glenties	III.	113
4	Tully Beg	72 1 27	Donegal	Inishowen East	Clonca	Inishowen	III.	117
44, 52	Tully Beg	135 3 9b	Donegal	Kilmacrenan	Gartan	Letterkenny	III.	128
36, 45	Tully Beg	240 2 0c	Donegal	Kilmacrenan	Tullyfern	Millford	III.	133
9, 10	Tully Beg	187 0 39d	Galway	Ballynahinch	Ballynakill	Clifden	IV.	12
16	Tullybeg	213 2 12	King's Co.	Ballycowan	Rahan	Tullamore	I.	129
89, 90	Tully Beg	64 2 31e	Mayo	Carra	Drum	Castlebar	IV.	128
90	Tully Beg	114 1 28f	Mayo	Clanmorris	Balla	Castlebar	IV.	132
20,21,26,27	Tully Beg	155 3 8	Sligo	Tirerrill	Kilross	Sligo	IV.	241
90, 100	Tullybeg Glebe	24 2 38	Mayo	Clanmorris	Mayo	Claremorris	IV.	135
16, 29	Tullybeg North	63 0 2	Galway	Dunmore	Tuam	Tuam	IV.	36
16, 29	Tullybeg South	151 0 36	Galway	Dunmore	Tuam	Tuam	IV.	36
19	Tullybellina	47 1 30	Fermanagh	Clanawley	Cleenish	Ballyshannon	III.	191
60, 66	Tullyblety	328 0 39	Tyrone	Dungannon Lower	Aghaloo	Dungannon	III.	297
32	Tullyboard	310 1 35	Down	Ards Upper	Ballyphilip	Downpatrick	III.	160
54	Tullybogly	176 3 28	Donegal	Raphoe	Raymoghy	Letterkenny	III.	142
38	Tullyboy	373 0 22	Cavan	Clanmahon	Kilbride	Cavan	III.	78
48	Tullyboy	174 1 16	Londonderry	Loughinsholin	Derryloran	Magherafelt	III.	240
10	Tullyboy	166 0 1	Roscommon	Boyle	Estersnow	Boyle	IV.	195
8, 9	Tullybrack	192 1 13	Cavan	Tullyhaw	Templeport	Bawnboy	III.	96
20, 25	Tullybrack or Ora More	443 0 39g	Fermanagh	Clanawley	Cleenish	Enniskillen	III.	191
32	Tullybradan	144 1 7	Leitrim	Mohill	Mohill	Mohill	IV.	108
49	Tullybranigan	1,213 0 18	Down	Upper Iveagh, Lr. pt.	Kilcoo	Kilkeel	III.	173
128, 129	Tullybrattan	79 2 29	Galway	Kiltartan	Beagh	Gort	IV.	46
29	Tullybrick	209 0 16	Cavan	Clankee	Enniskeen	Bailieborough	III.	73
28	Tullybrick	209 2 24	Cavan	Clankee	Shercock	Bailieborough	III.	75
17, 18	Tullybrick	209 2 22	Cavan	Tullygarvey	Drumgoon	Cootehill	III.	88
16	Tullybrick	74 3 33	Cavan	Tullygarvey	Drung	Cootehill	III.	89
40, 45	Tullybrick	2,257 2 36	Londonderry	Loughinsholin	Ballynascreen	Magherafelt	III.	239
15	Tullybrick Etra or Bondville	298 1 3	Armagh	Tiranny	Tynan	Armagh	III.	60
15	Tullybrick (Hamilton)	263 0 17	Armagh	Tiranny	Tynan	Armagh	III.	60
15	Tullybrisland	152 3 12	Londonderry	Tirkeeran	Faughanvale	Londonderry	III.	250
20	Tullybrone	265 0 23	Armagh	Fews Upper	Lisnadill	Armagh	III.	49
100	Tullybrook or Tullyleague	138 2 13	Donegal	Tirhugh	Drumhome	Donegal	III.	147
58, 59	Tullybroom	198 3 2	Tyrone	Clogher	Clogher	Clogher	III.	293
9	Tullybryan	151 3 9	Monaghan	Monaghan	Kilmore	Monaghan	III.	276
59	Tullybryan	150 1 28	Tyrone	Clogher	Errigal Keerogue	Clogher	III.	295
15	Tullybuck	90 1 24h	Cavan	Upper Loughtee	Castleterra	Cavan	III.	83
14	Tullybuck	115 2 1	Monaghan	Cremorne	Clontibret	Monaghan	III.	261
20	Tullycaghny	394 0 36	Monaghan	Cremorne	Muckno	Castleblayney	III.	262
11	Tullycahan	266 1 35	Louth	Louth	Louth	Dundalk	I.	185
29	Tullycall	322 1 30	Tyrone	Dungannon Upper	Derryloran	Cookstown	III.	307
6, 7	Tullycallick	96 2 5	Monaghan	Trough	Donagh	Monaghan	III.	283
11, 15	Tullycallidy	366 3 29	Armagh	Armagh	Derrynoose	Armagh	III.	44
5, 6	Tullycallrick	113 3 29	Fermanagh	Lurg	Magheraculmoney	Lowtherstown	III.	208
41, 46	Tullycanna	384 2 10	Wexford	Bargy	Ambrosetown	Wexford	I.	304
41	TULLYCANNA T.	—	Wexford	Bargy	Ambrosetown	Wexford	I.	304
11, 12	Tullycapple	196 0 4	Antrim	Lower Dunluce	Dunluce	Ballymoney	III.	17
14, 22	Tullycar	854 2 18i	Tyrone	Omagh West	Termonamongan	Castlederg	III.	317
14, 15	Tullycarbry	108 0 7	Fermanagh	Magheraboy	Devenish	Enniskillen	III.	211
105	Tullycarn	161 3 11	Donegal	Tirhugh	Templecarn	Donegal	III.	149
20	Tullycarn	267 3 5	Down	Lower Iveagh, Up. pt.	Donaghcloney	Lurgan	III.	169
32	Tullycarnan	294 0 15	Down	Ards Upper	Witter	Downpatrick	III.	161
45	Tullycarnan	154 0 5	Down	Lecale Lower	Ardglass	Downpatrick	III.	178
5	Tullycarnet	270 0 32	Down	Castlereagh Lower	Knockbreda	Belfast	III.	163
24	Tullycarragh	287 3 13	Monaghan	Cremorne	Clontibret	Castleblayney	III.	261
22, 23	Tullycartron	114 1 35j	Roscommon	Roscommon	Elphin	Strokestown	IV.	210
52	Tullychullion	189 2 19	Donegal	Kilmacrenan	Conwal	Letterkenny	III.	127
4	Tullychurry	521 2 20k	Fermanagh	Lurg	Belleek	Ballyshannon	III.	203
16	Tullyclea	113 3 10	Fermanagh	Lurg	Derryvullan	Lowtherstown	III.	205
73, 74	Tullycleave Beg	243 0 29	Donegal	Boylagh	Inishkeel	Glenties	III.	113

(a) Including 100A. 2R. 1F. water.
(b) Including 21A. 2R. 22P. water.
(c) Including 3A. 1R. 15P. water.
(d) Including 6A. 3R. 1F. water.

(e) Including 0A. 3R. 20P. water.
(f) Including 10A. 1R. 28P. water.
(g) Including 15A. 3R. 2P. water.
(h) Including 1A. 2R. 1F. water.

(i) Including 2A. 3R. 24P. water.
(j) Including 6A. 2R. 21P. water.
(k) Including 11A. 0R. 4P. water.

No. of Sheet of the Ordnance Survey Maps.	Townlands and Towns.	Area in Statute Acres.	County.	Barony.	Parish.	Poor Law Union in 1857.	Townland Census of 1851, Part I.	
		A. R. P.					Vol.	Page
73, 74	Tullycleave More	770 2 3	Donegal	Boylagh	Inishkeel	Glenties	III.	113
16	Tullyclevaun	311 3 14	Leitrim	Drumahaire	Inishmagrath	Manorhamilton	IV.	97
50	Tullyclunagh	357 0 13	Tyrone	Omagh East	Dromore	Omagh	III.	311
21	Tullycoe	203 0 2	Cavan	Tullygarvey	Larah	Cootehill	III.	91
25	Tullycoe	145 2 28	Cavan	Upper Loughtee	Annagelliff	Cavan	III.	82
20	Tullycollive	250 0 17	Monaghan	Cremorne	Muckno	Castleblayney	III.	262
15	Tullycoly	161 1 35	Leitrim	Drumahaire	Killanummery	Manorhamilton	IV.	98
10	Tullycommon	962 2 18	Clare	Inchiquin	Killinaboy	Corrofin	II.	27
69, 78	Tully Commons	437 2 31a	Mayo	Carra	Aglish	Castlebar	IV.	124
27, 34	Tullyconnaught	448 1 26	Down	Upper Iveagh, Up. pt.	Seapatrick	Banbridge	III.	176
8, 17	Tullyconnell	295 2 12b	Donegal	Kilmacrenan	Clondavaddog	Millford	III.	125
39	Tullyconnell	192 2 19	Tyrone	Dungannon Upper	Artrea	Cookstown	III.	306
11	Tullyconor	424 3 4c	Galway	Ballynahinch	Ballynakill	Clifden	IV.	12
20	Tullycoora	241 3 3d	Monaghan	Cremorne	Muckno	Castleblayney	III.	262
17, 24	Tullycore	138 0 7	Down	Dufferin	Killinchy	Downpatrick	III.	166
18, 20	Tullycorka	381 1 32	Leitrim	Drumahaire	Inishmagrath	Manorhamilton	IV.	97
51, 58	Tullycorker	304 1 4	Tyrone	Clogher	Clogher	Clogher	III.	293
4, 6	Tullycrafton	277 2 13	Cavan	Tullyhaw	Kinawley	Enniskillen	III.	93
44, 50	Tullycreenaght	180 0 2	Antrim	Upper Toome	Antrim	Antrim	III.	33
58	Tullycreen Lower	733 2 39	Clare	Clonderalaw	Kilmurry	Kilrush	II.	18
58	Tullycreen Upper	823 2 0	Clare	Clonderalaw	Kilmurry	Kilrush	II.	18
15, 21	Tullycreevy	257 1 21	Fermanagh	Magheraboy	Devenish	Enniskillen	III.	211
11, 15	Tullycreevy	80 0 20	Leitrim	Drumahaire	Killarga	Manorhamilton	IV.	99
9	Tullycroman	176 1 26	Monaghan	Monaghan	Tedavnet	Monaghan	III.	280
25	Tullycross	147 2 33	Down	Ards Upper	Castleboy	Downpatrick	III.	160
29	Tullycross	298 2 27	Westmeath	Brawny	St. Mary's	Athlone	I.	260
46	Tullycullion	105 1 29	Tyrone	Dungannon Middle	Drumglass	Dungannon	III.	303
10	Tullycumasky	152 0 36	Monaghan	Cremorne	Clontibret	Monaghan	III.	261
93	Tullycumber	253 1 7	Donegal	Banagh	Inver	Donegal	III.	108
42	Tullycunny	130 2 27e	Tyrone	Omagh East	Drumragh	Omagh	III.	313
31, 37	Tullycusheen Beg	264 1 20	Sligo	Leyny	Achonry	Tobercurry	IV.	229
31, 37	Tullycusheen More	429 1 23	Sligo	Leyny	Achonry	Tobercurry	IV.	230
6	Tullydagan	119 3 20	Armagh	Oneilland East	Shankill	Lurgan	III.	51
6, 7	Tullydermot	180 2 5	Cavan	Tullyhaw	Kinawley	Bawnboy	III.	93
5	Tullyderrin	161 0 21	Leitrim	Rosclogher	Rossinver	Manorhamilton	IV.	112
21, 22	Tullydevenish	103 3 34	Fermanagh	Magheraboy	Devenish	Enniskillen	III.	211
18	Tullydonnell	684 1 7	Louth	Ardee	Drumcar	Ardee	I.	172
31	Tullydonnell (Gage)	257 1 15	Armagh	Fews Upper	Creggan	Dundalk	III.	48
69	Tullydonnell Lower	146 2 15	Donegal	Raphoe	Raphoe	Strabane	III.	141
31	Tullydonnell (O'Callaghan)	586 2 26	Armagh	Fews Upper	Creggan	Dundalk	III.	48
61, 69	Tullydonnell Upper	214 0 7	Donegal	Raphoe	Raphoe	Strabane	III.	141
16	Tullydoortans	338 1 19	Tyrone	Strabane Lower	Urney	Strabane	III.	323
62	Tullydowey	205 2 38	Tyrone	Dungannon Middle	Clonfeacle	Dungannon	III.	300
46	Tullydraw	144 1 37	Tyrone	Dungannon Middle	Donaghmore	Dungannon	III.	302
10	Tullydrum	95 3 33	Louth	Ardee	Killanny	Dundalk	I.	173
118	Tullyduff	155 0 33	Mayo	Kilmaine	Kilmainemore	Ballinrobe	IV.	156
29	Tullydush Lower	454 3 17	Donegal	Inishowen West	Fahan Lower	Inishowen	III.	120
29, 38	Tullydush Upper	722 1 21	Donegal	Inishowen West	Fahan Lower	Inishowen	III.	120
27, 34	Tullyear	561 0 10	Down	Upper Iveagh, Up. pt.	Seapatrick	Banbridge	III.	176
99, 100	Tullyearl	188 2 12	Donegal	Tirhugh	Drumhome	Donegal	III.	147
22,23,27,28	Tully East	1,166 2 36	Kildare	Offaly East	Tully	Naas	I.	71
30	Tullyegan	113 1 19	Mayo	Tirawley	Kilmoremoy	Ballina	IV.	170
12	Tullyelmer	55 2 14	Armagh	Armagh	Armagh	Armagh	III.	43
21	Tullyeskar	267 3 6	Louth	Ferrard	Ballymakenny	Drogheda	I.	179
4	Tullyfad	107 2 17f	Fermanagh	Lurg	Belleek	Ballyshannon	III.	204
39	Tullyfaughan	43 3 10	Tyrone	Dungannon Middle	Donaghenry	Cookstown	III.	301
38, 39	Tullyfoyle Lower	114 3 5g	Down	Lecale Lower	Kilclief	Downpatrick	III.	179
38, 39	Tullyfoyle Upper	109 3 12h	Down	Lecale Lower	Kilclief	Downpatrick	III.	179
55	Tullyframe	759 3 24	Down	Mourne	Kilkeel	Kilkeel	III.	183
100	Tullygallan	167 2 15	Donegal	Tirhugh	Drumhome	Donegal	III.	147
95, 100, 101	Tullygallan, Tullywee, and Oughtnadrin Barr	1,434 2 38i	Donegal	Tirhugh	Drumhome	Donegal	III.	147
6	Tullygally	278 0 14	Armagh	Oneilland East	Shankill	Lurgan	III.	51
82	Tullyganny	319 1 1j	Mayo	Costello	Kilmovee	Swineford	IV.	142
9	Tullygarden	168 3 21	Armagh	Oneilland West	Kilmore	Armagh	III.	53
29	Tullygare	60 3 11	Tyrone	Dungannon Upper	Derryloran	Cookstown	III.	307
8, 12	Tullygarran	185 3 31	Armagh	Armagh	Grange	Armagh	III.	45
29	Tullygarran	163 3 10	Kerry	Trughanacmy	Ballymacelligott	Tralee	II.	207
10, 16	Tullygarvan	466 0 38k	Down	Castlereagh Lower	Comber	Newtownards	III.	162
93	Tullygarvan East	907 2 22	Clare	Corcomroe	Kilmanaheen	Ennistimon	II.	21
23	Tullygarvan West	308 0 12	Clare	Corcomroe	Kilmanaheen	Ennistimon	II.	21

(a) Including 38A. 3R. 20P. water.
(b) Including 22A. 1R. 29P. water.
(c) Including 3A. 2R. 0P. water.
(d) Including 4A. 3R. 35P. water.

(e) Including 4A. 1R. 8P. water.
(f) Including 1A. 1R. 2P. water.
(g) Including 9A. 1R. 8P. water.
(h) Including 10A. 1R. 32P. water.

(i) Including 15A. 2R. 7P. water.
(j) Including 7A. 1R. 23P. water.
(k) Including 2A. 2R. 30P. water.

No. of Sheet of the Ordnance Survey Maps.	Townlands and Towns.	Area in Statute Acres.			County.	Barony.	Parish.	Poor Law Union in 1857.	Townland Census of 1851, Part I.	
		A.	R.	P.					Vol.	Page
52,53,60,61	Tullygay . .	766	0	39	Donegal . .	Kilmacrenan . .	Conwal . . .	Letterkenny .	III.	127
13, 19, 20	Tullygerravra .	481	0	3	Fermanagh .	Clanawley . .	Boho . . .	Ballyshannon .	III.	189
13	Tullygillen .	126	0	6	Monaghan .	Monaghan . .	Kilmore . .	Monaghan .	III.	276
61	Tullygiven . .	360	0	24a	Tyrone . .	Dungannon Middle	Clonfeacle .	Dungannon .	III.	300
51, 61	Tullyglass . .	278	3	27	Clare . .	Bunratty Lower .	Clonloghan . .	Ennis . .	II.	3
121	Tullyglass . .	202	0	20	Cork, W.R. .	East Carbery (W.D.)	Kilmeen . . .	Dunmanway .	II.	134
95, 96, 109	Tullyglass . .	218	0	11	Cork, W.R. .	Kinalmeaky . .	Kilbrogan . .	Bandon . .	II.	152
95, 109	Tullyglass . .	872	1	18	Cork, W.R. .	Kinalmeaky . .	Murragh . .	Bandon . .	II.	152
17	Tullyglass . .	149	3	27	Limerick . .	Shanid . .	Kilfergus . .	Glin . .	II.	256
27	Tullyglass . .	286	3	37b	Monaghan .	Cremorne . .	Aghnamullen .	Castleblayney .	III.	258
20, 24	Tullyglush . .	1,131	3	0c	Armagh . .	Armagh . . .	Keady . . .	Armagh . .	III.	45
27, 28	Tullyglush . .	518	1	9	Down . .	Lower Iveagh, Lr. pt.	Dromore . .	Banbridge .	III.	168
52	Tullyglush . .	184	2	2	Tyrone . .	Clogher . .	Errigal Keerogue .	Clogher . .	III.	296
15	Tullyglush (Kane) .	280	0	31	Armagh . .	Tiranny . .	Tynan . . .	Armagh . .	III.	61
15	Tullyglush (Nevin) .	255	1	37	Armagh . .	Tiranny . .	Tynan . . .	Armagh . .	III.	61
61	Tullygoney . .	207	1	34	Tyrone . .	Dungannon Middle	Clonfeacle .	Dungannon .	III.	300
6, 9	Tullygony . .	111	1	21	Monaghan .	Monaghan . .	Tedavnet . .	Monaghan .	III.	280
10	Tullygony . .	21	2	32	Monaghan .	Monaghan . .	Tehallan . .	Monaghan .	III.	280
8	Tullygoonigan .	158	3	36	Armagh . .	Armagh . . .	Grange . .	Armagh . .	III.	45
35	Tullygorey . .	198	0	3	Kildare . .	Narragh&RebanWest	Kilberry . .	Athy . .	I.	68
37	Tullygowan . .	133	2	22	Antrim . .	Lower Toome . .	Ahoghill . .	Ballymena .	III.	32
10	Tullygowan . .	140	0	38	Louth . .	Ardee . .	Killanny . .	Dundalk .	I.	173
41	Tullygullin . .	416	2	18	Cavan . .	Clanmahon . .	Drumlumman .	Granard .	III.	77
46	Tullygun . .	82	0	34	Tyrone . .	Dungannon Middle	Drumglass . .	Dungannon .	III.	303
45	Tully Hall . .	72	0	27	Donegal . .	Kilmacrenan .	Tullyfern . .	Millford . .	III.	133
22	Tullyhappy . .	731	2	31	Armagh . .	Orior Lower . .	Killevy . .	Newry . .	III.	56
20	Tullyharnet . .	264	0	18	Monaghan .	Cremorne . .	Muckno . .	Castleblayney .	III.	262
27	Tullyharney . .	93	1	4	Fermanagh .	Tirkennedy . .	Derrybrusk .	Enniskillen .	III.	220
43	Tullyheeran . .	275	3	33	Tyrone . .	Omagh East . .	Clogherny . .	Omagh . .	III.	310
21	Tullyherron . .	325	1	1	Armagh . .	Orior Lower . .	Loughgilly . .	Newry . .	III.	57
19, 20	Tullyherron . .	841	3	23	Down . .	Lower Iveagh, Up. pt.	Donaghcloney .	Lurgan . .	III.	169
1	Tullyhill . .	99	2	16	Westmeath .	Fore . .	Foyran . .	Granard .	I.	270
27	Tullyhinan . .	426	0	38	Down . .	Lower Iveagh, Lr. pt.	Magherally . .	Banbridge .	III.	168
19	Tullyhirm . .	381	2	29	Armagh . .	Tiranny . . .	Derrynoose .	Armagh . .	III.	59
9	Tullyhirm . .	180	2	39	Monaghan .	Monaghan . .	Monaghan . .	Monaghan .	III.	277
9	Tullyhoe . .	58	3	28	Londonderry .	Keenaght . .	Tamlaght Finlagan .	New T.n Limavady	III.	238
38, 39	Tullyhog . .	120	2	10	Tyrone . .	Dungannon Upper .	Desertcreat .	Cookstown .	III.	308
23	Tullyhogan . .	46	0	15	Westmeath .	Kilkenny West .	Kilkenny West .	Athlone .	I.	273
38	TULLYHOG T. . .	—			Tyrone . .	Dungannon Upper .	Desertcreat .	Cookstown .	III.	308
21	Tullyholvin Lower .	19	1	9	Fermanagh .	Clanawley . .	Boho . .	Enniskillen .	III.	189
21	Tullyholvin Upper .	17	0	23	Fermanagh .	Clanawley . .	Boho . .	Enniskillen .	III.	189
4, 5	Tullyhommon . .	122	3	27	Fermanagh .	Lurg . .	Drumkeeran .	Lowtherstown .	III.	207
32	Tullyhona . .	277	3	6	Fermanagh .	Clanawley . .	Killesher . .	Enniskillen .	III.	193
60	Tullyhonour . .	1,019	0	32	Donegal . .	Raphoe . .	Conwal . .	Stranorlar .	III.	137
74, 83	Tullyhonwar . .	247	3	4	Donegal . .	Boylagh . .	Killybegs Lower .	Glenties .	III.	114
107	Tullyhorky . .	329	2	33d	Donegal . .	Tirhugh . .	Kilbarron . .	Ballyshannon .	III.	148
10, 16	Tullyhubbert . .	474	3	8e	Down . .	Castlereagh Lower .	Comber . .	Newtownards .	III.	162
14	Tullyhugh . .	629	0	39	Armagh . .	Orior Lower . .	Ballymore . .	Banbridge .	III.	55
32	Tullyhugh . .	412	0	27	Sligo . .	Leyny . .	Achonry . .	Tobercurry .	IV.	230
16, 21	Tullyhumphry .	126	0	36	Monaghan .	Dartree . .	Currin . .	Clones . .	III.	266
16, 23	Tullyhumphrys .	21	2	28	Westmeath .	Kilkenny West .	Kilkenny West .	Athlone . .	I.	274
39	Tullyhurken . .	67	2	14	Tyrone . .	Dungannon Upper .	Artrea . .	Cookstown .	III.	306
40	Tullyillan . .	79	3	38f	Donegal . .	Boylagh . .	Templecrone .	Glenties .	III.	116
48	Tullyillan Island .	3	3	32	Donegal . .	Boylagh . .	Templecrone .	Glenties .	III.	116
37	Tullykane . .	141	0	13	Meath . .	Lower Deece . .	Kilmessan .	Dunshaughlin .	I.	192
36	Tullykeeran . .	276	3	1	Londonderry .	Loughinsholin .	Killelagh .	Magherafelt .	III.	241
32	Tullykeeran Mountain .	771	2	34	Londonderry .	Loughinsholin .	Killelagh .	Magherafelt .	III.	241
21	Tullykelter . .	104	3	24	Fermanagh .	Magheraboy . .	Devenish . .	Enniskillen .	III.	211
24	Tullykenneye . .	204	0	4	Fermanagh .	Magherastephana .	Aghalurcher .	Lisnaskea .	III.	217
9, 13	Tullykenny . .	142	3	15	Monaghan .	Monaghan . .	Drumsnat . .	Monaghan .	III.	275
8	Tullykevan . .	81	3	20	Armagh . .	Armagh . . .	Clonfeacle .	Armagh . .	III.	44
12	Tullykevin . .	464	0	31	Down . .	Ards Lower . .	Greyabbey . .	Newtownards .	III.	158
31	Tullykin . .	492	3	23	Down . .	Dufferin . .	Killyleagh . .	Downpatrick .	III.	167
23, 27, 28	Tullykittagh Lower	425	3	3	Antrim . .	Kilconway . .	Dunaghy . .	Ballymena .	III.	26
23,24,27,28	Tullykittagh Upper	662	2	28	Antrim . .	Kilconway . .	Dunaghy . .	Ballymena .	III.	26
21	Tullylackan Beg .	125	3	23	Leitrim . .	Carrigallen . .	Oughteragh .	Bawnboy . .	IV.	93
21	Tullylackan More .	141	0	16	Leitrim . .	Carrigallen . .	Oughteragh .	Bawnboy . .	IV.	93
38	Tullylagan . .	124	3	35	Tyrone . .	Dungannon Upper .	Desertcreat .	Cookstown .	III.	308
10, 11	Tullylammy . .	155	3	34	Fermanagh .	Lurg . .	Derryvullan .	Lowtherstown .	III.	205
110, 111	Tullyland . .	506	2	14	Cork, W.R. .	East Carbery (E.D.)	Ballinadee .	Bandon . .	II.	126
110	Tullyland . .	348	0	21	Cork, W.R. .	East Carbery (E.D.)	Ballymodan .	Bandon . .	II.	127
16, 23	Tullylanesborough .	40	0	36	Westmeath .	Kilkenny West .	Kilkenny West .	Athlone .	I.	274

(a) Including 2A. 1R. 15P. water.   (c) Including 39A. 1R. 39P. water.   (e) Including 1A. 1R. 30P. water.
(b) Including 20A. 1R. 38P. water.   (d) Including 11A. 0R. 38P. water.   (f) Including 9A. 1R. 29P. water.

No. of Sheet of the Ordnance Survey Maps.	Townlands and Towns.	Area in Statute Acres.	County.	Barony.	Parish.	Poor Law Union in 1857.	Townland Census of 1851, Part I.	
		A. R. P.					Vol.	Page
27	Tullylannan	264 1 9a	Leitrim	Leitrim	Kiltoghert	Carᵏ. on Shannon	IV.	103
102	Tullylark	198 3 39	Donegal	Tirhugh	Templecarn	Donegal	III.	149
17, 26	Tullyleague	1,178 1 22	Limerick	Shanid	Kilfergus	Glin	II.	256
11	Tullyleague	96 3 31	Roscommon	Boyle	Tumna	Carᵏ. on Shannon	IV.	198
100	Tullyleague or Tullybrook	138 2 13	Donegal	Tirhugh	Drumhome	Donegal	III.	147
48	Tullyleak	141 2 15	Limerick	Coshlea	Kilbreedy Major	Kilmallock	II.	239
61, 62	Tullylcarn	150 2 27	Tyrone	Dungannon Middle	Clonfeacle	Dungannon	III.	300
6	Tullylease	251 1 7	Cork, E.R.	Duhallow	Tullylease	Kanturk	II.	76
46	Tullyleek	281 2 35	Tyrone	Dungannon Middle	Donaghmore	Dungannon	III.	302
13	Tullyleer	124 1 9	Monaghan	Monaghan	Monaghan	Monaghan	III.	277
47	Tullylig	131 1 28	Tyrone	Dungannon Middle	Donaghenry	Cookstown	III.	301
16, 17, 23	Tullylin or Ballyfeenaun	1,498 3 29	Sligo	Tireragh	Castleconor	Dromore West	IV.	232
42	Tullylinkisay	407 2 38	Londonderry	Loughinsholin	Magherafelt	Magherafelt	III.	243
17, 18	Tullylinn	189 3 36	Armagh	Orior Lower	Ballymore	Newry	III.	55
52	Tullylinton	176 1 19	Tyrone	Clogher	Errigal Keerogue	Clogher	III.	296
26	Tullylish	513 1 34	Down	Lower Iveagh, Up. pt.	Tullylish	Banbridge	III.	171
10	Tullylish	90 0 3	Monaghan	Monaghan	Tehallan	Monaghan	III.	280
16	Tullylone	139 1 11	Fermanagh	Tirkennedy	Trory	Enniskillen	III.	224
6	Tullylone	162 2 0	Monaghan	Monaghan	Tedavnet	Monaghan	III.	280
13	Tullyloob	299 0 22	Down	Lower Iveagh, Up. pt.	Moira	Lurgan	III.	170
22, 27, 28	Tullylorcan	434 0 19b	Cavan	Clankee	Knockbride	Cootehill	III.	74
94, 100	Tullyloskan	126 2 29	Donegal	Tirhugh	Donegal	Donegal	III.	145
12	Tullylost	32 2 23	Armagh	Armagh	Armagh	Armagh	III.	43
17, 22	Tullylost	452 3 39	Kildare	Offaly East	Rathangan	Edenderry	I.	71
20	Tullylough	103 3 32	Cavan	Upper Loughtee	Annagelliff	Cavan	III.	82
4	Tullylough	71 3 9c	Fermanagh	Lurg	Belleek	Ballyshannon	III.	204
13, 14	Tullyloughdaugh	198 3 4	Fermanagh	Magheraboy	Inishmacsaint	Ballyshannon	III.	213
28	Tullylougherny	57 1 16	Monaghan	Farney	Donaghmoyne	Carrickmacross	III.	271
30	Tullylougherny	162 1 37	Monaghan	Farney	Magheracloone	Carrickmacross	III.	273
8, 9	Tullyloughfin	224 3 25	Cavan	Tullyhaw	Templeport	Bawnboy	III.	96
20, 21	Tully Lower	195 0 9	Londonderry	Tirkeeran	Clondermot	Londonderry	III.	248
16, 22, 23	Tullyloyd	218 3 28d	Roscommon	Roscommon	Elphin	Strokestown	IV.	210
30	Tullylusk	183 1 10	Wicklow	Arklow	Dunganstown	Rathdrum	I.	344
14, 18	Tullymacann	295 0 19	Armagh	Orior Lower	Ballymore	Banbridge	III.	55
20, 27	Tullymacarath	184 3 38	Down	Lower Iveagh, Lr. pt.	Dromore	Banbridge	III.	168
18	Tullymackan	186 3 23e	Clare	Inchiquin	Ruan	Corrofin	II.	28
28	Tullymackilmartin	107 2 17f	Monaghan	Farney	Donaghmoyne	Carrickmacross	III.	271
24	Tullymacnous	208 3 6g	Down	Dufferin	Killyleagh	Downpatrick	III.	167
28	Tullymacreeve	593 1 0	Armagh	Orior Upper	Forkill	Newry	III.	57
49	Tullymagough	113 1 29	Tyrone	Omagh East	Donacavey	Lowtherstown	III.	311
9	Tullymain	60 1 36	Londonderry	Tirkeeran	Faughanvale	NewTⁿLimavady	III.	250
25, 32	Tullymally	356 3 5	Down	Ards Upper	Ballyphilip	Downpatrick	III.	160
21	Tullymargy	163 3 31	Fermanagh	Magheraboy	Devenish	Enniskillen	III.	211
6	Tullyminister	57 2 21	Cavan	Tullyhaw	Templeport	Enniskillen	III.	96
9	Tullymoan	381 3 21	Tyrone	Strabane Lower	Urney	Strabane	III.	323
20	Tullymongan Lower	26 3 15	Cavan	Upper Loughtee	Urney	Cavan	III.	86
20, 25	Tullymongan Upper	74 3 6h	Cavan	Upper Loughtee	Urney	Cavan	III.	86
33	Tullymore	363 1 34	Antrim	Lower Antrim	Skerry	Ballymena	III.	5
12	Tullymore	62 2 9	Armagh	Armagh	Armagh	Armagh	III.	43
9	Tullymore	367 0 34	Armagh	Oneilland West	Kilmore	Armagh	III.	53
73, 74	Tully More	632 0 19i	Donegal	Boylagh	Inishkeel	Glenties	III.	113
4	Tully More	176 2 29	Donegal	Inishowen East	Clonca	Inishowen	III.	117
44, 52	Tully More	110 1 35	Donegal	Kilmacrenan	Gartan	Letterkenny	III.	128
45	Tully More	159 3 35	Donegal	Kilmacrenan	Tullyfern	Milford	III.	133
107	Tullymore	302 3 3	Donegal	Tirhugh	Kilbarron	Ballyshannon	III.	148
24	Tullymore	144 3 16	Down	Dufferin	Killinchy	Downpatrick	III.	166
33, 40	Tullymore	448 3 0	Down	Upper Iveagh, Up. pt.	Donaghmore	Newry	III.	175
8, 13	Tullymore	327 0 18	Fermanagh	Magheraboy	Inishmacsaint	Ballyshannon	III.	213
10	Tully More	345 3 27j	Galway	Ballynahinch	Ballynakill	Clifden	IV.	12
90	Tully More	282 1 18k	Mayo	Clanmorris	Balla	Castlebar	IV.	132
26, 27	Tully More	231 3 6	Sligo	Tirerrill	Kilross	Sligo	IV.	241
7, 8	Tullymore Agowan	196 1 33l	Armagh	Tiranny	Eglish	Armagh	III.	59
7	Tullymore Etra	310 1 22	Armagh	Tiranny	Eglish	Armagh	III.	60
7	Tullymore Otra	306 0 32	Armagh	Tiranny	Eglish	Armagh	III.	60
16	Tullymorerahan	122 2 1	King's Co.	Ballycowan	Rahan	Tullamore	I.	129
8, 16	Tullymorerahan or Derrynanagh	119 0 4	King's Co.	Ballycowan	Rahan	Tullamore	I.	129
100	Tullymornin	55 0 24	Donegal	Tirhugh	Drumhome	Donegal	III.	147
45	Tully Mountain	135 2 5	Donegal	Kilmacrenan	Tullyfern	Milford	III.	133
37	Tullynoy	248 0 26	Sligo	Leyny	Kilmacteige	Tobercurry	IV.	231
25	Tullymuck	804 3 18	Tyrone	Strabane Lower	Ardstraw	Omagh	III.	319

(a) Including 12A. 0R. 21P. water.
(b) Including 7A. 3R. 4P. water.
(c) Including 2A. 0R. 2P. water.
(d) Including 11A. 3R. 21P. water.

(e) Including 53A. 2R. 24P. water.
(f) Including 2A. 0R. 16P. water.
(g) Including 18A. 1R. 8P. Clay Lake South.
(h) Including 4A. 1R., 33P. water.

(i) Including 11A. 0R. 12P. water.
(j) Including 52A. 1R. 16P. water.
(k) Including 10A. 2R. 1P. water.
(l) Including 7A. 0R. 37P. water.

No. of Sheet of the Ordnance Survey Maps.	Townlands and Towns.	Area in Statute Acres.	County.	Barony.	Parish.	Poor Law Union in 1857.	Townland Census of 1851, Part I.	
		A. R. P.					Vol.	Page
18, 20	Tullymurray . .	329 2 24	Leitrim .	Drumahaire . .	Inishmagrath . .	Manorhamilton .	IV.	97
109, 110,} 122, 123 }	Tullymurrihy .	665 0 38	Cork, W.R.	East Carbery (E.D.)	Desertserges . .	Bandon . .	II.	128
37	Tullymurry . .	275 0 25	Down .	Lecale Upper .	Down . .	Downpatrick .	III.	181
41	Tullymurry . .	184 3 18	Down .	Upper Iveagh, Up. pt.	Donaghmore .	Newry . .	III.	175
14	Tullynabeherny .	8 3 10	Cavan .	Tullyhunco .	Kildallan .	Bawnboy . .	III.	97
4	Tullynabohoge .	156 0 37a	Fermanagh .	Lurg . . .	Belleek . .	Ballyshannon .	III.	204
3, 10	Tullynabratilly .	974 0 16	Donegal .	Inishowen East .	Clonmany .	Inishowen .	III.	117
6	Tullynacleigh .	59 1 15	Cavan .	Tullyhaw .	Templeport .	Enniskillen .	III.	96
8	Tullynaconspod .	135 2 4	Cavan .	Tullyhaw .	Templeport .	Bawnboy . .	III.	96
20, 25	Tullynacor . .	196 3 7	Fermanagh .	Clanawley .	Cleenish . .	Enniskillen .	III.	191
30	Tullynacree . .	854 0 6	Down .	Kinelarty .	Kilmore . .	Downpatrick .	III.	177
32	Tullynacrew . .	66 1 32	Down .	Ards Upper .	Ballyphilip .	Downpatrick .	III.	160
18	Tullynacross . .	254 2 8	Armagh .	Orior Lower .	Ballymore .	Newry . .	III.	55
16	Tullynacross . .	112 3 24	Cavan .	Tullygarvey .	Drung . .	Cootehill .	III.	89
6	Tullynacross . .	183 1 6	Cavan .	Tullyhaw .	Templeport .	Enniskillen .	III.	96
8, 9	Tullynacross . .	459 1 30	Down .	Castlereagh Upper .	Lambeg . .	Lisburn . .	III.	166
20	Tullynacross . .	268 2 24	Down .	Lower Iveagh, Up. pt.	Magheralin .	Lurgan . .	III.	170
15	Tullynacross . .	80 1 27	Leitrim .	Drumahaire .	Killarga . .	Manorhamilton .	IV.	99
28	Tullynacross . .	84 0 37	Monaghan .	Farney . .	Donaghmoyne .	Carrickmacross .	III.	271
8	Tullynadall . .	117 3 4b	Donegal .	Kilmacrenan .	Clondavaddog .	Milford . .	III.	125
11	Tullynadall . .	449 0 33c	Tyrone .	Strabane Upper .	Bodoney Upper .	Gortin . .	III.	324
15	Tullynadall East .	50 0 33	Fermanagh .	Magheraboy .	Inishmacsaint .	Enniskillen .	III.	213
15	Tullynadall West .	71 2 17	Fermanagh .	Magheraboy .	Inishmacsaint .	Enniskillen .	III.	213
3, 5	Tullynafreave . .	297 3 2	Cavan .	Tullyhaw .	Killinagh .	Enniskillen .	III.	92
5, 6	Tullynagardy .	353 0 26	Down .	Castlereagh Lower .	Newtownards .	Newtownards .	III.	163
11	Tullynagarn . .	79 0 2	Fermanagh .	Lurg . . .	Derryvullan .	Lowtherstown .	III.	205
16	Tullynagee . .	865 1 16d	Down .	Castlereagh Lower .	Kilmood .	Newtownards .	III.	163
46	Tullynagee . .	393 0 29	Londonderry .	Loughinsholin .	Desertlyn .	Magherafelt .	III.	240
15	Tullynageer . .	316 0 16	Monaghan .	Cremorne .	Muckno . .	Castleblayney .	III.	262
16	Tullynagin . .	188 3 15	Armagh .	Fews Upper .	Lisnadill . .	Armagh . .	III.	49
84	Tullynaglack . .	122 0 7	Donegal .	Banagh . .	Inver . .	Donegal . .	III.	108
83	Tullynaglaggan .	856 1 28	Donegal .	Boylagh . .	Inishkeel .	Glenties . .	III.	113
23	Tullynaglug . .	43 3 28	Fermanagh .	Tirkennedy .	Enniskillen .	Enniskillen .	III.	222
15	Tullynagowan .	97 1 8	Fermanagh .	Magheraboy .	Inishmacsaint .	Enniskillen .	III.	213
23	Tullynagowan .	332 1 16	Fermanagh .	Magherastephana .	Aghavea . .	Lisnaskea .	III.	219
14	TullynagrackenNorth	54 0 27	Sligo .	Carbury . .	St. Johns .	Sligo . .	IV.	223
14, 20	TullynagrackenSouth	209 3 3	Sligo .	Carbury . .	St. Johns .	Sligo . .	IV.	223
84, 93	Tullynagreana .	882 0 36	Donegal .	Banagh . .	Inver . .	Donegal . .	III.	108
15	Tullynagrow . .	221 2 4	Monaghan .	Cremorne .	Muckno . .	Castleblayney .	III.	262
84, 93	Tullynaha . .	277 0 4	Donegal .	Banagh . .	Inver . .	Donegal . .	III.	108
18, 19, 21	Tullynabaia . .	1,555 3 24	Leitrim .	Drumahaire .	Drumreilly .	Cark. on Shannon	IV.	95
20	Tullynabattina .	361 1 5e	Monaghan .	Cremorne .	Muckno . .	Castleblayney .	III.	262
2	Tullynahaw . .	482 2 27	Roscommon .	Boyle . .	Kilronan .	Boyle . .	IV.	197
16, 17	Tullynahearka .	82 2 23	Roscommon .	Roscommon .	Aughrim . .	Carb. on Shannon	IV.	207
24	Tullynahinnera .	396 1 13f	Monaghan .	Cremorne .	Aghnamullen .	Castleblayney .	III.	258
31	Tullynahinnion .	465 0 14	Antrim .	Lower Toome .	Ahoghill . .	Ballymena .	III.	32
72	Tullynahoo . .	743 3 35g	Mayo .	Gallen . .	Kilconduff .	Swineford .	IV.	148
11, 17	Tullynakill . .	317 2 10	Down .	Castlereagh Lower .	Tullynakill .	Newtownards .	III.	163
3, 7	Tullynally or Paken-hamhall .	471 3 27	Westmeath .	Fore . . .	Mayne . .	Granard . .	I.	271
1	Tullynaloob . .	125 3 35	Fermanagh .	Lurg . . .	Drumkeeran .	Lowtherstown .	III.	207
16, 20	Tullynamalloge .	410 2 39	Armagh .	Armagh . .	Keady . .	Armagh . .	III.	45
24, 27	Tullynamalra . .	297 0 20	Monaghan .	Cremorne .	Aghnamullen .	Castleblayney .	III.	258
20	Tullynamalra . .	213 1 9	Monaghan .	Cremorne .	Muckno . .	Castleblayney .	III.	262
9	Tullynamoltra .	100 1 10	Cavan .	Tullyhaw .	Templeport .	Bawnboy . .	III.	96
3, 5	Tullynamoyle .	876 2 4h	Cavan .	Tullyhaw .	Killinagh .	Enniskillen .	III.	92
15, 16	Tullynamoyle .	644 1 25	Leitrim .	Drumahaire .	Killarga . .	Manorhamilton .	IV.	99
17, 22	Tullynample . .	247 1 20	Monaghan .	Dartree .	Currin . .	Cootehill .	III.	266
17	Tullynamuckduff .	190 2 14	Leitrim .	Drumahaire .	Inishmagrath .	Manorhamilton .	IV.	97
37, 43	Tullynamullan .	381 2 37	Antrim .	Lower Antrim .	Connor . .	Ballymena .	III.	4
24, 27	Tullynanegish .	298 0 13i	Monaghan .	Cremorne .	Aghnamullen .	Castleblayney .	III.	258
10	Tullynanure . .	72 1 30	Monaghan .	Monaghan .	Tehallan . .	Monaghan .	III.	280
18, 19	Tullynaputlin .	216 0 31	Leitrim .	Drumahaire .	Drumreilly .	Carb. on Shannon	IV.	95
13	Tullynarney . .	167 1 22	Monaghan .	Monaghan .	Kilmore . .	Monaghan .	III.	276
18	Tullynaroog . .	77 0 0	Leitrim .	Drumahaire .	Inishmagrath .	Manorhamilton .	IV.	97
14, 17	Tullynascreen .	1,035 3 14	Leitrim .	Drumahaire .	Killanummery .	Manorhamilton .	IV.	98
1	Tullynashammer .	241 3 15	Fermanagh .	Lurg . . .	Drumkeeran .	Lowtherstown .	III.	207
67	Tullynashane . .	153 1 10j	Tyrone .	Dungannon Lower .	Aghaloo . .	Armagh . .	III.	297
15	Tullynasharragh .	145 1 14	Leitrim .	Drumahaire .	Killarga . .	Manorhamilton .	IV.	99
7	Tullynasharragh .	46 3 35	Leitrim .	Rosclogher .	Killasnet .	Manorhamilton .	IV.	110
34	Tullynaskeagh .	387 2 36	Cavan .	Clankee .	Moybolgue .	Bailieborough .	III.	74
38	Tullynaskeagh .	223 0 7	Down .	Lecale Lower .	Dunsfort .	Downpatrick .	III.	179

(a) Including 1A. 1R. 37P. water.
(b) Including 12A. 3R. 0P. water.
(c) Including 0A. 2R. 34P. water.
(d) Including 20A. 2R. 16F. water.

(e) Including 7A. 1R. 8P. water.
(f) Including 8A. 0R. 22P. water.
(g) Including 29A. 0R. 38P. water.

(h) Including 6A. 2R. 18P. water.
(i) Including 60A. 1R. 13P. water.
(j) Including 3A. 1R. 18P. water.

No. of Sheet of the Ordnance Survey Maps.	Townlands and Towns.	Area in Statute Acres.	County.	Barony.	Parish.	Poor Law Union in 1857.	Townland Census of 1851, Part I.	
		A. R. P.					Vol.	Page
31	Tullynaskeagh East	265 1 2a	Monaghan	Farney	Killanny	Carrickmacross	III.	272
31	Tullynaskeagh West	197 3 15	Monaghan	Farney	Killanny	Carrickmacross	III.	272
42	Tullynasoo	523 0 17b	Down	Upper Iveagh, Lr. pt.	Kilcoo	Kilkeel	III.	173
14, 20	Tullynasrahan	577 3 6	Fermanagh	Magheraboy	Devenish	Ballyshannon	III.	211
27, 28	Tullynavall	846 0 37	Armagh	Fews Upper	Creggan	Castleblayney	III.	48
21, 31	Tullynavinn	894 3 36c	Donegal	Inishowen East	Moville Upper	Inishowen	III.	119
11, 12	Tullyneagh	31 3 34	Armagh	Tiranny	Eglish	Armagh	III.	60
134, 135	Tullyneasky East	305 3 28	Cork, W.R.	Ibane and Barryroe	Kilkerranmore	Clonakilty	II.	149
134, 135	Tullyneasky West	315 3 22	Cork, W.R.	Ibane and Barryroe	Kilkerranmore	Clonakilty	II.	149
47	Tullyneeny	182 1 39	Roscommon	Athlone	Taghboy	Athlone	IV.	184
34	Tullyneevin	95 1 27	Fermanagh	Magherastephana	Aghalurcher	Lisnaskea	III.	217
59	Tullynewbane	333 1 12	Antrim	Upper Massereene	Glenavy	Lisburn	III.	30
59	Tullynewbank	241 1 27	Antrim	Upper Massereene	Glenavy	Lisburn	III.	30
27	Tullynewy	258 0 26	Antrim	Kilconway	Dunaghy	Ballymena	III.	26
8, 12	Tullynichol	157 1 5	Armagh	Armagh	Eglish	Armagh	III.	44
49	Tullynincrin	226 0 34	Tyrone	Omagh East	Kilskeery	Lowtherstown	III.	314
35	Tullynisk or Woodfield	624 0 12	King's Co.	Eglish	Eglish	Parsonstown	I.	135
21	Tullynore	314 2 30	Down	Lower Iveagh, Up.pt.	Hillsborough	Lisburn	III.	170
18	Tully North	435 2 3	Antrim	Upper Dunluce	Loughguile	Ballymoney	III.	20
28	Tully North	234 3 37	Fermanagh	Magherastephana	Aghalurcher	Lisnaskea	III.	217
26	Tully North	244 3 15d	Leitrim	Carrigallen	Carrigallen	Bawnboy	IV.	90
45, 46, 48	Tullynure	540 0 1	Londonderry	Loughinsholin	Lissan	Magherafelt	III.	242
28, 35	Tullynure	743 0 37	Sligo	Tirerrill	Kilmactranny	Boyle	IV.	240
46, 54	Tullynure	151 0 38e	Tyrone	Dungannon Middle	Donaghmore	Dungannon	III.	302
17, 25	Tullyodea	243 2 32	Clare	Inchiquin	Ruan	Corrofin	II.	28
46	Tullyodonnell	76 1 23	Tyrone	Dungannon Middle	Drumglass	Dungannon	III.	303
38	Tullyodonnell	295 0 4	Tyrone	Dungannon Upper	Desertcreat	Cookstown	III.	308
25, 28	Tullyogallaghan	501 1 3	Armagh	Fews Upper	Newtownhamilton	Castleblayney	III.	49
32, 33	Tullyoran	97 2 2	Leitrim	Mohill	Cloone	Mohill	IV.	106
33	Tullyoran	81 0 38	Leitrim	Mohill	Mohill	Mohill	IV.	108
38, 39	Tullyoran or Mount Prospect	135 2 9	Fermanagh	Knockninny	Kinawley	Lisnaskea	III.	202
34	Tullyorior	981 3 0f	Down	Upper Iveagh, Lr. pt.	Garvaghy	Banbridge	III.	173
25	Tullyoscar	116 2 23	Leitrim	Carrigallen	Oughteragh	Bawnboy	IV.	93
63	Tullyowen	152 1 25	Donegal	Raphoe	Taughboyne	Strabane	III.	144
5	Tullypole	232 2 21	Meath	Lower Kells	Moynalty	Kells	I.	204
41	Tullyquilly	461 2 16	Down	Upper Iveagh, Up. pt.	Drumgath	Newry	III.	175
58	Tullyquin Glebe	240 2 33	Tyrone	Clogher	Clogher	Clogher	III.	293
20	Tullyrahan	264 1 1g	Monaghan	Cremorne	Muckno	Castleblayney	III.	262
27	Tullyrain	508 3 26	Down	Lower Iveagh, Lr. pt.	Magherally	Banbridge	III.	168
19, 26, 27	Tullyrain	494 0 32	Down	Lower Iveagh, Up. pt.	Tullylish	Banbridge	III.	171
16	Tullyrain	300 3 0	Fermanagh	Tirkennedy	Magheracross	Enniskillen	III.	223
27	Tullyrain	276 3 0h	Monaghan	Cremorne	Aghnamullen	Castleblayney	III.	259
10	Tullyraine	118 2 33	Louth	Ardee	Killanny	Dundalk	I.	173
70	Tullyrap	166 3 13	Donegal	Raphoe	Taughboyne	Strabane	III.	144
31	Tullyratty	223 3 23i	Down	Lecale Lower	Ballyculter	Downpatrick	III.	178
30, 39	Tullyraw	63 2 27	Tyrone	Dungannon Upper	Artrea	Cookstown	III.	306
27	Tullyreagh	189 0 35	Antrim	Lower Toome	Kirkinriola	Ballymena	III.	33
23	Tullyreagh	258 1 26	Fermanagh	Magherastephana	Aghavea	Lisnaskea	III.	219
17	Tullyreas	100 0 1	Monaghan	Dartree	Killeevan	Clones	III.	268
38	Tullyreavy	242 0 14	Tyrone	Dungannon Upper	Desertcreat	Cookstown	III.	308
43, 49	Tullyree	366 0 28	Down	Upper Iveagh, Lr. pt.	Kilcoo	Kilkeel	III.	173
7	Tullyree	140 1 5j	Monaghan	Trough	Donagh	Monaghan	III.	283
61, 67	Tullyremon	205 2 37	Tyrone	Dungannon Lower	Aghaloo	Armagh	III.	297
4, 8	Tullyroan	695 2 26	Armagh	Oneilland West	Clonfeacle	Armagh	III.	51
41	Tullyroan	322 2 15	Londonderry	Loughinsholin	Kilcronaghan	Magherafelt	III.	241
38	Tullyroan	73 0 6	Tyrone	Dungannon Upper	Kildress	Cookstown	III.	309
15	Tullyroane	135 3 19k	Cavan	Lower Loughtee	Annagh	Cavan	III.	79
33	Tullyroe	292 2 17	Galway	Killian	Killeroran	Mountbellew	IV.	44
71	Tullyroe	59 0 16	Mayo	Gallen	Meelick	Swineford	IV.	150
23	Tullyroe	713 1 26	Queen's Co.	Cullenagh	Abbeyleix	Abbeyleix	I.	238
41, 42	Tullyroe	149 3 24	Roscommon	Athlone	Kilmeane	Roscommon	IV.	182
6	Tullyronnelly	51 3 14	Armagh	Oneilland East	Shankill	Lurgan	III.	51
19, 20	Tullyrossmearan	117 0 22	Fermanagh	Clanawley	Cleenish	Ballyshannon	III.	191
50, 51	Tullyrush	198 3 34	Tyrone	Clogher	Donacavey	Omagh	III.	295
43	Tullyrush	480 2 35	Tyrone	Omagh East	Clogherny	Omagh	III.	310
59	Tullyrusk	1,043 3 4	Antrim	Upper Massereene	Tullyrusk	Lisburn	III.	31
7, 8, 11, 12	Tullysaran	100 1 19	Armagh	Tiranny	Eglish	Armagh	III.	60
13	Tullyshelferty	169 2 4	Monaghan	Monaghan	Kilmore	Monaghan	III.	276
11, 12	Tullyskeherny	1,046 0 24	Leitrim	Drumahaire	Cloonclare	Manorhamilton	IV.	94
5, 8	Tullyskeherny	568 0 13	Leitrim	Roslogher	Rossinver	Manorhamilton	IV.	112
20, 25	Tullyskerry	143 1 37	Monaghan	Cremorne	Clontibret	Castleblayney	III.	261
30, 39	Tullysleva	284 2 24	Mayo	Tirawley	Kilbelfad	Ballina	IV.	168

(a) Including 9A. 3R. 13P. water.
(b) Including 0A. 1R. 12P. water.
(c) Including 2A. 1R. 32P. water.
(d) Including 4A. 2R. 8P. water.

(e) Including 11A. 0R. 20P. water.
(f) Including 4A. 2R. 28P. Corbet Lough.
(g) Including 3A. 2R. 0P. water.
(h) Including 42A. 2R. 18P. water.

(i) Including 10A. 0R. 39P. Great Dam.
(j) Including 12A. 1R. 19P. water.
(k) Including 10A. 2R. 1P. water.

No. of Sheet of the Ordnance Survey Maps.	Townlands and Towns.	Area in Statute Acres.			County.	Barony.	Parish.	Poor Law Union in 1857.	Townland Census of 1851, Part I.	
		A.	R.	P.					Vol.	Page
18, 19	Tully South	400	1	11a	Antrim	Upper Dunluce	Loughguile	Ballymoney	III.	20
34	Tully South	123	2	8b	Fermanagh	Magherastephana	Aghalurcher	Lisnaskea	III.	217
34	Tully South	515	2	7c	Leitrim	Carrigallen	Carrigallen	Mohill	IV.	90
13, 19	Tullysranadeega	291	2	5	Fermanagh	Magheraboy	Devenish	Ballyshannon	III.	211
1	Tullystown	477	1	5	Westmeath	Fore	Foyran	Granard	I.	270
1, 2	Tullytawen	681	0	7	Roscommon	Boyle	Kilronan	Boyle	IV.	197
6	Tullytiernan	59	3	21	Cavan	Tullyhaw	Templeport	Enniskillen	III.	96
25	Tullytramon	263	3	7	Down	Ards Upper	Castleboy	Downpatrick	III.	160
8, 9	Tullytrasna	124	3	30	Cavan	Tullyhaw	Templeport	Bawnboy	III.	96
84, 93	Tullytrasna	138	2	11	Donegal	Banagh	Inver	Donegal	III.	108
60, 68	Tullytrasna	808	3	14	Donegal	Raphoe	Kilteevoge	Stranorlar	III.	140
26, 32	Tullytreane	226	1	5	Cavan	Upper Loughtee	Denn	Cavan	III.	84
17, 23	Tullyullagh	223	2	31	Fermanagh	Tirkennedy	Enniskillen	Enniskillen	III.	222
17	Tullyunshin	92	2	10	Cavan	Tullygarvey	Drumgoon	Cootehill	III.	88
22, 27	Tullyunshin	762	2	33d	Cavan	Tullygarvey	Larah	Cootehill	III.	91
21	Tully Upper	161	2	17	Londonderry	Tirkeeran	Clondermot	Londonderry	III.	248
3, 4, 6	Tullyval	156	0	9	Roscommon	Boyle	Ardcarn	Boyle	IV.	193
20,24,25,27	Tullyvallan	4,655	0	33	Armagh	Fews Upper	Newtownhamilton	Castleblayney	III.	49
24,25,27,28	Tullyvallan (Hamilton) East	294	3	13	Armagh	Fews Upper	Newtownhamilton	Castleblayney	III.	49
24, 27	Tullyvallan (Hamilton) West	81	2	21	Armagh	Fews Upper	Newtownhamilton	Castleblayney	III.	49
27, 28	Tullyvallan (Macullagh)	181	3	31	Armagh	Fews Upper	Newtownhamilton	Castleblayney	III.	49
28	Tullyvallan (Tipping) East	151	2	4	Armagh	Fews Upper	Newtownhamilton	Castleblayney	III.	49
27, 28	Tullyvallan (Tipping) West	204	1	36	Armagh	Fews Upper	Newtownhamilton	Castleblayney	III.	49
43, 51	Tullyvally	283	0	31	Tyrone	Clogher	Donacavey	Omagh	III.	295
53	Tullyvannon	448	1	15	Tyrone	Dungannon Lower	Killeeshil	Dungannon	III.	298
20	Tullyvanus	198	0	10	Monaghan	Cremorne	Muckno	Castleblayney	III.	262
59, 60	Tullyvar	313	3	35	Tyrone	Dungannon Lower	Carntcel	Clogher	III.	298
28	Tullyvaragh Lower	174	3	1e	Monaghan	Farney	Donaghmoyne	Carrickmacross	III.	271
28	Tullyvaragh Upper	158	3	28f	Monaghan	Farney	Donaghmoyne	Carrickmacross	III.	271
51, 61	Tullyvarraga	226	0	12	Clare	Bunratty Lower	Clonloghan	Ennis	II.	3
51, 61	Tullyvarraga	255	1	17	Clare	Bunratty Lower	Drumline	Ennis	II.	3
29, 36	Tullyvarran	455	2	37	Roscommon	Roscommon	Lissonuffy	Strokestown	IV.	212
4	Tullyvarrid	92	3	15	Fermanagh	Lurg	Templecarn	Lowtherstown	III.	209
18, 19, 21	Tullyveacan	592	0	34	Leitrim	Drumahaire	Drumreilly	Cark. on Shannon	IV.	95
39	Tullyveagh	158	3	13	Tyrone	Dungannon Upper	Artrea	Cookstown	III.	306
54	Tullyvealnaslee	58	2	24	Galway	Moycullen	Kilcummin	Oughterard	IV.	68
18	Tullyveame	69	0	8	Leitrim	Drumahaire	Inishmagrath	Manorhamilton	IV.	97
8	Tullyveela	503	1	26	Cavan	Tullyhaw	Templeport	Bawnboy	III.	96
23, 24	Tullyveery	783	0	4g	Down	Dufferin	Killyleagh	Downpatrick	III.	167
24	TULLYVEERY T.	—			Down	Dufferin	Killyleagh	Downpatrick	III.	167
24, 31	Tullyvellia	1,890	2	38h	Sligo	Leyny	Achonry	Tobercurry	IV.	230
58	Tullyvernan	171	3	16	Tyrone	Clogher	Clogher	Clogher	III.	293
15	Tullyverry	279	1	8	Londonderry	Tirkeeran	Faughanvale	Newt'nLimavady	III.	250
17	Tullyvin	160	1	12	Cavan	Tullygarvey	Kildrumsherdan	Cootehill	III.	90
25	Tullyvin	140	2	36	Monaghan	Cremorne	Clontibret	Castleblayney	III.	261
70	Tullyvinny	174	0	29	Donegal	Raphoe	Raphoe	Strabane	III.	141
17	TULLYVIN T.	—			Cavan	Tullygarvey	Kildrumsherdan	Cootehill	III.	90
4	Tullyvocady	371	3	3i	Fermanagh	Lurg	Templecarn	Lowtherstown	III.	209
34	Tullyvoghan	343	0	29j	Clare	Bunratty Upper	Kilraghtis	Ennis	II.	9
4	Tullyvogy	554	0	4k	Fermanagh	Lurg	Belleek	Ballyshannon	III.	204
6, 9	Tullyvogy	158	2	20	Monaghan	Monaghan	Tedavnet	Monaghan	III.	280
10	Tullyvohaun	244	0	9	Roscommon	Boyle	Estersnow	Boyle	IV.	195
35	Tullyvoheen	364	2	36l	Galway	Ballynahinch	Omey	Clifden	IV.	15
98	Tullyvoos	257	0	33	Donegal	Banagh	Inver	Donegal	III.	108
17	Tullyvrane	337	1	2m	Longford	Ratheline	Ratheline	Longford	I.	165
54	Tullyvrick	60	3	28	Galway	Moycullen	Kilcummin	Oughterard	IV.	68
27	Tullywaltry	277	0	12	Cavan	Clankee	Knockbride	Bailieborough	III.	74
21	Tullywana	263	1	10	Leitrim	Carrigallen	Oughteragh	Bawnboy	IV.	93
22	Tullywasnacunagh	584	1	25n	Down	Castlereagh Upper	Saintfield	Lisburn	III.	166
8, 9	Tullywaum	179	0	3	Cavan	Tullyhaw	Templeport	Bawnboy	III.	96
99, 100	Tullywee	167	3	2	Donegal	Tirhugh	Drumhome	Donegal	III.	147
49	Tullywee	133	2	39	Tyrone	Omagh East	Dromore	Lowtherstown	III.	311
24	Tullyweel	135	3	25	Fermanagh	Tirkennedy	Enniskillen	Lisnaskea	III.	222
2	Tullyweel	175	2	24	Meath	Lower Kells	Kilmainham	Kells	I.	203
30, 39	Tullyweery	68	3	31	Tyrone	Dungannon Upper	Artrea	Cookstown	III.	306
95, 100, 101	Tullywee, Tullygallan, and Oughtnadrin Barr	1,434	2	38o	Donegal	Tirhugh	Drumhome	Donegal	III.	147
22, 27	Tully West	624	2	19	Kildare	Offaly East	Tully	Naas	I.	71
9, 16	Tullywhisker	517	1	3	Tyrone	Strabane Lower	Urney	Strabane	III.	323

(a) { Including 156A. 1R. 23P. detached portion. / Including 40A. 1R. 28P. detached portion.
(b) Including 11A. 1R. 37P. water.
(c) Including 13A. 3R. 12P. water.
(d) Including 18A. 3R. 23P. water.
(e) Including 6A. 0R. 31P. water.

(f) Including 4A. 3R. 36P. water.
(g) Including Clay Lakes.
(h) Including 31A. 2R. 18P. water.
(i) Including 10A. 1R. 16P. water.
(j) Including 3A. 0R. 22P. water.

(k) Including 6A. 0R. 4P. water.
(l) Including 8A. 0R. 6P. water.
(m) Including 17A. 2R. 20P. water.
(n) Including 24A. 0R. 31P. water.
(o) Including 15A. 2R. 7P. water.

No. of Sheet of the Ordnance Survey Maps.	Townlands and Towns.	Area in Statute Acres.			County.	Barony.	Parish.	Poor Law Union in 1857.	Townland Census of 1851, Part I.	
		A.	R.	P.					Vol.	Page
38	Tullywiggan . .	159	0	12	Tyrone . .	Dungannon Upper .	Derryloran . .	Cookstown .	III.	307
25	Tullywinny . .	514	0	39	Armagh . .	Orior Upper . .	Loughgilly . .	Newry . .	III.	58
59, 60	Tullywinny . .	195	0	3	Tyrone . .	Dungannon Lower .	Carnteel . . .	Clogher . .	III.	298
49	Tullywolly . .	177	2	27	Tyrone . .	Omagh East . .	Kilskeery . .	Lowtherstown .	III.	314
29, 30	Tullywood . .	275	2	0	Westmeath . .	Clonlonan . .	Ballyloughloe .	Athlone . .	I.	261
12	Tullyworgle . .	23	2	8	Armagh . .	Armagh . . .	Armagh . . .	Armagh . .	III.	43
28, 29	Tulnacross . .	543	1	30	Tyrone . .	Dungannon Upper .	Kildress . .	Cookstown .	III.	309
46	Tulnagall . .	227	1	25	Tyrone . .	Dungannon Middle .	Pomeroy . . .	Dungannon .	III.	304
22	Tulnashane . .	560	2	19a	Tyrone . .	Omagh West . .	Termonamongan .	Castlederg .	III.	317
44,45,52,53	Tulnavern . .	896	2	22b	Tyrone . .	Dungannon Lower .	Carnteel . . .	Dungannon .	III.	298
102	Tulrohaun . .	47	0	18	Mayo . .	Costello . . .	Annagh . . .	Claremorris .	IV.	138
29, 43	Tulrush . . .	240	3	18	Galway . .	Clare . . .	Killower . .	Tuam . .	IV.	21
53	Tulrush . . .	208	0	30c	Roscommon . .	Moycarn . . .	Creagh . . .	Ballinasloe .	IV.	206
28, 32	Tulrusk . . .	167	2	21	Leitrim . .	Mohill . . .	Mohill . . .	Mohill . .	IV.	108
22, 28	Tulsk . . .	76	0	12	Roscommon . .	Roscommon . .	Ogulla . . .	Strokestown .	IV.	212
22	Tulsk T. . .	—			Roscommon . .	Roscommon . .	Ogulla . . .	Strokestown .	IV.	212
7	Tumbeagh . .	562	3	23	King's Co. .	Garrycastle . .	Lemanaghan .	Parsonstown .	I.	137
50, 62	Tumgesh . . .	687	2	5	Mayo . .	Gallen . . .	Killasser . .	Swineford .	IV.	149
61	Tummerillaun .	148	1	22	Galway . .	Killian . . .	Ahascragh . .	Ballinasloe .	IV.	43
49	Tummery . . .	819	1	36	Tyrone . .	Omagh East . .	Dromore . .	Lowtherstown .	III.	311
7, 11	Tumna . . .	182	1	20	Roscommon . .	Boyle . . .	Tumna . . .	Car^k. on Shannon	IV.	198
68, 81	Tumnasrah . .	165	1	36	Galway . .	Moycullen . .	Moycullen . .	Galway . .	IV.	71
27	Tumneenaun .	300	0	0	Galway . .	Ross . . .	Cong . . .	Oughterard .	IV.	73
47	Tumpher . . .	146	0	0	Tyrone . .	Dungannon Middle .	Clonoe . . .	Dungannon .	III.	300
11	Tunker . . .	128	0	37	Cavan . .	Tullygarvey . .	Annagh . . .	Cavan . .	III.	87
39	Tunnagh . . .	191	0	23	Sligo . .	Corran . . .	Kilshalvy . .	Boyle . .	IV.	227
27	Tunnagh . . .	387	1	37d	Sligo . .	Tirerrill . . .	Ballynakill . .	Sligo . .	IV.	237
84, 96	Tuocusheen . .	279	0	38	Cork, E.R. .	East Muskerry . .	Knockavilly . .	Bandon . .	II.	105
12, 20, 21	Tuogh . . .	787	0	1	Limerick . .	Kenry . . .	Adare . . .	Croom . .	II.	248
15	Tuogh . . .	733	2	6	Limerick . .	Owneybeg . .	Tuogh . . .	Limerick . .	II.	251
15	Turagh . . .	412	0	19	Limerick . .	Owneybeg . .	Tuogh . . .	Limerick . .	II.	251
122	Turavaghla . .	74	0	36	Galway . .	Kiltartan . .	Kilmacduagh .	Gort . .	IV.	48
6	Turavoggaun . .	334	0	6	Tipperary, N.R. .	Lower Ormond .	Terryglass . .	Borrisokane .	II.	288
19, 20	Turbeagh . . .	519	1	37	Cork, E.R. .	Condons&Clangibbon	Brigown . .	Mitchelstown .	II.	60
21	Turbeha . . .	249	2	22	Waterford . .	Decies without Drum	Affane . . .	Lismore . .	II.	353
34	Turbot Island .	147	2	19	Galway . .	Ballynahinch . .	Omey . . .	Clifden . .	IV.	15
3	Turbotstown . .	305	1	32	Westmeath . .	Fore . . .	Mayne . . .	Granard . .	I.	271
8, 12	Turcarra . . .	339	0	13e	Armagh . .	Oneilland West .	Loughgall . .	Armagh . .	III.	54
10, 14	Ture . . .	238	3	13f	Cavan . .	Lower Loughtee .	Drumlane . .	Cavan . .	III.	81
2	Ture . . .	115	2	17	Cavan . .	Tullyhaw . .	Killinagh . .	Enniskillen .	III.	92
30, 39	Ture . . .	1,165	1	16	Donegal . .	Inishowen West .	Muff . . .	Londonderry .	III.	121
16, 17	Ture . . .	40	2	37	Monaghan . .	Dartree . . .	Killeevan . .	Clones . .	III.	268
13	Tureagh . . .	1,086	1	35	Antrim . .	Cary . . .	Armoy . . .	Ballycastle .	III.	11
40, 46	Tureagh . . .	915	3	16	Antrim . .	Lower Belfast .	Raloo . . .	Larne . .	III.	9
27	Turfad . . .	374	1	16g	Cavan . .	Clankee . . .	Knockbride . .	Cootehill .	III.	74
7	Turfahun . .	427	2	28	Antrim . .	Lower Dunluce .	Billy . . .	Coleraine .	III.	16
28, 34	Turfarney . .	255	1	4	Queen's Co. .	Clarmallagh . .	Coolkerry . .	Abbeyleix .	I.	237
38	Turin . . .	192	0	39	Cavan . .	Clanmahon . .	Ballymachugh .	Cavan . .	III.	76
121, 122	Turin . . .	389	3	31	Mayo . .	Kilmaine . .	Kilmainemore .	Ballinrobe .	IV.	156
17	Turkenagh . .	445	0	38h	Clare . .	Inchiquin . .	Kilkeedy . .	Corrofin .	II.	26
20, 21	Turkenagh Mountain	1,913	1	11	Clare . .	Tulla Upper . .	Moynoe . .	Scarriff . .	II.	40
149	Turkhead . .	88	0	17	Cork, W.R. .	West Carbery (E.D.)	Aghadown .	Skibbereen .	II.	137
4, 5	Turkinstown . .	82	3	33	Dublin . .	Balrothery East .	Balrothery . .	Balrothery .	I.	19
86, 98	Turksland . .	136	0	20	Galway . .	Kilconnell . .	Killaan . .	Ballinasloe .	IV.	41
34, 38	Turksland . .	117	1	27	Roscommon . .	Ballymoe . .	Oran . . .	Roscommon .	IV.	192
39, 42	Turkstown . .	260	1	23	Kilkenny . .	Iverk . . .	Fiddown . .	Carrick on Suir	I.	105
11	Turkstown . .	143	2	6	Meath . .	Upper Kells . .	Dulane . . .	Kells . .	I.	205
32, 33	Turkyle . . .	142	0	13	Wexford . .	Ballaghkeen . .	St. Nicholas .	Enniscorthy .	I.	298
45	Turlagh . . .	249	1	8	Roscommon . .	Athlone . .	Rahara . . .	Roscommon .	IV.	183
6	Turlagh . . .	17	1	35i	Roscommon . .	Boyle . . .	Ardcarn . .	Boyle . .	IV.	193
10, 16	Turlagh . . .	59	3	32	Roscommon . .	Frenchpark . .	Creeve . . .	Car^k. on Shannon	IV.	203
8, 9, 14, 15	Turlagharee . .	121	2	18	Roscommon . .	Frenchpark . .	Tibohine . .	Castlereagh .	IV.	205
51	Turlaghmore . .	250	3	14	Roscommon . .	Athlone . .	Taghmaconnell .	Athlone . .	IV.	185
15	Turlaghnamaddy	78	3	12	Roscommon . .	Frenchpark . .	Tibohine . .	Castlereagh .	IV.	205
33	Turlaghyraun .	58	3	21	Sligo . .	Corran . . .	Kilmorgan . .	Sligo . .	IV.	227
55, 62	Turleenan . .	153	1	2	Tyrone . .	Dungannon Middle .	Clonfeacle . .	Dungannon .	III.	300
3, 6	Turlough . .	1,276	1	29	Clare . .	Burren . . .	Oughtmama . .	Ballyvaghan .	II.	14
7	Turlough . .	614	1	27	Galway . .	Ballymoe . .	Kilcroan . .	Glennamaddy .	IV.	9
52, 65	Turlough . .	3,078	1	11j	Galway . .	Moycullen . .	Kilcummin . .	Oughterard .	IV.	68
70	Turlough . .	240	2	35	Mayo . .	Carra . . .	Turlough . .	Castlebar .	IV.	131
92	Turlough . .	151	2	31k	Mayo . .	Costello . .	Bekan . . .	Claremorris .	IV.	139
96	Turloughalanger .	104	3	14	Galway . .	Athenry . .	Athenry . .	Loughrea .	IV.	4
122	Turloughanbaun .	94	2	33	Mayo . .	Kilmaine . .	Kilmainemore .	Ballinrobe .	IV.	156

(a) Including 8A. 0R. 36P. water.
(b) Including 260A. 3R. 18P. detached portion.
(c) Including 10A. 1R. 8P. water.
(d) Including 20A. 1R. 30P. water.

(e) Including 9A. 0R. 8P. water.
(f) Including 26A. 1R. 28P. water.
(g) Including 10A. 2R. 37P. water.
(h) Including 107A. 3R. 5P. water.

(i) Including 2A. 3R. 26P. water.
(j) Including 269A. 3R. 20P. water.
(k) Including 2A. 2R. 26P. water.

No. of Sheet of the Ordnance Survey Maps.	Townlands and Towns.	Area in Statute Acres.			County.	Barony.	Parish.	Poor Law Union in 1857.	Townland Census of 1851, Part I.	
		A.	R.	P.					Vol.	Page
65, 78	Turloughbeg	269	3	25	Galway	Moycullen	Kilcummin	Oughterard	IV.	68
57	Turloughcartron	33	1	27	Galway	Clare	Cummer	Tuam	IV.	19
56	Turloughcor	222	1	37	Galway	Clare	Killeany	Tuam	IV.	20
56	Turloughgarve	339	3	20	Galway	Clare	Annaghdown	Tuam	IV.	17
113	Turloughkeeloge	128	0	27	Galway	Kiltartan	Kinvarradoorus	Gort	IV.	49
57	Turloughmartin	129	2	3a	Galway	Clare	Cummer	Tuam	IV.	19
10	Turloughmore	406	2	6	Clare	Inchiquin	Kilkeedy	Corrofin	II.	26
70	Turloughmore Common	105	3	21	Galway	Clare	Lackagh	Galway	IV.	23
114	Turloughnacloghdoo Commons	48	1	0	Galway	Loughrea	Kilthomas	Loughrea	IV.	65
43	Turloughnaroyey or Common	93	3	4	Galway	Clare	Belclare	Tuam	IV.	17
43, 57	Turloughour	111	1	21	Galway	Clare	Cummer	Tuam	IV.	19
57	Turloughrevagh	145	2	23	Galway	Clare	Kilmoylan	Tuam	IV.	22
24, 30, 31	Turmeel	654	2	17	Londonderry	Keenaght	Dungiven	Newtᵃ Limavady	III.	236
30, 31	Turmennan	607	3	22	Down	Lecale Lower	Inch	Downpatrick	III.	179
46, 47	Turmore	374	2	4	Down	Lordship of Newry	Newry	Newry	III.	182
6	Turmoyra	278	1	13	Armagh	Oneilland East	Seagoe	Lurgan	III.	50
37, 45	Turnabarson	607	3	13	Tyrone	Dungannon Middle	Pomeroy	Cookstown	III.	304
46	Turnaface	243	1	11	Londonderry	Loughinsholin	Lissan	Magherafelt	III.	242
18	Turnagrove	516	1	2	Antrim	Upper Dunluce	Loughguile	Ballymoney	III.	20
8	Turnakibeck	71	0	3	Londonderry	North East Liberties of Coleraine	Kildollagh	Coleraine	III.	246
26, 27	Turnalaydan	295	1	14	Sligo	Tirerrill	Drumcolumb	Sligo	IV.	238
80	Turnamucka	278	1	37	Kerry	Iveragh	Caher	Cahersiveen	II.	194
14	Turnapin Great	206	3	18	Dublin	Coolock	Santry	Dublin North	I.	29
14	Turnapin Little	78	3	2	Dublin	Coolock	Santry	Dublin North	I.	29
13	Turnarobert	262	2	38	Antrim	Cary	Armoy	Ballycastle	III.	11
81	Turnaspidogy	827	1	35	Cork, W.R.	West Muskerry	Inchigeelagh	Macroom	II.	158
18	Turnavedog	435	2	28	Antrim	Upper Dunluce	Loughguile	Ballymoney	III.	20
30	Turnersglaster	73	3	38	King's Co.	Garrycastle	Lusmagh	Parsonstown	I.	137
35	Turnerstown	131	2	13	Kildare	Narragh & Reban East	Moone	Athy	I.	66
14	Turnings	52	2	4	Kildare	Naas North	Whitechurch	Naas	I.	63
14	Turnings Lower	523	2	22b	Kildare	Naas North	Whitechurch	Naas	I.	63
14	Turnings Upper	278	0	30	Kildare	Naas North	Whitechurch	Naas	I.	63
97	Turoe	392	3	1	Galway	Athenry	Kiltullagh	Loughrea	IV.	5
17	Turpaun	63	3	17	Leitrim	Drumahaire	Inishmagrath	Manorhamilton	IV.	97
24, 26	Turra	257	0	28	Carlow	St. Mullins Lower	St. Mullins	New Ross	I.	13
31	Turra	689	1	6	Queen's Co.	Slievemargy	Killabban	Carlow	I.	245
123	Turra Beg	52	3	12	Galway	Kiltartan	Kilbeacanty	Gort	IV.	47
45, 46	Turraheen Lower	1,153	1	21	Tipperary, S.R.	Kilnamanagh Lower	Clogher	Cashel	II.	322
39,40,45,46	Turraheen Upper	1,925	1	5	Tipperary, S.R.	Kilnamanagh Lower	Clogher	Cashel	II.	322
8	Turraloskin	217	2	18	Antrim	Cary	Ramoan	Ballycastle	III.	15
123	Turra More	67	2	31	Galway	Kiltartan	Kilbeacanty	Gort	IV.	47
15	Turraun	979	0	31	King's Co.	Garrycastle	Wheery or Killagally	Parsonstown	I.	139
17, 21	Turreen	285	0	27	Longford	Rathcline	Rathcline	Longford	I.	165
13	*Turret Island*	1	0	33	King's Co.	Garrycastle	Clonmacnoise	Parsonstown	I.	135
44, 47	Turrock	690	3	34c	Roscommon	Athlone	Taghboy	Athlone	IV.	184
11	Turry	160	1	19	Armagh	Tiranny	Tynan	Armagh	III.	61
19	Tursalla	42	2	22	Queen's Co.	Stradbally	Stradbally	Athy	I.	248
44	Tursallagh	117	0	26	Tyrone	Omagh East	Termonmaguirk	Omagh	III.	315
22, 29, 30	Tursillagh	550	1	1	Kerry	Trughanacmy	Ballymacelligott	Tralee	II.	207
17	Turtane	211	0	27	Carlow	Forth	Myshall	Carlow	I.	5
41, 47	Turtulla	790	1	12	Tipperary, N.R.	Eliogarty	Fertiana	Thurles	II.	269
41	Turtulla	34	3	36	Tipperary, N.R.	Eliogarty	Thurles	Thurles	II.	273
27	Turtulla	28	3	26	Tipperary, N.R.	Upper Ormond	Dolla	Nenagh	II.	290
8, 12	Turvey	273	3	34	Dublin	Balrothery East	Lusk	Balrothery	I.	21
8, 12	Turvey	312	0	38	Dublin	Nethercross	Donabate	Balrothery	I.	30
53	*Tuskar Rock*	—			Wexford	Forth	St. Margaret's	Wexford	I.	314
25, 28	Tusker	222	0	28	Monaghan	Farney	Donaghmoyne	Carrickmacross	III.	271
48	Twelveacre	22	2	15	Wexford	Forth	Ballybrennan	Wexford	I.	308
21, 24	Twenties	156	1	26	Louth	Drogheda	St. Peter's	Drogheda	I.	175
9	Twenty Acres	129	3	6	Antrim	Cary	Culfeightrin	Ballycastle	III.	14
44	Twentyacres	34	3	3	Galway	Clare	Killererin	Tuam	IV.	21
18	Twenty Acres	35	1	37	Londonderry	Coleraine	Desertoghill	Coleraine	III.	231
14, 19	Twentyacres	16	3	22	Longford	Ardagh	Ardagh	Longford	I.	151
14	Twentyacres	69	0	12	Longford	Ardagh	Templemichael	Longford	I.	154
42	Twentyacres	28	2	24	Wexford	Forth	Kildavin	Wexford	I.	310
38, 44	Twentypark	174	0	7	Meath	Ratoath	Ratoath	Dunshaughlin	I.	219
7	Twigspark	40	2	10	Leitrim	Rosclogher	Killasnet	Manorhamilton	IV.	110
20	Two Acres and Half	24	0	0	Antrim	Lower Glenarm	Ardclinis	Larne	III.	21
24	Two Gneeves	71	2	13	Cork, E.R.	Duhallow	Castlemagner	Kanturk	II.	67
29	Two Gneeves	199	0	27	Cork, E.R.	Duhallow	Cullen	Millstreet	II.	71

(a) Including 7ᴀ. 2ʀ. 15ᴘ. water.   (b) Including 1ᴀ. 2ʀ. 22ᴘ. water.   (c) Including 31ᴀ. 2ʀ. 8ᴘ. water.

5 X 2

No. of Sheet of the Ordnance Survey Maps.	Townlands and Towns.	Area in Statute Acres.			County.	Barony.	Parish.	Poor Law Union in 1857.	Townland Census of 1851. Part I.	
		A.	R.	P.					Vol.	Page
106	*Two Headed Island* .	22	2	36	Kerry . .	Dunkerron South .	Kilcrohane . .	Cahersiveen .	II.	184
42	TWOMILEBORRIS T.	—			Tipperary, N.R.	Eliogarty . .	Twomileborris .	Thurles . .	II.	274
83	Twomilebridge .	185	1	8a	Tipperary, S.R.	Iffa and Offa East .	Kilgrant . .	Clonmel . .	II.	314
30, 31, 35	Twomilebridge .	193	3	32	Waterford .	Decies without Drum	Dungarvan . .	Dungarvan .	II.	356
103, 107	Twomilestone .	60	3	8	Donegal . .	Tirhugh . .	Kilbarron . .	Ballyshannon .	III.	148
25	Twopothouse .	411	2	13	Cork, E.R. .	Fermoy . .	Caherduggan .	Mallow . .	II.	77
29, 30	Twyford . .	535	1	2b	Westmeath .	Clonlonan . .	Ballyloughloe .	Athlone . .	I.	261
33	Tyanee . .	1,719	1	11	Londonderry .	Loughinsholin .	Tamlaght O'Crilly .	Magherafelt .	III.	244
52, 59	Tycanny . .	615	2	1	Tyrone . .	Clogher . .	Clogher . .	Clogher . .	III.	293
12	Tyfarnham .	313	0	32	Westmeath .	Corkaree . .	Tyfarnham .	Mullingar .	I.	264
15	Tygore . .	141	0	3	Londonderry .	Tirkeeran . .	Faughanvale .	Londonderry .	III.	250
54, 61	Tyhan . .	216	3	3	Tyrone . .	Dungannon Middle .	Clonfeacle . .	Dungannon .	III.	300
30	Tylagh . .	412	3	35	Kerry . .	Trughanacmy .	O'Brennan . .	Tralee . .	II.	212
70	Tyleford . .	21	1	20	Donegal . .	Raphoe . .	Clonleigh . .	Strabane . .	III.	135
22	Tymon North .	483	1	26	Dublin . .	Uppercross .	Tallaght . .	Dublin South .	I.	42
22	Tymon South .	105	1	1	Dublin . .	Uppercross .	Tallaght . .	Dublin South .	I.	42
39	Tynacocka .	47	1	19	Limerick . .	Coshma . .	Uregare . .	Kilmallock .	II.	244
116, 117	Tynagh . .	232	1	12	Galway . .	Leitrim . .	Tynagh . .	Portumna .	IV.	56
117	TYNAGH T.	—			Galway . .	Leitrim . .	Tynagh . .	Portumna .	IV.	56
11, 15	Tynan . .	375	3	9	Armagh . .	Tiranny . .	Tynan . .	Armagh . .	III.	61
11	TYNAN T.	—			Armagh . .	Tiranny . .	Tynan . .	Armagh . .	III.	61
21	Tyone . .	97	1	29	Tipperary, N.R.	Upper Ormond .	Ballynaclogh .	Nenagh . .	II.	290
21	Tyone . .	265	3	27	Tipperary, N.R.	Upper Ormond .	Lisbunny . .	Nenagh . .	II.	292
20, 21	Tyone . .	298	1	19	Tipperary, N.R.	Upper Ormond .	Nenagh . .	Nenagh . .	II.	293
26, 27	Tyredagh Lower .	198	3	34	Clare . .	Tulla Upper .	Tulla . .	Tulla . .	II.	42
27	Tyredagh Upper .	1,089	1	25	Clare . .	Tulla Upper .	Tulla . .	Tulla . .	II.	42
44	Tyrella North .	420	0	10	Down . .	Lecale Upper .	Tyrella . .	Downpatrick .	III.	181
44	Tyrella South .	459	0	39	Down . .	Lecale Upper .	Tyrella . .	Downpatrick .	III.	181
103	Tyrone . .	267	1	17	Galway . .	Dunkellin .	Drumacoo . .	Gort . .	IV.	28
12	Tyross or Legagilly	47	0	6	Armagh . .	Armagh . .	Armagh . .	Armagh . .	III.	43
33, 38, 39	Tyrrellspass .	398	2	33	Westmeath .	Fartullagh .	Clonfad . .	Mullingar .	I.	268
39	TYRRELLSPASS T. .	—			Westmeath .	Fartullagh .	{ Clonfad . .	} Mullingar .	I.	{ 268
							Newtown . .			269
34, 35	Tyrrellstown .	259	3	1c	Kildare . .	Narragh&RebanWest	Kilberry . .	Athy . .	I.	68
26	Tyrrellstown .	368	0	23d	Westmeath .	Fartullagh .	Moylisker . .	Mullingar .	I.	269
13	Tyrrelstown .	427	2	2	Dublin . .	Castleknock .	Mulhuddart .	Dublin North .	I.	25
8	Tyrrelstown Big .	282	3	22e	Dublin . .	Balrothery East .	Lusk . .	Balrothery .	I.	21
8	Tyrrelstown Little .	254	2	8	Dublin . .	Balrothery East .	Lusk . .	Balrothery .	I.	21
67	Uggool . .	1,254	3	18f	Galway . .	Moycullen .	Killannin . .	Galway . .	IV.	70
81	Uggool . .	150	1	26	Galway . .	Moycullen .	Moycullen .	Galway . .	IV.	71
73	Uggool . .	821	1	29	Mayo . .	Costello . .	Kilmovee . .	Swineford .	IV.	142
27, 36	Uggool . .	3,204	2	15g	Mayo . .	Erris . .	Kilcommon .	Belmullet .	IV.	145
105, 115	Uggool . .	584	3	31	Mayo . .	Murrisk . .	Kilgeever . .	Westport .	IV.	161
27	Uggoon Lower .	92	2	32	Clare . .	Tulla Upper .	Tulla . .	Tulla . .	II.	42
19, 27	Uggoon Upper .	1,084	2	4h	Clare . .	Tulla Upper .	Tulla . .	Tulla . .	II.	42
5	Ughtyneill .	172	0	18	Meath . .	Lower Kells .	Moynalty . .	Kells . .	I.	204
131	Ulicksmountain .	387	0	23	Galway . .	Leitrim . .	Ballynakill .	Loughrea .	IV.	52
42, 43	Ullagha . .	123	1	14	Kerry . .	Corkaguiny .	Kilmalkedar .	Dingle . .	II.	178
58, 59	Ullanes East .	356	3	12	Cork, W.R. .	West Muskerry .	Ballyvourney .	Macroom .	II.	154
58	Ullanes West .	614	0	3	Cork, W.R. .	West Muskerry .	Ballyvourney .	Macroom .	II.	154
25	Ullard . .	637	1	26i	Kilkenny . .	Gowran . .	Ullard . .	Thomastown .	I.	100
17	Ullard Beg .	179	1	8	Carlow . .	Forth . .	Myshall . .	Carlow . .	I.	5
5	Ullard or Controversyland .	223	3	24	Queen's Co. .	Portnahinch .	Lea . .	Mountmellick .	I.	244
17	Ullard More .	284	1	23	Carlow . .	Forth . .	Myshall . .	Carlow . .	I.	5
84	Ullauns . .	1,587	3	19	Kerry . .	Magunihy .	Killarney . .	Killarney .	II.	204
42, 43	Ullid . .	579	0	34	Kilkenny . .	Iverk . .	Ullid . .	Waterford .	I.	107
24	Ullinagh . .	256	3	31	Monaghan .	Cremorne .	Aghnamullen .	Castleblayney .	III.	259
41	Ulrith . .	118	3	34	Galway . .	Clare . .	Killursa . .	Tuam . .	IV.	22
116	Ulusker . .	83	0	33	Cork, W.R. .	Bear . .	Kilcaskan .	Castletown .	II.	123
42	Umberstown Great .	437	3	11	Meath . .	Lower Moyfenrath .	Laracor . .	Trim . .	I.	210
42	Umberstown Little .	155	1	22	Meath . .	Lower Moyfenrath .	Laracor . .	Trim . .	I.	210
2	Umbra . .	87	1	7	Londonderry .	Keenaght .	Magilligan .	NewTⁿLimavady .	III.	237
32	*Umfin Island* .	17	3	3	Donegal . .	Kilmacrenan .	Tullaghobegly .	Dunfanaghy .	III.	132
2, 4	Umgall . .	461	2	36j	Donegal . .	Inishowen East .	Clonca . .	Inishowen .	III.	117
56	Umgall, Grange of .	753	2	19	Antrim . .	Upper Belfast .	Templepatrick .	Antrim . .	III.	10
12	Umgola . .	63	3	33	Armagh . .	Armagh . .	Armagh . .	Armagh . .	III.	43
16,17,26,27	Umlagh . .	403	1	38	Donegal . .	Kilmacrenan .	Mevagh . .	Millford .	III.	130
23	Umma Beg or Moneynamanagh .	207	3	20	Westmeath .	Rathconrath .	Ballymore .	Athlone .	I.	282
23	Umma More .	387	2	27	Westmeath .	Rathconrath .	Ballymore .	Athlone .	I.	282

(a) Including 3A. 3R. 12P. water.
(b) Including 11A. 1R. 36P. water.
(c) Including 7A. 2R. 4P. water.
(d) Including 4A. 0R. 10P. water.

(e) Including 85A. 2R. 9P. detached portion.
(f) Including 16A. 1R. 17P. water.
(g) Including 12A. 2R. 0P. Lough Nambrakkeagh.

(h) Including 3A. 2R. 32P. water.
(i) Including 15A. 1R. 10P. River Barrow.
(j) Including 18A. 1R. 33P. detached portion.

No. of Sheet of the Ordnance Survey Maps.	Townlands and Towns.	Area in Statute Acres.			County.	Barony.	Parish.	Poor Law Union in 1857.	Townland Census of 1851, Part I.	
		A.	R.	P.					Vol.	Page
17, 23	Ummer	116	3	16a	Fermanagh	Tirkennedy	Enniskillen	Enniskillen	III.	223
71	Ummera	1,117	3	10	Cork, W.R.	East Muskerry	Aghinagh	Macroom	II.	154
123	Ummera	159	3	1	Cork, W.R.	Ibane and Barryroe	Timoleague	Clonakilty	II.	151
41	Ummera	106	3	0	Fermanagh	Knockninny	Tomregan	Lisnaskea	III.	203
16, 18	Ummera	146	3	29	Leitrim	Drumahaire	Inishmagrath	Manorhamilton	IV.	97
32	Ummera	77	1	8	Leitrim	Mohill	Annaduff	Mohill	IV.	105
21	Ummera	179	0	19	Tipperary, N.R.	Upper Ormond	Ballymackey	Nenagh	II.	290
29	Ummeraboy East	371	2	37	Cork, E.R.	Duhallow	Kilmeen	Millstreet	II.	73
29	Ummeraboy West	709	0	13	Cork, E.R.	Duhallow	Kilmeen	Millstreet	II.	73
28	Ummeracam (Ball) North	414	0	34	Armagh	Fews Upper	Creggan	Castleblayney	III.	48
28	Ummeracam (Ball) South	44	2	19	Armagh	Fews Upper	Creggan	Castleblayney	III.	48
28	Ummeracam (Johnston)	396	3	5b	Armagh	Fews Upper	Creggan	Castleblayney	III.	48
16	Ummeracly East	185	2	4	Galway	Dunmore	Addergoole	Tuam	IV.	33
16	Ummeracly West	174	3	10	Galway	Dunmore	Addergoole	Tuam	IV.	33
26	Ummerafad	216	3	6	Donegal	Kilmacrenan	Clondahorky	Dunfanaghy	III.	123
27	Ummerafree	367	2	23	Monaghan	Farney	Magheross	Carrickmacross	III.	274
13, 20	Ummerantarry	1,104	1	27	Mayo	Tirawley	Kilfian	Killala	IV.	169
21	Ummeras Beg	162	2	29	Kildare	Offaly West	Lackagh	Athy	I.	73
21	Ummeras More	595	1	17	Kildare	Offaly West	Lackagh	Athy	I.	73
96	Ummerawirrinan	197	2	24	Donegal	Banagh	Glencolumbkille	Glenties	III.	106
25, 28	Ummerinvore	210	0	16	Armagh	Fews Upper	Newtownhamilton	Castleblayney	III.	49
27,28,34,35	Ummeryroe	434	0	39	Sligo	Tirerrill	Shancough	Boyle	IV.	241
60, 61	Ummoon	376	2	8c	Mayo	Gallen	Templemore	Swineford	IV.	151
19, 29	Umrycam	645	0	6	Donegal	Inishowen West	Fahan Lower	Inishowen	III.	120
17	Umrycam	314	0	8	Donegal	Kilmacrenan	Clondavaddog	Milford	III.	125
30	Umrycam	467	3	5	Londonderry	Tirkeeran	Banagher	Londonderry	III.	247
47	Umrygar	573	2	34	Wicklow	Shillelagh	Carnew	Shillelagh	I.	357
90, 96	Umuskan	401	1	24	Donegal	Banagh	Kilcar	Glenties	III.	109
29	Unagh	349	2	14	Tyrone	Dungannon Upper	Lissan	Cookstown	III.	30
107	Underhill	31	3	33	Cork, W.R.	East Carbery (W.D.)	Fanlobbus	Dunmanway	II.	132
22, 23	Ungwee	655	1	37d	Galway	Ballynahinch	Ballynakill	Clifden	IV.	12
5, 10	Unicarval	148	1	24	Down	Castlereagh Lower	Dundonald	Newtownards	III.	162
47	Unicks	65	2	12	Tyrone	Dungannon Middle	Donaghenry	Cookstown	III.	301
20	Union	1,155	1	16e	Sligo	Tirerrill	Ballysadare	Sligo	IV.	238
142	UNIONHALL T.	—			Cork, W.R.	West Carbery (E.D.)	Myross	Skibbereen	II.	141
14, 15	Unshanagh	231	3	6	Antrim	Lower Glenarm	Layd	Ballycastle	III.	23
17, 22	Unshinagh	780	2	30	Antrim	Kilconway	Finvoy	Ballymoney	III.	26
5	Unshinagh	75	1	28	Armagh	Oneilland West	Drumcree	Lurgan	III.	52
9, 13, 14	Unshinagh	172	0	12	Armagh	Orior Lower	Kilmore	Banbridge	III.	56
5	Unshinagh	108	3	35f	Cavan	Tullyhaw	Killinagh	Enniskillen	III.	92
21	Unshinagh	120	0	33	Cavan	Upper Loughtee	Castleterra	Cavan	III.	83
30	Unshinagh	51	0	5	Leitrim	Carrigallen	Carrigallen	Bawnboy	IV.	90
22, 25	Unshinagh	164	1	29	Leitrim	Carrigallen	Oughteragh	Bawnboy	IV.	93
20	Unshinagh	48	0	30	Leitrim	Drumahaire	Inishmagrath	Manorhamilton	IV.	97
1	Unshinagh	337	2	30	Leitrim	Rosclogher	Rossinver	Ballyshannon	IV.	112
18	Unshinagh	168	3	4	Monaghan	Dartree	Ematris	Cootehill	III.	267
33, 34, 42	Unshinagh	772	2	14	Tyrone	Omagh West	Longfield East	Omagh	III.	316
79	Unshinagh Lower	94	3	14g	Donegal	Raphoe	Clonleigh	Strabane	III.	135
25, 29	Unshinagh Mountain	635	1	5	Antrim	Lower Glenarm	Tickmacrevan	Larne	III.	24
25, 29	Unshinagh North	122	3	39	Antrim	Lower Glenarm	Tickmacrevan	Larne	III.	24
29	Unshinagh South	194	1	3	Antrim	Lower Glenarm	Tickmacrevan	Larne	III.	24
70, 79	Unshinagh Upper	80	2	35	Donegal	Raphoe	Clonleigh	Strabane	III.	135
15	Unshog	197	1	32	Armagh	Tiranny	Tynan	Armagh	III.	61
1, 2, 3, 4	Unshogagh	460	1	19	Cavan	Tullyhaw	Killinagh	Enniskillen	III.	92
14	Upper Broghindrummin or Dira	186	0	37	Antrim	Lower Glenarm	Grange of Layd	Ballycastle	III.	22
20, 25	Upper Glenariff Mountain East	986	2	15h	Antrim	Lower Glenarm	Ardclinis	Larne	III.	21
25	Upper Glenariff Mountain West	313	1	16i	Antrim	Lower Glenarm	Ardclinis	Larne	III.	21
19	Upper Gortnagross or Issbawn	244	0	9	Antrim	Lower Glenarm	Layd	Ballycastle	III.	22
10, 11	Upper Kiltinny	666	0	37	Londonderry	Coleraine	Macosquin	Coleraine	III.	233
32, 33	Upperland	568	2	14	Londonderry	Loughinsholin	Maghera	Magherafelt	III.	243
16, 24	Upperthird	187	0	35	Tyrone	Omagh West	Ardstraw	Castlederg	III.	315
15	Uppertown	229	1	13	Wicklow	Lower Talbotstown	Dunlavin	Baltinglass	I.	360
23,24,27,28	Upper Tullykittagh	662	2	28	Antrim	Kilconway	Dunaghy	Ballymena	III.	26
13	Upperwood Demesne	283	3	7	Kilkenny	Crannagh	Freshford	Kilkenny	I.	85
22	Upton	219	2	19	Wexford	Ballaghkeen	Kilmuckridge	Gorey	I.	297
41	Upton	116	3	30	Wexford	Shelmaliere West	Taghmon	New Ross	I.	335
16	Upton or Ballyhubbock	260	2	14	Carlow	Idrone East	Fennagh	Carlow	I.	7

(a) Including 5A. 0R. 30P. water.
(b) Including 11A. 1R. 0P. water.
(c) Including 12A. 1R. 31P. water.

(d) Including 10A. 1R. 12P. water.
(e) Including 55A. 3R. 15P. water.
(f) Including 4A. 2R. 27P. water.

(g) Including 1A. 2R. 32P. water.
(h) Including 9A. 2R. 14P. water.
(i) Including 3A. 3R. 24P. water.

No. of Sheet of the Ordnance Survey Maps.	Townlands and Towns.	Area in Statute Acres.	County.	Barony.	Parish.	Poor Law Union in 1857.	Townland Census of 1851, Part I.	
		A. R. P.					Vol.	Page
14	Uragh	117 3 1a	Cavan	Lower Loughtee	Drumlane	Cavan	III.	81
7	Uragh	147 3 32	Cavan	Tullyhaw	Kinawley	Bawnboy	III.	93
101, 109	Uragh	1,086 2 18b	Kerry	Glanarought	Tuosist	Kenmare	II.	189
1	Uragh	985 3 29	Leitrim	Rosclogher	Rossinver	Ballyshannon	IV.	112
43	Urard	1,043 2 8	Tipperary, S.R.	Slievardagh	Fennor	Urlingford	II.	333
12	Urbal	412 0 11	Antrim	Lower Dunluce	Billy	Ballymoney	III.	16
31, 37	Urbal	388 3 17	Cavan	Clanmahon	Ballintemple	Cavan	III.	75
92	Urbal	145 3 38	Donegal	Banagh	Killaghtee	Donegal	III.	110
18	Urbal	117 1 13	Leitrim	Drumahaire	Drumreilly	Carᵏ. on Shannon	IV.	95
30, 39	Urbal	240 1 37	Tyrone	Dungannon Upper	Tamlaght	Cookstown	III.	309
19	Urbal Barr	138 0 22	Leitrim	Drumahaire	Drumreilly	Carᵏ. on Shannon	IV.	95
74	Urbaldeevan	660 1 24c	Donegal	Boylagh	Inishkeel	Glenties	III.	114
13	Urbalkirk	271 3 30	Monaghan	Monaghan	Monaghan	Monaghan	III.	277
16	Urbal or Mossfield	238 3 19	Fermanagh	Tirkennedy	Trory	Enniskillen	III.	224
6	Urbalreagh	186 3 9	Antrim	Lower Dunluce	Dunluce	Coleraine	III.	17
2, 4	Urbalreagh	545 3 39	Donegal	Inishowen East	Clonca	Inishowen	III.	117
39	Urbalreagh	57 3 11	Tyrone	Dungannon Middle	Donaghenry	Cookstown	III.	301
17	Urbalreagh	537 3 26d	Tyrone	Strabane Lower	Ardstraw	Strabane	III.	319
36	Urbalshinny	104 2 37	Donegal	Kilmacrenan	Tullyfern	Milford	III.	133
99	Urbalshinny	19 0 36	Donegal	Tirhugh	Drumhome	Donegal	III.	147
30, 31	Urcher	494 1 27	Armagh	Fews Upper	Creggan	Castleblayney	III.	48
34	Urcher	342 3 11	Cavan	Clankee	Bailieborough	Bailieborough	III.	71
13, 18	Urcher	163 1 13	Monaghan	Monaghan	Kilmore	Monaghan	III.	276
39, 40	Uregare	343 2 21	Limerick	Coshma	Uregare	Kilmallock	II.	244
2, 3, 7, 8	Urglin or Rutland	726 2 11	Carlow	Carlow	Urglin	Carlow	I.	3
9	Urhannagh	68 0 23	Cavan	Tullyhaw	Templeport	Bawnboy	III.	96
114	Urhin	1,480 0 21	Cork, W.R.	Bear	Kilcatherine	Castletown	II.	124
40	*Urkaunbeg*	5 3 10	Galway	Moycullen	Kilcummin	Oughterard	IV.	69
40	*Urkaunmore*	8 2 35	Galway	Moycullen	Kilcummin	Oughterard	IV.	69
51	Urlan Beg	204 0 18	Clare	Bunratty Lower	Kilmaleery	Ennis	II.	6
51	Urlan More	332 1 29	Clare	Bunratty Lower	Kilmaleery	Ennis	II.	6
8	Urlar	317 2 31	Sligo	Carbury	Drumcliff	Sligo	IV.	222
73, 82	Urlaur	1,714 0 3e	Mayo	Costello	Kilmovee	Swineford	IV.	142
5	Urlee	520 1 32	Kerry	Iraghticonnor	Lisselton	Listowel	II.	192
12	Urlingford	347 2 37	Kilkenny	Galmoy	Urlingford	Urlingford	I.	93
12	URLINGFORD T.	—	Kilkenny	Galmoy	Urlingford	Urlingford	I.	93
3	Urlish	46 2 14	Monaghan	Trough	Errigal Trough	Clogher	III.	285
25, 31	Urney	246 1 14	Cavan	Clanmahon	Kilmore	Cavan	III.	78
15	Urney	142 1 0f	Cavan	Upper Loughtee	Urney	Cavan	III.	86
26	Urney	484 3 25	King's Co.	Upper Philipstown	Ballykean	Mountmellick	I.	143
4, 9	Urney	188 0 27	Tyrone	Strabane Lower	Urney	Strabane	III.	323
4, 9	Urney Glebe	124 0 13g	Tyrone	Strabane Lower	Urney	Strabane	III.	323
9, 14	Urra	618 3 29h	Tipperary, N.R.	Lower Ormond	Killodiernan	Borrisokane	II.	285
15, 16	Urracly	596 2 38i	Galway	Dunmore	Kilconla	Tuam	IV.	35
21, 22, 29, 30	Urraghilbeg	417 2 34	Cork, E.R.	Duhallow	Kilmeen	Kanturk	II.	73
21, 29, 30	Urraghilmore East	439 3 33	Cork, E.R.	Duhallow	Kilmeen	Millstreet	II.	73
29	Urraghilmore West	416 0 1	Cork, E.R.	Duhallow	Kilmeen	Millstreet	II.	73
87	Urraghry	635 2 14	Galway	Clonmacnowen	Clontuskert	Ballinasloe	IV.	25
19	Urrasaun	228 1 14	Roscommon	Frenchpark	Tibohine	Castlereagh	IV.	205
9, 10, 19	Urrismenagh	1,564 1 10	Donegal	Inishowen East	Clonmany	Inishowen	III.	117
39, 48	Urrohogal	502 1 31	Kerry	Trughanacmy	Currans	Killarney	II.	209
15	Urros	60 2 11	Fermanagh	Magheraboy	Inishmacsaint	Enniskillen	III.	213
24	Ushnagh Hill	251 2 32	Westmeath	Rathconrath	Conry	Mullingar	I.	282
32	Usk	565 1 32	Kildare	Narragh & RebanEast	Usk	Naas	I.	67
7	Uskane	350 3 21	Tipperary, N.R.	Lower Ormond	Uskane	Borrisokane	II.	288
6, 11	Uskerty	1,222 3 2	Kilkenny	Fassadinin	Dysart	Castlecomer	I.	89
32	Usk Little	53 3 17	Kildare	Narragh & RebanEast	Usk	Naas	I.	67
6, 7	Usna	201 3 33	Roscommon	Boyle	Tumna	Boyle	IV.	198
44	Usnagh	317 3 0	Tyrone	Omagh East	Clogherny	Omagh	III.	310
32	Ussaun	48 2 9	Leitrim	Mohill	Mohill	Mohill	IV.	108
7	Ussey	377 1 14j	Galway	Ballymoe	Ballynakill	Glennamaddy	IV.	5
40	Uttony	51 3 1	Fermanagh	Clankelly	Clones	Clones	III.	197
10	Valleymount or Cross	187 0 30	Wicklow	Lower Talbotstown	Boystown	Baltinglass	I.	359
54	Veagh	400 2 39	Donegal	Raphoe	Raymoghy	Letterkenny	III.	142
26, 32	Veldonstown	339 0 19	Meath	Lower Duleek	Kentstown	Navan	I.	196
17	Velvetstown	709 0 2	Cork, E.R.	Orrery and Kilmore	Buttevant	Mallow	II.	107
52	Ventry	192 2 8	Kerry	Corkaguiny	Ventry	Dingle	II.	180
52	VENTRY T.	—	Kerry	Corkaguiny	{ Kildrum / Ventry }	Dingle	II.	{ 177 / 190 }
12	Verdanthill	39 3 23	Tipperary, N.R.	Ikerrin	Corbally	Roscrea	II.	275

(a) Including   4A. 1R. 3P. water.   (e) Including 269A. 2R. 0P. water.   (h) Including 7A. 3R. 24P. water.
(b) Including 138A. 1R. 24P. water.   (f) Including 15A. 0R. 16P. water.   (i) Including 67A. 3R. 9P. water.
(c) Including 58A. 2R. 20P. water.   (g) Including   8A. 2R. 24P. water.   (j) Including 3A. 0R. 21P. water.
(d) Including 20A. 0R. 5P. water.

No. of Sheet of the Ordnance Survey Maps.	Townlands and Towns.	Area in Statute Acres.	County.	Barony.	Parish.	Poor Law Union in 1857.	Townland Census of 1851, Part I.	
		A. R. P.					Vol.	Page
15, 18	Verdonstown .	181 2 26	Louth . .	Ardee . . .	Drumcar . .	Ardee . .	I.	172
4, 9	Vermount .	312 3 26	Carlow . .	Rathvilly . .	Clonmore . .	Shillelagh .	I.	10
45	Vernegly .	239 0 37	Wexford . .	Bargy . .	Bannow . .	Wexford .	I.	304
29	Verosland .	16 0 31	Wexford .	Bantry . .	St. Mary's .	New Ross .	I.	302
50	Vesingstown .	415 3 9	Meath . .	Dunboyne . .	Dunboyne . .	Dunshaughlin .	I.	199
23, 29	Vesnoy . .	189 1 24	Roscommon .	Roscommon . .	Bumlin . .	Strokestown .	IV.	208
30	Vessingtown .	230 2 28	Meath . .	Upper Navan .	Tullaghanoge .	Trim . .	I.	217
74	Vicarsacre and Freagh	22 2 29	Cork, E.R. .	Cork . .	St. Finbars .	Cork . .	II.	66
43	Vicarschoral Land .	70 0 10	Galway . .	Clare . .	Tuam . .	Tuam . .	IV.	23
9	Vicarsfield Glebe .	26 1 7	Longford . .	Granard . .	Clonbroney . .	Granard . .	I.	155
62	Vicarstown . .	546 3 19	Cork, E.R. .	East Muskerry .	Matehy . .	Cork . .	II.	105
52	Vicarstown .	58 2 0	Kerry . .	Corkaguiny .	Dunquin . .	Dingle . .	II.	176
15	Vicarstown .	141 3 33	King's Co. .	Garrycastle .	Wheery or Killagally	Parsonstown .	I.	139
23	Vicarstown .	99 1 28	Longford . .	Shrule . .	Agharra . .	Ballymahon .	I.	166
14	Vicarstown (Cosby)	781 1 15a	Queen's Co. .	Stradbally . .	Moyanna . .	Athy . .	I.	247
14	Vicarstown (Dodd)	1,278 0 16b	Queen's Co. .	Stradbally . .	Moyanna . .	Athy . .	I.	247
22	Vicarstown North .	136 2 8	Waterford .	Decies without Drum	Modelligo . .	Dungarvan .	II.	359
22	Vicarstown South .	164 3 16	Waterford .	Decies without Drum	Modelligo . .	Dungarvan .	II.	359
36	Viewmount or Court-land .	24 0 17	King's Co. .	Ballybritt . .	Seirkieran .	Parsonstown .	I.	126
26	Vilanstown .	600 0 31	Westmeath .	Fartullagh .	Lynn . .	Mullingar .	I.	269
29	Villierstown .	190 1 33	Waterford .	Decies within Drum	Aglish . .	Dungarvan .	II.	349
29	VILLIERSTOWN T. .	—	Waterford .	Decies within Drum	Aglish . .	Dungarvan .	II.	349
46	Vinepark . .	7 0 17	Cork, E.R. .	Kinnatalloon .	Mogeely . .	Fermoy . .	II.	99
27	Vinesgrove . .	173 3 26	Kilkenny .	Kells . .	Dunnamaggan .	Callan . .	I.	108
36, 44	Violethill .	71 1 39	Clare .	Tulla Lower .	Killuran . .	Tulla . .	II.	36
44	Violethill .	216 3 33	Clare . .	Tulla Lower .	Kilseily . .	Limerick .	II.	37
18	Violethill Great .	50 3 5	Dublin .	Coolock . .	Glasnevin . .	Dublin North .	I.	27
18	Violethill Little .	33 3 13	Dublin .	Coolock . .	Glasnevin . .	Dublin North .	I.	27
23, 27	Viperkells .	168 2 18	Kilkenny .	Shillelogher .	Kells . .	Callan . .	I.	115
39	Virginia . .	244 2 24	Cavan . .	Castlerahan .	Lurgan . .	Oldcastle .	III.	70
39	VIRGINIA T. . .	—	Cavan . .	Castlerahan .	Lurgan . .	Oldcastle . .	III.	70
24	Volvenstown .	88 3 26	Meath . .	Upper Kells .	Balrathboyne .	Kells . .	I.	204
21, 22	Vow . .	337 0 17	Antrim . .	Kilconway .	Finvoy . .	Ballymoney .	III.	26
14	Wad . . .	93 0 30	Dublin . .	Coolock . . .	Glasnevin . .	Dublin North .	I.	27
48	Waddingsland .	67 1 25	Wexford . .	Forth . .	Kilrane . .	Wexford . .	I.	311
42	Waddingstown .	319 3 16	Kilkenny . .	Iverk . .	Rathkieran .	Waterford .	I.	107
41	Waddingtown .	230 3 28	Wexford . .	Bargy . .	Ballyconnick .	Wexford . .	I.	304
20	Wadestown .	80 0 29	Westmeath .	Farbill . .	Killucan . .	Mullingar .	I.	267
23	Walderstown .	402 0 20	Westmeath .	Kilkenny West .	Drumraney . .	Ballymahon .	I.	273
19	Walkinslough .	71 3 33	Kilkenny . .	Kilkenny, Municipal Borough of .	St. Canice .	Kilkenny . .	I.	117
7	Walk Mill . .	73 2 2	Antrim . .	Lower Dunluce .	Dunluce . .	Coleraine . .	III.	18
45	Walkmill . .	103 2 17	Antrim . .	Upper Antrim .	Kilbride . .	Antrim . .	III.	6
24	WALLACE'S Row T. .	—	Louth . .	Drogheda . .	St. Peter's .	Drogheda .	I.	175
3	Waller's Island .	1 2 22	Limerick . .	Kenry . . .	Kilcornan . .	Rathkeale .	II.	249
61	Waller's-lot .	153 0 0	Tipperary, S.R. .	Middlethird .	St. John Baptist .	Cashel . .	II.	330
75	Wallingstown .	377 1 31	Cork, E.R. .	Barrymore . .	Little Island .	Cork . .	II.	56
98	Wallscourt .	321 2 24	Galway . .	Leitrim . .	Kilreekill . .	Loughrea .	IV.	55
23, 24	Wallslough .	205 2 25	Kilkenny . .	Shillelogher .	Grangekilree .	Kilkenny .	I.	114
23	Wallslough .	262 3 35	Kilkenny .	Shillelogher . ' .	Outrath . .	Kilkenny .	I.	115
18, 26	Wallstown .	565 0 9	Cork, E.R. .	Fermoy . .	Wallstown . .	Mallow . .	II.	83
13, 18	Wallstown .	393 3 10	Kilkenny .	Crannagh . .	Ballinamara .	Kilkenny .	I.	84
14	Walnutgrove .	38 2 36	Dublin . .	Coolock . .	Glasnevin . .	Dublin North .	I.	27
43, 48	Walsheslough .	170 3 31	Wexford . .	Forth . .	Rosslare . .	Wexford . .	I.	313
72, 73	Walshestown .	303 3 38c	Cork, E.R. .	East Muskerry .	Athnowen . .	Cork . .	II.	101
7, 16	Walshestown .	438 0 29	Cork, E.R. .	Orrery and Kilmore	Churchtown .	Mallow . .	II.	107
31	Walshestown .	421 2 0	Down . .	Lecale Lower .	Saul . .	Downpatrick .	III.	179
4	Walshestown .	427 3 33	Dublin . .	Balrothery East .	Lusk . .	Balrothery .	I.	21
23	Walshestown .	667 2 28d	Kildare . .	Connell . .	Greatconnell .	Naas . .	I.	55
24	Walshestown .	106 3 2	Kildare . .	Naas North .	Rathmore . .	Naas . .	I.	63
24	Walshestown .	160 3 31	Kildare . .	Naas South .	Tipperkevin .	Naas . .	I.	65
36	Walshestown .	230 3 12	Limerick . .	Glenquin . .	Mahoonagh . .	Newcastle .	II.	246
18, 19, 22	Walshestown .	217 0 0	Louth . .	Ferrard . .	Rathdrumin .	Drogheda .	I.	182
47, 52, 53	Walshestown .	75 3 24	Wexford . .	Forth . .	Ishartmon . .	Wexford . .	I.	310
47	Walshestown .	146 1 22	Wexford . .	Forth . . .	Rathmacnee .	Wexford . .	I.	313
18	Walshestown North	327 2 13e	Westmeath .	Moyashel and Magh-eradernon .	Mullingar . .	Mullingar .	I.	275
18, 19	Walshestown South	898 1 18	Westmeath .	Moyashel and Magh-eradernon .	Mullingar . .	Mullingar .	I.	275
41, 46	Walshgraigue . .	87 2 25	Wexford . .	Bargy . .	Ambrosetown .	Wexford . .	I.	304
19, 27	Walshisland . .	700 1 30	King's Co. .	Upper Philipstown .	Geashill . .	Edenderry .	I.	144

(a) Including 3A. 2R. 22P. River Barrow.   (c) Including 6A. 3R. 16P. water.   (e) Including 20A. 0R. 21P. detached portion.
(b) Including 11A. 1R. 36P. River Barrow.   (d) Including 17A. 2R. 19P. water.

No. of Sheet of the Ordnance Survey Maps.	Townlands and Towns.	Area in Statute Acres.	County	Barony.	Parish.	Poor Law Union in 1857.	Townland Census of 1851. Part I. Vol.	Page
		A. R. P.						
5	Walshpark	809 0 19	Tipperary, N.R.	Lower Ormond	Dorrha	Parsonstown	II.	283
90	Walshpool	311 3 5a	Mayo	Carra	Drum	Castlebar	IV.	128
70, 71	Walshsbog	474 3 21	Tipperary, S.R.	Middlethird	Kiltinan	Clonmel	II.	328
69	Walsh's Island	2 2 6	Galway	Clare	Annaghdown	Galway	IV.	17
55	Walsh's Island	3 3 32	Galway	Clare	Killeany	Tuam	IV.	20
23, 25	Walshstown or Bally-nabranagh	465 0 6	Carlow	St. Mullins Lower	St. Mullins	New Ross	I.	13
99, 107	Walshtown	260 0 16	Galway	Longford	Killoran	Ballinasloe	IV.	59
54, 65	Walshtown Beg	918 1 18	Cork, E.R.	Barrymore	Templenacarriga	Middleton	II.	58
65	Walshtownmore	52 2 4	Cork, E.R.	Barrymore	Ballyspillane	Middleton	II.	51
54, 65	Walshtown MoreEast	290 1 34	Cork, E.R.	Barrymore	Templenacarriga	Middleton	II.	58
54, 65	WalshtownMoreWest	567 1 31	Cork, E.R.	Barrymore	Templenacarriga	Middleton	II.	58
54, 65	WALSHTOWN T.	—	Cork, E.R.	Barrymore	Templenacarriga	Middleton	II.	58
23	Waltersland	37 2 7	Dublin	Rathdown	Stillorgan	Rathdown	I.	38
76, 88	Walterstown	330 3 2	Cork, E.R.	Barrymore	Templerobin	Cork	II.	58
24	Walterstown	324 2 29	Kildare	Naas South	Carnalway	Naas	I.	64
27	Walterstown	1,039 1 7	Kildare	Offaly West	Walterstown	Athy	I.	74
11, 12	Walterstown	317 2 7	Louth	Louth	Dromiskin	Dundalk	I.	183
53	Walterstown	144 0 10	Meath	Dunboyne	Dunboyne	Dunshaughlin	I.	199
37	Walterstown	284 3 25	Meath	Lower Deece	Galtrim	Trim	I.	191
5, 11	Walterstown	417 1 31	Meath	Lower Kells	Moynalty	Kells	I.	204
32	Walterstown	356 0 1	Meath	Skreen	Monktown	Navan	I.	221
33	Walterstown	206 2 1	Westmeath	Fartullagh	Carrick	Mullingar	I.	267
10, 16	Walterstown	139 1 26	Wicklow	Lower Talbotstown	Hollywood	Baltinglass	I.	361
27	Walterstown Lower	265 0 11	Kildare	Offaly West	Walterstown	Athy	I.	74
27, 28	Walton's Grove or Mountjuliet	536 0 6b	Kilkenny	Knocktopher	Jerpointchurch	Thomastown	I.	111
9	Walworth	337 0 27	Londonderry	Keenaght	Tamlaght Finlagan	NewTᵉLimavady	III.	238
9	Walworth	259 2 31	Londonderry	Tirkeeran	Faughanvale	NewTᵉLimavady	III.	250
20, 21	Warbleshinny	218 2 31	Londonderry	Tirkeeran	Clondermot	Londonderry	III.	248
7, 11	Warblestown	31 0 27	Dublin	Nethercross	Killossery	Balrothery	I.	31
20, 21	Wardenstown	184 2 37	Westmeath	Farbill	Killucan	Mullingar	I.	267
1	Wardhouse	674 2 5	Leitrim	Rosclogher	Rossinver	Ballyshannon	IV.	112
10, 11	Ward Lower	285 3 29	Dublin	Castleknock	Ward	Dublin North	I.	25
9, 15	Wards of Tober	165 1 20	Wicklow	Lower Talbotstown	Tober	Baltinglass	I.	361
24, 30	Wardstown	631 0 36	Meath	Lune	Athboy	Trim	I.	207
11, 14	Ward Upper	212 1 0	Dublin	Castleknock	Ward	Dublin North	I.	25
20	WARINGSTOWN T.	—	Down	Lower Iveagh, Up. pt.	Donaghcloney	Lurgan	III.	169
20	Warren	22 3 18	Antrim	Lower Glenarm	Ardclinis	Larne	III.	21
20	Warren	57 1 30	Antrim	Lower Glenarm	Layd	Larne	III.	23
46	Warren	121 1 39	Roscommon	Athlone	St. Johns	Athlone	IV.	184
22	Warren and Bog	97 0 1	Wexford	Ballaghkeen	Donaghmore	Gorey	I.	293
6	Warren or Drum	581 0 3	Roscommon	Boyle	Boyle	Boyle	IV.	194
29, 30	Warren High	283 3 38	Westmeath	Clonlonan	Ballyloughloe	Athlone	I.	261
29	Warren Lower	72 3 31c	Westmeath	Clonlonan	Ballyloughloe	Athlone	I.	261
38, 43	Warren Lower	197 1 38	Wexford	Forth	Rosslare	Wexford	I.	313
43	Warren Middle	53 2 2	Wexford	Forth	Rosslare	Wexford	I.	313
29	Warrensfields	6 0 16	Westmeath	Brawny	St. Mary's	Athlone	I.	260
83	Warrensgrove	138 3 39	Cork, E.R.	East Muskerry	Moviddy	Bandon	II.	105
54	WARRENSPOINT T.	—	Down	Upper Iveagh, Up. pt.	Warrenspoint	Newry	III.	176
8	Warrenstown	50 2 36	Kilkenny	Galmoy	Erke	Urlingford	I.	92
8, 12	Warrenstown	701 3 19	Kilkenny	Galmoy	Fertagh	Urlingford	I.	92
50	Warrenstown	417 0 7	Meath	Dunboyne	Dunboyne	Dunshaughlin	I.	199
37, 38, 43	Warrenstown	701 0 10	Meath	Lower Deece	Knockmark	Dunshaughlin	I.	192
44	Warrenstown	127 0 37	Meath	Ratoath	Rathbeggan	Dunshaughlin	I.	219
43, 49, 50	Warrenstown	270 0 16	Meath	Upper Deece	Culmullin	Dunshaughlin	I.	193
20	WARREN T.	—	Antrim	Lower Glenarm	Layd	Larne	III.	23
43,44,51,52	Warrentown	443 3 31	Donegal	Kilmacrenan	Gartan	Letterkenny	III.	128
43	Warrentown Mountain North	380 1 15	Donegal	Kilmacrenan	Gartan	Dunfanaghy	III.	128
43, 51	Warrentown Mountain South	425 2 24	Donegal	Kilmacrenan	Gartan	Letterkenny	III.	128
19, 20	Warrington	487 2 32d	Kilkenny	Shillelogher	St. Patrick's	Kilkenny	I.	116
23	Washers Bog	26 3 24	Kilkenny	Shillelogher	Burnchurch	Callan	I.	113
11	Waste	154 0 38	Wexford	Scarawalsh	Toome	Gorey	I.	326
4	WATCH HOUSE T.	—	Wexford	Scarawalsh	Moyacomb	Shillelagh	I.	325
29	Watercastle	284 1 7	Queen's Co.	Clarmallagh	Abbeyleix	Abbeyleix	I.	235
69, 70	Waterdale	679 3 0	Galway	Clare	Claregalway	Galway	IV.	18
18	Waterdyke	160 2 37	Cork, E.R.	Fermoy	Templeroan	Mallow	II.	82
43, 44	Wateresk	661 0 35	Down	Lecale Upper	Kilmegan	Downpatrick	III.	181
20	Waterford or Bellisk	22 3 7	Antrim	Lower Glenarm	Layd	Ballycastle	III.	22
9, 22	WATERFORD CITY	—				Waterford	II.	377
22	Watergrange	368 3 18	Kildare	Offaly East	Grangeclare	Edenderry	I.	70
53	WATERGRASSHILL T.	—	Cork, E.R.	Barrymore	Ardnageehy / Kilquane	Fermoy / Cork	II.	51 / 56

(a) Including 58A. 3R. 36P. water.
(b) Including 13A. 3R. 8P. River Nore.
(c) Including 3A. 1R. 36P. water.
(d) Including 9A. 1R. 12P. River Nore.

No. of Sheet of the Ordnance Survey Maps.	Townlands and Towns.	Area in Statute Acres. A. R. P.	County.	Barony.	Parish.	Poor Law Union in 1857.	Townland Census of 1851, Part I. Vol.	Page
17	Waterhouse	224 3 11	Cork, E.R.	Orrery and Kilmore	Buttevant	Mallow	II.	107
8	Waterland	75 2 1	Kilkenny	Galmoy	Erke	Urlingford	I.	92
36, 37	Waterpark	463 1 22a	Cork, E.R.	Condons&Clangibbon	Lismore and Mocollop	Fermoy	II.	62
6	Waterpark	178 2 22	Limerick	Clanwilliam	Killeenagarriff	Limerick	II.	224
65, 76	Water-rock	349 0 12	Cork, E.R.	Barrymore	Carrigtohill	Middleton	II.	52
7	Waterside	565 1 9	Londonderry	Coleraine	Killowen	Coleraine	III.	232
32	Waterside Great	218 0 29	Meath	Skreen	Rathfeigh	Dunshaughlin	I.	221
32	Waterside Little	130 2 33	Meath	Skreen	Rathfeigh	Dunshaughlin	I.	221
112	Waters-land North	196 0 0	Cork, E.R.	Kinsale	Ringcurran	Kinsale	II.	100
112	Waters-land South	71 3 27	Cork, E.R.	Kinsale	Ringcurran	Kinsale	II.	100
4	Waterstown	196 1 23	Carlow	Rathvilly	Rathvilly	Baltinglass	I.	12
19	Waterstown	438 3 25b	Kildare	Clane	Bridechurch	Naas	I.	53
22	Waterstown	904 2 18c	Westmeath	Kilkenny West	Kilkenny West	Athlone	I.	274
98	Waterville	161 3 33	Kerry	Iveragh	Dromod	Cahersiveen	II.	195
20, 24	Watree	301 1 30	Kilkenny	Gowran	Gowran	Kilkenny	I.	95
17	*Watson's Island*	1 1 30	Down	Castlereagh Lower	Tullynakill	Newtownards	III.	164
7	Watts Town	116 0 38	Londonderry	North East Liberties of Coleraine	Coleraine	Coleraine	III.	246
11	Wattstown	284 0 8	Westmeath	Corkaree	Portloman	Mullingar	I.	263
50	Waynestown	263 2 29	Meath	Ratoath	Ballymaglassan	Dunshaughlin	I.	217
90, 100	Weatherfort	292 0 8d	Mayo	Carra	Rosslee	Ballinrobe	IV.	130
40, 41	Weatherstown	493 0 34	Kilkenny	Ida	Kilcoan	Waterford	I.	102
43	Weatherstown	70 2 24	Meath	Upper Deece	Kilmore	Dunshaughlin	I.	193
10	Webbsborough	271 1 5	Kilkenny	Fassadinin	Mothell	Castlecomer	I.	90
112	*Weir Island*	0 1 32	Galway	Kiltartan	Kinvarradoorus	Gort	IV.	50
68, 77	Welchtown	465 1 39e	Donegal	Raphoe	Kilteevoge	Stranorlar	III.	140
39	Wellfield	25 0 11	Limerick	Coshma	Dromin	Kilmallock	II.	243
20, 21	Wellington	36 0 6	Tipperary, N.R.	Lower Ormond	Knigh	Nenagh	II.	285
82, 94	Wellpark	19 3 16	Galway	Galway	St. Nicholas	Galway	IV.	38
125, 126	Wellpark	58 1 2	Galway	Leitrim	Ballynakill	Portumna	IV.	52
15, 16	Wells	702 2 7f	Carlow	Idrone West	Wells	Carlow	I.	10
21	Wells	360 3 38	Wexford	Ballaghkeen	Killincooly	Gorey	I.	295
21	Wells	37 0 25	Wexford	Ballaghkeen	Kilnamanagh	Gorey	I.	297
21	Wellshill	238 2 9	Wexford	Ballaghkeen	Killincooly	Gorey	I.	295
46	Weneytown	70 2 38	Wexford	Bargy	Duncormick	Wexford	I.	305
30	Westaston Demesne	206 1 23	Wicklow	Arklow	Dunganstown	Rathdrum	I.	344
30	Westaston Hill	147 1 0	Wicklow	Arklow	Dunganstown	Rathdrum	I.	344
22, 26	Westcourt Commons	118 3 32	Kilkenny	Callan	Callan	Callan	I.	84
26	Westcourt Demesne	140 2 20	Kilkenny	Callan	Callan	Callan	I.	84
22, 26	Westcourt North	466 1 21	Kilkenny	Callan	Callan	Callan	I.	84
26	Westcourt South	19 1 15	Kilkenny	Callan	Callan	Callan	I.	84
46,51,52,57	West Division	6,739 2 14	Antrim	Carrickfergus	Carrickfergus	Larne	III.	11
11	Westercave	0 3 5	Dublin	Nethercross	Finglas	Balrothery	I.	31
11	Westereave	170 3 3g	Dublin	Nethercross	Killeek	Balrothery	I.	31
18	West Farm or Slutsend	125 0 12h	Dublin	Coolock and Municipal Borough	Glasnevin	Dublin North	I.	27
89	Westland	263 3 23	Mayo	Carra	Ballyhean	Castlebar	IV.	126
13, 17	Westmanstown	437 0 8i	Dublin	Newcastle	Leixlip	Celbridge	I.	33
21	Westmanstown	101 1 31	Dublin	Newcastle	Rathcoole	Celbridge	I.	34
31	Westmoreland	145 1 12	Kilkenny	Knocktopher	Aghaviller	Thomastown	I.	111
61	Weston	270 0 12	Galway	Clonmacnowen	Ahascragh	Ballinasloe	IV.	24
46	Westonslot	46 3 39	Tipperary, S.R.	Kilnamanagh Lower	Clonoulty	Cashel	II.	323
4	Westown	525 3 1	Dublin	Balrothery West	Naul	Balrothery	I.	23
19	Westown	155 2 39	Kildare	Naas North	Johnstown	Naas	I.	62
7	Westpalstown	373 0 27	Dublin	Balrothery West	Westpalstown	Balrothery	I.	23
6	West Park	180 0 30	Antrim	Lower Dunluce	Dunluce	Coleraine	III.	18
76,77,87,88	Westport Demesne	1,070 3 3	Mayo	Burrishoole	Kilmeena	Westport	IV.	122
88	Westport Demesne	272 2 39j	Mayo	Murrisk	Oughaval	Westport	IV.	162
88	WESTPORT QUAY T.	—	Mayo	Murrisk	Oughaval	Westport	IV.	162
88	WESTPORT T.	—	Mayo	Murrisk	Oughaval	Westport	IV.	162
114	Westquarter	493 3 32k	Mayo	Murrisk	Inishbofin	Clifden	IV.	159
5, 9, 10	West Torr	587 1 36	Antrim	Cary	Culfeightrin	Ballycastle	III.	14
26	Westtown	343 1 27	Waterford	Middlethird	Drumcannon	Waterford	II.	366
19	Wetland	65 2 22	Kilkenny	Shillelogher	St. Patrick's	Kilkenny	I.	116
47	Wetmeadows	52 1 37	Wexford	Bargy	Kilmannan	Wexford	I.	306
32	Wevil	23 2 1	Kildare	Offaly West	Ballyshannon	Athy	I.	312
37	WEXFORD T.	—	Wexford	Forth	Maudlinstown St. Bridget's St. Doologue's St. Iberius St. John's St. Mary's St.Michael's of Feagh St. Patrick's St. Peter's St. Selskar's	Wexford	I.	315 314 315

(a) Including 9A. 3R. 8P. water.
(b) Including 9A. 3R. 34P. River Liffey.
(c) Including 114A. 2R. 0P. water.
(d) Including 15A. 3R. 24P. water.
(e) Including 6A. 3R. 13P. water.
(f) Including 4A. 1R. 32P. River Barrow.
(g) Including 0A. 3R. 29P. detached portion.
(h) { Within the Municipal Boundary, 0A. 2R. 15P. / Without the Municipal Boundary, 124A. 1R. 37P.
(i) Including 0A. 1R. 20P. River Liffey.
(j) Including 15A. 3R. 5P. water.
(k) Including 8A. 1R. 18P. water.

No. of Sheet of the Ordnance Survey Maps.	Townlands and Towns.	Area in Statute Acres. A. R. P.	County.	Barony.	Parish.	Poor Law Union in 1857.	Vol.	Page
38	Whappstown . .	634 3 7	Antrim . .	Lower Antrim .	Connor . . .	Antrim . .	III.	4
14, 15	Wheatfield Lower .	204 2 28	Kildare . .	South Salt . .	Castledillon .	Celbridge .	I.	76
15	Wheatfield Upper .	136 2 30	Kildare . .	South Salt . .	Castledillon .	Celbridge .	I.	76
26, 32	Wheathill . .	135 3 26	Fermanagh .	Clanawley . .	Killesher . .	Enniskillen .	III.	193
14, 15	Wheathill Glebe .	139 2 23	Fermanagh .	Magheraboy .	Inishmacsaint .	Enniskillen .	III.	213
14	Wheelagower . .	860 1 36	Wexford . .	Scarawalsh .	Templeshanbo .	Enniscorthy .	I.	326
17, 18	Wheelam . .	417 2 4	Kildare . .	Connell . .	Feighcullen .	Naas . .	I.	55
14, 15	Wheery . .	40 3 0	King's Co. .	Garrycastle .	Wheery or Killagally	Parsonstown .	I.	139
38, 39	Wherrew . .	74 1 27	Mayo . .	Tirawley . .	Kilbelfad . .	Ballina . .	IV.	168
44, 45	Whigamstown .	149 3 37	Down . .	Lecale Upper .	Bright . .	Downpatrick .	III.	180
30	Whigsborough .	985 0 20a	King's Co. .	Eglish . .	Eglish . .	Parsonstown .	I.	135
27, 33	Whilliter . .	190 1 9b	Fermanagh .	Tirkennedy .	Cleenish . .	Enniskillen .	III.	220
27	Whinnigan Glebe .	50 0 17	Fermanagh .	Tirkennedy .	Cleenish . .	Enniskillen .	III.	220
27	Whinnigan Glebe .	35 1 23	Fermanagh .	Tirkennedy .	Derrybrusk .	Enniskillen .	III.	220
22	Whinning . .	239 1 14	Westmeath .	Kilkenny West .	Bunown . .	Athlone . .	I.	272
44, 50	Whin Park . .	136 2 11	Antrim . .	Upper Antrim .	Antrim . .	Antrim . .	III.	5
25	Whistlemount .	72 1 36	Meath . .	Lower Navan .	Liscartan . .	Navan . .	I.	215
57	White Abbey . .	406 3 34	Antrim . .	Lower Belfast .	Carnmoney .	Belfast . .	III.	8
57	WHITE ABBEY T. .	—	Antrim . .	Lower Belfast .	Carnmoney .	Belfast . .	III.	8
67	Whitebarn . .	48 3 4	Cork, E.R. .	Imokilly . .	Youghal . .	Youghal . .	II.	91
19,20,27,28	Whitebog . .	633 1 25	Cork, E.R. .	Condons&Clangibbon	Kilworth . .	Fermoy . .	II.	62
20	Whitebog . .	283 2 5	Queen's Co. .	Ballyadams .	Ballyadams .	Athy . .	I.	231
31	Whitecastle . .	109 0 15	Donegal . .	Inishowen East .	Moville Upper .	Inishowen .	III.	119
52, 63	Whitechurch .	532 1 24	Cork, E.R. .	Cork . .	Whitechurch .	Cork . .	II.	66
12	Whitechurch .	673 2 8	Down . .	Ards Upper .	Ballywalter .	Newtownards .	III.	160
22	Whitechurch . .	60 1 6	Dublin . .	Rathdown . .	Whitechurch .	Dublin South .	I.	38
14	Whitechurch . .	72 1 23	Kildare . .	Naas North .	Whitechurch .	Naas . .	I.	63
38	Whitechurch . .	273 1 22	Kilkenny . .	Iverk . .	Whitechurch .	Carrick on Suir	I.	107
81	Whitechurch . .	296 1 24	Tipperary, S.R.	Iffa and Offa West .	Whitechurch .	Clogheen .	II.	322
30	Whitechurch . .	49 1 37	Waterford .	Decies without Drum	Whitechurch .	Dungarvan .	II.	362
34, 39	Whitechurch . .	747 1 21	Wexford . .	Shelburne . .	Whitechurch .	New Ross .	I.	329
11, 17	Whitecommons .	100 0 12	Meath . .	Upper Kells .	Kells . .	Kells . .	I.	206
11	Whitecross . .	128 1 37	Louth . .	Louth . .	Louth . .	Dundalk . .	I.	185
28	Whitecross . .	54 3 20	Meath . .	Upper Duleek .	Ballygarth .	Drogheda .	I.	197
28	Whitecross Glebe .	8 1 7	Meath . .	Upper Duleek .	Moorechurch .	Drogheda .	I.	198
57, 65	Whitefield . .	295 1 14c	Kerry . .	Dunkerron North .	Knockane . .	Killarney .	II.	182
11	Whitefield . .	178 3 3	Queen's Co. .	Upperwoods .	Offerlane . .	Mountmellick .	I.	252
29, 35	Whitefield . .	616 2 14	Tipperary, N.R.	Eliogarty . .	Loughmoe West .	Thurles . .	II.	271
25	Whitefield . .	170 2 30	Waterford .	Middlethird .	Islandikane .	Waterford .	II.	367
38	Whitefield . .	130 3 1	Wicklow . .	Ballinacor South .	Kilcommon .	Shillelagh .	I.	349
46, 47	Whitefort . .	142 1 11	Tipperary, N.R.	Eliogarty . .	Holycross . .	Thurles . .	II.	270
32	Whitefort . .	85 1 31	Wexford . .	Shelmaliere East .	Artramon . .	Wexford . .	I.	330
32	Whitefort . .	34 2 28	Wexford . .	Shelmaliere East .	Ballynaslaney .	Enniscorthy .	I.	330
32	Whitefort . .	32 1 16	Wexford . .	Shelmaliere East .	Kilpatrick .	Wexford . .	I.	331
134, 135	Whitegate . .	264 2 35d	Galway . .	Leitrim . .	Clonrush . .	Scarriff . .	IV.	53
117	Whitegates . .	28 3 6	Galway . .	Longford . .	Killimorbologue .	Portumna .	IV.	59
88	WHITEGATE T. .	—	Cork, E.R. .	Imokilly . .	{ Aghada . . Corkbeg . . }	Middleton .	II.	{ 85 86 }
149	Whitehall . .	142 2 6	Cork, W.R. .	West Carbery (E.D.)	Aghadown .	Skibbereen .	II.	137
22	Whitehall . .	189 0 11	Dublin . .	Rathdown . .	Rathfarnham .	Dublin South .	I.	37
22	Whitehall . .	128 0 9	Dublin . .	Uppercross .	Crumlin . .	Dublin South .	I.	40
21	Whitehall . .	122 2 29	Dublin . .	Uppercross .	Tallaght . .	Dublin South .	I.	42
14	Whitehall . .	99 2 12	Limerick . .	Clanwilliam .	Carrigparson .	Limerick . .	II.	223
36	Whitehall . .	42 3 33	Meath . .	Upper Navan .	Trim . .	Trim . .	I.	217
8, 11	Whitehall . .	98 1 17	Tipperary, N.R.	Lower Ormond .	Ballingarry .	Borrisokane .	II.	282
8	White Hall or Gort-amaddy .	82 3 8	Antrim . .	Cary . .	Ramoan . .	Ballycastle .	III.	14
47	White Head . .	278 2 31	Antrim . .	Lower Belfast .	Templecorran .	Larne . .	III.	9
52	Whitehill . .	258 3 17	Donegal . .	Kilmacrenan .	Conwal . .	Letterkenny .	III.	127
44	Whitehill . .	422 0 10e	Donegal . .	Kilmacrenan .	Gartan . .	Letterkenny .	III.	128
78	Whitehill . .	68 1 0	Donegal . .	Raphoe . .	Donaghmore .	Stranorlar .	III.	138
63	Whitehill . .	267 1 15	Donegal . .	Raphoe . .	Taughboyne .	Strabane .	III.	144
100	Whitehill . .	58 2 24	Donegal . .	Tirhugh . .	Donegal . .	Donegal . .	III.	145
21	Whitehill . .	104 3 26	Fermanagh .	Magheraboy .	Devenish . .	Enniskillen .	III.	211
14	Whitehill . .	181 3 1	Londonderry .	Tirkeeran .	Faughanvale .	NewTnLimavady	III.	250
40	Whitehill . .	159 2 2	Sligo . .	Tirerrill . .	Aghanagh .	Boyle . .	IV.	237
34	Whitehill . .	313 2 13	Sligo . .	Tirerrill . .	Tawnagh . .	Sligo . .	IV.	241
14, 15	Whitehill or Knock-anbaun .	563 1 32	Longford . .	Granard . .	Clonbroney .	Granard . .	I.	155
10, 11	Whitehill North .	96 0 9	Fermanagh .	Lurg . .	Derryvullan .	Lowtherstown .	III.	205
38	Whitehills . .	82 1 16f	Down . .	Lecale Lower .	Saul . .	Downpatrick .	III.	179
20	Whitehills . .	154 0 33	Wicklow . .	Upper Talbotstown .	Ballynure .	Baltinglass .	I.	362
16	Whitehill South .	85 2 25	Fermanagh .	Lurg . .	Derryvullan .	Lowtherstown .	III.	205

(a) Including 61A. 0R. 3P. water.
(b) Including 14A. 2R. 29P. water.
(c) Including 5A. 2R. 38P. water.
(d) Including 22A. 0R. 4P. water.
(e) Including 4A. 2R. 37P. water.
(f) Including 5A. 1R. 29P. water.

No. of Sheet of the Ordnance Survey Maps.	Townlands and Towns.	Area in Statute Acres.	County.	Barony.	Parish.	Poor Law Union in 1857.	Townland Census of 1851, Part I.	
		A. R. P.					Vol.	Page
15	Whitehouse	62 2 16	Antrim	Cary	Culfeightrin	Ballycastle	III.	14
57	White House	366 0 14	Antrim	Lower Belfast	Carnmoney	Belfast	III.	8
55	Whitehouse	112 2 36	Donegal	Raphoe	Killea	Londonderry	III.	139
28, 32	Whitehouse	223 1 25	Kildare	Offaly West	Fontstown	Athy	I.	72
22	Whitehouse	251 0 32	Kilkenny	Shillelogher	Killaloe	Callan	I.	115
16, 24	Whitehouse	271 0 12	Tyrone	Strabane Lower	Ardstraw	Castlederg	III.	319
43	Whitehouse	37 0 27	Wexford	Forth	Rosslare	Wexford	I.	313
13, 20	White House or Ballymagrorty	1,072 0 1	Londonderry	North West Liberties of Londonderry	Templemore	Londonderry	III.	247
5	Whitehousequarter	69 1 8	Waterford	Glenahiry	Kilronan	Clonmel	II.	366
57	WHITE HOUSE T.	—	Antrim	Lower Belfast. Upper Belfast.	Carnmoney. Shankill	Belfast	III.	8 10
10	White Island	60 1 35	Fermanagh	Lurg	Magheraculmoney	Lowtherstown	III.	208
15	White Island	29 2 18	Fermanagh	Tirkennedy	Trory	Enniskillen	III.	224
27	White Island	33 3 29	Galway	Ross	Ross	Oughterard	IV.	74
10	White Island	20 1 15	Limerick	Connello Lower	Tomdeely	Rathkeale	II.	230
6	White Island	3 0 17	Longford	Granard	Columbkille	Granard	I.	156
3	White Island	12 2 24	Longford	Granard	Killoe	Granard	I.	157
20	White Island	13 0 15	Monaghan	Cremorne	Muckno	Castleblayney	III.	262
7	White Island	59 2 39	Monaghan	Trough	Donagh	Monaghan	III.	283
76	Whiteland	220 0 33	Tipperary, S.R.	Middlethird	Outeragh	Cashel	II.	329
29	Whiteleas	129 3 25	Kildare	Naas South	Ballybought	Naas	I.	64
33, 34	Whiteleas	153 0 9	Meath	Upper Duleek	Stamullin	Drogheda	I.	199
4	Whitemill	110 2 39	Louth	Lower Dundalk	Ballymascanlan	Dundalk	I.	176
37	Whitemill North	29 0 31	Wexford	Forth	St. Peter's	Wexford	I.	314
37	Whitemill South	42 1 12	Wexford	Forth	St. Peter's	Wexford	I.	314
63, 64	White Mountain	484 2 18	Antrim	Upper Massereene	Derryaghy	Lisburn	III.	30
3, 4	White Park	170 1 38	Antrim	Cary	Ballintoy	Ballycastle	III.	12
73	Whitepark	322 3 10	Galway	Kilconnell	Ballymacward	Ballinasloe	IV.	39
100	Whitepark	96 2 26	Mayo	Carra	Touaghty	Ballinrobe	IV.	130
12	Whitepark	164 1 25	Tipperary, N.R.	Ikerrin	Roscrea	Roscrea	II.	276
3	Whitepark	131 1 9	Wexford	Gorey	Kilgorman	Gorey	I.	318
87	WHITE POINT T.	—	Cork, E.R.	Barrymore	Clonmel	Cork	II.	53
12	Whiterath	390 0 25	Louth	Louth	Dromiskin	Dundalk	I.	183
17,18,20,21	Whiteriver	326 0 26	Louth	Ardee	Mosstown	Ardee	I.	174
76	Whiterock	202 0 5	Cork, E.R.	Imokilly	Middleton	Middleton	II.	89
25	Whiterock	29 3 19	Leitrim	Carrigallen	Drumreilly	Bawnboy	IV.	91
14	Whiterock	226 2 6	Longford	Ardagh	Templemichael	Longford	I.	154
38	Whiterock	419 3 16	Wicklow	Ballinacor South	Kilcommon	Shillelagh	I.	349
37, 42	Whiterock North	27 1 0	Wexford	Forth	Maudlintown	Wexford	I.	312
9	Whiterocks	109 3 21	Fermanagh	Magheraboy	Inishmacsaint	Ballyshannon	III.	213
37, 42	Whiterock South	171 0 28	Wexford	Forth	Maudlintown	Wexford	I.	312
31	Whitescastle Lower	127 0 9	Kilkenny	Knocktopher	Knocktopher	Thomastown	I.	112
31	Whitescastle Upper	27 0 21	Kilkenny	Knocktopher	Knocktopher	Thomastown	I.	112
1, 5	Whitesfort	223 0 21a	Waterford	Glenahiry	Kilronan	Clonmel	II.	366
26	Whitesland	106 0 26	Kilkenny	Callan	Callan	Callan	I.	84
50, 51	Whitesland	40 1 10	Meath	Dunboyne	Dunboyne	Dunshaughlin	I.	200
22	Whitesland East	111 0 30	Kildare	Offaly East	Kildare	Naas	I.	70
22	Whitesland West	143 3 16	Kildare	Offaly East	Kildare	Naas	I.	70
5, 6	Whitespots	1,016 2 37	Down	Ards Lower	Newtownards	Newtownards	III.	159
4	Whitestown	241 1 12b	Dublin	Balrothery East	Balscaddan	Balrothery	I.	20
8	Whitestown	264 0 27	Dublin	Balrothery East	Lusk	Balrothery	I.	21
7	Whitestown	228 2 37	Dublin	Balrothery West	Palmerstown	Balrothery	I.	23
21	Whitestown	240 3 35	Dublin	Uppercross	Tallaght	Dublin South	I.	42
9	Whitestown	358 1 12	Louth	Lower Dundalk	Carlingford	Dundalk	I.	177
15, 16	Whitestown	330 1 21	Waterford	Decies without Drum	Rossmire	Kilmacthomas	II.	360
42	Whitestown	108 0 39	Wexford	Forth	Rathaspick	Wexford	I.	313
7, 8	Whitestown East	510 0 38	Waterford	Upperthird	Mothel	Carrick on Suir	II.	371
21	Whitestown Lower	426 2 9	Wicklow	Upper Talbotstown	Donaghmore	Baltinglass	I.	364
42, 43	Whitestown Lower or Hermitage	37 3 7	Wexford	Forth	Drinagh	Wexford	I.	309
9	WHITES TOWN T.	—	Louth	Lower Dundalk	Carlingford	Dundalk	I.	177
42, 43	Whitestown Upper	34 1 31	Wexford	Forth	Drinagh	Wexford	I.	309
21	Whitestown Upper	308 3 14	Wicklow	Upper Talbotstown	Donaghmore	Baltinglass	I.	364
7	Whitestown West	676 3 31	Waterford	Upperthird	Mothel	Carrick on Suir	II.	371
3	Whiteswall	977 1 31	Kilkenny	Galmoy	Erke	Urlingford	I.	92
46	Whitetown	124 3 35	Tyrone	Dungannon Middle	Tullyniskan	Dungannon	III.	305
26, 33	Whitewell	403 3 18	Westmeath	Fartullagh	Kilbride	Mullingar	I.	268
37	Whitewell	12 0 14	Wexford	Forth	St. Michael's of Feagh	Wexford	I.	315
11, 16	Whitewell	158 1 15	Wexford	Scarawalsh	Toome	Gorey	I.	326
5	Whitewood	500 1 8c	Meath	Morgallion	Nobber	Kells	I.	210
17	Whitfield North	339 1 29	Waterford	Middlethird	Lisnakill	Waterford	II.	368

(a) Including 4A. 2R. 24P. water.   (b) Including 20A. 2R. 1P. detached portion.   (c) Including 35A. 0R. 0P. water.

No. of Sheet of the Ordnance Survey Maps.	Townlands and Towns.	Area in Statute Acres.			County.	Barony.	Parish.	Poor Law Union in 1857.	Townland Census of 1851, Part I.	
		A.	R.	P.					Vol.	Page
17	Whitfield South	109	2	22	Waterford	Middlethird	Lisnakill	Waterford	II.	368
10	Whitstone	185	1	2	Tipperary, N.R.	Lower Ormond	Ardcrony	Borrisokane	II.	282
46	Whittyshill	105	0	5	Wexford	Bargy	Kilcavan	Wexford	I.	305
25	Wicklow	22	0	23a	Wicklow	Newcastle	Rathnew	Rathdrum	I.	354
25	WICKLOW T.	—			Wicklow	{ Arklow { Arklow { Newcastle	Drumkay) Kilpoole . } Rathnew .)	Rathdrum	I.	{343 {345 {354
11	Wildfield	290	1	21	Kilkenny	Fassadinin	Muckalee	Castlecomer	I.	91
11, 15	Wildfield	200	3	7	Kilkenny	Gowran	Kilmadum	Castlecomer	I.	97
67	Wilford	13	1	12	Mayo	Burrishoole	Burrishoole	Newport	IV.	120
18, 22	Wilkinstown	148	0	0	Dublin	Uppercross	Crumlin	Dublin South	I.	40
12, 18	Wilkinstown	900	2	33	Meath	Morgallion	Kilberry	Navan	I.	209
44	Wilkinstown	175	2	26b	Meath	Ratoath	Rathbeggan	Dunshaughlin	I.	219
36	Wilkinstown	706	1	0	Wexford	Bantry	Whitechurchglynn	Wexford	I.	303
18	WILKINSTOWN T.	—			Meath	Morgallion	Kilberry	Navan	I.	209
22	Willbrook	58	3	24	Dublin	Rathdown	Rathfarnham	Dublin South	I.	37
22	WILLBROOK T.	—			Dublin	Rathdown	Rathfarnham	Dublin South	I.	37
4	Williamstown	1,112	0	26	Carlow	Rathvilly	Rathvilly	Baltinglass	I.	12
67	Williamstown	21	2	4	Cork, E.R.	Imokilly	Youghal	Youghal	II.	91
23	Williamstown	114	2	29	Dublin	Rathdown	Booterstown	Rathdown	I.	35
3, 8	Williamstown	376	2	28	Kildare	Carbury	Nurney	Edenderry	I.	53
22	Williamstown	25	2	37	Limerick	Clanwilliam	Caheravally	Limerick	II.	221
22	Williamstown	99	2	28	Limerick	Clanwilliam	Fedamore	Limerick	II.	223
15	Williamstown	534	3	34	Louth	Ardee	Kilsaran	Ardee	I.	173
15	Williamstown	194	1	2	Meath	Fore	Diamor	Oldcastle	I.	200
12	Williamstown	106	3	0	Meath	Morgallion	Drakestown	Navan	I.	209
11, 17	Williamstown	277	0	6	Meath	Upper Kells	Dulane	Kells	I.	205
49	Williamstown	709	3	28	Tipperary, S.R.	Slievardagh	Ballingarry	Callan	II.	332
24	Williamstown	312	2	0	Waterford	Decies without Drum	Stradbally	Kilmacthomas	II.	361
17, 18	Williamstown	549	2	12	Waterford	Gaultiere	Ballynakill	Waterford	II.	362
30	Williamstown	321	0	9	Westmeath	Clonlonan	Ballyloughloe	Athlone	I.	261
1	Williamstown	490	0	25	Westmeath	Fore	Foyran	Granard	I.	270
3, 7	Williamstown	224	1	9	Westmeath	Fore	Mayne	Granard	I.	271
10, 17	Williamstown	762	0	10	Westmeath	Rathconrath	Piercetown	Ballymahon	I.	284
31	Williamstown or Bawn	265	2	13	Meath	Lower Navan	Ardsallagh	Navan	I.	214
13	Williamstown (Briscoe)	244	3	24	Westmeath	Delvin	Killulagh	Castletowndelvin	I.	266
17	Williamstown New	291	1	20	Westmeath	Rathconrath	Piercetown	Ballymahon	I.	284
13	Williamstown (Rochford)	163	3	5	Westmeath	Delvin	Killulagh	Castletowndelvin	I.	266
23	WILLIAMSTOWN T.	—			Dublin	{ Dublin { Rathdown }	Booterstown	Rathdown	I.	{30 {35
12	Willisson	79	1	28	Tipperary, N.R.	Ikerrin	Roscrea	Roscrea	II.	276
15, 18	Willistown	312	3	26	Louth	Ardee	Drumcar	Ardee	I.	172
33	Willmount	189	3	3	Tyrone	Omagh West	Longfield West	Castlederg	III.	316
9, 15	Willowbrook	100	2	27	Sligo	Carbury	Calry	Sligo	IV.	220
99	Willowhill	298	2	27	Cork, E.R.	Kinalea	Kilpatrick	Kinsale	II.	95
14	Willsborough	46	3	3	Dublin	Coolock	Coolock	Dublin North	I.	27
25	Willsborough	217	3	32	Roscommon	Castlereagh	Kiltullagh	Castlereagh	IV.	202
10	Willsborough	81	2	27	Tipperary, N.R.	Lower Ormond	Ardcrony	Borrisokane	II.	282
10	Willsbrook	178	2	5	Longford	Granard	Granard	Granard	I.	157
26	Willsbrook	465	3	33	Roscommon	Castlereagh	Kilkeevin	Castlereagh	IV.	201
35	Willsgrove	81	2	1	Kildare	Narragh & Reban West	Kilberry	Athy	I.	68
27	Willsgrove	711	3	1	Roscommon	Castlereagh	Ballintober	Castlereagh	IV.	198
8, 9	Willville	540	2	1	Louth	Lower Dundalk	Carlingford	Dundalk	I.	177
68	*Willyrogue Island*	0	3	38	Galway	Moycullen	Killannin	Oughterard	IV.	70
10, 11	Wilmount	51	1	14	Meath	Upper Kells	Dulane	Kells	I.	205
69	Wilson's Fort or Killynure	356	3	33	Donegal	Raphoe	Convoy	Stranorlar	III.	136
7	Wilton	164	0	38	King's Co.	Kilcoursey	Kilmanaghan	Tullamore	I.	141
15	Wilton	93	0	38	Tipperary, N.R.	Upper Ormond	Ballymackey	Nenagh	II.	290
25	Wilton	596	2	31	Wexford	Bantry	Clonmore	Enniscorthy	I.	300
7	Wimbletown	367	1	1	Dublin	Balrothery East	Lusk	Balrothery	I.	21
32, 46	Windfield	404	0	24	Galway	Killian	Killian	Mountbellew	IV.	45
58, 59	Windfield Demesne	691	2	34	Galway	Tiaquin	Moylough	Mountbellew	IV.	80
59	Windfield Lower	252	1	16	Galway	Tiaquin	Moylough	Mountbellew	IV.	80
59	Windfield Upper	177	0	31	Galway	Tiaquin	Moylough	Mountbellew	IV.	80
35, 36	Windgap	300	3	33	Waterford	Decies without Drum	Dungarvan	Dungarvan	II.	356
3	Windgap or Ardmore	76	0	36	Waterford	Upperthird	Dysert	Carrick on Suir	II.	369
30	WINDGAP T.	—			Kilkenny	Kells	Killamery	Callan	I.	109
8	Windgate	122	1	7	Wicklow	Rathdown	Delgany	Rathdown	I.	355
10	Windgates	331	0	13	Kildare	North Salt	Taghadoe	Celbridge	I.	76
5, 8	Windmill	282	2	12	Kildare	Carbury	Kilmore	Edenderry	I.	52
18	Windmill	68	1	30	Louth	Ferrard	Dunleer	Ardee	I.	181
18	Windmill	167	1	6	Louth	Ferrard	Dysart	Drogheda	I.	181

(*a*) Including 0A. 2R. 13P. detached portion.   (*b*) Including 6A. 0R. 20P. detached portion.

No. of Sheet of the Ordnance Survey Maps.	Townlands and Towns.	Area in Statute Acres.			County.	Barony.	Parish.	Poor Law Union in 1857.	Townland Census of 1851, Part I.	
		A.	R.	P.					Vol.	Page
60, 61	Windmill	299	2	31	Tipperary, S.R.	Middlethird	St. Patricksrock	Cashel	II.	331
26, 33	Windmill or Black-islands	152	0	29	Westmeath	Fartullagh	Enniscoffey	Mullingar	I.	268
20, 21	Windmillhill	155	0	5	Dublin	Newcastle	Newcastle	Celbridge	I.	34
22	Windmill Hill	91	2	28a	Fermanagh	Magheraboy	Rossory	Enniskillen	III.	214
11	Windmill Lands	159	0	13	Dublin	Nethercross	Swords	Balrothery	I.	32
16	Windmillpark or Chanterland	103	2	6	Roscommon	Roscommon	Elphin	Strokestown	IV.	209
85	Windsor	692	2	12	Cork, E.R.	East Muskerry	Kilnaglory	Cork	II.	104
70, 79	Windsor or Breandrum	215	1	3	Mayo	Carra	Breaghwy	Castlebar	IV.	127
16	Windsor or Cappagh-nahoran	269	3	4	Queen's Co.	Upperwoods	Offerlane	Abbeyleix	I.	252
37, 43	Windtown	211	3	30	Meath	Lower Deece	Galtrim	Trim	I.	191
25	Windtown	258	0	21	Meath	Lower Navan	Donaghmore	Navan	I.	214
7, 8	Windtown	497	0	7	Westmeath	Fore	St. Feighins	Castletowndelvin	I.	272
26, 27	Windtown	470	2	17	Westmeath	Moyashel and Magheradernon	Mullingar	Mullingar	I.	275
5, 6	Windtown	158	2	33	Westmeath	Moygoish	Rathaspick	Granard	I.	280
5, 6	Windtown North	114	1	9	Westmeath	Moygoish	Russagh	Granard	I.	280
6	Windtown South	190	0	30	Westmeath	Moygoish	Russagh	Granard	I.	280
33	Windygap	123	2	22	Tipperary, N.R.	Upper Ormond	Dolla	Nenagh	II.	290
53	Windyhall	209	1	35	Donegal	Kilmacrenan	Conwal	Letterkenny	III.	127
7	Windy Hall	99	1	35	Londonderry	North East Liberties of Coleraine	Coleraine	Coleraine	III.	246
22	WINDY HARBOUR T.	—			Dublin	Rathdown	Taney	Rathdown	I.	38
2, 5	Windyhill	150	0	5	Tyrone	Strabane Lower	Donaghedy	Strabane	III.	321
21	Winetavern	421	1	26	Wicklow	Upper Talbotstown	Rathbran	Baltinglass	I.	365
8	Wingfield	176	0	13	Tipperary, N.R.	Lower Ormond	Loughkeen	Parsonstown	II.	286
2	Wingfield	326	1	34	Wexford	Gorey	Kilpipe	Gorey	I.	320
7, 8	Wingfield	115	0	30	Wicklow	Rathdown	Kilmacanoge	Rathdown	I.	356
4	Winnings	59	1	13	Dublin	Balrothery West	Naul	Balrothery	I.	23
45	Winningtown	240	3	35	Wexford	Shelbourne	Fethard	New Ross	I.	327
62, 70	Winnyhaw	265	1	19	Donegal	Raphoe	Raphoe	Strabane	III.	141
93, 94	Winterhill	141	2	16	Donegal	Banagh	Killymard	Donegal	III.	112
111	Wintsmills	11	0	1	Cork, E.R.	Kinsale	Tisaxon	Kinsale	II.	101
22	Woaghternerry	172	3	34	Fermanagh	Tirkennedy	Enniskillen	Enniskillen	III.	223
20, 29	Wolfesburgess East	131	1	13b	Limerick	Connello Lower	Rathkeale	Rathkeale	II.	230
29	Wolfesburgess West	144	0	31	Limerick	Connello Lower	Rathkeale	Rathkeale	II.	230
20, 25	Wolfestown	452	2	10	Kildare	Naas North	Rathmore	Naas	I.	63
25, 31	Wolfhill	156	0	32	Queen's Co.	Ballyadams	Rathaspick	Athy	I.	232
7	Wolganstown	224	0	15	Dublin	Balrothery West	Clonmethan	Balrothery	I.	22
7	Wolganstown	17	2	24	Dublin	Balrothery West	Palmerstown	Balrothery	I.	23
23	Wonderhill	252	3	29	Limerick	Smallcounty	Kilteely	Kilmallock	II.	260
70, 79	Wood	44	3	25	Donegal	Raphoe	Clonleigh	Strabane	III.	135
4	Wood	295	1	1	King's Co.	Warrenstown	Ballyburly	Edenderry	I.	144
86	Woodberry	103	3	8	Galway	Kilconnell	Killallaghtan	Ballinasloe	IV.	41
32, 46	Woodbrook	233	3	6	Galway	Killian	Killian	Mountbellew	IV.	45
7, 10, 11	Woodbrook	351	0	38	Roscommon	Boyle	Tumna	Cark on Shannon	IV.	198
18	Woodbrook	413	0	26	Tyrone	Strabane Upper	Bodoney Lower	Gortin	III.	324
18, 19	Woodbrook Demesne	235	2	33	Wexford	Bantry	Killann	Enniscorthy	I.	300
52, 62	Woodcockhill	799	3	0	Clare	Bunratty Lower	Killeely	Limerick	II.	5
43, 44, 49, 50	Woodcockstown	260	0	6	Meath	Upper Deece	Culmullen	Dunshaughlin	I.	193
19, 20	Wooddown	906	2	21	Westmeath	Farbill	Killucan	Mullingar	I.	267
15	Woodenboley	390	0	7	Wicklow	Lower Talbotstown	Hollywood	Baltinglass	I.	361
5	Woodend	277	1	24c	Tyrone	Strabane Lower	Leckpatrick	Strabane	III.	322
17	Woodfarm	61	2	26	Dublin	Uppercross	Palmerston	Dublin South	I.	40
14, 15	Woodfarm	156	0	16	Limerick	Clanwilliam	Caherconlish	Limerick	II.	222
43	Woodfield	286	3	3	Clare	Tulla Lower	Kilseily	Limerick	II.	37
60, 61	Woodfield	213	0	19	Cork, W.R.	East Muskerry	Aghabullogue	Macroom	II.	153
134, 135	Woodfield	601	1	27	Cork, W.R.	Ibane and Barryroe	Kilkerranmore	Clonakilty	II.	149
5, 6, 17, 18, 107, 108, 117, 118	Woodfield	1,189	1	24	Galway	Ballymoe	Boyounagh	Glennamaddy	IV.	6
54	Woodfield	257	1	3	Galway	Longford	Kilquain	Portumna	IV.	60
54	Woodfield	121	1	21	Limerick	Connello Upper	Dromcolliher	Newcastle	II.	233
81	Woodfield	338	2	13d	Mayo	Costello	Aghamore	Swineford	IV.	137
3	Woodfield	281	3	13	Roscommon	Boyle	Ardcarn	Boyle	IV.	193
33	Woodfield	97	3	29	Sligo	Corran	Emlaghfad	Sligo	IV.	226
21	Woodfield	158	2	24	Sligo	Tirerrill	Killerry	Sligo	IV.	239
27	Woodfield	280	3	19	Wicklow	Upper Talbotstown	Baltinglass	Baltinglass	I.	362
2	Woodfield or Curraghboy	624	3	23	King's Co.	Kilcoursey	Kilbride	Tullamore	I.	141
27	Woodfieldglen	185	1	4	Wicklow	Upper Talbotstown	Baltinglass	Baltinglass	I.	362
35	Woodfield or Tully-nisk	624	0	12	King's Co.	Eglish	Eglish	Parsonstown	I.	135

(a) { Including 3A. 2R. 37P. Castle Island.
     { Including 19A. 0R. 15P. water.

(b) Including 2A. 2R. 8P. water.
(c) Including 1A. 2R. 0P. water.

(d) Including 21A. 0R. 16P. water.

No. of Sheet of the Ordnance Survey Maps.	Townlands and Towns.	Area in Statute Acres.			County.	Barony.	Parish.	Poor Law Union in 1857.	Townland Census of 1851, Part I.	
		A.	R.	P.					Vol.	Page
125, 131	Woodford	607	2	14	Galway	Leitrim	Ballynakill	Loughrea	IV.	52
52	Woodford	144	2	4	Tipperary, S.R.	Kilnamanagh Lower	Clonoulty	Cashel	II.	323
26	Woodford Demesne	351	2	8a	Leitrim	Carrigallen	Carrigallen	Bawnboy	IV.	90
125, 131	WOODFORT T.	—			Galway	Leitrim	Ballynakill	Loughrea	IV.	52
46	Woodgraigue	189	0	0	Wexford	Bargy	Ambrosetown	Wexford	I.	304
30, 37	Woodgrange	1,016	0	28b	Down	Lecale Upper	Down	Downpatrick	III.	181
73,74,82,83	Woodhill	62	2	4	Donegal	Banagh	Killybegs Lower	Glenties	III.	110
16	Woodhill	110	1	34c	Donegal	Kilmacrenan	Clondahorky	Dunfanaghy	III.	123
62	Woodhill	149	0	26	Donegal	Raphoe	Raymoghy	Letterkenny	III.	142
4	Woodhill	164	1	11	Fermanagh	Lurg	Templecarn	Lowtherstown	III.	209
46	Woodhill	61	3	13	Tyrone	Dungannon Middle	Tullyniskan	Dungannon	III.	305
33, 39	Woodhill or Knock-nakillew	311	3	29	Sligo	Corran	Cloonoghil	Tobercurry	IV.	225
18	Woodhouse	37	1	28	Louth	Ardee	Mosstown	Ardee	I.	174
61, 62	Woodhouse	303	0	24	Tipperary, S.R.	Middlethird	Magorban	Cashel	II.	328
22	Woodhouse	104	1	21	Waterford	Decies without Drum	Modelligo	Dungarvan	II.	359
24, 32	Woodhouse	394	2	24	Waterford	Decies without Drum	Stradbally	Kilmacthomas	II.	361
29, 30, 35	Woodhouse or Tinakilly	464	2	7	Waterford	Decies within Drum	Kilmolash	Dungarvan	II.	351
69, 76	Woodinstown	459	2	13	Tipperary, S.R.	Middlethird	Knockgraffon	Cashel	II.	328
71	Wood Island	39	2	1	Donegal	Raphoe	Clonleigh	Strabane	III.	135
17	Wood Island	23	1	16	Down	Castlereagh Lower	Tullynakill	Newtownards	III.	164
26	Wood Island	3	1	24	Galway	Ross	Ross	Oughterard	IV.	74
30	Woodland	147	2	1	Cavan	Tullyhunco	Killashandra	Cavan	III.	99
53	Woodland	205	2	28	Donegal	Kilmacrenan	Aghanunshin	Letterkenny	III.	122
23	Woodland	101	2	14	Dublin	Rathdown	Stillorgan	Rathdown	I.	38
18	Woodland	123	3	31	Louth	Ferrard	Dunleer	Ardee	I.	181
44	Woodland	211	0	6	Meath	Ratoath	Rathregan	Dunshaughlin	I.	219
31, 32	Woodland or Garragh	209	1	5	Queen's Co.	Slievemargy	Killabban	Carlow	I.	245
14	Woodlands	187	2	23	Carlow	St. Mullins Upper	Moyacomb	Carlow	I.	14
139, 140	Woodlands	267	1	7	Cork, W.R.	West Carbery (W.D.)	Skull	Skull	II.	147
62	Woodlands	287	0	31	Donegal	Raphoe	Taughboyne	Strabane	III.	144
13, 17	Woodlands	571	2	23d	Dublin	Castleknock	Clonsilla	Celbridge	I.	24
19, 23	Woodlands	234	1	12	Kilkenny	Shillelogher	Castleinch or Inchyo-laghan	Kilkenny	I.	114
22	Woodlands	50	1	38	Tipperary, N.R.	Upper Ormond	Aghnameadle	Nenagh	II.	289
32	Woodlands	71	0	15e	Wexford	Ballaghkeen	Ballynaslaney	Enniscorthy	I.	292
19	Woodlands	632	3	7	Wexford	Scarawalsh	Monart	Enniscorthy	I.	325
8, 13	Woodlands	229	3	29	Wicklow	Newcastle	Kilcoole	Rathdrum	I.	352
38, 40	Woodlands East	398	1	5	Kildare	Kilkea and Moone	Castledermot	Athy	I.	59
109	Woodlands or Kil-honerush	116	3	35	Galway	Longford	Meelick	Portumna	IV.	61
37,38,39,40	Woodlands West	389	3	26	Kildare	Kilkea and Moone	Castledermot	Athy	I.	59
73, 86	Woodlawn	1,368	1	23	Galway	Kilconnell	Killaan	Ballinasloe	IV.	41
66	Woodlawn	67	1	2	Kerry	Magunihy	Killarney	Killarney	II.	204
18	Woodlawn	89	0	38	Longford	Moydow	Killashee	Longford	I.	162
23	Woodmount	184	3	0	Clare	Corcomroe	Kilmanaheen	Ennistimon	II.	21
9, 17	Wood of O	774	3	11	King's Co.	Lower Philipstown	Ballycommon	Tullamore	I.	142
51	Woodpark	184	1	13	Clare	Bunratty Lower	Bunratty	Ennis	II.	3
44	Woodpark	102	0	16	Clare	Tulla Lower	Killokennedy	Limerick	II.	36
32	Woodpark	277	0	4f	Cork, E.R.	Duhallow	Ballyclogh	Mallow	II.	67
53, 61	Woodpark	92	0	6	Donegal	Raphoe	Leck	Letterkenny	III.	140
7	Woodpark	102	3	39	Dublin	Balrothery East	Lusk	Balrothery	I.	21
23	Woodpark	171	3	13	Dublin	Rathdown	Kill	Rathdown	I.	36
69	Woodpark	276	1	20	Galway	Clare	Annaghdown	Galway	IV.	17
136	Woodpark	201	3	8	Galway	Leitrim	Inishcaltra	Scarriff	IV.	54
1, 6	Woodpark	158	0	23	Limerick	Clanwilliam	Stradbally	Limerick	II.	226
102, 103	Woodpark	172	2	39	Mayo	Costello	Annagh	Claremorris	IV.	138
50	Woodpark	211	2	22g	Meath	Dunboyne	Dunboyne	Dunshaughlin	I.	200
14	Woodpark	18	1	13	Sligo	Carbury	Killaspugbrone	Sligo	IV.	222
9, 10, 14, 15	Woodpark	204	2	5	Tipperary, N.R.	Lower Ormond	Cloghprior	Borrisokane	II.	283
11	Woodpark	120	3	6	Wexford	Gorey	Liskinfere	Gorey	I.	321
15	Wood Park or Bally-nameta	234	3	27	Armagh	Tiranny	Tynan	Armagh	III.	60
10, 16	Woodpole	343	2	14	Meath	Upper Kells	Loughan or Castlekeeran	Kells	I.	207
27, 36	Woodquarter	682	0	20	Donegal	Kilmacrenan	Kilmacrenan	Millford	III.	130
20, 21	Woodquarter	63	2	18	Kilkenny	Gowran	Gowran	Kilkenny	I.	95
29	Woodquay	581	3	30	Galway	Clare	Belclare	Tuam	IV.	18
6	Woodroad	134	1	32	Limerick	Clanwilliam	Stradbally	Limerick	II.	226
76	Woodrooff	611	2	26	Tipperary, S.R.	Iffa and Offa East	Inishlounaght	Clonmel	II.	313
76	Woodrooff	135	1	7	Tipperary, S.R.	Iffa and Offa East	Newchapel	Clonmel	II.	315
76	Woodrooff	277	1	30	Tipperary, S.R.	Iffa and Offa West	Derrygrath	Clonmel	II.	318
72	Woods	476	3	2h	Mayo	Gallen	Kilconduff	Swineford	IV.	148
80, 81	Woods	549	0	26	Mayo	Gallen	Killedan	Swineford	IV.	150
12	Woodsgift	491	1	31	Kilkenny	Crannagh	Clomantagh	Urlingford	I.	85

(a) Including 57A. 2R. 18P. water.
(b) Including 12A. 3R. 10P. water.
(c) Including 17A. 2R. 12P. water.

(d) { Including 13A. 3R. 20P. Pond.
{ Including 4A. 0R. 35P. River Liffey.
(e) Including 6A. 1R. 2P. detached portion.

(f) Including 4A. 2R. 0P. water.
(g) Including 8A. 2R. 12P. detached portions.
(h) Including 4A. 0R. 22P. water.

No. of Sheet of the Ordnance Survey Maps.	Townlands and Towns.	Area in Statute Acres.			County.	Barony.	Parish.	Poor Law Union in 1857.	Townland Census of 1851, Part I.	
		A.	R.	P.					Vol.	Page
4	Woodside	116	3	23	Carlow	Rathvilly	Hacketstown	Shillelagh	I.	11
73	Woodside	181	3	26	Cork, E.R.	East Muskerry	Carrigrohanebeg	Cork	II.	102
22, 25	Woodside	154	3	0	Dublin	Rathdown	Kilgobbin	Rathdown	I.	35
30, 36	Woodside	34	1	36	Meath	Upper Navan	Trim	Trim	I.	217
23	Woodside	252	2	10a	Tyrone	Omagh West	Termonamongan	Castlederg	III.	317
64, 65, 76	Woodstock	581	2	17	Cork, E.R.	Barrymore	Carrigtohill	Middleton	II.	52
29	Woodstock	27	1	16	Limerick	Connello Upper	Ballingarry	Croom	II.	231
112	Woodstock	409	3	29	Mayo	Clanmorris	Crossboyne	Claremorris	IV.	133
29, 30	Woodstock	302	2	2	Waterford	Decies without Drum	Kilmolash	Dungarvan	II.	357
13	Woodstock Demesne	213	0	23	Wicklow	Newcastle	Newcastle Lower	Rathdrum	I.	353
35	Woodstock North	231	0	24	Kildare	Narragh&RebanWest	Churchtown	Athy	I.	67
35	Woodstock South	225	0	32	Kildare	Narragh&RebanWest	Churchtown	Athy	I.	67
6	Woodstown	188	2	36	Limerick	Clanwilliam	Killeenagarriff	Limerick	II.	224
25	Woodstown	414	3	7	Waterford	Middlethird	Islandikane	Kilmacthomas	II.	367
9, 17	Woodstown	437	2	27	Waterford	Middlethird	Killoteran	Waterford	II.	367
18	Woodstown Lower	271	2	4	Waterford	Gaultiere	Kilmacomb	Waterford	II.	364
18	Woodstown Upper	292	3	20	Waterford	Gaultiere	Kilmacomb	Waterford	II.	364
45	Woodtown	142	2	31	Donegal	Kilmacrenan	Conwal	Letterkenny	III.	127
22, 25	Woodtown	488	3	33	Dublin	Uppercross	Cruagh	Dublin South	I.	39
2, 6	Woodtown	187	0	4	Londonderry	Keenaght	Magilligan	New Tn Limavady	III.	237
14	Woodtown	325	0	20	Louth	Louth	Mansfieldstown	Ardee	I.	185
30	Woodtown	124	0	29	Meath	Lune	Athboy	Trim	I.	207
29, 35	Woodtown	19	0	31	Meath	Lune	Kildalkey	Trim	I.	208
43	Woodtown	947	1	9	Meath	Upper Deece	Culmullin	Dunshaughlin	I.	193
42	Woodtown	97	1	13	Wexford	Bargy	Kilmannan	Wexford	I.	306
47	Woodtown	83	1	25	Wexford	Forth	Mayglass	Wexford	I.	312
43	Woodtown	109	2	27	Wexford	Forth	Rosslare	Wexford	I.	313
36	Woodtown (Abbott)	392	3	29	Meath	Lune	Kildalkey	Trim	I.	208
6	Woodtown Lower	201	2	38	Meath	Lower Slane	Siddan	Ardee	I.	224
6	Woodtown Upper	349	2	35	Meath	Lower Slane	Siddan	Ardee	I.	224
29	Woodtown West	260	3	10	Meath	Lune	Kildalkey	Trim	I.	208
46	Woodview	36	1	31	Cork, E.R.	Kinnatalloon	Mogeely	Fermoy	II.	99
17	Woodville	124	3	10b	Dublin	Newcastle	Esker	Celbridge	I.	33
21	Woodville	118	0	30	Kilkenny	Gowran	Kilmacahill	Kilkenny	I.	97
29	Woodville	324	2	6	Mayo	Tirawley	Kilfian	Ballina	IV.	169
29	Woodville	83	0	37	Tipperary, N.R.	Eliogarty	Templemore	Thurles	II.	272
15,16,21,22	Woodville	516	2	20	Tipperary, N.R.	Upper Ormond	Ballymackey	Nenagh	II.	290
20	Woodville	141	0	17c	Waterford	Coshmore&Coshbride	Lismore and Mocollop	Lismore	II.	348
43	Woodworths Island	2	1	14	Cavan	Castlerahan	Lurgan	Oldcastle	III.	70
21,22,26,27	Woody, Mullaghree, or Ashwoods	168	1	9	Fermanagh	Magheraboy	Rossorry	Enniskillen	III.	214
24, 28	Woollengrange	729	2	33d	Kilkenny	Gowran	Woollengrange	Thomastown	I.	100
16	Worlough	36	3	18	Wexford	Scarawalsh	Kilbride	Enniscorthy	I.	323
55, 68	Wormhole	325	3	11	Galway	Moycullen	Killannin	Oughterard	IV.	70
30	Woteraghy	328	1	22	Cavan	Clanmahon	Ballintemple	Cavan	III.	75
45	Wotton	317	1	1	Meath	Ratoath	Donaghmore	Dunshaughlin	I.	218
15	Wottonstown	285	1	27	Louth	Louth	Mansfieldstown	Ardee	I.	185
2	Wranglestown	123	0	23	Queen's Co.	Tinnahinch	Kilmanman	Mountmellick	I.	249
41	Wrensborough	79	2	25	Tipperary, N.R.	Eliogarty	Thurles	Thurles	II.	273
37	Wrightown or Ardbrackan	258	3	1	Meath	Lower Deece	Scurlockstown	Trim	I.	192
7	Wyanstown	439	0	27	Dublin	Balrothery West	Clonmethan	Balrothery	I.	22
19	Wyanstown	241	2	0	Louth	Ferrard	Port	Drogheda	I.	182
6, 7	Wyestown	382	1	12	Dublin	Balrothery West	Ballymadun	Dunshaughlin	I.	22
40	Yardland	90	1	9	Wicklow	Arklow	Arklow	Rathdrum	I.	341
24	Yellowbatter	562	1	30e	Louth	Drogheda and Municipal Borough	St. Peter's	Drogheda	I.	175
28	Yellowbogcommon	289	3	3	Kildare	Kilcullen	Kilcullen	Naas	I.	58
67, 78	Yellowford	173	2	13	Cork, E.R.	Imokilly	Kilmacdonogh	Youghal	II.	88
26	YELLOW FURZE T.	—			Meath	Lower Duleek	Painstown	Navan	I.	196
109	Yellow Island	0	2	24	Galway	Longford	Meelick	Portumna	IV.	62
20	Yellow Island	16	1	32	Meath	Lower Duleek	Donore	Drogheda	I.	195
48	Yellow Island Large	1	2	4	Roscommon	Athlone	Kiltoom	Athlone	IV.	183
48	Yellow Island Little	0	1	32	Roscommon	Athlone	Kiltoom	Athlone	IV.	183
12	Yellowleas	131	2	29	Meath	Morgallion	Castletown	Navan	I.	209
17	Yellowmeadows	65	3	31	Dublin	Uppercross	Clondalkin	Dublin South	I.	39
38	Yellowshar	56	2	17	Meath	Skreen	Kilmoon	Dunshaughlin	I.	221
10, 13	Yellow Walls	137	1	2	Dublin	Castleknock	Mulhuddart	Dublin North	I.	25
12	Yellow Walls	405	0	0	Dublin	Coolock	Malahide	Balrothery	I.	28
17	Yellow Walls	51	1	31	Dublin	Uppercross	Palmerston	Dublin South	I.	40
30	Yellow Walls	152	1	16	Meath	Upper Navan	Moymet	Trim	I.	216

(a) Including 2A. 2R. 11P. water.
(b) Including 3A. 0R. 27P. water.
(c) Including 10A. 2R. 28P. water.
(d) Including 10A. 1R. 21F. River Nore.
(e) { Within the Municipal Boundary, 77A. 2R. 15P.
　　{ Without the Municipal Boundary, 484A. 3R. 15P.

No. of Sheet of the Ordnance Survey Maps.	Townlands and Towns.	Area in Statute Acres.	County.	Barony.	Parish.	Poor Law Union in 1857.	Townland Census of 1851, Part I.	
		A. R. P.					Vol.	Page
18, 19	Yeomanstown . .	426 1 35a	Kildare . .	Clane . . .	Carragh . . .	Naas . .	I.	53
19	Yewer Glebe . .	137 2 18b	Cavan . .	Tullyhunco . .	Killashandra . .	Cavan . .	III.	99
126	*Yew Islands* . {	0 3 24 / 1 0 9 }	Galway . .	Longford . .	Lickmolassy . .	Portumna .	IV.	61
41	Yolegrew . .	81 3 36	Wexford . .	Shelmaliere West .	Coolstuff . .	Wexford . .	I.	333
41	Yolegrew . .	29 1 13	Wexford . .	Shelmaliere West .	Taghmon . .	Wexford . .	I.	335
46, 47	Yoletown . .	113 3 16	Wexford . .	Bargy . . .	Kilcowan . .	Wexford . .	I.	305
48	Yoletown . .	84 3 28	Wexford . .	Forth . . .	Ballybrennan . .	Wexford . .	I.	308
47	Yoletown . .	125 1 19	Wexford . .	Forth . . .	Ballymore . .	Wexford . .	I.	308
48, 53	Yoletown . .	120 2 21	Wexford . .	Forth . . .	Tacumshin . .	Wexford . .	I.	315
40	Yoletown . .	531 0 36	Wexford . .	Shelburne . .	Owenduff . .	New Ross . .	I.	328
25	Yorkfield . .	47 2 24	Westmeath .	Moyashel and Magh-eradernon . .	Dysart . . .	Mullingar . .	I.	274
14, 20	Youghal . . .	224 1 34	Tipperary, N.R.	Owney and Arra .	Youghalarra . .	Nenagh . .	II.	298
67	Youghal-lands .	424 2 0	Cork, E.R. .	Imokilly . . .	Youghal . . .	Youghal . .	II.	91
56, 67	Youghal Park .	526 1 10	Cork, E.R. .	Imokilly . . .	Ardagh . . .	Youghal . .	II.	83
67	Youghal Park .	394 2 8	Cork, E.R. .	Imokilly . . .	Clonpriest . .	Youghal . .	II.	85
135	Youghals . .	109 3 30	Cork, W.R. .	East Carbery (E.D.)	Island . . .	Clonakilty . .	II.	128
135	Youghals . .	177 0 2	Cork, W.R. .	East Carbery (E.D.)	Kilgarriff . .	Clonakilty . .	II.	129
67	YOUGHAL T. . .	—	Cork, E.R. .	Imokilly . . .	Youghal . . .	Youghal . .	II.	91
14, 20	Youghalvillage .	267 1 22	Tipperary, N.R.	Owney and Arra .	Youghalarra . .	Nenagh . .	II.	298
90	Youngfield . .	308 0 36	Cork, W.R. .	Bear . . .	Kilcaskan . .	Bantry . .	II.	123
65	Young-grove . .	577 3 19	Cork, E.R. .	Barrymore . .	Dungourney . .	Middleton . .	II.	54
136	*Young's Island* .	2 1 3	Galway . .	Leitrim . . .	Inishcaltra . .	Scarriff . .	IV.	54
31	Youngstown . .	304 3 25	Kildare . .	Narragh&RebanWest	Narraghmore . .	Athy . .	I.	68
41	Youngstown . .	300 0 5	Wexford . .	Shelmaliere West .	Coolstuff . .	Wexford . .	I.	333

(*a*) Including 10A. 0R. 0P. water.   (*b*) Including 20A. 2R. 12P. water.

END OF TOWNLAND INDEX.

GENERAL ALPHABETICAL INDEX

TO THE

PARISHES OF IRELAND,

With the Number of the Sheet of the Ordnance Survey Maps on which they appear; the Areas of the Parishes in Statute Measure; the Counties, Baronies, and Poor Law Unions in which they are situated; also the Volume and Page of the Townland Census of 1851, which contains the Number of Houses in 1841 and 1851, and the Poor Law Valuation in 1851.

No. of Sheet of the Ordnance Survey Maps.	Parishes.	Area in Statute Measure.	County.	Barony.	Poor Law Union in 1857.	Townland Census of 1851, Part I.	
		A. R. P.				Vol.	Page
3, 5, 6	Abbey	4,714 1 32a	Clare	Burren	Ballyvaghan	II.	11
34, 35, 42, 43, 51, 52	Abbeyfeale	18,149 3 20b	Limerick	Glenquin	Newcastle	II.	244
98, 99, 106, 107	Abbeygormacan	3,439 2 12 / 8,317 2 28	Galway	Leitrim / Longford	Ballinasloe / Loughrea / Portumna	IV.	50 / 56
44, 45, 58, 59, 71	Abbeyknockmoy	1,473 1 23c / 10,912 3 22d	Galway	Clare / Tiaquin	Galway / Tuam	IV.	16 / 75
6, 10, 11, 16	Abbeylara	9,150 0 5e	Longford	Granard	Granard	I.	154
1, 5 / 17, 23, 24, 29, 30	Abbeyleix	680 2 30f / 1,475 0 26 / 11,245 3 25g / 144 1 29	Kilkenny / Queen's Co.	Fassadinin / Clarmallagh / Cullenagh / Maryborough West	Castlecomer / Abbeyleix	I.	88 / 235 / 238 / 242
123, 136, 145	Abbeymahon	4,481 3 3	Cork. W.R.	Ibane and Barryroe	Clonakilty	II.	148
23, 24, 27	Abbeyshrule	2,340 1 19h	Longford	Shrule	Ballymahon	I.	165
132, 133, 141, 142, 150, 151	Abbeystrowry	9,395 2 34i	Cork. W.R.	West Carbery (E.D.)	Skibbereen	II.	136
6, 7, 14, 15 / 32, 33, 38, 39	Abington	3,041 3 23 / 16,373 3 36 / 10,984 1 11	Limerick / Tipperary, N.R.	Clanwilliam / Owneybeg / Owney and Arra	Limerick / Nenagh	II.	221 / 250, 251 / 295
41, 42, 43, 53, 54, 55, 56, 65, 66, 75	Achill	51,521 2 19j	Mayo	Burrishoole	Newport	IV.	117
24, 25, 31, 32, 33, 37, 38, 42, 43	Achonry	60,896 0 26k	Sligo	Leyny	Tobercurry	IV.	228, to 230
30, 31, 35, 36	Adamstown	8,133 3 25	Wexford	Bantry	New Ross	I.	299
11, 12, 20, 21, 30	Adare	1,004 0 37 / 6,631 1 8l / 4,358 1 3m	Limerick	Connello Upper / Coshma / Kenry	Croom / Rathkeale	II.	230 / 241 / 248
4, 5, 16	Addergoole	8,441 3 35n	Galway	Dunmore	Tuam	IV.	32, 33
38, 46, 47, 48, 58, 59, 60, 68	Addergoole	36,629 2 28o	Mayo	Tirawley	Ballina / Castlebar	IV.	162,163
17	Aderrig	759 0 33p	Dublin	Newcastle	Celbridge	I.	32
12, 13, 21, 22, 29, 30	Affane	7,772 2 15	Waterford	Decies without Drum	Dungarvan / Lismore	II.	353
12, 16	Agha	4,183 2 18q	Carlow	Idrone East	Carlow	I.	6
21, 22, 23, 28, 29, 31	Aghaboe	6,510 1 21 / 12,192 1 3r	Queen's Co.	Clandonagh / Clarmallagh	Abbeyleix / Donaghmore	I.	232,233 / 235,236
12, 13, 17, 18, 22	Aghabog	11,543 2 19s	Monaghan	Dartree	Clones / Cootehill / Monaghan	III.	263,264
49, 60, 61, 71, 72	Aghabulloge	18,733 1 21	Cork. W.R.	East Muskerry	Macroom	II.	153
51	Aghacrew	1,230 1 27	Tipperary, S.R.	Kilnamanagh Lower	Tipperary	II.	322
18, 19	Aghacross	355 0 23	Cork. E.R.	Condons & Clangibbon	Mitchelstown	II.	59
88	Aghada	2,458 1 33t	Cork. E.R.	Imokilly	Middleton	II.	83
13, 17, 18	Aghade	1,697 3 24	Carlow	Forth	Carlow / Enniscorthy	I.	3
26, 27, 33, 34, 40, 41	Aghaderg	1,077 2 14 / 12,841 2 17u	Down	Lower Iveagh, Lr. pt. / Upper Iveagh, Up. pt.	Banbridge	III.	167 / 173,174
50, 58, 59, 60, 65, 66, 67, 68, 74, 76	Aghadoe	4,095 0 36v / 15,793 1 36w	Kerry	Dunkerron North / Magunihy	Killarney	II.	181 / 199

		A. R. P.				A. R. P.				A. R. P.
(a)	Including	25 3 12 Lough Luirk.	(h)	Including	43 1 37 of River Inny.	(o)	Including	2,927 0 31 of Lough Conn.		
(b)	Including	87 1 25 of water.	(i)	Including	462 1 13 detached portion. / 28 3 16 of Lough Abisdealy. / 21 2 5 of River Ilen tideway.			438 2 27 of Beltra Lough. / 397 0 17 of small loughs.		
(c)	Including	350 1 17 detached portion.				(p)	Including	111 1 11 detached portion.		
(d)	Including	4 2 32 of water.	(j)	Including	35,283 1 14 Achill Island. / 754 0 9 of water.			6 2 16 of River Liffey.		
(e)	Composed of 4 parts, viz.:—				143 0 29 of Easky Lough.	(q)	Including	18 1 39 of River Barrow.		
	1st Part	4,856 2 13 land. / 44 2 34 of River Inny. / 94 3 30 Derragh Lough. / 214 1 22 of Lough Kinale.	(k)	Including	35 0 27 Templehouse Lake. / 107 2 16 of small loughs.	(r)	Including	2,733 3 0 detached portion.		
						(s)	Including	222 2 37 of water.		
	2nd Part	2,267 0 24 land. / 272 1 2 of Lough Gowna.	(l)	Including	34 0 10 of River Maigue tideway.	(t)	Including	8 3 23 of water.		
	3rd Part	1,108 0 26 land.	(m)	Including	20 2 11 of River Maigue tideway. / 33 3 28 Curragh Chase Lough.	(u)	Including	119 1 3 of water.		
	4th Part	291 3 14 land.				(v)	Including	1,200 0 20 of Lough Leane. / 5 0 32 of River Laune.		
(f)	Including	249 0 20 detached portion.	(n)	Including	2,303 0 11 detached portion. / 67 1 19 of water.					
(g)	Including	1,548 3 13 detached portion.				(w)	Including	5,530 2 2 detached portions. / 1,761 3 35 of Lough Leane. / 31 0 32 of Rivers Flesk & Laune.		

No. of Sheet of the Ordnance Survey Maps.	Parishes.	Area in Statute Measure. A. R. P.	County.	Barony.	Poor Law Union in 1857.	Townland Census of 1851, Part I. Vol.	Page
10, 11, 12, 18, 19	Aghadowey	16,348 2 5a	Londonderry	Coleraine	{Ballymoney / Coleraine}	III.	229,230
140, 141, 149, 150	Aghadown	8,952 1 6b	Cork, W.R.	West Carbery (E.D.)	Skibbereen	II.	136,137
62, 66	Aghagallon	7,885 0 15c	Antrim	Upper Massereene	Lurgan	III.	29
77, 87, 88, 89, 97, 98, 99, 106, 107, 108, 115, 116	Aghagower	12,930 3 14d / 42,116 2 37e	Mayo	{Burrishoole / Murrisk}	Westport	IV.	{117,118 / 158,159}
62, 63, 66, 67	Aghalee	2,499 2 37f	Antrim	Upper Massereene	Lurgan	III.	29
60, 61, 66, 67	Aghaloo	19,521 0 33g	Tyrone	Dungannon Lower	{Armagh / Clogher / Dungannon}	III.	296,297
23, 24, 27, 28, 29, 30, 33, 34, 35, 39 / 64, 68	Aghalurcher	43,307 2 24h / 4,708 1 31i	Fermanagh / Tyrone	Magherastephana / Clogher	Lisnaskea / Clogher	III.	{214, to 218 / 291}
72, 81, 82, 92, 93	Aghamore	22,820 0 1j	Mayo	Costello	{Claremorris / Swineford}	IV.	136,137
34, 40, 45	Aghanagh	8,838 2 0k	Sligo	Tirerrill	Boyle	IV.	237
38, 39, 42, 43	Aghancon	4,621 2 1 / 922 2 25	King's Co.	{Ballybritt / Clonlisk}	Roscrea	I.	{124 / 129}
5, 6, 9, 10	Aghanloo	8,251 0 39l	Londonderry	Keenaght	New Tn Limavady	III.	233,234
45, 53, 54	Aghanunshin	4,011 2 6m	Donegal	Kilmacrenan	Letterkenny	III.	122
23, 24	Agharra	2,595 0 35n	Longford	Shrule	Ballymahon	I.	166
2, 3, 5, 6	Aghavallen	16,743 0 0o	Kerry	Iraghticonnor	Listowel	II.	189
23, 24, 28, 29, 34	Aghavea	17,142 0 3p	Fermanagh	Magherastephana	Lisnaskea	III.	218,219
31, 35	Aghaviller	5,670 3 26	Kilkenny	Knocktopher	{Carrick on Suir / Thomastown}	I.	110,111
37, 42, 43, 48, 49	Agher	768 3 4 / 1,293 3 22	Meath	{Lower Deece / Upper Deece}	Trim	I.	{191 / 192}
36, 45, 54	Aghern	3,489 0 15	Cork, E.R.	Kinnatalloon	Fermoy	II.	97
60, 71	Aghinagh	9,420 1 0q	Cork, W.R.	East Muskerry	Macroom	II.	153,154
28, 29, 34, 35	Aghmacart	9,600 3 5	Queen's Co.	Clarmallagh	Abbeyleix	I.	236
21, 22, 27, 28	Aghnameadle	10,322 1 10r	Tipperary, N.R.	Upper Ormond	Nenagh	II.	288,289
18,23,24,25,26,27,28	Aghnamullen	30,710 0 19s	Monaghan	Cremorne	{Carrickmacross / Castleblayney / Cootehill}	III.	{257, to 259}
37, 42, 43	Aghowle	8,139 3 38	Wicklow	Shillelagh	Shillelagh	I.	356,357
12, 19	Agivey	1,725 1 31t	Londonderry	Coleraine	Coleraine	III.	230
72, 84	Aglish	6,770 2 30u	Cork, E.R.	East Muskerry	{Bandon / Macroom}	II.	101
48, 57, 58	Aglish	4,857 0 2	Kerry	Magunihy	Killarney	II.	199,200
42, 43, 45, 46	Aglish	1,343 2 10	Kilkenny	Iverk	Waterford	I.	105
59,69,70,78,79,89	Aglish	14,794 0 13v	Mayo	Carra	Castlebar	IV.	123,124
29, 30, 34, 35	Aglish	6,856 0 33	Waterford	Decies within Drum	Dungarvan	II.	349
4, 5, 7, 8	Aglishcloghane	5,897 3 22	Tipperary, N.R.	Lower Ormond	Borrisokane	II.	281
23, 24, 33	Aglishcormick	1,141 1 29 / 574 1 19	Limerick	{Clanwilliam / Coonagh}	{Limerick / Tipperary}	II.	{221 / 233}
7, 8	Aglishdrinagh	3,309 3 4w	Cork, E.R.	Orrery and Kilmore	Kilmallock	II.	106
1, 2, 3, 4, 5, 6, 8	Ahamlish	16,413 2 2x	Sligo	Carbury	Sligo	IV.	219,220
4, 5, 9, 10 / 35	Aharney	5,546 1 21 / 1,392 2 27	Kilkenny / Queen's Co.	Galmoy / Clarmallagh	Urlingford / Abbeyleix	I.	{91 / 236}
47, 60, 61, 74	Ahascragh	6,315 2 13y / 2,776 0 10 / 8,250 1 27z	Galway	{Clonmacnowen / Kilconnell / Killian}	{Ballinasloe / Mountbellew}	IV.	{23, 24 / 38, 39 / 42, 43}
26,27,31,32,36,37	Ahoghill	2,801 2 21aa / 315 1 18 / 29,869 1 18bb / 2,431 3 19	Antrim	{Kilconway / Lower Antrim / Lower Toome / Upper Toome}	Ballymena	III.	{25 / 3 / 31, 32 / 33}
46, 47, 54, 55	Allsaints	9,673 3 6cc	Donegal	Raphoe	{Letterkenny / Londonderry}	III.	133,134
41, 46	Ambrosetown	2,197 0 31	Wexford	Bargy	Wexford	I.	303,304
30, 31	Anhid	980 2 36	Limerick	Coshma	Croom	II.	241
34, 35, 41	Annaclone	6,544 1 34	Down	Upper Iveagh, Up. pt.	Banbridge	III.	174
27,28,31,32,35, 37	Annaduff	5,329 1 6dd / 5,640 3 39ee	Leitrim	{Leitrim / Mohill}	{Carᵏ.on Shannon / Mohill}	IV.	{99,100 / 105}
20, 21, 25, 26	Annagelliff	8,260 1 7ff	Cavan	Upper Loughtee	Cavan	III.	81,82
11, 12, 15, 16	Annagh	6,805 1 9gg / 12,339 3 30hh	Cavan	{Lower Loughtee / Tullygarvey}	{Cavan / Cootehill}	III.	{78,79 / 87}
28, 29, 37, 38	Annagh	4,082 1 10 / 9,674 0 31ii	Kerry	{Corkaguiny / Trughanacmy}	Tralee	II.	{173 / 205}

A. R. P.

(a) Including 42 0 39 of River Bann.
(b) Including { 379 1 35 detached portion. / 11 0 28 Lough Marsh. }
(c) Including 2,415 0 21 of Lough Neagh.
(d) Including 153 0 25 of water.
(e) Including 493 3 13 of water.
(f) Including 39 0 15 Broad Water.
(g) Including 140 0 26 of water.
(h) Including { 2,556 1 12 of Upper Lough Erne. / 574 0 10 of small loughs. }
(i) Including 27 0 18 of water.
(j) Including { 309 3 18 of Mannin Lake. / 708 2 20 of small loughs. }
(k) Including 1,091 0 24 of Lough Arrow.
(l) Including 50 3 0 of water.

(m) Including 184 1 37 of tideway.
(n) Including { 890 0 29 detached portion. / 31 1 34 of River Inny. }
(o) Including { 231 1 38 Carrig Island, / 45 2 38 detached portion. }
(p) Including 17 2 16 of water.
(q) Including 63 0 1 of River Lee.
(r) Including 2,069 2 16 detached portion.
(s) Including 1,643 3 13 of water.
(t) Including 55 0 14 of River Bann.
(u) Including 53 3 39 of River Inny.
(v) Including { 377 0 29 of Lannagh or Castlebar / 368 2 27 of small loughs. }
(w) Including 773 0 25 detached portion.
(x) Including 22 2 35 of Cloonty Lough.

(y) Including 37 1 25 of water.
(z) Including 75 0 16 of water.
(aa) Including 16 0 20 of water.
(bb) Including { 129 2 37 of River Bann / 102 0 22 of water. }
(cc) Including 233 3 9 of small loughs.
(dd) Including { 191 0 24 of River Shannon. / 233 3 9 of small loughs. }
(ee) Including { 1,103 0 4 of River Shannon. / 48 3 38 of small loughs. }
(ff) Including 70 1 12 of water.
(gg) Including { 62 0 37 of Lough Erne. / 775 0 0 of water. }
(hh) Including { 65 0 25 of Lough Erne. / 367 2 13 of water. }
(ii) Including 471 0 21 detached portion.

No. of Sheet of the Ordnance Survey Maps.	Parishes.	Area in Statute Measure. A. R. P.	County.	Barony.	Poor Law Union in 1857.	Vol.	Page
92, 93, 102, 103, 112, 113	Annagh	20,315 2 3a	Mayo	Costello	Claremorris	IV.	137,138
42,43,56,57,69,70,82	Annaghdown	23,729 2 26b	Galway	Clare	Galway / Tuam	IV.	16, 17
15, 21, 22	Annahilt	708 1 27 / 6,069 0 5c	Down	Kinelarty / Lower Iveagh, Lr. pt.	Lisburn	III.	176 / 167
43, 44, 49, 50	Antrim	5,369 2 4 / 3,514 3 13d	Antrim	Upper Antrim / Upper Toome	Antrim	III.	5 / 33
48 / 30,31,39,40,47,48	Arboe	1,358 2 35 / 32,146 0 22e	Londonderry / Tyrone	Loughinsholin / Dungannon Upper	Magherafelt / Cookstown	III.	238 / 305
55, 56, 66, 67	Ardagh	7,880 0 23	Cork, E.R.	Imokilly	Youghal	II.	83
27, 28, 35, 36	Ardagh	626 1 15 / 8,404 0 8f	Limerick	Glenquin / Shanid	Newcastle / Rathkeale	II.	244 / 254,255
14, 19, 20	Ardagh	9,805 0 26g / 1,611 2 34	Longford	Ardagh / Moydow	Longford	I.	151 / 160
22, 29, 30, 38, 39	Ardagh	5,494 0 31h	Mayo	Tirawley	Ballina	IV.	163,164
2, 3, 6	Ardagh	2,357 3 19i / 1,311 1 14	Meath	Lower Slane / Morgallion	Kells	I.	222 / 209
12, 17	Ardamine	4,214 3 32	Wexford	Ballaghkeen	Gorey	I.	291
24, 25, 30, 31	Ardbraccan	6,490 3 18	Meath	Lower Navan	Navan	I.	214
36, 37	Ardcandrisk	1,226 3 2	Wexford	Shelmaliere West	Wexford	I.	332
3, 4, 12	Ardcanny	3,099 2 5j	Limerick	Kenry	Rathkeale	II.	248
3, 4, 6, 7, 10	Ardcarn	19,962 3 26k	Roscommon	Boyle	Boyle / Carᵏ. on Shannon	IV.	192,193
27, 33	Ardcath	4,380 1 34	Meath	Upper Duleek	Drogheda / Dunshaughlin	I.	197
32, 33, 37, 38	Ardcavan	2,457 2 14	Wexford	Shelmaliere East	Wexford	I.	329,330
20, 24, 25, 29	Ardclinis	15,691 2 24l	Antrim	Lower Glenarm	Larne	III.	21
32, 33, 37, 38	Ardcolm	2,232 0 3	Wexford	Shelmaliere East	Wexford	I.	330
10, 14, 15	Ardcrony	6,428 3 35	Tipperary, N.R.	Lower Ormond	Borrisokane / Nenagh	II.	281,282
4, 7, 8	Ardea	7,726 0 0	Queen's Co.	Portnahinch	Mountmellick	I.	243,244
14, 17	Ardee	4,884 2 19	Louth	Ardee	Ardee	I.	171
42	Arderra	776 3 23	Kilkenny	Iverk	Waterford	I.	105
14, 19, 20, 21, 28, 29	Ardfert	6,796 0 5m / 3,336 2 2n	Kerry	Clanmaurice / Trughanacmy	Tralee	II.	167 / 205,206
135, 144	Ardfield	2,645 0 21o	Cork, W.R.	Ibane and Barryroe	Clonakilty	II.	148
82,88	Ardfinnan	1,812 3 18p	Tipperary, S.R.	Iffa and Offa West	Clogheen	II.	316,317
45	Ardglass	1,137 0 38	Down	Lecale Lower	Downpatrick	III.	178
17, 18, 24, 25	Ardkeen and Islands	4,800 2 27q	Down	Ards Upper	Downpatrick / Newtownards	III.	159
3, 8, 9	Ardkill	5,848 1 12r	Kildare	Carbury	Edenderry	I.	51
52, 53, 60	Ardmayle	4,940 2 2	Tipperary, S.R.	Middlethird	Cashel	II.	324
30, 35, 36, 37 / 38, 39, 40	Ardmore	24,215 1 38s	Waterford	Decies within Drum	Dungarvan / Youghal	II.	349, to 351
25, 26	Ardmulchan	3,582 1 39t	Meath	Skreen	Navan	I.	220
34, 35, 43, 44, 52, 53	Ardnageehy	16,334 2 32u	Cork, E.R.	Barrymore	Cork / Fermoy	II.	50,51
2 / 24, 31, 32, 37, 38	Ardnurcher or Horseleap	2,812 3 15 / 9,199 2 9	King's Co. / Westmeath	Kilcoursey / Moycashel	Mullingar / Tullamore	I.	140 / 276,277
8, 9,13,14,17,18 / 37, 42	Ardoyne	4,646 1 20 / 131 0 35 / 1,800 0 4	Carlow / / Wicklow	Forth / Rathvilly / Shillelagh	Carlow / / Shillelagh	I.	3 / 10 / 357
48, 56	Ardpatrick	624 0 13v	Limerick	Coshlea	Kilmallock	II.	236
24, 25, 31, 32	Ardquin and Islands	3,043 0 8w	Down	Ards Upper	Downpatrick	III.	159
103, 104, 113 / 114, 115, 122 / 123, 124	Ardrahan	10,239 2 6 / 3,077 2 36x / 4,630 1 33	Galway	Dunkellin / Kiltartan / Loughrea	Gort / Loughrea	IV.	26, 27 / 45 / 62, 63
35	Ardree	323 1 30y	Kildare	Kilkea and Moone	Athy	I.	59
8, 13	Ardristan	1,570 3 31	Carlow	Rathvilly	Carlow	I.	10
31	Ardsallagh	1,738 2 24z	Meath	Lower Navan	Navan	I.	214
3, 8	Ardskeagh	1,928 2 24	Cork, E.R.	Fermoy	Mallow	II.	76
5, 9, 10, 11, 16, 17, 18, 23, 24, 25, 32, 33, 34	Ardstraw	6,727 3 8aa / 44,974 1 3bb	Tyrone	Omagh West / Strabane Lower	Castlederg / Gortin / Omagh / Strabane	III.	315 / 318,319

A. R. P.

(a) Including 25 3 34 of water.
(b) Including 73 0 1 Lough Afoor. / 4,179 1 1 of Lough Corrib.
(c) Including 87 3 9 of water.
(d) Including 523 0 27 of Lough Neagh. / 56 1 3 detached portion.
(e) Including 2 2 19 Islands. / 21,000 0 39 of Lough Neagh.
(f) Including 2,370 3 17 detached portions.
(g) Including 89 3 16 of Glen Lough.
(h) Including 64 3 3 of water.
(i) Including 53 3 25 of Ballyhoe Lough. / 2 0 8 of Rahans Lough.

A. R. P.

(j) Including 70 0 37 of River Maigue tideway. / 56 1 5 of loughs.
(k) Including 553 3 27 of Lough Key. / 234 0 13 of River Boyle. / 295 2 10 of small loughs. / 634 1 16 land. (detached portion) / 75 0 19 of River Boyle. / 1 2 36 of Lough Naseer.
(l) Including 91 3 32 of water. / 1,371 1 39 detached portions.
(m) Including 52 2 11 of water.
(n) Including 218 0 17 detached portion.
(o) Including 99 3 9 detached portion.

A. R. P.

(p) Including 26 1 24 of River Suir.
(q) Including 33 3 28 of water.
(r) Including 3 0 10 of water.
(s) Including 225 1 33 detached portions.
(t) Including 25 0 20 of River Boyne.
(u) Including 5 1 16 detached portion.
(v) Including 154 0 30 detached portion.
(w) Including 80 2 15 of water.
(x) Including 20 0 7 of Caherglassaun Lough.
(y) Including 5 3 20 of River Barrow.
(z) Including 20 1 26 of River Boyne.
(aa) Including 30 2 17 of water.
(bb) Including 537 1 36 of water.

No. of Sheet of the Ordnance Survey Maps.	Parishes.	Area in Statute Measure.	County.	Barony.	Poor Law Union in 1857.	Townland Census of 1851, Part I.	
		A. R. P.				Vol.	Page
40, 45	Arklow . . .	8,126 3 0a	Wicklow . .	Arklow . . .	Rathdrum . .	I.	341
12	Armagh . .	{ 3,555 1 36 / 1,051 1 1b }	Armagh . .	{ Armagh . . / Oneilland West . }	Armagh . .	III. {	43 / 51
8, 9, 13, 14	Armoy . .	{ 8,522 1 33 / 1,143 0 31 }	Antrim . .	{ Cary . . . / Upper Dunluce . }	{ Ballycastle / Ballymoney }	III. {	11 / 18
14, 15, 18, 19	Artaine . .	953 2 7c	Dublin . .	Coolock . .	Dublin North .	I.	26
32, 37	Artramon .	2,376 3 16	Wexford . .	Shelmaliere East .	Wexford . .	I.	330
42,43,46,47,48,49 ⎱ 30,39 ⎰	Artrea . .	{ 18,616 3 11d / 2,283 2 23 }	Londonderry . Tyrone . .	Loughinsholin . Dungannon Upper .	{ Magherafelt / Cookstown }	III. {	238 / 305,306
2, 3, 10, 11, 19, 20	Askeaton . .	6,520 2 12e	Limerick . .	Connello Lower .	Rathkeale . .	II.	226,227
31, 37	Assey . .	1,218 2 24f	Meath . .	Lower Deece .	Navan . .	I.	191
60, 68, 75	Athassel and Relickmurry .	{ 12,207 2 37 / 561 2 3 }	Tipperary, S.R.	{ Clanwilliam . / Middlethird . }	{ Cashel . . / Tipperary . }	II. {	309,310 / 330
23, 24, 29, 30	Athboy . .	11,884 0 39	Meath . .	Lune . . .	Trim . .	I.	207
57, 70, 71, 83, 84 ⎱ 95, 96 ⎰	Athenry . .	{ 13,198 1 22 / 8,797 0 8g / 2,955 1 31 }	Galway . .	{ Athenry . . / Clare . . . / Dunkellin . }	{ Galway . . / Loughrea . }	IV. {	3, 4 / 17 / 27
31, 39	Athlacca . .	5,511 0 27	Limerick . .	Coshma . .	{ Croom . . / Kilmallock }	II.	241
19, 20, 32, 33 ⎱ 39, 41, 44 ⎰	Athleague .	{ 4,975 2 35h / 8,036 1 3i }	Galway . . Roscommon .	Killian . . Athlone . .	{ Mountbellew / Roscommon }	IV. {	43 / 179
25	Athlumney .	2,453 3 32j	Meath . .	Skreen . .	Navan . .	I.	220
40, 48	Athneasy .	{ 1,836 0 33 / 1,000 2 33 }	Limerick . .	{ Coshlea . . / Smallcounty . }	Kilmallock .	II. {	237 / 258
35, 41	Athnid . .	854 2 22	Tipperary, N.R.	Eliogarty . .	Thurles . .	II.	269
72, 73, 84, 85	Athnowen .	4,837 3 1k	Cork, E.R. .	East Muskerry .	{ Bandon . . / Cork . . }	II.	101
1, 4, 5 ⎱ 29, 35 ⎰	Attanagh .	{ 1,930 0 22 / 630 2 14 }	Kilkenny . . Queen's Co. .	Fassadinin . Clarmallagh .	{ Castlecomer / Abbeyleix . }	I. {	88 / 237
39, 40, 48, 49	Attymass .	11,154 1 24l	Mayo . .	Gallen . .	Ballina . .	IV.	146,147
28, 37, 45, 46, 53,54	Aughnish .	9,194 2 24m	Donegal . .	Kilmacrenan .	{ Letterkenny / Milford }	III.	122
86, 87, 98, 99	Aughrim. .	{ 2,021 1 2 / 5,230 3 36n }	Galway . .	{ Clonmacnowen / Kilconnell }	Ballinasloe .	IV. {	24 / 39
11, 16, 17	Aughrim. .	8,254 2 7o	Roscommon .	Roscommon .	Cark. on Shannon	IV.	207
27, 28, 33, 34	Bailieborough .	{ 40 3 10 / 12,375 0 11p }	Cavan . .	{ Castlerahan . / Clankee . }	Bailieborough .	III. {	67 / 71
5, 8	Baldongan .	857 3 11	Dublin . .	Balrothery East .	Balrothery .	I.	19
15	Baldoyle . .	1,235 3 39	Dublin . .	Coolock . .	Dublin North .	I.	26
49	Balfeaghan .	1,617 1 13	Meath . .	Upper Deece .	Celbridge .	I.	193
15	Balgriffin .	1,052 2 2	Dublin . .	Coolock . .	Dublin North .	I.	26
79, 80, 90, 91	Balla . .	5,509 1 25q	Mayo . .	Clanmorris .	Castlebar .	IV.	131,132
39, 40	Ballaghmoon .	2,177 3 27r	Kildare . .	Kilkea and Moone .	Athy . .	I.	59
31, 38, 45	Ballee . .	6,427 3 1	Down . .	Lecale Lower .	Downpatrick .	III.	178
8, 9	Balleen . .	2,559 1 4	Kilkenny . .	Galmoy . .	Urlingford .	I.	91
85, 86, 97, 98	Ballinaboy . .	{ 649 2 31 / 1,527 3 30 / 2,834 1 22 / 2,960 2 6 }	Cork, E.R. .	{ Cork . . . / East Muskerry . / Kerrycurrihy . / Kinalea . }	{ Cork . . / Kinsale . }	II. {	63 / 101 / 91 / 93
7	Ballinacarrig .	2,605 1 12	Carlow . .	Carlow . . .	Carlow . .	I.	1
22,23,28,29,30,34,	Ballinacor .	17,448 3 10s	Wicklow . .	Ballinacor South .	Rathdrum . .	I.	347,348
83, 110, 111, 124	Ballinadee .	{ 7,637 0 35 / 697 1 20t }	Cork, W.R. .	{ East Carbery, (E.D.) / West Muskerry . }	{ Bandon . . / Macroom . }	II. {	126 / 154
13, 18	Ballinamara .	3,839 1 23	Kilkenny . .	Crannagh . .	Kilkenny . .	I.	84
23, 32	Ballinard .	1,441 3 29	Limerick . .	Smallcounty .	Kilmallock .	II.	259
3, 12, 13 ⎱ 117,118,120, 121 ⎰	Ballinchalla .	{ 6,776 1 21u / 8,418 3 39v }	Galway . . Mayo . .	Ross . . . Kilmaine . .	Ballinrobe .	IV. {	72 / 151,152
31,32,40,41,49,50	Ballincuslane .	39,737 2 36	Kerry . .	Trughanacmy .	Tralee . .	II.	206
59, 62, 63, 67	Ballinderry .	10,891 1 26w	Antrim . .	Upper Massereene .	{ Lisburn . . / Lurgan . }	III.	29
47, 49 ⎱ 30, 31 ⎰	Ballinderry .	{ 5,907 1 1x / 2,268 2 16y }	Londonderry . Tyrone . .	Loughinsholin . Dungannon Upper .	{ Magherafelt / Cookstown }	III. {	239 / 306
34,35,36,48,49,50,62	Ballindoon and Islands	20,033 0 32z	Galway . .	Ballynahinch . .	Clifden . .	IV.	10,11
47, 48, 55, 56	Ballingaddy .	5,998 1 39	Limerick . .	Coshlea . .	Kilmallock .	II.	237
29, 30, 37, 38	Ballingarry .	17,732 1 1aa	Limerick . .	Connello Upper .	{ Croom . . / Newcastle . }	II.	230,231

No. of Sheet of the Ordnance Survey Maps.	Parishes.	Area in Statute Measure.	County.	Barony.	Poor Law Union in 1857.	Townland Census of 1851, Part I. Vol.	Page
		A. R. P.					
48, 49, 57	Ballingarry	6,113 2 30	Limerick	Coshlea	Kilmallock	II.	237
7, 8, 11	Ballingarry	6,683 1 10a	Tipperary, N.R.	Lower Ormond	{Borrisokane {Parsonstown}	II.	282
48, 49, 54, 55, 56	Ballingarry	13,714 1 33	Tipperary, S.R.	Slievardagh	Callan	II.	331,332
40, 41	Ballingly	765 0 39	Wexford	Shelmaliere West	Wexford	I.	332
32, 33	Ballinlough	2,340 0 31	Limerick	Smallcounty	Kilmallock	II.	259
3, 13, 14 109, 110, 117, 118	Ballinrobe	9,362 0 8b 17,540 3 32c	Galway Mayo	Ross Kilmaine	Ballinrobe	IV.	72 152,153
24, 25, 30, 31, 37	Ballintemple	10,657 3 2d	Cavan	Clanmahon	Cavan	III.	75
88, 89	Ballintemple	2,659 3 10e	Cork, E.R.	Imokilly	Middleton	II.	84
51, 52, 59, 60	Ballintemple	4,207 3 2	Tipperary, S.R.	Kilnamanagh Lower	Cashel	II.	322
39, 40	Ballintemple	4,087 1 23	Wicklow	Arklow	Rathdrum	I.	342
77, 88, 89, 90, 98, 99, 100, 108	Ballintober	730 1 19 22,236 1 21f	Mayo	{Burrishoole {Carra}	{Ballinrobe {Castlebar {Westport}	IV.	118 124,125
26, 27, 34	Ballintober	6,351 3 10	Roscommon	Castlereagh	Castlereagh	IV.	198
3, 4, 7, 8	Ballintoy	12,753 2 22g	Antrim	Cary	Ballycastle	III.	11,12
36,44,45,46,52,54,55	Ballinvoher	16,661 0 20h	Kerry	Corkaguiny	Dingle	II.	173,174
13, 17	Ballon	3,700 0 28	Carlow	Forth	Carlow	I.	3
19, 20, 25, 26	Ballyadams	6,513 2 19i 395 1 1	Queen's Co.	{Ballyadams {Stradbally}	Athy	I.	231 246
3	Ballyaghran	3,894 0 1	Londonderry	North East Liberties of Coleraine	Coleraine	III.	244,245
23, 24, 29, 30	Ballyanne	4,577 2 17	Wexford	Bantry	New Ross	I.	299
87, 88, 90, 91	Ballybacon	11,120 0 3j	Tipperary, S.R.	Iffa and Offa West	Clogheen	II.	317
7, 12	Ballybarrack	1,018 1 25	Louth	Upper Dundalk	Dundalk	I.	177
18, 19, 23, 24	Ballybay	8,560 0 22k 181 0 13	Monaghan	{Cremorne {Monaghan}	Castleblayney	III.	259 274
46, 47, 52	Ballyboggan	6,222 1 16	Meath	Upper Moyfenrath	Edenderry	I.	212
7	Ballyboghil	2,789 1 0	Dublin	Balrothery West	Balrothery	I.	22
29	Ballybought	1,440 3 32	Kildare	South Naas	Naas	I.	64
23, 24, 31, 32	Ballyboy	14,274 0 38l	King's Co.	Ballyboy	Parsonstown	I.	123
5, 7, 8	Ballyboys	1,435 3 6	Louth	Lower Dundalk	Dundalk	I.	175
26, 27, 30, 31	Ballybrackan	3,057 0 38m	Kildare	West Offaly	Athy	I.	71
34, 39	Ballybrazil	2,370 1 38	Wexford	Shelburne	New Ross	I.	327
43, 48	Ballybrennan	1,041 0 34n	Wexford	Forth	Wexford	I.	308
23	Ballybrood	2,355 0 0	Limerick	Clanwilliam	Limerick	II.	221
23	Ballybur	667 1 33	Kilkenny	Shillelogher	Kilkenny	I.	113
3, 4, 10, 11	Ballyburly	2,435 0 0o 5,433 0 6p	King's Co.	{Lower Philipstown {Warrenstown}	Edenderry	I.	142 144
22	Ballycahane	1,780 3 20q 637 2 39	Limerick	{Pubblebrien {Smallcounty}	Croom	II.	251 259
40, 41	Ballycahill	2,495 0 24 1,348 3 17	Tipperary, N.R.	{Eliogarty {Kilnamanagh Upper}	Thurles	II.	269 277
18, 19, 22	Ballycallan	6,834 1 26	Kilkenny	Crannagh	{Callan {Kilkenny}	I.	84, 85
11, 12, 16, 17	Ballycanew	3,627 2 26	Wexford	Gorey	Gorey	I.	315,316
9, 10, 14, 15, 20	Ballycarney	8,233 2 11r	Wexford	Scarawalsh	Enniscorthy	I.	322
76, 77	Ballyclerahan	1,044 0 16s	Tipperary, S.R.	Iffa and Offa East	Clonmel	II.	312
39, 40, 47, 48	Ballyclog	7,796 3 2t	Tyrone	Dungannon Upper	Cookstown	III.	306
24, 32	Ballyclogh	4,635 3 33u 5,074 3 6	Cork, E.R.	{Duhallow {Orrery and Kilmore}	{Kanturk {Mallow}	II.	67 106
32, 33, 37, 38	Ballyclug	8,268 3 18	Antrim	Lower Antrim	Ballymena	III.	3
9, 10, 17, 18	Ballycommon	6,641 0 30	King's Co.	Lower Philipstown	Tullamore	I.	142
41, 46	Ballyconnick	1,610 2 31	Wexford	Bargy	Wexford	I.	304
5, 9, 10	Ballyconry	1,205 3 20	Kerry	Iraghticonnor	Listowel	II.	190
39, 40, 45, 46	Ballycor	7,329 3 35	Antrim	Upper Antrim	{Antrim {Larne}	III.	6
7	Ballycrogue	370 1 22	Carlow	Carlow	Carlow	I.	1
31, 32, 38, 39	Ballyculter and Islands	5,177 1 24v	Down	Lecale Lower	Downpatrick	III.	178
53, 64, 65	Ballycurrany	3,939 0 12	Cork, E.R.	Barrymore	Middleton	II.	51
64, 75	Ballydeloher	2,101 1 20	Cork, E.R.	Barrymore	Cork	II.	51
19	Ballydeloughy	1,999 3 14	Cork, E.R.	Fermoy	Mitchelstown	II.	76
34, 35, 43, 44	Ballyduff	6,983 1 39w	Kerry	Corkaguiny	Dingle	II.	174
13, 17, 19, 22, 23	Ballyellin	744 0 24x 2,691 1 3y 1,522 1 35	Carlow	{Forth {Idrone East {St. Mullin's Lower}	{Carlow {New Ross}	I.	4 6 13

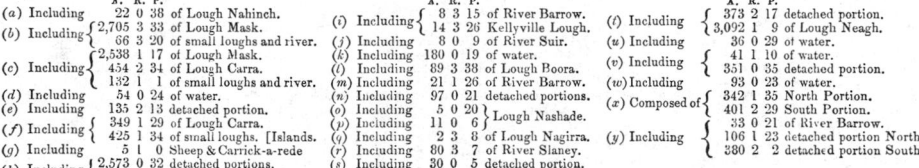

No. of Sheet of the Ordnance Survey Maps.	Parishes.	Area in Statute Measure.	County.	Barony.	Poor Law Union in 1857.	Townland Census of 1851, Part I.	
		A. R. P.				Vol.	Page
98, 112	Ballyfeard	3,461 3 25	Cork, E.R.	Kinalea	Kinsale	II.	93
17, 18	Ballyfermot	1,183 1 16a	Dublin	Uppercross	Dublin South	I.	39
112, 113	Ballyfoyle	2,882 2 4	Cork, E.R.	Kinalea	Kinsale	II.	94
28	Ballygarth	798 3 6b	Meath	Upper Duleek	Drogheda	I.	197
15, 16	Ballygibbon	3,293 3 27	Tipperary, N.R.	Upper Ormond	{ Borrisokane } { Nenagh }	II.	289
52, 60	Ballygriffin	2,862 0 34	Tipperary, S.R.	Clanwilliam	{ Cashel } { Tipperary }	II.	305
10, 18	Ballygunner	2,266 0 30	Waterford	Gaultiere	Waterford	II.	362
37, 41	Ballygurrim	1,923 3 29	Kilkenny	Ida	New Ross	I.	101
12, 18, 25	{ Ballyhalbert (alias) } { St. Andrews Islands }	4,011 3 39	Down	Ards Upper	Newtownards	III.	161
2, 3, 7, 8	Ballyhay	{ 2,438 1 15 } { 2,397 2 33c }	Cork, E.R.	{ Fermoy } { Orrery and Kilmore }	{ Kilmallock } { Mallow }	II.	{ 76 } { 106 }
78, 79, 89, 90	Ballyhean	7,674 3 27d	Mayo	Carra	Castlebar	IV.	125,126
8, 13, 14	Ballyheige	11,260 3 19e	Kerry	Clanmaurice	Tralee	II.	167,168
31, 32	Ballyhoge	{ 2,779 1 32 } { 1,489 1 26f }	Wexford	{ Bantry } { Shelmaliere West }	Enniscorthy,	I.	{ 299 } { 332 }
26, 27, 34, 35, 43	Ballyhooly	5,252 3 13	Cork. E.R.	Fermoy	Fermoy	II.	76
20, 21, 26, 27	Ballyhuskard	7,947 2 22	Wexford	Ballaghkeen	Enniscorthy	I.	291,292
25, 26, 27, 33, 34	Ballykean	{ 711 2 24 } { 12,201 2 37 }	King's Co.	{ Geashill } { Upper Philipstown }	{ Mountmellick } { Tullamore }	I.	{ 139 } { 143 }
29, 30, 34, 35, 39, 40	Ballykine	11,053 2 7	Wicklow	Ballinacor South	Rathdrum	I.	348
37, 44	Ballykinler	2,038 2 13	Down	Lecale Upper	Downpatrick	III.	180
49, 57	Ballylanders	7,717 1 19	Limerick	Coshlea	Mitchelstown	II.	237
15, 24, 25, 32	Ballylaneen	6,314 3 29g	Waterford	Decies without Drum	Kilmacthomas	II.	354
40, 45	Ballylannan	2,493 1 5	Wexford	Shelmaliere West	New Ross	I.	332
13	Ballylarkin	1,394 0 20	Kilkenny	Crannagh	Kilkenny	I.	85
28	Ballylinch	1,167 1 24h	Kilkenny	Gowran	Thomastown	I.	93
45, 51, 52	Ballylinny	5,683 3 22i	Antrim	Lower Belfast	Antrim	III.	7
22, 23, 29, 30	Ballyloughloe	13,577 2 38j	Westmeath	Clonlonan	Athlone	I.	260,261
35, 36, 38, 39	Ballymacart	2,538 0 33k	Waterford	Decies within Drum	{ Dungarvan } { Youghal }	II.	351
22, 29, 30, 38, 39	Ballymacelligott	14,018 0 5	Kerry	Trughanacmy	Tralee	II.	206,207
37, 38, 41, 42	Ballymachugh	7,728 2 3l	Cavan	Clanmahon	Cavan	III.	75, 76
15, 16, 21, 22, 27	Ballymackey	9,713 0 20	Tipperary, N.R.	Upper Ormond	Nenagh	II.	289,290
13, 14, 18, 19	Ballymacormick	{ 4,035 1 6 } { 4,890 2 32 }	Longford	{ Ardagh } { Moydow }	Longford	I.	{ 152 } { 160, 161 }
59, 60, 72, 73, 85, 86	Ballymacward	{ 7,987 1 37 } { 9,271 0 17m }	Galway	{ Kilconnell } { Tiaquin }	{ Ballinasloe } { Loughrea } { Mountbellew }	IV.	{ 39 } { 75, 76 }
4, 11, 12	Ballymacwilliam	4,976 2 11	King's Co.	Warrenstown	Edenderry	I.	144
3, 6, 7	Ballymadun	3,438 2 20	Dublin	Balrothery West	Dunshaughlin	I.	22
32	Ballymagarvey	915 1 28	Meath	Lower Duleek	Navan	I.	194
44, 50	Ballymaglassan	3,476 1 7	Meath	Ratoath	Dunshaughlin	I.	217
21, 24	Ballymakenny	{ 848 1 7n } { 732 3 10 }	Louth	{ Drogheda } { Ferrard }	Drogheda	I.	{ 175 } { 179 }
23	Ballymany	506 2 34	Kildare	East Offaly	Naas	I.	69
50, 51, 56	Ballymartin	{ 385 2 0 } { 2,421 0 37o }	Antrim	{ Lower Belfast } { Upper Belfast }	Antrim	III.	{ 7 } { 9 }
97, 98, 111, 112	Ballymartle	{ 5,067 2 4 } { 435 1 21 }	Cork, E.R.	{ Kinalea } { Kinsale }	Kinsale	II.	{ 94 } { 99 }
1, 4, 5, 7, 8	Ballymascanlan	{ 15,820 0 29p } { 177 1 11 }	Louth	{ Lower Dundalk } { Upper Dundalk }	Dundalk	I.	{ 175,176 } { 177 }
40, 41	Ballymitty	1,364 3 38	Wexford	Shelmaliere West	Wexford	I.	332
96, 109, 110	Ballymodan	{ 3,114 0 16 } { 4,966 1 5 }	Cork, W.R.	{ East Carbery (E.D.) } { Kinalmeaky }	Bandon	II.	{ 126,127 } { 151 }
108, 109, 121	Ballymoney	7,309 3 17q	Cork, W.R.	East Carbery (E.D.)	Dunmanway	II.	127
11, 12, 16, 17, 22 }	Ballymoney	{ 753 0 38 } { 21,303 3 27r } { 632 1 18s }	Antrim	{ Kilconway } { Upper Dunluce } { North-East Liberties of Coleraine }	Ballymoney	III.	{ 25 } { 18, 19 } { 245 }
8, 12	Londonderry						
13, 14, 17, 18, 22	Ballymore	14,158 3 32t	Armagh	Orior Lower	{ Banbridge } { Newry }	III.	55, 56
16, 17, 23, 24, 30, 31	Ballymore	10,465 2 7u	Westmeath	Rathconrath	{ Athlone } { Ballymahon }	I.	281,282
47, 48, 52	Ballymore	2,525 1 21	Wexford	Forth	Wexford	I.	308
24, 25, 29	Ballymore Eustace	4,203 2 2v	Kildare	South Naas	Naas	I.	64

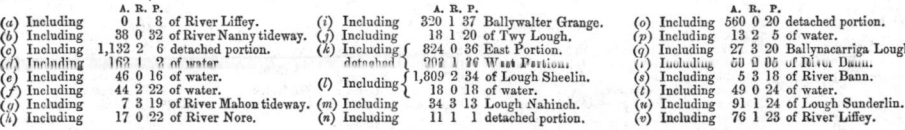

No. of Sheet of the Ordnance Survey Maps.	Parishes.	Area in Statute Measure. A. R. P.	County.	Barony.	Poor Law Union in 1857.	Townland Census of 1851, Part I. Vol.	Page
17, 24	Ballymorin	2,204 3 22	Westmeath	Rathconrath	Mullingar	I.	282
42, 47, 48, 53, 54	Ballymurreen	3,845 3 39a	Tipperary, N.R.	Eliogarty	Thurles	II.	269
20, 21, 24, 25	Ballymyre	7,381 1 18	Armagh	Fews Upper	Newry	III.	48
24	Ballynaclogh	1,091 3 25b	Limerick	Coonagh	Tipperary	II.	233,234
21, 27	Ballynaclogh	3,869 2 4	Tipperary, N.R.	Upper Ormond	Nenagh	II.	290
94, 95, 102, 103	Ballynacourty & Islands	6,293 0 22c	Galway	Dunkellin	Galway	IV.	27
35, 44, 45, 54, 55	Ballynacourty	5,318 1 17d	Kerry	Corkaguiny	Dingle	II.	174
1, 3	Ballynadrumny	4,285 1 20	Kildare	Carbury	Edenderry	I.	51
9, 13	Ballynafagh	4,154 3 5e	Kildare	Clane	Naas	I.	53
30, 39, 48, 60	Ballynahaglish	12,658 3 11f	Mayo	Tirawley	Ballina	IV.	164
28	Ballynahaglish	3,005 1 29	Kerry	Trughanacmy	Tralee	II.	207
6, 7, 8, 18, 19 }	Ballynakill	12,571 1 6g	Galway	} Ballymoe	{ Castlereagh	IV.	5
34, 38		2,006 3 8h	Roscommon		{ Glennamaddy { Roscommon		191
9,10,11,22,23,24,37	Ballynakill & Islands	49,052 3 6i	Galway	Ballynahinch	Clifden	IV.	11,12
32, 45, 46	Ballynakill	5,220 3 19j	Galway	Killian	Mountbellew	IV.	43
115,116,117,124, 125,126,130,131, 132, 134, 135 }	Ballynakill	59,606 2 19k	Galway	Leitrim	{ Loughrea { Portumna	IV.	50 to 52
11, 12, 18, 19, 20	Ballynakill	6,760 3 17l	King's Co.	Coolestown	Edenderry	I.	132
27	Ballynakill	4,589 2 22m	Sligo	Tirerrill	Sligo	IV.	237
9, 10, 17, 18	Ballynakill	1,877 0 22	Waterford	Gaultiere	Waterford	II.	362
32	Ballynamona	1,497 3 37	Limerick	Smallcounty	Kilmallock	II.	259
35,36,39,40,41,44,45	Ballynascreen	32,520 1 8	Londonderry	Loughinsholin	Magherafelt	III.	238,239
32	Ballynaslaney	1,765 2 29 / 879 3 6	} Wexford	{ Ballaghkeen { Shelmaliere East	Enniscorthy	I.	292 / 330
45, 46, 54, 55	Ballynoe	7,715 2 27	Cork, E.R.	Kinnatalloon	Fermoy	II.	97
40, 45, 46, 51, 52	Ballynure	8,540 3 11n	Antrim	Lower Belfast	{ Antrim { Larne	III.	7
14, 20, 21, 26	Ballynure	7,404 1 21	Wicklow	Upper Talbotstown	Baltinglass	I.	361,362
66, 76, 77, 89	Ballyoughtera	4,532 1 29o	Cork, E.R.	Imokilly	Middleton	II.	84
98, 99, 100, 108, 109, 110, 117 }	Ballyovey	27,622 1 7p	Mayo	Carra	Ballinrobe	IV.	126
25, 32	Ballyphilip	2,430 0 17	Down	Ards Upper	Downpatrick	III.	159,160
6, 7, 11, 12 }	Ballyrashane	2,689 0 13	Antrim	Lower Dunluce	{ Ballymoney	III.	15
3, 4, 7, 8 }		3,656 0 23	Londonderry	North-East Liberties of Coleraine	{ Coleraine		245
18, 23, 24, 30	Ballyroan	9,682 0 1	Queen's Co.	Cullenagh	Abbeyleix	I.	239
19, 20, 25, 26, 33	Ballysadare	7,560 3 4q / 8,464 1 2r	} Sligo	{ Leyny { Tirerrill	{ Sligo { Tobercurry	IV.	230 / 237,238
21, 22, 29, 30	Ballysakeery	12,692 0 2s	Mayo	Tirawley	Ballina	IV.	164,165
23, 27, 28	Ballysax	7,207 2 3t	Kildare	East Offaly	{ Athy { Naas	I.	69
41, 49	Ballyscaddan	943 1 38	Limerick	Coshlea	Kilmallock	II.	238
36, 42 }	Ballyscullion	2,132 3 4u	Antrim	Upper Toome	Ballymena	III.	33
33, 37, 38, 42 }		11,035 2 2v	Londonderry	Loughinsholin	Magherafelt		239,240
36, 37, 42, 43	Ballyscullion, Grange of	4,279 1 0w	Antrim	Upper Toome	Ballymena	III.	33
29, 30, 38, 39	Ballyseedy	3,489 0 18	Kerry	Trughanacmy	Tralee	II.	207,208
22, 27, 28, 31, 32	Ballyshannon	564 1 4x / 2,250 3 6	Kildare	{ East Offaly { West Offaly	{ Athy { Naas	I.	69 / 72
47, 53, 61	Ballysheehan	9,215 2 2	Tipperary, S.R.	Middlethird	Cashel	II.	324,325
65	Ballyspillane	2,088 0 37	Cork, E.R.	Barrymore	Middleton	II.	51
21, 27, 28	Ballysumaghan	4,216 2 24y	Sligo	Tirerrill	Sligo	IV.	238
42	Ballytarsney	895 3 25	Kilkenny	Iverk	Waterford	I.	105
26, 27, 30, 31	Ballytobin	2,393 2 3	Kilkenny	Kells	Callan	I.	107
25, 32	Ballytrustan	1,681 3 12z	Down	Ards Upper	Downpatrick	III.	160
33, 27, 28, 33	Ballyvaldon	3,911 0 37	Wexford	Ballaghkeen	Enniscorthy	I.	292
33	Ballyvalloo	1,891 2 13	Wexford	Ballaghkeen	Enniscorthy	I.	292
57,58,59,68,69,70	Ballyvourney	26,602 2 6	Cork, W.R.	West Muskerry	Macroom	II.	154
7, 12, 18	Ballywalter	3,378 3 33aa	Down	Ards Upper	Newtownards	III.	160
2, 6 }	Ballywillin	1,616 3 37bb	Antrim	Lower Dunluce	} Coleraine	III.	15, 16
3, 4 }		3,056 2 20	Londonderry	North East Liberties of Coleraine			245
5, 10	Balraheen	3,374 1 32	Kildare	Ikeathy & Oughterany	Celbridge	I.	56
16, 17, 23, 24	Balrathboyne }	3,392 1 27 / 599 2 23	} Meath	{ Upper Kells { Lower Navan	} Kells	I.	204 / 214
1, 2, 4, 5, 8	Balrothery	6,884 1 38	Dublin	Balrothery East	Balrothery	I.	19

A. R. P.

(a) Including 160 1 10 detached portion.
(b) Including 241 0 21 detached portions.
(c) Including 172 1 20 detached portion.
(d) Including 28 2 5 of water.
(e) Including 44 1 8 of reservoir.
(f) Including { 41 0 8 of Lough Conn. 656 0 13 of Lough Cuilin. 261 1 12 of River Moy & small loughs.
(g) Including 104 3 38 of water.
(h) Including 27 1 36 River Suck.
(i) Including { 416 3 1 Kylemore Lough. 432 1 28 Lough Fee. 240 3 24 of Lough Inagh. 606 1 24 of small loughs.

(j) Including 4 2 31 of water.
(k) Including { 137 3 16 of small loughs. 3,980 3 1 of Lough Derg.
(l) Composed of { 3,350 2 14 East Portion. 3,410 1 3 West Portion.
(m) Including 43 0 5 of water.
(n) Including 22 0 22 of water.
(o) Including { 84 3 2 detached portion. 29 0 14 Lough Aderry.
(p) Including { 6,602 3 26 of Lough Mask. 1,177 0 39 of Lough Carra. 313 1 22 of small loughs.
(q) Including 38 2 0 of water.
(r) Including { 4 2 27 of t'deway. 187 0 20 of loughs and river.

(s) Including 190 1 37 of water.
(t) Including 2,141 1 30 Part of the Curragh.
(u) Including 1,203 0 32 of Lough Beg.
(v) Including { 847 0 0 of Lough Beg. 73 1 13 of River Bann. 11 0 10 of River Bann.
(w) Including 4 3 32 of Lough Beg.
(x) Including 189 1 25 detached portion.
(y) Including 14 1 38 Castle Lough.
(z) Including 3 detached portions, viz., { 236 0 39 East part. 181 0 34 Middle part. 460 0 30 West part.
(aa) Including 366 1 3 detached portion.
(bb) Including 24 1 9 Skerry Islands.

No. of Sheet of the Ordnance Survey Maps.	Parishes.	Area in Statute Measure.			County.	Barony.	Poor Law Union in 1857.	Townland Census of 1851, Part I.	
		A.	R.	P.				Vol.	Page
1, 4, 5	Balscaddan	3,948	0	38	Dublin	Balrothery East	Balrothery	I.	20
31, 37	Balsoon	1,269	1	5a	Meath	Lower Deece	Navan / Trim	I.	191
10, 16, 17, 25	Balteagh	10,408	3	3b	Londonderry	Keenaght	New Tⁿ Limavady	III.	234
4 / 26, 27, 32 }	Baltinglass	234 / 6,149	0 / 0	5 / 26	Carlow / Wicklow	Rathvilly / Upper Talbotstown	} Baltinglass	I.	10 / 362
23, 24, 30, 31, 34, 35	Banagher	17,747 / 6,158	1 / 2	2 / 10	} Londonderry	Keenaght / Tirkeeran	Londonderry / New Tⁿ Limavady	III.	234 / 247
1, 2, 3, 5, 6 / 45, 46, 50 }	Bangor and Islands	12,957 / 4,069	0 / 3	31 / 0c	} Down	Ards Lower / Lower Castlereagh	} Newtownards	III.	157 / 161
	Bannow	6,551	0	23	Wexford	Bargy	Wexford	I.	304
70, 77	Baptistgrange	2,857	3	37d	Tipperary, S.R.	Middlethird	Cashel / Clonmel	II.	325
87	Barnahely	894	3	2	Cork, E.R.	Kerrycurrihy	Cork	II.	91
28, 29	Barnane-ely	2,166	3	5	Tipperary, N.R.	Ikerrin	Roscrea	II.	274
17, 18, 20, 21, 23	Barragh	11,458 / 1,838	0 / 3	7e / 15f	} Carlow	Forth / St. Mullin's Upper	Carlow / Enniscorthy / Shillelagh	I.	4 / 14
69, 70	Barrettsgrange	1,051	3	37	Tipperary, S.R.	Middlethird	Cashel	II.	325
10, 19, 20	Barr of Inch or Mintiaghs	3,258	2	26g	Donegal	Inishowen West	Inishowen	III.	121
6	Barronstown	2,208	2	25h	Louth	Upper Dundalk	Dundalk	I.	177
20, 21, 22, 27, 28	Baslick	15,395	3	22	Roscommon	Castlereagh	Castlereagh	IV.	199
122,123,128,129,133	Beagh	14,581	3	15i	Galway	Kiltartan	Gort	IV.	46
24, 25	Beaulieu	1,228	0	9j	Louth	Ferrard	Drogheda	I.	180
30, 31	Bective	3,385	3	4k	Meath	Upper Navan	Navan	I.	216
92, 93, 102, 103	Bekan	15,372	3	17l	Mayo	Costello	Claremorris	IV.	138,139
36, 38	Belan	1,197	2	10	Kildare	Kilkea and Moone	Athy	I.	59
28, 29, 42, 43, 56, 57	Belclare	7,847	0	35m	Galway	Clare	Tuam	IV.	17, 18
3, 4, 8, 9	Belleek and Islands	12,848	2	8n	Fermanagh	Lurg	Ballyshannon	III.	203,204
3, 7, 8, 12	Billy	8,069 / 9,260	0 / 3	16o / 13p	} Antrim	Cary / Lower Dunluce	Ballycastle / Ballymoney / Coleraine	III.	12, 13 / 16
35, 36, 38	Birr	7,217	2	11	King's Co.	Ballybritt	Parsonstown	I.	125
15, 19, 20	Blackrath	1,758	2	27q	Kilkenny	Gowran	Kilkenny	I.	93
20, 24	Blanchvilleskill	854	1	4	Kilkenny	Gowran	Kilkenny	I.	93
8, 14, 15 / 64, 67, 68 }	Blaris	4,805 / 3,064 / 2,827	3 / 0 / 1	22r / 7s / 6t	} Down / Antrim	Lower Iveagh, Up. pt. / Upper Castlereagh / Upper Massereene	} Lisburn	III.	169 / 164 / 30
1, 5, 6, 10, 11	Blessington	15,780	3	7	Wicklow	Lower Talbotstown	Naas	I.	358
14, 19	Bodenstown	2,831	3	7u	Kildare	North Naas	Naas	I.	62
11, 12, 13, 18, 19, / 20, 26, 27, 28 }	Bodoney Lower	47,921	3	10v	Tyrone	Strabane Upper	Gortin	III.	323,324
7, 8, 10, 11, 12, 13, / 17, 18, 19 }	Bodoney Upper	38,208	1	25w	Tyrone	Strabane Upper	Gortin	III.	324
77, 89	Bohillane	1,096	2	39	Cork, E.R.	Imokilly	Middleton	II.	84
13,14,19,20,21,25,26	Boho	8,907 / 6,151	1 / 1	38x / 18y	} Fermanagh	Clanawley / Magheraboy	Ballyshannon / Enniskillen	III.	189 / 209,210
71, 80	Bohola	8,674	1	18	Mayo	Gallen	Castlebar / Swineford	IV.	147
23	Booterstown	70 / 471	0 / 0	35 / 13	} Dublin	Dublin / Rathdown	} Rathdown	I.	30 / 35
28	Bordwell	113 / 2,690	2 / 2	13 / 30z	} Queen's Co.	Clandonagh / Clarmallagh	Abbeyleix / Donaghmore	I.	233 / 237
7, 8, 12, 13, 18	Borris	7,049	1	28	Queen's Co.	Maryborough East	Mountmellick	I.	240,241
8, 12	Borrismore	1,271	1	16	Kilkenny	Galmoy	Urlingford	I.	92
46, 47 / 22, 28 }	Borrisnafarney	1,382 / 3,157	3 / 1	4 / 6	} King's Co. / Tipperary, N.R.	Clonlisk / Ikerrin	} Roscrea	I. / II.	129 / 274
6, 7, 9, 10	Borrisokane	5,128	1	21	Tipperary, N.R.	Lower Ormond	Borrisokane	II.	282
17, 18, 22, 23, 24	Bourney	12,981	1	38aa	Tipperary, N.R.	Ikerrin	Roscrea	II.	274
16, 17, 23, 24, 25, 30	Bovevagh	18,005	1	26bb	Londonderry	Keenaght	New Tⁿ Limavady	III.	235
1, 3, 5, 6, 9, 10	Boyle	20,736	2	21cc	Roscommon	Boyle	Boyle	IV.	193,194
5, 6, 7, 17, 18, 19	Boyounagh	11,917 / 3,914	2 / 1	7dd / 18	} Galway	Ballymoe / Tiaquin	} Glennamaddy	IV.	6 / 76
5, 6, 9, 10, 11, 16, 17	Boystown	25,134	2	3ee	Wicklow	Lower Talbotstown	Baltinglass / Naas	I.	359
68	Boytonrath	991	2	23	Tipperary, S.R.	Middlethird	Cashel	II.	325
28, 29	Brannockstown	888	3	18ff	Kildare	South Naas	Naas	I.	64

	A.	R.	P.				A.	R.	P.				A.	R.	P.	
(a) Including {	17 / 33	2 / 0	0 of River Boyne. / 4 detached portion.		(m) Including {	2,133 / 0	0 / 1	13 detached portions. / 12 of water.		(w) Including	150	2	9 of water.				
(b) Including	14	3	12 of water.		(n) Including {	511 / 2,064	2 / 1	34 of River Erne & small loughs. / 37 of Lower Lough Erne.		(x) Including	61	3	27 of water.				
(c) Including	22	2	35 of water.							(y) Including	96	0	31 of water.				
(d) Including	1,140	2	17 detached portion.		(o) Including	11	0	10 of water.		(z) Including	27	1	20 Grantstown Lough.				
(e) Including	13	2	14 of River Slaney.		(p) Including	19	2	24 of water.		(aa) Including	803	2	34 detached portion.				
(f) Including	8	1	14 of River Slaney.		(q) { North Portion, / South Portion,	839 / 918	3 / 3	13 / 14		(bb) Including	1,039	2	10 detached portion.				
(g) Including	59	3	26 of water.		Including	0	0	38 of River Nore.		(cc) Including {	743 / 218 / 325 / 151	2 / 3 / 3 / 1	0 of Lough Key. / 9 of Lough Gara. / 12 detached portion. / 4 of Lough Arrow.				
(h) Including	4	3	36 of Cortial Lough.			7	1	21 of River Nore.									
(i) Including {	274 / 742	2 / 3	20 of small loughs. / 28 of Lough Cooter.		(r) Including	19	1	7 of water.									
(j) Including {	218 / 9	3 / 0	32 of River Boyne tideway. / 16 Lake Beaulieu.		(s) Including	20	2	2 of water.			134	1	25 of small loughs.				
(k) Including	31	1	29 of River Boyne.		(t) Including	28	1	31 of water.		(dd) Including	18	2	2 of water.				
(l) Including {	170 / 637	2 / 0	36 of Mannin Lake. / 12 of small loughs.		(u) Including	33	1	0 of River Liffey.		(ee) Including	38	0	25 of water.				
					(v) Including	178	2	4 of water.		(ff) Including	24	2	36 of River Liffey.				

No. of Sheet of the Ordnance Survey Maps.	Parishes.	Area in Statute Measure.	County.	Barony.	Poor Law Union in 1857.	Townland Census of 1851, Part I.	
		A. R. P.				Vol.	Page
4, 7, 8	Bray . .	2,985 3 34	Wicklow . .	Rathdown . .	Rathdown . .	I.	354,355
70, 78, 79	Breaghwy . .	5,265 3 1a	Mayo . .	Carra . .	Castlebar . .	IV.	126,127
16	Bregoge . .	1,332 3 0	Cork, E.R. .	Orrery and Kilmore .	Mallow . .	II.	106
61	Brickendown .	1,254 1 24	Tipperary, S.R. .	Middlethird . .	Cashel . .	II.	325
13, 14, 18, 19	Brideschurch .	2,217 0 24b	Kildare . .	Clane . .	Naas . .	I.	53
26, 34, 43	Bridgetown . .	3,239 2 30c	Cork, E.R. .	Fermoy . .	Fermoy . .	II.	77
37, 38, 44, 45	Bright . .	5,544 1 0d	Down . .	Lecale Upper . .	Downpatrick .	III.	180
10, 11, 19, 20	Brigown . .	15,212 1 2	Cork, E.R. .	Condons & Clangibbon	Mitchelstown .	II.	59,60
96, 97	Brinny . .	{ 853 0 26	Cork, E.R. .	Kinalea . .	} Bandon . .	II. {	94
		{ 308 0 14	} Cork, W.R. .	{ East Carbery (E.D.)			127
		{ 3,707 0 35		{ Kinalmeaky . .			151,152
45, 54	Britway . .	{ 3,670 2 0	} Cork, E.R. .	{ Barrymore . .	{ Fermoy . . }	II. {	51, 52
		{ 339 1 11		{ Kinnatalloon . .	{ Middleton }		98
23, 24, 31, 32	Brosna . .	11,959 2 35e	Kerry . .	Trughanacmy . .	Tralee . .	II.	208
26, 32	Brownstown . .	1,198 3 9	Meath . .	Skreen . .	Navan . .	I.	220
31, 32, 39, 40	Bruff . .	1,330 2 19	Limerick . .	Coshma . .	Kilmallock .	II.	242
66, 73	Bruis . .	3,698 2 19	Tipperary, S.R. .	Clanwilliam . .	Tipperary . .	II.	305
38, 39, 46, 47	Bruree . .	{ 6,685 0 19	} Limerick . .	{ Connello Upper .	} Kilmallock .	II. {	231
		{ 2,209 3 27		{ Coshma . .			242
97, 98	Bullaun . .	1,728 3 20	Galway . .	Loughrea . .	Loughrea . .	IV.	63
23, 24, 29, 30	Bumlin . .	6,582 1 12f	Roscommon .	Roscommon . .	Strokestown .	IV.	208
15, 22	Bunown . .	6,887 3 27g	Westmeath . .	Kilkenny West .	Athlone . .	I.	272
51, 52, 61, 62	Bunratty and Islands	2,754 2 29h	Clare . .	Bunratty Lower .	Ennis . .	II.	3
42, 43, 48, 49	Buolick . .	7,116 1 11	Tipperary, S.R. .	Slievardagh . .	Urlingford .	II.	332
5, 9, 10	Burgage . .	1,876 3 16i	Wicklow . .	Lower Talbotstown .	Naas . .	I.	359
19, 20, 25, 26	Burgesbeg . .	4,980 1 31	Tipperary, N.R. .	Owney and Arra .	Nenagh . .	II.	293,294
22, 23, 27	Burnchurch . .	3,363 2 37	Kilkenny . .	Shillelogher . .	Callan . .	I.	113
89, 90, 99, 100, 110	Burriscarra . .	5,760 1 30j	Mayo . .	Carra . .	{ Ballinrobe . } Castlebar	IV. {	127
							118
45, 46, 56, 57, 58, 65,66,67,68,76,77 }	Burrishoole . .	55,239 2 4k	Mayo . .	Burrishoole . .	Newport . .	IV.	to 120
16, 17, 23	Burry . .	3,694 2 27	Meath . .	Upper Kells . .	Kells . .	I.	205
38, 39, 46, 47	Burt . .	10,672 2 26	Donegal . .	Inishowen West .	Londonderry .	III.	119,120
16, 17, 24, 25	Buttevant . .	11,582 3 22	Cork, E. R. .	Orrery and Kilmore .	Mallow . .	II.	107
3, 4	Cadamstown . .	5,032 3 8	Kildare . .	Carbury . .	Edenderry .	I.	51
69, 79, 80, 88, 89	Caher . .	19,100 1 17l	Kerry . .	Iveragh . .	Cahersiveen .	II.	193,194
75, 76, 81, 82	Caher . .	{ 133 2 35	} Tipperary, S.R. .	{ Iffa and Offa East .	{ Clonmel . . }	II. {	312
		{ 13,513 1 34m		{ Iffa and Offa West .	{ Clogheen . . }		317,318
118, 119, 131, } 132, 133, 141 }	Caheragh . .	{ 1,406 0 7	} Cork, W.R. .	{ West Carbery (E.D.)	} Skibbereen .	II. {	137
		{ 22,119 3 4		{ West Carbery (W.D.)			141,142
13, 22	Caheravally . .	3,833 1 29n	Limerick . .	Clanwilliam . .	Limerick . .	II.	221
14, 15, 23	Caherconlish . .	8,172 3 5	Limerick . .	Clanwilliam . .	Limerick . .	II.	222
23, 32	Cahercorney . .	1,546 0 36	Limerick . .	Smallcounty . .	Kilmallock .	II.	259
17, 24, 25	Caherduggan . .	6,131 1 39	Cork, E.R. .	Fermoy . .	Mallow . .	II.	77
23	Caherelly . .	2,718 3 23	Limerick . .	Clanwilliam . .	Limerick . .	II.	222
64, 74, 75	Caherlag . .	3,556 3 16o	Cork, E.R. .	Barrymore . .	{ Cork . . } Middleton	II. {	52
13, 14, 22, 23	Cahernarry . .	2,478 0 38	Limerick . .	Clanwilliam . .	Limerick . .	II.	222,223
6, 7, 8, 11, 12, } 13, 17, 18 }	Calary . .	{ 11,352 1 7p	} Wicklow . .	{ Ballinacor North .	{ Rathdrum . . }	I. {	346
		{ 5,153 0 3		{ Newcastle . .	{ }		350
		{ 3,078 2 3		{ Rathdown . .	{ Rathdown . . }		355
22, 26	Callan . .	5,633 3 36	Kilkenny . .	Callan . . .	Callan . .	I.	83, 84
8, 9, 14, 15	Calry . .	11,510 2 11q	Sligo . .	Carbury . .	Sligo . .	IV.	220
44, 45, 47,48	Cam . .	12,403 1 13r	Roscommon .	Athlone . .	Athlone . .	IV.	179,180
55, 58, 59	Camlin . .	6,417 1 25s	Antrim . .	Upper Massereene .	Antrim . .	III.	30
4, 5, 10	Camus . .	7,505 2 37t	Tyrone . .	Strabane Lower .	Strabane . .	III.	320
71, 72, 83	Cannaway . .	5,225 0 38u	Cork, E.R. .	East Muskerry . .	Macroom . .	II.	102
20	Cappagh . .	1,267 2 23v	Limerick . .	Connello Lower .	Rathkeale .	II.	227
17, 18, 25, 26, 27, } 34, 35, 36, 43 }	Cappagh . .	{ 3,871 2 12w	} Tyrone . .	{ Omagh East . .	} Omagh . .	III. {	310
		{ 33,798 3 17x		{ Strabane Upper .			325
18	Cappoge . .	1,283 2 14	Louth . .	Ardee . .	Ardee . .	I.	171
3, 7, 8, 12	Carbury . .	4,796 3 9y	Kildare . .	Carbury . .	Edenderry .	I.	51
41, 42, 55, 56	Cargin . .	3,609 2 10z	Galway . .	Clare . .	Tuam . .	IV.	18
1, 2, 4, 5, 8, 9	Carlingford . .	20,049 3 15aa	Louth . .	Lower Dundalk .	Dundalk . .	I.	176,177

	A. R. P.					A. R. P.			A. R. P.
(a) Including	54 0 2 of water.				(r) Including	570 0 39 of water.			
(b) Including	21 3 0 of River Liffey.				(s) Including	708 1 4 of Lough Neagh.			
(c) Including	36 1 9 of water.	(k) Including	{ 26 3 20 of Beltra Lough.			{ 20 2 26 Lyon's Island.			
(d) Including	17 0 14 of water.		{ 1,036 2 12 Lougl. Feeagh.		(t) Including	{ 103 3 19 of River Mourne.			
(e) Including	53 1 16 of water.		{ 426 0 15 Furnace Lough.			{ 5 3 24 of tideway.			
(f) Including	20 0 36 of water.		{ 314 0 19 of small loughs.		(u) Including	62 1 34 of River Lee.			
(g) Including	{ 3,529 2 36 of Lough Ree.	(l) Including	{ 5,933 0 9 detached portion.		(v) Including	116 1 10 detached portion.			
	{ 23 2 16 of Creggan Lough.		{ 217 1 32 Beginish Island.		(w) Including	64 2 39 of water.			
(h) Including	7 0 17 of Owenogarney River	(m) Including	77 3 35 of River Suir.		(x) Including	2:12 0 14 of water.			
(i) Including	35 2 22 of water. [tideway.	(n) Including	134 1 11 detached portion.		(y) Including	19 1 8 of water.			
(j) Including	{ 1,403 3 26 of Lough Carra.	(o) Including	753 0 37 detached portion.		(z) Including	742 2 12 of Lough Corrib.			
	{ 136 3 28 of small loughs.	(p) Including	99 2 27 of water.		(aa) Including	65 1 24 of tideway.			
		(q) Including	{ 1,536 0 2 of Lough Gill.						
			{ 98 1 32 of small loughs.						

No. of Sheet of the Ordnance Survey Maps.	Parishes.	Area in Statute Measure.			County.	Barony.	Poor Law Union in 1857.	Townland Census of 1851, Part I.	
		A.	R.	P.				Vol.	Page
2, 7	Carlow . .	3,330	1	34a	Carlow .	Carlow . .	Carlow .	I.	1
28	Carn . .	1,457	1	38	Kildare .	East Offaly .	{ Athy . } { Naas . }	I.	69
53	Carn . .	1,963	1	22	Wexford .	Forth .	Wexford .	I.	309
30, 34, 35	Carnagh . .	2,106	0	39	Wexford .	Bantry .	New Ross .	I.	299
23, 24, 28, 29	Carnalway .	3,840	3	1b	Kildare .	South Naas .	Naas . .	I.	64
29, 30, 34, 35	Carncastle .	9,725	2	25	Antrim .	Upper Glenarm .	Larne . .	III.	24
2, 5, 6, 10 43, 46, 47 }	Carnew . .	{ 560 7,555 15,350 }	{ 1 1 1 }	{ 14c 16 26 }	Wexford . Wicklow .	{ Gorey . } { Scarawalsh . } { Shillelagh . }	{ Gorey } { Shillelagh . }	I.	{ 316 322 357 }
51, 52, 56, 57	Carnmoney .	8,937	1	12	Antrim .	Lower Belfast .	Belfast . .	III.	7, 8
44, 45, 52, 53, 59, 60, 61, 66 }	Carnteel .	13,431	2	31d	Tyrone .	Dungannon Lower .	{ Clogher . } { Dungannon }	III.	297,298
13, 18, 19	Carragh .	3,733	3	19c	Kildare .	Clane .	Naas . .	I.	53
6, 9, 10,	Carran .	14,460	2	4	Clare .	Burren .	{ Ballyvaghan } { Corrofin . }	II.	11, 12
2, 3, 7, 8	Carrick . .	5,196	1	26	Kildare .	Carbury .	Edenderry .	I.	51, 52
16, 17, 24, 25	Carrick .	5,337	1	21	Londonderry .	Keenaght .	NewTⁿLimavady	III.	{ 234,235, 237,238* }
84, 85	Carrick .	2,426	0	3f	Tipperary, S.R. .	Iffa and Offa East .	Carrick-on-Suir .	II.	312,313
25, 26, 32, 33	Carrick .	2,957	0	18g	Westmeath .	Fartullagh .	Mullingar .	I.	267
37, 42	Carrick .	3,009	0	37	Wexford .	Shelmaliere West .	Wexford .	I.	332
18, 21	Carrickbaggot .	826	1	0	Louth .	Ferrard .	Drogheda .	I.	180
46, 47, 51, 52, 53, 57	Carrickfergus .	16,700	1	34h	Antrim .	Carrickfergus .	Larne . .	III.	11
74, 75, 86 87, 98, 99 }	Carrigaline .	{ 6,146 7,950 404 }	{ 0 2 0 }	{ 26i 23j 8 }	Cork, E.R. .	{ Cork . } { Kerrycurrihy . } { Kinalea . }	{ Cork . } { Kinsale . }	II.	{ 63,64 92 94 }
25, 26, 30, 34	Carrigallen .	18,104	1	18k	Leitrim .	Carrigallen .	{ Bawnboy } { Mohill }	IV.	89,90
18, 19, 26, 27	Carrigdownane .	797	0	9	Cork, E.R. .	Fermoy .	{ Fermoy } { Mitchelstown }	II.	77
25, 26, 33, 34	Carrigleamleary .	3,320	0	5l	Cork, E.R. .	Fermoy .	Mallow .	II.	77
13, 14	Carrigparson .	1,449	1	31	Limerick .	Clanwilliam .	Limerick .	II.	223
73, 74	Carrigrohane .	{ 1,605 1,053 }	{ 1 0 }	{ 18m 9n }	Cork, E.R. .	{ Cork . } { East Muskerry }	Cork .	II.	{ 64 102 }
73	Carrigrohanebeg	2,061	1	36o	Cork, E.R. .	East Muskerry .	Cork .	II.	102
64, 65, 75, 76	Carrigtohill .	10,318	2	33p	Cork, E.R. .	Barrymore .	{ Cork . } { Middleton . }	II.	52
17, 18, 21, 22, 25, 26	Cashel and Islands	22,150	2	20q	Longford .	Rathcline .	{ Ballymahon } { Longford . }	I.	163,164
25	Castleboy .	1,358	0	38r	Down .	Ards Upper .	Downpatrick .	III.	160
1, 3, 4, 8	Castlebrack .	9,275	3	24	Queen's Co. .	Tinnahinch .	Mountmellick .	I.	248
1, 2, 5, 6, 11	Castlecomer .	21,592	0	1	Kilkenny .	Fassadinin .	Castlecomer .	I.	88, 89
16, 17, 22, 23	Castleconor .	16,677	3	39	Sligo .	Tireragh .	{ Ballina } { Dromore West }	IV.	232
37, 38, 39, 40	Castledermot .	7,497	2	13s	Kildare .	Kilkea and Moone .	{ Athy } { Baltinglass } { Carlow }	I.	59
10, 11, 14, 15	Castledillon .	1,133	1	14t	Kildare .	South Salt .	Celbridge .	I.	76
27, 33	Castle-ellis .	5,603	1	35	Wexford .	Ballaghkeen .	Enniscorthy .	I.	293
133, 141, 142, 150, 151 }	Castlehaven .	10,542	1	0u	Cork, W.R. .	West Carbery (E.D.) .	Skibbereen .	II.	137,138
19, 23	Castleinch or Inchy- olaghan .	2,366	3	19	Kilkenny .	Shillelogher .	Kilkenny .	I.	114
23, 30, 31, 39, 40, 49	Castleisland .	29,635	1	36	Kerry .	Trughanacmy .	Tralee .	II.	208,209
3, 4, 10, 11, 19 }	Castlejordan .	{ 1,801 11,052 4,518 }	{ 2 3 1 }	{ 7 18v 4 }	King's Co. . Meath .	{ Coolestown . } { Warrenstown . } { Upper Moyfenrath . }	{ Edenderry . }	I.	{ 132 145 212 }
43, 44	Castlekeeran or Loughan .	3,613	0	4w	Cavan .	Castlerahan .	Kells .	III.	69
10, 16	Castleknock .	5,114	2	25	Meath .	Upper Kells .	Oldcastle .	I.	206, 207
13, 14, 17, 18	Castleknock .	7,123	2	29x	Dublin .	Castleknock .	Dublin North .	I.	23, 24
33, 34, 39	Castlelost .	9,457	1	3	Westmeath .	Fartullagh .	Mullingar .	I.	268
35, 36, 44, 45	Castlelyons .	{ 9,720 2,998 }	{ 1 0 }	{ 1y 38z }	Cork, E.R. .	{ Barrymore . } { Condons & Clangibbon }	Fermoy .	II.	{ 53 60 }
30, 35, 40	Castlemacadam .	10,843	0	1	Wicklow .	Arklow .	Rathdrum .	I.	342
23, 24, 31, 32	Castlemagner .	7,880	1	26aa	Cork, E.R. .	Duhallow .	Kanturk .	II.	67
63, 64, 73, 74, 83 14 }	Castlemore .	{ 6,805 2,107 }	{ 2 1 }	{ 35 7 }	Mayo . Roscommon .	{ Costello . } { Frenchpark . }	Castlereagh .	IV.	{ 139,140 202 }
32, 38, 39, 42, 43	Castlerahan .	10,315	0	6bb	Cavan .	Castlerahan .	Oldcastle .	III.	67

	A. R. P.		A. R. P.		A. R. P.
(a) Including {	47 1 1 of River Barrow. 76 0 20 detached portion.	(k) Including {	364 0 36 of Garadice Lough. 786 1 2 of small loughs.	(r) Including {	12 3 17 of water. 115 3 9 detached portion.
(b) Including	49 0 34 of water.	(l) Including	29 1 10 of water.	(s) Including	27 0 39 detached portion.
(c) Including	204 2 2 detached portion.	(m) Including	25 1 2 of River Lee.	(t) Including	19 0 20 of River Liffey.
(d) Including	60 3 23 of water.	(n) Including	15 2 25 of River Lee.	(u) Including	84 1 28 of water.
(e) Including	21 3 0 of River Liffey.	(o) Including	33 0 24 of River Lee.	(v) Including	1,552 1 0 detached portion.
(f) Including	12 0 14 of River Suir.	(p) Including {	550 1 6 detached portion. 221 2 24 of Foaty Island.	(w) Including	637 1 30 detached portion.
(g) Including	853 0 39 of Lough Ennell.			(x) Including	19 0 2 of water.
(h) Including	89 3 22 Lough Mourne.	(q) Including {	6,290 3 23 of Lough Ree. 147 0 34 of small loughs.	(y) Including	324 1 6 detached portion.
(i) Including	285 2 31 detached portion.			(z) Including	24 3 31 of water.
(j) Including	2 0 21 of tideway.			(aa) Including	28 2 12 of water.
				(bb) Including	102 2 3 of Lough Ramor.

* This new Parish is composed of the following eleven Townlands, viz. : Ballyquin, Carrick East, and Maine South, from Balteagh Parish, page 234 ; Carrick and Templemoyle, from Bovevagh Parish, page 235 ; Ballyderg, Ballymore, Largy, Moys, Mulkeragh, and Terrydrum, from Tamlaght-Finlagan Parish, pages 237 and 238.

No. of Sheet of the Ordnance Survey Maps.	Parishes.	Area in Statute Measure.			County.	Barony.	Poor Law Union in 1857.	Townland Census of 1851, Part I.	
		A.	R.	P.				Vol.	Page
41, 42, 47	Castlerickard	119 3,314	1 2	19a 31b	Meath	Lune / Upper Moyfenrath	Trim	I.	207 213
15, 16, 20, 21	Castleterra	9,980	3	7c	Cavan	Upper Loughtee	Cavan	III.	82, 83
15, 16, 24, 25	Castletown	1,724	2	13	Limerick	Coonagh	Tipperary	II.	234
4, 6, 7	Castletown	562 2,047	3 3	35 18d	Louth	Lower Dundalk / Upper Dundalk	Dundalk	I.	177
5, 6, 11, 12	Castletown	4,067	2	19	Meath	Morgallion	Kells / Navan	I.	209
13, 14, 19, 20	Castletownarra	9,273	3	15e	Tipperary, N.R.	Owney and Arra	Nenagh	II.	294
4, 8, 9, 13, 14	Castletowndelvin	18,282	1	28f	Westmeath	Delvin	Castletowndelvin	I.	264, 265
45, 46, 47	Castletownely	1,803	1	24g	King's Co.	Clonlisk	Roscrea	I.	129
24, 25, 31, 32, 38	Castletownkindalen	11,398	2	11h	Westmeath	Moycashel	Mullingar	I.	277
26	Castletownroche	6,484	2	23	Cork, E.R.	Fermoy	Fermoy / Mallow	II.	77, 78
121, 122, 134, 135, 143	Castleventry	3,491 1,262	0 2	13 17i	Cork, W.R.	East Carbery (W.D.) / Ibane and Barryroe	Clonakilty	II.	131 148
24, 25, 30, 31	Chapel	3,588	0	36	Wexford	Bantry	Enniscorthy	I.	299
18	Chapelizod	532	2	35j	Dublin	Castleknock	Dublin North	I.	24
3, 4, 11, 12	Chapelrussell	633	3	25	Limerick	Kenry	Rathkeale	II.	248
13, 14	Charlestown	2,699	2	26	Louth	Ardee	Ardee	I.	171
18	Christ Church (Liberties of)	1	2	19	Dublin	City of Dublin	Dublin South	I.	44, 45
7, 15, 16	Churchtown	1,077 6,969	3 1	25 20	Cork, E.R.	Duhallow / Orrery and Kilmore	Kanturk / Mallow	II.	67 107
30, 34, 35	Churchtown	7,330	2	27k	Kildare	Narragh & Reban West	Athy	I.	67
30, 31	Churchtown	1,336	1	29	Meath	Lower Navan	Navan	I.	214
18, 24, 25	Churchtown	5,302	0	25l	Westmeath	Rathconrath	Mullingar	I.	282
9, 10, 13, 14	Clane	4,663	2	26m	Kildare	Clane	Naas	I.	53, 54
15, 20	Clara	3,201	1	9	Kilkenny	Gowran	Kilkenny	I.	94
33, 34, 41, 42	Clareabbey and Islands	7,028	2	36n	Clare	Islands	Ennis	II.	29
69, 70, 82, 83	Claregalway	5,431 7,020	3 2	27o 26	Galway	Clare / Dunkellin	Galway	IV.	18 27, 28
13	Clashacrow	999	1	13	Kilkenny	Crannagh	Kilkenny	I.	85
34, 35, 37, 38	Clashmore	7,201	3	20p	Waterford	Decies within Drum	Youghal	II.	351
153	Clear-island	1,504 30,636	3 2	2q 13r	Cork, W.R.	West Carbery (E.D.)	Skibbereen	II.	138
19, 20, 21, 23, 25, 26, 27, 28, 33	Cleenish and Islands	150 936 4,898	0 1 0	4 18s 22t	Fermanagh	Clanawley / Magheraboy / Magherastephana / Tirkennedy	Ballyshannon / Enniskillen / Lisnaskea	III.	189 to 192 210 219 219, 220
25, 26, 33	Clenor	4,289	0	38	Cork, E.R.	Fermoy	Mallow	II.	78
25,26,34,35,43,44,45,53	Cloghane	17,572	1	38u	Kerry	Corkaguiny	Dingle	II.	174, 175
19, 22	Clogher	1,861	1	16	Louth	Ferrard	Drogheda	I.	180
39, 40, 45, 46, 52	Clogher	8,119	0	25	Tipperary, S.R.	Kilnamanagh Lower	Cashel	II.	322
51, 52, 57, 58, 59, 63, 64, 65, 68	Clogher	49,761	0	20v	Tyrone	Clogher	Clogher	III.	291 to 293
21, 28, 29	Clogherbrien	3,410	0	25	Kerry	Trughanacmy	Tralee	II.	209
35, 36, 43, 44, 51, 52	Clogherny	17,791	2	5w	Tyrone	Omagh East	Omagh	III.	310
9, 10, 14, 15	Cloghprior	3,724	1	17x	Tipperary, N.R.	Lower Ormond	Borrisokane / Nenagh	II.	282, 283
13, 14	Cloghran	778	0	30	Dublin	Castleknock	Dublin North	I.	24
11, 12, 14, 15	Cloghran	1,557	2	31	Dublin	Coolock	Balrothery	I.	26
8, 9, 12, 13	Clomantagh	3,703	3	9	Kilkenny	Crannagh	Urlingford	I.	85
3, 4, 7, 8	Clonagam	4,939	3	30	Waterford	Upperthird	Carrick-on-Suir	II.	369
19, 28	Clonagh	2,427	1	28	Limerick	Connello Lower	Glin & Rathkeale	II.	227
6, 7, 11, 12, 13, 16, 17, 18, 23, 24	Clonagheen and Clonenagh	773 4,645 41,770	3 1 1	23 16 10y	Queen's Co.	Cullenagh / Maryborough East / Maryborough West	Abbeyleix / Mountmellick		239 241 242, 243
15	Clonaghlis	477	3	18z	Kildare	South Salt	Celbridge	I.	76
47, 50, 51, 54	Clonallan	11,658	0	33aa	Down	Upper Iveagh, Up. pt.	Newry	III.	174
33, 34, 39	Clonalvy	3,125	1	2	Meath	Upper Duleek	Drogheda	I.	197
33	Clonamery	3,390	1	38	Kilkenny	Ida	Thomastown		101
40, 41, 46, 47	Clonard	13,324	0	34bb	Meath	Upper Moyfenrath	Edenderry / Trim	I.	213
8, 9	Clonarney	2,307	2	23	Westmeath	Delvin	Castletowndelvin	I.	265
66, 67, 73, 74, 80	Clonbeg	15,112	1	27cc	Tipperary, S.R.	Clanwilliam	Tipperary	II.	305

	A.	R.	P.				A.	R.	P.				A.	R.	P.	
(a) Including	7	1	32	} of River Boyne.	(n) Including	{	5	1	36	of Ardsollus River tideway.	(u) Including	{	154	1	17	detached portion.
(b) Including	14	3	12				99	0	15	of loughs.			196	0	15	of water.
(c) Including	151	1	27	of water.	(o) Including	{	93	0	0	detached portion.	(v) Including		213	1	6	of water.
(d) Including	47	0	20	Newtownbalregan Lough.			468	2	9	of Lough Corrib.	(w) Including	{	2,368	1	20	detached portion.
(e) Including	2,469	0	30	of Lough Derg.	(p) Including	1,932	3	4		detached portions.			21	3	33	of water.
(f) Including	{ 2,135	0	5	detached portion.	(q) Including	11	1	23		Lough Errul.	(x) Including	{	31	1	26	of Lough Ourna.
	79	2	25	of water.	(r) Including	{	1,051	0	9	of Upper Lough M'Nean.			19	1	38	Clarce Lough.
(g) Including	794	0	3	detached portions.			492	2	3	of Lower Lough M'Nean.	(y) Including		26	0	0	Ballyfin Lough.
(h) Including	20	2	34	of Lough Ennell.			552	1	1	of River Erne & small loughs.	(z) Including		55	3	7	detached portions.
(i) Including	169	1	11	detached portion.	(s) Including	{	197	3	21	of Upper Lough Erne.	(aa) Including	{	66	3	20	of fresh water.
(j) Including	8	2	16	of River Liffey.			65	0	27	of River Erne & small loughs.			166	2	8	of tideway.
(k) Including	43	0	26	of River Barrow.	(t) Including	{	1,250	2	4	of Upper Lough Erne.	(bb) Including	{	31	1	4	of River Boyne.
(l) Including	8	1	8	of Mount Dalton Lough.			194	0	18	of River Erne & small loughs.			10	2	2	of Croboy Lough.
(m) Including	22	3	7	of River Liffey.							(cc) Including		21	0	35	of water.

No. of Sheet of the Ordnance Survey Maps.	Parishes.	Area in Statute Measure.	County.	Barony.	Poor Law Union in 1857.	Townland Census of 1851, Part I.	
		A. R. P.				Vol.	Page
17, 18, 30, 31	Clonbern	10,461 2 30a	Galway	Ballymoe	{Glennamaddy / Tuam}	IV.	6, 7
5, 9, 10, 14, 15	Clonbroney	{482 3 33 / 12,224 3 28b}	Longford	{Ardagh / Granard}	Granard	I.	152 / 154,155
67, 68, 74, 75	Clonbullogue	3,954 3 8	Tipperary, S.R.	Clanwilliam	Tipperary	II.	306
1, 2, 3, 4, 5, 11, 12	Clonca	19,643 0 18c	Donegal	Inishowen East	Inishowen	III.	116,117
29, 37	Cloncagh	4,543 0 12	Limerick	Connello Upper	Newcastle	II.	231
45, 54	Cloncrew	1,714 3 31	Limerick	Connello Upper	Newcastle	II.	232
12, 17	Cloncurry	5,419 2 31	Kildare	East Offaly	{Edenderry / Naas}	I.	69
4, 5, 9, 10	Cloncurry	8,390 0 9	Kildare	Ikeathy & Oughterany	Celbridge	I.	56, 57
40, 41, 48, 49, 50	Clondagad and Islands	16,978 0 17d	Clare	Islands	Killadysert	II.	29
15, 16, 25, 26, 34, 35	Clondahorky	29,632 2 21e	Donegal	Kilmacrenan	Dunfanaghy	III.	122 to 124
17, 18, 21, 22	Clondalkin	{157 1 13 / 4,776 2 22}	Dublin	{Newcastle / Uppercross}	{Celbridge / Dublin South}	I.	33 / 39
8, 9, 17, 18, 27, 28	Clondavaddog	27,367 1 18f	Donegal	Kilmacrenan	Millford	III.	124,125
13, 14, 20, 21, 22	Clondermot	21,606 1 4g	Londonderry	Tirkeeran	Londonderry	III.	247,248
47, 48, 49, 58, 59, 60, 69, 70, 71	Clondrohid	27,114 1 28	Cork, W.R.	West Muskerry	Macroom	II.	155
42, 47, 48, 51, 52	Clonduff	21,241 2 38h	Down	Upper Iveagh, Lr. pt.	Newry	III.	171
27, 28, 35, 36	Clondulane	4,926 2 14i	Cork, E.R.	Condons & Clangibbon	Fermoy	II.	60
15, 20	Clone	6,266 2 28j	Wexford	Scarawalsh	Enniscorthy	I.	322
23, 31, 32	Clonea	2,108 0 15k	Waterford	Decies without Drum	Dungarvan	II.	354
62, 63, 70, 71	Cloneen	{5,684 1 26 / 1,858 3 10}	Tipperary, S.R.	{Middlethird / Slievardagh}	{Callan / Cashel}	II.	325 / 332
28, 29, 36, 37	Clonelty	3,748 3 35	Limerick	Glenquin	{Newcastle / Rathkeale}	II.	245
6, 7, 11, 12, 13, 16, 17, 18, 23, 24	Clonenagh and Clonagheen	{773 3 23 / 4,645 1 16 / 41,770 1 10l}	Queen's Co.	{Cullenagh / Maryborough East / Maryborough West}	{Abbeyleix / Mountmellick}		239 / 241 / 242,243
29, 30, 35, 36, 40	Clones	27,581 1 29m	Fermanagh	Clankelly	Clones	III.	194 to 197
5, 8, 11, 12, 13, 16, 17		{10,782 0 35n / 4,514 0 2o}	Monaghan	{Dartree / Monaghan}	Monaghan	III.	264,265 / 274,275
25, 32, 33, 38, 39	Clonfad	4,872 0 8p	Westmeath	Fartullagh	Mullingar	I.	268
4, 8 / 54, 55, 61, 62, 67	Clonfeacle	{2,323 1 33 / 2,312 2 12 / 21,644 1 0q}	{Armagh / Tyrone}	{Armagh / Oneilland West / Dungannon Middle}	{Armagh / Dungannon}	III.	{43, 44 / 51 / 298 to 300}
4,5,6,13,14,15,21,22,23	Clonfert	62,109 2 10	Cork, E.R.	Duhallow	Kanturk	II.	67 to 69
88, 100, 101, 108, 109	Clonfert	24,876 2 22r	Galway	Longford	{Ballinasloe / Portumna}	IV.	56, 57
35, 40	Clongeen	5,379 1 38s	Wexford	Shelmaliere West	New Ross	I.	332,333
4, 8, 9, 13	Clongesh	12,832 2 14t	Longford	Longford	Longford	I.	157,158
11, 17, 18	Clongill	2,387 2 9	Meath	Morgallion	Navan	I.	209
14	Clonkeehan	605 0 11u	Louth	Louth	Ardee	I.	183
59, 72, 85	Clonkeen	8,213 3 5	Galway	Tiaquin	{Loughrea / Mountbellew}	IV.	76
6, 14	Clonkeen	1,144 2 10	Limerick	Clanwilliam	Limerick	II.	223
13, 14	Clonkeen	4,321 2 11	Louth	Ardee	Ardee	I.	172
35, 43, 52, 53	Clonlea	8,833 2 36v	Clare	Tulla Lower	{Limerick / Tulla}	II.	34, 35
62, 63, 70, 71, 79	Clonleigh	12,517 1 27w	Donegal	Raphoe	Strabane	III.	134 to 136
24, 30	Clonleigh	2,716 3 17	Wexford	Bantry	New Ross	I.	300
51, 61	Clonloghan	2,951 0 36	Clare	Bunratty Lower	Ennis	II.	3
24, 30	Clonmacduff	2,540 2 1	Meath	Upper Navan	Trim	I.	216
5, 6, 13, 14	Clonmacnoise	22,417 0 23x	King's Co.	Garrycastle	Parsonstown	I.	135
3, 4, 9, 10, 11, 18, 19	Clonmany	23,375 3 30y	Donegal	Inishowen East	Inishowen	III.	117
23, 31, 32, 40, 49	Clonmeen	20,075 2 32z	Cork, E.R.	Duhallow	Kanturk	II.	69, 70
75, 87	Clonmel	3,197 0 25aa	Cork, E.R.	Barrymore	Cork	II.	53
7, 12	Clonmelsh	3,146 2 10bb	Carlow	Carlow	Carlow	I.	1
7, 11	Clonmethan	3,027 3 19	Dublin	Balrothery West	Balrothery	I.	22
40, 45	Clonmines	1,379 3 20	Wexford	Shelburne	New Ross	I.	327
4, 5, 9, 10	Clonmore	6,029 1 38	Carlow	Rathvilly	Shillelagh	I.	10
39, 42	Clonmore	2,091 2 7	Kilkenny	Iverk	Carrick on Suir	I.	105

A. R. P.
(a) Including 3,703 2 8 detached portion.
(b) Including 130 3 39 of water.
(c) Including 124 2 16 of water.
(d) Including { 21 1 21 of water. |tideway, / 3 2 10 of Owenshieve River / 45 0 9 of loughs.
(e) Including 421 2 2 of water.
(f) Including 627 2 38 of water.
(g) Including 140 0 10 of water.
(h) Including 6 1 2 of water.
(i) Including 78 0 2 of water.
(j) Including 11 1 0 of River Slaney.

A. R. P.
(k) Including 112 3 22 detached portions.
(l) Including 26 0 0 Ballyfin Lough.
(m) Including 348 1 31 of water.
(n) Including 202 1 20 of water.
(o) Including 66 0 3 of water.
(p) Including 223 1 18 of Lough Ennell.
(q) Including { 127 1 10 of water. / 62 1 7 Mullaghmossog Glebe. / 38 0 36 of River Suck.
(r) Including 430 1 26 of River Shannon.
(s) Including 974 3 12 detached portion.
(t) Including 296 1 36 of River Shannon.
(u) Including 9 0 16 of water.

A. R. P.
(v) Including { 140 3 3 of Lough Cullaunyheeda. / 12 2 32 of Doon Lough. / 361 3 0 of small loughs.
(w) Including { 150 0 3 of River Foyle tideway. / 24 2 23 of water.
(x) Including { 186 0 0 Fin Lough. / 498 1 9 of River Shannon.
(y) Including 127 1 16 of water.
(z) Including 115 1 5 of water.
(aa) Including 544 3 33 of Footy Island.
(bb) Including { 7 0 20 of River Barrow. / 466 3 39 detached portion.

No. of Sheet of the Ordnance Survey Maps.	Parishes.	Area in Statute Measure.			County.	Barony.	Poor Law Union in 1857.	Townland Census of 1851, Part I.	
		A.	R.	P.				Vol.	Page
18, 19	Clonmore	1,905	0	16	Louth	Ferrard	Drogheda	I.	180
25, 26, 31, 32	Clonmore	{ 4,821 1,945	3 0	30 35	Wexford	{ Bantry Shelmaliere West	Enniscorthy	I.	{ 300 333
54, 55, 66	Clonmult	{ 3,329 694 578	1 1 2	39 6 1	Cork, E.R.	{ Barrymore Imokilly Kinnatalloon	{ Middleton Fermoy	II.	{ 53 84 98
47, 48, 55	Clonoe	12,070	2	38a	Tyrone	Dungannon Middle	Dungannon	III.	300
45, 46, 52, 60	Clonoulty	{ 234 10,900	1 1	3 38	Tipperary, S.R.	{ Clanwilliam Kilnamanagh Lower	{ Tipperary Cashel	II.	{ 306 322,323
66, 67	Clonpet	2,450	0	5	Tipperary, S.R.	Clanwilliam	Tipperary	II.	306
66, 67, 78	Clonpriest	7,302	0	35h	Cork. E.R.	Imokilly	Youghal	II.	84, 85
134, 135, 136, 137	Clonrush	11,850	0	31c	Galway	Leitrim	Scarriff	IV.	52, 53
19, 20, 27, 28, 34	Clonsast	23,557	2	19	King's Co.	Coolestown	Edenderry	I.	132,133
5, 9, 10	Clonshanbo	2,021	0	20	Kildare	Ikeathy & Oughterany	Celbridge	I.	57
20, 21	Clonshire	1,517	0	11	Limerick	Connello Lower	Rathkeale	II.	227
13, 17	Clonsilla	3,256	1	7d	Dublin	Castleknock	Celbridge	I.	24
15, 18, 19	Clontarf	1,189	3	0e	Dublin	Coolock	Dublin North	I.	26
111, 112	Clontead	3,097	2	26	Cork, E.R.	Kinsale	Kinsale	II.	99
10,14,15,19,20,24,25	Clontibret	26,553	1	17f	Monaghan	Cremorne	{ Castleblayney Monaghan	III.	{ 259 to 261
14, 18	Clonturk	1,244	0	10	Dublin	Coolock	Dublin North	I.	26, 27
87, 88, 99, 100	Clontuskert	{ 9,988 5,521	1 1	18g 19h	Galway	{ Clonmacnowen Longford	Ballinasloe	IV.	{ 24, 25 58
19, 22	Clonygoose	4,699	3	14i	Carlow	Idrone East	Carlow	I.	6
33, 34	Clonyhurk	11,747	1	30	King's Co.	Upper Philipstown	Mountmellick	I.	143
7, 8, 9, 11, 12, 13, 16	Clonclare	{ 22,677 10,313	0 0	26j 4k	Leitrim	{ Drumahaire Rosclogher	Manorhamilton	IV.	{ 93, 94 109
16, 17, 18, 23	Clooncraff	5,454	1	30l	Roscommon	Roscommon	{ Cark. on Shannon Strokestown	IV.	208
25,28,29,30,32,33, 34,35,36,37,38	Cloone	{ 9,366 32,157	0 0	19m 8n	Leitrim	{ Carrigallen Mohill	Mohill	IV.	{ 90 105,106
18, 26, 27, 34, 35	Clooney	10,656	0	31o	Clare	Bunratty Upper	{ Ennis Tulla	II.	7, 8
15, 16, 23, 24	Clooney	10,225	2	36p	Clare	Corcomroe	{ Corrofin Ennistimon	II.	18
23, 28, 29, 36	Cloonfinlough	7,814	0	26q	Roscommon	Roscommon	{ Roscommon Strokestown	IV.	208,209
7, 11, 12, 15, 16	Cloonlogher	6,444	0	5	Leitrim	Drumahaire	Manorhamilton	IV.	94
32, 33, 38, 39	Cloonoghil	7,097	3	27r	Sligo	Corran	Tobercurry	IV.	225
36, 37, 40	Cloontuskert	7,465	1	10s	Roscommon	Ballintober South	Roscommon	IV.	188
27, 28, 34, 35	Cloonygormican	8,543	2	29t	Roscommon	Ballymoe	{ Castlereagh Roscommon	IV.	191
6, 7, 11, 12 37	Cloydagh	{ 1,265 2,889 788	2 2 0	11u 29v 28w	Carlow Queen's Co.	{ Carlow Idrone West Slievemargy	Carlow	I.	{ 1 9 245
76, 77, 88, 89, 100	Cloyne	9,969	3	28x	Cork, E.R.	Imokilly	Middleton	II.	85, 86
24, 29	Coghlanstown	1,515	1	22y	Kildare	South Naas	Naas	I.	64
3, 7, 8	Coleraine	4,860	0	15z	Londonderry	North East Liberties of Coleraine	Coleraine	III.	246
22, 30	Colligan	3,784	2	38	Waterford	Decies without Drum	Dungarvan	II.	354
17, 20, 21 13	Collon	{ 6,768 2,945	1 0	39aa 30	Louth Meath	{ Ferrard Upper Slane	Ardee	I.	{ 180 224
69, 70, 76, 77	Colman	2,737	2	11	Tipperary, S.R.	Middlethird	Cashel	II.	325
46, 47	Colmanswell	2,811	0	35	Limerick	Connello Upper	Kilmallock	II.	232
20, 21, 27	Colp	5,785	2	35bb	Meath	Lower Duleek	Drogheda	I.	194,195
28, 29, 32	Columbkille	4,473	0	7cc	Kilkenny	Gowran	Thomastown	I.	94
2, 3, 5, 6, 7, 9, 10	Columbkille	20,313	3	32dd	Longford	Granard	{ Granard Longford	I.	155,156
5,6,9,10,11,15,16	Comber	{ 16,133 1,286	3 0	28ee 15	Down	{ Lower Castlereagh Upper Castlereagh	{ Lisburn Newtownards	III.	{ 161,162 164
6, 11	Confey	1,128	2	3	Kildare	North Salt	Celbridge	I.	74
25,26,27,38,39,40 117, 120, 121, 123	Cong	{ 22,840 14,888	3 3	4ff 5gg	Galway Mayo	{ Ross Kilmaine	{ Ballinrobe Oughterard	IV.	{ 72,73 153,154
37, 38, 43, 44	Connor	17,135	2	35hh	Antrim	Lower Antrim	{ Antrim Ballymena	III.	3, 4
24, 25, 31	Conry	3,696	3	28	Westmeath	Rathconrath	Mullingar	I.	282
60, 61, 68, 69, 70, 78	Convoy	20,982	0	8ii	Donegal	Raphoe	Stranorlar	III.	136

	A.	R.	P.				A.	R.	P.				A.	R.	P.
(a) Including	29	1	20 of River Blackwater.				387	3	8 of River Shannon.	(w) Including		245	2	33 detached portion.
(b) Including	2,940	2	33 of Lough Neagh.	(l) Including	207	2	5 of Lough Nablahy.			0	1	32 of River Barrow.
	317	2	20 of tideway.		332	2	24 of small loughs.	(x) Including	1,907	2	5 detached portions.
(c) Including	148	1	0 of small loughs.	(m) Including	211	1	11 of water.	(y) Including	3	0	16 of River Liffey.
	4,459	0	36 of Lough Derg.	(n) Including	1,524	1	15 of water.	(z) Including	22	0	23 of River Bann.
(d) Including	10	0	34 of River Liffey.		60	2	17 of water.	(aa) Including	21	3	6 Lake Oriel.
	13	3	20 of pond.	(o) Including	502	1	15 detached portion.	(bb) Including	367	3	21 of River Boyne tideway.
(e) Including	114	2	34 detached portion.		17	0	26 of water.	(cc) Including	18	3	6 of River Nore.
	120	3	21 of North Bull.	(p) Including	3,411	3	11 detached portion.	(dd) Including	1,747	1	15 of Lough Gowna.
(f) Including	333	3	28 of Muckno Lake.	(q) Including	352	3	31 of water.		55	3	4 of small loughs.
	193	2	30 of small loughs.		108	1	0 of Templeouse Lake.	(ee) Including	8	0	8 of water.
(g) Including	9	3	12 of water.	(r) Including	177	3	23 Cloonacleigha Lough.	(ff) Including	1,764	0	31 of Lough Corrib.
(h) Including	69	3	35 of River Suck.	(s) Including	1,388	2	26 of Lough Ree.		1	0	21 of river.
(i) Including	14	3	4 of River Barrow.		96	0	8 of River Shannon.	(gg) Including	1,292	2	19 of Lough Mask.
(j) Including	624	1	24 of Lough Macnean Upper.	(t) Including	45	1	33 of water.		1,835	3	19 of Lough Corrib.
	89	2	23 of small loughs.	(u) Including	27	1	32 of River Barrow.		48	1	13 of small loughs and river.
(k) Including	12	1	24 of Lough Macnean Upper.	(v) Including	22	0	8 of River Barrow.	(hh) Including	0	2	17 of water.
	48	1	34 of small loughs.					(ii) Including	25	3	14 of Lough Deele.

No. of Sheet of the Ordnance Survey Maps.	Parishes.	Area in Statute Measure. (A. R. P.)	County.	Barony.	Poor Law Union in 1857.	Townland Census of 1851, Part I. Vol.	Page
44, 45, 51, 52, 53, 59, 60, 61	Conwal	32,715 0 1a / 12,555 0 5b	Donegal	Kilmacrenan / Raphoe	Letterkenny / Millford / Stranorlar	III.	125 to 127
39, 45	Cookstown	1,238 1 18	Meath	Ratoath	Dunshaughlin		137
26, 30	Coolaghmore	5,504 2 23	Kilkenny	Kells	Callan	I.	217
4, 8, 9, 13, 14	Coolbanagher	9,621 0 26c	Queen's Co.	Portnahinch	Mountmellick	I.	107,108
8, 9	Coolcashin	1,670 2 30	Kilkenny	Galmoy	Urlingford	I.	92
9, 10, 13, 14	Coolcraheen	743 3 26 / 1,764 2 19	Kilkenny	Crannagh / Fassadinin	Kilkenny	I.	85 / 89
36, 45	Coole	1,152 2 0	Cork, E.R.	Barrymore	Fermoy	II.	53
54, 62	Cooleagh	2,557 3 21	Tipperary, S.R.	Middlethird	Cashel	II.	326
2, 7	Cooliney	1,152 1 11	Cork, E.R.	Orrery and Kilmore	Kilmallock	II.	108
28, 34	Coolkerry	4 2 12 / 1,615 2 6d	Queen's Co.	Clandonagh / Clarmallagh	Abbeyleix / Donaghmore	I.	233 / 237
70, 71	Coolmundry	1,688 1 17e	Tipperary, S.R.	Middlethird	Cashel	II.	326
14, 15	Coolock	1,734 1 26	Dublin	Coolock	Dublin North	II.	27
36, 37, 41, 42	Coolstuff	3,347 0 2	Wexford	Shelmaliere West	Wexford	I.	333
85	Corbally	869 0 13	Cork, E.R.	East Muskerry	Cork	II.	102
42, 43, 45	Corbally	418 1 15f / 449 1 37	King's Co.	Ballybritt / Clonlisk	Roscrea	I.	125 / 129
12, 17, 18		11,879 2 5g	Tipperary, N.R.	Ikerrin		II.	275
27	Corbally	725 0 27	Waterford	Gaultiere	Waterford	II.	362
2	Corcomohide	439 3 13	Cork, E.R.	Orrery and Kilmore	Kanturk	II.	108
37, 38, 45, 46		9,572 3 14	Limerick	Connello Upper	Croom / Kilmallock	II.	232
67, 74	Cordangan	3,905 3 22	Tipperary, S.R.	Clanwilliam	Tipperary	II.	306
87, 88, 99, 100	Corkbeg	2,660 3 7	Cork, E.R.	Imokilly	Middleton	II.	86
59, 67	Corroge	868 1 23	Tipperary, S.R.	Clanwilliam	Tipperary	II.	306
49, 54	Cranfield	3,526 0 19h	Antrim	Upper Toome	Antrim	III.	33
141, 142, 149, 150	Creagh	7,058 0 21i	Cork, W.R.	West Carbery (E.D.)	Skibbereen	II.	138,139
53, 54, 56	Creagh	8,867 2 37j	Roscommon	Moycarn	Ballinasloe	IV.	206
12, 13, 21, 22	Crecora	3,012 2 13	Limerick	Pubblebrien	Croom / Limerick	II.	252
9 / 37	Crecrin	926 2 34 / 1,544 0 4	Carlow / Wicklow	Rathvilly / Shillelagh	Shillelagh	I.	11 / 357
10, 11, 16, 17, 23	Creeve	3,828 3 35k / 745 1 37l	Roscommon	Frenchpark / Roscommon	Carr.on Shannon / Strokestown	IV.	203 / 209
27, 28, 30, 31 / 3, 6	Creggan	21,823 1 32m	Armagh	Fews Upper	Castleblayney	III.	48, 49
9, 15	Crehelp	2,991 3 16	Louth	Upper Dundalk	Dundalk	I.	177,178
38, 39	Crickstown	2,214 3 31	Wicklow	Lower Talbotstown	Baltinglass	I.	359
20, 21, 29, 30	Croagh	1,431 2 28	Meath	Ratoath	Dunshaughlin	I.	217
		7,220 2 14n	Limerick	Connello Lower	Rathkeale	II.	227,228
3, 10	Croghan	5,794 0 23	King's Co.	Lower Philipstown	Edenderry	I.	142
54, 55, 63	Crohane	5,434 0 34	Tipperary, S.R.	Slievardagh	Callan / Urlingford	II.	332
18	Crooke	1,935 1 11	Waterford	Gaultiere	Waterford	II.	362
12, 21, 22, 30, 31 / 38, 39	Croom	288 0 30 / 10,805 3 19 / 2,343 0 14o	Limerick	Connello Upper / Coshma / Pubblebrien	Croom / Limerick	II.	232 / 242 / 252
101,102,111,112,119	Crossboyne	16,234 1 24p	Mayo	Clanmorris	Claremorris	IV.	132,133
25, 31, 32, 37, 38	Crosserlough	11,729 3 5q / 4,445 1 35r / 261 2 17	Cavan	Castlerahan / Clanmahon / Upper Loughtee	Cavan / Oldcastle	III.	67,68 / 76 / 83
27, 28, 29, 30, 36, / 37, 38, 39, 45, 46, / 47, 48, 58, 59 / 2	Crossmolina	67,201 0 2s	Mayo	Tirawley	Ballina	IV.	165 to 167
43, 44	Crosspatrick	1,793 2 14 / 117 1 8 / 2,736 2 16	Wexford / Wicklow	Gorey / Ballinacor South / Shillelagh	Gorey / Shillelagh	I.	316 / 348 / 357
22, 25	Cruagh	4,460 1 9	Dublin	Uppercross	Dublin South	I.	39
5, 11	Cruicetown	1,863 1 8t	Meath	Lower Kells	Kells	I.	202
18, 22	Crumlin	1,817 0 38	Dublin	Uppercross	Dublin South	I.	39,40
2,4,5,11,12,13,20,21	Culdaff	20,089 1 28u	Donegal	Inishowen East	Inishowen	III.	118
5, 9, 10, 14, 15, 19	Culeightrin	26,337 3 21v	Antrim	Cary	Ballycastle	III.	13,14
29, 30, 38, 39	Cullen	12,674 1 19w	Cork, E.R.	Duhallow	Millstreet	II.	70,71
98, 112	Cullen	4,249 3 24	Cork, E.R.	Kinalea	Kinsale	II.	94
58	Cullen	1,985 3 24	Tipperary, S.R.	Clanwilliam	Tipperary	II.	306,307

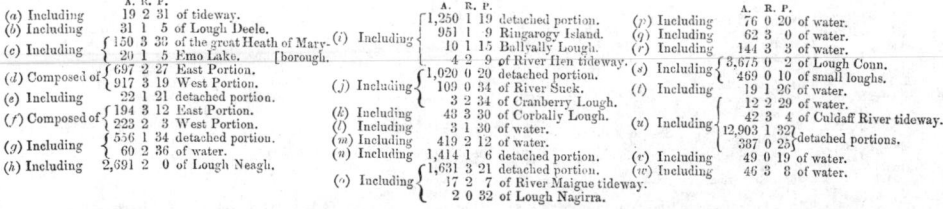

(a) Including 19 2 31 of tideway.
(b) Including 31 1 5 of Lough Deele.
(c) Including { 150 3 33 of the great Heath of Maryborough. / 20 1 5 Emo Lake. }
(d) Composed of { 697 2 27 East Portion. / 917 3 19 West Portion. }
(e) Including 22 1 21 detached portion.
(f) Composed of { 194 3 12 East Portion. / 222 2 3 West Portion. }
(g) Including { 556 1 34 detached portion. / 60 2 36 of water. }
(h) Including 2,691 2 0 of Lough Neagh.

(i) Including { 1,250 1 19 detached portion. / 951 1 9 Ringarogy Island. / 10 1 15 Ballyvally Lough. / 4 2 9 of River Ilen tideway. }
(j) Including { 1,020 0 20 detached portion. / 109 0 34 of River Suck. / 3 2 34 of Cranberry Lough. }
(k) Including 43 3 30 of Corbally Lough.
(l) Including 3 1 30 of water.
(m) Including 419 2 12 of water.
(n) Including 1,414 1 6 detached portion.
(o) Including { 1,631 3 21 detached portion. / 17 2 7 of River Maigue tideway. / 2 0 32 of Lough Nagirra. }

(p) Including 76 0 20 of water.
(q) Including 62 3 0 of water.
(r) Including 144 3 3 of water.
(s) Including { 3,675 0 2 of Lough Conn. / 469 0 10 of small loughs. }
(t) Including 19 1 26 of water.
(u) Including { 12 2 29 of water. / 42 3 4 of Culdaff River tideway. / 12,903 1 32 detached portions. / 387 0 25 }
(v) Including 49 0 19 of water.
(w) Including 46 3 8 of water.

No. of Sheet of the Ordnance Survey Maps	Parishes.	Area in Statute Measure.			County.	Barony.	Poor Law Union in 1857.	Townland Census of 1851. Part I.	
		A.	R.	P.				Vol.	Page
44, 45, 46, 47	Cullenwaine .	4,087	2	23	King's Co. .	Clonlisk . . .	Roscrea . .	I.	129
16, 22		657	0	22	Tipperary, N.R.	Ikerrin . . .		II.	275
43, 44, 49, 50	Culmullin .	156	1	27	Meath . .	Ratoath . . .	Dunshaughlin .	I.	218
		5,409	0	16		Upper Deece . .			193
14, 15, 22, 23	Cumber Lower .	14,466	2	3	Londonderry .	Tirkeeran . .	Londonderry .	III.	248, 249
22,23,24,28,29,30,	Cumber Upper .	17,597	2	2	Londonderry .	Tirkeeran . .	Londonderry . Newt^nlimavady	III.	249
6, 7		3,129	1	37	Tyrone . .	Strabane Lower .	Gortin . .		320
43, 44, 56, 57, 58	Cummer . .	9,314	3	4a	Galway . .	Clare . . .	Tuam . .	IV.	18, 19
14, 19	Curraclone . .	3,644	3	1b	Queen's Co. .	Stradbally . .	Athy . .	I.	246
38, 39, 47, 48	Currans . .	723	2	17	Kerry . .	Magunihy . .	Killarney . .	II.	200
		5,221	0	28		Trughanacmy . .			209
43	Currin . .	385	0	0	Fermanagh .	Clankelly . .	Clones . .	III.	197
16, 17, 21, 22		10,987	0	10c	Monaghan .	Dartree . .	Cootehill .		265, 266
62, 73, 74	Currykippane .	2,709	1	18d	Cork, E.R. .	Cork . . .	Cork . .	II.	64
32, 33, 39	Cushinstown .	1,199	3	38	Meath . .	Skreen . . .	Dunshaughlin .	I.	220
23	Dalkey . .	467	0	10e	Dublin . .	Rathdown . .	Rathdown .	I.	35
23, 24, 27, 28	Danesfort . .	5,062	2	27f	Kilkenny .	Shillelogher . .	Thomastown .	I.	114
26, 32	Danestown .	445	2	0	Meath . .	Lower Duleek . .	Navan . .	I.	195
		1,197	2	35		Skreen . . .			220
60, 68	Dangandargan .	422	3	20	Tipperary, S.R..	Clanwilliam . .	Tipperary .	II.	307
		663	3	26		Middlethird . .	Cashel .		326
55, 66	Dangandonovan	2,928	3	14	Cork, E.R. .	Imokilly . .	Middleton . Youghal	II.	86
48, 49, 56, 57, 59	Darragh . .	6,712	3	32	Limerick .	Coshlea . .	Kilmallock .	II.	238
11, 12, 14, 15	Darver . .	1,992	0	3	Louth . .	Louth . . .	Dundalk .	I.	183
28, 32, 36	Davidstown .	3,905	2	35g	Kildare . .	Narragh & Reban East	Athy . .	I.	66
8, 13	Delgany . .	3,977	3	36	Wicklow .	Rathdown . .	Rathdown .	I.	355
25, 26, 31, 32, 38	Denn . .	1,711	3	23h	Cavan . .	Castlerahan . .	Cavan .	III.	68
		2,113	3	18i		Clanmahon . .	Oldcastle .		76
		7,774	2	11j		Upper Loughtee .			83, 84
59, 60, 63, 64, 68	Derryaghy .	5,621	3	17	Antrim . .	Upper Belfast . .	Lisburn .	III.	10
		6,857	3	19		Upper Masereene .			30
16, 17, 22, 23, 27	Derrybrusk .	283	0	1k	Fermanagh .	Magherastephana .	Lisnaskea .	III.	219
		4,373	0	32l		Tirkennedy . .	Enniskillen .		220
5, 6, 13, 14	Derrygalvin .	1,719	1	15m	Limerick .	Clanwilliam . .	Limerick .	II.	223
76, 82	Derrygrath .	3,777	0	0	Tipperary, S.R..	Iffa and Offa West .	Clogheen . Clonmel	II.	318
7, 12, 13	Derrykeighan .	7,643	0	33	Antrim . .	Lower Dunluce .	Ballymoney .	III.	16, 17
48	Derryloran .	2,444	3	20	Londonderry .	Loughinsholin . .	Magherafelt .	III.	240
21, 29, 30, 38, 39		9,656	1	30	Tyrone . .	Dungannon Upper .	Cookstown .		306, 307
11, 12, 16, 17, 18,	Derrylossary .	41,341	3	17n	Wicklow . .	Ballinacor North .	Rathdrum .	I.	346
22, 23, 24, 30		4,623	3	23o		Newcastle . .			351
31, 32, 35, 36	Derrynahinch .	8,339	3	29	Kilkenny .	Knocktopher . .	Thomastown .	I.	111
11,12,15,16,19,20,	Derrynoose .	9,653	3	16	Armagh .	Armagh . .	Armagh .	III.	44
23		5,395	0	20p		Tiranny . .			59
37, 43	Derrypatrick .	1,951	0	13	Meath . .	Lower Deece . .	Dunshaughlin .	I.	191
18, 19, 27	Derryvillane .	693	3	36	Cork, E.R. .	Condons & Clangibbon	Mitchelstown .	II.	60
		1,133	3	32		Fermoy . .			78
6, 10, 11, 15, 16	Derryvullan .	15,070	2	38q	Fermanagh .	Lurg . . .	Lowtherstown .	III.	204, 205
22, 23, 27, 28, 33		8,575	0	17r		Tirkennedy . .	Enniskillen .		220, 221
135	Desert . .	450	1	12	Cork, W.R. .	East Carbery (E.D.) .	Clonakilty .	II.	127
		274	2	17		Ibane and Barryroe .			148
37, 38, 39, 46	Desertcreat .	14,399	1	20s	Tyrone . .	Dungannon Upper .	Cookstown .	III.	307, 308
9, 10, 18, 19, 28, 29	Desertegny .	7,577	0	10	Donegal . .	Inishowen West .	Inishowen .	III.	120
41, 46, 48	Desertlyn . .	5,561	0	5	Londonderry .	Loughinsholin . .	Magherafelt .	III.	240
41, 46	Desertmartin .	9,579	0	13	Londonderry .	Loughinsholin . .	Magherafelt .	III.	240, 241
72, 84, 85	Desertmore .	3,943	0	5	Cork, E.R. .	East Muskerry .	Bandon .	II.	102
18, 19, 26, 27, 32	Desertoghill .	11,466	0	21	Londonderry .	Coleraine . .	Ballymoney . Coleraine	III.	230, 231
108, 109, 110, 121,	Desertserges .	11,614	2	33	Cork, W.R. .	East Carbery (E.D.) .	Bandon .	II.	127, 128
122, 123		4,114	3	9		Kinalmeaky . .	Clonakilty .		152
13,14,15,16,19,20,	Devenish .	32,243	1	2t	Fermanagh .	Magheraboy . .	Ballyshannon . Enniskillen	III.	210 to 212
21, 22									
9, 15, 16	Diamor . .	5,463	0	2	Meath . .	Fore . . .	Oldcastle . .	I.	200

	A. R. P.			A. R. P.			A. R. P.
(a) Including 599 1 21 of Clonkeen Lough.			(h) Including 63 3 25 of water.		(q) Including	60 3 4 of small loughs.	
(b) Including 3 1 12 of River Barrow.			(i) Including 25 2 13 of water.			2,567 0 11 of Lower Lough Erne.	
(c) Including 126 0 36 Tullyhumphry Townland. / 131 0 19 of water.			(j) Including 35 3 32 of water.			Islands and detached portion.	
(d) Including 24 2 39 of River Lee. / 14 1 13 of Blarney Lake.			(k) Including 23 3 24 of water.		(r) Including 510 1 3 of water.		
(e) Including 21 2 27 Dalkey Island.			(l) Including 217 3 2 of water.		(s) Including 13 3 7 of water.		
(f) Including 36 2 14 of River Nore.			(m) Including 681 2 39 detached portion.		(t) Including	1,426 1 1 of Lower Lough Erne.	
(g) Including 531 3 12 detached portion.			(n) Including 506 1 1 of water.			193 2 25 of Lough Melvin.	
			(o) Including 242 0 5 detached portion.			312 3 4 of small loughs.	
			(p) Including 19 2 39 of water.				

No. of Sheet of the Ordnance Survey Maps.	Parishes.	Area in Statute Measure.	County.	Barony.	Poor Law Union in 1857.	Townland Census of 1851, Part I.	
		A. R. P.				Vol.	Page
34, 42, 43, 53	Dingle	9,097 0 27a	Kerry	Corkaguiny	Dingle	II.	175,176
45, 51	Doagh Grange of	2,304 2 7b	Antrim	Upper Antrim	Antrim	III.	6
68	Dogstown	406 1 30	Tipperary, S.R.	Middlethird	Cashel	II.	326
26, 27, 32, 33, 38, 39	Dolla	7,354 0 32	Tipperary, N.R.	Upper Ormond	Nenagh	II.	290
8, 12	Donabate	2,714 2 16	Dublin	Nethercross	Balrothery	I.	30
42, 43. 50, 51, 57, 58	Donacavey	18,342 1 8 / 4,710 0 33	Tyrone	Clogher / Omagh East	Clogher / Omagh	III.	294,295 / 310
9, 10	Donadea	2,110 0 25	Kildare	Ikeathy & Oughterany	Celbridge	I.	57
4,10,11,19,20,21,30	Donagh	25,259 0 35	Donegal	Inishowen East	Inishowen	III.	118 / 281
3, 4, 5, 6, 7, 9, 10	Donagh	16,202 1 11c	Monaghan	Trough	Monaghan	III.	281 to 283
2, 3, 6, 7, 11, 12	Donaghadee	9,593 0 7d	Down	Ards Lower	Newtownards	III.	157,158
19, 20, 27	Donaghcloney	6,697 3 32	Down	Lower Iveagh, Up. pt.	Lurgan	III.	169
11, 14, 15	Donaghcumper	261 3 24e / 2,090 1 37f	Kildare	North Salt / South Salt	Celbridge	I.	74 / 76
1, 2, 3, 5, 6, 7, 10, 11, 12	Donaghedy	39,398 1 35g	Tyrone	Strabane Lower	Gortin / Strabane	III.	320,321
38, 39, 46, 47	Donaghenry	7,154 2 22h	Tyrone	Dungannon Middle	Cookstown / Dungannon	III.	300,301
49, 50, 51, 60, 61, 62	Donaghmore	5,011 2 11 / 17,297 0 29	Cork, E.R.	Barretts / East Muskerry	Cork / Macroom	II.	49 / 102,103
136	Donaghmore	312 1 20	Cork, W.R.	Ibane and Barryroe	Clonakilty	II.	148
69, 70, 77, 78, 79, 86, 87, 88, 95	Donaghmore	46,378 0 3i	Donegal	Raphoe	Strabane / Stranorlar	III.	137, 138
33, 40, 41, 46	Donaghmore	8,396 1 13j	Down	Upper Iveagh, Up. pt.	Newry	III.	175
6, 11	Donaghmore	301 0 37	Kildare	North Salt	Celbridge	I.	74
4, 5, 9, 10	Donaghmore	5,270 1 28	Kilkenny	Fassadinin	Castlecomer	I.	89
13	Donaghmore	942 2 39	Limerick	Clanwilliam	Limerick	II.	223
18, 25	Donaghmore	3,955 0 9k	Meath	Lower Navan	Navan	I.	214
39, 45	Donaghmore	3,413 0 20	Meath	Ratoath	Dunshaughlin	I.	218
22, 27, 28	Donaghmore	3,528 3 22	Queen's Co.	Clandonagh	Donaghmore	I.	233
70, 77	Donaghmore	652 2 4 / 1,144 0 21	Tipperary, S.R.	Iffa and Offa East / Middlethird	Clonmel / Cashel	II.	313 / 326
45, 46, 53, 54, 60, 61	Donaghmore	18,410 2 10l	Tyrone	Dungannon, Middle	Dungannon	III.	301,302
17, 22	Donaghmore	7,423 2 25m / 54 2 0	Wexford	Ballaghkeen / Gorey	Gorey	I.	293, 294 / 316
15, 16, 21, 22, 27, 28	Donaghmore	23,427 2 39	Wicklow	Upper Talbotstown	Baltinglass	I.	362 to 364
25, 27, 28, 29, 31, 32	Donaghmoyne	25,603 3 30n	Monaghan	Farney	Carrickmacross / Castleblayney	III.	269 to 271
28, 42	Donaghpatrick	10,342 0 26o	Galway	Clare	Tuam	IV.	19
17, 18, 24, 25	Donaghpatrick	568 1 10 / 3,459 3 33p	Meath	Lower Navan / Upper Kells	Kells / Navan	I.	214 / 205
100, 108	Donananghta	2,634 1 2	Galway	Longford	Portumna	IV.	58
15, 16, 21	Donard	4,808 2 13	Wicklow	Lower Talbotstown	Baltinglass	I.	359, 360
85, 86, 93, 94, 95, 99, 100	Donegal	23,260 0 0q	Donegal	Tirhugh	Donegal	III.	144, 145
44, 45, 50, 51	Donegore	6,650 0 12	Antrim	Upper Antrim	Antrim	III.	6
8, 9, 17, 18, 25, 26	Doneraile	20,441 3 21	Cork, E.R.	Fermoy	Mallow	II.	78,79
18, 19, 22, 23	Donnybrook	1,313 2 9 / 363 3 26 / 10 2 0	Dublin	Dublin / Rathdown / Uppercross	Dublin South	I.	30 / 35 / 40
45, 51, 52, 59	Donohill	3,787 3 23 / 10,126 1 25	Tipperary, S.R.	Clanwilliam / Kilnamanagh Lower	Cashel / Tipperary	II.	307 / 323
20, 27	Donore	3,661 3 38r	Meath	Lower Duleek	Drogheda	I.	195
7, 8, 15, 16, 24, 25, 33	Doon	15,237 0 15s / 4,318 2 2	Limerick	Coonagh / Owneybeg	Limerick	II.	234 / 251
38, 39, 44, 45	Doon	8,127 0 35	Tipperary, N.R.	Kilnamanagh Upper	Tipperary	II.	277
19, 20, 28, 29	Doondonnell	1,394 0 20	Limerick	Connello Lower	Rathkeale	II.	228
5, 6, 7, 12, 13, 14	Doonfeeny	31,251 0 6t	Mayo	Tirawley	Killala	IV.	167
31	Doonooney	1,081 0 39	Wexford	Bantry	Wexford	I.	300
33, 34, 42	Doora	5,927 3 37u	Clare	Bunratty Upper	Ennis	II.	8
1, 2, 4, 5	Dorrha	15,798 0 39v	Tipperary, N.R.	Lower Ormond	Parsonstown	II.	283
31	Dowdstown	869 1 36w	Meath	Skreen	Navan	I.	220
30, 31, 37, 38, 44	Down	11,484 2 7x	Down	Lecale Upper	Downpatrick	III.	180,181

No. of Sheet of the Ordnance Survey Maps	Parishes.	Area in Statute Measure. A. R. P.	County.	Barony.	Poor Law Union in 1857.	Townland Census of 1851, Part I. Vol.	Page
13, 18	Downings	4,728 3 1a	Kildare	Clane	Naas	I.	54
19, 20	Dowth	1,463 2 3b	Meath	Upper Slane	Drogheda	I.	224
11, 12	Drakestown	2,692 3 9	Meath	Morgallion	Navan	I.	209
55, 62, 63	Drangan	5,427 1 25	Tipperary. S. R.	Middlethird	Cashel	II.	326
21, 30	Drehidtarsna	{ 455 0 16 / 545 1 14	Limerick	{ Connello Upper / Coshma	{ Croom / Rathkeale	II. {	232 / 242
17, 18, 22	Drimnagh	732 0 18	Dublin	Uppercross	Dublin South	I.	40
108, 120, 121, 133	Drinagh	{ 4,887 0 14c / 7,981 2 7d	Cork, W.R.	{ (East Carbery (W.D.) / West Carbery (E.D.)	{ Dunmanway / Skibbereen	II. {	131 / 139
42, 43	Drinagh	1,170 2 36	Wexford	Forth	Wexford	I.	309
38, 39, 47, 48	Drishane	{ 2,434 2 25e / 30,649 3 12f	Cork, E.R. / Cork, W.R.	{ Duhallow / West Muskerry	{ Millstreet	II. {	71 / 155, 156
28, 29, 34, 35	Drom	4,480 0 36	Tipperary, N.R.	Eliogarty	Thurles	II.	269
21, 22, 28, 29, 35, 36	Dromara	{ 7,024 1 15g / 6,027 0 33h / 8,141 0 15i	Down	{ Kinelarty / Lower Iveagh, Lr. pt. / Upper Iveagh, Lr. pt.	{ Banbridge / Downpatrick / Lisburn	III. {	176 / 167, 168 / 172
13, 19, 20	Dromard	7,422 1 28j	Sligo	Tireragh	Dromore West	IV.	233
45, 54	Dromcolliher	4,846 0 0	Limerick	Connello Upper	Newcastle	II.	232, 233
106, 107, 119, 120, 132, 133	Dromdaleague	18,708 0 33k	Cork, W.R.	West Carbery (E.D.)	Skibbereen	II.	139, 140
24, 32	Dromdowney	659 1 24	Cork, E.R.	Orrery and Kilmore	Mallow	II.	108
31, 39	Dromin	4,095 2 37	Limerick	Coshma	Kilmallock	II.	243
17, 18	Dromin	2,042 1 18	Louth	Ardee	Ardee	I.	172
14	Dromineer	2,425 3 12l	Tipperary, N.R.	Lower Ormond	Nenagh	II.	283
11, 12, 15	Dromiskin	5,312 0 8	Louth	Louth	Dundalk	I.	183
14, 15, 23, 24	Dromkeen	859 2 21	Limerick	Clanwilliam	Limerick	II.	223
71, 80, 81, 88, 89, 90, 97, 98, 99	Dromod	50,701 0 26m	Kerry	Iveragh	Cahersiveen	II.	194, 195
20, 21, 22, 27, 28	Dromore	20,488 1 5n	Down	Lower Iveagh, Lr. pt.	{ Banbridge / Lisburn	III.	168
41, 42, 49, 50, 57	Dromore	25,492 1 34o	Tyrone	Omagh East	{ Lowtherstown / Omagh	III.	311
23, 30, 31, 39, 40	Dromtarriff	15,224 1 17p	Cork, E.R.	Duhallow	{ Kanturk / Millstreet	II.	71
79, 89, 90, 100	Drum	7,767 2 19q	Mayo	Carra	Castlebar	IV.	127, 128
48, 49, 51, 52, 54, 55	Drum	16,148 2 30r	Roscommon	Athlone	Athlone	IV.	180
6, 9, 10, 16, 17	Drumachose	11,682 0 36s	Londonderry	Keenaght	New Tn. Limavady	III.	235
102, 103	Drumacoo, and Islands	1,931 3 21	Galway	Dunkellin	{ Galway / Gort	IV.	28
2 } / 26, 27, 33, 34 }	Drumatemple	{ 1,258 0 39 / 5,272 3 20	Galway / Roscommon	Ballymoe / Ballymoe	{ Castlereagh / Glennamaddy	IV. {	7 / 191
34, 35, 41, 42	Drumballyroney	12,338 2 23t	Down	Upper Iveagh, Lr. pt.	{ Banbridge / Newry	III.	172
64 } / 9, 15 }	Drumbeg	{ 1,517 3 28 / 1,186 2 37	Antrim / Down	Upper Belfast / Upper Castlereagh	Lisburn	III. {	10 / 164
9, 10, 14, 15	Drumbo	13,793 1 25u	Down	Upper Castlereagh	Lisburn	III.	164, 165
17, 18, 26, 27	Drumcannon	{ 89 2 11 / 7,582 1 25	Waterford	{ Gaultiere / Middlethird	Waterford	II. {	362 / 366
15, 18	Drumcar	4,041 1 36v	Louth	Ardee	Ardee	I.	172
25, 33, 41	Drumcliff	9,967 2 22w	Clare	Islands	Ennis	II.	29, 30
4, 5, 6, 7, 8, 9, 14, 15	Drumcliff	26,598 1 32x	Sligo	Carbury	Sligo	IV.	220 to 222
26, 27, 34, 40	Drumcolumb	4,528 2 39y	Sligo	Tirerrill	{ Boyle / Sligo	IV.	238
3, 6	Drumcondra	7,925 3 4z	Meath	Lower Slane	{ Ardee / Kells	I.	222, 223
5, 9, 10, 13	Drumcree	13,385 2 32aa	Armagh	Oneilland West	Lurgan	III.	51, 52
2, 3, 5	Drumcreehy	6,285 0 36	Clare	Burren	Ballyvaghan	II.	12
30, 31, 35, 36	Drumcullen	13,904 1 17bb	King's Co.	Eglish	Parsonstown	I.	134
41, 42, 47, 48	Drumgath	5,330 1 37cc	Down	Upper Iveagh, Up. pt.	Newry	III.	175
46, 54	Drumglass	3,503 3 15dd	Tyrone	Dungannon Middle	Dungannon	III.	302, 303
35, 36, 42, 43	Drumgooland	19,653 0 19ee	Down	Upper Iveagh, Lr. pt.	Banbridge	III.	172
17, 18, 22, 23, 27	Drumgoon	{ 8,121 3 27ff / 7,353 1 5gg	Cavan	{ Clankee / Tullygarvey	Cootehill	III. {	72 / 87, 88
94, 95, 99, 100, 101, 103, 104	Drumhome	35,433 0 12hh	Donegal	Tirhugh	{ Ballyshannon / Donegal	III.	146, 147

	A. R. P.		A. R. P.		A. R. P.
(a) Including	2 2 35 of Reservoir.	(n) Including	107 3 0 of water.	(y) Including {	2,822 1 25 detached portions. / 17 0 27 of water.
(b) Including	30 3 23 of River Boyne.	(o) Including	42 0 21 of water.		76 2 23 of Ballyhoe Lough.
(c) Including {	34 0 30 of Curraghalicky Lake. / 8 1 15 of Lough Atarriff.	(p) Including	92 0 10 of water.	(z) Including {	31 2 24 of small loughs.
(d) Including	38 1 23 of water.	(q) Including	206 1 21 of water.	(aa) Including	93 3 37 of water.
(e) Including	5 1 4 of water.	(r) Including {	665 1 34 detached portion. / 157 2 23 of River Shannon. / 8 2 20 Lough Clettiagh.	(bb) Including	34 2 35 of water.
(f) Including	48 0 10 of water.			(cc) Including	15 3 19 of water.
(g) Including	35 3 2 of water.	(s) Including	24 3 11 of water.	(dd) Including	15 2 11 of water.
(h) Including	30 0 27 of water.	(t) Including	112 2 3 of water.	(ee) Including	133 2 30 of water.
(i) Including	25 3 18 of water.	(u) Including	19 1 6 of water.	(ff) Including	310 1 24 of water.
(j) Including	8 3 37 Lough Doo.	(v) Including	18 2 8 of River Glyde.	(gg) Including	293 2 32 of water.
(k) Including	13 3 35 of water.	(w) Including {	29 3 14 of River Fergus tideway. / 96 1 9 of loughs.	(hh) Including	669 3 3 of small loughs.
(l) Including	686 2 12 of Lough Derg.				
(m) Including {	1,774 3 28 of Lough Currane. / 601 0 20 Derriana Lough. / 703 0 24 of small loughs.	(x) Including {	112 2 39 of Glencar Lake. / 66 2 0 of small loughs.		

6 B

No. of Sheet of the Ordnance Survey Maps.	Parishes.	Area in Statute Measure.	County.	Barony.	Poor Law Union in 1857.	Townland Census of 1851, Part I. Vol.	Page
		A. R. P.					
25, 31	Drumkay	1,654 2 33a / 7 1 34	Wicklow	Arklow / Newcastle	Rathdrum	I.	342,343 / 351
1, 2, 4, 5, 6, 10	Drumkeeran, & Islands	27,159 0 0b	Fermanagh	Lurg	Lowtherstown	III.	205 to 207
10, 11, 14, 15, 19, 20	Drumlane	20,056 0 30c	Cavan	Lower Loughtee	Bawnboy / Cavan	III.	79 to 81
43, 49	Drumlargan	1,276 0 31	Meath	Upper Deece	Trim	I.	193
6, 7, 10, 11, 14, 15	Drumlease	15,271 1 7d	Leitrim	Drumahaire	Manorhamilton	IV.	94, 95
51, 61	Drumline	2,954 3 10	Clare	Bunratty Lower	Ennis	II.	3
30, 31, 36, 37, 41	Drumlumman	17,147 3 11e	Cavan	Clanmahon	Cavan / Granard	III.	76, 77
37,42,43,44,48,49,54	Drummaul	32,394 0 14f	Antrim	Upper Toome	Antrim / Ballymena	III.	33, 34
40, 42, 43 / 11, 16	Drummully	1,760 2 21 / 3,450 1 23g / 2,427 3 28h	Fermanagh / Monaghan	Clankelly / Coole / Dartree	Clones	III.	197 / 199 / 266
25, 34, 35, 42, 43	Drumragh	20,163 3 39i	Tyrone	Omagh East	Omagh	III.	312,313
23, 30	Drumraney	9,102 1 39	Westmeath	Kilkenny West	Athlone / Ballymahon	I.	272,273
39, 40, 44, 45	Drumrat	3,730 2 3j	Sligo	Corran	Boyle	IV.	225,226
8 / 16, 18, 19, 20, 21 / 22, 25, 26, 29, 30	Drumreilly	3,178 1 38 / 14,218 3 2k / 16,276 0 24l	Cavan / Leitrim	Tullyhaw / Carrigallen / Drumahaire	Bawnboy / Cart on Shannon	III. / IV. / IV.	91 / 90, 91 / 95
19, 21, 22	Drumshallon	3,585 2 0m	Louth	Ferrard	Drogheda	I.	180
8, 9, 12, 13	Drumsnat	5,019 1 2n	Monaghan	Monaghan	Monaghan	III.	275
7, 8, 12, 13	Drumtullagh, Grange of	3,753 1 23	Antrim	Cary	Ballycastle	III.	14
12, 16, 17, 21, 22	Drung	11,475 0 9o	Cavan	Tullygarvey	Cootehill	III.	88, 89
11, 12, 17, 18, 23	Duagh	16,724 0 16p / 2,977 0 0q	Kerry	Clanmaurice / Iraghticonnor	Listowel	II.	168,169 / 190
10, 11, 16, 17	Dulane	4,242 3 18r	Meath	Upper Kells	Kells	I.	205
19, 20, 26, 27, / 32, 33,	Duleek	10,568 1 21s / 5,985 1 38	Meath	Lower Duleek / Upper Duleek	Drogheda	I.	195 / 197,198
27, 33	Duleek Abbey	1,029 2 17	Meath	Upper Duleek	Drogheda	I.	198
19, 23, 24, 27, 28	Dunaghy	13,743 1 18	Antrim	Kilconway	Ballymena	III.	25, 26
7, 8, 19, 20 / 38, 39	Dunamon	2,373 0 14t / 2,282 3 29u	Galway / Roscommon	Ballymoe / Ballymoe	Roscommon	IV.	7 / 191
16, 19	Dunany	1,661 3 5	Louth	Ferrard	Ardee	I.	180
20, 24	Dunbell	2,578 2 5v	Kilkenny	Gowran	Kilkenny	I.	94
6, 7, 11, 12	Dunbin	2,169 1 2	Louth	Upper Dundalk	Dundalk	I.	178
2, 3, 6, 7	Dunboe	10,577 2 8	Londonderry	Coleraine	Coleraine	III.	231,232
44, 45, 50, 51, 53	Dunboyne	13,685 2 18	Meath	Dunboyne	Dunshaughlin	I.	199, 200
39, 44, 45, 49, 50	Dunbrody & St. James	8,489 1 20	Wexford	Shelburne	New Ross	I.	328
42, 43, 51, 52, 63	Dunbulloge	16,532 2 15 / 249 3 38	Cork, E.R.	Barrymore / Cork	Cork	II.	54 / 64
41, 46	Duncormick	5,710 3 18	Wexford	Bargy	Wexford	I.	304, 305
4, 7, 12	Dundalk	6,201 3 26w	Louth	Upper Dundalk	Dundalk	I.	178
23, 27	Dundermot, Grange of	3,003 3 4	Antrim	Kilconway	Ballymena	III.	26, 27
85, 97, 111	Dunderrow	2,734 0 18 / 2,343 3 4x / 1,356 3 19	Cork, E.R.	East Muskerry / Kinalea / Kinsale	Cork / Kinsale	II.	103 / 94, 95 / 99
5, 10	Dundonald	4,635 0 37	Down	Lower Castlereagh	Belfast / Newtownards	III.	162
42, 43, 48, 49, 54	Duneane	13,128 1 38y	Antrim	Upper Toome	Antrim / Ballymena	III.	34, 35
21, 22, 26, 27	Duneany	3,084 2 0z	Kildare	West Offaly	Athy	I.	72
3, 4, 9	Dunfierth	5,548 1 11	Kildare	Carbury	Edenderry	I.	52
30, 31, 35, 36	Dunganstown	14,287 1 30	Wicklow	Arklow	Rathdrum	I.	343,344
24, 25, 28, 29	Dungarvan	5,881 1 10	Kilkenny	Gowran	Kilkenny / Thomastown	I.	94
30, 31, 35, 36	Dungarvan	9,413 1 5aa	Waterford	Decies without Drum	Dungarvan	II.	354 to 356
17,24,25,30,31,32,35	Dungiven	29,298 1 26	Londonderry	Keenaght	New Tn Limavady	III.	236
54, 55, 65, 66	Dungourney	6,513 0 3 / 1,717 2 13	Cork, E.R.	Barrymore / Imokilly	Middleton	II.	54 / 86
16, 25	Dunhill	6,287 0 5	Waterford	Middlethird	Kilmacthomas / Waterford	II.	366,367

(a) Including 558 1 35 detached portion.
(b) Including 3,497 3 23 of Lower Lough Erne.
(c) Including { 622 0 7 of Lough Erne. / 643 1 2 of Lough Oughter. / 1,809 0 4 of water. }
(d) Including { 498 2 18 of Lough Gill. / 208 1 10 of small loughs. }
(e) Including { 541 1 9 of Lough Sheelin. / 121 0 5 of Lough Kinale. / 140 1 1 of Lough Gowna. / 200 1 29 of water. }
(f) Including { 11,471 3 23 of Lough Neagh. / 171 1 4 of River Main. }
(g) Including { 348 3 3 of Upper Lough Erne. / 130 2 15 of River Erne & small loughs. }

(h) Including 26 2 37 of water.
(i) Including 161 2 28 of water.
(j) Including 134 0 85 detached portion.
(k) Including { 742 0 0 of Garadice Lough. / 350 0 30 of small loughs. }
(l) Including { 1,792 1 25 of Lough Allen. / 26 2 19 of small loughs. }
(m) Including { 372 0 26 Labanstown Townland [detached] / 9 2 32 Kircock Lough. }
(n) Including 41 0 16 of water.
(o) Including 316 2 2 detached portion.
(p) Including 77 3 20 of water.
(q) Including 45 3 8 of River Feale.

(r) Including 6 2 0 Red Bog Lough.
(s) Including 24 2 0 of River Boyne.
(t) Including 82 3 8 of water.
(u) Including 37 1 4 of River Suck.
(v) Including 14 0 34 of River Nore.
(w) Including 25 3 16 of Castletown River.
(x) Composed of { 1,468 1 0 North Portion. / 875 2 4 South Portion. }
(y) Including { 1,682 1 11 of Lough Neagh. / 415 3 30 of Lough Beg. / 29 2 26 of River Bann. }
(z) Including 945 0 12 detached portion.
(aa) Composed of { 3,508 3 7 East Portion. / 406 3 30 Middle Portion. / 5,497 2 8 West Portion. }

No. of Sheet of the Ordnance Survey Maps.	Parishes.	Area in Statute Measure.	County.	Barony.	Poor Law Union in 1857.	Townland Census of 1851, Part I.	
		A. R. P.				Vol.	Page.
106, 107, 116	Duniry	5,470 1 1 / 358 0 17	Galway	Leitrim / Longford	Loughrea / Portumna	IV.	53 / 58
71, 83	Dunisky	1,186 2 20a	Cork, W.R.	West Muskerry	Macroom	II.	156
41, 42, 44, 45, 47	Dunkerrin	7,769 3 11	King's Co.	Clonlisk	Roscrea	I.	130
40, 43	Dunkitt	6,773 1 25b	Kilkenny	Ida	Waterford	I.	101
14, 15, 21	Dunlavin	5,594 3 10 / 257 3 11	Wicklow	Lower Talbotstown / Upper Talbotstown	Baltinglass	I.	360 / 364
16, 17, 19, 20	Dunleckny	7,956 1 30c	Carlow	Idrone East	Carlow	I.	6,7
18	Dunleer	2,378 3 30	Louth	Ferrard	Ardee	I.	180,181
2, 3, 6, 7, 11, 12	Dunluce	9,380 3 25	Antrim	Lower Dunluce	Ballymoney / Coleraine	III.	17,18
27, 35	Dunmahon	37 1 15 / 2,265 1 19	Cork, E.R.	Condons & Clangibbon / Fermoy	Fermoy	II.	60 / 79
37, 39	Dunmanoge	2,961 1 14d	Kildare	Kilkea and Moone	Athy	I.	59
18, 25	Dunmoe	975 2 26e	Meath	Lower Navan	Navan	I.	215
4, 5, 6, 16, 17, 18, 29, 30, 31, 44, 45	Dunmore	15,424 3 31f	Galway	Ballymoe	Glennamaddy	IV.	7,8
		19,514 1 25g		Dunmore	Tuam		33, 34
14	Dunmore	2,379 2 1h	Kilkenny	Fassadinin	Kilkenny	I.	89
18, 19, 27, 28	Dunmoylan	6,189 3 30i	Limerick	Shanid	Glin / Newcastle / Rathkeale	II.	255
9	Dunmurraghill	501 3 30	Kildare	Ikeathy & Oughterany	Celbridge	I.	57
17, 22	Dunmurry	1,100 2 13	Kildare	East Offaly	Naas	I.	69
27, 31	Dunnamaggan	3,547 2 1 / 4 1 22	Kilkenny	Kells / Knocktopher	Callan / Thomastown	I.	108 / 111
42, 51, 52, 61	Dunquin	4,396 2 12j	Kerry	Corkaguiny	Dingle	II.	176
37, 38	Dunsany	964 0 26	Meath	Skreen	Dunshaughlin	I.	220
38, 39, 45	Dunsfort	4,238 3 34k	Down	Lecale Lower	Downpatrick	III.	179
38, 44	Dunshaughlin	5,263 2 28	Meath	Ratoath	Dunshaughlin	I.	218
33, 42	Dunurlin	4,699 3 18	Kerry	Corkaguiny	Dingle	II.	176
4		668 2 9	Kilkenny	Galmoy	Urlingford		92
8, 9, 16, 17	Durrow	7,513 3 37	King's Co.	Ballycowan	Tullamore	I.	127
29, 35		5,859 3 29	Queen's Co.	Clarmallagh	Abbeyleix		237
37, 38, 40		2,259 0 27l	Westmeath	Moycashel	Tullamore		277
117, 118, 130, 131	Durrus	1,587 0 3 / 9,551 1 16	Cork, W.R.	Bantry / West Carbery (W.D.)	Bantry	II.	119 / 142,143
5, 6, 10, 11	Dysart	7,938 1 16	Kilkenny	Fassadinin	Castlecomer	I.	89
18, 19	Dysart	1,911 2 31	Louth	Ferrard	Drogheda	I.	181
47, 48, 50	Dysart	6,568 2 32m	Roscommon	Athlone	Athlone	IV.	180,181
18, 25, 32	Dysart	5,834 2 31n / 1,245 3 34o / 336 0 24	Westmeath	Moyashel and Magheradernon / Moycashel / Rathconrath	Mullingar	I.	274 / 278 / 283
13, 14, 18, 19	Dysartenos	2,523 2 27 / 3,572 1 18	Queen's Co.	Maryborough East / Stradbally	Mountmellick / Athy	I.	241 / 247
24, 25, 30, 31	Dysartgallen	10,781 0 38p	Queen's Co.	Cullenagh	Abbeyleix	I.	239
32, 33, 36, 37	Dysartmoon	6,207 2 27	Kilkenny	Ida	New Ross	I.	101,102
24, 25, 33	Dysert	7,250 3 28q	Clare	Inchiquin	Corrofin / Ennis	II.	24
9, 10, 15, 16	Dysert	4,029 2 0r / 2,119 0 10s	Kerry	Clanmaurice / Iraghticonnor	Listowel	II.	169 / 190
39, 40, 48, 49, 59	Dysert	6,073 3 23t	Kerry	Trughanacmy	Killarney / Tralee	II.	210
21, 30	Dysert	909 3 32	Limerick	Coshma	Croom	II.	243
2, 3	Dysert	5,396 1 12u	Waterford	Upperthird	Carrick on Suir / Clonmel	II.	369
23, 26, 27	Earlstown	2,938 0 29	Kilkenny	Shillelogher	Callan	I.	114
10, 11, 17, 23	Easky	13,285 3 18v	Sligo	Tireragh	Dromore West	IV.	233, 234
26, 32	Edermine	4,130 2 23	Wexford	Ballaghkeen	Enniscorthy	I.	294
47, 55	Effin	1,980 2 3 / 3,286 2 36	Limerick	Coshlea / Coshma	Kilmallock	II.	238 / 243
7, 8, 11, 12	Eglish	3,428 3 23 / 7,145 3 34w	Armagh	Armagh / Tiranny	Armagh	III.	44 / 59, 60
22, 23, 30, 31, 35	Eglish	14,799 3 4x	King's Co.	Eglish	Parsonstown	I.	134, 135
16, 17, 21, 22, 23	Elphin	12,544 1 39y	Roscommon	Roscommon	Castlereagh / Strokestown	IV.	209, 210

	A. R. P.		A. R. P.			A. R. P.
(a) Including	4 0 39 of water.	(j) Including	1,020 3 12 Great Blasket Island.			33 3 8 of River Feale tidal portion.
(b) Including	7 3 0 of Lough Cullin.	(k) Including	53 3 1 Guns Island.	(s) Including		34 1 18 of River Feale freshwater.
(c) Including	2 1 20 of River Barrow.	(l) Including	510 3 38 detached portion.			9 3 6 of Galey River tideway.
(d) Including	23 2 16 of River Barrow.	(m) Including	176 1 24 of water.			2,384 1 11 North Portion.
(e) Including	17 3 21 of River Boyne.	(n) Including	843 3 17 detached portions. / 960 0 16 of Lough Ennell.	(t) Composed of		509 1 23 Middle Portion. / 3,180 0 29 South Portion.
(f) Including	1,149 1 27 detached portion. / 48 1 16 of water.	(o) Including	214 1 25 of Lough Ennell.	(u) Including		47 0 22 of River Suir. / 7 1 18 of lake.
(g) Including	2,508 0 5 detached portion. / 16 3 5 of water.	(p) Including	13 2 26 of water.	(v) Including		4 3 0 of Lough Scorrew.
(h) Including	15 1 4 of River Nore.	(q) Including	169 0 2 of water.	(w) Including		11 2 12 of water.
(i) Including	436 2 36 detached portions.	(r) Including	43 1 14 of River Feale tideway. / 7 2 22 of River Brick tideway.	(x) Including		164 1 10 of water.
				(y) Including		426 3 9 of water.

No. of Sheet of the Ordnance Survey Maps.	Parishes.	Area in Statute Measure.	County.	Barony.	Poor Law Union in 1857.	Townland Census of 1851, Part I. Vol.	Page
		A. R. P.					
17, 18, 22, 23	Ematris	12,297 3 17a	Monaghan	Dartree	Cootehill	III.	266, 267
11, 17	Emlagh	2,118 2 9	Meath	Lower Kells	Kells	I.	202
26, 33, 39,	Emlaghfad	9,453 1 7b	Sligo	Corran	{Boyle / Sligo / Tobercurry}	IV.	226
57, 58, 65, 66	Emly	9,183 2 35	Tipperary, S.R.	Clanwilliam	Tipperary	II.	307, 308
40, 48	Emlygrennan	2,513 0 37	Limerick	Coshlea	Kilmallock	II.	238
35, 36, 40, 41	Ennereilly	3,213 2 4	Wicklow	Arklow	Rathdrum	I.	344
26, 27, 33, 34	Enniscoffey	4,466 2 23c	Westmeath	Fartullagh	Mullingar	I.	268
28, 29, 34, 35		14,410 2 18d	Cavan	Clankee	Bailieborough	III.	72, 73
2, 3, 5, 6	Enniskeen	{2,103 1 8e / 4,295 3 17f}	Meath	{Lower Kells / Morgallion}	Kells	I.	{202 / 209}
		53 1 34g		Magheraboy	{Enniskillen		212
16, 17, 18, 22, 23,	Enniskillen	26,386 3 32h	Fermanagh	Tirkennedy		III.	221
24, 27					Lisnaskea		to 223
23, 27	Ennisnag	{233 3 3 / 1,502 0 28}	Kilkenny	{Knocktopher / Shillelogher}	Thomastown	I.	{111 / 114}
3, 7, 8, 12		12,595 0 10	Kilkenny	Galmoy	Urlingford	I.	92
33, 34	Erke	{3,685 0 8 / 2,304 1 16}	Queen's Co.	{Clandonagh / Clarmallagh}	Donaghmore	I.	{233 / 237}
10, 11, 17, 18, 25, 26, 31, 32	Errigal	19,625 1 13	Londonderry	Coleraine	Coleraine	III.	232
44, 45, 52, 53, 59, 60	Errigal Keerogue	21,139 3 13i	Tyrone	Clogher	{Clogher / Dungannon}	III.	{295 / 296}
1, 2, 3, 4, 5, 6	Errigal Trough	21,174 1 14j	Monaghan	Trough	{Clogher / Monaghan}	III.	{283 / to 285 / 296}
59, 65		3,617 3 11k	Tyrone	Clogher			
53	Erry	1,857 0 2	Tipperary, S.R.	Middlethird	Cashel	II.	326
17	Esker	{2,366 3 24l / 141 2 35}	Dublin	{Newcastle / Uppercross}	{Celbridge / Dublin South}	I.	{33 / 40}
9, 10, 15	Estersnow	6,457 0 16m	Roscommon	Boyle	Boyle	IV.	194, 195
38, 39, 42, 43	Ettagh	{1,131 3 21 / 5,970 0 13}	King's Co.	{Ballybritt / Clonlisk}	Roscrea	I.	{125 / 130}
19, 20, 28, 29, 30, 38	Fahan Lower	24,782 2 24n	Donegal	Inishowen West	Inishowen	III.	120
29, 38, 39	Fahan Upper	10,040 1 12	Donegal	Inishowen West	Londonderry	III.	121
108, 118	Fahy	3,823 3 17o	Galway	Longford	Portumna	IV.	58
10, 18	Faithlegg	1,494 0 38	Waterford	Gaultiere	Waterford	II.	362
28, 32	Famma	492 1 25p	Kilkenny	Gowran	Thomastown	I.	94
93, 94, 106, 107, 108 120, 121	Fanlobbus	35,605 3 17q	Cork, W.R.	East Carbery (W.D.)	Dunmanway	II.	131, 132
9, 18	Farahy	{1,195 2 28 / 4,298 0 27}	Cork, E.R.	{Condons & Clangibbon / Fermoy}	{Mallow / Mitchelstown}	II.	{60 / 79}
7, 8, 12, 13	Faughalstown	7,050 1 13r	Westmeath	Fore	{Castletowndelvin / Granard}	I.	269, 270
9, 14, 15, 16, 23, 24	Faughanvale	20,496 3 30s	Londonderry	Tirkeeran	{Londonderry / Newt'n Limavady}	III.	249, 250
3, 4, 7	Faughart	2,480 1 36	Louth	Upper Dundalk	Dundalk	I.	178
37	Feagh, St Michael's of	99 2 25	Wexford	Forth	Wexford	I.	315
12, 13, 19, 20, 27, 28	Feakle	36,972 0 11t	Clare	Tulla Upper	{Scarriff / Tulla}	II.	38 to 40
13, 22, 23, 31	Fedamore	{901 1 33 / 5,836 2 7}	Limerick	{Clanwilliam / Smallcounty}	{Croom / Limerick}	II.	{223 / 259}
51, 52, 62	Feenagh	2,854 1 8u	Clare	Bunratty Lower	{Ennis / Tulla}	II.	4
17, 18, 23	Feighcullen	{3,042 2 17v / 1,133 0 37}	Kildare	{Connell / East Offaly}	{Naas / Edenderry}	I.	{55 / 70}
24, 25, 28, 29	Fenagh	{122 0 22 / 6,859 2 31w / 2,783 0 34x}	Leitrim	{Carrigallen / Leitrim / Mohill}	{Bawnboy / Mohill}	IV.	{91 / 100 / 106}
28	Fenit	685 2 28	Kerry	Trughanacmy	Tralee	II.	210
8, 12, 13, 16, 17, 19, 20	Fennagh	{1,565 1 38y / 7,241 3 14z / 1,716 2 29}	Carlow	{Forth / Idrone East / Rathvilly}	Carlow	I.	{4 / 7 / 11}
19, 26	Fennor	1,127 0 14aa	Meath	Lower Duleek	Navan	I.	196
36, 42, 43, 48	Fennor	7,917 3 23bb	Tipperary, S.R.	Slievardagh	{Thurles / Urlingford}	II.	333
3, 4, 7	Fenoagh	3,613 1 25	Waterford	Upperthird	Carrick on Suir	II.	369, 370
27, 35	Fermoy	3,480 3 25cc	Cork, E.R.	Condons & Clangibbon	Fermoy	II.	60, 61

A. R. P.	A. R. P.	A. R. P.
(a) Including 590 1 32 of water.	(m) Including 296 0 13 of water.	(v) Including 516 3 23 detached portion.
(b) Including {143 3 12 of Templehouse Lake. / 66 2 20 of Ardrea Lough and Owen}	(n) Including 16 0 14 of water.	(w) Including 999 0 38 of water.
(c) Including 12 2 32 of water. [more River.	(o) Including 45 0 38 of River Shannon.	(x) Including 220 2 8 of water.
(d) Including 44 0 1 of water.	(p) Including 21 3 0 of River Nore.	(y) Composed {including 0 1 21 of water in / 548 2 1 East Portion. / 1,016 3 37 West Portion.}
(e) Including 28 0 10 of Ervey Lough.	(q) Including 52 0 20 of water.	
(f) Including 18 1 9 of Newcastle Lough.	(r) Including {898 0 26 of Lough Derravaragh. / 37 2 28 of small loughs.}	(z) Composed of {3,805 1 8 North Portion. / 3,436 2 6 South Portion.}
(g) Including 14 2 30 of River Erne.	(s) Including 60 0 8 of water.	
(h) Including 667 0 20 of water.	(t) Including {972 3 24 Lough Graney. / 171 0 37 of small loughs. [tideway. / 14 2 10 of Owenogarney River}	(aa) Including 36 2 12 of River Boyne.
(i) Including 5 3 35 of water.		(bb) Including 2,168 1 7 detached portion.
(j) Including 50 1 20 of water.		(cc) Including 56 2 16 of water.
(k) Including 51 2 13 of water.	(u) Including 0 2 20 of Rosroe Lough.	
(l) Including 11 1 14 of River Liffey.		

No. of Sheet of the Ordnance Survey Maps.	Parishes.	Area in Statute Measure.	County.	Barony.	Poor Law Union in 1857.	Townland Census of 1851. Part I.	
		A. R. P.				Vol.	Page.
10, 11, 15, 16, 20	Ferns . .	609 3 16 / 9,802 3 25	Wexford . .	Gorey . . . / Scarawalsh . .	Enniscorthy / Gorey . .	I.	316 / 323
8, 9, 12, 13	Fertagh . .	1,273 3 7 / 5,446 0 7	Kilkenny . .	Crannagh . . . / Galmoy . . .	Urlingford . .	I.	85 / 92
41, 47	Fertiana . .	3,606 3 26	Tipperary, N.R.	Eliogarty . .	Cashel / Thurles .	II.	269
70	Fethard . .	1,530 0 30	Tipperary, S.R.	Middlethird . .	Cashel . .	II.	326,327
45, 50	Fethard . .	3,929 2 32	Wexford . .	Shelburne . .	New Ross . .	I.	327
14, 15	Fews . .	6,817 3 15	Waterford . .	Decies without Drum	Kilmacthomas .	II.	356
35, 38, 39, 42	Fiddown . .	9,688 0 0 / 1,421 0 31	Kilkenny . .	Iverk . . . / Knocktopher . .	Carrick on Suir	I.	105 / 111
11, 13, 14, 18	Finglas . .	3,717 0 14a / 979 2 10	Dublin . .	Castleknock . . / Nethercross . .	Dublin North / Balrothery	I.	24, 25 / 30, 31
45, 47	Finglas . .	702 0 8	King's Co. . .	Clonlisk . .	Roscrea . .	I.	130
6, 9, 10	Finnoe . .	5,053 3 7b	Tipperary, N.R.	Lower Ormond .	Borrisokane .	II.	283,284
10, 11, 16, 17	Finuge . .	3,743 0 16c	Kerry . .	Clanmaurice . .	Listowel . .	II.	169
16, 17, 21, 22, 23, 26	Finvoy . .	16,474 1 9d	Antrim . .	Kilconway . .	Ballymoney .	III.	26
60, 61, 73, 74	Fohanagh . .	308 2 5 / 8,377 3 17	Galway . .	Clonmacnowen . / Kilconnell . .	Ballinasloe / Mountbellew	IV.	25 / 39, 40
25, 26, 31, 32	Follistown . .	653 0 33	Meath . .	Skreen . .	Navan . .	I.	220
28, 31, 32	Fontstown . .	2,242 1 35 / 3,037 0 15e	Kildare . .	Narragh & Reban East / West Offaly . .	Athy . .	I.	66 / 72
19	Forenaghts . .	563 3 31	Kildare . .	South Salt . .	Naas . .	I.	77
23, 27	Forgney . .	5,454 2 22f	Longford . .	Shrule . . .	Ballymahon .	I.	166
21, 22, 25, 28, 29, 31, 32	Forkill . .	152 1 5 / 12,437 3 8g / 9,853 0 18	Armagh . .	Orior Lower . . / Orior Upper . . / Cullenagh . .	Castleblayney / Newry . .	III.	56 / 57 / 240
18, 19, 24, 25	Fossy or Timahoe	137 2 1 / 663 1 24	Queen's Co. .	Maryborough East . / Stradbally . .	Abbeyleix . / Athy . .	I.	241 / 247
1, 3	Foyran . .	6,255 2 28h	Westmeath .	Fore . . .	Granard . .	I.	270
9, 13	Freshford . .	2,171 1 8i	Kilkenny . .	Crannagh . . .	Kilkenny . .	I.	85
15, 21	Freynestown . .	1,568 2 6	Wicklow . .	Upper Talbotstown .	Baltinglass .	I.	364
34, 35, 38, 39, 41	Fuerty . .	13,475 3 8j	Roscommon .	Athlone . . .	Roscommon .	IV.	181
47, 52, 53	Gaile . .	2,480 0 12	Tipperary, S.R.	Middlethird . .	Cashel . .	II.	327
41, 49, 50, 57, 58	Galbally . .	15,457 0 37	Limerick . .	Coshlea . . .	Mitchelstown .	II.	238, 239
41, 47, 48	Galbooly . .	1,267 3 3	Tipperary, N.R.	Eliogarty . .	Thurles . .	II.	270
5, 6, 9, 10, 11	Galey . .	12,604 2 28k	Kerry . .	Iraghticonnor . .	Listowel . .	II.	190
14, 15, 21, 22, 23, 30	Gallen . .	19,226 2 18l	King's Co. .	Garrycastle . .	Parsonstown .	I.	135, 136
34,35,39,40,42,43	Galloon, and Islands	9,341 0 24m / 15,513 1 13n / 432 2 3o	Fermanagh .	Clankelly . . . / Coole . . . / Knockninny . .	Clones . . / Lisnaskea . .	III.	198 / 199, 200 / 201
49	Gallow . .	2,583 2 12	Meath . .	Upper Deece . .	Trim . .	I.	193
37, 43	Galtrim . .	4,128 3 8p	Meath . .	Lower Deece . .	Trim . .	I.	191
43, 44, 53	Garfinny . .	3,915 1 19	Kerry . .	Corkaguiny . .	Dingle . .	II.	176, 177
9	Garranamanagh	529 0 6	Kilkenny . .	Crannagh . . .	Urlingford . .	I.	86
76, 88	Garranekinnefeake .	1,571 0 0	Cork, E.R. .	Imokilly . .	Middleton . .	II.	86
71, 72, 78, 79	Garrangibbon .	3,007 0 12 / 1,705 2 34	Tipperary, S.R.	Iffa and Offa East . / Slievardagh . .	Carrick on Suir / Clonmel . .	II.	313 / 333
3, 4, 6, 7	Garristown . .	5,345 1 19	Dublin . .	Balrothery West .	Dunshaughlin .	I.	22
62, 63, 73	Garrycloyne .	868 2 23 / 4,996 2 31q	Cork, E.R. .	Barretts . . . / East Muskerry . .	Cork . .	II.	49 / 103
77, 89	Garryvoe . .	1,698 1 13	Cork, E.R. .	Imokilly . .	Middleton . .	II.	86,87
34, 35, 43, 44, 50, 51, 52, 58, 59	Gartan . .	44,124 0 19r	Donegal . .	Kilmacrenan . .	Dunfanaghy / Letterkenny	III.	127, 128
27, 28, 34, 35	Garvaghy . .	3,807 3 39 / 6,448 2 1s	Down . .	Lower Iveagh, Lr. pt. / Upper Iveagh, Lr. pt.	Banbridge . .	III.	168 / 172, 173
40, 43	Gaulskill . .	1,302 2 21t	Kilkenny . .	Ida . . .	Waterford . .	I.	102
17, 18, 19, 24, 25, 26, 27, 32, 33	Geashill . .	30,162 2 29 / 13,147 1 19	King's Co. .	Geashill . . . / Upper Philipstown .	Edenderry . / Mountmellick / Tullamore .	I.	139, 140 / 144
15	Gernonstown . .	1,301 3 32u	Louth . .	Ardee . .	Ardee . .	I.	172
12, 18, 19	Gernonstown . .	2,837 3 1	Meath . .	Upper Slane . .	Navan . .	I.	224
8, 12, 13, 17	Gilbertstown . .	3,169 0 33v	Carlow . .	Forth . . .	Carlow . .	I.	4
28, 29, 33	Gilltown . .	4,869 0 13w	Kildare . .	South Naas . .	Naas . .	I.	65
23, 24	Girley . .	5,060 0 27x	Meath . .	Upper Kells . .	Castletowndelvin / Kells . .	I.	205

A. R. P.		A. R. P.		A. R. P.	
(a) Including 1,181 3 7 detached portions.		(i) Including 171 0 4 detached portion.		(p) Including 6 1 10 detached portions.	
(b) Including 15 0 19 of Lough Avan.		(j) Including 171 1 24 of water.		(q) Including 13 3 24 of Blarney Lake.	
(c) Including { 2 2 0 of River Feale tidal portion. / 98 0 14 of River Feale freshwater.		(k) Including 2 2 11 of Galey River tideway.		(r) Including 1,590 1 2 of water.	
(d) Including { 90 3 39 of River Bann. / 3 1 12 of small loughs.		(l) Including { 9 3 4 of Lough Boora. / 60 2 0 of River Shannon.		(s) Including 26 0 17 of water.	
(e) Including 595 0 4 detached portion.		(m) Including 137 3 3 of water.		(t) Including 1 3 36 of Lough Cullin.	
(f) Including 40 2 36 of River Inny.		(n) Including { 1,270 2 30 of Upper Lough Erne. / 934 1 26 of small loughs.		(u) Including 17 0 18 of River Glyde.	
(g) Including 11 3 24 of water.		(o) Including 184 3 17 of Upper Lough Erne.		(v) Including 217 3 1 detached portion.	
(h) Including { 803 2 23 of Lough Sheelin. / 74 3 18 of Lough Kinale. / 24 2 10 of Inny River.				(w) Including 5 3 25 of River Liffey.	
				(x) Including 10 1 0 of water.	

No. of Sheet of the Ordnance Survey Maps.	Parishes.	Area in Statute Measure. A. R. P.	County.	Barony.	Poor Law Union in 1857.	Townland Census of 1851, Part I. Vol.	Page
55, 63, 64, 70, 71, 72, 81, 82	Glanbehy	30,807 2 1a	Kerry	Iveragh	Cahersiveen / Killarney	II.	195, 196
19, 26, 27	Glanworth	3,478 3 9 / 6,201 2 26	Cork, E.R.	Condons & Clangibbon / Fermoy	Fermoy / Mitchelstown	II.	61 / 79
3, 4, 8, 9 / 34, 35	Glashare	2,326 0 22 / 432 1 27	Kilkenny / Queen's Co.	Galmoy / Clarmallagh	Urlingford / Abbeyleix	I.	92 / 238
14, 18	Glasnevin	4 0 27 / 995 2 35	Dublin	City of Dublin / Coolock	Dublin North	I.	44, 45 / 27
58, 59, 62, 63	Glenavy	16,786 0 5b	Antrim	Upper Massereene	Antrim / Lisburn / Lurgan	III.	30
58, 66	Glenbane	943 1 5	Tipperary, S.R.	Clanwilliam	Tipperary	II.	308
72, 80, 81, 89, 90, 96	Glencolumbkille	32,182 0 15c	Donegal	Banagh	Glenties	III.	105, 106
24, 25, 30, 31	Glenealy	3,086 1 35 / 5,011 3 4	Wicklow	Arklow / Newcastle	Rathdrum	I.	344 / 351
1, 2	Gleninagh	4,291 2 34	Clare	Burren	Ballyvaghan	II.	12
27, 28, 33, 34, 40	Glenkeen	14,495 2 7	Tipperary, N.R.	Kilnamanagh Upper	Thurles	II.	278, 279
22, 31, 39	Glenogra	4,252 2 20	Limerick	Smallcounty	Croom	II.	259, 260
33, 34, 38, 39	Glenwhirry	11,368 1 13	Antrim	Lower Antrim	Ballymena	III.	4
40, 41, 46, 47	Glynn	4,484 1 28	Antrim	Lower Belfast	Larne	III.	8
44, 45, 53, 54	Gortroe	9,043 0 1	Cork, E.R.	Barrymore	Fermoy / Middleton	II.	54, 55
20, 21, 24, 25	Gowran	6,347 1 26	Kilkenny	Gowran	Kilkenny	I.	95
25, 29, 33	Graiguenamanagh	12,422 3 10d	Kilkenny	Gowran	Thomastown	I.	95
4, 7	Grallagh	791 3 31	Dublin	Balrothery West	Balrothery	I.	22
6, 7, 10, 11, 15, 16	Granard	500 3 21 / 17,772 2 33e	Longford	Ardagh / Granard	Granard	I.	152 / 156, 157
38, 40	Graney	5,228 2 25f	Kildare	Kilkea and Moone	Athy / Baltinglass	I.	60
8, 12	Grange	4,383 3 32g / 2,411 2 3h	Armagh	Armagh / Oneilland West	Armagh	III.	44, 45 / 52
85, 86, 97, 98	Grange	3,754 2 28 / 941 2 27	Galway	Kilconnell / Loughrea	Loughrea	IV.	40 / 63
18, 19, 22, 23	Grange	1,934 2 24	Kilkenny	Shillelogher	Kilkenny	I.	114
28, 36	Grange	2,838 2 6	Limerick	Glenquin	Newcastle	II.	245
22	Grangeclare	532 3 8	Kildare	East Offaly	Edenderry / Naas	I.	70
8	Grangeford	3,503 1 26	Carlow	Carlow	Carlow	I.	2
12, 13, 19	Grangegeeth	4,447 2 15	Meath	Upper Slane	Ardee	I.	224
18	Grangegorman	326 0 8 / 552 0 25	Dublin	City of Dublin / Coolock	Dublin North	I.	44, 45 / 27
23, 24	Grangekilree	991 2 7i	Kilkenny	Shillelogher	Kilkenny	I.	114
9, 10, 14	Grangemaccomb	3,485 3 37j	Kilkenny	Fassadinin	Castlecomer / Kilkenny / Urlingford	I.	89
71, 72	Grangemockler	2,803 2 8	Tipperary, S.R.	Slievardagh	Carrick on Suir	II.	333
36, 37, 42, 43	Grange of Ballyscullion	4,279 1 0k	Antrim	Upper Toome	Ballymena	III.	33
45, 51	Grange of Doagh	2,304 2 7l	Antrim	Upper Antrim	Antrim	III.	6
7, 8, 12, 13	Grange of Drumtullagh	3,753 1 23	Antrim	Cary	Ballycastle	III.	14
23, 27	Grange of Dundermot	3,003 3 4	Antrim	Kilconway	Ballymena	III.	26, 27
10, 14, 15	Grange of Inispollan	933 1 35	Antrim	Lower Glenarm	Ballycastle	III.	21
35, 40	Grange of Killyglen	2,295 2 14	Antrim	Upper Glenarm	Larne	III.	24
14, 15, 19	Grange of Layd	7,834 0 3	Antrim	Lower Glenarm	Ballycastle	III.	22
49, 50, 54, 55	Grange of Muckamore	5,440 0 36m	Antrim	Lower Massereene	Antrim	III.	28, 29
50, 51	Grange of Nilteen	2,737 2 22	Antrim	Upper Antrim	Antrim	III.	6, 7
43, 44	Grange of Shilvodan	3,546 2 1	Antrim	Upper Toome	Antrim	III.	35
35, 38, 40	Grange or Lisgenan	5,709 3 0n	Waterford	Decies within Drum	Youghal	II.	352
35, 36, 37, 38	Grangerosnolvan	1,392 2 30	Kildare	Kilkea and Moone	Athy	I.	60
21, 25	Grangesilvia	4,807 0 26o	Kilkenny	Gowran	Kilkenny / Thomastown	I.	95, 96
47, 48, 53, 54, 61, 62	Graystown	908 2 30 / 6,893 0 35p	Tipperary, S.R.	Middlethird / Slievardagh	Callan / Cashel / Urlingford	II.	327 / 333
15, 23, 24, 33	Grean	1,511 0 27 / 5,680 0 10	Limerick	Clanwilliam / Coonagh	Limerick / Tipperary	II.	224 / 235
23, 24, 28	Greatconnell	4,847 2 22q	Kildare	Connell	Naas	I.	55
45	Greenoge	1,488 1 6	Meath	Ratoath	Dunshaughlin	I.	218
42, 51, 62	Grenagh	13,202 3 25 / 354 3 4	Cork, E.R.	Barretts / East Muskerry	Cork	II.	49 / 103
6, 11, 12	Greyabbey, and Islands	7,689 0 29	Down	Ards Lower	Newtownards	III.	158
7, 8	Guilcagh	3,949 2 9	Waterford	Upperthird	Carrick on Suir	II.	370

A. R. P.
(a) Including 548 2 37 of Lough Caragh. / 470 1 28 of small loughs.
(b) Including 6 3 23 Rams Island. / Duck Island. / 342 2 6 of Portmore Lough. / 9,219 1 23 of Lough Neagh.
(c) Including 329 1 25 of water.
(d) Including 46 0 23 of River Barrow.

A. R. P.
(e) Including 235 3 33 of Lough Kinale. / 71 3 19 of small loughs.
(f) Including 938 3 22 detached portion.
(g) Including 24 1 35 detached portion.
(h) Including 35 3 9 of water.
(i) Including 4 3 30 of River Nore.
(j) Including 401 3 12 detached portion.

A. R. P.
(k) Including 11 0 10 of River Bann. / 4 3 32 of Lough Beg.
(l) Including 9 2 7 of water.
(m) Including 1,518 3 21 of Lough Neagh.
(n) Including 1,076 3 30 detached portion.
(o) Including 40 2 29 of River Barrow.
(p) Including 334 0 21 detached portion.
(q) Including 82 1 12 of River Liffey.

No. of Sheet of the Ordnance Survey Maps.	Parishes.	Area in Statut. Measure.	County.	Barony.	Poor Law Union in 1857.	Townland Census of 1851, Part I.	
		A. R. P.				Vol.	Page
4, 5, 9, 10	Hacketstown .	5,451 3 37	Carlow . .	Rathvilly . . .	Baltinglass	I.	11
28, 33, 38		6,165 3 31	Wicklow . .	Ballinacor South .	Shillelagh . .		348, 349
3	Hackmys .	63 1 35	Cork, E.R. .	Orrery and Kilmore	Kilmallock . .	II.	108
46, 47		2,248 3 18	Limerick . .	Coshma . .			243
7, 12	Haggardstown .	1,400 0 21	Louth . .	Upper Dundalk .	Dundalk . .	I.	178
4, 9	Haroldstown .	2,833 3 22	Carlow . .	Rathvilly . . .	Shillelagh . .	I.	11
27, 31	Harristown .	4,680 1 36a	Kildare . .	West Offaly . .	Athy . .	I.	72
19, 20	Haynestown .	459 0 22	Kildare . .	South Salt . .	Naas . .	I.	77
11, 12	Haynestown .	1,980 1 29	Louth . .	Upper Dundalk .	Dundalk . .	I.	178
14, 15, 21, 22	Hillsborough .	8,484 2 34b	Down . .	Lower Iveagh, Up. pt.	Lisburn . .	III.	169, 170
4, 7	Hollywood .	3,997 ? 14	Dublin . .	Balrothery West .	Balrothery .	I.	23
9, 10, 15, 16, 17, 22	Hollywood .	10,383 2 4c	Wicklow . .	Lower Talbotstown .	Baltinglass	I.	360, 361
					Naas		
5	Holmpatrick .	2,131 0 36d	Dublin . .	Balrothery East .	Balrothery .	I.	20
40, 41, 46, 47, 52, 53	Holycross .	6,321 3 21	Tipperary, N.R. .	Eliogarty . .	Cashel . .	II.	270
		1,816 0 33	Tipperary, S.R. .	Middlethird . .	Thurles . .		327
74	Holy Trinity .	97 1 9e	Cork, E.R. .	City of Cork . .	Cork . .	II.	111
1, 4, 5	Holywood .	8,064 1 14	Down . .	Lower Castlereagh .	Belfast . .	III.	162, 163
49, 54	Hook . .	1,065 0 28	Wexford . .	Shelburne . .	New Ross .	I.	327
60, 61	Horeabbey .	1,520 0 7	Tipperary, S.R. .	Middlethird . .	Cashel . .	II.	327
35, 36, 40, 41	Horetown .	3,991 0 27	Wexford . .	Shelmaliere West .	New Ross .	I.	333
2	Horseleap or Ard-	2,812 3 15	King's Co. .	Kilcoursey . .	Mullingar .	I.	140
24, 31, 32, 37, 38	nurcher . .	9,199 2 9	Westmeath . .	Moycashel . .	Tullamore .		276, 277
32, 33, 40, 41	Hospital . .	3,999 0 7	Limerick . .	Smallcounty . .	Kilmallock .	II.	260
15, 16, 19	Howth . .	2,669 2 3f	Dublin . .	Coolock . .	Dublin North .	I.	27, 28
66, 77, 78	Ightermurragh .	5,555 2 4g	Cork, E.R. .	Imokilly . .	Middleton . .	II.	87
7, 8, 16, 17	Imphrick .	3,145 0 36	Cork, E.R. .	Fermoy . .	Mallow . .	II.	80
		966 2 5		Orrery and Kilmore	Kilmallock .		108
23, 24, 31, 32, 33	Inagh . .	19,887 3 9h	Clare . .	Inchiquin . .	Ennistimon .	II.	24, 25
76, 88, 89, 100	Inch . .	3,822 2 6i	Cork, E.R. .	Imokilly . .	Middleton . .	II.	87
37, 38, 46, 47	Inch . .	3,099 0 20	Donegal . .	Inishowen West .	Londonderry .	III.	121
34, 35, 40, 41	Inch . .	4,889 0 23	Tipperary, N.R. .	Eliogarty . .	Thurles . .	II.	270
2, 3, 7	Inch . .	5,943 0 7	Wexford . .	Gorey . .	Gorey . .	I.	316
40, 45		859 3 24	Wicklow . .	Arklow . .	Rathdrum .		344
35, 40	Inch . .	1,388 3 3	Wexford . .	Shelmaliere West .	New Ross .	I.	333
30, 31, 37	Inch, and Islands	6,494 1 12j	Down . .	Lecale Lower .	Downpatrick .	III.	179
18, 19, 26, 27, 34	Inchicronan .	17,438 1 34k	Clare . .	Bunratty Upper .	Ennis	II.	8, 9
					Gort .		
					Tulla		
68, 69, 70, 80,	Inchigeelagh .	5,576 1 17l	Cork, W.R. .	East Carbery (W.D.)	Dunmanway	II.	132
81, 82, 92, 93		39,839 0 4m		West Muskerry .	Macroom .		156 to 158
65, 66, 76, 77	Inchinabacky .	1,475 1 22	Cork, E.R. .	Barrymore . .	Middleton . .	II.	55
14, 23	Inch St. Lawrence .	2,203 0 27	Limerick . .	Clanwilliam . .	Limerick . .	II.	224
19, 23	Inchyolaghan or Castleinch .	2,366 3 19	Kilkenny . .	Shillelogher . .	Kilkenny . .	I.	114
85, 96, 97, 110, 111	Inishannon .	4,320 0 29	Cork, E.R. .	Kinalea . .	Bandon . .	II.	95
		2,831 0 34	Cork, W.R. .	East Carbery (E.D.)			128
11, 12, 17, 18, 24, 25	Inishargy, and Islands	5,516 0 26	Down . .	Ards Upper . .	Newtownards .	III.	160
104, 114	Inishbofin .	3,151 3 1n	Mayo . .	Murrisk . .	Clifden . .	IV.	159
29	Inishcaltra .	684 0 14o	Clare . .	Tulla Upper . .	Scarriff . .	II.	40
131, 134, 136		10,599 3 29p	Galway . .	Leitrim . .		IV.	53, 54
61, 62, 72, 73	Inishcarra .	10,190 0 6q	Cork, E.R. .	East Muskerry .	Cork . .	II.	103, 104
119, 120	Inisheer . .	1,400 0 12r	Galway . .	Aran . .	Galway . .	IV.	3
50, 58, 59, 64, 65,	Inishkeel, and Islands	21,627 2 27s	Donegal . .	Banagh . .	Glenties . .	III.	106
66, 67, 72, 73, 74,		80,453 3 9t		Boylagh . .			112
75, 78, 81, 82, 83,							to 114
84, 91, 92		86 1 3		Louth . .			184
6, 11	Inishkeen .	1,116 2 21u	Louth . .	Upper Dundalk .	Dundalk . .	I.	179
29, 32		4,989 3 17	Monaghan . .	Farney . .		III.	271
73, 74, 85, 86	Inishkenny .	2,899 2 15	Cork, E.R. .	Cork . .	Cork . .	II.	64
		958 2 16		East Muskerry .			104
76, 77, 82, 83	Inishlounaght .	6,407 3 23v	Tipperary, S.R. .	Iffa and Offa East .	Clogheen	II.	313
1		2,970 0 37w	Waterford . .	Glenahiry . .	Clonmel		365
119	Inishmaan . .	2,252 3 0x	Galway . .	Aran . .	Galway . .	IV.	3

	A. R. P.			A. R. P.			A. R. P.
(a) Including	1 3 32 detached portion.	(j) Including	80 1 9 of water.	(s) Including	198 3 22 of water.
(b) Including	62 1 35 of water.	(k) Including	597 1 28 of water.	(t) Including	730 1 14 of the Gweebarra tideway.
(c) Including	13 1 2 of water.	(l) Including	6 2 37 of water.		1,671 0 38 of loughs.
(d) Including	28 2 38 detached portion.	(m) Including	506 2 31 of water.	(u) Including	1 0 0 detached portion.
	38 0 29 Islands.	(n) Including	41 2 29 of water.		0 3 34 of Drumcah Lough.
(e) Including	15 0 10 of River Lee tideway.	(o) Including	279 1 0 of Lough Derg.	(v) Including	530 0 38 detached portion.
(f) Including	53 0 24 Ireland's Eye.	(p) Including	1,532 3 4 of Lough Derg.		50 3 6 of water.
(g) Including	12 3 20 Ballyhonock Lough.	(q) Including	48 2 25 of River Lee.	(w) Including	39 3 1 of River Suir.
(h) Including	231 1 6 of water.	(r) Including	16 2 27 Lough More.	(x) Including	16 1 24 Sandhead Lough.
(i) Including	1,570 3 5 detached portions.				

No. of Sheet of the Ordnance Survey Maps.	Parishes.	Area in Statute Measure.			County.	Barony.	Poor Law Union in 1857.	Townland Census of 1851, Part I.	
		A.	R.	P.				Vol.	Page
106, 107, 109, 110 7,8,9,10,12,13,14,15	Inishmacsaint, and Islands	7,126 45,867	3 0	30a 32b	Donegal Fermanagh	Tirhugh Magheraboy	Ballyshannon Enniskillen	III.	147 212,213
12, 15, 16, 17, 18,20	Inishmagrath	27,439	0	12c	Leitrim	Drumahaire	Manorhamilton	IV.	95 to 97
110, 111, 119	Inishmore, and Islands	7,635	0	5d	Galway	Aran	Galway	IV.	3
6, 7	Inishmot	1,437	2	6	Meath	Lower Slane	Ardee	I.	223
10, 14, 15	Inispollan, Grange of	933	1	35	Antrim	Lower Glenarm	Ballycastle	III.	21
28, 29, 32, 33, 36	Inistioge	9,741	1	19e	Kilkenny	Gowran	Thomastown	I.	96
40	Inver	1,773	0	28	Antrim	Lower Belfast	Larne	III.	8
75,83,84,92,93,98,99	Inver	36,810	3	3f	Donegal	Banagh	Donegal	III.	106 to 108
104, 105, 114	Isertkelly	1,894	0	6g	Galway	Loughrea	Loughrea	IV.	63
63	Isertkieran	1,428	2	10	Tipperary, S.R.	Slievardagh	Callan	II.	333
47, 48, 52, 53	Ishartmon	965	3	0h	Wexford	Forth	Wexford	I.	309,310
122, 135, 144	Island	1,367 1,309	0 1	16 27	Cork, W.R.	East Carbery (E.D.) Ibane and Barryroe	Clonakilty	II.	128 149
58, 59, 68, 69 77, 78, 88, 89	Islandeady	8,941 15,998	0 2	27i 16j	Mayo	Burrishoole Carra	Castlebar Westport	IV.	121 128,129
25, 26	Islandikane	4,537	2	1k	Waterford	Middlethird	Kilmacthomas Waterford	II.	367
41, 47	Island Magee	7,036	2	26l	Antrim	Lower Belfast	Larne	III.	8, 9
3, 11	Iveruss	2,765	0	24	Limerick	Kenry	Rathkeale	II.	248,249
29	Jago	1,520	3	13m	Kildare	South Naas	Naas	I.	65
28, 32	Jerpointabbey	1,008	0	23n	Kilkenny	Gowran	Thomastown	I.	96
27, 28, 31, 32, 36	Jerpointchurch	5,994	2	34o	Kilkenny	Knocktopher	Thomastown	I.	111
28, 32, 33, 36, 37	Jerpointwest	1,819 1,167 2,529	1 0 3	35p 38 39	Kilkenny	Gowran Ida Knocktopher	Thomastown New Ross	I.	96 102 111
14, 19	Johnstown	1,243	0	28	Kildare	North Naas	Naas	I.	62
29, 32	Jonesborough	2,185	3	14	Armagh	Orior Upper	Newry	III.	57
20, 21, 27, 28	Julianstown	2,782 283	1 1	12q 21r	Meath	Lower Duleek Upper Duleek	Drogheda	I.	196 198
3, 4, 6, 7	Kane	749	2	18	Louth	Upper Dundalk	Dundalk	I.	179
16, 19, 20, 23, 24	Keady	13,226 2,125	2 1	0s 12t	Armagh	Armagh Tiranny	Armagh	III.	45 60
7, 8, 12, 13, 17	Kellistown,	2,662 1,742	3 2	39 33u	Carlow	Carlow Forth	Carlow	I.	2 4, 5
23, 27	Kells	3,820 589	0 3	27 15v	Kilkenny	Kells Shillelogher	Callan	I.	108 115
10, 11, 16, 17	Kells	8,597	0	32w	Meath	Upper Kells	Kells	I.	205, 206
83, 84, 92, 93, 94, 102, 103	Kenmare	22,507	2	5x	Kerry	Glanarought	Kenmare	II.	185, 186
26, 32	Kentstown	2,521	0	3	Meath	Lower Duleek	Navan	I.	196
14, 19	Kerdiffstown	703	0	27	Kildare	North Naas	Naas	I.	62
42	Kerloge	268	3	32	Wexford	Forth	Wexford	I.	310
64, 65, 71, 72	Kilballyowen	10,835	0	19	Clare	Moyarta	Kilrush	II.	31,32
15	Kilbarrack	740	0	14	Dublin	Coolock	Dublin North	I.	28
89, 103, 104, 106, 107, 108, 110	Kilbarron	23,932	3	36y	Donegal	Tirhugh	Ballyshannon Glenties	III.	148
135 6, 9	Kilbarron	814 10,529	2 0	8z 4aa	Galway Tipperary, N.R.	Leitrim Lower Ormond	Scarriff Borrisokane	IV. II.	54 284
9, 17	Kilbarry	2,631	1	26	Waterford	Gaultiere	Waterford	II.	363
16, 25	Kilbarrymeaden	6,263	3	12bb	Waterford	Decies without Drum	Kilmacthomas	II.	356
123, 129	Kilbeacanty	12,473	2	33cc	Galway	Kiltartan	Gort	IV.	47
36, 40	Kilbeacon	3,402	2	33	Kilkenny	Knocktopher	Waterford	I.	111, 112
51, 52, 62, 63, 64 72, 73, 74	Kilbeagh	33,824	3	22dd	Mayo	Costello	Castlereagh Swineford	IV.	140, 141
5, 11	Kilbeg	5,184	3	30ee	Meath	Lower Kells	Kells	I.	202, 203
32, 37, 38	Kilbeggan	6,085	3	26	Westmeath	Moycashel	Tullamore	I.	278
7, 19, 20, 32	Kilbegnet	10,867	2	36ff	Galway	Ballymoe	Glennamaddy Roscommon	IV.	8
50, 57, 58, 60	Kilbeheny	15,376	1	29	Limerick	Coshlea	Mitchelstown	II.	239
29,30,38,39,47,48,60	Kilbelfad	13,515	1	12gg	Mayo	Tirawley	Ballina	IV.	167, 168

	A. R. P.			A. R. P.			A. R. P.
(a) Including	27 3 10 of River Erne.			615 0 10 of Beltra Lough.	(u) Including		0 0 37 of water.
(b) Including	8,002 3 39 of Lower Lough Erne. 886 2 16 of Lough Melvin. 507 0 11 of River Duue and small loughs.	(j) Including		140 1 38 of Islandeady Lough. 90 2 8 of Lannagh or Castlebar 100 0 07 of small loughs. [Lanagh.	(v) Including (w) Including (x) Including		168 2 18 detached portion. 44 1 32 of water. 10 0 5 of water.
(c) Including	4,026 0 8 of Lough Allen. 844 2 36 detached portion. 54 2 23 of small loughs.	(k) Including (l) Including		11 2 0 of Ballyscanlan Lough. 11 0 39 Isle of Muck. 54 1 16 of water.	(y) Including (z) Including		915 1 31 of River Erne and small 599 3 12 of Lough Derg. [loughs. 38 3 24 of small loughs.
(d) Including	10 2 1 Porthowroogh Lough.	(m) Including		14 1 33 of River Liffey.	(aa) Including		2,822 3 28 of Lough Derg.
(e) Including	30 3 20 of River Nore.	(n) Including		4 1 8 of River Nore.	(bb) Including		0 2 6 of River Mahon tideway.
(f) Including	205 1 13 of water.			1,345 1 10 detached portion.	(cc) Including		63 1 31 of small loughs.
(g) Including	667 1 9 detached portion.	(o) Including		25 0 28 of River Nore.			247 1 7 of Lough Cooter.
(h) Including detached	238 1 3 North portion. 100 0 7 South portion.	(p) Including		399 3 27 detached portion. 15 1 35 of River Nore.	(dd) Including (ee) Including		95 1 37 of water. 5 1 8 of water.
(i) Including	1,825 0 27 detached portion. 329 2 20 of Islandeady Lough. 301 1 16 of small loughs.	(q) Including (r) Including (s) Including (t) Including		45 3 7 of River Nanny tideway. 1 0 1 of River Nanny tideway. 208 0 4 of water. 40 1 13 of water.	(ff) Including (gg) Including		80 0 15 of water. 5,846 3 21 of Lough Conn. 407 2 35 of Lough Cullin. 161 1 28 of small loughs.

No. of Sheet of the Ordnance Survey Maps.	Parishes.	Area in Statute Measure. A. R. P.	County.	Barony.	Poor Law Union in 1857.	Townland Census of 1851, Part I. Vol.	Page
15, 16, 29	Kilbennan	7,656 1 20a	Galway	Dunmore	Tuam	IV.	34
30, 31, 34, 35	Kilberry	10,539 2 16b	Kildare	Narragh&RebanWest	Athy	I.	67, 68
12, 18	Kilberry	4,818 1 28	Meath	Morgallion	Navan	I.	209
6, 10, 11, 18	Kilbixy	6,493 1 4c	Westmeath	Moygoish	Mullingar	I.	279, 280
1, 2, 6, 7	Kilbolane	9,885 0 5	Cork, E.R.	Orrery and Kilmore	Kanturk	II.	108
54		129 2 28	Limerick	Connello Upper	Newcastle		233
84, 96	Kilbonane	4,709 3 32	Cork, E.R.	East Muskerry	Bandon	II.	104
47, 48, 57, 58, 65, 66	Kilbonane	8,668 2 11d	Kerry	Magunihy	Killarney	II.	200
19, 20, 28	Kilbradran	117 2 7	Limerick	Connello Lower	Glin	II.	228
		2,784 2 4		Shanid	Rathkeale		255
61, 69	Kilbragh	1,099 2 9	Tipperary, S.R.	Middlethird	Cashel	II.	327
39, 40, 48	Kilbreedy-major	3,363 1 26	Limerick	Coshlea	Kilmallock	II.	239
		21 0 22		Smallcounty			260
47	Kilbreedy-minor	2,110 1 13	Limerick	Coshma	Kilmallock	II.	243
38, 39	Kilbrew	2,530 2 4	Meath	Ratoath	Dunshaughlin	I.	218
44, 45, 51	Kilbride	5,641 0 15e	Antrim	Upper Antrim	Antrim	III.	6
38, 42	Kilbride	8,316 1 25f	Cavan	Clanmahon	Cavan	III.	77, 78
8, 9		1,025 1 32	Meath	Fore	Oldcastle	I.	200
21	Kilbride	846 0 24	Dublin	Newcastle	Celbridge	I.	33
36, 40, 41	Kilbride	1,696 2 28	Kilkenny	Ida	Waterford	I.	102
8, 9, 16, 17, 25	Kilbride	10,152 2 36	King's Co.	Ballycowan	Tullamore	I.	127, 128
2, 8	Kilbride	7,617 2 19	King's Co.	Kilcoursey	Tullamore	I.	141
7, 14	Kilbride	4,457 1 1	Mayo	Tirawley	Killala	IV.	168
45, 51	Kilbride	3,096 1 3	Meath	Dunboyne	Dunshaughlin	I.	200
28, 29, 35, 36, 39, 40	Kilbride	18,802 0 18g	Roscommon	Ballintober South	Roscommon	IV.	188, 189
		485 0 23h		Roscommon	Strokestown		210
17, 26	Kilbride	1,800 2 34	Waterford	Middlethird	Waterford	II.	367
26, 33	Kilbride	1,980 0 38	Westmeath	Fartullagh	Mullingar	I.	268
15, 16	Kilbride	4,473 2 33	Wexford	Scarawalsh	Enniscorthy Gorey	I.	323
35, 40, 41	Kilbride	6,754 0 8i	Wicklow	Arklow	Rathdrum	I.	344, 345
1, 2, 5, 6	Kilbride	11,640 2 27	Wicklow	Lower Talbotstown	Naas	I.	361
36, 37, 41, 42	Kilbrideglynn	4,109 3 25	Wexford	Shelmaliere West	Wexford	I.	334
27, 33, 34	Kilbride, Pass of,	4,031 3 28j	Westmeath	Fartullagh	Mullingar	I.	269
15, 16, 23, 24	Kilbrin	12,630 3 17	Cork, E.R.	Duhallow	Kanturk	II.	71, 72
110, 111, 123, 124	Kilbrittain	4,750 1 18	Cork, W.R.	East Carbery (E.D.)	Bandon	II.	128
95, 96, 109, 110	Kilbrogan	7,577 1 34	Cork, W.R.	Kinalmeaky	Bandon	II.	152
7, 16, 17	Kilbroney	1,876 1 32	Cork, E.R.	Orrery and Kilmore	Mallow	II.	109
51, 52, 54, 55	Kilbroney	13,208 1 13	Down	Upper Iveagh, Up. pt.	Kilkeel Newry	III.	175, 176
3, 6, 10	Kilbryan	3,852 0 20k	Roscommon	Boyle	Boyle	IV.	195
9, 17	Kilburne	3,514 3 30	Waterford	Middlethird	Waterford	II.	367
81, 82, 90, 91, 96, 97	Kilcar	18,883 1 17	Donegal	Banagh	Glenties	III.	108, 109
15, 16	Kilcaragh	2,910 3 12	Kerry	Clanmaurice	Listowel	II.	169
18	Kilcaragh	651 3 36	Waterford	Gaultiere	Waterford	II.	363
25, 31, 32	Kilcarn	2,337 0 23l	Meath	Skreen	Navan	I.	220
71, 78	Kilcash	3,753 2 14	Tipperary, S.R.	Iffa and Offa East	Clonmel	I.	313
90, 91, 103, 104, 105, 116, 117	Kilcaskan	35,104 3 22m	Cork, W.R.	Bear	Bantry Castletown	II.	122, 123
101, 102, 103, 109, 110		16,386 2 3	Kerry	Glanarought	Kenmare		186, 187
101, 102, 114, 115	Kilcatherine	21,778 1 3n	Cork, W.R.	Bear	Castletown	II.	123, 124
2, 3, 6, 7	Kilcavan	641 3 24	Wexford	Ballaghkeen	Gorey	I.	294
		8,887 1 7		Gorey			317
40, 41, 45, 46	Kilcavan	3,204 2 10	Wexford	Bargy	New Ross Wexford	I.	305
104, 105, 114, 115	Kilchreest	1,378 2 13	Galway	Dunkellin	Loughrea	IV.	28
		2,040 2 10		Loughrea			63
49, 50, 59, 60	Kilchreest, & Islands	7,061 2 8o	Clare	Clonderalaw	Killadysert	II.	14, 15
29, 30, 35, 36	Kilcleagh	15,264 1 10p	Westmeath	Clonlonan	Athlone	I.	261, 262
31, 32, 37, 38, 39, 45	Kilclief	1,853 1 8q	Down	Lecale Lower	Downpatrick	III.	179
		571 0 39		Lecale Upper			181
35, 36	Kilclonagh	758 3 39	Tipperary, N.R.	Eliogarty	Thurles	II.	270
49, 50	Kilclone	2,717 1 20	Meath	Upper Deece	Dunshaughlin	I.	193
9, 10, 18, 19	Kilconfert	10,266 3 15r	King's Co.	Lower Philipstown	Tullamore	I.	142
16, 17, 20, 21	Kilclooney	12,041 1 33s	Armagh	Fews Lower	Armagh	III.	46
		792 0 26		Orior Lower			56

A. R. P.
(a) Including 142 2 28 of water.
(b) Including 73 1 8 of River Barrow.
(c) Including 252 3 24 of Lough Iron. / 51 1 34 of Inny River.
(d) Including 39 0 29 of River Laune.
(e) Including 5 3 16 of water.
(f) Including 564 0 31 of Lough Sheelin.
(g) Including 34 3 36 of water.

A. R. P.
(h) Including 4 0 13 Loughanrah.
(i) Including 59 2 32 of tideway.
(j) Including 21 0 12 of water.
(k) Including 974 2 8 of Lough Key. / 222 0 7 detached portion. / 6 1 31 of River Boyle. / 31 3 29 of small loughs.
(l) Including 12 2 8 of River Boyne.

A. R. P.
(m) Including 339 0 3 of water.
(n) Including 173 2 21 Glanbeg Lough. / 55 0 5 of small loughs.
(o) Including 1 1 24 of Owenslieve River tideway.
(p) Including 22 2 0 of River Shannon.
(q) Including 19 3 0 of water.
(r) Including 3,307 2 5 detached portion.
(s) Including 9 3 8 of water.

6 C

No. of Sheet of the Ordnance Survey Maps.	Parishes.	Area in Statute Measure.	County.	Barony.	Poor Law Union in 1857.	Townland Census of 1851, Part I.	
		A. R. P.				Vol.	Page
74, 87, 88	Kilcloony . .	7,289 0 33a	Galway . .	Clonmacnowen .	Ballinasloe .	IV.	25
37, 40, 41	Kilcoan . .	1,583 0 19	Kilkenny .	Ida . . .	Waterford . .	I.	102
5, 10	Kilcock . .	4,064 0 9	Kildare . .	Ikeathy & Oughterany	Celbridge . .	I.	57
29, 34, 37	Kilcockan . .	4,537 3 34	Waterford .	Coshmore & Coshbride	Lismore . .	II.	343
131, 132, 140, 141	Kilcoe . .	5,272 0 21b	Cork, W.R. .	West Carbery (W.D.)	Skull . .	II.	143
9, 10, 15, 16	Kilcolagh . .	7,217 1 39c	Roscommon .	Frenchpark .	Boyle . .	IV.	203
103, 104, 113	Kilcolgan, and Islands	5,548 1 16d	Galway . .	Dunkellin . .	Gort . .	IV.	28
46, 47, 56, 57	Kilcolman . {	1,982 0 27 / 5,776 1 21e	Kerry . .	Magunihy . / Trughanacmy .	Killarney . .	II. {	200 / 210
38, 39, 42	Kilcolman . {	2,846 1 21 / 5,356 1 11	King's Co. .	Ballybritt . / Clonlisk . .	Parsonstown .	I. {	125 / 130
18, 19, 27, 28	Kilcolman .	2,761 3 28	Limerick . .	Shanid . .	Glin . . / Newcastle .	II.	255
80, 91, 92, 101, 102, 112	Kilcolman .	23,739 1 28f	Mayo . .	Clanmorris .	Claremorris .	IV.	133,134
63, 64, 74, 83 / 8, 14 / 44, 45, 46, 47	Kilcolman . {	10,953 2 8g / 1,628 1 12 / 5,511 2 1h	Mayo . . / Roscommon . / Sligo . .	Costello . . / Frenchpark . / Coolavin .	Castlereagh / Boyle . .	IV. {	141 / 203 / 223,224
13, 18	Kilcolmanbane	638 1 23 / 3,054 3 22	Queen's Co. .	Cullenagh . / Maryborough East .	Abbeyleix . / Mountmellick	I. {	240 / 241
18	Kilcolmanbrack	905 3 26	Queen's Co. .	Cullenagh .	Abbeyleix .	I.	240
40, 41, 43, 44	Kilcolumb .	8,274 0 21i	Kilkenny .	Ida . . .	Waterford . .	I.	102,103
5, 6, 10, 11, 16	Kilcomb .	5,441 0 6	Wexford . .	Scarawalsh .	Gorey . .	I.	323
25, 31, 37	Kilcomenty .	6,943 0 17j	Tipperary, N.R.	Owney and Arra	Nenagh . .	II.	294,295
41, 42, 44, 45	Kilcomin .	3,583 0 19	King's Co. .	Clonlisk . .	Roscrea . .	I.	130,131
18, 22, 23	Kilcommock . {	4,865 1 18k / 6,141 3 30l / 864 3 11	Longford . .	Moydow . . / Rathcline . . / Shrule . .	Ballymahon .	I. {	161 / 164 / 166
1, 3, 4, 5, 10, 11, 12, 13, 17, 18, 19, 20, 25, 26, 27, 34, 35, 36, 43, 44, 45, 55, 56, 57	Kilcommon .	203,396 0 0m	Mayo . .	Erris . .	Belmullet . / Newport .	IV. {	143 to 145
110, 111, 118, 119, 122	Kilcommon .	17,395 3 13n	Mayo . .	Kilmaine .	Ballinrobe . / Claremorris .	IV. {	154,155
24, 30, 35	Kilcommon . {	1,431 1 38 / 3,376 1 9	Wicklow . .	Arklow . . / Newcastle .	Rathdrum . .	I. {	345 / 351
33, 38, 39, 43	Kilcommon .	11,209 0 34	Wicklow . .	Ballinacor South	Shillelagh . .	I.	349
61, 62, 71, 72, 81	Kilconduff, .	16,522 2 31o	Mayo . .	Gallen . .	Swineford .	IV.	147,148
97, 104, 105	Kilconickny, . {	244 1 25 / 3,096 0 28 / 5,012 0 29	Galway . .	Athenry . . / Dunkellin . . / Loughrea . .	Loughrea . .	IV. {	4 / 29 / 63
84, 96, 97	Kilconierin . {	2,496 2 27 / 2,819 3 31 / 161 2 5	Galway . .	Athenry . . / Dunkellin . . / Loughrea . .	Loughrea . .	IV. {	4 / 29 / 64
15, 16, 28, 29	Kilconla . .	9,677 2 19p	Galway . .	Dunmore . .	Tuam . .	IV.	35
1, 2, 4, 5	Kilconly . .	5,742 0 18	Kerry . .	Iraghticonnor .	Listowel . .	II.	191
73, 74, 86, 87	Kilconnell .	6,082 0 33q	Galway . .	Kilconnell .	Ballinasloe .	IV.	40
54, 61, 62	Kilconnell .	2,344 1 39r	Tipperary, S.R.	Middlethird .	Cashel . .	II.	327
50, 51, 60, 61	Kilconry, and Islands	2,926 2 12	Clare . .	Bunratty Lower	Ennis . .	II.	4
42, 43, 48, 49, 52	Kilcoo . .	18,205 2 36s	Down . .	Upper Iveagh, Lr. pt.	Kilkeel . .	III.	173
8, 12, 13	Kilcoole . .	4,476 1 21	Wicklow . .	Newcastle .	Rathdrum . .	I.	351,352
22, 28	Kilcouley, . .	3,476 3 24t	Roscommon .	Roscommon .	Strokestown .	IV.	210
106	Kilcooly . .	1,616 0 12	Galway . .	Leitrim . .	Loughrea . .	IV.	54
12, 17	Kilcooly . {	328 1 23 / 2,515 3 26	Kilkenny . / Tipperary, N.R.	Crannagh . / Eliogarty .	Kilkenny . . / Thurles . .	I. / II. {	86 / 270
36, 42, 43 / 48, 49, 54	Kilcooly . {	8,664 1 36u	Tipperary, S.R.	Slievardagh .	Cashel . / Urlingford .	II. {	333,334
30, 31, 36, 37	Kilcooly . .	2,455 1 11v	Meath . .	Upper Navan .	Trim . .	I.	216
42, 56	Kilcoona . .	6,057 0 30w	Galway . .	Clare . .	Tuam . .	IV.	19, 20
18	Kilcop . .	388 3 7	Waterford .	Gaultiere . .	Waterford . .	II.	363
15, 23	Kilcorcoran .	1,292 0 10	Cork, E.R. .	Duhallow . .	Kanturk . .	II.	72
15, 21, 22	Kilcorkey . .	9,090 0 25	Roscommon .	Castlereagh .	Castlereagh .	IV.	199,200
15, 16, 20, 21, 27	Kilcormick . {	5,810 3 1 / 4,244 1 31	Wexford . {	Ballaghkeen . / Gorey . .	Enniscorthy . / Gorey . .	I. {	294 / 317
3, 11, 12, 20, 21	Kilcornan . .	9,345 3 33x	Limerick . .	Kenry . .	Rathkeale . .	II.	249
58, 66	Kilcornan . .	1,157 1 2	Tipperary, S.R.	Clanwilliam .	Tipperary . .	II.	308
5, 6, 9, 10	Kilcorney . .	3,352 2 4	Clare . .	Burren . .	Ballyvaghan .	II.	12

	A. R. P.			A. R. P.			A. R. P.
(a) Including	88 3 2 of water.	(i) Including	15 3 16 of Lough Cullin.	(q) Including	29 1 0 of water.
(b) Including	355 1 24 detached portion.	(j) Including	51 0 9 of River Shannon.	(r) Including	901 0 12 detached portions.
(c) Including {	1,605 1 9 detached portion. / 252 2 24 Lough Bally.	(k) Including	19 3 24 of Lough Bannow.	(s) Including	96 2 2 of water.
	988 2 17 detached portion.	(l) Including	78 2 8 of water.	(t) Including	56 3 38 of water.
(d) Including {	52 1 10 of water.	(m) Including {	2,436 1 12 Carrowmore Lake. / 1,107 0 36 of Owenmore River / and small loughs.	(u) Including {	2,917 0 27 detached portions. / 10 2 19 of water.
(e) Including	7 1 9 of River Maine tideway.			(v) Including	26 3 37 of River Boyne.
(f) Including	203 0 37 of water.	(n) Including	76 3 39 of water.	(w) Including	334 0 36 of Lough Corrib.
(g) Including	106 3 16 of Lough Gara.	(o) Including	89 3 25 of water.	(x) Including	31 1 10 of water.
(h) Including {	959 1 30 of Lough Gara. / 9 0 11 of Loughanboy.	(p) Including	132 3 39 of water.		

No. of Sheet of the Ordnance Survey Maps.	Parishes.	Area in Statute Measure. (A. R. P.)	County.	Barony.	Poor Law Union in 1857.	Townland Census of 1851, Part I. (Vol.)	(Page)
39, 40, 48, 49	Kilcorney	8,836 1 23	Cork, W.R.	West Muskerry	Millstreet	II.	158
46, 47	Kilcowan	2,082 1 34	Wexford	Bargy	Wexford	I.	305
25, 31	Kilcowanmore	2,760 1 4	Wexford	Bantry	Enniscorthy	I.	300
77, 78, 89	Kilcredan	1,014 0 27	Cork, E.R.	Imokilly	Middleton	II.	87
48, 58	Kilcredane	2,486 0 23	Kerry	Magunihy	Killarney	II.	200
1, 2, 6, 7	Kilcroan	7,701 1 4a	Galway	Ballymoe	Glennamaddy	IV.	8, 9
117, 129, 130, 138, 139	Kilcrohane	14,587 2 11b	Cork, W.R.	West Carbery (W.D.)	Bantry	II.	143,144
82, 90, 91, 92, 98, 99, 100, 101, 105, 106, 107, 108	Kilcrohane	63,701 2 3c	Kerry	Dunkerron South	{Cahersiveen, Kenmare}	II.	183,184
36, 40, 41	Kilcronaghan	7,979 2 5	Londonderry	Loughinsholin	Magherafelt	III.	241
19, 27, 28, 35, 36	Kilcrumper	1,827 1 10d / 1,688 2 24	Cork, E.R.	{Condons&Clangibbon, Fermoy}	Fermoy	II.	61 / 80
32	Kilcullane	1,389 3 25	Limerick	Smallcounty	Kilmallock	II.	260
23, 28, 29, 32, 33	Kilcullen	7,344 3 35e	Kildare	Kilcullen	Naas	I.	58
9, 10	Kilculliheen	2,137 2 34 / 100 2 3	Waterford	{Gaultiere, Waterford City}	Waterford	II.	363 / 373
63	Kilcully	1,759 3 39	Cork, E.R.	Cork	Cork	II.	64
26, 34	Kilcummer	2,612 2 36f	Cork, E.R.	Fermoy	Fermoy	II.	80
48, 49, 50, 58, 59, 60, 66, 67, 68, 76	Kilcummin	38,952 2 39g	Kerry	Magunihy	Killarney	II.	201,202
7, 8, 14, 15	Kilcummin	4,195 1 34h	Mayo	Tirawley	Killala	IV.	168
27, 38, 39, 40, 41, 52, 53, 54, 55, 65, 66, 67, 68, 77, 78, 79, 89, 90, 91	Kilcummin, Islands & detached portions	108,791 0 6i	Galway	Moycullen	{Galway, Oughterard}	IV.	66 to 69
8, 13	Kilcumny	2,921 0 13j	Westmeath	Delvin	Castletowndelvin	I.	265
1, 2	Kilcumreragh	2,293 2 8k	King's Co.	Kilcoursey	Tullamore	I.	141
24, 30, 31		1,642 1 15l / 5,321 0 30	Westmeath	{Clonlonan, Moycashel}	Athlone	I.	262 / 278
70, 71, 79, 80	Kildacommoge	2,896 3 28m / 4,656 1 10n	Mayo	{Carra, Gallen}	Castlebar	IV.	129 / 148
29, 30, 35, 36	Kildalkey	10,415 2 15	Meath	Lune	Trim	I.	208
13, 14, 19	Kildallan	11,989 1 16o	Cavan	Tullyhunco	{Bawnboy, Cavan}	III.	96,97
27	Kildangan	988 2 11	Kildare	West Offaly	Athy	I.	72
22, 23, 24, 27, 28	Kildare	878 0 0p / 8,337 2 26q	Kildare	{Connell, East Offaly}	{Edenderry, Naas}	I.	55 / 70
42, 47	Kildavin	3,411 1 17	Wexford	Forth	Wexford	I.	310
22, 28	Kildellig	1,251 0 28	Queen's Co.	Clarmallagh	Donaghmore	I.	238
17, 20	Kildemock	3,246 1 9	Louth	Ardee	Ardee	I.	172,173
15, 20	Kilderry	2,192 1 36	Kilkenny	Gowran	Kilkenny	I.	96
4, 11, 12	Kildimo	6,182 2 39r	Limerick	Kenry	{Croom, Rathkeale}	II.	249,250
11 / 7, 8, 12	Kildollagh	22 2 18 / 1,962 0 6s	Antrim / Londonderry	Upper Dunluce / North East Liberties of Coleraine	Coleraine	III.	19 / 246
9, 18	Kildorrery	2,934 3 25 / 401 2 15	Cork, E.R.	{Condons&Clangibbon, Fermoy}	Mitchelstown	II.	61 / 80
20,21,28,29,37,38	Kildress	26,251 2 37t	Tyrone	Dungannon Upper	Cookstown	III.	308,309
11	Kildrought	1,843 3 17u	Kildare	North Salt	Celbridge	I.	74
42, 43, 52, 53	Kildrum	2,888 1 25v	Kerry	Corkaguiny	Dingle	II.	177
16, 17, 22, 27	Kildrumsherdan	16,618 2 9w	Cavan	Tullygarvey	Cootehill	III.	89,90
24, 28, 29	Kilfane	3,971 2 12	Kilkenny	Gowran	Thomastown	I.	96,97
22, 23, 30, 31	Kilfarboy	13,981 1 32x	Clare	Ibrickan	Ennistimon	II.	22
133, 134, 142, 143	Kilfaughnabeg	3,126 2 19y	Cork, W.R.	East Carbery (W.D.)	{Clonakilty, Skibbereen}	II.	132,133
59, 60, 67, 68	Kilfeakle	6,500 2 11	Tipperary, S.R.	Clanwilliam	Tipperary	II.	308
46, 55, 56, 57, 66	Kilfearagh	9,870 2 38z	Clare	Moyarta	Kilrush	II.	32
15, 16, 17, 22, 23	Kilfeighny	11,408 0 38	Kerry	Clanmaurice	Listowel	II.	169,170
8, 9, 15, 16	Kilfenora	10,776 3 20aa	Clare	Corcomroe	{Corrofin, Ennistimon}	II.	18, 19
19, 20, 23, 24	Kilferagh	964 2 22bb	Kilkenny	Shillelogher	Kilkenny	I.	115
9, 17, 18, 26, 27	Kilfergus	14,207 0 39	Limerick	Shanid	Glin	II.	255,256
13, 14, 19, 20, 21, 29, 30	Kilfian	28,735 2 31	Mayo	Tirawley	{Ballina, Killala}	IV.	169
48, 49, 58, 59, 69	Kilfiddane	13,733 1 4cc	Clare	Clonderalaw	{Killadysert, Kilrush}	II.	15

(a) Including 10 1 11 of water.
(b) Including 10 3 15 Glan Lough.
(c) Including { 789 1 20 of Lough Currane. / 186 2 27 of small loughs.
(d) Including { 684 1 12 detached portion. / 14 3 10 of water.
(e) Including 27 0 25 of River Liffey.
(f) Including 32 1 5 of water.
(g) Including 16 3 37 of water.
(h) Including 20 1 6 of water.
(i) Including { 10,281 1 19 of Lough Corrib. / 4,729 2 25 of small loughs.

(j) Including 24 0 1 of water.
(k) Including 7 3 0 of Ballinderry Lough.
(l) Including 23 0 12 of water.
(m) Including 50 0 32 of water.
(n) Including { 2,094 0 32 detached portions. / 3 3 39 of water.
(o) Including { 10 2 9 of Lough Oughter. / 201 0 3 of water.
(p) Including 7 3 0 of River Liffey.
(q) Including 2,744 0 13 of The Curragh.
(r) Including { 71 3 35 of River Maigue tideway. / 76 0 33 of loughs.

(s) Including 25 1 34 of River Bann.
(t) Including 28 2 33 of water.
(u) Including 17 1 0 of River Liffey.
(v) Including 1,129 1 34 detached portion.
(w) Including 107 1 23 of water.
(x) Including 42 0 37 of water.
(y) Including 11 2 3 Cloonties Lake.
(z) Including 59 0 15 of water.
(aa) Including 218 2 35 of water.
(bb) Including 24 0 12 of River Nore.
(cc) Including 46 1 6 of water.

No. of Sheet of the Ordnance Survey Maps.	Parishes.	Area in Statute Measure.	County.	Barony.	Poor Law Union in 1857.	Townland Census of 1851, Part I. Vol.	Page
		A. R. P.					
43, 52	Kilfinaghta	8,109 2 36a	Clare	Bunratty Lower	{Ennis . Limerick . Tulla}	II.	4
48, 49, 56	Kilfinnane	6,487 1 10	Limerick	Coshlea	Kilmallock	II.	239,240
30	Kilfinny	2,437 3 11	Limerick	Connello Upper	{Croom Rathkeale}	II.	233
52, 62	Kilfintinan, & Islands	6,115 0 12b	Clare	Bunratty Lower	Limerick	II.	5
28, 34	Kilfithmone	1,330 2 1	Tipperary, N.R.	Eliogarty	Thurles	II.	270
15, 21, 22	Kilflyn	6,696 2 20	Kerry	Clanmaurice	{Listowel Tralee}	II.	170
56, 59	Kilflyn	4,818 3 16	Limerick	Coshlea	Kilmallock	II.	240
39, 43, 44, 45, 46	Kilfree	14,313 3 10c	Sligo	Coolavin	Boyle	IV.	224
40, 41	Kilrush	1,525 3 13	Limerick	Smallcounty	Kilmallock	II.	260
122, 135	Kilgarriff	{3,454 1 25 872 2 39}	Cork, W.R.	{East Carbery (E.D.) Ibane and Barryroe}	Clonakilty	II.	{128,129 149}
37, 38, 46, 47	Kilgarrylander	14,630 0 7	Kerry	Trughanacmy	{Dingle Tralee}	II.	210,211
74, 75, 84, 85, 86, 93, 94, 95, 103	Kilgarvan	43,631 3 39d	Kerry	Glanarought	{Kenmare Killarney}	II.	187,188
31, 32, 40, 49	Kilgarvan	19,879 1 36e	Mayo	Gallen	Ballina	IV.	148
31, 35, 36	Kilgarvan	4,275 0 8	Wexford	Shelmaliere West	New Ross	I.	334
75, 84, 85, 86, 94, 95, 96, 97, 104, 105, 106, 107, 115	Kilgeever	58,098 1 8f	Mayo	Murrisk	Westport	IV.	{159 to 161}
36	Kilgefin	6,060 1 8	Roscommon	Ballintober South	Roscommon	IV.	189
73, 74, 86, 87	Kilgerrill	{6,356 2 35 475 3 0}	Galway	{Clonmacnowen Kilconnell}	Ballinasloe	IV.	{25, 26 40}
19, 20, 23, 24	Kilglass	{1,609 1 10 2,307 3 10 1,826 3 23}	Longford	{Ardagh Moydow Shrule}	{Ballymahon Longford}	I.	{152 161 166}
17, 18, 23, 24, 29, 30	Kilglass	{15,511 2 2g 458 3 39}	Roscommon	{Ballintober North Roscommon}	Strokestown	IV.	{186 210}
10, 11, 16, 17, 23	Kilglass	12,884 2 35h	Sligo	Tireragh	Dromore West	IV.	234
36, 37, 45, 46	Kilgobban	10,415 3 13	Kerry	Corkaguiny	Tralee	II.	177
22, 23, 25, 26	Kilgobbin	3,257 2 28	Dublin	Rathdown	Rathdown	I.	35
13, 14, 22, 23, 30, 31	Kilgobnet	16,108 2 23i	Waterford	Decies without Drum	Dungarvan	II.	357
3, 7	Kilgorman	5,164 2 26j	Wexford	Gorey	Gorey	I.	318
77, 83	Kilgrant	3,071 0 13k	Tipperary, S.R.	Iffa and Offa East,	Clonmel	II.	314
7	Kilgrogan	231 1 21	Cork, E.R.	Orrery and Kilmore	Mallow	II.	109
19, 27	Kilgullane	{3,369 0 38 164 2 32}	Cork, E.R.	{Condons & Clangibbon Fermoy}	{Mitchelstown Fermoy}	II.	{61 80}
37, 38	Kilkea	3,096 1 28	Kildare	Kilkea and Moone	Athy	I.	60
21, 22, 27, 28	Kilkeary	2,726 2 9l	Tipperary, N.R.	Upper Ormond	Nenagh	II.	290
31, 35, 36	Kilkeasy	3,317 3 17	Kilkenny	Knocktopher	Thomastown	I.	112
6, 7, 10, 11, 17, 18	Kilkeedy	18,629 1 1m	Clare	Inchiquin	Corrofin	II.	25, 26
4, 12, 13	Kilkeedy	8,880 3 9n	Limerick	Pubblebrien	Limerick	II.	252
48,49,52,53,55,56,57	Kilkeel	47,882 3 19o	Down	Mourne	Kilkeel	III.	182,183
19,20,21,25,26,27,33	Kilkeevin	27,007 1 9p	Roscommon	Castlereagh	Castlereagh	IV.	200,201
15, 16, 22, 23, 29	Kilkenny West	10,047 3 32q	Westmeath	Kilkenny West	{Athlone Ballymahon}	I.	273,274
121, 134, 135, 144	Kilkerranmore	{652 0 1 5,475 1 18}	Cork, W.R.	{East Carbery, W.D. Ibane and Barryroe}	{Clonakilty Dunmanway}	II.	{133 149}
18, 19, 31, 32, 45, 46	Kilkerrin	20,246 3 31r	Galway	Tiaquin	Glennamaddy	IV.	76, 77
14, 15	Kilkieran	1,105 3 21	Kilkenny	Gowran	Kilkenny	I.	97
41, 42, 56	Kilkilvery	2,735 2 3s	Galway	Clare	Tuam	IV.	20
23, 26	Kill	2,702 2 28	Dublin	Rathdown	Rathdown	I.	35, 36
14, 19, 20, 24	Kill	{1,448 2 33 3,401 3 15}	Kildare	{South Naas South Salt}	Naas	I.	{65 77}
73, 86, 98	Killaan	{6,400 1 16 1,466 0 12}	Galway	{Kilconnell Loughrea}	{Ballinasloe Loughrea}	IV.	{41 64}
25, 26, 31, 32, 36, 37	Killabban	{7,290 3 3t 18,705 0 6}	Queen's Co.	{Ballyadams Slievemargy}	{Athy Carlow}	I.	{231 245}
102, 114, 115, 116, 127, 128, 129	Killaconenagh	19,294 1 24u	Cork, W.R.	Bear	Castletown	II.	124,125
29, 35, 36, 41	Killaconnigan	11,561 1 22v	Meath	Lune	Trim	I.	208
10, 18	Killaderry	5,554 2 14	King's Co.	Lower Philipstown	Tullamore	I.	142,143
10, 11, 14, 15	Killadoon	1,765 2 25w	Kildare	North Salt	Celbridge	I.	74, 75
34, 35, 40	Killadoon	3,879 3 24x	Sligo	Tirerrill	Boyle	IV.	238,239

	A. R. P.			A. R. P.			A. R. P.
(a) Including	119 1 9 of water.	(h)	Including	8 0 11 of Lough Scorrew.	(q)	Including	{535 2 7 of Lough Ree. 254 1 2 of small loughs.}
(b) Including	{16 2 4 of Owenogarney River tideway. 9 0 22 Lough Gorteen.}	(i)	Including	673 1 5 detached portions.	(r)	Including	281 0 12 of water.
(c) Including	{295 1 4 of Lough Gara. 7 0 26 of small loughs.}	(j)	Including	5 3 8 Kilpatrick Lough.	(s)	Including	{394 0 6 detached portion. 9 2 15 of water.}
(d) Including	42 2 5 of water.	(k)	Including	14 2 28 of River Suir.	(t)	Including	15 3 27 of River Barrow.
(e) Including	51 1 4 of water.	(l)	Including	992 0 18 detached portion.	(u)	Including	4,372 0 4 Bear Island.
(f) Including	{3,959 0 21 Clare Island. 1,451 2 22 Inishturk. 895 2 16 of water.}	(m)	Including	936 2 38 of water.	(v)	Including	29 2 1 of River Boyne.
		(n)	Including	153 0 22 of River Maigue tideway.	(w)	Including	20 0 32 of River Liffey.
(g) Including	{1,167 2 8 of River Shannon. 583 2 29 Kilglass Lough. 113 3 11 of small loughs.}	(o)	Including	36 3 0 of water.	(x)	Including	{535 0 20 of Lough Arrow. 51 2 17 of small loughs.}
		(p)	Including	{103 2 10 of Lough O'Flyn. 51 0 11 Drumalough. 11 2 22 Cottage Lough.}			

No. of Sheet of the Ordnance Survey Maps.	Parishes.	Area in Statute Measure.			County.	Barony.	Poor Law Union in 1857.	Townland Census of 1851, Part I.	
		A.	R.	P.				Vol.	Page
49, 50, 59, 60, 69	Killadysert, & Islands	12,859	1	4a	Clare	Clonderalaw	Killadysert	II.	15, 16
46, 47, 51, 52	Killag	1,953	0	1	Wexford	Bargy	Wexford	I.	306
6, 14, 15, 23	Killagally or Wheery	17,556	3	22b	King's Co.	Garrycastle	Parsonstown	I.	139
17, 18, 22, 23	Killagan	2,431	2	9	Antrim	Kilconway	Ballymoney	III.	27
		1,406	0	24		Upper Dunluce			19
13, 20, 21	Killagh	2,010	2	8	Westmeath	Delvin	Castletowndelvin	I.	265
44, 45, 53, 54	Killagholehane	4,846	3	12	Limerick	Glenquin	Newcastle	II.	245
82, 83, 91, 92, 97, 98	Killaghtee	13,368	0	0c	Donegal	Banagh	Donegal / Glenties	III.	109,110
67,68,75,76,77,85,86	Killaha	35,259	3	17d	Kerry	Magunihy	Killarney	II.	202
15, 21	Killahan	4,544	3	9e	Kerry	Clanmaurice	Listowel / Tralee	II.	170
39, 40, 44, 45	Killahurler	3,735	3	15	Wicklow	Arklow	Rathdrum	I.	345
12, 13, 17, 18	Killahy	1,584	2	16	Kilkenny	Crannagh	Urlingford	I.	86
35, 36, 39, 40		2,803	2	18		Knocktopher	Waterford		112
14, 15, 21, 22	Killala	5,634	1	10f	Mayo	Tirawley	Killala	IV.	169,170
73, 86, 87, 98, 99	Killallaghtan	2,771	3	21	Galway	Clonmacnowen	Ballinasloe	IV.	26
		9,097	2	14		Kilconnell			41
15, 16, 22, 23	Killallon	7,614	0	24g	Meath	Fore	Oldcastle	I.	200,201
77, 78, 83, 84	Killaloan	1,178	3	35h	Tipperary, S.R.	Iffa and Offa East	Clonmel	II.	314
2		2,029	1	0i	Waterford	Upperthird			370
36, 37, 45, 54	Killaloe	10,707	2	20j	Clare	Tulla Lower	Limerick / Scarriff	II.	35
	Killaloe	19	0	9	Kilkenny	Callan	Callan	I.	84
22, 26		489	2	30		Crannagh			86
		4,926	0	32		Shillelogher			115
26, 30, 34	Killamery	6,525	2	8	Kilkenny	Kells	Callan	I.	108,109
15, 22	Killaney	2,859	0	16k	Down	Upper Castlereagh	Lisburn	III.	165
13, 18, 19, 24, 25	Killann	11,424	1	14	Wexford	Bantry	Enniscorthy	I.	300
40,41,54,55,56,66, 67,68,69,77,78,79, 80, 89, 90, 91, 92	Killannin, Islands & detached portions	71,463	1	21l	Galway	Moycullen	Galway / Oughterard	IV.	69, 70
10	Killanny	1,939	0	27m	Louth	Ardee	Dundalk	I.	173
31, 32, 34		5,188	0	19n	Monaghan	Farney	Carrickmacross	III.	271,272
86	Killanully	951	0	2	Cork, E.R.	Cork	Cork	II.	64
		1,105	0	15		Kerrycurrihy			92
14, 15, 17	Killanummery	14,086	2	0	Leitrim	Drumahaire	Manorhamilton	IV.	97, 98
45, 46, 47	Killaraght	9,331	3	16o	Sligo	Coolavin	Boyle	IV.	224,225
38, 46, 47, 56, 57	Killard	17,022	1	1p	Clare	Ibrickan	Kilrush	II.	23
67, 68, 75	Killardry	5,623	2	10q	Tipperary, S.R.	Clanwilliam	Tipperary	II.	308
17, 24, 31	Killare	11,281	3	38r	Westmeath	Rathconrath	Ballymahon / Mullingar	I.	283
11, 12, 15, 16, 17	Killarga	14,893	1	28s	Leitrim	Drumahaire	Manorhamilton	IV.	98, 99
59,66,67,74,75,84,85	Killarney	38,151	1	9t	Kerry	Magunihy	Killarney	II.	202 to 204
28	Killarney	155	0	34	Kilkenny	Gowran	Thomastown	I.	97
12, 13	Killary	6,205	3	15	Meath	Lower Slane	Ardee	I.	223
13, 19, 24, 25, 30	Killashandra	22,241	0	11u	Cavan	Tullyhunco	Bawnboy / Cavan	III.	97 to 99
19, 23, 24	Killashee	146	1	34v	Kildare	North Naas	Naas	I.	62
		3,998	2	23		South Naas			65
8, 12, 13, 17, 18, 22	Killashee	3,701	0	7w	Longford	Longford	Ballymahon / Longford	I.	158
		10,726	0	20x		Moydow			161,162
3, 4, 6, 7, 8, 10, 11	Killasnet	26,918	1	10y	Leitrim	Rosclogher	Manorhamilton	IV.	109,110
7, 8, 13, 14, 20	Killaspugbrone	5,623	3	1	Sligo	Carbury	Sligo	IV.	222
15	Killaspuglonane	3,547	3	37	Clare	Corcomroe	Ennistimon	II.	19
53, 64	Killaspugmullane	1,852	0	13	Cork, E.R.	Barrymore	Cork	II.	55
49, 50, 61, 62	Killasser	19,677	0	14z	Mayo	Gallen	Swineford	IV.	149
27, 34, 35	Killathy	3,217	0	30aa	Cork, E.R.	Fermoy	Fermoy	II.	80
23, 24, 29, 30	Killavinoge	8,159	3	25	Tipperary, N.R.	Ikerrin	Roscrea / Thurles	II.	275
47, 55	Killea	1,869	0	22	Donegal	Raphoe	Londonderry	III.	138,139
22, 23, 28, 29	Killea	4,772	3	37	Tipperary, N.R.	Ikerrin	Roscrea	II.	275,276
18, 27	Killea	3,953	0	24	Waterford	Gaultiere	Waterford	II.	363
49, 50, 54, 55, 56, 58, 59, 60	Killead	42,836	1	16bb	Antrim	Lower Massereene	Antrim	III.	28
55, 66, 67, 77	Killeagh	5,854	1	14	Cork, E.R.	Imokilly		Middleton / Youghal	II.	88

No. of Sheet of the Ordnance Survey Maps.	Parishes.	Area in Statute Measure. A. R.	County.	Barony.	Poor Law Union in 1857.	Townland Census of 1851, Part I. Vol.	Page
8, 9, 14, 15	Killeagh	8,094 3 1 7c	Meath	Fore	Oldcastle	I.	201
5, 8, 9	Killeany	3,306 3 8	Clare	Burren	Ballyvaghan	II.	13
42, 55, 56	Killeany	5,711 1 38 i	Galway	Clare	Tuam	IV.	20
71, 72, 80, 81, 91	Killedan	14,515 0 10c	Mayo	Gallen	Swineford	IV.	149,150
36,43,44,45,52,53,54	Killeedy	25,456 1 10d	Limerick	Glenquin	{ Kanturk / Newcastle }	II.	245,246
11	Killeek	807 2 6e	Dublin	Nethercross	Balrothery	I.	31
52, 53, 62, 63	Killeely	5,012 3 35	Clare	Bunratty Lower			5
4, 5	Killeely	113 2 30f / 1,480 0 34g	Limerick	{ Limerick City / Pubblebrien }	Limerick	II.	262 / 253
95, 96, 103, 104	Killeely	6,232 2 30	Galway	Dunkellin	Gort	IV.	29, 30
37, 38	Killeen	3,346 3 26	Meath	Skreen	Dunshaughlin	I.	221
105, 115, 124, 130	Killeenadeema	24,503 3 23h	Galway	Loughrea	Loughrea	IV.	64
6, 14	Killeenagarriff	4,454 2 29	Limerick	Clanwilliam	Limerick	II.	224
68	Killeenasteena	729 2 23	Tipperary, S.R.	Middlethird	Cashel	II.	327
103, 113	Killeenavarra, and Islands	5,173 3 14i	Galway	Dunkellin	Gort	IV.	30
95, 96, 103, 104,	Killeeneen	4,966 3 25	Galway	Dunkellin	{ Gort / Loughrea }	IV.	30
19, 27	Killeenemer	414 2 5	Cork, E.R.	Fermoy	Mitchelstown	II.	80
21, 22	Killeenoghty	103 2 34 / 754 1 37j	Limerick	{ Coshma / Pubblebrien }	Croom	II.	243 / 253
39,40,48,49,58,59	Killeentierna	1,211 0 10 / 9,020 0 39	Kerry	{ Magunihy / Trughanacmy }	{ Killarney / Tralee }	II.	204 / 211
44, 45, 53, 60	Killeeshil	9,839 2 21k	Tyrone	Dungannon Lower	{ Clogher / Dungannon }	III.	298
12, 13, 16, 17, 21	Killeevan	11,571 3 19l	Monaghan	Dartree	{ Clones / Cootehill / Monaghan }	III.	267,268
39, 45	Killegland	716 1 11	Meath	Ratoath	Dunshaughlin	I.	218
24, 25, 30	Killegney	6,685 3 6	Wexford	Bantry	Enniscorthy	I.	301
4, 5, 9	Killehenny	4,664 0 31	Kerry	Iraghticonnor	Listowel	II.	191
26, 31, 32, 36	Killelagh	13,303 3 15	Londonderry	Loughinsholin	Magherafelt	III.	241
36, 37, 38, 39, 40	Killelan	7,378 2 36m	Kildare	Kilkea and Moone	{ Athy / Baltinglass }	I.	60
79,87,88,96,97,104,105	Killemlagh	11,859 2 17n	Kerry	Iveragh	Cahersiveen	II.	196
11, 12, 16, 17	Killenagh	3,232 1 12	Wexford	Ballaghkeen	Gorey	I.	295
48, 54, 62	Killenaule	7,711 1 15	Tipperary, S.R.	Slievardagh	Cashel	II.	334
9, 13, 14	Killenny	945 3 12	Queen's Co.	Stradbally	Mountmellick	I.	247
30,43,44,45,57,58	Killererin	674 3 2 / 10,307 3 38 / 1,634 1 10 / 1,918 0 7o	Galway	{ Ballymoe / Clare / Dunmore / Tiaquin }	Tuam	IV.	9 / 20,21 / 35 / 77
28, 29	Killermogh	2,764 3 36	Queen's Co.	Clarmallagh	Abbeyleix	I.	238
19, 32, 33, 46, 47	Killeroran	12,595 0 3p	Galway	Killian	Mountbellew	IV.	43, 44
2, 3, 7, 8, 12	Killerrig	5,318 3 28q	Carlow	Carlow	Carlow	I.	2
15, 21, 27, 28	Killerry	9,094 1 36r	Sligo	Tirerrill	Sligo	IV.	239
25, 26, 27, 31, 32} 33, 37	Killesher. & Islands in L. Macnean Lr.	24,936 1 11s	Fermanagh	Clanawley	Enniskillen	III.	192,193
31, 32, 36, 37	Killeshin	10,905 1 21t	Queen's Co.	Slievemargy	Carlow	I.	245,246
39, 44	Killesk	2,820 0 29	Wexford	Shelburne	New Ross	I.	327
14, 15, 18, 19	Killester	279 1 16	Dublin	Coolock	Dublin North	I.	28
18,21,22,25,26,} 28, 29, 32 }	Killevy	3,583 1 33 / 24,590 3 0u	Armagh	{ Orior Lower / Orior Upper }	Newry	III.	56 / 57, 58
32, 33, 46 47	Killian	13,564 3 37v	Galway	Killian	Mountbellew	IV.	44, 45
42, 43	Killiane	1,074 0 10	Wexford	Forth	Wexford	I.	310
27, 33	Killila	1,810 3 34	Wexford	Ballaghkeen	Enniscorthy	I.	295
4, 8, 14, 15,	Killilagh	12,357 1 15w	Clare	Corcomroe	Ennistimon	II.	19, 20
57, 58, 67, 68	Killimer	6,302 3 30x	Clare	Clonderalaw	Kilrush	II.	16
107, 117	Killimorbologue	9,220 0 16	Galway	Longford	Portumna	IV.	58, 59
72, 85, 86, 97,	Killimordaly	1,799 0 35 / 7,750 2 0 / 662 3 17	Galway	{ Athenry / Kilconnell / Tiaquin }	Loughrea	IV.	4 / 42 / 77
9, 10, 16, 17	Killinaboy	17,967 0 32y	Clare	Inchiquin	Corrofin	II.	26, 27
1, 2, 3, 4, 5	Killinagh	24,783 2 30z	Cavan	Tullyhaw	Enniskillen	III.	91, 92
104, 114, 115, 124	Killinan	815 1 0 / 4,945 1 14	Galway	{ Dunkellin / Loughrea }	Loughrea	IV.	30 / 64
11, 12, 15, 16	Killinane	380 0 8aa / 1,884 1 4bb	Carlow	{ Idrone East / Idrone West }	Carlow	I.	7 / 9

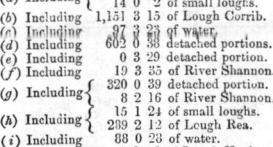

A. R. P.
(a) Including { 1,161 0 26 of Lough Sheelin. / 14 0 2 of small loughs.
(b) Including 1,151 3 15 of Lough Corrib.
(c) Including 27 3 32 of water.
(d) Including 663 0 33 detached portions.
(e) Including 0 3 29 detached portion.
(f) Including 19 3 35 of River Shannon.
(g) Including { 320 0 39 detached portion. / 8 2 16 of River Shannon. / 15 1 24 of small loughs.
(h) Including 289 2 12 of Lough Rea.
(i) Including 88 0 23 of water.
(j) Including 5 1 8 of Lough Nagirra.
(k) Including 241 1 13 detached portion.

A. R. P.
(l) Including { 127 2 15 detached portion. / 55 3 5 of water.
(m) Including 1,804 1 18 detached portions.
(n) Including 125 1 20 Puffin Island.
(o) Including 7 3 24 of water.
(p) Including 51 1 26 of water.
(q) Including 1,132 2 39 detached portions.
(r) Including { 193 2 13 detached portion. / 844 3 14 of Lough Gill. / 8 2 35 Lough Lumman.
(s) Including { 642 1 24 of Lr. Lough Macnean. / 24 1 17 of River Erne and small loughs.

A. R. F.
(t) Including 31 3 31 of River Barrow.
(u) Including { 16 2 0 of tideway. / 96 0 52 of fresh water.
(v) Including 14 3 23 of water.
(w) Including 22 3 12 of water.
(x) Including 36 0 7 of water.
(y) Including 554 0 30 of water.
(z) Including { 806 0 27 of Up. Lough Macnean. / 42 2 33 of Lr Lough Matnean. / 133 3 16 of water.
(aa) Including 2 3 0 of River Barrow.
(bb) Including 24 2 8 of River Barrow.

No. of Sheet of the Ordnance Survey Maps.	Parishes.	Area in Statute Measure.	County.	Barony.	Poor Law Union in 1857.	Townland Census of 1851, Part I.	
		A. R. P.				Vol.	Page
62, 63, 69, 70, 71, 79, 80, 81	Killinane	26,868 0 0a	Kerry	Iveragh	Cahersiveen	II.	197
16, 17, 23, 24	Killinchy, & Islands	6,437 1 5b / 3,281 0 17 / 4,147 2 34c	Down	Dufferin / Lower Castlereagh / Upper Castlereagh	Downpatrick / Newtownards	III.	166 / 163 / 165
11, 12	Killincoole	1,397 1 8	Louth	Louth	Dundalk	I.	184
21, 22, 27, 28,	Killincooly	4,430 2 20d	Wexford	Ballaghkeen	Enniscorthy / Gorey	I.	295
23, 26	Killiney	1,334 2 7	Dublin	Rathdown	Rathdown	I.	36
19,26,27,35,36,44,45 42, 43, 47, 48	Killiney .	14,955 3 31e	Kerry	Corkaguiny	Dingle	II.	177,178
	Killinick .	1,283 3 18f	Wexford	Forth	Wexford	I.	310
27, 32, 33, 34, 39, 40	Killinkere	12,078 0 36g / 3,883 3 33h	Cavan	Castlerahan / Upper Loughtee	Bailieborough / Cavan / Oldcastle	III.	68, 69 / 84
112, 113, 121,122,	Killinny .	6,117 1 13i	Galway	Kiltartan	Gort	IV.	47
42, 43, 45	Killinvoy .	6,554 2 1j	Roscommon	Athlone	Athlone / Roscommon	IV.	181,182
26, 27, 32, 33	Killisk .	4,037 2 5	Wexford	Ballaghkeen	Enniscorthy	I.	296
18, 19, 24, 25	Killiskey .	9,231 1 1	Wicklow	Newcastle	Rathdrum	I.	352
9, 14	Killodiernan .	4,562 1 38k	Tipperary, N.R.	Lower Ormond	Borrisokane / Nenagh	II.	284,285
1, 2, 3, 4, 5, 6, 8, 9, 14	Killoe	7,219 1 15l / 34,221 1 22m	Longford .	Granard / Longford .	Granard / Longford	I.	157 / 158,159
58, 59, 68, 69, 75	Killofin	6,692 2 7n	Clare	Clonderalaw	Killadysert	II.	16, 17
104, 105	Killogilleen .	2,845 1 23 / 759 1 35	Galway,	Dunkellin / Loughrea .	Loughrea .	IV.	31 / 64
36, 44, 53	Killokennedy .	11,656 0 1	Clare	Tulla Lower	Limerick .	II.	35, 36
1, 2, 4, 5	Killonaghan .	7,350 3 3	Clare	Burren	Ballyvaghan	II.	13
12, 21, 22	Killonahan .	872 3 8 / 1,195 3 17	Limerick .	Coshma / Pubblebrien	Croom / Limerick	II.	243 / 253
33, 41	Killone .	5,718 3 5o	Clare	Islands	Ennis	II.	30
96, 104	Killora .	5,372 0 38	Galway	Dunkellin	Loughrea .	IV.	31
98, 99, 106, 107	Killoran .	415 3 28 / 804 0 34p / 4,174 0 7	Galway	Clonmacnowen . / Leitrim . / Longford .	Ballinasloe / Loughrea	IV.	26 / 54 / 59
19, 25, 26, 32	Killoran .	13,999 0 28q	Sligo .	Leyny	Sligo / Tobercurry	IV.	230,231
55, 56, 57, 63, 64, 65,72,73	Killorglin .	12,924 2 7r / 5,743 3 20s / 3,117 2 29t / 9,402 0 4u	Kerry	Dunkerron North / Iveragh . / Magunihy / Trughanacmy .	Cahersiveen / Killarney	II.	181 / 197,198 / 204 / 211
45, 46, 59, 60, 72	Killoscobe	8,208 1 20	Galway	Tiaquin	Mountbellew	IV.	77, 78
25, 26, 31, 32	Killoscully	14,439 0 24	Tipperary, N.R.	Owney and Arra	Nenagh	II.	295
28, 34	Killoskehan .	2,541 3 14	Tipperary, N.R.	Ikerrin	Roscrea .	II.	276
46, 47, 60, 61	Killosolan .	3,592 1 25 / 7,890 1 38	Galway	Kilconnell / Tiaquin	Mountbellew	IV.	42 / 78
7, 11	Killossery	2,731 0 29c	Dublin	Nethercross	Balrothery	I.	31
9, 17	Killoteran .	2,493 0 32	Waterford	Middlethird	Waterford	II.	367
15,16,23,24,25,31,32	Killoughy	18,132 2 8w	King's Co.	Ballyboy	Tullamore .	I.	123,124
95, 109	Killowen	1,263 3 12	Cork, W.R.	Kinalmeaky	Bandon .	II.	152
3, 7	Killowen	1,806 0 26	Londonderry	Coleraine	Coleraine .	III.	232
28, 29, 42, 43	Killower .	3,596 2 22x	Galway	Clare	Tuam .	IV.	21
17	Kill St. Lawrence .	308 1 25	Waterford .	Gaultiere .	Waterford .	II.	363
10, 18, 27	Kill St. Nicholas	2,883 3 26y	Waterford	Gaultiere .	Waterford	I.	364
9, 14	Killua .	5,259 1 0z	Westmeath	Delvin	Castletowndelvin	I.	265,266
19,20,21,26,27,28,34	Killucan .	136 1 22 / 35,453 1 23aa	Westmeath	Delvin / Farbill	Castletowndelvin / Mullingar .	I.	266 / 266,267
10, 11	Killukin .	4,831 0 1bb	Roscommon	Boyle	Boyle / Carᵏ.on Shannon	IV.	195,196
22, 23, 28, 29	Killukin . .	5,956 3 3cc	Roscommon	Roscommon	Strokestown	IV.	210,211
8, 13, 14, 21	Killulagh	8,145 1 38dd	Westmeath	Delvin	Castletowndelvin	I.	266
10, 11, 16	Killummod	5,159 3 35ee	Roscommon	Boyle	Boyle / Carᵏ.on Shannon	IV.	196
35, 36, 43, 44	Killuran .	7,103 1 6ff	Clare	Tulla Lower	Limerick . / Tulla	II.	36
17, 18	Killure .	627 1 18	Waterford	Gaultiere .	Waterford .	II.	364
31, 32, 36, 37	Killurin .	1,873 2 32	Wexford	Shelmaliere West	Enniscorthy / Wexford	I.	334
40, 41, 42, 54, 55	Killursa .	8,877 2 18gg	Galway	Clare	Tuam .	IV.	21, 22

(a) Including 22 1 31 of water.	(k) Including { 1,255 0 29 of Lough Derg. / 54 3 28 of small loughs.	(w) Including { 111 0 29 of Annaghmore Lough. / 82 2 29 Pallas Lough.	
(b) Including 75 2 39 of water.		(x) Including 67 1 20 of water.	
(c) Including 50 1 22 of water.	(l) Including { 259 0 10 of Lough Gowna. / 150 0 1 of small loughs.	(y) Including 381 1 14 detached portion.	
(d) Including { 334 2 21 East / 810 0 14 Middle } portions. / 1,253 1 19 West	(m) Including 329 0 37 of water.	(z) Including 51 1 37 of water.	
	(n) Including 10 2 32 of water.	(aa) Including 20 1 18 of water.	
detached { 928 3 24 detached portion.	(o) Including 40 0 5 of water.	(bb) Including 78 2 21 of River Shannon.	
(e) Including { 302 0 13 of Lough Gill. / 88 0 20 small loughs.	(p) Composed of { 360 0 8 North Portion. / 444 0 26 South Portion.	(cc) Including 307 3 7 of water.	
(f) Composed of { 696 1 26 North Portion. / 587 1 32 South Portion.	(q) Including 44 1 38 of water.	(dd) Including 46 3 29 of water.	
	(r) Including 146 2 24 of water.	(ee) Including { 92 2 26 of River Shannon. / 208 1 23 of loughs.	
(g) Including 98 3 33 of water.	(s) Including { 341 2 35 of Lough Caragh. / 91 0 20 of small loughs.	(ff) Including { 293 0 11 of Doon Lough. / 127 2 25 of small loughs.	
(h) Including 32 1 2 of water.			
(i) Including 3 2 8 of Caherglassaun Lough.	(t) Including 18 3 35 of River Laune.	(gg) Including { 2,506 3 11 of Lough Corrib. / 16 3 27 of small loughs.	
(j) Including { 911 3 4 of Lough Ree. / 5 0 24 Lough Collog.	(u) Including 175 0 16 of water.		
	(v) Including 216 2 29 detached portion.		

No. of Sheet of the Ordnance Survey Maps.	Parishes.	Area in Statute Measure.			County.	Barony.	Poor Law Union in 1857.	Townland Census of 1851, Part I.	
		A.	R.	P.				Vol.	Page
8, 9, 14, 15	Killury	11,090	0	31	Kerry	Clanmaurice	Listowel	II.	170,171
13, 14	Killybegs	2,628	3	7	Kildare	Clane	Naas	I.	54
73, 74, 75, 82, 83	Killybegs Lower	11,074	1	18a	Donegal	Banagh / Boylagh	Glenties	III.	110
		4,304	1	11					114
82, 91, 92, 97	Killybegs Upper	15,583	2	18b	Donegal	Banagh	Glenties	III.	110,111
28, 37	Killygarvan	9,132	1	12c	Donegal	Kilmacrenan	Milford	III.	128
35, 40	Killyglen, Grange of	2,295	2	14	Antrim	Upper Glenarm	Larne	III.	24
23, 24, 30, 31	Killyleagh, & Islands	988	1	36	Down	Dufferin / Upper Castlereagh	Downpatrick	III.	167
		10,771	0	30d					165
1, 4	Killyman	3,154	3	36e	Armagh	Oneilland West	Armagh	III.	53
46, 47, 54, 55		7,404	2	15f	Tyrone	Dungannon Middle	Dungannon		303
75,76,84,85,93,94,99	Killymard	28,229	3	33g	Donegal	Banagh	Donegal	III.	111,112
35, 40, 41, 47	Killyon	4,316	2	5h	Meath	Upper Moyfenrath	Edenderry / Trim	I.	213
120,133,134,142,143	Kilmacabea,	9,484	3	24i	Cork, W.R.	East Carbery (W.D.) / West Carbery (E.D.)	Skibbereen	II.	133
		4,271	2	12j					140
15, 16, 20, 21	Kilmacahill	4,583	0	15	Kilkenny	Gowran	Kilkenny	I.	97
26, 27, 28, 34, 40	Kilmacallan	9,928	0	7k	Sligo	Tirerrill	Boyle / Sligo	IV.	239,240
3, 4, 7, 8	Kilmacanoge	5,401	1	9	Wicklow	Rathdown	Rathdown	I.	355,356
5, 10	Kilmacar	4,815	2	21	Kilkenny	Fassadinin	Castlecomer	I.	90
66, 67, 77, 78	Kilmacdonogh	6,376	0	36l	Cork, E.R.	Imokilly	Middleton / Youghal	II.	88
113, 122, 128	Kilmacduagh	8,804	1	37m	Galway	Kiltartan	Gort	IV.	47, 48
38, 39, 47, 48, 57, 58	Kilmacduane	166	1	27	Clare	Ibrickan / Moyarta	Kilrush	II.	23
		16,701	2	36n					32, 33
68, 77	Kilmaclasser	6,865	2	21o	Mayo	Burrishoole	Westport	IV.	121
18, 26, 27	Kilmacleague	3,462	1	19p	Waterford	Gaultiere	Waterford	II.	364
24	Kilmaclenine	1,042	0	8	Cork, E.R.	Orrery and Kilmore	Mallow	II.	109
10, 11, 17, 18	Kilmacnevan	5,016	0	7q	Westmeath	Moygoish	Mullingar	I.	280
18, 27	Kilmacomb	2,400	2	22r	Waterford	Gaultiere	Waterford	II.	364
40, 42, 43, 46	Kilmacow	4,445	0	5	Kilkenny	Iverk	Waterford	I.	105,106
14, 19, 20	Kilmacowen	3,548	1	36s	Sligo	Carbury	Sligo	IV.	222
6, 11	Kilmacredock	479	0	26	Kildare	North Salt	Celbridge	I.	75
42, 43, 47	Kilmacree	1,112	1	8	Wexford	Forth	Wexford	I.	311
14, 15, 22, 23	Kilmacreby	7,493	0	1t	Clare	Corcomroe	Ennistimon	II.	20
26, 27, 35, 36, 44, 45, 52, 53	Kilmacrenan, and detached portions	35,617	0	7u	Donegal	Kilmacrenan	Dunfanaghy / Leiterkenny / Millford	III.	128 to 130
11,12,17,18,23,24,30	Kilmacshalgan	26,008	2	31v	Sligo	Tireragh	Dromore West	IV.	234,235
17, 20, 21	Kilmactalway	2,492	2	20	Dublin	Newcastle	Celbridge	I.	33
23,24,30,31,36,37,42	Kilmacteige	32,533	0	20w	Sligo	Leyny	Tobercurry	IV.	231
28, 34, 35, 40, 41	Kilmactranny	13,447	0	23x	Sligo	Tirerrill	Boyle	IV.	240,241
22, 23	Kilmacud	286	1	15	Dublin	Rathdown	Rathdown	I.	36
10, 15, 16	Kilmacumsy	5,454	0	15	Roscommon	Frenchpark	Boyle	IV.	203,204
10, 14	Kilmademoge	1,726	1	36	Kilkenny	Fassadinin	Kilkenny	I.	90
10, 11, 14, 15	Kilmadum	903	3	24	Kilkenny	Fassadinin / Gowran	Castlecomer / Kilkenny	I.	90
		2,521	1	5					97
30, 31, 34, 35	Kilmaganny	7,454	3	10	Kilkenny	Kells	Callan / Carrick on Suir	I.	109
77, 89	Kilmahon	2,849	0	38y	Cork, E.R.	Imokilly	Middleton	II.	89
17	Kilmahuddrick	181	1	1	Dublin	Newcastle	Dublin South	I.	33
121, 122, 123	Kilmainebog	3,613	3	37z	Mayo	Kilmaine	Ballinrobe	IV.	155
118, 119, 121, 122	Kilmainemore	13,792	1	18aa	Mayo	Kilmaine	Ballinrobe	IV.	155,156
2, 5	Kilmainham	3,716	0	15bb	Meath	Lower Kells	Kells	I.	203
40, 41	Kilmakevoge	3,231	3	10	Kilkenny	Ida	Waterford	I.	103
6, 7, 11, 12	Kilmakilloge	2,009	2	25	Wexford	Ballaghkeen / Gorey	Gorey	I.	296
		3,303	3	0					318
50, 51	Kilmaleery, & Islands	2,956	3	18cc	Clare	Bunratty Lower	Ennis	II.	5, 6
31,32,33,39,40,41,49	Kilmaley	23,736	3	33dd	Clare	Islands	Ennis / Killadysert	II.	30, 31
117, 118, 127	Kilmalinoge	3,552	2	18ee	Galway	Longford	Portumna	IV.	59
33, 34, 42, 43	Kilmalkedar	5,819	3	39	Kerry	Corkaguiny	Dingle	II.	178
20, 28, 32, 33	Kilmallock	4,693	3	28	Wexford	Ballaghkeen	Enniscorthy,	I.	296
110, 122, 123	Kilmaloda	7,854	1	6ff	Cork, W.R.	East Carbery (E.D.)	Bandon / Clonakilty	II.	129

	A.	R.	P.			A.	R.	P.			A.	R.	P.			A.	R.	P.	
(a) Including	51	0	27	of water.	(l) Including	133	2	29	of tideway.	(w) Including	170	3	17	of Easky Lough.	(a) Including				

(a) Including { 51 0 27 of water. / 1,626 2 29 detached portion.
(b) Including 41 2 39 of water.
(c) Including 29 2 22 of water.
(d) Including 123 2 12 of water.
(e) Including 49 0 35 of water.
(f) Including 56 0 32 of water.
(g) Including { 472 0 24 of Lough Eask. / 202 1 4 of small loughs. / 681 1 19 detached portion.
(h) Including { 28 1 27 detached portion. / 13 3 8 of River Boyne.
(i) Including 46 0 27 of water.
(j) Including 44 1 5 of water.
(k) Including { 283 3 12 of Lough Arrow. / 39 2 28 of small loughs.

(l) Including 133 2 29 of tideway.
(m) Including 112 0 18 of water.
(n) Including { 206 0 17 detached portion. / 24 3 26 of water.
(o) Including 78 3 17 of water.
(p) Including 3 0 0 of Bally Lough.
(q) Including 57 0 22 of Fany River.
(r) Including 52 2 32 of Bally Lough.
(s) Including { 4 2 27 of tideway. / 13 3 21 of loughs.
(t) Including { 702 0 22 detached portion. / 4 3 24 of water.
(u) Including { 5 3 20 of River Lackagh tideway. / 782 0 27 of small loughs.
(v) Including { 24 2 15 of Easky Lough. / 34 1 0 of small loughs.

(w) Including { 170 3 17 of Easky Lough. / 326 1 17 of small loughs.
(x) Including { 1,667 1 17 of Lough Arrow. / 114 0 2 of small loughs.
(y) Including 134 1 26 detached portion.
(z) Including 549 3 38 detached portion.
(aa) Including { 1,223 1 37 detached portion. / 106 0 28 of water.
(bb) Including { 27 1 14 of Newcastle Lough / 14 0 16 of Whitewood Lough.
(cc) Including 13 0 2 of water.
(dd) Including 142 2 32 of water.
(ee) Including 77 0 12 of River Shannon.
(ff) Including 6 3 0 of Argideen River tideway.

No. of Sheet of the Ordnance Survey Maps.	Parishes.	Area in Statute Measure. (A. R. P.)	County.	Barony.	Poor Law Union in 1857.	Vol.	Page
18, 22	Kilmanagh	5,620 2 39	Kilkenny	Crannagh	Callan	I.	86
1, 2, 7, 8 / 30, 31, 36	Kilmanaghan	6,563 3 18 / 1,633 0 30a	King's Co. / Westmeath	Kilcoursey / Clonlonan	Tullamore / Athlone	I.	141 / 262
15, 16, 22, 23, 31	Kilmanaheen	8,177 0 11b	Clare	Corcomroe	Ennistimon	II.	21
1, 2, 3, 6	Kilmanman	16,848 3 19c	Queen's Co.	Tinnahinch	Mountmellick	I.	248,249
41, 42, 46, 47	Kilmannan	4,251 0 36	Wexford	Bargy	Wexford	I.	306
19, 25, 26, 31	Kilmastulla	4,805 1 24	Tipperary, N.R.	Owney and Arra	Nenagh	II.	295
8, 9, 16, 17	Kilmeadan	6,934 2 0 / 2,308 1 25	Waterford	Middlethird / Upperthird	Waterford / Carrick on Suir	II.	368 / 370
12, 13, 17, 18	Kilmeage	10,535 0 34 / 346 0 32	Kildare	Connell / East Offaly	Naas	II.	55 / 70
40, 41, 42, 43, 44	Kilmeane	8,966 0 29d	Roscommon	Athlone	Roscommon	IV.	182
37, 45, 46	Kilmeedy	9,036 1 21	Limerick	Connello Upper	Croom / Newcastle	II.	233
4, 12, 13, 21, 22, 23, 29, 30, 31	Kilmeen	36,710 0 5	Cork, E.R.	Duhallow	Kanturk / Millstreet	II.	72, 73
121, 122	Kilmeen	7,305 1 13e / 1,362 0 26	Cork, W.R.	East Carbery (W.D.) / Ibane and Barryroe	Clonakilty / Dunmanway	II.	133,134 / 149
98, 105, 106	Kilmeen	3,672 0 28 / 135 2 33	Galway	Leitrim / Loughrea	Loughrea	IV.	54 / 65
76, 77, 87, 88	Kilmeena	10,762 0 3f	Mayo	Burrishoole	Newport / Westport	IV.	121 to 123
36, 43, 44, 49	Kilmegan	1,792 3 29 / 5,983 2 10g / 6,195 0 26h	Down	Kinelarty / Lecale Upper / Upper Iveagh, Lr. pt.	Downpatrick	III.	176 / 181 / 173
4, 5	Kilmenan	1,008 1 6	Kilkenny	Fassadinin	Castlecomer	I.	90
31, 37	Kilmessan	3,336 3 36	Meath	Lower Deece	Dunshaughlin	I.	192
70,81,82,83,93,94,95	Kilmichael	4,412 2 12 / 16,455 3 0i	Cork, W.R.	East Carbery (W.D.) / West Muskerry	Dunmanway / Macroom	II.	134 / 158, 159
39,40,47,48,49,58,59	Kilmihil	18,772 3 2j	Clare	Clonderalaw	Ennis / Kilrush	II.	17
79, 80, 91, 92, 93, 104, 105, 106, 107, 117, 118, 119, 131	Kilmocomoge	57,629 1 4k / 1,206 2 7 / 5,750 2 34	Cork, W.R.	Bantry / East Carbery (W.D.) / West Carbery (W.D.)	Bantry	II.	119 to 122 / 134 / 144
138, 139, 146, 147, 148, 152, 153	Kilmoe	13,974 0 22l	Cork, W.R.	West Carbery (W.D.)	Skull	II.	144, 145
39	Kilmokea	3,420 1 23	Wexford	Shelburne	New Ross	I.	327
118, 121	Kilmolara	3,961 0 23	Mayo	Kilmaine	Ballinrobe	IV.	156, 157
29, 30, 35	Kilmolash	1,768 2 20 / 1,919 3 2	Waterford	Decies within Drum / Decies without Drum	Dungarvan / Lismore	II.	351 / 357
3	Kilmoleran	1,937 2 30	Waterford	Upperthird	Carrick on Suir	II.	370
86, 87, 98, 99	Kilmoney	1,430 2 37	Cork, E.R.	Kerrycurrihy	Kinsale	II.	92
112, 125	Kilmonoge	3,060 3 31	Cork, E.R.	Kinalea	Kinsale	II.	95
10, 16, 17	Kilmood	4,634 1 39m	Down	Lower Castlereagh	Newtownards	III.	163
4, 5, 8, 9	Kilmoon	6,461 0 16	Clare	Burren	Ballyvaghan / Ennistimon	II.	13
32, 33, 38, 39	Kilmoon	1,834 0 7	Meath	Skreen	Dunshaughlin	I.	221
8, 9, 10, 12, 13, 14	Kilmore	12,474 2 27 / 4,799 3 16n	Armagh	Oneilland West / Orior Lower	Armagh / Banbridge	III.	53 / 56
19, 20, 24, 25, 26, 31	Kilmore	3,937 0 5o / 12,948 3 28p	Cavan	Clanmahon / Upper Loughtee	Cavan	III.	78 / 84, 85
22, 23, 29, 30, 37	Kilmore	6,387 3 19q / 6,466 0 29r	Down	Kinelarty / Upper Castlereagh	Downpatrick	III.	177 / 165
3, 7, 8	Kilmore	1,908 0 13	Kildare	Carbury	Edenderry	I.	52
2, 3, 9, 10, 16, 17, 23, 24, 33	Kilmore	29,492 3 15s	Mayo	Erris	Belmullet	IV.	145, 146
43, 49	Kilmore	6,607 3 16t	Meath	Upper Deece	Dunshaughlin	I.	193
9, 13, 14, 18, 19	Kilmore	8,689 1 37u	Monaghan	Monaghan	Monaghan	III.	275, 276
11, 12, 17, 18	Kilmore	9,316 3 19v	Roscommon	Ballintober North	Car^k. on Shannon	IV.	186, 187
20, 26, 27, 32, 33	Kilmore	13,535 0 39	Tipperary, N.R.	Upper Ormond	Nenagh	II.	290, 291
51, 52, 60	Kilmore	2,004 1 15w	Tipperary, S.R.	Kilnamanagh Lower	Cashel	II.	323
46, 47, 51, 52	Kilmore	4,233 3 9x	Wexford	Bargy	Wexford	I.	306, 307
30 / 22, 29	Kilmoremoy	4,338 0 38y / 7,992 3 39z	Mayo / Sligo	Tirawley / Tireragh	Ballina	IV.	170 / 235
26, 27, 33, 34, 40	Kilmorgan	5,768 1 21aa	Sligo	Corran	Sligo	IV.	226, 227
63,72,73,74,81,82,83	Kilmovee	20,756 2 18bb	Mayo	Costello	Swineford	IV.	141, 142
43,44,57,58,70,71	Kilmoylan	8,567 3 5cc	Galway	Clare	Tuam	IV.	22
10, 18, 19, 26, 27	Kilmoylan	15,091 0 5dd	Limerick	Shanid	Glin / Rathkeale	II.	256

(a) Including 24 1 12 of water.
(b) Including { 463 1 5 detached portion. / 5 2 22 of water.
(c) Including 96 3 1 of Annamore Lough.
(d) Including 964 2 9 of Lough Ree.
(e) Including 9 0 16 of Lough Atarriff.
(f) Including 147 1 36 of water.
(g) Including 22 1 0 of water.
(h) Including 107 0 13 of water.
(i) Including 11 1 14 of water.
(j) Including 142 2 15 of water.
(k) Including { 1,000 3 1 Whiddy Island. / 192 3 22 of water.

(l) Including 7 1 5 Dun Lough.
(m) Including 34 0 25 of water.
(n) Including 13 1 9 of water.
(o) Including 55 0 20 of water.
(p) Including { 2,154 0 0 of Lough Oughter. / 125 0 39 of water.
(q) Including 89 0 36 of water.
(r) Including 5 0 18 of water.
(s) Including 381 2 17 of water.
(t) Including 14 3 19 of water.
(u) Including { 334 0 38 detached portion. / 15 3 8 of water.

(v) Including { 763 1 13 of River Shannon. / 154 1 19 of small loughs.
(w) Including 829 0 26 detached portion.
(x) Including { 226 0 17 detached portion. / 309 0 32 Saltee Islands.
(y) Including 11 1 13 of River Moy.
(z) Including 31 3 16 of River Moy.
(aa) Including 33 2 37 of water.
(bb) Including 451 3 15 of water.
(cc) Including 8 1 19 of water.
(dd) Including 4,786 3 3 detached portions.

No. of Sheet of the Ordnance Survey Maps.	Parish.	Area in Statute Measure.	County.	Barony.	Poor Law Union in 1857.	Townland Census of 1851, Part I.	
		A. R. P.				Vol.	Page
14, 15, 20, 21	Kilmoyly	7,743 0 7	Kerry	Clanmaurice	Tralee	II.	171
59	Kilmucklin	588 0 0	Tipperary, S.R.	Clanwilliam	Tipperary	II.	309
21, 22, 27, 28	Kilmuckridge	3,898 3 1la	Wexford	Ballaghkeen	Enniscorthy / Gorey	I.	296, 297
42, 43, 51, 52	Kilmurry	2,917 1 14b	Clare	Bunratty Lower	Tulla	II.	6
58, 68	Kilmurry	10,457 3 39	Clare	Clonderalaw	Killadysert / Kilrush	II.	17, 18
71, 83, 95	Kilmurry	159 1 30 / 8,949 2 37c	Cork, E.R. / Cork, W.R.	East Muskerry / West Muskerry	Bandon / Macroom	II. {	104 / 159
5, 6, 13, 14	Kilmurry	3,570 0 38d	Limerick	Clanwilliam	Limerick	II.	224, 225
78, 79, 84, 85	Kilmurry	7,275 3 34e	Tipperary, S.R.	Iffa and Offa East	Carrick on Suir	II.	314
30,31,32,38,39,40,47	Kilmurry, and Islands	25,857 3 28f	Clare	Ibrickan	Ennistimon / Kilrush	II.	23, 24
38, 41, 42	Kilmurryely	5,385 2 24	King's Co.	Clonlisk	Roscrea	I.	131
73, 85	Kilnaglory	879 0 14 / 3,062 3 25	Cork, E.R.	Cork / East Muskerry	Cork	II. {	65 / 104
122, 135, 136	Kilnagross	3,764 1 5	Cork, W.R.	East Carbery (E.D.)	Clonakilty	II.	129
2, 5, 6, 7, 11	Kilnahue	15,360 2 32	Wexford	Gorey	Gorey	I.	318, 319
114, 126, 127	Kilnamanagh	13,808 3 28g	Cork, W.R.	Bear	Castletown	II.	125, 126
8, 9, 10, 15	Kilnamanagh	7,621 1 2h	Roscommon	Frenchpark	Boyle / Castlereagh	IV.	204
21, 22	Kilnamanagh	2,678 2 21i	Wexford	Ballaghkeen	Gorey	I.	297
69, 70, 82	Kilnamartery	11,680 1 16	Cork, W.R.	West Muskerry	Macroom	II.	159, 160
24, 25, 32, 33	Kilnamona	5,418 1 33j	Clare	Inchiquin	Ennis	II.	27
47, 48, 57	Kilnanare	5,137 3 35k	Kerry	Magunihy	Killarney	II.	204
27, 33	Kilnaneave	6,607 2 24	Tipperary, N.R.	Upper Ormond	Nenagh	II.	291
25, 31, 32, 37, 38	Kilnarath	10,449 2 37l	Tipperary, N.R.	Owney and Arra	Nenagh	II.	295, 296
42, 50, 51	Kilnasoolagh	5,138 2 24m	Clare	Bunratty Lower	Ennis	II.	6
2, 3, 6	Kilnaughtin	9,164 2 4n	Kerry	Iraghticonnor	Glin	II.	191, 192
1, 2, 3	Kilnenor	6,435 3 5	Wexford	Gorey	Gorey	I.	319, 320
27, 28, 35, 36	Kilnoe	10,512 2 31o	Clare	Tulla Upper	Scarriff / Tulla	II.	40
99	Kilpatrick	719 1 10p / 1,951 1 8q	Cork, E.R.	Kerrycurrihy / Kinalea	Kinsale	II. {	92 / 95
8, 12	Kilpatrick	7,076 1 20	Kildare	Carbury	Edenderry	I.	52
51, 59	Kilpatrick	2,785 0 4	Tipperary, S.R.	Kilnamanagh Lower	Cashel	II.	324
7, 8, 12, 13	Kilpatrick	1,892 1 6	Westmeath	Fore	Castletowndelvin	I.	270
32, 37	Kilpatrick	2,739 1 2	Wexford	Shelmaliere East	Enniscorthy / Wexford	I.	330, 331
22	Kilpeacon	181 3 38 / 1,032 0 27	Limerick	Pubblebrien / Smallcounty	Croom	II. {	253 / 260
19	Kilphelan	523 3 6r	Cork, E.R.	Condons & Clangibbon	Mitchelstown	II.	62
1, 2	Kilpipe	3,477 0 39	Wexford	Gorey	Gorey		320
34, 38, 39, 43, 44	Kilpipe	12,153 3 12	Wicklow	Ballinacor South	Rathdrum / Shillelagh	I.	349
25, 31	Kilpoole	3,028 2 13	Wicklow	Arklow	Rathdrum	I.	345
107, 108, 117, 118	Kilquain	6,858 3 24	Galway	Longford	Portumna	IV.	60
53, 64	Kilquane	6,046 2 7	Cork, E.R.	Barrymore	Cork	II.	55, 56
3, 8	Kilquane	425 3 38	Cork, E.R.	Fermoy	Mallow	II. {	80
55	Kilquane	2,350 0 2	Limerick	Coshlea	Kilmallock		240
25, 33, 34, 43	Kilquane	9,708 3 37	Kerry	Corkaguiny	Dingle	II.	179
18, 26, 33, 34	Kilraghtis	5,587 3 15s	Clare	Bunratty Upper	Ennis	II.	9
12, 13, 17, 18, 22	Kilraghts	5,132 1 22t	Antrim	Upper Dunluce	Ballymoney	III.	19, 20
1, 2, 3	Kilrainy	2,617 2 38	Kildare	Carbury	Edenderry	I.	52
48	Kilrane	2,047 3 17	Wexford	Forth	Wexford	I.	311
27, 32	Kilranelagh	4,470 2 3	Wicklow	Upper Talbotstown	Baltinglass	I.	364
19, 27, 33	Kilrea	1,061 1 37u / 5,252 0 35v	Londonderry	Coleraine / Loughinsholin	Ballymoney	III. {	232 / 241
27, 31	Kilree	1,947 1 24	Kilkenny	Kells	Callan	I.	109
97, 98, 106	Kilreekill	5,947 1 22	Galway	Leitrim	Ballinasloe / Loughrea	IV.	54, 55
124, 125	Kilroan	245 2 6w / 894 2 37	Cork, E.R. / Cork, W.R.	Kinsale / Courceys	Kinsale	II. {	100 / 147
23	Kilroe	919 0 38	Cork, E.R.	Duhallow	Kanturk	II.	73, 74
1, 2, 3, 4	Kilronan	16,356 1 17x	Roscommon	Boyle	Boyle	IV.	196, 197
1, 5, 6, 13	Kilronan	16,701 3 4y	Waterford	Glenahiry	Clogheen / Clonmel	II.	365, 366

A. R. P.
(a) Including 21 0 0 of Leary's Lough.
(b) Including { 13 1 38 of Lough Cullaunyheeda. / 334 0 32 of small loughs.
(c) Including 7 0 18 of water.
(d) Including 65 1 3 of River Shannon.
(e) Including 19 2 14 of River Suir.
(f) Including { 331 2 20 Lough Doo. / 40 2 29 of small loughs.
(g) Including 1,403 0 2 Dursey Island.
(h) Including { 746 1 19 of Lough Gara. / 29 2 12 Loughanlea. / 7 1 21 of Lung River.

A. R. P.
(i) Composed of { 1,298 3 6 North Portion. / 1,379 3 15 South Portion.
(j) Including { 213 2 39 detached portion. / 54 1 24 of water.
(k) Including 7 2 20 of River Maine tideway.
(l) Including 1,228 3 25 detached portion.
(m) Including { 7 3 32 of Ardsollus River tideway. / 33 0 33 Dromoland Lough. / 63 0 35 Tarbert Island.
(n) Including 319 1 13 of water.
(o) Including 4 1 2 of tideway.
(p) Including

A. R. P.
(q) Including 2 0 30 of tideway.
(r) Including 22 2 30 detached portion.
(s) Including 113 2 33 of water.
(t) Including 5 0 24 of water.
(u) Including 21 3 31 of River Bann.
(v) Including 116 2 30 of River Bann.
(w) Including 18 1 29 Sandycove Island.
(x) Including { 1,315 0 9 of Lough Allen. / 38 0 27 of River Shannon. / 313 3 14 Lough Meelagh. / 14 2 26 Cuilbalkeen Lough.
(y) Including 46 3 32 of River Suir.

No. of Sheet of the Ordnance Survey Maps.	Parish.	Area in Statute Measure.	County.	Barony.	Poor Law Union in 1857.	Townland Census of 1851, Part I. Vol.	Page
		A. R. P.					
17	Kilronan	546 1 17	Waterford	Middlethird	Waterford	II.	368
47, 53	Kilroot	2,418 0 14	Antrim	Lower Belfast	Larne	III.	9
20, 21, 26, 27	Kilross	3,932 1 32a	Sligo	Tirerrill	Sligo	IV.	241
14, 15, 23, 24, 31, 32	Kilrossanty	17,416 1 21	Waterford	Decies without Drum	Kilmacthomas	II.	357,358
15, 21	Kilruane	{ 1,029 3 2b { 2,881 0 18c	} Tipperary, N.R.	{Lower Ormond {Upper Ormond	{Borrisokane {Nenagh	} II. {	285 292
27, 28, 31, 32	Kilrush	4,076 2 12	Kildare	West Offally	Athy	I.	72,73
30, 31	Kilrush	1,522 3 28	Waterford	Decies without Drum	Dungarvan	II.	358
4, 5, 9, 10, 15	Kilrush	11,385 3 15d	Wexford	Scarawalsh	Enniscorthy	I.	324
56, 57, 58, 66, 67	Kilrush, and Islands	15,658 3 15e	Clare	Moyarta	Kilrush	II.	33
11, 14	Kilsallaghan	2,730 3 38	Dublin	Nethercross	Balrothery	I.	31
15, 18	Kilsaran	3,393 2 10f	Louth	Ardee	Ardee	I.	173
35	Kilscanlan	1,154 0 32	Wexford	Bantry	New Ross	I.	301
28, 29, 36	Kilscannell	3,203 1 14	Limerick	Connello Lower	Rathkeale	II.	228
48	Kilscoran	2,151 3 5	Wexford	Forth	Wexford	I.	311
36, 43, 44, 52, 53	Kilseily	11,102 1 19g	Clare	Tulla Lower	Limerick	II.	36, 37
39, 44, 45	Kilshalvy	5,505 1 15h	Sligo	Corran	{Boyle {Tobercurry	} IV.	227
44, 53	Kilshanahan	4,842 1 38	Cork, E.R.	Barrymore	Fermoy	II.	56
67	Kilshane	1,424 1 35	Tipperary, S.R.	Clanwilliam	Tipperary	II.	309
31, 32, 33, 40, 41, 42, 49, 50	Kilshannig	27,594 3 33i	Cork, E.R.	Duhallow	Mallow	II.	74
8, 15	Kilshanny	5,805 0 24j	Clare	Corcomroe	Ennistimon	II.	21, 22
27	Kilsharvan	{ 1,528 1 31 { 568 0 21	} Meath	{Lower Duleek {Upper Duleek	} Drogheda	} I. {	196 198
77, 78, 83, 84	Kilsheelan	{ 4,348 3 29k { 4,629 0 1l	Tipperary, S.R. Waterford	Iffa and Offa East Upperthird	{Carrick on Suir {Clonmel	} II. {	314,315 370
2, 6							
10,16,17,22,23,30,31	Kilshenane	13,478 1 17m	Kerry	Clanmaurice	Listowel	II.	171,172
11, 12, 17, 18	Kilshine	1,543 2 10n	Meath	Morgallion	Navan	I.	210
136	Kilsillagh	244 2 7	Cork, W.R.	Ibane and Barryroe	Clonakilty	II.	149
9, 10, 15, 16, 23	Kilskeer	11,724 0 25	Meath	Upper Kells	{Kells {Oldcastle	} I.	206
49, 50, 56, 57	Kilskeery	20,438 3 27o	Tyrone	Omagh East	{Enniskillen {Lowtherstown	} III.	313,314
37	Kiltale	1,018 0 37	Meath	Lower Deece	Dunshaughlin	I.	192
38, 47	Kiltallagh	4,756 1 39p	Kerry	Trughanacmy	Tralee	II.	212
113, 114, 122, 123	Kiltartan	5,725 1 32q	Galway	Kiltartan	Gort	IV.	48
13, 14	Kilteale	{ 1,991 2 12r { 1,561 3 34	} Queen's Co.	{Maryborough East {Stradbally	{Athy {Mountmellick	} I. {	241 247
15, 20	Kilteel	3,435 1 20	Kildare	South Salt	Naas	I.	77
23, 24, 32, 33	Kilteely	{ 1,655 0 36 { 1,529 1 29	} Limerick	{Coonagh {Smallcounty	{Kilmallock {Tipperary	} II. {	235 260
40, 42	Kilteevan	8,411 0 32s	Roscommon	Ballintober South	Roscommon	IV.	189,190
59, 60, 67, 68, 76, 77, 85, 86	Kilteevoge	41,131 3 22t	Donegal	Raphoe	Stranorlar	III.	139,140
4	Kiltegan	{ 815 3 6 { 4,203 1 15 { 10,931 3 10	Carlow Wicklow	Rathvilly {Ballinacor South {Upper Talbotstown	} Baltinglass	} I. {	11 350 364,365
27, 28, 32, 33							
77, 83	Kiltegan	1,069 1 24	Tipperary, S.R.	Iffa and Offa East	Clonmel	II.	315
53, 54, 63	Kiltenanlea	7,627 1 19u	Clare	Tulla Lower	Limerick	II.	37
19, 20, 22, 23	Kiltennell	11,170 0 25	Carlow	Idrone East	{Carlow {New Ross	} I.	7, 8
7, 12	Kiltennell	4,125 3 19	Wexford	Ballaghkeen	Gorey	I.	297
105, 106, 115, 116	Kilteskill	{ 2,979 0 34 { 1,716 2 31	} Galway	{Leitrim {Loughrea	} Loughrea	} IV. {	55 65
114,123,124,129,130	Kilthomas	{ 4,584 3 3v { 7,125 1 8	} Galway	{Kiltartan {Loughrea	{Gort {Loughrea	} IV. {	49 65
25, 26, 27	Kiltiernan	3,165 2 26	Dublin	Rathdown	Rathdown	I.	36
70, 71, 77, 78	Kiltinan	5,102 1 29	Tipperary, S.R.	Middlethird	{Cashel {Clonmel	} II.	328
20, 21, 23, 24, 27, 28, 31, 32	Kiltoghert	30,494 3 2w	Leitrim	Leitrim	Cark. on Shannon	IV.	100 to 103
9, 15, 16, 21	Kiltomy	5,865 3 1x	Kerry	Clanmaurice	{Listowel {Tralee	} II.	172
45, 46, 48, 49, 52	Kiltoom	13,246 0 14y	Roscommon	Athlone	Athlone	IV.	182,183
16	Kiltoraght	3,091 3 25z	Clare	Corcomroe	{Corrofin {Ennistimon	} II.	22
99, 100, 107, 108	Kiltormer	6,898 0 6	Galway	Longford	Ballinasloe	IV.	60

No. of Sheet of the Ordnance Survey Maps.	Parish.	Area in Statute Measure.	County.	Barony.	Poor Law Union in 1857.	Townland Census of 1851, Part I.	
		A. R. P.				Vol.	Page
17, 21, 22	Kiltrisk . .	41 0 13	} Wexford . .	{ Ballaghkeen . .	} Gorey . .	I. }	297
17, 23		3,243 3 18		Gorey . .			320
17, 23	Kiltrustan .	6,339 0 35a	Roscommon .	Roscommon . .	Strokestown .	IV.	211
21, 23, 24, 27, 28	Kiltubbrid .	15,608 0 23b	Leitrim . .	Leitrim . .	Carᵏ. on Shannon	IV.	103,104
84, 85, 96, 97	Kiltullagh .	7,776 0 30	} Galway . .	{ Athenry . .	} Loughrea . .	IV. }	4, 5
		1,171 3 27		Kilconnell . .			42
19, 25, 26, 31, 32, 33	Kiltullagh .	24,713 1 18c	Roscommon .	Castlereagh .	Castlereagh .	IV.	201,202
47, 52	Kilturk . .	2,206 3 20d	Wexford . .	Bargy . .	Wexford . .	I.	307
51, 52	} Kilturra . .	3,645 0 23e	Mayo . .	Costello . .	Swineford .	IV. }	142
38, 39		3,238 0 30	Sligo . .	Corran . .	Tobercurry .		227,228
25, 26, 32, 33	Kilvarnet .	6,696 1 5f	Sligo . .	Leyny . .	Tobercurry .	IV.	231,232
31, 37, 38	Kilvellane .	8,678 2 22	Tipperary, N.R.	Owney and Arra .	Nenagh . .	II.	296
63, 64, 71, 72	Kilvemnon .	10,551 1 15	Tipperary, S.R.	Slievardagh .	{ Callan . . } Carrick on Suir }	II.	334,335
102, 112, 113	Kilvine . .	5,426 0 22	Mayo . .	Clanmorris .	Claremorris .	IV.	134
28, 29, 33, 34	Kilwatermoy .	6,556 3 1g	Waterford .	Coshmore & Coshbride	Lismore . .	II.	343,344
34, 35, 39, 40, 46	Kilwaughter .	9,803 2 17h	Antrim . .	Upper Glenarm .	Larne . .	III.	25
19, 20, 27, 28	Kilworth .	5,457 3 9	Cork, E.R. .	Condons & Clangibbon	Fermoy . .	II.	62
43, 44, 53, 54	Kinard . .	5,001 3 26i	Kerry . .	Corkaguiny .	Dingle . .	II.	179
4, 6, 7, 9	} Kinawley .	15,346 1 3	Cavan . .	Tullyhaw . .	{ Bawnboy . . }	III. }	92, 93
32, 33, 34, 37,		8,686 2 16j	} Fermanagh .	{ Clanawley . .	Enniskillen .		193,194
38, 39, 41, 42		26,970 3 5k		Knockninny .	Lisnaskea . .		201 to 203
3	} Kineagh . .	3,289 2 23	Carlow . .	Rathvilly . .	} Baltinglass .	I. }	11, 12
38, 40		3,008 2 38l	Kildare . .	Kilkea and Moone .			60, 61
94, 95, 108, 109	Kinneigh .	15,095 2 3	Cork, W.R. .	East Carbery, W.D. .	{ Bandon . . } Dunmanway }	II.	134,135
36, 37, 39, 40	Kinnitty .	13,894 2 10	King's Co. .	Ballybritt . .	Parsonstown .	I.	125,126
112, 125	Kinsale . .	377 3 17	Cork, E.R. .	Kinsale . .	Kinsale . .	II.	100
37, 38, 40	Kinsalebeg .	5,789 0 29	Waterford .	Decies within Drum .	Youghal . .	II.	351,352
11, 12, 15	Kinsaley .	2,129 3 27	Dublin . .	Coolock . .	Balrothery .	I.	28
112, 125	Kinure . .	1,987 2 38	Cork, E.R. .	Kinalea . .	Kinsale . .	II.	95, 96
102, 112, 113, 121	Kinvarradoorus .	11,289 2 2m	Galway . .	Kiltartan . .	Gort . .	IV.	49, 50
27, 32, 33, 37	Kirkinriola .	6,390 1 15	Antrim . .	Lower Toome .	Ballymena .	III.	32, 33
22	Knavinstown .	618 3 25	Kildare . .	West Offaly .	Athy . .	I.	73
14, 15, 20, 21	Knigh . .	4,514 2 26n	Tipperary, N.R.	Lower Ormond .	Nenagh . .	II.	285
80, 81, 91, 92, 102	} Knock . .	1,736 3 0o	} Mayo . .	{ Clanmorris .	} Claremorris .	IV. }	135
		9,967 3 19p		Costello . .			142,143
12	Knock . .	975 3 20	Meath . .	Morgallion .	Navan . .	I.	210
32, 40	Knockainy .	9,248 1 29q	Limerick . .	Smallcounty .	Kilmallock .	II.	260,261
57, 64, 65, 66, 72, 73, 74, 81, 82,	} Knockane .	55,726 1 29r	} Kerry . .	{ Dunkerron North .	{ Cahersiveen } Kenmare . }	II. }	181,182
83, 84, 90, 91		2,266 2 11s		Dunkerron South .	Killarney .		184
11, 12, 17	Knockanure .	5,950 0 9t	Kerry . .	Iraghticonnor .	Listowel . .	II.	192
84, 85, 96, 97	Knockavilly .	3,661 3 1	} Cork, E.R. .	{ East Muskerry, .	} Bandon . .	II. }	104,105
		2,548 0 37		Kinalea . .			96
4, 5, 9, 10	Knockbreda .	1,129 2 24	} Down . .	{ Lower Castlereagh .	{ Belfast . . } Lisburn . }	III. }	163
		6,968 2 24u		Upper Castlereagh .			165
22, 23, 27, 28, 33	Knockbride .	18,693 1 22v	Cavan . .	Clankee . .	{ Bailieborough } Cootehill . }	III.	73,74
19, 26	Knockcommon .	3,500 0 7w	Meath . .	Lower Duleck .	Navan . .	I.	196
68, 69, 75, 76	Knockgraffon .	9,873 1 27x	Tipperary, S.R.	Middlethird .	{ Cashel . . } Tipperary . }	II.	328
40, 41, 48, 49	Knocklong .	4,442 1 13	Limerick . .	Coshlea . .	Kilmallock .	II.	240
37, 38, 43, 44	Knockmark .	2,876 2 24	Meath . .	Lower Deece .	Dunshaughlin .	I.	192
36, 37, 45, 46	Knockmourne .	953 1 2y		{ Barrymore .	} Fermoy . .	II. }	56
		1,996 0 12	} Cork, E.R. .	Condons & Clangibbon			62
		5,886 2 5		Kinnatalloon .	} Lismore . .		98
13, 22	Knocknagaul .	2,171 3 18	Limerick . .	Pubblebrien .	Limerick . .	II.	253
22, 23, 24, 28, 29, 30	} Knockrath .	15,617 0 1z	} Wicklow . .	{ Ballinacor North .	} Rathdrum .	II. }	347
		3,237 1 37aa		Ballinacor South .			350
6, 7, 15, 16	Knocktemple .	4,618 1 13	Cork, E.R. .	Duhallow . .	{ Kanturk . } Mallow . }	II.	75
27, 28, 31, 32, 35	Knocktopher .	4,722 1 37	Kilkenny . .	Knocktopher .	Thomastown .	I.	112
15, 21	Kyle . .	7,145 3 33bb	Queen's Co. .	Clandonagh .	{ Donaghmore } Roscrea . }	I.	233

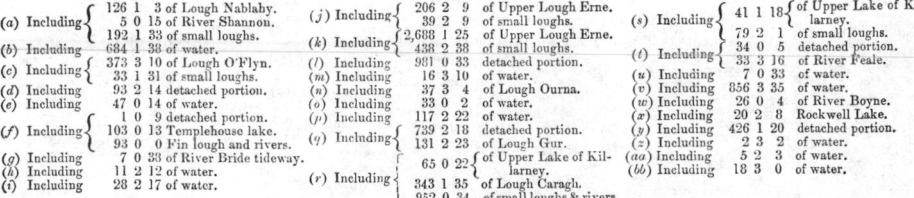

A. R. P.
(a) Including { 126 1 3 of Lough Nablahy. / 5 0 15 of River Shannon. / 192 1 33 of small loughs.
(b) Including 684 1 38 of water.
(c) Including { 373 3 10 of Lough O'Flyn. / 33 1 31 of small loughs.
(d) Including 93 2 14 detached portion.
(e) Including 47 0 14 of water.
(f) Including { 1 0 9 detached portion. / 103 0 13 Templehouse lake. / 93 0 0 Fin lough and rivers.
(g) Including 7 0 33 of River Bride tideway.
(h) Including 11 2 12 of water.
(i) Including 28 2 17 of water.

A. R. P.
(j) Including { 206 2 9 of Upper Lough Erne. / 39 2 9 of small loughs.
(k) Including { 2,688 1 25 of Upper Lough Erne. / 438 2 38 of small loughs.
(l) Including 981 0 33 detached portion.
(m) Including 16 3 10 of water.
(n) Including 37 3 4 of Lough Ourna.
(o) Including 33 0 2 of water.
(p) Including 117 2 22 of water.
(q) Including { 739 2 18 detached portion. / 131 2 23 of Lough Gur.
(r) Including { 65 0 22 of Upper Lake of Killarney. / 343 1 35 of Lough Caragh. / 952 0 34 of small loughs & rivers.

A. R. P.
(s) Including { 41 1 18 of Upper Lake of Killarney. / 79 2 1 of small loughs.
(t) Including { 33 3 16 of River Feale. / 34 0 5 detached portion.
(u) Including 7 0 33 of water.
(v) Including 356 3 35 of water.
(w) Including 26 0 4 of River Boyne.
(x) Including 20 2 8 Rockwell Lake.
(y) Including 426 1 20 detached portion.
(z) Including 2 3 2 of water.
(aa) Including 5 2 3 of water.
(bb) Including 18 3 0 of water.

No. of Sheet of the Ordnance Survey Maps.	Parish.	Area in Statute Measure.	County.	Barony.	Poor Law Union in 1857.	Townland Census of 1851, Part I.	
		A. R. P.				Vol.	Page
69, 70, 71, 83, 84	Lackagh . .	12,996 2 28a	Galway . .	Clare . . .	Galway . } Tuam . }	IV.	22, 23
21, 22	Lackagh . . .	8,316 2 5	Kildare . .	West Offaly . .	Athy . .	I.	73
7, 8, 14, 15	Lackan . . .	7,338 2 13	Mayo . . .	Tirawley . .	Killala . .	IV.	170,171
6, 11	Lackan . . .	3,202 1 9b	Westmeath .	Corkaree . .	Mullingar . .	I.	262
7, 16	Lackeen . . .	279 3 19	Cork, E.R. .	Orrery and Kilmore .	Mallow . .	II.	109
48, 53	Ladysisland .	597 1 7	Wexford . .	Forth . . .	Wexford . .	I.	311
18, 19, 23, 24	Ladytown . .	2,682 1 28c	Kildare . .	Connell . .	Naas . .	I.	55
64, 68 }	Lambeg . .	188 3 16 187 3 26 }	Antrim . .	Upper Belfast . . Upper Massereene . }	Lisburn .	III.	10 31
8, 9, 14, 15		1,190 0 38	Down . . .	Upper Castlereagh .			166
36, 37, 42, 43, 49	Laracor . . .	8,335 0 7d	Meath . .	Lower Moyfenrath .	Trim . .	I.	210
5, 6, 10, 11	Laraghbryan .	8,040 3 11e	Kildare . .	North Salt . .	Celbridge . .	I.	75
21, 22, 26, 27	Larah . .	12,115 3 24f 5,166 2 31g }	Cavan . .	Tullygarvey . . Upper Loughtee . }	Cavan . . Cootehill . }	III.	90, 91 85
35, 40	Larne . . .	2,209 3 37	Antrim . .	Upper Glenarm .	Larne . .	III.	25
27, 28	Latteragh . .	4,065 1 11	Tipperary, N.R.	Upper Ormond .	Nenagh . .	II.	292
66	Lattin . . .	2,276 0 3	Tipperary, S.R.	Clanwilliam . .	Tipperary . .	II.	309
21, 26, 27, 32, 33	Lavey . . .	10,678 3 30h	Cavan . .	Upper Loughtee .	Cavan . .	III.	85,86
14, 15, 19, 20, 24, 25	Layd . . .	20,476 1 14	Antrim . .	Lower Glenarm .	Ballycastle } Larne }	III.	22,23
14, 15, 19	Layd, Grange of	7,834 0 3	Antrim . .	Lower Glenarm .	Ballycastle .	III.	22
4, 5, 8, 9, 14	Lea . . .	18,488 0 31i	Queen's Co. .	Portnahinch . .	Mountmellick .	I.	244
23, 29, 30, 34	Learmount . .	14,484 2 6	Londonderry .	Tirkeeran . .	Londonderry .	III.	*247,249
53, 54, 61, 62	Leck . . .	10,744 3 19j	Donegal . .	Raphoe . .	Letterkenny .	III.	140
2, 5, 6, 10	Leckpatrick .	13,451 0 16k	Tyrone . .	Strabane Lower .	Strabane . .	III.	321,322
97, 111	Leighmoney .	2,716 1 39	Cork, E.R. .	Kinalea . .	Kinsale . .	II.	96
28, 36	Leitrim . .	5,910 0 8l	Cork, E.R. .	Condons & Clangibbon	Fermoy . .	II. }	62
19		1,217 3 27m	Waterford . .	Coshmore & Coshbride	Lismore . .		344
106, 116	Leitrim . . .	4,098 2 39	Galway . .	Leitrim . .	Loughrea . .	IV.	55
13, 17	Leixlip . .	1,506 1 26n	Dublin . .	Newcastle . .	Celbridge .	I. }	33
6, 11		1,695 3 5o	Kildare . .	North Salt . .			75
6, 7, 14, 15, 23	Lemanaghan .	19,615 1 28	King's Co. .	Garrycastle . .	Parsonstown } Tullamore }	I.	136,137
6, 11, 12	Leny . . .	4,231 2 20p	Westmeath .	Corkaree . .	Mullingar . .	I.	262,263
31, 32, 36, 37, 39	Letterluna . .	8,430 0 11q	King's Co. .	Ballybritt . .	Parsonstown .	I.	126
50,51,57,58,65,66	Lettermacaward	20,800 2 19r	Donegal . .	Boylagh . .	Glenties . .	III.	114
18	Liberties of Christ Church . }	1 2 19	Dublin . .	City of Dublin .	Dublin South .	I.	44,45
18	Liberties of St. Patrick's	9 0 4	Dublin . .	City of Dublin .	Dublin South .	I.	44,45
1, 2, 3	Lickbla . .	8,837 3 11s	Westmeath .	Fore . . .	CastleTⁿDelvin } Granard . }	I.	270
97	Lickerrig . .	267 0 22	Galway . .	Athenry . .	Loughrea . .	IV.	5
96, 97, 104, 105	Lickerrig .	2,524 1 2 1,677 1 12t }	Galway . .	Dunkellin . . Loughrea . . }	Loughrea . .	IV. }	31 65
48, 54	Lickfinn . .	679 3 4	Tipperary, S.R.	Slievardagh . .	Urlingford .	II.	335
117, 118, 126, 127	Lickmolassy .	12,112 2 36u	Galway . .	Longford . .	Portumna . .	IV.	60, 61
12, 13, 22	Lickoran . .	2,414 3 5	Waterford . .	Decies without Drum	Lismore . .	II.	358
20, 21	Lisbunny . .	4,393 2 17	Tipperary, N.R.	Upper Ormond .	Nenagh . .	II.	292
7, 15, 16	Liscarroll . .	4,027 2 15	Cork, E.R. .	Orrery and Kilmore .	Mallow . .	II.	109
17, 18, 24, 25	Liscartan . .	1,303 2 1	Meath . .	Lower Navan . .	Navan . .	I.	215
86, 87, 98	Liscleary . .	4,304 3 6v	Cork, E.R. .	Kerrycurrihy . .	Cork . } Kinsale }	II.	92
37, 42	Liscolman . .	2,483 0 3	Wicklow . .	Shillelagh . .	Shillelagh . .	I.	357
35, 38, 40	Lisgenan or Grange	5,709 3 0w	Waterford . .	Decies within Drum	Youghal . .	II.	352
53, 54, 64, 65	Lisgoold . .	3,153 3 0	Cork, E.R. .	Barrymore . .	Middleton . .	II.	56
4, 15, 16, 29	Liskeevy . .	7,206 2 32x	Galway . .	Dunmore . .	Tuam . .	IV.	35
11, 12, 16	Liskinfere . .	5,380 2 38	Wexford . .	Gorey . . .	Gorey . .	I.	320, 321
136, 137, 145	Lislee . . .	6,302 1 21	Cork, W.R. .	Ibane and Barryroe .	Clonakilty .	II.	149, 150
10, 19, 20	Lismakeery .	3,031 3 20	Limerick . .	Connello Lower .	Rathkeale .	II.	228
55, 56, 63	Lismalin . .	4,241 2 2	Tipperary, S.R.	Slievardagh . .	Callan . .	II.	335
35	Lismateige . .	1,643 2 17	Kilkenny . .	Knocktopher . .	Thomastown .	I.	113
36, 37 }	Lismore and Mo- collop }	1,293 1 38y	Cork, E.R. .	Condons & Clangibbon	Fermoy . }	II. {	62
11, 12, 19, 20, } 21, 28, 29, 34 } }		62,743 3 21z	Waterford . .	Coshmore & Coshbride	Lismore . }		344 to 348
31, 32	Lismullin . .	938 3 11	Meath . .	Skreen . .	Navan . .	I.	221
11,12,16,17,20,24	Lisnadill . .	4,529 1 0 8,203 2 3aa } 5,824 0 35 }	Armagh . .	Armagh . . Fews Lower . . Fews Upper . . }	Armagh . .	III. {	45 46, 47 49
16, 17	Lisnakill . .	2,534 1 0	Waterford . .	Middlethird . .	Waterford . .	II.	368
77	Lisronagh . .	3,046 1 20	Tipperary, S.R.	Iffa and Offa East .	Clonmel . .	II.	315

A. R. P.		A. R. P.		A. R. P.	
(a) Including 1,175 1 33 detached portion.	(k) Including { 56 3 34 of water. 104 0 29 of tideway. }	(s) Including 89 2 16 of water.
(b) Including { 75 0 24 of Lough Derravaragh. 61 3 32 of River Inny. }	(l) Including 25 0 11 of water.	(t) Including 331 3 35 detached portion.
(c) Including { 235 3 32 detached portion. 6 1 25 of River Liffey. }	(m) Including 18 2 14 of River Blackwater.	(u) Including { 57 3 27 of River Shannon. 2,167 0 28 of Lough Derg. }
(d) Including 11 3 16 of River Boyne.	(n) Including 18 1 20 of River Liffey.	(v) Including 692 1 21 detached portion.
(e) Including 42 0 32 of water.	(o) Including 12 2 34 of River Liffey.	(w) Including 1,076 3 30 detached portion.
(f) Including 116 0 17 of water.	(p) Including { 175 3 18 of Lough Owel. 259 0 18 of Lough Iron. 23 2 2 of Inny River and small lough. }	(x) Including 200 3 2 detached portion.
(g) Including 64 1 25 of water.		(y) Including { 93 1 28 of water. 9 3 8 of water. }
(h) Including 76 2 20 of water.		(z) Including { 26 2 30 of River Bride tideway. 196 2 28 of River Blackwater. }
(i) Including 28 2 7 of River Barrow.	(q) Including 279 1 12 of detached portion.	(aa) Including 6 2 16 of water.
(j) Including 263 3 27 of tideway.	(r) Including { 512 0 3 of Gweebarra River tideway. 503 2 1 of loughs. }	

* This *new Parish* is composed of the following 19 Townlands, viz.: Altinure Lower, Altinure Upper, Clagan, Dreen, Eden, Kilcreen, Loughtilube, Money-hoghan, Straid, Tamnagh, and Terrydreen, from *Banagher Parish*, page 247; Teenaght, from *Cumber Lower Parish*, page 249; Ballyrory, Carnanbane, Carnan-reagh, Gortscreagan, Kilgort, Lear, and Tireighter, from *Cumber Upper Parish*, page 249.

No. of Sheet of the Ordnance Survey Maps.	Parish.	Area in Statute Measure. (A. R. P.)	County.	Barony.	Poor Law Union in 1857.	Townland Census of 1851, Part I. — Vol.	Townland Census of 1851, Part I. — Page
40, 41, 45, 46, 48	Lissan	11,767 2 8a	Londonderry	Loughinsholin	Magherafelt	III.	242
20, 21, 29,		12,917 2 3b	Tyrone	Dungannon Upper	Cookstown		309
4, 5, 9, 10	Lisselton	6,882 1 0	Kerry	Iraghticonnor	Listowel	II.	192
29, 30, 36, 37	Lissonuffy	11,665 1 8c	Roscommon	Roscommon	Strokestown	IV.	211, 212
36, 37, 40, 41	Listerlin	3,161 3 7	Kilkenny	Ida	New Ross	I.	103
		2,270 2 2		Knocktopher			113
6, 10, 11	Listowel	21 2 0d	Kerry	Clanmaurice	Listowel	II.	172
		8,232 3 0e		Iraghticonnor			192, 193
27, 35	Litter	2,732 2 16f	Cork, E.R.	Condons & Clangibbon	Fermoy	II.	62
		2,671 2 35g		Fermoy			80, 81
75	Little Island	1,691 2 17h	Cork, E.R.	Barrymore	Cork	II.	56
9, 17, 18	Loghill	5,153 2 12i	Limerick	Shanid	Glin	II.	256, 257
25, 33, 34, 41, 42	Longfield East	9,716 1 5j	Tyrone	Omagh West	Omagh	III.	315, 316
24, 25, 32, 33, 34, 41	Longfield West	23,906 3 2k	Tyrone	Omagh West	Castlederg	III.	316
1, 3, 4, 5, 7	Lorrha	16,520 3 29l	Tipperary, N.R.	Lower Ormond	Borrisokane / Parsonstown	II.	285
16, 19	Lorum	5,345 1 22m	Carlow	Idrone East	Carlow	I.	8
43, 44	Loughan or Castle-keeran	3,613 0 4n	Cavan	Castlerahan	Kells	III.	69
10, 16		5,114 2 25	Meath	Upper Kells	Oldcastle	I.	206, 207
3, 6	Loughbrackan	2,159 3 0o	Meath	Lower Slane	Ardee	I.	223
9, 15, 22	Loughcrew	5,981 3 29p	Meath	Fore	Oldcastle	I.	201
4, 5, 8, 9, 12, 13	Loughgall	2,449 2 23	Armagh	Armagh	Armagh	III.	45, 46
		8,474 3 1q		Oneilland West			53, 54
17, 18, 21, 22, 25	Loughgilly	1,611 3 16r	Armagh	Fews Lower	Armagh	III.	47
		8,441 1 5s		Orior Lower	Banbridge		56, 57
		5,976 2 17		Orior Upper	Newry		58
12, 13, 14, 18, 19, 23, 24	Loughguile	6,466 0 32	Antrim	Kilconway	Ballymoney	III.	27
		23,373 1 11t		Upper Dunluce			20
29, 30, 36, 37, 43, 44	Loughinisland	12,485 3 14u	Down	Kinelarty	Downpatrick	III.	177
5, 8	Loughkeen	10,661 0 10	Tipperary, N.R.	Lower Ormond	Borrisokane / Parsonstown	II.	286
29, 35	Loughmoe East	6,014 1 27v	Tipperary, N.R.	Eliogarty	Thurles	II.	271
29, 35, 41	Loughmoe West	4,865 1 25	Tipperary, N.R.	Eliogarty	Thurles	II.	271
97, 98, 105, 106	Loughrea	6,436 1 11w	Galway	Loughrea	Loughrea	IV.	65, 66
6, 7, 10, 11, 12, 14	Louth	2,081 1 11	Louth	Ardee	Ardee	I.	173
		13,894 0 39x		Louth	Dundalk		184, 185
		1,867 0 30		Upper Dundalk			179
17	Lucan	1,125 2 16y	Dublin	Newcastle	Celbridge	I.	33
14, 23	Ludden	1,954 0 14	Limerick	Clanwilliam	Limerick	II.	225
12, 17	Lullymore	2,656 1 22	Kildare	East Offaly	Edenderry	I.	70
32, 33, 38, 39, 40, 43, 44	Lurgan	11,327 3 23z	Cavan	Castlerahan	Oldcastle	III.	69, 70
4, 5, 7, 8, 12	Lusk	16,183 2 28aa	Dublin	Balrothery East	Balrothery	I.	20, 21
21, 29, 30, 35	Lusmagh	8,919 3 26bb	King's Co.	Garrycastle	Parsonstown	I.	137
16, 17, 24, 25	Lynally	5,998 3 39cc	King's Co.	Ballycowan	Tullamore	I.	128
19, 26	Lynn	5,020 0 39dd	Westmeath	Fartullagh	Mullingar	I.	269
11, 14, 15	Lyons	1,634 3 23ee	Kildare	South Salt	Celbridge	I.	77
32, 38	Macetown	1,991 1 15	Meath	Skreen	Dunshaughlin	I.	221
70, 71, 82, 83	Macloneigh	3,808 1 8	Cork, W.R.	West Muskerry	Macroom	II.	160
6, 7, 8, 10, 11, 12	Macosquin	17,812 2 27ff	Londonderry	Coleraine	Coleraine	III.	232, 233
20, 28	Macroney	8,370 2 10	Cork, E.R.	Condons & Clangibbon	Fermoy	II.	63
48, 49, 59, 60, 70, 71	Macroom	12,666 2 31	Cork, W.R.	West Muskerry	Macroom	II.	160
43, 49	Maghera	3,214 1 10	Down	Upper Iveagh, Lr. pt.	Kilkeel	III.	173
31, 32, 33, 35, 36 / 37, 41, 42	Maghera	21,755 1 6	Londonderry	Loughinsholin	Magherafelt	III.	242, 243
30, 31, 33, 34	Magheracloone	14,951 3 32gg	Monaghan	Farney	Carrickmacross	III.	272, 273
11, 16, 17, 22	Magheracross	170 1 15	Fermanagh	Lurg	Enniskillen	III.	207
		9,938 0 23hh	Fermanagh	Tirkennedy	Lowtherstown		223
56		343 3 11	Tyrone	Omagh East	Lowtherstown		314
2, 5, 6, 10, 11	Magheraculmoney, and Islands	18,576 3 22ii	Fermanagh	Lurg	Lowtherstown	III.	207 to 209
22, 29, 30, 36	Magheradrool	11,923 2 13jj	Down	Kinelarty	Downpatrick	III.	177
		628 2 3		Lower Iveagh, Lr. pt.	Lisburn		168
41, 42, 46, 47	Magherafelt	8,291 3 37	Londonderry	Loughinsholin	Magherafelt	III.	243
63, 64, 67, 68	Magheragall	6,555 2 35	Antrim	Upper Massereene	Lisburn	III.	31
6	Magheralin	486 1 22	Armagh	Oneilland East	Lurgan	III.	49
13, 19, 20		7,807 0 29kk	Down	Lower Iveagh, Up. pt.			170

	A. R. P.			A. R. P.			A. R. P.
(a) Including	69 3 38 of Lough Fea.		(m) Including	12 2 0 of River Barrow.		(aa) Including	136 2 30 detached portion.
(b) Including	78 2 7 of Lough Fea.		(n) Including	637 1 30 detached portion.		(bb) Including	187 1 34 of River Shannon.
(c) Including	155 3 0 of River Shannon. / 4 2 8 Loughanlea.		(o) Including	25 1 8 Lough Brackan.		(cc) Including	54 2 10 of water.
(d) Including	5 0 2 of water.		(p) Including	15 2 8 of water.		(dd) Including	293 0 28 of Lough Ennell.
(e) Including	54 3 6 of River Feale. / 1 0 22 of Galey River tideway.		(q) Including	59 2 4 of water.		(ee) Including	150 3 37 detached portion. / 22 2 12 of water.
(f) Including	16 1 22 of water.		(r) Including	39 0 9 of water.		(ff) Including	64 0 25 of River Bann.
(g) Including	28 0 1 of water.		(s) Including	41 1 32 of water.		(gg) Including	336 1 23 of water.
(h) Including	69 2 23 Harpers Island.		(t) Including	59 2 13 of water.		(hh) Including	71 2 13 of water.
(i) Including	216 2 12 detached portions.		(u) Including	124 3 7 of water.		(ii) Including	3,843 2 18 of Lower Lough Erne. / 41 3 17 of small loughs.
(j) Including	22 1 14 of water.		(v) Including	267 2 17 detached portion.		(jj) Including	176 2 35 of water.
(k) Including	175 3 31 of water.		(w) Including	479 1 20 of Lough Rea.		(kk) Including	7 2 6 of water.
(l) Including	542 3 33 of Lough Derg. / 298 0 10 of River Shannon. / 10 3 36 Friars Lough.		(x) Including	31 0 35 of water.			
			(y) Including	18 2 16 of River Liffey.			
			(z) Including	774 1 29 of Lough Ramor. / 148 1 30 of water.			

No. of Sheet of the Ordnance Survey Maps.	Parish.	Area in Statute Measure.			County.	Barony.	Poor Law Union in 1857.	Townland Census of 1851, Part I.	
		A.	R.	P.				Vol.	Page
27, 34	Magherally . .	5,243	3	16a	Down . .	Lower Iveagh, Lr. pt.	Banbridge . .	III.	168
67	Magheramesk . .	3,149	2	13	Antrim . .	Upper Massereene .	Lisburn . .	III.	31
27, 28, 30, 31	Magheross . .	16,702	0	30b	Monaghan . .	Farney . . .	Carrickmacross .	III.	273,274
1, 2, 5, 6	Magilligan, or Tam-laght-ard . . }	13,129	2	29c	Londonderry .	Keenaght . . .	New Tⁿ Limavady	III.	236,237
61, 62	Magorban . .	4,149	0	5	Tipperary, S.R.	Middlethird . .	Cashel . .	II.	328
61, 71, 72	Magourney . .	5,868	2	7d	Cork, E.R. .	East Muskerry . .	Macroom . .	II.	105
54, 55, 62, 63	Magowry . .	1,931	2	13	Tipperary, S.R.	Middlethird . .	Cashel . .	II.	328
36, 37, 44, 45	Mahoonagh . .	12,687	0	33	Limerick . .	Glenquin . . .	Newcastle . .	II.	246
9, 10, 14	Mainham . .	2,823	2	1	Kildare . .	Ikeathy & Oughterany	Celbridge . .	I.	58
12	Malahide . .	1,125	3	2	Dublin . .	Coolock . . .	Balrothery . .	I.	28
26, 27	Mallardstown .	2,525	2	16	Kilkenny . .	Kells . . .	Callan . .	I.	110
24, 25, 32, 33	Mallow . . {	484	3	30e	} Cork, E.R. .	{ Duhallow . .	} Mallow . .	II. {	75
		8,335	1	13f		Fermoy . .			81
14, 15	Mansfieldstown .	2,417	2	33g	Louth . .	Louth . . .	Ardee . .	I.	185
79, 90	Manulla . .	5,464	0	35h	Mayo . .	Carra . . .	Castlebar .	IV.	129
14	Mapastown . .	1,446	1	14	Louth . .	Ardee . . .	Ardee . .	I.	173
42	Marhin . . .	2,794	1	11i	Kerry . .	Corkaguiny . .	Dingle . .	II.	179
18, 21	Marlestown . .	758	3	6	Louth . .	Ferrard . . .	Drogheda . .	I.	181
75, 87	Marmullane . .	529	1	8	Cork, E.R. .	Kerrycurrihy . .	Cork . . .	II.	92
10, 19	Marshalstown .	7,290	3	17	Cork, E.R. .	Condons & Clangibbon	Mitchelstown .	II.	63
17, 24	Martry . . .	3,890	3	7	Meath . .	Lower Navan . .	Kells . .	I.	215
51, 61, 62, 73	Matehy . . .	7,096	2	23	Cork, E.R. .	East Muskerry . .	Cork . .	II.	105
37, 38, 42, 43	Maudlintown . .	841	0	5	Wexford . .	Forth . . .	Wexford . .	I.	312
47	Mayglass . .	3,528	1	3	Wexford . .	Forth . . .	Wexford . .	I.	312
10, 14	Mayne . . .	1,940	3	28	Kilkenny . .	Fassadinin . .	Kilkenny . .	I.	90
19, 22	Mayne . . .	1,060	2	23	Louth . .	Ferrard . . .	Drogheda . .	I.	181
2, 3, 6, 7	Mayne . . .	7,148	1	3j	Westmeath .	Fore . . .	Granard . .	I.	271
90, 91, 100, 101	Mayo . . {	9,768	3	24k	} Mayo . .	{ Clanmorris . .	{ Ballinrobe . . Castlebar . Claremorris . }	IV. {	135
		2,079	1	19l		Kilmaine . .			157
108, 109, 118	Meelick . . .	4,292	2	9m	Galway . .	Longford . .	Portumna . .	IV.	61, 62
61, 71, 72	Meelick . . .	8,062	1	10n	Mayo . .	Gallen . . .	Swineford . .	IV.	150
21, 27	Meelnagh . .	4,189	0	27	Wexford . .	Ballaghkeen . .	{ Enniscorthy Gorey }	I.	297,298
7, 8, 16, 17, 26, 27, 35, 36 }	Mevagh . . .	21,026	2	4o	Donegal . .	Kilmacrenan . .	Milford . .	III.	130,131
65, 76, 77	Middleton . .	5,712	0	5p	Cork, E.R. .	Imokilly . . .	Middleton . .	II.	89
44, 53, 54	Minard . . .	6,055	2	36q	Kerry . .	Corkaguiny . .	Dingle . .	II.	179,180
10, 19, 20	Mintiaghs or Barr) of Inch . . }	3,258	2	26r	Donegal . .	Inishowen West .	Inishowen . .	III.	121
6, 12	Mitchelstown . .	973	2	10	Meath . .	Lower Slane . .	Ardee . .	I.	223
36, 37 11, 12, 19, 20, 21, 28, 29, 34 }	Mocollop & Lismore {	1,293	1	38s	Cork, E.R. .	Condons & Clangibbon	Fermoy . .	II. . {	62 344 to 348
		62,743	3	21t	Waterford . .	Coshmore & Coshbride	Lismore . .		
12, 13, 21, 22, 30	Modelligo . .	7,518	1	32	Waterford . .	Decies without Drum	{ Dungarvan . Lismore . }	II.	359
55, 56, 63, 64	Modeshil . .	3,100	2	33	Tipperary, S.R.	Slievardagh . .	Callan . .	II.	335
10, 11, 15, 16	Modreeny . .	12,165	1	0	Tipperary, N.R.	Lower Ormond . .	Borrisokane .	II.	286,287
66, 77	Mogeely . .	6,429	3	25	Cork, E.R. .	Imokilly . . .	Middleton . .	II.	89, 90
37, 46, 55	Mogeely . . .	9,708	3	26	Cork, E.R. .	Kinnatalloon . .	{ Fermoy . Lismore . Youghal . }	II.	98, 99
65, 75, 76	Mogeesha . {	3,007	3	28	} Cork, E.R. .	{ Barrymore . .	} Middleton . .	II. {	57
		481	0	24		Imokilly . .			90
28, 29, 32, 33, 35, 36, 37, 38 }	Mohill . {	3,373	3	37u	} Leitrim . .	{ Leitrim . .	{ Carᵏ. on Shannon Mohill . }	IV. {	104 107 to 109
		23,452	1	24v		Mohill . .			
4, 8	Moira . . . {	3,715	2	17w	Longford . .	Longford . .	Longford . .	I.	159,160
13, 14, 20, 21	Moira . . .	6,096	1	26x	Down . .	Lower Iveagh, Up. pt.	Lurgan . .	III.	170
38, 47, 48, 58	Molahiffe . .	9,807	2	29y	Kerry . .	Magunihy . .	Killarney . .	II.	204,205
88	Molough . .	1,625	2	2z	Tipperary, S.R.	Iffa and Offa West .	Clogheen . .	II.	318
35, 36, 43, 44, 53	Monagay . .	22,790	2	30aa	Limerick . .	Glenquin . .	Newcastle . .	II.	247
9, 10, 13, 14	Monaghan . .	13,547	2	0bb	Monaghan . .	Monaghan . .	Monaghan . .	III.	276,277
17, 18	Monamintra . .	356	2	1	Waterford . .	Gaultiere . .	Waterford . .	II.	364
16, 17, 21, 22	Monamolin . {	2,716	0	1	} Wexford . .	{ Ballaghkeen . .	} Gorey . .	I. {	298
		5,792	2	8		Gorey . .			321
26, 33, 34, 42, 43	Monanimy . .	8,831	0	12cc	Cork, E.R. .	Fermoy . .	Mallow . .	II.	81, 82
14, 15, 19, 20	Monart . . .	13,029	1	39dd	Wexford . .	Scarawalsh . .	Enniscorthy .	I.	324,325

	A. R. P.			A. R. P.			A. R. P.
(a) Including	22 2 13 of water.	(l) Including	12 2 24 of water.	(u) Including	41 3 27 of Lough Machugh.
(b) Including	298 3 34 of water.	(m) Including	178 0 6 of River Shannon.	(v) Including {	25 2 36 of River Shannon.
(c) Including	46 2 5 of water.	(n) Including	99 2 23 of water.		512 2 1 of loughs.
(d) Including	37 3 16 of River Lee.	(o) Including {	5 3 22 of River Lackagh tideway.	(w) Including	392 0 23 of River Shannon.
(e) Including	9 1 24 of water.		376 2 28 of small loughs.	(x) Including	26 1 1 of water.
(f) Including	62 2 24 of water.	(p) Including	20 0 14 of water.	(y) Including	2 3 10 of River Maine tideway
(g) Including	8 2 21 of River Glyde.	(q) Including	5 3 6 of water.	(z) Including	36 1 31 of River Suir.
(h) Including	465 3 37 of water.	(r) Including	59 3 26 of water.	(aa) Including	4,672 1 13 detached portions.
(i) Including	208 1 6 detached portion.	(s) Including	9 3 8 of water.	(bb) Including	26 2 6 of water.
(j) Including {	644 0 16 of Lough Derravaragh.	(t) Including {	26 2 30 of River Bride tideway.	(cc) Including	80 0 34 of water.
	37 0 35 of Inny River.		196 2 28 of River Blackwater.	(dd) Including	11 1 25 of River Slaney.
(k) Including {	604 0 38 detached portion.				
	102 0 9 of water.				

No. of Sheet of the Ordnance Survey Maps.	Parish.	Area in Statute Measure.	County.	Barony.	Poor Law Union in 1857.	Townland Census of 1851, Part I.	
		A. R. P.				Vol.	Page
22, 23, 30, 31, 32, 39	Monasteranenagh	650 0 22 / 2,848 1 8a / 4,120 3 31b	Limerick	Coshma / Pubblebrien / Smallcounty	Croom / Kilmallock	II.	243 / 253 / 261
21	Monasterboice	2,316 2 7	Louth	Ferrard	Drogheda	I.	181
21, 22, 26, 27	Monasterevin	7,142 0 1	Kildare	West Offaly	Athy	I.	73
10, 11, 12, 18, 19, 20	Monasteroris	15,762 1 14c	King's Co.	Coolestown	Edenderry	I.	133
58, 59, 71, 72, 84, 85	Monivea	1,653 3 5 / 2,121 1 31 / 18,157 0 27d	Galway	Clare / Kilconnell / Tiaquin	Galway / Loughrea / Tuam	IV.	23 / 42 / 78, 79
13, 19, 26	Monknewtown	3,673 1 23e	Meath	Upper Slane	Drogheda	I.	224
26, 32	Monksgrange	863 2 2f	Queen's Co.	Ballyadams	Athy	I.	231
24, 25	Monksland	2,118 1 15g	Waterford	Decies without Drum	Kilmacthomas	II.	359
75, 87	Monkstown	1,540 3 8	Cork, E.R.	Kerrycurrihy	Cork	II.	93
23	Monkstown	3 1 1 / 2,048 1 0	Dublin	Dublin / Rathdown	Rathdown	I.	30 / 36, 37
26, 32	Monktown	1,869 3 36	Meath	Skreen	Navan	I.	221
14, 20	Monsea	5,160 1 30h / 721 3 26	Tipperary, N.R.	Lower Ormond / Owney and Arra	Nenagh	II.	287 / 296
2, 3, 5, 6	Montiaghs, and Islands	18,098 1 15i	Armagh	Oneilland East	Lurgan	III.	49, 50
22, 31, 35, 36, 38	Moone	166 3 11 / 4,617 1 8 / 2,497 2 19	Kildare	East Offaly / Kilkea and Moone / Narragh & Reban East	Naas / Athy	I.	70 / 61 / 66
50, 51, 53, 54, 55, 56	Moore	21,013 1 21j	Roscommon	Moycarn	Ballinasloe	IV.	206, 207
27, 28, 33, 34	Moorechurch	5,290 3 18k	Meath	Upper Duleek	Drogheda	I.	198
121, 122	Moorgagagh	1,789 1 5l	Mayo	Kilmaine	Ballinrobe	IV.	157
69, 70, 76	Mora	3,623 0 4	Tipperary, S.R.	Middlethird	Cashel	II.	329
10	Morgans	1,227 2 32m	Limerick	Connello Lower	Rathkeale	II.	228
18, 23	Morristownbiller	3,672 1 29n	Kildare	Connell	Naas	I.	56
75, 76	Mortlestown	1,839 2 15	Tipperary, S.R.	Iffa and Offa West	Clogheen	II.	318, 319
17, 18, 20, 21	Mosstown	3,817 2 25o	Louth	Ardee	Ardee	I.	174
14, 15, 19, 20	Mostrim	10,943 0 30	Longford	Ardagh	Granard	I.	152, 153
3, 6, 7, 8, 14, 15	Mothel	20,740 1 25p	Waterford	Upperthird	Carrick on Suir	II.	370, 371
10, 11, 14, 15	Mothell	6,846 1 30q / 245 2 5	Kilkenny	Fassadinin / Gowran	Castlecomer / Kilkenny	I.	90 / 97
32,33,41,42,43,50,51	Mourneabbey	10,055 0 31 / 1,380 3 10r	Cork, E.R.	Barretts / Fermoy	Mallow	II.	50 / 82
71, 72, 83, 84, 95	Moviddy	6,132 1 39	Cork, E.R.	East Muskerry	Bandon	II.	105
12, 13, 21, 22	Moville Lower	15,950 1 21s	Donegal	Inishowen East	Inishowen	III.	118, 119
12, 20, 21, 30, 31	Moville Upper	19,081 2 31t	Donegal	Inishowen East	Inishowen	III.	119
55	Mowney	1,521 3 0	Tipperary, S.R.	Slievardagh	Callan	II.	335
14, 18 / 4, 5, 9 / 42, 43, 46, 47	Moyacomb	5,945 2 33 / 5,810 0 32u / 5,678 2 33	Carlow / Wexford / Wicklow	St. Mullin's Upper / Scarawalsh / Shillelagh	Carlow / Enniscorthy / Shillelagh	I.	14 / 325 / 358
39, 40, 46	Moyaliff	8,021 2 11v	Tipperary, N.R.	Kilnamanagh Upper	Cashel / Thurles	II.	279
9, 14	Moyanna	6,824 1 6w	Queen's Co.	Stradbally	Athy / Mountmellick	I.	247
55, 56, 65, 66, 72	Moyarta, and Islands	15,613 1 3	Clare	Moyarta	Kilrush	II.	34
34, 40	Moybolgue	2,555 2 39	Cavan	Clankee	Bailieborough	III.	74
1, 2, 4, 5	Moybolgue	4,205 2 2x	Meath	Lower Kells	Kells	I.	203
47, 53	Moycarky	3,835 2 39	Tipperary, N.R.	Eliogarty	Thurles	II.	271
67, 68, 69, 80, 81, 82, 92, 93	Moycullen	35,824 2 8y	Galway	Moycullen	Galway	IV.	70 to 72
18, 19	Moydow	4,626 0 20	Longford	Moydow	Ballymahon / Longford	I.	162
19, 20, 21, 27, 28, 29	Moygawnagh	20,269 0 9z	Mayo	Tirawley	Killala	IV.	171
49, 50, 53	Moyglare	4,558 3 17	Meath	Upper Deece	Celbridge / Dunshaughlin	I.	194
8, 9, 14, 15, 22	Moylagh	7,457 0 18aa	Meath	Fore	Oldcastle	I.	201
25, 26, 33	Moylisker	2,183 0 39bb	Westmeath	Fartullagh	Mullingar	I.	269
31, 32, 44, 45, 46, 58, 59, 60, 71, 72	Moylough	2,647 0 3cc / 20,739 3 8dd	Galway	Killian / Tiaquin	Glennamaddy / Mountbellew / Tuam	IV.	45 / 79, 80
30, 36	Moymet	3,255 0 30	Meath	Upper Navan	Trim	I.	216
1, 2, 4, 5, 10, 11	Moynalty	12,678 3 9	Meath	Lower Kells	Kells	I.	203, 204
35, 36, 42	Moyne	9,514 1 8	Tipperary, N.R.	Eliogarty	Thurles	II.	271, 272
22, 28, 29, 33, 34, 38	Moyne	8,461 2 5	Wicklow	Ballinacor South	Shillelagh	I.	350
13, 20, 21, 28, 29	Moynoe	9,848 1 36ee	Clare	Tulla Upper	Scarriff	II.	40

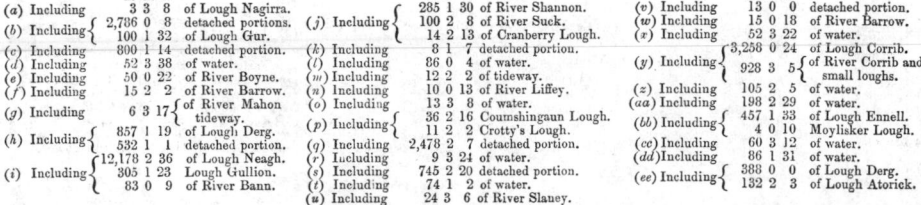

	A. R. P.				A. R. P.			A. R. P.	
(a) Including	3 3 8	of Lough Nagirra.	(j) Including	285 1 30	of River Shannon.	(v) Including	13 0 0	detached portion.
(b) Including	2,786 0 8 / 100 1 32	detached portions. / of Lough Gur.		100 2 8 / 14 2 13	of River Suck. / of Cranberry Lough.	(w) Including	15 0 18	of River Barrow.
(c) Including	800 1 14	detached portion.	(k) Including	8 1 7	detached portion.	(x) Including	52 3 22	of water.
(d) Including	52 3 38	of water.	(l) Including	36 0 4	of water.	(y) Including	3,258 0 24 / 928 3 5	of Lough Corrib. / of River Corrib and small loughs.
(e) Including	50 0 22	of River Boyne.	(m) Including	12 2 2	of tideway.			
(f) Including	15 2 2	of River Barrow.	(n) Including	10 0 13	of River Liffey.	(z) Including	105 2 5	of water.
(g) Including	6 3 17	of River Mahon tideway.	(o) Including	13 3 8	of water.	(aa) Including	198 2 29	of water.
			(p) Including	36 2 16 / 11 2 2	Counshingaun Lough. / Crotty's Lough.	(bb) Including	457 1 33 / 4 0 10	of Lough Ennell. / Moylisker Lough.
(h) Including	857 1 19 / 532 1 1 / 12,178 2 36	of Lough Derg. / detached portion. / of Lough Neagh.	(q) Including	2,478 2 7	detached portion.	(cc) Including	60 3 12	of water.
(i) Including	305 1 23 / 83 0 9	Lough Gullion. / of River Bann.	(r) Including	9 3 24	of water.	(dd) Including	86 1 31	of water.
			(s) Including	745 2 20	detached portion.	(ee) Including	388 0 0 / 132 2 3	of Lough Derg. / of Lough Atorick.
			(t) Including	74 1 2	of water.			
			(u) Including	24 3 6	of River Slaney.			

No. of Sheet of the Ordnance Survey Maps.	Parishes.	Area in Statute Measure. A. R. P.	County.	Barony.	Poor Law Union in 1857.	Townland Census of 1851, Part I. Vol.	Page
23, 24, 25, 35, 36, 37, 38, 49, 50, 51, 52, 62, 63, 64, 65, 75, 76, 77, 78, 89	Moyrus, *and Islands*	101,510 3 8a	Galway	Ballynahinch	Clifden	IV.	12 to 14
10, 11	Muckalee	3,706 0 16	Kilkenny	Fassadinin	Castlecomer	I.	90, 91
35, 39	Muckalee	1,141 1 29 / 1,570 2 32	Kilkenny	Iverk / Knocktopher	Carrick-on-Suir	I.	106 / 113
49, 50, 54, 55	Muckamore, Grange of	5,440 0 36b	Antrim	Lower Massereene	Antrim	III.	28, 29
15, 20, 25	Muckno	17,194 0 8c	Monaghan	Cremorne	Castleblayney	III.	261, 262
29, 30, 38, 39	Muff	15,030 0 9	Donegal	Inishowen West	Inishowen / Londonderry	III.	121
10, 13, 14	Mulhuddart	4,067 0 34	Dublin	Castleknock	Dublin North / Dunshaughlin	I.	25
33, 34. 39, 40, 44	Mullagh	12,872 3 24d	Cavan	Castlerahan	Bailieborough / Kells / Oldcastle	III.	70
12, 13, 16, 17	Mullaghbrack	7,900 3 38e / 3,656 0 8f	Armagh	Fews Lower / Oneilland West	Armagh / Banbridge	III.	47 / 54
18, 20, 21	Mullary	3,635 3 1	Louth	Ferrard	Ardee / Drogheda	I.	181, 182
37, 38, 42, 43	Mullinacuff	6,616 0 1	Wicklow	Shillelagh	Shillelagh	I.	358
12, 18, 19, 25, 26, 27	Mullingar	971 1 32 / 21,351 1 34g	Westmeath	Fartullagh / Moyashel and Magheradernon	Mullingar	I.	269 / 275
47	Mulrankin	2,433 1 19	Wexford	Bargy	Wexford	I.	307
6, 7, 11, 12	Multyfarnham	4,895 0 12h	Westmeath	Corkaree	Mullingar	I.	263
4, 5, 12, 13	Mungret	6,149 0 8	Limerick	Pubblebrien	Limerick	II.	253, 254
39, 43, 44	Munterconnaught	7,432 2 34i	Cavan	Castlerahan	Oldcastle	III.	71
6, 7, 11, 12	Murher	10,698 2 18	Kerry	Iraghticonnor	Glin / Listowel	II.	193
83, 95, 96, 109	Murragh	1,518 3 37 / 7,236 1 6	Cork, W.R.	East Carbery (W.D.) / Kinalmeaky	Bandon	II.	135 / 152
3, 4, 8, 9	Mylerstown	3,846 0 26	Kildare	Carbury	Edenderry	I.	52
142, 151	Myross	4,119 1 14j	Cork, W.R.	West Carbery (E.D.)	Skibbereen	II.	140, 141
16, 17, 20	Myshall	8,893 3 11 / 565 3 17	Carlow	Forth / Idrone East	Carlow	I.	5 / 8
19, 24	Naas	5,526 3 17k	Kildare	North Naas	Naas	I.	62
11, 20, 26, 29, 34	Nantinan	6,591 2 18l / 1,330 0 3	Limerick	Connello Lower / Shanid	Rathkeale / Glin	II.	228, 229 / 257
31, 32, 35, 36	Narraghmore	2,114 1 5 / 8,234 2 25 / 1,921 0 34	Kildare	Kilkea and Moone / Narragh & Reban East / Narragh & Reban West	Athy / Baltinglass	I.	61 / 66 / 68
1, 4	Naul	2,627 2 21	Dublin	Balrothery West	Balrothery	I.	23
25, 31	Navan	3,344 3 0m	Meath	Lower Navan	Navan	I.	215
82, 88	Neddans	2,384 3 5n	Tipperary, S.R.	Iffa and Offa West	Clogheen	II.	319
14, 20, 21, 26, 27	Nenagh	2,020 2 13 / 1,861 0 2	Tipperary, N.R.	Lower Ormond / Upper Ormond	Nenagh	II.	287 / 292, 293
30, 35	Newbawn	2,657 0 8 / 4,880 0 4	Wexford	Bantry / Shelmaliere West	New Ross	I.	301 / 334
20, 21	Newcastle	4,282 1 32	Dublin	Newcastle	Celbridge	I.	34
27, 28, 35, 36	Newcastle	5,257 1 4 / 167 3 37	Limerick	Glenquin / Shanid	Newcastle	II.	247, 248 / 257
88, 91	Newcastle	10,854 2 37o	Tipperary, S.R.	Iffa and Offa West	Clogheen	II.	319
8, 16	Newcastle	305 1 24 / 3,656 1 5	Waterford	Decies without Drum / Middlethird	Kilmacthomas / Waterford	II.	359 / 368
13, 19	Newcastle Lower	4,750 0 4	Wicklow	Newcastle	Rathdrum	I.	353
12, 13, 18, 19	Newcastle Upper	7,025 2 7	Wicklow	Newcastle	Rathdrum	I.	353
76, 77, 82	Newchapel	4,873 1 17	Tipperary, S.R.	Iffa and Offa East	Clonmel	II.	315
9, 22, 26, 29 / 35, 40, 41, 46, 47 / 50, 51	Newry	968 1 33 / 4,501 3 16p / 16,141 3 7q / 878 3 31	Armagh / Down	Oneilland West / Orior Upper / Lordship of Newry / Upper Iveagh, Lr. pt.	Armagh / Newry / Banbridge	III.	54 / 58, 59 / 182 / 173
11	Newtown	1,103 0 7	Meath	Lower Kells	Kells	I.	204
32, 33, 38, 39	Newtown	3,399 1 28 / 6,848 3 32	Westmeath	Fartullagh / Moycashel	Mullingar	I.	269 / 278, 279
1, 2, 5, 6, 11	Newtown Ards	8,222 3 28 / 6,580 3 32	Down	Ards Lower / Lower Castlereagh	Newtownards	III.	158, 159 / 163

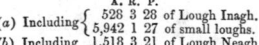

A. R. P.
(a) Including { 528 3 26 of Lough Inagh. / 5,942 1 27 of small loughs.
(b) Including 1,518 3 21 of Lough Neagh.
(c) Including { 577 3 0 of Muckno Lake. / 163 0 9 of small loughs.
(d) Including 140 3 8 of water.
(e) Including 40 2 20 of water.
(f) Including 53 0 19 of water.

A. R. P.
(g) Including { 739 1 36 of Lough Owel. / 580 3 19 of Lough Ennell. / 131 0 39 of small loughs.
(h) Including 922 0 39 of Lough Derravaragh.
(i) Including 965 2 8 of Lough Ramor.
(j) Including 44 3 9 of water.
(k) Including 15 3 2 of River Liffey.

A. R. P.
(l) Including { 540 1 17 detached portions. / 14 1 29 of Doohyle Lough.
(m) Including 20 2 1 of River Boyne.
(n) Including 35 2 33 of River Suir.
(o) Including 21 2 23 of River Suir.
(p) Including { 206 1 8 of tideway. [water. / 40 0 23 of small loughs and fresh
(q) Including 104 3 5 of fresh water.

No. of Sheet of the Ordnance Survey Maps.	Parishes.	Area in Statute Measure.			County.	Barony.	Poor Law Union in 1857.	Townland Census of 1851, Part I.	
		A.	R.	P.				Vol.	Page
30, 36	Newtownclonbun	566	0	7a	Meath	Upper Navan	Trim	I.	216
23, 24	Newtown Crommelin	3,445	2	33	Antrim	Kilconway	Ballymena	III.	27
20, 24, 25, 27, 28	Newtownhamilton	12,404	2	8b	Armagh	Fews Upper	Castleblayney	III.	49
72, 79, 85	Newtownlennan {	4,156	0	16	Tipperary, S.R. { Iffa and Offa East / Slievardagh		Carrick on Suir	II. {	315 / 335
		1,618	0	6					
50, 51	Nilteen, Grange of	2,737	2	22	Antrim	Upper Antrim	Antrim	III.	6,7
3, 5, 6, 11, 12	Nobber {	1,088	3	6	Meath { Lower Kells / Morgallion		Kells	I. {	204 / 210
		9,399	1	25c					
112, 113	Nohaval	2,568	2	0	Cork, E.R.	Kinalea	Kinsale	II.	96
30, 39	Nohaval	3,204	1	17	Kerry	Trughanacmy	Killarney / Tralee	II.	212
12, 13, 21, 29, 38	Nohavaldaly {	11,543	2	8d	Cork, E.R.	Duhallow	Kanturk / Millstreet / Killarney	II. {	75 / 205
50, 60, 68		5,828	3	10	Kerry	Magunihy			
9, 16	Noughaval	4,661	1	9	Clare	Burren	Ballyvaghan / Corrofin	II.	13, 14
26, 27	Noughaval {	331	2	35e	Longford	Rathcline	Athlone	I. {	164
		3,232	0	3f		Shrule	Ballymahon		166
15, 16, 22, 23		11,588	1	5g	Westmeath	Kilkenny West			274
		785	0	28		Carlow			2
12	Nurney {	142	3	3	Carlow	Forth	Carlow	I. {	5
		1,795	0	18h		Idrone East			8
2, 3, 8	Nurney	2,130	1	18	Kildare	Carbury	Edenderry	I.	53
27, 31	Nurney	1,798	1	24	Kildare	West Offaly	Athy	I.	74
22, 30	O'Brennan	6,547	0	12	Kerry	Trughanacmy	Tralee	II.	212
36, 37 / 44, 45, 52, 53, 54	O'Briensbridge	11,425	0	29i	Clare	Tulla Lower	Limerick / Scarriff	II.	37, 38
13, 14	Odagh {	4,113	0	26	Kilkenny { Crannagh / Fassadinin		Kilkenny	I. {	86 / 91
		428	3	25					
15, 21	O'Dorney	7,227	1	30	Kerry	Clanmaurice	Tralee	II.	172,173
6,10,11,12,15,16, 17, 21, 22, 23	Offerlane	48,926	2	14	Queen's Co.	Upperwoods	Abbeyleix / Donaghmore / Mountmellick	I.	250 to 252
29, 36, 37	Ogonnelloe	9,925	2	9j	Clare	Tulla Lower	Scarriff	II.	38
21, 22, 23, 28	Ogulla	6,213	2	3k	Roscommon	Roscommon	Strokestown	IV.	212
9, 10, 15	Oldcastle	7,907	3	33	Meath	Fore	Oldcastle	I.	202
26, 28	Oldconnaught	1,978	0	6	Dublin	Rathdown	Rathdown	I.	37
18, 23	Oldconnell	3,987	0	8l	Kildare	Connell	Naas	I.	56
11, 12, 15, 16	Oldleighlin	9,920	1	16	Carlow	Idrone West	Carlow	I.	9
29, 30, 34, 35	Oldross	10,653	0	22	Wexford	Bantry	New Ross	I.	301
21,22,23,34,35,36	Omey, and Islands	20,835	2	38m	Galway	Ballynahinch	Clifden	IV.	14, 15
24, 25, 33	Oola	6,858	1	35n	Limerick	Coonagh	Tipperary	II.	235,236
34, 35, 38, 39	Oran	5,181	1	8o	Roscommon	Ballymoe	Roscommon	IV.	192
69,81,82,83,94,95	Oranmore, & Islands {	9,989	2	14	Galway { Dunkellin / Galway		Galway	IV. {	31,32 / 37
		9,349	1	23p					
77,86,87,88,96,97,107	Oughaval	33,695	0	28q	Mayo	Murrisk	Westport	IV.	161,162
19, 21, 22, 24, 25	Oughteragh	21,689	3	20r	Leitrim	Carrigallen	Bawnboy / Mohill	IV.	91 to 93
14, 15, 19, 20	Oughterard	2,919	2	22	Kildare	South Salt	Naas	I.	78
52, 60	Oughterleague {	735	1	38	Tipperary, S.R. { Clanwilliam / Kilnamanagh Lower		Tipperary / Cashel	II. {	309 / 324
		1,881	1	22					
2, 3, 5, 6	Oughtmama, & Islands	9,843	1	14s	Clare	Burren	Ballyvaghan / Gort	II.	14
69, 75, 76	Outeragh	1,547	2	24	Tipperary, S.R.	Middlethird	Cashel	II.	329
19, 23	Outrath	2,050	0	26	Kilkenny	Shillelogher	Kilkenny	I.	115
34, 35, 39, 40	Owenduff	7,980	1	7	Wexford	Shelburne	New Ross	I.	328
34, 35, 38, 39	Owning	4,030	2	13	Kilkenny	Iverk	Carrick on Suir	I.	106
2 / 39	Painestown {	1,855	1	3t	Carlow	Carlow	Carlow	I. {	2
		288	1	15u	Kildare	Kilkea and Moone	Athy		61
19, 25, 26	Painestown	3,511	0	30v	Meath	Lower Duleek	Navan	I.	196
17, 18	Palmerston	1,517	3	7w	Dublin	Uppercross	Dublin South	I.	40
6, 7	Palmerstown	1,580	2	34	Dublin	Balrothery West	Balrothery	I.	23
19	Parsonstown	524	0	6	Louth	Ferrard	Drogheda	I.	182
48, 55, 56, 59	Particles	8,496	3	4	Limerick	Coshlea	Kilmallock	II.	240,241

A. R. P.

(a) Including 4 2 25 of River Boyne.
(b) Including 20 3 23 of water.
(c) Including { 70 2 19 of Whitewood Lough. / 6 2 33 of small loughs.
(d) Including 20 0 35 of water.
(e) Including { 36 2 16 of Lough Ree. / 10 0 3 of River Inny.
(f) Including 28 2 6 of River Inny.
(g) Including { 1,433 3 31 detached portion. / 2,391 3 26 of Lough Ree. / 181 2 8 of Inny River and small loughs.

(h) Including 10 2 16 of River Barrow.
(i) Including { 2,772 2 19 detached portion. / 56 1 23 of River Shannon.
(j) Including 3,353 0 0 of Lough Derg.
(k) Including { 753 1 28 detached portion. / 116 1 34 of water.
(l) Including 54 2 6 of River Liffey.
(m) Including 513 0 7 of water.
(n) Including 1,455 3 10 detached portion.
(o) Including 11 2 24 of River Suck.

(p) Including { 1,638 3 0 of Lough Corrib. / 193 2 22 of small loughs and River Corrib.
(q) Including 358 1 22 of water.
(r) Including 485 0 30 of water.
(s) Including { 2,244 1 9 detached portions. / 34 3 27 Lough Murree.
(t) Including { 15 0 30 of New Lake. / 20 0 0 of New Lake.
(u) Including 8 0 0 of River Barrow.
(v) Including 17 3 13 of River Boyne.
(w) Including 22 3 8 of River Liffey.

No. of Sheet of the Ordnance Survey Maps.	Parishes.	Area in Statute Measure.	County.	Barony.	Poor Law Union in 1857.	Townland Census of 1851, Part I.	
		A. R. P.				Vol.	Page
27, 33, 34	Pass of Kilbride	4,031 3 28a	Westmeath	Fartullagh	Mullingar	I.	269
62, 63, 70	Peppardstown	4,779 1 29	Tipperary, S.R.	Middlethird	Cashel	II.	329
10, 11, 13, 14	Philipstown	3,659 3 32	Louth	Ardee	Ardee	I.	174
21, 24	Philipstown	268 1 29	Louth	Ferrard	Drogheda	I.	182
3, 6	Philipstown	1,035 3 15	Louth	Upper Dundalk	Dundalk	I.	179
26, 32, 33, 39	Piercetown	{ 635 2 5 / 1,895 3 28 } Meath	{ Lower Duleek / Upper Duleek }	{ Navan / Dunshaughlin }	I.	{ 196 / 198 }
10, 17	Piercetown	4,230 2 1b	Westmeath	Rathconrath	{ Ballymahon / Mullingar }	I.	283,284
28, 32	Pleberstown	898 0 14c	Kilkenny	Gowran	Thomastown	I.	97
23	Pollardstown	1,249 3 6	Kildare	East Offaly	Naas	I.	70
39, 42, 45	Pollrone	3,596 0 24	Kilkenny	Iverk	{ Carrick on Suir / Waterford }	I.	106
37, 38, 45, 46	Pomeroy	15,950 3 29	Tyrone	Dungannon Middle	{ Cookstown / Dungannon }	III.	303,304
15, 16, 18, 19	Port	1,803 2 10	Louth	Ferrard	Drogheda	I.	182
11, 12, 18, 19	Portloman	2,617 1 36d	Westmeath	Corkaree	Mullingar	I.	263
12, 14, 15	Portmarnock	2,084 1 2e	Dublin	Coolock	Balrothery	I.	28
42, 45, 46	Portnascully	2,452 3 20	Kilkenny	Iverk	Waterford	I.	106
11, 12	Portnashangan	3,635 3 37f	Westmeath	Corkaree	Mullingar	I.	263
8, 9, 12	Portraine	2,185 2 19g	Dublin	Nethercross	Balrothery	I.	31
2, 3, 6, 7, 12	Powerscourt	18,938 0 37h	Wicklow	Rathdown	Rathdown	I.	356
25	Powerstown	5,432 2 25i	Kilkenny	Gowran	Thomastown	I.	97, 98
33, 34, 38, 39	Preban	4,265 0 16	Wicklow	Ballinacor South	Shillelagh	I.	350
88, 97, 105	Prior	11,795 0 12	Kerry	Iveragh	Cahersiveen	II.	198
34, 35, 42, 43	Quin	9,584 3 31j	Clare	Bunratty Upper	{ Ennis / Tulla }	II.	9, 10
28,29,32,33,34,38,39	Racavan	17,563 0 36k	Antrim	Lower Antrim	Ballymena	III.	4
25, 33, 34, 42, 43	Rahan	10,082 3 36l	Cork, E.R.	Fermoy	Mallow	II.	82
7, 8, 15, 16, 24	Rahan	14,985 3 6	King's Co.	Ballycowan	Tullamore	I.	128,129
41, 42, 44, 45	Rahara	5,362 2 24m	Roscommon	Athlone	{ Athlone / Roscommon }	IV.	183
35, 36, 41, 42, 47	Rahelty	4,875 0 38n	Tipperary, N.R.	Eliogarty	Thurles	II.	272
15, 19	Raheny	920 1 19	Dublin	Coolock	Dublin North	I.	28, 29
1, 3, 4	Rahill	2,684 1 38	Carlow	Rathvilly	Baltinglass	I.	12
81, 82, 93, 94	Rahoon, and Islands	{ 11,014 3 5o / 4,154 1 25p } Galway	{ Galway / Moycullen }	Galway	IV.	{ 37,38 & 81 / 72 }
38, 39, 40	Rahugh	4,973 2 15	Westmeath	Moycashel	{ Mullingar / Tullamore }	I.	279
61, 69	Railstown	904 1 31	Tipperary, S.R.	Middlethird	Cashel	II.	329
40, 46	Raloo	6,105 3 20	Antrim	Lower Belfast	Larne	III.	9
4, 5, 8, 9, 14	Ramoan	12,066 1 35	Antrim	Cary	Ballycastle	III.	14, 15
61, 62, 69, 70	Raphoe	13,224 2 3	Donegal	Raphoe	{ Letterkenny / Strabane / Stranorlar }	III.	140,141
22, 23, 26, 27, 31	Rasharkin	19,337 3 5q	Antrim	Kilconway	{ Ballymena / Ballymoney }	III.	27,28
38, 39, 44, 45	Rashee	6,460 2 11r	Antrim	Upper Antrim	Antrim	III.	7
30, 31	Rataine	1,631 3 11	Meath	Lower Navan	Navan	I.	215
21, 22, 29, 30, 38	Ratass	6,982 2 23	Kerry	Trughanacmy	Tralee	II.	213
16, 17, 24, 25	Rath	8,488 3 38s	Clare	Inchiquin	{ Corrofin / Ennistimon }	II.	27, 28
12,16,17,21,22	Rathangan	{ 11,480 0 5 / 50 1 19 } Kildare	{ East Offaly / West Offaly }	{ Edenderry / Naas / Athy }	I.	{ 70, 71 / 74 }
2	Rathaspick	689 3 30	Kilkenny	Fassadinin	Castlecomer		91
25, 31	Rathaspick	{ 4,138 3 17 / 3,438 2 15 } Queen's Co.	{ Ballyadams / Slievemargy }	{ Athy / Carlow }	I.	{ 232 / 246 }
5, 6, 10, 11	Rathaspick	7,664 1 3t	Westmeath	Moygoish	{ Granard / Mullingar }	I.	280
42	Rathaspick	2,804 1 31	Wexford	Forth	Wexford	I.	312,313
134, 135, 143, 144	Rathbarry	{ 375 2 23 / 4,358 3 0u } Cork, W.R.	{ East Carbery (W.D.) / Ibane and Barryroe }	Clonakilty	II.	{ 135 / 150 }

A. R. P.

(a) Including 21 0 12 of water.
(b) Including 6 3 27 of Inny River.
(c) Including 9 2 2 of River Nore.
(d) Including 707 2 0 of Lough Owel.
(e) Including 16 1 13 of detached portion.
(f) Including { 904 1 31 of Lough Owel. / 7 2 17 of Lough Iron. / 29 0 16 of small loughs. }
(g) Including 595 3 0 Lambay Island.
(h) Including { 64 3 0 Lough Bray Lower. / 26 2 24 Lough Bray Upper. }

A. R. P.

(i) Including 11 2 37 of River Barrow.
(j) Including { 232 1 32 of Lough Cullaunyheeda. / 72 3 37 of small loughs. }
(k) Including 0 2 25 detached portion.
(l) Including 31 0 0 of water.
(m) Including 161 1 38 of Lough Funshinagh.
(n) Including 1,358 0 5 detached portion.
(o) Including { that portion which is within the Town of Galway, and / 232 3 8 of water. }

A. R. P.

(p) Including 28 0 19 of water.
(q) Including { 84 1 29 of River Bann. / 2 2 16 of small lough. }
(r) Including 5 1 5 of water.
(s) Including 151 1 37 of water.
(t) Including { 134 0 24 of Lough Iron. / 193 3 39 of Glen Lough. / 48 0 0 of Inny River. }
(u) Including { 52 2 32 Kilkeran Lake. / 15 2 39 Lough Rahavarrig. }

No. of Sheet of the Ordnance Survey Maps.	Parishes.	Area in Statute Measure. A. R. P.	County.	Barony.	Poor Law Union in 1857.	Townland Census of 1851, Part I. Vol.	Page
9, 10	Rathbeagh	354 1 28 / 2,469 0 33	Kilkenny	Fassadinin / Galmoy	Castlecomer / Urlingford	I.	91 / 93
44	Rathbeggan	2,865 3 24	Meath	Ratoath	Dunshaughlin	I.	219
2, 5, 9	Rathborney	9,633 0 39	Clare	Burren	Ballyvaghan	II.	14
20, 21, 26, 27	Rathbran	5,831 3 1	Wicklow	Upper Talbotstown	Baltinglass	I.	365
123, 124, 136	Rathclarin	5,915 3 5a	Cork, W.R.	East Carbery (E.D.)	Bandon	II.	129,130
12, 17, 18, 21, 22	Rathcline, and Islands	12,883 1 7b	Longford	Rathcline	Ballymahon / Longford	I.	164,165
12. 13, 19, 20	Rathconnell	15,659 1 12c	Westmeath	Moyashel and Magheradernon	Mullingar	I.	276
10, 17, 18, 24, 25	Rathconrath	8,745 3 7d	Westmeath	Rathconrath	Ballymahon / Mullingar	I.	284
61, 62, 69, 70	Rathcool	5,904 0 8	Tipperary, S.R.	Middlethird	Cashel	II.	329
20, 21, 24	Rathcoole	4,705 1 30	Dublin	Newcastle	Celbridge	I.	34
11, 14, 15	Rathcoole	3,672 3 25e	Kilkenny	Gowran	Kilkenny	I.	98
63, 64, 74, 75	Rathcooney	5,152 2 12	Cork, E.R.	Cork	Cork	II.	65
42, 47, 48, 49	Rathcore	12,804 0 26 / 1,078 2 26	Meath	Lower Moyfenrath / Upper Deece	Trim	I.	211 / 194
35, 43, 44, 53	Rathcormack	13,995 1 36f	Cork, E.R.	Barrymore	Fermoy	II.	57
21, 22, 27, 28, 33, 34	Rathdowney	17,116 2 28g / 108 2 18h	Queen's Co.	Clandonagh / Clarmallagh	Abbeyleix / Donaghmore	I.	234 / 238
24 29, 30, 35	Rathdrum	5,798 3 14	Wicklow	Ballinacor North	Rathdrum	I.	347
18, 19, 21, 22	Rathdrumin	1,211 0 27	Louth	Ferrard	Drogheda	I.	182
13, 17, 18	Rathernan	5,140 1 36i	Kildare	Connell	Naas	I.	56
18, 22	Rathfarnham	2,581 0 36 / 200 2 39	Dublin	Rathdown / Uppercross	Dublin South	I.	37 / 40
32	Rathfeigh	2,887 3 25	Meath	Skreen	Dunshaughlin	I.	221
1, 3, 7	Rathgarve	6,024 1 22j	Westmeath	Fore	Castletowndelvin / Granard	I.	271
2, 3, 7, 8	Rathgoggan	3,317 2 9	Cork, E.R.	Orrery and Kilmore	Kilmallock	II.	109
2, 3, 6, 7, 14	Rathgormuck	17,965 3 19	Waterford	Upperthird	Carrick on Suir / Clonmel	II.	371
23, 32	Rathjordan	1,063 3 33	Limerick	Clanwilliam	Limerick	II.	225
19, 20, 28, 29, 37	Rathkeale	12,095 1 20k	Limerick	Connello Lower	Croom / Rathkeale	II.	229,230
46	Rathkennan	786 2 26	Tipperary, S.R.	Kilnamanagh Lower	Cashel	II.	324
12, 18	Rathkenny	5,496 0 10	Meath	Upper Slane	Navan	I.	225
39, 40, 42, 43	Rathkieran	3,478 3 38l	Kilkenny	Iverk	Carrick on Suir / Waterford	II.	106,107
1	Rathlin Island	3,398 3 10m	Antrim	Cary	Ballycastle	III.	15
8	Rathlogan	484 3 7	Kilkenny	Galmoy	Urlingford	I.	93
59, 60	Rathlynin	2,781 3 30	Tipperary, S.R.	Clanwilliam	Tipperary	II.	309
42, 47	Rathmacknee	1,861 0 4	Wexford	Forth	Wexford	I.	313
26	Rathmichael	2,808 0 9	Dublin	Rathdown	Rathdown	I.	37
36, 41, 42, 47, 48	Rathmolyon	9,782 3 28	Meath	Lower Moyfenrath	Trim	I.	211
3	Rathmore	815 0 39	Carlow	Rathvilly	Baltinglass	I.	12
19, 20, 24, 25	Rathmore	7,756 1 8	Kildare	North Naas	Naas	I.	62,63
23, 24, 30	Rathmore	5,345 2 25	Meath	Lune	Trim	I.	208
26, 27	Rathmoylan	2,455 2 20n	Waterford	Gaultiere	Waterford	II.	364
37, 38, 44, 45	Rathmullan	319 2 8 / 3,050 0 33o	Down	Lecale Lower / Lecale Upper	Downpatrick	III.	179 / 181
16, 17, 22, 23	Rathnaveoge	5,152 3 9	Tipperary, N.R.	Ikerrin	Roscrea	II.	276
19, 24, 25	Rathnew	8,640 2 13p	Wicklow	Newcastle	Rathdrum	I.	354
43, 44, 46, 47	Rathpatrick	4,479 1 38	Kilkenny	Ida	Waterford	I.	103
19, 20, 24	Rathreagh	4,023 2 4q	Longford	Ardagh	Ballymahon	I.	153
14, 21	Rathreagh	4,164 0 3	Mayo	Tirawley	Killala	IV.	171
44, 50	Rathregan	2,577 1 19	Meath	Ratoath	Dunshaughlin	I.	219
39, 40, 44, 45	Rathroe	2,396 2 33	Wexford	Shelburne	New Ross	I.	328
19, 26, 27, 28, 34, 35	Rathronan	18,117 0 3r	Limerick	Shanid	Glin / Newcastle / Rathkeale	II.	257
76, 77, 82, 83	Rathronan	2,641 0 13s	Tipperary, S.R.	Iffa and Offa East	Clonmel	II.	316
14, 15, 20, 21	Rathsallagh	1,776 1 21	Wicklow	Upper Talbotstown	Baltinglass	I.	365
27, 28, 33	Rathsaran	2,291 0 22	Queen's Co.	Clandonagh	Donaghmore	I.	234,235
20	Rathtoole	692 1 8	Wicklow	Upper Talbotstown	Baltinglass	I.	365
1, 3, 4, 8, 9	Rathvilly	9,212 1 12	Carlow	Rathvilly	Baltinglass	I.	12
38, 39, 44, 45, 51	Ratoath	9,331 3 23	Meath	Ratoath	Dunshaughlin	I.	219

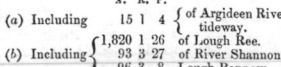

A. R. P.
(a) Including 15 1 4 { of Argideen River tideway.
(b) Including { 1,820 1 26 of Lough Ree. / 93 3 27 of River Shannon. / 96 3 8 Lough Bannow.
(c) Including 231 2 39 of water.
(d) Including 51 1 33 of Mount Dalton Lough.
(e) Including 285 0 33 detached portion.
(f) Including 13 3 4 of water.

A. R. P.
(g) Including 1,585 0 12 detached portion.
(h) Including 102 1 23 detached portion.
(i) Including 1,376 3 6 detached portion.
(j) Including 47 0 22 of Lough Glore.
(k) Including { 322 2 30 detached portion. / 33 1 27 of water.
(l) Composed of { 1,527 3 32 North Portion. / 1,951 0 6 South Portion.

A. R. P.
(m) Including 30 2 14 of water.
(n) Including 661 3 16 detached portion.
(o) Including 9 2 10 of water.
(p) Including 207 3 0 Broad Lough.
(q) Including 31 2 22 of River Inny.
(r) Including 4,175 3 6 detached portion.
(s) Including 792 1 19 detached portion.

No. of Sheet of the Ordnance Survey Maps.	Parishes.	Area in Statute Measure.			County.	Barony.	Poor Law Union in 1857.	Townland Census of 1851. Part I.	
		A.	R.	P.				Vol.	Page
9, 10, 15	Rattoo	7,042	0	1a	Kerry	{ Clanmaurice	Listowel	II.	173
		1,188	1	21b		Iraghticonnor			193
46, 53, 54, 61, 62	Raymoghy	15,286	3	29c	Donegal	Raphoe	{ Letterkenny / Londonderry / Strabane	III.	141,142
15, 24, 25, 26, 34	Raymunterdoney & detached portions	12,613	2	10d	Donegal	Kilmacrenan	Dunfanaghy	III.	131
1, 2, 3, 6, 7	Rearymore	13,943	2	7e	Queen's Co.	Tinnahinch	Mountmellick	I.	249,250
70	Redcity	722	2	28	Tipperary, S.R.	Middlethird	Cashel	II.	329
30, 31, 35, 36	Redcross	6,247	3	14	Wicklow	Arklow	Rathdrum	I.	345,346
16, 17, 25, 26	Reisk	3,826	2	12f	Waterford	Middlethird	{ Kilmacthomas / Waterford	II.	368,369
60, 68, 75	Relickmurry and Athassel	12,207	2	37	Tipperary, S.R.	{ Clanwilliam	{ Tipperary	II.	309,310
		561	2	3		Middlethird	Cashel		330
21, 22, 29, 30, 35	Reynagh	8,826	2	20g	King's Co.	Garrycastle	Parsonstown	I.	137,138
14, 15, 17, 18	Richardstown	1,089	2	38	Louth	Ardee	Ardee	I.	174
31, 36	Ringagonagh	3,246	1	16	Waterford	Decies within Drum	Dungarvan	II.	352,353
97, 98, 111, 112, 125	Ringcurran	1,361	3	2	Cork, E.R.	{ Kinalea	{ Kinsale	II.	96
		4,056	0	38h		Kinsale			100
		1,514	2	19	Cork, E.R.	Kinsale	Kinsale		100,101
111,112,124,125,137	Ringrone	5,371	3	38	Cork, W.R.	{ Courceys	{ Kinsale	II.	147
		2,353	2	27		East Carbery (E.D.)			130
100, 110, 111, 118	Robeen	10,907	0	26i	Mayo	Kilmaine	Ballinrobe	IV.	157,158
9, 10, 18, 19	Robertstown	5,905	3	33j	Limerick	Shanid	{ Glin / Rathkeale	II.	257,258
3, 4, 7	Roche	3,305	1	17	Louth	Upper Dundalk	Dundalk	I.	179
22, 23	Rochestown	1,164	3	10	Limerick	Clanwilliam	Limerick	II.	225
81, 82	Rochestown	1,063	1	36k	Tipperary, S.R.	Iffa and Offa West	Clogheen	II.	319
49	Rodanstown	1,621	0	3	Meath	Upper Deece	Celbridge	I.	194
37, 41	Rosbercon	2,674	2	4	Kilkenny	Ida	New Ross	I.	103
39, 40, 41, 42	Roscommon	9,819	0	3	Roscommon	Ballintober South	Roscommon	IV.	190
39, 43	Roscomroe	5,965	2	11	King's Co.	Ballybritt	{ Parsonstown / Roscrea	I.	126
1, 5	Rosconnell	761	1	25	Kilkenny	Fassadinin	Castlecomer		91
29, 30, 35		1,214	2	34	Queen's Co.	{ Clarmallagh	{ Abbeyleix	I.	238
		214	0	20		Cullenagh			240
42, 43, 45	Roscrea	3,642	3	19	King's Co.	{ Ballybritt	{ Roscrea	I.	126
		2,182	2	27l		Clonlisk			131
12, 17		4,829	3	2	Tipperary, N.R.	Ikerrin		II.	276
3, 4, 6, 7, 8	Rosenallis	14,118	3	5	Queen's Co.	Tinnahinch	Mountmellick	I.	250
121, 133, 134, 143	Ross	12,403	0	19	Cork, W.R.	{ East Carbery (W.D.)	Clonakilty	II.	135,136
		947	0	35		Ibane and Barryroe			150
11, 12, 13, 14, 24, 25, 26, 27, 38, 39	Ross	59,651	1	25m	Galway	Ross	{ Ballinrobe / Oughterard	IV.	73, 74
18, 19, 25, 31	Rossdroit	8,166	1	18	Wexford	Bantry	Enniscorthy	I.	301,302
18	Rossduff	196	3	16	Waterford	Gaultiere	Waterford	II.	364
40, 43	Rossinan	1,705	1	2	Kilkenny	{ Ida	{ Waterford	I.	104
		2,628	0	39		Knocktopher			113
1, 2, 3, 4, 5, 7, 8	Rossinver	48,843	0	21n	Leitrim	Rosclogher	{ Ballyshannon / Manorhamilton	IV.	110 to 112
3, 5, 6		7,932	3	14	Sligo	Carbury	Sligo		223
31, 32	Rosskeen	1,674	2	38o	Cork, E.R.	Duhallow	Kanturk	II.	75
38, 43, 48	Rosslare	2,532	0	8	Wexford	Forth	Wexford	I.	313
90, 100	Rosslee	3,700	2	7p	Mayo	Carra	{ Ballinrobe / Castlebar	IV.	130
6, 11	Rossminoge	4,549	1	10	Wexford	Gorey	Gorey	I.	321
7, 8, 15, 16, 24, 25	Rossmire	8,017	0	5	Waterford	{ Decies without Drum	{ Kilmacthomas	II.	359,360
		143	2	12		Upperthird			371
21, 22, 26, 27	Rossory	2,302	0	34q	Fermanagh	{ Clanawley	{ Enniskillen	III.	194
		5,201	3	1r		Magheraboy			214
88, 100	Rostellan	2,258	1	29s	Cork, E.R.	Imokilly	Middleton	II.	90
17, 18, 25, 26	Ruan	10,744	1	22t	Clare	Inchiquin	Corrofin	II.	28
5, 6	Russagh	2,568	2	19u	Westmeath	Moygoish	{ Granard / Mullingar	I.	280
20, 21, 24	Saggart	4,453	0	12v	Dublin	Newcastle	Celbridge	I.	34, 35
18	St. Andrew's	45	0	31w	Dublin	Dublin City	Dublin South	I.	44, 45
12, 18, 25	St. Andrews (alias) Ballyhalbert and Islands	4,011	3	39	Down	Ards Upper	Newtownards	III.	161
18	St. Anne's	70	3	17	Dublin	Dublin City	Dublin South	I.	44, 45

		A.	R.	P.				A.	R.	P.				A.	R.	P.	
(a) Including		8	0	29	of River Brick tideway.	(k) Including		10	2	30	of River Suir.	(q) Including		180	2	39	of River Erne and small loughs.
(b) Including		10	0	23	of River Feale tideway.	(l) Composed of		1,076	3	6	North portion.	(r) Including		165	3	31	of River Erne and small loughs.
		9	2	28	of Galey River tideway.			1,105	3	21	South portion.			745	3	5	detached portion.
(c) Including		97	0	38	of tideway.			5,430	0	26	of Lough Mask.	(s) Including		8	3	2	of water.
(d) Including		17	1	4	of water.	(m) Including		226	2	24	of Lough Corrib.	(t) Including		756	3	26	of water.
(e) Including		11	3	19	Lough Duff.			630	1	7	Lough Nafooey.	(u) Including		118	1	32	of water.
(f) Including		12	1	38	of Ballyscanlan Lough.			106	3	5	of small loughs.	(v) Including		452	0	18	detached portions.
(g) Including		112	2	36	of River Shannon.	(n) Including		4,460	3	10	of Lough Melvin	(w) Including		2	2	36	of tideway.
(h) Including		519	1	2	detached portion.			71	2	3	of small loughs.						
(i) Including		667	0	9	of Lough Carra.	(o) Including		35	0	3	of water.						
		82	24		of small loughs and river.	(p) Including		68	3	14	of water.						
(j) Including		221	1	33	of tideway.												

No. of Sheet of the Ordnance Survey Maps.	Parishes.	Area in Statute Measure.	County.	Barony.	Poor Law Union in 1857.	Townland Census of 1851, Part I.	
		A. R. P.				Vol.	Page
63, 74	St. Anne's-shandon	1,855 0 16a 1,346 3 22b	Cork, E.R.	Cork Cork City	Cork	II.	65 111
18	St. Audoen's	33 2 17c	Dublin	Dublin City	Dublin South	I.	44, 45
18	St. Bridget's	37 1 38	Dublin	Dublin City	Dublin South	I.	44, 45
37	St. Bridget's	9 1 13	Wexford	Forth	Wexford	I.	315
13, 14, 18, 19, 23	St. Canice	6,003 0 8d 458 1 21e 454 1 5	Kilkenny	Crannagh Kilkenny City Shillelogher	Kilkenny	I.	87 117 115
18	St. Catherine's	288 3 14 188 0 15	Dublin	Dublin City Uppercross	Dublin South	I.	44, 45 40
37	St. Doologe's	3 3 17	Wexford	Forth	Wexford	I.	315
1, 3, 4, 7, 8, 13	St. Feighins	11,082 2 34f	Westmeath	Fore	Castletowndelvin	I.	271,272
9, 15, 16, 22, 23	Saintfield	13,333 2 26g	Down	Upper Castlereagh	Downpatrick Lisburn	III.	166
73, 74, 75, 85, 86	St. Finbar's	8,436 2 22h 447 2 19i 878 0 30	Cork, E.R.	Cork Cork City East Muskerry	Cork Bandon	II.	65, 66 111 106
18	St. George's	309 1 21 344 1 29	Dublin	Coolock Dublin City	Dublin North	I.	29 44, 45
48	St. Helen's	670 3 8	Wexford	Forth	Wexford	I.	313,314
48, 53	St. Iberius	891 0 12	Wexford	Forth	Wexford	I.	314
37	St. Iberius (In Town of Wexford)	15 2 10	Wexford	Forth	Wexford	I.	315
18	St. James'	547 2 0j 517 2 11k 905 1 36l	Dublin	Castleknock Dublin City Uppercross	Dublin North Dublin South	I.	25 44, 45 41
39, 44, 45, 49, 50	St. James & Dunbrody	8,489 1 20	Wexford	Shelburne	New Ross	I.	328
54,60,61,62,68,69	St. Johnbaptist	4,675 1 23m 941 1 13	Tipperary, S.R.	Middlethird Slievardagh	Cashel	II.	330 336
18	St. John's	14 0 33n	Dublin	Dublin City	Dublin South	I.	44, 45
34, 35, 37 20	St. John's	1,021 0 31o 101 3 36	Kildare Queen's Co.	Narragh & Reban West Ballyadams	Athy	I.	68 232
14, 15, 19, 20	St. John's	5,259 2 31p 262 2 31q 9 0 4r	Kilkenny	Gowran Kilkenny City Shillelogher	Kilkenny	I.	98 117 115
5	St. John's	10 0 6 123 3 6s	Limerick	Clanwilliam Limerick City	Limerick	II.	225 262
42, 43, 45, 46	St. Johns	11,634 3 34t	Roscommon	Athlone	Athlone Roscommon	IV.	183,184
14, 15, 20, 21	St. Johns	7,256 1 39u	Sligo	Carbury	Sligo	IV.	223
19, 20, 25, 26	St. John's	2,206 2 13	Wexford	Bantry	Enniscorthy	I.	302
37	St. John's	525 0 10	Wexford	Forth	Wexford	I.	315
54, 62	St. Johnstown	2,180 1 11	Tipperary, S.R.	Middlethird	Cashel	II.	330
9	St. John's Within	13 0 33	Waterford	Waterford City	Waterford	II.	373
9, 10, 17	St. John's Without	732 0 15 187 2 19	Waterford	Gaultiere Waterford City	Waterford	II.	365 373
5	St. Lawrence's	219 2 35 60 0 25	Limerick	Clanwilliam Limerick City	Limerick	II.	225 262
18	St. Luke's	38 2 20	Dublin	Dublin City	Dublin South	I.	44, 45
11, 14	St. Margaret's	2,400 3 7	Dublin	Coolock	Dublin North	I.	29
33, 38	St. Margaret's	142 3 29 2,281 2 6	Wexford	Ballaghkeen Shelmaliere East	Wexford	I.	298 331
48, 53	St. Margaret's	467 2 7	Wexford	Forth	Wexford	I.	314
18	St. Mark's	31 0 12 318 3 25v	Dublin	Dublin Dublin City	Dublin South	I.	30 44, 45
19, 20	St. Martin's	782 1 37w	Kilkenny	Gowran	Kilkenny	I.	98, 99
18	St. Mary's	154 1 31x	Dublin	Dublin City	Dublin North	I.	44, 45
19	St. Mary's	65 3 24y	Kilkenny	Kilkenny City	Kilkenny	I.	117
5	St. Mary's	49 3 30z	Limerick	Limerick City	Limerick	II.	262
24 20	St. Mary's	145 0 23aa 1,203 2 29aa	Louth Meath	Drogheda Town Drogheda	Drogheda	I.	185 194
22, 29, 35	St. Marys	11,455 3 36bb	Westmeath	Brawny	Athlone	I.	259,260
4, 8	St. Marys	4,289 3 39cc	Westmeath	Fore	Castletowndelvin	I.	272
29, 34	St. Mary's	4,922 1 27	Wexford	Bantry	New Ross	I.	302
37	St. Mary's	11 2 1	Wexford	Forth	Wexford	I.	315
83	St Mary's, Clonmel	1,370 3 15dd	Tipperary, S.R.	Iffa and Offa East	Clonmel	II.	316
1, 2, 5, 6		9,017 1 16ee	Waterford	Upperthird			371,372
20, 26	St. Mary's, Enniscorthy	2,990 2 21ff	Wexford	Scarawalsh	Enniscorthy	I.	325
8, 9, 14	St. Mary's, New- townbarry	8,284 1 10gg	Wexford	Scarawalsh	Enniscorthy	I.	325

	A. R. P.			A. R. P.			A. R. P.	
(a) Including	308 2 32	detached portion.	(j) Including	26 0 0	of water.	(w) Including	4 0 20	of River Nore.
(b) Including	58 2 19	of River Lee tideway.	(k) Including	17 0 28	of tideway.	(x) Including	3 3 39	of tideway.
(c) Including	3 2 39	of tideway.	(l) Including	14 2 19	of River Liffey.	(y) Including	2 1 16	of River Nore.
(d) Including	28 0 0	of River Nore.	(m) Including	205 0 0	detached portions.	(z) Including	4 2 0	of Abbey River.
(e) Including	4 2 9	of River Nore.	(n) Including	2 1 17	of tideway.			of River Boyne tideway
(f) Including	1,004 3 27	of Lough Lene.	(o) Including	55 3 14	detached portions.	(aa) Exclusive of	78 0 3	which has not been ap-
	203 3 14	of small loughs.		11 1 32	of River Barrow.			portioned.
(g) Including	508 0 32	detached portion.	(p) Including	29 2 25	of River Nore.	(bb) Including	1,206 2 24	of Lough Ree.
	166 1 21	of water.	(q) Including	16 1 20	of River Nore.		179 0 12	of River Shannon.
(h) Including	33 1 5	of River Lee.	(r) Including	0 2 2	of River Nore.	(cc) Including	99 2 4	of Lough Lene.
	17 3 27	Lough of Cork.	(s) Including	0 3 3	of Abbey River.		160 1 11	of small loughs.
(i) Including	256 0 37	of River Lee tidal portion.	(t) Including	3,616 0 20	of Lough Ree.	(dd) Including	15 3 22	of River Suir.
				38 2 11	of Lough Funshinagh.	(ee) Including	31 1 29	of River Suir.
	7 2 19	of River Lee fresh- water portion.	(u) Including	750 2 3	of Lough Gill.	(ff) Including	34 2 28	of River Slaney.
			(v) Including	29 0 29	of tideway.	(gg) Including	29 1 33	of River Slaney.

No. of Sheet of the Ordnance Survey Maps.	Parishes.	Area in Statute Measure.	County.	Barony.	Poor Law Union in 1857.	Townland Census of 1851, Part I.	
		A. R. P.				Vol.	Page
62, 63, 73, 74	St. Mary's-shandon	2,106 1 1a 282 0 33b	Cork, E.R.	Cork Cork City	Cork	II.	66 111
19	St. Maul's .	243 3 12 68 2 15	Kilkenny	Gowran Kilkenny City	Kilkenny .	I.	99 117
52, 63	St. Michael's .	1,303 1 36 689 3 7	Cork, E.R.	Barrymore Cork	Cork	II.	57 66
18	St. Michael's .	5 3 11c	Dublin	Dublin City	Dublin South	I.	44, 45
35	St. Michaels .	566 3 22 1,314 0 32d	Kildare	Kilkea and Moone Narragh & Reban West	Athy .	I.	61 68
5, 13	St. Michael's .	578 2 16e 989 3 14	Limerick	Limerick City Pubblebrien	Limerick .	II.	262 254
9	St. Michael's .	5 2 28	Waterford	Waterford City	Waterford .	II.	373
48	St. Michael's .	387 0 24	Wexford .	Forth	Wexford .	I.	314
37	St. Michael's of Feagh	99 2 25	Wexford	Forth	Wexford .	I.	315
18	St. Michan's .	126 0 36f	Dublin	Dublin City	Dublin North	I.	44, 45
22, 23, 24, 25, 26 18, 23, 24	St. Mullin's .	17,853 1 37g 3,347 1 38	Carlow Wexford .	St. Mullin's Lower . Bantry .	New Ross .	I.	13 303
52, 53, 62, 63 5	St. Munchin's .	2,826 2 31 245 3 8h 1,510 3 2	Clare Limerick .	Bunratty Lower Limerick City Pubblebrien	Limerick .	II.	6 262 254
18, 26	St. Nathlash .	1,024 1 27 572 2 33	Cork, E.R.	Fermoy . Cork	Mitchelstown .	II.	82 66
73, 74, 85	St. Nicholas .	445 3 36i 331 1 15 1,509 2 22	Cork, E.R.	Cork City East Muskerry Clanwilliam	Cork .	II.	111 106 225
5, 13	St. Nicholas' .	319 2 6j 59 1 22	Limerick .	Limerick City Pubblebrien	Limerick .	II.	262 254
32, 33	St. Nicholas .	1,213 2 18	Wexford	Ballaghkeen	Enniscorthy	I.	298
82, 94	St. Nicholas, and Islands .	3,767 1 35k	Galway .	Galway .	Galway .	IV.	38, 81
18	St. Nicholas' Within	5 0 11	Dublin	Dublin City	Dublin South	I.	44, 45
18	St. Nicholas' Without	58 1 9 5 0 19	Dublin	Dublin City Uppercross	Dublin South	I.	44, 45 41
9	St. Olave's .	3 2 14	Waterford .	Waterford City	Waterford .	II.	373
53, 63 5	St. Patrick's .	3,894 1 8l 793 0 13m 722 0 12n	Clare . Limerick .	Bunratty Lower Clanwilliam Limerick City	Limerick .	II.	6, 7 225 262
19, 20	St. Patrick's .	65 2 30 4,121 0 14o	Kilkenny	Kilkenny City Shillelogher	Kilkenny .	I.	117 116
9	St. Patrick's .	8 3 22	Waterford	Waterford City	Waterford .	II.	373
37	St. Patrick's .	7 0 8	Wexford	Forth	Wexford .	I.	315
18	St. Patrick's (Liberties of) .	9 0 4	Dublin	Dublin City	Dublin South	I.	44, 45
52, 53, 60, 61, 68, 69	St. Patricksrock	10,561 3 9p	Tipperary, S.R. .	Middlethird	Cashel	II.	330, 331
74	St. Paul's .	25 0 22q	Cork, E.R.	Cork City	Cork .	II.	111
18	St. Paul's .	114 2 28r	Dublin	Dublin City	Dublin North	I.	44, 45
39, 40, 47, 48	St. Paul's & St. Peter's	4,074 0 37s	Limerick .	Kilmallock	Kilmallock	II.	250
74	St. Peter's .	40 1 10t	Cork, E.R.	Cork City	Cork .	II.	111
18, 22	St. Peter's .	226 1 1 501 1 38u 1,206 2 3	Dublin .	Dublin Dublin City Uppercross	Dublin South	I.	30 44, 45 41
21, 24	St. Peter's .	3,209 0 36v 269 1 26v	Louth	Drogheda Drogheda Town	Drogheda .	I.	175 185
48, 49, 51, 52, 55	St. Peters .	7,617 0 0w	Roscommon	Athlone	Athlone	IV.	184
9	St. Peter's .	3 2 24	Waterford .	Waterford City	Waterford .	II.	373
37, 42	St. Peter's .	1,405 0 11x	Wexford	Forth	Wexford .	I.	314
39, 40, 47, 48	St. Peter's & St. Paul's	4,074 0 37y	Limerick .	Kilmallock	Kilmallock	II.	250
37	St. Selskar's . .	21 0 18	Wexford	Forth	Wexford .	I.	315
9	St. Stephen's Within	5 0 33	Waterford .	Waterford City	Waterford .	II.	373
9	St. Stephen's Without	12 3 11 17 3 9	Waterford .	Gaultiere . Waterford City	Waterford .	II.	365 373
18	St. Thomas' .	774 1 16z	Dublin	Dublin City	Dublin North	I.	44, 45
18	St. Werburgh's .	16 2 22aa	Dublin	Dublin City	Dublin South	I.	44, 45
15, 16, 19	Salterstown .	1,047 3 17	Louth	Ferrard	Ardee .	I.	182
14, 15	Santry .	4,726 0 1	Dublin	Coolock	Dublin North	I.	29
31, 38	Saul, and Islands	5,272 1 6bb	Down .	Lecale Lower	Downpatrick .	III.	179, 180
30, 36	Scrabby . . .	6,661 0 14cc	Cavan .	Tullyhunco	Cavan Granard .	III.	99

	A. R. P.			A. R. P.			A. R. P.	
(a) Including	5 1 29	of River Lee.	(k) Including		that portion which is within the Town of Galway, and	(v) Exclusive of	26 1 14	of River Boyne tideway, which has not been apportioned.
(b) Including	10 2 0	of River Lee tidal portion.		127 1 11	of water.			
	3 1 33	of River Lee fresh-water portion.	(l) Including	34 2 22	of River Shannon.	(w) Including	2,615 2 33	detached portion.
(c) Including	0 1 11	of tideway.	(m) Including	9 0 17	of River Shannon.		224 1 27	of River Shannon.
(d) Including	11 2 3	of River Barrow.	(n) Including	71 3 13	of River Shannon.		11 0 14	of Canal.
(e) Including	1 0 30	of Abbey River.		11 0 35	of Abbey River.	(x) Including	23 3 4	detached portion.
(f) Including	3 2 30	of tideway.	(o) Including	20 3 14	of River Nore.	(y) Including	25 3 6	Ash Hill Lough.
(g) Including	90 0 18	of River Barrow.	(p) Including	1,231 1 32	detached portion.	(z) Including	144 0 22	of tideway.
(h) Including	22 3 30	of River Shannon.	(q) Including	2 2 27	of River Lee tideway.	(aa) Including	0 3 30	of tideway.
	6 1 1	of Abbey River.	(r) Including	6 1 31	of tideway.	(bb) Including	1,228 2 11	detached portion.
(i) Including	73 0 12	of River Lee tideway.	(s) Including	25 3 6	Ash Hill Lough.		20 3 3	of water.
(j) Composed of	255 0 17	North Portion.	(t) Including	3 1 9	of River Lee tideway.	(cc) Including	1,182 0 11	of Lough Gowna.
	64 1 29	South Portion.	(u) Including	1 1 9	detached portion.		195 3 38	of water.

No. of Sheet of the Ordnance Survey Maps.	Parishes.	Area in Statute Measure.	County.	Barony.	Poor Law Union in 1857.	Townland Census of 1851, Part I.	
		A. R. P.				Vol.	Page
4, 9	Scullogestown	2,468 0 12	Kildare	Ikeathy & Oughterany	Celbridge	I.	58
36, 37	Scurlockstown	2,589 2 28a	Meath	Lower Deece	Trim	I.	192
3, 5, 6, 9, 10	Seagoe	10,982 0 39b	Armagh	Oneilland East	Lurgan	III.	50
19, 20, 26, 27, 34	Seapatrick	2,715 1 16c / 425 2 0 / 4,441 2 32	Down	Lower Iveagh, Lr. pt. / Lower Iveagh, Up. pt. / Upper Iveagh, Up. pt.	Banbridge / Lurgan	III.	169 / 171 / 176
35, 36, 38, 39, 43	Seirkieran	5,825 0 38d	King's Co.	Ballybritt	Parsonstown / Roscrea	I.	126,127
5, 6, 12, 13, 14, 22	Seskinan	16,876 2 16	Waterford	Decies without Drum	Dungarvan / Lismore	II.	360
9, 10, 18, 19	Shanagolden	4,233 1 23e	Limerick	Shanid	Glin / Rathkeale	II.	258
37, 41	Shanbogh	1,802 1 26	Kilkenny	Ida	New Ross	I.	104
27, 28, 34, 35	Shancough	5,441 1 4	Sligo	Tirerrill	Boyle	IV.	241
1, 2, 6, 7	Shandrum	13,451 0 2	Cork, E.R.	Orrery and Kilmore	Kanturk / Kilmallock	II.	109,110
56, 57, 60, 61, 64, 65	Shankill	4,081 2 3 / 1,147 2 3 / 14,255 3 0f	Antrim	Belfast Town / Lower Belfast / Upper Belfast	Belfast / Lisburn	III.	35 / 9 / 10
3, 6, 10 / 13	Shankill	4,931 2 25g / 1,652 1 20h	Armagh / Down	Oneilland East / Lower Iveagh, Up. pt.	Lurgan	III.	50, 51 / 171
15, 16, 20, 21	Shankill	6,489 0 26	Kilkenny	Gowran	Kilkenny	I.	99
15, 16, 21, 22	Shankill	6,610 2 33i	Roscommon	Roscommon	Boyle / Castlereagh / Strokestown	IV.	212,213
14, 17	Shanlis	2,038 1 14j	Louth	Ardee	Ardee	I.	174
74, 80, 81, 86, 87, 89, 90	Shanrahan	24,922 3 19	Tipperary, S.R.	Iffa and Offa West	Clogheen	II.	319,320
9	Sheffin	787 0 4 / 1,701 0 14	Kilkenny	Crannagh / Galmoy	Urlingford	I.	86 / 93
23, 28, 29	Shercock	8,221 0 4k	Cavan	Clankee	Bailieborough	III.	74, 75
14, 19	Sherlockstown	917 2 12	Kildare	North Naas	Naas	I.	63
43, 44	Shilvodan, Grange of	3,546 2 1	Antrim	Upper Toome	Antrim	III.	35
41, 42	Shinrone	4,868 2 14l	King's Co.	Clonlisk	Roscrea	I.	131
58, 66	Shronell	2,805 3 12	Tipperary, S.R.	Clanwilliam	Tipperary	II.	310
22, 23, 26, 27	Shrule	6,922 1 37m	Longford	Rathcline	Ballymahon	I.	165
121, 122, 123	Shrule	11,600 2 32n	Mayo	Kilmaine	Ballinrobe	IV.	158
32	Shrule	982 1 24o	Queen's Co.	Slievemargy	Carlow	I.	246
35, 41	Shyane	909 0 34	Tipperary, N.R.	Eliogarty	Thurles	II.	272
6, 7, 12, 13,	Siddan	5,163 3 5	Meath	Lower Slane	Ardee	I.	223,224
24, 25, 27, 28 / 29, 32, 33	Skerry	26,176 0 9	Antrim	Lower Antrim	Ballymena	III.	4, 5
21, 22, 27, 28	Skirk	3,337 0 6	Queen's Co.	Clandonagh	Donaghmore	I.	235
31, 32, 37, 38	Skreen	4,521 2 36	Meath	Skreen	Dunshaughlin	I.	221
12, 13, 18, 19, 24, 25	Skreen	13,237 2 39p	Sligo	Tireragh	Dromore West	IV.	235,236
33	Skreen	836 1 1 / 530 0 26	Wexford	Ballaghkeen / Shelmaliere East	Wexford	I.	298 / 331
130, 131, 132, / 138, 139, 140, / 148, 149	Skull	37,922 3 27q	Cork, W.R.	West Carbery, W.D.	Skull	II.	145 to 147
12, 13, 18, 19	Slane	5,947 1 1r	Meath	Upper Slane	Navan	I.	225
25, 32	Slanes	946 1 21	Down	Ards Upper	Downpatrick	III.	161
32	Sleaty	671 0 11s	Queen's Co.	Slievemargy	Carlow	I.	246
16, 19, 20	Sliguff	6,755 3 14t	Carlow	Idrone East	Carlow	I.	8
17, 20	Smarmore	1,595 3 27	Louth	Ardee	Ardee	I.	174
51, 58, 59	Solloghodbeg	2,201 1 29	Tipperary, S.R.	Clanwilliam	Tipperary	II.	310
50, 51, 58, 59	Solloghodmore	6,657 1 15	Tipperary, S.R.	Clanwilliam	Tipperary	II.	310,311
14, 15, 17, 18	Stabannan	4,376 3 11	Louth	Ardee	Ardee	I.	174
18, 19, 25, 26	Stackallan	2,351 0 30u	Meath	Upper Slane	Navan	I.	225
11	Stacumny	568 3 18	Kildare	South Salt	Celbridge	I.	78
26, 32	Staffordstown	616 3 7	Meath	Skreen	Navan	I.	221
11	Staholmog	2,109 0 12	Meath	Lower Kells	Kells	I.	204
27, 28, 33, 34	Stamullin	5,144 1 37	Meath	Upper Duleek	Drogheda	I.	198,199
14, 17	Stickillin	1,361 3 10	Louth	Ardee	Ardee	I.	175
23	Stillorgan	689 3 23v	Dublin	Rathdown	Rathdown	I.	37, 38
27, 31	Stonecarthy	55 0 36 / 210 2 33 / 1,224 0 5	Kilkenny	Kells / Knocktopher / Shillelogher	Thomastown	I.	110 / 113 / 115

No. of Sheet of the Ordnance Survey Maps.	Parishes.	Area in Statute Measure.	County.	Barony.	Poor Law Union in 1857.	Townland Census of 1851. Part I. Vol.	Page
7, 12	Stonehall	3,106 0 16a	Westmeath	Corkaree	Mullingar	I.	263
3, 8	Straboe	1,104 0 24	Carlow	Rathvilly	Baltinglass	I.	12
8, 18	Straboe	5,757 2 31	Queen's Co.	Maryborough East	Mountmellick	I.	241,242
95, 103	Stradbally	4,167 2 1b	Galway	Dunkellin	Galway / Gort	IV.	32
19, 26, 27, 35	Stradbally	4,103 1 13c	Kerry	Corkaguiny	Dingle	II.	180
1, 6	Stradbally	6,678 1 31d	Limerick	Clanwilliam	Limerick	II.	226
14, 19	Stradbally	2,466 3 6	Queen's Co.	Stradbally	Athy	I.	247,248
15, 23, 24, 31, 32,	Stradbally	10,917 1 2	Waterford	Decies without Drum	Kilmacthomas	II.	360,361
10, 14	Straffan	2,286 2 18e	Kildare	North Salt	Celbridge	I.	75,76
68,69,77,78,85,86	Stranorlar	15,508 3 27f	Donegal	Raphoe	Stranorlar	III.	142,143
15, 16 }	Street	3,377 0 4	Longford	Ardagh	Granard }	I. {	153
2, 6, 7 }		13,345 3 3g	Westmeath	Moygoish	Mullingar }		281
23, 24	Subulter	741 2 7	Cork, E.R.	Duhallow	Kanturk	II.	75
7, 8, 11, 12, 14, 15	Swords	5 3 29	Dublin	Coolock }	Balrothery	I. {	29
		9,668 3 31		Nethercross }			32
47, 48, 52, 53	Tacumshin	3,153 3 34h	Wexford	Forth	Wexford	I.	314,315
10, 11, 14	Taghadoe	4,126 1 35	Kildare	North Salt	Celbridge	I.	76
47, 61 }	Taghboy	5,134 2 9i	Galway	Killian	Mountbellew }	IV. {	45
44, 47 }		8,861 3 0j	Roscommon	Athlone	Athlone / Roscommon		184
100, 101, 110, 111	Tagheen	6,837 0 38k	Mayo	Clanmorris	Claremorris	IV.	135,136
47,48, 50, 51, 53, 54	Taghmaconnell	18,826 3 33l	Roscommon	Athlone	Athlone / Ballinasloe	IV.	185
12, 13	Taghmon	3,452 3 2m	Westmeath	Corkaree	Mullingar	I.	264
36, 41, 42	Taghmon	1,386 3 0	Wexford	Bargy	New Ross }	I. {	307
		8,738 0 37n		Shelmaliere West	Wexford }		334,335
18, 19, 22, 23	Taghsheenod	5,491 3 26	Longford	Moydow }	Ballymahon	I. {	162
		221 1 7		Shrule }			166
23, 27	Taghshinny	409 3 0o	Longford	Rathcline }	Ballymahon	I. {	165
		4,470 3 3p		Shrule }			167
21, 22, 24, 25, 27,	Tallaght	21,868 1 3	Dublin	Uppercross	Dublin South / Naas	I.	41,42
11, 13, 14	Tallanstown	3,210 0 25q	Louth	Ardee	Ardee	I.	175
28, 33	Tallow	5,026 3 27r	Waterford	Coshmore & Coshbride	Lismore	II.	348
47, 48, 49 }	Tamlaght	2,506 3 22	Londonderry	Loughinsholin	Magherafelt }	III. {	243
30, 39 }		2,447 3 17	Tyrone	Dungannon Upper	Cookstown		309
1, 2, 5, 6	Tamlaght-ard or Magilligan	13,129 2 29s	Londonderry	Keenaght	Newtⁿlimavady	III.	236,237
5, 9, 16, 24	Tamlaght Finlagan	16,467 1 24t	Londonderry	Keenaght	Newtⁿlimavady	III.	237,238
26, 27, 32, 33, 37	Tamlaght O'Crilly	1,334 2 14	Londonderry	Coleraine }	Ballymoney }	III. {	233
		15,501 2 29u		Loughinsholin }	Magherafelt }		243,244
22, 23, 25	Taney	6 0 17	Dublin	Dublin }	Rathdown	I. {	30
		4,556 3 19		Rathdown }			38
35, 37 }}	Tankardstown	4,437 0 10v	Kildare	Kilkea and Moone }	Athy	I. {	61
		440 3 17	Kildare	Narragh & Reban East }			66
20, 26 }		3,472 0 13w	Queen's Co.	Ballyadams			232
39, 47	Tankardstown	1,710 1 39	Limerick	Coshma	Kilmallock	II.	244
31, 32, 37, 38	Tara	3,364 0 15	Meath	Skreen	Navan	I.	222
1, 2, 4, 5, 9	Tartaraghan	11,612 0 35x	Armagh	Oneilland West	Armagh / Lurgan	III.	54, 55
54, 55, 62, 63, 70	Taughboyne	15,773 3 7	Donegal	Raphoe	Londonderry / Strabane	III.	143,144
27, 34	Tawnagh	3,234 3 36y	Sligo	Tirerrill	Sligo	IV.	241
19, 25	Tecolm	1,022 3 11	Queen's Co.	Ballyadams	Athy	I.	232
5, 6, 8, 9	Tedavnet	26,502 0 3z	Monaghan	Monaghan	Monaghan	III.	278 to 280
7, 9, 10	Tehallan	823 1 10	Monaghan	Cremorne }	Monaghan	III. {	262
		5,126 1 0		Monaghan }			280
34, 35, 39	Tellarought	1,653 3 38	Wexford	Shelburne	New Ross	I.	328
11, 17	Teltown	4,266 0 34	Meath	Upper Kells	Kells	I.	207
19, 25, 31	Templeachally	10,038 3 12aa	Tipperary, N.R.	Owney and Arra	Nenagh	II.	297
39, 40	Templebeg	3,427 1 22bb	Tipperary, N.R.	Kilnamanagh Upper	Thurles	II.	279
53, 54, 65	Templebodan	4,735 3 7	Cork, E.R.	Barrymore	Fermoy / Middleton	II.	58
11, 12, 13, 18, 24	Templeboy	9,112 2 18cc	Sligo	Tireragh	Dromore West	IV.	236
33 }	Templebredon	1,408 0 13	Limerick	Coonagh }	Tipperary }	II. {	236
57 }		1,046 2 29	Tipperary, S.R.	Clanwilliam }			311

	A. R. P.	
(a) Including {	106 0 36	of Lough Derravaragh.
	14 0 4	Lough Patrick.
(b) Including	144 2 38	detached portion.
(c) Including {	1,205 0 17	detached portions.
	82 2 6	of Lough Gill.
	14 0 3	Lough Acummeen.
(d) Including	190 1 6	of River Shannon.
(e) Including	24 3 19	of River Liffey.
(f) Including	158 3 26	of water.
(g) Including {	390 3 0	of Lough Derravaragh.
	156 2 32	of Inny River and small loughs.
(h) Including	11 2 4	of water.
(i) Including	104 1 26	of water.

	A. R. P.	
(j) Including	129 3 33	of water.
(k) Including	60 0 32	of water.
(l) Including	215 1 22	of water.
(m) Including	14 3 10	of Lough Derravaragh.
(n) Including	1,812 2 0	detached portion.
(o) Including	6 3 32	of River Inny.
(p) Including	23 0 26	of River Inny.
(q) Including	15 3 27	of water.
(r) Including	12 0 0	of River Bride tideway.
(s) Including	46 2 5	of water.
(t) Including {	1,002 1 4	Ballykelly Level (Intake).
	661 2 39	Myroe Level (Intake).
	102 1 7	of water.

	A. R. P.	
(u) Including	49 0 34	of River Bann.
(v) Including	40 3 0	of River Barrow.
(w) Including	26 1 34	of River Barrow.
(x) Including {	1,917 2 34	of Lough Neagh.
	204 3 21	of small loughs.
(y) Including	15 2 10	of Loughymeenaghan.
(z) Including	163 0 12	of water.
(aa) Including {	1,009 0 13	of Lough Derg.
	87 2 8	of River Shannon.
(bb) Including	1,221 2 1	detached portion.
(cc) Including	384 3 33	detached portion.

6 F

No. of Sheet of the Ordnance Survey Maps.	Parishes.	Area in Statute Measure.	County.	Barony.	Poor Law Union in 1857.	Townland Census of 1851, Part I.	
		A. R. P.				Vol.	Page
99	Templebreedy . .	2,654 0 21	Cork, E.R. .	Kerrycurrihy . .	Kinsale . .	II.	93
122, 135	Templebryan . .	1,188 3 26a	Cork, W.R. .	East Carbery (E.D.)	Clonakilty . .	II.	130
95,100,101,102, } 104, 105 }	Templecarn and Islands . .	38,149 1 20b	Donegal . .	Tirhugh . . .	Donegal . .	III. {	148,149
1, 4, 5, 9, 10 }		7,815 0 18c	Fermanagh .	Lurg . . .	Lowtherstown }		209
46, 47, 53	Templecorran . .	4,744 1 24	Antrim . .	Lower Belfast .	Larne . .	III.	9
32, 40, 41, 48, } 49, 50, 56, } 57, 58 }	Templecrone . .	52,921 0 0d	Donegal . .	Boylagh . .	Glenties . .	III. {	114 to 116
27, 33, 39	Templederry . .	6,998 1 9	Tipperary, N.R.	Upper Ormond .	Nenagh . .	II.	293
21, 22, 27	Templedowney .	1,850 0 4e	Tipperary, N.R.	Upper Ormond .	Nenagh . .	II.	293
71, 77, 78	Temple-etney . .	6,677 0 6	Tipperary, S.R.	Iffa and Offa East .	Clonmel . .	II.	316
44, 45	Templeharry . .	4,589 2 34	King's Co. .	Clonlisk . .	Roscrea . .	I.	132
31, 32	Templekeeran .	1,067 1 39f	Meath . .	Skreen . .	Navan . .	I.	222
18, 23, 24	Templeludigan .	8,177 1 30	Wexford . .	Bantry . .	New Ross . .	I.	303
25, 26, 33, 34	Templemaley . .	4,648 3 23g	Clare . .	Bunratty Upper .	Corrofin } Ennis }	II. {	10, 11
83, 84, 95, 96	Templemartin .	7,515 0 33	Cork, W.R. .	Kinalmeaky . .	Bandon . .	II.	152,153
97	Templemichael .	2,064 1 25	Cork, E.R. .	Kinalea . .	Kinsale . .	II.	96
8, 9, 13, 14	Templemichael .	5,445 3 1 } 3,669 0 28h }	Longford . {	Ardagh . . Longford . . }	Longford . . {	I. {	153,154 160
71, 72, 79	Templemichael .	2,869 3 14	Tipperary, S.R.	Slievardagh . .	Callan } Carrick on Suir }	II. {	336
33, 34, 37	Templemichael .	8,215 2 12	Waterford .	Coshmore & Coshbride	Youghal . .	II.	348,349
9, 10, 18, 19	Templemolaga .	4,395 2 29	Cork, E.R. .	Condons & Clangibbon	Mitchelstown .	II.	63
13, 14, 20, 21	Templemore . .	12,772 2 3i	Londonderry .	North West Liberties } of Londonderry }	Londonderry .	III.	246,247
60, 61,70,71,79,80	Templemore . .	9,462 3 36j	Mayo . .	Gallen . .	Castlebar . } Swineford . }	IV.	151
23, 29	Templemore . .	6,441 0 27k } 2,030 1 22 }	Tipperary, N.R. {	Eliogarty . . Ikerrin . . }	Roscrea . } Thurles . }	II. {	272 276
14, 15	Templemurry . .	2,240 3 25l	Mayo . .	Tirawley . .	Killala . .	IV.	171,172
54, 65	Templenacarriga	5,208 1 30	Cork, E.R. .	Barrymore . .	Middleton . .	II.	58
67, 68, 74, 75, 80	Templeneiry . .	12,840 1 8m	Tipperary, S.R.	Clanwilliam . .	Tipperary . .	II.	311
82,83,84,91,92,93,101	Templenoe . .	1,276 3 1 } 31,151 2 34n }	Kerry . . {	Dunkerron North } Dunkerron South }	Kenmare . . {	II. {	182 185
59, 67	Templenoe . .	2,729 3 33	Tipperary, S.R.	Clanwilliam . .	Tipperary . .	II.	311,312
135, 136	Templeomalus .	1,931 2 0	Cork, W.R. .	Ibane and Barryroe .	Clonakilty . .	II.	150,151
11, 18	Templeoran . .	5,188 3 33o	Westmeath .	Moygoish . .	Mullingar . .	I.	281
50, 51, 55, 56, 60	Templepatrick .	4,835 0 30p } 8,969 3 9q }	Antrim . . {	Lower Belfast . } Upper Belfast . }	Antrim . } Belfast . }	III. {	9 10, 11
17	Templepatrick .	2,151 0 31	Westmeath .	Rathconrath . .	Ballymahon .	I.	284
12, 13	Templepeter . .	1,045 3 6	Carlow . .	Forth . .	Carlow . .	I.	5
3, 4, 5, 6, 7, 8, 9, } 10, 13, 14 }	Templeport . .	42,171 3 31r	Cavan . .	Tullyhaw . .	Bawnboy . } Enniskillen }	III.	93 to 96
122, 123, 135, 136	Templequinlan .	922 1 20 } 1,345 2 3 }	Cork, W.R. . {	East Carbery (E.D.) } Ibane and Barryroe . }	Clonakilty . .	II. {	130 151
29, 30, 35	Templeree . .	4,241 0 10	Tipperary, N.R.	Ikerrin . .	Thurles . .	II.	277
9, 18, 26	Templeroan . .	3,865 2 16	Cork, E.R. .	Fermoy . .	Mallow . .	II.	82
75,76,87,88	Templerobin . .	3,594 1 9s	Cork, E.R. .	Barrymore . .	Cork . .	II.	58, 59
19, 25	Templescoby . .	1,707 1 12	Wexford . .	Bantry . .	Enniscorthy .	I.	303
8, 9, 13, 14, 18, 19	Templeshanbo .	19,516 1 8	Wexford . .	Scarawalsh . .	Enniscorthy .	I.	326
20, 26	Templeshannon .	3,601 0 36t } 1,381 2 24u }	Wexford . {	Ballaghkeen . } Scarawalsh . . }	Enniscorthy . {	I. {	298,299 326
80, 86, 89	Templetenny . .	18,181 2 28	Tipperary, S.R.	Iffa and Offa West .	Clogheen . .	II.	320
1, 2, 5, 6	Templetogher .	13,705 3 18v	Galway . .	Ballymoe . .	Glennamaddy .	IV.	9, 10
24, 29, 30, 35, 36	Templetouhy .	1,226 2 5 } 7,234 1 24 }	Tipperary, N.R. {	Eliogarty . . } Ikerrin . . }	Thurles . . {	II. {	273 277
44, 49, 50	Templetown . .	4,156 3 11	Wexford . .	Shelburne . .	New Ross . .	I.	328,329
124, 137	Templetrine . .	2,546 1 2 } 2,328 1 12 }	Cork, W.R. . {	Courceys . . } East Carbery (E.D.) }	Kinsale . . {	II. {	147 130
52, 53, 63, 64, 75	Templeusque .	4,601 2 10	Cork, E.R. .	Barrymore . .	Cork . .	II.	59
14,15,22,23,24,32,33	Termonamongan	45,399 0 13w	Tyrone . .	Omagh West . .	Castlederg .	III.	316,317
18, 24, 30	Termonbarry .	9,295 0 12x	Roscommon .	Ballintober North .	Strokestown .	IV.	187,188
36, 37, 41, 42	Termoneeny .	4,801 0 13	Londonderry .	Loughinsholin .	Magherafelt .	III.	244
21, 22, 24, 25	Termonfeckin .	6,382 0 4y	Louth . .	Ferrard . .	Drogheda . .	I.	182,183
27, 28, 35, 36, 37, } 43, 44, 45 }	Termonmaguirk	39,725 2 15z } 1,352 3 6aa }	Tyrone . . {	Omagh East . . } Strabane Upper . }	Omagh . . {	III. {	314,315 326

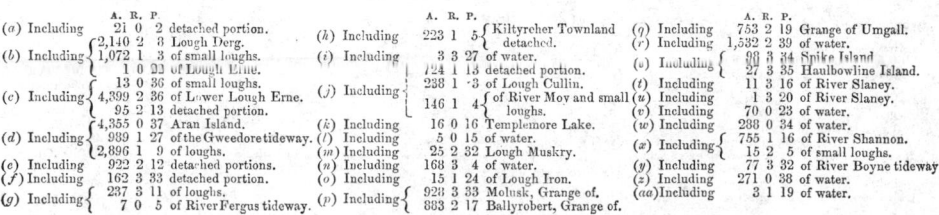

No. of Sheet. of the Ordnance Survey Maps.	Parishes.	Area in Statute Measure.	County.	Barony.	Poor Law Union in 1857.	Townland Census of 1851, Part I.	
		A. R. P.				Vol.	Page
3, 4, 6, 7	Terryglass . .	9,761 3 27a	Tipperary, N.R.	Lower Ormond .	Borrisokane .	II.	287,288
33, 37	The Rower . .	10,758 0 20	Kilkenny . .	Ida	{ New Ross . } { Thomastown }	I.	104
17, 22	Thomastown . .	853 1 0	Kildare . .	East Offaly . .	Edenderry .	I.	71
28, 32	Thomastown . .	2,041 3 33b	Kilkenny . .	Gowran . .	Thomastown .	I.	99
35, 41, 42, 47	Thurles . .	8,268 2 24	Tipperary, N.R.	Eliogarty . .	Thurles . .	II.	273
38, 39	Tibberaghny . .	1,147 2 18	Kilkenny . .	Iverk . .	Carrick on Suir	I.	107
8, 9, 13, 14, 15, 19, 20, 21	Tibohine . .	44,092 3 3c	Roscommon .	Frenchpark .	{ Castlereagh } { Swineford . }	IV.	204,205
25, 29, 30, 34, 35, 39	Tickmacrevan .	20,506 3 22	Antrim . .	Lower Glenarm .	Larne . .	III.	23, 24
32, 37	Tikillin . .	2,866 2 37d	Wexford . .	Shelmaliere East .	Wexford . .	I.	331
8, 9, 12, 13	Timahoe . .	9,896 0 39e	Kildare . .	Clane . .	Naas . . .	I.	54
18, 19, 24, 25	Timahoe or Fossy	{ 9,853 0 18 } { 137 2 1 } { 663 1 24 }	Queen's Co. .	{ Cullenagh . . } { Maryborough East . } { Stradbally . . }	{ Abbeyleix . } { Athy . . . }	I.	{ 240 } { 241 } { 247 }
19	Timogue . .	2,490 3 32	Queen's Co. .	Stradbally . .	Athy . . .	I.	248
123, 136	Timoleague .	{ 708 0 24 } { 2,184 1 1f }	Cork, W.R. .	{ East Carbery (E.D.) } { Ibane and Barryroe . }	Clonakilty .	II.	{ 130 } { 151 }
36	Timolin . .	2,289 2 31	Kildare . .	Narragh & Reban East	Baltinglass .	I.	67
26, 32, 33	Timoole . .	1,033 0 34	Meath . .	Skreen . . .	Dunshaughlin .	I.	222
39, 40, 45	Tiuntern . .	6,863 0 39	Wexford . .	Shelburne . .	New Ross . .	I.	329
19, 20, 24	Tipper . .	3,288 1 27	Kildare . .	North Naas . .	Naas . . .	I.	63
58, 59, 66, 67	Tipperary . .	4,362 2 10g	Tipperary, S.R.	Clanwilliam . .	Tipperary . .	II.	312
24, 25	Tipperkevin . .	3,751 2 15	Kildare . .	South Naas . .	Naas . . .	I.	65
108, 118	Tiranascragh .	3,629 0 31h	Galway . .	Longford . .	Portumna . .	IV.	62
13, 14, 21, 22	Tisaran . .	7,316 2 12i	King's Co. . .	Garrycastle . .	Parsonstown .	I.	138,139
111, 124	Tisaxon . .	1,346 2 31	Cork, E.R. .	Kinsale . .	Kinsale . .	II.	101
11, 15, 20	Tiscoffin . .	4,708 2 5	Kilkenny . .	Gowran . .	Kilkenny . .	I.	99
41, 44, 45	Tisrara . .	8,482 1 4j	Roscommon .	Athlone . .	Roscommon .	IV.	185,186
88, 100	Titeskin . .	1,144 2 37k	Cork, E.R. .	Imokilly . .	Middleton . .	II.	90
9, 15	Tober . . .	1,423 0 15	Wicklow . .	Lower Talbotstown .	Baltinglass .	I.	361
39, 44, 45, 50, 51	Toem . .	{ 11,666 2 25 } { 610 3 20 }	Tipperary, N.R. Tipperary, S.R.	Kilnamanagh Upper Clanwilliam .	} Tipperary .	II.	{ 280 } { 312 }
10, 11	Tomdeely . .	1,324 1 13l	Limerick . .	Connello Lower .	Rathkeale .	II.	230
42, 43, 51	Tomfinlough . .	6,736 0 2m	Clare . .	Bunratty Lower .	Ennis . .	II.	7
13, 20, 28, 29, 36, 37	Tomgraney . .	14,181 0 12n	Clare . .	Tulla Upper .	Scarriff . .	II.	40, 41
47, 52	Tomhaggard . .	2,180 0 16	Wexford . .	Bargy . .	Wexford . .	I.	307,308
9, 10, 14	Tomregan .	{ 2,256 1 22o } { 5,221 0 12p } { 3,200 2 39q }	Cavan . . Fermanagh .	{ Lower Loughtee } { Tullyhaw . } { Knockninny . }	{ Bawnboy . } { Cavan . } { Lisnaskea . }	III.	{ 81 } { 96 } { 203 }
38, 41							
11, 15, 16	Toome . .	{ 3,500 1 34 } { 2,479 0 28 }	Wexford . .	{ Gorey . . } { Scarawalsh . }	} Gorey . .	I.	{ 321 } { 326 }
48, 49, 60, 61	Toomore . .	6,787 1 29r	Mayo . .	Gallen . .	Swineford . .	IV.	151
33, 34, 39, 40, 44, 45	Toomour . .	10,834 2 3s	Sligo . .	Corran . .	{ Boyle . } { Sligo . }	IV.	228
100	Touaghty . .	3,067 1 38t	Mayo . .	Carra . .	Ballinrobe . .	IV.	130
100	Trabolgan . .	830 0 34	Cork, E.R. .	Imokilly . .	Middleton . .	II.	90
98, 99, 112, 113	Tracton . .	5,867 3 21u	Cork, E.R. .	Kinalea . .	Kinsale . .	II.	97
21, 29	Tralee . .	4,604 2 24	Kerry . .	Trughanacmy . .	Tralee . .	II.	213,214
24	Treadingstown	{ 692 3 2v } { 18 3 36w }	Kilkenny . .	{ Gowran . . } { Shillelogher . }	} Thomastown .	I.	{ 99 } { 116 }
38	Trevet . .	{ 1,207 1 12 } { 2,962 1 27 }	Meath . .	{ Ratoath . } { Skreen . . }	} Dunshaughlin .	I.	{ 220 } { 222 }
30, 35, 36, 41, 42	Trim . . .	{ 9,391 0 23x } { 4,034 2 6y }	Meath . .	{ Lower Moyfenrath } { Upper Navan . }	} Trim . . .	I.	{ 211,212 } { 216,217 }
9	Trinity Within .	14 2 33	Waterford . .	Waterford City .	Waterford . .	II.	373
9, 17	Trinity Without	{ 896 0 23 } { 171 2 39z }	Waterford . .	{ Middlethird . } { Waterford City . }	} Waterford . .	II.	{ 369 } { 373 }
10, 15, 16, 22	Trory, and Islands	{ 1,564 2 25aa } { 4,504 0 3sbb }	Fermanagh .	{ Lurg . . } { Tirkennedy . }	{ Enniskillen } { Lowtherstown }	III.	{ 209 } { 223,224 }
31, 37	Trubley . .	854 3 24cc	Meath . .	Lower Deece .	Trim . . .	I.	192
16, 17, 29, 30, 43, 44	Tuam . .	{ 2,316 0 31dd } { 5,819 3 3ee } { 16,879 3 21ff }	Galway . .	{ Ballymoe . . } { Clare . . } { Dunmore . . }	} Tuam . .	IV.	{ 10 } { 23 } { 35, 36 }
39, 42	Tubbrid . .	1,004 1 2	Kilkenny . .	Iverk . .	Carrick on Suir .	I.	107
74, 80, 81, 82, 87, 88	Tubbrid . .	12,572 3 37gg	Tipperary, S.R.	Iffa and Offa West .	Clogheen . .	II.	320,321
12, 13, 17	Tubbridbritain .	4,140 0 4	Kilkenny . .	Crannagh . .	Urlingford .	I.	87

	A. R. P.			A. R. P.			A. R. P.	
(a) Including	1,989 2 7	of Lough Derg.						
(b) Including	26 0 8	of River Nore.	(n) Including	{ 22 1 24 } { 238 2 6 }	of Lough Derg. of small loughs.	(y) Including	{ 28 1 11 } { 29 2 22 }	detached portion. of River Boyne.
(c) Including	667 1 19	of water.	(o) Including	161 1 38	of water.	(z) Including	35 2 16	detached portion.
(d) Including	799 2 6	detached portion.	(p) Including	89 2 39	of water.	(aa) Including	641 1 33	of Lower Lough Erne.
(e) Including	10 0 30	of Reservoir. [way.	(q) Including	23 3 23	of water.		{ 1,190 2 22 }	of Lower Lough Erne.
(f) Including	19 0 0	of Argideen River tide-	(r) Including	102 3 23	of water.	(bb) Including	{ 135 2 27 }	of River Erne and small
(g) Including	14 2 26	Carrownreddy Lough.	(s) Including	101 1 18	of water.		{ }	loughs. [tached.
(h) Including	41 1 20	of River Shannon.	(t) Including	109 1 3	of water.		{ 106 3 37 }	DrumgarrowTownland,de-
(i) Including	106 3 38	of River Shannon.	(u) Including	6 0 8	of tideway.	(cc) Including	10 0 8	of River Boyne.
(j) Including	135 3 30	of water.		{ 7 1 2 }	detached portion.	(dd) Including	93 1 22	of water.
(k) Including	317 2 14	detached portion.	(v) Including	{ 11 0 35 }	of River Nore.	(ee) Including	153 0 22	of Cloonkeen Lough.
(l) Including	34 3 3	of River Deel tideway.	(w) Including	0 1 37	of River Nore.	(ff) Including	{ 7 0 4 } { 40 2 32 }	detached portion. of water.
(m) Including	613 1 32	of water.	(x) Including	109 3 39	of River Boyne.	(gg) Including	12 2 26	of River Suir.

No. of Sheet of the Ordnance Survey Maps.	Parishes.	Area in Statute Measure.	County.	Barony.	Poor Law Union in 1857.	Townland Census of 1851, Part I.	
		A. R. P.				Vol.	Page
19, 26, 27, 34, 35, 43	Tulla . . .	24,531 3 27a	Clare . . .	Tulla Upper . .	Tulla . .	II.	41, 42
31, 32	Tullabracky .	2,044 2 36 / 1,163 3 13	Limerick .	Coshma . .) Smallcounty . }	Croom .) Kilmallock }	II. {	244 / 261
149, 150, 153	Tullagh . .	5,349 0 38b	Cork, W.R. .	West Carbery (E.D.)	Skibbereen .	II.	141
22, 23	Tullaghanbrogue {	1,160 0 21 / 2,327 1 30 }	Kilkenny .	Crannagh) Shillelogher }	Callan .	I. {	87 / 116
30	Tullaghanoge .	1,414 2 10	Meath . .	Upper Navan . .	Trim . .	I.	217
11, 12	Tullaghgore . .	432 2 0	Antrim . .	Upper Dunluce .	Ballymoney .	III.	20
82, 88	Tullaghmelan .	2,695 2 35c	Tipperary, S.R.	Iffa and Offa West .	Clogheen .	II.	321
6, 14, 23, 24, 25, 32) 33, 34, 41, 42 } 43, 49, 50, 51)	Tullaghobegly .	68,608 2 21d	Donegal . .	Kilmacrenan .	Dunfanaghy .	III.	131,132
87, 90	Tullaghorton .	6,889 0 36e	Tipperary, S.R.	Iffa and Offa West .	Clogheen .	II.	321
24, 28	Tullaherin .	5,052 0 6	Kilkenny .	Gowran . .	Thomastown .	I.	100
30, 34, 35	Tullahought .	4,601 3 21	Kilkenny .	Kells . . .	Callan .) Carrick on Suir }	I.	110
61, 69	Tullamain .	2,217 0 13f	Tipperary, S.R.	Middlethird .	Cashel .	II.	331
22, 23, 26, 27	Tullamaine .	1,171 3 39	Kilkenny . .	Shillelogher .	Callan .	I.	116
13, 17, 18	Tullaroan .	12,359 2 10	Kilkenny . .	Crannagh .	Kilkenny .	I.	87, 88
19, 25, 31	Tullomoy . {	677 3 32 / 5,330 1 20 }	Queen's Co.	Ballyadams) Stradbally }	Athy .	I. {	232 / 248
6, 11, 12	Tullowcreen .	5,899 0 33g	Carlow . .	Idrone West .	Carlow .	I.	9, 10
7, 12	Tullowmagimma {	3,360 0 24 / 703 2 35 }	Carlow .	Carlow .) Forth . }	Carlow .	I. {	2 / 5
3, 8, 9, 13	Tullowphelim .	7,989 2 36	Carlow . .	Rathvilly .	Carlow .	I.	12
22, 23, 25, 26	Tully . .	3,285 3 31	Dublin . .	Rathdown .	Rathdown .	I.	38
17, 18, 22, 23, 27, 28	Tully . . {	4,017 1 30h / 1,147 1 34 }	Kildare .	East Offaly) Kilcullen . }	Athy .) Naas . }	I. {	71 / 58
20, 21, 23, 24, 25) } 13, 19)	Tullyallen . {	26 0 37 / 7,317 3 25i / 949 3 11 }	Louth . . / Meath . .	Drogheda Borough .) Ferrard . } Upper Slane . .	Drogheda .	I. {	185 / 183 / 225
13, 14, 18, 19	Tullycorbet .	1,588 3 22 / 6,324 1 30j	Monaghan .	Cremorne .) Monaghan . }	Monaghan .	III.	262,263 / 280,281
27, 28, 36, 37, 45, 46	Tullyfern .	16,612 0 10k	Donegal .	Kilmacrenan .	Milltown .	III.	132,133
5, 6, 15	Tullylease . {	7,005 1 28 / 1,286 2 12 }	Cork, E.R.	Duhallow) Orrery and Kilmore . }	Kanturk .	II. {	76 / 110
19, 20, 26, 27	Tullylish .	11,707 0 1l	Down . .	Lower Iveagh, Up. pt.	Banbridge .) Lurgan . }	III.	171
10, 11, 16, 17	Tullynakill .	2,923 1 22m	Down . .	Lower Castlereagh .	Newtownards .	III.	163,164
46, 47, 55	Tullyniskan .	4,461 1 3n	Tyrone . .	Dungannon Middle .	Dungannon .	III.	304,305
59, 60	Tullyrusk .	4,779 2 17	Antrim . .	Upper Masserecne .	Lisburn .	III.	31
4, 6, 7, 10, 11	Tumna . .	9,188 3 13o	Roscommon .	Boyle . .	Boyle .) Cark.onShannon }	IV.	197,198
7, 15, 24	Tuogh . .	6,518 2 33	Limerick .	Owneybeg .	Limerick .	II.	251
24, 33	Tuoghcluggin .	2,093 2 11p	Limerick .	Coonagh .	Tipperary .	II.	236
92, 93, 100, 101, 102,) 108, 109, 111 }	Tuosist . .	39,340 2 37q	Kerry . .	Glanarought .	Kenmare .	II.	188,189
48, 59, 60, 69, 70, 79	Turlough .	24,566 3 6r	Mayo . .	Carra . .	Castlebar .	IV.	130,131
41, 42, 47, 48	Twomileborris .	11,939 2 38	Tipperary, N.R.	Eliogarty .	Thurles .	II.	273,274
7, 11, 12, 18	Tyfarnham .	1,818 3 29s	Westmeath .	Corkaree .	Mullingar .	I.	264
106, 107, 116, 117, 126	Tynagh . {	9,286 0 31t / 3,233 3 35 }	Galway .	Leitrim .) Longford . }	Loughrea .) Portumna . }	IV. {	55, 56 / 62
11, 15, 19	Tynan . {	4,314 2 23 / 12,731 1 12u }	Armagh .	Armagh .) Tiranny . }	Armagh .	III. {	46 / 60, 61
44	Tyrella .	1,999 1 32	Down .	Lecale Upper .	Downpatrick .	III.	181
22, 24) } 25, 29)	Ullard . . {	72 2 0v / 2,588 0 5w / 3,186 3 18x }	Carlow . / Kilkenny .	Idrone East .) St. Mullin's Lower . } Gowran . .	Carlow .) New Ross . } Thomastown .	I. {	8 / 13 / 100
39, 40, 42, 43	Ullid . .	2,248 3 25	Kilkenny .	Iverk . .	Waterford .	I.	107
33, 34, 39, 40	Upperchurch .	12,902 3 29	Tipperary, N.R.	Kilnamanagh Upper .	Nenagh .) Thurles . }	II.	280,281
32, 39, 40	Uregare . . {	3,004 0 18 / 1,840 0 33 }	Limerick .	Coshma .) Smallcounty . }	Kilmallock .	II. {	244 / 261
2, 3, 7, 8	Urglin . .	3,149 1 13	Carlow . .	Carlow . .	Carlow .	I.	3
8, 12	Urlingford .	3,497 3 26	Kilkenny . .	Galmoy . .	Urlingford .	I.	93

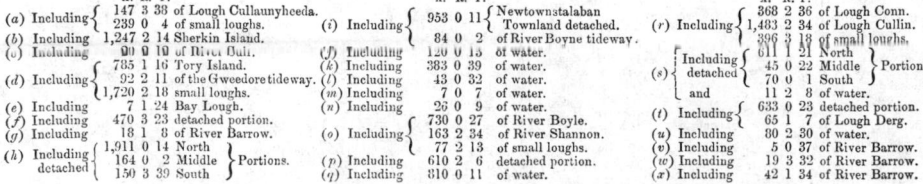

A. R. P.
(a) Including { 147 3 38 of Lough Cullaunyheeda. / 239 0 4 of small loughs.
(b) Including 1,247 2 14 Sherkin Island.
(c) Including 90 0 10 of River Gub.
(d) Including { 785 1 16 Tory Island. / 92 2 11 of the Gweedore tideway. / 1,720 2 18 small loughs.
(e) Including 7 1 24 Bay Island.
(f) Including 470 3 23 detached portion.
(g) Including 18 1 8 of River Barrow.
(h) Including { 1,911 0 14 North / 164 0 2 Middle } Portions. detached { 150 3 39 South }

A. R. P.
(i) Including { 953 0 11 Newtownstalaban Townland detached.
(j) Including 84 0 2 of River Boyne tideway.
(k) Including 120 0 15 of water.
(l) Including 383 0 39 of water.
(m) Including 43 0 32 of water.
(n) Including 7 0 7 of water. / 26 0 9 of water.
(o) Including { 730 0 27 of River Boyle. / 163 2 34 of River Shannon. / 77 2 13 of small loughs.
(p) Including 610 2 6 detached portion.
(q) Including 810 0 11 of water.

A. R. P.
(r) Including { 368 2 36 of Lough Conn. / 1,483 2 34 of Lough Cullin. / 396 3 18 of small loughs.
(s) Including detached { 611 1 21 North / 45 0 22 Middle } Portions. / 70 0 1 South } and 11 2 8 of water.
(t) Including { 633 0 23 detached portion. / 65 1 7 of Lough Derg.
(u) Including 80 2 30 of water.
(v) Including 5 0 37 of River Barrow.
(w) Including 19 3 32 of River Barrow.
(x) Including 42 1 34 of River Barrow.

No. of Sheet of the Ordnance Survey Maps	Parishes.	Area in Statute Measure. A. R. P.	County.	Barony.	Poor Law Union in 1857.	Townland Census of 1851, Part I. Vol.	Page
15, 20, 25	Urney	440 2 24a / 7,493 2 2b	Cavan	Lower Loughtee / Upper Loughtee	Cavan	III.	81 / 86
79, 88 / 4, 5, 9, 10, 15, 16, 23, 24	Urney	5,204 3 36c / 7,558 1 14d / 9,284 1 33e	Donegal / Tyrone	Raphoe / Omagh West / Strabane Lower	Castlederg / Strabane	III.	144 / 318 / 322,323
32	Usk	1,763 0 8	Kildare	Narragh & Reban East	Naas	I.	67
7, 8, 10, 11	Uskane	7,656 1 10f	Tipperary, N.R.	Lower Ormond	Borrisokane	II.	288
78, 79, 87, 88	Valencia	6,371 1 7	Kerry	Iveragh	Cahersiveen	II.	198
42, 52	Ventry	4,439 0 26g	Kerry	Corkaguiny	Dingle	II.	180
17, 18, 26	Wallstown	3,056 1 12	Cork, E.R.	Fermoy	Mallow	II.	83
27	Walterstown	1,501 2 22	Kildare	West Offaly	Athy	I.	74
10, 11, 13, 14	Ward	1,349 1 8	Dublin	Castleknock	Dublin North	I.	25
51, 54	Warrenspoint	1,110 0 13h	Down	Upper Iveagh, Up. pt.	Newry	III.	176
11, 12, 15, 16, 19 / 21	Wells	2,472 2 39i / 253 0 36	Carlow / Kilkenny	Idrone West / Gowran	Carlow / Kilkenny	I.	10 / 100
7	Westpalstown	1,595 3 36	Dublin	Balrothery West	Balrothery	I.	23
6, 14, 15, 23	Wheery or Killagally	17,556 3 22j	King's Co.	Garrycastle	Parsonstown	I.	139
51, 52, 62, 63, 74	Whitechurch	2,623 2 17 / 740 2 23 / 7,150 1 8	Cork, E.R.	Barretts / Barrymore / Cork	Cork	II.	50 / 59 / 66
22, 25	Whitechurch	2,873 1 27	Dublin	Rathdown	Dublin South	I.	38
14, 15	Whitechurch	3,165 3 5k	Kildare	North Naas	Naas	I.	63
34, 38	Whitechurch	2,186 2 39	Kilkenny	Iverk	Carrick on Suir	I.	107
74, 75, 81	Whitechurch	3,921 2 20	Tipperary, S.R.	Iffa and Offa West	Clogheen	II.	321,322
22, 30, 35	Whitechurch	9,951 3 9	Waterford	Decies without Drum	Dungarvan / Lismore	II.	361,362
34, 39	Whitechurch	765 0 15 / 4,577 0 32	Wexford	Bantry / Shelburne	New Ross	I.	303 / 329
31, 32, 36, 37	Whitechurchglynn	7,165 2 13 / 22 0 24	Wexford	Bantry / Shelmaliere West	Wexford	I.	303 / 335
25, 32, 39	Witter	2,529 2 23l	Down	Ards Upper	Downpatrick	III.	161
24, 25, 28	Woolengrange	1,663 2 25m	Kilkenny	Gowran	Thomastown	I.	100
67	Youghal	4,830 2 22	Cork, E.R.	Imokilly	Youghal	II.	90, 91
13, 14, 19, 20, 25, 26	Youghalarra	8,356 0 24n	Tipperary, N.R.	Owney and Arra	Nenagh	II.	297,298

A. R. P.
(a) Including   72 3 33 of water.
(b) Including { 452 2 13 of Lough Oughter. / 530 2 7 of water.
(c) Including   32 2 6 of water.
(d) Including   46 1 4 of water.
(e) Including   99 1 25 of water.

A. R. P.
(f) Including   9 2 8 of water.
(g) Including   10 1 1 Mount Eagle Lough.
(h) Including   68 1 21 of tideway.
(i) Including { 45 2 4 of River Barrow. / 691 0 24 detached portion.
(j) Including   8 1 8 of Lough Boora.

A. R. P.
(k) Including   16 0 12 of River Liffey.
(l) { Detached 690 0 22 portion. / including 17 0 1 of water. [detached.
(m) Including { 83 2 37 Baronsland Townland, / 20 0 12 of River Nore.
(n) Including   560 0 13 of Lough Derg.

END OF PARISH INDEX.

GENERAL ALPHABETICAL INDEX

TO THE

BARONIES OF IRELAND,

With the Number of the Sheet of the Ordnance Survey Maps in which they appear; the Areas of the Baronies in Statute Measure; the Counties and Poor Law Unions in which they are situated; also the Volume and Page of the Townland Census of 1851, which contains the Population and the Number of Houses in 1841 and 1851, and the Poor Law Valuation in 1851.

No. of Sheet of the Ordnance Survey Maps.	Baronies.	Area in Statute Measure.			County.	Poor Law Union in 1857.	Townland Census of 1851, Part I.	
		A.	R.	P.			Vol.	Page
24, 25, 27, 28, 29, 32, 33, 34, 37, 38, 39, 43, 44	Antrim Lower . . .	80,827	2	9a	Antrim . . .	Antrim . Ballymena .	III.	3 to 5
38, 39, 40, 44, 45, 46, 50, 51	Antrim Upper . . .	36,493	1	26b	Antrim . . .	Antrim . Larne .	III.	5 to 7
110, 111, 119, 120	Aran	11,287	3	17c	Galway . . .	Galway . .	IV.	3
9, 10, 13, 14, 15, 16, 19, 20, 23, 24	Ardagh	40,223	0	15d	Longford . .	Ballymahon . Granard . Longford .	I.	151 to 154
6, 10, 11, 13, 14, 15, 17, 18, 20, 21	Ardee	53,832	1	9e	Louth . . .	Ardee . Dundalk .	I.	171 to 175
1, 2, 3, 5, 6, 7, 11, 12	Ards Lower . . .	38,462	1	15f	Down . . .	Newtownards .	III.	157 to 159
7, 11, 12, 17, 18, 24, 25, 31, 32, 39	Ards Upper . . .	29,697	0	4g	Down . . .	Downpatrick . Newtownards .	III.	159 to 161
25, 30, 31, 35, 36, 39, 40, 41, 44, 45	Arklow . . .	67,356	3	38h	Wicklow . .	Rathdrum .	I.	341 to 346
4, 8, 11, 12, 15, 16, 19, 20, 24	Armagh . . .	47,865	2	26i	Armagh . .	Armagh . .	III.	43 to 46
71, 83, 84, 85, 95, 96, 97	Athenry . . .	25,782	0	1	Galway . .	Galway . Loughrea .	IV.	3 to 5
34, 35, 38, 39, 40, 41, 42, 43, 44, 45, 46, 47, 48, 49, 50, 51, 52, 53, 54, 55	Athlone . . .	146,185	0	25j	Roscommon .	Athlone . Ballinasloe . Roscommon .	IV.	179 to 186
7, 11, 12, 16, 17, 20, 21, 22, 26, 27, 28, 32, 33	Ballaghkeen . .	86,539	0	32k	Wexford . . .	Enniscorthy . Gorey . . Wexford . .	I.	291 to 299
6, 7, 11, 12, 16, 17, 18, 22, 23, 24, 29, 30, 35	Ballinacor North .	74,109	3	39l	Wicklow . .	Rathdrum .	I.	346, 347
22, 23, 28, 29, 30, 33, 34, 35, 38, 39, 40, 43, 44	Ballinacor South .	78,316	0	15m	Wicklow . .	Baltinglass . Rathdrum . Shillelagh .	I.	347 to 350
11, 12, 17, 18, 23, 24, 29, 30	Ballintober North .	34,123	1	33n	Roscommon .	Carrick on Shannon Strokestown .	IV.	186 to 188
28, 29, 35, 36, 37, 39, 40, 41, 42	Ballintober South .	50,557	3	31o	Roscommon .	Roscommon . Strokestown .	IV.	188 to 190
19, 20, 25, 26, 31, 32	Ballyadams . .	24,081	2	13p	Queen's Co. .	Athy . . Carlow . .	I.	231, 232
15, 16, 23, 24, 25, 31, 32	Ballyboy . . .	32,406	3	6q	King's Co. .	Parsonstown . Tullamore .	I.	123, 124
31, 32, 35, 36, 37, 38, 39, 40, 43	Ballybritt . . .	53,993	3	38	King's Co. .	Parsonstown . Roscrea .	I.	124 to 127
7, 8, 9, 15, 16, 17, 24, 25	Ballycowan . .	38,651	1	38r	King's Co. .	Tullamore .	I.	127 to 129
1, 2, 5, 6, 7, 8, 17, 18, 19, 20, 30, 31, 32, 44, 45	Ballymoe . . .	89,272	2	18s	Galway . . .	Glennamaddy . Roscommon . Tuam . .	IV.	5 to 10
26, 27, 28, 33, 34, 35, 38, 39	Ballymoe . .	23,287	2	14t	Roscommon . .	Castlereagh . Glennamaddy . Roscommon .	IV.	191, 192
9, 10, 11, 21, 22, 23, 24, 25, 34, 35, 36, 37, 38, 48, 49, 50, 51, 52, 62, 63, 64, 65, 75, 76, 77, 78, 89	Ballynahinch . . .	191,432	2	4u	Galway . . .	Clifden . .	IV.	10 to 15

	A.	R.	P.			A.	R.	P.			A.	R.	P.	
(a) Including	0	2	17	of water.	(h) Including	76	1	0	of tideway.	(o) Including	2,479	2	13	of water.
(b) Including	20	2	28	of water.	(i) Including	208	0	4	of water.	(p) Including	81	2	24	of water.
(c) Including	43	2	12	of water.	(j) Including	10,396	3	32	of water.	(q) Including	283	3	16	of water.
(d) Including	121	1	38	of water.	(k) Including	180	0	39	of water.	(r) Including	54	2	10	of water.
(e) Including	80	1	15	of water.	(l) Including	603	2	30	of water.	(s) Including	639	2	14	of water.
(f) Including	32	1	39	of water.	(m) Including	16	1	37	of water.	(t) Including	121	3	17	of water.
(g) Including	144	1	21	of water.	(n) Including	3,553	2	21	of water.	(u) Including	10,750	1	11	of water.

No. of Sheet of the Ordnance Survey Maps.	Baronies.	Area in Statute Measure.	County.	Poor Law Union in 1857.	Townland Census of 1851, Part I.	
		A.　R.　P.			Vol.	Page
1, 2, 4, 5, 7, 8, 12	Balrothery East	30,005　1　31	Dublin	Balrothery	I.	19 to 21
1, 3, 4, 6, 7, 11	Balrothery West	25,195　0　34	Dublin	Balrothery / Dunshaughlin	I.	22, 23
72, 73, 74, 75, 76, 80, 81, 82, 83, 84, 85, 89, 90, 91, 92, 93, 94, 96, 97, 98, 99	Banagh	177,759　3　13a	Donegal	Donegal / Glenties	III.	105 to 112
79, 80, 91, 92, 93, 104, 105, 106, 117, 118, 119	Bantry	59,216　1　7b	Cork, W.R.	Bantry	II.	119 to 122
13, 18, 19, 20, 23, 24, 25, 26, 29, 30, 31, 32, 34, 35, 36, 37	Bantry	101,987　2　22c	Wexford	Enniscorthy / New Ross / Wexford	I.	299 to 303
40, 41, 42, 45, 46, 47, 50, 51, 52	Bargy	40,002　0　8	Wexford	New Ross / Wexford	I.	303 to 308
33, 41, 42, 43, 50, 51, 52, 61, 62	Barretts	31,761　3　27	Cork, E.R.	Cork / Mallow	II.	49, 50
34, 35, 36, 42, 43, 44, 45, 51, 52, 53, 54, 55, 63, 64, 65, 66, 74, 75, 76, 77, 87, 88	Barrymore	152,834　2　22d	Cork, E.R.	Cork / Fermoy / Middleton	II.	50 to 59
90, 91, 101, 102, 103, 104, 105, 114, 115, 116, 117, 126, 127, 128, 129	Bear	89,986　1　37e	Cork, W.R.	Bantry / Castletown	II.	122 to 126
40, 41, 45, 46, 47, 51, 52, 53, 56, 57	Belfast Lower	56,092　3　18f	Antrim	Antrim / Belfast / Larne	III.	7 to 9
50, 51, 55, 56, 57, 60, 61, 64, 65	Belfast Upper	37,119　2　18g	Antrim	Antrim / Belfast / Lisburn	III.	9 to 11
32, 40, 41, 48, 49, 50, 51, 56, 57, 58, 59, 64, 65, 66, 67, 72, 73, 74, 75, 76, 83, 84	Boylagh	158,479　2　39h	Donegal	Glenties	III.	112 to 116
1, 2, 3, 4, 5, 6, 7, 9, 10, 11, 15, 16	Boyle	86,544　3　29i	Roscommon	Boyle / Carrick on Shannon	IV.	192 to 198
22, 29, 35	Brawny	11,455　3　36j	Westmeath	Athlone	I.	259, 260
41, 42, 43, 50, 51, 52, 53, 60, 61, 62, 63	Bunratty Lower	69,082　1　20k	Clare	Ennis / Limerick / Tulla	II.	3 to 7
18, 19, 25, 26, 27, 33, 34, 35, 42, 43,	Bunratty Upper	53,844　1　11l	Clare	Corrofin / Ennis / Gort / Tulla	II.	7 to 11
1, 2, 3, 4, 5, 6, 8, 9, 10, 16	Burren	74,360　3　39m	Clare	Ballyvaghan / Corrofin / Ennistimon / Gort	II.	11 to 14
41, 42, 43, 45, 46, 53, 54, 55, 56, 57, 58, 65, 66, 67, 68, 75, 76, 77, 78, 87, 88, 89, 98, 99, 108	Burrishoole	146,991　0　27n	Mayo	Newport / Westport	IV.	117 to 123
22, 26	Callan	5,653　0　5	Kilkenny	Callan	I.	83, 84
96, 97, 108, 109, 110, 111, 121, 122, 123, 124, 135, 136, 137	Carbery East (E.D.)	67,691　0　34o	Cork, W.R.	Bandon / Clonakilty / Dunmanway / Kinsale	II.	126 to 130
92, 93, 94, 95, 106, 107, 108, 109, 120, 121, 122, 133, 134, 135, 142, 143	Carbery East (W.D.)	105,141　2　19p	Cork, W.R.	Bandon / Bantry / Clonakilty / Dunmanway / Skibbereen	II.	131 to 136
106, 107, 119, 120, 121, 132, 133, 140, 141, 142, 149, 150, 151, 153	Carbery West (E.D.)	80,841　3　10q	Cork, W.R.	Skibbereen	II.	136 to 141
117, 118, 119, 129, 130, 131, 132, 138, 139, 140, 141, 146, 147, 148, 149, 152	Carbery West (W.D.)	109,178　2　15r	Cork, W.R.	Bantry / Skibbereen / Skull	II.	141 to 147
1, 2, 3, 4, 7, 8, 9, 12	Carbury	48,286　3　1s	Kildare	Edenderry	I.	51 to 53
1, 2, 3, 4, 5, 6, 7, 8, 9, 13, 14, 15, 19, 20, 21	Carbury	78,884　0　15t	Sligo	Sligo	IV.	219 to 223
2, 3, 7, 8, 12, 13	Carlow	31,353　2　10u	Carlow	Carlow	I.	1 to 3

	A.　R.　P.			A.　R.　P.			A.　R.　P.
(a) Including	1,573　1　1 of water.	(i) Including	6,755　1　4 of water.	(o) Including	367　3　39 of water.
(b) Including	192　3　22 of water.	(j) Including	1,206　2　24 of Lough Reé.	(p) Including	168　0　28 of water.
(c) Including	389　0　15 of tideway.		179　0　12 of River Shannon.	(q) Including	1,866　1　32 of water.
(d) Including	4,148　0　34 of water.	(k) Including	12,890　1　18 of water.	(r) Including	18　0　20 of water.
(e) Including	567　2　29 of water.	(l) Including	1,331　2　39 of water.	(s) Including	22　1　18 of water.
(f) Including	76　1　38 of water.	(m) Including	60　2　39 of water.	(t) Including	2,605　1　39 of water.
(g) Including	85　1　9 of water.	(n) Including	3,568　0　29 of water.	(u) Including	117　0　3 of water.
(h) Including	7,302　3　12 of water.				

No. of Sheet of the Ordnance Survey Maps.	Baronies.	Area in Statute Measure.	County.	Poor Law Union in 1857.	Townland Census of 1851, Part I.	
		A. R. P.			Vol.	Page
48, 58, 59, 60, 68, 69, 70, 77, 78, 79, 89, 90, 98, 99, 100, 108, 109, 110, 117	Carra	146,816 0 8a	Mayo	Ballinrobe / Castlebar / Westport	IV.	123 to 131
46, 47, 51, 52, 53, 57	Carrickfergus	16,700 1 34b	Antrim	Larne	III.	11
19, 21, 22, 24, 25, 26, 29, 30, 33, 34, 36	Carrigallen	63,501 1 1c	Leitrim	Bawnboy / Mohill	IV.	89 to 93
1, 3, 4, 5, 7, 8, 9, 10, 12, 13, 14, 15, 19	Cary	74,901 3 0d	Antrim	Ballycastle / Coleraine	III.	11 to 15
10, 11, 13, 14, 17, 18	Castleknock	21,371 3 37e	Dublin	Celbridge / Dublin North / Dunshaughlin	I.	23 to 25
27, 31, 32, 33, 34, 37, 38, 39, 40, 42, 43, 44	Castlerahan	71,122 1 5f	Cavan	Bailieborough / Cavan / Kells / Oldcastle	III.	67 to 71
15, 19, 20, 21, 22, 25, 26, 27, 28, 31, 32, 33, 34	Castlereagh	82,558 2 4g	Roscommon	Castlereagh	IV.	198 to 202
1, 2, 4, 5, 6, 9, 10, 11, 15, 16, 17	Castlereagh Lower	51,452 3 13h	Down	Belfast / Newtownards	III.	161 to 164
4, 5, 8, 9, 10, 14, 15, 16, 22, 23, 30	Castlereagh Upper	55,367 2 7i	Down	Belfast / Downpatrick / Lisburn / Newtownards	III.	164 to 166
13, 19, 20, 21, 22, 25, 26, 27, 31, 32, 33, 37, 38	Clanawley	75,469 0 32j	Fermanagh	Ballyshannon / Enniskillen	III.	189 to 194
15, 21, 22, 27, 28, 33, 34	Clandonagh	43,733 1 5k	Queen's Co.	Donaghmore / Roscrea	I.	232 to 235
8, 9, 10, 12, 13, 14, 18, 19	Clane	32,023 1 1l	Kildare	Naas	I.	53, 54
17, 18, 22, 23, 27, 28, 29, 33, 34, 35, 40	Clankee	64,377 3 1m	Cavan	Bailieborough / Cootehill	III.	71 to 75
29, 30, 34, 35, 36, 39, 40, 43	Clankelly	39,068 0 34n	Fermanagh	Clones / Lisnaskea	III.	194 to 198
24, 25, 30, 31, 36, 37, 38, 41, 42	Clanmahon	54,346 3 19o	Cavan	Cavan / Granard / Oldcastle	III.	75 to 78
8, 9, 10, 11, 13, 14, 15, 16, 17, 18, 19, 20, 21, 22, 23, 28, 29, 30, 31	Clanmaurice	120,872 1 34p	Kerry	Listowel / Tralee	II.	167 to 173
79, 80, 90, 91, 92, 100, 101, 102, 110, 111, 112, 113, 119	Clanmorris	69,252 1 1q	Mayo	Ballinrobe / Castlebar / Claremorris	IV.	131 to 136
1, 5, 6, 13, 14, 15, 22, 23, 24, 32	Clanwilliam	55,891 3 21r	Limerick	Limerick / Tipperary	II.	221 to 226
50, 51, 52, 57, 58, 59, 60, 65, 66, 67, 68, 73, 74, 75, 80	Clanwilliam	115,960 1 10s	Tipperary, S.R.	Cashel / Tipperary		305 to 312
28, 29, 30, 40, 41, 42, 43, 44, 54, 55, 56, 57, 58, 69, 70, 71, 82, 83, 84	Clare	136,870 0 29t	Galway	Galway / Tuam	IV.	16 to 23
22, 23, 28, 29, 30, 34, 35	Clarmallagh	43,533 3 19u	Queen's Co.	Abbeyleix / Donaghmore	I.	235 to 238
42, 43, 44, 45, 50, 51, 52, 53, 57, 58, 59, 60, 63, 64, 65, 68	Clogher	97,569 2 3v	Tyrone	Clogher / Dungannon / Omagh	III.	291 to 296
39, 40, 47, 48, 49, 50, 57, 58, 59, 60, 67, 68, 69, 70, 75	Clonderalaw	98,541 1 6w	Clare	Ennis / Killadysert / Kilrush	II.	14 to 18
38, 39, 41, 42, 43, 44, 45, 46, 47	Clonlisk	49,053 3 34x	King's Co.	Parsonstown / Roscrea	I.	129 to 132
22, 23, 29, 30, 31, 35, 36	Clonlonan	32,117 2 13y	Westmeath	Athlone	I.	260 to 262
61, 73, 74, 86, 87, 88, 98, 99, 100	Clonmacnowen	35,467 1 35z	Galway	Ballinasloe / Mountbellew	IV.	23 to 26
2, 3, 6, 7, 8, 10, 11, 12, 17, 18, 19, 25, 26, 27, 31, 32	Coleraine	86,342 0 34aa	Londonderry	Ballymoney / Coleraine	III.	229 to 233
3, 4, 7, 8, 12	Coleraine, North East Liberties of	18,334 2 19bb	Londonderry	Ballymoney / Coleraine	III.	244 to 246
9, 10, 11, 18, 19, 20, 27, 28, 35, 36, 37	Condons and Clangibbon	78,481 1 8cc	Cork, E.R.	Fermoy / Mitchelstown	II.	59 to 63
12, 13, 17, 18, 19, 23, 24, 28	Connell	34,785 3 14dd	Kildare	Naas	I.	55, 56
2, 3, 10, 11, 19, 20, 21, 28, 29, 30, 36, 37	Connello Lower	50,599 2 6ee	Limerick	Croom / Glin / Rathkeale	II.	226 to 230
21, 29, 30, 37, 38, 39, 45, 46, 47, 54	Connello Upper	61,256 3 15	Limerick	Croom / Kilmallock / Newcastle / Rathkeale	II.	230 to 233

	A. R. P.			A. R. P.			A. R. P.	
(a) Including	15,475 2 32 of water.		(l) Including	123 2 0 of water.		(v) Including	297 3 32 of water.	
(b) Including	89 3 22 Lough Mourne.		(m) Including	1,835 1 6 of water.		(w) Including	23,028 2 12 of water.	
(c) Including	2,939 0 29 of water.		(n) Including	486 0 34 of water.		(x) Including	1 2 22 of Lough Nahinch.	
(d) Including	90 3 3 of water.		(o) Including	3,674 2 27 of water.		(y) Including	88 1 4 of water.	
(e) Including	77 0 30 of water.		(p) Including	715 3 39 of water.		(z) Including	155 3 39 of water.	
(f) Including	2,357 1 16 of water.		(q) Including	564 3 6 of water.		(aa) Including	505 0 17 of water.	
(g) Including	573 2 4 of water.		(r) Including	264 2 26 of River Shannon.		(bb) Including	326 3 5 of River Bann.	
(h) Including	180 3 35 of water.		(s) Including	61 2 15 of water.		(cc) Including	225 2 20 of water.	
(i) Including	420 1 34 of water.		(t) Including	10,506 3 37 of water.		(dd) Including	161 0 16 of River Liffey.	
(j) Including	3,251 1 18 of water.		(u) Including	27 1 20 Grantstown Lough.		(ee) Including	2,797 1 11 of water.	
(k) Including	18 3 0 of water.							

No. of Sheet of the Ordnance Survey Maps.	Barony.	Area in Statute Measure.	County.	Poor Law Union in 1857.	Townland Census of 1851, Part I.	
		A. R. P.			Vol.	Page
39, 43, 44, 45, 46, 47	Coolavin . . .	29,157 0 27a	Sligo . . .	Boyle . . .	IV.	223 to 225
34, 35, 39, 40, 42, 43	Coole . . .	18,963 2 36b	Fermanagh . .	Clones . . / Lisnaskea . .	III.	199, 200
10,11,12,18,19,20,27,28,34	Coolestown . .	47,882 1 17	King's Co. . .	Edenderry . .	I.	132, 133
11, 12, 14, 15, 16, 18, 19	Coolock . . .	27,907 0 36	Dublin . . .	Balrothery . / Dublin North .	I.	26 to 29
7, 8, 15, 16, 23, 24, 25, 33	Coonagh . . .	36,323 1 17	Limerick . .	Kilmallock . / Limerick . . / Tipperary . .	II.	233 to 236
4, 8, 9, 14, 15, 16, 22, 23, 24, 31	Corcomroe . . .	61,385 0 9c	Clare . . .	Corrofin . . / Ennistimon . .	II.	18 to 22
51, 52, 62, 63, 64, 73, 74, 75, 85, 86, 87	Cork	45,310 1 10d	Cork, E.R. . .	Cork . . .	II.	63 to 66
19, 25, 26, 27, 28, 33, 34, 35, 36, 37, 42, 43, 44, 45, 46, 51, 52, 53, 54, 55, 61	Corkaguiny . .	138,990 1 17e	Kerry . . .	Dingle . . / Tralee . .	II.	173 to 180
6, 7, 11, 12, 13, 18, 19	Corkaree . . .	26,960 1 1f	Westmeath . .	Mullingar . .	I.	262 to 264
26, 27, 32, 33, 34, 38, 39, 40, 44, 45	Corran . . .	45,628 0 26g	Sligo . . .	Boyle . . / Sligo . . / Tobercurry . .	IV.	225 to 228
39, 40, 41, 47, 48, 49, 50, 55, 56, 57, 58, 59, 60	Coshlea . . .	95,232 1 21	Limerick . .	Kilmallock . / Mitchelstown .	II.	236 to 241
12, 21, 22, 30, 31, 32, 38, 39, 40, 46, 47, 55	Coshma . . .	49,052 2 3h	Limerick . .	Croom . . / Kilmallock . / Rathkeale .	II.	241 to 244
11, 12, 19, 20, 21, 28, 29, 33, 34, 37	Coshmore and Coshbride .	89,402 3 2i	Waterford . .	Lismore . . / Youghal . .	II.	343 to 349
51, 52, 62, 63, 64, 72, 73, 74, 80, 81, 82, 83, 91, 92, 93, 102, 103, 112, 113	Costello . . .	144,462 0 26j	Mayo . . .	Castlereagh . / Claremorris . / Swineford .	IV.	136 to 143
111, 124, 125, 137	Courceys . . .	9,011 1 32k	Cork, W.R. . .	Kinsale . .	II.	147
8, 9, 10, 12, 13, 14, 17, 18, 19, 22	Crannagh . . .	58,075 1 39l	Kilkenny . .	Callan . / Kilkenny . . / Urlingford .	I.	84 to 88
10, 14, 15, 18, 19, 20, 23, 24, 25, 26, 27, 28	Cremorne . . .	85,429 3 18m	Monaghan . .	Carrickmacross / Castleblayney . / Cootehill . . / Monaghan . .	III.	257 to 263
18, 19, 23, 24, 25, 29, 30, 31	Cullenagh . .	44,094 2 14n	Queen's Co. .	Abbeyleix . .	I.	238 to 240
8, 11, 12, 13, 16, 17, 18, 21, 22, 23	Dartree . . .	59,610 2 8o	Monaghan . .	Clones . . / Cootehill . . / Monaghan . .	III.	263 to 268
29, 30, 31, 34, 35, 36, 37, 38, 39, 40	Decies within Drum . .	58,907 0 35p	Waterford . .	Dungarvan . / Youghal . .	II.	349 to 353
5, 6, 7, 8, 12, 13, 14, 15, 16, 21, 22, 23, 24, 25, 29, 30, 31, 32, 35, 36	Decies without Drum .	137,699 0 31q	Waterford . .	Dungarvan . / Kilmacthomas . / Lismore . .	II.	353 to 362
31, 36, 37, 38, 43, 44	Deece Lower . .	20,013 0 3r	Meath . . .	Dunshaughlin . / Navan . . / Trim . .	I.	191, 192
42, 43, 44, 48, 49, 50, 53	Deece Upper . .	28,763 3 16s	Meath . . .	Celbridge . . / Dunshaughlin . / Trim . .	I.	192 to 194
4, 8, 9, 13, 14, 20, 21	Delvin . . .	39,062 3 12t	Westmeath . .	Castletowndelvin .	I.	264 to 266
21, 24	Drogheda . . .	4,498 1 26u	Louth . . .	Drogheda . .	I.	175
20	Drogheda . . .	1,203 2 29v	Meath . . .	Drogheda . .	I.	194
6, 7, 8, 9, 10, 11, 12, 13, 14, 15, 16, 17, 18, 19, 20, 21	Drumahaire . .	117,087 2 22w	Leitrim . .	Carrick on Shannon / Manorhamilton .	IV.	93 to 99
18, 19, 22, 23	Dublin . . .	1,650 1 35	Dublin . . .	Dublin South . / Rathdown .	I.	30
16, 17, 23, 24, 30, 31	Dufferin . . .	17,208 1 35x	Down . . .	Downpatrick . / Newtownards .	III.	166, 167
4, 5, 6, 7, 12, 13, 14, 15, 16, 21, 22, 23, 24, 29, 30, 31, 32, 33, 38, 39, 40, 41, 42, 49, 50	Duhallow . . .	232,328 2 14y	Cork, E.R. . .	Kanturk . / Mallow . . / Millstreet .	II.	67 to 76
19, 20, 21, 25, 26, 27, 28, 32, 33	Duleek Lower . .	36,982 2 24z	Meath . . .	Drogheda . . / Navan . .	I.	194 to 196
27, 28, 33, 34, 39	Duleek Upper . .	28,502 1 22aa	Meath . . .	Drogheda . . / Dunshaughlin .	I.	197 to 199
44, 45, 50, 51, 53	Dunboyne . . .	16,781 3 21	Meath . . .	Dunshaughlin . .	I.	199, 200

A. R. P.			
(a) Including 3,707 2 23 of water.	(l) Including 28 0 0 of River Nore.		
(b) Including 2,668 3 19 of water.	(m) Including 3,097 1 19 of water.		
(c) Including 292 3 26 of water.	(n) Including 13 2 26 of water.	(u) Including 26 1 14	of River Boyne tideway, and all the Town of Drogheda, except portion of river referred to in note (v).
(d) Including 1,617 2 16 of water.	(o) Including 1,242 3 5 of water.		
(e) Including 838 1 33 of water.	(p) Including 1,581 2 6 of River Blackwater tideway.		
(f) Including 3,313 0 15 of water.	(q) Including 151 3 2 of tideway.	(v) Exclusive of part of 78 0 8	of River Boyne tideway which has not been apportioned.
(g) Including 639 3 33 of water.	(r) Including 61 1 32 of River Boyne.		
(h) Including 34 0 10 of River Maigue tideway.	(s) Including 14 3 19 of water.	(w) Including 7,709 0 18 of water.	
(i) Including 1,364 3 30 of water.	(t) Including 202 0 12 of water.	(x) Including 199 1 17 of water.	
(j) Including 2,671 0 24 of water.		(y) Including 445 3 4 of water.	
(k) Including 198 1 35 of Bandon River tideway.		(z) Including 621 3 36 of water.	
		(aa) Including 39 0 33 of River Nanny tideway.	

6 G

No. of Sheet of the Ordnance Survey Maps.	Barony.	Area in Statute Measure.	County.	Poor Law Union in 1857.	Townland Census of 1851, Part I.	
		A. R. P.			Vol.	Page
1, 2, 4, 5, 7, 8, 9	Dundalk Lower	37,868 3 5a	Louth	Dundalk	I.	175 to 177
3, 4, 6, 7, 11, 12	Dundalk Upper	30,750 3 30b	Louth	Dundalk	I.	177 to 179
44, 45, 52, 53, 59, 60, 61, 66, 67	Dungannon Lower	42,792 2 5c	Tyrone	{ Armagh { Clogher { Dungannon	III.	296 to 298
37, 38, 39, 45, 46, 47, 48, 53, 54, 55, 60, 61, 62, 67	Dungannon Middle	90,600 3 12d	Tyrone	{ Cookstown { Dungannon	III.	298 to 305
20, 21, 28, 29, 30, 31, 37, 38, 39, 40, 46, 47, 48	Dungannon Upper	110,168 0 10e	Tyrone	Cookstown	III.	305 to 309
69, 70, 82, 83, 94, 95, 96, 97, 102, 103, 104, 105, 113, 114, 115	Dunkellin	83,371 1 21f	Galway	{ Galway { Gort { Loughrea	IV.	26 to 32
56, 57, 64, 65, 66, 72, 73, 74, 81, 82, 83, 90, 91	Dunkerron North	74,035 1 1g	Kerry	{ Cahersiveen { Kenmare { Killarney	II.	181, 182
73, 74, 82, 83, 84, 90, 91, 92, 93, 98, 99, 100, 101, 105, 106, 107, 108	Dunkerron South	97,119 3 8h	Kerry	{ Cahersiveen { Kenmare { Killarney	II.	183 to 185
2, 3, 6, 7, 11, 12, 13	Dunluce Lower	30,591 0 1i	Antrim	{ Ballymoney { Coleraine	III.	15 to 18
11, 12, 13, 14, 16, 17, 18, 19, 22, 23	Dunluce Upper	52,814 0 13j	Antrim	{ Ballymoney { Coleraine	III.	18 to 20
4, 5, 15, 16, 17, 28, 29, 30, 43, 44	Dunmore	71,011 1 2k	Galway	Tuam	IV.	32 to 36
22, 23, 30, 31, 35, 36	Eglish	28,704 0 21l	King's Co.	Parsonstown	I.	134, 135
23, 28, 29, 30, 34, 35, 36, 40, 41, 42, 46, 47, 48, 52, 53, 54	Eliogarty	90,257 2 3m	Tipperary, N.R.	{ Cashel { Roscrea { Thurles	II.	269 to 274
1, 2, 3, 4, 5, 9, 10, 11, 12, 13, 16, 17, 18, 19, 20, 23, 24, 25, 26, 27, 33, 34, 35, 36, 43, 44, 45, 55, 56, 57	Erris	232,888 3 15n	Mayo	{ Belmullet { Newport	IV.	143 to 146
19, 20, 21, 26, 27, 28, 34	Farbill	35,453 1 23o	Westmeath	{ Castletowndelvin { Mullingar	I.	266, 267
25, 27, 28, 29, 30, 31, 32, 33, 34	Farney	67,436 0 8p	Monaghan	{ Carrickmacross { Castleblayney { Dundalk	III.	269 to 274
19, 25, 26, 27, 32, 33, 34, 38, 39	Fartullagh	39,339 2 16q	Westmeath	Mullingar	I.	267 to 269
1, 2, 4, 5, 6, 9, 10, 11, 14, 15	Fassadinin	68,174 0 23r	Kilkenny	{ Castlecomer { Kilkenny { Urlingford	I.	88 to 91
2, 3, 7, 8, 9, 16, 17, 18, 19, 24, 25, 26, 27, 32, 33, 34, 35, 42, 43	Fermoy	121,561 2 32s	Cork, E.R.	{ Fermoy { Mallow { Mitchelstown	II.	76 to 83
15, 16, 17, 18, 19, 20, 21, 22, 23, 24, 25	Ferrard	49,212 3 28t	Louth	{ Ardee { Drogheda	I.	179 to 183
12, 13, 16, 17, 20, 21	Fews Lower	29,757 3 10u	Armagh	Armagh	III.	46, 47
16, 20, 21, 24, 25, 27, 28, 30, 31	Fews Upper	47,433 2 13v	Armagh	{ Armagh { Castleblayney { Dundalk { Newry	III.	48, 49
8, 9, 10, 14, 15, 16, 22, 23	Fore	43,549 1 29w	Meath	Oldcastle	I.	200 to 202
1, 2, 3, 4, 6, 7, 8, 12, 13	Fore	52,581 1 36x	Westmeath	{ Castletowndelvin { Granard	I.	269 to 272
8, 12, 13, 14, 17, 18, 20, 21, 23	Forth	39,510 0 22y	Carlow	{ Carlow { Enniscorthy	I.	3 to 5
37, 38, 42, 43, 47, 48, 52, 53	Forth	38,849 1 36z	Wexford	Wexford	I.	308 to 315
8, 9, 10, 11, 13, 14, 15, 16, 17, 19, 20, 21	Frenchpark	71,950 0 33aa	Roscommon	{ Boyle { Carrick on Shannon { Castlereagh { Swineford	IV.	202 to 205
31, 32, 39, 40, 48, 49, 50, 60, 61, 62, 70, 71, 72, 79, 80, 81, 91	Gallen	119,392 0 18bb	Mayo	{ Ballina { Castlebar { Swineford	IV.	146 to 151
3, 4, 5, 7, 8, 9, 10, 12	Galmoy	40,236 1 39	Kilkenny	Urlingford	I.	91 to 93
69, 81, 82, 93, 94, 95	Galway	24,131 2 23cc	Galway	Galway	IV.	37, 38
5, 6, 7, 13, 14, 15, 21, 22, 23, 29, 30, 35	Garrycastle	103,879 0 29dd	King's Co.	{ Parsonstown { Tullamore	I.	135 to 139
9, 10, 17, 18, 26, 27	Gaultiere	32,993 3 2ee	Waterford	Waterford	II.	362 to 365

	A. R. P.		A. R. P.		A. R. P.
(a) Including	78 3 29 of water.	(l) Including	199 0 5 of water.	(v) Including	449 1 0 of water.
(b) Including	78 3 26 of water.	(m) Including	16 0 16 Templemore Lake.	(w) Including	1,394 3 6 of water.
(c) Including	201 0 9 of water.	(n) Including	3,925 0 25 of water.	(x) Including	4,125 2 5 of water.
(d) Including	2,779 0 20 of water.	(o) Including	90 1 10 of water.	(y) Including	20 0 03 of water.
(e) Including	24,535 2 37 of water.	(p) Including	1,101 3 39 of water.	(z) Including	11 2 4 of water.
(f) Including	140 1 38 of water.	(q) Including	1,865 0 12 of water.	(aa) Including	1,952 1 5 of water.
(g) Including	2,725 0 15 of water.	(r) Including	15 1 4 of River Nore.	(bb) Including	1,641 3 18 of water.
(h) Including	1,265 2 30 of water.	(s) Including	381 3 24 of water.	(cc) Including	2,192 2 1 of water.
(i) Including	19 2 24 of water.	(t) Including	421 2 0 of water.	(dd) Including	1,170 0 9 of water.
(j) Including	118 1 32 of water.	(u) Including	96 0 13 of water.	(ee) Including	1,462 0 35 of water.
(k) Including	493 3 31 of water.				

No. of Sheet of the Ordnance Survey Maps.	Barony.	Area in Statute Measure.	County.	Poor Law Union in 1857.	Townland Census of 1851, Part I.	
		A. R. P.			Vol.	Page
17, 18, 24, 25, 26, 32	Geashill . . .	30,874 1 13	King's Co. . .	Tullamore . .	I.	139, 140
74, 75, 83, 84, 85, 86, 92, 93, 94, 95, 100, 101, 102, 103, 108, 109, 110, 111	Glanarought . .	121,866 3 4a	Kerry . . .	Kenmare . . / Killarney . .	II.	185 to 189
1, 5, 6, 13	Glenahiry . . .	19,672 0 1b	Waterford . .	Clogheen . . / Clonmel . .	II.	365, 366
10, 14, 15, 19, 20, 24, 25, 29, 30, 34, 35, 39	Glenarm Lower . .	65,442 1 18c	Antrim . . .	Ballycastle . / Larne . .	III.	21 to 24
29, 30, 34, 35, 39, 40, 46	Glenarm Upper . .	24,034 3 13d	Antrim . . .	Larne . . .	III.	24, 25
27, 28, 29, 34, 35, 36, 37, 42, 43, 44, 45, 51, 52, 53, 54	Glenquin . . .	96,402 0 5e	Limerick . .	Kanturk . / Newcastle . / Rathkeale .	II.	244 to 248
1, 2, 3, 5, 6, 7, 11, 12, 15, 16, 17, 20, 21, 22	Gorey . . .	81,931 3 5f	Wexford . . .	Enniscorthy . / Gorey . . / Shillelagh .	I.	315 to 321
11, 14, 15, 16, 19, 20, 21, 24, 25, 28, 29, 32, 33, 36	Gowran . . .	111,772 0 35g	Kilkenny . .	Castlecomer . / Kilkenny . . / Thomastown .	I.	93 to 100
1, 2, 3, 5, 6, 7, 9, 10, 11, 14, 15, 16	Granard . . .	66,680 3 38h	Longford . .	Granard . . / Longford . .	I.	154 to 157
121, 122, 123, 134, 135, 136, 137, 143, 144, 145	Ibane and Barryroe .	35,310 1 15i	Cork, W.R. . .	Clonakilty . .	II.	148 to 151
22, 23, 30, 31, 32, 38, 39, 40, 46, 47, 56, 57	Ibrickan . . .	57,028 0 8j	Clare . . .	Ennistimon . / Kilrush . .	II.	22 to 24
32, 33, 36, 37, 40, 41, 43, 44, 46, 47	Ida	61,703 3 33k	Kilkenny . .	New Ross . / Thomastown . / Waterford .	I.	101 to 104
12, 13, 16, 17, 19, 20, 22, 23	Idrone East . . .	52,857 3 23l	Carlow . . .	Carlow . . / New Ross .	I.	6 to 8
6, 7, 11, 12, 15, 16, 19	Idrone West . . .	23,066 1 1m	Carlow . . .	Carlow . .	I.	9, 10
71, 72, 76, 77, 78, 79, 82, 83, 84, 85	Iffa and Offa East . .	57,219 0 5n	Tipperary, S.R. .	Carrick on Suir / Clogheen . . / Clonmel .	II.	312 to 316
74, 75, 76, 80, 81, 82, 86, 87, 88, 89, 90, 91	Iffa and Offa West .	117,175 2 5o	Tipperary, S.R. .	Clogheen . . / Clonmel . .	II.	316 to 322
4, 5, 9, 10, 14	Ikeathy and Oughterany .	25,753 1 18	Kildare . . .	Celbridge . .	I.	56 to 58
12, 16, 17, 18, 22, 23, 24, 28, 29, 30, 34, 35, 36	Ikerrin . . .	69,805 1 19p	Tipperary, N.R. .	Roscrea . . / Thurles . .	II.	274 to 277
55, 56, 65, 66, 67, 76, 77, 78, 87, 88, 89, 99, 100	Imokilly . . .	95,317 3 31q	Cork, E.R. . .	Middleton . / Youghal . .	II.	83 to 91
6, 7, 9, 10, 11, 16, 17, 18, 23, 24, 25, 26, 31, 32, 33	Inchiquin . . .	88,387 0 3r	Clare . . .	Corrofin . / Ennis . . / Ennistimon .	II.	24 to 28
1, 2, 3, 4, 5, 9, 10, 11, 12, 13, 18, 19, 20, 21, 22, 30, 31	Inishowen East . .	123,399 3 3s	Donegal . .	Inishowen . .	III.	116 to 119
9, 10, 18, 19, 20, 28, 29, 30, 37, 38, 39, 46, 47	Inishowen West .	74,460 2 7t	Donegal . . .	Inishowen . / Londonderry .	III.	119 to 121
1, 2, 3, 4, 5, 6, 7, 9, 10, 11, 12, 16, 17, 18	Iraghticonnor . .	102,017 0 5u	Kerry . . .	Glin . . / Listowel . .	II.	189 to 193
25, 31, 32, 33, 34, 39, 40, 41, 42, 48, 49, 50	Islands . . .	67,101 1 34v	Clare . . .	Ennis . . / Killadysert .	II.	29 to 31
15, 20, 21, 22, 26, 27, 28, 29, 33, 34, 35	Iveagh Lower, Lower part	46,057 3 11w	Down . . .	Banbridge . / Lisburn . .	III.	167 to 169
13, 14, 15, 19, 20, 21, 22, 26, 27	Iveagh Lower, Upper part	47,677 0 4x	Down . . .	Banbridge . / Lisburn . . / Lurgan . .	III.	169 to 171
27, 28, 29, 34, 35, 36, 41, 42, 43, 47, 48, 49, 51, 52	Iveagh Upper, Lower part	96,317 0 39y	Down . . .	Banbridge . / Downpatrick . / Kilkeel . . / Newry . .	III.	171 to 173
26, 27, 33, 34, 35, 40, 41, 42, 46, 47, 48, 50, 51, 52, 54, 55	Iveagh Upper, Upper part	63,491 2 4z	Down . . .	Banbridge . / Kilkeel . . / Newry . .	III.	173 to 176
55, 56, 62, 63, 64, 69, 70, 71, 72, 78, 79, 80, 81, 82, 87, 83, 89, 90, 93, 97, 98, 99, 104, 105	Iveragh . . .	163,246 3 20aa	Kerry . . .	Cahersiveen . / Killarney . .	II.	193 to 198
34, 35, 38, 39, 40, 42, 43, 45, 46	Iverk . . .	41,368 2 32bb	Kilkenny . .	Carrick on Suir / Waterford . .	I.	105 to 107

A. R. P.	A. R. P.	A. R. P.
(a) Including 871 2 21 of water.	(k) Including 1,596 3 12 of water.	(t) Including 76 0 0 of water.
(b) Including 86 2 33 of River Suir.	(l) Including 138 3 34 of River Barrow.	(u) Including 14,080 1 32 of water.
(c) Including 91 3 32 of water.	(m) Including 110 1 28 of River Barrow.	(v) Including 3,932 1 17 of water.
(d) Including 11 2 12 of water.	(n) Including 255 3 15 of water.	(w) Including 253 3 12 of water.
(e) Including 87 1 25 of water.	(o) Including 257 2 7 of water.	(x) Including 296 3 24 of water.
(f) Including 5 3 8 Kilpatrick Lough.	(p) Including 60 2 36 of water.	(y) Including 503 0 5 of water.
(g) Including 439 3 11 of water.	(q) Including 1,519 0 33 of water.	(z) Including 423 3 19 of water.
(h) Including 3,270 3 26 of water.	(r) Including 2,854 0 3 of water.	(aa) Including 4,553 2 23 of water.
(i) Including 87 1 31 of water.	(s) Including { 235 2 28 of water. / 42 3 4 of Culdaff River tideway.	(bb) Including 840 0 34 of River Suir tideway.
(j) Including 598 1 9 of water.		

6 G 2

No. of Sheet of the Ordnance Survey Maps.	Barony.	Area in Statute Measure.	County.	Poor Law Union in 1857.	Townland Census of 1851, Part I.	
		A. R. P.			Vol.	Page
1, 2, 5, 6, 9, 10, 16, 17, 23, 24, 25, 30, 31, 32, 34, 35	Keenaght . . .	130,327 3 1a	Londonderry . .	Newtownlimavady	III.	233 to 238
23, 26, 27, 30, 31, 34, 35	Kells . . .	38,376 1 9	Kilkenny . .	Callan . . / Carrick on Suir / Thomastown .	I.	107 to 110
1, 2, 4, 5, 10, 11, 17	Kells Lower . .	36,171 1 26b	Meath . . .	Kells . . . / Castletowndelvin	I.	202 to 204
9, 10, 11, 15, 16, 17, 18, 23, 24, 25	Kells Upper . .	49,552 1 8c	Meath . . .	Kells . . / Navan . . / Oldcastle .	I.	204 to 207
2, 3, 4, 11, 12, 20, 21	Kenry . . .	30,937 3 36d	Limerick . .	Croom . . / Rathkeale .	II.	248 to 250
75, 85, 86, 87, 97, 98, 99	Kerrycurrihy . .	24,244 2 17e	Cork, E.R. .	Cork . . / Kinsale .	II.	91 to 93
46, 47, 60, 61, 72, 73, 74, 84, 85, 86, 87, 97, 98, 99	Kilconnell . .	64,819 0 34f	Galway . . .	Ballinasloe . / Loughrea . / Mountbellew .	IV.	38 to 42
16, 17, 18, 19, 21, 22, 23, 24, 26, 27, 28, 31, 32	Kilconway . .	68,457 2 9g	Antrim . . .	Ballymena . / Ballymoney .	III.	25 to 28
1, 2, 7, 8	Kilcoursey . .	19,287 3 20h	King's Co. . .	Tullamore .	I.	140, 141
23, 28, 29, 32, 33	Kilcullen . . .	8,492 1 29i	Kildare . . .	Athy . . / Naas . .	I.	58
35, 36, 37, 38, 39, 40	Kilkea and Moone .	46,286 3 31j	Kildare . . .	Athy . . / Baltinglass . / Carlow .	I.	59 to 61
15, 16, 22, 23, 29, 30	Kilkenny West . .	37,626 2 23k	Westmeath . .	Athlone . / Ballymahon .	I.	272 to 274
19, 20, 32, 33, 45, 46, 47, 59, 60, 61, 74	Killian . . .	52,388 2 13l	Galway . . .	Ballinasloe . / Mountbellew .	IV.	42 to 45
6, 7, 8, 9, 14, 15, 16, 17, 18, 23, 24, 25, 26, 27, 28, 32, 33, 34, 35, 36, 37, 41, 42, 43, 44, 45, 46, 49, 50, 51, 52, 53, 54, 58, 59, 60, 61	Kilmacrenan . .	310,655 1 33m	Donegal . . .	Dunfanaghy . / Letterkenny . / Millford . / Stranorlar .	III.	122 to 133
100, 109, 110, 111, 117, 118, 119, 120, 121, 122, 123	Kilmaine . . .	105,988 2 9n	Mayo . . .	Ballinrobe . / Claremorris . / Oughterard .	IV.	151 to 158
39, 40, 47, 48	Kilmallock . .	4,074 0 37o	Limerick . .	Kilmallock .	II.	250
39, 40, 45, 46, 51, 52, 59, 60	Kilnamanagh Lower .	42,041 2 24	Tipperary, S.R.	Cashel . . / Tipperary .	II.	322 to 324
27, 28, 33, 34, 38, 39, 40, 44, 45, 46, 50, 51	Kilnamanagh Upper .	59,990 0 26	Tipperary, N.R.	Cashel . . / Nenagh . / Thurles . / Tipperary .	II.	277 to 281
102, 112, 113, 114, 121, 122, 123, 124, 128, 129, 130, 133	Kiltartan . . .	66,654 3 11p	Galway . . .	Gort . . / Loughrea .	IV.	45 to 50
85, 86, 96, 97, 98, 99, 111, 112, 113, 125	Kinalea . . .	50,941 1 36q	Cork, E.R. .	Bandon . . / Kinsale .	II.	93 to 97
83, 84, 95, 96, 97, 109, 110, 123	Kinalmeaky . .	36,381 0 14	Cork, W.R. .	Bandon .	II.	151 to 153
15, 22, 23, 29, 30, 36, 37, 43, 44	Kinelarty . . .	40,322 3 37r	Down . . .	Downpatrick . / Lisburn .	III.	176, 177
36, 37, 45, 46, 54, 55	Kinnatalloon . .	27,718 0 5	Cork, E.R. .	Fermoy . / Lismore . / Youghal .	II.	97 to 99
98, 111, 112, 124, 125	Kinsale . . .	13,032 2 17s	Cork, E.R. .	Kinsale .	II.	99 to 101
33, 34, 37, 38, 39, 41, 42	Knockninny . .	30,604 0 7t	Fermanagh . .	Enniskillen . / Lisnaskea .	III.	201 to 203
27, 28, 31, 32, 35, 36, 39, 40, 43	Knocktopher . .	46,765 1 14u	Kilkenny . .	Carrick on Suir / New Ross . / Thomastown . / Waterford .	I.	110 to 113
30, 31, 32, 37, 38, 39, 45	Lecale Lower . .	30,920 3 11v	Down . . .	Downpatrick .	III.	178 to 180
30, 31, 36, 37, 38, 43, 44, 45, 49	Lecale Upper . .	30,671 3 14w	Down . . .	Downpatrick .	III.	180, 181
97, 98, 105, 106, 107, 115, 116, 117, 124, 125, 126, 130, 131, 132, 134, 135, 136, 137	Leitrim . . .	120,185 0 20x	Galway . . .	Ballinasloe . / Loughrea . / Portumna . / Scarriff .	IV.	50 to 56
20, 21, 23, 24, 25, 27, 28, 29, 31, 32, 35	Leitrim . . .	61,665 3 19y	Leitrim . . .	Carrick on Shannon / Mohill .	IV.	99 to 104
19, 20, 23, 24, 25, 26, 30, 31, 32, 33, 36, 37, 38, 42, 43	Leyny . . .	121,685 2 3z	Sligo . . .	Sligo . . / Tobercurry .	IV.	228 to 232

	A. R. P.			A. R. P.			A. R. P.
(a) Including	1,247 2 20 of water.	(j) Including	87 0 20 of water.	(s) Including	601 3 0 of tideway.
(b) Including	147 0 16 of water.	(k) Including	6,916 2 15 of water.	(t) Including	3,335 3 23 of water.
(c) Including	61 0 32 of water.	(l) Including	459 3 36 of water.	(u) Including	25 0 22 of River Nore.
(d) Including	4,912 5 26 of water.	(m) Including	6,248 2 21 of water.	(v) Including	162 0 22 of water.
(e) Including	287 0 8 of tideway.	(n) Including	11,408 2 32 of water.	(w) Including	174 0 21 of water.
(f) Including	42 3 13 of water.	(o) Including	25 3 6 Ash Hill Lough.	(x) Including	10,903 3 38 of water.
(g) Including	197 1 36 of water.	(p) Including	1,542 0 39 of water.	(y) Including	4,874 2 4 of water.
(h) Including	7 3 0 of Ballinderry Lough.	(q) Including	248 3 23 of tideway.	(z) Including	1,062 0 37 of water.
(i) Including	27 0 25 of River Liffey.	(r) Including	426 2 0 of water.		

No. of Sheet of the Ordnance Survey Maps.	Barony.	Area in Statute Measure.	County.	Poor Law Union in 1857.	Townland Census of 1851, Part I.	
		A. R. P.			Vol.	Page
13, 14, 20, 21	Londonderry, North West Liberties of	13,800 1 19a	Londonderry .	Londonderry .	III.	246, 247
88, 98, 99, 100, 101, 106, 107, 108, 109, 117, 118, 126, 127	Longford .	99,504 0 7b	Galway .	Ballinasloe . Loughrea . Portumna .	IV.	56 to 62
1, 2, 3, 4, 5, 6, 8, 9, 12, 13, 14	Longford .	58,139 3 8c	Longford .	Granard . Longford .	I.	157 to 160
26, 27, 31, 32, 33, 35, 36, 37, 38, 39, 40, 41, 42, 43, 44, 45, 46, 47, 48, 49	Loughinsholin .	177,822 1 14d	Londonderry .	Ballymoney . Magherafelt .	III.	238 to 244
96, 97, 98, 104, 105, 106, 114, 115, 123, 124, 130	Loughrea .	65,175 1 29e	Galway .	Gort . Loughrea .	IV.	62 to 66
10, 11, 14, 15, 19, 20	Loughtee Lower	29,568 2 5f	Cavan .	Bawnboy . Cavan .	III.	78 to 81
15, 16, 19, 20, 21, 24, 25, 26, 27, 31, 32, 33	Loughtee Upper	66,449 1 6g	Cavan .	Bailieborough . Cavan . Oldcastle .	III.	81 to 86
6, 10, 11, 12, 14, 15	Louth .	25,704 2 25h	Louth .	Ardee . Dundalk .	I.	183 to 185
23, 24, 29, 30, 35, 36, 41	Lune .	39,326 1 0i	Meath .	Trim .	I.	207, 208
1, 2, 3, 4, 5, 6, 8, 9, 10, 11, 15, 16	Lurg .	83,205 1 6j	Fermanagh .	Ballyshannon . Lowtherstown .	III.	203 to 209
7, 8, 9, 10, 12, 13, 14, 15, 16, 19, 20, 21, 22, 26, 27	Magheraboy .	89,667 0 18k	Fermanagh .	Ballyshannon . Enniskillen .	III.	209 to 214
23, 24, 27, 28, 29, 30, 33, 34, 35, 39	Magherastephana	61,729 0 6l	Fermanagh .	Lisnaskea .	III.	214 to 219
38, 39, 47, 48, 49, 50, 56, 57, 58, 59, 60, 65, 66, 67, 68, 74, 75, 76, 77, 84, 85, 86	Magunihy .	171,995 2 39m	Kerry .	Killarney .	II.	199 to 205
7, 8, 12, 13, 14, 17, 18	Maryborough East .	25,160 0 17	Queen's Co. .	Abbeyleix . Mountmellick .	I.	240 to 242
6, 7, 11, 12, 16, 17, 18, 23, 24	Maryborough West .	41,914 2 39n	Queen's Co. .	Abbeyleix . Mountmellick .	I.	242, 243
49, 50, 54, 55, 56, 58, 59, 60	Massereene Lower .	48,276 2 12o	Antrim .	Antrim .	III.	28, 29
55, 58, 59, 60, 62, 63, 64, 66, 67, 68	Massereene Upper .	68,837 2 24p	Antrim .	Antrim . Lisburn . Lurgan .	III.	29 to 31
46, 47, 52, 53, 54, 55, 60, 61, 62, 63, 68, 69, 70, 71, 75, 76, 77, 78	Middlethird .	113,641 3 24q	Tipperary, S.R.	Callan . Cashel . Clonmel . Tipperary .	II.	324 to 331
8, 9, 16, 17, 18, 25, 26, 27	Middlethird .	45,120 0 1r	Waterford .	Kilmacthomas . Waterford .	II.	366 to 369
24, 25, 28, 29, 32, 33, 35, 36, 37, 38	Mohill .	64,033 2 25s	Leitrim .	Carrick on Shannon . Mohill .	IV.	105 to 109
5, 6, 7, 8, 9, 10, 12, 13, 14, 18, 19	Monaghan .	69,904 0 7t	Monaghan .	Castleblayney . Monaghan .	III.	274 to 281
2, 3, 5, 6, 11, 12, 17, 18	Morgallion .	31,492 1 31u	Meath .	Kells . Navan .	I.	209, 210
48, 49, 52, 53, 55, 56, 57	Mourne .	47,882 3 19v	Down .	Kilkeel .	III.	182, 183
38, 39, 46, 47, 48, 55, 56, 57, 58, 64, 65, 66, 67, 71, 72, 73	Moyarta .	83,151 3 8w	Clare .	Kilrush .	II.	31 to 34
12, 13, 18, 19, 20, 25, 26, 27	Moyashel and Magheradernon .	42,845 1 37x	Westmeath .	Mullingar .	I.	274 to 276
50, 51, 53, 54, 55, 56	Moycarn .	29,881 0 18y	Roscommon .	Ballinasloe .	IV.	206, 207
24, 25, 30, 31, 32, 33, 37, 38, 39, 40	Moycashel .	47,332 3 24z	Westmeath .	Athlone . Mullingar . Tullamore .	I.	276 to 279
27, 38, 39, 40, 41, 52, 53, 54, 55, 56, 65, 66, 67, 68, 69, 77, 78, 79, 80, 81, 82, 89, 90, 91, 92, 93	Moycullen .	220,233 1 20aa	Galway .	Galway . Oughterard .	IV.	66 to 72
12, 13, 14, 17, 18, 19, 22, 23	Moydow .	34,519 3 0bb	Longford .	Ballymahon . Longford .	I.	160 to 162
35, 36, 37, 41, 42, 43, 47, 48, 49	Moyfenrath Lower .	40,313 1 4cc	Meath .	Trim .	I.	210 to 212
35, 40, 41, 42, 46, 47, 52	Moyfenrath Upper .	31,696 0 10dd	Meath .	Edenderry . Trim .	I.	212, 213
2, 5, 6, 7, 10, 11, 17, 18	Moygoish .	40,276 3 29ee	Westmeath .	Granard . Mullingar .	I.	279 to 281

A. R. P.	A. R. P.	A. R. P.
(a) Including 1,031 3 3 of water.	(l) Including 3,434 3 30 of water.	(v) Including 36 3 0 of water.
(b) Including 3,105 1 28 of water.	(m) Including 5,926 0 10 of water.	(w) Including 14,603 2 12 of water.
(c) Including 1,225 2 10 of water.	(n) Including 26 0 0 Ballyfin Lough.	(x) Including 2,643 1 29 of water.
(d) Including 6,232 0 22 of water.	(o) Including 21,313 2 11 of Lough Neagh.	(y) Including 513 1 39 of water.
(e) Including 784 1 16 of water.	(p) Including 13,036 1 30 of water.	(z) Including 235 0 19 of Lough Ennell.
(f) Including 4,146 0 1 of water.	(q) Including 20 2 8 Rockwell Lake.	(aa) Including 26,409 3 6 of water.
(g) Including 3,693 1 17 of water.	(r) Including 531 0 15 of water.	(bb) Including 69 0 13 of water.
(h) Including 48 3 32 of water.	(s) Including 3,235 0 22 of water.	(cc) Including 121 3 15 of River Boyne
(i) Including 36 3 33 of River Boyne.	(t) Including 432 2 23 of water.	(dd) Including 70 1 26 of water.
(j) Including 17,641 3 9 of water.	(u) Including 95 2 21 of water.	(ee) Including 1,423 3 31 of water.
(k) Including 11,698 2 26 of water.		

No. of Sheet of the Ordnance Survey Maps.	Barony.	Area in Statute Measure.	County.	Poor Law Union in 1857.	Townland Census of 1851, Part I.	
		A. R. P.			Vol.	Page
75, 77, 84, 85, 86, 87, 88, 94, 95, 96, 97, 98, 104, 105, 106, 107, 108, 114, 115, 116	Murrisk . . .	137,061 3 34a	Mayo . . .	Clifden . . Westport . .	IV.	158 to 162
49, 50, 51, 60, 61, 62, 63, 71, 72, 73, 83, 84, 85, 95, 96, 97, 98	Muskerry East .	94,720 3 28b	Cork, E.R. . .	Bandon . . Cork . . Macroom . .	II.	101 to 106
		28,153 2 21c	Cork, W.R. . .			153, 154
38, 39, 40, 47, 48, 49, 57, 58, 59, 60, 68, 69, 70, 71, 80, 81, 82, 83, 92, 93, 94, 95	Muskerry West .	188,487 0 5d	Cork, W.R. . .	Dunmanway . Macroom . . Millstreet .	II.	154 to 160
14, 15, 19, 20, 24, 25	Naas North . . .	25,579 2 5e	Kildare . . .	Naas . . .	I.	62, 63
19, 23, 24, 25, 28, 29, 33	Naas South . . .	27,478 1 12f	Kildare . . .	Naas . . .	I.	64, 65
28, 31, 32, 35, 36	Narragh and Reban East .	21,374 0 10	Kildare . . .	Athy . . Baltinglass . Naas . .	I.	66, 67
30, 31, 34, 35, 37	Narragh and Reban West .	22,126 3 20g	Kildare . . .	Athy . . .	I.	67, 68
17, 18, 24, 25, 30, 31	Navan Lower . . .	25,835 1 28h	Meath . . .	Kells . . Navan . .	I.	214, 215
24, 30, 31, 36, 37	Navan Upper . . .	17,651 3 29i	Meath . . .	Navan . . Trim . .	I.	216, 217
7, 8, 9, 11, 12, 14, 15	Nethercross . . .	21,818 1 29	Dublin . . .	Balrothery .	I.	30 to 32
13, 17, 20, 21, 24	Newcastle . . .	22,876 1 31j	Dublin . . .	Celbridge . . Dublin South .	I.	32 to 35
8, 12, 13, 18, 19, 24, 25, 30, 31	Newcastle	52,296 0 39k	Wicklow . . .	Rathdrum . .	I.	350 to 354
40, 41, 46, 47, 50, 51	Newry, Lordship of .	16,279 2 7l	Down . . .	Newry . . .	III.	182
12, 16, 17, 18, 21, 22, 23, 27, 28	Offaly East . . .	47,029 3 20	Kildare . . .	Athy . . Edenderry . Naas . .	I.	69 to 71
21, 22, 26, 27, 28, 30, 31, 32	Offaly West . . .	40,603 1 14m	Kildare . . .	Athy . .	I.	71 to 74
25, 27, 28, 34, 35, 36, 37, 41, 42, 43, 44, 45, 49, 50, 51, 52, 56, 57	Omagh East . . .	132,538 0 16n	Tyrone . . .	Enniskillen . Lowtherstown . Omagh . .	III.	310 to 315
14, 15, 16, 22, 23, 24, 25, 32, 33, 34, 41, 42	Omagh West . . .	93,308 1 2o	Tyrone . . .	Castlederg . Omagh . .	III.	315 to 318
2, 3, 5, 6, 9, 10	Oneilland East . .	34,498 2 21p	Armagh . . .	Lurgan . .	III.	49 to 51
1, 2, 4, 5, 8, 9, 10, 12, 13, 17	Oneilland West . .	59,502 0 28q	Armagh . . .	Armagh . . Banbridge . Lurgan . .	III.	51 to 55
9, 10, 13, 14, 17, 18, 21, 22	Orior Lower . . .	31,927 3 37r	Armagh . . .	Armagh . . Banbridge . Newry . .	III.	55 to 57
21, 22, 25, 26, 28, 29, 31, 32	Orior Upper . . .	49,692 3 15s	Armagh . . .	Castleblayney . Newry . .	III.	57 to 59
1, 2, 3, 4, 5, 6, 7, 8, 9, 10, 11, 13, 14, 15, 16, 20, 21	Ormond Lower . .	135,723 0 32t	Tipperary, N.R. .	Borrisokane . Nenagh . . Parsonstown .	II.	281 to 288
15, 16, 20, 21, 22, 26, 27, 28, 32, 33, 38, 39	Ormond Upper . .	79,471 3 26	Tipperary, N.R. .	Borrisokane . Nenagh . .	II.	288 to 293
1, 2, 3, 6, 7, 8, 15, 16, 17, 24, 25, 32	Orrery and Kilmore .	69,346 1 16	Cork, E.R. . .	Kanturk . . Kilmallock . Mallow . .	II.	106 to 110
13, 14, 19, 20, 25, 26, 31, 32, 33, 37, 38, 39	Owney and Arra . .	89,671 2 3u	Tipperary, N.R. .	Nenagh . . .	II.	293 to 298
6, 7, 8, 14, 15, 24	Owneybeg	27,211 0 31	Limerick . .	Limerick . . .	II.	250, 251
3, 9, 10, 11, 17, 18, 19	Philipstown Lower .	30,691 3 2v	King's Co. . .	Edenderry . Tullamore .	I.	142, 143
18, 19, 26, 27, 33, 34	Philipstown Upper .	37,096 2 6	King's Co. . .	Edenderry . Mountmellick . Tullamore .	I.	143, 144
4, 5, 7, 8, 9, 13, 14	Portnahinch . . .	35,835 1 17w	Queen's Co. . .	Mountmellick . .	I.	243, 244
4, 5, 12, 13, 21, 22, 30, 31	Pubblebrien . . .	34,582 1 15x	Limerick . .	Croom . . Limerick . .	II.	251 to 254

	A. R. P.		A. R. P.		A. R. P.
(a) Including	1,789 2 0 of water.	(i) Including	92 2 33 of River Boyne.	(q) Including	2,424 2 0 of water.
(b) Including	307 2 23 of water.	(j) Including	54 3 26 of River Liffey.	(r) Including	103 3 30 of water.
(c) Including	63 0 1 of River Lee.	(k) Including	207 3 0 Broad Lough.	(s) Including	271 0 7 of water.
(d) Including	624 0 26 of water.	(l) Including	242 2 5 of water.	(t) Including	8,740 2 25 of water.
(e) Including	65 0 14 of River Liffey.	(m) Including	21 1 26 of River Barrow.	(u) Including	4,176 3 33 of water.
(f) Including	178 3 7 of water.	(n) Including	591 2 38 of water.	(v) Including	5 0 20 of Lough Nashade.
(g) Including	139 1 29 of River Barrow.	(o) Including	563 1 20 of water.	(w) Including	48 3 12 of water.
(h) Including	82 1 17 of River Boyne.	(p) Including	14,136 1 21 of water.	(x) Including	1,416 2 22 of water.

No. of Sheet of the Ordnance Survey Maps.	Barony.	Area in Statute Measure.	County.	Poor Law Union in 1857.	Townland Census of 1851, Part I.	
		A. R. P.			Vol.	Page
46, 47, 52, 53, 54, 55, 59, 60, 61, 62, 63, 67, 68, 69, 70, 71, 76, 77, 78, 79, 85, 86, 87, 88, 95	Raphoe . . .	220,723 1 6a	Donegal . . .	Letterkenny . Londonderry . Strabane . Stranolar .	III.	133 to 144
12, 17, 18, 21, 22, 23, 25, 26, 27	Rathcline . . .	48,839 3 9b	Longford . .	Ballymahon . Longford .	I.	163 to 165
10, 16, 17, 18, 23, 24, 25, 30, 31	Rathconrath . .	48,415 0 23c	Westmeath . .	Athlone . Ballymahon . Mullingar .	I.	281 to 284
18, 22, 23, 25, 26, 27, 28	Rathdown . . .	32,870 2 24	Dublin . .	Dublin South . Rathdown .	I.	35 to 38
2, 3, 4, 6, 7, 8, 12, 13	Rathdown . . .	34,381 3 39d	Wicklow . .	Rathdown . .	I.	354 to 356
1, 3, 4, 5, 8, 9, 10, 13	Rathvilly . . .	44,806 1 9	Carlow . . .	Baltinglass . Carlow . . Shillelagh .	I.	10 to 12
38, 39, 44, 45, 50, 51	Ratoath . . .	35,697 1 27	Meath . .	Dunshaughlin .	I.	217 to 220
1, 2, 3, 4, 5, 6, 7, 8, 9, 10, 11, 12	Rosclogher . .	86,074 1 35e	Leitrim . .	Ballyshannon . Manorhamilton .	IV.	109 to 112
11, 15, 16, 17, 18, 21, 22, 23, 24, 28, 29, 30, 36, 37	Roscommon . .	82,601 3 39f	Roscommon . .	Boyle . . Carrick on Shannon Castlereagh . Roscommon . Strokestown .	IV.	207 to 213
3, 11, 12, 13, 14, 24, 25, 26, 27, 38, 39, 40	Ross . . .	98,630 2 18g	Galway . . .	Ballinrobe . Oughterard .	IV.	72 to 74
22, 23, 24, 25, 26	St. Mullin's Lower .	21,963 3 37h	Carlow . . .	New Ross . .	I.	13
14, 17, 18, 20, 21	St. Mullin's Upper .	7,784 2 8i	Carlow . . .	Carlow . . Shillelagh .	I.	14
5, 6, 10, 11, 14, 15	Salt North . .	21,930 0 1j	Kildare . .	Celbridge . .	I.	74 to 76
10, 11, 14, 15, 19, 20	Salt South . .	16,685 1 20k	Kildare . . .	Celbridge . . Naas . .	I.	76 to 78
4, 5, 6, 8, 9, 10, 11, 13, 14, 15, 16, 18, 19, 20, 26	Scarawalsh . .	106,659 0 16l	Wexford . . .	Enniscorthy . Gorey . . Shillelagh .	I.	322 to 326
2, 9, 10, 17, 18, 19, 20, 26, 27, 28, 34, 35, 36	Shanid . . .	92,505 0 12m	Limerick . .	Glin . . Newcastle . Rathkeale .	II.	254 to 258
34,35,39,40,44,45,49,50,54	Shelburne . . .	53,102 1 26n	Wexford . . .	New Ross . .	I.	327 to 329
32, 33, 37, 38	Shelmaliere East .	16,746 3 24o	Wexford . . .	Enniscorthy . Wexford .	I.	329 to 331
25, 26, 31, 32, 35, 36, 37, 40, 41, 42, 45	Shelmaliere West .	50,769 2 13p	Wexford . . .	Enniscorthy . New Ross . Wexford .	I.	332 to 335
37, 38, 42, 43, 44, 46, 47	Shillelagh . . .	44,348 3 5	Wicklow . . .	Shillelagh . .	I.	356 to 358
18, 19, 20, 22, 23, 24, 26, 27, 28, 31	Shillelogher . .	36,684 3 32q	Kilkenny . .	Callan . Kilkenny . Thomastown .	I.	113 to 116
19, 22, 23, 24, 26, 27	Shrule . . .	21,006 0 3r	Longford . .	Ballymahon .	I.	165 to 167
25, 26, 31, 32, 33, 37, 38, 39	Skreen . . .	40,891 2 29s	Meath . . .	Dunshaughlin . Navan .	I.	220 to 222
2, 3, 6, 7, 12, 13	Slane Lower . .	26,224 0 19t	Meath . . .	Ardee . Kells .	I.	222 to 224
12, 13, 18, 19, 20, 25, 26	Slane Upper . .	29,211 3 4u	Meath . . .	Ardee . Drogheda . Navan .	I.	224, 225
36, 42, 43, 48, 49, 53, 54, 55, 56, 61, 62, 63, 64, 71, 72, 78, 79	Slievardagh . .	90,772 3 16v	Tipperary, S.R. .	Callan . Carrick on Suir Cashel . Thurles . Urlingford .	II.	331 to 336
25, 26, 31, 32, 36, 37	Slievemargy . .	35,490 2 25w	Queen's Co. . .	Carlow . .	I.	245, 246
13, 22, 23, 24, 31, 32, 33, 39, 40, 41	Smallcounty . .	44,424 3 21x	Limerick . .	Croom . Kilmallock . Limerick .	II.	258 to 261
1, 2, 3, 4, 5, 6, 7, 9, 10, 11, 12, 16, 17, 18, 24, 25, 34	Strabane Lower .	118,380 1 25y	Tyrone . . .	Castlederg . Gortin . Omagh . Strabane .	III.	318 to 323
7, 8, 10, 11, 12, 16, 17, 18, 19, 20, 25, 26, 27, 28, 34, 35, 36	Strabane Upper .	121,281 3 18z	Tyrone . . .	Gortin . Omagh .	III.	323 to 326
9, 13, 14, 18, 19, 25, 31	Stradbally . .	27,895 3 34aa	Queen's Co. . .	Athy . Mountmellick .	I.	246 to 248

	A. R. P.			A. R. P.			A. R. P.	
(a) Including	2,082 3 38	of water.	(k) Including	70 2 18	of water.	(s) Including	78 2 30	of River Boyne.
(b) Including	8,320 2 37	of water.	(l) Including	229 2 16	of River Slaney.	(t) Including	189 2 8	of water.
(c) Including	207 3 33	of water.	(m) Including	8,430 0 11	of water.	(u) Including	135 2 11	of River Boyne.
(d) Including	93 1 24	of water.	(n) Including	1,998 3 36	of River Barrow tideway.	(v) Including	10 2 39	of water.
(e) Including	4,990 0 4	of water.				(w) Including	52 2 39	of River Barrow.
(f) Including	3,023 3 11	of water.	(o) Including	382 3 34	of River Slaney tideway.	(x) Including	232 0 15	Lough Gur.
(g) Including	21,610 1 12	of water.	(p) Including	469 3 31	of River Slaney tideway.	(y) Including	1,699 0 17	of water.
(h) Including	110 0 10	of River Barrow.	(q) Including	87 1 29	of River Nore.	(z) Including	534 2 6	of water.
(i) Including	8 1 14	of River Slaney.	(r) Including	167 1 19	of River Inny.	(aa) Including	18 1 30	of River Barrow.
(j) Including	120 2 5	of water.						

No. of Sheet of the Ordnance Survey Maps.	Barony.	Area in Statute Measure.			County.	Poor Law Union in 1857.	Townland Census of 1851, Part I.	
		A.	R.	P.			Vol.	Page
1, 2, 5, 6, 9, 10, 11, 14, 15, 16, 17, 21, 22	Talbotstown Lower	86,857	3	6a	Wicklow	{ Baltinglass { Naas	I.	358 to 361
14, 15, 16, 20, 21, 22, 26, 27, 28, 32, 33	Talbotstown Upper	62,510	1	26	Wicklow	Baltinglass	I.	361 to 365
6, 18, 19, 31, 32, 44, 45, 46, 58, 59, 60, 71, 72, 73, 84, 85	Tiaquin	110,135	3	10b	Galway	Ballinasloe Galway Glennamaddy Loughrea Mountbellew Tuam	IV.	75 to 80
1, 2, 3, 4, 6, 7, 8	Tinnahinch	54,187	0	15c	Queen's Co.	Mountmellick	I.	248 to 250
7, 8, 11, 12, 15, 19, 20, 23, 24	Tiranny	27,397	2	38d	Armagh	Armagh	III.	59 to 61
5, 6, 7, 8, 12, 13, 14, 15, 19, 20, 21, 22, 27, 28, 29, 30, 36, 37, 38, 39, 45, 46, 47, 48, 58, 59, 60, 68	Tirawley	261,029	2	8e	Mayo	Ballina Castlebar Killala	IV.	162 to 172
10, 11, 12, 13, 16, 17, 18, 19, 20, 22, 23, 24, 25, 29, 30	Tireragh	106,802	0	8f	Sligo	Ballina Dromore West	IV.	232 to 236
15, 20, 21, 26, 27, 28, 33, 34, 35, 40, 41, 45	Tirerrill	79,596	0	9g	Sligo	Boyle Sligo Tobercurry	IV.	237 to 241
85, 86, 89, 93, 94, 95, 99, 100, 101, 102, 103, 104, 105, 106, 107, 108, 109, 110	Tirhugh	127,964	0	21h	Donegal	Ballyshannon Donegal Glenties	III.	144 to 149
9, 13, 14, 15, 16, 20, 21, 22, 23, 24, 28, 29, 30, 34	Tirkeeran	95,687	1	30i	Londonderry	Londonderry Newtownlimavady	III.	247 to 250
11, 15, 16, 17, 18, 22, 23, 24, 27, 28, 33	Tirkennedy	58,675	3	1j	Fermanagh	Enniskillen Lisnaskea Lowtherstown	III.	219 to 224
26, 27, 31, 32, 33, 36, 37	Toome Lower	36,259	2	33k	Antrim	Ballymena	III.	31 to 33
36, 37, 42, 43, 44, 44, 48, 49, 50, 54	Toome Upper	64,953	3	28l	Antrim	Antrim Ballymena	III.	33 to 35
1, 2, 3, 4, 5, 6, 7, 9, 10	Trough	37,376	2	25m	Monaghan	Clogher Monaghan	III.	281 to 285
20, 21, 22, 23, 24, 28, 29, 30, 31, 32, 37, 38, 39, 40, 41, 46, 47, 48, 49, 50, 55, 56, 57, 58, 59, 64	Trughanacmy	195,773	0	38n	Kerry	Dingle Killarney Tralee	II.	205 to 214
29, 35, 36, 37, 43, 44, 45, 52, 53, 54, 63	Tulla Lower	78,381	0	19o	Clare	Limerick Scarriff Tulla	II.	34 to 38
12, 13, 19, 20, 21, 26, 27, 28, 29, 34, 35, 36, 37, 43	Tulla Upper	96,730	1	11p	Clare	Scarriff Tulla	II.	38 to 42
11, 12, 15, 16, 17, 18, 21, 22, 23, 26, 27	Tullygarvey	59,902	2	37q	Cavan	Cavan Cootehill	III.	87 to 91
1, 2, 3, 4, 5, 6, 7, 8, 9, 10, 13, 14	Tullyhaw	90,701	1	34r	Cavan	Bawnboy Enniskillen	III.	91 to 96
13, 14, 19, 24, 25, 30, 36	Tullyhunco	40,891	2	1s	Cavan	Bawnboy Cavan Granard	III.	96 to 99
17, 18, 21, 22, 24, 25, 27	Uppercross	39,013	3	20t	Dublin	Dublin South Naas	I.	39 to 42
1, 2, 3, 4, 5, 6, 7, 8, 14, 15, 16	Upperthird	77,089	0	17u	Waterford	Carrick on Suir Clonmel Kilmacthomas	II.	369 to 372
6, 10, 11, 12, 15, 16, 17, 21, 22, 23	Upperwoods	48,926	2	14	Queen's Co.	Abbeyleix Donaghmore Mountmellick	I.	250 to 252
3, 4, 10, 11, 12	Warrenstown	21,462	1	35v	King's Co.	Edenderry	I.	144, 145

	A.	R.	P.			A.	R.	P.			A.	R.	P.	
(a) Including	87	0	9	of water.	(i) Including	1,110	0	5	of water.	(p) Including	2,911	0	29	of water.
(b) Including	467	3	30	of water.	(j) Including	4,237	1	29	of water.	(q) Including	1,027	3	10	of water.
(c) Including	108	2	20	of water.	(k) Including	129	2	37	of River Bann.	(r) Including	2,605	0	34	of water.
(d) Including	152	1	14	of water.	(l) Including	18,204	3	35	of water.	(s) Including	2,801	3	9	of water.
(e) Including	15,931	1	22	of water.	(m) Including	292	1	27	of water.	(t) Including	37	2	35	of River Liffey.
(f) Including	327	2	24	of water.	(n) Including	854	1	34	of water.	(u) Including	596	3	38	of water.
(g) Including	4,397	1	31	of water.	(o) Including	5,416	0	1	of water.	(v) Including	11	0	6	of Lough Nashade.
(h) Including	5,544	3	27	of water.										

DUBLIN: Printed by ALEX. THOM & SONS, 87 & 88, Abbey-street,
For Her Majesty's Stationery Office.